Canadian Environmental Resource Guide

Guide des ressources environnementales canadiennes

VOLUME 2

Industry Resources: Associations, Libraries, Law Firms, Research Centres

Government Listings

Ten Indexes

Additional Publications

For more detailed information or to place an order, see the back of the book.

CANADIAN PARLIAMENTARY GUIDE 2013
Guide parlementaire canadien

1266 pages, 6 x 9, Hardcover
ISBN 978-1-61925-148-9
ISSN 0315-6168

Published annually since before Confederation, this indispensable guide to government in Canada provides information on federal and provincial governments, with biographical sketches of government members, descriptions of government institutions, and historical text and charts. With significant bilingual sections, the Guide covers elections from Confederation to the present, including the most recent provincial elections.

FINANCIAL SERVICES CANADA 2013-2014
Services financiers au Canada

1684 pages, 8 1/2 x 11, Softcover
16th edition, April 2013
ISBN 978-1-61925-146-5
ISSN 1484-2408

This directory of Canadian financial institutions and organizations includes banks and depository institutions, non-depository institutions, investment management firms, financial planners, insurance companies, accountants, major law firms, government and regulatory agencies, and associations. Fully indexed.

CANADIAN ALMANAC & DIRECTORY 2013
Répertoire et almanach canadien

2366 pages, 8 1/2 x 11, Hardcover
166th edition, November 2012
ISBN 978-1-59237-988-0
ISSN 0068-8193

A combination of textual material, charts, colour photographs and directory listings, the Canadian Almanac & Directory provides the most comprehensive picture of Canada, from physical attributes to economic and business summaries to leisure and recreation.

GOVERNMENTS CANADA SUMMER/FALL 2013
Gouvernements du Canada

1042 pages, 8 ½ x 11, Softcover
Summer/Fall 2013
ISBN 978-1-61925-149-6
ISSN 1493-3918

Governments Canada provides a solution to finding the departments and people that you are searching for within our federal and provincial political system.

ASSOCIATIONS CANADA 2013
Associations du Canada

2104 pages, 8 1/2 x 11, Hardcover
33th edition, February 2013
ISBN 978-1-61925-145-8
ISSN 1186-9798

Nearly 20,000 entries profile Canadian and international organizations active in Canada. Over 2,000 subject classifications index activities, professions and interests served by associations. Includes listings of NGOs, institutes, coalitions, social agencies, federations, foundations, trade unions, fraternal orders, political parties. Fully indexed by subject, geographic location, electronic addresses, executive name, acronym, mailing list availability, conferences and publications.

LIBRARIES CANADA 2013-2014
Bibliothèques Canada

1000 pages, 8 1/2 x 11, Softcover
28th edition, May 2013
ISBN 978-1-61925-147-2
ISSN 1920-2849

Libraries Canada offers comprehensive information on Canadian libraries, resource centres, business information centres, professional associations, regional library systems, archives, library schools, government libraries, and library technical programs.

HEALTH GUIDE CANADA 2013-2014
Guide canadien de la santé

944 pages, 8 1/2 x 11, Softcover
1st edition, May 2013
ISBN: 978-1-61925-185-4

Health Guide Canada contains thousands of ways to deal with the many aspects of chronic or mental health disorder. It includes associations, government agencies, libraries and resource centres, educational facilities, hospitals and publications.

18th Edition

2013-2014

Canadian Environmental Resource Guide

Guide des ressources environnementales canadiennes

VOLUME 2

Industry Resources: Associations, Libraries, Law Firms, Research Centres

Government Listings

Ten Indexes

GREY HOUSE PUBLISHING CANADA

Grey House Publishing Canada
PUBLISHER: Leslie Mackenzie
GENERAL MANAGER: Bryon Moore
MANAGING EDITOR: Tannys Williams
ASSOCIATE EDITORS: Elysia Cheung, Sarah Elshater, Jill McCullough, Stuart Paterson
OPERATIONS AND
MARKETING COORDINATORS: Christelle Agboka, Caitlin Beatty, Demi Dina

Grey House Publishing New York
EDITORIAL DIRECTOR: Laura Mars
MARKETING DIRECTOR: Jessica Moody
COMPOSITION: Kristen Thatcher

Grey House Publishing Canada
555 Richmond Street West, Suite 301
Toronto, ON M5V 3B1
866-433-4739
FAX 416-644-1904
www.greyhouse.ca
e-mail: info@greyhouse.ca

Grey House Publishing Canada is a wholly owned subsidiary of Grey House Publishing, Inc. USA.

18th edition published 2013
Printed in Canada by Webcom, Inc.

ISBN: 978-1-61925-144-1
ISSN: 1920-2725

Cataloguing in Publication Data is available from Libraries and Archives Canada.

Table of Contents

VOLUME 1

Environmental Update 2013

Environmental Products & Services Buyer's Guide

VOLUME 2

Environmental Resources

Environmental Government Listings

Indexes

Introduction

This is the 18th edition of the *Canadian Environmental Resource Guide,* previously *Canadian Environmental Directory.* It is the seventh edition to be published by Grey House Publishing Canada.

As its name indicates, this reference book is so much more than a directory. It includes colour maps, charts, rankings, recent events, descriptions of environmental issues and prominent researchers, plus valuable profiles of government and private agencies, educational and research facilities, foundations, law firms, manufacturers and service providers—over 10,000 ways to access information and knowledge about the environment in Canada. The wealth of information in this annual resource guide—essential for any business or agency with an interest in a wide spectrum of environmental issues—is arranged into four main sections and 22 subsections. All profiles include current contact information and key executives, plus valuable details, such as number of employees, financial and membership data, additional services and more. In addition, there are 14 indexes: one all-inclusive at the end of the second volume—Entry Index—and 13 others, arranged throughout the two volumes for quick and easy navigation.

Volume 1:

Environmental Update 2013

This section offers a current look at the Canadian environmental picture. With revised and expanded **Chronology, Statistics** and more, Update 2013 includes Ranking Charts from Environmental Performance Indicators that show how Canada compares with the rest of the world in significant environmental issues. It also gives an update on the Canada-U.S. Air Quality Agreement. You'll find 26 **Biographies** of prominent Canadian environmentalists, 16 full-colour environmental **Maps, Abbreviations** of environmental terms, and updated and expanded **Trade Show, Conference & Seminar** profiles.

Environmental Products & Services Buyer's Guide

The manufacturers and service providers listed here offer products that deal with environmental issues from Absorbents to Wood Recycling, from Agriculture Management to Wind Energy Conversion. Company profiles are current and comprehensive, with descriptions, corporate details and key executives. This valuable information is further accessed by four indexes: **Subject, Geographic, Executive** (5,198 names) and **ISO**.

Volume 2:

Environmental Government Listings

Arranged in six subsections, this section starts with a **Quick Reference Guide** to environmental government agencies, followed by **Government Acts & Regulations** as they relate to environmental issues. Next is current, comprehensive information on all **Federal, Provincial** and **Municipal** agencies that deal with environmental concerns. Municipal listings include detailed descriptions on water and waste treatment information, landfill statistics and more. It also includes updated information on **Intergovernmental Offices & Councils** and **Environmental Trade Representatives Abroad**.

Environmental Resources

This section includes 2315 **Associations**, 896 **Special Libraries & Resource Centres**, and private and government environment **Publications**. You'll also find environmental **Educational Programs, Foundations & Grants** and **Research Centres**, all arranged by province. Rounding out this section are **Law Firms** across Canada with an interest in environmental law. Volume 2 includes nine volume-specific indexes: Three for Associations; Educational Programs; Foundations & Grants; Law Firms; Libraries & Resource Centres; Research Centres; and Executive (16,441 names). This volume ends with a master, two-volume Entry Name Index (7,127 entries).

This reference work is also available as part of **Canada's Information Resource Centre (CIRC)** on the web (information available at www.greyhouse.ca). Subscribers have full access to this rich database right at their computer. Trial subscriptions to the CIRC database are available when you call 866-433-4739.

Grey House Publishing Canada also publishes annual editions of the *Canadian Parliamentary Guide, Canadian Almanac & Directory, Associations Canada, Financial Services Canada, Libraries Canada, Governments Canada & Health Services Canada.*

Every effort has been made to assure the accuracy of the information included in this edition of the *Canadian Environmental Resource Guide.* We acknowledge the valuable contributions of those individuals and organizations that have responded to our information gathering process. Your help and responses to our phone calls, faxes and questionnaires are greatly appreciated. Do not hesitate to contact us with comments, or with revisions if necessary.

Industry Resources

L'Académie canadienne du génie *See* The Canadian Academy of Engineering

Acadia Environmental Society

c/o Acadia Students' Union, PO Box 1269, Wolfville NS B0P 1Z0
Tel: 902-585-2150
e-mail: aes@acadiau.ca
Overview: A small local organization founded in 1989
Mission: To provide an information resource on environmental issues; to encourage & help the Acadia community to adopt & maintain environmentally sound & sustainable practices
Chief Officer(s):
James Patterson, Coordinator
Finances: *Annual Operating Budget:* Less than $50,000; *Funding Sources:* Acadia Students' Union
Membership: *Committees:* Events Coordination; Fundraising & Membership; Finance; Education & Networking

The Acadian Entomological Society (AES)

Natural Resources Canada, Canadian Forest Service, PO Box 4000, Atlantic Forestry Centre, 1350 Regent St., Fredericton NB E3B 597
e-mail: b35ckp@mun.ca
www.acadianes.org/aes.html
Overview: A small local organization founded in 1915
Mission: To bring about a close association of entomologists & those interested in entomology in the four Atlantic provinces & the neighbouring New England States; To cooperate with, & to support the Entomological Society of Canada; Affiliation(s): Entomological Society of Canada
Chief Officer(s):
Carolyn Parsons, President, 709-772-5640
b35ckp@mun.ca
Peggy Dixon, Vice-President
dixonpl@agr.gc.ca
Rob Johns, Sec./Treas.
Finances: *Annual Operating Budget:* Less than $50,000; *Funding Sources:* Membership dues; Entomological Society of Canada
Staff: 5 volunteer(s)
Membership: 50; *Fees:* Regular: $20; Student: $10; *Committees:* Archives; Memberships; Pest Management; Public Education
Meetings/Conferences:
For more information see Trade Shows, Conferences and Seminars Chapter
The Acadian Entomological Society 2013 Annual Meeting
July 2013
Publications:
•The Journal of the Acadian Entomological Society
Editor: Don Ostaff; *ISSN:* 1710-4033

Acoustical Association Ontario (AAO)

32 Vancho Cres., Toronto ON M9A 4Z2
Tel: 905-738-1733; *Fax:* 416-240-1465
e-mail: aao@bellnet.ca
www.aao-online.ca
Overview: A small provincial organization founded in 1963
Mission: The Acoustical Association Ontario (AAO) is an association representing unionized employers engaged in Acoustic and Drywall construction in the Industrial, Commercial and Institutional sector of the construction industry in the Province of Ontario.
Chief Officer(s):
Joseph De Caria, Executive Secretary
Membership: 55; *Member Profile:* Unionized contractors engaged in interior finishing construction

Action Patrimoine

82, Grande-Allée ouest, Québec QC G1R 2G6
Tél: 418-647-4347; *Téléc:* 418-647-6483
Ligne sans frais: 800-494-4347
Courriel: info@actionpatrimoine.ca
www.actionpatrimoine.ca
Aperçu: *Dimension:* petite; *Envergure:* provinciale; fondée en 1975
Membre(s) du bureau directeur:
Louise Mercier, Présidente
Charles Méthé, Vice-président
Guy Drouin, Trésorier
Membre: *Critères d'admissibilite:* Ouvert à toute personne intéressée par la sauvegarde et la mise en valeur du patrimoine du Québec
Activités: *Listes de destinataires:* Oui; *Bibliothèque:*

Action to Restore a Clean Humber (ARCH)

147 Stephenson Cres., Richmond Hill ON L4C 5T3
Tel: 416-326-0726
Overview: A small local organization founded in 1991
Mission: To clean up & conserve the Humber watersheds
Chief Officer(s):
Luciano Martin, Executive Director

Action Volunteers for Animals (AVA)

PO Box 64578, Unionville ON L3R 0M9
Tel: 416-439-8770
e-mail: ava2009@actionvolunteersforanimals.com
www.actionvolunteersforanimals.com
Overview: A medium-sized local charitable organization founded in 1972
Mission: To abolish all cruelty against & suffering of non-human animals
Chief Officer(s):
Josephine Polk
Shana Mortimer-Gibson
Carol Lawson
Finances: *Annual Operating Budget:* $50,000-$100,000
Staff: 20 volunteer(s)
Membership: 600; *Fees:* $25; *Committees:* Stray Animals; Vet Fund; Anti-Fur; Fundraising
Activities: Meetings, demonstrations, membership parties, lectures, fundraising events; *Library:* AVA Library; Open to public

Advanced Foods & Materials Network / Réseau des aliments et des matériaux d'avant-garde

#215, 150 Research Lane, Guelph ON N1G 4T2
Tel: 519-822-6253; *Fax:* 519-824-8453
www.afmnet.ca
Also Known As: AFMNet
Overview: A medium-sized national organization
Member of: Networks of Centres of Excellence
Chief Officer(s):
Rickey Yada, Scientific Director, 519-824-4120 Ext. 58915, Fax: 519-824-6631
rickey.yada@afmnet.ca

Aerospace Industries Association of Canada (AIAC) / Association des industries aérospatiales du Canada

#703, 255 Albert St., Ottawa ON K1P 6A9
Tel: 613-232-4297; *Fax:* 613-232-1142
e-mail: info@aiac.ca
www.aiac.ca
Previous Name: Air Industries Association of Canada
Overview: A large national organization founded in 1962
Mission: To promote & facilitate the continued success & growth of this strategic industry; To establish & maintain a public policy environment that enables sustained aerospace industry growth; To strengthen the international competitiveness of all aerospace firms in Canada; To strengthen Canadian aerospace SME capabilities & position them as "suppliers of choice"; To represent & involve the full range of aerospace companies that operate in Canada
Chief Officer(s):
Jim Quick, President & CEO
David Schellenberg, Chair
Membership: 400; *Committees:* International Exhibition; Technology Council; Defence Procurement Council; Suppliers Development; Space; Civil Aviation; Public Affairs
Meetings/Conferences:
For more information see Trade Shows, Conferences and Seminars Chapter
2013 Canadian Aerospace Summit
October 2013 Ottawa, ON

African Violet Society of Canada

c/o 349 Hyman Dr., Dollard-des-Ormeaux QC H9B 1L5
e-mail: other@avsc.ca
www.avsc.ca
Overview: A small national organization
Chief Officer(s):
Paul F. Kroll, President
Membership: 400+; *Fees:* $15 annual
Publications:
•Chatter
Type: Magazine; *Frequency:* Quarterly

African Wildlife Foundation (AWF)

#120, 1400 Sixteenth St. NW, Washington DC 20036 USA
Tel: 202-939-3333; *Fax:* 202-939-3332
Toll-Free: 888-494-5354
e-mail: africanwildlife@awf.org
www.awf.org
www.facebook.com/AfricanWildlifeFoundation
twitter.com/AWF_Official?ref=nf
www.youtube.com/AfricanWildlife
Overview: A large international organization
Mission: To promote conservation of Africa's wildlife & natural resources; to promote belief that the survival of African wildlife lies in a working knowledge of the relationship between man, his economics & his environment; to promote, establish & support grassroots & institutional programs in conservation education, wildlife management & training, & management of threatened conservation areas; to manage projects aimed at saving endangered species (eg. the African Elephant, Mountain Gorilla, Rhinoceros)
Chief Officer(s):
Patrick J. Bergin, CEO
Helen W. Gichohi, President
Jeff Chrisfield, CFO
Publications:
•African Heartland News
Type: Newsletter; *Frequency:* Quarterly
Profile: For AWF's technical partners
•African Wildlife News
Type: Newsletter; *Frequency:* Quarterly
Profile: For AWF members

Agence internationale de l'énergie atomique *See* International Atomic Energy Agency

Aggregate Producers' Association of Ontario *See* Ontario Stone, Sand & Gravel Association

Agricultural Alliance of New Brunswick (AANB) / Alliance agricole du Nouveau-Brunswick Parent Name: Canadian Federation of Agriculture

#303, 259 Brunswick St., Fredericton NB E3B 1G8
Tel: 506-452-8101; *Fax:* 506-452-1085
e-mail: alliance@fermenbfarm.ca
www.fermenbfarm.ca
Previous Name: New Brunswick Federation of Agriculture
Overview: A medium-sized provincial charitable organization founded in 1876 overseen by Canadian Federation of Agriculture
Mission: To promote & advance the social & economic conditions of those engaged in agricultural pursuits; to formulate & promote agricultural policies to meet changing economic conditions; *Member of:* Atlantic Farmers Council
Chief Officer(s):
Nicole Arseneau, Office Manager
Mélanie Godin, Coordinator, Environmental Farm Plan
Finances: *Annual Operating Budget:* $100,000-$250,000; *Funding Sources:* Membership fees
Staff: 3 staff member(s); 12 volunteer(s)
Membership: 1,200 individual; *Fees:* $150-500; *Member Profile:* Farmers maintaining specified level of specific commodity; *Committees:* Training; Sustainable Agriculture; Farm Safety; Farm Finance
Activities: *Speaker Service:* Yes; *Library:*

Agricultural Groups Concerned About Resources & the Environment

Ontario AgriCentre, #106, 100 Stone Rd. West, Guelph ON N1G 5L3
Tel: 519-837-1326
e-mail: agcare@agcare.org
www.agcare.org
www.facebook.com/FarmFoodCare
twitter.com/farmfoodcare
www.youtube.com/user/FarmandFoodCare
Also Known As: AGCare
Overview: A medium-sized provincial organization

Affiliation(s): Christian Farmers' Federation of Ontario; Federated Women's Institutes of Ontario; Ontario Beekeepers' Association; Ontario Canola Growers' Association; Ontario Soybean Growers; Ontario Fruit & Vegetable Growers' Association; Ontario Corn Producers' Association; Ontario Wheat Producers' Marketing Board; Ontario Potato Board; Ontario Processing Vegetable Growers; Ontario Bean Producers' Marketing Board; Ontario Seed Growers' Association; Ontario Soil & Crop Improvement Association; Ontario Federation of Agriculture; Flowers Canada (Ontario); Ontario Flue-Cured Tobacco Growers' Marketing Board
Chief Officer(s):
Lilian Schaer, Executive Director
lschaer@agcare.org
Kelly Daynard, Program Manager
kdaynard@ofac.org
Finances: *Funding Sources:* Funded by all major Ontario farm organizations involved in crop production
Membership: 45,000 Ontario horticultural & field crop producers
Activities: Our Farm Environmental Agenda (drafted by a coalition of AGCare, the Christian Farmers' Federation of Ontario, the Ontario Farm Animal Council & the Ontario Federation of Agriculture) outlines the strong commitment of farmers, through Environmental Farm Plans, to document present environmental conditions on their farms, develop a strategy for making appropriate changes, document actual farm practices & use that data for the development of new farm environmental initiatives

Agricultural Institute of Canada (AIC) / Institut agricole du Canada

#900, 9 Corvus Crt., Ottawa ON K2E 7Z4
Tel: 613-232-9459; *Fax:* 613-594-5190
Toll-Free: 888-277-7980
e-mail: office@aic.ca
www.aic.ca
Overview: A large national organization founded in 1920
Mission: To provide the voice for national knowledge & expertise; To promote the creation, production, & delivery of safe foods & sustainable use of related national resources in Canada & beyond; Affiliation(s): Canadian Agricultural Economics; Canadian Consulting Agrologists' Association; Canadian Society of Agronomy; Canadian Society of Animal Science; Canadian Society for Horticultural Science; Canadian Society of Soil Science; Canadian Society of Agrometeorology; British Columbia Institute of Agrologists; Alberta Institute of Agrologists; Saskatchewan Institute of Agrologists; Manitoba Institute of Agrologists; Ontario Institute of Agrologists; New Brunswick Institute of Agrologists; Nova Scotia Institute of Agrologists; PEI Institute of Agrologists; Newfoundland/Labrador Institute of Agrologists
Chief Officer(s):
Lynn Lashuk, PAg, President, 250-766-2080
Lianne Dwyer, PhD, Vice-President
ldwyer2416@rogers.com
Frances Rodenburg, Manager, Administration & Communications
frodenburg@aic.ca
Finances: *Annual Operating Budget:* $100,000-$250,000; *Funding Sources:* Membership fees
Staff: 8 staff member(s)
Membership: 9 provincial institutes + 8 agriculture-related scientific societies; *Fees:* $125 individual; $500 corporate; $1,000 association
Activities: News service; international program
Publications:
•AIC [Agricultural Institute of Canada] Monthly Report
Type: Newsletter; *Frequency:* Monthly
•GEM (Gender Equality Mainstreaming) Digest [a publication of the Agricultural Institute of Canada]
Type: Newsletter; *Frequency:* Monthly
•Sustainable Futures [a publication of the Agricultural Institute of Canada]
Type: Magazine
Profile: No longer published, but back-issues are archived on AIC's website

Agricultural Institute of Canada Foundation (AICF)

#900, 9 Corvus Crt., Ottawa ON K2E 7Z4
Tel: 613-232-9459; *Fax:* 613-594-5190
Toll-Free: 888-277-7980
e-mail: aicf@aic.ca
www.aic.ca/about/foundation.cfm
Overview: A large national charitable organization founded in 1987
Mission: To enhance agriculture & the role it plays in providing Canadians with a safe, affordable, nutritious food supply; Affiliation(s): Agricultural Institute of Canada
Chief Officer(s):
Corrina Dawe, PAg, President
Frances Rodenburg, General Manager
frodenburg@aic.ca
Finances: *Annual Operating Budget:* Less than $50,000; *Funding Sources:* Personal donations; corporate sponsorship
Staff: 1 staff member(s)
Publications:
•Connections [a publication of the Agricultural Institute of Canada Foundation]
Type: Newsletter

Agricultural Manufacturers of Canada (AMC)

Evraz Place, Stockman's Arena, PO Box 636, Stn. Main, Regina SK S4P 3A3
Tel: 306-522-2710; *Fax:* 306-781-7293
e-mail: amc@a-m-c.ca
www.a-m-c.ca
Previous Name: Prairie Implement Manufacturers Association; PIMA - Agricultural Manufacturers of Canada
Overview: A medium-sized local licensing charitable organization founded in 1970
Mission: To foster & promote the growth & development of the agricultural equipment manufacturing industry; to identify industry problems & take remedial action; to encourage governments to enact legislation & offer programs that enhance the growth potential of industry; to provide a forum for members to exchange ideas & discuss their industry as it relates to the national & international economy
Chief Officer(s):
James Umlah, Chair, 204-453-6833
Jerry Engel, President
Finances: *Annual Operating Budget:* $250,000-$500,000; *Funding Sources:* Membership fees; special projects
Staff: 9 staff member(s)
Membership: 200 regular + 5 affiliate + 300 associate; *Fees:* Schedule available; *Member Profile:* Regular - manufacturer of farm & ranch equipment; associate - supplier of goods & services; *Committees:* Alberta Provincial; Saskatchewan Provincial; Manitoba Provincial; Ontario Provincial

Agricultural Producers Association of Saskatchewan (APAS)
Parent Name: Canadian Federation of Agriculture

#100, 2400 College Ave., Regina SK S4P 1C8
Tel: 306-789-7774; *Fax:* 306-789-7779
e-mail: info@apas.ca
www.apas.ca
Overview: A medium-sized provincial organization overseen by Canadian Federation of Agriculture
Mission: To provide farmers & ranchers with a democratically elected, grassroots, non-partisan producer organization based on rural municipal boundaries
Chief Officer(s):
Nial Kuyek, General Manager
nkuyek@apas.ca
Membership: 114 rural municipalities; *Member Profile:* Producers in rural municipalities of Saskatchewan

Agricultural Research & Extension Council of Alberta (ARECA)

#211, 2 Athabascan Ave., Sherwood Park ON T8A 4E3
Tel: 780-416-6046; *Fax:* 780-416-8915
www.areca.ab.ca
Overview: A medium-sized provincial organization
Mission: To provide agricultural producers with access to field research and new technology, in order to enhance & improve their operations
Chief Officer(s):
Gerald Keufler, Chair
Ty Faechner, Executive Director
faechner@areca.ab.ca
Finances: *Funding Sources:* Government; sponsors
Publications:
•ARECA [Agricultural Research & Extension Council of Alberta] E-Newsletter
Type: Newsletter; *Frequency:* Monthly

Agricultural Technologists Association Inc. ***Voir*** Association des technologues en agroalimentaire

AgriVenture International Rural Placements

PO Box 165, Annaheim SK SOK 0G0
Fax: 306-598-4416
Toll-Free: 888-598-4415
e-mail: canada@agriventure.com
www.agriventure.com
www.facebook.com/people/AgriVenture-Iaea/724272279
twitter.com/AgriVenture
Previous Name: International Agricultural Exchange Association
Overview: A small international organization
Mission: To administer agricultural exchange for young people
Chief Officer(s):
Allison Sarauer, Manager
Membership: 5,000 in 14 countries

Air & Waste Management Association (A&WMA) / Association pour la prévention de la contamination de l'air et du sol

One Gateway Center, 420 Fort Duquesne Blvd., 3rd Fl., Pittsburgh PA 15222-1435 USA
Tel: 412-232-3444; *Fax:* 412-232-3450
Toll-Free: 800-270-3444
e-mail: info@awma.org
www.awma.org
www.linkedin.com/company/445959
www.facebook.com/groups/33499462923
twitter.com/AirandWaste
Previous Name: Air Pollution Control Association
Overview: A large international organization founded in 1907
Mission: To improve environmental knowledge & decisions; To assist members in critical environmental decision making & professional development; To provide a neutral forum for exchanging information & developing networking opportunities; To increase public education & outreach; *Member of:* International Union of Air Pollution Prevention & Environmental Protection Associations; Affiliation(s): Canadian Prairie & Northern Section (www.cpans.org); Ontario Section (www.awma.on.ca); Québec Section (www.apcas.qc.ca); Ottawa Valley Chapter (www.awma-ovc.ca); Pacific Northwest International Section (www.pnwis.org)
Environmental Activity: Promoting global environmental responsibility
Chief Officer(s):
Merlyn L. Hough, President
Jim Powell, Executive Director/Secretary, 412-904-6007
jpowell@awma.org
Amy Gilligan, Treasurer
Membership: 5,000+ in 65 countries; *Fees:* $40 students; $75 emeritus members; $105 young professional members; $200 individuals; $480 primary organizational members; *Member Profile:* Environmental professionals; *Committees:* Councils: Education; Sections & Chapters; Technical; Young Professionals
Awards:
•S. Smith Griswold Outstanding Air Pollution Control Official Award (Award)
•Frank A. Chambers Excellence in Air Pollution Control Award (Award)
Awarded to individuals who make an exceptional contribution to any technical aspect of air pollution control
•J. Deane Sensenbaugh Environmental Technology Award (Award)
Presented every year to a firm, company, or corporation that has made outstanding achievements in air pollution control or waste management; the recipient's contribution to the state of the art must be one that has been recognized & accepted in the field
Meetings/Conferences:
For more information see Trade Shows, Conferences and Seminars Chapter
Air & Waste Management Association 2013 Annual Conference & Exhibition
June 2013 Chicago, IL
Publications:
•Air & Waste Management Association Membership Directory
Type: Directory
Profile: Contact information for members
•EM, The Magazine for Environmental Managers
Type: Magazine; *Frequency:* Monthly; *Accepts Advertising*; *Price:* $180 individuals; $265 nonprofit organization & government agencies; $405 all others
Profile: Management, policy, & regulatory perspective
•Journal of the Air & Waste Management Association
Type: Journal; *Frequency:* Monthly; *Editor:* Tim Keener
Profile: Peer reviewed, technical environmental journal

Air Industries Association of Canada ***See*** Aerospace Industries Association of Canada

Air Pollution Control Association ***See*** Air & Waste Management Association

Air Transport Association of Canada (ATAC) / Association du transport aérien du Canada

#700, 255 Albert St., Ottawa ON K1P 6A9
Tel: 613-233-7727; *Fax:* 613-230-8648
e-mail: atac@atac.ca
www.atac.ca
Overview: A medium-sized national organization founded in 1934
Mission: To advance the issues that affect members from the commercial aviation & flight training industries as well as avaiation industry suppliers
Environmental Activity: Working to reduce emissions, as part of Canada's commitment to the International Civil Aviation Organization goal of achieving carbon neutral growth by 2020
Chief Officer(s):
John McKenna, President & Chief Executive Officer
jmckenna@atac.ca
Fred Gaspar, Vice-President, Policy & Strategic Planning, 613-233-7727 Ext. 314
fgaspar@atac.ca
Bill Boucher, Vice-President, Flight Operations
bboucher@atac.ca
Wayne Gouveia, Vice-President, Commercial General Aviation
wgouveia@atac.ca
Cedric Paillard, Vice-President, Communications & Marketing
cpaillard@atac.ca
Mike Skrobica, Vice-President, Industry Monetary Affairs
mikes@atac.ca
Brian Whitehead, Vice-President, Technical Operations
bwhitehead@atac.ca
Membership: 200; *Member Profile:* Operators; Associates; Affiliates
Activities: Engaging in lobbying activities; *Speaker Service:* Yes
Meetings/Conferences:
For more information see Trade Shows, Conferences and Seminars Chapter
Air Transport Association of Canada 2013 79th Annual General Meeting & Trade Show
November 2013 Montréal, QC
Air Transport Association of Canada 2013 Annual Spring Event
May 2013 Ottawa, ON
Air Transport Association of Canada 2014 80th Annual General Meeting & Trade Show
2014 Vancouver, BC
Publications:
•@ATAC [Air Transport Association of Canada] Newsletter
Type: Newsletter
Profile: Association activities, such as events, awards, & membership information
•Air Transport Association of Canada Annual Report
Type: Magazine; *Frequency:* Annually
•Flightplan
Type: Magazine; *Price:* Free with Air Transport Association of Canada membership

Air Waste Management Association - Québec Section ***Voir*** Association pour la prévention de la contamination de l'air et du sol

Alameda Agricultural Society

PO Box 103, Alameda SK S0C 0A0
Tel: 306-489-4913
Overview: A small local charitable organization
Chief Officer(s):
Melissa Gervais, President
Jamie Neuman, Secretary
Finances: *Funding Sources:* Donations
Activities: Hosting a summer fair, 4-H show, & flower show

Alberni Valley Outdoor Club

c/o Ursula Knoll, 3941 - 9th Ave., Port Alberni BC V9Y 4V1
Tel: 250-723-6883
e-mail: uschik@telus.net
www.mountainclubs.org/AVOC.htm
Overview: A small local organization
Member of: Federation of Mountain Clubs of British Columbia
Chief Officer(s):
Harold Carlson, Chairperson, 250-724-4535
Membership: *Fees:* Single: $25; Family: $45; Associate: $5

Alberta & Northwest Territories Lung Association Parent Name: Canadian Lung Association

PO Box 4500, Stn. South, #208, 17420 Stony Plain Rd., Edmonton AB T5E 6K2
Tel: 780-488-6819; *Fax:* 780-488-7195
Toll-Free: 888-566-5864
e-mail: info@ab.lung.ca
www.ab.lung.ca
www.facebook.com/group.php?gid=192015860715
Overview: A medium-sized provincial charitable organization founded in 1939 overseen by Canadian Lung Association
Mission: To educate the public & medical professionals about lung health
Chief Officer(s):
Anne Marie Downey, Chair
Kate Hurlburt, Vice-Chair
Tom Watts, Secretary
Paul Borrett, Treasurer
Finances: *Funding Sources:* Donations; Fundraising; Sponsorships
Membership: *Fees:* $25
Activities: Providing indepth information about asthma, COPD, sleep apnea, tuberculosis, & other lung conditions, as well as smoking & clean air; Organizing & promoting events about lung health to support the association; Funding medical research; *Awareness Events:* Radon Awareness Campaign; Northwest Territories Asthma & Allergies Door-to-Door Campaign, May
Meetings/Conferences:
For more information see Trade Shows, Conferences and Seminars Chapter
Alberta & Northwest Territories Lung Association 2013 9th Annual Alberta Sleep Forum
October 2013 Edmonton, AB
Alberta & Northwest Territories Lung Association 2013 4th Annual Tobacco Stakeholders Workshop
2013, AB
Alberta & Northwest Territories Lung Association 2013 Annual General Meeting
2013
Publications:
•Alberta & Northwest Territories Lung Association Annual Report
Type: Yearbook; *Frequency:* Annually
Profile: Highlights of fundraising activities, advocacy activities, & patient support programs

Alberta Agricultural Economics Association (AAEA)

Dept. of Rural Economy, University of Alberta, 515 General Services Bldg., Edmonton AB T6G 2H1
Tel: 780-422-3122
e-mail: info@aaea.ab.ca
www.aaea.ab.ca
Overview: A small provincial charitable organization founded in 1984
Mission: To provide an opportunity for communication among those interested in the agricultural & rural social sciences; To provide a forum for the discussion of issues affecting the rural economy; To encourage research & dissemination of research results & other information relating to Alberta's rural economy; To provide avenues for continuing education & professional upgrading
Chief Officer(s):
Bodo Steiner, President, 780-492-0819
bsteiner@ualberta.ca
Diane McCann-Hiltz, Secretary, 780-422-6081
diane.mccann-hiltz@gov.ab.ca
Finances: *Annual Operating Budget:* Less than $50,000
Membership: 200; *Fees:* $30
Activities: Annual 'Visions' Conference in May; regional seminars & luncheon speakers; newsletter; undergraduate & graduate scholarships in agricultural economics at University of Alberta

Alberta Aquaculture Association

PO Box 26, Site 3, RR#1, Red Deer AB T4N 5E1
Tel: 403-342-5206; *Fax:* 403-342-2646
e-mail: info@affa.ab.ca
www.affa.ab.ca
Previous Name: Alberta Fish Farmers Association
Overview: A small local organization
Mission: To support the pursuit of aquaculture promotion & education; *Member of:* Canadian Aquaculture Producers' Council
Chief Officer(s):
Dan Menard, Treasurer
rdmenard@telusplanet.net
Victoria Page, Sec.-Treas.
Membership: *Fees:* $10 Assoc.; $100 Full; $250 Corporate; $250 Ed. Inst.

Alberta Association of Agricultural Societies (AAAS)

J.G. O'Donoghue Building, #200, 7000 - 113 St., Edmonton AB T6H 5T6
Tel: 780-427-2174; *Fax:* 780-422-7755
e-mail: aaas@gov.ab.ca
www.albertaagsocieties.ca
Overview: A medium-sized provincial organization founded in 1947
Mission: To preserve & enhance the viability of agricultural societies in Alberta
Environmental Activity: Encouraging environmental responsibility
Chief Officer(s):
Tim Carson, Chief Executive Officer
tim.carson@xplornet.com
Lisa Hardy, Executive Director
lisa.hardy@gov.ab.ca
Monica Bradley, Treasurer
monica.bradley@shaw.ca
Membership: 294+; *Fees:* $150 service membership; $200 agricultural societies; *Member Profile:* Agricultural societies & communities in Alberta
Activities: Presenting education programs; Lobbying government; Providing information; Facilitating networking
Meetings/Conferences:
For more information see Trade Shows, Conferences and Seminars Chapter
Alberta Association of Agricultural Societies 2013 Annual Meeting & Convention
February 2013 Edmonton, AB
Alberta Association of Agricultural Societies 2013 Regional Meetings
2013, AB
Publications:
•Across the Fence [a publication of the Alberta Association of Agricultural Societies]
Type: Newsletter; *Frequency:* Quarterly; *Accepts Advertising*; *Price:* Free with Alberta Association of Agricultural Societies membership
Profile: Contents include the chief executive officer's message, industry topics, conventions, awards, grant opportunities, & regionalissues
•Alberta Association of Agricultural Societies Membership Directory
Type: Directory; *Price:* Free access on request, with Alberta Association of Agricultural Societies membership

Alberta Association of Landscape Architects (AALA)

PO Box 21052, Edmonton AB T6R 2V4
Tel: 780-435-9902; *Fax:* 780-413-0076
e-mail: aala@aala.ab.ca
www.aala.ab.ca
Overview: A medium-sized provincial organization founded in 1970
Mission: To advance the quality of the professional practice of landscape architecture in Alberta; *Member of:* Canadian Society of Landscape Architects
Environmental Activity: Teaching about environmental construction; Promoting the planning, designing, & managing of land to protect the natural environment
Chief Officer(s):
Jill Lane, Manager
Mark Nolan, Registrar, 780-428-4000
mnolan7@hotmail.com
Brian Charanduk, Treasurer, 780-917-7219
brian.charanduk@stantec.com
Michelle Lefebre, Secretary
Finances: *Funding Sources:* Membership dues; Sponsorships
Membership: *Fees:* $50; *Committees:* Registration; Discipline & Practice Review; Website; Grievance; Promotions; Continuing Education; Examining Board; Calgary; Edmonton
Activities: Offering a continuing education program; *Internships:* Yes; *Library:* Alberta Association of Landscape Architects Resource Library
Meetings/Conferences:
For more information see Trade Shows, Conferences and Seminars Chapter
Alberta Association of Landscape Architects 2013 Annual General Meeting
2013, AB
Alberta Association of Landscape Architects 2013 Alberta Sustainable Building Symposium
May 2013 Edmonton, AB
Publications:
•Alberta Association of Landscape Architects Newsletter

Type: Newsletter
Profile: Association activities & forthcoming events

Alberta Association of Municipal Districts & Counties (AAMDC)

2510 Sparrow Dr., Nisku AB T9E 8N5
Tel: 780-955-3639; *Fax:* 780-955-3615
Toll-Free: 855-548-7233
e-mail: aamdc@aamdc.com
www.aamdc.com
twitter.com/aamdc
www.flickr.com/photos/45829734@N03
Overview: A medium-sized provincial organization founded in 1909
Member of: Federation of Canadian Municipalities
Chief Officer(s):
Bob Barss, President, 780-842-7309
bbarss@aamdc.com
Gerald Rhodes, Executive Director, 780-955-4076
Finances: *Annual Operating Budget:* $500,000-$1.5 Million
Staff: 13 staff member(s)
Membership: 69 regular; 650 associate; *Member Profile:* Rural municipalities, counties & municipal districts in Alberta
Meetings/Conferences:
For more information see Trade Shows, Conferences and Seminars Chapter
Alberta Association of Municipal Districts & Counties Spring 2013 Convention & Trade Show
March 2013 Edmonton, AB
Alberta Association of Municipal Districts & Counties Fall 2013 Convention & Trade Show
November 2013 Edmonton, AB
Alberta Association of Municipal Districts & Counties Spring 2014 Convention & Trade Show
March 2014 Edmonton, AB
Alberta Association of Municipal Districts & Counties Fall 2014 Convention & Trade Show
November 2014 Edmonton, AB
Alberta Association of Municipal Districts & Counties Spring 2015 Convention & Trade Show
March 2015 Edmonton, AB
Alberta Association of Municipal Districts & Counties Fall 2015 Convention & Trade Show
November 2015 Edmonton, AB
Alberta Association of Municipal Districts & Counties Spring 2016 Convention & Trade Show
March 2016 Edmonton, AB
Alberta Association of Municipal Districts & Counties Fall 2016 Convention & Trade Show
November 2016 Edmonton, AB
Alberta Association of Municipal Districts & Counties Spring 2017 Convention & Trade Show
March 2017 Edmonton, AB
Alberta Association of Municipal Districts & Counties Fall 2017 Convention & Trade Show
November 2017 Edmonton, AB

Alberta Beef Producers (ABP)

#320, 6715 - 8th St. NE, Calgary AB T2E 7H7
Tel: 403-275-4400; *Fax:* 403-274-0007
e-mail: abpfeedback@albertabeef.org
www.albertabeef.org
Previous Name: Alberta Cattle Commission
Overview: A medium-sized provincial organization founded in 1969
Mission: To strengthen the sustainability & competitiveness of the beef industry; To produce beef in an environmentally sustainable manner; To support responsible animal care & handling; *Member of:* Canadian Cattlemen's Association (CCA)
Environmental Activity: Promoting beneficial environmental management practices; Supporting policies, programs, & educational efforts related to environmental stewardship; Recognizing producers who have incorporated environmental protection into their management strategy
Chief Officer(s):
Rich Smith, General Manager, 403-451-1183
RichS@albertabeef.org
Lori Creech, Manager, Communications, 403-451-1179
loric@albertabeef.org
Barb Sweetland, Manager, Promotions, 403-451-1178
BarbS@albertabeef.org
Fred Hays, Policy Analyst, 403-451-1181
fredh@albertabeef.org
Membership: 15,000-49,999
Activities: Influencing government policy; Improving the beef industry's public image; Engaging in research activities; Providing landowners with information on rangeland health
Publications:
•Beneficial Management Practices: Envrionmental Manual for Alberta Cow/Calf Producers
Price: Free to all Alberta cattleproducers
Profile: Developed in partnership with Alberta Beef Producers (ABP) & Alberta Agriculture, Food, & Rural Development
•Recommended Code of Practice for the Care & Handling of Farm Animals: Beef Cattle Edition
Type: Booklet; *Price:* Free

Alberta Blonde d'Aquitaine Association

PO Box 5959, Westlock AB T7P 2P7
Tel: 780-348-5308
e-mail: aba@clearwave.ca
www.albertablondecattle.com
Overview: A small provincial organization
Mission: To represent breeders of Blonde d'Aquitaine cattle in Alberta
Chief Officer(s):
Reed Rigney, President, 780-348-5308
Ken Mackenzie, Vice-President, 780-542-2268
kenkb@telus.net
Dave Kamelchuk, Treasurer, 780-675-1227
littlecreekagroforestry@gmail.com
Membership: *Member Profile:* Breeders of Blonde d'Aquitaine cattle from Alberta
Activities: Providing information for breeders of Blonde d'Aquitaine cattle; Organizing field days
Publications:
•Blonde Bullet [a publication of the Alberta & Manitoba / Saskatchewan Blonde d'Aquitaine Associations]
Type: Newsletter; *Accepts Advertising*

Alberta Bottle Depot Association (ABDA)

#202, 17850 - 105 Ave., Edmonton AB T5S 2H5
Tel: 780-454-0400; *Fax:* 780-454-0424
www.albertadepot.ca
www.facebook.com/142558085810395
twitter.com/AlbertaDepot
Overview: A small provincial organization
Mission: To educate about industry & to standardize the practices for depot operation
Environmental Activity: Waste management; advancing the efficiency of the bottle depot system in Alberta
Chief Officer(s):
Jeff Linton, Executive Director
Finances: *Funding Sources:* Membership dues
Staff: 2 staff member(s); 14 volunteer(s)
Membership: 184
Activities: ; *Library:* Open to public

Alberta Building Envelope Council (South) (ABEC)

PO Box 61152, Stn. Kensington, Calgary AB T2N 4S6
Tel: 403-246-4500; *Fax:* 403-246-4220
www.abecsouth.org
Overview: A small provincial organization founded in 1983
Mission: ABEC is interested in design, construction, performance, evaluation, testing, renovation, restoration and maintenance of building envelopes.; *Member of:* National Building Envelope Council
Chief Officer(s):
Mike Dietrich, President
mdietrich@morrisonhershfield.com
Randy Smith, Secretary, 403-263-2393
rsmith@adwilliams.com
Gene LaVallee, Treasurer, 403-560-8627
gwlavallee@dryvit.ca
Finances: *Annual Operating Budget:* Less than $50,000; *Funding Sources:* Membership dues
Staff: 8 volunteer(s)
Membership: 148; *Fees:* Individual: $48; Corporate: $65; Student: $10
Activities: The link between architects, building owners, engineers & contractors; *Speaker Service:* Yes

Alberta Camping Association (ACA)
Parent Name: Canadian Camping Association

Percy Page Centre, 11759 Groat Rd., Edmonton AB T5M 3K6
Tel: 780-427-6605; *Fax:* 780-427-6695
e-mail: info@albertacamping.com
www.albertacamping.com
www.facebook.com/AlbertaCampingAssociation
Overview: A medium-sized provincial charitable organization founded in 1949 overseen by Canadian Camping Association
Mission: To promote & coordinate organized camping in Alberta by providing camp information & leadership direction as well as promoting high standards of camp programs & activities for all populations; to take a leading role in the recognition & promotion of professional standards for organized camps in Alberta
Chief Officer(s):
Jon Olfert, President
Les Waite, Secretary-Treasurer
Finances: *Annual Operating Budget:* $50,000-$100,000; *Funding Sources:* Lotteries; community development; recreation; Parks & Wildlife Foundation
Staff: 1 staff member(s); 18 volunteer(s)
Membership: 20 corporate + 400 individual + 100 camps; *Fees:* $15 student; $35 general; $150 camps; $100 commercial; *Committees:* Conference & Education; Marketing & Fundraising; Standards; Research & Development; Newsletter
Activities: *Speaker Service:* Yes; *Rents Mailing List:* Yes; *Library:* ACA Resource Centre; Open to public

Alberta Canola Producers Commission (ACPC)

#170, 14315 - 118 Ave., Edmonton AB T5L 4S6
Tel: 780-454-0844; *Fax:* 780-465-5473
Toll-Free: 800-551-6652
e-mail: web@canola.ab.ca
www.canola.ab.ca
www.facebook.com/albertacanola
twitter.com/albertacanola
www.youtube.com/albertacanola
Overview: A medium-sized provincial organization founded in 1989
Mission: To provide leadership in a vibrant canola industry for the benefit of Alberta canola producers; to strive to improve the long-term profitability of Alberta canola producers; *Member of:* Canola Council of Canada; Food Safety Info Society; Agriculture Education Network; Affiliation(s): Canadian Canola Growers Association
Chief Officer(s):
Ward Toma, General Manager, 780-454-0844
ward.toma@canola.ab.ca
Finances: *Annual Operating Budget:* $500,000-$1.5 Million
Staff: 3 staff member(s)
Membership: 26,000; *Fees:* Based on sale of canola seed; *Committees:* Administration & Finance; Market Development; Member Relation & Extension; Research
Activities: *Speaker Service:* Yes

Alberta Cattle Commission *See* Alberta Beef Producers

Alberta Centre for Boreal Studies

PO Box 52031, 8210 - 109 St., Edmonton AB T6G 2T5
e-mail: contact@borealcentre.ca
www.borealcentre.ca
Overview: A small provincial organization
Mission: To promote the involvement & effectiveness of the public in decision-making on boreal issues, enabling them to promote the conservation of biodiversity more effectively
Chief Officer(s):
Richard Schneider, Executive Director

Alberta Chamber of Resources

#1940, 10180 - 101 St., Edmonton AB T5J 3S4
Tel: 780-420-1030; *Fax:* 780-425-4623
e-mail: admin@acr-alberta.com
www.acr-alberta.com
Overview: A medium-sized provincial organization
Chief Officer(s):
Gord Ball, President

Alberta Cogenerators Council

Postal Bag 1020, Grande Prairie AB T8V 3A9
Tel: 403-539-8069; *Fax:* 403-539-8597
Toll-Free: 866-953-0530
e-mail: kim.logan@weyerhaeuser.com
Overview: A small provincial organization
Chief Officer(s):
Kim Logan

Alberta Conservation Association (ACA)

#101, 9 Chippewa Rd., Sherwood Park AB T8A 6J7
Tel: 780-410-1999; *Fax:* 780-464-0990
Toll-Free: 877-969-9091
e-mail: info@ab-conservation.com
www.ab-conservation.com
Overview: A medium-sized provincial charitable organization founded in 1997
Mission: To envision an Alberta where citizens understand & support good stewardship of natural biological resources, &

where future generations can value, enjoy & use these natural biological resources
Environmental Activity: Maintaining habitat integrity; Encouraging government, business, & citizens to work together for nature conservation
Chief Officer(s):
Todd Zimmerling, President/CEO
Finances: *Funding Sources:* Alberta conservationists: Hunters; Anglers; corporate partners
Staff: 75 staff member(s)
Membership: 1-99
Activities: *Speaker Service:* Yes

Alberta Conservation Tillage Society II (ACTS)
#211, 2 Athabasca Ave., Sherwood Park AB T8A 4E3
Tel: 780-416-6046; *Fax:* 780-416-8915
e-mail: admin@areca.ab.ca
www.areca.ab.ca/site/acts
Overview: A medium-sized provincial organization founded in 1978
Mission: To protect & enhance soil productivity by promoting environmentally responsible conservation farming systems; to address soil & related water conservation resource concerns including government policy & programming, research, environmental & food safety issues, public awareness, & education; *Member of:* Soil Conservation Council of Canada
Chief Officer(s):
Ty Faechner, Executive Director
Finances: *Annual Operating Budget:* $500,000-$1.5 Million; *Funding Sources:* Government; industry; membership dues
Staff: 1 staff member(s); 16 volunteer(s)
Membership: 400 + 4,000 associate; *Fees:* $30; *Member Profile:* Interest in soil conservation
Activities: Alberta Reduced Tillage Initiative; Reduced Tillage Courses; Direct Seeding Demonstration Days; Farm Tours; *Speaker Service:* Yes; *Rents Mailing List:* Yes; *Library:* Open to public by appointment
Awards:
•Provincial Conservation Farm Family Award (Award)

Alberta Construction Association (ACA)
Parent Name: Canadian Construction Association
18012 - 107 Ave., Edmonton AB T5S 2J5
Tel: 780-455-1122; *Fax:* 780-451-2152
e-mail: info@abconst.org
www.albertaconstruction.net
Overview: A medium-sized provincial organization founded in 1958 overseen by Canadian Construction Association
Chief Officer(s):
Ken Gibson, Executive Director
Shelley Andrea, Director, Administration
Finances: *Funding Sources:* Membership dues
Staff: 120 volunteer(s)
Membership: 1,663
Activities: *Speaker Service:* Yes; *Rents Mailing List:* Yes

Alberta Development Officers Association
PO Box 2232, Stn. Main, Stony Plain AB T7Z 1X7
Tel: 780-913-4214; *Fax:* 780-963-9762
e-mail: admin@adoa.net
www.adoa.net
Overview: A small provincial organization founded in 1984
Chief Officer(s):
Jerry Brett, President
Betty Ann Fountain, Vice-President
Cheryl Callihoo, Secretary
Diane Burtnick, Treasurer
Membership: 301; *Fees:* $75; *Member Profile:* Development Officers from rural & urban municipalities in Alberta; Municipal & independent planners; Engineers; Surveyors
Activities: Establishing a certified training course through the University of Alberta
Meetings/Conferences:
For more information see Trade Shows, Conferences and Seminars Chapter
Alberta Development Officers Association 2013 Conference September 2013 Lac La Biche, AB
Alberta Development Officers Association 2014 Conference 2014, AB
Publications:
•The Communicator [a publication of the Alberta Development Officers Association]
Editor: Carol-Lynn Gilchrist
Profile: Association activities, conferences, training, & articles

Alberta Environmental Network (AEN)
Parent Name: Canadian Environmental Network
PO Box 4541, Edmonton AB T6E 5G4
Tel: 780-757-4872; *Fax:* 866-868-5563
e-mail: admin@aenweb.ca
www.aenweb.ca
twitter.com/ABEnvNet
Overview: A medium-sized provincial organization founded in 1987 overseen by Canadian Environmental Network
Mission: To facilitate communication & cooperation among environmental groups in Alberta in order to contribute to the enhancement & protection of the environment
Chief Officer(s):
Nashina Shariff, Chair
Membership: 70; *Fees:* $30-$200; *Member Profile:* Alberta Environmental NGOs; *Committees:* Clean Air/Energy; Forest; Waste Avoidance/Toxics
Activities: *Rents Mailing List:* Yes

Alberta Falconry Association
22 Chilcotin Way West, Lethbridge AB T1K 7L8
e-mail: info@albertafalconry.com
www.albertafalconry.com
Overview: A small local organization founded in 1965
Mission: In addition to providing guidance for any Alberta resident who is interested in falconry & the care of falcons, the aims of the association are to promote the conservation of raptors and their prey, & to perpetuate the highest standards of the practice.
Chief Officer(s):
Alex Stokes, Contact
Membership: 35; *Fees:* $70; $35 renewal

Alberta Farm Fresh Producers Association (AFFPA)
PO Box 56, Kelsey AB T0B 2K0
Tel: 780-373-2503; *Fax:* 780-373-2297
Toll-Free: 800-661-2642
e-mail: jag@syban.net
www.albertafarmfresh.com
Overview: A small provincial organization
Mission: To develop a sustainable & profitable farm direct marketing industry; To support the production of farm direct market vegetable, berry, & fruit crops, perennials, herbs, flowers, & bedding plants, meat, poulty, & eggs, & other specialty items; To contribute to the health & economic well-being of Albertans
Chief Officer(s):
Jim Hill, President, 403-887-3778, Fax: 403-887-3768
hilljl@telusplanet.net
Nelson Boychuk, Vice-President, 780-398-2123, Fax: 780-398-2123
rrlc@telus.net
Don Gregorwich, Secretary, 780-373-2503, Fax: 780-373-2297
dgregorwich@syban.net
Grace Fedak, Treasurer, 403-934-2412
fedakg@telus.net
Joan Gregorwich, Contact, Administration, 780-373-2503
dgregorwich@syban.net
Membership: 162; *Fees:* $145; *Member Profile:* Agri-preneuers in Alberta
Activities: Promoting the farm direct market industry; Providing educational opportunities, such as courses & workshops; Supporting horticultural research; Collaborating with industry partners & government; Arranging insurance; Branding Alberta products from members; Offering networking opportunities with growers acrossAlberta
Publications:
•Come To Our Farm Guide
Type: Guide; *Price:* Free
Profile: Contact & product information about Alberta Farm Fresh Producers Association members
•Direct Currents [a publication of the Alberta Farm Fresh Producers Association]
Type: Newsletter; *Frequency:* Quarterly; *Accepts Advertising*; *Price:* Free with Alberta Farm Fresh Producers Association membership
Profile: Association updates

Alberta Farmers' Market Association (AFMA)
Parent Name: Farmers' Markets Canada
PO Box 69071, 13040 - 137 Ave., Edmonton AB T5L 5E3
Fax: 780-669-5779
Toll-Free: 866-754-2362
e-mail: info@albertamarkets.com
www.albertamarkets.com
Overview: A small provincial organization founded in 1994 overseen by Farmers' Markets Canada
Mission: To provide direction & support to members; To assist Alberta Approved Farmers' Markets in playing a major role in the establishment of vibrant communities; To advocate for farmers' markets in Alberta; *Member of:* Alberta Farm Fresh Producers Association; Growing Alberta; Dine Alberta; Alberta Association of Agricultural Societies; GO Organic; Affiliation(s): Alberta Farmers' Market Program; Alberta Agriculture & Rural Development; RBC Agencies/The Cooperators; Times Two Gifts & Promotions; Whytespace
Chief Officer(s):
Darlene Cavanaugh, Director, 780-644-5377
director@albertamarkets.com
Becky Lipton, Coordinator, Training & Communications, 780-427-6403
becky@albertamarkets.com
Membership: *Member Profile:* Alberta Approved Farmers' Markets in Alberta; Vendors; Managers; Boards; Sponsors; Persons who support the principles by which farmers' markets operate
Activities: Promoting Alberta's farmers' markets; Providing education for members, such as regional workshops & market manager training; Offering networking opportunities; Funding & establishing surveys; Advising government organizations regarding guidelines for markets; Arranging market & vendor group liability insurance; *Awareness Events:* Alberta Farmers' Market Awareness Week
Publications:
•Market Express
Type: Newsletter; *Frequency:* Quarterly
Profile: Feature articles, recipes, & reports from executive members, committess, & regional directors

Alberta Fish & Game Association (AFGA)
Parent Name: Canadian Wildlife Federation
6924 - 104 St., Edmonton AB T6H 2L7
Tel: 780-437-2342; *Fax:* 780-438-6872
e-mail: office@afga.org
www.afga.org
Overview: A medium-sized provincial organization overseen by Canadian Wildlife Federation
Mission: To ensure fish & wildlife habitat & resources in Alberta
Environmental Activity: Promoting conservation & utilization of fish & wildlife
Chief Officer(s):
Conrad Fennema, President
Martin Sharren, Executive Vice-President
Sandie Buwalda, Coordinator, Programs
Brad Fenson, Coordinator, Habitats
Kerry Grisley, Co-Manager, Operation Grassland Community
Susan Skinner, Co-Manager, Operation Grassland Community
Finances: *Funding Sources:* Membership fees; Donations
Membership: 20,000 members in 100+ clubs; *Fees:* $35 individuals; $55 families; *Committees:* Finance; Environment; Fishing; Hunting; Programs
Activities: Providing educational programs; Liaising with government, industry, & other organizations
Meetings/Conferences:
For more information see Trade Shows, Conferences and Seminars Chapter
Alberta Fish & Game Association 2013 Annual General Meeting 2013, AB

Alberta Fish Farmers Association ***See*** Alberta Aquaculture Association

Alberta Forest Products Association (AFPA)
#500, 10709 Jasper Ave., Edmonton AB T5J 3N3
Tel: 780-452-2841; *Fax:* 780-455-0505
www.albertaforestproducts.ca
Overview: A medium-sized provincial licensing organization founded in 1942
Mission: To represent companies that manufacture forest products throughout Alberta
Environmental Activity: Providing members with services & information in the areas of forestry, the environment, health & safety, transportation, & lumber grading; Increasing public awareness of environmental & social values
Chief Officer(s):
Neil Shelly, Executive Director
Brady Whittaker, President & Chief Executive Officer
Norm Dupuis, Director, Grade Bureau, 780-452-2841 Ext. 235
Brock Mulligan, Director, Communications, 780-452-2841 Ext. 229
Keith Murray, Director, Policy & Regulation, 780-452-2841 Ext. 227

Carola von Sass, Director, Health & Safety, 780-452-2841 Ext. 237
Finances: *Funding Sources:* Membership fees; Sponsorships
Membership: *Member Profile:* Manufacturers of pulp & paper, lumber, panelboard, & secondary manufactured wood products in Alberta
Meetings/Conferences:
For more information see Trade Shows, Conferences and Seminars Chapter
Alberta Forest Products Association 2013 71st Annual General Meeting & Conference
September 2013 Jasper, AB
Alberta Forest Products Association 2014 72nd Annual General Meeting & Conference
2014, AB

Alberta Greenhouse Growers Association (AGGA)
#200, 10331 - 178 St., Edmonton AB T5S 1R5
Tel: 780-489-1991; *Fax:* 780-444-2152
www.agga.ca
Overview: A small provincial organization
Mission: To strengthen the greenhouse growing industry in Alberta; To act as the voice of the industry, in areas such as taxation, natural gas rebates, disaster relief, & electricity costs
Chief Officer(s):
Michiel Verheul, President, 780-939-7490
Albert Cramer, Vice-President, 403-526-3059
Carol Maier, Secretary, 780-467-5784
Dietrich Kuhlmann, Treasurer, 780-475-7500
Membership: *Fees:* $27.30 students; $54.60 associates & individuals; $168 growers; $180.60 allied trades people; $105 new member; *Member Profile:* Growers; Allied trades people; Educators; Students; Individuals with an interest in horticulture
Activities: Promoting the greenhouse growing industry in Alberta; Providing workshops & seminars; Conducting research; Liaising with related organizations, such as the Canadian Horticultural Council & the Alberta Professional Horticultural Growers Congress Foundation; Increasing cooperation; Assisting members in marketing
Publications:
•Alberta Greenhouse Growers Association Newsletter
Type: Newsletter; *Frequency:* Quarterly; *Editor:* Peter Johnston-Berresford
Profile: Association activities, & greenhouse growing industry research, developments, & policy
•Regional Crop Reports

Alberta Historical Resources Foundation (AHRF)
Old St. Stephen's College, 8820 - 112 St., Edmonton AB T6G 2P8
Tel: 780-431-2300; *Fax:* 780-427-5598
culture.alberta.ca/ahrf/default.aspx
Overview: A medium-sized provincial organization founded in 1976
Mission: To assist in the preservation of Alberta's historic sites, buildings & objects; to encourage & promote public awareness of the province's past; grants are awarded in the spring & fall at each year to a wide variety of community-based heritage initiatives
Chief Officer(s):
David Link, Director
david.link@gov.ab.ca
Finances: *Annual Operating Budget:* $3 Million-$5 Million; *Funding Sources:* Alberta Lotteries
Staff: 3 staff member(s)
Membership: *Committees:* Geographical Names
Activities: Alberta Main Street Programme; Heritage Preservation Grants; Heritage Awareness Grants
Awards:
•Roger Soderstrom Scholarship in Historical Preservation (Scholarship)
Encourages professional development & advanced studies in the field of heritage conservation in Alberta; for university students at the graduate level in disciplines relating to heritage preservation & research, focussing on Alberta; includes studies in architectural restoration; area conservation & research preservation planning &/or interpretive development of archaeological, historical or palaeontological sites in the province, as well as related thematic work *Eligibility:* Canadian citizen or landed immigrant & a resident of Alberta for at least six months prior to applying *Deadline:* February & September *Amount:* up to $3,000 *Contact:* Community Resources Officer

Alberta Institute of Agrologists
Parent Name: Agricultural Institute of Canada
#249, 2055 Premier Way, Sherwood Park AB T8H 0G2
Tel: 780-464-9797; *Fax:* 780-464-1171
e-mail: info@aia.ab.ca
www.albertaagrologists.ca
Overview: A small provincial licensing organization founded in 1947 overseen by Agricultural Institute of Canada
Mission: To serves as a regulatory body within the province for matters related to agrology
Chief Officer(s):
Twlya Jones, Chair
David Lloyds, CEO & Registrar
dlloyd@aia.ab.ca
Finances: *Funding Sources:* Membership fees
Membership: 1,500; *Member Profile:* Professional Agrologists (P.Ag.); Articling Agrologists (A.Ag.)
Activities: In-training programs
Meetings/Conferences:
For more information see Trade Shows, Conferences and Seminars Chapter
The Ninth Annual Alberta Institute of Agrologists Banff Conference
March 2013 Banff, AB
Publications:
•AIA [Alberta Institute of Agrologists] Bulletin
Profile: Events of interest to Agrologists
•News Update [a publication of the Alberta Institute of Agrologists]
Type: Newsletter
Profile: Update on Institute issues

Alberta Irrigation Projects Association (AIPA)
#909, 400 - 4 Ave. South, Lethbridge AB T1K 7H5
Tel: 403-328-3063; *Fax:* 403-327-1043
e-mail: info@aipa.org
www.aipa.org
Overview: A medium-sized provincial organization founded in 1946
Mission: To advance understanding of the value of irrigation to Alberta; To promote progressive water management practices; Affiliation(s): Canadian Water Resources Association
Environmental Activity: Ensuring water conservation; Monitoring water quality; Publishing reports on collaborative decision making, conservation, efficiency, & productivity, & the value of water
Chief Officer(s):
Richard Phillips, Chair
Ron McMullin, Executive Director, 403-328-3063, Fax: 403-327-1043
ron.mcmullin@aipa.org
Vicky Kress, Administrator, 403-328-3063, Fax: 403-327-1043
vicky.kress@aipa.org
Membership: *Member Profile:* Incorporated Irrigation Districts in Alberta; Associate members; Honorary members
Activities: Participating in education & outreach activities; Developing policy; Researching; Providing information to federal, provincial, & local government officials, departments & agencies, water management stakeholders, members, the public, & the media; Promoting the benefits of Alberta's irrigations infrastructure; Developing partnerships

Alberta Lake Management Society (ALMS)
PO Box 4283, Edmonton AB T6E 4T3
Tel: 780-702-2567; *Fax:* 501-423-6381
e-mail: info@alms.ca
www.alms.ca
www.facebook.com/176278492417652
twitter.com/AlbertaLake
Also Known As: Lakewatch
Overview: A small provincial charitable organization founded in 1991
Mission: To promote understanding & comprehensive management of lakes & reservoirs & their watersheds; *Member of:* North American Lake Management Society
Chief Officer(s):
Stephanie Neufeld, President
sneufeld@gmail.com
Sheldon Helbert, Vice-President
7shelbert7@gmail.com
Finances: *Annual Operating Budget:* Less than $50,000; *Funding Sources:* Government; workshops
Staff: 16 volunteer(s)
Membership: 100+; *Fees:* $50 associations; $25 individual; $15 student; *Member Profile:* Private citizens; municipalities; government organizations
Activities: Water sampling; conservation & lake management; *Speaker Service:* Yes; *Library:* ALMS Library; by appointment

Alberta Land Surveyors' Association (ALSA)
Parent Name: Professional Surveyors Canada
#1000, 10020 - 101A Ave., Edmonton AB T5J 3G2
Tel: 780-429-8805; *Fax:* 780-429-3374
Toll-Free: 800-665-2572
e-mail: info@alsa.ab.ca
www.alsa.ab.ca
Overview: A medium-sized provincial organization founded in 1910 overseen by Professional Surveyors Canada
Mission: The ALSA is a self-governing professional association which regulates the practice of land surveying.
Chief Officer(s):
Brian Munday, Executive Director
munday@alsa.ab.ca
David McWilliam, Registrar
alsaregistrar@shaw.ca
Brian D. Ross, President
John Haggerty, Secretary-Treasurer
Finances: *Funding Sources:* Membership fees; products
Staff: 9 staff member(s)
Activities: ; *Library:*
Meetings/Conferences:
For more information see Trade Shows, Conferences and Seminars Chapter
Alberta Land Surveyors' Association 2013 Annual General Meeting
April 2013 Jasper, AB
Alberta Land Surveyors' Association 2014 Annual General Meeting
April 2014 Banff, AB

Alberta Medical Association (AMA)
Parent Name: Canadian Medical Association
12230 - 106 Ave. NW, Edmonton AB T5N 3Z1
Tel: 780-482-2626; *Fax:* 780-482-5445
Toll-Free: 800-272-9680
e-mail: amamail@albertadoctors.org
www.albertadoctors.org
Overview: A medium-sized provincial organization founded in 1905 overseen by Canadian Medical Association
Mission: To advocate on behalf of its physician members; to provide leadership & support for their role in the provision of quality health care
Chief Officer(s):
R. Michael Giuffre, President
Michael A. Gormley, Executive Director
michael.gormley@albertadoctors.org
Cameron N. Plitt, Chief Financial Officer
cameron.plitt@albertadoctors.org
Finances: *Annual Operating Budget:* $3 Million-$5 Million
Membership: 4,400
Activities: ; *Library:* Open to public

Alberta Milk
1303 - 91 St. SW, Edmonton AB T6X 1H1
Tel: 780-453-5942; *Fax:* 780-455-2196
Toll-Free: 877-361-1231
e-mail: cblatz@albertamilk.com
www.albertamilk.com
www.facebook.com/MoreAboutMilk
twitter.com/MoreAboutMilk
www.youtube.com/user/albertamilk
Previous Name: Dairy Nutrition Council of Alberta
Overview: A small E organization founded in 2002
Mission: To promote the sustainability of the dairy industry in Alberta; Affiliation(s): Dairy Farmers of Canada
Chief Officer(s):
Bill Feenstra, Chair, 403-335-9290
Gerald Weiss, Executive Director, 403-527-0063
Mike Southwood, General Manager, 780-577-3300
msouthwood@albertamilk.com
Denise Brattinga, Manager, Finance, 780-577-3320
dbrattinga@albertamilk.com
Ray Grapentine, Manager, Industry & Member Services, 780-577-3313
rgrapentine@albertamilk.com
Katherine Loughlin, Manager, Market Development, 780-577-3326
kloughlin@albertamilk.com
Gerd Andres, Manager, Policy & Transportation, 780-577-3308
gandres@albertamilk.com
Membership: *Member Profile:* Milk producers of Alberta; *Committees:* Executive; Animal Health & Environment Advisory; Canadian Milk Supply Management; Corporate Affairs; Dairy Advisory; Dairy Farmers of Canada; Finance; Market Development Advisory; Milk Quality, Component &

Measurement Advisory; Research & Extension Advisory; Transportation Advisory; Western Milk Pool Coordinating
Activities: Providing industry-specific information to producers, such as Canadian Quality Milk & production reports; Offering nutritional & educational resources to the public; Supporting research
Publications:
•Alberta Milk Annual Report
Type: Yearbook; *Frequency:* Annually
•Alberta Milk Producer Handbook
Type: Handbook
•Milking Times
Type: Newsletter; *Frequency:* Monthly; *Accepts Advertising*; *Number of Pages:* 12
Profile: Information for Alberta's dairy producers & their industry partners

Alberta Motor Transport Association (AMTA)
Parent Name: Canadian Trucking Alliance

#1, 285005 Wrangler Way, Rocky View AB T1X 0K3
Fax: 403-243-4610
Toll-Free: 800-267-1003
e-mail: amtamsc@amta.ca
www.amta.ca
Merged from: Alberta Trucking Industry Safety Association; Alberta Trucking Association
Overview: A medium-sized provincial organization overseen by Canadian Trucking Alliance
Mission: To take a leadership role in fostering a healthy, vibrant industry; *Member of:* Canadian Council of Motor Transport Administrators
Chief Officer(s):
Don Wilson, Executive Director, 403-214-3429
Lorri Christensen, Director, Partners in Compliance, 403-214-3430
Peter Vaudry, Director, Corporate Services, 403-214-3438
Kathleen Brown, Administrator, Registration & Certificates, 403-214-3437
William Raccah, Administrator, Program Development, 403-214-3428
Membership: 12,000; *Member Profile:* All sectors of the highway transportation industry; *Committees:* Injury Reduction & Training; Compliance & Regulatory Affairs; Member Services
Meetings/Conferences:
For more information see Trade Shows, Conferences and Seminars Chapter
Alberta Motor Transport Association 2013 Annual General Meeting & Conference
April 2013 Banff, AB

Alberta Native Plant Council (ANPC)

PO Box 52099, Stn. Garneau Postal Outlet, Edmonton AB T6G 2T5
www.anpc.ab.ca
Overview: A small provincial organization founded in 1987
Mission: To increase knowledge of native plants in Alberta among individuals, government, & industry; To conserve Alberta's native plant species
Environmental Activity: Preserving plant species & habitats in Alberta; Supporting legislation to protect native plants; Acting as environmental stewards for important sites around Alberta
Membership: *Fees:* $10 students & seniors; $15 individuals; $25 families; $50 corporate memberships; $500 lifetime memberships; *Member Profile:* Individuals interested in ecology, natural history, conservation, photography, drawing, & hiking; *Committees:* Education & Information; Rare Plants; Reclamation & Horticulture; Conservation Action
Activities: Promoting awareness of native plant issues; Organizing field trips & species counts; Developing collection, salvage, & management guidelines; Providing information about uses for native plants; Awarding grants
Publications:
•Alberta Native Plant Council Guidelines on Plant Recues
•Alberta Native Plant Council Guidelines for Rare Plant Surveys in Alberta
•Alberta Native Plant Council Guidelines for the Purchase & Use of Wildflower Seed Mixes
•Dandelion Recipes: 34 great recipes for salads, jellies, beverages, & appetizers!
•IRIS: The Alberta Native Plant Council Newsletter
Type: Newsletter; *Frequency:* 3-4 pa; *Price:* Free with Alberta Native Plant Council membership
Profile: ANPC activities, articles, & plant happenings
•Plant Collection Guidelines for Horticultural Use of Native Plants
•Plant Collection Guidelines for Researchers, Students, & Consultants
•Plant Collection Guidelines for Wildcrafters

Alberta Natural History Society ***See*** Red Deer River Naturalists

Alberta Organic Producers Association (AOPA)

RR#1, Morinville AB T8R 1P4
Tel: 780-939-5808; *Fax:* 780-939-6738
e-mail: aopa@cruzinternet.com
www.albertaorganicproducers.org
Previous Name: Organic Crop Improvement Association - Alberta Chapter #1
Overview: A small local organization founded in 1990
Affiliation(s): Organic Crop Improvement Association International (OCIA) Inc.
Chief Officer(s):
Sam Godwin, President
samhillent@hotmail.com
Val Schafers, Vice-President, 780-674-4166
Membership: 100-499;; *Fees:* $50; *Member Profile:* Individuals interested in the production, processing, marketing, & consumption of organic products in Alberta
Activities: Offering a certificate to producers who meet the special organic criteria; Providing workshops & seminars
Publications:
•Alberta Organic Producers Association Chapter Binder
Type: Manual
Profile: Information for first time organic producers, with examples of forms & documents
•AOPA [Alberta Organic Producers Association] Newsletter
Type: Newsletter
Profile: Association updates & upcoming events

Alberta Plastics Recycling Association (APRA)

PO Box 56092, #115, 1935 - 32nd Ave. NE, Calgary AB T2E 8K5
Tel: 780-690-3667
e-mail: albertaplastics@gmail.com
www.albertaplasticsrecycling.com
Overview: A medium-sized provincial organization founded in 1991
Mission: To minimize plastic waste to landfill in Alberta; Affiliation(s): Canadian Plastics Industry Association (CPIA)
Environmental Activity: Developing sustainable programs to manage plastics waste
Chief Officer(s):
Grantland M. Cameron, Executive Director
Dave Schwass, President
Otto Parets, Vice-President
Guy West, Secretary-Treasurer
Membership: *Member Profile:* Plastics resin producers; Plastic manufacturers, fabricators, & converters; Packagers & fillers of plastic products; Wholesalers & retailers of plastic products & products in plastics packaging; Plastics recyclers & the recycling community; Industry associations; Interested members of the public
Activities: Collaborating with industry, environmental interest groups, & all levels of government; Providing resources to companies, groups, & individuals
Publications:
•Alberta Plastics Recycling Association News
Type: Newsletter
Profile: Highlights & accomplishments of the Alberta Plastics Recycling Association
•Alberta Post-Consumer Plastics Recycling Strategy, Recycled Plastic Audit
Number of Pages: 36
Profile: An initiative of the Alberta Plastics Recycling Association in partnership with Alberta Environment

Alberta Professional Outfitters Society (APOS)

#103, 6030 - 88 St., Edmonton AB T6E 6G4
Tel: 780-414-0249; *Fax:* 780-465-6801
e-mail: info@apos.ab.ca
www.apos.ab.ca
Previous Name: Professional Outfitters Association of Alberta
Overview: A small provincial organization founded in 1997
Mission: To provide leadership & direction in the continuing development of Alberta's outfitter-hunting industry; strives for long term sustainability in its approach to wildlife management, business opportunities & global competitiveness; Affiliation(s): Safari Club International; Foundation for North American Wild Sheep; Rocky Mountain Elk Foundation
Chief Officer(s):
Glenn Brown, President, 403-443-5718
bluebronna@gmail.com
Vacant, Managing Director
Mabel Brick, Administration Manager
mabel@apos.ab.ca
Finances: *Annual Operating Budget:* $500,000-$1.5 Million
Staff: 3 staff member(s); 30 volunteer(s)
Membership: 400; *Fees:* OG permit $107
Activities: Provides all administrative services to the industry; government liaison; cooperative marketing; disciplinary function

Alberta Public Health Association (APHA)
Parent Name: Canadian Public Health Association

c/o University of Alberta, 4075 RTF, 8308 - 114th St., Edmonton AB T6G 2E1
Tel: 780-492-6014; *Fax:* 780-492-7154
e-mail: info@apha.ab.ca
www.apha.ab.ca
Overview: A medium-sized provincial charitable organization founded in 1943 overseen by Canadian Public Health Association
Mission: To promote & protect the health of the public through advocacy, partnerships, & education
Chief Officer(s):
Cathy Gladwin, Contact, 780-492-9218
cgladwin@ualberta.ca
Finances: *Annual Operating Budget:* $100,000-$250,000; *Funding Sources:* Membership dues; conferences; charitable donations; grants
Staff: 15 volunteer(s)
Membership: 300; *Fees:* $50 regular; student/retired $22; *Member Profile:* Public health practitioners; professionals from NGOs; educators, government & citizens interested in advocating for, promoting & protecting the health of the public; *Committees:* Conference; Program; Communications; Membership

Alberta Recreation & Parks Association (ARPA)
Parent Name: Canadian Parks & Recreation Association

11759 Groat Rd., Edmonton AB T5M 3K6
Tel: 780-415-1745; *Fax:* 780-451-7915
Toll-Free: 877-544-1747
e-mail: arpa@arpaonline.ca
arpaonline.ca
www.facebook.com/arpaonline; twitter.com/#!/arpaonline
Overview: A medium-sized provincial charitable organization overseen by Canadian Parks & Recreation Association
Mission: To promote accessibility to recreation & parks & their benefits to Albertans; To work toward economic sustainability, natural resource protection, & conservation within provincial parks & natural environments
Environmental Activity: Working to build healthy environments & citizens throughout Alberta
Chief Officer(s):
Rick Curtis, Executive Director, 780-415-1745
rcurtis@arpaonline.ca
Steve Allan, Manager, Finance & Operations
sallan@arpaonline.ca
Shelley Shea, President
shelley.shea@calgary.ca
Carol Petersen, Manager, Recreation & Community Development
cpetersen@arpaonline.ca
Terry Welsh, Secretary
twelsh@brooks.ca
Judi Frank, Treasurer
judfra@medicinehat.ca
Lisa Tink, Manager, Children & Youth Programs
ltink@arpaonline.ca
Mandi Wise, Coordinator, Communications
mwise@arpaonline.ca
Membership: 1,300+; *Member Profile:* Students; Municipal elected officials, staff, volunteers & stakeholders; Business staff, suppliers & clients; Eductional institution staff; Non-profit association & government agency elected officials, staff, volunteers & stakeholders; Individuals interested in or working in areas of recreation, parks, leisure, & tourism
Activities: Providing leadership to Alberta's recreation & parks industry; Facilitating communication & information networking; Maximizing human & financial resources for recreation & parks services; Establishing relations with the provincial government; Advocating recreational safety, fair play & gender equity; Increasing public awareness of recreation & active lifestyles; Monitoring development of formal post-secondary educational opportunities for recreation & parks; Research & preparing position papers on various issues; *Awareness Events:* Recreation & Parks Month, June; Communities in Bloom; Community Choosewell Challenge

Meetings/Conferences:
For more information see Trade Shows, Conferences and Seminars Chapter
Alberta Recreation & Parks Association 2013 Annual Conference & Energize Workshop & IFPRA World Congress
October 2013 Lake Louise, AB
Alberta Recreation & Parks Association 2013 Parks Forum
March 2013 Canmore, AB
Alberta Recreation & Parks Association 2014 Biennial Youth Development Through Recreation Services Symposium
2014 Banff, AB
Alberta Recreation & Parks Association 2015 Parks Forum
2015, AB
Publications:
•Alberta Recreation & Parks Association Recreation Buyers Guide
Type: Booklet; *Accepts Advertising*
Profile: Advertisements with contact information
•REConnect [a publication of the Alberta Recreation & Parks Association]
Type: Newsletter; *Frequency:* Monthly
Profile: News about recreation & parks related issues in Alberta

Alberta Registered Professional Foresters Association *See* College of Alberta Professional Foresters

Alberta Rural Municipal Administrators Association
6027 - 4th St. NE, Calgary AB T2K 4Z5
Tel: 403-275-0622; *Fax:* 403-275-8179
www.armaa.ca
Overview: A medium-sized provincial organization founded in 1922
Chief Officer(s):
Valerie Schmaltz, Sec.-Treas.
Ross Rawlusyk, President
Finances: *Annual Operating Budget:* Less than $50,000; *Funding Sources:* Membership dues; grant
Membership: 95; *Fees:* $120; *Member Profile:* Rural municipal administrator; *Committees:* Various Ad Hoc
Meetings/Conferences:
For more information see Trade Shows, Conferences and Seminars Chapter
Alberta Rural Municipal Administrators' Association 2013 Conference
September 2013 Lethbridge, AB

Alberta Safety Council
4831 - 93 Ave. NW, Edmonton AB T6B 3A2
Tel: 780-462-7300; *Fax:* 780-462-7318
Toll-Free: 800-301-6407
e-mail: info@safetycouncil.ab.ca
www.safetycouncil.ab.ca
www.facebook.com/group.php?gid=189043441145255
Overview: A medium-sized provincial organization founded in 1946
Mission: To create awareness & provide educational & training programs to citizens of Alberta on how to maintain a safe environment at home, in traffic, at work & at play; Affiliation(s): Canada Safety Council; National Safety Council; Safety Services Canada
Chief Officer(s):
Laurie Billings, Executive Director
Finances: *Annual Operating Budget:* $1.5 Million-$3 Million
Staff: 12 staff member(s); 100 volunteer(s)
Membership: 280; *Fees:* $195 corporate/group; $50 individual; *Member Profile:* Companies, organizations, agencies which promote safety
Activities: *Speaker Service:* Yes; *Library:* Open to public

Alberta Society of Engineering Technologists *See* Association of Science & Engineering Technology Professionals of Alberta

Alberta Society of Petroleum Geologists *See* Canadian Society of Petroleum Geologists

Alberta Society of Professional Biologists (ASPB)
PO Box 21104, Edmonton AB T6R 2V4
Tel: 780-434-5765; *Fax:* 780-413-0076
e-mail: pbiol@aspb.ab.ca
www.aspb.ab.ca
Overview: A medium-sized provincial organization founded in 1975
Mission: To promote excellence in the practice of biology; To provide a voice for professional biologists in Alberta
Chief Officer(s):
P. Ross Bradford, Executive Director, 780-469-6196
Executivedirector@aspb.ab.ca
Robin Leech, Executive Director
releech@telusplanet.net
Bette Beswick, Registrar, 403-560-4357
bette_beswick@golder.com
Carol Engstrom, President
carol.engstrom@huskyenergy.ca
Gary Ash, Treasurer
gash@golder.com
Monika Burak, Coordinator, Finance, 780-434-5765
monika@managewise.ca
Shauna Prokopchuk, Coordinator, Membership & Communications, 780-434-5765
shauna@managewise.ca
Joy Sager, Coordinator, Association & Events, 780-434-5765
joy@managewise.ca
Membership: *Fees:* $25 student biologists; $50 biologists in training; $250 professional biologists; *Member Profile:* Persons from all disciplines of biology, such as aquatic biology, botany, ecology, genetics, biotechnology, entomology, physiology, & zoology; Student biologists; *Committees:* Discipline, Practice Review; Communications
Activities: Upholding the code of ethics; Organizing seminars for practitioners; Offering a mentorship program
Meetings/Conferences:
For more information see Trade Shows, Conferences and Seminars Chapter
Alberta Society of Professional Biologists 2013 Annual Conference & General Meeting
April 2013 Calgary, AB
Alberta Society of Professional Biologists 2014 Annual Conference & General Meeting
April 2014 Edmonton, AB
Publications:
•BIOS [a publication of the Alberta Society of Professional Biologists]
Type: Newsletter; *Frequency:* 3 pa; *Editor:* Linda Zimmerling (lindazim@shaw.ca)
Profile: Articles to inform & educate members of the society & the public

Alberta Society of Surveying & Mapping Technologies (ASSMT)
PO Box 68168, 28 Crowfoot Terrace NW, Calgary AB T3G 3N8
Tel: 403-214-7504
e-mail: manager@assmt.ab.ca
www.assmt.ab.ca
Overview: A medium-sized provincial organization founded in 1970
Mission: To promote the knowledge, skill & proficiency of technicians & technologists involved in the field of surveying & mapping in Alberta; Affiliation(s): Alberta Land Surveyors' Association
Chief Officer(s):
Ray Heilman, President
president@assmt.ab.ca
Finances: *Annual Operating Budget:* Less than $50,000
Staff: 1 staff member(s); 15 volunteer(s)
Membership: 30 student; 250 individual; 10 associate; *Fees:* $75 individual; $40 associate; students free; *Committees:* Legislation; Education; Membership; Publication; Nominating
Activities: Regional meetings; Annual general meeting; certification

Alberta Special Waste Services Association *See* Environmental Services Association of Alberta

Alberta Speleological Society (ASS)
c/o Andrea Corlett, #1606 924 - 14 Ave. SW, Calgary AB T2R 0N7
e-mail: info@caving.ab.ca
www.caving.ab.ca
Overview: A medium-sized provincial organization founded in 1968
Mission: To promote cave conservation; To facilitate cave explorations, primarily in the Canadian Rockies, with some activities throughout Western Canada & internationally; *Member of:* Federation of Alberta Naturalists
Chief Officer(s):
Jeremy Burns, President
Finances: *Funding Sources:* Membership fees
Activities: ; *Library:* Open to public by appointment
Meetings/Conferences:
For more information see Trade Shows, Conferences and Seminars Chapter
Alberta Speleological Society 2013 Semi-Annual General Meeting
June 2013, AB
Alberta Speleological Society 2013 Weymerfest
July 2013 Tahsis, BC
Alberta Speleological Society 2013 Annual General Meeting
2013, AB
Publications:
•Journal of Subterranean Metaphysics
Type: Newsletter; *Frequency:* Quarterly
Profile: A publication in both paper & digital formats, with articles about exploration, as well as society administrative information & event announcements

Alberta Sulphur Research Ltd. (ASRL)
Center for Applied Catalysts & Industrial Sulfur Chemistry, #6, 3535 Research Rd. NW, Calgary AB T2L 2K8
Tel: 403-220-5346; *Fax:* 403-284-2054
e-mail: asrinfo@ucalgary.ca
www.chem.ucalgary.ca/asr
Overview: A small international organization founded in 1964
Mission: Provides technological support for producers & users of sulfur; research & technology training through seminars & courses; provides contact between industry & academia for applied catalysis & industrial sulfur chemistry; examination of the chemistry & technology of sulfur & its compunds; emphasis on research relevant to sour gas, sulfur & refining industries; Affiliation(s): Chemistry Dept., Univ. of Calgary
Chief Officer(s):
Richard Surprenant, President & Chair
Terry Crooks, CFO & Treasurer
Finances: *Annual Operating Budget:* $500,000-$1.5 Million; *Funding Sources:* Membership research contributions
Staff: 21 staff member(s)
Membership: 62; *Member Profile:* Sulphur producers & users; *Committees:* Technical Advisory; Finance; Executive
Activities: ; *Library:* Open to public by appointment
Publications:
•ASRL Alberta Sulphur Research Ltd.] Board Newsletter
Type: Newsletter

Alberta Underwater Council (AUC)
Percy Page Building, 11759 Groat Rd., 2nd Fl., Edmonton AB T5M 3K6
Tel: 780-427-9125; *Fax:* 780-427-8139
Toll-Free: 888-307-8566
e-mail: info@albertaunderwatercouncil.com
www.albertaunderwatercouncil.com
www.facebook.com/?sk=2361831622
Overview: A medium-sized local organization founded in 1962
Mission: To represent responsible participation in & awareness of underwater activities; Affiliation(s): Canadian Federation of Underwater Activities; Alberta Underwater Archaeology Society; Canadian Underwater Games Association
Environmental Activity: Preserving the aquatic environment; Participating in lake clean-up
Chief Officer(s):
Cathie McCuaig, Executive Director, 780-427-9125, Fax: 780-427-8139
Finances: *Funding Sources:* Alberta Gaming; Alberta Sport Recreation Parks & Wildlife Foundation
Membership: 600 individual; *Fees:* $15
Activities: *Awareness Events:* Divescapes

Alberta Urban Municipalities Association (AUMA)
#300, 8616 15 Ave., Edmonton AB T6E 6E6
Tel: 780-433-4431; *Fax:* 780-433-4454
Toll-Free: 800-310-2862
e-mail: main@auma.ca
www.auma.ca
twitter.com/theauma
Overview: A medium-sized provincial organization founded in 1905
Mission: To provide leadership in advocating local government interests to the provincial government & other organizations, & to provide services that address the needs of its membership
Chief Officer(s):
John McGowan, CEO
jmcgowan@auma.ca
Finances: *Funding Sources:* Membership dues
Staff: 23 staff member(s)
Membership: 284 municipalities; *Fees:* $474 + GST affiliate/associate; *Committees:* 15 Committees & Task Forces
Activities: *Rents Mailing List:* Yes; *Library:*
Meetings/Conferences:
For more information see Trade Shows, Conferences and

Seminars Chapter
Alberta Urban Municipalities Association Convention & AMSC Trade Show 2013
November 2013 Calgary, AB
Alberta Urban Municipalities Association Convention & AMSC Trade Show 2014
September 2014 Edmonton, AB
Alberta Urban Municipalities Association Convention & AMSC Trade Show 2015
September 2015 Calgary, AB
Alberta Urban Municipalities Association Convention & AMSC Trade Show 2016
October 2016 Edmonton, AB

Alberta Water & Wastewater Operators Association (AWWOA)

11810 Kingsway Ave., Edmonton AB T5G 0X5
Tel: 780-454-7745; *Fax:* 780-454-7748
Toll-Free: 877-454-7745
e-mail: awwoa@telus.net
www.awwoa.ab.ca
www.facebook.com/group.php?gid=157981630910194
twitter.com/awwoa
Overview: A small provincial organization founded in 1976
Mission: To contribute to the training & upgrading of persons employed in the water & wastewater field in Alberta; To encourage the best possible operation of water & wastewater facilities; Affiliation(s): Western Canada Water & Wastewater Association
Environmental Activity: Sponsoring Alberta Environment training programs
Chief Officer(s):
John Voyer, Executive Director, Fax: 780-451-6451
awwoa1@telus.net
Cathie Monson, Coordinator, Training Program, Fax: 780-454-7748
awwoa@telus.net
Laura Selcho, Training Course Registrar, Fax: 780-454-7758
awwoa2@telus.net
Activities: Providing manuals to operators
Awards:
•Alberta Water & Wastewater Operators Association Outreach Student Applicant Bursaries (Scholarship)
Available to students entering the Water & Wastewater Technician program at the Northern Alberta Institute of Technology *Eligibility:* Applicant must provide a copy of the Alberta Enviornment approved course completion certificate *Amount:* $300 *Contact:* AWWOA Outreach Student Bursaries, Address: 11810 Kingway Ave., Edmonton, AB T5G 0X5
•Alberta Water & Wastewater Operators Association Steve Blonsky Honorary Life Membership Award (Award)
For persons retired from the water or sewage field *Deadline:* October *Contact:* Kathy Abramowski, Awards Chair, Phone: 780-427-5204; E-mail: Kathy.Abramowski@gov.ab.ca
•Alberta Water & Wastewater Operators Association NAIT Achievement Award (Award)
Eligibility: The student enrolled in the Northern Alberta Institute of Technology's full time Water & Wastewater Technician Program, who achieves the highest marks *Amount:* $500
•Alberta Water & Wastewater Operators Association Operator of the Year Award (Award)
Eligibility: A member in good standing of the Alberta Water & Wastewater Operators Association who has provided exemplary service to the water or wastewater operations field over an extended period of time *Deadline:* January *Contact:* Kathy Abramowski, Awards Chair, Phone: 780-427-5204; E-mail: Kathy.Abramowski@gov.ab.ca
•Alberta Water & Wastewater Operators Association Ron Bayne Service Award (Award)
To recognize outstanding service to the Alberta Water & Wastewater Operators Association & contribution to the water & wastewater operartions field *Deadline:* January *Contact:* Kathy Abramowski, Awards Chair, Phone: 780-427-5204; E-mail: Kathy.Abramowski@gov.ab.ca
•Alberta Water & Wastewater Operators Association NAIT North Scholarship (Scholarship)
To honour academically outstanding individuals who have made significant contributions in extracurricular or community activities *Eligibility:* Registration in the full-time Water & Wastewater Technician program at the Edmonton Campus of the Northern Alberta Institute of Technology *Amount:* $3,000 *Contact:* Alberta Water & Wastewater Operators Assn, 11810 Kingsway Ave., Edmonton, AB, T5G 0X5
•Alberta Water & Wastewater Operators Association NAIT South Scholarship (Scholarship)
To recognize academic credentials, personal leadership activities, excellence in extracurricular activities, & notable contributions to the community *Eligibility:* Registration in the full-time Water & Wastewater Technician program at the Calgary Campus of the Northern Alberta Institute of Technology *Amount:* $3,000 *Contact:* Alberta Water & Wastewater Operators Assn, 11810 Kingsway Ave., Edmonton, AB, T5G 0X5
Meetings/Conferences:
For more information see Trade Shows, Conferences and Seminars Chapter
Alberta Water & Wastewater Operators Association 2013 Pre-Seminar Workshops
March 2013 Banff, AB
Alberta Water & Wastewater Operators Association 2013 38th Annual Operators Seminar
March 2013 Banff, AB
Alberta Water & Wastewater Operators Association 2014 39th Annual Operators Seminar
2014, AB
Publications:
•Alberta Utility Operator Newsletter
Type: Newsletter; *Frequency:* 3 pa; *Editor:* Gayle Sacuta
Profile: Information about Alberta's water & wastewater operations, outstanding service, new technologies, research, regulatory changes, & trainingopportunities

Alberta Water Council

Petroleum Plaza, South Tower, #1400, 9915 - 108 St., Edmonton AB T5K 2G8
Tel: 780-644-7380
www.albertawatercouncil.ca
Overview: A medium-sized provincial organization
Mission: The Alberta Water Council is a stakeholder partnership that provides leadership, expertise and advocacy, to engage and empower individuals, organizations, business and governments to achieve the outcomes of the Water for Life strategy.
Chief Officer(s):
Gord Edwards, Executive Director
g.edwards@awchome.ca
Membership: 24 institutional

Alberta Water Well Drilling Association (AWWDA) Parent Name: Canadian Ground Water Association

PO Box 130, Lougheed AB T0B 2V0
Tel: 780-386-2335; *Fax:* 780-386-2344
e-mail: awwda@telusplanet.net
www.awwda.com
Overview: A medium-sized provincial organization founded in 1958 overseen by Canadian Ground Water Association
Mission: The AWWDA is a non-profit, non-sectarian organization with certain objectives including: assisting, promoting, encouraging, and supporting the interest and welfare of the water well industry in all of its phases; fostering aid and promote scientific education, standard research, and technique in order to improve methods of well construction and development and advance the science of groundwater in the province of Alberta.
Chief Officer(s):
Brad Meyers, Secretary Manager, 403-938-4961, Fax: 403-938-3324
aarondrill@telus.net

Alberta Wilderness Association (AWA)

PO Box 6398, Stn. D, 455 - 12 St. NW, Calgary AB T2N 1Y9
Tel: 403-283-2025; *Fax:* 403-270-2743
Toll-Free: 866-313-0713
e-mail: awa@shaw.ca
albertawilderness.ca
www.facebook.com/AlbertaWilderness
twitter.com/ABWilderness
www.youtube.com/user/AlbertaWilderness
Overview: A large provincial charitable organization founded in 1965
Mission: To promote the protection of Alberta's rivers & wildlands areas; To restore the natural ecosystems of Alberta; To educate Albertans on wilderness conservation & sustainable use of natural lands & waters; *Member of:* Alberta Environment Network; Environmental Law Centre; Calgary & Area Outdoor Council; Volunteer Centre of Calgary; Affiliation(s): Environmental Resource Centre
Chief Officer(s):
Richard Secord, President
Christyann Olson, Executive Director
awa@abwild.ca
Finances: *Annual Operating Budget:* $250,000-$500,000; *Funding Sources:* Provincial grants; Fundraising events; Membership fees; Donations
Staff: 4 staff member(s); 250 volunteer(s)
Membership: 2,500 individual + 110 organizations; *Fees:* $25 single; $30 family
Activities: Researching wilderness issues; *Awareness Events:* Climb & Run for Wilderness, April; *Speaker Service:* Yes; *Library:* Wilderness Resource Centre; Open to public
Publications:
•Bighorn Wildland [a publication of the Alberta Wilderness Association]
Type: Book; *ISBN:* 0-920074-20-0
•Elbow Sheep Wilderness [a publication of the Alberta Wilderness Association]
Type: Book
•Recall of the Wild [a publication of the Alberta Wilderness Association]
Profile: A supplement to the Wild Lands Advocate
•Rivers on Borrowed Time [a publication of the Alberta Wilderness Association]
Type: Book
•Wild Lands Advocate [a publication of the Alberta Wilderness Association]
Type: Journal; *Frequency:* 6 pa.; *Editor:* Ian Urquhart
•Willmore Wilderness Park [a publication of the Alberta Wilderness Association]
Type: Book

Aldergrove Daylily Society

24642 - 51 Ave., Langley BC V2Z 1H9
Tel: 604-856-5758
e-mail: pamela1@istar.ca
www.distinctly.on.ca/chs/aldergrove.html
Overview: A small local organization founded in 1991
Chief Officer(s):
Pam Erikson, President
Membership: *Fees:* $10 individual; $15 family

Algoma Manitoulin Environmental Awareness (AMEA)

RR#1, Kagawong ON P0P 1J0
Tel: 705-282-2886
Overview: A small local organization
Mission: To encourage participation in envionmental matters in the Algoma Manitoulin region of Ontario; *Member of:* Ontario Clean Air Alliance
Environmental Activity: Engaging in advocacy activities related to environmental issues

AllerGen NCE Inc.

Michael DeGroote Centre for Learning & Discovery, McMaster University, #3120, 1200 Main St. West, Hamilton ON L8N 2A5
Tel: 905-525-9140; *Fax:* 905-524-0611
e-mail: info@allergen-nce.ca
www.allergen-nce.ca
Overview: A medium-sized national organization founded in 2004
Mission: To support research, capacity building activities, & networking regarding allergic disease in Canada; To reduce the morbidity, mortality & socio-economic impacts of allergy, asthma, & related immune diseases
Environmental Activity: Conducting research programs in the areas of gene-environment interactions, diagnostics & therapeutics, & public health, ethics, policy, & society
Chief Officer(s):
Judah Denburg, CEO & Scientific Director, 905-525-9140 Ext. 26502
Diana Royce, Chief Operating Officer & Managing Director, 905-525-9140 Ext. 26502
Mark Mitchell, Manager, Research & Partnerships, 905-525-9140 Ext. 26092
Marta Rudyk, Manager, Communications & Coordinator, Knowledge Mobilization, 905-525-9140 Ext. 26641
Allison Brown, Coordinator, Research, 905-525-9140 Ext. 26553
Michelle Harkness, Coordinator, Highly Qualified Personnel & Events, 905-525-9140 Ext. 26633
Finances: *Funding Sources:* Government of Canada, through the Networks of Centres of Excellence (NCE) Program
Meetings/Conferences:
For more information see Trade Shows, Conferences and Seminars Chapter
AllerGen NCE Inc. 2013 8th Annual Conference
2013
AllerGen NCE Inc. 2013 Scientific Meeting
June 2013 King City, ON

Publications:
•Agenda [a publication of AllerGen NCE Inc.]
Type: Newsletter
Profile: An overview of research, training, partnerships, & networking
•AirWays [a publication of AllerGen NCE Inc.]
Type: Newsletter
Profile: News about training & professional development opportunities
•AllerGen NCE Inc. Annual Report
Type: Yearbook; *Frequency:* Annually
Profile: Highlights of the year & a financial overview
•AllerGen Network Newsletter
Type: Newsletter; *Frequency:* Quarterly
Profile: Information about the management of the network for board & committee members & investigators
•ReAction [a publication of AllerGen NCE Inc.]
Type: Newsletter
Profile: Partnership, training, & networking opportunities

Allergie Asthme association d'information ***See*** Allergy Asthma Information Association

Allergy & Environmental Health Association ***See*** Environmental Health Association of Ontario

Allergy Asthma Information Association (AAIA) / Allergie Asthme association d'information
#118, 295 The West Mall, Toronto ON M9C 4Z4
Tel: 416-621-4571; *Fax:* 416-621-5034
Toll-Free: 800-611-7011
e-mail: admin@aaia.ca
www.aaia.ca
www.facebook.com/AllergyAsthmaInformationAssociation
Overview: A large national charitable organization founded in 1964
Mission: To create a safer environment for Canadians with allergies, asthma, & anaphylaxis; To assist persons coping with allergies; To act as a national voice for individuals affected by allergy, asthma, & anaphylaxis; Affiliation(s): Canadian Society of Allergy & Immunology
Chief Officer(s):
Sharon Van Gyzen, Chair
Mary Allen, CEO
quebec@aaia.ca
Louis Isabella, Treasurer
Finances: *Funding Sources:* Donations; Corporate partnerships
Membership: *Fees:* $35/one year; $60/two years
Activities: Providing education; Raising money for research; Working with related organizations, government, & the food industry; Engaging in advocacy activities; Offering food allergy summer camps; *Awareness Events:* Walk to Axe Anaphylaxis
Publications:
•Allergy Asthma Information Association Newsletter
Type: Newsletter; *Frequency:* Quarterly
Profile: Information for persons affected by allergy, asthma, & anaphylaxis

AAIA Atlantic
70 Snowy Owl Dr., Bedford NS B4A 3L3
Tel: 902-835-1344
Toll-Free: 888-453-0088
e-mail: atlantic@aaia.ca
Chief Officer(s):
Ruth Roberts, Regional Coordinator

AAIA BC/Yukon
4730 Redridge Rd., Kelowna BC V1W 3A6
Tel: 250-764-7507; *Fax:* 250-764-7587
Toll-Free: 877-500-2242
e-mail: bc@aaia.ca
Chief Officer(s):
Yvonne Rousseau, Regional Coordinator

AAIA Ontario
30 Patton St., Collingwood ON L9Y 0E4
Tel: 705-444-0477; *Fax:* 705-445-7054
Toll-Free: 888-250-2298
e-mail: ontario@aaia.ca
Chief Officer(s):
Monika Gibson, Regional Coordinator

AAIA Prairies/NWT
16531 - 114 St., Edmonton AB T5X 3V6
Tel: 780-456-6651; *Fax:* 780-456-6651
Toll-Free: 866-456-6651
e-mail: prairies@aaia.ca
Chief Officer(s):
Lilly Byrtus, Regional Coordinator

AAIA Québec
172, rue Andover, Beaconsfield QC H9W 2Z8
Tel: 514-694-0679; *Fax:* 514-694-9814
Toll-Free: 866-694-0679
e-mail: quebec@aaia.ca
Chief Officer(s):
Mary Allen, Regional Coordinator

Allergy, Asthma & Immunology Society of Ontario
2 Demaris Ave., Toronto ON M3N 1M1
Tel: 416-633-2215
e-mail: inquiry@allergyasthma.on.ca
www.allergyasthma.on.ca
Previous Name: Ontario Allergy Society
Overview: A small provincial organization founded in 1958
Mission: To strive to provide high quality medical services to the public, through consultation by referral from other physicians, as well as through public service education
Membership: *Member Profile:* Practicing physicians
Activities: *Speaker Service:* Yes

Alliance agricole du Nouveau-Brunswick ***See*** Agricultural Alliance of New Brunswick

Alliance animale du Canada ***See*** Animal Alliance of Canada

L'Alliance canadienne des victimes d'accidents et de maladies du travail ***See*** Canadian Injured Workers Alliance

L'Alliance canadienne du camionnage ***See*** Canadian Trucking Alliance

Alliance de l'industrie canadienne de l'aquiculture ***See*** Canadian Aquaculture Industry Alliance

Alliance for Sustainability
Hillel Centre, 1521 University Ave. SE, Minneapolis MN 55414 USA
Tel: 612-331-1099; *Fax:* 612-379-9004
e-mail: iasa@mtn.org
www.afors.org
Also Known As: International Alliance for Sustainable Agriculture
Overview: A medium-sized international charitable organization founded in 1983
Mission: Supporting ecologically sound, economically viable, socially just & humane projects on a personal, organizational & planetary level
Chief Officer(s):
Sean Gosiewski, Program Director
sean@allianceforsustainabilty.com
Finances: *Annual Operating Budget:* Less than $50,000; *Funding Sources:* Membership; foundations; donors; corporations; religious groups; fundraising; revenue from public speaking, sale of publications, shirts, & buttons
Staff: 1 staff member(s); 5 volunteer(s)
Membership: 800; *Fees:* $25; *Member Profile:* Farmers; consumers; business & government leaders; environmentalists; educators & scientists
Activities: Natural Step Network meetings; introductory presentations; slide shows; seminars; support projects overseas; *Internships:* Yes; *Speaker Service:* Yes; *Library:* Sustainability Resource Center; Open to public

Alliance for the Wild Rockies (AWR)
PO Box 505, Helena MT 59624 USA
Tel: 406-459-5936
e-mail: awr@wildrockiesalliance.org
www.wildrockiesalliance.org
www.facebook.com/148406678172
twitter.com/awr_nrepa
www.myspace.com/awrnrepa
Overview: A medium-sized international organization founded in 1988
Mission: To protect wildlands & wildlife habitat in the Wild Rockies Bioregion, containing parts of Alberta, British Columbia, Montana, Idaho, Wyoming, Oregon, Washington; to protect threatened, endangered & sensitive species; to promote sound ecosystem protection & sustainable economic development; to promote ecosystem-based land management based on scientific principles
Chief Officer(s):
Gary Macfarlane, President
Finances: *Annual Operating Budget:* $250,000-$500,000; *Funding Sources:* Membership dues; fundraising; donations; foundations
Staff: 2 staff member(s); 10 volunteer(s)
Membership: 3,500 individual + 1,000 organizational; *Fees:* (USD) Habitat Sponsor: $25; Watershed Sponsor: $50; Ecosystem Sponsor: $100; Bioregion Sponsor: $1000
Activities: *Internships:* Yes; *Library:* Ecosystem Defense; Open to public

Alliance of Foam Packaging Recyclers (AFPR)
#201, 1298 Cronson Blvd., Crofton MD 21114 USA
Tel: 410-451-8340; *Fax:* 410-451-8343
e-mail: info@epscentral.org
www.epspackaging.org
Overview: A small international organization founded in 1991
Mission: To provide leadership to the EPS foam packaging industry through activities that promote the development of recycling; To maintain a network for the collection, reprocessing, & reuse of foam packaging; *Member of:* Institute of Packaging Professionals
Finances: *Funding Sources:* Manufacturers of expanded polystyrene packaging
Membership: 45; *Fees:* $1,000-$36,000

Alliance of Manufacturers & Exporters Canada ***See*** Canadian Manufacturers & Exporters

Alouette Field Naturalists (AFN)
12554 Grace St., Maple Ridge BC V2X 5N2
Tel: 604-463-8743
Overview: A small local organization founded in 1973
Mission: To promote the enjoyment of nature through environmental appreciation & conservation; To encourage wise use & conservation of natural resources & environmental protection; *Member of:* Federation of BC Naturalists
Membership: 30-35; *Fees:* $16-30; *Committees:* Pitt Polder Preservation Society; Blue Mountain-Kanata Creek Conservation Committee
Activities: Rivers Day, Nature Day, with displays; hiking, camping, birding, botanizing, mycologizing; *Awareness Events:* Earth Day, April; Annual Christmas Bird Count, December

Alpine Garden Club of BC
c/o 14776 - 90th Ave., Surrey BC V3R 1A4
Tel: 604-580-3219
www.agc-bc.ca
Overview: A small local organization
Mission: To promote the propagation & display of plants suitable for the alpine garden & alpine house, rare & unusual species of hardy plants, trees, shrubs & ferns, plants suitable for the art of bonsai; to promote an interest in the native plants of British Columbia & their preservation; *Member of:* North American Rock Garden Society
Chief Officer(s):
Linda Verbeek, President, 604-526-6656
Membership: 500; *Fees:* $25
Activities: Seed exchange; open gardens; field trips; plants sales; *Library:* Open to public
Publications:
•The Bulletin
Type: Newsletter; *Frequency:* Quarterly

The Aluminum Association
#600, 1525 Wilson Blvd., Arlington VA 22209 USA
Tel: 703-358-2960; *Fax:* 703-358-2961
www.aluminum.org
www.facebook.com/AluminumAssociation?v=wall
www.twitter.com/AluminumNews
Previous Name: Aluminum Recycling Association
Overview: A small national organization
Mission: To enhance aluminum's position in a world of proliferating materials, increase its use as the "material of choice" remove impediments to its fullest use & assist in achieving the industry's environmental, societal, & economic objectives
Chief Officer(s):
Heidi Biggs Brock, President
hbrock@aluminum.org
Membership: *Member Profile:* Producers of primary aluminum, recyclers & semi-fabricated aluminum products, as well as suppliers to the industry

Aluminum Recycling Association ***See*** The Aluminum Association

Amalgamated Conservation Society (ACS)
PO Box 8741, Victoria BC V8W 3S3
Tel: 250-382-8502
acsbc.ca

Previous Name: Amalgamated Lower Islands Sportsmen's Association
Overview: A small local organization founded in 1963
Mission: To promote the conservation of fish, game & natural resources; To provide the machinery necessary to put up a united front to combat any program by which the democratic rights of individuals may be threatened; To provide a permanent council through which such joint action may be directed
Chief Officer(s):
Charles Nisbet, President
Wayne Zaccarelli, Sec.-Treas., 250-391-1844
Finances: *Annual Operating Budget:* Less than $50,000; *Funding Sources:* Donations; government grants
Staff: 3 volunteer(s)
Membership: 8 organizations representing 3,000 individuals; *Fees:* $30; *Member Profile:* Membership restricted to associations with similar objectives; *Committees:* Projects
Activities: Salmonid Enhancement Projects; *Speaker Service:* Yes

Amalgamated Construction Association of British Columbia *See* Vancouver Regional Construction Association

Amalgamated Lower Islands Sportsmen's Association *See* Amalgamated Conservation Society

American Association for the Advancement of Science (AAAS)

1200 New York Ave. NW, Washington DC 20005 USA
Tel: 202-326-6440
e-mail: membership@aaas.org
www.aaas.org
Overview: A large national organization founded in 1848
Mission: To advance science, engineering, & innovation around the world to benefit all people; To provide a voice for science on societal issues; Affiliation(s): 262 affiliated societies & academies of science
Chief Officer(s):
Nina V. Fedoroff, Chair
Phillip A. Sharp, President
Alan I. Leshner, Chief Executive Officer
David E. Shaw, Treasurer
Membership: *Member Profile:* Open to all
Activities: Offering international programs; Providing science education; Publishing books & reports; Promoting the integrity of science & its responsible use in public policy; Facilitating communication among scientists, engineers, & the public; Raising public engagement with science & technology
Meetings/Conferences:
For more information see Trade Shows, Conferences and Seminars Chapter
American Association for the Advancement of Science 2013 Annual Meeting: The Beauty & Benefits of Science
February 2013 Boston, MA
American Association for the Advancement of Science 2014 Annual Meeting
February 2014 Chicago, IL
American Association for the Advancement of Science 2015 Annual Meeting
February 2015 San Jose, CA
American Association for the Advancement of Science 2016 Annual Meeting
February 2016 Washington, DC
American Association for the Advancement of Science 2017 Annual Meeting
February 2017 Boston, MA
Publications:
•AAAS [American Association for the Advancement of Science] Annual Report
Type: Yearbook; *Frequency:* Annually
•AAAS [American Association for the Advancement of Science] Advances
Type: Newsletter
Profile: A members only newsletter with updates on American Association for the Advancement of Science research
•AAAS [American Association for the Advancement of Science] Policy Alert
Type: Newsletter; *Frequency:* Weekly
Profile: News about science policy
•Science [a publication of the American Association for the Advancement of Science]
Type: Journal; *Frequency:* Weekly; *Editor:* Bruce Alberts
Profile: Original scientific research & global news
•Science Books & Films [a publication of the American Association for the Advancement of Science]
Type: Journal
Profile: A critical review journal of educational materials for science teachers
•Science Roundup [a publication of the American Association for the Advancement of Science]
Type: Newsletter
Profile: A members only newsletter with updates on American Association for the Advancement of Science research & programs
•Science Signaling [a publication of the American Association for the Advancement of Science]
Type: Journal; *Frequency:* Weekly; *Editor:* Michael B. Yaffe, M.D., Ph.D; *ISSN:* 1937-9145
Profile: Information for experts & novices in cell signaling
•Science Translational Medicine [a publication of the American Association for the Advancement of Science]
Type: Journal; *Editor:* Katrina L. Kelner, Ph.D.
Profile: Information for basic translational, & clinical research practitioners & trainees

American Association of Bovine Practitioners (AABP)

PO Box 3610, #802, 3320 Skyway Dr., Auburn AL 36831-3610 USA
Tel: 334-821-0442; *Fax:* 334-821-9532
e-mail: aabphq@aabp.org
www.aabp.org
Overview: A medium-sized international organization
Mission: To enhance the professional lives of international veterinarians; To improve the well-being of cattle; To help the economic success of cattle owners
Chief Officer(s):
Roger Saltman, President
M. Gatz Riddell, Executive Vice-President
mgriddell@aabp.org
Membership: *Member Profile:* International veterinarians engaged in the general field of bovine medicine or those who are interested in bovine medicine; Honorary members are persons who have made outstanding contributions to bovine practice; Veterinary students; *Committees:* Amstutz Scholarship; Animal Welfare; Beef Production Management; Biological Risk Management & Preparedness; Bovine Respiratory Disease; Food Quality, Safety, & Security; Distance Education; Information Management; Lameness; Milk Quality & Udder Health; Membership; Nutrition; Pharmaceutical & Biological Issues; Reproduction
Activities: Offering continuing education programs; Providing networking opportunities with fellow veterinarians; Improving career opportunities in bovine medicine; Increasing awareness of issues in the cattle industry; Promoting leadership on critical issues in the cattle business;
Meetings/Conferences:
For more information see Trade Shows, Conferences and Seminars Chapter
The American Association of Bovine Practitioners 2013 Annual Conference
September 2013 Milwaukee, WI
The American Association of Bovine Practitioners 2014 Annual Conference
September 2014 Albuquerque, NM
The American Association of Bovine Practitioners 2015 Annual Conference
September 2015 New Orleans, LA
The American Association of Bovine Practitioners 2016 Annual Conference
September 2016 Charlotte, NC
The American Association of Bovine Practitioners 2017 Annual Conference
September 2017 Omaha, NE
Publications:
•American Association of Bovine Practitioners Newsletter
Type: Newsletter; *Frequency:* Monthly; *Price:* Free with American Association of Bovine Practitioners membership
Profile: Updates from the association
•American Association of Bovine Practitioners Annual Membership Directory
Type: Directory; *Frequency:* Annually; *Price:* Free with American Association of Bovine Practitioners membership
•The Bovine Practitioner
Type: Journal; *Frequency:* Semiannually; *Accepts Advertising*; *Price:* Free with American Association of Bovine Practitioners membership
•Proceedings of the American Association of Bovine Practitioners Annual Conference
Type: Yearbook; *Frequency:* Annually; *Price:* Free with American Association of Bovine Practitioners membership

The American Association of Petroleum Geologists (AAPG)

PO Box 979, 1444 South Boulder, Tulsa OK 74101-0979 USA
Tel: 918-584-2555; *Fax:* 918-560-2665
Toll-Free: 800-364-2274
e-mail: postmaster@aapg.org
www.aapg.org
Overview: A small national organization
Affiliation(s): Canadian Society of Petroleum Geologists
Chief Officer(s):
Richard (Rick) D. Fritz, Executive Director
Scott W. Tinker, President
Awards:
•Grants-in-Aid (Scholarship)
Postgraduate research projects leading to the M.S. degree in geology, geophysics, engineering, environmental studies, earth sciences, chemistry, mineralogy or science for Canadian, landed immigrant or visa students *Amount:* $2,000 maximum

American Birding Association, Inc. (ABA)

1618 West Colorado Ave., Colorado Springs CO 80904 USA
Tel: 719-578-9703; *Fax:* 719-578-1480
Toll-Free: 800-850-2473
e-mail: member@aba.org
www.americanbirding.org
www.facebook.com/birders
twitter.com/aba
www.youtube.com/user/AmericanBirding
Overview: A large national organization founded in 1969
Mission: To provide leadership to field birders by increasing their knowledge, skills & enjoyment of birding & by contributing to bird conservation; *Member of:* Partners in Flight; American Bird Conservancy; Bird Conservation Alliance
Chief Officer(s):
Louis M. Morrell, Chair
Jeffrey A. Gordon, President
jgordon@aba.org
Finances: *Annual Operating Budget:* $500,000-$1.5 Million
Staff: 18 staff member(s)
Membership: 22,000; *Fees:* US$55 individual; US$63 family
Activities: Youth Education; Conservation Programs; *Rents Mailing List:* Yes; *Library:* Open to public
Publications:
•Big Day Report & List Report [a publication of American Birding Association, Inc.]
Frequency: Annual
Profile: Formerly in print, now the Report is online
•Birding [a publication of American Birding Association, Inc.]
Type: Magazine; *Frequency:* s-m.; *Editor:* Ted Floyd
•Gear Guide [a publication of American Birding Association, Inc.]
Frequency: Annual
•North American Birds [a publication of American Birding Association, Inc.]
Type: Journal; *Frequency:* q.; *Editor:* Ned Brinkley
•Winging It [a publication of American Birding Association, Inc.]
Type: Newsletter; *Editor:* Michael Retter

American Cave Conservation Association (ACCA)

PO Box 409, 119 Main St. East, Horse Cave KY 42749 USA
Tel: 270-786-1466; *Fax:* 270-786-1467
www.cavern.org
Also Known As: American Cave & Karst Center
Overview: A small international organization founded in 1977
Mission: To protect & preserve caves, karstlands & groundwater; to bring together information about cave & karst resources from across the nation & make it available to those who are working to protect these resources
Chief Officer(s):
David G. Foster, Executive Director
acca@cavern.org
Finances: *Annual Operating Budget:* $250,000-$500,000
Staff: 7 staff member(s)
Membership: 500; *Fees:* Regular: $25-30; Student: $25; Family: $35, Supporter: $50; Sustainer: $100; Guarantor: $200; Benefactor: $500; Patron: $1000
Activities: Operates National Cave Management Training program & The American Cave Museum; provides outreach educational programs; constructs cave gates; *Library:* Open to public by appointment
Publications:
•American Caves

American Chemistry Council (ACC)

700 Second St. NE, Washington DC 20002 USA
Tel: 202-249-7000; *Fax:* 202-249-6100
www.americanchemistry.com

Overview: A medium-sized national organization
Chief Officer(s):
Calvin M. Dooley, President & Chief Executive Officer
Raymond J. O'Bryan, Chief Financial Officer & CAO
Dell Perelman, Chief of Staff & General Counsel
Roger D. Bernstein, Vice-President, State Affairs & Grassroots
Walter Moore, Vice-President, Federal Affairs
Steve Russell, Vice-President, Plastics
Robert J. Simon, Vice-President, Chemical Products & Technology & Chlorine Chemistry
Michael P. Walls, Vice-President, Regulatory & Technical Affairs
Anne Womack Kolton, Vice-President, Communications
Activities: Conducting research & development activities

American Council for an Energy-Efficient Economy (ACEEE)

#600, 529 14th St. NW, Washington DC 20045-1000 USA
Tel: 202-507-4000; *Fax:* 202-429-2248
www.aceee.org
www.facebook.com/67449893973
twitter.com/ACEEEdc
Overview: A medium-sized national organization founded in 1980
Mission: To advance energy-conserving technology & policies; to assist utilities & regulators to implement cost-effective conservation programs; to support the adoption of comprehensive new policies for increasing energy efficiency; to show how energy efficiency improvements can protect the environment; to analyse & promote technologies & policies for increasing vehicle fuel efficiency & reducing vehicle use; to help developing & Eastern European countries undertake energy efficiency programs
Chief Officer(s):
Steven Nadel, Executive Director
snadel@aceee.org
Activities: ; *Library:*

American Farmland Trust (AFT)

#800, 1200 - 18th St. NW, Washington DC 20036 USA
Tel: 202-331-7300; *Fax:* 202-659-8339
e-mail: info@farmland.org
www.farmland.org
www.facebook.com/AmericanFarmland
www.twitter.com/farmland
Overview: A large national charitable organization founded in 1980
Mission: To stop the loss of productive farmland & to promote farming practices that lead to a healthy environment
Chief Officer(s):
Miranda M. Kaiser, Chair
Membership: 20,000; *Fees:* $25
Activities: Public education; technical assistance in policy development; direct farmland protection projects; sustainable agriculture projects
Publications:
•American Farmland
Type: Magazine; *Frequency:* Biannually

American Fisheries Society (AFS)

5410 Grosvenor Lane, Bethesda MD 20814-2199 USA
Tel: 301-897-8616; *Fax:* 301-897-8096
www.fisheries.org
www.facebook.com/group.php?gid=39804224812
twitter.com/AmFisheriesSoc
www.flickr.com/photos/americanfisheriessociety
Overview: A large international organization founded in 1870
Mission: To advance fisheries science & the conservation of renewable aquatic resources; To promote & evaluate the educational, scientific, & technological development & advancement of all branches of fisheries science & practice, including aquatic biology, engineering, economics, fish culture, limnology, oceanography, & technology; To gather & disseminate technical & other information on fish, fishing, fisheries, & all phases of fisheries science & practice; To encourage the teaching of all phases of fisheries science
Chief Officer(s):
Bill Franzin, President
Gus Rassam, Executive Director
Finances: *Annual Operating Budget:* $1.5 Million-$3 Million; *Funding Sources:* Donations; Grants; Membership fees; Publication sales
Staff: 24 staff member(s)
Membership: 8,500+ fisheries & aquatic science professionals & students; *Fees:* $80 North America; $95 outside North America; *Member Profile:* Open to anyone interested in the progress of fisheries science & education & the conservation & management of fisheries resources; *Committees:* Arrangements; Award of Excellence; Board of Appeals; Board of Professional Certification; Budget & Finance; Continuing Education; Mail Ballot Tally; Membership; Membership Concerns; Names of Fishes; Names of Aquatic Invertebrates; Nominating; Program; Publications Overview; Resolutions; Resource Policy; Time & Place
Activities: *Rents Mailing List:* Yes
Awards:
•The AFS Award of Excellence (Award)
Given to recognize outstanding scientists in the fields of fisheries & aquatic biology
•The Carl R. Sullivan Fisheries Conservation Award (Award)
Given annually to an individual or organization, professional or non-professional, for outstanding contributions to the conservation of fishery resources
•Award for Excellence in Fisheries Education (Award)
Presented annually to an individual to recognize excellence in organized teaching & advising in a field of fisheries
•Presidents' Fishery Conservation Award (Award)
Presented annually, one or more awards if warranted, in one of two categories: (1) an AFS individual or unit or (2) a non-AFS individual or entity, for a singular accomplishment or activity that advancces aquatic resource conservation at the regional or Society level
•William E. Ricker Resource Conservation Award (Award)
Given to any entity for a singular accomplishment or activity in resource conservation that is significant at the U.S., continental, or international level
•Excellence in Public Outreach (Award)
Awarded annually to an AFS member who goes "the extra mile" in sharing the value of fisheries science/research with the general public through the popular media & other communication channels
Meetings/Conferences:
For more information see Trade Shows, Conferences and Seminars Chapter
American Fisheries Society Annual Meeting
September 2013 Little Rock, AR
American Fisheries Society Annual Meeting
August 2014 Québec, QC
American Fisheries Society Annual Meeting
August 2015 Portland, OR
Publications:
•Fisheries
Editor: Sarah Gilbert Fox
Profile: Monthly Magazine

American Forest & Paper Association (AF&PA)

#800, 1111 - 19th St. NW, Washington DC 20036 USA
Tel: 202-463-2700
Toll-Free: 800-878-8878
e-mail: info@afandpa.org
www.afandpa.org
Previous Name: American Paper Institute
Overview: A large international organization founded in 1993
Mission: To act as a leading voice for the forest products industry
Environmental Activity: Advancing policies that promote a sustainable forest products industry, such as recycling, clean air, & clean water
Chief Officer(s):
Alexander Toeldte, Chair
Donna A. Harman, President & Chief Executive Officer
Jan Poling, Vice-President, General Counsel & Secretary
Membership: 157; *Member Profile:* Companies & associations that produce forest, paper, & wood products; *Committees:* North American Forest Carbon Standards; Environment Resource; Energy Resource; Air Quality; Printing-Writing; Timber Purchasers
Activities: Providing advice & counsel about the forest products industry; Operating a statistics program in the paper & packaging industry

American Industrial Hygiene Association (AIHA)

#250, 2700 Prosperity Ave., Fairfax VA 22031 USA
Tel: 703-849-8888; *Fax:* 703-207-3561
e-mail: infonet@aiha.org
www.aiha.org
Overview: A medium-sized international organization founded in 1939
Mission: To serve the needs of occupational & environmental health professionals; To achieve high professional standards; To promote certification of industrial hygienists
Chief Officer(s):
Peter J. O'Neil, Executive Director, 703-846-0760
Mary Ellen Brennan, Director, Human Resources, 703-846-0760
Mary Ann Latko, Director, Scientific & Technical Initiatives, 703-846-0786
mlatko@aiha.org
Cheryl Morton, Director, Laboratory Quality Assurance Programs, 703-846-0789
cmorton@aiha.org
Connie Paradise, Director, Communications & Product Development, 703-846-0742
cparadise@aiha.org
Aaron Trippler, Director, Government Affairs, 703-846-0730
atrippler@aiha.org
Vicky Yobp, Director, Member Services & Special Interest Groups, 703-846-0769
vyobp@aiha.org
Membership: 10,460; *Member Profile:* International occupational & environmental health & safety professionals, who practise industrial hygiene in industry, academic institutions, government, & independent organizations
Activities: Administering education programs; Operating laboratory accreditation programs based on high international standards; Providing networking opportunities; Engaging in advocacy activities
Meetings/Conferences:
For more information see Trade Shows, Conferences and Seminars Chapter
American Industrial Hygiene Conference & Exposition 2013
May 2013 Montréal, QC
Publications:
•American Industrial Hygiene Association Member Directory
Type: Directory
•Journal of Occupational & Environmental Hygiene
Type: Journal; *Accepts Advertising*; *Editor:* Sheila Brown
Profile: A peer-reviewed publication to enhance the knowledge & practice of occupational & environmental hygiene & safety
•The Synergist
Type: Magazine; *Frequency:* Monthly; *Accepts Advertising*; *Editor:* Ed Rutkowski
Profile: Information about the occupational & environmental health & safety fields & the industrial hygiene profession, including industry trends, government activities, technical information, &association news

American Iron & Steel Institute (AISI)

#705, 1140 Connecticut Ave. NW, Washington DC 20036 USA
Tel: 202-452-7100; *Fax:* 202-463-6573
e-mail: webmaster@steel.org
www.steel.org
Overview: A small international organization
Mission: To advance steel as the material of choice and to enhance the competitiveness of member companies and the North American steel industry.
Chief Officer(s):
Ward J. Timken Jr., Chair
Membership: *Member Profile:* Producer companies - including integrated, electric furnace & reconstituted mills; associate companies - suppliers to or customers of the industry; affiliate organizations - downstream steel producers of products such as cold rolled strip, pipe & tube, coated sheet

American Lung Association (ALA)

Washington Office, #800, 1301 Pennsylvania Ave. NW, Washington DC 20004 USA
Tel: 202-785-3355; *Fax:* 202-452-1805
Toll-Free: 800-732-9339
e-mail: info@lungusa.org
www.lungusa.org
www.facebook.com/lungusa
twitter.com/lungassociation
www.youtube.com/user/americanlung
Overview: A large international charitable organization founded in 1904
Mission: To prevent lung disease & promote lung health; Affiliation(s): American Thoracic Society
Chief Officer(s):
Kathryn A. Forbes, Chair
Finances: *Annual Operating Budget:* Greater than $5 Million; *Funding Sources:* Donations; Grants
Staff: 105 staff member(s)
Membership: 130,000 volunteers

American Medical Association

515 North State St., Chicago IL 60610 USA
Tel: 312-464-5000; *Fax:* 312-464-5543
Toll-Free: 800-621-8335
www.ama-assn.org

www.linkedin.com/groups?mostPopular=&gid=76194&trk=myg_ugrp_ovr
www.facebook.com/AmericanMedicalAssociation
twitter.com/AmerMedicalAssn
plus.google.com/107410187242660838577
Overview: A large international organization founded in 1847
Chief Officer(s):
Michael D. Maves, Exec. Vice President & CEO
Membership: *Fees:* Physician: $84-420; Intern/Resident/Fellow: $45-160; Student: $20-68
Activities: Council on Scientific Affairs - major contributions in the area of environmental health; Dept. of Environmental, Public & Occupational Health (these responsibilities are now with the Dept. of Risk Assessment in the Division of Biomedical Science)
Publications:
•JAMA [The Journal of the American Medical Association]
Type: Journal

American Ornithologists' Union (AOU)

5405 Villa View Dr., Farmington NM 87402 USA
Tel: 505-326-1579
e-mail: aou@aou.org
www.aou.org
Overview: A medium-sized national organization founded in 1883
Mission: To be devoted to the scientific study of birds in North America
Chief Officer(s):
Scott Gillihan, Executive Director
John R. Faaborg, President
president@aou.org
Sara R. Morris, Secretary
secretary@aou.org
Membership: 4,500; *Fees:* Regular: $85; Student: $27; Lifetime: $2550
Activities: Supporting individual research projects; Providing funds for graduate students to attend annual meetings; Presenting several annual awards for excellence in research; *Rents Mailing List:* Yes
Publications:
•The Auk [a publication of the American Ornithologists' Union]
Type: Journal; *Frequency:* Quarterly
Profile: A journal of ornithology

American Paper Institute *See* American Forest & Paper Association

American Planning Association (APA)

#750 West, 1030 15th St. NW, Washington DC 20005-1503 USA
Tel: 202-872-0611; *Fax:* 202-872-0643
e-mail: customerservice@planning.org
www.planning.org
www.linkedin.com/groups?gid=116818
www.facebook.com/AmericanPlanningAssociation
twitter.com/APA_Planning
www.youtube.com/user/AmericanPlanningAssn
Overview: A large national organization founded in 1909
Mission: To provide members with systematic ways to work on problems in common & to affect national planning policies
Chief Officer(s):
Mitch Silver, President
Paul Farmer, Executive Director
Finances: *Annual Operating Budget:* $3 Million-$5 Million
Staff: 66 staff member(s)
Membership: 29,000
Activities: Environment, Natural Resources & Energy Division - to bring sound planning principles to the protection, management or conservation of environmental, natural & energy resources, as well as national forests & public lands; Small town & Rural Planning Division - oriented toward improving the quality & extent of planning in small communities & rural areas with a focus on protection of natural resources; *Rents Mailing List:* Yes; *Library:* APA Library; by appointment
Publications:
•JAPA [The Journal of the American Planning Association]
Type: Journal
•Planning
Type: Magazine

American Public Gardens Association (APGA)

351 Longwood Rd., Kennet Square PA 19348 USA
Tel: 610-708-3010; *Fax:* 610-444-3594
www.publicgardens.org
Overview: A medium-sized international organization founded in 1940
Mission: To support North American botanical gardens & arboreta, public horticultural organizations, their staff & trustees by: promoting the value of botanical gardens, arboreta & public horticultural organizations involved in the display, study & conservation of plants for public benefit; setting, promoting & recognizing professional standards; facilitating the exchange of information; advocating the collective interests of the association's members; promoting membership services
Chief Officer(s):
Casey Sclar, Interim Executive Director, 610-708-3016
csclar@publicgardens.org
Finances: *Annual Operating Budget:* $250,000-$500,000; *Funding Sources:* Membership dues; meetings; publication sales
Staff: 8 staff member(s)
Membership: 2,400; *Fees:* $65-80 regular; $35 student; $50 library subscription; institutional dues based on operating budget; *Member Profile:* Anyone who works or volunteers for public gardens, zoos, horticultural societies, arboreta or historic house gardens
Activities: *Internships:* Yes; *Rents Mailing List:* Yes; *Library:* by appointment
Publications:
•The Public Garden
Profile: Quarterly Magazine

American Public Works Association (APWA)

#700, 2345 Grand Blvd., Kansas City MO 64108-2625 USA
Tel: 816-472-6100; *Fax:* 816-472-1610
Toll-Free: 800-848-2792
e-mail: apwa@apwa.net
www.apwa.net
www.facebook.com/AmericanPublicWorksAssociation
twitter.com/apwatweets
www.youtube.com/apwatv
Overview: A medium-sized international organization founded in 1938
Mission: To provide high quality public works goods & services
Chief Officer(s):
Peter King, Executive Director
pking@apwa.net
Cindy Long, Assistant to the Exec. Director, 816-595-5220
clong@apwa.net
Finances: *Annual Operating Budget:* Greater than $5 Million; *Funding Sources:* Membership dues; Federal grants; Products
Staff: 50 staff member(s); 250 volunteer(s)
Membership: 26,000; *Fees:* Schedule available; *Member Profile:* Public agencies, private sector companies, & individuals engaged in public works services; *Committees:* Transportation; Solid Waste; Water Resources; Engineering & Technology; Management & Leadership; Emergency Management; Fleet Services; Facilities & Grounds; Utility & Public Right of Way

American Rivers

#1400, 1101 - 14th St. NW, Washington DC 20005 USA
Tel: 202-347-7550; *Fax:* 202-347-9240
e-mail: outreach@americanrivers.org
www.americanrivers.org
www.facebook.com/AmericanRivers
twitter.com/AmericanRivers
www.youtube.com/AmericanRivers
Previous Name: American Rivers Conservation Council
Overview: A medium-sized national organization founded in 1973
Mission: To preserve & restore America's river systems; to foster a river stewardship ethic
Chief Officer(s):
William Robert (Bob) Irvin, President
Swep Davis, Chair
Finances: *Annual Operating Budget:* $1.5 Million-$3 Million
Staff: 25 staff member(s); 7 volunteer(s)
Membership: *Fees:* $20
Activities: Policy manuals; *Internships:* Yes; *Speaker Service:* Yes

American Rivers Conservation Council *See* American Rivers

American Society for Environmental History (ASEH)

Interdisciplinary Arts & Sciences Program, University of Washington, PO Box 358436, 1900 Commerce St., Tacoma WA 98402-3100 USA
Tel: 206-465-0630
e-mail: director@aseh.net
www.aseh.net
Overview: A small international charitable organization founded in 1977
Mission: To promote interdisciplinary study of past environmental change; to promote the study of environmental history in all disciplines; *Member of:* American Council of Learned Societies; Affiliation(s): International Consortium of Environmental History Organizations
Chief Officer(s):
Harriet Ritvo, President
ritvo@mit.edu
Lisa Mighetto, Executive Director
Membership: *Committees:* Executive; Nominating; Diversity; Outreach; Conference Site Selection; Publications; Education; Conference Program; Conference Local Arrangements; George Perkins Marsh Prize; Alice Hamilton Prize; Rachel Carson Prize; Leopold-Hidy Prize; H-Evironment
Awards:
•Leopold-Hidy Prize for Best Article in Environmental History (Award)
•Alice Hamilton Prize for Best Article, Outside the journal, Environmental History (Award)
•Rachel Carson Prize for Best Dissertation in Environmental History (Award)
•George Perkins March Prize for Best Book in Environmental History (Award)
Publications:
•ASEH [American Society for Environmental History] News
Type: Newsletter; *Frequency:* Quarterly
•Environmental History
Type: Journal
Profile: Published jointly with the Forest History Society

American Society of Heating, Refrigerating & Air Conditioning Engineers (ASHRAE)

1791 Tullie Circle NE, Atlanta GA 30329 USA
Tel: 404-636-8400; *Fax:* 404-321-5478
Toll-Free: 800-527-4723
e-mail: ashrae@ashrae.org
www.ashrae.org
www.facebook.com/pages/ashrae/106136469528
Overview: A medium-sized international organization founded in 1894
Mission: ASHRAE is an international organization with a mission of advancing heating, ventilation, air conditioning & refrigeration. It promotes a sustainable environment through research, standards writing, publishing & continuing education.
Chief Officer(s):
Ronald Jarnagin, President
Jeff H. Littleton, Exec. Vice-Pres.
Membership: 50,000; *Fees:* Regular/Student: $165; Associate: $165; Affiliate: $40
Awards:
•ASHRAE Engineers Grant-in-Aid (Scholarship)
Graduate level studies in the areas of heating, cooling, refrigeration, air conditioning, energy conservation, air quality
Deadline: February *Amount:* $6,000 US; 12 awards available
Contact: Manager of Research, ASHRAE
Meetings/Conferences:
For more information see Trade Shows, Conferences and Seminars Chapter
13th Annual International Conference for Enhanced Building Operations (ICEBO)
October 2013 Montréal, QC
Publications:
•ASHRAE [American Society of Heating, Refrigerating & Air Conditioning Engineers] Journal
Type: Journal; *Frequency:* Monthly

British Columbia Chapter

PO Box 43016, 111 - 3790 Canada Way, Burnaby BC V5C 4S2
ashrae.bc.ca/bc
Chief Officer(s):
Chris Collett, President

Chapitre de Québec Chapter

CP 8652, Succ. Ste-Foy, Québec QC G1V 4N6
www.ashraequebec.org
Chief Officer(s):
Andréa Daigle, Président, 418-688-2161, Fax: 418-688-7807
andrea.daigle@honywell.com

Chapitre Montréal Chapter

CP 81, Boucherville QC J4B 5E6
Tél: 514-990-3953; *Téléc:* 866-532-0444
Courriel: info@ashrae-mtl.org
www.ashrae-mtl.org
Chief Officer(s):

Caroline Paquet, Présidente, 514-383-3747 Ext. 223, Fax: 514-383-8760

Halifax Chapter

c/o CBCL Ltd., PO Box 606, Stn. Central, 1489 Hollis St., Halifax NS B3J 3M5
Tel: 902-421-7241; *Fax:* 902-423-3938
www.halifax-ashrae.org
Chief Officer(s):
Conrad LeLievre, President
lelievreeng@ns.sympatico.ca

Hamilton Chapter

c/o Union Gas, PO Box 340, 603 Kumpf Dr., Waterloo ON N2J 4A4
Tel: 519-885-7460; *Fax:* 519-885-7540
e-mail: ashrae@vaxxine.com
www.vaxxine.com/ashrae
Chief Officer(s):
Mike Krewski, President
mkrewski@uniongas.com

London Chapter

c/o Aquatech, 4390 Paletta Ct., Burlington ON L7L 5R2
Tel: 905-631-5815; *Fax:* 905-637-8655
londoncanada.ashraechapters.org
Chief Officer(s):
Jason Vanderberghe, President
jasonv@aquatech.ws

Manitoba Chapter

c/o epp siepman engineering inc., 303, 100 Osborne St. South, Winnipeg MB R3L 1Y5
Tel: 204-453-1080; *Fax:* 204-453-1335
www.ashraemanitoba.ca
Chief Officer(s):
Johann Baetsen, President
jbaetsen@eppsiepman.com

New Brunswick/PEI Chapter

PO Box 1629, Moncton NB E1C 9X4
www.ashraenbpei.com
Chief Officer(s):
Kevin Clannon, President, 506-382-8625, Fax: 506-382-8626
kclannon@master.ca

Northern Alberta Chapter

PO Box 42066, Stn. Milbourne, Edmonton AB T6K 4C4
e-mail: admin@ashraenac.org
ashraenac.org
Chief Officer(s):
Lindsay Austrom, President, 780-720-2222

Ottawa Valley Chapter

PO Box 21088, 1166 Bank St., Ottawa ON K1S 5N1
e-mail: contact@ashrae.ottawa.on.ca
www.ashrae.ottawa.on.ca
Chief Officer(s):
christine Kemp, President
christine@walmar.net

Regina Chapter

c/o HVAC Sales (1997) Ltd., 1362 Lorne St., Regina SK S4R 2K1
Tel: 306-721-7980
e-mail: ashraeregina@accesscomm.ca
regina.ashraechapters.org
Chief Officer(s):
Jason Danyliw, President

Saskatoon Chapter

Saskatoon SK
Tel: 306-477-0678
e-mail: reply@ashraesaskatoon.ca
www.ashraesaskatoon.ca
Chief Officer(s):
Jonathan Bushman, President, 306-651-6372

Southern Alberta Chapter

PO Box 76006, Calgary AB T2Y 2Z9
Tel: 403-201-4454
e-mail: chapter.administrator@sac-ashrae.com
www.sac-ashrae.com
Chief Officer(s):
Don Blacklock, President, 403-541-5547, Fax: 403-229-0506
dblacklock@designdialog.ca

Toronto Chapter

c/o #201, 2800 Skymark Ave., Mississauga ON L4W 5A6
Tel: 905-602-4714
www.torontoashrae.com
Chief Officer(s):
Michael Khaw, President
m.khaw@isothermengineering.com
Sabrina Tai, Contact
stai@hrai.ca

Vancouver Island Chapter

c/o HVAC Systems & Solutions Ltd., #202, 4030 Quadra St., Victoria BC V8X 1K2
Tel: 250-590-3737; *Fax:* 250-590-3711
www.ashrae.bc.ca/vi
Chief Officer(s):
Alfredo Munoz, President
amunoz@hvacsystems.ca

Windsor Chapter

c/o Univ. of Windsor, Crystal Hall Tower, #610, 401 Sunset Ave., Windsor ON N9B 3P4
windsor.ashraechapters.org
Chief Officer(s):
Bill Davis, President, 519-250-2355
Dan Castellan, Contact, 519-253-3000 Ext. 2164, Fax: 519-561-1404
danc@uwindsor.ca

American Society of Mechanical Engineers (ASME)

3 Park Ave., New York NY 10016-5990 USA
Tel: 800-843-2763*Tel:* 973-882-1170
e-mail: customercare@asme.org
www.asme.org
www.facebook.com/ASME.org
twitter.com/ASMEmembership
Overview: A large international organization founded in 1880
Mission: To promote the art, science, & practice of multidisciplinary engineering; To focus on the technical, educational, & research issues of the engineering & technology community; To help the engineering community develop solutions to improve the quality of life
Environmental Activity: Promoting environmental engineering to help make the land, air, & water safer for humans
Chief Officer(s):
Thomas G. Loughlin, Executive Director
execdirector@asme.org
Marc Goldsmith, President
marc@mgallc.net
Warren DeVries, Secretary-Treasurer
wdevries@umbc.edu
David Soukup, Managing Director, Governance, 212-591-7397
soukupd@asme.org
Finances: *Funding Sources:* Publications; Meetings; Standards accreditation
Membership: 120,000+ in 150+ countries; *Fees:* Schedule available; *Member Profile:* Students; Engineers; Technical professionals; Researchers; Project managers; Academic leaders; Corporate executives; *Committees:* Finance & Investment; Honors; Organization & Rules; Past Presidents; Governance & Strategy; Executive Director Evaluation & Staff Compensation
Activities: Promoting multidisciplinary engineering & allied science throughout the world; Engaging in research; Liaising with government; Enabling knowledge sharing; Offering continuing education & professional development in mechanical engineering; Maintaining codes & standards; Promoting the technical competency of members; Offering a mentoring program; *Library:* American Society of Mechanical Engineers e-Library; Open to public
Meetings/Conferences:
For more information see Trade Shows, Conferences and Seminars Chapter
American Society of Mechanical Engineers 2013 Annual Meeting
June 2013 Indianapolis, IN
American Society of Mechanical Engineers 2013 Pressure Vessels & Piping Conference
July 2013 Paris
American Society of Mechanical Engineers 2013 International Mechanical Engineering Congress & Exposition
November 2013
American Society of Mechanical Engineers 2013 58th Turbo Expo
June 2013 San Antonio, TX
Publications:
•Applied Mechanics Reviews
Type: Journal; *Frequency:* Bimonthly; *Editor:* Harry Dankowicz; *ISSN:* 0003-6900
Profile: An international review journal featuring topics such as heat transfer, vibration, & dynamics
•ASME [American Society of Mechanical Engineers] Capitol Update
Type: Newsletter; *Frequency:* Weekly
Profile: Legislative & regulatory news of interest to the engineering community
•History & Heritage Newsletter [a publication of the American Society of Mechanical Engineers]
Type: Newsletter; *Frequency:* Semiannually
Profile: Notable accomplishments in mechanical engineering history
•Journal of Applied Mechanics
Type: Journal; *Frequency:* Bimonthly; *Editor:* Yonggang Huang; *ISSN:* 0021-8936
Profile: Peer-reviewed research papers covering subjects such as wave propagation, turbulence, stress analysis, structures, hydraulics, & flow & fracture
•Journal of Biomechanical Engineering
Type: Journal; *Frequency:* Monthly; *Editor:* Beth Winkelstein; *ISSN:* 0148-0731
Profile: Research papers on topics such as cellular mechanics, the design & control of biological systems, bioheat transfer, biomaterials, & biomechanics
•Journal of Computational & Nonlinear Dynamics
Type: Journal; *Frequency:* Quarterly; *Editor:* Ahmed A. Shabana, Ph.D.; *ISSN:* 1555-1415
Profile: Technical briefs & research papers cover bio-mechanical dynamics, design & design optimization dynamical analysis & method, vehicular dynamics,stability, & aerospace applications
•Journal of Computing & Information Science in Engineering
Type: Journal; *Frequency:* Quarterly; *Editor:* Bahram Ravani; *ISSN:* 1530-9827
Profile: Research papers & technical briefs about virtual environments & haptics, tolerance mondeling & computational metrology, reverse engineering,& internet-aided design, manufacturing, & commerce
•Journal of Dynamic Systems, Measurement, & Control
Type: Journal; *Frequency:* Bimonthly; *Editor:* Karl Hedrick; *ISSN:* 0022-0434
Profile: Articles on design innovation, research papers, & technical briefs address aerospace systems, energy systems & control, manufacturing technology,power systems, production systems, signal processing, & transportation
•Journal of Electronic Packaging
Type: Journal; *Frequency:* Quarterly; *Editor:* Bahgat Sammakia; *ISSN:* 1043-7398
Profile: Papers to address mechanical, materials, & reliability problems encountered in the design, manufacturing, & operation of electronic, optoelectronic, & photonicsystems
•Journal of Energy Resources Technology
Type: Journal; *Frequency:* Quarterly; *Editor:* Hameed Metghalchi; *ISSN:* 0195-0738
Profile: Research on topics such as extraction of energy from natural resources, enerty resource recovery from biomass & solid wastes, technology for energygenerations, offshore & deepwater mechanics, petroleum engineering, natural gas technology, & rock & material mechanics for energy resources
•Journal of Engineering for Gas Turbines & Power
Type: Journal; *Frequency:* Monthly; *Editor:* Dilip R. Ballal; *ISSN:* 0742-4795
Profile: Technical briefs & research examime nuclear engineering, coal, biomass & alternative fuels, energy production & conversion, & oil & gasapplications
•Journal of Engineering Materials & Technology
Type: Journal; *Frequency:* Quarterly; *Editor:* Hussein M. Zbib; *ISSN:* 0094-4289
Profile: Topics include environmental effects, fatigue, fracture, high temperature creep, & phase transformations in materials
•Journal of Fluids Engineering
Type: Journal; *Frequency:* Monthly; *Editor:* Malcolm J. Andrews; *ISSN:* 0098-2202

Profile: Contents include cavitation erosion, flow in biolgical systems, fluid transients & wave motion, naval hydrodynamics, pumps, pipelines, turbines, propulsion systems,& water hammers
•Journal of Fuel Cell Science & Technology
Type: Journal; *Frequency:* Bimonthly; *Editor:* Nigel M. Sammes; *ISSN:* 1550-624X
Profile: Subjects include durability & damage tolerance, aging, system design & manufacturing, & fuel cell applications
•Journal of Heat Transfer
Type: Journal; *Frequency:* Monthly; *Editor:* Terrence W. Simon; *ISSN:* 0022-1481
Profile: Featuring research on environmental issues, low temperature & the Arctic, aircraft, & energy technology & systems
•Journal of Manufacturing Science & Engineering
Type: Journal; *Frequency:* Bimonthly; *Editor:* Y. Lawrence Yao; *ISSN:* 1087-1357
Profile: Subjects include rail transportation, inspection & quality control, material removal by machining, production systems optimization, textileproduction, & sensors
•Journal of Mechanical Design
Type: Journal; *Frequency:* Monthly; *Editor:* Panos Y. Papalambros; *ISSN:* 1050-0472
Profile: Technical briefs & research papers address design theory & methodology, design automation, & design of direct contact systems
•Journal of Mechanisms & Robotics
Type: Journal; *Frequency:* Quarterly; *Editor:* J. Michael McCarthys; *ISSN:* 1942-4302
Profile: Research covers the theory, algorithms, & applications for robotic & machine systems
•Journal of Medical Devices
Type: Journal; *Frequency:* Quarterly; *Editor:* Arthur G. Erdman; Gerald E. Miller; *ISSN:* 1932-6181
Profile: Design innovation articles & research papers focus upon new medical devices or instrumentation that improve diagnostic interventional & therapeutictreatments
•Journal of Micro & Nano Manufacturing
Type: Journal
•Journal of Microelectromechanical Systems (MEMS)
Type: Journal; *Frequency:* 6 pa.; *Editor:* William Trimmer
•Journal of Nanotechnology in Engineering & Medicine
Type: Journal; *Frequency:* Quarterly; *Editor:* Vijay K. Varadan; *ISSN:* 1949-2944
Profile: The impact of nanotechnology upon medicine & the direction of research & development
•Journal of Offshore Mechanics & Arctic Engineering
Type: Journal; *Frequency:* Quarterly; *Editor:* Solomon C. Yim; *ISSN:* 0892-7219
Profile: Articles highlight Arctic exploration & drilling, permafrost engineering & Arctic thermal design, offshore structures, ice structure interaction, &marine geotechnique
•Journal of Pressure Vessel Technology
Type: Journal; *Frequency:* Bimonthly; *Editor:* G. E. Otto Widera; *ISSN:* 0094-9930
Profile: Technology reviews & research papers cover codes & standards, pressure vessel & piping, fatigue & fracture prediction, elevated temperature analysis &design, lifeline earthquake engineering, & safety & reliability
•Journal of Solar Energy Engineering
Type: Journal; *Frequency:* Quarterly; *Editor:* Gilles Flamant; *ISSN:* 0199-6231
Profile: Research papers & technical information about solar collectors, solar optics, solar chemistry & bioconversion, solar thermal power, energy storage, conservation,solar buildings, solar space applications, wind energy, emerging technologies, & energy policy
•Journal of Thermal Science & Engineering Applications
Type: Journal; *Frequency:* Quarterly; *Editor:* Michael Jensen; *ISSN:* 1948-5085
Profile: Subjects addressed include applications in areas such as defense systems, aerospace systems, energy systems, refrigeration & air conditioning,petrochemical processing, combustion systems, & medical systems
•Journal of Tribology
Type: Journal; *Frequency:* Quarterly; *Editor:* Michael Khonsari; *ISSN:* 0742-4787
Profile: Technical information & research cover tribological systems, bearing design & technology, gears, seals, & friction & wear
•Journal of Turbomachinery
Type: Journal; *Frequency:* Quarterly; *Editor:* David C. Wisler; *ISSN:* 0889-504X
Profile: Research papers examine fluid dynamics & heat transfer phenomena in compressor & turbine components
•Journal of Vibration & Acoustics
Type: Journal; *Frequency:* Bimonthly; *Editor:* Noel C. Perkins; *ISSN:* 1048-9002
Profile: Subjects include areas such as machinery dynamics & noise, structural acoustics, acoustic emission, noise control, & vibration suppression
•ME Today [a publication of the American Society of Mechanical Engineers]
Type: Newsletter; *Frequency:* Quarterly
Profile: Information of interest to early career engineers
•Mechanical Engineering [a publication of the American Society Of Mechanical Engineers]
Type: Magazine; *Frequency:* Monthly; *Editor:* John G. Falconi
Profile: Engineering trends & breakthroughs
•Member Savvy [a publication of the American Society of Mechanical Engineers]
Type: Newsletter; *Frequency:* Monthly
Profile: The benefits of membership in the American Society of Mechanical Engineer
•Standards & Certification Update [a publication of the American Society of Mechanical Engineers]
Type: Newsletter; *Frequency:* Quarterly
Profile: Information about American Society of Mechanical Engineers standards & certification activities, including newpublications, professional development, & conformity assessment

American Society of Mining & Reclamation (ASMR)

3134 Montavesta Rd., Lexington KY 40502-3548 USA
Tel: 859-351-9032; *Fax:* 859-335-6529
ces.ca.uky.edu/asmr
Overview: A medium-sized international charitable organization founded in 1983
Mission: To encourage any agency, institution, organization, or individual in their efforts to protect, re-establish or enhance the surface resources of land disturbances associated with mineral extraction; to promote, support & assist in research & studies; to encourage communication between the research scientist, regulatory agencies, organizations & others who seek assistance; to promote & support related educational programs; Affiliation(s): International Affiliation of Land Reclamationists
Chief Officer(s):
Bruce Buchanan, President
Finances: *Annual Operating Budget:* $50,000-$100,000; *Funding Sources:* Membership dues
Staff: 1 staff member(s); 1 volunteer(s)
Membership: 400; *Fees:* $100 sustaining; $50 regular; $10-25 student; *Member Profile:* Sustaining - agency, department, organization, corporation, or individual representation; regular - individual representation; student - full-time students at accredited colleges; *Committees:* Publication Policy & Review Board; Awards; National Meeting; Membership; Memorial Scholarship Fund; National Register of Research & Demonstration
Activities: Small independent professional groups affiliated with the Society have been organized to concentrate on a particular aspect of surface mining or reclamation: International Tailings Reclamation, Landscape Architecture, Soil & Overburden, Ecology, Geotechnical Engineering, Meter Management, Forestry & Wildlife
Awards:
•Reclamation Researcher of the Year (Award)
Awarded to research scientists who have made substantive contributions to the advancement of reclamation science &/or technology, or contributed meaningful information relating to the economic, social, environmental or ecological effects of surface mining
•William T. Plass Award (Award)
Awarded irregularly; recognizes outstanding contributions in the areas of mining, teaching, research, &/or regulating authority as they relate to land reclamation. Those nominated should be recognized nationally & internationally for their contibutions covering a significant portion of their career
•Reclamationist of the Year (Award)
Awarded to individuals demonstrating outstanding accomplishments in the practical application or evaluation of reclamation technology

American Society of Plant Biologists (ASPB)

15501 Monona Dr., Rockville MD 20855-2768 USA
Tel: 301-251-0560; *Fax:* 301-279-2996
e-mail: info@aspb.org
www.aspb.org
Overview: A medium-sized international organization founded in 1924
Mission: To advance the plant sciences; To promote the development & outreach of plant biology as a pure & applied science
Chief Officer(s):
Crispin Taylor, Executive Director
ctaylor@aspb.org
Kim Kimnach, Executive Director
kKimnach@aspb.org
Gordon Gordon, Manager, Executive & Governance Affairs
dgordon@aspb.org
Membership: *Member Profile:* Plant biology researchers, educators, & students from any nation; Any person concerned with the physiology, molecular biology, environmental biology, cell biology, & biophysics of plants; *Committees:* Awards; Constitution & Bylaws; Education; Executive; International; Membership; Minority Affairs; Nominating; Operations Subcommitee; Program; Public Affairs; Publications; Women in Plant Biology
Publications:
•ASPB [American Society of Plant Biologists] News
Type: Newsletter; *Frequency:* Bimonthly; *Price:* Free for American Society Of Plant Biologists members; $30 non-members
•The Plant Cell
Type: Journal; *Frequency:* Monthly; *Accepts Advertising*; *Editor:* John Long; *ISSN:* 1040-4651
Profile: Primary research in the plant sciences
•Plant Physiology
Type: Journal; *Frequency:* Monthly; *Accepts Advertising*; *Editor:* John Long; *ISSN:* 0032-0889
Profile: Physiology, biochemistry, cellular & molecular biology, genetics, biophysics, & environmental biology of plants

American Society of Plumbing Engineers (ASPE)

2980 River Rd. South, Des Plaines IL 60018 USA
Tel: 847-296-0002; *Fax:* 847-296-2963
e-mail: info@aspe.org
www.aspe.org
Overview: A medium-sized international organization founded in 1964
Chief Officer(s):
Jim Kendzel, Executive Director Ext. 222
jkendzel@aspe.org
Membership: 6,500

British Columbia Chapter
PO Box 2201, Vancouver BC V6B 3W2
Tel: 604-696-8078
e-mail: ecrowdis@stantec.com
sites.google.com/site/aspebcchapter
Chief Officer(s):
Kevin Der, President
kevin.aspebc@gmail.com

Chapitre de Montréal
CP 20024, 8610, Boul St-Laurent, MontréAl QC H2P 3A4
Tél: 514-237-6559; *Téléc:* 514-383-8760
Courriel: aspemtl@videotron.ca
www.aspe.org/Montreal/
Chief Officer(s):
Daniel Marchand, Président, 514-383-3747
dmarchand@bpa.ca

Québec
1937 rue Delisle, Saint-Nicolas QC G7A 2E3
Tel: 418-834-4040
www.aspequebec.com
Chief Officer(s):
Dave Morin, Président, 418-654-9600
dave.morin@roche.ca

American Society of Safety Engineers (ASSE)

1800 East Oakton St., Des Plaines IL 60018-2187 USA
Tel: 847-699-2929; *Fax:* 847-768-3434
e-mail: customerservice@asse.org
www.asse.org
www.facebook.com/ASSESafety
www.twitter.com/asse_safety
Overview: A large international organization founded in 1911
Mission: To promote the advancement of the safety profession & to foster the technical, scientific, managerial & ethical knowledge, skills & competency of safety professionals; Affiliation(s): Canadian Society of Safety Engineering, Inc.
Chief Officer(s):
Fred J. Fortman, Executive Director

Membership: 30,000; *Fees:* Regular: $160; Student: $135
Activities: Providing a Professional Development Conference & Exposition; Offering continuing education & training seminars; Presenting technical publications & audio-visual training courses; *Awareness Events:* National Safety Week, June; *Rents Mailing List:* Yes
Publications:
•Profofessional Safety
Profile: Monthly journal

American Water Resources Association (AWRA)

PO Box 1626, 4 Federal St. West, Middleburg VA 20118-1626 USA
Tel: 540-687-8390; *Fax:* 540-687-8395
e-mail: info@awra.org
www.awra.org
www.linkedin.com/groups?gid=769747&trk=myg_ugrp_ovr
www.facebook.com/pages/American-Water-Resources-Association/1114740355
twitter.com/AWRAHQ
Overview: A large national organization founded in 1964
Mission: To advance research, planning, management, development & education in water resources; provides a focal point for the collection, organization & dissemination of ideas & information in the physical, biological, economic, social, political, legal & engineering aspects of water-related problems; to provide a forum for communication among disciplines with a common interest in water supply, quality, use, development & conservation
Chief Officer(s):
Kenneth D. Reid, Executive Vice President
ken@awra.org
Finances: *Annual Operating Budget:* $500,000-$1.5 Million
Staff: 8 staff member(s)
Membership: 3,000 worldwide; *Fees:* Schedule available; *Member Profile:* Regular - persons interested in any aspect of water resources; student - full-time student engaged in study of any aspect of water resources at a college or university; institutional - universities, governmental agencies & institutions; corporate - consulting firms & business concerns
Activities: Technical Committees provide a focus for special interests; *Rents Mailing List:* Yes
Publications:
•JAWRA [Journal of the American Water Resources Association]
Type: Journal

American Water Works Association (AWWA)

6666 West Quincy Ave., Denver CO 80235 USA
Tel: 303-794-7711; *Fax:* 303-347-0804
Toll-Free: 800-926-7337
e-mail: custsvc@awwa.org
www.awwa.org
www.linkedin.com/groups?gid=733277&trk=hb_side_g
www.facebook.com/AmericanWaterWorksAssociation
twitter.com/AWWAACE
www.youtube.com/user/AmericanWaterWorks
Overview: A large international organization founded in 1881
Mission: To advance public health & safety through the improvement of water quality & supply throughout North America & beyond; To provide standards for the design, manufacturing, installation, & performance of water industry products; To advance & protect the interests of the water industry
Environmental Activity: Advocating to improve the quality & supply of water in North America & beyond
Chief Officer(s):
Charles F. Anderson, President
Dave E. Rager, Treasurer
David B. LaFrance, Executive Director
Susan Franceschi, Chief Membership Officer
Robert Huff, Chief Information Officer
Kevin Mann, Chief Financial Officer
April DeBaker, Director, Conferences & Events
adebaker@awwa.org
Liz Haigh, Director, Publishing
Jane Johnson, Director, Sales & Research
jjohnson@awwa.org
Cynthia Lane, Director, Engineering & Technical Services
rmartinez@awwa.org
Membership: 60,000+; *Fees:* Schedule available; *Member Profile:* Treatment plant operators & managers; Scientists; Environmentalists; Manufacturers; Academics; Regulators; Others interested in water supply & public health; *Committees:* 250 committees
Activities: Providing information about the water industry; *Library:* American Water Works Association Water Library
Meetings/Conferences:
For more information see Trade Shows, Conferences and Seminars Chapter
American Water Works Association 2013 Membrane Technology Conference & Exposition
February 2013 San Antonio, TX
American Water Works Association 2013 Utility Management Conference
March 2013 Glendale, AZ
American Water Works Association 2013 Sustainable Water Management Conference
April 2013 Nashville, TN
American Water Works Association 2013 132nd Annual Conference & Exposition
June 2013 Denver, CO
American Water Works Association 2013 Water Quality Technology Conference & Exposition
November 2013 Long Beach, CA
American Water Works Association 2014 133rd Annual Conference & Exposition
June 2014 Boston, MA
American Water Works Association 2015 134th Annual Conference & Exposition
June 2015 Anaheim, CA
American Water Works Association 2016 135th Annual Conference & Exposition
June 2016 Chicago, IL
American Water Works Association 2017 136th Annual Conference & Exposition
June 2017 Philadelphia, PA
American Water Works Association 2018 137th Annual Conference & Exposition
June 2018 Las Vegas, NV
American Water Works Association 2019 138th Annual Conference & Exposition
June 2019 Denver, CO
American Water Works Association 2020 139th Annual Conference & Exposition
June 2020 Orlando, FL
American Water Works Association 2021 140th Annual Conference & Exposition
2021
Publications:
•American Water Works Association Officers & Committee Directory
Type: Directory
Profile: Director, trustee, officer, & staff management information, plus the AWWA strategic plan & statements of policy
•AWWA [American Water Works Association] Standards
Profile: A print set of the current standards of the American Water Works Association
•Journal AWWA [American Water Works Association]
Type: Journal; *Frequency:* Monthly; *Editor:* Marcia Lacey; *ISSN:* 1551-8833; *Price:* Free with individual, utility, & service provider membership in AWWA
Profile: Peer-reviewed information about water quality, resources, & supply, in addition to professional & scholarly articles about themanagement & operation of water utilities
•Opflow [a publication of the American Water Works Association]
Type: Magazine; *Frequency:* Monthly; *Accepts Advertising*; *Editor:* John Hughes; *ISSN:* 1551-8701; *Price:* Free with individual, utility, & service provider membership in AWWA
Profile: Practical publication for water supply operators
•The Water Dictionary: A Comprehensive Reference of Water Terminology
Type: Book; *Number of Pages:* 716; *Editor:* Nancy McTigue; *ISBN:* 978-1-58321-741-2
Profile: Definitions for 15,000 water-related words, acronyms, & formulas

American Wilderness Alliance *See* American Wildlands

American Wildlands (AWL)

PO Box 6669, #418, 321 East Main St., Bozeman MT 59771 USA
Tel: 406-586-8175
www.facebook.com/pages/American-Wildlands/188400107836676
Previous Name: American Wilderness Alliance
Overview: A medium-sized international organization founded in 1977
Mission: To insure the responsible management & protection of forests, wildlife, wilderness, wetlands, watersheds, rivers & fisheries
Finances: *Annual Operating Budget:* $250,000-$500,000
Staff: 6 staff member(s); 6 volunteer(s)
Membership: 2,500; *Fees:* $40
Activities: *Internships:* Yes; *Speaker Service:* Yes; *Rents Mailing List:* Yes

American Zoo & Aquarium Association (AZA)

#710, 8403 Colesville Rd., Silver Spring MD 20910-3314 USA
Tel: 301-562-0777; *Fax:* 301-562-0888
www.aza.org
www.facebook.com/AssociationOfZoosAndAquariums
twitter.com/zoos_aquariums
Overview: A medium-sized national organization founded in 1924
Mission: To help preserve the world's rare & endangered species; to advance zoological parks & aquariums through conservation, education, scientific studies & recreation; to cooperate with government agencies & international conservation groups in matters dealing with the health & welfare of wildlife in captivity; Affiliation(s): World Wildlife Fund - USA; Species Survival Commission of IUCN - World Conservation Union; Captive Breeding Specialist Group; International Species Information System; Wildlife Conservation International; American Committee for International Conservation; Centre for Marine Conservation; International Union of Directors of Zoological Gardens; International Association of Zoo Educators
Chief Officer(s):
Jim Maddy, President & CEO
Finances: *Annual Operating Budget:* $500,000-$1.5 Million
Staff: 20 staff member(s)
Membership: 5,500; *Fees:* Associate: $70; Affiliate: $95; Fellow: $195; *Member Profile:* Comprises zoological institutions, related organizations, societies, zoological staff employees, commercial concerns that provide products & services to zoological facilities & other interested individuals; open to anyone interested in animal welfare, protection of wildlife & the development of better zoos & aquariums for the good of animals & people; *Committees:* Accreditation; Animal Data Information Systems; Animal Health; Animal Welfare; Aquatic Advisory; Board of Regents; Charter & Bylaws; Conference; Conservation Education; Diversity; Ethics; Field Conservation; Finance & Investments; Government Affairs; Honors & Awards; Information Trends; Marketing; Membership; National Awareness Campaign; Nominating; Operations; Public Relations; Wildlife Conservation & Management
Activities: Species Survival Plan - a strategy for the long-term survival of certain endangered species; International Species System (ISIS) - to promote healthy gene pools; computerized inventory of over 60,000 living animals in order to enable zoos to locate the best individuals for their breeding programs; *Rents Mailing List:* Yes

Les Ami(e)s de la Terre Canada *See* Friends of the Earth Canada

Les AmiEs de la Terre de Québec (ATQ)

Centre Frédéric-Back Culture et Environnement, #210, 870, rue Salaberry, Québec QC G1R 2T9
Tél: 418-524-2744
Courriel: info@atquebec.org
www.atquebec.org
Aperçu: *Dimension:* petite; *Envergure:* locale; Organisme sans but lucratif; fondée en 1978
Mission: Conscientiser la population à la crise écologique mondiale versus le droit de tous à un environnement sain; éduquer les gens à leur propre prise en charge personnelle et collective face à cette crise; améliorer les communications entre écologistes aussi bien qu'entre ceux-ci et la population qu'ils desservent; renforcer la qualité de la vie associative chez-nous aussi bien qu'ailleurs dans la région et au Québec; *Membre de:* Réseau Québécois des Groupes Écologistes (RQGE); Regroupement d'éducation populaire en action communautaire (Répac)
Membre(s) du bureau directeur:
Yan Grenier, Président
Renaud Blais, Administrator
Finances: *Budget de fonctionnement annuel:* Moins de $50,000
Personnel: 9 membre(s) du personnel
Membre: 250 *Montant de la cotisation:* 10$ travailleur; 5$ non-travailleur; *Comités:* Paix; Environnement et mondialisation; Écologie et santé; Eau; Forêt
Activités: RadioTerre; émission hebdomadaire d'écologie politique diffusée sur les ondes de CKIA FM (Québec); une conférence par mois sur des thèmes reliés à l'écologie; *Service de conférenciers:* Oui; *Bibliothèque:* Centre documentation des ATQ

Amis des parc nationaux du Mont-Revelstoke et des Glaciers ***See*** Friends of Mount Revelstoke & Glacier National Parks

Les Amis du Jardin botanique de Montréal / Friends of the Montréal Botanical Garden

#206A, 4101, rue Sherbrooke est, Montréal QC H1X 2B2
Tél: 514-872-1493; *Téléc:* 514-872-3765
Courriel: amisjardin@ville.montreal.qc.ca
www.amisjardin.qc.ca
www.facebook.com/LesAmisduJardinbotaniquedeMontreal
Nom précédent: Société d'animation du Jardin et de l'Institut botanique
Aperçu: *Dimension:* moyenne; *Envergure:* locale; Organisme sans but lucratif; fondée en 1975
Membre de: Fédération des sociétés d'horticulture et d'écologie du Québec (FSHEQ); Flora Québec
Membre(s) du bureau directeur:
Céline Couture, Secrétaire-Réceptionniste
Paule Lamontagne, Présidente
Membre: 28 000 *Montant de la cotisation:* 30$ étudiant/ainé; 45$ individu; 60$ familial; $180 corporatif
Activités: Cours et ateliers donnés par des spécialistes; Conférences; Visites guidées et excursions; Voyages

Les Amis du Parc Awenda ***See*** The Friends of Awenda Park

Analystes des minéraux canadiens ***See*** Canadian Mineral Analysts

Animal Alliance of Canada (AAC) / Alliance animale du Canada

#101, 221 Broadview Ave., Toronto ON M4M 2G3
Tel: 416-462-9541; *Fax:* 416-462-9647
e-mail: contact@animalalliance.ca
www.animalalliance.ca
www.facebook.com/132125293547127
Overview: A medium-sized national organization founded in 1990
Mission: To preserve & protect all animals; to promote harmonious relationship between people, animals & the environment; to address issues including pound seizure, cosmetic & product testing, puppy mills, pet overpopulation, exotic pet trade, the fur trade, sport hunting, factory farming, animals as "entertainment"
Chief Officer(s):
Shelly Hawley-Yan, Editor, 519-940-4712
shelly@animalalliance.ca
George Dupras, Director
Jacqui Barnes, Director
Marie Crawford, Director
Barry Kent MacKay, Director
Liz White, Director
Finances: *Funding Sources:* Private donations; garage sales; merchandise; information & displays
Staff: 5 staff member(s); 130 volunteer(s)
Membership: 20,000
Activities: Promoting cruelty-free, environmentally friendly biodegradable products; currently involved in working to ban pound seizure; information displays; National Wolf Campaign; Endangered Species Campaign; working to end the destruction of over 1,000,000 companion animals (abandoned & unwanted pets) in Canada each year through legislation, spay/neuter programs & public education; working to ban the keeping of exotic animals as pets; *Awareness Events:* "Literary Lions" annual literary benefit; "Animal Magnetism" annual music benefit; *Library:* Animal Alliance Resource Centre

Animal Defence & Anti-Vivisection Society of BC (ADAV)

PO Box 391, Stn. A, Vancouver BC V6C 2N2
vivisectionresearch.ca
Overview: A small provincial organization
Chief Officer(s):
Anne Birthistle, Director
shamrockstudio@shaw.ca
John Pranger, Director, 604-564-1432
prangerjohn@yahoo.ca
Finances: *Funding Sources:* Private
Staff: 6 staff member(s)
Membership: 200; *Fees:* $5 student/senior; $10 individual; $50 lifetime

Animal Defence League of Canada (ADLC)

PO Box 3880, Stn. C, Ottawa ON K1Y 4M5
Tel: 613-233-6117; *Fax:* 613-233-6117
animal-defence.ncf.ca
Overview: A medium-sized national organization founded in 1958
Mission: To promote animal welfare/rights; To disseminate information; To encourage spaying & neutering of cats & dogs; To increase public awareness of oppression of animals & how to prevent or alleviate animal exploitation, cruelty & suffering; *Member of:* World Society for the Protection of Animals
Chief Officer(s):
J. Bélair, Office Manager
Finances: *Annual Operating Budget:* $50,000-$100,000; *Funding Sources:* Donations; Membership fees
Membership: 2,050; *Fees:* $50 lifetime; $10 individual; $5 senior/student; *Committees:* Companion Animals; Food Animals; Experimentation; Wildlife Protection
Activities: *Speaker Service:* Yes; *Library:* Open to public

Animal Nutrition Association of Canada (ANAC) / Association de nutrition animale du Canada

#1301, 150 Metcalfe St., Ottawa ON K2P 1P1
Tel: 613-241-6421; *Fax:* 613-241-7970
e-mail: info@anacan.org
www.anacan.org
Previous Name: Canadian Feed Industry Association
Overview: A large national organization founded in 1929
Mission: ANAC advocates on behalf of the livestock & poultry feed industry with government regulators & policy-makers, & works to maintain high standards of feed & food safety.; *Member of:* International Feed Industry Federation (IFIF); Affiliation(s): Canola Council of Canada; Canada Grains Council; Canadian Egg Marketing Agency; Canadian Chicken Marketing Agency; Canadian Turkey Marketing Agency
Chief Officer(s):
Peter Bennett, Chair
Graham Cooper, Executive Director
gcooper@anacan.org
Finances: *Funding Sources:* Membership fees
Staff: 3 staff member(s)
Membership: 170 organizations; *Fees:* Variable; *Member Profile:* Manufacturers & suppliers of animal nutrition products to Canada's livestock & poultry industries; *Committees:* FFA; GMP; Certification
Activities: FeedAssure program; Canadian Feed Industry Advisor Certification Program; Canadian Feed Technology Seminar; Canadian Feed Industry Commodity Supplier Course; promotion of environment & animal care issues, & regulations & legislation pertaining to feed products, manufacturing, food safety & salmonella control; monitors regulations pertaining to agricultural trade & international & interprovincial import & export
Meetings/Conferences:
For more information see Trade Shows, Conferences and Seminars Chapter
Animal Nutrition Association of Canada Annual General Meeting & Convention 2013
April 2013 Toronto, ON
2013 Eastern Nutrition Conference
May 2013 Quebec City, QC
Publications:
•Directory of Members [a publication of the Animal Nutrition Association of Canada]
Type: Directory

Animal Welfare Foundation of Canada (AWF) / Fondation du bien-être animal du Canada

#343, 300 Earl Grey Dr., Ottawa ON K2T 1C1
e-mail: info@awfc.ca
www.awfc.ca
Overview: A small national charitable organization founded in 1965
Mission: The Animal Welfare Foundation of Canada is a registered charity, supported by donors and administered by a volunteer Board of Directors. The Foundation seeks to improve the quality of life for animals in this country. Since the 1960s the Foundation, an independent watchdog organization, has been at the forefront of issues of humane care of animals in Canada.; Affiliation(s): World Society for the Protection of Animals
Chief Officer(s):
Alice Crook, President & Chair
Frances Rodenberg, Secretary
Finances: *Annual Operating Budget:* $100,000-$250,000
Staff: 14 volunteer(s)
Activities: *Speaker Service:* Yes

Antarctic & Southern Ocean Coalition (ASOC)

1630 Connecticut Ave., 3rd Fl., Washington DC 20009 USA
Tel: 202-234-2480; *Fax:* 202-387-4823
e-mail: antarctica@igc.org
www.asoc.org
www.facebook.com/38924681853
twitter.com/ASOC1
Also Known As: Secretariat, The Antarctica Project
Overview: A medium-sized international organization founded in 1977
Mission: To protect the biological diversity & pristine wilderness of Antarctica, including its oceans & marine life; to work for the passage of strong measures which protect the marine ecosystem from the harmful effects of overfishing; to ensure that the integrity of the southern ocean whale sanctuary is maintained & internationally respected; Affiliation(s): World Wildlife Fund Canada; World Society for the Protection of Animals; Friends of the Earth; Greenpeace; Sierra Club
Chief Officer(s):
Jim Barnes, Executive Director
Finances: *Annual Operating Budget:* $250,000-$500,000; *Funding Sources:* Foundation grants; membership dues
Staff: 9 staff member(s); 2 volunteer(s)
Membership: 235
Activities: Conducts legal & policy research & analysis; testifies at Congressional hearings; produces educational materials; works with the key users of Antarctica, including scientists, tourists, & governments, to ensure that activities have a minimal environmental impact; attends all Antarctic Treaty Consultative Meetings & all CCAMLR meetings; *Library:* by appointment

Anti-Tuberculosis Society ***See*** British Columbia Lung Association

Applied Science Technologists & Technicians of British Columbia (ASTTBC)
Parent Name: Canadian Council of Technicians & Technologists

10767 - 148 St., Surrey BC V3R 0S4
Tel: 604-585-2788; *Fax:* 604-585-2790
e-mail: techinfo@asttbc.org
www.asttbc.org
www.youtube.com/user/ASTTBC
Previous Name: Society of Engineering Technologists of BC
Overview: A large provincial organization founded in 1958 overseen by Canadian Council of Technicians & Technologists
Mission: To advance the profession of applied science technology & the professional recognition of applied science technologists, certified technician, & other members in a manner that serves & protects the public interest; *Member of:* Canadian Council of Technicians & Technologists
Chief Officer(s):
Bill MacPherson, AScT, President
John E. Leech, AScT, CAE, Executive Director
jleech@asttbc.org
Cindy Aitken, Manager, Governance & Events
caitken@asttbc.org
Garry Gaudet, Manager, Media Relations
ggaudet@asttbc.org
Jason Jung, Manager, Member & Program Development
jjung@asttbc.org
Nicky Malli, Manager, Finance
nmalli@asttbc.org
Geoff Sale, AScT, Manager, Internationally Trained Professionals
gsale@asttbc.org
Anne Sharp, BA, Manager, Marketing & Exec. Dir., ASTTBC Foundation
asharp@asttbc.org
Robert Stitt, AScT, Manager, Special Projects
rstitt@asttbc.org
Karen Taylor, DipBM, Manager, Operations
ktaylor@asttbc.org
Finances: *Funding Sources:* Membership dues; Accreditation; Member services; Advertising; Education
Staff: 250 volunteer(s)
Membership: 8,600; *Fees:* $255; *Committees:* Construction Safety Certification Panel; Fire Protection Certification Board; Public Works Inspection Certification Board
Activities: *Internships:* Yes; *Rents Mailing List:* Yes
Publications:
•Member Compensation Survey [a publication of Applied Science Technologists & Technicians of British Columbia]
Type: Report
•Member Satisfaction Survey [a publication of Applied Science Technologists & Technicians of British Columbia]
Type: Report

Aquaculture Association of Canada (AAC) / Association Aquacole du Canada

16 Lobster Lane, St. Andrews NB E5B 3T6
Tel: 506-529-4766; *Fax:* 506-529-4609
e-mail: aac@dfo-mpo.gc.ca
www.aquacultureassociation.ca
Overview: A medium-sized national charitable organization founded in 1984
Mission: To foster an aquaculture industry in Canada; To encourage & support the educational, technological, & scientific advancement of aquaculture
Environmental Activity: Promoting sustainable aquaculture
Chief Officer(s):
Susan Waddy, Manager, Association Office, 506-529-4766
Susan.Waddy@dfo-mpo.gc.ca
Tim Jackson, President, 506-636-3728, Fax: 506-636-3479
timothy.jackson@nrc-cnrc.gc.ca
Tim DeJager, Vice-President, 250-751-0634
dejagert@co3.ca
Joy Wade, Vice-President, 250-754-6884
joy2004wade@yahoo.ca
Shelley King, Secretary, 902-421-5646, Fax: 902-421-2733
sking@genomeatlantic.ca
Caroline Graham, Treasurer
cpgraham@rogers.com
Finances: *Funding Sources:* Donations
Membership: 900+; *Member Profile:* Students; Educators; Producers; Suppliers; Scientists; Government representatives; *Committees:* Election; Finance; Rules; Time & Place; Arrangements; Program; Publications; Awards; Student Affairs; Membership; Business Development
Activities: Promoting the study of aquaculture & related sciences; Providing scientific & technical information related to aquaculture; Increasing public awareness & understanding of aquaculture; Liaising with goverment & industry; Providing networking opportunities; Conducting seminars
Meetings/Conferences:
For more information see Trade Shows, Conferences and Seminars Chapter
Aquaculture Canada 2013: The Aquaculture Association of Canada's Annual Conference & General Meeting
June 2013 Guelph, ON
Aquaculture Canada 2014: The Aquaculture Association of Canada's Annual Conference & General Meeting
2014
Aquaculture Canada 2015: The Aquaculture Association of Canada's Annual Conference & General Meeting
2015
Publications:
•Aquaculture Canada Abstracts
Profile: Conference program guides, featuring conference sessions
•Aquaculture Canada Proceedings of Contributed Papers
Profile: Proceedings of the contributed papers of the annual meetings of the Aquaculture Association of Canada
•Bulletin of the Aquaculture Association of Canada
Type: Newsletter
Profile: Topics have included sea-urchin aquaculture, application of genome science to sustainable aquaculture, proceedings of the scallop aquaculture session, fish health,aquaculture public awareness & education, water movement & aquatic animal health, aquaculture biotechnology, & progress in cod farming
•The Watermark [a publication of the Aquaculture Association of Canada]
Type: Newsletter; *Frequency:* 3 pa; *Editor:* Gregor Reid; Candace Durston
Profile: Aquaculture Association of Canada updates, such as donations, awards, & meetings

Aquaculture Association of Nova Scotia (AANS)

c/o Starlite Gallery, #215, 7071 Bayers Rd., Halifax NS B3L 2C2
Tel: 902-422-6234; *Fax:* 902-422-6248
e-mail: info@aansonline.ca
www.aansonline.ca
twitter.com/AANSOnline
www.youtube.com/user/aansonline
Overview: A small provincial organization founded in 1977
Member of: Canadian Aquaculture Industry Alliance
Chief Officer(s):
Bruce Hancock, Executive Director
bhancock@seafarmers.ca
Finances: *Funding Sources:* Membership fees
Staff: 3 staff member(s)
Membership: 40; *Fees:* Producers $500-10,000; Suppliers/Processors $375-10,000; Friends $150; Students $25; *Member Profile:* Not-for-profit association of growers, suppliers & industry supporters; *Committees:* Nova Scotia Aquaculture Environmental Coordinating Committee
Meetings/Conferences:
For more information see Trade Shows, Conferences and Seminars Chapter
Sea Farmers Conference 2013
January 2013 Halifax, NS

AquaNet - Network in Aquaculture

Ocean Sciences Centre, Memorial University of Newfoundland, St. John's NL A1C 5S7
Tel: 709-737-3245; *Fax:* 709-737-3500
e-mail: info@aquanet.ca
www.aquanet.ca
Overview: A medium-sized national organization
Mission: To foster a sustainable aquaculture sector in Canada through high quality research & education; *Member of:* Networks of Centres of Excellence

Arbres Canada *See* Tree Canada Foundation

Archaeological Institute of America (AIA) / Institut Archéologique d'Amérique

Boston University, 656 Beacon St., 6th Fl, Boston MA 02215-2006 USA
Tel: 617-353-9361; *Fax:* 617-353-6550
e-mail: aia@aia.bu.edu
www.archaeological.org
www.facebook.com/Archaeological.Institute
twitter.com/archaeology_aia
youtube.com/archaeologytv
Overview: A large international charitable organization founded in 1879
Mission: To encourage & support archaeological research & publication; To encourage protection of world's cultural heritage; *Member of:* American Council of Learned Societies; Affiliation(s): Fédération internationale des associations d'études classiques
Chief Officer(s):
Peter Herdrich, CEO
pherdrich@aia.bu.edu
Elizabeth Bartman, President
Finances: *Annual Operating Budget:* Greater than $5 Million; *Funding Sources:* Membership dues; donations; subscription income
Staff: 25 staff member(s)
Membership: 9,000; *Fees:* Schedule available; *Committees:* AIA Tours; American Committee on the Corpus Vasorum Antiquorum; Archaeology in Higher Education; Archives; Audit; Conservation & Site Preservation; Corresponding Members; Development; Digital Technology; Education; Executive; Fellowship; Gold Medal; Governance; Lecture Program; Museums and Exhibitions; Nominating; Personnel; Professional Responsibilities; Publication Subvention; Societies
Activities: Provides over 250 lectures within the US each year; *Speaker Service:* Yes; *Rents Mailing List:* Yes
Publications:
•American Journal of Archaeology
Editor: Naomi Norman
Profile: Quarterly academic journal
•Archaeology
Editor: Peter A. Young
Profile: Bi-monthly magazine

The Architectural Conservancy of Ontario (ACO)

#403, 10 Adelaide St. East, Toronto ON M5C 1J3
Tel: 416-367-8075; *Fax:* 416-367-8630
Toll-Free: 877-264-8937
e-mail: manager@arconserv.ca
www.arconserv.ca
Overview: A medium-sized provincial charitable organization founded in 1933
Mission: To preserve buildings & structures of architectural merit & places of natural beauty or interest; Affiliation(s): Ontario Heritage Alliance
Chief Officer(s):
Lloyd Alter, President
Finances: *Annual Operating Budget:* $100,000-$250,000; *Funding Sources:* Donations; government grants; membership dues; fundraising activities
Staff: 2 staff member(s); 81 volunteer(s)
Membership: 1,025 + 25 branches & groups; *Fees:* $35; *Committees:* Advisory Board & various Planning Committees
Activities: Technical consulting service for property owners, groups & municipalities; neighbourhood & garden tours; conferences & workshops; capital fundraising for repair & restoration work; architectural research; property acquisition
Meetings/Conferences:
For more information see Trade Shows, Conferences and Seminars Chapter
Architectural Conservancy of Ontario 2013 Annual General Meeting
June 2013 Penetanguishene, ON

Architectural Heritage Society of Saskatchewan (AHSS)

202 - 1275 Broad St., Regina SK S4R 1Y2
Tel: 306-359-0933; *Fax:* 306-359-3899
e-mail: sahs@sasktel.net
www.ahsk.ca
Overview: A small provincial organization founded in 1987
Mission: To promote, support & facilitate the preservation, conservation, restoration & reuse of distinct architectural & historical heritage properties (designated or potential) throughout the province, ensuring that our built heritage is maintained for present & future citizens to appreciate the contributions & craftsmanship of past generations; to enhance the current social, economic & environmental quality of life; *Member of:* Saskatchewan Council of Cultural Organizations; Canadian Heritage Network; National Preservation Trust
Finances: *Annual Operating Budget:* $50,000-$100,000; *Funding Sources:* Private & public sector funding
Staff: 1 staff member(s)
Membership: 230; *Fees:* $20; *Committees:* Membership; Finance; Administration; Policy

Arctic Council

Foreign Affairs Canada, 125 Sussex Dr., Ottawa ON K1A 0G2
Tel: 613-995-1874; *Fax:* 613-644-1852
e-mail: media@international.gc.ca
www.arctic-council.org
Mission: To operate as an intergovernmental forum; To address common concerns & challenges by the member states of Canada, Denmark (including Greenland & the Faroe Islands), Finland, Iceland, Norway, the Russian Federation, Sweden & the United States; To address environmental, social & economic issues; To carry out scientific work in five expert working groups, focusing on such issues as monitoring, assessing & preventing pollution in the Arctic, climate change, biodiversity conservation & sustainable use, emergency preparedness, & prevention; To meet every two years, with the secretariat rotating among the member states
Environmental Activity: Acting as a a regional forum for sustainable development
Chief Officer(s):
Magnus Jóhannesson, Director of the Secretariat
magnus@arctic-council.org
Membership: *Member Profile:* Member states include Canada, Denmark (including Greenland & the Faroe Islands), Finland, Iceland, Norway, the Russian Federation, Sweden & the United States; Permananent participants are the Arctic Athabascan Council, the Aleut International Association, the Gwich'in Council International, the Inuit Circumpolar Council, the Russian Association of Indigenous Peoples of the North, and the Saami Council
Activities: Five working groups are as follows: Sustainable Development Working Group; Arctic Monitoring & Assessment Programme; Protection of the Marine Environment; Conservation of Arctic Flora & Fauna; Emergency, Prevention, Preparedness & Response

Arctic Institute of North America (AINA)

University of Calgary, 2500 University Dr. NW, Calgary AB T2N 1N4
Tel: 403-220-7515; *Fax:* 403-282-4609
e-mail: arctic@ucalgary.ca
www.arctic.ucalgary.ca
Overview: A medium-sized local organization founded in 1945
Mission: To encourage & support scientific research pertaining to the polar regions; Affiliation(s): The University of Alaska
Chief Officer(s):
Michel Scott, Board Chair
Benoît Beauchamp, Executive Director
Membership: 1,000-4,999
Awards:
•Jennifer Robinson Memorial Scholarship (Scholarship)
For Master's or Ph.D. students; must submit a brief statement of research objectives *Deadline:* December 1 *Amount:* $5,000
•Lorraine Allison Scholarship (Scholarship)
Granted on the basis of academic standing, commitment to northern Canadian research & benefit to Northerners; Master's or Ph.D. students from the Yukon & NWT are encouraged to apply *Deadline:* May 1 *Amount:* $2,000

ArcticNet Inc.
Pavillon Alexandre-Vachon, Université Laval, #4081, 1045, av de la Médecine, Québec QC G1V 0A6
Tel: 418-656-5830; *Fax:* 418-656-2334
e-mail: arcticnet@arcticnet.ulaval.ca
www.arcticnet-ulaval.ca
Overview: A medium-sized national organization founded in 2003
Mission: To study the impacts of climate change in the coastal Canadian Arctic; To engage Inuit organizations, northern communities, universities, research institutes, industry, government, & international agencies as partners in the scientific process; *Member of:* Network of Centres of Excellence of Canada
Environmental Activity: Formulating strategies to face the impacts of climate change & globalization in the Arctic
Chief Officer(s):
Martin Fortier, Executive Director, 418-656-5233
martin.fortier@arcticnet.ulaval.ca
Louis Fortier, Scientific Director, 418-656-5646
louis.fortier@bio.ulaval.ca
Réal Choquette, Administrative Director, 418-656-2445
real.choquette@arcticnet.ulaval.ca
Jean-Luc Bernier, Officer, Communications, 418-656-7106
jean-luc.bernier@arcticnet.ulaval.ca
Keith Levesque, Coordinator, Ship-based Research, 418-656-3071
keith.levesque@arcticnet.ulaval.ca
Josée Michaud, Coordinator, Data, 418-656-2411
Josee.Michaud@arcticnet.ulaval.ca
Finances: *Funding Sources:* Government of Canada, through the Networks of Centres of Excellence programs
Membership: 1-99; *Member Profile:* Educational institutions; *Committees:* Executive; Communications; Audit & Finance; Environmental Review; Industrial Partnership; Inuit Partnership; Research Management; Inuit Advisory
Activities: Conducting Integrated Regional Impact Studies on marine & terrestrial coastal ecosystems & societies in the Eastern Canadian Arctic, the Canadian High Arctic & in Hudson Bay; Disseminating knowledge; Facilitating networking opportunities
Publications:
•ArcticNet Inc. Annual Report
Type: Yearbook; *Frequency:* Annually
•ArcticNet Newsletter
Type: Newsletter; *Frequency:* .

ARK II
PO Box 687, Stn. Q, Toronto ON M4T 2N5
Tel: 416-536-2308
e-mail: info@ark-ii.com
www.ark-ii.com
www.facebook.com/group.php?gid=2355091568
twitter.com/ARKII_TO
Also Known As: Animal Rights Kollective
Overview: A small local charitable organization
Mission: To promote & protect the rights of all animals & foster their individual liberties through direct action, political action, & public awareness campaigns
Membership: *Fees:* Annual: $10; Lifetime: $50
Activities: Anti-fur campaigns, Veganism/Vegetarianism promotion, Anti-animal experimentation campaigns

Arrowsmith Natural History Society *See* Arrowsmith Naturalists

Arrowsmith Naturalists
PO Box 1542, Parksville BC V9P 2H4
Tel: 250-752-0445
e-mail: arrowsmithnats@gmail.com
www.arrowsmithnats.org
Previous Name: Arrowsmith Natural History Society
Overview: A small local organization founded in 1970
Mission: To further the understanding & conservation of nature; *Member of:* Federation of BC Naturalists; Affiliation(s): B.C. Nature; Nature Canada
Finances: *Annual Operating Budget:* Less than $50,000
Membership: 110; *Fees:* $25 individual; $35 family; $12 junior (up to 18); *Member Profile:* Interest in nature; *Committees:* Botany; Birds; Outings

Arusha Centre Society
The Old "Y" Bldg., #106, 223 - 12 Ave. SW, Calgary AB T2R 0G6
Tel: 403-270-3200; *Fax:* 403-270-8832
e-mail: arusha@arusha.org
www.arusha.org
www.facebook.com/ArushaCentre?ref=ts
www.twitter.com/ArushaCentre
Overview: A small local charitable organization founded in 1972
Mission: To provide opportunities for, & remove barriers to, individual & community participation, self-determination & empowerment, especially for those who have been marginalized; To acknowledge, respect & actively value diversity, based on the belief in inherent human dignity; To challenge unjust internal & external assumptions & structures & work toward socially just alternatives; To connect social, economic & ecological issues, both locally & globally; to create a meaningful partnership that fosters social justice internally & externally; *Member of:* Volunteer Centre of Calgary; Parklands Institute
Chief Officer(s):
Sharon Stevens, Info-activee Coordinator
Finances: *Annual Operating Budget:* $250,000-$500,000; *Funding Sources:* Federal & provincial government; donations; United Way
Staff: 7 staff member(s); 75 volunteer(s)
Membership: 225; *Fees:* $10; *Member Profile:* Calgary community; *Committees:* Finance; Fundraising; Membership; Programming; Marketing
Activities: ; *Library:* Resource Centre; Open to public

Ashmont & District Agricultural Society
PO Box 23, Ashmont AB T0A 0C0
Tel: 780-726-3897
Overview: A small local organization founded in 1984
Chief Officer(s):
Jenny Bespalko, Contact
jbsbespalko@yahoo.com
Finances: *Funding Sources:* Fundraising; donations
Staff: 30 volunteer(s)
Membership: 60; *Fees:* $1; *Committees:* Economic Development; Agricultural Services; Aspen Grove Seniors Lodge; Agri-Plex Management; Heritage Day; Minor Sports; Continuing Education; Government Liaison

Asia Pacific Foundation of Canada (APFC) / Fondation Asie Pacifique du Canada
#220, 890 West Pender St., Vancouver BC V6C 1J9
Tel: 604-684-5986; *Fax:* 604-681-1370
e-mail: info@asiapacific.ca
www.asiapacific.ca
www.facebook.com/asiapacificfoundationofcanada
twitter.com/AsiaPacificFdn
Also Known As: APF Canada
Overview: A medium-sized international organization founded in 1984
Mission: Independent think tank on Canada's relations with Asia; to bring together people & knowledge to provide the most current & comprehensive research, analysis & information on Canada's transpacific relations; to promote dialogue on economic, security, political & social issues, helping to influence public policy & foster informed decision-making in the Canadian public, private & non-governmental sectors
Chief Officer(s):
Yuen Pau Woo, President & CEO
president@asiapacific.ca
Jill Price, Executive Director
jill.price@asiapacific.ca
Finances: *Annual Operating Budget:* $1.5 Million-$3 Million; *Funding Sources:* Federal & provincial government
Staff: 30 staff member(s)
Activities: Business; media; education; public policy; research; *Internships:* Yes

Asia-Pacific Centre for Environmental Law (APCEL)
Faculty of Law, Ntl. University of Singapore, Eu Tong Sen Bldg., 469G Bukit Timah Rd., Singapore 259776 Singapore
Tel: 65-6516-6246; *Fax:* 65-6872-1937
e-mail: lawapcel@nus.edu.sg
law.nus.edu.sg/apcel/
Overview: A small international organization
Chief Officer(s):
Koh Kheng-Lian, Director
Shirley Mak, Secretary
lawmaksy@nus.edu.sg

Asociación Nacional de la Industria Química, A.C *See* National Association of the Chemistry Industry

ASPHME
#301, 2271, boul Fernand-Lafontaine, Longueuil QC J4G 2R7
Tél: 450-442-7763; *Téléc:* 450-442-2332
Courriel: info@aspme.org
www.asphme.org
Nom précédent: Association paritaire pour la santé et la sécurité du travail - Habillement
Aperçu: *Dimension:* grande; *Envergure:* provinciale; Organisme sans but lucratif; fondée en 1986
Mission: To prevent work-related injuries in the apparel sector. Full name: Association sectorielle paritaire pour la santé et la sécurité du travail du secteur de la fabrication de produits en métal, de la fabrication de produits électriques et des industries de l'habillement
Membre(s) du bureau directeur:
Normand Durocher, Coprésident
Denis Dufour, Coprésident
Alain Plourde, Directeur général
Finances: *Budget de fonctionnement annuel:* $500,000-$1.5 Million
Personnel: 7 membre(s) du personnel
Activités: *Stagiaires:* Oui; *Service de conférenciers:* Oui

Assemblée des Premières Nations *See* Assembly of First Nations

Assembly of First Nations (AFN) / Assemblée des Premières Nations (APN)
Trebla Building, 473 Albert St., Ottawa ON K1R 5B4
Tel: 613-241-6789; *Fax:* 613-241-5808
Toll-Free: 866-869-6789
e-mail: imcleod@afn.ca
www.afn.ca
www.facebook.com/AFN.APN
twitter.com/AFN_Updates
www.youtube.com/user/afnposter
Previous Name: National Indian Brotherhood
Overview: A large national organization
Mission: The AFN Secretariat acts as an advocate for First Nations on many issues, including Aboriginal & Treaty Rights, economic development, education, languages & literacy, health, housing, social development, justice, land claims & the environment
Chief Officer(s):
Shawn Atleo, National Chief
Finances: *Funding Sources:* Federal grants
Staff: 100 staff member(s)
Membership: 633 First Nations in Canada

Assiniboine Park Conservancy
55 Pavilion Cres., Winnipeg MB R3P 2N7
Tel: 204-927-6001
e-mail: info@assiniboinepark.ca
www.zoosociety.com
www.facebook.com/assiniboineparkzoo
twitter.com/assiniboinepark
www.youtube.com/user/AssiniboinePark
Previous Name: Zoological Society of Manitoba
Overview: A small provincial charitable organization founded in 1956
Mission: To redevelop & manage the Park's operations & ongoing financial viability.
Environmental Activity: Conservation & research programs
Chief Officer(s):
Hartley Richardson, Chair
Margaret Redmond, President & CEO
Finances: *Annual Operating Budget:* $1.5 Million-$3 Million
Membership: *Fees:* $10-$95
Activities: School & group programs; workshops & classes; outreach & sleepovers; day campsl guided tours;

Associated Country Women of the World
Mary Sumner House, 24 Tufton St., London SW1P 3RB United Kingdom
Tel: 44-20-7799-3875; *Fax:* 44-20-7340-9950
e-mail: info@acww.org.uk
www.acww.org.uk
www.facebook.com/133340763410423
twitter.com/acww_news
www.youtube.com/user/ACWWnews
Overview: A large international organization
Mission: To raise the standards of living & education of women & their families all over the world through community development projects & training; To promote international goodwill, friendship & understanding between women everywhere; To work for equal opportunites for women by the elimination of discrimination because of gender, race, nationality, religion or marital status; To act as a forum on international affairs for rural women, speaking for them with an informed voice in the Councils of the world
Environmental Activity: Funds for water resources
Chief Officer(s):

May Kidd, World President
Membership: *Fees:* £20 annual; £50 three-year; *Committees:* Promotion & Publications; United Nations; Projects
Activities: Funding more than 900 projects around the world, including the Water for All Fund, the Women Feed the World Fund, & the Projects Fund
Meetings/Conferences:
For more information see Trade Shows, Conferences and Seminars Chapter
Associated Country Women of the World 27th Triennial Conference
September 2013 Chennai
Publications:
•ACWW [Associated Country Women of the World] Annual Report
Type: Yearbook; *Frequency:* Annually
•All About ACWW [Associated Country Women of the World]
Type: Brochure
•The Country Woman [a publication of the Associated Country Women of the World]
Type: Magazine; *Frequency:* q.
Profile: Up-to-date association news & stories

Associated Environmental Site Assessors of Canada Inc. (AESAC)

PO Box 490, Fenelon Falls ON K0M 1N0
Tel: 877-512-3722
Toll-Free: 877-512-3722
e-mail: info@aesac.ca
www.aesac.ca
Overview: A small national organization founded in 1992
Mission: To provide services to assist site assessors in meeting the needs of potential clients such as lenders & major property owners; To assist practitioners from many different professional backgrounds in identifying & maintaining appropriate standards for conducting site assessments
Chief Officer(s):
Bruno Luzak, President

Association Aquacole du Canada ***See*** Aquaculture Association of Canada

Association botanique du Canada ***See*** Canadian Botanical Association

Association canadienne d'énergie éolienne ***See*** Canadian Wind Energy Association Inc.

Association canadienne d'énergie fluide ***See*** Canadian Fluid Power Association

L'Association canadienne d'ergonomie ***See*** Association of Canadian Ergonomists

Association canadienne d'études environnementales ***See*** Environmental Studies Association of Canada

Association canadienne d'experts-conseils en patrimoine ***See*** Canadian Association of Heritage Professionals

Association canadienne d'hydrographie ***See*** Canadian Hydrographic Association

Association canadienne de cartographie ***See*** Canadian Cartographic Association

Association canadienne de droit et société ***See*** Canadian Law & Society Association

Association canadienne de droit maritime ***See*** Canadian Maritime Law Association

Association canadienne de l'autobus ***See*** Canadian Bus Association

Association canadienne de l'électricité ***See*** Canadian Electricity Association

Association canadienne de l'emballage ***See*** Packaging Association of Canada

Association canadienne de l'hydroélectricité ***See*** Canadian Hydropower Association

Association canadienne de l'imprimerie ***See*** Canadian Printing Industries Association

Association canadienne de l'industrie de la peinture et du revêtement ***See*** Canadian Paint & Coatings Association

Association canadienne de l'industrie des plastiques ***See*** Canadian Plastics Industry Association

Association canadienne de l'industrie du caoutchouc ***See*** The Rubber Association of Canada

Association canadienne de la construction ***See*** Canadian Construction Association

Association canadienne de la gestion de l'innovation ***See*** Innovation Management Association of Canada

Association canadienne de la gestion parasitaire ***See*** Canadian Pest Management Association

Association canadienne de la médecine du travail et de l'environnement ***See*** Occupational & Environmental Medical Association of Canada

Association canadienne de méchanique des roches ***See*** Canadian Rock Mechanics Association

Association canadienne de pipelines d'énergie ***See*** Canadian Energy Pipeline Association

Association canadienne de radioprotection ***See*** Canadian Radiation Protection Association

Association canadienne de recherches en évaluation non-destructive ***See*** Canadian Association for Research in Nondestructive Evaluation

Association canadienne de réhabilitation des sites dégradés ***See*** Canadian Land Reclamation Association

Association canadienne de santé publique ***See*** Canadian Public Health Association

Association canadienne de sécurité agricole ***See*** Canadian Agricultural Safety Association

Association canadienne de technologie de pointe ***See*** Canadian Advanced Technology Alliance

Association canadienne de transport industriel ***See*** Canadian Industrial Transportation Association

L'Association canadienne de vérification ***See*** Auditing Association of Canada

Association canadienne des agronomes-conseils ***See*** Canadian Consulting Agrologists Association

Association canadienne des aliments de santé ***See*** Canadian Health Food Association

Association canadienne des automobilistes ***See*** Canadian Automobile Association

Association canadienne des barrages ***See*** Canadian Dam Association

Association canadienne des boissons ***See*** Canadian Beverage Association

Association canadienne des carburants ***See*** Canadian Fuels Association

Association canadienne des carburants ***See*** Canadian Fuels Association

Association canadienne des carburants ***See*** Canadian Fuels Association

Association canadienne des carburants ***See*** Canadian Fuels Association

Association canadienne des carburants renouvelables ***See*** Canadian Renewable Fuels Association

Association canadienne des chefs de pompiers ***See*** Canadian Association of Fire Chiefs

Association canadienne des constructeurs d'habitations ***See*** Canadian Home Builders' Association

Association canadienne des distributeurs de produits chimiques ***See*** Canadian Association of Chemical Distributors

Association canadienne des eaux potables et usées ***See*** Canadian Water & Wastewater Association

Association canadienne des eaux souterraines ***See*** Canadian Ground Water Association

L'Association canadienne des éleveurs de porcs ***See*** Canadian Swine Breeders' Association

Association canadienne des embouteilleurs d'eau ***See*** Canadian Bottled Water Association

Association canadienne des entrepreneurs en mousse de polyuréthane ***See*** Canadian Urethane Foam Contractors Association

Association canadienne des entreprises de géomatique ***See*** Geomatics Industry Association of Canada

Association canadienne des exportateurs d'équipement et services miniers ***See*** Canadian Association of Mining Equipment & Services for Export

Association canadienne des fabricants de produits chimiques ***See*** Canadian Chemical Producers' Association

Association canadienne des fabricants de tuyaux de béton ***See*** Canadian Concrete Pipe Association

Association canadienne des fournisseurs de produits sanitaires ***See*** Canadian Sanitation Supply Association

Association canadienne des géographes ***See*** Canadian Association of Geographers

Association canadienne des industries du recyclage ***See*** Canadian Association of Recycling Industries

Association canadienne des laboratoires d'essais ***Voir*** Association des consultants et laboratoires experts

Association canadienne des manufacturiers de palettes et contenants ***See*** Canadian Wood Pallet & Container Association

Association canadienne des médecins vétérinaires ***See*** Canadian Veterinary Medical Association

Association canadienne des palynologues ***See*** Canadian Association of Palynologists

Association canadienne des parcs et loisirs ***See*** Canadian Parks & Recreation Association

Association canadienne des producteurs d'acier ***See*** Canadian Steel Producers Association

Association canadienne des producteurs de semences ***See*** Canadian Seed Growers' Association

Association canadienne des producteurs pétroliers ***See*** Canadian Association of Petroleum Producers

Association canadienne des prospecteurs & entrepreneurs ***See*** Prospectors & Developers Association of Canada

Association canadienne des rédacteurs scientifiques ***See*** Canadian Science Writers' Association

Association canadienne des ressources hydriques ***See*** Canadian Water Resources Association

Association canadienne des sciences géomatiques ***See*** Canadian Institute of Geomatics

Association canadienne des sciences régionales (ACSR) / Canadian Regional Science Association (CRSA)

a/s INRS-Urbanisation, 3465, rue Durocher, Montréal QC H2X 2C6
Tél: 514-499-4052; *Téléc:* 514-499-4065
geog.utm.utoronto.ca/crsa-acsr
Aperçu: *Dimension:* petite; *Envergure:* nationale; fondée en 1977
Mission: Favoriser la circulation des idées et promouvoir les études canadiennes portant sur les régions en se servant d'instruments, de méthodes et de cadres théoriques; propos aux sciences régionales comme ceux mis en avant par les diverses sciences, sociales ou autres; *Membre de:* Humanities & Social Sciences Federation of Canada
Membre(s) du bureau directeur:
Bill Anderson, Président
bander@uwindsor.ca
Richard Shearmur, Vice-président
richard.shearmur@ucs.inrs.ca
Pierre-Marcel Desjardins, Directeur exécutif
pierre-marcel.desjardins@umoncton.ca
Finances: *Budget de fonctionnement annuel:* Moins de $50,000
Membre: 245 *Montant de la cotisation:* 60$ individuel; 25$ étudiant/sans emploi
Activités: *Listes de destinataires:* Oui

Association canadienne des soins de santé ***See*** Canadian Healthcare Association

Association canadienne des surintendants de golf ***See*** Canadian Golf Superintendents Association

Association canadienne des techniciens et technologistes en santé animale ***See*** Canadian Association of Animal Health Technologists & Technicians

Association canadienne des travaux publics ***See*** Canadian Public Works Association

Association canadienne des tunnels ***See*** Tunnelling Association of Canada

Association Canadienne des Vétérinaires Porcins ***See*** Canadian Association of Swine Veterinarians

Association canadienne du bison ***See*** Canadian Bison Association

Association canadienne du camionnage d'entreprise ***See*** Private Motor Truck Council of Canada

Association canadienne du cartonnage ondulé et du carton-caisse ***See*** Canadian Corrugated Containerboard Association

Association canadienne du ciment ***See*** Cement Association of Canada

Association canadienne du commerce des semences ***See*** Canadian Seed Trade Association

Association canadienne du droit de l'environnement ***See*** Canadian Environmental Law Association

Association canadienne du gaz ***See*** Canadian Gas Association

Association canadienne du marketing ***See*** Canadian Marketing Association

Association canadienne du propane ***See*** Canadian Propane Association

Association canadienne du transport urbain ***See*** Canadian Urban Transit Association

Association canadienne française pour l'avancement des sciences ***Voir*** Association francophone pour le savoir

Association canadienne pour les énergies renouvelables ***See*** Canadian Association for Renewable Energies

Association canadienne pour les études sur la coopération ***See*** Canadian Association for Studies in Co-operation

Association canadienne pour les Nations-Unies ***See*** United Nations Association in Canada

Association Canadienne pour les Plantes Fourragères ***See*** Canadian Forage & Grassland Association

Association canadienne sur la qualité de l'eau ***See*** Canadian Association on Water Quality

Association canadienne Tourbe de Sphaigne ***See*** Canadian Sphagnum Peat Moss Association

Association chasse et pêche du Lac Brébeuf

247, ch du Lac Brébeuf, Saint-Félix-d'Otis QC G0V 1M0
Tél: 418-544-4884; *Téléc:* 418-544-7456
Aperçu: *Dimension:* petite; *Envergure:* locale
Mission: S'occupe de ce territoire protégé et contrôlé de chasse, de pêche et de villégiature; Affiliation(s): Regroupement régional de gestionnaires de Zec
Finances: *Budget de fonctionnement annuel:* $100,000-$250,000; *Fonds:* Gouvernement provincial
Personnel: 4 membre(s) du personnel; 10 bénévole(s)
Membre: 400 individu *Montant de la cotisation:* 22$ & 25$ individu

Association d'archéologie canadienne ***See*** Canadian Archaeological Association

Association d'isolation du Québec (AIQ)

#102, 4099, boul St-Jean-Baptiste, Montréal QC H1B 5V3
Tél: 514-354-9877; *Téléc:* 514-354-7401
Ligne sans frais: 800-711-2381
Courriel: info@isolation-aiq.ca
www.isolation-aiq.ca
Nom précédent: Association des entrepreneurs en isolation de la Province de Québec
Aperçu: *Dimension:* petite; *Envergure:* provinciale; fondée en 1959
Mission: L'AIQ fait la promotion du respect des règles de l'art du métier et de l'utilisation de l'isolation dans les secteurs commerciaux, industriels et institutionnels.
Membre(s) du bureau directeur:
Linda Wilson, Directrice générale
linda.wilson@isolation-aiq.ca
Membre: *Montant de la cotisation:* 700 $ - 1 073.24 $; *Critères d'admissibilite:* Entrepreneurs; fabricants; distributeurs

Association de chasse et pêche nordique, inc.

148, rue St-Marcellin Ouest, Les Escoumins QC G0T 1K0
Tél: 418-233-3062; *Téléc:* 418-233-3083
Aperçu: *Dimension:* petite; *Envergure:* locale; fondée en 1978
Affiliation(s): Fédération québécoise des gestionnaires de Zec
Membre(s) du bureau directeur:
Donald Tremblay, Responsable
Finances: *Budget de fonctionnement annuel:* $100,000-$250,000; *Fonds:* Gouvernement régional
Membre: 600 *Montant de la cotisation:* 12$

L'Association de l'efficacité énergétique du Canada ***See*** Canadian Energy Efficiency Alliance

Association de l'exploration minière de Québec (AEMQ)

#203, 132, avenue du Lac, Rouyn-Noranda QC J9X 4N5
Tél: 819-762-1599; *Téléc:* 819-762-1522
Courriel: aemq@aemq.org
www.aemq.org
Nom précédent: Association des prospecteurs du Québec
Aperçu: *Dimension:* moyenne; *Envergure:* provinciale; fondée en 1975
Mission: Développer, défendre et promouvoir l'exploration minière au Québec
Membre(s) du bureau directeur:
Ghislain Poirier, Président
Mélissa Desrochers, Vice-présidente, Communications
Finances: *Budget de fonctionnement annuel:* $100,000-$250,000
Personnel: 2 membre(s) du personnel; 20 bénévole(s)
Membre: 1 510 membres individuels, incluant 184 entreprises *Montant de la cotisation:* 20$ étudiant - 2 000$ entreprises; *Critères d'admissibilite:* Oeuvrer en exploration minière

Association de l'industrie touristique du Nouveau-Brunswick inc. ***See*** Tourism Industry Association of New Brunswick Inc.

Association de la construction navale du Canada ***See*** Shipbuilding Association of Canada

Association de la santé et de la sécurité des pâtes et papiers et des industries de la forêt du Québec (ASSIFQ-ASSPPQ)

Place Iberville II, #210, 1175, av Lavigerie, Sainte-Foy QC G1V 4P1
Tél: 418-657-2267; *Téléc:* 418-651-4622
Ligne sans frais: 888-632-9326
Courriel: info@santesecurite.org
www.santesecurite.org
Aperçu: *Dimension:* moyenne; *Envergure:* provinciale; fondée en 2010
Mission: A pour mission de soutenir et d'accompagner les entreprises dans l'amélioration continue de la santé et de la sécurité du travail; Affiliation(s): Association des entrepreneurs en travaux sylvicoles du Québec; Association des fabricants des meubles du Québec; Association des manufacturiers de palettes et contenants du Québec; Conseil de l'industrie forestière du Québec; Fédération québécoise des coopératives forestières; Regroupement des sociétés d'aménagement du Québec; Commission de la santé et de la sécurité du travail
Membre(s) du bureau directeur:
Jacques Laroche, Président-directeur général
jlaroche@santesecurite.org
Suzanne Lavoie, Adjointe administrative
slavoie@santesecurite.org
Finances: *Budget de fonctionnement annuel:* $1.5 Million-$3 Million
Personnel: 35 membre(s) du personnel
Membre: 600 entreprises *Montant de la cotisation:* Barème; *Critères d'admissibilite:* Oeuvrer dans le domaine des industries de la forêt ou des pâtes et papiers
Activités: Information; formation; expertise-conseil et impartition; mutuelles de prévention; activités régionales; *Stagiaires:* Oui; *Bibliothèque:*

Association de nutrition animale du Canada ***See*** Animal Nutrition Association of Canada

Association de ventes directes du Canada ***See*** Direct Sellers Association of Canada

Association des administrateurs municipaux du Nouveau-Brunswick ***See*** Association of Municipal Administrators of New Brunswick

Association des affaires publiques du Canada ***See*** The Public Affairs Association of Canada

Association des Allergologues et Immunologues du Québec

Parent Name: Fédération des médecins spécialistes du Québec

CP 216, Succ. Desjardins, #3000, 2, Complexe Desjardins, Montréal QC H5B 1G8
Tél: 514-350-5101; *Téléc:* 514-350-5146
Courriel: jdelisle@fmsq.org
www.allerg.qc.ca
Aperçu: *Dimension:* moyenne; *Envergure:* provinciale surveillé par Fédération des médecins spécialistes du Québec
Membre de: Fédération des medecins spéialistes du Québec
Membre(s) du bureau directeur:
Normand Dubé, Président

Association des Aménagistes Régionaux du Québec (AARQ)

#105, 870, av de Salaberry, Québec QC G1R 2T9
Tél: 418-524-4666; *Téléc:* 418-524-3666
Ligne sans frais: 888-771-4559
Courriel: secretariat@aarq.qc.ca
www.aarq.qc.ca
Aperçu: *Dimension:* petite; *Envergure:* provinciale; Organisme sans but lucratif; fondée en 1983
Membre(s) du bureau directeur:
Marie-Josée Casaubon, Présidente
Finances: *Budget de fonctionnement annuel:* $50,000-$100,000
Personnel: 1 membre(s) du personnel; 12 bénévole(s)
Membre: 120 *Montant de la cotisation:* 330 $ avant taxes; *Critères d'admissibilite:* Aménagiste travaillant au sein d'une M.R.C.; *Comités:* Vigie; réprésentation; évaluation; opérations
Activités: Lieu d'échange entre les professionnels de l'aménagement du territoire oeuvrant au sein des municipalités régionales de comté (M.R.C.)

Association des architectes paysagistes du Canada ***See*** Canadian Society of Landscape Architects

Association des architectes paysagistes du Québec (AAPQ)

4655, De Lorimier, Montréal QC H2H 2B4
Tél: 514-990-7731; *Téléc:* 877-990-7731
Courriel: info@aapq.org
www.aapq.org
Aperçu: *Dimension:* petite; *Envergure:* provinciale; fondée en 1965
Mission: Promouvoir la création et la valorisation du paysage en milieu naturel et construit dans le but de constituer un cadre de vie sain, fonctionnel, esthétique, axé sur les besoins de la population et répondant aux exigences écologiques; Affiliation(s): Association des Architectes Paysagistes du Canada
Membre(s) du bureau directeur:
Marie-Claude Robert, Directrice générale
Finances: *Budget de fonctionnement annuel:* $50,000-$100,000
Membre: 100-499; *Montant de la cotisation:* Barème; *Comités:* Admission; Nomination; Affaires légales et éthique professionelle; Promotion; Formation continue; Pratique privée; Action - réaction; Bulletin

Association des arpenteurs des terres du Canada ***See*** Association of Canada Lands Surveyors

Association des arpenteurs-géomètres du Nouveau-Brunswick ***See*** Association of New Brunswick Land Surveyors

Association des camps du Canada ***See*** Canadian Camping Association

Association des chefs de services d'incendie du Québec ***Voir*** Association des chefs en sécurité incendie du Québec

Association des chefs en sécurité incendie du Québec (ACSIQ) / Québec Association of Fire Chiefs

5, rue Dupré, Beloeil QC J3G 3J7
Tél: 450-464-6413; *Téléc:* 450-467-6297
Ligne sans frais: 888-464-6413
www.acsiq.qc.ca
Nom précédent: Association des chefs de services d'incendie du Québec

Aperçu: *Dimension:* moyenne; *Envergure:* provinciale; Organisme sans but lucratif; fondée en 1968
Mission: Regroupe les personnes détanant un poste de commande dans le domaine de la prévention et de la lutte contre les incendies
Membre(s) du bureau directeur:
Jean-Claude Bolduc, Président
Finances: *Budget de fonctionnement annuel:* $250,000-$500,000
Personnel: 3 membre(s) du personnel
Membre: 1 000 *Montant de la cotisation:* 195$; *Critères d'admissibilite:* Chefs de service incendie de municipalités ou de brigade en industries; *Comités:* Mise en candidature; vérification des politiques; évaluation du rendement du directeur général; finances; consultatif; comités ad hoc; prévention; consultatif en sécurité incendie
Activités: *Evénements de sensibilisation:* Congrès annuel

Association des consommateurs du Canada ***See*** Consumers' Association of Canada

Association des consommateurs industriels de gaz ***See*** Industrial Gas Users Association Inc.

Association des consultants et laboratoires experts (ACLE)

#211, 6360, rue Jean-Talon Est, Saint-Léonard QC H1S 1M8
Tél: 514-253-2878; *Téléc:* 514-253-6825
Courriel: info@acle.qc.ca
www.acle.qc.ca
Nom précédent: Association canadienne des laboratoires d'essais
Aperçu: *Dimension:* moyenne; *Envergure:* nationale; Organisme sans but lucratif; fondée en 1959
Mission: Developper, promouvoir et sauvegarder les intérêts techniques et commerciaux communs des membres et de leurs clients
Membre(s) du bureau directeur:
Ronald Blackburn, Président
blackburn.ronald@qualitas.qc.ca
Finances: *Budget de fonctionnement annuel:* $50,000-$100,000
Personnel: 1 membre(s) du personnel
Membre: 90 firmes, laboratoires associés et succursales; *Critères d'admissibilite:* Entreprises indépendantes réparties en trois divisions - Ingénierie des Sols et Matériaux; Services Analytiques et Environnement; Toiture et Étanchéité

Association des directeurs généraux des municipalités du Québec

#129, 10, rue Hugues-Pommier, Beauport QC G1E 4T9
Tél: 418-660-7591; *Téléc:* 418-660-0848
Courriel: adgmq@adgmq.qc.ca
www.adgmq.qc.ca/
Aperçu: *Dimension:* moyenne; *Envergure:* provinciale; fondée en 1973
Mission: Permettre l'amélioration des connaissances et du statut de ses membres et la promotion de la formule de gestion conseil/directeur général
Membre(s) du bureau directeur:
Jacques Poulin, Président
Jacques Alain, Directeur Exécutif
Membre: 200 *Montant de la cotisation:* 365$; *Critères d'admissibilite:* Directeur général d'une municipalité gérée par la loi des cités et villes

Association des eaux souterraines du Québec ***Voir*** Association des enterprises spécialiseés en eau du Québec

Association des écoles forestières universitaires du Canada ***See*** Association of University Forestry Schools of Canada

Association des embouteilleurs d'eau du Québec (AEEQ) / Québec Water Bottlers' Association

#102, 200, rue MacDonald, Saint-Jean-sur-Richelieu QC J3B 8J6
Tél: 450-349-1521; *Téléc:* 450-349-6923
Courriel: info@conseiltac.com
www.aeeq.org
Aperçu: *Dimension:* moyenne; *Envergure:* provinciale; fondée en 1975
Mission: L'association des embouteilleurs d'eau du Québec (AEEQ) est le porte-parole de l'industrie québécoise de l'embouteillage de l'eau de source et de l'eau minérale; *Membre de:* Canadian Bottled Water Federation
Membre(s) du bureau directeur:
Daniel Colpron, Président
Pierre Gagné, Vice-président
Membre: 24 *Montant de la cotisation:* 1000$ régulier; 1,500$ privilégié; *Critères d'admissibilite:* Entreprises spécialisées dans le commerce de l'eau embouteillée; fournisseurs de services et d'équipments

Association des enterprises spécialiseés en eau du Québec

Parent Name: Canadian Ground Water Association
5930, boul Louis-H. Lafontaine, MontréAl QC H1M 1S7
Tél: 514-353-9960; *Téléc:* 514-353-3393
Ligne sans frais: 800-468-8160
Courriel: contact@aeseq.com
www.aeseq.com
Nom précédent: Association des eaux souterraines du Québec
Aperçu: *Dimension:* moyenne; *Envergure:* provinciale surveillé par Canadian Ground Water Association
Mission: L'AESEQ est la seule association qui regroupe les entrepreneurs de construction oeuvrant dans tous les secteurs du cycle de l'eau décentralisé au Québec
Membre(s) du bureau directeur:
Daniel Schanck, Directeur général
Membre: 148; *Critères d'admissibilite:* Entrepreneurs puisatiers; entrepreneurs en installation de pompe, ou en assainissement autonome, ou en traitement d'eau potable; fournisseurs d'équipement et de matériaux; consultants; organismes publics et parapublics

Association des entomologistes amateurs du Québec inc. (AEAQ)

302, rue Gabrielle Roy, Varennes QC J3X 1L8
Courriel: info@aeaq.ca
www.aeaq.ca
www.facebook.com/group.php?gid=114179175276983
Aperçu: *Dimension:* petite; *Envergure:* provinciale; Organisme sans but lucratif; fondée en 1973
Mission: Promouvoir l'entomologie comme loisir scientifique; favoriser l'échange d'informations entre les membres lors des réunions; publier les travaux et les observations entomologiques des membres; veiller à la protection et à la conservation de l'entomofaune et du patrimoine entomologique du Québec; initier les nouveaux membres à l'étude des insectes à l'aide de séances d'identification, d'excursions et de rencontres avec des spécialistes; Affiliation(s): Société d'entomologie du Québec; Corporation Entomofaune du Québec; Amis de l'Insectarium de Montréal
Membre(s) du bureau directeur:
Claude Chantal, Président
Finances: *Budget de fonctionnement annuel:* Moins de $50,000
Personnel: 10 bénévole(s)
Membre: 200 *Montant de la cotisation:* 30$ régulière, Canada

Association des entrepreneurs en isolation de la Province de Québec ***Voir*** Association d'isolation du Québec

Association des entrepreneurs en mécanique du Canada ***See*** Mechanical Contractors Association of Canada

Association des entrepreneurs en mécanique du N.-B. ***See*** Mechanical Contractors Association of New Brunswick

Association des expositions agricoles du Québec (AEAQ)

#22A, 1175 boul. Charest ouest, Montmagny QC G1N 2C9
Tél: 418-527-1196; *Téléc:* 418-527-1196
Ligne sans frais: 800-267-2579
Courriel: info@expoduquebec.com
expoduquebec.com
www.facebook.com/group.php?gid=203811642990737
Aperçu: *Dimension:* petite; *Envergure:* provinciale; fondée en 1940
Mission: D'offrir aux agriculteurs et aux éleveurs des événements professionnels spécialisés et bien organisés; et de présenter au grand public des événements populaires, éducatifs, divertissants et sécuritaires.
Membre(s) du bureau directeur:
Benoît Boulanger, Secrétaire
Finances: *Budget de fonctionnement annuel:* $500,000-$1.5 Million
Membre: 41 *Montant de la cotisation:* 50$

Association des fabricants internationaux d'automobiles du Canada ***See*** Association of International Automobile Manufacturers of Canada

Association des fermières de l'Ontario (AFO)

CP 190, 5095, rue Fatima, Saint-Eugène ON K0B 1P0
Tél: 613-674-2035; *Téléc:* 613-674-1176
Courriel: cerclefermieres@cnwl.igs.net
Aperçu: *Dimension:* moyenne; *Envergure:* provinciale; Organisme sans but lucratif; fondée en 1969
Mission: Travailler aux intérêts des femmes et jeunes filles dans les paroisses, en artisanat, au progrès spirituel, social, culturel, économique et technique; Affiliation(s): Association canadienne-française de l'Ontario
Membre(s) du bureau directeur:
Denise Dupont, Présidente
Laurence Demers, Vice-présidente
Louise Myner, Sec.-trés.
Finances: *Budget de fonctionnement annuel:* Moins de $50,000
Personnel: 10 bénévole(s)
Membre: 300 *Montant de la cotisation:* 6$; *Critères d'admissibilite:* Femme de 20 ans (en moyenne) et plus, interessée à sa santé, bien-être, culture (artisanat), connaissances générales, économie, loi etc.
Activités: Exposition artisanale annuelle; *Service de conférenciers:* Oui

L'Association des firmes d'ingénieurs-conseils - Canada ***See*** Association of Consulting Engineering Companies - Canada

Association des fonderies canadiennes ***See*** Canadian Foundry Association

Association des forestiers agréés du Nouveau-Brunswick ***See*** Association of Registered Professional Foresters of New Brunswick

L'Association des fruiticulteurs et des maraîchers de l'Ontario ***See*** Ontario Fruit & Vegetable Growers' Association

Association des herboristes de la province de Québec

CP 80, 7, av 70e ouest, Blainville QC J7C 1R7
Tél: 450-435-2979
Courriel: herbesunivers@bellnet.ca
Aperçu: *Dimension:* petite; *Envergure:* provinciale
Membre: 100-499

Association des industries aérospatiales du Canada ***See*** Aerospace Industries Association of Canada

Association des industries CANDU ***See*** Organization of CANDU Industries

Association des industries de l'automobile du Canada ***See*** Automotive Industries Association of Canada

L'Association des industries de l'environnement du Nouveau-Brunswick ***See*** New Brunswick Environment Industry Association

Association des ingénieurs et géoscientifiques du Nouveau-Brunswick ***See*** Association of Professional Engineers & Geoscientists of New Brunswick

Association des ingénieurs municipaux du Québec (AIMQ) / Association of Québec Municipal Engineers

CP 792, Succ. B, Montréal QC H3B 3K5
Tél: 514-845-5303
Courriel: aimg.rlamarche@videotron.ca
www.aimq.net
Aperçu: *Dimension:* moyenne; *Envergure:* provinciale; fondée en 1963
Mission: Améliorer les connaissances et le statut de l'ingénieur municipal par l'échange d'information, la coopération entre ingénieurs municipaux et avec d'autres associations professionnelles et la promotion des intérêts communs des membres de l'Association
Membre(s) du bureau directeur:
Dany Lachance, Président
Finances: *Budget de fonctionnement annuel:* $100,000-$250,000
Personnel: 15 bénévole(s)
Membre: 200 *Montant de la cotisation:* 225.75$; *Critères d'admissibilite:* Membre de l'Ordre des ingénieurs du Québec; employé d'une administration municipale ou régionale
Activités: Séminaire de formation annuel; *Listes de destinataires:* Oui

Association des ingénieurs-conseils du Québec (AICQ) / Consulting Engineers of Québec

Parent Name: Association of Consulting Engineering Companies - Canada
#930, 1440, rue Ste-Catherine ouest, Montréal QC H3G 1R8
Tél: 514-871-2229; *Téléc:* 514-871-9903
Courriel: info@aicq.qc.ca

www.aicq.qc.ca
www.linkedin.com/company/association-des-ing-nieurs-conseils-du-qu-bec
www.facebook.com/forumAICQ
www.youtube.com/aicqtv
Aperçu: *Dimension:* grande; *Envergure:* provinciale; fondée en 1974 surveillé par Association of Consulting Engineering Companies - Canada
Mission: Promouvoir et développer l'industrie du génie-conseil en regroupant des membres qui offrent des services de qualité
Membre(s) du bureau directeur:
Marc Tremblay, ing., Président du Conseil
Johanne Desrochers, Présidente-directrice générale, 514-871-2229
jdesrochers@aicq.qc.ca
Pierre Nadeau, Directeur, Communications, 514-871-0589 Ext. 28
pnadeau@aicq.qc.ca
Membre: 280 bureaux; *Comités:* Bâtiment; Énergie; Environnement; Industrie; Municipal; Télécommunications et nouvelles technologies; Transport
Activités: *Listes de destinataires:* Oui; *Bibliothèque:* rendez-vous

Association des ingénieurs-professeurs des sciences appliquées (AIPSA)

c/o Université de Sherbrooke, 2500, boul Université, Sherbrooke QC J1K 2R1
Tél: 819-821-7929; *Téléc:* 819-821-7955
Courriel: aipsa@usherbrooke.ca
pages.usherbrooke.ca/aipsa/
Aperçu: *Dimension:* petite; *Envergure:* locale; Organisme sans but lucratif; fondée en 1970
Mission: Négocier la convention collective des ingénieur-professeurs; représenter les ingénieur-professeurs au sens du code du travail
Membre(s) du bureau directeur:
François Boone, Président
aipsa@usherbrooke.ca
Finances: *Budget de fonctionnement annuel:* Moins de $50,000
Personnel: 6 membre(s) du personnel
Membre: 95 *Montant de la cotisation:* 0.75% du salaire régulier annuel; *Critères d'admissibilite:* Membre de l'ordre des ingénieurs du QC; salarié affecté à une tâche d'enseignement ou de recherche à l'Université de Sherbrooke

Association des jardins du Québec / Québec Gardens Association

82, Grande-Allée ouest, Québec QC G1R 2G6
Tél: 418-692-0886
www.jardinsduquebec.com
www.facebook.com/9180555411
Aperçu: *Dimension:* petite; *Envergure:* provinciale
Mission: L'Association des jardins du Québec a comme mission de regrouper en corporation les jardins du Québec ouverts au public afin d'aider à leur développement et à leur promotion et de souligner leur apport à la culture et au patrimoine québécois
Membre(s) du bureau directeur:
Geneviève David, Chargée de projet en communication
gdavid@tapagecreation.com
Membre: 20

Association des jeunes ruraux du Québec (AJRQ)

65, rang 3 est, Princeville QC G6L 4B9
Tél: 819-364-5606; *Téléc:* 819-364-5006
Courriel: info@ajrq.qc.ca
www.ajrq.qc.ca
Aperçu: *Dimension:* moyenne; *Envergure:* provinciale; fondée en 1974
Mission: Promouvoir la formation auprès de nos membres; soutenir leur sentiment d'appartenance au milieu rural; *Membre de:* Regroupement Loisir Québec; Affiliation(s): Conseil des 4-H du Canada
Membre(s) du bureau directeur:
Josiane Chabot, Présidente
Annie Chabot, Directrice générale
Finances: *Budget de fonctionnement annuel:* $100,000-$250,000
Personnel: 2 membre(s) du personnel; 300 bénévole(s)
Membre: 1 200 *Montant de la cotisation:* 5$
Activités: *Stagiaires:* Oui; *Listes de destinataires:* Oui

Association des manufacturiers de bois de sciage de l'Ontario *See* Ontario Lumber Manufacturers' Association

Association des manufacturiers de bois de sciage du Québec *Voir* Conseil de l'industrie forestière du Québec

Association des manufacturiers de produits alimentaires du Québec *Voir* Conseil de la transformation agroalimentaire et des produits de consommation

Association des médecins biochimistes du Canada *See* Canadian Association of Medical Biochemists

Association des médecins biochimistes du Québec (AMBQ)
Parent Name: Fédération des médecins spécialistes du Québec

#3000, 2, Complexe Desjardins, Montréal QC H5B 1G8
Tél: 514-350-5105; *Téléc:* 514-350-5151
Courriel: ambq@fmsq.org
www.ambq.med.usherbrooke.ca
Aperçu: *Dimension:* petite; *Envergure:* provinciale surveillé par Fédération des médecins spécialistes du Québec
Mission: Promouvoir l'utilisation optimale des tests de laboratoire au Québec en offrant, au professionnel de la santé et au patient, les meilleurs services de diagnostic et de dépistage de maladies grâce à des techniques biochimiques et immunologiques
Membre(s) du bureau directeur:
Elaine Letendre, Présidente

Association des médecins spécialistes en santé communautaire du Québec (AMSSCQ)
Parent Name: Fédération des médecins spécialistes du Québec

#3000, 2, Complexe Desjardins, Montréal QC H5B 1G8
Tél: 514-350-5138; *Téléc:* 514-350-5151
Courriel: amsscq@fmsq.org
www.amsscq.org
Aperçu: *Dimension:* petite; *Envergure:* provinciale; fondée en 1982 surveillé par Fédération des médecins spécialistes du Québec
Mission: L'association a pour rôle de promouvoir les intérêts professionnels et économiques de ses membres
Membre(s) du bureau directeur:
Jacques Ringuet, Président
Marc Rhainds, Vice-président

Association des microbiologistes du Québec (AMQ)

5094A, av. Charlemagne, Montréal QC H1X 3P3
Tél: 514-728-1087; *Téléc:* 514-374-3988
Courriel: amq@microbiologistes.ca
www.microbiologistes.ca
Aperçu: *Dimension:* moyenne; *Envergure:* provinciale; fondée en 1975
Mission: L'association regroupe les microbiologistes du Québec oeuvrant principalemtn en environnement, en alimentaire et en pharmaceutique. Elle a pour but d'étudier, de protéger et de développer les intérêts économiques, sociaux et professionnels des microbiologistes et de promouvoir l'essor de la microbiologie en général; est impliquée au niveau de l'accréditation des laboratoires d'analyses microbiologiques et elle est représentée au sein de plusieurs comités ou associations.
Membre(s) du bureau directeur:
Stéphane Bourget, Président
stephane.bourget@microbiologistes.ca
Finances: *Budget de fonctionnement annuel:* Moins de $50,000
Personnel: 7 bénévole(s)
Membre: 500 *Montant de la cotisation:* Barème; *Critères d'admissibilite:* 30 crédits universitaires en microbiologie

Association des mines de métaux du Québec inc. *Voir* Association minière du Québec

Association des pompiers professionnels de l'Ontario (ind.) *See* Ontario Professional Fire Fighters Association

Association des Praticiens de la santé naturelle du Canada *See* Natural Health Practitioners of Canada Association

Association des produits forestiers du Canada *See* Forest Products Association of Canada

L'Association des produits forestiers du Nouveau-Brunswick *See* New Brunswick Forest Products Association Inc.

Association des prospecteurs du Québec *Voir* Association de l'exploration minière de Québec

Association des recycleurs de pièces d'autos et de camions (ARPAC) / Association of Auto Part Recyclers

#101, 37, rue de la Gare, St-Jérôme QC J7Z 2B7
Tel: 450-504-8315; *Fax:* 450-504-8313
Toll-Free: 855-504-8315
e-mail: info@arpac.org
arpac.org
www.facebook.com/pages/ARPAC/106847846016208
www.youtube.com/user/ARPACpiecesvertes
Overview: A medium-sized provincial organization
Member of: Automotive Recyclers of Canada
Chief Officer(s):
Simon Matte, Président-directeur général
Membership: 88

Association des sciences de la santé de l'Alberta (ind.) *See* Health Sciences Association of Alberta

Association des sciences de la santé de la Saskatchewan (ind.) *See* Health Sciences Association of Saskatchewan

Association des spécialistes en extermination du Québec *Voir* Association québécoise de la gestion parasitaire

Association des technologistes agro-alimentaires inc. *Voir* Association des technologues en agroalimentaire

Association des technologues en agroalimentaire (ATA) / Agricultural Technologists Association Inc.

a/s Ordre des technologues professionnels du Québec, #720, 1265, rue Berri, Montréal QC H2L 4X4
Tél: 514-845-3247; *Téléc:* 514-845-3643
Ligne sans frais: 800-561-3459
www.otpq.qc.ca
Nom précédent: Association des technologistes agro-alimentaires inc.
Aperçu: *Dimension:* moyenne; *Envergure:* provinciale; Organisme sans but lucratif; fondée en 1964
Mission: Défense des intérêts professionnels; promouvoir la profession et le perfectionnement des membres; *Membre de:* Ordre des technologues professionnels du Québec
Membre(s) du bureau directeur:
Sylvain Biron, Président
Finances: *Budget de fonctionnement annuel:* Moins de $50,000
Personnel: 1 membre(s) du personnel; 5 bénévole(s)
Membre: 300 *Montant de la cotisation:* 396.68$

Association des terrains de camping du Québec *Voir* Camping Québec

Association des transports du Canada *See* Transportation Association of Canada

Association des zoos et aquariums du Canada *See* Canadian Association of Zoos & Aquariums

Association du barreau canadien *See* Canadian Bar Association

Association du barreau du comté de Carleton *See* Carleton County Law Association

Association du camionnage du Québec inc. (ACQ) / Québec Trucking Association Inc.
Parent Name: Canadian Trucking Alliance

#200, 6450, rue Notre Dame ouest, Montréal QC H4C 1C4
Tél: 514-932-0377; *Téléc:* 514-932-1358
Ligne sans frais: 800-361-5813
Courriel: info@carrefour-acq.org
www.carrefour-acq.org
Aperçu: *Dimension:* moyenne; *Envergure:* provinciale; Organisme sans but lucratif; fondée en 1951 surveillé par Canadian Trucking Alliance
Mission: Favoriser l'amélioration des normes de sécurité, d'efficacité et d'éthique dans l'industrie du camionnage; maintenir un contact avec l'autorité gouvernementale, les usagers des services de camionnage et le public en général; soutenir le perfectionnement professionnel; soutenir les entreprises dans la défense de leurs intérêts.; Affiliation(s): Union Internationale des Transports Routiers - Genève; American Trucking Association - Washington, DC
Membre(s) du bureau directeur:
Éric Gignac, Président du conseil
Michel Robert, 1er vice-président du conseil
René Rouillard, Secrétaire du conseil
Bernard Boutin, Trésorier du conseil
Jean-Claude Fortin, Vice-President
Yves Marchand, Vice-President
Finances: *Budget de fonctionnement annuel:* $500,000-$1.5 Million
Personnel: 13 membre(s) du personnel

Membre: 600 sociétés + 251 associés; *Critères d'admissibilite:* transporteurs et locateurs publics & privés
Activités: *Stagiaires:* Oui

L'Association du saumon Nepisiguit ***See*** Nepisiguit Salmon Association

Association du transport aérien du Canada ***See*** Air Transport Association of Canada

Association du transport aérien international ***See*** International Air Transport Association

Association for Canadian Educational Resources (ACER)

#44, 3665 Flamewood Dr., Mississauga ON L4Y 3P5
Tel: 905-275-7685; *Fax:* 905-275-9420
e-mail: acerinfo@rogers.com
www.acer-acre.org
www.facebook.com/pages/ACER/113442745413630
twitter.com/AcerAcre
Overview: A small national organization founded in 1991
Mission: To promote & to help create Canadian materials for classroom life early learners
Environmental Activity: Helping students become more aware of environmental issues; Planting for Change; Measuring our Resources; Let's Plant, Measure & Mulch; Go Blobal; Youth Stewardship Project
Chief Officer(s):
Alice Casselman, President
Ana Maria Martinez, Program Coordinator
Finances: *Annual Operating Budget:* Less than $50,000; *Funding Sources:* Membership fees; donations; grants
Staff: 1 staff member(s); 30 volunteer(s)
Membership: 50; *Fees:* $30 adult; $20 retired person; $10 student; *Member Profile:* Volunteers from all sectors especially retired educators
Activities: Schools, community groups volunteer as part of Environment Canada delivery of mentoring system; community outreach; training workshops; displays at conferences

Association for Canadian Registered Safety Professionals ***See*** Board of Canadian Registered Safety Professionals

Association for Literature, Environment, and Culture in Canada (ALECC) / Association pour la littérature, l'environnement et la culture au Canada

c/o Department of English, University of Calgary, 2500 University Dr. NW, 11th Fl., Calgary AB T2N 1N4
e-mail: contactus@alecc.ca
www.alecc.ca
Overview: A small national organization founded in 2005
Mission: To promote and support artistic, critical and cultural studies work on a wide range of environmental issues.
Chief Officer(s):
Pamela Banting, President
pbanting@ucalgary.ca
Membership: *Fees:* $25-$40

Association for Mineral Exploration British Columbia (AMEBC)

#800, 889 West Pender St., Vancouver BC V6C 3B2
Tel: 604-689-5271; *Fax:* 604-681-2363
e-mail: info@amebc.ca
www.amebc.ca
Previous Name: British Columbia & Yukon Chamber of Mines
Overview: A medium-sized provincial organization founded in 1912
Mission: To promote & assist development & growth of mining of mineral exploration in BC; Affiliation(s): Mining Association of Canada; Mining Association of BC
Chief Officer(s):
Gavin C. Dirom, President & CEO
Finances: *Annual Operating Budget:* $250,000-$500,000; *Funding Sources:* Membership dues
Staff: 6 staff member(s)
Membership: 3,605 individual + 179 corporate; *Fees:* $50 individual; *Member Profile:* Member of mining community; *Committees:* Many-Land Use; Mining Law; Safety
Activities: ; *Library:* Charles S. Ney Library; Open to public

Association for Mountain Parks Protection & Enjoyment (AMPPE)

PO Box 2999, Banff AB T1L 1C7
Tel: 403-762-3800; *Fax:* 403-762-3828
e-mail: info@amppe.org
www.amppe.org
www.facebook.com/158883817584661
twitter.com/amppe
Overview: A small provincial organization founded in 1994
Mission: To champion & promote sustainable tourism, a vibrant mountain economy, & responsible human use in mountain parks
Chief Officer(s):
Monica Andreeff, Executive Director
Membership: *Fees:* $50

Association forestière canadienne ***See*** Canadian Forestry Association

Association forestière canadienne du Nouveau-Brunswick ***See*** Canadian Forestry Association of New Brunswick

Association forestière de l'Ontario ***See*** Ontario Forestry Association

Association francophone pour le savoir (ACFAS)

425, rue de la Gauchetière est, Montréal QC H2L 2M7
Tél: 514-849-0045; *Téléc:* 514-849-5558
www.acfas.ca
linkedin.com/company/acfas—-association-francophone-pour-le-savoir
www.facebook.com/33532707807
twitter.com/_Acfas
Nom précédent: Association canadienne française pour l'avancement des sciences
Aperçu: *Dimension:* moyenne; *Envergure:* nationale; fondée en 1923
Mission: Promouvoir et soutenir la science et la technologie pour encourager le développement culturel et économique de la société
Membre(s) du bureau directeur:
Esther Gaudreault, Directrice générale, 514-849-0045 Ext. 232
esther.gaudreault@acfas.ca
Finances: *Budget de fonctionnement annuel:* $500,000-$1.5 Million
Personnel: 8 membre(s) du personnel
Membre: 8 000 individu; 40 institutionnel *Montant de la cotisation:* 45$
Prix, Bouses: •Prix J.-Armand-Bombardier (Bourse d études)
Award for technological innovation *Amount:* $2,500
•Prix Urgel-Archambault (Bourse d études)
Award for physics, mathematics or engineering; sponsored by Alcan *Amount:* $2,500
•Prix Michel-Jurdant (Bourse d études)
Award recognizes research in environmental sciences; sponsored by Hydro-Québec *Amount:* $2,500

Association géologique du Canada ***See*** Geological Association of Canada

Association internationale des pompiers (FAT-COI/CTC) ***See*** International Association of Fire Fighters (AFL-CIO/CLC)

Association internationale du droit nucléaire ***See*** International Nuclear Law Association

Association médicale canadienne ***See*** Canadian Medical Association

Association médicale du Québec (AMQ) / Québec Medical Association (QMA)
Parent Name: Canadian Medical Association

#3200, 380, rue Saint-Antoine ouest, Montréal QC H2Y 3X7
Tél: 514-866-0660; *Téléc:* 514-866-0670
Ligne sans frais: 800-363-3932
Courriel: admin@amq.ca
www.amq.ca
www.facebook.com/Association.medicale.du.Quebec
Aperçu: *Dimension:* moyenne; *Envergure:* provinciale; Organisme sans but lucratif; fondée en 1922 surveillé par Canadian Medical Association
Mission: Rassembler et soutenir les médecins du Québec afin de garantir à la population québécoise des conditions et des soins de santé de qualité
Membre(s) du bureau directeur:
Claudette Duclos, Directrice générale
Membre: 8 500 *Montant de la cotisation:* 136-765, schedule; *Critères d'admissibilite:* Etre médecin et être membre de la Corporation professionnelle des médecins du Québec; *Comités:* Soins et promotion de la santé; Économique et politique de la santé; Éducation; Éthique; Mises en candidatures; Finances

Association minéralogique du Canada ***See*** Mineralogical Association of Canada

Association minière du Canada ***See*** Mining Association of Canada

L'Association minière du Nouveau-Brunswick ***See*** New Brunswick Mining Association

Association minière du Québec (AMQ) / Québec Mining Association (QMA)
Parent Name: Mining Association of Canada

Place de la Cité - Tour Belle Cour, #720, 2590, boul Laurier, Québec QC G1V 4M6
Tél: 418-657-2016; *Téléc:* 418-657-2154
Courriel: mines@amq-inc.com
www.amq-inc.com
Nom précédent: Association des mines de métaux du Québec inc.
Aperçu: *Dimension:* grande; *Envergure:* provinciale; Organisme sans but lucratif; fondée en 1936 surveillé par Mining Association of Canada
Mission: Promouvoir le développement de l'industrie des mines, de la métallurgie et des industries connexes; défendre les intérêts généraux de ses membres; soutenir les efforts de ses membres quant au bien-être, à la sécurité et à la prévention des accidents au travail
Membre(s) du bureau directeur:
Dan Tolgyesi, Président
dtolgyesi@amq-inc.com
Josée Méthot, Présidente-directrice générale
jmethot@amq-inc.com
Finances: *Budget de fonctionnement annuel:* $500,000-$1.5 Million
Personnel: 9 membre(s) du personnel
Membre: 1-99; *Critères d'admissibilite:* Toutes les compagnies opérant dans le secteur minier ou dans un secteur connexe; *Comités:* Environnement; Prévention des accidents; Santé; Relations publiques; Fiscalité; Contrôle de terrain; Sauvetage minier (catamine); Entretien

Association nationale pour la conservation de l'énergie ***See*** National Energy Conservation Association Inc.

Association nucléaire canadienne ***See*** Canadian Nuclear Association

Association of Alberta Agricultural Fieldmen (AAAF)

c/o Municipal District of Rocky View, 911 - 32nd Ave. NE, Calgary AB T2E 6X6
Tel: 403-230-1401
e-mail: info@aaaf.ab.ca
www.aaaf.ab.ca
Overview: A small provincial organization
Mission: Committed to the enhancement, promotion & protection of the agricultural resources of Alberta
Chief Officer(s):
Pat Dirk, President, 403-362-4343
dirkp@countyofnewell.ab.ca
Kim Butler, Supervisor, Agricultural Services
kbutler@rockyview.ca
Finances: *Annual Operating Budget:* Less than $50,000
Membership: 107; *Fees:* $125; *Member Profile:* Agricultural fieldmen develop, implement, and control programs that adhere to the priorities and policies set by the Agricultural Service Board across the province.; *Committees:* Education; Policy; Soils; Weed Control

Association of Alberta Coordinated Action for Recycling Enterprises

5212 - 49 St., Leduc AB T9E 7H5
Tel: 780-980-0035; *Fax:* 780-980-0232
Toll-Free: 866-818-2273
www.albertacare.org
Also Known As: Alberta CARE
Overview: A medium-sized provincial organization founded in 2010
Mission: To support waste management & recycling activities at the community level in Alberta
Environmental Activity: Coordinating recycling & waste management activities; Promoting recycling; Raising awareness of recycling initiatives
Chief Officer(s):
Linda McDonald, Executive Director
executivedirector@albertacare.org
Membership: *Fees:* $52.50 associate, non-voting membership; $105 non-profit; $262.50 corporate; $272 goverment; $105-$525 municipality, based on population; *Member Profile:* Non-profit organizations; Governments; Municipalities; Businesses

Activities: Organizing partnerships; Establishing & operating programs such as Electronic Waste Recycling, Regional Concrete & Asphalt Crushing, Regional Scrap Metals Recycling, Alberta CARE Ink Recycle, Paper Fibre Recycling, Fluorescent Tube Recycling, Wood Waste Grinding
Meetings/Conferences:
For more information see Trade Shows, Conferences and Seminars Chapter
Alberta CARE 2013 Annual Alberta Recycling Conference
September 2013 Slave Lake, AB
Publications:
•Reuse / Recycle Directory
Type: Directory; *Number of Pages:* 122
Profile: A list of organizations & companies that offer alternatives to throwing garbage in landfills

Association of American Geographers (AAG)
1710 - 16 St. NW, Washington DC 20009-3198 USA
Tel: 202-234-1450; *Fax:* 202-234-2744
e-mail: gaia@aag.org
www.aag.org
Overview: A medium-sized national organization founded in 1904
Mission: To advance professional studies in geography & to encourage the application of geographic research in education, government & business; to promote discussion among its members & with scholars in related fields; to support the publication of scholarly studies; *Member of:* American Council of Learned Societies
Chief Officer(s):
Douglas Richardson, Executive Director
drichardson@aag.org
Finances: *Annual Operating Budget:* $1.5 Million-$3 Million
Staff: 10 staff member(s)
Membership: 7,100 individual + 800 institutional; *Fees:* Schedule available; *Member Profile:* Members include students & professionals with backgrounds in a wide variety of geographic subfields such as urban geography, geographic information systems, cartography, remote sensing, historical geography, geomorphology, political geography, planning, environmental studies, & area studies
Activities: Specialty groups (comprised of geographers who share a professional interest in a systematic or topical specialty or in a major region of the world) sponsor sessions at the annual meetings, publish newsletters or other communications, & develop workshops & other projects to advance their professional interests; AAG manages several funded projects; AAG supports special symposia; *Internships:* Yes; *Rents Mailing List:* Yes
Publications:
•The Professional Geographer
Editor: Sharmistha Bagchi-Sen
Profile: Annual journal

Association of Applied Geochemists (AEG)
PO Box 26099, 72 Robertson Rd., Nepean ON K2H 9R0
Tel: 613-828-0199; *Fax:* 613-828-9288
e-mail: office@appliedgeochemists.org
www.appliedgeochemists.org
Previous Name: Association of Exploration Geochemists
Overview: A medium-sized international organization founded in 1970
Mission: To promote interest in the applications of geochemistry to mineral & petroleum exploration, resource evaluation & related fields; Affiliation(s): International Union of Geological Sciences (IUGS)
Chief Officer(s):
David R. Cohen, President
Betty Arseneault, Business Manager
Finances: *Annual Operating Budget:* $50,000-$100,000; *Funding Sources:* Membership dues; publisher rebates
Staff: 2 staff member(s); 70 volunteer(s)
Membership: 650; *Fees:* US$100; *Committees:* New Membership; Admissions; Awards and Medals; Education; Symposia
Activities: *Speaker Service:* Yes
Meetings/Conferences:
For more information see Trade Shows, Conferences and Seminars Chapter
26th International Applied Geochemistry Symposium (IAGS 2013)
November 2013 Rotorua

Association of Auto Part Recyclers ***See*** Association des recycleurs de pièces d'autos et de camions

Association of British Columbia Forest Professionals (ABCFP)
#330 - 321 Water St., Vancouver BC V6B 1B8
Tel: 604-687-8027; *Fax:* 604-687-3264
e-mail: info@abcfp.ca
www.abcfp.ca
www.facebook.com/79659811198
twitter.com/abcfp
Previous Name: Association of British Columbia Professional Foresters
Overview: A medium-sized provincial licensing organization founded in 1947
Mission: To protect the public interest in the practice of professional forestry by ensuring the competence, independence & integrity of its members; to ensure that every person practising professional forestry is accountable to the association & to the public; *Member of:* Canadian Federation of Professional Foresters Association
Chief Officer(s):
Sharon Glover, Chief Executive Officer, 604-331-2323
sglover@abcfp.ca
Finances: *Annual Operating Budget:* $500,000-$1.5 Million; *Funding Sources:* Membership dues
Staff: 12 staff member(s); 300 volunteer(s)
Membership: 5,300; *Fees:* $300-330 + GST; *Member Profile:* Individual - membership is mandatory for all who practise professional forestry in the province of British Columbia; *Committees:* ABCFP Forestrust
Activities: Policy review seminars; Professional Foresters' Network; Forest Capital of BC

Association of British Columbia Land Surveyors (ABCLS)
Parent Name: Professional Surveyors Canada
#301, 2400 Bevan Ave., Sidney BC V8L 1W1
Tel: 250-655-7222; *Fax:* 250-655-7223
Toll-Free: 800-332-1193
e-mail: office@abcls.ca
www.abcls.ca
Also Known As: Association of BC Land Surveyors
Previous Name: Corporation of BC Land Surveyors
Overview: A medium-sized provincial licensing organization founded in 1905 overseen by Professional Surveyors Canada
Mission: To protect the public interest & the integrity of the survey system in British Columbia by regulating & governing the practice of land surveying in the province.; *Member of:* Professional Surveyors Canada; Affiliation(s): Canadian Society of Association Executives
Chief Officer(s):
Nigel Hemingway, BCSL, President
Chuck Salmon, Secretary & Treasurer
csalmon@abcls.ca
Ian Lloyd, BCLS, Vice-President
Gamble Gordon, Practice Advisory Manager, 250-729-3852
ggamble@abcls.ca
Palecek Debbie, Technical Assistant, 604-560-2777
cpalecek@abcls.ca
Finances: *Annual Operating Budget:* $500,000-$1.5 Million; *Funding Sources:* Membership dues; Electronic Checklist Registry
Staff: 6 staff member(s)
Membership: 600; *Fees:* Various; *Member Profile:* Land Surveyors
Activities: Conducting examining for admission; Performing legal surveys in British Columbia; Providing professional development opportunities; *Internships:* Yes; *Library:* BC Land Surveyors Foundation Anna Papove Memorial; Open to public by appointment
Meetings/Conferences:
For more information see Trade Shows, Conferences and Seminars Chapter
Association of British Columbia Land Surveyors 2013 108th Annual General Meeting
March 2013 Whistler, BC
Association of British Columbia Land Surveyors 2014 109th Annual General Meeting
March 2014 Richmond, BC
Publications:
•The Land Surveyor
Type: Newsletter; *Editor:* Janice Henshaw
Profile: Articles about land surveying in British Columbia
•The Link
Type: Magazine; *Frequency:* 3 pa; *Accepts Advertising*; *Editor:* Dave Morton, BCLS
Profile: Articles & news relevant to British Columbia land surveyors

Association of British Columbia Professional Foresters ***See*** Association of British Columbia Forest Professionals

Association of Canada Lands Surveyors / Association des arpenteurs des terres du Canada
100E, 900 Dynes Rd., Ottawa ON K2C 3L6
Tel: 613-723-9200; *Fax:* 613-723-5558
www.acls-aatc.ca
Previous Name: Canadian Institute of Surveying
Overview: A medium-sized national organization
Mission: To establish & maintain standards of qualification for Canada Lands Surveyors; to regulate Canada Lands Surveyors; To establish & maintain standards of conduct, knowledge & skill among members of the Association & permit holders; to govern the activities of members of the Association & permit holders; To cooperate with other organizations for the advancement of surveying; To perform the duties & exercise the powers that are imposed or conferred on the Association by the Act
Chief Officer(s):
Jean-Claude Tétreault, Executive Director
jctetreault@acls-aatc.ca
Meetings/Conferences:
For more information see Trade Shows, Conferences and Seminars Chapter
Association of Canada Lands Surveyors 2013 9th National Surveyor's Conference (in conjunction with Professional Surveyors Canada)
June 2013 Niagara Falls, ON

Association of Canadian Ergonomists (ACE) / L'Association canadienne d'ergonomie
#1003, 105-150 Crowfoot Cres. NW, Calgary AB T3G 3T2
Tel: 403-219-4001; *Fax:* 403-451-1503
Toll-Free: 888-432-2223
e-mail: info@ace-ergocanada.ca
www.ace-ergocanada.ca
Previous Name: Human Factors Association of Canada
Overview: A small national organization founded in 1968
Mission: To advance human factors/ergonomics through encouraging a high quality of practice, education & research; To facilitate communication among members; To represent the discipline; To increase awareness of human factors/ergonomics; To identify resources; *Member of:* International Ergonomics Association
Chief Officer(s):
Margo Fraser, Executive Director
margo@ace-ergocanada.ca
Brenda Mallat, President
Finances: *Annual Operating Budget:* $100,000-$250,000; *Funding Sources:* Membership dues; annual conference
Staff: 2 staff member(s)
Membership: 600 individuals; *Fees:* $150 full; $75 affiliate; $34 student; *Member Profile:* Engineers; medical practitioners; safety specialists; research scientists; architects; designers; educators; managers; consultants; kinesiologists; psychologists; ergonomists
Activities: *Speaker Service:* Yes

Association of Canadian Port Authorities (ACPA)
#1502, 85 Albert St., Ottawa ON K1P 6A4
Tel: 613-232-2036; *Fax:* 613-232-9554
e-mail: leroux@acpa-ports.net
www.acpa-ports.net
Previous Name: Canadian Port & Harbour Association
Overview: A medium-sized national organization founded in 1958
Mission: To encourage, mentor & stimulate the development of excellence within Canadian ports; Affiliation(s): American Association of Port Authorities
Chief Officer(s):
Gary Leroux, Executive Director
leroux@acpa-ports.net
Finances: *Annual Operating Budget:* $50,000-$100,000; *Funding Sources:* Membership fees; seminars
Staff: 1 staff member(s)
Membership: 18 corporate + 17 associate; *Fees:* $750 associate & affiliate; $100 individual; *Committees:* Constitution; Finance & Administration; Marketing; Public Relations; Operations & Environment; Past Presidents; Real Property Management
Activities: Annual conferences where papers are given by experts in the field of port operations & where members inspect the host port's dock & industrial facilities; port-related research; special seminars; *Speaker Service:* Yes

Association of Canadian Universities for Northern Studies (ACUNS) / Association universitaire canadienne d'études nordiques
Parent Name: Association of Universities & Colleges of Canada

#405, 17 York St., Ottawa ON K1N 9J6
Tel: 613-562-0515; *Fax:* 613-562-0533
e-mail: office@acuns.ca
www.acuns.ca
twitter.com/acunsaucen
Overview: A small national charitable organization founded in 1977 overseen by Association of Universities & Colleges of Canada
Mission: The Association encourages the government & private sector to support polar scholarship, fostering programs to increase public awareness of polar sciences & research. It represents its member universities & colleges, encouraging the establishment of funds & resources to ensure a network of trained researchers, regional managers & educators.
Chief Officer(s):
Robert C. Baily, President
Peter Geller, Vice-President
Michael Goodyear, Sec.-Treas.
Heather Cayouette, Program Manager
Finances: *Annual Operating Budget:* $100,000-$250,000; *Funding Sources:* University dues
Staff: 1 staff member(s)
Membership: 32 universities/colleges; *Fees:* $1,082
Activities: Maintaining a network of circumpolar contacts; providing education & public awareness programs; triennial Student Conference on Northern Studies
Awards:
•Caribou Research Award (Award)
Awarded to students enrolled in a recognized Canadian community college or university pursuing studies that will contribute to the understanding of the Beverly & Qamanirjuaq Barren Ground Caribou (& their habitat) in Canada *Deadline:* January 31 *Amount:* Up to $1,500
•Studentships in Northern Studies (Scholarship)
Research culminating in a thesis or similar document involving direct northern experience; for students enrolled in graduate & undergraduate degree programs or other courses of study recognized at a Canadian university with special relevance to Canada's northern territories & adjacent regions *Deadline:* January 31 *Amount:* $10,000
•Cooperative Award (Award)
Awarded to a student whose studies will contribute to the understanding & development of cooperatives in NWT; applicants who are not northern residents must be full-time students at the Cooperative College of Canada, a recognized Canadian community college, or a Canadian university *Deadline:* January 31 *Amount:* $2,000
•Research Support Opportunity in Arctic Environmental Studies (Award)
Preference is given to environmental research proposals in the physical &/or biological sciences for which location at the High Arctic Weather Stations would be advantageous; graduate level studies *Deadline:* January 31 *Amount:* Logistical support

Association of Certified Engineering Technicians & Technologists of Prince Edward Island (ACETTPEI)
Parent Name: Canadian Council of Technicians & Technologists

PO Box 1436, 92 Queen St., Charlottetown PE C1A 7N1
Tel: 902-892-8324
e-mail: info@acettpei.ca
www.techpei.ca
Previous Name: Prince Edward Island Society of Certified Engineering Technologists
Overview: A small provincial organization founded in 1972 overseen by Canadian Council of Technicians & Technologists
Mission: To benefit society by advancing the professions of applied science & engineering technology in Prince Edward Island; Affiliation(s): Island Technology Professionals
Chief Officer(s):
Trent Collicutt, President
Alan Robison, Vice-President
Delbert Reeves, Treasurer
Tom MacDonald, Registrar
Activities: Certifying engineering / applied science technicians & technologists; Conferring the designations C.Tech., C.E.T., & A.Sc.T.; *Awareness Events:* Career Options Day, November; National Skilled Trades Day, November; National Technology Week, November
Publications:
•AtlanTECH News
Type: Newsletter
Profile: Information for technology professionals in New Brunswick, Prince Edward Island, & Newfoundland & Labrador

Association of Consulting Engineering Companies - Canada (ACEC) / L'Association des firmes d'ingénieurs-conseils - Canada (AFIC)

#420, 130 Albert St., Ottawa ON K1P 5G4
Tel: 613-236-0569; *Fax:* 613-236-6193
Toll-Free: 800-565-0569
e-mail: info@acec.ca
www.acec.ca
twitter.com/ACECCanada
Previous Name: Association of Consulting Engineers of Canada
Overview: A large national organization founded in 1925
Mission: To assist in promoting satisfactory business relations between its Member Firms & their clients; To promote cordial relations among the various consulting engineering firms in Canada & to foster the interchange of professional, management & business experience & information among them; To safeguard the interest of the consulting engineer; To further the maintenance of high professional standards in the consulting engineering profession; *Member of:* International Federation of Consulting Engineers
Chief Officer(s):
Murray Thompson, Chair
murray.thompson@urs.com
John D. Gamble, CET, P.Eng., President
jgamble@acec.ca
Jean-Marc Carrière, Vice-President, Finance & Administration, 613-236-0569 Ext. 209
jmcarriere@acec.ca
Susie Grynol, CAE, Vice-President, Policy & Public Affairs, 613-236-0569 Ext. 203
sgrynol@acec.ca
Membership: 600 independent consulting engineering companies & 11 provincial and territorial member organizations; *Fees:* Based on annual revenue; *Member Profile:* Firms which have passed a thorough membership screening process: proven technical capability, necessary experience as consultants, adherence to rules of ethical practice & professional responsibility; membership is voluntary & is limited to those firms primarily engaged in providing independent consulting engineering services to the public; *Committees:* Executive Directors' Coordination; Member Organization Chairs; Budget & Finance; General Reserve Investment; International; Federal/Industry Real Property Advisory Council; DND/DCC Liaison; Student Outreach Advisory Group; Canadian Engineering Leadership Forum; Contracts; Allen D. Williams Scholarship Foundation; Public-Private Partnerships (P3) Task Force
Activities: Federal government lobbying on major public policy issues; Negotiations with government departments re: contracting-out of public work, selection of consultants & remuneration; Negotiations with other industry organizations re: establishment of guidelines for contracts; International market development; *Awareness Events:* National Engineering Month; *Speaker Service:* Yes; *Rents Mailing List:* Yes; *Library:* Open to public
Meetings/Conferences:
For more information see Trade Shows, Conferences and Seminars Chapter
Association of Consulting Engineering Companies (ACEC) Summit 2013
June 2013 Lake Louise, AB
Publications:
•Concept [a publication of the Association of Consulting Engineering Companies - Canada]
Number of Pages: 4
•Source [a publication of the Association of Consulting Engineering Companies - Canada]
Type: Newsletter; *Frequency:* Monthly
•Source Express [a publication of the Association of Consulting Engineering Companies - Canada]
Type: Newsletter

Association of Consulting Engineering Companies - New Brunswick (ACEC-NB)
Parent Name: Association of Consulting Engineering Companies - Canada

183 Hanwell Rd., Fredericton NB E3B 2R2
Tel: 506-470-9211; *Fax:* 506-451-9629
e-mail: info@acec-nb.ca
www.acec-nb.ca
Overview: A medium-sized provincial organization founded in 1983 overseen by Association of Consulting Engineering Companies - Canada
Mission: To develop & support member firms; To improve the business environment for member firms & their clients; To further the professional standards of the consulting engineering profession
Chief Officer(s):
John Fudge, Executive Director
David McAllister, President
Christy Cunningham, Secretary
Karen Robichaud, Treasurer
Activities: Advocating for consulting engineering companies in New Brunswick; Providing training opportunities
Meetings/Conferences:
For more information see Trade Shows, Conferences and Seminars Chapter
Association of Consulting Engineering Companies - New Brunswick 2013 6th Annual Deputy Ministers' Dinner & Information Session
2013, NB
Association of Consulting Engineering Companies - New Brunswick 2013 16th Annual General Meeting, Trade Show, Conference, & Awards Gala
2013, NB
Publications:
•CE [Consulting Engineers] News
Type: Newsletter; *Frequency:* Bimonthly
Profile: Information for Association of Consulting Engineering Companies - New Brunswick members

Association of Consulting Engineers of Canada *See*
Association of Consulting Engineering Companies - Canada

Association of Consulting Engineers of Saskatchewan *See*
Consulting Engineers of Saskatchewan

Association of Engineering Technicians & Technologists of Newfoundland & Labrador (AETTNL)
Parent Name: Canadian Council of Technicians & Technologists

Donovan's Industrial Park, PO Box 790, 22 Sagona Ave., Mount Pearl NL A1N 2Y2
Tel: 709-747-2868; *Fax:* 709-747-2869
Toll-Free: 888-238-8600
e-mail: aettnl@aettnl.com
www.aettnl.com
Overview: A small provincial organization founded in 1968 overseen by Canadian Council of Technicians & Technologists
Mission: AETTNL's mission is to advance the profession of Applied Science/Engineering Technology & the professional recognition of Certified Technicians & Technologists. It regulates the standards of training & practice, & protects the interests of its members & the public.
Chief Officer(s):
Tony Scott, President
Linda Hayward, Office Manager
Finances: *Annual Operating Budget:* Less than $50,000
Membership: 1200; *Fees:* Schedule available; *Committees:* Certification/Registration Board; Constitution/Bylaws; Accreditation Board; Act; Public Relations

Association of Environmental Engineering & Science Professors (AEESP)

2303 Naples Ct., Champaign IL 61822-3510 USA
Tel: 217-398-6969; *Fax:* 217-355-9232
e-mail: joanne@aeesp.org
www.aeesp.org
Overview: A medium-sized international organization founded in 1963
Mission: To assist members in the development & dissemination of knowledge in environmental engineering & science; to strengthen & advance the environmental field through cooperation amongst academic & other communities
Chief Officer(s):
Amy Childress, President
Joanne Fetzner, Manager, Business Office
Finances: *Annual Operating Budget:* $50,000-$100,000
Membership: 700; *Fees:* $15 student; $75 professor
Activities: *Rents Mailing List:* Yes

Association of Equipment Manufacturers - Canada (AEM-Canada)

World Exchange Plaza, PO Box 81067, #880, 111 Albert St., Ottawa ON K1P 1B1

Tel: 613-566-4568; *Fax:* 613-566-2026
www.aem.org
Previous Name: Canadian Farm & Industrial Equipment Institute
Overview: A small national organization founded in 1966
Mission: The Association acts as a voice for its members to the public & on a governmental level. It is also a regulatory body setting standars for safety, offering a variety of educational programs & seminars. AEM also serves as a disseminating body providing it members with current information & news on the industry.
Chief Officer(s):
Dennis Slater, President, 414-298-4140
dslater@aem.org
Howard Mains, Canada Consultant, Public Policy
hmains@aem.org
Membership: 750 companies; *Fees:* Based on sales; *Member Profile:* Manufacturers & distributors of equipment, & those who offer services, in the agriculture, construction, forestry, mining & utility industries.

Association of Exploration Geochemists ***See*** Association of Applied Geochemists

Association of Fish & Wildlife Agencies

#725, 444 North Capitol St. NW, Washington DC 20001 USA
Tel: 202-624-7890; *Fax:* 202-624-7891
e-mail: info@fishwildlife.org
www.fishwildlife.org
Previous Name: International Association of Fish & Wildlife Agencies
Overview: A small international organization founded in 1902
Mission: The Association works cooperatively to guide its members toward long term conservation of renewable natural resources by employing conservation science & research.
Chief Officer(s):
Ron Regan, Executive Director
rregan@fishwildlife.org
Curtis Taylor, President
Finances: *Annual Operating Budget:* $500,000-$1.5 Million
Staff: 25 staff member(s)
Membership: *Member Profile:* Conservationists; Governments & government agencies; Regional associations; Organizations with similar objectives or supportive of the Association; Sportsmen; Individuals with varied backgrounds
Activities: All bird conservation; Agency information database; Automated wildlife data systems; Conservation education; Conservation Leadership Institute; Farm Bill program; Furbearer management; International relations; Legislation; National Fish Habitat Action Plan; Science & Research; Teaming with wildlife; Wildlife conflict

Association of Great Lakes Outdoor Writers (AGLOW)

PO Box 35, Benld IL 62009 USA
Toll-Free: 877-472-4569
e-mail: edir@AGLOW.INFO
www.aglow.info
Overview: A small local organization founded in 1954
Mission: Dedicated to communicating the outdoor experience in word & image
Chief Officer(s):
Curt Hicken, Executive Director
Bob Whitehead, President
OGMBOBW@aol.com
Finances: *Annual Operating Budget:* Less than $50,000; *Funding Sources:* Membership dues; fundraising
Staff: 2 staff member(s)
Membership: 330; *Fees:* $45-135

Association of Heritage Consultants ***See*** Canadian Association of Heritage Professionals

Association of Independent Corrugated Converters

PO Box 73063, Stn. White Shields, 2300 Lawrence Ave. East, Toronto ON M1P 4Z5
Tel: 905-727-9405; *Fax:* 905-727-1061
e-mail: info@aicc11.com
www.aiccbox.org
Also Known As: AICC Canada
Overview: A small national organization founded in 1975
Mission: To provide a forum for the independent corrugated converter on legitimate matters of mutual interest; To enhance the level of professionalism of the independent converter in the operation of his/her business; To implement democratically determined goals on matters civil & governmental which have a positive effect on all independent corrugated converters; *Member of:* AICC International - Alexandria, Virginia
Environmental Activity: Member of the Paper & Paperboard Packaging Environmental Council (PPEC)
Finances: *Annual Operating Budget:* $50,000-$100,000; *Funding Sources:* Membership fees
Staff: 2 staff member(s); 10 volunteer(s)
Membership: 65 regular + 35 associate; *Fees:* Levels based on gross sales or total number of staff; *Member Profile:* Sheet plant owners & associated members; *Committees:* Education, Program, Hall of Fame, Golf Tournament, Industry Lobby Committee

Association of International Automobile Manufacturers of Canada (AIAMC) / Association des fabricants internationaux d'automobiles du Canada Parent Name: The Canadian Association of Importers & Exporters

PO Box 5, #1804, 2 Bloor St. West, Toronto ON M4W 3E2
Tel: 416-595-8251; *Fax:* 416-595-2864
e-mail: auto@aiamc.com
www.aiamc.com
Previous Name: Automobile Importers of Canada
Overview: A medium-sized national organization founded in 1973 overseen by The Canadian Association of Importers & Exporters
Mission: To represent before federal, provincial, & territorial governments the interests of members engaged in the manufacturing, importation, distribution, & servicing of light-duty vehicles
Chief Officer(s):
David C. Adams, President
Mary Hogarth, Director, Policy Development & Corporate Affairs
Andrew Morin, Director, Technical & Regulatory Affairs
Finances: *Funding Sources:* Membership dues
Staff: 100 volunteer(s)
Membership: 25; *Committees:* Executive; Consumer Relations; Custom; Finance & Taxation; Financial Services; Government Relations; Legal; Logistics; Parts; Show Exhibitors; Statistical; Technical
Activities: ; *Library:* Open to public

Association of Local Official Health Agencies (ALOHA) ***See*** Association of Local Public Health Agencies

Association of Local Public Health Agencies (ALPHA)

#1306, 2 Carlton St., Toronto ON M5G 1T6
Tel: 416-595-0006; *Fax:* 416-595-0030
e-mail: info@alphaweb.org
www.alphaweb.org
Previous Name: Association of Local Official Health Agencies (ALOHA)
Overview: A medium-sized provincial organization founded in 1986
Mission: To provide leadership in public health management to health units in Ontario; To assist local public health units in the provision of efficient & effective services; Affiliation(s): ANDSOOHA - Public Health Nursing Management; Association of Ontario Public Health Business Administrators; Association of Public Health Epidemiologists in Ontario; Association of Supervisors of Public Health Inspectors of Ontario; Health Promotion Ontario; Ontario Association of Public Health Dentistry; Ontario Society of Nutrition Professionals in Public Health
Environmental Activity: Providing information on issues related to public health
Chief Officer(s):
Linda Stewart, Executive Director
linda@alphaweb.org
Gordon Fleming, Manager, Public Health Issues
gordon@alphaweb.org
Tannisha Lambert, Manager, Administrative & Association Services
tannisha@alphaweb.org
Membership: 36 health units; *Member Profile:* Board of health members of health units in Ontario; Medical & associate medical officers of health; *Committees:* Advocacy
Activities: Advocating for public health policies, programs, & services
Meetings/Conferences:
For more information see Trade Shows, Conferences and Seminars Chapter
Association of Local Public Health Agencies 2013 Winter Symposium
February 2013 Toronto, ON
Association of Local Public Health Agencies 2013 Annual General Meeting
June 2013, ON
Association of Local Public Health Agencies 2013 Fall Symposium
2013, ON
Publications:
•Public Health Pulse
Type: Newsletter; *Frequency:* Quarterly; *Editor:* Tannisha Lambert
Profile: Association activities, affiliate information, conference highlights, & upcoming events

Association of Major Power Consumers in Ontario (AMPCO)

Thomson Bldg., #1510, 65 Queen St. West, Toronto ON M5H 2M5
Tel: 416-260-0280; *Fax:* 416-260-0442
www.ampco.org
www.linkedin.com/profile/view?id=11277536
twitter.com/powerconsumer
Overview: A large provincial organization founded in 1975
Mission: To represent Ontario's electricity-intensive companies; To ensure reliability of power supply to support the economy of Ontario; To advocate a fair & equitable pricing system for electricity; To present views on energy matters to such groups as the Ontario Energy Board, the Ontario Government, Ontario Hydro, the news media, & the general public; To provide decision makers with recommendations on resolving issues
Chief Officer(s):
Adam White, President
awhite@ampco.org
Fareeda Heeralal, Contact
Finances: *Funding Sources:* Membership fees
Membership: 43; *Fees:* Based on electrical energy usage; *Member Profile:* Companies that are major manufacturers, employers, & power consumers (represents key industries - mining, pulp & paper, automobile manufacturing, petro-chemicals, metals, consumer products, steel, etc.)
Publications:
•AMPCO [Association of Major Power Consumers in Ontario] Bulletins
Type: Newsletter

Association of Manitoba Land Surveyors Parent Name: Professional Surveyors Canada

#202, 83 Gary St., Winnipeg MB R3C 4J9
Tel: 204-943-6972; *Fax:* 204-957-7602
e-mail: amls@mts.net
www.amls.ca
Overview: A medium-sized provincial licensing organization founded in 1881 overseen by Professional Surveyors Canada
Mission: To license qualified persons becoming commissioned land surveyors; To protect public interests concerning land boundary matters; Affiliation(s): Canadian Institute of Surveying & Mapping; Western Canadian Board of Examiners for Land Surveyors
Chief Officer(s):
Kelly Tole, Executive Officer
Finances: *Annual Operating Budget:* $100,000-$250,000; *Funding Sources:* Membership fees
Membership: 10 student + 13 lifetime + 64 individual; *Fees:* Schedule available; *Member Profile:* Commissioned land surveyor in Manitoba; *Committees:* Board of Examiners; Continuing Education; Executive Council; Legislation; Nominating; Professional Standards & Ethics; Public Relations; Restoration
Activities: *Internships:* Yes; *Speaker Service:* Yes; *Rents Mailing List:* Yes; *Library:* Open to public by appointment

Association of Manitoba Municipalities (AMM)

1910 Saskatchewan Ave. West, Portage la Prairie MB R1N 0P1
Tel: 204-857-8666; *Fax:* 204-856-2370
e-mail: amm@amm.mb.ca
www.amm.mb.ca
www.facebook.com/124665930946719
twitter.com/AMMManitoba
Merged from: Union of Manitoba Municipalities; Manitoba Association of Urban Municipalities
Overview: A medium-sized provincial organization founded in 1905
Mission: To provide communications link between municipalities; to lobby for municipal governments with senior levels of government; *Member of:* Federation of Canadian Municipalities
Chief Officer(s):

Joe Masi, Executive Director, 204-856-2360
Doug Dobrowolski, President
Finances: *Annual Operating Budget:* $500,000-$1.5 Million; *Funding Sources:* Membership fees
Staff: 6 staff member(s)
Membership: 165 municipalities
Activities: ; *Library:* Open to public
Meetings/Conferences:
For more information see Trade Shows, Conferences and Seminars Chapter
Municipal Officials Seminar & MTCML Trade Show 2013
April 2013 Brandon, MB
Municipal Officials Seminar & MTCML Trade Show 2014
April 2014 Brandon, MB
Municipal Officials Seminar & MTCML Trade Show 2015
April 2015 Brandon, MB

Association of Municipal Administrators of New Brunswick (AMANB) / Association des administrateurs municipaux du Nouveau-Brunswick (AAMNB)

20 Courtney St., Douglas NB E3G 8A1
Tel: 506-453-4229; *Fax:* 506-444-5452
e-mail: amanb@nb.aibn.com
www.amanb-aamnb.ca
Overview: A medium-sized provincial organization founded in 1977
Mission: To promote & advance status of persons employed in field of municipal administration; to advance quality of administration of municipal services; to encourage closer official & personal relationship among members to facilitate interchange of ideas & experience; to establish & maintain standards of performance for members; to assist in provision of formal training & educational facilities
Chief Officer(s):
Cynthia Geldart, President, 506-451-3333
Danielle Charron, Executive Director
Finances: *Annual Operating Budget:* Less than $50,000
Staff: 1 staff member(s)
Membership: 226 municipal + 23 associate; *Committees:* Legislation; Education; Membership
Meetings/Conferences:
For more information see Trade Shows, Conferences and Seminars Chapter
Association of Municipal Administrators of New Brunswick 2013 Annual Conference and Annual General Meeeting
June 2013 Sheiac, NB

Association of Municipal Administrators, Nova Scotia (AMANS)

CIBC Building, #1106, 1809 Barrington St., Halifax NS B3J 3K8
Tel: 902-423-2215; *Fax:* 902-425-5592
e-mail: amans@eastlink.ca
www.amans.ca
Overview: A medium-sized provincial organization founded in 1970
Mission: To improve the quality of local government in Nova Scotia through the development of educational programs; To provide a forum for the exchange of ideas; to provide a resource to municipal officials; To provide service to members to improve their professional capabilities
Chief Officer(s):
Janice Wentzell, Executive Director, 902-423-8323, Fax: 902-425-5592
jwentzell@amans.ca
Kristy Hardie, Administrative Assistant, 902-423-2215, Fax: 902-425-5592
khardie@amans.ca
Finances: *Funding Sources:* Membership dues; Conference surplus
Membership: 165; *Fees:* $175

Association of Municipal Recycling Coordinators *See* Municipal Waste Association

Association of Municipalities of Ontario (AMO)

#801, 200 University Ave., Toronto ON M5H 3C6
Tel: 416-971-9856; *Fax:* 416-971-6191
Toll-Free: 877-426-6527
e-mail: amo@amo.on.ca
www.amo.on.ca
Overview: A medium-sized provincial organization founded in 1899
Mission: To support & enhance strong & effective municipal government in Ontario; To represent almost all of Ontario's 444 municipal governments; *Member of:* Federation of Canadian Municipalities
Chief Officer(s):
Pat Vanini, Executive Director, 416-971-9856 Ext. 316
pvanini@amo.on.ca
Nancy Plumridge, Director, Administration & Business Development
NPlumridge@amo.on.ca
Monika Turner, Director, Policy
MTurner@amo.on.ca
Finances: *Funding Sources:* Membership fees; Sales of services & products; Sponsorships
Membership: 100-499; *Member Profile:* Ontario municipalities; Related non-profit organizations & private corporations
Activities: Developing policy positions; Reporting on issues; Liaising with the Ontario provincial government; Informing & educating the media & the public; Marketing services to the municipal sector
Meetings/Conferences:
For more information see Trade Shows, Conferences and Seminars Chapter
Association of Municipalities of Ontario 2013 Urban Symposium
April 2013 Mississauga, ON
Association of Municipalities of Ontario 2013 Annual Conference
August 2013 Ottawa, ON
Association of Municipalities of Ontario 2013 Counties, Regions, & Single Tiers Symposium
October 2013 Oshawa, ON
Publications:
•AMO Watch File e-Newstter
Type: Newsletter
•Association of Municipalities of Ontario Annual Report
Type: Yearbook; *Frequency:* Annually

Association of New Brunswick Land Surveyors (ANBLS) / Association des arpenteurs-géomètres du Nouveau-Brunswick (AA-GN-B)
Parent Name: Professional Surveyors Canada

#312, 212, Queen St., Fredericton NB E3B 1A8
Tel: 506-458-8266; *Fax:* 506-458-8267
e-mail: anbls@nbnet.nb.ca
www.anbls.nb.ca
Overview: A small provincial licensing organization founded in 1954 overseen by Professional Surveyors Canada
Mission: To regulate & govern the practice of land surveying in New Brunswick; To develop & maintain standards of knowledge, skill, & professional ethics
Chief Officer(s):
Louise McSheffrey, Executive Director
lmcsheffrey@nb.aibn.com
Membership: 140; *Member Profile:* Individuals who comply with the requirements as specified in the New Brunswick Land Surveyors Act, 1986, & By-Laws
Activities: Increasing public awareness of the role of the association; Liaising with other professional organizations
Meetings/Conferences:
For more information see Trade Shows, Conferences and Seminars Chapter
Association of New Brunswick Land Surveyors 2014 Annual General Meeting
January 2014, NB
Publications:
•Surveyor-In-Training Manual
Type: Manual

Association of Newfoundland Land Surveyors
Parent Name: Professional Surveyors Canada

#203, 62-64 Pippy Pl., St. John's NL A1B 4H7
Tel: 709-722-2031; *Fax:* 709-722-4104
e-mail: anls@nf.aibn.com
www.surveyors.nf.ca
Overview: A small provincial licensing organization founded in 1953 overseen by Professional Surveyors Canada
Mission: To establish & maintain standards of knowledge, skill, & professional conduct in the practice of land surveying, in order to serve & protect the public interest in Newfoundland; to regulate & govern the practice of land surveying in the province
Chief Officer(s):
Robin Davis, President, 709-646-2776
rcdavis@nf.sympatico.ca
Paula Baggs, Executive Director
paulabaggs@surveyors.nf.ca
Membership: *Committees:* Annual General Meeting; Archives; Board of Examiners; By-laws & Regulations; Discipline; Executive Directory; Finance; Land Surveyors Act; Liability Insurance; Liaison; Nominating; Professional Development; Regional Representatives; Representatives
Activities: Advancing & protecting the interests of members; Improving the knowledge & skill of members; Liaising with other professional organizations

Association of Nova Scotia Land Surveyors (ANSLS)
Parent Name: Professional Surveyors Canada

325A Prince Albert Rd., Dartmouth NS B2Y 1N5
Tel: 902-469-7962; *Fax:* 902-469-7963
e-mail: ansls@accesswave.ca
www.ansls.ca
Overview: A medium-sized provincial licensing organization founded in 1951 overseen by Professional Surveyors Canada
Mission: To establish & maintain standards of professional ethics among its members, student members & holders of a certificate of authorization, in order that the public interest may be served & protected; & knowledge & skills among its members, student members & holders of a certificate of authorization; to regulate the practice of professional land surveying & govern the profession in accordance with the Act, the regulations & the by-laws; & to communicate & cooperate with other professional organizations for the advancement of the best interests of the surveying profession
Chief Officer(s):
Fred Hutchinson, Executive Director
Finances: *Funding Sources:* Membership dues
Staff: 3 staff member(s); 30 volunteer(s)
Membership: 172 regular + 19 life + 39 retired + 24 student; *Fees:* $800 regular; $120 retired; $80 student; *Member Profile:* Examinations & apprenticeship; licensed professionals
Activities: *Internships:* Yes; *Speaker Service:* Yes; *Library:* Open to public

Association of Nova Scotia Museums (ANSM)

1113 Marginal Rd., Halifax NS B3H 4P7
Tel: 902-423-4677; *Fax:* 902-422-0881
Toll-Free: 800-355-6873
e-mail: admin@ansm.ns.ca
ansm.ns.ca
www.facebook.com/113166268748419
Previous Name: Federation of Nova Scotian Heritage
Overview: A medium-sized provincial organization founded in 1976
Mission: The Association of Nova Scotia Museums, using a consultative regional representative model, proactively champions museums through education, outreach, networking and advocacy to achieve excellence.; Affiliation(s): Heritage Canada; Canadian Museums Association; Association for State & Local History
Chief Officer(s):
Anita Price, Managing Director
director@ansm.ns.ca
Membership: 50 organizational + 25 individual + 1 student + 2 lifetime; *Fees:* $50 organizational; $25 individual; $15 student
Activities: Training & Education Program; Heritage Studies Certificate; applied learning workshops; seminars

Association of Ontario Land Economists

#205, 555 St. Clair Ave. West, Toronto ON M4V 2Y7
Tel: 416-283-0440; *Fax:* 416-283-1399
e-mail: admin@aole.org
www.aole.org
Overview: A medium-sized provincial organization founded in 1962
Mission: To continue attracting membership-quality professionals engaged in land economics pursuits; To broaden & enrich the professional development of members; To promote & maintain high ethical work standards throughout our membership; To make submissions to government for improvements in law & public administration bearing on land economics
Chief Officer(s):
Andrea Calla, President, 416-736-2610
acalla@tridel.com
John Blackburn, Vice-President & Secretary, 416-948-6969
johnblackburn@brightstarcorp.ca
Naomi Irizawa, Treasurer, 416-283-0440
naomiiriz@yahoo.ca
Membership: 215; *Fees:* $144.45; *Member Profile:* Architects; Certified Property Managers; Economists; Land Use Planners; Management Consultants; Mortgage Brokers; Municipal Assessors; Ontario Land Surveyors; Engineers; Property Tax Agents; Quantity Surveyors; Real Estate Brokers; Real Property Appraisers

Association of Ontario Land Surveyors (AOLS)
Parent Name: Professional Surveyors Canada

1043 McNicoll Ave., Toronto ON M1W 3W6
Tel: 416-491-9020; *Fax:* 416-491-2576
Toll-Free: 800-268-0718
e-mail: blain@aols.org
www.aols.org
Overview: A medium-sized provincial licensing organization founded in 1892 overseen by Professional Surveyors Canada
Mission: AOLS is responsible for the licensing and governance of professional land surveyors, in accordance with the Surveyors Act. The self-governing association ensures that public interest is paramount.
Chief Officer(s):
Blain W. Martin, Executive Director
William D. Buck, Registrar
bill@aols.org
Finances: *Funding Sources:* Membership fees
Staff: 8 staff member(s)
Membership: 500-999;; *Fees:* $56.50 associate; *Member Profile:* Individuals with a degree in Geomatics from an accredited university program, followed bu a term of articles & professional examinations
Activities: Providing continuing education; *Speaker Service:* Yes
Meetings/Conferences:
For more information see Trade Shows, Conferences and Seminars Chapter
Association of Ontario Land Surveyors 2013 Annual General Meeting
February 2013 Toronto, ON
Association of Ontario Land Surveyors 2014 Annual General Meeting
February 2014 Niagara Falls, ON

Association of Postconsumer Plastic Recyclers (APR)

#500 west, 1001 - G St. NW, Washington DC 20001 USA
Tel: 202-316-3046
e-mail: info@plasticsrecycling.org
www.plasticsrecycling.org
Overview: A small national organization founded in 1992
Mission: The Association represents companies who acquire, reprocess & sell post-consumer plastic. It strives to enhance the plastics recycling industry by promoting cooperative testing for the development of new packaging, improving the quality of plastics, encouraging better recycling guidelines, & presenting awards for advancements in the industry.
Chief Officer(s):
Steve Alexander, Executive Director
salexander@cmrgroup4.com
Finances: *Annual Operating Budget:* $100,000-$250,000; *Funding Sources:* Related associations; membership dues
Staff: 1 staff member(s)
Membership: 103; *Fees:* $800-3,500; *Member Profile:* PCR reclaimers; *Committees:* Market Development; Technical; Executive
Activities: Design for Recyclability Programs; Champions for Change

Association of Power Producers of Ontario (APPrO)

PO Box 1084, Stn. F, #1602, 25 Adelaide St. East, Toronto ON M5C 3A1
Tel: 416-322-6549; *Fax:* 416-481-5785
e-mail: appro@appro.org
www.appro.org
Previous Name: Independent Power Producers Society of Ontario (IPPSO)
Overview: A medium-sized provincial organization founded in 1986
Mission: To act as the voice of electricity generators in Ontario; To support a reliable & secure electricity supply in Ontario
Environmental Activity: Promoting use of renewable energy generation
Chief Officer(s):
Jake Brooks, Executive Director
jake.brooks@appro.org
David Butters, President
david.butters@appro.org
Carole Kielly, Manager, Sales & Marketing, 416-322-6549 Ext. 222
carole.kielly@appro.org
Soraya Rivera, Manager, Registration & Data
soraya.rivera@appro.org
Karla Martinez, Manager, Office
karla.martinez@appro.org
Membership: 100+; *Member Profile:* Companies involved in the generation of electricity in Ontario, including suppliers of services & consulting services
Activities: Advocating for generators; Offering resources to assist business, government, utilities, & researchers; Organizing educational programs;
Meetings/Conferences:
For more information see Trade Shows, Conferences and Seminars Chapter
Association of Power Producers of Ontario 2013: 25th Annual Canadian Power
November 2013, ON
Association of Power Producers of Ontario 2014: 26th Annual Canadian Power Conference & Power Networking Centre
November 2014, ON
Association of Power Producers of Ontario 2015: 27th Annual Canadian Power Conference & Power Networking Centre
November 2015, ON
Publications:
•APPrO [Association of Power Producers of Ontario] Conference Proceedings
Type: Yearbook; *Frequency:* Annually; *Price:* $40
•Canadian Power Directory
Type: Directory
Profile: Contact information for organizations involved in all aspects of electricity generation in Canada, such as developers, equipment & service suppliers, utilities, & resource groups
•IPPSO FACTO: Magazine of the Association of Power Producers of Ontario
Type: Magazine; *Frequency:* Bimonthly; *Accepts Advertising*; *Price:* Free with Association of Power Producers of Ontario membership
Profile: Ontario, national, international, & regulatory news

Association of Prince Edward Island Land Surveyors (APEILS)
Parent Name: Professional Surveyors Canada

PO Box 20100, Charlottetown PE C1A 9E3
Tel: 902-566-9966
e-mail: info@apeils.ca
www.apeils.ca
Overview: A small provincial licensing organization overseen by Professional Surveyors Canada
Chief Officer(s):
Wayne Tremblay, Sec.-Treas.
wtremblay@mles.ca

Association of Professional Community Planners of Saskatchewan
Parent Name: Canadian Institute of Planners

2424 College Ave., Regina SK S4P 1C8
Tel: 306-584-3879; *Fax:* 306-352-6913
e-mail: president@apcps.ca
www.apcps.ca
Overview: A medium-sized provincial organization founded in 1963 overseen by Canadian Institute of Planners
Mission: To promote & maintain professionalism in planning field; Affiliation(s): Canadian Institute of Planners
Chief Officer(s):
Marilyn Steranka, Executive Director, 306-584-3879, Fax: 306-352-6913
msteranka@sasktel.net
Bill Delainey, Secretary, 306-975-1663, Fax: 306-242-6965
Ryan Walker, Treasurer, 306-966-5664, Fax: 306-966-5680
Membership: 24 student + 78 individual + 11 non-resident; *Committees:* Program; Education; Membership
Activities: *Speaker Service:* Yes; *Rents Mailing List:* Yes
Meetings/Conferences:
For more information see Trade Shows, Conferences and Seminars Chapter
Association of Professional Community Planners of Saskatchewan 2013 Conference
September 2013 Regina, SK
Association of Professional Community Planners of Saskatchewan 2014 Conference
2014

Association of Professional Engineers & Geoscientists of British Columbia (APEGBC)
Parent Name: Engineers Canada

#200, 4010 Regent St., Burnaby BC V5C 6N2
Tel: 604-430-8035; *Fax:* 604-430-8085
Toll-Free: 888-430-8035
e-mail: apeginfo@apeg.bc.ca
www.apeg.bc.ca
twitter.com/APEGBC
Overview: A large provincial licensing organization founded in 1920 overseen by Engineers Canada
Mission: To protect the public interest in matters related to geoscience & engineering; To regulate & govern the professions of professional engineers & geoscientists in British Columbia, according to the Engineers & Geoscientists Act; To strive for professional excellence, by establishing academic, experience, & professional practice standards; *Member of:* Engineers Canada
Environmental Activity: Establishing an Environment Committee to provide advice on environmental matters
Chief Officer(s):
Michael Isaacson, P.Eng., PhD, President
president@apeg.bc.ca
Ann English, P.Eng., CEO & Registrar, 604-412-4850 Ext. 4850
aenglish@apeg.bc.ca
Tony Chong, P.Eng., Chief Regulatory Officer & Deputy Registrar, 604-412-6058 Ext. 6058
tchong@apeg.bc.ca
Janet Sinclair, COO, 604-412-4874 Ext. 4874
jsinclair@apeg.bc.ca
Jennifer Cho, CGA, Director, Finance & Administration, 604-412-4870 Ext. 4870
jcho@apeg.bc.ca
Peter Mitchell, P.Eng., Director, Professional Practice, Standards, & Development, 604-412-4853 Ext. 4853
pmitchell@apeg.bc.ca
Gillian Pichler, P.Eng., Director, Registration, 604-412-4857 Ext. 4857
gpichler@apeg.bc.ca
Geoff Thiele, LLB, Director, Legislation, Ethics & Compliance, 604-412-4852 Ext. 4852
gthiele@apeg.bc.ca
Megan Archibald, Associate Director, Communications & Stakeholder Engagement, 604-412-4883 Ext. 4883
marchibald@apeg.bc.ca
Don Gamble, Associate Director, Information Systems, 604-412-4867 Ext. 4867
dgamble@apeg.bc.ca.ca
Deesh Olychick, Associate Director, Member Services, 604-412-4882 Ext. 4882
dolychick@apeg.bc.ca
Membership: *Committees:* Audit; Branches; Discipline; Executive; Geoscience; Registration; Structural Qualifications Bd.; Applications; Bd. of Examiners; Registration Task Force; Professional Renewal Task Force; ABCPF/APEGBC Joint Practice Bd.; Building Codes; Building Enclosure; Consulting Practice; Environment; Investigation; Practice Review; Sustainability; Continuing Professional Dev.; Editorial Bd.; Mentoring; Standing Awards; Div. for Advancement of Woman in Engineering & Geoscience; Div. of Engineers & Geoscientists in the Resource Sector; Municipal Engineers Div.; and others...
Activities: Maintaining practice standards; Upholding the code of ethics; Publishing brochures, position papers, & other association documents; Promoting the professions; Protecting members' interests; Establishing the Engineers Benevolent Fund to assist members; Setting up Foundation Trustees to support education through scholarships & bursaries & to promote professional development opportunities;
Meetings/Conferences:
For more information see Trade Shows, Conferences and Seminars Chapter
Association of Professional Engineers & Geoscientists of British Columbia 2013 Conference & Annual General Meeting
2013, BC
Publications:
•APEGBC [Association of Professional Engineers & Geoscientists of British Columbia] Membership Directory
Type: Directory
Profile: Rosters of professional engineers & professional geoscientists with contact information & scope of practice
•APEGBC [Association of Professional Engineers & Geoscientists of British Columbia] Professional Practice Guidelines
Type: Guides
Profile: Examples of guidelines are as follows: APEGBC/CEBC Budget Guidelines for Engineering Services; Guidelinesfor Terrain Stability Assessments in the Forest Sector; & Guidelines for Legislated Landslide Assessments for Proposed Residential Development in British Columbia
•Association of Professional Engineers & Geoscientists of British Columbia Compensation Survey
Profile: Information on APEGBC members' compensation & benefits

•Association of Professional Engineers & Geoscientists of British Columbia Annual Report
Type: Yearbook; *Frequency:* Annually
Profile: A yearly review, featuring reports from the association's executive director & president, as well as the auditor
•Association of Professional Engineers & Geoscientists of British Columbia Technical Bulletins
Type: Bulletins
Profile: Examples of technical bulletins are as follows: Assessment of Seismic Slope Stability; Engineering Modifications to FireTested & Listed Assemblies; & Addressing Smoke & CO Control in Elevator Machine Rooms
•Bylaws of the Association [a publication of the Association of Professional Engineers & Geoscientists of British Columbia]
Type: Booklet
Profile: Information about items such as conduct of meetings, election of council, finances, & membership
•Connections E-news [a publication of the Association of Professional Engineers & Geoscientists of British Columbia]
Type: Newsletter; *Frequency:* Monthly
Profile: Currents happenings in the association & in the professions of engineers & geoscientists in BritishColumbia
•Innovation [a publication of the Association of Professional Engineers & Geoscientists of British Columbia]
Type: Magazine; *Frequency:* Bimonthly; *Accepts Advertising*; *Editor:* Melinda Lau
Profile: Information circulated to more than 26,000 British Columbia registered professionalengineers & geoscientists, industry & government reporesentatives, educational institutions, as well as the general public

Burnaby/New West Branch

e-mail: bn@apeg.bc.ca
apeg.bc.ca/services/branches/bn.html
Chief Officer(s):
Mike Samilski, P.Eng, Chair

Central Interior Branch

e-mail: ci@apeg.bc.ca
apeg.bc.ca/services/branches/ci.html
Chief Officer(s):
Brendon Masson, P.Eng, Chair, 250-561-2229
bmasson@mcelhanney.com

East Kootenay Branch

e-mail: ek@apeg.bc.ca
apeg.bc.ca/services/branches/ek.html
Chief Officer(s):
Sean Abram, Chair, 250-489-8188
sean@abramcs.com

Fraser Valley Branch

e-mail: fv@apeg.bc.ca
apeg.bc.ca/services/branches/fv.html
Chief Officer(s):
Bernadette Currie, P.Eng, Chair
daweg.past.chair.fv.exec@gmail.com

Northern Branch

e-mail: no@apeg.bc.ca
apeg.bc.ca/services/branches/no.html
Chief Officer(s):
Anatasia Ledwon, P.Geo., Chair

Okanagan Branch

e-mail: ok@apeg.bc.ca
apeg.bc.ca/services/branches/ok.html

Peace River Branch

e-mail: pr@apeg.bc.ca
apeg.bc.ca/services/branches/pr.html
Chief Officer(s):
Adel Morhart, EIT, Chair

Richmond/Delta Branch

e-mail: rd@apeg.bc.ca
apeg.bc.ca/services/branches/rd.html
Chief Officer(s):
Ravee Ramakrishnan, MBA, P.Eng, Chair

Sea-to-Sky Branch

e-mail: ss@apeg.bc.ca
apeg.bc.ca/services/branches/seatosky/index.html
Chief Officer(s):
Piotr Mazur, P.Eng, Chair

South Central Branch

e-mail: sc@apeg.bc.ca
apeg.bc.ca/services/branches/sc.html
Chief Officer(s):
Eric Sears, EIT, Chair
sc@apeg.bc.ca

Tri-City Branch

e-mail: tc@apeg.bc.ca
apeg.bc.ca/services/branches/tc/index.html
Chief Officer(s):
Stella Chiu, P.Eng, Chair

Vancouver Branch

e-mail: van@apeg.bc.ca
apeg.bc.ca/services/branches/van/index.html
Chief Officer(s):
Ben Skillings, P.Eng., Chair

Vancouver Island Branch

e-mail: vi@apeg.bc.ca
apeg.bc.ca/services/branches/vi.html
Chief Officer(s):
Lee Rowley, P.Eng, Chair, 250-751-8558
lrowley@HeroldEngineering.com

Victoria Branch

e-mail: vic@apeg.bc.ca
apeg.bc.ca/services/branches/vic.html
Chief Officer(s):
Richard Summers, P.Eng, Chair
Richard.Summers@forces.gc.ca

West Kootenay Branch

e-mail: wk@apeg.bc.ca
apeg.bc.ca/services/branches/wk.html
Chief Officer(s):
Mark Sirges, P.Eng, Chair & Treasurer, 250-365-4230
msirges@telus.net

Association of Professional Engineers & Geoscientists of British Columbia Foundation

#200, 4010 Regent St., Burnaby BC V5C 6N2
Tel: 604-430-8035; *Fax:* 604-430-8085
Toll-Free: 888-430-8035
www.apeg.bc.ca/services/foundation.html
Also Known As: APEGBC Foundation
Overview: A medium-sized provincial charitable organization founded in 1994
Mission: To operate at arms-length from the APEGBC & to promote education in engineering & geoscience through the granting of bursaries & scholarships

Association of Professional Engineers & Geoscientists of Manitoba (APEGM)
Parent Name: Engineers Canada

870 Pembina Hwy., Winnipeg MB R3M 2M7
Tel: 204-474-2736; *Fax:* 204-474-5960
Toll-Free: 866-227-9600
e-mail: apegm@apegm.mb.ca
www.apegm.mb.ca
Overview: A large provincial organization founded in 1920 overseen by Engineers Canada
Mission: To serve & protect the public interest by governing & advancing the practice of engineering in accordance with the Engineering Profession Act of Manitoba; *Member of:* Engineers Canada
Environmental Activity: Establishing the Sustainable Development Task Force
Chief Officer(s):
Grant Koropatnick, P.Eng., Executive Director & Registrar, 204-474-2736 Ext. 234
GKoropatnick@apegm.mb.ca
Sharon E. Sankar, Director, Admissions, 204-474-2736 Ext. 229
SSankar@apegm.mb.ca
Michael Gregoire, P.Eng., Officer, Professional Standards, 204-474-2736 Ext. 225
MGregoire@apegm.mb.ca
William C. Boyce, Manager, Operations & Finance, 204-474-2736 Ext. 231
WBoyce@apegm.mb.ca
Lorraine Dupas, Coordinator, Admissions, 204-474-2736 Ext. 228
LDupas@apegm.mb.ca
Angela Moore, Coordinator, Events & Communications, 204-474-2736 Ext. 233
AMoore@apegm.mb.ca
Diana Vander Aa, Coordinator, Volunteers, 204-474-2736 Ext. 233
Volunteer@apegm.mb.ca
Finances: *Annual Operating Budget:* $500,000-$1.5 Million
Membership: 3,500; *Fees:* $218

Association of Professional Engineers & Geoscientists of New Brunswick (APEGNB) / Association des ingénieurs et géoscientifiques du Nouveau-Brunswick (AINB)
Parent Name: Engineers Canada

183 Hanwell Rd., Fredericton NB E3B 2R2
Tel: 506-458-8083; *Fax:* 506-451-9629
Toll-Free: 888-458-8083
e-mail: info@apegnb.com
www.apegnb.com
twitter.com/APEGNB
Also Known As: Engineers & Geoscientists New Brunswick
Overview: A large provincial licensing organization founded in 1920 overseen by Engineers Canada
Mission: To establish, maintain & develop standards of knowledge & skill, qualification & practice, & professional ethics; To promote public awareness of the role of the association; *Member of:* Engineers Canada
Chief Officer(s):
Jean Boudreau, P.Eng., President
Mark Bellefleur, P.Eng., Vice-President
Andrew McLeod, FEC (Hon.), CEO
mcleod@apegnb.com
Finances: *Funding Sources:* Membership fees
Membership: 5,500; *Fees:* Schedule available; *Committees:* Council; Admissions; Board of Examiners; Discipline; Internship; Legislation; Nominating; Professional Conduct; Annual Meeting; Awards; Association Affairs; Continuing Competency Assurance; Lay Councillor Appointment; Professional Development; Scrutineers
Meetings/Conferences:
For more information see Trade Shows, Conferences and Seminars Chapter
Association of Professional Engineers & Geoscientists of New Brunswick Annual Meeting 2013
February 2013 Fredericton, NB
Publications:
•APEGNB [Association of Professional Engineers & Geoscientists of New Brunswick] Annual Meeting Magazine
Type: Magazine; *Frequency:* Annual; *Editor:* Melissa Mertz
•Association of Professional Engineers & Geoscientists of New Brunswick Annual Report
Type: Yearbook; *Frequency:* Annual
•Engenuity [a publication of the Association of Professional Engineers & Geoscientists of New Brunswick]
Type: Newsletter; *Frequency:* 3 pa; *Editor:* Melissa Mertz
•Member Salary Survey [Association of Professional Engineers & Geoscientists of New Brunswick]
Type: Report; *Frequency:* Annual

Association of Professional Engineers & Geoscientists of Newfoundland ***See*** Professional Engineers & Geoscientists Newfoundland & Labrador

Association of Professional Engineers & Geoscientists of Saskatchewan (APEGS)
Parent Name: Engineers Canada

#104, 2255 - 13 Ave., Regina SK S4P 0V6
Tel: 306-525-9547; *Fax:* 306-525-0851
Toll-Free: 800-500-9547
e-mail: apegs@apegs.sk.ca
www.apegs.sk.ca
Overview: A large provincial licensing organization founded in 1930 overseen by Engineers Canada
Mission: To achieve a safe & prosperous future through engineering & geoscience; *Member of:* Engineers Canada
Chief Officer(s):
Leon C. Botham, P.Eng., President

Dennis Paddock, P.Eng., FEC, Executive Director & Registrar
dkpaddock@apegs.sk.ca
Patti Kindred, P.Eng., FEC, Director, Education & Compliance
pkindred@apegs.sk.ca
Barb Miller, Director, Finance & Operations
barbmiller@apegs.sk.ca
Kate MacLachlan, Ph.D., P.Geo., Director, Academic Review
katem@apegs.sk.ca
Tina Maki, P.Eng., FEC, Director, Registration
tmaki@apegs.sk.ca
Bob McDonald, P.Eng., FEC, LL, Director, Membership & Legal Services
rhmcdonald@apegs.sk.ca
Chris Wimmer, P.Eng., Director, Professional Standards
cwimmer@apegs.sk.ca
Finances: *Funding Sources:* Membership dues
Staff: 125 volunteer(s)
Membership: 3,070; *Fees:* Schedule available; *Committees:* Education Board (Professional Development, Student Development, K-12, Environment & Sustainability); Governance Board (Academic Review, Experience Review, Professional Practice Exam, Licensee Admissions, Registrar's Advisory); Image & Identity Board (Awards, Communications & Public Relations, Connection & Involvement, Professional Edge, Equality & Divserity); Discipline; Investigation; Executive
Activities: *Internships:* Yes; *Speaker Service:* Yes
Publications:
•APEGS [Association of Professional Engineers & Geoscientists of Saskatchewan] Salary Survey
Type: Report
•Association of Professional Engineers & Geoscientists of Saskatchewan Annual Report
Type: Yearbook; *Frequency:* Annual
•The Professional Edge [a publication of the Association of Professional Engineers & Geoscientists of Saskatchewan]
Type: Magazine; *Accepts Advertising*; *Editor:* Lyle Hewitt

Association of Professional Engineers of Ontario *See* Professional Engineers Ontario

Association of Professional Engineers of Prince Edward Island (APEPEI)
Parent Name: Engineers Canada
549 North River Rd., Charlottetown PE C1E 1J6
Tel: 902-566-1268; *Fax:* 902-566-5551
e-mail: info@engineerspei.com
www.engineerspei.com
Also Known As: Engineers PEI
Overview: A small provincial licensing charitable organization founded in 1955 overseen by Engineers Canada
Mission: Engineers PEI regulates the practice of professional engineering in the province, with authority over members, licensees, engineers-in-training, & holders of certificates of authorization.; *Member of:* Engineers Canada
Chief Officer(s):
Mark E. Victor, President
Jim Landrigan, Executive Director/Registrar
Finances: *Annual Operating Budget:* $100,000-$250,000; *Funding Sources:* Membership dues
Staff: 2 staff member(s); 35 volunteer(s)
Membership: 275; *Fees:* $200; *Member Profile:* Open to those with B.Sc. (Engineering) from an accredited institution & four years acceptable engineering experience
Activities: Bridge Building Contest for students, grades 5-12; *Awareness Events:* National Engineering Month, March; *Internships:* Yes

Association of Professional Engineers of the Government of Québec (Ind.) *Voir* Association professionnelle des ingénieurs du gouvernement du Québec (ind.)

Association of Professional Engineers of the Yukon Territory (APEY)
Parent Name: Engineers Canada
312B Hanson St., Whitehorse YT Y1A 1Y6
Tel: 867-667-6727; *Fax:* 867-668-2142
e-mail: staff@apey.yk.ca
www.apey.yk.ca
Overview: A medium-sized provincial licensing organization founded in 1955 overseen by Engineers Canada
Mission: To establish, maintain & develop standards of knowledge & skill, standards of qualification & practice & standards of professional ethics; to promote public awareness of the role of the association; *Member of:* Engineers Canada
Chief Officer(s):
Gord Hamilton, President
Richard Trimble, Registrar
Sandy Birrell, Sec.-Treas.
Finances: *Funding Sources:* Membership fees
Membership: *Fees:* $240 + $45 for a stamp + GST, Registered Professional Engineer; $72.50 + GST Engineer in Training; *Member Profile:* Persons with a degree in engineering from an accredited university & with 4 years of experience
Activities: Annual Bridge Building Competition; Professional development; National Secondary Professional Liability Insurance Program; *Awareness Events:* Engineering Week
Publications:
•Association of Professional Engineers of Yukon Newsletter
Type: Newsletter; *Frequency:* 3 pa

Association of Professional Geoscientists of Nova Scotia (APGNS)
PO Box 232, 53 Queen St., Dartmouth NS B2Y 1C2
Tel: 902-420-9928; *Fax:* 902-463-1419
e-mail: info@geoscientistsns.ca
www.apgns.ns.ca
Overview: A small provincial organization
Mission: To ensure high standards of practice within the geoscience community; To promote & advance the profession; To work with associated organizations across Canada to facilitate the registration of APGNS members in other provinces
Chief Officer(s):
David C. Carter, Executive Director & Registrar
exec.director@geoscientistsns.ca
Membership: *Fees:* $200 Member-in-Training; $400 License to Practice; $450 Member;

Association of Professional Geoscientists of Ontario (APGO)
#1100, 25 Adelaide St. East, Toronto ON M5C 3A1
Tel: 416-203-2746; *Fax:* 416-203-6181
Toll-Free: 877-557-2746
e-mail: info@apgo.net
www.apgo.net
www.linkedin.com/groups?gid=4495029&trk=myg_ugrp_ovr
www.facebook.com/489636501070336
Overview: A small provincial organization founded in 2000
Mission: To govern the practice of professional geoscience in Ontario, in accordance with The Professional Geoscientists Act, 2000, in order to protect the public & investors; To develop standards of knowledge & skills for association members; Affiliation(s): Canadian Council of Professional Geoscientists; Canadian Geoscience Standards Board; National Professional Practice & Ethics Exam Advisory Committee; CCPG Licensure Compliance Committee
Chief Officer(s):
Gord White, CEO
gwhite@apgo.net
Ian Macdonald, President
imac@wesa.ca
Andrew Cheatle, Vice-President
amcheatle@mac.com
Finances: *Funding Sources:* Sponsorships
Membership: 1,389 practising members + 12 temporary members + 10 limited members + 12 non-practising members + 60 geoscientists in training + 24 student members; *Committees:* Discipline; Complaints; Registration; Executive; Finance; Nomination; Non-Member Appointment; Insurance Advisory; Governance; Professional Practice; Enforcement & Compliance; Communications & Public Awareness
Activities: Reporting to Ontario's Minister of Northern Development & Mines; Accepting registration for the licensure to practice professional geoscience in Ontario; Disciplining members for professional misconduct; Organizing continuing professional development programs
Publications:
•Association of Professional Geoscientists of Ontario Annual Report
Type: Yearbook; *Frequency:* Annually
•Field Notes: Association of Professional Geoscientists of Ontario Newsletter
Type: Newsletter; *Frequency:* Bimonthly; *Editor:* Wendy Diaz, M.Sc., P.Geo.
Profile: Association reports, meetings, awards, & news for all APGO members

Association of Quantity Surveyors of Alberta (AQSA)
Kingsway Mall, PO Box 34062, Edmonton AB T5G 3G4
Tel: 780-628-7324
e-mail: info@aqsa.ca
www.aqsa.ca
Overview: A small provincial organization founded in 1979
Mission: To promote & advance the professional status of quantity surveyors & certified cost estimators; To establish & maintain high standards of professional competence; *Member of:* International Cost Engineering Council; Pacific Association of Quantity Surveyors; Affiliation(s): Canadian Institute of Quantity Surveyors (CIQS); Australian Institute of Quantity Surveyors (Reciprocal Agreement); Canadian Construction Association (Reciprocal Agreement); Appraisal Institute of Canada (Memoranda of Understanding); Royal Institution of Chartered Surveyors - Canada (Memoranda of Understanding)
Chief Officer(s):
Dave Burns, President
president@aqsa.ca
Dave Moller, Vice-President
vicepresident@aqsa.ca
Doug Eastwell, Registrar
registrar@aqsa.ca
Membership: *Member Profile:* Professional Quantity Surveyors (PQS) & Construction Estimator Certifieds (CEC), from areas such as construction companies, private practice, & government organizations, in the provinces of Alberta, Saskatchewan, & Manitoba, as well as the Northwest Territories & Nunavut
Activities: Offering continuing professional development programs; Facilitating networking opportunities & the exchange of knowledge; Providing professional costing, value, & estimating advice; Disciplining members; Collaborating with other organizations
Publications:
•Association of Quantity Surveyors of Alberta Newsletter
Type: Newsletter; *Price:* Free with association membership
Profile: Association reports, chapter news, forthcoming events, & Canadian Institute of Quantity Surveyors (CIQS) updates
•Consultants Directory [a publication of the Association of Quantity Surveyors of Alberta]
Type: Directory
Profile: Listing of firms, with one or more principals who are Professional Quantity Surveyors (PQS) &, which are operating in privatepractice in Alberta, Saskatchewan, Manitoba, the Northwest Territories, or Nunavut

Association of Québec Municipal Engineers *Voir* Association des ingénieurs municipaux du Québec

Association of Registered Professional Foresters of New Brunswick (ARPFNB) / Association des forestiers agréés du Nouveau-Brunswick (AFANB)
#221, 1350 Regent St., Fredericton NB E3C 2G6
Tel: 506-452-6933; *Fax:* 506-450-3128
e-mail: arpf@nbnet.nb.ca
www.arpfnb.ca
Overview: A small provincial organization founded in 1937
Mission: To manage the forest resources of New Brunswick for the sustained development of these resources; To assure the proficiency & competency of Registered Professional Foresters in New Brunswick; Affiliation(s): Canadian Federation of Professional Foresters Association (CFPFA)
Chief Officer(s):
Edward Czerwinski, Executive Director
Steven Spears, President
Jasen Golding, Secretary-Treasurer
Membership: 300; *Member Profile:* Registered Professional Foresters eligible to practice Forestry in New Brunswick, including forestry consultants, & federal & provincial public servants
Activities: Improving forestry practice in New Brunswick; Increasing understanding of forestry issues; Promoting the knowledge & skill of association members
Meetings/Conferences:
For more information see Trade Shows, Conferences and Seminars Chapter
Association of Registered Professional Foresters of New Brunswick Annual General Meeting 2013
February 2013 Fredericton, NB
Association of Registered Professional Foresters of New Brunswick Annual General Meeting 2014
2014, NB

Association of Saskatchewan Forestry Professionals (ASFP)
#102C, 1061 Central Ave., Prince Albert SK S6V 4V4
Tel: 306-960-8682; *Fax:* 306-764-7461
e-mail: registrar@asfp.ca
www.asfp.ca
Overview: A small provincial organization founded in 2006

Mission: To promote the profession of forestry & its members; to satisfy the public demand for competent & ethical management of the province's forests
Chief Officer(s):
Roman Ornyik, Registrar
David Stevenson, Vice-President
Finances: *Annual Operating Budget:* Less than $50,000; *Funding Sources:* Membership dues
Membership: 166; *Member Profile:* Registered Professional Foresters & Forest Technologists; Foresters-in-training & forest technologists-in-training; *Committees:* Admissions; Finance; Continuing Competence; Professional Conduct; Discipline

Association of Science & Engineering Technology Professionals of Alberta (ASET)
Parent Name: Canadian Council of Technicians & Technologists

Phipps-McKinnon Building, #1630, 10020 - 101A Ave. NW, Edmonton AB T5J 3G2
Tel: 780-425-0626; *Fax:* 780-424-5053
Toll-Free: 800-272-5619
www.aset.ab.ca
Previous Name: Alberta Society of Engineering Technologists
Overview: A large provincial organization founded in 1963 overseen by Canadian Council of Technicians & Technologists
Mission: To benefit the public & the profession by regulating & promoting safe, high quality, professional technology practice; To focus on the engineering technology, applied science, & information technology fields; To issue credentials to qualified individuals; To accredit training programs. There are 9 chapters across the province; *Member of:* Canadian Council of Technicians & Technologists
Chief Officer(s):
Norman Kyle, R.E.T., P.L.(En, President
Barry Cavanaugh, CEO & General Counsel
Jennifer McNeil Betrand, BA, Director, Education & Special Projects
Russifer Medvedev, MA, Director, Communications & Member Benefits
Heather Shewchuk, B.Comm., Director, Corporate & Government Relations
Norman Viegas, CMA, CAE, Director, Finance & Administration
Membership: 16,500
Activities: Awarding Engineering Technology Scholarship Foundation of Alberta (ETSFA) scholarships; *Speaker Service:* Yes
Publications:
•Salary Survey [a publication of the Association of Science & Engineering Technology Professionals of Alberta]
•Technology Alberta [a publication of the Association of Science & Engineering Technology Professionals of Alberta]
Frequency: 5 pa

Association of Supervisors of Public Health Inspectors of Ontario (ASPHIO)

c/o Durham Region Health Dept., 101 Consumers Dr., 2nd Fl., Whitby ON L1N 1C4
Tel: 905-723-3818; *Fax:* 905-666-1887
e-mail: Ken.Gorman@region.durham.on.ca
Overview: A medium-sized provincial organization founded in 1982
Mission: To provide a recognized organization which can bring together persons immediately responsible for public health inspection programs for discussion on matters of public interest; to promote public health inspection programs affecting the Ministry of Health, other ministers & local health agencies; to represent all members in liaison with other associations or societies; to provide regular updates of information on the activities of the association to each of the directors of member health units; to act as a resource group on all matters that fall within the competence of the association; *Member of:* Ontario Public Health Association; Affiliation(s): Association of Local Public Health Agencies (alPHa)
Chief Officer(s):
Chris Munn, President, 519-376-9420
c.munn@publichealthgreybruce.on.ca
Donna Taylor, Vice President, 519-271-7600
dtaylor@pdhu.on.ca
Andrew Braton, Secretary, 519-376-9420
a.barton@publichealthgreybruce.on.ca
Angela Newman, Treasurer, 519-376-9420
a.newman@publichealthgreybruce.on.ca
Chad Ikert, Logistics Coordinator, 519-383-8331
chad.ikert@county-lambton.on.ca
Finances: *Annual Operating Budget:* Less than $50,000; *Funding Sources:* Membership fees
Staff: 15 volunteer(s)
Membership: 138; *Fees:* $100; *Member Profile:* Persons immediately responsible for giving direction to Public Health Inspection Programs of Local Health Agencies in Ontario; voting privileges will be restricted to one vote per local official agency
Activities: *Internships:* Yes; *Speaker Service:* Yes; *Rents Mailing List:* Yes; *Library:* Open to public by appointment

Association of the Chemical Profession of Alberta (ACPA)

PO Box 21017, Edmonton AB T6R 2V4
Tel: 780-413-0004; *Fax:* 780-413-0076
www.pchem.ca
Overview: A small national organization founded in 1992
Mission: To provides a legal definition of chemistry; To promote & increase the knowledge, skills, & proficiency of members in all things relating to chemistry
Chief Officer(s):
Roger Cowles, President
Membership: *Fees:* $150 Professional Chemist; $75 Chemist-in-Training; $50 Retired Member. Associate Member; Student Members free
Publications:
•Association of the Chemical Profession of Alberta Newsletter
Type: Newsletter; *Frequency:* Irregular

Association of the Chemical Profession of Ontario (ACPO)

#1801, 1 Yonge St., Toronto ON M5E 1W7
Tel: 416-364-4609; *Fax:* 416-369-0515
Toll-Free: 800-260-0992
e-mail: info@acpo.on.ca
www.acpo.on.ca
Overview: A medium-sized provincial organization founded in 1958
Mission: To promote & increase the knowledge, skills & proficiency of its members in all things relating to chemistry & to establish standards of chemical practice for its members; provides a legal definition of chemistry & of those practising chemistry in Ontario
Chief Officer(s):
T. Obal, President
Finances: *Annual Operating Budget:* Less than $50,000
Membership: 1,200; *Fees:* $40-$140; *Member Profile:* Honours degree with work experience deemed acceptable by the association; 3-year chemistry degree with 5 years experience; 6 years experience & written examinations set by the association; *Committees:* Professional Affairs; Membership; Environmental
Activities: *Speaker Service:* Yes

Association of University Forestry Schools of Canada (AUFSC) / Association des écoles forestières universitaires du Canada
Parent Name: Association of Universities & Colleges of Canada

c/o Faculté de foresterie, Université Laval, QuéBec QC G1K 7P8
Tel: 418-656-2116; *Fax:* 418-656-5411
www.aefuc-aufsc.ca
Overview: A medium-sized national organization overseen by Association of Universities & Colleges of Canada
Chief Officer(s):
Robert Beauregard, Chair
doyen@ffgg.ulaval.ca
Membership: 9

Association of Yukon Communities (AYC)

#15, 1114 - 1st Ave., Whitehorse YT Y1A 1A3
Tel: 867-668-4388; *Fax:* 867-668-7574
www.ayc-yk.ca
Previous Name: Association of Yukon Municipalities
Overview: A medium-sized provincial organization founded in 1974
Mission: To further the establishment of responsible government at the community level; To provide a united approach to issues affecting local governments; To advance ambitions & goals of member communities by developing a shared common vision of the future; To represent members in matters affecting them & the welfare of their communities; To provide programs & services of common interest & benefit to members; Affiliation(s): Federation of Canadian Municipalities
Chief Officer(s):
John Pattimore, Executive Director
ayced@northwestel.net
Finances: *Funding Sources:* Membership dues; Government
Membership: 52; *Fees:* Schedule available; *Member Profile:* Yukon communities & elected officials; *Committees:* Energy; Municipal Act Review

Association of Yukon Municipalities *See* Association of Yukon Communities

Association ontarienne des éleveurs de bovins *See* Ontario Cattlemen's Association

Association paritaire pour la santé et la sécurité du travail - Administration provinciale

#10, 1220, boul Lebourgneuf, Québec QC G2K 2G4
Tél: 418-624-4801; *Téléc:* 418-624-4858
Courriel: apssap@apssap.qc.ca
www.apssap.qc.ca
Aperçu: *Dimension:* moyenne; *Envergure:* provinciale
Mission: L'Association a pour mission de supporter la prise en charge paritaire de la prévention en matière de santé, de sécurité et d'intégrité physique des personnes du secteur de l'Administration provinciale.
Membre(s) du bureau directeur:
Colette Trudel, Directrice générale

Association paritaire pour la santé et la sécurité du travail - Affaires municipales (APSAM)

#710, 715, carré Victoria, Montréal QC H2Y 2H7
Tél: 514-849-8373; *Téléc:* 514-849-8873
Ligne sans frais: 800-465-1754
Courriel: info@apsam.com
www.apsam.com
Aperçu: *Dimension:* moyenne; *Envergure:* provinciale; fondée en 1985
Mission: Développer et promouvoir les moyens nécessaires pour protéger la santé et la sécurité des personnes à l'emploi des municipalités et des organismes qui y sont reliés, dans l'ensemble du Québec; fournir aux employeurs et travailleurs des municipalités du Québec des services de formation, d'information, de recherche et de conseil
Membre(s) du bureau directeur:
Alain Langlois, Directeur général
Finances: *Budget de fonctionnement annuel:* $500,000-$1.5 Million
Membre: 3 000
Activités: *Service de conférenciers:* Oui; *Listes de destinataires:* Oui; *Bibliothèque:* rendez-vous

Association paritaire pour la santé et la sécurité du travail - Affaires sociales

#950, 5100, rue Sherbrooke est, Montréal QC H1V 3R9
Tél: 514-253-6871; *Téléc:* 514-253-1443
Ligne sans frais: 800-361-4528
Courriel: info@asstsas.qc.ca
www.asstsas.qc.ca
Aperçu: *Dimension:* moyenne; *Envergure:* provinciale
Mission: Une association sectorielle paritaire vouée exclusivement à la prévention en santé et en sécurité du travail dans le secteur de la santé et des services sociaux
Membre(s) du bureau directeur:
Diane Parent, Directrice générale

Association paritaire pour la santé et la sécurité du travail - Habillement *Voir* ASPHME

Association paritaire pour la santé et la sécurité du travail - Imprimerie et activités connexes

#450, 7450, boul Galeries d'Anjou, Anjou QC H1M 3M3
Tél: 514-355-8282; *Téléc:* 514-355-6818
Courriel: info@aspimprimerie.qc.ca
www.aspimprimerie.qc.ca
Également appelé: ASP Inprimerie
Aperçu: *Dimension:* moyenne; *Envergure:* provinciale; Organisme sans but lucratif; fondée en 1983
Mission: Fournir aux employeurs et aux travailleurs du secteur imprimerie et activités connexes des services d'information, de formation, de conseil et de recherche pour favoriser la prise en charge de la prévention dans les entreprises
Membre(s) du bureau directeur:
Marie Ménard, Directrice générale
mmenard@aspimprimerie.qc.ca
Finances: *Budget de fonctionnement annuel:* $500,000-$1.5 Million
Personnel: 8 membre(s) du personnel
Membre: 1-99
Activités: Formations de groupe: Action sur les machines: Évacuation en cas d'incendie; Introduction à la prévention; Superviser avec diligence; Enquête accident; Formateur chariot; Formation de formateurs SIMDUT; *Stagiaires:* Oui; *Bibliothèque:* rendez-vous

Association paritaire pour la santé et la sécurité du travail - Mines et services miniers (APSM)
#570, 979, av de Bourgogne, Sainte-Foy QC G1W 2L4
Tél: 418-653-1933; *Téléc:* 418-653-7726
Courriel: info@apsam.com
www.apsam.com
Aperçu: *Dimension:* moyenne; *Envergure:* provinciale; fondée en 1986
Membre(s) du bureau directeur:
Pierre Lapointe, Directeur général
Finances: *Budget de fonctionnement annuel:* $500,000-$1.5 Million
Membre: 100 *Montant de la cotisation:* .13$/100$ de masse salariale

Association paritaire pour la santé et la sécurité du travail - Produits en métal et électriques
#301, 2271, boul Fernand-Lafontaine, Longueuil QC J4G 2R7
Tél: 450-442-7763; *Téléc:* 450-442-2332
Courriel: jarsenault@aspme.org
www.aspme.org
Aperçu: *Dimension:* moyenne; *Envergure:* provinciale
Membre(s) du bureau directeur:
Jocelyne Arsenault, Conseillère en gestion
jarsenault@asphme.org
Éric Bélanger, Conseiller technique

Association paritaire pour la santé et la sécurité du travail - Services automobiles
#150, 8, rue de la Place-Du-Commerce, Brossard QC J4W 3H2
Tél: 450-672-9330; *Téléc:* 450-672-4835
Ligne sans frais: 800-363-2344
Courriel: info@autoprevention.qc.ca
www.autoprevention.qc.ca
Également appelé: Auto Prévention
Aperçu: *Dimension:* moyenne; *Envergure:* provinciale
Mission: Depuis 1983, Auto Prévention aide les travailleurs et les employeurs du secteur des services automobiles à prendre en charge la santé et la sécurité au travail, afin d'éliminer les risques d'accidents et de maladies professionnelles.
Membre(s) du bureau directeur:
Jean-Guy Trottier, Directeur général

Association pour l'amélioration des cultures biologiques (international) ***See*** Organic Crop Improvement Association (International)

Association pour l'amélioration des sols et des récoltes de l'Ontario ***See*** Ontario Soil & Crop Improvement Association

Association pour l'amélioration du sol et des cultures du Nouveau-Brunswick ***See*** New Brunswick Soil & Crop Improvement Association

Association pour l'enseignement de la géographie et de l'environnement en Ontario ***See*** Ontario Association for Geographic & Environmental Education

Association pour la littérature, l'environnement et la culture au Canada ***See*** Association for Literature, Environment, and Culture in Canada

Association pour la prévention de la contamination de l'air et du sol (APCAS) / Air Waste Management Association - Québec Section
CP 49527, 5122, Côte des Neiges, Montréal QC H3T 2A5
Tél: 514-355-2675; *Téléc:* 514-355-4159
Courriel: apcas@apcas.qc.ca
www.apcas.qc.ca
Aperçu: *Dimension:* petite; *Envergure:* provinciale
Mission: La formation professionnelle dans les domaines de la qualité et du traitement de l'air, de la gestion des matières résiduelles, des sols contaminés
Membre(s) du bureau directeur:
Anne-Marie Bourgeois, Présidente
Finances: *Budget de fonctionnement annuel:* Moins de $50,000
Membre: 100-499

Association pour la prévention de la contamination de l'air et du sol ***See*** Air & Waste Management Association

Association pour la prévention des infections à l'hôpital et dans la communauté - Canada ***See*** Community & Hospital Infection Control Association Canada

Association pour la protection des intérêts des consommateurs de la Côte-Nord
872, rue de Puyjalon St., 2e étage, Baie-Comeau QC G5C 1N1
Tél: 418-589-7324; *Téléc:* 418-589-7088
Courriel: apic@globetrotter.net
Également appelé: APIC Côte-Nord
Aperçu: *Dimension:* petite; *Envergure:* locale; Organisme sans but lucratif; fondée en 1978
Mission: Promouvoir les intérêts des consommateurs dans tous les aspects de la consommation; grouper les consommateurs de la région Côte-Nord; *Membre de:* Coalition des associations de consommateurs du Québec
Membre(s) du bureau directeur:
Colette Savard, Responsable
Finances: *Budget de fonctionnement annuel:* $50,000-$100,000
Personnel: 2 membre(s) du personnel; 12 bénévole(s)
Membre: 1199 *Montant de la cotisation:* 5$ individu
Activités: Aide de planification budgétaire; ateliers; centre de documentation; traitement des plaintes; informations; *Bibliothèque:*

Association pour la santé publique de l'Ontario ***See*** Ontario Public Health Association

Association pour la santé publique du Québec (ASPQ) / Québec Public Health Association Parent Name: Canadian Public Health Association
#200, 4126, rue St-Denis, Montréal QC H2W 2M5
Tél: 514-528-5811; *Téléc:* 514-528-5590
Courriel: info@aspq.org
www.aspq.org
Aperçu: *Dimension:* moyenne; *Envergure:* provinciale; Organisme sans but lucratif; fondée en 1943 surveillé par Canadian Public Health Association
Mission: Favoriser un regard critique sur les enjeux de santé publique au Québec en constituant un regroupement volontaire, autonome, multidisciplinaire et multisectoriel de personnes et d'organisations provenant des milieux tant institutionnels et professionnels que communautaires. L'Association constitue un forum qui offre un espace à ses membres pour développer des prises de position communes ou concertées, appuyer des politiques favorables à la santé et au bien-être et développer des coalitions et des projets en collaboration avec d'autres partenaires de santé publique ou du milieu.
Membre(s) du bureau directeur:
Lucie Granger, Directrice Générale, 514-528-5811 Ext. 225
Martine Deschênes, Adjointe administrative
Finances: *Budget de fonctionnement annuel:* $100,000-$250,000
Personnel: 16 membre(s) du personnel
Membre: 170 *Montant de la cotisation:* 46$ pour un an

Association professionnelle des géographes du Québec (APGQ)
Dept. de géographie - UQAM, CP 8888, Succ. Centre-Ville, Montréal QC H3C 3P8
Tél: 514-987-3000; *Téléc:* 514-987-6784
Courriel: apgq@uqam.ca
Aperçu: *Dimension:* petite; *Envergure:* provinciale; fondée en 1962
Mission: Promouvoir la géographie comme discipline de même que la pratique professionnelle de ses membres
Membre(s) du bureau directeur:
Guy Mercier, Président
Guy.Mercier@ggr.ulaval.ca
Membre: *Montant de la cotisation:* 85$ (membre régulier); *Comités:* Scientifique; Environnement; Affaires internationales; Recrutement
Activités: Représentation auprès des gouvernements et des entreprises privées; bottin des membres; colloque annuel, congrès;

Association professionnelle des ingénieurs du gouvernement du Québec (ind.) (APIGQ) / Association of Professional Engineers of the Government of Québec (Ind.)
Complexe Iberville, #600, 2954, boul Laurier, Sainte-Foy QC G1V 4T2
Tél: 418-683-3633; *Téléc:* 418-683-6878
Courriel: lepont@apigq.qc.ca
www.apigq.qc.ca
Aperçu: *Dimension:* moyenne; *Envergure:* provinciale; fondée en 1986
Mission: Association professionnelle des ingénieurs du Gouvernement de Québec.
Membre(s) du bureau directeur:
Michel Gagnon, Président
Finances: *Budget de fonctionnement annuel:* $250,000-$500,000
Personnel: 2 membre(s) du personnel
Membre: 1 000; *Critères d'admissibilite:* Ingénieur; *Comités:* CE (Comité exécutif); CRS (Conseil des représentants de section)

Association provinciale des constructeurs d'habitations du Québec inc. (APCHQ) / Provincial Association of Home Builders of Québec
5930, boul Louis-H.-Lafontaine, Anjou QC H1M 1S7
Tél: 514-353-9960; *Téléc:* 514-353-4825
Ligne sans frais: 800-468-8160
www.apchq.com
Aperçu: *Dimension:* moyenne; *Envergure:* provinciale; fondée en 1950
Mission: Depuis 1997, l'APCHQ est la plus importante gestionnaire de mutuelles de prévention du domaine de la construction. Étant le seul agent négociateur patronal des relations de travail dans le secteur résidentiel, elle défend les intérêts de quelque 12 000 employeurs et 25 000 travailleurs
Membre(s) du bureau directeur:
Marc Savard, Directeur général
nsavard@apchqmontreal.ca
Frédéric Birtz, Directeur des opérations
fbirtz@apchqmontreal.ca
Membre: 3 600

Association pulmonaire du Canada ***See*** Canadian Lung Association

Association pulmonaire du Nouveau-Brunswick ***See*** New Brunswick Lung Association

Association pulmonaire du Québec ***See*** Québec Lung Association

Association québécoise d'urbanisme (AQU)
CP 655, Succ. Saint-Jacques, Montréal QC H3C 2T8
Tél: 514-277-0228; *Téléc:* 514-277-0093
Courriel: info@aqu.qc.ca
www.aqu.qc.ca
Aperçu: *Dimension:* petite; *Envergure:* provinciale; Organisme sans but lucratif; fondée en 1978
Mission: La promotion de l'urbanisme et de l'aménagement du territoire
Membre(s) du bureau directeur:
Noël Pelletier, Président
Finances: *Budget de fonctionnement annuel:* Moins de $50,000
Personnel: 1 membre(s) du personnel; 1 bénévole(s)
Membre: 700 *Montant de la cotisation:* 35$ étudiant; 100$ individuel; 370$ collectif

Association québécoise de l'industrie de la pêche (AQIP) / Québec Fish Processors Association
#860, 2600, boul Laurier, Sainte-Foy QC G1V 4W2
Tél: 418-654-1831; *Téléc:* 418-654-1376
Courriel: aqip@globetrotter.net
www.quebecweb.com/aqip
Aperçu: *Dimension:* moyenne; *Envergure:* provinciale; fondée en 1978
Mission: Défendre les intérêts professionnels des industries québécoises de la transformation des produits marins; travailler au développement des services; aider à l'amélioration de la productivité en usines; *Membre de:* CRCD Gaspésie des Iles
Finances: *Budget de fonctionnement annuel:* $250,000-$500,000
Membre: 40 industriels *Montant de la cotisation:* 1 000-3 000$; *Comités:* Comité sur la rationnalisation des usines; Comité sur les approvisionnements extérieurs; Comité sur le transport des produits marins
Activités: Négociations des plans conjoints

Association québécoise de la gestion parasitaire (AQGP)
CP 32, #410, 7400, boul Les Galeries d'Anjou, Anjou QC H1M 3M2
Tél: 514-355-3757; *Téléc:* 514-355-4159
Ligne sans frais: 800-663-2730
Courriel: aqgp@spg.qc.ca
www.spg.qc.ca/aqgp/index.php
Nom précédent: Association des spécialistes en extermination du Québec
Aperçu: *Dimension:* petite; *Envergure:* provinciale; fondée en 1968
Mission: Promouvoir le professionnalisme de ses membres - en les représentant auprès des instances régissant l'industrie de l'extermination et du public en général; en s'assurant de la conformité de ses membres par l'élaboration de normes et de règlements spécifiques; en contribuant à l'accroissement de leurs connaissances techniques et scientifiques par l'accès à

l'information et l'élaboration de programmes de formation adaptés; *Membre de:* Canadian Pest Management Association
Membre(s) du bureau directeur:
Nathalie Juteau, Présidente
service@parasitech.com
Pierre St-Louis, Vice-président
pierrestlouis@videotron.ca
Membre: 125

Association québécoise de lutte contre la pollution atmosphérique (AQLPA)

CP 26, 489A, rue Principale, Saint-Léon-de-Standon QC G0R 4L0
Tél: 418-642-1322; *Téléc:* 418-642-1323
Ligne sans frais: 888-819-7330
Courriel: info@aqlpa.com
www.aqlpa.com
Aperçu: *Dimension:* petite; *Envergure:* provinciale; fondée en 1982
Mission: L'Association québécoise de lutte contre la pollution atmosphérique (AQLPA) est un organisme qui s'est donnée pour mandat de contribuer à la protection de l'air et de l'atmosphère entourant notre planète, à la fois pour la santé des humains et des écosystèmes qu'elle abrite
Membre(s) du bureau directeur:
André Belisle, Président
andre.belisle@aqlpa.com
Membre: 415

Association québécoise des groupes d'ornithologues ***Voir*** Regroupement QuébecOiseaux

Association québécoise des organismes de coopération internationale (AQOCI) / Québec Association of International Cooperation

#540, 1001, rue Sherbrooke Est, Montréal QC H2L 1L3
Tél: 514-871-1086; *Téléc:* 514-871-9866
Courriel: aqoci@aqoci.qc.ca
www.aqoci.qc.ca
www.facebook.com/aqoci
twitter.com/aqoci
www.youtube.com/aqoci
Aperçu: *Dimension:* moyenne; *Envergure:* internationale; fondée en 1976
Mission: Soutenir le travail des membres afin de permettre leur développement en s'inspirant des principes de solidarité et de coopération; favoriser l'échange pour mieux coordonner les actions communautaires; regrouper des organismes de coopération et d'éducation à la solidarité oeuvrant au Québec; *Membre de:* Canadian Council for International Cooperation; Conseil canadien pour la coopération internationale.; Affiliation(s): Réseau québécois sur l'intégration continentale; Conseil canadien pour la coopération internationale
Membre(s) du bureau directeur:
Gervais L'Heureux, Directeur général, 514-871-1086 Ext. 202
glheureux@aqoci.qc.ca
Denis Labelle, Président
Finances: *Budget de fonctionnement annuel:* $250,000-$500,000
Personnel: 5 membre(s) du personnel
Membre: 68 *Montant de la cotisation:* Selon revenu; *Critères d'admissibilite:* Regroupements d'organismes de coopération internationale; *Comités:* Comité québécois femmes et développement (CQFD)
Activités: *Stagiaires:* Oui; *Service de conférenciers:* Oui

Association québécoise des techniques de l'environnement ***Voir*** Réseau environnement

Association québécoise du gaz naturel (AQGN)

#207, 560, boul Henri-Bourassa ouest, Montréal QC H3L 1P4
Tél: 514-339-9399; *Téléc:* 514-339-9353
Courriel: aqgn@aqgn.com
www.aqgn.com
Aperçu: *Dimension:* petite; *Envergure:* provinciale
Mission: L'Association Québécoise du Gaz Naturel regroupe les gens d'affaires intéressés par le développement de l'industrie du gaz naturel au Québec
Membre(s) du bureau directeur:
Ginette Gamache, Directrice générale
Membre: *Montant de la cotisation:* 450$ régulier; 2 500$ aviseur

Association québécoise du transport aérien (AQTA)

Aéroport international Jean-Lesage, 600, 6e av de l'Aéroport, Québec QC G2G 2T5
Tél: 418-871-4635; *Téléc:* 418-871-8189
Courriel: aqta@aqta.ca
www.aqta.ca
www.linkedin.com/groups?home=&gid=2588987
www.facebook.com/group.php?gid=119190028092054
Aperçu: *Dimension:* moyenne; *Envergure:* provinciale; Organisme sans but lucratif; fondée en 1975
Mission: Voué à la défense et la promotion des intérêts de tous les secteurs du transport aérien
Membre(s) du bureau directeur:
Éric Lippé, Président-directeur général
Membre: 155 *Montant de la cotisation:* Barème; *Critères d'admissibilite:* Transporteurs aériens et fournisseurs de produits et services liés à l'aviation

Association québécoise du transport et des routes inc. (AQTR)

Bureau de Montréal, #200, 1255, rue University, Montréal QC H3B 3B2
Tél: 514-523-6444; *Téléc:* 514-523-2666
www.aqtr.qc.ca
Aperçu: *Dimension:* grande; *Envergure:* provinciale; fondée en 1965
Mission: Assumer un leadership technique; définir des règles en matière de sécurité et d'environnement; Favoriser l'échange international des expertises; promouvoir la recherche et le développement des expertises et des produits en transport; promouvoir la formation dans le domaine des transports; Assumer la représentativité de l'AQTR par la participation aux principaux forums sur les transports; Contribuer à servir la société par l'éducation et l'information du grand public
Membre(s) du bureau directeur:
Jean Mastropietro, Président
Dominique Lacoste, Présidente-directrice générale
Mathieu Charbonneau, Directeur général adjoint
Finances: *Budget de fonctionnement annuel:* $500,000-$1.5 Million
Personnel: 7 membre(s) du personnel; 100 bénévole(s)
Membre: 950 *Montant de la cotisation:* 270 $; *Critères d'admissibilite:* Secteur privé - Ingénieur conseils; Entrepreneurs; Fournisseurs et manufacturiers; Laboratoires; Transporteurs; Architectes et urbanistes; Étudiants; Spécialistes en environnement; Secteur public et parapublic - Ministères; Municipalités; Maisons d'enseignement; Sociétés de transport; Autres sociétés, départements et services publics; *Comités:* Directions techniques - Infrastructures de transport; Transport des personnes; Circulation; Sécurité dans les transports; Transport aérien; Recherche et développement; Comités - Transport des marchandises; Environnement; Revue; Congrès; Activités municipales
Activités: Regrouper les personnes impliquées dans les techniques du transport; Encourager les échanges multidisciplinaires et favoriser la collaboration entre différents secteurs; Recommander toute mesure permettant de développer des techniques du transport; *Listes de destinataires:* Oui
Meetings/Conferences:
For more information see Trade Shows, Conferences and Seminars Chapter
Le 48e Congrès annuel de l'Association québécoise du transport et des routes inc. - Vers une mobilité intégrée
March 2013 Montréal, QC
Publications:
•Routes et Transports [a publication of Association québécoise du transport et des routes inc.]
Type: Revue

Association québécoise pour l'évaluation d'impacts (AQEI)

CP 785, Succ. Place d'Armes, Montréal QC H2Y 3J2
Tél: 514-990-2193
Courriel: mondorf@aqei.qc.ca
www.aqei.qc.ca
Aperçu: *Dimension:* moyenne; *Envergure:* provinciale
Mission: Regrouper toute personne, professionnelle ou non, intéressée par l'évaluation d'impacts et à son utilisation dans le processus de planification et de prise de décision; Affiliation(s): International Association for Impact Assessment
Membre(s) du bureau directeur:
Eric Giroux, Président
Membre: *Montant de la cotisation:* Barème

Association québécoise pour l'hygiène, la santé et la sécurité du travail (AQHSST)

CP 52, 89, boul de Bromont, Bromont QC J2L 1A9
Tél: 450-776-2169
Ligne sans frais: 888-355-3830
Courriel: info@aqhsst.qc.ca
www.aqhsst.qc.ca
Aperçu: *Dimension:* moyenne; *Envergure:* provinciale; Organisme sans but lucratif; fondée en 1978
Mission: Promouvoir les connaissances relatives à l'hygiène industrielle par l'échange et la vulgarisation de l'information; Faire la promotion des connaissances dans des domaines connexes pouvant avoir un impact sur la santé et la sécurité du travail tels la sécurité, l'ergonomie et l'environnement; étudier les législations pertinentes et toute action gouvernementale relatives à ses champs d'activités et faire les représentations qu'elle juge à propos; Encourager la reconnaissance de la compétence de ses membres
Membre(s) du bureau directeur:
Nicolas Perron, Président, 450-774-9131, Fax: 450-261-2107
Amélie Trudel, Vice-présidente, 514-849-8373, Fax: 514-849-8873
France de Repentigny, Secrétaire, 514-982-2553, Fax: 514-283-6737
Christine Venditto, Trésorière
Membre: *Montant de la cotisation:* 30$ membre étudiant; 115$ membre individuel; 325$ membre corporatif
Activités: ; *Bibliothèque:* UNF Library; Bibliothèque publique

Association québécoise pour la maîtrise de l'énergie (AQME) / Québec Association of Energy Managers (QAEM)

#750, 255, boul. CréMazie est, Montréal QC H2M 1L5
Tél: 514-866-5584; *Téléc:* 514-874-1272
Courriel: info@aqme.org
www.aqme.org
Aperçu: *Dimension:* moyenne; *Envergure:* provinciale; Organisme sans but lucratif; fondée en 1985
Mission: Contribuer à la promotion de la maîtrise de l'énergie au Québec pour une utilisation et une exploitation optimale des ressources et pour le respect de l'environnement
Membre(s) du bureau directeur:
Jean Lacroix, Président/directeur général
jlacroix@aqme.org
Finances: *Budget de fonctionnement annuel:* $500,000-$1.5 Million
Personnel: 5 membre(s) du personnel; 100 bénévole(s)
Membre: 700 *Montant de la cotisation:* 160$; *Critères d'admissibilite:* Utilisateur ou fournisseur d'énergie; *Comités:* Bâtiment; Municipalité; Industrie
Activités: Congrès annuel, concours Énergia, party homards, tournois de golf; *Stagiaires:* Oui; *Bibliothèque:* rendez-vous

Association scientifique canadienne de la viande ***See*** Canadian Meat Science Association

Association SeCan ***See*** SeCan Association

Association sectorielle - Fabrication d'équipement de transport et de machines (ASFETM) / Sectorial Association - Transportation Equipment & Machinery Manufacturing (SATEMM)

#202, 3565, rue Jarry est, Montréal QC H1Z 4K6
Tél: 514-729-6961; *Téléc:* 514-729-8628
Ligne sans frais: 888-527-3386
Courriel: info@asfetm.com
www.asfetm.com
Aperçu: *Dimension:* grande; *Envergure:* provinciale; Organisme sans but lucratif; fondée en 1983
Mission: Aider les employeurs et les travailleurs à prévenir les accidents du travail et les maladies professionnelles, en faisant pour eux de la recherche, en leur dispensant de l'information, de la formation et de l'assistance technique qui visent essentiellement à rendre impossibles les accidents et les maladies au travail, et en privilégiant, à cette fin, l'élimination de cette possibilité à sa source même selon un processus de participation paritaire; *Membre de:* National Safety Council (USA); Association du camionnage du Québec
Membre(s) du bureau directeur:
Arnold Dugas, Directeur général
adugas@asfetm.com
Suzanne Ready, Chargée de l'information
sready@asfetm.com
Finances: *Budget de fonctionnement annuel:* $500,000-$1.5 Million
Personnel: 20 membre(s) du personnel
Membre: 8 groupes corporatifs - 3 patronaux + 5 syndicaux; *Critères d'admissibilite:* Etre une association patronale ou syndicale du secteur
Activités: Programme d'action annuel (30 projets); journées de sessions et de formation; colloques; *Bibliothèque:* Centre de documentation; Bibliothèque publique rendez-vous

Publications:
•Fiches techniques [a publication of Association sectorielle - Fabrication d'équipement de transport et de machines]
•Santé + Sécurité [a publication of Association sectorielle - Fabrication d'équipement de transport et de machines]
Type: Magazine

Association technique des pâtes et papiers du Canada *See* Pulp & Paper Technical Association of Canada

Association universitaire canadienne d'études nordiques *See* Association of Canadian Universities for Northern Studies

Atlantic Canada Centre for Environmental Science (ACCES)
Saint Mary's University, 923 Robie St., Halifax NS B3H 3C3
www.smu.ca
Overview: A medium-sized local organization founded in 1991
Mission: To foster interdisciplinary research related to the environment
Environmental Activity: Conducting research in areas such as climate change, geothermal energy, pollution, impacts of mining, coastal zone management, fisheries management, & conservation
Chief Officer(s):
G. Pe-Piper, Contact, 902-420-5744, Fax: 902-496-8104
gpiper@smu.ca
Liette Vasseur, Contact
Membership: *Member Profile:* Saint Mary's University faculty members; Professionals interested in environmental science

Atlantic Canada Fish Farmers Association (ACFFA)
226 Limekiln Rd., Letang NB E5C 2A8
Tel: 506-755-3526; *Fax:* 506-755-6237
e-mail: info@atlanticfishfarmers.com
atlanticfishfarmers.com
www.facebook.com/group.php?gid=150506105026651
twitter.com/AtlFishFarmers
Previous Name: New Brunswick Salmon Growers Association
Overview: A small provincial organization founded in 1987
Mission: To act as the voice of Atlantic Canada's salmon farming industry; To implement fish health initiatives to produce high-quality finfish; Affiliation(s): Atlantic Canada Aquaculture Industry Research & Development Network (ACAIRDN)
Environmental Activity: Promoting environmental stewardship; Supporting research to ensure sustainability of the aquaculture industry in Atlantic Canada; Collaborating with conservation organizations, such as the North Atlantic Salmon Conservation Organization
Chief Officer(s):
Pamela Parker, Executive Director
Sybil Smith, Director, Operations
Betty House, Coordinator, Research & Development
Jim Hanley, Manager, Wharf
Membership: *Member Profile:* Salmon farming producers in New Brunswick; Companies & organizations that support the industry
Activities: Liaising with governments; Promoting fish health & welfare & social responsibility; Developing training programs; Fostering a positive image for finfish aquaculture in Atlantic Canada; Participating in management & research initiatives with related organizations, such as the Aquaculture Association of Canada, the National Fish Health Working Group, the Bay of Fundy Marine Resource Planning, & the Musquash Marine Protected Area Steering Committee

Atlantic Canada Water & Wastewater Association (ACWWA)
PO Box 41002, Dartmouth NS B2Y 4P7
Tel: 902-434-6002; *Fax:* 902-435-7796
e-mail: acwwa@hfx.andara.com
www.acwwa.ca
Overview: A medium-sized local organization
Mission: To improve drinking water in Atlantic Canada; *Member of:* American Water Works Association (AWWA); Water Environment Federation (WEF)
Chief Officer(s):
Ensor Nicholson, Chair
ensor.nicholson@moncton.org
Willard D'Eon, Secretary-Treasurer
willardd@cbcl.ca
Darrell Fisher, Director, Communications
dfisher@adi.ca
Membership: 430+; *Member Profile:* Water professionals in Atlantic Canada, from areas such as service provision, contracting, utility management, operations, system design, consulting, & academia; *Committees:* Education; Membership; Newsletter; Technical Papers; CWWA & CAC; Cross Connection Control; Young Professionals; Water for People; Government Affairs; Conference; Operator Involvement; Volunteers; Website
Activities: Providing training & information about the water & wastewater industry to members; Enhancing government relations; Offering networking opportunities
Meetings/Conferences:
For more information see Trade Shows, Conferences and Seminars Chapter
Atlantic Canada Water & Wastewater Association 2013 66th Annual Conference
September 2013 Fredericton, NB
Atlantic Canada Water & Wastewater Association 2014 67th Annual Conference
2014
Atlantic Canada Water & Wastewater Association 2015 68th Annual Conference
2015
Publications:
•ACWWA [Atlantic Canada Water & Wastewater Association] Newsletter
Type: Newsletter
Profile: Association activities
•AWWA Wastewater Operator Field Guide
Type: Booklet; *Price:* $55
Profile: Information used daily by wastewater system operators
•AWWA Water Operator Field Guide
Type: Booklet; *Price:* $55
Profile: Information for water treatment plant operators & water distribution operators
•Operator Certification Study Guide [a publication of the Atlantic Canada Water & Wastewater Association]
Type: Booklet; *Price:* $75
Profile: Information for water treatment & water distribution operators
•Wastewater Operator Certification Study Guide
Type: Booklet; *Price:* $75
Profile: Sample questions & answer for wastewater operator certification exams

Atlantic Canadian Organic Regional Network (ACORN) / Réseau régional du l'industrie biologique du Canada atlantique
PO Box 6343, Sackville NB E4L 1G6
Toll-Free: 866-322-2676
e-mail: admin@acornorganic.org
www.acornorganic.org
www.facebook.com/group.php?gid=153617164641
twitter.com/acornorganic
Overview: A medium-sized local organization founded in 2000
Mission: To act as the voice of organics in Atlantic Canada; *Member of:* Volunteer Canada; Organic Materials Review Institute; Affiliation(s): Canadian Organic Growers
Chief Officer(s):
Beth McMahon, Executive Director
Membership: 300; *Fees:* $30

Atlantic Dairy Council (ADC)
PO Box 9410, Stn. A, #700, 6009 Quinpool Rd., Halifax NS B3K 5S3
Tel: 902-425-2445; *Fax:* 902-425-2441
e-mail: info@adcrecycles.com
www.adcrecycles.com
Overview: A medium-sized local organization
Mission: To maintain good relations among those engaged in dairy processing & distribution industries; to provide opportunities for industry training courses; & to enable united action on any matter concerning the welfare of the dairy trade
Chief Officer(s):
John K. Sutherland, Executive Secretary
Membership: 80

Atlantic Pest Management Association (APMO)
51 Duke St., Bedford NS B4A 2Z2
Tel: 902-835-2304; *Fax:* 902-835-0953
pestworldapma.net/apma/
Overview: A small local organization
Member of: Canadian Pest Management Association
Chief Officer(s):
Don McCarthy, President
microkil@ns.sympatico.ca

Atlantic Planners Institute (API) / Institut des Urbanistes de l'atlantique (IVA)
Parent Name: Canadian Institute of Planners
57 Parkside Dr., Charlottetown PE C1E 1N1
Tel: 902-892-3684
Toll-Free: 800-207-2138
e-mail: krlewis@pei.eastlink.ca
www.atlanticplanners.org
Overview: A medium-sized provincial organization overseen by Canadian Institute of Planners
Mission: Represents professional planners in New Brunswick, Prince Edward Island, Nova Scotia, Newfoundland & Labrador. They provide the processing of membership applications, maintenance of the membership roster, production of a regularly-scheduled newsletter, funding guarantess for the annual conference organizing committee.; Affiliation(s): Canadian Institute of Planners
Chief Officer(s):
Kingsley Lewis
Finances: *Annual Operating Budget:* Less than $50,000; *Funding Sources:* Membership fees
Membership: 100-499; *Member Profile:* Professional planner in the four Atlantic Provinces of Canada; New Brunswick, Newfoundland and Labrador, Nova Scotia, and Prince Edward Island.
Meetings/Conferences:
For more information see Trade Shows, Conferences and Seminars Chapter
2013 Atlantic Planners Institute Annual Conference
October 2013 Charlottetown, PE

Atlantic Provinces Association of Landscape Architects (APALA)
PO Box 653, Stn. Halifax CRO, Halifax NS B3J 2Z1
e-mail: info@apala.ca
www.apala.ca
Overview: A medium-sized local organization
Mission: To promote, improve & advance the profession; to maintain standards of professional practice & conduct consistent with the need to serve & to protect the public interest; to support improvement &/or conservation of the natural, cultural, social & built environment
Chief Officer(s):
Edward Versteeg, Sec.-Treas.
Gordon Smith, President
Membership: 56

Atlantic Provinces Council on the Sciences; Atlantic Provinces Inter-University Committee on the Sciences *See* Science Atlantic

Atlantic Provinces Trucking Association (APTA)
Parent Name: Canadian Trucking Alliance
#400, 725 Champlain St., Dieppe NB E1A 1P6
Tel: 506-855-2782; *Fax:* 506-853-7424
Toll-Free: 866-866-1679
e-mail: apta@apta.ca
www.apta.ca
Overview: A medium-sized local organization founded in 1950 overseen by Canadian Trucking Alliance
Mission: To promote an efficient, safe & environmentally sound trucking industry in Atlantic Canada. PUBLICATIONS: Atlantic Trucking Magazine (quaterly); Atlantic Report Newsletter (monthly) (only to members).
Chief Officer(s):
Ralph Boyd, President
Peter Nelson, Executive Director
Georgia Smallwood, Marketing/Membership Services
Chris McKee, Managing Editor- Atlantic Trucking
Shane Esson, Chairperson
Membership: 400 corporate & individual; *Member Profile:* Open to anyone having an interest in the trucking industry in Atlantic Canada, including common carriers, owner-operators & private fleets; *Committees:* Accident Review; Associated Trades Council; Broker; Common Carrier; Group Insurance; Marine; Membership; New Brunswick Legislative; Newfoundland Legislative; Nova Scotia Legislative; Prince Edward Island Legislative; Safety Council; Workers Compensation
Activities: Infrastructure improvements; complete twinning of the highway between Halifax & Saint John; elimination of motor carrier plates & fees; simplification of multiple registration & other tax collection systems in North America to allow for "one-stop shipping"; establishment of training programs; Annual Meeting & Convention; Atlantic Truck Show; Spring Maintenance Seminar; *Rents Mailing List:* Yes

Atlantic Salmon Federation (ASF) / Fédération du saumon atlantique
PO Box 5200, St. Andrews NB E5B 3S8
Tel: 506-529-4581; *Fax:* 506-529-1070
Toll-Free: 800-565-5666

e-mail: savesalmon@asf.ca
www.asf.ca
www.facebook.com/pages/Atlantic-Salmon-Federation/143596265564
twitter.com/SalmonNews
www.youtube.com/user/ASFatlanticsalmon
Overview: A large international charitable organization founded in 1948
Mission: To protect, conserve & restore wild Atlantic salmon & their ecosystems
Environmental Activity: Encouraging stewardship of watersheds
Chief Officer(s):
Bill Taylor, President & Chief Executive Officer, 506-529-1034
btaylor@asf.ca
Todd Dupuis, Executive Director, Regional Programs, 902-628-4349
tdupuis@upei.ca
Jonathan Carr, Director, Research & Environment, 506-529-1385
jcarr@asf.ca
Bill Mallory, Executive Vice-President & CFO, 506-529-1386
wmallory@asf.ca
Rob Beatty, Vice-President, Development, 506-529-1031
rbeatty@asf.ca
Sue Ann Scott, Vice-President, Communications, 506-529-1027
sscott@asf.ca
Muriel Ferguson, Manager, Public Information, 506-529-1033
mferguson@asf.ca
Martin Silverstone, Editor, Atlantic Salmon Journal, 514-457-8737
martinsilverstone@videotron.ca
Finances: *Annual Operating Budget:* Greater than $5 Million; *Funding Sources:* Donations from individuals, corporations, & foundations
Staff: 25 staff member(s); 40,0 volunteer(s)
Membership: 8,000; *Fees:* Schedule available
Activities: Sharing knowledge with adults & children about wild Atlantic salmon; Conducting scientific research; *Internships:* Yes; *Library:* Interpretive Centre (summer)
Awards:
•Olin Fellowships (Scholarship)
Presented annually to individuals who seek to improve their knowledge & skills while searching for solutions to challenges in Atlantic salmon biology, conservation, & management *Deadline:* March 15 *Amount:* $1,000-3,000 *Contact:* Olin Fellowships, Atlantic Salmon Federation, PO Box 5200, St. Andrews, NB, EOG 2X0
•T.B. (Happy) Fraser Award (Award)
Presented annually to an individual who has made outstanding contributions to wild Atlantic salmon conservation at a regional or national level
•Lee Wulff Conservation Award (Award)
Presented annually to an individual who has made outstanding contributions to wild Atlantic salmon conservation
•Atlantic Salmon Federation Roll Of Honor (Award)
Presented annually to individuals who demonstrate outstanding commitment to wild Atlantic salmon conservation at the grass-roots level
•Affiliate of the Year Award (Award)
To recognize outstanding leadership in wild Atlantic salmon conservation within the Atlantic Salmon Federation's affiliate structure
Publications:
•Atlantic Salmon Federation Annual Report
Type: Yearbook; *Frequency:* Annually
Profile: Information about the federation's current projects that impact Atlantic salmon restoration plus future strategies
•Atlantic Salmon Federation Newsletter
Type: Newsletter
Profile: Updates on activities of the Federation
•Atlantic Salmon Journal
Type: Journal; *Accepts Advertising*; *Editor:* Martin Silverstone
Profile: Issues surrounding wild Atlantic salmon, including protection of the species
•Incidence & Impacts of Escaped Farmed Atlantic Salmon "Salmo Salar" in Nature
Type: Report; *Number of Pages:* 114; *Author:* Eva B. Thorstad et al.
Profile: The impacts of escaped farmed salmon
•Prince Edward Island Nitrate Report
Type: Report
Profile: The problem of nitrates entering streams & lakes
•State of the Population - Atlantic Salmon
Type: Report
Profile: A backgrounder on the Atlantic salmon population, featuring statistics, tables, & graphs

Newfoundland & Labrador Regional Office
305-20 Linden Pl., St. John's NL A1B 2S8
Tel: 709-753-2930
e-mail: donaldhustins@hotmail.com
Chief Officer(s):
Donald Hustins, President

Nova Scotia Regional Office
PO Box 396, Chester NS B0J 1J0
Tel: 902-466-3024
e-mail: nssalmo@yahoo.ca
www.novascotiasalmon.ns.ca
Chief Officer(s):
Carl Purcell, President
c.purcell@ns.sympatico.ca

Prince Edward Island Regional Office
88 Upper Tea Hill Cres., Stratford PE C1B 2V2
Tel: 902-368-7865
e-mail: mjlanigan@eastlink.ca
www.asf.ca/regions.php?id=5
Chief Officer(s):
Mark Langian, President

Atlantic Turfgrass Research Foundation (ATRC)
Nova Scotia Agricultural College, 20 Rock Garden Rd., Truro NS B2N 5E3
Tel: 902-456-8571
Overview: A small provincial organization founded in 1992
Mission: To advance the turfgrass industry in Atlantic Canada
Chief Officer(s):
David Davey, President
Kevin Wentzell, Secretary
Activities: Researching turfgrass systems, in areas such as irrigation efficiency & water conservation & management

Auditing Association of Canada (AAC) / L'Association canadienne de vérification
PO Box 3093, Stn. Lapierre, LaSalle QC H8N 3H2
Tel: 866-582-9595
e-mail: admin@auditingcanada.com
www.auditingcanada.com
Previous Name: Canadian Environmental Auditing Association
Overview: A medium-sized international organization
Mission: To represent & promote the auditing profession; To advance public interest by enabling members to provide quality services
Environmental Activity: Furthering the professional development of auditors in the areas of the environment & health & safety; Developing & maintaining ISO standards
Chief Officer(s):
Guy Brisebois, Executive Director
Jean-Pierre Fry, President
Membership: 375+; *Fees:* $25 plus GST student members; $195 plus GST general members; $1000-$10,000 corporations; *Member Profile:* Auditors in environmental, health & safety, & related areas from across Canada, such as ISO 14001 & OHSAS 18001 registration auditors; Students who are interested in environmental & health & safety auditing; Corporations that support association activities
Activities: Certifying auditors; Upholding a code of ethics; Offering educational programs; Providing opportunities to network with colleagues; Offering information about government legislation & activities; Partnering with similar organizations
Publications:
•Auditing Association of Canada Membership Directory
Type: Directory

Ausable Bayfield Conservation Foundation
71108 Morrison Line, RR#3, Exeter ON N0M 1S5
Tel: 519-235-2610; *Fax:* 519-235-1963
Toll-Free: 888-286-2610
e-mail: info@abca.on.ca
www.abca.on.ca
Overview: A small local organization founded in 1974
Mission: Raising funds for conservation, preservation & protection of the natural landscapes of the Ausable River, Bayfield River & Packhill Creek watersheds
Chief Officer(s):
Tom Prout, General Manager/Sec.-Treas., 519-235-261 Ext. 234
Finances: *Annual Operating Budget:* Less than $50,000
Staff: 2 staff member(s); 9 volunteer(s)
Membership: 1-99
Activities: Conservation Dinner Auction

Australian Association for Environmental Education (AAEE)
PO Box 560, Bellingen 2454 Australia
Tel: 61-2-6655-1865
e-mail: admin@aaee.org.au
www.aaee.org.au
Overview: A small national organization founded in 1980
Mission: To promote environmental education
Chief Officer(s):
Phil Smith, President
rephilled@hotmail.com
Finances: *Annual Operating Budget:* $50,000-$100,000; *Funding Sources:* Fees; grants; sponsorship; subsidies
Staff: 1 staff member(s); 30 volunteer(s)
Membership: 500; *Fees:* $90-$99 individual; $120 family; $240 corporate; $140 school/NGO; $896-$985 lifetime; *Member Profile:* Professionals; *Committees:* Special interest groups

AUTO21 - The Automobile of the 21st Century *See* AUTO21 Network of Centres of Excellence

AUTO21 Network of Centres of Excellence
754 California Ave., Windsor ON N9B 2Z2
Tel: 519-253-3000; *Fax:* 519-971-3626
e-mail: info@auto21.ca
www.auto21.ca
www.linkedin.com/groups?about=&gid=2804256&trk=anet_ug_grppro
www.facebook.com/AUTO21
twitter.com/auto21nce
www.youtube.com/user/AUTO21NCE
Also Known As: AUTO21
Previous Name: AUTO21 - The Automobile of the 21st Century
Overview: A medium-sized national organization founded in 2001
Mission: To partner the public & private secotrs in applied automotive R&D; *Member of:* Networks of Centres of Excellence
Chief Officer(s):
Peter Frise, CEO & Scientific Director
Michelle Watters, COO & Executive Director
Stephanie Campeau, Director, Public Affairs & Communications
Finances: *Annual Operating Budget:* Greater than $5 Million; *Funding Sources:* Federal government; Private sector
Staff: 11 staff member(s)
Membership: 200 researchers + 120 industry & government partners
Activities: Automotive research; *Internships:* Yes

Automobile Importers of Canada *See* Association of International Automobile Manufacturers of Canada

Automotive Industries Association of Canada (AIAC) / Association des industries de l'automobile du Canada
1272 Wellington St. West, Ottawa ON K1Y 3A7
Fax: 613-728-6021
Toll-Free: 800-808-2920
e-mail: info@aia@aiacanada.com
www.aiacanada.com
www.facebook.com/AIAofCanada
Overview: A large national organization founded in 1964
Mission: To represent the automotive aftermarket industry in Canada; To promote, educate, & represent members
Chief Officer(s):
John P. MacDonald, Chair
john.macdonald@aiacanada.com
Marc Brazeau, President & CEO
marc.brazeau@aiacanada.com
Therese Santostefano, Director, Operations & Finance
therese.santostefano@aiacanada.com
Andrew Shepherd, Director, Collision Training
andrew.shepherd@aiacanada.com
Patty Kettles, Manager, Marketing & Communications
patty.kettles@aiacanada.com
Finances: *Funding Sources:* Membership dues
Staff: 300 volunteer(s)
Membership: 1,400 organizations; *Fees:* Dues based on the confirmed sales volumes of the individual members; *Member Profile:* Open to wholesalers, warehouse distributors, mass merchandizers, specialty groups & oil company headquarters, manufacturers, rebuilders, national distributors, manufacturers' agents, international exporters, allied organizations that supply goods &/or services to members of the association not for resale to warehouse distributors or wholesalers; *Committees:* Government Relations; Market Research; Audit & Finance; Paint, Body & Equipment; Yobe Car Care Aware Advisory

Activities: Offering correspondence courses (parts specialist training; sales training; jobber management; dangerous goods, WHMIS & hazardous waste); Providing insurance services (benefits & pensions); government relations; *Awareness Events:* Car Care Month, May; Car Safety Month, October; *Speaker Service:* Yes

Automotive Parts Manufacturers' Association (APMA)

#801, 10 Four Seasons Pl., Toronto ON M9B 6H7
Tel: 416-620-4220; *Fax:* 416-620-9730
e-mail: info@apma.ca
www.apma.ca
www.linkedin.com/groups?home=&gid=2654454
www.facebook.com/APMACanada
twitter.com/APMACanada
Overview: A large national organization founded in 1952
Mission: To promote the manufacture in Canada of automotive parts, systems, components, materials, tools, equipment & supplies, & also the provision of services used in the automotive industry & in particular for the original equipment market; To engage in activities in support of the welfare of the members of the Association
Chief Officer(s):
Steve Rodgers, President
Vincent Guglielmo, Vice-President, 416-620-4220 Ext. 233
Shaun Cott, Manager, Marketing, 416-620-4220 Ext. 224
Membership: 400+ corporate; *Fees:* Schedule available; *Member Profile:* Canadian producers of parts, components, systems, tools, equipment & services for the automotive & truck manufacturing industries worldwide; 3 categories: Regular - manufacturers in Canada independent of vehicle companies; Canadian manufacturers which are divisions or affiliates of vehicle companies; International associates - manufacturers outside Canada interested or involved in the Canadian market & industry; Other associates - not manufacturers but interested in keeping in touch with industry trends & developments; *Committees:* Annual Conference; Environment, Energy, Health & Safety; Human Resources Development; Innovation & Technology; Marketing & Strategic Initiatives; Strategic Purchasing
Activities: Conducting an emissions survey
Meetings/Conferences:
For more information see Trade Shows, Conferences and Seminars Chapter
Automotive Parts Manufacturers' Association 2013 Annual Conference & Exhibition
June 2013 Windsor, ON
Publications:
•APMA [Automotive Parts Manufacturers' Association] Bulletins
Type: Bulletin
Profile: Information on issues, opportunities, & events
•APMA [Automotive Parts Manufacturers' Association] eNews Brief
Type: Newsletter
Profile: APMA activities, issues & news delivered electronically

Automotive Recyclers of Canada (ARC)

134 Langarth St. E., London ON N6C 1Z5
Tel: 519-858-8761
e-mail: info@autorecyclers.ca
www.autorecyclers.ca
twitter.com/autorecyclersCA
www.youtube.com/user/SRFletcher21
Overview: A large national organization founded in 1997
Mission: To act as the national voice for provincial member automotive recycling associations
Chief Officer(s):
Wally Dingman, Chair
Steve Fletcher, Managing Director
Membership: 7 associations; *Member Profile:* Automotive recycling associations
Publications:
•Canadian Auto Recyclers [a publication of Automotive Recyclers of Canada]
Type: Magazine; *Frequency:* Annually; *Editor:* Mike Raine

The Avian Preservation Foundation (APF)

PO Box 123, Chemainus BC V0R 1K0
Tel: 250-246-4803; *Fax:* 250-246-4912
e-mail: exec@aacc.ca
www.aacc.ca/apf.htm
Overview: A medium-sized national charitable organization
Mission: To support recognized expert aviculturists who are endeavouring to breed rare & endangered avian species; to establish a Canadian breeding centre for rare & endangered avian species; to establish a monitoring body for captive avian stocks in Canada through surveys & computer software; to create & maintain a breeding program throughout Canada for avian species currently listed as endangered; to create a captive preservation program for rare & endangered species within zoos, bird parks & sanctuaries where re-introduction into the natural habitat is not possible or practical; *Member of:* Avicultural Advancement Council of Canada
Chief Officer(s):
Mark S. Curtis, Executive Director
Finances: *Annual Operating Budget:* Less than $50,000
Staff: 12 volunteer(s)
Membership: 250; *Fees:* $35

Avicultural Advancement Council of Canada (AACC)

28 Greene Dr., Brampton ON L6V 2R6
www.aacc.ca
Overview: A medium-sized national licensing organization founded in 1972
Mission: To establish & maintain a national association of interested societies & individuals to promote the advancement of aviculture in Canada; To represent the Canadian avicultural community internationally; To disseminate information; to support recognized expert aviculturalists; To assist all levels of government in preparing informed legislation & policy relating to aviculture; To establish standards for the exhibition of birds in Canada; To provide a national identification leg band registry; To establish an avian species preservation program in Canada; Affiliation(s): American Singer Canary Club of Canada; Assoc. des amateurs d'oiseaux de la Mauricie; Assoc. des éléveurs d'oiseaux de Montréal; BC Avicultural Society; BC Exotic Bird Society; Budgerigar & Foreign Bird Society; Cage Bird Society of Hamilton; Calgary Canary Club; Canadian Dove Assoc.; Canadian Gloster Club; Cowichan Valley & Upper Island Cage Bird Club; Durham Avicultural Society; Edmonton Avicultural Association; Essex-Kent Cage Bird Society; Feather Fanciers Club; Golden Triangle Parrot Club; Kamloops Aviculturalist Society; London & District Cage Bird Society; Manitoba Canary & Finch Club
Chief Officer(s):
Dunstan H. Browne, President
hdbrowne@shaw.ca
Denise Antler, Ring Registrar
antler3795@rogers.com
Roslynne Webb, Secretary
rozwebb@telus.net
Finances: *Annual Operating Budget:* Less than $50,000; *Funding Sources:* Membership dues; Donations
Staff: 12 volunteer(s)
Membership: 300 individual + 40 institutional; *Fees:* $30 individual; $70 club; *Member Profile:* Breeders, exhibitors & fanciers of birds; Clubs thaa subscribe to the principles of association
Activities: ; *Library:* Open to public

Bancroft Gem & Mineral Club

PO Box 1749, Bancroft ON K0L 1C0
Overview: A small local charitable organization
Mission: To foster an interest in the earth sciences & related lapidary arts; *Member of:* Central Canadian Federation of Mineralogical Societies
Chief Officer(s):
Frank Melanson, President, 613-332-1032
wfmelanson@sympatico.ca
Finances: *Funding Sources:* Gem & Mineral Club Show admission; Donations
Activities: Hosting monthly meetings (except August & December); Organizing field trips; Presenting displays; *Awareness Events:* Bancroft Gem & Mineral Club Annual Gem & Mineral Show

Barrhead Animal Rescue Society (BARS)

c/o Terry Colborne, PO Box 4702, Barrhead AB T7N 1A5
Tel: 780-307-6590
www.barrheadanimalrescue.org
www.facebook.com/BarrheadAnimalRescueSociety
Overview: A medium-sized local charitable organization founded in 2010
Mission: Dedicated to ensuring the humane treatment of all animals in the Town of Barrhead, the County of Barrhead and surrounding areas.
Chief Officer(s):
Terry Colbourne, President
Finances: *Funding Sources:* Private donations

Barrie Agricultural Society

PO Box 217, #3, 199 Essa Rd., Barrie ON L4M 4T2
Tel: 705-737-3670; *Fax:* 705-737-2581
e-mail: info@essaagriplex.ca
www.eventcentre.ca
www.facebook.com/pages/Barrie-Fair/122250804475473
Also Known As: Event Centre
Overview: A small local charitable organization founded in 1853
Mission: To encourage an awareness of agriculture; To promote improvements in the quality of life for persons living in our community, rural & urban; To organize & operate the Barrie Fair & other similar events; To provide a venue where exhibitors can showcase, compete & market their products, crops or livestock
Chief Officer(s):
Henry VanderWielen, President
Wayne Hawke, Executive Director
Cindy Vecchiarelli, Administrator
cindy@essaagriplex.ca
Finances: *Annual Operating Budget:* $250,000-$500,000; *Funding Sources:* Sponsors; Rental revenue; Barrie Fair
Staff: 4 staff member(s); 150 volunteer(s)
Membership: 1,000-4,999;; *Fees:* $5

Barrow Bay & District Sports Fishing Association (BB&DSFA)

PO Box 987, Lions Head ON N0H 1W0
Fax: 519-793-3363
e-mail: barrowbayfishing@hotmail.com
www.bltg.com/bbdsfa/
Overview: A small local organization founded in 1993
Member of: Ontario Federation of Anglers & Hunters
Environmental Activity: Stream restoration; tree planting; farm fencing; bank stabilization; spawning lanes; monitoring; egg collection
Finances: *Annual Operating Budget:* $50,000-$100,000; *Funding Sources:* Membership dues; fundraising; government grants
Staff: 35 volunteer(s)
Membership: 92; *Member Profile:* Local sport fishers & environmentalists
Publications:
•Barrow Bay & District Sports Fishing Association Newsletter
Type: Newsletter

Bâtiments Durables Canada ***See*** Sustainable Buildings Canada

Battle River Research Group (BRRG)
Parent Name: Agricultural Research & Extension Council of Alberta

PO Box 339, 4804 - 43 Ave., Forestburg AB T0B 1N0
Tel: 780-582-7308; *Fax:* 780-582-7312
Toll-Free: 866-828-6774
e-mail: brrg@cciwireless.ca
www.areca.ab.ca/brrghome.html
Overview: A small local organization overseen by Agricultural Research & Extension Council of Alberta
Mission: To support agricultural research, in order to make agriculture more sustainable; *Member of:* Agricultural Research & Extension Council of Alberta
Chief Officer(s):
Alvin Eyolfson, P.Ag., Manager & Agrologist
brrgmgr@cciwireless.ca
Vicki Heidt, Agrologist, Forage & Livestock
brrgfl@cciwireless.ca
Membership: *Fees:* $20 individual (annual); $50 individual (3 years); $100 corporate
Publications:
•Over the Fence [a publication of the Battle River Research Group]
Type: Newsletter

Battlefords Agricultural Society (BAS)

PO Box 668, North Battleford SK S9A 2Y9
Tel: 306-445-2024; *Fax:* 306-445-3352
e-mail: b.agsociety@sasktel.net
agsociety.com
Previous Name: Battlefords Exhibition Association
Overview: A small local charitable organization founded in 1884
Mission: To promote improvements in agriculture & community development; to provide facilities for educational & leisure programs; *Member of:* Saskatchewan Association of Agricultural Societies & Exhibitions
Chief Officer(s):
Gordon Craig, President
Jocelyn Ritchie, General Manager
Finances: *Annual Operating Budget:* $500,000-$1.5 Million
Staff: 4 staff member(s); 130 volunteer(s)

Membership: 125; *Fees:* $15; *Member Profile:* Families, ages 16-85
Activities: Trade shows, quarter horse shows, raffles, chuckwagon races, 4H Regional Show, children's festival

Battlefords Exhibition Association *See* Battlefords Agricultural Society

BC Biotech *See* LifeSciences British Columbia

BC Motels, Campgrounds, Resorts Association *See* British Columbia Lodging & Campgrounds Association

BC Motor Transport Association *See* British Columbia Trucking Association

Bear Biology Association *See* International Association for Bear Research & Management

Beaverhill Bird Observatory (BBO)
PO Box 1418, Edmonton AB T5J 2N5
www.beaverhillbirds.com
Overview: A small local charitable organization
Mission: To promote study of resident & migratory birds & other aspects of natural history at Beaverhill Lake & elsewhere
Environmental Activity: Acting as a steward of the Beaverhill Natural Area
Chief Officer(s):
Charles Priestley, Chair
charles@ualberta.ca
Lisa Takats Priestley, Executive Director
lisa@beaverhillbirds.com
Membership: *Fees:* $10 one year; $20 two year; $25 family/club; *Member Profile:* Biologists; Nature lovers
Activities: Documenting & monitoring changes in the avian species that utilize the Beaverhill area; Promoting an interest in the conservation of birds; Encouraging nature activities
Publications:
•The Willet [a publication of the Beaverhill Bird Observatory]
Type: Newsletter

Bedeque Bay Environmental Management Association (BBEMA)
PO Box 8310, Emerald PE C0B 1M0
Tel: 902-886-3211
www.bbema.ca
Overview: A small local organization founded in 1992
Mission: To provide a framework for citizen-based education and action that reduced soil erosion, maintained water quality and improved the ecosystem.

Bengough Agricultural Society
PO Box 411, Bengough SK S0C 0K0
Tel: 306-268-2855
e-mail: benagsoc@hotmail.com
Overview: A small local charitable organization founded in 1915
Mission: To improve agriculture & the quality of life in the community by educating members & the community; to provide a community forum for discussing agricultural issues; to foster community development & community spirit; to help provide markets for Saskatchewan products; to encourage conservation of natural resources, including soil conservation, reforestation, rural & urban beautification; *Member of:* Saskatchewan Association of Agricultural Societies & Exhibitions
Chief Officer(s):
Rocky Kaufman, President, 306-268-4248
Finances: *Annual Operating Budget:* Less than $50,000
Staff: 12 volunteer(s)
Membership: 60 individual; *Fees:* $3; *Member Profile:* Area residents striving to promote our community through education & entertainment
Activities: Horse show & fair; trade show; farmers market

Big Rideau Lake Association (BRLA)
PO Box 93, Hwy. 15, Portland ON K0G 1V0
Tel: 613-272-3629
e-mail: brla@brla.on.ca
www.brla.on.ca
Overview: A medium-sized local organization founded in 1911
Mission: The Big Rideau Lake Association (BRLA) is a non-profit organization committed to long-term environmental protection and service to all who use Big Rideau Lake and share its resources.
Environmental Activity: Water testing; Wildlife monitoring
Chief Officer(s):
Peter Copestake, President
Membership: *Fees:* $60

Bikes Without Borders (BWB)
25 Havelock St., Toronto ON M6H 3B3
Tel: 416-432-4801
e-mail: info@bikeswithoutborders.org
bikeswithoutborders.org
www.facebook.com/bikeswithoutborders
twitter.com/BWB_Canada
www.youtube.com/user/bikeswithoutborders/videos
Overview: A small international charitable organization founded in 2008
Mission: Uses bikes and bike-related solutions as a tool for development in marginalized communities.
Chief Officer(s):
Tanya Smith, Executive Director
Tanya@bikeswithoutborders.org
Activities: The Bicycle Ambulance; Pedal Powered Hope Project

Binbrook Agricultural Society (BAS)
PO Box 244, 2600, RR #56, Binbrook ON L0R 1C0
Tel: 905-692-4003; *Fax:* 905-692-1434
e-mail: info@binbrookagriculturalsociety.org
www.binbrookagriculturalsociety.org
twitter.com/BinbrookFair
Overview: A small local organization founded in 1854
Affiliation(s): Ontario Association of Agricultural Societies; Canadian Association of Exhibitions
Finances: *Annual Operating Budget:* Less than $50,000; *Funding Sources:* Regional government
Staff: 1 staff member(s); 140 volunteer(s)
Membership: 175 individual; 18 associate; *Fees:* $5 individual; $5 associate
Activities: Annual Fall Fair; agricultural education & awareness programs;

Bio-dynamic Agricultural Society of British Columbia
2478 East 23rd Ave., Vancouver BC V5R 1A2
Tel: 778-869-4060
e-mail: bdcertification@yahoo.ca
Overview: A small provincial licensing organization
Affiliation(s): Certified Organic Associations of BC
Chief Officer(s):
Doug Helmer, Treasurer
Grant Watson, Administrator

Biophysical Society of Canada (BSC) / La société de biophysique du Canada
Parent Name: Canadian Federation of Biological Societies
a/s Dept. de chimie, Univ. Laval, 1045 Avenue de la médecine, Québec QC G1V 0A6
Tel: 418-656-3393; *Fax:* 418-656-7916
e-mail: info@biophysicalsociety.ca
www.biophysicalsociety.ca
Overview: A medium-sized national organization founded in 1985 overseen by Canadian Federation of Biological Societies
Mission: To promote biophysical research & education; to encourage cross-feeding of ideas between the physical & biological sciences; to foster & support scientific meetings, workshops & discussions in biophysics; to represent Canadian biophysics & biophysicists
Chief Officer(s):
Bruce C. Hill, President
Finances: *Annual Operating Budget:* Less than $50,000; *Funding Sources:* Membership dues
Staff: 10 volunteer(s)
Membership: 80; *Fees:* $84.20
Activities: *Speaker Service:* Yes

BIOQuébec / Québec Bio-Industries Business Network
#120, 500, Boul Cartier ouest, Laval QC H7V 5B7
Tél: 450-781-3965; *Téléc:* 450-781-3966
Courriel: info@bioquebec.com
www.bioquebec.com
Nom précédent: Conseil des bio-industries du Québec; Association québécoise des bio-industries
Aperçu: *Dimension:* moyenne; *Envergure:* provinciale; Organisme sans but lucratif; fondée en 1997
Mission: Ôtre le porte-parole des entreprises biotechnologiques du Québec; favoriser le développement et la mise en valeur des biotechnologies et des bioindustries québécoises, et ce au bénéfice de ses membres; To promote the development & the upgrading of biotechnologies; to supply strategic information of technical & economical content as well as carry out projects, events & activities; to stimulate collaboration between private industry, governments & universities; to stimulate the growth of structuring economical activities in this field; to act as a spokesman for the bio-industry in Québec
Membre(s) du bureau directeur:
Gilles R. Gagnon, Président
Mario Lebrun, Directeur général
brun@bioquebec.com
Finances: *Budget de fonctionnement annuel:* $500,000-$1.5 Million; *Fonds:* Federal Office of Regional Development - Québec; membership fees; Laval Technopole
Personnel: 1 membre(s) du personnel; 4 bénévole(s)
Membre: 240 companies *Montant de la cotisation:* 385$ (corporatif 1-5 employés); *Comités:* Environnement d'affaires; Conseil de l'innovation biopharmaceutique
Activités: Colloques, conférences, expositions

BIOTECanada
#600, 1 Nicholas St., Ottawa ON K1N 7B7
Tel: 613-230-5585; *Fax:* 613-563-8850
e-mail: info@biotech.ca
www.biotech.ca
www.linkedin.com/company/biotecanada
twitter.com/biotecanada
Previous Name: Canadian Institute of Biotechnology; Industrial Biotechnology Association of Canada
Overview: A medium-sized national organization founded in 1987
Mission: To provide a unified voice fostering an environment that responds to the needs of the biotechnology industry & research community, both nationally & internationally
Chief Officer(s):
Brad Thompson, Chair
Andrew Casey, President & CEO, 613-230-5585 Ext. 229
andrew.casey@biotech.ca
Finances: *Annual Operating Budget:* $1.5 Million-$3 Million; *Funding Sources:* Membership dues; government; sponsorship
Staff: 10 staff member(s)
Membership: 250 institutional; *Fees:* Schedule available; *Member Profile:* Biotechnology industry & regional groups; *Committees:* Agriculture; Human Health Care; Environment; Finance; Intellectual Property; Ethics; Communications; Government Relations; Science
Activities: Policy & regulatory advocacy; communications; human resources; *Rents Mailing List:* Yes

Bird Studies Canada (BSC)
PO Box 160, 115 Front St., Port Rowan ON N0E 1M0
Fax: 519-586-3532
Toll-Free: 888-448-2473
e-mail: generalinfo@birdscanada.org
www.bsc-eoc.org
twitter.com/BirdStudiesCan
Previous Name: Long Point Bird Observatory
Overview: A small provincial charitable organization founded in 1960
Mission: To advance the understanding, appreciation & conservation of wild birds & their habitats, in Canada & elsewhere, through studies that engage the skills, enthusiasm, & support of its members volunteers, staff & the interested public; *Member of:* Federation of Ontario Naturalists; Affiliation(s): Ontario Bird Banding Association; James L. Baillie Memorial Fund
Chief Officer(s):
Art Martell, Chair
Finances: *Annual Operating Budget:* $1.5 Million-$3 Million
Staff: 34 staff member(s)
Membership: 5,000-14,999;; *Fees:* $25 student; $35 individual; $50 family; $100 contributing; $175 sustaining; $1000 lifetime; $2500 patron
Activities: *Internships:* Yes; *Library:* by appointment
Meetings/Conferences:
For more information see Trade Shows, Conferences and Seminars Chapter
BirdLife World Congress 2013
June 2013 Ottawa, ON

Black Creek Conservation Project
PO Box 324, Stn. A, Toronto ON M3M 3A6
Tel: 416-661-6000; *Fax:* 416-667-6278
www.bccp.ca
Previous Name: Black Creek Project of Toronto Inc.
Overview: A small local organization founded in 1982
Mission: To preserve & rehabilitate the Black Creek watershed; To support a healthy, diverse, & sustainable ecosystem; *Member of:* Federation of Ontario Naturalists
Chief Officer(s):

Amy Maurer, Contact
amaurer@trca.on.ca
Finances: *Annual Operating Budget:* $50,000-$100,000; *Funding Sources:* Government; private
Staff: 1 staff member(s); 2500 volunteer(s)
Membership: 45; *Fees:* $15
Activities: Tree planting; garbage clean-up; environmental lectures; erosion control; wetland creation

Black Creek Project of Toronto Inc. ***See*** Black Creek Conservation Project

Blomidon Naturalists Society (BNS)
PO Box 2350, Wolfville NS B4P 2N5
e-mail: members@blomidonnaturalists.ca
blomidonnaturalists.ca
Overview: A small local charitable organization founded in 1974
Mission: To encourage & develop an understanding & appreciation of nature; *Member of:* Nature Nova Scotia, Nature Canada
Chief Officer(s):
John Owen, President
john.owen@ns.sympatico.ca
Helen Archibald, Secretary
hfarchibald@ns.sympatico.ca
Finances: *Annual Operating Budget:* $50,000-$100,000; *Funding Sources:* Membership dues
Staff: 15 volunteer(s)
Membership: 250; *Fees:* $20 adult, family; $1 Junior
Activities: Monthly meetings; field trips; bird counts; astronomy sessions
Publications:
•Blomidon Naturalists Society Newsletter
Type: Newsletter; *Frequency:* Quarterly; *Number of Pages:* 48
Profile: Published once every season of the year around the equinoxes & solstices.

Bluewater Recycling Association (BRA)
415 Canada Ave., Huron Park ON N0M 1Y0
Tel: 519-228-6678; *Fax:* 519-228-6656
e-mail: info@bra.org
www.bra.org
Overview: A small local organization founded in 1989
Mission: To provide ethical, innovative, effective resource-management services; To carry out our mission efficiently, safely & in an environmentally responsible manner, ultimately enabling our members to meet their environmental commitments
Finances: *Annual Operating Budget:* Greater than $5 Million
Staff: 55 staff member(s)
Membership: 21; *Fees:* Schedule available; *Member Profile:* Municipalities
Activities: *Speaker Service:* Yes
Publications:
•Bluewater Recycling Newsletter
Type: Newsletter

Board of Canadian Registered Safety Professionals (BCRSP) / Conseil canadien des professionnels en securité agréés
6519B Mississauga Rd., Mississauga ON L5N 1A6
Tel: 905-567-7198; *Fax:* 905-567-7191
Toll-Free: 888-279-2777
e-mail: info@bcrsp.ca
www.bcrsp.ca
Previous Name: Association for Canadian Registered Safety Professionals
Overview: A medium-sized national licensing organization founded in 1976
Mission: To protect & promote occupational health & safety, environmental safety, & public safety, through the registration of qualified health & safety professionals committed to a code of ethics
Chief Officer(s):
Ron Durdle, Chair
Nicola Wright, Executive Director
Finances: *Annual Operating Budget:* $250,000-$500,000; *Funding Sources:* Membership dues
Staff: 5 staff member(s); 130 volunteer(s)
Membership: 2,000; *Fees:* $125; *Member Profile:* Successfully completed high school or equivalency; three years of continuous safety experience & current employment of at least 50% in a safety practitioners role
Activities: CRSP designation (the Board evaluates qualifications of candidates & members against established standards);

Boating Ontario
15 Laurier Rd., Penetanguishene ON L9M 1G8
Tel: 705-549-1667; *Fax:* 705-549-1670
Toll-Free: 888-547-6662
e-mail: info@boatingontario.ca
www.boatingontario.ca
Previous Name: Ontario Marine Operators Association
Overview: A medium-sized provincial organization founded in 1967
Mission: To promote recreational boating throughout Ontario
Environmental Activity: Employing a director of environmental services; Offering a guide to environment-friendly boating
Chief Officer(s):
Dick Peever, President, 519-524-4409, Fax: 519-524-2301
Graham Lacey, Vice-President, 705-383-2295, Fax: 705-383-2243
Al Donaldson, Executive Director, 705-549-1667, Fax: 705-549-1670
Ed Leeman, Secretary, 613-583-7973
Bob Eaton, Director, Environmental Services, 705-326-9359, Fax: 705-326-3827
Membership: 460+ individual marinas + 160 trade members; *Member Profile:* Ontario marinas; Yacht clubs; Marine dealers; Associated companies
Activities: Lobbying on behalf of the industry; Providing information; Encouraging safe boating; Participating in boat shows; Offering workshops
Publications:
•Boating Ontario: Marinas & Destination Guide
Type: Directory; *Frequency:* Annually
Profile: A guide to more than 450 marina members of the Ontario Marine Operators Association, with information about their facilities & services
•Enviro Boater
Type: Manual
Profile: Suggestions for environment-friendly boating, produced by the Ontario Marine Operators Association, the Canadian Power & Sail Squadrons, & other interested organizations
•Marina News
Type: Newsletter; *Frequency:* 8 pa; *Price:* Free with membership in the Ontario Marine Operators Association
Profile: Business suggestions & industry news, for members of the Ontario Marine Operators Association

Bonn Agreement (BONN)
Victoria House, 37-63 Southampton Row, London WC1B 4DA United Kingdom
Tel: 44-20-7430-5200; *Fax:* 44-20-7430-5225
e-mail: secretariat@bonnagreement.org
www.bonnagreement.org
Overview: A small international organization founded in 1969
Mission: To provide a cooperation forum for dealing with accidental marine pollution of the North Sea & marine pollution aerial surveillance
Chief Officer(s):
M. Michel Aymeric, Chair
Membership: 9 European & EU countries; *Fees:* Annual contribution

Boreal Institute for Northern Studies (1960-1990) ***See*** Canadian Circumpolar Institute

Boundary Organic Producers Association (BOPA)
PO Box 675, Grand Forks BC V0H 1H0
Tel: 250-442-5840
Overview: A small local licensing organization
Affiliation(s): Certified Organic Associations of BC
Chief Officer(s):
Karl Lilgert, President
Christine Carlson, Administrator
christine@slowkettle.org
Finances: *Annual Operating Budget:* Less than $50,000
Staff: 1 staff member(s)
Membership: 10-15 certified organic operators & associate members; *Fees:* $25; *Member Profile:* Organic producers & processors; *Committees:* Certification
Activities: Organic certification of producers & processors

Bowen Nature Club
RR#1, CL-27, Bowen Island BC V0N 1G0
Tel: 604-947-9562
e-mail: bowennatureclub@gmail.com
bowennatureclub.blogspot.ca
Overview: A small local organization founded in 1985
Mission: To promote the enjoyment of nature through environmental appreciation & conservation; To encourage wise use & conservation of natural resources & environmental protection; *Member of:* Federation of BC Naturalists
Membership: *Fees:* $18 individual; $22 family

Brampton Horticultural Society
PO Box 92546, 160 Main St. South, Brampton ON L6W 4R1
e-mail: bramhort@hotmail.com
bramptonhort.org
Overview: A small local charitable organization founded in 1895
Member of: Ontario Horticultural Association
Chief Officer(s):
Fran Caldwell, President
Wendy Lovegrove, Secretary
Membership: *Fees:* $19 single; $26 family; $14 senior single; $20 senior family; $2.50 junior

Brantford Lapidary & Mineral Society Inc. (BLMS)
1 Sherwood Dr., Brantford ON N3T 1N3
e-mail: brantfordlapclub@live.ca
www.brantfordlapidarymineral.ca
Overview: A small local organization founded in 1964
Mission: To increase interest in the earth sciences & related lapidary arts
Chief Officer(s):
Ernie Edmonds, President, 519-583-9457
John Moons, Vice-President, 519-752-9756
Campbell.moons@silomail.com
Kim LeBlanc, Secretary, 519-442-7372
marcell@execulink.com
Darren Gage, Treasurer, 519-758-8426
darren_gage@hotmail.com
Russ McCrory, Librarian, 905-389-6526
russelldavid.mccrory@sympatico.ca
Membership: *Fees:* $15 single membership; $18 family
Activities: Offering lapidary training; Providing equipment access; Organizing monthly meetings; Arranging field trips; *Library:* Brantford Lapidary & Mineral Society Library
Publications:
•The Telephone City Crystal [a publication of the Brantford Lapidary & Mineral Society, Inc.]
Type: Newsletter; *Editor:* Marcel LeBlanc
Profile: Information about lapidary & minerals, equipment advice, & forthcoming events

Brereton Field Naturalists' Club Inc. (BFN)
PO Box 1084, Barrie ON L4M 5E1
www.breretonfieldnaturalists.org
Overview: A small local charitable organization founded in 1951
Mission: To acquire & disseminate knowledge of natural history; to protect & preserve wildlife; to stimulate public interest in nature & its preservation; Affiliation(s): Federation of Ontario Naturalists
Chief Officer(s):
Brian Gibbon, Contact, 705-726-8969
bwg@backland.net
Finances: *Annual Operating Budget:* Less than $50,000; *Funding Sources:* Membership fees
Staff: 95 volunteer(s)
Membership: 125; *Fees:* $10 student; $15 corresponding; $25 individual; $30 family; *Committees:* Conservation; Education; Field Trips; Newsletter; Program
Activities: Bird-watching outings; nature strolls; lunches; *Speaker Service:* Yes; *Library:* BFN Library; Open to public by appointment
Publications:
•The Blue Heron
Type: Newsletter; *Frequency:* Annually

British Columbia & Yukon Chamber of Mines ***See*** Association for Mineral Exploration British Columbia

British Columbia Agriculture Council
Parent Name: Canadian Federation of Agriculture
#230, 32160 South Fraser Way, Abbotsford BC V2T 1W5
Tel: 604-854-4454; *Fax:* 604-854-4485
Toll-Free: 866-522-3477
e-mail: bcac@bcagcouncil.com
www.bcac.bc.ca
Overview: A medium-sized provincial organization founded in 1997 overseen by Canadian Federation of Agriculture
Mission: To provide leadership in representing, promoting, & advocating the collective interests of all agriculture producers in the province of British Colombia; To foster cooperation & a collective response to matters affecting the future of agriculture in the province; To facilitate programs & service delivery for a number of programs that benefit the industry

British Columbia Association for Regenerative Agriculture (BCARA)
PO Box 1601, Aldergrove BC V4W 2V1
Tel: 778-240-8746
e-mail: bcara.admin@gmail.com
newcity.ca/Pages/regener_agricult.html
Overview: A small provincial organization
Affiliation(s): Certified Organic Associations of BC
Chief Officer(s):
Sarah Davidson, Administrator
Susan Davidson, President
Membership: 100-499

British Columbia Association of Agricultural Fairs & Exhibitions (BCAAFE)
18231 - 60th Ave., Surrey BC V3S 1V7
Tel: 778-574-4082
e-mail: info@bcfairs.ca
www.bcfairs.ca
www.facebook.com/BCFairs
twitter.com/BCFairs
Previous Name: The Provincial Agricultural Fairs Association
Overview: A small provincial organization founded in 1910
Mission: To celebrate the importance of agriculture in British Columbia; To represent agricultural fairs, exhibitions, & related events throughout British Columbia
Environmental Activity: Increasing awareness of agriculture in communities throughout British Columbia
Chief Officer(s):
Janine Saw, Executive Director
jbsaw@bcfairs.ca
Leah North Hryko, President, 250-338-0165
lhryko@shaw.ca
Pamela Brenner, Chair, Finance, 604-823-2109, Fax: 604-852-6631
pamela.agrifair@telus.net
Finances: *Funding Sources:* Fundraising; Sponsorships
Membership: *Committees:* Agriculture Awareness & Education; Annual Awards Program; B.C. 4-H Liaison; BCAAFE Annual Scholarship; By-laws, Constitution, & Board Policies; Conference & Annual General Meeting; Evaluation Program; Finance; Fundraising & Sponsorship; Government & Corporate Relations; Media & Public Relations; Nominating; Membership
Activities: Educating the public about the importance of agriculture; Offering resources & services to agricultural exhibitions & fairs; Providing networking opportunities;
Publications:
•BC Fairs LiveWire
Type: Newsletter; *Frequency:* Quarterly; *Accepts Advertising*
Profile: Developments on the agricultural fair circuit across British Columbia

British Columbia Automobile Association (BCAA)
Parent Name: Canadian Automobile Association
4567 Canada Way, Burnaby BC V5G 4T1
Toll-Free: 877-325-8888; *Crisis Hot-Line: 800-222-4357*
www.bcaa.com
Overview: A large provincial organization founded in 1906 overseen by Canadian Automobile Association
Mission: To provide motoring, travel, & insurance services to members in British Columbia & the Yukon; *Member of:* Canadian Automobile Association (CAA); American Automobile Association (AAA)
Environmental Activity: Implementing office recycling programs, staff carpooling, & road service fleet motoroil recycling; Serving as a member of several joint government/business air quality committees
Chief Officer(s):
Timothy J. Condon, President & CEO
Brenda Lowden, Senior Vice-President, People & Community
Collin MacKinnon, Senior Vice-President & Chief Risk Officer
Ken Ontko, Senior Vice-President & CIO
Greg Oyhenart, Sr. VP & Chief Member Experience Officer
Heidi Worthington, Sr. Vice-President & Chief Marketing Officer
Finances: *Annual Operating Budget:* Greater than $5 Million; *Funding Sources:* Membership fees
Staff: 1000 staff member(s)
Membership: 790,000; *Committees:* Human Resources; Finance & Investment; Audit; Governance
Activities: *Internships:* Yes
Publications:
•BCAA [British Columbia Automobile Association] Newsletter
Type: Newsletter

British Columbia Bottle Depot Association (BCBDA)
9850 King George Hwy., Surrey BC V3T 4Y3
Tel: 604-930-0003; *Fax:* 604-930-0060
e-mail: bcbda@telus.net
www.bcbda.com
Overview: A small provincial organization founded in 1997
Mission: To further the interests of association members through representation; To support a healthy environment by promoting recycling programs
Chief Officer(s):
Corinne Atwood, Executive Director
Grant Robertson, Chair
grobertson@bcbda.com
Kulbir Rana, Secretary-Treasurer
krana@bcbda.com
Finances: *Funding Sources:* Membership fees
Membership: *Member Profile:* Bottle depots in British Columbia
Activities: Liaising with government & industry partners; Assisting the public by maintaining a website with information about depot locations, sales, & what each depot accepts for recycling

British Columbia Camping Association
Parent Name: Canadian Camping Association
c/o Sasamat Outdoor Centre, 3302 Senkler Rd., Belcarra BC V3H 4S3
Tel: 604-931-6449; *Fax:* 604-939-8522
e-mail: info@bccamping.org
www.bccamping.org
Overview: A medium-sized provincial organization overseen by Canadian Camping Association
Mission: To facilitate the development of organized camping in order to provide educational, character-building & constructive recreational experiences for all people; to develop awareness & appreciation of the natural environment
Chief Officer(s):
Hart Banack, President
Activities: *Rents Mailing List:* Yes

British Columbia Cattlemen's Association (BCCA)
#4, 10145 Dallas Dr., Kamloops BC V2C 6T4
Tel: 250-573-3611; *Fax:* 250-573-5155
Toll-Free: 877-688-2333
e-mail: info@cattlemen.bc.ca
www.cattlemen.bc.ca
Also Known As: BC Cattlemen
Overview: A medium-sized provincial organization founded in 1929
Mission: To develop & protect the cattle industry in British Columbia; To act as the official voice of the beef cattle industry in British Columbia; To act in an environmentally responsible manner; To provide quality beef products to consumers; Affiliation(s): Canadian Cattlemen's Association
Environmental Activity: Providing the the Environmental Farm Planning Program; Offering the Farmland-Riparian Interface Stewardship Program to assist ranchers to achieve best management practices; Promoting environmental stewardship
Chief Officer(s):
Roland Baumann, President
Kevin Boon, General Manager, 250-573-3611
bccattle@kamloops.net
Elaine Stovin, Coordinator, Communications, 250-573-3611
estovin@kamloops.net
Finances: *Funding Sources:* Sponsorships
Membership: 1,300; *Fees:* $101; *Member Profile:* Cattle producers in British Columbia; *Committees:* Land Stewardship & Aboriginal Affairs; Environmental Stewardship; Public Affairs, Education & Research; Livestock Industry Protection; Finance & Taxation
Activities: Providing input on government regulations related to ranching; Advocating for cattle producers; Liaising with local, provincial, & federal government officials; Sponsoring courses at the Rangeland Management School; Providing industry information; Increasing awarenss of the beef industry & its issues; Offering various programs, such as the Dam Inspection Program & the BC Highways Fencing Program; Researching; Collaborating with the Canadian Beef Export Federation to expand foreign markets; Protecting landowner rights;
Publications:
•Beef In BC
Type: Magazine; *Frequency:* 7 pa; *Accepts Advertising*; *Editor:* Diane Edstrom; *Price:* $24 Canada; $34 USA
Profile: Association reports & articles about issues important to the cattle production industry
•British Columbia Cattlemen's Association Newsletter
Type: Newsletter; *Frequency:* Monthly

British Columbia Chicken Growers' Association (BCCGA)
PO Box 581, Abbotsford BC V2T 6Z8
Tel: 604-859-9332; *Fax:* 604-853-4808
e-mail: bccga@telus.net
www.bcchicken.ca
Overview: A small provincial organization founded in 1957
Mission: To represent chicken producers in British Columbia; To work towards a stable industry; Affiliation(s): BC Chicken Marketing Board; BC Agriculture Council; BC Poultry Association; BC Sustainable Poultry Farming Group
Environmental Activity: Serving on biosecurity, food safety, & animal welfare committees
Chief Officer(s):
Ravi Bathe, President
Margret Duin, Administrator
Membership: 340; *Member Profile:* Commercial chicken growers in British Columbia
Activities: Distributing information to chicken growers; Engaging in lobbying activities; Developing a Poultry in Motion mobile barn in partnership with the BC Broiler Hatching Egg Producers' Association to educate consumers & raise public awareness

British Columbia Conservation Foundation (BCCF)
#206, 17564 - 56A Ave., Surrey BC V3S 1G3
Tel: 604-576-1433; *Fax:* 604-576-1482
e-mail: hoffice@bccf.com
www.bccf.com
Overview: A medium-sized provincial organization founded in 1969
Mission: The British Columbia Conservation Foundation (BCCF) was founded and incorporated under the Society Act of British Columbia in 1969, by the Directors of the BC Wildlife Federation, to contribute significantly to the perpetuation and expansion of fish and wildlife populations through the efficient implementation of projects in the field. They are a federally registered charity dedicated to the conservation and stewardship of British Columbia's ecosystems and species.
Membership: 30
Activities: Four regional offices

British Columbia Construction Association (BCCA)
Parent Name: Canadian Construction Association
#401, 655 Tyee Rd., Victoria BC V9A 6X5
Tel: 250-475-1077; *Fax:* 250-475-1078
www.bccassn.com
www.facebook.com/WeBuildBC
twitter.com/WeBuildBC
www.youtube.com/user/BCCASSN
Overview: A large provincial organization founded in 1969 overseen by Canadian Construction Association
Mission: To provide excellence in the representation of & service to British Columbia's construction industry
Chief Officer(s):
Manley McLachlan, President & CEO
Abigail Fulton, Vice-President, Government Relations
Warren Perks, Vice-President & Director, Industry Practices
Jen Reid, Coordinator, Marketing & Communications
Finances: *Funding Sources:* Membership dues; Group benefit plan; Industry forms; Publications
Staff: 13 volunteer(s)
Membership: 2,000 companies + 4 regional associations
Publications:
•British Columbia Construction Association Member Bulletin
Type: Bulletin
•Construction File [a publication of the British Columbia Construction Association]
Type: Newsletter
•Green Building Market Update [a publication of the British Columbia Construction Association]
Type: Newsletter
•Issue Update [a publication of the British Columbia Construction Association]
Type: Newsletter

British Columbia Environment Industry Association (BCEIA)
#400, 602 West Hastings St., Vancouver BC V6B 1P2
Tel: 604-683-2751; *Fax:* 604-677-5960
e-mail: info@bceia.com
www.bceia.com
twitter.com/BCEIA_
Previous Name: Canadian Environment Industry Association - British Columbia Chapter
Overview: A medium-sized provincial organization founded in 1992

Mission: To develop the environmental industry in British Columbia; To promote technological development
Environmental Activity: Increasing awareness of the environmental industry
Chief Officer(s):
Frank Came, President
frank.came@bceia.com
Charles Bois, Secretary-Treasurer
Membership: *Member Profile:* Engineering & environmental service companies; Research organizations; Technology providers; Disaster response organizations; Environmental law firms; Environmental analysts & consultants; Government agencies; *Committees:* Contaminated sites & Brownfields; Hazardous waste; Executive; Energy conservation & efficiency; Eduction & professional development; First Nations; International affairs; Business development; Task forces
Activities: Networking within the environmental industry; Engaging in advocacy activities; Providing market & regulatory information; Offering professional development seminars on environmental related topics
Publications:
•British Columbia Environment Industry Association Newsletter
Type: Newsletter; *Frequency:* Weekly; *Price:* Free with British Columbia Environment Industry Association membership
Profile: Association announcements & upcoming events
•Environmental Product & Services Directory
Type: Directory; *Accepts Advertising*
Profile: Comprehensive listings available to British Columbia Environment Industry Association members

British Columbia Environmental Network (BCEN)
Parent Name: Canadian Environmental Network

#461, 1755 Robson St., Vancouver BC V6G 3B7
Tel: 604-515-1969
www.ecobc.org
Overview: A medium-sized provincial organization founded in 1979 overseen by Canadian Environmental Network
Mission: To facilitate communication among environmental groups & individuals so that ecological sustainability & economic stability prevail, & biological diversity & human health remain viable
Chief Officer(s):
David Boehm, Treasurer
Finances: *Annual Operating Budget:* $50,000-$100,000
Staff: 2 staff member(s); 15 volunteer(s)
Membership: 419 groups; *Fees:* $40 for groups under 100 individuals; $80 for groups over 100 individuals; *Member Profile:* Open to non-profit environmental groups promoting environmental integrity; *Committees:* Steering
Activities: *Speaker Service:* Yes; *Rents Mailing List:* Yes

British Columbia Farm Industry Review Board (BCFIRB)

PO Box 9129, Stn. Prov. Govt., 1007 Fort St., 3rd Fl., Victoria BC V8W 9B5
Tel: 250-356-8945; *Fax:* 250-356-5131
e-mail: firb@gov.bc.ca
www.firb.gov.bc.ca
Previous Name: British Columbia Marketing Board (BCMB)
Merged from: British Columbia Marketing Board (BCMB) & The Farm Practices Board (FPB)
Overview: A medium-sized provincial organization founded in 1934
Mission: To act in accordance with the Natural Products Marketing (BC) Act, the Agricultural Produce Grading Act, & the Farm Practices Protection (Right to Farm) Act; To supervise regulated marketing boards; To hear complaints regarding agriculture or aquaculture operations; To hear appeals from those who have had grading licenses refused, suspended, or revoked; To serve & protect the public interest
Chief Officer(s):
Jim Collins, Executive Director
Ron Kilmury, Chair
Shane Ford, Manager, Issues & Planning
Activities: Studying & reporting on farm practices in British Columbia; Promoting cooperation between urban & agricultural interests; Meeting regularly with commodity boards
Publications:
•British Columbia Farm Industry Review Board Strategic Plan

British Columbia Farm Machinery & Agriculture Museum Association

9131 King St., Fort Langley BC V1M 2R9
Tel: 604-888-2273
e-mail: bcfm@telus.net
www.bcfma.com
Also Known As: BC Farm Museum
Overview: A small provincial charitable organization founded in 1958
Member of: British Columbia Museums Association
Chief Officer(s):
Syd Pickerell, P.Ag (Ret)., President
Membership: *Fees:* $10
Activities: Operating a museum with a collection of farm artifacts, such as carriages, wagons, & tractors, a sawmill, & a blacksmith shop; *Library:* British Columbia Farm Machinery & Agriculture Museum Library; Open to public

British Columbia Food Technolgists (BCTF)
Parent Name: Canadian Institute of Food Science & Technology

c/o Nilmini Wijewickreme, SGS Canada, 50-655 West Kent Ave. North, Vancouver BC V6P 6T7
e-mail: info@bcft.ca
www.bcft.ca
www.facebook.com/group.php?gid=180485308680605
twitter.com/bcfoodtech
Overview: A small provincial organization overseen by Canadian Institute of Food Science & Technology
Mission: To advance food science & technology in British Columbia; *Member of:* Canadian Institute of Food Science & Technology; Institute of Food Technologists; Affiliation(s): Packaging Association of British Columbia; British Columbia Food Protection Association; British Columbia Nutraceutical Network
Environmental Activity: Promoting the quality & safety of the food supply by applying science & technology
Chief Officer(s):
Reena Mistry, Chair
chair@bcft.ca
Jenny Li, Secretary
jli@shafer-haggart.com
Thu Pham, Treasurer
Erin Friesen, Chair, Membership
membership@bcft.ca
Peter Taylor, Chair, Program, Banquet, & Suppliers' Night Committee
taylor58@telus.net
Nilmini Wijewickreme, Chair, Advertising
nilmini_wijewickreme@sgs.com
Membership: *Member Profile:* Scientists & technologists from government, academia, & industry; *Committees:* Advertising; Banquet; Membership; Program
Activities: Engaging in advocacy activities; Offering networking opportunities
Meetings/Conferences:
For more information see Trade Shows, Conferences and Seminars Chapter
British Columbia Food Technologists 2013 Annual Suppliers' Night
February 2013 Burnaby, BC
Publications:
•Tech Talk: The British Columbia Food Technolgists Newsletter
Type: Newsletter; *Frequency:* Monthly; *Accepts Advertising*; *Editor:* Brian Jang; *Price:* Free with membership in British Columbia Food Technolgists
Profile: Association information, meetings, & food-related activities on the local & international scene, for persons involved in areas suchas food processing, research, product development, quality control, sales, & management

British Columbia Fruit Growers' Association

1473 Water St., Kelowna BC V1Y 1J6
Tel: 250-762-5226; *Fax:* 250-861-9089
e-mail: info@bcfga.com
www.bcfga.com
www.facebook.com/pages/BC-Fruit-Growers-Association/20833 1935875260
Overview: A medium-sized provincial organization
Mission: To represent fruit growers' interests in British Columbia
Chief Officer(s):
Joe Sardinha, President
Membership: *Member Profile:* Fruit growers in British Columbia
Activities: Lobbying the government for positive change to risk management programs, such as crop insurance & the Net Income Stablization Program; Providing services & products to growers
Meetings/Conferences:
For more information see Trade Shows, Conferences and Seminars Chapter
BC Fruit Growers Association Special General Meeting 2013
November 2013 Kelowna, BC

British Columbia Fuchsia & Begonia Society

c/o #17, 910 Fort Fraser Rise, Port Coquitlam BC V3C 6K3
e-mail: info@bcfuchsiasociety.com
www.bcfuchsiasociety.com
Overview: A small provincial organization founded in 1961
Mission: The Society encourages the cultivation & promotion of fuchsias, begonias, ferns, gesneriads & all other shade-loving plants.; *Member of:* BC Council of Garden Clubs
Chief Officer(s):
Fran Carter, President
Lorna Herchenson, Int'l Corresponding Secretary
lherchenson@telus.net
Diane Rudd, Membership Contact
Finances: *Annual Operating Budget:* Less than $50,000; *Funding Sources:* Membership dues; plant sales; raffles
Staff: 185 volunteer(s)
Membership: 185; *Fees:* $18 single; $23 family
Activities: Meetings; workshops; plant sales; speaking to the community & other garden clubs; *Awareness Events:* Annual Show & Competition; *Speaker Service:* Yes; *Library:* Open to public

British Columbia Ground Water Association (BCGWA)
Parent Name: Canadian Ground Water Association

1708 - 197A St., Langley BC V2Z 1K2
Tel: 604-530-8934; *Fax:* 604-530-8934
e-mail: secretary@bcgwa.org
www.bcgwa.org
Overview: A small provincial organization overseen by Canadian Ground Water Association
Affiliation(s): Canadian Ground Water Association
Chief Officer(s):
Joan Perry, Secretary
Membership: *Member Profile:* Corporations that employ persons who work in water well contracting, manufacturing, or supplying materials & equipment; Individuals employed by a company or who belong to an association affiliated with the ground water industry
Activities: Offering workshops & seminars; Promoting research & standards in water well construction; Liaising with government agencies
Publications:
•British Columbia Ground Water Association Newsletter
Type: Newsletter; *Frequency:* Quarterly

British Columbia Herb Growers Association (BCHGA)

998 Skeena Dr., Kelowna BC V1V 2K7
Tel: 604-824-2833
Overview: A small provincial organization founded in 1997
Mission: To promote & enhance herb growing in British Columbia; To represent herb growers
Finances: *Funding Sources:* Sponsorships
Membership: 50; *Fees:* $50 individuals; $75 foreign memberships; $125 corporations; *Member Profile:* Individuals & corporations involved in the herb business, such asresearchers, educators, growers, manufacturers, processors, buyers, distributors, retailers, & service providers
Activities: Facilitating research; Providing networking opportunities; Offering market information; Organizing workshops; Supporting herb marketing
Publications:
•BCHGA [British Columbia Herb Growers Association] Newsletter
Type: Newsletter; *Frequency:* Quarterly; *Accepts Advertising*
Profile: Upcoming meetings, trade shows, & educational opportunities, association reports, & articles
•British Columbia Herb Growers Association Annual Report
Type: Yearbook; *Frequency:* Annually
•British Columbia Herb Growers Association Directory
Type: Directory
Profile: Listing of association members with contact information

British Columbia Institute of Agrologists (BCIA)
Parent Name: Agricultural Institute of Canada

2777 Claude Rd., Victoria BC V9B 3T7
Tel: 250-380-9292; *Fax:* 250-380-9233
Toll-Free: 877-855-9291
e-mail: p.ag@bcia.com
www.bcia.com
Overview: A medium-sized provincial licensing organization founded in 1947 overseen by Agricultural Institute of Canada
Chief Officer(s):
Kelly McLaughlin, Financial Officer
Robert Moody, Executive Director

Finances: *Annual Operating Budget:* $250,000-$500,000; *Funding Sources:* Membership dues
Staff: 2 staff member(s); 20 volunteer(s)
Membership: 950; *Fees:* $150; *Member Profile:* Professional agrologists
Activities: *Internships:* Yes
Meetings/Conferences:
For more information see Trade Shows, Conferences and Seminars Chapter
British Columbia Institute of Agrologists 66th Annual General Meeting & Conference 2013
April 2013 Cranbrook, BC

British Columbia Investment Agriculture Foundation (IAF)
PO Box 8248, 808 Douglas Victoria, 3rd Fl., Victoria BC V8W 2Z7
Tel: 250-356-1662; *Fax:* 250-953-5162
e-mail: info@iafbc.ca
www.iafbc.ca
Also Known As: Investment Agriculture Foundation of BC
Overview: A medium-sized provincial organization founded in 1996
Mission: To encourage growth & innovation in the agriculture & agri-food industry across British Columbia
Chief Officer(s):
Peter Levelton, Chair
Peter Donkers, Executive Director, 250-356-6654
pdonkers@iafbc.ca
Finances: *Funding Sources:* Federal & provincial government
Publications:
•Growing Tomorrow [a publication of British Columbia Investment Agriculture Foundation]
Type: Newsletter; *Frequency:* 3 pa

British Columbia Landscape & Nursery Association (BCLNA)
Parent Name: Canadian Nursery Landscape Association
#102, 5783 - 176A St., Surrey BC V3S 6S6
Tel: 604-575-3500; *Fax:* 604-574-7773
Toll-Free: 800-421-7963
www.bclna.com
Previous Name: British Columbia Nursery Trades Association
Overview: A medium-sized provincial organization founded in 1953 overseen by Canadian Nursery Landscape Association
Mission: To work together to improve quality & standards of the industry; *Member of:* BC Agriculture Council
Chief Officer(s):
Lesley Tannen, Executive Director
ltannen@bclna.com
Finances: *Annual Operating Budget:* $1.5 Million-$3 Million; *Funding Sources:* Membership dues; CanWest Horticultural Show
Staff: 10 staff member(s)
Membership: 800; *Fees:* $370-$980, based on gross sales; *Member Profile:* Nurserymen, garden centre operators, landscape & maintenance contractors, sod growers, arborists & suppliers from across British Columbia
Activities: Educational seminars; certification programs

British Columbia Lodging & Campgrounds Association (BCLCA)
#209, 3003 St. John's St., Port Moody BC V3H 2C4
Tel: 778-383-1037; *Fax:* 604-945-7606
www.bclca.com
www.facebook.com/TravellinginBritishColumbia
twitter.com/TravellinginBC
Previous Name: BC Motels, Campgrounds, Resorts Association
Overview: A medium-sized provincial organization founded in 1944
Mission: To promote the public's utilization of member lodging & campground businesses; to monitor & make representation to governments on legislation affecting the interests of British Columbia's lodging & campground businesses; to speak for the membership on matters of general or specific interest; to encourage members to strive for excellence in accommodation & service
Chief Officer(s):
Joss Penny, Executive Director
jpenny@bclca.com
Finances: *Annual Operating Budget:* $250,000-$500,000
Staff: 3 staff member(s)
Membership: 625; *Fees:* $280; *Member Profile:* Motels; resorts; campgrounds
Activities: Marketing & promotion; group purchasing discounts; lobbying; education & industry standards

British Columbia Lung Association (BCLA)
Parent Name: Canadian Lung Association
2675 Oak St., Vancouver BC V6H 2K2
Tel: 604-731-5864; *Fax:* 604-731-5810
Toll-Free: 800-665-5864
e-mail: info@bc.lung.ca
www.bc.lung.ca
www.facebook.com/home.php?#!/BCLungAssociation
Previous Name: Anti-Tuberculosis Society
Overview: A medium-sized provincial charitable organization founded in 1906 overseen by Canadian Lung Association
Mission: To support lung health research, education, prevention, & advocacy; To help people manage respiratory diseases, including asthma, COPD (chronic bronchitis and emphysema), lung cancer, sleep apnea, & tuberculosis
Environmental Activity: Providing information on lung health & air quality issues
Chief Officer(s):
Scott McDonald, Executive Director
Kelly Ablog-Morrant, Director, Health Education & Program Services
Chris Lam, Manager, Development
Katrina van Bylandt, Manager, Communications
Debora Wong, Manager, Finance & Administration
Marissa McFadyen, Coordinator, Specia Events
Finances: *Funding Sources:* Donations; Sponsorships; Fundraising
Membership: *Committees:* Executive; Medical Advisory
Activities: Providing money to physicians & scientists doing research in British Columbia on lung diseases; Offering breathing test events; *Awareness Events:* The Stairclimb for Clean Air, February; The Bicycle Trek for Life & Breath, September
Meetings/Conferences:
For more information see Trade Shows, Conferences and Seminars Chapter
British Columbia Lung Association 2013 10th Annual Air Quality & Health Workshop
February 2013 Vancouver, BC
British Columbia Lung Association 2013 Annual General Meeting 2013, BC
Publications:
•British Columbia Lung Association Annual Report
Type: Yearbook; *Frequency:* Annually
•Your Health
Type: Magazine; *Frequency:* Semiannually; *Editor:* Katrina van Bylandt; Destin Haynes
Profile: Health information for medical & health promoters, educators, donors to the Lung Association, & persons interested in respiratory health

British Columbia Marine Trades Association (BCMTA)
#300, 1275 West 6th Ave., Vancouver BC V6H 1A6
Tel: 604-683-5191; *Fax:* 604-893-8808
e-mail: info@bcmta.com
www.bcmta.com
Overview: A medium-sized provincial organization
Mission: To act as the voice of the BC recreational marine industry
Chief Officer(s):
Alan Stovell, President
stovell@westernmarine.com
Kim Barbero, Executive Director, 604-683-5191, Fax: 604-893-8808
kim@bcmta.com
Chris Goulder, Treasurer, 604-872-7511, Fax: 604-872-4606
christopher.goulder@volvo.com
Finances: *Annual Operating Budget:* $50,000-$100,000
Membership: 300 corporate; *Fees:* $295-395

British Columbia Marketing Board (BCMB) *See* British Columbia Farm Industry Review Board

British Columbia Medical Association (BCMA)
Parent Name: Canadian Medical Association
#115, 1665 West Broadway, Vancouver BC V6J 5A4
Tel: 604-736-5551; *Fax:* 604-736-4566
Toll-Free: 800-665-2262
e-mail: communications@bcma.bc.ca
www.bcma.org
Overview: A medium-sized provincial organization founded in 1900 overseen by Canadian Medical Association
Mission: To promote a social, economic & political climate in which members can provide the citizens of British Columbia with the highest standard of health care while achieving maximum professional satisfaction & fair economic reward.
Chief Officer(s):
Brian Brodie, President
president@bcma.bc.ca
Membership: 11,000; *Committees:* Environmental Health
Activities: Programs to explore & articulate concerns regarding environmental health issues in a fashion which will best enable an informed public to participate in an open, valid, scientifically based analysis of issues involved; to assist society in development of policies dealing with environmental health issues; to enhance public health & harmony between humans & nature; Waste Management; Water Quality; Air Quality; *Internships:* Yes; *Speaker Service:* Yes; *Rents Mailing List:* Yes; *Library:*

British Columbia Nature (Federation of British Columbia Naturalists) (FBCN)
c/o Parks Heritage Centre, 1620 Mount Seymour Rd., North Vancouver BC V7G 2R9
Tel: 604-985-3057
e-mail: manager@bcnature.ca
www.bcnature.ca
Previous Name: Nature Council of British Columbia
Overview: A medium-sized provincial organization founded in 1969
Mission: To protect biodiversity, species at risk, & natural areas throughout British Columbia; To present a unified voice on conservation & environmental issues
Environmental Activity: Implementing conservation & stewardship projects; Fostering awareness & understanding of the natural environment; Providing a means of communication between British Columbia naturalists; Offering field trips, such as birding & marine biology outings
Chief Officer(s):
Betty Davison, Office Manager, 604-985-3057
manager@bcnature.ca
Bev Ramey, President
bevramey@telus.net
Rosemary Fox, Chair, Conservation
foxikrj@bulkley.net
Elisa Kreller, Treasurer
elisakreller@shaw.ca
Maria Hamann, Office Manager
Joan Snyder, Chair, Education
snowdance@columbiawireless.ca
Pat Westheuser, Chair, Awards
hughwest@shaw.ca
Finances: *Funding Sources:* Membership fees; Donations; Fundraising
Membership: 50+ local nature clubs; *Fees:* $20; *Member Profile:* Naturalists, biologists, academics, environmentalists, nature experts, local natural history groups, & nature clubs throughout British Columbia; *Committees:* Conservation; Education; Awards
Activities: Providing educational opportunities; Coordinating stewardship projects
Meetings/Conferences:
For more information see Trade Shows, Conferences and Seminars Chapter
British Columbia Nature (Federation of British Columbia Naturalists) 2013 Nature Conference & Annual General Meeting
May 2013 Abbotsford, BC
British Columbia Nature (Federation of British Columbia Naturalists) 2014 Nature Conference & Annual General Meeting
2014, BC
Publications:
•BC Nature Magazine
Type: Magazine; *Frequency:* Quarterly; *Accepts Advertising*; *Price:* Free with membership in the British Columbia Nature (Federation of BC Naturalists)
Profile: Club news, conservation information, & book reviews

British Columbia Nursery Trades Association *See* British Columbia Landscape & Nursery Association

British Columbia Oyster Growers' Association *See* British Columbia Shellfish Growers Association

British Columbia Paint Manufacturers' Association (BCPMA)
c/o Cloverdale Paint Inc., 6950 King George Blvd., Surrey BC V3W 4Z1
Tel: 604-596-6261; *Fax:* 604-597-2677
e-mail: helpdesk@cloverdalepaint.com

Overview: A small provincial organization founded in 1933
Mission: To act as the voice of paint manufacturers in British Columbia; To promote the welfare of association members
Chief Officer(s):
Ed Linton, President, 604-596-6261, Fax: 604-597-2677
Ron Vanderdrift, Vice-President, 604-521-7779, Fax: 604-521-2323
Deryk Pawsey, Secretary, 604-541-2569
Yvon Poitras, Treasurer, 604-575-3188, Fax: 604-575-3184
Membership: 1-99; *Member Profile:* Paint manufacturing companies in British Columbia
Activities: Engaging in advocacy activities related to the paint manufacturing industry in British Columbia; Liaising with various levels of government

British Columbia Ready Mixed Concrete Association Parent Name: Canadian Ready Mixed Concrete Association

26162 - 30A Ave., Aldergrove BC V4W 2W5
Tel: 604-626-4141; *Fax:* 604-626-4143
e-mail: ccampbell@bcrmca.bc.ca
www.bcrmca.bc.ca
Overview: A medium-sized provincial organization overseen by Canadian Ready Mixed Concrete Association
Mission: To work cooperatively with all levels of government to ensure the ready-mix concrete industry operates with a focus on the communities & the environment
Chief Officer(s):
Carolyn Campbell, Executive Director

British Columbia Recreation & Parks Association (BCRPA) Parent Name: Canadian Parks & Recreation Association

#101, 4664 Lougheed Hwy., Burnaby BC V5C 5T5
Tel: 604-629-0965; *Fax:* 604-629-2651
Toll-Free: 866-929-0965
e-mail: bcrpa@bcrpa.bc.ca
www.bcrpa.bc.ca
Overview: A medium-sized provincial charitable organization founded in 1958 overseen by Canadian Parks & Recreation Association
Mission: To establish & sustain healthy lifestyles & communities in British Columbia
Environmental Activity: Fostering economic & environmental sustainability
Chief Officer(s):
Dean Gibson, President
Suzanne Allard Strutt, Chief Executive Officer
sstrutt@bcrpa.bc.ca
Holly-Ann Burrows, Manager, Communication
hburrows@bcrpa.bc.ca
Sandra Couto, Manager, Finance
scouto@bcrpa.bc.ca
Kara Misra, Manager, Parks & Recreation
kmisra@bcrpa.bc.ca
Misty Thomas, Manager, Fitness Program
mthomas@bcrpa.bc.ca
Finances: *Funding Sources:* Membership fees; Donations
Membership: *Fees:* Free, 1st year students; $60 individual goverment members; $245 individual independent members; Schedule based on population for local governments; *Member Profile:* Local governments, such as municipalities & regional districts; Corporations or commercial organizations; Not-for-profit organizations & educational institutions, connected to park, recreation, & cultural sectors; Individuals who work for or who are connected to a local government member; Students
Activities: Advocating accessibility & inclusiveness to recreation & physical activity; Providing training & resources; Distributing manuals on topics such as fitness theory, aquatic fitness group fitness, weight training, & yoga fitness
Meetings/Conferences:
For more information see Trade Shows, Conferences and Seminars Chapter
British Columbia Recreation & Parks Association 2013 36th Annual ProvincialParks & Grounds Spring Training Conference
February 2013 Surrey, BC
British Columbia Recreation & Parks Association 2013 Symposium: Building Healthy, Creative & Green Communities
May 2013 Whistler, BC
British Columbia Recreation & Parks Association 2013 Provincial Ripple Effects Aquatics Conference
2013, BC
Publications:
•British Columbia Recreation & Parks Association Annual Report
Type: Yearbook
•Recreation & Parks BC
Type: Magazine; *Frequency:* Quarterly
Profile: Happenings in the parks & recreation sector

British Columbia Salmon Farmers Association (BCSFA)

#201, 909 Island Hwy., Campbell River BC V9W 2C2
Tel: 250-286-1636
Toll-Free: 800-661-7256
e-mail: info@salmonfarmers.org
www.salmonfarmers.org
www.facebook.com/SalmonFarmers?ref=ts
twitter.com/BCSalmonFarmers
www.youtube.com/bcsalmonfarmers;
pinterest.com/bcsalmonfarmers
Overview: A small provincial organization founded in 1984
Mission: To act as the voice of British Columbia's farmed salmon industry; To advance the competitiveness & sustainable growth of the salmon farming industry
Environmental Activity: Requiring environmental stewardship, sustainability, & transparency of members
Chief Officer(s):
Mary Ellen Walling, Executive Director
mwalling@salmonfarmers.org
Colleen Dane, Manager, Communications, 250-286-1636 Ext. 225
colleen.dane@telus.net
Valerie Lamirande, Coordinator, Events
valerie.lamirande@telus.net
David Minato, Coordinator, Community & Member Relations, 250-286-1636 Ext. 224
david.minato@telus.net
Membership: *Member Profile:* Salmon farmers from British Columbia; Supply & service companies that support the salmon farming industry
Activities: Liaising with government; Educating the public
Publications:
•Catch! [a publication of the British Columbia Salmon Farmers Association]
Type: Newsletter; *Frequency:* Quarterly
Profile: Information for members & forthcoming events

British Columbia Shellfish Growers Association (BCSGA)

2002 Comox Ave., Unit F, Comox BC V9M 3M6
Tel: 250-890-7561; *Fax:* 250-890-7563
www.bcsga.ca
Previous Name: British Columbia Oyster Growers' Association
Overview: A small provincial organization founded in 1949
Mission: Advancing the sustainable growth & prosperity of the BC shellfish industry in a global economy by providing leadership & advocacy to members & stakeholders while maintaining the integrity of the marine environment; *Member of:* Canadian Aquaculture Industry Alliance; Aquaculture Association of Canada
Chief Officer(s):
Roberta Stevenson, Executive Director
roberta@bcsga.ca
Finances: *Annual Operating Budget:* $100,000-$250,000; *Funding Sources:* Membership fees
Staff: 2 staff member(s)
Membership: 181; *Fees:* $500
Activities: Advocacy; research & development; marketing; member services; *Library:* Open to public

British Columbia Society of Landscape Architects (BCSLA)

#110, 355 Burrard St., Vancouver BC V6C 2G8
Tel: 604-682-5610; *Fax:* 604-681-3394
e-mail: admin@bcsla.org
www.bcsla.org
Overview: A medium-sized provincial licensing organization founded in 1964
Mission: To promote, improve & advance the profession; to maintain standards of professional practice & conduct consistent with the need to serve & protect the public interest; to support the improvement &/or conservation of the natural, cultural, social & built environment.; *Member of:* Canadian Society of Landscape Architects
Chief Officer(s):
Pawel Gradowski, President
Finances: *Funding Sources:* Membership dues; special events; sponsors
Staff: 1 staff member(s); 13 volunteer(s)
Membership: 370; *Fees:* $550 landscape architect; $159 associate; $36 student; *Member Profile:* Must have university degree in landscape architecture followed by two years experience working for registered landscape architect; must complete series of exams.; *Committees:* Urban Issues; Membership; Ethics; Standards; Annual General Meeting; Promotion; Continuing Education
Activities: *Internships:* Yes

British Columbia Spaces for Nature

PO Box 673, Gibsons BC V0N 1V0
www.spacesfornature.org
Overview: A medium-sized provincial charitable organization founded in 1989
Mission: To protect British Columbia's wilderness resource
Environmental Activity: Providing education about caring for nature & conservation issues in British Columbia; Implementing the Tourism Zonation System, a land use planning approach that allows tourism in an environmentally sensitive & economically viable manner
Chief Officer(s):
Robert Ballantyne, Executive Member
Chloe O'Loughlin, Executive Member
Loretta Woodcock, Executive Member
Activities: Leading campaigns to protect wilderness areas throughout British Columbia; *Library:* British Columbia Spaces for Nature Library
Publications:
•Jobs & Environment: Moving British Columbia into the 21st Century
Type: Report; *Number of Pages:* 74
Profile: Policy options & recommendations for British Columbia's future
•Keeping the Special in Special Management Zones: A Citizens Guide [a publication of British Columbia Spaces for Nature]
Type: Report; *Number of Pages:* 143
Profile: Information about special management zones, or government designated land use planning areas, whereconservation is emphasized in management decisions
•Klinaklini Resource Analysis [a publication of British Columbia Spaces for Nature]
Type: Report; *Number of Pages:* 87
Profile: Suggestions for safeguarding the biodiversity of this interior-to-coastal watershed
•West Chilcotin Demonstration Project [a publication of British Columbia Spaces for Nature]
Type: Report; *Number of Pages:* 73
Profile: Collaboration between First Nations, the local community, the tourism industry, & the forest industry to create a sustainablefuture for the West Chilcotin

British Columbia Sustainable Energy Association (BCSEA)

#5, 4217 Glanford Ave., Victoria BC V8Z 4B9
Tel: 250-744-2720
e-mail: info@bcsea.org
www.bcsea.org
www.facebook.com/BCSEA
Overview: A medium-sized provincial organization founded in 2004
Mission: To empower British Columbians to build a clean, renewable energy future; *Member of:* Canadian Renewable Energy Alliance; Canadian Solar Industries Ass'n; Canadian Wind Energy Ass'n; Climate Action Network Canada; KyotoPLUS; Livable Region Coalition; Oil Free Coast Alliance; Organizing for Change: Priorities for Environmental Leadership
Environmental Activity: Offering the SolarBC project, Climate Change Showdown program, Clean Energy Classroom progject, & the Green Landlords program
Chief Officer(s):
Guy Dauncey, President
Finances: *Funding Sources:* Donations
Membership: *Fees:* Schedule available; *Member Profile:* Individuals & organizations
Activities: Providing education through programs & webinars
Meetings/Conferences:
For more information see Trade Shows, Conferences and Seminars Chapter
The Water Show 2013
October 2013 Abbotsford, BC

British Columbia Technology Industries Association (BCTIA)

#900, 1188 West Georgia St., Vancouver BC V6E 4A2
Tel: 604-683-6159; *Fax:* 604-683-3879
e-mail: info@bctia.org
www.bctia.org

Also Known As: BC Technology Industries Association
Merged from: Electronic Manufacturers' Association of BC & the Information Technology Assn of Canada, BC Chapter
Overview: A medium-sized provincial organization founded in 1993
Mission: To support the growth of a strong knowledge economy in British Columbia; To act as the voice of the technology industry
Chief Officer(s):
Bill Tam, President & Chief Executive Officer, 604-602-5230
btam@bctia.org
Cindy Pearson, Vice-President & Chief Operating Officer, 604-602-5234
cpearson@bctia.org
Peter Payne, Director, Business Intelligence, 604-602-5266
ppayne@bctia.org
Rebecca Clark, Coordinator, Program & Events, 604-602-5241
rclark@bctia.org
Caylee Stewart, Coordinator, Administration & Membership, 604-602-5233
cstewart@bctia.org
Wendy Turnbull, Specialist, Marketing Communications, 604-602-5231
wturnbull@bctia.org
Membership: 2700+ companies; *Member Profile:* Companies of all sizes, from all sectors
Activities: Offering professional development activities; Delivering programs, such as Xcelerate, an executive education program & PODIUM, an industry promotion program; Advocating on behalf of the industry; Facilitating partnerships; Increasing public awareness

British Columbia Trucking Association (BCTA) Parent Name: Canadian Trucking Alliance

#100, 20111 - 93A Ave., Langley BC V1M 4A9
Tel: 604-888-5319
e-mail: bcta@bctrucking.com
www.bctrucking.com
Previous Name: BC Motor Transport Association
Overview: A large provincial organization founded in 1913 overseen by Canadian Trucking Alliance
Mission: To act as the recognised voice of the commercial road transportation industry in British Columbia, by consulting & communicating with the industry, government, & the public; To promote a prosperous, safe, efficient & responsible road transportation industry; To provide programs & services to members
Chief Officer(s):
Louise Yako, President & Chief Executive Officer
Trace Acres, Vice-President
Greg Kolesniak, Director, Policy
Michele Nicol, Director, Business Operations
Veena Nanubhai, Coordinator, Accounting
Sandra Stashuk, Coordinator, Member Services
Shelley McGuinness, Specialist, Communications
Finances: *Funding Sources:* Membership dues
Membership: 1,000 corporate; *Fees:* $325-$400; *Member Profile:* Trucking company operating in BC; Supplier to trucking industry; *Committees:* Convention; Insurance; International; Labour; Freight Claims & Hazardous Goods; Safety; Truxpo; Vehicle Standards
Activities: *Speaker Service:* Yes; *Rents Mailing List:* Yes; *Library:* by appointment
Meetings/Conferences:
For more information see Trade Shows, Conferences and Seminars Chapter
British Columbia Trucking Association 2013 100th Annual General Meeting & Management Conference
June 2013 Kelowna, BC

British Columbia Water & Waste Association (BCWWA)

#221, 8678 Greenall Ave., Burnaby BC V5J 3M6
Tel: 604-433-4389; *Fax:* 604-433-9859
Toll-Free: 877-433-4389
e-mail: contact@bcwwa.org
www.bcwwa.org
www.facebook.com/group.php?gid=21435804125
Overview: A medium-sized provincial organization founded in 1964
Mission: To safeguard public health & the environment through the sharing of skills, knowledge, experience & education; To provide a voice for the water & waste community in British Columbia & the Yukon; *Member of:* American Water Works Association (AWWA); Water Environment Federation (WEF); Canadian Water & Wastewater Association (CWWA)
Chief Officer(s):
Daisy Foster, Chief Executive Officer, 604-433-7824
dfoster@bcwwa.org
David Icharia, Director, Operations, 604-433-0093
dicharia@bcwwa.org
Judy Zhang, Manager, Finance, 604-433-6941
jzhang@bcwwa.org
Sarah Vaughan, Manager, Communications, 604-630-0011
svaughan@bcwwa.org
Kimberly Perreault, Coordinator, Member Services, 604-433-4389
kperreault@bcwwa.org
TBA, Coordinator, Education & Technology
Finances: *Funding Sources:* Membership fees; Courses; Seminars; Annual conference
Membership: *Fees:* $25 students; $35 operators; $60 full members; *Member Profile:* British Columbia & Yukon professionals & students in the water & wastewater fields; *Committees:* Young Professionals; Climate Change; Cross Connection Control; Decentralized Wastewater Management; Drinking Water; Energy Management; Infrastructure Management; Residuals Management; Small Water Systems; SCADA & Information Technology; Vancouver Island; Wastewater Collection; Wastewater Management; Wastewater Source Control; Water Sustainability; Watershed (Stormwater) Management; Yukon; Small Wastewater Systems; Small Water Systems; Wastewater Treatment; Water Distribution; Water Treatment; Awards; Elections; Governance; Nominations; Leadership Council
Activities: Promoting dialogue & information dissemination on environmental matters; Offering operator education & training opportunities (online training now available); Providing networking opportunities such as our Annual Conference; Certifying backflow assembly testers in British Columbia & Yukon through our Cross Connection Control program; Creating awareness of the value of water through Drinking Water Week, which occurs annually in May.; *Awareness Events:* Drinking Water Week, May; *Library:* British Columbia Water & Waste Association Library
Meetings/Conferences:
For more information see Trade Shows, Conferences and Seminars Chapter
British Columbia Water & Waste Association 2013 41st Annual Conference & Trade Show
April 2013 Kelowna, BC
British Columbia Water & Waste Association 2014 42nd Annual Conference & Trade Show
May 2014 Whistler, BC
British Columbia Water & Waste Association 2015 43rd Annual Conference & Trade Show
2015, BC
Publications:
•Watermark
Type: Magazine; *Frequency:* Quarterly; *Accepts Advertising*; *Editor:* Carol Campbell
Profile: Calendar of events, product listings, new member listings, employment opportunities, informative articles, & reports on the annual conference, technical seminars & symposia

British Columbia Waterfowl Society

5191 Robertson Rd., RR#1, Delta BC V4K 3N2
Tel: 604-946-6980; *Fax:* 604-946-6980
www.reifelbirdsanctuary.com/bcws2.html
Also Known As: Reifel Bird Sanctuary
Overview: A medium-sized provincial charitable organization founded in 1961
Mission: To encourage conservation of wetlands; to spur public awareness on importance of conservation of estuaries; to operate George C. Reifel Migratory Bird Sanctuary.
Chief Officer(s):
Kathleen Fry, Acting Manager
Jack Bates, President
Finances: *Annual Operating Budget:* $100,000-$250,000
Staff: 2 staff member(s); 40 volunteer(s)
Membership: 2,000; *Fees:* $20 single; $40 family; $500 life; *Committees:* Conservation; Publicity & Promotion; Operations; Membership Services
Activities: *Awareness Events:* Snow Goose Festival, Nov.; *Speaker Service:* Yes; *Library:* Open to public

British Columbia Women's Institutes (BCWI) Parent Name: Federated Women's Institutes of Canada

#203B, 750 Cottonwood Ave., Kamloops BC V2B 3X2
Tel: 250-554-5406; *Fax:* 250-554-5406
e-mail: info@bcwi.org
www.bcwi.org
Overview: A medium-sized provincial charitable organization founded in 1909 overseen by Federated Women's Institutes of Canada
Mission: To help discover, stimulate & develop leadership among women; to assist, encourage & support women to become knowledgeable & responsible citizens; to ensure basic human rights for women & to work towards their equality; to be a strong voice through which matters of utmost concern can reach the decision makers; to network with organizations sharing similar objectives; to promote the improvement of agricultural & other rural communities & to safeguard the environment; *Member of:* Associated Country Women of the World; Affiliation(s): BC Federation of Agriculture
Finances: *Annual Operating Budget:* $50,000-$100,000; *Funding Sources:* Membership dues; grants
Staff: 1 staff member(s)
Membership: 1,800; *Fees:* $15
Activities: *Awareness Events:* Women's Institutes Week, Feb.; *Speaker Service:* Yes; *Library:* Open to public by appointment

British Columbia Wood Specialities Group Association

#200, 9292 - 200th St., Langley BC V1M 3A6
Tel: 604-882-7100; *Fax:* 604-882-7300
Toll-Free: 877-422-9663
e-mail: info@bcwood.com
www.bcwood.com
twitter.com/BC_Wood
Also Known As: BC Wood
Overview: A medium-sized provincial charitable organization founded in 1989
Mission: To assist BC manufacturers of value-added products achieve global competitiveness by providing essential marketing services to capitalize on new market opportunities
Chief Officer(s):
Brian Hawrysh, CEO Ext. 244
Finances: *Annual Operating Budget:* $1.5 Million-$3 Million; *Funding Sources:* Membership dues; provincial government; federal government
Staff: 12 staff member(s)
Membership: 260; *Fees:* $500-$2,000; *Member Profile:* Manufacturers of value-added wood products in BC; *Committees:* Marketing
Activities: *Speaker Service:* Yes; *Library:* BC Wood Resource Library; by appointment

British Council - Canada

#2800, 777 Bay St., Toronto ON M5G 2G2
e-mail: educatioinfo@ca.britishcouncil.org
www.britishcouncil.org/canada
www.linkedin.com/company/british-council
www.facebook.com/BritishCouncilCanada
twitter.com/britishcouncil
www.youtube.com/user/britishcouncilcanada
Overview: A small international charitable organization
Mission: To encourage cultural, scientific, technological & educational cooperation between Britain & Canada
Activities: Education, arts, science & information
Awards:
•British Chevening Scholarships (Award)
One year's postgraduate study at a British university in disciplines including: environmental studies, science, international relations, engineering

Bruce Peninsula Environment Group (BPEG)

PO Box 1072, Lions Head ON N0H 1W0
e-mail: info@bpeg.ca
www.bpeg.ca
Overview: A small local organization founded in 1989
Mission: BPEG is a group of people concerned about the environment & committed to preserving the unique ecology of the Bruce Peninsula. It promotes awareness of the region's diverse flora, fauna, geology & cultural history, & monitors human impact on them. It has planted trees, helped with water quality issues on farmland, encouraged wildlife with habitat improvement, & has been active in legislating for better forestry practices.; *Member of:* Great Lakes United; Ontario Environment Network; Durham Nuclear Awareness; Canadian Environmental Network; Grey-Bruce Power Council
Chief Officer(s):
Tony Barton, Chair, 519-534-2355
Finances: *Annual Operating Budget:* Less than $50,000; *Funding Sources:* Membership fees; donations

Staff: 8 volunteer(s)
Membership: 125; *Fees:* $25 family, $15 single; *Member Profile:* Residents of the Bruce Peninsula; *Committees:* Alternate Energy; Dark Sky; Media; Recycling; Sustainable Forestry
Activities: Earth Day; energy tour; monthly meetings; tree planting; road clean-ups; recycling; environmental awards; *Awareness Events:* Energy Tour, June 4; *Library:* by appointment

The Bruce Trail Association ***See*** The Bruce Trail Conservancy

The Bruce Trail Conservancy

PO Box 857, Hamilton ON L8N 3N9
Tel: 905-529-6821; *Fax:* 905-529-6823
Toll-Free: 800-665-4453
e-mail: info@brucetrail.org
www.brucetrail.org
www.facebook.com/group.php?gid=111645892194726
Previous Name: The Bruce Trail Association
Overview: A medium-sized provincial charitable organization founded in 1963
Mission: To secure, develop & manage the Bruce Trail as a public footpath along the Niagara Escarpment from Queenston to Tobermory, thereby promoting preservation of the escarpment's ecological & cultural integrity & fostering an appreciation of its natural beauty. The Bruce Trail, designated as a UNESCO World Biosphere Reserve, is Canada's oldest and longest footpath.; *Member of:* Hike Ontario; Affiliation(s): Ontario Trails Council; Coalition on the Niagara Escarpment; Federation of Ontario Naturalists; Hike Ontario
Chief Officer(s):
Beth Kümmling, Executive Director
bkummling@brucetrail.org
Finances: *Annual Operating Budget:* $250,000-$500,000; *Funding Sources:* Memberships; donations; sales
Staff: 14 staff member(s); 1050 volunteer(s)
Membership: 8,500; *Fees:* $50
Activities: Land conservation; trail management & development; environmental hikes; *Awareness Events:* Bruce Trail Day, Oct.; *Speaker Service:* Yes; *Library:* by appointment

Beaver Valley
PO Box 3251, Meaford ON N4L 1A5
www.beavervalleybrucetrail.org
Chief Officer(s):
Linda Murray, President, 519-538-1445
linmur@bmts.com

Blue Mountains
PO Box 91, Collingwood ON L9Y 3Z4
e-mail: hart@bmbtc.org
www.bmbtc.org
Chief Officer(s):
Peter McDonald, President, 705-444-8294
mcd106@hotmail.com

Caledon Hills
PO Box 65, Stn. Caledon Village, Caledon ON L7K 3L3
e-mail: info@caledonbrucetrail.org
www.caledonbrucetrail.org
Chief Officer(s):
Jean Kerins, President
Joan Richard, Vice President
Robert Gillespie, Secretary

Dufferin Hi-Land
PO Box 698, Alliston ON L9R 2V9
www.dufferinbrucetrailclub.org
Chief Officer(s):
Tony Hopkins, President
ahopkins@primus.ca

Iroquoia
PO Box 71057, Burlington ON L7T 4J8
e-mail: info@iroquoia.on.ca
www.iroquoia.on.ca
Chief Officer(s):
Gary Wrathall, President

Niagara
PO Box 176, Niagara-on-the-Lake ON L0S 1J0
e-mail: niagarabrucetrailclub@gmail.com
www.niagarabrucetrail.org
Chief Officer(s):
Trudy Senesi, President, 905-935-9777
trudykp@becon.org

Peninsula
PO Box 2, Tobermory ON N0H 2R0
e-mail: pbtc@amtelecom.net
www.pbtc.ca
Chief Officer(s):
Don McIlraith, President, 519-793-3768
donmcilraith@amtelecom.net

Sydenham
PO Box 431, Owen Sound ON N4K 5P7
e-mail: info@sydenhambrucetrail.ca
www.sydenhambrucetrail.ca
Chief Officer(s):
Frank Schoenhoeffer, President, 519-395-4935
franksch3@gmail.com

Toronto
PO Box 44, Stn. D, Toronto ON M6P 3J5
Tel: 416-763-9061
e-mail: information@torontobrucetrailclub.org
www.torontobrucetrailclub.org
Chief Officer(s):
Peter Leeney, President

Buffalo Lake Naturalists Club

PO Box 1802, Stettler AB T0C 2L0
Tel: 403-747-2221
e-mail: clipskic@rttinc.com
Overview: A small local organization founded in 1973
Mission: To promote the enjoyment of nature through environmental appreciation & conservation; To encourage wise use & conservation of natural resources & environmental protection; *Member of:* Federation of Alberta Naturalists
Finances: *Annual Operating Budget:* Less than $50,000; *Funding Sources:* Membership fees
Staff: 26 volunteer(s)
Membership: 30; *Fees:* $10 single; *Committees:* Environmental Protection; Program; Trail
Activities: Bird, plant & butterfly identification field trips; community projects; park planning & cleanup; *Library:*

Building Energy Management Manitoba (BEMM)

#309, 23 - 845 Dakota St., Winnipeg MB R2M 5M3
Tel: 204-452-2098
e-mail: info@bemm.ca
www.bemm.ca
Overview: A medium-sized provincial organization
Mission: To promote energy efficiency & management in the various building sectors
Chief Officer(s):
Monica Samuda Poitras, Chair, 204-261-0718
monica@samudaenergy.com
Robert Bisson, Treasurer, 204-945-8452
robert.bisson@gov.mb.ca
Kent Glenday, Contact, Membership, 204-669-3346, Fax: 204-669-3350
kent.glenday@philips.com
Membership: *Fees:* $85; *Member Profile:* Engineers, architects, property managers, contractors & energy management professionals; government, school boards, hospitals & utility representatives
Meetings/Conferences:
For more information see Trade Shows, Conferences and Seminars Chapter
Building Energy Management Manitoba 2013 Better Buildings Conference
April 2013 Winnipeg, MB

Building Supply Industry Association of British Columbia (BSIA of BC)

#2, 19299 - 94th Ave., Surrey BC V4N 4E6
Tel: 604-513-2205; *Fax:* 604-513-2206
Toll-Free: 888-711-5656
www.bsiabc.ca
Overview: A medium-sized provincial organization founded in 1938
Mission: To act as the official voice of the building supply industry in British Columbia; To provide services to members
Environmental Activity: Addressing environmental issues affecting the building supply industry in British Columbia; Providing information about health & safety in the workplace; Printing & distributing the Occupational Health & Safety Policy & Procedures Manual
Chief Officer(s):
Thomas Foreman, President
thomas@bsiabc.ca
Marijoel Chamberlain, Coordinator, Member Services, & Manager, Trade Show
marijoel@bsiabc.ca
Jackie Trafton, Administrator
jackie@bsiabc.ca
Membership: *Fees:* $169 wholesale branches; $199 retail stores & manufacturer's agents; $399 associates & retail & wholesale head offices; *Member Profile:* Manufacturers; Wholesalers; Suppliers; Retailers who operate lumber yards, hardware stores, & home centres
Activities: Promoting the building supply industry in British Columbia; Liaising with government; Addressing concerns within the industry; Providing information to members; Hosting product knowledge evenings at the BSIA office
Meetings/Conferences:
For more information see Trade Shows, Conferences and Seminars Chapter
Westcoast Building & Hardware Trade Show & Conference 2013
October 2013 Whistler, BC
Publications:
•BSIA e-news
Type: Newsletter; *Frequency:* Monthly; *Accepts Advertising*; *Price:* Free with membership in the Building Supply Industry Association of British Columbia
Profile: Industry & association news
•BSIA News Magazine
Type: Magazine; *Frequency:* 5 pa; *Accepts Advertising*; *Price:* Free with membership in the Building Supply Industry Association of British Columbia
Profile: A 40 to 60 page magazine, featuring association activities & in-depth articles for building supply dealers & suppliers throughout British Columbia, who retail a wide range of home improvement supplies& materials
•Building Supply Industry Association of British Columbia Directory
Type: Directory; *Frequency:* Annually; *Accepts Advertising*; *Price:* Free with membership in the Building SupplyIndustry Association of British Columbia
Profile: An alphabetical & city listing of British Columbia's building material & hardware retailers & suppliers
•Building Supply Industry Association of British Columbia Retail Product Buying Guide
Type: Guide; *Frequency:* Annually; *Accepts Advertising*; *Price:* Free with membership in the Building Supply Industry Association of BritishColumbia
Profile: Information about industry related vendors & suppliers
•Occupational Health & Safety Policy & Procedures Manual
Type: Manual; *Price:* Free with membership in the BSIA of British Columbia; $19.95 non-members
Profile: A generic guide to the development of a specific manual for each business
•Retail Job Descriptions Handbook
Type: Handbook

Bulkley Valley Naturalists

PO Box 4209, Smithers BC V0J 2N0
Tel: 250-847-3727
e-mail: hoekjh@mail.bulkley.net
Overview: A small local organization
Mission: To promote the enjoyment of nature through environmental appreciation & conservation; To encourage wise use & conservation of natural resources & environmental protection.; *Member of:* Federation of BC Naturalists; Affiliation(s): Federation of BC Naturalists.
Membership: *Fees:* $15 individual; $20 family
Activities: Participating in Christmas bird count and midwinter Bald Eagle count; participating on advisory committees on land use; developing nature education programs, field trips for schools

Bureau canadien de reconnaissance professionnelle des spécialistes de l'environnement ***See*** Canadian Environmental Certification Approvals Board

Bureau d'assurance du Canada ***See*** Insurance Bureau of Canada

Bureau of International Recycling (BIR)

24, av Franklin Roosevelt, Brussels B-1050 Belgium
Tel: 32-2-627-5770; *Fax:* 32-2-627-5773
e-mail: bir@bir.org
www.bir.org
Overview: A medium-sized international organization founded in 1948
Mission: To promote recycling & a recyclability, thereby conserving natural resources, protecting the environment, &

facilitating free trade of recyclables in an environmentally sound manner
Chief Officer(s):
Dominique Maguin, President
Membership: *Fees:* ī1460-1820

Burke Mountain Naturalists
PO Box 52540, Stn. Coquitlam Centre, Coquitlam BC V3B 7J4
Tel: 604-937-3483; *Fax:* 604-937-3483
e-mail: burkemtnnats@gmail.com
www.bmn.bc.ca
Overview: A small local charitable organization founded in 1989
Mission: The group is a non-profit society that promotes the enjoyment of nature through environmental appreciation & conservation. It advocates accessibility & maintenance of natural areas, particularly local ones. It is a registered charity, BN: 873847966RR0001.; *Member of:* BC Nature
Chief Officer(s):
Ian McArthur, President, 604-939-4039
imcart@telus.net
Carole Edwards, Treasurer, 604-461-3864
caroleedwards@shaw.ca
Membership: 450; *Fees:* $25 single; $30 family/group
Activities: Monthly meetings; field trips & hikes; recording bird/flora sightings; preparing natural history brochures

BurlingtonGreen Environmental Association
3281 Myers Lane, Burlington ON L7N 1K6
Tel: 905-466-2171
www.burlingtongreen.org
www.facebook.com/burlington.green.environment
Overview: A medium-sized local organization
Mission: To advocate for local environmental issues
Environmental Activity: Hosting events on eco-topics; Providing information to the public about environmental issues
Chief Officer(s):
Amy Schnurr, Executive Director
Finances: *Funding Sources:* Membership fees; Donations
Membership: *Fees:* $5 students; $20 individuals; $25 families; *Member Profile:* Citizens for a greener community
Activities: Establishing the BurlingtonGreen Youth Network which meets monthly; *Awareness Events:* BurlingtonGreen Eco-Film Festival
Publications:
•BurlingtonGreen Environmental Association Newsletter
Type: Newsletter; *Frequency:* Annually
Profile: Information, eco-event listings, stories, & special bulletins
•BurlingtonGreen Youth Network Bulletin
Type: Newsletter
Profile: Information about volunteering, events, competitions, & scholarships
•Greening Tips
Type: Newsletter; *Frequency:* Monthly

Burrard Inlet Environmental Action Program & Fraser River Estuary Management Program (BIEAP/FREMP)
#501, 5945 Kathleen Ave., Burnaby BC V5H 4J7
Tel: 604-775-5756; *Fax:* 604-431-6739
e-mail: info@bieapfremp.org
bieapfremp.org
Overview: A small local organization founded in 1985
Mission: To establish a management framework to facilitate activities to protect & improve the environmental quality of Burrard Inlet & the Fraser River Estuary; To promote the balance between the environment & the economy
Chief Officer(s):
Annemarie De Andrade, Program Manager, 604-775-5755
manager@bieapfremp.org
Michelle Gaudry, Policy Coordinator, 604-775-5195
mgaudry@bieapfremp.org
Finances: *Annual Operating Budget:* $250,000-$500,000; *Funding Sources:* Federal, provincial & regional government
Staff: 3 staff member(s)
Membership: *Committees:* Partners; Management; BIEAP Plan Implementation; Water & Land Use; FREMP Environmental Review; Burrard Environmental Review

Business Council of British Columbia
#810, 1050 Pender St. West, Vancouver BC V6E 3S7
Tel: 604-684-3384; *Fax:* 888-488-5376
e-mail: info@bcbc.com
www.bcbc.com
www.linkedin.com/company/business-council-of-british-columbia
twitter.com/BizCouncilBC
Previous Name: Employers' Council of BC
Overview: A large provincial organization founded in 1966
Mission: To build a competitive & growing economy that provides opportunities for all who invest, work, & live in British Columbia
Chief Officer(s):
Hank Ketcham, Chair
Greg D'Avignon, President & CEO
greg.davignon@bcbc.com
Jock Finlayson, Executive VP & Chief Policy Officer
jock.finlayson@bcbc.com
Herb Eibensteiner, COO & Vice-President, Membership
herb.eibensteiner@bcbc.com
Ken Peacock, Chief Economist & Vice-President
ken.peacock@bcbc.com
Finances: *Funding Sources:* Membership fees
Membership: 260 organizations; *Fees:* Schedule available; *Committees:* Environment; Employee Relations; Membership; Competitiveness; Innovation; Energy Policy; Human Capital; Aboriginal Affairs
Publications:
•BC Economic Index [a publication of Business Council of British Columbia]
Frequency: q.
•BC Economic Review & Outlook [a publication of Business Council of British Columbia]
•Environment & Energy Bulletin [a publication of Business Council of British Columbia]
Type: Bulletin
•Human Capital Law & Policy [a publication of Business Council of British Columbia]
•Industrial Relations Bulletin [a publication of Business Council of British Columbia]
Type: Bulletin
•Policy Perspectives [a publication of Business Council of British Columbia]
Type: Newsletter

Calgary Field Naturalists' Society (CFNS)
Parent Name: Federation of Alberta Naturalists
PO Box 981, Stn. M, Calgary AB T2P 2K4
Tel: 403-239-6444
e-mail: naturecalgary@cfns.fanweb.ca
www.naturecalgary.com
www.facebook.com/naturecalgary
Also Known As: Nature Calgary
Overview: A small local charitable organization founded in 1955 overseen by Federation of Alberta Naturalists
Mission: To promote enjoyment of nature through environmental appreciation & conservation; To encourage wise use & conservation of natural resources & environmental protection; *Member of:* Calgary Area Outdoor Council; Alberta Environmental Network
Chief Officer(s):
Jamie Noakes, Contact, 403-243-7232
Hart Andrew, Contact, 403-279-5209
Finances: *Annual Operating Budget:* Less than $50,000; *Funding Sources:* Membership dues; donations; publications sale
Staff: 185 volunteer(s)
Membership: 100-499;; *Fees:* $20 regular; $25 family; *Committees:* Bird Study; Botany & Fungi Study; Nature Photography; Endangered Species; Natural Areas
Activities: 35 slide shows/presentations & over 100 field trips a year; *Speaker Service:* Yes; *Library:* Open to public by appointment

Calgary Horticultural Society (CHS)
208 - 50 Ave. SW, Calgary AB T2S 2S1
Tel: 403-287-3469; *Fax:* 403-287-6986
e-mail: office@calhort.org
www.calhort.org
Overview: A medium-sized provincial organization founded in 1907
Mission: To educate, promote & encourage gardening in the Calgary area; Affiliation(s): Royal Horticultural Society
Chief Officer(s):
Christina Smith, President
Elizabeth Jolicoeur, General Manager
Finances: *Annual Operating Budget:* $250,000-$500,000; *Funding Sources:* Membership fees; committee activities
Staff: 5 staff member(s); 650 volunteer(s)
Membership: 5,000+; *Fees:* $37 individual; $50 family; $200 corporate; *Committees:* Advertising; Books & Library; Bus Tours; CHS Book Committee; Clinics; Finance; Flower Show; Fundraising; Garden Competition; Garden Design Competition; Garden Viewing (Open Gardens); Home Show; Membership; Newsletter; Plant Exchange; Programs; Properties; Public Relations; Research & Development; Social; Volunteers
Activities: Gardeners Fair; garden competition; plant exchanges; *Speaker Service:* Yes; *Library:* Open to public

Calgary Zoological Society
1300 Zoo Rd. NE, Calgary AB T2E 7V6
Tel: 403-232-9300; *Fax:* 403-237-7582
Toll-Free: 800-588-9993
e-mail: comments@calgaryzoo.ab.ca
www.calgaryzoo.org
www.facebook.com/thecalgaryzoo
www.youtube.com/calgaryzoo1
Overview: A large provincial charitable organization founded in 1929
Mission: To operate the Calgary Zoo, Botanical Garden & Prehistoric Park; to advocate on behalf of animals; *Member of:* Canadian Association of Zoos & Aquariums (CAZA); Association of Zoos & Aquariums (AZA); Affiliation(s): Amphibian Ark; Tourism Calgary
Environmental Activity: Conserving endangered species, habitats, & ecosystems in Canada & throughout the world; Conducting scientific research in zoos & in the wild through The Calgary Zoo's Centre for Conservation Research; Participatign in Species Survival Plans
Chief Officer(s):
Greg Turnbull, Chair
Clément Lanthier, President & CEO
Finances: *Annual Operating Budget:* $100,000-$250,000; *Funding Sources:* Donations; Sponsorships; Admission
Activities: Offering educational programs; Providing the Calgary Zoo's Endangered Species Reintroduction Research program
Meetings/Conferences:
For more information see Trade Shows, Conferences and Seminars Chapter
Calgary Zoological Society 2013 Annual General Meeting 2013, AB
Publications:
•Calgary Zoological Society eMagazine
Frequency: Quarterly

California Institute of Public Affairs (CIPA)
PO Box 189040, Sacramento CA 95818 USA
Tel: 916-442-2472; *Fax:* 916-442-2478
e-mail: info@interenvironment.org
www.interenvironment.org/cipa
Overview: A small international organization founded in 1969
Mission: To promote lateral communication & cooperation across professions, academic disciplines, governmental agencies & other sectors of society; to help define the public interest by bringing together people with disparate interests to find common ground; serves as the headquarters of the International Center for the Environment & Public Policy (ICEP), established in 1993 to provide a focus for CIPA international activities that started in 1972; Affiliation(s): Claremont Graduate School; IUCN - The World Conservation Union
Chief Officer(s):
Thaddeus C. Trzyna, President
Elisabeth K. Kersten, Senior Associate
Finances: *Annual Operating Budget:* $100,000-$250,000
Staff: 3 staff member(s)
Publications:
•The Urban Imperative: Urban Outreach Strategies for Protected Area Agencies
Number of Pages: 168; *Editor:* Ted Trzyna; *Price:* $35

Campground Owners Association of Nova Scotia (COANS)
Parent Name: Canadian Camping Association
c/o Arm of Gold Campground, 24 Church Rd., Little Bras d'Or, Cape Breton NS B1Y 2Y2
Tel: 902-736-6671
e-mail: info@campingnovascotia.com
www.campingnovascotia.com
Previous Name: Camping Association of Nova Scotia
Overview: A medium-sized provincial organization founded in 1941 overseen by Canadian Camping Association
Mission: To provide the best camping experience possible throughout our diverse province; to improve standards at all the province's campgrounds; to provide leadership to this important segment of the provincial economy.
Chief Officer(s):
John Brennick, President, 902-736-6671
camp@armofgoldcamp.com
Chris Miller, Vice-President
campshubie@ns.sympatico.ca

Finances: *Annual Operating Budget:* Less than $50,000; *Funding Sources:* Membership dues; conferences; government grants
Staff: 10 volunteer(s)
Membership: 69; *Committees:* Membership; Newsletter; Marketing & Promotion; Nomination; Publication

Camping Association of Nova Scotia ***See*** Campground Owners Association of Nova Scotia

Camping Québec

#700, 2001, rue de la Metropole, Longueuil QC J4G 1S9
Tél: 450-651-7396; *Téléc:* 450-651-7397
Ligne sans frais: 800-363-0457
www.destinationcamping.ca
Nom précédent: Association des terrains de camping du Québec
Aperçu: *Dimension:* moyenne; *Envergure:* provinciale; fondée en 1962
Mission: Défendre les intérêts de nos membres; offrir des services de publications et promotion, des activitées, des escomptes sur achats et programmes divers.
Membre(s) du bureau directeur:
Maryse Catellier, Vice-président exécutif
Finances: *Budget de fonctionnement annuel:* $500,000-$1.5 Million
Personnel: 4 membre(s) du personnel
Membre: 430 *Montant de la cotisation:* 400$; *Critères d'admissibilite:* Exploitants de terrains de camping

CAMPUT, Canada's Energy & Utility Regulators (CAMPUT)

#646, 200 North Service Rd. West, Oakville ON L6M 2Y1
Tel: 905-827-5139; *Fax:* 905-827-3260
e-mail: info@camput.org
www.camput.org
Previous Name: Canadian Association of Members of Public Utility Tribunals / Association canadienne des membres des tribunaux d'utilité publique
Overview: A small national organization founded in 1976
Mission: To improve public utility regulation in Canada
Chief Officer(s):
Terry Rochefort, Executive Director, 905-827-5139
rochefort@camput.org
Lise Duquette, Chair, 514-873-2452
lise.duquette@regie-energie.qc.ca
Carolyn Dahl Rees, Secretary-Treasurer, 414-592-4534
carolyn.dahlrees@auc.ab.ca
Membership: *Member Profile:* Any Canadian tribunal, board, commission, or agency that is responsible for the economic regulation of utilities; Any Canadian energy tribunal, board, commission, or agency that makes binding decisions through adjudicative or quasi-judicial processes; *Committees:* Regulatory Affairs; Education
Activities: Educating & training commissioners & staff of public utility tribunals; Communicating with members; Liaising with parallel regulatory organizations
Meetings/Conferences:
For more information see Trade Shows, Conferences and Seminars Chapter
CAMPUT, Canada's Energy & Utility Regulators 2013 Conference: Serving the Public Interest - The Regulator's Balancing Act
May 2013 Niagara Falls, ON
CAMPUT, Canada's Energy & Utility Regulators 2013 Annual General Meeting
September 2013 St. John's, NL
CAMPUT, Canada's Energy & Utility Regulators 2014 Conference
May 2014 Halifax, NS
CAMPUT, Canada's Energy & Utility Regulators 2014 Annual General Meeting
2014
CAMPUT, Canada's Energy & Utility Regulators 2015 Conference
May 2015 Calgary, AB

Canada - Newfoundland & Labrador Offshore Petroleum Board (C-NLOPB)

TD Place, 140 Water St., 5th Fl., St. John's NL A1C 6H6
Tel: 709-778-1400; *Fax:* 709-778-1473
e-mail: information@cnlopb.nl.ca
www.cnlopb.nl.ca
Mission: To apply the provisions of the *Atlantic Accord* & the *Atlantic Accord Implementation Acts*; To regulate the oil & gas industry for the Newfoundland & Labrador Offshore Area
Environmental Activity: Overseeing operator activity for legislative & regulatory compliance in the areas of environmental protection, resource management, & offshore safety; Verifying that operators perform an environmental assessment pursuant to Canadian regulations
Chief Officer(s):
Max Ruelokke, P.Emg, Chair, CEO, & Chief Conservation Officer, 709-778-1456
David Wells, Deputy Chief Executive Officer, 709-778-1452
John P. Andrews, Manager, Legal & Land, 709-778-1458
Mike Baker, Manager, Support Services, 709-778-1464
Jeffrey M. Bugden, P.Eng., Manager, Industrial Benefits, 709-778-1448
Dave Burley, Manager, Environmental Affairs, 709-778-1403
Nicholle Carter, P.Geo., Manager, Exploration, 709-778-1428
Daniel B. Chicoyne, MSS, Manager, Safety, 709-778-4262
Sean Kelly, Manager, Public Relations, 709-778-1418, Fax: 709-689-0713
skelly@cnlopb.nl.ca
Jeff O'Keefe, Manager, Resource Management, 709-778-1406
Howard L. Pike, P.Eng., Manager, Operations, 709-778-1412
Activities: Facilitating the exploration for & development of hydrocarbon resources
Publications:
•Canada - Newfoundland & Labrador Offshore Petroleum Board Annual Report
Type: Yearbook; *Frequency:* Annually
Profile: Contents include the board's role, objectives, & financial statements

Canada - Nova Scotia Offshore Petroleum Board (CNSOPB)

TD Centre, 1791 Barrington St., 18th Fl., Halifax NS B3J 3K9
Tel: 902-422-5588; *Fax:* 902-422-1799
e-mail: postmaster@cnsopb.ns.ca
www.cnsopb.ns.ca
twitter.com/CNSOPB
Mission: To regulate petroleum activities in the Nova Scotia Offshore Area
Environmental Activity: Overseeing the protection of the environment, the health & safety of offshore workers, & the management & conservation of offshore petroleum resources
Chief Officer(s):
Stuart Pinks, P.Eng., Chief Executive Officer, 902-496-3206
spinks@cnsopb.ns.ca
Steve Bigelow, P.Eng., Chief Conservation Officer & Director, Resources & Rights, 902-429-1816
sbigelow@cnsopb.ns.ca
Keith Landra, Director, Operations, Health, Safety, & Environment, 902-496-0723
klandra@cnsopb.ns.ca
Michael S. McPhee, Director, General Counsel, Secretary, & Mgr., Regulatory Policy, 902-496-0739
mmcphee@cnsopb.ns.ca
Kim Nauss, Director, Industrial Benefits, 902-496-0751
knauss@cnsopb.ns.ca
Troy MacDonald, Director, Information Services, 902-496-0734
tmacdonald@cnsopb.ns.ca
Tanya T. White, Director, Public Relations & Administration, 902-496-0750
twhite@cnsopb.ns.ca
Activities: Issuing licences for offshore exploration & development; Collecting & distributing data
Publications:
•Canada - Nova Scotia Offshore Petroleum Board Annual Report
Type: Yearbook; *Frequency:* Annually
Profile: A summary of offshore activities, healthy & safety initiatives, environmental protection, information services, & financial statements

Canada Beef Export Federation

#235, 6715 - 8th St. NE, Calgary AB T2E 7H7
Tel: 403-274-0005; *Fax:* 403-274-7275
e-mail: canada@cbef.com
www.cbef.com
Overview: A medium-sized national organization founded in 1989
Mission: The Canada Beef Export Federation facilitates the expansion of strategic global markets for Canadian beef products and identifies and develops key export markets to increase the sale of Canadian beef products. Their objective revolves around securing and increasing markets outside the USA for Canadian beef products in order to decrease export dependence on the United States.
Chief Officer(s):
Ted Haney, President
canada@cbef.com
Gib Drury, Chairman

Canada East Equipment Dealers' Association (CEEDA)

580 Bryne Dr, #C1, Barrie ON L4N 9P6
Tel: 705-726-2100; *Fax:* 705-726-2187
e-mail: www.ceeda.ca
www.orfeda.com
twitter.com/@ceedaCanadaEast
Previous Name: Ontario Retail Farm Equipment Dealers' Association
Overview: A medium-sized provincial organization founded in 1945
Mission: To promote the welfare of equipment trade retailers in the Maritimes & Ontario; To represent dealer interests in government legislation & regulation; To foster cooperation among manufacturers & distributors; To promote high standards for the retail equipment industry; Affiliation(s): North American Equipment Dealers' Association (NAEDA)
Chief Officer(s):
Craig Smith, Chair, 905-572-6714
oneils@mountaincable.net
Keith Stoltz, 1st Vice-Chair, 519-291-2151
keith@stoltzsales.com
Beverly J. Leavitt, President & CEO, 905-841-6888
bev@ceeda.ca
Carol Schoen, Secretary-Treasurer, 519-638-3317
cschoen2003@yahoo.com
Membership: *Member Profile:* Farmstead, agricultural, powersport, & outdoor power equipment dealers from Ontario & the Maritimes
Activities: Liaising with educational institutions, equipment manufacturers, & provincial & federal governments; Providing training seminars; Collecting industry statistics; Disseminating timely information; Offering insurance counselling; Promoting safety
Meetings/Conferences:
For more information see Trade Shows, Conferences and Seminars Chapter
Canada East Equipment Dealers' Association 2013 Annual Meeting & Convention
2013

Canada Green Building Council (CaGBC) / Conseil du bâtiment durable du Canada (CBDCa)

#202, 47 Clarence St., Ottawa ON K1N 9K1
Tel: 613-241-1184; *Fax:* 613-241-4782
Toll-Free: 866-941-1184
e-mail: info@cagbc.org
www.cagbc.org
www.linkedin.com/groups?mostPopular=&gid=1333997
www.facebook.com/pages/CaGBC/168202776539520
twitter.com/CaGBC
www.youtube.com/user/CaGBC
Overview: A small national organization founded in 2002
Mission: To create buildings, homes, & communities across Canada that are environmentally responsible & high-performing; To advocate for green buildings
Environmental Activity: Promoting sustainable building across Canada; Encouraging energy efficiency; Offering in formaton about the LEED Canada program, Green Up program, Smart Growth program, & the Living Building Challenge
Chief Officer(s):
Lisa Bate, Chair
Joanne Weir, Secretary
Anthony Exposti, Treasurer
Finances: *Funding Sources:* Sponsorships
Activities: Developing best design practices; Providing educational materials for members
Meetings/Conferences:
For more information see Trade Shows, Conferences and Seminars Chapter
Canada Green Building Council 2013 National Conference & Expo
June 2013 Vancouver, BC
Canada Green Building Council 2013 Annual General Meeting
June 2013 Vancouver, BC
Canada Green Building Council 2014 National Conference & Expo
2014
Canada Green Building Council 2015 National Conference & Expo
2015

Canada Nature ***See*** Nature Canada

Canada Safety Council (CSC) / Conseil canadien de la sécurité (CCS)

1020 Thomas Spratt Pl., Ottawa ON K1G 5L5
Tel: 613-739-1535; *Fax:* 613-739-1566
e-mail: csc@safety-council.org
www.canadasafetycouncil.org
www.facebook.com/canada.safety
twitter.com/CanadaSafetyCSC
Overview: A large national charitable organization founded in 1968
Chief Officer(s):
Jack Smith, President
jack.smith@safety-council.org
Raynard Marchand, General Manager
raynald.marchand@safety-council.org
Publications:
•Famille Avertie
Frequency: Quarterly
•Living Safety
Type: Magazine; *Frequency:* Quarterly; *Price:* $11.25
Profile: CSC news, CSC initiatives, & traffic, occupational & public safety

Canadian 4-H Council / Conseil des 4-H du Canada

Central Experimental Farm, #26, 930 Carling Ave., Ottawa ON K1A 0C6
Tel: 613-234-4448; *Fax:* 613-234-1112
www.4-h-canada.ca
www.facebook.com/4HCanada
twitter.com/4HCanada
www.youtube.com/4hcanada
Previous Name: Canadian Council on 4-H Clubs
Overview: A large national charitable organization founded in 1933
Mission: To inspire youth across Canada to become contributing leaders in their communities; To support the development of Canada's rural youth
Chief Officer(s):
Roger Shier, Interim Chief Executive Officer
Tammy Oswick-Kearney, Officer, Special Projects
Finances: *Funding Sources:* Memberhip fees; Sponsorships; Donations; Wills & Bequests
Membership: *Committees:* Youth Advisory
Activities: Offering exchanges & scholarships which focus on citizenship; Providing leadership development opportunities
Publications:
•L'avantage 4-H Advantage
Type: Magazine; *Frequency:* Semiannually; *Price:* Free
Profile: Coverage of national programs & 4-H activities across Canada
•Canadian 4-H Council Annual Report
Type: Yearbook; *Frequency:* Annually
Profile: Annual Report of the Canadian 4-H Council & Canadian 4-H Foundation

Alberta - Airdrie Office

Airdrie Office, 97 East Lake Ramp NE, Airdrie AB T4A 0C3
Tel: 403-948-8501; *Fax:* 403-948-2069
e-mail: rob.g.smith@gov.ab.ca
www.4h.ab.ca
Chief Officer(s):
Margarite Stark, Head, 403-948-8510, Fax: 403-948-2069
margarite.stark@gov.ab.ca

British Columbia

#1, 904 Maud St., Enderby BC V0E 1V0
Tel: 250-376-0373; *Fax:* 250-554-2723
Toll-Free: 866-776-0373
e-mail: mail@bc4h.bc.ca
www.bc4h.bc.ca

Manitoba

1129 Queens Ave, Brandon MB R7A 1L9
Tel: 204-726-6412; *Fax:* 204-726-6260
e-mail: 4hdirector@mymts.net
www.4h.mb.ca
Chief Officer(s):
Clayton Robins, Executive Director

New Brunswick

#5, 267 Connell St., Woodstock NB E7M 1L2
Tel: 506-324-6244; *Fax:* 506-325-9266
e-mail: nb4h@nb4h.com
www.nb4h.com
Chief Officer(s):
Linda Porter

Newfoundland

PO Box 23047, St. John's NL A1B 4J9
Tel: 709-722-2112
www.4hnl.ca
Gerry Sullivan, President
gerry@4hnl.ca

Nova Scotia

PO Box 550, 157 College Rd., Truro NS B2N 5E3
Tel: 902-893-6587; *Fax:* 902-893-2757
e-mail: pickaa@gov.ns.ca
www.gov.ns.ca/agri/4h
Chief Officer(s):
Arthur Pick, Acting Manager

Ontario

5653 Hwy. 6, RR#5, Guelph ON N1H 6J2
Tel: 519-824-0101; *Fax:* 519-824-8759
Toll-Free: 877-410-8748
e-mail: inquiries@4-hontario.ca
www.4-hontario.ca
www.facebook.com/4hontario
twitter.com/4hontario
Chief Officer(s):
John denHaan, President
Wraychel Horne, Executive Director

Prince Edward Island

PO Box 2000, Charlottetown PE C1A 7N8
Tel: 902-368-4833; *Fax:* 902-368-6289
e-mail: pei4h@gov.pe.ca
www.pei4h.pe.ca
Chief Officer(s):
Robert Holmes, Administrative Director
rmholmes@gov.pe.ca

Saskatchewan

Rural Service Centre, 3830 Thatcher Ave., Saskatoon SK S7K 2H6
Tel: 306-933-7727; *Fax:* 306-933-7730
e-mail: webmaster@4-h.sk.ca
www.4-h.sk.ca
Chief Officer(s):
Valerie Pearson, Executive Director, 306-933-7729
valerieAT4-h.sk.ca

The Canadian Academy of Engineering (CAE) / L'Académie canadienne du génie (ACG)

#1402, 180 Elgin St., Ottawa ON K2P 2K3
Tel: 613-235-9056; *Fax:* 613-235-6861
e-mail: info@acad-eng-gen.ca
www.acad-eng-gen.ca
Overview: A medium-sized national charitable organization founded in 1987
Mission: To ensure that Canadian engineering expertise is applied to the benefit of all Canadians; *Member of:* International Council of Academies of Engineering & Technological Sciences (CAETS); Affiliation(s): Council of Canadian Academies
Chief Officer(s):
Michael A. Ball, Executive Director
Finances: *Funding Sources:* Sponsorships
Staff: 2 staff member(s)
Membership: 517; *Member Profile:* Accomplished engineers, nominated & elected by their peers
Activities: Increasing awareness of engineering in society; Promoting industrial competitiveness & environmental preservation; Advising on engineering education, research, & innovation; Developing relations with other professional engineering organizations
Publications:
•Canadian Academy of Engineering Newsletter / Communiqué
Type: Newsletter; *Frequency:* Quarterly
Profile: Reports, updates, upcoming events, & activities of the Academy & its Fellows

Canadian Administrative Housekeepers Association ***See*** Canadian Association of Environmental Management

Canadian Advanced Technology Alliance (CATA Alliance) / Association canadienne de technologie de pointe

National Headquarters, #416, 207 Bank St., Ottawa ON K2P 2N2
Tel: 613-236-6550
e-mail: info@cata.ca
www.cata.ca
www.facebook.com/groups/5391503953
twitter.com/CATAAlliance
Overview: A large national organization founded in 1978
Mission: To provide members with a network to establish partnerships, to match up with global business opportunities; To offer communication & advocacy services, notably in dealing with the government; To work to ensure that policies are favourable to Canadian technology companies; To maintain a research repository where members can access information to advance their agendas; Affiliation(s): Canadian Association of Internet Providers (CAIP)
Chief Officer(s):
John Reid, President & CEO
jreid@cata.ca
Barry Gander, Executive Vice-President, 613-340-0701
bgander@cata.ca
Charles Duffet, Senior Vice-Presient & CIO Advisor
cduffett@cata.ca
Russ Roberts, Senior Vice-President, Tax & Finance
roberts-bishop@sympatico.ca
Kevin Wennekes, Vice-President, Research
kwennekes@cata.ca
Membership: *Member Profile:* Corporations with Canadian offices, engaged in research & development activities; International corporations in a collaboration with CATA; User industries; Service companies
Activities: Engaging in advocacy activities; Providing original & timely information for members & stakeholders; Supporting research projects

Canadian Aeronautical Institute (CAI) ***See*** Canadian Aeronautics & Space Institute

Canadian Aeronautics & Space Institute (CASI) / Institut aéronautique et spatial du Canada

#104, 350 Terry Fox Dr., Ottawa ON K2K 2W5
Tel: 613-591-8787; *Fax:* 613-591-7291
e-mail: casi@casi.ca
www.casi.ca
Previous Name: Canadian Aeronautical Institute (CAI)
Merged from: Institute of Aircraft Technicians; Ottawa Aeronautical Society; US Institute of Aeronautical Science
Overview: A medium-sized national licensing organization founded in 1954
Mission: To advance the art, science, engineering, & applications of aeronautics & associated technologies in Canada; To promote Canadian competence & international competitiveness; Affiliation(s): Canadian Air Cushion Technology Society; Canadian Navigation Society; Canadian Remote Sensing Society
Chief Officer(s):
Geoff Languedoc, Executive Director
April Duffy, Coordinator, Publications, Information & Membership Services
Membership: 1,600; *Fees:* $36.75 juniors; $63 seniors; $94.50 associates & individuals
Activities: Facilitating communications among the Canadian aeronautics & space community; Developing members' skills
Meetings/Conferences:
For more information see Trade Shows, Conferences and Seminars Chapter
Canadian Aeronautics & Space Institute 2013 60th Aeronautics Conference & Annual General Meeting: Aerospace Clusters - Where Are We Headed?
April 2013 Toronto, ON
Canadian Aeronautics & Space Institute 65th International Astronautical Congress 2014
September 2014 Toronto, ON
Publications:
•Canadian Aeronautics & Space Journal (CASJ)
Type: Journal; *Frequency:* 4 pa; *Accepts Advertising*; *Editor:* Dr. Steven Zan; *Price:* Free to members & corporate
Profile: Fundamental & applied research, new technologies, & developments in the aerospace sciences & related fields
•Canadian Journal of Remote Sensing (CJRS)
Type: Journal; *Frequency:* 6 pa; *Accepts Advertising*; *Editor:* Nicholas Coops; *Price:* Free to members & corporatepartners
Profile: Technical research articles, notes, & review papers on topics such as information processing methods, data acquisition, & applications
•CASI [Canadian Aeronautics & Space Institute] Clipper
Frequency: Bimonthly
Profile: Information about the aeronautics, space, & remote sensing communities, produced & distributed to members & corporate partners
•CASI [Canadian Aeronautics & Space Institute] Log
Type: Newsletter

Profile: Information about events & branches, produced & distributed to members & corporate partners

Canadian Agricultural Economics & Farm Management Society *See* Canadian Agricultural Economics Society

Canadian Agricultural Economics Society (CAES) / Société canadienne d'agroéconomie (SCAE)

University Of Victoria, PO Box 1700, Stn. CSC, Rm. 360, Business & Economics Bldg., Victoria BC V8W 2Y2
Fax: 866-543-7613
caes.usask.ca/
Previous Name: Canadian Agricultural Economics & Farm Management Society
Overview: A medium-sized national organization
Mission: To address problems related to the economics of food production & marketing & the quality of rural life through extension, research, teaching, & policy making in government & private industry; Affiliation(s): Agricultural Institute of Canada
Chief Officer(s):
Valerie Johnson, Executive Director
valcaes@telus.net
Membership: 488; *Fees:* Schedule available; *Member Profile:* Individuals with interest in agricultural economics
Publications:
•Canadian Agricultural Economics Society Newsletter
Type: Newsletter
Profile: CAES news & activities
•Canadian Journal of Agricultural Economics / Revue Canadienne d'Agroéconomie
Type: Journal; *Frequency:* 4 pa; *Price:* Free to members
Profile: International peer-reviewed journal about agricultural & resource economics

Canadian Agricultural Safety Association (CASA) / Association canadienne de sécurité agricole (ACSA)

3325-C Pembina Hwy., Winnipeg MB R3V 0A2
Tel: 204-452-2272; *Fax:* 204-261-5004
Toll-Free: 877-452-2272
e-mail: info@casa-acsa.ca
www.casa-acsa.ca
www.facebook.com/group.php?gid=161720997195550
twitter.com/planfarmsafety
Overview: A medium-sized national organization founded in 1993
Mission: To address problems of illness, injuries & accidental death in farmers, their families & agricultural workers; To improve health & safety conditions of those that live or work on Canadian farms
Chief Officer(s):
Marcel L. Hacault, Executive Director
Dean Anderson, Chair
John Gordon, Vice-Chair
Denis Bilodeau, Second Vice President General
Lauranne Sanderson, Treasurer
Finances: *Annual Operating Budget:* $1.5 Million-$3 Million
Staff: 6 staff member(s)
Membership: *Fees:* $50 personal, not-profit; $250 academia, producer, government, service/supply industry
Meetings/Conferences:
For more information see Trade Shows, Conferences and Seminars Chapter
Canadian Agricultural Safety Association's Conference & AGM 2013
October 2013 Québec, QC
Canadian Agricultural Safety Association's Conference & AGM 2014
2014
Publications:
•CASA [Canadian Agricultural Safety Association] / ACSA [Association canadienne de sécurité agricole] Liaison
Type: Newsletter; *Frequency:* Monthly
Profile: News for members & interested individuals
•CASA [Canadian Agricultural Safety Association] Annual Report
Type: Yearbook; *Frequency:* Annually
Profile: Long term objectives of the association & financial statements

Canadian Agri-Marketing Association (Alberta) (CAMA)

c/o CAMA, 22 Guyers Dr., RR#3, Port Elgin ON N0H 2C7
e-mail: Alberta@cama.org
www.cama.org/alberta/AlbertaHome.aspx
Also Known As: CAMA Alberta
Overview: A medium-sized provincial organization founded in 1978
Mission: To increase knowledge of ideas related to agri-marketing; To promote high professional standards of agricultural marketing; Affiliation(s): National Agri-Marketing Association (NAMA); CAMA Saskatchewan; CAMA Manitoba; CAMA Ontario; CAMA Québec
Chief Officer(s):
Jenn Norrie, CAMA AB Treasurer
Membership: *Fees:* $140
Activities: Offering professional development seminars; Providing networking opportunities
Publications:
•CAMA [Canadian Agri-Marketing Association] Membership Directory
Type: Directory
Profile: Contact information for CAMA members throughout Canada
•MarketNews [a publication of the Canadian Agri-Marketing Association]
Type: Newsletter; *Frequency:* 5 pa
Profile: Association events & industry information for members

Canadian Agri-Marketing Association (Manitoba)

210 - 1600 Kenaston Blvd., Winnipeg MB R3P 0Y4
Tel: 204-799-2019; *Fax:* 204-257-5651
e-mail: camamb@mts.net
www.cama.org/manitoba/ManitobaHome.aspx
Also Known As: CAMA Manitoba
Overview: A small provincial organization founded in 1985
Mission: To promote excellence in agrimarketing; Affiliation(s): CAMA Ontario; CAMA Alberta; CAMA Saskatchewan
Chief Officer(s):
David Lazarnko, President
dlazarenko@bcg.ca
Finances: *Annual Operating Budget:* Less than $50,000
Staff: 1 staff member(s); 12 volunteer(s)
Membership: 125 individual; *Fees:* $100 individual; $25 student

Canadian Airports Council (CAC) / Conseil des aéroports du Canada

#600, 116 Lisgar St., Ottawa ON K2P 0C2
Tel: 613-560-9302; *Fax:* 613-560-6599
www.cacairports.ca
Overview: A medium-sized national organization founded in 1991
Mission: To act as the voice for Canadian airports on a great range of important issues; *Member of:* Airports Council International - North America (ACI-NA); Affiliation(s): Air Transport Association of Canada (ATAC); Canadian International Freight Forwarders Association (CIFFA); Canadian Chamber of Commerce; Canadian Tourism Commission; Tourism Industry Association of Canada (TIAC)
Chief Officer(s):
Daniel-Robert Gooch, President, 613-560-9302 Ext. 16
daniel.gooch@cacairports.ca
Nicole Larocque, Administrative Assistant, 613-560-9302 Ext. 14
nicole.larocque@cacairports.ca
Finances: *Funding Sources:* Sponsorships
Membership: 48; *Member Profile:* Canadian airports (CAC members are also members of Airports Council International - North America)
Activities: Preparing submissions to governmental bodies & agencies
Publications:
•The Airport Voice: News & Views
Type: Newsletter
Profile: National & international news affecting Canadian airports
•The Canadian Airports Council Annual Report
Type: Yearbook; *Frequency:* Annually
Profile: Significant developments at the CAC & in the industry during the year

Canadian Animal Health Institute (CAHI) / Institut canadien de la santé animale (ICSA)

#102, 160 Research Lane, Guelph ON N1G 5B2
Tel: 519-763-7777; *Fax:* 519-763-7407
e-mail: cahi@cahi-icsa.ca
www.cahi-icsa.ca
Overview: A medium-sized national organization founded in 1968
Mission: To work closely with allied industry groups for the betterment of Canadian agriculture; To foster & maintain a regulatory & legislative climate which will encourage member companies to develop & market useful animal health products & services; To promote the proper use of animal health & nutrition products by livestock & poultry farmers through user education information programs; To develop a public information program which enhances appreciation of the contributions the animal health & nutrition industry makes to the economy & society
Chief Officer(s):
Jean Szkotnicki, President
Tracey Firth, Director, Programs
Finances: *Funding Sources:* Membership dues
Staff: 3 staff member(s)
Membership: 60 organizations
Meetings/Conferences:
For more information see Trade Shows, Conferences and Seminars Chapter
Canadian Animal Health Institute 2013 Annual Meeting 2013
Publications:
•CAHI [Canadian Animal Health Institute] Resource Directory
Type: Directory; *Frequency:* Biennially
Profile: Listings of CAHI members, veterinary associations, government agencies related to animal health, commodity organizations, & CAHI's foreign sisterorganizations
•Inforum [a publication of the Canadian Animal Health Institute]
Type: Newsletter; *Frequency:* 4 pa
Profile: Distributed to Canadian veterinarians in the Canadian Veterinary Journal

Canadian Aquaculture Industry Alliance (CAIA) / Alliance de l'industrie canadienne de l'aquiculture

PO Box 81100, Stn. World Exchange Plaza, #705, 116 Albert St., Ottawa ON K1P 1B1
Tel: 613-239-0612; *Fax:* 613-239-0619
e-mail: info@aquaculture.ca
www.aquaculture.ca
Overview: A medium-sized national organization founded in 1987
Mission: To represent the interests of aquaculture operators, feed companies, suppliers, & provincial finfish & shellfish aquaculture associations on both the national & international scenes; To ensure the international competitiveness of the Canadian aquaculture industry
Chief Officer(s):
Ruth Salmon, Executive Director, 613-239-0612, Fax: 613-239-0619
ruth.salmon@aquaculture.ca
Sherry Sadler, Coordinator, Projects
sherry.sadler@aquaculture.ca
Membership: *Member Profile:* Aquaculture operators; Feed companies; Suppliers; Provincial shellfish & finfish aquaculture associations
Activities: Advocating for Canadian aquaculture issues; Fostering cooperation among various aquaculture interests; Promoting a positive image of the Canadian aquaculture industry; Encouraging the consumption of aquaculture products from Canada

Canadian Archaeological Association (CAA) / Association d'archéologie canadienne

c/o William Ross, 189 Peter St., Thunder Bay ON P7A 5H8
Tel: 807-345-2733
www.canadianarchaeology.com
Overview: A small national charitable organization founded in 1968
Mission: To publish & disseminate archaeological knowledge in Canada; To encourage archaeological research & conservation efforts; To promote cooperation among archaeological societies & agencies
Chief Officer(s):
William Ross, President, 807-345-2733
wiross@tbaytel.net
Jennifer Birch, Vice-President
jabirch@uga.edu
Jeff Hunston, Secretary-Treasurer, 867-667-5363
keeperaustraliamt@klondiker.com
Membership: *Fees:* $35 students; $75 regular; $100 institutional & supporting; *Member Profile:* Professional, avocational, & student archaeologists; General public; *Committees:* Heritage & Legislation Policy; Aboriginal Heritage; Student's; Membership; Cultural Resource Management; Financial Advisory; Public Communication Awards; Comité du Prix Weetaluktuk Award; James & Margaret Pendergast Award; Smith-Wintemberg Award
Activities: Fostering cooperation with aboriginal groups; Promoting activities advantageous to archaeology; Advocating nationally
Publications:
•CAA [Canadian Archaeological Association] Newsletter / Bulletin de l'ACA [Association d'archéologie canadienne
Type: Newsletter; *Frequency:* Semiannually; *Editor:* Karen Ryan; *Price:* Free with membership in the CanadianArchaeological

Association
Profile: A spring & fall publication
•Canadian Journal of Archaeology / Journal canadien d'archéologie
Type: Journal; *Frequency:* Semiannually; *Editor:* Dr. Gerry Oetelaar; *Price:* Free with membership in the Canadian ArchaeologicalAssociation
Profile: Documents the processes & results of Canadian archaeology

Canadian Associated Air Balance Council (CAABC)

Tel: 905-886-6513; *Fax:* 905-886-6513
e-mail: mail@designtest.ca
www.caabc.org
Overview: A small national organization founded in 1970
Mission: To promote independent testing & balancing of mechanical systems; to produce standards to advance the industry; Affiliation(s): Associated Air Balance Council
Chief Officer(s):
Surrinder S. Sahota, President
Finances: *Funding Sources:* Membership fees
Staff: 1 staff member(s); 18 volunteer(s)
Membership: 20; *Fees:* $3,000; *Committees:* Membership; Technical; Standards

Canadian Association for Humane Trapping (CAHT)

PO Box 7115, Stn. Maplehurst, Burlington ON L7T 4J8
e-mail: caht1@cogeco.ca
www.caht.ca
Overview: A medium-sized national charitable organization founded in 1954
Mission: To reduce & eliminate suffering of animals trapped for whatever reason; To work with governments, trappers, the commercial fur industry, animal welfare organizations & the public-at-large to bring about actual trapping improvements; *Member of:* World Conservation Union; Fur Institute of Canada; World Wildlife Fund; Canadian Nature Federation; Canadian Federation of Humane Societies
Chief Officer(s):
James H. Bandow, Executive Director
Donald Mitton, Project Director
Donna Bandow, Coordinator, Grants & Fundraising
Finances: *Funding Sources:* Membership fees; Bequests; Donations
Membership: 750; *Fees:* $10; *Committees:* Trap research & development
Activities: *Speaker Service:* Yes
Publications:
•The CAHT [Canadian Association for Humane Trapping] Bulletin
Type: Newsletter; *Number of Pages:* 16

Canadian Association for Laboratory Accreditation Inc. (CALA)

#310, 1565 Carling Ave., Ottawa ON K1Z 8R1
Tel: 613-233-5300; *Fax:* 613-233-5501
e-mail: ecummins@cala.ca
www.cala.ca
www.facebook.com/group.php?gid=161209647296775
Overview: A medium-sized national organization founded in 1989
Mission: To provide internationally-recognized accreditation services; To assist laboratories in the achievement of high levels of scientific & management excellence; To improve environmental quality & public health & safety; *Member of:* Asia Pacific Laboratory Accreditation Cooperation; International Laboratory Accreditation Cooperation
Chief Officer(s):
Charlie Brimley, President & CEO
cbrimley@cala.ca
Brenda Dashney, Chief Financial Officer
bdashney@cala.ca
Ned Gravel, Manager, Quality & Training
ngravel@cala.ca
Ken Middlebrook, Manager, Proficiency Testing
kmiddlebrook@cala.ca
Andrew Morris, Manager, Data & Information
amorris@cala.ca
Membership: *Fees:* $15 students; $50 associates & individual (voting); $4500 institutional (voting); *Member Profile:* Individuals, consultants, institutions, industrial organizations, regulatory agencies, laboratory equipment suppliers, & user groups interested in the work of environmental analytical laboratories
Activities: Advocating for change in protecting public health & safety; Educating the public & raising awareness of laboratory accreditation; Offering training opportunities, such as workshops & web-based education; Conducting site audits & proficiency testing to evaluate the performance of laboratories; Granting accreditation to laboratories, based on decisions of the CALA Accreditation Council;
Meetings/Conferences:
For more information see Trade Shows, Conferences and Seminars Chapter
Canadian Association for Laboratory Accreditation 2013 Annual General Meeting
June 2013 Moncton, NB
Canadian Association for Laboratory Accreditation 2014 Conference and Tradeshow
2014
Publications:
•Canadian Association for Laboratory Accreditation Inc. Annual Report
Type: Yearbook; *Frequency:* Annually

Canadian Association for Laboratory Animal Science (CALAS)

#640, 144 Front St., Toronto ON M5J 2L7
Tel: 416-593-0268; *Fax:* 416-979-1819
e-mail: office@calas-acsal.org
www.calas-acsal.org
Overview: A small national organization founded in 1962
Mission: To elevate standards of laboratory animal science; To promote excellence in research; To eliminate inhumane & unnecessary use of animals in research; To enhance animal welfare
Chief Officer(s):
Teresa McKernan, President
tmckernan@calas-acsal.org
Michelle Gillespie, Vice-President
tmckernan@calas-acsal.org
Wendy Ansell, Administrator
Claire Smits, Treasurer
claire.smits@hli.ubc.ca
Khadijah Hewitt, Coordinator, Membership & Registry
Finances: *Funding Sources:* Membership fees; Sponsorships
Membership: 1,000; *Member Profile:* Veterinarians; Physicians; Researchers; Technicians; Administrators; Students; Institutions; *Committees:* Awards; Marketing; Membership; Educational; Regional Chapter; Symposium; Continuing Education
Activities: Providing information about the animal science industry; Offering networking opportunities; Providing continuing education to advance the knowledge & skills of persons who work with laboratory animals
Publications:
•Canadian Association for Laboratory Animal Science Members' Magazine
Type: Magazine; *Frequency:* Bimonthly; *Price:* Free with membership in the Canadian Association for Laboratory Animal Science

Canadian Association for Mine & Explosive Ordnance Security (CAMEO)

1009 Oak Cres., Cornwall ON K6J 2N2
Tel: 613-937-0686; *Fax:* 613-937-4643
e-mail: frank.jewsbury@rogers.com
www.cameo.org
Also Known As: CAMEO Landmine Clearance
Overview: A small international charitable organization
Mission: To engage in humanitarian mine clearance; to engage in humanitarian explosive ordnance disposal; to engage in live-firing area clearance & environmental clean-up; to engage in land mine & explosive ordnance awareness training; to engage in land mine & battle area surveys; to provide training & assistance to others in the carrying out of all of the above activities
Chief Officer(s):
James D. McGill, Executive Director
megill@cameo.org
Membership: 100-499
Activities: Landmine clearance in Southern Sudan; *Speaker Service:* Yes

Canadian Association for Renewable Energies (CARE) / Association canadienne pour les énergies renouvelables

7885 Jock Trail, Ottawa ON K0A 2Z0
Fax: 613-822-4987
www.renewables.ca
Also Known As: we c.a.r.e
Overview: A small national organization founded in 1998
Mission: To promote feasible applications of renewable energies
Chief Officer(s):
Bill Eggertson, Executive Director
eggertson@renewables.ca
Finances: *Funding Sources:* Membership fees
Membership: *Fees:* $214 personal; $321 corporate; $1,070 institutional; *Member Profile:* Supporters of renewable energies
Activities: Undertaking research to optimize renewable energy technologies
Publications:
•Refocus Weekly [a publication of the Canadian Association for Renewable Energies]
Type: Newsletter; *Frequency:* Weekly; *Accepts Advertising*
Profile: News, reports, & events from around the world
•Renewable Energy Focus
Type: Magazine; *Accepts Advertising*
Profile: Debate & dialogue between industry, research, government agencies, & financial organizations throughout the world on topics such as biomass, biogass, hydroelectricity, wind, waves, solararchitecture, & fuel cells

Canadian Association for Research in Nondestructive Evaluation (CARNDE) / Association canadienne de recherches en évaluation non-destructive (ACREND)

75, boul de Montagne, Boucherville QC J4B 6Y4
Tel: 450-641-5252; *Fax:* 450-641-5106
e-mail: jean.bussiere@nrc.ca
www.nrc.ca
Overview: A small national organization founded in 1987
Mission: To foster, coordinate & disseminate results of research, development & application of new or advanced NDE techniques in Canada; to promote technology transfer by encouraging collaboration between universities, research organizations & industrial or governmental users; to raise the profile of NDE research in Canada by publicizing the need for & economic benefits arising from advances in NDE
Chief Officer(s):
Jean Bussière, Research Editor
Membership: 100; *Member Profile:* Open to applied scientists & engineers who have a professional interest in conductor application of research in NDE
Activities: *Rents Mailing List:* Yes

Canadian Association for Studies in Co-operation (CASC) / Association canadienne pour les études sur la coopération (ACEC)

c/o Centre for the Study of Co-operatives, University of Saskatchewan, 101 Diefenbaker Pl., Saskatoon SK S7N 5B8
Tel: 306-966-8509; *Fax:* 306-966-8517
e-mail: casc.acec@usask.ca
www.coopresearch.coop
Overview: A small national organization founded in 2000
Mission: To promote research on co-operatives in Canada
Chief Officer(s):
Darryl Reed, President
Monica Adler, Vice-President
Membership: *Member Profile:* Researchers, scholars, & practitioners working in the area of co-operatives
Awards:
•Lemaire Co-operative Studies Award (Scholarship)
Postgraduate & undergraduate awards to encourage students to undertake studies which will help them to contribute to the development of co-operatives in Canada or elsewhere; disciplines include: housing, planning, environmental studies, engineering, geography, science, architecture *Amount:* $1,000 - $3,000
•Alexander Fraser Laidlaw Fellowship (Scholarship)
Postgraduate award for students in: housing, environmental studies, planning, geography, science, architecture, civil engineering, engineering; the fellowship is awarded on the basis of the applicant's academic record & the importance of the proposed research activities to the development of the co-operative movement in Canada or elsewhere *Amount:* $1,000
•Amy & Tim Dauphinee Scholarships for Studies in Co-operation (Scholarship)
For graduate students in the following disciplines: cooperatives, housing, planning, environmental studies, geography, science, architecture, civil engineering, engineering; awards based on the applicant's academic records & on the importance of the proposed research activities to the development of the co-operative movement in Canada or abroad *Amount:* $3,000
Publications:
•CASC [Canadian Association for Studies in Co-operation] Newsletter
Type: Newsletter

The Canadian Association for the Prevention of Consumption & Other Forms of Tuberculosis; The Canadian Tuberculosis & Respiratory Disease Associa ***See*** Canadian Lung Association

Canadian Association for the Study of Humanities and the Environment

c/o Institute for Governance Studies, Simon Fraser University, Burnaby BC V5A 1S6
Tel: 778-782-4293; *Fax:* 778-782-4786
e-mail: igs@sfu.ca
www.sfu.ca/igs/cashe.html
Overview: A small national organization
Chief Officer(s):
Rebecca Raglon, Secretary
Publications:
•Journal of Ecocriticism
Type: online; *Frequency:* Biannual; *Editor:* Michael Howlett
Profile: A new journal of Nature, Society and Literature

Canadian Association of Aerial Surveyors ***See*** Geomatics Industry Association of Canada

Canadian Association of Agri-Retailers (CAAR)

#628, 70 Arthur St., Winnipeg MB R3B 1G7
Tel: 204-989-9300; *Fax:* 204-989-9306
Toll-Free: 800-463-9323
e-mail: info@caar.org
www.caar.org
www.facebook.com/group.php?gid=142300712530309
Previous Name: Western Fertilizer & Chemical Dealers Association
Overview: A medium-sized national organization founded in 1978
Mission: To represent & protect the interests of Canadian agricultural retailers
Chief Officer(s):
Delaney Ross, Manager, Communications & Marketing, 204-989-9305
delaney@caar.org
Irene O'Dell, Office Coordinator, 204-989-9300
irene@caar.org
Lynda Nicol, Coordinator, Communications & Research, 204-989-9304
lynda@caar.org
Membership: *Member Profile:* Canadian agricultural retailer members, who provide farmers with the products & services required for agricultural production; Canadian suppliers, who manufacture the products sold by retailers; *Committees:* Executive Council; Finance; Membership Development & Services; Facility & Transport Logistics; Convention; Communication & Public Relations; Stewardship & Agronomy; Government Affairs & Industry Relations
Activities: Liaising with provincial & national governments; Engaging in advocacy actitivities; Offering networking opportunities for agricultural suppliers & retailers; Providing information & training events
Meetings/Conferences:
For more information see Trade Shows, Conferences and Seminars Chapter
Canadian Association of Agri-Retailers 2013 18th Annual Convention & Trade Show
February 2013 Banff, AB
Canadian Association of Agri-Retailers 2014 19th Annual Convention & Trade Show
February 2014 Montréal, QC
Publications:
•CAAR [Canadian Association of Agri-Retailers] Communicator
Type: Magazine; *Frequency:* 5 pa; *Accepts Advertising*
Profile: Information about government regulations, industry initiatives, & new technology for recipients throughout Canada & the United States
•CAAR [Canadian Association of Agri-Retailers] Roster
Type: Directory
Profile: A networking tool with hundreds of listings of businesses & organizations, as well as the Supplier's Guide & the CAARPerk$ Guide (formerly the Member BenefitsGuide)
•CCA [Certified Crop Advisors] Examiner
Type: Newsletter; *Frequency:* Quarterly
Profile: Distributed with the Canadian Association of Agri-Retailers Input newsletter
•Fast Facts [a publication of the Canadian Association of Agri-Retailers]
Type: Newsletter; *Frequency:* Monthly
Profile: Events, services, & information for association members
•Input [a publication of the Canadian Association of Agri-Retailers]
Type: Newsletter; *Frequency:* Quarterly
Profile: Information about the association & the industry for members only
•Retail Compensation Survey [a publication of the Canadian Association of Agri-Retailers]
Type: Newsletter

Canadian Association of Animal Health Technologists & Technicians (CAAHTT) / Association canadienne des techniciens et technologistes en santé animale (ACTTSA)

339 Booth St., Ottawa ON K1R 7K1
Tel: 800-567-2862
e-mail: info@caahtt-acttsa.ca
www.caahtt-acttsa.ca
Overview: A medium-sized national organization founded in 1989
Mission: To provide coordination & resources to support members in the delivery of animal health care services; *Member of:* International Veterinary Nurses & Technicians Association (IVNTA); Affiliation(s): Canadian Veterinary Medical Association; National Association of Veterinary Technicians in America (NAVTA)
Chief Officer(s):
Phyllis Mierau, Executive Director
Michele Moroz, President
Chantal Cormier, Vice-President
Finances: *Funding Sources:* Provincial association fees; Corporate sponsorship
Membership: *Committees:* Professional Development; Veterinary Technician Testing; CVMA Animal Health Technology / Veterinary Technician Program Accreditation; CVMA Professional Development
Activities: Facilitating communication links; Providing informational updates; Lobbying to protect & promote the profession; Coordinating national & provincial activities; Promoting Doggone Safe, a national dog bit prevention program; *Awareness Events:* Veterinary Technician Week; Animal Health Week
Meetings/Conferences:
For more information see Trade Shows, Conferences and Seminars Chapter
Canadian Association of Animal Health Technologists & Technicians 2013 24th Annual General Meeting
July 2013 Victoria, BC
Canadian Association of Animal Health Technologists & Technicians 2014 25th Annual General Meeting
2014
Publications:
•Canadian Association of Animal Health Technologists & Technicians Annual Report
Type: Yearbook; *Frequency:* Annually
•TechLife [a publication of the Canadian Association of Animal Health Technologists & Technicians]
Type: Journal
Profile: Continuing education publication for animal health technicians

Canadian Association of Chemical Distributors (CACD) / Association canadienne des distributeurs de produits chimiques (ACDPC)

349 Davis Rd., #A, Oakville ON L6J 2X2
Tel: 905-844-9140; *Fax:* 905-844-5706
www.cacd.ca
www.linkedin.com/company/canadian-association-of-chemical-distributors
www.facebook.com/group.php?gid=339092806129805
www.youtube.com/user/CatherineCACD
Overview: A medium-sized national organization founded in 1986
Chief Officer(s):
Cathy Campbell, President, 905-844-9140 Ext. 21
ccampbell@cacd.ca
Membership: 46 companies; *Fees:* Schedule available based on sales; *Member Profile:* Chemical distributing companies; *Committees:* Financial Reporting; Health & Safety; Montréal Chapter; Operation & Logistics; Regulatory Affairs; Responsible Distribution; Western Chapter; You be The Chemist
Activities: Collaborating with government to establish policies
Meetings/Conferences:
For more information see Trade Shows, Conferences and Seminars Chapter
Canadian Association of Chemical Distributors 2013 27th Annual General Meeting
May 2013 Niagara-on-the-Lake, ON
Canadian Association of Chemical Distributors 2014 28th Annual General Meeting
2014
Publications:
•The Chemunicator
Type: Magazine; *Frequency:* 3 pa; *Accepts Advertising*; *Editor:* Catherine Wieckowska
Profile: Canadian Association of Chemical Distributors reports, plus news & information for the chemical distribution industry

Canadian Association of Drilling Engineers (CADE)

#560, 400 - 5 Ave. SW, Calgary AB T2P 0L2
Tel: 403-532-0220; *Fax:* 403-263-2722
e-mail: info@cade.ca
www.cade.ca
twitter.com/cade_can
Overview: A medium-sized national organization founded in 1974
Mission: To provide a forum for the exchange of technical drilling knowledge & expertise; Affiliation(s): Canadian Association of Oilwell Drilling Contractors
Chief Officer(s):
Eric Schmelzl, President, 403-862-0870
Jeff Arvidson, Chair, Technical, 403-232-7478
Mike Buker, Chair, Education, 403-213-3615
John Burnell, Chair, Membership, 403-265-4973
Graham Evans, Chair, Information Technology
Finances: *Funding Sources:* Membership dues
Staff: 11 volunteer(s)
Membership: 620 corporate + 2 institutional + 8 student + 8 senior/lifetime; *Fees:* $10 student; $47.50 retiree; $95 full member; *Member Profile:* Open to those who work in the petroleum industry
Meetings/Conferences:
For more information see Trade Shows, Conferences and Seminars Chapter
Canadian Association of Drilling Engineers 2013 Presentation
2013
Publications:
•CADEnews [a publication of the Canadian Association of Drilling Engineers]
Type: Newsletter; *Editor:* Glenn Mencer

Canadian Association of Environmental Law Societies (CAELS)

e-mail: info@caels.org
caels.org
facebook.com/CAELSorg
www.twitter.com/CAELSorg
Overview: A medium-sized national organization
Mission: The Canadian Association of Environmental Law Societies (CAELS) is a networking project connecting environmental law students across the country. CAELS will allow law students to interact with their peers and professors, practitioners and environmental professionals.
Meetings/Conferences:
For more information see Trade Shows, Conferences and Seminars Chapter
Canadian Association of Environmental Law Societies 2013 Conference
February 2013 Ottawa, ON

Canadian Association of Environmental Management

c/o Homewood Health Centre, 150 Delhi St., Guelph ON N1E 6K9
Tel: 519-824-1010; *Fax:* 519-824-1827
www.caenvironmentalmanagement.com
Previous Name: Canadian Administrative Housekeepers Association
Overview: A small national organization founded in 1972
Mission: CAEM promotes the professional growth & development of its members & helps them improve the environmental & housekeeping services they offer.
Chief Officer(s):
Keith Sopha, President Ext. 2380
sophkeit@homewood.org
Finances: *Annual Operating Budget:* Less than $50,000; *Funding Sources:* Advertising; membership dues
Membership: 250; *Fees:* $80 individual; $140 organization; $40 additional member; *Member Profile:* Managers, supervisors, self-employed people, corporate & associate members involved in the environmental services field
Activities: Conference & trade shows; *Speaker Service:* Yes

Meetings/Conferences:
For more information see Trade Shows, Conferences and Seminars Chapter
Canadian Association of Environmental Management 2013 Conference & Trade Show
September 2013 Ottawa, ON

Alberta
David Thompson Health Region, 5430 - 47th Ave., Lacombe AB T4L 1G8
Tel: 403-782-8830; *Fax:* 403-782-2818
e-mail: amcbain@dthr.ab.ca
www.caenvironmentalmanagement.com
Chief Officer(s):
Ann McBain, Director, Public/Internal Relations

Eastern Passage
Ocean View Manor Society, 1909 Caldwell Rd., Eastern Passage NS B3G 1M4
Tel: 902-465-6020; *Fax:* 902-465-4929
Chief Officer(s):
Jacob Hillier, Director of Membership
jhillier@ovm.ca

Nova Scotia
Aberdeen Hospital, 835 East River Rd., New Glasgow NS B2H 3S6
Tel: 902-752-7600; *Fax:* 902-755-3975
Chief Officer(s):
Rosemary Gillis-Bowers, Sec.-Treas.

Canadian Association of Equipment Distributors (CAED)

4531 Southclark Pl., Ottawa ON K1T 3V2
Tel: 613-822-8861; *Fax:* 613-822-8862
www.caed.org
Overview: A small national organization founded in 1943
Mission: To represent the equipment industry in Canada; To promote cooperation between distributors & manufacturers; To encourage environmentally sound business practices; Affiliation(s): Associated Equipment Distributors (USA)
Environmental Activity: Establishing an industry focused Environment, Health, & Safety committee to promote best practices
Chief Officer(s):
Mike Christodoulou, Chair
michael.n.christodoulou@cummins.com
Nancy Ellen Leu, President
nleu@caed.org
Finances: *Funding Sources:* Sponsorships
Membership: 1,500; *Member Profile:* Canadian firms that provide equipment to the construction, forestry, mining, marine, & oil &-gas industries across Canada & throughout the world; Other organizations, such as manufacturers, trade media, financial organizations, & specialized service firms, are allied members
Activities: Liaising with federal & provincial governments & other industry associations; Implementing & harmonzing regulations; Facilitating communication among members; Offering learning materials
Publications:
•CAED [Canadian Association of Equipment Distributors] - Ontario Membership Newsletter
Type: Newsletter
Profile: Articles of interest to Ontario chapter members
•Showcase Newsletter: News from the Canadian Association of Equipment Distributors
Type: Newsletter; *Frequency:* Monthly
Profile: CAED reports, industry news, & forthcoming events

Canadian Association of Fire Chiefs (CAFC) / Association canadienne des chefs de pompiers (ACCP)

#702, 280 Albert St., Ottawa ON K1P 5G8
Tel: 613-270-9138
Toll-Free: 800-775-5189
www.cafc.ca
ca.linkedin.com/pub/canadian-association-of-fire-chiefs/2a/a05/8 2b
twitter.com/cafc2
Overview: A medium-sized national organization
Mission: To lead & represent the Canadian Fire Service on public safety issues with the vision of being nationally recognized as the fire service voice of authority; Affiliation(s): International Association of Fire Chiefs
Chief Officer(s):
Robert Simonds, President
Pierre Voisine, Secretary
Lee Grant, Treasurer
Membership: 1,000; *Fees:* $190 + GST
Activities: *Rents Mailing List:* Yes; *Library:* Fire Services Resource Centre; Open to public
Meetings/Conferences:
For more information see Trade Shows, Conferences and Seminars Chapter
Canadian Association of Fire Chiefs 2013 Fire Rescue Canada Conference
September 2013 Regina, SK
Canadian Association of Fire Chiefs 2014 Fire Rescue Canada Conference
September 2014
Canadian Association of Fire Chiefs 2015 Fire Rescue Canada Conference
September 2015
Publications:
•Canadian Association of Fire Chiefs Directory of Members
Type: Directory; *Frequency:* Annually
Profile: Includes CAFC leadership listings & updated bylaws
•Fire Chief Magazine
Type: Magazine; *Frequency:* Quarterly
Profile: Important issues about fire services

Canadian Association of Geographers (CAG) / Association canadienne des géographes

Department of Geography, McGill University, #425, 805, rue Sherbrooke ouest, Montréal QC H3A 2K6
Tel: 514-398-4946; *Fax:* 514-398-7437
e-mail: valerie.shoffey@cag-acg.ca
www.cag-acg.ca
Overview: A medium-sized national organization founded in 1951
Mission: To promote the discipline of geography in Canada & internationally; *Member of:* Humanities & Social Science Federation of Canada; Canadian Federation of Earth Sciences; International Geographical Union; Affiliation(s): L'l'association professionelle des géographes du Québec; Association of American Geographers; Institute of British Geographers
Chief Officer(s):
Anne Godlewska, President
anne.godlewska@queensu.ca
Mary-Louise Byrne, Secretary-Treasurer
mlbyrne@wlu.ca
Ian MacLachlan, Editor, The Canadian Geographer
TCG.editor@cag-acg.ca
Valerie Shoffey, Editor, The CAG Newsletter
valerie.shoffey@cag-acg.ca
Membership: *Member Profile:* Practicing geographers from the public & private sectors & universities across Canada & internationally; Students
Activities: Promoting geographic education; Disseminating geographic research; Collaborating with other national & international geographic organizations
Meetings/Conferences:
For more information see Trade Shows, Conferences and Seminars Chapter
Canadian Association of Geographers 2013 Annual Meeting & Conference
August 2013 St. John's, NL
Canadian Association of Geographers 2014 Annual Meeting & Conference
May 2014 St Catharines, ON
Canadian Association of Geographers 2015 Annual Meeting & Conference
June 2015 Sackville, NB
Canadian Association of Geographers 2016 Annual Meeting & Conference
2016 Toronto, ON
Publications:
•The CAG [Canadian Association of Geographers] Newsletter
Type: Newsletter; *Frequency:* Quarterly; *Editor:* Valerie Shoffey; *Price:* Free with membership in the Canadian Association of Geographers
Profile: News about members, employment opportunities & announcements, technical features, Statistics Canada news, research highlights, & studentinformation
•The CAG [Canadian Association of Geographers] Annual Directory
Type: Directory; *Frequency:* Annually; *Editor:* Kim Falcigno (kimfalcigno@shaw.ca); *Price:* Free with membership in the Canadian Association of Geographers
Profile: Listings of CAG members, academic staff, research activities, & current publications of Canadian university geographydepartments & government agencies
•The Canadian Geographer (TCG) / Le Géographe canadien (LGC)
Type: Journal; *Frequency:* Quarterly; *Editor:* Ian MacLachlan; *Price:* Free with membership in theCanadian Association of Geographers
Profile: Philosophical, theoretical, & methodological subjects of interest to scholars & geographers in Canada & worldwide

Atlantic Division
c/o James Boxall, GIS Centre, Killam Library, Dalhousie University, 6225 University Ave., Halifax NS B3H 4H8
community.smu.ca/acag
Chief Officer(s):
Colin Laroque, President
claroque@mta.ca
James Boxall, Secretary-Treasurer
James.Boxall@Dal.ca

Ontario Division
c/o Marilyne Jollineau, Dept. of Geography, Faculty of Social Sciences, Brock University, St Catharines ON L2S 3A1
www.geography.ryerson.ca/cagont
Chief Officer(s):
Marilyn Jollineau, President, 905-688-5550 Ext. 4556
mjollineau@brocku.ca
Wayne Forsythe, Vice-President, 416-979-5000 Ext. 7141, Fax: 416-979-5362
Randy Dirszowsky, Secretary-Treasurer, 705-675-1151 Ext. 3358, Fax: 705-675-4893

Prairie Division
c/o D. Eberts, J.R. Brodie Science Ctr., Dept of Geography, Brandon U., #4-09, 270 - 18th St., Brandon MB R7A 6A9
pcag.uwinnipeg.ca
Chief Officer(s):
Dirk de Boer, President
dirk.deboer@usask.ca
Derrek Eberts, Secretary-Treasurer
ebertsd@BrandonU.ca

Western Division
c/o H. Jiskoot, Water & Environmental Science Bldg., U. of Lethbridge, 4401 University Dr., Lethbridge AB T1K 3M4
www.geog.uvic.ca/dept/wcag
Theresa Garvin, President
Theresa.Garvin@ualberta.ca
Craig Coburn, Secretary-Treasurer
hester.jiskoot@uleth.ca

Canadian Association of Geophysical Contractors (CAGC)

#1045, 1015 - 4 St. SW, Calgary AB T2R 1J4
Tel: 403-265-0045; *Fax:* 403-265-0025
e-mail: info@cagc.ca
www.cagc.ca
Overview: A small national organization founded in 1977
Mission: To act as the voice of business in the Canadian seismic industry; To promote the Canadian geophysical industry
Environmental Activity: Promoting the protection of the natural environment in geophysical operations
Chief Officer(s):
Forrest Burkholder, Chair
Forrest.Burkholder@cggveritas.com
Mike Doyle, President
mjd@cagc.ca
Marvin Lebeau, Chair, Health, Safety, & Environment
mjd@cagc.ca
Activities: Working with governments, stakeholders, & communities; Promoting hight ethical standards throughout the geophysical industry; Providing health & safety training
Publications:
•The Source: The Voice of Business in the Canadian Seismic Industry
Type: Magazine; *Frequency:* Quarterly
Profile: Canadian Association of Geophysical Contractors membership news, awards, & upcoming events

Canadian Association of Heritage Professionals (CAPHC) / Association canadienne d'experts-conseils en patrimoine (ACECP)

George Brown House, #211, 50 Baldwin St., Toronto ON M5T 1L4
Tel: 416-515-7450; *Fax:* 416-515-0961
e-mail: admin@cahp-acecp.ca
www.caphc.ca

Previous Name: Association of Heritage Consultants
Overview: A medium-sized national organization founded in 1987
Mission: To represent & further the professional interests of heritage consultants active in both the private & public sectors; To establish & maintain principles & standards of practice for heritage consultants; To enhance awareness & appreciation of heritage resources, & the contribution of heritage consultants; To foster communication among private practitioners, public agencies, & the public at large in matters related to heritage conservation; Affiliation(s): ICOMOS International (International Council on Monuments & Sites); ICOMOS Canada - English-Speaking Committee
Chief Officer(s):
Fernando Pellicer, President & Chair, Communications Committee
Eileen Costello, Treasurer & Secretary
Membership: 210; *Fees:* $50; *Member Profile:* Practitioners active in either private or public sector in fields allied to heritage conservation; *Committees:* Advocacy; Professional Conduct & Ethics; Communications; Membership Services; Strategic Business Development
Activities: Offering the following range of services by members: archaeology, anthropology, conservation, curation, design & planning, education, heritage administration, landscape design, photography, illustration & recording, & restoration
Publications:
•Canadian Association of Professional Heritage Consultants Forum
Type: Newsletter; *Accepts Advertising*
Profile: Articles on conservation, CAPHC / ACECP news & events
•CAPHC [Canadian Association of Professional Heritage Consultants] Membership Directory
Type: Directory; *Accepts Advertising*

Canadian Association of Medical Biochemists (CAMB) / Association des médecins biochimistes du Canada (AMBC)

774 Echo Dr., Ottawa ON K1S 5N8
Tel: 613-730-8177; *Fax:* 613-730-1116
Toll-Free: 800-668-3740
e-mail: camb@rcpsc.edu
www.camb-ambc.ca
Overview: A small national organization founded in 1975
Chief Officer(s):
Danièle Saintonge, Association Manager
Membership: *Fees:* $100 ordinary members; $15 emeritus & student members

Canadian Association of Members of Public Utility Tribunals / Association canadienne des membres des tribunaux d'utilité publique *See* CAMPUT, Canada's Energy & Utility Regulators

Canadian Association of Mining Equipment & Services for Export (CAMESE) / Association canadienne des exportateurs d'équipement et services miniers

#101, 345 Renfrew Dr., Markham ON L3R 9S9
Tel: 905-513-0046; *Fax:* 905-513-1834
e-mail: minesupply@camese.org
www.camese.org
www.facebook.com/pages/CAMESE/137206069649085
twitter.com/miningsuppliers
Overview: A medium-sized international organization founded in 1981
Member of: Prospectors & Developers Association of Canada (PDAC); Canadian Institute of Mining, Metallurgy & Petroleum (CIM); Mining Association of Canada (MAC)
Chief Officer(s):
Jon Baird, Managing Director
baird@camese.org
Roy Jakola, Director, Business Development
jakola@camese.org
Spencer Ramshaw, Director, Information & Communication
ramshaw@camese.org
Linda Collins, Manager, Office
collins@camese.org
Dolores Wharton, Manager, Exhibition
wharton@camese.org
Finances: *Funding Sources:* Memnbership dues; Special projects
Staff: 7 staff member(s); 10 volunteer(s)
Membership: 300; *Fees:* Schedule available; *Member Profile:* Organizations, with an office or employee in Canada, that seek to export goods & services to the global mining industry; Organizations that assist others to export goods & services; *Committees:* Membership; Finance
Activities: Providing selling advice to members; Participating in international mining trade exhibitions; Networking with other firms in the mining sector; Researching target makets for member firms
Publications:
•CAMESE [Canadian Association of Mining Equipment & Services for Export] Bulletin
Type: Newsletter; *Frequency:* Semimonthly
Profile: Market conditions, export sales opportunities, & upcoming events in the mining sector
•Compendium of Canadian Mining Suppliers
Type: Yearbook; *Frequency:* Annually; *Editor:* Bonnie Toews

Canadian Association of Oilwell Drilling Contractors (CAODC)

#2050, 717 - 7th Ave. SW, Calgary AB T2P 0Z3
Tel: 403-264-4311; *Fax:* 403-263-3796
e-mail: info@caodc.ca
www.caodc.ca
twitter.com/markascholz
www.youtube.com/user/TheCAODC
Overview: A large national organization founded in 1949
Mission: To represent drilling rig contractors; to provide ongoing means of communication between drilling & well servicing contractors, governments, other industry sector participants, & the general public; To improve standards for safety & training, equipment & technical procedures; To coordinate programs between government bodies & contractors; To oversee the Rig Technician Trade & Apprenticeship Program in Alberta, British Columbia, & Saskatchewan
Chief Officer(s):
W. Ross Pickering, Chair
Wade McGowan, Vice-Chair
Membership: 44 Drilling Rig Division + 2 Atlantic Division + 73 Service Rig Division + 198 Associate Division; *Fees:* Schedule available; *Member Profile:* Upstream Canadian petroleum drilling contractors (land-based & offshore) service rig contractors & associate companies; *Committees:* Accounting & Taxation (Drilling); Engineering & Technical; Finance/Audit; Forecasting; Government & Public Relations; Health, Safety & Environment (Drilling); Human Resources & Training; Information Technology; Legal & Contract (Drilling); Manpower; Rig Technician Apprenticeship
Activities: ; *Library:* Open to public by appointment
Publications:
•CAODC [Canadian Association of Oilwell Drilling Contractors] Oil Driller
Type: Magazine; *Frequency:* 3 pa; *Accepts Advertising*; *Editor:* Cindy Soderstrom
Profile: Reports on issues about Canada's oil industry. drilling forecasts, & CAODC committee updates
•CAODC [Canadian Association of Oilwell Drilling Contractors] Members Directory & Buyers Guide
Type: Directory; *Frequency:* Annual
Profile: Available in print & online

Canadian Association of Palynologists (CAP) / Association canadienne des palynologues

c/o Dr. Mary A. Vetter, Luther College, University of Regina, Regina SK S4S 0A2
www.scirpus.ca/cap/cap.shtml
Overview: A small national organization founded in 1979
Mission: To advance all aspects of palynology in Canada; Affiliation(s): International Federation of Palynological Societies (IFPS)
Chief Officer(s):
Matthew Peros, President
mperos@uottawa.ca
Mary A. Vetter, Secretary-Treasurer
mary.vetter@uregina.ca
Terri Lacourse, Editor, CAP Newsletter
tlacours@uvic.ca
Finances: *Funding Sources:* Membership dues
Membership: 57; *Fees:* $10; *Member Profile:* Palynologists from universities, government agencies, & industries; Persons with an interest in Canadian palynology
Activities: Promoting cooperation between palynologists & persons in related fields of study; *Library:* CAP Library;
Publications:
•CAP [Canadian Association of Palynologists] Newsletter
Type: Newsletter; *Frequency:* Semiannually; *Editor:* Dr. Terri Lacourse; *Price:* Free with membership in theCanadian Association of Palynologists
Profile: Reports about fieldwork, analytical methods, & research in Canadian palynology, plus essays & conference information

Canadian Association of Petroleum Landmen (CAPL)

#350, 500 - 5 Ave. SW, Calgary AB T2P 3L5
Tel: 403-237-6635; *Fax:* 403-263-1620
e-mail: reception@landman.ca
www.landman.ca
Overview: A medium-sized national organization founded in 1948
Mission: To enhance all facets of the land profession
Chief Officer(s):
Margaret Ariss, President
margaret.ariss@pxx.ca
John Covey, Vice-President
jcovey@shaw.ca
Gloria Boogmans, Director, Member Services
gboogmans@shaw.ca
Joan Dornian, Director, Communications
joan.dornian@mcmillan.ca
Kevin Egan, Director, Education
kevin.egan@huskyenergy.com
Chris Lamb, Director, Public Relations
clamb@atha.com
Nikki Sitch, Director, Finance
nsitch@barrick-energy.com
Membership: 1,500+
Activities: Liaising with government departments & other resource based associations; Communicating with members; Providing professional development opportunities; Offering networking events
Meetings/Conferences:
For more information see Trade Shows, Conferences and Seminars Chapter
Canadian Association of Petroleum Landmen 2013 Annual Conference
2013
Publications:
•Canadian Association of Petroleum Landmen Membership Directory
Type: Directory; *Price:* Free access with membership in the Canadian Association of Petroleum Landmen
•CAPL [Canadian Association of Petroleum Landmen] Annual Report
Type: Yearbook; *Frequency:* Annually
•The Negotiator: The Magazine of the Canadian Association of Petroleum Landmen
Type: Magazine; *Frequency:* 10 pa; *Accepts Advertising*; *Editor:* K. Rennie, M. Innes, & J. Frese; *Price:* Free with membership in the CanadianAssociation of Petroleum Landmen
Profile: Feature articles, CAPL conference information, & CAPL news & events

Canadian Association of Petroleum Producers (CAPP) / Association canadienne des producteurs pétroliers

#2100, 350 - 7 Ave. SW, Calgary AB T2P 3N9
Tel: 403-267-1100; *Fax:* 403-261-4622
e-mail: communication@capp.ca
www.capp.ca
www.linkedin.com/groupRegistration?gid=2632445
www.facebook.com/OilGasCanada
twitter.com/oilgascanada
www.youtube.com/cappvideos
Merged from: Canadian Petroleum Association; Independent Petroleum Association of Canada
Overview: A large national organization founded in 1992
Mission: To represent companies that produce Canada's natural gas & crude oil; To enhance the economic sustainability of the Canadian upstream petroleum industry; To ensure work is conducted in a safe & environmentally & socially responsible manner; To work with government to develop regulatory requirements
Environmental Activity: Offering Energy in Action, with activities that bring industry & communities together to care for the environment; Facilitating development of performance measures for environmental stewardship; Maintaining environmental operating guidelines
Chief Officer(s):
David Collyer, President
dave.collyer@capp.ca
Janet Annesley, Vice-President, Communications
janet.annesley@capp.ca
Bob Bleaney, Vice-President, External Relations
bob.bleaney@capp.ca

David Pryce, Vice-President, Operations
pryce@capp.ca
Nick Schultz, Vice-President, Pipeline Regulation
schultz@capp.ca
Greg Stringham, Vice-President, Oil Sands & Markets
stringham@capp.ca
Membership: 100+ producer members + 150 associate members; *Member Profile:* Producer members range from two person operations to internationally recognized corporations employing thousands; Associate members provide services, such as drilling, baniking, & computing, for Canada's oil & gas industry; *Committees:* Industry Equalization Steering Committee
Activities: Reviewing, analyzing, & recommending industry policy positions; Participating in regulatory change dialogues; Representing the industry on multi-sector international, federal, & provincial consultation bodies; Communicating with governments, regulators, stakeholders, & the public; Offering seminars & workshops; Providing industry trends, statistics, & research information; Informing members of industry standards & guidelines; Monitoring pipeline expansions; Improving coordinated land use planning processes
Meetings/Conferences:
For more information see Trade Shows, Conferences and Seminars Chapter
Canadian Association of Petroleum Producers (CAPP) Scotiabank Investment Symposium 2014
April 2014 Toronto, ON

Canadian Association of Physicians for the Environment (CAPE)

#301, 130 Spadina Ave., Toronto ON M5V 2L4
Tel: 416-306-2273; *Fax:* 416-960-9392
e-mail: info@cape.ca
www.cape.ca
twitter.com/CAPE_Doctors
Overview: A small national organization founded in 1994
Mission: To act as a national voice of physicians on issues surrounding health & the environment; To address issues of environmental degradation to protect & promote human health; Affiliation(s): International Society of Doctors for the Environment (ISDE)
Chief Officer(s):
Kapil Khatter, President
John Howard, Chair
Finances: *Funding Sources:* Membership fees; Donations
Membership: *Fees:* $100 physicians; $50 non-physicians; $25 students/retirees/limited income persons; $50 member organizations; *Member Profile:* Physicians; Health care workers; Citizens across Canada
Activities: Providing educational opportunities; Liaising with other national & international organizations; Designing the online resource, Children's Environmental Health Project; Advocating for laws, standards, & policies to promote health & protect the environment;
Publications:
•CAPE [Canadian Association of Physicians for the Environment] News
Type: Newsletter
Profile: Association news & information on the health implications of environmental issues

Canadian Association of Recycling Industries (CARI) / Association canadienne des industries du recyclage (ACIR)

#1, 682 Monarch Ave., Ajax ON L1S 4S2
Tel: 905-426-9313; *Fax:* 905-426-9314
www.cari-acir.org
Overview: A medium-sized national organization founded in 1941
Mission: To address issues facing the recycling industry in Canada & internationally; To promote commercial recycling activities
Environmental Activity: Advocating on behalf of Canada's recycling industry; Promoting the recycling industry to the public & the government
Chief Officer(s):
Bertrand Van Dorpe, President, 450-658-2183, Fax: 450-658-1461
rouvillestation@videotron.ca
Len Shaw, Executive Director
len@cari-acir.org
Donna Turner, Association Manager, 905-426-9313, Fax: 905-426-9314
donna@cari-acir.org
Tracy Shaw, Manager, Communications & Membership
tracy@cari-acir.org
Chris Cassell, Secretary-Treasurer, 613-283-5230, Fax: 613-283-9529
chirsc@glenviewiron.ca
Membership: 260+; *Member Profile:* Canadian companies in the recycling sector, from small scrap yards to large processing plants
Activities: Providing information on government legislation, environment & safety regulations, & new technology; Organizing networking events; Working to solve scrap metal theft; Developing cost cutting services for members; *Speaker Service:* Yes
Meetings/Conferences:
For more information see Trade Shows, Conferences and Seminars Chapter
Canadian Association of Recycling Industries (CARI) 2013 72nd Annual General Meeting & Convention
June 2013 Halifax, NS
Canadian Association of Recycling Industries (CARI) 2013 16th Annual Consumer's Night
2013
Canadian Association of Recycling Industries (CARI) 2014 73rd Annual General Meeting & Convention
2014
Publications:
•Canadian Association of Recycling Industries Membership Directory
Type: Directory; *Frequency:* Annually
Profile: Listings of contact information for the recycling industry
•The Prompt [a publication of the Canadian Association of Recycling Industries]
Type: Newsletter; *Accepts Advertising*
Profile: Information about business opportunities & forthcoming events
•The Pulse [a publication of the Canadian Association of Recycling Industries]
Type: Newsletter; *Frequency:* Monthly; *Accepts Advertising*
Profile: Information for CARI members & industry leaders concerning recycling industry issues & opportunities, including market trends, governmentallegislation, & technology advancements

Canadian Association of Swine Veterinarians (CASV) / Association Canadienne des Vétérinaires Porcins (ACVP)

Tel: 519-273-7170
www.casv-acvp.ca
Overview: A small national organization founded in 2003
Mission: To support members; To discuss issues affecting members; To offer a nation voice on issues that affect pork production; To enhance knowledge of animal welfare, herd health management, & food safety
Chief Officer(s):
John Harding, Chair, 306-966-7070
john.harding@usask.ca
George Charbonneau, President, 519-273-7170
gcharbon@swineservices.ca
Membership: *Member Profile:* Canadian veterinarians who have a special interest in swine; Persons in industry, academia, & government
Activities: Facilitating networking opportunities; Encouraging professional development; Promoting communications among organizations with similar interests

Canadian Association of Zoological Parks & Aquariums ***See*** Canadian Association of Zoos & Aquariums

Canadian Association of Zoos & Aquariums (CAZA) / Association des zoos et aquariums du Canada (AZAC)

#400, 280 Metcalfe St., Ottawa ON K2P 1R7
Tel: 613-567-0099; *Fax:* 613-233-5438
Toll-Free: 888-822-2907
e-mail: info@caza.ca
www.caza.ca
Previous Name: Canadian Association of Zoological Parks & Aquariums
Overview: A medium-sized national charitable organization founded in 1975
Mission: To promote the welfare of animals; To provide input into legislative matters & government policy affecting the zoo & aquarium industry; *Member of:* IUCN, International Union for Conservation of Nature; The World Association of Zoos & Aquariums; Canadian Museums Association
Environmental Activity: Encouraging the advancement of conservation & science; Initiating a national awareness campaign about the preservation of biodiversity in the Arctic; Increasing awareness about endangered species in Canada & throughout the world
Chief Officer(s):
Robin Hale, President
rhale@torontozoo.ca
Bill Peters, National Director, 613-567-0099 Ext. 242
bpeters@caza.ca
Greg Tarry, Manager, Special Projects
gtarry@caza.ca
Serge Lussier, Secretary-Treasurer
slussier@lionsafari.com
Finances: *Funding Sources:* Donations
Membership: *Member Profile:* Zoo & aquarium professionals; *Committees:* Executive; Nominating; Ethics; Awards; Conservation & Education; National Awareness; Policy; Accreditation; Business Development; Government Relations; Membership Services; Finance; Arctic Biodiversity; Conference
Activities: Administering the CAZA Accreditation Program; Upholding the CAZA Code of Professional Ethics; Promoting education; Offering a mentoring program for institutions
Meetings/Conferences:
For more information see Trade Shows, Conferences and Seminars Chapter
Canadian Association of Zoos & Aquariums 2013 Annual Conference
September 2013 Saskatoon, SK
Publications:
•Canadian Association of Zoos & Aquariums Membership Directory
Type: Directory
Profile: A listing of institutional, commercial, & affiliate members of the Canadian Association of Zoos & Aquariums
•CAZA [Canadian Association of Zoos & Aquariums] News
Type: Newsletter; *Frequency:* Bimonthly; *Editor:* G. Tarry; *Price:* Free with Canadian Association of Zoos & Aquariums membership
•CAZA [Canadian Association of Zoos & Aquariums] Annual Report
Type: Yearbook; *Frequency:* Annually
•Connecting Canadians to Nature: Strategic Plan [a publication of the Canadian Association of Zoos & Aquariums
Type: Report; *Number of Pages:* 16

Canadian Association on Water Pollution Research & Control ***See*** Canadian Association on Water Quality

Canadian Association on Water Quality (CAWQ) / Association canadienne sur la qualité de l'eau (ACQE)

PO Box 5050, 867 Lakeshore Rd., Burlington ON L7R 4A6
Tel: 905-336-4513; *Fax:* 905-336-6444
www.cawq.ca
Also Known As: Canadian National Committee of the International Association on Water Quality
Previous Name: Canadian Association on Water Pollution Research & Control
Overview: A medium-sized national charitable organization founded in 1967
Mission: To promote research on scientific, technological, legal & administrative aspects of water pollution research & control; To further the exchange of information & the practical application of such research for public benefit; *Member of:* International Association on Water Quality
Chief Officer(s):
Clayton Tiedemann, President, 780-412-3830, Fax: 780-412-7679
CTiedema@epcor.ca
Yves Comeau, Secretary, 514-340-4711 Ext. 3728, Fax: 514-340-5918
yves.comeau@polymtl.ca
Peter Jones, Treasurer, 819-821-8000 Ext. 62165, Fax: 819-821-7955
peter.jones@usherbrooke.ca
Finances: *Funding Sources:* Membership fees; Subscriptions; Grants
Membership: 10 corporate + 210 individual; *Fees:* Schedule available; *Member Profile:* Joint or individual - engaged in water quality & pollution research & control; Corporate - organizations engaged in water quality & pollution research & control; Sustaining - individuals & organizations interested in support & results of water quality & pollution research & control; Joint or student - students engaged in full-time study on water quality & pollution research & control
Meetings/Conferences:
For more information see Trade Shows, Conferences and Seminars Chapter

Canadian Association on Water Quality 2013 Central Canadian Symposium on Water Quality Research
March 2013 Hamilton, ON
Publications:
•Canadian Association on Water Quality Annual Report
Frequency: Annually
•IWA's Water 21
Type: Newsletter; *Frequency:* Bimonthly
•Water Quality Research Journal of Canada
Type: Journal; *Frequency:* Quarterly; *Editor:* Ronnie Gehr; *Price:* Free for individual CAWQ members; $250 Canada & USA; $295 International
Profile: Peer-reviewed scholarly & review articles & original research on topics such as the impact of pollutants & contaminants on aquatic ecosystems,aquatic species at risk, water treatment & quality, conservation, & water pollution policies

Canadian Automobile Association (CAA) / Association canadienne des automobilistes

National Office, #200, 1145 Hunt Club Rd., Ottawa ON K1V 0Y3
Toll-Free: 800-564-6222
www.caa.ca
twitter.com/CAA
www.youtube.com/TheCAAChannel
Overview: A large national organization founded in 1913
Mission: To promote, develop & implement programs & information related to the rights, responsibilities, & needs of the motorist as a consumer; Affiliation(s): Alliance internationale de tourisme; Fédération internationale de l'automobile; Federacion interamericana de touring y automovil-clubes; Commonwealth Motoring Conference; American Automobile Association
Chief Officer(s):
Tim Shearman, President
Jeff Walker, Vice-President & Chief Strategy Officer, Public Affairs
Ian Jack, Managing Director, Communications & Government Relations, 613-247-0117 Ext. 2007
ijack@national.caa.ca
Alayne Crawford, Manager, Public Affairs, 613-247-0117 Ext. 2006
acrawford@national.caa.ca
Finances: *Funding Sources:* Membership dues
Membership: 9 clubs serving 5,000,000+ members
Activities: Roadside assistance; driver training; insurance; travel packages; Savings & Rewards program; *Speaker Service:* Yes; *Library:*

Canadian Automobile Association South Central Ontario

Parent Name: Canadian Automobile Association
60 Commerce Valley Dr. East, Thornhill ON L3T 7P9
Tel: 905-771-3000; *Fax:* 905-771-3101
Toll-Free: 866-988-8878
e-mail: info@caasco.ca
www.caasco.com
www.facebook.com/106112779480473
twitter.com/caasco
www.youtube.com/caasouthcentralON
Also Known As: CAA South Central Ontario
Previous Name: Canadian Automobile Association Toronto
Overview: A large local organization founded in 1903 overseen by Canadian Automobile Association
Mission: To enrich the driving experience of members by providing travel, insurance & automotive services & information
Environmental Activity: Organizing a Recycle Drive for drained car, household, & marine batteries, used motor oil, & old tires
Chief Officer(s):
Dina Palozzi, BA, MBA, ICD.D, Chair
Nick Parks, President & CEO
Silvana Aceto, Specialist, Media & Public Relations, 905-771-3194
sace@caasco.ca
Jeff LeMoine, Consultant, Communications, 905-771-4709
jlem@caasco.ca
Finances: *Funding Sources:* Membership fees
Membership: 800,000
Activities: Offering roadside services, CAA driver training, CAA-approved vehicle repair facilities, insurance services, & travel services;
Publications:
•CAA [Canadian Automobile Association] eLetter
Type: Newsletter; *Frequency:* Monthly
Profile: CAA programs, advice, consumer information, & membership savings
•CAA [Canadian Automobile Association] Waves
Type: Newsletter; *Frequency:* Monthly
Profile: Tavel newsletter with information such as destinations, deals, & tips
•CAA [Canadian Automobile Association South Central Ontario] Magazine
Type: Magazine; *Frequency:* Quarterly; *Editor:* Tracy Howard
Profile: Publication for members includes CAA, automotive, insurance, travel, & lifestyle information
•Extraordinary Explorations [a publication of the Canadian Automobile Association]
Frequency: Quarterly
Profile: Travel ideas & vacation experiences

Canadian Automobile Association Toronto ***See*** Canadian Automobile Association South Central Ontario

Canadian Avalanche Association (CAA)

PO Box 2759, 110 MacKenzie Ave., Revelstoke BC V0E 2S0
Tel: 250-837-2435; *Fax:* 250-837-4624
Toll-Free: 800-667-1105
e-mail: info@avalanche.ca
www.avalanche.ca
Overview: A medium-sized national organization founded in 1982
Mission: To foster & support a professional environment for avalanche safety operations in Canada; To represent the avalanche community to stakeholders
Environmental Activity: Operating as a repository for snow science & avalanche research
Chief Officer(s):
Ian Tomm, Executive Director
itomm@avalanche.ca
Mary Clayton, Director, Communications
mclayton@avalanche.ca
Kristin Anthony-Malone, Manager, Operations
kmalone@avalanche.ca
Emily Grady, Manager, Industry Training Program
egrady@avalanche.ca
Finances: *Funding Sources:* Donations
Activities: Establishing technical standards; Providing technical training courses for professional avalanche workers, wilderness guiding operations, government programs (Parks Canada & provincial parks), & highway, railway, mining, forestry, & construction operations
Meetings/Conferences:
For more information see Trade Shows, Conferences and Seminars Chapter
Canadian Avalanche Association 2013 Spring Conference & Meetings
2013
Publications:
•Avalanche Accidents in Canada
Profile: Volume 1 - 1955 to 1976; Volume 2 - 1943 to 1978; Volume 3 - 1978 to 1984; Volume 4 - 1984 to 1996; Volume 5 - 1996 to 2007
•avalanche.ca
Type: Journal; *Frequency:* Quarterly; *Accepts Advertising*; *Price:* $30 Canada; $40 USA; $45 international
Profile: Research, reports from alpine countries, publication & product reviews, plus techniques, tools, & tips for avalanche safety
•Guidelines for Snow Avalanche Risk Determination & Mapping in Canada
Type: Guide; *Price:* $20
Profile: A technical reference for avalanche consultants & others, featuring concepts for the determination of avalanche risks, plus guidelines for avalanchemapping & acceptable risks
•Land Managers Guide for Snow Avalanche Hazards in Canada
Type: Guide; *Price:* $20
Profile: A guide to help land managers & consultants recognize & mitigate potential snow avalanche hazards
•Observation Guidelines & Recording Standards for Weather, Snowpack, & Avalanches (OGRS)
Type: Guide
Profile: A technical guide for professional avalanche safety operations & research in Canada

Canadian Bar Association (CBA) / Association du barreau canadien

#500, 865 Carling Ave., Ottawa ON K1S 5S8
Tel: 613-237-2925; *Fax:* 613-237-0185
Toll-Free: 800-267-8860
e-mail: info@cba.org
www.cba.org
www.linkedin.com/company/canadian-bar-association
www.facebook.com/CanadianBarAssociation
twitter.com/CBA_News
www.youtube.com/user/cbaspin
Overview: A large national organization founded in 1921
Mission: To promote improvements in the law; to promote improvements in the administration of justice; to promote individual lawyer training; to advocate in the public interest; to represent the profession on a national & international level; to promote the interests of the CBA; to promote equality in the profession; Affiliation(s): Canadian Association of Law Teachers; Canadian Law Information Council; Commonwealth Bar Association; Inter-American Bar Association; International Bar Association; Union internationale des avocats
Chief Officer(s):
John Hoyles, Chief Executive Officer
Robert Brun, President
Finances: *Annual Operating Budget:* Greater than $5 Million
Staff: 70 staff member(s)
Membership: 37,000; *Member Profile:* Open to lawyers, notaries, judges, law students, persons with a recognized law degree but not licensed to practise or retired from active practice of law, law administrators; membership is voluntary in all but British Columbia & New Brunswick; *Committees:* Awards; Communications; Continuing Legal Education; Equality; Ethics & Professional Issues; International Development; Judicial Compensation & Benefits Commitee; Law Day; Legal Aid; Legislation & Law Reform; Membership; Resolutions, Constitution & ByLaws; Supreme Court of Canada
Activities: Law for the Future Fund; legal aid; law reform initiatives; insurance & financial services for members; advocacy; Canadian Bar Foundation; *Awareness Events:* National Law Day, April
Meetings/Conferences:
For more information see Trade Shows, Conferences and Seminars Chapter
Canadian Bar Association 2013 Annual National Environmental, Energy and Resources Law Summit
June 2013 Yellowknife, NT
Canadian Bar Association Mid-Winter Meeting of Council 2013
February 2013 Mont Tremblant, QC
Canadian Bar Association Canadian Legal Conference & Expo 2013
August 2013 Saskatoon, SK

Canadian Beverage Association / Association canadienne des boissons

WaterPark Place, 20 Bay St., 11th Fl., Toronto ON M5J 2N8
Tel: 416-362-2424; *Fax:* 416-362-3229
e-mail: info@canadianbeverage.ca
www.canadianbeverage.ca
Previous Name: Refreshments Canada; Canadian Bottlers of Carbonated Beverages; Canadian Soft Drink Association
Overview: A medium-sized national organization founded in 1942
Mission: To represent soft drink bottlers, distributors, franchise houses & industry suppliers on a variety of issues
Chief Officer(s):
Jim Goetz, President
jim@canadianbeverage.ca
Stephanie Baxter, Senior Director, Communications
stephanie@canadianbeverage.ca
Anthony Van Heyningen, Senior Director, Research & Policy
anthony@canadianbeverage.ca
Finances: *Annual Operating Budget:* $500,000-$1.5 Million
Staff: 8 staff member(s)
Membership: 45 organizations; *Member Profile:* Manufacturers & distributors of carbonated soft drinks & their suppliers
Activities: ; *Library:* Open to public by appointment

Canadian Biochemical Society ***See*** Canadian Society for Molecular Biology

Canadian Bioethics Society (CBS) / Société canadienne de bioéthique

561 Rocky Ridge Bay NW, Calgary AB T3G 4E7
Tel: 403-208-8027
e-mail: info@bioethics.ca
www.bioethics.ca
www.facebook.com/groups/2393214575
Merged from: Canadian Society of Bioethic; Société canadienne de la bioéthique médicale
Overview: A small national organization founded in 1988
Mission: To facilitate knowledge sharing related to bioethics; To discover solutions to bioethical problems by promotion of research & dissemination of information
Chief Officer(s):

Susan (Sue) MacRae, President, 604-786-8043
sue.macrae@utoronto.ca
Marika Warren, Treasurer, 902-470-2764
marika.warren@dal.ca
Holly Longstaff, Officer, Communications, 778-279-4007
longstaf@exchange.ubc.ca
Finances: *Funding Sources:* Donations
Membership: 600+; *Fees:* $36 student; $127 individual; $500 supporting organization; *Member Profile:* Professional individuals & institutions interested in ethics & health research & practice
Activities: Promoting teaching of bioethics
Publications:
•Canadian Bioethics Society Newsletter
Type: Newsletter; *Accepts Advertising*; *Editor:* Stacey Page
Profile: Articles. book reviews, CBS activities, & upcoming events of interest to CBS members

Canadian Bison Association (CBA) / Association canadienne du bison

PO Box 3116, #200, 1660 Pasqua St., Regina SK S4P 3G7
Tel: 306-522-4766; *Fax:* 306-522-4768
e-mail: cba1@sasktel.net
www.canadianbison.ca
Overview: A medium-sized national licensing charitable organization founded in 1984
Mission: To develop the bison industry; to maintain the production of bison in a natural state (no growth hormones, chemicals, feed lots, free-range management); to be the voice for commercial breeders; to assist in the formation of regulations & guidelines in commercial production & management of Canadian Plains Bison & to promote the product & awareness of the bison industry; *Member of:* Canadian Livestock Records Corp.; Affiliation(s): National Bison Association - USA; BC Interior Bison Association; Peace Country Bison Association; Alberta, Saskatchewan, Manitoba, Ontario Bison Association; Québec Bison Union
Chief Officer(s):
Gavin Conacher, Executive Director
Finances: *Funding Sources:* Membership fees; convention; show & sale
Staff: 3 staff member(s); 10 volunteer(s)
Membership: 1,300 active + 100 associate; *Fees:* Schedule available; *Member Profile:* Active - own bison; associate - interest in bison industry; *Committees:* Research; Promotions; Disease; Grading; Food Safety
Activities: Bison Show & Sale; Annual Convention

Canadian Botanical Association (CBA) / Association botanique du Canada (ABC)

PO Box 160, Aberdeen SK S0K 0A0
Tel: 613-364-4074; *Fax:* 613-364-4027
e-mail: lconsaul@mus-nature.ca
www.cba-abc.ca
Overview: A small national organization founded in 1965
Mission: Representing Canadian Botany & botanists nationally & internationally, the Association responds quickly & professionally on matters that are of concern to Canadian botanists.; Affiliation(s): Botanical Society of America
Chief Officer(s):
Hugues Massicotte, President, 250-960-5813
hugues@unbc.ca
Marian Munro, Vice-President, 902-424-3564
zinckmc@gov.ns.ca
Laurie Consaul, Secretary
Jane Young, Treasurer, 250-960-5861
youngj@unbc.ca
Finances: *Annual Operating Budget:* Less than $50,000; *Funding Sources:* Membership
Membership: *Fees:* $55 regular; $25 student & retired; *Member Profile:* Professional botanists; academics; research scientists; *Committees:* Conservation; Science Policy; Development; Membership
Activities: Ecology; Mycology; Structure & development; Systematics & phytogeography; Teaching; *Library:* Open to public
Publications:
•Botany
Type: Journal; *Frequency:* Monthly; *Editor:* Cecily Pearson; *ISSN:* 1480-3305
•CBA [Canadian Botanical Association] / ABC [Association botanique du Canada] Bulletin
Type: Bulletin; *Frequency:* 3 pa; *Editor:* Christine D. Maxwell

Canadian Botanical Conservation Network (CBCN) / Le Réseau canadien pour la conservation de la flore

c/o Science Department, Royal Botanical Gardens, PO Box 399, 680 Plains Rd., Hamilton ON L8N 3H8
Tel: 905-527-1158; *Fax:* 905-577-0375
www.rbg.ca/cbcn
www.facebook.com/pages/Royal-Botanical-Gardens/140038459379746
twitter.com/RBGCanada#
www.youtube.com/user/royalbotanicalgarden
Overview: A small national organization founded in 1994
Mission: To preserve the biological diversity of Canada's rare & endangered native plant species, wild habitats & ecosystems
Membership: *Member Profile:* Individuals & organizations with an interest in conservation of plant diversity
Activities: Promoting preservation of native plant species, wild habitats, & ecosystems through education & conservation programs; *Library:* CBCN Library
Publications:
•CBCN [Canadian Botanical Conservation Network] Newsletter
Type: Newsletter; *Frequency:* Quarterly; *Editor:* Dr. David A. Galbraith; *ISSN:* 1480-8218
Profile: Plant conservation & biodiversity news, CNCN member news, & upcoming events

Canadian Bottled Water Association (CBWA) / Association canadienne des embouteilleurs d'eau

#203-1, 70 East Beaver Creek Rd., Richmond Hill ON L4B 3B2
Tel: 905-886-6928; *Fax:* 905-886-9531
e-mail: info@cbwa.ca
www.cbwa.ca
Overview: A medium-sized national licensing organization founded in 1992
Mission: To represent the Canadian bottled water industry; To ensure a high standard of quality for bottled water; *Member of:* International Council of Bottled Water Associations
Environmental Activity: Ensuring that members are committed to environmentally responsible practices
Chief Officer(s):
Elizabeth Griswold, Executive Director
griswold@cbwa.ca
Membership: *Member Profile:* Canadian bottled water companies; Equipment manufacturers; Suppliers; Distributors
Activities: Providing educational opportunities
Meetings/Conferences:
For more information see Trade Shows, Conferences and Seminars Chapter
Canadian Bottled Water Association 2013 25th Annual Canadian Bottled Water Convention & Trade Show
2013
Publications:
•WaterPower
Type: Magazine; *Frequency:* Semiannually; *Accepts Advertising*
Profile: Information & news for the bottled water industry in Canada

Canadian Bus Association (CBA) / Association canadienne de l'autobus

c/o #2001, 45 O'Connor St., Ottawa ON K1P 1A4
Tel: 613-238-1800; *Fax:* 613-241-4936
e-mail: mresnick@rothwellgroup.ca
Previous Name: Canadian Motor Coach Association
Overview: A medium-sized national organization founded in 1936
Mission: To act as the national voice of the Canadian bus industry; to act as a national forum for the discussion of bus-related issues & the establishment of positions in relation to industry-wide areas of concern; to function as a technical & operational information gathering & exchange mechanism; to further the objectives of safety, convenience & quality of the motor coach industry.
Membership: 100 companies

Canadian Camping Association (CCA) / Association des camps du Canada (ACC)

c/o Stillwood Camp & Conference Centre, 43975 Watt Rd., Lindell Beach BC V2R 4X9
Toll-Free: 877-427-6958
www.ccamping.org
www.facebook.com/CanadianCampingAssociation
twitter.com/ccampingorg
Overview: A large national charitable organization founded in 1936
Mission: To develop & promote organized camping for all populations across Canada; To further the interests & welfare of children, youth, & adults through camping; To encourage high standards in camping; Affiliation(s): International Camping Fellowship; American Camp Association; Outdoor Council of Canada; Canadian Canoe Museum; SmartBoater.ca
Chief Officer(s):
Harry Edwards, President
hedwards@stillwood.ca
Finances: *Funding Sources:* Provincial Camping Associations, corporate sponsors and private contributions.
Membership: 9 provincial camping associations, representing more than 700 camps throughout Canada; *Member Profile:* Provincial camping associations
Activities: Providing information about camping developments & regulations; Engaging in advocacy activities; Guiding camping leaders

Canadian Carbonization Research Association (CCRA)

PO Box 2460, Burlington ON L8N 3J5
Tel: 905-548-4796
www.cancarb.ca
Overview: A small national organization founded in 1965
Mission: To fund coke & coal research in Canada for benefit of member companies
Chief Officer(s):
Ted Todoschuk, Chairman
G.A. Chapman, Treasurer
Finances: *Annual Operating Budget:* $500,000-$1.5 Million; *Funding Sources:* Membership fees
Membership: 6 corporate; *Member Profile:* Coal producer, coke producer or related to coal/coke products; *Committees:* Technical

Canadian Cartographic Association (CCA) / Association canadienne de cartographie

c/o Department of Geography, University of Victoria, PO Box 3050, Stn. CSC, Victoria BC V8W 3P5
e-mail: awood@mun.ca
www.cca-acc.org
Overview: A small national organization founded in 1975
Mission: To promote interest in cartographic materials; To encourage research in the field of cartography; To advance education in cartography; Affiliation(s): International Cartographic Association
Chief Officer(s):
Alberta Auringer Wood, Secretary
secretary@cca-acc.org
Paul Heersink, Treasurer, 905-477-7408
Membership: *Fees:* $45 students, retired members, & institutions; $90 regular members; $110 family membership; $200 corporate; *Member Profile:* Individuals with an interest in mapping
Activities: Facilitating the exchange of information; Organizing a biannual exhibit of Canadian cartography; Collaborating with sister organizations
Meetings/Conferences:
For more information see Trade Shows, Conferences and Seminars Chapter
Canadian Cartographic Association 2013 Conference
June 2013 Calgary, AB
Canadian Cartographic Association 2014 Conference
2014
Publications:
•Cartographica
Type: Journal; *Frequency:* Quarterly; *ISSN:* 0317-7173; *Price:* Free with CCA membership
Profile: Cartographica also appears as a monograph on a single topic
•Cartouche
Type: Newsletter; *Frequency:* Quarterly; *Editor:* Patricia Connor Reid; *Price:* Free with CCA membership
Profile: Association activities, forthcoming events, articles, products, & news

Canadian Cattle Breeders' Association (CCBA) / Société des éleveurs de bovins canadiens (SEBC)

4865, boul Laurier ouest, Saint-Hyacinthe QC J2S 3V4
Tel: 450-774-2775; *Fax:* 450-774-9775
e-mail: info@cqrl.org
www.clrc.ca/canadiancattle.shtml
Overview: A medium-sized national organization founded in 1895
Chief Officer(s):
Angèle Hébert, Sec.-trés.
Finances: *Annual Operating Budget:* $50,000-$100,000; *Funding Sources:* Membership dues, casino
Staff: 1 staff member(s)

Membership: 93; *Fees:* $40 regular; $15 supportive; *Committees:* Genetic Classification

Canadian Cattlemen's Association (CCA)

#310, 6715 - 8 St. NE, Calgary AB T2E 7H7
Tel: 403-275-8558; *Fax:* 403-274-5686
e-mail: feedback@cattle.ca
www.cattle.ca
Overview: A large national organization founded in 1932
Mission: To act as the national voice of beef producers across Canada; To produce high-quality beef products; To maintain a profitable Canadian beef industry; To use management practices that protect the health of the animal & protect the environment
Environmental Activity: Administering the Greenhouse Gas Mitigation Program for Canadian Agriculture with three other national organizations; Promoting environmental stewardship; Presenting the Environmental Stewardship Award; Participating in the protection of birds
Chief Officer(s):
Martin Unrau, President
Dennis Laycraft, Executive Director
Rob McNabb, General Manager, Operations
Fawn Jackson, Manager, Environmental Affairs
Finances: *Funding Sources:* Fee assessments to provincial cattle organization members; National Check-off Agency
Membership: *Committees:* Environment; Animal Care; Animal Health & Meat Inspection; Value Creation & Competitiveness; Foreign Trade; Domestic Ag-Policy & Regulations; Convention; Executive & Finance
Activities: Collaborating with other agricultural sectors & food industries on matters of mutual concern; Providing a mentorship program
Meetings/Conferences:
For more information see Trade Shows, Conferences and Seminars Chapter
Canadian Cattlemen's Association 2013 Annual General Meeting
March 2013 Ottawa, ON
Canadian Cattlemen's Association 2013 Semi-Annual Meeting & Convention
2013
Publications:
•Canadian Cattlemen's Association By-laws
Number of Pages: 20
•Canadian Cattlemen's Association Policy Manual
Type: Manual; *Number of Pages:* 26
Profile: Topics include animal care, animal health, meat inspection, environment, finance, foreign trade, value creation, & competitiveness
•CCA [Canadian Cattlemen's Association] Monthly Report
Type: Report; *Frequency:* Monthly
Profile: CCA news & information about the beef producing industry
•CCA [Canadian Cattlemen's Association] Annual Report
Frequency: Annually
Profile: Executive, division, committee, provincial association, & financial reports
•CCA [Canadian Cattlemen's Association] News
Type: Newsletter; *Frequency:* Semimonthly; *Price:* Free
Profile: Recent association & industry information

Ottawa Office
#1207, 350 Sparks St., Ottawa ON K1R 7S8
Tel: 613-233-9375; *Fax:* 613-233-2860
Chief Officer(s):
John Masswohl, Director, Government & International Relations

Canadian Centre for Creative Technology ***See*** Shad Valley International

Canadian Centre for Emergency Preparedness (CCEP)

#210, 860 Harrington Ct., Burlington ON L7N 3N4
Tel: 905-331-2552; *Fax:* 905-331-1641
e-mail: info@ccep.ca
www.ccep.ca
Overview: A small national organization founded in 1993
Mission: To develop a disaster resilient Canada; To prepare small businesses, non-profit organizations, & disaster management professionals; To foster the establishment & maintenance of professional standards & certification for the disaster management community
Environmental Activity: Encouraging the balance of environmental, social, & economic considerations in formulating government policy
Chief Officer(s):
Adrian Gordon, President & Chief Executive Officer
agordon@ccep.ca
Gary Mohr, Executive Vice-President
gemohr@ccep.ca
Mary-Ellen Heiman, Director, Development & Funding
meheiman@ccep.ca
Richard Kinchlea, Director, Operations
rkinchlea@ccep.ca
Activities: Advocating for disaster resilient communities; Liaising with all levels of government; Providing information & emergency preparedness programs; Sharing knowledge with international disaster management organizations
Publications:
•CCEP [Canadian Centre for Emergency Preparedness] Newsletter
Type: Newsletter; *Frequency:* Quarterly; *Price:* Free
•Disaster Management Canada (DMC)
Type: Magazine; *Frequency:* Quarterly; *Accepts Advertising*; *Price:* Free to qualified disaster management professionals withCanadian addresses
Profile: Timely, practical information from across the disaster management spectrum for emergency management & business continuity readers

Canadian Centre for Energy Information / Centre info-énergie

#201, 322 - 11th Ave. SW, Calgary AB T2R 0C5
Tel: 403-263-7722; *Fax:* 403-237-6286
Toll-Free: 877-606-4636
www.centreforenergy.com
Also Known As: Centre for Energy
Overview: A medium-sized national organization founded in 2002
Mission: To provide information about the Canadian energy system & energy-related issues
Chief Officer(s):
Pierre Alvarez, Chair
Thomas Cotter, Secretary
David Luff, Treasurer
Activities: Raising awareness & understanding about the Canadian energy system; Providing learning resources for teachers & students; *Speaker Service:* Yes
Publications:
•Energy Research & Innovation Directory
Type: Directory
Profile: Highlights of energy research projects, developed in partnership with the Department of Foreign Affairs & International Trade

Canadian Centre for Fisheries Innovation (CCFI) / Centre canadien d'innovations des pêches

PO Box 4920, Stn. C, Ridge Rd., St. John's NL A1C 5R3
Tel: 709-778-0517; *Fax:* 709-778-0516
e-mail: ccfi@mi.mun.ca
www.ccfi.ca
Previous Name: Centre for Fisheries Innovation
Overview: A medium-sized national organization founded in 1989
Mission: To work with the fishing industry to improve productivity & profitability of fishery through science & technology; *Member of:* Newfoundland Ocean Industries Association; Aquaculture Association of Canada; Fisheries Council of Canada; St. John's Board of Trade; Affiliation(s): Memorial University of Newfoundland; Marine Institute
Chief Officer(s):
Robert Verge, Managing Director
Robert.Verge@mi.mun.caa
Gabe Gregory, Chair
ggregory@nl.rogers.com
Activities: Efforts of the Centre are concentrated in four main areas: aquaculture, harvesting, processing & equipment development; the pursuit of excellence in these areas is addressed through demonstration projects, & research & development projects which pool the expertise of industry, educational institutions & governments; the Centre plays a leading role in technology transfer & information dissemination initiatives so that the fishing industry may benefit from scientific discoveries & state-of-the-art equipment

Canadian Centre for Occupational Health & Safety (CCOHS) / Centre canadien d'hygiène et de sécurité au travail (CCHST)

135 Hunter St. East, Hamilton ON L8N 1M5
Tel: 905-572-2981; *Fax:* 905-572-2206
Toll-Free: 800-668-4284
e-mail: clientservices@ccohs.ca
www.ccohs.ca
www.linkedin.com/company/canadian-centre-for-occupational-health-and-s
www.facebook.com/CCOHS
twitter.com/ccohs
Overview: A large national charitable organization founded in 1978
Mission: Promotes the total well-being—physical, psychological & mental health—of working Canadians by providing information, training, education, management systems & solutions that support health, safety, & wellness programs
Chief Officer(s):
S. Len Hong, President/CEO, 905-572-2981 Ext. 4433
Patabendi K. Abeytunga, Vice-President, 905-572-2981 Ext. 4537
Finances: *Annual Operating Budget:* Greater than $5 Million; *Funding Sources:* Government & revenue from product sales
Staff: 85 staff member(s)
Membership: *Fees:* Optional membership packages from $25 - $500/ yr.; customized membership packages can include consulting, customized training, database development
Activities: Provides a variety of both public service initiaties at no charge to user, such as OSH Answers, Inquiry Service, Newsletters, Webinars & Podcasts. Services for specialty resources provided on a cost recovery basis include databases, publications & training & education; *Speaker Service:* Yes; *Library:* Documentation Resources; by appointment
Publications:
•The Health & Safety Report
Type: Newsletter; *Frequency:* Monthly; *Price:* Free
Profile: Workplace health & safety news, plus information & tips
•Liaison [a publication of the Canadian Centre for Occupational Health & Safety]
Type: Newsletter; *Frequency:* Bimonthly
Profile: CCOHS developments, resources, & initiatives

Canadian Centre for Policy Alternatives (CCPA) / Centre canadien de politique alternative

#205, 75 Albert St., Ottawa ON K1P 5E7
Tel: 613-563-1341; *Fax:* 613-233-1458
e-mail: ccpa@policyalternatives.ca
www.policyalternatives.ca
Overview: A medium-sized national organization founded in 1980
Mission: To promote research on economic & social issues facing Canada; to monitor current developments in economy & study important trends that affect Canadians; to demonstrate thoughtful alternatives to the limited perspectives of business, research institutes & government agencies; to put forward research that reflects concerns of women & men, labour & business, churches, cooperatives & voluntary agencies, governments, minorities, disadvantaged & fortunate individuals
Chief Officer(s):
Bruce Campbell, Executive Director
Diane Touchette, Director, Operations
Finances: *Annual Operating Budget:* $500,000-$1.5 Million
Staff: 15 staff member(s)
Membership: 3,600 individual + 150 organizations; *Fees:* $1000 director's circle; $500 editor's circle; $300 sponsor; $100 sustaining; $35 student/low income; *Member Profile:* open
Activities: Publishes research reports & books; organizes public symposiums & conferences
Publications:
•The CCPA Monitor
Type: Magazine; *Frequency:* Monthly; *Price:* Free to CCPA members
Profile: Research articles
•Our Schools / Our Selves
Type: Journal; *Frequency:* Quarterly
Profile: Articles on educational issues such as social justice, action, pedagogy, & educational content

Canadian Centre for Pollution Prevention (C2P2) / Centre canadien pour la prévention de la pollution

#134, 215 Spadina Ave., Toronto ON M5T 2C7
Tel: 905-822-4133; *Fax:* 416-979-3936
Toll-Free: 800-667-9790
e-mail: info@c2p2online.com
www.c2p2online.com
Overview: A small national organization founded in 1992
Mission: To shape the future of production & consumption; To catalyze behavioural change in order to increase sustainable practices, a healthier environment, & competitiveness
Environmental Activity: Applying sound pollution prevention technologies, methods, & practices
Chief Officer(s):

Fred Granek, Chief Operating Officer, 905-822-4133 Ext. 224
fred@c2p2online.com
Leah Nielsen, Coordinator, Projects
Shari Russell, Coordinator, Projects
Activities: Providing training opportunities; Sharing knowledge with governments, businesses, academia, & organizations
Meetings/Conferences:
For more information see Trade Shows, Conferences and Seminars Chapter
Canadian Pollution Prevention 2013 3rd Annual Sustainability Applied Event
2013
Publications:
•At the Source [a publication of the Canadian Centre for Pollution Prevention]
Type: Newsletter; *Frequency:* 3 pa
Profile: Highlights of pollution prevention activities
•What's New in P2
Type: Newsletter; *Frequency:* Monthly
Profile: National & international pollution prevention news, upcoming conferences, & recent publications

The Canadian Chamber of Commerce / La Chambre de commerce du Canada

#420, 360 Albert St., Ottawa ON K1R 7X7
Tel: 613-238-4000; *Fax:* 613-238-7643
e-mail: info@chamber.ca
www.chamber.ca
www.facebook.com/CanadianChamberofCommerce
twitter.com/CdnChamberofCom
www.youtube.com/user/CdnChamberofCommerce
Overview: A large national organization founded in 1925
Mission: To create a climate for competitiveness, profitability & job creation for enterprises of all sizes in all sectors across Canada. Offices in Ottawa, Toronto, Montreal & Calgary; *Member of:* International Chamber of Commerce; Affiliation(s): Business and Industry Advisory Committee; Canadian Services Coalition; Canadian Society of Association Executives; C.D. Howe Institute; Chamber of Commerce Executives of Canada; Forum for International Trade Training; International Chamber of Commerce; World Chambers Federation
Chief Officer(s):
Pat Horgan, Chair
Perrin Beatty, President & CEO
pbeatty@chamber.ca
Michel Barsalou, Executive Vice-President, Communications & Services
mbarsalou@chamber.ca
Membership: 420+ chambers of commerce + 192,000 businesses across Canada; *Fees:* Schedule available; *Committees:* Competition Law & Policy; Economic Policy; Innovations; Energy & Environment; Intellectual Property; International Affairs; Ottawa Liaison; Taxation; Transportation; Small & Medium-Sized Business

Canadian Chemical Producers' Association (CCPA) / Association canadienne des fabricants de produits chimiques

#805, 350 Sparks St., Ottawa ON K1R 7S8
Tel: 613-237-6215; *Fax:* 613-237-4061
www.ccpa.ca
Overview: A medium-sized national organization founded in 1962
Mission: To represent the interests of chemical manufacturers; To promote the ethic, "Responsible Care"; To act responsibly, with accountability & openness
Chief Officer(s):
Richard Paton, President & CEO
Michael Bourque, Vice-President, External Relations
David Podruzny, Vice-President, Business & Economics
Gordon Lloyd, Vice-President, Technical Affairs
Bob Masterson, Vice-President, Responsible Care
Membership: 60+; *Member Profile:* Companies that manufacture or formulate chemicals, with a commitment to ethics & codes; Companies that directly manage chemicals; Companies that supply goods or services to the chemical industry; Responsible care partnership associations & responsible care supporting associations
Activities: Communicating values & concerns of the chemcial producing industry to member companies, governments, & the public; Supporting & sharing successful practices; Promoting improved safety & environmental performance; *Library:* Canadian Chemical Producers' Association Library
Publications:
•Catalyst
Frequency: Quarterly; *Accepts Advertising*; *Editor:* Michael Bourque
Profile: Feature articles & departments about the management of chemicals throughout their life cycle

Alberta Regional Office
#223, 97 - 53017 Range Rd., Androssan AB T8E 2M3
Tel: 780-922-5902
Chief Officer(s):
Al Schulz, Regional Director
alschulz@telusplanet.net

British Columbia Regional Office
#13, 1238 Cardero St., Vancouver BC V6G 2H6
Tel: 778-888-6461
Chief Officer(s):
Lorna Young, Regional Director
lyoung@canadianchemistry.ca

Ontario Regional Office
41 Cornerbrook Dr., Toronto ON M3A 1H5
Tel: 416-445-9353
Chief Officer(s):
Norm Huebel, Regional Director
nhuebel@sympatico.ca

Québec Regional Office
8910, rue Deschambault, Saint-Léonard QC H1R 2C4
Tel: 514-324-1308
Chief Officer(s):
Jules Lauzon, Regional Director
jlauzon@videotron.ca

Canadian Circumpolar Institute (CCI) / Institut circumpolaire canadien

University of Alberta, #1-42, Pembina Hall, Edmonton AB T6G 2H8
Tel: 780-492-4512; *Fax:* 780-492-1153
www.uofaweb.ualberta.ca/CCI
Previous Name: Boreal Institute for Northern Studies (1960-1990)
Overview: A small international organization founded in 1990
Mission: To promote & support research, education, & training related to the boreal & circumpolar regions of the Arctic & Antactica; To enhance awareness of polar environments; *Member of:* University of Alberta
Environmental Activity: Promoting sustainability of circumpolar areas, including northern Canada, the Arctic, & Antarctic
Chief Officer(s):
Marianne S. Douglas, Director, 780-492-0055, Fax: 780-492-1153
marianne.douglas@ualberta.ca
Anita Dey Nuttall, Associate Director, Research Advancement, 780-492-9089, Fax: 780-492-1153
anitad@ualberta.ca
Lindsay Johnston, Circumpolar Librarian & Public Service Mgr, Cameron Library, 780-492-5946
lindsay.johnston@ualberta.ca
Elaine L. Maloney, Managing Editor, CCI Press, 780-492-4999, Fax: 780-492-1153
elaine.maloney@ualberta.ca
Finances: *Funding Sources:* Grants; Donations
Membership: 500-999
Activities: Developing & facilitating interdisciplinary circumpolar research & education; Facilitating communication among northern researchers; Awarding grants & scholarships; Providing outreach programs; Publishing three to five titles each year in subject areas related to the north; Disseminating information about circumpolar areas; *Library:* The Canadian Circumpolar Collection (CCC), U of Alberta Library; Open to public
Publications:
•Canadian Circumpolar Institute Occasional Publications Series
Type: Monographs; *Editor:* Elaine L. Maloney, CCI Press; *ISSN:* 0068-0303
Profile: Conference proceedings & collections of papers
•Circumpolar Research Series
Type: Monographs; *Editor:* Elaine L. Maloney, CCI Press; *ISSN:* 0838-133X
Profile: Scholarly research on circumpolar situations & concerns
•Northern Hunter-Gatherers Research Series
Editor: Elaine L. Maloney, CCI Press; *ISSN:* 1707-522X
Profile: Interdisciplinary research about the hunting & gathering peoples of arctic, boreal, & sub-arctic regions
•Northern Reference Series [publications of the Canadian Circumpolar Institute]
Editor: Elaine L. Maloney, CCI Press; *ISSN:* 1192-5620
Profile: Bibliographies, literature reviews, annotated bibliographies, & review papers
•Solstice Series [publications of the Canadian Circumpolar Institute]
Editor: Elaine L. Maloney, CCI Press; *ISSN:* 1709-5824
Profile: Case studies & community-based models

Canadian Clean Power Coalition (CCPC)

64 Chapala Heath, Calgary AB T2X 3P9
Tel: 403-606-0973; *Fax:* 403-256-0424
www.canadiancleanpowercoalition.com
Overview: A medium-sized national organization
Mission: To secure a future for coal-fired electricity generation, along with a mix of fuels such as solar, wind, hydro, & nuclear; To research & develop clean coal technology
Chief Officer(s):
Don Wharton, Chair
Bob Stobbs, Executive Director, 306-566-3326
bstobbs@saskpower.com
Membership: *Member Profile:* Canadian coal & coal-fired electricity producers
Activities: Addressing environmental issues with governments & stakeholders

Canadian Coalition for Nuclear Responsibility (CCNR) / Regroupement pour la surveillance du nucléaire (RSN)

PO Box 236, Stn. Snowdon, Montréal QC H3X 3T4
Fax: 514-489-5118
e-mail: ccnr@web.ca
www.ccnr.org
Overview: A small national organization founded in 1975
Mission: Dedicated to education and research on all issues related to nuclear energy, whether civilian or military — including non-nuclear alternatives — especially those pertaining to Canada.; Affiliation(s): Environment Liaison Centre - International; Friends of the Earth - Canada; Canadian Peace Alliance; Abolition 2000
Chief Officer(s):
Gordon Edwards, President
Marc Chénier, Sec.-Treas.
Finances: *Annual Operating Budget:* Less than $50,000

Canadian Concrete Pipe Association (CCPA) / Association canadienne des fabricants de tuyaux de béton (ACTB)

205 Miller Dr., Halton Hills ON L7G 6G4
Tel: 905-877-5369; *Fax:* 905-877-5369
e-mail: info@ccpa.com
www.ccpa.com
www.facebook.com/group.php?gid=106265401921
Overview: A medium-sized national organization founded in 1992
Mission: To coordinate research & development, promotion, education & federal government relations programs pertaining to the marketing of high quality precast concrete waste water & storm drainage products in Canada.; *Member of:* Federation of Canadian Municipalities; Affiliation(s): Ontario Concrete Pipe Association; Tubecon; American Concrete Pipe Association
Chief Officer(s):
John Greer, Chair
Finances: *Annual Operating Budget:* Less than $50,000; *Funding Sources:* Membership dues; research grants
Staff: 2 staff member(s); 30 volunteer(s)
Membership: 35; *Member Profile:* Manufacturers of concrete pipes & related products; suppliers to manufacturers
Activities: Software development; product development; market research; *Speaker Service:* Yes; *Library:* Data Centre; Open to public

Canadian Construction Association (CCA) / Association canadienne de la construction (ACC)

#1900, 275 Slater St., Ottawa ON K1P 5H9
Tel: 613-236-9455; *Fax:* 613-236-9526
e-mail: cca@cca-acc.com
www.cca-acc.com
www.linkedin.com/company/canadian-construction-association—-associati
twitter.com/ConstructionCAN
www.youtube.com/user/ConstructionCAN
Overview: A large national organization founded in 1918
Mission: To act as the national voice of the construction industry; To serve, promote, & enhance the construction industry by acting on behalf of its members in matters of national concern
Chief Officer(s):
John Schubert, Chair
Michael Atkinson, President
mikea@cca-acc.com

Pierre Boucher, COO
pierre@cca-acc.com
Eric Lee, Senior Director, Industry Practices
ericlee@cca-acc.com
Mark Belton, Director, Finance
mbelton@cca-acc.com
Bill Ferreira, Director, Government Relations & Public Affairs
bferreira@cca-acc.com
Chantal Montpetit, Director, Meetings & Conferences
chantal@cca-acc.com
Kirsi O'Connor, Director, Marketing & Communications
koconnor@cca-acc.com
Aneel Rangi, Director, Legal & Research Services
aneel@cca-acc.com
Membership: 17,000 firms + 70 partner associations; *Committees:* Executive; Governance; Standard Practices; Innovation & Technology; Business & Market Development; Industry Advocacy & Regulatory Affairs; Gold Seal; Canadian Design-Build Institute; Operations & Maintenance Council; Canadian Construction Documents; Institute for BIM in Canada
Meetings/Conferences:
For more information see Trade Shows, Conferences and Seminars Chapter
Canadian Construction Association 95th Annual Conference
March 2013 La Malbaie, QC
Canadian Construction Association 96th Annual Conference
March 2014
Publications:
•CCA [Canadian Construction Association] Weekly
Type: Newsletter; *Frequency:* Weekly

Canadian Consulting Agrologists Association (CCAA) / Association canadienne des agronomes-conseils

PO Box 20, 2004 - 401 Bay St., Toronto ON M5H 2Y4
Tel: 416-860-1515; *Fax:* 416-860-1535
Toll-Free: 800-268-1148
e-mail: info@ccaa.bz
www.ccaa.bz
Overview: A small national organization founded in 1973
Mission: To provide excellence in agricultural consulting; To promote standards of competency; To maintain Standards of Ethical Conduct
Chief Officer(s):
Adele Buettner, Executive Director
Terry Betker, President, 204-775-4531, Fax: 204-783-8329
terry.betker@mnp.ca
Membership: *Fees:* Schedule available; *Member Profile:* Professional agrology consultants who offer consulting services to agricultural sectors around the world
Activities: Promoting certification; Offering professional development & networking opportunities; Advocating for the profession of agricultural consulting; Promoting member services to national & international agricultural sectors
Awards:
•Lifetime Achievement Award (Award)
•Distinguished Certified Agricultural Consultant (Award)
•CCAA Fellow Award (Award)
Publications:
•CCAA [Canadian Consulting Agrologists Association] Member Directory
Type: Directory
•CCAA [Canadian Consulting Agrologists Association] Newsletter
Type: Newsletter; *Frequency:* Quarterly
Profile: Current industry practices & trends & professional development

Canadian Consumer Specialty Products Association (CCSPA)

#800, 130 Albert St., Ottawa ON K1P 5G4
Tel: 613-232-6616; *Fax:* 613-233-6350
e-mail: assoc@ccspa.org
www.ccspa.org
twitter.com/CCSPA_ACPCS
Previous Name: Canadian Manufacturers of Chemical Specialties Association
Overview: A medium-sized national organization founded in 1958
Mission: Represents the specialty chemical & formulated products industry; promotes the interests of member companies by providing a national voice, encouraging ethical practices, negotiating with government, & fostering industry cooperation
Chief Officer(s):
Shannon Coombs, Executive Director, 613-232-6616 Ext. 18
coombss@ccspa.org
Nancy Hitchins, Director, Administration & Member Services, 613-232-6616 Ext. 12
hitchinsn@ccspa.org
Finances: *Annual Operating Budget:* $250,000-$500,000
Staff: 6 staff member(s)
Membership: 60+ corporate; *Committees:* Technical: Soap & Detergent; Antimicrobial Chemicals; Pest Control Products; Waxes & Polishes; Occupational Health & Safety; Pesticides; Automotive Chemicals; Aerosols; Environmental; Non-Technical: Executive; Public Relations; Membership Recruitment; Ontario Golf
Activities: *Rents Mailing List:* Yes
Publications:
•The Formulator [a publication of the Canadian Consumer Specialty Products Association]
Type: Magazine; *Frequency:* Annually; *Editor:* Ali Mintenko
Profile: Feature articles & CCSPA information
•Microgram [a publication of the Canadian Consumer Specialty Products Association]
Type: Newsletter; *Frequency:* Quarterly
Profile: CCSPA new for members only

Canadian Co-operative Wool Growers Ltd. (CCWG)

PO Box 130, 142 Franktown Rd., Carleton Place ON K7C 3P3
Tel: 613-257-2714; *Fax:* 613-257-8896
Toll-Free: 800-488-2714
e-mail: ccwghq@wool.ca
www.wool.ca
Overview: A medium-sized national organization founded in 1918
Mission: To operate as a producer-owned wool marketing cooperative; To collect, grade, & market, the majority of the Canadian wool clip to the global market; To retail farm supplies & animal health & identification products
Chief Officer(s):
Eric Bjergso, General Manager
ericb@wool.ca
Membership: 1,200

Canadian Corrugated Containerboard Association / Association canadienne du cartonnage ondulé et du carton-caisse
Parent Name: Paper & Paperboard Packaging Environmental Council

#3, 1995 Clark Blvd., Brampton ON L6T 4W1
Tel: 905-458-1247; *Fax:* 905-458-2052
e-mail: info@cccabox.org
www.cccabox.org
Previous Name: Paper Packaging Canada
Overview: A medium-sized national organization overseen by Paper & Paperboard Packaging Environmental Council
Mission: To represent containerboard mill sites, corrugator plants, sheet plants & related industries; to work together with other players in the paper industry to develop an agenda of common concerns & issues
Chief Officer(s):
Rob Latter, Chair
John Mullinder, President & CEO, 905-458-0087
ppec@ppec-paper.com
Membership: 1-99
Activities: Networking & information sharing; seminars; conference & trade fair; annual golf tournament; *Awareness Events:* Golf Tournament, June

Canadian Council for Human Resources in the Environment Industry *See* Environmental Careers Organization of Canada

Canadian Council for International Co-operation (CCIC) / Conseil canadien pour la coopération internationale

#200, 450 Rideau St., Ottawa ON K1N 5Z4
Tel: 613-241-7007; *Fax:* 613-241-5302
e-mail: info@ccic.ca
www.ccic.ca
www.facebook.com/ccciccic
twitter.com/CCCICCIC
www.youtube.com/user/CCICable
Overview: A large national organization founded in 1968
Mission: To work globally to achieve sustainable human development; To seek to end global poverty; To promote social justice & human dignity for all
Chief Officer(s):
Jim Cornelius, Chair
Janice Hamilton, Treasurer
Julia Sánchez, President & CEO
jsanchez@ccic.ca
Anna Campos, Officer, Finance & Administration
acampos@ccic.ca
Chantal Havard, Officer, Government Relations & Communications
chavard@ccic.ca
Fraser Reilly-King, Policy Analyst, Aid & International Co-operation
freillyking@ccic.ca
Finances: *Funding Sources:* Federal government through CIDA
Staff: 4 volunteer(s)
Membership: 100 organizations; *Fees:* Schedule available; *Member Profile:* Non-profit organizations working in Canada & overseas, including religious & secular development groups, professional associations, & labour unions; These work with NGOs, cooperatives, & citizens' groups in Africa, Asia, & Latin America to meet basic needs for food, shelter, education, health, & sanitation; Many groups conduct policy research & campaign with their southern partners for fair trade, global security, children's rights, biodiversity, or the forgiveness of multilateral debt; Some members work exclusively in Canada, designing education materials for use in classrooms & resource centres; All members must adhere to a Code of Ethics which governs their financial management, communications with the public, & administration
Activities: Monitoring & analyzing federal policies on foreign affairs, aid, trade, debt & defence & communicating findings to members & the public; Engaging Canadians in a collective search for development alternatives; *Internships:* Yes; *Speaker Service:* Yes
Publications:
•Au Courant [a publication of the Canadian Council for International Co-operation]
Type: Newsletter; *Frequency:* Semiannually; *ISSN:* 118-604X
Profile: News, analysis, & opinion about domestic & international economic policy, development aid, & foreign policy
•Who's Who in International Development [a publication of the Canadian Council for International Co-operation]
Type: Directory
Profile: Listing of CCIC members working to end global poverty

Canadian Council for Tobacco Control (CCTC) / Conseil canadien pour le contrôle du tabac

192 Bank St., Ottawa ON K2P 1W8
Tel: 613-567-3050; *Fax:* 613-567-2730
Toll-Free: 800-267-5234
e-mail: infoservices@cctc.ca
www.cctc.ca
Previous Name: Canadian Council on Smoking & Health
Overview: A medium-sized national charitable organization founded in 1974
Mission: To envision a strong & effective tobacco control movement; To diminish the adverse impact to the health of Canadians caused by tobacco industry products; To increase the effectiveness & capacity of individuals & organizations involved in tobacco control, to achieve a smoke free society in Canada; To prevent tobaccco use; To persuade & help smokers to stop using tobacco products; To educate Canadians about the marketing strategies & tactics of the tobacco industry & the adverse effects tobacco products have on the health of Canadians
Environmental Activity: Striving to eliminate exposure to second-hand smoke
Chief Officer(s):
Robert Walsh, Executive Director
Jocelyne Koepke, Manager, Operations
Finances: *Annual Operating Budget:* $500,000-$1.5 Million; *Funding Sources:* Federal & provincial governments
Staff: 7 staff member(s)
Membership: *Fees:* $40 student; $75 individual; $500 Organizational up to 10 members
Activities: *Awareness Events:* National Non-Smoking Week/Weedless Wednesday, Jan.; World No Tobacco Day, May; *Speaker Service:* Yes; *Library:* National Clearing House for Tobacco & Health; Open to public

Canadian Council of Engineering Technicians and Technologists (CCETT) *See* Canadian Council of Technicians & Technologists

Canadian Council of Food & Nutrition (CCFN) / Conseil canadien des aliments et de la nutrition

2810 Matheson Blvd. East, 1st Fl., Mississauga ON L4W 4X7
Tel: 905-625-5746; *Fax:* 905-265-9372
e-mail: info@ccfn.ca
www.ccfn.ca

Previous Name: Canadian Institute of Food & Nutrition; Canadian Food Information Council
Overview: A medium-sized national organization founded in 2004
Mission: The multi-sectoral trusted voice for science-based food & nutrition policy & information in Canada.
Chief Officer(s):
Francey Pillo-Blocka, President & CEO
Finances: *Annual Operating Budget:* $250,000-$500,000
Staff: 2 staff member(s)
Membership: 30 active members; *Fees:* based on annual sales active; patron national $2,500, provincial $1,350; *Member Profile:* Active members from agri-food industry corporations; patron members from agri-food trade associations & marketing boards, pharma, retail grocery, pr firms.
Activities: ; *Library:* Resource Centre; Open to public

Canadian Council of Forest Ministers (CCFM) / Conseil canadien des ministres des forêts

c/o Policy, Economics & Industry Branch, Natural Resources Canada, 580 Booth St., 11th Fl., Ottawa ON K1A 0E4
Tel: 613-947-9099; *Fax:* 613-947-9033
www.ccfm.org
Mission: The Canadian Council of Ministers (CCFM) was established in 1985 to give sufficient attention to forest issues. CCFM stimulates the development of policies & initiatives for strengthening the forest sector, including the forest resource & its use. It provides leadership, addresses national & international issues & sets the direction for stewardship & sustainable management of Canada's forests. The CCFM is composed of the 14 federal, provincial & territorial ministers responsible for forests. The CCFM undertakes activities primarily through ad hoc fora, committees & working groups. CCFM initiatives include: International Forest Issues Working Group; International Forestry Partnerships Program; Sustainable Forest Management Working Group; Canadian Wildland Fire Strategy; National Forest Information System; National Forestry Database Program; Science & Technology Working Group; Forest Communities Working Group. The Council also cooperates with the Canadian Wildland Fire Strategy Declaration, a federal-provincial-territorial initiative to address the management of wildland fires. National Forestry Database Program: nfdp.ccfm.org/; National Forest Information System: nfis.org
Chief Officer(s):
Martine Ouellet, Minister, Natural Resources & Wildlife
ministre@mrnf.gouv.qc.ca
Mario Gibeault, Sous-ministre, Forêts
mario.gibeault@bmmb.gouv.qc.ca

Canadian Council of Independent Laboratories (CCIL) / Conseil canadien des laboratoires indépendants

PO Box 41027, Ottawa ON K1G 5K9
Tel: 613-746-3919; *Fax:* 613-746-4324
e-mail: ccil@magma.ca
www.ccil.com
Overview: A medium-sized national licensing organization founded in 1993
Chief Officer(s):
Alnoor Nathoo, Vice-President; Secretary-Treasurer
David Hope, President
Membership: 51
Activities: *Speaker Service:* Yes

Canadian Council of Ministers of the Environment (CCME) / Conseil canadien des ministres de l'environnement

#360, 123 Main St., Winnipeg MB R3C 1A3
Tel: 204-948-2090; *Fax:* 204-948-2125
Toll-Free: 800-805-3025
e-mail: info@ccme.ca
www.ccme.ca
Mission: CCME is comprised of the environment ministers from the federal, provincial and territorial governments. These 14 ministers normally meet at least once a year to discuss national environmental priorities and determine work to be carried out under the auspices of CCME. The Council seeks to achieve positive environmental results, focusing on issues that are national in scope and that require collective attention by a number of governments. CCME aims to assist its members to meet their mandate of protecting Canada's environment. As with any association, each member can accomplish more by working together than by working alone. CCME serves as a principal forum for members to develop national strategies, norms, and guidelines that each environment ministry across the country can use. Since environment is constitutionally speaking an area of shared jurisdiction, it makes sense to work together to promote effective results. CCME is not another level of government regulator, but a council of government ministers holding similar responsibilities
Chief Officer(s):
James Arreak, President, 867-924-6423, Fax: 867-924-6429
jarreak@assembly.nu.ca
Michael Goeres, Executive Director, 204-948-2172
mgoeres@ccme.ca
David Akeeagok, Chair, Management & Deputy Ministers Committees
Kelvin Leary, Chair, Environmental Planning & Protection Committee
Finances: *Annual Operating Budget:* $1.5 Million-$3 Million; *Funding Sources:* Federal, provincial & territorial governments
Staff: 8 staff member(s)
Membership: 1-99; *Committees:* Environmental Planning & Protection

Canadian Council of Motor Transport Administrators (CCMTA) / Conseil canadien des administrateurs en transport motorisé (CCATM)

2323 St. Laurent Blvd., Ottawa ON K1G 4J8
Tel: 613-736-1003; *Fax:* 613-736-1395
e-mail: ccmta-secretariat@ccmta.ca (general information & membership)
www.ccmta.ca
Overview: A medium-sized national charitable organization founded in 1940
Mission: To coordinate operational matters dealing with the administration, regulation, & control of motor vehicle transportation & highway safety
Chief Officer(s):
Ward Keith, President
Methusalah Kunuk, Vice-President
Finances: *Funding Sources:* Member assessments; Special projects; Membership fees
Membership: 100-499;; *Fees:* $433.50 associate; *Member Profile:* Members include representatives of provincial, territorial, & federal governments, & associate members from transportation related organizations.; *Committees:* Drivers & Vehicles; Compliance & Regulatory Affairs; Road Safety Research & Policies
Activities: Developing strategies & programs; Managing a communications network, called the Interprovincial Record Exchange system; *Rents Mailing List:* Yes
Meetings/Conferences:
For more information see Trade Shows, Conferences and Seminars Chapter
Canadian Council of Motor Transport Administrators 2013 Annual Meeting: Northern Reality Meets Modern Transportation
May 2013 Iqaluit, NU
Canadian Council of Motor Transport Administrators 2014 Annual Meeting
2014
Publications:
•AAMVA / CCMTA Inspection Handbook
Type: Handbook
Profile: Recommended inspection procedures & standards for all types of vehicles in the United States & Canada
•CCMTA [Canadian Council of Motor Transport Administrators] News
Type: Newsletter; *Frequency:* Semiannually; *Editor:* Harvey Chartrand; *ISSN:* 1192-747X; *Price:* Free for all government & assoicate members
Profile: Current projects & initiatives of CCMTA
•CCMTA [Canadian Council of Motor Transport Administrators] Directory
Type: Directory; *Price:* Free CD-ROM for associatemembers with membership renewal
Profile: Bilingual list of names, addresses, telephone & fax numbers, & e-mail addresses of over 600 contacts
•Commercial Vehicle Inspections in Canada
Type: Manual
Profile: An outline of Canadian commercial vehicle inspection requirements, availble in hard copy or CD-ROM
•Periodic Commercial Motor Vehicle Inspections
Type: Handbook

Canadian Council of Professional Engineers ***See*** Engineers Canada

Canadian Council of Professional Fish Harvesters (CCPFH) / Conseil canadien des pêcheurs professionnels (CCPP)

#712, 1 Nicholas St., Ottawa ON K1N 7B7
Tel: 613-235-3474; *Fax:* 613-231-4313
www.ccpfh-ccpp.org
Overview: A medium-sized national organization founded in 1995
Mission: To represent the interests of professional fish harvesters across Canada in their dealings with the federal, provincial & territorial governments on national issues of common concern; To provide organizational structure & leadership for the development of a program of professionalization for fish harvesters in collaboration with the organizations representing professional fishers across Canada; To act as a national industry sector council to plan & implement training & adjustment programs for the fish harvesting industry in Canada
Chief Officer(s):
John Sutcliffe, Executive Director
Earle McCurdy, President
Dan Edwards, Vice-President
Ronnie Heighton, Vice-President
Daniel Landry, Secretary
O'Neil Cloutier, Treasurer
Membership: *Member Profile:* Fish harvesters; Captains & crew members
Publications:
•Canadian Council of Professional Fish Harvesters Newsletter
Type: Newsletter; *Frequency:* Quarterly
Profile: News & information from the council & industry

Canadian Council of Technicians & Technologists (CCTT) / Conseil canadien des techniciens et technologues

#155, 955 Green Valley Cres., Ottawa ON K2C 3V4
Tel: 613-238-8123; *Fax:* 613-238-8822
Toll-Free: 800-891-1140
e-mail: ccttadm@cctt.ca
www.cctt.ca
twitter.com/CCTTCanada
Previous Name: Canadian Council of Engineering Technicians and Technologists (CCETT)
Overview: A large national organization founded in 1973
Mission: To advocate on behalf of Canada's certified technicians & technologists; To establish & maintain national competency standards
Chief Officer(s):
Robert Okabe, CET, Chair
Isidore J. LeBlond, CEO
ileblond@cctt.ca
Rick Tachuk, Director, Communications & Marketing
rtachuk@cctt.ca
Valery Vidershpan, Manager, Project
vvidershpan@cctt.ca
Marisa Sosa, Coordinator, Program
msosa@cctt.ca
Activities: Government relations; accreditation; insurance services; trade mark protection; *Awareness Events:* National Technology Week, Nov.
Meetings/Conferences:
For more information see Trade Shows, Conferences and Seminars Chapter
Canadian Council of Technicians & Technologists (CTTT) 2013 National Technology Conference
September 2013 Winnipeg, MB
Publications:
•Innovation [a publication of the Canadian Council of Technicians & Technologists]
Type: Newsletter; *Frequency:* Monthly
Profile: News for technology professionals across Canada, including credential information, awards, & awareness activities

Canadian Council on 4-H Clubs ***See*** Canadian 4-H Council

Canadian Council on Animal Care (CCAC) / Conseil canadien de protection des animaux (CCPA)

#1510, 130 Albert St., Ottawa ON K1P 5G4
Tel: 613-238-4031; *Fax:* 613-238-2837
e-mail: ccac@ccac.ca
www.ccac.ca
Overview: A medium-sized national organization founded in 1968
Mission: To act on behalf of the people of Canada to ensure, through programs of education, assessment & persuasion, that the use of animals in Canada, where necessary for research, teaching & testing, employs physical & psychological care according to acceptable scientific standards; To promote an increased level of knowledge, awareness, & sensitivity to the relevant ethical principles

Chief Officer(s):
Clément Gauthier, Executive Director, 613-238-4031 Ext. 224
cgauthier@ccac.ca
Michael Baar, Director, Assessment & Certification Program, 613-238-4031 Ext. 226
mbaar@ccac.ca
Gilly Griffin, Director, Guidelines & Three Rs Programs, 613-238-4031 Ext. 225
ggriffin@ccac.ca
Pascale Belleau, Coordinator, Education, Training, & Communications, 613-238-4031 Ext. 234
pbelleau@ccac.ca
Emily Verlinden, Coordinator, Publications, 613-238-4031 Ext. 231
everlinden@ccac.ca
Membership: 22 organizations; *Committees:* Planning & Priorities; Finance; Guidelines; Education & Training; Assessments
Activities: ; *Library:* Open to public by appointment
Publications:
•Canadian Council on Animal Care Workshop Proceedings
•CCAC [Canadian Council on Animal Care] Annual Report
Frequency: Annually
•CCAC [Canadian Council on Animal Care] Guidelines
Frequency: Irregular
Profile: Topics include procurement of animals used in science, laboratory animal facilities, the care and use of wildlife, antibody production, institutional animal user training,transgenic animals, & animal use protocol review
•CCAC [Canadian Council on Animal Care] Guide to the Care & Use of Experimental Animals
•Resource: The Newsletter of the Canadian Council on Animal Care (CCAC)
Type: Newsletter; *Frequency:* Semiannually; *Editor:* Clément Gauthier, PhD; *ISSN:* 0700-5237
Profile: Articles about laboratory animal science; news about current issues & events related to the CCAC

Canadian Council on Ecological Areas (CCEA)
c/o Environmental Stewardship Branch, Environment Canada, #3, 351, boul St. Joseph, Gatineau QC K1A 0H3
Tel: 819-934-6064; *Fax:* 819-994-4445
e-mail: mark.richardson@ec.gc.ca
www.ccea.org
Overview: A small national organization founded in 1982
Mission: To facilitate the establishment of a comprehensive network of protected areas which are linked together in a system that will protect Canada's terrestrial & aquatic diversity in perpetuity
Chief Officer(s):
Mark Richardson, Sec.-Manager

Canadian Council on Electrotechnologies *Voir* Conseil Canadien des Électrotechnologies

Canadian Council on International Law (CCIL) / Conseil canadien de droit international (CCDI)
275 Bay St., Ottawa ON K1R 5Z5
Tel: 613-235-0442; *Fax:* 613-232-8228
e-mail: manager@ccil-ccdi.ca
www.ccil-ccdi.ca
Overview: A small international charitable organization founded in 1972
Mission: To bring together scholars of international law & organizations engaged in teaching & research at Canadian universities; To encourage & conduct studies in international law with a view to its progressive development & codification; To foster the study of legal aspects of Canada's international problems & to advocate their solution in accordance with existing or developing principles of international law.; Affiliation(s): Société québécoise de droit international; American Society of International Law; Japanese Association of International Law
Chief Officer(s):
Craig Forcese, President
Elizabeth Macaulay, Manager
manager@ccil-ccdi.ca
Finances: *Annual Operating Budget:* $50,000-$100,000; *Funding Sources:* Membership fees, donations, government project funding
Staff: 1 staff member(s); 24 volunteer(s)
Membership: 400; *Fees:* $85 individual; $45 student; *Member Profile:* Leading scholars; students of international law; government & practising lawyers from both public & private sectors
Activities: Speakers series; *Speaker Service:* Yes; *Library:*

Canadian Council on Smoking & Health *See* Canadian Council for Tobacco Control

Canadian Crude Quality Technical Association (CCQTA)
www.ccqta.com
Overview: A medium-sized national organization
Mission: The CCQTA facilitates the resolution of common crude oil quality issues by establishing direct lines of communications among crude oil stakeholders. Note: CCQTA does not have a permanent office location
Membership: 75; *Fees:* $1,000-$2,000; *Member Profile:* Any subscriber that is engaged in any commercial activity of the petroleum industry and who pays the initial and subsequent annual fees.
Meetings/Conferences:
For more information see Trade Shows, Conferences and Seminars Chapter
Canadian Crude Quality Technical Association (CCQTA) 2013 Annual General Meeting
June 2013 Calgary, AB
Oil Sands and Heavy Oil Technologies Conference & Exhibition 2013
July 2013 Calgary, AB

Canadian Dam Association (CDA) / Association canadienne des barrages (ACB)
PO Box 2281, Moose Jaw SK S6TH 7W6
www.cda.ca
Merged from: Canadian National Committee on Large Dams
Overview: A small national organization founded in 1989
Mission: To monitor the technical, environmental, social, economic, legal, & administrative aspects of dams in Canada; To ensure the safe operation of dams across Canada; *Member of:* Society of the Engineering Institute of Canada; International Commission on Large Dams
Environmental Activity: Providing for the exchange of ideas & experiences regarding dam safety, public safety, & the protection of the environment in Canada; Monitoring coastal zone & shoreline protection
Chief Officer(s):
Wayne Phillips, Executive Director
Finances: *Funding Sources:* Membership fees; Conferences; Advertising
Membership: *Fees:* $5 students; $40 individuals; $350 corporate members; $700 corporate sponsors; *Member Profile:* Individuals, students, & corporations with an interest in dam safety, such as dam owners, engineers, technologists, researchers, government agencies, hydro companies, & equipment manufacturers & suppliers
Activities: Promoting the adoption of regulatory policies & safety guidelines for dams & reservoirs in Canada; Fostering inter-provincial cooperation; Offering education & outreach about dams
Meetings/Conferences:
For more information see Trade Shows, Conferences and Seminars Chapter
Canadian Dam Association 2013 Annual Conference
October 2013 Montréal, QC
Canadian Dam Association 2014 Annual Conference
October 2014 Banff, AB
Canadian Dam Association 2015 Annual Conference
October 2015
Publications:
•Canadian Dam Association Bulletin
Type: Magazine; *Frequency:* Quarterly; *Accepts Advertising*; *Editor:* A. Kirkham (allan.kirkham@opg.com); *Price:* Free with membership in the Canadian Dam Association
Profile: Information from the Canadian Dam Association to help members remain informed about the association, the board, awards, conferences, & suppliers &buyers
•Dam Safety Guidelines
Type: Guidelines; *Number of Pages:* 82; *Price:* $60 each, plus GST, for CDA members; $100 each, plus GST, for non-members
Profile: A Canadian Dam Association publication, with a companion series of English language technical bulletins (235 pages)
•Dams in Canada
Type: CD; *Price:* $60 each, plus GST, for CDA members; $100 each, plus GST, for non-members
Profile: Featuring chapters, with photographs, drawings, & text, on water resources, water supply, irrigation, hydroelectric dams, & flood control dams, plus the Dams in Canada Register, with information about over 900dams

Canadian Direct Marketing Association *See* Canadian Marketing Association

Canadian Earth Energy Association *See* Earth Energy Society of Canada

Canadian Egg Marketing Agency *See* Egg Farmers of Canada

Canadian Electricity Association (CEA) / Association canadienne de l'électricité (ACE)
#1100, 350 Sparks St., Ottawa ON K1R 7S8
Tel: 613-230-9263; *Fax:* 613-230-9326
e-mail: info@electricity.ca
www.electricity.ca
twitter.com/CDNElectricity
Overview: A medium-sized national organization founded in 1891
Mission: To act as the voice of the Canadian electricity business
Environmental Activity: Implementing Sustainable Electricity, an industry-wide intitiative
Chief Officer(s):
Jim Burpee, President & CEO, 613-230-4762
burpee@electricity.ca
Francis Bradley, Vice-President, Policy Development, 613-230-5027
bradley@electricity.ca
Sandra Schwartz, Vice-President, Policy Advocacy, 613-230-9876
schwartz@electricity.ca
Tracy Walden, Director, Communications, 613-627-4333
Angela Macleod, Corporate Secretary, 613-230-7384
macleod@electricity.ca
Richard Lussier, Controller, 613-688-2065
Membership: *Member Profile:* Members generate, transmit, & distribute electrical energy to residential, commercial, institutional, & industrial customers throughout Canada
Activities: Analyzing national & international business issues; Providing a national forum for the electricity business; Advocating industry views; Helping companies in evolving markets; Communicating findings about concerns such as mercury emissions & electric & magnetic fields
Meetings/Conferences:
For more information see Trade Shows, Conferences and Seminars Chapter
Annual Smart Grid Interoperability 2013 4th Annual Summit
June 2013 Toronto, ON
Annual Smart Grid Interoperability 2014 5th Annual Summit
February 2014
Publications:
•Annual Service Continuity Report on Distribution System Performance in Electrical Utilities
Type: Yearbook; *Frequency:* Annually
Profile: Produced by the Performance Excellence & Benchmarking program of the Canadian Electricity Association, the report containsinformation about industry standard metrics for electricity distribution, including system average interruption frequency index & the system average interruption duration index
•The CEA [Canadian Electricity Association] Member Directory
Type: Directory; *Frequency:* Annually; *Price:* $15 members; $65 non-members
Profile: Contact information for the Canadian electricity industry's major players, in addition to information about the operations of the Canadian ElectricityAssociation's member companies
•Electricity Annual
Type: Yearbook; *Frequency:* Annually
Profile: The Canadian Electricity Association's yearly industry review
•Forced Outage Performance of Transmission Equipment [a publication of the Canadian Electricity Association]
Type: Yearbook; *Frequency:* Annually
Profile: Produced by the Performance Excellence & Benchmarking program of the Canadian Electricity Association, thereport addresses the performance of transmission equipment in Canada
•Generation Equipment Status [a publication of the Canadian Electricity Association]
Type: Yearbook; *Frequency:* Annually
Profile: Produced by the Performance Excellence & Benchmarking program of the Canadian Electricity Association, the report features informationon the performance of electrical generating units in Canada

Canadian Energy Efficiency Alliance (CEEA) / L'Association de l'efficacité énergétique du Canada
#402, 2800 Skymark Ave., Mississauga ON L4W 5A6

Tel: 905-614-1641
Toll-Free: 866-614-1641
e-mail: alliance@energyefficiency.org
www.energyefficiency.org
Overview: A medium-sized national organization founded in 1995
Mission: To become the leading energy efficiency advocate in Canada; To work in partnership with industry, environmental & consumer leaders to promote energy efficiency programs & policies that will move Canada toward a more sustainable future; Affiliation(s): Canadian Energy Efficiency Centre
Chief Officer(s):
Ken Elsey, President/CEO
kenelsey@energyefficiency.org
Finances: *Annual Operating Budget:* $250,000-$500,000; *Funding Sources:* Membership dues & projects
Staff: 14 volunteer(s)
Membership: 40; *Fees:* $1,500 corporate; $15,000 leader; *Committees:* Codes & Standards; Executive; Government Relations
Activities: Establishing a National Energy Efficiency Centre to be North America's energy technology showcase; promoting/advocating energy efficiency; breakfast policy updates; annual meeting

Canadian Energy Pipeline Association (CEPA) / Association canadienne de pipelines d'énergie

#200, 505 - 3rd St. SW, Calgary AB T2P 3E6
Tel: 403-221-8777; *Fax:* 403-221-8760
e-mail: aboutpipelines@cepa.com
www.cepa.com
www.facebook.com/aboutpipelines
twitter.com/aboutpipelines
www.youtube.com/aboutpipelines;
www.slideshare.net/aboutpipelines
Overview: A medium-sized national organization founded in 1993
Mission: To represent Canada's transmission pipeline companies; To ensure a strong transmission pipeline industry
Environmental Activity: Promoting social & environmental stewardship & the safe operation of pipelines
Chief Officer(s):
Brenda Kenny, President & Chief Executive Officer
Kim McCaig, Vice-President & Chief Operating Officer
Philippe Reicher, Vice-President, External Communications
Ziad Saad, Vice-President, Safety & Sustainability
Amanda Affonso, Director, Regulatory & Financial
Thomas Linder, Director, Safety
Vanessa Coates-Humen, Administrator & Work Group Analyst
Sandra Burns, Manager, Communications, 403-221-8764
sburns@cepa.com
Cathy Hay, Manager, Industry Information, Research, & Analysis, 403-221-8762
chay@cepa.com
Donna Menuz, Accountant, 403-221-8775
dmenuz@cepa.com
Carole Brownlees, Secretary
Membership: *Member Profile:* Canada's pipeline companies that transport natural gas & crude oil throughout North America; *Committees:* Damage Prevention Regulations; Emergency Security Management; Environment; Health & Safety; Land Issues Task Force; Pipeline Integrity; Aboriginal Affairs; Climate Change; Corporate Tax; Commodity Tax; Pipeline Abandonment Obligations; Pipeline Economics; Property Tax; Regulatory Accounting; Regulatory Policy
Activities: Liaising with government regarding industry practices
Awards:
•Environmental Management Award (Award)
•Environmental Achievement Award (Award)
•Spill Prevention Award (Award)

Canadian Energy Research Institute (CERI)

#150, 3512 - 33 St. NW, Calgary AB T2L 2A6
Tel: 403-282-1231; *Fax:* 403-284-4181
e-mail: info@ceri.ca
www.ceri.ca
Overview: A medium-sized national organization founded in 1975
Mission: To provide the public, industry, & the government with information concerning all aspects of energy
Chief Officer(s):
Peter Howard, President & Chief Executive Officer
David McWhinney, Director, Accounting & Operations
Dinara Millington, Director, Research
Jon Rozhon, Senior Researcher
Thorn Walden, Senior Economist
Membership: 150
Activities: *Speaker Service:* Yes; *Library:* I.N. McKinnon Memorial Library
Meetings/Conferences:
For more information see Trade Shows, Conferences and Seminars Chapter
Canadian Energy Research Institute 2013 Natural Gas Conference: Short-term Survival & Future Gas Pathways
March 2013 Calgary, AB
Canadian Energy Research Institute 2013 Oil Conference
April 2013 Calgary, AB
Canadian Energy Research Institute 2013 Petrochemical Conference
June 2013 Kananaskis, AB
Canadian Energy Research Institute 2014 Natural Gas Conference
2014 Calgary, AB
Canadian Energy Research Institute 2014 Oil Conference
2014 Calgary, AB

Canadian Environment Industry Association (CEIA)

119, Concession 6 Rd., Fisherville ON NOA 1G0
Tel: 416-410-0432; *Fax:* 416-362-5231
Overview: A large national organization
Mission: To promote the interests and development of Canadian companies supplying environmental technologies, products and services.
Chief Officer(s):
Christopher Henderson, Chair
Membership: 1,500

Canadian Environment Industry Association - British Columbia Chapter ***See*** British Columbia Environment Industry Association

Canadian Environment Industry Association - Ontario Chapter ***See*** Ontario Environment Industry Association

Canadian Environmental Auditing Association ***See*** Auditing Association of Canada

Canadian Environmental Certification Approvals Board (CECAB) / Bureau canadien de reconnaissance professionnelle des spécialistes de l'environnement

#200, 308 - 11th Ave. SE, Calgary AB T2G 0Y2
Tel: 403-233-7484; *Fax:* 403-264-6240
e-mail: certification@eco.ca
www.cecab.org
Overview: A small national licensing organization founded in 1998
Mission: CECAB is a professional autonomous body providing national certification for Canadian environmental practitioners.
Chief Officer(s):
Lou Locatelli, Vice Chair
Finances: *Annual Operating Budget:* $250,000-$500,000; *Funding Sources:* Industry; HRDC; CCHREI
Staff: 3 staff member(s)
Membership: 700+; *Fees:* CEDIT $50; CCEP $150-300; *Member Profile:* Environmental practitioners from all provinces & territories, representing all disciplines.; *Committees:* Certification; Discipline; Ethics; Professional Development

Canadian Environmental Defence Fund ***See*** Environmental Defence

Canadian Environmental Grantmakers' Network (CEGN) / Réseau canadien des subventionneurs en environnement (RCSE)

#300, 70 The Esplanade, Toronto ON M5E 1R2
Tel: 647-288-8891; *Fax:* 416-979-3936
e-mail: pegi_dover@cegn.org
www.cegn.org
Overview: A medium-sized national organization founded in 1995
Mission: Works to develop an effective network of environmental grantmakers in Canada by facilitating information-sharing, collaboration, training & professional development, research, & communications
Chief Officer(s):
Pegi Dover, Executive Director
pegi_dover@cegn.org
Membership: *Member Profile:* Private, community, public & corporate foundations; government & corporate funding programs that give grants in support of Canadian environment
Meetings/Conferences:
For more information see Trade Shows, Conferences and Seminars Chapter
Canadian Environmental Grantmakers' Network Annual Conference and CFC Conference 2013
June 2013 Winnipeg, MB

Canadian Environmental Law Association (CELA) / Association canadienne du droit de l'environnement

#301, 130 Spadina Ave., Toronto ON M5V 2L4
Tel: 416-960-2284; *Fax:* 416-960-9392
e-mail: articling@cela.ca (legal inquiries)
www.cela.ca
Overview: A medium-sized national organization founded in 1970
Mission: To advocate for environmental law reform; To act in court or during hearings on behalf of citizens' groups & individuals who would otherwise be unable to afford legal assistance
Chief Officer(s):
Theresa McClenaghan, Executive Director & Counsel
theresa@cela.ca
Mary Anderson, Manager, Finance
mary@cela.ca
Tracy Tucker, Manager, Office
tracy@cela.ca
Kathleen Cooper, Senior Researcher
kcooper@cela.ca
Burgandy Dunn, Counsel, Public Legal Education
bdunn@cela.ca
Finances: *Funding Sources:* Legal Aid Ontario
Staff: 1 volunteer(s)
Membership: 23
Activities: ; *Library:* Resource Library for the Environment & the Law; by appointment

Canadian Environmental Network (RCEN) / Réseau canadien de l'environnement

39 McArthur Ave., Level 1-1, Ottawa ON K1L 8L7
Tel: 613-728-9810; *Fax:* 613-728-2963
e-mail: info@rcen.ca
rcen.ca
www.facebook.com/CanadianEnvironmentalNetwork
twitter.com/RCEN
Overview: A large national organization founded in 1977
Mission: To promote ecologically sound ways of life; To enhance members' work to restore, protect, & promote a clean & sustainable environment
Environmental Activity: Working with organizations & citizens to protect, preserve, & restore the environment; Affecting how people think about environmental issues; Coordinating projects to strengthen the environmental movement across Canada
Chief Officer(s):
Daniel Casselman, Coordinator, National Caucus, 613-728-9810 Ext. 236
daniel@rcen.ca
Jessie Sadler, Coordinator, National Caucus, 613-728-9810 Ext. 224
jessie@rcen.ca
Joséphine Hénault, Administrator, Office & Events, 613-728-9810 Ext. 221
josephine@rcen.ca
Membership: 600+ organizations; *Member Profile:* Canadian non-profit, non-governmental organizations with a focus on environmental concerns; *Committees:* Atmosphere & Energy; Agriculture; Biodiversity; Environmental Planning & Assessment; Health; International Program; Mining; Toxics; Water, Fisheries & Oceans; Youth
Activities: Providing communication & networking services for members; *Awareness Events:* Environment Week, June
Meetings/Conferences:
For more information see Trade Shows, Conferences and Seminars Chapter
Canadian Environmental Network / Réseau canadien de l'environnement 2013 Annual Conference on the Environment
2013
Publications:
•Getting Answers: A Guide to the Environmental Petitions Process
Type: Guide; *Number of Pages:* 27
•Ideas for a More Effective Environmental Movement in Canada
Number of Pages: 17; *Author:* Jerry DeMarco
•Mercury . . . A Global Toxin: Perspectives on Initiatives & Programs on Coal-Fired Power Plants & Mercury Emissions
Number of Pages: 114; *Author:* Anna Tilman
Profile: Coal-fired Power Plants - Mercury Emissions; Canada-wide Standards for Mercury Electric PowerGenerating Sector; Strategies & Control Technologies for Reducing Mercury

Emissions; Mercury Emission Trading; U.S. Regulatory Action on Mercury & Coal-Fired Plants; Global Initiatives on Mercury
•Mercury . . . A Public Concern, including Analysis of Mercury Emissions from Coal-Fired Power Plants & Canada-Wide Standards
Number of Pages: 198; *Author:* Anna Tilman
Profile: Government Programs-Mercury; Canada-wide Standards for Mercury Electric Power GeneratingSector; Mercury Data from Coal-Fired Plants; Cumulative Emissions-The True Loading Picture; U.S. Regulatory Action on Mercury & Coal-Fired Plants; Recommendations for Canada-wide Standards for Mercury
•Participating in Federal Public Policy: A Guide for the Voluntary Sector
Type: Guide
Profile: A resource to assist voluntary organizations participate in the federal public policy development process
•RCEN [Canadian Environmental Network] e-Bulletin
Type: Newsletter; *Frequency:* Weekly
Profile: Up-to-date information about RCEN activities & news of interest for RECEN members
•RCEN [Canadian Environmental Network] Annual Report
Type: Yearbook; *Frequency:* Annually
Profile: A review of the network's activities & audited financial statements
•RCEN [Canadian Environmental Network] Youth Friendly Guide: Youth Guide to Policy Change for Intergenerational Partnerships
Type: Guide
Profile: A guidebook of interest to organizations wanting to make their operations youth-friendly
•RCEN [Canadian Environmental Network] Biodiversity Best Practices Handbook
Type: Handbook

Canadian Environmental Technology Advancement Corporation - West (CETAC)

3608 - 33rd St. NW, Calgary AB T2L 2A6
Tel: 403-777-9595; *Fax:* 403-777-9599
e-mail: cetac@cetacwest.com
cetacwest.com
www.facebook.com/431936763529236
Also Known As: CETAC-West
Overview: A medium-sized national organization founded in 1994
Mission: Established by Environment Canada, CETAC-West is a private sector, not-for-profit corporation committed to helping small & medium-sized enterprises that are engaged in the development & commercialization of new environmental technologies. To this end, it has created a network of technology producers, industry experts, & investment sources.
Finances: *Funding Sources:* Provincial & federal government
Staff: 8 staff member(s)
Activities: Specialist advisors provide technical research assistance, regulatory counsel & a range of consulting & referral services; focuses on technologies for natural resource conservation, pollution prevention & control, waste reductions & management, & environmental protection & remediation
Publications:
•CETAC [Canadian Environmental Technology Advancement Corporation] Focus
Type: Newsletter; *Frequency:* Quarterly

Canadian Farm & Industrial Equipment Institute ***See*** Association of Equipment Manufacturers - Canada

Canadian Farm Animal Care Trust

#306, 92 Caplan Ave., Barrie ON L4N 0Z7
Tel: 705-436-5776; *Fax:* 705-436-3551
e-mail: canfact@rogers.com
www.canfact.ca
Also Known As: CANFACT
Overview: A small national charitable organization founded in 1989
Mission: To encourage the development & use of systems that subject farm animals to the minimum amount of stress, distress or injury in the rearing, transportation & slaughter of these animals
Chief Officer(s):
Tom Hughes, President
Finances: *Annual Operating Budget:* $50,000-$100,000
Staff: 15 volunteer(s)
Activities: *Speaker Service:* Yes

Canadian Farm Writers' Federation (CFWF)

PO Box 250, Ormstown QC J0S 1K0
Fax: 450-829-2226
Toll-Free: 877-782-6456
e-mail: office@cfwf.ca
www.cfwf.ca
Overview: A small national organization founded in 1955
Mission: To serve the interests of agricultural journalists; Affiliation(s): British Columbia Farm Writers' Association (BCFWA); Alberta Farm Writers' Association (AFWA); Saskatchewan Farm Writers' Association (SFWA); Manitoba Farm Writers' & Broadcasters' Association; Eastern Canada Farm Writers' Association (ECFWA)
Chief Officer(s):
Myrna Stark-Leader, President
m.starkleader@sasktel.net
Tamara Leigh, Vice-President
tamara.leigh@agr.gc.ca
Hugh Maynard, Secretary-Treasurer
hugh@quanglo.ca
Christina Franc, Administrator
christina@quanglo.ca
Membership: 380+; *Member Profile:* Agricultural journalists, such as editors, reporters, & broadcasters; Journalists in business & government who are responsible for agricultural communications
Activities: Providing networking opportunities; Offering professional development
Meetings/Conferences:
For more information see Trade Shows, Conferences and Seminars Chapter
Canadian Farm Writers' Federation 2013 Annual General Meeting & Conference
2013
Publications:
•The Farm Journalist: Newsletter of the Canadian Farm Writers' Federation
Type: Newsletter; *Frequency:* Bimonthly; *Editor:* Christina Franc
Profile: News for farm jouralists, information sources, events, launches, awards, & professional development information

Canadian Federation for Humanities & Social Sciences (CFHSS) / Fédération canadienne des sciences humaines (FCSH)

#300, 275 Bank St., Ottawa ON K2P 2I6
Tel: 613-238-6112; *Fax:* 613-238-6114
e-mail: fedcan@fedcan.ca
www.fedcan.ca
www.linkedin.com/company/canadian-federation-for-the-humanit ies-and-so
www.facebook.com/fedcan?ref=nf
twitter.com/fedcan
Previous Name: Humanities & Social Sciences Federation of Canada
Merged from: Social Science Federation of Canada (SSFC); Canadian Federation for the Humanities (CFH)
Overview: A large national charitable organization founded in 1996
Mission: The Federation represents the Canadian research community by working to support & advance research in the humanities & social sciences in Canada.; Affiliation(s): Canadian Federation of Students (CFS); Canadian Association of Research Libraries (CARL); Canadian Research Knowledge Network (CRKN); Association of Canadian Deans of Education (ACDE); American Council of Learned Societies (ACLS); Frontier College
Chief Officer(s):
Antonia Maioni, President
president@fedcan.ca
Jean-Marc Mangin, Executive Director, 613-238-6112 Ext. 306
jmmangin@fedcan.ca
Finances: *Annual Operating Budget:* $3 Million-$5 Million; *Funding Sources:* Membership fees; Congress revenue; Funding from SSHRC; Donations
Membership: 80 scholarly associations + 79 universities & colleges + 6 affiliates, with 85,000+ individuals; *Fees:* Schedule available, based upon size of association or institution; *Member Profile:* Scholarly associations; Universities & colleges; Practitioners; Scholars; Students
Activities: Publishing scholarly books; Conducting a series of lectures to increase awareness of humanities & social science research among policy makers
Meetings/Conferences:
For more information see Trade Shows, Conferences and Seminars Chapter
Congress of the Humanities & Social Sciences 2013
June 2013 Victoria, BC
Canadian Federation for the Humanities & Social Sciences 2013 Annual Conference
2013
Congress of the Humanities & Social Sciences 2014
May 2014 St Catharines, ON
Congress of the Humanities & Social Sciences 2015
2015
Publications:
•The Academy as Community: A Manual of Best Practices for Meeting the Needs of New Scholars
Type: Manual; *Number of Pages:* 31; *ISBN:* 0-920052-46-0
Profile: Prepared by the Canadian Federation for the Humanities & Social Sciences' Task Force on New Scholars
•Best Practice Manual: A Guide for Scholarly Associations in Canada
Type: Manual; *Number of Pages:* 61
Profile: Information to maintain & strengthen scholarly societies in Canada
•Canadian Federation for the Humanities & Social Science Annual Report
Type: Yearbook; *Frequency:* Annually
Profile: A year of the federation in review
•Communiqué [a publication of the Canadian Federation for the Humanities & Social Science]
Type: Newsletter
Profile: News, events, & opportunities for CFHSS members
•Renewing Scholarly Associations: Knowledge Networks for the Next Generation
Number of Pages: 51; *ISBN:* 0-920052-47-9
Profile: Prepared by the Canadian Federation for the Humanities & Social Sciences' Scholarly Associations Task Force

Canadian Federation of Agriculture (CFA) / Fédération canadienne de l'agriculture (FCA)

21 Florence St., Ottawa ON K2P 0W6
Tel: 613-236-3633; *Fax:* 613-236-5749
e-mail: info@cfafca.ca
www.cfa-fca.ca
www.facebook.com/cfafca
twitter.com/CFAFCA
Overview: A large national organization founded in 1935
Mission: To coordinate the efforts of agricultural producer organizations throughout Canada for the purpose of promoting their common interests through collective action; to promote & advance the social & economic conditions of those engaged in agricultural pursuits; to assist in formulating & promoting national agricultural policies to meet changing national & international conditions; *Member of:* International Federation of Agriculture Producers; Affiliation(s): BC Agriculture Council; Keystone Agricultural Producers (Manitoba); Ontario Federation of Agriculture; L'Union des producteurs agricoles (Québec); Coopérative fédérée de Québec; NS Federation of Agriculture; PEI Federation of Agriculture; Agriculture Producers Assoc. of New Brunswick; Newfoundland & Labrador Federation of Agriculture; Dairy Farmers of Canada; Canadian Egg Marketing Agency; Chicken Farmers of Canada; Canadian Turkey Marketing Agency; Canadian Broiler Hatching Egg Marketing Agency; Canadian Sugar Beet Producers' Assoc.; Canadian Pork Council; Wild Rose Agricultural Producers
Chief Officer(s):
Ron Bonnett, President
president@cfafca.ca
Errol Halkai, Executive Director
errol@cfafca.ca
Jessica Goodfellow, Director, Communications
communications@cfafca.ca
Finances: *Annual Operating Budget:* $500,000-$1.5 Million; *Funding Sources:* Membership fees
Staff: 8 staff member(s)
Membership: 22 provincial farm organizations, national/regional commodity organizations; *Member Profile:* Farm organization or farmer co-op
Activities: *Awareness Events:* Food Freedom Day, Feb. 12; *Internships:* Yes; *Library:* by appointment
Meetings/Conferences:
For more information see Trade Shows, Conferences and Seminars Chapter
Canadian Federation of Agriculture 2013 Annual General Meeting
February 2013 Ottawa, On

Canadian Federation of Earth Sciences (CFES) / Fédération canadienne des sciences de la Terre

c/o Managing Director, 210 Main St., Wolfville NS B4P 1C4

Tel: 902-542-6125
e-mail: cfes@magma.ca
www.geoscience.ca
Previous Name: Canadian Geoscience Council
Overview: A medium-sized national organization founded in 1972
Mission: To promote coordination & cooperation in activities in Canadian geoscientific education; to advise on science policy involving the earth sciences; to provide an informed opinion to the public of Canada on matters of public concern.
Chief Officer(s):
Bill Mercer, President
bmercer_cfes@magma.ca
Finances: *Annual Operating Budget:* $100,000-$250,000; *Funding Sources:* Geological Survey of Canada; member societies
Membership: 20,000 individuals + 13 societies + 5 associate organizations

Canadian Federation of Engineering Students (CFES) / Fédération canadienne des étudiants et étudiantes en génie

c/o Engineers Canada, #1100, 180 Elgin St., Ottawa ON K2P 2K3
e-mail: info@cfes.ca
www.cfes.ca
twitter.com/FCEEG_CFES
Overview: A medium-sized national organization founded in 1969
Mission: To act as a unified voice for engineering students both nationally & internationally; To assist engineering students in both personal & professional growth; To be aware of & communicate changes in society which affect the engineering profession & engineering students; Affiliation(s): BEST (Board of European Students of Technology)
Chief Officer(s):
Nicolas Blanchet, CFES President
president@cfes.ca
Alexandra Dozzi, Vice-President, Finances & Administration
vpfa@cfes.ca
Lauren Brunet, Vice-President, Communications
vpcomm@cfes.ca
Finances: *Funding Sources:* Sponsorships
Membership: 60,000; *Member Profile:* Engineering students across Canada; *Committees:* Education; Official Languages; Information Technology; Outreach
Activities: Facilitating the exchange of information between members; Recognizing student achievements; Supporting an all-encompassing education for engineering students; Offering complementary education courses
Publications:
•CFES [Canadian Federation of Engineering Students] eBulletin
Type: Newsletter
Profile: Federation activities, commissioner reports, & upcoming events
•Project [a publication of the Canadian Federation of Engineering Students]
Type: Magazine; *Frequency:* Semiannually; *Accepts Advertising*; *Editor:* Shaunvir Sidhu; *Price:* Distributed to schools for engineering students
Profile: Relevant articles for engineering students across Canada

Canadian Federation of Humane Societies (CFHS) / Fédération des sociétés canadiennes d'assistance aux animaux

#102, 30 Concourse Gate, Ottawa ON K2E 7V7
Tel: 613-224-8072; *Fax:* 613-723-0252
Toll-Free: 888-678-2347
e-mail: info@cfhs.ca
www.cfhs.ca
www.linkedin.com/company/canadian-federation-of-humane-societies
www.facebook.com/HumaneCanada
twitter.com/cfhs/
www.youtube.com/user/CanadianHumane
Overview: A large national charitable organization founded in 1957
Mission: As the national voice of societies and SPCAs, the CFHS supports its member animal welfare organizations across Canada in promoting respect & humane treatment toward all animals
Chief Officer(s):
Barbara Cartwright, CEO
Kim Elmslie, Communications Coordinator
Shelagh MacDonald, Program Director
Finances: *Annual Operating Budget:* $250,000-$500,000; *Funding Sources:* Donations
Staff: 6 staff member(s)
Membership: 40 organizations; *Member Profile:* Any society devoted to the prevention of cruelty to or suffering of animals; *Committees:* Farm Animal; Companion Animal; Member Services; Bills & Legislation; Wildlife & Habitat
Activities: *Internships:* Yes; *Speaker Service:* Yes; *Library:* Open to public by appointment
Publications:
•Animal Welfare in Focus
Type: Newsletter; *Frequency:* Semiannually; *Editor:* Tanya O'Callaghan; *Price:* Free for CFHS member societies, donors, & the public upon request
Profile: Up-to-date information about the CFHS & member societies, & animal welfare news from Canada & abroad
•Canadian Federation of Humane Societies Factsheets
Price: Free
Profile: Information about companion animals, wildlife, & farm animal welfare issues
•CFHS [Canadian Federation of Humane Societies] Annual Report
Type: Yearbook; *Frequency:* Annually

Canadian Federation of Independent Grocers (CFIG) / Fédération canadienne des épiciers indépendants

#902, 2235 Sheppard Ave. East, Toronto ON M2J 5B5
Tel: 416-492-2311; *Fax:* 416-492-2347
Toll-Free: 800-661-2344
e-mail: info@cfig.ca
www.cfig.ca
www.facebook.com/CFIGFCEI
twitter.com/cfigfcei
Overview: A large national organization founded in 1962
Mission: To equip & enable independent, franchised, & specialty grocers for sustainable success; To act as a united voice for independent grocers across Canada
Environmental Activity: Working with local governments across Canada on environmental issues, usch as packaging & plastic bags
Chief Officer(s):
Francois Bouchard, Chair
John F.T. Scott, President & Chief Executive Officer, 416-492-2311 Ext. 229
jftscott@cfig.ca
Ward Hanlon, Vice-President, Industry Relations, 416-492-2311 Ext. 225
whanlon@cfig.ca
Fran Nielsen, Vice-President, Finance & Administration, 416-492-2311 Ext. 236
fran@cfig.ca
Gary Sands, Vice-President, Government Relations, 416-492-2311 Ext. 230
garys@cfig.ca
Sacha Lalla, Director, Member Services, 416-492-2311 Ext. 222
slalla@cfig.ca
Eden Minty, Director, Events, 416-492-2311 Ext. 224
eminty@cfig.ca
Irina Costachescu, Tradeshow Operations Manager, Expositions, 416-492-2311 Ext. 234
icostachescu@cfig.ca
Dan Leggieri, Manager, Communications, 416-492-2311 Ext. 231
dleggieri@cfig.ca
Rolster Taylor, Tradeshow Manager, Sales, 416-492-2311 Ext. 223
rtaylor@cfig.ca
Membership: 4,000+; *Member Profile:* Independent, franchised, & specialty grocery retailers throughout Canada
Activities: Providing educational & training programs; Offering information about the food industry
Meetings/Conferences:
For more information see Trade Shows, Conferences and Seminars Chapter
Canadian Federation of Independent Grocers Grocery Showcase West 2013
April 2013 Vancouver, BC
Canadian Federation of Independent Grocers Grocery Innovations Canada 2013
September 2013 Toronto, ON
Canadian Federation of Independent Grocers Grocery Showcase West 2014
2014 Vancouver, BC
Canadian Federation of Independent Grocers Grocery Innovations Canada 2014
2014 Toronto, ON
Publications:
•The Canadian Retail Food Safety Manual
Type: Manual
Profile: Retail food safety practices & procedures, produced in collaboration with the Canadian Council of Grocery Distributors
•CFIG [Canadian Federation of Independent Grocers] Emergency Food Recall Registry
Profile: Current food re-calls & government announcements available to CFIG members
•CFIG's [Canadian Federation of Independent Grocers] Crisis Communication & Pandemic Planning Manual
Type: Manual
•Independent Grocer Magazine
Type: Magazine; *Accepts Advertising*
Profile: CFIG programs, activities, & member achievements, & industry & government updates, for CFIG members only
•President's Notes Newsletter [a publication of the Canadian Federation of Independent Grocers]
Type: Newsletter
Profile: Headlines plus highlights of government policies, available to CFIG members
•Privacy Guide [a publication of the Canadian Federation of Independent Grocers]
Price: Free to CFIG members
Profile: Available to CFIG members

Canadian Federation of Mayors & Municipalities *See* Federation of Canadian Municipalities

Canadian Federation of Woodlot Owners

#304, 259 Brunswick St., Fredericton NB E3B 1G8
Tel: 506-459-2990; *Fax:* 506-459-3515
e-mail: nbfwo@nbnet.nb.ca
Overview: A medium-sized national organization founded in 1989
Chief Officer(s):
Peter de Marsh, President

Canadian Feed Industry Association *See* Animal Nutrition Association of Canada

Canadian Fertilizer Institute (CFI) / Institut canadien des engrais

#907, 350 Sparks St., Ottawa ON K1R 7S8
Tel: 613-230-2600; *Fax:* 613-230-5142
e-mail: info@cfi.ca
www.cfi.ca
Overview: A medium-sized national organization
Chief Officer(s):
Roger L. Larson, President, 613-230-2600
president@cfi.ca
Dave Finlayson, Vice-President, Science & Risk Management, 613-786-3031
dfinlayson@cfi.ca
Clyde Graham, Vice-President, Strategy & Alliances, 613-786-3033
cgraham@cfi.ca
Kristian Stephens, Senior Manager, Technical Affairs, 613-786-3035
kstephens@cfi.ca
Robert Godfrey, Manager, Policy, 613-786-3034
Catherine King, Manager, Communications, 613-786-3026
Monique MacDonald, Manager, Finance & Corporate Services, 613-786-3032
Membership: 70 organizations
Meetings/Conferences:
For more information see Trade Shows, Conferences and Seminars Chapter
Joint Canadian Fertilizer Institute 68th Annual Conference & North American Fertilizer Transportation Forum
August 2013 Banff, AB
Canadian Fertilizer Institute 69th Annual Conference
August 2014 Ottawa, ON
Canadian Fertilizer Institute 70th Annual Conference
August 2015 Vancouver, BC
Canadian Fertilizer Institute 71st Annual Conference
August 2016 Mont-Tremblant, QC

Canadian Fire Safety Association (CFSA)

#310, 2175 Sheppard Ave. East, Toronto ON M2J 1W8
Tel: 416-492-9417; *Fax:* 416-491-1670
e-mail: cfsa@taylorenterprises.com
www.canadianfiresafety.com

Overview: A medium-sized national organization founded in 1971
Mission: To promote fire safety through seminars, safety training courses, scholarships & regular meetings.
Chief Officer(s):
Leo Grellette, President, 905-832-8510 Ext. 8218
leo.grellette@vaughan.ca
Finances: *Funding Sources:* Membership fees
Staff: 10 volunteer(s)
Membership: 350; *Fees:* $390-$1290 corporate; $80 individual; *Member Profile:* Membership represents a broad cross-section of government, business & education including architects, engineers, fire officials, building officials, fire protection consultants, manufacturers, the insurance industry, teachers & students.

Canadian Fisheries Association *See* Fisheries Council of Canada

Canadian Fluid Power Association (CFPA) / Association canadienne d'énergie fluide
#310, 2175 Sheppard Ave. East, Toronto ON M2J 1W8
Tel: 416-499-1416; *Fax:* 416-491-1670
e-mail: info@cfpa.ca
www.cfpa.ca
Overview: A medium-sized national organization founded in 1974
Mission: To build public awareness of fluid power technology; To provide a forum for the exchange of information & opinion; To represent the Canadian fluid power industry to government, educational institutions & other organizations; To ensure that members' concerns are known to those in government; To ensure that students are able to be properly prepared for careers in the fluid power industry; To ensure that members are kept abreast of the latest developments in the fluid power industry; *Member of:* National Fluid Power Association
Chief Officer(s):
Carolyne Vigon, Administrator
carolyne@taylorenterprises.com
Mary Lou Murray, Registrar, Events
maryloum@taylorenterprises.com
Finances: *Funding Sources:* Membership fees; Sponsorships
Staff: 10 volunteer(s)
Membership: 80 corporate; *Fees:* $588.50 large corporation; $401.25 small corporation; $160.50 individual; *Member Profile:* Open to manufacturers, distributors, assemblers, educators, consultants & designers of fluid power components, systems & services; *Committees:* Communications; Membership
Activities: Representing the fluid power industry on the Canadian advisory committee with regard to the drafting of international standards; Representing the fluid power industry in the formulation of applicable national standards; *Speaker Service:* Yes
Meetings/Conferences:
For more information see Trade Shows, Conferences and Seminars Chapter
Canadian Fluid Power Association 2013 Annual General Meeting
September 2013 Niagara-on-the-Lake, ON

Canadian Forage & Grassland Association (CFGA) / Association Canadienne pour les Plantes Fourragères (ACPF)
125 Patterson Cres., Brandon MB R7A 6T7
Tel: 204-726-9393; *Fax:* 204-726-9703
www.canadianfga.ca
Overview: A small national organization
Mission: The CFGA/ACPF is the national voice for all sectors of the forage and grassland industry. Its main role is to uphold our robust forage industry and realize the potential of the domestic and export forage market.
Chief Officer(s):
Wayne Digby, Executive Director
w_digby@canadianfga.ca
Membership: *Fees:* $1500 overseas exporters; $250 US exporters, patrons; *Committees:* Producer/User; Forage Export & Domestic Development; Research & Extension

Canadian Forestry Association (CFA) / Association forestière canadienne
1027 Pembroke St. East, Pembroke ON K8A 3M4
Tel: 613-732-2917; *Fax:* 613-732-3386
Toll-Free: 866-441-4006
www.canadianforestry.com
Overview: A large national charitable organization founded in 1900
Mission: To advocate for the wise use & protection of Canada's forest, water, & wildlife resources; To nurture economic & environmental health, through the management & conservation of forest resources; To provide a national voice for provincial forestry agencies
Environmental Activity: Promoting sustainable forest development, management, & conservation; Coordinatign the Logging for Wildlife program; Administering tree planting programs
Chief Officer(s):
Barry Waito, Chair
Kathy Abusow, President & Chief Executive Officer
Finances: *Funding Sources:* Donations
Activities: Advising the federal government of forest policy; Increasing public awareness about the protection of forests; *Awareness Events:* National Forest Week, September
Publications:
•Canadian Forestry Association Teaching Kit, Volume 1: Canada's Forests - Learning from the Past, Building for the Future
Type: Kit; *Number of Pages:* 32
Profile: A tool for educators to help young people in junior to senior grades understand the importance ofprotecting & conserving forests
•Canadian Forestry Association Teaching Kit, Volume 2: Canada's Forests - A Breath of Fresh Air
Type: Booklet; *Number of Pages:* 40
Profile: An exploration of climate change & its effects on Canadian forests
•Canadian Forestry Association Teaching Kit, Volume 3: Canada's Forests - All Things Big & Small
Type: Booklet; *Number of Pages:* 40
Profile: An examination of biodiversity in Canada's forests for the junior to intermediate grade levels
•Canadian Forestry Association Teaching Kit, Volume 4: Canada's Forests - Source of Life
Type: Booklet; *Number of Pages:* 48
Profile: Information about forest sustainability for students from grade 4 to 7
•Canadian Forestry Association Teaching Kit, Volume 5: Canada's Forest - A Fine Balance
Type: Booklet; *Number of Pages:* 44
Profile: Information & activities about the decline of wildlife habitat & species at risk, for students from grade 4 to grade 12
•Canadian Forestry Association Teaching Kit, Volume 6: Canada's Forests & Wetlands - Our Natural Water Filters
Type: Booklet; *Number of Pages:* 40
Profile: Forest, wetland, & water issues presented for children in grades 5 to 8
•Canadian Forestry Association Teaching Kit, Volume 7: The Boreal Forest - A Global Legacy
Type: Booklet; *Number of Pages:* 48
Profile: A teaching kit about the boreal forest intended for students from age 5 to 18
•Canadian Forestry Association Teaching Kit, Volume 8: Canada's Boreal Forest - Tradition & Transition
Type: Booklet; *Number of Pages:* 44
Profile: An exploration of the boreal forest & the interdependence that exists between the forest & Canadians
•Canadian Forestry Association Teaching Kit User Guide
Type: Guide
Profile: Activities for the entire class, group activities, activities for partners, games, outdoor activities, research, student presentations, & activities with Aboriginalcontent

Canadian Forestry Association of BC; British Columbia Forestry Association *See* For Ed BC

Canadian Forestry Association of New Brunswick (CFANB) / Association forestière canadienne du Nouveau-Brunswick (AFCNB)
Parent Name: Canadian Forestry Association
#248, 1350 Regent St., Fredericton NB E3C 2G6
Tel: 506-452-1339; *Fax:* 506-452-7950
Toll-Free: 866-405-7000
e-mail: info@cfanb.ca
www.cfanb.ca
Also Known As: The Tree House
Overview: A medium-sized provincial charitable organization founded in 1939 overseen by Canadian Forestry Association
Mission: To champions trees & forests of New Brunswick; To promote environmental, commercial, recreational, & inspirational benefits; To encourages conservation & wise use of natural resources
Chief Officer(s):
Christopher Dickie, President
Valerie Archibald, Associate Director
Jennifer Geneau, Secretary
Jamie Morrison, Treasurer
Finances: *Funding Sources:* Membership fees; Government grants; Foundation support
Staff: 20 volunteer(s)
Membership: 75; *Fees:* Schedule available; Individual membership $25; *Member Profile:* Open
Activities: *Awareness Events:* National Forest Week, September; Arbor Day, May

Canadian Foundation for Climate & Atmospheric Sciences (CFCAS) / Fondation canadienne pour les sciences du climat et de l'atmosphère (FCSCA)
#901, 350 Sparks St., Ottawa ON K1R 7S8
Tel: 613-238-2223; *Fax:* 613-238-2227
e-mail: info@cfcas.org
www.cfcas.org
Overview: A medium-sized national charitable organization founded in 2000
Mission: To fund university-based research on climate, & atmospheric & related oceanic work in Canada
Chief Officer(s):
Dawn Conway, Executive Director
conway@cfcas.org
Denny Alexander, Officer, Communications
alexander@cfcas.org
Tim Aston, Officer, Science
aston@cfcas.org
Finances: *Annual Operating Budget:* Greater than $5 Million
Activities: Responding to national needs or scientific imperatives; Providing grants
Publications:
•CFCAS [Canadian Foundation for Climate & Atmospheric Sciences] News
Type: Newsletter
Profile: Foundation happenings, research news, & grant information

Canadian Foundation for Healthcare Improvement (CFHI) / Fondation canadienne pour l'amélioration des services de santé (FCASS)
#700, 1565 Carling Ave., Ottawa ON K1Z 8R1
Tel: 613-728-2238; *Fax:* 613-728-3527
e-mail: info@cfhi-fcass.ca
www.cfhi-fcass.ca
www.facebook.com/group.php?gid=107329739320566
twitter.com/cfhi_fcass
www.youtube.com/user/CHSRF
Previous Name: Canadian Health Services Research Foundation
Overview: A large national organization founded in 1996
Mission: To funds management & policy research in health services; To support applied health services & nursing researchers; To support the synthesis & dissemination of research results; To support the use of research results by decision makers in the health system
Chief Officer(s):
Brian D. Postl, Chair
Maureen O'Neil, President, 613-728-2238 Ext. 237
maureen.oneil@cfhi-fcass.ca
Nancy Quattrocchi, Vice-President, Corporate Services
nancy.quattrocchi@cfhi.fcass.ca
Stephen Samis, Vice-President, Programs
stephen.samis@cfhi-fcass.ca
Finances: *Annual Operating Budget:* Greater than $5 Million; *Funding Sources:* Government grants & endowments
Activities: Collaborating with regions, provinces, territories to improve healthcare systems; *Awareness Events:* CEO Forum; *Internships:* Yes; *Speaker Service:* Yes
Meetings/Conferences:
For more information see Trade Shows, Conferences and Seminars Chapter
CEO Forum 2013
February 2013 Montréal, QC
Taming of the Queue 2013, Beyond the Queue: A systems approach to addressing the root causes of wait times
March 2013 Ottawa, ON
CEO Forum 2014
2014
CEO Forum 2015
2015
Publications:
•@CFHI-FCASS [Canadian Foundation for Healthcare Improvement] Bulletin
Type: Newsletter; *Frequency:* Monthly

Profile: Current reports & activities from the Canadian Foundation for Healthcare Improvement
•Canadian Foundation for Healthcare Improvement Annual Report
Type: Yearbook; *Frequency:* Annually
Profile: Organizational highlights from the past year
•CFHI [Canadian Foundation for Healthcare Improvement] Strategic Directions 2009-2013
Profile: An outline of activities & initiatives
•Pass it on! [a series of publications from the Canadian Foundation for Healthcare Improvement]
Profile: Innovative approaches to successful changes in healthcare

Canadian Foundry Association (CFA) / Association des fonderies canadiennes (AFC)

#1500, 1 Nicholas St., Ottawa ON K1N 7B7
Tel: 613-789-4894; *Fax:* 613-789-5957
www.foundryassociation.ca
Overview: A medium-sized national organization founded in 1975
Mission: To assist & represent the membership in dealing with government on industry specific issues; To communicate information to the industry, which will assist its members in strengthening their own competitive position & ensuring a strong Canadian foundry industry; *Member of:* Canadian Society of Association Executives
Environmental Activity: Establishing an environment committee & an occupational health & safety program
Chief Officer(s):
Judith Arbour, Executive Director
judy@foundryassociation.ca
William Monaghan, Secretary-Treasurer
Membership: 50 organizations; *Fees:* Fees based on sales volume; *Member Profile:* Pour metal castings or supplier to the industry; *Committees:* Education; Environment; Membership; Occupational Health & Safety
Activities: *Rents Mailing List:* Yes
Meetings/Conferences:
For more information see Trade Shows, Conferences and Seminars Chapter
Canadian Foundry Association 2013 Issues Meeting
March 2013 Hamilton, ON
Canadian Foundry Association 2013 Annual Meeting
September 2013 Hamilton, ON

Canadian Fuels Association / Association canadienne des carburants

#1000, 275 Slater St., Ottawa ON K1P 5H9
Tel: 613-232-3709; *Fax:* 613-236-4280
www.cppi.ca
Previous Name: Canadian Petroleum Products Institute
Overview: A large national organization founded in 1989
Mission: With chapters in Western Canada, Ontario, Quebec, & Eastern Canada, the Institute represents its membership to governments on issues related to business, the environment, & health & safety in the petroleum products sector. CPPI ensures its own adherence to the Competition Act, & provides a competition compliance program & training sessions to all staff & members
Environmental Activity: Environmental, health & safety guidelines; recycling programs for used petroleum products; brownfield development initiatives; environmental protection strategies & systems
Chief Officer(s):
Peter Boag, President
Membership: 10; *Member Profile:* Companies engaged in petroleum refining, marketing & distribution
Activities: Training & education; news releases, reports & technical documents; Driver Certification Program for petroleum transport drivers
Publications:
•Fuel for Thought [a publication of the Canadian Fuels Association]
Type: Newsletter
•Fuels for Life [a publication of the Canadian Fuels Association]
Type: Report; *Number of Pages:* 60
Profile: Discussion paper on Canada's future transportation fuels choices

Eastern Canada Division
#1000, 275 Slater St., Toronto ON K1P 5H9
Tel: 514-284-7754; *Fax:* 514-284-3301

Ontario Division
#901, 20 Adelaide East, Toronto ON M5C 256
Tel: 416-492-5677; *Fax:* 416-492-2514
Chief Officer(s):
Faith Goodman, Vice-President

Western Division
#2100, 350 - 7th Ave. SW, Calgary AB T2P 3N9
Tel: 403-266-7565
Chief Officer(s):
Brian Ahearn, Vice-President

Canadian Gas Association (CGA) / Association canadienne du gaz

#809, 350 Sparks St., Ottawa ON K1R 7S8
Tel: 613-748-0057; *Fax:* 613-748-9078
e-mail: info@cga.ca
www.cga.ca
twitter.com/GoSmartEnergy
Overview: A large national organization founded in 1907
Mission: To act as the voice of the natural gas distribution industry in Canada
Environmental Activity: Promoting natural gas as a clean, safe, & reliable energy choice
Chief Officer(s):
Timothy M. Egan, President & Chief Executive Officer, 613-748-0057 Ext. 300
tegan@cga.ca
Paula Dunlop, Director, Public Affairs & Strategy, 613-748-0057 Ext. 341
pdunlop@cga.ca
Bryan Gormely, Director, Policy, Economics, & Information, 613-748-0057 Ext. 315
bgormley@cga.ca
Jim Tweedie, Director, Operations, Safety, & Integrity Management, 613-748-0057 Ext. 311
jtweedie@cga.ca
Valerie Prokop, Manager, Finance & Corporate Services, 613-748-0057 Ext. 309
vprokop@cga.ca
Membership: *Member Profile:* Equipment manufacturers; Distribution companies; Transmission companies; Service providers
Activities: Advancing policy positions with federal & provincial decision makers; Developing educational information
Meetings/Conferences:
For more information see Trade Shows, Conferences and Seminars Chapter
Canadian Gas Association 2013 Operations Conference
March 2013 Québec, QC
Canadian Gas Association 2013 Engineering Conference
April 2013 Winnipeg, MB
Publications:
•Canadian Gas Association Market Updates
Profile: Topics include natural gas markets pre-heating season, post-heating season, supply, & demographics
•Canadian Gas Association Membership Directory
Type: Directory
Profile: Available for current CGA members
•Canadian Natural Gas Magazine
Type: Magazine; *Frequency:* Semiannually; *Accepts Advertising*; *Editor:* Suzy Richardson
Profile: CGA news, feature articles, & a buyers' guide for the natural gas distribution industry in Canada

Canadian Gas Processors Association ***See*** Gas Processing Association Canada

Canadian General Standards Board (CGSB) / Office des normes générales du Canada (ONGC)

CGSB, #6B1, Place Du Portage III, Gatineau QC K1A 1G6
Tel: 819-956-0425; *Fax:* 819-956-1634
Toll-Free: 800-665-2472
www.ongc-cgsb.gc.ca
Previous Name: Canadian Government Specifications Board
Overview: A medium-sized national organization founded in 1934
Mission: To develop standards, through accreditation with the Standards Council of Canada; To offer conformity assessment services, including product certification & registration of quality & environmental management systems, conforming to ISO standards; *Member of:* American Society for Quality; Business Forms Management Association; Canadian Safe Boating Council; Standards Engineering Society; Affiliation(s): Standards Council of Canada; National Standards Authority of Ireland; Standards & Industrial Research Institute of Malaysia; Business & Institutional Furniture Manufacturers' Association; American Society for Testing & Materials; Canadian Centre for Occupational Health & Safety; Information Handling Services; Canadian International Development Agency; Canadian Society for Nondestructive Testing, Inc.; Techstreet; Provincial Territorial Committee on Building Standards; Canadian Council of Fire Marshals & Fire Commissioners
Chief Officer(s):
Terrence Davies, Acting Director
Finances: *Annual Operating Budget:* $3 Million-$5 Million
Staff: 53 staff member(s); 5000 volunteer(s)
Membership: 1,000-4,999
Activities: ; *Library:* Sales Centre; Open to public

Canadian GeoExchange Coalition (CGC) / Coalition canadienne de l'énergie géothermique

#405, 1030, rue Cherrier, Montréal QC H2L 1H9
Tel: 514-807-7559; *Fax:* 514-807-8221
www.geo-exchange.ca
Overview: A medium-sized national organization
Mission: To develop industry standards; To expand the market for geoexchange technology in Canada; *Member of:* Energy Dialogue Group
Chief Officer(s):
Denis Tanguay, President & Chief Executive Officer
Ted Kantrowitz, Vice-President, 514-807-7559 Ext. 34
ted.kantrowitz@geo-exchange.ca
Pierre Jolicoeur, Comptroller, 514-807-7559 Ext. 22
pierre.jolicoeur@geo-exchange.ca
Anis Boubaker, Manager, Information Technology, 514-807-7559 Ext. 27
anis.boubaker@geo-exchange.ca
Membership: *Committees:* Training; Technology
Activities: Providing information, training, & certification; Increasing public awareness; Working with stakeholders to foster the growth of the Canadian geoexchange industry; Liaising with provincial ministries of energy in Canada
Meetings/Conferences:
For more information see Trade Shows, Conferences and Seminars Chapter
2013 Canadian GeoExchange Conference and Trade Show
May 2013 Burnaby, BC
11th International Energy Agency Heat Pump Conference
May 2014 Montréal, QC
12th International Energy Agency Heat Pump Conference
2017

Canadian Geophysical Union (CGU) / Union géophysique canadienne (UGC)

c/o Dept. of Geology & Geophysics, University of Calgary, ES #278, 2500 University Dr. NW, Calgary AB T2N 1N4
Tel: 403-220-5596; *Fax:* 403-284-0074
e-mail: cgu@ucalgary.ca
www.cgu-ugc.ca
Overview: A medium-sized national organization founded in 1973
Mission: To bring together & promote the geophysical sciences; To provide a focus for geophysicists at Canadian universities, government agencies, & industry in fields of study encompassing the composition & processes of the whole earth, including hydrology, space studies, & geology
Chief Officer(s):
Gail Atkinson, President
gatkins6@uwo.ca
Jim Craven, Treasurer
Masaki Hayashi, Secretary
Finances: *Annual Operating Budget:* Less than $50,000
Staff: 1 staff member(s); 12 volunteer(s)
Membership: 500; *Fees:* $30 full; $15 associate
Publications:
•Elements: The Newsletter of the Canadian Geophysical Union / Le Bulletin de l'union géophysique canadienne
Type: Newsletter; *Frequency:* Semiannually; *Accepts Advertising*; *Editor:* Ed S. Krebes; *Price:* Free to CGUmembers
Profile: CGU information, announcements, events, awards, officers, & section & committee news

Canadian Geoscience Council ***See*** Canadian Federation of Earth Sciences

Canadian Golf Superintendents Association (CGSA) / Association canadienne des surintendants de golf

#205, 5520 Explorer Dr., Mississauga ON L4W 5L1
Tel: 905-602-8873; *Fax:* 905-602-1958
Toll-Free: 800-387-1056
e-mail: cgsa@golfsupers.com
www.golfsupers.com
www.facebook.com/group.php?gid=151227228150
twitter.com/GolfSupers
Overview: A medium-sized national organization founded in 1966

Mission: To promote excellence in golf course management & environmental responsibility; To uphold the Canadian Golf Superintendents Association Principles Of Professional Practice & Code of Ethics & Conduct; *Member of:* Canadian Turfgrass Research Foundation
Chief Officer(s):
Kenneth S. Cousineau, Executive Director, 905-602-8873 Ext. 222, Fax: 905-602-1958
kcousineau@golfsupers.com
Tim Kubash, President, 250-832-8834
tkubash@salmonarmgolf.com
John Mills, Vice-President, 902-243-2119
jwmills@ns.sympatico.ca
Christian Pilon, Secretary-Treasurer, 450-653-1265
cpilon_mbcc@bellnet.ca
Finances: *Funding Sources:* Sponsorships
Membership: 1,500; *Fees:* $421 superintendents & course management; $330 assistant superintendents; $199 golf course maintenance; $179 equipment technicians; $61 students; *Member Profile:* Golf course superintendents & turfgrass specialists in Canada; *Committees:* Environment; Communications, Marketing, & Public Relations; Professional Development & Research; Conference & Events; Member Services; Equipment Technicians Advisory
Activities: Providing continuing professional development opportunities for members; Sponsoring research projects; Establishing the Master Superintendent Designation Program; Offering networking opportunities; *Awareness Events:* Canadian International Turfgrass Conference and Trade Show, annual; *Library:* CGSA Office Library
Meetings/Conferences:
For more information see Trade Shows, Conferences and Seminars Chapter
Canadian International Turfgrass 2013 46th Annual Conference & Trade Show
January 2013 Toronto, ON
Publications:
•CGSA [Canadian Golf Superintendents Association] Membership Directory
Type: Directory; *Frequency:* Annually; *Price:* Free with Canadian Golf Superintendents Association membership
Profile: Listings of CGSA members, members' clubs, & industry affiliates, for members only
•Environmental Management Resource Manual [a publication of the Canadian Golf Superintendents Association]
Type: Manual
•GreenMaster
Type: Magazine; *Frequency:* Bimonthly; *Price:* Free with Canadian Golf Superintendents Association membership
Profile: Informative articles of interest to golf course superintendents
•Greenmatter E-News [a publication of the Canadian Golf Superintendents Association]
Type: Newsletter; *Frequency:* Monthly
Profile: Current issues, regional news, & product information

Canadian Government Specifications Board *See* Canadian General Standards Board

Canadian Ground Water Association (CGWA) / Association canadienne des eaux souterraines
#100-409, 1600 Bedford Hwy., Bedford NS B4A 1E8
Tel: 902-845-1885; *Fax:* 902-845-1886
e-mail: info@cgwa.org
www.cgwa.org
Previous Name: Canadian Water Well Association
Overview: A medium-sized national organization founded in 1976
Mission: To act as the national voice of the ground water industry in Canada; To encourage the management & protection of ground water
Environmental Activity: Serving as stewards of the Canadian ground water resource
Chief Officer(s):
Kevin Constable, President, 905-778-9888, Fax: 905-778-1999
kevinconstable@zing-net.ca
Wayne C. MacRae, Executive Director, 902-845-1885, Fax: 902-845-1886
cgwa@ns.sympatico.ca
Finances: *Funding Sources:* Sponsorships
Activities: Promoting the development of ground water guidelines & strategies; Providing education about ground water for members & the public
Meetings/Conferences:
For more information see Trade Shows, Conferences and Seminars Chapter
Canadian Ground Water Association CanWell 2014: Canada's National Ground Water Symposium
June 2014 Kelowna, BC
Canadian Ground Water Association CanWell 2016: Canada's National Ground Water Symposium
2016
Publications:
•Guidelines for Water Well Construction
Profile: Construction requirements, according to provincial standards, for the construction of a water well

Canadian Hay Association (CHA)
1274 - 3rd Ave. South, Lethbridge AB T1J 0J9
Tel: 403-320-2727; *Fax:* 403-320-2855
www.canadianhay.com
Overview: A small national organization founded in 1987
Mission: To promote the development of Canada's hay industry for the benefit of its members
Chief Officer(s):
Marc Lavoie, President, 780-624-2850
John van Hierden, Vice-President, 403-327-9941
Albert VanGenderen, Secretary Treasurer, 403-380-6667
Finances: *Annual Operating Budget:* $50,000-$100,000; *Funding Sources:* Membership service fee & dues
Staff: 1 staff member(s); 8 volunteer(s)
Membership: 154; *Fees:* $150 (voting); $50 (non-voting); $300 (corporate); *Member Profile:* Producers, processor companies, marketers & brokers, & industry suppliers such as equipment manufacturers, seed companies, chemical companies

Canadian Health Food Association (CHFA) / Association canadienne des aliments de santé
#302, 235 Yorkland Blvd., Toronto ON M2J 4Y8
Tel: 416-497-6939; *Fax:* 905-479-3214
Toll-Free: 800-661-4510
e-mail: info@chfa.ca
www.chfa.ca
www.facebook.com/group.php?gid=12940324924
Previous Name: Health Food Dealers Association
Overview: A medium-sized national organization founded in 1964
Mission: To act as the voice of the natural products industry; To promote natural & organic products as an integral part of health & well-being; To ensure the growth of the natural & organic industry
Chief Officer(s):
Deborah Callbreath, Chair, 416-497-6939 Ext. 501
board@chfa.ca
Natalie Cajic, Specialist, Communications
ncajic@chfa.ca
Membership: 1,000+; *Member Profile:* Suppliers of natural products &/or organics; Retailers of natural health products &/or health foods; Associate members, such as farmers, organic certification providers, health practitioners, gyms, industry consultants, & media
Activities: Supporting & empowering members; Seeking scientific advice from the Expert Scientific Advisory Panel; Engaging in advocacy & outreach activities; Offering education; Providing networking opportunities; *Awareness Events:* National Health Food Month, November
Meetings/Conferences:
For more information see Trade Shows, Conferences and Seminars Chapter
Canadian Health Food Association (CHFA) Québec 2013
February 2013 Montréal, QC
Canadian Health Food Association (CHFA) Expo West 2013
April 2013 Vancouver, BC
Canadian Health Food Association (CHFA) Expo East 2013
October 2013 Toronto, ON
Canadian Health Food Association (CHFA) Expo West 2014
2014
Canadian Health Food Association (CHFA) Expo East 2014
2014
Canadian Health Food Association (CHFA) Québec 2014
2014, QC
Publications:
•Canadian Health Food Association Annual Report
Type: Yearbook; *Frequency:* Annually
Profile: Activities of the association during the past year
•Canadian Health Food Association Asssociate Member Directory
Type: Directory; *Frequency:* Monthly; *Editor:* Eva Chen
Profile: A membership directory exclusively for members
•Canadian Health Food Association e-News
Type: Newsletter; *Frequency:* Weekly; *Price:* Free with membership in the Canadian Health Food Association
Profile: Latest developments in the natural health & organic products industry
•Canadian Health Food Association Member Bulletins
Type: Newsletter; *Frequency:* Irregular; *Price:* Free with membership in the Canadian Health Food Association
Profile: Recent news in the natural health & organic products industry
•Canadian Health Food Association Retail Member Directory
Type: Directory; *Frequency:* Monthly; *Editor:* Eva Chen
Profile: A listing with contact information
•Canadian Health Food Association Supplier Member Directory
Type: Directory; *Frequency:* Monthly; *Editor:* Eva Chen
Profile: A membership directory exclusively for members
•Membership that Matters! [a publication of the Canadian Health Food Association]
Type: Newsletter; *Price:* Free with membership in the Canadian Health Food Association
Profile: Information for members to help their businesses prosper
•The Natural Voice [a publication of the Canadian Health Food Association]
Type: Newsletter; *Frequency:* Quarterly; *Price:* Free with membership in the Canadian Health Food Association
Profile: Association & industry news
•Research & Your Health
Type: Newsletter; *Frequency:* Quarterly; *Number of Pages:* 8; *Price:* Free with membership in the Canadian Health Food Association
Profile: Abstracts about the value of natural health products

Canadian Health Services Research Foundation *See* Canadian Foundation for Healthcare Improvement

Canadian Healthcare Association (CHA) / Association canadienne des soins de santé
#100, 17 York St., Ottawa ON K1N 9J6
Tel: 613-241-8005; *Fax:* 613-241-5055
e-mail: tneuman@cha.ca
www.cha.ca
www.facebook.com/166008030086000
twitter.com/CHA_ACS
Previous Name: Canadian Hospital Association
Merged from: Canadian Association for Community Care; Canadian Healthcare Association
Overview: A large national charitable organization founded in 1931
Mission: To improve the delivery of health services in Canada through policy development, advocacy & leadership; Affiliation(s): American Hospital Association; Canadian Council on Health Services Accreditation
Chief Officer(s):
Pamela C. Fralick, President/CEO, 613-241-8005 Ext. 202
Teresa Neuman, Communications Specialist
tneuman@cha.ca
Finances: *Annual Operating Budget:* $1.5 Million-$3 Million; *Funding Sources:* Membership fees; Services
Staff: 22 staff member(s)
Membership: 13; *Fees:* Schedule available; *Member Profile:* Federation of 13 provinicial & territorial hospital/health associations & serves as a voice for over 1,200 health care facilities & health service agencies
Activities: *Rents Mailing List:* Yes
Meetings/Conferences:
For more information see Trade Shows, Conferences and Seminars Chapter
Canadian Healthcare Association 2013 Annual General Meeting
June 2013 Niagara Falls, ON
Canadian Healthcare Assn & Canadian College of Health Leaders 2013 National Health Leadership Conference
June 2013 Niagara Falls, ON
Canadian Healthcare Association 2014 Annual General Meeting
2014
Canadian Healthcare Assn & Canadian College of Health Leaders 2014 National Health Leadership Conference
2014

Canadian Heavy Oil Association (CHOA)
#400, 500 - 5th Ave. SW, Calgary AB T2P 3L5
Tel: 403-269-1755; *Fax:* 403-453-0179
e-mail: office@choa.ab.ca
www.choa.ab.ca
Overview: A medium-sized national organization
Mission: To provide a technical, educational, & social forum for people employed in, or associated with, the oil sands & heavy oil industries
Chief Officer(s):

Barry Lappin, President, 403-232-1141
Maureen Armitage, Executive Director, 403-453-0178 Ext. 302, Fax: 403-453-0179
Maureen.Armitage@choa.ab.ca
Gerald Bruce, Vice-President, 403-775-1835, Fax: 403-264-1711
Bill Whitelaw, Secretary, 403-209-3500, Fax: 403-245-8666
Tracy Grills, Treasurer, 403-208-1674
Georgia A. Hasapes, Coordinator, Events, 403-269-1755, Fax: 403-453-0179
office@choa.ab.ca
Finances: *Funding Sources:* Membership fees; Sponsorships
Membership: 1,200+; *Fees:* $25 plus GST students; $100 plus GST regular members; *Member Profile:* Individuals employed in heavy oil exploration & production, service & supply, consulting, & government; Students
Activities: Providing continuing education; Offering networking opportunities with industry peers; *Library:* Canadian Heavy Oil Association Library; Open to public by appointment
Publications:
•CHOA [Canadian Heavy Oil Association] Handbook
Type: Handbook; *Price:* $60
Profile: Topics include markets & logistics, environment & regulatory best management practices, geology & geophysics, geostatistics, geomechanics, reservoir & wellbore simulation,drilling & completions, field testing, bitumen / heavy oil upgrading, & heavy oil research
•Journal of the Canadian Heavy Oil Association
Type: Journal; *Accepts Advertising*; *Editor:* Deborah Jaremko
Profile: Feature articles, technology information, news from the association, scholarship winners, volunteer recognition, & sponsor information

Canadian Hemerocallis Society

16 Douville Ct., Toronto ON M5A 4E7
Tel: 416-362-1682
www.distinctly.on.ca/chs
Also Known As: National Daylily Society of Canada
Overview: A small national organization
Mission: To promote, encourage & foster the development & improvement of the genus Hemerocallis
Chief Officer(s):
John P. Peat, President
jpeat@distinctly.on.ca
Membership: *Fees:* $25

The Canadian Heritage of Québec ***Voir*** L'Héritage canadien du Québec

Canadian Home Builders' Association (CHBA) / Association canadienne des constructeurs d'habitations

#500, 150 Laurier Ave. West, Ottawa ON K1P 5J4
Tel: 613-230-3060; *Fax:* 613-232-8214
e-mail: chba@chba.ca
www.chba.ca
Previous Name: Housing & Urban Development Association of Canada
Overview: A large national organization founded in 1943
Mission: To assist its members in serving the needs & meeting the aspirations of Canadians for housing; To be the voice of the residential construction industry in Canada; To achieve an environment in which members can operate profitably; To promote affordability & choice in housing for all Canadians; To support the professionalism of members
Chief Officer(s):
Nichael Gough, National Coordinator, Association Services, 613-230-3060 Ext. 227
Jack Mantyla, National Coordinator, Education & Training, 613-230-3060 Ext. 226
John Kenward, Chief Operating Officer
Don Johnston, Senior Director, Technology & Policy, 613-230-3060 Ext. 225
Lynda Barrett, Director, Conferences & Special Events, 905-954-0730
John Bos, Director, Finance, 613-230-3060 Ext. 238
David Crenna, Director, Urban Issues, 613-230-3060 Ext. 236
David Foster, Director, Environmental Affairs, 613-230-3060 Ext. 232
Membership: *Member Profile:* New home builders; Renovators; Trade contractors; Leading manufacturers; Suppliers; Warranty program providers; Government housing agents; Service people; Professionals; *Committees:* Technical Research; National Education & Training; National Marketing; Governance
Activities: Promoting the interests of housing consumers; Liaising with all levels of government; Working to influence decision-makers on issues such as taxation & regulatory reform; Developing courses & workshops; Distributing industry news; *Awareness Events:* Renovation Month, October; New Homes Month
Meetings/Conferences:
For more information see Trade Shows, Conferences and Seminars Chapter
Canadian Home Builders' Association 2013 70th National Conference
2013
Canadian Home Builders' Association 2014 71st National Conference
April 2014 Whistler, BC
Publications:
•Canadian Home Builders' Association Builders' Manual
Type: Book; *Number of Pages:* 400; *Price:* $65
Profile: A guide to building energy-efficient housing
•Connecting with Customers [a publication of the Canadian Home Builders' Association]
Type: Book; *Price:* $15
Profile: Practical information & strategies for new home builders to sell homes, including market research & marketing plans
•How to Manage Risk: A Canadian Home Builders' Association Guide for New Home Builders & Renovators
Type: Book; *Price:* $15
Profile: Featuring topics such as main insurance coverages & financial assurance instruments
•The Marketing Advantage: A Guide For Professional Home Renovators
Type: Book; *Price:* $15
Profile: Advice for home renovators, including information on advertising & presentations
•The National [a publication of the Canadian Home Builders' Association]
Type: Newspaper; *Frequency:* Quarterly; *Editor:* Kerry Gibbens
Profile: Current events in the housing industry

Canadian Home Builders' Association - British Columbia (CHBA BC)

Parent Name: Canadian Home Builders' Association
c/o Bldg. NW5, British Columbia Institute of Technology Campus, 3700 Willingdon Ave., Burnaby BC V5G 3H2
Tel: 604-432-7112; *Fax:* 604-432-9038
Toll-Free: 800-933-6777
e-mail: info@chbabc.org
www.chbabc.org
Overview: A medium-sized provincial organization founded in 1967 overseen by Canadian Home Builders' Association
Mission: To act as the voice of British Columbia's residential construction industry; to foster an environment for effectiveness & professionalism in the industry; to maintain affordability & profitability in British Columbia's housing industry
Environmental Activity: Launching the Built Green BC program, an energy efficiency & sustainability program for residential housing
Chief Officer(s):
Bob Deeks, President, 604-932-3618
bob@rdcfinehomes.com
M.J. Whitemarsh, CEO
mjwhitemarsh@chbabc.org
Membership: *Committees:* Renovation Council; Technical Council; Education & Training
Activities: Liaising with the provincial government on province-wide initiatives; offering courses for Master Builder credential; providing government information & reference materials; offering technical support services; *Library:* CHBA BC Technical & Video Library
Publications:
•BC Homes Magazine
Type: Magazine; *Frequency:* Bimonthly; *Accepts Advertising*; *Editor:* Scott Whitemarsh
Profile: Issue in British Columbia's housing industry

Canadian Horticultural Council (CHC) / Conseil canadien de l'horticulture

9 Corvus Ct., Ottawa ON K2E 7Z4
Tel: 613-226-4880; *Fax:* 613-226-4497
e-mail: webmaster@hortcouncil.ca
www.hortcouncil.ca
Overview: A large national organization founded in 1922
Mission: To improve horticultural & allied industries including production, grading, packing, transportation, storage & marketing; *Member of:* CanAgPlus; Affiliation(s): Canadian Potato Council; International Federation for Produce Standards; Potatoes Canada
Chief Officer(s):
Murray Porteous, President
Anne Fowlie, Executive Vice-President
afowlie@hortcouncil.ca
Finances: *Annual Operating Budget:* $500,000-$1.5 Million
Staff: 10 staff member(s)
Membership: 120+ organizations; *Fees:* Amount based on national farm cash receipts; *Member Profile:* Organizations promoting development of horticultural industry; horticultural commodity organizations; federal & provincial government agriculture departments; *Committees:* Apple & Fruit; Crop, Plant Protection & Environment; Finance & Marketing; Food Safety; Greenhouse Production; Human Resources; Potato; Research & Technology; Science Advisory; Trade & Industry Standards; Vegetable
Activities: ; *Library:*
Meetings/Conferences:
For more information see Trade Shows, Conferences and Seminars Chapter
Canadian Horticultural Council 91st Annual General Meeting 2013
March 2013 Ottawa, ON
Publications:
•Fresh Thinking [a publication of the Canadian Horticultural Council]
Type: Magazine; *Frequency:* s-a.
•Hort Shorts [a publication of the Canadian Horticultural Council]
Type: Newsletter

Canadian Horticultural Therapy Association

100 Westmount Rd., Guelph ON N1H 5H8
Tel: 519-822-9842
e-mail: admin@chta.ca
www.chta.ca
Overview: A small national organization
Mission: To promote the use & awareness of horticulture as a therapeutic modality; horticultural therapy is a process which uses plants, horticultural activities, & the natural world to promote awareness & well-being by improving the body, mind, & spirit
Chief Officer(s):
Ann Kent, Chair
chair@chta.ca
Membership: *Fees:* $25 student; $55 individual; $75 corporate; *Member Profile:* Professionals such as occupational therapists, physiotherapists, recreation therapists, social workers, nurses, psychologists, landscape architects & designers, horticulturists, & people who have a passion for gardening

Canadian Hospital Association ***See*** Canadian Healthcare Association

Canadian Hydrogen & Fuel Cell Association (CHFCA)

4250 Wesbrook Mall, Vancouver BC V6T 1W5
Tel: 604-822-9178; *Fax:* 604-822-8106
e-mail: info@chfca.ca
www.chfca.ca
Merged from: Canadian Hydrogen Association (CHA) & Hydrogen & Fuel Cells Canada (H2FCC)
Overview: A small national organization founded in 2009
Mission: To act as the collective voice of the hydrogen & fuel cell technologies & products sector; To support Canadian corporations, educational institutions, & governments which develop & deploy hydrogen & fuel cell products & services in Canada
Chief Officer(s):
John W. Tak, President & Chief Executive Officer
Terry Kimmel, Vice-President, 613-230-8484
tkimmel@chfea.ca
Michael Dujardin, Controller, 604-822-0170
mdujardin@chfca.ca
Javis Lui, Manager, Communications & Member Relations, 604-822-0841
jlui@chfca.ca
Sarah Richards, Manager, Conferences & Workshops, 604-822-1736
srichardschfca.ca
Membership: 70 organizations; *Fees:* Schedule available, based upon number of employees; *Member Profile:* Hydrogen & fuel cell technology & component firms; Fuelling system organizations; Fuel storage services; Engineering firms; Financial services
Activities: Increasing awareness of the economic, environmental, & social benefits of hydrogen & fuel cells; Supporting the development of regulations, codes, & standards; Facilitating demonstration projects, such as Hydrogen Village & the Hydrogen Highway; Supporting the safe & widespread

application & commercialization of hydrogen & fuel cell products; Engaging in advocacy activities; Liasing with government stakeholders; Providing information to governments, media & the pubblic; Offering networking opportunities for members
Meetings/Conferences:
For more information see Trade Shows, Conferences and Seminars Chapter
6th Annual Hydrogen + Fuel Cells 2013 International Conference
June 2013 Vancouver, BC
Publications:
•Canadian Capabilities Guide: Canada's Hydrogen & Fuel Cell Industry
Type: Guide
Profile: Profiles & critical information about companies & organizations in Canada's hydrogen & fuel cell sector
•Canadian Fuel Cell Commercialization Roadmap Update: Progress of Canada's Hydrogen & Fuel Cell Industry
Type: Guide
Profile: ISSN: 978-1-100-10468-360537E
•Canadian Hydrogen & Fuel Cell Association Newsletter
Type: Newsletter; *Frequency:* Quarterly
Profile: Association member news & successes
•Canadian Hydrogen & Fuel Cell Sector Profile
Type: Guide
Profile: Statistics about Canada's hydrogen & fuel cell sector

Canadian Hydrographic Association (CHA) / Association canadienne d'hydrographie
867 Lakeshore Rd., Burlington ON L7R 4A6
Tel: 905-336-4491
www.hydrography.ca
Overview: A small national organization founded in 1966
Mission: The scientific & technical group has the following objectives: to advance the development of hydrography & associated activities in Canada; to further the knowledge & professional development of members; to enhance & demonstrate the public need for hydrography; & to help the development of hydrographic sciences in developing countries; & to embrace the desciplines of marine cartography, hydrographic surveying, offshore exploration, marine geodesy, & tidal studies.; *Member of:* International Federation of Hydrographic Societies; Affiliation(s): Canadian Institute of Geomatics (formal affiliation); The Hydrographic Society (informal affiliation)
Chief Officer(s):
George McFarlane, National President, 416-512-5764
george.mcfarlane@pwgsc.gc.ca
Terese Herron, National Secretary, 905-336-4832
Terese.Herron@dfo-mpo.gc.ca
Christine Delbridge, National Treasurer, 905-336-4745
Christine.Delbridge@dfo-mpo.gc.ca
Finances: *Funding Sources:* Membership dues; Conferences & seminars; Sponsorships
Membership: 200+; *Fees:* $40 individual; $150 corporate; $20 student; *Member Profile:* Hydrographers; Workers in associated disciplines; persons interested in hydrography & marine cartography
Activities: Operating a Student Award Program; *Library:* Gerry Wade Memorial Library; by appointment
Publications:
•Lighthouse: The Journal of the Canadian Hydrographic Association
Type: Journal; *Frequency:* Semiannually; *Number of Pages:* 60; *Price:* $20 Canada; $25international
Profile: Timely scientific, technical, & non-technical articles about hydrography in Canada, news from the industry, & CHA activities & events

Canadian Hydropower Association (CHA) / Association canadienne de l'hydroélectricité
#1300, 340 Albert St., Ottawa ON K1R 7Y9
Tel: 613-751-6655; *Fax:* 613-751-4465
e-mail: info@canhydropower.org
www.canhydropower.org
Overview: A small national organization founded in 1998
Mission: To provide leadership for the responsible growth & prosperity of the Canadian hydropower industry
Membership: 16 generators; 21 industry; 8 associate; *Member Profile:* Hydroelectic generation; hydroelectric industry; Associated associations and organizations
Meetings/Conferences:
For more information see Trade Shows, Conferences and Seminars Chapter
13th Annual Forum on Hydropower 2013
May 2013 Ottawa, ON

Canadian Industrial Transportation Association (CITA) / Association canadienne de transport industriel (ACTI)
#405, 580 Terry Fox Dr., Ottawa ON K2L 4C2
Tel: 613-599-3283; *Fax:* 613-599-1295
e-mail: info@cita-acti.ca
www.cita-acti.ca
Overview: A medium-sized national organization
Mission: CITA-ACTI actively promotes a competitive and cost effective North American transportation system serving Canada and its NAFTA allies. Their vision is to be recognized as the "National Voice" of industrial transportation in Canada through increased membership and member representation in all regions of the county.
Chief Officer(s):
Bob Ballantyne, President
Denise Fata, Manager, Marketing and Events
Cindy Hick, Vice-President
Finances: *Annual Operating Budget:* $250,000-$500,000; *Funding Sources:* Membership dues
Staff: 3 staff member(s)
Membership: 400 major shippers
Activities: Advocacy; education; *Speaker Service:* Yes; *Library:* Open to public
Meetings/Conferences:
For more information see Trade Shows, Conferences and Seminars Chapter
Canadian Industrial Transportation Association 46th Annual Conference
May 2013 Mississauga, ON

Canadian Injured Workers Alliance (CIWA) / L'Alliance canadienne des victimes d'accidents et de maladies du travail (ACVAMT)
PO Box 10098, 1201 Jasper Dr., Thunder Bay ON P7B 6T6
Tel: 807-345-3429; *Fax:* 807-344-8683
Toll-Free: 877-787-7010
www.ciwa.ca
Overview: A medium-sized national organization founded in 1990
Mission: To support & strengthen the work of local & provincial groups by providing a forum for exchanging information & experiences; To provide training & educational resources in partnership with these groups to ensure that injured workers maintain control over their destinies & that the groups themselves be democratically controlled by the workers
Chief Officer(s):
Bill Cheodore, National Coordinator
Finances: *Annual Operating Budget:* $100,000-$250,000
Staff: 3 staff member(s); 20 volunteer(s)
Membership: 8; *Member Profile:* Provincial injured workers organizations
Activities: Offering conferences & workshops; Providing leadership training; Conducting a survey on the re-employment of injured workers; Engaging in research; *Speaker Service:* Yes; *Library:* Resource Centre; Open to public
Publications:
•Highlights [a publication of the Canadian Injured Workers Alliance]
Type: Newsletter; *Frequency:* Quarterly; *Price:* $5 injured worker & unemployed;$10 individual; $15 organization
Profile: Information about provincial & national developments, government policies, & CIWA projects for injured workers' groups

Canadian Innovation Centre (CIC)
c/o Waterloo Research & Technology Park, #15, 295 Hagey Blvd., Waterloo ON N2L 6R5
Tel: 519-885-5870; *Fax:* 519-513-2421
Toll-Free: 800-265-4559
e-mail: info@innovationcentre.ca
www.innovationcentre.ca
Overview: A medium-sized national organization founded in 1981
Mission: To advance innovation by helping our clients make better business decisions through information, education & commercialization.
Chief Officer(s):
Ted Cross, Chair & CEO
Activities: ; *Library:* by appointment
Awards:
•Market Research Services (Grant)
Assists individuals & established companies in commercializing their technologies & business ventures; will conduct preliminary & detailed market research, evaluate commercial potential, manage development & testing, assist in venture planning, provide training & education programs, & promote international technologies available for license *Eligibility:* Individual entrepreneurs, inventors/innovators & small businesses
•The Inventor's Assistance Program (Grant)
Provides an objective evaluation of a new idea which considers technical feasibility, available legal protection & market competition *Eligibility:* Individual entrepreneurs, inventors/innovators or small businesses

The Canadian Institute (CI) / L'Institut canadien
1329 Bay St., Toronto ON M5R 2C4
Tel: 416-927-7936; *Fax:* 416-927-1563
Toll-Free: 877-927-7936
e-mail: customerservice@canadianinstitute.com
www.canadianinstitute.com
Overview: A small national organization
Mission: To monitor trends in public policy, the law, & major industry sectors; To provide business intelligence for Canadian decision-makers; Affiliation(s): American Conference Institute (New York); C5 (London, UK)
Chief Officer(s):
Patricia Fletcher, Managing Director
Finances: *Funding Sources:* Sponsorships; Conference fees
Activities: Organizing conferences, executive briefings, & summits for senior delegates; Publishing materials for conferences
Meetings/Conferences:
For more information see Trade Shows, Conferences and Seminars Chapter
CI Energy Group's 16th Annual BC Natural Gas Symposium
June 2013 Vancouver, BC
CI Energy Group's 17th Annual BC Natural Gas Symposium
2014, BC

Canadian Institute for Energy Training (CIET) / Institut canadien de formation de l'énergie
#200, 160, rue Saint-Paul, Québec QC G1K 3W1
Tel: 418-692-2592; *Fax:* 418-692-4899
Toll-Free: 800-461-7618
e-mail: info@cietcanada.com
www.cietcanada.com
Overview: A medium-sized national organization founded in 1994
Mission: To focus on the advancement of energy efficiency in industrial, commercial, & public sector organizations; To provide effective training solutions for the incorporation of energy management into organizational management priorities
Chief Officer(s):
Douglas Tripp, President
Finances: *Funding Sources:* Fees for service
Activities: Offers the following training courses: Certified Energy Manager (CEM); Certification à l'utilisation du logiciel de simulation RETScreenr; Certified Energy Auditor (CEA); Techniques d'amélioration de l'efficacité énergétique; Certified Measurement and Verification Professional (CMVP); Certified in the Use of RETScreenr (CRU); Mesurage et ciblage énergétique; & Certification CEM

Canadian Institute for Health Information (CIHI) / Institut canadien d'information sur la santé (ICIS)
#600, 495 Richmond Rd., Ottawa ON K2A 4H6
Tel: 613-241-7860; *Fax:* 613-241-8120
e-mail: communications@cihi.ca
www.cihi.ca
Overview: A small national organization founded in 1994
Mission: To collect, analyze, & provide information about the health system in Canada & the health of Canadians; To support persons who use data for health & health-services research
Chief Officer(s):
John Wright, President & Chief Executive Officer, 613-694-6500
JWright@cihi.ca
Louis Barré, Vice-President, Strategy, Planning & Outreach
LBarre@cihi.ca
Jean-Marie Berthelot, Vice-President, Programs
JBerthelot@cihi.ca
Anne McFarlane, Vice-President, Western Canada & Developmental Initiatives
AMcFarlane@cihi.ca
Louise Ogilvie, Vice-President, Corporate Services
LOgilvie@cihi.caca
Jeremy Veillard, Vice-President, Research & Analysis
JVeillard@cihi.ca
Finances: *Funding Sources:* Federal, provincial, & territorial governments

Activities: Maintaining health databases, measurements, & standards; Developing reports; Raising awareness about services; *Speaker Service:* Yes
Publications:
•Canadian Institute for Health Information Annual Report
Type: Yearbook; *Frequency:* Annually
•CIHI [Canadian Institute for Health Information] Directions ICIS [Institut canadien d'information sur la santé]
Type: Newsletter; *ISSN:* 1201-0383

Canadian Institute for NDE

135 Fennell Ave. West, Hamilton ON L8N 3T2
Tel: 905-387-1655; *Fax:* 905-574-6080
Toll-Free: 800-964-9488
e-mail: info@cinde.ca
www.cinde.ca
www.facebook.com/297023083473
Also Known As: CINDE
Merged from: Canadian Society for Nondestructive Testing; NDE Institute of Canada
Overview: A medium-sized national organization founded in 1964
Mission: To advance scientific, engineering, technical knowledge in the field of nondestructive testing; to gather & disseminate information relating to nondestructive testing useful to individuals & beneficial to the general public; to promote nondestructive testing through courses of instruction, lectures, meetings, publications, conferences, etc.; *Member of:* NDE Institute of Canada
Chief Officer(s):
Larry Cote, President & CEO
l.cote@cinde.ca
Finances: *Annual Operating Budget:* $100,000-$250,000
Staff: 1 staff member(s)
Membership: 50 corporate + 20 associate + 20 student + 20 senior/lifetime + 1,000 individual + 50 subscriptions; *Fees:* $60 individual; $160 sustaining; $475 corporate
Meetings/Conferences:
For more information see Trade Shows, Conferences and Seminars Chapter
Canadian Institute for NDE NDT in Canada 2013 Conference
October 2013 Calgary, AB
Publications:
•CINDE [Canadian Institute for NDE] Journal
Type: Journal; *Frequency:* Bimonthly; *Accepts Advertising*; *Price:* Free with Canadian Institute for NDE membership; $80 Canada; $110 USA; $135 overseas
Profile: Canadian Institute for NDE chapter reports, conferences, members, & board of directors, industry & international news, business directory, & new products supplies & services

Canadian Institute for Photonics Innovations (CIPI)

Université Laval, Pavillion d'optique-photonique, #2111, 2375 rue de la Terrasse, Québec QC G1V 0A6
Tel: 418-656-3013; *Fax:* 418-656-2995
e-mail: cipi@cipi.ulaval.ca
www.cipi.ulaval.ca
Overview: A medium-sized national organization
Mission: Photonics - science of generating, manipulating, transmitting & detecting light; *Member of:* Networks of Centres of Excellence
Chief Officer(s):
Robert Corriveau, President
robert.corriveau@cipi.ulaval.ca

Canadian Institute for Radiation Safety *See* Radiation Safety Institute of Canada

Canadian Institute of Biotechnology; Industrial Biotechnology Association of Canada *See* BIOTECanada

Canadian Institute of Energy (CIE)

#26, 181 Ravine Dr., Port Moody BC V3H 4T3
Tel: 604-949-1346; *Fax:* 604-469-3717
e-mail: cienergybc@gmail.com
www.cienergy.org
Overview: A medium-sized national organization founded in 1979
Mission: To provide a Canadian perspective on energy technology, business & policy, nationally & internationally, for those affected professionally or personally by energy issues; To encourage energy research, education & dissemination of topical information; To provide an unbiased forum for discussion & debate
Chief Officer(s):
Penny Cochrane, Chair
Melissa McArthur, Administrator
John Oliver, Treasurer
Finances: *Funding Sources:* Membership fees
Staff: 6 volunteer(s)
Membership: 500; *Fees:* $60; *Member Profile:* Professionally involved in all aspects of energy, whether in exploring for sources, conducting energy research, converting or using energy, or in energy planning
Activities: *Speaker Service:* Yes; *Rents Mailing List:* Yes
Awards:
•Energy Scholarship Award (Award)
•Energy Research & Development Award (Award)
•Applied Energy Innovation Award (Award)

Canadian Institute of Food & Nutrition; Canadian Food Information Council *See* Canadian Council of Food & Nutrition

Canadian Institute of Food Science & Technology (CIFST) / Institut canadien de science et technologie alimentaires (ICSTA)

#1311, 3-1750 The Queensway, Toronto ON M9C 5H5
Tel: 905-271-8338; *Fax:* 905-271-8344
e-mail: cifst@cifst.ca
www.cifst.ca
Overview: A medium-sized national organization founded in 1951
Mission: To advance food science & technology; To act as a voice for scientific issues related to the Canadian food industry; Affiliation(s): British Columbia Food Technolgists
Environmental Activity: Promoting the quality & safety of the food supply by applying science & technology
Chief Officer(s):
Carol Ann Burrell, Executive Director, 905-271-8338, Fax: 905-271-8344
caburrell@cifst.ca
Charles Powell, President, 204-795-8613, Fax: 204-746-2932
charles.powell@gov.mb.ca
Finances: *Funding Sources:* Sponsorships
Membership: 1,200+; *Member Profile:* Food industry professionals from across Canada, such as scientists & technologists in industry, academia, & government; *Committees:* Awards; Executive; National Symposium; Conference; International Liaison; Membership; Nominations; Fellow Selection
Activities: Exchanging scientific, educational, & business information; Engaging in advocacy activities; Liaising with related national & international organizations, such as Agriculture & Agri-Food Canada (AAFC) & the International Union of Food Science & Technology (IUFoST); Promoting professional development; Establishing Subject Interest Divisions, such as food process engineering, functional foods, government & regulatory affairs, microbiology, nutrition, packaging, & sensory evaluation
Meetings/Conferences:
For more information see Trade Shows, Conferences and Seminars Chapter
2014 World Congress of Food Science of Technology
August 2014 Montréal, QC

Alberta Section

Michael Gänzle, University of Alberta, 4-10 Ag/For Centre, Edmonton AB
www.cifst.ca
Chief Officer(s):
Michael Gänzle, Chair, 780-492-0774, Fax: 780-492-4265
mgaenzle@ualberta.ca
Mirko Betti, Secretary-Treasurer, 780-248-1598
mirko.betti@ales.ualberta.ca
Hisham Karami, Director, Membership, 780-710-2071
hishamkarami@hotmail.com

Atlantic Section

c/o Jim Smith, Executive Director, P.E.I. Food Technology Centre, PO Box 2000, 101 Belvedere Ave., Charlottetown PE C1A 7N8
Tel: 902-368-5767
e-mail: jsmith@gov.pe.ca (Jim Smith, Past Chair)
www.cifst.ca
Chief Officer(s):
Yaw Dako, Chair, 902-569-7699, Fax: 902-368-5549
yadako@foodtechnologycentre.ca
Jessica Dunfield, Vice-Chair, 506-433-8155, Fax: 506-433-5689
j.dunfield@agrapoint.ca
H.P. Vasantha Rupasinghe, Secretary-Treasurer, 902-893-6623, Fax: 902-893-1404
vrupasinghe@nsac.ca

Guelph Section

c/o Judy Chow, Maple Leaf Consumer Foods, 321 Courtland Ave. East, Kitchener ON N2G 3X8
Tel: 519-741-5000
e-mail: jychow@rogers.com
www.cifst.ca
Chief Officer(s):
Judy Chow, Chair, 519-741-5000 Ext. 7321
judy.chow@mapleleaf.com
Victoria Hudson, Treasurer, 519-824-4120
vhudson@uoguelph.ca

Manitoba Section

c/o A. Tezcucano, Manitoba Agriculture, Food & Rural Initiatives, PO Box 100, 229 Main St. South, Morris MB R0G 1K0
e-mail: manitobasection@cifst.ca
www.cifst.ca
Chief Officer(s):
Aline Tezcucano, Chair, 204-795-7968, Fax: 204-746-2932
aline.tezcucano@gov.mb.ca
Prabal Ghosh, Secretary, 204-239-3164, Fax: 204-239-3180
Prabal.Ghosh@gov.mb.ca
David Adamik, Treasurer
adamik22@mts.net
Ketie Sandhu, Chair, Programs
ksandhu@gourmetbaker.com

Québec Section

c/o Carole Désautels, Section Administrator, 414, rue Champlain, Beloeil QC J3G 4M3
Tel: 450-464-2171; *Fax:* 450-464-3457
e-mail: caroledesautels@mac.com
www.cifst.ca
Chief Officer(s):
Nicole Rodrigue, Chair, 514-421-0754, Fax: 514-421-9829
nrodrigue@cic-can.net
Carole Désautels, Section Administrator, 450-464-2171, Fax: 450-464-3457
caroledesautels@mac.com
Stéphane Lachambre, Treasurer, 450-659-3768, Fax: 450-659-5174
slachambre@ecomcanada.com
Marc Poirier, Director, Communication, 819-758-5229, Fax: 819-758-5220
marcp@selwarwick.com

Toronto Section

c/o Christine Baily, Toronto Section Administrator, 5 Fenwook Circle, Peterborough ON K9J 6M4
Tel: 866-437-6030; *Fax:* 866-719-5396
e-mail: TorontoSection@cifst.ca
www.cifst.ca
Chief Officer(s):
Robert Kowal, Chair, 905-567-8361, Fax: 905-567-0097
rkowal@kriscor.ca
Christine Baily, Administrator, 866-437-6030, Fax: 866-719-5396
Heather Paterson, Treasurer, 905-457-5523, Fax: 905-450-5955
heather.paterson@psi-inc.biz
Paul Hebbel, Director, Marketing, 905-815-8158 Ext. 224, Fax: 905-815-9194
phebbel@cic-can.net
Saqib Javaid, Director, Programs, 416-502-8218 Ext. 232, Fax: 416-505-8217
saqib.javaid@shandiz.ca
Marlene McClure, Director, Science & Technology, 905-838-5416, Fax: 905-843-3334
marlene.mcclure@gmail.com
James Summers, Editor, SciTech, 416-964-1280
jsummers@FoodScienceSolutions.com

Canadian Institute of Forestry / Institut forestier du Canada

c/o The Canadian Ecology Centre, PO Box 430, 6905 Hwy. 17 West, Mattawa ON P0H 1V0
Tel: 705-744-1715; *Fax:* 705-744-1716
e-mail: admin@cif-ifc.org
www.cif-ifc.org
www.facebook.com/groups/53806339292
twitter.com/cif_ifc
www.youtube.com/user/CIFtube
Previous Name: Canadian Society of Forest Engineers
Overview: A large national organization founded in 1908
Mission: To act as the national voice of forest practitioners; *Member of:* International Union of Societies of Foresters

Environmental Activity: Advancing the stewardship of Canada's forest resources; Examining topics such as biodiversity & species at risk & climate change adaptation; Presenting the Tree of Life Award for contributions to forest renewal & sustainable forest management
Chief Officer(s):
John Pineau, Chief Executive Officer
Matt Meade, Executive Director
Michel Vallée, President
Tattersall Smith, Vice-President
Finances: *Funding Sources:* Membership dues; Sponsorships
Membership: 2,200; *Fees:* $39.55 students; $67.80 retired members; $50 sustaining individuals; $111.87 active members & spousal; $192.10 current active members; *Member Profile:* Foresters; Forest technicians & technologists; Educators; Scientists, such as biologists & ecologists; Students; Others with a professional interest in forestry; *Committees:* National board of Directors; Executive; Awards; Silver Ring Accreditation
Activities: Providing national leadership in forestry; Promoting competence & knowledge of forestry for professionals; Presenting a national electronic lecture series; Providing workshops & seminars; Fostering public awareness & understanding of forestry issues; Presenting rings to graduates of Canadian forest technical & forestry baccalaureate programs; Offering field tours; Establishing demonstration forests; Providing networking opportunities; Liaising with the Canadian Council of Forest Ministers; *Speaker Service:* Yes
Awards:
•International Forestry Achievement Award (Award)
To recognize outstanding achievement in international forestry
•James M. Kitz Award (Award)
To honour contributions of forest practitioners who are new to the profession
•Canadian Forest Management Group Achievement Award (Award)
To honour outstanding achievement by teams & groups of natural resource managers, researchers, & NGO groups in the field of forest resource related activities in Canada
•Canadian Forestry Achievement Award (Award)
To recognize outstanding achievement in forestry in Canada
•Canadian Forestry Scientific Achievement Award (Award)
To honour unique achievement in forestry research in Canada
Meetings/Conferences:
For more information see Trade Shows, Conferences and Seminars Chapter
Canadian Institute of Forestry / Institut forestier du Canada 2013 105th Annual General Meeting & Conference
September 2013 Corner Brook, NL
Canadian Institute of Forestry / Institut forestier du Canada 2014 106th Annual General Meeting & Conference
2014
Publications:
•Canadian Institute of Forestry Annual Report
Type: Yearbook; *Frequency:* Annually
•Canadian Institute of Forestry E-news
Type: Newsletter; *Frequency:* Bimonthly
Profile: Information about the Institute, such as conferences, section updates, & member resources
•The Forestry Chronicle: The Official Journal of the Canadian Institute of Forestry
Type: Journal; *Frequency:* Bimonthly; *Accepts Advertising*; *Editor:* Brian Haddon; *Price:* $100 personal electronic & print; $300multi-users electronic & print
Profile: Practical & applied science & information for forest management planning & operations

Canadian Institute of Geomatics (CIG) / Association canadienne des sciences géomatiques

#100D, 900 Dynes Rd., Ottawa ON K2C 3L6
Tel: 613-224-9851; *Fax:* 613-224-9577
e-mail: admincig@magma.ca
www.cig-acsg.ca
Overview: A medium-sized national organization founded in 1882
Mission: Geomatics is commonly defined as a "discipline aimed at managing geographic data by means of the science & technology used to acquire, store, process, display & distribute them"; to advance the development of geomatics sciences in Canada; to enhance & demonstrate the public usefulness of geomatics; to further the professional development of its members; to foster cooperation between & promote unity of purpose among Canadian geomatics organizations; to represent & promote Canadian interests in geomatics internationally; Affiliation(s): International Federation of Surveyors; International Society for Photogrammetry & Remote Sensing; International Cartographic Association; Commonwealth Association of Canada Lands Surveyors; Canadian Council of Land Surveyors; Canadian Hydrographic Association
Chief Officer(s):
David R. Stafford, Executive Director
exdircig@magma.ca
Lucie Lebrun-Ginn, Office Administrator
Finances: *Annual Operating Budget:* $100,000-$250,000; *Funding Sources:* Membership fees; events; contributions
Staff: 3 staff member(s); 30 volunteer(s)
Membership: 1,500; *Fees:* $95 member; $500 sustaining; $40 student; *Committees:* Cartography; Education; Engineering & Mining; Geodesy; Geospatial Data Infrastructures; Hydrography; GPS; Land Surveying; Land Information Management; Photogrammetry; Remote Sensing; Urban Regional Information; Annual Conferences
Activities: Geographical information systems (GIS); global positioning systems & remote sensing as tools & techniques in environmental monitoring & planning (ie. sustainable development); *Library:* by appointment
Publications:
•Geomatica
Type: Journal; *Frequency:* Quarterly; *Accepts Advertising*; *Price:* $275
Profile: Formerly the CISM Journal ACSGC, the surveying & mapping publication features both scientific & practical information, conferences, reviews, industry news, & new products

Canadian Institute of International Affairs / Institut canadien des affaires internationales *See* Canadian International Council

Canadian Institute of Mining & Metallurgy *See* Canadian Institute of Mining, Metallurgy & Petroleum

Canadian Institute of Mining, Metallurgy & Petroleum (CIM) / Institut canadien des mines, de la métallurgie et du pétrole

CIM National Office, #1250, 3500, boul de Maisonneuve ouest, Westmount QC H3Z 3C1
Tel: 514-939-2710; *Fax:* 514-939-2714
e-mail: cim@cim.org
www.cim.org
Previous Name: Canadian Institute of Mining & Metallurgy
Overview: A large national organization founded in 1898
Mission: To act as a source of leadership for its members, by offering conferences & courses, liaising with government departments, commissioning special volumes & reports, & publishing technical papers
Chief Officer(s):
Jean Vavrek, Executive Director, 514-939-2710 Ext. 1301, Fax: 513-939-2714
jvavrek@cim.org
Chuck Edwards, President
chuck.edwards@amec.com
Jean-Marc Demers, Deputy Executive Director
jmdemers@cim.org
Lise Bujold, Director, Conferences & Exhibitions
lbujold@cim.org
Marjolaine Dugas, Director, Membership
mdugas@cim.org
Gérard Hamel, Director, Information Technology
ghamel@cim.org
Angela Hamlyn, Director, Media & Communications
ahamlyn@cim.org
Serge Major, Director, Finance & Admininstration
smajor@cim.org
Deborah Sauvé, Manager, Canadian Mining Metallurgical Foundation
dsauve@cim.org
Membership: 12,000+; *Member Profile:* Professionals in the Canadian minerals, metals, materials, & energy sectors, from industry, government, & academia; *Committees:* Central Publications; Audit; Bulletin; By-Laws; CIM Valuation of Mineral Properties; Education; Estimation Guidelines; Human Resources; International Advisory Liaison; Membership; President Elect Nominating; Public Affairs; Special Volumes
Activities: Providing technical forums & professional networking opportunities; Offering continuing education; Recognizing excellent programs; *Speaker Service:* Yes; *Library:* Canadian Institute of Mining, Metallurgy & Petroleum Library
Awards:
•CIM Awards (Award)
The institute administers 27 awards recognizing achievement in mining, metallurgy & petroleum industries
Meetings/Conferences:
For more information see Trade Shows, Conferences and Seminars Chapter
Canadian Institute of Mining, Metallurgy & Petroleum 2013 Annual Conference & Exhibition
May 2013 Toronto, ON
23rd World Mining Congress & Expo
August 2013 Montréal, QC
30th International Symposium on Automation and Robotics in Construction (ISARC 2013)
August 2013 Montréal, QC
Canadian Institute of Mining, Metallurgy & Petroleum MassMin 2016: 7th Intl Conference & Exhibition on Mass Mining
2016 Sydney
Publications:
•CIM [Canadian Institute of Mining, Metallurgy & Petroleum] Magazine
Type: Magazine; *Frequency:* 7 pa; *Accepts Advertising*; *ISSN:* 1718-4177; *Price:* Free for members; $160 non-members in Canada
Profile: Editorials, technical information, industry events, & industry information
•CIM [Canadian Institute of Mining, Metallurgy & Petroleum] Directory
Type: Directory; *Frequency:* Annually
Profile: Listing of individual & corporate CIM members
•CIM [Canadian Institute of Mining, Metallurgy & Petroleum] Reporter
Frequency: Annually
Profile: Official publication of the annual CIM Conference & Exhibition, for all registered delegates & visitors
•CIM [Canadian Institute of Mining, Metallurgy & Petroleum] Canadian Metallurgical Quarterly
Frequency: Quarterly; *ISSN:* 0008-4433
Profile: Publishes original contributions on all aspects of metallurgy and materials science, including mineral processing,hydrometallurgy, pyrometallurgy, materials processing, physical metallurgy and the service behaviour of materials.

Canadian Institute of Planners (CIP) / Institut canadien des urbanistes (ICU)

#1112, 141 Laurier Ave. West, Ottawa ON K1P 5J3
Tel: 613-237-7526; *Fax:* 613-237-7045
Toll-Free: 800-207-2138
e-mail: general@cip-icu.ca
www.cip-icu.ca
Overview: A medium-sized national organization founded in 1919
Mission: To advance professional planning excellence, through the delivery of membership & public services in Canada & abroad; Affiliation(s): Alberta Association, Canadian Institute of Planners; Association of Professional Community Planners of Saskatchewan; Atlantic Planners Institute; Manitoba Professional Planners Institute; Ontario Professional Planners Institute; Ordre des urbanistes du Québec; Planning Institute of British Columbia
Chief Officer(s):
Steven Brasier, CAE, Executive Director
sbrasier@cip-icu.ca
Finances: *Funding Sources:* Membership fees
Membership: 7,000; *Member Profile:* Professional community & regional planners employed in the private sector in the consulting & land development industries & in the public sector at all levels of government.
Activities: *Awareness Events:* World Town Planning Day; *Internships:* Yes; *Rents Mailing List:* Yes
Meetings/Conferences:
For more information see Trade Shows, Conferences and Seminars Chapter
Canadian Institute of Planners 2013 Conference: Infuse Vancouver 2013
July 2013 Vancouver, BC
Canadian Institute of Planners 2014 Conference
2014

Canadian Institute of Plumbing & Heating (CIPH) / Institut canadien de plomberie et de chauffage

#504, 295 The West Mall, Toronto ON M9C 4Z4
Tel: 416-695-0447; *Fax:* 416-695-0450
Toll-Free: 800-639-2474
e-mail: info@ciph.com
www.ciph.com
www.facebook.com/pages/CIPH/355926634482039
twitter.com/ciphnews
Overview: A large national organization founded in 1933

Mission: To act as a unified voice for plumbing, heating, hydronic, PVF, & waterworks across Canada
Environmental Activity: Promoting clean technologies
Chief Officer(s):
Ralph Suppa, President & General Manager
r.suppa@ciph.com
Elizabeth McCullough, General Manager, Trade Shows
e.mccullough@ciph.com
Kevin Wong, Coordinator, Member Services
k.wong@ciph.com
Stephen Apps, Contact, Education & Training
s.apps@ciph.com
Ken Tomihiro, Contact, Hydronics, Codes, & Standards
k.tomihiro@ciph.com
Membership: *Member Profile:* Companies throughout Canada that manufacture, sell, & distribute plumbing, heating, hydronic, PVF, & waterworks products & services; *Committees:* Executive / Finance; Nominating; Membership; Government Affairs; Region Hydronics; Charity Committee for Habitat for Humanity Canada; Manufacturers' Agents; Wholesalers' Division; Manufacturers' Division; Education & Training Council; Plumbing Industry Advisory Council; Canadian Hydronics Council; Industrial Pipe, Valve, & Fittings Council
Activities: Liaising with governments & organizations; Influencing the development of standards & codes; Raising awareness of safety; Providing education; Offering networking opportunities to share best practices
Meetings/Conferences:
For more information see Trade Shows, Conferences and Seminars Chapter
Canadian Institute of Plumbing & Heating 2013 Annual Business Conference: Pathways to Relevance
June 2013 Halifax, NS
Canadian Institute of Plumbing & Heating 2013 Annual General Meeting
June 2013 Halifax, NS
CMX CIPHEX 2014
March 2014 Toronto, ON
Canadian Institute of Plumbing & Heating 2014 Annual General Meeting
June 2014 Kelowna, BC
Canadian Institute of Plumbing & Heating 2014 Annual General Meeting
June 2015 Québec, QC
Publications:
•Advocacy Link [a publication of the Canadian Institute of Plumbing & Heating]
Type: Newsletter
Profile: A summary of information about the Canadian Institute of Plumbing & Heating. the Industrial Pipes, Valves, & Fittings Council, & theCanadian Hydronics Council, involving code & standards, public safety, & education
•Canadian Institute of Plumbing & Heating Member Directory
Type: Directory
Profile: Listing of members by head office, plus further information such as sales offices & contacts
•CIPH [Canadian Institute of Plumbing & Heating] EconoLink
Profile: Results from surveys
•CIPH [Canadian Institute of Plumbing & Heating] Wholesalers Sales Statistics
Frequency: Monthly; *Price:* $325
Profile: A summary of sales survey results in six regions by product groups
•Pipeline
Type: Newsletter; *Frequency:* 3-4 pa
Profile: Information about the hydronics, plumbing, & PVF industries, educational products, trade shows, & association activities for Canadian Institute of Plumbing & Heating members, industry stakeholders, &government

Atlantic Region
c/o John Sutherland, PO Box 9410, Stn. A, #700, 6009 Quinpool Rd., Halifax NS B3K 5S3
Tel: 902-425-2445; *Fax:* 902-425-2441
www.ciph.com
Chief Officer(s):
Rob Barrett, Region President, 506-693-8630
barrett4@nb.aibn.com
John Sutherland, Region Coordinator
jsutherland@pathfinder-group.com

British Columbia Region
c/o Kathryn Fallis, 15316 Sequoia Dr., Surrey BC V3S 8N4
Tel: 778-867-5956; *Fax:* 604-594-5091
e-mail: ciphbc@shaw.ca
www.ciph.com
Chief Officer(s):
Randy Kolstad, President, 604-444-2000
randyk@barobinson.ca
Ed Chubb, Treasurer
ed.chubb@mphsupply.com
Kathryn Fallis, Region Coordinator, 778-867-5956, Fax: 604-594-5091
ciphbc@shaw.ca

Calgary, Alberta Region
PO Box 4520, Stn. C, Calgary AB T2T 5N3
Tel: 403-244-4487; *Fax:* 403-244-2340
www.ciph.com
Chief Officer(s):
Mike Stringer, President, 403-256-4900, Fax: 403-256-1208
sales@stringersales.com
Connie Pruden, Region Coordinator, 403-244-4487, Fax: 403-244-2340
conniep@associationsplus.ca

Edmonton, Alberta, Region
c/o Linda Wood Edwards, PO Box 11021, Stn. Main, Edmonton AB T5J 3K3
Tel: 780-466-9938; *Fax:* 780-468-4449
www.ciph.com
Chief Officer(s):
Linda Wood Edwards, Region Coordinator
lue42@shaw.ca
Stephen Lee, Region President
stephenl@barobinson.com

Manitoba Region
PO Box 2737, Winnipeg MB R3C 4B3
Tel: 204-832-1512; *Fax:* 204-897-8094
www.ciph.com
Chief Officer(s):
Dan Jones, Region President, 204-632-6221
dan@jonesgoodridge.ca
Lise Carbonneau, Region Coordinator
whirlwind@shaw.ca

Newfoundland Region
c/o Sheri Slaney, 16 Argus Pl., St. John's NL A1A 5N2
Tel: 709-753-4222; *Fax:* 709-753-6641
e-mail: ciph.nl@gmail.com
www.ciph.com
Chief Officer(s):
Ron Neary, Region President, 709-747-7473
ron.neary@ipexna.com
Sheri Slaney, Region Coordinator, 709-753-4222

Ontario Region
c/o Nancy Barden, 5827 - 6th Line, RR#1, Hillsburgh ON N0B 1Z0
Tel: 519-855-6474; *Fax:* 519-855-1747
www.ciph.com
Chief Officer(s):
Jon Leeson, Region President, 416-213-1585 Ext. 144
jleeson@desco.ca
Nancy Barden, Region Coordinator
barden@sympatico.ca

Québec Region
Claude Robitaille, #106, 4460, ch des Cageux, Montréal QC H7W 2S7
Tél: 514-989-1002; *Téléc:* 514-681-1941
www.ciph.com
Chief Officer(s):
Claude Robitaille, Region Coordinator
claude.robitaille@mtaplus.com
Raymond Beauchemin, Region President, 819-563-7171
rbeauchemin@maburco.com

Saskatchewan Region
c/o Audrey Price, #202, 1275 Broad St., Regina SK S4R 1Y2
Tel: 306-585-3948; *Fax:* 306-585-1765
www.ciph.com
Chief Officer(s):
Wes Sapieha, Region President, 306-933-1033
wes.sapieha@wolseleyinc.ca
Audrey Price, Region Coordinator
audrey.price@b-creative.ca

Canadian Institute of Resources Law (CIRL) / Institut canadien du droit des ressources

Murray Fraser Hall, University of Calgary, #3353, 2500 University Dr. NW, Calgary AB T2N 1N4
Tel: 403-220-3200; *Fax:* 403-282-6182
e-mail: cirl@ucalgary.ca
www.cirl.ca
Overview: A small national charitable organization founded in 1979
Mission: To undertake and promote research, education and publication on the law relating to Canada's renewable and non-renewable natural resources.
Chief Officer(s):
Allan Ingelson, Executive Director, 403-220-3200
Clifford D. Johnson, Chair
Finances: *Funding Sources:* Public and Private Sectors; Non-Governmental Organizations
Staff: 9 staff member(s)
Activities: Sponsoring conferences, workshops & courses on aspects of resources law; *Library:* Open to public by appointment
Publications:
•Canada Energy Law Service
Profile: Looseleaf guide to the regulatory regimes administered by the National Energy Board & the Alberta Energy & Utilities Board
•CIRL [Canadian Institute of Resources Law] Annual Report
Type: Yearbook; *Frequency:* Annually
•Resources [a publication of the Canadian Institute of Resources Law]
Type: Newsletter; *Frequency:* Quarterly; *ISSN:* 0714-5918; *Price:* Free
Profile: Commentary on matters of concern in natural resources law & policy, developments in resources case & statute law, & CIRL new publications,courses, & conferences

Canadian Institute of Steel Construction (CISC) / Institut canadien de la construction en acier (ICCA)

#200, 3760 - 14th Ave., Markham ON L3R 3T7
Tel: 905-946-0864; *Fax:* 905-946-8574
e-mail: info@cisc-icca.ca
www.cisc-icca.ca
www.linkedin.com/company/986081?trk=tyah
www.facebook.com/cisc.icca.ca
twitter.com/cisc_icca
Overview: A medium-sized national organization founded in 1942
Mission: To promote good design & safety, together with efficient & economical use of steel as a means of expanding the construction markets for structural steel, joists & platework; *Member of:* Standards Council of Canada; Canadian Standards Association; Canadian Welding Bureau; Welding Institute of Canada; Canadian Steel Trade & Employment Congress; Canadian Construction Association; Construction Specifications Canada; Transportation Association of Canada; Affiliation(s): Canadian Steel Construction Council; Steel Structures Education Foundation
Chief Officer(s):
E. Whalen, President
Membership: 448
Activities: *Speaker Service:* Yes; *Library:* by appointment

Canadian Institute of Surveying *See* Association of Canada Lands Surveyors

Canadian Institute of Traffic & Transportation (CITT) / Institut canadien du trafic et du transport

#400, 10 King St. East, Toronto ON M5C 1C3
Tel: 416-363-5696; *Fax:* 416-363-5698
e-mail: info@citt.ca
www.citt.ca
www.facebook.com/group.php?gid=148552441716
Overview: A medium-sized national organization founded in 1958
Mission: Designation granting body in logistics management.
Chief Officer(s):
Patrick K. Bohan, Chair
Catherine Viglas, President
cviglas@citt.ca
Chrissy Aitchison, Marketing Manager
caitchison@citt.ca
Jennifer Barry, Membership/Events Coordinator
jbarry@citt.ca
Maria Murjani, Customer Service Representative
mmurjani@citt.ca
Sue MacMillan, Program Manager
smacmillan@citt.ca
Membership: 2,000; *Fees:* $275; *Member Profile:* Members must complete course of study to hold the designation, CITT
Activities: Offers the CITT Diploma Program

Canadian Institute of Treated Wood *See* Wood Preservation Canada

Canadian Intergovernmental Conference Secretariat (CICS) / Secrétariat des conférences intergouvernementales canadiennes

PO Box 488, Stn. A, 222 Queen St., 10th Fl., Ottawa ON K1P 5V9
Tel: 613-995-2341; *Fax:* 613-996-6091
e-mail: info@scics.gc.ca
www.scics.gc.ca
Mission: CICS was established in 1973 by the First Ministers as an agency of the federal & provincial governments. Governments recognized a need for a mechanism to serve on a continuing basis conferences of First Ministers & a growing number of intergovernmental meetings. CICS serves federal-provincial First Ministers' meetings, the Annual Premiers' Conference, the Eastern Canadian Premiers' & New England Governors' Conference & the Western Premiers' Conference. The core of the Secretariat's work is providing services to multilateral meetings of Ministers & Deputy Ministers in virtually every sector of government activity. The Secretariat's services are available to federal, provincial & territorial departments that are called upon to organize & chair such meetings. The agency's mandate & sole program are designed to relieve its clients of the numerous & various technical & administrative tasks associated with the planning & conduct of senior level intergovernmental conferences. The CICS maintains through its Information Services section, a document archives for the use of governments & the general public. Containing over 25,000 conference-related documents spanning every sector of conference activity, this collection is unique. The information contained in the archives is made available, as appropriate, to government institutions at the federal, provincial & territorial levels while unclassified material is also available to the public on request.
Chief Officer(s):
André McArdle, Secretary, 613-995-2345
Louise Seaward-Gagnon, Director, 613-995-4328
Louise.Seaward-Gagnon@scics.gc.ca

Canadian International Council (CIC) / Conseil international du Canada

#210, 45 Willcocks St., Toronto ON M5S 1C7
Tel: 416-946-7209; *Fax:* 416-946-7319
e-mail: info@opencanada.org
www.opencanada.org
www.facebook.com/CanadianInternationalCouncil
twitter.com/TheCIC
www.youtube.com/user/onlinecicvideos
Previous Name: Canadian Institute of International Affairs / Institut canadien des affaires internationales
Overview: A medium-sized international charitable organization founded in 1928
Mission: To strengthen Canada's role in international affairs; To advance research & dialogue on international affairs
Chief Officer(s):
Jennifer Jeffs, President, 416-946-7209
Laura Sunderland, Vice-President, Programs, 416-946-7071
lsunderland@opencanada.org
Deborah Shields, Director, Operations, 416-946-7273
dshields@opencanada.org
Kathryn McBride, Administrator, Office, 416-946-7209
kmcbride@opencanada.org
Finances: *Funding Sources:* Private supporters
Membership: *Fees:* $75 regular members; $35 students; *Member Profile:* Individuals & organizations interested in international affairs
Activities: Conducting policy research; Offering a fellowship program; Presenting seminars, discussions, & study groups
Publications:
•Behind the Headlines [a publication of the Canadian International Council]
Editor: Robert Johnstone; *Price:* Free for CIC members
Profile: Articles on international issues, with an emphasis on their implications for Canada
•Foreign Policy for Canada's Tomorrow
Profile: Preliminary papers to outline critical issues which have not yet been peer reviewed
•International Insights
Profile: Canada's role in international security issues
•International Journal
Type: Journal; *Editor:* Rima Berns-McGown
Profile: Scholarly articles on international relations
•Strategic Datalink [a publication of the Canadian International Council]
Profile: Analytical paper on a timely, policy-relevant international security issue

Canadian Iris Society (CIS)

c/o Ed Jowett, 1960 Sideroad 15, RR#2, Tottenham ON L0G 1W0
Tel: 905-936-9941
e-mail: cdn-iris@rogers.com
www.cdn-iris.ca
Overview: A small national organization founded in 1946
Mission: To encourage, improve & extend the cultivation of the Iris & to collaborate with other societies for this purpose, as well as to regulate the nomenclature & colour classification of this flower.
Chief Officer(s):
Ed Jowett, President
ed.jowett@hotmail.com
Ann Granatier, Secretary, 519-647-9746
ann@trailsendiris.com
Finances: *Funding Sources:* Membership dues; iris auctions
Membership: 600; *Fees:* $15; *Member Profile:* Amateur gardeners; gardening experts; horticulturists
Activities: June Iris Shows: Royal Botanical Gardens, Hamilton; Iris sales & auctions; *Awareness Events:* June Iris Shows

Canadian Labour Congress (CLC) / Congrès du travail du Canada (CTC)

National Headquarters, 2841 Riverside Dr., Ottawa ON K1V 8X7
Tel: 613-521-3400; *Fax:* 613-521-4655
www.canadianlabour.ca
www.facebook.com/clc.ctc
twitter.com/canadianlabour
www.youtube.com/canadianlabour
Overview: A large national licensing organization founded in 1956
Mission: To represent the interests of affiliated workers across Canada; To act as an umbrella organization for affiliated regional labour councils, provincial federations, Canadian unions, & international unions
Chief Officer(s):
Ken Georgetti, President
Barbara Byers, Executive Vice-President
Marie Clarke Walker, Executive Vice-President
Hassan Yussuff, Secretary-Treasurer
Karl Flecker, Director, Anti-Racism & Human Rights, 613-521-3400 Ext. 236
Andrew Jackson, Director, Social & Economic Policy, 613-521-3400 Ext. 262
Daniel Mallett, Director, Political Action, 613-521-3400 Ext. 322
Lucien Royer, Director, International, 613-521-3400 Ext. 270
Colleen Kilty, Manager, Human Resources, 613-521-3400 Ext. 325
Dennis Gruending, Contact, Communications, Media Calls, 613-526-7431
Membership: 3,000,000+; *Member Profile:* Affiliated workers in various occupations throughout Canada
Activities: Lobbying politicians; Organizing campaigns & rallies; Representing the Canadian labour movement when dealing with the media & business
Meetings/Conferences:
For more information see Trade Shows, Conferences and Seminars Chapter
Canadian Labour Congress 2014 National Convention
May 2014

Canadian Land Reclamation Association (CLRA) / Association canadienne de réhabilitation des sites dégradés (ACRSD)

PO Box 61047, RPO Kensington, Calgary AB T2N 4S6
Tel: 403-289-9435; *Fax:* 403-289-9435
e-mail: clra@telusplanet.net
www.clra.ca
Overview: A small national organization founded in 1975
Mission: To rehabilitate disturbed lands & waterways; *Member of:* International Affiliation of Land Reclamationists
Chief Officer(s):
David Polster, President
dpolster@telus.net
Tracy Patterson, Vice-President
tracy@aqilapublish.com
Linda Jones, Secretary-Treasurer
clra@telusplanet.net
Finances: *Funding Sources:* Membership fees; Sponsorships
Membership: *Fees:* $15 full-time students & retirees; $50 regular members; $200 corporate members; *Member Profile:* Individuals & corporations interested in or engaged in reclamation activities
Activities: Facilitating the exchange of information & experience; Encouraging education in the field of land reclamation
Awards:
•Dr. Edward M. Watkin Award (Award)
To recognize contributions that advance the progress of reclamation or the association
•Noranda Land Reclamation Award (Award)
To recognize outstanding achievement in land reclamation in Canada
Meetings/Conferences:
For more information see Trade Shows, Conferences and Seminars Chapter
Canadian Land Reclamation Association / Association canadienne de réhabilitation des sites dégradés 2013 38th Annual General Meeting
September 2013 Whitehorse, YT
Publications:
•Canadian Land Reclamation Association Annual Meeting Proceedings
Type: Yearbook; *Frequency:* Annually
•Canadian Reclamation
Type: Magazine; *Frequency:* Semiannually; *Accepts Advertising*; *Editor:* Tracy Patterson
Profile: Articles & illustrations
•Reclamation Newsletter
Type: Newsletter; *Frequency:* Semiannually
Profile: Articles & updates on all aspects of reclamation

Canadian Law & Society Association (CLSA) / Association canadienne de droit et société (ACDS)

c/o Dept. of Law, Carleton University, 1125 Colonel Bay Dr., Ottawa ON K1S 5B6
e-mail: info@acds-clsa.org
www.acds-clsa.org
Overview: A small national organization founded in 1985
Mission: To encourage socio-legal inquiry both domestically & internationally; *Member of:* Canadian Federation for the Humanities & Social Sciences
Membership: *Fees:* Annually, $100 individual; $30 student; $50 Emeritus; *Member Profile:* Scholars from many disciplines, with an interst in the place of law in economic political, cultural, social life
Activities: Awaring prizes for scholarship
Publications:
•Canadian Journal of Law & Society / La Revue Canadienne Droit et Société (CJLS / RCDS)
Type: Journal; *Frequency:* Semiannually; *Accepts Advertising*; *Editor:* D. Moore; M. Valverde; M. Coutu; *ISSN:* 0829-3201; *Price:* Free with CLSA / ACDSmembership; $90 Canada; $110 International
Profile: Original academic research in the field of law & society scholarship
•The CLSA / ACDS Bulletin
Type: Newsletter; *Frequency:* Semiannually; *Editor:* Kimberley White; *Price:* Free with CLSA / ACDS membership
Profile: Forum for for CLSA members to share information on developments & issues affecting Canadian law & society research

Canadian Lung Association (CLA) / Association pulmonaire du Canada

National Office, #300, 1750 Courtwood Cres., Ottawa ON K2C 2B5
Tel: 613-569-6411; *Fax:* 613-569-8860
Toll-Free: 800-566-5864
e-mail: info@lung.ca
www.lung.ca
www.facebook.com/canadianlungassociation
www.twitter.com/canlung
www.youtube.com/user/TheLungAssociation
Previous Name: The Canadian Association for the Prevention of Consumption & Other Forms of Tuberculosis; The Canadian Tuberculosis & Respiratory Disease Association
Overview: A large national charitable organization founded in 1900
Mission: To improve & promote lung health across Canada
Environmental Activity: Informing the public about the health effects of air pollution; Encouraging laws & policies that promote clean air
Chief Officer(s):
Mary-Pat Shaw, Acting President & Chief Executive Officer
Connie Côté, Senior Director, National Lung Health Framework
Claudia Gongora, Director, Finance

Janis Hass, Director, Marketing & Communications
Janet Sutherland, Director, Canadian Thoracic Society/Canadian Respiratory Health Professiona
Anne Van Dam, Director, Research & Knowledge Translation
Christopher Wilson, Director, Public Affairs & Advocacy
Finances: *Funding Sources:* Donations; Fundraising; Sponsorships
Activities: Advocating for improvements to care for lung disease patients; Providing lung health information to governments & the public; Funding medical research; Coordinating the Christmas Seal campaign; *Awareness Events:* National Non-Smoking Week, January; Lung Cancer Month, November; COPD Awareness Week, November
Meetings/Conferences:
For more information see Trade Shows, Conferences and Seminars Chapter
Canadian Respiratory Conference 2013
April 2013 Québec, QC
Publications:
•Canadian Lung Association Annual Report
Type: Yearbook; *Frequency:* Annually

Canadian Manufacturers & Exporters (CME) / Manufacturiers et Exportateurs Canada

#1500, 1 Nicholas St., Ottawa ON K1N 7B7
Tel: 613-238-8888; *Fax:* 613-563-9218
www.cme-mec.ca
www.linkedin.com/companies/100367/Canadian+Manufacturers+%26+Exporters
twitter.com/cme_mec
www.youtube.com/manufacturingTV
Previous Name: Alliance of Manufacturers & Exporters Canada
Merged from: Canadian Manufacturers' Association (1871); Canadian Exporters' Association (1943)
Overview: A large national organization founded in 1996
Mission: To continuously improve the competitiveness of Canadian industry & to expand export business by: aggressive, effective advocacy to government at all levels; delivering timely, relevant information, programs & support of superior quality & value; providing opportunities for education, learning & professional growth; & promoting the development & implementation of advanced technology
Chief Officer(s):
Jayson Myers, President & Chief Executive Officer, 613-238-8888 Ext. 4231
jayson.myers@cme-mec.ca
Jeff Sholdice, Chief Financial Officer & Vice-President, Operations, 613-238-8888 Ext. 3245
jeff.sholdice@cme-mec.ca
Jeff Brownlee, Vice-President, Public Affairs & Partnerships, 613-238-8888 Ext. 4233
jeff.brownlee@cme-mec.ca
Joanne Heighway, Vice-President, Organizational Excellence, 613-238-8888 Ext. 3294
joanne.heighway@cme-mec.ca
John Knox, Vice-President, Sales & Marketing, 613-238-8888 Ext. 3258
john.knox@cme-mec.ca
Jean-Michel Laurin, Vice-President, Global Business Policy, 613-238-8888 Ext. 4238
jean-michel.laurin@cme-mec.ca
Craig Williams, Vice-President, National Programs, 604-713-7844
craig.williams@cme-mec.ca
Mathew Wilson, Vice-President, National Policy, 905-672-3466 Ext. 3242
mathew.wilson@cme-mec.ca
Finances: *Funding Sources:* Membership fees; Publication sales; Services
Membership: 5,000-14,999;; *Fees:* Schedule available; *Member Profile:* Manufacturers, exporters, exporting companies, businesses & institutions servicing the manufacturing & exporting sectors; *Committees:* Environmental Quality; Export Financing; Insurance; Export Issues Roundtable; Export Promotion; Development Aid; Legislation; Market Access & Customs; Science & Technology; Service Exporters; Standards; Taxation & Financial Issues; Transportation
Activities: *Awareness Events:* Canadian Manufacturing Week, 2nd week of Oct.; *Speaker Service:* Yes; *Library:* Open to public
Publications:
•20/20: Canada's Industry Association Magazine
Type: Magazine; *Frequency:* Bimonthly; *Accepts Advertising*; *Editor:* Marie Morden
Profile: Information for Canadian industry to compete in the global economy, on subjects such as global competitiveness, workforce capability, energy, environment &efficiency, financial services, logistics, innovation, & CME strategy
•CME [Canadian Manufacturers & Exporters] Newsletter
Type: Newsletter

Alberta Division

#531, 10060 Jasper Ave., Edmonton AB T5J 3R8
Tel: 800-642-3871; *Fax:* 780-426-1509
www.cme-mec.ca
Chief Officer(s):
Neil Kaarsemaker, Director, Operations
neil.kaarsemaker@cme-mec.ca

Association des manufacturiers et des exportateurs du Québec

#210, 2000, rue Peel, Montréal QC H3A 2W5
Tél: 514-866-7774; *Téléc:* 514-866-9447
Ligne sans frais: 800-363-0226
Courriel: info@meq.ca
qc.cme-mec.ca
Chief Officer(s):
Simon Prévost, Président
simon.prevost@meq.ca
José Jacome, Directeur général
jose.jacome@meq.ca

British Columbia Division

#540, 688 West Hastings St., Vancouver BC V6B 1P1
Tel: 604-713-7800; *Fax:* 604-713-7801
www.cme-mec.ca
Chief Officer(s):
Peter Jeffrey, Vice-President, 604-713-7804
peter.jeffrey@cme-mec.ca

Manitoba Division

110 Lowson Cres., Winnipeg MB R3P 2H8
Tel: 204-949-1454; *Fax:* 204-943-3476
www.cme-mec.ca
Chief Officer(s):
Ron Koslowsky, Vice-President
ron.koslowsky@cme-mec.ca

New Brunswick & Prince Edward Island Division

PO Box 7129, #12, 567 Coverdale Rd., Riverview NB E1B 4T8
Tel: 506-861-9071; *Fax:* 506-857-3049
www.cme-mec.ca
Chief Officer(s):
David Plante, Vice-President
david.plante@cme-mec.ca

Newfoundland & Labrador Division

Parsons Building, 90 O'Leary Ave., 1st Fl., St. John's NL A1B 2C7
Tel: 709-772-3682; *Fax:* 709-772-3213
www.cme-mec.ca
Chief Officer(s):
David Haire, Vice-President
david.haire@cme-mec.ca

Nova Scotia Division

Collins' Bank Building, #305, 1869 Upper Water St., Halifax NS B3J 1S9
Tel: 902-422-4477; *Fax:* 902-422-9563
Ann Janega, Vice President
ann.janega@cme-mec.ca

Ontario Division

#200, 6725 Airport Rd., Mississauga ON L4V 1V2
Tel: 800-268-9684; *Fax:* 905-672-1764
www.cme.mec.ca
Chief Officer(s):
Ian Howcroft, Vice-President
ian.howcroft@cme-mec.ca

Canadian Manufacturers of Chemical Specialties Association ***See*** Canadian Consumer Specialty Products Association

Canadian Marine Manufacturers Association ***See*** National Marine Manufacturers Association Canada

Canadian Maritime Industries Association ***See*** Shipbuilding Association of Canada

Canadian Maritime Law Association / Association canadienne de droit maritime

#900, 1000, rue de la Gauchetiére ouest, Montréal QC H3B 5H4
Tel: 514-849-4161; *Fax:* 514-849-4167
e-mail: cmla@cmla.org
www.cmla.org
Overview: A medium-sized national organization founded in 1951
Mission: To represent all Canadian commercial maritime interests for the uniform development of Canadian & international maritime law affecting marine transportation & related aspects; *Member of:* Comité maritime international
Chief Officer(s):
Robert C. Wilkins, Secretary-Treasurer
rwilkins@blg.com
Christopher J. Giaschi, President
giaschi@admiraltylaw.com
John G. O'Connor, National Vice-President
john.oconnor@lkd.ca
Finances: *Funding Sources:* Membership fees
Membership: 318 individual + 20 organizations; *Fees:* $105 individual; $500 organization; *Member Profile:* Individual, association, or corporate body resident in Canada; *Committees:* Executive; Liaison; Limitation of Liability; Marine Insurance; Special Liaison; Tanker Safety

Canadian Marketing Association (CMA) / Association canadienne du marketing (ACM)

#607, 1 Concorde Gate, Toronto ON M3C 3N6
Tel: 416-391-2362; *Fax:* 416-441-4062
e-mail: info@the-cma.org
www.the-cma.org
www.linkedin.com/groups?mostPopular=&gid=47336
www.facebook.com/cdnmarketing
twitter.com/Cdnmarketing
Previous Name: Canadian Direct Marketing Association
Overview: A large national organization founded in 1967
Mission: To be the pre-eminent marketing association in Canada representing the integration & convergence of all marketing disciplines, channels & technologies; Affiliation(s): European Direct Marketing Association; Direct Marketing Association - USA
Chief Officer(s):
John Gustavson, President & CEO
Peg Hunter, Chair
Finances: *Annual Operating Budget:* $1.5 Million-$3 Million; *Funding Sources:* Membership dues; events
Staff: 28 staff member(s); 400 volunteer(s)
Membership: 800 corporate; 1,200 total; *Member Profile:* Membership includes corporations & organizations which encompass Canada's major business sectors & which represent the integration & convergence of all marketing disciplines, channels & technologies; supports 480,000 jobs & generates more than $51 billion in overall annual sales; *Committees:* Special Interest Councils - Branding & Strategic Planning; Customer Relationship Management; Database & Marketing Technology; Integrated Marketing Communications; Not-for-Profit; Contact Centre; Direct Mail; E-Marketing
Activities: Responds to public policy issues; participates in a variety of government-led task forces & working groups on issues such as privacy, electronic commerce, consumer protection, the prevention of telemarketing fraud, & unsolicited bulk e-mail; forms internal task forces to develop self-regulatory policies on standards of business practice, ethics, privacy, & marketing to children & teenagers; enforces Code of Ethics & Standards of Practice & Privacy Code; *Rents Mailing List:* Yes
Publications:
•Canadian Marketing Association Membership Directory & Buyers' Guide
Type: Directory; *Accepts Advertising*
Profile: Listing of companies & their services
•CMA [Canadian Marketing Association] Guide to E-mail Marketing
Type: Guide
Profile: Theory, best practices & practical advice, for marketers
•CMA [Canadian Marketing Association] Fundraiser's Handbook
Type: Handbook; *Number of Pages:* 35; *Price:* $15 members; $25 non-members
Profile: A guide to measurement & evaluation

Manitoba Chapter

PO Box 1973, Winnipeg MB R3C 3R3
Tel: 204-284-5642
www.cmamanitoba.com

Canadian Meat Council (CMC) / Conseil des viandes du Canada

#407, 1545 Carling Ave., Ottawa ON K1Z 8P9

Tel: 613-729-3911; *Fax:* 613-729-4997
e-mail: info@cmc-cvc.com
www.cmc-cvc.com
Previous Name: Meat Packers Council of Canada
Overview: A medium-sized national organization founded in 1919
Mission: To express the views of the membership with government, all elements of the food industry, consumer organizations, the research & academic community, & the media; To foster high standards of industry integrity, & a vast range of wholesome, nutritional meat products
Chief Officer(s):
James M. Laws, Executive Director, 613-729-3911 Ext. 24
jiml@cmc-cvc.com
Ray Price, First Vice President-Treasurer
Finances: *Funding Sources:* Membership dues
Staff: 6 staff member(s)
Membership: 66; *Member Profile:* Federally inspected packers & processors of meat; *Committees:* Beef, Veal & Lamb; Pork; Technical, Processed Meats, Environment; Foodservice; Special Events; Annual Conference; Administrative Committees
Activities: Responding to members' needs; Contributing to the competitiveness of the industry at both domestic & international levels; Providing a forum for members to discuss & consider matters relating to government regulations & activities, competitiveness, & dealings with other national trade associations; Working towards a free & expanding market environment; *Speaker Service:* Yes; *Library:* Council Library
Meetings/Conferences:
For more information see Trade Shows, Conferences and Seminars Chapter
Canadian Meat Council 2013 93rd Annual Conference
May 2013 Banff, AB
Publications:
•Food Service Meat Manual / Manuel des vaindes pour les services alimenaires
Type: Manual; *Number of Pages:* 40+; *Price:* $30 for 1-9 copies; $25 for 10+copies
Profile: The third revised edition that outines the cutting & trimming techniqes for 86 cuts of meat

Canadian Meat Science Association (CMSA) / Association scientifique canadienne de la viande (ASCB)

Dept. of Agricultural, Food & Nutritional Science, Univ. of Alberta, #4-10, Agriculture / Forestry Centre, Edmonton AB T6G 2P5
Tel: 780-492-3651; *Fax:* 780-492-5771
e-mail: ruth.ball@ales.ualberta.ca
www.cmsa-ascv.ca
Overview: A medium-sized national organization
Mission: To promote the application of science & technology to the production, processing, packaging, distribution, preparation, evaluation, & utilization of all meat & meat products; To develop & promote useful, coordinated research, educational techniques, & service activities
Chief Officer(s):
Peter Purslow, President, 519-824-4120 Ext. 52099
ppurslow@uoguelph.ca
Sandra Gruber, President-Elect, 403-671-0781
gruber_sandra@lilly.com
Manuel Juárez, Sec.-Treas., 403-782-8118
manuel.juarez@agr.gc.ca
Sylvain Fournaise, Director at Large, 514-858-9000
sylvainfournaise@olymel.com
Membership: 13 corporate members; *Fees:* $60 professional; $200 corporate; $0 students; *Member Profile:* Individuals & corporations with an interest in the science of meat & meat products; *Committees:* Promotion & Membership; Education; Newsletter; Nominations & Elections; Symposium; Website & Electronic Communications; Audit
Activities: Providing forums & networking opportunities for discussion & dissemination of information; Promoting recognition of people engaged in meat science
Meetings/Conferences:
For more information see Trade Shows, Conferences and Seminars Chapter
Canadian Meat Science Association 2013 Annual Meeting
June 2013 Banff, AB
Canadian Meat Science Association 2013 Technical Symposium
May 2013 Banff, AB
Canadian Meat Science Association 2014 Annual Meeting
2014
Publications:
•Canadian Meat Science Association Membership Directory
Type: Directory; *Frequency:* Annually
Profile: A listing of persons & organizations throughout Canada with an interest in meat science
•CMSA [Canadian Meat Science Association] News
Type: Newsletter; *Frequency:* Quarterly
Profile: Activities of the meat sector & the association for CMSA members

Canadian Medical & Biological Engineering Society (CMBES) / Société canadienne de génie biomédical inc. (SCGB)

1485 Laperrière Ave., Ottawa ON K1Z 7S8
Tel: 613-728-1759
e-mail: secretariat@cmbes.ca
www.cmbes.ca
Overview: A medium-sized national organization founded in 1965
Mission: To advance the theory & practice of medical device technology; To advance individuals who are engaged in interdisciplinary work involving medicine, engineering, & the life sciences; To represent the interests of biomedical & clinical engineering to government agencies; Affiliation(s): International Federation for Medical and Biological Engineering (IFMBE)
Chief Officer(s):
Murat Firat, President
murat.firat@uhn.on.ca
Mike Capuano, Chair, Professional Affairs
capuamik@hhsc.ca
Tim J. Zakutney, Chair, Awards
tzakutney@ottawaheart.ca
Martin Poulin, Treasurer
martin.poulin@viha.ca
Melanie Chayra, Secretariat, 613-728-1759
secretariat@cmbes.ca
Membership: 100-499;; *Fees:* $35 students; $130 full members; $150 student institutional; Schedule for corporate members, based upon number of members per group
Activities: Offering continuing education; Providing networking opportunities; *Awareness Events:* Biomedical / Clinical Engineering Appreciation Week
Meetings/Conferences:
For more information see Trade Shows, Conferences and Seminars Chapter
Canadian Medical & Biological Engineering Society 2013 36th Annual National Conference
May 2013 Ottawa, ON
Canadian Medical & Biological Engineering Society 2014 37th Annual National Conference
May 2014 Vancouver, BC
Canadian Medical & Biological Engineering Society 2015 38th Annual National Conference
June 2015 Toronto, ON
The World Congress on Medical Physics & Biomedical Engineering: IUPESM 2015 (hosted by the Canadian Medical & Biological Engineering Society)
June 2015 Toronto, ON
Publications:
•Canadian Medical & Biological Engineering Society Conference Proceedings & Abstracts
•Canadian Medical & Biological Engineering Society Career Booklet
Type: Booklet
Profile: Information for guidance counselors & employment centers
•Clinical Engineering Standards of Practice [a publication of the Canadian Medical & Biological Engineering Society]
Type: Guide; *Price:* Free with Cdn. Medical & Biological Engineering Society membership; $50 non-members
Profile: Criteria for health care institutions on the management of medical devices, the education & certificationrequirements for clinical engineers & biomedical engineering technologists & technicians & the promotion of professional development
•CMBES [Canadian Medical & Biological Engineering Society Inc.] Newsletter
Type: Newsletter; *Editor:* Dr. Gnahoua Zoabli; Pamela Wilson; *ISSN:* 1499-4089
Profile: Society activities, conferences, events, awards, chapters, & events

Canadian Medical Association (CMA) / Association médicale canadienne (AMC)

1867 Alta Vista Dr., Ottawa ON K1G 5W8
Tel: 613-731-8610; *Fax:* 613-236-8864
Toll-Free: 888-855-2555
e-mail: cmamsc@cma.ca
www.cma.ca
twitter.com/CMA_Docs
www.youtube.com/user/CanadianMedicalAssoc
Overview: A large national organization founded in 1867
Mission: To act as the national voice of physicians in Canada; To serve the Canadian medical community; To promote the highest standards of health & health care; *Member of:* World Medical Association; Affiliation(s): Assn. of Cdn. Medical Colleges; Cdn. Anesthesiologists' Soc.; Cdn. Assn. of Medical Biochemists; Cdn. Assn. of Physicians with Disabilities; Cdn. Assn. of Physicians for the Environment; Cdn. Assn. of Radiation Oncologists; Cdn. Fedn. of Medical Students; Cdn. Infectious Disease Soc.; Cdn. Neurological/Neurosurgical/Clinical Neurophysiologists Societies; Cdn. Ophthalmological Soc.; Cdn. Orthopaedic Assn.; Cdn. Paediatric Soc.; Cdn. Psychiatric Assn; Cdn. Rheumatology Assn.; Cdn. Soc. of Addiction Medicine; Cdn. Soc. of Internal Medicine; Cdn. Soc. of Nuclear Medicine; Cdn. Soc. of Otolaryngoly
Environmental Activity: Protecting & promoting health, through the Office for Public Health, by addressing the environmental, physical, & mental health concerns of the population
Chief Officer(s):
Anne Reid, President
Michael Golbey, Chair
Louis Francescutti, President Elect
Membership: Over 50,000; *Member Profile:* Practising physicians; Residents; Retired physicians; Students; *Committees:* Ethics; Political Action; Health Care & Promotion; Health Policy & Economics; Education & Professional Development
Activities: Providing national & provincial advocacy; Offering practice management solutions; Providing courses through the CMA's Physician Management Institute, a leadership development program designed for physicians in the Canadian health care system;
Meetings/Conferences:
For more information see Trade Shows, Conferences and Seminars Chapter
Canadian Medical Association 2013 146th Annual Meeting
August 2013 Calgary, AB
Canadian Medical Association 2014 147th Annual Meeting
August 2014 Ottawa, ON
Canadian Medical Association 2015 148th Annual Meeting
2015
Publications:
•Canadian Health Magazine
Type: Magazine; *Frequency:* Quarterly; *Accepts Advertising*; *Editor:* Diana Swift; *Price:* $12 / year
Profile: A health & wellness resource for patients in a physician's waiting room
•Canadian Journal of Surgery (CJS)
Type: Journal; *Frequency:* Bimonthly; *Accepts Advertising*; *Editor:* E.J. Harvey, MD; G.L. Warnock, MD; *ISSN:* 0008-428X; *Price:* $35 Canadian students & residents; $175 Canadian individuals; $270 institutions
Profile: Continuing medical education for Canadian surgical specialists
•Canadian Medical Association Complete Home Medical Guide
Type: Book; *ISSN:* 1-55363-054-8; *Price:* $51.95 members
Profile: An 1104 page authoritative & user-friendly resource for physicians to recommend to patients
•Canadian Medical Association Conference Updates
Profile: The latest news from major clinical meetings
•Canadian Medical Association Journal (CMAJ)
Type: Journal; *Frequency:* Semimonthly; *Accepts Advertising*; *Editor:* Paul C. Hébert; *ISSN:* 0820-3946; *Price:* $35 / issue Canadian; $40 / issue USA
Profile: Peer-reviewed original research, review articles, practice updates, drug alerts, health news, & commentaries for clinicians, available online& in print
•CMA [Canadian Medical Association] Bulletin
Type: Newsletter; *Frequency:* Semimonthly; *Editor:* Patrick Sullivan; Steve Wharry
Profile: A communication from the Canadian Medical Association, with news stories of interest to Canadian physicians, inserted in the Canadian MedicalAssociation Journal
•CMA [Canadian Medical Association] Driver's Guide: Determining Medical Fitness to Operate Motor Vehicles
Type: Guide; *Price:* Free for Canadian Medical Association members
Profile: Examples of sections include the following: Functional assessment - emerging emphasis; Reporting - when & why; Drivingcessation; Aging; Vision; Respiratory diseases; Psychiatric illness; Cardiovascular diseases; Seat belts & air

bags; Motorcycles & off-road vehicles; Aviation; Railway; & Appendices
•CMA [Canadian Medical Association] Leadership Series: MD Pulse
Type: Magazine; *Price:* $8.95 / copy members; $14.95 nonmembers
Profile: Results of the National Physician Survey, prepared by the Canadian Medical Association in collaboration with the College of Family Physicians of Canada & theRoyal College of Physicians & Surgeons of Canada
•CMA [Canadian Medical Association] Leadership Series: Primary Care Reform
Type: Magazine; *Editor:* Dr. Albert Schumacher
Profile: An outline of primary care reform initiatives throughout Canada
•CMA [Canadian Medical Association] Leadership Series: Elder Care - Issues & Options
Type: Magazine; *Price:* $8.95 / copy members; $14.95 nonmemebers
Profile: An examination of the medical, social, & ethical dimensions of care for older patients
•CMA [Canadian Medical Association] Leadership Series: Women's Health - Research & Practice Issues for Canadian Physicians
Type: Magazine; *Price:* $8.95 / copy members; $14.95 nonmemebers
Profile: Published by the Canadian Medical Association in partnership with the Centre for Research inWomen's Health
•CMA [Canadian Medical Association] Complete Book of Mother & Baby Care
Type: Book; *Number of Pages:* 264; *Editor:* Anne Biringer MD, CCFP,FCFP; *ISBN:* 978-1-55363-154-5; *Price:* $24 members
Profile: Care for a mother & her baby, from conception to age three
•Future Practice
Type: Magazine; *Frequency:* Irregular; *Editor:* Pat Rich
Profile: Information for physicians about health information technology in Canada
•History of the Canadian Medical Association, 1954-94
Type: Book; *Number of Pages:* 388; *Author:* John Sutton Bennett, MD; *ISBN:* 0-920169-83-X; *Price:* $19.95 members
Profile: A comprehensive account of important events that continue to affect medicine in Canada
•Honour Due: the Story of Dr. Leonora Howard King
Type: Book; *Number of Pages:* 236; *Author:* Margaret I. Negodaeff-Tomsik; *ISBN:* 0-920169-33-3; *Price:* $19.95 members
Profile: The story of the first Canadian to work as a physician in China
•Lessons Learned: Reflections of Canadian Physician Leaders
Type: Book; *Number of Pages:* 123; *Editor:* Chris Carruthers, MD; *ISBN:* 978-1-897490-09-9; *Price:* $16.95 members
•MD Lounge
Type: Magazine; *Editor:* Dr. Francine Lemire et al.
Profile: Information & advice to strengthen relations between general practitioners, family physicians, & other specialists, published by the Canadian Medical Association in partnership withThe Royal College of Physicians & Surgeons of Canada & the College of Family Physicians of Canada
•PMI [Physician Management Institute] Newsletter: Leadership for Physicians
Type: Newsletter
Profile: Information about leadership theories & techniques

Canadian Meteorological & Oceanographic Society (CMOS) / Société canadienne de météorologie et d'océanographie (SCMO)

PO Box 3211, Stn. D, Ottawa ON K1P 6H7
Tel: 613-990-0300; *Fax:* 613-990-1617
e-mail: cmos@cmos.ca
www.cmos.ca
www.facebook.com/groups/338431655320
Previous Name: Canadian Meteorological Society
Overview: A large national charitable organization founded in 1967
Mission: To advance meteorology & oceanography in Canada; *Member of:* Canadian Consortium for Research; Partnership Group for Science & Engineering
Chief Officer(s):
Ian D. Rutherford, Executive Director
exec-dir@cmos.ca
Peter Bartello, President
president@cmos.ca
Bourque Sheila, Director, Education & Outreach
education@cmos.ca
Qing Liao, Office Manager, 613-991-4494
accounts@cmos.ca
Finances: *Annual Operating Budget:* $500,000-$1.5 Million; *Funding Sources:* Membership fees; Donations; Congress resignation fees
Staff: 3 staff member(s); 3 volunteer(s)
Membership: 800; *Fees:* $80; *Member Profile:* Meteorologists & oceanographers; Persons interested in meteorology & oceanography; Corporations & institutions; Government organizations; Students; *Committees:* Accreditation; Students; External Relations; Fellows; Awards: Scholarships; Scientific; Audit; Nominating
Activities: Participating in School Science Fairs; Accrediting consultants in meteorology & oceanography; Providing advice & suggestions to government & its departments on meteorological & oceanographic issues; Publications; Scholarships; Prizes & Awards; Public lectures; *Speaker Service:* Yes
Awards:
•The J.P. Tully Medal in Oceanography (Award)
May be awarded each year to a person whose scientific contributions have had a significant impact on Canadian oceanography
•The President's Prize (Award)
May be awarded each year to a member or members of the Society for a recent paper or book of special merit in the fields of meteorology or oceanography. *Eligibility:* Paper must have been published in Atmosphere-Ocean, The CMOS bulletin, SCMO or another referred journal
•François J. Saucier Prize in Applied Oceanography (Award)
May be awarded each year to a member or members of the Society for an outstanding contribution to the application of oceanography in Canada
•The Rube Hornstein Medal in Operational Meteorology (Award)
May be awarded each year to an individual for outstanding operational meteorological service. The work for which the prize is granted may be cumulative over a period of years or may be a single notable achievement
•Dr. Andrew Thomson Prize in Applied Meteorology (Award)
May be awarded each year to a member or members of the Society for an outstanding contribution to the application of meteorology in Canada
•Neil J. Campbell Award for Exceptional Volunteer Service (Award)
The award may be made for an exceptional contribution in a single year or for contributions over an extended period.
Meetings/Conferences:
For more information see Trade Shows, Conferences and Seminars Chapter
Canadian Meteorological & Oceanographic Society Congress 2013 Joint Scientific Congress
May 2013 Saskatoon, SK
Publications:
•Atmosphere-Ocean
Type: Journal; *Frequency:* Quarterly; *ISSN:* 0705-5900; *Price:* $50 individual; $125 institution
Profile: Scientific journal with original research, survey articles, & comments on published papers in the fields of atmospheric, oceanographic, & hydrological sciences
•Canadian Meteorological & Oceanographic Society Annual Review
Frequency: Annually; *Price:* Free with Canadian Meteorological & OceanographicSociety membership
Profile: Summaries of the Canadian Meteorological & Oceanographic Society yearly activities & the audited financial statement
•Canadian Meteorological & Oceanographic Society Annual Congress Program & Abstracts
Type: Yearbook; *Frequency:* Annually; *Price:* Free withCMOS membership; $50 non-members & institutions
Profile: Guide to the Canadian Meteorological & Oceanographic Society Annual Congress sessions & abstracts of papers to be presented
•CMOS [Canadian Meteorological & Oceanographic Society] Bulletin SCMO [Société canadienne de météorologie et d'océanographie]
Frequency: Bimonthly; *Accepts Advertising*; *Editor:* Paul-André Bolduc; *Price:* Free with CMOS / SCMO membership; $80 non-members & institutions
Profile: Technical articles, conferences, & events related to meteorology, oceanography,climatology, & meteorological & oceanographic history
•The Edmonton Tornado & Hailstorm: A Decade of Research
Author: R. Charlton, B. Kachman, L. Wojtiw; *Price:* $10
•Numerical Methods in Atmospheric & Oceanic Modelling: The André J. Robert Memorial Volume
Number of Pages: 634; *Editor:* C. Lin, R. Laprise, & H. Ritchie; *ISBN:* 0-9698414-4-2; *Price:* $39.95
Profile: Refereed papers by scientists on the art & science of numerical modelling, for students &researchers

Canadian Meteorological Society *See* Canadian Meteorological & Oceanographic Society

Canadian Micro-Mineral Association

21 Hathway Dr., Toronto ON M1P 4L4
Tel: 416-438-8908
e-mail: bill.lechner@rogers.com
canadianmicrominerals.ca
Overview: A small national organization founded in 1964
Mission: To promote education & interest in micromineralogy & to encourage fellowship & goodwill among its members; *Member of:* Gem & Mineral Federation of Canada
Chief Officer(s):
Bill Lechner, President
Membership: 1-99;; *Fees:* $15
Activities: Micro Symposium; Micro Workshop

Canadian Mineral Analysts (CMA) / Analystes des minéraux canadiens

444 Harold Ave. West, Winnipeg MB R2C 2E2
Tel: 204-224-1443
www.canadianmineralanalysts.com
Overview: A small national organization founded in 1969
Mission: To promote communication among analysts in the mining industry & persons engaged in analytical procedures & the development of methods
Chief Officer(s):
John Gregorchuk, Managing Secretary, 204-224-1443
jgregorchuk@mts.net
Sean Murry, Treasurer, 604-270-2252
smurry@anachemia.com
Eric Arseneault, Executive Secretary, 506-522-7143
EArseneault@xstrata.com
Membership: *Fees:* $25 students & retired individuals; $40 new & renewing members; $1000 corporate members; *Member Profile:* Analysts employed in the mineral industry; Technical personnel connected with the provision of analyses
Activities: Providing educational opportunities; Assisting in the development of methods for element analysis; Compiling methods manuals for members; Liaising with laboratories of the Canadian mining industry; Supporting the Certified Assayers Foundation of British Columbia
Publications:
•Alchemist Digest: The CMA / SMA [Canadian Mineral Analysts / Analystes des minéraux canadiens] Newsletter
Type: Newsletter; *Editor:* Mark Lewis; *Price:* Free with CMA / SMA membership
•Proceedings of the Canadian Mineral Analysts / Analystes des minéraux canadiens Annual Meeting
Type: Yearbook; *Frequency:* Annually; *Price:* Free with CMA / SMA membership
•QC / QA Manual [a publication of the Canadian Mineral Analysts]
Type: Manual; *Price:* $30

Canadian Mining Industry Research Organization (CAMIRO)

1545 Maley Dr., Sudbury ON P3A 4R7
Tel: 705-673-6595; *Fax:* 705-673-6588
e-mail: info@camiro.org
www.camiro.org
Overview: A small national organization
Mission: To manage collaborative mining research in the divisions of exploration, mining, & metallurgical processing; To contribute to the safety, growth, & competitiveness of the Canadian mineral industry
Chief Officer(s):
Larry Urbanoski, Director, Research, Metallurgical Division
LUrbanoski@XstrataZinc.ca
Tom Lane, Director, Research Development, Exploration Division
tom.lane@sympatico.ca
Charles Graham, Contact, Mining Division
Membership: *Member Profile:* Corporations & organizations who wish to further the objects of the association
Activities: Initiating applied research

Canadian Motor Coach Association *See* Canadian Bus Association

Canadian National Committee for Irrigation & Drainage (CANCID)

9 Corvus Crt., Ottawa ON K2E 7Z4
Tel: 613-237-9363; *Fax:* 613-594-5190
e-mail: executivedirector@cwra.org
www.cwra.org
twitter.com/cwraed
Previous Name: International Commission on Irrigation & Drainage - Canadian National Committee
Overview: A small international organization
Mission: To promote research, development, & application of technology among those interested in irrigation, drainage, & flood control; Affiliation(s): Canadian Water Resources Association (CWRA); International Commission on Irrigation & Drainage (ICID); Canadian Committee on Irrigation and Drainage; Canadian Society for Hydrologic Sciences; Student and Young Professionals
Chief Officer(s):
Brent Paterson, President, 403-381-5515, Fax: 403-381-5765
brent.paterson@gov.ab.ca
Laurie Tollefson, Secretary-Treasurer, 306-867-5404, Fax: 306-867-9656
tollefsonl@agr.gc.ca
Activities: Disseminating news about technical information & CANCID & ICID activities; Liaising with other ICID committees & related organizations

Canadian Nature Federation *See* Nature Canada

Canadian Network for Environmental Education & Communication (EECOM) / Réseau canadien d'éducation et de communication relatives à l'environnement

c/o 336 Rosedale Ave., Winnipeg MB R3L 1L8
e-mail: nswayze@eecom.org
www.eecom.org
Overview: A small national charitable organization founded in 1993
Mission: To advance environmental learning in Canada; To promote environmental literacy & environmental stewardship; To contribute to a sustainable future
Chief Officer(s):
Natalie Swayzer, Executive Director, 204-221-2007
Grant Gardner, Chair, 709-737-8155
Rick Wishart, Treasurer, 204-467-3254
Finances: *Funding Sources:* Donations
Membership: *Fees:* $10 associates; $20 students; $40 individuals; $115 not-for-profit organizations; $280 corporations & government; *Member Profile:* Environmental educators, practitioners, researchers, scientists, administrators, & business representatives
Activities: Offering networking opportunities; Providing professional development resources & activities; Liaising with other organizations
Awards:
•EECom Awards for Excellence in Environmental Education (Award)
Publications:
•EECOM News
Type: Newsletter; *Frequency:* Bimonthly; *Editor:* Sue Wallace; *Price:* Free with Canadian Network for Environmental Education & Communication membership
Profile: Conferences, members, regional reports, awards, & announcements

Canadian Network of Toxicology Centres (CNTC) / Réseau canadien des centres de toxicologie

Bovey Bldg., 2nd Fl., Gordon St., Guelph ON N1G 2W1
Tel: 519-824-4120; *Fax:* 519-837-3861
uoguelph.ca/ses/content/canadian-network-toxicology-centres
Overview: A medium-sized national organization founded in 1983
Mission: To be recognized & respected for excellence in research, training, analysis & communication of information focused on critical toxicology issues for ecosystem & human health; to achieve this through innovative, multi-disciplinary teamwork & partnerships between the public & private sector; Affiliation(s): Metals in the Environment Research Network
Chief Officer(s):
Len Ritter, Executive Director
lritter@uoguelph.ca
Donna Warner, Program Coordinator
dwarner@uoguelph.ca
Finances: *Annual Operating Budget:* $1.5 Million-$3 Million; *Funding Sources:* Environment Canada; grants from government & industrial companies & associations
Staff: 4 staff member(s)
Activities: 4 themes - Human Health & Environmental Risk Assessment; Metal Speciation at the Biological Interface; Endocrine Disrupters & Reproductive/Endocrines Toxicology; Immunotoxicology; also conducts research on a contract basis for government or industry, develops educational materials on toxicology for secondary school programs across Canada; risk assessments of complex mixtures
Publications:
•CNTC [Canadian Network of Toxicology Centres] News
Type: Newsletter
Profile: Communication among CNTC member scientists & the public to increase education about toxicology
•CNTC [Canadian Network of Toxicology Centres] Science Briefs
Type: Newsletter
•CNTC [Canadian Network of Toxicology Centres] Annual Report
Type: Yearbook; *Frequency:* Annually
•CNTC [Canadian Network of Toxicology Centres] Annual Symposium Report
Type: Yearbook; *Frequency:* Annually

Canadian Nuclear Association (CNA) / Association nucléaire canadienne

#1610, 130 Albert St., Ottawa ON K1P 5G4
Tel: 613-237-4262; *Fax:* 613-237-0989
www.cna.ca
www.facebook.com/TalkNuclear
twitter.com/talknuclear
www.youtube.com/talknuclear
Overview: A large national organization founded in 1960
Mission: To promote the orderly & sound development of nuclear energy for peaceful purposes in Canada & abroad; To promote & foster an environment favourable to the healthy growth of the uses of nuclear energy & radioisotopes; To encourage cooperation between various industries, utilities, educational institutions, government departments & agencies, which may have a common interest in the development of economic nuclear power & the uses of radioisotopes; To provide a forum for the discussion & resolution of problems which are of concern to the members, the industry, or the Canadian public; To stimulate cooperation with other associations with similar objectives & purposes
Chief Officer(s):
Heather Kleb, Acting President & Chief Executive Officer, 613-237-4262 Ext. 111
klebh@cna.ca
Steve Coupland, Director, Environmental Affairs, 613-237-4262 Ext. 107
couplands@cna.ca
George Christidis, Director, Government Affairs, 613-237-4262 Ext. 108
georgec@cna.ca
Laura Allardyce, Officer, Communications & Digital Media, 613-237-4262 Ext. 110
allardycel@cna.ca
John Stewart, Director, Policy & Research, 613-237-4262 Ext. 103
stewartj@cna.ca
Marie-danielle Davis, Corporate Secretary/Director, Member Services, 613-237-4262 Ext. 102
davism@cna.ca
Finances: *Funding Sources:* Membership fees
Membership: 112; *Fees:* Based on company size & activity; *Member Profile:* Industries & enterprises interested in the development & application of nuclear energy for peaceful purposes including uranium producers, reactor manufacturers, electrical utilities, engineering companies, banks, employee unions, departments of federal & provincial governments, educational establishments; *Committees:* Communications; Regulatory Affairs; Climate Change
Activities: ; *Library:*
Publications:
•Nuclear Canada
Type: Newsletter; *Editor:* Colin G. Hunt
Profile: CNA activities & news about nuclear energy in Canada
•Nuclear Canada Yearbook
Type: Yearbook; *Frequency:* Annually
Profile: Information about the Canadian nuclear industry & a buyers' guide of nuclear products & services
•Nuclear Energy Handbook
Profile: Basic & factual information about nuclear energy

Canadian Nuclear Society (CNS) / Société nucléaire canadienne (SNC)

655 Bay St., 17th Fl., Toronto ON M5G 2K4
Tel: 416-977-7620; *Fax:* 416-977-8131
e-mail: cns-snc@on.aibn.com
www.cns-snc.ca
Previous Name: The technical society of the Canadian Nuclear Association (CNA)
Overview: A medium-sized national organization founded in 1979
Mission: To promote the exchange of information about nuclear science & technology & its applications; To foster the beneficial utilization of nuclear science; *Member of:* Engineering Institute of Canada (EIC)
Environmental Activity: Encouraging information exchange on topics such as uranium mining & refining, the management of radioactive wastes, used fuel, & environmental & occupational radiation protection
Chief Officer(s):
Adriaan Buijs, President
K.L. (Ken) Smith, Financial Administrator
Denise Rouben, Office Manager
cns-snc@on.aibn.com
Finances: *Funding Sources:* Sponsorships
Membership: *Fees:* $27.81 students; $48.41 retirees; $82.40 regular members; *Member Profile:* Individuals directly involved with nuclear technology; Students; Persons interested in nuclear topics; *Committees:* Program; CNA Interface; WIN Interface; COG Interface; OCI Interface; Branch Affairs; Education & Communication; Membership; Bulletin; Finance; Past Presidents'; Climate Change, The Nuclear Future, & Communication Advisory; Fusion; Honours & Awards; Universities / UNENE; Inter-society Relations; Young Generation; Representative to PAGSE
Activities: Providing education; Offering opportunities to network with colleagues in Canada & internationally
Meetings/Conferences:
For more information see Trade Shows, Conferences and Seminars Chapter
Canadian Nuclear Society 2013 34rd Annual Conference & 37th Annual CNS / CNA Student Conference
June 2013 Toronto, ON
Canadian Nuclear Society 2014 35th Annual Conference & 38th Annual CNS / CNA Student Conference
2014
Publications:
•Canadian Nuclear Society Bulletin
Type: Journal; *Frequency:* Quarterly; *Editor:* Ric Fluke; *Price:* Free with Canadian Nuclear Society membership
Profile: Society news, conference reports, technical papers, articles, & letters
•Canadian Nuclear Society Proceedings
Profile: Information from Canadian Nuclear Society conferences or symposia

Canadian Nursery Landscape Association (CNLA)

Stn. Main, 7856 Fifth Line South, R.R.#4, Milton ON L9T 2X8
Tel: 905-875-1399; *Fax:* 905-875-1840
Toll-Free: 888-446-3499
e-mail: info@canadanursery.com
www.canadanursery.com
twitter.com/cnlavictor
Previous Name: Canadian Nursery Trades Association; Landscape Canada
Overview: A medium-sized national organization founded in 1968
Mission: To coordinate provincial member groups in the Canadian horticultural industry; to set national standards; to work with government; to develop national priorities; Affiliation(s): Flowers Canada; Canadian Ornamental Plant Foundation; Associated Landscape Contractors of America; International Garden Centres Association; North American Plant Protection Organization; American Nursery & Landscape Association; International Ornamental Growers Association; Canadian Plant Protection Advisory Committee; Canadian Horticultural Council
Chief Officer(s):
Victor Santacruz, Executive Director
victor@canadanursery.com
Finances: *Annual Operating Budget:* $500,000-$1.5 Million; *Funding Sources:* Membership dues; publications; management fees
Staff: 8 staff member(s); 21 volunteer(s)
Membership: 3,210; *Fees:* $115.23; *Member Profile:* Must be a supplier, active or associate member of one of the provincial

organizations; *Committees:* Certification; Garden Centres; Growers; Human Resources; Insurance; Landscape
Awards:
•Award of Excellence for Landscape Construction/Installation (Award)
•Award of Excellence for Landscape Maintenance (Award)
Publications:
•Canadian Standards for Nursery Stock
Price: Free with CNLA membership
Profile: A set of minimum professional standards for for the nursery industry
•CNLA [Canadian Nursery Landscape Association] Newsbrief
Type: Newsletter; *Frequency:* Bimonthly; *Price:* Free with CNLA membership
Profile: National news about the industry & the association
•CNLA [Canadian Nursery Landscape Association] Membership Directory
Type: Directory; *Frequency:* Annually; *Price:* Free with CNLA membership

Canadian Nursery Trades Association; Landscape Canada
See Canadian Nursery Landscape Association

Canadian Oil Heat Association (COHA)
#202, 115 Apple Creek Blvd., Markham ON L3R 6C9
Tel: 905-946-0264; *Fax:* 905-946-0316
Toll-Free: 800-257-1593
e-mail: oilheat@coha.ca
www.coha.ca
Overview: A small national organization founded in 1983
Mission: A voluntary membership organization, COHA serves as the industry's voice to provincial and federal regulators and government decision makers on matters of policy, safety, and certification. COHA works with government and other stakeholders to foster a sustainable business environment for its members.; *Member of:* Canadian Association Executives
Chief Officer(s):
Veronica Yu, President & CEO
Finances: *Annual Operating Budget:* $250,000-$500,000
Staff: 3 staff member(s)
Membership: 400; *Fees:* $300 - $18,000; *Member Profile:* Oil companies; HVAC manufacturers & suppliers; service contractors; *Committees:* Technical Development & Education; Marketing; Membership; Certification & Training
Activities: Promoting the benefits of residential fuel oil to the consumer public
Publications:
•COHA [Canadian Oil Heat Association] Directory
Type: Directory
Profile: Listing of equipment wholesalers & manufacturers, fuel oil suppliers, & service contractors
•Today's Oilheat Newsletter
Type: Newsletter

Canadian Oil Sands Network for Research & Development Inc. (CONRAD)
3608 - 33 St. NW, Calgary AB T2L 2A6
Tel: 403-210-5221; *Fax:* 403-210-5380
e-mail: info@conrad.ab.ca
www.conrad.ab.ca
Overview: A large international organization founded in 1994
Mission: CONRAD is a network organized to faciliatate collaborative research in science & technology for Alberta oilsands.; Affiliation(s): WADE Canada
Environmental Activity: Focus on bitumen production & bitumen upgrading
Chief Officer(s):
Carolyn Preston, CEO & Executive Director, Administration
preston@conrad.ab.ca
Stephanie Sutton, Executive Assistant, Administration
stephanie@conrad.ab.ca
Roger Melley, Treasurer, Administration
Finances: *Annual Operating Budget:* Greater than $5 Million; *Funding Sources:* Industry
Staff: 6 staff member(s); 50 volunteer(s)
Membership: 35 associations; *Fees:* $10,000-$50,000 general members; *Member Profile:* Regular members consist of universities, government agencies and companies involved in oilsands industry.
Activities: *Awareness Events:* CONRAD Clay Conference, bi-annual; CONRAD Water Conference & Workshops, bi-annual

Canadian Organic Growers Inc. (COG) / Cultivons Biologique Canada
#7519 - 1145 Carling Ave., Ottawa ON K1Z 7K4
Tel: 613-216-0741; *Fax:* 613-236-0743
Toll-Free: 888-375-7383
e-mail: office@cog.ca
www.cog.ca
www.facebook.com/pages/Canadian-Organic-Growers/277231516329
www.twitter.com/CanadianOrganic
Overview: A medium-sized national charitable organization founded in 1975
Mission: To conduct research into alternatives to traditional chemical & energy-intensive food growing practices; To provide a resource base & a forum open to all farmers & food growers interested in alternative agriculture; To foster the goals of a decentralized, bio-regionally-based food system; To endorse practices which promote & maintain long-term soil fertility, reduce fossil fuel uses, reduce pollution, recycle wastes & conserve non-renewable resources; To assist the farmer, grower, food processor & consumer, through education & demonstration, in understanding the value of organic foods; *Member of:* Canadian Environmental Network; Affiliation(s): International Federation of Organic Agriculture Movements; Organic Trade Association
Chief Officer(s):
Laura Telford, Executive Director
Finances: *Funding Sources:* Membership dues; Publications sale; Foundations; Governments
Membership: 2,000; *Fees:* $40-250; *Member Profile:* Farmers; Gardeners; Consumers; Environmentalists; Writers; Wholesale marketers
Activities: ; *Library:* Mail-Lending Library; Open to public
Awards:
•Mary Perlmutter Scholarship (Scholarship)
Awarded annually to a graduate student whose work within a recognized research institution is deemed beneficial to organic growers
Publications:
•The Canadian Organic Grower
Price: $18 + HST
Profile: Canada's voice for organics-reaching over 2,500 farmers, gardeners and consumers across Canada.
•
•Organic Statistics
Profile: Statistical overview of the Canadian organic sector for Canada & by province
•Practical Skills Handbooks
Profile: Resources for organic, transitioning, & conventional farmers on topics such as organic field crops & organic livestock

Durham
4720 Old Scugog Rd., RR#1, Bowmanville ON L1C 3K2
Tel: 905-263-9907
e-mail: info@durhamorganicgardeners.com
durhamorganicgardeners.com
twitter.com/cogdurham
Chief Officer(s):
Vincent Powers, Contact

Essex-Kent-Lambton
c/o 11016 Pinehurst Line, RR2, Kent Bridge ON N0P 1V0
Tel: 519-676-2885
e-mail: cogelk@hotmail.com
Chief Officer(s):
Chris White, Contact

Hamilton
201 Dumbarton Ave., Hamilton ON L8K 5C1
Tel: 905-544-3587
e-mail: greaterhamilton@cog.ca
Chief Officer(s):
Sapphire Singh, Chapter Chair

Island Natural Growers (Gulf Islands)
106 Old Scott Rd., Salt Spring Island BC V8K 2L6
Tel: 250-537-5511
Chief Officer(s):
Patricia Reichert, Chapter Chair, 250-537-4282
Anne Macey, Secretary

New Brunswick
c/o 267 South Knowlesville Rd., Knowlesville NB E7L 4S3
Tel: 506-375-4574
Chief Officer(s):
Katherine McCord, Chapter Chair, 506-529-4576
kathmccord@gmail.com
Beryl de Beaupré, Treasurer
beryl_de_beaupre@hotmail.com

Organic Food Council of Manitoba
PO Box 68082, Stn. Osborne Village, Winnipeg MB R3L 2V9
Tel: 204-779-8546
e-mail: ofcm@cog.ca
organicfoodcouncil.org
Chief Officer(s):
Janine Gibson, Chapter Chair

Ottawa
Ottawa ON
e-mail: ottawachapter@cog.ca
Chief Officer(s):
Margaret Tourond-Townsend, Chapter Chair, 613-244-4000 Ext. 4

Perth/Waterloo/Wellington
5420 Hwy. 6 North, RR5, Guelph ON N1H 6J8
Tel: 226-251-3012
Chief Officer(s):
T. Schumilas, Contact

Toronto
Toronto ON
e-mail: torontochapter@cog.ca
Chief Officer(s):
Chrumka Elizabeth, Chapter Chair

Vancouver Island
8973 Mainwaring Rd., North Saanich BC V8L 1J8
Tel: 250-656-7529
Chief Officer(s):
Tina Baynes, Chapter Chair
tinajfraser@shaw.ca

Yukon
PO Box 20228, Whitehorse YT
Tel: 867-393-4628
Chief Officer(s):
Joanne Jackson Johnson, Chapter Chair
jjj@northwestel.net

Canadian Ornamental Plant Foundation (COPF) / Fondation canadienne des plantes ornementales
5A - #218, 975 McKeown Ave., North Bay ON P1B 9P2
Tel: 705-495-2563; *Fax:* 705-495-1449
Toll-Free: 800-265-1629
e-mail: info@copf.org
www.copf.org
Overview: A small national organization founded in 1964
Mission: To encourage new plant development by strengthening relations between growers & breeders for the benefit of the horticulture industry; *Member of:* Canadian Horticultural Council; International Plant Propagators Society
Chief Officer(s):
Peggy Walsh Craig, Managing Director
peggy@copf.org
Finances: *Annual Operating Budget:* $100,000-$250,000
Staff: 7 staff member(s); 12 volunteer(s)
Membership: 650; *Fees:* Schedule available
Activities: *Rents Mailing List:* Yes

Canadian Paint & Coatings Association (CPCA) / Association canadienne de l'industrie de la peinture et du revêtement
#608, 170 Laurier Ave. West, Ottawa ON K1P 5V5
Tel: 613-231-3604; *Fax:* 613-231-4908
e-mail: cpca@cdnpaint.org
www.cdnpaint.org
Overview: A medium-sized national organization founded in 1913
Mission: To represent the paint industry among the provincial, federal & municipal governments
Chief Officer(s):
Dale Constantinoff, Chair
Finances: *Annual Operating Budget:* $500,000-$1.5 Million
Staff: 5 staff member(s)
Membership: 105 organizations
Activities: Seminars; annual convention; government relations
Meetings/Conferences:
For more information see Trade Shows, Conferences and Seminars Chapter
Canadian Paint and Coating Association 100th Annual Conference
October 2013 Ottawa, ON

Canadian Pallet Council (CPC) / Conseil des palettes du Canada
239 Division St., Cobourg ON K9A 3P9

Tel: 905-372-1871; *Fax:* 905-373-0230
e-mail: info@cpcpallet.com
www.cpcpallet.com
Overview: A medium-sized national organization founded in 1977
Chief Officer(s):
Belinda Junkin, President/CEO, 905-372-1871 Ext. 105
bjunkin@cpcpallet.com
Finances: *Funding Sources:* Membership fees; royalties
Staff: 3 staff member(s)
Membership: 1,300+; *Fees:* $485-$5,665
Publications:
•CPC [Canadian Pallet Council] Communiqué
Type: Newsletter; *Frequency:* Bimonthly; *Price:* Free with CPC membership
Profile: Pallet issues & topics of interest for members

Canadian Parks & Recreation Association (CPRA) / Association canadienne des parcs et loisirs

PO Box 83069, 1180 Walkley Rd., Ottawa ON K1V 2M5
Tel: 613-523-5315
e-mail: info@cpra.ca
www.cpra.ca
www.facebook.com/168910893249240?ref=hl
twitter.com/CPRA_ACPL
Overview: A large national charitable organization founded in 1945
Mission: To advocate on the benefits of parks & recreation services
Environmental Activity: Contributing to healthy communities; Collaborating with environmental & public health organizations
Chief Officer(s):
Jennifer Reynolds, President
CJ Noble, Executive Director, 613-523-5315
cjnoble@cpra.ca
Sarah Wayne, Accountant, 613-523-5315
swayne@cpra.ca
Membership: 2,600+; *Member Profile:* Parks & recreation professionals; *Committees:* Finance; Strategic Development; Communications; Awards
Activities: Influencing policy direction; Promoting the benefits of parks & recreation; Providing information to members; Offering professional development opportunities; *Awareness Events:* Recreation & Parks Month, June
Awards:
•Claude Langelier Award for Young Professionals (Award)
•Award of Merit (Award)
•Citation of Outstanding Achievement (Award)
•Award of Excellence for Innovation (Award)
Publications:
•The Benefits Catalogue
Type: Catalogue; *Number of Pages:* 200
Profile: Research outlining why parks, recreation, fitness, arts, & culture are important to the development of healthy individuals & communities
•Canadian Parks & Recreation Association Annual Report
Type: Yearbook; *Frequency:* Annually
•Canadian Parks & Recreation Association Research Reports
Profile: Topics include A Workbook on Child Health & Poverty: A Shared Vision for Health Children; Recreation & Children & Youth Living in Poverty: Barriers, Benefits & SuccessStories; & Bridging the Recreation Divide: Listening to Youth & Parents from Low-income Families across Canada
•CPRA [Canadian Parks & Recreation Association] E-News
Type: Newsletter; *Frequency:* Quarterly; *Price:* Free with CPRA membership
Profile: CPRA activities, conferences, awards, news, resources, initiatives, & research
•CPRA [Canadian Parks & Recreation Association] Tool Kits
Type: Kit
Profile: Topics of tool kits include Making All Recreation Safe, Relevant Recreation, & Everybody Gets to Play

Canadian Parks & Wilderness Society (CPAWS) / Société pour la nature et les parcs du Canada (SNAP)

#506, 250 City Centre Ave., Ottawa ON K1R 6K7
Tel: 613-569-7226; *Fax:* 613-569-7098
Toll-Free: 800-333-9453
e-mail: info@cpaws.org
www.cpaws.org
www.facebook.com/cpaws; twitter.com/#!/cpaws
Previous Name: National & Provincial Parks Association (NPPAC)
Overview: A medium-sized national charitable organization founded in 1963
Mission: To act as the Canadian voice for public wilderness protection
Environmental Activity: Creating protected areas in Canada; Conducting research in conservation biology
Chief Officer(s):
Alison Woodley, National Director, Conservation
Ellen Adelberg, Director, Communications & Marketing, 613-569-7226 Ext. 234
media@cpaws.org
Chris Henschel, National Manager, Domestic & International Affairs
Sabine Jessen, National Manager, Oceans & Great Freshwater Lakes Program
sabine@cpawsbc.org
Chris Miller, National Manager, Wilderness Conservation & Climate Change
Finances: *Funding Sources:* Donations; Fundraising
Staff: 50 staff member(s)
Membership: 20,000
Activities: Increasing awareness & understanding of ecological principles; Providing educational programs; Liaising with government, First Nations, business, & other organizations
Awards:
•J.B. Harkin Medal (Award)
To honour individuals who have made a significant contribution to the conservation of Canada's parks & wilderness
Publications:
•Canadian Wilderness
Type: Newsletter; *Frequency:* Semiannually; *Price:* Free with Canadian Parks & Wilderness Society membership
Profile: Wilderness conservation news & views from across Canada for Canadian Parks & Wilderness Society members
•Community Atlas Initiative [a publication of the Canadian Parks & Wilderness Society]
Profile: CPAWS works with communities near national parks to produce atlases about land use & the natural environment, such as the Gulf IslandsCommunity Atlas, the Riding Mountain Community Atlas, the St. Lawrence Islands Atlas, & the Bruce Penninsula Community Atlas
•CPAWS [Canadian Parks & Wilderness Society] Annual Report
Type: Yearbook; *Frequency:* Annually
Profile: CPAWS yearly highlights & financial information
•CPAWS [Canadian Parks & Wilderness Society] Research Reports
Frequency: Irregular
Profile: Conservation biology scientific report topics include Grizzly Challenge; Special Marine Areas in Newfoundland & Labrador; Ontario's Timber Harvesting Levels: Scienceor Wishful Thinking?; The State of the Alberta Parks & Protected Areas; & Uncertain Future: Woodland Caribou & Canada's Boreal Forest
•Gatineau Park: A Threatened Treasure
Type: Booklet; *Number of Pages:* 28
Profile: Information to ensure a sustainable future for Gatineau Park & its ecosystems
•More Than Trees: A Citizen's Guide to Making Conservation a Bigger Part of Forest Management
Type: Guide; *Number of Pages:* 91; *Editor:* Chris Henschel; Dave Pearce
Profile: A guide featuring advice fact sheets, compliance checklists, & the forest guardians reporting form
•Nahanni: Protected Forever
Type: Booklet; *Number of Pages:* 16
Profile: The expansion of the Nahanni National Park Reserve

Calgary - Southern Alberta Chapter
Kahanoff Centre, ?425 - 78th Ave. SW, Calgary AB T2V 5K5
Tel: 403-232-6686; *Fax:* 403-232-6988
e-mail: infosab@cpaws.org
cpaws-southernalberta.org
facebook.com/cpawssab
twitter.com/cpawssab
www.youtube.com/cpawsnational
Chief Officer(s):
Grégoire Belland, Executive Director
gbelland@cpawscalgary.org
Gord James, Chair

Edmonton - Northern Alberta Chapter
PO Box 52031, #202, 8540 - 109 St., Edmonton AB T6G 2T5
Tel: 780-424-5128; *Fax:* 780-424-5133
e-mail: infonab@cpaws.org
www.cpawsnab.org
www.facebook.com/cpaws.northernalberta
twitter.com/cpawsnab
Chief Officer(s):
Catherine Shier, Executive Director
Jeannette Gysbers, Chair
Wally Friesen, Secretary

Fredericton - New Brunswick Chapter
180 St John St., Fredericton NB E3B 4A9
Tel: 506-452-9902
e-mail: cpawsnb@nb.sympatico.ca
www.cpawsnb.org
www.facebook.com/CPAWSNewBrunswick
twitter.com/RCnature
Chief Officer(s):
Roberta Clowater, Executive Director

Halifax - Nova Scotia Chapter
#101, 5435 Portland Pl., Halifax NS B3K 6R7
Tel: 902-446-4155; *Fax:* 902-446-4156
cpawsns.org
www.facebook.com/CPAWSNS
twitter.com/cpawsnovascotia
www.youtube.com/cpawsns;
www.flickr.com/photos/64626833@N02
Chief Officer(s):
Martin Willison, President & Chair
Chris Miller, Biologist, National Conservation
cmiller@cpaws.org
Rodrigo Menafra, Coordinator, Marine Conservation
marine@cpawsns.org

Montréal - Québec Chapter
#303, 727, St-Urbain, Montréal QC H2R 2Y5
Tél: 514-278-7627
www.snapqc.org
www.facebook.com/pages/SNAP-Québec/107424984239
twitter.com/snapqc
www.youtube.com/channel/UCrE5HMtv8GnNtZCxplQVlsw
Chief Officer(s):
Brigitte Voss, Présidente
Patrick Nadeau, Directeur général, 514-278-7627 Ext. 226
Marie-Eve Allaire-Hébert, Coordonnatrice, Relations avec la communauté, 514-278-7627 Ext. 221
Jérôme Spaggiari, Coordonnateur, Conservation, 581-307-7627

Ottawa - Ottawa Valley Chapter
190 Bronson Ave., Ottawa ON K1R 6H4
Tel: 613-232-7297; *Fax:* 613-569-7098
www.cpaws-ov-vo.org
www.facebook.com/cpawsov
twitter.com/cpaws_ottawa
www.youtube.com/user/cpawsov
Chief Officer(s):
John McDonnell, Executive Director
jmcdonnell@cpaws.org

St. John's - Newfoundland & Labrador Chapter
The Environmental Gathering Place, PO Box 1027, Stn. C, 172 Military Rd., 3rd Fl., St. John's NL A1C 5M3
Tel: 709-726-5800; *Fax:* 709-726-2764
e-mail: nlcoordinator@cpaws.org
www.cpawsnl.org
www.facebook.com/pages/CPAWS-NL/184526941575823
twitter.com/cpawsnl
www.youtube.com/user/cpawsnl;
www.flickr.com/photos/cpaws-nl
Chief Officer(s):
Suzanne Dooley, Co-Executive Director
Tanya Edwards, Co-Executive Director
Leah Mahoney, Coordinator, Marine

Saskatoon - Saskatchewan Chapter
PO Box 25106, Stn. River Hts., Saskatoon SK S7K 2B1
Tel: 306-469-7876
www.cpaws-sask.org
www.facebook.com/cpaws.sask
twitter.com/cpawsSK
Chief Officer(s):
Sue Michalsky, Chair
Gord Vaadeland, Executive Director
gvaadeland@cpaws.org
Kjelti Anderson, Coordinator, Communications & Project
kanderson@cpaws.org

Toronto - CPAWS Wildlands League Chapter
#380, 401 Richmond St. West, Toronto ON M5V 3A8
Tel: 416-971-9453; *Fax:* 416-979-3155
Toll-Free: 866-510-9453
e-mail: info@wildlandsleague.org

www.wildlandsleague.org
www.facebook.com/259132727038
Kim Statham, B.Sc., M.E.S., President
Janet Summer, Executive Director
janet@wildlandsleague.org

Vancouver - British Columbia Chapter
#410, 698 Seymour St., Vancouver BC V6B 3K6
Tel: 604-685-7445; *Fax:* 604-685-6449
e-mail: info@cpawsbc.org
www.cpawsbc.org
www.facebook.com/cpawsbc
twitter.com/CPAWSbc
www.youtube.com/user/CPAWSinBC/videos
Chief Officer(s):
Chloe O'Loughlin, Executive Director
Robert Penrose, President
Michaeln Barkusky, Treasurer

Whitehorse - Yukon Chapter
PO Box 31095, 211 Main St., Whitehorse YT Y1A 5P7
Tel: 867-393-8080; *Fax:* 867-393-8081
e-mail: info@cpawsyukon.org
cpawsyukon.org
www.facebook.com/CPAWS.Yukon
twitter.com/CPAWSYukon
www.youtube.com/cpawsyukon
Jill Pangman, Chair
Mike Dehn, Executive Director

Winnipeg - Manitoba Chapter
#3, 303 Portage Ave., Winnipeg MB R3B 2B4
Tel: 204-949-0782
e-mail: info@cpawsmb.org
cpawsmb.org
www.facebook.com/cpawsmb.org
twitter.com/cpawsmb
Chief Officer(s):
Amanda Karst, President
Ron Thiessen, Executive Director

Yellowknife - Northwest Territories Chapter
PO Box 1934, 5020 - 52nd St., Yellowknife NT X1A 2P5
Tel: 867-873-9893; *Fax:* 867-873-9593
e-mail: nwtadmin@cpaws.org
cpawsnwt.org
Chief Officer(s):
Kris Brekke, Executive Director
Erica Janes, Coordinator, Conservation Outreach

Canadian Parks Partnership (CPP) / Partenaires des parcs canadiens

#360, 1414 - 8th St. SW, Calgary AB T2R 1J6
Tel: 613-567-0099
Overview: A medium-sized national organization founded in 1986
Mission: To support the overall enhancement of Canada's parks, historic sites & canals system & to foster public awareness, appreciation, understanding of & involvement in the system
Finances: *Annual Operating Budget:* Less than $50,000
Staff: 3 staff member(s)
Membership: Over 60 associations across Canada which work on an individual level with their partner national & provincial park or historic site
Activities: Direct Volunteer Support Program - to help cooperating associations to be strong & effective partners to their local national/provincial parks & historic sites & other protected area sites across Canada; National Education Programs - reaching beyond the park gate to encourage public awareness, appreciation of & involvement in supporting our special places; Canadian Parks Partnership Fund - was established in 1992 to act as a community foundation; *Speaker Service:* Yes; *Rents Mailing List:* Yes; *Library:* Open to public

Canadian Partnership for Children's Health and Environment (CPCHE) / Le Partenariat canadien pour la santé des enfants et l'environnement (PCSEE)

#301, 130 Spadina Ave., Toronto ON M5V 2L4
Tel: 416-960-2284
e-mail: info@healthyenvironmentforkids.ca
www.healthyenvironmentforkids.ca
Overview: A medium-sized national organization
Mission: The Canadian Partnership for Children's Health and Environment (CPCHE) is an affiliation of groups with overlapping missions to improve children's environmental health in Canada. Working across traditional boundaries, CPCHE provides common ground for organizations working to protect children's health from environmental contaminants.
Chief Officer(s):
Erica Phipps, Director
erica@healthyenvironmentforkids.ca

Canadian Pest Control Association *See* Canadian Pest Management Association

Canadian Pest Management Association (CPMA) / Association canadienne de la gestion parasitaire (ACGP)

PO Box 1748, Moncton NB E1C 9X5
Fax: 866-957-7378
Toll-Free: 866-630-2762
e-mail: cpma@pestworld.org
www.pestworldcanada.org
Previous Name: Canadian Pest Control Association
Overview: A medium-sized national organization founded in 1943
Mission: To provide pest management information; To act as the voice of the pest management industry throughout Canada; Upholding the association's Code of Ethics; Affiliation(s): National Pest Management Association; Leadership Development Group; Minorities in Pest Management; Professional Women in Pest Management
Environmental Activity: Speaking with legislators & formulators to ensure the industry has environmentally friendly legislation & tools
Chief Officer(s):
Bill Melville, President
bmelville@orkincanada.com
Karen Furgiuele-Percy, Director, Business Development
kfurgiuele@gardexinc.com
Randy Hobbs, Director, Government Affairs
rhobbs@braemargroup.ca
Sean Rollo, Treasurer
srollo@pcocanada.com
Membership: *Member Profile:* Members of provincial & regional pest management associations; Suppliers
Activities: Offering training & networking opportunities; Conducting research; Offering assistance to consumers seeking a professional pest control company
Meetings/Conferences:
For more information see Trade Shows, Conferences and Seminars Chapter
Pest Management Canada 2013
March 2013 Toronto, ON
Publications:
•Canada ePestWorld
Type: Newsletter; *Frequency:* Monthly; *Price:* Free with Canadian Pest Management Association membership
Profile: Timely national industry news & happenings, membership bulletins, & articles
•Pest Gazette
Type: Newsletter; *Frequency:* Quarterly; *Number of Pages:* 4
Profile: Educational information about seasonal pests for pest management consumers
•PestWorld
Type: Newsletter; *Frequency:* Bimonthly; *Price:* Free with Canadian Pest Management Association membership
Profile: Business techniques & tips, analysis of the pest management industry, field stories, technical updates, & legislative news

Canadian Petroleum Law Foundation

PO Box 4143, Stn. C, Calgary AB T2T 5M9
Tel: 403-237-2423
e-mail: lara.h.pella@esso.ca
www.cplf.org
Overview: A small national organization founded in 1963
Mission: To study oil & gas laws
Chief Officer(s):
Ben Rogers, President
ben.rogers@blakes.com
Miles Pittman, Treasurer
miles.pittman@fmc-law.com

Canadian Petroleum Products Institute *See* Canadian Fuels Association

Canadian Physiological Society (CPS) / Société canadienne de physiologie

Parent Name: Canadian Federation of Biological Societies
c/o Dr. Melanie Woodin, Dept. of Cell & Systems Biology, U. of Toronto, 25 Harbord St., Toronto ON M5S 3G5
www.cpsscp.ca
Overview: A medium-sized national charitable organization founded in 1935 overseen by Canadian Federation of Biological Societies
Mission: To disseminate & discuss scientific information of interest to researchers in physiology & biological sciences
Chief Officer(s):
Steven Barnes, President
Melanie Woodin, Secretary, 416-978-8646, Fax: 416-978-8532
m.woodin@utoronto.ca
Membership: *Fees:* $25 students; $65 associates; $100 regular; *Committees:* Nominating; Web Resources
Activities: Encouraging reseaerch in the physiological sciences; Fostering communication within the scientific community in Canada
Meetings/Conferences:
For more information see Trade Shows, Conferences and Seminars Chapter
Canadian Physiological Society 2013 Annual Winter Meeting 2013
Canadian Physiological Society 2014 Annual Winter Meeting 2014

Canadian Phytopathological Society (CPS) / Société Canadienne de Phytopathologie (SCP)

c/o Crop Protection & Food Research Ctr Agriculture & Agri-Food Canada, 1391 Sandford St., London ON N5V 4T3
e-mail: connk@agr.gc.ca
www.cps-scp.ca
Overview: A medium-sized national organization founded in 1929
Mission: To encourage & support research, education, & dissemination of knowledge on the nature, cause, & control of plant diseases; To promote communication among plant pathologists; To broaden educational opportunities for members
Chief Officer(s):
Kenneth Conn, Contact
Finances: *Funding Sources:* Membership fees
Meetings/Conferences:
For more information see Trade Shows, Conferences and Seminars Chapter
Canadian Phytopathological Society 2013 84th Annual Meeting
June 2013 Edmonton, AB
Publications:
•Canadian Journal of Plant Pathology / Revue canadienne de phytopathologie
Type: Journal; *Frequency:* Quarterly; *Editor:* Zamir K. Punja; *ISSN:* 0706-0661; *Price:* $85 Canada individuals; $140 Canada institutions; $95-$105international individuals
Profile: Scientific research, reviews & information about plant pathology
•Canadian Plant Disease Survey / Inventaire des maladies des plantes au Canada
Editor: Dr. Robin Morrall, Coordinator
Profile: Records of plant diseases in Canada & assessments of losses from disease
•Diseases & Pests of Vegetable Crops in Canada
Number of Pages: 554; *Editor:* R. Howard, J. Garland, & W. Seaman
Profile: Joint publication of the Canadian Phytopathological Society & the Entomological Society of Canada
•Diseases of Field Crop Crops in Canada
Number of Pages: 304; *Editor:* Bailey, Gossen, Gugel & Morrall; *ISBN:* 0-9691627-6-6; *Price:* $35
Profile: Thorough, illustrated guide to identifying diseases of forage, pulse, oilseed, cereal, & specialty crops
•The Pest Management Research Report (PMRR)
Editor: Andrea Labaj
Profile: Information about integrated pest management (IPM) for researchers & advisors

Canadian Plastics Industry Association (CPIA) / Association canadienne de l'industrie des plastiques

#125, 5955 Airport Rd., Mississauga ON L4V 1R9
Tel: 905-678-7748; *Fax:* 905-678-0774
www.plastics.ca
www.linkedin.com/company/1087578
www.facebook.com/IntelligentPlastics
twitter.com/CPIA_ACIP
Previous Name: Society of the Plastics Industry of Canada
Overview: A large national organization founded in 1997

Mission: To advance the prosperity & international competitiveness of the Canadian plastics industry in an environmentally & socially responsible manner
Environmental Activity: Recycling & energy recovery programs
Chief Officer(s):
Paul Cohen, Chair
Carol Hochu, President & CEO, 905-678-7748 Ext. 229
Michael Hill, Director, Membership Development, 905-678-7748 Ext. 281
Finances: *Funding Sources:* Membership fees
Staff: 30 staff member(s)
Membership: 500; *Fees:* $1,000-$16,000; *Member Profile:* Companies involved in Canadian plastics industry; *Committees:* Composites; Construction; EH&S; EPIC; Machinery; Mould Makers; Natural Composites; Vinyl
Activities: P3 Sustainability Management Program; Intelligent Plastics Campaign; *Speaker Service:* Yes; *Rents Mailing List:* Yes; *Library:* Technical Information Resource Centre; Open to public by appointment
Publications:
•Canadian Plastics Industry Association Executive Summary
Type: Newsletter
Profile: Internal newsletter of the CPIA President & CEO for CPIA members only
•CPIA [Canadian Plastics Industry Association] Annual Report
Type: Yearbook; *Frequency:* Annually
•CPIA [Canadian Plastics Industry Association] Membership Directory
Type: Directory
•CPIA [Canadian Plastics Industry Association] Plastics Machinery & Moulds Export Directory
Type: Directory
•CPIA [Canadian Plastics Industry Association] NewsBrief
Type: Newsletter
•Green Building
Type: Newsletter
Profile: Publication of the Green Building Task Force of the Canadian Plastics Industry Association
•Member to Member [a publication of Canadian Plastics Industry Association]
Type: Newsletter
•News & Views [a publication of Canadian Plastics Industry Association]
Type: Newsletter
•Plastics in Class [a publication of Canadian Plastics Industry Association]
Type: Newsletter
•Plastics Perspectives [a publication of Canadian Plastics Industry Association]
Type: Newsletter

Atlantic Region
1 Research Dr., Dartmouth NS B2Y 4M9
Tel: 902-424-2742; *Fax:* 902-466-6889
e-mail: dcross@cpia.ca
Chief Officer(s):
Duncan Cross, Executive Director

Ontario Region
#712, 5915 Airport Rd., Mississauga ON L4V 1T1
Tel: 905-678-7748; *Fax:* 905-678-0774
e-mail: ontario@cpia.ca
Chief Officer(s):
Atul Sharma, Director

Région du Québec
#117, 75, boul de Mortagne, Boucherville QC J4B 6Y4
Tél: 450-641-5922; *Téléc:* 450-641-5921
Chief Officer(s):
Denise Lacas, Chargée de projets

Western Region - Alberta
Mission Hills Plaza, Stn. 65066, St Albert AB T8N 5Y3
Tel: 780-418-2604
e-mail: rkelsey@cpia.ca
Chief Officer(s):
Ray Kelsey, Manager

Canadian Plastics Sector Council (CPSC) / Conseil canadien sectoriel des plastiques
#1, 200 Colonnade Rd., Ottawa ON K2E 7M1
Tel: 613-231-4470; *Fax:* 613-231-3775
e-mail: info@cpsc-ccsp.ca
www.cpsc-ccsp.ca
www.linkedin.com/groups?home=&gid=3122682&trk=anet_ug_hm
www.facebook.com/170596692956657
twitter.com/PlasticsHR
youtube.com/CanadianPlastics
Overview: A small national organization founded in 2000
Mission: To explore & address emerging human resources issues in the plastics processing industry
Chief Officer(s):
Amelia Siva, Executive Director
a.siva@cpsc-ccsp.ca
Finances: *Annual Operating Budget:* $500,000-$1.5 Million
Staff: 4 staff member(s)
Publications:
•CPSC [Canadian Plastics Sector Council] Newsletter / Bulletin du CCSP [Conseil canadien sectoriel des plastiques]
Type: Newsletter; *Frequency:* 3 pa; *Editor:* Jérôme Bourgault
Profile: Feature articles & CPSC activities

Canadian Plumbing & Mechanical Contractors Association, BC Branch ***See*** Mechanical Contractors Association of British Columbia

Canadian Plywood Association
735 - 15 St. West, North Vancouver BC V7M 1T2
Tel: 604-981-4190; *Fax:* 604-985-0342
e-mail: info@canply.org
www.canply.org
Also Known As: CANPLY
Overview: A medium-sized national organization
Mission: Canadian plywood organization.
Chief Officer(s):
Judy White, Office Manager
James F. Shaw, President
Finances: *Annual Operating Budget:* $1.5 Million-$3 Million
Staff: 14 staff member(s)
Membership: 1-99

Canadian Polystyrene Recycling Alliance (CPRA)
260 Peter St., Port Hope ON L1A 3V6
www.cpracanada.ca
Overview: A medium-sized national organization founded in 1989
Mission: To operate a vertically integrated polystyrene recycling facility to recycle polystyrene into picture frames & mouldings
Chief Officer(s):
Sam Alavy, President & Chief Executive Officer

Canadian Port & Harbour Association ***See*** Association of Canadian Port Authorities

Canadian Portland Cement Association ***See*** Cement Association of Canada

Canadian Precast / Prestressed Concrete Institute (CPCI) / Institut canadien du béton préfabriqué et précontraint
#100, 196 Bronson Ave., Ottawa ON K1R 6H4
Tel: 613-232-2619; *Fax:* 613-232-5139
Toll-Free: 877-937-2724
e-mail: info@cpci.ca
www.cpci.ca
www.facebook.com/121188924614844
Overview: A medium-sized national organization founded in 1961
Mission: To stimulate & advance the common interests & general welfare of the structural precast/prestressed concrete industry, the architectural precast concrete industry & the post-tensioned concrete industry in Canada
Chief Officer(s):
Rob Burak, President
robert.burak@cpci.ca
Finances: *Annual Operating Budget:* $500,000-$1.5 Million
Staff: 3 staff member(s)
Membership: 31 institutional
Activities: ; *Library:* Open to public
Publications:
•CPCI [Canadian Precast / Prestressed Concrete Institute] Imagineering
Type: Magazine; *Accepts Advertising*; *Editor:* Jeanne Fronda
Profile: Feature articles, industry updates, member directory, "tech talk", marketing information, president's messages

Canadian Printing Industries Association (CPIA) / Association canadienne de l'imprimerie (ACI)
#1110, 151 Slater St., Ottawa ON K1P 5H3
Tel: 613-236-7208; *Fax:* 613-232-1334
Toll-Free: 800-267-7280
e-mail: info@cpia-aci.ca
www.cpia-aci.ca
www.linkedin.com/company/canadian-printing-industries-association
Previous Name: Graphic Arts Industries Association; Canadian Printing & Imaging Association
Overview: A medium-sized national organization founded in 1939
Mission: To advance the quality of management in the printing & allied trades; to offer services through a network of local & related organizations including representations to various sectors; to enhance the image & profile of the industry; Affiliation(s): Printing Industries of America
Chief Officer(s):
Anateresa Mendes-Collins, Executive Assistant
anateresa@cpia-aci.ca
Bob Elliott, President
belliott@cpia-aci.ca
Jamie Barbieri, Secretary-Treasurer
james.barbieri@groupepdi.com
Finances: *Annual Operating Budget:* $250,000-$500,000; *Funding Sources:* Membership dues
Staff: 2 staff member(s); 25 volunteer(s)
Membership: 300; *Member Profile:* Owners/senior executives of companies in pre-press, press, bindery & allied industries; *Committees:* Government Affairs; Membership
Activities: ; *Library:* Open to public

Canadian Printing Ink Manufacturers Association (CPIMA)
Tel: 905-556-1808; *Fax:* 647-439-1572
e-mail: mconnolly@cpima.org
www.cpima.org
Overview: A medium-sized national organization founded in 1936
Mission: To exchange information that will be of benefit to members, the ink industry, & the printing industry; Affiliation(s): Society of British Ink Manufacturers; National Association of Printing Ink Manufacturers
Chief Officer(s):
Vivy DaCosta, President
Finances: *Annual Operating Budget:* Less than $50,000; *Funding Sources:* Membership dues
Staff: 1 staff member(s)
Membership: 5; *Fees:* Based on sales; *Member Profile:* Canadian ink manufacturers; *Committees:* Management; Technical
Publications:
•Canadian Printing Ink Manufacturers Association Technical Bulletins
Type: Newsletter; *Frequency:* Irregular
Profile: Topics include environmental issues, printing inks & food packaging, scrap ink, & UV inks health & saftey

Canadian Process Control Association (CPCA)
2100 Banbury Cres., Oakville ON L6H 5P6
Tel: 905-844-6822; *Fax:* 905-901-9913
e-mail: cpca@cpca-assoc.com
www.cpca-assoc.com
Previous Name: Industrial Instrument Manufacturers Association
Overview: A medium-sized national organization
Mission: To promote the industry & its members to customers, academia, & public bodies; To provide a forum to exchange technical, industry, & regulatory information; To develop industry statistics; To encourage professional & ethical behaviour & quality standards among members
Finances: *Annual Operating Budget:* Less than $50,000
Membership: 52 corporate

Canadian Propane Association (CPA) / Association canadienne du propane (ACP)
#616, 130 Albert St., Ottawa ON K1P 5G4
Tel: 613-683-2270; *Fax:* 613-683-2279
e-mail: info@propane.ca
www.propane.ca
twitter.com/Propanedotca
Merged from: Propane Gas Association of Canada Inc.; Ontario Propane Association
Overview: A medium-sized national licensing organization founded in 2011
Mission: To act as the national voice of the Canadian propane industry; To supports its members in the development of a safe, environmentally responsible Canadian propane industry; Affiliation(s): Propane Training Institute (PTI), a division of the CPA; Liquefied Petroleum Gas Emergency Response Corporation, a wholly owned subsidiary of the CPA
Chief Officer(s):

Jim Facette, President & CEO
jimfacette@propane.ca
Steven Sparling, Chair
Allison Mallette, Manager, Research & Communications, 647-340-2208
allisonmallette@propane.ca
Peter Maddox, Regional Manager, Ontario, 416-903-8518
petermaddox@propane.ca
Finances: *Funding Sources:* Membership dues
Staff: 7 staff member(s)
Membership: 400+; *Fees:* Schedule available; *Member Profile:* Producers; Wholesalers; Retailers; Transporters; Manufacturers of appliances, cylinders, & equipment; Associates
Activities: Providing industry related training & emergency response; Promoting the interests of the industry; Engaging in regulatory relations
Meetings/Conferences:
For more information see Trade Shows, Conferences and Seminars Chapter
Canadian Propane Association (CPC) Annual General Meeting 2013
June 2013 Regina, SK
Canadian Propane Association (CPC) 2014 Leadership Summit
May 2014 Ottawa, ON
Publications:
•CPA Bulletin
Type: Newsletter; *Frequency:* Bimonthly
Profile: For members
•CPA Newsletter
Type: Newsletter; *Frequency:* Monthly
Profile: For members

Calgary Office
#800, 717 - 7th Ave. SW, Calgary AB T2P 0Z3
Tel: 403-543-6500; *Fax:* 403-543-6508
Toll-Free: 877-784-4636
e-mail: info@propane.ca
www.propane.ca
Chief Officer(s):
Bill Egbert, Senior Director, 403-543-6506
billegbert@propane.ca

Canadian Public Health Association (CPHA) / Association canadienne de santé publique (ACSP)

#300, 1565 Carling Ave., Ottawa ON K1Z 8R1
Tel: 613-725-3769; *Fax:* 613-725-9826
e-mail: info@cpha.ca
www.cpha.ca
www.facebook.com/group.php?gid=159289860285?ref
twitter.com/CPHA_ACSP
Overview: A large national charitable organization founded in 1910
Mission: To represent public health in Canada; To support universal & equitable access to the necessary conditions to achieve health for all Canadians; To provide links to the international public health community; Affiliation(s): World Health Organization; World Federation of Public Health Associations
Environmental Activity: Guiding intitiatives to safeguard the personal & community health of Canadians
Chief Officer(s):
Debra Lynkowski, Chief Executive Officer
Erica Di Ruggiero, Chair
James Chauvin, Director, Policy Development, 613-725-3769 Ext. 160
Ian Culbert, Director, Communications & Development, 613-725-3769 Ext. 142
Greg Penney, Director, Public Health Knowledge Centre, 613-725-3769 Ext. 150
Sarah Pettenuzzo, Manager, Conferences, 613-725-3769 Ext. 153
Finances: *Funding Sources:* Membership fees; Donations
Membership: 2,000; *Fees:* $88 students, retired persons, & low income individuals; $107 international students; $185 regular members; $200 regular international members; *Member Profile:* Individuals who support Canadian Public Health Association objectives, & who are engaged or interested in community or public health activities, such as professionals in public health practice, researchers, professors, & government workers
Activities: Advising decision-makers about public health system reform; Liaising with provincial & territorial public health associations & national & international agencies & organizations; Publishing & disseminating research results; *Speaker Service:* Yes
Meetings/Conferences:
For more information see Trade Shows, Conferences and Seminars Chapter
Canadian Public Health Association 2013 Conference: Moving Public Health Forward - Evidence, Policy, Practice
June 2013 Ottawa, ON
Publications:
•The Canadian Journal of Public Health
Type: Journal; *Frequency:* Bimonthly; *Accepts Advertising*; *Editor:* Debra Lynkowski; *Price:* Free with membership in the Canadian Public Health Association
Profile: Articles on public health, including epidemiology, nutrition, family health, environmental health, sexually transmitted diseases, gerontology, behavioural medicine,rural health, health promotion, & public health policy
•Canadian Public Health Association Annual Report
Type: Yearbook; *Frequency:* Annually
•CPHA [Canadian Public Health Association] Health Digest
Frequency: Quarterly; *Editor:* Debra Lynkowski; *ISBN:* 0703-5624; *Price:* Free with membership inthe Canadian Public Health Association
Profile: Incorporates the international newsletter, Partners Around the World, plus articles from across Canada & around the world

Canadian Public Health Association - NB/PEI Branch
Parent Name: Canadian Public Health Association

#34, 2865 Rothesay Rd., Rothesay NB E3B 4P2
Tel: 506-847-0311; *Fax:* 506-847-0311
e-mail: nbpei.pha@gmail.com
Overview: A small provincial organization founded in 1952 overseen by Canadian Public Health Association
Chief Officer(s):
Cristin Muecke, President
Ann Harling, Secretary-Treasurer

Canadian Public Health Association - NWT/Nunavut Branch (NTNUPHA)
Parent Name: Canadian Public Health Association

PO Box 1709, Yellowknife NT X1A 2P3
Overview: A small provincial organization overseen by Canadian Public Health Association
Chief Officer(s):
Faye Stark, President

Canadian Public Works Association (CPWA) / Association canadienne des travaux publics

797 Somerset St. West, Ottawa ON K1R 6R3
Tel: 202-408-9541; *Fax:* 202-408-9542
Toll-Free: 800-848-2792
e-mail: cpwa@cpwa.net
www.cpwa.net
Overview: A medium-sized national organization founded in 1986
Mission: To improve the quality of public works services for Canadian citizens; To share information about public works issues that are unique to Canada
Chief Officer(s):
Peter King, Executive Director
pking@apwa.net
Gail Clark, Manager, International Affairs
gclark@apwa.net
Brent Colbert, Consultant, Government Relations
bcolbert@tactix.ca
Laura Bynum, Contact, Media Relations
lbynum@apwa.net
Membership: *Member Profile:* Public works employees in Canada who are members of the American Public Works Association; Any person or organization in Canada with an interest in infrastructure & public works issues
Activities: Engaging in advocacy projects; Producing position statements; Facilitating the exchange of information for public works employees

Canadian Pulp & Paper Association ***See*** Forest Products Association of Canada

Canadian Pulp & Paper Association - Technical Section ***See*** Pulp & Paper Technical Association of Canada

Canadian Pulp & Paper Network for Innovation in Education & Research; Mechanical Wood-Pulps Network ***See*** Pulp & Paper Centre

Canadian Radiation Protection Association (CRPA) / Association canadienne de radioprotection (ACRP)

PO Box 83, Carleton Place ON K7C 3P3
Tel: 613-253-3779; *Fax:* 888-551-0712
e-mail: secretariat2007@crpa-acrp.ca
www.crpa-acrp.ca
Overview: A small national organization founded in 1982
Mission: To develop scientific knowledge for protection from the harmful effects of radiation; To encourage research; To assist in the development of professional standards in the discipline; Affiliation(s): International Radiation Protection Association (IRPA).
Chief Officer(s):
Lois Sowden-Plunkett, President
lsowden@uottawa.ca
Christine Dehm, Treasurer
christine.dehm@uregina.ca
Membership: *Fees:* $565 corporate members; $140 full or associate members; $25 students; $70 retired; *Member Profile:* Individuals with training who are engaged in the science & practice of radiation protection
Activities: Promoting educational opportunities
Publications:
•CRPA [Canadian Radiation Protection Association] Bulletin
Type: Newsletter; *Frequency:* Quarterly
Profile: For Canadian Radiation Protection Association members only

Canadian Recreational Canoeing Association ***See*** Paddle Canada

Canadian Regional Science Association ***Voir*** Association canadienne des sciences régionales

Canadian Remote Sensing Society (CRSS) / Société canadienne de télédétection

c/o Canadian Aeronautics & Space Institute, #104, 350 Terry Fox Dr., Kanata ON K2K 2W5
Tel: 613-591-8787; *Fax:* 613-591-7291
e-mail: casi@casi.ca
www.casi.ca/cdn-remote-sensing-society
Overview: A small national organization founded in 1978
Mission: To advance the art, science, engineering, & application of remote sensing in Canada; To uphold the Society's Code of Ethics; *Member of:* Canadian Aeronautics & Space Institute (CASI)
Chief Officer(s):
Monique Bernier, Chair
Anne Smith, Vice-Chair
Richard Fournier, Secretary-Treasurer
Activities: Disseminating technical remote sensing information; Developing a program for certification of remote sensing scientists & mapping scientists in GIS & photogrammetry
Meetings/Conferences:
For more information see Trade Shows, Conferences and Seminars Chapter
Canadian Remote Sensing Society 2013 34th Canadian Symposium on Remote Sensing
2013
Publications:
•Canadian Journal of Remote Sensing (CJRS) / Journal canadien de télédétection (JCT)
Type: Journal; *Frequency:* Bimonthly; *Accepts Advertising*; *Editor:* Nicholas Coops; *Price:* $211.68 Canada; $206.30 USA; $217.20 International
Profile: Research articles & notes, technical notes, & review papers on topics such asinformation processing methods, data acquisition, & applications

Canadian Renewable Energy Alliance (CanREA)

new.canrea.ca/site
Previous Name: Canadian Renewable Energy Association
Overview: A large national organization
Mission: To promote a global transition to energy conservation & efficiency, & the use of renewable energy. A founding member of the North American Alliance for Renewable Energy, CanREA & its members advocate to all levels of government & work with like-minded organizations worldwide to recommend new policy directions & practical strategies.; Affiliation(s): BC Sustainable Energy Association; David Suzuki Foundation; Ecolology Action Centre; Environmental Coalition of Prince Edward Island; The Falls Brook Centre; Green Communities Canada; Greenpeace Canada; Nova Scotia Cooperative Council; Ontario Sustainable Energy Association; Canadian Institute for Sustainable Living; Pembina Institute; Sierra Club Canada; Saskatchewan Environmental Society; Toronto Renewable Energy Coop; Windfall Ecology Centre
Chief Officer(s):
Jose Etcheverry, President
rejose@yorku.ca
Membership: 16; *Member Profile:* Registered & incorporated not-for-profit organizations which actively promote renewable energy policy & implementation & are in good standing under applicable laws

Activities: Conferences

Canadian Renewable Energy Association ***See*** Canadian Renewable Energy Alliance

Canadian Renewable Fuels Association (CRFA) / Association canadienne des carburants renouvelables

#605, 350 Sparks St., Ottawa ON K1R 7S8
Tel: 613-594-5528; *Fax:* 613-594-3076
e-mail: l.ehman@greenfuels.org
www.greenfuels.org
Overview: A medium-sized national organization founded in 1984
Mission: To promote renewable fuel development & usage
Environmental Activity: Providing information about the development & use of renewable fuel
Chief Officer(s):
Gordon Quaiattini, President
g.quaiattini@greenfuels.org
Deborah Elson, Director, Member Relations & Industry Promotions
D.Elson@greenfuels.org
Debby Marandola, Director, Operations
D.Marandola@greenfuels.org
Alison Ouellet, Director, Government Affairs
A.Ouellet@greenfuels.org
Finances: *Funding Sources:* Membership dues
Membership: 1-99;; *Fees:* Schedule available based upon company's litres of production; $15,000 associate members; $5,000 supporting members; *Member Profile:* Representatives from all levels of the ethanol & biodiesel industries
Activities: Liaising with government; Promoting policy initiatives advantageous to ethanol & biodiesel fuel development; Increasing awareness of ethanol & biodiesel; Conducting research
Meetings/Conferences:
For more information see Trade Shows, Conferences and Seminars Chapter
Canadian Renewable Fuels 2013 10th Annual Summit
December 2013 Montréal, QC
Canadian Renewable Fuels 2014 11th Annual Summit
2014

Canadian Research Management Association ***See*** Innovation Management Association of Canada

Canadian Respiratory Health Professionals (CRHP) Parent Name: Canadian Lung Association

#300, 1750 Courtwood Cres., Ottawa ON K2C 2B5
Tel: 613-569-6411; *Fax:* 613-569-8860
e-mail: crhpinfo@lung.ca
www.lung.ca/crhp
Merged from: Cdn Nurses Respiratory, Cdn Physiotherapy Cardio-Respiratory, & Respiratory Therapy Societies
Overview: A small national organization founded in 2004 overseen by Canadian Lung Association
Mission: To promote lung health & the prevention of lung disease; Affiliation(s): Canadian Thoracic Society
Membership: *Fees:* $30 associate member; $45 full member; *Member Profile:* A multidisciplinary health professional section of The Canadian Lung Association, consisting of respiratory therapists, cardio-pulmonary physiotherapists, nurses, pharmacists, & other health professionals who work in the respiratory field
Activities: Advising the Canadian Lung Association on scientific matters, as well as professional & public education; Administering a research & fellowship program; Facilitating interprofessional collaboration
Meetings/Conferences:
For more information see Trade Shows, Conferences and Seminars Chapter
Canadian Respiratory Health Professionals 2013 Annual General Meeting
2013
Publications:
•Airwaves - The Newsletter of the Canadian Respiratory Health Professionals
Type: Newsletter; *Price:* Free with CRHP membership
Profile: Information for Canadian Respiratory Health Professionals members

Canadian Rock Mechanics Association (CARMA) / Association canadienne de méchanique des roches

c/o Civil Engineering Department, University of Toronto, 35 St. George St., Toronto ON M5S 1A4
www.carma-rocks.ca
Overview: A medium-sized national organization founded in 1980
Mission: To represent Canada to the international community of engineers working in the mining & civil engineering aspects of rock mechanics engineering; *Member of:* Canadian Geotechnical Society; Canadian Institute of Mining & Metallurgy; Affiliation(s): International Society for Rock Mechanics
Chief Officer(s):
John Hadjigeorgiou, Chair
john.hadjigeorgiou@utoronto.ca
Luc Beauchamp, Secretary-Treasurer
lucbeauchamp@workplacesafetynorth.ca
Membership: 165

Canadian Rose Society (CRS)

#100, Chancellor Ave., Victoria BC V8Z 1R4
Tel: 416-266-6303
e-mail: info@canadianrosesociety.org
www.canadianrosesociety.org
Previous Name: Rose Society of Ontario
Overview: A medium-sized national charitable organization founded in 1955
Mission: To provide information about rose growing, speakers, judges, nurseries & suppliers, & rose shows; To correspond with people with similar interests throughout Canada & around the world; *Member of:* World Federation of Rose Societies; Affiliation(s): World Federation of Rose Societies
Chief Officer(s):
Barb Munton, Membership Sec.-Treas.
Finances: *Annual Operating Budget:* Less than $50,000; *Funding Sources:* Donations, membership fees, sales of goods & services
Membership: 500-999;; *Fees:* $20 regular; $25 family; $30 affiliate society, nursery, institute;$35 U.S.A. members; $50 foreign; $15 all electronic subscriptions
Activities: *Speaker Service:* Yes; *Library:* Rose Book Library & Rose Slide Library
Publications:
•Canadian Rose Society Newsletter: Sharing your love of roses
Type: Newsletter
Profile: Business of the Canadian Rose Society & world rose news

Canadian Sanitation Standards Association ***See*** Canadian Sanitation Supply Association

Canadian Sanitation Supply Association (CSSA) / Association canadienne des fournisseurs de produits sanitaires

PO Box 10009, 910 Dundas St. West, Whitby ON L1P 1P7
Tel: 905-665-8001; *Fax:* 905-430-6418
Toll-Free: 866-684-8273
www.cssa.com
www.facebook.com/group.php?gid=183837499478
twitter.com/CSSA_Canada
Previous Name: Canadian Sanitation Standards Association
Overview: A large national organization founded in 1957
Mission: To provide a high degree of professionalism, technical knowledge & business ethics within the membership; To promote greater public awareness, appreciation & understanding of the sanitation industry
Chief Officer(s):
Mike Nosko, Executive Director
mike@cssa.com
Catherine Fedak, Contact, Sales
cathie@cssa.com
Diane Mason, Contact, Accounting
dcm@cssa.com
Membership: 395 corporate + 10 associate + 15 senior/lifetime; *Fees:* Schedule available; *Member Profile:* Manufacturer or distributor of sanitation products & services; *Committees:* Long Range Planning; Government Liaison
Activities: ; *Library:* by appointment
Publications:
•Canadian Sanitation Supply Association Update
Type: Newsletter; *Price:* Free with CSSA membership
Profile: CSSA activities, awards, chapter news, & events
•Canadian Sanitation Supply Association Bulletin
Type: Newsletter; *Price:* Free with CSSA membership
Profile: Information for CSSA members important to their business

Canadian Science Writers' Association (CSWA) / Association canadienne des rédacteurs scientifiques

PO Box 75, Stn. A, Toronto ON M5W 1A2
Toll-Free: 800-796-8595
e-mail: office@sciencewriters.ca
www.sciencewriters.ca
Overview: A small national organization founded in 1971
Mission: To foster excellence in science communication; To increase public awareness of Canadian science & technology
Chief Officer(s):
Kristina Bergen, Executive Director
Stephen Strauss, President
president@sciencewriters.ca
Membership: 450+; *Fees:* $75 regular members; $35 students; *Member Profile:* Professional science communicators in all media, who communicate science & technology to non-specialist audiences
Activities: Providing networking opportunities for communications officers in science & technology institutions, media professionals, educators, & technical writers; Offering workshops & public meetings; Encouraging awareness of the need for science coverage
Awards:
•Science in Society Journalism Awards (Award)
•Medal For Excellence In Health Research Journalism (Award)
Publications:
•Canadian Science Writers' Association Membership Directory
Type: Directory
Profile: For CSWA / ACRS members
•Science Link [a publication of the Canadian Science Writers' Association]
Type: Newsletter; *Editor:* Peter McMahon
Profile: Information for CSWA / ACRS members

Canadian Seed Growers' Association (CSGA) / Association canadienne des producteurs de semences

PO Box 8455, #202, 240 Catherine St., Ottawa ON K1G 3T1
Tel: 613-236-0497; *Fax:* 613-563-7855
e-mail: seeds@seedgrowers.ca
www.seedgrowers.ca
Overview: A medium-sized national organization founded in 1904
Chief Officer(s):
Dale Apolphe, Executive Director, 613-236-0497 Ext. 224
adolphed@seedgrowers.ca
Membership: 4,300
Meetings/Conferences:
For more information see Trade Shows, Conferences and Seminars Chapter
Canadian Seed Growers' Association's 2013 Annual General Meeting
July 2013 Halifax, NS

Canadian Seed Trade Association (CSTA) / Association canadienne du commerce des semences (ACCS)

#505, 39 Robertson Rd., Ottawa ON K2H 8R2
Tel: 613-829-9527; *Fax:* 613-829-3530
e-mail: csta@cdnseed.org
www.cdnseed.org
www.facebook.com/cdnseed
twitter.com/SeedInnovation
Overview: A medium-sized national organization founded in 1923
Mission: The Canadian Seed Trade Association (CSTA) is committed to fostering an environment conducive to research, developing, distributing, and trading seed and associated technologies; with the goal of bettering the choices and successes of our members and their customers. Their five key goals are as follows; fostering innovation; support for a science based regulatory system; increase the use of pedigreed seed; support the understanding and use of indentity preserved systems; improve market access and understanding for the trade of seed
Chief Officer(s):
W.C. Leask, Executive Vice-President, 613-829-9527 Ext. 222
bleask@cdnseed.org
David Sippell, President, 519-461-0072
dave.sippell@syngenta.com
Finances: *Funding Sources:* Membership fees
Staff: 2 staff member(s)
Membership: 128
Meetings/Conferences:
For more information see Trade Shows, Conferences and Seminars Chapter
Canadian Seed Trade Association 90th Annual Meeting
July 2013 Québec City, QC

Canadian Sheep Breeders' Association (CSBA) / La société canadienne des éleveurs de moutons
333 Ontario St., Toronto ON M5A 2V8
Fax: 416-972-1023
Toll-Free: 866-956-1116
www.sheepbreeders.ca
Overview: A medium-sized national organization
Chief Officer(s):
Trenholm Nelson, President, 819-826-3066
nelson@abacom.com
Kim MacDougall, Vice President, 306-545-6190, Fax: 306-543-3919
kmacdougall@supremebasics.com
Membership: 1,100; *Fees:* $50

Canadian Sheet Steel Building Institute (CSSBI) / Institut canadien de la tôle d'acier pour le bâtiment (ICTAB)
#2A, 652 Bishop St. North, Cambridge ON N3H 4V6
Tel: 519-650-1285; *Fax:* 519-650-8081
e-mail: info@cssbi.ca
www.cssbi.ca
Overview: A medium-sized national organization founded in 1961
Mission: The CSSBI's vision statement is to make steel the material of choice for building construction in Canada.
Membership: 27 corporate; *Member Profile:* Producers, fabricators & associates involved in the structural sheet steel industry

Canadian Society for Analytical Sciences & Spectroscopy
PO Box 46122, 2339 Ogilvie Rd., Ottawa ON K1J 9M7
Fax: 204-954-5984
www.csass.org
Previous Name: Spectroscopy Society of Canada
Overview: A medium-sized national organization founded in 1957
Mission: To organize programs of scientific & general interest for the educational benefit of members & the public; to organize annual scientific conferences & workshops on various aspects of pure & applied spectroscopy in the chemical, biological, geochemical & metallurgical sciences; Affiliation(s): Society for Applied Spectroscopy - USA; Colloquium Spectroscopicum Internationale; Chemical Institute of Canada; Canadian Society of Forensic Science
Chief Officer(s):
Graeme Spiers, President
gspiers@mirarco.org
Ana Delgado, Treasurer
ana.delgado@nrc.gc.ca
Finances: *Annual Operating Budget:* $50,000-$100,000
Staff: 25 volunteer(s)
Membership: 500; *Fees:* Schedule available; *Committees:* National Executive

Canadian Society for Bioengineering (CSBE) / Société canadienne de génie agroalimentaire et de bioingénierie (SCGAB)
2028 Calico Crescent, Orleans ON K4A 4L7
Tel: 613-590-0975
e-mail: bioeng@shaw.ca
www.bioeng.ca
Previous Name: Canadian Society for Engineering in Agricultural, Food & Biological Systems
Overview: A medium-sized national organization founded in 1958
Mission: To provide expertise in the areas of farm power & machinery, structures & environment, soil & water & electrical power & processing; Affiliation(s): American Society of Agricultural & Biological Engineers
Chief Officer(s):
James S. Townsend, Secretary
Ron MacDonald, President
rmacdonald@agviro.com
Finances: *Annual Operating Budget:* Less than $50,000; *Funding Sources:* Annual dues
Staff: 1 staff member(s); 17 volunteer(s)
Membership: 500 full + 200 students; *Fees:* Schedule available
Activities: Canadian Society for Bioengineering Foundation
Meetings/Conferences:
For more information see Trade Shows, Conferences and Seminars Chapter
Canadian Society for Bioengineering Conference for Interdisciplinary Engineering and CSBE/SCGAB Annual General Meeting 2013
July 2013 Saskatoon, SK
Publications:
•Canadian Biosystems Engineering Journal / Le Journal de la Société Canadienne de Génie Agroalimentaire et de Bioingénierie
Type: Journal; *Editor:* Ranjan Sri Ranjan; *Price:* $50 Canada non-members; $30 Canada CSBE / SCGAB members
Profile: Peer-reviewed papers
•Canadian Society for Bioengineering Annual Meeting Papers
Frequency: Annually
Profile: Presentations from conferences
•Perspectives: The Newsletter of CSBE [Canadian Society for Bioengineering] / Les Nouvelles de SCGAB
Type: Newsletter
Profile: Canadian Society for Bioengineering / Société canadienne de génie agroalimentaire et de bioingénierie activities,awards, chapter news, job opportunities, & events
•Resource [a publication of the Canadian Society for Bioengineering]
Type: Magazine; *Accepts Advertising*
Profile: Industry news & trends

Canadian Society for Civil Engineering (CSCE) / Société canadienne de génie civil
Parent Name: The Engineering Institute of Canada
4877, rue Sherbrooke ouest, Montréal QC H3Z 1G9
Tel: 514-933-2634; *Fax:* 514-933-3504
e-mail: info@csce.ca
www.csce.ca
Overview: A medium-sized national organization founded in 1887 overseen by The Engineering Institute of Canada
Mission: To develop & maintain high standard of civil engineering practice in Canada; To enhance the public image of the civil engineering profession
Environmental Activity: Establishing environmental & transportation technical divisions; Providing leadership in sustainable infrastructure
Chief Officer(s):
Doug Salloum, Executive Director
doug.salloum@csce.ca
Mahmoud Lardjane, Manager, Programs
mahmoud@csce.ca
Louise Newman, Manager, Communications
louise@csce.ca
Andrea Grimaud, Officer, Membership Liaison
membership@csce.ca
Membership: *Fees:* Schedule available; *Committees:* Infrastructure Renewal; Innovations & IT; International Affairs; Sustainable Development; Career Development; Honours & Fellowships; History
Activities: Offering continuing education & networking opportunities; Working with sister organizations; Promoting civil engineering
Meetings/Conferences:
For more information see Trade Shows, Conferences and Seminars Chapter
Canadian Society for Civil Engineering 2013 Annual General Meeting & Conference
May 2013 Montréal, QC
Publications:
•Canadian Civil Engineer (CCE)
Type: Magazine; *Frequency:* 5 pa; *Accepts Advertising*; *Editor:* Louise Newman; *ISSN:* 9825-7515; *Price:* $35 Canada & U.S.A.; $45 other countries
Profile: Technical activity reports, technical articles, corporate & personal achievement items, & networking news
•Canadian Journal of Civil Engineering (CJCE)
Type: Journal
Profile: Technical journal featuring scholarly papers devoted to civil engineering
•Canadian Society for Civil Engineering Annual Report
Type: Yearbook; *Frequency:* Annually
Profile: Reports from executives such as the president, the president-elect, the executive director, vice-president, committees, & the CSCE Foundation, in addition to theauditor's report & financial statements
•Canadian Society for Civil Engineering E-Bulletin
Type: Newsletter; *Frequency:* Monthly; *Accepts Advertising*
Profile: Featuring current industry & society news, trends, & forthcoming events of interest to over 7,000 subscribers
•Canadian Society for Civil Engineering President's E-Letter
Type: Newsletter; *Frequency:* Monthly
Profile: Information for members of the Canadian Society for Civil Engineering, including forthcoming programs & conferences
•Canadian Society for Civil Engineering Conference Proceedings
Type: Yearbook; *Frequency:* Annually
Profile: Proceedings usually include an abstract book & CD-ROM with details of the society's annual conference
•A Civil Society - A brief personal history of the CSCE [Canadian Society for Civil Engineering]

Canadian Society for Engineering in Agricultural, Food & Biological Systems *See* Canadian Society for Bioengineering

Canadian Society for Horticultural Science (CSHS) / Société canadienne de science horticole (SCSH)
c/o Dept. of Plant & Animal Sciences, Nova Scotia Agricultural College, PO Box 550, Truro NS B2N 5E3
Tel: 902-893-6032; *Fax:* 902-897-9762
www.cshs.ca
Overview: A small national organization founded in 1956
Mission: To advance research, teaching, information, & technology related to all horticultural crops
Chief Officer(s):
Samir C. Debnath, President
samir.debnath@agr.gc.ca
Kris Pruski, Ph.D., Secretary-Treasurer
kpruski@nsac.ca
Membership: *Member Profile:* Scientists; Educators; Extension agents; Industry personnel; Students
Activities: Providing professional development opportunities; Organizing an annual conference & scientific meeting
Publications:
•Canadian Journal of Plant Science (CJPS)
Type: Journal; *Frequency:* Quarterly; *Editor:* Vaino Poysa
Profile: Shared with the Canadian Society of Agronomy (CSA)
•CSHS [Canadian Society for Horticultural Science] Newsletter
Type: Newsletter; *Frequency:* Quarterly
Profile: Society activities, issues, & events
•CSHS [Canadian Society for Horticultural Science] Membership Directory
Type: Directory; *Frequency:* Annually
Profile: Listings of Society members, plus information about governance, committees, & awards
•Program & Abstracts of the CSHS [Canadian Society for Horticultural Science] Annual Conference
Type: Yearbook; *Frequency:* Annually
Profile: The latest horticultural research

Canadian Society for International Health (CSIH) / Société canadienne de la santé internationale
#1105, 1 Nicholas St., Ottawa ON K1N 7B7
Tel: 613-241-5785
e-mail: csih@csih.org
www.csih.org
www.linkedin.com/groups/CSIH-Global-Health-Forum-3671985
www.facebook.com/CSIH.org
twitter.com/globalsante
Previous Name: Canadian Society for Tropical Medicine & International Health
Overview: A medium-sized international charitable organization founded in 1977
Mission: To promote international health & development through mobilization of Canadian resources; To advocate & facilitate research, education, & service activities in international health; To further Canadian strengths of progressive health policy & programming in all fields where global & domestic health concerns meet; To contribute to the evolving global understanding of health & development; *Member of:* Canadian Coalition for Global Health Research
Chief Officer(s):
Karam Ramotar, Co-Chair
Colleen Cash, Co-Chair
Janet Hatcher-Roberts, Executive Director, 613-241-5785 Ext. 302
Finances: *Annual Operating Budget:* $1.5 Million-$3 Million; *Funding Sources:* Membership fees; Contracts; CIDA; Competitive bids
Staff: 11 staff member(s); 30 volunteer(s)
Membership: 400; *Fees:* $50 regular; $25 student/retired/non-wage-earner; *Member Profile:* Persons with interest in health development, tropical medicine, health systems strengthening, & capacity building; *Committees:* Communication; Advocacy; Research
Activities: *Internships:* Yes; *Library:*
Publications:
•Synergy Online
Type: Newsletter; *Frequency:* Monthly
Profile: International health & development information, news bulletins, awards, conference information, & job listings

Canadian Society for Mechanical Engineering (CSME) / Société canadienne de génie mécanique (SCGM)
Parent Name: The Engineering Institute of Canada

1295 Hwy. 2 East, Kingston ON K7L 4V1
Tel: 613-547-5989; *Fax:* 613-547-0195
e-mail: csme@cogeco.ca
www.csme-scgm.ca
Overview: A medium-sized national charitable organization founded in 1970 overseen by The Engineering Institute of Canada
Mission: To benefit Canada & the world by fostering excellence in the practice of mechanical engineering; To support members; Affiliation(s): Engineering Institute of Canada
Chief Officer(s):
Rama B. Bhat, President
Membership: *Fees:* $15 students; $45 retired members; $85 first year membership; $115 professional affiliate; $125 full membership; *Member Profile:* Mechnical engineering personnel; Engineers in other disciplines who are interested in mechanical engineering; *Committees:* Executive; Regional Vice Presidents; Chairs Special; Chairs Standing; Chairs Technical
Activities: Providing continuing education; Arranging networking opportunities
Meetings/Conferences:
For more information see Trade Shows, Conferences and Seminars Chapter
Canadian Society for Mechanical Engineering 2013 24th Biennial Canadian Congress of Applied Mechanics (CANCAM) 2013
Canadian Society for Mechanical Engineering 2014 Congress 2014
Canadian Society for Mechanical Engineering 2015 25th Biennial Canadian Congress of Applied Mechanics (CANCAM) 2015
Publications:
•CSME [Canadian Society for Mechanical Engineering] Bulletin
Type: Newsletter; *Frequency:* 3 pa; *Editor:* Kamran Siddiqui, PhD; *Price:* Free with membership in theCanadian Society for Mechanical Engineering
Profile: News & articles of a general technical nature, covering all aspects of the practice of mechanical engineering
•From Steam to Space. . . Contributions of Mechanical Engineering to Canadian Development
Number of Pages: 400; *Editor:* Andrew H. Wilson; *Price:* $25 softcover; $50 hardcover
Profile: Essays, memoirs, & photographs
•Transactions of the Canadian Society for Mechanical Engineering
Type: Journal; *Frequency:* Quarterly; *Editor:* Paul J. Zsombor-Murray; *ISSN:* 0315-8977; *Price:* $40 / yearfor members of the Canadian Society for Mechanical Engineering
Profile: Scholarly papers of a reference or archival nature in the field of mechanical engineering or related disciplines

Canadian Society for Molecular Biology (CSBM) / Société canadienne de biologie moléculaire
Parent Name: Canadian Federation of Biological Societies

c/o Rofail Conference & Management Services, 17 Dossetter Way, Ottawa ON K1G 4S3
Tel: 613-421-7229; *Fax:* 613-421-9811
e-mail: contact@csmb-scbm.ca
www.csmb-scbm.ca
Previous Name: Canadian Biochemical Society
Merged from: Canadian Society for Biochemistry & Molecular & Cellular Biology and Genetics Society of Canada
Overview: A medium-sized national organization founded in 1958 overseen by Canadian Federation of Biological Societies
Chief Officer(s):
James Davie, President
Arthur Hilliker, Vice President
Finances: *Annual Operating Budget:* $100,000-$250,000; *Funding Sources:* Membership fees
Staff: 12 volunteer(s)
Membership: 100 student + 50 senior/lifetime + 650 other; *Member Profile:* Demonstrated interest in biochemistry research
Activities: *Internships:* Yes; *Rents Mailing List:* Yes
Publications:
•CSBMCB [The Canadian Society of Biochemistry, Molecular & Cellular Biology] Bulletin
Type: Newsletter
Profile: CSBMCB activites, meeting minutes, lectures, awards, & news from member departments

Canadian Society for the Study of Allergy; Canadian Academy of Allergy *See* Canadian Society of Allergy & Clinical Immunology

Canadian Society for the Study of Practical Ethics (CSSPE) / Société canadienne pour l'étude de l'éthique appliquée (SCEEA)

c/o Dept. of Philosophy, #618, Jorgenson Hall, Ryerson Univ., 350 Victoria St., Toronto ON M5B 2K3
Tel: 416-979-5000; *Fax:* 416-979-5362
www.csspe.ca
Overview: A small national organization founded in 1987
Mission: To study all areas of practical ethics, including environmental ethics, health care ethics, bioethics, & business ethics
Chief Officer(s):
Philip MacEwen, President
pmacewen@yorku.ca
Sandra Tomsons, Vice-President
stomsons@mts.net
Angela White, Secretary-Treasurer
awhite33@uwo.ca
Membership: *Member Profile:* Persons interested in practical ethics, from a variety of fields, such as academia, business, & the civil service
Activities: Addressing ethical issues which arise in areas of learning & activitiy, such as the social sciences & professions

Canadian Society for Tropical Medicine & International Health *See* Canadian Society for International Health

Canadian Society of Agronomy

S.C. Sheppard, PO Box 637, Pinawa MB R0E 1L0
Tel: 204-753-2747; *Fax:* 204-753-8478
e-mail: sheppards@ecomatters.com
www.agronomycanada.com
Overview: A medium-sized national organization
Mission: The mission of The Canadian Society of Agronomy is dedicated to enhancing cooperation and coorindation among agronomists, to recognizing significant achievements in agronomy and to providing the oppourtunity to report and evaluate information pertinent to agronomy in Canada. The goals and objects include networking; external relations and awareness; and internal communications and coordination.; *Member of:* Agricultural Institute of Canada
Chief Officer(s):
Steve Sheppard, Executive Director
sheppards@ecomatters.com
Membership: 300

Canadian Society of Air Safety Investigators (CSASI)

139 West 13th Ave., Vancouver BC V5Y 1V8
e-mail: avsafe@shaw.ca
www.beyondriskmgmt.com
Overview: A small international organization founded in 1975
Mission: To ensure air safety through investigation; Affiliation(s): International Society of Air Safety Investigators
Chief Officer(s):
Barbara M. Dunn, President
Elaine M. Parker, Vice-President
Membership: *Fees:* $100 annual fee; $65 initiation fee; $25 student annual fee; $20 student initiation fee; *Member Profile:* Canadian aircraft accident investigators; Students
Publications:
•Canadian Society of Air Safety Investigators Proceedings
Price: Free with CSASA membership
Profile: Papers presented at each seminar
•Canadian Society of Air Safety Investigators Newsletter
Type: Newsletter; *Price:* Free with CSASA membership
•ISASI Forum
Frequency: Quarterly; *Price:* Free with CSASA membership

Canadian Society of Allergy & Clinical Immunology (CSACI) / Société canadienne d'allergie et d'immunologie clinique

PO Box 51045, Orleans ON K1E 3W4
Tel: 613-986-5869; *Fax:* 866-839-7501
e-mail: info@csaci.ca
www.csaci.ca
Previous Name: Canadian Society for the Study of Allergy; Canadian Academy of Allergy
Overview: A small national organization founded in 1945
Mission: To ensure optimal patient care by advancing the knowledge & practice of allergy, clinical immunology, & asthma
Chief Officer(s):
Paul Keith, President
Sandy Kapur, Vice-President
David Fischer, Secretary-Treasurer
Finances: *Funding Sources:* Donations; Sponsorships
Membership: 475+; *Member Profile:* Clinical immunologists; Allergists; Asthma specialists; Allied health professionals; Medical students; Persons interested in the research & treatment of allergic diseases
Activities: Conducting research; Engaging in advocacy activities; Offering continuing professional development; Providing education to the public
Publications:
•Allergy, Asthma & Clinical Immunology: Official Journal of the Canadian Society of Allergy & Clinical Immunology
Type: Journal; *Frequency:* Quarterly; *Editor:* Richard Warrington
Profile: Articles to further the understanding & treatment of allergic &immunologic disease
•CSACI [Canadian Society of Allergy & Clinical Immunology] Newsletter / Bulletin CSAIC
Type: Newsletter; *Frequency:* Bimonthly
Profile: CSACI activities, events, & awards

Canadian Society of Animal Science (CSAS) / Société canadienne de science animale

c/o Agriculture & Agri-Food Canada Research Station, CP 90, #2000, rte 108 est, Sherbrooke QC J1M 1Z3
Tél: 819-565-9171; *Téléc:* 819-564-5507
Courriel: info@aic.ca
www.csas.net
Aperçu: *Dimension:* moyenne; *Envergure:* nationale; fondée en 1951
Mission: To provide opportunities to discuss the problems of the Canadian animal & poultry industries, with the objective of furthering advancements in these industries; To assist in the coordination of research, teaching & technology transfer related to the animal & poultry industries; To encourage publication of scientific information; To provide an annual forum for professionals in the agricultural industry to meet & discuss the most recent technological advancements in the field of animal & poultry science; *Membre de:* Agricultural Institute of Canada
Membre(s) du bureau directeur:
Karen Schwartzkopf-Genswein, President, 403-317-3354, Fax: 403-382-3156
karen.genswein@agr.gc.ca
Marie-France Palin, Secretary-Treasurer, 819-565-9174 Ext. 207, Fax: 819-564-5507
mariefrance.palin@agr.gc.ca
Membre: 500-999; *Critères d'admissibilite:* Membership is open to persons currently or previously employed in research, teaching, administration, extension, production, marketing, or otherwise interested in any field pertaining to the animal industry. There are three categories for membership; regular, retired, or student members (undergraduate or graduate).; *Comités:* Awards; Membership

Canadian Society of Clinical Chemists (CSCC) / Société canadienne des clinico-chimistes

PO Box 1570, #310, 4 Cataraqui St., Kingston ON K7K 1Z7
Tel: 613-531-8899; *Fax:* 866-303-0626
e-mail: office@cscc.ca
www.cscc.ca
Overview: A medium-sized national organization founded in 1965
Mission: To establish standards for diagnostic services in the practice of clinical biochemistry & clinical laboratory medicine
Chief Officer(s):
Edward Randell, President
Elizabeth Hooper, Executive Director
Ronald Booth, Treasurer
Membership: *Member Profile:* Clinical biochemists throughout Canada
Activities: Providing leadership, education, & research in the practice of clinical biochemistry & clinical laboratory medicine; Liaising with goverment, industry, & healthcare associations; Engaging in advocacy activities
Meetings/Conferences:
For more information see Trade Shows, Conferences and Seminars Chapter
2013 Joint Canadian Society of Clinical Chemists-American Association for Clinical Chemistry Conference
July 2013 Houston, TX
2014 Canadian Society of Clinical Chemists Conference
June 2014 Charlottetown, PE
Publications:
•Canadian Society of Clinical Chemists Member Handbook
Type: Yearbook; *Frequency:* Annually
•Clinical Biochemistry
Type: Journal; *Editor:* Edgard E. Delvin; *ISSN:* 0009-9120

Profile: Analytical & clinical investigative articles related to molecular biology, chemistry, biochemistry, immunology, clinical investigation, diagnosis, therapy, & monitoring humandisease, for chemists, immunologists, biologists, & biochemists
•The CSCC [Canadian Society of Clinical Chemists] News
Type: Newsletter
Profile: Society activities & information for CSCC members

Canadian Society of Environmental Biologists (CSEB) / Société canadienne des biologistes de l'environnement

PO Box 962, Stn. F, Toronto ON M4Y 2N9
www.cseb-scbe.org
Overview: A medium-sized national charitable organization founded in 1943
Mission: To further the conservation of natural resources of Canada & to promote the prudent management of these resources so as to minimize adverse environmental effects; to ensure high professional standards in education, research & management related to resources & environment; to advance the education of the public & to protect public interest on matters pertaining to the use of natural resources & the protection & management of the environment; to undertake environmental research & education programs; to assess & evaluate administrative & legislative policies having ecological significance in terms of conservation of resources & quality of the environment; to develop & promote policies that seek to achieve balance among resource management & utilization, protection of the environment & quality of life; to foster liaison among environmental biologists working within governmental, industrial & educational frameworks across Canada
Chief Officer(s):
Robert Stedwill, President, 306-585-1854
rstedwill@live.ca
Finances: *Annual Operating Budget:* Less than $50,000; *Funding Sources:* Membership dues
Staff: 2 staff member(s); 30 volunteer(s)
Membership: 500; *Fees:* $35; *Member Profile:* Regular - graduate from college or university in discipline of biological sciences, professionally engaged in teaching, management or research related to natural resources & the environment; Student - persons enrolled in accredited college or university in discipline of biological sciences & preparing themselves for professional work in teaching, management or research related to natural resources; Associate - supporters in general
Activities: *Speaker Service:* Yes; *Rents Mailing List:* Yes
Publications:
•CSEB [Canadian Society of Environmental Biologists] National Newsletter / Bulletin
Type: Newsletter; *Frequency:* Quarterly; *Accepts Advertising*; *Editor:* Gary Ash; *ISSN:* 0318-5133; *Price:* Free with Canadian Society of Environmental Biologistsmembership
Profile: CSEB activities, & national & regional news, for members

Canadian Society of Exploration Geophysicists (CSEG)

#600, 640 - 8th Ave. SW, Calgary AB T2P 1G7
Tel: 403-262-0015
e-mail: cseg.office@shaw.ca
www.cseg.ca
Overview: A medium-sized national organization founded in 1949
Mission: To promote the science of geophysics; Affiliation(s): Society of Exploration Geophysicists (USA); European Association of Geoscientists & Engineers
Chief Officer(s):
John Townsley, President
jtownsley@arcresources.com
Larry Herd, Vice-President
larryh@boydpetro.com
Jim Racette, Managing Director, 403-262-0015, Fax: 403-262-7383
jimra@shaw.ca
John Fernando, Director, Educational Services
john.fernando@sait.ca
Kelly Jamison, Director, Finance
kelly.jamison@divestco.com
Kristy Manchul, Director, Communications
kristy.manchul@cggveritas.com
Dave Nordin, Director, Member Service
denordin@telusplanet.net
Finances: *Funding Sources:* Membership fees
Membership: 1,800; *Member Profile:* Geophysicists involved in hydrocarbon exploration; Geologists; Field specialists; Technical specialists; Academics; Interested industry personnel; Corporate members
Activities: Offering a mentorship program; Exchanging technical information; Providing networking activities
Meetings/Conferences:
For more information see Trade Shows, Conferences and Seminars Chapter
Canadian Society of Exploration Geophysicists, Canadian Society of Petroleum Geologists & Canadian Well Logging Society 2013 Joint Annual Convention
2013
Canadian Society of Exploration Geophysicists, Canadian Society of Petroleum Geologists & Canadian Well Logging Society 2014 Joint Annual Convention
2014
Publications:
•Canadian Society of Exploration Geophysicists Annual Report
Type: Yearbook; *Frequency:* Annually
•The CSEG / CSPG Geophysical Atlas of Western Canadian Hydrocarbon Pools
Type: Atlas; *Editor:* Leonard V. Hills
•Recorder
Type: Magazine; *Frequency:* Monthly; *Accepts Advertising*
Profile: Canadian Society of Exploration Geophysicists membership news, & events, plus articles related to geophysics

Canadian Society of Forest Engineers *See* Canadian Institute of Forestry

Canadian Society of Landscape Architects (CSLA) / Association des architectes paysagistes du Canada (AAPC)

PO Box 13594, Ottawa ON K2K 1X6
Tel: 866-781-9799; *Fax:* 866-871-1419
e-mail: info@csla.ca
www.csla.ca
Overview: A medium-sized national organization founded in 1934
Mission: To support the improvement &/or conservation of the natural, cultural, social & built environment; to promote visibility, recognition, acceptance & understanding of the profession by communicating its value in relation to that of the public good; Affiliation(s): International Federation of Landscape Architects; Landscape Alliance
Chief Officer(s):
Elizabeth A. Sharpe, Executive Director
executive-director@csla.ca
Finances: *Annual Operating Budget:* $100,000-$250,000; *Funding Sources:* Membership dues
Staff: 40 volunteer(s)
Membership: 1,250 individuals; *Fees:* $115; *Member Profile:* Qualified & experienced landscape architects who practise their profession by providing a variety of services ranging from advice, consultation & design to preparing working drawings, contract documents & supervising the implementation of various size construction projects
Meetings/Conferences:
For more information see Trade Shows, Conferences and Seminars Chapter
2014 Canadian Society of Landscape Architects Congress
May 2014 Ottawa, ON
Publications:
•CSLA [Canadian Society of Landscape Architects] Bulletin
Type: Newsletter; *Frequency:* Monthly
Profile: News & events related to landscape architecture in Canada
•CSLA [Canadian Society of Landscape Architects] Membership Directory
Type: Directory
•CSLA [Canadian Society of Landscape Architects] Annual Report
Type: Yearbook; *Frequency:* Annually
•Landscapes / Paysages
Type: Journal; *Frequency:* Quarterly; *Accepts Advertising*
Profile: Articles about the professional practice of landscape architecture in Canada, related to culture, design, & the environment

Canadian Society of Microbiologists (CSM) / Société canadienne des microbiologistes

CSM-SCM Secretariat, 17 Dossetter Way, Ottawa ON K1G 4S3
Tel: 613-421-7229; *Fax:* 613-421-9811
e-mail: info@csm-scm.org
www.csm-scm.org
Overview: A medium-sized national organization founded in 1958
Mission: To advance microbiology in all its aspects; to facilitate interchange of ideas between microbiologists; Affiliation(s): Youth Science Foundation; International Union of Microbiological Societies
Chief Officer(s):
Ivan Oresnik, President
Ayush Kumar, Secretary-Treasurer
Finances: *Annual Operating Budget:* $100,000-$250,000
Staff: 2 staff member(s)
Membership: 450; *Fees:* $75; *Member Profile:* open; *Committees:* Education; Manpower Placement; Science Policy; Regulatory Issues
Meetings/Conferences:
For more information see Trade Shows, Conferences and Seminars Chapter
The Canadian Society of Microbiologists 63rd Annual Conference
June 2013 Ottawa, ON
Publications:
•Canadian Society of Microbiologists Call for Abstracts
Type: Booklet; *Frequency:* Annually
Profile: Published in advance of the Annual General Meeting in November / December
•Canadian Society of Microbiologists Programme & Abstracts
Frequency: Annually
Profile: Published for the Annual General Meeting each May
•Canadian Society of Microbiologists Graduate Studies & Membership Directory
Type: Directory; *Frequency:* Biennially
•CSM [Canadian Society of Microbiologists] Newsletter
Type: Newsletter; *Frequency:* 3 pa

Canadian Society of Petroleum Geologists (CSPG)

#110, 333 - 5th Ave. SW, Calgary AB T2P 1G7
Tel: 403-264-5610; *Fax:* 403-264-5898
e-mail: cspg@cspg.org
www.cspg.org
www.linkedin.com/groups/Canadian-Society-Petroleum-Geologists-4153517
www.facebook.com/CSPGOnline
Previous Name: Alberta Society of Petroleum Geologists
Overview: A medium-sized national organization founded in 1929
Mission: To advance the science of geology, especially as it relates to petroleum, natural gas & other fossil fuels; to promote the technology of exploration for finding & producing these resources; to foster the spirit of scientific research; to develop a sense of pride & community among Canadian Petroleum Geologists; to provide the means to ensure that the Canadian Petroleum Geologist is the best trained, best supported & most skillful practitioner in the world
Chief Officer(s):
Lis Bjeld, Executive Director, 403-513-1235
lis.bjeld@cspg.org
Finances: *Annual Operating Budget:* $250,000-$500,000; *Funding Sources:* Membership dues; publications; programs; trust fund
Staff: 3 staff member(s); 300 volunteer(s)
Membership: 3,500; *Fees:* $65; $20 students; $500 corporate
Activities: Education trust fund; member programs
Awards:
•CSPG Graduate Scholarships (Scholarship)
Three scholarships available (Atlantic, Ontario/Québec & Western) in petroleum geology, one in marine geoscience; awarded to a second year graduate student *Deadline:* May *Amount:* $1,500
Publications:
•The Bulletin of Canadian Petroleum Geology
Type: Journal; *Frequency:* Quarterly; *Accepts Advertising*; *Editor:* Denise Then; *ISSN:* 0007-4802; *Price:* $120 Canada; $140USA; $170 International
Profile: Peer-reviewed scientific articles, technical papers, book reviews, & debates of interest to the Canadian petroleum geoscience community
•Canadian Society of Petroleum Geologists Calendar
Frequency: Annually
Profile: Photographs & CSPG, CSEG, APEGGA, & CWLS events
•Digital Atlas: Geological Atlas of the Western Canada Sedimentary Basin
Profile: Created by CSPG & the Alberta Geologic Survey (AGS)
•Reservoir [a publication of the Canadian Society of Petroleum Geologists]
Type: Magazine; *Frequency:* 11 pa; *Accepts Advertising*; *Editor:* Heather Tyminski; *Price:* $60 Canada; $70 USA;

$80International
Profile: Industry articles & commentaries, conferences, upcoming events, & awards of interest to CSPG members

Canadian Society of Plant Physiologists (CSPP) / Société canadienne de physiologie végétale (SCPV)

c/o Dr. Harold Weger, Department of Biology, University of Regina, 3737 Wascana Pkwy., Regina SK S4S 0A2
www.cspp-scpv.ca
twitter.com/cspbscbv
Overview: A small national organization founded in 1958
Mission: To promote the teaching & public awareness of plant physiology in Canada
Chief Officer(s):
Rob Guy, Senior Director
seniordirector@cspp-scpvca.ca
Bill Plaxton, President
president@cspp-scpvca.ca
Barry Micallef, Secretary
secretary@cspp-scpvca.ca
Harold G. Weger, Treasurer
treasurer@cspp-scpvca.ca
Membership: *Member Profile:* Plant scientists in Canada; Retired members; Students; Persons who live outside Canada are eligible for corresponding membership; *Committees:* Society (Gold) Medal Award; C.D. Nelson Award; David J. Gifford Tree Physiology Award; Gleb Krotkov Award; Ann Oaks Scholarship; Ragai Ibrahim Award; Communications; Education; Meeting Site; Nominating; Auditors
Activities: Facilitating the exchange of information; Promoting the importance of research in plant sciences; Liaising with other educational, non-profi, or governmental agencies or organizations to develop the science of plant physiology
Publications:
•Canadian Society of Plant Physiologists Membership List
•CSPP [Canadian Society of Plant Physiologists] / SCPV [Société canadienne de physiologie végétale] Bulletin
Type: Newsletter; *Frequency:* Semiannually; *Editor:* Gordon Gray; *ISSN:* 1183-9597
Profile: Issues related to plant biology, & CSPP / SCPV events, activites, awards, & financialinformation, of interest to society members

Canadian Society of Safety Engineering, Inc. (CSSE) / Société canadienne de la santé et de la sécurité, inc.

39 River St., Toronto ON M5A 3P1
Tel: 416-646-1600; *Fax:* 416-646-9460
www.csse.org
www.linkedin.com/groups?gid=1558517
www.facebook.com/39373429711
twitter.com/csse
Previous Name: Ontario Society of Safety Engineering
Overview: A medium-sized national organization founded in 1949
Mission: To be the voice of safety in Canada; Affiliation(s): American Society of Safety Engineers
Chief Officer(s):
Wayne Glover, Executive Director
wglover@csse.org
Peter Sturm, President
president@csse.org
Finances: *Annual Operating Budget:* $250,000-$500,000; *Funding Sources:* Membership dues; educational programs
Staff: 7 staff member(s); 50 volunteer(s)
Membership: 30 associate + 100 student + 45 senior/lifetime + 2,000 individual; *Fees:* $150; *Member Profile:* Open to those employed full-time in occupational health, safety & environment work
Activities: Certification program for Health & Safety Consultant; *Awareness Events:* Canadian Occupational Health & Safety Week, 1st week of June; *Speaker Service:* Yes; *Rents Mailing List:* Yes
Meetings/Conferences:
For more information see Trade Shows, Conferences and Seminars Chapter
Canadian Society of Safety Engineering (CSSE) 2013 Professional Development Conference
September 2013 Montréal, QC
Publications:
•CSSE [Canadian Society of Safety Engineering, Inc.] Contact
Type: Newsletter; *Frequency:* Quarterly; *Price:* Free with CSSE membership; $100 non-members

Canadian Society of Soil Science (CSSS) / Société canadienne de la science du sol

Business Office, PO Box 637, Pinawa MB R0E 1L0
Tel: 204-753-2747; *Fax:* 204-753-8478
e-mail: sheppards@ecomatters.com
www.csss.ca
Overview: A medium-sized national charitable organization
Mission: To be actively engaged in land use, soils research, & classification; *Member of:* Agricultural Institute of Canada; Affiliation(s): International Union of Soil Science
Chief Officer(s):
Gordon Price, President
gprice@nsac.ca
Barbara Cade-Menun, Secretary
barbara.cade-menun@agr.gc.ca
Paul Bullock, Treasurer
bullockp@ms.umanitoba.ca
Finances: *Funding Sources:* Membership dues
Membership: 100-499; *Member Profile:* Open to those concerned with farming practices as they affect soil quality & the development of soil conserving cropping practices, or those concerned with non-agricultural uses of soils, including forestry, engineering, & reclamation
Activities: *Speaker Service:* Yes
Publications:
•Canadian Journal of Soil Science
Type: Journal; *Frequency:* Quarterly; *Editor:* Dr. F.J. Larney
Profile: International peer-reviewed original research related to the development, structure, use, & management of soils
•CSSS [Canadian Society of Soil Science] Newsletter
Type: Newsletter; *Frequency:* 3 pa; *Price:* Free with CSSS membership
Profile: CSSS activities, awards, events, & reports

Canadian Society of Zoologists (CSZ) / Société canadienne de zoologie (SCZ)

c/o Biology Department, University of Western Ontario, London ON N6A 5B7
Tel: 519-661-3869
www.csz-scz.ca
Overview: A medium-sized national organization founded in 1961
Mission: To promote advancement & public awareness of zoology; To facilitate sharing of knowledge & ideas among all persons interested in science & practice of zoology; To organize discussions & debates of general interest; Affiliation(s): Canadian Council on Animal Care; Canadian Federation of Biological Societies
Chief Officer(s):
Helga Guderley, Secretary, 418-656-2131 Ext. 3184, Fax: 418-656-2043
helga.guderley@bio.ulaval.ca
Louise Milligan, President
milligan@uwo.ca
Finances: *Funding Sources:* Membership fees
Membership: 373; *Fees:* $80 regular; $20 student, associate, & emeritus; *Member Profile:* Working in zoology; *Committees:* Membership; Recognition; Science Policy; Biodiversity; Animal Care Advisory; Collections Advisory; Outstanding Ph.D. Thesis; Communications; Nominating
Awards:
•CSZ Public Awarensss Award - Public Education Prize (Award)
Intended to recognize excellent in public education about zoology *Amount:* $300
•Helen Battle Award (Award)
Cash prize & scroll, given for the best student poster at the Annual Conference *Amount:* $200
•Leo Margolis Scholarship (Scholarship)
Presented to a Canadian who is registered in a graduate studies program at a Canadian university, whose research is in the field of fisheries biology *Amount:* $500
•CSZ Student Research Grant (Grant)
To assist students & post-doctoral fellows from Canadian Universities to conduct zoological research *Amount:* Up to $500
•CSZ Public Awareness Award; Best issue driven popular press article (Award)
Cash prize & scroll, intended to encourage & stimulate members to increase public awarenss of zoology through articles in the popular press *Amount:* $500
•Fry Award - Outstanding Biologist of the Year (Award)
Receives the Fry Medal, delivers the Fry Lecture at the AGM, full travel expenses are reimbursed
•Fry Award & Medal - Outstanding Zoologist of the Year (Award)
Recipient receives the Fry Medal, delivers the Fry Lecture at the Annual Meeting
•CSZ Distinguished Service Medal (Award)
Scroll & medal, presented at the AGM; recogizing members who have contributed to the well being of zoology in Canada, by working hard for the CSZ
•T.W.M. Cameron Outstanding Ph.D. Thesis Award (Award)
Recipient is invited to present a lecture of their dissertation to the AGM
•Hoar Award (Award)
Cash prize & scroll given for the best student paper presented orally at the Annual Conference *Amount:* $500
•CSZ New Investigator Award (Award)
Scroll & cash award to an individual, who since professional appointment, has made a significant contribution to zoology & may be considered a 'rising star' in their field *Amount:* Up to $500
Meetings/Conferences:
For more information see Trade Shows, Conferences and Seminars Chapter
Canadian Society of Zoologists 2013 52nd Annual Congress
May 2013 Guelph, ON
Publications:
•Canadian Society of Zoologists / Société canadienne de zoologie Bulletin
Type: Newsletter; *Frequency:* 3 pa; *Editor:* Sally Leys; *ISSN:* 0319-6674; *Price:* Free with CSZ / SCZ membership
Profile: CSZ / SCZ reports, events, articles, & interviews

Canadian Solar Industries Association

#605, 150 Isabella St., Ottawa ON K1S 1V7
Tel: 613-736-9077; *Fax:* 613-736-8938
Toll-Free: 866-522-6742
e-mail: info@cansia.ca
www.cansia.ca
www.linkedin.com/groups/Canadian-Solar-Industries-Association-4208965
www.facebook.com/cansia
twitter.com/CanadianSIA
Also Known As: CanSIA
Overview: A medium-sized national organization founded in 1978
Mission: To develop a strong Canadian solar energy industry; To act as the voice for the solar energy industry in Canada
Environmental Activity: Promoting the sustainable growth of solar energy throughout Canada; Researching & developing renewable energy policy options; Producing Solar in Canada fact sheets & brochures
Chief Officer(s):
Michelle Chislett, Chair
John A. Gorman, President, 613-736-9077 Ext. 223
Wesley Johnston, Director, Policy & Research, 613-736-9077 Ext. 224
David Samuel, Director, Member Services & Operations, 613-736-9077 Ext. 225
Tiffany Shields, Administrator, Services & Communications, 613-736-9077 Ext. 228
Membership: 650 companies; *Member Profile:* Solar energy companies across Canada
Activities: Offering education & networking events for members; Liaising with federal & provincial governments
Meetings/Conferences:
For more information see Trade Shows, Conferences and Seminars Chapter
Canadian Solar Industries Association 2013 Game Changer Awards Gala
2013
Canadian Solar Industries Association 2013 Solar West Conference & Showcase
October 2013 Calgary, AB
Canadian Solar Industries Association 2013 Solar Canada Conference & Exposition
December 2013 Toronto, ON
Canadian Solar Industries Association 2014 Solar West Conference & Showcase
2014
Canadian Solar Industries Association 2014 Solar Canada Conference & Exposition
2014
Publications:
•Canadian Solar Industries Association Member Directory
Type: Directory; *Accepts Advertising*
Profile: A buyers' guide of companies & organizations across Canada involved in solar thermal & photovoltaics (PV) technologies

•Solar Beat Newsletter
Type: Newsletter; *Frequency:* Bimonthly
Profile: News from the solar industry
•SOLutions Magazine [a publication of the Canadian Solar Industries Association]
Type: Magazine; *Frequency:* Semiannually; *Accepts Advertising*
Profile: Information from the Canadian Solar Industries Association

Canadian Space Society (CSS) / La société canadienne de l'espace

Bldg. E, PO Box 70009, Stn. Rimrock Plaza, 1115 Lodestar Rd., Toronto ON M3J 0H3
www.css.ca
Overview: A small national organization founded in 1983
Mission: To conduct technical & outreach projects; to promote the involvement of Canadians in space development
Chief Officer(s):
Kevin Shortt, President
president@css.ca
Marc Fricker, Vice-President
vp@css.ca
Gary McQueen, Treasurer
treasurer@css.ca
Membership: *Fees:* $75 professional; $40 students; *Member Profile:* Professionals & individuals interested in the exploration of the solar system, including engineers, teachers, environmentalists, & writers
Activities: Increasing knowledge of space & space-related technologies among members & the public; Providing feedback to the government on legislation that impacts Canadian space development
Publications:
•Canadian Space Gazette
Frequency: Quarterly; *Accepts Advertising*
Profile: Current affairs in space development & exploration of interest to the Canadian space community

Canadian Special Crops Association (CSCA)

#1215, 220 Portage Ave., Winnipeg MB R3C 0A5
Tel: 204-925-3780; *Fax:* 204-925-4454
e-mail: office@specialcrops.mb.ca
www.specialcrops.mb.ca
Overview: A medium-sized national organization founded in 1987
Mission: To encourage sustainable growth in the pulse industry by facilitating relations with growers
Membership: 110+; *Fees:* Schedule available; *Member Profile:* Companies involved in the merchandising of Canadian pulse & special crops

Canadian Sphagnum Peat Moss Association (CSPMA) / Association canadienne Tourbe de Sphaigne

#2208, 13 Mission Ave., St Albert AB T8N 1H6
Tel: 780-460-8280; *Fax:* 780-459-0939
e-mail: cspma@peatmoss.com
www.peatmoss.com
Overview: A medium-sized national organization founded in 1988
Mission: To promote the benefits of peat moss to horticulturists and home gardeners throughout North America.; *Member of:* Canadian Society of Association Executives
Environmental Activity: Restoration & restoration research
Chief Officer(s):
Paul Short, President
Finances: *Annual Operating Budget:* $250,000-$500,000; *Funding Sources:* Membership dues
Staff: 2 staff member(s)
Membership: 18 producers; *Member Profile:* Producer/broker of Canadian peat moss; supplier to industry
Meetings/Conferences:
For more information see Trade Shows, Conferences and Seminars Chapter
Canadian Sphagnum Peat Moss Association (CSPMA) 25th Annual General Meeting
November 2013 Montréal, QC

Canadian Standards Association (CSA)

#100, 5060 Spectrum Way, Mississauga ON L4W 5N6
Tel: 416-747-4000; *Fax:* 416-747-2473
Toll-Free: 800-463-6727
e-mail: member@csa.ca
www.csa.ca
Overview: A medium-sized national organization
Mission: To develop new standards & codes to meet needs, such as public health & safety & the facilitation of trade; To contribute to the global harmonization of standards; To serve government, industry, business, & consumers in Canada & the worldwide marketplace; *Member of:* CSA Group
Environmental Activity: Establishing standards which will help to preserve the environment
Chief Officer(s):
Bonnie Rose, President
Finances: *Funding Sources:* Sponsorships
Activities: Presenting e-learning, seminars, & training opportunities, through the CSA Learning Centre, to assist people to understand standards; Reviewing & considering adopted & adapted standards from other organizations & countries
Meetings/Conferences:
For more information see Trade Shows, Conferences and Seminars Chapter
Canadian Standards Association 2013 Annual Conference & Committee Week
June 2013 Calgary, AB
Canadian Standards Association 2014 Annual Conference & Committee Week
June 2014 Charlottetown, PE
Publications:
•Canadian Standards Association Annual Report
Type: Yearbook; *Frequency:* Annually
Profile: A review of the association's activities for the past year
•Perspectives [a publication of the Canadian Standards Association]
Type: Newsletter; *Editor:* James Harrison
Profile: Current information about standards development initiatives for members

Canadian Steel Construction Council (CSCC) / Conseil canadien de la construction en acier

#300, 201 Consumers Rd., Toronto ON M2J 4G8
Tel: 416-491-9898; *Fax:* 416-491-6461
Previous Name: Canadian Steel Industries Construction Council
Overview: A medium-sized national organization founded in 1960
Mission: To represent the manufacturers of steel products, including: open-web steel joists, steel platework, corrugated steel pipe, sheet steel, & steel fasteners; to promote the use of steel in construction through research & engineering; Affiliation(s): Canadian Institute of Steel Construction; Steel Structures Education Foundation
Membership: 9; *Committees:* Codes & Standards; Fire Protection
Activities: *Speaker Service:* Yes; *Library:*

Canadian Steel Industries Construction Council *See* Canadian Steel Construction Council

Canadian Steel Partnership Council (CSPC)

#407, 350 Sparks St., Ottawa ON K1R 7S8
Tel: 613-238-6049; *Fax:* 613-238-1832
Overview: A small national organization
Mission: To address the global competitiveness & sustainability of the Canadian steel industry; Affiliation(s): Canadian Steel Producers Association
Chief Officer(s):
Ron Watkins, President, CSPA

Canadian Steel Producers Association (CSPA) / Association canadienne des producteurs d'acier (ACPA)

#906, 350 Sparks St., Ottawa ON K1R 7S8
Tel: 613-238-6049; *Fax:* 613-238-1832
e-mail: info@canadiansteel.ca
www.canadiansteel.ca
www.facebook.com/220022834730294
twitter.com/CSPA_ACPA
Overview: A medium-sized national organization founded in 1986
Mission: To represent the steel producers that melt & pour steel in Canada
Chief Officer(s):
Ron Watkins, President
Finances: *Annual Operating Budget:* $500,000-$1.5 Million; *Funding Sources:* Membership dues
Staff: 4 staff member(s)
Membership: 17; *Committees:* Communications; Environment; Climate Change; Statistics; Trade; Research & Development

Canadian Sugar Beet Producers' Association Inc. (CSBPA)

Parent Name: Canadian Federation of Agriculture
4900 - 50 St., Taber AB T1G 1T3
Tel: 403-223-1110; *Fax:* 403-223-1022
e-mail: sugarmb@telusplanet.net
Overview: A medium-sized national organization founded in 1943 overseen by Canadian Federation of Agriculture
Mission: To represent interests of Canadian sugar beet growers on provincial & federal government levels & on an international level through the World Association of Beet & Cane Growers; to raise public profile of the beet sugar industry.; Affiliation(s): World Association of Beet & Cane Growers
Chief Officer(s):
Bruce Webster, General Manager
sugarmb@telusplanet.net
Finances: *Annual Operating Budget:* $250,000-$500,000
Staff: 2 staff member(s)
Membership: 470; *Member Profile:* Member must be sugar beet grower.; *Committees:* Executive

Canadian Swine Breeders' Association (CSBA) / L'Association canadienne des éleveurs de porcs

Bldg 54, Central Experiemental Farm, 930 Carling Ave., Ottawa ON K1A 0C6
Tel: 613-731-5531; *Fax:* 613-233-8903
e-mail: canswine@canswine.ca
www.canswine.ca
Previous Name: Purebred Swine Breeders' Association of Canada
Overview: A medium-sized national organization founded in 1889
Mission: To improve & promote Canadian purebred swine; to lobby on behalf of purebred swine breeders in Canada; to direct & regulate purebred swine industry; to be involved in registration & transfer of following breeds: Berkshire, British Saddleback, Chester White, Duroc, Hampshire, Large Black, Pietrain, Poland China, Spotted, Tamworth, Welsh, Yorkshire, Landrace, Lacombe, Red Wattle (registration forms can be obtained from Canadian Livestock Records Corporation).
Chief Officer(s):
Brian Sullivan, General Manager
brian@canswine.ca
Finances: *Annual Operating Budget:* $100,000-$250,000
Staff: 3 staff member(s)
Membership: 120; *Fees:* Schedule available; *Member Profile:* Four classes: honorary, life, annual, non-resident; *Committees:* Promotion

Canadian Swine Exporters Association (CSEA)

#2, 408 Dundas St., Woodstock ON N4S 1B9
Tel: 519-421-0997; *Fax:* 519-421-0887
e-mail: csea@rogers.com
www.canadianswine.com
Overview: A small national organization
Mission: To assist the Canadian swine industry promote & market swine genetics worldwide
Chief Officer(s):
Rosemary Smart, Intl Marketing Programs Coordinator
Membership: 19; *Member Profile:* Represents the top exporters from Canada

Canadian Transport Tariff Bureau Association *See* Freight Carriers Association of Canada

Canadian Transportation Research Forum (CTRF) / Groupe de recherches sur les transports au Canada

PO Box 23033, Woodstock ON N4T 1R0
Tel: 519-421-9701; *Fax:* 519-421-9319
e-mail: feedback@ctrf.ca, cawoudsma@ctrf.ca
www.ctrf.ca
Overview: A medium-sized national charitable organization founded in 1967
Mission: To promote the development of research in transportation & related fields; to publish research papers through media & through national & regional forum meetings.
Chief Officer(s):
Doug Johnson, President
Carole Ann Woudsma, Secretary
Malcolm Cairns, Executive Vice-President
Mark Hemmes, Vice-President External
Gerry Kolaitis, VP Finance/Treasurer
Vijay Gill, Vice-President Program/Publications
Linda McAusland, Vice-President Meetings
Gordon E. Tufts, VP Organization/Development
Finances: *Annual Operating Budget:* Less than $50,000
Staff: 21 volunteer(s)
Membership: 320; *Fees:* $129; *Member Profile:* Open to anyone interested in any aspect of transportation; membership is individual rather than corporate; present membership is drawn from carriers, shippers, consultants & suppliers in the

commercial sector, the policy, regulatory, planning & research environments at all levels of government, students & professors at universitites & community colleges

Canadian Trucking Alliance (CTA) / L'Alliance canadienne du camionnage (ACC)

324 Somerset St. West, Ottawa ON K2P 0J9
Tel: 613-236-9426; *Fax:* 866-823-4076
e-mail: info@cantruck.ca
www.cantruck.com
Overview: A medium-sized national organization founded in 1937
Mission: To promote business excellence in trucking; to participate in the development of public policy which supports the economic growth, safety & prosperity of the industry; to provide services, including research, development, products & information to meet the needs of the industry.
Chief Officer(s):
Dietmar Krause, Chairperson
Paul Landry, President/CEO
Louise Yako, Director Policy/Communications
Michele Nicol, Director Business Programs
Sandra Stashuk, Member Services Coordinator
Susan Van Egdom, Accounting Coordinator
Membership: *Member Profile:* Motor carriers & associated trades
Activities: *Speaker Service:* Yes

Canadian University Service Overseas ***See*** CUSO-VSO

Canadian Urban Transit Association (CUTA) / Association canadienne du transport urbain (ACTU)

#1401, 55 York St., Toronto ON M5J 1R7
Tel: 416-365-9800; *Fax:* 416-365-1295
www.cutaactu.ca
Overview: A large national organization founded in 1904
Mission: To represent the public transit community throughout Canada; To strengthen the industry
Environmental Activity: Strengthening public transit's contributions to the environment & health
Chief Officer(s):
Michael W. Roschlau, President & Chief Executive Officer, 416-365-9800 Ext. 104
Becky Benaissa, Director, Finance & Administration, 416-365-9800 Ext. 108
Patrick Leclerc, Director, Marketing & Public Affairs, 613-788-7982
Paré Jean, Director, Research & Technical Services, 416-365-9800 Ext. 109
Nancy Ortenburg, Director, Training & Membership Development, 416-365-9800 Ext. 102
Maureen Shuell, Director, Events & Publications, 416-365-9800 Ext. 105
Membership: 503; *Member Profile:* Transit systems; Manufacturers & suppliers of transit equipment; Federal, provincial, & municipal government agencies; Consultants; Affiliated individuals & companies; *Committees:* Business Members; Communications & Public Affairs; Human Resources; Technical Services; Transit Board Members
Activities: Conducting research & preparing statistics; Providing technical & operational information; Liaising with government; Partnering with other transportation associations & community development stakeholders; Engaging in advocacy activities; Raising public awareness of transit's contributions to communities; *Library:* Canadian Urban Transit Association Library; Open to public
Meetings/Conferences:
For more information see Trade Shows, Conferences and Seminars Chapter
Canadian Urban Transit Association 2013 Annual Conference
June 2013 St. John's, NL
Canadian Urban Transit Association 2013 Fall Conference & Trans-Expo
November 2013 Calgary, AB
Canadian Urban Transit Association 2014 Annual Conference
June 2014 Gatineau, QC
Canadian Urban Transit Association 2014 Fall Conference & Trans-Expo
November 2014 Niagara Falls, ON
Canadian Urban Transit Association 2015 Annual Conference
May 2015 Winnipeg, MB
Canadian Urban Transit Association 2015 Fall Conference & Trans-Expo
November 2015 Montréal, QC
Canadian Urban Transit Association 2016 Annual Conference
2016 Halifax, NS
Canadian Urban Transit Association 2016 Fall Conference & Trans-Expo
2016 Vancouver, BC
Publications:
•Canadian Transit Forum
Type: Magazine; *Frequency:* Y
Profile: Transit industry news in Canada, plus special conference issues in May/June & November/December
•Canadian Urban Transit Association's Buyer's Guide
Type: Guide
Profile: Products & services organized by categories
•CUTA Membership Directory
Type: Directory; *Frequency:* Annually; *Accepts Advertising*; *Price:* $50
Profile: Specific contact details for transit systems, suppliers, government agencies, consultants, & affiliate members
•EXPRESSions
Type: Newsletter; *Frequency:* Semimonthly
Profile: Association activities & forthcoming events
•Transit Vision 2040
Number of Pages: 74
Profile: An industry vision of the role of public transit in Canada

Canadian Urethane Foam Contractors Association (CUFCA) / Association canadienne des entrepreneurs en mousse de polyuréthane

3200 Wharton Way, Mississauga ON L4X 2C1
Fax: 877-416-3626
Toll-Free: 866-467-7729
e-mail: cufca@cufca.ca
www.cufca.ca
Overview: A small national licensing organization founded in 1985
Mission: To champion the polyurethane foam industry in Canada; To maintain high standards in the industry; to ensure the professionalism & profitability of the industry
Chief Officer(s):
Ryan Dalgleish, Executive Director
Andrew B. Cole, Chair
Jean Doucet, Secretary-Treasurer, 418-679-0497
Membership: *Fees:* $500 general membership & contractors; $3,500 manufacturers; *Member Profile:* Manufacturers; Contractors
Activities: Liaising with government agencies; Encouraging professional development; Providing a quality assurance program; Promoting use of ray polyurethane foam; Facilitating research; Publishing; Implementing standards for materials;

Canadian Urethane Manufacturers Association (CUMA)

PO Box 5281, Penetanguishene ON L9M 2G4
Tel: 705-427-5383; *Fax:* 705-549-8197
www.cumahome.org
Overview: A medium-sized national organization founded in 1974
Chief Officer(s):
Scott Woodworth, President
Noel Campbell, Manager
manager@cumahome.org
Finances: *Annual Operating Budget:* Less than $50,000
Membership: 45 corporate; *Fees:* $375; *Member Profile:* Urethane processors & suppliers; *Committees:* Health; Safety; Environmental
Meetings/Conferences:
For more information see Trade Shows, Conferences and Seminars Chapter
Canadian Urethane Manufacturers Association & Polyurethane Manufacturers Association 2013 Joint Annual General Meeting
May 2013 Las Vegas, NV

Canadian Veterinary Medical Association (CVMA) / Association canadienne des médecins vétérinaires (ACMV)

339 Booth St., Ottawa ON K1R 7K1
Tel: 613-236-1162; *Fax:* 613-236-9681
e-mail: admin@cvma-acmv.org
www.canadianveterinarians.net
twitter.com/CanVetMedAssoc
Overview: A medium-sized national organization founded in 1948
Mission: To represent the interests of the veterinary profession in Canada; commits to excellence within the profession & to the well-being of animals; promotes public awareness of the contribution of animals & veterinarians to society
Chief Officer(s):
Jost Am Rhyn, Executive Director, 613-236-1162 Ext. 114
Suzanne Lavictoire, Director, Membership Services & Communications, 613-236-1162 Ext. 118
slavictoire@cvma-acmv.org
Finances: *Annual Operating Budget:* $1.5 Million-$3 Million
Staff: 17 staff member(s)
Membership: *Member Profile:* Graduates in veterinary medicine; *Committees:* National Issues; Animal Welfare; Business Management; Animal Health Technology/Veterinary Technician Accreditation Program; Professional Development; Environmental Advisory Group; National Examination Board; Editorial; Students of the CVMA; Student Liaison Advisory Group; CVMA Insurance Advisory Group
Activities: *Awareness Events:* Animal Health Week, Oct.
Publications:
•Canadian Journal of Veterinary Research
Type: Journal; *Frequency:* Quarterly
•Canadian Veterinary Journal
Type: Journal; *Frequency:* Monthly

Canadian Water & Wastewater Association (CWWA) / Association canadienne des eaux potables et usées (ACEPU)

#11, 1010 Polytek St., Ottawa ON K1J 9H9
Tel: 613-747-0524; *Fax:* 613-747-0523
e-mail: tdellison@cwwa.ca
www.cwwa.ca
Overview: A medium-sized national organization founded in 1986
Mission: To represent the common interests of Canadian municipal water & wastewater systems to federal & interprovincial bodies; *Member of:* Canadian National Committee for the International Water Association
Environmental Activity: Addressing Canadian water & wastewater issues at the national level
Chief Officer(s):
Schmidt Thomas, President
Membership: *Member Profile:* Utility members are owners or operators of municipal infrastructure or services; Associate members are the private sector & academics; Subscription members are federal, provincial, or territorial government departments or agencies; *Committees:* Wastewater & Stormwater; National Water Efficiency; Drinking Water Quality; Water Protection Information; Biosolids; Energy
Activities: Monitoring policies, legislation, & standards; Liaising with federal & interprovincial organizations; Hosting workshops; Facilitating networking opportunities; Increasing & improving public awareness; Cooperating with regional water & wastewater associations
Meetings/Conferences:
For more information see Trade Shows, Conferences and Seminars Chapter
Canadian Water & Wastewater Association 2013 Canadian Wastewater Management Conference & Central Canadian Symposium on Water Quality Research
March 2013 Hamilton, ON
Canadian Water & Wastewater Association 2013 Water Efficiency & Conservation Conference
October 2013 Calgary, AB
Canadian Water & Wastewater Association 2013 16th Drinking Water Canadian National Conference & 7th Policy Forum: Assessing & Managing Risk
2013
Publications:
•Canadian Municipal Water News & Review / Journal et faits sur l'eau municipale canadienne
Type: Magazine; *Frequency:* Semiannually; *Accepts Advertising*
Profile: National & international news & events
•Canadian Water & Wastewater Association Conference Proceedings
•CWWA [Canadian Water & Wastewater Association] Membership Directory
Type: Directory; *Accepts Advertising*
Profile: Directory acts as association information as well as a buyers' guide
•CWWA [Canadian Water & Wastewater Association] Bulletin
Type: Newsletter; *Frequency:* 10 pa; *Accepts Advertising*
Profile: National information on water & wastewater developments, for CWWA members
•CWWA Members' Briefing Book: Current National Issues & Topics Concerning Water & Wastewater Management in Canada
Frequency: Quarterly
Profile: Briefing notes on current management topics that are national in nature, to assist managers & operators

•Directory of Sources of Contaminants Entering Municipal Sewer Systems
Type: Directory
Profile: Aid in identifying industrial, commercial, & institutional sources of contaminants entering municipal sewage treatment plants
•Guideline on Sampling, Handling, Transporting, & Analyzing Legal Wastewater Samples
•Meters Made Easy: A Guide to the Economic Appraisal of Alternative Metering Investment Strategies
Type: Guidebook
Profile: A tool to assist system owners & operators determine whether the introduction of meters will produce long-term savings intheir community
•Municipal Water & Wastewater Rate Manual
Type: Manual
Profile: New & alternative approaches to traditional & current rate setting methods
•Municipal Water & Wastewater Rates Primer
Type: Monograph
Profile: An overview of topics on rate setting
•National Water Works Operator Training Manuals
Type: Manual
•Survey on Chloramine in Drinking Water Disinfection
•Water Safety Plans for Municipal Drinking Water Systems
Profile: Hazard Analysis & Critical Control Points (HACCP) plan for the source, treatment, & distribution of drinking water in Canada
•Water Treatment Principles & Applications

Canadian Water Network (CWN) / Réseau canadien de l'eau

University of Waterloo, 200 University Ave. West, Waterloo ON N2L 3G1
Tel: 519-888-4567; *Fax:* 519-883-7574
e-mail: info@cwn-rce.ca
www.cwn-rce.ca
www.linkedin.com/company/canadian-water-network
www.facebook.com/CanadianWaterNetwork
twitter.com/CdnWaterNetwork
Overview: A medium-sized national organization founded in 2001
Mission: To create a national partnership in innovation that promotes environmentally responsible stewardship & opportunities with respect to Canada's water resources resulting in sustained prosperity & improved quality of life for Canadians.; *Member of:* Networks of Centres of Excellence
Chief Officer(s):
Bernadette Conant, Executive Director, 519-888-4567
bconant@cwn-rce.ca
Mark Servos, Scientific Director, 519-888-4567 Ext. 36034
mservos@uwaterloo.ca
Finances: *Annual Operating Budget:* $3 Million-$5 Million
Staff: 8 staff member(s)
Membership: 48 industrial, 65 government, 120 researchers, 200 students; *Fees:* None
Activities: Research funding, student development, national networking; *Internships:* Yes

Canadian Water Quality Association (CWQA)

#330, 295 The West Mall, Toronto ON M9C 4Z4
Tel: 416-695-3068; *Fax:* 416-695-2945
Toll-Free: 866-383-7617
e-mail: k.wong@cwqa.com
www.cwqa.com
www.linkedin.com/groups/Canadian-Water-Quality-Association-3948494
Overview: A medium-sized national organization founded in 1967
Mission: To promote the individual right to quality water; To educate water quality professionals; To promote the growth of the water quality improvement industry; To serve as a unified voice in government & public relations; To provide a role in consumer education
Chief Officer(s):
Kevin Wong, Executive Director
Membership: 106 dealers/distributors + 16 manufacturers/suppliers + 10 associates; *Fees:* $355 associate; Based on volume for dealer/distributor & manufacturer/supplier
Meetings/Conferences:
For more information see Trade Shows, Conferences and Seminars Chapter
Canadian Water Quality Association 2013 Spring Event
2013
Publications:
•Canadian Water Quality Association Membership Directory
Type: Directory
Profile: A listing of members by their head office or main facility, for use by Canadian Water Quality Association members only
•Communiqué [a publication of the Canadian Water Quality Association]
Frequency: 11 pa

Canadian Water Resources Association (CWRA) / Association canadienne des ressources hydriques (ACRH)

c/o Membership Office, 9 Covus Crt., Ottawa ON K2E 7Z4
Tel: 613-237-9363; *Fax:* 613-594-5190
e-mail: services@aic.ca
www.cwra.org
Overview: A large national charitable organization founded in 1948
Mission: To encourage recognition of the high priority & value of water; Affiliation(s): Canadian Water & Wasterwater Association; International Water Resources Association; American Water Resources Association; British Hydological Society; American Institute of Hydrology
Environmental Activity: Promoting effective water management
Chief Officer(s):
F.A. (Rick) Ross, Executive Director & Editor, Water News, 403-317-0017
executivedirector@cwra.org
André Saint-Hilaire, President, 418-654-3113
andre_st-hilaire@ete.inrs.ca
Paul H. Whitfield, Co-Editor, Canadian Water Resources Journal, 604-664-9238, Fax: 604-664-9004
paul.whitfield@ec.gc.ca
Brenda Toth, Secretary
Ed Dean, Treasurer
Membership: *Member Profile:* Individuals & organizations interested in the management of Canada's water resources, including private & public sector water resource managers, administrators, scientists, academics, students, & users
Activities: Increasing awareness & understanding of Canada's water resources; Providing a forum for the exchange of information; Participating with appropriate agencies in international water management activities
Meetings/Conferences:
For more information see Trade Shows, Conferences and Seminars Chapter
2013 Joint Scientific Congress: Bridging Environmental Science, Policy & Resource Management
May 2013 Saskatoon, SK
Publications:
•Canadian Perspectives on Integrated Water Resources Management
Type: Book; *Number of Pages:* 123; *Editor:* Dan Shrubsole; *Price:* $23
•Canadian Water Resources Association Conference Proceedings
•Canadian Water Resources Journal
Type: Journal; *Frequency:* Quarterly; *Editor:* Paul H. Whitfield; *ISSN:* 0701-1784
Profile: Research articles, technical notes, & review papers
•CWRA [Canadian Water Resources Association] Water News
Type: Newsletter; *Frequency:* Quarterly; *Editor:* F.A. (Rick) Ross
Profile: National & branch activities, international water resource information, a technical supplement, & a profile article
•Hydroscan: Airborne Laser Mapping of Hydrological Features & Resources
Type: Book; *Editor:* Chris Hopkinson et al.; *Price:* $15
•Predictions in Ungauged Basins
Type: Book; *Editor:* C. Spence et al.; *Price:* $15
•Reflections on Water: CWRA 1947 - 1997
Type: Book; *Author:* B. Mitchell; Robert de Loe; *Price:* $20

Canadian Water Well Association ***See*** Canadian Ground Water Association

Canadian Well Logging Society (CWLS)

Scotia Centre, #2200, 700 - 2nd St. SW, Calgary AB T2P 2W1
Tel: 403-269-9366; *Fax:* 403-269-2787
www.cwls.org
Overview: A medium-sized national organization founded in 1957
Chief Officer(s):
Mike Seifert, Membership Chair, 403-269-3644
seifertm@telus.net
Harold S. Hovdebo, President, 403-750-5058
harold.hovdebo@huskyenergy.ca
Finances: *Annual Operating Budget:* Less than $50,000; *Funding Sources:* Membership fees; corporate sponsors
Membership: 500; *Fees:* $40; *Member Profile:* Oil industry petrophysical interests
Publications:
•CWLS [Canadian Well Logging Society] InSite
Type: Newsletter; *Frequency:* Quarterly; *Accepts Advertising*; *Editor:* Tyler Maksymchuk & Kelly Skuce; *Price:* Free with CWLS membership
Profile: Short articles, & upcoming events to inform CWLS members
•CWLS [Canadian Well Logging Society] Journal
Type: Journal; *Frequency:* Biennially; *Price:* Free with CWLS membership
Profile: Formal papers for people interested in formation evaluation
•CWLS [Canadian Well Logging Society] Annual Report
Type: Yearbook; *Frequency:* Annually; *Price:* Free with Canadian Well Logging Society membership

Canadian Wildflower Society ***See*** North American Native Plant Society

Canadian Wildlife Federation (CWF) / Fédération canadienne de la faune

350 Michael Cowpland Dr., Kanata ON K2M 2W1
Tel: 613-599-9594; *Fax:* 613-599-4428
Toll-Free: 800-563-9453
e-mail: info@cwf-fcf.org
www.cwf-fcf.org
www.facebook.com/pages/Canadian-Wildlife-Federation/7787249430
twitter.com/CWF_FCF
www.youtube.com/user/CanadianWildlifeFed
Overview: A large national charitable organization founded in 1961
Mission: To promote the conservation of fish & wildlife, wildlife habitat & quality aquatic environments; To foster an understanding of natural processes; To ensure adequate stocks of wildlife for the use & enjoyment of all Canadians; To sponsor research; To cooperate with legislators, government & non-government agencies in achieving conservation objectives; *Member of:* World Conservation Union
Chief Officer(s):
Dave Powell, President
Lloyd Lintott, First Vice-President
Bob Morris, Second Vice-President
Guy Vezina, Secretary
John Ford, Treasurer
Finances: *Funding Sources:* Membership fees; Sales of merchandise; Donations
Membership: 300,000; *Fees:* $25; *Committees:* Affiliate; Associate Member; Audit; Awards; Constitution; Credentials; Energy; Environment; Fisheries; Forestry; Native Affairs; Nominating; Parks; Resolutions; Wildlife
Activities: Offering educational programs; Engaging in advocacy activities concerning national & international conservation & environmental issues; *Awareness Events:* National Wildlife Week, April; Canadian Rivers Day, June; *Speaker Service:* Yes; *Rents Mailing List:* Yes; *Library:* Open to public by appointment
Awards:
•Doug Clarke Memorial Award (Award), Canadian Conservation Achievement Awards Program
Presented annually to a Canadian Wildlife Federation affiliate for the most outstanding conservation project completed during the previous year by the affiliate or its clubs or members *Contact:* Sandy Baugartner
•Stan Hodgkiss Outdoorsman of the Year Award (Award), Canadian Conservation Achievement Awards Program
Presented annually to an outdoorsperson who has demonstrated an active commitment to conservation in Canada
•Roland Michener Conservation Award (Award), Canadian Conservation Achievement Awards Program
A trophy is given annually in recognition of an individual's outstanding achievement in the field of conservation in Canada
•Roderick Haig-Brown Memorial Award (Award), Canadian Conservation Achievement Awards Program
Awarded annually to an individual who has made a significant contribution to furthering the sport of angling &/or conservation & wise use of Canada's recreational fisheries resources
•Past Presidents' Canadian Legislator Award (Award), Canadian Conservation Achievement Awards Program
Presented annually to an elected provincial, territorial or federal legislator in recognition of a significant contribution toward the conservation of wildlife in Canada *Contact:* Sandy Baugartner

Publications:
•Biosphère [a publication of the Canadian Wildlife Federation]
Frequency: Bimonthly
Profile: French language edition of Canadian Wildlife, for young adults & adults
•Canadian Wildlife [a publication of the Canadian Wildlife Federation]
Type: Magazine; *Frequency:* Bimonthly
Profile: Stories about Canadian & international wildlife, plus CWF news & reports, for young adults & adults
•Wild [a publication of the Canadian Wildlife Federation]
Type: Magazine; *Frequency:* 8 pa
Profile: Educational information & games, for children between the ages of 6 & 12
•Your Big Backyard
Type: Magazine; *Frequency:* Monthly
Profile: Easy-to-read nature information, puzzles, & games, for children between the ages of 3 & 5

Canadian Wind Energy Association Inc. (CanWEA) / Association canadienne d'énergie éolienne

#810, 170 Laurier Ave. West, Ottawa ON K1P 5V5
Tel: 613-234-8716; *Fax:* 613-234-5642
Toll-Free: 800-922-6932
e-mail: info@canwea.ca
www.canwea.ca
twitter.com/canwindenergy
Overview: A small national organization founded in 1984
Mission: To promote the social, economic, & environmental benefits of wind energy in Canada; To encourage the appropriate development & application of wind energy; To create suitable environmental policy
Environmental Activity: Advocating for the responsible & sustainable growth of wind energy; Developing policy with different levels of government; Providing education, such as Wind Matters seminars
Chief Officer(s):
Robert Hornung, President
Chris Forrest, Vice-President, Communications & Marketing
Sean Whittaker, Vice-President, Policy
Penelope Feather, Director, Finance
Janice Taylor, Director, Conference & Events
Finances: *Funding Sources:* Membership fees; Conference & workshop fees
Membership: 420; *Member Profile:* Organizations & individuals who are involved in the development & application of wind energy technology, products, & services in Canada
Activities: Providing information about wind energy; Offering networking opportunities for all stakeholders; Facilitating research; Forming strategic alliances; *Library:* Canadian Wind Energy Association Library; by appointment
Meetings/Conferences:
For more information see Trade Shows, Conferences and Seminars Chapter
Canadian Wind Energy Association (CanWEA) 29th Annual Conference and Exhibition
October 2013 Toronto, ON
Canadian Wind Energy Association (CanWEA) 30th Annual Conference and Exhibition
October 2014 Montréal, QC
Canadian Wind Energy Association (CanWEA) 31st Annual Conference and Exhibition
October 2015 Toronto, ON
Publications:
•CanWEA Members Directory
Type: Directory
Profile: Contact information & a profile of each CanWEA member
•WindLink
Type: Newsletter; *Frequency:* Semimonthly
Profile: Issues & events that affect the Canadian wind energy for CanWEA members, policymakers, & the public
•WindSight
Type: Magazine; *Frequency:* Quarterly
Profile: Detailed articles on Canadian wind energy projects & policy

Canadian Wood Council (CWC) / Conseil canadien du bois (CCB)

#400, 99 Bank St., Ottawa ON K1P 6B9
Tel: 613-747-5544; *Fax:* 613-747-6264
www.cwc.ca
Overview: A large national organization founded in 1959
Mission: To represent Canadian manufacturers of wood products; To insure market access for wood products; To communicate technical information; To organize educational programs for students & construction professionals
Chief Officer(s):
Michael Giroux, President
Helen Griffin, Vice-President, Codes & Engineering
Étienne Lalonde, Vice-President, Market Development
Ioana Lazea, Manager, Events
Natalie Tarini, Manager, Communications
Membership: 15 corporate; *Fees:* Schedule available; *Member Profile:* Manufacturers of Canadian wood products used in construction; *Committees:* Management: Audit, Finance & Risk Management; Membership; HR; Nominating. Operations: U.S. Affairs; Lumber Properties Steering Committee; Market Development; Fire & Structural Design; Canadian Wood Industries Forum on Market Access; Canadian Sustainable Building Partnership. Other: WoodWORKS!; Advisory Groups; Chairmen's Club
Activities: *Awareness Events:* Annual Wood WORKS! Awards Gala; Wood Solutions Fairs; *Library:* by appointment
Publications:
•Canadian Wood Council Awards Book
Type: Yearbook; *Frequency:* Annually
Profile: Compilation of best projects submitted to the Wood Design Awards program
•Canadian Wood Council Technical Publications
Profile: Topics include the Wood Design Manual, Span Books, & Engineering Guides
•The CWC [Canadian Wood Council] Newsletter
Type: Newsletter; *Frequency:* Weekly
Profile: Trends & events that affect the wood products industry
•Wood Design & Building
Type: Magazine; *Frequency:* Quarterly; *Accepts Advertising*; *Editor:* Bernadette Johnson; *Price:* $24
Profile: Wood use in architecture & construction
•Wood WORKS!
Type: Newsletter; *Frequency:* Monthly
Profile: Resources for technical support, training opportunities, & educational events

Canadian Wood Pallet & Container Association (CWPCA) / Association canadienne des manufacturiers de palettes et contenants (ACMPC)

#11, 1884 Merivale Rd., Ottawa ON K2G 1E6
Tel: 613-521-6468; *Fax:* 613-521-1835
Toll-Free: 877-224-3555
e-mail: info@canadianpallets.com
www.canadianpallets.com
twitter.com/canadianpallets
Overview: A small national organization founded in 1967
Mission: To promote the general welfare of the wooden pallet & container manufacturing industry; to improve services directly or otherwise; to cooperate with officers of government & business in any program considered essential to the national welfare or economy; to engage in any other lawful activities & enjoy powers, rights & privileges granted or conferred upon associations of a similar nature.; *Member of:* Partners in Protection; Affiliation(s): National Wooden Pallet & Container Association; Western Pallet Association
Environmental Activity: National Packaging Protocol
Chief Officer(s):
Bill Eggertson, Executive Director
bill.eggertson@canadianpallets.com
Lori Devlin, Director, Member Services
lori.devlin@canadianpallets.com
Stephanie Poirier, CWPCP
Blair McEwen, President
bowmanvillewoodproducts@bellnet.ca
Finances: *Annual Operating Budget:* $500,000-$1.5 Million
Staff: 3 staff member(s)
Membership: 550; *Fees:* $595 corporate; $525 associate; *Member Profile:* Active manufacturers & suppliers within wood pallet & container industry; *Committees:* Wood Waste Standards; Workers Compensation; Education
Activities: *Speaker Service:* Yes; *Library:* Open to public

Canadian Wood Preservers Bureau (WPC) / Préservation du bois Canada

#202, 2141 Thurston Dr., Ottawa ON K1G 6C9
Tel: 613-737-4337; *Fax:* 613-247-0540
e-mail: info@woodpreservation.ca
www.woodpreservation.ca
Previous Name: Canadian Wood Preservers Bureau
Overview: A small national organization founded in 1988
Mission: To provide a quality assurance program for the treated wood industry
Chief Officer(s):
Henry Walthert, Executive Director
Finances: *Annual Operating Budget:* Less than $50,000; *Funding Sources:* Membership dues
Staff: 1 staff member(s); 7 volunteer(s)
Membership: 11 corporate + 4 institutional; *Member Profile:* Treated wood producers; consumer groups

Canadian Wood Preservers Bureau *See* Canadian Wood Preservers Bureau

Canadians for Ethical Treatment of Food Animals (CETFA)

PO Box 18024, 2225 - 41 Ave. West, Vancouver BC V6M 4L3
e-mail: care@cetfa.com
www.cetfa.com
www.facebook.com/cetfa.news
Overview: A medium-sized national organization founded in 1990
Mission: CETFA is an investigation-based, farm animal advocacy organization that promotes the humane treatment of animals raised for food. It works to educate the public about Canada's food industry by providing information on factory farming practices.
Chief Officer(s):
Patricia Oswald, President
Twyla Francois, Head, Investigation, 204-296-1375
twyla.1@mts.net
Membership: *Fees:* $10

Canadians for Responsible & Safe Highways (CRASH)

PO Box 1042, Stn. B, Ottawa ON K1P 5R1
Tel: 613-860-0529; *Fax:* 613-567-6204
Toll-Free: 800-530-9945
Overview: A small national organization
Mission: CRASH strives to ensure that safety, environmental & economic concerns are fully considered by governments when the latter establish & administer regulations pertaining to trucking operations on public highways.
Chief Officer(s):
Harry Gow, President

Can-Am Border Trade Alliance

PO Box 929, Lewiston NY 14092 USA
Tel: 716-754-8824; *Fax:* 716-754-8824
e-mail: canambta@aol.com
www.canambta.org
Overview: A medium-sized international organization
Mission: To maximize global commercial activity and ensure continued growth of two-way cross border trade along the entire common U.S./Canadian border and assure efficient, productive border crossing capabilities; and also to provide unified leadership for border concern, operations and needs and to act as an effective, proactive and focused border issues resource.
Chief Officer(s):
James D. Phillips, President & CEO

Canards Illimités Canada *See* Ducks Unlimited Canada

Carleton County Law Association (CCLA) / Association du barreau du comté de Carleton (ABCC)

Law Library, Ottawa Courthouse, #2004, 161 Elgin St., Ottawa ON K2P 2K1
Tel: 613-233-7386; *Fax:* 613-238-3788
Toll-Free: 866-637-3888
www.ccla-abcc.ca
www.linkedin.com/company/county-of-carleton-law-association
www.facebook.com/CCLA.ABCC
twitter.com/ccla_abcc
Overview: A small local organization founded in 1888
Mission: To advance the interests of it members; to promote the administration of justice
Chief Officer(s):
Jaye E. Hooper, President
hooper@williamsmcenery.com
Rick Haga, Executive Director
rhaga@ccla-abcc.ca
Wanda Walters, Administrator, Finance
wwalters@ccla-abcc.ca
Jennifer Walker, BAH, BEd, MLIS, Head Librarian
jwalker@ccla-abcc.ca
Membership: *Fees:* $52.50 - $309.75; *Member Profile:* Ottawa & Eastern Ontario lawyers
Activities: Offering continuing education programs; Providing networking opportunities; *Library:* County of Carleton Law Association Ottawa Courthouse Law Library

Publications:
•CCLA [Carleton County Law Association] Bulletin
Type: Newsletter; *Frequency:* Bimonthly
Profile: Updated policies & procedures for CCLA members
•Ottawa & Eastern Ontario Lawyers' Directory
Type: Directory; *Frequency:* Annually; *Accepts Advertising*; *Price:* $55 - $65

Carolinian Canada Coalition
Grosvenor Lodge, 1017 Western Rd., London ON N6G 1G5
Tel: 519-433-7077; *Fax:* 519-913-2449
e-mail: info@carolinian.org
www.carolinian.org
Overview: A medium-sized local organization
Mission: To promote the protection and conservation of the Carolinian Life Zone of Southwestern Ontario.
Chief Officer(s):
Gordon Nelson, Chair
Membership: *Fees:* $20 individual; $50 organization

Carp Agricultural Society
PO Box 188, Carp ON K0A 1L0
Tel: 613-839-2172; *Fax:* 613-839-1961
e-mail: info@carpfair.ca
www.carpfair.ca
Overview: A medium-sized local charitable organization founded in 1863
Mission: To improve agriculture & the quality of life in the community by educating members & the community; To provide a community forum for discussing agricultural issues; To foster community development & community spirit; To help provide markets for Ontario products; To encourage conservation of natural resources, including soil conservation, reforestation, rural & urban beautification; *Member of:* Carp BIA
Chief Officer(s):
Joyce Trafford, General Manager
Paul Caldwell, President, Agriculture
Heather Johnston, President, Homecraft
Membership: 500-999; *Committees:* Concessions; Light Horse; Heavy Horse; Gate; Parking; Dairy; Beef Cattle; Sheep; 4-H Club; Field Crops; Fruit & Vegetables; Grains & Seeds; Honey & Maple Syrup; Wine & Beer; Flowers; Domestic Science; Junior Department; Sewing, Needlework, & Crafts; Antiques; Story Book Farm

Carrying Capacity Network (CCN)
PO Box 457, San Francisco CA 94104-0457 USA
Tel: 202-296-4548; *Fax:* 202-296-4609
Toll-Free: 800-466-4866
e-mail: info@carryingcapacity.org
www.carryingcapacity.org
Overview: A large international organization founded in 1989
Mission: "Carrying Capacity" refers to the number of individuals who can be supported without degrading the physical, ecological, cultural & social environment (ie without reducing the ability of the environment to sustain the desired quality of life over the long term); CCN functions as a clearinghouse of information for participants, a forum for discussion of controversial issues & as a catalyst for cooperation among diverse groups involved in carrying capacity issues; CCN's objective is to facilitate the understanding of the crucial linkages between population & the environment by exchanging information, disseminating news & encouraging cooperation among environmental, resource conservation, growth control & population stabilization organizations & activists
Finances: *Annual Operating Budget:* $500,000-$1.5 Million
Staff: 8 staff member(s)
Membership: *Fees:* $20 senior/student; $25 adult; $40 sustaining; $100 major; $250 sponsor; $500 benefactor; $1,000 patron
Activities: Resource Bank (a catalogue of resources to aid participants in their search for information); Speakers/Writers Bureau (a database of individuals & organizations that would speak or write on the wide range of carrying capacity issues); *Speaker Service:* Yes

Castle-Crown Wilderness Coalition (CCWC)
PO Box 2621, #202, 696 Kettles St., Pincher Creek AB T0K 1W0
Tel: 403-627-5059
e-mail: office@ccwc.ab.ca
www.ccwc.ab.ca
www.facebook.com//269184503160443
Overview: A small local organization founded in 1989
Mission: To restore & maintain the Castle Wilderness within the Crown of the Continent Ecosystem
Chief Officer(s):
Gordon Petersen, President & Treasurer
Carolyn Aspeslet, Executive Director, 403-627-5059
James Tweedie, Director, Conservation
james@ccwc.ab.ca
Finances: *Funding Sources:* Membership fees; Donations; Conservation organizations; Fisheries & Oceans Canada
Membership: 500+; *Fees:* $10 individuals; $15 families; $25 groups; $110 supporting members; $250 life members
Activities: Sponsoring a stewardship program to monitor & restore the Castle Wilderness; Conducting hikes to raise awareness of the area; *Awareness Events:* Annual West Castle Wetland Ecological Reserve Weed Pull, July
Publications:
•Bringing it Back: A Restoration Framework for the Castle Wilderness
•The Castle Wilderness Environmental Inventory
•Castle Wilderness News
Type: Newsletter; *Frequency:* Quarterly; *Editor:* Judy Huntley
•The State of the Castle Wilderness: Annual Report
Type: Yearbook; *Frequency:* Annually

C.D. Howe Institute / Institut C.D. Howe
#300, 67 Yonge St., Toronto ON M5E 1J8
Tel: 416-865-1904; *Fax:* 416-865-1866
e-mail: cdhowe@cdhowe.org
www.cdhowe.org
Overview: A medium-sized international organization founded in 1973
Mission: Research & educational institute identifying current & emerging economic & social policy issues facing Canadians; to recommend particular policy options; to communicate conclusions of research to domestic & international audiences.
Chief Officer(s):
Finn Poschmann, Vice-President, Research
Kevin Fleming, Editor
William B.P. Robson, President & CEO
Finances: *Annual Operating Budget:* $1.5 Million-$3 Million; *Funding Sources:* Membership dues
Staff: 18 staff member(s)
Membership: 215 corporate + 50 institutional; *Fees:* Schedule available; *Member Profile:* Participation in & support of its activities from business, organized labor, associations, professions & interested individuals; *Committees:* British-North American; North-American
Activities: *Speaker Service:* Yes; *Library:* by appointment

Cement Association of Canada (CAC) / Association canadienne du ciment
#502, 350 Sparks St., Ottawa ON K1R 7S8
Tel: 613-236-9471; *Fax:* 613-563-4498
www.cement.ca
Previous Name: Canadian Portland Cement Association
Overview: A medium-sized national organization
Mission: Represents all of Canada's cement producers; aims to improve & extend the uses of cement & concrete through market development, engineering, research, education, & public affairs work
Chief Officer(s):
Michael McSweeney, President & CEO
mmcsweeney@cement.ca
Membership: 10 companies; *Member Profile:* 100% of the manufacturers of Portland cement in Canada

Center for Health, Environment & Justice (CHEJ)
PO Box 6806, Falls Church VA 22040-6806 USA
Tel: 703-237-2249; *Fax:* 703-237-8389
e-mail: chej@chej.org
www.chej.org
Previous Name: Citizens Clearinghouse for Hazardous Wastes
Overview: A medium-sized national charitable organization founded in 1981
Mission: To help communities win environmental justice
Chief Officer(s):
Lois Marie Gibbs, Executive Director/Founder
Sharon Franklin, Finance/Administrative Director
Finances: *Annual Operating Budget:* $500,000-$1.5 Million; *Funding Sources:* Membership dues; donations
Staff: 14 staff member(s)
Membership: 25,000 individual + 7,500 groups; *Fees:* $30 individual; $100 group
Activities: Provides science, organizing & technical assistance to citizens concerned with dioxin, toxic waste, chemical poisons, etc. in their communities; site visits by staff; 130+ self-help guides & fact packs; campaigns: Stop Dioxin Exposure; childproofing communities; BESAFE; *Awareness Events:* March into Spring, March; *Internships:* Yes; *Speaker Service:* Yes; *Library:* Open to public

Center for Marine Conservation; Center for Environmental Education ***See*** The Ocean Conservancy

Center for Plant Conservation
PO Box 299, St. Louis MO 63166-0299 USA
Tel: 314-577-9450; *Fax:* 314-577-9465
e-mail: cpc@mobot.org
www.centerforplantconservation.org
Overview: A medium-sized international organization founded in 1984
Mission: To create a systematic, comprehensive national program of plant conservation, research & education within existing institutions, as a complement to the preservation of genetic diversity through habitat protection; to strengthen its collaborative ties with countries contiguous to the US & its territories - Canada, Mexico & nations of the Greater Antilles; to develop & maintain comprehensive & broadly accessible information systems, national networks & databases concerning the biology, horticulture & conservation status of all nationally endangered native plants of the US
Chief Officer(s):
Kathryn Kennedy, President & Executive Director
Activities: The National Collection of Endangered Species consists of living plant materials collected from the wild, representing to the greatest extent possible the genetic diversity found in natural populations; Participating Institutions - affiliated botanical gardens & arboreta around the US; Priority Regions - areas facing a major plant extinction crisis; Integrated Conservation; Conservation Research; Information & Data Systems; Economic Plant Research; International Conservation

Central British Columbia Railway & Forest Industry Museum Society
850 River Rd., Prince George BC V2L 5S8
Tel: 250-563-7351; *Fax:* 250-563-3697
e-mail: trains@pgrfm.bc.ca
www.pgrfm.bc.ca
Also Known As: Railway & Forestry Museum
Overview: A small local charitable organization founded in 1983
Mission: Administers Prince George Railway & Forest Industry Museum; *Member of:* Canadian Railway Historical Association; Canadian Museum Association; British Columbia Museum Association; American Railway Museum Association
Chief Officer(s):
Laura Williams, General Manager
Finances: *Annual Operating Budget:* $50,000-$100,000
Staff: 6 staff member(s); 15 volunteer(s)
Membership: 75; *Fees:* $15-$40
Activities: *Awareness Events:* Steam Day; Forester Day; Family Carnival; *Library:* Canfor Library; by appointment

Central Canadian Federation of Mineralogical Societies (CCFMS)
c/o Natural History, Mineralogy, 100 Queen's Park, Toronto ON M5S 2C6
e-mail: info@ccfms.ca
www.ccfms.ca
Overview: A medium-sized national organization founded in 1969
Mission: To act as the voice for amateur rock, mineral, & lapidary clubs in central Canada
Chief Officer(s):
Russell Bruce, President, 416-284-9797
bruce12@bell.net
Ray Hainsworth, Secretary
eyciboy@yahoo.ca
Faye Meadows, Treasurer
fayemeadows@rogers.com
Membership: 25 clubs; *Member Profile:* Rock, mineral, & lapidary clubs for hobbyists in central Canada
Activities: Promoting the earth sciences; Encouraging exchange of information between societies, federations, & institutions; Educating rock & mineral collectors; Protecting collecting sites; *Speaker Service:* Yes

Central Interior Logging Association (CILA)
#201, 850 River Rd., Prince George BC V2L 5S8
Tel: 250-562-3368; *Fax:* 250-563-3697
Toll-Free: 877-562-5668
e-mail: cila@pgonline.com
www.cila.bc.ca
www.facebook.com/280253495363132
Previous Name: Prince George & District Truck Loggers Association

Overview: A medium-sized local charitable organization founded in 1966
Mission: To present the views of members to all levels of government, its agencies, & the corporate sector
Chief Officer(s):
MaryAnne Arcand, Executive Director
maryanne@cila.ca
Membership: *Fees:* $413.40-$3174.70; *Member Profile:* Companies & individuals directly or indirectly engaged in logging or log hauling; manufacturers & suppliers of goods &/or services to the logging industry

Central Okanagan Naturalists Club (CONC)

PO Box 21128, Stn. Orchard Park, Kelowna BC V1Y 9N8
Tel: 250-768-3334
e-mail: guilds@telus.net
www.okanagannature.org
Overview: A small local charitable organization founded in 1962
Mission: To promote the enjoyment of nature through environmental appreciation & conservation; To encourage wise use & conservation of natural resources & environmental protection.; *Member of:* Federation of BC Naturalists
Chief Officer(s):
Don Guild, President
Finances: *Annual Operating Budget:* Less than $50,000
Staff: 9 staff member(s); 70 volunteer(s)
Membership: 200; *Fees:* $14 student; $30 single; $42 family; *Member Profile:* Retirees; *Committees:* Education; Ecological Reserves; Forestry
Activities: Hiking; skiing; botany; ornithology; participating with City of Kelowna in environmental events; conservation; *Library:* CONC Library; Open to public
Publications:
•Central Okanagan Naturalist Newsletter
Type: Newsletter; *Frequency:* 10 pa; *Editor:* Teresa Smith

Central Ontario Orchid Society (COOS)

PO Box 40074, 75 King St. South, Waterloo ON N2J 4V1
retirees.uwaterloo.ca/~jerry/coos
Overview: A small local organization founded in 1985
Mission: To promote & train people about growing orchids
Chief Officer(s):
Gerhard Kompter, Interim President, 519-745-3815
Christine Williams, Secretary, 519-747-1087
cwilliams3740@yahoo.caca
Finances: *Annual Operating Budget:* Less than $50,000
Membership: 100+; *Fees:* $15 individual; $20 family
Activities: Promote & train people about growing orchids; *Speaker Service:* Yes; *Library:* Open to public
Publications:
•The COOS [Central Ontario Orchid Society] Newsletter
Type: Newsletter; *Editor:* Cathy Ralston

Central Valley Naturalists

PO Box 612, Abbotsford BC V2T 6Z8
Tel: 604-853-4283
e-mail: haroos@shaw.ca
www.centralvalleynaturalists.org
Overview: A small local organization
Affiliation(s): Federation of BC Naturalists
Chief Officer(s):
Hank Roos, President
Membership: 120; *Fees:* $30 individual; $35 family

Centre canadien d'hygiène et de sécurité au travail *See* Canadian Centre for Occupational Health & Safety

Centre canadien d'innovations des pêches *See* Canadian Centre for Fisheries Innovation

Centre canadien de politique alternative *See* Canadian Centre for Policy Alternatives

Centre canadien pour la prévention de la pollution *See* Canadian Centre for Pollution Prevention

Centre de formation en entreprise et récupération Normand-Maurice

605, rue Notre-Dame est, Victoriaville QC G6P 6Y9
Tél: 819-758-4789; *Téléc:* 819-752-3488
Courriel: cfer@csbf.qc.ca
Aperçu: *Dimension:* moyenne; *Envergure:* provinciale
Mission: Offrir aux jeunes en difficultés une formation préparatoire au marché du travail; initier les enfants du primaire aux grandes problématiques environnementales; développer une conscience environnementale chez les jeunes
Membre(s) du bureau directeur:
Marie Chaput, Présidente
Yves Couture, Directeur

Centre de recherche sur la vie marine de Grand Manan *See* Grand Manan Whale & Seabird Research Station

Centre de recherches pour le développement international *See* International Development Research Centre

Centre for Environmental Law & Development *See* Foundation for International Environmental Law & Development

Centre for Fisheries Innovation *See* Canadian Centre for Fisheries Innovation

Centre for Indigenous Environmental Resources, Inc. (CIER)

245 McDermot Ave., 3rd Fl., Winnipeg MB R3B 0S6
Tel: 204-956-0660; *Fax:* 204-956-1895
www.cier.ca
Overview: A small national organization
Chief Officer(s):
Roger Augustine, Chair
Phil Fontaine, Secretary

Centre info-énergie *See* Canadian Centre for Energy Information

Centre international d'informations de sécurité et de santé au travail *See* International Occupational Safety & Health Information Centre

Centre québécois du droit de l'environnement (CQDE) / Québec Environmental Law Centre

454, av Laurier Est, Montréal QC H2J 1E7
Tél: 514-861-7022
Courriel: info@cqde.org
www.cqde.org
Aperçu: *Dimension:* petite; *Envergure:* provinciale; Organisme sans but lucratif; fondée en 1989
Mission: Promouvoir le droit de l'environnement comme outil de protection de la santé publique et du patrimoine collectif
Membre(s) du bureau directeur:
Jean-François Girard, Président
Anna-Léa Scollan, Vice-présidente
Anne-Marie Robichaud, Secrétaire
Finances: *Budget de fonctionnement annuel:* $100,000-$250,000
Membre: 120 *Montant de la cotisation:* 10$ étudiant; 20$ membre individuel; 50$ entreprise
Activités: *Service de conférenciers:* Oui; *Bibliothèque:* Bibliothèque publique rendez-vous

Le Cercle Saint-François *See* The Kindness Club

Cercles des jeunes naturalistes (CJN)

Jardin botanique de Montréal, #262, 4101, rue Sherbrooke est, Montréal QC H1X 2B2
Tél: 514-252-3023; *Téléc:* 514-254-8744
Courriel: info@jeunesnaturalistes.org
www.jeunesnaturalistes.org
www.facebook.com/161347170575251
Aperçu: *Dimension:* grande; *Envergure:* nationale; Organisme sans but lucratif; fondée en 1931
Mission: Nous initions les jeunes à l'étude des sciences de la nature et à la protection de l'environnement; *Membre de:* Regroupement Loisir Québec
Membre(s) du bureau directeur:
André St-Arnaud, Président
Vicky Lesieur, Coodonnatrice générale
Finances: *Fonds:* Gouvernement provincial pour la gestion du Siège social
Personnel: 2 membre(s) du personnel; 4 bénévole(s)
Membre: 1 300 membres; 135 animateurs bénévoles *Montant de la cotisation:* 35$ individuel; 50$ famille
Activités: Camps nature; animations dans les cercles avec les Jeunes Naturalistes sur les sciences de la nature; activités parascolaires et dans les écoles; formation pour animateurs; trousses d'animations; festival provincial annuel; *Bibliothèque:* Bibliothèque publique
Publications:
•Les Naturalistes [a publication of Cercles des jeunes naturalistes]
Type: Revue

Certified Organic Associations of British Columbia (COABC)

#202, 3002 - 32nd Ave., Vernon BC V1T 2L7
Tel: 250-260-4429; *Fax:* 250-260-4436
e-mail: office@certifiedorganic.bc.ca
www.certifiedorganic.bc.ca
Overview: A medium-sized provincial organization founded in 1994
Mission: To maintain a credible set of organic production & processing standards
Chief Officer(s):
Sarah Clark, Administrator
Kristy Wipperman, Office Manager
Activities: Cyber-Help; Canadian Organic Initiative; Organic Environmental Farm Program; Organic Harvest Awards; Organic Sector Development Program; Standards
Publications:
•BC Organic Grower
Frequency: Quarterly

Certified Technicians & Technologists Association of Manitoba (CTTAM)
Parent Name: Canadian Council of Technicians & Technologists

#602, 1661 Portage Ave., Winnipeg MB R3J 3T7
Tel: 204-784-1088; *Fax:* 204-784-1084
e-mail: admin@cttam.com
www.cttam.com
Previous Name: Manitoba Society of Certified Engineering Technicians & Technologists Inc.
Overview: A medium-sized provincial organization founded in 1965 overseen by Canadian Council of Technicians & Technologists
Mission: To advance the professional recognition & development of certified applied science technicians & technologists in a manner that serves the public interest; *Member of:* Science & Technology Awareness Network
Chief Officer(s):
Tracey Kucheravy, CET, President
president@cttam.com
Terry Gifford, CAE, Executive Director, 204-784-1080
Robert B. Chochinov, CET, Registrar, 204-784-1081
Finances: *Funding Sources:* Membership fees
Membership: 2,600; *Fees:* $155; *Member Profile:* Open to those employed in all aspects of engineering technology (civil, mechanical, electrical, electronic, computer, instrumentation, surveying, design & drafting, structural, construction) provided they meet the academic requirements
Activities: *Internships:* Yes

Ceta-Research Inc.

PO Box 10, Trinity NL A0C 2S0
Tel: 709-464-3269; *Fax:* 709-464-3700
e-mail: beamish@oceancontact.com
www.oceancontact.com/research/research.html
Overview: A medium-sized local organization founded in 1990
Mission: To undertake the rescue of entrapped whales & dolphins; to conduct research on whales; To organize a discovery in animal communication using Rhythm Bases Communication
Chief Officer(s):
Peter Beamish, Co-Director
Christine Beamish, Co-Director
Finances: *Annual Operating Budget:* $100,000-$250,000
Staff: 30 staff member(s)
Membership: 5,000 individual

La Chaine bleue mondiale *See* World Blue Chain for the Protection of Animals & Nature

Chamber of Mineral Resources of Nova Scotia (CMRNS)

PO Box 2171, Windsor NS B0N 2T0
Tel: 902-798-0187; *Fax:* 902-798-2141
e-mail: terry.daniels@ns.sympatico.ca
Overview: A medium-sized provincial organization founded in 1981
Mission: To ensure Nova Scotia is recognized internationally as having mineral resources worthy of investment; to develop mineral deposits; to work for government policies that provide a framework for a competitive mining industry within the global marketplace; to promote mining as a corporate industry creating wealth & long-term stable employment, with responsible environmental & social attitudes; Affiliation(s): Mining Association of Canada
Chief Officer(s):
Terry Daniels, Managing Director
Finances: *Annual Operating Budget:* Less than $50,000
Membership: 150

Activities: *Awareness Events:* Mining Week; *Library:* by appointment

Chamber of Mines of Eastern British Columbia

215 Hall St., Nelson BC V1L 5X4
Tel: 250-352-5242; *Fax:* 250-352-7227
e-mail: chamberofminesebc@netidea.com
www.cmebc.com
Overview: A medium-sized provincial organization founded in 1921
Mission: To act as advocate for the mining industry in British Columbia; to provide a collective voice on behalf of prospectors & miners; to provide information on exploration & mining; to educate the public through accessibility to mineral museum & library.; *Member of:* BC Mining Association; BC/Yukon Chamber of Mines
Chief Officer(s):
Jack Denny, President
Dennis Llewellyn, Chamber Manager
Finances: *Annual Operating Budget:* Less than $50,000
Staff: 1 staff member(s)
Membership: 175; *Fees:* $40 individual; $100-$500 corporate
Activities: ; *Library:*

La Chambre de commerce du Canada ***See*** The Canadian Chamber of Commerce

The Chartered Institute of Logistics & Transport in North America (CILT) / Institut agréé de la logistique et des transports Amérique du Nord

#900, 275 Slater St., Ottawa ON K1P 5H9
Tel: 613-688-1438; *Fax:* 613-688-0966
e-mail: requestinfo@ciltna.com
www.ciltna.com
Also Known As: CILT in North America
Previous Name: Chartered Institute of Transport Canadian Division
Overview: A medium-sized international organization founded in 1919
Mission: To promote, encourage, coordinate study & advancement of science & art of transportation.; *Member of:* Chartered Institute of Transport
Chief Officer(s):
David Collenette, Vice-Chairman
Ed Coylits, Executive Director
Edgar Courtemanch, Vice-Chairman
Tom Maville, Treasurer
Gilles Legault, Chair
Finances: *Funding Sources:* Membership fees, conferences, workshop revenue
Staff: 1 staff member(s); 15 volunteer(s)
Membership: 250; *Fees:* Schedule available; *Member Profile:* Individuals with experience, interest & education in the transportation field.; *Committees:* Regional
Activities: *Internships:* Yes; *Library:*

Chartered Institute of Transport Canadian Division ***See*** The Chartered Institute of Logistics & Transport in North America

Chemical Institute of Canada (CIC) / Institut de chimie du Canada

#550, 130 Slater St., Ottawa ON K1P 6E2
Tel: 613-232-6252; *Fax:* 613-232-5862
Toll-Free: 888-542-2242
e-mail: info@cheminst.ca
www.cheminst.ca
www.linkedin.com/company/chemical-institute-of-canada
www.facebook.com/ChemicalInstituteOfCanada
fr.twitter.com/CIC_ChemInst
www.flickr.com/photos/61234653@N08
Overview: A large national organization founded in 1945
Mission: To maintain all branches of the professions of chemical sciences & chemical engineering in their proper status among other learned & scientific professions; To encourage original research & develop & maintain high standards in profession; To enhance usefulness of profession to the public; Affiliation(s): Canadian Society for Chemical Engineering; Canadian Society for Chemical Technology; Canadian Society for Chemistry
Chief Officer(s):
Roland Andersson, Executive Director, 613-232-6252 Ext. 222
randersson@cheminst.ca
Joan Kingston, Director, Finance & Administration, 613-232-6252 Ext. 225
jkingston@cheminst.ca
Gale Thirlwall, Manager, Awards & Local Sections, 613-232-6252 Ext. 223
gthirlwall@cheminst.ca
Luke Andersson, Coordinator, Marketing, 613-232-6252 Ext. 227
landersson@cheminst.ca
Angie Moulton, Coordinator, Membership Services, 613-232-6252 Ext. 230
amoulton@cheminst.ca
Anne Campbell, Officer, Conference Programs, 613-232-6252 Ext. 235
acampbell@cheminst.ca
Finances: *Funding Sources:* Membership fees
Membership: 6,000; *Fees:* Schedule available; *Member Profile:* Open to those interested in chemistry & chemical technology & engineering with appropriate background; *Committees:* Finance; Fellowship
Activities: *Awareness Events:* National Chemistry Week; *Speaker Service:* Yes; *Rents Mailing List:* Yes
Awards:
•The Chemical Institute of Canada Award for Environmental Improvement (Award)
A plaque & certificate & up to $500 travel assistance awarded to a company, individual, team or organization in Canada for a significant achievement in pollution prevention, treatment or remediation in Canada *Contact:* Awards Manager, E-mail: awards@cheminst.ca
•Chemical Institute of Canada Awards (Award)
The institute administers several awards & scholarships in chemistry, chemical engineering, & macromolecular science or engineering
•Pestcon Graduate Scholarship (Scholarship)
For M.Sc. or Ph.D. students for research into alternate pest control strategies *Deadline:* March *Amount:* $3,000
Meetings/Conferences:
For more information see Trade Shows, Conferences and Seminars Chapter
96th Canadian Chemistry Conference & Exhibition
May 2013 Québec, QC
63rd Canadian Chemical Engineering Conference: Resources, Energy, Environment
October 2013 Fredericton, NB
97th Canadian Chemistry Conference & Exhibition
June 2014 Vancouver, BC
64th Canadian Chemical Engineering Conference
October 2014 Niagara Falls, ON
98th Canadian Chemistry Conference & Exhibition
June 2015 Ottawa, ON
65th Canadian Chemical Engineering Conference
2015 Calgary, AB
Publications:
•Canadian Chemical News
Type: Magazine; *Frequency:* Bimonthly
•The Canadian Journal of Chemical Engineering
Type: Journal

Chicken Farmers of Saskatchewan (CFS) Parent Name: Chicken Farmers of Canada

Rumley Building, #201, 224 Pacific Ave., Saskatoon SK S7K 1N9
Tel: 306-242-3611; *Fax:* 306-242-3286
www.saskatchewanchicken.ca
Overview: A medium-sized provincial organization founded in 1966 overseen by Chicken Farmers of Canada
Affiliation(s): Chicken Farmers of Canada
Chief Officer(s):
Gale Kellington, Office Manager
Gale@saskatchewanchicken.ca
Finances: *Funding Sources:* Levy system for chicken producers
Staff: 5 staff member(s)
Membership: 70; *Committees:* Saskatchewan Chicken Industry Development Fund (SCIDF)

Chilliwack Field Naturalists

#216, 45598 McIntosh Dr., Chilliwack BC V2P 1J3
Tel: 604-796-9182
e-mail: postmaster@chilliwackfieldnaturalists.freeservers.com
www.chilliwackfieldnaturalists.com
Overview: A small local organization founded in 1970
Mission: To promote the enjoyment of nature through environmental appreciation & conservation; To encourage wise use & conservation of natural resources & environmental protection; *Member of:* Federation of BC Naturalists
Chief Officer(s):
Janne Perrin, President
djperrin@uniserve.com
Membership: 60 individual; *Fees:* $25 individual; $35 family; *Committees:* Conservation; Education
Activities: Field trips; meetings & speakers; education; *Awareness Events:* Christmas Bird Count, December; *Library:* Open to public

Chinook Applied Research Association (CARA) Parent Name: Agricultural Research & Extension Council of Alberta

PO Box 690, Oyen AB T0J 2J0
Tel: 403-664-3777; *Fax:* 403-664-3007
e-mail: cara-1@telus.net
www.areca.ab.ca/carahome.html
Overview: A small local organization overseen by Agricultural Research & Extension Council of Alberta
Mission: To expand agricultural research; *Member of:* Agricultural Research & Extension Council of Alberta
Chief Officer(s):
Dianne Westerlund, Manager
cara-dw@telus.net
Audrey Bamber, Agrologist, Crops
cara-ab@telus.net
Lacey Ryan, Agrologist, Forage
cara-ca@telus.net
Membership: *Fees:* $20 (annual); $80 (5 years)
Publications:
•Grain, Grass & Growth [a publication of Chinook Applied Research Association]
Type: Newsletter

Christian Farmers Federation of Ontario (CFFO)

7660 Mill Rd., RR#4, Guelph ON N1H 6J1
Tel: 519-837-1620; *Fax:* 519-824-1835
e-mail: cffomail@christianfarmers.org
www.christianfarmers.org
twitter.com/CFFOnt
www.youtube.com/user/ChristianFarmers
Overview: A large provincial organization founded in 1954
Mission: A professional organization for Christian family farm entrepreneurs; a general farm organization with an interest in a broad range of agricultural, rural & social issues that impact upon the quality of the family life & family businesses of members; as a professional organization, committed to enabling members as producers, as marketers & as citizens, developing both the entrepreneurial & community leadership of members; through involvement in public policy, promotes a family farm & stewardship perspective; as a confessional organization, committed to being upfront about the Christian value system that motivates members, in order to make the wisdom of the Christian faith available to farm practice & farm policy; Affiliation(s): AG Care; Christian Farmers Federation of Alberta; Christian Environmental Council; Rural Development Advisory Committee
Chief Officer(s):
Lorne Small, President
Nathan Stevens, Interim Manager & Director, Policy Development
stevens@christianfarmers.org
Finances: *Annual Operating Budget:* $500,000-$1.5 Million; *Funding Sources:* Membership fees
Staff: 5 staff member(s)
Membership: 4,172; *Fees:* $157.50; *Member Profile:* Full-time commercial family farm entrepreneurs; part-time, hobby & lifestyle farmers; all those who have directed their farm organization fee to CFFO when they register with the Ontario Ministry of Agriculture, Food & Rural Affairs as part of the farm business registration process; *Committees:* Supply Management; Pork Producers; Sheep Producers; Stewardship & Policy East; Stewardship & Policy West
Activities: Our Farm Environmental Agenda (drafted by a coalition of Christian Farmers Federation of Ontario, AGCare, Ontario Federation of Agriculture, & the Ontario Farm Animal Council) outlines the strong commitment of farmers, through farm plans, to document present environmental conditions on their farms, develop a strategy for making appropriate changes, document actual farm practices & use that data for the development of new farm environmental initiatives; *Speaker Service:* Yes

Christmas Tree Farmers of Ontario (CFTO)

#1, 9251 County Rd., Palgrave ON L0N 1P0
Fax: 905-729-0548
Toll-Free: 800-661-3530
e-mail: ctfo@christmastrees.on.ca
www.christmastrees.on.ca
Overview: A small provincial organization founded in 1950

Mission: CFTO is an association devoted to farmers who specialize in Christmas tree growing.; *Member of:* Canadian Christmas Tree Growers Association
Chief Officer(s):
Shirley Brennan, Executive Director
Membership: 200; *Fees:* Member $195; Senior member $250; Plus member $360; Associate member $130; Subscriber $80; *Member Profile:* Christmas tree farmers; *Committees:* Public Relations; Membership

Chrysotile Institute / Instit du Chrysotile
#1640, 1200, av McGill College, Montréal QC H3B 4G7
Tel: 514-877-9797; *Fax:* 514-877-9717
e-mail: info@chrysotile.com
www.chrysotile.com
Overview: A medium-sized national organization founded in 1984
Mission: To promote the implementation & enforcement of effective regulations, standards, work practices & techniques for the safe use of asbestos.
Chief Officer(s):
Denis Hamel, Director General
Activities: Participates in international missions by providing information, consultation, or training of a technical, medical & scientific nature for processors & users in other countries; gathers & disseminates medical, scientific & technical data about asbestos & substitute fibres; *Library:* by appointment

Citizen Scientists
c/o Rouge Valley Conservation Centre, 1749 Meadowvale Rd., Toronto ON M1B 5W8
e-mail: info@citizenscientists.ca
www.citizenscientists.ca
www.facebook.com/group.php?gid=2259994028
Overview: A medium-sized local organization founded in 2001
Mission: To monitor local watersheds, foster local environmental stewardship, and educate volunteers and the public.
Membership: 11 institutional

Citizens Clearinghouse for Hazardous Wastes *See* Center for Health, Environment & Justice

Citizens for a Safe Environment (CSE)
Tel: 416-461-1092
e-mail: info@csetoronto.org
www.csetoronto.org
Overview: A medium-sized local organization founded in 1983
Mission: To promomote waste management practices that protect the health of Toronto citizens, their communities and the environment.; *Member of:* Ontario Environmental Network
Environmental Activity: School Programs
Activities: *Awareness Events:* Green Tea Parties; *Speaker Service:* Yes

Citizens' Clearinghouse on Waste Management (CCWM)
17 Major St., Kitchener ON N2H 4R1
www.citizenswasteinfo.org
Overview: A small national organization founded in 1989
Mission: To help citizens gain access to information that will help them solve waste management problems in their communities and across Ontario.
Chief Officer(s):
John Jackson, Coordinator
jjackson@web.net

Citizens' Environment Alliance of Southwestern Ontario (CEA)
1950 Ottawa St., Windsor ON N8Y 1R7
Tel: 519-973-1116; *Fax:* 519-973-8360
e-mail: ceaadmin@cogeco.net
www.citizensenvironmentalliance.org
www.facebook.com/group.php?gid=4417742199
Previous Name: Citizens' Environment Alliance of Southwestern Ontario
Overview: A small local charitable organization founded in 1985
Mission: CEA is a non-profit, grass-roots, international, education & research organization that aims to protect, restore & enhance the quality of the local environment in the Detroit-St. Clair Rivers corridor & in the Essex-Kent regions of the Great Lakes Basin; educate the public about environmental problems & solutions as they relate to the Great Lakes ecosystems & in particular to Southwestern Ontario. It is a registered charity, BN: 899837850RR0001.; *Member of:* Canadian Environmental Network; Ontario Environment Network; Environmental Action Ontario; Affiliation(s): Canadian Environmental Network (RCEN); Ontario Environmental Network (OEN); Lake Erie Millennium Network (LEMN); Ontario Water Conservation Alliance
Finances: *Annual Operating Budget:* $50,000-$100,000
Staff: 20 volunteer(s)
Membership: 100-499;; *Fees:* Donations; *Committees:* Endangered Species; Toxic Trackers; Air Quality; Area Clean-up Team
Activities: "State of the Detroit River" boat tour; annual "Weenie Award" night; endangered natural spaces; toxic trackers; air quality; Detroit River clean-up; waste management; *Speaker Service:* Yes; *Rents Mailing List:* Yes; *Library:* Environmental & Resource Library; Open to public

Citizens' Environment Alliance of Southwestern Ontario *See* Citizens' Environment Alliance of Southwestern Ontario

Citizens' Environment Watch (CEW)
#204, 147 Spadina Ave., Toronto ON M5V 2L7
Tel: 647-258-3280; *Fax:* 416-637-2717
e-mail: info@citizensenvironmentwatch.org
www.citizensenvironmentwatch.org
Overview: A medium-sized national organization founded in 1996
Mission: To provide communities the tools for education, monitoring and influencing positive change and to encourage people to take an active role in restoring and sustaining nature.
Chief Officer(s):
Meredith Cochrane, Executive Director
Finances: *Annual Operating Budget:* $250,000-$500,000; *Funding Sources:* Government, Foundations
Staff: 4 staff member(s)

Citizens' Opposed to Paving the Escarpment (COPE)
PO Box 20014, 2211 Brant St., Burlington ON L7P 0A4
e-mail: mail@cope-nomph.org
www.cope-nomph.org
www.facebook.com/pages/Highway-No-Way/146644585393483?v=wall
twitter.com/StopHwy
Overview: A large local organization
Mission: To preserve the Niagara Escarpment, by ensuring that no new highway corridors are paved across the Niagara Escarpment & that all viable alternatives to the proposed Mid-Peninsula Highway are fully considered; Affiliation(s): Coalition on the Niagara Escarpment; Sierra Club
Membership: 1000+; *Fees:* Donations of $10 or more

City Farmer - Canada's Office of Urban Agriculture
PO Box 74567, Stn. Kitsilano, Vancouver BC V6K 4P4
Tel: 604-685-5832
e-mail: cityfarm@interchange.ubc.ca
www.cityfarmer.org
cityfarmer.info
Overview: A small national organization founded in 1978
Mission: City Farmer encourages gardening in an urban environment. The website carries information for communities & schools about organic farming, composting, pest control.
Chief Officer(s):
Michael Levenston, Executive Director
Activities: Research Garden functions as the City of Vancouver's Compost Demonstration Garden & site of the Compost Hotline: 604-736-2250

CIVICUS: World Alliance for Citizen Participation
Stn. 933, 24 Gwigwi Mrwebi St., Johannesburg 2135 South Africa
Tel: +27 11 833 5959; *Fax:* +27 11 833 7997
e-mail: info@civicus.org
www.civicus.org
Overview: A small international organization
Mission: To strengthen citizen action & civil society around the globe towards a more just & equitable world; To promote the rights of citizens to organize & act collectively; To foster interaction between civil society & other institutions
Chief Officer(s):
Ingrid Srinath, Secretary General
Katsuji Imata, Deputy Secretary General, Programs
Sebastian Njagi Runguma, Manager, Planning & Learning
Sandra Pires, Manager, Membership
Devendra Tak, Manager, Communications & Media
Membership: 450+; *Member Profile:* Citizens from 110 countries, including individuals, youth, business associates, citizen organizations, & nongovernmental grantmaking organizations
Activities: Advocating for citizen participation; Amplifying the opinions of ordinary people; Increasing the effectiveness of civil society organizations
Meetings/Conferences:
For more information see Trade Shows, Conferences and Seminars Chapter
CIVICUS: World Alliance for Citizen Participation 2013 12th World Assembly
2013
Publications:
•Affinity Group of National Associations (AGNA) Newsletter
Type: Newsletter
•Civil Society Index (CSI) Newsletter
Type: Newsletter; *Frequency:* Quarterly
Profile: Project updates
•Civil Society Watch (CSW) Monthly Bulletin
Type: Newsletter; *Frequency:* Monthly
•e-CIVICUS [a publication of CIVICUS: World Alliance for Citizen Participation]
Type: Newsletter; *Frequency:* Weekly
Profile: Developments in civil society organizations around the world

Clean Air Foundation *See* Summerhill Impact

Clean Air Strategic Alliance (CASA)
10035 - 108 St., 10th Fl., Edmonton AB T5J 3E1
Tel: 780-427-9793; *Fax:* 780-422-3127
e-mail: casa@casahome.org
www.casahome.org
www.facebook.com/group.php?gid=38613321574
Overview: A medium-sized provincial organization founded in 1994
Mission: To manage strategic issues of air quality in Alberta; To represent three levels of government, as well as industry & NGOs; To plan for, organize, & commit resources related to air quality in Alberta; Operating the Comprehensive Air Quality Management System (CAMS)
Environmental Activity: Working towards a vision of air that will be odourless, tasteless, look clear, & have no measurable short- or long-term adverse effects on people, animals, or the environment
Chief Officer(s):
Kerra Chomlak, Executive Director
Finances: *Annual Operating Budget:* $500,000-$1.5 Million; *Funding Sources:* Industry; Government; Donations
Staff: 200 volunteer(s)

Clean Annapolis River Project (CARP)
PO Box 395, Annapolis Royal NS B0S 1A0
Tel: 902-532-7533; *Fax:* 902-532-3038
Toll-Free: 888-547-4344
e-mail: carp@annapolisriver.ca
www.annapolisriver.ca
www.facebook.com/183264721694056
twitter.com/CARPAnnapolis
Overview: A medium-sized local charitable organization founded in 1990
Mission: To promote, encourage & assist with the wise use of the resources of the Annapolis Watershed; Water quality monitoring program
Chief Officer(s):
Monik Richard, Executive Director
monikrichard@annapolisriver.ca
Finances: *Annual Operating Budget:* $250,000-$500,000; *Funding Sources:* Private & public
Staff: 12 staff member(s); 60 volunteer(s)
Membership: 100; *Fees:* $5 student; $7 individual; $10 family; $25 NGO; $100 lifetime
Activities: Environment monitoring; habitat restoration; climate change issues; water quality issues; public awareness; *Internships:* Yes; *Speaker Service:* Yes; *Library:* by appointment

Clean Calgary Association *See* Green Calgary

Clean Energy BC
#354, 409 Granville St., Vancouver BC V6C 1T2
Tel: 604-568-4778; *Fax:* 604-568-4724
Toll-Free: 855-568-4778
www.cleanenergybc.org
twitter.com/CleanEnergyBC
Previous Name: Independent Power Association of BC
Overview: A small provincial organization founded in 1992
Mission: To ensure that British Columbia's independent power producer industry is a contributor to the electricity market in the province

Environmental Activity: Promoting clean energy solutions throughout British Columbia
Chief Officer(s):
Paul Kariya, Executive Director
paul.kariya@cleanenergybc.org
Loch McJannett, Vice-President
loch.mcjannett@cleanenergybc.org
Lisa Bateman, Coordinator, Events
lisa.bateman@cleanenergybc.org
Kristen McIntyre, Contact, Membership Services, Registration, & Administration
kristen.mcintyre@cleanenergybc.org
Membership: *Committees:* Conference; First Nations; Hydro; Market Development; Public Affairs; Regulatory; Thermal; Transmission; Wind
Activities: Engaging in policy implementation
Meetings/Conferences:
For more information see Trade Shows, Conferences and Seminars Chapter
Clean Energy BC 2013 11th Annual Conference
October 2013 Vancouver, BC
Clean Energy BC 2014 12th Annual Conference
2014, BC

Clean North
736A Queen St. East, Sault Ste Marie ON P6A 2A9
Tel: 705-945-1573
e-mail: info@cleannorth.org
www.cleannorth.org
Also Known As: The Sault & District Recycling Association
Overview: A small provincial organization founded in 1989
Mission: This citizens' group promotes environmental protection through reduction, reuse & recycling of residential & industrial waste in Sault Ste. Marie & the Algoma District.; *Member of:* Northwatch; Ontario Environmental Network; Affiliation(s): Ontario Environment Network; Northwatch
Environmental Activity: Planting trees
Finances: *Annual Operating Budget:* $50,000-$100,000; *Funding Sources:* Membership dues; fundraising; foundations; grants
Staff: 210 volunteer(s)
Membership: 350; *Fees:* $10 & $15
Activities: Recycling phone books; dry cells; Christmas trees; *Internships:* Yes; *Speaker Service:* Yes; *Library:* Environmental Resource Room; Open to public

Clean Nova Scotia (CNS)
126 Portland St., Dartmouth NS B2Y 1H8
Tel: 902-420-3474; *Fax:* 902-424-5334
Toll-Free: 888-380-5008
e-mail: cns@clean.ns.ca
www.clean.ns.ca
www.facebook.com/pages/Clean-Nova-Scotia/117505381665669
twitter.com/CleanNovaScotia
www.youtube.com/user/CleanNovaScotia1
Previous Name: The Clean Nova Scotia Foundation
Overview: A medium-sized provincial charitable organization founded in 1988
Mission: To inspire positive environmental change in Nova Scotia
Environmental Activity: Effecting change in air quality, climate change, waste, water, energy, & health
Chief Officer(s):
Judy McMullen, Executive Director, 902-420-3476
judym@clean.ns.ca
Jill Murphy, Director, Finance, 902-420-7939
jmurphy@clean.ns.ca
Marlene Parsons, Director, Human Resources, 902-420-7945
mparsons@clean.ns.ca
Gina Patterson, Director, Programs, 902-420-7937
patterson@clean.ns.ca
Katie Abriel, Manager, Climate Change Education Programs, 902-420-7936
kabriel@clean.ns.ca
Joe Moar, Manager, Home Energy Evaluations, 902-420-7928
jmoar@clean.ns.ca
David Ashley, Coordinator, Ship to Shore Program, 902-420-7940
adavid@clean.ns.ca
Neil Bailey, Coordinator, Waste Programs, 902-420-7943
nbailey@clean.ns.ca
Steve Fairbairn, Coordinator, Green Schools Nova Scotia, 902-420-7948
sfairbairn@clean.ns.ca
Spencer Fowlie, Coordinator, Farms-to-School, 902-420-7933
sfowlie@clean.ns.ca
Valerie Francella, Coordinator, Adopt-a-Watershed, 902-420-3473
vfrancella@clean.ns.ca
Derek Gillis, Coordinator, Drive Wiser / Fleet Wiser Program, 902-420-7944
Wiserdgillis@clean.ns.ca
Leann Grosvold, Coordinator, Communications, 902-420-8803
lgrosvold@clean.ns.ca
Lisa Privett, Coordinator, Environmental Home Assessment Program, 902-420-6593
Kari Riddell, Coordinator, Litterless Road Tour, 902-420-7924
riddell@clean.ns.ca
Finances: *Funding Sources:* Donations; Sponsorships
Membership: *Member Profile:* Persons & businesses committed to the creation of a sustainable & healthy environment in Nova Scotia
Activities: Providing environmental education & information; *Awareness Events:* Commuter Challenge; Clean Across Nova Scotia
Meetings/Conferences:
For more information see Trade Shows, Conferences and Seminars Chapter
Clean Nova Scotia 2013 Annual General Meeting
2013, NS
Clean Nova Scotia 2014 Annual General Meeting
2014, NS
Publications:
•A Carbon Offsetting Primer
Author: Gina Patterson
•Clean & Green Newsletter
Type: Newsletter; *ISSN:* 1715-7897; *Price:* Free with Clean Nova Scotia membership
Profile: Environmental articles & tips, plus a list of interesting websites
•Clean Nova Scotia Annual Report
Type: Yearbook; *Frequency:* Annually
•Clean Nova Scotia Strategic Plan
Profile: A direction for the organization's activities during the next three to five years
•A Guide to Energy Efficiency for Religious Buildings in Nova Scotia
Type: Guide; *Number of Pages:* 50
Profile: Sections of the guide include getting started, the walk-through audit, how to do a greenhouse gas inventory, youth group engagement, energy efficiencyimprovements, a case study, a master checklist, resources for churches, & references

The Clean Nova Scotia Foundation ***See*** Clean Nova Scotia

Clean Water Action
#400, 1010 Vermont Ave. NW, Washington DC 20005-4918 USA
Tel: 202-895-0420; *Fax:* 202-895-0438
e-mail: cwa@cleanwater.org
www.cleanwateraction.org
www.facebook.com/pages/Clean-Water-Action/22907478728?ref=nf
twitter.com/cleanh2oaction
www.youtube.com/cleanwateraction
Overview: A large international organization founded in 1971
Mission: A national organization of diverse people and groups working together for clean water, protection of health, creation of jobs and making democracy work for environmental causes.
Chief Officer(s):
Robert Wendelgass, President & CEO
bwendelgass@cleanwater.org
Membership: 1,200,000

Climate Action Network - Canada
#412, 1 Nicholas St., Ottawa ON K1N 7B7
Tel: 613-241-4413
Toll-Free: 866-373-2990
e-mail: info@climateactionnetwork.ca
www.climateactionnetwork.ca
www.facebook.com/climate.action.network.canada
twitter.com/CANRACCanada
www.youtube.com/user/CANRACCanada
Overview: A small national organization
Mission: To support & empower Canada's governments, private sector, labour & civil society by designing, developing & implementing effective strategies to reduce greenhouse gas emissions at international, national & local levels; To prevent dangerous levels of human interference with the global climate system
Chief Officer(s):
Christian Holz, Executive Director
cholz@climateactionnetwork.ca
Membership: *Fees:* $40

Climate Institute
1785 Massachusetts Ave., NW, Washington DC 20036 USA
Tel: 202-547-0104; *Fax:* 202-547-0111
e-mail: info@climate.org
www.climate.org
Overview: A medium-sized international charitable organization founded in 1986
Mission: To help maintain the balance between climate & life on earth; To strive to be a source of objective, reliable information & a trustworthy facilitator of dialogue among scientists, policy makers, business executives, & citizens
Environmental Activity: Conducting projects on energy efficiency & cities, climate change in developing countries, & environmental refugees
Chief Officer(s):
John C. Topping Jr., President/CEO
Crispin Tickell, Chair (Emeritus)
Finances: *Annual Operating Budget:* $500,000-$1.5 Million; *Funding Sources:* Foundation; US government; Corporations
Staff: 8 staff member(s)
Membership: 1,500; *Fees:* $95 member; $200 associate; $1,000 patron; $2,500 sponsor; $5,000 benefactor; *Member Profile:* Scientists & environmentalists of many nationalities; *Committees:* Leadership Council
Activities: *Internships:* Yes; *Speaker Service:* Yes; *Library:* by appointment
Publications:
•Climate Alert
Editor: Corrine Kisner
Profile: Quarterly Newsletter
•Sudden & Disruptive Climate Change: Exploring the Real Risks & How We Can Avoid Them
Type: Book; *Editor:* Michael C. MacKracken et al.
Profile: An outline of the risks of & solutions to climate change

Le Club de gemmologie et de minérlogie de Montréal ***Voir*** Montréal Gem & Mineral Club

Club de naturalistes de Prince George ***See*** Prince George Naturalists

Club des ornithologues de Québec inc. (COQ)
Domaine de Maizerets, 2000, boul Montmorency, Québec QC G1J 5E7
Tél: 418-661-3544
Courriel: coq@coq.qc.ca
www.coq.qc.ca
Aperçu: *Dimension:* petite; *Envergure:* provinciale; fondée en 1955
Membre(s) du bureau directeur:
Norbert Lacroix, Président
nlacroix@mat.ulaval.ca
Marguerite Larouche, Vice-président
marlarou@sympatico.ca
Louis Messely, Secrétaire
lmessely@mediom.qc.ca
Norbert Lacroix, Président
Publications:
•Bulletin ornithologique
Editor: Pierre Otis

Clubs 4-H du Québec
#202, 6500 boul. Arthur-Sauvé, Laval QC H7R 3X7
Tél: 450-314-1942; *Téléc:* 450-314-1952
Courriel: info@clubs4h.qc.ca
www.clubs4h.qc.ca
Aperçu: *Dimension:* moyenne; *Envergure:* provinciale; fondée en 1942
Mission: Susciter et développer, chez le jeune, une préoccupation active pour la conservation de l'arbre, du milieu forestier et de l'environnement; développer le sens des autres, le sens des responsabilités, l'esprit d'initiative, la créativité, le sens de l'émerveillement et le respect pour tout ce qui vit; contribuer à répandre dans le public une mentalité de conservation envers l'environnement, en posant des gestes concrets pour l'amélioration de la qualité de la vie; *Membre de:* Regroupement Loisir Québec; Conseil québecois du loisir
Membre(s) du bureau directeur:
Andrée Gignac, Directrice
agignac@clubs4h.gc.ca

Finances: *Budget de fonctionnement annuel:* $100,000-$250,000; *Fonds:* Financement municipal, provincial, et fédéral; les frais d'adhésion; collecte de fonds
Personnel: 4 membre(s) du personnel; 300 bénévole(s)
Membre: 30 institutionnel; 1 000 individu *Montant de la cotisation:* $100/club
Activités: *Evénements de sensibilisation:* Mois de l'arbre et des forêts, mai

Coady International Institute (CII)
St. Francis Xavier University, PO Box 5000, Antigonish NS B2G 2W5
Tel: 902-867-3960; *Fax:* 902-867-3907
Toll-Free: 866-820-7835
e-mail: coady@stfx.ca
www.coady.stfx.ca
www.facebook.com/coady.international.institute
twitter.com/coadystfx
www.youtube.com/user/CoadyInstitute
Overview: A large international charitable organization founded in 1959
Mission: Promotes learning in individuals & organizations engaged in community-driven action to achieve wellbeing, global justice, peace & participating democracy; *Member of:* Canadian Council for International Cooperation
Environmental Activity: Environment & Development course taught as part of 6-month diploma course in Social Development
Chief Officer(s):
John Gaventa, Director
Finances: *Annual Operating Budget:* $1.5 Million-$3 Million
Staff: 28 staff member(s)
Membership: *Committees:* University Advisory
Activities: Conferences & presentations; publishes occasional papers; *Awareness Events:* Coady Celebrates, Nov 1; *Internships:* Yes; *Library:* Marie Michael Library; Open to public

Coalition canadienne de l'énergie géothermique *See* Canadian GeoExchange Coalition

Coalition des communautés en santé de l'Ontario *See* Ontario Healthy Communities Coalition

Coalition for a Smoke-Free Nova Scotia
PO Box 822, Lower Sackville NS B4V 3V3
Tel: 902-864-9633; *Fax:* 902-864-6946
Toll-Free: 866-777-7374
e-mail: carivanlingen@smokefreens.ca
www.smokefreens.ca
Also Known As: Smoke-Free Nova Scotia
Previous Name: Nova Scotia Council on Smoking & Health
Overview: A small provincial organization
Mission: Committed to the achievement of a tobacco-free Nova Scotia; *Member of:* Canadian Council on Smoking & Health
Finances: *Annual Operating Budget:* Less than $50,000; *Funding Sources:* Provincial government grants; Membership fees
Membership: 28; *Fees:* $20-200; *Member Profile:* Health professionals; Health agencies; Individuals
Activities: Media strategies; Public presentaions; Educational material; Consultations with government; *Awareness Events:* National Non-Smoking Week; World No Tobacco Day

Coalition for Education in the Outdoors
PO Box 2000, S.U.N.Y. Cortland, Cortland NY 13045 USA
Tel: 607-753-4971; *Fax:* 607-753-5982
e-mail: info@outdooredcoalition.org
www.outdooredcoalition.org
Overview: A medium-sized international organization founded in 1987
Mission: To assist in identifying the networking needs of its affiliates & to seek ways to meet those needs
Finances: *Annual Operating Budget:* Less than $50,000
Staff: 2 staff member(s)
Membership: 70 affiliates; *Fees:* $60-$250; *Member Profile:* A network of agencies, institutions, associations, centres, businesses & organizations linked & communicating in support of the broad purposes of education in, for, & about the outdoors
Activities: *Speaker Service:* Yes
Publications:
•Taproot
Profile: Quarterly Journal

Coalition Jeunesse Sierra *See* Sierra Youth Coalition

Coalition of Rail Shippers (CRS)
#405, 580 Terry Fox Dr., Ottawa ON K2L 4C2
Tel: 613-599-3283; *Fax:* 613-599-1295
Overview: A medium-sized national organization founded in 2005
Mission: CRS provides input to government on matters affecting Canadian, rail freight transportation.
Chief Officer(s):
Robert H. Ballantyne, Chair
Membership: *Member Profile:* Shipping industry associations

Coalition to Save the Elms *See* Trees Winnipeg

Coast Forest & Lumber Association *See* Coast Forest Products Association

Coast Forest Products Association (CFPA)
#1200, 1090 Pender St. West, Vancouver BC V6E 2N7
Tel: 604-891-1237; *Fax:* 604-682-8641
e-mail: info@coastforest.org
www.coastforest.org
Also Known As: Coast Forest
Previous Name: Coast Forest & Lumber Association
Overview: A medium-sized international organization founded in 1994
Mission: To promote the interests & protect the rights of those engaged in the coast forest industry in BC; *Member of:* Canadian Wood Council; Business Council of BC; Vancouver Board of Trade
Chief Officer(s):
Rick Jeffrey, President/CEO
Finances: *Annual Operating Budget:* $3 Million-$5 Million; *Funding Sources:* Coast Forest Industry; Partnership funding for lumber promotion in Japan & China
Staff: 3 staff member(s)
Membership: 20; *Fees:* Production related; *Member Profile:* Logging companies &/or lumber manufacturing companies
Activities: User-pay menu programs; log security; Japan & China lumber promotion

Coast Waste Management Association (CWMA)
1185 Rolmar Cres., Cobble Hill BC V0R 1L4
Tel: 250-733-2213; *Fax:* 250-733-2214
Toll-Free: 886-386-2962
e-mail: info@cwma.bc.ca
www.cwma.bc.ca
Overview: A small local organization
Mission: To facilitate communication between members; to provide networking & educational opportunities
Chief Officer(s):
Malcolm Harvey, Chair, 604-831-7203
malcolm_harvey@telus.net
Will Burrows, Executive Director
info@cwma.bc.ca
Membership: 115; *Member Profile:* Members of the solid waste industry on Vancouver Island, the Gulf Islands & the Sunshine Coast
Publications:
•CWMA [Coast Waste Management Association] News
Type: Newsletter; *Frequency:* q.
•CWMA [Coast Waste Management Association] E-bulletins
Type: Bulletin

Coastal Ecosystems Research Foundation
General Delivery, Dawson's Landing BC V0N 1M0
Tel: 44-0-7745-730873; *Fax:* 815-327-0173
e-mail: info@cerf.bc.ca
www.cerf.bc.ca
Overview: A small local organization founded in 1995
Mission: To fund ecological research through eco-tourism
Chief Officer(s):
William Megill, Ph.D., Research Director
Finances: *Annual Operating Budget:* $50,000-$100,000; *Funding Sources:* Provincial & national government
Staff: 4 staff member(s)
Membership: 120
Activities: Week-long "research adventure" in which people can participate in all aspects of our research while living a wilderness adventure along the southern Central Coast of British Columbia; this program almost completely funds our research focused on grey & humpback whales studies of the subtidal intertidal & coastal forest zones

CODE
321 Chapel St., Ottawa ON K1N 7Z2
Tel: 613-232-3569; *Fax:* 613-232-7435
Toll-Free: 800-661-2633
e-mail: codehq@codecan.org
www.codecan.org
www.facebook.com/code.org
www.youtube.com/user/TheCodecan
Also Known As: Canadian Organization for Development through Education
Overview: A large international charitable organization founded in 1959
Mission: To enable people to learn by developing partnerships that provide resources for learning, to promote awareness & understanding & to encourage self-reliance; To support training for teachers & librarians; To coordinate book donations from North American publishers to schools & libraries in the developing world; *Member of:* Canadian Council for International Cooperation; Affiliation(s): International Book Bank; CODE Europe; CODE Inc.; CODE Foundation
Chief Officer(s):
Scott Walter, Executive Director, 613-232-3569 Ext. 230
Brian Coburn, Director, Finance & Administration, 613-232-3569 Ext. 224
Ann Collins, Director, Marketing & Public Engagment, 613-232-3569 Ext. 232
Sean Maddox, Director, Development, 613-232-3569 Ext. 236
Dominique Naud, Manager, Communications, 613-232-3569 Ext. 252
Finances: *Funding Sources:* Individual; Corporate donations; CIDA
Staff: 4500 volunteer(s)
Membership: 30; *Fees:* $20; *Committees:* Governance; Audit; Human Resources
Activities: Organizing Adopt a Library to support a community library in Tanzania, Ethiopia or Malawi;

Cole Harbour Rural Heritage Society (CHRHS)
471 Poplar Dr., Dartmouth NS B2W 4L2
Tel: 902-434-0222; *Fax:* 902-462-0154
e-mail: farm.museum@ns.aliantzinc.ca
www.coleharbourfarmmuseum.ca/chrhs.html
Overview: A small local charitable organization founded in 1973
Mission: To protect & increase awareness of the natural history & cultural resources of Cole Harbour & the surrounding area; To foster appreciation & respect for the resources of the Cole Harbour region
Finances: *Funding Sources:* Community support
Membership: *Fees:* $20 individuals; $30 families
Activities: Administering the Cole Harbour Rural Heritage Farm Museum, a community museum that preserves & interprets the agricultural history of Cole Harbour; Preserving the former Methodist Chapel, now known as the Cole Harbour Meeting House; Advocating for the protection of natural history in the Cole Harbour area; Providing education about the ecosystem of the region; Promoting careful use of sensitive lands around Cole Harbour

College of Alberta Professional Foresters
#209, 10544 - 106 St., Edmonton AB T5H 2X6
Tel: 780-432-1177; *Fax:* 780-432-7046
e-mail: office@capf.ca
www.capf.ca
Previous Name: Alberta Registered Professional Foresters Association
Overview: A medium-sized provincial licensing organization founded in 1988
Mission: To maintain an accurate register of registered professional foresters in Alberta; To set standards of professional conduct & competence for members; To administer the title, Registered Professional Forester (RPF); *Member of:* Canadian Federation of Professional Foresters Associations; Affiliation(s): Alberta Forest Technologists Association; Canadian Institute of Forestry
Chief Officer(s):
Ted Gooding, President
Finances: *Funding Sources:* Membership fees
Staff: 1 staff member(s); 14 volunteer(s)
Membership: 630+; *Fees:* $285 Registered Professional Forester (RPF); $261 Forester-in-Training (FIT); $52 retired; $142.50 non-resident; $52 Syllabus member; *Member Profile:* B.Sc. in Forestry + professional examination + 2 yr. Forester-in-Training period; *Committees:* Executive; Discipline; Competence; Registration; Policy, Act, Regulation & Bylaws: Finance; Nominating

College of Applied Biology British Columbia
#205, 733 Johnson St., Victoria BC V8W 3C7
Tel: 250-383-3306; *Fax:* 250-383-2400
e-mail: cab@cab-bc.org
www.cab-bc.org
Overview: A small provincial licensing organization

Associations / Organizations

Mission: To uphold & protect the public interest by: preserving & protecting the scientific methods & principles that are the foundation of the applied bilogical sciences; To uphold the principles of stewardship of aquatic & terrestrial ecosystems & biological resources; To ensure the integrity, objectivity & expertise of its members
Chief Officer(s):
Brian Churchill, President
Pierre Lachetti, Executive Director
Finances: *Annual Operating Budget:* $250,000-$500,000
Staff: 4 staff member(s); 30 volunteer(s)
Membership: 1,500

Colonial Waterbird Society ***See*** The Waterbird Society

Comité canadien des Électrotechnologies ***Voir*** Conseil Canadien des Électrotechnologies

Comité intergouvernemental de recherches urbaines et régionales ***See*** Intergovernmental Committee on Urban & Regional Research

Comité maritime international (CMI) / International Maritime Committee
Everdijstraat 43, Antwerpen B-2000 Belgium
Tel: 32-3-227-3526; *Fax:* 32-3-227-3528
e-mail: admini@cmi-imc.org
www.comitemaritime.org
Overview: A medium-sized international organization founded in 1897
Mission: To contribute by all appropriate means & activities to the unification of maritime law; Affiliation(s): Canadian Maritime Law Association
Chief Officer(s):
Karl-Johan Gombrii, President
Nigel Frawley, Secretary General, 416-923-0333, Fax: 416-944-9020
nhfrawley@earthlink.net
Membership: 50 associations
Activities: ; *Library:* CMI-Secretariat; Open to public by appointment

Commercial Seed Analysts Association of Canada Inc. (CSAAC)
#208, 301 Rothesay St., Douglas MB R0K 0K0
Tel: 204-763-4610
e-mail: csaacexecutivedirector@gmail.com
www.seedanalysts.ca
Overview: A medium-sized national licensing organization founded in 1944
Mission: To help determine the future of the seed industry; to enhance professionalism through ongoing education; to provide customers with seed analysis services & information
Chief Officer(s):
Christine DeRooy, President
cderooy@hylandseeds.com
Betty Girard, Executive Director
csaacexecutivedirector@gmail.com
Membership: 100+; *Fees:* $60-$350; *Committees:* Membership; Research & Review; Historical; Special; Technical; Ethics; Exam; CSI Reps; CSGA Standard & Stock Seed; Nomination; CSAAC By-law Review
Activities: Exams & accreditation
Publications:
•Breaking Dormancy [a publication of the Commercial Seed Analysts Association of Canada Inc.]
Type: Newsletter; *Frequency:* Monthly

Commission Coopération Environnementale ***See*** Commission for Environmental Cooperation

Commission de coopération environnementale ***See*** Commission for Environmental Cooperation

Commission des Grands Lacs ***See*** Great Lakes Commission

Commission for Environmental Cooperation (CEC) / Commission Coopération Environnementale
Secretariat, #200, 393, rue St-Jacques ouest, Montréal QC H2Y 1N9
Tel: 514-350-4300; *Fax:* 514-350-4314
e-mail: info@cec.org
www.cec.org
Mission: The Commission for Environmental Cooperation (CEC) is an international organization created by Canada, Mexico & the United States under the North American Agreement on Environmental Cooperation (NAAEC). The CEC was established to address regional environmental concerns, help prevent potential trade & environmental conflicts & to promote the effective enforcement of environmental law. The Agreement complements the environmental provisions of the North American Free Trade Agreement (NAFTA).
Chief Officer(s):
Irasema Coronado, Executive Director
Marco Antonio Heredia Fragoso, Program Manager, Environmental Law, 514-350-4302
maheredia@cec.org
Orlando Cabrera-Rivera, Program Manager, Air Quality & PRTR, 514-350-4323
ocabrera@cec.org
Heidy G. Rivasplata, Project Coordinator, Chemicals Management, 514-350-4378
hrivasplata@cec.org

Commission for Environmental Cooperation (CEC) / Commission de coopération environnementale (CCE)
#200, 393, St-Jacques St. West, Montréal QC H2Y 1N9
Tel: 514-350-4300; *Fax:* 514-350-4314
e-mail: info@cec.org
www.cec.org
Overview: A medium-sized international organization founded in 1995
Mission: Created by Canada, Mexico & the United States to address regional environmental concerns; to help prevent potential trade & environmental conflicts, & to promote the effective enforcement of environmental law
Chief Officer(s):
Evan Lloyd, Executive Director
Nathalie Daoust, Secretary, 514-350-4310
Finances: *Annual Operating Budget:* Greater than $5 Million; *Funding Sources:* Three NAFTA governments, Canada, Mexico, United States
Staff: 55 staff member(s)
Membership: 1-99
Activities: *Internships:* Yes; *Library:*

Mexico Office
Progreso #3, Viveros de Coyoacán, Mexico DF 04110 Mexico
Tel: 52-555 659 5021; *Fax:* 52-555-659 5023
Chief Officer(s):
Juan Rafael Elvira Quesada

Commission internationale de la santé au travail ***See*** International Commission on Occupational Health

Commission internationale des irrigations & du drainage ***See*** International Commission on Irrigation & Drainage

Commission Internationale du Genie Rural ***See*** International Commission of Agricultural & Biosystems Engineering

Commission on Sustainable Development (CSD)
Dept. of Economic & Social Affairs, UN Secretariat Bldg., #405, 42nd East St., New York NY 10017 USA
Tel: 212-963-8102; *Fax:* 212-963-4260
e-mail: dsd@un.org
sustainabledevelopment.un.org
Mission: To operate as a functional commission of the UN Economic & Social Council, composed of members elected for terms of office for three years; To meet annually; To be guided by a multi-year (2004-2017) program of work which outlines seven two-year cycles, with each two-year cyle focused on themes; To review progress at the international, regional & national levels in the implementation of recommendations & commitments contained in Agenda 21 & the Rio Declaration on Environment & Development
Chief Officer(s):
Nikhil Seth, Director
Membership: *Member Profile:* Members of the intergovernmental body are elected by the Economic & Social Council from memberstates of the United Nations & its specialized agencies
Activities: Promoting dialogue & building partnerships for sustainable development with governments, the international community & the major groups who have a role to play in the transition toward sustainable development, including women, youth, indigenous peoples, non-governmental organizations, local authorities, workers & trade unions, business & industry, the scientific community & farmers

Committee for the National Institutes for the Environment ***See*** National Council for Science & the Environment

Committee on Nutrition in the Commonwealth ***See*** Commonwealth Human Ecology Council

Commonwealth Association of Surveying & Land Economy (CASLE)
c/o Faculty of the Built Environment, Univ. of West England, Coldharbour Lane, Bristol BS16 1QY United Kingdom
Tel: 44-117-750440; *Fax:* 44-117-750440
www.casle.org
Overview: A medium-sized international organization founded in 1969
Mission: To maintain & strengthen professional links between Commonwealth countries, with the aim of assisting each country to achieve the scale, quality & integrity of surveying services that it requires; to foster the establishment of professional societies in countries where none exists & to promote their usefulness for the public advantage
Chief Officer(s):
Jacob Opadeyi, President
Susan M. Spedding, Secretary
Brian Waldy, Secretary General
Finances: *Annual Operating Budget:* $50,000-$100,000
Membership: 40 societies; *Member Profile:* Open to leading society in each surveying discipline in each Commonwealth country; *Committees:* Management Board
Activities: Conferences/seminars; research into sustainable development

Commonwealth Engineers' Council (CEC)
The Institution of Civil Engineers, One Great George St., London SW1P 3AA United Kingdom
Tel: 44-20-7665-2156; *Fax:* 44-20-7223-1806
www.ice.org.uk/cec/
Overview: A small international organization founded in 1946
Member of: World Federation of Engineering Organizations; Affiliation(s): Canadian Council of Professional Engineers
Chief Officer(s):
Tom Foulkes, Secretary General
Tony Ridley, President
Oivind Grimsmo, Deputy Secretary
Finances: *Funding Sources:* Membership fees; Commonwealth Foundation
Staff: 3 staff member(s)
Membership: 42

Commonwealth Forestry Association - Canadian Chapter (CFA)
c/o Faculty of Forestry, University of BC, #2045, 2424 Main Mall, Vancouver BC V6T 1Z4
Tel: 604-822-6761; *Fax:* 604-822-9106
www.cfa-international.org
Overview: A small international organization founded in 1921
Mission: To promote the conservation and sustainable management of the world's forests and the contribution they make to peoples' livelihoods; *Member of:* Commonwealth Forestry Association, UK
Chief Officer(s):
John Innes, Regional Director, The Americas
john.innes@ubc.ca
Finances: *Annual Operating Budget:* Less than $50,000
Staff: 1 volunteer(s)
Membership: 60; *Fees:* $108; *Member Profile:* Professional foresters

Commonwealth Geographical Bureau (CGB)
c/o Dept. of Geography, 1 Arts Link, National Univ. of Singapore, Singapore 117570 Singapore
Tel: 65-6874-3855; *Fax:* 65-6777-3091
www.commonwealthgeography.org
Overview: A small international organization founded in 1968
Mission: CGB promotes the study & practice of geography at all levels within the Commonwealth, especially in developing countries. It aims to disseminate information to Commonwealth geographers & effect the exchange of staff between member countries.; Affiliation(s): International Geographical Union
Chief Officer(s):
Victor R. Savage, President
geosava@nus.edu.sg
Denis Dwyer, Treasurer
Finances: *Annual Operating Budget:* Less than $50,000; *Funding Sources:* Commonwealth Foundation
Staff: 4 volunteer(s)
Membership: 5,000-14,999; *Member Profile:* Commonwealth geographers; *Committees:* Management; Small Island Development
Activities: Organizing workshops

Commonwealth Human Ecology Council (CHEC)
Church House, Newton Rd., Bayswater, London W2 5LS United Kingdom

Tel: 44 (0) 207 7925934; *Fax:* 44 (0) 207 7925948
e-mail: chec@btopenworld.com
www.checinternational.org
Previous Name: Committee on Nutrition in the Commonwealth
Overview: A medium-sized international charitable organization founded in 1969
Mission: CHEC is a human ecology network with links in many Commonwealth countries. The Council challenges governments to create policies in support of ecological & sustainable communities, & has successfully implemented projects in countries as diverse as Kenya, Bangladesh, Hong Kong, Malta, New Zealand, India, Canada, Guyana, Barbados, Sierra Leone, Pakistan, Nigeria, Australia, & Sri Lanka. It promotes discussion & action programmes with emphasis on the joint responsibilities of government, civil society & the individual to alleviate poverty. It is recognized in Britain as an international charity.; Affiliation(s): In consultative status with UN ECOSOC (Economic & Social Council)
Chief Officer(s):
Zena Daysh, Executive Vice-Chair
Finances: *Annual Operating Budget:* $100,000-$250,000; *Funding Sources:* Commonwealth Foundation; UK Government; UK Lottery; Comic Relief
Staff: 4 staff member(s); 2 volunteer(s)
Membership: 500; *Fees:* £20 individual; £50 corporate; *Member Profile:* Government; non-government; professionals; cross section of communities & civil society; *Committees:* Executives; Finance; Governing Board; Projects

Canadian Contact
c/o Interstice Consulting Corporation, 34 Whippoorwill Dr., Ottawa ON K1J 8P2
Tel: 613-749-7293
e-mail: info@intersticeconsulting.com
www.intersticeconsulting.com
Chief Officer(s):
Mohan Prabhu, Contact

Communications, Energy & Paperworkers Union of Canada (CEP) / Syndicat canadien des communications, de l'énergie et du papier (SCEP)

301 Laurier Ave. West, Ottawa ON K1P 6M6
Tel: 613-230-5200; *Fax:* 613-230-5801
Toll-Free: 877-230-5201
e-mail: info@cep.ca
www.cep.ca
www.facebook.com/group.php?gid=14453572223
twitter.com/CEPinfoSCEP
www.youtube.com/user/CEPunionSCEP
Overview: A large national organization founded in 1992
Mission: To improve pay & working conditions through collective bargaining & to represent members at grievance hearings; To present a common front with other unions & community groups to governments on issues that affect all workers, from minimum wage to medicare; Affiliation(s): Canadian Labour Congress
Chief Officer(s):
Gaétan Ménard, Sec.-Treas.
gmenard@cep.ca
Dave Coles, President
dcoles@cep.ca
Finances: *Annual Operating Budget:* Greater than $5 Million; *Funding Sources:* Membership dues
Staff: 150 staff member(s)
Membership: 110,000; *Committees:* Health & Safety; Pensions; Women's; Special Committees
Activities: Education Program; *Library:*
Meetings/Conferences:
For more information see Trade Shows, Conferences and Seminars Chapter
Communciation, Energy & Paperworkers Union of Canada 2013 Convention
2013
Publications:
•The Activist
Type: Newsletter; *Frequency:* Monthly

Community & Hospital Infection Control Association Canada / Association pour la prévention des infections à l'hôpital et dans la communauté - Canada

PO Box 46125, Stn. Westdale, Winnipeg MB R3R 3S3
Tel: 204-897-5990; *Fax:* 204-895-9595
Toll-Free: 866-999-7111
e-mail: chicacanada@mts.net
www.chica.org
Also Known As: CHICA-Canada
Overview: A medium-sized national charitable organization founded in 1976
Mission: To promote excellence in the practice of infection prevention & control; to employ evidence based practice & application of epidemiological principles to improve the health of Canadians; *Member of:* International Federation of Infection Control (IFIC)
Chief Officer(s):
Jim Gauthier, President, 613-548-5567 Ext. 5754
gauthij2@providencecare.ca
Membership: 1,700; *Fees:* $195
Activities: Education; Communication; Standards; Research; Consumer awareness; *Library:*
Publications:
•Canadian Journal of Infection Control
Type: Journal; *Frequency:* Quarterly; *Editor:* Pat Piaskowski, RN, HBScN, CIC; *Price:* Free with CHICA-Canada membership
Profile: Information relevant to the practice of infection control in hospitals & communities
•Community & Hospital Infection Control Association Canada Annual Member & Source Guide
Type: Yearbook; *Frequency:* Annually; *Price:* Free with CHICA-Canada membership

Community Energy Association (CEA)

#1400, 333 Seymour St., Vancouver BC V6B 5A6
Tel: 604-628-7076; *Fax:* 778-786-1613
e-mail: info@communityenergy.bc.ca
www.communityenergy.bc.ca
Overview: A medium-sized provincial charitable organization founded in 1993
Mission: To support local governments in British Columbia in energy conservation & climate change activities
Environmental Activity: Delivering & supporting programs such as Community Action on Energy & Emissions & Green Buildings BC for Local Governments
Chief Officer(s):
Dale Littlejohn, Executive Director
dlittlejohn@communityenergy.bc.ca
Patricia Bell, Senior Community Energy Planner
pbell@communityenergy.bc.ca
Megan Lohmann, Senior Energy Planner, 250-423-7212
Finances: *Funding Sources:* Membership revenues; Fundraising
Activities: Communicating with elected officials, municipal & regional district staff, & First Nations in British Columbia; Offering advisory services to local governments regarding energy innovations; Promoting energy efficiency & renewable energy for infrastructure; Encouraging local governments to consider energy in land planning & development; Conducting research on energy related topics; *Speaker Service:* Yes
Publications:
•Community Energy Association Directory
Type: Directory
Profile: Listings of association members
•Energy Brief for Elected Officials
Type: Guide
Profile: Information for local government leaders
•Heating Our Communities
Type: Guide
Profile: A renewable energy guide produced for local government leaders

Compost Council of Canada / Conseil canadien du compost

16 Northumberland St., Toronto ON M6H 1P7
Tel: 416-535-0240; *Fax:* 416-536-9892
Toll-Free: 877-571-4769
e-mail: info@compost.org
www.compost.org
www.facebook.com/people/Compost-Council/100001137258465
Overview: A medium-sized national organization founded in 1991
Mission: To advance organics residuals recycling & compost use; To contribute to environmental sustainability
Environmental Activity: Advocating for organics residuals recycling; Offering composting & other greening advice; Promoting composting & compost usage; Developing a greenhouse gas protocol for centralized costing facilities in Canada
Chief Officer(s):
Susan Antler, Executive Director
Activities: Providing resources for the Canadian compost industry; *Awareness Events:* Compost Week, May
Meetings/Conferences:
For more information see Trade Shows, Conferences and Seminars Chapter
Compost Council of Canada 2013 Regional Workshop: Compost Matters!
January 2013 Mississauga, ON
Compost Council of Canada 2013 23rd Annual National Compost Conference
September 2013 Toronto, ON
Compost Council of Canada 2013 Compost Garden Party 2013
Compost Council of Canada 2014 24th Annual National Compost Conference
2014
Publications:
•Compost Matters
Type: Newsletter
Profile: Information for members of the Compost Council of Canada, such as regulations, members, grants, workshops, conferences, & awareness events

Compressed Gas Association, Inc. (CGA)

#103, 14501 George Carter Way, Chantilly VA 20151 USA
Tel: 703-788-2700; *Fax:* 703-961-1831
e-mail: cga@cganet.com
www.cganet.com
Overview: A small international organization founded in 1913
Mission: To develop & promote safety standards for the industrial gas industry
Environmental Activity: Promoting practices for safe, secure, & environmentally responsible manufacture, transportation, storage, & disposal of industrial & medical gases & their containers; Organizing seminars about industry safety & environmental practices
Membership: *Member Profile:* Manufacturers, suppliers, distributors, & transporters of gases, cryogenic liquids, & related products in Canada & the United States; *Committees:* Canadian Cylinder Specification; Canadian Medical, Food, & Beverage Gases & Equipment; Canadian Pressure Vessels & Piping Sys.; Canadian Health, Safety, & Environment; Canadian Transportation; Acetylene; Atmospheric Gases & Equipment; Bulk Distribution Equipment & Standards; Carbon Dioxide; Compressed Gas Emergency Action Plan; Cylinder Specifications; Cylinder Valve; Distribution & Fleet Safety; Environmental; Food Gases; Hazard Comm.; Hazardous Materials Codes; Hydrogen Tech.; HYCO; Industrial Gases Apparatus; Liquefied Petroleum Gas; Medical Equipment; Medical Gases; Security; Safety/Health
Activities: Working with governmental agencies to produce standards & regulations; Promoting compliance with regulations in the workplace; Providing access to edcuational publications & videos; Offering networking opportunities
Publications:
•Compressions [a publication of the Compressed Gas Association]
Type: Newsletter; *Frequency:* Quarterly; *Price:* Free with Compressed Gas Association membership
Profile: Association & industry news

Concerned Educators Allied for a Safe Environment (CEASE)

55 Frost St., Cambridge MA 2140 USA
Tel: 617-661-8347
e-mail: info@peaceeducators.org
www.peaceeducators.org
Overview: A small national organization founded in 1979
Mission: To create safe world for children; to seek to end the violence in society & remove the root causes of violence by advocating for peace, justice & economic opportunity; *Member of:* Survival Education Fund; Affiliation(s): National Association for the Education of Young Children
Chief Officer(s):
Lucy Stroock
Susan Hopkins
Chris Lamm
Lucy Stroock, Sec.-Treas.
Finances: *Annual Operating Budget:* Less than $50,000; *Funding Sources:* Subscriptions; membership dues; donations
Staff: 6 volunteer(s)
Membership: 1,000; *Fees:* $10; $5 student; *Member Profile:* Early childhood educators & trainers
Activities: Workshops; seminars

Le Conference Board du Canada *See* The Conference Board of Canada

The Conference Board of Canada / Le Conference Board du Canada

255 Smyth Rd., Ottawa ON K1H 8M7
Tel: 613-526-3280; *Fax:* 613-526-4857
Toll-Free: 866-711-2262
www.conferenceboard.ca
Overview: A medium-sized national organization founded in 1954
Mission: To be dedicated to applied research, notably in public policy, economic trends, & organizational performance
Chief Officer(s):
Anne Golden, President & CEO
Glen Hodgson, Sr. VP & Chief Economist
Perry Eisenschmid, Vice-President, Marketing, Sales & IT
Finances: *Funding Sources:* Fees for service to the public & private sectors
Activities: The Business & Environment Research Program provides research & networking facilities for business & government in the economics, business management & public policy aspects of environmental issues. Other activities include conferences, publishing & disseminating research, & facilitating networking & training for leadership; *Library:* Information Centre; by appointment

Conférence des coopératives forestières du Québec *Voir* Fédération québécoise des coopératives forestières

Conférence des Nations Unies sur le commerce et le développement *See* United Nations Conference on Trade & Development

Conference of New England Governors & Eastern Canadian Premiers

Council Secretariat, PO Box 2044, #1006, 5161 George St., Halifax NS B3J 2Z1
Tel: 902-424-7590; *Fax:* 902-424-8976
e-mail: info@cap-cpma.ca
www.cap-cpma.ca
Mission: To expand economic ties among the Atlantic provinces, Québec, & six New England states; To foster energy exchanges; To coordinate numerous policies & programs, in areas such as transportation, forest management, tourism, small-scale agriculture & fisheries; To enact policy resolutions that call on actions by the state & provincial governments, as well as by the two national governments; To promote natural gas, resource & infrastructure development
Environmental Activity: Advocating for environmental issues & & sustainable development; Adopting an acid rain action plan & a mercury action plan; Collaborating with environmental departments & agencies
Membership: *Member Profile:* Premiers of the Atlantic provinces & Québec; Governors of six New England States
Activities: Hosting conferences of the Premiers & Governors to discuss issues of common interest; Convening meetings of state & provincial officials; Organizing workshops & roundtables; Preparing reports & studies; Monitoring & acting on common issues in the northeast region, such as electric restructuring

Congrès du travail du Canada *See* Canadian Labour Congress

Congrès mondiaux du pétrole *See* World Petroleum Congress

Connexions Information Sharing Services

#305, 489 College St., Toronto ON M6G 1A5
Tel: 416-964-1511; *Fax:* 416-964-8763
e-mail: connexions@connexions.org
www.connexions.org
www.facebook.com/ConnexionsOnline
Overview: A small national organization founded in 1975
Mission: To link people striving to create positive solutions to social, environmental, economic & international problems; To encourage development of a more just & democratic society; To disseminate information & ideas that contribute to this goal; *Member of:* Ontario Environment Network
Chief Officer(s):
Ulli Diemer, Coordinator
Finances: *Annual Operating Budget:* Less than $50,000
Staff: 3 staff member(s); 12 volunteer(s)
Activities: *Internships:* Yes; *Speaker Service:* Yes; *Rents Mailing List:* Yes; *Library:* by appointment

Conseil canadien de droit international *See* Canadian Council on International Law

Conseil canadien de l'énergie *See* Energy Council of Canada

Conseil canadien de l'horticulture *See* Canadian Horticultural Council

Conseil canadien de la construction en acier *See* Canadian Steel Construction Council

Conseil canadien de la fourrure *See* The Fur Council of Canada

Conseil canadien de la lutte antiparasitaire en milieu urbain *See* Urban Pest Management Council of Canada

Conseil canadien de la sécurité *See* Canada Safety Council

Conseil canadien de protection des animaux *See* Canadian Council on Animal Care

Conseil canadien des administrateurs en transport motorisé *See* Canadian Council of Motor Transport Administrators

Conseil canadien des aliments et de la nutrition *See* Canadian Council of Food & Nutrition

Conseil canadien des directeurs provinciaux et des commissaires des incendies *See* Council of Canadian Fire Marshals & Fire Commissioners

Conseil Canadien des Électrotechnologies (CCE) / Canadian Council on Electrotechnologies (CCE)

600, av de la Montagne, Shawinigan QC G9N 7N5
Tél: 819-539-1560; *Téléc:* 819-539-1558
Nom précédent: Comité canadien des Électrotechnologies
Aperçu: *Dimension:* moyenne; *Envergure:* nationale; fondée en 1986
Mission: Transfert technologique en vue de l'utilisation rationnelle et optimale de l'électricité
Membre(s) du bureau directeur:
Richard Clayton, President-CCE
rick.h.clayton@ca.pwcglobal.com
Michael P. Dudar, Vice Président-CCE
mpdudar@hydro.mb.ca
Membre: 20 *Montant de la cotisation:* 500$; *Critères d'admissibilite:* Industriels, ingénieurs, chercheurs, professeurs, producteurs et distributeurs d'électricité
Activités: Groupes technologie, éducation, information; *Service de conférenciers:* Oui; *Bibliothèque:* Bibliothèque publique rendez-vous

Conseil canadien des laboratoires indépendants *See* Canadian Council of Independent Laboratories

Conseil canadien des ministres de l'environnement *See* Canadian Council of Ministers of the Environment

Conseil canadien des ministres des forêts *See* Canadian Council of Forest Ministers

Conseil canadien des pêcheurs professionnels *See* Canadian Council of Professional Fish Harvesters

Conseil canadien des professionnels en securité agréés *See* Board of Canadian Registered Safety Professionals

Conseil canadien des techniciens et technologues *See* Canadian Council of Technicians & Technologists

Conseil canadien du bois *See* Canadian Wood Council

Conseil canadien du commerce de détail *See* Retail Council of Canada

Conseil canadien du compost *See* Compost Council of Canada

Conseil canadien pour la coopération internationale *See* Canadian Council for International Co-operation

Conseil canadien pour le contrôle du tabac *See* Canadian Council for Tobacco Control

Conseil canadien sectoriel des plastiques *See* Canadian Plastics Sector Council

Conseil de conservation de l'Ontario *See* Conservation Council of Ontario

Conseil de l'industrie forestière du Québec (CIFQ) / Québec Forestry Industry Council (QFIC)

#200, 1175, av Lavigerie, Sainte-Foy QC G1V 4P1
Tél: 418-657-7916; *Téléc:* 418-657-7971
Courriel: info@cifq.qc.ca
www.cifq.qc.ca
Nom précédent: Association des manufacturiers de bois de sciage du Québec
Aperçu: *Dimension:* grande; *Envergure:* provinciale
Mission: Représente la très grande majorité des entreprises de sciage résineux, de pâtes, papiers, cartons et panneaux oeuvrant au Québec; se consacre à la défense des intérêts de ces entreprsies, à la promotion de leur contribution au développement socio-économique, à la gestion intégrée et à l'aménagement durable des forêts, de même qu'à l'utilisation optimale des ressources naturelles; oeuvre auprès des instances gouvernementales, des organismes publics et parapublics, des organisations et de la population; encourage un comportement responsable de ses membres en regard des dimensions environnementales, économiques et sociales de leurs activités.
Environmental Activity: Comité Environnement
Membre(s) du bureau directeur:
André Tremblay, Président-CEO
Membre: 200 compagnies; *Critères d'admissibilite:* Membres réguliers - compagnies possédant une ou des usines de sciage ou de rabotage ou papetière; membres remanufacturiers - compagnies dont la fonction consiste à transformer le bois en provenance d'une scierie; membres associés - grossistes, manufacturiers d'équipements, consultants, sociétés financières dont les activités sont reliées à celles des membres réguliers
Activités: *Listes de destinataires:* Oui
Publications:
•Fibrexpression
Type: Bulletin

Conseil de la conservation du Nouveau-Brunswick *See* Conservation Council of New Brunswick

Conseil de la transformation agroalimentaire et des produits de consommation (CTAC) / Council of Food Processing & Consumer Products

#102, 200, rue MacDonald, Saint-Jean-sur-Richelieu QC J3B 8J6
Tél: 450-349-1521; *Téléc:* 450-349-6923
Courriel: info@conseiltac.com
www.conseiltac.com
www.linkedin.com/company/1237456
Nom précédent: Association des manufacturiers de produits alimentaires du Québec
Merged from: Conseil de la boulangerie du Québec; Association des abattoirs avicoles du Québec
Aperçu: *Dimension:* moyenne; *Envergure:* provinciale; Organisme sans but lucratif; fondée en 1954
Mission: Le porte-parole officiel des manufacturiers de produits alimentaires du Québec qui s'y regroupent à titre de membres fabricants; canalise les représentations des manufacturiers, en particulier auprès des gouvernements; coordonne l'action des membres en vue de promouvoir leurs intérêts économiques, sociaux et professionnels; suscite l'éducation des consommateurs sur les valeurs d'une bonne alimentation; favorise la promotion des produits fabriqués par les membres; établit des liaisons entre les manufacturiers, les producteurs, les fournisseurs, les distributeurs, les consommateurs et les autres maillons de la chaîne alimentaire; encourage la recherche dans les domaines de l'agriculture, de l'alimentation et du marketing
Membre(s) du bureau directeur:
Sylvie Cloutier, Présidente-directrice générale
Finances: *Budget de fonctionnement annuel:* $500,000-$1.5 Million
Personnel: 5 membre(s) du personnel
Membre: 400; *Critères d'admissibilite:* Fabricants; fournisseurs; distributeurs; *Comités:* Activités sociales; Agriculture; Environnement; Mise en marché; Négociations; Nomination; Recrutement; Santé et securité du travail; Travail

Conseil des 4-H du Canada *See* Canadian 4-H Council

Conseil des aéroports du Canada *See* Canadian Airports Council

Conseil des bio-industries du Québec; Association québécoise des bio-industries *Voir* BIOQuébec

Conseil des fabricants de bois *See* Wood Manufacturing Council

Conseil des palettes du Canada *See* Canadian Pallet Council

Conseil des ressources humaines de l'industrie minière *See* Mining Industry Human Resources Council

Conseil des viandes du Canada *See* Canadian Meat Council

Conseil du bâtiment durable du Canada *See* Canada Green Building Council

Conseil du Manitoba pour la coopération internationale ***See*** Manitoba Council for International Cooperation

Conseil du recyclage de l'Ontario ***See*** Recycling Council of Ontario

Conseil international des Monuments et des Sites ***See*** International Council on Monuments & Sites

Conseil international des sciences de l'animal de laboratoire ***See*** International Council for Laboratory Animal Science

Conseil international du Canada ***See*** Canadian International Council

Conseil international du droit de l'environnement ***See*** International Council of Environmental Law

Conseil Mondial de l'Energie ***See*** World Energy Council

Conseil National de l'Enveloppe du Bâtiment ***See*** National Building Envelope Council

Conseil patronal de l'environnement du Québec (CPEQ)

#206, 640, rue Saint-Paul ouest, Montréal QC H3C 1L9
Tél: 514-393-1122; *Téléc:* 514-393-1146
Courriel: info@cpeq.qc.ca
www.cpeq.qc.ca
Aperçu: *Dimension:* moyenne; *Envergure:* provinciale
Mission: To promote the interests of industry & business in environmental matters
Membre(s) du bureau directeur:
Hélène Lauzon, Présidente

Conseil régional de l'environnement de la Gaspésie et des Iles-de-la-Madeleine (CREGIM)

#103, 106-A, Port Royal, Bonaventure QC G0C 1E0
Tél: 418-534-4498
Ligne sans frais: 877-534-4498
Courriel: cregim@globetrotter.net
www.cregim.org
Aperçu: *Dimension:* petite; *Envergure:* locale; fondée en 1995
Mission: Regrouper et représenter des organismes proenvironnementaux et des individus voués à la protection et la mise en valeur de l'environnement, auprès de toutes les instances concernées; favoriser la concertation et assurer l'établissement de priorités et de suivi en matière d'environnement; favoriser et promouvoir des stratégies d'actions concertées; agir à titre d'organisme ressource aux services des intervenants régionaux; Affiliation(s): Regroupement national des Conseils régionaux en environnement
Membre(s) du bureau directeur:
Caroline Duchesne, Directrice
caroline.cregim@globetrotter.net
Maryève Charland-Lallier, Présidente
Monette Bujold, Secrétaire adjointe-administrative
monette.cregim@globetrotter.net
Finances: *Budget de fonctionnement annuel:* $50,000-$100,000; *Fonds:* Gouvernement provincial; gouvernement régional; gouvernement municipal
Personnel: 4 membre(s) du personnel; 9 bénévole(s)
Membre: 119 *Montant de la cotisation:* 100$ institutionnel; 10$ individu; 30$ associé

Conservation Council of New Brunswick (CCNB) / Conseil de la conservation du Nouveau-Brunswick

180 St. John St., Fredericton NB E3B 4A9
Tel: 506-458-8747; *Fax:* 506-458-1047
e-mail: info@ccnbaction.ca
www.conservationcouncil.ca
Overview: A medium-sized provincial charitable organization founded in 1969
Mission: To generate awareness of the ecological foundations of our quality of life; To promote public policies with respect to the integrity of natural systems & to contribute to a sustainable society; To advocate appropriate remedies to pressing environmental problems such as ground water contamination & hazardous wastes; *Member of:* New Brunswick Environmental Network; Canadian Environmental Networks; Affiliation(s): Friends of the Earth Canada
Chief Officer(s):
Jamie Watson, Executive Director
Stephanie Coburn, President
Finances: *Annual Operating Budget:* $100,000-$250,000; *Funding Sources:* Enterprise activities; Special events; Contracts for special projects
Staff: 3 staff member(s)
Membership: 550; *Fees:* Schedule available
Activities: *Rents Mailing List:* Yes; *Library:*

Conservation Council of Ontario (CCO) / Conseil de conservation de l'Ontario

#132, 215 Spadina Ave., Toronto ON M5T 2C7
Tel: 416-533-1635; *Fax:* 416-979-3936
e-mail: cco@web.ca
www.weconserve.ca/cco
Overview: A medium-sized provincial charitable organization founded in 1951
Mission: To build a strong conservation movement across Ontario
Environmental Activity: Promoting conservation solutions
Chief Officer(s):
Ben Marans, President
Chris Winter, Executive Director
cco@web.ca
Karen Sun, Secretary
Membership: *Member Profile:* Municipalities, businesses, organizations, & individuals dedicated to conservation & a healthy environment
Activities: Increasing public awareness of conservation; Developing a provincial fund to support conservation efforts throughout Ontario
Meetings/Conferences:
For more information see Trade Shows, Conferences and Seminars Chapter
Conservation Council of Ontario 2013 Annual Meeting
2013, ON

Conservation de la faune au Canada ***See*** Wildlife Preservation Canada

Conservation Foundation of Greater Toronto

5 Shoreham Dr., Toronto ON M3N 1S4
Tel: 416-667-6279; *Fax:* 416-667-6275
e-mail: fdn@trca.on.ca
www.trca.on.ca
Also Known As: The Living City Foundation
Previous Name: The Metropolitan Toronto & Region Conservation Foundation; The Conservation Foundation of Greater Toronto
Overview: A small local charitable organization founded in 1961
Mission: To acquire & manage regional greenspace & watershed conservation lands; To support watershed management, reforestation, wildlife habitats, public access & recreation, historic sites, & environmental rehabilitation of natural spaces; Affiliation(s): The Toronto & Region Conservation Authority
Chief Officer(s):
Linda Craib, Admin Coordinator & Sr. Researcher
lcraib@trca.on.ca
David Love, Executive Director
dlove@trca.on.ca
Finances: *Annual Operating Budget:* $250,000-$500,000; *Funding Sources:* Donors include businesses, industries, other foundations, estates, conservation organizations & individuals
Staff: 20 volunteer(s)
Membership: 20; *Committees:* Board; Campaign; Executive; Members
Activities: Tree For Life Program; Kortright Centre for Conservation; Conservation Education Field Centres (conservation education schools at Albion Hills, Cold Creek & Claremont Conservation Areas); conservation libraries & scholarships; Don River; Greenspace Strategy (the authority's conservation vision for the 21st century - urges greater cooperation between the authority, the province & the municipalities in managing the regional watershed; also advocates protection of the Oak Ridges Moraine complex

Conservation Halton Foundation

2596 Britannia Rd. West, Burlington ON L7P 0G3
Tel: 905-336-1158; *Fax:* 905-336-7014
e-mail: web@hrca.on.ca
www.conservationhalton.on.ca
www.facebook.com/ConservationHalton
twitter.com/CH_Comm
Previous Name: Halton Foundation
Overview: A small local charitable organization
Mission: To raise funds for Conservation Halton projects & programs that protect & enhance the natural environment
Chief Officer(s):
Jim A. Sweetlove, Chair, Conservation Halton Foundation
John Vice, Chair, Conservation Halton
Brian Hobbs, Director, Development, Conservation Halton Foundation
Finances: *Annual Operating Budget:* $100,000-$250,000
Publications:
•Focus on Conservation [a publication of Conservation Halton Foundation]
Type: Newsletter

Conservation International (CI)

#500, 2011 Crystal Dr., Arlington VA 22202 USA
Tel: 703-341-2400
Toll-Free: 800-429-5660
www.conservation.org
www.facebook.com/conservation.intl
twitter.com/ConservationOrg
Overview: A large international charitable organization founded in 1987
Mission: To conserve the Earth's living natural heritage, our global biodiversity, & to demonstrate that human societies are able to live harmoniously with nature
Chief Officer(s):
Peter Seligmann, Chairman/Chief Executive Officer
Russell A. Mittermeier, President
Barbara DiPietro, CFO
Finances: *Annual Operating Budget:* Greater than $5 Million; *Funding Sources:* Private; government; agencies; foundations
Staff: 1200 staff member(s)
Membership: 5,000; *Fees:* $35; *Member Profile:* Scientists; economists; communicators; educators; conservation professionals
Activities: Center for Applied Biodiversity Science; Critical Ecosystem Partnership Fund; Global Conservation Fund; Center for Environmental Leadership in Business; Field Support; Resources & Communications; *Internships:* Yes; *Library:* Open to public

Conservation Ontario

Box 11, 120 Bayview Pkwy., Newmarket ON L3R 4W3
Tel: 905-895-0716; *Fax:* 905-895-0751
e-mail: info@conservationontario.ca
www.conservation-ontario.on.ca
www.facebook.com/home.php?sk=group_33621230329
Also Known As: Association of Conservation Authorities of Ontario
Overview: A medium-sized provincial organization founded in 1946
Mission: To represent & support a network of community-based environmental organizations; To ensure conservation, restoration, & responsible management of Ontario's wetlands, woodlands, & natural habitat
Environmental Activity: Raising awareness of the importance of healthy watersheds; Delivering watershed-based ecosystem resources & services; Conducting a water resources information project; Ensuring that rivers, lakes, & streams are properly safeguarded
Chief Officer(s):
Dick Hibma, Chair, 905-895-0716
info@conservationontario.ca
Don Pearson, General Manager
dpearson@conservationontario.ca
Bonnie Fox, Manager, Policy & Planning
bfox@conservationontario.ca
Charley Worte, Manager, Source Water Protection Planning
cworte@conservationontario.ca
Jo-Anne Rzadki, Coordinator, Watershed Stewardship
jrzadki@conservationontario.ca
Chris Wilkinson, Coordinator, Water Resources Information Project (WRIP)
cwilkinson@conservationontario.ca
Jane Lewington, Specialist, Marketing & Communications
jlewington@conservationontario.ca
Finances: *Funding Sources:* Levies provided by the conservation authorities
Membership: 36 organizations; *Member Profile:* Ontario's conservation authorities; Community-based watershed management agencies
Activities: Developing programs to protect life & property from natural hazards, such as erosion & flooding; Encouraging watershed stewardship practices; Promoting teh expertise of conservation authorities in managing Ontario's environment
Meetings/Conferences:
For more information see Trade Shows, Conferences and Seminars Chapter
2013 A.D. Latornell Conservation Symposium
November 2013 Alliston, ON

Publications:
•Adaptive Management of Stream Corridors in Ontario
Type: Report
Profile: A planning & design guide
•An Evaluation of Water Resource Monitoring Efforts in Support of Agricultural Stewardship in Watersheds of the Great Lakes
Type: Report
Profile: Produced by Conservation Ontario in partnership with the Ontario Ministry of Agriculture, Food &Rural Affairs
•Conservation Ontario Annual Report
Type: Yearbook; *Frequency:* Annually
•Conservation Ontario E-Bulletin
Type: Newsletter
Profile: Information & updates on issues about conservation authorities
•Cost Benefit Analysis of Agricultural Source Water Protection Beneficial Management Practices
Type: Report
Profile: Agricultural beneficial management practices such as plant buffers, soile testing, crop covers, & crop rotation to protect thequality & supply of water
•Guide to Conservation Areas
Type: Guide; *Number of Pages:* 64
Profile: A guide to 261 conservation areas among 36 conservation authorities in Ontario
•Innovations in Water Management
Type: Report
Profile: Place-based environmental management approaches
•Navigating Ontario's Future: A Water Budget Overview for Ontario
Type: Report; *Number of Pages:* 36
•Navigating Ontario's Future: Overview of Integrated Watershed Management in Ontario
Type: Report; *Number of Pages:* 122
•Navigating Ontario's Future: Water Management Framework
Type: Report; *Number of Pages:* 32
Profile: Contents include the need for a framework, developing the water management framework, the use of the framework in Ontario, & next steps
•Ontario Drinking Water Stewardship Program Outreach & Education Toolkit
Type: Kit
Profile: A communication toolkit for each Source Protection Region & Source Protection Area in Ontario
•Protecting People & Property: A Business Case for Investing in Flood Prevention & Control
Type: Report; *Number of Pages:* 56; *Author:* M. Fortin
Profile: Subjects addressed include the evolution of flood management, accomplishments, flood frequency & severity, responding tofuture risks, & costs & benefitis of improvements
•Sensitivity Mapping & Local Watershed Assessments for Climate Change Detection & Adaptation Monitoring
Type: Report; *Number of Pages:* 77
Profile: Topics include Ontario sensitivity assessment using GIS mapping, climate change detection monitoring, & climatechange adaptation monitoring
•Walkerton Inquiry
Type: Report
Profile: A summary of Conservation Ontario's participation in part II of the Walkerton Inquiry, including a position paper entitled "The Importance of Watershed Management in Protecting Ontario's Drinking WaterSupplies"
•Water Resources Information Project
Type: Report
Profile: The current state of water information in Ontario

Conserver Society of Hamilton & District Inc.

c/o EcoHouse, 22 Veevers Dr., Hamilton ON L8K 5P5
e-mail: contact@conserversociety.ca
www.conserversociety.ca
Overview: A small local charitable organization founded in 1969
Mission: To promote a healthy, sustainable environment in Hamilton, Ontario & the surrounding area; To provide public education about environmental issues
Environmental Activity: Advocating for environmental responsibility; Carrying out environmental projects; Supporting research related to the environment
Chief Officer(s):
Pete Wobschall, Chair, 905-540-8787 Ext. 117
Finances: *Funding Sources:* Donations; Membership fees; Sponsorships
Membership: *Fees:* $10 individuals; $20 families; $40 organizations
Activities: Partnering with like-minded organizations
Publications:
•Environmental Advocate
Type: Newsletter; *Price:* Free with membership in the Conserver Society of Hamilton & District Inc.
Profile: Information related to envrionmental issues

Construction Association of New Brunswick Inc. (CANB)
Parent Name: Canadian Construction Association

59 Avonlea Ct., Fredericton NB E3C 1N8
Tel: 506-459-5770; *Fax:* 506-457-1913
e-mail: canb1@nbnet.nb.ca
www.constructnb.ca
Overview: A small provincial organization founded in 1971 overseen by Canadian Construction Association
Mission: CANB is designed to perform a co-ordinating function for reaching consensus to effectively present the Industry's collective views to various client groups, partic-ularly to relevant departments and agencies of the provincial government.
Chief Officer(s):
Hilary Howes, Executive Director

Construction Association of Prince Edward Island (CAPEI)
Parent Name: Canadian Construction Association

PO Box 728, #223, 40 Enman Cres., Charlottetown PE C1E 1E6
Tel: 902-368-3303; *Fax:* 902-894-9757
e-mail: admin@capei.ca
www.capei.ca
Overview: A medium-sized provincial organization overseen by Canadian Construction Association
Mission: To foster, promote & advance the interests & efficiency of Prince Edward Island's construction industry
Chief Officer(s):
Ross D. Barnes, General Manager
ross@capei.ca
Craig Ling, President
cling@hewitt.ca
Publications:
•CAPEI [Construction Association of Prince Edward Island] Project Newsletter
Type: Newsletter; *Frequency:* Weekly
•Construction Association of Prince Edward Island Membership Directory
Type: Directory
Profile: Guide for public of CAPEI members' company information
•Working for You [a publication of the Construction Association of Prince Edward Island]
Type: Newsletter

Construction Safety Association of Manitoba (CSAM)

1447 Waverly St., Winnipeg MB R3T 0P7
Tel: 204-775-3171; *Fax:* 204-779-3505
e-mail: safety@constructionsafety.ca
www.constructionsafety.ca
Overview: A small provincial organization founded in 1989
Mission: To promote safe work practices & procedures throughout Manitoba's construction industry; To provide news about changes to health & safety regulations; To offer information about accident prevention methods; *Member of:* Canadian Federation of Construction Safety Associations
Environmental Activity: Providing specialized training in areas such as emergency preparedness & response, inspections, & investigations
Chief Officer(s):
Sean Scott, Executive Director
sean@constructionsafety.ca
Derek Pott, Manager, Client Services
derek@constructionsafety.ca
Tara Zukewich, Program Manager
tara@constructionsafety.ca
Mitch Calvert, Coordinator, Marketing & Innovations
mitch@constructionsafety.ca
Marla Fillion, Coordinator, Training & Program
marla@constructionsafety.ca
Finances: *Funding Sources:* Manitoba contractors, through a surchrge on a percentage of their assessment premiums collected by the Workers Compensation Baord
Activities: Developing training programs; Working with the Workers Compensation Board of Manitoba & the Workplace Saftey & Health Branch
Meetings/Conferences:
For more information see Trade Shows, Conferences and Seminars Chapter
Construction Safety Association of Manitoba 2013 Safety Conference
February 2013 Winnipeg, MB
Construction Safety Association of Manitoba 2013 19th Annual Westman Safety Conference
March 2013 Brandon, MB
Publications:
•Construction Safety Association of Manitoba Newsletter
Type: Newsletter; *Price:* Free, as part of themandate to assist construction employers in safety matters
Profile: Information & education about safety regulatory matters & accident prevention methods for building construction employers throughout Manitoba

Construction Specifications Canada (CSC) / Devis de construction Canada

#312, 120 Carlton St., Toronto ON M5A 4K2
Tel: 416-777-2198; *Fax:* 416-777-2197
e-mail: info@csc-dcc.ca
www.csc-dcc.ca
www.linkedin.com/groups?mostRecent=&gid=1911916&trk=eml-anet_dig-h_gn-
www.facebook.com/120516191352386?ref=ts
Previous Name: Specification Writers Association of Canada
Overview: A large national organization founded in 1954
Mission: To improve communication, contract documentation, & technical information in the construction industry; Affiliation(s): Construction Specification Foundation; Construction Specifications Canada/Alberta Section Training Trust Fund; Construction Specifications Institute; Canadian Standards Assoc.; Mechanical Contractors Assoc. of Canada; Ontario Bid Depository Council; Alberta Building Envelope Council; Alberta Roofing Contractor's Assoc.; Canadian Institute of Plumbing & Heating; Assoc. of Professional Engineers of Canada; Royal Architectural Institute of Canada; Canadian Construction Assoc.; Toronto Construction Assoc.; Society of the Plastics Industry of Canada; Thermal Insulation Assoc. of Canada
Chief Officer(s):
Claude Giguère, President
cgiguere@pageaumorel.com
Finances: *Annual Operating Budget:* $500,000-$1.5 Million; *Funding Sources:* Sale of technical documents; membership fees
Staff: 4 staff member(s)
Membership: 650 specifier architects & engineers + 750 industrial manufacturers, suppliers & contractors; *Fees:* $235; $50 student; *Member Profile:* Interested & involved in the dissemination of construction specifications & related documentation; incorporates specifiers, architects, engineers, construction product manufacturers & distributors, general & trade contractors; chapter-based association with chapters in Halifax, Quebéc, Montréal, Ottawa, Toronto, Hamilton/ Niagara, Grand Valley, London, Winnipeg, Regina, Saskatoon, Edmonton, Calgary & Vancouver; *Committees:* Awards; Conferences; Executive; Finance; French Language Publications; Legislative; Professional Development & Education; Technical Studies
Activities: National education programs consists of Technical Documents Programs including Home Study Course for Architectural Specifiers, & courses leading to the Registered Specification Writer (RSW) designation; *Speaker Service:* Yes; *Rents Mailing List:* Yes
Meetings/Conferences:
For more information see Trade Shows, Conferences and Seminars Chapter
Construction Specifications Canada Conference 2013
May 2013 Calgary, AB
Construction Specifications Canada Conference 2014
2014
Publications:
•Construction Canada
Type: Magazine

Consultative Group on International Agricultural Research (CGIAR)

Secretariat, 1818 H St. NW, MSN-G6-601, Washington DC 20433 USA
Tel: 202-473-8951; *Fax:* 202-473-8110
e-mail: cgiar@cgiar.org
www.cgiar.org
Overview: A medium-sized international organization founded in 1971
Mission: To achieve sustainable food security and reduce poverty in developing countries through scientific research and research-related activities in the fields of agriculture, forestry, fisheries, policy, and environment.

Chief Officer(s):
Ren Wang, Director
Finances: *Annual Operating Budget:* Greater than $5 Million
Membership: 64
Activities: ; *Library:* Information Center; by appointment

Consulting Engineers of Alberta (CEA)
Parent Name: Association of Consulting Engineering Companies - Canada

Phipps-McKinnon Building, #870, 10020 - 101A Ave., Edmonton AB T5J 3G2
Tel: 780-421-1852; *Fax:* 780-424-5225
e-mail: info@cea.ca
www.cea.ca
Overview: A medium-sized provincial organization founded in 1978 overseen by Association of Consulting Engineering Companies - Canada
Mission: To provide leadership to foster a positive business environment for the consulting engineering firms in Alberta; To promote the engineering industry; To enhance interests & opportunities of CEA members; To provide society with high standards of engineering design & safety
Environmental Activity: Working to make significant contributions to the environment, society, & the economy; Establishing an environmental committee to provide further information on items such as the Alberta Water Act & its effect upon the work of engineers
Chief Officer(s):
Wendy Cooper, Executive Director
Gord Johnston, President
gord.johnston@stantec.com
Ken Pilip, Registrar
Sharon Moroskat, Manager, Finance & Administration
smoroskat@cea.ca
Hiju Song, Manager, Events & Communications
hsong@cea.ca
Finances: *Funding Sources:* Membership fees; Sponsorships
Membership: *Committees:* Board of Directors; Buildings; City of Calgary Liaison; City of Edmonton Liaison; Environmental; Industrial; Municipal Liaison; Small Firm; Transportation; Transportation Conference; Young Professionals' Group
Activities: Protecting legislative & regulatory interests; Offering a forum to exchange ideas; Providing training programs & information; *Speaker Service:* Yes
Meetings/Conferences:
For more information see Trade Shows, Conferences and Seminars Chapter
Consulting Engineers of Alberta 2013 16th Annual Tri-Party Transportation Conference & Trade Show Exhibition
March 2013 Red Deer, AB
Consulting Engineers of Alberta 2013 Infrastructure Partners Conference
2013, AB
Consulting Engineers of Alberta 2013 35th Annual General Meeting
2013, AB
Consulting Engineers of Alberta 2013 Annual Luncheon with the City of Edmonton Council
2013, AB
Publications:
•Bullet [a publication of the Consulting Engineers of Alberta]
Type: Newsletter
Profile: Information for Consulting Engineers of Alberta, such as forthcoming meetings, sponsorship opportunities, & social events
•CEA [Consulting Engineers of Alberta] Progress Report on Salaries
Frequency: Annually
Profile: Salary recommendations
•CEA [Consulting Engineers of Alberta] Annual Report
Type: Yearbook; *Frequency:* Annually
•Consulting Engineers of Alberta Directory of Members
Type: Directory
Profile: Listing of members, including location & size of firms
•Consulting Engineers Rate Guidelines
Profile: Standard hourly rates for engineers, technicians, & technologists in Alberta

Consulting Engineers of British Columbia (CEBC)
Parent Name: Association of Consulting Engineering Companies - Canada

#1258, 409 Granville St., Vancouver BC V6C 1T2
Tel: 604-687-2811; *Fax:* 604-688-7110
e-mail: info@acec-bc.ca
www.acec-bc.ca
Overview: A medium-sized provincial organization founded in 1976 overseen by Association of Consulting Engineering Companies - Canada
Mission: To improve the commercial environment for consulting engineering firms
Environmental Activity: Hosting conferences to address issues such as reducing greenhouse gas & adapting to climate change
Chief Officer(s):
Glenn Martin, Executive Director
glenn@cebc.org
Jack Lee, President
Glen Martin, Executive Director
Alla Samusevich, Coordinator, Accounting & Events
alla@cebc.org
Membership: *Member Profile:* Consulting engineering firms across British Columbia that provide services to the built & natural environment; *Committees:* Building Engineering; Municipal Engineering; Resource & Energy; Transportation; Business Practice; Membership Affairs; Young Professsionals' Group; Okanagan/Thompson Liaison; Vancouver Island Liaison
Activities: Lobbying to policymakers in districts, provincial & municipal governments, & private sector clients; Coordinating a common industry approach to issues; Promoting CEBC members' consulting services; Providing networking, educational, & professional development opportunities
Meetings/Conferences:
For more information see Trade Shows, Conferences and Seminars Chapter
Consulting Engineers of British Columbia 2013 Annual Transportation Conference
January 2013 Vancouver, BC
Consulting Engineers of British Columbia 2013 Awards Gala
April 2013 Vancouver, BC
Consulting Engineers of British Columbia 2013 Member / Industry Dinner
2013, BC
Consulting Engineers of British Columbia 2013 Client Mixers
2013, BC
Consulting Engineers of British Columbia 2013 Government Relations Day
2013, BC
Consulting Engineers of British Columbia 2013 Young Professionals' Group Seminars
2013, BC
Consulting Engineers of British Columbia 2013 Annual General Meeting
2013, BC
Consulting Engineers of British Columbia 2014 Annual Transportation Conference
2014, BC
Publications:
•Consulting Engineers of British Columbia Annual Report
Type: Yearbook; *Frequency:* Annually
Profile: The association's profile, reports from the president, executive director, treasurer, & the committees, the minutes from the annual general meeting, awards, &events
•Directory of CEBC [Consulting Engineers of British Columbia] Member Firms
Type: Directory
Profile: Listings of Consulting Engineers of British Columbia members, available for the public

Consulting Engineers of Manitoba Inc. (CEM)
Parent Name: Association of Consulting Engineering Companies - Canada

PO Box 1547, Stn. Main, Winnipeg MB R3C 2Z4
Tel: 204-774-5258; *Fax:* 204-779-0788
acec-mb.ca
twitter.com/acec_manitoba
Overview: A medium-sized provincial organization founded in 1978 overseen by Association of Consulting Engineering Companies - Canada
Mission: To promote & enhance the business interests of the consulting engineers of Manitoba; to lead in the application of technology for the benefit of society.; Affiliation(s): Association of Professional Engineers of Manitoba; International Federation of Consulting Engineers; Manitoba Association of Architects
Chief Officer(s):
Shirley E. Tillett, Executive Director
cemca@shaw.ca
H. Pankratz, President
Finances: *Annual Operating Budget:* $50,000-$100,000; *Funding Sources:* Membership dues
Membership: 31 firms; *Member Profile:* Offer primarily consulting engineering services to public; *Committees:* City of Winnipeg; First Nations; Golf Tournament; MWSB/PFRA; Private Industry Liasion; Public Relations; Transportation
Activities: *Speaker Service:* Yes

Consulting Engineers of Nova Scotia (CENS)
Parent Name: Association of Consulting Engineering Companies - Canada

PO Box 613, Stn. M, Halifax NS B3J 2R7
Tel: 902-461-1325; *Fax:* 902-461-1321
e-mail: cens@eastlink.ca
www.cens.org
Previous Name: Nova Scotia Consulting Engineers Association
Overview: A medium-sized provincial organization founded in 1973 overseen by Association of Consulting Engineering Companies - Canada
Mission: To enable the consulting engineering industry in Nova Scotia to capitalize on opportunities to grow; To promote employment of member firms
Membership: 50 companies; *Member Profile:* Nova Scotia based companies in the business of engineering & related services
Activities: Maintaining high professional standards in the industry; Increasing awareness about the work & employment of consulting engineers
Meetings/Conferences:
For more information see Trade Shows, Conferences and Seminars Chapter
Consulting Engineers of Nova Scotia (CENS) 2013 40th Annual General Meeting
April 2013 Halifax, NS

Consulting Engineers of Ontario (CEO)
Parent Name: Association of Consulting Engineering Companies - Canada

#405, 10 Four Seasons Pl., Toronto ON M9B 6H7
Tel: 416-620-1400; *Fax:* 416-620-5803
e-mail: staff@ceo.on.ca
www.ceo.on.ca
Overview: A medium-sized provincial organization founded in 1975 overseen by Association of Consulting Engineering Companies - Canada
Mission: To further the maintenance of high professional standards in consulting engineering profession; to promote cordial relations among various consulting firms in Ontario; to foster interchange of professional management & business experience & information among consulting engineers; to develop regional representation & participation in affairs of the association.
Chief Officer(s):
Saskia Martini-Wong, Manager, Operations & Finance, 416-620-1400 Ext. 225
David Amm, Chair
Finances: *Annual Operating Budget:* $250,000-$500,000
Staff: 4 staff member(s)
Membership: 250 firms
Activities: Co-sponsor "Living Earth" exhibit at Ontario Science Centre; *Speaker Service:* Yes
Meetings/Conferences:
For more information see Trade Shows, Conferences and Seminars Chapter
Consulting Engineers of Ontario 2013 Annual General Meeting
June 2013 Toronto, ON

Consulting Engineers of Québec *Voir* Association des ingénieurs-conseils du Québec

Consulting Engineers of Saskatchewan (CES)
Parent Name: Association of Consulting Engineering Companies - Canada

#12, 2010 - 7 Ave., Regina SK S4R 1C2
Tel: 306-359-3338; *Fax:* 306-522-5325
e-mail: ces@sasktel.net
www.ces.sk.ca
Previous Name: Association of Consulting Engineers of Saskatchewan
Overview: A small provincial organization founded in 1977 overseen by Association of Consulting Engineering Companies - Canada
Mission: To further the maintenance of high professional standards in consulting engineering profession; To promote cordial relations among various consulting firms in Saskatchewan; To foster interchange of professional management & business experience & information among consulting engineers; To develop regional representation & participation in affairs of the association
Chief Officer(s):
Mel Leu, P.Eng, Chair

Beverly MacLeod, Executive Director
Finances: *Annual Operating Budget:* $50,000-$100,000
Staff: 2 staff member(s); 100+ volunteer(s)
Membership: 49 firms + 9 associates; *Committees:* Building; Communications; Environment/Water Resources; Human Resources; Industry Resources; Transportation; Young Professionals Group (YPG); CEG Task Groups
Meetings/Conferences:
For more information see Trade Shows, Conferences and Seminars Chapter
Consulting Engineers of Saskatchewan (CES) 2013 Annual General Meeting
May 2013 Elbow, SK

Consulting Engineers of Yukon (CEY) Parent Name: Association of Consulting Engineering Companies - Canada

c/o EBA Engineering Consultants Ltd., #6, 151 Industrial Rd., Whitehorse YT Y1A 2V3
Tel: 867-668-3068; *Fax:* 867-668-4349
e-mail: cey@eba.ca
www.cey.ca
Overview: A small provincial organization founded in 1983 overseen by Association of Consulting Engineering Companies - Canada
Mission: To maintain high professional standards in the consulting engineering profession; To promote cordial relations among various consulting firms in the Yukon; to foster interchange of professional management & business experience & information among consulting engineers; To develop regional representation & participation in affairs of the association
Chief Officer(s):
Richard Trimble, Executive Director
Membership: 21 firms

Consulting Foresters of British Columbia

PO Box 98, Pender Island BC V0N 2M0
Tel: 250-656-8818
e-mail: info@cfbc.bc.ca
www.cfbc.bc.ca
Overview: A small provincial organization founded in 1968
Mission: To maintain high professional standards in forestry consulting; To advance contact between its members, client groups, & the public at large
Chief Officer(s):
Jonathan Lok, President
jonathan.lok@sfmi.ca
Vacant, Vice-President
Membership: 80; *Fees:* $200-$1000

Consumer Policy Institute (CPI)

225 Brunswick Ave., Toronto ON M5S 2M6
Tel: 416-964-9223; *Fax:* 416-964-8239
e-mail: cpi@eprf.ca
www.c-p-i.org/cpi/index.cfm
Overview: A small local organization founded in 1980
Mission: A project of the Energy Probe Research Foundation (EPRF), CPI focuses on the force of the individual consumer, the empowerment of the general public brought about by the communications revolution & trade liberalization, circumstances that are eroding the power of traditional authorities in society. CPI understands this individual empowerment must be rooted in a sense of responsibility to other people & to the environment. The Institute is activly involved in a number of campaigns, covering a wide range of such fields as health care, tranportation, economic policy, automobile insurance & airports.
Chief Officer(s):
Lawrence Solomon, Executive Director
lawrence.solomon@nextcity.com

Consumers International (CI)

24 Highbury Cres., London N5 1RX United Kingdom
Tel: 44-20-7226-6663; *Fax:* 44-20-7354-0607
e-mail: consint@consint.org
www.consumersinternational.org
Overview: A medium-sized international organization founded in 1960
Mission: To protect consumer interests worldwide through institution building, education, research & lobbying of international decision making bodies
Chief Officer(s):
Richard Lloyd, Director General
Finances: *Annual Operating Budget:* $1.5 Million-$3 Million; *Funding Sources:* Membership fees; Project funding
Staff: 80 staff member(s)
Membership: links the activities of more than 220 consumer groups in 115 countries; *Fees:* Schedule available
Activities: Special services available only to IOCU members, volunteers, correspondents, networks & participants of like-minded organizations: Consumer Alert (a hazard notification issued by the Consumer Interpol; Consumer Interpol seeks to protect consumers from hazardous products, technologies & wastes); Consumer Interpol Memo (disseminates news on health & safety issues); Pesticide Monitor (disseminates information on the work of the Pesticide Action Network, a global network which aims to curb indiscriminate use; *Internships:* Yes; *Speaker Service:* Yes

Consumers' Association of Canada (CAC) / Association des consommateurs du Canada

436 Gilmour St., 3rd Fl., Ottawa ON K2P 0R8
Tel: 613-238-2533; *Fax:* 613-238-2538
e-mail: info@consumer.ca
www.consumer.ca
Overview: A large national organization founded in 1947
Mission: To represent & articulate the best interests of Canadian consumers to all levels of government & to all sectors of society by continually earning recognition as the trusted voice of the consumer on a national basis; to inform & educate consumers on marketplace issues; To work with government & industry to solve marketplace problems; To focus its work in the areas of food, health, trade, standards, financial services, communications industries & other marketplace issues as they emerge
Chief Officer(s):
Bruce Cran, President
Mel Fruitman, Vice-President
Finances: *Funding Sources:* Membership fees; project grants; donations
Staff: 6 staff member(s); 350 volunteer(s)
Membership: 16,000; *Fees:* $25; *Member Profile:* Open; *Committees:* Financial Services; Communications; Food & Agriculture - Supply Management Task Force & Biotechnology Task Force; Health; Marketplace Issues - Standards, Environment Network, Energy Network
Activities: Consumer literacy program; consumer referral, information, education; consumer representation - standards development & implementation, multi-stakeholder working groups & advisory committees, special purpose task forces; *Speaker Service:* Yes

Corporation des agronomes du Québec *Voir* Ordre des agronomes du Québec

Corporation des entreprises de traitement de l'air et du froid (CETAF) / Corporation of Air Treatment & Cold Processing Enterprises

#301, 6525, boul Décarie, Montréal QC H3W 3E3
Tél: 514-735-1131; *Téléc:* 514-735-3509
Ligne sans frais: 866-402-3823
Courriel: cetaf@cetaf.qc.ca
www.cetaf.qc.ca
Aperçu: *Dimension:* moyenne; *Envergure:* provinciale; Organisme sans but lucratif; fondée en 1964
Mission: Représenter et défendre les intérêts de ses membres; règlementer leur discipline et leur conduite professionnelle; favoriser et encourager la formation permanente
Membre(s) du bureau directeur:
Chantal Demers, Directrice générale
chantal.demers@cetaf.qc.ca
Finances: *Budget de fonctionnement annuel:* $250,000-$500,000
Personnel: 3 membre(s) du personnel; 16 bénévole(s)
Membre: 300 entreprises *Montant de la cotisation:* 660$; *Critères d'admissibilite:* Détenir une licence de la RBQ #4230.1, 4230.2, 4230.3, 4234, 4250.4 ou 4509
Activités: Mecanex-Climatex: Exposition commerciale - le carrefour annuel des professionnels de l'installation, de la vente et du service, dans l'industrie du traitement de l'air et du froid; séminaires; programme de formation et de perfectionnement; tournoi de golf annuel; *Bibliothèque:* Bibliothèque publique rendez-vous
Publications:
•ClimaPresse
Profile: Une revue technique et professionnelle d'expression française, publiée 6 fois l'an

Corporation des maîtres mécaniciens en tuyauterie du Québec (CMMTQ) / Corporation of Master Pipe Mechanics of Québec

8175, boul St-Laurent, Montréal QC H2P 2M1
Tél: 514-382-2668; *Téléc:* 514-382-1566
Ligne sans frais: 800-465-2668
www.cmmtq.org
Aperçu: *Dimension:* moyenne; *Envergure:* provinciale; Organisme sans but lucratif; fondée en 1949
Mission: Augmenter la compétence et l'habilité de ses membres en vue d'assurer au public une plus grande sécurité et protection au point de vue de l'hygiène et de la santé; *Membre de:* Heating, Refrigeration & Air Conditioning Institute of Canada
Membre(s) du bureau directeur:
André Bergeron, Directeur général
Alain Daigle, Président
Finances: *Budget de fonctionnement annuel:* $500,000-$1.5 Million
Personnel: 21 membre(s) du personnel
Membre: 2 200 *Montant de la cotisation:* 660$; *Critères d'admissibilite:* Entrepreneur en mécanique du bâtiment
Activités: Mécanex
Publications:
•L'Entre-Presse
Type: Newsletter; *Frequency:* Biweekly

Corporation des officiers municipaux agréés du Québec (COMAQ) / Corporation of Chartered Municipal Officers of Québec

Édifice Lomer-Gouin, #R02, 575, rue Saint-Amable, Québec QC G1R 2G4
Tél: 418-527-1231; *Téléc:* 418-527-4462
Ligne sans frais: 800-305-1031
Courriel: info@comaq.qc.ca
www.comaq.qc.ca
Aperçu: *Dimension:* moyenne; *Envergure:* provinciale; fondée en 1968
Mission: Regrouper les cadres municipaux des cités et villes du Québec; promouvoir la formation professionnelle par l'organisation de cours; protéger les intérêts sociaux-économiques des membres.
Membre(s) du bureau directeur:
Erick Parent, Secrétaire général
Finances: *Budget de fonctionnement annuel:* $250,000-$500,000
Personnel: 2 membre(s) du personnel; 100 bénévole(s)
Membre: 600 officiers municipaux *Montant de la cotisation:* 405$; *Critères d'admissibilite:* Gestionnaires municipaux; *Comités:* Comité de formation professionnelle, des communications, des retraités, des technologies de l'information, de législation et scrutins, des finances et fiscalité municipales
Activités: Cours aménagement et urbanisme; scrutins municipaux; rédaction d'articles - information; étude des lois municipales des cités et villes; *Listes de destinataires:* Oui

Corporation of Air Treatment & Cold Processing Enterprises *Voir* Corporation des entreprises de traitement de l'air et du froid

Corporation of BC Land Surveyors *See* Association of British Columbia Land Surveyors

Corporation of Chartered Municipal Officers of Québec *Voir* Corporation des officiers municipaux agréés du Québec

Corporation of Master Pipe Mechanics of Québec *Voir* Corporation des maîtres mécaniciens en tuyauterie du Québec

Corporation professionnelle des technologues professionnelles du Québec *Voir* Ordre des technologues professionnels du Québec

Corrugated Steel Pipe Institute (CSPI) / Institut pour tuyaux de tôle ondulée

#2A, 652 Bishop St. North, Cambridge ON N3H 4V6
Tel: 519-650-8080; *Fax:* 519-650-8081
e-mail: info@cspi.ca
www.cspi.ca
Overview: A medium-sized national organization
Mission: To promote & encourage general & wider use of corrugated steel pipe for drainage & other uses across Canada; to initiate & support research, marketing, promotion, public relations & advertising programs designed to broaden the markets for CSP products; to cooperate with public & private agencies engaged in the formulation of specifications & designs for drainage & other underground structures; to provide the industry & the public with documented experience & up-to-date technical information on CSP products & their proper use & application; to enhance, through responsible public relations practices, the reputation & image of the Canadian CSP industry; to cooperate with allied industry & government authorities; to encourage & participate in educational endeavours in colleges & universities.
Chief Officer(s):
David J. Penny, Marketing Manager

Membership: 9 active (manufacturers) + 4 associate (materials) + 2 affiliate (non-domestic) + 1 special (equipment)
Activities: ; *Library:* Open to public

Couchiching Institute on Public Affairs (CIPA)
#301, 250 Consumers Rd., Willowdale ON M2J 4V6
Tel: 416-642-6374; *Fax:* 416-495-8723
Toll-Free: 866-647-6374
e-mail: couch@couchichinginstitute.ca
www.couchichinginstitute.ca
www.facebook.com/couchichinginstitute
twitter.com/couchiching
Overview: A small international charitable organization founded in 1931
Mission: To bring together interested Canadians to discuss important public policy issues with experts & other members of the general public
Chief Officer(s):
Rima Berns-McGown, President
Shannon Bott, Executive Director, 416-494-1440 Ext. 229
sbott@couchichinginstitute.ca
Finances: *Annual Operating Budget:* $100,000-$250,000; *Funding Sources:* Charitable, corporate, personal & government donations; membership & conference fees
Staff: 6 staff member(s)
Membership: 350 individual; *Fees:* $100 family; $75 individual; $25 student; *Member Profile:* Individuals interested in public affairs; *Committees:* Program; Communications; Membership; Fundraising; Youth; Big Picture; Partnerships

Council of Atlantic Premiers (CAP)
Council Secretariat, PO Box 2044, #1006, 5161 George St., Halifax NS B3J 2Z1
Tel: 902-424-7590; *Fax:* 902-424-8976
e-mail: info@cap-cpma.ca
www.cap-cpma.ca
Mission: The mandate of the Council is to promote Atlantic Canadian interests on national issues. To accomplish this, the Council seeks to establish common views & positions to ensure that Atlantic Canadians & their interests are well represented in national debates. The work of the Council of Atlantic Premiers builds on the ongoing work of the Council of Maritime Premiers & the Conference of Atlantic Premiers. The premiers are committed to work together on behalf of Atlantic Canadians to strengthen the economic competitiveness of the region, improve the quality of public services to Atlantic Canadians and/or improve the cost-effectiveness of delivering public services to Atlantic Canadians.
Chief Officer(s):
Tim Porter, Secretary to Council, 902-424-7600
tporter@cap-cpma.ca
Membership: *Member Profile:* Premiers of New Brunswick, Newfoundland & Labrador, Nova Scotia & Prince Edward Island

Council of Biology Editors ***See*** Council of Science Editors

Council of Canadian Fire Marshals & Fire Commissioners (CCFMFC) / Conseil canadien des directeurs provinciaux et des commissaires des incendies
c/o 491 McLeod Hill Rd., Fredericton NB E3A 6H6
Tel: 506-453-1208; *Fax:* 506-457-0793
e-mail: CCFMFC@rogers.com
www.ccfmfc.ca
Overview: A medium-sized national organization founded in 1921
Mission: To contribute to a reduction in the number of fire deaths
Environmental Activity: Promoting fire safety awareness
Chief Officer(s):
Ben Laroche, President
Christopher Jones, Vice-President
Philippa Gourley, Secretary-Treasurer
Activities: Advising on & promoting legislation, policies, & procedures; Participating in the development of standards & codes; Arranging national fire loss statistics; Supporting professional development of the Canadian fire service; Identifying trends related to the causes of fire; Providing a forum for the exchange of information on fire safety matters; Offering advice to accredited agencies involved in the testing & certification of fire protection equipment

Council of Food Processing & Consumer Products ***Voir*** Conseil de la transformation agroalimentaire et des produits de consommation

Council of Forest Industries (COFI)
Pender Place I Business Building, #1501, 700 Pender St. West, Vancouver BC V6C 1G8
Tel: 604-684-0211; *Fax:* 604-687-4930
e-mail: info@cofi.org
www.cofi.org
Also Known As: Canadian Forest Industries Council
Overview: A medium-sized provincial organization
Mission: To be the voice of the British Columbia interior forest industry; To offer member companies services in areas such as international market & trade development, community relations, public affairs, quality control, & forest policy
Environmental Activity: Preserving sensitive ecosystems, through old growth conservation, a limited working forest, regulated & limited logging, & full restoration
Chief Officer(s):
Ken Higginbotham, Chair
John Allan, President & Chief Executive Officer
Paul J. Newman, Executive Director, Market Access & Trade
newman@cofi.org
Doug Routledge, Vice-President, Forestry & Northern Operations
routledge@cofi.org
Anne Mauch, Director, Regulatory Issues
mauch@cofi.org
Membership: *Member Profile:* Companies that operate production facilities in forest dependent communities in the interior of British Columbia
Activities: Advocating for British Columbia's forest industry; Liaising with government about the development & implementation of policies related to British Columbia's forest sector; Increasing public awareness about the importance of the forest sector;
Meetings/Conferences:
For more information see Trade Shows, Conferences and Seminars Chapter
Council of Forest Industries 2013 Annual Convention
April 2013 Prince George, BC
Publications:
•British Columbia Forest Industry Fact Book
Type: Book
Profile: Sections include the world's forests & forest industry; Canada's forests & forest industry; competitiveness; land use, forest management, & the environment; & British Columbiaforest industry statistical tables
•COFI [Council of Forest Industries] News: Month in Review
Type: Newsletter
Profile: Council of Forest Industries events & British Columbia forest industry news
•Council of Forest Industries Annual Report
Type: Yearbook; *Frequency:* Annually
Profile: A review of operations & the financial report
•Quarterly Stumpage Update [a publication of the Council of Forest Industries]
Profile: Including British Columbia stumpage parameters & average stumpage prices

Council of Great Lakes Governors (CGLG)
#2700, 20 North Wacker Dr., Chicago IL 60606
Tel: 312-407-0177; *Fax:* 312-407-0038
e-mail: cglg@cglg.org
www.cglg.org
Overview: A small international organization founded in 1990
Mission: To facilitate economic growth in the Great Lakes region, including Ontario, Québec, & the Great Lakes states of Illinois, Indiana, Michigan, Minnesota, New York, Ohio, Pennsylvania, & Wisconsin
Environmental Activity: Encouraging environmentally responsible economic growth in Ontario, Québec, & the eight Great Lakes states; Participating in projects such as Great Lakes protection & restoration, water management, & aquatic invasive species
Chief Officer(s):
Mitchell E. Daniels, Co-Chair; Governor of Indiana
Pat Quinn, Co-Chair; Governor of Illinois
David Naftzger, Executive Director
dnaftzger@cglg.org
Toby McCarrick, Executive Director, Great Lakes USA
tmccarrick@cglg.org
Zoë Munro, Program Manager
zmunro@cglg.org
Michael Piskur, Program Manager
mpiskur@cglg.org
Finances: *Funding Sources:* Donations
Activities: Hosting webinars for Great Lakes companies; Leading multi-sector trade missions
Publications:
•The Compass [a publication of the Council of Great Lakes Governors]
Type: Newsletter; *Frequency:* Quarterly
Profile: Information about the ongoing work of the Council of Great Lakes Governors, such as trade missions & trade offices

Council of Marine Carriers
#215, 3989 Henning Dr., Burnaby BC V5C 6P8
Tel: 604-687-9677; *Fax:* 604-687-1788
e-mail: cmc@comc.cc
www.comc.cc
Overview: A small national organization founded in 1972
Chief Officer(s):
Leo Stradiotti, President
ole@dccnet.com

Council of Ontario Construction Associations (COCA)
#2001, 180 Dundas St. West, Toronto ON M5G 1Z8
Tel: 416-968-7200; *Fax:* 416-968-0362
e-mail: info@coca.on.ca
www.coca.on.ca
www.linkedin.com/company/2397076?trk=tyah
www.facebook.com/172643879452017
www.twitter.com/ICIconstruction
Overview: A large provincial organization founded in 1974
Mission: To contribute to the long-term growth & profitability of the construction industry in Ontario; To speak with a unified voice to government, the industry & the public.
Chief Officer(s):
Ian Cunningham, President, 416-968-7200 Ext. 224
icunningham@coca.on.ca
Membership: 32 organizations; *Committees:* Labour Legislation; Environment; WSIB; Taxation; Occupational Health & Safety; Employment Practices; Human Resources
Activities: *Speaker Service:* Yes

Council of Outdoor Educators of Ontario (COEO)
3 Concorde Gate, Toronto ON M3C 3N7
e-mail: info@coeo.org
www.coeo.org
Overview: A medium-sized provincial charitable organization founded in 1969
Mission: To promote outdoor education in a safe manner; to develop environmental awareness of the outdoors; to act as a professional body for outdoor educators in Ontario; *Member of:* North American Association of Environmental Educators
Finances: *Annual Operating Budget:* Less than $50,000
Staff: 20 volunteer(s)
Membership: 30 student + 10 senior/lifetime + 200 individual; *Fees:* $35 student; $50 individual; $60 family
Activities: *Speaker Service:* Yes
Meetings/Conferences:
For more information see Trade Shows, Conferences and Seminars Chapter
Council of Outdoor Educators of Ontario (COEO) 2013 91st Annual Conference
September 2013 Sundridge, ON

Council of Science Editors
#304, 10200 W. 44th Ave., Wheat Ridge CO 80033 USA
Tel: 720-881-6046; *Fax:* 303-422-8894
e-mail: cse@councilscienceeditors.org
www.councilscienceeditors.org
www.facebook.com/CouncilofScienceEditors?ref=ts
Previous Name: Council of Biology Editors
Overview: A small international organization
Mission: To improve communications in the life sciences; to educate authors, editors & publishers; to promote effective communication practices in primary & secondary publishing in any form
Chief Officer(s):
David Stumph, Executive Director
Membership: 1,200; *Fees:* $164; $43 student

Council of the Haida Nation - Haida Fisheries Program (HFP)
PO Box 87, 2143 Collison Ave., Old Masset BC V0T 1M0
Tel: 250-626-3302; *Fax:* 250-626-3309
Toll-Free: 888-638-7778
e-mail: hfpm.reception@haidanation.net
www.haidanation.ca/Pages/Programs/Fish/Fish.html
Overview: A small local organization

Mission: The Program provides advice to the Council of the Haida Nation about actions, political or otherwise, on the marine habitat & environment. It assesses all commerical/recreational fisheries & any plans affecting marine resources. Its priority is the protection of Aboriginal rights & title of the Haida people.
Chief Officer(s):
Marvin Collison, Receptionist
Activities: Pallant Creek hatchery; Integrated Marine Use Plan; abalone stewardship

Council on Hemispheric Affairs (COHA)
#1C, 1250 Connecticut Ave. NW, Washington DC 20036 USA
Tel: 202-223-4975; *Fax:* 202-223-4979
Toll-Free: 888-922-9261
e-mail: coha@coha.org
www.coha.org
Overview: A medium-sized international organization founded in 1975
Mission: To monitor US-Canadian-Latin American relations in the areas of economics, politics, human rights, trade & diplomacy through public statements, critical analyses & media appearances
Chief Officer(s):
Larry Birns, Director
Finances: *Annual Operating Budget:* $100,000-$250,000; *Funding Sources:* Subscription revenue; private donations
Staff: 4 staff member(s); 25 volunteer(s)
Membership: 1,500; *Fees:* $100
Activities: Issue press releases, submit op-eds to national newspapers for publication; publish biweekly Washington Report on the Hemisphere; provide congressional testimony & media resource; representatives frequently appear on radio & tv programs to analyze news stories; *Internships:* Yes; *Speaker Service:* Yes; *Library:*

The Cousteau Society (TCS) / Société Cousteau
#707E, 732 Eden Way North, Chesapeake VA 23320 USA
Tel: 212-532-2588
e-mail: communication@cousteau.org
www.cousteau.org
www.youtube.com/user/cousteauenglish
Overview: A large international charitable organization founded in 1973
Mission: Dedicated to the protection & wise management of natural resources & the improvement of life for present & future generations; to promote an increased awareness & knowledge of the beauty & fragility of the planet's resources
Chief Officer(s):
Francine Cousteau, President
Finances: *Annual Operating Budget:* Greater than $5 Million; *Funding Sources:* Membership fees; production contracts
Staff: 32 staff member(s); 5 volunteer(s)
Membership: 50,000 worldwide including sister organization Equipe Cousteau; *Fees:* $30 individual; $40 family
Activities: Produces television films, filmstrips & books on important environmental concerns for the general public

Cowichan Valley Naturalists' Society (CVNS)
PO Box 361, Duncan BC V9L 3X5
Tel: 250-746-6141
e-mail: cvns at naturecowichan.net
www.naturecowichan.net/CVNS
Overview: A small local organization founded in 1962
Affiliation(s): BC Nature: The Federation of British Columbia Naturalists
Environmental Activity: Participating in conservation activities
Chief Officer(s):
John Scull, Vice-President
Membership: *Fees:* $25 families of Young Naturalists Club members; $30 individuals; $35 families; *Member Profile:* Naturalists in the Cowichan Valley of British Columbia
Activities: Providing educational programs; Organizing nature hikes
Publications:
•Valley Naturalist [a publication of the Cowichan Valley Naturalists' Society]
Type: Newsletter; *Price:* Free with memberships in the Cowichan Valley Naturalists' Society
Profile: Information & events for naturalists in the Cowichan Valley

Credit Valley Conservation Foundation
1255 Old Derry Rd. West, Mississauga ON L5N 6R4
Tel: 905-670-1615; *Fax:* 905-670-2210
Toll-Free: 800-668-5557
e-mail: cvc@creditvalleyca.ca
www.creditvalleyca.ca
www.facebook.com/creditvalleyconservation
twitter.com/cvc_ca
www.youtube.com/user/CreditValleyCA;
www.flickr.com/photos/cvca
Overview: A small local organization founded in 1954
Mission: To raise funds & awareness in support of Credit Valley Conservation's goal of an environmentally healthy river for economically & socially healthy communities
Chief Officer(s):
Pat Mullin, Chair, 905-896-5200
Lou Maieron, Vice-Chair
Finances: *Funding Sources:* 67% from member municipalities; 20% generated by Credit Valley Conservation Foundation
Activities: Publishing a coffee table book; raising funds for the development of the Elora Cataract Trailway & Glassford Arboretum Trail; provides an annual bursary to a student at the University of Guelph & University of Toronto (Erindale); *Library:* Resource Library
Publications:
•Credit Cascades [a publication of the Credit Valley Conservation Foundation]
Frequency: Quarterly
Profile: Updates on work being done by the CVC.
•Currents [a publication of the Credit Valley Conservation Foundation]
Frequency: s-a.
Profile: A means of connecting the public to the Credit River Watershed.
•The Source [a publication of the Credit Valley Conservation Foundation]
Frequency: Monthly
Profile: Credit River Watershed news, profiles, tips, & opportunities.

Creelman Agricultural Society
PO Box 46, Creelman SK S0G 0X0
Tel: 306-722-3735; *Fax:* 306-722-3740
e-mail: CreelmanKid@gmail.com
www.creelmanagsociety.ca
www.facebook.com/CreelmanAgSociety
Overview: A small local organization
Mission: To improve agriculture & the quality of life in the community by educating members & the community; To provide a community forum for discussion of agricultural issues; To encourage conservation of natural resources; *Member of:* Saskatchewan Association of Agricultural Societies & Exhibitions
Chief Officer(s):
Christine Procyk, Secretary
cmprocyk@yahoo.ca
Activities: *Awareness Events:* Creelman Fair, July

Crop Protection Institute of Canada ***See*** CropLife Canada

CropLife Canada
#627, 21 Four Seasons Pl., Toronto ON M9B 6J8
Tel: 416-622-9771
www.croplife.ca
Previous Name: Crop Protection Institute of Canada
Overview: A medium-sized national organization founded in 1952
Mission: To represent Canada's plant science industry; To foster the developmment of the industry; To build Canadians' trust & appreciation for plant science innovations; *Member of:* CropLife International
Environmental Activity: Protecting human health & the environment through safe & effective technology; Supporting innovative & sustainable agriculture in Canada; Offering Stewardship First initiatives, including Biotech Stewardship, Urban Stewardship & Chemistry Stewardship
Chief Officer(s):
Lorne Hepworth, President, 613-230-9881 Ext. 3225
hepworth@croplife.ca
Pierre Petelle, Executive Director, Regulatory Affairs & Non-Ag Uses
Nadine Sisk, Executive Director, Communications & Member Services
siskn@croplife.ca
Russel Hurst, Managing Director, Stewardship & Sustainability
hurstr@croplife.ca
Cam Davreux, Vice-President, Stewardship
davreuxc@croplife.ca
Annie Hsu, Vice-President, Finance & Administration
hsua@croplife.ca
Peter MacLeod, Vice-President, Chemistry
macleodp@croplife.ca
Dennis Prouse, Vice-President, Government Affairs, 613-230-9881 Ext. 3226
Janice Tranberg, Vice-President, Western Canada, 306-373-4052
tranbergj@croplife.ca
Finances: *Funding Sources:* Sponsorships
Membership: *Member Profile:* Developers, manufacturers, & distributors of plant science innovations
Activities: Conducting research; Promoting the code of conduct
Meetings/Conferences:
For more information see Trade Shows, Conferences and Seminars Chapter
GrowCanada Conference 2013
December 2013 Calgary, AB

Croplife International
PO Box 35, 326, av Louise, Brussels 1050 Belgium
Tel: 32-2-542-0410; *Fax:* 32-2-542-0419
e-mail: croplife@croplife.org
www.croplife.org
Previous Name: Global Crop Protection Federation; International Group of National Associations of Manufacturers of Agrochemical Products
Overview: A medium-sized international charitable organization
Mission: To act as an ambassador for the pan science industry, encouraging understanding & dialogue whilst promoting agricultural technology in the context of sustainable development

Chief Officer(s):
Christian Verschueren, Director General
Membership: 1-99; *Member Profile:* Regional crop protection associations

Cultivons Biologique Canada ***See*** Canadian Organic Growers Inc.

Cumulative Environmental Management Association (CEMA)
Morrison Center, #214, 9914 Morrison St., Fort McMurray AB T9H 4A4
Tel: 780-799-3947; *Fax:* 780-714-3081
e-mail: info@cemaonline.ca
www.cemaonline.ca
Overview: A medium-sized national organization founded in 2000
Mission: To study the cumulative environmental effects of industrial development in the region and produce guidelines and management frameworks.
Chief Officer(s):
Glen Semenchuk, Executive Director
glen.semenchuk@cemaonline.ca
Membership: 44 institutional

CUSO-VSO
200-44 Eccles St., Ottawa ON K1R 6S4
Tel: 613-829-7445; *Fax:* 613-829-7996
Toll-Free: 888-434-2876
e-mail: questions@cusointernational.org
www.cusointernational.org
www.facebook.com/cusovso
twitter.com/CusoIntl
www.youtube.com/cusointernational
Previous Name: Canadian University Service Overseas
Overview: A large international charitable organization founded in 1961
Mission: CUSO-VSO is a non-profit development agency that works through skilled volunteers to aid global social justice; to address poverty, human rights violations, HIV/AIDS, inequity & environmental degradation; to give Canadians information, the experiences & the tools they need to become active global citizens.; *Member of:* VSO International; Canadian Council for International Cooperation; Global Campaign for Education (GCE); Global Citizens for Change Coalition; Canadian Make Poverty History Campaign; Affiliation(s): CJEO Youth Avenue Internationale; El Salvador Cultural Partnership; International Model Forest Partnership; Canadian Community Economic Development Network (CCEDNet); Marbek Resource Consultants
Chief Officer(s):
Derek Evans, Executive Director
derek.evans@cusointernational.org
Finances: *Annual Operating Budget:* Greater than $5 Million; *Funding Sources:* Largest donor is Canadian International Development Agency (CIDA)
Staff: 140 staff member(s); 400 volunteer(s)

Activities: Works in over 40 countries, Canada's largest volunteer-sending agency; *Internships:* Yes; *Speaker Service:* Yes

Dairy Farmers of Manitoba (DFM) / Producteurs Laitiers du Manitoba

PO Box 724, 36 Scurfield Blvd., Winnipeg MB R3C 2K3
Tel: 204-488-6455; *Fax:* 204-488-4772
Toll-Free: 800-567-1671
e-mail: general@milk.mb.ca
www.milk.mb.ca
Previous Name: Manitoba Milk Producers
Overview: A small provincial organization founded in 1974
Mission: To represent the interests of dairy farmers of Manitoba at the provincial & national levels; To produce milk according to the highest standards; To sell milk from Manitoba's dairy farmers to processors
Chief Officer(s):
David Wiens, Chair
Finances: *Funding Sources:* Manitoba's dairy farmers
Membership: *Member Profile:* Dairy farmers in Manitoba
Activities: Developing advertising programs

Dairy Farmers of New Brunswick (DFNB) / Producteurs laitiers du Nouveau-Brunswick

PO Box 5034, Sussex NB E4E 5L2
Tel: 506-432-4330; *Fax:* 506-432-4333
e-mail: nbmilk@nbmilk.org
www.nbmilk.org
Overview: A small provincial organization
Mission: To represent the interests of dairy farmers in New Brunswick; To produce high quality milk
Environmental Activity: Operating sustainable farms in New Brunswick
Chief Officer(s):
Steve Michaud, General Manager
stevem@nbmilk.org
Danielle Kennedy, Contact, Producer Services
danielle@nbmilk.org
Veronica McEwen, Contact, Transportation
veronica@nbmilk.org
Cassandra Murray, Contact, Producer Services
cassandra@nbmilk.org
Finances: *Funding Sources:* Dairy farmers of New Brunswick
Membership: *Member Profile:* New Brunswick's dairy farmers
Activities: Marketing raw milk

Dairy Nutrition Council of Alberta ***See*** Alberta Milk

Dangerous Goods Advisory Council

#740, 1100 H St. NW, Washington DC 20005 USA
Tel: 202-289-4550; *Fax:* 202-289-4074
e-mail: info@dgac.org
www.hmac.org
Also Known As: Hazardous Materials Advisory Council
Overview: A medium-sized international organization founded in 1978
Mission: To promote improvement in the safe transportation of hazardous materials/dangerous goods globally by providing education, assistance & information to the private & public sectors, through our unique status with regulatory bodies, & the diversity & technical strengths of our membership; Affiliation(s): Canadian Government
Chief Officer(s):
Mike Morrissette, President
Loretta Saunders, Office Manager
Membership: *Fees:* Schedule available; *Member Profile:* Shippers; carriers; container manufacturers & reconditioners; emergency response/waste clean-up companies; trade associations

David Suzuki Foundation (DSF)

#219, 2211 - 4th Ave. West, Vancouver BC V6K 4S2
Tel: 604-732-4228; *Fax:* 604-732-0752
Toll-Free: 800-453-1533
e-mail: contact@davidsuzuki.org
www.davidsuzuki.org
www.facebook.com/DavidSuzuki
twitter.com/DavidSuzukiFDN
Overview: A small national organization founded in 1991
Mission: To seek out & commission the best, most up-to-date research to help reveal ways we can live in balance with nature; to support the implementation of ecologically sustainable models - from local projects, such as habitat restoration, to international initiatives, such as better frameworks for economic decisions; to ensure the solutions developed through research & application to reach the widest possible audience, & help mobilize broadly supported change; to urge decision makers to adopt policies which encourage & guide individuals & businesses, so their daily decisions reflect the need to act within nature's constraints; *Member of:* Canadian Renewable Energy Alliance
Chief Officer(s):
Tara Cullis, President
David Suzuki, Chair
Peter Robinson, CEO
Membership: 45,000

Defense environmentale ***See*** Environmental Defence

Developing Countries Farm Radio Network ***See*** Farm Radio International

Devis de construction Canada ***See*** Construction Specifications Canada

Direct Marketing Association (DMA)

1120 Avenue of the Americas, New York NY 10036-6700 USA
Tel: 212-768-7277; *Fax:* 212-302-6714
e-mail: customerservice@the-dma.org
www.the-dma.org
www.linkedin.com/groups?gid=1620437
www.facebook.com/pages/Direct-Marketing-Association-DMA/60905377232?r
twitter.com/dma_usa
Overview: A large international organization
Chief Officer(s):
Linda A. Woolley, Acting President & CEO
Finances: *Funding Sources:* Membership dues
Staff: 120 staff member(s)
Membership: 3,600
Activities: *Speaker Service:* Yes; *Rents Mailing List:* Yes; *Library:* by appointment

Direct Sellers Association of Canada (DSA) / Association de ventes directes du Canada

#250, 180 Attwell Dr., Toronto ON M9W 6A9
Tel: 416-679-8555; *Fax:* 416-679-1568
e-mail: info@dsa.ca
www.dsa.ca
Overview: A small national organization founded in 1954
Mission: The Association represents companies that manufacture & distribute goods & services through independent sales contractors, away from a fixed retail location; encourages strong consumer protection, through Codes of Ethics & Business Practices; engages in discussion with government & industry; acts as the voice of the direct selling industry to government in pursuit of better business opportunities for Canadian entrepreneurs.
Chief Officer(s):
Greg Neath, Chair
Ross Creber, President & Secretary
Membership: 48

Division de l'Atlantique de l'association Canadienne des Géographes ***See*** Canadian Association of Geographers

Doctors Manitoba
Parent Name: Canadian Medical Association

20 Desjardins Dr., Winnipeg MB R3X 0E8
Tel: 204-985-5888; *Fax:* 204-985-5844
Toll-Free: 888-322-4242
www.docsmb.org
Previous Name: Manitoba Medical Association
Overview: A medium-sized provincial organization founded in 1908 overseen by Canadian Medical Association
Mission: To advocate for Manitoba physicians, representing their professional & economic interests.
Chief Officer(s):
Debbie Bride, Communications Officer
John A. Laplume, CEO
Finances: *Annual Operating Budget:* $1.5 Million-$3 Million; *Funding Sources:* Membership dues
Staff: 16 staff member(s)
Membership: 2,272; *Member Profile:* Manitoba physicians, medical students & residents; *Committees:* Public Health Issues; Aboriginal Health; Ethics; Insurance

Doctors Nova Scotia
Parent Name: Canadian Medical Association

25 Spectacle Lake Dr., Dartmouth NS B3B 1X7
Tel: 902-468-1866; *Fax:* 902-468-6578
e-mail: info@doctorsns.com
www.doctorsns.com
Previous Name: Medical Society of Nova Scotia
Overview: A medium-sized provincial organization founded in 1862 overseen by Canadian Medical Association
Mission: To maintain the integrity of the medical profession; To represent members; To promote high quality health care & disease prevention in Nova Scotia; *Member of:* Canadian Medical Association
Chief Officer(s):
Nancy MacCready-Williams, CEO
John Chiasson, President
Membership: 2,200 physicians + 700 medical students & residents; *Member Profile:* Doctors, medical students, & residents in Nova Scotia
Activities: Educating the public on healthy lifestyle choices; Partnering with organizations; Offering the Youth Running for Fun Program; Voicing physician concerns with the health-care system; Advising on health-related policies & legislation

DRS Earthwise Society; Delta Recycling Society ***See*** Earthwise Society

Ducks Unlimited Canada (DUC) / Canards Illimités Canada

PO Box 1160, Stonewall MB R0C 2Z0
Fax: 204-467-9028
Toll-Free: 800-665-3825
e-mail: webfoot@ducks.ca
www.ducks.ca
www.facebook.com/ducksunlimitedcanada
twitter.com/ducanada
www.youtube.com/user/DucksUnlimitedCanada?feature=watch
Also Known As: DU Canada
Overview: A large national charitable organization founded in 1937
Mission: To conserve, restore, & manage wetlands & associated habitats, for the benefit of waterfowl, which in turn provide healthy environments for wildlife & people; Affiliation(s): North American Waterfowl Management Plan (NAWMP)
Environmental Activity: Working to change policy in favour of wetland & habitat conservation; Delivering environmental education programs; Working with landowners to make land use more sustainable
Chief Officer(s):
Gregory E. Siekaniec, Chief Executive Officer
Tom Worden, President
James A. Fortune, Chief Operating Officer
Sandy Gousseau, National Director, Communications & Marketing
Grant Monck, National Director, Development
Henry Murkin, National Director, Conservation
Loraine Nyokong, National Director, Fundraising & Membership
Gary Goodwin, Executive Corporate Secretary & Counsel
Finances: *Funding Sources:* Donations; Fundraising; Corporate partners
Membership: *Committees:* Executive; Governance; Risk & Finance; Conservation Planning; Membership & Revenue; Personnel Policy; Nominating
Activities: Conducting wetland & waterfowl research to guide conservation work; *Library:* Ducks Unlimited Film & Video Library
Publications:
•Conservator
Type: Magazine; *Frequency:* 5 pa; *Accepts Advertising*; *Editor:* D. Morrison (d_morrison@ducks.ca)
Profile: Feature articles from the world of wetland & waterfowl conservation
•Ducks Unlimited Canada Annual Report
Type: Yearbook; *Frequency:* Annually
Profile: A yearly tracking of Ducks Unlimited Canada's scientific research, conservation programs, partnerships, volunteers, & supporters

Alberta Provincial Office
17915 - 118th Ave., Edmonton AB T5S 1L6
Tel: 780-489-2002; *Fax:* 780-489-1856
Toll-Free: 866-479-3825
e-mail: du_edmonton@ducks.ca

British Columbia Provincial Office
#511, 13370 - 78th Ave., Surrey BC V3W 0H6
Tel: 604-592-0987; *Fax:* 604-592-0930
Toll-Free: 800-665-3825
e-mail: du_surrey@ducks.ca

Manitoba Provincial Office
#2, 545 Conservation Dr., Brandon MB R7A 7L8
Tel: 204-729-3500; *Fax:* 204-727-6044
e-mail: du_brandon@ducks.ca

New Brunswick Provincial Office
752 Union St., Fredericton NB E3A 3P2
Tel: 506-458-8848; *Fax:* 506-458-9921
Toll-Free: 888-920-3330
e-mail: du_fredericton@ducks.ca

Newfoundland & Labrador Provincial Office
19 Conway St., Grand Falls-Windsor NL A2A 2P4
Tel: 709-486-7674; *Fax:* 709-489-1554
Toll-Free: 877-516-1554
e-mail: du_newfoundland@ducks.ca
Chief Officer(s):
Ian Barnett, Director, Regional Operations

Northwest Territories Office
PO Box 1438, #4A, 4921 - 49th St., Yellowknife NT X1A 2P1
Tel: 867-873-6744

Nova Scotia Provincial Office
PO Box 430, #64, Hwy. 6, Amherst NS B4H 3Z5
Tel: 902-667-8726; *Fax:* 902-667-0916
Toll-Free: 866-903-8257
e-mail: du_amherst@ducks.ca
Chief Officer(s):
Mark Gloutney, Provincial Manager

Ontario Provincial Office
#1, 740 Hurontario Rd., Barrie ON L4N 6C6
Tel: 705-721-4444; *Fax:* 705-721-4999
Toll-Free: 888-402-4444
e-mail: du_barrie@ducks.ca

Prince Edward Island Provincial Office
Farm Centre, #113, 420 University Ave., Charlottetown ON C1A 7Z5
Tel: 902-569-4544; *Fax:* 902-569-4674
e-mail: du_charlottetown@ducks.ca
Chief Officer(s):
Jamie Fortune, Director, Regional Operations

Québec Provincial Office
#260, 710, rue Bouvier, Québec QC G2J 1C2
Tél: 418-623-1650; *Téléc:* 418-623-0420
Courriel: du_quebec@ducks.ca
Chief Officer(s):
Bernard Filion, Directeur provincial

Saskatchewan Provincial Office
PO Box 4465, 1030 Winnipeg St., Regina SK S4R 8P8
Tel: 306-569-0424; *Fax:* 306-565-3699
Toll-Free: 866-252-3825
e-mail: du_regina@ducks.ca

Yukon Territory Office
PO Box 31775, 308 Hanson St., Whitehorse YT Y1A 6L3
Tel: 867-668-3824

Ducks Unlimited Inc. (DU)
1 Waterfowl Way, Memphis TN 38120 USA
Tel: 901-758-3825
Toll-Free: 800-459-8257
e-mail: webmaster@ducks.org
www.ducks.org
Overview: A medium-sized international organization founded in 1937
Mission: To fulfill the annual life cycle needs of North American waterfowl by protecting, enhancing, restoring & managing important wetlands & associated uplands
Chief Officer(s):
Don A. Young, Executive Vice-President
Publications:
•Ducks Unlimited Magazine
Editor: Tom Fulgham
Profile: Bimonthly magazine

Durham Avicultural Society of Ontario (DAS)
ON
www.birdclub.ca
Overview: A small local organization founded in 1977
Mission: To serve breeders in Durham & surrounding area; To improve fellowship among breeders & between clubs; To exchange ideas & educate members for betterment of the fancy through breeding & exhibiting; To encourage members to deal fairly with fellow breeders; To keep birds in good physical condition & not overextend breeding; *Member of:* Avicultural Advancement Council of Canada
Chief Officer(s):
Jacquie Blackburn, Secretary
jacquies.parrots@sympatico.ca
Membership: 150; *Fees:* $15 junior; $35 individual/family; $25 senior
Activities: ; *Library:*

EAGLE (Environmental-Aboriginal Guardianship through Law & Education)
6520 Salish Dr., Vancouver BC V6N 2C7
Tel: 604-536-6261; *Fax:* 604-536-6221
e-mail: eagle@eaglelaw.org
www.eaglelaw.org
Overview: A small national charitable organization
Mission: EAGLE is a national organization that assists Aboriginal Peoples in protecting & restoring the natural environment. It also promotes the understanding of Aboriginal Rights & responsibilities as cultural stewards of the land.
Chief Officer(s):
Gibby Jacob, Chair
Deanie Kolybabi, Executive Director
dkolybabi@eaglelaw.org
Activities: Litigation Program; Education Program

Earth Day Canada (EDC) / Jour de la terre Canada
#503, 111 Peter St., Toronto ON M5V 2H1
Tel: 416-599-1991; *Fax:* 416-599-3100
Toll-Free: 888-283-2784
e-mail: info@earthday.ca
www.earthday.ca
www.facebook.com/EarthDayCanada
twitter.com/earthdaycanada
www.youtube.com/user/EarthDayCanada
Overview: A medium-sized national charitable organization founded in 1991
Mission: To improve the state of the environment by motivating & helping Canadians to achieve local solutions; Affiliation(s): Earth Day Network; 3,500 community-based organizations
Chief Officer(s):
Jed Goldberg, President
jgoldberg@earthday.ca
Keith Treffry, Director, Communications
keith@earthday.ca
Paul Bubelis, Chair
Finances: *Funding Sources:* Sponsorships; Donations
Membership: 5,000 organizations
Activities: Coordinating & promoting Earth Day; Circulating educational materials; Initiating & coordinating environmental projects; Offering programs, such as EcoKids; *Awareness Events:* Earth Day, April; Earth Month

Earth Energy Society of Canada (EESC) / Société canadienne de l'énergie du sol (SCES)
7885 Jock Trail, Richmond ON K0A 2Z0
Tel: 613-822-4987; *Fax:* 613-822-4987
e-mail: info@earthenergy.ca
www.earthenergy.ca
Also Known As: GeoCanada
Previous Name: Canadian Earth Energy Association
Overview: A medium-sized national organization founded in 1985
Mission: To represent the ground-source/geothermal heat pump industry by promoting quality installations & earth energy technology
Chief Officer(s):
Bill Eggertson, Consultant, 613-222-6920
Eggertson@EarthEnergy.ca

Earth Island Institute (EII)
#460, 2150 Allston Way, Berkeley CA 94704-1375 USA
Tel: 510-859-9100; *Fax:* 510-859-9091
www.earthisland.org
www.facebook.com/groups/26250703694
twitter.com/earthisland
Overview: A large international organization founded in 1982
Mission: To develop innovative projects for the conservation, preservation & restoration of the global environment
Chief Officer(s):
Martha Davis, President
John Knox, Executive Director, 510-859-9108
johnknox@earthisland.org
Finances: *Annual Operating Budget:* $3 Million-$5 Million; *Funding Sources:* Membership dues; grants; contributions
Staff: 65 staff member(s); 25 volunteer(s)
Membership: 15,000; *Fees:* US$25 regular; US$15 student/limited income
Activities: Operating more than 40 projects, including: Baikal Watch; Borneo Project; Campaign to Safeguard America's Waters; Centre for Safe Energy; Global Service Corps; International Marine Mammal Project; Women's Earth Alliance; *Library:* by appointment
Publications:
•Earth Island Journal
Type: Magazine; *Frequency:* q.
•IslandWire [a publication of Earth Island Institute]
Type: Newsletter
Profile: Campaign updates

Earth Voice
2100 L St. NW, Washington DC 20037 USA
Tel: 202-778-6146; *Fax:* 202-778-6134
e-mail: earthvoice@earthvoice.org
www.earthvoice.org
Overview: A small international organization
Mission: To preserve the biological support systems upon which all life depends, including but not limited to forests, topsoils, coral reefs & wetlands; to promote attitudes & policies which will seek to prevent the abuse & suffering of all living creatures & protect them from becoming threatened or endangered; to stabilize the growth of human population so that it will not exceed the carrying capacity of the land or displace other forms of life; to choose a renewable energy path that will not destroy the forests, pollute the waters, degrade the atmosphere, or endanger wildlife; to support an agricultural system that is sustainable, equitable & humane; to promote pollution prevention by reusing, repairing & recycling wherever possible
Chief Officer(s):
Jan A. Hartke, Executive Director

Earthroots
#410, 401 Richmond St. West, Toronto ON M5V 3A8
Tel: 416-599-0152; *Fax:* 416-340-2429
e-mail: info@earthroots.org
www.earthroots.org
www.facebook.com/groups/16937496801
www.myspace.com/156509574
Previous Name: Earthroots Coalition; Temagami Wilderness Society
Overview: A medium-sized local organization founded in 1986
Mission: To preserve Ontario's ancient forests & other threatened ecosystems; Affiliation(s): Temagami Wilderness Society
Chief Officer(s):
Amber Ellis, Executive Director
amber@earthroots.org
Josh Garfinkel, Senior Campaigner
joshg@earthroots.org
Finances: *Annual Operating Budget:* $250,000-$500,000; *Funding Sources:* Individual donors
Staff: 5 staff member(s); 40 volunteer(s)
Membership: 12,000; *Fees:* $40 donation
Activities: Works to protect wilderness, wildlife & watersheds through research, education & action; *Library:* by appointment

Earthroots Coalition; Temagami Wilderness Society *See*
Earthroots

Earthsave Canada (ESC) / SauveTerre
PO Box 2213, Stn. Terminal, #106 - 1850 Lorne St., Vancouver BC V6B 3W2
Tel: 604-731-5885; *Fax:* 604-731-5805
e-mail: office@earthsave.ca
earthsavecanada.wildapricot.org
www.youtube.com/earthsavecanada
www.facebook.com/EarthsaveCanada
twitter.com/earthsavecanada
Overview: A small national charitable organization founded in 1990
Mission: To promote awareness of the health, ethical & environmental consequences of our food choices; To advocate transition to a plant-based diet for better health, a cleaner environment & a more compassionate world; Affiliation(s): EarthSave International
Chief Officer(s):
David Steele, President
Carolyn Mill, Office Manager
Finances: *Annual Operating Budget:* $100,000-$250,000; *Funding Sources:* BC Gaming; Individual donations; Memberships; Retail sales
Staff: 2 staff member(s); 250 volunteer(s)
Membership: 500; *Fees:* $24 senior; $36 individual; $48 family; $96 corporate; $12 youth/student
Activities: Wellness Show; Healthy Living Expo; monthly potlucks; monthly dine-outs; Healthy School Lunch Program; Taste of Health; Vegeterian Food Festival; *Awareness Events:*

Taste of Health, Vegetarian Food Festival, Oct.; World Veg Week Fundraiser, Nov.; Vegstock; *Library:* Open to public
Publications:
•Canada Earthsaver [a publication of Earthsave Canada]
Type: Newsletter; *Frequency:* Quarterly

Earthwatch Europe
256 Banbury Rd., Oxford OX2 7DE United Kingdom
Tel: 44-1865-318-838; *Fax:* 44-1865-311-383
e-mail: info@earthwatch.org.uk
www.earthwatch.org/europe
Overview: A large international charitable organization
Mission: To engage people worldwide in scientific field research & education
Environmental Activity: Promoting the understanding & actions necessary for a sustainable environment
Chief Officer(s):
Nigel Winser, Executive Director
Ed Wilson, President & CEO
Finances: *Annual Operating Budget:* Greater than $5 Million
Staff: 50 staff member(s); 5 volunteer(s)
Membership: 5,000-14,999
Activities: *Internships:* Yes; *Speaker Service:* Yes

Earthwise Society
6400 - 3rd Ave., Delta BC V4L 1B1
Tel: 604-946-9828
e-mail: info@earthwisesociety.bc.ca
www.earthwisesociety.bc.ca
www.facebook.com/earthwisebc
twitter.com/EarthwiseBC
Previous Name: DRS Earthwise Society; Delta Recycling Society
Overview: A small local organization
Chief Officer(s):
Kathy Martin, President
Activities: Market Day; Root to Rise: Yoga Event; Music in the Garden; Family Harvest Box; workshops; Ecotours; education resources

East African Wild Life Society (EAWLS)
PO Box 20110-00200, Nairobi 00200 Kenya
Tel: 254-2-574-145; *Fax:* 254-2-570-335
e-mail: info@eawildlife.org
www.eawildlife.org
Overview: A medium-sized international organization founded in 1956
Mission: To promote the conservation & wise use of wildlife & the environment in East Africa; *Member of:* World Conservation Union
Chief Officer(s):
Nigel Derek Hunter, Executive Director
Finances: *Funding Sources:* Membership fees; shop fund; donations
Staff: 40 staff member(s); 7 volunteer(s)
Membership: 5,500; *Fees:* Schedule available; *Committees:* Conservation; Fundraising; Executive
Activities: Education & awareness; advocacy; monitoring of species; field projects; *Speaker Service:* Yes; *Library:* by appointment

East Kootenay Chamber of Mines
#201, 12 - 11th Avenue South, Cranbrook BC V1C 2P1
Tel: 250-489-2255; *Fax:* 250-426-8755
www.ekcm.org/chamber2
Overview: A small local organization
Chief Officer(s):
Ross Stanfield, President

Eastern Canada Orchid Society (ECOS)
699, rue Cardinal, Mont-Saint-Hilaire QC J3H 3Z5
Tel: 514-684-3904
e-mail: info@ecosorchids.ca
www.ecosorchids.ca
Overview: A small national organization founded in 1953
Mission: ECOS is a non-profit group of orchid hobbyists dedicated to promoting the art, science & culture of raising orchids in the Montréal area.; Affiliation(s): Canadian Orchid Congress; American Orchid Society
Chief Officer(s):
Brian Dunbar, President
Membership: *Fees:* $25 individual; $30 couple
Activities: Orchidfête; *Library:* Open to public

Eastern Ontario Model Forest
PO Box 2111, 10 Campus Dr., Kemptville ON K0G 1J0
Tel: 613-258-8241; *Fax:* 613-258-8363
e-mail: modelforest@eomf.on.ca
www.eomf.on.ca
Overview: A small local organization
Mission: To demonstrate how partners, representing a diversity of forest values, can work together to achieve sustainable forest management using innovative, region-specific approaches; *Member of:* Canadian Model Forest Network
Chief Officer(s):
Jim McCready, President
Elizabeth Holmes, General Manager
eholmes@eomf.on.ca

Eau Vive *See* WaterCan

Éco Entreprises Québec (EEQ)
#600, 1600, boul René-Lévesque ouest, Montréal QC H3H 1P9
Tél: 514-987-1491; *Téléc:* 514-987-1598
Courriel: service@ecoentreprises.qc.ca
www.ecoentreprises.qc.ca
Aperçu: *Dimension:* petite; *Envergure:* provinciale; fondée en 2003
Mission: Organisme privé sans but lucratif; représenter les entreprises assujetties à la Loi sur la qualité de l'environnement qui mettent sur le marché québécois des contenants et emballages et des imprimés.
Membre(s) du bureau directeur:
Maryse Vermette, Présidente-directrice générale
mvermette@ecoentreprises.qc.ca
Marie-Andrée Prénoveau, Directrice, Affaires corporatives, relations externes et communications
mprenoveau@ecoentreprises.qc.ca

Ecoforestry Institute Society (EIS)
PO Box 5070, Stn. B, Victoria BC V8R 6N3
Tel: 604-595-0655
www.ecoforestry.ca
Overview: A small national charitable organization founded in 1992
Mission: To provide ecologically sound alternatives to current ruinous industrial forestry practices; To support preservation of ancient & natural forests; to encourage restoration of plantation tree farms to natural forest status; *Member of:* BC Environmental Network; Forest Stewardship Council
Chief Officer(s):
Sharon Chow, Treasurer
martchow@islandnet.com
Finances: *Annual Operating Budget:* $50,000-$100,000; *Funding Sources:* Foundations; donations; subscriptions
Staff: 1 staff member(s); 12 volunteer(s)
Membership: 250; *Fees:* $10
Activities: Provides community outreach through conferences, videos & publications; helps community watershed & land trusts set up ecoforestry programs; *Speaker Service:* Yes
Publications:
•Ecoforestry
Editor: Irv Penner
Profile: No longer published, but back-copies are available.

Ecojustice Canada Society
#214, 131 Water St., Vancouver BC V6B 4M3
Tel: 604-685-5618; *Fax:* 604-685-7813
Toll-Free: 800-926-7744
www.ecojustice.ca
www.facebook.com/ecojustice
twitter.com/ecojustice_ca
Also Known As: Ecojustice
Previous Name: Sierra Legal Defence Fund
Overview: A medium-sized national charitable organization founded in 1990
Mission: To provide legal representation to environmental groups that cannot afford to go to court against large institutions when important wilderness values are at stake; to bring selected cases with the ultimate goal of establishing an aggregate of strong legal precedents that recognize environmental values; to provide professional advice on the development of environmental legislation
Chief Officer(s):
Cathy Wilkinson, President & Chair
Deborah Curran, Vice-Chair
Mike Cormack, Treasurer
Ronald H. Pearson, Secretary
Devon Page, Executive Director
Finances: *Annual Operating Budget:* $1.5 Million-$3 Million; *Funding Sources:* Individual donors; private foundations
Staff: 49 staff member(s); 10 volunteer(s)
Membership: 5,000-14,999
Activities: Free legal services; litigation; *Internships:* Yes

Alberta Office
#900, 1000 - 5th Ave. SW, Calgary AB T2P 4V1
Tel: 403-705-0202; *Fax:* 403-264-8399

Ecojustice Clinic at the University of Ottawa
c/o University of Ottawa, Faculty of Law, #107, 35 Copernicus St., Ottawa ON K1N 6N5
Tel: 613-562-5800; *Fax:* 613-562-5319

Toronto Office
Centre for Green Cities, #401, 550 Bayview Ave., Toronto ON M4W 3X8
Tel: 416-368-7533; *Fax:* 416-363-2746

Ecological Agriculture Projects (EAP) / Projets pour une agriculture écologique (PAE)
Macdonald Campus of McGill University, Sainte-Anne-de-Bellevue QC H9X 3V9
Tel: 514-398-7771; *Fax:* 514-398-7621
e-mail: ecological.agriculture@mcgill.ca
eap.mcgill.ca
Overview: A small national organization founded in 1974
Mission: To facilitate the establishment of nutritional, just, & sustainable food systems worldwide; Affiliation(s): International Federation of Organic Agriculture Movements
Finances: *Annual Operating Budget:* $100,000-$250,000
Staff: 1 staff member(s)
Membership: *Fees:* $40 individual; $60 organization; $500 sustaining; $1,250 organization
Activities: *Speaker Service:* Yes; *Library:* Open to public by appointment
Meetings/Conferences:
For more information see Trade Shows, Conferences and Seminars Chapter
33rd Annual Guelph Organic Conference & Expo 2014
January 2014 Guelph, ON

Ecological Farmers of Ontario (EFO)
5420 Hwy. 6 North, RR#5, Guelph ON N1H 6J2
Tel: 519-822-8606; *Fax:* 519-822-5681
Toll-Free: 877-822-8606
e-mail: info@efao.ca
www.efao.ca
Overview: A medium-sized provincial charitable organization founded in 1979
Mission: To provide information about ecological farming practices in Ontario
Environmental Activity: Promoting ecological & organic farming
Chief Officer(s):
Chris Litster, President
Shauna Bloom, Manager, Programs
programs@efao.ca
Caitlin Hill, Coordinator, Communications & Outreach
outreach@efao.ca
Karen Maitland, Coordinator, Membership Services
Smith Dave, Treasurer
Finances: *Funding Sources:* George Cedric Metcalf Foundation; Ontario Trillium Foundation; Friends of Greenbelt Foundation
Membership: *Member Profile:* Ontario farmers; *Committees:* Energy & farming; Peak oil; Soil & carbon
Activities: Providing access to advice; Organizing farm tours
Meetings/Conferences:
For more information see Trade Shows, Conferences and Seminars Chapter
Ecological Farmers of Ontario 2013 Two-Day Course: Essentials to Ecological Agriculture
2013,
Ecological Farmers of Ontario 2013 Two-Day Course: Transition to Organic Farming
2013
Publications:
•Ecological Farmers of Ontario Newsletter
Type: Newsletter; *Editor:* Fiona Wagner

Ecological Society of America (ESA)
#700, 1990 M St. NW, Washington DC 20036 USA
Tel: 202-833-8773; *Fax:* 202-833-8775
e-mail: esahq@esa.org
www.esa.org
Overview: A medium-sized international organization founded in 1915
Mission: To stimulate & publish research on the interrelations of organisms & their environment; to facilitate an exchange of ideas among those interested in ecology; to instill ecological principles

in the decision-making of society at large; provides Professional Certification which constitutes recognition by the Society that an applicant meets the minimum educational, experience & ethical standards adopted by ESA for professional ecologists; Affiliation(s): American Association for the Advancement of Science; American Institute of Biological Sciences; National Resources Council; National Research Council; Council of Scientific Society Presidents; Renewable Natural Resources Foundation
Chief Officer(s):
Katherine S. McCarter, Executive Director
ksm@esa.org
Finances: *Annual Operating Budget:* $3 Million-$5 Million
Staff: 30 staff member(s)
Membership: 7,800; *Fees:* Schedule available
Activities: Maintains sections for ecologists with special needs & interests: Paleoecology, Aquatic, Physiological, Statistical, Applied Ecology, Vegetation, Education, Long-Term Studies; Professional Certification (constitutes recognition by the Society that an applicant meets the minimum educational experience & ethical standards adopted by ESA for professional ecologists); *Internships:* Yes; *Rents Mailing List:* Yes
Awards:
•The MacArthur Award (Award)
Given for outstanding research contributions by an established ecologist
•Eminent Ecologist Award (Award)
Given to senior ecologist for distinguished contributions
•Corporate Award (Award)
Given to a corporation, business, program or individual of a company for incorporating sound ecological concepts in operating procedures

Ecology Action Centre (EAC)
2705 Fern Lane, Halifax NS B3K 4L3
Tel: 902-429-2202; *Fax:* 902-405-3716
e-mail: info@ecologyaction.ca
www.ecologyaction.ca
www.facebook.com/EcologyActionCentre
twitter.com/ecologyaction
Overview: A medium-sized provincial organization founded in 1971
Mission: To act as a voice for Nova Scotia's environment; To build a healthier, more sustainable Nova Scotia; *Member of:* Canadian Renewable Energy Alliance
Chief Officer(s):
Maggy Burns, Internal Director, 902-429-5287
centre@ecologyaction.ca
Tim Roberts, Co-Chair
Karen Hollett, Co-Chair
Finances: *Funding Sources:* Membership dues; Donations
Staff: 30 staff member(s); 200 volunteer(s)
Membership: 1,000+; *Committees:* Marine Issues; Transportation; Wilderness Issues; Coastal Issues; Energy Issues; Food Action; Built Environment; Climate Change
Activities: Communication; Education and Programming; Research; Advocacy; *Awareness Events:* Annual Awards; *Internships:* Yes; *Speaker Service:* Yes; *Library:* Open to public

Ecology North
5013 - 51 St. St., Yellowknife NT X1A 2N4
Tel: 867-873-6019
e-mail: admin@ecologynorth.ca
www.ecologynorth.ca
Overview: A small local organization founded in 1971
Mission: To promote appreciation & protection of the natural environment of the Northwest Territories; To foster public awareness through seminars & outdoor activities; To provide a forum for communication of ideas on environmental issues between the scientific community, government & the peoples of the Northwest Territories; *Member of:* Canadian Environmental Network
Chief Officer(s):
John Carr, Board Member
Dawn Tremblay, Program Coordinator
Christine Wenman, Coordinator, Northern Waters Program
Finances: *Annual Operating Budget:* $50,000-$100,000
Staff: 2 staff member(s)
Membership: 200; *Fees:* $25 individual; $40 family; *Committees:* Recycling; Botanical Gardens/Volunteer Development; Endangered Species
Activities: Participates in environmental hearings; reviews legislation & policy; sponsors a wide range of activities such as bird walks & nature hikes; public education seminars on various aspects of the northern environment; community recycling programs such as Rent-a-Plate; *Awareness Events:* Earth Week, April; Folk on the Rocks; *Library:* Recycling Resource Centre

EcoPerth
2196 Old Brooke Rd., RR#2, Maberry ON K0H 2B0
Tel: 613-267-6463; *Fax:* 613-268-2907
e-mail: info@ecoperth.on.ca
www.ecoperth.on.ca
Overview: A small local organization
Mission: To promote local projects that are environmentally sustainable and economically efficient in the Perth, Ontario area.
Chief Officer(s):
Bob Argue, Executive Director
bob@ecoperth.on.ca

EcoSource Mississauga
Clarke Hall, 161 Lakeshore Rd. West, 2nd Fl., Mississauga ON L5H 1G3
Tel: 905-274-6222; *Fax:* 905-274-4387
e-mail: info@ecosource.ca
www.ecosource.ca
www.facebook.com/pages/Ecosource/248354978560089
twitter.com/EcoSourceGreen
Overview: A small local charitable organization founded in 1979
Mission: To offer education & programs related to the environment
Environmental Activity: Promoting environmentally responsible personal action
Chief Officer(s):
Lea Ann Mallett, Executive Director
lmallett@ecosource.ca
Stephanie Crocker, Associate Director
scrocker@ecosource.ca
Carolyn Bailey, Manager, Urban Agriculture Program
cbailey@ecosource.ca
Sierra Frank, Manager, School Programs
sfrank@ecosource.ca
Monika Kokoszka, Coordinator, Healthy Roots Program
mkokoszka@ecosource.ca
Jessica Kukac, Coordinator, Waste Reduction
jkukac@ecosource.ca
Finances: *Funding Sources:* Donations; Foundations; Municipal government agencies; Corporations
Publications:
•Gardens & Agriculture
Type: Newsletter; *Editor:* Carolyn Bailey
Profile: Updates about community projects through the EcoSource Urban Agriculture & Community Gardens initiatives
•Peel Environmental Youth Alliance (PEYA)
Type: Newsletter; *Frequency:* Semimonthly; *Editor:* Rahul Mehta
Profile: Environmental events & opportunities for students in the Region of Peel
•Trailblazers
Type: Newsletter
Profile: Information for Region of Peel educators about environmental teaching resources & events

EcoWatch Canada (EWC)
e-mail: seeds@telusplanet.net
www.ecowatchcanada.org
www.linkedin.com/company/ecowatch-canada
www.facebook.com/ecowatchcanada
twitter.com/ecowatchcanada
ecowatchcanada.wordpress.com
Overview: A medium-sized national charitable organization founded in 2008
Mission: To improve the environmental quality, to educate our future generations, and to raise awareness among our community by partnering with local businesses, community leaders, government officials, schools and neighbors.
Chief Officer(s):
Carmen Ng, Executive Director

Edmonton Association of Sheet Metal & Air Conditioning Contractors *See* Sheet Metal Contractors Association of Alberta

Edmonton Space & Science Foundation (ESSF)
11211 - 142 St., Edmonton AB T5M 4A1
Tel: 780-452-9100; *Fax:* 780-455-5882
e-mail: info@telusworldofscienceedmonton.com
www.telusworldofscienceedmonton.com
www.facebook.com/EdmontonScience
twitter.com/twosedm
Also Known As: Telus World of Science - Edmonton
Overview: A small local organization founded in 1978
Mission: To inspire & motivate people to learn about & contribute to science & technology advances that strengthen themselves, their family & community
Chief Officer(s):
George Smith, President & CEO
Finances: *Annual Operating Budget:* $3 Million-$5 Million; *Funding Sources:* Revenue; donations; grants
Staff: 82 staff member(s); 265 volunteer(s)
Membership: 5,000-14,999;; *Fees:* Schedule available
Activities: Community courses; Mobile Astronomy program; Challenger Missions; Summer camps; IMAX films; full-dome shows; observatory; *Library:* by appointment

Egg Farmers of Canada (EFC) / Producteurs d'oufs du Canada
Parent Name: Canadian Federation of Agriculture
21 Florence St., Ottawa ON K2P 0W6
Tel: 613-238-2514; *Fax:* 613-238-1967
e-mail: info@eggs.ca
www.eggs.ca
www.facebook.com/eggs
www.youtube.com/getcracking
Previous Name: Canadian Egg Marketing Agency
Overview: A large national organization founded in 1972 overseen by Canadian Federation of Agriculture
Mission: To forcast demand for eggs; to promote eggs nationally; to develop national standards for egg farming; *Member of:* Canadian Federation of Agriculture; Affiliation(s): World Trade Organization (WTO)
Chief Officer(s):
Peter Clarke, Chair
Tim Lambert, CEO
Membership: 1,000 farm families
Publications:
•Dedicated to Quality [a publication of the Egg Farmers of Canada]

Electric Mobility Canada (EMC) / Mobilité Électrique Canada
#309, 9-6975 Meadowvale Town Centre Circle, Mississauga ON L5N 2V7
Tel: 905-301-5950; *Fax:* 905-826-0157
www.emc-mec.ca
www.linkedin.com/pub/al-cormier/15/985/559
www.facebook.com/240477292643669?ref=ts
twitter.com/EMC_MEC
www.youtube.com/user/ElectricMobilityCA
Overview: A small national organization
Mission: Electric Mobility Canada is a national membership-based not-for-profit organization dedicated exclusively to the promotion of electric mobility as a readily available and important solution to Canada's emerging energy and environmental issues.
Chief Officer(s):
Chris Hill, President & CEO
chris.hill@emc-mec.ca
Membership: 125; *Committees:* Government Relations; Working Group on PEV Readiness; Electric Bus
Meetings/Conferences:
For more information see Trade Shows, Conferences and Seminars Chapter
5th Annual Electric Vehicles Conference & Trade Show 2013
October 2013 Gatineau, QC

Electric Vehicle Council of Ottawa (EVCO)
PO Box 4044, Stn. E, Ottawa ON K1S 5B1
e-mail: info@evco.ca
www.evco.ca
www.youtube.com/EVCOdotCA
Overview: A small local organization founded in 1980
Mission: To promote the use of electric vehicles as a viable transportation alternative
Environmental Activity: Promoting awareness of electric vehicles, which are ecologically friendly
Chief Officer(s):
Darryl McMahon, President
president@evco.ca
Barry Hoover, Vice-President
bhoover@evco.ca
David French, Treasurer
dfrench@evco.ca
Activities: Offering technical literature; Organizing displays, demonstrations, talks, & competitions; Hosting monthly meetings; Participating in advocacy projects; *Library:* Electric Vehicle Council of Ottawa Print & Video Library

Publications:
•EV Circuit
Type: Newsletter
Profile: Information for members of the Electric Vehicle Council of Ottawa

Electric Vehicle Society of Canada (EVS)
21 Burritt Rd., Toronto ON M1R 3S5
Tel: 416-755-4324; *Fax:* 416-755-4324
e-mail: info@evsociety.ca
www.evsociety.ca
Overview: A medium-sized national organization founded in 1991
Mission: To investigate & promote clean transportation technologies
Environmental Activity: Encouraging electric vehicle conversions
Chief Officer(s):
Howard W. Hutt, President
hhutt@rogers.com
Joel Clemens, Treasurer
Emile Stevens, Contact, Membership
Robert Weekley, Editor, EVSurge
editor@evsociety.ca
Membership: *Fees:* $20 students, spouses, & seniors; $30 adults; $50 families; $100 corporations; *Member Profile:* Engineers; Environmentalists; Enthusiasts for electric energy for propulsion
Activities: Providing a forum for member discussions; Examining modes of electric transportation
Publications:
•Electric Vehicle Conversion Manual: A Workshop Guide for High Schools
Type: Manual; *Number of Pages:* 85; *Author:* Neil Gover et al.
Profile: Contents include the move to sustainable transportation, getting started, basics of electrical energy & electricity, starting theconversion, & EV performance & evaluation
•EVSurge [a publication of the Electric Vehicle Society of Canada]
Type: Newsletter; *Frequency:* Bimonthly; *Editor:* Robert Weekley; *Price:* Free with Electric VehicleSociety of Canada membership
Profile: Electric Vehicle Society of Canada events, membership information, & articles about activities in the EV world

Electricity Distributors Association (EDA)
#1100, 3700 Steeles Ave. West, Vaughan ON L4L 8K8
Tel: 905-265-5300; *Fax:* 905-265-5301
Toll-Free: 800-668-9979
e-mail: email@eda-on.ca
www.eda-on.ca
www.facebook.com/EDAMembersAssistSandy
Previous Name: Municipal Electric Association
Overview: A large provincial organization founded in 1986
Mission: To be the voice of Ontario's electricity distributors, the publicly & privately owned companies that deliver electricity to Ontario homes, businesses & public institutions. Focus is on advocacy & representation to government, analysis of legislation & market regulations, communication & networking among members & industry colleagues
Chief Officer(s):
Charlie Macaluso, President & CEO
John Loucks, Vice President, Corporate & Member Affairs
Teresa Sarkesian, Vice President, Policy & Government Affairs
Finances: *Annual Operating Budget:* Greater than $5 Million; *Funding Sources:* Membership dues
Staff: 18 staff member(s); 100 volunteer(s)
Membership: 256; *Fees:* $750 commercial member; *Member Profile:* Public & privately owned electricity distributors

Electro-Federation Canada Inc. (EFC)
#300, 180 Attwell Dr., Toronto ON M9W 6A9
Tel: 905-602-8877; *Fax:* 905-602-5686
Toll-Free: 866-602-8877
e-mail: info@electrofed.com
www.electrofed.com
twitter.com/EFC_Tweets
Overview: A medium-sized national organization founded in 1995
Mission: To represent members provincially, federally, & internationally on issues affecting the electro-technical business
Chief Officer(s):
Milos Jancik, President/CEO
mjancik@electrofed.com
Ken Frankum, Chair
Harald Henze, Treasurer
Larry Moore, Vice-President, Consumer Councils
lmoore@electrofed.com
Joseph Neu, Vice-President, Engineering, Codes & Standards
jneu@electrofed.com
Membership: 300 companies; *Member Profile:* Companies that manufacture, distribute, & service electrical, electronics, & telecommunications products; *Committees:* Canadian Appliance Manufacturers Association; Consumer Electronics Marketers of Canada; Electrical Equipment Manufacturers Association of Canada; Supply & Manufacturers' Reps Councils; Installation Maintenance & Repair Sector Council & Trade Association; Electro-Federation Canada Alumni Association
Activities: Collecting & disseminating market data; Providing networking opportunities; Hosting annual conferences; Researching; Offering educational programs; Communicating with members; Promoting the industry; Conducting surveys;

Electronics Product Stewardship Canada
#600, 15 Allstate Parkway, Markham ON L3R 5B4
Tel: 905-415-4591
e-mail: info@epsc.ca
www.epsc.ca
Overview: A medium-sized national organization founded in 2003
Mission: To design, promote & implement sustainable solutions for electronics waste
Chief Officer(s):
Shelagh Kerr, President/CEO
Nathan B. MacDonald, Director, Environmental Programs
nathan@epsc.ca
Membership: 16 leading electronics manufacturers

Elora Centre for Environmental Excellence *See* Elora Environment Centre

Elora Environment Centre
PO Box 1100, 75 Melville St., 2nd Fl., Elora ON N0B 1S0
Tel: 519-846-8464; *Fax:* 519-846-8464
Toll-Free: 866-865-7337
e-mail: info@eloraenvironmentcentre.ca
www.ecee.on.ca
Previous Name: Elora Centre for Environmental Excellence
Overview: A small local charitable organization founded in 1993
Mission: The Centre a not-for-profit organization focused on providing leadership in community-based environmental initiatives for both urban & rural communities. Areas of experience include: energy efficiency, greenhouse gas reduction, water efficiency, sustainable transportation, environmental education. It is a registered charity, BN: 138373196RR0001.; *Member of:* Green Communities Canada; Affiliation(s): Ontario Environmental Network; Centre for Applied Renewable Energy; GreenPathways; several municipal governments & hydro-electric companies
Chief Officer(s):
Jennifer McLellan, Chair
Lynda Bausinger, Acting General Manager
wellaware@eloraenvironmentcentre.ca
Finances: *Annual Operating Budget:* $50,000-$100,000; *Funding Sources:* Fees from clients; Natural Resources Canada
Staff: 7 staff member(s)
Activities: Home energy evaluations; NeighbourWoods tree steward program; *Speaker Service:* Yes

Elsa Wild Animal Appeal of Canada
PO Box 45051, 2482 Yonge St., Toronto ON M4P 3E3
Tel: 416-489-8862; *Fax:* 416-489-4769
e-mail: info@elsacanada.com
www.elsacanada.com
Also Known As: Elsa Canada
Overview: A small national charitable organization founded in 1972
Mission: To help save endangered wildlife species in Canada
Chief Officer(s):
Betty Henderson, President
Finances: *Annual Operating Budget:* Less than $50,000; *Funding Sources:* Donations; membership fees; fundraising
Staff: 15 volunteer(s)
Membership: 150; *Fees:* $25

Employers' Council of BC *See* Business Council of British Columbia

Énergie Solaire Québec
CP 540, Succ. St-Laurent, Ville St-Laurent QC H4L 4V7
Tél: 514-392-0095
www.esq.qc.ca
Aperçu: *Dimension:* petite; *Envergure:* provinciale
Mission: Promouvoir l'utilisation de l'énergie solaire au Québec
Membre: *Montant de la cotisation:* 40$ individuel
Activités: Souper solaire; clinique solaire; concours Cocktail Transport

Energy Action Council of Toronto (EnerACT)
51 Wolseley St., 5th Fl., Toronto ON M5T 1A4
Tel: 416-488-3966; *Fax:* 416-203-3121
Overview: A small local organization
Mission: To accelerate the change in society's usage of energy away from environmentally inappropriate forms towards conservation & renewable energy; To encourage the further application of technologies which contribute to energy conservation & the wider use of renewable energy; To broaden society's understanding of the relationship between energy & the environment & the potential for meeting society's energy needs through conservation & renewable energy technologies; To assist in the development of public policies which encourage energy conservation & the use of renewable energy
Chief Officer(s):
Mark Fernandez, Project Coordinator
Fraser Stewart, Executive Director
Membership: *Fees:* Schedule available

Energy Council of Canada / Conseil canadien de l'énergie
#608, 350 Sparks St., Ottawa ON K1R 7S8
Tel: 613-232-8239; *Fax:* 613-232-1079
e-mail: krystal.piamonte@energy.ca
www.energy.ca
Previous Name: World Energy Council - Canadian Member Committee
Overview: A medium-sized national organization founded in 1924
Mission: To foster a greater understanding of energy issues; To enhance the effectiveness of the Canadian energy strategy; *Member of:* World Energy Council
Chief Officer(s):
Murray J. Stewart, President
murray.stewart@energy.ca
Brigitte Svarich, Director, Operations
brigitte.svarich@energy.ca
Membership: 75+; *Member Profile:* Representatives from all facets of Canada's energy sector
Activities: Providing networking opportunities; Sponsoring forums & conferences; Disseminating current energy reports & information; Contributing to the development of the Canadian energy policy

Energy Probe Research Foundation (EPRF)
225 Brunswick Ave., Toronto ON M5S 2M6
Tel: 416-964-9223; *Fax:* 416-964-8239
e-mail: webadmin@eprf.ca
www.eprf.ca
www.facebook.com/EnergyProbeResearchFoundation
Overview: A large national charitable organization founded in 1980
Mission: To educate Canadians about the benefits of conservation & renewable energy; to help Canada secure long-term energy self-sufficiency in the shortest possible time with the fewest disruptive effects & with the greatest societal, environmental & economic benefits; to provide business, government & the public with information on energy & energy-related issues; to help Canada contribute to global harmony & prosperity; recipient of the 1990 Lieutenant Governor's Conservation Award, the first time that an environmental organization has been so honoured; divisions include Energy Probe, Probe International, Environment Probe, Margaret Laurence Fund, Consumer Policy Institute, Environmental Bureau of Investigations, Urban Renaissance Institute; Affiliation(s): Energy Probe; Probe International; Environment Probe; Consumer Policy Institute; Urban Renaissance Institute; Environmental Bureau of Investigation; Three Gorges Probe; Canadian Environmental News Network
Chief Officer(s):
Patricia Adams, President
Elizabeth Brubaker, Executive Director, Environment Probe
Finances: *Annual Operating Budget:* $1.5 Million-$3 Million; *Funding Sources:* Donations
Staff: 15 staff member(s); 10 volunteer(s)
Membership: 50,000 supporters
Activities: Policy research & education; *Internships:* Yes; *Speaker Service:* Yes; *Library:* Open to public
Awards:
•The Margaret Laurence Fund (Grant)
Grants & scholarships are made to foster an understanding of

peace & the environment upon which the fate of the planet rests
Eligibility: Recipients of the grants & scholarships are limited to students, authors, researchers, & publishers, working with the foundation in collaborative projects approved by the directors

Enform: The Safety Association for the Upstream Oil & Gas Industry

Head Office, 5055 - 11th St. NE, Calgary AB T2E 8N4
Tel: 403-516-8000; *Fax:* 403-516-8166
Toll-Free: 800-667-5557
e-mail: customerservice@enform.ca
www.enform.ca
Previous Name: Petroleum Industry Training Service
Overview: A large national licensing charitable organization founded in 2005
Mission: To improve the Canadian upstream oil & gas industry's safety performance; To prevent work-related injuries in the upstream oil & gas industry in Canada; Affiliation(s): Canadian Association of Geophysical Contractors (CAGC); Canadian Association of Oilwell Drilling Contractors (CAODC); Canadian Association of Petroleum Producers (CAPP); Canadian Energy Pipeline Association (CEPA); Petroleum Services Association of Canada (PSAC); Small Explorers & Producers Association of Canada (SEPAC); Petroleum Human Resources Council of Canada; Western Canadian Spill Services
Environmental Activity: Offering training programs in environmental management
Chief Officer(s):
Duane Mather, Chair
Cameron MacGillivray, President & CEO
L. Harman, Vice President, Operations
R. Ogilvie, Vice President, Corporate Services
Activities: Providing training courses; Offering saftey information; Promoting shared safety practices in the Canadian oil & gas industry; Providing the Small Employers Certificate of Recognition (SECOR), the Certificate of Recognition (COR), & the Petroleum Competency Program
Publications:
•Enform Insider
Type: Newsletter

British Columbia Office

#1240, 9600 - 93rd Avenue, Fort St. John BC V1J 5Z2
Tel: 250-785-6009; *Fax:* 250-785-6013
Toll-Free: 855-436-3676

Genesee - Enform Ignition Training Facility

Genesee AB
Tel: 780-955-7770

Nisku Training Facility

1020 - 20th Ave., Nisku AB T9E 7Z6
Tel: 780-955-7770; *Fax:* 780-955-2454
Toll-Free: 800-667-5557

Saskatchewan Office

1912 Prince of Wales Dr., Regina BC S4Z 1A4
Tel: 306-337-9600; *Fax:* 306-337-9610
Toll-Free: 877-336-3676

The Engineering Institute of Canada (EIC) / L'Institut canadien des ingénieurs (ICI)

1295 Hwy. 2 East, RR#1, Kingston ON K7L 4V1
Tel: 613-547-5989; *Fax:* 613-547-0195
e-mail: jplant1@cogeco.ca
www.eic-ici.ca
Overview: A large national charitable organization founded in 1887
Mission: To further the development of engineering in Canada; to stimulate the advancement of the quality & scope of Canadian engineering; to meet regularly with other engineering organizations & industries to promote understanding & improvement of the profession, the diffusion of engineering information & to provide Canadian representation in specialized engineering fields; to interact with government agencies & departments for the purpose of influencing decision making on matters relating to engineering & technology; to cooperate with the provincial engineering licensing bodies, The Canadian Council of Professional Engineering, The Association of Consulting Engineers of Canada, The Canadian Academy of Engineering & other engineering organizations in matters of common interest; to promote interaction with specific interest groups; to collaborate with universities & educational institutions; Affiliation(s): Engineers Canada; Association of Canadian Engineering Companies; Canadian Academy of Engineering; International Association for Continuing Education & Training (IACET); Internation Association for Continuing Engineering Education (IACEE)
Chief Officer(s):
Tony Bennett, P.Eng, President
John Plant, PhD, FCAE, FIEE, Executive Director
Xiaohua Wu, PhD, Treasurer
Jean Zu, PhD, PEng, Vice-President
Louise McNamara, Office Manager, 613-547-5989
louisem@cogeco.ca
Finances: *Annual Operating Budget:* $100,000-$250,000; *Funding Sources:* Membership fees; Con Ed quality, Assurance program, Career Site
Staff: 1 staff member(s); 20 volunteer(s)
Membership: 11 member societies; *Fees:* $2.50 per regular member of the member society; *Member Profile:* Join one of the member societies: Canadian Society for Civil Engineering; Canadian Society for Mechanical Engineering; Canadian Geotechnical Society; Canadian Society for Engineering in Management; IEEE - Canada; Canadian Society for Chemical Engineering; *Committees:* Executives, Council, Honours & Awards; History & Archives; Life Members Organization
Activities: Promotes the creation, exchange & dissemination of technical information; organizes conferences & symposia & promotes continuing education for engineers; supports engineering student advancement; maintains an official Registry of Continuing Education Units & Professional Development Activities; *Library:* Archives at University of Ontario Inst.; Open to public

Engineers Canada / Ingénieurs Canada

#1100, 180 Elgin St., Ottawa ON K2P 2K3
Tel: 613-232-2474; *Fax:* 613-230-5759
Toll-Free: 877-408-9273
e-mail: info@engineerscanada.ca
www.engineerscanada.ca
www.facebook.com/EngineersCanada
twitter.com/engineerscanada
www.youtube.com/user/EngineersCanada
Previous Name: Canadian Council of Professional Engineers
Overview: A large national organization founded in 1936
Mission: To establish & maintain a common bond between constituent associations; To assist constituent associations to meet their common needs & those of their members by coordinating standards, procedures, & programs across Canada; To represent the engineering profession with respect to national & international affairs; To increase the profile & prestige of the engineering profession; Affiliation(s): World Federation of Engineering Organizations
Chief Officer(s):
Kim Allen, FEC, P.Eng., CEO
kim.allen@engineerscanada.ca
Marie Carter, FEC, P.Eng., COO
marie.carter@engineerscanada.ca
Marc Bourgeois, FIC (Hon.), Director, Communications & Public Affairs
marc.bourgeois@engineerscanada.ca
Gordon Griffith, FEC, P.Eng, ing, Director, Education
gordon.griffith@engineerscanada.ca
Ken McMartin, FEC, P.Eng., Director, Professional & International Affairs
ken.mcmartin@engineerscanada.ca
Finances: *Funding Sources:* Membership dues
Membership: 10 provincial + 2 territorial associations representing 250,000 professional engineers; *Committees:* Canadian Engineering Accreditation Board (CEAB); Canadian Engineering Qualifications Board (CEQB); International; Awards
Activities: *Awareness Events:* National Engineering Month, March
Awards:
•Gold Medal Award (Award)
•Young Engineer Achievement Award (Award)
Awarded for outstanding contribution in a field of engineering by an engineer 35 years of age or younger
•Medal for Distinction in Engineering Education (Scholarship)
Awarded for exemplary contribution to engineering teaching at a Canadian University
•Gold Medal Award (Award)
Awarded for exceptional individual achievement & distinction in a field of engineering
•Gold Medal Student Award (Award)
•National Award for an Engineering Project or Achievement (Award)
•Engineers Canada Fellowship (Award)
Meetings/Conferences:
For more information see Trade Shows, Conferences and Seminars Chapter
Engineers Canada Board Meeting & AGM
June 2013 Yellowknife, NT
Engineers Canada Board Meeting & AGM 2014
2014
Publications:
•Engineers Canada Newsletter
Type: Newsletter

Engineers Nova Scotia

Parent Name: Engineers Canada
1355 Barrington St., Halifax NS B3J 1Y9
Tel: 902-429-2250; *Fax:* 902-423-9769
Toll-Free: 888-802-7367
e-mail: info@engineersnovascotia.ca
www.engineersnovascotia.ca
Overview: A medium-sized provincial licensing organization founded in 1920 overseen by Engineers Canada
Mission: To establish, maintain & develop standards of knowledge & skill, standards of qualification & practice, & standards of professional ethics; To promote public awareness of the role of the association; *Member of:* Engineers Canada
Chief Officer(s):
Len White, P.Eng., Chief Executive Officer & Registrar
Perry Mitchelmore, P.Eng., President
Finances: *Funding Sources:* Membership dues
Staff: 230 volunteer(s)
Membership: 5,000+; *Committees:* Public Relations; Student Affairs; Awards; Building; Professional Development; Professional Practice; Construction; Consulting Practice; Zones; Engineering Week; Finance; Publications; Information Highway; Salary; Employee Engineers
Activities: *Awareness Events:* National Engineering Week, March; *Internships:* Yes; *Speaker Service:* Yes
Meetings/Conferences:
For more information see Trade Shows, Conferences and Seminars Chapter
Engineers Nova Scotia 2013 Annual General Meeting
2013, NS

Engineers Without Borders (EWB) / Ingénieurs sans Frontières (ISF)

#601, 366 Adelaide St. West, Toronto ON M5V 1R9
Tel: 416-481-3696; *Fax:* 416-352-5360
Toll-Free: 866-481-3696
e-mail: info@ewb.ca
www.ewb.ca
Overview: A small international organization
Mission: To promote human development through access to technology
Chief Officer(s):
Parker Mitchell, Co-CEO
parkermitchell@ewb.ca
George Roter, Co-CEO
georgeroter@ewb.ca
Brenna Donoghue, Director of Operations
brennadonoghue@ewb.ca

Entomological Society of Alberta (ESA)

Dept. of Agricultural, Food & Nutritional Science, U of Alberta, 410 Ag/For Bldg., Edmonton AB T6G 2P5
Tel: 780-492-6893; *Fax:* 780-492-4265
www.entsocalberta.ca/esa.htm
Overview: A small provincial organization founded in 1952
Mission: To foster the advancement, exchange & dissemination of the knowledge of insects in relation to their importance in agriculture, forestry, public health & industry; *Member of:* Entomological Society of Canada
Chief Officer(s):
Lloyd Dosdall, President
lloyd.dosdall@ualberta.ca
Caroline Whitehouse, Treasurer, 780-492-3929, Fax: 780-492-9234
cmw7@ualberta.ca
Finances: *Annual Operating Budget:* Less than $50,000
Membership: 108; *Fees:* $10

Entomological Society of British Columbia (ESBC)

e-mail: info@entsocbc.ca
blogs.sfu.ca/groups/esbc
www.linkedin.com/groups/Entomological-Society-British-Columbia-4760901
www.facebook.com/groups/135038946598013
twitter.com/EntSocBC

Overview: A small provincial organization founded in 1902
Member of: Entomological Society of Canada
Chief Officer(s):
Ward Strong, President
Leo Rankin, Secretary
scholarships@entsocbc.ca
Max Salomon, Treasurer
membership@entsocbc.ca
Membership: 230; *Fees:* $20; *Member Profile:* Professional; amateur; student entomologists
Activities: ; *Library:* Pacific Forestry Centre
Awards:
•Student Research Presentation Awards (Award)
•Graduate Student Travel Grants (Grant)

Entomological Society of Manitoba Inc. (ESM)
Agriculture Canada, Research Station, 195 Dafoe Rd., Winnipeg MB R3T 2M9
Tel: 204-983-1450; *Fax:* 204-983-4604
e-mail: iwise@agr.gc.ca
home.cc.umanitoba.ca/~fieldspg
Overview: A small provincial charitable organization founded in 1945
Mission: To encourage & promote the field of entomology; To provide a forum to enable individuals with an interest in entomology to acquire & share information; Affiliation(s): Entomological Society of Canada
Chief Officer(s):
David Wade, Secretary
Bob Lamb, President
Finances: *Annual Operating Budget:* Less than $50,000; *Funding Sources:* Donations; membership fees; interest income; fundraising
Staff: 25 volunteer(s)
Membership: 106; *Fees:* $25; *Member Profile:* Professional & amateur entomologists; *Committees:* Endowment Fund; Finance; Scientific Program; Newsletter; Youth Encouragement & Public Education; Social; Scholarships & Awards; Fundraising; Nomination; Membership; Scrtineers; Archivist; Common Names of Insects; Web Page
Activities: Scientific paper symposia; public education presentations on entomology; *Library:* Agriculture & Agrifood Canada Resource Centre; Open to public

Entomological Society of Ontario (ESO)
c/o Vista Centre, PO Box 83025, 1830 Bank St., Ottawa ON K1V 1A3
Tel: 603-736-3393
www.entsocont.ca
Overview: A small provincial organization founded in 1863
Mission: To foster interest in entomology
Chief Officer(s):
Bruce Gill, President, 613-759-1842, Fax: 613-759-6938
bruce.gill@inspection.gc.ca
Nicole McKenzie, Secretary
nicole_mckenzie@hc-sc.gc.ca
Finances: *Annual Operating Budget:* Less than $50,000
Membership: 100-499; *Member Profile:* Amateurs & professionals
Activities: ; *Library:*
Meetings/Conferences:
For more information see Trade Shows, Conferences and Seminars Chapter
Entomological Society of Ontario 2013 150th Annual General Meeting
2013, ON
Publications:
•Journal of the Entomological Society of Ontario
Type: Journal; *Frequency:* Annually

Entomological Society of Saskatchewan (ESS)
c/o Agriculture & Agri-Food Canada, 107 Science Pl., Saskatoon SK S7N OX2
Tel: 306-956-7287; *Fax:* 306-956-7247
www.usask.ca/biology/ess/ess.html
Overview: A small provincial organization founded in 1952
Mission: The Society promotes the significance of entomology to the general public & provides a forum for those interested in the field to communicate. It also works in conjunction with other similar societies.; *Member of:* Entomological Society of Canada
Chief Officer(s):
Ruwandi Andrahennadi, President
ruwandi.andra@usask.ca
Finances: *Annual Operating Budget:* Less than $50,000
Membership: *Fees:* $20; $5 student; *Member Profile:* Amateurs & professionals

Activities: North American butterfly count; insect inventory of endangered/protected ecosystems; talks & presentations, displays at schools; *Speaker Service:* Yes; *Rents Mailing List:* Yes; *Library:*

Enviro-Accès Inc.
Place Andrew-Paton, #150, 85, rue Belvédère nord, Sherbrooke QC J1H 4A7
Tél: 819-823-2230; *Téléc:* 819-823-6632
Courriel: enviro@enviroaccess.ca
www.enviroaccess.ca
Également appelé: Centre pour l'avancement des technologies environnementales
Aperçu: *Dimension:* moyenne; *Envergure:* provinciale; fondée en 1993
Mission: Supporter les petites et moyennes entreprises qui oeuvrent dans le domaine de l'environnement en leur offrant les services professionnels nécessaires au développement de leurs projets et de leurs affaires.
Membre(s) du bureau directeur:
Manon Laporte, Présidente-directrice générale
mlaporte@enviroaccess.ca
Finances: *Budget de fonctionnement annuel:* $1.5 Million-$3 Million
Personnel: 10 membre(s) du personnel
Membre: 1-99

Environment Resources Managament Association
PO Box 857, Grand Falls-Windsor NL A2A 2P7
Tel: 709-489-7350
www.exploitsriver.ca/association.php
Overview: A medium-sized national organization founded in 1984
Mission: To promote the development of the Exploits River as a major Atlantic Salmon producing river.

Environmental & Outdoor Education Council of Alberta *See* Global, Environmental & Outdoor Education Council

Environmental Abatement Council of Ontario (EACO)
70 Leek Cres., Richmond Hill ON L4B 1H1
Tel: 416-499-4000; *Fax:* 416-499-8752
e-mail: mthorburn@tcanetworks.com
www.eacoontario.com
Previous Name: Ontario Asbestos Removal Contractors Association
Overview: A medium-sized provincial organization founded in 1992
Mission: To collect, generate & disseminate information concerning environmental abatement & other hazardous environmental health issues
Chief Officer(s):
Mary Thorburn, Secretary/Manager Ext. 114
mthorburn@tcaconnect.com
Finances: *Annual Operating Budget:* Less than $50,000; *Funding Sources:* Membership dues
Staff: 10 staff member(s); 30 volunteer(s)
Membership: 25 corporate; *Fees:* $625 general/contractor; $75 associate

Environmental Action Barrie - Living Green
Barrie ON
www.livinggreenbarrie.com
twitter.com/livinggreenbarr
Overview: A small local charitable organization founded in 1990
Mission: To provide education & awareness about environmental issues for the people of Barrie, Ontario & neighbouring communities; To promote environmentally friendly practices
Chief Officer(s):
Mike Fox, Executive Director
Erich Jacoby-Hawkins, Board Member
erich@livinggreenbarrie.com; erich@livinggreen.info
Finances: *Funding Sources:* Donations
Activities: Carrying out eco-projects; Providing articles related to environmental issues; Offering environmental information & activities through a web site, as a web site based organization; *Speaker Service:* Yes

Environmental Bankers Association (EBA)
#410, 510 King St., Alexandria VA 22314 USA
Tel: 703-549-0977; *Fax:* 703-548-5945
e-mail: eba@envirobank.org
www.envirobank.org
Overview: A medium-sized international organization founded in 1994

Mission: To assist the financial services industry in developing environmental risk management policies & procedures
Environmental Activity: Responding to the need for due diligence policies & procedures, sustainable development, & environmental risk management in financial institutions
Chief Officer(s):
Rick Ferguson, President, Policy
richardr.ferguson@usbank.com
Sharon Valverde, Vice-President, Programs
sharon.s.valverde@chase.com
Tacy Telego, Co-Executive Director
Tacytelego@envirobank.org
D. Jeffrey Telego, Co-Executive Director
jefftelego@envirobank.org
Membership: 1-99;; *Fees:* Schedule available based upon asset size of financial institutions; *Member Profile:* Members of the financial services industry, such as bank & non-bank financial institutions, asset management firms, insurers, & those who provide services to them; Environmental consultants, appraisers, environmental attorneys, & environmental information management firms; *Committees:* Policy; Finance & Budget; Communications & Programs; Business Development & Membership; Legal & ASTM; Trust; Risk Management; Global Issues; Technical
Activities: Facilitating networking opportunities

Environmental Careers Organization of Canada / L'Organisation pour les carrières en environnement du Canada
#200, 308 - 11th Ave. SE, Calgary AB T2G 0Y2
Tel: 403-233-0748; *Fax:* 403-269-9544
e-mail: info@eco.ca
www.eco.ca
www.facebook.com/ecocanada
twitter.com/ecocanada
Also Known As: ECO Canada
Previous Name: Canadian Council for Human Resources in the Environment Industry
Overview: A medium-sized national organization founded in 1992
Mission: To provide services to all participants in the environmental sector, including educators, students, practitioners, & employers
Chief Officer(s):
Hubert Bourque, Chair
Jon Ogryzlo, Sec.-Treas.
Grant S. Trump, President/CEO
Michael Kerford, Vice-President
Janelle Thomlinson, Director, Marketing & Communications
Finances: *Funding Sources:* Government of Canada's Sector Council Program
Activities: Providing career information & a job board; Recruiting; Offering ECO Canada internships; Providing professional development opportunities to practitioners; Offering employee retention strategies to employers; Providing tools for career change & career development; Disseminating human resource statistics & trends; Increasing Aboriginal employment in the environment sector through career awareness, training, & employment resources

The Environmental Coalition of PEI
126 Richmond St., Charlottetown PE C1A 1H9
Tel: 902-566-4696; *Fax:* 902-566-4037
e-mail: energy@ecopei.ca
www.ecopei.ca
Also Known As: ECO-PEI
Overview: A medium-sized provincial organization founded in 1988
Mission: To preserve & enhance the environment for all living things; *Member of:* PEI Environmental Network; Canadian Environmental Network
Chief Officer(s):
Kate McDonald, Energy Coordinator
Finances: *Annual Operating Budget:* $100,000-$250,000
Staff: 15 volunteer(s)
Membership: 150; *Fees:* $10

Environmental Coalition of Prince Edward Island (ECO-PEI)
c/o Voluntary Resource Centre, 81 Prince St., Charlottetown PE C1A 4R3
Tel: 902-651-2575
e-mail: mail@ecopei.ca
www.ecopei.ca
Overview: A small provincial organization founded in 1988

Mission: To work in partnership in order to understand & improve the Island's environment; *Member of:* Canadian Renewable Energy Alliance
Chief Officer(s):
Gary Schneider, Co-Chair
Membership: *Fees:* $10 basic; $25 supporting; $100 corporate
Publications:
•ECO-NEWS [a publication of the Environmental Coalition of Prince Edward Island]
Type: Newsletter

Environmental Data Research Institute *See* Resources for Global Sustainability

Environmental Defence / Defense environmentale
#705, 317 Adelaide St. West, Toronto ON M5V 1P9
Tel: 416-323-9521; *Fax:* 416-323-9301
Toll-Free: 877-399-2333
e-mail: info@environmentaldefence.ca
www.environmentaldefence.ca
Previous Name: Canadian Environmental Defence Fund
Overview: A medium-sized national charitable organization founded in 1985
Mission: To protect the environment & human health; To research, educate, & initiate action in the courts when necessary; *Member of:* Canadian Environmental Network
Environmental Activity: Ensuring clean air, safe food, & thriving ecosystems nationwide
Chief Officer(s):
Rick Smith, Executive Director
Finances: *Annual Operating Budget:* $500,000-$1.5 Million
Staff: 25 volunteer(s)

Environmental Defense
Membership & Public Information, #600, 1875 Connecticut Ave., NW, Washington DC 20009 USA
Tel: 212-505-2100; *Fax:* 212-505-2375
Toll-Free: 800-684-3322
www.edf.org
www.linkedin.com/company/environmental-defense
www.facebook.com/EnvDefenseFund
twitter.com/EnvDefenseFund
Previous Name: Environmental Defense Fund
Overview: A large international organization founded in 1967
Mission: To protect environmental rights for all people — clean air, clean water, healthy food, & flourishing ecosystems; To work to create practical solutions, guided by science, that win lasting political, economic & social support
Environmental Activity: Initiating legal action on environmental matters; Conducting educational campaigns
Chief Officer(s):
Fred Krupp, President
Finances: *Annual Operating Budget:* Greater than $5 Million; *Funding Sources:* Donations; foundations
Staff: 340 staff member(s)
Membership: 750,000+
Activities: Areas of focus include climate, oceans, ecosystems & health
Publications:
•Earth: The Sequel - The Race to Reinvent Energy and Stop Global Warming
Number of Pages: 256; *Author:* Fred Krupp, Miriam Horn; *Price:* $24.95

Environmental Defense Fund *See* Environmental Defense

Environmental Education Association of the Yukon (EEAY)
Whitehorse YT
e-mail: eeyukon@gmail.com
taiga.net/YukonEE
Overview: A small provincial organization
Mission: To promote environmental education in the Yukon and foster communication between individuals and groups with and interest in environmental education.; *Member of:* EENorth; Canada's Arctic Environmental Education Network

Environmental Education Ontario (EEON)
32 Springdale Dr., Kitchener ON N2K 1P9
Tel: 519-579-3097
e-mail: admin@eeon.org
www.eeon.org
www.facebook.com/group.php?gid=103171483071910&ref=ts
Overview: A small local charitable organization founded in 2000
Mission: EEON promotes in Ontario the facilitation, development & implementation of education on sustainable environments. It is a registered charity, BN: 864934617RR0001.; *Member of:* Education Alliance for a Sustainable Ontario
Chief Officer(s):
David Arthur, President
Jane Forbes, Treasurer
Finances: *Annual Operating Budget:* Less than $50,000; *Funding Sources:* Federal & provincial governments; foundations
Staff: 12 volunteer(s)
Membership: *Member Profile:* Environmental & ecological educators, concerned citizens, parents, & representatives from non-governmental organizations & government agencies; *Committees:* Fundraising; Research; Education; Tracking
Activities: Listserv; meetings; representations; *Speaker Service:* Yes
Meetings/Conferences:
For more information see Trade Shows, Conferences and Seminars Chapter
Environmental Education Ontario Spring Event and Annual General Meeting 2013
April 2013 Toronto, ON

Environmental Educators' Provincial Specialist Association (EEPSA)
c/o British Columbia Teachers' Federation, #100, 550 - 6th Ave. West, Vancouver BC V5Z 4P2
Tel: 604-871-2283
eepsa.org
www.facebook.com/eepsa.bc
twitter.com/EEPSA
Overview: A medium-sized provincial organization founded in 1972
Mission: To promote, through public education, greater awareness, understanding & appreciation of the environment & to encourage global citizenship through the development of active decision making; *Member of:* BC Teachers' Federation
Chief Officer(s):
Selina Metcalfe, President
selmet@shaw.ca
Finances: *Funding Sources:* Membership dues
Membership: 200; *Fees:* $15 student; $25 BCTF members; $45.68 associate

Environmental Health Association of British Columbia (EHABC)
PO Box 30033, Stn. Saanich Centre, Victoria BC V8X 5E1
Tel: 250-658-2027
www.ehabc.org
Overview: A medium-sized provincial organization founded in 2008
Mission: To raise awareness within the medical community, educational institutions, and the general public to prevent further cases of environmental sensitivity from occurring.; Affiliation(s): EHA Nova Scotia; EHA Québec; EHA Ontario; EHA Alberta
Membership: *Fees:* $25

Environmental Health Association of Nova Scotia (EHANS)
PO Box 31323, Halifax NS B3K 5Y5
Toll-Free: 800-449-1995
e-mail: ehans@environmentalhealth.ca
www.environmentalhealth.ca
www.facebook.com/165405756830794
Previous Name: Nova Scotia Allergy & Environmental Health Association
Overview: A small provincial organization founded in 1985
Chief Officer(s):
Eric Slone, President
Membership: *Fees:* $25 individual; $35 family; $75 supporting

Environmental Health Association of Ontario (EHA Ontario)
PO Box 33023, Ottawa ON K2C 3Y9
Tel: 613-860-2342
e-mail: helpline@ehaontario.ca
www.ehaontario.ca
Previous Name: Allergy & Environmental Health Association
Overview: A small provincial charitable organization founded in 1975
Mission: EHA Ontario is a volunteer, not-for-profit, self-help organization for persons with chemical & environmental allergies. It promotes awareness of environmental conditions that may be harmful to human health, & advocates less-contaminated sources of food, water, clothing, personal & home care products, home furnishings & building materials. It also disseminates information to its members, as well as the general public concerning allergies & environmental health-related issues. It is a registered charity, BN 132737099RR0001.; *Member of:* Human Ecology Foundation of Canada; Affiliation(s): EHA Nova Scotia; EHA Québec; EHA Alberta; EHA BC
Chief Officer(s):
Carol Lebel, Executive Director
office@ehaontario.ca
Finances: *Funding Sources:* Donations; Membership fees
Membership: 300; *Fees:* $28 new member; $25 pa renewal; *Member Profile:* Individuals with environmental sensitivities & their families; *Committees:* Membership; Newsletter
Activities: ; *Library:* AEHA-Ottawa Library; Open to public

Environmental Health Foundation of Canada (EHFC) Parent Name: Canadian Institute of Public Health Inspectors
Stn. #720, 999 West Broadway Ave., Vancouver BC V5Z 1K5
www.ehfc.ca
Overview: A small national charitable organization founded in 1989 overseen by Canadian Institute of Public Health Inspectors
Mission: The research & educational arm of the Canadian Institute of Public Health Inspectors; Dedicated to advancing environmental health in Canada through the development & implementation of education & research initiatives
Chief Officer(s):
Tim Roark, Treasurer
Membership: *Member Profile:* Members of the environmental public health profession; industry representatives; educational institutions; government

Environmental Industry Associations (EIA)
#300, 4301 Connecticut Ave., Washington DC 20008-2304 USA
Tel: 202-244-4700; *Fax:* 202-966-4818
Toll-Free: 800-424-2869
www.envasns.org
Overview: A medium-sized national organization
Chief Officer(s):
Bruce J. Parker, President & CEO
bparker@nswma.org

Environmental Information Association
#306, 6935 Wisconsin Ave., Chevy Chase MD 20815-6112 USA
Tel: 301-961-4999; *Fax:* 301-961-3094
Toll-Free: 888-343-4342
e-mail: info@eia-usa.org
www.eia-usa.org
Previous Name: National Asbestos Council
Overview: A small international organization
Mission: To protect public health & safety; To provide information about environmental health hazards to occupants of buildings, industrial sites, & other facility operations
Chief Officer(s):
Michael Breu, President
michaelbreu@hotmail.com
Brent Kynoch, Managing Director
bkynoch@eia-usa.org
Mike Schrum, Secretary
mwschrum@terracon.com
Kevin Cannan, Treasurer
ktc@aac-contracting.com
Kim Goodman, Manager, Membership & Marketing
kgoodman@kynoch.com
Kelly Ruttman, Manager, Development & Communications
krutt@kynoch.com
Membership: *Fees:* $1,000 executive; $500 organization; $125 individual; *Committees:* Conference; Membership / Marketing; Publications; Strategic Planning; Training; Asbestos; EMS / ESA; Indoor Air Quality; Lead Paint; Sampling & Analysis
Activities: Offering professional development opportunities; Providing networking events
Publications:
•Indoor Environment Connections
Type: Newsletter; *Price:* Free with Environmental Information Association membership
•Inside EIA [Environmental Information Association]
Type: Newsletter; *Accepts Advertising*; *Price:* Free with Environmental Information Association membership
•Net News [a publication of the Environmental Information Association]
Type: Newsletter; *Frequency:* Weekly; *Price:* Free with Environmental Information Association membership

The Environmental Law Centre (Alberta) Society (ELC)
#800, 10025 - 106 St., Edmonton AB T5J 1G4
Tel: 780-424-5099; *Fax:* 780-424-5133
Toll-Free: 800-661-4238
e-mail: elc@elc.ab.ca

www.elc.ab.ca
www.facebook.com/environmentallawcentre
twitter.com/ELC_Alberta
www.youtube.com/ELCAlberta
Overview: A small provincial charitable organization founded in 1981
Mission: To conduct research in environmental & natural resources law, policy & procedure; to educate the public on environmental law; to operate an environmental law information & referral service for the benefit of the public; to monitor relevant municipal, provincial & federal environmental laws, policies & procedures, & make recommendations for reform; *Member of:* Alberta Environmental Network
Chief Officer(s):
Cindy Chiasson, Executive Director
Finances: *Annual Operating Budget:* $500,000-$1.5 Million; *Funding Sources:* Funded in part by the Alberta Law Foundation & through public support
Staff: 9 staff member(s)
Membership: 13
Activities: *Speaker Service:* Yes; *Rents Mailing List:* Yes; *Library:*
Awards:
•Sir John A. Mactaggart Essay Prize (Scholarship)
Open to undergraduate & graduate students attending a recognized law school in Canada; prizes will be awarded for essays of high quality which address an issue in environmental law which is orginal, significant & relevant to Canada *Amount:* First prize is $500 plus a bound volume of the author's choice from Carswell; winning essay will als

Environmental Law Institute

#620, 2000 L St. NW, Washington DC 20036 USA
Tel: 202-939-3800; *Fax:* 202-939-3868
e-mail: law@eli.org
www.eli.org
Overview: A medium-sized international organization
Mission: To advance environmental protection by improving law, policy & management; to research pressing problems; to educate professionals & citizens about the nature of these issues; to convene all sectors in forging effective solutions; to achieve society's goals for improving the health of the biosphere & its inhabitants
Chief Officer(s):
Leslie Carothers, President
Finances: *Annual Operating Budget:* Greater than $5 Million; *Funding Sources:* Subscriptions; fees; grants
Staff: 52 staff member(s)
Membership: 1,000-4,999
Activities: *Internships:* Yes; *Speaker Service:* Yes; *Library:*

Environmental Managers Association of British Columbia (EMABC)

PO Box 3741, Vancouver BC V6B 3Z8
Tel: 604-998-2226; *Fax:* 604-998-2226
e-mail: info@emaofbc.com
www.emaofbc.com
Overview: A medium-sized provincial organization
Mission: To encourage education, share knowledge among members and create a forum for environmental management issues in the industrial, commercial and institutional sectors, serve as a key resource of environmental information for members and explore existing and emerging environmental issues.
Chief Officer(s):
Patrick Novak, President
Krista Hennebury, Executive Director
Membership: 67 corporate; *Fees:* $450

Environmental Protection UK

44 Grand Parade, Brighton BN2 9QA United Kingdom
Tel: 01273 878770; *Fax:* 01273 606626
e-mail: admin@environmental-protection.org.uk
www.environmental-protection.org.uk
Previous Name: National Society for Clean Air
Overview: A medium-sized international organization founded in 1898
Mission: To bring together organisations across the public, private & voluntary sectors to promote a balanced & innovative approach to understanding & solving environmental problems
Chief Officer(s):
James Grugeon, Chief Executive Officer
james.grugeon@environmental-protection.org.uk
Finances: *Funding Sources:* Funded by members' subscriptions, donations, & money raised by activities
Staff: 10 staff member(s)
Membership: 344 individuals; *Member Profile:* Open to local authorities, universities & colleges, professional & learned institutions, the energy industries, industrial companies & private individuals; *Committees:* Noise; Technical; Finance & Administration; Conference & Promotions
Activities: *Rents Mailing List:* Yes; *Library:* Open to public by appointment

Environmental Services Association of Alberta (ESAA)

#102, 2528 Ellwood Dr. SW, Edmonton AB T6X 0A9
Tel: 780-429-6363; *Fax:* 780-429-4249
Toll-Free: 800-661-9278
e-mail: info@esaa.org
www.esaa.org
Previous Name: Alberta Special Waste Services Association
Overview: A medium-sized provincial organization founded in 1987
Mission: To act as the voice of Alberta's environment industry
Environmental Activity: Monitoring & informing members of changes in environmental regulations
Chief Officer(s):
Craig Robertson, President
Randy Neumann, Secretary
Skip Kerr, Treasurer
Joe Barraclough, Director, Industry & Government Relations, 780-429-6363 Ext. 224
Joe Chowaniec, Director, Program & Event Development, 780-429-6363 Ext. 223
chowaniec@esaa.org
Membership: 200+ organizations; *Fees:* $475
Activities: Communicating with all levels of government; Providing networking opportunities; Offering market & industry information
Meetings/Conferences:
For more information see Trade Shows, Conferences and Seminars Chapter
Environmental Services Association of Alberta 2013 Remediation Technologies (RemTech) Symposium
October 2013 Banff, AB
Environmental Services Association of Alberta 2013 Water Technology (WaterTech) Symposium
April 2013 Banff, AB
Environmental Services Association of Alberta 2014 Water Technology (WaterTech) Symposium
2014, AB
Environmental Services Association of Alberta 2014 Remediation Technologies (RemTech) Symposium
2014, AB
Publications:
•B.I.D.S. (Business Initiative Development Service)
Type: Newsletter; *Frequency:* Weekly
Profile: Environmental business opportunities, news, & marketing information for the buyers & sellers of environmental goods & services
•Environmental Association of Alberta Annual Report
Type: Yearbook; *Frequency:* Annually
•The ESAA [Environmental Services Association of Alberta] Weekly News
Type: Newsletter; *Frequency:* Weekly; *Accepts Advertising*
Profile: Association happenings, such as conferences & job opportunities, for Environmental Services Association of Alberta members
•The Regulatory Review [a publication of the Environmental Services Association of Alberta]
Frequency: Monthly
Profile: Current information on environmental policies & law, produced by the Environmental Services Association of Alberta & the EnvironmentalLaw Center

Environmental Services Association of Nova Scotia (ESANS)

Woodside Industrial Park, #211-2, 1 Research Dr., Dartmouth NS B2Y 4M9
Tel: 902-463-3538; *Fax:* 902-466-6889
e-mail: contact@esans.ca
www.esans.ca
Also Known As: Nova Scotia Environmental Business Network
Overview: A medium-sized provincial organization founded in 1994
Mission: ESANS is a province-wide business organization dedicated to the promotion of environmental products, services & organizations within the environmental industry.
Chief Officer(s):
Adam Cooney, President
Finances: *Annual Operating Budget:* $100,000-$250,000; *Funding Sources:* Membership; projects; government
Staff: 1 staff member(s)
Membership: 100-499;; *Fees:* Schedule available; *Member Profile:* Individuals & companies/organizations involved in the environmental industry; *Committees:* Communications; Membership; Business Development; Government Liaison; Finance; Nominating
Activities: *Awareness Events:* Membership Appreciation Social; *Internships:* Yes; *Rents Mailing List:* Yes

Environmental Studies Association of Canada (ESAC) / Association canadienne d'études environnementales

c/o Dean's Office, Faculty of Environmental Studies, Univ. of Waterloo, Waterloo ON N2L 3G1
Tel: 519-888-4442; *Fax:* 519-746-0292
Toll-Free: 866-437-2587
www.esac.ca
www.facebook.com/group.php?gid=218543575398
Overview: A small national organization founded in 1993
Mission: To to advance research & teaching activities in areas related to environmental studies in Canada
Chief Officer(s):
André Roy, Dean, Environmental Studies, U. of Waterloo, 519-888-4567 Ext. 32884
agroy@uwaterloo.ca
Membership: *Fees:* $45 student & unwaged & small NGO; $95 faculty & professional; $125 institutional; *Member Profile:* Members include individuals, who are interested in social science & humanities approaches to environmental issues, from educational institutions, government agencies, & private sector & non-profit organizations.
Meetings/Conferences:
For more information see Trade Shows, Conferences and Seminars Chapter
The Environmental Studies Association of Canada (ESAC) 2013 Conference
June 2013 Victoria, BC
Publications:
•Directory of ESAC [Environmental Studies Association of Canada] Members
Type: Directory; *Frequency:* Annually
Profile: Listing of ESAC members, with their areas of interest & research
•Rhizome [a publication of the Environmental Studies Association of Canada]
Type: Newsletter; *Editor:* Angela Waldie
Profile: Information about conferences, research projects, events, new publications, & teaching materials

Environmental Youth Alliance (EYA)

#517, 119 Pender St. West, Vancouver BC V6B 1S5
Tel: 604-689-4446
e-mail: info@eya.ca
www.eya.ca
www.facebook.com/EnvironmentalYouthAlliance
twitter.com/EnviroYA
www.youtube.com/user/EnviroYouthAlliance
Overview: A small local organization founded in 1989
Mission: To save the earth through non-violent means; To promote change by educating people on our interconnectedness with Nature & involving youth in action projects; To create a youth movement that is activist-oriented & works towards environmental respect & protection.
Chief Officer(s):
Hartley Rosen, Managing Director
hartley@eya.ca
Finances: *Annual Operating Budget:* $100,000-$250,000; *Funding Sources:* Federal, provincial & municipal government; foundations
Staff: 2 staff member(s); 25 volunteer(s)
Membership: 10,000
Activities: Stewardship of urban sites; *Speaker Service:* Yes; *Library:* by appointment

Environnement jeunesse

454, rue Laurier est, Montréal QC H2J 1E7
Tél: 514-252-3016; *Téléc:* 514-254-5873
Ligne sans frais: 866-377-3016
Courriel: infoenjeu@enjeu.qc.ca
www.enjeu.qc.ca
Également appelé: ENJEU
Aperçu: *Dimension:* moyenne; *Envergure:* provinciale; fondée en 1979

Mission: Promouvoir la conservation et l'amélioration de la qualité de l'environnement; développer chez les jeunes les qualités favorisant leur implication sociale.; Affiliation(s): Réseau québécois des groupes écologistes; Association québécoise pour la promotion de l'éducation relative à l'environnement
Membre(s) du bureau directeur:
Jérôme Normand, Directeur général
Finances: *Budget de fonctionnement annuel:* $250,000-$500,000
Personnel: 5 membre(s) du personnel; 40 bénévole(s)
Membre: 400 individu; 300 associations
Activités: Tient une assemblée générale annuelle; organise un colloque annuel, La Bise D'Automne; tient des comités inter-groupes; réalise L'Écologie en Action, un vaste projet d'éducation et d'action relatifs à l'environnement; offre un Service d'Activités en Formation et en Éducation Relatives à l'Environnement; produit une panoplie d'outils de qualité visant à soutenir l'action des groupes membres; participe à des processus de consultation publique; *Service de conférenciers:* Oui

Eskasoni Fish & Wildlife Commission (EFWC)
4115 Shore Rd., Eskasoni NS B1W 1C2
Tel: 902-379-2024; *Fax:* 902-379-2159
e-mail: info@efwc.ca
www.efwc.ca
Overview: A small local organization founded in 1991
Mission: To facilitate the Aboriginal Fisheries Strategy agreement; to create partnerships with other agencies & organizations dealing with fish & wildlife

ETC Group
ETC Headquarters, #206, 180 Metcalfe St., Ottawa ON K2P 1P5
Tel: 613-241-2267; *Fax:* 613-241-2506
e-mail: etc@etcgroup.org
www.etcgroup.org
www.linkedin.com/company/2587794
www.facebook.com/theetcgroup
plus.google.com/115793847250050059887#115793847250050059887/posts
Also Known As: Action Group on Erosion, Technology & Concentration
Previous Name: Rural Advancement Foundation International
Overview: A small international organization founded in 1985
Chief Officer(s):
Mooney Pat Roy, Executive Director
Activities: ; *Library:* ETC Group Resource Library; by appointment

European Association of Geoscientists & Engineers (EAGE)
PO Box 59, Houten 3990 DB Netherlands
Tel: 31-30-635-4055; *Fax:* 31-30-634-3524
e-mail: eage@eage.org
www.eage.nl
Overview: A medium-sized international organization founded in 1951
Mission: To promote exploration geophysics; to foster fellowship & cooperation among those working, studying, or being otherwise interested in the field; comprised of EAEG Division (formerly European Association of Exploration Geophysicists) & EAPG Division (formerly European Association of Petroleum Geoscientists & Engineers); Affiliation(s): Society of Exploration Geophysicists
Chief Officer(s):
Phil Christie, President
Membership: 6,000; *Fees:* 50 euros general; 25 euros student; *Committees:* Technical Program; Awards; Publications; Executive
Activities: *Speaker Service:* Yes; *Library:* by appointment

European Geophysical Union ***See*** European Geosciences Union

European Geosciences Union (EGS)
5, rue René Descartes, Strasbourg 67084 France
Tel: 33-3-88450191; *Fax:* 33-3-88603887
e-mail: egu@eost.u-strasbg.fr
www.egu.eu
Previous Name: European Geophysical Union
Overview: A medium-sized international organization founded in 2002
Mission: To promote geophysics including planetary & space sciences by assisting cooperation among scientists, laboratories, institutes & individual research workers; Affiliation(s): Canadian Geophysical Union
Chief Officer(s):
Tuija Pulkkinen, President
Membership: 6,000; *Fees:* Schedule available; *Member Profile:* Scientists
Activities: Organization of conferences; meetings & workshops; publication of scientific journals & books

European Solidarity Towards Equal Participation of People / Solidarité européenne pour une égale participation des peuples
115, rue Stévin, Brussels B-1000 Belgium
Tel: 32-2-231-1659; *Fax:* 32-2-230-3780
e-mail: admin@eurostep.org
www.eurostep.org
Also Known As: EUROSTEP
Overview: A small international organization founded in 1990
Mission: To co-ordinate the policy work of its members at European level & to influence the policy & practice of the European Union; with a focus on the EU's cooperation with other countries, particularly in Africa, Asia, & Latin America, Eurostep uses its membership base in 15 European countries & the secretariat located in Brussels to present common policy approaches to the European Commission, European Parliament & Member States governments
Chief Officer(s):
Simon Stocker, Director
Finances: *Annual Operating Budget:* $250,000-$500,000
Activities: *Internships:* Yes

Evergreen
#300, 550 Bayview Ave, Toronto ON M4W 3X8
Tel: 416-596-1495; *Fax:* 416-596-1443
Toll-Free: 888-426-3138
e-mail: info@evergreen.ca
www.evergreen.ca
Previous Name: The Evergreen Foundation
Overview: A medium-sized national charitable organization founded in 1991
Mission: To bring communities & nature together for the benefit of both; To create sustaining, healthy, dynamic outdoor spaces by engaging people & encouraging local stewardship
Chief Officer(s):
Geoff Cape, Executive Director
gcape@evergreen.ca
Seana Irvine, Chief Operating officer
seana@evergreen.ca
Finances: *Funding Sources:* Donations; Sponsorships
Activities: Creating innovative resources; Transforming school grounds & home landscapes; Conserving publicly accessible land; Hosting conferences; *Library:*

Québec Office
5764, av Monkland, CP 107, Montréal QC H4A 1E9
Tel: 888-426-3138; *Fax:* 416-596-1443
e-mail: infoqc@evergreen.ca
Chief Officer(s):
Kathleen Usher, Contact, Evergreen Québec

Vancouver Office
#107, 555 Great Northern Way, Vancouver BC V5T 1E2
Tel: 604-689-0766; *Fax:* 604-669-6222
e-mail: infobc@evergreen.ca
Chief Officer(s):
Bill Sinclair, Regional Director, Western Canada

The Evergreen Foundation ***See*** Evergreen

Evergreen Party of Alberta
Parent Name: Green Party of Canada
#428, 300, 8120 Beddington Blvd. NW, Calgary AB T2K 2A8
Tel: 403-293-4593
e-mail: information@evergreenparty.ca
albertagreens.ca
www.facebook.com/EverGreenParty
twitter.com/evergreenparty
Also Known As: The Green Party of Alberta
Overview: A small provincial organization founded in 1990 overseen by Green Party of Canada
Mission: To encourage the development of an attitude that everyone is part of the land; to encourage strict control of all forms of pollution; to promote programs teaching consensus & facilitation; to facilitate the process of all interested community members becoming involved in education, both learning & teaching, guided by the long-term sustainability of the Earth community; to create the opportunity for Albertans to become involved in the strategic planning process
Chief Officer(s):
David Crowe, Treasurer/Chief Financial Officer
Susan Stratton, President
Janet Keeping, Party Leader
Finances: *Funding Sources:* Donations; membership
Membership: *Member Profile:* Environmentally & socially concerned Albertans
Activities: Organizing for provincial elections; education; raising awareness of issues; *Speaker Service:* Yes

Explorer's Club (Canadian Chapter)
171 Brentwood Rd. North, Toronto ON M8X 2C8
Tel: 416-239-8840
e-mail: explorersclubcanada@hotmail.com
www.explorersclub.ca
Overview: A medium-sized national organization founded in 1979
Mission: To promote field sciences & exploration of land, sea, air & space; Affiliation(s): Explorer's Club (New York)
Chief Officer(s):
Jason Schoonover, Communications Director
Simon Donato, Chair
simon@adventurescience.ca
Finances: *Annual Operating Budget:* Less than $50,000
Staff: 11 staff member(s)
Membership: 110; 3,000 worldwide; *Fees:* US$120-450; *Member Profile:* Field scientists; *Committees:* Exploration; Student Recruitment; Events; Membership; Communications; Executive; Regional
Activities: *Speaker Service:* Yes

Expo agricole de Chicoutimi
CP 8222, Succ. Racine, 350, boul Université est, Chicoutimi QC G7H 5B7
Tél: 418-545-8597; *Téléc:* 418-545-9243
Courriel: info@expoagricoledechicoutimi.com
www.expoagricoledechicoutimi.com
Nom précédent: Société d'agriculture de Chicoutimi
Aperçu: *Dimension:* petite; *Envergure:* locale
Affiliation(s): Association des expositions agricoles du Québec
Membre(s) du bureau directeur:
Louis-Joseph Jean, Directeur général
expoagricole@qc.aira.com
Finances: *Fonds:* Gouvernement régional
Personnel: 1 membre(s) du personnel; 6 bénévole(s)
Membre: 70 individu; 5 associé *Montant de la cotisation:* 10$ individu; 100$ associé
Activités: Exposition agricole

Fabricants de produits alimentaires du Canada ***See*** Food Processors of Canada

Fairview Applied Research Association ***See*** Peace Agricultural Research & Demonstration Association

Falls Brook Centre
125 South Knowlesville Rd., Knowlesville NB E7L 1B1
Tel: 506-375-8143; *Fax:* 506-375-4221
e-mail: ja@fallsbrookcentre.ca
www.fallsbrookcentre.ca
Overview: A small local organization
Mission: Situated on 400 acres of rural forest and farmland, the Centre is a sustainable community demonstration and training centre. On-site activities and features include solar and wind energy systems, organic gardening, forest trails, herbariums and tree nurseries, and a conference centre. The Centre promotes sustainability and collaborates with the community to provide alternatives.; *Member of:* Canadian Renewable Energy Alliance; Affiliation(s): Canadian Coalition for Biodiversity
Environmental Activity: Forest Stewardship; Organic Agriculture; Appropriate Technology
Chief Officer(s):
Jean Arnold, Executive Director
Activities: Education and Outreach; Community Development; International Work; workshops and workbees

Farm Radio International / Radios Rurales Internationales
1404 Scott St., Ottawa ON K1Y 4M8
Tel: 613-761-3650; *Fax:* 613-798-0990
Toll-Free: 888-773-7717
e-mail: info@farmradio.org
www.farmradio.org
www.linkedin.com/company/farm-radio-international
www.facebook.com/farmradio
twitter.com/farmradio
www.youtube.com/farmradioint
Previous Name: Developing Countries Farm Radio Network

Overview: A medium-sized international charitable organization founded in 1979
Mission: To increase food supplies & to improve the nutrition, health & quality of life of small-scale farmers in developing countries through a coordinating network of broadcasters & others who exchange information about simple, practical sustainable farming techniques & health practices; To support broadcasters to strengthen small scale farmers & rural life; *Member of:* Canadian Centre for Philanthropy; Ontario Council for International Cooperation; Canadian Council for International Cooperation
Chief Officer(s):
Kevin Perkins, Executive Director
kperkins@farmradio.org
Finances: *Annual Operating Budget:* $250,000-$500,000; *Funding Sources:* Private donations; government grants; CIDA
Staff: 6 staff member(s); 10 volunteer(s)
Membership: 500; *Fees:* Free to radio stations in developing countries; *Member Profile:* Rural radio broadcasters in developing countries
Publications:
•Network News
Type: Newsletter
Profile: Provides information about the program and the people involved in the organization, as well as updates on Canada's international development program.

Farmers of North America (FNA)
#318, 111 Research Dr., Saskatoon SK S7N 3R2
Tel: 306-665-2294; *Fax:* 306-651-0444
Toll-Free: 877-362-3276
e-mail: info@fna.ca
www.fna.ca
Overview: A large national organization founded in 1998
Mission: To improve farm profitability across Canada
Membership: 10,000

Farmers of North America Strategic Agriculture Institute (FNA-SAG)
Parent Name: Canadian Federation of Agriculture
Head Office, #318, 111 Research Dr., Saskatoon SK S7N 3R2
Tel: 306-665-5032; *Fax:* 306-665-4513
www.fnastrategicag.ca
Overview: A large national organization founded in 2008 overseen by Canadian Federation of Agriculture
Mission: To identify new methods for farm profitability; to identify policy & regulatory issues affecting profitability, & to help advocate for change; to identify areas of needed research; *Member of:* Canadian Federation of Agriculture
Chief Officer(s):
Bob Friesen, CEO
bfriesen@fna.ca
Jonathan Warnock, Director, Research
jwarnock@fna.ca

FarmFolk CityFolk
#203, 1661 Duranleau St., Vancouver BC V6H 3S3
Tel: 604-730-0450
Toll-Free: 877-730-0452
e-mail: info@farmfolkcityfolk.ca
wwww.farmfolkcityfolk.ca
www.facebook.com/FarmFolkCityFolk
twitter.com/ffcf
Previous Name: FarmFolk/CityFolk Society
Overview: A small local charitable organization founded in 1993
Mission: To work with others for a local, sustainable food system; to make connection between farm & city, producer & consumer, grower & eater that creates sustainable communities; To protect foodlands, support farmers & food producers, & connect communities
Chief Officer(s):
Heather Johnstone, Chair
Nicholas Scapillati, Execxutive Director
Finances: *Annual Operating Budget:* $100,000-$250,000; *Funding Sources:* Foundations; memberships; donations
Staff: 4 staff member(s); 80 volunteer(s)
Membership: 15 institutional; 200 student; 200 individual; 20 associate; *Fees:* $500+ corporate; $100 farm; $50 family; $30 individual; *Member Profile:* Not-for-profit, charitable organization
Activities: Events, projects, education; *Awareness Events:* "Feast of Fields" Fundraiser, Sept.; *Library:* FarmFolk/CityFolk Resource Library; Open to public

FarmFolk/CityFolk Society ***See*** FarmFolk CityFolk

Farming Smarter (SARA)
Parent Name: Agricultural Research & Extension Council of Alberta
#100, 5401 - 1st Ave. South, Lethbridge AB T1J 4V6
Tel: 403-381-5118; *Fax:* 403-382-4526
e-mail: sara.research@connectcomm.ca
www.farmingsmarter.com
www.facebook.com/farmingsmarter
twitter.com/farmingsmarter
www.youtube.com/farmingsmarter
Overview: A small local organization founded in 1994 overseen by Agricultural Research & Extension Council of Alberta
Mission: To improve sustainability & efficiency of farming methods throughout Southern Alberta; *Member of:* Agricultural Research & Extension Council of Alberta
Chief Officer(s):
Ron Lamb, Chair
Ken Coles, General Manager, 403-317-0757
ken@farmingsmarter.com
Publications:
•Farming Smarter Newsletter
Type: Newsletter

FaunENord
313, 3e Rue, 2e étage, Chibougamau QC G8P 1N4
Tél: 418-748-4441; *Téléc:* 418-748-1110
www.faunenord.icr.qc.ca
Aperçu: *Dimension:* petite; *Envergure:* locale
Mission: Une entreprise vouée à la promotion & à l'aménagement durable des ressources fauniques & des écosystèmes
Membre(s) du bureau directeur:
Justine Desmeules
jdesmeules.faunenord.lino.com

Fédération canadienne de l'agriculture ***See*** Canadian Federation of Agriculture

Fédération canadienne de la faune ***See*** Canadian Wildlife Federation

Fédération canadienne des épiciers indépendants ***See*** Canadian Federation of Independent Grocers

Fédération canadienne des étudiants et étudiantes en génie ***See*** Canadian Federation of Engineering Students

Fédération canadienne des municipalités ***See*** Federation of Canadian Municipalities

Fédération canadienne des sciences de la Terre ***See*** Canadian Federation of Earth Sciences

Fédération canadienne des sciences humaines ***See*** Canadian Federation for Humanities & Social Sciences

Fédération d'agriculture biologique du Québec (FABQ)
#100, 555, boul Roland-Therrien, Longueuil QC J4H 3Y9
Tél: 450-679-0530; *Téléc:* 450-670-4867
Courriel: fabq@upa.qc.ca
www.fabqbio.ca
Aperçu: *Dimension:* petite; *Envergure:* provinciale; fondée en 1989
Mission: Promouvoir l'étude, la défense et le développement des intérêts économiques, sociaux et moraux de ses membres; administrer tout le programme de la mise en marché; étudier des problèmes relatifs à la production; coopérer à la vulgarisation des techniques de production biologique; renseigner le producteur sur la production et la vente de produits biologiques certifiés
Membre(s) du bureau directeur:
Gérard Bouchard, Président
Finances: *Budget de fonctionnement annuel:* $50,000-$100,000
Personnel: 1 membre(s) du personnel; 7 bénévole(s)
Membre: 200 *Montant de la cotisation:* 125$; *Critères d'admissibilite:* Producteurs agricoles biologiques
Activités: Promotion générique; développement de marchés; information

Fédération de la faune du Nouveau-Brunswick ***See*** New Brunswick Wildlife Federation

Fédération des agricultrices du Québec (FAQ)
555, boul Roland-Therrien, Longueuil QC J4H 4E7
Tél: 450-679-0540; *Téléc:* 450-463-5228
Courriel: fed.agricultrices@upa.qc.ca
www.agricultrices.com
Aperçu: *Dimension:* moyenne; *Envergure:* provinciale; Organisme sans but lucratif; fondée en 1987
Mission: Valoriser la profession; créer un réseau entre les femmes; avoir une force politique capable de défendre les intérêts des agricultrices; prodiguer de la formation; *Membre de:* L'Union des producteurs agricoles
Membre(s) du bureau directeur:
Marcel Groleau, Présidente
Membre: 1,000-4,999; *Critères d'admissibilite:* Agricultrice, membre de soutien

La Fédération des producteurs de bois du Québec (FPBQ)
#565, 555, boul Roland-Therrien, Longueuil QC J4H 4E7
Tél: 450-679-0530; *Téléc:* 450-679-4300
Courriel: bois@upa.qc.ca
www.fpbq.qc.ca
Aperçu: *Dimension:* moyenne; *Envergure:* provinciale; fondée en 1970
Mission: Défendre les intérêts de l'ensemble des propriétaires de boisés du Québec ainsi que l'élaboration et la promotion des politiques souhaitables et nécessaires pour atteindre cet objectif; représenter les propriétaires de boisés privés auprès des pouvoirs publics et des autres groupes de la société au niveau provincial et national; coordonner l'ensemble des activités des Syndicats et Offices de producteurs de bois ainsi que l'établissement, le maintien et le développement entre eux d'une étroite collaboration; Affiliation(s): Union des producteurs agricoles
Membre(s) du bureau directeur:
Marc-André Côté, Directeur
macote@upa.qc.ca
Finances: *Budget de fonctionnement annuel:* $500,000-$1.5 Million
Personnel: 9 membre(s) du personnel

Fédération des producteurs de cultures commerciales du Québec (FPCCQ)
#505, 555, boul Roland-Therrien, Longueuil QC J4H 3Y9
Tél: 450-679-0540; *Téléc:* 450-679-6372
Courriel: fpccq@fpccq.qc.ca
www.fpccq.qc.ca
Aperçu: *Dimension:* petite; *Envergure:* provinciale; fondée en 1975
Affiliation(s): Union des producteurs agricoles (UPA)
Membre(s) du bureau directeur:
Christian Overbeek, Président
Membre: 11 syndicats

Fédération des propriétaires de lots boisés du Nouveau-Brunswick inc. ***See*** New Brunswick Federation of Woodlot Owners Inc.

Fédération des sociétés canadiennes d'assistance aux animaux ***See*** Canadian Federation of Humane Societies

Fédération des sociétés d'horticulture et d'écologie du Québec (FSHÉQ)
CP 1000, Succ. M, 4545, av Pierre-de-Coubertin, Montréal QC H1V 3R2
Tél: 514-252-3010; *Téléc:* 514-251-8038
Courriel: fsheq@fsheq.com
www.fsheq.com
Aperçu: *Dimension:* moyenne; *Envergure:* provinciale; Organisme sans but lucratif; fondée en 1978
Mission: Regrouper tous les organismes voués à l'horticulture; faire la promotion de l'horticulture.
Membre(s) du bureau directeur:
Thérèse Tourigny, Directrice générale
Finances: *Budget de fonctionnement annuel:* $50,000-$100,000
Personnel: 3 bénévole(s)
Membre: 280 *Montant de la cotisation:* 90$; *Critères d'admissibilite:* Sociétés d'horticulture
Activités: *Service de conférenciers:* Oui

Fédération du personnel de l'enseignement privé (FPEP)
9405, rue Sherbrooke est, Montréal QC H1L 6P3
Tél: 514-356-8888; *Téléc:* 514-356-1866
Courriel: fpep@csq.qc.net
www.fpep.csq.qc.net
Aperçu: *Dimension:* moyenne; *Envergure:* provinciale; Organisme sans but lucratif; fondée en 1986
Membre de: Centrale des syndicats du Québec
Environmental Activity: Comité sur l'environnement
Membre(s) du bureau directeur:

Francine Lamoureux, Présidente, 514-356-8888 Ext. 2810
lamoureux.francine@csq.qc.net
Martine Dion, Première Vice-Présidente, 514-356-8888 Ext. 2813
dion.martine@csq.qc.net
Denis Benoit, Deuxième Vice-Président
fpep@csq.qc.net
Lévis Stéphane, Secrétaire
fpep@csq.qc.net
Noël Marie-Josée, Trésorerie
fpep@csq.qc.net
Finances: *Fonds:* Grille tarifaire
Personnel: 11 membre(s) du personnel
Membre: 2 700 individu; 42 unités *Montant de la cotisation:* 0.576% du salaire; *Critères d'admissibilite:* Organisation syndicale; *Comités:* Élections; Élèves handicapés ou en difficulté d'adaptation ou d'apprentissage (HDAA); Comité du personnel professionnel et de soutien (CPPS); Environnement; Action professionnel
Activités: Relations du travail et d'action professionnelle

Fédération du saumon atlantique ***See*** Atlantic Salmon Federation

Fédération internationale des Amis de la Terre ***See*** Friends of the Earth International

Fédération internationale des architectes paysagistes ***See*** International Federation of Landscape Architects

Fédération Internationale des Associations de Professeurs de Sciences ***See*** International Council of Associations for Science Education

Fédération internationale des géomètres ***See*** International Federation of Surveyors

Fédération internationale des mouvements d'agriculture biologique ***See*** International Federation of Organic Agriculture Movements

Fédération internationale pour l'habitation, l'urbanisme et l'aménagement des territoires ***See*** International Federation for Housing & Planning

Federation of Alberta Naturalists (FAN)

11759 Groat Rd., Edmonton AB T5M 3K6
Tel: 780-427-8124; *Fax:* 780-422-2663
e-mail: info@fanweb.ca
www.fanweb.ca
Overview: A medium-sized provincial charitable organization founded in 1970
Mission: To encourage Albertans to increase knowledge & understanding of natural history & ecological processes; to provide a unified voice for naturalists on conservation issues; to organize field meetings, conferences, nature camps, research symposia, & other activities.; *Member of:* Canadian Nature Federation
Finances: *Annual Operating Budget:* $50,000-$100,000; *Funding Sources:* Donations; grants; projects
Staff: 3 volunteer(s)
Membership: 5,000 individual + 42 clubs; *Fees:* $20

Federation of Calgary Communities (FCC)

#301, 1609 - 14 St. SW, Calgary AB T3C 1E4
Tel: 403-244-4111; *Fax:* 403-244-4129
e-mail: fcc@calgarycommunities.com
www.calgarycommunities.com
www.facebook.com/FederationofCalgaryCommunities
twitter.com/FedYYC
www.youtube.com/user/FederationCalgary
Overview: A small local licensing organization founded in 1961
Mission: To enhance Calgary communities
Chief Officer(s):
Leslie Evans, Executive Director
leslie.evans@calgarycommunities.com
Melanie McDonald, President
Finances: *Annual Operating Budget:* $100,000-$250,000
Staff: 1 staff member(s); 25 volunteer(s)
Membership: 114
Activities: *Rents Mailing List:* Yes; *Library:* Open to public

Federation of Canadian Municipalities (FCM) / Fédération canadienne des municipalités

24 Clarence St., Ottawa ON K1N 5P3
Tel: 613-241-5221; *Fax:* 613-241-7440
e-mail: federation@fcm.ca
www.fcm.ca
www.linkedin.com/company/federation-of-canadian-municipalities
www.facebook.com/pages/FCM/201746766534992
twitter.com/FCM_online
Previous Name: Canadian Federation of Mayors & Municipalities
Overview: A large national organization founded in 1901
Mission: FCM is the national voice of municipal government that represents the interests of municipalities on policy & program matters that fall within federal jurisdiction. Its goal in serving elected municipal officials is the improvement of the quality of life in all communities.
Chief Officer(s):
Berry Vrbanovic, President
ceo@fcm.ca
Basil L. Stewart, President
Finances: *Funding Sources:* Membership fees; advertising; trade show; market research
Membership: 1,600+; *Fees:* Schedule available based on population; *Member Profile:* Members include Canada's cities, small urban & rural communities, & provincial & territorial municipal associations.; *Committees:* Standing Committees: Increasing Women's Participation in Municipal Government; Community Safety & Crime Prevention; Environmental Issues & Sustainable Development; International Relations; Municipal Finance & Intergovernmental Arrangements; Municipal Infrastructure & Transportation Policy; Northern Forum; Rural Forum; Social Economic Development
Activities: Promoting strong, effective, & accountable municipal government; *Rents Mailing List:* Yes
Meetings/Conferences:
For more information see Trade Shows, Conferences and Seminars Chapter
Federation of Canadian Municipalities 2013 Sustainable Communities Conference and Trade Show
February 2013 Windsor Essex, ON
Federation of Canadian Municipalities 2013 Annual Conference & Trade Show
May 2013 Vancouver, BC
Publications:
•Federation of Canadian Municipalities Annual Report
Type: Yearbook; *Frequency:* Annually
•Forum: Canada's National Municipal Magazine
Type: Magazine; *Frequency:* Bimonthly; *Accepts Advertising*; *Editor:* Robert Ross
Profile: Recent municipal-sector developments

Federation of Northern Ontario Municipalities (FONOM)

PO Box 2175, Stn. A, Sudbury ON P3A 4S1
Tel: 705-586-9120; *Fax:* 705-586-9195
e-mail: fonom@eastlink.ca
www.fonom.org
Overview: A medium-sized local organization founded in 1960
Mission: To act as the voice for the people of northeastern Ontario communities; To work for the betterment of municipal government by striving for improved legislation respecting local government in northern Ontario; *Member of:* Association of Municipalities of Ontario
Chief Officer(s):
Lynne Reynolds, Executive Director
Al Spacek, President
Finances: *Funding Sources:* Membership fees; Provincial grants; Sponsorships
Membership: 111; *Member Profile:* Municipal governments from the following districts: Cochrane, Algoma, Manitoulin, Nipissing, Parry Sound, Sudbury, & Timiskaming
Meetings/Conferences:
For more information see Trade Shows, Conferences and Seminars Chapter
Federation of Northern Ontario Municipalities 2013 53rd Annual Conference
May 2013 Parry Sound, ON
Federation of Northern Ontario Municipalities 2014 54th Annual Conference
May 2014 Sault Ste Marie, ON

Federation of Nova Scotia Naturalists ***See*** Nature Nova Scotia (Federation of Nova Scotia Naturalists)

Federation of Nova Scotian Heritage ***See*** Association of Nova Scotia Museums

Federation of Ontario Cottagers' Associations (FOCA)

#201, 159 King St., Peterborough ON K9J 2R8
Tel: 705-749-3622; *Fax:* 705-749-6522
e-mail: info@foca.on.ca
www.foca.on.ca
Overview: A medium-sized provincial organization founded in 1963
Mission: To ensure a healthy future for waterfront Ontario; To support the interests of Ontario's cottagers
Environmental Activity: Engaging in freshwater advocacy activities; Promoting sustainable waterfront communities; Encouraging environmental stewardship
Chief Officer(s):
Terry Rees, Executive Director, 705-749-3622 Ext. 4
trees@foca.on.ca
Tracy Logan, Contact, Programs, 705-749-3622 Ext. 3
programs@foca.on.ca
Finances: *Funding Sources:* Membership fees; Sponsorships; Donations
Membership: 550+; *Fees:* $37.50 individuals; $75 associations; *Member Profile:* Ontario cottagers' associations; Individuals, such as waterfront property owners; *Committees:* Property Tax
Activities: Providing information about issues that affect cottage properties; Offering networking opportunities
Meetings/Conferences:
For more information see Trade Shows, Conferences and Seminars Chapter
Federation of Ontario Cottagers' Associations 2013 Spring Annual General Meeting
March 2013 Toronto, ON
Federation of Ontario Cottagers' Associations 2014 Spring Annual General Meeting
2014, ON
Publications:
•Federation of Ontario Cottagers' Associations Report to Members
Type: Newsletter; *Price:* Free with Federation of Ontario Cottagers' Associations membership
Profile: Federation activities
•Lake Stewards Newsletter
Type: Newsletter; *Frequency:* Annually; *Price:* Free with Federation of Ontario Cottagers' Associations membership

Federation of Ontario Naturalists ***See*** Ontario Nature

Federation of Prince Edward Island Municipalities Inc. (FPEIM)

1 Kirkdale Rd., Charlottetown PE C1E 1R3
Tel: 902-566-1493; *Fax:* 902-566-2880
e-mail: info@fpeim.ca
www.fpeim.ca
Overview: A large provincial organization founded in 1957
Mission: To represent the interests of the cities, towns & communities within PEI; To secure united action for the protection of individual municipalities & municipal interests as a whole; To act as a clearing house for the collection, exchange & dissemination of information of concern & interest to member municipalities; To provide training, education & development opportunities for elected & appointed municipal officials; *Member of:* Federation of Canadian Municipalities; Affiliation(s): Association of Municipal Administrators, PEI
Chief Officer(s):
John Dewey, Executive Director
jdewey@fpeim.ca
Bruce MacDougall, President
president@fpeim.ca
Finances: *Annual Operating Budget:* $100,000-$250,000; *Funding Sources:* Small government grant; membership fees
Staff: 2 staff member(s); 13 volunteer(s)
Membership: 43 municipalities; *Fees:* Per capita fee; *Member Profile:* Incorporated municipality; *Committees:* Finance; Resolutions; Constitution; Annual Meeting; Semi-Annual Meeting; Transportation; Membership; Nominating; Resolutions; Policy
Activities: Monthly board meetings; 2 full membership meetings per year; bi-monthly information updates to membership; liaising with provincial municipal associations across Canada as well as provincial & federal government departments; *Awareness Events:* Municipal Government Week; *Library:* by appointment

Federation of Saskatchewan Surface Rights Association (FSSRA)

Lone Rock SK
Tel: 306-387-6650; *Fax:* 306-387-6650
Overview: A small provincial organization founded in 1982
Mission: To aid in reclamation concerns in land, gas lines, rail lines, compensation, environmental issues & legislation; Affiliation(s): Alberta Surface Rights Federation

Chief Officer(s):
Terry Crush, Contact
Membership: 1-99; *Member Profile:* Farmers
Activities: *Speaker Service:* Yes

Federation of Sewage Works Associations; Federation of Sewage & Industrial Wastes Associations; Water Pollution Control Federation ***See*** Water Environment Federation

Fédération québécoise de camping et de caravaning inc. (FQCC)
CP 100, 1560, rue Eiffel, Boucherville QC J4B 5Y1
Tél: 450-650-3722; *Téléc:* 450-650-3721
Ligne sans frais: 877-650-3722
Courriel: info@fqcc.ca
www.fqcc.ca
www.facebook.com/LaFQCC
Aperçu: *Dimension:* grande; *Envergure:* provinciale; fondée en 1967
Mission: Unir les adepts du camping et du caravaning; entreprendre et coordonner des actions relatives au camping et au caravaning.; *Membre de:* Fédération internationale de camping et de caravaning
Membre(s) du bureau directeur:
Martin Healey, Président
Michel Quintal, Trésorier
Finances: *Budget de fonctionnement annuel:* $500,000-$1.5 Million
Personnel: 10 membre(s) du personnel
Membre: 45 000 familles membres *Montant de la cotisation:* 45$
Activités: *Service de conférenciers:* Oui

Fédération québécoise de la faune ***Voir*** Fédération québécoise des chasseurs et pêcheurs

Fédération québécoise de la montagne et de l'escalade (FQME)
CP 1000, Succ. M, 4545, av Pierre-de-Coubertin, Montréal QC H1V 3R2
Tél: 514-252-3004; *Téléc:* 514-252-3201
Ligne sans frais: 866-204-3763
Courriel: fqme@fqme.qc.ca
www.fqme.qc.ca
Aperçu: *Dimension:* petite; *Envergure:* provinciale; Organisme sans but lucratif; fondée en 1969
Mission: Regrouper les adeptes de l'escalade et de l'alpinisme au Québec; promouvoir l'escalade (rocher et glace) et le ski de l'alpinisme et de randonnée en montagne; promouvoir une pratique sécuritaire de ces activités; protéger et rendre accessibles les différents sites d'escalade et de grande randonnée à skis au Québec; *Membre de:* Canadian Avalanche Association; Outdoor Recreation Coalition of America (ORCA); Affiliation(s): Union internationale des associations d'alpinisme
Membre(s) du bureau directeur:
André St-Jacques, Directeur des opérations
Finances: *Budget de fonctionnement annuel:* $100,000-$250,000
Membre: 2 000 *Montant de la cotisation:* 30$ adulte; 10$ jeune; *Comités:* Formation; Site; Expédition
Activités: Amateur d'activités montagnes; *Stagiaires:* Oui; *Bibliothèque:* Centre de documentation; rendez-vous

Fédération québécoise des chasseurs et pêcheurs
Parent Name: Canadian Wildlife Federation
162, rue du Brome, Saint-Augustin-de-Desmaures QC G3A 2P5
Tél: 418-878-8901; *Téléc:* 418-878-8980
Ligne sans frais: 888-523-2863
Courriel: info@fedecp.qc.ca
www.fedecp.qc.ca
www.facebook.com/116805682100
twitter.com/FederationCP
Nom précédent: Fédération québécoise de la faune
Aperçu: *Dimension:* moyenne; *Envergure:* provinciale; fondée en 1946 surveillé par Canadian Wildlife Federation
Mission: Contribuer, dans le respect de la faune et de ses habitats, à la gestion du développement et à la perpétuation de la chasse et de la pêche comme activités traditionnelles et sportives
Membre(s) du bureau directeur:
Pierre Latraverse, Président
Marjorie Alain, Responsable des relations publiques
marjoriealain@fedecp.qc.ca
Membre: 200 associations *Montant de la cotisation:* 39,95$ membre individuel; *Critères d'admissibilite:* Chasseurs, pêcheurs

Fédération québécoise des coopératives forestières (FQCF)
#200, 3188, ch Sainte-Foy, Québec QC G1X 1R4
Tél: 418-651-0388; *Téléc:* 418-651-3860
www.fqcf.coop
Nom précédent: Conférence des coopératives forestières du Québec
Aperçu: *Dimension:* moyenne; *Envergure:* provinciale; fondée en 1985
Mission: La Fédération québécoise des coopératives forestières (FQCF) regroupe et représente dans des domaines d'intérêts communs l'ensemble des coopératives forestières de travailleurs, les coopératives de travailleurs actionnaires et les coopératives de solidarité actives dans le milieu forestier, et ce dans toutes les régions du Québec
Membre(s) du bureau directeur:
Jocelyn Lessard, Directeur général
j.lessard@fqcf.coop
Cathy Gagnon, Adjointe administrative
cathyg@fqcf.coop
Finances: *Budget de fonctionnement annuel:* $500,000-$1.5 Million
Personnel: 4 membre(s) du personnel
Membre: 44

Fédération Québécoise des Municipalités (FQM)
#560, 2954, boul Laurier, Sainte-Foy QC G1V 4T2
Tél: 418-651-3343; *Téléc:* 418-651-1127
Courriel: fqm@fqm.ca
www.fqm.ca
Nom précédent: Union des municipalités régionales de comté et des municipalités locales du Québec
Aperçu: *Dimension:* moyenne; *Envergure:* provinciale; fondée en 1944
Mission: Etre la porte-parole des régions; défendre les intérêts de ses membres
Membre(s) du bureau directeur:
Bernard Généreux, Président
Membre: 1000 municipalités et presque la totalité des MRC; *Critères d'admissibilite:* Municipalités
Activités: *Service de conférenciers:* Oui

Fédération québécoise du canot camping inc ***Voir*** Fédération québécoise du canot et du kayak

Fédération québécoise du canot et du kayak (FQCK)
CP 1000, Succ. M, 4545, av Pierre-de Coubertin, Montréal QC H1V 3R2
Tél: 514-252-3001; *Téléc:* 514-252-3091
Courriel: info@canot-kayak.qc.ca
www.canot-kayak.qc.ca
www.facebook.com/group.php?gid=254842564559812
Nom précédent: Fédération québécoise du canot camping inc
Aperçu: *Dimension:* moyenne; *Envergure:* provinciale; Organisme sans but lucratif; fondée en 1976
Mission: Regrouper les organismes et individus intéressés à la pratique du canotage récréatif et du canot-camping et de promouvoir la pratique de ces activités en utilisant le canot ouvert de type amérindien autrement appelé Canot Canadien
Environmental Activity: Fonds de préservation des rivières
Membre(s) du bureau directeur:
Pierre Trudel, Directeur général
Bernard Hugonnier, Directeur, Technique
Magalie Bernard, Agente, L'Information et aux communications
Philippe Pelland, Agent, Développement
Membre: 4 000 *Montant de la cotisation:* 40$; *Comités:* Cartographie; Formation
Activités: *Stagiaires:* Oui; *Service de conférenciers:* Oui

Fédération québécoise pour le saumon atlantique (FQSA)
42B, rue Racine, Québec QC G2B 1C6
Tél: 418-847-9191; *Téléc:* 418-847-9279
Ligne sans frais: 888-847-9191
Courriel: secretariat@saumon-fqsa.qc.ca
www.FQSA.ca
Aperçu: *Dimension:* moyenne; *Envergure:* provinciale; fondée en 1984
Mission: Organisme à but non lucratif dont la raison d'être est d'unir et de représenter les intérêts de l'ensemble des saumoniers du Québec
Membre(s) du bureau directeur:
Michel Jean, Directeur général
mjean@saumon-fqsa.qc.ca
Membre: 1 000 *Montant de la cotisation:* 40$
Activités: *Service de conférenciers:* Oui; *Bibliothèque:* Bibliothèque publique rendez-vous

FEESA - An Environmental Education Society ***See*** Inside Education

Fiducie du patrimoine ontarien ***See*** Ontario Heritage Trust

Fiducie foncière Vallée de Ruiter ***See*** Ruiter Valley Land Trust

Field Botanists of Ontario (FBO)
c/o W.D. McIlveen, RR#1, Acton ON L7J 2L7
e-mail: wmcilveen@sympatico.ca
aww.trentu.ca/fbo
www.facebook.com/group.php?gid=7783788221#/group.php?gid=7783788221
Overview: A small provincial organization founded in 1983
Mission: To increase documentation of the flora of Ontario; To encourage interest in botany & conservation in the province of Ontario
Environmental Activity: Promoting conservation
Chief Officer(s):
Bill Crowley, President
fisheye@eagle.ca
Chris Zoladeski, Vice-President
chriszoladeski@savanta.ca
Nancy Falkenberg, Secretary
falken@rogers.ca
Bill Draper, Treasurer
william.draper@sympatico.ca
Julia Marko Dunn, Newsletter Editor
jmarkodunn@gmail.com
Leaf Lefler, Contact, Field Trips
fbo.trips@gmail.com
Bill McIlveen, Contact, Memberships
wmcilveen@sympatico.ca
Membership: 300; *Fees:* $15 individuals; $18 families; $250 life memberships; *Member Profile:* Amateur & professional botanists of all ages
Activities: Offering field trips; Providing education & workshops; Offering botanical expertise; Encouraging the exchange of botanical information; Facilitating networking opportunities
Publications:
•Field Botanists of Ontario Newsletter
Type: Newsletter; *Frequency:* Quarterly; *Editor:* Cheryl Hendrickson
Profile: Articles, meeting information, & field trip reports

Film & Bag Federation
#1000, 1667 K St. NW, Washington DC 20006 USA
Tel: 202-974-5218; *Fax:* 202-296-7675
www.plasticbag.com
Previous Name: Plastic Bag Association; Plastic Bag Information Clearing House
Overview: A small national organization
Chief Officer(s):
Donna Dempsey, Executive Director
ddempsey@socplas.org

Fire Prevention Canada (FPC)
PO Box 47037, Ottawa ON K1B 5P9
Tel: 613-749-3844; *Fax:* 613-749-0109
Toll-Free: 877-906-6651
e-mail: info@fiprecan.ca
www.fiprecan.ca
Also Known As: Fiprecan
Overview: A medium-sized national charitable organization
Mission: Working with the public & private sectors to achieve fire safety through education.
Chief Officer(s):
E. David Hodgins, President

First Nations Environmental Network
Parent Name: Canadian Environmental Network
PO Box 394, Tofino BC V0R 2Z0
Tel: 250-726-5265; *Fax:* 250-725-2357
e-mail: councilfire@hotmail.com
www.fnen.org
Overview: A small national organization overseen by Canadian Environmental Network
Mission: The First Nations Environmental Network is a circle of First Nations people committed to protecting, defending, and restoring the balance of all life by honouring traditional Indigenous values and the path of our ancestors. We encourage the work of protecting, defending and healing Mother Earth. We desire and need to link grassroots Indigenous people nationally and internationally to support each other on environmental struggles and concerns. We are obligated to leave footprints for our children to follow by striving to live our life with traditional values.

Chief Officer(s):
Steve Lawson, Coordinator
wolf@lincsat.com

Fish Harvesters Resource Centres (FRC)
PO Box 1242, Stn. C, 2 Steers Cove, St. John's NL A1C 5M9
Tel: 709-576-0292; *Fax:* 709-576-0339
www.frc.nf.ca
Overview: A small provincial organization founded in 1993
Mission: The Centres assist & support the restructuring of the Newfoundland & Labrador fishing industry by providing information & resources to fish harvesters in the province. They offer business counselling & technical assistance to encourage entrepreneurship among harvesters.; Affiliation(s): FFAW/CAW Fish; Food & Allied Workers Union; Atlantic Canada Opportunities Agency (ACOA)
Chief Officer(s):
Richard Moores, Executive Director
rmoores@frc.nf.ca
Rose Walsh, Program Coordinator
rwalsh@frc.nf.ca

Fisheries Council of British Columbia *See* Fisheries Council of Canada - British Columbia Representative

Fisheries Council of Canada (FCC)
#900, 170 Laurier Ave. West, Ottawa ON K1P 5V5
Tel: 613-727-7450; *Fax:* 613-727-7453
e-mail: info@fisheriescouncil.org
www.fisheriescouncil.ca
Previous Name: Canadian Fisheries Association
Overview: A large national organization founded in 1915
Mission: To represent Canada's fish & seafood industry
Environmental Activity: Conserving fishing resources to ensure a sustainable future for the fishing industry; Providing information on environmental issues such as species at risk & ocean use; Promoting a healthy resource; Protecting the marine environment
Chief Officer(s):
Patrick McGuinness, President
pmcguinness@fisheriescouncil.org
Membership: *Fees:* $600 associate members; $5000 special purpose associations; *Member Profile:* Enterprises & associations that harvest, handle, process, distribute, & market fish & seafood; Associate institutions & firms that provide a product or service to the fish & seafood industry
Activities: Developing an economically sound & competitive industry; Liaising with government departments & agencies
Meetings/Conferences:
For more information see Trade Shows, Conferences and Seminars Chapter
Fisheries Council of Canada 2013 68th Annual Conference
October 2013 Halifax, NS
Fisheries Council of Canada 2014 69th Annual Conference
2014
Publications:
•Building a Fishery that Works: Ottawa Update
Type: Newsletter; *Frequency:* Monthly
Profile: Updates on the Council's activities, environmental issues, Canadian & international fisheries issues, & market reports
•Fisheries Council of Canada Annual Fish & Seafood Products & Services Directory
Type: Directory; *Frequency:* Annually
Profile: Listings to promote members' products & services

Fisheries Council of Canada - British Columbia Representative
4214 - 199A St., Langley BC V3A 4V6
Tel: 604-530-7258; *Fax:* 604-530-2015
e-mail: gjconsult@telus.net
Previous Name: Fisheries Council of British Columbia
Overview: A medium-sized provincial organization
Member of: Fisheries Council of Canada
Chief Officer(s):
Patrick McGuinness, President

Fishermen and Scientists Research Society (FSRS)
PO Box 25125, Halifax NS B3M 4H4
Tel: 902-876-1160; *Fax:* 902-876-1320
www.fsrs.ns.ca
Overview: A medium-sized provincial organization
Mission: To establish and maintain a network of fishermen and scientific personnel that are concerned with the long-term sustainability of the marine fishing industry in the Atlantic Region.
Chief Officer(s):
Patricia King, General Manager
Membership: *Member Profile:* Fishermen; Research scientists

Flax Canada 2015 Inc.
#465, 167 Lombard Ave., Winnipeg MB R3B 0T6
Tel: 204-942-2115; *Fax:* 204-982-2128
e-mail: kelley@fc2015.ca
www.fc2015.ca
Overview: A small national organization
Mission: To position flax as one of the main drivers of the Canadian bio-economy by the year 2015; To develop health care strategies based on flaxseed; To increase research & commercialization of new products from flax; To ensure utilization of value-added components from seed & straw; To develop a "branding strategy" for flax; To capture opportunities provided by the multiple end-uses of flax to increase net farm income; To improve agricultural sustainability & to enhance Canada's rural communities
Chief Officer(s):
Kelley C. Fitzpatrick, Director
kelleyf@shaw.ca

Flax Council of Canada
#465, 167 Lombard Ave., Winnipeg MB R3B 0T6
Tel: 204-982-2115; *Fax:* 204-942-1841
e-mail: flax@flaxcouncil.ca
www.flaxcouncil.ca
Overview: A medium-sized national organization founded in 1985
Mission: To provide a central focus for industry, producers, government, research institutions & marketing organizations; to promote flax worldwide through crop, market & product development.
Chief Officer(s):
M. Barry Hall, President
Finances: *Annual Operating Budget:* $500,000-$1.5 Million
Membership: 60 corporate; *Fees:* $200; *Committees:* Communications; Market Development; Research & Technical
Activities: ; *Library:* Open to public

Fleurs Canada *See* Flowers Canada

Flowers Canada (FC) / Fleurs Canada
Retail & Distribution Sector, #305, 99 Fifth Ave., Ottawa ON K1S 5P5
Fax: 866-671-8091
Toll-Free: 800-447-5147
e-mail: flowers@flowerscanada.org
www.flowerscanada.org
Also Known As: Association of the Canadian Floral Industry
Overview: A medium-sized national organization founded in 1897
Mission: To act as the voice of the Canadian floriculture industry; To improve the Canadian floriculture industry
Chief Officer(s):
James Fuller, Chairman
Membership: 1,000; *Fees:* $200 associates; $265 retailers; $500 distributors & wholesalers; *Member Profile:* Flower growers; Distributors; Retailers; Educators; Associates
Activities: Establishing partnerships; Researching; Developing consumers; Taking legislative action; Encouraging professional accreditation; Providing education; Offering business services; Giving sales & marketing support; Organizing conferences; Communicating with members; Developing standards; Conducting research; Identifying & sharing best practices; Promoting e-business; Presenting awards; *Library:* Flowers Canada Library; Open to public

FogQuest
448 Monarch Pl., Kamloops BC V2E 2B2
Tel: 250-374-1745; *Fax:* 250-374-1746
e-mail: info@fogquest.org
www.fogquest.org
Overview: A small international charitable organization founded in 1987
Mission: To plan & implement water projects for rural communities located in developing countries
Environmental Activity: Producing clean water through fog collection in developing countries
Chief Officer(s):
Robert Schemenauer, Executive Director
Melissa Rosato, Associate Executive Director
Finances: *Funding Sources:* Grants; donations; membership fees
Membership: *Fees:* $40

Foire agricole royale d'hiver *See* Royal Agricultural Winter Fair Association

Fondation Asie Pacifique du Canada *See* Asia Pacific Foundation of Canada

Fondation canadienne des plantes ornementales *See* Canadian Ornamental Plant Foundation

Fondation canadienne pour l'amélioration des services de santé *See* Canadian Foundation for Healthcare Improvement

Fondation canadienne pour les sciences du climat et de l'atmosphère *See* Canadian Foundation for Climate & Atmospheric Sciences

Fondation de la faune du Québec (FFQ)
#420, 1175, av Lavigerie, Sainte-Foy QC G1V 4P1
Tél: 418-644-7926; *Téléc:* 418-643-7655
Ligne sans frais: 877-639-0742
Courriel: ffq@fondationdelafaune.qc.ca
www.fondationdelafaune.qc.ca
www.facebook.com/fondationdelafauneduquebec
Aperçu: *Dimension:* moyenne; *Envergure:* provinciale; Organisme sans but lucratif; fondée en 1985
Mission: Promouvoir la conservation et la mise en valeur de la faune et de son habitat
Membre(s) du bureau directeur:
André Martin, Président-directeur général
direction@fondationdelafaune.qc.ca
Finances: *Budget de fonctionnement annuel:* $3 Million-$5 Million
Personnel: 17 membre(s) du personnel
Membre: 4 500 *Montant de la cotisation:* 20$
Activités: Programmes de subvention: amélioration de la qualité des habitats aquatiques; faire connaître nos habitats fauniques; programme d'aide à la protection des habitats; pêche en herbe, faune en danger; programme de mise en valeur des cours d'eau en milieu agricole

Fondation des amis de l'environnement TD *See* TD Friends of the Environment Foundation

Fondation du bien-être animal du Canada *See* Animal Welfare Foundation of Canada

Fondation du sentier transcanadian *See* Trans Canada Trail Foundation

Fondation Harmonie du Canada *See* Harmony Foundation of Canada

Fondation Héritage Canada *See* Heritage Canada Foundation

Fondation Hydro-Québec pour l'environnement / Hydro-Québec Foundation for the Environment
740, rue Notre-Dame Ouest, 8e étage, Montréal QC H3C 3X6
Tél: 514-289-5384; *Téléc:* 514-289-2079
Courriel: fondation_environnement@hydro.qc.ca
www.hydroquebec.com/fondation_environnement
Aperçu: *Dimension:* petite; *Envergure:* provinciale
Mission: Promouvoir la conservation, la restauration et la mise en valeur de la faune, de la flore et des habitats naturels; soutenir les besoins locaux en matière de prise en charge de l'environnement; contribuer à l'utilisation responsable et durable des ressources naturelles
Membre(s) du bureau directeur:
Marie-José Nadeau, Présidente

Fondation pour la conservation de l'environnement *See* Foundation for Environmental Conservation

Fondation pour la protection des sites naturels du Nouveau-Brunswick *See* Nature Trust of New Brunswick

Fondation Québec Labrador du (Canada) inc. *See* Québec-Labrador Foundation (Canada) Inc.

Fondation québécoise en environnement / Québec Environment Foundation
#706, 1255 carré Phillips, Montréal QC H3B 3G1
Tél: 514-849-3323; *Téléc:* 514-849-0028
Ligne sans frais: 800-361-2503
Courriel: info@fqe.qc.ca
www.fqe.qc.ca
www.facebook.com/FQEnvironnement
twitter.com/fqe
Aperçu: *Dimension:* moyenne; *Envergure:* provinciale; Organisme sans but lucratif; fondée en 1987
Mission: Sensibiliser les Québécoises et les Québécois à l'égard de l'environnement par l'information et l'éducation; créer

une synergie entre l'économie et l'écologie; favoriser la recherche et la mise en place de solutions concrètes et efficaces
Membre(s) du bureau directeur:
Louis-Paul Allard, Président
Claude Hill, Directeur général
chill@fge.qc.ca
Finances: *Budget de fonctionnement annuel:* $500,000-$1.5 Million
Personnel: 5 membre(s) du personnel; 35 bénévole(s)
Membre: 210 membres; 10 000 ami(e)s *Montant de la cotisation:* 25$; *Comités:* Environnement
Activités: Journées éducatives, colloques, conférences, plantations d'arbres; *Service de conférenciers:* Oui

Fonds international pour la protection des animaux ***See*** International Fund for Animal Welfare Canada

Fonds mondial pour la nature ***See*** World Wildlife Fund - USA

Fonds mondial pour la nature ***See*** World Wildlife Fund - Canada

Food & Consumer Products of Canada (FCPC) / Produits alimentaires et de consommation du Canada (PACC)
100 Sheppard Ave E., Toronto ON m2n 6Z1
Tel: 416-510-8024; *Fax:* 416-510-8043
e-mail: info@fcpc.ca
www.fcpc.ca
www.linkedin.com/company/2609609?trk=tyah
twitter.com/FCPC1
Previous Name: Grocery Products Manufacturers of Canada; Food & Consumer Products Manufacturers of Canada
Overview: A large national organization founded in 1959
Mission: To represent the food & consumer products industry, from small privately-owned companies to big glboal multinationals
Environmental Activity: Working with government, regulatory bodies, & retail & foodservice partners on issues such as food safety; Providing environmental & safety issue information
Chief Officer(s):
Nancy Croitoru, President & Chief Executive Officer
Glenda Costa, Vice-President, Finance & Administration
Errol Cerit, Senior Director, Industry Affairs & Membership
Rachel Kagan, Vice-President, Environment & Sustainability Policy
Janice Emery-Carter, Manager, Education Centre
Derek Nighbor, Senior Vice-President, Public & Regulatory Affairs
Heather Spencer, Coordinator, Member Services
Heather.Spencer@fcpc.ca
Jami Nirenberg, Coordinator, Events
Membership: *Member Profile:* Companies that make & market retailer & national brands
Activities: Offering educational opportunities; Engaging in advocacy activities; Advising members about government policy changes; Offering networking opportunities
Meetings/Conferences:
For more information see Trade Shows, Conferences and Seminars Chapter
Canadian Grocery & Consumer Goods Leadership Symposium 2013
JUne 2013 Toronto, ON

Food Institute of Canada ***See*** Food Processors of Canada

Food Processors of Canada (FPC) / Fabricants de produits alimentaires du Canada
#900, 350 Sparks St., Ottawa ON K1R 7S8
Tel: 613-722-1000; *Fax:* 613-722-1404
e-mail: fpc@foodprocessors.ca
www.foodnet.fic.ca
Previous Name: Food Institute of Canada
Overview: A medium-sized national organization founded in 1989
Mission: To provide professional services & advice to members on matters such as manufacturing, trade, & commerce
Chief Officer(s):
Christopher J. Kyte, President
Mel Fruitman, Vice-President
Membership: *Member Profile:* Canadian food industry executives who own or manage food processing companies
Activities: Maintaining relationships with government departments to affect policies, programs, & regulations; Organizing conferences; Providing networking opportunities
Meetings/Conferences:
For more information see Trade Shows, Conferences and Seminars Chapter
Food Processors of Canada Annual Executives Meeting 2013
May 2013 Ottawa, ON

Foodservice & Packaging Institute (FPI)
#204, 150 Washington St. South, Falls Church VA 22046 USA
Tel: 703-538-2800; *Fax:* 703-538-2187
e-mail: fpi@fpi.org
www.fpi.org
Overview: A small national organization founded in 1933
Chief Officer(s):
John Burke, President
Beth Phillips, Director, Member Services & Administration
Lynn Rosseth, Director, Market Development & Programs
Finances: *Annual Operating Budget:* $500,000-$1.5 Million; *Funding Sources:* Membership fees
Staff: 3 staff member(s)
Membership: 25; *Fees:* Varies by sales; *Member Profile:* Serves the single-use foodservice packaging industry; is the material-neutral trade association for manufacturers, suppliers & distributors of single-use foodservice packaging products; *Committees:* Market Development; Marketing & Communiciations; Public Affairs; Safety Management; Technical; Standards Council
Activities: Market development; marketing & communications; member services; public affairs & technical programs

Foothills Forage & Grazing Association (FFGA) Parent Name: Agricultural Research & Extension Council of Alberta
PO Box 5145, High River AB T1V 1M3
Tel: 403-652-4900; *Fax:* 403-652-4090
www.foothillsforage.com
www.facebook.com/166272723417016
twitter.com/FoothillsForage
Overview: A small local organization founded in 1972 overseen by Agricultural Research & Extension Council of Alberta
Mission: To provide forage & livestock information to producers; to partner with industry, government & the agricultural community; *Member of:* Agricultural Research & Extension Council of Alberta
Chief Officer(s):
Laura Gibney, Manager
laura@foothillsforage.com
Membership: *Fees:* $31.50; *Member Profile:* Any individual or firm involved in the production of forage
Publications:
•Grassroots News & Views [a publication of Foothills Forage & Grazing Association]
Type: Newsletter

Foothills Model Forest ***See*** Foothills Research Institute

Foothills Research Institute
PO Box 6330, Hinton AB T7V 1X6
Tel: 780-865-8330; *Fax:* 780-865-8331
foothillsresearchinstitute.ca
Previous Name: Foothills Model Forest
Overview: A small local organization founded in 1992
Mission: Plays a key role in establishing Alberta & Canada's reputation as a world leader in sustainable forest management; *Member of:* Canadian Model Forest Network
Chief Officer(s):
Bill Tinge, General Manager
btinge@foothillsri.ca
Rick Bonar, President
rick.bonar@westfraser.com
Finances: *Annual Operating Budget:* $3 Million-$5 Million
Membership: 1-99; *Member Profile:* Industry, government, environmental non-governmental offices, academics, aboriginals, researchers

For Ed BC
Parent Name: Canadian Forestry Association
#213, 4438 - 10th Ave. West, Vancouver BC V6R 4R8
Tel: 604-737-8555; *Fax:* 604-737-8598
e-mail: info@foredbc.org
www.landscapesmag.com
Previous Name: Canadian Forestry Association of BC; British Columbia Forestry Association
Overview: A medium-sized provincial charitable organization founded in 1925 overseen by Canadian Forestry Association
Mission: To provide education to lifelong learners in all segments of society about the environment & its resources to achieve better environmental decisions & health outcomes; To engage citizens, communities, & volunteers to rehabilitate, protect, & enhance the environment
Chief Officer(s):
Cheryl Ziola, President
cheryl@foredbc.org
Sandra Ulmer, Contact, Education
education@foredbc.org
Helen Sutherland, Contact, Administration
admin@foredbc.org
Finances: *Funding Sources:* Donations
Activities: Offering field service programs; Providing information resources about sustainability; Supporting youth volunteer groups; Providing community participation models for First Nations; Increasing public awareness about conservation, stewardship, economic diversification, & volunteerism; Providing resource packages to community groups, youth leaders, teachers, & volunteers involved in environmental activities; Giving workshops; Consulting with communities & youth groups; *Awareness Events:* National Forest Week, September

Foreign Agricultural Resource Management Services (FARMS)
Parent Name: Canadian Federation of Agriculture
#706, 5995 Avebury Rd., Mississauga ON L5R 3P9
Tel: 905-568-4500
Toll-Free: 866-271-0826
www.farmsontario.ca
www.facebook.com/FARMSCANADA
twitter.com/FARMSCanada
Overview: A medium-sized international organization founded in 1987 overseen by Canadian Federation of Agriculture
Mission: To facilitate & coordinate requests for foreign seasonal agricultural workers; *Member of:* Canadian Federation of Agriculture
Chief Officer(s):
Ken Forth, President
Sue Williams, General Manager
Membership: *Member Profile:* Participating countries: Barbados, Eastern Caribbean, Jamaica, Mexico & Trinidad & Tobago
Activities: Operating CanAg Travel Services; providing forms & information online

Forest Action Network (FAN)
PO Box 625, Bella Coola BC V0T 1C0
e-mail: info@fanweb.org
fanweb.org
Overview: A small local organization founded in 1993
Mission: To campaign to save British Columbia's coastal temperate rainforest & other ancient forests
Finances: *Annual Operating Budget:* Less than $50,000
Membership: 100-499
Activities: Public education & civil disobedience against clearcutting & other industrial deforestation

Forest Engineering Research Institute of Canada, A Division of FPInnovations ***See*** FPInnovations

Forest Products Association of Canada (FPAC) / Association des produits forestiers du Canada
#410, 99 Bank St., Ottawa ON K1P 6B9
Tel: 613-563-1441; *Fax:* 613-563-4720
e-mail: ottawa@fpac.ca
www.fpac.ca
Previous Name: Canadian Pulp & Paper Association
Overview: A medium-sized national organization founded in 1913
Mission: To be the voice of Canada's wood, pulp & paper producers nationally & internationally in the areas of government, trade, & environmental affairs; To advance the Canadian forest products industry's global competitiveness & sustainable stewardship; To operate in a mannner which is economically viable, environmentally responsible, & socially desirable
Environmental Activity: Regenerating harvested areas; Participating in recovery & recycling; Promoting carbon neutrality; Reducing greenhouse gas emissions in the pulp & paper industry; Operating according to government-approved forest management plans
Chief Officer(s):
Avrim Lazar, President & Chief Executive Officer
Andrew Casey, Vice-President, Public Affairs & International Trade
Jean-Pierre Martel, Sr. Vice-President, Sustainability
Catherine Cobden, Vice-President, Economics & Regulatory Affairs
Lori Harop, Executive Director, Environmental Reputation Project

Isabelle Des Chênes, Vice-President, Market Relations & Communications
Mark Hubert, Vice-President, Climate Change Leadership
Susan Murray, Executive Director, Public Relations, 613-563-1441 Ext. 313
smurray@fpac.ca
David Church, Director, Transportation & Recycling
Roger Cook, Director, Environment
Andrew DeVries, Director, Conservation Biology & Aboriginal Affairs
Jon Flemming, Director, Ecomonics & Trade Policy
Paul Lansbergen, Director, Energy, Economics, & Climate Change
Joel Neuheimer, Director, Market Affairs
Étienne Bélanger, Manager, Forestry Issues
George Wamala, Manager, Government Relations & Policy
Membership: *Member Profile:* Canadian producers of forest products, with third-party certification of member companies' forest practices
Activities: Liaising with governments, non-governmental organizations (NGOs), & multi-stakeholder groups; Conducting advertising campaigns; *Library:* Forest Products Association of Canada Resource Centre
Publications:
•A Buyers' Guide to Canada's Sustainable Forest Products
Type: Guide; *Number of Pages:* 32
Profile: Contents include sustainable procurement, key issues related to sustainable procurement, sample forest products procurement, green building with Canada's forestproducts, FPAC member companies, a glossary, useful links, reference guides, & standards, & environmental performance data
•Canadian Wood, Renewable by Nature, Sustainable by Design
Type: Report; *Number of Pages:* 22
Profile: Information about sustainable forest management in Canada
•Forest Certification in Canada: The Programs, Similarities, & Achievements
Type: Report; *Number of Pages:* 26
Profile: Contents include an introduction to certification, Canada, a world leader in forest certification, & key elements of certification programs
•Forest Products Association of Canada Annual Report
Type: Yearbook; *Frequency:* Annually
•FPAC [Forest Products Association of Canada] Sustainability Report
Type: Report; *Frequency:* Biennially
•The New Face of the Canadian Forest Industry: The Emerging Bio-revolution (The Bio-pathways Project)
Type: Report
Profile: An examination of the market potential of emerging bio-energy, bio-chemical, & bio-products
•Tackle Climate Change, Use Wood
Type: Report; *Number of Pages:* 22
Profile: Managing forests to mitigate climate change
•Transforming Canada's Forest Products Industry: Summary of Findings from the Future Bio-Pathways Project
Type: Report
Profile: Forest Products Association of Canada investigators & their partner, FPInnovations, examine traditional & emergingbio-industries to assess how wood fibre can create bio-products such as bio-energy & bio-chemicals
•Woodland Caribou Recovery: Audit of Operatinig Practices & Mitigation Measures Employed within Woodland Caribou Ranges
Type: Report; *Author:* Golder Associates
Profile: An audit commissioned by the Forest Products Association of Canada & the CaribouLandscape Management Association

Forest Products Association of Nova Scotia (FPANS)

PO Box 696, Truro NS B2N 5E5
Tel: 902-895-1179; *Fax:* 902-893-1197
www.fpans.ca
Previous Name: Nova Scotia Forest Products Association
Overview: A medium-sized provincial organization founded in 1934
Mission: To act as the voice of the forest industry in Nova Scotia; To cooperate with industry, federal, provincial, & municipal governments, & other stakeholders to ensure adherence to forest management & stewardship policies; To promote sustainable management & viability of the forest industry
Environmental Activity: Offering programs in forest stewardship; Supporting forest sustainability, wildlife habitat, & watercourse protection regulations; Presenting the Don Eldridge Memorial Award for sustainable forest stewardship practices
Chief Officer(s):
Steve Talbot, Executive Director
stalbot@fpans.ca
Jeff Bishop, Coordinator, Communications
jbishop@fpans.ca
Membership: 500-999;; *Fees:* Schedule available; *Member Profile:* Representatives from the logging sector of the trucking industry; Pulp & paper manufacturers; Sawmill operators; Forest equipment operators; Woodlot owners; Small & large landowners; Maple product producers; Silviculture & harvesting contractors; Christmas tree producers; *Committees:* Forest management; Gas tax access road; Annual meeting; Communications; Energy; Environment; Safety training & worker's compensation; Transportation; Ad hoc gypsy moth
Activities: Enhancing training standards; Providing educational programs in schools; *Awareness Events:* National Forest Week
Meetings/Conferences:
For more information see Trade Shows, Conferences and Seminars Chapter
Forest Products Association of Nova Scotia 2013 Annual Meeting
January 2013 Halifax, NS
Publications:
•Forest Products Association of Nova Scotia Newsletter
Type: Newsletter
Profile: Updates for association members

Fort Saskatchewan Fish & Game Association

PO Box 3038, Fort Saskatchewan AB T8L 2T1
Tel: 780-998-0062
e-mail: fortfishngame@hotmail.com
www.fsfga.com
Overview: A small local organization founded in 1958
Mission: To promote through education, lobbying & programs the conservation & utilization of fish & wildlife; protect & enhance the habitat they depend on; *Member of:* Alberta Fish & Game Association
Chief Officer(s):
Gord Blize, President
Finances: *Funding Sources:* Fundraising
Staff: 500 volunteer(s)
Membership: 500; *Fees:* $25
Activities: Monthly club meetings; various events for members & families; *Awareness Events:* Kid's Ice Fishing Derby, March; Fishing Derby, June; Family Fun Day & Fishing Derby, Dec.

FortWhyte Alive

1961 McCreary Rd., Winnipeg MB R3P 2K9
Tel: 204-989-8355; *Fax:* 204-895-4700
e-mail: info@fortwhyte.org
www.fortwhyte.org
www.facebook.com/pages/FortWhyte-Alive/471614835647?ref=ts
Previous Name: Wildlife Foundation of Manitoba; Fort Whyte Centre for Environmental Education
Overview: A small local organization founded in 1966
Mission: FortWhyte Alive is dedicated to providing programming, natural settings and facilities for environmental education and outdoor recreation. In so doing, FortWhyte promotes awareness and understanding of the natural world and actions leading to sustainable living.
Chief Officer(s):
Bill Elliott, President/CEO
Membership: 2,000; *Fees:* Schedule available

Foundation for Educational Exchange Between Canada & the United States of America

#2015, 350 Albert St., Ottawa ON K1R 1A4
Tel: 613-688-5540; *Fax:* 613-237-2029
e-mail: info@fulbright.ca
www.fulbright.ca
www.facebook.com/pages/Fulbright-Canada/193768967190
twitter.com/FulbrightPrgrm
www.youtube.com/user/FulbrightCanada
Also Known As: Canada-U.S. Fulbright Program
Overview: A medium-sized international charitable organization founded in 1990
Mission: To support outstanding graduate students, faculty, professionals, & independent researchers in order to enhance understanding between the people of Canada & the United States
Chief Officer(s):
Michael K. Hawes, Executive Director
mhawes@fulbright.ca
Ava Kovats, Sr. Finance Officer
akovats@fulbright.ca
Finances: *Funding Sources:* Department of Foreign Affairs and International Trade Canada; United States Department of State; Public sector partners; Private sector partners
Activities: Presenting grants & scholarships to Canadian & American scholars, post-doctoral researchers, experienced professionals, junior professionals, executives of the Government of Canada, & Canadian & American teachers; *Internships:* Yes

Foundation for Environmental Conservation (FEC) / Fondation pour la conservation de l'environnement

1148 Moiry, Switzerland
Fax: 41-21-8666-6616
e-mail: envcons@ncl.ac.uk
www.ncl.ac.uk/icef
Overview: A small international organization founded in 1975
Mission: To undertake, in cooperation with appropriate individuals, organizations & other groups, all possible activities to further environmental conservation & global sustainability
Chief Officer(s):
Nicholas V.C. Polunin, Editor
Membership: *Committees:* Awards
Activities: International Conferences on Environmental Future (ICEFs); specialist workshops

Foundation for International Environmental Law & Development (FIELD)

3 Endsleigh St., London WC1H 0DD United Kingdom
Tel: 44-20-7872-7200; *Fax:* 44-20-7388-2826
e-mail: field.org@field.org.uk
www.field.org.uk
Previous Name: Centre for Environmental Law & Development
Overview: A small international organization founded in 1989
Mission: To help vulnerable countries, communities, & campaigners negotiate for fairer international environmental laws
Chief Officer(s):
Joy Hyvarinen, Director
Finances: *Annual Operating Budget:* $500,000-$1.5 Million; *Funding Sources:* Foundations; Consultancy work
Staff: 13 staff member(s); 8 volunteer(s)
Membership: *Member Profile:* Public international lawyers
Activities: *Internships:* Yes

FPInnovations

580, boul Saint-Jean, Pointe-Claire QC H9R 3J9
Tel: 514-630-4100; *Fax:* 514-630-4134
e-mail: info@fpinnovations.ca
www.feric.ca
Previous Name: Forest Engineering Research Institute of Canada, A Division of FPInnovations
Overview: A medium-sized national organization founded in 1975
Mission: To develop & assist with the implementation of innovative & safe forest operational solutions, which encompass areas such as the engineering, environmental, & human aspects of forestry & wildland fire operations; To improve sustainable forest operations in Canada; To provide members with knowledge & technology, based on research, to conduct cost-competitive, quality forest operations
Chief Officer(s):
Lynn M. Dyer, President
Finances: *Funding Sources:* Forestry companies; Government of Canada; Provincial & territorial governments
Staff: 100 staff member(s)
Membership: *Member Profile:* Forestry companies; Canadian forestry equipment manufacturers & distributors (CFEMD); *Committees:* Strategic Advisory; Advisory Committeeon Forest Engineering Research; Advisory Committee on Wildland Fire Operations Research
Activities: Researching, in consultation with members & partners, which focuses on silvicultural operations, harvesting, wildland fire operations, transportation & roads, & precision forestry; Providing Feric workshops & seminars; *Library:* FERIC Library

Western Division
2601 East Mall, Vancouver BC V6T 1Z4
Tel: 604-228-1555; *Fax:* 604-228-0999
e-mail: admin@vcr.feric.ca
www.feric.ca
Chief Officer(s):
John W. Mann, Vice-President, Western Region

Fraser Basin Council (FBC)
Basin-Wide Office, 470 Granville St., 1st Fl., Vancouver BC V6C 1V5
Tel: 604-488-5350; *Fax:* 604-488-5351
e-mail: info@fraserbasin.bc.ca
www.fraserbasin.bc.ca
Overview: A medium-sized local organization founded in 1997
Mission: To advance sustainability in the Fraser River Basin & across British Columbia
Environmental Activity: Aboriginal partnerships; climate programs; flood hazard management program; invasive plant strategy program; Sustainability Purchasing Network; water governance program; youth & sustainability program
Chief Officer(s):
David Marshall, Executive Director
dmarshall@fraserbasin.bc.ca
Charlotte Argue, Assistant Manager, Climate Change & Air Quality Program
cargue@fraserbasin.bc.ca
Publications:
•Basin News [a publication of the Fraser Basin Council]
Type: Newsletter; *Frequency:* 2 pa

Cariboo-Chilcotin Regional Office
#104, 197 Second Ave. North, Williams Lake BC V2G 1Z5
Tel: 250-392-1400; *Fax:* 250-305-1004
Chief Officer(s):
Maureen LeBourdais, Regional Manager & Sr. Program Manager, Smart Planning for Communities
mlebourdais@fraserbasin.bc.ca

Fraser Valley Regional Office
PO Box 3006, Mission BC V2V 4J3
Tel: 604-826-1661; *Fax:* 604-826-6848
Chief Officer(s):
Marion Town, Senior Regional Manager, GVSS & Fraser Valley
mtown@fraserbasin.bc.ca
Marion Robinson, Regional Manager
mrobinson@fraserbasin.bc.ca

Greater Vancouver Sea to Sky Regional Office (GVSS)
470 Granville St., 1st Fl., Vancouver BC V6C 1V5
Tel: 604-488-5365; *Fax:* 604-488-5351
Chief Officer(s):
Marion Town, Senior Regional Manager, GVSS & Fraser Valley
mtown@fraserbasin.bc.ca

Thompson Regional Office
#200A, 1383 McGill Rd., Kamloops BC V2C 6K7
Tel: 250-314-9660; *Fax:* 250-828-2597
Chief Officer(s):
Mike Simpson, Senior Regional Manager
msimpson@fraserbasin.bc.ca

Upper Fraser Regional Office
#207, 155 George St., Prince George BC V2L 1P8
Tel: 250-612-0252; *Fax:* 250-564-6514
Chief Officer(s):
Terry Robert, Regional Manager & Program Manager, Climate Change & Air Quality
trobert@fraserbasin.bc.ca

Fraser Valley Labour Council
Parent Name: British Columbia Federation of Labour
#202, 9292 - 200th St., Langley BC V1M 3A6
Tel: 604-314-9867; *Fax:* 604-430-6762
e-mail: bharder@usw.ca
www.fvlc.ca
www.facebook.com/group.php?gid=242003131602&ref=mf
Overview: A small local organization founded in 2007 overseen by British Columbia Federation of Labour
Mission: To advance the economic, social, & political life of persons in British Columbia's Fraser Valley; To act as the unified voice for workers to ensure workers' rights, such as fair wages & safe working conditions
Environmental Activity: Working to ensure a sustainable environment
Chief Officer(s):
Brian Harder, President
bharder@usw.ca
Pamela Willingshofer, Secretary
kidogo@shaw.ca
Karen Porter, Treasurer
kporter64@shaw.ca
Membership: 12,000; *Member Profile:* Members of unions from the Fraser Valley region of British Columbia, such as Chilliwack, Hope, Abbotsford, Mission, Lytton, & Harrison
Activities: Lobbying governments about worker's issues; Providing labour education; Conducting campaigns to support the issues of working families; Supporting local organizations, such as the United Way
Meetings/Conferences:
For more information see Trade Shows, Conferences and Seminars Chapter
Fraser Valley Labour Council 2013 Annual General Meeting
January 2013 Abbotsford, BC

Fredericton Fish & Game Association (FFGA)
PO Box 1083, Stn. A, Fredericton NB E3B 5C2
Tel: 506-474-0458
www.freewebs.com/fishandgame
www.facebook.com/165642576892091
Overview: A small local organization founded in 1924
Mission: To foster sound management & wise use of natural resources so that economic, recreational & aesthetic values may continue to benefit future generations; *Member of:* New Brunswick Wildlife Federation
Chief Officer(s):
Rod Currie, President
president@frederictonfishandgame.org
Finances: *Annual Operating Budget:* Less than $50,000
Staff: 30 volunteer(s)
Membership: 140; *Fees:* $25 single; $40 family; *Member Profile:* Individuals concerned about natural resources & willing to assist in conservation; *Committees:* Jr. Branch; Education; Environment; Conservation Lottery; Wildlife; Newsletter
Activities: Adopt-A-Stream; Youth Fishing Tournament; Fishing & Hunting Enhancement Project; education & speakers

Freight Carriers Association of Canada (FCA)
#3-4, 427 Garrison Rd., Fort Erie ON L2A 6E6
Tel: 905-994-0560; *Fax:* 905-994-0117
Toll-Free: 800-559-7421
e-mail: info@fca-natc.org
www.fca-natc.org
Previous Name: Canadian Transport Tariff Bureau Association
Overview: A medium-sized national organization founded in 1939
Mission: To provide quality information, products & services to users, providers & third parties involved in motor carrier transportation; Affiliation(s): North American Transportation Council
Chief Officer(s):
David J. Sirgey, President, 800-559-7421 Ext. 214
Ken Leising, Manager Rate Research/Development
Diane Sheppard, Accountant
Jon Ainsworth, Senior Analyst/Programmer
Mary Anne Vehrs, Sales/Marketing
Finances: *Annual Operating Budget:* $1.5 Million-$3 Million; *Funding Sources:* Membership fees; sales of publications & software
Staff: 17 staff member(s)
Membership: 100; *Fees:* Based on revenues; *Member Profile:* For-hire motor carriers; *Committees:* Tariff Advisory; Québec Comité Consultatif
Activities: Carrier meetings; seminars; research; info gathering & dissemination; *Speaker Service:* Yes

Fresh Outlook Foundation (FOF)
12510 Ponderosa Rd., Lake Country BC V4V 2G9
Tel: 250-766-1777; *Fax:* 250-766-1767
www.freshoutlookfoundation.org
www.facebook.com/FreshOutlookFoundation?ref=website
www.twitter.com/FreshOutlook
Overview: A small national charitable organization founded in 2007
Mission: The Fresh Outlook Foundation (FOF) builds sustainable communities through a focus on the social, cultural, environmental, and economic aspects of community sustainability.
Environmental Activity: Climate Change Program; The Green School Program; The Heat Challenge; May Bird Count Challenge
Chief Officer(s):
Joanne de Vries, CEO
jo@freshoutlookfoundation.org
Finances: *Funding Sources:* Donations (industry, business); government (federal/provincial, less than 5%); private foundations
Activities: Green School Program, environmental action program for elementary school students; Challenge Programs; Water & Clean Air; Writing & Bird challenges for elementary & junior high school students; Creating a Climate of Change Multimedia Program; Energy Literacy Series; Taking Action on Climate Change
Meetings/Conferences:
For more information see Trade Shows, Conferences and Seminars Chapter
2013 Building SustainAble Communities Conference
November 2013 Kelowna, BC
2014 Building SustainAble Communities Conference
2014

Freshwater Fisheries Society of British Columbia (FFSBC)
#101, 80 Regatta Landing, Victoria BC V9A 7S2
Tel: 250-414-4200; *Fax:* 250-414-4211
Toll-Free: 888-601-4200
e-mail: fish@gofishbc.com
www.gofishbc.com
Overview: A medium-sized provincial organization
Mission: To stock eggs & fish into lakes & streams across British Columbia; To support sturgeon & steelhead recovery programs; To operate hatcheries & visitor's centres
Environmental Activity: Restoring & conserving wild fish populations; Working with the Ministry of Environment to create fisheries & to manage existing fisheries
Chief Officer(s):
Don Peterson, President
Evert Van Eerden, Chair
Rob Adkin, Secretary-Treasurer
Activities: Providing information related to freshwater fishing & freshwater ecosystems in British Columbia; Partnering with organizations such as the Ministry of Environment to offer the Go Fish program so that children can experience fishing & foster an appreciation for the environment

Friends of Abandoned Pets
PO Box 67052, Ottawa ON K2A 4E4
Tel: 613-729-9820
e-mail: information@foap.on.ca
www.foap.on.ca
Overview: A small local organization founded in 1992
Mission: To prevent cruelty to animals by caring for stray & abandoned animals
Chief Officer(s):
Berni Conn, President
Membership: 400 individual; *Fees:* $30 individual; $50 family
Publications:
•Pet Talk
Type: Newsletter; *Frequency:* Semiannually; *Editor:* Pat Winter, Jean Burns

The Friends of Algonquin Park
PO Box 248, Whitney ON K0J 2M0
Tel: 613-637-2828; *Fax:* 613-637-2138
www.algonquinpark.on.ca/friends
Overview: A small local charitable organization founded in 1983
Mission: To further the educational & interpretive programs in Algonquin Park; Affiliation(s): Canadian Parks Partnership; Ontario Parks
Chief Officer(s):
Lee Pauzé, General Manager
Finances: *Annual Operating Budget:* $500,000-$1.5 Million
Staff: 7 staff member(s); 197 volunteer(s)
Membership: 3,000; *Fees:* $7 student; $12 individual; $17 family
Activities: *Speaker Service:* Yes

Friends of Animals (FoA)
#205, 777 Post Rd., Darien CT USA
Tel: 203-656-1522; *Fax:* 203-656-0267
Toll-Free: 800-321-7387
e-mail: info@friendsofanimals.org
friendsofanimals.org
www.facebook.com/FriendsOfAnimalsOrg
twitter.com/pferal
www.youtube.com/user/FriendsofAnimals
Overview: A large national charitable organization founded in 1957
Mission: To free animals from cruelty & institutionalized exploitation around the world; works to cultivate a respectful view of nonhuman animals, free-living & domestic. Branch offices in New York & Victoria, BC.
Environmental Activity: Protects national wildlife refuges & public lands

Chief Officer(s):
Carol Fleischmann, Chair
Priscilla Feral, President
feral@friendsofanimals.org
Finances: *Annual Operating Budget:* $3 Million-$5 Million; *Funding Sources:* Membership dues; bequests; grants; donations
Staff: 23 staff member(s); 185 volunteer(s)
Membership: 200,000; *Fees:* US$25; $30 international
Activities: Low-cost spay/neuter program; anti-fur, anti-wolf & anti-ivory campaigns; opposes all hunting & & international animal trade; supports marine mammal protection; assists & supports programs in Africa for chimpanzees & other animals; anti-vivisection; advocates vegan, plant-based diets
Publications:
•ActùionLine [a publication of Friends of Animals]
Type: Magazine

The Friends of Awenda Park / Les Amis du Parc Awenda
c/o Awenda Provincial Park, PO Box 5004, Penetanguishene ON L9M 2G2
Tel: 705-549-6378; *Fax:* (
e-mail: awenda@csolve.net
www.awendapark.ca
Overview: A small local organization founded in 1991
Mission: Dedicated to the preservation, understanding & interpretation of Awenda's biological, geological & cultural treasurers

The Friends of Bon Echo Park
16151 Highway 41, RR#1, Cloyne ON K0H 1K0
Tel: 613-336-0830; *Fax:* 613-336-2712
e-mail: fobecho@mazinaw.on.ca
www.mazinaw.on.ca/fobecho
Overview: A small local charitable organization
Mission: To preserve the natural & cultural heritage of Bon Echo Provincial Park
Chief Officer(s):
E. Helen Yanch, Operations Manager
Finances: *Annual Operating Budget:* $100,000-$250,000
Staff: 90 volunteer(s)
Membership: 200; *Fees:* $10 individual; $15 family; $25 corporate; $100 life
Activities: Annual Art Show & Sale, July

The Friends of Bonnechere Parks
RR#5, 4024 Round Lake Rd., Killaloe ON K0J 2A0
Tel: 613-732-9273
e-mail: bettyb@nrtco.net
www.bonnecherepark.on.ca
www.facebook.com/bonnecherepark
twitter.com/bonnechere
Overview: A small local organization founded in 1992
Mission: To encourage & support programs for interpretive, educational, scientific, historical, protection & preservation purposes related to the natural & historic resources of the Little Bonnechere River in the Ottawa Valley
Chief Officer(s):
Betty Biesenthal, Director of Publicity

The Friends of Charleston Lake Park
148 Woodvale Rd., RR#4, Lansdowne ON K0E 1L0
e-mail: info@friendsofcharlestonlake.ca
www.friendsofcharlestonlake.ca
Overview: A small local organization
Mission: To help people enjoy Charleston Lake Park, this unique & beautiful place & to help keep it that way
Chief Officer(s):
Steve Psge, Chair

Friends of Clayoquot Sound (FOCS)
PO Box 489, 331 Neill St., Tofino BC V0R 2Z0
Tel: 250-725-4218
e-mail: info@focs.ca
www.focs.ca
Overview: A medium-sized local charitable organization founded in 1979
Mission: To be peaceful & courageous advocates for the earth, air & waters of Clayoquot Sound & all temperate rainforests; To dramatically reduce economic reliance upon raw resource extraction by developing sustainability in rural & urban cultures; To oppose logging on ancient temperate rainforests, as well as the export of raw (unprocessed) logs; To support ecoforestry in second growth forest; To promote reduced wood & paper consumption & support the use of ecologically sustainable, tree-free alternatives to wood & wood-fibre products; To advocate taking fish farms out of wild waters & putting them in on-land closed containment systems; *Member of:* BC Environmental Network; Coastal Alliance for Aquaculture Reform (CAAR); Affiliation(s): Greenpeace; Sierra Club; Natural Resources Defence Council; Western Canada Wilderness Committee (WCWC)
Chief Officer(s):
Dan Lewis, Executive Director
dan@focs.ca
Finances: *Annual Operating Budget:* $100,000-$250,000; *Funding Sources:* Individual donors; foundation grants
Staff: 4 staff member(s)
Membership: 3,000; *Fees:* $25
Activities: *Speaker Service:* Yes; *Library:* FOCS Resource Centre

Friends of Devonian Botanic Garden
University of Alberta, Edmonton AB T6G 2R3
Tel: 780-987-3054; *Fax:* 780-987-4141
e-mail: friends@ualberta.ca
www.devonian.ualberta.ca
www.facebook.com/DevonianBotanicGarden
Overview: A medium-sized local charitable organization founded in 1971
Chief Officer(s):
Lee Foote, Director Ext. 2233
lee.foote@ualberta.ca
Finances: *Annual Operating Budget:* $50,000-$100,000; *Funding Sources:* Membership fees; donations
Staff: 14 staff member(s); 300 volunteer(s)
Membership: 800; *Fees:* $50 families; $45 individuals; $35 seniors/students
Activities: Sponsors lectures, courses, papers, seminars, publishes material on botanical & horticultural matters; promotes & finances construction of gardens, path, signs, structures & other facilities; raises funds for projects of the society; *Library:* Open to public by appointment

Friends of Ecological Reserves (FER)
PO Box 8477, Stn. Central, Victoria BC V8W 3S1
Tel: 250-361-1694
e-mail: ecoreserves@hotmail.com
www.ecoreserves.bc.ca
Overview: A small local charitable organization founded in 1982
Mission: To promote the interests of British Columbia's ecological reserves program
Environmental Activity: Raising public awareness about the importance of ecological reserves
Chief Officer(s):
Michael Fenger, President
Stephen Ruttan, Vice-President
Finances: *Funding Sources:* Donations; Fundraising
Membership: *Fees:* $15 students & seniors; $20 individuals; $25 families & institutions
Activities: Supporting research in the area of ecological reserves; Organizing field trips
Publications:
•The Log [a publication of the Friends of Ecological Reserves]
Type: Newsletter; *Frequency:* Semiannually; *Editor:* Louise Beinhauer; *Price:* Free to members of Friends ofEcological Reserves
Profile: Information about the establishment, management, & maintenance of ecological reserves in British Columbia

Friends of Ferris
PO Box 504, Campbellford ON K0L 1L0
Tel: 705-653-3575
e-mail: info@friendsofferris.ca
www.friendsofferris.ca
Overview: A small local organization founded in 1994
Mission: The Friends of Ferris is a non-profit group of volunteers who are hard at work, constantly bringing to Ferris special events and promotions unique to the Provincial Park.
Chief Officer(s):
Doreen Sharpe, President
Membership: *Fees:* $10 individual; $17 family

The Friends of Frontenac Park
PO Box 2237, Kingston ON K7L 5J8
e-mail: frontenacpark@frontenacpark.ca
www.frontenacpark.ca
www.facebook.com/frontenacpark
twitter.com/frontenacpark
Overview: A small local organization

The Friends of Killarney Park
c/o Killarney Provincial Park, Killarney ON P0M 2A0
Tel: 705-287-2800; *Fax:* 705-287-2922
friendsofkillarneypark.ca
www.facebook.com/group.php?gid=9103598236
www.youtube.com/user/friendsofkillarney
Overview: A small local organization founded in 1986
Mission: To enhance the interpretive, educational & recreational objectives of Killarney Park
Chief Officer(s):
Kris Puhvel, Executive Director

The Friends of MacGregor Point
c/o MacGregor Point Provincial Park, RR#1, Port Elgin ON N0H 2C5
Tel: 519-389-6232; *Fax:* 519-389-2444
e-mail: fompp@bmts.com
www.friendsofmacgregor.org
Overview: A small local organization
Mission: To supplement & enhance the interpretive & educational programs in the park; to stimulate community interest in & understanding of the park & its resources; to support research of the park's natural & cultural resources
Membership: *Fees:* $15 individual; $20 family; $30 corporate

Friends of Mashkinonje Park
Site 8, Box 1, 99 Langs Landing, Monetville ON P0M 2K0
e-mail: mashkinonje@hotmail.com
www.mashkinonje.com
Overview: A small local organization founded in 2000
Mission: To maintain & share the beauty of this unique area of scenic shorelines & wonderful wetlands
Chief Officer(s):
Angela Martin, President
Membership: *Fees:* $15 individual; $25 family; $50 organization
Publications:
•The Wetlands Observer
Type: Newsletter; *Frequency:* Semiannually

Friends of Mount Revelstoke & Glacier National Parks (FMRG) / Amis des parc nationaux du Mont-Revelstoke et des Glaciers
#102, 103 First St. East, Revelstoke BC V0E 2S0
Tel: 250-837-2010; *Fax:* 250-837-2050
e-mail: fmrg@telus.net
www.friendsrevglacier.com
www.facebook.com/revelstoke.glacier
Overview: A small local charitable organization founded in 1987
Mission: To promote the protection, appreciation, enjoyment & understanding of Mount Revelstoke & Glacier National Parks; Affiliation(s): Friends in High Places
Environmental Activity: National Parks projects
Chief Officer(s):
A. Neills Kristensen, Executive Director
Finances: *Annual Operating Budget:* $100,000-$250,000; *Funding Sources:* Grants; Membership dues; Book store
Staff: 6 staff member(s); 40 volunteer(s)
Membership: 46 individual; 45 family; 63 lifetime; *Fees:* $20 individual; $30 family & non-profit; $100 corporate; $160 lifetime; *Committees:* Naturalist & Environment; Mountain Club; Volunteer & Membership; Marketing; Speaker Series
Activities: Education program, hiking, interpretation, speaker evenings; *Speaker Service:* Yes; *Library:*
Publications:
•Between Friends [a publication of Friends of Mount Revelstoke & Glacier]
Type: Newsletter; *Frequency:* Semiannually

The Friends of Nancy Island Historic Site & Wasaga Beach Park
11 - 22nd St. North, Wasaga Beach ON L9Z 2V9
Tel: 705-429-2516; *Fax:* 705-429-7983
www.wasagabeachpark.com
Overview: A small local organization
Mission: To further the educational & interpretive programs of Wasaga Beach Provincial Park & Nancy Island Historic Site

Friends of Nature Conservation Society
PO Box 281, Chester NS B0J 1J0
Tel: 902-275-3361
e-mail: info@friends-of-nature.ca
www.friends-of-nature.ca
Overview: A small local organization founded in 1954
Mission: To preserve the balance of nature for the mutual benefit of people & their plant & animal friends; *Member of:* Nova Scotia Environmental Network; Nova Scotia Public Lands Coalition; Affiliation(s): Nature Canada; Friends of Nature, Incorporated
Chief Officer(s):

Martin R. Haase, Executive Secretary
Finances: *Annual Operating Budget:* Less than $50,000
Membership: 100-499;; *Fees:* $10
Activities: ; *Library:* Friends of Nature: Environmental Library;

The Friends of Pinery Park

c/o The Visitor Centre, Pinery Provincial Park, RR#2, Grand Bend ON N0M 1T0
Tel: 519-243-2220
www.pinerypark.on.ca/friends.html
Overview: A small local organization founded in 1989
Mission: Dedicated to the development of interpretive, educational, historical & scientific projects & programs to ensure that Pinery Provincial Park's natural legacy will remain for future generations

The Friends of Presqu'ile Park

PO Box 1442, Brighton ON K0K 1H0
Tel: 613-475-2209
e-mail: info@friendsofpresquile.on.ca
www.friendsofpresquile.on.ca
Overview: A small local organization
Mission: To enhance the educational, interpretive, & scientific research programs at Presqu'ile Provincial Park

The Friends of Rondeau Park

RR#1, Morpeth ON N0P 1X0
Tel: 519-674-1777
e-mail: info@rondeauprovincialpark.ca
www.rondeauprovincialpark.ca
www.facebook.com/pantsgloydi
Overview: A small local organization
Mission: To raise funds on a continuing basis in order to encourage & support programs for interpretive, educational, scientific, historical, protection & preservation purposes related to the natural & historical resources of Rondeau Provincial Park & other Ontario Provincial Parks

The Friends of Sandbanks Park

PO Box 20007, 97 Main St., Picton ON K0K 0A0
e-mail: friends@friendsofsandbanks.org
friendsofsandbanks.org
Overview: A small local organization founded in 1993
Mission: To protect & preserve the natural & cultural history of provincial park through interpretation, education, & scientific & historic research
Publications:
•Between Friends
Type: Newsletter

Friends of Short Hills Park

PO Box 236, Fonthill ON L0S 1E0
www.friendsofshorthillspark.ca
Overview: A small local organization
Mission: To preserve the cultural & natural integrity of Short Hills Provincial Park through liaison with Ontario Parks, volunteer work, public education & fundraising activities
Membership: *Fees:* $20

The Friends of Sleeping Giant

PO Box 29031, Thunder Bay ON P7B 6P9
e-mail: info@thefriendsofsleepinggiant.ca
www.thefriendsofsleepinggiant.ca
Overview: A small local organization founded in 1993
Mission: To assist in conserving & fostering an appreciation for Sleeping Giant Provincial Park

Friends of the Coves Subwatershed Inc. (FOTCSI)

111 Elmwood Ave. East, London ON N6C 1J4
Tel: 519-640-5397; *Fax:* 519-640-5780
e-mail: contact@thecoves.ca
www.thecoves.ca
Overview: A small local organization
Mission: A group supporting the protection, conservation & stewardship of the Coves Environmentally Significant Area and surrounding watershed
Chief Officer(s):
Heather Popham, Program Manager
Membership: *Fees:* $25, individual; $35, family; $75, non-profit organization; $200, corporate
Activities: *Awareness Events:* Christmas Bird Count, December

Friends of the Delta Marsh Field Station

c/o University Field Station, University of Manitoba, 239 Machray Hall, Winnipeg MB R3T 2N2
Tel: 204-474-9297
e-mail: delta_marsh@umanitoba.ca
www.umanitoba.ca/faculties/science/delta_marsh/friends
Previous Name: Friends of the Field Station (Delta Marsh)
Overview: A small local organization founded in 1992
Mission: To further the development & use of the University of Manitoba field stations
Chief Officer(s):
Harry Duckworth, President
harry_duckworth@umanitoba.ca
Gordon Goldsborough, Director, Field Station
ggoldsb@cc.umanitoba.ca
Finances: *Annual Operating Budget:* Less than $50,000
Staff: 3 staff member(s); 10 volunteer(s)
Membership: 1-99;; *Fees:* $15 individual; $25 family; $40 three years; $150 lifetime

Friends of the Earth Canada (FoE) / Les Ami(e)s de la Terre Canada

#300, 260 St. Patrick St., Ottawa ON K1N 5K5
Tel: 613-241-0085; *Fax:* 613-241-7998
Toll-Free: 888-385-4444
e-mail: foe@foecanada.org
www.foecanada.org
www.facebook.com/foe.canada
twitter.com/FoE_Canada
www.flickr.com/photos/foecanada
Overview: A large international charitable organization founded in 1978
Mission: To serve as a national voice for the environment, working with others to inspire the renewal of our communities & the earth, through research, education, advocacy & cooperation; *Member of:* Friends of the Earth International; Canadian Council for International Cooperation; Affiliation(s): Canadian Environmental Network
Chief Officer(s):
Beatrice Olivastri, CEO
Geoff Love, President
Finances: *Annual Operating Budget:* $250,000-$500,000; *Funding Sources:* 52% individuals; 19% corporate; 5% foundation; 11% government; 13% earned income/merchandise
Staff: 6 staff member(s); 10 volunteer(s)
Membership: 1,000-4,999; *Committees:* Campaigns: Stop Global Warming; Universal Water Security; Stop Devils Lake Outlet; Environmental Justice
Activities: *Speaker Service:* Yes

Friends of the Earth International (FoEI) / Fédération internationale des Amis de la Terre

International Secretariat, PO Box 19199, Amsterdam 1000 GD Netherlands
Tel: 31-20-622-1369; *Fax:* 31-20-639-2181
e-mail: foei@foei.org
www.foei.org
Also Known As: Amigos de la Tierra
Overview: A medium-sized international organization founded in 1971
Mission: To promote that environmental problems do not respect geographical & political boundaries; To cooperate with other organizations; To raise awareness that environmental, social, economic & political issues are interdependent; To encourage positive alternatives to policies & practices which cause ecological degradation; *Member of:* International Union for the Conservation of Nature; Affiliation(s): International Rivers Network; Rainforest Action Network; Rainforest Information Centre; EcoPeace; Action for Solidarity, Equality Environment & Development Europe
Environmental Activity: Creating networks of environmental, consumer, & human rights organizations worldwide
Chief Officer(s):
Meena Raman, Chair
Marijke Torfs, International Coordinator
Isis Alvarez, Office Coordinator
Finances: *Annual Operating Budget:* $250,000-$500,000; *Funding Sources:* Fees; Donations; Subsidies
Staff: 12 staff member(s); 4 volunteer(s)
Membership: Over 50,000; *Member Profile:* Comprises 71 member organizations, with a combined membership of nearly one million; the European member groups have formed FoE European Coordination with its own structure & offices in Brussels; each country member group is an autonomous body responsible for their own funding & campaigning strategies
Activities: Workshops on specific campaigns; Political lobbying; Information distribution

Friends of the Environment Foundation ***See*** TD Friends of the Environment Foundation

Friends of the Field Station (Delta Marsh) ***See*** Friends of the Delta Marsh Field Station

Friends of the Forestry Farm House Inc. (FFFH)

1903 Forestry Farm Dr., Saskatoon SK S7N 1G9
Tel: 306-249-1315
www.fffh.ca
Overview: A small local charitable organization founded in 1996
Mission: To restore the superintendent's residence of the Sutherland Forest Nursery Station which, from 1913 to 1965, distributed millions of trees to prairie farmers, who planted these trees on their land to create the miles of shelterbelts; Affiliation(s): Saskatoon Tourism; Saskatchewan Tourism
Chief Officer(s):
Bernie Cruikshank, President
maxic@yourlink
Finances: *Annual Operating Budget:* Less than $50,000; *Funding Sources:* Saskatchewan Heritage Foundation; City of Saskatoon Heritage Conservation Program
Staff: 3 staff member(s); 20 volunteer(s)
Membership: 1-99;; *Fees:* $10
Activities: Historical walking tour brochure; Victoria Day High Tea; Haunted House Program; Old Fashioned Christmas Party; *Speaker Service:* Yes

Friends of the Montréal Botanical Garden ***Voir*** Les Amis du Jardin botanique de Montréal

Friends of the Oldman River (FOR)

615 Deer Croft Way SE, Calgary AB T2J 5V4
Tel: 403-271-1408
Overview: A small local organization founded in 1987
Mission: To defend the Oldman River from environmentally destructive activities; to protect the Oldman River & decommission the Oldman Dam; *Member of:* Alberta Environmental Network; Affiliation(s): Canadian Environmental Network
Finances: *Annual Operating Budget:* Less than $50,000; *Funding Sources:* Membership dues; donations
Staff: 8 volunteer(s)
Membership: 1,000; *Fees:* $5
Activities: Sustainable community/watershed project in Cameroon; legal actions on water issues; *Speaker Service:* Yes

Friends of the Stikine Society (FOS)

#502, 620 View St., Victoria BC V8W 1J6
Tel: 250-383-5677
e-mail: stikine@islandnet.com
Overview: A small local organization founded in 1981
Mission: To maintain a free-flowing Stikine; to protect the integrity of the Stikine watershed & her peoples & the biodiversity of life & habitats within it; to achieve Canadian Heritage River status for the entire mainstream Stikine River; Affiliation(s): BC Environmental Network; Environmental Mining Council of BC; Outdoor Recreation Council of BC; Canadian Nature Federation; Canadian Environmental Network
Chief Officer(s):
Stan Tomandi, Co-Chair
Finances: *Annual Operating Budget:* Less than $50,000; *Funding Sources:* Membership fees; donations
Staff: 3 volunteer(s)
Membership: 100; *Fees:* $35
Activities: *Speaker Service:* Yes

Friends of the Trent-Severn Waterway (FTSW)

PO Box 572, Peterborough ON K9J 6Z6
Tel: 705-742-2251; *Fax:* 705-742-9644
Toll-Free: 800-663-2628
e-mail: info@ftsw.com
Overview: A small local organization founded in 1982
Mission: To assist Parks Canada to protect, preserve & interpret the natural historical, recreational & cultural resources of the Trent Severn Waterway; to encourage awareness & appreciation, develop & support programs to further enhance awareness; *Member of:* Canadian Parks Partnership
Chief Officer(s):
Mark Doherty, Contact
Finances: *Annual Operating Budget:* $50,000-$100,000
Staff: 1 staff member(s); 50 volunteer(s)
Membership: 275; *Fees:* $20 family; $50 corporate; *Committees:* Volunteer; Selection; Publicity; Trust; Environment; Marine Safety; Speakers Bureau; Tourism
Activities: *Speaker Service:* Yes

The Friends of West Kootenay Parks Society (FWKP)

PO Box 212, Nelson BC V1L 5P9
e-mail: contactus@fwkp.kics.bc.ca
www.fwkp.kics.bc.ca
Overview: A small local organization founded in 1988

Mission: To promote conservationist & recreational use of British Columbia parks in the West Kootenay area
Chief Officer(s):
Bill Bryce, Chair
Membership: *Fees:* $10
Activities: Kokanee Glacier Alpine Campaign; advocacy for parks; construction projects; fundraising; publicizing parks issues

Fundy Model Forest
#2, 701 Main St., Sussex NB E4E 7H7
Tel: 506-432-7575; *Fax:* 506-432-7562
e-mail: info@fundymodelforest.net
www.fundymodelforest.net
Overview: A small local organization
Member of: Canadian Model Forest Network
Chief Officer(s):
Nairn Hay, General Manager
Membership: 30

The Fur Council of Canada (FCC) / Conseil canadien de la fourrure
#1270, 1435, rue Saint-Alexandre, Montréal QC H3A 2G4
Tel: 514-844-1945; *Fax:* 514-844-8593
e-mail: info@furcouncil.com
www.furcouncil.com
Overview: A medium-sized national organization founded in 1964
Mission: To promote all aspects of the fur trade
Chief Officer(s):
Alan Herscovici, Executive Director
Angela Gurley, Secretary
Paula Lishman, President
Activities: Public education; fashion promotion & advertising; market development

Fur Institute of Canada (FIC) / Institut de la fourrure du Canada (IFC)
#701, 331 Cooper St., Ottawa ON K2P 0G5
Tel: 613-231-7099; *Fax:* 613-231-7940
e-mail: info@fur.ca
www.fur.ca
Overview: A medium-sized national organization founded in 1983
Mission: To promote the sustainable & wise use of Canadian fur resources; *Member of:* International Fur Trade Federation; World Conservation Union; International Association of Fish & Wildlife Agencies
Chief Officer(s):
Robert B. Cahill, Executive Director
rcahill@fur.ca
Bruce Williams, Chair
Mary Baskin, Manager, Corporate & Communications
mbaskin@fur.ca
Finances: *Funding Sources:* Membership dues; Donations
Membership: *Member Profile:* Trappers; Fur Farmers; Wholesale Fur Dealers; Fur Manufacturers & Processors; Fur Retailers; Aboriginal Organizations; Conservation Organizations; Animal Welfare Associations; Support Industries; Government of Canada; Provincial & Territorial Governments; *Committees:* Trap Research & Development; National Communications; Aboriginal Communications; External Communications
Activities: Coordinating the implementation of the Agreement on International Humane Trapping Standards in Canada; Presenting awards; Offering programs such as trap research & testing, conservation, international relations, communication, aboriginal communications, & funding; Researching; Promoting conservation efforts

Fur-Bearer Defenders (FBD)
#215, 3989 Henning Dr., Burnaby BC V5C 6P8
Tel: 604-435-1850; *Fax:* 604-435-1840
e-mail: fbd@banlegholdtraps.com
furbearerdefenders.com
www.facebook.com/FURfree?ref=ts
twitter.com/FurBearers
www.youtube.com/furbearerdefenders
Also Known As: The Association for the Protection of Fur-Bearing Animals
Previous Name: The Fur-Bearers
Overview: A medium-sized national charitable organization founded in 1944
Mission: To stop trapping cruelty & protect fur-bearing animals
Chief Officer(s):
Lesley Fox, Executive Director
lesley@furbearerdefeners.com
Finances: *Funding Sources:* Donations; Membership dues
Staff: 3 staff member(s)
Membership: *Fees:* $25; $200 lifetime
Activities: Providing information to government, media, activists, & the public; Launching campaigns to create awareness
Meetings/Conferences:
For more information see Trade Shows, Conferences and Seminars Chapter
3rd Annual Living with Wildlife 2013
September 2013 Vancouver, BC

The Fur-Bearers *See* Fur-Bearer Defenders

Furriers Guild of Canada
#211, 4174 Dundas St. West, Toronto ON M8X 1X3
Tel: 416-234-9494; *Fax:* 416-234-2244
e-mail: furriersguildca@ica.net
Merged from: Fur Trade Association of Canada (Ontario) Inc.; Retail Furriers Guild of Canada
Overview: A medium-sized national organization
Mission: To promote Canadian fur retailers
Membership: *Member Profile:* Canadian fur retailers
Activities: Providing programs such as community outreach

FutureWatch Environment & Development Education Partners
3101 Dundas St. West, Toronto ON M6P 1Z9
Tel: 416-926-1985; *Fax:* 416-926-0618
e-mail: info@futurewatch.net
www.futurewatch.net
Also Known As: FutureWatch
Overview: A small local organization founded in 1993
Mission: To foster the creation of healthy & sustainable communities locally & internationally
Chief Officer(s):
Lidia Ferreira, Executive Director
lidiaf@futurewatch.net

Ganaraska Hiking Trail Association (GHTA)
PO Box 693, 12 King St., Orillia ON L3V 6K7
Tel: 705-487-6457; *Fax:* 705-487-6459
e-mail: admin@ganaraska-hiking-trail.ca
www.ganaraska-hiking-trail.ca
Overview: A small local charitable organization founded in 1969
Mission: To construct & maintain a hiking trail from Port Hope to Glen Huron; to encourage recreational hiking & respect for the environment; *Member of:* Hike Ontario; Ontario Nature
Chief Officer(s):
Mike Pidwerbecki, President
mike@siberi-inn.ca
Finances: *Annual Operating Budget:* Less than $50,000; *Funding Sources:* Membership dues; donations
Staff: 120 volunteer(s)
Membership: 500; *Fees:* $20; *Committees:* Landowners; Trail; Guidebook
Activities: On the edge of the Laurentian Shield, within reach of Ontario's major cities, the trail forms a vital link in the National Trail network (500 km)

The Garden Clubs of Ontario (GCO)
PO Box 399, Hamilton ON L8N 3H8
www.gardenclubsofontario.ca
www.facebook.com/GardenClubsOfOntario
Overview: A small provincial organization founded in 1954
Mission: To stimulate knowledge & love of gardening amongst amateurs; to aid in the protection of native plants, trees, birds & soil; to encourage civic planning; *Member of:* Ontario Horticultural Association; World Association of Flower Arrangers
Chief Officer(s):
Janice Middleton, Contact
Finances: *Annual Operating Budget:* $50,000-$100,000
Staff: 15 volunteer(s)
Membership: 1,500 individual; *Committees:* Archives; Judges; National & International Liaison
Activities: Coordinates activities of 12 Garden Clubs in Ontario; Tour of Summer Gardens

Garden Institute of Alberta
#1406, 5328 Calgary Trail, Edmonton AB T6H 4J8
Tel: 780-461-9958; *Fax:* 780-469-6314
e-mail: slrempel@shaw.ca
Overview: A small provincial organization founded in 1997
Mission: To promote organic urban agriculture & gardening
Chief Officer(s):
Nancy Finlayson, Founder
Sharon Rempel, Founder & Project Manager
oldwheat@shaw.ca
Finances: *Annual Operating Budget:* $50,000-$100,000; *Funding Sources:* Fundraising projects
Membership: 1-99
Activities: *Speaker Service:* Yes

Gas Processing Association Canada (GPAC)
#400, 1040 - 7th Ave. SW, Calgary AB T2P 3G9
Tel: 403-244-4487; *Fax:* 403-244-2340
e-mail: info@gpacanada.com
www.gpacanada.com
Previous Name: Canadian Gas Processors Association
Overview: A medium-sized national organization founded in 1960
Mission: To promote interaction & exchange of ideas & technology that will add value to those who are involved with or affected by the hydrocarbon processing industry; Affiliation(s): Gas Processors Association (USA)
Chief Officer(s):
Josh Carter, President
Jeff McPhail, Director, Safety
Rob Nadalutti, Director, Academic
Erika Rauser, Coordinator, Events
Finances: *Funding Sources:* Membership dues
Staff: 17 volunteer(s)
Membership: 450 individual; *Fees:* $75 Regular, $9 Retired; *Member Profile:* Open to those employed in companies processing gaseous & liquid hydrocarbons; *Committees:* Safety; Research; Environment; Membership; Publications
Activities: ; *Library:*
Meetings/Conferences:
For more information see Trade Shows, Conferences and Seminars Chapter
Gas Processing Association Canada 25th Annual Operation & Maintenance Conference & Tradeshow
May 2013 Calgary, AB

Gateway Research Organization (GRO) Parent Name: Agricultural Research & Extension Council of Alberta
PO Box 5865, 10336 - 106 St., Westlock AB T7P 2G1
Tel: 780-349-4546; *Fax:* 780-349-5399
e-mail: grohome@telus.net
www.areca.ab.ca/grohome.html
Overview: A small local organization overseen by Agricultural Research & Extension Council of Alberta
Mission: To meet the changing needs of the agriculture industry in Alberta by working with producers & industry stakeholders; *Member of:* Agricultural Research & Extension Council of Alberta
Chief Officer(s):
Glen Pidsadowski, Chair
Reed Rigney, B.Sc., Office Manager
Michelle Holden, Agronomist, Crops Research, 780-307-5219
grocrops@telus.net
Membership: *Fees:* $30
Publications:
•Hayshaker [a publication of the Gateway Research Organization]
Type: Newsletter; *Frequency:* 2 pa

Gem & Mineral Club of Scarborough (GMCS)
#1B, 10 Chichester Pl., Toronto ON M1T 1G5
e-mail: scarbgemclub@gmail.com
www.scarbgemclub.ca
www.facebook.com/group.php?gid=181294731911802
Overview: A small local organization founded in 1963
Mission: To promote collecting & studying rocks, minerals, fossils, & lapidary work; *Member of:* Central Canadian Federation of Mineralogical Societies (CCFMS)
Environmental Activity: Encouraging conservation of natural resources
Membership: *Fees:* $15 single members; $20 families; *Member Profile:* Collectors & mineral enthusiasts in Scarborough, Ontario
Activities: Hosting monthly meetings from September to June; Exchanging information about the hobby; Organizing exhibits; Presenting auctions; Planning mineral & fossil collecting field trips; Providing workshops; *Awareness Events:* Gem Show, September; *Library:* Gem & Mineral Club of Scarborough Library
Publications:
•Strata Data: GMCS [Gem & Mineral Club of Scarborough] Newsletter
Type: Newsletter; *Frequency:* 10 pa
Profile: Upcoming events & articles about the hobby

Genome Canada
#2100, 150 Metcalfe St., Ottawa ON K2P 1P1
Tel: 613-751-4460; *Fax:* 613-751-4474
e-mail: info@genomecanada.ca

www.genomecanada.ca
www.facebook.com/GenomeCanada
twitter.com/genomecanada
www.youtube.com/genomecanada
Overview: A medium-sized national organization
Mission: To develop & implement a national strategy in genomics & proteomics research for the benefit of all Canadians; to enable Canada to become a world leader in genomics & proteomics research in key selected areas as agriculture, environment, fisheries, forestry & health
Chief Officer(s):
Pierre Meulien, President & CEO
pmeulien@genomecanada.ca

Geochemical Society

c/o Earth & Planetary Sciences Department, Washington University, #CB 11691, Brookings Dr., St. Louis MO 63130-4899 USA
Tel: 314-935-4131; *Fax:* 314-935-4121
e-mail: gsoffice@geochemsoc.org
www.geochemsoc.org
Overview: A medium-sized international organization
Mission: To encourage the application of chemistry to the solution of geological & cosmological problems; Affiliation(s): American Association for the Advancement of Science; International Union of Geological Sciences; Council of Scientific Society Presidents; Geological Society of America
Chief Officer(s):
Martin Goldhaber, President
mgold@usgs.gov
Samuel Mukasa, Vice-President
mukasa@umich.edu
Neil Sturchio, Secretary
sturchio@uic.edu
Louise Criscenti, Treasurer
ljcrisc@sandia.gov
Seth Davis, Manager, Business
seth.davis@geochemsoc.org
Membership: *Member Profile:* An international membership with interests in fields such as high & low-temperature geochemistry, fluid-rock interaction, organic geochemistry, petrology, isotope geochemistry, & meteoritics; *Committees:* Joint Publications; Nominations; Program; V.M. Goldschmidt Award; F.W. Clarke Award; C.C. Patterson Award; Geochemical Fellows; OGD Executive; Alfred Treibs Award; OGD Best Paper Award; AAAS Liaison
Meetings/Conferences:
For more information see Trade Shows, Conferences and Seminars Chapter
Goldschmidt Conference 2013
August 2013 Florence
Goldschmidt Conference 2014
June 2014 Sacramento, CA
Goldschmidt Conference 2015
August 2015 Prague
Goldschmidt Conference 2016
2016 Yokohama
Publications:
•Elements Magazine [a publication of the Geochemical Society]
Type: Journal; *Frequency:* Bimonthly; *Price:* Free with membership in the Geochemical Society
Profile: Theme issues with peer-reviewed invited papers related to the mineral & geochemical sciences
•GCA: Geochimica et Cosmochimica Acta
Type: Journal; *Frequency:* Biweekly; *Editor:* Dr. Frank Podosek
Profile: Scientific contributions related to geochemistry & cosmochemistry
•G-Cubed (Geochemistry, Geophysics, Geosystems)
Type: Journal
Profile: Research papers on the chemistry, physics, & biology of earth & planetary processes
•Geochemical News
Type: Newsletter; *Frequency:* Quarterly; *Editor:* Stephen Komor
Profile: News of the Geochemical Society
•Geochemical Society Special Publication Series
Profile: Scientifically significant collections of related, original papers on topics such as magmatic processes, fluid-mineral interactions, stable isotope geochemistry, mineralspectroscopy, mantle petrology, & volcanic, geothermal, & ore-forming fluids

Geological Association of Canada (GAC) / Association géologique du Canada (AGC)

Department of Earth Sciences, Memorial University of Newfoundland, #ER4063, Alexander Murray Bldg., St. John's NL A1B 3X5
Tel: 709-737-7660; *Fax:* 709-737-2532
e-mail: gac@mun.ca
www.gac.ca
Overview: A large national organization founded in 1947
Mission: To advance the wise use of geoscience in academic, professional, & public circles; *Member of:* Canadian Federation of Earth Sciences; Affiliation(s): American Geophysical Union; Atlantic Geoscience Society; Canadian Geophysical Union; Canadian Quaternary Association; Canadian Society of Petroleum Geologists; Toronto Geological Discussion Group
Chief Officer(s):
Peter Bobrowsky, President, 613-947-0333
pbobrows@nrcan.gc.ca
Richard Wardle, Vice-President, 709-753-2074
richwardle@nl.rogers.com
Toby Rivers, Secretary-Treasurer, 709-864-8392
trivers@mun.ca
Karen Johnston, Manager, Finance & Administration, 709-864-2399
kajohnston@mun.ca
Karen Dawe, Director, Publications, 709-864-2151
kfmdawe@mun.ca
Finances: *Funding Sources:* Membership fees; Publication sales
Membership: 1,000-4,999;; *Fees:* $10 students & teachers; $20 spousal; $70 - $80 seniors & unemployed; $105 - $120 full members; $250 universities; $500 supporters; $1000 sponsors; *Committees:* Science Program; Finance; Publications; Communications
Activities: Providing professional development opportunities for members; Disseminating information about geoscience; Offering networking opportunities; *Internships:* Yes; *Speaker Service:* Yes
Meetings/Conferences:
For more information see Trade Shows, Conferences and Seminars Chapter
Geological Association of Canada (GAC) & the Mineralogical Association of Canada (MAC) 2013 Joint Annual Meeting
May 2013 Winnipeg, MB
Geological Association of Canada (GAC) & the Mineralogical Association of Canada (MAC) 2014 Joint Annual Meeting
May 2014 Fredericton, NB
Publications:
•Geolog
Type: Magazine; *Frequency:* Quarterly; *Accepts Advertising*; *Price:* Free with membership in the Geological Association of Canada
Profile: News items & short articles of interest to Geological Association of Canada members
•Geological Association of Canada Membership Directory
Type: Directory
•Geoscience Canada
Type: Journal; *Frequency:* Quarterly; *Accepts Advertising*; *Editor:* R.A. Wilson (reg.wilson@gnb.ca); *Price:* Free with membership in the GeologicalAssociation of Canada
Profile: A general interest, earth-science journal featuring review papers, topical articles, conference reports, book reviews, & commentary

Edmonton Section

c/o Jill Weiss, Twin Atria Building, Alberta Geological Survey, 4999 - 98 Ave., 4th Fl., Edmonton AB T6B 2X3
www.egs.ab.ca
Chief Officer(s):
Heather Budney, President
Rob L'Heureux, Treasurer
Matt Grobe, Manager, Publications, 780-427-2843
matt.grobe@ercb.ca

Newfoundland & Labrador Section

c/o Heather Rafuse, Department of Natural Resources, Geological Survey, PO Box 8700, St. John's NL A1B 4J6
gac.esd.mun.ca/nl/nfsection.htm
Chief Officer(s):
Sam Bentley, President
sbentley@mun.ca
Joe McQuaker, Vice-President
jmacquaker@mun.ca
Larry Hicks, Secretary-Treasurer
larryhicks@gov.nl.ca
Andrew Kerr, Chair, Technical Program
andykerr@gov.nl.ca

Québec Section

c/o Pierre Cousineau, Sciences appliquées, U. du Québec à Chicoutimi, 555, boul de l'Université, Pavillon principal, Chicoutimi QC G7H 2B1
gac.esd.mun.ca/AQUEST/index_anglais.htm
Chief Officer(s):
Robert Marquis, Contact, Membership
robert.marquis@mrnf.gouv.qc.ca

Vancouver (Cordilleran) Section

Bentall Centre, PO Box 398, Stn. A, Vancouver BC V6C 2N2
e-mail: webmaster@gac-cs.ca
www.gac-cs.ca
Chief Officer(s):
Jim Ryan, President
Peter Friz, Treasurer

Winnipeg Section

#360, 1395 Ellice Ave., Winnipeg MB R3G 3P2
Tel: 204-945-6561; *Fax:* 204-945-1406
e-mail: wgs-gac@hotmail.com
www.umanitoba.ca/faculties/science/geological_sciences/gac wpg/
Chief Officer(s):
Scott Anderson, Contact
scott.anderson@gov.mb.ca

Geomatics for Informed Decisions Network

Pavillon Louis-Jacques-Casault, Cité Universitaire, #2306, 1055, av du Séminaire, Québec QC G1V 0A6
Tel: 418-656-7758; *Fax:* 418-656-2611
e-mail: info@geoide.ulaval.ca
www.geoide.ulaval.ca
Also Known As: GEOIDE
Overview: A medium-sized national organization
Member of: Networks of Centres of Excellence
Chief Officer(s):
Chantal Arguin, President
Nicholas Chrisman, Scientific Director
Nicholas.Chrisman@geoide.ulaval.ca

Geomatics Industry Association of Canada (GIAC) / Association canadienne des entreprises de géomatique

Covent Glen, PO Box 62009, 6491 Jeanne D'Arc Blvd., Ottawa ON K1C 2S0
Fax: 613-851-1256
e-mail: dhtessier@giac.ca
www.giac.ca
Previous Name: Canadian Association of Aerial Surveyors
Overview: A medium-sized national organization founded in 1961
Mission: To strengthen business climate; to maintain cooperative relations with government; to promote expanded role for members in provision of geomatics products & services; to encourage adoption by governments of improved policies & practices for procurement of geomatics products & services; to promote member firms as source of high quality, professional services; to promote Canadian geomatics industry abroad.; *Member of:* Alliance of Manufacturers & Exporters Canada
Chief Officer(s):
Dave Gariepy, Chairman
Finances: *Annual Operating Budget:* $100,000-$250,000; *Funding Sources:* Membership fees
Staff: 2 staff member(s)
Membership: 100 firms; *Committees:* Export

Géomètres professionnels du Canada ***See*** Professional Surveyors Canada

Geotechnical Society of Edmonton (GSE)

c/o City of Edmonton, Engineering Services Section, 11004 - 190 St. NW, Edmonton AB T5S 0G9
Tel: 780-944-7653
e-mail: gse@geotechnical.ca
www.geotechnical.ca
Overview: A small local organization founded in 1969
Chief Officer(s):
Kristen Tappenden, President
Membership: 190; *Fees:* $15
Activities: Student presentations; lecture series & talks; professional development events; Reinforced Soil Wall Competition

Glass Packaging Institute (GPI)

#510, 700 North Fairfax St., Alexandria VA 22314 USA
Tel: 703-684-6359; *Fax:* 703-299-1543
e-mail: info@gpi.org
www.gpi.org

Overview: A medium-sized national organization
Chief Officer(s):
Joseph J. Cattaneo, President
jcattaneo@gpi.org

Global Crop Protection Federation; International Group of National Associations of Manufacturers of Agrochemical Products *See* Croplife International

Global, Environmental & Outdoor Education Council (GEOEC)
c/o Barnett House, Alberta Teachers' Association, 11010 - 142 St. NW, Edmonton AB T5N 2R1
Tel: 780-987-7315; *Fax:* 780-455-6481
Toll-Free: 800-232-7208
e-mail: info@geoec.org
www.geoec.org
Previous Name: Environmental & Outdoor Education Council of Alberta
Overview: A small provincial organization founded in 1976
Mission: To encourage professional development for teachers in the area of global, environmental, & outdoor education; *Member of:* Alberta Teachers' Association
Chief Officer(s):
Rita Poruchny, President, 403-949-3444
reporuchny@cbe.ab.ca
Chenoa Marcotte, Secretary
chenoamarcotte@hotmail.com
Karen Whitehead, Treasurer
kuntzhead@shaw.ca
Membership: *Fees:* $12.50 students; $25 regular & life memberships; $30 subscription; *Member Profile:* Active members of the Alberta Teachers' Association; Students members of the Alberta Teachers' Association; Individuals or corporations ineligible for active or associate membership in the Alberta Teachers' Association, such as teaching assistants, parents, & libraries
Activities: Providing workshops
Publications:
•Connections [a publication of the Global, Environmental & Outdoor Education Council]
Type: Newsletter; *Frequency:* Quarterly; *Editor:* Noel Jantzie; *Price:* Free with membership in the Global,Environmental & Outdoor Education Council
Profile: Articles & features related to global, environmental, & outdoor education

GLOBE Foundation
World Trade Centre, #578, 999 Canada Pl., Vancouver BC V6C 3E1
Tel: 604-695-5001; *Fax:* 604-695-5019
Toll-Free: 800-274-6097
e-mail: info@globe.ca
www.globe.ca
Overview: A medium-sized national organization founded in 1993
Mission: To strive to find practical business-oriented solutions to environmental problems; To assist companies & individuals realize the value of economically viable environmental business opportunities
Environmental Activity: Promoting the business case for sustainable development
Chief Officer(s):
John D. Wiebe, President & Chief Executive Officer
ceo@globe.ca
Freddie Frankling, Vice-President, International Relations
freddie.frankling@globe.ca
Nancy Wright, Vice-President, Marketing
nancy.wright@globe.ca
Cindy Leung, Director, Finance & Administration
cindy.leung@globe.ca
John Gough, Manager, Information Technology
john.gough@globe.ca
Zahida Kanani, Manager, Registration & Database
zahida.kanani@globe.ca
Finances: *Funding Sources:* Sponsorships
Activities: Researching & consulting; Managing projects; Providing opportunities for communication; Developing partnerships
Meetings/Conferences:
For more information see Trade Shows, Conferences and Seminars Chapter
GLOBE Foundation 2013 7th Annual EPIC Sustainable Living Festival
July 2013 Vancouver, BC
GLOBE Foundation 2013 1st Annual EPIC: The Sustainable Living Expo, Dubai
2013 Dubai
GLOBE 2014 13th Biennial Conference & Trade Fair on Business & the Environment
March 2014 Vancouver, BC
Publications:
•GLOBE-Net Environmental Business E-Newsletter
Type: Newsletter; *Frequency:* Weekly

Government Refuse Collection & Disposal Association *See* Solid Waste Association of North America

Grain Elevator & Processing Society (GEAPS)
4248 Park Glen Rd., Minneapolis MN 55416 USA
Tel: 952-928-4640; *Fax:* 952-929-1318
e-mail: info@geaps.com
www.geaps.com
Overview: A medium-sized international organization founded in 1937
Mission: To provide a forum for the analysis & exchange of information affecting the industries; to advance educational & professional qualifications of the members; to represent the interests of the members in governmental activities; to foster good business ethics & social responsibility throughout the membership; to communicate with the trade media & general public concerning the issues of interest to the members & the industries; to provide technical information on grain handling & storage
Chief Officer(s):
David Krejci, Executive Vice-President
Finances: *Annual Operating Budget:* $500,000-$1.5 Million; *Funding Sources:* Membership dues; publications
Staff: 7 staff member(s)
Membership: 2,500 individual; *Fees:* US$185; *Member Profile:* Individuals across the grain operations industry worldwide; *Committees:* Grain Handling & Storage, Facility Design; Safety & Health; Environmental Responsibility
Activities: Publications; education & training; trade shows; conferences; *Awareness Events:* International Technical Conference & Expositions; *Speaker Service:* Yes; *Rents Mailing List:* Yes

Grain Farmers of Ontario
Ontario AgriCentre, #201, 100 Stone Rd. West, Guelph ON N1G 5L3
Fax: 519-767-9713
Toll-Free: 800-265-0550
e-mail: info@gfo.ca
www.gfo.ca
Merged from: Ontario Soybean Growers; Ontario Corn Producers' Association; Ontario Wheat Producers' Marketing Bd.
Overview: A medium-sized provincial organization
Mission: To develop an innovative & successful business environment to benefit farmer members; To promote the Ontario grain industry to become a global leader
Chief Officer(s):
Barry Senft, Chief Executive Officer
bsenft@gfo.ca
Ryan Brown, Vice-President, Operations
rbrown@gfo.ca
John Cowan, Vice-President, Strategic Development
jcowan@gfo.ca
Todd Austin, Manager, Marketing
taustin@gfo.ca
Crosby Devitt, Manager, Research & Market Development
cdevitt@gfo.ca
Tom Farfaras, Manager, Finance & Administration
tfarfaras@gfo.ca
Erin Fletcher, Manager, Public Affairs & Communications
efletcher@gfo.ca
Brenda Miller-Sanford, Manager, Projects
bmsanford@gfo.ca
Membership: 15,000-49,999; *Member Profile:* Ontario's growers of soybeans, corn, & wheat
Activities: Researching; Expanding markets; Encouraging new uses for Ontario grains; Engaging in advocacy activities
Meetings/Conferences:
For more information see Trade Shows, Conferences and Seminars Chapter
Grain Farmers of Ontario 2013 March Classic: Driving Ontario's Grain Industry to Global Leadership
March 2013 London, ON

Grand Manan Whale & Seabird Research Station (GMWSRS) / Centre de recherche sur la vie marine de Grand Manan
24 Rte. 776, Grand Manan NB E5G 1A1
Tel: 506-662-3804
e-mail: info@gmwsrs.org
www.gmwsrs.org
www.facebook.com/122376994520768
twitter.com/GMWSRS
Overview: A small local charitable organization founded in 1981
Mission: To conduct research on the Bay of Fundy ecosystem, concentrating on marine mammals & seabirds; To operate a public display of Bay of Fundy Marine Fauna; *Member of:* New Brunswick Environmental Network
Chief Officer(s):
Laurie Murison, Managing Director
Finances: *Annual Operating Budget:* $50,000-$100,000
Staff: 4 volunteer(s)
Activities: *Speaker Service:* Yes; *Library:* Gaskin Memorial Library; by appointment

Grand Manan Wildlife Association
PO Box 926, 212 Ingalls Head Rd., Grand Manan NB E5G 4M1
Tel: 506-662-3508; *Fax:* 506-662-3508
Overview: A small local organization founded in 1975
Member of: New Brunswick Wildlife Federation
Chief Officer(s):
Brian Urquhart, President
John Cunningham, Secretary, 506-662-3837
Membership: 75; *Fees:* $30

Grand River Conservation Foundation (GRCF)
PO Box 729, 400 Clyde Rd., Cambridge ON N1R 5W6
Tel: 519-621-2761; *Fax:* 519-621-4844
Toll-Free: 877-294-7263
e-mail: foundation@grandriver.ca
www.grandriver.ca
www.facebook.com/grandriverconservation
twitter.com/grandriverca
www.youtube.com/user/grandriverca
Previous Name: Grand River Foundation
Overview: A small local charitable organization founded in 1965
Mission: To provide leadership & support within the community of the Valley of the Grand River for the protection, conservation, responsible use & management of its natural resources, in response to the needs & wishes & for the ongoing enjoyment of its residents, as well as of the broader community of our province & country
Chief Officer(s):
Joe Farwell, P.Eng, CAO
jfarwell@grandriver.ca
Sara Wilbur, Executive Director, Development
swilbur@grandriver.ca
Finances: *Annual Operating Budget:* Less than $50,000; *Funding Sources:* Individuals, groups & corporations
Staff: 1 staff member(s); 22 volunteer(s)
Membership: 1-99
Activities: *Speaker Service:* Yes
Awards:
•S.C. Johnson & Son Ltd. Environmental Scholarship (Scholarship)
Annual award for a student enrolled in an environmental sciences program with an emphasis on manufacturing, eocnomics, business, chemistry or related applications at a university in the Grand River watershed area *Amount:* $1,500

Grand River Foundation *See* Grand River Conservation Foundation

Graphic Arts Industries Association; Canadian Printing & Imaging Association *See* Canadian Printing Industries Association

Grasslands Naturalists (GN)
Police Point Park Nature Centre, PO Box 2491, Police Point Dr. NE, Medicine Hat AB T1A 8G8
Tel: 403-529-6225; *Fax:* 403-526-6408
www.natureline.info/gn/index.php
Also Known As: Society of Grasslands Naturalists
Overview: A small local charitable organization founded in 1991
Member of: Nature Alberta; Affiliation(s): Canadian Nature Federation
Environmental Activity: Promoting environmental research & consulting; Encouraging conservation projects
Chief Officer(s):
Marty Drut, Contact

Membership: 140; *Fees:* $20 individuals; $25 families; *Committees:* Land; Wildlife
Activities: Offering educational opportunities, such as field trips & lectures; Publishing a bi-weekly newspaper column; *Library:* Police Point Park Nature Centre Resource Centre

Great Lakes Commission / Commission des Grands Lacs

Eisenhower Corporate Park, #100, 2805 Industrial Way South, Ann Arbor MI 48104-6791 USA
Tel: 734-971-9135; *Fax:* 734-971-9150
www.glc.org
Mission: The Commission is a binational, public agency dedicated to the use, management & protection of water, land & other natural resources of the Great Lakes-St. Lawrence system. In partnership with 8 Great Lakes states & provinces of Ontario & Québec, the Commission applies sustainable development principles addressing issues of resource management, environmental protection, transportation & sustainable development. The Commission provides information on public policy issues; a forum for developing & coordinating public policy; & a unified, system-wide voice to advocate member interests.
Chief Officer(s):
Kenneth G. Johnson, Chair
Tim A. Eder, Executive Director
teder@glc.org

Great Lakes Institute for Environmental Research (GLIER)

401 Sunset Ave., Windsor ON N9B 3P4
Tel: 519-253-3000; *Fax:* 519-971-3616
e-mail: glier@uwindsor.ca
www.uwindsor.ca/glier
Overview: A small local organization founded in 1981
Mission: Multidisciplinary facility with members from many disciplines, including biology, geology, chemistry, engineering, marine biology, molecular biology, genetics and ecology.
Chief Officer(s):
Brian Fryer, Contact
bfryer@uwindsor.ca

The Great Lakes Research Consortium (GLRC)

SUNY College of Environmental Science & Forestry, 253 Baker Labs, 1 Forestry Dr., Syracuse NY 13210 USA
Tel: 315-470-6720; *Fax:* 315-470-6970
e-mail: glrc@esf.edu
www.esf.edu/glrc
Overview: A medium-sized international organization founded in 1986
Mission: To facilitate research & scholarship on Great Lakes problems; to provide opportunities for training & education of students; to disseminate important information & research findings
Chief Officer(s):
Greg Boyer, Executive Director
glboyer@esf.edu
Heather Carringon, Coordinator, Great Lakes Research Consortium
Finances: *Annual Operating Budget:* $100,000-$250,000
Staff: 2 staff member(s)
Membership: 18 institutional; *Fees:* $500-1,000 per campus; *Member Profile:* New York State colleges & universities + 9 Ontario universities
Activities: Speakers exchange; task forces; small grants program; annual student/faculty conferences; *Speaker Service:* Yes

Great Lakes United (GLU) / Union Saint Laurent Grands Lacs

#302, 260 Patrick St., Ottawa ON K1N 5K5
Tel: 519-591-7503
e-mail: glu@glu.org
www.glu.org
Overview: A small international charitable organization founded in 1982
Mission: To ensure a healthy, safe, & sustainable St. Lawrence River & Great Lakes region
Environmental Activity: Working to protect the Great Lakes & St. Lawrence River freshwater ecosystem
Chief Officer(s):
John Jackson, Executive Director & Director, Clean Production & Toxics
jjackson@glu.org
Bonnie Danni, Director, Finance & Development
bonnie@glu.org
Jennifer Nalbone, Director, Navigation & Invasive Species
jen@glu.org
Sylvie Trudel, Director, Québec Operations
sylvie@glu.org
Lauren Cheal, Contractor, Communications
lcheal@glu.org
Brent Gibson, Contact, Press Inquiries, 613-482-1324 Ext. 509
Finances: *Funding Sources:* Donations; Membership fees
Membership: *Fees:* $50 individuals; $75 supporting individuals; $35 - $125 organizations (based upon annual budget)
Activities: Engaging in advocacy activities; Conducting campaigns around issues such as invasive species, navigation, restoration, energy, & water levels & flows

Greater Hamilton Technology Enterprise Centre *See* Hamilton Technology Centre

Greater Toronto Rose & Garden Society Parent Name: Ontario Horticultural Association

9 Tarlton Rd., Toronto ON M5P 2M5
Tel: 416-485-5907
e-mail: GTRoses@aol.com
www.gardenontario.org/site.php/rosegarden
Also Known As: Toronto Rose
Previous Name: York Rose & Garden Society
Overview: A small local organization founded in 1979 overseen by Ontario Horticultural Association
Mission: Dedicated to cultivation & enjoyment of roses; *Member of:* Canadian Rose Society, American Rose Society, Ontario Horticultural Association
Chief Officer(s):
Iris Hazen, Contact
Membership: 150; *Fees:* $10 regular; $15 family
Activities: Annual "Roses" garden tour; lectures; public meetings

Greater Toronto Water Garden & Horticultural Society (GTWGHS)

4691 Hwy. 7A, RR#1, Nestleton Station ON L0B 1L0
Tel: 416-438-4862
e-mail: info@onwatergarden.com
www.onwatergarden.com
Previous Name: Ontario Water Garden Society
Overview: A small provincial organization
Member of: Ontario Horticultural Association
Chief Officer(s):
Laura Grant, Contact, 416-422-2164, Fax: 416-422-2820
Joachim G. Doehler, President
Peter Poot, Secretary
Membership: *Fees:* $20 single; $25 family

Green Action Centre (RCM)

303 Portage Ave., 3rd Fl., Winnipeg MB R3B 2B4
Tel: 204-925-3777; *Fax:* 204-942-4207
Toll-Free: 866-394-8880
www.resourceconservation.mb.ca
www.facebook.com/group.php?gid=134760813229244
Previous Name: Recycling Council of Manitoba; Resource Conservation Manitoba Inc.
Overview: A medium-sized provincial organization founded in 1985
Mission: To promote ecological sustainability by developing alternatives to currently unsustainable practices; our principal activity is environmental education; our partners & clients include businesses, schools, non-profit groups, governments, recyclers, home gardeners & general public; *Member of:* Canadian Environment Network; Manitoba Eco-Network; Manitoba Environmental Industries Association
Chief Officer(s):
Randall McQuaker, Executive Director, 204-925-3770
Finances: *Annual Operating Budget:* $100,000-$250,000; *Funding Sources:* 3 levels of government; corporate; private foundations; membership dues
Staff: 11 staff member(s); 20 volunteer(s)
Membership: 200; *Committees:* Membership; Policy
Activities: Public Infoline; Environmental Speaker's Bureau; The R-Report; Public Forums; Green Commuting Program; Composting Education Program; *Speaker Service:* Yes; *Library:* Resource Centre

The Green Brick Road (GBR)

#408, 429 Danforth Ave., Toronto ON M4K 1P1
Tel: 416-421-9816; *Fax:* 416-537-7518
Toll-Free: 800-473-3638
e-mail: gbr@look.ca
Overview: A small local organization founded in 1990
Mission: To distribute teaching materials related to environmental & global education for all grade levels
Chief Officer(s):
John Tersigni, Executive Director

Green Calgary

#100, 301 - 14th St. NW, Calgary AB T2N 2A1
Tel: 403-230-1443; *Fax:* 403-230-1458
e-mail: info@greencalgary.org
www.greencalgary.org
www.facebook.com/home.php#!/pages/Green-Calgary/136497856363082
twitter.com/greencalgary
Previous Name: Clean Calgary Association
Overview: A medium-sized local charitable organization founded in 1978
Mission: To provide educational programs which assist Calgarians to develop an environmentally friendly lifestyle; *Member of:* Alberta Environmental Network; Ecotrust; City of Calgary Environment Advisory Committee
Chief Officer(s):
Patricia Cameron, Executive Director
patricia@greencalgary.org
Finances: *Annual Operating Budget:* $250,000-$500,000; *Funding Sources:* Municipal government; corporate; casino; goods & services
Staff: 8 staff member(s); 125 volunteer(s)
Membership: 90; *Fees:* $15 low-income/student; $50 individual; $75 non-profit; $200 business; *Member Profile:* Concern for environment & positive, proactive programs
Activities: Waste reduction & water conservation; *Speaker Service:* Yes

Green Communities Association *See* Green Communities Canada

Green Communities Canada (GCC)

PO Box 928, 416 Chambers St., 2nd Fl., Peterborough ON K9J 7A5
Tel: 705-745-7479; *Fax:* 705-745-7294
e-mail: info@greencommunitiescanada.org
www.gca.ca
Previous Name: Green Communities Association
Overview: A small national organization founded in 1995
Mission: To support member organizations in achieving environmental sustainability; *Member of:* Canadian Renewable Energy Alliance
Chief Officer(s):
Clifford Maynes, Executive Director, 705-745-7479 Ext. 118
Beth Jones, Associate Director & Manager, EcoDriver, 705-745-7479 Ext. 152
Jacky Kennedy, Director, Walking Programs, 416-488-7263, Fax: 416-488-2296
Bhim Subba, Director, Home Energy, 705-745-9183
Heather Kirby, Manager, Well Aware, 705-745-7479 Ext. 114
Bruce Roxburgh, Manager, Green Information Technology, 705-745-7479 Ext. 117
Membership: *Fees:* $500 full membership; $250 associate membership; *Member Profile:* Non-profit community-based organizations that deliver environmental programs
Activities: Sharing information & resources; joint member projects; Water Programs; Energy Programs; Walking Programs/Safe Routes to School; Green IT
Publications:
•Green Community News
Type: Newsletter; *Frequency:* Weekly
Profile: Association activities, resources, & events

Green Kids Inc.

#251, 162-2025 Corydon Ave., Winnipeg MB R3P 0N5
Tel: 204-940-4745; *Fax:* 204-201-0676
Toll-Free: 800-441-6751
e-mail: jeff@greenkids.com
www.greenkids.com
Overview: A small national charitable organization founded in 1991
Mission: To empower children to take positive action & change the world
Chief Officer(s):
Daina Leitold, Tour Manager
Finances: *Annual Operating Budget:* $100,000-$250,000
Staff: 5 staff member(s); 4 volunteer(s)
Activities: Educates children (K-8) about environmental issues in schools using interactive theatre;

Green Party of Canada (GPC) / Parti vert du Canada

PO Box 997, Stn. B, #204, 396 Cooper St., Ottawa ON K1P 5R1

Tel: 613-562-4916; *Fax:* 613-482-4632
Toll-Free: 888-868-3447
e-mail: info@greenparty.ca
www.greenparty.ca
twitter.com/canadiangreens
Overview: A medium-sized national organization founded in 1983
Mission: To promote a platform that includes debt reduction, eco-jobs, saving Canada's forests, supporting small business, use of soft energies, sovereignty for First Nations, & a guarantee of full rights for women; *Member of:* CanAmex; World Greens Coordination
Chief Officer(s):
Elizabeth May, Leader
leader@greenparty.ca
Maureen Murphy, Executive Director
maureen.murphy@greenparty.ca
Finances: *Annual Operating Budget:* $50,000-$100,000; *Funding Sources:* Individual contributions
Staff: 1 staff member(s); 40 volunteer(s)
Membership: 4,000; *Fees:* $10+; *Committees:* Election Coordinating; Officer/Functionary Review; Finance/Administration; Green Convenors
Activities: *Speaker Service:* Yes

The Green Party of Manitoba
Parent Name: Green Party of Canada
PO Box 26023, Stn. Maryland, 120 Sherbrook St., Winnipeg MB R3C 3R3
Tel: 204-488-2831
Toll-Free: 866-742-4292
e-mail: info@greenparty.mb.ca
www.greenparty.mb.ca
facebook.com/profile.php?id=43307539939
twitter.com/Green_Party_MB
www.youtube.com/user/GreenPartyofManitoba
Also Known As: Manitoba Greens
Overview: A medium-sized provincial organization founded in 1996 overseen by Green Party of Canada
Chief Officer(s):
James Beddome, President
James R. Beddome, Party Leader
Membership: *Fees:* $5

Green Party of New Brunswick / Parti Vert du Nouveau Brunswick
Parent Name: Green Party of Canada
PO Box 3723, Stn. B, 403 Regent St., Bottom Fl., Fredericton NB E3A 5L8
Tel: 506-447-8499; *Fax:* 506-447-8489
Toll-Free: 888-662-8683
e-mail: info@greenpartynb.ca
www.greenpartynb.ca
Overview: A small provincial organization overseen by Green Party of Canada
Chief Officer(s):
David Coon, Party Leader

Green Party of Nova Scotia
Parent Name: Green Party of Canada
PO Box 36044, 5665 Spring Garden Rd., Halifax NS B3J 3S9
e-mail: gpns@greenparty.ns.ca
www.greenparty.ns.ca
Overview: A small provincial organization overseen by Green Party of Canada
Chief Officer(s):
John Percy, Party Leader
leader@greenparty.ns.ca

The Green Party of Ontario (GPO) / Parti Vert d'Ontario
Parent Name: Green Party of Canada
PO Box 1132, Stn. F, #035, 67 Mowat Ave., Toronto ON M4Y 2T8
Tel: 416-977-7476; *Fax:* 416-977-5476
Toll-Free: 888-647-3366
e-mail: admin@gpo.ca
www.gpo.ca
Previous Name: The Ontario Greens
Overview: A small provincial organization founded in 1983 overseen by Green Party of Canada
Chief Officer(s):
Mike Schreiner, Leader
Becky Smit, Executive Director, 647-830-6486
Finances: *Funding Sources:* Membership dues
Staff: 1 staff member(s); 900 volunteer(s)
Membership: 1,000; *Fees:* $25; *Committees:* Policy; Candidate Facilitation
Activities: Annual Fall Meeting; *Library:* by appointment

Green Party of Prince Edward Island
Parent Name: Green Party of Canada
PO Box 104, 101 Kent St., Charlottetown PE C1A 7K2
Tel: 902-569-2068
e-mail: peigreens@gmail.com
greenparty.pe.ca
Overview: A small provincial organization overseen by Green Party of Canada
Chief Officer(s):
Peter Bevan Baker, Party Leader

Green Party of Québec ***Voir*** Parti Vert du Québec

Green Party Political Association of British Columbia (GPBC)
Parent Name: Green Party of Canada
PO Box 8088, Stn. Central, Victoria BC V8W 3R7
Toll-Free: 888-473-3686
e-mail: info@greenparty.bc.ca
www.greenparty.bc.ca
www.facebook.com/groups/bcgreens
twitter.com/janesterk
Also Known As: Green Party of BC
Overview: A medium-sized provincial charitable organization founded in 1983 overseen by Green Party of Canada
Mission: To form healthy communities with diverse economies by involving the citizens of British Columbia in the political process; To offer voters in British Columbia fiscal responsibility, socially progressive policies, & environmental sustainability
Chief Officer(s):
Rebecca Helps, Executive Director
execdirector@greenparty.bc.ca
Jane Sterk, Leader
David Pearce, Treasurer & Financial Agent
Finances: *Funding Sources:* Donations
Membership: 4,000; *Fees:* Donation; *Member Profile:* Residents of British Columbia, fourteen years of age & older, who are not members of any other provincial political party; *Committees:* Fundraising; Administration; Media; Organizing; Membership

Green Roofs for Healthy Cities (GRHC)
406 King St. East, Toronto ON M5A 1L4
Tel: 416-971-4494; *Fax:* 416-971-9844
www.greenroofs.org
Overview: A medium-sized international organization founded in 1999
Mission: To promote the green roof industry throughout North America
Chief Officer(s):
Jeffrey Bruce, Chair
Steven Peck, President
speck@greenroofs.org
Dan Slone, Secretary
Paul Sheehy, Treasurer
Membership: *Member Profile:* Corporate suppliers & manufacturers; Individuals who practise the art of living architecture; Supporters (LAM subscribers); *Committees:* Research; Policy; Membership; Training & Accreditation; Corporate Members; Technical; GreenSave Calculator; Conference; Green Walls; Integrated Building Water Management; Growing Medium
Activities: Increasing awareness of the environmental, economic, & social benefits of green roofs & green walls; Providing education; Offering networking opportunities
Publications:
•Living Architecture Monitor
Type: Magazine; *Frequency:* Quarterly; *Accepts Advertising*; *Editor:* Caroline Nolan
Profile: For Green Roofs for Healthy Cities members only

Greenest City
220 Cowan Ave., Toronto ON M6K 2N6
Tel: 647-438-0038
e-mail: info@greenestcity.ca
www.greenestcity.ca
www.facebook.com/GreenestCityToronto
www.twitter.com/Greenest_City
pinterest.com/greenestcity
Overview: A small local organization
Mission: To reduce pollution; To regenerate urban life; To promote social equity
Chief Officer(s):
Sandi Trillo, Secretary
Activities: Walk to School Day; Active & Safe Routes to School; Walking School Bus; projects & campaigns embrace community diversity & engage people in finding locally appropriate solutions to global environmental problems

Greenpeace Canada
33 Cecil St., Toronto ON M5T 1N1
Tel: 416-597-8408; *Fax:* 416-597-8422
Toll-Free: 800-320-7183
e-mail: supporter.ca@greenpeace.org
www.greenpeace.org/canada
www.facebook.com/greenpeace.canada
twitter.com/greenpeaceCA
www.youtube.com/user/GreenpeaceCanada
Overview: A large international charitable organization founded in 1971
Mission: Greenpeace is an independent, non-profit organization best known for non-violent direct actions to raise awareness on issues such as biodiversity, pollution of the Earth, nuclear threats & disarmament; it brings public opinion to bear on decisions makers. Public protest is only one of many Greenpeace strategies; it conducts scientific, economic & political research, publicizes environmental problems, recommends environmentally sound solutions & lobbies for change.; *Member of:* Greenpeace International; Canadian Renewable Energy Alliance
Environmental Activity: Campaigns: Climate Change; Tar Sands; Nuclear Power; Boreal Forest; Great Bear Rainforest; Marine Fish; GMO Foods
Chief Officer(s):
Bruce Cox, Executive Director
Ann Rowan, Chair
Finances: *Annual Operating Budget:* $1.5 Million-$3 Million; *Funding Sources:* Donations; shop sales
Staff: 35 staff member(s)
Membership: 100,000+ in Canada + over 2.5 million internationally; *Fees:* $30
Activities: Communications; e-news; reports; *Speaker Service:* Yes; *Library:* Information Office; Open to public
Publications:
•Forest Views [a publication of Greenpeace Canada]
Type: Newsletter
•Greenpeace Canada Annual Report
Type: Yearbook
•Greenpeace Canada E-News
Type: Newsletter

Edmonton Office
6328 - 104 St. NW, Edmonton AB T6H 2K9
Tel: 780-430-9202; *Fax:* 780-430-9282

Montréal Office
454, Laurier est, 3e étage, Montréal QC H2J 1E7
Tel: 514-933-0021; *Fax:* 514-933-1017

Vancouver Office
1726 Commercial Dr., Vancouver BC V5N 4A3
Tel: 604-253-7701; *Fax:* 604-253-0114

Greenpeace International
Ottho Heldringstraat 5, Amsterdam 1066 AZ Netherlands
Tel: 31-20-718-2000; *Fax:* 31-20-718-2002
e-mail: supporter.services.int@greenpeace.org
www.greenpeace.org
www.facebook.com/greenpeace.international
twitter.com/Greenpeace
www.youtube.com/greenpeacevideo
Also Known As: Stichting Greenpeace Council
Overview: A large international organization founded in 1971
Mission: To protect the environment from the threats of pollution, global warming, & the depletion of natural resources; To protect endangered species, such as whales, dolphins, & seals
Environmental Activity: Climate change; forests; oceans; agriculture; toxic pollution; nuclear
Chief Officer(s):
Ana Toni, Chair
Kumi Naidoo, Executive Director
Finances: *Annual Operating Budget:* $1.5 Million-$3 Million
Staff: 175 staff member(s)
Membership: 40 countries
Activities: Campaigning; non-violent direct action; publishing environmental reports
Publications:
•Greenpeace Annual Report
Type: Yearbook

Greenpeace USA

#300, 702 H St. NW, Washington DC 20001 USA
Tel: 202-462-1177; *Fax:* 202-462-4507
Toll-Free: 800-326-0959
e-mail: info@wdc.greenpeace.org
www.greenpeaceusa.org
www.facebook.com/greenpeaceusa
twitter.com/greenpeaceusa
www.youtube.com/profile?user=greenpeaceusa
Overview: A large international charitable organization founded in 1971
Mission: To use non-violent confrontation to expose global environmental problems & to promote solutions essential to a green & peaceful future; to protect biodiversity in all its forms; to end the nuclear threat & promote global disarmament; Affiliation(s): Greenpeace International
Chief Officer(s):
Kumi Naidoo, International Executive Director
Phil Radford, Executive Director
Finances: *Annual Operating Budget:* Greater than $5 Million
Membership: 4 million; *Fees:* $30
Activities: *Internships:* Yes; *Speaker Service:* Yes; *Rents Mailing List:* Yes

Greenspace Alliance of Canada's Capital

PO Box 55085, 240 Sparks St., Ottawa ON K1P 1A1
e-mail: greenspace@greenspace-alliance.ca
www.greenspace-alliance.ca
Overview: A medium-sized local organization founded in 1997
Mission: To preserve green spaces in the National Capital area.
Chief Officer(s):
Cheryl Doran, Chair
Membership: *Fees:* $15 group; $5 student; $30 associate

Grey Wooded Forage Association (GWFA) Parent Name: Agricultural Research & Extension Council of Alberta

PO Box 1448, 5039 - 45 St., Rocky Mountain House AB T4T 1B1
Tel: 403-844-2645; *Fax:* 403-844-2624
e-mail: gwfa1@telus.net
www.areca.ab.ca/gwfahome.html
Overview: A small local organization overseen by Agricultural Research & Extension Council of Alberta
Mission: To create awareness about the uses of forages; to help the agricultural community be more environmentaly & economically sustainable through knowledge & innovation; *Member of:* Agricultural Research & Extension Council of Alberta
Chief Officer(s):
Albert Kuipers, Manager
gwfa2@telus.net
Muriel Finkbeiner, Office Manager
Membership: *Fees:* $20
Publications:
•The Blade [a publication of the Grey Wooded Forage Association]
Type: Newsletter; *Frequency:* Monthly
•The Newsletter [a publication of the Grey Wooded Forage Association]
Type: Newsletter; *Frequency:* 2 pa

Grocery Products Manufacturers of Canada; Food & Consumer Products Manufacturers of Canada *See* Food & Consumer Products of Canada

Groundfish Enterprise Allocation Council

1362 Revell Rd., Manotick ON K4M K84
Tel: 613-692-8249; *Fax:* 613-692-8250
e-mail: bchapman@sympatico.ca
www.geaconline.com
Overview: A medium-sized national organization founded in 1997
Mission: To generally promote the common interests of its members; to promote the wise use, development & conservation of the Atlantic Canadian groundfish resource; To provide an organization that permits Atlantic groundfish enterprise allocation license holders to speak with a unified voice to the general public & all levels of government on matters of broad concern to the members; To provide an organization that permits groundfish enterprise allocation license holders to interface with similar organizations in Canada; To conduct research that has the potential to produce information & data that will be helpful or useful to the members; to monitor regional, national & international corporate & political activities which have a bearing on the members; To provide a platform for the views of members with regard to these activities
Chief Officer(s):
Bruce Chapman, Executive Director

Groupe de recherche d'intérêt public de l'Ontario *See* Ontario Public Interest Research Group

Groupe de recherche d'intérêt public du Québec - McGill *Voir* Québec Public Interest Research Group - McGill

Groupe de recherche en écologie sociale (GRESOC) / Social Ecology Research Group (SERG)

Dépt. de Sociologie, Université de Montréal, CP 6128, Succ. Centre, Montréal QC H3C 3J7
Tél: 514-343-5959; *Téléc:* 514-343-5722
Aperçu: *Dimension:* petite; *Envergure:* locale; Organisme sans but lucratif; fondée en 1978
Mission: Le GRESOC est constitué de chercheurs universitaires qui s'intéressent à l'écologie sociale, à l'écosociologie et à la sociologie de l'environnement; les recherches en cours portent sur le mouvement vert (écologisme et environnementalisme), le développement durable, les pluies acides, les déchets, et les aspects sociaux des changements environnementaux globaux; plusieurs rapports de recherches, livres, chapitres et articles ont été publiés; *Membre de:* Réseau des Groupes Écologistes Québécois; Conseil Régional de l'Environnement de Montréal
Membre(s) du bureau directeur:
Jean-Guy Vaillancourt, Directeur
Finances: *Budget de fonctionnement annuel:* Moins de $50,000; *Fonds:* Hydro-Québec; Agence de l'éfficacité energétique; étalez votre science
Personnel: 2 bénévole(s)
Membre: 25; *Critères d'admissibilite:* Chercheurs universitaires
Activités: *Stagiaires:* Oui; *Bibliothèque:* Bibliothèque publique

Groupe de recherches sur les transports au Canada *See* Canadian Transportation Research Forum

Gulf of Maine Council on the Marine Environment

c/o New Brunswick Dept. of Environment & Local Government, PO Box 6000, 850 Lincoln Rd., Fredericton NB E3B 5H1
Tel: 506-457-8946; *Fax:* 506-457-7823
www.gulfofmaine.org
Mission: This U.S.-Canadian partnership of government & non-government organizations works to maintain & enhance environmental quality in the Gulf of Maine to allow for sustainable resource use. The Council organizes conferences & workshops; offers grants & recognition awards; conducts environmental monitoring; provides science translation to management; raises public awareness about the Gulf. The secretariat rotates annually among the member jurisdictions. Initiatives include: Gulf of Maine Mapping Initiative (GOMMI), comprehensive seafloor imaging, mapping & biological & geological surveys; habitat restoration grants program (U.S. only); Action Plan grants program; Gulf of Maine Times, a quarterly newspaper; Gulfwatch Monitoring Program, which helps to assess the fate & impacts of toxic contaminants in the Gulf of Maine.; Affiliation(s): ME State Planning Office; NB Department of Environment; naturesource communications, NH; NH Department of Environmental Services; NS Department of Fisheries & Aquaculture
Chief Officer(s):
Robert Capozi, New Brunswick Contact
robert.capozi@gnb.ca
Sophia Foley, Nova Scotia Contact
foleysm@gov.ns.ca

Habitat Acquisition Trust (HAT)

PO Box 8552, Victoria BC V8W 3S2
Tel: 250-995-2428; *Fax:* 250-920-7975
e-mail: hatmail@hat.bc.ca
www.hat.bc.ca
www.facebook.com/HabitatAcqTrust
twitter.com/HabitatAcqTrust
Overview: A small local charitable organization founded in 1996
Mission: To promote the preservation of the natural environment on Southern Vancouver Island & the Southern Gulf Island by: conserving habitats by acquisition, conservation coverants or other legal mechanisms; & promoting habitat stewardship, education & research; *Member of:* Land Trust Alliance of British Columbia; Affiliation(s): Victoria Natural History Society
Chief Officer(s):
Jennifer Eliason, Executive Director
Finances: *Annual Operating Budget:* $250,000-$500,000; *Funding Sources:* Private; foundations; provincial & municipal government
Staff: 4 staff member(s); 100 volunteer(s)
Membership: 100-499;; *Fees:* $30 regular; $45 family; $100 corporate; $20 Victoria Natural History Society member
Activities: Land purchase; conservation covenants (easements); environmental education; *Library:* Bob Ogilvie Bioregional Resource Library; Open to public by appointment

Habitat faunique Canada *See* Wildlife Habitat Canada

Halifax Field Naturalists (HFN)

c/o Nova Scotia Museum of Natural History, 1747 Summer St., Halifax NS B3H 3A6
e-mail: hfninfo@yahoo.ca
halifaxfieldnaturalists.ca/hfnWP
Overview: A small local charitable organization founded in 1975
Mission: To promote the enjoyment & preservation of Nova Scotia's history & natural areas through education, discussion & fellowship; *Member of:* Federation of Nova Scotia Naturalists; Affiliation(s): Canadian Nature Federation; Canadian Parks & Wilderness Society; The Nature Conservancy of Canada
Chief Officer(s):
Janet Dalton, President
Finances: *Annual Operating Budget:* Less than $50,000; *Funding Sources:* Membership dues; sales; donations
Membership: 120; *Fees:* $15 student; $20 individual; $25 family; $30 supporting/institutional; $5 Nature Nova Scotia; *Committees:* Programme; Newsletter; Conservation; Colin Stewart Conservation Award; Membership; Socials; Web Site
Activities: Presentations, field trips; *Speaker Service:* Yes
Publications:
•The Halifax Field Naturalist
Type: Newsletter; *Frequency:* Quarterly

Halton Foundation *See* Conservation Halton Foundation

Hamilton Industrial Environmental Association (HIEA)

PO Box 35545, Hamilton ON L8H 7S6
Tel: 905-561-4432
e-mail: info@hiea.org
www.hiea.org
Overview: A medium-sized local organization
Mission: To improve the local environment - air, land and water - through joint and individual activities, and by partnering with the community to enhance future understanding of environmental issues and help establish priorities for action.
Chief Officer(s):
Jim Stirling, Chair
Membership: 15 companies

Hamilton Naturalists' Club (HNC)

PO Box 89052, Hamilton ON L8S 4R5
Tel: 905-381-0329
e-mail: info@hamiltonnature.org
www.hamiltonnature.org
www.facebook.com/386408715600
Overview: A small local charitable organization founded in 1919
Mission: To promote the enjoyment of nature through environmental appreciation & conservation; To foster public interest & education in the appreciation & study of nature; To encourage wise use & conservation of natural resources; to promote environmental protection; *Member of:* Federation of Ontario Naturalists; Affiliation(s): Canadian Nature Federation
Chief Officer(s):
Michael Fischer, President, 905-526-0325
fischermj@sympatico.ca
Finances: *Annual Operating Budget:* Less than $50,000; *Funding Sources:* Donations; membership dues; grants
Staff: 80 volunteer(s)
Membership: 500; *Fees:* $30 senior/student; $35 individual/institution; $40 family; $750 lifetime; *Committees:* Bird Study Group; Conservation; Hamilton Bird Records; Education; Sanctuary; Newsletter; Plant Study Group
Activities: Monthly public meetings from Sept.-May; public hikes; *Speaker Service:* Yes

Hamilton Technology Centre (HIT)

#200, 7 Innovation Dr., Flamborough ON L9H 7H9
Tel: 905-689-2400; *Fax:* 905-689-2200
e-mail: penny.gardiner@hamilton.ca
www.hitcentre.ca
www.linkedin.com/groups/Hamilton-Economic-Development-3932028
www.facebook.com/HamiltonEcDev
twitter.com/hamiltonecd
Previous Name: Greater Hamilton Technology Enterprise Centre
Overview: A small local organization founded in 1977

Mission: To create wealth-generating jobs by helping form & grow technology-focussed business; *Member of:* City of Hamilton
Chief Officer(s):
Penny Gardiner, Facilities Director
Finances: *Annual Operating Budget:* $250,000-$500,000; *Funding Sources:* City of Hamilton
Staff: 2 staff member(s)
Activities: Incubating, mentoring & coaching tech business start-ups

Hanley & District Agricultural Society

PO Box 172, c/o 320 Walter Scott St., Hanley SK S0G 2E0
Overview: A small local organization founded in 1982
Mission: The Society works to improve agriculture & the quality of life in the community by providing a forum for discussion of agricultural issues. It also encourages conservation of natural resources.; *Member of:* Saskatchewan Association of Agricultural Societies & Exhibitions
Chief Officer(s):
Patti Prosofsky, President, 306-544-2226
Finances: *Annual Operating Budget:* Less than $50,000
Staff: 30 volunteer(s)
Activities: Agricultural & domestic displays; beef show; light horse show; co-ed slow pitch; men's fastball; children's activities

Harmony Foundation of Canada / Fondation Harmonie du Canada

PO Box 50022, #15, 1594 Fairfield Rd., Victoria BC V8S 1G1
Tel: 250-380-3001; *Fax:* 250-380-0887
e-mail: harmony@islandnet.com
www.harmonyfdn.ca
www.facebook.com/117724434937243
www.youtube.com/user/harmonyfdn
Overview: A medium-sized international charitable organization founded in 1985
Mission: To encourage development which is socially & environmentally sustainable; To strive towards ecological stability, long-term prosperity, & social harmony
Chief Officer(s):
Michael Bloomfield, Founder & Executive Director
Robert Bateman, Honorary Chair
Jean-Pierre Soublière, President
Nick Mosky, Secretary
Robert Van Tongerloo, Treasurer
Finances: *Funding Sources:* Donations; Sponsorships
Activities: Working with organizations & individuals around the world through the Building Sustainable Societies Program; Improving environmental practices in workplaces; Providing community service opportunities for young people; Publishing action guides for homes, workplaces, & communities; Implementing training programs; Forming partnerships to establish meaningful results around environment & development issues; Educating about sustainable development & global change

Hawk Migration Association of North America (HMANA)

C/O John Weeks, Membership Secretary, 51 Pheasant Run, North Granby CT 06060 USA
www.hmana.org
Overview: A medium-sized international organization founded in 1974
Mission: To conserve raptor populations through the scientific study, enjoyment & appreciation of hawk migration
Chief Officer(s):
Iain MacLeod, Chair
Finances: *Annual Operating Budget:* Less than $50,000
Membership: 900; *Fees:* US$25; family US$40; club US$50; benefactor US$100; corporate US$250; life US$500
Activities: *Speaker Service:* Yes

Health & Safety Conference Society of Alberta (HSCSA)

PO Box 38009, Calgary AB T3K 5G9
Tel: 403-236-2225; *Fax:* 780-455-1120
e-mail: info@hsconference.com
www.hsconference.com
Overview: A small provincial organization
Mission: To promote the importance of health & safety for safer workplaces
Chief Officer(s):
Guy Clyne, President
Arlene Ledi-Thom, Vice-President
Dianne Paulson, Secretary
Jerald Richelhoff, Treasurer
Finances: *Funding Sources:* Sponsorships
Membership: 1-99; *Member Profile:* Health & safety associations; Professional societies; Employer associations
Activities: Hosting an annual multi-partner conference; Providing health & safety education
Meetings/Conferences:
For more information see Trade Shows, Conferences and Seminars Chapter
Alberta Health & Safety 2013 12th Annual Conference & Trade Fair
October 2013 Calgary, AB

Health Food Dealers Association *See* Canadian Health Food Association

Health Sciences Association of Alberta (HSAA) / Association des sciences de la santé de l'Alberta (ind.)

10212 - 112 St., Edmonton AB T5K 1M4
Tel: 780-488-0168; *Fax:* 780-488-0534
Toll-Free: 800-252-7904
www.hsaa.ca
Overview: A medium-sized provincial organization founded in 1971
Mission: To conduct activities as a labour union to enhance the quality of life for HSAA members & society
Chief Officer(s):
Elisabeth Ballermann, President
elisabethb@hsaa.ca
Patricia Heffel, Director, Administrative Services
patriciah@hsaa.ca
Lynette McAvoy, Director, Labour Relations
lynettem@hsaa.ca
Roni Hermanutz, Manager, Human Resources
ronih@hsaa.ca
Joanne Monro, Officer, Occupational Health & Safety
joannem@hsaa.ca
Scott Pattison, Officer, Communications, 780-405-4684
scottpat@hsaa.ca
Finances: *Funding Sources:* Membership dues; Merchandise sales
Membership: 17,000; *Member Profile:* Professional, paramedical technical, general support, & EMS employees in the public & private health care sectors of Alberta; *Committees:* Bylaws & Resolutions; Community Relations; Elections/Credentials; EMAC; Environmental; Finance; Human Rights & Equality; Labour Relations Appeals; Members' Benefits; OHS&W; Political Action / Education
Activities: Offering educational workshops; Awarding bursaries
Meetings/Conferences:
For more information see Trade Shows, Conferences and Seminars Chapter
Health Sciences Association of Alberta 2013 42nd Annual General Meeting
April 2013 Banff, AB
Publications:
•HSAA Challenger
Type: Magazine; *Frequency:* Quarterly; *Accepts Advertising*; *Editor:* Scott Pattison (scottpat@hsaa.ca)
Profile: Feature articles, labour relations updates, HSAA activities, affiliate & member news, forthcoming workshops & events

Health Sciences Association of Saskatchewan (HSAS) / Association des sciences de la santé de la Saskatchewan (ind.)

#42, 1736 Quebec Ave., Saskatoon SK S7K 1V9
Tel: 306-955-3399; *Fax:* 306-955-3396
Toll-Free: 888-565-3399
e-mail: hsasstoon@sasktel.net
www.hsa-sk.com
www.facebook.com/124779960928913
Overview: A medium-sized provincial organization founded in 1972
Mission: To conduct activities as an independent union representing its members who are health sciences professionals in Saskatchewan
Chief Officer(s):
Karen Wasylenko, President
president@hsa-sk.com
Anne Robins, Vice-President
mt@hsa-sk.com
Cara McDavid, Secretary
sw3@hsa-sk.com
Karen Kinar, Treasurer
respiratory@hsa-sk.com
Bill Craik, Executive Director, 306-585-7757
bill@hsa-sk.com
Membership: 2,900+; *Member Profile:* Health professionals from all health regions in Saskatchewan; *Committees:* Annual Convention; Constitutional; Emergency Fund; Grievance; Charitable Donations / Professional Contributions; Communications; Education Fund; Regional Council Development; Provincial Negotiating; Finance
Activities: Conducting public relations campaigns to increase public awareness about the profession; Presenting bursaries & scholarships

Healthy Indoors Partnership (HIP) / Partenariat pour des environnements intérieurs sains

2699 Priscilla St., Ottawa ON K2B 7E1
Tel: 613-224-3800
e-mail: mail@cullbridge.com
www.cullbridge.com/Projects/Healthy_Indoors.htm
Overview: A small national organization
Mission: To involve private, public & not-for-profit organizations & individuals in the development, implementation & financing of a broad range of collaborative actions to improve indoor environments in Canada
Chief Officer(s):
Jay Kassirer, President
kassirer@healthyindoors.com
Membership: *Fees:* $100

Heating, Refrigeration & Air Conditioning Institute of Canada (HRAI) / Institut canadien du chauffage, de la climatisation et de la réfrigération (ICCCR)

Bldg. 1, #201, 2800 Skymark Ave., Mississauga ON L4W 5A6
Tel: 905-602-4700; *Fax:* 905-602-1197
Toll-Free: 800-267-2231
e-mail: hraimail@hrai.ca
www.hrai.ca
www.facebook.com/pages/HRAI/322711681086830
twitter.com/HRAI_Canada
www.youtube.com/hraichannel
Overview: A large national organization founded in 1969
Mission: To serve the HRAI membership & HVACR industry in Canada by facilitating industry solutions, coordinating a strong national membership, representing the industry to their publics, conducting accountable association activities, providing quality member/customer services, & educating & training industry members
Chief Officer(s):
Warren J. Heeley, President
Martin Luymes, Vice-President
Andrew Hall, Director, Energy Conservation/Demand Management Programs
Joanne Spurrell, Director, Education & Market Development
Heather Grimoldby-Campbell, Manager, Administration & Wholesalers Division
Daisy Del Prado, Communications Coordinator
Finances: *Annual Operating Budget:* $1.5 Million-$3 Million; *Funding Sources:* Membership dues; education programs
Staff: 24 staff member(s)
Membership: 900 corporate; *Member Profile:* Voting members divided into three divisions based on industry sector - manufacturers, wholesalers & contractors; Associate members include utilities, municipalities, manufacturers' agents & distributors, builders, educational institutions, building maintenance, other associations, & consultants; *Committees:* C.M.X. Show; Technical; Education
Activities: Owns the Canadian Mechanicals Exposition (C.M.X.), a national trade show held every two years in Toronto at the end of March; educational programs provide industry members with the technical & management competence required to design & install HVAC systems & operate successful HVAC businesses

British Columbia - Regional Chapter

Refrigeration & Air Conditioning Contractors Assn. of BC, 26121 Fraser Hwy., Aldergrove BC V4X 2E3
e-mail: raccabc@hrai.ca
Chief Officer(s):
Blaire Masztalar, Chapter President, 604-856-8644

Manitoba - Regional Chapter

c/o Refrigeration & Air Conditioning Contractors Assn. of Manitoba, 807 McLeod Ave., Winnipeg MB R2G 0Y4
Chief Officer(s):
Ryan Dalgleish, Regional Manager, 204-956-5888
rdalgleish@hrai.ca
Dave Derksen, Site Contact, 204-949-2788

Ontario - Brant/Haldimand/Norfolk Chapter
c/o Bowser Technical Ltd., 200 St. George St., Brantford ON N3R 1W4
e-mail: brant@hrac.ca
www.hracbrant.com
Chief Officer(s):
Dave Murtland, President, 519-428-4000, Fax: 519-428-2591
Dara Bowser, Secretary, 519-756-9116, Fax: 519-756-9227

Ontario - Essex/Kent/Lambton Chapter
c/o Ideal Heating & Cooling Ltd, PO Box 1030, Stn. A, 1900 North Talbot Rd., Windsor ON N9A 6P4
e-mail: essex_kent_lambton@hrai.ca
Chief Officer(s):
Peter Steffes, Chapter President, 519-737-6797

Ontario - Golden Horseshoe Chapter
c/o Arvin Air Systems, 331 Glover Rd., Stoney Creek ON L8E 5M2
e-mail: goldenhorseshoe@hrai.ca
Chief Officer(s):
Joe Muchynski, Site Contact, 905-643-6646

Ontario - Greater Toronto Area Chapter
c/o Carrier Canada Ltd., 1515 Drew Rd., Mississauga ON L5S 1Y8
Chief Officer(s):
Marisa Soulis, Chapter Meeting Manager, 905-405-3201

Ontario - Huronia Chapter
c/o LifeBreath Indoor Air Systems, 511 McCormick Blvd., Oro Station ON N5W 4C8
Chief Officer(s):
Wayne Fischer, Chapter President, 705-791-3418
wfischer@airiabrands.com

Ontario - Kawartha Lakes Chapter
c/o Coulter Heating & Air Conditioning, 89 West St., Fenelon Falls ON K0M 1N0
Chief Officer(s):
Laverne Coulter, Chapter President, 705-887-5559

Ontario - London Chapter
c/o Lennox Industries (Canada) Ltd., #5, 1 Adelaide St. North, London ON N6B 3P4
Chief Officer(s):
Sean Dinel, Chapter Secretary, 519-433-5581
sean.dinel@lennoxind.com

Ontario - Loyalist Chapter
c/o McKeown & Wood Ltd., 373 Centre St. North, Napanee ON K7R 1P7
Chief Officer(s):
James Wood, Chapter President, 613-354-6505

Ontario - National Capital Region Chapter
c/o E.N. Blue Ltd., PO Box 535, Stittsville ON K2S 1A6
Chief Officer(s):
Darrell McCagg, Chapter President, 613-831-1430, Fax: 613-831-2969
enblue@enblue.com

Ontario - Waterloo/Wellington Chapter
c/o BRC Mechanical Inc., 92 Woolwich St. South, Breslau ON N0B 1M0
Chief Officer(s):
Janette Smith, Chapter Secretary, 519-648-2222

Québec - Montréal Chapter
c/o Corporation des maîtres mécaniciens en tuyauterie du Québec, 8175, boul Saint-Laurent, Montréal QC H2P 2M1
Chief Officer(s):
André Bergeron, Site Contact, 514-382-2668

Helicopter Association of Canada (HAC)

#500, 130 Albert St., Ottawa ON K1P 5G4
Tel: 613-231-1110; *Fax:* 613-369-5097
www.h-a-c.ca
Overview: A small national organization
Mission: To ensure the financial viability of the Canadian civil helicopter industry; To promote flight safety; To expand utilization of helicopter transport
Chief Officer(s):
Teri Northcott, Chair
teri_northcott@telus.net
Fred L. Jones, BA LLB, President & Chief Executive Officer, 613-231-1110 Ext. 239, Fax: 613-236-2361
Fred.Jones@h-a-c.ca
Sylvain Seguin, Vice-President & Director, Marketing
sseguin@canadianhelicopters.com
Gary McDermid, Secretary
gary.mcdermid@helifor.com
Maureen Crockett, Treasurer
mcrockett@dt-avn.com
Membership: *Member Profile:* Individuals who operate helicopters in Canada; Non-operator organizations; *Committees:* Air Taxi; Finance; Flight Training Units; Heli Logging; IFR / EMS; Law Enforcement; Maintenance & Manufacturing; Oil & Gas Producers; Safety; Utility Flight Operations
Activities: Educating members, civil servants, & the public about issues important to the industry; Providing opportunities for members to exchange maintenance practices & common issues
Meetings/Conferences:
For more information see Trade Shows, Conferences and Seminars Chapter
Helicopter Association of Canada 2013 17th Annual Convention & Trade Show
November 2013 Vancouver, BC
Helicopter Association of Canada 2014 18th Annual Convention & Trade Show
2014
Publications:
•Class "D" External Loads Training Guidelines
Type: Guide
Profile: An outline of industry training guidelines to support operations specifications allowing carriage of class D external loads
•HAC [Helicopter Association of Canada] Newsletter
Type: Newsletter
Profile: Association & general information updates
•Helicopter Association of Canada Utility Flight Operations Committee Best Practices Safety Guide for Helicopter Operators
Type: Guide; *Number of Pages:* 90
Profile: Chapters include background information, basic utility infrastructure, helicopter patrol safeguidelines, power line construction & maintenance, safety guide for utilities in evaluating & selecting qualified helicopter contractors, & safety guide for utilities performing utility flight operations
•Helicopter Guidelines for Canadian Onshore Seismic Operations
Type: Guide; *Number of Pages:* 89
Profile: Sections include safety management systems (SMS), program operations, training, competency, & staffing levels, personal protective equipment (PPE), helicopterperformance & role equipment standards, & base camp / staging area / helipad requirements
•Heli-skiing Guidelines
Type: Guide
Profile: Information about performance, weight management, ski baskets, pilot flight & duty time, weather, training, safety briefings, & flagging
•Mountain Flying Training Guidelines
Type: Guide
Profile: Helicopter Association of Canada recommended guidelines for mountain fluying training
•Pilot Competencies for Helicopter Wildfire Operations - Best Practices Training & Evaluation
Type: Guide; *Number of Pages:* 26
Profile: Guidance for members of the Helicopter Association of Canada, prepared by the Air Tax Committee, Pilot Qualifications WorkingGroup

Henry A. Wallace Center for Agricultural & Environmental Policy at Winrock International

#1200, 1621 Kent St. North, Arlington VA 22209-2134 USA
Tel: 703-525-9430; *Fax:* 703-525-1744
e-mail: wallacecenter@winrock.org
www.winrock.org/wallace
Also Known As: Wallace Center
Previous Name: Institute for Alternative Agriculture
Overview: A small national charitable organization founded in 1983
Mission: To serve as publisher of reliable scientific information on alternative agriculture; to sponsor research & education outreach programs; to be a voice for alternative agriculture; to act as a contact for farmers & others who seek information on diversified, sustainable farming systems; to encourage & facilitate the adoption of low-cost, resource-conserving & environmentally sound farming methods
Chief Officer(s):
Erin Caricofe, Program Assistant
John Fisk, Director
Finances: *Annual Operating Budget:* $500,000-$1.5 Million
Staff: 10 staff member(s)
Membership: 995; *Fees:* US$16 individual; *Member Profile:* Farmers, researchers, Extension personnel, policy makers & consumers
Activities: Research; policy analysis & development; education & outreach; scientific & general audience publications; symposia;

Herb Society of Manitoba

PO Box 61004, RPO Grant Park, Winnipeg MB R3M 3X8
Tel: 204-785-8690
e-mail: herbs@herbsocietymb.com
www.herbsocietymb.com
Overview: A small national organization founded in 1995
Mission: To promote knowledge, use & enjoyment of herbs through education, programs, research & sharing the experience of its members with the community
Chief Officer(s):
Vera Paul, President
pres@herbsocietymb.com
Membership: 100; *Fees:* $25
Activities: *Awareness Events:* International Herb Day, Oct. 14; *Library:* The Bev Lloyd Memorial Library; Open to public
Publications:
•Prairie Sage Quarterly
Type: Newsletter; *Frequency:* Quarterly
Profile: Available to members

Heritage Agricultural Society

PO Box 2188, 5411 - 51 St., Stony Plain AB T7Z 1X7
Tel: 780-963-2777; *Fax:* 780-963-0233
www.multicentre.org
Also Known As: Multicultural Heritage Centre
Overview: A small local charitable organization founded in 1974
Mission: The Society is a non-profit organization dedicated to the preservation of the region's cultural heritage. It acts as custodian to the Multicultural Heritage Centre, a living museum of 2 historic buildings which reflect local history & Western Canadian pioneer life. The Society is a registered charity, BN: 107478760RR0001.
Chief Officer(s):
Rebecca Still, Museum Manager
rebecca@multicentre.org
Finances: *Annual Operating Budget:* $500,000-$1.5 Million; *Funding Sources:* Alberta Museums Association; Donations
Staff: 20 staff member(s); 180 volunteer(s)
Membership: 250; *Fees:* $10
Activities: Tours; School programs for classes K-12; Farm demonstrations; Farmers' market; Canada Day; *Library:* Wild Rose Library; Open to public

Heritage Association of Antigonish

20 East Main St., Antigonish NS B2G 2E9
Tel: 902-863-6160
e-mail: antheritage@parl.ns.ca
www.heritageantigonish.ca
Overview: A small local organization founded in 1982
Member of: Federation of the Nova Scotian Heritage
Membership: 60; *Fees:* $7 individual; $10 family

Heritage Canada Foundation (HCF) / Fondation Héritage Canada

190 Bronson Ave., Ottawa ON K1R 6H4
Tel: 613-237-1066; *Fax:* 613-237-5987
Toll-Free: 866-964-1066
e-mail: heritagecanada@heritagecanada.org
www.heritagecanada.org
www.facebook.com/heritagecanadafoundation
twitter.com/HeritageCanada
Overview: A large national charitable organization founded in 1973
Mission: To foster & ensure the understanding, protection & sustainable evolution of Canada's heritage buildings & historic places; Affiliation(s): Canadian Heritage Network
Chief Officer(s):
Ross Keith, Chair
Natalie Bull, Executive Director, 613-237-1066 Ext. 222
nbull@heritagecanada.org
Carolyn Quinn, Director, Communications & Editor, 613-237-1066 Ext. 229
cquinn@heritagecanada.org
Finances: *Annual Operating Budget:* Greater than $5 Million; *Funding Sources:* Grants; individuals; corporate; endowment
Staff: 20 staff member(s); 3 volunteer(s)
Membership: 2,400 voting members; 100,000 network members; *Fees:* $40 individual; $25 student; $70 family; $150 organization

Activities: *Awareness Events:* Heritage Day, 3rd Monday of Feb.; National Flag of Canada Day, Feb. 15; *Internships:* Yes; *Speaker Service:* Yes; *Library:* Building Stories; by appointment
Awards:
•Gabrielle Léger Award for Lifetime Achievement in Heritage Conservation (Award)
Recognizes outstanding work in architectural conservation in Canada; this is an annual national award to an individual who has contributed outstanding community service in the cause of heritage conservation
•The National Achievement Awards (Award)
Established 1989, these awards recognize individuals or groups for achievements in the conservation of heritage in the natural or cultural environments; designed to be presented jointly by Heritage Canada & established provincial or territorial umbrella groups or associations that are members of Heritage Canada & that have juried awards programs & awards ceremonies; each group or association, called a partner, will be fully responsible for choosing its candidate within prescribed criteria & eligibility rules; in this way, Heritage Canada also recognizes these partners for their dedication & commitment to excellence in heritage preservation
•Lieutenant Governor's Award for Outstanding Achievement in Heritage Conservation at the Provincial/Territorial Level (Award)
Established 1979 to recognize outstanding work in architectural conservation on a provincial level by an individual or group
Eligibility: It must be demonstrated that the applicant's continuous efforts in the field of heritage conservation have benefited the province where the foundation's annual meeting is being held; applicants must be sponsored by an organized heritage group &/or elected officials at any level of government
Publications:
•Annual Report [a publication of the Heritage Canada Foundation]
Type: Report; *Frequency:* a.
•Built Heritage: Assessing a Tourism Resource [a publication of the Heritage Canada Foundation]
Type: Report; *Editor:* Veronica Vaillancourt; *ISBN:* 0-88814-207-2
•Exploring The Connection Between Built & Natural Heritage [a publication of the Heritage Canada Foundation]
Type: Report; *Editor:* Veronica Vaillancourt; *ISBN:* 0-88814-204-8
•Heritage [a publication of the Heritage Canada Foundation]
Type: Magazine; *Frequency:* q.; *Price:* $40/year subscription
•Human Resource Issues in the Preservation of Heritage Buildings [a publication of the Heritage Canada Foundation]
Type: Report; *Editor:* Carolyn Quinn; *ISBN:* 0-88814-209-9

L'Héritage canadien du Québec (HCQ) / The Canadian Heritage of Québec (CHQ)

#1202, 1350, rue Sherbrooke ouest, Montréal QC H3G 1J1
Tél: 514-393-1417; *Téléc:* 514-393-9444
Courriel: chq@total.net
www.hcq-chq.org/french/
Aperçu: *Dimension:* petite; *Envergure:* provinciale; fondée en 1960
Mission: Organisme qui se consacre à la préservation des terrains & des constructions revêtant une valeur historique/architecturale dans la province du Québec
Membre(s) du bureau directeur:
John Molson, Président
Finances: *Budget de fonctionnement annuel:* $250,000-$500,000
Personnel: 1 membre(s) du personnel
Membre: 250 *Montant de la cotisation:* $50 (Ami/Amie)

Heritage Foundation of Newfoundland & Labrador (HFNL)

The Newman Building, PO Box 5171, 1 Springdale St., St. John's NL A1C 5V5
Tel: 709-739-1892; *Fax:* 709-739-5413
Toll-Free: 888-739-1892
e-mail: info@heritagefoundation.ca
www.heritagefoundation.ca
Overview: A small provincial charitable organization founded in 1984
Mission: To stimulate an understanding of & appreciation for the architectural heritage of Newfoundland & Labrador; To support & contribute to the preservation, maintenance & restoration of buildings of architectural or historical significance; To designate buildings & structures as Registered Heritage Structures; may make grants for purpose of preservation, maintenance, or restoration (Deadline for submitting grant application is Mar. 1 & Sept. 1 of each year); *Member of:* Heritage Canada; Newfoundland & Labrador Homebuilders Association; Heritage Coalition of Newfoundland & Labrador; Newfoundland Historic Trust
Chief Officer(s):
George Chalker, Executive Director
george@heritagefoundation.ca
Kenneth Flynn, Chairperson
Finances: *Annual Operating Budget:* $100,000-$250,000; *Funding Sources:* Provincial government; private
Staff: 3 staff member(s)
Membership: 11; *Member Profile:* Appointed Board by Lt. Governor in council; *Committees:* Buildings; Grants; Finance; Public Relations; Policy
Activities: Education & advisory service in restoration of older structures; *Library:* by appointment

Héritage Montréal (HM)

#0500, 100, rue Sherbrooke est, Montréal QC H2X 1C3
Tél: 514-286-2662; *Téléc:* 514-286-1661
www.heritagemontreal.org
www.facebook.com/heritagemontreal
twitter.com/heritagemtl
Également appelé: Fondation Héritage Montréal
Aperçu: *Dimension:* moyenne; *Envergure:* locale; Organisme sans but lucratif; fondée en 1975
Mission: Encourager auprès des décideurs publics et privés la transformation des attitudes et favoriser l'introduction et la mise en oeuvre des méthodes et des stratégies permettant la conservation du patrimoine urbain architectural de Montréal, le patrimoine naturel, les espaces publics ainsi que l'environnement culturel et social; *Membre de:* Forum québécois du patrimoine; Conseil régional de l'environnement de Montréal; Affiliation(s): International Council on Monuments & Sites
Membre(s) du bureau directeur:
Marie Senécal-Tremblay, Directrice générale
Finances: *Budget de fonctionnement annuel:* $250,000-$500,000
Personnel: 5 membre(s) du personnel; 30 bénévole(s)
Membre: 700 *Montant de la cotisation:* 50$ (individuel); 125-500 (corporatif); *Comités:* Patrimoine et aménagement
Activités: Promenades architecturales; cours de rénovation; conférences; recherches; publications; *Bibliothèque:* Bibliothèque publique

Heritage Society of British Columbia

914 Garthland Pl. West, Victoria BC V9A 4J5
Tel: 250-384-4840
e-mail: hsbc@islandnet.com
www.heritagebc.ca
www.facebook.com/pages/Heritage-BC/191841050874008
Also Known As: Dogwood Heritage Society of British Columbia
Overview: A medium-sized provincial organization founded in 1981
Mission: To represent groups involved with heritage projects & issues; Affiliation(s): Heritage Canada
Chief Officer(s):
Rick Goodacre, Executive Director
rgoodacre@heritagebc.ca
Eric Pattison, President
eric@eparchitect.ca
Jan Thomas, Office Manager, Surrey, 604-582-1332
jthomas@heritagebc.ca
Activities: Presenting awards; Organizing conferences; Preserving historical sites, such as trails; Restoring the built environment; Funding community participation in workshops; *Awareness Events:* Heritage Week, February

Heritage Trust of Nova Scotia (HTNS)

PO Box 36111, Stn. RPO Spring Garden, 1588 Barrington St., Halifax NS B3J 3S9
Tel: 902-423-4807; *Fax:* 902-423-3977
e-mail: contact@htns.ca
www.htns.ca
Overview: A medium-sized provincial charitable organization founded in 1959
Mission: To promote interest in the preservation of historic structures & sites in Nova Scotia; *Member of:* Federation of the Nova Scotian Heritage; Affiliation(s): Heritage Canada
Chief Officer(s):
Peter Delefes, President, 902-826-2087
president@htns.ca
Finances: *Annual Operating Budget:* $100,000-$250,000; *Funding Sources:* Donations; federal funding; membership dues; sales of goods & services
Membership: 450; *Fees:* $5 student; $15 single; $20 family; $10 senior; $15 senior couple; $25 group/institutions; $500 life membership; *Member Profile:* Individuals & groups who are committed to the protection & rehabilitation of Nova Scotia's heritage; *Committees:* Buildings-at-Risk; Communities; Education; Events/Programs; HRM; Quarterly; Painted Rooms; Publications; Public Relations; Religious Buildings; Tax Incentives
Activities: Providing a public lecture series; Offering input on legislative policy at the municipal & provincial levels; *Speaker Service:* Yes; *Library:* Open to public
Awards:
•Heritage Trust of Nova Scotia Built Heritage Award (Award)
Presented for outstanding contribution to building restoration
Contact: Joyce McCulloch, HTNS Awards Chair
Publications:
•The Griffin [a publication of the Heritage Trust of Nova Scotia]
Type: Newsletter; *Frequency:* Quarterly; *Price:* Free with Heritage Trust of Nova Scotia membership

Heritage Winnipeg Corp. (HW)

#509, 63 Albert St., Winnipeg MB R3B 1G4
Tel: 204-942-2663; *Fax:* 204-942-2094
e-mail: info@heritagewinnipeg.com
www.heritagewinnipeg.com
Overview: A small local charitable organization founded in 1978
Mission: To promote & encourage preservation of historic sites & structures in Winnipeg; To educate the public on heritage issues & make them aware of the richness of their material culture; To advocate & lobby on behalf of heritage related issues; *Member of:* Heritage Canada; Manitoba Historical Society; St. Boniface Historical Society; Manitoba Heritage Federation; Affiliation(s): Downtown Biz; Exchange Biz, Destination Winnipeg; Parks Canada; City of Winnipeg; Province of Manitoba
Chief Officer(s):
Cindy Tugwell, Executive Director
Penny McMillan, President
Finances: *Annual Operating Budget:* Less than $50,000; *Funding Sources:* Private donations; provincial government; city of Winnipeg; membership dues; fundraisers
Staff: 1 staff member(s)
Membership: 170; *Fees:* $20 individual; $15 student/senior; $30 family/organization; corporate $100-$1,000; *Committees:* Public Service & Information; Legal & Economic Instruments; Advocacy; Preservation Awards; Education
Activities: Museum & Heritage Exposition; heritage auctions; annual preservation awards; school presentations; walking tours; Manitoba Day events; heritage fairs; Doors Open Winnipeg; *Awareness Events:* Heritage Preservation Awards; Doors Open Winnipeg; 3rd Mon. in Feb.; *Speaker Service:* Yes; *Library:* Open to public by appointment
Publications:
•Illustrated Guide to Winnipeg's Exchange District
Type: Brochure

Hike Ontario

#800, 165 Dundas St. West, Mississauga ON L5B 2N6
Tel: 905-277-4453
Toll-Free: 800-894-7249
e-mail: info@hikeontario.com
www.hikeontario.com
Overview: A medium-sized provincial charitable organization founded in 1974
Mission: To act as the voice for hikers & walkers in Ontario; To encourage hiking, walking & trail development in Ontario; To promote trail maintenance. best practices, & safe hiking; To enhance environmental awareness, conservation & sustainable trails; Affiliation(s): Ontario Trails Council (OTC); Hike Canada En Marche
Chief Officer(s):
Bill Wilson, President
Fran Rawlings, Secretary
Asvin Parsad, Treasurer
Finances: *Funding Sources:* Membership dues; Grants; Sponsorships; Donations
Membership: *Member Profile:* Not-for-profit trail building & hiking organizations; Individuals; Corporations, government agencies, & organizations other than hiking or trail building organizations
Activities: Providing hiking information & services throughout Ontario; Offering the Hike Leader Certification Program & the Young Hikers Program; Supporting trails across the province; Advocating for clubs; Liaising with government; Promoting research & education into the health benefits of walking & hiking; Presenting awards to celebrate dedicated hikers; *Awareness Events:* Ontario Hiking Week, September

Hope for Wildlife Society
PO Box 1, 5909 Hwy. 207, #14 R.R.#2, Head of Chezzetcook NS B0J 1N0
Tel: 902-452-3339
e-mail: info@hopeforwildlife.net
www.hopeforwildlife.net
Overview: A small provincial organization founded in 1997
Mission: Specializing in the care, treatment and rehabilitation of injured or orphaned native fur bearing mammals, sea birds and songbirds both indigenous to the Nova Scotia area as well as non-indigenous species and pets.
Chief Officer(s):
Hope Swinimer, Founder & Director

Horticulture Nova Scotia (HORT NS)
Kentville Agricultural Centre, 32 Main St., Kentville NS B4N 1J5
Tel: 902-678-9335; *Fax:* 902-678-1280
e-mail: hortns@ns.sympatico.ca
www.hortns.com
Previous Name: Vegetable & Potato Producers' Association of Nova Scotia
Merged from: Vegetables NS and Berries NS
Overview: A small provincial organization founded in 1998
Mission: To enhance collaborative efforts among members which will strengthen & provide leadership to the horticultural industry; Affiliation(s): NS Federation of Agriculture; Canadian Horticultural Council
Chief Officer(s):
Donna Crawford, Administrative Coordinator
hortns@ns.sympatico.ca
Lloyd Evans, President
Finances: *Annual Operating Budget:* $50,000-$100,000; *Funding Sources:* Membership fees
Staff: 2 staff member(s); 8 volunteer(s)
Membership: 100+; *Fees:* Scale based on acreage & gross income; *Member Profile:* Vegetable & berry growers; agribusiness; *Committees:* Research; Human Resources; Agriculture Awareness; Marketing; Conference
Activities: Administers NS Potato Marketing Board;

Hospitality New Brunswick *See* Tourism Industry Association of New Brunswick Inc.

Housing & Urban Development Association of Canada *See* Canadian Home Builders' Association

H.R. MacMillan Space Centre Society (HRMSC)
1100 Chestnut St., Vancouver BC V6J 3J9
Tel: 604-738-7827; *Fax:* 604-736-5665
e-mail: info@spacecentre.ca
www.spacecentre.ca
twitter.com/AskAnAstronomer
www.youtube.com/user/MacMillanSpaceCentre
Also Known As: H.R. MacMillan Planetarium
Previous Name: Pacific Space Centre Society
Overview: A medium-sized local charitable organization founded in 1968
Mission: To educate, inspire & evoke a sense of wonder about the universe, our planet & space exploration; *Member of:* Canadian Association of Science Centres; Affiliation(s): Canadian Museums Association
Chief Officer(s):
Rob Appleron, Executive Director
Denise Mathie, Contact, Marketing & Communications
Finances: *Annual Operating Budget:* $1.5 Million-$3 Million; *Funding Sources:* Government; foundations; corporate sponsors; individuals; admissions to facility
Staff: 40 staff member(s)
Membership: 1,000-4,999;; *Fees:* $30 individual; $55 couple; $80 family
Activities: New star show productions; teacher workshops; classroom activities; community astronomy; Starlab; video-conferences

HUDAM *See* Manitoba Home Builders' Association

Human Factors Association of Canada *See* Association of Canadian Ergonomists

Humanities & Social Sciences Federation of Canada *See* Canadian Federation for Humanities & Social Sciences

Hydrographic Society *See* International Federation of Hydrographic Societies

Hydro-Québec Foundation for the Environment *Voir* Fondation Hydro-Québec pour l'environnement

ICOMOS Canada
PO Box 737, Stn. B, Ottawa ON K1P 5P8
Tel: 613-749-0971; *Fax:* 613-749-0971
e-mail: canada@icomos.org
canada.icomos.org
Also Known As: International Council on Monuments & Sites Canada
Overview: A medium-sized international organization founded in 1975
Mission: To further the conservation, protection, rehabilitation, & enhancement of monuments, groups of buildings & sites; To encourage primary research in many important fields; Affiliation(s): UNESCO; International Centre for the Study of the Preservation & Restoration of Cultural Property (ICCROM)
Chief Officer(s):
Dinu Bumbaru, President
Alain Dejeans, Vice-président, Comité francophone
John Ward, Vice President, English Speaking Committee
Finances: *Annual Operating Budget:* Less than $50,000
Staff: 1 staff member(s)
Membership: 500; *Fees:* $85 individual; $30 students & friends; institutional available; *Member Profile:* Conservation professionals & advocates concerned with developing & promoting, through international exchange, the highest professional standards of practice in the conservation of the built environment; *Committees:* National Committees which bring together professionals in each country
Activities: Researching; Communicating; Providing professional services
Publications:
•eCOMoS [a publication of the ICOMOS Canada]
Type: Newsletter

Independent Lumber Dealers Co-operative (ILDC)
#100, 596 Kingston Rd. West, Ajax ON L1T 3A2
Tel: 905-428-0690; *Fax:* 905-428-0690
e-mail: ildc@ildc.com
www.ildc.com
Overview: A small local organization founded in 1964
Member of: SPANCAN
Chief Officer(s):
A. Battagliotti, General Manager
P. Bonhomme, President
Finances: *Annual Operating Budget:* $250,000-$500,000
Membership: 20; *Member Profile:* Independent home improvement chains

Independent Power Association of BC *See* Clean Energy BC

Independent Power Producers Society of Alberta (IPPSA)
#2600, 144 - 4th Ave. SW, Calgary AB T2P 3N4
Fax: 403-256-8342
www.ippsa.com
Overview: A small provincial organization founded in 1993
Mission: To represent Alberta's major power producers; To encourage dialogue among power producers in Alberta
Chief Officer(s):
Evan Bahry, Executive Director, 403-282-8811, Fax: 403-256-8342
Evan.Bahry@ippsa.com
Joe Novecosky, Contact, Membership & Events, 403-256-1587, Fax: 403-256-8342
joeno@telusplanet.net
Membership: 100+; *Fees:* $10,000 power member; $5,000 junior power member; $1,000 corporate member; $250 associate member; *Member Profile:* Operators of Alberta's power supply
Activities: Engaging with Alberta's government & its agencies in policy development; Reviewing legislation, regulations, & market rules; Promoting competition in Alberta's electrical market; Providing news about the industry; Sponsoring a bursary for a student at the University of Calgary's Schulich School of Engineering (Electricity Department)
Meetings/Conferences:
For more information see Trade Shows, Conferences and Seminars Chapter
Independent Power Producers Society of Alberta 2013 19th Annual Conference
March 2013 Banff, AB
Independent Power Producers Society of Alberta 2014 20th Annual Conference
March 2014 Banff, AB
Publications:
•IPPSA [Independent Power Producer Society of Alberta] News
Type: Newsletter; *Frequency:* 5 pa
Profile: Industry happenings for IPPSA members

Independent Power Producers Society of Ontario (IPPSO)
See Association of Power Producers of Ontario

Indian Agricultural Program of Ontario (IAPO)
PO Box 100, 220 North St., Stirling ON K0K 3E0
Tel: 613-395-5505; *Fax:* 613-395-5510
Toll-Free: 800-363-0329
e-mail: iapo-lambeth@on.aibn.com
www.indianag.on.ca
Overview: A small provincial organization founded in 1984
Mission: IAPO is a non-profit corporation that fosters sustainable economic growth of Ontario First Nations People through agricultural programs involved in all sectors, including dairy, beef, swine, poultry, crops, farm retail, repair, & agri-forestry.
Chief Officer(s):
William J. Brant, Chair
Beth Wismer, General Manager
beth@indianag.on.ca
Membership: *Member Profile:* Status Indians registered in Ontario with businesses on or off reserve
Activities: Loans program; agriculture advisory service; seminars; conferences
Publications:
•Native Agri Update
Type: Newsletter; *Frequency:* Monthly

Western/Southern Office
PO Box 83, Stn. Lambeth, 6453 Hamlyn St., London ON N6P 1P9
Tel: 519-652-2440; *Fax:* 519-652-0085
Toll-Free: 800-663-6912
Chief Officer(s):
Mary McFarlane, Programs Officer
iapo-mary@on.aibn.com

Industrial Accident Victims Group of Ontario (IAVGO)
#203, 489 College St., Toronto ON M6G 1A5
Tel: 416-924-6477
Toll-Free: 877-230-6311
www.iavgo.org
www.facebook.com/167369409975545
Overview: A medium-sized provincial charitable organization founded in 1975
Mission: Our community legal clinic provides free services to injured workers in Ontario including legal advice, legal representation, public legal education, advocacy training and community development.
Chief Officer(s):
Mary DiNucci, Coordinator
Finances: *Annual Operating Budget:* $100,000-$250,000
Staff: 8 staff member(s)
Membership: *Fees:* $10
Activities: ; *Library:* by appointment

Industrial Gas Users Association Inc. (IGUA) / Association des consommateurs industriels de gaz (ACIG)
#502, 350 Sparks St., Ottawa ON K1R 7S8
Tel: 613-236-8021; *Fax:* 613-230-9531
www.igua.ca
Overview: A medium-sized national organization founded in 1973
Mission: To provide a coordinated & effective voice for industrial firms depending on natural gas as fuel or feedstock; to represent industrial users of natural gas before regulatory boards & governments
Chief Officer(s):
Murray Newton, President
mnewton@igua.ca
Ghislaine Carrière, Manager, Accounting & Office Services
gcarriere@igua.ca
Finances: *Annual Operating Budget:* $500,000-$1.5 Million; *Funding Sources:* Membership dues
Staff: 3 staff member(s)
Membership: 39 corporate; *Fees:* Based on gas consumption, $1,200-$36,099; *Member Profile:* Open to end users of natural gas

Industrial Instrument Manufacturers Association *See* Canadian Process Control Association

Industrial Truck Association (ITA)
#460, 1750 K St. NW, Washington DC 20006 USA
Tel: 202-296-9880; *Fax:* 202-296-9884
www.indtrk.org

Overview: A medium-sized international organization
Mission: Represents the manufacturers of lift trucks & their suppliers who do business in Canada, the United States or Mexico
Chief Officer(s):
William Montwieler, Executive Director
Finances: *Annual Operating Budget:* $1.5 Million-$3 Million
Staff: 5 staff member(s)
Membership: 100; *Fees:* Varies; *Member Profile:* Manufacturers of forklifts & suppliers

l'Industrie forestière de l'Ontario ***See*** Ontario Forest Industries Association

INFORM Inc.

5 Hanover Sq., 19th Fl., New York NY 10004 USA
Tel: 212-361-2400; *Fax:* 212-361-2412
e-mail: ramsey@informinc.org
www.informinc.org
www.facebook.com/199694845376
twitter.com/informinc
Overview: A medium-sized international charitable organization founded in 1974
Mission: To examine the effects of business practices on the environment & human health; *Member of:* Earthshare
Environmental Activity: Identifying ways of doing business that ensure environmentally sustainable economic growth
Chief Officer(s):
Virginia Ramsey, Executive Director
Finances: *Annual Operating Budget:* $1.5 Million-$3 Million; *Funding Sources:* Individual donors; Foundations; Government; Corporate contributions; Book sales
Staff: 25 staff member(s); 5 volunteer(s)
Membership: 1,000; *Fees:* $35
Activities: Researching strategies to prevent chemical hazards & to develop sustainable products & practices; *Internships:* Yes; *Speaker Service:* Yes

Infrastructure Health & Safety Association (IHSA)

Centre for Health & Safety Innovation, #400, 5110 Creekbank Rd., Mississauga ON L4W 0A1
Tel: 905-625-0100; *Fax:* 905-625-8998
Toll-Free: 800-263-5024
e-mail: info@ihsa.ca
www.ihsa.ca
ca.linkedin.com/pub/ihsa-news/41/986/aa3
twitter.com/IHSAnews
Merged from: CSAO; E&USA; THSAO
Overview: A medium-sized provincial organization founded in 2010
Mission: To serve the utilities, electrical, natural gas, aggregates, ready-mix, construction, & transportation industries in Ontario; To develop prevention solutions for work environments
Chief Officer(s):
Al Beattie, Chief Executive Officer & President
Membership: *Committees:* Advisory Councils; CVOR Review Panel; Fleet Safety Council; Labour - Management Committees; Section 21 Committees
Activities: Providing training that meets regulatory requirements & compliance standards
Meetings/Conferences:
For more information see Trade Shows, Conferences and Seminars Chapter
Infrastructure Health & Safety Association 2013 Annual General Meeting
2013, ON
Publications:
•Infrastructure Health & Safety Association Annual Report
Type: Yearbook; *Frequency:* Annually
Profile: Departmental updates & financial statements

Ingénieurs Canada ***See*** Engineers Canada

Ingénieurs sans Frontières ***See*** Engineers Without Borders

Ingersoll District Nature Club

RR#1, Salford ON N0J 1W9
www.ingersollnature.ca
Overview: A small local charitable organization
Mission: To promote the enjoyment of nature through environmental appreciation & conservation; To encourage wise use & conservation of natural resources; to promote environmental protection; *Member of:* Federation of Ontario Naturalists
Chief Officer(s):
Ruth Bucknell, Treasurer
Ken Whiteford, Contact, 519-539-5234
kenwhiteford@sympatico
John Bomans, Contact, 519-485-7575
bomansj@msn.com
Finances: *Annual Operating Budget:* Less than $50,000; *Funding Sources:* Donations
Membership: 45; *Fees:* $10 youth; $15 single; $25 family
Activities: Adopt-a-Bird program;

L'Initiative torontoise de biotechnologie ***See*** Toronto Biotechnology Initiative

Innovation Management Association of Canada (IMAC) / Association canadienne de la gestion de l'innovation (ACGI)

c/o CATAAlliance, #416, 207 Bank St., Ottawa ON K2P 2N2
Tel: 613-236-6550; *Fax:* 613-236-8189
e-mail: info@cata.ca
www.cata.ca/imac/
Previous Name: Canadian Research Management Association
Overview: A small national organization founded in 1996
Mission: To enhance the productivity & effectiveness of Canadian research development & technology-based innovations
Chief Officer(s):
Cathi Malette, Membership Coordinator
cmalette@cata.ca
Finances: *Annual Operating Budget:* $50,000-$100,000
Membership: 240; *Fees:* $225 individual; *Member Profile:* Research, technology management & innovation leaders; *Committees:* Program; Research Practices

Inside Education

11428 - 100 Ave., Edmonton AB T5K 0J4
Tel: 780-421-1497; *Fax:* 780-425-4506
Toll-Free: 888-421-1497
e-mail: info@insideeducation.ca
www.insideeducation.ca
www.linkedin.com/company/1409777
www.facebook.com/InsideEducation
twitter.com/insideeducation
www.youtube.com/user/InsideEducation
Previous Name: FEESA - An Environmental Education Society
Overview: A medium-sized provincial charitable organization founded in 1985
Mission: To empower all Albertans to make informed choices about the environment by providing bias-balanced environmental education; to communicate, coordinate & initiate the development & support of bias-balanced environmental education in Alberta through a variety of programs & services; to ensure that the views of business, industry, government, the environment & community sector are represented in any programming or communication; *Member of:* Environmental Outdoor Education Council; Alberta Environmental Network; Canadian Environmental Network; Affiliation(s): North American Association for Environmental Education; EECOM
Chief Officer(s):
Steve McIsaac, Executive Director
smcisaac@insideeducation.ca
Finances: *Annual Operating Budget:* $500,000-$1.5 Million; *Funding Sources:* Industry 50%; government 40%; private/users 10%
Staff: 9 staff member(s); 1000 volunteer(s)
Membership: 300 associates; 18 members (Board); *Fees:* $15 student; $25 individual; $50 institution; $250 corporate
Activities: Promotion of environmental education in formal & public education areas; presentations, conferences & conventions; coordination & development of education resources that focus on a variety of environmental & educational needs; teacher-training institutes focusing on a variety of environmental issues; *Awareness Events:* Environment Week, 1st week of June

Calgary
#205, 1117 - 1st St. SW, Calgary AB T2R 0T9
Tel: 403-263-7720; *Fax:* 403-263-7709

Instit du Chrysotile ***See*** Chrysotile Institute

Institut aéronautique et spatial du Canada ***See*** Canadian Aeronautics & Space Institute

Institut agréé de la logistique et des transports Amérique du Nord ***See*** The Chartered Institute of Logistics & Transport in North America

Institut agricole du Canada ***See*** Agricultural Institute of Canada

Institut Archéologique d'Amérique ***See*** Archaeological Institute of America

L'Institut canadien ***See*** The Canadian Institute

Institut canadien d'information sur la santé ***See*** Canadian Institute for Health Information

Institut canadien de formation de l'énergie ***See*** Canadian Institute for Energy Training

Institut canadien de la construction en acier ***See*** Canadian Institute of Steel Construction

Institut canadien de la santé animale ***See*** Canadian Animal Health Institute

Institut canadien de la tôle d'acier pour le bâtiment ***See*** Canadian Sheet Steel Building Institute

Institut canadien de plomberie et de chauffage ***See*** Canadian Institute of Plumbing & Heating

Institut canadien de science et technologie alimentaires ***See*** Canadian Institute of Food Science & Technology

Institut canadien des engrais ***See*** Canadian Fertilizer Institute

L'Institut canadien des ingénieurs ***See*** The Engineering Institute of Canada

Institut canadien des mines, de la métallurgie et du pétrole ***See*** Canadian Institute of Mining, Metallurgy & Petroleum

Institut canadien des urbanistes ***See*** Canadian Institute of Planners

Institut canadien du béton préfabriqué et précontraint ***See*** Canadian Precast / Prestressed Concrete Institute

Institut canadien du chauffage, de la climatisation et de la réfrigération ***See*** Heating, Refrigeration & Air Conditioning Institute of Canada

Institut canadien du droit des ressources ***See*** Canadian Institute of Resources Law

Institut canadien du trafic et du transport ***See*** Canadian Institute of Traffic & Transportation

Institut C.D. Howe ***See*** C.D. Howe Institute

Institut circumpolaire canadien ***See*** Canadian Circumpolar Institute

Institut de chimie du Canada ***See*** Chemical Institute of Canada

Institut de développement urbain du Canada ***See*** Urban Development Institute of Canada

Institut de l'énergie et de l'environnement de la Francophonie (IEPF)

56, rue St-Pierre, 3e étage, Québec QC G1K 4A1
Tél: 418-692-5727; *Téléc:* 418-692-5644
www.iepf.org
Aperçu: *Dimension:* moyenne; *Envergure:* internationale; Organisme sans but lucratif; fondée en 1988
Mission: Contribuer au renforcement des capacités nationales et au développement des partenariats dans les domaines de l'énergie et de l'environnement; *Membre de:* Agence de la Francophonie
Membre(s) du bureau directeur:
Fatimata Dia Touré, Directrice
Finances: *Budget de fonctionnement annuel:* $3 Million-$5 Million
Personnel: 17 membre(s) du personnel
Activités: ; *Bibliothèque:* Service information et documentation

Institut de la fourrure du Canada ***See*** Fur Institute of Canada

Institut de radioprotection du Canada ***See*** Radiation Safety Institute of Canada

Institut de recherche en biologie végétale (IRBV) / Plant Biology Research Institute (PBRI)

4101, rue Sherbrooke est, Montréal QC H1X 2B2
Tél: 514-343-2121
Courriel: irbv@irbv.umontreal.ca
www.irbv.umontreal.ca
Aperçu: *Dimension:* petite; *Envergure:* locale; Organisme sans but lucratif; fondée en 1990
Mission: To develop a centre of excellence in plant biology; both in fundamental research and its applicaitons; train students

in plant biology at the master, doctoral, and post-doctoral levels; further training and knowledge of its researchers and technical personnel; promote the technological transfer of its scientific research results to users; provide complementary services to the community in fields relevant to plant biology, where expertise in the field is lacking.
Membre(s) du bureau directeur:
Anne Bruneau, Directrice
Finances: *Budget de fonctionnement annuel:* $1.5 Million-$3 Million
Personnel: 100 membre(s) du personnel
Membre: 1-99
Activités: *Service de conférenciers:* Oui; *Bibliothèque:* Bibliothèque publique

Institut de recherche en politiques publiques ***See*** Institute for Research on Public Policy

Institut de recherche et de développement en agroenvironnement ***See*** Research & Development Institute for the Agri-Environment

Institut de recherche Robert-Sauvé en santé et en sécurité du travail (IRSST) / Robert Sauvé Occupational Health & Safety Research Institute

505, boul de Maisonneuve ouest, 15e étage, Montréal QC H3A 3C2
Tél: 514-288-1551; *Téléc:* 514-288-7636
Courriel: communications@irsst.qc.ca
www.irsst.qc.ca
www.facebook.com//207703664186
twitter.com/IRSST
Aperçu: *Dimension:* moyenne; *Envergure:* provinciale; fondée en 1980
Mission: Contribuer par la recherche et le développement à l'amélioration de la santé et de la sécurité des travailleurs et plus spécifiquement, à l'élimination à la source des dangers pour leur santé, leur sécurité et leur intégrité physique ainsi qu'à la réadaptation des travailleurs victimes d'accidents ou de maladies professionnelles; fournir au Réseau public québécois de la prévention en santé et en sécurité du travail - composé de CSST, des Centres locaux de services communautaires, des Régies de la santé et des services sociaux et des associations sectorielles paritaires - les services et l'expertise nécessaires à leur action; diffuser les connaissances issues de ces recherches et de ces expertises auprès des milieux de travail et en favoriser le transfert; accorder des bourses d'études supérieures en santé et en sécurité du travail; agir comme laboratoire de référence au Québec, dans le domaine de l'hygiene industrielle.; Affiliation(s): International Occupational Safety & Health Information Centre
Membre(s) du bureau directeur:
Marie Larue, Présidente/Directrice générale
Finances: *Budget de fonctionnement annuel:* Plus de $5 Million*Fonds:* Près de 85 % des revenus proviennent d'une subvention de la Commission de la santé et de la sécurité du travail du Québec (CSST)
Personnel: 130 membre(s) du personnel
Activités: ; *Bibliothèque:* Bibliothèque publique

Institut de recherche sur le travail et la santé ***See*** Institute for Work & Health

L'Institut des agronomes du Nouveau-Brunswick ***See*** New Brunswick Institute of Agrologists

Institut des planificateurs professionnels de l'Ontario ***See*** Ontario Professional Planners Institute

Institut des Urbanistes de l'atlantique ***See*** Atlantic Planners Institute

Institut forestier du Canada ***See*** Canadian Institute of Forestry

Institut international de l'ocean ***See*** International Ocean Institute

Institut international du développement durable ***See*** International Institute for Sustainable Development

Institut pour tuyaux de tôle ondulée ***See*** Corrugated Steel Pipe Institute

Institute for Alternative Agriculture ***See*** Henry A. Wallace Center for Agricultural & Environmental Policy at Winrock International

Institute for Local Self-Reliance (ILSR)

#570, 2001 S St. NW, Washington DC 20009 USA
Tel: 202-898-1610
e-mail: info@ilsr.org
www.ilsr.org
Overview: A medium-sized international organization founded in 1974
Mission: To provide innovative strategies & models to support environmentally sound community development; To work with citizens & policymakers to meet local needs; To provide the tools to increase economic effectiveness, to reduce waste & decrease impacts on the environment, & provide for local ownership of infrastructure & resources; Affiliation(s): Healthy Building Network; Black Environment Justice Network; GrassRoots Recycling Network
Chief Officer(s):
Neil Seldman, President
nseldman@ilsr.org
David Morris, Vice-President
dmorris@ilsr.org
Sarah Pickell, Director, Finance
dmorris@ilsr.org
Brenda Platt, Director, Waste to Wealth & Sustainable Plastics Program
Stacy Mitchell, Senior Researcher
smitchell@ilsr.org
Finances: *Funding Sources:* Foundations; Individuals; Speaking; Technical assistance
Staff: 1 volunteer(s)
Activities: *Internships:* Yes; *Speaker Service:* Yes

Institute for Research on Public Policy / Institut de recherche en politiques publiques

#200, 1470, rue Peel, Montréal QC H3A 1T1
Tel: 514-985-2461; *Fax:* 514-985-2559
e-mail: irpp@irpp.org
www.irpp.org
Overview: A medium-sized national organization founded in 1972
Mission: To improve public policy in Canada by generating research, providing insight, & sparking debate that will contribute to the public policy decision-making process & strengthen the quality of public policy decisions made by Canadian governments, citizens, institutions, & organizations
Chief Officer(s):
Graham Fox, President, 514-787-0741
gfox@irpp.org
Activities: ; *Library:* Open to public

Institute for Risk Research (IRR)

University of Waterloo, 200 University Ave. West, Waterloo ON N2L 3G1
Tel: 519-885-4027
e-mail: irr-neram@uwaterloo.ca
www.irr-neram.ca
Overview: A small local organization founded in 1982
Mission: To promote safety for Canadians by improving the understanding of risk & risk policy decisions
Chief Officer(s):
John Shortreed, Director
shortree@uwaterloo.ca
Finances: *Funding Sources:* Corporations; government grants & contracts
Staff: 3 staff member(s)
Membership: 185; *Fees:* $25
Activities: Includes Environmental Risk Management shortcourse; environmental conferences; *Speaker Service:* Yes; *Library:* Open to public by appointment

Institute for Sustainable Energy, Economy & Environment Student's Association (ISEEESA)

Scrubfield Hall, #199B, 2500 University Dr., Calgary AB T2N 1N4
e-mail: info@iseeesa.ca
www.iseeesa.ca
www.facebook.com/groups/iseeesa
twitter.com/iseeesa
flickr.com/iseeesa
Overview: A large national organization founded in 2006
Mission: To promote and create initiatives that reflect the growing movement to obtain a cleaner energy supply, healthy environment, and efficient economy.
Chief Officer(s):
Pasley Weeks, President

Institute for Work & Health (IWH) / Institut de recherche sur le travail et la santé

#800, 481 University Ave., Toronto ON M5G 2E9
Tel: 416-927-2027; *Fax:* 416-927-4167
e-mail: info@iwh.on.ca
www.iwh.on.ca
Previous Name: Ontario Workers' Compensation Institute
Overview: A medium-sized provincial organization founded in 1990
Mission: To conduct & share research with workers, labour, employers, clinicians & policy-makers to promote, protect & improve the health of working people
Chief Officer(s):
Cameron Mustard, President & Senior Scientist
Ian Anderson, Chair
Finances: *Annual Operating Budget:* $3 Million-$5 Million; *Funding Sources:* Public & private sector; research grants
Staff: 75 staff member(s)
Activities: *Awareness Events:* Alf Nachemson Memorial Lecture; *Library:* Open to public

Institute of Electrical & Electronics Engineers Inc. (IEEE)

445 Hoes Lane, Piscataway NJ 8855 USA
Tel: 732-981-0060; *Fax:* 732-981-9667
e-mail: customer-service@ieee.org
www.ieee.org
www.linkedin.com/groups?home=&gid=23804
www.facebook.com/IEEE.org
twitter.com/IEEEorg
Overview: A large international organization founded in 1884
Mission: The world's largest technical professional society; to advance theory & practice of electrical engineering, electronics, radio & allied branches of engineering & related arts & sciences; to publish documents in order to enhance the quality of life for all peoples through improved public awareness of the influences & applications of its technologies; to advance the standing of the engineering profession & its members; to provide leadership in areas ranging from aerospace, computers & communications to biomedical technology, electric power & consumer electronics
Chief Officer(s):
Gordon W. Day, President & CEO
Membership: 365,000 worldwide; 39 technical societies; 4 councils; *Fees:* Schedule available
Activities: Has published more than 130 transactions, magazines & journals; global network of over 90 branches worldwide, providing local focus for engineering, including events, lectures & company visits; *Internships:* Yes; *Library:*

Institute of Electrical & Electronics Engineers Inc. - Canada

PO Box 63005, Stn. University PO, Shoppers Drug Mart #742, 102 Plaza Dr., Dundas ON L9H 4H0
Tel: 905-628-9554; *Fax:* 905-628-9554
e-mail: admin@ieee.ca
www.ieee.ca
www.facebook.com/group.php?gid=182255135157013
Also Known As: IEEE Canada
Overview: A medium-sized national charitable organization founded in 1884
Mission: To advance the theory & practice of electrical, electronics, & computer engineering & computer science; *Member of:* Institute of Electrical and Electronics Engineers (IEEE); Affiliation(s): The Engineering Institute of Canada
Chief Officer(s):
Cathie Lowell, IEEE Canada Administrator
cathie.lowell@gmail.com
Om Malik, President
maliko@ieee.org
Keith Brown, President Elect
Gerard Dunphy, Treasurer
Finances: *Funding Sources:* Membership dues; Publications; Sponsorship; Sale of products & services
Membership: 13,000; *Member Profile:* Professional engineers or technologists; *Committees:* Awards; Conferences; Membership; Publications; Professional Activities; Student Activities; Educational Activites; Industry Relations; Other Societies; Sections/Chapter Support; GOLD (Graduates of the Last Decade); Life Members; Women in Engineering; Standards
Activities: Sponsoring technical conferences, symposia & local meetings worldwide; Providing resources to assist members in increasing their professional skills; Facilitating networking capabilities
Publications:
•Canadian Journal of Electrical & Computer Engineering
Type: Journal; *Frequency:* Quarterly; *Editor:* Witold Kinsner; Xavier Maldague; *ISSN:* 0840-8688; *Price:* $30 IEEE member; $60 other individual; $90institution

Profile: Refereed scientific papers in all areas of electrical & computer engineering
•IEEE [Institute of Electrical & Electronics Engineers Inc.] Canada Newsletter / Bulletin de IEEE Canada
Type: Newsletter; *Frequency:* Monthly; *Editor:* Alex Bot
Profile: IEEE activities & industry trends
•IEEE [Institute of Electrical & Electronics Engineers Inc.] Canadian Review / La revue canadienne de l'IEEE
Type: Magazine; *Frequency:* 3 pa; *Accepts Advertising*; *Editor:* Eric Holdrinet; *ISSN:* 1481-2002; *Price:* Free to members in Canada; $35 non-members; $37.50 corporations & libraries

Institute of Food Technologists (IFT)

#1000, 525 West Van Buren, Chicago IL 60607
Tel: 312-782-8424; *Fax:* 312-782-8348
Toll-Free: 800-438-3663
e-mail: info@ift.org
www.ift.org
www.linkedin.com/groups/Institute-Food-Technologists-IFT-36409
www.facebook.com/events/193978063950994
twitter.com/IFT
www.youtube.com/user/IFTlive
Overview: A large international organization founded in 1939
Mission: To advance food & health through science
Environmental Activity: Striving to ensure a safe & abundant food supply to contribute to health & wellness
Chief Officer(s):
John Ruff, President
Kelley Ahuja, CAO
kahuja@ift.org
Mark Barenie, CFO
mbarenie@ift.org
Jerry Bowman, Vice-President, Communications & Media Relations
jmbowman@ift.org
Will Fisher, Vice-President, Science & Policy Initiatives
wfisher@ift.org
Amanda Perl, Vice-President, Development
aperl@ift.org
Finances: *Funding Sources:* Membership fees; Sponsorships
Membership: *Member Profile:* Food science & technology professionals from over 90 countries
Activities: Engaging in advocacy activities; Fostering technology development & supporting innovation in food science; Facilitating the exchange of information & ideas among the food community; Offering professional development activities; Increasing the understanding & application of the science of food; Publishing science reports of interest to members, government officials, scientific constituencies, government officials, the media, & the public; Publishing books through IFT Press, a joint publishing venture with Wiley-Blackwell
Meetings/Conferences:
For more information see Trade Shows, Conferences and Seminars Chapter
Institute of Food Technologists 2013 Annual Wellness Conference
February 2013 Rosemont, IL
Institute of Food Technologists 2013 Annual Meeting & Food Expo
July 2013 Chicago, IL
Institute of Food Technologists 2014 Annual Wellness Conference
March 2014
Institute of Food Technologists 2014 Annual Meeting & Food Expo
June 2014 New Orleans, LA
Institute of Food Technologists 2015 Annual Meeting & Food Expo
July 2015 Chicago, IL
Publications:
•Comprehensive Reviews in Food Science & Food Safety
Type: Journal; *Frequency:* Bimonthly; *Editor:* Daryl B. Lund
Profile: A peer-reviewed journal, covering topics such as nutrition, physiology, microbiology, engineering, & regulations
•Eat Your Words
Type: Newsletter; *Frequency:* Monthly
Profile: Food science & technology stories for new professionals in the industry
•Express Connect
Type: Newsletter; *Frequency:* Monthly
Profile: Happenings at the Institute of Food Technologists, for members only
•Food Technology
Type: Magazine; *Frequency:* Monthly; *Accepts Advertising*; *Editor:* Bob Swientek (bswientek@ift.org)
Profile: Industry news, research developments, consumer product innovations, & professional opportunities
•Institute of Food Technologists Annual Meeting & Food Expo Preview
Type: Newsletter; *Frequency:* Annually
Profile: A preview of the annual educational event, which attracts food scientists, technologists, sellers, & buyers from around the globe
•Institute of Food Technologists Annual Meeting & Food Expo Wrap-up
Type: Newsletter; *Frequency:* Annually
Profile: A review of the annual event, which features over 21,500 attendees, as well as more than 900 exhibitors who present recent products & innovations inthe food industry
•Journal of Food Science
Type: Journal; *Frequency:* 9 pa; *Editor:* Daryl B. Lund (dlund@cals.wisc.edu)
Profile: A peer-reviewed journal, featuring original research, & reviews of all aspects of food science
•Journal of Food Science Education
Type: Journal; *Editor:* Daryl B. Lund (dlund@cals.wisc.edu)
Profile: Information of interest to persons in the field of food science education at all levels, including primary, secondary, undergraduate & graduate,continuing, & workplace education
•Nutraraceutical Newsletter
Type: Newsletter
Profile: News & current research from the nutraceutical & functional foods sector
•The Weekly Newsletter
Type: Newsletter; *Frequency:* Weekly
Profile: Industry news & highlights from the food science, technology, & regulatory sectors
•The World of Food Science
Type: Journal; *Editor:* Ken Buckle (k.buckle@unsw.edu.au)
Profile: A publication of current research on sensors & biosensors & its potential application in the food & technology industry, presented to readers by the Institute ofFood Technologists & the International Union of Food Science & Technology

Institute of Industrial Engineers (IIE)

#200, 3577 Parkway Lane, Norcross GA 30092 USA
Tel: 770-449-0461; *Fax:* 770-441-3295
e-mail: cs@iienet.org
www.iienet2.org
www.linkedin.com/groups?mostPopular=&gid=75670
www.facebook.com/group.php?gid=26148220561
twitter.com/iienet
Overview: A large national licensing organization founded in 1948
Mission: To advance the technical & managerial excellence of industrial engineers, concerned with the design, installation & improvement of integrated systems of people, material, information, equipment & energy; Affiliation(s): Organized into three societies: Society for Health Systems (SHS); Society for Engineering & Management Systems (SEMS); Aerospace & Defense Society (ADS)
Chief Officer(s):
Don Greene, Executive Director
Finances: *Annual Operating Budget:* $3 Million-$5 Million
Staff: 35 staff member(s)
Membership: 24,000 internationally in 200 senior & 140 university chapters; *Fees:* $30-$139 USD; *Committees:* Divisions: Energy, Environment & Plant Engineering; Engineering Economy; Ergonomics; Facilities Planning & Design; Financial Services; Industrial & Labour Relations; Operations Research; Quality Control & Reliability; Utilities; Work Measurement & Methods Engineering; Interest Groups; Computer & Information Systems; Consultants; Electronics Industry; Engineering Design; Government; Maintenance; Process Industries; Production & Inventory Control; Retail; Transportation & Distribution
Activities: Provides continuing education opportunities through professional trade books, periodicals, journals, technical publications, conferences, seminars & workshops; Conferences: International Industrial Engineering, Industrial Engineering Research & International Maintenance; Material Handling Management Course; Management, Maintenance, Quality & Manufacturing Seminars; *Speaker Service:* Yes; *Rents Mailing List:* Yes; *Library:* by appointment
Meetings/Conferences:
For more information see Trade Shows, Conferences and Seminars Chapter
Institute of Industrial Engineers Annual IE Conference & Expo 2013
May 2013 San Juan

Institute of Packaging Professionals (IoPP)

#123, 1833 Centre Point Circle, Naperville IL 60563 USA
Tel: 800-432-4085
e-mail: info@iopp.org
www.iopp.org
www.linkedin.com/groups?gid=77086&mostPopular=
www.facebook.com/groups/253022814142
twitter.com/IoPP_Pros
www.youtube.com/user/iopppack1
Overview: A medium-sized national organization
Mission: To create networking & educational opportunities to help packaging professionals succeed
Chief Officer(s):
Barbara Dykes, Manager, Member Services, 630-544-5050 Ext. 114
bdykes@iopp.org
Finances: *Funding Sources:* Corporate sponsors
Membership: 5,000; *Fees:* $150; *Member Profile:* Packaging professionals
Publications:
•IoPP [Institute of Packaging Professionals] Update
Type: Newsletter; *Frequency:* Biweekly
Profile: Institute information, such as awards competitions, scholarships, publications surveys, & professional development activities

Institute of Power Engineers (IPE)

PO Box 878, Burlington ON L7R 3Y7
Tel: 905-333-3348; *Fax:* 905-333-9328
e-mail: ipenat@nipe.ca
www.nipe.ca
Overview: A medium-sized national organization founded in 1940
Mission: To promote business relations, social activities & mutual understanding among power engineers
Chief Officer(s):
Jude Rankin, National President
Bruce King, 1st National Vice President
Don Purser, National Secretary
Finances: *Annual Operating Budget:* $50,000-$100,000
Staff: 1400 volunteer(s)
Membership: 1,420; *Fees:* $60; *Member Profile:* Persons holding certificates of qualification as recognized by the Institute; persons enrolled in recognized power engineering courses; persons engaged in any pursuit identified or allied with power engineering

Institute of Scrap Recycling Industries, Inc. (ISRI)

#600, 1615 I St. NW, Washington DC 20036-5610 USA
Tel: 202-662-8500; *Fax:* 202-626-0900
www.isri.org
www.linkedin.com/company/563629
www.facebook.com/isri1987
twitter.com/ISRI
www.youtube.com/user/ISRI1987
Overview: A medium-sized national organization
Mission: To provide education, advocacy, compliance training; to promote public awareness of the value & importance of recycling to the produciton of the world's goods & services
Chief Officer(s):
Robin K. Wiener, President
robinwiener@isri.org
Membership: 1,250; 21 chapters across the US; *Fees:* Schedule available; *Member Profile:* North American companies that process, broker & consume srap commodities; associate memberships available for international members outside Canada, Mexico & the US, as well as to equipment & service providers of the scrap recycling industry
Activities: *Internships:* Yes; *Speaker Service:* Yes

Institute of Space & Atmospheric Studies (ISAS)

University of Saskatchewan, 116 Science Pl., Saskatoon SK S7N 5E2
Tel: 306-966-6401; *Fax:* 306-966-6428
e-mail: isas.office@usask.ca
www.usask.ca/physics/isas
Overview: A small national organization
Mission: Focus is on space & atmospheric studies, solar terrestrial physics, space weather, & atmospheric change
Chief Officer(s):
J.-P. St-Maurice, Chair, 306-966-2906
jp.stmaurice@usask.ca

Alan Manson, Executive Secretary, 306-966-6449
alan.manson@usask.ca
Membership: 1-99; *Member Profile:* Professors, research associates, post-doctoral fellow, research engineers

Institute of Transportation Engineers (ITE)

#600, 1627 Eye St. NW, Washington DC 20006 USA
Tel: 202-785-0060; *Fax:* 202-785-0609
e-mail: ite_staff@ite.org
www.ite.org
www.linkedin.com/groups?gid=166463
www.facebook.com/74169838900
twitter.com/ITEHQ
plus.google.com/116119105398656508668
Overview: A large international organization founded in 1930
Mission: To facilitate the application of technology & scientific principles for modes of ground transportation
Chief Officer(s):
Rock E. Miller, International President
Membership: 10,750; *Member Profile:* Transportation professionals with the responsibilities for meeting mobility & safety needs, such as transportation educators, researchers, consultants, planners, & engineers
Activities: Promoting professional development; Supporting education; Encouraging research; Increasing public awareness; Exchanging professional information
Meetings/Conferences:
For more information see Trade Shows, Conferences and Seminars Chapter
Institute of Transportation Engineers 2013 Technical Conference & Exhibit
March 2013 San Diego, CA
Institute of Transportation Engineers 2013 Annual Meeting & Exhibit
August 2013 Boston, MA
Institute of Transportation Engineers 2014 Technical Conference & Exhibit
March 2014 Miami, FL
Institute of Transportation Engineers 2014 Annual Meeting & Exhibit
August 2014 Seattle, WA
Institute of Transportation Engineers 2015 Technical Conference & Exhibit
March 2015 Tucson, AZ
Institute of Transportation Engineers 2015 Annual Meeting & Exhibit
August 2015 Hollywood, FL
Institute of Transportation Engineers 2016 Annual Meeting & Exhibit
August 2016 Anaheim, CA
Institute of Transportation Engineers 2017 Annual Meeting & Exhibit
July 2017 Toronto, ON
Publications:
•Context Sensitive Solutions in Designing Major Urban Thoroughfares for Walkable Communities
Profile: An ITE Proposed Recommended Practice
•Parking Generation: An ITE Informational Report
•Traffic Engineering Handbook
•Traffic Signal Timing Manual
•Transportation Impact Analyses for Site Development: An ITE Proposed Recommended Practice
•Transportation Planning Handbook
•Trip Generation: An ITE Informational Report
•Urban Street Geometric Design Handbook

Institute of Urban Studies (IUS)

University of Winnipeg, #103, 520 Portage Ave., Winnipeg MB R3C 0G2
Tel: 204-982-1140; *Fax:* 204-943-4695
e-mail: ius@uwinnipeg.ca
ius.uwinnipeg.ca
Overview: A medium-sized national organization founded in 1969
Mission: To undertake policy-oriented research in the field of Urban Studies; to serve as a resource centre for the community; to provide educational services to the University community & the community-at-large.; *Member of:* National Housing Research Committee
Chief Officer(s):
Jino Distasio, Director
j.distasio@uwinnipeg.ca
Finances: *Funding Sources:* University of Winnipeg; contracts
Staff: 5 staff member(s)
Activities: Areas of expertise include: housing, planning, urban Aboriginal issues, sustainable development, municipal government & finance, & socio-economic & demographic analysis; Research services include: trend analysis, market analysis, cost/benefit analysis, database development, survey & data analysis, community needs assessment, program/policy development & evaluation, community consultation & consensus building, & literature search & review, bibliography development; conference, workshop & publishing services; *Library:* by appointment

Institution of Mechanical Engineers (IMechE)

1 Birdcage Walk, London SW1H 9JJ United Kingdom
Tel: 44-(0)20-7222-7899; *Fax:* 44-(0)20-7222-4557
e-mail: enquiries@imeche.org
www.imeche.org
www.linkedin.com/e/vgh/2265081/
www.facebook.com/imeche
twitter.com/imeche
Overview: A medium-sized international organization founded in 1847
Mission: To educate, train & promote the professional development of engineers; to act as an international centre for technology transfer in mechanical engineering
Chief Officer(s):
Rod Smith, President
president@imeche.org
Finances: *Annual Operating Budget:* $3 Million-$5 Million; *Funding Sources:* Subscriptions & earnings
Staff: 180 staff member(s)
Membership: 75,000+
Activities: *Speaker Service:* Yes; *Library:* by appointment

Insurance Council of Canada *See* Insurance Bureau of Canada

Integrated Vegetation Management Association of British Columbia (IVMA of BC)

#720, 999 West Broadway, Vancouver BC V5Z 1K5
e-mail: reception@ivma.com
www.ivma.com
Overview: A small provincial organization
Mission: The organization is dedicated to the responsible practice of all aspects of vegetation management
Chief Officer(s):
Gwen Shrimpton, President
Membership: *Member Profile:* Independent contractors, consultants, manufacturers, suppliers

Intergovernmental Committee on Urban & Regional Research (ICURR) / Comité intergouvernemental de recherches urbaines et régionales (CIRUR)

#210, 40 Wynford Dr., Toronto ON M3C 1J5
Tel: 647-345-6454; *Fax:* 647-345-6991
www.muniscope.ca
Overview: A medium-sized national organization founded in 1967
Mission: ICURR supports local and regional governments, as well as private and non-profit companies through subsidized information and networking services. Muniscope is Canada's national resource on municipal issues, with subscription-based research and library services available on economic development, finance and taxation, housing and infrastructure, transportation, planning, and sustainability.
Chief Officer(s):
Katherine d'Entremont, Director
kdentremont@icurr.org
Finances: *Funding Sources:* Canadian Mortgage & Housing Corporation
Staff: 6 staff member(s)
Activities: Information exchange & research; *Rents Mailing List:* Yes; *Library:*

International Academy of Energy, Minerals, & Materials (AEMM)

Esprit Dr., Ottawa ON K4A 4Z1
Tel: 613-322-1029; *Fax:* 613-830-8371
e-mail: info@iaemm.com
iaemm.com
Overview: A medium-sized international organization
Mission: To provide information about technological advancements in the fields of energy, minerals, & materials to academia & industry
Environmental Activity: Offering training in matters related to energy, minerals, & materials
Chief Officer(s):
Lyne Bourgault, Adjointe administrative
Meetings/Conferences:
For more information see Trade Shows, Conferences and Seminars Chapter
International Academy of Energy, Minerals, & Materials 2013 International Conference & Exhibition on Advanced & Nano Materials
August 2013 Québec, QC
International Academy of Energy, Minerals, & Materials 2013 International Conference on Clean Energy
September 2013 Ottawa, ON
Publications:
•Additives & Surfactants
Price: $185
•Anode Materials for Lithium Ion Batteries — Patent Review, Market Trends, & Mmore
Price: $350
•Hard Metal Process, Application & Analysis
Price: $235
•Hydrometallurgy
Price: $225
•Ore Analysis, Handling, & Preparation
Price: $225
•Physical & Chemical Separation
Price: $225
•Plant Optimisation & Control
Price: $225
•Pyrometallurgy
Price: $225

International Academy of Science, Engineering & Technology

#414, 1376 Bank St., Ottawa ON K1H 7Y3
Tel: 613-695-3040
e-mail: info@international-aset.com
www.international-aset.com
www.linkedin.com/company/1169039
www.facebook.com/207827708283
twitter.com/ASET_INC
www.youtube.com/user/InternationalASET
Also Known As: International ASET Inc.
Overview: A medium-sized international organization
Mission: The International Academy of Science, Engineering and Technology (International ASET Inc.) is a young, growing and independent institution created to serve in the matters of education involving science and engineering.
Meetings/Conferences:
For more information see Trade Shows, Conferences and Seminars Chapter
ICEPR 2013: 3rd International Conference on Environmental Pollution and Remediation
July 2013 Toronto, ON
MHCI 2013: International Conference on Multimedia and Human-Computer Interaction
July 2013 Toronto, ON
ICMEM 2013: 2nd International Conference on Mechanical Engineering and Mechatronics
August 2013 Toronto, ON
ICNFA 2013: 4th International Conference on Nanotechnology: Fundamentals and Applications
August 2013 Toronto, ON
NTTP 2014: New Trends in Transport Phenomena
May 2014 Ottawa, ON
DSC 2014: Canadian Conference on Dynamic Systems and Control
May 2014 Ottawa, ON
MHCI 2014: 2nd International Conference on Multimedia and Human Computer Interaction
August 2014 Prague
ICEPR 2014: 4th International Conference on Environmental Pollution and Remediation
August 2014 Prague
ICMEM 2014: 3rd International Conference on Mechanical Engineering and Mechatronics
August 2014 Prague
ICNFA 2014: 5th International Conference on Nanotechnology: Fundamentals and Applications
August 2014 Prague

International Agricultural Exchange Association *See* AgriVenture International Rural Placements

International Air Transport Association (IATA) / Association du transport aérien international

PO Box 113, 800, Place Victoria, Montréal QC H4Z 1M1
Tel: 514-874-0202; *Fax:* 514-874-1753
www.iata.org

www.linkedin.com/groups?mostPopular=&gid=3315879
twitter.com/iata
www.youtube.com/iatatv
Overview: A small international organization founded in 1945
Mission: To promote safe, regular & economical air transport for the benefit of the peoples of the world; to foster air commerce; to study the problems connected with air transport; to provide a means for collaboration among the air transport enterprises engaged directly or indirectly in international air transport service; to cooperate with the International Civil Aviation Organization & other international organizations; to furnish for governments a forum for developing industry working standards &, as appropriate, coordinating international fares & rates; to simplify the travelling process for the general public; Affiliation(s): International Civil Aviation Organization
Chief Officer(s):
Tony Tyler, Director General
Membership: *Committees:* Avionics & Telecommunications; Engineering & Environment; Airports; Flight Operations; Medical; Security; Air Law; Financial; Traffic Coordination; Traffic Services

International Arctic Science Committee (IASC)

Telegrafenberg A43, Postdam DE-14473 Germany
Tel: 49-331-288-2214; *Fax:* 49-331-288-2215
e-mail: iasc@iasc.info
iasc.info
www.facebook.com/groups/343786799008379
Overview: A large international organization founded in 1990
Mission: To encourage & facilitate cooperation in all aspects of arctic research, in all countries engaged in arctic research & in all areas of the arctic region; to provide scientific advice on arctic issues including environmental & technological matters; Affiliation(s): Canadian Polar Commission
Chief Officer(s):
David Hik, President
Jackie Grebmeier, Vice-President
Volker Rachold, Executive Secretary
Finances: *Annual Operating Budget:* $250,000-$500,000; *Funding Sources:* Government of Norway: the IASC Secretariat
Staff: 2 staff member(s); 150 volunteer(s)
Membership: 18 countries; *Fees:* $7,000-9,000; *Member Profile:* Significant arctic research for a period of at least 5 years
Activities: Circum-Arctic research planning; 12 project groups; Developing Arctic EIA Guidelines under the Arctic Environmental Protection Strategy & International Arctic Environmental Data Directory; *Awareness Events:* Arctic Science Summit Week; *Internships:* Yes

International Association for Bear Research & Management (IBA)

c/o Terry While, USGS-SAFL, University of Tennessee, 274 Ellington Hall, Knoxville TN 37996 USA
Fax: 865-974-3555
e-mail: tdwhite@utk.edu
www.bearbiology.com
Also Known As: IUCN/SSC Bear Specialist Group
Previous Name: Bear Biology Association
Overview: A small international charitable organization founded in 1968
Mission: To support the scientific management of bears & their habitats, through research & distribution of information
Environmental Activity: Promoting the conservation & restoration of the world's bears; Supporting innovative solutions to bear conservation; Developing sound stewardship through population & habitat management
Chief Officer(s):
Frank van Manen, President
vanmanen@utk.edu
Harry Reynolds, Vice-President, Americas
hreynolds@reynoldsalaska.com
Diana Doan-Crider, Secretary
d-crider@tamu.edu
Cecily Costello, Treasurer
ccostello@bresnan.net
Membership: 550+ from 50+ countries; *Member Profile:* Professional biologists with an interest in bears; Wildlife managers; Others dedicated to the conservation of all bear species; *Committees:* Conference; Publications; Membership; Website
Activities: Encouraging communication & collaboration across scientific disciplines; Increasing public awareness & understanding of bear ecology; Maintaining high standards of professional ethics; Building an endowment & a future funding base; Sponsoring workshops & conferences on bear ecology, management, & biology;
Publications:
•International Bear News
Type: Newsletter; *Frequency:* Quarterly; *Editor:* Tanya Rosen; *ISSN:* 1064-1564; *Price:* Free for members of the International Association forBear Research & Management
Profile: Articles about biology, conservation, & management of the world's eight bear species, plus reviews of books on bears
•Ursus [a publication of the International Association for Bear Research & Management]
Type: Journal; *Frequency:* Semiannually; *Editor:* Richard B. Harris; *Price:* Free for members of theInternational Association for Bear Research & Management
Profile: A peer-reviewed journal with articles on all aspects of bear management & research worldwide

International Association for Earthquake Engineering (IAEE)

Central Office, Ken chiku-kaikan Bldg., 3rd Fl., Minatoku Shiba 5, Chome 26-20, Tokyo 108-0014 Japan
Fax: 81-3-3453-0428
e-mail: secretary@iaee.or.jp
www.iaee.or.jp
Overview: A medium-sized international organization founded in 1963
Mission: To promote international cooperation among scientists, engineers & other professionals in the broad field of earthquake engineering through interchange of knowledge, ideas, results of research & practical experience
Chief Officer(s):
Manabu Yoshimura, Secretary General
Polat Gulkan, President
Membership: 54 countries

International Association for Ecology (INTECOL)

Dean of Faculty of Pure Science, Dept. of Animal & Plant Sciences, Univ. of Sheffield, Sheffield S10 2TN United Kingdom
e-mail: kimeuns@kookmin.ac.kr
www.intecol.net
Overview: A medium-sized international organization founded in 1967
Mission: To promote the development of the science of ecology & the application of ecological principles to global needs; to collect, evaluate & disseminate information about ecology; to promote international actions in ecological research; *Member of:* Union of Biological Societies
Chief Officer(s):
Alan P. Covich, President
Membership: 1,000; *Fees:* $25

International Association for Environmental Hydrology (IAEH)

2607 Hopeton Dr., San Antonio TX 78230 USA
Tel: 201-984-7583; *Fax:* 201-564-8581
e-mail: hydroweb@gmail.com
www.hydroweb.com
Overview: A medium-sized international organization founded in 1991
Mission: To provide a place to share technical information & exchange ideas; To provide a source of inexpensive tools for the environmental hydrologist, especially hydrologists & water resource engineers in developing countries
Membership: 450; *Fees:* US$75
Publications:
•Journal of Environmental Hydrology
Type: Journal; *Frequency:* Monthly; *ISSN:* 1058-3912
Profile: Covering the fields of hydrology, environmental hydrology, urban hydrology, groundwater, groundwater pollution, groundwater contamination, & groundwater remediation

International Association for Great Lakes Research (IAGLR)

4840 South State Rd., Ann Arbor MI 48108 USA
Tel: 734-665-5303; *Fax:* 734-741-2055
e-mail: office@iaglr.org
www.iaglr.org
Overview: A small international organization
Mission: To promote all aspects of Great Lakes research & the dissemination of research information through publications & meetings
Chief Officer(s):
Wendy Foster, Business Manager
Matt F. Simcik, President
Membership: 1,000; *Fees:* $70 individual; $37 student; $200 library; $1,000 life
Activities: Annual four-day Conference on Great Lakes Research to exchange information on all aspects of research applicable to the understanding of large lakes of the world & to the human societies surrounding them
Awards:
•IAGLR Scholarship (Scholarship)
To a M.Sc or PhD student whose proposed research topic is relevant to large lake research *Amount:* US$2,000

International Association for Hydrogen Energy (IAHE)

#303, 5794 40th St. SW, Miami FL 33155 USA
e-mail: info@iahe.org
www.iahe.org
Overview: A medium-sized international organization
Mission: To provide information about the role of hydrogen energy
Environmental Activity: Promoting the exchange of information about hydrogen energy in the planning of a clean energy system
Chief Officer(s):
T. Nejat Veziroglu, President
veziroglu@iahe.org
David Sanborn Scott, Vice-President, North America
davidsanbornscott@scottpoint.ca
Ayfer Veziroglu, Comptroller
ayfer@iahe.org
Membership: *Member Profile:* Professional persons in fields related to hydrogen energy; Laypersons with an interest in hydrogen energy; IAHE Fellows; Emeritus members; Students
Meetings/Conferences:
For more information see Trade Shows, Conferences and Seminars Chapter
5th World Hydrogen Technology Convention (WHTC 2013)
September 2013 Shanghai
20th World Hydrogen Energy Conference (WHEC 2014)
June 2014 Gwangju Metropolitan City
6th World Hydrogen Technology Convention (WHTC 2015)
2015 Sydney,
21st World Hydrogen Energy Conference (WHEC 2016)
2016 Zaragoza
7th World Hydrogen Technology Convention (WHTC 2017)
2017 Prague
Publications:
•International Journal of Hydrogen Energy
Type: Journal; *Editor:* Emre A. Veziroglu; *ISBN:* 0360-3199
Profile: Ideas in the field of hydrogen energy for environmentalists, chemists, energy researchers, energy companies, & engineering students

International Association for Impact Assessment (IAIA)

1330 - 23rd St. South, #C, Fargo ND 58103-3705 USA
Tel: 701-297-7908; *Fax:* 701-297-7917
e-mail: info@iaia.org
www.iaia.org
www.linkedin.com/company/international-association-for-impact-assessme
www.facebook.com/iaia.impact.assessment
www.iaia.org/iaia-connect.aspx
Overview: A small international organization founded in 1980
Mission: To be a forum for advancing innovation, development & communication of best practice in impact assessment; to promote the development of local & global capacity for the application of environmental assessment in which sound science & full public participation provide a foundation for equitable & sustainable development; Affiliation(s): International Society of City & Regional Planners; Environment Institute of Australia & New Zealand; South Asian Regional Environment Assessment Association; Japan Society for Impact Assessment; Chinese Association of Environmental Protection Industry
Chief Officer(s):
Rita R. Hamm, CEO, 701-297-7912
rita@iaia.org
Nick Taylor, President
Finances: *Annual Operating Budget:* $500,000-$1.5 Million; *Funding Sources:* Membership fees; meeting registration
Staff: 6 staff member(s)
Membership: 1,600 in more than 120 countries; *Fees:* $US110 individual (base rate); $55 student; *Member Profile:* Corporate planners & managers; public interest advocates; government planners & administrators; private consultants & policy analysts; college teachers; students; *Committees:* Awards; Financial; Program; Board Nominations; Publications; Training & Professional Development; Conferences; Affiliates; Editorial Board; Conference Sponsorship
Activities: Presentation of papers, posters, plenary sessions, exhibits, technical tours, pre-meeting training courses

International Association for Impact Assessment - Western & Northern Canada

PO Box 2619, Stn. Bankview, 14 Street SW, Calgary AB T2T 5X6
Tel: 403-245-6404
e-mail: IAIA-WNC@praxis.ca
www.iaiawnc.org
Overview: A small local organization
Chief Officer(s):
Alan Ehrlich, President
aehrlich@mveirb.nt.ca

International Association for Public Participation (IAP2)

#124 PMB 54, 13762 Colorado Blvd., Thornton CO 80602 USA
Tel: +61 8 8120 0669; *Fax:* 1-303-255-2382
e-mail: iap2hq@iap2.org
www.iap2.org
www.facebook.com/group.php?gid=11982150193
Previous Name: International Association of Public Participation Practitioners
Overview: A medium-sized international organization founded in 1990
Mission: To serve the learning needs of members through events, publications, & communication technology; To advocate for public participation throughout the world; to promote research; To provide technical assistance
Chief Officer(s):
Moira Deslandes, Executive Director
moira@iap2.org
Geoff Wilson, President
president@iap2.org
Antonietta Cacciani, Manager, Professional Development
antonietta@iap2.org
Membership: 1,100; *Fees:* $975 individual; *Member Profile:* Public participation designers & facilitators; Policymakers; Project managers; Representatives from government agencies; Members of advocacy groups & professional organizations; trainers; Mediators; Citizen activists

International Association of Agricultural Economists (IAAE)

#1100, 555 East Wells St., Milwaukee WI 53202 USA
Tel: 414-918-3199; *Fax:* 414-276-3349
e-mail: iaae@execinc.com
www.iaae-agecon.org
Overview: A medium-sized international organization founded in 1929
Mission: To foster the application of agricultural economics to improve rural economic & social conditions; to advance knowledge of agriculture's economic organization; to facilitate communication & information exchange among those concerned with rural welfare; Affiliation(s): Canadian Council - International Association of Agricultural Economists
Chief Officer(s):
Walter J. Armbruster, Sec.-Treas., 630-271-1679, Fax: 630-908-3384
walt@farmfoundation.org
David R. Colman, President
Finances: *Annual Operating Budget:* $50,000-$100,000
Membership: 1,700; *Fees:* US$60-US$175; *Member Profile:* A worldwide confederation of agricultural economists & others concerned with agricultural economic problems
Activities: *Rents Mailing List:* Yes

International Association of Educators for World Peace (IAEWP Canada)

#100-209, 2 Bloor St. West, Toronto ON M4W 3E2
Tel: 416-924-4449; *Fax:* 416-924-4094
www.homeplanet.org
Overview: A large international organization founded in 1969
Mission: To promote peace through education; to promote a universal declaration of human rights & responsibilities; to promote global citizenship; to promote World Water Day; to promote the Vision Changer Project, TOPS Program & homeplanet.org; Affiliation(s): NGO status with UNESCO, UNICEF, UNDPI, UNCED & United Nations
Chief Officer(s):
Mitchell Gold, Secretary General & Executive Director, Homeplanet Alliance
mgold@homeplanet.org
Finances: *Annual Operating Budget:* $50,000-$100,000; *Funding Sources:* Programs; grants
Staff: 1 staff member(s); 200 volunteer(s)
Membership: 35,000 worldwide; *Fees:* $50
Activities: Regional workshops; exchanges; community outreach projects; UNESCO clubs; lectures; seminars; Home Planet Alliance; TOPS Program; *Awareness Events:* Vision Changer Project; *Speaker Service:* Yes

International Association of Environmental Analytical Chemistry (IAEAC)

c/o Dr. Montserrat Filella, Institut F.- A. Forel, Route de Suisse, Versoix 1290 Switzerland
Tel: 41 22 379 03 00; *Fax:* 41 22 379 03 29
e-mail: iaeac@dplanet.ch
www.iaeac.com
Overview: A small international organization founded in 1977
Mission: To support regular exchange of experiences between experts in the field of analytical chemistry of pollutants & related areas; To orient its members about recent advances in the field; To address relevant problems of environmental analysis & on questions related to environmental protection & control
Chief Officer(s):
Montserrat Filella, Secretary
montserrat.filella@unige.ch
José A.C. Broekaert, President
jose.broekaert@chemie.uni-hamburg.de
Membership: 110-130; *Fees:* SFR 110-300

International Association of Fire Fighters (AFL-CIO/CLC) (IAFF) / Association internationale des pompiers (FAT-COI/CTC)

#300, 1750 New York Ave. NW, Washington DC 20006-5395 USA
Tel: 202-737-8484; *Fax:* 202-737-8418
e-mail: membership@iaff.org
www.iaff.org
www.facebook.com/IAFFonline
twitter.com/iaffnewsdesk
Overview: A large international organization founded in 1918
Mission: To establish professional standards for the North American fire service with active political & legislative programs, & with experts in the fields of occupational health & safety, fire-based emergency medical services & hazardous materials training; to provide a voice in the development & implementation of new training & equipment; to work to ensure the staffing of fire & EMS departments
Chief Officer(s):
Harold A. Schaitberger, General President
Thomas H. Miller, General Secretary-Treasurer
Tim Burns, Press Secretary, tburn@iaff.org, 202-824-1566
Membership: 300,000+ fire fighters & paramedics in the U.S. & Canada + 3,200 affiliates; *Member Profile:* full-time professional fire fighters & paramedics
Activities: ; *Library:*
Publications:
•International Fire Fighter [a publication of the International Association of Fire Fighters (AFL-CIO/CLC)]
Type: Magazine; *Frequency:* 5 pa

Canadian Office
#403, 350 Sparks St., Ottawa ON K1R 7S8
Tel: 613-567-8988; *Fax:* 613-567-8986
www.iaff.org/canada
Chief Officer(s):
Scott Marks, Asst. to President, Canadian Operations
smarks@iaff.org

International Association of Fish & Wildlife Agencies *See* Association of Fish & Wildlife Agencies

International Association of Geochemistry & Cosmochemistry *See* International Association of GeoChemistry

International Association of Hydrogeologists (IAH)

IAH Secretariat, PO Box 4130, Stn. Goring, Reading RG8 6BJKOA 1L0 UK
Tel: +44 870 762 4462; *Fax:* +44 870 762 8462
e-mail: info@iah.org
www.iah.org
Overview: A medium-sized international organization founded in 1956
Mission: To advance the science of hydrogeology & exchange hydrogeologic information internationally; Affiliation(s): UNESCO; International Union of Geological Sciences
Chief Officer(s):
John Chilton, Executive Manager, IAH Secretariat
jchilton@iah.org
Membership: 4,000 in 135 countries; 300 in Canada
Meetings/Conferences:
For more information see Trade Shows, Conferences and Seminars Chapter
International Association of Hydrogeologists & Gowen Environmental Limited 18th Annual Contaminated & Hazardous Waste Site Management Course
June 2013 Toronto, ON
International Association of Hydrogeologists 2013 40th Congress: Solving the Groundwater Challenges of the 21st Century
September 2013 Perth
International Association of Hydrogeologists 2014 41st Congress: Groundwater: Challenges & Strategies
September 2014 Marrakech,

International Association of Hydrogeologists - Canadian National Chapter (IAH-CNC)

c/o WESA, 3108 Carp Rd., Carp ON K0A 1L0
Tel: 613-839-3053
www.iah.ca
Overview: A medium-sized national organization founded in 1972
Mission: To advance the science of hydrogeology & exchange hydrogeologic information internationally; *Member of:* Canadian Geoscience Council; Affiliation(s): International Union of Geological Congresses
Chief Officer(s):
Nell van Walsum, Secretary
Finances: *Annual Operating Budget:* Less than $50,000
Membership: 300 across Canada; *Fees:* $120; schedule
Activities: *Speaker Service:* Yes

International Association of Public Participation Practitioners *See* International Association for Public Participation

International Association of Science & Technology for Development (IASTED)

Bldg B6, #101, 2509 Dieppe Ave. SW, Calgary AB T3E 7J9
Tel: 403-288-1195; *Fax:* 403-247-6851
e-mail: calgary@iasted.com
www.iasted.org
www.facebook.com/pages/IASTED/130963346917239
twitter.com/IASTED_Calgary
Overview: A medium-sized international organization founded in 1977
Mission: To further economic development by promoting science & technology
Finances: *Annual Operating Budget:* $500,000-$1.5 Million
Staff: 3 staff member(s); 100 volunteer(s)
Membership: 250; *Fees:* US$110 individual; US$190 corporate
Activities: Interchange & circulation of information on science & technology; organizing international conferences, symposia, courses
Meetings/Conferences:
For more information see Trade Shows, Conferences and Seminars Chapter
The 24th International Association of Science & Technology for Development (IASTED) International Conference on Modelling and Simulation
July 2013 Banff, AB
The 15th International Association of Science & Technology for Development (IASTED) International Conference on Signal and Image Processing
July 2013 Banff, AB
The 15th International Association of Science & Technology for Development (IASTED) International Conference on Control and Applications
August 2013 Honolulu, HI
The International Association of Science & Technology for Development (IASTED) International Symposium on Power and Energy
November 2013 Marina del Rey, CA
Publications:
•Control & Intelligent Systems
Type: Journal; *Frequency:* Quarterly; *Editor:* Prof. Clarence W. de Silva
•International Journal of Computational Bioscience
Type: Journal; *Frequency:* Quarterly; *Editor:* Dr. L. Elnitski; Prof. L.R. Welch
•International Journal of Computers and Applications
Type: Journal; *Frequency:* Quarterly; *Editor:* Dr. L. Monticone
•International Journal of Modelling and Simulation
Type: Journal; *Frequency:* Quarterly; *Editor:* Prof. A. Houshyar
•International Journal of Power and Energy Systems
Type: Journal; *Frequency:* Quarterly; *Editor:* Dr. A/ Domijan, Jr.

•International Journal of Robotics and Automation
Type: Journal; *Frequency:* Quarterly

International Association of Sedimentologists (IAS)

c/o Universita' di Sassari, Via Piandanna 4, Sassari 07100 Italy
www.sedimentologists.org
Overview: A medium-sized international organization founded in 1952
Mission: To promote the study of sedimentology by publication, discussion & comparison of research results; to encourage the interchange of research, particularly where international cooperation is desirable; to promote integration with other disciplines. Canadian Correspondent: Dr. A. Guy Plint, Dept. of Earth Sciences, University of Western Ontario, London, ON N6A 5B7, email gplint@uwo.ca; *Member of:* International Union of Geological Sciences
Chief Officer(s):
Vincenzo Pascucci, General Secretary, Universita' di Sassari
pascucci@uniss.it
Poppe de Boer, President, Utrecht University
pdeboer@geo.uu.nl
Marc De Batist, Treasurer, Ghent University, Belgium
marc.debatist@ugent.be
Finances: *Annual Operating Budget:* $500,000-$1.5 Million; *Funding Sources:* Membership dues; sales of books
Staff: 1 staff member(s)
Membership: 1,700; *Fees:* EUR 30 full member; EUR 15 student
Publications:
•Basin Research
Type: Journal
Profile: Published by Blackwell
•Journal of Petroleum Geology
Type: Journal
Profile: Published by Blackwell
•Sedimentology
Type: Journal
Profile: Published by Blackwell

International Association of Theoretical and Applied Limnology; Societas Internationalis Limnologiae, SIL ***See*** International Society of Limnology

International Association on Water Quality; International Association on Water Pollution Research & Control ***See*** International Water Association

International Atomic Energy Agency (IAEA) / Agence internationale de l'énergie atomique

Vienna International Centre, PO Box 100, Wagramer Strasse 5, Vienna A-1400 Austria
Tel: 43-1 2600-0; *Fax:* 43-1 2600-7
e-mail: official.mail@iaea.org
www.iaea.org
www.facebook.com/iaeaorg
twitter.com/iaeaorg
www.youtube.com/user/IAEAvideo
Overview: A large international organization founded in 1957
Mission: An independent intergovernmental organization within the UN system; to accelerate & enlarge the contribution of atomic energy to peace, health & prosperity throughout the world; to ensure that assistance provided is not used to further any military purpose; Affiliation(s): United Nations
Chief Officer(s):
Yukiya Amano, Director General
Janice Dunn Lee, Deputy Director General, Management
Finances: *Annual Operating Budget:* Greater than $5 Million; *Funding Sources:* Member states contributions
Staff: 2300 staff member(s)
Membership: 158 sovereign states; *Fees:* Percentage of share of regular budget is fixed by UN General Assembly; *Member Profile:* Intergovernmental organization; *Committees:* Board of Governors composed of 35 member states
Activities: Verification in framework of Nuclear Non-Proliferation Treaty (NPT) that over 1,000 nuclear facilities in over 60 non-nuclear weapon states are used for peaceful purposes only; *Library:* by appointment
Publications:
•Animal Production & Health Newsletter [a publication of the International Atomic Energy Agency]
Type: Newsletter; *Editor:* Gerrit Johannes Viljoen; *ISSN:* 1011-2529
•Education & Training in Radiation, Transport & Waste Safety Newsletter
Type: Newsletter; *Editor:* Andrea Luciani; *ISSN:* 2304-5744
•Food & Environmental Protection Newsletter [a publication of the International Atomic Energy Agency]
Type: Newsletter; *Editor:* David Henry Byron; *ISSN:* 1020-6671
•Fuel Cycle & Waste Newsletter [a publication of the International Atomic Energy Agency]
Type: Newsletter; *Editor:* Hiroko Ratcliffe; *ISSN:* 1816-9287
•IAEA [International Atomic Energy Agency] Bulletin
Type: Magazine
•Insect Pest Control Newsletter [a publication of the International Atomic Energy Agency]
Type: Newsletter; *Editor:* Jorge Hendrichs; *ISSN:* 1011-274X
•Nuclear Data Newsletter [a publication of the International Atomic Energy Agency]
Type: Newsletter; *Editor:* Janet Roberts; *ISSN:* 0257-6376
•Nuclear Fusion [a publication of the International Atomic Energy Agency]
Type: Journal; *Editor:* Sophy Le Masurier
•Nuclear Information & Knowledge [a publication of the International Atomic Energy Agency]
Type: Newsletter; *Editor:* Bruna Lecossois; *ISSN:* 1819-9186
•Nuclear Power Newsletter [a publication of the International Atomic Energy Agency]
Type: Newsletter; *Editor:* Elisabeth Dyck; *ISSN:* 1816-9295
•Water & Environment News [a publication of the International Atomic Energy Agency]
Type: Newsletter; *Editor:* Luis Jesus Araguas Araguas; *ISSN:* 1020-7120
•XRF Newsletter [a publication of the International Atomic Energy Agency]
Type: Newsletter; *ISSN:* 1608-4632

International Bottled Water Association (IBWA)

#650, 1700 Diagonal Rd., Alexandria VA 22314 USA
Tel: 703-683-5213; *Fax:* 703-683-4074
Toll-Free: 800-928-3711
e-mail: info@bottledwater.org
www.bottledwater.org
www.facebook.com/bottledwatermatters
twitter.com/BottledWaterOrg
www.youtube.com/user/BottledWaterMatters
Overview: A large international organization founded in 1958
Mission: To assure that safe, clean, good-tasting bottled water is produced & marketed to consumers
Chief Officer(s):
Joseph K. Doss, President
jdoss@bottledwater.org
Membership: 1,200; *Fees:* Schedule available
Activities: IBWA works closely with its member companies & with government officials; takes active role at all levels of local, state & federal governments to assist in the development of regulations for bottled water

International Centre for Conservation Education (ICCE)

Brocklebank, Butts Lane, Woodmancote, Cheltenham GL52 9QH United Kingdom
Tel: 44-1242-674-839
www.icce.org.uk
Overview: A small international organization founded in 1984
Mission: To promote greater understanding of conservation, the environment & sustainable development through education & communication, placing particular emphasis on the needs of Africa; *Member of:* World Conservation Union (IUCN)
Chief Officer(s):
Mark Boulton, Honorary Director
Finances: *Annual Operating Budget:* Less than $50,000; *Funding Sources:* Earned income; some charitable funds
Activities: Produces wide range of educational materials; distributes audiovisual presentations worldwide; manages an environmental photolibrary; undertakes conservation education consultancy services; provides EE Consultancy services worldwide; *Internships:* Yes

International Centre for Research in Agroforestry (ICRAF) ***See*** World Agroforestry Centre

International Centre for Sustainable Cities (ICSC)

#205, 1525 West 8th Ave., Vancouver BC V6J 1T5
Tel: 604-569-0965; *Fax:* 604-569-0975
e-mail: info@icsc.ca
www.sustainablecities.net
Overview: A small international charitable organization founded in 1993
Mission: To support sustainable city projects around the world through demonstration projects using Canadian experience & expertise
Chief Officer(s):
Jane McRae, CEO
jcmcrae@icsc.ca
Beth Johnson, Chair
Finances: *Annual Operating Budget:* $500,000-$1.5 Million; *Funding Sources:* Projects
Staff: 5 staff member(s); 2 volunteer(s)
Membership: 36; *Committees:* Sustainable Cities Foundation; ICSC Management
Activities: Supports sustainable urban development demonstration projects in India, China, Columbia, Thailand, SE Asia (Thailand, Indonesia, Philippines), Turkey, Poland, Slovakia, Hungary: Plus-30 Network; *Internships:* Yes; *Library:* Open to public by appointment

International Coalition of Fisheries Associations (ICFA)

c/o National Fisheries Institute, #700, 7918 Jones Branch Dr., McLean VA 22102 USA
Tel: 703-752-8880; *Fax:* 703-752-7583
www.icfa.net
Overview: A small international organization founded in 1988
Mission: To provide a unified voice for the world's commercial fishing industries in international forums; to preserve & maintain the oceans as a major source of food for the people of the world; Affiliation(s): Fisheries Council of Canada
Membership: 1,000

International Commission of Agricultural & Biosystems Engineering / Commission Internationale du Genie Rural (CIGR)

c/o Dr. Takaaki Maekawa, School of Life & Environmental Sciences, 1-1-1 Tennodai, University of Tsukuba, Tsukuba, Ibaraki Japan
Tel: +81-29-875-6380; *Fax:* +81-29-875-6381
e-mail: biopro@sakura.cc.tsukuba.ac.jp
www.cigr.org
Overview: A medium-sized international organization
Mission: To ensure food security & the sustainable use of natural resources, through the application of principles of technology & engineering science
Chief Officer(s):
Soren Pedersen, President
Takaaki Maekawan, Secretary General
biopro@sakura.cc.tsukuba.ac.jp
Yutaka Kitamura, Secretary
kitamura@sakura.cc.tsukuba.ac.jp
Membership: *Member Profile:* National organizations, such as the Canadian Society for Bioengineering; Regional organizations; Individuals; Corporations
Activities: Providing networking opportunities for regional & national societies of agricultural engineering, as well as for private & public companies & individuals throughout the world
Meetings/Conferences:
For more information see Trade Shows, Conferences and Seminars Chapter
International Commission of Agricultural & Biosystems Engineering XVIII 2014 World Congress
September 2014 Beijing
International Commission of Agricultural & Biosystems Engineering 2016 4th International Conference of Agricultural Engineering (CIGR-AgEng2016)
June 2016 Aarhus
Publications:
•Agricultural Engineering International: The CIGR Journal of Scientific Research & Development
Type: Journal; *Editor:* Fedro S. Zazueta Ranahan
•CIGR [Commission Internationale du Genie Rural] Newsletter / Bulletin de la CIGR
Type: Newsletter; *Frequency:* Quarterly
Profile: Available in English, French, Arabic, Chinese, Russian, & Spanish

International Commission on Irrigation & Drainage (ICID) / Commission internationale des irrigations & du drainage

48 Nyaya Marg, Chanakyapuri, New Delhi 110021 India
Tel: 91-11-26116837; *Fax:* 91-11-26115962
e-mail: icid@icid.org
www.icid.org
Overview: A small international organization founded in 1950
Mission: To stimulate & promote development & application of arts, sciences & techniques of engineering, agriculture, economics, ecology & social science in managing water & land resources for irrigation, drainage, flood control & river training &/or for research in a more comprehensive manner adopting up-to-date techniques; to help produce more food from irrigated

agriculture on a global basis to alleviate want & hunger without disturbing the environment adversely; Affiliation(s): International Commission on Irrigation & Drainage - Canadian National Committee
Environmental Activity: Working Group on Environmental Impacts of Irrigation, Drainage & Flood Control Porjects
Chief Officer(s):
Avinash C. Tyagi, Secretary General
tyagi@icid.org
S.A. Kulkarni, Executive Secretary
kulkarni@icid.org
Membership: 107 countries
Activities: ; *Library:*

International Commission on Irrigation & Drainage - Canadian National Committee ***See*** Canadian National Committee for Irrigation & Drainage

International Commission on Occupational Health (ICOH) / Commission internationale de la santé au travail (CIST)
INAIL, Italian Workers' Compensation Authority, Occupational Medicine, Via Fontana Candida 1, Monteporzio Catone, Rome I-00040 Italy
Tel: 39-06-941-815-06; *Fax:* 39-06-941-815-56
e-mail: icoh@inail.it
www.icohweb.org
Overview: A small international organization founded in 1906
Mission: To foster scientific progress, knowledge & development of occupational health & safety in all its aspects; Affiliation(s): International Association of Agricultural Medicine & Rural Health; International Federation of Associations of Specialists in Occupational Safety & Industrial Hygiene; International Social Security Association; ISSA International Section on Prevention of Occupational Risks in the Iron & Metal Industry
Chief Officer(s):
Kazutaka Kogi, President
k.kogi@isl.or.jp
Sergio Iavicoli, Secretary General
S.Iavicoli@inail.it
Finances: *Annual Operating Budget:* $100,000-$250,000
Staff: 2 staff member(s)
Membership: 1,900 individual + 19 sustaining + 31 affiliate (in 93 countries); *Member Profile:* Individual & collective members; sustaining - organization, society, industry, or enterprise; affiliate - professional organization or a scientific society; *Committees:* 36 scientific committees & working groups
Activities: International congresses; special meetings; collaboration with international & national bodies & societies having similar aims

International Commission on Radiological Protection (ICRP)
PO Box 1046, Stn. B, 280 Slater St., Ottawa ON K1P 5S9
Tel: 613-947-9750
e-mail: admin@icrp.org
www.icrp.org
Overview: A small international charitable organization founded in 1928
Mission: To advance for the public benefit the science of radiological protection, in particular by providing recommendations & guidance on all aspects of protection against ionisary radiation
Chief Officer(s):
Christopher Clement, Scientific Secretary
Finances: *Annual Operating Budget:* $250,000-$500,000; *Funding Sources:* Grants from intergovernmental/governmental organizations & national sources
Staff: 2 staff member(s); 100 volunteer(s)
Membership: 1-99; *Committees:* Radiation Effects; Doses from Exposures; Protection in Medicine; Application of the Commission's Recommendations; Radiological Protection of the Environment
Meetings/Conferences:
For more information see Trade Shows, Conferences and Seminars Chapter
ICRP 2013
October 2013 Abu Dhabi

International Confederation for Thermal Analysis & Calorimetry (ICTAC)
SONY Inst. of Higher Education, Dept. of Informatics & Media Tech., Atsugi, Kanagawa 243-8501 Japan
Tel: 81-46-247-3131; *Fax:* 81-46-250-8936
www.ictac.org
Overview: A large international organization founded in 1965
Mission: To promote the use of thermal analysis in science & technology; to strengthen the collaboration between scientists & technicians from different parts of the world; *Member of:* International Union of Pure & Applied Chemistry
Chief Officer(s):
Andrzej Malecki, President
malecki@agh.edu.pl
Riko Ozao, Membership Secretary
ozao@ei.shohoku.ac.jp
Finances: *Annual Operating Budget:* Less than $50,000
Staff: 6 volunteer(s)
Membership: 500 full + 5,000 affiliate; *Fees:* US$20 student; US$100 individual; US$200 corporate; US$320 affiliate with less than 100 members; US$480 affiliate with more than 100 members; *Member Profile:* Open to scientists & technicians who are involved in thermal analysis; *Committees:* ICTAC Advisory; ICTAC Scientific Awards; ICTAC Congress Organising; Education; Environmental Safety; Geosciences; Kinetics; Lifetime Prediction of Materials; Nomenclature; Pharmaceuticals; Polymers; Sample Controlled Thermal Analysis; Standardization; Temperature Modulated Calorimetry; Thermal Analysis Combined Approach to Food Work; Thermal Reactivity; Thermochemistry
Activities: Scientific congress every four years

International Cooperative Alliance (ICA)
15, route des Morillons, Grand Saconnex, Geneva 1218 Switzerland
Tel: 41-22-929-8838; *Fax:* 41-22-798-4122
e-mail: ica@ica.coop
www.coop.org
Overview: A small international organization founded in 1895
Mission: To unite, represent & serve cooperatives worldwide
Chief Officer(s):
Ivano Barberini, President
Membership: 233 national & international cooperative

International Council for Applied Mineralogy (ICAM)
Federal Institute for Geosciences & Natural Resources, B4.15 Inorganic Geochemistry, Stilleweg 2, Hannover D-30655 Germany
Tel: 49-511-643-2565; *Fax:* 49-511-643-3685
e-mail: icam2000@bgr.de
www.bgr.de/icam
Overview: A small international organization founded in 1981
Mission: To promote scientific & technical interests of applied mineralogy by providing an international forum for exchange of ideas; Affiliation(s): National Mineralogical Association - USA, Australia, South Africa, Europe, Brazil, South America, Poland; International Mineralogical Association
Chief Officer(s):
Dieter Rammlmair, Secretary General
rammlmair@bgr.de
Finances: *Annual Operating Budget:* Less than $50,000; *Funding Sources:* Meeting registrations; donations
Membership: 20; *Member Profile:* Professionals in the field
Meetings/Conferences:
For more information see Trade Shows, Conferences and Seminars Chapter
11th International Congress for Applied Mineralogy
July 2013 Mianyang

International Council for Archaeozoology (ICAZ)
c/o University Of Sheffield, Department of Archaeology, Northgate House, West St., Sheffield S1 4ET England
e-mail: icaz@alexandriaarchive.org
www.alexandriaarchive.org/icaz/
Overview: A small international charitable organization founded in 1976
Mission: To develop & stimulate archaeozoological research; To strengthen cooperation among archaeozoologists; To foster cooperation with archaeologists & scientists working in related fields; To promote high ethical & scientific standards for archaeozoological work; Affiliation(s): International Union of Prehistoric & Protohistoric Sciences
Chief Officer(s):
László Bartosiewicz, President
h10459bar@ella.hu
Umberto Albarella, Secretary
u.albarella@sheffield.ac.uk
Finances: *Annual Operating Budget:* Less than $50,000; *Funding Sources:* Membership fees
Membership: 383; *Fees:* US$15; *Member Profile:* University staff; museums; freelance; *Committees:* Working Groups; Fish Remains; Bird Remains; Archaeozoology of Southwestern Asia & Adjacent Areas; Camelid; Animal Pathology; Worked Bone; North Atlantic Bioarchaeological Organization

International Council for Laboratory Animal Science (ICLAS) / Conseil international des sciences de l'animal de laboratoire
PO Box 296, Stn. 1900, La Plata Argentina
Tel: 54-221-421-1276; *Fax:* 54-221-421-1276
e-mail: ccarbone@fcv.unlp.edu.ar
www.iclas.org
Overview: A small international organization founded in 1956
Mission: To promote the humane use of animals in research through recognition of ethical principles & scientific responsibilities; to be an advocate for the advancement of laboratory animal science & biological research resources throughout the world; to promote international collaboration as a worldwide resource of knowledge in laboratory animal science; to promote the production & monitoring of high-quality laboratory animals by establishing standards & providing support resources; Affiliation(s): Canadian Association for Laboratory Animal Science
Chief Officer(s):
Gilles Demers, President
Cecilia Carbone, Secretary General
Membership: *Fees:* Schedule available; *Committees:* Communications & Publications; Complementary Methods; Constitution & By-Laws; Education & Training; Finance; Historical; International Genetics; Nominations Reference & Monitoring Centers; Regional Assistance: Europe, French-speaking Africa, English-speaking Africa, InterAmerica, Australia, Oceania & India
Activities: Scientific meetings; reference & monitoring centres; training courses; publications

International Council for Local Environmental Initiatives (ICLEI)
World Secretariat, Kaiser-Friedrich-Str. 7, Bonn 53113
Tel: 49-228/97 62 99-0; *Fax:* 49-228/97 62 99-01
e-mail: iclei@iclei.org
www.iclei.org
Overview: A small international organization founded in 1990
Mission: To build & serve a worldwide movement of local governments to achieve tangible improvements in global environmental & sustainable development conditions through cumulative local actions; Affiliation(s): International Union of Local Authorities
Chief Officer(s):
David Cadman, President
Martha Delgado-Peralta, Vice-President
Finances: *Annual Operating Budget:* Greater than $5 Million; *Funding Sources:* Membership dues; project funding
Staff: 50 staff member(s)
Membership: 360; *Fees:* Schedule available
Activities: ; *Library:* by appointment

International Council of Associations for Science Education (ICASE) / Fédération Internationale des Associations de Professeurs de Sciences (FIAPS)
e-mail: info@icaseonline.net
www.icaseonline.net
Overview: A small international organization founded in 1973
Mission: To improve science education worldwide by assisting member organizations; Affiliation(s): Canadian Association for Science Education
Chief Officer(s):
Beverley Cooper, Secretary
bcooper@waikato.ac.nz
Teresa J. Kennedy, President
tkennedy@uttyler.edu
Dennis Chisman, Treasurer
Finances: *Annual Operating Budget:* Less than $50,000; *Funding Sources:* Membership fees
Staff: 1 staff member(s); 14 volunteer(s)
Membership: 155 organizations; *Fees:* Schedule available; *Member Profile:* Organization involved in science education
Activities: Project 2000+, providing appropriate science & technology education for all; exchange of teaching resources; science education research & its application in teaching; exchanges of science teaching personnel;

International Council of Environmental Law (ICEL) / Conseil international du droit de l'environnement (CIDE)
Godesberger Allee 108-112, Bonn D-53175 Germany
Tel: 49-228-2692-240; *Fax:* 49-228-2692-251
e-mail: icel@intlawpol.org
www.i-c-e-l.org

Overview: A small international organization founded in 1969
Mission: Promoting the exchange of information on the legal, administrative and policy aspects of environmental conservation and sustainable development, to support new initiatives in this field, and to encourage advice and assistance through its network.; *Member of:* The World Conservation Union
Chief Officer(s):
Wolfgang E. Burhenne, Executive Governor
Finances: *Funding Sources:* Donations
Membership: 340
Activities: ICEL Reference to Environmental Policy & Law Literature; Bulletin online; *Library:* by appointment

International Council on Monuments & Sites (ICOMOS) / Conseil international des Monuments et des Sites

#49, 51, rue de la Fédération, Paris 75015 France
Tel: 33-1-45-67-67-70; *Fax:* 33-1-45-66-06-22
e-mail: secretariat@icomos.org
www.icomos.org
twitter.com/icomos
Overview: A medium-sized international organization founded in 1965
Mission: ICOMOS works for the conservation and protection of cultural heritage places, with a focus on the application of theory, methodology and scientific techniques for conservation.
Chief Officer(s):
Gustavo Araoz, President
Bernadette Bertel-Rault, Secretary General
Membership: 9,500 worldwide; *Member Profile:* Architects & specialists in the conservation & renovation of built heritage
Activities: ; *Library:* UNESCO-ICOMOS Documentation Centre; Open to public

International Development Research Centre (IDRC) / Centre de recherches pour le développement international

PO Box 8500, 150 Kent St., Ottawa ON K1G 3H9
Tel: 613-236-6163; *Fax:* 613-238-7230
e-mail: info@idrc.ca
www.idrc.ca
www.facebook.com/IDRC.CRDI
twitter.com/idrc_crdi
www.youtube.com/user/IDRCCRDI
Overview: A large international organization founded in 1970
Mission: To help scientists in developing countries identify long-term, practical solutions to pressing development problems; support is given directly to scientists in universities, private enterprise, government & non-profit organizations; priority given to equitable & sustainable development; projects are designed to maximize the use of local materials & to strengthen human & institutional capacity; research is undertaken by Third World recipients independently or in collaboration with Canadian partners; Affiliation(s): Regional offices in Asia & Africa
Chief Officer(s):
David M. Malone, President
Aboudou Karim Adjibade, Regional Director, Middle East & North Africa, Cairo, Egypt
Federico Burone, Regional Director, Latin America & the Caribbean, Montevideo, Uruguay
Simon Carter, Regional Director, Eastern & Southern Africa, Nairobi, Kenya
Kathryn Touré, Regional Director, West & Central Africa, Dakar, Senegal
Finances: *Annual Operating Budget:* Greater than $5 Million
Staff: 408 staff member(s)
Activities: Environment & natural resource management; social & economic equity; information & communication technologies for development; innovation, policy & science; *Internships:* Yes; *Library:* IDRC Library; Open to public
Awards:
•Ecosystem Approaches to Human Health Training Awards (Award)
Supports research that focuses on ecosystem management interventions leading to the improvement of human health & well-being while simultaneously maintaining or improving the condition of the ecosystem as a whole. Awards will be granted for training & research linked to the Ecosystem Approaches to Human Health Program Initiatives of the Centre. Priority will be give to proposals for research on ecosystems that are stressed through agriculture, urbanization or mining activities *Eligibility:* Citizens of developing countries &/or Canadian citizens or landed immigrants students currently enrolled in a graduate programme at a recognized university in Canada or in a developing country. Relevant language proficiency for site of study *Deadline:* May 31 *Amount:* Up to 6 awards for a maximum of $15,000 *Contact:* Centre Training & Awards Unit, 613/236-6163 ext 2098; Fax: 563-0815; Email: cta@idrc.da
•John G. Bene Fellowship: Community Forestry, Trees & People (Award)
Contributes to the expenses of Canadian graduate students undertaking field research in social forestry in a developing country *Eligibility:* Applicants must be Canadian citizens or hold permanent residency status; be registered in a Canadian university at the master's or doctoral level; have an academic background that combines forestry or agroforestry with social sciences. Applicants from interdisciplinary programs (e.g. environmental studies) may also be eligible, provided their programs contain the specified elements *Deadline:* March *Amount:* $15,000 per year *Contact:* Centre Training & Awards Unit, 613/236-6163 ext. 2098; Fax: 613/563-0815; Emails cta@irdc.ca
•Bentley Fellowship: Use of Fertility Enhancing Food, Forage & Cover Crops in Sustainably Managed Agroecosystems (Award)
Supports applied research of Canadian graduate students on how increased use of forage crops in cropping systems can improve agricultural production by farmers in developing countries *Eligibility:* Applicants must be Canadian citizens or hold permanent residency status; be registered in a Canadian university at the master's or doctoral level; have an academic background in agriculture or biology undertaking research on the role of forage crops in improved sustainable tropical farming. Applicants from interdisciplinary programs (e.g. environmental studies) may be eligible provided their programs contain the specified elements *Deadline:* October *Amount:* $20,000 *Contact:* Centre Training & Awards Unit, 613/236-6163 ext 2098; Fax: 613/563-0815; Email: cta@idrc.ca
Publications:
•IDRC [International Development Research Centre] Bulletin
Type: Newsletter

International Energy Foundation (IEF)

Clear Mountain Estates, PO Box 64, Site 8, RR#1, Okotoks AB T1S 1A1
Tel: 403-938-6210; *Fax:* 403-938-6210
www.ief-energy.org
Overview: A medium-sized international charitable organization founded in 1989
Mission: To facilitate the transfer of research & technology in all areas of energy with special emphasis on developing countries; interested in better ways to produce, transmit & conserve energy; to sponsor & conduct research studies, surveys & state-of-the-art studies; to undertake consulting projects & organize training programs for the interchange of knowledge & expertise amongst the international community; to provide scholarships for the education of students in fields of interest consistent with the objectives of the Foundation; to administer awards for the purpose of recognition & encouragement of outstanding achievement in areas of study consistent with objectives of the Foundation; to recommend standards to existing national & international associations & promote adoption of such approved standards for energy consumption, production & conservation; *Member of:* International Standards Organization
Chief Officer(s):
Peter J. Catania, Chair
Finances: *Annual Operating Budget:* $100,000-$250,000; *Funding Sources:* Contributions, donations, subventions, aids & grants made by donors & benefactors; fees for membership
Staff: 50 volunteer(s)
Membership: fellows in 49 countries, committee members in 175 countries; *Member Profile:* Open to all professionals, educational institutes, industries, governmental or quasi-governmental bodies operating in the field of energy; *Committees:* Constitution & Bylaws; External Administrative Centres; External & Internal Meetings; Finance; Goals & Objectives; Membership; Publications & Public Relations
Activities: Conferences, symposiums, workshops; *Speaker Service:* Yes

International Ergonomics Association

Department of Industrial Engineering, National Tsing Hua University, 101, Sec. 2 Guang Fu Rd., Hsinchu 30013 Taiwan
Tel: 886-3-574-2649; *Fax:* 886-3-572-6153
www.iea.cc
Overview: A small international organization
Mission: To elaborate & advance ergonomics science & practice & to improve the quality of life by expanding its scope of application & contribution to society
Chief Officer(s):
Eric Min-yang Wang, Secretary General
mywang@ie.nthu.edu.tw
Membership: *Committees:* Policy & Planning; Professional Standards & Education; Science, Technology & Practice; Communications & Public Relations; Industrially Developing Countries; Awards

International Erosion Control Association (IECA)

#3500, 3401 Quebec St., Denver CO 80207 USA
Tel: 1-303-640-7554; *Fax:* 866-308-3087
Toll-Free: 800-455-4322
e-mail: ecinfo@ieca.org
www.ieca.org
www.facebook.com/erosioncontrol
Overview: A medium-sized international organization founded in 1972
Mission: Serves as a global resource for environmental education & exchange of information; represents, leads & unifies a diverse group of people worldwide who share a common responsibility for the causes, prevention & control of erosion
Chief Officer(s):
Philip Handley, President
Finances: *Annual Operating Budget:* $500,000-$1.5 Million; *Funding Sources:* Membership dues; conferences; courses; publications
Staff: 10 staff member(s)
Membership: 3,500 members in 52 countries; *Fees:* Schedule available; *Member Profile:* 17 Professional Fields of Practice: Academic, Consultant, Contractor, Developer, Engineer, Government Agency, Landscape Architect, Library, Mining, Non-Profit, Publisher, Ski Industry, Supplier, Utility Company, & Other
Activities: Professional development courses; field trips & tours throughout the world; training bureau; scholarship program; research grant program & an erosion control material standards program; *Speaker Service:* Yes

International Federation for Cell Biology (IFCB)

www.ifcbiol.org
Overview: A medium-sized international organization founded in 1972
Mission: To promote cooperation & to contribute to the advancement of cell biology in all its branches; Affiliation(s): International Union of Biological Sciences; International Cell Research Organization
Chief Officer(s):
Denys Wheatley, President, United Kingdom
pat028@abdn.ac.uk
Hernandez F. Carvalho, Secretary General, Brazil
hern@unicamp.br
Membership: 15 member organizations representing 60 nations; *Fees:* US$200

International Federation for Housing & Planning (IFHP) / Fédération internationale pour l'habitation, l'urbanisme et l'aménagement des territoires (FIHUAT)

Binckhorstlaan 36, M04-03, The Hague 2516 BE Netherlands
Tel: 31-70-324-4557; *Fax:* 31-70-328-2085
e-mail: info@ifhp.org
www.ifhp.org
www.facebook.com/50479462167
twitter.com/ifhp
Previous Name: International Garden Cities & Town Planning Association
Overview: A medium-sized international organization founded in 1913
Mission: To plan & organize activities; To create opportunities for an exchange of professional knowledge & experience
Chief Officer(s):
Derek Martin, Secretary General
d.martin@ifhp.org
Membership: 500-999; *Member Profile:* Organizations or individuals who support the aims & objectives of IFHP, & who wish to participate in a worldwide network
Activities: Offering conferences, seminars, symposia, & study tours; Organizing student & film & video competitions
Publications:
•IFHP [International Federation for Housing & Planning] Membership List & Directory
Type: Directory; *Number of Pages:* 77; *Price:* Free for members only

International Federation for Medical & Biological Engineering (IFMBE)

e-mail: office@ifmbe.org
www.ifmbe.org
Overview: A medium-sized international organization founded in 1959

Mission: To reflect the interests & initiatives of national affiliated organizations; to generate & disseminate information of interest to the medical & biological engineering community & international organizations; to provide an international forum for the exchange of ideas & concepts; to encourage & foster research & application of medical & biological engineering knowledge & techniques in support of life quality & cost-effective health care; to stimulate international cooperation & collaboration on medical & biological engineering matters; to encourage educational programs that develop scientific & technical expertise in medical & biological engineering. IFMBE Secretariat currently located in Stockholm, Sweden.; Affiliation(s): International Union of Physical & Engineering Sciences in Medicine; International Organization for Medical Physics
Chief Officer(s):
Herbert F. Voigt, President, Boston University, USA
hfv@bu.edu
Ratko Magjarevic, Vice President, University of Zagreb, Croatia
ratko.magjarevic@fer.hr
Membership: 48 countries; *Fees:* Schedule available; *Committees:* Finance; Constitution & Bylaws; Secretaries; Working Groups: Asian Pacific Activities; Developing Countries; European Activities; Women in MBE; Regional Liaisons; International Liaisons; Nominating; Publication & Publicity; Federation Journal
Meetings/Conferences:
For more information see Trade Shows, Conferences and Seminars Chapter
World Congress on Medical Physics and Biomedical Engineering 2015
2015 Toronto, ON
World Congress on Medical Physics and Biomedical Engineering 2018
2018 Prague

International Federation of Hydrographic Societies
PO Box 103, Plymouth PL4 7YP United Kingdom
Tel: 44-175-222-3512; *Fax:* 44-175-222-3512
e-mail: helen@hydrographicsociety.org
www.hydrographicsociety.org
Previous Name: Hydrographic Society
Overview: A small international charitable organization founded in 1972
Mission: To promote the science of surveying afloat & related sciences; to promote better education & training of persons engaged or intending to engage in the study of hydrography & related sciences; to accumulate, extend & disseminate information, knowledge & expertise
Finances: *Annual Operating Budget:* $100,000-$250,000
Staff: 1 staff member(s); 10 volunteer(s)
Membership: From over 70 countries; *Fees:* Available on application; *Member Profile:* Individuals & organizations with an interest in any aspect of surveying afloat; *Committees:* Educational Award Scheme
Activities: Publications, conferences, seminars, workshops

International Federation of Landscape Architects (IFLA) / Fédération internationale des architectes paysagistes
c/o Christine Bavassa, Tour Louise - Ave Louise 149/24, Brussels 1050 Belgium
Tel: 32-0-497-63-05-50
e-mail: admin@iflaonline.org
www.iflaonline.org
Also Known As: IFLA
Overview: A small international charitable organization founded in 1948
Mission: To develop the profession of landscape architecture; To assist in identifying & preserving the intricate balance of ecological systems; To promote education & encourage scientific research in landscape architecture; To assist all levels of government in establishing & improving legislation connected with the profession of landscape architecture
Chief Officer(s):
Radmila Fingerova, Secretary-General
secgen@iflaonline.org
Desiree Martinez Uriarte, President
IFLA_president@iflaonline.org
John Easthope, Treasurer
john@jea.com.au
Membership: 1-99; *Member Profile:* National associations of professional landscape architects, individuals & corporations; *Committees:* Executive; Finance; Foundation
Activities: Offering world congresses, regional conferences, symposia & seminars; Organizing an international student design competition & educational programs
Publications:
•Guide to International Opportunities in Landscape Architecture, Education & Internships
Profile: Listing of international opportunities sorted by country
•IFLA Journal
Type: Journal; *Editor:* Thomas Jakob
Profile: Selected articles from landscape architecture magazines from around the world

International Federation of Organic Agriculture Movements (IFOAM) / Fédération internationale des mouvements d'agriculture biologique
Charles-de-Gaulle-Str.5, Bonn 53113 Germany
Tel: 49-228-926-5010; *Fax:* 49-228-926-5099
e-mail: headoffice@ifoam.org
www.ifoam.org
Overview: A small international charitable organization founded in 1972
Mission: To lead, assist, & unite the organic movement in its full diversity; To promote the worldwide adoption of ecologically, socially, & economically sound systems that are based on the principles of organic agriculture; *Member of:* Consumers Choice Council; Affiliation(s): Association interprofessionnelle pour le développement agrobiologique; Canadian Organic Growers; International Development Research Center; Ecological Agriculture Projects; Université écologique internationale; Mouvement pour l'agriculture biologique au Québec
Finances: *Annual Operating Budget:* $500,000-$1.5 Million
Staff: 10 staff member(s)
Membership: 750 member organizations & corporate associates in 105 countries; *Fees:* Schedule available; *Committees:* Standards; Third World; Accreditation; Criteria Revision
Activities: *Internships:* Yes; *Speaker Service:* Yes; *Library:* by appointment

International Federation of Surveyors (IFS) / Fédération internationale des géomètres (FIG)
Kalvebod Brygge 31-33, Copenhagen 1780 Denmark
Tel: 45 3886 1081; *Fax:* 45 3886 0252
e-mail: FIG@fig.net
www.fig.net
Overview: A medium-sized international organization founded in 1878
Mission: To ensure that the disciplines of surveying and all who practise them meet the needs of the markets and communities that they serve.; Affiliation(s): Canadian Institute of Surveying and Mapping
Chief Officer(s):
CheeHai Teo, President
chteo.surveyor@gmail.com
Membership: 200,000

International Flying Farmers (IFF)
PO Box 309, Mansfield IL 61854 USA
Tel: 217-489-9300; *Fax:* 217-489-9280
e-mail: iff1944@hotmail.com
www.internationalflyingfarmers.org
Overview: A medium-sized international organization founded in 1944
Mission: To provide a personalized, unique & economical opportunity to experience agriculture & aviation in a family environment in Canada & the United States
Chief Officer(s):
Marilyn Brohman, President
Membership: 1,100; *Fees:* US$60 per family

International Fund for Animal Welfare Canada (IFAW) / Fonds international pour la protection des animaux
#612, 1 Nicholas St., Ottawa ON K1N 7B7
Tel: 613-241-8996; *Fax:* 613-241-0641
Toll-Free: 888-500-4329
www.ifaw.org
Overview: A small international organization founded in 1969
Mission: Works to improve the welfare of wild & domestic animals throughout the world by reducing the commercial exploitation of animals, protecting wildlife habitats & assisting animals in distress; seeks to motivate the public to prevent cruelty to animals; promotes animal welfare & conservation policies that advance the well-being of animals & people
Chief Officer(s):
Fred O'Regan, President
Olivier Bonnet, Canadian Director
Finances: *Annual Operating Budget:* $500,000-$1.5 Million
Staff: 12 staff member(s)
Membership: 45,000
Activities: Campaigns against the commercial seal hunt in Canada, supporting anti-cruelty legislations for Canada

International Garden Cities & Town Planning Association
See International Federation for Housing & Planning

International Genetics Federation (IGF)
Dept. of Evolution & Ecology, University of California - Davis, 1 Shields Ave., Davis CA 95616-8554 USA
Tel: 530-752-4085; *Fax:* 530-752-1449
e-mail: info@meiosis.org
www.meiosis.org
Overview: A small international organization founded in 1968
Mission: To promote the advancement of the science of genetics; *Member of:* International Union of Biological Sciences; Affiliation(s): Genetics Society of Canada
Chief Officer(s):
Alfred Nordheim, President
alred.nordheim@uni-tuebingen.de
Charles H. Langley, Secretary-General
chlangley@ucdavis.edu
Membership: 63 national genetics societies

International Geographic Union (IGU) / Union géographique internationale
2246N Pollard St., Arlington VA 22207-3805 USA
Fax: 703-527-3227
www.igu-online.org
Overview: A small international organization founded in 1922
Mission: The IGU has the following objectives: to promote the study of geographical problems; to initiate & coordinate geographical research; to provide for the participation of geographers in the work of international organizations; to facilitate the collection & diffusion of geographical data & documentation; & to promote international standardization or compatibility of methods, nomenclature & symbols employed in geography.; *Member of:* International Social Science Council; Affiliation(s): International Council of Science
Chief Officer(s):
Michael Meadows, Secretary-General
mmeadows@mweb.co.za
Adalberto Vallega, President
Membership: 1-99
Activities: ; *Library:* Archives, Royal Geographical Society in London
Publications:
•IGU [International Geographic Union] Newsletter
Type: Newsletter; *Frequency:* Quarterly; *Editor:* Ronald F. Abler
Profile: Announcements, information, calls for participation in scientific events, programs, & projects

International Geographical Union - Canadian Committee
Simon Fraser Univ., Dept. of Geography, 8888 University Dr., Burnaby BC V5A 1S6
Tel: 604-291-3321; *Fax:* 604-291-5841
e-mail: agill@sfu.ca
www.igu-net.org/uk/what_is_igu/nationalcommittees.html
Overview: A small national organization
Mission: To promote international programs in geography within Canada; to promote activities within IGU programs relevant to Canada & to coordinate Canadian participation; to formulate Canadian position & advise the National Research Council on Canadian participation in IGU activities
Chief Officer(s):
Alison Gill
Finances: *Annual Operating Budget:* Less than $50,000; *Funding Sources:* National Research Council; SSHRCC
Staff: 10 volunteer(s)

International Geosynthetics Society (IGS)
IGS Secretariat, #4, 1934 Commerce Lane, Jupiter FL 33458 USA
Tel: 561-768-9489; *Fax:* 561-828-7618
e-mail: igssec@geosyntheticssociety.org
www.geosyntheticssociety.org
Overview: A medium-sized international organization founded in 1984
Mission: To be dedicated to the scientific & engineering development of geotextiles, geomembranes, related products, & associated technologies
Chief Officer(s):
Jorge G. Zornberg, President
zornberg@mail.utexas.edu
Finances: *Funding Sources:* Membership dues
Staff: 10 volunteer(s)

Membership: 31 chapters; 2,279 individuals; 128 corporate members from 68 countries; 156 student members; *Fees:* Schedule available; *Member Profile:* Geosynthetics professionals; *Committees:* Awards; Chapters; Corporate; Education; Technical
Publications:
•IGS (International Geosynthetics Society) News
Type: Newsletter; *Editor:* Gerhard Bräu
Profile: General information for IGS members, news from IGS chapters, conference reports, & a calendar of events

International Heavy Haul Association (IHHA)
2808 Forest Hills Crt., Virginia Beach 23454-1236 USA
Tel: 757-496-8288; *Fax:* 757-496-2622
www.ihha.net
Overview: A large international organization
Mission: To pursue excellence in heavy haul railway operations, engineering, technology & maintenance
Chief Officer(s):
Michael Roney, Chair
W. Scott Lovelace, CEO
scottlovelace@verizon.net
Finances: *Funding Sources:* Membership fees; Sponsorships
Membership: *Member Profile:* Railway organizations; National & state organizations; Private railway systems; Advocates for the world's heavy haul rail operations; *Committees:* Finance; Strategic Planning
Activities: Organizing specialist seminars & specialist technical sessions; Offering networking opportunities
Meetings/Conferences:
For more information see Trade Shows, Conferences and Seminars Chapter
International Heavy Haul Association 2013 International Conference
February 2013 New Delhi
International Heavy Haul Association 2015 Specialist Technical Session
2015 Perth
International Heavy Haul Association 2017 International Conference
2017
Publications:
•Guidelines To Best Practices For Heavy Haul Railway Operations - Infrastructure Construction & Maintenance Issues
Price: $125
•Guidelines To Best Practices For Heavy Haul Railway Operations - Wheel & Rail Interface Issues
Price: $80
•International Heavy Haul Association Conference Proceedings

International Institute for Applied Systems Analysis (IIASA)
Schlossplatz 1, Laxenburg A-2361 Austria
Tel: 43-2236-807-0; *Fax:* 43-2236-71-313
e-mail: inf@iiasa.ac.at
www.iiasa.ac.at
www.facebook.com/IIASA
twitter.com/IIASAVienna
Overview: A medium-sized international organization founded in 1972
Mission: To initiate & support individual & collaborative research on problems associated with social, economic, technological & environmental change, & thereby assist scientific, industrial & policy communities throughout the world in tackling such problems; current principal focus: scientific study of sustainability & the human dimensions of global change; to bring together scientists from various countries & disciplines to conduct research in a setting that is non-political & scientifically rigorous; to provide policy-oriented research results that deal with issues transcending national boundaries; to coordinate research projects, working in collaboration with worldwide networks of researchers, policy makers & research organizations; *Member of:* International Council for Science; International Federation of Institutes for Advanced Study; Affiliation(s): Canadian Committee for IIASA
Chief Officer(s):
Detlof von Winterfeldt, Director
detlof@iiasa.ac.at
Finances: *Annual Operating Budget:* Greater than $5 Million
Staff: 180 staff member(s)
Membership: 16; *Member Profile:* International & national research & policy institutes, organizations, & universities; *Committees:* Executive; Finance; Program; Membership; Advisory; Science; Steering
Activities: Policy-relevant research carried out by international, interdisciplinary teams, based on the following related themes: 1. Energy & Technology, including studies of environmentally compatible energy strategies, economic transition & integration, decision analysis & support, dynamic systems, & risk, modeling & policy; 2. Natural Resources & the Environment, including modeling land-use & land-cover changes in Europe & Northern Asia, sustainable boreal forest resources, transboundary air pollution, & adaptive dynamics; *Library:* by appointment

International Institute for Conservation of Historic & Artistic Works (IIC)
#209, 3 Birdcage Walk, Westminster, london SW1H 9JJ UK
Tel: +44 (0)20 7799 5500; *Fax:* +44 (0)20 7799 5800
e-mail: iic@iiconservation.org
www.iiconservation.org
Overview: A medium-sized international organization founded in 1950
Mission: To coordinate & improve the knowledge, methods, & working standards needed to protect, preserve & maintain the condition & integrity of historic & artistic works
Chief Officer(s):
Graham Voce, Executive Secretary
iic@iiconservation.org
Valerie Compton-Taylor, Membership Secretary
membership@iiconservation.org
Membership: *Fees:* £49 individual; £19 student; £70 fellow; £170 institution; *Member Profile:* Restorers; Conservators; Conservation scientists; Educators; Students; Architects; Collection managers; Curators; Art historians; Cultural heritage professionals

International Institute for Energy Conservation (IIEC)
#100, 10005 Leamoore Lane, Vienna VA 22181 USA
Tel: 703-281-7263; *Fax:* 703-938-5153
e-mail: iiec@iiec.org
www.iiec.org
Overview: A medium-sized international organization founded in 1984
Mission: To bring the power of sustainable energy solutions to developing countries & economies in transition
Chief Officer(s):
Robert L. Pratt, Chair
Nitin Pandit, Ph.D., President

International Institute for Sustainable Development (IISD) / Institut international du développement durable (IIDD)
161 Portage Ave. East, 6th Fl., Winnipeg MB R3B 0Y4
Tel: 204-958-7700; *Fax:* 204-958-7710
e-mail: info@iisd.ca
www.iisd.org
Overview: A large international organization founded in 1990
Mission: To promote sustainable development in decision-making in Canada & abroad by undertaking sustainable development research, advising government, business & organizations, analyzing & reporting on issues & events, & publishing & disseminating sustainable development information. Offices in Winnipeg, Ottawa, New York, & Geneva.
Chief Officer(s):
Franz Tattenbach, President/CEO
William H. Glanville, Vice-President & COO
Finances: *Annual Operating Budget:* Greater than $5 Million; *Funding Sources:* Federal & provincial government; government of other countries; philanthropic foundations
Staff: 80 staff member(s)
Activities: Trade & sustainable development; community adaptation & sustainable livelihoods; greening national budgets; business & industry accountability; Great Plains Sustainable Development; sustainable development measurement & indicators; *Internships:* Yes; *Speaker Service:* Yes; *Library:* Open to public by appointment

International Institute for Transportation & Ocean Policy Studies; Oceans Institute of Canada ***See*** International Oceans Institute of Canada

International Institute of Concern for Public Health (IICPH)
PO Box 40017, 292 Dupont St., Toronto ON M5R 0A2
Tel: 905-906-6128
e-mail: info@iicph.org
www.iicph.org
Overview: A medium-sized international charitable organization founded in 1984
Mission: To engage in advocacy on health issues; to assist in promoting & protecting people in their work & living environment in Ontario; to provide expertise on health, scientific & environmental issues; *Member of:* Ontario Environment Network; Earth Appeal; Nuclear Waste Watch
Chief Officer(s):
Marion Odell, Contact
Finances: *Annual Operating Budget:* Less than $50,000; *Funding Sources:* Private donations
Staff: 7 volunteer(s)
Activities: *Speaker Service:* Yes

International Institute of Fisheries Economics & Trade (IIFET)
Agricultural & Resource Economics, Oregon State University, 220 Ballard Hall, Corvallis OR 97331-3601 USA
Tel: 541-737-1416; *Fax:* 541-737-2563
e-mail: iifet@oregonstate.edu
www.oregonstate.edu/Dept/IIFET/
Overview: A small international charitable organization founded in 1982
Mission: To promote discussion of factors which affect international trade in seafoods & fisheries policy questions
Chief Officer(s):
Dan Holland, President
dholland@gmri.org
Ann L. Shriver, Executive Director
ann.l.shriver@oregonstate.edu
Membership: 100-499;; *Fees:* $75 regular; $25 student; $500 corporate/institutional; *Member Profile:* International Fisheries Economists; *Committees:* Executive
Activities: *Rents Mailing List:* Yes

International Law Association - Canadian Branch
c/o Bloomfield & Associés, #1720, 1080, Côte du Beaver Hall Hill, Montréal QC H2Z 1S8
Tel: 514-871-9571; *Fax:* 514-397-0816
e-mail: ila@fieldbloom.com
www.ila-canada.ca
Overview: A medium-sized national organization founded in 1967
Mission: Is a body for the study & advancement of international law in all its forms, commercial & interpersonal. Membership of the Association which is at present over 3,500 is spread among 50 Branches in every continent.
Chief Officer(s):
Janet Walker, President
Finances: *Annual Operating Budget:* Less than $50,000
Membership: *Committees:* International Committees
Activities: *Awareness Events:* Biennial Conference

International Lilac Society
1510, rue Pine, Mascouche QC J7L 2M4
Tel: 450-477-3797
e-mail: info@lilacs.freeservers.com
www.internationallilacsociety.org
Overview: A small international organization
Mission: To promote & stimulate interest in the genus Syringa
Chief Officer(s):
Nicole Jordan, President
njordan236@aol.com
Brad Bittorf, Executive Vice-President
ilsexecvp@gmail.com
Karen McCauley, Treasurer & Membership Secretary
mccauleytk@aol.com

International Maritime Committee ***See*** Comité maritime international

International Maritime Organization (IMO) / Organisation maritime internationale
4 Albert Embankment, London SE1 7SR United Kingdom
Tel: 44-20-7735-7611; *Fax:* 44-20-7587-3210
e-mail: info@imo.org
www.imo.org
www.facebook.com/IMOHQ
twitter.com/imohq
www.youtube.com/user/IMOHQ
Overview: A large international organization founded in 1948
Mission: To encourage the adoption of high standards in matters concerning maritime safety, security, efficiency of navigation & control of marine pollution from ships
Environmental Activity: Oil Pollution Co-ordination Centre
Chief Officer(s):
Koji Sekimizu, Secretary General
Lee Adamson, Manager, Public Information
Finances: *Annual Operating Budget:* Greater than $5 Million; *Funding Sources:* Government
Staff: 300 staff member(s)

Membership: 170 member states + 3 associate; *Fees:* Based on shipping fleet tonnage; *Committees:* Maritime Safety; Marine Environment Protection; Legal; Technical Cooperation; Facilitation
Activities: *Awareness Events:* Day of the Seafarer, June; *Library:* by appointment

International Network for Environmental Management (INEM)

Osterstrasse 58, Hamburg 20259 Germany
Tel: 49-89-18935-200; *Fax:* 49-89-18935-199
e-mail: l.karg@inem.org
www.inem.org
Overview: A small international organization founded in 1991
Mission: To be committed to the implementation of environmental management in businesses worldwide, including small- & medium-sized enterprises; To promote clean technologies
Chief Officer(s):
Ludwig Karg, Chair
Membership: *Member Profile:* Autonomous & non-profit business associations concerned with environmental management

International Nuclear Law Association (INLA) / Association internationale du droit nucléaire

Square de Meeûs 29, Brussels B-1000 Belgium
Tel: 32-2-547-5841; *Fax:* 32-2-503-0440
e-mail: info@aidn-inla.be
www.aidn-inla.be
Overview: A small international organization founded in 1970
Mission: To promote international studies of legal problems related to the peaceful use of nuclear energy
Chief Officer(s):
Rafael Manovil, President
Patrick Reyners, Secretary General
Membership: 500; *Committees:* Safety and Regulation; Nuclear Liability and Inurance; International Nuclear Trade; Radiological Protection; Waste Management; Radioisotopes

International Occupational Safety & Health Information Centre / Centre international d'informations de sécurité et de santé au travail

International Labour Office/CIS, Geneva CH-1211 Switzerland
Tel: 41-22-799-67-40; *Fax:* 41-22-799-85-16
e-mail: cis@ilo.org
www.ilo.org/cis/
Also Known As: Centro Internacional de Informacion sobre Seguridad y Salud en el Trabajo
Overview: A small international organization founded in 1959
Mission: To collect & disseminate world information that can contribute to the prevention of occupational accidents & diseases; Affiliation(s): Canadian Centre for Occupational Health & Safety; Canada Safety Council; Institut de recherche en santé et en sécurité de travail - Québec
Chief Officer(s):
J. Somavia, Director General
Finances: *Annual Operating Budget:* $1.5 Million-$3 Million
Staff: 12 staff member(s)
Membership: 183 national centres; *Fees:* CHF 26-315
Activities: CIS Information Service (personalized searches on any OSH topic); CIS factual microcomputer databases (covering important OSH topics); CIS Information Sheets (chemical, medical, technical, ergonomic); CIS microfiche service (reproduction of abstracted documents no longer obtainable from original sources); Directory of OSH Institutions (complete international OSH contact information); CIS Glossary of OSH Terms (OSH words & expressions: English, French, Spanish, German, Russian); CIS Bibliographies; *Library:* Open to public

International Ocean Institute (IOI) / Institut international de l'ocean

PO Box 3, Gzira GZR 1000 Malta
Tel: 356-21-346-529; *Fax:* 356-21-346-502
e-mail: ioihq@ioihq.org.mt
www.ioinst.org
Overview: A small international organization founded in 1972
Mission: To promote education, training & research to enhance the peaceful uses of ocean space & its resources, their management & regulation as well as the protection & conservation of the marine environment, guided by the principle of the common heritage of mankind
Chief Officer(s):
Awni Behnam, President
awni.behnam@ioihq.org.mt
Finances: *Annual Operating Budget:* $1.5 Million-$3 Million; *Funding Sources:* Donations; UN & government funding agencies; private foundations; endowment fund
Staff: 35 staff member(s); 200 volunteer(s)
Membership: 25 operational centres worldwide; *Committees:* Directors; Governing Board
Activities: Policy research; training; advisory services; *Speaker Service:* Yes; *Library:* IOI, Malta HQ Library; Open to public

International Oceans Institute of Canada (IOIC)

c/o Dalhousie Univ., 1226 LeMarchant St., Halifax NS B3H 3P7
Tel: 902-494-6918; *Fax:* 902-494-1334
e-mail: ioi@dal.ca
internationaloceaninstitute.dal.ca
Previous Name: International Institute for Transportation & Ocean Policy Studies; Oceans Institute of Canada
Overview: A small national organization founded in 1976
Mission: To promote responsible management of the world's oceans & sustainable development of marine resources; to protect the integrity of the ocean environment; to promote sustainable resource development; to improve the quality of ocean-dependent human life, including health & safety of maritime communities; to further these objectives, all aspects of the ocean environment are pursued - resource management & development, marine environmental quality, ocean law & policy, high seas management, coastal zone management, marine transportation, ocean science & technology, tourism & recreation, ocean industries & maritime boundary delimitation; Affiliation(s): International Oceans Institute; Atlantic Coastal Zone Information Steering Committee
Membership: 50
Activities: Services of the institute are available nationally & internationally for governments, organizations & private sector concerns, including industry, special interest groups & foundations; services include project development & management, policy development, education & training, conference & workshop coordination, research & information

International Organization for Standardization (ISO) / Organisation internationale de normalisation

PO Box 56, 1, ch. de la Voie-Creuse, Geneva 20 1211 Switzerland
Tel: 41-22-749-01-11; *Fax:* 41-22-733-34-30
e-mail: central@iso.org
www.iso.org
www.linkedin.com/company/iso-international-organization-for-standardiz
www.facebook.com/isostandards
twitter.com/isostandards
plus.google.com/+iso#+iso/posts
Overview: A small international organization founded in 1947
Mission: To promote the development of standardization & related activities in the world with a view to facilitating the international exchange of goods & services; developing cooperation in the spheres of intellectual, scientific, technological & economic activity; the results of ISO's technical work are published as "International Standards"; Affiliation(s): Standards Council of Canada
Chief Officer(s):
Terry Hill, President
Sadao Takeda, Vice-President, Policy
Finances: *Funding Sources:* 62% member bodies + 38% subscriptions + publications income + other services
Staff: 154 staff member(s)
Membership: 162; *Member Profile:* National body, representative of standardization in its country; *Committees:* 192 technical committees which develop international standards in a wide range of technological areas; the secretariat for a number of committees is held by the ISO member body for Canada (Standards Council of Canada, Ottawa)
Activities: ; *Library:* Reference Library; Open to public

International Peat Society (IPS)

Kauppakatu 19 D 31, Jyväskylä FIN-40100 Finland
Tel: 358-40-418-4075; *Fax:* 358-14-3385-410
e-mail: ips@peatsociety.org
www.peatsociety.org
Overview: A small international organization founded in 1968
Mission: IPS works toward the advancement & communication of scientific, technical, & social knowledge for the wise use of peatlands & peat.; Affiliation(s): UNESCO
Chief Officer(s):
Jaakko Silpola, Secretary General
Markku Mäkelä, President
markku.makela@gsf.fi
Membership: 1,450 from 36 countries; *Fees:* Schedule available; *Member Profile:* Scientific, industrial, commercial, & other organizations; Individuals interested in the study, conservation, & utilization of peat & peatlands
Activities: Organizing congresses, symposia & workshops; Publishing scientific publications; *Library:*
Meetings/Conferences:
For more information see Trade Shows, Conferences and Seminars Chapter
International Peat Society (IPS) Annual Assembly & ISHS-IPS International Symposium on Growing Media & Soilless Cultivation
June 2013 Leiden
International Peat Technology Conference 2014
August 2014 Riga
15th International Peat Congress: Peatland in Harmony - Agriculture, Industry, Nature
August 2016 Kuching
Publications:
•Mires & Peat
Type: Journal; *Editor:* Dr. Olivia Bragg; Prof. Jack Rieley
Profile: A joint scientific journal of the International Peat Society & the International Mire Conservation Group, featuring peer-reviewed academic papers on research related tomires, peatlands, & peat throughout the world
•Peat News
Type: Newsletter; *Frequency:* Monthly; *Editor:* Susann Warnecke
•Peatlands International
Type: Magazine; *Frequency:* Semiannually; *Accepts Advertising*; *Number of Pages:* 60; *Price:* Free for members
Profile: Background reports on peat & peatlands, reviews of conferences & books, research findings, business reports, & internal information about the IPS
•Proceedings
Profile: Proceedings of IPS conferences, symposia, & workshops

International Peat Society - Canadian National Committee

c/o Coastal Zones Research Institute, 232B, av de l'Eglise, Shippagan NB E8S 1J2
Tel: 506-336-6600; *Fax:* 506-336-6601
e-mail: jydaigle@umcs.ca
www.peatsociety.org
Overview: A small national organization founded in 1970
Mission: Dedicated to fostering the advancement, exchange and communication of scientific, technical and social knowledge and understanding for the wise use of peatlands and peat.; Affiliation(s): International Peat Society
Chief Officer(s):
Jean-Yves Daigle, President
Gerry Hood, Secretary
ghood@peatmoss.com
Finances: *Annual Operating Budget:* Less than $50,000; *Funding Sources:* Membership fees
Membership: 41 institutional/corporate + 3 senior/lifetime + 11 individual; *Fees:* $200 institutional/corporate; $30 individual
Activities: *Rents Mailing List:* Yes

International Permafrost Association (IPA)

c/o H. Lantuit, Alfred Wegener Institute for Polar & Marine Research, Telefrafenberg A43, Potsdam 14473 Germany
Tel: +49-331-288-2162; *Fax:* +49-331-288-2188
e-mail: contact@ipa-permafrost.org
ipa.arcticportal.org
twitter.com/ipapermafrost
Overview: A medium-sized international organization founded in 1983
Mission: To disseminate knowledge concerning permafrost; To promote cooperation among persons & national or international organizations engaged in scientific investigation & enginering work on permafrost; Affiliation(s): International Union of Geological Science
Chief Officer(s):
Hugues Lantuit, International Secretariat
Hugues.Lantuit@awi.de
Hans-W. Hubberten, President
hans-wolfgang.hubberten@awi.de
Hanne H. Christiansen, Vice-President
hanne.christiansen@unis.no
Antoni G. Lewkowicz, Vice-President
alewkowi@uottawa.ca
Membership: *Committees:* Standing Committee on Data, Information & Communications; International Advisory Committee for ICOP

Activities: Assembling the following working groups: Antarctic Permafrost & Periglacial Environments; Coastal & Offshore Permafrost Dynamics; Cryosol; Glaciers & Permafrost Hazards in High Mountain Slopes; Isotopes & Geochemistry of Permafrost; Periglacial Landforms, Processes & Climate; Permafrost & Climate; Planetary Permafrost & Astrobiology; Permafrost Engineering
Meetings/Conferences:
For more information see Trade Shows, Conferences and Seminars Chapter
International Permafrost Association 2016 11th International Conference on Permafrost
2016 Potsdam
Publications:
•Frozen Ground: The News Bulletin of the International Permafrost Association
Type: Yearbook; *Frequency:* Annually; *ISSN:* 2076-7463
Profile: Member news, current events, working group & task force reports, calendar, & publications
•Permafrost & Periglacial Processes
Type: Journal; *Frequency:* Semiannually
Profile: Reports from the International Permafrost Association
•Proceedings of the International Conferences on Permafrost
Type: Yearbook; *Frequency:* Annually
Profile: Peer-reviewed conference proceedings

International Plant Nutrition Institute (IPNI)
#550, 3500 Parkway Lane, Norcross GA 30092 USA
Tel: 770-447-0335; *Fax:* 770-448-0439
e-mail: info@ipni.net
www.ipni.net
Previous Name: Potash & Phosphate Institute/Potash & Phosphate Institute of Canada
Overview: A medium-sized international organization founded in 1935
Mission: To assist in the design & implementation of agronomic research; to obtain scientific facts & education programs to tell those facts about balanced fertilization, particularly in relation to agricultural production systems; to conduct & provide on-site support of field experiments worldwide
Chief Officer(s):
Terry L. Roberts, President
troberts@ipni.net
Tom Jensen, Northern Great Plains Director, (Saskatchewan)
tjensen@ipni.net
Tom Bruulsema, N. American-Northeastern Director, (Ontario)
tom.bruulsema@ipni.net
Finances: *Annual Operating Budget:* Greater than $5 Million; *Funding Sources:* North American potash & phosphate producers; Government of Saskatchewan
Staff: 6 staff member(s)
Membership: 16 corporate; 6 affiliate companies; *Member Profile:* North American potash or phosphate producer
Activities: ; *Library:* Open to public

Northern Great Plains Region - Saskatoon
#102-411 Downey Rd., Saskatoon SK S7N 4L8
Tel: 306-652-3467; *Fax:* 306-664-8941
Chief Officer(s):
Tom Jensen, Director

International Plant Propagators Society, Inc. (IPPS)
4 Hawthorn Court., Castle PA 17015-7930 USA
Tel: 717-243-7685; *Fax:* 717-243-7691
e-mail: Secretary@ipps.org
www.ipps.org
Overview: A medium-sized international organization founded in 1951
Mission: To seek & share information about the art & science of plant propagation
Chief Officer(s):
David Cliffe, Chair
d.cliffe@bigpond.net.au
Finances: *Annual Operating Budget:* $100,000-$250,000; *Funding Sources:* Membership dues
Membership: 3,200 individual; *Fees:* Varies with region; *Member Profile:* Open to individuals for commercial purposes or to those involved in research, teaching or extension activities

International Primate Protection League (IPPL)
PO Box 766, Summerville SC 29484 USA
Tel: 843-871-2280; *Fax:* 843-871-7988
e-mail: info@ippl.org
www.ippl.org
Overview: A medium-sized international charitable organization founded in 1973
Mission: To encourage & contribute to a better understanding of matters relating to the conservation of non-human primates & their habitats; to promote relevant training & educational activities with reference to non-human primates; to promote & enhance the welfare of non-human primates; to support primate protection projects; to investigate smuggling of primates; *Member of:* Monitor Consortium; Summit for the Animals; International Union for Conservation of Nature; Civicus
Chief Officer(s):
Dianne Taylor-Snow, Chair
Shirley McGreal, Executive Director
Jean Martin, Secretary-Treasurer
Finances: *Annual Operating Budget:* $500,000-$1.5 Million; *Funding Sources:* Membership dues; foundation grants; bequests
Staff: 7 staff member(s); 4 volunteer(s)
Membership: 15,000 in over 60 countries; *Fees:* $20 regular; $10 student; $50 sustaining; $100 patron

International Reference Centre for Community Water Supply & Sanitation *See* IRC International Water & Sanitation Centre

International Research Group on Wood Protection (IRG)
IRG Secretariat, PO Box 5609, Stockholm SE-114 86 Sweden
Tel: 46-8-101-453; *Fax:* 46-8-108-081
e-mail: irg@sp.se
www.irg-wp.com
Overview: A small international organization founded in 1969
Mission: To promote research throughout the world on the subject of wood protection; to facilitate collaborative research projects; to promote the exchange of technical information on wood protection
Chief Officer(s):
Jöran Jermer, Secretary General
Finances: *Annual Operating Budget:* $100,000-$250,000; *Funding Sources:* Membership & conference fees; sponsorships
Membership: 350; *Fees:* 900 SEK (Swedish Kroner) - regular; 450 SEK - student; *Member Profile:* Open to all persons with appropriate qualifications or research experience who are active or interested in wood protection research; *Committees:* Executive; Finance; Scientific Program; Membership; Ron Cockcroft Award; IRG Travel Awards; Electronic Communications
Activities: 4-day conference; workshops; plenary meetings; *Rents Mailing List:* Yes; *Library:* by appointment

International Sanitary Supply Association, Inc. (ISSA)
7373 Lincoln Ave. North, Lincolnwood IL 60712-1799 USA
Tel: 847-982-0800; *Fax:* 847-982-1012
Toll-Free: 800-225-4772
e-mail: info@issa.com
www.issa.com
www.linkedin.com/groups?gid=1799553
www.facebook.com/issaworldwide
twitter.com/issaworldwide
Previous Name: National Sanitary Supply Association
Overview: A large international organization founded in 1923
Mission: To link resources & expertise of everyone in the cleaning & maintenance products industry through an ongoing program of training & education, regional & national conferences, publications & the industry's largest annual trade show; to act as one voice before government agencies; to increase product quality, service & value to the customer; to promote the highest standards of public health & sanitation
Chief Officer(s):
John P. Garfinkel, Executive Director
Barbara Bornmann, Executive Assistant
barbara@issa.com
Finances: *Annual Operating Budget:* Greater than $5 Million; *Funding Sources:* Convention revenue; membership dues; educational materials
Staff: 24 staff member(s); 15 volunteer(s)
Membership: 5,700 companies in 83 countries; *Fees:* Schedule available; *Member Profile:* Firms which have been continuously engaged in the manufacture &/or distribution of cleaning & maintenance supplies & related products & services; classes of membership are distributor, wholesaler, manufacturer, associate, manufacturer representative, publisher; *Committees:* ISSA/INTERCLEAN; YES Coordinators
Activities: *Awareness Events:* Operation Clean Sweep; *Library:*

International Society for Ecological Economics (ISEE)
PO Box 44194, West Allis WI 53214 USA
Tel: 414-453-0030
e-mail: secretariat@ecoeco.org
www.ecoeco.org
www.facebook.com/iseeorg; twitter.com/ISEEORG
Overview: A medium-sized international organization founded in 1988
Mission: To extend & integrate the study & management of "nature's household" (ecology) & "humankind's household" (economics)
Chief Officer(s):
Marsha Kopan, Secretariat
Peter May, President
president@ecoeco.org
Finances: *Annual Operating Budget:* $100,000-$250,000; *Funding Sources:* Membership fees; grants
Staff: 4 staff member(s)
Membership: 2,008; *Fees:* $15-$130; *Committees:* Curriculum Development; Policy

International Society for Ecological Modelling (ISEM)
PMB 255, 550 M Ritchie Hwy., Severna Park MD 21146 USA
www.isemna.org
Overview: A small international organization founded in 1975
Mission: To promote the international exchange of ideas, scientific results, & general knowledge in the area of the application of systems analysis & simulation in ecology & natural resource management
Chief Officer(s):
Sven E. Jorgensen, President
msijapan@hotmail.com
Membership: *Fees:* $10 student; $20 individual; $100 institution

International Society for Environmental Biotechnology (ISEB)
ISEB Secretariat, Dept. of Chemical Engineering, U. of Waterloo, Waterloo ON N2L 3G1
Fax: 519-746-4979
e-mail: iseb@cape.uwaterloo.ca
www3.inecol.edu.mx/iseb/
Overview: A small international organization founded in 1992
Mission: To facilitate the development & promotion of environmental biotechnology worldwide
Chief Officer(s):
Eugenia Olguin, President
eugenia.olguin@inecol.edu.mx

International Society for Environmental Epidemiology (ISEE)
c/o ISEE Secretariat, JSI Research & Training Institute, 44 Farnsworth St., Boston MA 2210 USA
Tel: 617-482-9485; *Fax:* 617-482-0617
www.iseepi.org
Overview: A small international organization founded in 1989
Mission: To provide a forum for the discussion of problems unique to the study of health & the environment, such as environmental exposures, health effects, methodology, environment-gene interactions, & ethics & law; *Member of:* International Society of Exposure Analysis
Chief Officer(s):
Carol Rougvie, Secretariat
Daniel Wartenberg, President
dew@eohsi.rutgers.edu
Francine Laden, Sec.-Treas.
francine.laden@channing.harvard.edu
Membership: 500-999;; *Fees:* US$220 full member; US$145 basic; US$55 developing country & student; *Member Profile:* Members include epidemiologists, toxicologists, exposure analysts & others with an interest in environmental epidemiology, from academia, local, state & federal government, industry, & community organizations.; *Committees:* Nominations; Annual Conference; Awards; Membership; Communications; Ethics & Philosophy; Capacity Building in Developing Countries
Activities: *Rents Mailing List:* Yes
Publications:
•Epidemiology
Type: Journal; *Frequency:* Bimonthly; *Editor:* Allen J. Wilcox; *ISSN:* 1044-3983
Profile: A peer-reviewed scientific journal featuring original research on the full spectrum of epidemiologic topics
•International Society for Environmental Epidemiology Directory of Members
Type: Directory
Profile: Includes all ISEE members

International Society for Environmental Ethics (ISEE)

c/o Mark Woods, Philosophy Department, University of San Diego, 5998 Alcala Park, San Diego CA 92110
www.cep.unt.edu/ISEE.html
Overview: A small international organization founded in 1990
Chief Officer(s):
Emily Brady, President
Emily.Brady@ed.ac.uk
Philip J. Cafaro, Vice-President, 970-491-2061, Fax: 970-491-4900
philip.cafaro@colostate.edu
Mark Woods, Secretary, 619-260-6865, Fax: 619-260-7950
mwoods@sandiego.edu
Marion Hourdequin, Treasurer, 719-227-8331
marion.hourdequin@coloradocollege.edu
Membership: *Fees:* $25 regular membership (US); $15 students (US); $25 regular international member
Activities: Providing information about environmental ethics; Maintaining a bibliography on environmental ethics; Offering educational events
Publications:
•Environmental Ethics Syllabus Project
Editor: Robert Hood; *ISSN:* 1564-001
Profile: Information about courses in environmental philosophy & environmental ethics
•International Society for Environmental Ethics Newsletter
Frequency: 3 pa; *Editor:* Mark Woods; *Price:* Free with International Society for Environmental Ethics membership
Profile: Society activities & announcements, plus articles

International Society for Evolutionary Protistology (ISEP)

c/o Andrew J. Roger, President, Dalhousie University, 5850 College St., #8B1, Halifax NS B3H 1X5
Tel: 902-494-2620; *Fax:* 902-494-1355
www.isepsociety.com
Overview: A small international organization
Chief Officer(s):
Andrew Roger, President
Membership: *Fees:* $35 per 2-year period

International Society for Plant Pathology

c/o Secretary General, PO Box 412, Jamison ACT 2612 Australia
Tel: 61-2-62515658
www.isppweb.org
twitter.com/Food_Security
Overview: A small international charitable organization founded in 1968
Mission: To promote the worldwide development of plant pathology & the dissemination of knowledge about plant diseases & plant health management; *Member of:* International Union of Biological Sciences; International Union of Microbiological Sciences
Chief Officer(s):
M. Lodovica Gullino, President
issp.president@isppweb.org
Thomas Evans, Treasurer
ispp.treasurer@isppweb.org
Membership: *Member Profile:* Open to persons interested in or involved in plant pathology

International Society for Rock Mechanics (ISRM)

c/o Laboratório Nacional de Engenharia Civil, 101 Av. do Brasil, Lisbon 1700-066 Portugal
Tel: 351-21-844-3419; *Fax:* 351-21-844-3021
e-mail: secretariat.isrm@lnec.pt
www.isrm.net
Overview: A medium-sized international organization founded in 1962
Mission: The non-profit scientific association encourages & coordinates international cooperation in the area of rock mechanics. It maintains liaison with other organizations dealing with fields of science related to rock mechanics, such as geology, geophysics, soil mechanics, mining engineering, petroleum engineering & civil engineering.; *Member of:* International Union of Geological Societies; Affiliation(s): Canadian Rock Mechanics Association; Canadian Geotechnical Society
Chief Officer(s):
Luís Lamas, Secretary General
llamas@lnec.pt
John A. Hudson, President
john.a.hudson@gmail.com
Finances: *Funding Sources:* Membership fees; Grants that do not impair the Society's free action
Membership: 5,000 members + 46 national groups; *Member Profile:* Rock mechanics practitioners & corporations; *Committees:* Joint Technical Committee on Landslides & Engineered Slopes; Joint Technical Committee on Representation of Geo-engineering Data in Electronic Form; Joint Technical Committee on Education & Training; Joint Technical Committee on Professional Practice; Joint Technical Committee on Sustainable Use of Underground Space; Joint Technical Committee on Ancient Monuments & Historical Sites; Joint Technical Committee on Soft Rocks & Indurated Soils
Activities: Encouraging teaching, research, & advancement of knowledge in rock mechanics; Operating commissions for studying scientific & technical matters; Sponsoring international & regional symposia; *Library:* by appointment
Meetings/Conferences:
For more information see Trade Shows, Conferences and Seminars Chapter
International Society for Rock Mechanics 13th International Congress on Rock Mechanics
2015 Montréal, QC
Publications:
•International Journal of Rock Mechanics & Mining Sciences
Type: Journal
•ISRM [International Society for Rock Mechanics] News Journal
Type: Journal
Profile: Information about technology related to rock mechanics & news on activities in the rock mechanics community
•ISRM [International Society for Rock Mechanics] Newsletter
Type: Newsletter
•Journal of Rock Mechanics & Rock Engineering
Type: Journal

International Society for Soil Mechanics & Foundation Engineering ***See*** International Society for Soil Mechanics & Geotechnical Engineering

International Society for Soil Mechanics & Geotechnical Engineering (ISSMGE) / Société Internationale de Mécanique des Sols et de la Géotechnique (SIMSG)

City University, Northampton Square, London EC1V 0HB United Kingdom
Tel: 44-20-7040-8154; *Fax:* 44-20-7040-8832
e-mail: secretariat@issmge.org
www.issmge.org
Previous Name: International Society for Soil Mechanics & Foundation Engineering
Overview: A medium-sized international organization
Affiliation(s): International Society for Soil Mechanics & Geotechnical Engineering - Canadian Section; Canadian Geotechnical Society
Chief Officer(s):
R. N. (Neil) Taylor, Secretary General
Jean-Louis Briaud, President
Finances: *Annual Operating Budget:* $250,000-$500,000
Membership: 15,000-49,999; *Committees:* 25 active international Technical Committees working in various specialist areas of geotechnics

International Society of Arboriculture

PO Box 3129, Champaign IL 61821-3129 USA
Tel: 217-355-9411; *Fax:* 217-355-9516
e-mail: isa@isa-arbor.com
www.isa-arbor.com
Overview: A medium-sized international organization founded in 1924
Mission: To foster research & education that promotes the care & the benefits of trees; office located at 2101 West Park Court, Champaign IL
Chief Officer(s):
Tim Gamma, President
tgammatree@aol.com
Jim Skiera, Executive Director
jskiera@isa-arbor.com

International Society of Biometeorology (ISB) / Société internationale de biométéorolgy

Secretariat, Dept. of Geography, Univ. of Wisconsin-Milwaukee, Milwaukee WI 53201-0413 USA
Tel: 414-229-3740; *Fax:* 414-229-3981
www.biometeorology.org
Overview: A small international organization founded in 1956
Mission: To promote international collaboration of physicists, biologists, meteorologists & other scientists & the development of the field of meteorology in relation to humans, animals & plants
Chief Officer(s):
Paul Beggs, President
paul.beggs@mq.edu.au
Mark D. Schwartz, Secretary
mds@uwm.edu
Finances: *Annual Operating Budget:* Less than $50,000; *Funding Sources:* Membership fees
Membership: 240; *Fees:* US$85; *Committees:* Standing; Membership; Nomination; Election; Finance; Publication
Activities: ; *Library:* ISB Archive

International Society of Citriculture (ISC)

Dept. of Botany & Plant Sciences, University of California, Riverside CA 92521-0124 USA
Tel: 951-827-4663; *Fax:* 951-827-4437
e-mail: iscucr@ucr.edu
www.crec.ifas.ufl.edu/societies/ISC
Overview: A large international organization founded in 1976
Mission: To promote & encourage research, exchange of information & education, in all aspects of citrus production, harvesting, handling, & distribution of both fresh fruit & products; Affiliation(s): International Society for Horticultural Science
Chief Officer(s):
Luis Navarro, President
lnavarro@ivia.es
Carol J. Lovatt, Sec.-Treas.
Finances: *Funding Sources:* Membership dues; Sales of congress proceedings
Membership: 1,000-4,999;; *Fees:* US$30/4 years; *Member Profile:* Any individual, corporation, unincorporated association, or organization interested in an aspect of citrus culture, handling, marketing, processing, transportation, research, or education
Publications:
•ISC [International Society of Citriculture] Proceedings
Profile: Papers presented at previous meetings
•ISC [International Society of Citriculture] Newsletter
Type: Newsletter
Profile: Archived newsletters from 1995-2003

International Society of City & Regional Planners

PO Box 983, The Hague 2501 CZ Netherlands
Tel: 31-70-346-2654; *Fax:* 31-70-361-7909
e-mail: isocarp@isocarp.org
www.isocarp.org
Also Known As: ISOCARP
Overview: A small international licensing organization founded in 1965
Mission: To improve cities & territories through planning practice, training, education, & research; Affiliation(s): UNESCO; Council of Europe; UN/ECOSOC; UNCHS/Habitat
Chief Officer(s):
Milica Bajic Brkovic, President
Alex Macgregor, Secretary General
Manfred Schrenk, Treasurer
Finances: *Funding Sources:* Membership fees
Membership: 100-499;; *Fees:* Schedule available; *Member Profile:* Professional planners; Stakeholders involved in the development & maintenance of the built environment
Activities: Promoting the planning profession; Facilitating exchange between planners from different countries; Providing information on major planning issues; Evaluating developments & trends in planning practice
Meetings/Conferences:
For more information see Trade Shows, Conferences and Seminars Chapter
49th ISOCARP Congress - Brisbane, Australia
October 2013 Brisbane
Publications:
•International Manual of Planning Practice (IMPP)
Editor: Judith Ryser; Teresa Franchini
Profile: Reference guide to the key features of the spatial planning systems
•International Society of City & Regional Planners Annual Congress Report
Type: Yearbook; *Frequency:* Annually
Profile: Final report of each congress
•ISOCARP [International Society of City & Regional Planners] NET
Type: Newsletter; *Editor:* Judy van Hemert
•ISOCARP [International Society of City & Regional Planners] Review
Profile: Complement to the research efforts prepared for the annual ISOCARP Congresses

International Society of Indoor Air Quality & Climate (ISIAQ)

c/o Gina Bendy, 2548 Empire Grade, Santa Cruz CA 95060 USA
Tel: 831-426-0148; *Fax:* 831-426-6522
e-mail: info@isiaq.org
www.isiaq.org
Overview: A medium-sized international organization founded in 1992
Mission: To support the establishment of healthy, productivity-encouraging indoor environments
Environmental Activity: Providing information about the latest developments in indoor air quality & climate; Developing guidelines to improve indoor air quality & climate
Chief Officer(s):
Richard Shaughnessy, President
rjstulsau@aol.com
Anne Hyvärinen, Secretary
anne.hyvarinen@thl.fi
Carl-Gustaf Bornehag, Treasurer
carl-gustaf.bornehag@kau.se
Finances: *Funding Sources:* Membership fees; Donations; Sponsorships
Membership: *Fees:* US $15 - $30 /year students; US $135 / year individuals; US $700 / year corporate members; *Member Profile:* Individuals, such as scientist involved in indoor air quality research, occupational health professionals, government & regulatory professionals, & architects; Corporations; Students; *Committees:* Task force on the control of moisture & mould problems in cold climate; Task force on the vocabulary of the indoor air sciences; Task force on the IAQ & climate in cultural & heritage collections; Task force on the criteria for cleaning of air handling systems; Task force on the performance of portable air cleaners; Task force on the education for healthier buildings; Task force on the effect of the indoor environment on productivity in offices; Task force on indoor air research & building practice
Activities: Facilitating international & interdisciplinary communication; Liaising with governments & other agencies with interests in indoor environment
Meetings/Conferences:
For more information see Trade Shows, Conferences and Seminars Chapter
Indoor Air 2014: The Triennial Conference of the International Society of Indoor Air Quality & Climate
July 2014 Hong Kong
International Society of Indoor Air Quality & Climate Healthy Buildings 2015
2015
Publications:
•Indoor Air: The International Journal of Indoor Environment & Health
Type: Journal; *Frequency:* Bimonthly; *Accepts Advertising*; *Editor:* Jan Sundell; William Nazaroff; *Price:* Free with International Society of Indoor Air Quality & Climate membership
Profile: Original research about indoor environments
•International Society of Indoor Air Quality & Climate Conference Proceedings
Profile: Proceedings of Healthy Buildings & Indoor Air conferences
•International Society of Indoor Air Quality & Climate Task Force Reports
•International Society of Indoor Air Quality & Climate Newsletter
Type: Newsletter; *Accepts Advertising*; *Price:* Free with International Society of Indoor Air Quality & Climate membership
Profile: Society activities
•Vocabulary of the Indoor Air Sciences

International Society of Limnology (IATAL) / Societas Internationalis Limnologiae (SIL)

c/o Denise L. Johnson, GSGPH, 135 Dauer Dr., ESE, 148 Rosenau Hall, University of North Carolina, Chapel Hill NC 27599-7431 USA
Tel: 336-376-9362; *Fax:* 336-376-8825
e-mail: denisej@email.unc.edu
www.limnology.org
Previous Name: International Association of Theoretical and Applied Limnology; Societas Internationalis Limnologiae, SIL
Overview: A medium-sized international organization founded in 1922
Mission: The Society promotes communication between limnologists of all countries & all disciplines to increase understanding of inland aquatic ecosystems & their management.; Affiliation(s): Canadian Society of Limnology
Chief Officer(s):
Brian Moss, President, (United Kingdom)
brmoss@liverpool.ac.uk
Morten S›ndergaard, General Sec.-Treas., (Denmark)
msondergaard@bi.ku.dk
Membership: *Fees:* US$55 regular; US$110 institutional; *Member Profile:* Open to those with an interest in limnology, the study of inland water ecosystems (rivers, lakes, streams, reservoirs, fish ponds, aquifers, & bogs); Members have varied interests which include physics of water movements, water chemistry, plankton & water plants, invertebrate ecology, fish & fisheries, watershed & reservoir management, pollution of inland waters, & modelling of aquatic ecosystems; *Committees:* Baldi Memorial; Conservation; International; Kilham Memorial; Limnology in Developing Countries; Naumann-Thienemann Medal; Nominating; Publication Advisory; Tonolli Memorial; Working Groups

International Society of Soil Science *See* International Union of Soil Sciences

International Soil Reference & Information Centre (ISRIC)

PO Box 353, #101, Droevendaalsesteeg 3, Wageningen 6700 AJ Netherlands
Tel: 31-317-483-735
e-mail: soil.isric@wur.nl
www.isric.org
Overview: A small international organization founded in 1966
Mission: To contribute to the challenge of providing sufficient food for the growing world populations while preserving the biophysical potential of natural resources & minimizing environmental degradation; *Member of:* World Data Centres of International Council of Sciences; World Data Centre for Soils; Affiliation(s): Wageningen University & Research Centre
Chief Officer(s):
Ir P.S. Bindraban, Director
Prem.Bindraban@wur.nl
Finances: *Annual Operating Budget:* $500,000-$1.5 Million; *Funding Sources:* Dutch government, international/bilateral project donor organizations
Staff: 25 staff member(s)
Membership: 1-99
Activities: ; *Library:* Open to public by appointment

International Solar Energy Society (ISES)

International Headquarters, Villa Tannheim, Wiesentalstrasse 50, Freiburg 79115 Germany
Tel: 49-761-459-06-0; *Fax:* 49-761-459-06-99
e-mail: hq@ises.org
www.ises.org
Overview: A medium-sized international charitable organization founded in 1954
Mission: A United Nations accredited NGO, with members in 50+ countries worldwide; goals include the promotion of renewable energy, with solar energy being a focus, sustainable development, and research; *Member of:* International Renewable Energy Alliance
Chief Officer(s):
Eduardo A. Rincón Mejía, Secretary, (Mexico)
rinconsolar@hotmail.com
Monica V. Oliphant, President, (Australia)
oliphant@adam.com.au
Membership: 4,000; *Fees:* Schedule available; *Member Profile:* Persons engaged in the research development & utilisation of solar energy & persons who have an interest in advancing the purposes of the society
Activities: All aspects of solar energy, including characteristics, effects & methods of use; international congresses on solar energy
Awards:
•Achievement through Action Award (Award)
Monetary, biennial; awarded to an individual, a group, or corporate body that has made an important contribution to the harnessing of solar energy for practical use or is proposing a new concept, development or product for the same purpose
•Farrington Daniel Award (Award)
Recognition for outstanding intellectual leadership in the field of solar energy
Publications:
•Solar Energy
Type: Journal; *Frequency:* Monthly; *Editor:* Dr. D. Yogi Goswami

International Solid Waste Association (ISWA)

Auerspergstrasse 15, Top 41, Vienna 1080 Austria
Tel: +43 1 253 6001; *Fax:* +43 1 523 6001 99
e-mail: iswa@iswa.dk
www.iswa.org
www.facebook.com/group.php?gid=123367611068687
Overview: A medium-sized international organization founded in 1931
Mission: To promote efficiency in environmental practice
Environmental Activity: Advancing waste management through training
Chief Officer(s):
Hermann Koller, Managing Director
hkoller@iswa.org
Greg Vogt, Managing Director
gvogt@iswa.dk
Gerfried Habenicht, Manager, Communications
Niels Jorn Hahn, President
njh@r98.dk
Alfred Holzschuster, Manager, Finance & Member Services
Morten Sandbakken, Treasurer
morten.sandbakken@fias.no
Rachael Williams, Technical Manager
Finances: *Funding Sources:* Sponsorships
Membership: *Member Profile:* Non-profit waste management associations representing the waste management industry in a particular country; Organizations or companies associated with or working in the field of waste management
Activities: Promoting professionalism; Supporting developing countries
Meetings/Conferences:
For more information see Trade Shows, Conferences and Seminars Chapter
International Solid Waste Association 2013 Annual World Congress
October 2013 Vienna
Publications:
•Global News [a publication of the International Solid Waste Association]
Type: Newsletter
Profile: Contents include news from the association president, conference information, awards, news from around the world, & forthcoming events
•International Solid Waste Association Conference Proceedings
Type: Yearbook; *Frequency:* Annually
Profile: Information from the International Solid Waste Association Annual Congress, the Beacon Conference, & other conferences organized by the association
•International Solid Waste Association Annual Report
Type: Yearbook; *Frequency:* Annually
•Waste Management & Research
Type: Journal; *Frequency:* Monthly; *Editor:* Jens Aage Hansen
Profile: The theory & practice of waste management & research
•Waste Management World
Type: Magazine; *Frequency:* Bimonthly; *Accepts Advertising*; *Editor:* Tom Freyberg
Profile: Incorporates the International Directory of Solid Waste Management, with a listing of ISWA members & waste management companies

International Titanium Association (ITA)

#100, 11674 Huron St., Northglenn CO 80234 USA
Tel: 303-404-2221; *Fax:* 303-404-9111
e-mail: ita@titanium.org
www.titanium.org
Overview: A large international organization founded in 1984
Mission: To connect the public with titanium specialists throughout the world, who can offer technical & sales assistance
Chief Officer(s):
Jennifer Simpson, Executive Director
jsimpson@titanium.org
Stacey Blicker, Contact, Member Services
sblicker@titanium.org
Membership: 195 companies; *Fees:* Schedule available based on previous year's shipments (producers), receipts (users & consumers); $500-$4,500 non-voting; *Committees:* Education; Safety; Conference Planning; Trade Show; Achievement Award; Grant; Applications
Activities: Offering titanium literature; Sponsoring educational workshops & seminars
Meetings/Conferences:
For more information see Trade Shows, Conferences and Seminars Chapter
Titanium Europe 2013
March 2013 Hamburg
Titanium 2013
October 2013 Las Vegas, NV
Publications:
•Titanium Update Newsletter

Type: Newsletter; *Price:* Free
Profile: Titanium news, awards, & membership information

International Union for Conservation of Nature (IUCN)

28, rue Mauverney, Gland 1196 Switzerland
Tel: 41-22-999-0000; *Fax:* 41-22-999-0002
e-mail: mail@iucn.org
www.iucn.org
www.facebook.com/iucn.org
twitter.com/IUCN
www.youtube.com/user/IUCN
Previous Name: The World Conservation Union; International Union for Conservation of Nature & Natural Resources
Overview: A large international organization founded in 1948
Mission: To find solutions to environment & development challenges; To conserve the integrity & diversity of nature; To ensure the use of natural resources is equitable & ecologically sustainable
Environmental Activity: Promoting the value & conservation of nature; Providing authoritative information on the environment & sustainable development
Chief Officer(s):
Zhang Xinsheng, President
president@iucn.org
Patrick de Henry, Treasurer
Finances: *Funding Sources:* Member organizations; Governments; Foundations; Bilateral & multilateral agencies; Corporations
Staff: 1000 staff member(s)
Membership: 1,200+ government organizations & NGOs + 11,000 volunteer scientist from over 160 countries; *Member Profile:* Government organizations; NGOs; Volunteer scientists
Activities: Supporting scientific research; Managing field projects; Coordinatingpersons & organization to develop & implement policies, laws, & best practices; Publishing over 100 books, reports, documents, & guidelines each year
Publications:
•Arborvitae [a publication of the International Union for Conservation of Nature]
Type: Newsletter; *Frequency:* 3 pa
Profile: Issues affecting how forest resources are used & governed
•Building Bridges [a publication of the International Union for Conservation of Nature]
Type: Newsletter; *Frequency:* Quarterly
Profile: Conservation & the private sector
•Conservation Made Clear [a publication of the International Union for Conservation of Nature]
Type: Newsletter; *Frequency:* Monthly
Profile: Information about environmental issues & sustainable solutions
•European Newsletter [a publication of the International Union for Conservation of Nature]
Type: Newsletter; *Frequency:* q.
Profile: Provides updates on IUCN's work in Europe
•Off the Shelf [a publication of the International Union for Conservation of Nature]
Type: Newsletter; *Frequency:* Monthly
Profile: International Union for Conservation of Nature's latest & most notable publications
•UNFCCC Newsletter
Type: Newsletter; *Frequency:* Semiannually
Profile: International Union for Conservation of Nature's contributions to the UN Framework Convention on Climate Change
•World Conservation [a publication of the International Union for Conservation of Nature]
Type: Magazine; *Frequency:* 2 - 3 pa
Profile: An examinations of conservation, development, economics, & society

International Union of Architects ***See*** Union internationale des architectes

International Union of Biological Sciences (IUBS) / Union internationale des sciences biologiques

Secretariat, Bat 442 Université Paris-Sud 11, Orsay cedex, Paris 91 405 France
Tel: 33 1 69 15 50 27; *Fax:* 33 1 69 15 79 47
e-mail: secretariat@iubs.org
www.iubs.org
Overview: A medium-sized international charitable organization founded in 1919
Mission: To promote the study of biological sciences; to initiate, facilitate & coordinate research & other scientific activities that require international cooperation; to ensure the discussion & dissemination of the results of cooperative research; to promote the organization of international conferences & to assist in the publication of their reports
Chief Officer(s):
Nathalie Fomproix, Executive Director
Membership: 44 ordinary + 80 scientific (associations, societies or commissions); *Fees:* Schedule available; *Member Profile:* National science academies; International scientific organizations
Activities: *Speaker Service:* Yes
Publications:
•Biology International
Type: Journal; *Frequency:* Quarterly

International Union of Food Science & Technology (IUFoST)

IUFoST Secretariat, PO Box 61021, #19, 511 Maple Grove Dr., Oakville ON L6J 6X0
Tel: 905-815-1926; *Fax:* 905-815-1574
e-mail: secretariat@iufost.org
www.iufost.org
www.linkedin.com/company/2754293
www.facebook.com/437738436247543
Overview: A large international organization
Mission: To improve the distribution & conservation of the world's food supply; To promote international cooperation among food technologists & scientists; Affiliation(s): Institute of Food Technologists
Chief Officer(s):
Pingfan Rao, President
Rickey Yada, President-Elect
Judith Meech, Secretary-General & Treasurer
Gustavo Barbosa-Canovas, Chair, Scientific Council
Membership: *Member Profile:* Food scientists, technologists, & engineers from around the world; *Committees:* Food Safety; Food Security Task Force
Activities: Promoting training in food science & technology; Sponsoring international conferences & workshops; Fostering the international exchange of knowledge in the food science & technology community
Meetings/Conferences:
For more information see Trade Shows, Conferences and Seminars Chapter
International Union of Food Science & Technology 2013 International Forum on Food Safety
April 2013 Beijing
Publications:
•International Union of Food Science & Technology Scientific Information Bulletins (SIBs)
Type: Bulletin
Profile: Food science issues, presented by scientific experts & reviewed & approved by the IUFoST Scientific Council, for members of IUFoSTadhering bodies, legislators, food scientists & technologists, & consumers
•IUFoST [International Union of Food Science & Technology] Newsline
Type: Newsletter; *Frequency:* Irregular
Profile: The official newsletter of the International Union of Food Science & Technology, featuring activities of the General Assembly, theBoard, the Governing Council, the International Academy, & adhering bodies, for adhering bodies in more than 100 countries around the world
•Sustainable Development at Risk: Ignoring the Past
Type: Book; *Author:* Robert D. Reichert; *ISBN:* 9788175965218
Profile: The challenge of improving third world nations, while conserving critical resources & protecting the environment
•The Textbook of Food Science & Technology
Type: Book; *Editor:* Geoffrey Campbell-Platt; *ISBN:* 978-0-632-06421-2
Profile: Chapters from international industry researchers, experts, & teachers, written for students, teachers, & professionals in the food industry
•Trends in Food Science & Technology [a publication of the International Union of Food Science & Technology]
Type: Journal; *ISSN:* 0924-2244
Profile: A peer-reviewed journal, featuring critical synopses of advances in food research
•Using Food Science & Technology to Improve Nutrition & Promote National Development: Selected Case Studies
Type: Book; *Editor:* Gordon Robertson & John Lupien; *ISBN:* 978-0-9810247-0-7
Profile: A handbook about the application of food science & technology toimprove nutrition & promote national development in developing countries
•World of Food Science [a publication of the International Union of Food Science & Technology]
Profile: A joint publication of the IUFoST & the Institute of Food Technologists (IFT)

International Union of Forest Research Organizations (IUFRO) / Union internationale des instituts de recherches forestières

IUFRO Secretariat, Mariabrunn (BFW), Hauptstrasse 7, Vienna A-1140 Austria
Tel: 43-1-877-01-510; *Fax:* 43-1-877-01-5150
e-mail: office@iufro.org
www.iufro.org
Overview: A medium-sized international organization founded in 1892
Mission: To promote international cooperation in scientific studies embracing the whole field of research related to forestry & forest products by facilitating exchanges of ideas, methods, data & results among researchers throughout the world
Chief Officer(s):
Peter Mayer, Executive Director, (Austria)
mayer@iufro.org
Don K. Lee, President, (Korea)
leedk@plaza.snu.ac.kr
Membership: 15,000 scientists in 700 member organizations in 110 countries worldwide; *Fees:* Schedule available; *Member Profile:* Open to organizations conducting research related to forestry, including government agencies, universities, private institutions, natural resource associations; associate - individuals
Activities: Environmental change; forests in sustainable mountain development; internet resources; sustainable forest management; management & conservation of forest gene resources; water & forests; on-line reference library; *Library:* Open to public
Awards:
•Student Award for Excellence in Forest Service (Award)

International Union of Geodesy & Geophysics (IUGG) / Union géodésique et géophysique internationale

University Of Karlsruhe, Geophysical Institute, Hertzstrasse 16 Geb. 06.36, Karlsruhe 76187 Germany
www.iugg.org
Overview: A medium-sized international organization founded in 1919
Mission: To promote & coordinate studies of the Earth & its environment in space
Chief Officer(s):
Alik Ismail-Zadeh, Secretary General
secretariat@iugg.org
Membership: 67 member countries; *Member Profile:* 8 member associations: International Assn of Cryospheric Sciences; International Assn of Geodesy; International Assn of Geomagnetism & Aeronomy; International Assn of Hydrological Sciences; International Assn of Meteorology & Atmospheric Sciences; International Assn of the Physical Sciences of the Ocean; International Assn of Seismology & Physics of the Earth's Interior; and International Assn of Volcanology & Chemistry of the Earth's Interior

International Union of Microbiological Societies

Centralbureau voor Schimmelcultures, PO Box 85167, Utrecht 3508AD Netherlands
Tel: 31-30-21-22-600; *Fax:* 31-30-251-2097
www.iums.org
Overview: A small international organization
Affiliation(s): International Council of Scientific Unions
Chief Officer(s):
Robert A. Samson, Secretary General
r.samson@cbs.knaw.nl
Membership: *Member Profile:* National & international societies & other organizations having a common interest in microbiological sciences
Meetings/Conferences:
For more information see Trade Shows, Conferences and Seminars Chapter
International Union of Microbiological Societies 2014 XIV Congress
July 2014 Montréal, QC

International Union of Nutritional Sciences

c/o UCLA School of Public Health, PO Box 951772, Los Angeles CA 90095-1772 USA
Tel: 310-206-9639; *Fax:* 310-794-1805
e-mail: info@iuns.org
www.iuns.org

Overview: A medium-sized international organization founded in 1948
Mission: To accomplish extensive international cooperation among scientists in nutrition-related research & education
Chief Officer(s):
Richard Uauy, President
ricardo.uauy@lshtm.ac.uk
Osman Galal, Secretary General
ogalal@ucla.edu
Suzanne Murphy, Treasurer
suzanne@crch.hawaii.edu
Finances: *Annual Operating Budget:* Less than $50,000; *Funding Sources:* International Council of Scientific Unions; UNESCO; membership
Membership: 81 adhering bodies + 15 affiliated bodies

International Union of Pure & Applied Chemistry (IUPAC)
IUPAC Secretariat, Bldg. 19, PO Box 13757, 104 T.W. Alexander Park, Research Triangle Park NC 27709-3757 USA
Fax: 919-485-8706
e-mail: secretariat@iupac.org
www.iupac.org
Overview: A small international organization founded in 1919
Mission: To advance the worldwide aspects of the chemical sciences & to contribute to the application of chemistry in the service of mankind; *Member of:* International Council of Scientific Unions; Affiliation(s): World Health Organization; UN Food & Agricultural Organization; United Nations Education, Scientific & Cultural Organization; International Organization for Standardization; Organization internationale de métrologie légale
Chief Officer(s):
Kazuyuki Tatsumi, President
John D. Petersen, Executive Director
jpetersen@iupac.org
Finances: *Annual Operating Budget:* $1.5 Million-$3 Million
Staff: 6 staff member(s); 1000 volunteer(s)
Membership: 49 National Adhering Organizations which represent the chemists of different member countries; *Fees:* Variable - min. US$1,400; *Member Profile:* Adhering organizations are the members of the Union & they may be a national chemical council, a national society representing chemistry, a national academy of science, or any institution or association of institutions representative of national chemical interests; *Committees:* Divisions: Physical & Biophysical, Inorganic, Organic & Biomolecular, Polymer, Analytical, Chemistry & the Environment, Chemistry & Human Health, Chemical Nomenclature & Structure Representation; Standing Committees: Chemical Research Applied to World Needs, Chemistry Education, Chemistry & Industry, Printed & Electronic Publications, Terminology Nomenclature & Symbols, Finance, Project, Evaluation

International Union of Societies for Biomaterials Science & Engineering (IUSBSE)
c/o Prof. Nicholas A. Peppas, The University of Texas at Austin, #C-0400, 1 University Station, Austin TX 78712-0231 USA
Tel: 512-471-6644; *Fax:* 512-471-8227
e-mail: peppas@che.utexas.edu
www.worldbiomaterials.org
Overview: A medium-sized international organization
Mission: To advance biomaterials, surgical implants, prosthetics, artificial organs, tissue engineering, & regenerative medicine
Chief Officer(s):
Nicholas A. Peppas, President
Membership: *Member Profile:* National & multi-national groups from Canada, the United States, the European Union, China, Japan, Korea, India, & Australia
Meetings/Conferences:
For more information see Trade Shows, Conferences and Seminars Chapter
Biomaterials 2016 10th World Congress
May 2016 Montréal, QC

International Union of Soil Sciences (IUSS) / Union internationale de la science du sol
c/o Dept. of Soil Science, Univ. of Reading, PO Box 233, Stn. Whiteknights, Reading RG6 6DW United Kingdom
Tel: 44 (0) 118378 6559; *Fax:* 44 (0) 118378 6666
e-mail: iuss@reading.ac.uk
www.iuss.org
Previous Name: International Society of Soil Science
Overview: A medium-sized international charitable organization founded in 1924
Member of: International Council of Scientific Unions; Affiliation(s): Canadian Society of Soil Science
Chief Officer(s):
Roger Swift, President, (Australia)
deannravs@uq.edu.au
Stephen Nortcliff, Secretary General
Finances: *Annual Operating Budget:* $50,000-$100,000; *Funding Sources:* Membership fees
Staff: 1 staff member(s); 3 volunteer(s)
Membership: 50,000 in 146 countries; *Fees:* According to number of members in national societies; *Member Profile:* National soil science societies; *Committees:* Soil Physics; Soil Zoology; World Soils & Terrain Digital Data Base; Committee on Statute & Structure
Activities: *Rents Mailing List:* Yes; *Library:*

International Water Association (IWA)
Alliance House, 12 Caxton St., London SW1H 0QS United Kingdom
Tel: 44-20-7654-5500; *Fax:* 44-20-7654-5555
e-mail: water@iwahq.org
www.iwahq.org
www.linkedin.com/company/international-water-association
twitter.com/IWAwaternews
Previous Name: International Association on Water Quality; International Association on Water Pollution Research & Control
Overview: A large international organization founded in 1999
Mission: To advance the science & practice of water management internationally
Chief Officer(s):
Glen Daigger, President & Chair
Ger Bergkamp, Interim Executive Director
ger.bergkamp@iwahq.org
Finances: *Annual Operating Budget:* $250,000-$500,000
Staff: 20 staff member(s)
Membership: 9,000; *Committees:* Executive; Finance & Investment; Renumeration; Program; Publications; Young Professionals
Activities: Wastewater treatment processes; hazardous wastes & source control; impacts of pollutants on receiving waters; environmental restoration
Meetings/Conferences:
For more information see Trade Shows, Conferences and Seminars Chapter
International Water Association 3rd Development Congress & Exhibition 2013
October 2013 Nairobi
International Water Association 10th Leading Edge Conference on Water & Waste Water Technologies 2013
June 2013 Bordeaux
International Water Association World Water Congress & Exhibition 2014
September 2014 Lisbon
International Water Association World Water Congress & Exhibition 2016
September 2016 Brisbane,
International Water Association World Water Congress & Exhibition 2018
2018
Publications:
•Hydrology Research [a publication of the International Water Association]
Type: Journal; *Editor:* Ian Littlewood & Chong-Yu Xu; *ISSN:* 0029-1277
Profile: Official journal of the Nordic Association for Hydrology, British Hydrological Society, German HydrologicalSociety, & Italian Hydrological Society
•Journal of Hydroinformatics [a publication of the International Water Association]
Type: Journal; *Editor:* Professor Dragan Savic; *ISSN:* 1464-7141
Profile: Devoted to the application of information technology to problems of the aquatic environment
•Journal of Water & Health [a publication of the International Water Association]
Type: Journal; *Editor:* Morteza Abbaszadegan; *ISSN:* 1477-8920
Profile: Promotes research into the challenges of harnessing water for health in developing & developed countries
•Journal of Water Reuse & Desalination [a publication of the International Water Association]
Type: Journal; *Frequency:* q.; *Editor:* Blanca Jiménez Cisneros; *ISSN:* 2220-1319
•Journal of Water Supply: Research and Technology - Aqua [a publication of the International Water Association]
Type: Journal; *Editor:* Rolf Gimbel; *ISSN:* 0003-7214
Profile: Research & development in water supply technology & management
•Journal of Water, Sanitation & Hygiene for Development [a publication of the International Water Association]
Type: Journal; *Editor:* Barbara Evans; *ISSN:* 2043-9083
Profile: Science, policy & practice of drinking-water supply, sanitation & hygiene
•Water Asset Management International [a publication of the International Water Association]
Type: Newsletter; *Editor:* Dr. John Bridgeman; *ISSN:* 1814-5434
Profile: Asset management in water & wastewater utilities
•Water Practice & Technology [a publication of the International Water Association]
Type: Journal; *Editor:* Dr.-Ing. Burkhard Teichgräber; *ISSN:* 1751-231X
Profile: Online journal under the control of the Water Science & Technology Editorial Board
•Water21 [a publication of the International Water Association]
Type: Magazine; *Frequency:* 6 pa.; *ISSN:* 1561-9508
Profile: Official magazine of the International Water Association

International Whaling Commission (IWC)
The Red House, 135 Station Rd., Impington, Cambridge CB4 9NP United Kingdom
Tel: 441-223-233-971; *Fax:* 441-223-232-876
e-mail: secretariat@iwcoffice.org
www.iwcoffice.org
Overview: A medium-sized international organization founded in 1946
Mission: To keep under review & revise as necessary those measures which provide for the complete protection of certain species of whales; to designate specified areas as whale sanctuaries; to set limits on the maximum numbers of whales which may be taken in one season; to prescribe open & closed seasons & areas for whaling; to set limits on the size of whales that may be killed; to prohibit the capture of suckling calves & female whales accompanied by calves; to encourage, coordinate & fund whale research; to publish results of research & other scientific research; to promote studies into related matters. Canada is not currently a member.
Chief Officer(s):
William Hogarth, Chair, USA
Membership: 88 whaling governments; *Member Profile:* Open to any country in the world that formally adheres to the 1946 Convention; *Committees:* Scientific; Technical; Finance & Administration
Activities: *Speaker Service:* Yes; *Library:* Open to public by appointment

International Wildlife Coalition (IWC)
70 Falmouth Hwy. East, Falmouth MA 2536 USA
Tel: 508-548-8328; *Fax:* 508-457-1988
Overview: A medium-sized international charitable organization founded in 1982
Mission: To prevent cruelty & killing of animals & the destruction of wildlife habitat; Affiliation(s): Canadian Federation of Humane Societies
Finances: *Annual Operating Budget:* $250,000-$500,000
Staff: 5 staff member(s)
Activities: *Internships:* Yes; *Rents Mailing List:* Yes

Canada
PO Box 461, Stn. Port Credit, Mississauga ON L5G 4M1
Tel: 905-306-7216; *Fax:* 905-306-7217
e-mail: etex@iwc.org

International Wildlife Rehabilitation Council (IWRC)
PO Box 3197, Eugene OR 97403 USA
Tel: 866-871-1869
Toll-Free: 866-871-1869
e-mail: info@iwrc-online.org
www.iwrc-online.org
www.linkedin.com/companies/the-international-wildlife-rehabilitation-c
www.facebook.com/theiwrc
twitter.com/theiwrc
Overview: A small international charitable organization founded in 1972
Mission: To further knowledge & experience in the field of wildlife rehabilitation, through education, networking, & professional standards of review; to preserve our wildlife & its habitat
Chief Officer(s):
Kai Williams, Executive Director
director@theiwrc.org

Finances: *Annual Operating Budget:* $250,000-$500,000; *Funding Sources:* Membership dues; course fees; private donations; sales of literature; annual conference
Staff: 3 staff member(s); 12 volunteer(s)
Membership: 1,850; *Fees:* $49 individual; $59 family; $75 organization; $32 library; *Member Profile:* Individual - persons actively working in the field of wildlife rehabilitation in administration, conservation, management, education, research, humane work, or veterinary or allied professional practice; Family - two or more active rehabilitators residing at the same address; Organizational/Institutional - non-profit corporations or public agencies affiliated with a branch of local, state, or federal government actively supporting or operating wildlife rehabilitation programs; Affiliate/Corporate - small & large businesses or foundations that are not actively involved in wildlife rehabilitation but wish to provide financial support for IWRC programs; Library/Agency: Accredited library or government, state, provincial agency
Activities: Nationwide certification program which includes a series of hands-on training seminars in state-of-the-art wildlife rehabilitation techniques, from beginner through advanced levels;

International WWOOF Association
PO Box 2675, Lewes BN7 1RB United Kingdom
www.wwoof.org
Also Known As: World-Wide Opportunities on Organic Farms
Overview: A small international organization
Mission: To help those who would like to volunteer on organic farms internationally
Chief Officer(s):
Sally Antill, Administrator

IRC International Water & Sanitation Centre
PO Box 82327, The Hague 2508 EH Netherlands
Tel: 31-70-304-4000; *Fax:* 31-70-304-4044
www.irc.nl
Previous Name: International Reference Centre for Community Water Supply & Sanitation
Overview: A small international organization founded in 1968
Mission: The IRC helps people in developing countries to get the best water & sanitation services they can afford
Chief Officer(s):
L. de Waal, Chairman, Supervisory Board
Michel van der Leest, Office Coordinator, Services Section
Finances: *Annual Operating Budget:* $1.5 Million-$3 Million
Staff: 38 staff member(s)
Activities: *Internships:* Yes; *Library:* by appointment

Is Five Foundation
#302, 161 Eglinton Ave. East, Toronto ON M4P 1J5
Tel: 416-480-2408; *Fax:* 416-480-2546
Overview: A small local organization

Island Nature Trust (INT)
PO Box 265, Charlottetown PE C1A 7K4
Tel: 902-566-9150; *Fax:* 902-628-6331
e-mail: intrust@eastlink.ca
www.islandnaturetrust.ca
www.facebook.com/pages/Island-Nature-Trust/190787204315860
Also Known As: Prince Edward Island Nature Trust
Overview: A small provincial charitable organization founded in 1979
Mission: To acquire & manage natural areas on PEI; *Member of:* Tourism Industry Association of PEI; Affiliation(s): Canadian Nature Federation; Tree Canada Foundation
Chief Officer(s):
Bruce Smith, Executive Director
Finances: *Annual Operating Budget:* $100,000-$250,000; *Funding Sources:* Donations; fundraising; contract work
Staff: 4 staff member(s); 100 volunteer(s)
Membership: 350; *Fees:* $20; *Committees:* Acquisition; Fundraising; Program Development
Activities: Educational programs; acquisition, protection & management of natural areas; *Speaker Service:* Yes

Islands Organic Producers Association (IOPA)
3490 Glenora Rd., Duncan BC V9L 6S2
Tel: 250-748-2791; *Fax:* 250-748-2741
e-mail: admin@iopa.ca
www.iopa.ca
Overview: A small local organization founded in 1990
Affiliation(s): Certified Organic Associations of BC
Finances: *Funding Sources:* Membership fees
Staff: 30 volunteer(s)
Membership: 60; *Member Profile:* Organic farmers

Jack Miner Migratory Bird Foundation, Inc.
PO Box 39, 360 RR#3 WeEst, Kingsville ON N9Y 2E5
Tel: 519-733-4034
Toll-Free: 877-289-8328
e-mail: info@jackminer.com
www.jackminer.com
www.facebook.com/JackMinerMigratoryBirdSanctuary
Overview: A small local charitable organization founded in 1904
Mission: The sanctuary provides food, shelter & protection to migratory water fowl, tags birds & tracks migration patterns
Chief Officer(s):
Kirk W. Miner, Executive Director
Finances: *Funding Sources:* Private
Staff: 3 staff member(s); 12 volunteer(s)

The Jane Goodal Institute of Canada (JGI)
c/o University of Toronto Mailroom, 565 Spadina Cres., Toronto ON M5S 2J7
Tel: 416-978-3711; *Fax:* 416-978-3713
Toll-Free: 888-882-4467
e-mail: info@janegoodall.ca
www.janegoodall.ca/roots-shoots.php
www.facebook.com/rootsandshoots.canada
twitter.com/JaneGoodallCAN
www.youtube.com/user/RootsanShoots
Also Known As: Roots & Shoots
Overview: A small local organization founded in 1994
Mission: To support wildlife research, education, & conservation
Chief Officer(s):
Jane Lawton, CEO
Jane Goodall, Founder
Finances: *Funding Sources:* Donations
Activities: Providing training in environmental & humanitarian education; Raising awareness of endangered animals; Promoting activities to aid the well-being of wild & captive chimpanzees
Publications:
•Jane Goodall Institute of Canada eNewsletter
Type: Newsletter
Profile: Canadian news, news from the field, & ways to become involved
•Roots & Shoots Canada eNewsletter
Type: Newsletter
Profile: Events, activities, parnerships, & resources

The Jane Goodall Institute for Wildlife Research, Education & Conservation
#600, 4245 North Fairfax Dr., Arlington VA 22203 USA
Tel: 703-682-9220; *Fax:* 703-682-9312
www.janegoodall.org
Overview: A small international organization founded in 1977
Mission: To increase primate habitat conservation; to increase awareness of, support for & training in issues related to our relationship with each other, the environment & other animals (leading to behaviour change); to expand non-invasive research program on chimpanzees & other primates; to promote activities that ensure the well-being of chimpanzees, other primates & animal welfare activities in general
Chief Officer(s):
Robert G. Menzi, CFO & Executive Vice-President
Bill Johnston, President
Activities: Gombe Stream Research Centre; ChimpanZoo Project; reforestation projects; conservation centres; educational & communcation resources

The Jane Goodall Institute of Canada
c/o University of Toronto Mailroom, 563 Spadina Cres., Toronto ON M5S 2J7
Tel: 416-978-3711; *Fax:* 416-978-3713
Toll-Free: 888-882-4467
e-mail: info@janegoodall.ca
www.janegoodall.ca
www.facebook.com/JaneGoodallCAN
twitter.com/JaneGoodallCAN
www.youtube.com/user/jgicanada
Overview: A small national charitable organization founded in 1994
Mission: To support wildlife research, education & conservation; to promote informed & compassionate action to improve the environment shared by all Earth's living creatures; Affiliation(s): The Jane Goodall Institute - USA; The Jane Goodall Institute - UK
Chief Officer(s):
John Wall, Chair
Jane Lawton, Executive Director
Finances: *Annual Operating Budget:* $250,000-$500,000; *Funding Sources:* Private donations; lecture honorariums
Staff: 8 staff member(s); 32 volunteer(s)
Membership: 100-499
Activities: Chimp Guardian Program - sponsor orphan chimpanzees; Roots & Shoots - Jane Goodall Institute's global environmental & humanitarian program; *Awareness Events:* Earth Day, April 22; Peace Day, Sept. 21; *Internships:* Yes
Publications:
•Jane Goodall Institute of Canada eNewsletter
Type: Newsletter; *Frequency:* 2 pa; *Price:* Free online
•Roots & Shoots Canada eNewsletter [a publication of the Jane Goodall Institute of Canada]
Type: Newsletter; *Price:* Free online

Jardin zoologique du Québec (JZQ)
9300, rue de la Faune, Charlesbourg QC G1G 5H9
Tél: 418-622-0312; *Téléc:* 418-646-9239
Aperçu: *Dimension:* moyenne; *Envergure:* provinciale; fondée en 1931
Mission: Contribuer à l'étude, à la mise en valeur et à la conservation de la faune et de son environnement.; *Membre de:* Société des musées québécois
Environmental Activity: Activités éducatives, programmes de recherche et de conservation
Membre(s) du bureau directeur:
Jean-Paul Bédard, Directeur
Finances: *Budget de fonctionnement annuel:* $1.5 Million-$3 Million
Personnel: 25 membre(s) du personnel; 140 bénévole(s)
Activités: *Stagiaires:* Oui; *Service de conférenciers:* Oui; *Listes de destinataires:* Oui; *Bibliothèque:*

Les jardins botaniques royaux ***See*** Royal Botanical Gardens

Jasper Environmental Association (JEA)
PO Box 2198, Jasper AB T0E 1E0
Tel: 780-852-4152; *Fax:* 780-852-4152
e-mail: jea2@telus.net
www.jasperenvironmental.org
Overview: A medium-sized local organization
Mission: To support Parks Canada in administering Jasper National Park in accordance with Canadian legislation, Parks Canada principles and policies and the wishes of the Canadian public.
Membership: *Fees:* $5

Joint Centre for Bioethics
University of Toronto, 88 College St., Toronto ON M5G 1L4
Tel: 416-978-2709; *Fax:* 416-978-1911
e-mail: jcb.info@utoronto.ca
www.utoronto.ca/jcb
Overview: A small national organization
Chief Officer(s):
Rhonda Martin, Executive Assistant

Jour de la terre Canada ***See*** Earth Day Canada

Junior Farmers' Association of Ontario (JFAO)
Ontario AgriCentre, #206, 100 Stone Rd. West, Guelph ON N1G 5L3
Tel: 519-780-5326; *Fax:* 519-821-8810
e-mail: info@jfao.on.ca
www.jfao.on.ca
www.facebook.com/group.php?gid=2212763210
Overview: A medium-sized provincial organization founded in 1944
Mission: To build future rural leaders through self-help & community betterment
Chief Officer(s):
Sarah McLaren, President
president@jfao.on.ca
Meetings/Conferences:
For more information see Trade Shows, Conferences and Seminars Chapter
Junior Farmers' Association of Ontario 2013 Winter Games
February 2013 Pembroke, ON
Junior Farmers' Association of Ontario 2013 Annual General Meeting & Conference
March 2013 London, ON

Kamloops Exploration Group
#1100, 235 First Ave., Kamloops BC V2C 3J4
Tel: 250-828-2585
e-mail: info@keg.bc.ca
www.keg.bc.ca
Overview: A small local organization

Mission: To generally promote the interests of mining & prospecting for minerals, metals, & petroleum to the general public; to further the member's knowledge of mineral exploration & mining by offering informational lectures to members & the general public; to hold prospecting classes & promote other educational projects in connection with mining & prospecting;to further the general public's knowledge on the subject of Geoscience
Chief Officer(s):
Mike Cathro, President

Kamloops Naturalist Club (KNC)
Parent Name: Federation of BC Naturalists

PO Box 625, Kamloops BC V2C 5L7
Tel: 250-554-1285
e-mail: marggraham@shaw.ca
www.kamloopsnaturalistclub.ca
Overview: A small local charitable organization founded in 1981 overseen by Federation of BC Naturalists
Mission: To promote the enjoyment of nature through environmental appreciation & conservation; to encourage wise use & conservation of natural resources & environmental protection; *Member of:* Canadian Nature Federation; Affiliation(s): Nature Canada
Finances: *Annual Operating Budget:* Less than $50,000; *Funding Sources:* Membership fees; grants; raffles
Membership: 1-99;; *Fees:* $25 single; $35 family; *Member Profile:* All ages, but predominately retired
Activities: Field trips; workshops; monthly meetings; speakers

Kamloops Wildlife Park Society

9077 Dallas Dr., Kamloops BC V2C 6V1
Tel: 250-573-3242; *Fax:* 250-573-2406
e-mail: info@bczoo.org
www.bczoo.org
www.facebook.com/group.php?gid=216392988374473
Also Known As: BC Wildlife Park
Overview: A small local charitable organization founded in 1965
Mission: To encourage the appreciation of & respect for BC's wildlife; to assist in preserving biodiversity through education, research, captive breeding & rehabilitation service; Affiliation(s): Canadian Association of Zoos & Aquariums
Chief Officer(s):
Glenn Grant, Operations Manager, 250-573-3242 Ext. 231
glenn@bczoo.org
Jeff Stone, President
Jack Madryga, 1st Vice-President
Rod Simmons, 2nd Vice-President
Don Bogie, Treasurer
Finances: *Annual Operating Budget:* $500,000-$1.5 Million; *Funding Sources:* Regional government; self-generated revenue
Staff: 15 staff member(s); 200 volunteer(s)
Membership: 2,000; *Fees:* $32 adults; $24 seniors; $20 children (age 3-17); $99 family (up to 5 members); *Member Profile:* Families from Kamloops region
Activities: Captive breeding for release endangered Burrowing Owls; *Awareness Events:* BC Hydro Wildlights, Dec.-Jan.; Family Farm, May-Sept.; BC Wildlife Day, Ist Mon. in Aug.; *Internships:* Yes; *Speaker Service:* Yes; *Library:* by appointment

Kawartha World Issues Centre (KWIC)

PO Box 895, Peterborough ON K9J 7A2
Tel: 705-748-1680; *Fax:* 705-748-1681
e-mail: kwic@trentu.ca
www.trentu.ca/kwic
Overview: A small international charitable organization founded in 1988
Mission: To further an understanding of global issues; to create links between global & local community development; to promote analysis & action for positive social change; *Member of:* Eastern Ontario Coalition of Internationally-Minded NGOs; Ontario Council for International Cooperation
Chief Officer(s):
Julie Cosgrove, Coordinator
Finances: *Funding Sources:* Public donations; Trent student donations; CIDA; special grants
Staff: 1 staff member(s); 50 volunteer(s)
Membership: 150; *Fees:* $20 individual; $20 - $50 group; $100 institutional
Activities: Public Programming on global issues; skills training; networking; special projects: Person's Day Breakfast, International Development Week; One World (Vegetarian) Dinner; Global Youth Day, Volunteer Recruitment & Training, Annual Secondary School Symposium; *Speaker Service:* Yes; *Library:* Open to public

Kennebecasis Naturalists' Society

c/o Ms. H. Folkins, 827 Main St., Sussex NB E4E 2N1
www.macbe.com/kns/
Overview: A small local organization
Chief Officer(s):
Gart Bishop, Chair
Membership: 80
Activities: Field trips

Keystone Agricultural Producers (KAP)
Parent Name: Canadian Federation of Agriculture

#203, 1700 Ellice Ave., Winnipeg MB R3H 0B1
Tel: 204-697-1140; *Fax:* 204-697-1109
e-mail: kap@kap.mb.ca
www.kap.mb.ca
Previous Name: Manitoba Farm Bureau
Overview: A medium-sized provincial organization founded in 1985 overseen by Canadian Federation of Agriculture
Mission: To be a democratic & effective policy organization, promoting the social, economic & physical well-being of all Manitoban agricultural producers
Chief Officer(s):
Yvonne Rideout, General Manager
Ian Wishart, President
Finances: *Annual Operating Budget:* $250,000-$500,000
Staff: 5 staff member(s)
Membership: 5,000; *Fees:* $150 per farm unit
Meetings/Conferences:
For more information see Trade Shows, Conferences and Seminars Chapter
Keystone Agricultural Producers 2014 Annual Meeting
January 2014 Winnipeg, MB
Publications:
•Manitoba Farmers' Voice
Type: Journal; *Frequency:* Quarterly

The Kindness Club / Le Cercle Saint-François

65 Brunswick St., Fredericton NB E3B 1G5
Tel: 506-459-3379; *Fax:* 506-450-3703
e-mail: kindness@nb.aibn.com
www.kindnessclub.nb.ca
Overview: A small international charitable organization founded in 1959
Mission: To educate children to be kind to animals & people & to respect the environment; *Member of:* Canadian Federation of Humane Societies; Affiliation(s): Canadian Nature Federation; Zoocheck Canada; New Brunswick Naturalists
Finances: *Annual Operating Budget:* $50,000-$100,000; *Funding Sources:* Donations; interest from small capital
Staff: 2 staff member(s); 6 volunteer(s)
Membership: 2,300; *Fees:* $5 child; $10 adult
Activities: Essay contest for students, grades 4-8; pet shows; displays; weekly column in 6 New Brunswick newspapers; liaison teacher program; *Library:*

Kingston Field Naturalists (KFN)

PO Box 831, Kingston ON K7L 4X6
e-mail: info@kingstonfieldnaturalists.org
kingstonfieldnaturalists.org
Overview: A small local charitable organization founded in 1949
Mission: To acquire, record & disseminate knowledge of natural history; To stimulate public interest in nature & in the protection & preservation of wildlife; *Member of:* Ontario Nature; Affiliation(s): Canadian Nature Federation; Thousand Islands-Frontenac Arch Biosphere Reserve Network
Chief Officer(s):
Gaye Beckwith, President, 613-376-3716
Finances: *Annual Operating Budget:* Less than $50,000; *Funding Sources:* Membership fees
Membership: 500; *Fees:* $30 individual; $32 family; $20 young adult/junior; $800 life; *Committees:* Conservation; Education; Bird Records; Field Trips; Nature Reserves
Activities: Junior naturalists club (6-12); bird counts; Helen Quillam Sanctuary; Amherst Island Reserve; teen naturalists (13-17); habitat protection projects; *Awareness Events:* Spring/Fall Leisure Shows - Kingston

Kingston Lapidary & Mineral Club

623 King St. West, Kingston ON K7M 2E7
www.mineralclub.ca
Overview: A small local organization founded in 1962
Mission: To encourage the growth of silversmithing work, & mineral, fossil, & crystal collecting; *Member of:* The Central Canadian Federation of Mineralogical Societies (CCFMS)
Chief Officer(s):
Paul Blaney, President, 613-544-5138
paulrichardblaney@hotmail.com
Eileen Moss, Vice-President, Social & Publicity, 613-384-4439
emoss@cogeco.net
Wendy Dawes, Secretary, 613-876-2505
wdawes1@cogeco.ca
Membership: *Fees:* $10 junior; $15 adult; $20 family; *Member Profile:* Rockhounds; Lapidary enthusiasts; Silversmiths
Activities: Hosting meetings & workshops; Organizing field trips; *Library:* Kingston Lapidary & Mineral Club Library
Publications:
•The Streak Plate: The Kingston Lapidary & Mineral Club Newsletter
Type: Newsletter; *Frequency:* 5 pa; *Editor:* John Casnig
Profile: Upcoming events & articles about the hobby

Kitchener-Waterloo Field Naturalists

317 Highland Rd. East, Kitchener ON N2M 3W6
www.kwfn.ca
Overview: A small local charitable organization founded in 1934
Mission: To promote the enjoyment of nature through environmental appreciation & conservation; To encourage wise use & conservation of natural resources; *Member of:* Federation of Ontario Naturalists
Chief Officer(s):
Janet Ozaruk, President, 519-893-0490
janeto@golden.net
Finances: *Annual Operating Budget:* Less than $50,000
Membership: 250; *Fees:* $20
Activities: Walks; speakers; social; photography; plant study; *Library:* Open to public

Kitimat Valley Naturalists

12 Farrow St., Kitimat BC V8C 1E2
Tel: 250-632-7632; *Fax:* 250-632-2543
www.bcnature.ca/pages/local_clubs/kitimat_valley_naturalists.html
Overview: A small local organization
Mission: Interests include birding, wildflowers, ecology, & environmental issues related to wildlife.
Chief Officer(s):
April Macleod
Membership: *Fees:* $16.10

Klondike Placer Miners' Association

3151B Third Ave., Whitehorse YT Y1A 1G1
Tel: 867-667-2267; *Fax:* 867-668-7127
e-mail: kpma@kpma.ca
www.kpma.ca
Overview: A small provincial organization
Chief Officer(s):
Mike McDougall, President
Membership: *Fees:* $159-$3210

The Ladies of the Lake

ON
Tel: 905-476-4045
e-mail: ladies@lakeladies.ca
www.lakeladies.ca
Overview: A small local organization founded in 2005
Mission: To promote a greater sense of connection with Lake Simcoe; to get people involved in what the future brings - both in terms of the lake itself & for those who share it; to offer a set of possible actions to restore the Lake to health for the communities around the Lake & watershed
Chief Officer(s):
Jane Meredith, Contact
Membership: 100+; *Member Profile:* Women of all ages who are working to rescue Lake Simcoe and its watershed.
Activities: Calendar; "Naked Truth" series of events

Lake Abitibi Model Forest

PO Box 129, 143 - 3rd St., Cochrane ON P0L 1C0
Tel: 705-272-7800; *Fax:* 705-272-2744
e-mail: office@lamf.net
www.lamf.net
Overview: A small local organization
Member of: Canadian Model Forest Network
Chief Officer(s):
Jacynthe Peever, Business Administrator
Wayne D. Young, General Manager

Lake Simcoe Region Conservation Foundation

PO Box 282, 120 Bayview Pkwy., Newmarket ON L3Y 4X1
Tel: 905-895-1281
e-mail: foundation@lsrca.on.ca
www.lsrca.on.ca/Foundation/index.html
Overview: A small local organization

Mission: The Lake Simcoe Conservation Foundation (LSCF) invests in projects designed to protect and restore Lake Simcoe. Working in partnership with the Lake Simcoe Region Conservation Authority (LSRCA), watershed municipalities and other partners, they enable vital work to be done that maintains the natural environment, and in many places return the land and the rivers and the streams to a natural state.
Chief Officer(s):
Kimberley Mackenzie, Executive Director
k.mackenzie@lsrca.on.ca
Activities: Undertaken a million dollar fundraising campaign to help restore the lake

Lakeland Agricultural Research Association (LARA) Parent Name: Agricultural Research & Extension Council of Alberta

PO Box 7068, Bonnyville AB T9N 2H4
Tel: 780-826-7260; *Fax:* 780-826-7099
e-mail: livestock.lara@mcsnet.ca
www.areca.ab.ca/larahome.html
Overview: A small local organization overseen by Agricultural Research & Extension Council of Alberta
Mission: To achieve a profitable & sustainable future for agricultural producers by conducting agricultural research programs; *Member of:* Agricultural Research & Extension Council of Alberta
Chief Officer(s):
Janet Montgomery, Manager
manager.lara@mcsnet.ca
Kellie Nichiporik, Coordinator, Conservation
sustainag.lara@mscnet.ca
Publications:
•LARA [Lakeland Agricultural Research Association] Newsletter
Type: Newsletter

Lambton Industrial Society: An Environmental Co-operative
See Sarnia-Lambton Environmental Association

Lambton Wildlife Inc. (LWI)

PO Box 681, Sarnia ON N7T 7J7
Tel: 519-542-7914
e-mail: info@lambtonwildlife.com
www.lambtonwildlife.com
Overview: A small local charitable organization founded in 1966
Mission: To preserve our natural heritage for present & future generations; Particularly concerned with the natural history of Lambton County & the establishment & care of conservation areas & wildlife sanctuaries therein; *Member of:* Federation of Ontario Naturalists; Affiliation(s): Canadian Nature Federation
Chief Officer(s):
Janet Bremner, President
Finances: *Annual Operating Budget:* Less than $50,000; *Funding Sources:* Membership fees; donations
Staff: 75 volunteer(s)
Membership: 210; *Fees:* $20 individual; $25 family; *Committees:* Adopt-a-Highway; Arbor Week; Ausable Trail; Binational Public Advisory; Bluebird Nesting; Conservation; Education; Environment; Indoor; Mandaumin Woods; Outdoor; Rural Lambton Stewardship; Wawanosh Wetlands Management; Wildlife Inventory; Woodlot Protection; Howard Watson Nature Trail; Port Franks Property Management
Activities: Education programs in environmental studies & natural history; lectures in natural history at Lambton County schools & other organizations; special public lectures; regular field trips; sponsors the annual Audubon Christmas Bird census in Lambton area; purchase & management of Mandaumin Woods Nature Reserve; establishment of Ausable Trail; sponsorship of the World Wildlife studies of the Port Franks Karner Blue Butterfly & the Walpole Island Life Science Inventory

Land Improvement Contractors of Ontario

231 Dimson Rd., Guelph ON N1G 3C7
Tel: 519-836-1386; *Fax:* 519-836-4059
e-mail: john.johnston@gto.net
www.drainage.org
Overview: A small provincial organization founded in 1995
Mission: An association of professional contractors, suppliers of drainage pipe and equipment, engineers and municipal drainage superintendents principally concerned with agriculture and the land drainage industry of Ontario, Canada.
Chief Officer(s):
Gerald Neeb, President, 519-656-2618
John Johnston, Sec.-Treas.
Finances: *Annual Operating Budget:* Less than $50,000
Membership: *Fees:* $146.90 general membership

Land Trust Alliance (LTA)

#1100, 1660 L St. NW, Washington DC 20036 USA
Tel: 202-638-4725; *Fax:* 202-638-4730
e-mail: info@lta.org
www.lta.org
www.facebook.com/landtrustalliance
twitter.com/ltalliance
Overview: A large international organization founded in 1982
Mission: To strengthen the land trust movement & ensure that land trusts have the information, skills & resources they use to save land
Chief Officer(s):
Rand Wentworth, President
rwentworth@lta.org
Mary Pope Hutson, Exec. Vice President
mpmhutson@lta.org
Marilyn Ayres, Chief Operating
mayres@lta.org
Finances: *Annual Operating Budget:* $3 Million-$5 Million
Staff: 32 staff member(s)
Membership: 1,000
Activities: *Awareness Events:* National Land Trust Rally; *Internships:* Yes
Publications:
•Saving Land
Type: Magazine; *Frequency:* Quarterly; *Number of Pages:* 40

Landscape Alberta Nursery Trades Association (LANTA) Parent Name: Canadian Nursery Landscape Association

#200, 10331 - 178 St., Edmonton AB T5S 1R5
Tel: 780-489-1991; *Fax:* 780-444-2152
Toll-Free: 800-378-3198
e-mail: info@landscape-alberta.com
www.landscape-alberta.com
Overview: A medium-sized provincial organization founded in 1957 overseen by Canadian Nursery Landscape Association
Mission: To advance the Alberta ornamental horticulture industry through unity, education & professionalism; Affiliation(s): Saskatchewan Nursery Landscape Association
Chief Officer(s):
Nigel Bowles, Executive Director
nigel.bowles@landscape-alberta.com
Finances: *Annual Operating Budget:* $100,000-$250,000; *Funding Sources:* Membership fees; fundraising programs
Staff: 4 staff member(s)
Membership: 350; *Fees:* Schedule available; *Member Profile:* Must be engaged in the horticultural industry or a supplier

Landscape Newfoundland & Labrador (LNL) Parent Name: Canadian Nursery Landscape Association

PO Box 8062, St. John's NL A1B 3M9
Tel: 709-726-5651; *Fax:* 709-726-8441
e-mail: davek@nl.rogers.com
www.landscapenf.org
Overview: A small provincial organization founded in 1992 overseen by Canadian Nursery Landscape Association
Mission: Our vision is one that promotes professionalism at all levels of the Industry, and achieves the highest standards of excellence in delivery of services and products across all sectors of our industry.
Chief Officer(s):
David Kiell, Executive Director
Membership: 75; *Fees:* $50 individual; $125 affiliated; $310 associate/active

Landscape Nova Scotia Parent Name: Canadian Nursery Landscape Association

Executive Plus Business Centre, #44, 201 Brownlow Ave., Dartmouth NS B3B 1W2
Tel: 902-463-0519; *Fax:* 902-463-6308
Toll-Free: 877-567-4769
e-mail: info@landscapenovascotia.ca
www.landscapenovascotia.ca
Overview: A medium-sized provincial organization overseen by Canadian Nursery Landscape Association
Mission: Landscape Nova Scotia's mission is to promote high standards in product quality, professional service and conduct in the landscape and horticulture industry. We have been a voice for the landscape and horticultural industry for more than 20 years in Nova Scotia, and are committed to providing consumers with options to make informed decisions.
Chief Officer(s):
Scott Mosher, President

Landscape Ontario Horticultural Trades Association (LOHTA) Parent Name: Canadian Nursery Landscape Association

7856 Fifth Line South, RR#4, Milton ON L9T 2X8
Tel: 905-875-1805; *Fax:* 905-875-3942
Toll-Free: 800-265-5656
www.horttrades.com
Overview: A medium-sized provincial organization founded in 1973 overseen by Canadian Nursery Landscape Association
Mission: To be a leader in representing, promoting & fostering a favourable environment for the advancement of the horticultural industry in Ontario; Affiliation(s): Horticultural Human Resource Council
Chief Officer(s):
Tony DiGiovanni, Executive Director
tonydigiovanni@landscapeontario.com
Finances: *Annual Operating Budget:* $1.5 Million-$3 Million; *Funding Sources:* Membership dues; congress
Staff: 23 staff member(s)
Membership: 2,100 members in 9 chapters; *Fees:* $470 active; $281 interim; $572 associate; $150 horticultural; *Member Profile:* Active - firms with at least 3 years experience in the field; Interim/Active - firms with at least 1 year but less than 3 years experience in the field; Associate - suppliers to the industry & the association
Activities: *Speaker Service:* Yes

Langley Field Naturalists Society (LFN)

PO Box 56052, Stn. Valley Centre, Langley BC V3A 8B3
e-mail: Langleyfieldnaturalists@shaw.ca
www.langleyfieldnaturalists.org
Overview: A small local organization founded in 1973
Mission: To promote the enjoyment of nature; to learn about natural history; to promote preservation of the environment through active participation in conservation projects; *Member of:* The Federation of BC Naturalists; Canadian Nature Federation
Finances: *Annual Operating Budget:* Less than $50,000; *Funding Sources:* Langley Arts Council Grant; membership fees
Membership: 60-70; *Fees:* $25 single; $30 family; *Committees:* Conservation education; Watson nature reserve
Activities: Monthly field trips from Sept.-June, weekly walks July-Aug.; Maintenance of Brydan Lagoon & Irene Pearce Trail; *Awareness Events:* Rivers Day; Earth Day; Campbell Valley Country Celebration

Lansdowne Outdoor Recreational Development Association (LORDA)

PO Box 591, Westville NS B0K 2A0
Tel: 902-396-4470; *Fax:* 902-396-1399
e-mail: contact@lorda.org
www.lorda.org
Overview: A small local organization
Chief Officer(s):
Dave Leese, Contact
dave@lorda.org
Activities: Operates senior citizen & disabled persons park; facilities: fishing ponds, nature trails, bocce court, trailer parking, picnic benches, screened gazebo, croquet court, tenting area

LEAD Canada Inc.

PO Box 250, 3202 Tullochgorum, Ormstown QC J0S 1K0
Toll-Free: 866-532-3539
e-mail: president@leadcanada.net
www.leadcanada.net
Also Known As: Leadership for Environment & Development Canada
Overview: A small national organization
Chief Officer(s):
Carole Therrien, President
Membership: *Fees:* $35

Learning for a Sustainable Future (LSF)

York University, 343 York Lanes, Toronto ON M3J 1P3
Toll-Free: 877-250-8202
e-mail: info@lsf-lst.ca
www.lsf-lst.ca
www.facebook.com/lsf.lst.ca
twitter.com/LSF_LST
Overview: A medium-sized national charitable organization founded in 1991
Mission: LSF is a non-profit Canadian organization that was created to integrate sustainability education into Canada's education system.
Chief Officer(s):

Lisa Roy, Chair
liseroy@health.nb.ca

Lethbridge & District Japanese Garden Society

PO Box 751, Lethbridge AB T1J 3Z6
Tel: 403-328-3511; *Fax:* 403-328-0511
e-mail: info@nikkayuko.com
www.nikkayuko.com
Also Known As: Nikka Yuko Japanese Garden
Overview: A small local organization founded in 1965
Mission: To acquaint visitors with cultural & historical background; to create support for garden philosophy of authenticity & meditative/contemplative setting; to create a unique attraction drawing large numbers to foster economic betterment of the community; to contribute to education fields such as arts, botany & general gardening; *Member of:* Lethbridge Chamber of Commerce; Affiliation(s): Chinook Tourist Association; Community Volunteer Centre
Chief Officer(s):
Amanda M. Jensen, Manager
Finances: *Annual Operating Budget:* $100,000-$250,000
Staff: 15 staff member(s); 29 volunteer(s)
Membership: 700; *Fees:* $25 single; $35 family; *Committees:* Budget; Personnel; Strategic Planning; Fundraising; Marketing; Gardening

Lethbridge Naturalists' Society

PO Box 1691, Stn. Main, Lethbridge AB T1J 4K4
Tel: 403-328-8977
Overview: A small local organization founded in 1970
Mission: To encourage knowledge & appreciation of natural history & understanding of ecological processes; To organize lectures, visual presentations & field trips; to conduct research on natural history; To become involved in environmental issues relating to conservation of the natural environment; *Member of:* Federation of Alberta Naturalists
Finances: *Annual Operating Budget:* Less than $50,000; *Funding Sources:* Membership fees
Membership: *Fees:* $10 family/individual; $6 student
Activities: Winter programs; summer field trips

Lifeforce Foundation

PO Box 3117, Vancouver BC V6B 3X6
Tel: 604-649-5258
e-mail: lifeforcesociety@hotmail.com
www.lifeforcefoundation.org
Also Known As: Lifeforce
Overview: A small international charitable organization founded in 1981
Mission: Dedicated to raising public awareness of the interrelationship of human, animal & environmental problems; to urge society to address & solve problems by taking into consideration the long-term effects on all parts of the ecosystem
Chief Officer(s):
Peter Hamilton, Founder
Finances: *Annual Operating Budget:* Less than $50,000; *Funding Sources:* Donations; membership fees; bequests
Staff: 1 staff member(s)
Membership: 500; *Fees:* $25 individual; $15 seniors/students; $50 family; $250 business; *Committees:* Ecology Issues
Activities: Whale & dolphin hotline; Orca research; Lifewatch program distributes whale watching regulations & stops boaters who harass marine mammals; Marine Wildlife Rescue; educational materials & displays; all animal rights & issues;

LifeSciences British Columbia

#900, 1188 West Georgia St., Vancouver BC V6E 4A2
Tel: 604-669-9909; *Fax:* 604-669-9912
e-mail: info@lifesciencesbc.ca
www.lifesciencesbc.ca/
www.facebook.com/lifesciencesbc
twitter.com/lifesciences_bc
Previous Name: BC Biotech
Overview: A medium-sized provincial organization founded in 1991
Mission: To improve the climate in which the business of biotechnology is conducted in BC; To be an advocate for the industry; To improve the level of awareness & understanding of biotechnology
Chief Officer(s):
Don Enns, President
denns@lifesciencesbc.ca
Karimah Es Sabar, President
Finances: *Annual Operating Budget:* $250,000-$500,000; *Funding Sources:* Membership fees
Staff: 4 staff member(s)
Membership: 260; *Fees:* $50 students; $250 individuals; $750+ corporations, depending on membership categories; *Member Profile:* Producers & users of biotechnology, including companies, colleges & universities, government agencies & students; *Committees:* Communications; Finance; Human Resources; Public Policies; Research & Development

Lifewater Canada

#194, 307 Euclid Ave., Thunder Bay ON P7E 6G6
Tel: 807-622-4848; *Fax:* 807-577-9798
Toll-Free: 888-543-3426
www.lifewater.ca
Overview: A small international organization
Mission: Christian organization dedicated to ensuring that people everywhere have access to adequate supplies of safe water; to train & equip Nationals with drill rigs & hand pumps so they can solve their own water problems; to place as many technical documents on-line as possible so they can benefit people everywhere, regardless of affiliation
Chief Officer(s):
Alanna Drost, Contact
Membership: *Member Profile:* Hydrogeologists, well drillers, educators, engineers, environmental scientists, businessmen & many other people with diverse skills & training

Ligue de sécurité de l'Ontario *See* Ontario Safety League

Lloydminster Agricultural Exhibition Association (LAEA)

PO Box 690, 5521 - 49 Ave., Lloydminster SK S9V 0Y7
Tel: 306-825-5571; *Fax:* 306-825-7017
e-mail: lloydexh@lloydexh.com
www.lloydexh.com
www.facebook.com/pages/Lloydminster-Exhibition-Association/56114974626
Overview: A small local charitable organization founded in 1904
Mission: Dedicated in continuing to foster and develop the tourism industry of Lloydminster, and providing support to the business, social and cultural sectors of the reason.; *Member of:* Saskatchewan Association of Agricultural Societies & Exhibitions; Affiliation(s): Alberta Association of Agricultural Associations; Canadian Association of Fairs & Exhibitions; International Association of Fairs & Exhibitions
Chief Officer(s):
Michael Sidoryk, Manager
Owen Noble, President
Finances: *Annual Operating Budget:* $1.5 Million-$3 Million
Staff: 15 staff member(s); 300 volunteer(s)
Membership: 100-499;; *Fees:* $10 with $40 on demand
Activities: Agricultural activities; rentals; seminars; livestock sales & shows; social receptions

Local Government Management Association of British Columbia (LGMA)

Central Building, 620 View St., 7th Fl., Victoria BC V8W 1J6
Tel: 250-383-7032; *Fax:* 250-384-4879
e-mail: office@lgma.ca
www.lgma.ca
Previous Name: Municipal Officers' Association of British Columbia
Overview: A medium-sized provincial organization founded in 1919
Mission: To promote professional management & leadership excellence in local government; To create awareness of local government officers' roles in the community
Chief Officer(s):
Tom MacDonald, Executive Director, 250-383-7032 Ext. 223, Fax: 250-383-4879
tmacdonald@lgma.ca
Elizabeth Brennan, Coordinator, Internship Program, 250-383-7032 Ext. 231, Fax: 250-383-4879
ebrennan@lgma.ca
Ana Fuller, Coordinator, Program, 250-383-7032 Ext. 227, Fax: 250-383-4879
afuller@lgma.ca
Renee Johansson, Accountant, 250-383-7032, Fax: 250-383-4879
rjohansson@lgma.ca
Finances: *Funding Sources:* Membership dues; Conference fees; Workshop fees; Sponsorships
Membership: *Fees:* $125 retired; $275 regular; $325 affiliate; fee for corporate membership based on number of members; *Member Profile:* Municipal & regional district managers, administrators, clerks, treasurers, & other local government officials in the province of British Columbia; Persons with an interest in local government administration may be affiliate members; *Committees:* Operations & Member Services; Education; Special Initiatives & External Relations; LGMA Policy 004
Activities: Providing educational programs for local government professionals to encourage fellowship & networking; Offering career transition counselling services; Providing personal pension & retirement planning counselling services for members
Meetings/Conferences:
For more information see Trade Shows, Conferences and Seminars Chapter
Local Government Management Association of British Columbia 2013 CAO (Chief Administrative Officers) Forum
February 2013 Victoria, BC
Local Government Management Association of British Columbia 2013 Annual General Meeting & Conference
June 2013 Kelowna, BC
Local Government Management Association of British Columbia 2013 Administrative Professionals Conference
October 2013, BC
Local Government Management Association of British Columbia 2014 Annual General Meeting & Conference
June 2014 Vancouver, BC
Local Government Management Association of British Columbia 2015 Annual General Meeting & Conference
2015, BC
Publications:
•Exchange
Type: Magazine; *Frequency:* Quarterly; *Accepts Advertising*
Profile: A magazine, featuring best practices, ideas, & professional development, distributed to more than 1,000 local government managers, mayors, & regional district chairs throughout British Columbia, as well asbusiness affiliates
•Local Government Elections Manual
Type: Manual; *Price:* $175
Profile: Ready-to-use forms, plus a CD ROM with sample bylaws
•Local Government Management Association of British Columbia Annual Report
Type: Yearbook; *Frequency:* Annually
Profile: A review of the year's activities, including chapter reports & financial statements
•Local Government Management Association of British Columbia Guide for Approving Officers
Type: Manual; *Price:* $150 CD ROM; $225 print version, including the CD ROM
Profile: An updated edition to reflect new & amended legislation & court decisions
•Local Government Management Association of British Columbia Records Management Manual for Local Government
Type: Manual; *Price:* $150 CD ROM; $225 print version, including the CD ROM
Profile: Standards & best practices for records management

Lower Mainland Chapter

c/o Jennifer Kooistra, City of Chilliwack, 8550 Young Rd., Chilliwack BC V2P 8A4
www.lgma.ca
Chief Officer(s):
Lynda Floyd, President, 604-937-4100, Fax: 604-939-5034
lfloyd@belcarra.ca
Lisa Parkes, Vice-President, 604-927-3000, Fax: 604-927-3015
lparkes@coquitlam.ca
Siobhian Heaney, Secretary, 604-873-7011, Fax: 604-873-7419
siobhian.heaney@vancouver.ca
Jennifer Kooistra, Treasurer, 604-792-9311
jkooistra@chilliwack.com

North Central Chapter

c/o Ron Bowles, North Central Municipal Officers' Association, 3215 Eby St., Terrace BC V8G 2X8
Chief Officer(s):
Fred Banham, President, 250-784-3208, Fax: 250-784-3201
fred.banham@prrd.bc.ca
Janis Bell, Vice-President, 250-392-3351, Fax: 250-392-2812
jbell@cariboord.bc.ca
Kim Isaak, Secretary, 250-242-4242, Fax: 250-242-3993
tradmin@dtr.ca
Ron Bowles, Treasurer, 250-638-4725, Fax: 250-638-4777
rbowles@terrace.ca

Rocky Mountain Chapter

c/o Terry Melcer, District of Sparwood, PO Box 520, Sparwood BC V0B 2G0
Chief Officer(s):
Terry Melcer, President, 250-425-6271, Fax: 250-425-7277
tmelcer@sparwood.bc.ca

Curtis Helgesen, Vice-President, 250-865-4000, Fax: 250-865-4001
chelgesen@elkford.ca
Christopher Prosser, Secretary, 250-342-9281, Fax: 250-342-2934
cao@invermere.net

Thompson Okanagan Chapter
c/o Patti Bridal, 3400 - 30th St., Vernon BC VIT 5E6
Chief Officer(s):
Larry Randle, President, 250-679-6238, Fax: 250-679-3070
lrandle@chasebc.ca
Melinda Stickney, Vice-President, 250-546-3023, Fax: 250-546-3710
msticney@cityofarmstrong.bc.ca
Patti Bridal, Secretary-Treasurer, 250-550-3524, Fax: 250-545-7876
pbridal@vernon.ca

Vancouver Island Chapter
c/o Andrew Hicik, 2440 Sidney Ave., Sidney BC V8L 1Y7
Chief Officer(s):
Richard Kanigan, President, 250-339-2202, Fax: 250-339-7110
rkanigan@comox.ca
Sarah Jones, Vice-President, 250-708-2250, Fax: 250-727-9551
sjones@town.viewroyal.bc.ca
Davina Sparrow, Secretary, 250-720-2822, Fax: 250-723-1003
davina_sparrow@portalberni.ca
Andrew Hicik, Treasurer, 250-655-5470, Fax: 250-655-4508
ahicik@sidney.ca

West Kootenay Boundary Chapter
c/o Amy Gurnett, PO Box 510, Montrose BC V0G 1P0
Chief Officer(s):
Elaine Kumar, President, 250-368-9148, Fax: 250-368-3990
ekumar@rdkb.com
John Malcolm, Vice-President, 250-365-7227, Fax: 250-365-4810
jmalcolm@castlegar.ca
Amy Gurnett, Secretary-Treasurer, 250-367-7234, Fax: 250-367-7288
montvill@telus.net

London Regional Resource Centre for Heritage & the Environment
1017 Western Rd., London ON N6G 1G5
Tel: 519-645-2845; *Fax:* 519-645-0981
e-mail: info@grosvenorlodge.com
www.heritagelondonfoundation.org/IndexGrosvenor.htm
Also Known As: Grosvenor Lodge
Overview: A small local organization founded in 1992
Mission: To promote heritage & environmental activities & organizations in the London area; *Member of:* Heritage London Foundation
Chief Officer(s):
Jan Dickinson, Executive Director

Long Point Bird Observatory ***See*** Bird Studies Canada

Lower Mainland Wildlife Rescue Association ***See*** Wildlife Rescue Association of British Columbia

Lumber & Building Materials Association of Ontario (LBMAO)
#27, 5155 Spectrum Way, Mississauga ON L4W 5A1
Tel: 905-625-1084; *Fax:* 905-625-3006
Toll-Free: 888-365-2626
www.lbmao.on.ca
Previous Name: Ontario Retail Lumber Dealers Association
Overview: A medium-sized provincial organization founded in 1917
Mission: To promote the welfare of members so that they are able to build a competitive advantage & remain at the leading edge of the lumber & building materials industry
Chief Officer(s):
David W. Campbell, President
dwcampbell@lbmao.on.ca
Bob Lockwood, Chair
lockwoodbc@hotmail.com
Dwayne Sprague, Vice-Chair
Membership: *Member Profile:* Manufacturers; Distributors; Purchasing organizations; Wholesalers; Service firm
Activities: Providing educational opportunities; Offering support services; Engaging in advocacy activities

Lynn Canyon Ecology Centre
3663 Park Rd., North Vancouver BC V7J 3G3
Tel: 604-990-3755
e-mail: ecocentre@dnv.org
www.dnv.org/ecology/
Overview: A small local organization founded in 1971
Mission: To educate people about ecology
Chief Officer(s):
S.A. Kissinger
D. Robertson
Finances: *Funding Sources:* District of North Vancouver
Staff: 3 staff member(s); 12 volunteer(s)
Membership: 1,000-4,999; *Committees:* Stream Keepers - Maplewood Conservation Area
Activities: School & public education program; displays; leaflets;

Mackenzie Applied Research Association (MARA)
Parent Name: Agricultural Research & Extension Council of Alberta
PO Box 646, 1 River Road Experimental Farm, Fort Vermilion AB T0H 1N0
Tel: 780-927-3776; *Fax:* 780-927-4747
e-mail: mara3@telus.net
www.areca.ab.ca/marahome.html
Overview: A small local organization overseen by Agricultural Research & Extension Council of Alberta
Mission: To conduct agricultural research, trials & rural extension in Northern Alberta's Mackenzie county; *Member of:* Agricultural Research & Extension Council of Alberta

Macleod Institute
223, 20 Coachway Rd. SW, Calgary AB T3H 1E6
Tel: 403-240-2573; *Fax:* 403-246-1852
Toll-Free: 866-204-6123
e-mail: macleod@macleodinstitute.com
www.macleodinstitute.com
Previous Name: Macleod Institute for Environmental Analysis
Overview: A small national organization
Mission: To provide impartial advice on regulatory & environmental issues; Affiliation(s): University of Calgary
Chief Officer(s):
Elaine McCoy, President
Finances: *Annual Operating Budget:* $100,000-$250,000; *Funding Sources:* Contract
Staff: 5 staff member(s)
Membership: 1-99

Macleod Institute for Environmental Analysis ***See*** Macleod Institute

Madawaska Forest Products Marketing Board ***Voir*** Office de vente des produits forestiers du Madawaska

Maintenance, Engineering and Reliability (MER) Society
Parent Name: Canadian Institute of Mining, Metallurgy & Petroleum
c/o Chair, Brad Kingston, Wardrop Engineering Inc., 725 Hewitson St., Thunder Bay ON P7B 6B5
Tel: 807-345-5453
Previous Name: Mechanical-Electrical Division of The Canadian Institute of Mining, Metallurgy & Petroleum
Overview: A medium-sized national organization overseen by Canadian Institute of Mining, Metallurgy & Petroleum
Mission: To advance the theory & practice of electrical & mechanical arts & sciences in the mining industry; To improve mechanical-electrical standards
Environmental Activity: Offering an information interchange service to mine designers, engineers, suppliers, & operating personnel for the sound operation & maintenance of projects, mines, & facilities
Chief Officer(s):
Brad Kingston, Chair, 807-345-5453
brad.kingston@wardrop.com
Mel Harju, Director, Energy & Membership
mel.harju@sympatico.ca
Jacek Paraszczak, Director, Education, Student Papers, & Scholarships
jacek.paraszczak@gmn.ulaval.ca
Ed Patton, Secretary
emptech@sympatico.ca
R.A. (Dick) McIvor, Treasurer
dmcivor@sympatico.ca
Activities: Facilitating the exchange of information & data on electrical & mechanical subjects; Publishing technical papers; Providing educational assistance; Promoting methods & devices to increase safety
Meetings/Conferences:
For more information see Trade Shows, Conferences and Seminars Chapter
Maintenance & Engineering Society of The Canadian Institute of Mining, Metallurgy & Petroleum 2013 Maintenance Engineering/Mine Operators' Conference
2013
Maintenance & Engineering Society of The Canadian Institute of Mining, Metallurgy & Petroleum 2015 Maintenance Engineering/Mine Operators' Conference
2015

Manitoba Association of Landscape Architects (MALA)
131 Callum Cres., Winnipeg MB R2G 2C7
Tel: 204-663-4863; *Fax:* 204-668-5662
www.mala.net
Overview: A medium-sized provincial organization founded in 1973
Mission: To promote, improve & advance the profession; to maintain standards of professional practice & conduct consistent with the need to serve & protect public interest; to support improvement &/or conservation of the natural, cultural, social & built environment; *Member of:* Canadian Society of Landscape Architects
Chief Officer(s):
Emeka Nnadi, President
Finances: *Annual Operating Budget:* Less than $50,000
Staff: 1 staff member(s)
Membership: 49 individual + 5 honorary + 28 associate + 40 student affiliates + 4 friend; *Committees:* CSLA Awards/Annual Symposium; Communications; Examining Board; Ethics; University Liaison
Activities: *Internships:* Yes; *Rents Mailing List:* Yes

Manitoba Camping Association (MCA)
Parent Name: Canadian Camping Association
#302, 960 Portage Ave., Winnipeg MB R3G 0R4
Tel: 204-784-1134; *Fax:* 204-784-4177
e-mail: sunshinefund@mbcamping.ca
www.mbcamping.ca
www.facebook.com/sunshinefundmb
Overview: A medium-sized provincial organization founded in 1937 overseen by Canadian Camping Association
Mission: To act as a coordinating body for organized camping in Manitoba; To promote organized camping as an educational and recreational experience; *Member of:* Canadian Camping Association
Chief Officer(s):
Bryan Ezako, Executive Director
executivedirector@mbcamping.ca
Janis Banman, Coordinator, General Office Administration & Sunshine Fund Program, 204-784-1130, Fax: 204-784-4177
Finances: *Funding Sources:* Donations; Membership dues
Membership: *Member Profile:* Organizations & individuals who support organized childrens & family camps & the mission of the MCA
Activities: Developing standards for organized camping in Manitoba; Communicating information about regulations & developments that affect organized camping; Representing member camps to government agencies & to the public; Administering the Winnipeg Free Press Sunshine Fund which allows financially disadvantaged children to attend camps; Offering workshops; Providing networking opportunities; *Awareness Events:* Manitoba Parade of Camps

Manitoba Cattle Producers Association (MCPA)
154 Paramount Rd., Winnipeg MB R2X 2W3
Tel: 204-772-4542; *Fax:* 204-774-3264
Toll-Free: 800-772-0458
e-mail: feedback@mcpa.net
www.mcpa.net
twitter.com/ManitobaBeef
Overview: A medium-sized provincial organization
Mission: To act as the voice of the cattle industry in Manitoba; To ensure a sustainable future for the industry; *Member of:* Canadian Cattlemen's Association
Chief Officer(s):
Jay Fox, President
Sheila Mowat, General Manager
Audrey Treichel, Coordinator, Communications
Lauren Stone, Policy Analyst
Membership: *Member Profile:* Cattle producers in Manitoba; *Committees:* Executive; Animal Health; Annual Meeting; APF;

Communications; Crown Lands; Environment; Finance; Production Management; Quality Starts Here; Research; Resolutions
Activities: Engaging in advocacy activities; Researching; Providing education; *Awareness Events:* Manitoba Beef Week
Publications:
•Cattle Country: The Voice of Manitoba's Cattle Industry
Type: Magazine; *Frequency:* 8 pa; *Accepts Advertising*; *Editor:* Karen Emilson; *Price:* Free
Profile: Information for cattle producers & industry supporters in Manitoba & eastern Saskatchewan

Manitoba Christmas Tree Growers Association (MCTGA)
900 Corydon Ave., Winnipeg MB R3M 0Y4
Tel: 204-453-3128
e-mail: mctga@realchristmastrees.mb.ca
www.realchristmastrees.mb.ca
Overview: A small provincial organization
Mission: To assist membership in promoting benefits of Christmas trees
Environmental Activity: Promoting the use of Winnipeg's Let's Chip In recylcing program
Chief Officer(s):
Cliff Freund, President
Dorothy Freund, Treasurer

Manitoba Council for International Cooperation (MCIC) / Conseil du Manitoba pour la coopération internationale
#302, 280 Smith St., Winnipeg MB R3C 1K2
Tel: 204-987-6420; *Fax:* 204-956-0031
e-mail: info@mcic.ca
www.mcic.ca
www.facebook.com/mcic.ca
twitter.com/MCIC_CA
Overview: A medium-sized international charitable organization founded in 1974
Mission: To promote international development that protects the environment; To coordinate the development work of member agencies; *Member of:* Canadian Council for International Cooperation (CCIC)
Chief Officer(s):
Janice Hamilton, Executive Director
mcic@web.ca
Finances: *Funding Sources:* Donations; Member agencies; MB Gov't Matching Grant Program; MB Education, Citizenship & Youth, Gov't of MB; Canadian International Development Agency
Activities: Administering funds for international development; Supporting overseas projects; Providing development education in Manitoba; Increasing public awareness of international issues; Fostering member interaction
Meetings/Conferences:
For more information see Trade Shows, Conferences and Seminars Chapter
Manitoba Council for International Cooperation's Annual General Meeting 2013
June 2013 Winnipeg, MB

Manitoba Eco-Network Inc. (MEN) / Réseau écologique du Manitoba inc.
Parent Name: Canadian Environmental Network
#3, 303 Portage Ave., Winnipeg MB R3B 2B4
Tel: 204-947-6511; *Fax:* 204-989-8476
e-mail: info@mbeconetwork.org
www.mbeconetwork.org
Also Known As: Manitoba Environmental Network
Overview: A small provincial charitable organization founded in 1988 overseen by Canadian Environmental Network
Mission: To educate the public on environmental issues; to conduct research on environmental issues; to facilitate communications between environmental groups & the general public
Chief Officer(s):
Anne Lindsey, Executive Director
Finances: *Annual Operating Budget:* $100,000-$250,000; *Funding Sources:* Project work; donations; membership dues; grants
Staff: 6 staff member(s); 10 volunteer(s)
Membership: 55 groups; *Fees:* $50 organizations, agencies, government departments & corporation; *Member Profile:* Open to any non-profit non-governmental group which has as one of its objectives the enhancing or furthering of environmental quality, protecting the environment or environmental education
Activities: Sponsors public forums, speakers, workshops on a broad variety of issues; operates projects regarding climate change, water issues & organic lawn care; offers GIS & mapping services to environmental projects; meets regularly with officials of the provincial government; *Speaker Service:* Yes; *Library:* Alice Chambers Memorial Library; Open to public

Manitoba Environment Officers Association Inc. (MEOA)
147 Norcross Cres., Winnipeg MB R3X 1J2
e-mail: meoa@mts.net
www.meoa.ca
Overview: A medium-sized provincial organization
Mission: To enhance the public health and safety of Manitobans and to protect, maintain and rehabilitate Manitoba's environment ecosystems through the diligent duties of educated Environment Officers and to obtain for Environment Officers continued education and recognition of their efforts.
Chief Officer(s):
Bill Barr, President
Membership: *Fees:* $25

Manitoba Environmental Industries Association Inc. (MEIA)
#100, 62 Albert St., Winnipeg MB R3B 1E9
Tel: 204-783-7090; *Fax:* 204-783-6501
e-mail: admin@meia.mb.ca
www.meia.mb.ca
Overview: A medium-sized provincial organization founded in 1991
Mission: To assist members in the business of the environment; To connect business, government, & stakeholders with environmental issues
Environmental Activity: Liaising with the government to develop environmental policies, regulations, & standards; Increasing awareness of environmental practices & initiatives; Communicating with members regarding environmental developments
Chief Officer(s):
John Fjeldsted, Executive Director
Vaughn Bullough, President
Rosemary Deans, Coordinator, Education & Training
Deb Tardiff, Coordinator, Education & Training
Sheldon McLeod, Secretary
John Pikel, Treasurer
Finances: *Funding Sources:* Membership fees; Sponsorships
Membership: *Fees:* Schedule available, based upon number of employees & number of representatives; *Member Profile:* Professionals, companies, & organizations in Manitoba who practise in the area of environment & sustainable development; *Committees:* Executive; Member Services; Legislation & Regulation; Programs Development
Activities: Providing professional development training, including courses, MEIA learning sessions, & environment industry workshops; Collaborating with other organizations; Providing networking opportunities
Meetings/Conferences:
For more information see Trade Shows, Conferences and Seminars Chapter
Manitoba Environmental Industries Association Inc. 2013 Remediation & Renewal Conference
February 2013 Winnipeg, MB
Manitoba Environmental Industries Association Inc. 2013 Conference: Emerging Issues
2013, MB
Manitoba Environmental Industries Association Inc. 2013 Annual General Meeting
2013, MB
Publications:
•Manitoba Environmental Industries Association Inc. Members' Directory
Type: Directory
Profile: Contact information for association members
•MEIA [Manitoba Environmental Industries Association Inc.] Information Bulletin
Type: Newsletter; *Frequency:* Biweekly
Profile: Information for Manitoba Environmental Industries Association Inc. members about events, technology updates, & emerging regulatory & policyissues

Manitoba Farm Bureau *See* Keystone Agricultural Producers

Manitoba Forestry Association Inc.
Parent Name: Canadian Forestry Association
900 Corydon Ave., Winnipeg MB R3M 0Y4
Tel: 204-453-3182; *Fax:* 204-477-5765
e-mail: mfainc@mts.net
www.mbforestryassoc.ca
Previous Name: Prairie Provinces Forestry Association
Overview: A medium-sized provincial charitable organization founded in 1972 overseen by Canadian Forestry Association
Mission: To promote the wise use & management of all natural renewable resources, with emphasis on forests; to promote the planting of trees; to promote private land forestry (woodlots); to act as liaison among government, industry & the general public.
Chief Officer(s):
Patricia Pohrebnuk, Executive Director
Jennifer Lidgett, President
Finances: *Annual Operating Budget:* $100,000-$250,000; *Funding Sources:* Government; industry; individuals
Staff: 5 staff member(s); 34 volunteer(s)
Membership: 286 individual + 115 corporate; *Fees:* Individuals - $25 member; $50 contributing; $100 sustaining; Companies - $125 general; $250 contributing; $500 sustaining; *Committees:* Education & Public Information; Fundraising; Membership; National Forest Week; Special Events
Activities: School programs; forest centres; Private Land Forests Program; operates Forest Museum; conservation kits for use by teachers; wildfire prevention campaigns; *Awareness Events:* National Forest Week, May; *Speaker Service:* Yes; *Library:* Open to public
Awards:
•Alan B. Beaven Forestry Scholarship (Scholarship)
Manitoba resident; must be a recent graduate of high school, entering a Canadian university or technical school in forestry or an allied field *Deadline:* July *Amount:* $500

Manitoba Health Organizations *See* The Regional Health Authorities of Manitoba

Manitoba Heavy Construction Association (MHCA)
Parent Name: Canadian Construction Association
#3, 1680 Ellice Ave., Winnipeg MB R3G 0Z2
Tel: 204-947-1379; *Fax:* 204-943-2279
e-mail: info@mhca.mb.ca
www.mhca.mb.ca
twitter.com/ManitobaHeavy
Overview: A small provincial organization founded in 1943 overseen by Canadian Construction Association
Mission: To promote a safe workplace for employees in Manitoba's heavy construction industry; To represent the heavy construction industry in Manitoba
Environmental Activity: Offering safety, health & environmental training
Chief Officer(s):
Christopher Lorenc, President
Wendy Greund Summerfield, Manager, Finance
Greg Huff, Manager, MHC Training Academy
Christine Miller, Manager, Events & Membership, 204-947-1379
Jason Rosin, Manager, Communications
Membership: 340+ organizations & businesses; *Member Profile:* Heavy construction (heavy civil) & related industries in Manitoba; *Committees:* Safety Program; Winnipeg; Aggregate Producers; Highways; Events; Equipment Rental Rates; Education, Training, Education, Training, & Gold Seal; Membership
Activities: Providing government approved career & vocational training; Liaising with government; Facilitating networking opportunities
Meetings/Conferences:
For more information see Trade Shows, Conferences and Seminars Chapter
Manitoba Heavy Construction Association 2013 2nd Annual Expo
April 2013 Winnipeg, MB
Manitoba Heavy Construction Association 2013 Annual General Meeting & Chairman's Gala
2013, MB
Publications:
•Heavy News Weekly
Type: Newsletter; *Frequency:* Weekly
Profile: Articles about the heavy construction industry & association activities
•Manitoba Heavy Construction Association Annual Report
Type: Yearbook; *Frequency:* Annually
•Manitoba Heavy Construction Association Directory
Type: Directory; *Frequency:* Annually
Profile: Listings of Manitoba Heavy Construction Association member & a guide to equipment rental rates in Manitoba
•Perspectives [a publication of the Manitoba Heavy Construction Association]

Type: Magazine; *Frequency:* Annually; *Accepts Advertising*
Profile: Information about public policy, industry positions, & safety & environment related issues

Manitoba Home Builders' Association (MHBA)
Parent Name: Canadian Home Builders' Association

#1, 1420 Clarence Ave., Winnipeg MB R3T 1T6
Tel: 204-925-2560; *Fax:* 204-925-2567
e-mail: info@homebuilders.mb.ca
www.homebuilders.mb.ca
Previous Name: HUDAM
Overview: A small provincial organization founded in 1937 overseen by Canadian Home Builders' Association
Mission: To act as the voice of Manitoba's residential construction industry; To promote affordability & choice in housing in Manitoba; To uphold the MHBA Code of Ethics & the Code of Discipline; Affiliation(s): Canadian Home Builders' Association
Chief Officer(s):
Mike Moore, President
mmoore@homebuilders.mb.ca
Janet Constable, Coordinator, Special Events & Membership, 204-925-2578
jconstable@homebuilders.mb.ca
Jan Currier, Coordinator, Show, 204-925-2566
jcurrier@homebuilders.mb.ca
James Murphy, Coordinator, Training Program, 204-925-2572
jmurphy@homebuilders.mb.ca
Membership: *Member Profile:* Builders, conducting business in Manitoba, who have been members of a new home warranty program for two years, & who have completed COR registration, or have a Simplified Safety certificate; Renovators, conducting business in Manitoba, for at least two years, who are members of a new home warranty program, if they build complete new homes; Developers in Manitoba; Professionals registered to provide services to the housing industry; Sub-contractors; Suppliers to the housing industry; Manufacturers; Government; Persons employed by or enrolled in any educational institution, in study related to the housing industry; *Committees:* Government Liaison; Technical Research; Show Management; Education & Training; Workplace Safety & Health; Parade of Homes; Renovators; Nominating; Marketing; Membership Services; Past Chairman's Advisory
Activities: Offering information about the housing industry in Manitoba; Providing educational opportunities; Supporting Habitat for Humanity
Meetings/Conferences:
For more information see Trade Shows, Conferences and Seminars Chapter
Manitoba Home Builders' Association 2013 12th Annual Kitchen, Bath, & Renovation Show
January 2013 Winnipeg, MB
Manitoba Home Builders' Association 2013 Spring Parade of Homes
March 2013, MB
Manitoba Home Builders' Association 2013 39th Annual Home Expressions Home & Garden Show
March 2013 Winnipeg, MB
Manitoba Home Builders' Association 2013 Annual Housing Forum & Trade Show
2013, MB
Publications:
•Builders' Voice
Type: Newsletter
Profile: Association activities & forthcoming events

Manitoba Institute of Agrologists (MIA)
Parent Name: Agricultural Institute of Canada

#201, 38 Dafoe Ave., Winnipeg MB R3T 2N2
Tel: 204-275-3721; *Fax:* 888-315-6661
e-mail: mia@mts.net
www.mia.mb.ca
Overview: A small provincial organization founded in 1950 overseen by Agricultural Institute of Canada
Mission: To act in accordance with the Agrologists Act of Manitoba; To regulate the practice of agrology in Manitoba; To ensure the knowledge, competence, & integrity of institute members, in order to protect the public interest; To act as the voice of the agrology profession
Environmental Activity: Improving conditions in the agricultural industry
Chief Officer(s):
Richard Kieper, P.Ag., President
miapresident@mia.mb.ca
Jim Weir, Executive Director & Registrar
miaweir@mia.mb.ca ca
Estel Facundo, Officer, Administration
miaadmin@mia.mb.ca
Membership: *Member Profile:* Agricultural professionals in Manitoba; *Committees:* Finance; Education; Admission & Registration
Activities: Licensing agrologists; Promoting high standards in research; Advancing the professional status of members; Providing educational & networking opportunities
Meetings/Conferences:
For more information see Trade Shows, Conferences and Seminars Chapter
Manitoba Institute of Agrologists 2013 63rd Annual General Meeting & Professional Development Event
April 2013 Portage la Prairie, MB
Publications:
•MIA [Manitoba Institute of Agrologists] Bulletin
Type: Newsletter
Profile: Institute activities, member news, & events

Manitoba Lung Association
Parent Name: Canadian Lung Association

629 McDermot Ave., Winnipeg MB R3A 1P6
Tel: 204-774-5501; *Fax:* 204-772-5083
Toll-Free: 888-566-5864
e-mail: info@mb.lung.ca
www.mb.lung.ca
Overview: A small provincial charitable organization founded in 1904 overseen by Canadian Lung Association
Mission: To improve lung health
Environmental Activity: Providing information about pollution & air quality
Chief Officer(s):
Margaret Bernhardt-Lowdon, Executive Director & Director, Health Initiatives
margaret.bernhardt-lowdon@mb.lung.ca
Jo-anne Douglas, Director, Tobacco Reduction Initiatives
jo-anne.douglas@mb.lung.ca
Ron East, Director, Programming, Fund Development, & Marketing
ron.east@mb.lung.ca
Kris Kamenz, Director, Finance
kristopher.kamenz@mb.lung.ca
Finances: *Funding Sources:* Donations; Fundraising; Sponsorships
Activities: Providing information about lung health; Supporting & promoting research; Offering education programs in areas such as asthma, chronic obstructive pulmonary disease (COPD), & air quality
Publications:
•Manitoba Lung Association Annual Report
Type: Yearbook; *Frequency:* Annually

Manitoba Medical Association ***See*** Doctors Manitoba

Manitoba Milk Producers ***See*** Dairy Farmers of Manitoba

Manitoba Model Forest

PO Box 6500, Pine Falls MB R0E 1M0
Tel: 204-367-5232; *Fax:* 204-367-8897
e-mail: miette@granite.mb.ca
www.manitobamodelforest.net
Overview: A small provincial organization founded in 1992
Member of: Canadian Model Forest Network
Chief Officer(s):
Brian Kotak, General Manager

Manitoba Municipal Administrators' Association Inc.

533 Buckingham Rd., Winnipeg MB R3R 1B9
Tel: 204-255-4883; *Fax:* 204-255-2623
e-mail: mmaa@mts.net
www.mmaa.mb.ca
Overview: A medium-sized provincial organization
Mission: The Manitoba Municipal Administrators' Association (MMAA) is a dynamic, action-orientated organization for Municipal Employees. The MMAA focusses on the needs of our membership and are committed to their professional development.
Chief Officer(s):
Mel Nott, Executive Director

Manitoba Ozone Protection Industry Association (MOPIA)

1980B Main St., Winnipeg MB R2V 2B6
Tel: 204-338-0804; *Fax:* 204-338-0810
Toll-Free: 888-667-4203
e-mail: mopia@mts.net
www.mopia.ca
Overview: A medium-sized provincial organization
Mission: To work towards protection of the stratospheric ozone layer; To control, reduce, & eventually eliminate emissions of ozone depleting substances
Environmental Activity: Implementing the MOPIA Atmosphere Protection Program; Offering environmental certification training to persons in the air conditioning & refrigeration industry
Chief Officer(s):
Mark E. Miller, Executive Director
George Kurowski, Chair
John Kub, Secretary
Laverne Dalgleish, Treasurer
Activities: Liaising with industry, interest groups, & Manitoba Environment; Raising public awareness of the impact of ozone depleting substances
Meetings/Conferences:
For more information see Trade Shows, Conferences and Seminars Chapter
Manitoba Ozone Protection Industry Association 2013 19th Annual General Meeting
April 2013 Winnipeg, MB
Manitoba Ozone Protection Industry Association 2014 20th Annual General Meeting
April 2014, MB
Publications:
•Environmental Awareness Training for Ozone Depleting Substances (ODS) & Other Halocarbons
Type: Manual; *Price:* $45
Profile: A training manual for persons working on refrigeration or air conditioning equipment that contains a regulated substance
•Manitoba Ozone Protection Industry Association Annual Report
Type: Yearbook; *Frequency:* Annually
Profile: Featuring messages from the Chair of the Board of Directors & the Executive Director, reports from the treasurer & auditor, as well as highlights of the year
•MOPIA [Manitoba Ozone Protection Industry Association] E-Bulletin
Type: Newsletter; *Frequency:* Monthly; *Editor:* Mark Miller; Vanessa Krahn
Profile: Information for Manitoba Ozone Protection Industry Association members & select stakeholders

Manitoba Professional Planners Institute (MPPI)
Parent Name: Canadian Institute of Planners

137 Bannatyne Ave., 2nd Fl., Winnipeg MB R3B 0R3
Tel: 204-943-3637; *Fax:* 204-925-4624
e-mail: mjohnson@mts.net
www.mppi.mb.ca
Overview: A medium-sized provincial organization overseen by Canadian Institute of Planners
Mission: MPPI is responsible for handling membership applications and services, and for the enforcement of the Code of Professional Conduct. MPPI, along with the Association of Community Planners of Saskatchewan, jointly publishes the membership newsletter SCENARIO and sponsors workshops and seminars for the purpose of informing the membership of relevant developments and issues in the planning field.; Affiliation(s): Canadian Institute of Planners (CIP)
Chief Officer(s):
Valdene Buckley, President
Meetings/Conferences:
For more information see Trade Shows, Conferences and Seminars Chapter
Manitoba Professional Planners Institute 2013 Annual General Meeting
May 2013 Winnipeg, MB

Manitoba Public Health Association (MPHA)
Parent Name: Canadian Public Health Association

c/o Klinic Community Health Centre, 870 Portage Ave., Winnipeg MB R3G 0P1
e-mail: manitobapha@mts.net
www.manitobapha.ca
Overview: A small provincial organization founded in 1940 overseen by Canadian Public Health Association
Mission: To influence health, social, environmental, & economic policy decisions, in order to improve the well-being of people in Manitoba; To ensure that health promotion, health protection, & disease protection are part of services; *Member of:* Canadian Public Health Association (CPHA)
Chief Officer(s):
Barb Wasilewski, President
manitobapha@mts.net
Membership: *Fees:* $67 MPHA / CPHA memberships for students, & retired & low-income people; $140 regular MPHA / CPHA memberships

Activities: Advocating for healthy public policies; Liaising with community & professional associations & the government

Manitoba Pulse Growers Association Inc.

PO Box 1760, 38 - 4th Ave. NE, Carman MB R0G 0J0
Tel: 204-745-6488; *Fax:* 204-745-6213
Toll-Free: 866-226-9442
www.manitobapulse.ca
Overview: A medium-sized provincial organization founded in 1984
Mission: To provide production knowledge to members of the Manitoba pulse growers industry
Chief Officer(s):
Kyle Friesen, President
Michael Reimer, Acting Executive Director
Membership: 3,000; *Member Profile:* Farmers in Manitoba who grow edible beans, peas, lentils, chickpeas, faba beans & soybeans; *Committees:* Executive; Edible Bean; Finance; Market Development; MASC; Peas, Faba beans, Lentils & Chickpeas; Soybean; Variety Trial Results

Manitoba Regional Lily Society

PO Box 846, Neepawa MB R0J 1H0
e-mail: nigel@lilynook.mb.ca
www.manitobalilies.ca
Overview: A small provincial organization
Mission: To promote the growing and care of lillies in Manitoba.
Chief Officer(s):
Deborah Petrie, President
petrie@mymts.net
Membership: *Fees:* $10

Manitoba Safety Council ***See*** Safety Services Manitoba

Manitoba Society of Certified Engineering Technicians & Technologists Inc. ***See*** Certified Technicians & Technologists Association of Manitoba

Manitoba Trucking Association (MTA)
Parent Name: Canadian Trucking Alliance

25 Bunting St., Winnipeg MB R2X 2P5
Tel: 204-632-6600; *Fax:* 204-694-7134
e-mail: info@trucking.mb.ca
www.trucking.mb.ca
Overview: A medium-sized provincial organization founded in 1932 overseen by Canadian Trucking Alliance
Mission: Develops and maintains a safe and healthy business environment for its members; Affiliation(s): Canadian Trucking Alliance; Canadian Council of Motor Transport Administrators; Canadian Trucking Human Resource Council; Winnipeg Chamber of Commerce; Manitoba Chamber of Commerce; Infrastructure Council of Manitoba; Employers' Task Force on Workers' Compensation; Manitoba Employers' Council
Chief Officer(s):
Earl Coleman, President
Susan Snyder, 1st Vice President
Tom Payne, Jr., 2nd Vice President
Bob Dolyniuk, General Manager
Susan Green, Coordinator, Program & Member Services
Finances: *Funding Sources:* Membership dues & fundraising through services
Staff: 5 staff member(s)
Membership: 350 organizations; *Member Profile:* PSV Carriers; City Transportation; Private Fleet; Household Goods Carriers; Associated Trades; Vehicle Maintenance; *Committees:* Associated Trades (Members, Executive); Vehicle Maintenance Council; Maintenace Council Executive
Activities: *Speaker Service:* Yes; *Library:* Open to public by appointment
Publications:
•Western Canada Highway News
Type: Journal; *Frequency:* Quarterly

Manitoba Underwater Council (MUC)

PO Box 711, Winnipeg MB R3C 2K3
Tel: 204-632-8508
e-mail: info@manunderwater.com
www.manunderwater.com
Overview: A medium-sized provincial charitable organization founded in 1962
Mission: To coordinate, preserve, support & promote sport diving clubs & associations; to promote safety in diving; to exchange & disseminate information concerning the sport of skin & scuba diving & to foster conservation; *Member of:* Sport Manitoba
Finances: *Annual Operating Budget:* Less than $50,000; *Funding Sources:* Provincial Government & membership fees
Staff: 10 staff member(s); 10 volunteer(s)
Membership: 27 institutional + 150 individual; *Fees:* $20; *Member Profile:* Certified scuba divers, divers in training
Activities: Spear fishing competition, pumpkin dive, super dive, underwater football competition

Manitoba Water & Wastewater Association (MWWA)

PO Box 1600, #215, 9 Saskatchewan Ave. West, 2nd Fl., Portage la Prairie MB R1N 3P1
Tel: 204-239-6868; *Fax:* 204-239-6872
Toll-Free: 866-396-2549
e-mail: mwwa@mts.net
www.mwwa.net
www.facebook.com/group.php?gid=167933616574016
Overview: A small provincial organization founded in 1975
Mission: To provide operator members with educational opportunities for operating & maintaining water & wastewater treatment facilities & water distribution & wastewater collection systems; To promote operator certification & facility classification; *Member of:* Western Canada Water & Wastewater Association
Environmental Activity: To be dedicated to the stewardship of the environment & public health
Chief Officer(s):
Dale Scott, Chair
Iva Last, Executive Director
Activities: Exchnaging information & experiences
Meetings/Conferences:
For more information see Trade Shows, Conferences and Seminars Chapter
Manitoba Water & Wastewater Association 2013 Annual Conference & Trade Show
February 2013 Winnipeg, MB
Manitoba Water & Wastewater Association 2014 Annual Conference & Trade Show
February 2014 Portage la Prairie, MB
Manitoba Water & Wastewater Association 2015 Annual Conference & Trade Show
January 2015 Brandon, MB
Manitoba Water & Wastewater Association 2016 Annual Conference & Trade Show
January 2016 Winnipeg, MB
Publications:
•Waterways [a publication of the Manitoba Water & Wastewater Association]
Type: Newsletter
Profile: Information for members about upcoming conferences & educational opportunities

Manitoba Water Well Association (MWWA)
Parent Name: Canadian Ground Water Association

PO Box 1648, Winnipeg MB R3C 2Z6
Tel: 204-479-3777
e-mail: info@mwwa.ca
www.mwwa.ca
Overview: A medium-sized provincial organization founded in 1958 overseen by Canadian Ground Water Association
Mission: To promote & support the water well industry in Manitoba
Environmental Activity: Encouraging cooperation between association members & government agencies for the protection & management of the underground water supply in Manitoba
Chief Officer(s):
Jeff Bell, President
Ray Ford, Vice-President
Lynn Giersch, Business Manager
Marilyn Schneider, Secretary-Treasurer
Membership: *Member Profile:* Manufacturers; Technicians; Suppliers; Contractors
Activities: Offering workshops & seminars; Providing networking opportunities; Fostering & promoting scientific education, research, & standards
Meetings/Conferences:
For more information see Trade Shows, Conferences and Seminars Chapter
Manitoba Water Well Association 2013 Annual General Meeting
2013, MB
Publications:
•Manitoba Water Well Association Newsletter
Type: Newsletter; *Frequency:* Quarterly
Profile: Featuring the president's report, membership information

Manitoba Wildlife Federation (MWF)
Parent Name: Canadian Wildlife Federation

70 Stevenson Rd., Winnipeg MB R3H 0W7
Tel: 204-633-5967; *Fax:* 204-632-5200
e-mail: info@mwf.mb.ca
www.mwf.mb.ca
Overview: A medium-sized provincial charitable organization founded in 1944 overseen by Canadian Wildlife Federation
Mission: To devote members to the causes of conservation & the participation in the wise use of natural resources; To encourage the propagation of game & fish; To promote the enforcement of game laws; To cooperate with government departments
Environmental Activity: Educating members & the public, especially about conservation & safety; Supporting research on diseases in fish & wildlife; Acting as a voice for the progressive management of Manitoba's natural resources; Cleaning up rivers & streams
Chief Officer(s):
Reid Woods, President
President@mwf.mb.ca
Lori Thomas, Director, Administration
Rachelle Aime, Vice-President, Education
vpAngling@mwf.mb.ca
Ken MacMaster, Vice-President, Membership
vpMembership@mwf.mb.ca
Larry Millan, Vice-President, Environment & Habitat
vpEnvironment@mwf.mb.ca
Reg Wiebe, Coordinator, Hunter Education
Finances: *Funding Sources:* Membership fees; Donations; Sponsorships
Membership: 14,000; *Fees:* $7.50 youth (12 to 17 years of age); $25 individuals; $35 families; *Member Profile:* Anglers; Hunters; Outdoor enthusiasts; *Committees:* Education; Hunting; Environment & Habitat; Angling; Publicity; Program Coordination; Membership; Legislation Review; Internal Services
Activities: Offering hunting skills & firearms training programs; Developing the Hunters Sharing the Harvest program; Supporting the MWF Habitat Foundation
Publications:
•Outdoor Edge [a publication of the Manitoba Wildlife Federation]
Type: Magazine; *Frequency:* Bimonthly; *Price:* Free with Manitoba Wildlife Federation membership
Profile: Information for Manitoba's hunters & anglers

Manitoba Wildlife Rehabilitation Organization ***See*** Wildlife Haven Rehabilitation Centre

Manufacturiers et Exportateurs Canada ***See*** Canadian Manufacturers & Exporters

Marine Renewables Canada

121 Bird Sanctuary Dr., Nanaimo BC V9R 6H1
www.marinerenewables.ca
www.linkedin.com/groups/Marine-Renewables-Canada-2689413?home=&gid=268
www.facebook.com/marinerenewablescanada
twitter.com/Canadian_MRE
Previous Name: Ocean Renewable Energy Group
Overview: A medium-sized national charitable organization founded in 2004
Mission: Marine Renewables Canada aligns industry, academia and government to ensure that Canada is a leader in providing ocean energy solutions to a world market.
Chief Officer(s):
Chris Campbell, Exective Director, 250-754-0040
chris@marinerenewables.ca
Membership: *Fees:* $50 student; $300 individual; $500 organization; $1,000 government dept.; $2,500-$10,000 Ocean Energy Leader
Activities: Conferences
Meetings/Conferences:
For more information see Trade Shows, Conferences and Seminars Chapter
Marine Renewables Canada 2013 Annual Conference
November 2013 Ottawa, ON
5th International Conference on Ocean Energy (ICOE) 2014
November 2014 Halifax, NS

Atlantic Office
PO Box 34066, #400, 1533 Barrington St., Halifax NS B3J 3S1
Chief Officer(s):
Elisa Obermann, Atlantic Director, 902-817-4317
elisa@marinerenewables.ca

Marmot Recovery Foundation

PO Box 2332, Stn. A, Nanaimo BC V9R 6X6

Tel: 250-390-0006
Toll-Free: 877-462-7668
e-mail: marmots@telus.net
www.marmots.org
Overview: A small local organization founded in 1998
Mission: To manage the recovery effort for one of North America's most endangered mammals: the Vancouver Island marmot (Marmota vancouverensis); Affiliation(s): Vancouver Island Marmot Recovery Team
Chief Officer(s):
Viki Jackson, Executive Director

Master Insulators' Association of Ontario Inc.
Building 1, #101, 2600 Skymark Ave., Mississauga ON L4W 5B2
Tel: 905-279-6426; *Fax:* 905-279-6422
www.miaontario.org
Overview: A small provincial organization founded in 1942
Chief Officer(s):
Malcolm D. Haylock, Office Manager

McGregor Model Forest
PO Box 2640, Prince George BC V2N 4T5
Tel: 250-612-5840; *Fax:* 250-612-5848
www.mcgregor.bc.ca
Overview: A small local organization
Member of: Canadian Model Forest Network
Chief Officer(s):
Al Gorley, President
Dan Adamson, General Manager
dan.adamson@mcgregor.bc.ca

McIlwraith Field Naturalists
PO Box 24008, London ON N6H 5C4
Tel: 519-457-4593
e-mail: info@mcilwraith.ca
www.mcilwraith.ca
Overview: A small local organization founded in 1890
Mission: To promote the enjoyment of nature through environmental appreciation & conservation; to encourage wise use & conservation of natural resources; to promote environmental protection; Affiliation(s): Canadian Nature Federation; Federation of Ontario Naturalists
Finances: *Annual Operating Budget:* $50,000-$100,000
Membership: 5 institutional + 400 individual; *Fees:* $30 individual; $10 student; $50 contributing; $100 sustaining; *Member Profile:* Interest in natural world; *Committees:* Conservation; Education; Birding; Junior Naturalists
Activities: Field trips; tree & wild flower plantings; nature reserve; life science inventories; *Speaker Service:* Yes

Meat Packers Council of Canada **See** Canadian Meat Council

Mechanical Contractors Association of Alberta
Parent Name: Mechanical Contractors Association of Canada
#204, 2725 - 12 St. NE, Calgary AB T2E 7J2
Tel: 403-250-7237; *Fax:* 403-291-0551
Toll-Free: 800-251-0620
e-mail: vicky@mca-ab.com
www.mca-ab.com
Overview: A small provincial organization overseen by Mechanical Contractors Association of Canada
Mission: To promote plumbing & mechanical contractors; to provide educational programs to foster improved management & productivity in mechanical contracting; to represent mechanical contractors with their various publics - governments, design authorities, labour; to foster professional advancement & profitability of the plumbing, heating & mechanical contracting industry through its member services
Chief Officer(s):
Hans Tiedemann, Executive Director
hans@mcaalberta.com
Finances: *Annual Operating Budget:* $250,000-$500,000
Staff: 3 staff member(s)
Membership: 100-499;; *Fees:* $530 contractor; $424 affiliate

Mechanical Contractors Association of British Columbia (MCABC)
Parent Name: Mechanical Contractors Association of Canada
#223, 3989 Henning Dr., Burnaby BC V5C 6N5
Tel: 604-205-5058; *Fax:* 604-205-5075
Toll-Free: 800-663-8473
www.mcabc.org
Previous Name: Canadian Plumbing & Mechanical Contractors Association, BC Branch
Overview: A medium-sized provincial organization founded in 1905 overseen by Mechanical Contractors Association of Canada
Mission: To encourage, support & promote the advancement of the mechanical contracting industry; to provide leadership, assistance & training to members.
Chief Officer(s):
Dana Taylor, Executive Vice President
Finances: *Annual Operating Budget:* $250,000-$500,000
Staff: 3 staff member(s)
Membership: 14 senior/lifetime + 142 general + 63 associate; *Committees:* Contractor-Engineer; Joint Apprenticeship; Management Education
Activities: *Speaker Service:* Yes; *Library:*

Mechanical Contractors Association of Canada (MCAC) / Association des entrepreneurs en mécanique du Canada
#601, 280 Albert St., Ottawa ON K1P 5G8
Tel: 613-232-0492; *Fax:* 613-235-2793
e-mail: mcac@mcac.ca
www.mcac.ca
Overview: A medium-sized national organization founded in 1895
Mission: To promote plumbing & mechanical contractors; to provide educational programs to foster improved management & productivity in mechanical contracting; to represent mechanical contractors to their various publics - governments, design authorities, labour.; Affiliation(s): Council of Construction Trade Associations
Chief Officer(s):
Richard McKeagan, President
rick@mcac.ca
Membership: 800
Meetings/Conferences:
For more information see Trade Shows, Conferences and Seminars Chapter
Mechanical Contractors Association of Canada (MCAC) 72nd Annual National Conference 2013
September 2013 Winnipeg, MB
Mechanical Contractors Association of Canada (MCAC) 73rd Annual National Conference 2014
September 2014 St. John's, NL

Mechanical Contractors Association of Manitoba (MCAM)
Parent Name: Mechanical Contractors Association of Canada
#1, 860 Bradford St., Winnipeg MB R3H 0N5
Tel: 204-774-2404; *Fax:* 204-772-0233
e-mail: mcam@mts.net
www.mca-mb.com
Overview: A medium-sized provincial organization founded in 1970 overseen by Mechanical Contractors Association of Canada
Mission: To continually improve mechanical industry standards while providing a high level of value performance & customer service for our members
Chief Officer(s):
Betty McInerney, Executive Director

Mechanical Contractors Association of New Brunswick / Association des entrepreneurs en mécanique du N.-B.
Parent Name: Mechanical Contractors Association of Canada
c/o Moncton Northeast Construction Association, 297 Collishaw St., Moncton NB E1C 9R2
Tel: 506-857-4128; *Fax:* 506-857-8861
e-mail: bdixon@mneca.ca
www.mneca.ca
Also Known As: MCA New Brunswick Inc.
Previous Name: Plumbing & Mechanical Contractors Association of New Brunswick
Overview: A small provincial organization founded in 1976 overseen by Mechanical Contractors Association of Canada
Mission: To provide leadership & service to members; to act on behalf of members in labour relations matters, including collective bargaining; to advance & develop the industry, primarily in New Brunswick; to endeavour to improve legislation affecting the industry; to promote sound labour relations; Affiliation(s): Canadian Construction Association
Chief Officer(s):
Bill Dixon, Executive Director
Finances: *Annual Operating Budget:* $100,000-$250,000; *Funding Sources:* Membership fees
Staff: 1 staff member(s)
Membership: 28; *Fees:* $1,017 contractor/sub-contractor/supplier; $491.55 associate; *Member Profile:* Open to individual firms engaged in plumbing & related trades

Mechanical Contractors Association of Newfoundland & Labrador
Parent Name: Mechanical Contractors Association of Canada
PO Box 745, Stn. Mount Pearl, Mount Pearl NL A1N 2Y2
Tel: 709-747-5577; *Fax:* 709-368-5342
e-mail: ddawe@nfld.net
Overview: A small provincial organization overseen by Mechanical Contractors Association of Canada
Chief Officer(s):
David Dawe, Executive Director

Mechanical Contractors Association of Nova Scotia
Parent Name: Mechanical Contractors Association of Canada
c/o Construction Association of Nova Scotia, #3, 260 Brownlow Ave., Dartmouth NS B3B 1V9
Tel: 902-468-2267; *Fax:* 902-468-2470
e-mail: cans@cans.ns.ca
www.cans.ns.ca
Also Known As: Mechanical Contractors Section of The Construction Association of Nova Scotia (CANS)
Overview: A small provincial organization overseen by Mechanical Contractors Association of Canada
Chief Officer(s):
Donna Cruickshank, Manager

Mechanical Contractors Association of Ontario (MCAO)
Parent Name: Mechanical Contractors Association of Canada
#103, 10 Director Ct., Woodbridge ON L4L 7E8
Tel: 905-856-0342; *Fax:* 905-856-0385
e-mail: mcao@mcao.org
www.mcao.org
Overview: A medium-sized provincial organization overseen by Mechanical Contractors Association of Canada
Chief Officer(s):
Steve Coleman, Executive Vice-President
steve@mcao.org

Mechanical Contractors Association of Prince Edward Island
Parent Name: Mechanical Contractors Association of Canada
c/o Association of Commercial & Industrial Contractors of PEI, PO Box 1685, Charlottetown PE C1A 7N4
Tel: 902-566-3456; *Fax:* 902-368-2754
e-mail: wmm@wmm93.pe.ca
Overview: A small provincial organization overseen by Mechanical Contractors Association of Canada
Chief Officer(s):
Mary MacDonald, Contact

Mechanical Contractors Association of Saskatchewan Inc. (MCAS)
Parent Name: Mechanical Contractors Association of Canada
Heritage Business Park, #105, 2750 Faithfull Ave., Saskatoon SK S7K 6M6
Tel: 306-664-2154; *Fax:* 306-653-7233
e-mail: mca-sask@mca-sask.com
www.mca-sask.com
Overview: A small provincial organization founded in 1919 overseen by Mechanical Contractors Association of Canada
Mission: MCAS is a provincial non-profit, trade association that represents plumbing & heating contractors in relation to the construction industry, legislative departments of municipal & provincial government & other industry-related bodies.; Affiliation(s): Mechanical Contractors Association of Canada
Chief Officer(s):
Allan Awrey, President, 306-244-2941, Fax: 306-652-1423
Judy Nagus, Executive Director
judy@mca-sask.com
Finances: *Funding Sources:* Membership fees
Staff: 1 staff member(s)
Membership: 150; *Fees:* $350; *Member Profile:* Mechanical contractors

Mechanical-Electrical Division of The Canadian Institute of Mining, Metallurgy & Petroleum *See* Maintenance, Engineering and Reliability (MER) Society

Medical Society of Nova Scotia *See* Doctors Nova Scotia

Medical Society of Prince Edward Island (MSPEI)
Parent Name: Canadian Medical Association

2 Myrtle St., Stratford PE C1B 2W2
Tel: 902-368-7303; *Fax:* 902-566-3934
Toll-Free: 888-368-7303
www.mspei.org
Overview: A medium-sized provincial organization founded in 1855 overseen by Canadian Medical Association
Mission: To promote health & improvement of medical services; to prevent disease; to represent members at national bodies & government; to consider all matters concerning the professional welfare of members.
Chief Officer(s):
Kathy Maher, Communications Director
kathy@mspei.org
Sandy Irwin, Executive Director
airwin@mspei.org
Finances: *Annual Operating Budget:* $100,000-$250,000; *Funding Sources:* Membership dues
Staff: 6 staff member(s)
Membership: 352 physicians; *Member Profile:* Individuals licensed to practise medicine in PEI
Activities: *Internships:* Yes; *Library:* by appointment

Meewasin Valley Authority (MVA)

402 - 3rd Ave. South, Saskatoon SK S7K 3G5
Tel: 306-665-6887; *Fax:* 306-665-6117
e-mail: meewasin@meewasin.com
www.meewasin.com
Overview: A small local organization founded in 1979
Mission: To ensure a healthy & vibrant river valley with a balance between human use & conservation by: providing leadership in the management of its resources; promoting understanding, conservation & beneficial use of the valley; undertaking programs & projects in river valley development & conservation for the benefit of present & future generations
Chief Officer(s):
Susan Lamb, CEO
Finances: *Annual Operating Budget:* Greater than $5 Million; *Funding Sources:* Donations; Government of Saskatchewan; City of Saskatoon; University of Saskatchewan
Staff: 28 staff member(s)
Membership: *Committees:* Development Review; Resource Conservation Advisory; Design Advisory; Education Advisory
Activities: Clean-up Campaign; Stewardship Program; Dragon Boat Races

Melfort Agricultural Society

PO Box 816, Melfort SK S0E 1A0
Tel: 306-752-2240; *Fax:* 306-752-2240
e-mail: info@melfortex.com
www.melfortex.com
Overview: A small local charitable organization founded in 1906
Mission: To improve agriculture & the quality of life in the community by educating members & the community; to provide a community forum for discussing agricultural issues; to foster community development & community spirit; to help provide markets for Saskatchewan products; to encourage conservation of natural resources, including soil conservation, reforestation, rural & urban beautification; *Member of:* Saskatchewan Association of Agricultural Societies & Exhibitions; Canadian Association of Fairs & Exhibitions
Chief Officer(s):
Christy Vodicka, President
Finances: *Annual Operating Budget:* $100,000-$250,000; *Funding Sources:* Bingo; flea markets; exhibition; grants
Staff: 1 staff member(s); 101 volunteer(s)
Membership: 101; *Fees:* $5

Melville & District Agri-Park Association Inc.

PO Box 2678, Melville SK S0A 2P0
Tel: 306-728-5277; *Fax:* 306-728-4544
e-mail: agripark@sasktel.net
www.melvilleagripark.com
Also Known As: Melville Agri-Park
Overview: A small local organization founded in 1981
Mission: To promote agriculture events in Melville & surrounding district; *Member of:* Saskatchewan Association of Agricultural Societies & Exhibitions; Canadian Association of Exhibitions; Saskatchewan Horse Federation
Chief Officer(s):
Jamie D. McDonald, Manager
Finances: *Annual Operating Budget:* $50,000-$100,000
Staff: 1 staff member(s); 100 volunteer(s)
Membership: 200 senior/lifetime; *Fees:* $100; *Committees:* 4-H Organization; Horse Show; Showstoppers ATV; Archery Club; Homecrafts; Horse Racing; Rodeo; Cattle, Team Roping; Barrel Racing
Activities: *Internships:* Yes; *Rents Mailing List:* Yes

Metal Industries Association *See* Western Employers Labour Relations Association

Metallurgy & Materials Society of the Canadian Institute of Mining, Metallurgy & Petroleum (MetSoc)
Parent Name: Canadian Institute of Mining, Metallurgy & Petroleum

#1250, 3500, boul de Maisonneuve ouest, Montréal QC H3Z 3C1
Tel: 514-939-2710
www.metsoc.org
www.facebook.com/group.php?gid=77992627143
Overview: A medium-sized national organization founded in 1967 overseen by Canadian Institute of Mining, Metallurgy & Petroleum
Mission: To expand the professional horizons of society members in order to serve the metals & materials industry
Environmental Activity: Serving members, society, & researchers involved in the development of technologies for the environmentally responsible extraction, fabrication, utilization, & recycling of metals & materials
Chief Officer(s):
Greg Richards, President
greg.richards@teck.com
Brigitte Farah, Manager, Administration & Meetings, 514-939-2710 Ext. 1329, Fax: 514-939-2714
bfarah@cim.org
Ronona Saunders, Contact, Publications, Web, & Marketing, 514-939-2710 Ext. 1327, Fax: 514-939-2714
rsaunders@cim.org
Membership: *Member Profile:* Persons involved in the development & application of technologies for the extraction, fabrication, & utilization of metals & materials in Canada; *Committees:* CIM Journal; Student Activities; Historical Metallurgy; Membership Services; Publications; Trustees
Activities: Providing information to the government & the public; Offering continuing education; Recognizing excellence; Providing networking opportunities
Meetings/Conferences:
For more information see Trade Shows, Conferences and Seminars Chapter
Metallurgy & Materials Society of the Canadian Institute of Mining, Metallurgy & Petroleum COM 2013: 52nd Annual Conference of Metallurgists
October 2013 Montréal, QC
Metallurgy & Materials Society of the Canadian Institute of Mining, Metallurgy & Petroleum World Gold 2013 4th International Conference
2013
Metallurgy & Materials Society of the Canadian Institute of Mining, Metallurgy & Petroleum COM 2014: 53rd Annual Conference of Metallurgists
September 2014 Vancouver, BC
Metallurgy & Materials Society of the Canadian Institute of Mining, Metallurgy & Petroleum COM 2015: 54th Annual Conference of Metallurgists
2015
Metallurgy & Materials Society of the Canadian Institute of Mining, Metallurgy & Petroleum World Gold 2015 5th International Conference
2015
Publications:
•Canadian Metallurgical Quarterly: The Canadian Journal of Metallurgy & Materials Science
Type: Journal; *Frequency:* Quarterly; *Accepts Advertising*; *Editor:* Doug Boyd; *ISSN:* 0008-4433
Profile: Research in the areas of mineral processing, extraction, synthesis, processing, characterization properties, &performance of metals & materials
•mLink: The The Electronic Newsletter of the METSOC of CIM
Type: Newsletter
Profile: News for members & students about MetSoc meetings & publications

The Metropolitan Toronto & Region Conservation Foundation; The Conservation Foundation of Greater Toronto *See* Conservation Foundation of Greater Toronto

Middlesex Federation of Agriculture (MFA)
Parent Name: Ontario Federation of Agriculture

PO Box 820, Mount Brydges ON N0L 1W0
Tel: 519-457-8444; *Fax:* 519-264-9173
www.ofa.on.ca/middlesex
Overview: A small local organization founded in 1939 overseen by Ontario Federation of Agriculture
Mission: To advance agriculture & the rural community through partnerships, education & advocacy
Chief Officer(s):
Steve Fonger, President
Finances: *Annual Operating Budget:* $50,000-$100,000
Staff: 1 staff member(s); 50 volunteer(s)
Membership: 2500; *Committees:* Education; Communication; Special Events; Political Awareness

Millarville Racing & Agricultural Society (MRAS)

Box 68, Millarville AB T0L 1K0
Tel: 403-931-3411; *Fax:* 403-931-3485
www.millarville-ab.com
Overview: A small local organization founded in 1907
Mission: To build a strong community; *Member of:* Alberta Association of Agricultural Societies
Chief Officer(s):
Barb Castell, Staff
Don Stewart, President
Finances: *Annual Operating Budget:* $250,000-$500,000
Staff: 3 staff member(s); 300 volunteer(s)
Membership: 500; *Fees:* $40 general; $325 family; $225 individual
Activities: Organizing rodeos, races, farmers' markets, & fairs

Mineral Society of Manitoba (MSM)

c/o The Manitoba Museum, 190 Rupert Ave., Winnipeg MB R3B 0N2
e-mail: ysearle@mts.net
www.umanitoba.ca/geoscience/mineralsociety/index.htm
Overview: A small provincial organization founded in 1971
Mission: To promote the study of minerals, rocks, & fossils for both scientific & recreational purposes
Chief Officer(s):
Jack Bauer, Contact, Membership, 204-632-6934
jebauer@mts.net
Marion Foster, Contact, General Information, 204-775-0625
2mandm@mts.net
Yvonne Searle, Contact, School Programs, 204-663-6637
wsearle@mts.net
Membership: *Fees:* $15 individuals; $20 families
Activities: Hosting monthly meetings at the Manitoba Museum; organizing field trips; planning educational exhibits; guest speakers
Publications:
•The Mineral Vein: The Mineral Society of Manitoba Newsletter
Type: Newsletter; *Frequency:* 9 pa; *Editor:* Tony Smith
Profile: Upcoming events, presentation summaries, & articles about rockhounding & mineralogy

Mineralogical Association of Canada (MAC) / Association minéralogique du Canada

490, rue de la Couronne, Québec QC G1K 9A9
Tel: 418-653-0333; *Fax:* 418-653-0777
e-mail: office@mineralogicalassociation.ca
www.mineralogicalassociation.ca
Overview: A medium-sized national charitable organization founded in 1955
Mission: To promote & advance knowledge of mineralogy & the allied disciplines of petrology, crystallography, mineral deposits, & geochemistry
Chief Officer(s):
Iain M. Samson, President, 519-253-3000 Ext. 2489, Fax: 519-973-7081
ims@uwindsor.ca
Lee A. Groat, Vice-President, 604-822-1289, Fax: 604-228-6088
lgroat@eos.ubc.ca
Michelle DeWolfe, Secretary, 705-675-1151
mx_dewolfe@laurentian.ca
Marc Constantin, Treasurer, 418-656-2131 Ext. 3139, Fax: 418-656-7339
marc.constantin@ggl.ulaval.ca
Ronald C. Peterson, Chair, Finance Committee, 613-533-6180 Ext. 36180
peterson@geol.queensu.ca
Robert F. Martin, Principal Editor, The Canadian Mineralogist, 514-398-7370, Fax: 514-398-4680
robert.martin@mcgill.ca

Pierrette Tremblay, Managing Editor, Elements Magazine, 418-654-2606, Fax: 418-654-2525
Pierrette_Tremblay@inrs-ete.uquebec.ca
Membership: *Member Profile:* Individuals or organizations engaged or interested in mineralogy, crystallography, petrology, geochemistry, & economic geology
Activities: Organizing annual meetings & symposia; Providing short courses; Disseminating information about mineralogy; Providing reference books & textbooks in the mineral sciences; Presenting awards & scholarships; Increasing public awareness of science
Publications:
•The Canadian Mineralogist: The Journal of the Mineralogical Association of Canada
Type: Journal; *Frequency:* Bimonthly; *Editor:* Robert F. Martin
Profile: Subjects include mineralogy, mineral deposits, petrology, crystallography, & geochemistry
•Elements: An International Magazine of Mineralogy, Geochemistry, & Petrology
Type: Magazine; *Frequency:* Bimonthly; *Accepts Advertising*; *Editor:* Pierrette Tremblay; *ISSN:* 1811-5209; *Price:* Free with membership in the Mineralogical Association of Canada
Profile: An international magazine published by organizations such as the Mineralogical Association of Canada, theMineralogical Society of America, the Mineralogical Society of Great Britain & Ireland, the European Association of Geochemistry, the Clay Minerals Society, & the Geochemical Society

Mines Alerte Canada ***See*** MiningWatch Canada

Mining Association of British Columbia (MABC)
Parent Name: Mining Association of Canada
#900, 808 West Hastings St., Vancouver BC V6C 2X4
Tel: 604-681-4321; *Fax:* 604-681-5305
e-mail: mabcinfo@mining.bc.ca
www.mining.bc.ca
Overview: A medium-sized provincial organization founded in 1901 overseen by Mining Association of Canada
Mission: To speak on behalf of mineral producers; To represent the interests of British Columbia's mining industry; To communicate with senior government decision-makers, communities, NGOs, First Nations, & the media; To act as the industry's voice regarding issues such as environmental regulations, taxation, infrastructure demands, labour issues, health & safety, & international trade
Chief Officer(s):
Pierre Gratton, President/CEO
Zoe Younger, Vice-President, Corporate Affairs
Ben Chalmers, Vice-President, Environmental & Technical Affairs
Membership: *Member Profile:* Members include corporate members with producing operations within BC, service & supply organizations, institutions, & non-profit organizations.
Activities: Liaising with government legislators; Lobbying for regulatory advancement; Promoting the economic & social value of mining; Updating members on regulatory change; Facilitating exchange of information among members
Publications:
•Daily News [a publication of the Mining Association of British Columbia]
Type: Newsletter; *Frequency:* Daily
Profile: Mining related news, on provincial, national, & international levels, for members

Mining Association of Canada (MAC) / Association minière du Canada
#1105, 350 Sparks St., Ottawa ON K1R 7S8
Tel: 613-233-9392; *Fax:* 613-233-8897
e-mail: communications@mining.ca
www.mining.ca
www.facebook.com/group.php?gid=193636270672849
twitter.com/theminingstory
Overview: A large national organization founded in 1935
Mission: To represent the interests of member companies engaged in mineral exploration, extraction & refining; To work with governments on public policy pertaining to minerals
Environmental Activity: Environmental Policy & Guidelines; Environmental Research
Chief Officer(s):
Pierre Gratton, President & CEO
Marilyn Fortin, Office Manager & Member Services
Monique Laflèche, Executive Assistant
Finances: *Annual Operating Budget:* $1.5 Million-$3 Million; *Funding Sources:* Membership dues
Staff: 10 staff member(s)
Membership: 55
Activities: *Awareness Events:* National Mining Week, May; Mining Weeks in Canada, April - June

Mining Association of Manitoba Inc. (MAMI)
Parent Name: Mining Association of Canada
#700, 305 Broadway Ave., Winnipeg MB R3C 3J7
Tel: 204-989-1890
e-mail: pmarsden@mines.ca
www.mines.ca
Overview: A medium-sized provincial organization founded in 1940 overseen by Mining Association of Canada
Mission: To represent mining & exploration companies in Manitoba.
Chief Officer(s):
Ed Huebert, Executive Vice President
edhuebert@mines.ca
Finances: *Funding Sources:* Membership dues
Staff: 1 staff member(s)
Membership: 16; *Member Profile:* Mining companies with more than 50 employees; *Committees:* Environment; Exploration; Tax
Activities: *Speaker Service:* Yes; *Library:* by appointment

Mining Industry Human Resources Council (MIHR) / Conseil des ressources humaines de l'industrie minière (RHIM)
#401, 260 Hearst Way, Kanata ON K2L 3H1
Tel: 613-270-9696; *Fax:* 613-270-9399
e-mail: info@mihr.ca
www.mihr.ca
www.facebook.com/group.php?gid=103398309715163
Overview: A medium-sized national organization
Mission: Contributes to the strength, competitiveness & sustainability of the Canadian mining industry by collaborating with all communities of interest in the development & implementation of solutions to the industry's national human resource challenges
Chief Officer(s):
Patricia Dillon, Chair
Ryan Montpellier, Executive Director
Finances: *Annual Operating Budget:* $3 Million-$5 Million; *Funding Sources:* Government; Industry

Mining Society of Nova Scotia
Parent Name: Mining Association of Canada
88 Leeside Dr., Sydney NS B1R 1S6
Tel: 902-567-2147; *Fax:* 902-567-2147
e-mail: florence@ns.sympatico.ca
Overview: A small provincial organization founded in 1887 overseen by Mining Association of Canada
Affiliation(s): Canadian Institute of Mining, Metallurgy & Petroleum
Chief Officer(s):
Dan McLeod, President
Membership: 250; *Fees:* $90

Mining Suppliers, Contractors & Consultants Association of BC (MSCCA)
#900, 808 West Hastings St., Vancouver BC V6C 2X4
Tel: 604-681-4321; *Fax:* 604-681-5305
e-mail: tmulligan@mining.bc.ca
miningsuppliersbc.ca/
Overview: A medium-sized provincial licensing organization founded in 1986
Mission: To promote the development of a sustainable mining industry in BC; Affiliation(s): Mining Association of British Columbia
Chief Officer(s):
Terry B. Mulligan, Executive Director Ext. 111
Finances: *Annual Operating Budget:* $100,000-$250,000; *Funding Sources:* Membership dues; special events
Staff: 1 staff member(s); 3 volunteer(s)
Membership: 225 companies; *Fees:* Based on sales to BC mining
Activities: Networking functions with the mining industry

MiningWatch Canada / Mines Alerte Canada
City Centre Building, #508, 250 City Centre Ave., Ottawa ON K1R 6K7
Tel: 613-569-3439; *Fax:* 613-569-5138
e-mail: info@miningwatch.ca
www.miningwatch.ca
Overview: A small national organization founded in 1999
Mission: To address the urgent need for a coordinated public interest response to the threats to public health, water & air quality, fish & wildlife habitat & community interests posed by irresponsible mineral policies & practices in Canada & around the world; *Member of:* Canadian Environmental Network; Canadian Council for International Cooperation; Halifax Initiative
Chief Officer(s):
Catherine Coumans, Research Coordinator
Membership: 1-99;; *Fees:* Sliding scale; *Member Profile:* Aboriginal, labour, environmental, international groups

Mitlenatch Field Naturalists Society
PO Box 105, Quathiaski Cove BC V0P 1H0
Tel: 250-285-3570
Overview: A small local organization founded in 1970
Mission: To promote the enjoyment of nature through environmental appreciation & conservation; To encourage wise use & conservation of natural resources & environmental protection.; *Member of:* Federation of BC Naturalists
Membership: 40; *Fees:* $17

Mobilité Électrique Canada ***See*** Electric Mobility Canada

Model Forest of Newfoundland & Labrador (MFNL)
Humber Trust Building, PO Box 68, #11, 19 - 21 West St., Corner Brook NL A2H 6C3
Tel: 709-637-7300
Previous Name: Western Newfoundland Model Forest
Overview: A small local organization
Mission: The Model Forest is a not-for-profit corporation formed as a partnership of organizations & individuals working on the implementation of activities that advance their abilities to practice sustainable forest management & community-based economic development utilizing forest resources; *Member of:* Canadian Model Forest Network
Chief Officer(s):
Sean Dolter, General Manager
seandolter@mfnl.ca

Montréal Field Naturalists Club
42, av Ballantyne nord, Montréal QC H4X 2B8
Tel: 514-484-5664
montrealfieldnaturalists.wordpress.com
Overview: A small local organization founded in 1971
Mission: To increase knowledge of nature through outdoor & indoor activities; to act when nature seems to be threatened, by expressing protests, participating in meetings
Chief Officer(s):
Raymond Murphy, President
Membership: 150 individual; *Fees:* $15 individual

Montréal Gem & Mineral Club (MGMC) / Le Club de gemmologie et de minérlogie de Montréal
CP 32522, Succ. B, 2445 ch Lucern, Montréal QC H3R 2K5
Tél: 514-878-9110
Courriel: geminews@gmail.com
www.montrealgemmineralclub.ca
Aperçu: *Dimension:* petite; *Envergure:* locale; fondée en 1957
Mission: To provide information about gems & minerals; *Membre de:* Central Canadian Federation of Mineralogical Societies
Membre(s) du bureau directeur:
Mike Rooney, Contact
Membre: *Montant de la cotisation:* $20 individuals; $30 familiesy; *Critères d'admissibilite:* Rockhounds, collectors lapidaries, jewelers, & persons interested in learning about gems & minerals in the Montréal area
Activités: Organizing programs & field trips; Planning workshops; *Evénements de sensibilisation:* Annual Gem & Mineral Show; *Bibliothèque:* Montréal Gem & Mineral Club Library
Publications:
•Geminews
Type: Newsletter; *Frequency:* Monthly; *Price:* Free for Montréal Gem & Mineral Club members
Profile: Club activities & forthcoming events

Moose Jaw Wildlife Federation
1396 - 3rd Ave. NE, Moose Jaw SK S6H 0A1
Tel: 306-693-4047
e-mail: MJWildlife.Federation@gmail.com
sites.google.com/site/moosejawwildlife
www.facebook.com/groups/128957300560194
Overview: A small local organization
Member of: Saskatchewan Wildlife Federation
Chief Officer(s):
Doreen Dodd, Contact, 306-692-4148
doreendodd@sasktel.net

Mouvement féderalist mondial ***See*** World Federalist Movement

Municipal Electric Association ***See*** Electricity Distributors Association

Municipal Engineers Association (MEA)

#2, 6355 Kennedy Rd., Mississauga ON L5T 2L5
Tel: 905-795-2555; *Fax:* 905-795-2660
e-mail: info@municipalengineers.on.ca
www.municipalengineers.on.ca
Overview: A medium-sized provincial organization founded in 1974
Mission: To provide focus & unity for licensed engineers employed by municipalities in Ontario; To address issues of common concern to members; To facilitate the dissemination of information
Chief Officer(s):
Rick A. Kester, President, 905-795-2555, Fax: 905-795-2660
J. David Shantz, Executive Director
Gary Carroll, Vice-President
Trevor D. Lewis, Treasurer
Membership: *Member Profile:* Public sector professional engineers in full time employment of municipalities, who perform functions in the field of municipal engineering; *Committees:* Administrative & Seconded; Municipal Transportation Advisory; MEA/CEO Liaison; Development Engineering; MEA/MNR/CO Liaison; MEA Training; MEA/MOE Liaison; Ontario Works Network; Tri-Committee Board
Activities: Organizing training events; Advocating for sound municipal engineering; Championing positions on municipal engineering issues; Recognizing achievements of municipal engineers
Meetings/Conferences:
For more information see Trade Shows, Conferences and Seminars Chapter
Municipal Engineers Association 2013 Annual General Meeting & Workshop
November 2013
Municipal Engineers Association 2014 Annual General Meeting & Workshop
November 2014
Publications:
•Annual Report of the Municipal Engineers Association Administrative & Standing Committees
Type: Yearbook; *Frequency:* Annually
Profile: A review of the year's activities
•Municipal Engineers Association Members Directory
Type: Directory

Municipal Equipment & Operations Association (Ontario) Inc.

38 Summit Ave., Kitchener ON N2M 4W2
Tel: 519-741-2600; *Fax:* 519-741-2750
e-mail: admin@meoa.org
www.meoa.org
Also Known As: MEOA
Overview: A small provincial organization founded in 1965
Mission: To promote high standards & cost effectiveness in public services across Ontario
Chief Officer(s):
Greg Lancaster, Contact
Finances: *Funding Sources:* Annual membership dues
Membership: 250; *Member Profile:* Supervisory employees & management support staff from any government body; Suppliers of equipment & services used by municipal corporate organizations; Honorary members who have been beneficial to the association; Affiliate members who have an interest in the association
Activities: Offering education & training; Organizing field trips; Facilitating the exchange of information; Providing networking opportunities;
Meetings/Conferences:
For more information see Trade Shows, Conferences and Seminars Chapter
Municipal Equipment & Operations Association (Ontario) Inc. 2013 Annual Spring Meeting
2013, ON
Municipal Equipment & Operations Association (Ontario) Inc. 2013 Annual Professional Development Day
2013, ON
Municipal Equipment & Operations Association (Ontario) Inc. 2013 Annual Municipal & Contractor Fall Equipment Show
2013, ON

Municipal Officers' Association of British Columbia ***See*** Local Government Management Association of British Columbia

Municipal Waste Association (MWA)

#100, 127 Wyndham St. North, Guelph ON N1H 4E9
Tel: 519-823-1990; *Fax:* 519-823-0084
e-mail: carrie@municipalwaste.ca
www.municipalwaste.ca
Previous Name: Association of Municipal Recycling Coordinators
Overview: A medium-sized provincial organization founded in 1987
Mission: To expedite the flow of information regarding 3R programs to municipalities & other community & government groups; To act as an information forum for municipal recycling coordinators; To allow member municipalities to act as a unified voice in promoting progressive waste reduction & recycling alternatives; *Member of:* Recycling Council of Ontario
Chief Officer(s):
Vivian De Giovanni, Executive Director
vivian@municipalwaste.ca
Ben Bennett, Manager, Projects & Communications
ben@municipalwaste.ca
Finances: *Funding Sources:* Membership fees; Project sponsorship
Membership: 100-499;; *Fees:* $85 - $995, based on population; *Committees:* Household Hazardous Waste; Markets Operation & Contracts; Organic Waste Diversion; Policy & Program
Activities: *Speaker Service:* Yes
Meetings/Conferences:
For more information see Trade Shows, Conferences and Seminars Chapter
Municipal Waste Association 2013 Spring Workshop
May 2013 Mono, ON
Municipal Waste Association 2013 Annual General Meeting
2013, ON

Municipalities Newfoundland & Labrador

460 Torbay Rd., St. John's NL A1A 5J3
Tel: 709-753-6820; *Fax:* 709-738-0071
Toll-Free: 800-440-6536
e-mail: mnl@municipalitiesnl.com
www.municipalitiesnl.com
Previous Name: Newfoundland & Labrador Federation of Municipalities
Overview: A medium-sized provincial charitable organization founded in 1951
Mission: To assist communities in their endeavour to achieve & sustain strong & effective local government thereby improving the quality of life for all the people of this province.; *Member of:* Federation of Canadian Municipalities
Chief Officer(s):
Craig Pollett, Executive Director, 709-753-6110
executivedirector@municipalitiesnl.com
Christine Cave, Administrative Officer, 709-753-6821
administration@municipalitiesnl.com
Finances: *Annual Operating Budget:* $250,000-$500,000
Membership: 281 municipalities; *Fees:* Sliding scale based on population; *Member Profile:* Incorporated municipal governments in Newfoundland
Activities: *Internships:* Yes; *Rents Mailing List:* Yes

Muskoka Lakes Association

PO Box 289, 65 Joseph St., 2nd Fl., Port Carling ON P0B 1J0
Tel: 705-765-5723; *Fax:* 705-765-3203
e-mail: info@mla.on.ca
www.mla.on.ca
www.facebook.com/muskokalakesassociation
twitter.com/MuskokaLakes
Overview: A medium-sized local organization founded in 1894
Mission: To represent the interests of lakeshore residents in preserving the unique beauty of Muskoka
Chief Officer(s):
Lisa Noonan, Senior Manager
lisa@mla.on.ca
Membership: 2,458 members; *Fees:* $95 family; *Member Profile:* Permanent & seasonal residents of the Muskoka Lakes & area; anyone interested in the preservation & safety of the lakes

Muskoka Ratepayers' Association (MRA)

PO Box 336, Port Carling ON P0B 1J0
Tel: 705-765-0022; *Fax:* 705-765-0023
e-mail: muskokaratepayers@vianet.ca
www.tmlra.on.ca
Overview: A small local organization founded in 1976
Mission: Preservation, fairness & enhancement for & with property owners in the Township of Muskoka Lakes & beyond
Chief Officer(s):
J. Douglas Bryden, President

Musquodoboit Trailways Association

PO Box 336, Musquodoboit Harbour NS B0J 2L0
Tel: 902-889-3447
e-mail: pmcpers@eastlink.ca
www.mta-ns.ca
Overview: A small local organization founded in 1997
Mission: To provide world-class hiking & cycling trails while preserving the ecosystem & wildlife habitats of the area; *Member of:* Nova Scotia Regional Trails Federation; Trans Canada Trail
Chief Officer(s):
Peter McInroy, Chair
Membership: *Fees:* $10 individual; $15 family; $25 corporate
Activities: Manages & maintains 40 kms of non-motorized trails

NACE International (NACE)

1440 South Creek Dr., Houston TX 77084-4906 USA
Tel: 281-228-6200; *Fax:* 281-228-6300
Toll-Free: 800-797-6223
e-mail: firstservice@nace.org
www.nace.org
www.linkedin.com/groups?gid=868097&goback=%2Egna_868097
www.facebook.com/NACEinternational
twitter.com/NACEtweet
Previous Name: The National Association of Corrosion Engineers
Overview: A large international licensing charitable organization founded in 1943
Mission: To protect people, assets & the environment from the effects of corrosion. Northern Area sections include: Atlantic Canada, B.C., Calgary, Canadian National Capital Section, Edmonton, Montreal, Saskatchewan & Toronto
Chief Officer(s):
Bob Chalker, Executive Director
Jenny Been, Section Secretary/Treasurer, Northern Area
jenny.been@arc.ab.ca
Scott MacIntyre, Area Membership Chairman, Northern Area
scott.amc@ns.aliantzinc.ca
Finances: *Annual Operating Budget:* Greater than $5 Million; *Funding Sources:* Membership dues; registration fees; publication sales
Staff: 65 staff member(s)
Membership: 19,000 members in 100 countries; *Fees:* $130; *Member Profile:* Engineers & others involved in corrosion prevention & control
Activities: Technical training & certification; technical conferences; standards, publications & software; *Speaker Service:* Yes; *Rents Mailing List:* Yes; *Library:* Open to public
Publications:
•CorrDefense
Type: Magazine
•Corrosion Journal
Type: Journal; *Frequency:* Monthly
•InspectThis!
Type: Newsletter
•Materials Performance (MP)
Type: Journal; *Frequency:* Monthly
•NACE Corrosion Press
Type: Newsletter
•Stay Current
Type: Newsletter; *Frequency:* Monthly

Canadian Region - Atlantic Canada Section
c/o AMC Atlantic Met Consulting Ltd., #106, 11 Morris Dr., Dartmouth NS B3B 1M2
Tel: 902-405-3600
Chief Officer(s):
Glenn McRae, Section Trustee
gmcrae@mae.carleton.ca

Canadian Region - British Columbia Section
c/o Terasen Gas Inc., 3700 2nd Ave., Burnaby BC V5C 6S4
Chief Officer(s):
Scott Bowing, Section Chair
scott.bowing@terasengas.com

Canadian Region - Calgary Section
c/o Husky Energy, 707 8th Ave. SW, Calgary AB T2P 3G7
Tel: 403-840-1913
Chief Officer(s):
Thane Schaffer, Section Chair
chair@nacecalagry.com

Canadian Region - Edmonton Section

c/o CSI Coating Systems Inc., 556 Stewart Cres. SW, Edmonton AB T6X 0A8
Tel: 780-955-2856
Chief Officer(s):
Glenn MacIntosh, Section Chair

Canadian Region - Montréal Section
c/o CPI Corrosion Ltd., #300, 1200, boul St-Martin ouest, Laval QC H7S 2E4
Tél: 514-342-2828
Chief Officer(s):
Stephanie Dontigny, Section Chair

Canadian Region - National Capital Section
c/o CANMET Materials Technology Laboratory, 183 Longwood South, Hamilton ON L8P 0A5
Tel: 905-645-0688
Chief Officer(s):
Sankara Papavinasam, Section Chair
spapavin@nrcan.gc.ca

Canadian Region - Toronto Section
c/o Kinectrics Inc., #215, 800 Kipling Ave., Toronto ON M8Z 6C4
Tel: 416-207-6000
Chief Officer(s):
Joseph Beutler, Section Chair

NAID Canada

95 King St. East, 4th Fl., Toronto ON M5C 1G4
Toll-Free: 800-825-0864
e-mail: info@naidcanada.org
www.naidcanada.org
Also Known As: National Association for Information Destruction Canada
Overview: A small national organization
Mission: To raise awareness & understanding of the importance of secure information & document destruction; to ensure that private personal & business information is not used for purposes other than originally intended; to develop & implement industry standards & certification; to provide a range of member services which include advocacy, communication, education & professional development; *Member of:* National Association for Information Destruction in United States
Chief Officer(s):
Kevin Perry, Chair
Membership: *Member Profile:* Companies that specialize in secure information & document destruction

National & Provincial Parks Association (NPPAC) ***See*** Canadian Parks & Wilderness Society

National Aboriginal Forestry Association (NAFA)

#1426, 220 Laurier Ave. W, Ottawa ON K1P 5Z9
Tel: 613-233-5563; *Fax:* 613-233-4329
e-mail: hbombay@nafaforestry.org
www.nafaforestry.org
Overview: A medium-sized national organization founded in 1989
Mission: To promote & support increased Aboriginal involvement in forest management & related commercial opportunities; to assist Aboriginal communities in their quest to achieve a standard of land care which is balanced, sustainable & reflective of the traditional knowledge & forest values of Aboriginal peoples; to facilitate capacity-building in forest management through the development of human resource strategies & models for increased participation in natural resource decision making; to address the need for Aboriginal forest land rehabilitation & increased Aboriginal control over forest resources through the development of appropriate policy & programming
Chief Officer(s):
Harry M. Bombay, Executive Director
hbombay@nafaforestry.org
Peggy Smith, Senior Advisor
Janet Pronovost, Office Manager
janet@nafaforestry.org
Membership: *Fees:* Schedule available

National Asbestos Council ***See*** Environmental Information Association

National Association for Environmental Education (UK) (NAEE)

University of Wolverhampton, Walsall Campus, Gorway Rd., Walsall WS1 3BD United Kingdom
Tel: 44-922-631-200
e-mail: info@naee.org.uk
www.naee.org.uk
www.facebook.com/NAEEUK
twitter.com/NAEE_UK
Overview: A medium-sized international charitable organization founded in 1965
Mission: To promote environmental education for sustainability in the formal education sector by teachers for teachers; *Member of:* Council for Environmental Education
Chief Officer(s):
William Scott, President
Finances: *Annual Operating Budget:* Less than $50,000; *Funding Sources:* Dept. of Environment grant; membership dues; publication sales
Staff: 2 staff member(s)
Membership: 1,000; *Fees:* 50 Pounds overseas; 40 Pounds Europe; 30 Pounds UK; *Member Profile:* Educationalists
Activities: Conferences & courses which attempt to further environmental education in both its natural & human setting; seminars on current topics; publications; *Speaker Service:* Yes; *Library:* Open to public

National Association for Environmental Management (NAEM)

#1002, 1612 K St. NW, Washington DC 20006 USA
Tel: 202-986-6616; *Fax:* 202-530-4408
Toll-Free: 800-391-6236
e-mail: programs@naem.org
www.naem.org
www.linkedin.com/groups?home=&gid=151419
www.facebook.com/NAEM.org
twitter.com/thegreentie
Overview: A large international organization founded in 1990
Mission: To promote global sustainability; To advance environmental stewardship; To establish safe & healthy workplaces
Chief Officer(s):
Carol Singer Neuvelt, Executive Director
csinger@naem.org
Virginia Hoekenga, Deputy Director
Virginia@naem.org
Mike Mahanna, Manager, Programs
mike@naem.org
Elizabeth Ryan, Manager, Interactive Media & Communications
elizabeth@naem.org
Membership: *Fees:* $1,500-$7,500; *Member Profile:* Corporate environmental, health & safety, & sustainability decision-makers
Activities: Conducting research; Creating a knowledge sharing network; Offering educational webinars
Meetings/Conferences:
For more information see Trade Shows, Conferences and Seminars Chapter
National Association for Environmental Management 2013 21st Annual EHS Management Forum
October 2013 Montréal, QC
National Association for Environmental Management 2014 22nd Annual EHS Management Forum
October 2014 Austin, TX
Publications:
•Affiliates Council Guide [a publication of the National Association for Environmental Management]
Type: Guide
Profile: A guide to finding a service provider or consultant
•Green TIPS Guide
Type: Guide
Profile: A resource to engage others about a company's sustainability goals
•NAEM [National Association for Environmental Management] Network E-News
Type: Newsletter; *Frequency:* Biweekly
Profile: Relevant news for environmental, health & safety, & sustainability professionals

National Association for Information Destruction (NAID)

#350, 1951 W Camelback Rd., Phoenix AZ 85015 USA
Tel: 602-788-6243; *Fax:* 602-788-4144
e-mail: info@naidonline.org
www.naidonline.org
www.linkedin.com/groups?gid=3957595&trk=hb_side_g
www.facebook.com/NAIDHQ
twitter.com/NAIDinc
www.youtube.com/user/NAIDTV
Overview: A small international organization
Mission: NAID is the international, non-profit trade association of the information destruction industry. Its members are companies and individuals involved in providing information destruction services. NAID's mission is to educate business, industry and government of the importance of destroying discarded information and the value of contract destruction services
Chief Officer(s):
Robert Johnson, Executive Director
rjohnson@naidonline.org
Membership: *Fees:* Schedule available; *Member Profile:* Includes 50+ Canadian companies

National Association for PET Container Resources (NAPCOR)

PO Box 1327, Sonoma CA 95476 USA
Tel: 707-996-4207; *Fax:* 707-935-1998
Toll-Free: 800-762-7267
e-mail: information@napcor.com
www.napcor.com
Overview: A small national organization founded in 1987
Mission: To promote the usage of PET packaging & to facilitate the collection of PET plastic containers
Chief Officer(s):
Mike Schedler, Technical Advisor
Dennis Sabourin, Executive Director
Finances: *Funding Sources:* Membership dues
Membership: 13; *Member Profile:* PET bottle manufacturers & suppliers to the PET industry

The National Association of Corrosion Engineers ***See*** NACE International

National Association of Environmental Professionals (NAEP)

c/o Bower Management Services, LLC, PO Box 460, Collingswood NJ 08108 USA
Tel: 856-283-7816; *Fax:* 856-210-1619
e-mail: tbower@bowermanagementservices.com
www.naep.org
Overview: A medium-sized national organization founded in 1975
Mission: To promote a code of ethics & standard of practice among environmental professionals
Chief Officer(s):
Tim Bower, NAEP Headquarters
Ron Deverman, President
deverman415@comcast.net
Finances: *Annual Operating Budget:* $100,000-$250,000
Staff: 2 staff member(s); 30 volunteer(s)
Membership: 2,000; *Fees:* US$150 general membership; *Committees:* Working Groups: NEPA Working Group; Education Research & Science Working Group; Transportation Working Group; Sustainable Systems Working Group; Utility Working Group; Health Impact Assessment Working Group; committes include membership, publications, external relations, & career development...
Activities: *Rents Mailing List:* Yes

National Association of Sanitarians ***See*** National Environmental Health Association

National Association of the Chemistry Industry / Asociación Nacional de la Industria Química, A.C (ANIQ)

Angel Urraza No. 505, Col del Valle, Mexico 03100 DF Mexico
Tel: 52-55-5230-5100; *Fax:* 52-55-5230-5107
e-mail: anavarrete@aniq.org.mx
www.aniq.org.mx
Overview: A medium-sized national organization
Mission: To promote the sustainable development of the chemical sector, in harmony with the environment that surrounds it, as well as to look for joint solutions to common problems by dialogue & agreement, under strict rules of ethics & supported by specialized services, consulting, information, negotiation & diffusion
Chief Officer(s):
Miguel Benedetto Alexanderson, President
Finances: *Annual Operating Budget:* $500,000-$1.5 Million; *Funding Sources:* Membership fees & services
Staff: 50 staff member(s)
Membership: 223; *Member Profile:* Chemical producers & distributors; *Committees:* International Trade; Human Resources; Logistics & Transportation; Environment; Safety & Health; Communication & Information
Activities: National Forum of the Chemical Industry; *Internships:* Yes; *Speaker Service:* Yes; *Rents Mailing List:* Yes; *Library:* ANIQ's Information Centre; Open to public

National Association of Towns & Townships (NATaT)

#300, 1130 Connecticut Ave., Washington DC 20036 USA
Tel: 202-454-3950; *Fax:* 202-331-1598
www.natat.org
www.facebook.com/168130923318590
Overview: A large national organization founded in 1976
Mission: To help improve the quality of life for suburban and non-metro communities.
Environmental Activity: Guidbooks on waste & drinking water; lobbying
Chief Officer(s):
Jennifer Jimo, Federal Director
jimo@tfgnet.com.
Finances: *Annual Operating Budget:* $500,000-$1.5 Million
Staff: 5 staff member(s)
Membership: 13,000 towns; *Member Profile:* Small, generally rural, communities
Activities: Offers technical assistance, educational services & public policy support to local government officials from small communities across the USA; conducts research & develops public policy recommendations through National Center for Small Communities; *Awareness Events:* America's Town Meeting, 1st week Sept.
Publications:
•Washington Report
Type: Newsletter
Profile: A focus on legislative issues of importance to small governments.

National Audubon Society, Inc. (NAS)

225 Varick St., New York NY 10014 USA
Tel: 212-979-3000
www.audubon.org
www.facebook.com/NationalAudubonSociety
twitter.com/AudubonSociety
www.youtube.com/user/NationalAudubon
Overview: A large national charitable organization founded in 1905
Mission: To conserve & restore natural ecosystems, focusing on birds, other wildlife & their habitats for the benefit of humanity & the earth's biological diversity
Environmental Activity: Animal & environmental conservation
Chief Officer(s):
B. Holt Thrasher, Chair
David Yarnold, President & CEO
Susan Lunden, COO
Membership: 500,000; *Fees:* $20 USA; $45 Canada; $50 international
Activities: Seminars, educational events & workshops on various conservation topics
Publications:
•Audubon Magazine [a publication of the National Audubon Society, Inc.]
Type: Magazine; *Frequency:* s-m.
Profile: The magazine is a century old, & reaches 1.8 million readers
•Audubon Wingspan [a publication of the National Audubon Society, Inc.]
Type: Newsletter
Profile: Photographs, conservation news, & more
•National Audubon Society, Inc. Annual Report
Type: Yearbook; *Frequency:* Annual

National Building Envelope Council (NBEC) / Conseil National de l'Enveloppe du Bâtiment (CNEB)

c/o 5041 Regent St., Burnaby BC V5C 4H4
Tel: 604-473-9587
e-mail: nbec@cebq.org
www.nbec.net
Overview: A small national organization
Mission: To pursue excellence in the design, construction & performance of the building envelope
Chief Officer(s):
Dominique Derome, President Elect
Meetings/Conferences:
For more information see Trade Shows, Conferences and Seminars Chapter
14th Canadian Conference on Building Science and Technology October 2014 Toronto, ON

National Coalition Against the Misuse of Pesticides (NCAMP)

#200, 701 East St. SE, Washington DC 20003 USA
Tel: 202-543-5450; *Fax:* 202-543-4791
e-mail: info@beyondpesticides.org
www.beyondpesticides.org
www.facebook.com/beyondpesticides
twitter.com/bpncamp
www.youtube.com/bpncamp
Overview: A medium-sized national organization founded in 1981
Mission: To address the issue of hazards of pesticide use; to provide the public with clearinghouse of information on pesticides & pesticides issues; to promote alternative forms of pest management
Chief Officer(s):
Jay Feldman, Executive Director
jfeldman@beyondpesticides.org
Finances: *Annual Operating Budget:* $250,000-$500,000
Staff: 4 staff member(s); 1 volunteer(s)
Membership: 1,400
Activities: *Speaker Service:* Yes; *Library:*

National Council for Science & the Environment (NCSE)

#250, 1101 17th St. NW, Washington DC 20036 USA
Tel: 202-530-5810; *Fax:* 202-628-4311
e-mail: info@ncseonline.org
www.ncseonline.org
Previous Name: Committee for the National Institutes for the Environment
Overview: A medium-sized national organization founded in 1990
Mission: Improving the scientific basis for environmental decision making; Affiliation(s): Council of Environmental Deans & Directors; National Commission on Science for Sustainable Forestry
Chief Officer(s):
A. Karim Ahmed, Sec.-Treas.
ahmed@ncseonline.org
Peter D. Saundry, Executive Director
peter@ncseonline.org
Finances: *Annual Operating Budget:* $500,000-$1.5 Million
Staff: 12 staff member(s); 10 volunteer(s)
Membership: *Member Profile:* Open to any concerned individual or organization
Activities: National Conference on Science Policy & the Environment; education & outreach programs; *Library:* National Library for the Environment

National Electricity Roundtable (NER)

c/o Bryan Simonson, 148 Park Estates Pl. SE, Calgary AB T2J 3W5
Tel: 403-619-8967
e-mail: nationaler@shaw.ca
www.nationalelectricityroundtable.com
Overview: A medium-sized national organization founded in 1994
Mission: To act as a forum for companies operating in the Canadian electric power industry; to work with government to develop a sustainable industry
Chief Officer(s):
Richard Wunderlich, Chair, 416-294-5861
richard.wunderlich@siemens.com
Bryan Simonson, President
Membership: 20 companies + 6 federal departments

National Energy Conservation Association Inc. (NECA) / Association nationale pour la conservation de l'énergie

250 McDermot Ave., Winnipeg MB R3B 0S5
Tel: 204-956-5888; *Fax:* 204-956-5819
Toll-Free: 800-263-5974
www.neca.ca
Previous Name: National Insulation & Energy Conservation Contractors Association
Overview: A medium-sized national organization founded in 1983
Mission: To promote energy efficiency in the building sector; To work towards a sustainable future
Environmental Activity: Encouraging the use of energy efficient technology in existing & new buildings; Working with government agencies & utilities to develop energy conservation programs; Providing training in energy conservation & construction
Chief Officer(s):
Ryan Dalgleish, Contact, Business Development

National Environmental Health Association (NEHA)

#1000N, 720 South Colorado Blvd., Denver CO 80246 USA
Tel: 303-756-9090; *Fax:* 303-691-9490
Toll-Free: 866-956-2258
e-mail: staff@neha.org
www.neha.org
www.facebook.com/NEHA.org
twitter.com/nehaorg
Previous Name: National Association of Sanitarians
Overview: A medium-sized national charitable organization founded in 1937
Mission: To advance the environmental health & protection professional, in order to improve the environment throughout the world & provide a more healthful quality of life for all
Environmental Activity: Developing positions on serious environmental health concerns
Chief Officer(s):
Nelson Fabian, Executive Director
nfabian@neha.org
Mel Knight, President
melknight@sbcglobal.net
Brian Collins, President Elect
brianc@plano.gov
Membership: 4,500+; *Member Profile:* Environmental health practitioners in both the public & private sectors; Academia; Uniformed services, employed mainly by health departments
Activities: Providing national credential programs; Advocating for the profession; Offering networking opportunities; Working cooperatively with other national professional societies & government agencies
Meetings/Conferences:
For more information see Trade Shows, Conferences and Seminars Chapter
National Environmental Health Association 2013 77th Annual Conference & Exhibition
2013,
Publications:
•Journal of Environmental Health
Type: Journal; *Frequency:* 10 pa; *Accepts Advertising*; *Editor:* Nelson Fabian
Profile: Current issues, peer-reviewed research, products, & services in the area or environmental health

National Farmers Foundation

2717 Wentz Ave., Saskatoon SK S7K 4B6
Tel: 306-652-9465; *Fax:* 306-664-6226
e-mail: nationalfarmersfoundation@gmail.com
www.nfu.ca/about/national-farmers-foundation
Overview: A large national charitable organization founded in 1987
Mission: To stimulate rural/urban cooperation; to fund education & research that will further the progressive farm movement in Canada; Affiliation(s): National Farmers Union
Chief Officer(s):
Jim Phelps, President
Finances: *Funding Sources:* Fundraising; donations

National Farmers Union (NFU) / Syndicat national des cultivateurs

2717 Wentz Ave., Saskatoon SK S7K 4B6
Tel: 306-652-9465; *Fax:* 306-664-6226
e-mail: nfu@nfu.ca
www.nfu.ca
www.facebook.com/nfuCanada
twitter.com/NFUcanada
Overview: A large national organization founded in 1969
Mission: To improve economic & social well-being of rural people & rural communities; *Member of:* Rural Dignity of Canada; Affiliation(s): Action Canada Network
Chief Officer(s):
Terry Boehm, President
centaur2@sasktel.net
Joan Brady, Women's President
jbbrady@eastlink.ca
Cammie Harbottle, Youth President
cammie@waldegrave.org
Finances: *Annual Operating Budget:* $500,000-$1.5 Million; *Funding Sources:* Membership dues; fundraising; donations
Staff: 7 staff member(s); 300 volunteer(s)
Membership: 10,329; *Fees:* $195 family; $40 youth; $65 associate; *Committees:* Women's Advisory; Youth Advisory; International Program
Activities: *Speaker Service:* Yes; *Library:*
Publications:
•Union Farmer Monthly [a publication of the National Farmers Union]
Type: Newsletter; *Frequency:* Monthly
•Union Farmer Quarterly [a publication of the National Farmers Union]
Type: Magazine; *Frequency:* q.

Manitoba - Taxation Office
Newdale Shopping Centre, 2999B Pembina Hwy., Winnipeg MB R3T 2H5
Tel: 204-261-0500

Maritimes - NFU Financial Services
120 Bishop Dr., Summerside PE C1N 5Z8
Tel: 902-436-1872
Chief Officer(s):
Gayle Read, Contact

Maritimes - Taxation Office
559 Rte. 390, Rowena NB E7N 4N2
Tel: 506-273-4328; *Fax:* 506-273-4328
Chief Officer(s):
Judy Barr, Contact

Ontario Office
5420 Hwy. 6 North, RR#5, Guelph ON N1H 6J2
Tel: 705-738-3993
Toll-Free: 888-832-9638
e-mail: office@nfuontario.ca
nfuontario.ca
Chief Officer(s):
Ann Slater, Ontario NFU Coordinator
Sarah Bakker, Regional Office Administrator

National Ground Water Association (NGWA)
601 Dempsey Rd., Westerville OH 43081 USA
Tel: 614-898-7791; *Fax:* 614-898-7786
Toll-Free: 800-551-7379
e-mail: ngwa@ngwa.org
www.ngwa.org
Overview: A medium-sized international organization founded in 1948
Mission: Dedicated to advancing the expertise of all ground water professionals & furthering ground water awareness & protection through education & outreach; *Member of:* American Association for the Advancement of Science; Geological Society of America; Geoenvironmental Forum; Geothermal Heat Pump Consortium; Groundwater Foundation
Chief Officer(s):
Kevin McCray, Executive Director
kmmcray@ngwa.org
Paul Humes, Vice President, Operations
Finances: *Annual Operating Budget:* Greater than $5 Million
Staff: 34 staff member(s); 220 volunteer(s)
Membership: 13,000; *Fees:* Schedule available; *Member Profile:* Ground water scientists & engineers; water well drillers; pump installers; suppliers & manufacturers; *Committees:* Numerous committees, subcommittees & task forces
Activities: *Awareness Events:* Ground Water Awareness Week, March; *Speaker Service:* Yes; *Library:* National Ground Water Information Centre

National Indian Brotherhood *See* Assembly of First Nations

National Insulation & Energy Conservation Contractors Association *See* National Energy Conservation Association Inc.

National Marine Manufacturers Association (NMMA)
#5100, 200 E. Randolph Dr., Chicago IL 60601 USA
Tel: 312-946-6200
www.nmma.org
Overview: A medium-sized international organization
Mission: NMMA is dedicated to creating, promoting and protecting an environment where members can achieve financial success through excellence in manufacturing, in selling, and in servicing their customers.; Affiliation(s): National Association of Boat Manufacturers; National Association of Marine Products & Services; Association of Marine Engine Manufacturers
Chief Officer(s):
Thomas Dammrich, President, 312-946-6220
Linda Waddell, Vice President, Northern Shows, 905-951-4051
Finances: *Funding Sources:* Membership fees & shows
Staff: 5 staff member(s)
Membership: 1,400 corporate; *Member Profile:* Canadian/American manufacturer, distributor, or retailer of boating-related products
Activities: *Internships:* Yes

National Marine Manufacturers Association Canada (NMMA)
#8, 14 McEwan Dr., Bolton ON L7E 1H1
Tel: 905-951-0009; *Fax:* 905-951-0018
e-mail: sanghel@nmma.org
www.cmma.ca
Also Known As: NMMA Canada
Previous Name: Canadian Marine Manufacturers Association
Overview: A medium-sized national organization
Mission: The CMMA is committed to being a leader; in promoting boating, advocacy with government and providing value added services to foster the financial success of the marine industry.
Chief Officer(s):
Rick Layzell, Chair
rick_layzell@yamaha-motor.ca
Membership: *Member Profile:* Marine industry

National Oil Recyclers Association *See* NORA, An Association of Responsible Recyclers

National Parks Conservation Association (NPCA)
#700, 777 6th St. NW, Washington DC 20001-3723 USA
Tel: 202-223-6722; *Fax:* 202-659-0650
Toll-Free: 800-628-7275
e-mail: npca@npca.org
www.npca.org
www.facebook.com/NationalParks
twitter.com/npca
Overview: A large national organization founded in 1919
Mission: America's only private, non-profit advocacy organization dedicated to protecting, preserving & enhancing the National Park system; to protect & improve the quality of parks & to promote an understanding of, appreciation for, & sense of personal commitment to parklands
Chief Officer(s):
Thomas C. Kiernan, President
Theresa Pierno, Executive Vice-President
Finances: *Annual Operating Budget:* Greater than $5 Million
Membership: 460,000; *Fees:* $25; $18 students

National Recycling Coalition
#425, 805 15th St. NW, Washington DC 20005 USA
Tel: 202-789-1430; *Fax:* 202-789-1431
e-mail: info@nrc-recycle.org
www.nrc-recycle.org
Overview: A small national organization founded in 1978
Mission: To advance & improve recycling, source reduction, composting & reuse by providing technical information, education, training, outreach & advocacy services to its members in order to conserve resources & benefit the environment; Affiliation(s): California Resource Recovery Association; Northern California Recycling Association; Recycling Council of Alberta; Indiana Recycling Coalition; North Carolina Recycling Association; Oklahoma Recycling Association; Association of Oregon Recyclers; Pennsylvania Resources Council; Arizona Recycling Coalition; Arkansas Recycling Coalition; RECARIBE; Colorado Association for Recycling; Connecticut Recyclers Coalition; Recycle Florida Today; Illinois Recycling Association; Iowa Recycling Association; Kansas Recyclers Association; Louisiana Recycling Association
Chief Officer(s):
Ed Skernolis, Executive Director
eskernolis@nrc-recycle.org
Membership: 5,000+
Activities: *Internships:* Yes

National Sanitary Supply Association *See* International Sanitary Supply Association, Inc.

National Society for Clean Air *See* Environmental Protection UK

National Solid Wastes Management Association (NSWMA)
#300, 4301 Connecticut Ave. NW, Washington DC 20008 USA
Tel: 202-244-4700; *Fax:* 202-966-4824
Toll-Free: 800-424-2869
www.nswma.org
www.facebook.com/group.php?gid=130041787022156
Overview: A medium-sized international organization founded in 1962
Mission: To promote the environmentally responsible, efficient, profitable, & ethical management of waste
Chief Officer(s):
Bruce J. Parker, President & Chief Executive Officer
bparker@nswma.org
David Biderman, General Counsel & Director, Safety
davidb@nswma.org
Christine Hutcherson, Director, Member Services
chutcherson@nswma.org
Alice Jacobsohn, Director, Education
alicej@nswma.org
Thom Metzger, Director, Communications & Public Affairs
tmetzger@nswma.org
Ed Repa, Director, Environmental Programs
erepa@nswma.org
Catherine Maimon, Manager, Meetings
cmaimon@nswma.org
Membership: *Member Profile:* For-profit companies in North America that provide solid, hazardous, & medical waste collection, recycling, & disposal services; Companies that provide professional & consulting services to the waste services industry
Activities: Offering educational & training opportunities; Engaging in research; Facilitating networking; *Library:* National Solid Wastes Management Association Library
Meetings/Conferences:
For more information see Trade Shows, Conferences and Seminars Chapter
WasteExpo 2013 45th Conference & Tradeshow
May 2013 New Orleans, LA
Publications:
•NSWMA [National Solid Wastes Management Association] e-News
Type: Newsletter
Profile: Timely information to help businesses make decisions

National Sunflower Association of Canada (NSAC)
PO Box 1269, 38 - 4th Ave. NE, Carman MB R0G 0J0
Tel: 204-745-6776; *Fax:* 204-745-6122
www.canadasunflower.com
www.facebook.com/142997522440563
Overview: A small national organization founded in 1996
Mission: To ensure the profitability and long term growth of the sunflower crop through industry wide leadership
Chief Officer(s):
Kelly Dobson, President
Darcelle Graham, Executive Director
Membership: 950; *Fees:* $50 producers; $500 corporate

National Wildlife Federation (NWF)
PO Box 1583, Merrifield VA 22116-1583 USA
Tel: 703-438-6000; *Fax:* 703-438-6035
Toll-Free: 800-822-9919
www.nwf.org
www.facebook.com/NationalWildlife
twitter.com/nwf
www.youtube.com/user/NationalWildlife
Overview: A large national organization founded in 1936
Mission: NWF advances common-sense conservation policies through advocacy, education & litigation in concert with affiliate groups & other like-minded organizations across the country & around the world; efforts focus on the conservation of wildlife & wild places & the health of the environment upon which we all depend, with special emphasis on wetlands, water quality, endangered habitats, land stewardship & sustainable communities
Chief Officer(s):
Larry J. Schweiger, President & CEO
Finances: *Annual Operating Budget:* Greater than $5 Million; *Funding Sources:* Memberships; donations; bequests; magazine subscriptions; sales of nature education materials
Staff: 600 staff member(s)
Membership: Over 4 million members & supporters + 46 affiliated organizations + 11 field office locations; *Fees:* $15+
Activities: *Awareness Events:* National Wildlife Week; *Internships:* Yes; *Rents Mailing List:* Yes; *Library:*
Awards:
•The National Conservation Achievement Awards (Award)
Program that recognizes outstanding individual & group achievements in conservation
Meetings/Conferences:
For more information see Trade Shows, Conferences and Seminars Chapter
2013 for National Wildlife Federation's 77th Annual Meeting
March 2013 Albuquerque, NM

Native Fishing Association (NFA)
#110, 100 Park Royal South, West Vancouver BC V7T 1A2
Tel: 604-913-2997; *Fax:* 604-913-2995
e-mail: reception@shoal.ca
www.shoal.ca
www.facebook.com/native.fishing
twitter.com/nativefishing
Overview: A small local organization founded in 1985

Mission: To enhance, stabilize, & support Native participation in British Columbia's commercial fishing industry.
Chief Officer(s):
Mark Recalma, Co-Chair
Bill Wilson, Co-Chair
Violet Hill, Executive Director
vhill@shoal.ca

Native Orchid Conservation Inc.

117 Morier Ave., Winnipeg MB R2M 0C8
Tel: 204-947-9707
e-mail: adames@mts.net
www.nativeorchid.org
Overview: A small local organization
Mission: To protect unique mini-ecosystems & their plant communities
Chief Officer(s):
Doris Ames, President
Membership: *Fees:* $10 individual; $25 group

Natural Health Practitioners of Canada Association (NHPCA) / Association des Praticiens de la santé naturelle du Canada (PSNC)

#600, 10339 - 124 St., Edmonton AB T5N 3W1
Tel: 780-484-2010; *Fax:* 780-484-3605
Toll-Free: 888-711-7701
e-mail: growingtogether@nhpcanada.org
www.nhpcanada.org
www.facebook.com/group.php?gid=142729347410
Overview: A medium-sized national organization
Mission: To provide programs, services and products for members in the service of public wellness and to serve the public by promoting and advocating the wellness professions.
Chief Officer(s):
Colleen MacDougall, Executive Director & Registrar
Publications:
•Connections [a publication of the Natural Health Practitioners of Canada]
Type: Magazine; *Frequency:* Quarterly

Natural History Society of Manitoba; Manitoba Naturalists Society ***See*** Nature Manitoba

Natural History Society of Newfoundland & Labrador

c/o The Osprey, PO Box 1013, Stn. C, St. John's NL A1C 5M3
Tel: 709-754-0455
www.nhs.nf.ca
Overview: A small provincial charitable organization founded in 1963
Mission: The Natural History Society is a province-wide organization with a primary interest in promoting the enjoyment and protection of all wildlife and natural history resources in the Province of Newfoundland and Labrador and surrounding waters.; *Member of:* Canadian Nature Federation
Chief Officer(s):
Allan Stein, Acting Vice-President, 709-895-2056
arstein@mun.ca
Don Steele, Secretary
dsteele@mun.ca
Finances: *Annual Operating Budget:* Less than $50,000; *Funding Sources:* Membership fees; donations
Membership: 175; *Fees:* $25
Activities: Field trips; monthly meetings

Natural Resources Union (NRU)
Parent Name: Public Service Alliance of Canada (CLC)

#600, 233 Gilmour St., Ottawa ON K2P 0P2
Tel: 613-560-4378; *Fax:* 613-233-7012
www.nru-srn.com
Previous Name: Union of Energy, Mines & Resources Employees
Overview: A medium-sized national organization founded in 1978 overseen by Public Service Alliance of Canada (CLC)
Chief Officer(s):
Mike Sargent, National President
sargentm@nru-srn.com
Finances: *Annual Operating Budget:* $250,000-$500,000
Staff: 2 staff member(s)
Membership: 1,600 + 20 locals; *Member Profile:* Government employees, Natural Resources Canada, Canadian Space Agency & various other agencies & boards; *Committees:* Occupational Safety & Health; Equal Opportunities; Labour Management Consultation

Natural Step Canada

#203, 4 Florence St., Ottawa ON K2P 0W7
Tel: 613-748-3001; *Fax:* 613-748-1649
e-mail: info@naturalstep.ca
www.naturalstep.ca
www.linkedin.com/groups?mostPopular=&gid=1169257
www.facebook.com/TheNaturalStepCanada
twitter.com/thenaturalstep
www.youtube.com/user/naturalsteponline
Overview: A large national charitable organization
Mission: The Natural Step Canada is a non-profit organization that helps organizations and individuals understand and make meaningful progress toward sustainability.
Chief Officer(s):
Chad Park, Executive Director
Meetings/Conferences:
For more information see Trade Shows, Conferences and Seminars Chapter
Natural Step Canada Conference 2013
June 2013 Guelph, ON

Nature Canada / Canada Nature

#300, 75 Albert St., Ottawa ON K1P 5E7
Tel: 613-562-3447; *Fax:* 613-562-3371
Toll-Free: 800-267-4088
e-mail: info@naturecanada.ca
www.naturecanada.ca
www.facebook.com/NatureCanada
twitter.com/NatureCanada
www.youtube.com/user/NatureCanada1
Previous Name: Canadian Nature Federation
Overview: A large national charitable organization founded in 1971
Mission: To protect & conserve wildlife & habitats throughout Canada
Environmental Activity: Advocating on behalf of nature; Encouraging the development of parks & protected areas; Promoting biodiversity in Canada & abroad; Conserving bird habitat
Chief Officer(s):
Ian Davidson, Executive Director
idavidson@naturecanada.ca
Ruth Catana, Chief Operating Officer
rcatana@naturecanada.ca
Dave Spooner, Director, Finance & Administration
dspooner@naturecanada.ca
Chris Sutton, Director, Communications
csutton@naturecanada.ca
Ted Cheskey, Manager, Bird Conservation Programs
tcheskey@naturecanada.ca
Jodi Joy, Manager, Major & Planned Giving
jjoy@naturecanada.ca
Katherine Lim, Manager, Outreach & Engagement
klim@naturecanada.ca
Alex MacDonald, Manager, Protected Areas Campaigns
amacdonald@naturecanada.ca
Carla Sbert, Manager, Conservation Programs
csbert@naturecanada.ca
Andrew Van Iterson, Manager, Green Budget Coalition
avaniterson@naturecanada.ca
Finances: *Funding Sources:* Donations
Membership: 350+ organizations + 40,000 supporters; *Member Profile:* Natualist organizations across Canada; Individual supporters
Activities: Offering outreach & educational programs; Organizing action campaigns for nature
Awards:
•Affiliate Award (Award)
To recognize conservation efforts of a partner organization that support Nature Canada's conservation initiatives or mission
•Charles Labatiuk Scholarship (Scholarship)
Eligibility: Any student enrolled in an entrance level course or program at an accredited college or university in Canada, in the interdisciplinary study of natural environmental systems *Amount:* $2000
•Douglas H. Pimlott Award (Award)
Eligibility: An individual with outstanding contributions to Canadian conservation
Meetings/Conferences:
For more information see Trade Shows, Conferences and Seminars Chapter
Nature Canada 2013 Annual General Meeting
2013
Publications:
•The Nature Nation
Type: Newsletter; *Frequency:* Monthly
Profile: Action alerts, reports, polls, reading suggestions, & upcoming events

The Nature Conservancy of Canada (NCC) / Société canadienne pour la conservation de la nature

#400, 36 Eglinton Ave. West, Toronto ON M4R 1A1
Tel: 416-932-3202; *Fax:* 416-932-3208
Toll-Free: 800-465-0029
e-mail: nature@natureconservancy.ca
www.natureconservancy.ca
www.linkedin.com/company/the-nature-conservancy-of-canada
www.facebook.com/natureconservancy.ca
twitter.com/NatureConsCDA
www.youtube.com/user/NatureConsCDA
Overview: A large national charitable organization founded in 1962
Mission: To protect Canada's biodiversity through long-term stewardship & property securement
Environmental Activity: Purchasing, acquiring by donation, or placing conservation easements on ecologically significant lands
Chief Officer(s):
John Lounds, President & Chief Executive Officer
Jane Gilbert, Chief Communications Officer
Lynn Gran, Chief Development Officer & Vice-President, Strategic Philanthropy
Kamal Rajani, Chief Financial Officer
John Riley, Chief Science Officer & National Director, Strategies
Ian Barnett, Vice-President, Regional Operations
Michael Bradstreet, Vice-President, Conservation
Julie Wood, Vice-President, Corporate
Finances: *Funding Sources:* Donations
Membership: *Committees:* Executive; Governance & Nominating; Audit; Investment; Conservation
Activities: Partnering with landowners & corporations to protect Canada's natural areas
Publications:
•The Ark [a publication of The Nature Conservancy of Canada]
Type: Newsletter; *Frequency:* 3 pa; *Price:* A donation of $20+
Profile: A national newsletter, with updates on featured projects & properties, stewardship work, & threatened or vulnerable species
•The Nature Conservancy of Canada Annual Report to our Donors
Type: Yearbook; *Frequency:* Annually
Profile: The year in review for each region of Canada

Alberta & The North
#830, 1202 Centre St. South, Calgary AB T2G 5A5
Tel: 403-262-1253; *Fax:* 403-515-6987
Toll-Free: 877-262-1253
e-mail: alberta@natureconservancy.ca
Chief Officer(s):
Bob Demulder, Regional Vice President

Atlantic
#180, 924 Prospect St., Fredericton NB E3B 2T9
Tel: 506-450-6010; *Fax:* 506-450-6013
Toll-Free: 877-231-4400
e-mail: atlantic@natureconservancy.ca
Chief Officer(s):
Linda M. Stephenson, Regional Vice President

British Columbia
#200, 825 Broughton St., Victoria BC V8W 1E5
Tel: 250-479-3191; *Fax:* 250-479-0546
Toll-Free: 888-404-8428
e-mail: bcoffice@natureconservancy.ca
Chief Officer(s):
Jan Garnett, Regional Vice President

Manitoba
#200, 611 Corydon Ave., Winnipeg MB R3L 0P3
Tel: 204-942-6156; *Fax:* 204-942-1016
Toll-Free: 866-683-6934
e-mail: manitoba@natureconservancy.ca
Chief Officer(s):
Ursula Goeres, Regional Vice President

Ontario
PO Box 520, Port Rowan ON N0E 1M0
Tel: 519-586-7773; *Fax:* 519-586-9777
Toll-Free: 800-249-9598
e-mail: ontario@natureconservancy.ca
Chief Officer(s):
Donna Stewart, Regional Vice President

Québec
#1000, 55 av Mont-Royal Ouest, Montréal QC H2T 2S6

Tél: 514-876-1606; *Téléc:* 514-876-7901
Ligne sans frais: 877-876-5444
Courriel: quebec@conservationdelanature.ca
Chief Officer(s):
Nathalie Zinger, Regional Vice President

Saskatchewan
#100, 1777 Victoria Ave., Regina SK S4P 4K5
Tel: 306-347-0447; *Fax:* 306-347-2345
Toll-Free: 866-622-7275
e-mail: saskatchewan@natureconservancy.ca
www.natureconservancy.ca/en/where-we-work/saskatchewan
Chief Officer(s):
Carmen Leibel, Regional Vice President

Nature Council of British Columbia *See* British Columbia Nature (Federation of British Columbia Naturalists)

Nature Manitoba (MNS)

Hammond Building, #401, 63 Albert St., Winnipeg MB R3B 1G4
Tel: 204-943-9029; *Fax:* 204-943-9029
e-mail: info@naturemanitoba.ca
www.naturemanitoba.ca
www.facebook.com/pages/Nature-Manitoba/67945358869
Previous Name: Natural History Society of Manitoba; Manitoba Naturalists Society
Overview: A medium-sized provincial charitable organization founded in 1920
Mission: To foster the popular & scientific study of nature; To preserve the natural environment; To act as a voice for people interested in the outdoors & natural history
Environmental Activity: Providing programs to enhance awareness, understanding & appreciation for the natural environment; Working for environmental protection
Chief Officer(s):
Roger Turenne, President
Donald Himbeault, Executive Vice-President
Alain Louer, Secretary
Sean Worden, Treasurer
Susan McLarty, Office Administrator
Finances: *Funding Sources:* Donations; Nature Manitoba Store
Membership: *Fees:* $20 students; $35 seniors; $40 individuals; $55 families; *Member Profile:* Manitobans who share a passion for nature
Activities: Conducting research; Engaging in advocacy activities; Offering educational & recreational programs & field trips to observe botany, butterflies, & birds; *Library:* Nature Manitoba Library
Meetings/Conferences:
For more information see Trade Shows, Conferences and Seminars Chapter
Nature Manitoba 2013 Annual General Meeting
March 2013, MB
Nature Manitoba 2014 Annual General Meeting
2014, MB
Publications:
•The Birds of Manitoba
Type: Book; *Price:* $63.95
Profile: Information about & illustrations & photographs of the 382 species of birds known in Manitoba
•Checklist of the Birds of Manitoba
Price: $1
Profile: A checklist of 391 confirmed species in Manitoba
•Finding Birds in Southern Manitoba
Type: Guide; *Price:* $20
Profile: A birding guide for southern Manitoba, featuring photographs & maps
•Nature Manitoba News
Type: Newsletter; *Frequency:* Bimonthly; *Accepts Advertising*; *Editor:* Tommy Allen; *Price:* Free with membership in Nature Manitoba
Profile: Information about Nature Manitoba's meetings & workshops, activities, members, & nature in the news
•Naturescape Manitoba
Type: Book; *Number of Pages:* 200; *Price:* $24.95
Profile: A source book about native planting & water conservation for the Prairies Ecozone of Manitoba

Nature NB

#110, 924 Prospect St., Fredericton NB E3B 2T9
Tel: 506-459-4209; *Fax:* 506-459-4209
e-mail: nbfn@nb.aibn.com
www.naturenb.ca
Previous Name: New Brunswick Federation of Naturalists
Overview: A medium-sized provincial charitable organization founded in 1979
Mission: To preserve wildlife & protect its natural habitat; to promote a public interest in & a knowledge of natural history; to promote, encourage & cooperate with organizations & individuals who have similar interests & objectives; to consider matters of environmental concern.; *Member of:* Nature Canada
Chief Officer(s):
Vanessa Roy-McDougall, Executive Director
Membership: 1,000-4,999;; *Fees:* $25 individual; $30 family membership; *Member Profile:* 13 federated nature clubs

Nature Nova Scotia (Federation of Nova Scotia Naturalists)

c/o Nova Scotia Museum of Natural History, 1747 Summer St., Halifax NS B3H 3A6
Tel: 902-582-7176
e-mail: doug@fundymud.com
www.naturens.ca
Previous Name: Federation of Nova Scotia Naturalists
Overview: A medium-sized provincial charitable organization founded in 1990
Mission: To support the interests of naturalists clubs; To represent naturalists clubs throughout Nova Scotia; *Member of:* Nature Conservancy of Canada (NCC); Canadian Parks & Wilderness Society (CPAWS); Affiliation(s): Nature Canada
Environmental Activity: Establishing protected natural areas; Conserving species & spaces; Promoting the sustainable use of resources; Developing policies on issues such as ATVs, tidal power, & wind power
Chief Officer(s):
Bob Bancroft, President, 902-386-2501
Sue Abbot, Vice-President, 902-453-0435
Doug Linzey, Secretary, 902-582-7176
Jean Gibson, Treasurer, 902-678-4725
Finances: *Funding Sources:* Donations
Membership: *Fees:* $5 students & seniors; $20 single adults & families; *Member Profile:* Naturalists clubs & organizations within Nova Scotia; Members-at-large
Activities: Providing educational opportunities; Hosting field trips; Conducting research; Serving on committees & advisory boards involving issues that affect the health of the natural environment
Meetings/Conferences:
For more information see Trade Shows, Conferences and Seminars Chapter
Nature Nova Scotia 2013 Annual General Meeting & Conference
May 2013 Annapolis Royal, NS
Publications:
•Nature Nova Scotia Annual Report
Type: Yearbook; *Frequency:* Annually
Profile: A summary of Nature Nova Scotia's yearly activities

Nature Québec

#207, 870, av de Salaberry, Québec QC G1R 2T9
Tél: 418-648-2104; *Téléc:* 418-648-0991
Courriel: conservons@naturequebec.org
www.naturequebec.org
www.linkedin.com/company/nature-qu-bec?trx=hb_tab_compy_id_2794658
www.facebook.com/naturequebec
twitter.com/NatureQuebec
Nom précédent: Union québécoise pour la conservation de la nature
Aperçu: *Dimension:* moyenne; *Envergure:* provinciale; Organisme sans but lucratif; fondée en 1981
Mission: Regrouper les individus et les sociétés oeuvrant en sciences naturelles et en environnement; maintenir des processus écologiques essentiels; préserver la diversité génétique; utiliser soutenablement des espèces et des écosystèmes; *Membre de:* Union internationale pour la conservation de la nature
Membre(s) du bureau directeur:
Christian Simard, Directeur général, 418-648-2104 Ext. 2071
christian.simard@naturequebec.org
Finances: *Budget de fonctionnement annuel:* $500,000-$1.5 Million
Personnel: 8 membre(s) du personnel
Membre: 120 institutionnel; 5 000 individu *Montant de la cotisation:* 25$
Activités: *Stagiaires:* Oui; *Service de conférenciers:* Oui

Nature Saskatchewan

#206, 1860 Lorne St., Regina SK S4P 2L7
Tel: 306-780-9273; *Fax:* 306-780-9263
Toll-Free: 800-667-4668
e-mail: info@naturesask.ca
www.naturesask.ca
www.linkedin.com/pub/nature-sask-gary-seib/38/7b6/39a
www.facebook.com/NatureSask
twitter.com/naturesask
Also Known As: Saskatchewan Natural History Society
Overview: A medium-sized provincial charitable organization founded in 1949
Mission: To foster appreciation & understanding for the natural environment; To document & protect the biological diversity of Saskatchewan; To preserve the natural eco-systems of the province
Environmental Activity: Promoting conservation; Engaging in stewardship projects, such as Operation Burrowing Owl, Rare Plant Rescue, & Shrubs for Shrikes
Chief Officer(s):
Gary Seib, General Manager
gseib@naturesask.ca
Deanna Trowsdale-Mutafov, Manager, Conservation & Education
dtmutafov@naturesask.ca
Melissa Ranalli, Manager, Species at Risk
mranalli@naturesask.ca
Ellen Bouvier, Office Coordinator
rpr@naturesask.ca
Finances: *Annual Operating Budget:* $500,000-$1.5 Million; *Funding Sources:* Membership fees; Donations; Sponsorships
Staff: 7 staff member(s); 900 volunteer(s)
Membership: 1,000; *Fees:* $15 students; $20 seniors; $25 individuals; $30 families, institutions, & foreign members; $600 lifetime members; *Member Profile:* Naturalists in Saskatchewan
Activities: Conducting research; Providing education; Producing special publications, such as: Ferns & Fern Allies; Lilies, Irises & Orchids; Dragonflies & Damselflies in the Hand; Getting to know Saskatchewan Lichens; *Speaker Service:* Yes; *Library:* Nature Saskatchewan Resource Centre
Awards:
•Conservation Award (Award)
Publications:
•Blue Jay
Type: Journal; *Accepts Advertising*; *Editor:* Chris Somers; Vicky Kjoss; *Price:* $25 / year
Profile: Conservation, nature, & scientific research news, plus artwork & poetry
•Nature Views
Type: Newsletter; *Frequency:* Quarterly; *Accepts Advertising*; *Editor:* Robert Warnock; Angela Dohms; *Price:* Free with Nature Saskatchewan membership
Profile: Discussions of environmental issues, contributions from well known naturalists, & forthcoming events

Fort Qu'Appelle Branch
PO Box 757, Fort Qu'appelle SK S0G 1S0
Tel: 306-332-6783
Chief Officer(s):
Ron Hooper, President

Indian Head Nature Society
PO Box 995, Indian Head SK S0G 2K0
Chief Officer(s):
Lorne Scott, President, 306-695-3524

Kelsey Ecological Society
PO Box 1000, Preeceville SK S0A 3B0
Chief Officer(s):
Dave Weiman, President

Nature Moose Jaw
PO Box 2042, Moose Jaw SK S6H 3G7
Chief Officer(s):
Rod Moran, President, 306-692-4464
moran@sasktel.net

Nature Prince Albert
PO Box 235, Prince Albert SK S6V 5R5
Tel: 306-764-2347
e-mail: carman.dodge@sasktel.net
Chief Officer(s):
Carman Dodge, President

Nature Regina
PO Box 291, Regina SK S4P 3A1
Chief Officer(s):
Dale Hjertaas, President
beathiaume@sasktel.net

Saskatoon Nature Society
PO Box 448, RPO University, Saskatoon SK S7N 4J8
Tel: 306-665-1915
www.saskatoonnaturesociety.sk.ca

Chief Officer(s):
Donna Bruce, President

Southwest Naturalists
370 - 4th Ave. SE, Swift Current SK S9H 3L8
Tel: 306-778-2775
e-mail: info@swnaturalists.org
www.swnaturalists.org
Chief Officer(s):
Gerald Handley, President

Weyburn Nature Society
PO Box 131, McTaggart SK S0G 3G0
Chief Officer(s):
Val Thomas, Secretary, 306-842-5005
van_doyle_thomas@hotmail.com

Yellowhead Flyway Birding Trail Association
PO Box 460, Saltcoats SK S0A 4R0
yfbta.com
Chief Officer(s):
Rob Wilson, Secretary

Yorkton Natural History Society
45 Darlinton St. East, Yorkton SK S3N 0C3
Chief Officer(s):
Geoffrey Rushowick, President, 306-783-5898
rushg@sasktel.net

Nature Trust of New Brunswick (NTNB) / Fondation pour la protection des sites naturels du Nouveau-Brunswick

PO Box 603, Stn. A, 404 Queen St., 3rd Fl., Fredericton NB E3B 5A6
Tel: 506-457-2398; *Fax:* 506-450-2137
e-mail: naturetrust@ntnb.org
www.naturetrust.nb.ca
www.facebook.com/group.php?gid=2412803975
twitter.com/@naturetrustNB
Overview: A small provincial charitable organization founded in 1987
Mission: To identify, classify & preserve natural areas which are outstanding for their biological, geological or aesthetic value; to foster in the people of New Brunswick an awareness of their natural heritage & to educate persons in connection therewith
Chief Officer(s):
Renata Woodward, Executive Director
Don Dennison, President
Bill Anderson, Treasurer & Vice-President
Dorothy Diamond, Secretary
Finances: *Annual Operating Budget:* $100,000-$250,000; *Funding Sources:* Donations; Government grants; Membership dues
Membership: 100-499;; *Fees:* $25 individual; $35 family/group; $75 supporting; $150 sponsoring; $250 donor; $500 benefactor

Nature Vancouver

PO Box 3021, Vancouver BC V6B 3X5
Tel: 604-737-3074
e-mail: info@naturevancouver.ca
www.naturevancouver.ca
Previous Name: Vancouver Natural History Society
Overview: A small local charitable organization founded in 1918
Mission: To promote the enjoyment of nature; to foster public interest & education in appreciation & study of nature; To encourage wise use & conservation of natural resources; To work for complete protection of endangered species & ecosystems; To promote access to & maintenance of natural areas in vicinity of Vancouver; *Member of:* The Federation of BC Naturalists; Affiliation(s): Nature Canada
Finances: *Annual Operating Budget:* $50,000-$100,000; *Funding Sources:* Membership fees
Staff: 100 volunteer(s)
Membership: 700; *Fees:* $40 individual; $50 family; $20 student; *Committees:* Conservation; Birding; Botany; Marine Biology
Activities: Marsh & bog restoration; bird & plant survey; conservation - briefs, forums & public information meetings; monthly speakers; annual summer camp to allow participants to learn about a special wilderness area in the province

Nepisiguit Salmon Association (NSA) / L'Association du saumon Nepisiguit

789 Riverside Dr., Bathurst NB E2A 2M8
Tel: 506-546-5279
e-mail: nsa@nbnet.nb.ca
www.nbsalmoncouncil.com
Overview: A small local organization founded in 1976
Mission: To enhance & preserve Atlantic Salmon in general & in the Nepisiguit river in particular; to educate the public as to the value of this unique, renewable, natural resource; *Member of:* Atlantic Salmon Federation; Affiliation(s): New Brunswick Salmon Council; Nepisiguit Watershed Management Committee
Chief Officer(s):
J. Robert Chaisson, Vice-President
Bob Baker, President
Finances: *Annual Operating Budget:* $50,000-$100,000; *Funding Sources:* Donations; Grants; Programs; Fundraising
Membership: 300+; *Member Profile:* Anglers & those interested in salmon conservation
Activities: Salmon enchancement program

New Brunswick Environment Industry Association (NBEIA) / L'Association des industries de l'environnement du Nouveau-Brunswick (AIENB)

PO Box 637, Stn. A, Fredericton NB E3B 5B3
Tel: 506-455-0212; *Fax:* 506-452-0213
e-mail: nbeia@nbnet.nb.ca
www.nbeia.nb.ca
Overview: A medium-sized provincial organization founded in 1994
Mission: To promote the growth of environmental business in New Brunswick
Environmental Activity: Promoting high standards for environmental products & services
Chief Officer(s):
Pierre Landry, President
Eric Cook, Secretary-Treasurer
Membership: 130+; *Member Profile:* Companies & individuals from the environment sector, including manufacturing, engineering, technology development, laboratories, education, & consultation
Activities: Offering marketing & networking opportunities; Providing professional development for practitioners in the environmental sector
Publications:
•New Brunswick Environment Industry Association Newsletter
Type: Newsletter; *Frequency:* Quarterly; *Accepts Advertising*; *Editor:* Carol Tibbitts; Amy Brown
Profile: Environmental news, plus information about members' products & services

New Brunswick Environmental Network (NBEN) / Réseau environnemental du Nouveau-Brunswick (RENB)
Parent Name: Canadian Environmental Network

167 Creek Rd., Waterford NB E4E 4L7
Tel: 506-433-6101; *Fax:* 506-433-6111
e-mail: nben@nben.ca
www.nben.ca
www.facebook.com/pages/NBEN-RENB/134259049952351
Overview: A medium-sized provincial organization founded in 1991 overseen by Canadian Environmental Network
Mission: To strengthen the environmental movement throughout New Brunswick; To promote ecologically sound ways of life; Affiliation(s): Canadian Environmental Network
Environmental Activity: Improving cooperation among environmental groups, industry, & government
Chief Officer(s):
Mary Ann Coleman, Executive Director
Joanna Brown, Coordinator, Youth Outreach & Events
Raissa Marks, Coordinator, Education & Outreach Programs
Finances: *Funding Sources:* Environment Canada; Health Canada; NB Dept. of Environment; NB Dept. of Health; NB Dept. of Intergovernmental Affairs; NB Dept. of Natural Resources
Membership: *Member Profile:* Non-profit environmental organizations
Activities: Providing educational opportunities
Meetings/Conferences:
For more information see Trade Shows, Conferences and Seminars Chapter
New Brunswick Environmental Network 2013 Annual General Meeting
2013, NB
Publications:
•Greenprint: Towards a Sustainable New Brunswick
Type: Report; *Number of Pages:* 16
Profile: Lead organizations include the New Brunswick Environmental Network, Canadian Parks & Wilderness Society - New Brunswick Chapter, Conservation Council of New Brunswick,Falls Brook Centre, Meduxnekeag River Association Inc., & Petitcodiac Riverkeeper
•Legal Information for Environmental Groups
Type: Guide; *Number of Pages:* 20
Profile: Topics include civil disobedience, property law, endangered species, & international law

New Brunswick Federation of Agriculture ***See*** Agricultural Alliance of New Brunswick

New Brunswick Federation of Naturalists ***See*** Nature NB

New Brunswick Federation of Woodlot Owners Inc. / Fédération des propriétaires de lots boisés du Nouveau-Brunswick inc.

819 Royal Rd., Fredericton NB E3G 6M1
Tel: 506-459-2990; *Fax:* 506-459-3515
www.nbwoodlotowners.ca
Overview: A small provincial organization founded in 1965
Mission: To advocate for woodlot owners; To direct government policy as it affects private woodlots
Chief Officer(s):
Andrew Clark, President
Ken Hardie, Manager

New Brunswick Forest Products Association Inc. (NBFPA) / L'Association des produits forestiers du Nouveau-Brunswick (APFNB)

Hugh John Flemming Forestry Centre, 1350 Regent St., Fredericton NB E3C 2G6
Tel: 506-452-6930; *Fax:* 506-450-3128
e-mail: info@nbforestry.com
www.nbforestry.com
Overview: A small provincial organization founded in 1959
Mission: The New Brunswick Forest Products Association is a non-government, non-profit organization that represents its forest industry members by serving as a common voice in relations with the government and the public, promoting a healthy New Brunswick forest, raising public awareness of sustainable forest management practices, and providing a forum for the exchange of information, ideas, and concerns.
Chief Officer(s):
Mark Arsenault, President/CEO
Membership: 110 organizations

New Brunswick Fruit Growers Association Inc.

c/o NBFGA Scholarship Committee, #206, 1115 Regent St., Fredericton NB E3B 3Z2
e-mail: nbapple@nbnet.nb.ca
Overview: A small provincial organization founded in 1904
Chief Officer(s):
Euclide Bourgeois, President
Membership: *Committees:* Scholarship

New Brunswick Ground Water Association
Parent Name: Canadian Ground Water Association

31 Gray Rd., Penobsquis NB E4E 5S7
Tel: 506-433-6767; *Fax:* 506-432-6888
e-mail: nbgwa@nb.sympatico.ca
www.nbgwa.ca
Overview: A small provincial organization overseen by Canadian Ground Water Association
Mission: To preserve & protect New Brunswick's water; To promote education of members & the public; To encourage the development of ground water guidelines & strategies
Chief Officer(s):
Roger Roy, President
Terry Burpee, Sec.-Treas.
Finances: *Annual Operating Budget:* Less than $50,000; *Funding Sources:* Membership dues
Membership: 42; *Fees:* $300

New Brunswick Institute of Agrologists (NBIA) / L'Institut des agronomes du Nouveau-Brunswick (IANB)
Parent Name: Agricultural Institute of Canada

PO Box 3479, Stn. B, Fredericton NB E3B 5H2
Tel: 506-459-5536; *Fax:* 506-454-7837
www.ianbia.com
Overview: A small provincial organization founded in 1960 overseen by Agricultural Institute of Canada
Mission: To maintain high competency & professional standards for those practicing agrology in New Brunswick; To uphold the NBIA Code of Ethics; to offer advice to the public about agriculture & related areas; To formulate policies & improve the agriculture & food industry
Chief Officer(s):
Pat Toner, President
pat.toner@gnb.ca
Duncan Fraser, Secretary
duncan.fraser@gnb.ca

Rita Rattray, Office Administrator
nbia@nbagrologists.nb.ca
Membership: 200; *Fees:* $25; *Member Profile:* Professional agrologists in New Brunswick, with a degree in agriculture from a recognized university, plus three or more years of training or experience in the field; Individuals with a degree accepted by the Council; Articling agrologists; *Committees:* Admissions; Act / Bylaws; Scholarship; Professional Development; NBIA Strategy; Communication; Discipline; Complaints; Nominating; Executive
Activities: Participating in programs to benefit the agriculture & food industry; Analyzing issues & making recommendations to organizations; Improving standards of research; Providing professional development & networking opportunities; Offering information for members, the farming industry, & the public; Promoting the profession of agrology to famers
Meetings/Conferences:
For more information see Trade Shows, Conferences and Seminars Chapter
New Brunswick Institute of Agrologists 2013 Annual General Meeting
April 2013 Fredericton, NB

New Brunswick Lung Association / Association pulmonaire du Nouveau-Brunswick
Parent Name: Canadian Lung Association
65 Brunswick St., Fredericton NB E3B 1G5
Tel: 506-455-8961; *Fax:* 506-462-0939
Toll-Free: 800-565-5864
e-mail: nblung@nbnet.nb.ca
www.nb.lung.ca
Overview: A small provincial charitable organization overseen by Canadian Lung Association
Mission: To promote wellness throughout New Brunswick & prevent lung disease
Environmental Activity: Providing health & environment resources & programs to the public in New Brunswick
Chief Officer(s):
Barbara MacKinnon, President & Chief Executive Officer
Betty Barrett, Officer, Finance & Administration
Louise Steeves, Officer, Communications
Arthur Thomson, Director, Environmental Initiatives
Barbara Walls, Director, Health Initiatives
Finances: *Funding Sources:* Donations; Sponsorships; Fundraising
Activities: Engaging in advocacy activities; Offering education about respiratory health; Providing resources such as fact sheets, booklets, & audio-visual & program resources; Supporting respiratory research; Organizing fundraising events to support children & adults with lung disease; *Awareness Events:* Asthma Month, March; Sleep Apnea Week, March; Clean Air Month, June; *Library:* NB Lung Associations' Environment & Health Public Resource Svs.; Open to public

New Brunswick Medical Society (NBMS) / Société médicale du Nouveau-Brunswick
Parent Name: Canadian Medical Association
176 York St., Fredericton NB E3B 3N7
Tel: 506-458-8860; *Fax:* 506-458-9853
e-mail: nbms@nb.aibn.com
www.nbms.nb.ca
Overview: A medium-sized provincial organization founded in 1867 overseen by Canadian Medical Association
Mission: To advance medical science in all its branches; to promote improvement of medical services; to prevent disease in cooperation with health officers & all others engaged in such work; to maintain high scientific & professional status for its members; to promote medical science & related arts & sciences
Chief Officer(s):
Robert Rae, President
Finances: *Annual Operating Budget:* $250,000-$500,000
Staff: 8 staff member(s)
Membership: 20 student + 40 senior/lifetime + 1,100 individual; *Fees:* Schedule available; *Member Profile:* Licensed physician by College of Physicians & Surgeons of NB; *Committees:* Economics; Health Care; Medical Education; Communications
Activities: *Internships:* Yes; *Speaker Service:* Yes; *Rents Mailing List:* Yes

New Brunswick Mining Association / L'Association minière du Nouveau-Brunswick
Parent Name: Mining Association of Canada
#312, 236 St. George Blvd., Moncton NB E1C 1W1
Tel: 506-857-3056; *Fax:* 506-857-3059
Overview: A small provincial organization overseen by Mining Association of Canada
Chief Officer(s):
Blaine Lewis, Manager

New Brunswick Potato Agency *See* Potatoes New Brunswick

New Brunswick Safety Council Inc. *See* Safety Services New Brunswick

New Brunswick Salmon Council (NBSC)
PO Box 533, Stn. A, Fredericton NB E3B 5A6
Tel: 506-452-1875; *Fax:* 506-454-0336
e-mail: thenbsc@nbnet.nb.ca
www.nbsalmoncouncil.com
Overview: A small provincial organization
Affiliation(s): Atlantic Salmon Federation

New Brunswick Salmon Growers Association *See* Atlantic Canada Fish Farmers Association

New Brunswick Society of Certified Engineering Technicians & Technologists (NBSCETT) / Société des techniciens et des technologues agréés du génie du Nouveau-Brunswick (STTAGN-B)
Parent Name: Canadian Council of Technicians & Technologists
#2, 385 Wilsey Rd., Fredericton NB E3B 5N6
Tel: 506-454-6124; *Fax:* 506-452-7076
Toll-Free: 800-665-8324
e-mail: nbscett@nbscett.nb.ca
www.nbscett.nb.ca
Overview: A medium-sized provincial organization founded in 1968 overseen by Canadian Council of Technicians & Technologists
Mission: To grant certification to applied science & engineering technology technicians & technologists; to protect titles & powers of discipline for its members
Chief Officer(s):
David Sheaves, President
Jennifer Lawson, Executive Assistant
Edward F. Leslie, Executive Director
Finances: *Annual Operating Budget:* $100,000-$250,000; *Funding Sources:* Membership dues
Staff: 3 staff member(s)
Membership: 1,600; *Fees:* Schedule available; *Member Profile:* Certified - in field of engineering, applied science, technology & meets requirements for certification; Technology graduate in training - meet all of academic requirements for certification; Associate - employed in engineering technology field; *Committees:* Accreditation; Certification & Review; Finance; Human Resources
Activities: Awards; Scholarships; *Awareness Events:* Annual Awards; *Internships:* Yes; *Speaker Service:* Yes; *Library:* Open to public

New Brunswick Soil & Crop Improvement Association (NBSCIA) / Association pour l'amélioration du sol et des cultures du Nouveau-Brunswick
#302, 259 Brunswick St., Fredericton NB E3B 1G8
Tel: 506-454-1736; *Fax:* 506-453-1985
e-mail: nbscia@nbnet.nb.ca
www.nbscia.ca
Overview: A small provincial organization founded in 1978
Mission: To improve soil & crop sustainability in New Brunswick; To encourage research & innovation to advance the agricultural industry throughout the province; Affiliation(s): Agricultural Alliance of New Brunswick; Eastern Soil & Water Conservation Centre; Soil Conservation Council of Canada
Chief Officer(s):
Susannah Banks, General Manager
John Robinson, President, 506-432-6473
Membership: *Fees:* $20 provincial membership
Activities: Promoting environmental & economical agricultural practices in New Brunswick; Organizing field days & tours; Distributing educational information to New Brunswick farmers; Conducting research projects; Sponsoring research projects & new farming techniques; Liaising with government
Publications:
•New Brunswick Soil & Crop Improvement Association Newsletter
Type: Newsletter; *Frequency:* Quarterly; *Price:* Free with New Brunswick Soil & Crop Improvement Association membership

New Brunswick Wildlife Federation (NBWF) / Fédération de la faune du Nouveau-Brunswick
Parent Name: Canadian Wildlife Federation
576, rue Principale, St. Leonard NB E7E 2H5
www.nbwildlifefederation.org
Overview: A medium-sized provincial organization founded in 1924 overseen by Canadian Wildlife Federation
Mission: To foster sound management & wise use of the renewable & non-renewable natural resources of New Brunswick; to assist & encourage the enforcement of those game laws which are in keeping with the objectives of the Federation & to strive for better management & game laws where & when necessary; to educate membership & the public, with particular emphasis upon conservation & safety; to represent the interests & concerns of New Brunswick sportsmen; to cooperate with government departments & all related groups, where interests are mutual.; *Member of:* New Brunswick Salmon Council; Fur Institute of Canada
Chief Officer(s):
Roland Michaud, President, 506-475-3612
michaudr@nbnet.nb.ca
Rod Currie, Secretary, 506-458-5643
racurrie@nb.sympatico.ca
Finances: *Annual Operating Budget:* $100,000-$250,000
Membership: 44 clubs + 10,000 individual; *Fees:* $40 individual; $400 max. per club; *Committees:* Adopt-a-Stream; Constitution & By-Laws; Environment; Fisheries; Forestry; Master Angler; Membership; Memorial Cards, Merchandise & Prints; Outdoor Heritage Camps; Resolutions; Wildlife & Hunter Education; Fundraising; Becoming an Outdoors-Woman
Activities: *Speaker Service:* Yes

The New Directions Group (NDG)
PO Box 8105, Canmore AB T1W 2T8
Tel: 403-678-9956
e-mail: info@newdirectionsgroup.org
www.newdirectionsgroup.org
Overview: A small national organization founded in 1990
Mission: To provide a forum for leaders from Canadian businesses & NGO communities to debate sustainability issues
Chief Officer(s):
Paul Griss, Coordinator
Finances: *Funding Sources:* Corporate participants; Project support from governments
Activities: Advancing policy; Releasing reports on projects

Newfoundland & Labrador Association of Landscape Architects (NLALA)
77 Gower St., St. John's NL A1C 1N6
Tel: 709-579-7744
www.nlala.com
Overview: A medium-sized provincial organization
Chief Officer(s):
Jim Floyd, President
jfloyd@nnet.net
Membership: 12; *Member Profile:* Landscape architects & firms

Newfoundland & Labrador Association of Technology Companies (NLATC)
#5, 391 Empire Ave., St. John's NL A1E 1W6
Tel: 709-772-8324; *Fax:* 709-757-6284
e-mail: info@nati.net
www.nati.net
twitter.com/NATI_NL
Previous Name: Newfoundland Alliance of Technical Industries
Overview: A medium-sized provincial organization
Mission: To act collectively for technical organizations in Newfoundland industry in cooperation with educational & public sectors to promote the growth of innovative technical industries in Newfoundland & Labrador & the rest of Canada; Affiliation(s): Canadian Advanced Technology Association; Information Technology Association of Canada
Chief Officer(s):
Ron Taylor, Chief Executive Officer, 709-757-3252
ron@nati.net
Finances: *Annual Operating Budget:* $500,000-$1.5 Million; *Funding Sources:* Membership dues; government
Staff: 10 staff member(s); 30 volunteer(s)
Membership: 200; *Fees:* $130-$695
Activities: Leadership; corporate development; market development; networking & communications; *Library:* NATI Library; Open to public

Newfoundland & Labrador Camping Association
Parent Name: Canadian Camping Association
27 Earle Dr., Pasadena NL A0L 1K0
Tel: 709-686-2363; *Fax:* 709-639-1636
Overview: A medium-sized provincial organization overseen by Canadian Camping Association
Mission: To facilitate the development of organized camping in order to provide educational, character-building & constructive

recreational experiences for all people; to develop awareness & appreciation of the natural environment

Newfoundland & Labrador Construction Association (NLCA)
Parent Name: Canadian Construction Association
#201, 333 Pippy Pl., St. John's NL A1B 3X2
Tel: 709-753-8920; *Fax:* 709-754-3968
e-mail: info@nfld.com
www.nlca.ca
Overview: A small provincial organization founded in 1968 overseen by Canadian Construction Association
Mission: To act as the voice of the construction industry in Newfoundland & Labrador; To enhance the professionalism & productivity of members through the development of policies; *Member of:* Canadian Construction Association
Chief Officer(s):
Keith McCarthy, Chair, 709-834-7473, Fax: 709-834-7310
keithmccarthy@nf.aibn.com
Rhonda Neary, President & Chief Operating Officer
rneary@nlca.ca
Frank Collins, Secretary-Treasurer, 709-726-8453, Fax: 709-726-8488
f.collins@nl.rogers.com
Susan Casey, Coordinator, Events
scasey@nlca.ca
Adelle Connors, Coordinator, Member Services
aconnors@nlca.ca
Membership: *Fees:* Schedule available, based upon volume of construction related business; *Member Profile:* Contractors, builders, & suppliers in Newfoundland & Labrador's construction industry; *Committees:* Standard Practices; Safety; Membership; Education & Training; Conference Planning; Golf
Activities: Promoting safety practices in the workplace; Facilitating networking opportunities; Offering the Electronic Plans Room for members; Providing the Gold Seal Certification program; Selling CCA / CCDC construction documents & guides; Providing educational programs & seminars; Developing standard tendering & contractual practices & procedures; Awarding scholarships & bursaries; *Speaker Service:* Yes
Meetings/Conferences:
For more information see Trade Shows, Conferences and Seminars Chapter
Newfoundland & Labrador Construction Association 2013 44th Annual Conference & Annual General Meeting
February 2013 St. John's, NL
Newfoundland & Labrador Construction Association 2013 General Membership Meeting
2013, NL
Newfoundland & Labrador Construction Association 2013 3nd Annual Construction Career Expo & Opportunities Fair
2013, NL
Newfoundland & Labrador Construction Association 2013 Annual Awards Gala
2013, NL
Publications:
•Newfoundland & Labrador Construction Association Weekly Bulletin
Type: Newsletter; *Frequency:* Weekly
Profile: Updates for NLCA members
•Newfoundland & Labrador Construction Association Membership Directory
Type: Directory
Profile: Featuring a Trade Classification Section

Newfoundland & Labrador Environment Network (NLEN)
Parent Name: Canadian Environmental Network
Environmental Gathering Place, PO Box 5125, Stn. C, 172 Military Rd., St. John's NL A1A 5V5
Tel: 709-753-7898; *Fax:* 709-726-2764
e-mail: nlen.ed@gmail.com
www.nlen.ca
www.facebook.com/166529556721191
twitter.com/nl_environet
www.youtube.com/user/NLenvironet
Overview: A small provincial organization founded in 1990 overseen by Canadian Environmental Network
Mission: To take an active role in protecting, restoring & enhancing the environment; committed to taking an advocacy & activist role in our community; to educate the public on environmental issues
Chief Officer(s):
Chris Hogan, Executive Director
Finances: *Funding Sources:* Membership dues
Membership: *Fees:* $30-$90; *Member Profile:* Organizations interested in environmental issues

Newfoundland & Labrador Environmental Industry Association (NEIA)
Parsons Bldg., #101, 90 O'Leary Ave., St. John's NL A1B 2C7
Tel: 709-772-3333; *Fax:* 709-772-3213
e-mail: info@neia.org
www.neia.org
Overview: A medium-sized provincial organization founded in 1992
Mission: To promote the growth & development of the environmental industry of Newfoundland & Labrador; to promote ethical behavior & high standards for environmental products & services; to provide a strong, unified voice toward all private sector, government & non-profit entities involved in the Newfoundland environmental industry.
Chief Officer(s):
Linda Bartlett, Executive Director
linda@neia.org
Bill Scott, President
wascott@nl.rogers.com
Finances: *Funding Sources:* Government; luncheons; seminars
Staff: 4 staff member(s); 20 volunteer(s)
Membership: 173; *Member Profile:* Full - commercial enterprises that provide environmental products & services in Newfoundland & Labrador; associate - individuals & organizations supportive of the aims & objectives of NEIA; *Committees:* Policy; Programs; Membership/Communications; Trade Development; Finance

Newfoundland & Labrador Federation of Agriculture
Parent Name: Canadian Federation of Agriculture
PO Box 1045, 308 Brookfield Rd., Bldg. 4, Mount Pearl NL A1N 3C9
Tel: 709-747-4874; *Fax:* 709-747-8827
e-mail: info@nlfa.ca
www.nlfa.ca
Overview: A medium-sized provincial organization overseen by Canadian Federation of Agriculture
Mission: To act as the united voice of farmers in Newfoundland & Labrador; To improve the agricultural industry in Newfoundland & Labrador; To advance the economic & social conditions of those in the agricultural industry
Chief Officer(s):
Paul Connors, Executive Director
paul@nlfa.ca
Matthew Carlson, Officer, Communications
mcarlson@nlfa.ca
Kim O'Rourke, Administrative Assistant
kimorourke@nlfa.ca
Jamie Warren, Officer, Industry Development
jamie@nlfa.ca
Gerry Sullivan, Coordinator, Agriculture Awareness & Agri-Tourism
gerry@nlfa.ca
Christa Wright, Coordinator, Agriculture in the Classroom
christa@nlfa.ca
Finances: *Funding Sources:* Membership fees; Federal or provincial government programs
Membership: *Fees:* Schedule available, based upon farm gate revenue; *Member Profile:* Farmers & farmer groups in Newfoundland & Labrador
Activities: Assisting in the formulation of agricultural policies; Providing information about the state of the industry
Meetings/Conferences:
For more information see Trade Shows, Conferences and Seminars Chapter
Newfoundland & Labrador Federation of Agriculture 2013 Annual General Meeting
2013, NL
Publications:
•AgriView [a publication of Newfoundland & Labrador Federation of Agriculture]
Type: Newsletter; *Frequency:* Semiannually; *Accepts Advertising*; *Editor:* Matthew Carlson; *ISSN:* 1911-2297; *Price:* Free with Newfoundland & LabradorFederation of Agriculture membership
Profile: Feature articles, news, forthcoming events, & safety information

Newfoundland & Labrador Federation of Municipalities ***See*** Municipalities Newfoundland & Labrador

Newfoundland & Labrador Forest Protection Association
Parent Name: Canadian Forestry Association
PO Box 728, Mount Pearl NL A1N 2C2
Tel: 709-729-1012; *Fax:* 709-368-2740
e-mail: nlfpa@nfld.com
www.nlfpa.nfol.ca
Overview: A medium-sized provincial organization founded in 1910 overseen by Canadian Forestry Association
Mission: To maintain Newfoundland's forests as a productive & renewable resource;to increase public awareness, school education & natural appreciation of forests; to bring about better understanding of forests to people of all ages & backgrounds.
Chief Officer(s):
Doug Rex, Executive Director
William Furey, President
Finances: *Annual Operating Budget:* Less than $50,000
Membership: *Committees:* Public Education
Activities: *Awareness Events:* National Forest Week, May; *Speaker Service:* Yes

Newfoundland & Labrador Health Libraries Association (NLHLA)
Parent Name: Canadian Health Libraries Association
c/o Health Sciences Library, Memorial Univ. of Newfoundland, St. John's NL A1B 3V6
Tel: 709-777-8951
www.chla-absc.ca/?q=en/node/78
Overview: A medium-sized provincial organization founded in 1979 overseen by Canadian Health Libraries Association
Mission: To promote the provision of a high quality library service to the health community in Newfoundland & Labrador through mutual assistance & communication; to provide professional support to the membership by offering continuing education opportunities; Affiliation(s): Canadian Health Libraries Association
Chief Officer(s):
Shannon Gordon, President
sgordon@mun.ca
Finances: *Annual Operating Budget:* Less than $50,000
Membership: 35; *Fees:* $10; *Member Profile:* People who work in hospital & other health-related libraries & resource centres throughout Newfoundland & Labrador
Activities: NLHLA Lifeline (internet newsletter); initiate & coordinate projects to improve library services & information access in the health care field in Newfoundland

Newfoundland & Labrador Institute of Agrologists (NLIA)
Parent Name: Agricultural Institute of Canada
PO Box 978, Mount Pearl NL A1N 3C9
Tel: 709-772-4170
www.aic.ca/agrology/nlia.cfm
Overview: A small provincial licensing organization founded in 1988 overseen by Agricultural Institute of Canada
Mission: Dedicated to the professional aspects of Canadian agriculture.
Chief Officer(s):
Gary Bishop, President/Treasurer
gary.bishop@agr.gc.ca
Samir Debnath, Registrar
Finances: *Annual Operating Budget:* Less than $50,000
Membership: 40; *Fees:* $110

Newfoundland & Labrador Lung Association (NLLA)
Parent Name: Canadian Lung Association
Carnell Building, PO Box 13457, Stn. A, 15 Pippy Pl., 2nd Fl., St. John's NL A1B 4B8
Tel: 709-726-4664; *Fax:* 709-726-2550
Toll-Free: 888-566-5864
e-mail: info@nf.lung.ca
www.nf.lung.ca
Overview: A small provincial charitable organization founded in 1944 overseen by Canadian Lung Association
Mission: To achieve healthy breathing for the people of Newfoundland & Labrador
Environmental Activity: Increasing awareness of the link between air pollution & respiratory illness
Chief Officer(s):
Greg Noel, Acting Executive Director, 709-726-4664 Ext. 213
greg.noel@nf.lung.ca
Finances: *Funding Sources:* Donations; Fundraising; Sponsorships
Activities: Organizing fundraisers; Supporting research; Providing education; Offering support groups in areas such asthma, COPD, & smoking cessation; Engaging in advocacy

activities; *Awareness Events:* Idle Free School Program; Retire Your Ride
Publications:
•Newfoundland & Labrador Lung Association Newsletter
Type: Newsletter

Newfoundland & Labrador Medical Association (NLMA)
Parent Name: Canadian Medical Association
164 MacDonald Dr., St. John's NL A1A 4B3
Tel: 709-726-7424; *Fax:* 709-726-7525
Toll-Free: 800-563-2003
e-mail: nlma@nlma.nl.ca
www.nlma.nl.ca
Overview: A medium-sized provincial organization founded in 1924 overseen by Canadian Medical Association
Mission: To represent & support physicians in Newfoundland & Labrador; provide leadership in the promotion of good health & the provision of quality health care to the people of the province
Chief Officer(s):
Sandra Luscombe, President
president@nlma.nl.ca
Robert Ritter, Executive Director, 709-726-7424 Ext. 302
rritter@nlma.nl.ca
Finances: *Annual Operating Budget:* $500,000-$1.5 Million; *Funding Sources:* Membership dues
Staff: 11 staff member(s); 60 volunteer(s)
Membership: 1,600; *Fees:* $1,394; *Member Profile:* Physicians; medical students; residents; retired physicians

Newfoundland & Labrador Outfitters Association (NLOA)
Goodhouse Building, 93 West St., 2nd Fl., Corner Brook NL A2H 2Y5
Tel: 709-639-5926
Toll-Free: 866-420-6562
e-mail: janeshears@nloa.ca
www.nloa.ca
Overview: A small provincial organization
Mission: To assist hunting & fishing outfitters throughout Newfoundland & Labrador; To work with government departments & other organizations that impact the outfitting industry
Chief Officer(s):
Melissa Byrne, Coordinator, Project Support
melissa@nloa.ca
Keith Payne, Executive Director, 709-634-9962
keithpayne@nloa.ca
Membership: *Member Profile:* Licensed hunting & fishing outfitter operations in Newfoundland & Labrador that uphold the ethics & goals of the association
Activities: Providing information to hunting & fishing outfitters

Newfoundland & Labrador Parks & Recreation Association *See* Recreation Newfoundland & Labrador

Newfoundland & Labrador Public Health Association (NLPHA)
Parent Name: Canadian Public Health Association
PO Box 8172, St. John's NL A1B 3M9
Overview: A small provincial organization founded in 1978 overseen by Canadian Public Health Association
Mission: To advocate for the physical, emotional, social, & environmental well-being of Newfoundland & Labrador's people & communities; *Member of:* Canadian Public Health Association (CPHA)
Chief Officer(s):
Fay Matthews, President, 709-759-3359
fay.matthews@easternhealth.ca
Elizabeth Wright, Secretary
Pat Murray, Treasurer
Finances: *Funding Sources:* Donations
Membership: *Fees:* $20 direct NLPHA membership; $150 regular conjoint CPHA & NLPHA membership; $98 student conjoint CPHA & NLPHA membership; *Member Profile:* Individuals in Newfoundland & Labrador who are interested in public health & community activities, such as health & community service workers, researchers, & educators
Activities: Raising awareness of public health issues; Addressing public health issues, such as school nutrition, food security, mental health services, family life education, fetal alcohol syndrome, primary health care, & low level flying; Providing education; Offering prevention programming; Liaising with partners & community organizations to strengthen community health; Offering monthly business & educational teleconferences
Publications:
•Newfoundland & Labrador Public Health Association Newsletter
Type: Newsletter; *Editor:* Douglas Howse

Newfoundland & Labrador Safety Council *See* Safety Services Newfoundland and Labrador

Newfoundland & Labrador Water Well Corporation *See* Newfoundland/Labrador Ground Water Association

Newfoundland & Labrador Wildlife Federation (NWLF)
Parent Name: Canadian Wildlife Federation
15 Conran St., St. John's NL A1E 5L8
Tel: 709-368-6180
e-mail: ward.sampson@nf.sympatico.ca
www.nlwf.ca
Overview: A medium-sized provincial organization founded in 1962 overseen by Canadian Wildlife Federation
Mission: To foster awareness & enjoyment of the natural world; To promote the sustainable use of natural resources; To protect wildlife & its habitat through conservation & effective wildlife management; Affiliation(s): Over 15 affiliated conservation groups, including the Canadian Wildlife Federation (CWF), & Rod & Gun Clubs from St. John's, Bay Of Islands, Green Bay, Baie d'Espoir, Marystown, South East Placentia, & Grand Falls
Environmental Activity: Undertaking & sponsoring research related to wildlife & the environment; Recommending legislative changes for the benefit of wildlife & its habitat; Increasing understanding of the impact of human activities on the environment
Chief Officer(s):
Bernie Rumboldt, Contact, 709-364-8415
Membership: *Member Profile:* Clubs or organizations; Individuals; Associate members; Honorary members
Activities: Liaising with government agencies & organizations with similar goals; Conducting educational programs in conservation

Newfoundland Alliance of Technical Industries *See* Newfoundland & Labrador Association of Technology Companies

Newfoundland Aquaculture Industry Association (NAIA)
PO Box 23176, 20 Mount Scio Pl., St. John's NL A1B 4J9
Tel: 709-754-2854; *Fax:* 709-754-2981
www.naia.ca
Overview: A small provincial organization
Mission: To facilitate the commercial development of aquaculture in Newfoundland; To strive towards excellence in quality, safety, environmental sustainability, & profitability; To act as the voice of the industry in the province; *Member of:* Canadian Aquaculture Industry Alliance (CAIA); National Seafood Sector Council (NSSC)
Chief Officer(s):
Miranda Pryor, Executive Director
miranda@naia.ca
Job Halfyard, President, 709-675-2511
Robert Barry, Secretary, 709-576-7292
Jennifer Caines, Treasurer, 709-665-3168
Membership: *Fees:* $400 regular members; $200 associate members; *Member Profile:* Finfish & shellfish farmers in Newfoundland; Primary & secondary processors; Hatcheries producers; Supply & service companies; Academic institutions
Activities: Liaising with government; Offering training & advice; Providing business intelligence; *Awareness Events:* Aquaculture Week, June
Publications:
•Cold Harvester [a publication of the Newfoundland Aquaculture Industry Association]
Type: Magazine; *Frequency:* Quarterly
Profile: Information about the successes & challenges of the aquaculture industry for Newfoundland Aquaculture Industry Association members
•Newfoundland Aquaculture Industry Association Member Directory
Type: Directory

Newfoundland Horticultural Society
PO Box 28086, Stn. Avalon Mall, St. John's NL A1B 4J8
e-mail: NHSweb@nl.rogers.com
trenchfoot.2y.net/nfldhort
Overview: A small provincial organization founded in 1963
Mission: To encourage an interest in all aspects of gardening as related to Newfoundland conditions; Affiliation(s): Royal Horticultural Society
Chief Officer(s):
Frank Rose, Treasurer
Finances: *Annual Operating Budget:* Less than $50,000; *Funding Sources:* Membership fees
Membership: 104; *Fees:* $20
Activities: Monthly meetings; garden visits in summer; *Awareness Events:* Garden Show, August

Newfoundland/Labrador Ground Water Association
Parent Name: Canadian Ground Water Association
PO Box 160, Doyles NL A0N 1J0
Tel: 709-955-2561; *Fax:* 709-955-3402
e-mail: gwater@nf.sympatico.ca
Previous Name: Newfoundland & Labrador Water Well Corporation
Overview: A small provincial organization overseen by Canadian Ground Water Association
Mission: To promote the protection & management of ground water in Newfoundland & Labrador
Chief Officer(s):
Francis Gale, Contact
Activities: Increasing public awareness about ground water protection

Niagara Falls Nature Club (NFNC)
PO Box 901, Niagara Falls ON L2E 6V8
e-mail: rick.y@sympatico.ca
niagaranatureclub.tripod.com
Overview: A small local charitable organization founded in 1967
Mission: To promote awareness, understanding, preservation, & protection of the natural habitat of the Niagara area
Chief Officer(s):
Win Laar, Contact, 905-262-5057
Membership: *Fees:* $15 students; $25 single members; $35 families
Activities: Arranging programs & field trips; Conducting regular meetings at the Niagara Falls Public Library
Awards:
•R.W. Sheppard Award (Award)
To honour an individual or organization for their contribution, through education, conservation or research, in the field of nature
Publications:
•Nature Niagara News
Type: Newsletter; *Editor:* Margaret Pickles; *ISSN:* 0829-1241
Profile: Articles about local nature

Niagara Peninsula Conservation Foundation (NPCF)
250 Thorold Rd. West, 3rd Fl., Welland ON L3C 3W2
Tel: 905-788-3135; *Fax:* 905-788-1121
e-mail: info@npca.ca
www.conservation-niagara.on.ca
Also Known As: Conservation Niagara Foundation
Overview: A small local charitable organization founded in 1969
Mission: To raise funds in support of the Niagara Peninsula Conservation Authority in order to undertake programs designed to further the conservation, restoration, development and management of natural resources within the Niagara Watershe.; *Member of:* Canadian Centre for Philanthropy
Chief Officer(s):
Terry McDougall, Executive Director
Finances: *Annual Operating Budget:* $100,000-$250,000; *Funding Sources:* Donations; bequests; grants
Staff: 10 volunteer(s)
Membership: 15; *Member Profile:* Member must be approved by conservation authority
Activities: Grants; Donations; Bequests and Special Events; *Awareness Events:* Golf Tournament, June; Elimination Draw & Dinner, Nov.

Niagara Peninsula Geological Society (NPGS)
c/o Barry Douglas, 17 Lochinvar Dr., St Catharines ON L2T 2B5
www.ccfms.ca/Clubs/NPGS
Overview: A small local organization founded in 1962
Mission: To share knowledge in geology, mineralogy, petrology, palaeontology, & lapidary; *Member of:* Central Canadian Federation of Mineralogical Societies (CCFMS)
Chief Officer(s):
Patti Anderson, President
meriton@cogeco.ca
Darlene Sloggett, Vice-President
desleo2056@cogeco.ca
Dave Baker, Secretary
bbaker160@cogeco.ca
Barry Douglas, Treasurer
barry.douglas@cogeco.ca

Membership: *Fees:* $15 individuals; $20 families; *Member Profile:* Individuals interested in collecting rocks, minerals, & fossils & in jewellery making
Activities: Hosting monthly meetings from September to June; Arranging collecting field trips; Teaching lapidary techniques; Lending equipment, such as a rock splitter, & microscope; *Awareness Events:* Gem, Mineral, & Fossil Show & Sale, June; *Library:* Niagara Peninsula Geological Society Lending Library
Publications:
•The Pink Dolomite Saddle Bulletin
Type: Newsletter; *Frequency:* 10 pa; *Editor:* John Tordiff; *Price:* Free with NPGS membership; $10 non-members
Profile: Upcoming regional events, club activities, & general interest articles

Nickel Development Institute ***See*** Nickel Institute

Nickel Institute
Brookfield Place, #2700, 161 Bay St., Toronto ON M5J 2S1
Tel: 416-591-7999; *Fax:* 416-591-7987
e-mail: ni_toronto@nickelinstitute.org
www.nickelinstitute.org
Previous Name: Nickel Development Institute
Overview: A large national organization founded in 1984
Mission: Market development & applications oriented non-profit research organization of international nickel industry; to provide information for nickel users, designers, specifiers, educators & others interested in nickel-containing materials & their applications
Chief Officer(s):
Tim Aiken, Chairman
Kevin Bradley, President
Finances: *Annual Operating Budget:* Greater than $5 Million
Staff: 9 staff member(s)
Membership: 24 corporate; *Member Profile:* Nickel miner, smelter, refiner; *Committees:* Technical Program; Advisory
Activities: ; *Library:*

Niijkiwenhwag - Friends of Lake Superior Park
c/o Lake Superior Provincial Park, PO Box 267, Wawa ON P0S 1K0
Tel: 705-856-2284
e-mail: info@lakesuperiorpark.ca
www.lakesuperiorpark.ca
Overview: A small local organization founded in 1993
Mission: To achieve public awareness, knowledge & appreciation of the park's natural & cultural heritage; To coordinate special events & projects related to the park's theme; To support the development of park interpretive programs; To provide supplementary funds to complement park educational & scientific research projects
Chief Officer(s):
Christina Speer, Chair
Christina Speer, Chair
Membership: *Fees:* $10 individual; $15 family

Nipissing Environmental Watch (NEW)
PO Box 1543, North Bay ON P1B 8K6
Tel: 705-494-8935
www.nipissingenvironmentalwatch.org
Overview: A small local organization
Mission: A local, independent, non-profit, environmental group serving the Nipissing District

NOIA
Atlantic Place, #602, 215 Water St., St. John's NL A1C 6C9
Tel: 709-758-6610; *Fax:* 709-758-6611
www.noianet.com
Also Known As: Newfoundland & Labrador Oil & Gas Industries Association
Overview: A medium-sized provincial organization founded in 1977
Mission: To assist, promote & facilitate the participation of members in ocean industries, with particular emphasis on oil & gas, to enhance their growth & development; to promote the growth of ocean industry; to act as a focal point for representations to government bodies & agencies; to act as a source of information & education for members
Chief Officer(s):
Robert Cadigan, President & CEO
Finances: *Annual Operating Budget:* $500,000-$1.5 Million; *Funding Sources:* Membership fees; conferences, seminars & special events
Staff: 10 staff member(s); 100 volunteer(s)
Membership: 450; *Fees:* Schedule available; *Member Profile:* Those who develop, manufacture & market products & services in the oil & gas industry, both offshore & onshore; *Committees:* Board of Directors; Petroleum Research & Information; Membership Services & Internal Communications; External Relations; Finance & Human Resources; Policy & Positions
Activities: Promotes development of East Coast Canada's hydrocarbon resources & facilitates its membership's participation in oil & gas industries; *Library:* by appointment

NORA, An Association of Responsible Recyclers (NORA)
5965 Amber Ridge Rd., Haymarket VA 20169 USA
Tel: 703-753-4277; *Fax:* 703-733-2445
www.noranews.org
Previous Name: National Oil Recyclers Association
Overview: A medium-sized national licensing organization founded in 1984
Member of: American Society of Association Executives
Chief Officer(s):
Scott D. Parker, Executive Director
sparker@noranews.org
Finances: *Annual Operating Budget:* $250,000-$500,000
Staff: 4 staff member(s)
Membership: 200 companies; *Fees:* Based on company type; *Member Profile:* Liquid recyclers & vendors; *Committees:* Membership; Marketing; Conference; Governmental Affairs; Parts cleanin; Chemical Recycling; Used Oil Recycling; Ethics/Standards; Strategic Planning; Associate Advisory
Activities: *Rents Mailing List:* Yes

Norfolk County Agricultural Society
172 South Dr., Simcoe ON N3Y 1G6
Tel: 519-426-7280; *Fax:* 519-426-7286
www.norfair.com
Overview: A small local organization
Chief Officer(s):
Karen Matthews, General Manager
kmatthews@norfolkcountyfair.com

Norfolk Field Naturalists (NFN)
PO Box 995, Simcoe ON N3Y 5B3
Tel: 519-586-2603
e-mail: info@norfolkfieldnaturalists.org
www.norfolkfieldnaturalists.org
Overview: A small local organization founded in 1962
Mission: Dedicated to the acquisition & extension of knowledge of natural history & appreciation, enjoyment & stewardship of natural environment, especially within the region of Haldimand-Norfolk; *Member of:* Federation of Ontario Naturalists; Long Point Bird Observatory; Carolinian Canada
Chief Officer(s):
Bernie Solymar, President
solymar@nornet.on.ca
Finances: *Annual Operating Budget:* Less than $50,000; *Funding Sources:* Membership dues; donations; LPBO Birdathon
Staff: 10 volunteer(s)
Membership: 150; *Fees:* $20 single; $30 family; *Committees:* Local Environmental Protection; Waste Management
Activities: Field trips for birding; free identification; nature appreciation; local natural heritage sites; *Speaker Service:* Yes

Nornet-Yukon ***See*** Yukon Territory Environmental Network

North American Association for Environmental Education (NAAEE)
#540, 2000 P St. NW, Washington DC 20036 USA
Tel: 202-419-0412; *Fax:* 202-419-0415
e-mail: bredy@naaee.org
www.naaee.org
Overview: A medium-sized international organization founded in 1971
Mission: To promote education about environmental issues
Environmental Activity: Supporting the work of environmental educators
Chief Officer(s):
Brian A. Day, Executive Director
brian@naaee.org
Finances: *Funding Sources:* Donations
Membership: *Member Profile:* Practitioners in the fields of environmental education, outdoor education, & conservation education; Students in the field of environmental education
Activities: Providing professional development events; Offering networking opportunities
Publications:
•Conservation Education & Outreach Techniques
Number of Pages: 496; *Author:* S. Jacobson; M. McDuff; M.C. Monroe; *ISBN:* 0-19-856772-3
Profile: Case sudies & application exercises
•EE News [a publication of the North American Association for Environmental Education]
Type: Newsletter
•Elementary School Teachers' Beliefs About Teaching Environmental Education
Number of Pages: 48; *Author:* S. Middlestadt; R. Ledsky; *ISBN:* 1-884008-76-3
•Environmental Education at the Early Childhood Level
Number of Pages: 126; *Editor:* R. Wilson; *ISBN:* 1-884008-14-3
•Environmental Education in the Schools: Creating a Program That Works!
Number of Pages: 500; *Author:* J. Braus; D. Wood; *ISBN:* 1-884008-08-9
•Environmental Education Research, Special Issue on Significant Life Experiences
Number of Pages: 114; *Editor:* T. Tanner; *ISBN:* 1350-4622
•Environmental Education Undergraduate & Graduate Programs & Faculty in the United States
Author: Michaela Zint; Aimee Giles; *ISBN:* 1-884008-79-B
•Environmental Education: Academia's Response
Number of Pages: 96; *Author:* E. Kormondy; P.B. Corcoran; *ISBN:* 1-884008-51-8
•Environmental Literacy in the United States: What Should Be...What Is...Getting from Here to There
Number of Pages: 80; *Editor:* T. Volk; W. McBeth; *ISBN:* 1-884008-73-9
•Evaluating Your Environmental Education Programs: A Workbook for Practitioners
Author: J.A. Ernst; M.C. Monroe; B. Simmons
Profile: Case sudies & application exercises
•A Field Guide to Environmental Literacy: Making Strategic Investments in Environmental Education
Number of Pages: 110; *Author:* J.L. Elder; *ISBN:* 1-884008-87-9
•NAAEE [North American Association for Environmental Education] Communicator
Type: Newsletter
•North American Association for Environmental Education Conference Proceedings
•Preparing Effective Environmental Educators
Type: Monograph; *Number of Pages:* 89; *Editor:* Dr. Bora Simmons; *ISBN:* 1-884008-88-7
•Using a Logic Model to Review & Analyze an Environmental Education Program
Type: Monograph; *Number of Pages:* 72; *Editor:* Thomas C. Marcinkowski; *ISBN:* 1-884008-86-0
•What's Fair Got To Do With It: Diversity Cases from Environmental Educators
Number of Pages: 119; *Editor:* Tania J. Madfes; *ISBN:* 0-914409-20-4

North American Bird Conservation Initiative Canada (NABCI)
c/o Canadian Wildlife Service-Environment Canada, 351, boul. St-Joseph, 3e étage, Gatineau QC K1A 0H3
Tel: 819-994-0512; *Fax:* 819-994-4445
e-mail: nabci@ec.gc.ca
www.nabci.net
Mission: The NABCI is a coordinated effort among Canada, the United States & Mexico to maintain the diversity & abundance of all North American birds. National coordination of this effort in Canada occurs through the NABCI Canada Council, chaired by the Asst. Deputy Minister of Environment Canada's Environmental Conservation Service. Council members include representatives from provincial governments, non-government organizations, four bird plans (waterfowl, landbirds, shorebirds, waterbirds), & habitat joint ventures. In Canada, the joint venture conservation projects has three habitat joint ventures (Pacific Coast, Prairie Habitat, Eastern Habitat) & three species (Arctic Goose, Black Duck, Sea Duck.)

North American Native Plant Society (NANPS)
PO Box 84, Stn. D, Toronto ON M9A 4X1
Tel: 416-631-4438
e-mail: nanps@nanps.org
www.nanps.org
www.facebook.com/nativeplant
Previous Name: Canadian Wildflower Society
Overview: A medium-sized provincial charitable organization founded in 1984
Mission: Dedicated to the study, conservation & cultivation of North America's wild flora.; *Member of:* Federation of Ontario Naturalists
Chief Officer(s):
Ruth Zaugg, Secretary
Membership: *Fees:* $20/year

Activities: Members-only seed exchange; Native Garden Award; Native Plant Sale
Publications:
•Blazing Star [a publication of the North American Native Plant Society]
Type: Journal; *Frequency:* Quarterly

North American Recycled Rubber Association (NARRA)
#24, 1621 McEwen Dr., Whitby ON L1N 9A5
Tel: 905-433-7769; *Fax:* 905-433-0905
www.recycle.net/recycle/assn/narra
Overview: A small national organization founded in 1994
Mission: The Association provides a unified voice, as well as a communication network & research facility, for issues of concern to those involved in rubber recycling across North America.; *Member of:* Canadian Environment Industry Association; Ontario Automotive Recyclers Association; International Tire & Rubber Association
Chief Officer(s):
Diane Sarracini, Office Manager
Finances: *Annual Operating Budget:* $100,000-$250,000; *Funding Sources:* Membership dues; research
Staff: 1 staff member(s); 1 volunteer(s)
Membership: 100; *Fees:* $350
Activities: Provides specialized training & feasibility studies; annual convention (March) & newsletter; *Speaker Service:* Yes; *Library:* Rubber Recycling Library; Open to public by appointment

North American Society for Oceanic History (NASOH)
Texas Christian University, Department Of History, PO Box 297260, Fort Worth TX 76129 USA
www.nasoh.org
Overview: A small international organization founded in 1974
Mission: To provide a forum for maritime history; To study & promote naval & maritime history; To promote exchange of information among its members & others interested in history of seas, lakes & inland waterways; To call attention to books, articles, other publications & documents pertinent to naval & maritime history; to work with local, regional, national & international organizations as well as appropriate government agencies towards goal of fostering a more general awareness & appreciation for North America's naval & maritime heritage
Chief Officer(s):
Warren Reiss, President
Finances: *Annual Operating Budget:* Less than $50,000
Membership: 220; *Fees:* $65 US individual/corporate; $18 US student
Meetings/Conferences:
For more information see Trade Shows, Conferences and Seminars Chapter
North American Society for Oceanic History Annual Conference 2013
May 2013 Alpena, MI
North American Society for Oceanic History Annual Conference 2014
2014

North American Waterfowl Management Plan (NAWMP) / Le plan nord-américain de gestion de la sauvagine
c/o Canadian Wildlife Service, Place Vincent Massey, 351, boul St. Joseph, 7th Fl., Gatineau QC K1A 0H3
Tel: 819-934-6036; *Fax:* 819-934-6017
e-mail: nawmp@ec.gc.ca
www.nawmp.ca
Mission: The North American Waterfowl Management Plan is an international action plan to conserve migratory birds throughout the continent. The Plan's goal is toreturn waterfowl populations to their 1970's levels by conserving wetland and upland habitat. Canada & the United States signed the Plan in 1986 in reaction to critically low numbers of waterfowl. Mexico joined in 1994 making it a truly continental effort. The Plan is a partnership of federal, provincial/state & municipal governments, non-governmental organizations, private companies & many individuals, all working towards achieving better wetland habitat for the benefit of migratory birds, other wetland-associated species & people. The Plan's unique combination of biology, landscape conservation & partnerships comprise its exemplary conservation legacy. Plan projects are international in scope, but implemented at regional levels. These projects contribute to the protection of habitat & wildlife species across the North American landscape. In fact, the North American Waterfowl Management Plan is considered one of the most successful conservation initiatives in the world.
Awards:
•Great Blue Heron Award (Award)
Recognizes primary participants in the Plan who have made major, long-term national contributions that result in benefits to waterfowl & other bird populations of North America; for US nominations - Executive Director, N. American Waterfowl & Wetlands Office, US Fish & Wildlife Service, Rm.110, 4401 N. Fairfax Dr., Arlington VA 22203, ph. 703/358-1784; for Mexican nominations - Humberto Berlanga, Instituto Nacional de Ecolgis, Avenida Revoluclon 1425-19, Colonia Tlacopoc San Angel, Mexico D.F.01040, ph.(52-56)24-33-09-09; for Canadian nomination contact above address *Eligibility:* Nominees must demonstrate protection, maintenance, restoration or improvement of habitat for waterfowl & migratory bird populations; or initiation of legislation or major corporate or public policy that helped attain goals of the plan, & benefit waterfowl & migratory bird populations; or donation of a gift valued at $10,000 or more to any plan partner; or fostering of cooperation & coordination that contributes to plan goals *Deadline:* February *Amount:* A carving of a Great Blue Heron & a certificate
•International Canvasback Award (Award)
For individuals, corporations, & organizations who have made substantial, long-term international contributions to the implementation & continuation of the plan throughout North America *Deadline:* February *Amount:* An original decoy carving of a Canvasback & a certificate
Chief Officer(s):
Tasha Sargent, Coordinator, Canadian Wildlife Service
tasha_sargent@pcjv.org

Arctic Goose Joint Venture
e-mail: agvj@ec.gc.ca
www.agjv.ca
Chief Officer(s):
Deanna Dixon, Coordinator
deanna.dixon@ec.gc.ca

Black Duck Joint Venture
www.blackduckjv.org
Chief Officer(s):
Brigitte Collins, Coordinator
brigitte.collins@ec.gc.ca

Eastern Habitat Joint Venture
www.ehjv.ca
Chief Officer(s):
Patricia Edwards, Coordinator
patricia.edwards@ec.gc.ca

Pacific Coast Joint Venture
www.pcjv.org
Chief Officer(s):
Tasha Sargent, Coordinator
tasha_sargent@pcjv.org

Prairie Habitat Joint Venture
e-mail: phjv@ec.gc.ca
www.phjv.ca
Chief Officer(s):
Deanna Dixon
deanna.dixon@ec.gc.ca

North Central Local Government Association (NCLGA)
c/o Maxine Koppe, #206, 155 George St., Prince George BC V2L 1P8
Tel: 250-564-6585; *Fax:* 250-564-6514
ncma.enorthernbc.com
twitter.com/NCLGA
Overview: A small local organization
Mission: To address the issues of local governments; To mobilize initiatives to benefit member governments
Chief Officer(s):
Mitch Campsall, President
president@nclga.ca
Bruce D. Christensen, First Vice-President
Brian Frenkel, Second Vice-President
Maxine Koppe, Executive Director
mkoppe@nclga.ca
Membership: 40 municipalities; *Member Profile:* Elected officials from member regional municipalities, districts, cities, towns, & villages in the north area of British Columbia
Meetings/Conferences:
For more information see Trade Shows, Conferences and Seminars Chapter
North Central Local Government Association 2013 58th Annual General Meeting & Convention
May 2013 Quesnel, BC
Publications:
•Issues in Focus [a publication of the North Central Local Government Association]
Type: Newsletter; *Frequency:* 8 pa

North Okanagan Naturalists Club (NONC)
PO Box 473, Vernon BC V1T 6M4
Tel: 250-545-0490
www.nonc.ca
Overview: A small local charitable organization founded in 1951
Mission: To foster an interest in nature; to record data & sightings of flora & fauna; to educate young people; to hold land; *Member of:* The Federation of BC Naturalists; Canadian Nature Federation
Chief Officer(s):
Rod Drennan, President, 250-545-4999
Finances: *Annual Operating Budget:* Less than $50,000; *Funding Sources:* Dues; social activities; club sales
Staff: 3 volunteer(s)
Membership: 180; *Fees:* $35 adults; $50 family; *Committees:* Conservation; Education; Land Stewardship; Socials; Trips; Ways & Means
Activities: *Awareness Events:* Annual Field & Dinner Day, May

North Okanagan Organic Association (NOOA)
C76 Cedar Hill Rd., RR#1, Vernon BC V0E 1W0
Tel: 250-540-2557
e-mail: northorganics@gmail.com
Overview: A small local licensing organization
Mission: To encourage the practice of soil regeneration & sustainable food production, through the use of organic methods as per the Canadian definition; To certify members' food products that are organically grown in accordance with the association's guidelines; Affiliation(s): Certified Organic Associations of BC
Chief Officer(s):
Molly Thurston, President
Cara Nunn, Administrator
Finances: *Annual Operating Budget:* Less than $50,000
Membership: 101; *Fees:* $325; *Committees:* Certification; Standards
Activities: Certification of members' food products; monthly meeting for information on organic practices; *Library:* by appointment

North Peace Applied Research Association (NPARA) Parent Name: Agricultural Research & Extension Council of Alberta
PO Box 750, Manning AB T0H 2M0
Tel: 780-836-3354; *Fax:* 780-836-2670
e-mail: npara1@telus.net
www.areca.ab.ca/nparahome.html
Overview: A small local organization founded in 1988 overseen by Agricultural Research & Extension Council of Alberta
Mission: To conduct agricultural research, trials, extension & research plots; *Member of:* Agricultural Research & Extension Council of Alberta
Chief Officer(s):
Nora Paulovich, Manager & Coordinator, Research
Tom Fromme, Specialist, Cereal & Oilseed
npara6@telus.net
Membership: *Fees:* $20
Publications:
•NPARA [North Peace Applied Research Association] Newsletter
Type: Newsletter

North Saskatchewan Watershed Alliance
0504 - 49 St., Edmonton AB T6B 2M9
Tel: 780-442-6363; *Fax:* 780-495-0610
e-mail: water@nswa.ab.ca
www.nswa.ab.ca
Overview: A small local organization founded in 2000
Mission: To protect & improve water quality & ecosystem functioning in the North Saskatchewan Watershed within Alberta
Chief Officer(s):
David Trew, Executive Director, 780-496-3474
Tom Cottrell, IWMP Coordinator, 780-496-6962
tom.cottrell@edmonton.ca
Finances: *Annual Operating Budget:* $50,000-$100,000; *Funding Sources:* Industry; government; grants
Staff: 6 staff member(s)
Membership: 140

Activities: State of watershed reporting; watershed planning; education & awareness; stewardship; *Library:* by appointment

North Shore Forest Products Marketing Board
PO Box 386, Bathurst NB E2A 3Z3
Tel: 506-548-8958
e-mail: nsfpmb@nb.aibn.com
www.forestrysyndicate.com
Overview: A small local organization founded in 1973
Mission: To negotiate with industry & government on behalf of the private wood producers of the regulated area for fair prices for the products of the woodlots & to promote improved forest management; Affiliation(s): NB Forest Products Commission
Chief Officer(s):
Alain Landry, General Manager
Patrick Doucet, Sylviculture Manager
patrick.doucet@forestrysyndicate.com
Finances: *Annual Operating Budget:* Greater than $5 Million; *Funding Sources:* Regional Government
Staff: 10 staff member(s); 10 volunteer(s)
Membership: 2,000 individual
Activities: *Rents Mailing List:* Yes

North Shuswap Naturalists
Parent Name: Federation of BC Naturalists
Comp. 110, Site 11, RR#1, Chase BC V0E 1M0
Tel: 250-679-8763
Overview: A small local charitable organization overseen by Federation of BC Naturalists
Mission: To promote the enjoyment of nature through environmental appreciation & conservation; To encourage wise use & conservation of natural resources & environmental protection.
Chief Officer(s):
Rudy Vervoort, Contact
Finances: *Annual Operating Budget:* Less than $50,000; *Funding Sources:* Membership fees
Membership: 21; *Fees:* $20; *Member Profile:* Mostly seniors
Activities: Monthly meetings (Sept.-June); summer field trips

Northeast Avalon ACAP, Inc.
PO Box 1027, Stn. C, 172 Military Rd., St. John's NL A1C 5M3
Tel: 709-726-9673; *Fax:* 709-726-2764
e-mail: info@naacap.ca
www.naacap.ca
Also Known As: Atlantic Coastal Action Program
Previous Name: St. John's Harbour ACAP
Overview: A small local organization
Member of: NL Environmental Industries Association; NL Environment Network
Chief Officer(s):
Cal Baker, Chair
Patrick Wells, Secretary
Finances: *Annual Operating Budget:* $100,000-$250,000
Staff: 2 staff member(s); 25 volunteer(s)
Membership: 1-99
Activities: ; *Library:* Open to public by appointment

Northeast Organic Farming Association (NOFA)
Massachusetts Chapter, 411 Sheldon Rd., Barre MA 1005 USA
Tel: 978-355-2853; *Fax:* 978-355-4046
e-mail: nofa@nofamass.org
www.nofamass.org
Overview: A small local charitable organization founded in 1982
Mission: To educate members & the general public about the benefits of local organic systems based on complete cycles, natural materials & minimal waste for the health of individual beings, communities & the living planet
Chief Officer(s):
Julie Rawson, Executive Director
Finances: *Annual Operating Budget:* $250,000-$500,000; *Funding Sources:* Private donations; membership dues; conference fees
Staff: 17 staff member(s); 50 volunteer(s)
Membership: 865; *Fees:* US$30 individual; US$20 low income; US$40 family/institution; US$150 supporting
Activities: Educational conferences & workshops; videos on organic growing; information about apprenticeship programs matching farms seeking workers with people wanting to learn organic methods; Organic Food Guide map listing organic farmers in Massachusetts; bulk order of soil amendments; genetic engineering awareness; *Speaker Service:* Yes

Northern Interior Vegetation Management Association (NIVMA)
PO Box 460, Prince George BC V2L 4S6
Tel: 250-564-4115
Overview: A small local organization founded in 1988
Mission: To use common protocols & databases to adaptively & cost-effectively deliver defensible, effective, & ecologically sound practices that contribute to sustainable forest management
Chief Officer(s):
Naomi Donat, Manager
Finances: *Annual Operating Budget:* $100,000-$250,000
Staff: 1 staff member(s)
Membership: 16; *Fees:* Based on harvest levels; *Member Profile:* Forest industry & government, northern BC & Alberta

Northern Native Fishing Corporation (NNFC)
#160, 110 First Ave. West, Prince Rupert BC V8J 1A8
Tel: 250-627-8486; *Fax:* 250-624-6627
e-mail: nnfc@citytel.net
nnfc.coppermoon.ca
Overview: A small local organization founded in 1982
Mission: To preserve & enhance for individual native fishermen the economic opportunity to harvest & market marine resources by creating & ensuring access to the resources
Chief Officer(s):
Corinne McKay, General Manager
Activities: Fishing licenses

Northern Ontario Aquaculture Association
PO Box 124, 9050 Hwy. 6, #C, Little Current ON P0P 1K0
Tel: 705-368-1345; *Fax:* 705-368-0685
e-mail: ontarioaquaculture@manitoulin.net
www.ontarioaquaculture.com
Overview: A small local organization
Mission: The voice of Ontario's sustainable fish farming industry
Chief Officer(s):
Mike Meeker, President
Karen Tracey, Executive Director
noaa@manitoulin.net
Membership: 30; *Fees:* Non-voting members: $100 associate. Voting members: $500 supporting; $1,000 corporate; $4,000 patron; $2,000 sustaining

Northern Prospectors Association (NPA)
PO Box 535, Kirkland Lake ON P2N 3J5
Tel: 705-642-1982; *Fax:* 705-567-4426
www.northernprospectors.com
Overview: A small local organization founded in 1971
Mission: To act as a strong voice for the prospecting & mining industry; Affiliation(s): Ontario Prospectors Association
Chief Officer(s):
Dave Larocque, President
Membership: *Member Profile:* Members of the mining exploration community in the Kirkland Lake area, including prospectors & geologists
Activities: Offering courses on topics such as geology & geophysics; Hosting NPA gold panning events for tourists
Publications:
•The Explorationist [a publication of the Northern Prospectors Association & the Ontario Prospectors Association]
Type: Newsletter; *Frequency:* 10 pa; *Price:* Free with Northern Prospectors Association membership
Profile: Land use issues, the environment, & mining law, published in association with the Ontario ProspectorsAssociation

Northumberland Salmon Protection Association (NSPA)
#11042, Rte 430, Trout Brook NB E9E 1R4
Tel: 506-622-8834; *Fax:* 506-622-7691
www.nbsalmoncouncil.com/northumberland.htm
Overview: A small local organization
Member of: Atlantic Salmon Federation; Affiliation(s): New Brunswick Salmon Council
Chief Officer(s):
Debbie Norton, President, New Brunswick Salmon Council
adventures@upperoxbow.com
Membership: 200

Northwatch (NW)
PO Box 282, North Bay ON P1B 8H2
Tel: 705-497-0373; *Fax:* 705-476-7060
e-mail: northwatch@onlink.net
www.northwatch.org
Overview: A small local organization founded in 1988
Mission: To act as a representative body & to provide support to local citizens groups addressing environmental issues such as energy use, generation & conservation, forest conservation & wild areas protection, waste management & water quality issues, mining & militarization as well as other environmental concerns; to improve forest management, promote community involvement in mine monitoring & management & to prevent northeastern Ontario from becoming the receiving ground for foreign wastes, including Toronto's garbage, Ontario's biomedical waste, Canada's nuclear reactor fuel waste & PCBs from around the world; *Member of:* Canadian Environmental Network
Chief Officer(s):
B. Lloyd, Coordinator
Finances: *Annual Operating Budget:* Less than $50,000
Staff: 2 staff member(s); 100 volunteer(s)
Membership: 20 organizations; *Fees:* $10 individual; $25 group/supporting; *Committees:* Forest; Mining; Energy; Waste; Water
Activities: Advocacy; public education; regional meetings; workshops; tours; *Internships:* Yes; *Speaker Service:* Yes; *Library:* by appointment

Northwest Coalition for Alternatives to Pesticides (NCAP)
PO Box 1393, Eugene OR 97440-1393 USA
Tel: 541-344-5044; *Fax:* 541-344-6923
www.pesticide.org
www.facebook.com/pesticide.free
twitter.com/_ncap
www.youtube.com/user/NCAPVids
Overview: A medium-sized local charitable organization founded in 1977
Mission: Works to protect the health of people & the environment by advancing alternatives to pesticides
Chief Officer(s):
Kim Leval, Executive Director
kleval@pesticide.org
Betty McArdle, President
Finances: *Annual Operating Budget:* $250,000-$500,000; *Funding Sources:* Grants; donations
Staff: 9 staff member(s); 10 volunteer(s)
Membership: 2,300; *Fees:* $25; $15 limited income; $50 associate
Activities: Clean water for salmon; public education; sustainable agriculture; pesticide free parks; inert ingredient disclosure; *Internships:* Yes; *Library:* Open to public

Northwest Territories & Nunavut Association of Professional Engineers & Geoscientists (NAPEG)
Parent Name: Engineers Canada
#201, 4817 - 49 St., Yellowknife NT X1A 3S7
Tel: 867-920-4055; *Fax:* 867-873-4058
www.napeg.nt.ca
Overview: A medium-sized provincial licensing organization founded in 1978 overseen by Engineers Canada
Mission: To license professional engineers & professional geoscientists in the Northwest Territories & Nunavut; To regulate the practices of professional engineering & professional geoscience; To establish & maintain standards of knowledge, skill, care, & professional ethics among registrants; *Member of:* Engineers Canada
Chief Officer(s):
Hendrik Falck, President
Linda Golding, Executive Director
Victoria James, Coordinator, Registration
Finances: *Funding Sources:* Membership fees; Dues
Staff: 100 volunteer(s)
Membership: 397 + 781 Licensees; *Fees:* $300 registration; $220 annual dues; *Member Profile:* Accredited degree in engineering, geology or geophysics followed by 4 years of directly related experience in practice of engineering, geology & geophysics; Must pass Association's Professional Practice Examination; *Committees:* Council; Executive; Discipline; Membership/Enforcement; Professional Development; Public Relations; Newsletter; Professional Practice; Nominating; Planning; Environment; Finance
Activities: *Awareness Events:* National Engineering Week, March; National Science & Technology Week, October

Northwest Territories & Nunavut Chamber of Mines
PO Box 2818, #103, 5102-50 Ave., Yellowknife NT X1A 2R1
Tel: 867-873-5281; *Fax:* 867-920-2145
e-mail: info@miningnorth.com
www.miningnorth.com
Previous Name: Northwest Territories Chamber of Mines
Overview: A medium-sized provincial organization founded in 1967
Mission: To promote & assist the development & growth of mining & mineral exploration in NWT & Nunavut; Affiliation(s): Mining Association of Canada; Canadian Institute of Mining, Metallurgy & Petroleum
Chief Officer(s):

Tom Hoefer, Executive Director
executivedirector@miningnorth.com
Finances: *Annual Operating Budget:* $100,000-$250,000; *Funding Sources:* Membership fees
Staff: 2 staff member(s); 25 volunteer(s)
Membership: 200 corporate + 600 individual + 9 senior/lifetime; *Fees:* Schedule available; *Member Profile:* Persons & corporations interested in, or associated with, mining industry in NWT & Nunavut
Activities: *Awareness Events:* Mining Week, June; GeoScience Forum, Nov.; *Library:* Open to public by appointment

Northwest Territories Association of Communities (NWTAC)

Finn Hansen Bldg., #200, 5105 - 50th St., Yellowknife NT X1A 1S1
Tel: 867-873-8359; *Fax:* 867-873-3042
Toll-Free: 866-973-8359
www.nwtac.com
Overview: A medium-sized provincial organization founded in 1967
Mission: To promote the exchange of information amongst the community governments of the Northwest Territories and to provide a united front for the realization of goals.; *Member of:* Federation of Canadian Municipalities
Chief Officer(s):
Yvette Gonzalez, CEO
yvette@nwtac.com

Northwest Territories Association of Landscape Architects (NWTALA)

PO Box 1394, Yellowknife NT X1A 2P1
Tel: 867-920-2986; *Fax:* 867-920-2986
e-mail: atborow@internorth.com
Overview: A medium-sized provincial organization founded in 1991
Mission: To represent landscape architects in the Northwest Territories; Affiliation(s): Canadian Society of Landscape Architects (CSLA)
Membership: *Member Profile:* Landscape architects in the Northwest Territories

Northwest Territories Chamber of Mines *See* Northwest Territories & Nunavut Chamber of Mines

Northwest Territories Construction Association (NWTCA)
Parent Name: Canadian Construction Association

PO Box 2277, 4921 - 49th St., 3rd Fl., Yellowknife NT X1A 2P7
Tel: 867-873-3949; *Fax:* 867-873-8366
e-mail: director@nwtca.ca
www.nwtca.ca
Overview: A medium-sized provincial organization founded in 1976 overseen by Canadian Construction Association
Mission: To act as a voice for construction-related business in the Northwest Territories & Nunavut
Chief Officer(s):
Bob Doherty, President
bdoherty@ykfireprevention.ca
Niels Konge, Vice-President, Northwest Territories
nkonge@ssimicro.com
Brent Crooks, Vice-President, Nunavut
bcrooks@nig.ca
Trina Rentmeister, Secretary-Treasurer
drapes@ssimicro.com
Membership: *Fees:* $250; *Member Profile:* Construction-related businesses in the Northwest Territories & Nunavut
Activities: Lobbying governments on behalf of the construction industry

Northwest Territories Recreation & Parks Association (NWTRPA)
Parent Name: Canadian Parks & Recreation Association

PO Box 841, Yellowknife NT X1A 2N6
Tel: 867-873-5340; *Fax:* 867-669-6791
e-mail: admin@nwtrpa.org
www.nwtrpa.org
Overview: A small provincial organization founded in 1989 overseen by Canadian Parks & Recreation Association
Mission: To increase public awareness of recreation & parks; to enhance the quality of life of residents of the NWT through fostering the development of recreation & parks services; Affiliation(s): Sport North
Chief Officer(s):
Robin Langille, President, 867-777-8627
Geoff Ray, Executive Director
gray@nwtrpa.org
Finances: *Annual Operating Budget:* $50,000-$100,000; *Funding Sources:* Federal, territorial government
Staff: 6 staff member(s)
Membership: 100; *Fees:* $35 individual; $75 municipal or recreation committee; *Committees:* Executive; Corporate; Sponsorship
Activities: Recreation Code of Ethics; Recreation & Parks Resource Binder; Awards Program; Corporate Sponsorship; Active Living

Northwest Wildlife Preservation Society (NWPS)

#203, 5066 Kingsway, Burnaby BC V5H 2E7
Tel: 604-568-9160; *Fax:* 604-568-6152
e-mail: info@northwestwildlife.com
www.northwestwildlife.com
www.facebook.com/NorthwestWildlifePreservationSociety
twitter.com/NWwildlife
Overview: A small local organization founded in 1987
Mission: To ensure that healthy wildlife populations are preserved for their own intrinsic value & for the appreciation of all; To develop & provide educational, research & advisory services which can advance the public's awareness & knowledge about wildlife & wildlife systems in northwest North America; *Member of:* BC Endangered Species Coalition; Vancouver Urban Wildlife Committee; BC Environmental Network
Environmental Activity: Education & stewardship programs, including Wildlife in the Schools, Nature Walks & Workshops; & Youth Estuary Stewardship projects
Chief Officer(s):
Ann Peters, Executive Director, 604-568-9160, Fax: 604-568-6152
execdirector@northwestwildlife.com
Jim Pigott, President
Michele Kvarnstrom, Vice-President
James McBeath, Sec.-Treas.
Finances: *Annual Operating Budget:* $100,000-$250,000; *Funding Sources:* Donations; grants; honoria
Staff: 2 staff member(s); 60 volunteer(s)
Membership: 100+; *Fees:* $35 family; $20 individual; $15 senior/student; $100 corporate; *Committees:* Fundraising; Volunteer
Activities: *Awareness Events:* Green Ribbon Campaign, April; *Internships:* Yes; *Speaker Service:* Yes; *Library:* NWPS Wildlife Library; Open to public by appointment

Northwestern Ontario Municipal Association (NOMA)

PO Box 10308, Thunder Bay ON P7B 6T8
Tel: 807-683-6662
e-mail: admin@noma.on.ca
www.noma.on.ca
Overview: A medium-sized local organization founded in 1946
Mission: To consider matters of interest to municipalities in northwestern Ontario; To procure enactment of legislation which may be advantageous to northwestern Ontario's municipalities; *Member of:* Association of Municipalities of Ontario
Chief Officer(s):
Charla Robinson, Executive Director
Dennis Brown, President
Iain Angus, Vice-President
Finances: *Funding Sources:* Operating subsidy from the Ministry of Northern Development & Mines; Membership fees
Membership: 100-499;; *Fees:* $250 not-for-profit organizations; $500 businesses; *Member Profile:* Membership is attained from the Corporation of the City of Thunder Bay, the Kenora District Municipal Association, the Rainy River District Municipal Association, & the Thunder Bay District Municipal League; Associate membership is comprised of not-for-profit organizations & businesses
Activities: Advocating for northwestern Ontario's regional interests; Acting on matters where municipal rights may be affected; Promoting municipal interests; Offering opportunities for education & discussion to advance the standards of municipal government
Meetings/Conferences:
For more information see Trade Shows, Conferences and Seminars Chapter
Northwestern Ontario Municipal Association 2013 Annual General Meeting & Conference
April 2013 Thunder Bay, ON
Northwestern Ontario Municipal Association 2013 Annual Regional Conference
September 2013 Thunder Bay, ON

Not Far From The Tree

90 Croatia St., Toronto ON M6H 1K9
Tel: 416-363-6441
e-mail: info@notfarfromthetree.org
www.notfarfromthetree.org
Overview: A small local organization
Mission: The group operates a residential, fruit-picking program where teams of volunteers are dispatched to harvest fruit from trees that the owners would otherwise let go to waste. The fruit is divided equally among the ownners, volunteers & a local, community food distribution organization who can make good use of it.

Nova Forest Alliance

PO Box 208, 285 George St., Stewiacke NS B0N 2J0
Tel: 902-639-2921; *Fax:* 902-639-2981
e-mail: info@novaforestalliance.com
www.novaforestalliance.com
Overview: A small provincial organization

Nova Scotia Allergy & Environmental Health Association *See* Environmental Health Association of Nova Scotia

Nova Scotia Cattle Producers (NSCP)

#201, 332 Willow St., Truro NS B2N 5A5
Tel: 902-893-7455; *Fax:* 902-893-3397
e-mail: office@nscattle.ca
www.nscattle.ca
Previous Name: Nova Scotia Cattlemen's Association
Overview: A medium-sized provincial organization founded in 2004
Mission: To assist in the sustainable development of the beef production industry in Nova Scotia; *Member of:* Canadian Cattlemen's Association; Affiliation(s): National Check-off Agency; The Beef Cattle Research Agency; Beef Information Centre; Nappan Beef Research Committee; Maritime Beef Council; Maritime Beef Testing Society; The Nova Scotia Federation of Agriculture Council of Leaders
Environmental Activity: Focussing on food safety, environmental farm planning, animal welfare, & SRM disposal
Chief Officer(s):
David Oulton, Chair
John Tilley, Vice-Chair
William Cox, Chair, Finance
Membership: 1,300; *Member Profile:* Persons involved in Nova Scotia's beef & dairy production industry
Activities: Providing information about beef production & marketing; Promoting the beef industry in Nova Scotia; Monitoring & responding to issues in the industry; Advocating on behalf of producers
Publications:
•N.S.C.Action [a publication of Nova Scotia Cattle Producers]
Type: Newsletter

Nova Scotia Cattlemen's Association *See* Nova Scotia Cattle Producers

Nova Scotia Consulting Engineers Association *See* Consulting Engineers of Nova Scotia

Nova Scotia Council on Smoking & Health *See* Coalition for a Smoke-Free Nova Scotia

Nova Scotia Daylily Society

Newport RR#3 999 McKay Rd., Hants Co NS B0N 2A0
Tel: 902-757-2057
e-mail: cgharvey@eastlink.ca
www.nsdaylilysociety.com
Overview: A small provincial organization founded in 2003
Chief Officer(s):
Carla Heggie, President
heggiens@yahoo.ca
Membership: 110; *Fees:* $10

Nova Scotia Environmental Network (NSEN)
Parent Name: Canadian Environmental Network

3115 Veith St., Halifax NS B3K 3G9
Tel: 902-454-6846; *Fax:* 902-453-3633
e-mail: nsen@cen-rce.org
www.nsen.ca
Overview: A medium-sized provincial organization founded in 1991 overseen by Canadian Environmental Network
Mission: To conserve & enhance the natural environment; To achieve a sustainable future for Nova Scotia; To connect environmental & health organizations; Affiliation(s): Canadian Environmental Network (CEN)
Environmental Activity: Increasing community awareness of environmental conservation; Promoting sustainability; Presenting

Eco-Hero awards; Networking with other environmental & health organizations in Nova Scotia
Chief Officer(s):
Tamara Lorincz, Executive Director
Emma Boardman, Secretary & Agent
board_nsen@cen-rce.org
Finances: *Funding Sources:* Fundraising; Donations
Membership: *Fees:* Schedule available, based upon annual budget range; *Member Profile:* Non-profit groups, agencies, educational institutions, & individuals in Nova Scotia who share Nova Scotia Environmental Network's mission
Activities: Liaising with government at the provincial, national, & international levels; Organizing roundtables & conferences; Providing networking opportunities; Supporting members; Facilitating information exchange; Providing educational activities; *Internships:* Yes; *Library:* Nova Scotia Environmental Network Library
Meetings/Conferences:
For more information see Trade Shows, Conferences and Seminars Chapter
Nova Scotia Environmental Network 2013 Annual General Meeting
2013, NS
Nova Scotia Environmental Network 2013 Annual Roundtable
2013, NS
Nova Scotia Environmental Network 2013 Annual Book Club
2013, NS
Publications:
•By-Laws of the Nova Scotia Environmental Network (NSEN)
•Eco-Connections [a publication of the Nova Scotia Environmental Network]
Type: Newsletter; *Frequency:* Monthly; *Price:* Free with Nova Scotia Environmental Network membership
Profile: A bulletin about Nova Scotia Environmental Network's activities & environmental actions
•General Policies of the Nova Scotia Environmental Network (NSEN)
Profile: Topics include membership, the duties of the board, delegate selection, purchasing, the newsletter, mailing lists, meeting protocol, rights & responsibilities ofgeneral members, duties of the executive director, the caucus, working groups, & duties of the member representative
•Nova Scotia Environmental Network Annual Activity Report
Type: Yearbook; *Frequency:* Annually
Profile: A report of activities plus financial statements for the Canadian Environmental Network

Nova Scotia Federation of Agriculture (NSFA)
Parent Name: Canadian Federation of Agriculture

Covington Place, 332 Willow St., 2nd Fl., Truro NS B2N 5A5
Tel: 902-893-2293; *Fax:* 902-893-7063
e-mail: info@nsfa-fane.ca
www.nsfa-fane.ca
Overview: A medium-sized provincial organization founded in 1895 overseen by Canadian Federation of Agriculture
Mission: To act as the voice for the agricultural community in Nova Scotia; To ensure a competitive & sustainable future for agriculture in Nova Scotia; To build financially viable, ecologically sound, & socially responsible farm businesses in the province; *Member of:* Canadian Federation of Agriculture
Chief Officer(s):
Beth Densmore, President
Donna Langille, Manager, Operations
dlangille@nsfa-fane.ca
Membership: 1,800+; *Member Profile:* Individual farm businesses in Nova Scotia which represent all aspects of primary agriculture; Corporations
Activities: Reviewing legislative & regulatory issues & lobbying for change; Developing & delivering programs to meet the needs of the farm community, such a environmental farm planning services

Nova Scotia Fish Packers Association (NSFPA)

38B John St., Yarmouth NS B5A 3H2
Tel: 902-742-6168; *Fax:* 902-742-1620
e-mail: fishpackers@ns.aliantzinc.ca
www.fishpackers.com
Previous Name: Southwestern Nova Scotia Fish Packers Association
Overview: A small local organization founded in 1972
Mission: To ensure the survival of a competitive seafood processing industry in Nova Scotia; To provide leadership on industry issues, effective representation with government, R&D, project management, & volume discount purchases
Chief Officer(s):
Marc Surette, Executive Director
Finances: *Annual Operating Budget:* $50,000-$100,000
Staff: 1 staff member(s)
Membership: 60; *Fees:* $460-$2645 plus HST; *Member Profile:* Fish processing companies dealing with a wide variety of seafood for Canadian & export sales

Nova Scotia Forest Products Association ***See*** Forest Products Association of Nova Scotia

Nova Scotia Forest Technicians Association (NSFTA)

164 Forest Hills Dr., Truro NS B2N 2B7
e-mail: nsfta@nsfta.com
www.nsfta.ca
Overview: A small provincial organization
Chief Officer(s):
Lloyd Morgan, President
Finances: *Annual Operating Budget:* Less than $50,000
Staff: 12 volunteer(s)
Membership: 200 individual; *Fees:* $35 regular; $70 certified; *Member Profile:* Forest technicians; technologists
Activities: ; *Library:* Open to public

Nova Scotia Forestry Association (NSFA)
Parent Name: Canadian Forestry Association

PO Box 696, 430 Marney Rd. (Hilden), Truro NS B2N 5E5
Tel: 902-895-1179; *Fax:* 902-893-1197
www.nsfa.ca
www.facebook.com/pages/Envirothon-Nova-Scotia/1769011590 22332
twitter.com/envirothonns
Overview: A medium-sized provincial charitable organization founded in 1959 overseen by Canadian Forestry Association
Mission: To conserve Nova Scotia's forests; To promote the wise use & management of forest resources
Chief Officer(s):
Debbie Waycott, Contact
Finances: *Funding Sources:* Sponsorships
Activities: Conducting programs in schools, such as Envirothon; Advocating for the full development, utilization, & protection of forests in Nova Scotia; Promoting reforestation; *Awareness Events:* Arbor Day, September

Nova Scotia Fruit Growers' Association (NSFGA)

Kentville Agricultural Centre, 32 Main St., Kentville NS B4N 1J5
Tel: 902-678-1093; *Fax:* 902-679-1567
www.nsapples.com
www.facebook.com/173682379335493
Overview: A small provincial organization founded in 1863
Mission: To serve the interests of tree fruit growers in Nova Scotia; *Member of:* Canadian Horticulture Council; Affiliation(s): Nova Scotia Federation of Agriculture
Chief Officer(s):
Dela Erith, Executive Director
derith@nsapples.com
Finances: *Annual Operating Budget:* $100,000-$250,000
Staff: 10 staff member(s); 16 volunteer(s)
Membership: 220; *Fees:* $225.60-$1,804.84

Nova Scotia Ground Water Association (NSGWA)
Parent Name: Canadian Ground Water Association

#417, 3 - 644 Portland St., Dartmouth NS B2W 2M3
Fax: 902-435-0089
Toll-Free: 888-242-4440
e-mail: nsgwa@ns.aliantzinc.ca
www.nsgwa.ca
Previous Name: Nova Scotia Well Drillers Association
Overview: A medium-sized provincial organization overseen by Canadian Ground Water Association
Mission: To act as the voice of the industry to all levels of government; To encourage the management & protection of ground water; *Member of:* Canadian Ground Water Association
Chief Officer(s):
Arthur Jefferson, President
Noreene McGuire, Secretary-Treasurer
Membership: *Fees:* $100 associate, non-voting, non-certifed membership; $200 drillers, diggers, pump installers, suppliers, & technical personnel; *Member Profile:* Well drillers; Well diggers; Pump installers; Manufacturers; Suppliers; Technicians
Activities: Increasing public awareness; Encouraging partnerships; Providing continuing education; Presenting awards
Meetings/Conferences:
For more information see Trade Shows, Conferences and Seminars Chapter
Nova Scotia Ground Water Association 2013 Annual General Meeting
May 2013, NS
Publications:
•Water Talk [a publication of the Nova Scotia Ground Water Association]
Type: Newsletter; *Frequency:* Semiannually; *Accepts Advertising*
Profile: A publication for Nova Scotia's well drillers & diggers, pump installers, technical personnel, manufacturerer, & suppliers to the ground waterindustry, featuring association happenings & industry news

Nova Scotia Institute of Agrologists (NSIA)
Parent Name: Agricultural Institute of Canada

PO Box 550, 35 Tower Rd., Truro NS B2N 5E3
Tel: 902-897-6742
e-mail: nsagrologists@eastlink.ca
www.nsagrologists.ca
Overview: A medium-sized provincial licensing organization founded in 1953 overseen by Agricultural Institute of Canada
Finances: *Annual Operating Budget:* Less than $50,000; *Funding Sources:* Membership dues
Staff: 15 volunteer(s)
Membership: 300; *Fees:* $110
Activities: *Internships:* Yes; *Speaker Service:* Yes; *Library:* Open to public

Nova Scotia Mackerel Fishermen's Association

PO Box 34, RR#2, Hubbards NS B0J 1T0
Tel: 902-857-3619; *Fax:* 902-857-2057
Overview: A small provincial organization founded in 1992
Chief Officer(s):
Robert Conrad, President
rconrad91@hotmail.com

Nova Scotia Nature Trust (NSNT)

PO Box 2202, 2085 Maitland St., Halifax NS B3J 3C4
Tel: 902-425-5263; *Fax:* 902-429-5263
Toll-Free: 877-434-5263
e-mail: nature@nsnt.ca
www.nsnt.ca
Overview: A medium-sized provincial organization founded in 1994
Mission: To protect Nova Scotia's outstanding natural legacy through land conservation.
Chief Officer(s):
Nil d'Entremont, President
Bonnie Sutherland, Executive Director

Nova Scotia Public Interest Research Group (NSPIRG)

Student Union Building, Dalhousie University, #314, 6136 University Ave., Halifax NS B3H 4J2
Tel: 902-494-6662
e-mail: info@nspirg.org; board@nspirg.org
www.nspirg.org
www.facebook.com/NSPIRG
twitter.com/NSPIRG_Dal
Overview: A medium-sized local organization
Mission: To link research with social justice & environmental action
Chief Officer(s):
Andrew Jantzen, Coordinator, Outreach & Administration
alia@nspirg.org
Alia Saied, Coordinator, Resources & Administration
andrew@nspirg.org
Finances: *Annual Operating Budget:* Less than $50,000
Membership: 5,000-14,999;; *Fees:* $4; *Member Profile:* Dalhousie University students
Activities: *Speaker Service:* Yes; *Library:* Resource Library

Nova Scotia Safety Council; The Nova Scotia Highway Safety Council ***See*** Safety Services Nova Scotia

Nova Scotia Salmon Association (NSSA)

PO Box 396, Chester NS B0J 1J0
e-mail: nssalmo@yahoo.ca
www.novascotiasalmon.ns.ca
Overview: A medium-sized provincial charitable organization founded in 1963
Mission: To further the conservation & wise management of wild Atlantic salmon & trout; *Member of:* Atlantic Salmon Federation
Chief Officer(s):
Carl Purcell, President, 902-466-3024
c.purcell@ns.sympatico.ca
Finances: *Funding Sources:* Donations
Membership: *Fees:* $20; $5 junior; *Member Profile:* Individuals with an interest in the welfare of salmon & trout; Affiliate associations

Activities: Increasing public awareness; Offering educational activities; Conducting & supporting research; Administering programs, such as Adopt-A-Stream

Nova Scotia Swordfish Fishermen's Association

#9, 155 Chain Lake Dr., Halifax NS B3S 1B3
Tel: 902-875-2052; *Fax:* 902-875-1573
Overview: A small provincial organization
Chief Officer(s):
George Rennehan, Vice-President

Nova Scotia Well Drillers Association *See* Nova Scotia Ground Water Association

Nova Scotia Wild Flora Society

c/o Nova Scotia Museum, 1747 Summer St., Halifax NS B3H 3A6
Tel: 902-423-7032
e-mail: nswildflora@yahoo.ca
www.nswildflora.ca
Overview: A small provincial organization founded in 1990
Member of: Federation of Nova Scotia Naturalists; Affiliation(s): Canadian Wildflower Society
Chief Officer(s):
Charles Cron, President
ccron72@hotmail.com
Heather Drope, Secretary-Treasurer
Finances: *Annual Operating Budget:* Less than $50,000; *Funding Sources:* Membership dues
Staff: 2 volunteer(s)
Membership: 50; *Fees:* $15 individual; $20 family

Nova Scotian Institute of Science (NSIS)

Science Services, Killam Library, Dalhousie Univ., 6225 University Ave., Halifax NS B3H 4H8
Tel: 902-494-3621; *Fax:* 902-494-2062
e-mail: nsis@chebucto.ns.ca
www.chebucto.ns.ca/Science/NSIS
Overview: A medium-sized provincial organization founded in 1862
Mission: To provide a forum for scientists & those interested in science
Chief Officer(s):
John Rutherford, President
Michelle Paon, Vice-President
Linda Marks, Secretary
Elaine McCullogh, Treasurer
Membership: *Fees:* $20 regular; $10 student; $300 life members; *Member Profile:* Individual with an amateur or professional interest in science
Activities: Conducting the NSIS Student Essay Competition; Providing a public lecture series; *Library:* Killam Library, Dalhousie University, Halifax, NS;

NSERC/Petro-Canada Chair for Women in Science & Engineering

c/o Faculty of Engineering & Applied Sciences, Memorial University, St. John's NL A1B 3X5
Tel: 709-737-7960; *Fax:* 709-737-7658
e-mail: cwse@morgan.ucs.mun.ca
www.mun.ca/cwse/
Overview: A medium-sized national organization founded in 1977
Mission: To encourage women in Canada to enter careers in science, engineering, mathematics & computer sciences; to encourage women in Canada to attain high levels of professional achievement in these fields; to serve as an information centre for & about women in these fields; to make people aware of Canadian women scientists & engineers & of career opportunities available to them; to provide a forum for discussion of subjects of interest to members
Chief Officer(s):
Carolyn J. Emerson, Chair, Atlantic Region
Finances: *Annual Operating Budget:* Less than $50,000
Membership: 360; *Fees:* $250 corporate; $40 full; $25 associate; $10 student; $20 information (receives newsletter)
Activities: *Speaker Service:* Yes

British Columbia/Yukon

c/o The Jade Project, Dept. of Computer Science, #227, 2366 Main Mall, Vancouver BC V6T 1Z4
Tel: 604-822-5693; *Fax:* 604-822-5485
Chief Officer(s):
Anne Condon, NSERC/GM Canada, CWSE BC & Yukon

Ontario

c/o School of Engineering, Univ. of Guelph, Guelph ON N1G 2W1
Tel: 519-824-4120; *Fax:* 519-836-0227
www.cwse-on.ca
Chief Officer(s):
Valerie Davidson, Chair, NSERC/HP CWSE

Prairie Region

c/o Dept. of Computer Science, #110 Science Place, 176 Thorvaldson Bldg., Saskatoon SK S7N 5C9
Tel: 306-966-4901; *Fax:* 306-966-4884
wise.usask.ca/
Chief Officer(s):
Julita Vassileva, NSERC/Cameco CWSE, Prairie Region

WISE (Women in Science & Engineering) Newfoundland & Labrador

#293, 38 Pearson St., St. John's NL A1A 3R1
Tel: 709-754-1435; *Fax:* 709-738-8840
e-mail: wisenl@mun.ca
www.cdli.ca/wise/
www.facebook.com/group.php?gid=39236633023
Chief Officer(s):
Laura Halfyard, President

Nuclear Information & Resource Service (NIRS)

#340, 6930 Carroll St., Tacoma Park MD 20912 USA
Tel: 301-270-6477; *Fax:* 301-270-4291
e-mail: nirsnet@nirs.org
www.nirs.org
Overview: A small international organization founded in 1978
Affiliation(s): Nuclear Awareness Project
Chief Officer(s):
Don Keesing, Administrative Coordinator
Michael Mariotte, Executive Director
Finances: *Annual Operating Budget:* $500,000-$1.5 Million
Staff: 8 staff member(s)
Activities: *Internships:* Yes; *Speaker Service:* Yes; *Library:* by appointment

Nunavut Harvesters Association (NHA)

c/o Brian Zawadski, PO Box 249, Rankin Inlet NU X0C 0G0
Tel: 867-645-3170; *Fax:* 867-645-3755
e-mail: brian@ndcorp.nu.ca
www.harvesters.nu.ca
Overview: A small provincial organization
Mission: To develop & promote the sustainable harvesting of natural resources & wildlife in Nunavut
Chief Officer(s):
Brian Zawadski, Executive Director, 867-645-3170
brian@ndcorp.nu.ca
Activities: Promoting conservation of wildlife & natural resources in Nunavut; Administering & delivering the Agriculture & Agri-Food Canada program, entitled Advancing Canadian Agriculture & Agri-Food;

Oakville Community Centre for Peace, Ecology & Human Rights

PO Box 52007, Oakville ON L6J 7N5
Tel: 905-849-5501
e-mail: info@oakvillepeacecentre.org
www.oakvillepeacecentre.org
Overview: A small local organization
Chief Officer(s):
Stephen Dankowich, Executive Director

Occupational & Environmental Medical Association of Canada (OEMAC) / Association canadienne de la médecine du travail et de l'environnement (ACMTE)

#1430, 1101 Upper Middle Rd. East, Oakville ON L6H 5Z9
Tel: 905-849-9925; *Fax:* 905-338-8523
e-mail: oemac@oemac.org
www.oemac.org
Overview: A medium-sized national organization founded in 1983
Mission: To act as the voice of the Canadian occupational & environmental medicine sector; Affiliation(s): Canadian Medical Association; Canadian Board of Occupational Medicine; Royal College of Physicians & Surgeons of Canada
Chief Officer(s):
Howard Hamer, President
Finances: *Annual Operating Budget:* $50,000-$100,000; *Funding Sources:* Membership fees
Staff: 1 staff member(s); 12 volunteer(s)
Membership: 30 senior/lifetime + 282 individual; *Fees:* $250; *Member Profile:* Licensed physicians with an interest in occupational medicine
Activities: Exchanging scientific & professional information
Meetings/Conferences:
For more information see Trade Shows, Conferences and Seminars Chapter
Occupational & Environmental Medical Association of Canada (OEMAC) 31st Annual Scientific Conference
September 2013 Montréal, QC
Publications:
•Liaison [a publication of the Occupational & Environmental Medical Association of Canada]
Type: Newsletter; *Frequency:* Quarterly

Occupational Health Clinics for Ontario Workers (OHCOW)

#601, 15 Gervais Dr., Toronto ON M3C 1Y8
Tel: 416-510-8713; *Fax:* 416-443-9132
Toll-Free: 877-817-0336
e-mail: info@ohcow.on.ca
www.ohcow.on.ca
Overview: A medium-sized provincial organization
Mission: To prevent work-related illnesses & injuries; To improve workers' physical, mental & social well-being
Chief Officer(s):
Lyle Hargrove, President

Occupational Hygiene Association of Ontario (OHAO)

6519B Mississauga Rd., Mississauga ON L5N 1A6
Tel: 905-567-7196; *Fax:* 905-567-7191
e-mail: office@ohao.org
www.ohao.org
Overview: A medium-sized provincial organization founded in 1984
Mission: To protect people's health from hazards arising in or from the workplace; to develop & promote the profession of occupational hygiene; to sponsor professional development, training & research; to provide public education
Chief Officer(s):
Elizabeth A. Walpac, President
Richard Quenneville, Sec.-Treas.
Jason Boyer, Executive Manager
office@ohao.org
Finances: *Annual Operating Budget:* $50,000-$100,000; *Funding Sources:* Membership dues; seminars
Staff: 10 volunteer(s)
Membership: 300; *Fees:* $84 individual; $26.25 student; *Committees:* Education; Program; Membership; Public Affairs
Activities: Regional meetings; *Awareness Events:* Technical Symposia; *Speaker Service:* Yes; *Rents Mailing List:* Yes
Awards:
•Hugh Nelson Award (Award)
Presented to an individual who has made a significant long-term contribution to the advancement of occupational hygiene in Ontario

The Ocean Conservancy

1300 19th St. NW, 8th Fl., Washington DC 20036 USA
Tel: 202-429-5609; *Fax:* 202-872-0619
Toll-Free: 800-519-1541
e-mail: info@oceanconservancy.org
www.oceanconservancy.org
www.facebook.com/oceanconservancy
twitter.com/OurOcean
www.youtube.com/user/oceanconservancy
Previous Name: Center for Marine Conservation; Center for Environmental Education
Overview: A large international organization founded in 1972
Mission: To protect ocean ecosystems & conserve the global abundance & diversity of marine wildlife
Chief Officer(s):
Janis Searles Jones, President & CEO
jjones@oceanconservancy.org
Finances: *Annual Operating Budget:* $3 Million-$5 Million; *Funding Sources:* Bequests; contributions; grants
Staff: 40 staff member(s)
Membership: 110,000; *Fees:* Schedule available
Activities: Policy oriented research; promotion of public awareness through education; *Internships:* Yes

Ocean Net

276 Water St., St. John's NL A1C 1B7
Tel: 709-753-3680
www.oceannet.ca
Overview: A small provincial organization

Mission: To help reverse the polluting of the world's ocean's
Chief Officer(s):
Robert O'Brien, Founder/Chair
Membership: *Fees:* $20 individual; $25 family; $30 association; $150 corporate

Ocean Renewable Energy Group ***See*** Marine Renewables Canada

The Oceanography Society
PO Box 1931, Rockville MD 20849-1931 USA
Tel: 301-251-7708; *Fax:* 301-251-7709
e-mail: info@tos.org
www.tos.org
Overview: A small international organization founded in 1988
Chief Officer(s):
Jennifer Ramarui, Executive Director
Publications:
•Oceanography
Editor: Dr. Ellen Kappel; *ISSN:* 1042-8275
Profile: Monthly magazine; peer reviewed

Office de vente des produits forestiers du Madawaska / Madawaska Forest Products Marketing Board
CP 5, 870, rue Canada, Edmundston NB E3V 3X3
Tél: 506-739-9585; *Téléc:* 506-739-0859
Également appelé: Office de vente du Madawaska
Aperçu: *Dimension:* petite; *Envergure:* locale; Organisme sans but lucratif; fondée en 1962
Mission: Mise en marché des produits forestiers bruts; encourager les bonnes pratiques d'aménagement forestier; *Membre de:* La Fédération des Propriétaires de Lots Boissés du Nouveau Brunswick
Membre(s) du bureau directeur:
Claude A. Pelletier, Directeur général
Finances: *Budget de fonctionnement annuel:* $100,000-$250,000
Personnel: 7 membre(s) du personnel
Membre: 2 200 individu; 400 associé

Office des normes générales du Canada ***See*** Canadian General Standards Board

Office of Greening Government Operations (OGGO)
Tel: 416-241-4000
www.greeninggovernment.ca
Mission: Greening Government is an electronic information system developed by the Government of Canada for the internet. It is designed to provide a one-window access to sustainable development in government operations knowledge in the Government of Canada. This website was developed to support the Sustainable Development in Government Operations (SDGO) initiative, whose purpose is to coordinate the federal effort to green government operations & encourage the report of concrete results among the departments & agencies that prepare Sustainable Development Strategies (SDSs). There are seven priority areas of operations: Energy Efficiency/Buildings, Human Resources Management, Land Use Management, Procurement, Vehicle Fleet Management, Waste Management & Water Conservation & Wastewater Management
Chief Officer(s):
Nigel Marsh, President & Conference Director, 416-241-4000 Ext. 221
nigel.marsh@govpages.ca

Offshore Energy Research Association of Nova Scotia (OERA)
Bank of Montreal Building, #602, 5151 George St., Halifax NS B3J 1M5
Tel: 902-406-7010; *Fax:* 902-406-7019
Toll-Free: 888-257-8688
www.oera.ca
Merged from: Offshore Energy Environmental Research (OEER); Offshore Energy Technical Research (OETR)
Overview: A medium-sized provincial organization founded in 2012
Mission: To foster offshore energy & environmental research & development; To develop offshore petroleum exploration & development for Nova Scotia
Chief Officer(s):
Stephen Dempsey, Executive Director, 902-406-7011, Fax: 902-406-7019
Wanda Barrett, Manager, Operations, 902-406-7010, Fax: 902-406-7019
Jennifer Pinks, Manager, Research, 902-406-7013, Fax: 902-406-7019

Okanagan Mainline Municipal Association; Okanagan Valley Municipal Association; Okanagan Valley Mayors & Reeves Association ***See*** Southern Interior Local Government Association

Okanagan Similkameen Parks Society (OSPS)
PO Box 787, Summerland BC V0H 1Z0
Tel: 250-494-8996
okanagansimilkameenparkssociety.ca
Overview: A small local charitable organization founded in 1965
Member of: West Coast Environmental Law; Sierra Club; Affiliation(s): Friends of Stikine; Friends of Strathcona Park; Creston Wildlife; Okanagan Naturalists
Chief Officer(s):
Jeremy McCall, Executive Director
Finances: *Annual Operating Budget:* Less than $50,000; *Funding Sources:* Donations; membership fees; bequests; Penticton Foundation
Membership: 273; *Fees:* $10 single; $15 couple/family; $20 organization; *Member Profile:* Interest in parks; land & wildlife stewardship/conservation; historic trails; forestry practices; watershed protection; urban green spaces
Activities: Monthly meetings; special events; seminars; workshops; film; brochures & booklets; *Awareness Events:* Meadowlark Festival, Penticton - May

Oliver-Osoyoos Naturalists
PO Box 1181, Osoyoos BC V0H 1V0
Tel: 250-495-6907
e-mail: hwbking@telus.net
Overview: A small local organization founded in 1973
Mission: To cooperate and communicate with other naturalists. To foster an awareness, appreciation and understanding of our natural environment so that it may be wisely used and maintained for future generations.; *Member of:* The Federation of BC Naturalists
Finances: *Annual Operating Budget:* Less than $50,000
Membership: 75; *Fees:* $20 individual; $25 family; *Member Profile:* People interested in nature & the environment
Activities: Walks; hiking; bird watching; outdoor education; caretaking of two ecological reserves; environmental restoration; "clean-up" projects.

One Sky: Canadian Institute of Sustainable Living
PO Box 3352, 3768 2nd Ave., Smithers BC V0J 1N0
Tel: 250-877-6030
www.onesky.ca
Overview: A medium-sized national organization
Mission: A not-for-profit, non-governmental organization dedicated to a vision of an environmentally sustainable and socially just world, and the promotion of sustainable living globally. It seeks to inspire and promote solutions, provide practical solutions, and network across sectors with like-minded organizations.; *Member of:* Canadian Renewable Energy Alliance; Affiliation(s): BC Sustainable Energy Association
Chief Officer(s):
Michael Simpson, Executive Director
Finances: *Funding Sources:* Donations
Membership: *Fees:* $10
Activities: Current projects include: GO2 Carshare Cooperative; Leading from Within - Integral Leadership for Sustainable Development; Fire and Ice; Athletes for Africa

Ontario Agri Business Association (OABA)
#104, 160 Research Lane, Guelph ON N1G 5B2
Tel: 519-822-3004; *Fax:* 519-822-8862
e-mail: info@oaba.on.ca
www.oaba.on.ca
Merged from: Ontario Grain & Feed Association; Fertilizer Institute of Ontario
Overview: A medium-sized provincial organization founded in 1965
Mission: To serve & represent firms engaged in the crop inputs, country grain elevator, & feed & farm supply industy, plus related agricultural businesses operating within Ontario; *Member of:* Canadian Fertilizer Institute; Animal Nutrition Association of Canada
Chief Officer(s):
D.O. Buttenham, CEO
dave@oaba.on.ca
Gwen Paddock, President
Cory McDonald, Vice-President
Dale Cowan, Treasurer
Finances: *Funding Sources:* Annual membership dues from regular, branch, &c associate members
Membership: *Member Profile:* Country grain elevators in Ontario; Ontario crop input supply businesses; Feed manufacturing facilities in the province; Associated businesses that provide products & services to the crop input, grain, & feed industry
Activities: Delivering products, programs, & services to members; Promoting the crop input, grain, & feed industry; Coordinating services of member sectors in areas such as food safety & environmental stewardship; Providing educational opportunities; Liaising with stakeholders, consumers, & government; Studying legislation affecting members; Disseminating information to members; Engaging in & sponsoring research

Ontario Agri-Food Education Inc. (OAFE)
PO Box 460, 8560 Tremaine Rd., Milton ON L9T 4Z1
Tel: 905-878-1510; *Fax:* 905-878-0342
e-mail: info@oafe.org
www.oafe.org
Overview: A small provincial organization founded in 1991
Mission: To build awareness & understanding of the importance of an agriculture & food system; To provide high quality, objective & relevant agriculture & food related learning materials & services for Ontario educators to enhance the learning experiences of students in Ontario classrooms
Chief Officer(s):
Colleen Smith-Robinson, Executive Director
Membership: *Fees:* $50 individual

Ontario Agri-Food Technologies (OAFT)
#200, 120 Research Lane, Guelph ON N1G 0B4
Tel: 519-826-4195; *Fax:* 519-821-7361
e-mail: info@oaft.org
www.oaft.org
Overview: A medium-sized provincial organization founded in 1997
Mission: To generate wealth & sustainability for the Ontario agriculture & food industries by utilizing current technologies; Affiliation(s): Agriculture and Agri-Food Canada; Ontario Ministry of Agriculture and Food/Ministry of Rural Affairs; Ontario Ministry of Economic Development, Trade and Employment
Chief Officer(s):
Gord Surgeoner, President
Kathy Derksen, Office Manager
Membership: *Member Profile:* Grower organizations; industry; universities; government; affiliates

Ontario Allergy Society ***See*** Allergy, Asthma & Immunology Society of Ontario

Ontario Asbestos Removal Contractors Association ***See*** Environmental Abatement Council of Ontario

Ontario Association for Geographic & Environmental Education (OAGEE) / Association pour l'enseignement de la géographie et de l'environnement en Ontario (AÉGÉO)
#202, 10 Morrow Ave., Toronto ON M6R 2J1
www.oagee.org
Overview: A small provincial organization founded in 1949
Chief Officer(s):
Mark Lowry, President
Shawn Hughes, Vice-President, Membership Services, 705-742-9221
shawn_hughes@kprdsb.ca
Joe Maurice, Vice-President, Communications
Paul VanZant, Vice-President, Curriculum
Jennifer Farrell-Cordon, Secretary
Lew French, Treasurer
Membership: *Fees:* $25 university students & faculty; $30 retired members; $50 individuals; *Member Profile:* Teachers of geography from across Ontario
Activities: Providing information & resources to elementary & secondary school teachers of geography & environmental education
Publications:
•The Monograph Editor
Type: Journal; *Frequency:* Quarterly; *Editor:* Gary Birchall; *Price:* Free with Ontario Association of Geographic & Environmental Education membership
Profile: Lesson plans & activities, for geography courses, designed by teachers

Ontario Association for Impact Assessment (OAIA)
87 Irondale Dr., 2nd Fl., Toronto ON M9L 2S6
e-mail: info@oaia.on.ca
www.oaia.on.ca
Overview: A medium-sized provincial organization
Chief Officer(s):

Steven Rowe, President
Membership: *Fees:* $40 regular; $10 student

Ontario Association of Agricultural Societies (OAAS)

PO Box 189, Glencoe ON N0L 1M0
Tel: 519-287-3553; *Fax:* 519-287-2000
e-mail: oaas@bellnet.ca
www.ontariofairs.com
Overview: A medium-sized provincial organization founded in 1900
Mission: To provide education, information & leadership to members & to act as a single voice when dealing with members, media, public & government; *Member of:* Canadian Association of Fairs & Exhibitions; International Association of Fairs & Expositions
Chief Officer(s):
Harry Emmott, President
Finances: *Annual Operating Budget:* $50,000-$100,000
Staff: 3 staff member(s)
Membership: 234; *Fees:* Depends on size of fair; *Member Profile:* Open to agricultural fair or service manager

Ontario Association of Certified Engineering Technicians & Technologists (OACETT)

#404, 10 Four Seasons Pl., Toronto ON M9B 6H7
Tel: 416-621-9621; *Fax:* 416-621-8694
e-mail: info@oacett.org
www.oacett.org
Overview: A small provincial organization founded in 1957
Mission: To advance the profession of applied science & engineering technology through standards for society's benefit.; *Member of:* Canadian Council of Technicians & Technologists
Chief Officer(s):
David J. Thomson, CEO
dthomson@oacett.org
David Saunders, President
Finances: *Annual Operating Budget:* $1.5 Million-$3 Million
Staff: 18 staff member(s); 300 volunteer(s)
Membership: *Fees:* Schedule available
Activities: *Internships:* Yes; *Speaker Service:* Yes

Ontario Association of Landscape Architects (OALA)

#407, 3 Church St., Toronto ON M5E 1M2
Tel: 416-231-4181; *Fax:* 416-231-2679
e-mail: oala@oala.ca
www.oala.ca
Overview: A medium-sized provincial licensing organization founded in 1968
Mission: To promote, improve & advance the profession; to maintain standards of professional practice & conduct consistent with the need to serve & to protect the public interest; to support improvement &/or conservation of the natural, cultural, social & built environment; *Member of:* Canadian Society of Landscape Architects; Council of Landscape Architectural Registration Boards; Affiliation(s): American Society of Landscape Architects
Chief Officer(s):
Linda MacLeod, Registrar
Glenn O'Connor, President
Finances: *Annual Operating Budget:* $3 Million-$5 Million; *Funding Sources:* Membership dues
Staff: 2 staff member(s); 100 volunteer(s)
Membership: 690 full + 250 associate + 20 affiliate; *Fees:* $696.25 full; $150 associate; $141.75 affiliate; *Member Profile:* Professional landscape architects; *Committees:* Ethics; Honours, Awards & Protocol; Discipline; Continuing Education; Marketing
Activities: *Internships:* Yes; *Library:* Open to public
Awards:
•Emeritus & Honorary Award (Award)
Honorary members being non-landscape architects appointed by Council, nominated by another member
•Public Practice Award (Award)
Recognizes the outstanding leadership of a member of the profession in public practice who promotes & enhances landscape architecture by working for improved understanding & appreciation of the work of landscape architects in both public & private practice
•Carl Borgstrom Award for Service to the Environment (Award)
Given to an individual landscape architect or landscape architectural group, organization or agency to recognize & encourage a special or unusual contribution to the sensitive, sustainable design for human use of the environment
•OALA Award for Service to the Environment (Award)
Given to a non-landscape architectural individual, group, organization or agency to recognize & encourage a special or unusual contribution to the sensitive, sustainable design for human use of the environment
•Pinnacle Award for Landscape Architectural Excellence (Award)
Recognizes an OALA member and their professional work
•David Erb Memorial Award (Award)
Recognizes an OALA member who has made an exemplary vountary contribution to the work of the association

Ontario Automotive Recyclers Association (OARA)

#1, 1447 Upper James St., Hamilton ON L8W 3J6
Tel: 905-383-9788; *Fax:* 905-383-1904
Toll-Free: 800-390-8743
e-mail: admin@oara.com
www.oara.com
Overview: A small provincial organization founded in 1992
Mission: The association is the voice of the automotive recycling industry in Ontario. OARA works to improve recycling industry practices, and to promote the benefits of responsbile auto recycling to the general public, to stakeholders, and to local and provincial governments.; *Member of:* Automotive Recyclers of Canada
Chief Officer(s):
Steve Fletcher, Executive Director
Finances: *Funding Sources:* Membership fees
Staff: 3 staff member(s)
Membership: 170; *Fees:* $150-$500; *Member Profile:* Automotove recyclers; Direct Members must demonstrate compliance with the Ontario Certified Auto Recylcers Program; *Committees:* Government Affairs; Health & Safety; Meetings; Membership; Salvage & Licencing; Transportation; Budget & Audit; Nominations
Activities: *Rents Mailing List:* Yes

Ontario Beef Improvement Association ***See*** Ontario Cattlemen's Association

Ontario Camping Association ***See*** Ontario Camps Association

Ontario Camps Association (OCA)
Parent Name: Canadian Camping Association

#403, 250 Merton St., Toronto ON M4S 1B1
Tel: 416-485-0425; *Fax:* 416-485-0422
e-mail: info@ontariocamps.ca
www.ontariocamps.ca
Previous Name: Ontario Camping Association
Overview: A medium-sized provincial organization founded in 1937 overseen by Canadian Camping Association
Mission: To promote youth camping throughout Ontario; To maintain high standards for organized camping; To advocate on issues which impact members
Chief Officer(s):
Rick Howard, President
Aruna Ogale, Executive Director
aruna@ontariocamps.ca
Membership: *Member Profile:* Ontario camps which meet the association's standards; Individuals; Like-minded organizations & agencies
Activities: Enforcing camp standards, through inspections, in order to ensure sound camp operation & administration & safe camping experiences; Sharing information & ideas; Supporting training seminars & workshops; Informing the public about the benefits of camping & the role of the association; Conducting research, through the OCA Educational Research Task Force
Publications:
•Camp Health Issues
Price: $20
Profile: Articles about health & safety issues at camps
•How to be a Camp Counsellor . . . The Best Job in the World!
Author: Catherine Ross; *Price:* $19.95
Profile: Tips & tools to become a summer camp counsellor, such as leadership styles, teaching techniques, & behaviour management
•OCA [Ontario Camps Association] Bulletin
Type: Newsletter
•OCA [Ontario Camps Association] Camps Guide
Type: Directory; *Frequency:* Annually; *Accepts Advertising*
Profile: Listings & descriptions of accredited camps in Ontario
•OCA [Ontario Camps Association] Crisis Response & Management Plan
Price: $10.50
Profile: Information about managing a crisis, plus forms for camps to use, such as a crisis response log, & a parent / guardian call form
•Ontario Camps Association's Guidelines for Accreditation
Price: $15
Profile: Addressing aspects of a day or residential camp's operations, such as health & safety, facilities, & leadership

Ontario Cattlemen's Association (OCA) / Association ontarienne des éleveurs de bovins

130 Malcolm Rd., Guelph ON N1K 1B1
Tel: 519-824-0334; *Fax:* 519-824-9101
e-mail: ontbeef@cattle.guelph.on.ca
www.cattle.guelph.on.ca
Previous Name: Ontario Beef Improvement Association
Overview: A medium-sized provincial organization founded in 1963
Mission: To foster a sustainable & profitable beef industry in Ontario; To provide programs & serivces to support local cattlemen's associations & provincial cattlemen in general; To lobby on issues at the provincial & national level; *Member of:* Canadian Cattlemen's Association
Environmental Activity: Encouraging environmentally sustainable production methods; Analyzing government regulations related to water quality issues; Evaluating & advising on nutrient management legislation; Conducting research on environmental issues
Chief Officer(s):
Dave Stewart, Executive Director
Paul Stiles, Assistant Manager
Lianne Appleby, Manager, Communications
Jamie Thomas, Coordinator, Market Information
Lisa Turney, Coordinator, Research & Projects
Jen Snively, Policy Advisor
Membership: *Member Profile:* Cattle producers in Ontario; *Committees:* Cow / Calf; Feedlot; Research
Activities: Providing education & information to Ontario cattlemen; Engaging in advocacy activities on behalf of the Ontario beef industry; Liaising with government; Initiating studies, programs, & reviews; Encouraging economically sustainable production methods; Promoting Quality Starts Here programs to beef producers across Ontario; Developing domestic & export markets Promoting beef
Meetings/Conferences:
For more information see Trade Shows, Conferences and Seminars Chapter
2013 Ontario Cattlemen's Association Annual General Meeting
February 2013 Toronto, ON
Publications:
•OCA [Ontario Cattlemen's Association] Weekly Update
Type: Newsletter; *Frequency:* Weekly; *Editor:* Lianne Appleby
•Ontario Beef
Type: Magazine; *Frequency:* 5 pa; *Accepts Advertising*; *Editor:* Lianne Appleby; *Price:* Free for members of the OntarioCattlemen's Association
Profile: Information for producers, featuring articles of interest in the beef industry, research, market information, producer profiles, & current policy issues
•Ontario Cattlemen's Association Production Guides
Type: Guide
Profile: Production information of a wide variety of topics
•The Ontario Steakholder
Type: Newsletter; *Frequency:* Irregular; *Editor:* Lianne Appleby
Profile: A timely publication for Ontario's MPs & MPPs to connect them with Ontario's beef farmers

Ontario Centres of Excellence (OCE)

#200, 156 Front St. West, Toronto ON M5J 2L6
Tel: 416-861-1092; *Fax:* 416-971-7164
Toll-Free: 866-759-6014
e-mail: anne.wettlaufer@oce-ontario.org
www.oce-ontario.org
www.linkedin.com/groups/Ontario-Centres-Excellence-1811772
www.facebook.com/OCEInnovation
twitter.com/oceinnovation
www.youtube.com/ocediscovery
Previous Name: Ontario Centres of Excellence - Centre for Earth & Environmental Technologies
Overview: A large provincial organization founded in 1987
Mission: To create new jobs, products, services, technologies & businesses by creating partnerships between industry & academia; Affiliation(s): Accelerator Centre for Commercialization Excellence (ACE)
Chief Officer(s):
Michael J. Nobrega, Chair
Tom Corr, President & CEO
Tanya Dunn, Executive Assistant, Office of President
tanya.dunn@oce-ontario.org
Membership: *Committees:* Social Innovation Steering; Centre for Commercialization of Research Advisory Board; Advanced Health Technologies Sector Advisory Board; Advanced Manufacturing Sector Advisory Board; Energy & Environment

Sector Advisory Board; Information, Communications & Digital Media Sector Advisory Board
Activities: Ontario Network of Excellence (ONE); Industry-Academic Collaboration Program (IACP); Centre for Commercialization of Research (CCR); Networks of Centres of Excellence (NCE)
Publications:
•OCE [Ontario Centres of Excellence] Newsletter
Type: Newsletter

Ontario Centres of Excellence - Centre for Earth & Environmental Technologies ***See*** Ontario Centres of Excellence

Ontario Clean Air Alliance (OCAA)
#300, 160 John St., Toronto ON M5V 2E5
Tel: 416-260-2080; *Fax:* 416-598-9520
e-mail: contact@cleanairalliance.org
www.cleanairalliance.org
Overview: A medium-sized provincial organization founded in 1997
Mission: To ensure that Ontario's electricity needs are met by ecologically sustainable renewable sources
Environmental Activity: Advocating for the phase-out of coal-fired power plants in Ontario in order to reduce greenhouse gas; Promoting energy conservation & efficiency & green power; Campaigning for a renewable electricity future in Ontario
Chief Officer(s):
Jack Gibbons, Chair, 416-260-2080 Ext. 2
jack@cleanairalliance.org
Angela Bischoff, Director, Outreach, 416-260-2080 Ext. 1
Angela@cleanairalliance.org
Finances: *Funding Sources:* Donations
Membership: *Member Profile:* Organizations & individuals who work for cleaner air through a coal phase-out & a move to a renewable electricity future
Publications:
•Finishing the Coal Phase Out: An Historic Opportunity for Climate Leadership
Type: Report
Profile: A review of the Government of Ontario's coal phase-out to reduce greenhouse gas emission
•Increasing Productivity & Moving Towards a Renewable Future: A New Electricity Strategy for Ontario
Type: Report; *Number of Pages:* 60; *Author:* Jack Gibbons
•Ontario Clean Air Alliance E-Bulletin
Type: Newsletter; *Frequency:* Semimonthly
Profile: The most recent news & reports about energy issues & air quality
•The Ontario Power Authority's Coal Phase-Out Strategy: A Critical Review
Type: Report; *Number of Pages:* 13
•Ontario's Coal Phase-Out: A Major Climate Accomplishment Within Our Grasp
Type: Report; *Number of Pages:* 10
Profile: A review of the coal phase-out's progress
•Ontario's Green Future: How We Can Build a 100% Renewable Electricity Grid by 2027
Type: Report; *Number of Pages:* 32; *Author:* Jack Gibbons
Profile: An Ontario Clean Air Alliance report with recommendations
•Powerful Options: A Review of Ontario's Options for Replacing Aging Nuclear Plants
Type: Report; *Number of Pages:* 18
Profile: A presentation of options for replacing nuclear plants that are less expensive than building new nuclear reactors

Ontario Commercial Fisheries' Association (OCFA)
PO Box 2129, 45 James St., Blenheim ON N0P 1A0
Tel: 519-676-0488; *Fax:* 519-676-0944
Toll-Free: 800-461-7890
www.myfishquota.com
Overview: A medium-sized provincial organization founded in 1945
Mission: To be dedicated to the growth & continued strength of a responsible, competitive, & sustainable licensed commercial fishery in Ontario; To represent the industry's interests & its view to government, the media, & consumers
Chief Officer(s):
Peter Meisenheimer, Executive Director
Finances: *Annual Operating Budget:* $500,000-$1.5 Million; *Funding Sources:* Membership dues; Contractual programs
Staff: 22 staff member(s); 19 volunteer(s)
Membership: 267; *Fees:* $150; *Member Profile:* Licensed Ontario commercial fishing license holders; Federal registered processing plants
Activities: Maintaining a code of conduct for responsible fishing practices; Hosting an annual convention

Ontario Community Transit Association ***See*** Ontario Public Transit Association

Ontario Concrete Pipe Association (OCPA)
447 Frederick St., 2nd Fl, Kitchener ON N2H 2P4
Tel: 519-489-4488; *Fax:* 519-578-6060
e-mail: admin@ocpa.com
www.ocpa.com
Overview: A medium-sized provincial organization founded in 1957
Mission: To represent the concrete pipe & maintenance hole industry throughout Ontario; to promote engineered concrete products of permanence; *Member of:* Canadian Standards Association; Affiliation(s): Municipal Engineers Association; Canadian Concrete Pipe Association; Tubecon; American Concrete Pipe Association; Canadian Portland Cement Association; Water Environment Association of Ontario; Canadian Public Works Association; Ontario Sewer & Watermain Construction Association; Consulting Engineers of Ontario
Chief Officer(s):
Brian Wood, President, 800-668-7473, Fax: 519-763-1982
brwood@concastpipe.com
Mike Leathers, Vice President, 888-888-3222
mike.leathers.hanson.com
John Munro, Sec.-tres., 705-734-2892, Fax: 705-734-2920
jmunro@munroltd.com
Finances: *Annual Operating Budget:* $250,000-$500,000; *Funding Sources:* Membership dues
Staff: 2 staff member(s); 30 volunteer(s)
Membership: 40; *Member Profile:* Manufacturers of precast concrete pipe & associated products; *Committees:* Prequalification; Public Relations & Communications; Technical
Activities: *Awareness Events:* Construct Canada; Ontario Good Roads; *Speaker Service:* Yes; *Library:* by appointment

Ontario Creamerymen's Association
26 Dominion St., Alliston ON L9R 1L5
Tel: 705-435-6751; *Fax:* 705-435-6797
e-mail: allistoncreamery1@bellnet.ca
Overview: A small provincial organization founded in 1935
Chief Officer(s):
Lloyd Kennedy, President
Finances: *Annual Operating Budget:* Less than $50,000; *Funding Sources:* Membership dues
Staff: 3 volunteer(s)

Ontario Dairy Council (ODC)
6533D Mississauga Rd., Mississauga ON L5N 1A6
Tel: 905-542-3620; *Fax:* 905-542-3624
Toll-Free: 866-542-3620
e-mail: info@ontariodairies.ca
www.ontariodairies.ca
Overview: A medium-sized provincial organization founded in 1971
Mission: To represent interests of dairy product processors, marketers & distributors in Ontario; Affiliation(s): International Dairy Federation
Chief Officer(s):
Tom Kane, President
tomkane@ontariodairies.ca
Christina Lewis, Vice-President
clewis@ontariodairies.ca
Finances: *Annual Operating Budget:* $500,000-$1.5 Million; *Funding Sources:* Membership fees
Staff: 3 staff member(s)
Membership: 40 corporate + 50 associate; *Fees:* Schedule available; *Member Profile:* Licensed processor, marketer or distributor; *Committees:* Technical; Advisory; Environment; Policy & Technical
Activities: ; *Library:* by appointment

Ontario Daylily Society (ODS)
6798 9th Line, R R#2, Beeton ON L0G 1A0
Tel: 905-729-2718
e-mail: cgharvey@eastlink.ca
www.nsdaylilysociety.com
Overview: A small provincial organization founded in 1997
Chief Officer(s):
Faye Collins, President
president@ontariodaylily.on.ca
Membership: *Fees:* $8 youth; $20 individual; $25 family

Ontario Delphinium Club
c/o Christine Gill, 4691 Hwy. 7A, RR#1, Nestleton Station ON L0B 1L0
Tel: 905-986-0310
e-mail: ontdelphs@yahoo.ca
www.ondelphiniums.com
Overview: A small provincial organization
Membership: *Fees:* $10 family

Ontario Electrical League (OEL)
#300, 180 Attwell Dr., Toronto ON M9W 6A9
Tel: 905-238-1382; *Fax:* 905-238-1420
e-mail: communications@oel.org
www.oel.org
www.linkedin.com/oeleague
www.facebook.com/132812900129239?fref=ts
twitter.com/OEL3
Overview: A medium-sized provincial organization founded in 1966
Mission: To represent & strengthen the electrical industry in Ontario
Chief Officer(s):
Stephen Sell, President
stephen.sell@oel.org
Sheila Sage, Manager, Operations
sheila.sage@oel.org
Cynthia Kenth, Editor, Dialogue
dialogue@oel.org
Membership: 21 chapters, with 2,500+ members; *Member Profile:* Educators; Electricians; Electrical contractors; Electrical inspectors; Manufacturers; Consulting engineers; Distributors
Activities: Promoting Ontario's electrical industry; Providing educational opportunities
Publications:
•Contractor News [a publication of the Ontario Electrical League]
Type: Newsletter; *Frequency:* Monthly
Profile: Update on industry news, plus issues that affect contractors & their businesses
•Contractor Newsbrief [a publication of the Ontario Electrical League]
Type: Newsletter
Profile: Contractor Committee activities, for Ontario Electrical League contractor members
•Dialogue [a publication of the Ontario Electrical League]
Type: Magazine; *Frequency:* Quarterly; *Accepts Advertising*; *Price:* Free with membership in the Ontario Electrical League
Profile: League activities, member news, plus updates about industry & government issues
•Ontario Electrical League Chapter Newsletter
Type: Newsletter
Profile: Chapter committee update

Ontario Energy Association (OEA)
#202, 121 Rochmon St. West, Toronto ON M5H 2K1
Tel: 416-961-2339; *Fax:* 416-961-1173
e-mail: oea@energyontario.ca
www.energyontario.ca
www.linkedin.com/company/ontario-energy-association
twitter.com/ontarioenergy
Overview: A small provincial organization
Mission: To represent the energy industry of Ontario
Chief Officer(s):
Elise Herzig, President & Chief Executive Officer
Tina Arvanitis, Vice-President, Communications & Stakeholder Relations, 647-920-3269
tarvanitis@energyontario.ca
Finances: *Funding Sources:* Sponsorships
Membership: 150+ corporate members; *Member Profile:* Members of Ontario's energy industry, such as power producers, manufacturers, contractors, service providers, energy retailers, marketers, energy distributors, & energy consultants; *Committees:* Energy Markets Joint Sector; Environment Joint Sector; Government Relations Joint Sector; Green Energy & Conservation Joint Sector; Marketers & Retailers Sector; Utility Sector
Activities: Providing education & resources about the energy sector; Engaging in advocacy activities for members; Conducting research into energy matters; *Speaker Service:* Yes
Meetings/Conferences:
For more information see Trade Shows, Conferences and Seminars Chapter
Ontario Energy Association 2013 Annual Conference & Annual General Meeting
October 2013 Niagara Falls, ON
Energy Conference '13
September 2013 Toronto, ON

Ontario Energy Association 2014 Annual Conference & Annual General Meeting
2014, ON

Ontario Environment Industry Association (ONEIA)

#401, 215 Spadina Ave., Toronto ON M5T 2C7
Tel: 416-531-7884; *Fax:* 416-644-0116
e-mail: info@oneia.ca
www.oneia.ca
Previous Name: Canadian Environment Industry Association - Ontario Chapter
Overview: A medium-sized provincial organization founded in 1991
Mission: To promote the growth of environment business in Ontario; *Member of:* Canadian Environmental Auditing Association; CRESTech; Retail Council of Canada; Affiliation(s): Canadian Standards Association; Cements Association of Canada; Ontario Concrete Pipe Association; Ontario Sewer & Watermain Construtions Association; Ontario Environmental Training Consortium; Ontario Centre for Environmental Technology Advancement
Chief Officer(s):
Marjan Lahuis, Operations Manager, Membership Recruitment and Sponsor Relations
Alex Gill, Executive Director
Finances: *Annual Operating Budget:* $100,000-$250,000; *Funding Sources:* Membership dues; projects
Staff: 1 staff member(s); 12 volunteer(s)
Membership: 167; *Fees:* $395-$1,375; *Member Profile:* Ontario-based companies, business associations & organizations which actively provide environmental technologies & services that help protect or improve the environment & that help achieve sustainable development; *Committees:* Advocacy; Business Development; Member Services
Activities: Has been an active participant in a number of initiatives - the Green Industry Strategy for Ontario led by the Ministry of Energy in collaboration with MOE & MITT; the 3R's Municipal Infrastructure Task Force to implement the MOE's Waste Management Initiative; the CCME Task Force for a National Waste Management Strategy; the Canadian-American Environmental Marketing Council to establish a facilitation office in Washington DC for Canadian companies pursuing the USA environmental market; *Library:* by appointment

Ontario Environmental Network (OEN)
Parent Name: Canadian Environmental Network

PO Box 1412, Stn. Main, North Bay ON P1B 8K6
Tel: 705-840-2888
e-mail: oen@oen.ca
www.oen.ca
www.facebook.com/180386751992826
www.youtube.com/ontarioenvironment
Overview: A large provincial organization founded in 1981 overseen by Canadian Environmental Network
Mission: To encourage discussions of ways to protect the environment; To increase environmental awareness throughout Ontario; To serve the environmental non-profit, non-governmental community in Ontario; Affiliation(s): Canadian Environmental Network
Environmental Activity: Researching environmental matters; Providing envionmental education; Offering reference & referral services for environmentally-related inquiries; Establishing caucuses that work on issues such as energy, forest, & waste
Chief Officer(s):
Phillip Penna, Coordinator, 705-840-2888
Membership: 500+ environmental groups; *Fees:* $15 individuals; $30 government agencies & businesses; $40 organizations; *Member Profile:* Non-government, not-for-profit organizations in Ontario concerned with the preservation of the environment; Government agencies; Businesses; Individuals
Activities: Facilitating communication among environmental organizations; Maintaining a database of Ontario's environmental groups; Increasing awareness of environmental organizations; Operating the First Ontario TimeBank (firstontario.timebanks.org)
Meetings/Conferences:
For more information see Trade Shows, Conferences and Seminars Chapter
Ontario Environmental Network 2013 Annual General Meeting
2013, ON
Publications:
•OEN [Ontario Environmental Network] News
Type: Newsletter; *Frequency:* Semimonthly; *Accepts Advertising*; *Price:* Free with Ontario Environmental Network membership
Profile: Ontario Environment Network updates, events, & action alerts sent to member groups & subscribers
•Ontario Environmental Directory [a publication of the Ontario Environmental Directory]
Type: Directory; *Editor:* Peter Blanchard; *Price:* Free with Ontario EnvironmentalNetwork membership
Profile: Comprehensive information about Ontario environmental organizations & agencies

Ontario Farm & Country Accommodations Association (OFCA)

8724 Wellington Rd. 18, RR#5, Belwood ON N0J 1J0
Tel: 519-787-0346; *Fax:* 519-787-0946
e-mail: paul.faires@sympatico.ca
www.countryhosts.com
Overview: A small provincial organization founded in 1967
Mission: To be a self-supporting, accredited association whose members provide warm hospitality, country accommodations & farm tours, for guests seeking a unique getaway with the opportunity to experience rural culture, farming & the environment
Chief Officer(s):
Lore Schafer, President
Paul Faires, Secretary
Finances: *Annual Operating Budget:* Less than $50,000
Staff: 2090 volunteer(s)
Membership: 20; *Fees:* $115
Activities: *Speaker Service:* Yes; *Rents Mailing List:* Yes

The Ontario Farm Animal Council (OFAC)

#106, 100 Stone Rd. West, Guelph ON N1G 5L3
Tel: 519-837-1326; *Fax:* 519-837-3209
www.farmfoodcare.org
www.facebook.com/FarmFoodCare
twitter.com/farmfoodcare
Overview: A medium-sized provincial organization founded in 1988
Mission: To support & promote the responsible production & marketing of livestock & poultry by Ontario farmers & through a variety of initiatives, to better inform the public of the excellence of animal agriculture
Chief Officer(s):
John Maaskant, Chairman
Crystal Mackay, Executive Director
Finances: *Annual Operating Budget:* $250,000-$500,000; *Funding Sources:* Memberships; corporate sponsorships; grants
Staff: 3 staff member(s); 100 volunteer(s)
Membership: Represents both directly & indirectly the over 40,000 livestock & poultry producers & related agri-food businesses in Ontario; *Fees:* $35-$1,000
Activities: Consumer & producer displays; public speaking; agri-food spokespeople training; media relations; industry representation & services; referral & research; *Awareness Events:* Canadian National Exhibition Model Farm; *Speaker Service:* Yes; *Library:* by appointment

Ontario Federation of Agriculture (OFA)
Parent Name: Canadian Federation of Agriculture

Ontario AgriCentre, #206, 100 Stone Rd. West, London ON N1G 5L3
Tel: 519-821-8883; *Fax:* 519-821-8810
Toll-Free: 800-668-3276
e-mail: info@ofa.on.ca
www.ofa.on.ca
www.facebook.com/ontariofarms
twitter.com/ontariofarms
www.youtube.com/user/ontariofarms
Overview: A large provincial organization founded in 1936 overseen by Canadian Federation of Agriculture
Mission: To represent farm families throughout Ontario; to champion the interests of Ontario farmers; to work towards a sustainable future for farmers; *Member of:* Agricultural Credit Corporation; AgEnergy Co-operative Ltd.; Agricultural Adaptation Council; Biosolids Utilization Committee; Canadian Federation of Agriculture; Cooperators Insurance; Drains Action Working Group; Farm & Food Care Ontario; Guelph Chamber of Commerce; and more...; Affiliation(s): SHARE Agriculture Foundation
Chief Officer(s):
Mark Wales, President
Don McCabe, Vice-President
Debra Pretty-Straathof, Vice-President
Finances: *Funding Sources:* Membership fees; Sponsorships
Staff: 21 staff member(s)
Membership: 38,000 individual + 31 organizations; *Fees:* $220.35
Activities: Engaging in advocacy activities; providing networking opportunities
Meetings/Conferences:
For more information see Trade Shows, Conferences and Seminars Chapter
Ontario Federation of Agriculture 2013 Southwest Agricultural Conference
2013 Ridgetown, ON
Publications:
•Ag Buyer's Guide [a publication of the Ontario Federation of Agriculture]
Type: Guide
Profile: Information to assist Ontario farmers purchase equipment
•Better Farming
Type: Magazine; *Frequency:* Monthly; *Price:* Free with Ontario Federation of Agriculture membership
Profile: A business magazine about Ontario agriculture
•Country Guide
Type: Magazine
Profile: Suggestions to improve farm profitability plus innovative technologies
•Ontario Federation of Agriculture Policy Handbook
Type: Handbook; *Number of Pages:* 42; *Price:* Free with Ontario Federation of Agriculture membership
Profile: Topics addressed include animal welfare & control; education, schools, & training; energy; environment; farm implements; finance; labour, employment, & human resources;land use planning; marketing & production; rural affairs; science & technology; telecommunications; & transportation

Ontario Federation of Anglers & Hunters (OFAH)
Parent Name: Canadian Wildlife Federation

PO Box 2800, 4601 Guthrie Dr., Peterborough ON K9J 8L5
Tel: 705-748-6324; *Fax:* 705-748-9577
e-mail: ofah@ofah.org
www.ofah.org
www.facebook.com/127166042780
twitter.com/ofah
www.youtube.com/ofahcommunications
Overview: A medium-sized provincial charitable organization founded in 1928 overseen by Canadian Wildlife Federation
Mission: To save & defend from waste the natural resources of Ontario, its soils, minerals, air, water, forests & wildlife
Chief Officer(s):
Rob Hare, President
Mike Reader, Executive Director
Finances: *Funding Sources:* Membership fees; Donations
Membership: 83,000 individuals + 655 affiliated clubs; *Fees:* $45.50 adult; $57.50 family; $33.00 youth; $1,000 life; *Member Profile:* Interest in fish & wildlife conservation; *Committees:* Land Access; Forestry; Fisheries; Hunter Education
Activities: Ontario Family Fishing Weekend, July; Project Purple Week, Aug.
Meetings/Conferences:
For more information see Trade Shows, Conferences and Seminars Chapter
Ontario Federation of Anglers & Hunters 2013 Annual Get Outdoors Youth Leadership Conference
March 2013, ON
Ontario Federation of Anglers & Hunters 2013 85th Annual General Meeting & Fish & Wildlife Conference
2013, ON

Ontario Field Ornithologists (OFO)

PO Box 455, Stn. R, Toronto ON M4G 4E1
e-mail: membership@ofo.ca
www.ofo.ca
Overview: A medium-sized international charitable organization founded in 1982
Mission: To study bird life in Ontario
Chief Officer(s):
John Black, President & Director, Certificates & Convention, 905-684-0143
jblack3@brocku.ca
Robert Maciver, Vice-President & Director, Birdathon & Convention, 519-260-0729
robert.maciver@gmail.com
Lynne Freeman, Secretary & Director, Convention, 416-463-9540
lynnef@interlog.com
Brian Gibbon, Treasurer, 705-726-8969
bwg@backland.net
Marcie Jacklin, Director, Advertising
advertising@ofo.ca

David Milsom, Director, Publicity & Field Trips
fieldtrips@ofo.ca
Doug Woods, Director, Memberships, Mailbox, & Website, 416-466-4660
membership@ofo.ca
Finances: *Funding Sources:* Membership fees; Donations
Membership: *Fees:* $35 Canada; $40 USA; $45 international; $700 Canadian life membership; $800 USA life membership; $900 international life membership; *Member Profile:* Field ornithologists from Ontario & abroad; *Committees:* Annual Convention; Distinguished Ornithologist Award Nomination; Ontario Bird Records; OFO Website & Photo Page; ONTBIRDS Listserv
Activities: Offering field trips to birding spots in Ontario; Publishing site guides to birding areas of Ontario; Facilitating the exchange of information
Meetings/Conferences:
For more information see Trade Shows, Conferences and Seminars Chapter
Ontario Field Ornithologists 2013 Annual Convention
September 2013 Pt. Pelee, ON
Ontario Field Ornithologists 2014 Annual Convention
2014, ON
Publications:
•Field Checklist of Ontario Birds
Type: Booklet; *Price:* $2
•OFO [Ontario Field Ornithologists] News
Type: Newsletter; *Frequency:* 3 pa; *Editor:* Seabrooke Leckie; *Price:* Free with Ontario Field Ornithologists membership
Profile: Announcements, field trip reports, site guides, & Ontario Bird Records Committe reports
•Ontario Birds
Type: Journal; *Frequency:* 3 pa; *Editor:* R. James; G. Coady; D.V. Weseloh; *Price:* Free with Ontario Field Ornithologists membership
Profile: New information about the status, distribution, identification, & behaviour of birds in Ontario
•Ornithology in Ontario
Type: Book; *Number of Pages:* 400; *Editor:* Martin McNicholl; John Cranmer-Byng
Profile: Historical overview, archaeology, early naturalists, biographies, zoology, museums, bird banding, species accounts, & studies

Ontario Fire Buff Associates (OFBA)

PO Box 802, Stn. Q, Toronto ON M4T 2N7
e-mail: ontariofirebuffs@yahoo.ca
www.ofba.ca
Overview: A small provincial organization founded in 1971
Mission: To bring together people who share a common interest - the fire service of Ontario; *Member of:* International Fire Buff Associates
Chief Officer(s):
Rick Loiselle, President
Finances: *Annual Operating Budget:* Less than $50,000
Staff: 170 volunteer(s)
Membership: 100-499;; *Fees:* $15-$28; *Member Profile:* Open to any eligible individual or organization upon required recommendation, payment of fees & approval of the Board of Directors

Ontario Forest Industries Association (OFIA) / l'Industrie forestière de l'Ontario

#950, 20 Toronto St., Toronto ON M5C 2B8
Tel: 416-368-6188; *Fax:* 416-368-5445
e-mail: info@ofia.com
www.ofia.com
Overview: A medium-sized provincial organization founded in 1943
Mission: To act as a unified voice on behalf of member companies to ensure industry positions are considered; To respond to industry issues, such as economic, environmental, & technological developments
Environmental Activity: Working towards sustainable development, by balancing economic & environmental interests; Ensuring that member companies adhere to a Code of Forest Practices & a Statement of Environmental Policy
Chief Officer(s):
Jamie Lim, President/CEO, 416-368-6188
Mark Holmes, Manager, Public Affairs, 416-368-9196
Scott Jackson, Manager, Forest Policy
Membership: 13 member companies + 10 affiliate members; *Member Profile:* Companies, ranging from large multinational corporations to small businesses, that produce materials such as pulp, paper, paperboard, plywood, panelboard, veneer, & lumber
Activities: Liaising with government & other business sectors; Developinig partnerships, such as the Ontario Forestry Coalition; Raising awareness of the forest industry in Ontario; Providing opportunities for members to discuss industry issues
Publications:
•Canadian Forests: A Primer
Number of Pages: 50; *Author:* Dr. Ken Armson; *ISBN:* 1-895540-17-8
Profile: Part of the Environmental Literacy Series, the contents address the ownership & governance of forests, forest management, the economy

Ontario Forestry Association (OFA) / Association forestière de l'Ontario
Parent Name: Canadian Forestry Association

#700, 144 Front St. W., Toronto ON MSJ 2L7
Tel: 416-493-4565; *Fax:* 416-493-4608
Toll-Free: 800-387-0790
e-mail: info@oforest.ca
www.oforest.ca
www.linkedin.com/company/ontario-forestry-association
www.facebook.com/ontarioforestryassoc
twitter.com/ontforest
www.youtube.com/user/ontforest
Overview: A medium-sized provincial charitable organization founded in 1949 overseen by Canadian Forestry Association
Mission: To promote sound land use & full development protection & utilization of Ontario's forest resources for maximum public advantage; to increase public awareness, school education & natural appreciation of forests; to bring about better understanding of forests to people of all ages & backgrounds
Chief Officer(s):
Carla Grant, Executive Director
Finances: *Annual Operating Budget:* $250,000-$500,000
Staff: 4 staff member(s); 100 volunteer(s)
Membership: 1000; *Fees:* $50 individual, $25 student, $150 group, $85 educational institution, $1000 life; *Committees:* Public Forestry Education; Speakers Bureau; Trees Ontario; Woodland Owners; Honour Roll of Ontario Trees
Activities: Ontario Envirothon; National Forest Week; Focus on Forests First; Tree Bee; Forestry Careers Awareness; Forestry Connects; Invite a forester into your classroom; *Speaker Service:* Yes
Awards:
•James S. Miller Memorial Scholarship (Scholarship)
Eligibility: Student in Northern Ontario in final year of high school entering first year of post-secondary education in natural resources or related field *Deadline:* February *Contact:* Tracey Cooke
•John Wesley Beaver Memorial Awards (Scholarship)
Eligibility: Student of Native ancestry entering Ontario college or university for engineering, technology, environmental studies, forestry, biology, land use & environmental planning, or business *Amount:* $4000
•Bentley Cropping Systems Fellowship (Scholarship)
Eligibility: Student in graduate studies doing research related to agriculture, forestry or biology in developing countries *Amount:* $30,000
•William Peyton Hubbard Award (Scholarship)
Eligibility: African-Canadian student in 2nd, 3rd or 4th year in engineering, computer science, forestry or business *Amount:* $2,000-4,000

Ontario Fruit & Vegetable Growers' Association (OFVGA) / L'Association des fruiticulteurs et des maraîchers de l'Ontario

#105, 355 Elmira Rd. North, Guelph ON N1K 1S5
Tel: 519-763-6160; *Fax:* 519-763-6604
e-mail: info@ofvga.org
www.ofvga.org
Overview: A medium-sized provincial organization founded in 1859
Mission: Dedicated to the advancement of horticulture, working proactively through effective lobbying for the betterment of the industry & producers as a whole through advocacy, research, education, communication & marketing; *Member of:* Canadian Horticultural Council
Chief Officer(s):
Art Smith, CEO Ext. 115
artsmith@ofvga.org
Finances: *Annual Operating Budget:* $500,000-$1.5 Million; *Funding Sources:* Membership fees; advertising revenue
Staff: 7 staff member(s)
Membership: 7,500; *Fees:* $30
Activities: *Speaker Service:* Yes

Ontario Good Roads Association (OGRA)

#22, 1525 Cornwall Rd., Oakville ON L6J 0B2
Tel: 289-291-6472; *Fax:* 289-291-6477
e-mail: info@ogra.org
www.ogra.org
ca.linkedin.com/pub/ontario-good-roads-association/43/b08/829
twitter.com/Ont_Good_Roads
Overview: A medium-sized provincial organization founded in 1894
Mission: To represent the transportation & public works-related interests of Ontario's municipalities & First Nation communities; To deliver programs & services that meet the needs of members; To support municipalities in the provision of effective & efficient transportation systems throughout Ontario
Environmental Activity: Providing workshops about winter maintenance materials, such as salt
Chief Officer(s):
Joseph W. Tiernay, Executive Director
Brian Anderson, Manager, MEmber & Technical Services
Scott Butler, Manager, Policy & Research
Heather Crewe, Manager, Education & Training
Rayna Gillis, Manager, Finance & Administration
Colette Caruso, Coordinator, Communications & Marketing
Roni Kean, Coordinator, Curriculum
Cherry-Lyn Sales, Coordinator, Training Services
Fahad Shuja, Coordinator, Member Services & OPS
James Smith, Coordinator, Member Services & Infrastructure
Finances: *Funding Sources:* Membership fees; Sponsorships
Membership: 400+ municipalities; *Member Profile:* Ontario municipalities; First Nations communities; Corporations; Life & honourary members; *Committees:* Executive; Policy; Member Services; Nominating; Combined Conference; Companions Program
Activities: Advocating for the collective interests of municipal transportation & works departments; Analyzing policies; Reviewing legislation; Consulting with stakeholders & partners; Offering education & training opportunities
Meetings/Conferences:
For more information see Trade Shows, Conferences and Seminars Chapter
Ontario Good Roads Association / Rural Ontario Municipal Association 2013 Combined Conference
February 2013, ON
Ontario Good Roads Association / Rural Ontario Municipal Association 2014 Combined Conference
February 2014 Toronto, ON
Publications:
•Milestones [a publication of the Ontario Good Roads Association]
Type: Magazine; *Frequency:* 4 pa; *Accepts Advertising*; *Editor:* Colette Caruso; Scott Butler
Profile: Articles of interest to the municipal services sector, including a conference issue & a wintermaintenance issue
•Ontario Good Roads Association Annual Report
Type: Yearbook; *Frequency:* Annually

The Ontario Greenhouse Alliance (TOGA)

PO Box 175, #6, 76 Main St., Grimsby ON L3M 1S5
Tel: 905-945-9773; *Fax:* 905-945-5767
Toll-Free: 888-480-0659
e-mail: info@theontariogreenhousealliance.com
www.theontariogreenhousealliance.com
Overview: A small provincial organization founded in 2003
Mission: To provide an infrastructure & approach that will integrate all the current resources & future potential of the Ontario greenhouse stakeholders into a community & international marketplace presence, with the synergy & standards to be a world leader in greenhouse operations
Chief Officer(s):
Rejean Picard, Chair
Membership: *Member Profile:* Ontario's greenhouse vegetable, pepper & flower growers

The Ontario Greens ***See*** The Green Party of Ontario

Ontario Ground Water Association (OGWA)
Parent Name: Canadian Ground Water Association

48 Front St. East, Strathroy ON N7G 1Y6
Tel: 519-245-7194; *Fax:* 519-245-7196
www.ogwa.ca
Previous Name: Ontario Water Well Association
Overview: A medium-sized provincial organization founded in 1952 overseen by Canadian Ground Water Association
Mission: To protect & promote Ontario's ground water; To provide guidance to members, government representatives, & the public

Environmental Activity: Working to ensure the delivery of safe & clean water supplies throughout Ontario
Chief Officer(s):
Greg Bullock, President
Rob MacKinnon, Secretary-Treasurer
Anne Gammage, Office Manager, 519-245-7194, Fax: 519-245-7196
Finances: *Funding Sources:* Membership dues
Membership: *Member Profile:* Ground water professionals
Activities: Disseminating information & providing education about ground water; Promoting technical skills of ground water professional
Meetings/Conferences:
For more information see Trade Shows, Conferences and Seminars Chapter
Ontario Ground Water Association 61st Annual Convention & Trade Show: Drillapalooza 2013
April 2013 Hunstville, ON
Publications:
•The Source [a publication of the Ontario Ground Water Association]
Type: Newsletter; *Accepts Advertising*; *Editor:* Shannon Savory
Profile: Ontario Ground Water Association information, plus feature articles & industry news

Ontario Healthy Communities Coalition (OHCC) / Coalition des communautés en santé de l'Ontario
#1810, 2 Carlton St., Toronto ON M5B 1J3
Tel: 416-408-4841; *Fax:* 416-408-4843
Toll-Free: 800-766-3418
www.ohcc-ccso.ca
Overview: A medium-sized provincial charitable organization
Mission: To achieve social, environmental, economic & physical well-being for individuals, communities & local governments throughout Ontario
Chief Officer(s):
Anderson Rouse, Coordinator, Finance & Administration
Lorna Heidenheim, Executive Director
lorna@healthycommunities.on.ca
Finances: *Annual Operating Budget:* $250,000-$500,000; *Funding Sources:* Trillium Foundation; Ministry of Health & Long Term Care; Ministry of Environment
Staff: 10 staff member(s); 2 volunteer(s)
Membership: 94 organizations; *Member Profile:* Provincial associations; community; individuals; *Committees:* Diversity; Communication; Resource Develoment; Food Security
Activities: *Speaker Service:* Yes; *Library:* Open to public by appointment

Ontario Heritage Trust (OHT) / Fiducie du patrimoine ontarien
10 Adelaide St. East, Toronto ON M5C 1J3
Tel: 416-325-5000; *Fax:* 416-325-5071
e-mail: marketing@heritagefdn.on.ca
www.heritagetrust.on.ca
Overview: A medium-sized provincial charitable organization founded in 1967
Mission: Dedicated to the preservation, protection & promotion of Ontario's built, natural & cultural heritage for all of us to enjoy now & for others to experience in the future
Chief Officer(s):
Richard Moorhouse, Executive Director
Activities: Enters into conservation easement agreements with the owners of heritage properties to ensure that the significant heritage features of these properties are protected; holds provincially significant heritage properties & collections "in trust" on behalf of the people of Ontario; provides technical assistance to individuals & groups involved in heritage preservation; protects significant natural areas & geological land formations through Natural Heritage & Niagara Escarpment Programs

Ontario Horticultural Association (OHA)
448 Paterson Ave., London ON N5W 5C7
e-mail: secretary@gardenontario.org
www.gardenontario.org
www.facebook.com/home.php?sk=group_167342733299811
twitter.com/gardenontario
Overview: A medium-sized provincial charitable organization founded in 1906
Mission: To promote civic beautification, preservation of the environment, youth work & education of many aspects of horticulture
Chief Officer(s):
Carol Dunk, President
president@gardenontario.org
Finances: *Annual Operating Budget:* Less than $50,000; *Funding Sources:* Membership dues; grants; fundraising
Staff: 1 staff member(s)
Membership: 278 societies; 40,000 members; *Fees:* $1; *Member Profile:* Gardener

Ontario Hospital Association (OHA)
Parent Name: Canadian Healthcare Association
#2800, 200 Front St. West, Toronto ON M5V 3L1
Tel: 416-205-1300; *Fax:* 416-205-1301
Toll-Free: 800-598-8002
e-mail: info@oha.com
www.oha.com
Overview: A medium-sized provincial organization founded in 1924 overseen by Canadian Healthcare Association
Mission: To build a strong, innovative, & sustainable health care system that meets patient care needs throughout Ontario; To promote an efficent & effective health care system
Environmental Activity: Hosting conferences on healthy work environments & sustainable hospital practices
Chief Officer(s):
Kevin P.D. Smith, Chair
Tom Closson, President & Chief Executive Officer
Warren DiClemente, Chief Operating Officer & VP, Educational Services
Julie Giraldi, Chief Human Resources & Officer, Information Technology
Doug Miller, Chief Financial Officer
Paul Davies, Treasurer
Membership: 159 public hospitals; *Member Profile:* Public hospitals throughout Ontario; Affiliated associations & organizations
Activities: Engaging in advocacy activities to help shape health care policy in Ontario; Building partnerships; Providing opportunities for professional development;
Publications:
•Healthcare Governance Update
Type: Newsletter
Profile: Information from the Governance Centre of Excellence to maintain & increase trustees' knowledge of health care governance issues
•Hospital Perspectives
Type: Newsletter; *Editor:* Tamarah Harel; *ISSN:* 1198-0192
Profile: Articles about innovations in health care
•OHA [Ontario Hospital Association] Executive Report
Type: Newsletter; *Frequency:* Weekly; *Editor:* Alessandra Nigro; *Price:* Free with membership in the Ontario Hospital Association
Profile: Current health care news
•Ontario Hospital Association Annual Report
Type: Yearbook; *Frequency:* Annually

Ontario Industrial Fire Protection Association (OIFPA)
193 James St. South, Hamilton ON L8P 3A8
Tel: 905-527-0700; *Fax:* 905-527-6254
e-mail: oifpa@interlynx.net
www.oifpa.org
Overview: A medium-sized provincial organization founded in 1981
Mission: To unite individuals with a concern for fire protection within Ontario's industrial community
Chief Officer(s):
Roy Graham, President
Jim Belrose, Vice-President
Todd Wilson, 2nd Vice-President
George Fawcett, Treasurer
Finances: *Funding Sources:* Membership fees
Membership: *Member Profile:* Individuals from the chemical industry & the oil & gas industry; Consulting engineers; Emergency response personnel; Municipal fire departments & fire protection consultants; Government agencies; Industrial underwriters
Activities: Creating networking opportunities with members from organizations such as municipal fire departments & government agencies; Providing educational seminars, on topics such as Ontario Fire Code updates, explosion protection, & fire pump installation
Publications:
•Firewatch
Type: Newsletter
Profile: Information updates from the association

Ontario Institute of Agrologists (OIA)
Parent Name: Agricultural Institute of Canada
Ontario AgriCentre, #108, 100 Stone Rd. West, Guelph ON N1G 5L3
Tel: 519-826-4226; *Fax:* 519-826-4228
Toll-Free: 866-339-7619
e-mail: info@oia.on.ca
www.oia.on.ca
Overview: A medium-sized provincial organization founded in 1960 overseen by Agricultural Institute of Canada
Mission: OIA regulates Ontario's Professional Agrologists & ensures that competencies meet a Standard of Practice within a specific scope of agrology; ensures that business is conducted within a Code of Ethics; protects the public interest; grows the agri-life science industry; contributes to the excellence of colleagues; pursues professional development to enhance knowledge, skills & experience so they can practise science of agrology with skill, integrity & transparency.; Affiliation(s): Certified Crop Advisor Program; Ontario Agricultural Hall of Fame Association; Ontario Agricultural Training Institute; Ontario Farm Animal Council; Western Fair Association
Chief Officer(s):
Bruce Hobin, President
Phillis Chang, Director, Finance & Admin. Ext. 232
Pat Joannie, Project Manager Ext. 231
projectmanager@oia.on.ca
Terry Kingsmill, Registrar Ext. 230
registrar@oia.on.ca
Finances: *Annual Operating Budget:* $100,000-$250,000
Staff: 3 staff member(s)
Membership: 900 individual; *Fees:* Variable; *Member Profile:* B.Sc (Agriculture) from Canadian university or equivalent; *Committees:* Act to Regulate Agrologists; Articling Agrologist Committee; Board of Examiners; Internet; Membership; Professional Development; Professional Standards; Public Relations
Activities: *Internships:* Yes
Awards:
•Public Relations Award (Award)
Presented to a member who has made an outstanding contribution to promoting OIA
•Branch Newsletter Award (Award)
Presented to the branch newsletter editor deemed by the Membership Committee to produce the most effective branch newsletter for their members
•Cheryl Somerville Memorial Distinguished Young Agrologist Award (Award)
Presented annually to an individual under 40 years of age who has made significant contributions to the agriculture & food industry in this province, the profession of agrology &/or the OIA
•Distinguished Agrologist (Award)
Member individuals who have rendered signal service to the agricultural industry of Ontario &/or the affairs of the OIA
•Honourary Life Member (Award)
Individuals who have rendered signal service to the agricultural industry of Ontario
•President's Honour Roll (Award)
Member individuals who have contributed greatly to branch effectiveness during the year
Meetings/Conferences:
For more information see Trade Shows, Conferences and Seminars Chapter
The Canadian Greenhouse Conference (CGC) 2013
October 2013 Niagara Falls, ON
The Canadian Greenhouse Conference (CGC) 2014
October 2014, ON
The Canadian Greenhouse Conference (CGC) 2015
October 2015, ON

Ontario Lumber Manufacturers' Association (OLMA) / Association des manufacturiers de bois de sciage de l'Ontario
PO Box 97530, #1202, 55 York St., Toronto ON M1C 4Z1
Tel: 416-367-9717; *Fax:* 416-367-3415
e-mail: info@olma.ca
www.olma.ca
Overview: A medium-sized provincial organization founded in 1966
Mission: To ensure a sound & renewable forest economy; To oversee lumber grading licenses & quality control at member sawmills in Ontario; To ensure market access within Northern America, Europe, & Japan; Affiliation(s): Canadian Lumber Standards Accreditation Board; American Lumber Standards Committee, Inc.
Environmental Activity: Ensuring the role of forests in the envionment is protected
Chief Officer(s):
Dale Kaemingh, Chair
Hartley Multamaki, Vice-Chair

David G. Milton, President & Secretary
president@olma.ca
Hal Brindley, Treasurer
Andre G. Boucher, Chief Grading Inspector
inspection@olma.ca
Membership: *Member Profile:* Ontario sawmills, planing mills, lumber remanufacturers, & MSR & Fj manufacturers; Ontario companies engaged in equipment manufacturing, & lumber sales & distribution
Activities: Training persons to classify lumber; Supervising the grading of lumber; Authorizing manufacturing facilities to mark pieces of lumber with the OLMA facsimile stamp; Mediating disputes between sellers & buyers of lumber with the OLMA stamp; Promoting trade & diversification; Improving access to markets for Canadian softwood lumber; Reviewing forestry issues & policies; Liaising with government

Ontario Lung Association (OLA)
Parent Name: Canadian Lung Association

573 King St. East, Toronto ON M5A 4L3
Tel: 416-864-9911; *Fax:* 416-864-9916
Toll-Free: 888-344-5864
e-mail: olalung@on.lung.ca
www.on.lung.ca
www.facebook.com/OntarioLungAssociation?ref=ts
twitter.com/OntarioLung
www.youtube.com/user/ONLungAssociation
Overview: A large provincial charitable organization founded in 1945 overseen by Canadian Lung Association
Mission: To provide lung health information & support to people affected by lung disease; To prevent & control chronic lung disease
Environmental Activity: Offering indoor & outdoor air quality information
Chief Officer(s):
Hélène Michaud, Chair
George Habib, President & Chief Executive Officer
Eric Bentzen, Treasurer
Finances: *Funding Sources:* Donations; Fundraising; Sponsorships
Activities: Supporting lung health research; Providing education about asthma (Asthma Action Helpline) & chronic obstructive pulmonary disease (BreathWorks Program); Offering smoking cessation information; *Awareness Events:* Lungs Are For Life Program; The Amazing Pace; Tulip Day
Publications:
•Asthma Action
Type: Newsletter
•Breathworks
Type: Newsletter
•Oxygen
Type: Newsletter
Profile: Lung health information, donor & research profiles, & forthcoming events

Belleville Office (Hastings & Prince Edward Counties)

c/o Century Place, #107, 199 Front St., Belleville ON K8N 5H5
Tel: 613-969-0323; *Fax:* 613-969-0359
Toll-Free: 800-972-2636
e-mail: jobrien@on.lung.ca
www.on.lung.ca

Brantford Office (Brant County)

410 Colborne St., Lower Level, Brantford ON N3S 3N6
Tel: 519-753-4682; *Fax:* 519-753-4667
e-mail: brant@on.lung.ca
www.on.lung.ca

Hamilton Office (Hamilton, Niagara, & Waterloo & Wellington Regions)
#4, 1447 Upper Ottawa St., Hamilton ON L8W 3J6
Tel: 905-383-1616; *Fax:* 905-383-1213
e-mail: hamilton@on.lung.ca
www.on.lung.ca

Kingston Office (Kingston & the Thousand Islands)

c/o The Woolen Mill, #301, 4 Cataraqui St., Kingston ON K7L 1Z7
Tel: 613-545-3462; *Fax:* 613-545-1007
Toll-Free: 866-534-5514
e-mail: jobrien@on.lung.ca
www.on.lung.ca

London Office (Bluewater-Thames Valley)

480 Egerton St., London ON N5W 3Z6
Tel: 519-453-9086; *Fax:* 519-453-9184
e-mail: london@on.lung.ca
www.on.lung.ca

Ottawa Office (Ottawa, Renfrew County, & Cornwall Area)

#500, 2319 St. Laurent Blvd., Ottawa ON K1G 4J8
Tel: 613-230-4200; *Fax:* 613-230-5210
www.on.lung.ca

Sault Ste Marie Office (Algoma Area)

516 Queen St. East, Sault Ste Marie ON P6A 2A1
Tel: 705-256-2335; *Fax:* 705-256-1210
e-mail: gbriglio@on.lung.ca
www.on.lung.ca

Simcoe Office (Haldimand & Norfolk Counties)

203 John St., Simcoe ON N3Y 2Y6
Tel: 519-426-4973; *Fax:* 519-426-2729
e-mail: haldimand@on.lung.ca
www.on.lung.ca

Stratford Office (Huron-Perth)

c/o Jenny Trout Centre, #121, 342 Erie St., Stratford ON N5A 2N4
Tel: 519-271-7500; *Fax:* 519-271-7503
e-mail: dherman@on.lung.ca
www.on.lung.ca

Toronto Office (Greater Toronto Area West)

#118, 295 The West Mall, Toronto ON M9C 4Z4
Tel: 416-622-2566; *Fax:* 416-622-3847
Toll-Free: 866-525-5864
e-mail: peel@on.lung.ca
www.on.lung.ca
Chief Officer(s):
Janet Hatch, Contact

Windsor Office (Windsor-Essex & Chatham-Kent Area)

#104, 647 Ouellette Ave., Windsor ON N9A 4J4
Tel: 519-256-3433; *Fax:* 519-256-8179
e-mail: windsor@on.lung.ca
www.on.lung.ca

Ontario Marine Operators Association ***See*** Boating Ontario

Ontario Medical Association (OMA)
Parent Name: Canadian Medical Association

#900, 150 Bloor St. West, Toronto ON M5S 3C1
Tel: 416-599-2580; *Fax:* 416-340-2944
Toll-Free: 800-268-7215
e-mail: info@oma.org
www.oma.org
Overview: A large provincial organization founded in 1880 overseen by Canadian Medical Association
Mission: To represent the clinical, political, & economic interests of Ontario physicians; To promote an accessible, quality health-care system
Chief Officer(s):
Mark MacLeod, President
Catherine Flaman, Contact, Member Relations, Public Affairs & Communications, 416-340-2915, Fax: 416-340-2950
mentor@oma.org
Membership: 30,000+; *Member Profile:* Practicing physicians, residents, & students who are enrolled in one of Ontario's faculties of medicine
Activities: Advocating for the health of Ontarians; Promoting health care services throughout Ontario; Providing a continuing medical education program; Offering tools to manage an effective practice, such as legal advice & incorporation services
Meetings/Conferences:
For more information see Trade Shows, Conferences and Seminars Chapter
Ontario Medical Association, Sport Medicine Section 2013 Annual Symposium: Sport Med
January 2013 Toronto, ON
Publications:
•Ontario Medical Review
Type: Journal

Ontario Mineral Exploration Federation (OMEF) ***See*** Ontario Prospectors Association

Ontario Mining Association (OMA)
Parent Name: Mining Association of Canada

#520, 5775 Yonge St., Toronto ON M2M 4J1
Tel: 416-364-9301; *Fax:* 416-364-5986
e-mail: pmcbride@oma.on.ca
www.oma.on.ca
Overview: A medium-sized provincial organization founded in 1920 overseen by Mining Association of Canada
Mission: To help improve the competitiveness of the Ontario mineral industry
Chief Officer(s):
Chris Hodgson, President
Finances: *Annual Operating Budget:* $500,000-$1.5 Million; *Funding Sources:* Membership fees
Staff: 6 staff member(s)
Membership: 45; *Committees:* Environmental Steering Committee; Energy; Workers Health & Safety
Activities: *Awareness Events:* Ontario Mining Week, 1st week of May

Ontario Municipal Human Resources Association (OMHRA)

#307, 1235 Fairview St., Burlington ON L7S 2K9
Tel: 905-525-4000; *Fax:* 905-525-9833
e-mail: admin@omhra.ca
www.omhra.ca
Previous Name: Ontario Municipal Personnel Association
Overview: A medium-sized provincial organization founded in 1963
Mission: To provide direction on issues of human resources management; To represent the interests of the association, related to legislation & policies
Chief Officer(s):
Peggy Mellor, President
Kandy Webb, Vice-President
Christine A. Ball, Executive Officer
Finances: *Funding Sources:* Membership fees; Sponsorships
Membership: *Member Profile:* Ontario human resources professionals who are employed by municipalities, commissions, & local public sector boards
Activities: Facilitating the exchange of information from the field of human resources; Promoting education;

Ontario Municipal Management Development Board ***See*** Ontario Municipal Management Institute

Ontario Municipal Management Institute (OMMI)

618 Balmoral Dr., Oshawa ON L1J 3A7
Tel: 905-434-8885; *Fax:* 905-434-7381
www.ommi.on.ca
Previous Name: Ontario Municipal Management Development Board
Overview: A small provincial organization founded in 1979
Mission: To enhance management skills, in order to strengthen local government administration
Chief Officer(s):
Bill McKim, Executive Director
Shea-Lea Latchford, Administrative Assistant
Membership: 350; *Member Profile:* Local governments, including cities, towns, regions, & municipalities
Activities: Providing educational workshops & seminars; Conducting training opportunities; Certifying qualified candidates with the Certified Municipal Manager designation (CMM); Liaising with other professional local government associations
Publications:
•Councillor Development Resource Manual
Type: Manual
•You & Your Local Government
Type: Handbook

Ontario Municipal Personnel Association ***See*** Ontario Municipal Human Resources Association

Ontario Municipal Water Association (OMWA)

c/o Doug Parker, 43 Chelsea Cres., Belleville ON K8N 4Z5
Tel: 613-966-1100; *Fax:* 613-966-3024
Toll-Free: 888-231-1115
www.omwa.org
Overview: A medium-sized provincial organization
Mission: To act as the voice of municipal water supply in Ontario; To ensure the safety, quality, reliability, & sustainability of drinking water in Ontario; Affiliation(s): Ontario Water Works

Association (a section of the American Water Works Association)
Chief Officer(s):
Ed Houghton, President
ehoughton@collus.com
Douglas Parker, Executive Director, 613-966-1100, Fax: 613-966-3024
dparker@omwa.org
Membership: 180+ public drinking water authorities in Ontario; *Fees:* Schedule available, based upon population; *Member Profile:* Ontario's public water supply authorities
Activities: Reviewing policy, & legislative, & regulatory issues; Liaising with government, agencies, & associations to maintain safe & sustainable water sources; Lobbying to improve conditions; Promoting high standards of treatment, infrastructure, & operations; Offering technical training for operating authorities, operators, & owners of drinking water systems; Encouraging dissemination of information for public education
Meetings/Conferences:
For more information see Trade Shows, Conferences and Seminars Chapter
Ontario Water Works Association / Ontario Municipal Water Association 2013 Annual Joint Conference & Trade Show
2013, ON
Ontario Municipal Water Association 2nd Annual Drinking Water Leadership Summit (in partnership with MediaEDGE Communications)
October 2013 Toronto, ON
Publications:
•Councillors Handbook: Stewardship Responsibilities Under the Safe Drinking Water Act
Type: Handbook
•Ontario Municipal Water Association Members' Handbook
Type: Handbook

Ontario Nature

#612, 214 King St West, Toronto ON M5H 3S6
Tel: 416-444-8419; *Fax:* 416-444-9866
Toll-Free: 800-440-2366
e-mail: info@ontarionature.org
www.ontarionature.org
www.facebook.com/OntarioNature?ref=ts
twitter.com/ontarionature
www.youtube.com/user/ONNature
Previous Name: Federation of Ontario Naturalists
Overview: A large provincial charitable organization founded in 1931
Mission: To promote knowledge, understanding & respect for Ontario's natural heritage & commitment to its conservation & protection on the part of the FON membership, landowners, decision makers & the general public; To seek legislation, policies, practices & institutions which permanently protect Ontario's natural ecosystem & indigenous biodiversity, including the establishment of a comprehensive natural heritage system for Ontario with an enlarged system of parks & other protected areas linked by a network of existing & rehabilitated natural corridors; Affiliation(s): Coalition on the Niagara Escarpment; Conservation Council of Ontario; Great Lakes United; International Union for Conservation of Nature & Natural Resources; International Committee for Bird Preservation
Environmental Activity: Ontario Nature protects wild species and wild spaces through conservation, education & public engagement.
Chief Officer(s):
Nidhi Tandon, President
Caroline Schultz, Executive Director
Finances: *Annual Operating Budget:* $1.5 Million-$3 Million; *Funding Sources:* Private donations; membership dues; foundations
Staff: 24 staff member(s); 100 volunteer(s)
Membership: 30,000 individuals + 140 member groups; *Fees:* $50
Activities: ; *Library:* by appointment

Ontario Parks Association (OPA)

7856 - 5th Line South, RR#4, Milton ON L9T 2X8
Tel: 905-864-6182; *Fax:* 905-864-6184
Toll-Free: 866-560-7783
e-mail: opa@ontarioparksassociation.ca
www.ontarioparksassociation.ca
Overview: A medium-sized provincial charitable organization founded in 1936
Mission: To develop & protect parks & green spaces in Ontario
Environmental Activity: Advocating for the protection of parks & open spaces throughout Ontario; Conserving parks, open spaces, & the environment
Chief Officer(s):
Paul Ronan, Executive Director, 905-864-6182 Ext. 6730
paul@ontarioparksassociation.ca
Eric Trogdon, Executive Director
eric@opassoc.on.ca
Shelley May, Coordinator, Operations & Administration, 905-864-6182 Ext. 6710
opa@ontarioparksassociation.ca
Maureen Sinclair, President
msinclair@brantford.ca
Bill Harding, Vice-President
bhardin@toronto.ca
Finances: *Funding Sources:* Donations
Membership: *Fees:* $70 students & seniors; $130 individuals; $500 associates
Activities: Offering education to park professionals
Meetings/Conferences:
For more information see Trade Shows, Conferences and Seminars Chapter
Ontario Parks Association 2013 57th Annual Educational Forum
February 2013 Mississauga, ON
Ontario Parks Association 2013 Parks & Landscaping Equipment Safety Operations Program
2013, ON
Ontario Parks Association 2013 Playground Introductory Compliance & Hazard Analysis Workshop
2013, ON
Ontario Parks Association 2013 Ball Diamond Maintenance & Best Practices Workshop
2013, ON
Ontario Parks Association 2013 Parks Oriented Chainsaw Safety Awareness & Basic Chipper Operations & Handling Course
2013, ON
Ontario Parks Association 2013 Trails Specialist Workshop
2013, ON
Ontario Parks Association 2013 Supervisor Competency Program
2013, ON
Ontario Parks Association 2013 Accident / Incident Investigation Program
2013, ON
Ontario Parks Association 2013 Parks Equipment Safety Training & Train the Trainer Program
2013, ON
Ontario Parks Association 2013 Parks Confined Spaces Program
2013, ON
Ontario Parks Association 2013 Registered Playground Practitioner Program
2013, ON
Publications:
•OPA [Ontario Parks Association] Playability Tool Kit: Building Accessible Playspaces
Type: Kit
Profile: Creating playspaces that are accessible to persons with disabilities
•Urban Parks in Ontario
Type: Book; *Author:* Dr. J.R. Wright
Profile: The evolution of parks & open space development

Ontario Pest Control Association ***See*** Structural Pest Management Association of Ontario

Ontario Petroleum Institute Inc. (OPI)

#104, 555 Southdale Rd. East, London ON N6E 1A2
Tel: 519-680-1620; *Fax:* 519-680-1621
www.ontpet.com
Overview: A medium-sized provincial organization founded in 1963
Mission: To promote responsible exploration & development by Ontario's oil, gas, hydrocarbon storage, & solution-mining industries
Chief Officer(s):
Hugh Moran, Executive Director
Finances: *Funding Sources:* Sponsorships
Membership: *Member Profile:* Geologists in Ontario; Geophysicists; Explorationists; Producers; Contractors; Petroleum engineers; Companies involved in the oil & gas, hydrocarbon storage, & solution mining industries
Activities: Liaising with government agencies; Disseminating information to members; Increasing public awareness of the importance of the industry in Ontario; *Library:* Ontario Oil, Gas, & Salt Resources Library
Meetings/Conferences:
For more information see Trade Shows, Conferences and Seminars Chapter
Ontario Petroleum Institute 2013 52nd Conference & Trade Show
2013
Publications:
•Ontario Oil & Gas
Type: Magazine; *Accepts Advertising*; *Editor:* Carly Peters
Profile: Articles about the oil & gas industry & technical features
•Ontario Petroleum Institute Conference Proceedings
Frequency: Annually; *Price:* $50
Profile: Topics presented by guest speakers from around the world at the Institute's annual conference & trade show
•Ontario Petroleum Institute Membership Directory
Type: Directory; *Frequency:* Annually; *Accepts Advertising*
Profile: Listings & advertising are available to members of the Ontario Petroleum Institute only
•OPI [Ontario Petroleum Institute Inc.] Newsletter
Type: Newsletter; *Frequency:* Bimonthly; *Accepts Advertising*; *ISSN:* 14802201
Profile: Membership updates, reports, conferences, & legislation information

Ontario Pipe Trades Council

Confederation Square, #203, 45 Goderich Rd., Hamilton ON L8E 4W8
Tel: 905-573-3703; *Fax:* 905-573-0804
e-mail: info@optc.org
www.optc.org
Overview: A medium-sized provincial organization
Mission: To promote the many technical, commercial & environmental benefits of the Pipe Trades & maximize their use in the construction industry; to promote the interest of the plumbing, pipe fitting, sprinkler fitting & HVAC industry in the province of Ontario
Chief Officer(s):
Neil McCormack, Business Manager
Membership: 16 local unions

Ontario Plumbing Inspectors Association (OPIA)

129 Dumble Ave., Peterborough ON K9H 5A9
Tel: 705-748-0120
e-mail: opia@opia.info, secretary@opia.info
www.opia.info/members
Overview: A medium-sized provincial organization founded in 1920
Mission: To promote uniform enforcement of plumbing regulations; close liaison & interchange of ideas & knowledge between members of the OPIA & members of other associations; provide education & training to members & the industry; *Member of:* World Plumbing Council; Affiliation(s): Ontario Ministry of Municipal Affairs, Building Branch
Chief Officer(s):
Doug Flucker, President
Rainier Blundel, Vice President
Finances: *Annual Operating Budget:* $50,000-$100,000; *Funding Sources:* Membership fees
Staff: 14 volunteer(s)
Membership: 800; *Fees:* $60; *Committees:* Advisory; Auditors; Awards; Bulletin; Certification Review; Code Technical; Conference; Education; Election; Executive; Finance; Future Conference; Membership; Memorial; Nominations; Public Relations; Reciprocal Licensing; Resolutions; Special; Zone Meetings
Activities: CMX Show; CIPH Ex; Annual conference; *Library:* Open to public

Ontario Pollution Control Equipment Association (OPCEA)

PO Box 137, Midhurst ON L0L 1X0
Tel: 705-725-0917; *Fax:* 705-725-1068
e-mail: opcea@opcea.com
www.opcea.com
Previous Name: Ontario Sanitation Equipment Association
Overview: A small provincial organization founded in 1970
Mission: To assist members in the promotion of their services & equipment in Ontario; Affiliation(s): Water Environment Association of Ontario
Chief Officer(s):
Kelly Manden, Executive Administrator
Brian Allen, President, 416-743-3751, Fax: 416-743-2038
Wayne Harrison, Vice-President, 905-944-2777, Fax: 905-474-1660
Heinz Held, Treasurer, 905-791-1553, Fax: 905-791-2999
Finances: *Funding Sources:* Membership fees

Associations / Organizations

Membership: 160+; *Fees:* $339 initiation fee; $282 / year; *Member Profile:* Ontario firms that manufacture or distribute environmental & related equipment for the air & water pollution control marketplace
Publications:
•Influents [a publication of the Ontario Pollution Control Equipment Association]
Type: Magazine; *Accepts Advertising*; *Editor:* Cole Kelman
Profile: A combined publication of the Ontario Pollution Control Equipment Association & the Water Environment Association of Ontario,featuring information about forthcoming trade shows & events
•OPCEA [Ontario Pollution Control Equipment Association] Membership Directory & Buyers Guide
Type: Directory; *Frequency:* Annually; *Accepts Advertising*; *Editor:* Steve Davey
Profile: Listings of member companies, with their products & services, distributed to the Ontario marketplace

Ontario Printing & Imaging Association (OPIA)

#135, 3-1750 The Queensway, Toronto ON M9C 5H5
Tel: 905-602-4441; *Fax:* 905-602-9798
www.opia.on.ca
Overview: A medium-sized provincial organization
Mission: To provide leadership for a successful printing & imaging industry in Ontario; Affiliation(s): Canadian Printing Industries Association (CPIA); Printing Industries of America (PIA); Graphic Arts Technical Foundation (GATF)
Environmental Activity: Offering advice to businesses about environmental & safety concerns
Chief Officer(s):
Kim Stewart, Chair
Membership: *Committees:* Events; Government Affairs; Environment, Health & Safety; Human Resource Services; Membership; Communications; Strategic Planning
Activities: Providing technical advice; Facilitating the exchange of ideas; Offering print referral services

Ontario Professional Fire Fighters Association (OPFFA) / Association des pompiers professionnels de l'Ontario (ind.)

292 Plains Rd. East, Burlington ON L7T 2C6
Tel: 905-681-7111; *Fax:* 905-681-1489
www.opffa.org
Previous Name: Provincial Federation of Ontario Fire Fighters
Overview: A medium-sized provincial organization founded in 1997
Affiliation(s): International Association of Fire Fighters
Chief Officer(s):
Fred LeBlanc, President
Mark McKinnon, Executive Vice-President
Barry Quinn, Secretary-Treasurer
Jeff Braun-Jackson, Office Manager & Researcher
Membership: *Member Profile:* Full-time professional fire fighters throughout Ontario; *Committees:* Education; Health & Safety & Section 21; Finance; Workplace Safety & Insurance Board; Occupational Disease; Pension; Legislative; Human Relations
Activities: Educating members to negotiate & administer collective agreements
Meetings/Conferences:
For more information see Trade Shows, Conferences and Seminars Chapter
Ontario Professional Fire Fighters Association 2013 16th Annual Convention
June 2013, ON
Ontario Professional Fire Fighters Association 2013 Annual Legislative Conference
2013, ON
Ontario Professional Fire Fighters Association 2014 17th Annual Convention
2014, ON

Ontario Professional Foresters Association (OPFA)

#201, 5 Wesleyan St., Georgetown ON L7G 2E2
Tel: 905-877-3679; *Fax:* 905-877-6766
e-mail: opfa@opfa.ca
www.opfa.ca
Overview: A medium-sized provincial organization founded in 1957
Mission: To operate as a regulatory body for the practice of professional forestry in Ontario; To govern members in accordance with the Ontairo Professional Foresters Act 2000
Chief Officer(s):
Tony Jennings, R.P.F, Executive Director; Registrar
Finances: *Annual Operating Budget:* $100,000-$250,000; *Funding Sources:* Membership fees
Staff: 7 staff member(s)
Membership: 850; *Fees:* Schedule available; *Member Profile:* Registered professional foresters who are committed to services in relation to the development, management, conservation, & sustainability of forest & urban forests; *Committees:* Statutory Committees: Executive; Complaints, Discipline; Registration. Standing Committees: Annual General Meeting; Blue Ribbon Panel; By-Laws; Competency; Communications Working Group; Editorial Board; Finance; Membership Standards; Private Land Forestry Network; Recognition & Awards Website
Activities: *Speaker Service:* Yes
Meetings/Conferences:
For more information see Trade Shows, Conferences and Seminars Chapter
Ontario Professional Foresters Association 2013 Annual Meeting
April 2013 Ottawa, ON
Ontario Professional Foresters Association 2014 Annual Meeting
2014

Ontario Professional Planners Institute (OPPI) / Institut des planificateurs professionnels de l'Ontario
Parent Name: Canadian Institute of Planners

#201, 234 Eglinton Ave. East, Toronto ON M4P 1K5
Tel: 416-483-1873; *Fax:* 416-483-7830
Toll-Free: 800-668-1448
e-mail: info@ontarioplanners.on.ca
www.ontarioplanners.on.ca
Overview: A medium-sized provincial organization founded in 1986 overseen by Canadian Institute of Planners
Mission: To act as the voice of Ontario's planning profession; To provide leadership on policies related to planning & development; Affiliation(s): Canadian Institute of Planners (CIP)
Environmental Activity: Providing leadership on policy related to the environment
Chief Officer(s):
Sue Cumming, President
Mary Ann Rangam, Executive Director
Robert Fraser, Manager, Finance & Administration
Loretta Ryan, Manager, Policy & Communications
Ron Keeble, Registrar
Finances: *Funding Sources:* Membership fees; Program & activity revenue
Membership: 3,000+ planners + 500 students; *Member Profile:* Practising planners throughout Ontario; Students; *Committees:* Discipline; Nominations; Membership Services; Membership Outreach; Professional Development; Policy Development; Recognition; Student Liaison
Activities: Offering professional development courses; Preparing position statements, policy papers, & other documents of interest to planners; Presenting awards for excellence in planning; *Awareness Events:* World Town Planning Day
Meetings/Conferences:
For more information see Trade Shows, Conferences and Seminars Chapter
Ontario Professional Planners Institute 2013 Conference
September 2013 London, ON
Publications:
•Consultants' Directory [a publication of the Ontario Professional Planners Institute]
Type: Directory
Profile: A source used by OPPI members & potential clients
•Ontario Planning Journal
Type: Journal; *Frequency:* Bimonthly; *Accepts Advertising*; *Editor:* Glenn Miller; *Price:* $55 / year Canada; $65 / year International
Profile: Ontario Professional Planners Institute activities & planning issues
•OPPI [Ontario Professional Planners Institute] Members Update
Type: Newsletter; *Frequency:* Monthly; *Price:* Free with membership in the Ontario Professional Planners Institute
Profile: Recent news from the institute for members only
•Planning by Design: A Healthy Communities Handbook
Type: Handbook
Profile: Produced by the Ontario Professional Planners Institute in partnership with the Ministry of Municipal Affairs & Housing

Ontario Prospectors Association (OPA)

c/o Garry Clark, 1000 Alloy Dr., Thunder Bay ON P7B 6A5
Tel: 807-622-3284; *Fax:* 807-622-4156
Toll-Free: 866-259-3727
www.ontarioprospectors.com
Previous Name: Ontario Mineral Exploration Federation (OMEF)
Overview: A small provincial organization founded in 1987
Mission: To advance the interests of prospectors & the mineral exploration industry; To promote ethical standards among prospectors in Ontario; To ensure adherence by members to the code of conduct
Chief Officer(s):
Garry Clark, Executive Director
gjclark@ontarioprospectors.com
Wally Rayner, President
Roger Poulin, Vice-President
John McCance, Secretary:
Membership: 3,000; *Committees:* Audit; Membership; Symposium; Education; Land Use / Access; Issue Resolution; Communications; Policy; Finance
Activities: Engaging in lobbying activities; Designing prospector development initiatives; Providing information; Developing awareness of the industry; Offering networking opportunities; Presenting awards
Publications:
•Building a Dialogue with Aboriginal Communities: A Guide for Junior Exploration Companies & Prospectors
Type: Guide
•The Explorationist [a publication of the Northern Prospectors Association & the Ontario Prospectors Association]
Type: Newsletter; *Frequency:* 10 pa
Profile: Information distributed to OPA members, associates, & government personnel about Ontario's mineralexploration scene
•Ontario Mining & Exploration Directory
Type: Directory
•The Ontario Prospector
Type: Magazine; *Frequency:* Semiannually; *Accepts Advertising*; *Editor:* Cadence Hays
Profile: Conference reports, feature articles, & buyers' guide

Ontario Public Health Association (OPHA) / Association pour la santé publique de l'Ontario
Parent Name: Canadian Public Health Association

#1850, 439 University Ave., Toronto ON M5G 1Y8
Tel: 416-367-3313; *Fax:* 416-367-2844
Toll-Free: 800-267-6817
e-mail: info@opha.on.ca
www.opha.on.ca
Overview: A medium-sized provincial organization founded in 1949 overseen by Canadian Public Health Association
Mission: To provide leadership on issues affecting public health in Ontario; To strengthen the influence of persons involved in public & community health across Ontario; Affiliation(s): Canadian Public Health Association
Environmental Activity: Offering information related to community & public health; Promoting public health issues
Chief Officer(s):
Siu Mee Cheng, Exeuctive Director, 416-367-3313 Ext. 226
Magdalena Wasilewska, Research Assistant, 416-367-3313 Ext. 229
Finances: *Funding Sources:* Membership fees; Sponsorships
Membership: 3,000; *Fees:* $50 students, retired persons, unemployed individuals; $85 individuals; *Member Profile:* Individuals & constituent societies interested in advancing public health
Activities: Providing education opportunities; Analyzing policy; Advocating for public health policies to improve the health of Ontarians; Liaising with governments; Partnering with other organizations to address broader elements of public health issues
Meetings/Conferences:
For more information see Trade Shows, Conferences and Seminars Chapter
Ontario Public Health Association 2013 Annual Conference & General Meeting
2013, ON
Publications:
•Ontario Public Health Association E-Bulletin
Type: Newsletter; *Frequency:* Monthly
Profile: Current topics in public health & information about the association's workgroups & partnerships
•Public Health Today
Type: Magazine; *Price:* Free with membership in the Ontario Public Health Association

Ontario Public Interest Research Group (OPIRG) / Groupe de recherche d'intérêt public de l'Ontario

North Borden Building, #101, 563 Spadina Ave., Toronto ON M5S 2J7
Tel: 416-978-7770; *Fax:* 416-971-2292
e-mail: opirg.toronto@utoronto.ca
www.opirg.org

Overview: A medium-sized provincial organization founded in 1973
Mission: To make information available to the general public that enables them to make informed decisions on issues & understand & possibly influence decisions made by others on their behalf; to provide an alternative to the information provided by the academic community, government & business; to offer an analysis of environmental & social issues aimed at motivating change & placing issues in the broader social, economic & political perspective in which they need to be understood
Chief Officer(s):
, Chief Returning Officer
cro.opirgtoronto@gmail.com
Finances: *Annual Operating Budget:* $50,000-$100,000; *Funding Sources:* Student & community membership fees
Staff: 2 staff member(s); 50 volunteer(s)
Membership: 30,000; *Fees:* $1-$5; *Member Profile:* U of T students mostly; *Committees:* Environment; Anti-Racism; Education; Global
Activities: Activism; education; research; action; social & environmental justice; *Speaker Service:* Yes; *Library:* by appointment

OPIRG Brock
Brock University, Almuni Student Centre, #204, 500 Glenridge Ave., St Catharines ON L2S 3A1
Tel: 905-688-5555; *Fax:* 905-378-5701
e-mail: info@opirgbrock.org
www.opirgbrock.org
www.facebook.com/opirgbrock
twitter.com/opirgbrock/
plus.google.com/115989504119091960180
Chief Officer(s):
Em (Matthew) Heppler, Coordinator, Promotions & Public Relations

OPIRG Carleton
Carleton University, 326 Unicentre, 1125 Colonel By Dr., Ottawa ON K1S 5B6
Tel: 613-520-2757; *Fax:* 613-520-3989
e-mail: opirgadmin@gmail.com
www.opirg-carleton.org/opirghome.php

OPIRG Guelph
University of Guelph, 1 Trent Lane, Guelph ON N1G 2W1
Tel: 519-824-2091; *Fax:* 519-824-8990
e-mail: opirg@uoguelph.ca
www.opirgguelph.org
Chief Officer(s):
Mandy Hiscocks, Coordinator, Volunteer & Programming

OPIRG Kingston
Queens University, The Grey House, 51 Bader Lane, Kingston ON K7L 3N6
Tel: 613-533-3189
e-mail: info@opirgkingston.org
www.opirgkingston.org

OPIRG McMaster
McMaster University, PO Box 1013, 1280 Main St., Hamilton ON L8S 1C0
Tel: 905-525-9140
e-mail: opirg@mcmaster.ca
www.opirg.org/mcmaster

OPIRG Peterborough
751 George St. North, 1st Fl., Peterborough ON K9H ET2
Tel: 705-741-1208
e-mail: opirg@trentu.ca
www.opirgpeterborough.ca
Chief Officer(s):
Yolanda Jones, Coordinator

OPIRG Windsor
University Of Windsor, 252 Dillon Hall, Windsor ON N9B 3P4
Tel: 519-253-3000
e-mail: opirg@uwindsor.ca
opirg.uwindsor.ca
Chief Officer(s):
Samina Yousuf Esha, President

OPIRG York
York University, C449 Student Centre, 4700 Keele St., Toronto ON M3J 1P3
Tel: 416-736-5724; *Fax:* 416-650-8014
e-mail: opirg@yorku.ca
www.yorku.ca/opirg/

Waterloo PIRG
Univ. of Waterloo, Student Life Centre, #2139, 200 University Ave. West, Waterloo ON N2L 3G1
Tel: 519-888-4882; *Fax:* 519-725-3093
e-mail: info@wpirg.org
www.wpirg.org
Chief Officer(s):
Tammy Kovich, Coordinator, Programming & Volunteer Support
tammy@wpirg.org

Ontario Public Transit Association (OPTA)
#400, 1235 Bay St., Toronto ON M5R 3K4
Tel: 416-229-6222; *Fax:* 416-969-6222
www.ontariopublictransit.ca
Previous Name: Ontario Community Transit Association
Overview: A medium-sized provincial organization founded in 1997
Mission: To strengthen & improve public transit services in Ontario; To ensure excellence & sustainability in public transit
Chief Officer(s):
Kelly Paleczny, Chair
Dave Sherlock, Vice-Chair
Norman Cheesman, Chief Executive Officer
Alex Milojevic, Secretary
Pat Delmore, Treasurer
Membership: *Fees:* Annual fees for transportation service providers sales based on operating budget or net sales; $560 for affiliates; *Member Profile:* Representatives of public transit systems; Health & social service agency transportation providers; Government representatives; Suppliers to the industry; Consultants
Activities: Engaging in advocacy activities; Sharing information; *Awareness Events:* OTE, annual conference & trade show
Publications:
•OPTA [Ontario Public Transit Association] News
Type: Newsletter; *Frequency:* Quarterly
Profile: Association activities & upcoming events

Ontario Refrigeration & Air Conditioning Contractors Association (ORAC)
#43, 6770 Davand Dr., Mississauga ON L5T 2G3
Tel: 905-670-0010; *Fax:* 905-670-0474
e-mail: info@orac.ca
www.orac.ca
Overview: A medium-sized provincial organization
Mission: To represent Ontario's contractor practitioners in the refrigeration & air conditioning trade; To enhance quality & efficiency in the industry to benefit customers
Chief Officer(s):
David Irwin, President, 416-748-9872
irwin@xtramech.com
Grant Sheahan, Vice-President, 613-228-3612
grant.sheahan@honeywell.com
Dave Honsberger, Managing Director, 905-670-0010
Ted Martin, Treasurer, 416-465-7581
tedmartin@toromont.com
Membership: *Fees:* $1,500 initiation fee & $350 membership dues for provincial members; $1,500 initiation fee & $1,500 membership dues for associate members; *Member Profile:* Individuals, partnerships, & corporations in Ontario, who are engaged in selling, installing, repairing, & maintaining refrigeration & air conditioning equipment; Individuals, partnerships or corporations in Ontario, who provide materials, equipment, or training to the heating, ventilation, refrigeration & air conditioning industry
Activities: Liaising with government & other organizations that represent trade local, provincial, & national bodies; Managing a state of the art training centre; Educating the public about the profession

Ontario Respiratory Care Society (ORCS)
#401, 18 Wynford Dr., Toronto ON M3C 0K8
Tel: 416-864-9911; *Fax:* 416-864-9916
e-mail: orcs@on.lung.ca
www.on.lung.ca
Overview: A medium-sized provincial charitable organization
Mission: To improve lung health through the provision of excellent interdisciplinary respiratory care
Chief Officer(s):
Sheila Gordon-Dillane, Director, 416-864-9911 Ext. 236
Libby Groff, Chair, Volunteers
Janna Patrick, Administrative Assistant
Finances: *Funding Sources:* Sponsorships
Membership: *Member Profile:* Persons involved in respiratory care, such as pulmonary function technologists, nurses, occupational therapists & physiotherapists, dietitians, & social workers; *Committees:* Provincial; Research & Fellowship; Editorial Board; Education; Membership & Program Promotion
Activities: Funding graduate education & research in respiratory care; Providing education & disseminating information for health care professionals; Offering professional expertise to the Ontario Lung Association & other interested groups
Meetings/Conferences:
For more information see Trade Shows, Conferences and Seminars Chapter
Ontario Respiratory Care Society 2013 Annual Better Breathing Conference & Breathe! Gala
January 2013 Toronto, ON
Ontario Respiratory Care Society 2014 Annual Better Breathing Conference
2014, ON
Publications:
•ORCS [Ontario Respiratory Care Society] Update
Type: Newsletter; *Frequency:* 3 pa; *Price:* Free with membership in the Ontario Respiratory Care Society
Profile: ORCS activities & respiratory articles
•Research Review [a joint publication of the Ontario Respiratory Care Society & the Ontario Thoracic Society]
Frequency: Annually; *Price:* Free with membership in the Ontario Respiratory Care Society
Profile: Highlights of researchers & their studies
•RHEIG [Respiratory Health Educators Interest Group] Connections
Frequency: 3 pa; *Price:* Free with membership in the Ontario Respiratory Care Society
Profile: Published by the Respiratory Health Educators Interest Group for members of the group

Ontario Retail Farm Equipment Dealers' Association ***See*** Canada East Equipment Dealers' Association

Ontario Retail Lumber Dealers Association ***See*** Lumber & Building Materials Association of Ontario

Ontario Road Builders' Association
Parent Name: Canadian Construction Association
#1, 365 Brunel Rd., Mississauga ON L4Z 1Z5
Tel: 905-507-1107; *Fax:* 905-890-8122
www.orba.org
www.facebook.com/OntarioRoadBuildersAssociation
twitter.com/onroadbuilders
Overview: A medium-sized provincial organization founded in 1926 overseen by Canadian Construction Association
Mission: To act as the voice of the Ontario road building industry; To maintain high standards in the road building industry; To promote worker health & safety
Environmental Activity: Monitoring government environmental regulation; Educating members about environmental compliance; Presenting the Green Leadership & Sustainability Awards program
Chief Officer(s):
Geoff Wilkinson, Executive Director
Geoff@orba.org
Karen Renkema, Director, Government Relations
karen@orba.org
Kathryn Thomas, Director, Member Services
kathryn@orba.org
Kim Le Fort, Office Manager & Coordinator, Events
kim@orba.org
Patrick McManus, Policy Analyst
patrick@orba.org
Membership: 75+ road building contractors; 85+ associate members; *Fees:* Schedule available based upon annual civil contracting volume; *Member Profile:* Road building contractors across Ontario; Organizations that manufacture or supply products & services to the road building industry; *Committees:* Area Maintenance Contractor Council; Associate Members; Contacts & Documents; Education, Training, & Industry Promotion; Structures & Concrete Technical; Transportation & Equipment; Environment; Hot Mix Technical; Occupational Health & Safety; CCA Civil Infrastructure Council
Activities: Advocating for road building contractors throughout Ontario; Promoting the benefits of infrastructure investment; Providing education & training; Offering information & research
Meetings/Conferences:
For more information see Trade Shows, Conferences and Seminars Chapter
Ontario Road Builders' Association 2013 Annual Convention
February 2013 Toronto, ON
Ontario Road Builders' Association 2014 Annual Convention
February 2014 Toronto, ON

Publications:
•ORBA [Ontario Road Builders' Association] Directory
Type: Directory; *Frequency:* Annually; *Price:* Free with Ontario Road Builders' membership
Profile: Member contact information, plus product & services information
•Road Builder Magazine
Type: Magazine; *Frequency:* Semiannually
Profile: Industry issues, new technology, & articles about member companies for Ontario Road Builders' Association members, Ministry of Transporation staff, as well as consulting engineers

Ontario Rock Garden Society
88 Cottonwood Dr., Toronto ON M3C 2B4
www.onrockgarden.com
Overview: A small provincial organization founded in 1984
Mission: To promote the study & cultivation of alpine & related garden plants & the creation of rock gardens; *Member of:* North American Rock Garden Society
Chief Officer(s):
Merle Burston, Chair
Andrew Osyany, Secretary
Finances: *Annual Operating Budget:* Less than $50,000; *Funding Sources:* Membership fees; plant sales
Membership: 450; *Fees:* $25 individual; $30 family; $10 student
Activities: 10 meetings per year; spring & fall plant sales; seed exchange in Dec.; handbook listing members, gardens to visit, mail order & non-mail order services; *Speaker Service:* Yes

Ontario Safety League (OSL) / Ligue de sécurité de l'Ontario
#212, 2595 Skymark Ave., Mississauga ON L4W 4L5
Tel: 905-625-0556; *Fax:* 905-625-0677
www.ontariosafetyleague.com
Overview: A medium-sized provincial licensing charitable organization founded in 1913
Mission: Safety through education with an emphasis on traffic & child safety; Affiliation(s): Canada Safety Council; Provincial Safety Leagues/Councils
Chief Officer(s):
Brian J. Patterson, President & General Manager
Finances: *Annual Operating Budget:* $1.5 Million-$3 Million
Staff: 10 staff member(s)
Membership: 300; *Fees:* $30-$300
Activities: Video production sales; courses for instructors of all vehicle types & road safety professionals; safety services for commercial fleets; *Speaker Service:* Yes; *Library:* OSL Film & Video Library; Open to public

Ontario Sanitation Equipment Association ***See*** Ontario Pollution Control Equipment Association

Ontario Sewer & Watermain Construction Association (OSWCA)
#300, 5045 Orbitor Dr., Unit 12, Mississauga ON L4W 4Y4
Tel: 905-629-7766; *Fax:* 905-629-0587
e-mail: info@oswca.org
www.oswca.org
Overview: A small local organization
Mission: To represent sewer & watermain construction contractors throughout Ontario; To increase business opportunities for members
Environmental Activity: Promoting environmentally sound construction practices & safe working conditions in the sewer & watermain construction industry
Chief Officer(s):
Joe Accardi, P.Eng, Executive Director
joe.accardi@oswca.org
Susan McGovern, Assistant Executive Director
susan.mcgovern@oswca.org
Don Del Vecchio, Contact, Member Services
don.delvecchio@oswca.org
Mary Reuse, Contact, Financial Services
mary.reuse@oswca.org
Membership: 700+ companies; *Committees:* Young Executives; Government Relations; Members Services; Marketing Initiatives; Education Program; Administration
Activities: Liaising with the Government of Ontario & its agencies; Increasing public awareness about the maintenance of water & wastewater systems in Ontario; Providing apprenticeship training & upgrading training; Informing members of industry developments
Publications:
•Ontario Sewer & Watermain Construction Association Membership Directory
Type: Directory; *Frequency:* Annually; *Accepts Advertising*
Profile: A buyers' guide for products & services used by sewer & watermain construction contractors, municipalities, utilities, & engineers
•Undergrounder [a publication of the Ontario Sewer & Watermain Construction Association]
Type: Magazine; *Frequency:* 3 pa; *Accepts Advertising*
Profile: Association business, industry issues, & regulatory updates available in print or digital editions

Ontario Shade Tree Council ***See*** Ontario Urban Forest Council

Ontario Small Urban Municipalities (OSUM)
c/o Association of Municipalities of Ontario, #801, 200 University Ave., Toronto ON M5H 3C6
Tel: 416-971-9856; *Fax:* 416-971-6191
Toll-Free: 877-426-6527
e-mail: amo@amo.on.ca
www.osum.ca
Overview: A medium-sized provincial organization
Mission: To take matters which affect Ontario's small urban communities to the attention of the provincial & federal governments; *Member of:* Association of Municipalities of Ontario
Chief Officer(s):
Paul Grenier, Chair, 905-788-2624
Jim Collard, Vice-Chair & Conference Chair, 905-658-1977
Larry McCabe, Administrative Member, OSUM Executive Committee, 519-524-8344, Fax: 519-524-7209
lmccabe@goderich.ca
Finances: *Funding Sources:* Sponsorships
Membership: 100-499; *Member Profile:* Small urban municipalities in Ontario
Activities: Providing a forum for both elected & appointed municipal officials of Ontario's small urban municipalities to exchange information;
Meetings/Conferences:
For more information see Trade Shows, Conferences and Seminars Chapter
Ontario Small Urban Municipalities 2013 60th Annual Conference & Trade Show: OSUM Diamond Jubilee - A Brilliant Future
May 2013 New Tecumseth, ON
Ontario Small Urban Municipalities 2014 61th Annual Conference & Trade Show
April 2014 Parry Sound, ON

Ontario Society for Environmental Education
PO Box 587, Lakefield ON K0L 2H0
Tel: 705-652-0923
www.osee.org
Overview: A small provincial organization
Mission: To develop a population that is aware of, & concerned about, the environment & its associated problems, & which has the knowledge, skills, attitudes, motivations & commitment to work individually & collectively toward solutions of current problems & the prevention of new ones (from UNESCO)
Chief Officer(s):
Emily Addison, Membership Coordinator
Finances: *Annual Operating Budget:* Less than $50,000
Staff: 2 staff member(s); 10 volunteer(s)
Membership: *Fees:* $40 individual; $20 student; $57 overseas; $300 corporate; *Member Profile:* Teachers & outdoor education leaders

Ontario Society for Environmental Management (OSEM)
87 Irondale Dr., Toronto ON M9L 2S6
Tel: 416-746-9076; *Fax:* 416-743-3737
Toll-Free: 800-305-6736
e-mail: osem@rogers.com
Overview: A small provincial organization founded in 1976
Mission: To encourage the exchange of information on matters of environmental management through seminars, meetings, position papers, newsletter, etc.; to develop an interdisciplinary forum for information exchange with other professions; to help persons & institutions responsible for decisions affecting the environment to make & implement policy consistent with the Society's environmental management ethic; to encourage high standards of competence & ethics among environmental management practitioners; to encourage education in the field of environmental management; to encourage individuals to become environmental management practitioners
Chief Officer(s):
Sue Ruggero, Administrator
Finances: *Annual Operating Budget:* Less than $50,000
Staff: 1 staff member(s)
Membership: 120; *Fees:* $95 full; $20 student; *Member Profile:* Open to those professionally involved in environmental management; potential members must have appropriate academic &/or professional credentials; *Committees:* Membership; Events
Activities: Seminars; conferences

Ontario Society of Nutrition Professionals in Public Health (OSNPPH) / La société ontarienne des professionelles et professionnels de la nutrition en santé publique
c/o Ontario Public Health Association, #310, 700 Lawrence Ave. West, Toronto ON M6A 3B4
e-mail: info@osnpph.on.ca
www.osnpph.on.ca
Overview: A small provincial organization founded in 1977
Mission: To provide an official organization that will give nutrition personnel in public health a strong voice within public health & for commenting on public health issues; *Member of:* Ontario Public Health Association
Chief Officer(s):
Michael Hurd, Chair
Janice Stewart, Secretary
Bart Bartle, Chair
Finances: *Annual Operating Budget:* Less than $50,000
Staff: 36 volunteer(s)
Membership: 145; *Fees:* $100; *Member Profile:* Dietitians/nutritionists in public health departments/units
Activities: Annual Nutrition Exchange, 2-day conference

Ontario Society of Professional Engineers (OSPE)
#502, 4950 Yonge St., Toronto ON M2N 6K1
Tel: 416-223-9961; *Fax:* 416-223-9963
Toll-Free: 866-763-1654
e-mail: info@ospe.on.ca
www.ospe.on.ca
www.linkedin.com/e/vgh/1968967
www.facebook.com/140328494064
twitter.com/O_S_P_E
www.youtube.com/OSPETV
Overview: A large provincial organization
Mission: To advance the interests of professional engineers in Ontario by advocating on behalf of engineers & the profession; to provide members with a sense of belonging & mutual support; to supply valued & innovative services; to offer quality professional training
Chief Officer(s):
Nadine Miller, M.Eng., P.Eng., President & Chair
Mark Dietrich, CEO
mdietrich@ospe.on.ca
Membership: *Fees:* $165 professional; $83 professional (65+); $132 associate; $90 intern; $26 student; *Committees:* Advocacy; Environment; Women in Engineering Advisory; Ontario Professional Engineers Awards; PEO Chapter Liaison; Social; Membership Advisory; mployer Salary Survey Advisory; Fee Schedule; Audit & Investments; Executive; Finance; Human Resources; Nominations; PEO/OSPE Joint Relations
Activities: ; *Library:* Reports Library
Publications:
•Employer Salary Survey [a publication of the Ontario Society of Professional Engineers]
Type: Report; *Frequency:* Annually
•The OSPE [Ontario Society of Professional Engineers] Advocate
Type: Newsletter; *Frequency:* Weekly
Profile: Electronic newsletter
•OSPE [Ontario Society of Professional Engineers] Annual Report
Type: Yearbook; *Frequency:* Annually
•Society Notes [a publication of the Ontario Society of Professional Engineers]
Type: Newsletter; *Frequency:* Bi-weekly
Profile: Electronic newsletter
•The Voice [a publication of the Ontario Society of Professional Engineers]
Type: Magazine; *Frequency:* q.
Profile: Formerly a print newsletter, The Voice is now a full-colour magazine

Ontario Society of Safety Engineering ***See*** Canadian Society of Safety Engineering, Inc.

Ontario Soil & Crop Improvement Association (OSCIA) / Association pour l'amélioration des sols et des récoltes de l'Ontario
1 Stone Rd. West, Guelph ON N1G 4Y2

Tel: 519-826-4214; *Fax:* 519-826-4224
Toll-Free: 800-265-9751
e-mail: oscia@ontariosoilcrop.org
www.ontariosoilcrop.org
Overview: A medium-sized provincial organization founded in 1939
Mission: To communicate & facilitate the responsible management of soil, water, air, & crops
Environmental Activity: Providing information about Ontario stewardship programs
Chief Officer(s):
Harold Rudy, Executive Director, 519-826-4217
Julie Henderson, Administrator, Finance, 519-826-4221
Steven Nadeau, Administrator, Information Technology, 519-826-6059
Andrew Graham, Manager, Programs, 519-826-4216
John Laidlaw, Program Manager, Farm Business Management, 519-826-4218
Membership: *Member Profile:* Farmers & persons involved in agriculture in Ontario; *Committees:* Nomination; Resolutions; Finance; Research; Membership; Constitution & Bylaws; Annual Meeting; Ontario Soil Management Research; Soil & Water Quality Sub-Committee; Waste Utilization Sub-Committee; Field Crops Sub-Committee; Ontario Corn; Ontario Weed; Ontario Cereal Crop; Ontario Forage Crops; Ontario Oil & Protein; Biosolids Utilization; Ontario Forage Council; Ontario Agri-Food Education; AGCare; Ontario Field Crops Research Coalition; Canada's Outdoor Farm Show; Ontario Agri-Food Technologies; Soil Conservation Council of Canada
Activities: Offering information about agricultural management practices; Networking with farmers
Meetings/Conferences:
For more information see Trade Shows, Conferences and Seminars Chapter
Ontario Soil & Crop Improvement Association 2013 Provincial Annual Meeting
February 2013 London, ON
Ontario Soil & Crop Improvement Association 2014 Provincial Annual Meeting
2014, ON
Publications:
•New Crops, Old Challenges: Tips & Tricks for Managing New Crops!
Number of Pages: 76
Profile: Crop profiles
•Ontario Soil & Crop Improvement Association Newsletter
Type: Newsletter; *Frequency:* Quarterly; *Price:* Free with Ontario Soil & Crop Improvement Association membership
•Rotational Grazing in Extensive Pastures
Type: Report
Profile: Discusses using rotational grazing to increase health of pastures, cattle & the environment.

Ontario Stone, Sand & Gravel Association (OSSGA)

#103, 5720 Timberlea Blvd., Mississauga ON L4W 4W2
Tel: 905-507-0711; *Fax:* 905-507-0717
www.ossga.com
twitter.com/_OSSGA
Previous Name: Aggregate Producers' Association of Ontario
Overview: A medium-sized provincial organization founded in 1956
Chief Officer(s):
Moreen Miller, CEO
mmiller@ossga.com
Finances: *Annual Operating Budget:* $250,000-$500,000; *Funding Sources:* Membership dues
Staff: 7 staff member(s)
Membership: 200+ corporate

Ontario Streams

50 Bloomington Rd. West, Aurora ON L4G 3G8
Tel: 905-713-7399; *Fax:* 905-713-7361
www.ontariostreams.on.ca
Overview: A medium-sized provincial organization
Mission: To promote the conservation & rehabilitation of streams & wetlands, through education & community involvement
Chief Officer(s):
Doug Forder, Field Supervisor
doug.forder@ontariostreams.on.ca

Ontario Sustainable Energy Association (OSEA)

#201, 156 Front St. West, Toronto ON M5J 2L6
Tel: 416-977-4441; *Fax:* 416-977-4441
Toll-Free: 888-840-3447
e-mail: info@ontario-sea.org
www.ontario-sea.org
www.facebook.com/ontariosea
Overview: A small provincial organization founded in 2002
Mission: To represent & serve municipalities, First Nations, institutions, businesses, cooperatives, farms, & households; To support the work of local sustainable energy organizations
Environmental Activity: Enabling people to produce clean, sustainable enery in their homes & communities
Chief Officer(s):
Kristopher Stevens, Executive Director
Kristopher@ontario-sea.org
Harry French, Director, Community Power Services Group
harry@ontario-sea.org
Kate Holloway, Director, Business Development
kate@ontario-sea.org
Roberto Garcia, Coordinator, Community Power Services Group
roberto@ontario-sea.org
Craig Jackson, Coordinator, Community Power Services Group
craig@ontario-sea.org
Ian Jackson, Coordinator, Web, Data, & Social Media
ian@ontario-sea.org
Nicole Risse, Coordinator, Tradeshow, Events, & Logistics
ian@ontario-sea.org
Finances: *Funding Sources:* Sponsorships
Membership: *Fees:* $56.50 students; $113 minimum donation, friends; $565 - $1,695 supporters; $2,260 champions; $5,650 enablers
Activities: Engaging in advocacy activities, capacity building, & non-partisan policy work; Providing public outreach services
Meetings/Conferences:
For more information see Trade Shows, Conferences and Seminars Chapter
Ontario Sustainable Energy Association 2013 Annual All-Energy Canada Exhibition & Conference
October 2013 Toronto, ON
Ontario Sustainable Energy Association 2013 Annual General Meeting
2013, ON
Ontario Sustainable Energy Association 2014 Annual All-Energy Canada Exhibition & Conference
April 2014 Toronto, ON
Publications:
•Arts Revision Report: Renewables Without Limits [a publication of the Ontario Sustainable Energy Association]
Type: Report; *Price:* $1 + $13.50 shipping & handling, members; $10 +$13.50 S&H, non-members
Profile: A review of Ontario's Renewable Energy Standard Offer Program
•Community Power Financing Guidebook
Type: Manual; *Price:* $40 + $13.50 shipping & handling,members; $65 + $13.40 S&H, non-members
Profile: Contents include pre-development financing, land acquisition, legal contracting, permits & approvals, resource assessment, & community engagement
•The Community Power Guidebook
Type: Guide
Profile: A guide to the development of a community power project, from conception to commissioning
•Green Energy ACTion Kit
Type: Kit; *Price:* $10 + $13.50 shipping & handling, members; $20 + $13.40 S&H, non-members
Profile: Suggestions to help citizens advocate for green energy in Ontario
•Ontario Landowner's Guide to Wind Energy
Type: Guide; *Author:* Paul Gipe; James Murphy; *Price:* $10 + $13.50 shipping & handling, members; $20 + $13.50 S&H,non-members
Profile: A comprehensive manual for rural landowners & farmers who are interested in wind power
•Ontario Sustainable Energy Association E-Bulletin
Type: Newsletter; *Price:* Free with Ontario Sustainable Energy Association membership
Profile: Updates about the association & upcoming events
•OSEA [Ontario Sustainable Energy Association] Member Directory
Type: Directory
Profile: Contact information for members
•Permitting & Approvals Processes for CP Projects [a publication of the Ontario Sustainable Energy Association]
Type: Guide; *Price:* $40 + $13.50 shipping & handling, members; $65 + $13.50 S&H, non-members
Profile: An overview of the policy environment for biogas & wind projects in Ontario, of interest to municipal planners,project proponents, & the general public
•Powering Ontario Communities: Proposed Policy for Projects up to 10mw
Type: Study
Profile: Options to encourage small or community-owned renewable energy generation in Ontario
•Proposal for a Green Energy Act for Ontario
Profile: A proposal for renewable energy sources to protect the environment & to manage climate change
•Recommendations for Procuring Sustainable Energy: An Addendum to Renewables Without Limits
Profile: An update to recommendations from the Arts Revision Report: Renewable Without Limits
•Solar PV Community Action Manual
Type: Manual
Profile: Information for Canadian residents about residential-scale or small-scale commercial Solar PV installations, as well as related topics such as financing & home assessment
•Solar Thermal Community Action Manual
Type: Manual
Profile: Information for Canadians about residential-scale or small-scale commercial solar thermal installations, as well as the establishment of a community based organization

Ontario Telecommunications Association (OTA)

29 Peevers Cres., Newmarket ON L3Y 7T5
Tel: 519-595-3975; *Fax:* 519-595-3976
e-mail: ota@ota.on.ca
www.ota.on.ca
Previous Name: Ontario Telephone Association
Overview: A small provincial organization
Chief Officer(s):
Jonathan Holmes, Executive Director
jonathan.holmes@ota.on.ca
Finances: *Funding Sources:* Membership dues
Staff: 1 staff member(s)
Membership: 21
Activities: Liaising with government departments & agencies & industry associates, such as Bell Canada; Setting policies & compliance guidelines; Offering a forum to share expertise
Meetings/Conferences:
For more information see Trade Shows, Conferences and Seminars Chapter
Ontario Telecommunications Association 2013 48th Annual Convention
June 2013, ON
Ontario Telecommunications Association 2014 49th Annual Convention
June 2014, ON

Ontario Telephone Association *See* Ontario Telecommunications Association

Ontario Tender Fruit Producers

c/o Faye Clack Communications Inc., 170 Robert Speck Pkwy., Mississauga ON L4Z 3G1
Tel: 905-206-0577; *Fax:* 905-206-0581
e-mail: tenderfruit@fayeclack.com
www.ontariotenderfruit.com
Overview: A small provincial organization founded in 1979
Membership: 500 grower members

Ontario Tire Dealers Association

PO Box 516, 34 Edward St., Drayton ON N0G 1P0
Tel: 888-207-9059; *Fax:* 866-375-6832
www.otda.com
Overview: A medium-sized national organization
Mission: To represent & promote members; Affiliation(s): Tire Dealers Association of Canada; Tire Industry Association
Environmental Activity: Participating in the development of an environmentally friendly scrap tire management program
Chief Officer(s):
Robert Bignell, Executive Director
bbignell@otda.com
Glenn Warnica, President
gwarnica@sympatico.ca
Ron Spiewak, Secretary-Treasurer
rons@bellnet.ca
Eric Gilbert, Chair, Ontario Tire Dealers Associaton Committee
ericwaytire@primus.ca
Finances: *Funding Sources:* Membership fees; Fundraising
Activities: Educating members; Promoting standards of ethics; Engaging in lobbying activities
Meetings/Conferences:
For more information see Trade Shows, Conferences and Seminars Chapter

Ontario Tire Dealers Association 2013 Winter Conference
January 2013
Publications:
•Ontario Tire Dealers Association Membership Directory
Type: Directory
Profile: Contact information about Ontario's tire professionals
•Trends [a publication of the Ontario Tire Dealers Association]
Type: Newsletter; *Frequency:* Quarterly; *Accepts Advertising*
Profile: Information for members about industry issues

Ontario Traffic Council (OTC)

#2, 6355 Kennedy Rd., Mississauga ON L5T 2L5
Tel: 647-346-4050; *Fax:* 647-346-4060
e-mail: info@otc.org
www.otc.org
twitter.com/ontariotraffic
Overview: A medium-sized provincial organization
Mission: To improve traffic conditions & traffic safety in municipalities of Ontario
Chief Officer(s):
Marco D'Angelo, Executive Director
Ron Hamilton, President
Keith Haines, Vice-President
Mike Pelzowski, Secretary/Treasurer
Heide Schlegl, Director Engineering
Robyn Zutis, Director of Education
Kimberly Rossi, Director Marketing

Ontario Trails Council

PO Box 500, Deseronto ON K0K 1X0
e-mail: ontrails@gmail.com
www.ontariotrails.on.ca
www.facebook.com/OntarioTrails?ref=mf
twitter.com/ontrails
www.youtube.com/user/ontrails
Overview: A medium-sized provincial organization founded in 1988
Mission: To promote the creation, development, preservation, management & use of an integrated, recreational, multi-seasonal trail network in Ontario; To show interest in all types of trails for non-motorized & motorized (where applicable) use in all seasons; To acquire & convert Ontario's abandoned railway rights-of-way to linear greenways for year-round recreational activities for the people of Ontario; Affiliation(s): Bruce Trail Association; Canadian Motorcycling Association; Guelph Trail Club; Hike Ontario; Kawartha Rail-Trail; Ontario Federation of Snowmobile Clubs; Ontario Cycling Association; Ontario Competitive Trail Riders Association; Ontario Working Dog Association; Parry Sound Rail Line Task Force; Rideau Trail Association; Northland Associates; Ontario Trail Riders Association; Rails to Trails Conservancy - USA; Credit Valley Conservation Authority; Georgian Cycle & Ski Trail Association; Grand Valley Trail Association; Southeastern Ontario Rails to Tracks
Chief Officer(s):
Chris Laforest, President, 519-534-2092
claforest@brucecounty.on.ca
Forbes Symon, Vice-President, 613-258-9569
fsymon@northgrenville.on.ca
Patrick Connor, CAE, Executive Director, 613-396-3226, Fax: 613-396-2144
execdir@ontariotrails.on.ca
Damian Braley, Secretary, 705-559-6705
damian.bradley@gmail.com
Finances: *Annual Operating Budget:* Less than $50,000; *Funding Sources:* Membership fees; Corporate donations
Membership: 500,000 individuals + 21 groups; *Fees:* $26.50 individual; $106-$795 club/association + GST; *Member Profile:* Association or club with interest in recreational trail acquisition, maintenance & use; individuals concerned with environment & trail recreation; *Committees:* Government Relations; Public Affairs; Trails Development
Activities: ; *Library:*
Meetings/Conferences:
For more information see Trade Shows, Conferences and Seminars Chapter
Ontario Trails Council 2013 Trailhead Ontario
June 2013 Peterborough, ON
Publications:
•OTC [Ontario Trails Council] Newsletter
Type: Newsletter; *Frequency:* Monthly; *Price:* Free with membership in the Ontario Trails Council
Profile: Information about events, activities, & news from trails

Ontario Trucking Association (OTA)
Parent Name: Canadian Trucking Alliance

555 Dixon Rd., Toronto ON M9W 1H8
Tel: 416-249-7401; *Fax:* 866-713-4188
e-mail: publicaffairs@ontruck.org
www.ontruck.org
twitter.com/ontruck
Overview: A large provincial organization founded in 1926 overseen by Canadian Trucking Alliance
Mission: To represent companies & industry suppliers; To provide political advocacy, education, & information services to North American freight transport companies
Chief Officer(s):
Brian Taylor, Chair
David H. Bradley, President
Jeff Bryan, Secretary
Scott Tilley, Treasurer
Barrie Montague, Senior Policy Advisor
Doug Switzer, Manager Government Relations
Rebecka Torn, Manager Communications
Rolf VanderZwaag, Manager Maintenance/Tech. Issues
Finances: *Funding Sources:* Membership fees
Membership: 1,700 member companies; *Committees:* Axle Weight; Credit; Education; Executive; Social/Labour; Tech./Ops; Convention; Dues; Membership; Insurance; Finance; Environmental Issues
Activities: Offering training courses & seminars; *Speaker Service:* Yes; *Library:*

Ontario Urban Forest Council (OUFC)

Mount Pleasant Group of Cemeteries, #23/25, 1523 Warden Ave., Toronto ON M1R 4Z8
Tel: 416-936-6735; *Fax:* 416-291-5709
e-mail: info@oufc.org
www.oufc.org
Previous Name: Ontario Shade Tree Council
Overview: A medium-sized provincial organization founded in 1964
Mission: To promote & assist in the protection & preservation of shade trees; to cooperate with all associations, government agencies, industry & individuals with a mutual interest in preserving & developing Ontario's shade tree heritage & landscape; to promote management of urban forest in Ontario; Affiliation(s): Urban Forest Network
Chief Officer(s):
Jack Radecki, Executive Director
Finances: *Annual Operating Budget:* Less than $50,000
Staff: 11 volunteer(s)
Membership: 189 corporate + 9 senior/lifetime + 55 individual; *Fees:* Student: $25; Individual: $75; Group/Corporate: $150
Activities: *Speaker Service:* Yes

Ontario Vegetation Management Association (OVMA)

4 Spruce Blvd., Acton ON L7J 2Y2
Tel: 905-805-2294; *Fax:* 519-853-0352
e-mail: info@ovma.on.ca
www.ovma.on.ca
Overview: A small provincial organization founded in 1984
Chief Officer(s):
Tom McLean, President
Membership: *Fees:* $75 individual; $250 corporate gold; *Member Profile:* Promotes environmentally safe vegetation management

Ontario Waste Management Association (OWMA) / Société ontarienne de gestion des déchets

#3, 2005 Clark Blvd., Brampton ON L6T 5P8
Tel: 905-791-9500; *Fax:* 905-791-9514
e-mail: contact@owma.org
www.owma.org
Overview: A medium-sized provincial organization founded in 1977
Mission: To act as the voice of the private sector waste industry in Ontario; To protect the enviroment by properly managing waste & recyclable materials
Environmental Activity: Offering professional advice to members about environmental management issues; Providing educational materials to the public to increase awarement of waste management issues
Chief Officer(s):
Rob Cook, President
rcook@owma.org
Michele Goulding, Manager, Finance & Administration
mgoulding@owma.org
Membership: 300; *Member Profile:* Private sector independent companies in Ontario which provide waste & recycling services; Associate members include equipment manufacturers, suppliers, legal firms, & consultants; *Committees:* EFW & WDF; Environmental Affairs; Financial Business Analysis; Green Energy & Greenhouse Gas Task Group; Hazardous Waste; Membership; Organics Diversion & Composting; Programs; Public Affairs; Safety & Transportation; Soils Caucus; Standards & Accreditation; Waste Diversion & Recycling; Waste Transfer & Disposal
Activities: Monitoring & assessing regulatory & policy initiatives; Promoting new standards & regulatory policies to improve waste management services; Providing information to members about government initiatives, waste management, & business issues;

Ontario Water Garden Society *See* Greater Toronto Water Garden & Horticultural Society

Ontario Water Well Association *See* Ontario Ground Water Association

Ontario Water Works Association (OWWA)

#00, 1092 Islington Ave., Toronto ON M8Z 4R9
Tel: 416-231-1555; *Fax:* 416-231-1556
Toll-Free: 866-975-0575
e-mail: waterinfo@owwa.ca
www.owwa.com
Overview: A medium-sized provincial organization
Mission: To protect public health through the delivery of safe, sufficient, & sustainable drinking water in Ontario; *Member of:* American Water Works Association; Affiliation(s): Ontario Municipal Water Association; Ontario Water Works Equipment Association
Environmental Activity: Promoting water stewardship
Chief Officer(s):
Saad Jasim, President
jasims@windsor.ijc.org
Lee Anne E. Jones, Vice-President
ljones@toronto.ca
Bill Balfour, Executive Director, 905-642-5283
bbalfour@owwa.ca
Lesia Lachmaniuk, Manager, Marketing & Membership, 416-231-1555, Fax: 416-231-1556
llachmaniuk@owwa.ca
Glenn Powell, Director, Communications, 905-827-4508, Fax: 905-827-6483
gpowell@owwa.ca
Ray Miller, Secretary-Treasurer
rmiller@clowcanada.com
Membership: 1,100+; *Member Profile:* Drinking water professionals in Ontario, such as hydrogeologists, scientists, engineers, chemists, & managers & technicians employed by Ontario's municipal water systems; *Committees:* Climate Change; C-PAC; Conference Management; Continuing Education; Cross Connection Control; Distribution; Government Affairs; Groundwater; Joint OWWA / OMWA; Management; Membership; OWWA / WEAO Joint Asset Management; Publications; Small Systems; Source Water Protection; Training, Certification, & Safety; Treatment; University Forum; Water Efficiency; Water for People - Canada; Young Professionals; Youth Education
Activities: Improving technology, science & management; Influencing government policy; Providing education for members; *Library:* Ontario Water Works Association Library
Publications:
•Consultants' Listing [a publication of the Ontario Water Works Association]
Frequency: 3 pa; *Accepts Advertising*
•Ontario Pipeline
Type: Magazine; *Frequency:* 3 pa; *Accepts Advertising*
Profile: A joint publication of the Ontario Water Works Association, the Ontario Municipal Water Association, & the Ontario Water Works Equipment Association

Ontario Waterpower Association (OWA)

#264, 380 Armour Rd., Peterborough ON K9H 7L7
Fax: 705-743-1570
Toll-Free: 866-743-1500
e-mail: info@owa.ca
www.owa.ca
Overview: A medium-sized provincial organization
Mission: Promotes the achievement of sustainable development, provides a source for quality information about waterpower and grows and enhances the competitiveness of the Ontario waterpower industry.
Chief Officer(s):
Paul Norris, President, 866-743-1500 Ext. 22

Meetings/Conferences:
For more information see Trade Shows, Conferences and Seminars Chapter
13th Annual Power of Water Caanada Conference 2013
October 2013 Niagara-on-the-Lake, ON

Ontario Woodlot Association
RR#4, 275 County Rd. 44, Kemptville ON K0G 1J0
Tel: 613-258-0110; *Fax:* 613-258-0207
e-mail: info@ont-woodlot-assoc.org
www.ont-woodlot-assoc.org
Overview: A small provincial organization founded in 1992
Mission: To promote the wise & profitable use of Ontario's private land forest resource
Chief Officer(s):
Wade Knight, Executive Director
Pieter Leenhouts, President
Andrew Mack, Vice-President
Membership: 1,700; *Fees:* $40

Ontario Workers' Compensation Institute ***See*** Institute for Work & Health

Ordre des agronomes du Québec (OAQ)
#810, 1001, rue Sherbrooke est, Montréal QC H2L 1L3
Tél: 514-596-3833; *Téléc:* 514-596-2974
Ligne sans frais: 800-361-3833
Courriel: agronome@oaq.qc.ca
www.oaq.qc.ca
Nom précédent: Corporation des agronomes du Québec
Aperçu: *Dimension:* moyenne; *Envergure:* provinciale; Organisme sans but lucratif; fondée en 1937
Mission: Assure les utilisateurs de services agronomiques et les consommateurs de la compétence, du professionnalisme et de l'engagement des agronomes et ainsi favoriser le mieux-être de la société
Membre(s) du bureau directeur:
René Mongeau, Président
rene.mongeau@oaq.qc.ca
Finances: *Budget de fonctionnement annuel:* $500,000-$1.5 Million
Personnel: 10 membre(s) du personnel; 100 bénévole(s)
Membre: 3 189; *Critères d'admissibilite:* Agronomes

Ordre des arpenteurs-géomètres du Québec (OAGQ) / Québec Land Surveyors Association
Parent Name: Professional Surveyors Canada
Iberville Quatre, #350, 2954, boul Laurier, Québec QC G1V 4T2
Tél: 418-656-0730; *Téléc:* 418-656-6352
Courriel: oagq@oagq.qc.ca
www.oagq.qc.ca
Aperçu: *Dimension:* moyenne; *Envergure:* provinciale; fondée en 1882 surveillé par Professional Surveyors Canada
Mission: La protection du public et le contrôle de la profession; *Membre de:* Association de géomatique municipale; Affiliation(s): Fédération des arpenteurs-géomètres du Québec
Membre: 1 000 *Montant de la cotisation:* 830$; *Critères d'admissibilite:* BAC en géomatique; Stage d'un an; Examens de l'Ordre; *Comités:* Arbitrage; Assurances et sinistres; Discipline; Examinateurs; Formation; Inspection; Réglementation; Révision; Stages; Syndic
Activités: Ateliers divers; *Stagiaires:* Oui; *Listes de destinataires:* Oui
Meetings/Conferences:
For more information see Trade Shows, Conferences and Seminars Chapter
Ordre des arpenteurs-géomètres du Québec 2013 AGM
September 2013 Mont Saint-Sauveur, QC

Ordre des chimistes du Québec (OCQ)
Place du Parc, #2199, 300 rue Léo-Pariseau, Montréal QC H2X 4B3
Tél: 514-844-3644; *Téléc:* 514-844-9601
Courriel: information@ocq.qc.ca
www.ocq.qc.ca
Aperçu: *Dimension:* moyenne; *Envergure:* provinciale; Organisme de réglementation; fondée en 1926
Mission: L'Ordre est une corporation professionnelle dont la raison d'être est la protection du public
Membre(s) du bureau directeur:
Guy Collin, Président du Conseil d'administration
Finances: *Budget de fonctionnement annuel:* $500,000-$1.5 Million
Personnel: 5 membre(s) du personnel; 120 bénévole(s)
Membre: 2 500; *Critères d'admissibilite:* Chimistes, biochimistes; *Comités:* Réglementaires prévus par le code des professions (L.R.Q., chapitre C-26)

Ordre des ingénieurs du Québec (OIQ)
Parent Name: Engineers Canada
Gare Windsor, #350, 1100, av des Canadiens-de-Montréal, Montréal QC H3B 2S2
Tél: 514-845-6141; *Téléc:* 514-845-1833
Ligne sans frais: 800-461-6141
Courriel: info@oiq.qc.ca
www.oiq.qc.ca
Aperçu: *Dimension:* grande; *Envergure:* provinciale; fondée en 1920 surveillé par Engineers Canada
Mission: Faire de la promotion et s'assurer de la qualité des services rendus à la société par les ingénieurs, individuellement et collectivement, en tant que membres d'un corps professionnel; Favoriser leur épanouissement professionnel et personnel; Contribuer au développement socio-économique de la société; *Membre de:* Engineers Canada; Affiliation(s): Conseil Interprofessionnel du Québec
Membre(s) du bureau directeur:
Daniel Lebel, PMP, Président
Martin Lapointe, ing., Vice-président, Finances
Stéphane Bilodeau, ing., Vice-président, Affaires publiques
Éric Potvin, ing., Vice-président, Affaires professionnelles
Membre: 60 000 *Montant de la cotisation:* 180$; *Comités:* Discipline; Inspection professionnelle; Révision; Examinateurs; Surveillance des élections; Finances et de vérification; Gouvernance; Orientation des affaires publiques; Promotion et la valorisation de la profession et des femmes en génie; Surveillance de la pratique illégale; Assurance-responsabilité professionnelle; Liaison CODIQ-OIQ-CRÉIQ; Liaison des regroupements d'ingénieurs
Activités: Préparation d'avis, mémoires et de documents professionnels; Organisation ou préparation à des conférences; Groupes de travail sur: la gestion des déchets solides, l'eau de consommation, le bilan technologique, l'analyse technologique des secteurs d'activité économique du Québec, le transfert de technologie, le génie-conseil; *Evénements de sensibilisation:* Journée de l'ingénieur(e); *Stagiaires:* Oui; *Service de conférenciers:* Oui; *Bibliothèque:* Bibliothèque publique
Publications:
•Bulletins aux membres [a publication of the Ordre des ingénieurs du Québec]
Type: Bulletin
•PLAN [a publication of the Ordre des ingénieurs du Québec]
Type: Revue

Ordre des ingénieurs forestiers du Québec (OIFQ)
#110, 2750, rue Einstein, Québec QC G1P 4R1
Tél: 418-650-2411; *Téléc:* 418-650-2168
Courriel: oifq@oifq.com
www.oifq.com
Aperçu: *Dimension:* moyenne; *Envergure:* provinciale; Organisme sans but lucratif; Organisme de réglementation; fondée en 1921
Mission: Assurer la protection du public; assurer la qualité des services rendus au public québécois; favoriser l'amélioration continue de l'expertise et de la compétence des ingénieurs forestiers; mettre en place des actions favorisant la durabilité de l'aménagement forestier pour le bénéfice de l'ensemble de la société; *Membre de:* Conseil interprofessionnel du Québec; Affiliation(s): Fédération canadienne des associations d'ingénieurs forestiers
Membre(s) du bureau directeur:
Denis Villeneuve, Président
Finances: *Budget de fonctionnement annuel:* $500,000-$1.5 Million
Membre: 2 260 *Montant de la cotisation:* 435$; *Critères d'admissibilite:* Diplôme universitaire de premier cycle en foresterie
Activités: *Service de conférenciers:* Oui

Ordre des technologues professionnels du Québec (OTPQ)
Parent Name: Canadian Council of Technicians & Technologists
#720, 1265, rue Berri, Montréal QC H2L 4X4
Tél: 514-845-3247; *Téléc:* 514-845-3643
Ligne sans frais: 800-561-3459
Courriel: info@otpq.qc.ca
www.otpq.qc.ca
www.linkedin.com/groups?home=&gid=4134994
www.facebook.com/TechnologuesProfessionnels
twitter.com/otpq
Nom précédent: Corporation professionnelle des technologues professionnelles du Québec
Aperçu: *Dimension:* moyenne; *Envergure:* provinciale; fondée en 1927 surveillé par Canadian Council of Technicians & Technologists
Mission: Promouvoir et assurer la compétence des technologues professionnels dans l'intérêt public; *Membre de:* Conseil canadiens des techniciens et technologues
Membre(s) du bureau directeur:
Denis Beauchamp, Directeur général et secrétaire, 514-845-3247 Ext. 107
dbeauchamp@otpq.qc.ca
Finances: *Budget de fonctionnement annuel:* $500,000-$1.5 Million
Personnel: 9 membre(s) du personnel
Membre: 5 000; *Comités:* Admission; Discipline; Inspection professionnelle; Prix
Activités: *Stagiaires:* Oui; *Listes de destinataires:* Oui

Ordre des urbanistes du Québec (OUQ)
Parent Name: Canadian Institute of Planners
#410, 85, rue St-Paul ouest, Montréal QC H2Y 3V4
Tél: 514-849-1177; *Téléc:* 514-849-7176
Courriel: info@ouq.qc.ca
www.ouq.qc.ca
Nom précédent: Ordre professionnel des urbanistes du Québec
Aperçu: *Dimension:* moyenne; *Envergure:* provinciale; fondée en 1963 surveillé par Canadian Institute of Planners
Mission: Assurer la protection du public dans l'exercice de la profession par ses membres et la promotion de la pratique de l'urbanisme au Québec
Membre(s) du bureau directeur:
Claude Beaulac, Directeur général
cbeaulac@ouq.qc.ca
Odette Michaud, Secrétaire de l'Ordre
omichaud@ouq.qc.ca
Nathalie Corso, Coordonnatrice, Admission et qualité
ncorso@ouq.qc.ca
Membre: 700 *Montant de la cotisation:* 360$; *Comités:* Admission; Déontologie; Discipline; Formation Continue; Inspection Professionnelle

Ordre professionnel des urbanistes du Québec ***Voir*** Ordre des urbanistes du Québec

Organic Crop Improvement Association - Alberta Chapter #1 ***See*** Alberta Organic Producers Association

Organic Crop Improvement Association - New Brunswick (OCIA-NB)
2002 Cedar Camp Rd., South Beach Kings NB E4E 5E7
Tel: 506-433-3935
e-mail: ocianb@nbnet.nb.ca
Overview: A small provincial organization founded in 1987
Mission: To provide organic certification & crop improvement for New Brunswick farmers; *Member of:* OCIA International; Affiliation(s): New Brunswick Federation of Agriculture
Chief Officer(s):
Susan Tyler, Administrator
Membership: *Fees:* $30; *Member Profile:* Growers both in New Brunswick & northern Maine

Organic Crop Improvement Association - Québec & Ontario
25 Bryden Ave., Cornwall ON K6H 5M4
Tel: 613-933-6093; *Fax:* 613-933-6093
e-mail: ahoude@ocia.org
Also Known As: OCIA Québec & Ontario
Overview: A small provincial organization
Mission: To work as a farmer-owned & operated organization to support farmers with technical knowledge, skill & organizational aids to develop ecologically sound crop management systems; To administer the OCIA International certification program at the chapter level; To promote the OCIA seal & the principles of organic agriculture; *Member of:* Organic Crop Improvement Association (International)
Chief Officer(s):
Annie Houde, Regional Office Manager

Organic Crop Improvement Association (International) (OCIA) / Association pour l'amélioration des cultures biologiques (international)
1340 North Cotner, Lincoln NE 68505 USA
Tel: 402-477-2323; *Fax:* 402-477-4325
e-mail: info@ocia.org
www.ocia.org
Also Known As: OCIA International

Overview: A medium-sized international licensing organization founded in 1988
Mission: To support all farmers with the technical knowledge, skills & organizational aids they need to develop workable crop management systems capable of supplying the growing market demand for organic foods; to provide third party certification of organic foods; *Member of:* Organic Trade Association; Affiliation(s): International Federation of Organic Agriculture Movements; Japan Agriculture Standards; US National Organic Program; Conseil des Appelations Agroalimentaires du Québec; Costa Rica Ministry of Agriculture & Livestock; ISO Guide 65
Chief Officer(s):
Peggy Linzmeier, President
Finances: *Annual Operating Budget:* $1.5 Million-$3 Million; *Funding Sources:* Member-owned & funded
Staff: 30 staff member(s)
Membership: 3,000+; *Fees:* US$75 corporate & chapter level; individual chapter membership fees vary; *Member Profile:* Farmers, processors & merchants who are committed to seeking alternatives to conventional chemical & energy-intensive food system; *Committees:* By-Laws; Crop Improvement; Finance; Inspector Accreditation; Internal Review; Certification Analysis; International Certification; International Standards; Chapter Licensing; Promotions; AGMM; Canadian Organic Regulatory Committee; Research & Education
Activities: *Speaker Service:* Yes

Organic Crop Producers & Processors Ontario Inc. (OCPP)
PO Box 74, 2311 Elm Tree Rd., Cambray ON K0M 1E0
Tel: 705-374-5602; *Fax:* 705-374-5604
e-mail: ocpp@lindsaycomp.on.ca
www.ocpro.ca
Also Known As: OCPRO
Overview: A small provincial organization founded in 1991
Member of: International Federation of Organic Agriculture Movements; Affiliation(s): Pro-Cert Organic Systems
Chief Officer(s):
Larry Lenhardt
Activities: Organic food & community certification; *Speaker Service:* Yes

Organic Food Production Association of North America ***See*** Organic Trade Association

Organic Producers Association of Manitoba Co-operative Inc. (OPAM)
PO Box 279, Miniota MB R0M 1M0
Tel: 204-567-3745; *Fax:* 204-567-3749
www.opam-mb.com
Overview: A medium-sized provincial organization founded in 1988
Mission: To provide organic certification inspection service to farmers & processors; to teach & promote standards, methods & techniques for growing, producing & processing organically grown products
Membership: 881; *Fees:* $25 individual
Activities: Marketing seminars; farm tours; production seminars; AGM

Organic Trade Association (OTA)
#413, 28 Vernon St., Brattleboro VT 05301 USA
Tel: 802-275-3800; *Fax:* 802-275-3801
www.ota.com
Previous Name: Organic Food Production Association of North America
Overview: A medium-sized international organization founded in 1985
Mission: To encourage global sustainability through promoting & protecting the growth of diverse organic trade; *Member of:* International Federation of Organic Agriculture Movements
Chief Officer(s):
Christine Bushway, Executive Director
Finances: *Annual Operating Budget:* $500,000-$1.5 Million; *Funding Sources:* Membership fees; merchandise sales; fundraising
Staff: 22 staff member(s); 20 volunteer(s)
Membership: 1,500; *Fees:* Based on revenues; *Member Profile:* Organic food processors; certifiers; distributors; organic farm organizations; consultants; farmers; retail outlets; restaurants; *Committees:* Legislative; Quality Assurance; Marketing; International Relations; Organic Certifiers Council; Organic Fiber Council; Organic Suppliers Advisory Council; Canadian Council
Activities: Organic Harvest Month; *Awareness Events:* Organic Harvest Month, Sept.; *Speaker Service:* Yes

Organic Verification Organization of North America (OVONO US)
PO Box 146, Hitterdal MN 56552 USA
Tel: 218-962-3264
e-mail: info@organicfood.com
Overview: A small international organization
Mission: To provide certification services
Chief Officer(s):
Matthew Moe, Contact

Organisation de coopération et de développement économique ***See*** Organization for Economic Cooperation & Development

Organisation internationale de normalisation ***See*** International Organization for Standardization

Organisation maritime internationale ***See*** International Maritime Organization

Organisation météorologique mondiale ***See*** World Meteorological Organization

Organisation mondiale de la santé ***See*** World Health Organization

L'Organisation pour les carrières en environnement du Canada ***See*** Environmental Careers Organization of Canada

Organization for Economic Cooperation & Development (OECD) / Organisation de coopération et de développement économique (OCDE)
2, rue André-Pascal, Paris F-75775 France
Tel: 33-1-45-24-82-00; *Fax:* 33-1-45-24-85-00
e-mail: webmaster@oecd.org
www.oecd.org
www.facebook.com/theOECD
twitter.com/oecd
www.youtube.com/oecd
Overview: A large international organization founded in 1961
Mission: To achieve the highest sustainable economic growth & employment; To promote economic & social welfare throughout the OECD area by coordinating the policies of its member countries; To stimulate & harmonize its members' efforts in favour of developing countries; *Member of:* International Organization of Securities Commissions - Canada; Affiliation(s): International Energy Agency (IEA); Nuclear Energy Agency
Chief Officer(s):
Angel Gurría, Secretary General
Membership: 30 member countries
Activities: Provides a forum for monitoring economic trends & coordinating economic policies among its 30 member countries: the free-market democracies of North America, Western Europe & the Pacific; provides the largest source of comparative data on the industrial economies in the world; produces a wide range of publications, economic surveys, statistics, analyses & policy recommendations
Publications:
•OECD Observer
Type: Magazine

Organization of CANDU Industries (OCI) / Association des industries CANDU
#2, 1730 McPherson Ct., Pickering ON L1W 3E6
Tel: 905-839-0073; *Fax:* 905-839-7085
www.oci-aic.org
Overview: A medium-sized national organization founded in 1979
Mission: To represent companies in the Canadian private sector engaged in the supply of goods & services for CANDU power plants in export markets; to provide a focal point for industrial collaboration between the private sector of Canada's nuclear industry & foreign purchasers of a CANDU plant; functions separately from AECL, but participates with it in the design, manufacture, construction & commissioning of CANDU facilities in foreign countries; Affiliation(s): Atomic Energy of Canada
Chief Officer(s):
Ron Oberth, President
ron.oberth@oci-aic.org
Marina Oeyangen, Manager, Member Services
marina.oeyangen@oci-aic.org
Finances: *Annual Operating Budget:* Less than $50,000; *Funding Sources:* Membership dues
Staff: 3 staff member(s)
Membership: 105; *Fees:* Schedule available; *Member Profile:* Manufacturing & engineering companies engaged in supply of goods & services for CANDU nuclear steam plants

Oslo & Paris Commissions ***See*** OSPAR Commission

OSPAR Commission (OSPAR)
New Court, 48 Carey St., London WC2A 2JQ United Kingdom
Tel: 44-207-430-5200; *Fax:* 44-207-430-5225
e-mail: secretariat@ospar.org
www.ospar.org
Previous Name: Oslo & Paris Commissions
Overview: A small international organization founded in 1998
Mission: To control pollution of marine environment of the Northeast Atlantic
Chief Officer(s):
David Johnson, Executive Secretary
Finances: *Annual Operating Budget:* $500,000-$1.5 Million; *Funding Sources:* Membership
Staff: 12 staff member(s)
Membership: 15 European countries & EU; *Fees:* Annual contribution; *Committees:* Assessment & Monitoring; Eutophication; Hazardous Substances; Radioactive Substances; Biodiversity; Offshore Industry
Activities: Protection of the marine environment NE Atlantic

Ottawa Duck Club (ODC)
841 Kinsgmere Ave., Ottawa ON K2A 3J8
www.ottawaduckclub.com
Overview: A small local organization founded in 1966
Mission: To actively improve the nesting habitat for waterfowl and other birds along the Ottawa River.
Chief Officer(s):
Bill Bower, President, 613-824-9104
bigbuckbill@hotmail.com
Membership: *Fees:* $20 individual; $25 family

Ottawa Environmental Law Clinic ***See*** Ecojustice Canada Society

Ottawa Field-Naturalists' Club (OFNC)
PO Box 35069, Stn. Westgate, Ottawa ON K1Z 1A2
Tel: 613-722-3050
e-mail: ofnc@ofnc.ca
www.ofnc.ca
Overview: A small local charitable organization founded in 1879
Mission: To promote the preservation & conservation of Canada's natural heritage
Chief Officer(s):
Ann Mackenzie, President
Ken Young, Treasurer
Membership: *Fees:* $40 individuals; $45 families; *Member Profile:* Individuals who share an interest in nature; *Committees:* Birds; Education & Publicity; Excursions & Lectures; Nominations; Finance; Fletcher Wildlife Garden; Membership; Publications; Awards; Macoun Club for Young Naturalists
Activities: Encouraging research in all fields of natural history
Publications:
•Autobiography of John Macoun, Canadian Explorer & Naturalist, 1831-1920
Price: $20
•A Birder's Checklist of Ottawa
Price: $2
•The Canadian Field-Naturalist
Type: Journal; *Editor:* Carolyn Callaghan; *ISSN:* 0008-3550
•Checklist of the Butterflies of the Ottawa District
Price: $2
•A Guide to the Geology of the Gatineau-Lièvre District
Price: $5
•A Guide to the Geology of the Ottawa District
Price: $5
•Lichens of the Ottawa Region
Price: $10
•Nature & Natural Areas in Canada's Capital
Price: $5
•Trail & Landscape [a publication of the Ottawa Field-Naturalists' Club]
Type: Newsletter; *Frequency:* Quarterly; *Editor:* Karen McLachlan-Hamilton; *Price:* Free for OFNC members
Profile: Club activities & articles on the natural history of the Ottawa Valley

Ottawa Orchid Society
13 Sandringham Crt., Ottawa ON K2C 2H9
www.ottawaorchidsociety.com
www.facebook.com/pages/Ottawa-Orchid-Society/196485693713178
Overview: A small local organization founded in 1978
Mission: To promote knowledge, development, improvement, & conservation of orchids
Chief Officer(s):

Jean Hollebone, President
jhollebone@sympatico.ca
Janet Johns, Treasurer
Membership: *Fees:* $25
Activities: Offering programs about the care of orchids; *Awareness Events:* Annual Orchid Show; *Library:* Ottawa Orchid Society Library
Publications:
•Spike [a publication of the Ottawa Orchid Society]
Type: Newsletter; *Frequency:* Monthly; *Editor:* Rick Sobkowicz

Ottawa Valley Rock Garden & Horticultural Society

PO Box 9123, Stn. T, Ottawa ON K1G 3T8
e-mail: info@ovrghs.ca
www.ovrghs.ca
Overview: A small local organization founded in 1992
Affiliation(s): North American Rock Garden Society, Ontario Horticultural Association
Chief Officer(s):
Josie Pazdzior, President
josiepaz@rogers.com
Margaret Don, Membership Secretary
Membership: *Fees:* $20 individual, $25 family
Activities: Meetings held second Saturday of each month from Sept.-May at Woodroffe Campus of Algonquin College

Outdoor Writers of Canada

PO Box 934, Cochrane AB T4C 1B1
Tel: 403-932-3585; *Fax:* 403-851-0618
e-mail: outdoorwritersofcanada@shaw.ca
www.outdoorwritersofcanada.com
www.facebook.com/groups/31592177632
Overview: A small national organization founded in 1957
Mission: To promote high standards of craftsmanship in the portrayal of outdoor life
Environmental Activity: Cooperating with others to support responsible uses of natural resources
Chief Officer(s):
T.J. Schwanky, Executive Director
Membership: *Fees:* $40 student; $90 active & associate membership; $280 corporate; *Member Profile:* Professional communicators who specialize in the outdoor field, such as writers, photographers, artists, cinematographers, broadcasters, & government information officers; Corporate members that share the organization's goals; Students
Activities: Increasing appreciation of the outdoors
Meetings/Conferences:
For more information see Trade Shows, Conferences and Seminars Chapter
Outdoor Writers of Canada 2013 National Conference & Annual General Meeting
June 2013 Campbell River, BC
Publications:
•Inside Outdoors
Type: Newsletter; *Frequency:* 6 pa
Profile: Happenings of Outdoor Writers of Canada, corporate news, craft improvement articles, & new markets

Outdoors Unlittered ***See*** Pitch-In Canada

Outdoors Unlittered (Alberta) ***See*** Pitch-In Alberta

Outward Bound Canada

Centre for Green Cities, #404, 550 Bayview Ave., Toronto ON M4W 3X8
Fax: 705-382-5959
Toll-Free: 888-688-9273
e-mail: info@outwardbound.ca
www.outwardbound.ca
www.linkedin.com/company/outward-bound-canada
www.facebook.com/pages/Outward-Bound-Canada/8376438193?ref=ts
twitter.com/OutwardBoundCan
www.youtube.com/user/OutwardBoundCanada
Also Known As: Canadian Outward Bound Wilderness School
Overview: A small provincial charitable organization founded in 1976
Mission: To promote self-reliance, care & respect for others, responsibility to community & concern for the environment; *Member of:* Ontario Camping Association; Ontario Society for Training & Development; Association for Experiential Education; Council of Outdoor Educators of Ontario
Chief Officer(s):
Sarah Wiley, Executive Director
sarah_wiley@outwardbound.ca
Finances: *Annual Operating Budget:* $1.5 Million-$3 Million
Staff: 11 staff member(s); 20 volunteer(s)
Activities: Youth - 21-day Adventure courses available for 15-16 yrs. old & 22-day Voyageur programs for 17+ yrs.; Adults - courses vary from 7 - 24 days, including canoeing, sea-kayaking, hiking or dog-sledding & skiing; special courses for 50+ yrs., for women only & courses for managers & educators; leadership courses; *Internships:* Yes; *Speaker Service:* Yes

Oxford County Geological Society
Parent Name: Central Canadian Federation of Mineralogical Societies

820 Devonshire Ave., Woodstock ON N4S 7W2
e-mail: marion.eccleston@sympatico.ca
Overview: A small local organization founded in 1977 overseen by Central Canadian Federation of Mineralogical Societies
Mission: To arouse interest & knowledge in all fields of earth sciences; to ensure that all age-group needs are considered; *Member of:* Canadian Central Federation Minerals Society
Chief Officer(s):
Marion Eccleston, President
Grace Poole, Treasurer
Peter Nielsen, Secretary
Finances: *Funding Sources:* Membership dues
Staff: 5 volunteer(s)
Membership: 18 families; *Fees:* $18 family; $15 single; *Committees:* Field Trippers
Activities: Workshops; seminars; monthly meetings meetings 2nd Friday of the month; guest speakers; *Speaker Service:* Yes; *Library:* by appointment

Pacific NorthWest Economic Region (PNWER)

World Trade Center West, #460, 2200 Alaskan Way, Seattle WA 98121 USA
Tel: 206-443-7723; *Fax:* 206-443-7703
www.pnwer.org
Previous Name: Pacific Northwest Legislative Leadership
Overview: A medium-sized local organization founded in 1989
Mission: To promote greater collaboration among the seven state & provincial members in order to enhance the economic competitiveness of the region in international & domestic markets
Chief Officer(s):
Matt Morrison, Executive Director
matt@pnwer.org
Finances: *Annual Operating Budget:* $100,000-$250,000
Staff: 3 staff member(s); 6 volunteer(s)
Membership: 1,000-4,999;; *Fees:* $250 individual; $500 non-profit; $1000 corporate; *Member Profile:* Consists of the Pacific Northwestern states of Alaska, Idaho, Montana, Oregon & Washington & the provinces of Alberta, British Columbia & the Yukon Territory; includes Legislators, Governors/Premiers & private sector individuals
Activities: 9 Working Groups; *Internships:* Yes

Pacific Northwest Legislative Leadership ***See*** Pacific NorthWest Economic Region

Pacific Peoples Partnership (PPP)

#407, 620 View St., Victoria BC V8W 1J6
Tel: 250-381-4131; *Fax:* 250-388-5258
e-mail: info@pacificpeoplespartnership.org
www.pacificpeoplespartnership.org
Previous Name: South Pacific Peoples Foundation
Overview: A small international organization founded in 1975
Mission: To promote increased understanding of social justice, environment, development, health & other issues of importance to the people of the Pacific Islands; To support equitable, environmentally sustainable development & social justice in the region; *Member of:* Canadian Council for International Cooperation; British Columbia Council for International Cooperation; Affiliation(s): Nuclear Free & Independent Pacific Movement
Chief Officer(s):
April Ingham, Executive Director
director@pacificpeoplespartnership.org
Finances: *Annual Operating Budget:* $100,000-$250,000; *Funding Sources:* Membership dues; donors; sales; Canadian International Development Agency; professional service fees
Staff: 5 staff member(s); 15 volunteer(s)
Membership: 160; *Fees:* $35 regular; $45 family; $20 student; *Member Profile:* Supporter of SPPF's aims & objectives, Canadian citizen or a current resident of Canada, annual donation required; *Committees:* Program; Finance; Fundraising; Journal; Public Relations
Activities: Pacific Networking Conference, every two years; *Awareness Events:* One Wave Festival, September; *Speaker Service:* Yes; *Library:* Resource Centre; Open to public

Pacific Space Centre Society ***See*** H.R. MacMillan Space Centre Society

Pacific States/British Columbia Oil Spill Task Force

Environmental Emergencies Branch, BC Ministry of Environment, PO Box 9377, Stn. Prov Govt, 2975 Jutland Rd., 3rd Fl., Victoria BC V8W 9M6
Tel: 250-356-8383; *Fax:* 250-387-9935
www.oilspilltaskforce.org
Mission: The Pacific States/British Columbia Oil Spill Task Force was authorized by a Memorandum of Cooperation signed in 1989 by the Governors of Alaska, Washington, Oregon, and California and the Premier of British Columbia following the Nestucca and Exxon Valdez oil spills. These events highlighted their common concerns regarding oil spill risks and the need for cooperation across shared borders. In June 2001 a revised Memorandum of Cooperation was adopted to include the State of Hawaii and expand the focus to spill preparedness and prevention needs of the 21st century. Now in the second decade, the Task Force provides a forum where Members can work with stakeholders from the Western US and Canada to implement regional initiatives that protect 56,660 miles of coastline from Alaska to California and the Hawaiian archipelago. The Task Force Members are senior executives from the environmental agencies with oil spill regulatory authority in the states of Alaska, Washington, Oregon, California and Hawaii and the Province of British Columbia. Oil spill program managers from each member agency comprise the Task Force's Coordinating Committee, which oversees activities and projects as authorized by the Members when they adopt a Five Year Strategic Plan and Annual Work Plans. The Coordinating Committee convenes four times a year. The Task Force Members hold their Annual Meetings each summer, rotating locations among member jurisdictions.
Chief Officer(s):
Sarah Brace, Executive Coordinator, 206-409-3253
sarah@vedaenv.com

Pacific Urchin Harvesters Association (PUHA)

902 - 4th Street, New Westminster BC V3L 2W6
Tel: 604-524-0322; *Fax:* 604-524-1023
e-mail: info@puha.org
www.puha.org
www.facebook.com/153381171388169
twitter.com/puhaorg
Overview: A small local organization founded in 1994
Mission: To examine issues around the commercial dive fishery for Red Sea Urchins; to enhance the urchins' market profile & that of the Canadian seafood production industry in general
Chief Officer(s):
Mike Featherstone, President, 604-230-1686
president@puha.org
Ross Morris, Secretary-Treasurer, 604-524-0322
secretary@puha.org
Publications:
•Pacific Urchin Harvesters Association Newsletter
Type: Newsletter

Packaging Association of Canada (PAC) / Association canadienne de l'emballage

#607, 1 Concorde Gate, Toronto ON M3C 3N6
Tel: 416-490-7860; *Fax:* 416-490-7844
e-mail: pacinfo@pac.ca
www.pac.ca
www.linkedin.com/company/the-packaging-association
www.facebook.com/ThePackagingAssociation
twitter.com/PackagingAssoc
Overview: A large national organization founded in 1950
Mission: To represent both users & suppliers on the strength of environmental & economic policy
Chief Officer(s):
James D. Downham, President & CEO, 416-646-4637
jdd@leaderlinx.com
Jan McCallum, Communications Director, 416-646-4642
janmccallum@pac.ca
Finances: *Funding Sources:* Membership dues; Activities
Staff: 11 staff member(s)
Membership: 1,700+; *Fees:* Schedule available; *Member Profile:* Canadian packaging industry

Québec Office
CP 43010, Succ. Place Vilamont, 1839, René-Laënnec, Laval QC H7M 6A1
Tél: 450-990-0134; *Téléc:* 450-668-2691
Courriel: quebec@pac.ca

Paddle Canada (PC) / Pagaie Canada
PO Box 126, Stn. Main, Kingston ON K7L 4V6
Tel: 613-547-3196; *Fax:* 613-547-4880
Toll-Free: 888-252-6292
e-mail: info@paddlecanada.com
www.paddlingcanada.com
Previous Name: Canadian Recreational Canoeing Association
Overview: A large national licensing charitable organization founded in 1971
Mission: To promote all forms of recreational paddling to Canadians of diverse abilities, culture or age; to advocate for a healthy natural environment; To develop an appreciation for the canoe & the kayak in our Canadian heritage; Affiliation(s): Active Living Alliance for Canadians with a Disability; Girl Guides of Canada
Chief Officer(s):
Blair Doyle, President & Regional Director, Nova Scotia
president@paddlecanada.com
Rick Wise, Vice-President & Chair, Member Services Committee
vicepres@paddlecanada.com
Bryan Sarauer, Regional Director & Chair, Communications (Marketing & Promotions)
communications@paddlecanada.com
Graham Ketcheson, Executive Director
Finances: *Funding Sources:* Membership fees; Donations; Program delivery; Sponsorships
Staff: 80 volunteer(s)
Membership: 1,500 individual; *Fees:* $42 individual; *Committees:* Canoeing Program Development; River Kayaking Program Development; Sea Kayaking Program Development; SUP Board Program Development; Finance; Instruction & Safety; Communications (Marketing & Promotions); Member Services; Environment
Activities: Reviewing park management plans, hydroelectric developments & timber management plans; Promoting waterway conservation through the Waterwalker Film Festival; Providing educational programs; Increasing environmental awareness
Publications:
•Current Strokes [a publication of Paddle Canada]
Type: Newsletter

Pagaie Canada ***See*** Paddle Canada

Pan American Center for Sanitary Engineering & Environmental Sciences (CEPIS)
Urbanizacion Camacho, La Molina, PO Box 4337, Calle Los Pinos 259, Lima 12 Peru
Tel: 51-1-437-1077; *Fax:* 51-1-437-8289
Overview: A large international organization founded in 1968
Mission: To cooperate with the countries of the Americas to evaluate & manage environmental risk factors that, directly or indirectly, affect the health of the population
Finances: *Funding Sources:* PAHO; WHO; Peruvian government; other
Staff: 90 staff member(s)
Membership: Governments of 48 countries & territories
Activities: Carries out programs aimed at strengthening national capacities for protecting environmental health & the management of risks derived from man-made contamination; *Library:* Open to public

Panos Washington
Webster House, #T6, 1718 P St. NW, Washington DC 20036 USA
Tel: 202-429-0730
e-mail: washington@panoscaribbean.org
Overview: A medium-sized international organization founded in 1986
Mission: To provide information resources on sustainable development issues; *Member of:* Inter Action
Chief Officer(s):
Jan Voordouw, Executive Director
Finances: *Annual Operating Budget:* $250,000-$500,000; *Funding Sources:* Bilateral, multilateral & non-governmental organizations; private foundations
Staff: 4 staff member(s)
Activities: ; *Library:* Open to public

Paper & Paperboard Packaging Environmental Council (PPEC)
#3, 1995 Clark Blvd., Brampton ON L6T 4W1
Tel: 905-458-0087; *Fax:* 905-458-2052
e-mail: ppec@ppec-paper.com
www.ppec-paper.com
www.linkedin.com/company/2516029?trk=tyah
Overview: A medium-sized national organization
Mission: Represents member companies to various levels of government, as well as to environmental and consumer interest groups; networks with other players in the paper industry to establish common interests; promotes environmentally sound practices in manufacture and recovery.; Affiliation(s): American Forest & Paper Association; Fibre Box Association; Association of Independent Corrugated Converters (AICC)
Membership: *Member Profile:* Packaging mills, and packaging converters

Paper Packaging Canada ***See*** Canadian Corrugated Containerboard Association

Parcs et loisirs de l'Ontario ***See*** Parks & Recreation Ontario

Parks & Recreation Ontario (PRO) / Parcs et loisirs de l'Ontario
Parent Name: Canadian Parks & Recreation Association
#302, 1 Concorde Gate, Toronto ON M3C 3N6
Tel: 416-426-7142; *Fax:* 416-426-7371
e-mail: pro@prontario.org
www.prontario.org
Overview: A large provincial organization founded in 1984 overseen by Canadian Parks & Recreation Association
Mission: To enhance the quality of life, health & well-being of people, their communities & their environments; To advocate provincially for parks & recreation issues; To provide networking as well as multi-discipline professional development opportunities
Chief Officer(s):
Larry Ketcheson, CEO, 416-426-7143
lketcheson@prontario.org
Finances: *Annual Operating Budget:* $500,000-$1.5 Million; *Funding Sources:* Self-funding through programs; provincial grants for special projects; membership dues
Staff: 14 staff member(s); 100 volunteer(s)
Membership: 1,000; *Fees:* Schedule available; *Member Profile:* Individual; student; corporate; *Committees:* Anti-Harassment Policies; Day Care Reform; Government Relations; Benefits of Recreation; Violence in Recreation Activities
Activities: Recreation - An Essential Service; *Library:*
Meetings/Conferences:
For more information see Trade Shows, Conferences and Seminars Chapter
Parks & Recreation Ontario / Parcs et loisirs de l'Ontario 2013 Aquatics Conference & Trade Show
2013

Partenaires des parcs canadiens ***See*** Canadian Parks Partnership

Le Partenariat canadien pour la santé des enfants et l'environnement ***See*** Canadian Partnership for Children's Health and Environment

Partenariat pour des environnements intérieurs sains ***See*** Healthy Indoors Partnership

Parti Vert d'Ontario ***See*** The Green Party of Ontario

Parti vert du Canada ***See*** Green Party of Canada

Parti Vert du Nouveau Brunswick ***See*** Green Party of New Brunswick

Parti Vert du Québec (PVQ) / Green Party of Québec
Parent Name: Green Party of Canada
#220, 10000 rue Lajeunesse, Montréal QC H3L 2E1
Tél: 514-303-7750
Ligne sans frais: 888-998-8378
Courriel: info@partivertquebec.org
www.partivertquebec.org
www.facebook.com/partivert
twitter.com/claudesabourin_
Aperçu: *Dimension:* moyenne; *Envergure:* provinciale surveillé par Green Party of Canada
Membre(s) du bureau directeur:
Guy Rainville, Chef

Partners FOR the Saskatchewan River Basin (PFSRB)
402 - 3rd Ave. South, Saskatoon SK S7K 3G5
Tel: 306-665-6887; *Fax:* 306-665-6117
Toll-Free: 800-567-8007
e-mail: partners@saskriverbasin.ca
www.saskriverbasin.ca
Overview: A small local charitable organization founded in 1993
Mission: To promote watershed sustainability through awareness, linkages & stewardship
Chief Officer(s):
Ray Fast, Chair
Susan Lamb, Managing Partner
Lis Mack, Manager
Finances: *Annual Operating Budget:* $250,000-$500,000
Staff: 2 staff member(s); 50 volunteer(s)
Membership: 110; *Fees:* $25 individual/family; $50-$10,000 corporations/organizations based on budget; *Member Profile:* Individuals & organizations from all sectors of society & all the geographic areas of the basin - Alberta, Saskatchewan & Manitoba
Activities: Watershed monitoring; low water landscaping; storm drain marking; basin-wide stewardship program; aquatic restoration projects; integrated research; ecotourism development & marketing; watershed stewardship program for children
Publications:
•The River Current [a publication of Partners FOR the Saskatchewan River Basin]
Type: Newsletter; *Frequency:* Quarterly

Passons à l'action Canada ***See*** Pitch-In Canada

Peace & Environment Resource Centre
PO Box 4075, Stn. E, 174 First Ave., Ottawa ON K1S 5B1
Tel: 613-230-4590
e-mail: info@perc.ca
www.perc.ca
Overview: A small local charitable organization
Mission: To ensure peaceful, equitable, healthy, & sustainable local & global communities
Environmental Activity: Collaborating with local organizations in the area of environmental stewardship
Finances: *Funding Sources:* Donations; Fundraising
Activities: Developing community projects; Organizing workshops & events; *Library:* Peace & Environment Resource Centre Library; Open to public
Publications:
•The Peace & Environment News
Type: Newsletter; *Price:* Free
Profile: Information about critical issues for Canada & the world

Peace Agricultural Research & Demonstration Association (PARDA)
Parent Name: Agricultural Research & Extension Council of Alberta
PO Box 1551, Fairview AB T0H 1L0
Tel: 780-835-9158
e-mail: peaceagrd@gmail.com
www.areca.ab.ca/pardahome.html
www.facebook.com/pages/PARDA/105160659548217
Previous Name: Fairview Applied Research Association
Overview: A small local organization overseen by Agricultural Research & Extension Council of Alberta
Mission: To increase the profitability of grain producers in Northern Alberta through developing new technology & improving management practices; *Member of:* Agricultural Research & Extension Council of Alberta
Chief Officer(s):
Vacant, Manager, Research & Program
Membership: *Fees:* $20
Publications:
•PARDA [Peace Agricultural Research & Demonstration Association] Newsletter
Type: Newsletter

Peace Country Beef & Forage Association (PCGFA)
Parent Name: Agricultural Research & Extension Council of Alberta
PO Box 3000, Fairview AB T0H 1L0
Tel: 780-835-6799; *Fax:* 780-835-6626
www.areca.ab.ca/pcbfahome.html
Overview: A small local organization founded in 1982 overseen by Agricultural Research & Extension Council of Alberta
Mission: To demonstrate new forage varieties & technology; *Member of:* Agricultural Research & Extension Council of Alberta
Chief Officer(s):
Ryan Leiske, President
Morgan Hobin, Acting Manager
mhobin@gprc.ab.ca
Akim Omokanye, Coordinator, Program
aomokanye@gprc.ab.ca
Membership: 175; *Fees:* $25
Publications:
•Forage Facts [a publication of the Peace Country Beef &

Forage Association]
Type: Newsletter

High Prairie Office

PO Box 2803, 5226 - 53 Ave., High Prairie AB T0G 1E0
Tel: 780-523-4033; *Fax:* 780-523-6569
Chief Officer(s):
Karlah Rudolph, Coordinator, Extension/ASB
krudolph@gprc.ab.ca

Peace Parkland Naturalists
PO Box 1451, Grande Prairie AB T8V 4Z2
Tel: 780-539-6102
www.peacenaturalists.fanweb.ca
Overview: A small local organization founded in 1990
Mission: To promote awareness & appreciation of the natural history of the Peace Region of northwestern Alberta; *Member of:* Federation of Alberta Naturalists
Chief Officer(s):
Margot Hervieux, Contact
hervieux@telusplanet.net
Finances: *Annual Operating Budget:* Less than $50,000
Membership: 40; *Fees:* $10 individual; $15 family
Activities: Field trips; meetings
Publications:
•The Hooter [a publication of the Peace Parkland Naturalists]
Type: Newsletter
•Kleksun Hill: A Discovery Guide [a publication of the Peace Parkland Naturalists]
Type: Book; *Author:* Margot Hervieux; *Price:* $6

Peace Valley Environment Association (PVEA)
PO Box 6062, Fort St John BC V1J 4H6
e-mail: pvea@shaw.ca
www.peacevalley.ca
Overview: A small local organization
Mission: To protect and defend the natural environment of the Peace Valley area of British Columbia
Membership: *Fees:* $10

P.E.I. Cattlemen's Association *See* Prince Edward Island Cattle Producers

PEI Tuberculosis League *See* Prince Edward Island Lung Association

The Pembina Institute
219 - 19 St. NW, Calgary AB T2N 2H9
Tel: 403-269-3344; *Fax:* 403-269-3377
www.pembina.org
Overview: A medium-sized provincial charitable organization founded in 1985
Mission: To develop & promote public policy & educational programs which protect the environment & encourage environmentally sound resource management strategies; to implement a conserver society; *Member of:* Canadian Renewable Energy Alliance
Chief Officer(s):
Ed Whittingham, Executive Director
Membership: 32
Activities: Major program areas include Environmental Education & Publishing (teacher professional development; national environmental education resource cataloguing service; curricular materials for schools; classroom presentations & student workshops; community adult environmental education courses); Research, Development & Promotion of Environmental Policy (analyzing & developing municipal, provincial & federal energy-related environmental policy, as well as policy related to other conservation & recycling issues; *Speaker Service:* Yes; *Library:* Open to public by appointment

Pembroke Area Field Naturalists (PAFN)
PO Box 1242, Pembroke ON K8A 6Y6
www.pafn.on.ca
Overview: A small local charitable organization founded in 1983
Member of: Federation of Ontario Naturalists
Chief Officer(s):
Leo Boland, President
leoboland@pafn.on.ca
Finances: *Annual Operating Budget:* Less than $50,000; *Funding Sources:* Donations; fundraising
Membership: 50; *Fees:* $15 individual; $20 family; $10 student/senior
Activities: Nature walks; bird & insect counts; fundraisers

Pender Island Field Naturalists (PIFN)
1105 Ogden Rd., Pender Island BC V0N 2M1
Overview: A small local organization
Membership: 1-99;; *Fees:* $18/year; *Member Profile:* Birding & botany enthusiasts

Peninsula Field Naturalists (PFN)
PO Box 23031, Stn. Carlton, St Catharines ON L2R 7P6
Tel: 905-892-2566; *Fax:* 905-892-6401
e-mail: info@peninsulafieldnats.com
peninsulafieldnats.com
Overview: A small local charitable organization founded in 1954
Mission: To promote the enjoyment of nature through environmental appreciation & conservation; to encourage wise use & conservation of natural resources; to promote environmental protection; *Member of:* Ontario Nature; Affiliation(s): Canadian Nature Federation
Chief Officer(s):
John Potter, President
Finances: *Annual Operating Budget:* Less than $50,000; *Funding Sources:* Membership fees
Staff: 12 volunteer(s)
Membership: 100; *Fees:* $10 student; $25 adult; $35 family; *Member Profile:* Interest in natural history
Activities: Outdoor natural history walks; annual park clean-up; annual bird & plant inventories

People for the Ethical Treatment of Animals (PETA)
501 Front St., Norfolk VA 23510 USA
Tel: 757-622-7382; *Fax:* 757-628-0457
www.peta.org
www.linkedin.com/in/ingridnewkirk
www.facebook.com/officialpeta
twitter.com/peta
www.youtube.com/profile?user=officialpeta
Overview: A large international charitable organization founded in 1980
Mission: To protect animals from exploitation & cruelty; To bring positive changes in the ways humans regard other species; to expose animal abuse so it will not be perpetuated; To promote a world in which animals are respected & people are aware of & concerned with how their daily decisions affect the lives of other sentient beings
Chief Officer(s):
Ingrid E. Newkirk, President
Mary Beth Sweetland, Vice-President
Finances: *Annual Operating Budget:* Greater than $5 Million; *Funding Sources:* Contributions
Staff: 180 staff member(s); 40 volunteer(s)
Membership: 3,000,000+; *Fees:* US$16; $25 Cdn.
Activities: International campaigns on vegetarianism, against animal testing, against fur & dissection, against animal abuse in the entertainment industry; *Internships:* Yes; *Rents Mailing List:* Yes; *Library:* PETA Library; Open to public

People's Law School
#150, 900 Howe St., Vancouver BC V6Z 2M4
Tel: 604-331-5400; *Fax:* 604-331-5401
e-mail: staff@publiclegaled.bc.ca
www.publiclegaled.bc.ca
www.linkedin.com/company/2024453?trk=tyah
www.facebook.com/pages/Peoples-Law-School-BC/181366371905105
twitter.com/PLSBC
www.youtube.com/user/plsbc
Overview: A small provincial organization founded in 1972
Mission: To make law & legal system understandable & accessible to people of British Columbia; *Member of:* Public Legal Education Association of Canada
Chief Officer(s):
Terresa Augustine, Executive Director
info@publiclegaled.bc.ca
Activities: Produces public legal education and information publications

Pest Management Association of Alberta (PMAA)
c/o John Patton, #1550, 246 Stewart Green SW, Calgary AB T3H 3C8
Tel: 403-242-2467
e-mail: pmaa@telus.net
www.pmaapestworld.com
Previous Name: Structural Pest Management Association of Alberta
Overview: A small provincial organization
Mission: To improve & maintain standards of pest management services in the province; *Member of:* Canadian Pest Management Association; National Pest Management Association Inc.
Chief Officer(s):
John Patton, President
jpatton@japco.ca
Tom Schultz, Treasurer, 780-466-8535
edexterm@telusplanet.net
Susan Baker, Secretary, 780-446-7428
sbaker@telus.net
Membership: *Fees:* $385

Pesticide Action Network North America (PANNA)
#1200, 1611 Telegraph Ave., Oakland CA 94612 USA
Tel: 510-788-9020; *Fax:* 415-981-1991
e-mail: panna@panna.org
www.panna.org
www.facebook.com/pesticideactionnetwork
twitter.com/pesticideaction
www.youtube.com/user/pannavideo
Overview: A medium-sized international charitable organization founded in 1984
Mission: Works to replace pesticide use with ecologically sound & socially just alternatives; links local & international consumer, labor, health, environment & agriculture groups into an international citizens' action network; network challenges the global proliferation of pesticides, defends basic rights to health & environmental quality & works to insure the transition to a just & viable society
Chief Officer(s):
Jennifer Sokolove, President
Monica Moore, Founding Executive Director
Steve Scholl-Buckwald, CFO & Managing Director
Finances: *Annual Operating Budget:* $1.5 Million-$3 Million; *Funding Sources:* Grants & individual donors
Staff: 21 staff member(s); 5 volunteer(s)
Membership: 225 affiliate organizations; *Fees:* US$35 organizations with paid staff; US$20 all volunteer organizations
Activities: Campaign to stop pesticide drift; documenting pesticide body burden; holding corporations accountable for the use & promotion of pesticides & genetically engineered crops; campaign to transform agricultural development through the International Assessment of Agricultural Science & Technology for Development; California & Midwest pesticide use reduction; public education; farmworkers' rights campaign; promotion of alternatives to pesticides; *Internships:* Yes; *Library:* by appointment

Pesticide Education Network
web.ncf.ca/bf250/pen.html
Overview: A small local organization
Chief Officer(s):
John Sankey, Contact
johnsankey@ncf.ca
Finances: *Annual Operating Budget:* Less than $50,000
Staff: 20 volunteer(s)
Membership: 1-99
Activities: Reduction of pesticide use within urban areas; *Speaker Service:* Yes

Peterborough Field Naturalists (PFN)
Parent Name: Ontario Nature
PO Box 1532, Peterborough ON K9J 7H7
Tel: 705-742-1524
www.peterboroughnature.org
Overview: A small local organization founded in 1940 overseen by Ontario Nature
Mission: To promote the enjoyment of nature through environmental appreciation & conservation; To encourage wise use & conservation of natural resources & environmental protection
Chief Officer(s):
Martin Parker, President
mparker19@cogeco.ca
Jim Young, Head, Memberships
Membership: 200; *Fees:* $25 single; $30 family/couple; $15 student; *Committees:* Program, Project
Activities: Monthly meetings with guest speakers, nature walks, birding excursions;
Publications:
•The Orchid
Type: Newsletter; *Editor:* Rebecca Zeran

Petroleum Human Resources Council of Canada (PHRCC)
5055 - 11 St. NE, Calgary AB T2E 8N4
Tel: 403-516-8100; *Fax:* 403-516-8171
e-mail: info@petrohrsc.ca
www.petrohrsc.ca
Overview: A medium-sized national organization

Mission: Collaborative forum that addresses human resources issues within the petroleum industry

Petroleum Industry Training Service ***See*** Enform: The Safety Association for the Upstream Oil & Gas Industry

Petroleum Research Atlantic Canada (PRAC ***See*** Petroleum Research Newfoundland & Labrador

Petroleum Research Newfoundland & Labrador

Baine Johnston Centre, #802, 10 Fort William Pl., St. John's NL A1C 1K4
Tel: 709-738-7916; *Fax:* 709-738-7922
www.pr-ac.ca
Previous Name: Petroleum Research Atlantic Canada (PRAC
Overview: A small local organization founded in 1999
Mission: To fund & facilitate research & development on behalf of the offshore oil & gas industry of Newfoundland & Labrador
Environmental Activity: Funding research projects in areas such as health, safety, & the environment & Arctic & harsh environments
Chief Officer(s):
Doug Cook, Chief Executive Officer, 709-738-7920
doug.cook@petroleumresearch.ca
David Finn, Chief Operating Officer, 709-738-7917
dave.finn@petroleumresearch.ca
Susan Hunt, Program Manager, HSE, 709-738-7904
susan.hunt@petroleumresearch.ca
Lisa A. Hutchens, Manager, Business Services, 709-738-7921
lisa.hutchens@petroleumresearch.ca
Matilda Maddigan, Manager, Office, 709-738-7916
matilda.maddigan@petroleumresearch.ca
Metzi Prince, Manager, Project Delivery, 709-738-7919
metzi.prince@petroleumresearch.ca
Charles E. Smith, Senior Technical Advisor, 709-738-7918
charles.smith@petroleumresearch.ca
Robert Trask, Coordinator, Research Grants, 709-738-7974
robert.trask@petroleumresearch.ca
Membership: *Member Profile:* Representatives from the oil & gas industry

Petroleum Services Association of Canada (PSAC)

#1150, 800 - 6 Ave. SW, Calgary AB T2P 3G3
Tel: 403-264-4195; *Fax:* 403-263-7174
www.psac.ca
www.linkedin.com/groups/PSAC-Working-Energy-4706150
Overview: A large national organization founded in 1981
Mission: To represent the supply, manufacturing, & service sectors of the upstream petroleum industry
Environmental Activity: Developing a Community Partners program to address concerns related to oil & gas activity
Chief Officer(s):
Lucas Mezzano, Chair
Mark Salkeld, MBA, President & CEO
msalkeld@psac.ca
Elizabeth Aquin, CAE, Senior Vice-President
eaquin@psac.ca
Patrick J. Delaney, CRSP, Vice-President, Health & Safety
pdelaney@psac.ca
Kelly Morrison, Vice-President, Communications
kmorrison@psac.ca
Heather Doyle, Manager, Meetings & Events
hdoyle@psac.ca
Membership: 250+ companies; *Fees:* Schedule available; *Member Profile:* Petroleum services industry companies; *Committees:* Corporate Finance; Education Fund; Health & Safety; Human Resources; Special Events; Transportation Issues; Cathodic Protection; Drilling Fluids; Oilwell Perforators' Safety Training & Advisory; Snubbing Services; Well Testing
Activities: Engaging in lobbying activities; Providing educational opportunities
Meetings/Conferences:
For more information see Trade Shows, Conferences and Seminars Chapter
Petroleum Services Association of Canada 2013 Annual Spring Conference
April 2013 Red Deer, AB
Petroleum Services Association of Canada 2013 Annual Mid-Year Luncheon
April 2013 Calgary, AB
Petroleum Services Association of Canada 2013 Annual General Meeting, Canadian Drilling Activity Forecast Session, & Industry Dinner
2013
Petroleum Services Association of Canada 19th Annual STARS & Spurs Gala
January 2013 Calgary, AB
Petroleum Services Association of Canada 2014 Annual Spring Conference
April 2014 Red Deer, AB
Petroleum Services Association of Canada 2014 Annual Mid-Year Update
2014
Petroleum Services Association of Canada 2014 Annual General Meeting, Canadian Drilling Activity Forecast Session, & Industry Dinner
2014
Petroleum Services Association of Canada 2015 Annual Spring Conference
2015
Petroleum Services Association of Canada 2015 Annual Mid-Year Update
2015
Petroleum Services Association of Canada 2015 Annual General Meeting, Canadian Drilling Activity Forecast Session, & Industry Dinner
2015
Publications:
•Canadian Drilling Activity Forecast
Type: Yearbook; *Frequency:* Annually
Profile: Five years of historical data, plus forecasts for the coming year across Canada
•FAST-Line [a publication of the Petroleum Services Association of Canada]
Type: Newsletter; *Frequency:* Biweekly
Profile: Association news & upcoming events
•Petroleum Services Association of Canada Membership Directory
Type: Directory
Profile: Contact information for association members
•Petroleum Services Association of Canada Annual Report
Type: Yearbook; *Frequency:* Annually
Profile: A review of the association's activities, released at the end of each October in conjunction with the Canadian Drilling Activity Forecast & the Annual GeneralMeeting
•Petroleum Services News [a publication of the Petroleum Services Association of Canada]
Type: Magazine; *Frequency:* Quarterly; *Accepts Advertising*
Profile: Covering issues of importance to the upstream oil & gas industry
•Total Compensation Survey [a publication of the Petroleum Services Association of Canada]
Type: Yearbook; *Frequency:* Annually
Profile: An analysis of current salary & benefits practices in the petroleum service, supply, & manufacturing industry
•Well Cost Study
Type: Study
Profile: Geological, technical, & financial data on wells drilled across Canada

Petroleum Tank Management Association of Alberta (PTMAA)

#980, 10303 Jasper Ave., Edmonton AB T5J 3N6
Tel: 780-425-8265; *Fax:* 780-425-4722
Toll-Free: 866-222-8265
e-mail: ptmaa@ptmaa.ab.ca
www.ptmaa.ab.ca
Overview: A medium-sized provincial licensing charitable organization founded in 1994
Mission: To offer programs to enhance the management of petroleum storage tank systems in Alberta
Environmental Activity: Ensuring storage tank systems are designed, installed, upgraded or operated in accordance with the Alberta Fire Code; Monitoring of storage tank closures
Chief Officer(s):
Don Edgecombe, Operations Manager
Mark Tse, Chair
Randy Hall, Secretary
Sim Koopmans, Treasurer
Activities: Monitoring new storage tank installations; Inspecting existing storage tank installations; Investigating accidents & incidents

Petroleum Technology Alliance Canada (PTAC)

Chevron Plaza, #400, 500 - 5th Ave. SW, Calgary AB T2P 3L5
Tel: 403-218-7700; *Fax:* 403-920-0054
e-mail: info@ptac.org
www.ptac.org
Overview: A medium-sized national organization
Mission: To facilitate innovation, technology transfer & research & development in the upstream oil & gas industry
Chief Officer(s):
Soheil Asgarpour, President
sasgarpour@ptac.org

Pickering Naturalists

PO Box 304, Pickering ON L1V 2R6
Tel: 905-831-1639
e-mail: pnclub@pickeringnaturalists.org
www.pickeringnaturalists.org
Overview: A small local organization founded in 1977
Member of: Federation of Ontario Naturalists
Finances: *Funding Sources:* Membership dues
Membership: *Fees:* $21 individual; $25 family; $250 life
Publications:
•Pickering Naturalist [a publication of Pickering Naturalists]
Type: Newsletter; *Frequency:* Quarterly
Profile: Nature articles & information on upcoming events.

Pigeon Lake Regional Chamber of Commerce (PLRCC)

#6B Village Dr., RR#2, Westerose AB T0C 2V0
Tel: 780-586-6263; *Fax:* 780-586-3667
e-mail: info@pigeonlakechamber.ca
www.pigeonlakechamber.ca
Overview: A small local charitable organization founded in 1988
Mission: To build an economic base for permanent & seasonal residence that will provide services for tourists, while maintaining environmental characteristics & quality of life; To promote the commercial, industrial, social, & civic interests of the community; Affiliation(s): Alberta Chambers of Commerce
Environmental Activity: Protecting the environment
Chief Officer(s):
Doug McKenzie, President
dhmfin@telus.net
Sereda Bernadette, Manager
Finances: *Annual Operating Budget:* Less than $50,000; *Funding Sources:* Fundraising; Membership fees
Staff: 1 staff member(s); 70 volunteer(s)
Membership: 106; *Fees:* $60 + GST
Activities: Organizing dinner meetings & forums; *Library:* Tourist Booth; Open to public

Pipe Line Contractors Association of Canada (PLCAC)

#201, 1075 North Service Rd. West, Oakville ON L6M 2G2
Tel: 905-847-9383; *Fax:* 905-847-7824
e-mail: plcac@pipeline.ca
www.pipeline.ca
Overview: A small national organization founded in 1954
Mission: To represent contractors in labour relations
Chief Officer(s):
O.J. Kavanaugh, President
Neil G. Lane, Executive Director
Michael J. Gallardo, Assistant Executive Director
Membership: 35 regular members; 66 associate members; 18 honorary members; *Member Profile:* Employers engaged in contacting for the construction, installation, & maintenance of piplines; Corporations or individuals engages in manufacturing, supplying, & transporting material for the construction & maintenance of piplines; *Committees:* Convention Planning; Education & Training; Equipment Rental; Executive; Membership & Promotion; National Labour Relations; Negotiating - Distribution; Negotiating - Mainline; Pipeline Standards; Safety
Activities: Establishing training courses; Reviewing legislation;
Meetings/Conferences:
For more information see Trade Shows, Conferences and Seminars Chapter
Pipe Line Contractors Association of Canada 2013 59th Annual Convention
May 2013 Montréal, QC
Pipe Line Contractors Association of Canada 2014 60th Annual Convention
May 2014 Vancouver, BC
Publications:
•Canadian Pipeliner
Type: Newsletter; *Frequency:* 4 pa
Profile: News, industry information, & upcoming events
•PLCAC [Pipe Line Contractors Association of Canada] Membership Directory
Type: Directory; *Frequency:* Annually
Profile: Featuring membership profiles & contact information

Pitch-In Alberta (PIA)

PO Box 45011, RPO Ocean Park, White Rock BC V4A 9L1
Fax: 604-535-4653
Toll-Free: 877-474-8244
www.pitch-in.ca

Previous Name: Outdoors Unlittered (Alberta)
Overview: A medium-sized provincial charitable organization founded in 1974
Mission: To carry out promotional, educational & action programs aimed at reducing, reusing, recycling & properly managing & disposing of waste & solid wastes in particular; To initiate cleanup & beautification programs; To secure support of all levels of government, industry, media, other public sector organizations & the public for these objectives; *Member of:* Pitch-In Canada; Affiliation(s): Clean World International
Chief Officer(s):
Misha van Veen, Program Manager
Allard W. van Veen, Founder
Finances: *Annual Operating Budget:* $50,000-$100,000; *Funding Sources:* Local governments; foundations; industry; individuals
Staff: 2 staff member(s)
Activities: *Awareness Events:* Pitch-In Canada Week, May; Coastal Clean Up Campaign, Sept.; *Speaker Service:* Yes; *Library:* Open to public by appointment

Pitch-In Canada (PIC) / Passons à l'action Canada

PO Box 45011, RPO Ocean Park, White Rock BC V4A 9L1
Fax: 604-535-4653
Toll-Free: 877-474-8244
www.pitch-in.ca
Previous Name: Outdoors Unlittered
Overview: A medium-sized national charitable organization founded in 1967
Mission: To improve communities & the envionment by providing programs to reduce, re-use, recycle, & properly manage & dispose waste; Affiliation(s): Clean World International; Clean up the World
Environmental Activity: Initiating recycling & composting programs; Cleaning up areas; Offering The National Cell Phone Collection Program & the Shoreline Clean Up Program
Chief Officer(s):
Misha Cook, Executive Director, 877-474-8244 Ext. 1
misha@pitch-in.ca
Lisa Davis, Project Coordinator, 877-474-8244 Ext. 2
lisa@pitch-in.ca
Misha van Veen, Program Manager
misha@pitch-in.ca
Valerie S. Thom, Executive Director
vthom@pitch-in.ca
Finances: *Funding Sources:* Donations; Sponsorships; Grants; Fees for service; Merchandising of materials
Activities: Working with all levels of government & other organizations; *Awareness Events:* National Pitch-In Week; *Library:* Pitch-In Canada Resource Centre

Le plan nord-américain de gestion de la sauvagine ***See*** North American Waterfowl Management Plan

Planetary Association for Clean Energy, Inc. (PACE) / Société planétaire pour l'assainissement de l'énergie

#1001, 100 Bronson Ave., Ottawa ON K1R 6G8
Tel: 613-236-6265; *Fax:* 613-235-5876
e-mail: paceincnet@gmail.com
pacenet.homestead.com
Overview: A medium-sized international charitable organization founded in 1975
Mission: To steward & facilitate the implementation of clean energy systems worldwide
Chief Officer(s):
Andrew Michrowski, President
Finances: *Annual Operating Budget:* $100,000-$250,000; *Funding Sources:* Membership fees; donations
Staff: 2 staff member(s); 10 volunteer(s)
Membership: 3,600 in 60 countries; *Fees:* $50
Activities: Electromagnetic bioaffect, analyses & abatement; monitors unclean developments; peer review of new technologies; books, databases & technical reports; *Internships:* Yes; *Speaker Service:* Yes; *Library:* by appointment

The Planning Forum ***See*** Strategic Leadership Forum, The Toronto Society for Strategic Management

Planning Institute of British Columbia (PIBC) Parent Name: Canadian Institute of Planners

#110, 355 Burrard St., Vancouver BC V6C 2G8
Tel: 604-696-5031; *Fax:* 604-696-5032
Toll-Free: 866-696-5031
e-mail: info@pibc.bc.ca
www.pibc.bc.ca
Overview: A medium-sized provincial organization founded in 1958 overseen by Canadian Institute of Planners
Mission: To promote orderly use of land, buildings & natural resources; to maintain high standard of professional competence; to protect rights & interests of those engaged in planning profession
Chief Officer(s):
Lindsay Chase, President
Dave Crossley, Executive Director
dave.crossley@pibc.bc.ca
Finances: *Annual Operating Budget:* $50,000-$100,000
Staff: 2 staff member(s)
Membership: 1,300; *Fees:* $56.50-$255
Meetings/Conferences:
For more information see Trade Shows, Conferences and Seminars Chapter
Planning Institute of British Columbia 2013 Annual Conference
July 2013 Vancouver, BC

Plant Biology Research Institute ***Voir*** Institut de recherche en biologie végétale

Plant Engineering & Maintenance Association of Canada (PEMAC)

#402, 6 - 2400 Dundas St. West, Mississauga ON L5K 2R8
Tel: 905-823-7255; *Fax:* 905-823-8001
e-mail: mail@pemac.org
www.pemac.org
Overview: A medium-sized national licensing organization founded in 1989
Mission: To be recognized as a nationwide centre of excellence in plant engineering & maintenance; To form positive & constructive links with industry & service sectors, in support of local & nationwide developments & productivity; To deliver strongly identifiable services & commitments across the range of disciplines embraced by the association; to educate & introduce new concepts; To provide representation at all government levels; To provide career enhancement & networking opportunities; To promote research in the field of plant engineering & maintenance
Chief Officer(s):
Norm Clegg, Executive Director
Brian Malloch, President
Finances: *Annual Operating Budget:* $250,000-$500,000; *Funding Sources:* Membership fees; website; colleges
Staff: 1 staff member(s); 11 volunteer(s)
Membership: 2,000; *Fees:* Including GST: $50.85 student; $101.70 - full individual; $310.75 - allied; $621.50 - corporate; *Member Profile:* Maintenance professionals & practitioners; *Committees:* Strategic Planning; Communications; Bylaws & Constitution; Membership; Education & Research; Programming
Activities: Certification Program, MMP - Maintenance Management Professional; *Speaker Service:* Yes; *Library:* Open to public by appointment

Plastic Bag Association; Plastic Bag Information Clearing House ***See*** Film & Bag Federation

Plastic Loose Fill Council (PLFC)

PO Box 21040, Oakland CA 94620 USA
Tel: 510-654-0756; *Fax:* 510-654-0196
Toll-Free: 800-828-2214
www.loosefillpackaging.com
Overview: A small national organization
Mission: Promoted the reuse of plastic packing peanuts through its national collection program the Peanut Hotline, with over 240 drop-off sites in California
Chief Officer(s):
John D. Mellott
Membership: 4; *Member Profile:* Manufacturers of expanded polystyrene loose fill packaging
Activities: Operates the Peanut Hotline, the consumer reuse program in US for plastic packaging peanuts

Plumbing & Mechanical Contractors Association of New Brunswick ***See*** Mechanical Contractors Association of New Brunswick

Pollution Control Association of Ontario ***See*** Water Environment Association of Ontario

The Pollution Probe Foundation (PPF)

#402, 625 Church St., Toronto ON M4Y 2G1
Tel: 416-926-1907; *Fax:* 416-926-1601
e-mail: pprobe@pollutionprobe.org
www.pollutionprobe.org
www.facebook.com/PollutionProbe
twitter.com/PollutionProbe
Also Known As: Pollution Probe
Overview: A medium-sized national charitable organization founded in 1969
Mission: A registered Canadian charity which seeks to define environmental problems through research; to promote understanding through education & to press for practical solutions through advocacy. The organization is non-partison & works collaboratively with government agencies, other non-profit organizations, & private business to engage key issues & find solutions. Offices in Toronto & Ottawa; *Member of:* Canadian Environmental Network; Canadian Renewable Energy Alliance; Affiliation(s): Clean Air Network; Ontario Clean Air Alliance
Chief Officer(s):
Bob Oliver, CEO
boliver@pollutionprobe.org
Husam Mansour, COO
hmansour@pollutionprobe.org
Finances: *Annual Operating Budget:* $1.5 Million-$3 Million; *Funding Sources:* Individual & corporate charitable donations; foundation grants; publication sales; government grants
Staff: 16 staff member(s); 20 volunteer(s)
Membership: 100 corporate donors + 50 institutional
Activities: Programme areas include: Air, Water, Energy, Climate Change, Environment & Child Health, Mercury, Environmental Policy Development; *Awareness Events:* Clean Air Campaign & Commute

Ottawa
#101, 63 Sparks St., Ottawa ON K1P 5A6
Tel: 613-237-3786; *Fax:* 613-237-6111
e-mail: rfindlay@pollutionprobe.org
Chief Officer(s):
Rick Findlay, Director, Ottawa Office

Polystyrene Packaging Council (PSPC)

1300 Wilson Blvd., 8th Fl., Arlington VA 22209 USA
Tel: 703-741-5649; *Fax:* 703-741-5651
e-mail: pspc@plastics.org
www.polystyrene.org
Overview: A small international organization
Mission: To promote & defend the polystyrene industry by providing a forum for issues of importance to the polystyrene industry; keeping markets free by eliminating or amending anti-polystyrene legislation & regulation & avoiding future burdensome polystyrene legislation/regulation; & serving as the polystyrene industry communications voice to selected audiences & the general public
Chief Officer(s):
Michael H. Levy, Director
Finances: *Annual Operating Budget:* $500,000-$1.5 Million
Staff: 2 staff member(s)
Membership: 9; *Fees:* Schedule available; *Member Profile:* Major suppliers & manufacturers of polystyrene products

Pommes de terre Nouveau-Brunswick ***See*** Potatoes New Brunswick

Population Connection (PC)

#500, 2120 L St. NW, Washington DC 20037 USA
Tel: 202-332-2200; *Fax:* 202-332-2302
Toll-Free: 800-767-1956
e-mail: info@populationconnection.org
www.populationconnection.org
www.facebook.com/PopulationConnection
twitter.com/popconnect
www.youtube.com/user/populationconnection
Previous Name: Zero Population Growth
Overview: A large international organization founded in 1968
Mission: To advocate progressive action to stabilize world population at a level that can be sustained by Earth's resources
Chief Officer(s):
Marianne Gabel, Chair
John Seager, President & CEO
john@popconnect.org
Finances: *Annual Operating Budget:* $3 Million-$5 Million; *Funding Sources:* Memberships; foundations; private donations
Staff: 40 staff member(s); 20 volunteer(s)
Membership: 30,000; *Fees:* $25
Activities: Encourages better media coverage of population issues; Teachers PETNet (Population Education Trainers Network); roving reporters; legislative alert; campus organizing; *Speaker Service:* Yes
Publications:
•Congressional Report Card [a publication of Population Connection]
Type: Report; *Frequency:* Annual

•The Reporter [a publication of Population Connection]
Type: Magazine; *Frequency:* 3 pa; *Editor:* Marian Starkey
Profile: Covers environmental, social & health-related topics

Port Moody Rock & Gem Club

c/o The Kyle Centre, 125 Kyle St., Port Moody BC V3H 2N6
e-mail: info@portmoodyrockclub.com
www.portmoodyrockclub.com
Overview: A small local organization founded in 1978
Member of: Port Moody Arts Centre Society; ArtsConnect; British Columbia Lapidary Society; Gem & Mineral Federation of Canada
Chief Officer(s):
Lisa Elser, Co-Chair, 778-996-5620
Rose Kapp, Show Chair; Historian; Librarian, 604-941-3023
rock.show@portmoodyrockclub.com
Lynne Johnston, Contact, Field Trips, 604-945-6695
field.trips@portmoodyrockclub.com
Membership: *Fees:* $25 individuals; $45 families; *Member Profile:* Persons in the Port Moody British Columbia area who are interested in geology & the earth sciences as well as the hobbies of rock hunting, faceting, & lapidary
Activities: Offering weekly lapidary & faceting workshops; Hosting monthly meetings, except in July, August, & December; Arranging field trips; *Awareness Events:* Annual Rock & Gem Show, October

Potash & Phosphate Institute/Potash & Phosphate Institute of Canada ***See*** International Plant Nutrition Institute

Potatoes New Brunswick / Pommes de terre Nouveau-Brunswick

PO Box 7878, Grand Falls NB E3Z 3E8
Tel: 506-473-3036; *Fax:* 506-473-4647
e-mail: gfpotato@potatoesnb.com
www.potatoesnb.com
Previous Name: New Brunswick Potato Agency
Overview: A medium-sized provincial organization founded in 1979
Mission: To work in close collaboration with industry partners in advocating, coordinating, promoting, negotiating, & leading growth & development of New Brunswick potato producers; *Member of:* Canadian Horticultural Council
Chief Officer(s):
Joe Brennan, Chair
Matt Hemphill, Executive Director
Robert Corriveau, Director, Finance
Gisele Beardsley, Bookkeeper & Translator
Membership: 400 individual
Meetings/Conferences:
For more information see Trade Shows, Conferences and Seminars Chapter
Potatoes New Brunswick 2013 Conference & Trade Show
February 2013 Grand Falls, NB
Potatoes New Brunswick 2014 Conference & Trade Show
2014, NB

Prairie Agricultural Machinery Institute (PAMI)

PO Box 1150, 2215 - 8th Ave., Humboldt SK S0K 2A0
Tel: 306-682-2555; *Fax:* 306-682-5080
Toll-Free: 800-567-7264
e-mail: humboldt@pami.ca
www.pami.ca
Overview: A medium-sized local charitable organization founded in 1974
Mission: To serve manufacturers & farmers in Manitoba & Saskatchewan's agricultural sector through applied research, development, & testing; Affiliation(s): Manitoba Ministry of Agriculture, Food, & Rural Initiatives; Saskatchewan Ministry of Agricultue
Finances: *Funding Sources:* Fee-for-service work; Government
Staff: 45 staff member(s)
Activities: ; *Library:* Prairie Agricultural Machinery Institute Research Library
Publications:
•Direct Seeding Manual: A Farming System for the New Millennium
Price: $50 Manitoba, Saskatchewan, & Alberta; $55 elsewhere
•The Rancher's Guide to Elk & Bison Handling Facilities
Type: Book; *Number of Pages:* 35; *Price:* $20 Canada; $25 international
•The Stockman's Guide to Range Livestock Watering from Surface Sources
Type: Book; *Number of Pages:* 36; *Price:* $10 Canada; $12 international
Profile: Includes a workbook

Prairie Conservation Forum

c/o Southern Region, Alberta Environment, 200 - 5th Ave. South, 2nd Fl., Lethbridge AB T1J 4L1
Tel: 403-381-5562; *Fax:* 403-382-4428
e-mail: info@albertapcf.org
www.albertapcf.org
Overview: A small local organization
Mission: Conservation of native prairie & parkland environments in Alberta
Chief Officer(s):
Cheryl Dash, Secretary
cheryl.dash@gov.ab.ca
Activities: Alberta Prairie Conservation Action Plan

Prairie Fruit Growers Association (PFGA)

PO Box 2430, Altona MB R0G 0B0
Tel: 204-324-5058; *Fax:* 204-324-5058
e-mail: pfga@xplornet.com
www.pfga.com
Overview: A small local organization founded in 1974
Mission: To educate members, access quality planting stock, direct research & develop markets; *Member of:* North American Berry Association
Finances: *Annual Operating Budget:* $100,000-$250,000
Staff: 1 staff member(s)
Membership: 115; *Fees:* $195

Prairie Implement Manufacturers Association; PIMA - Agricultural Manufacturers of Canada ***See*** Agricultural Manufacturers of Canada

Prairie Provinces Forestry Association ***See*** Manitoba Forestry Association Inc.

Préservation du bois Canada ***See*** Wood Preservation Canada

Préservation du bois Canada ***See*** Canadian Wood Preservers Bureau

Prince Albert Model Forest Association Inc. (PAMF)

PO Box 2406, Prince Albert SK S6V 7G3
Tel: 306-922-1944; *Fax:* 306-763-6456
e-mail: pamf@sasktel.net
www.pamodelforest.sk.ca
Overview: A small provincial organization founded in 1993
Mission: To work towards sustainable forest management through development & testing of new forest management tools, sharing our successes, developing linkages & expanding the PAMF partnership; *Member of:* Saskatchewan Forestry Association; Canadian Model Forest Network; Affiliation(s): University of Saskatchewan; University of Regina
Chief Officer(s):
Susan Carr, General Manager
Finances: *Annual Operating Budget:* $250,000-$500,000; *Funding Sources:* Canadian Forest Service; partners; grants
Staff: 2 staff member(s)
Membership: *Committees:* Science & Technology; Communications & Outreach; Beyond our Boundaries; Planning & Operations
Activities: Applied research in sustainable forestry; technology transfer of research findings; *Library:* PAMF Reference Library; Open to public

Prince Edward Island Aquaculture Alliance (PEIAA)

101 Longworth Ave., 1st Fl., Charlottetown PE C1A 5A9
Tel: 902-368-2757; *Fax:* 902-626-3954
e-mail: peiaqua@aquaculturepei.com
www.aquaculturepei.com
Overview: A small provincial organization founded in 1998
Mission: To provide focus for the Prince Edward Island aquaculture industry; to enhance industry prosperity through its development as an effective world competitor; *Member of:* Canadian Aquaculture Industry Alliance
Chief Officer(s):
Gary Rogers, President
Ann Worth, Executive Director
ed@aquaculturepei.com
Finances: *Annual Operating Budget:* $100,000-$250,000; *Funding Sources:* Government; industry
Staff: 3 staff member(s)
Membership: 130+; *Fees:* $1,070 supporting; $267.50 supplier; $53.50 associate; *Member Profile:* Mussel, Oyster, Clam & Finfish culturists in PEI & companies which supply goods & services to them
Activities: Co-Host of International PEI Shellfish Festival; Co-Host of Great Atlantic Shellfish Exchange
Publications:
•Soundings [a publication of the Prince Edward Island Aquaculture Alliance]
Type: Newsletter; *Frequency:* Quarterly

Prince Edward Island Cattle Producers (PEICP)

420 University Ave., Charlottetown PE C1A 7Z5
Tel: 902-368-2229; *Fax:* 902-367-3082
e-mail: cattlemen@eastlink.ca
www.peicattleproducers.com
Previous Name: P.E.I. Cattlemen's Association
Overview: A medium-sized provincial organization founded in 1976
Mission: To support the beef industry in Prince Edward Island; To ensure a responsible production of safe, quality beef; To foster a profitable industry; *Member of:* Canadian Cattlemen's Association (CCA)
Environmental Activity: Fostering environmentally sustainable beef production through leadership, education, & cooperation; Promoting the ALUS program for PEI landowners & farmers to protect water, fish, & wildlife habitat
Chief Officer(s):
Peter Verleun, Chair
Rinnie Bradley, Executive Director
Justin Lawless, Coordinator, Atlantic Verified Beef Program
Brian Morrison, Secretary-Treasurer
Finances: *Funding Sources:* Mandatory levies; Membership fees
Membership: 550+; *Fees:* Levies collected by processing facilities or a $5 membership fee; *Member Profile:* Prince Edward Island beef producers
Activities: Representing the beef industry in Prince Edward Island; Providing education
Publications:
•Beef Newsletter
Type: Newsletter
Profile: Timely information for Prince Edward Island's beef producers
•PEI Cattle Producers Annual Report with Financial Statements
Type: Yearbook; *Frequency:* Annually

Prince Edward Island Cultured Mussel Growers Association (PEICMGA)

c/o PEI Aquaculture Alliance, 101 Longworth Ave., 1st Fl., Charlottetown PE C1A 5A9
Tel: 902-386-2757; *Fax:* 902-626-3954
www.aquaculturepei.com/pei_cultured_mussels.php
Also Known As: PEI Mussel Growers
Overview: A small local organization founded in 1981
Mission: To advance the well-being of the cultured mussel industry in Prince Edward Island; to provide a forum for mussel growers to discuss concerns; *Member of:* PEI Aquaculture Alliance
Chief Officer(s):
Martin MacDonald, President
Membership: 1-99
Activities: Promoting the cultured mussel industry in PEI; Liaising with the provincial government

Prince Edward Island Eco-Net (PEIEN)

Parent Name: Canadian Environmental Network
126 Richmond St., Charlottetown PE C1A 1H9
Tel: 902-566-4170; *Fax:* 902-566-4037
e-mail: peien@isn.net
www.peieconet.org
www.facebook.com/peieconet?ref=ts
Also Known As: Prince Edward Island Environmental Network
Overview: A medium-sized provincial organization founded in 1990 overseen by Canadian Environmental Network
Mission: To promote communication & cooperation among ENGO's (Environmental NGO's) & between ENGO's & governments; to provide referral services; to coordinate workshops & conferences; to provide consultations; to publish & distribute information
Chief Officer(s):
Susan Hawkins, Executive Director
Finances: *Annual Operating Budget:* Less than $50,000
Membership: 29; *Fees:* $25
Activities: *Speaker Service:* Yes; *Library:*

Prince Edward Island Federation of Agriculture (PEIFA)

Parent Name: Canadian Federation of Agriculture
420 University Ave., Charlottetown PE C1A 7Z5
Tel: 902-368-7289; *Fax:* 902-368-7204
www.peifa.ca
Overview: A medium-sized provincial organization founded in 1941 overseen by Canadian Federation of Agriculture
Mission: To provide a united voice for Island farmers

Chief Officer(s):
John Jaimeson, Executive Director
Finances: *Annual Operating Budget:* $100,000-$250,000
Staff: 4 staff member(s)
Membership: 500-999;

Prince Edward Island Finfish Association

c/o Dover Fish Hatchery, RR#2, Murray River PE C0A 1W0
Tel: 902-962-3446
Overview: A small provincial organization founded in 2000
Mission: To represent the interests of the finfish aquaculture sector in Prince Edward Island; Affiliation(s): Prince Edward Island Aquaculture Alliance (PEIAA)
Chief Officer(s):
Leon Moyaert, President
Dawn Runighan, Vice-President
Mike Murray, Secretary-Treasurer
Membership: 1-99; *Member Profile:* Prince Edward Island individuals & companies occupied in finfish farming, including the production of Rainbow Trout, Halibut, & Atlantic Salmon, plus eggs, fry, & smolt

Prince Edward Island Fishermen's Association (PEIFA)

#102, 420 University Ave., Charlottetown PE C1A 7Z5
Tel: 902-566-4050; *Fax:* 902-368-3748
e-mail: adminpeifa@pei.eastlink.ca
www.peifa.org
Overview: A small provincial organization
Mission: To represent fishermen across Prince Edward Island; To act as a single, united voice on behalf of Island fishers on industry issues
Chief Officer(s):
Michael McGeoghegan, President, 902-659-2264
Ed Frenette, Manager
managerpeifa@pei.eastlink.ca
Membership: *Fees:* $105; *Member Profile:* Prince Edward Island fishers from the following Locals: Central Northumberland Strait Fishermen's Association (CNSFA), Eastern Kings Fishermen's Association (EKFA), North Shore Fishermen's Association (NSFA), Prince County Fishermen's Association (PCFA), Southern Kings & Queens Fishermen's Association (SKQFA), & Western Gulf Fishermen's Association (WGFA)
Activities: Liaising with government; Facilitating networking opportunities; Collaborating with fisher organizations in other provinces

Prince Edward Island Forest Improvement Association (PEIFIA)
Parent Name: Canadian Forestry Association

RR#1, York PE C9A 1P0
Tel: 902-672-2114; *Fax:* 902-672-2620
Previous Name: Prince Edward Island Silvicultural Contractors Association
Overview: A medium-sized provincial organization overseen by Canadian Forestry Association
Chief Officer(s):
Wanson Hemphill, Contact
wm.hemphill@pei.sympatico.ca
Finances: *Annual Operating Budget:* Less than $50,000
Staff: 1 staff member(s); 17 volunteer(s)
Membership: *Fees:* $40 individual; $30 associate
Activities: Umbrella organization of PEI forest-related groups

Prince Edward Island Ground Water Association
Parent Name: Canadian Ground Water Association

PO Box 857, RR#2, Cornwall PE C0A 1H0
Tel: 902-675-2360; *Fax:* 902-675-2360
Overview: A small provincial organization overseen by Canadian Ground Water Association
Mission: To promote the protection of ground water in Prince Edward Island; Affiliation(s): Canadian Ground Water Association
Environmental Activity: Increasing public awareness of the management of ground water
Chief Officer(s):
Watson MacDonald, Contact
Activities: Encouraging education about ground water resources

Prince Edward Island Institute of Agrologists (PEIIA)
Parent Name: Agricultural Institute of Canada

PO Box 2712, Charlottetown PE C1A 8C3
Tel: 902-892-1943; *Fax:* 902-892-0443
e-mail: info@peiia.ca
www.peiia.ca
Overview: A small provincial organization overseen by Agricultural Institute of Canada
Mission: To safeguard the public by ensuring its members are qualified & competent to provide knowledge & advice on agriculture & related areas
Chief Officer(s):
Ronda Bellefontaine, President
ronda@prideoftheisle.ca
Elizabeth Maynard, Sec.-Treas.
elizabeth.maynard@fcc-fac.ca
Allison Weeks, Registrar
aaweeks@gov.pe.ca
Finances: *Annual Operating Budget:* Less than $50,000; *Funding Sources:* Membership fees
Staff: 7 staff member(s)
Membership: 81; *Fees:* $115 P.Ag.; $70 AIT; $75 Permit to Practice; *Committees:* Education; Honours & Awards; Program; Publicity
Activities: Professional development; *Internships:* Yes

Prince Edward Island Lung Association
Parent Name: Canadian Lung Association

#2, 1 Rochford St., Charlottetown PE C1A 9L2
Tel: 902-892-5957; *Fax:* 902-566-9901
Toll-Free: 888-566-5864
e-mail: info@pei.lung.ca
www.pei.lung.ca
Previous Name: PEI Tuberculosis League
Overview: A small provincial charitable organization founded in 1936 overseen by Canadian Lung Association
Mission: To improve the respiratory health of Islanders through education, advocacy & research; To raise funds to support medical research
Environmental Activity: Raising awareness of the health effects of indoor & outdoor air pollution; Advocating for clean air
Chief Officer(s):
Margaret Munro, President
Judy Hansen, Vice-President
Joanne Ings, Executive Director
Bev McCormick, Treasurer
Finances: *Funding Sources:* Donations; Fundraising; Sponsorships
Activities: Promoting lung health in Prince Edward Island; Helping people to stop smoking through the Provincial Cessation Program (QuitCare)

Prince Edward Island Salmon Association (PEISA)

PO Box 3315, Charlottetown PE C1A 8W5
Tel: 902-892-3635
e-mail: david.olafson@pei.sympatico.ca
Overview: A small provincial organization
Affiliation(s): Atlantic Salmon Federation
Chief Officer(s):
David Olafson, Contact

Prince Edward Island Silvicultural Contractors Association
See Prince Edward Island Forest Improvement Association

Prince Edward Island Society of Certified Engineering Technologists *See* Association of Certified Engineering Technicians & Technologists of Prince Edward Island

Prince Edward Island Wildlife Federation
Parent Name: Canadian Wildlife Federation

#103B, 420 University Ave., Charlottetown PE C1A 7Z5
Tel: 902-892-3332; *Fax:* 902-892-3334
Overview: A small provincial organization founded in 1906 overseen by Canadian Wildlife Federation
Mission: To foster sound management & wise use of the renewable resources of PEI; to assist & encourage the enforcement of those game laws which are in keeping with the objectives of the Federation & to strive for better management & game laws where & when necessary; to cooperate with government departments & related groups where interests are mutual; to educate membership & the public, with particular emphasis upon conservation & safety; to represent the interests & concerns of PEI sportsmen
Chief Officer(s):
Karl McCormack, President
Membership: 800
Activities: Assists with the Central Queens, O'Leary Wildlife & Souris Wildlife Federations

Prince George & District Truck Loggers Association *See* Central Interior Logging Association

Prince George Backcountry Recreation Society (PGBRS)

PO Box 26, Stn. A, Prince George BC V2L 4R9
Tel: 250-564-5256
e-mail: info@pgbrs.com
www.pgbrs.com
Overview: A small local organization founded in 1998
Mission: The primary mandate of the PGBRS is to promote and encourage safe non-motorized backcountry recreation in the Prince George region.; *Member of:* Federation of BC Naturalists
Chief Officer(s):
Marc Steynen, President
Membership: 1,700

Prince George Naturalists (PGNC) / Club de naturalistes de Prince George

PO Box 1092, Stn. A, Prince George BC V2L 4V2
Tel: 250-963-7709
e-mail: clive_keen@hotmail.com
Overview: A small local organization founded in 1969
Mission: To promote the enjoyment of nature through environmental appreciation & conservation; To encourage wise use & conservation of natural resources & environmental protection.; *Member of:* Federation of BC Naturalists
Finances: *Annual Operating Budget:* Less than $50,000
Membership: 48; *Fees:* $25 individual/family; $15 student
Activities: Monthly guest speakers; weekly field trips; birding; annual bird counts;

Prince George Recycling & Environmental Action Planning Society (REAPS)

PO Box 444, 1950 Gorse Street, Prince George BC V2L 4S6
Tel: 250-561-7324; *Fax:* 250-561-7324
e-mail: garden@reaps.org
www.reaps.org
www.facebook.com/group.php?gid=115633161790444
Overview: A small local organization founded in 1989
Mission: To educate the public on where & what can be recycled, how to compost & vermicompost, organic gardening, environmentally friendly alternatives & promotion of the 5 R's (Rethink, Refuse, Reduce, Recycle & Reuse); To provide educational programs to schools, daycares & committee groups; *Member of:* Recycling Council of British Columbia; Volunteer PG; Downtown Community Gardens
Environmental Activity: Education
Chief Officer(s):
Terri McClaymont, Executive Director, 250-561-7327, Fax: 250-561-7324
terri@reaps.org
Finances: *Annual Operating Budget:* $100,000-$250,000; *Funding Sources:* Regional District Fraser Fort George; Dept. Fisheries & Oceans; City of Prince George
Staff: 2 staff member(s); 20 volunteer(s)
Membership: 61; *Fees:* $25 institutional; $8 student; $8 individual; $15 family; *Committees:* EnhancePG, Recycling Council of BC; Civic Pride
Activities: Adopt-a-Worm Program; Dump the Overfed Landfill; Workshops on gardening, composting, recycling; Earth Day Celebration; Pitch-In Canada; Buy Nothing Day; *Awareness Events:* Earth Day, April 22; Composting Week, May 5; Buy Nothing Day, November 3; *Internships:* Yes; *Speaker Service:* Yes; *Library:* Open to public by appointment

Private Motor Truck Council of Canada (PMTC) / Association canadienne du camionnage d'entreprise (ACCE)

#115, 1660 North Service Rd. East, Oakville ON L6H 7G3
Tel: 905-827-0587; *Fax:* 905-827-8212
Toll-Free: 877-501-7682
e-mail: info@pmtc.ca
www.pmtc.ca
Overview: A medium-sized national organization founded in 1977
Mission: Recognized as the leader of the private trucking community in Canada; represents the varied interests of private fleet operators with integrity & sound business practices.; *Member of:* North American Private Truck Council; Affiliation(s): National Private Truck Council
Chief Officer(s):
Bruce J. Richards, President
trucks@pmtc.ca
Richard Lalonde, Québec Director
richard_lalonde@praxair.com
Finances: *Annual Operating Budget:* $250,000-$500,000; *Funding Sources:* Seminars; social events; membership fees
Staff: 4 staff member(s)

Membership: 400; *Member Profile:* Private truck fleets or suppliers to same; private truck fleets operated by companies whose principal business is other than transportation, but use their own truck fleets to further their business
Activities: Seminars; annual conference; benchmarking and best practices survey;National Vehicle Graphics Design Competition
Publications:
•The Counsellor [a publication of the Private Motor Truck Council of Canada]
Type: Magazine; *Frequency:* Quarterly
•NewsBriefs [a publication of the Private Motor Truck Council of Canada]
Type: Newsletter

Probe International (PI)
225 Brunswick Ave., Toronto ON M5S 2M6
Tel: 416-964-9223; *Fax:* 416-964-8239
e-mail: probeinternational@nextcity.com
journal.probeinternational.org
www.facebook.com/ProbeInternational
twitter.com/probeintl
Overview: A medium-sized international charitable organization founded in 1980
Mission: To educate Canadians about the environmental, social, & economic effects of Canada's aid & trade abroad; To monitor & expose the effects of projects financed by Canadian tax dollars (through international financial institutions, such as the World Bank & the Asian Development Bank, & through agencies such as CIDA & the Export Development Corp.) & by Canadian corporations; *Member of:* Energy Probe Research Foundation; Canadian Environmental Network; Affiliation(s): Environment Liaison Centre (International); International Organization of Consumers Unions; Energy Probe; Environment Probe; Consumer Policy Institute; Environmental Bureau of Investigation
Chief Officer(s):
Patricia Adams, Executive Director
Finances: *Annual Operating Budget:* $50,000-$100,000; *Funding Sources:* Private donations
Staff: 2 staff member(s)
Activities: *Speaker Service:* Yes; *Library:* by appointment

Product Care Association
12337 82A Ave., Surrey BC V3W 0L5
Tel: 604-592-2972; *Fax:* 604-592-2982
e-mail: contact@productcare.org
www.productcare.org
Overview: A medium-sized national organization
Mission: A national, not-for-profit industry association that manages product stewardship programs for household hazardous and special waste; the association's programs aim to divert leftover and end of life products from landfills, waterways and sewers, and to reuse or recycle collected products where possible. Product Care provides information and resources on responsible use, storage, recycling and disposal of products to conumers, retailers and local governments.
Chief Officer(s):
Mark Kruschner, President
Publications:
•The Circular
Type: Newsletter

Producteurs d'oufs du Canada ***See*** Egg Farmers of Canada

Producteurs Laitiers du Manitoba ***See*** Dairy Farmers of Manitoba

Producteurs laitiers du Nouveau-Brunswick ***See*** Dairy Farmers of New Brunswick

Produits alimentaires et de consommation du Canada ***See*** Food & Consumer Products of Canada

Professional Engineers & Geoscientists Newfoundland & Labrador (PEG-NL)
Parent Name: Engineers Canada
PO Box 21207, #203, 10 Fort William Pl., St. John's NL A1A 5B2
Tel: 709-753-7714; *Fax:* 709-753-6131
e-mail: main@pegnl.ca
www.pegnl.ca
Previous Name: Association of Professional Engineers & Geoscientists of Newfoundland
Overview: A medium-sized provincial licensing organization founded in 1952 overseen by Engineers Canada
Mission: To provide competent & ethical practice of engineering & geoscience in Newfoundland & Labrador; To ensure public confidence, sustainability, & stewardship of the professions; To provide leadership to enhance quality of life through the application & management of engineering & geoscience; *Member of:* Engineers Canada; Canadian Council of Professional Geoscientists
Environmental Activity: Establishing an Environmental Committee
Chief Officer(s):
Geoff Emberley, P. Eng., FEC, Chief Executive Officer & Registrar
Mark Fewer, B. Comm., Chief Operating Officer & Deputy Registrar
Leo White, P. Eng., Director, Professional Standards
Carl King, Councilor, Western District
Steve McLean, Executive Director
Finances: *Funding Sources:* Membership dues
Staff: 200 volunteer(s)
Membership: 2,500 individual + 286 student + 31 licensee + 296 corporate; *Fees:* $224 individual; $564-1,031 corporate; $530 licensee; *Member Profile:* Bachelor's degree in engineering or geoscience; *Committees:* Discipline; Board of Examiners; Awards; Professional Development & Education; Code of Ethics; Complaints; Conference; Environmental; Geoscience Issues; National Engineering Week; Endowment Fund
Activities: Administering The Engineers & Geoscientists Act in Newfoundland; *Awareness Events:* National Engineering Week; Science & Technology Week

Professional Engineers Ontario (PEO)
Parent Name: Engineers Canada
#101, 40 Sheppard Ave. West, Toronto ON M2N 6K9
Tel: 416-224-1100; *Fax:* 416-224-9527
Toll-Free: 800-339-3716
e-mail: financialservices@peo.on.ca
www.peo.on.ca
Previous Name: Association of Professional Engineers of Ontario
Overview: A large provincial licensing organization founded in 1922 overseen by Engineers Canada
Mission: To meet the needs of Ontario society by licensing & regulating the entire practice of professional engineering in an open, transparent, inclusive manner. There are 36 chapters across the province; *Member of:* Engineers Canada
Chief Officer(s):
Denis Dixon, P.Eng., FEC, President
Michael Price, P.Eng., MBA, Acting CEO & Registrar, 416-840-1060
mprice@peo.on.ca
Scott Clark, LL.B., CAO, 416-840-1126
sclark@peo.on.ca
Eric Brown, P.Eng., ISP, PM, Director, IT & Facilities Management, 416-840-1110
ebrown@peo.on.ca
Connie Mucklestone, Director, Communications, 416-840-1061
cmucklestone@peo.on.ca
Moody Samuel Farag, M.Eng., P.Eng., Manager, Admissions, 416-840-1055
mfarag@peo.on.ca
Brian MacEwen, P.Eng., Manager, Registration, 416-840-1056
bmacewen@peo.on.ca
Finances: *Funding Sources:* Membership fees
Staff: 700 volunteer(s)
Membership: 70,000; *Fees:* Schedule available; *Committees:* Executive; Audit; Finance; Human Resources; Legislation; Regional Councillors; Academic Requirements; Advisory Committee on Volunteers; Awards; Central Election & Search; Complaints; Complaints Review Councillor; Consulting Engineer Designation; Discipline; Education; Enforcement; Equity & Diversity; Experience Requirements; Fees Mediation; Government Liaison; Ontario Centre for Engineering & Public Policy Advisory Bd.; OSPE-PEO Joint Relations; Overlapping Practices; PEO-OAA Joint Liaison; Professional Standards; Registration; Regional
Activities: *Speaker Service:* Yes
Publications:
•Employer Salary Survey [a publication of the Professional Engineers Ontario]
Type: Report
•Engineering Dimensions [a publication of the Professional Engineers Ontario]
Type: Magazine; *Editor:* Jennifer Coombes
•Membership Salary Survey [a publication of the Professional Engineers Ontario]
Type: Report
•PEO [Professional Engineers Ontario] Practice Bulletins
Type: Bulletin
•Professional Engineers Ontario Annual Report
Type: Yearbook; *Frequency:* Annual

Professional Outfitters Association of Alberta ***See*** Alberta Professional Outfitters Society

Professional Petroleum Data Management Association (PPDM)
PO Box 22155, Stn. Bankers Hall, #860, 736 - 8th Ave. SW, Calgary AB T2P 4J5
Tel: 403-660-7817; *Fax:* 403-660-0540
e-mail: info@ppdm.org
www.ppdm.org
www.linkedin.com/groups?home=&gid=146440
www.facebook.com/group.php?gid=108325212519325
twitter.com/PPDMAssociation
Previous Name: Public Petroleum Data Model Association
Overview: A small national organization founded in 1991
Mission: To develop data management standards for the collection & exchange of data in the petroleum industry; To promote information standards
Chief Officer(s):
David Hood, Chair
dhood@geologic.com
Chellie Hailes, Secretary
Chellie.hailes@chevron.com
Peter MacDougall, Treasurer
peter.macdougall@ihs.com
Membership: *Committees:* Global Framework; Well Identification - US; Well Identification - Western Canada; Business Rules; Education Task Force
Activities: Increasing awareness of the value of data management; Providing training

Professional Surveyors Canada / Géomètres professionnels du Canada
#303, 1390 Prince of Wales Dr., Ottawa ON K2C 3N6
Tel: 613-695-8333
www.psc-gpc.ca/surveyors
Overview: A medium-sized national organization
Mission: To foster cooperation amongst surveyors in Canada; To advocate for an integrated Canadian surveying profession
Chief Officer(s):
Sarah Cornett, BSc, OLS, Executive Director

Programme des nations unies pour l'environnement ***See*** United Nations Environment Programme

Projets pour une agriculture écologique ***See*** Ecological Agriculture Projects

Prospectors & Developers Association of Canada (PDAC) / Association canadienne des prospecteurs & entrepreneurs
135 King St. East, Toronto ON M5C 1G6
Tel: 416-362-1969; *Fax:* 416-362-0101
e-mail: info@pdac.ca
www.pdac.ca
Overview: A medium-sized national organization founded in 1932
Mission: To protect & promote the interests of the Canadian mineral exploration & development sector
Environmental Activity: Encouraging high standards of technical, environmental, safety, & social practices domestically & internationally
Chief Officer(s):
Ross Gallinger, Executive Director
rgallinger@pdac.ca
Lisa J. McDonald, Chief Operations Officer
lmcdonald@pdac.ca
Philip Bousquet, Senior Program Director, Finance & Taxation & Securities
pbousquet@pdac.ca
Sheriden Barnett, Program Director, Land Use Planning & Resource Development
sbarnett@pdac.ca
Scott Cavan, Program Director, Aboriginal Affairs
scavan@pdac.ca
Nicole Sampson, Director, Convention
nsampson@pdac.ca
Steve Virtue, Director, Communications
svirtue@pdac.ca
Lesley Williams, Program Manager, Advvocacy & Issues Management
lwilliams@pdac.ca

Florence MacLeod, Coordinator, Membership
fmacleod@pdac.ca
Finances: *Funding Sources:* Membership fees
Membership: 6,000 individuals + 950 corporate members; *Member Profile:* Individuals, such as professional geoscientists, mining executives, prospectors, developers; geological consultants, & those working in the drilling, financial, investment, legal, & other related fields; Students; Corporate members, such as producing companies, junior non-producing exploration companies, & non-mining companies; *Committees:* Aboriginal Affairs; Audit; Awards; Convention Planning; Corporate Social Responsibility; Education; Environment; Executive; Finance & Taxation; Geosciences; Health & Safety; Human Resources Development; International; Lands & Regulations; Membership; Nomination; Public Affairs, Securities
Activities: Compiling statistics; Providing information; Offering continuing education; Engaging in advocacy activities; Providing networking opportunities; *Speaker Service:* Yes; *Library:* Open to public
Meetings/Conferences:
For more information see Trade Shows, Conferences and Seminars Chapter
Prospectors & Developers Association of Canada (PDAC) 2013 81st International Convention, Trade Show, & Investors Exchange Mining Investment Show
March 2013 Toronto, ON
Prospectors & Developers Association of Canada (PDAC) 2014 82nd International Convention, Trade Show, & Investors Exchange Mining Investment Show
March 2014 Toronto, ON
Prospectors & Developers Association of Canada (PDAC) 2015 83rd International Convention, Trade Show, & Investors Exchange Mining Investment Show
2015 Toronto, ON
Publications:
•Communiqué [a publication of the Prospectors & Developers Association of Canada]
Frequency: Irregular
Profile: Each occasional publication deals with a particular topic related to exploration & development
•Exploration & Development Highlights
Type: Yearbook; *Frequency:* Annually
Profile: Articles about exploration & development activities in each Canadian province & territory distributed to all members
•News & Activities [a publication of the Prospectors & Developers Association of Canada]
Type: Newsletter; *Frequency:* Monthly
Profile: Association activities & events of interest to members
•PDAC [Prospectors & Developers Association of Canada] Activities
Type: Yearbook; *Frequency:* Annually
Profile: Summary of the association's work distributed to all members
•PDAC [Prospectors & Developers Association of Canada] in Brief
Type: Newsletter; *Frequency:* Quarterly; *Editor:* Cameron Ainsworth-Vincze
Profile: Information about the association's activities for members

Protected Areas Association of Newfoundland & Labrador (PAA)

PO Box 1027, Stn. C, St. John's NL A1C 5M5
Tel: 709-726-2603; *Fax:* 709-726-2764
www.paanl.org
Overview: A small provincial charitable organization founded in 1989
Mission: To promote the establishment of a provincial network of reserves that preserve representative portions of all eco-regions & protect biodiversity; To promote sound ecological practices that support sustainable development; *Member of:* Newfoundland & Labrador Environment Network; Affiliation(s): World Wildlife Fund Canada; Canadian Parks & Wilderness Society
Chief Officer(s):
Ruth French, Development & Outreach Coordinator
rfrench@nf.aibn.com
Finances: *Annual Operating Budget:* $100,000-$250,000
Staff: 4 staff member(s); 45 volunteer(s)
Membership: 500; *Fees:* $20 individual; *Member Profile:* People interested in conservation of nature, wilderness; *Committees:* Lac Joseph-Atikonak; Main River
Activities: Issue-related public meetings; *Awareness Events:* Benefit Concert, Nov.

Provancher Society of Natural History of Canada *Voir* Société Provancher d'histoire naturelle du Canada

The Provincial Agricultural Fairs Association *See* British Columbia Association of Agricultural Fairs & Exhibitions

Provincial Association of Home Builders of Québec *Voir* Association provinciale des constructeurs d'habitations du Québec inc.

Provincial Federation of Ontario Fire Fighters *See* Ontario Professional Fire Fighters Association

The Public Affairs Association of Canada (PAAC) / Association des affaires publiques du Canada

#301, 250 Consumers Rd., Toronto ON M2J 4V6
Tel: 416-367-2223; *Fax:* 416-495-8723
e-mail: info@publicaffairs.ca
www.publicaffairs.ca
Overview: A medium-sized national organization founded in 1984
Mission: To improve the professionalism of members to enhance the relations of members' organizations with their publics
Chief Officer(s):
John Capobianco, President
Erika Mozes, Events Chair
Chris May, Sec.-Treas.
Finances: *Funding Sources:* Membership fees
Membership: 300; *Fees:* $200
Activities: *Rents Mailing List:* Yes

Public Health Association of British Columbia (PHABC)
Parent Name: Canadian Public Health Association

#210, 1027 Pandora Ave., Victoria BC V8V 3P6
Tel: 250-595-8422; *Fax:* 250-595-8622
e-mail: staff@phabc.org
www.phabc.org
Overview: A medium-sized provincial organization overseen by Canadian Public Health Association
Mission: To constitute a special resource in BC for the betterment & maintenance of the population's health at the community & personal level
Chief Officer(s):
Ted Bruce, President
Finances: *Annual Operating Budget:* $100,000-$250,000; *Funding Sources:* Membership dues; project grants
Staff: 2 staff member(s); 25 volunteer(s)
Membership: 300; *Fees:* $25 individual; $15 student; $50 organization
Activities: BC Healthy Communities Network

Public Health Association of Nova Scotia (PHANS)
Parent Name: Canadian Public Health Association

PO Box 33074, Halifax NS B3L 4T6
e-mail: info@phans.ca
www.phans.ca
Overview: A small provincial charitable organization overseen by Canadian Public Health Association
Mission: To build public health capacity & to make progress on the determinants of health in Nova Scotia; Affiliation(s): Canadian Public Health Association
Environmental Activity: Monitoring environmental developments that may influence public health
Membership: *Fees:* $20 students & retired persons; $40 regular members; *Member Profile:* Persons interested in health & health issues in Nova Scotia
Activities: Advocating for policy change on issues that affect health; Liaising with government departments & voluntary agencies; Increasing professional & public awareness of health issues; Providing education; Offering networking opportunities; Delivering updates on health policy issues

Public Legal Education Association of Saskatchewan, Inc. (PLEA Sask.)

#500, 333 - 25th St. East, Saskatoon SK S7K 0L4
Tel: 306-653-1868; *Fax:* 306-653-1869
e-mail: plea@plea.org
www.plea.org
Overview: A medium-sized provincial organization founded in 1980
Member of: Public Legal Education Association of Canada
Membership: *Fees:* $20
Activities: *Speaker Service:* Yes; *Library:* Public Legal Education Association of Saskatchewan Library; Open to public

Public Legal Information Association of Newfoundland (PLIAN)

Tara Place, #227, 31 Peet St., St. John's NL A1B 3W8
Tel: 709-722-2643; *Fax:* 709-722-0054
Toll-Free: 888-660-7788
e-mail: info@publiclegalinfo.com
www.publiclegalinfo.com
Overview: A small provincial organization founded in 1984
Mission: To provide plain language legal information to the general public of Newfoundland, in both official languages, through a telephone enquiry line, public speaking engagements, publications, & a lawyer referral service; *Member of:* Public Legal Information Association of Canada
Chief Officer(s):
Kristen O'Keefe, Executive Director
Finances: *Annual Operating Budget:* $100,000-$250,000; *Funding Sources:* Justice Canada; Newfoundland Dept. of Justice; Law Foundation of Newfoundland
Staff: 4 staff member(s); 3 volunteer(s)
Membership: 30
Activities: *Speaker Service:* Yes

Public Petroleum Data Model Association *See* Professional Petroleum Data Management Association

Pulp & Paper Centre

University of British Columbia, 2385 East Mall, Vancouver BC V6T 1Z4
Tel: 604-822-8560
e-mail: ppc-info@ubc.ca
www.ppc.ubc.ca
Previous Name: Canadian Pulp & Paper Network for Innovation in Education & Research; Mechanical Wood-Pulps Network
Overview: A medium-sized provincial organization
Mission: To act as a university-industry partnership for innovation & education; to house inter-disciplinary, cross-faculty post-graduate research programs; Affiliation(s): FPInnovations; PAPIER
Chief Officer(s):
James Olson, Ph.D., P.Eng., Director & Professor, Mechanical Engineering, 604-822-5705
James.Olson@ubc.ca
George Soong, Safety & Operations Officer, Building/Technical Inquiries, 604-822-2530
gsoong@mail.ubc.ca
Richard Kerekes, Director
kerekes@chml.ubc.ca
Membership: *Member Profile:* UBC faculty & students involved in teaching & research for the pulp & paper industry; members of the manufacturing, utilities & supplier industries, as well as consultants & government agencies
Publications:
•Canadian Pulp & Paper Network for Innovation in Education & Research Newsletter
Type: Newsletter; *Frequency:* Semiannually
Profile: Papier's recent activities, such as meetings & award presentations

Pulp & Paper Technical Association of Canada (PAPTAC) / Association technique des pâtes et papiers du Canada

#1070, 740, rue Notre-Dame ouest, Montréal QC H3C 3X6
Tel: 514-392-0265; *Fax:* 514-392-0369
e-mail: ccrotogino@paptac.ca
www.paptac.ca
Previous Name: Canadian Pulp & Paper Association - Technical Section
Overview: A medium-sized national organization founded in 1915
Mission: To provide means for the interchange of knowledge & expertise among its members; to improve the skill levels & effectiveness of present & future employees through training & education; to provide technical & practical information on pulp & paper manufacture & use
Chief Officer(s):
Greg Hay, Executive Director
ghay@paptac.ca
André Bernier, Chair
Finances: *Funding Sources:* Membership fees; Events
Publications:
•Journal of Pulp and Paper Science (JPPS)
Type: Journal; *Frequency:* Quarterly

Purebred Swine Breeders' Association of Canada *See* Canadian Swine Breeders' Association

Québec 4-H
6500, boulevard Arthur-Sauvé, bur. 202, Laval QC H7R 3X7
Tel: 450-314-1942; *Fax:* 450-314-1952
e-mail: info@clubs4h.qc.ca
www.clubs4h.qc.ca
Previous Name: Québec Young Farmers
Overview: A medium-sized provincial organization founded in 1969
Mission: To develop life skills, such as leadership, cooperation, responsibility, & independence, for the English speaking rural youth of Québec, through achievement & skill-development; *Member of:* Canadian 4-H Council; Québec Community Groups Network
Chief Officer(s):
Tammy Oswick-Kearney, Provincial Coordinator
Finances: *Annual Operating Budget:* $50,000-$100,000
Staff: 1 staff member(s); 10 volunteer(s)
Membership: 450; *Fees:* Schedule available; *Member Profile:* Must be 6-21 years of age & member of Québec 4-H; *Committees:* Lifestock Management Tour; Provincial Rally

Québec Association of Energy Managers ***Voir*** Association québécoise pour la maîtrise de l'énergie

Québec Association of Fire Chiefs ***Voir*** Association des chefs en sécurité incendie du Québec

Québec Association of International Cooperation ***Voir*** Association québécoise des organismes de coopération internationale

Québec Bio-Industries Business Network ***Voir*** BIOQuébec

Québec Environment Foundation ***Voir*** Fondation québécoise en environnement

Québec Environmental Law Centre ***Voir*** Centre québécois du droit de l'environnement

Québec Farmers' Association (QFA)
#255, 555, boul Roland-Therrien, Longueuil QC J4H 4E7
Tel: 450-679-0540; *Fax:* 450-463-5291
e-mail: qfa@upa.qc.ca
www.quebecfarmers.org
Overview: A medium-sized provincial organization founded in 1957
Member of: Quebec Community Groups Network
Chief Officer(s):
Ivan Hale, Executive Director
Wendy Jones, Director, Operations
Membership: 3,000; *Fees:* $56.98; *Member Profile:* Québec's English-speaking farmers & rural citizens

Québec Fish Processors Association ***Voir*** Association québécoise de l'industrie de la pêche

Québec Forestry Industry Council ***Voir*** Conseil de l'industrie forestière du Québec

Québec Gardens Association ***Voir*** Association des jardins du Québec

Québec Land Surveyors Association ***Voir*** Ordre des arpenteurs-géomètres du Québec

Québec Lung Association (QLA) / Association pulmonaire du Québec (APQ)
Parent Name: Canadian Lung Association
5790, av Pierre-de-Coubertin, Montréal QC H1N 1R4
Tel: 514-287-7400; *Fax:* 514-287-1978
Toll-Free: 888-768-6669
e-mail: info@pq.poumon.ca
www.pq.poumon.ca
www.linkedin.com/groups?gid=2111754
www.facebook.com/poumon.qc
www.youtube.com/user/PoumonAPQ
Overview: A medium-sized provincial charitable organization founded in 1938 overseen by Canadian Lung Association
Mission: To provide resources in Québec about lung cancer, chronic obstructive pulmonary disease, sarcoidosis, tuberculosis, asthma, chronic bronchitis, sleep apnea, pneumonia, & emphysema; *Member of:* World Health Organization; International Union against Tuberculosis & Lung Disease; American Lung Association; European Lung Association
Environmental Activity: Offering information about air pollution, smoking, ragweed, etc.
Chief Officer(s):
Dominique Massie, Executive Director, 514-975-5382 Ext. 224
dominique.massie@pq.poumon.ca
Raymond Jabbour, Chief Financial Officer & Director, Direct Marketing & Information Technology, 514-975-5382 Ext. 226
Carole Bouchard, Director, Development & Communications, 514-975-5382 Ext. 225
carole.bouchard@pq.poumon.ca
Lynda Monière, Coordinator, Media Relations & Major Events, 514-975-5382 Ext. 229
lynda.moniere@pq.poumon.ca
Lise Vaillancourt, Respiratory Therapist & Coordinator, Programs, 514-975-5382 Ext. 232
lise.vaillancourt@pq.poumon.ca
Finances: *Funding Sources:* Donations; Fundraising; Sponsorships
Staff: 15 staff member(s); 20 volunteer(s)
Activities: Supporting respiratory health research; Providing education about respiratory illness; Offering support groups for persons affected by lung disease; Organizing events to raise funds; *Awareness Events:* Provincial Ragweed Extermination Campaign
Publications:
•Le Bulletin de l'association pulmonaire du Québec
Type: Newsletter; *Editor:* Louis P. Brisson; *ISSN:* 0843-381X
Profile: Respiratory health information, plus donation news
•Le Rapport annuel de l'association pulmonaire du Québec
Type: Yearbook; *Frequency:* Annually

Québec Medical Association ***Voir*** Association médicale du Québec

Québec Mining Association ***Voir*** Association minière du Québec

Québec Public Health Association ***Voir*** Association pour la santé publique du Québec

Québec Public Interest Research Group - McGill / Groupe de recherche d'intérêt public du Québec - McGill
3647, rue Université, 3e étage, Montréal QC H3A 2B3
Tél: 514-398-7432; *Téléc:* 514-398-8976
Courriel: qpirg@ssmu.mcgill.ca
qpirgmcgill.org
www.facebook.com/QPIRG.GRIP.McGill
twitter.com/qpirgmcgill
Également appelé: QPIRG-McGill
Aperçu: *Dimension:* petite; *Envergure:* nationale
Mission: To work on social justice & environmental issues
Membre: *Critères d'admissibilite:* Students; *Comités:* Conflict Resolution & Complaints

Québec Rose Society ***Voir*** Société des roses du Québec

Québec Society for the Defense of Animals ***Voir*** Société québécoise pour la défense des animaux

Québec Society for the Protection of Plants ***Voir*** Société de protection des plantes du Québec

Québec Trucking Association Inc. ***Voir*** Association du camionnage du Québec inc.

Québec Water Bottlers' Association ***Voir*** Association des embouteilleurs d'eau du Québec

Québec Young Farmers ***See*** Québec 4-H

Québec-Labrador Foundation (Canada) Inc. (QLF (Canada)) / Fondation Québec Labrador du (Canada) Inc.
#901, 505, boul René Lévesque ouest, Montréal QC H2Z 1Y7
Tel: 514-395-6020; *Fax:* 514-395-4505
e-mail: montreal@qlf.org
www.qlf.org
Overview: A small national charitable organization founded in 1969
Mission: To promote local leadership & assist in improvement of human conditions in northern New England, Eastern Québec, & Canadian Atlantic provinces; to conserve cultural heritage & natural resources of region; To conduct scientific research; To enrich educational experience of Canadian & US students; Affiliation(s): Atlantic Centre for the Environment
Chief Officer(s):
Lawrence B. Morris, President
Finances: *Annual Operating Budget:* $500,000-$1.5 Million
Staff: 17 staff member(s)
Membership: 4,000 individual; 50 institutional

Quesnel Naturalists
3084 RedBluff Rd., Quesnel BC V2J 6C6
e-mail: shofmeie@goldcity.net
www.bcnature.ca/pages/local_clubs/quesnel_naturalists.html
Overview: A small local organization
Mission: To promote the enjoyment of nature through environmental appreciation & conservation; To encourage wise use & conservation of natural resources & environmental protection.; *Member of:* Federation of BC Naturalists
Membership: 40; *Fees:* $15 single; 20$ family

Quetico Foundation
#216, 642 King St. West, Toronto ON M5V 1M7
Tel: 416-941-9388; *Fax:* 416-941-9236
e-mail: office@queticofoundation.org
www.queticofoundation.org
Overview: A small provincial charitable organization founded in 1954
Mission: To preserve wilderness areas of Ontario for recreation & scientific use
Chief Officer(s):
Glenda McLachlan, Executive Director
Finances: *Funding Sources:* Endowment & donations
Staff: 1 staff member(s); 27 volunteer(s)
Membership: 28 trustees; *Fees:* $40; *Committees:* Executive; Finance; Investment; Funding; Publications
Activities: ; *Library:* John B. Ridley Research Library; Open to public
Publications:
•The Quetico
Type: Newsletter; *Frequency:* Quartley

Quidi Vidi Rennie's River Development Foundation (QVRRDF)
Nagle's Place, St. John's NL A1B 2Z2
Tel: 709-754-3474; *Fax:* 709-754-5947
e-mail: info@fluvarium.ca
www.fluvarium.ca
Overview: A small local organization founded in 1985
Mission: To promote responsible environmental stewardship; To raise awareness of the nature of freshwater systems; To provide leadership in urban watershed management; To operate The Fluvarium as a public centre for environmental education; *Member of:* Hospitality Newfoundland & Labrador; St. John's Board of Trade; Newfoundland & Labrador Environmental Industry Association
Chief Officer(s):
Deborah Picco Garland, Executive Director
Finances: *Annual Operating Budget:* $250,000-$500,000; *Funding Sources:* Admission fees; building rentals; catering services; corporate & private donations; fundraising
Staff: 7 staff member(s); 100 volunteer(s)
Membership: 200; *Fees:* $30.00; *Member Profile:* Friends of Rennie's River; *Committees:* Development; Education; Facilities & Operations; Finance; Science & Exhibitions
Activities: Environmental education; tourism; restoration & habitat enhancement; *Awareness Events:* River Dance, March; Duck Race, Sept.; Fish Fry, August

Radiation Safety Institute of Canada / Institut de radioprotection du Canada
Head Office & National Education Centre, #300, 165 Avenue Rd., Toronto ON M5R 3S4
Tel: 416-650-9090; *Fax:* 416-650-9920
Toll-Free: 800-263-5803
e-mail: info@radiationsafety.ca
www.radiationsafety.ca
www.facebook.com/group.php?gid=143472245714096
Previous Name: Canadian Institute for Radiation Safety
Overview: A medium-sized national charitable organization founded in 1981
Mission: To be an independent source for knowledge about radiation safety in the environment, the community, & the workplace
Environmental Activity: Promoting radiation safety
Chief Officer(s):
Fergal Nolan, President & Chief Executive Officer
R. Moridi, Vice-President, Chief Scientist
Bruce Sylvester, Vice-President, Finance & Administration
Mike Haynes, Scientific Director
Natalia Mozayani, Program Manager
Tara Hargreaves, Scientist & Coordinator, Training
Activities: Providing information about radiation & radiation safety
Meetings/Conferences:
For more information see Trade Shows, Conferences and Seminars Chapter
Radiation Safety Institute of Canada 2013 All About X-ray Safety

Employee Training Course
2013 Toronto, ON
Radiation Safety Institute of Canada 2013 All About Radiation Safety Employee Training Course
2013 Toronto, ON
Radiation Safety Institute of Canada 2013 Radiation Safety Awareness Education
2013
Radiation Safety Institute of Canada 2013 X-ray Safety Awareness Education
2013

Radios Rurales Internationales ***See*** Farm Radio International

Rainforest Action Network (RAN)

#500, 221 Pine St., San Francisco CA 94104 USA
Tel: 415-398-4404; *Fax:* 415-398-2732
Toll-Free: 800-989-7246
e-mail: rainforest@ran.org
www.ran.org
Overview: A medium-sized international organization founded in 1985
Mission: To protect the Earth's rainforests & support the rights of their inhabitants through campaigns that work to bring corporate & government policies into alignment with popular support for rainforest conservation; *Member of:* Friends of the Earth International; Affiliation(s): 150 Rainforest Action Groups (RAGs) in the US & Europe; the RAGs are informally affiliated with RAN, receiving support materials, but no funding; RAGs organize local community actions
Chief Officer(s):
Randall Hayes, President
Chris Hatch, Executive Director
Finances: *Annual Operating Budget:* $1.5 Million-$3 Million; *Funding Sources:* 45% membership; 55% grants & donations
Staff: 27 staff member(s); 21 volunteer(s)
Membership: 32,000; *Fees:* $35
Activities: Oil Exploration Campaign; Old Growth Wood Consumption Campaign; Traditional Forest Peoples Campaign; Education Campaign; Grass Roots Team; Zero Emissions Campaign; Global Finance Campaign; *Awareness Events:* World Rainforest Week; *Internships:* Yes; *Library:*

Rainforest Alliance (RA)

#500, 665 Broadway, New York NY 10012 USA
Tel: 212-677-1900; *Fax:* 212-677-2187
Toll-Free: 888-693-2784
e-mail: info@ra.org
www.rainforest-alliance.org
Overview: A medium-sized international charitable organization founded in 1987
Mission: To protect ecosystems & the people & wildlife that depend on them by transforming land-use practices, business practices & consumer behavior
Chief Officer(s):
Tensie Whelan, Executive Director
Finances: *Annual Operating Budget:* Greater than $5 Million
Staff: 100 staff member(s); 25 volunteer(s)
Membership: 31,000; *Fees:* $35+ donation
Activities: *Internships:* Yes; *Rents Mailing List:* Yes

Rare Breeds Canada (RBC)

2495 boul Perrot, N.D. de L'Ile Perrot ON J7V 8PA
Tel: 514-901-0999
e-mail: rbc@rarebreedscanada.ca
www.rarebreedscanada.ca
Overview: A medium-sized national charitable organization founded in 1986
Mission: To make Canadians more aware of their agricultural heritage; through education & niche marketing involve them in conserving endangered breeds of farm livestock & poultry; Affiliation(s): Canadian Coalition for Biodiversity
Chief Officer(s):
Pam Heath, Office Manager
Finances: *Annual Operating Budget:* Less than $50,000; *Funding Sources:* Membership dues
Staff: 1 staff member(s); 20 volunteer(s)
Membership: 600; *Fees:* $35 individual; $50 family; $100 corporate
Activities: *Speaker Service:* Yes

Island Heritage Livestock
c/o Margaret Thomson, Chair, 1432 North Beach Rd., Salt Spring Island BC V8K 1B2
Tel: 250-537-4669
www.islandsheritagelivestock.com
Chief Officer(s):
Wynnie Konkle, Contact
olderbonz@shaw.ca

Recreation & Parks Association of New Brunswick Inc. ***See*** Recreation New Brunswick

Recreation New Brunswick
Parent Name: Canadian Parks & Recreation Association

#34, 55 Whiting Rd., Fredericton NB E3B 5Y5
Tel: 506-459-1929; *Fax:* 506-450-6066
www.recreationnb.ca
www.facebook.com/RecreationNB
twitter.com/RecreationNB
Previous Name: Recreation & Parks Association of New Brunswick Inc.
Overview: A medium-sized provincial organization founded in 1987 overseen by Canadian Parks & Recreation Association
Mission: To develop a professional organization for members; To enhance the image of recreation to government & the general public; To develop liaisons with other recreation groups; To affect legislation in the field of recreation & parks; to expand the NB Skills Program for Management Volunteers; To promote the need for education for leisure
Chief Officer(s):
Sarah Wagner, Executive Director
rnb@recreationnb.ca
Finances: *Annual Operating Budget:* $100,000-$250,000
Membership: *Fees:* $87 general; $265-$565 municipal; $132 associate; $295 corporate
Activities: Annual conference; awards; resource centre; membership directory; workshops; counsellors conference; Canoe School; career videos for high schools

Recreation Newfoundland & Labrador
Parent Name: Canadian Parks & Recreation Association

Bldg. 810, Pleasantville, PO Box 8700, Stn. A, St. John's NL A1B 4J6
Tel: 709-729-3892; *Fax:* 709-729-3814
www.recreationnl.com
Previous Name: Newfoundland & Labrador Parks & Recreation Association
Overview: A medium-sized provincial organization founded in 1971 overseen by Canadian Parks & Recreation Association
Mission: To promote, foster & develop recreation; to provide a full range of services to enrich the concept of leisure throughout Newfoundland & Labrador; to enable individual citizens to improve their quality of life.; Affiliation(s): Provincial/Territorial parks & recreation associations
Chief Officer(s):
Wanda Wight, President
wwight@nf.aibn.com
Gary Milley, Executive Director
garymilley@recreationnl.com
Finances: *Annual Operating Budget:* $100,000-$250,000; *Funding Sources:* Membership fees; services; government grants; corporate
Staff: 4 staff member(s)
Membership: 300 individual; *Fees:* Schedule available; *Member Profile:* Municipalities, communities, individuals, non-profit groups, students or businesses interested or involved in recreation; *Committees:* Executive; Finance; Marketing/Membership; AGM & Conference; Constitution/Nominations; Recreation Practitioners/Facilities; Recreation Inclusion Commitee; Awards
Activities: Playground Training Workshops; *Awareness Events:* Annual General Meeting & Conference; Arena Operators Course; Recreation Month, June; *Library:* Open to public

Recycling Council of Alberta (RCA)

PO Box 23, Bluffton AB T0C 0M0
Tel: 403-843-6563; *Fax:* 403-843-4156
e-mail: info@recycle.ab.ca
www.recycle.ab.ca
www.facebook.com/RecyclingCouncilOfAlberta
twitter.com/3RsAB
Overview: A medium-sized provincial charitable organization founded in 1987
Mission: To promote & facilitate waste reduction, recycling, & resource conservation in Alberta
Environmental Activity: Encouraging policies that facilitate waste reduction, recycling, & resource conservation; Promoting industrial, commercial, & institutional waste reduction & stewardship; Encouraging market development for recycled materials & products
Chief Officer(s):
Jason London, President
Sharon Howland, Vice-President
Maegan Lukian, Secretary
Anne Auriat, Treasurer
Membership: *Fees:* Fee based upon sales for corporations & small businesses; Fee based upon population for municipalities & regional waste authorities; *Member Profile:* Corporations; Small Businesses; Institutions; Governments; Municipalities; Regional Waste Authorities; Not-for-Profit Organizations; Individuals; *Committees:* Leadership & Advocacy; Small & Rural Communities; Communications; Indstrial, Commercial, & Institutional Sector Issues
Activities: Facilitating the exchange of information between environmental groups, governments, industries, & consumers; Providing public education campaigns; Encouraging research in the recycling of waste materials; *Awareness Events:* Waste Reduction Week, October; *Speaker Service:* Yes
Meetings/Conferences:
For more information see Trade Shows, Conferences and Seminars Chapter
Recycling Council of Alberta Waste Reduction 2013 Conference
October 2013 Calgary, AB
Recycling Council of Alberta Waste Reduction 2014 Conference
October 2014 Lake Louise, AB
Publications:
•Connector [a publication of the Recycling Council of Alberta]
Type: Newsletter
Profile: RCA activities, member profiles, & success stories
•Enviro Business Guide
Type: Directory
Profile: Contact information & descriptions of businesses

Recycling Council of British Columbia (RCBC)

#10, 119 West Pender St., Vancouver BC V6B 1S5
Tel: 604-683-6009; *Fax:* 604-683-7255
Toll-Free: 800-667-4321
e-mail: rcbc@rcbc.bc.ca
www.rcbc.bc.ca
www.facebook.com/home.php?sk=group_10340005498
twitter.com/RecyclingBC
www.youtube.com/user/RCBCTrailerTrashed
Overview: A medium-sized provincial charitable organization founded in 1974
Mission: To promote the principles of zero waste; To decrease British Columbia's environmental footprint
Environmental Activity: Providing a recycling hotline with information on waste reduction; Operating the RCBC Materials Exchange program for the reuse & recycling of discarded products & materials
Chief Officer(s):
Brock Macdonald, Executive Director, 604-683-6009 Ext. 307
brock@rcbc.bc.ca
Anna Rochelle, Director, Finance, 604-683-6009 Ext. 302
anna@rcbc.bc.ca
Harvinder Gill, Manager, Information Services, 604-683-6009 Ext. 313
harv@rcbc.bc.ca
Ben Ramos, Manager, Member Services, 604-683-6009 Ext. 314
ben@rcbc.bc.ca
Finances: *Funding Sources:* Sponsorships; Donations
Membership: *Member Profile:* Individuals & corporations that support environmental sustainability
Activities: Conducting research; Providing information services; Participating in community-based events & activities; Establishing public policy positions; *Awareness Events:* Waste Reduction Week
Meetings/Conferences:
For more information see Trade Shows, Conferences and Seminars Chapter
Recycling Council of British Columbia 2013 Annual General Meeting & Conference
May 2013 Whistler, BC
Recycling Council of British Columbia 2014 Annual General Meeting & Conference
May 2014 Whistler, BC
Publications:
•Best Practices for Multi-Family Food Scraps Collection
Type: Report; *Number of Pages:* 18; *Author:* Jordan Best
Profile: Topics include barriers in the multi-family sector, materials collected, collection details, containers & liners, education & outreach, & incentives &policies
•Examining the Waste-to-Energy Option
Type: Report; *Number of Pages:* 24; *Author:* Jordan Best

Profile: A background paper examining environmental performance & compatibility with zero waste principles
•On the Road to Zero Waste: Priorities for Local Governments
Type: Report; *Number of Pages:* 16
Profile: Guidance for municipal & regional governments across British Columbia
•Organics Working Group Report: Recommendations for Residential Collection
Type: Report; *Number of Pages:* 16
Profile: Recommendations developed by the Organics Working Group to service single family homes
•RCBC [Recycling Council of British Columbia] Backgrounder: Degradable Plastic Bags
Type: Report
•Recycling Council of British Columbia Annual Report
Type: Yearbook; *Frequency:* Annually
Profile: Featuring the executive director's report, the auditor's report, & organizational information

Recycling Council of Manitoba; Resource Conservation Manitoba Inc. ***See*** Green Action Centre

Recycling Council of Ontario (RCO) / Conseil du recyclage de l'Ontario

#225, 215 Spadina Ave., Toronto ON M5T 2C7
Tel: 416-657-2797
Toll-Free: 888-501-9637
e-mail: rco@rco.on.ca
www.rco.on.ca
twitter.com/RCOntario
Overview: A medium-sized provincial charitable organization founded in 1978
Mission: To minimize impact on the environment by eliminating waste
Environmental Activity: Providing education about the efficient use of resources
Chief Officer(s):
Jo-Anne St. Godard, Executive Director, 416-657-2797 Ext. 3
joanne@rco.on.ca
Diane Blackburn, Manager, Events, 416-657-2797 Ext. 4
events@rco.on.ca; diane@rco.on.ca
David Hanson, Program Manager, Waste Diversion Certification Program, 416-657-2797 Ext. 8
david@rco.on.ca
Sarah Mills, Manager, Special Projects & Take Back the Light, 416-657-2797 Ext. 7
sarah@rco.on.ca
Lucy Robinson, Manager, Member Relations, 416-657-2797 Ext. 1
lucy@rco.on.ca; members@rco.on.ca
Catherine Leighton, Coordinator, Special Projects, 416-657-2797 Ext. 5
catherine@rco.on.ca
Andrew Reeves, Coordinator, Outreach & Communications, 416-657-2797 Ext. 10
andrew@rco.on.ca
Finances: *Funding Sources:* Donations; Sponsorships
Membership: *Fees:* Schedule available based upon annual gross sales for businesses & population for municipalities; *Member Profile:* Businesses; Municipalities; Communities; Educational organizations; Individuals; Students; Families; *Committees:* Executive / Finance; Membership / Communications; Policy / Advocacy; Program Development; Events
Activities: Liaising with all levels of government, environmental organizations, & industry; *Awareness Events:* Waste Reduction Week in Ontario; Waste Free Lunch Challenge
Awards:
•Visual Arts, Sculpture, & Arts Installation Award (Award)
•Business Award (Award)
•Communications Award (Award)
•Festivals & Events Award (Award)
•Municipal Awards (Award)
•Sustainable Product or Service Award (Award)
•Waste Diversion Program Operator Award (Award)
•Waste Reduction Week in Canada Participation Award (Award)
Meetings/Conferences:
For more information see Trade Shows, Conferences and Seminars Chapter
Recycling Council of Ontario 2013 Annual General Meeting & Policy Forum
January 2013 Toronto, ON
Publications:
•RCO [Recycling Council of Ontario] Highlights the Headlines
Price: Free with Recycling Council of Ontario membership
Profile: Information about local, national, & international environmental, waste management, & diversion issues
•Recycling Council of Ontario Annual Report
Type: Yearbook; *Frequency:* Annually
Profile: Operational highlights of the council
•Recycling Council of Ontario e-Newsletter
Type: Newsletter; *Price:* Free with Recycling Council of Ontario membership
•Recycling Council of Ontario Member Bulletin
Type: Newsletter; *Frequency:* Irregular; *Price:* Free with Recycling Council of Ontario membership

Red Deer River Naturalists (RDRN)

PO Box 785, Red Deer AB T4N 5H2
Tel: 403-347-8200; *Fax:* 403-347-8200
e-mail: rd.rn@hotmail.com
www.rdrn.fanweb.ca
Previous Name: Alberta Natural History Society
Overview: A small local charitable organization founded in 1906
Mission: To foster increased knowledge, understanding & appreciation of natural history; to support conservation measures dealing with environment, wildlife & natural resources; to cooperate with other clubs & organizations having similar views & objectives; *Member of:* Federation of Alberta Naturalists; Affiliation(s): Canadian Nature Federation
Chief Officer(s):
Don Wales, President
Finances: *Annual Operating Budget:* Less than $50,000; *Funding Sources:* Membership fees; donations; grants
Staff: 300 volunteer(s)
Membership: 300 individual; *Fees:* $15 individual; $20 family; *Committees:* Habitat Preservation
Activities: Field trips; Habitat Steward Program; educational programs; species counts

Refreshments Canada; Canadian Bottlers of Carbonated Beverages; Canadian Soft Drink Association ***See*** Canadian Beverage Association

Refrigeration & Air Conditioning Contractors Association of British Columbia (RACCA-BC)

26121 Fraser Hwy., Aldergrove BC V4X 2E3
Tel: 604-856-8644
e-mail: raccabc@hrai.ca
Overview: A medium-sized provincial organization
Mission: To act on behalf of the members to promote positive & effective employee development & labour relations
Chief Officer(s):
Blaire Masztalar, President
Finances: *Annual Operating Budget:* Less than $50,000
Staff: 1 staff member(s)
Membership: 15 corporate

Refrigeration Service Engineers Society (Canada) (RSES Canada)

PO Box 3, Stn. B, Toronto ON M9W 5K9
Tel: 905-842-9199
Toll-Free: 877-955-6255
www.rsescanada.com
Overview: A medium-sized national organization founded in 1952
Mission: To lead all segments of the HVAC industry by providing superior educational & training programs; to create an environment that encourages maximum member participation in the development & decision process of the Society; *Member of:* Refrigeration Service Engineers Society - International
Chief Officer(s):
David Chafe, President
dchafe@personainternet.com
Nick Reggi, Secretary
dreggi@cogeco.ca
Finances: *Annual Operating Budget:* $50,000-$100,000; *Funding Sources:* Membership dues; educational seminars
Staff: 2 volunteer(s)
Membership: 2,200; *Fees:* $125
Activities: Education program

Regina & District Labour Council (RDLC)
Parent Name: Saskatchewan Federation of Labour

2709 - 12th Ave., #E, Regina SK S4T 1J3
Tel: 306-757-7076; *Fax:* 306-585-2874
e-mail: rdlc@sasktel.net
www.rdlc.sasktelwebsite.net
Overview: A medium-sized local organization overseen by Saskatchewan Federation of Labour
Mission: To advance the economic & social welfare of workers in Regina & the surrounding region; To engage in political activity at the municipal level; Affiliation(s): Canadian Labour Congress (CLC)
Environmental Activity: Presenting issues of importance to workers & their families to the Regina City Council, such as a Green Agenda for Cities & Communities
Chief Officer(s):
Janice Bernier, President, 306-775-2333
jmbernier@sasktel.net
Laurie Temple, Secretary
Carol Mullaney, Treasurer
Membership: 25,560; *Member Profile:* Nineteen unions & forty locals from Regina & the surrounding region
Activities: Increasing the council's affiliate base; Promoting the interests of affiliates; Liaising with the city council to discuss issues of importance to affilitates; Hosting an annual Day of Mourning Ceremony to recognize workers killed on the job; Ensuring that occupational health & safety laws are enforced; Supporting local causes to make the community a better place to work & live; Establishing the Janice Bernier Endowment Fund for long-term food sustainability with the United Way; Coordinating lobbies in Regina ridings

Regina Wildlife Federation (RWF)

PO Box 594, Regina SK S4P 3A3
Tel: 306-359-7733
e-mail: rwf1@accesscomm.ca
nonprofits.accesscomm.ca/rwf
Overview: A medium-sized local charitable organization founded in 1962
Mission: The RWF is a non-profit wildlife conservation organization.; *Member of:* Saskatchewan Wildlife Federation
Chief Officer(s):
Gil White, President
gilwhite@sasktel.net
Finances: *Annual Operating Budget:* Less than $50,000
Membership: 1,200; *Fees:* $25 to $115
Activities: *Speaker Service:* Yes

The Regional Health Authorities of Manitoba (RHAM)
Parent Name: Canadian Healthcare Association

#2, 203 Duffield St., Winnipeg MB R3J 0H6
Tel: 204-833-1721; *Fax:* 204-940-2042
e-mail: mebbitt@rham.mb.ca
www.rham.mb.ca
Previous Name: Manitoba Health Organizations
Overview: A medium-sized provincial organization founded in 1998 overseen by Canadian Healthcare Association
Chief Officer(s):
Tom Kapac, Program Manager
Finances: *Annual Operating Budget:* $3 Million-$5 Million; *Funding Sources:* Membership fees; service fees
Staff: 12 staff member(s)
Membership: 11; *Fees:* Schedule available
Activities: *Rents Mailing List:* Yes

Registered Professional Foresters Association of Nova Scotia (RPFANS)

PO Box 1031, Truro NS B2N 5G9
Tel: 902-893-0099
e-mail: contact@rpfans.ca
www.rpfans.ca
Overview: A medium-sized provincial organization founded in 1999
Mission: To improve the holistic management of forest resources in Nova Scotia
Chief Officer(s):
Roger Aggas, Registrar
John Ross, President
Mike Brown, Treasurer
Membership: *Member Profile:* Professional foresters in Nova Scotia; Foresters-in-training & students
Activities: Disciplining members who fail to comply with the code of ethics; Ensuring that the public receives proper forest management advice; Encouraging further education
Meetings/Conferences:
For more information see Trade Shows, Conferences and Seminars Chapter
Registered Professional Foresters Association of Nova Scotia 2013 Annual General Meeting
2013, NS
Publications:
•Forest Steward [a publication of the Registered Professional Foresters Association of Nova Scotia]
Type: Newsletter
Profile: Contents include the message from the president & news from the association & forestry sector

Regroupement des associations forestières régionales du Québec
Parent Name: Canadian Forestry Association
#100, 138, rue Wellington nord, Sherbrooke QC J1H 5C5
Tél: 819-562-3388
Courriel: info@afce.qc.ca
www.afce.qc.ca
Aperçu: *Dimension:* moyenne; *Envergure:* provinciale surveillé par Canadian Forestry Association
Membre(s) du bureau directeur:
Daniel Archambault

Regroupement pour la surveillance du nucléaire *See* Canadian Coalition for Nuclear Responsibility

Regroupement QuébecOiseaux
CP 1000, Succ. M, 4545, av Pierre-de Coubertin, Montréal QC H1V 3R2
Tél: 514-252-3190; *Téléc:* 514-251-8038
Ligne sans frais: 866-583-4846
Courriel: info@quebecoiseaux.org
www.quebecoiseaux.org
Nom précédent: Association québécoise des groupes d'ornithologues
Aperçu: *Dimension:* moyenne; *Envergure:* provinciale; Organisme sans but lucratif; fondée en 1981
Mission: Favoriser le développement du loisir ornithologique; promouvoir l'étude des oiseaux; veiller à leur protection et à celle de leurs habitats
Membre(s) du bureau directeur:
Jean-Sébastien Guénette, Directeur général
Finances: *Budget de fonctionnement annuel:* $100,000-$250,000
Personnel: 4 membre(s) du personnel; 13 bénévole(s)
Membre: 6,000 *Montant de la cotisation:* 20$ non-membre d'un club; 15$ membre d'un club; 50$ Organismes sans but lucratif; 100$ autres membres associés; *Critères d'admissibilite:* Toute personne intéressée par l'observation des oiseaux
Activités: Banques de données; *Stagiaires:* Oui

Renewable Natural Resources Foundation (RNRF)
5430 Grosvenor Lane, Bethesda MD 20814-2142 USA
Tel: 301-493-9101; *Fax:* 301-493-6148
e-mail: info@rnrf.org
www.rnrf.org
Overview: A small national charitable organization founded in 1972
Mission: To advance sciences & public education in renewable natural resources; to promote the application of sound, scientific practices in managing & conserving renewable natural resources; to foster coordination & cooperation among professional, scientific & educational organizations having leadership responsibilities for renewable natural resources; to develop a Renewable Natural Resources Center
Chief Officer(s):
Robert D. Day, Executive Director
Membership: 12; *Member Profile:* Professional & scientific societies with interest in natural resources
Activities: Public policy roundtables, national congresses, annual awards, quarterly journal, internship program; *Internships:* Yes

Research & Development Institute for the Agri-Environment (IRDA) / Institut de recherche et de développement en agroenvironnement (IRDA)
Head Office & Research Center, PO Box 480, 3300, rue Sicotte, Saint-Hyacinthe QC J2S 7B8
Tel: 450-778-6522; *Fax:* 450-778-6539
www.irda.qc.c
Overview: A medium-sized national organization founded in 1998
Mission: To contribute to the sustainable development of agriculture, through research, knowledge acquisition, & transfer activities
Chief Officer(s):
Pierre Lemieux, President, Board
Gisèle Grandbois, President & Chief Executive Officer
Robert Doré, Director, Research Services & Human Resources
Activities: Publishing fact sheets, research reports, scientific papers, & technology transfer papers
Publications:
•Agro Solutions / Revue Agrosolutions [a publication of the Research & Development Institute for the Agri-Environment]
Editor: Marcel Giroux
•Research & Development Institute for the Agri-Environment Annual Report
Type: Yearbook; *Frequency:* Annually
•Research & Development Institute for the Agri-Environment Scientific Activity Report
Type: Yearbook

Réseau canadien d'éducation et de communication relatives à l'environnement *See* Canadian Network for Environmental Education & Communication

Réseau canadien de l'eau *See* Canadian Water Network

Réseau canadien de l'environnement *See* Canadian Environmental Network

Réseau canadien des centres de toxicologie *See* Canadian Network of Toxicology Centres

Réseau canadien des subventionneurs en environnement *See* Canadian Environmental Grantmakers' Network

Le Réseau canadien pour la conservation de la flore *See* Canadian Botanical Conservation Network

Réseau des aliments et des matériaux d'avant-garde *See* Advanced Foods & Materials Network

Réseau écologique du Manitoba inc. *See* Manitoba Eco-Network Inc.

Réseau environnement
#220, 911, rue Jean Talon est, Montréal QC H2R 1V5
Tél: 514-270-7110; *Téléc:* 514-270-7154
Courriel: info@reseau-environnement.com
www.reseau-environnement.com
Nom précédent: Association québécoise des techniques de l'environnement
Aperçu: *Dimension:* moyenne; *Envergure:* provinciale; Organisme sans but lucratif; fondée en 1959
Mission: Regrouper des entreprises spécialisées dans la gestion des déchets commerciaux, industriels et des services municipaux reliés à l'environnement; Assurer l'avancement des technologies et de la science, la promotion des expertises et le soutien des activités en environnement
Membre(s) du bureau directeur:
Stéphanie Myre, Présidente-directrice générale
smyre@reseau-environnement.com
Mario Laplante, Directeur général adjointé
mlaplante@reseau-environnement.com
Josianne Lafantaisie, Coordonnatrice principale, Communications et relations publiques
jlafantaisie@reseau-environnement.com
Romy Regis, Coordonnatrice, Événements
rregis@reseau-environnement.com
Lyne Dubois, Merlicom, 514-935-3830 Ext. 227
ldubois@merlicom.com
Mihaela Sandor, Comptable, 514-935-3830 Ext. 237
msandor@reseau-environnement.com
Membre: 364 corpratif

Réseau environnemental du Nouveau-Brunswick *See* New Brunswick Environmental Network

Réseau québécois des groupes écologistes (RQGE)
Parent Name: Canadian Environmental Network
1557-A, avenue Papineau, Montréal QC H2K 4H7
Tél: 514-392-0096
Courriel: info@rqge.qc.ca
www.rqge.qc.ca
Aperçu: *Dimension:* petite; *Envergure:* provinciale; Organisme sans but lucratif; fondée en 1983 surveillé par Canadian Environmental Network
Mission: Réseau de services et d'information pour les groupes écologiques du Québec; aider les groupes à communiquer entre eux
Membre(s) du bureau directeur:
Yvan Croteau, Président
presidence@rqge.qc.ca
Finances: *Budget de fonctionnement annuel:* $50,000-$100,000
Personnel: 7 membre(s) du personnel; 10 bénévole(s)
Membre: 80 *Montant de la cotisation:* 10$ individu; 35$ groupe local; 50$ groupe national
Activités: *Service de conférenciers:* Oui

Réseau régional du l'industrie biologique du Canada atlantique *See* Atlantic Canadian Organic Regional Network

Resource Efficient Agricultural Production (REAP Canada)
Glenaladale House, PO Box 125, 21111, ch Lakeshore, Sainte-Anne-de-Bellevue QC H9X 3V9
Tel: 514-398-7743; *Fax:* 514-398-7972
e-mail: info@reap-canada.com
www.reap-canada.com
Also Known As: Sustainable Farming
Overview: A medium-sized national charitable organization founded in 1988
Mission: To improve farm profits & productivity while minimizing adverse health & environmental effects; Affiliation(s): Canadian Organic Growers; Ecological Farmers Association of Ontario
Chief Officer(s):
Roger Samson, Executive Director
Finances: *Annual Operating Budget:* $250,000-$500,000
Staff: 4 staff member(s); 10 volunteer(s)
Membership: 500; *Fees:* $25 individual; $100 organization
Activities: Sustainable farming research into biomass energy on farm sustainable agriculture research for carbon dioxide reduction; *Speaker Service:* Yes; *Library:* by appointment

Resource Industry Suppliers Association (RISA)
#104, 14020 - 128th Ave., Edmonton AB T5L 4M8
Tel: 780-489-5900; *Fax:* 780-489-6262
e-mail: risa@resourcesuppliers.com
www.resourcesuppliers.com
www.linkedin.com/company/2369860
www.facebook.com/RISA.012
twitter.com/risa_allan
Overview: A medium-sized national organization
Mission: To source project information & contracts from members of the energy, mining, forest & bio-products industries
Chief Officer(s):
Allan Bartolcic, Executive Director
allan@resourcesuppliers.com

Resource Recycling Inc.
PO Box 42270, Portland OR 97242-0270 USA
Tel: 503-233-1305; *Fax:* 503-233-1356
e-mail: info@resource-recycling.com
www.resource-recycling.com
www.facebook.com/ResourceRecycling
twitter.com/rrecycling
Overview: A medium-sized international organization founded in 1982
Chief Officer(s):
Cara Bergeson, Publisher & Conference Manager
cara@resource-recycling.com
Finances: *Annual Operating Budget:* $500,000-$1.5 Million
Staff: 8 staff member(s)
Activities: *Rents Mailing List:* Yes
Publications:
•Resource Recycling
Editor: Jerry Powell; *Price:* $52 annual subscription
Profile: Monthly magazine

Resources for Global Sustainability (RGS)
PO Box 3665, Cary NC 27519-3665 USA
Fax: 919-363-9841
Toll-Free: 800-724-1857
Previous Name: Environmental Data Research Institute
Overview: A medium-sized local organization founded in 1996
Mission: To develop information about environmental funding; to compile, analyze & disseminate information on environmental funding; to broaden & deepen the knowledge base from which grant makers & others make decisions
Finances: *Annual Operating Budget:* $100,000-$250,000
Staff: 4 staff member(s)
Activities: Databases & information services; grants database contains information on environmental awards made by US grant makers since Jan. 1988; issues standard reports on funding patterns for the previous calendar year; prepares custom reports in specialized subject areas (on request)

Retail Council of Canada (RCC) / Conseil canadien du commerce de détail
#800, 1255 Bay St., Toronto ON M5R 2A9
Tel: 416-922-6678; *Fax:* 416-922-8011
Toll-Free: 888-373-8245
e-mail: info@retailcouncil.org
www.retailcouncil.org
www.facebook.com/retailcouncil
twitter.com/RetailCouncil
www.youtube.com/user/RetailCouncil
Overview: A large national organization founded in 1963
Mission: To be the best at delivering the services our retail members value most; To serve, promote & represent the diverse needs of Canada's retailing industry to the highest standards of quality; Affiliation(s): Canadian Health Food Association; Footwear Council of Canada; Le Conseil quebeçois du

commerce de rétail; Retail Merchants' Association of Alberta; Retail Merchants' Association of Manitoba
Chief Officer(s):
Kevin Macnab, Chair
Diane J. Brisebois, CAE, President & CEO
David Wilkes, Senior Vice-President, Grocery Division
Andrew Siegwart, Vice-President, Membership Services
Finances: *Annual Operating Budget:* $3 Million-$5 Million
Staff: 24 staff member(s)
Membership: 8,500 companies; *Fees:* Schedule available; *Member Profile:* Retailers of all sizes across Canada; *Committees:* Technology Committee; Resources Protection; Government Relations; Committees of the Board of Directors; Education Committee
Activities: *Speaker Service:* Yes; *Library:* Open to public by appointment

Rhododendron Society of Canada (RSC)
RR#2, St George Brant ON N0E 1N0
Tel: 519-448-1537
Overview: A small national charitable organization founded in 1971
Mission: To share information on rhododendrons; *Member of:* American Rhododendron Society
Chief Officer(s):
H.G. Hedges, Contact
Finances: *Annual Operating Budget:* Less than $50,000; *Funding Sources:* Membership dues; plant sales
Staff: 50 volunteer(s)
Membership: 400; *Fees:* $35; *Member Profile:* Growers of rhododendrons
Activities: Bulletins; flower shows; plant sales

Richard Ivey Foundation
#400, 11 Church St., Toronto ON M5E 1W1
Tel: 416-867-9229; *Fax:* 416-601-1689
e-mail: info@ivey.org
www.ivey.org
Overview: A medium-sized local charitable organization founded in 1947
Mission: To pursue & support excellence by making grants that will improve the well-being of Canadians. Today, the Conserving Canada's Forests Program provides critical support for environmental sustainability across the country.
Chief Officer(s):
Rosamond Ivey, Chair
Richard W. Ivey, Secretary-Treasurer
Bruce Lourie, President
Activities: Participating in the Conserving Canada's Forests program, by providing support to national or provincial charitable environmental organizations;

Richmond Agricultural Society
Parent Name: Ontario Association of Agricultural Societies
PO Box 1210, 6121 Perth St., Richmond ON K0A 2Z0
Tel: 613-838-3420; *Fax:* 613-838-3933
e-mail: richmondfair@sympatico.ca
www.richmondfair.ca
Overview: A small local charitable organization founded in 1841 overseen by Ontario Association of Agricultural Societies
Mission: To promote agricultural awareness to the community by hosting a Fall Agricultural Fair; *Member of:* Society of Composers, Authors & Music Publishers of Canada; Affiliation(s): Canadian Association of Fairs & Exhibitions; Ontario Association of Agricutural Societies
Chief Officer(s):
Dale Greene, General Manager/Secretary
Finances: *Annual Operating Budget:* $250,000-$500,000; *Funding Sources:* Federal, provincial & regional government; local businesses, individuals
Staff: 2 staff member(s); 450 volunteer(s)
Membership: 400 individual; *Fees:* $10 individual; *Member Profile:* To promote agricultural awareness to the community; *Committees:* Over 30, Livestock, Homecraft, Kiddyland, Entertainment, 4-H, Advertising, Consessions
Activities: Richmond Fair, Sept.; livestock shows; fundraising events

Richmond Hill Naturalists (RHN)
PO Box 33217, Stn. Harding Post Outlet, Richmond Hill ON L4C 9S3
Tel: 905-883-3047
e-mail: membership@rhnaturalists.ca
www.rhnaturalists.ca
Overview: A small local organization founded in 1955
Mission: To encourage interest in natural history; To preserve natural areas; To discover & appreciate the natural world
Environmental Activity: Participating in the Christmas Bird Count & the Great Backyard Bird Count
Chief Officer(s):
Marianne Yake, President, 905-883-3047
president@rhnaturalists.ca
Gene Denzel, Treasurer
treasurer@rhnaturalists.ca
Membership: *Fees:* $25 students; $30 individuals; $35 families
Activities: Offering field trips; Arranging programs on nature topics
Publications:
•The RHN [Richmond Hill Naturalists] Bulletin
Type: Newsletter; *Frequency:* 9 pa; *Accepts Advertising*; *Editor:* Denise Potter; *Price:* Free with Richmond Hill Naturalists membership
Profile: Organization activities, nature news, & forthcoming events

Rideau Environmental Action League (REAL)
PO Box 1061, Smiths Falls ON K7A 5A5
Tel: 613-283-9500; *Fax:* 613-283-9500
e-mail: info@realaction.ca
www.realaction.ca
Overview: A medium-sized local organization founded in 1989
Mission: To conduct community-wide environmental projects and promote environmental improvements within the Town of Smiths Falls and Lanark, Leeds and Grenville Counties.; Affiliation(s): Green Communities Canada; Ontario Environmental Network
Chief Officer(s):
Barb Hicks, President
dhicks11@cogeco.ca
Membership: 26 corporate; *Fees:* $15 individual; $20 family; $5 student; $25 associate; $50 corporate

Rideau Trail Association (RTA)
PO Box 15, Kingston ON K7L 4V6
Tel: 613-545-0823
e-mail: info@rideautrail.org
www.rideautrail.org
www.facebook.com/sharer.php?u=http%3A%2F%2Frideautrail.org&src=sp
Overview: A small local charitable organization founded in 1971
Mission: The Association is a non-profit organization that preserves & maintains a hiking trail from Kingston to Ottawa. It is comprised of 3 clubs - Kingston, Central (Perth), & Ottawa - that organize events year-round. It is a registered charity, BN: 119119485RR0001.; *Member of:* Hike Ontario
Finances: *Funding Sources:* Donations
Membership: 1200; *Fees:* $25 individual; $30 household; $500 life membership
Activities: Hiking, cross-country skiing, & snowshoeing
Awards:
•End-to-End (Award)
Amount: Certificate & badge for those completing the trail
Publications:
•Rideau Trail Association E-Letter
Type: Newsletter; *Frequency:* Biweekly; *Price:* Free with RTA membership
•Rideau Trail Association Newsletter
Type: Newsletter; *Frequency:* Quarterly; *Price:* Free with RTA membership
Profile: Hiking articles & club activities
•The Rideau Trail Guidebook
Number of Pages: 109; *Editor:* Ernie Trischuk; *ISBN:* 0-9693759-7-2; *Price:* $25.50 members; $39.95 non-members
Profile: Maps & trail directions & descriptions

Central Rideau Trail Club
PO Box 213, Perth ON K7H 3E4
Tel: 613-264-8338

Ottawa Rideau Trail Club
PO Box 4616, Stn. E, Ottawa ON K1S 5H8
Tel: 613-860-2225

Rideau Valley Conservation Authority (RVCA)
PO Box 599, 3889 Rideau Valley Dr., Manotick ON K4M 1A5
Tel: 613-692-3571; *Fax:* 613-692-0831
Toll-Free: 800-267-3504
e-mail: info@rvcf.ca
www.rvca.ca
www.facebook.com/group.php?gid=108941882522595
twitter.com/RideauValleyCA
Overview: A large local organization
Mission: To advocate for clean water, natural shorelines and sustainable land use throughout the Rideau Valley watershed.
Chief Officer(s):
Alan Arbuckle, Chair
Charles Billington, Executive Director
charles.billington@rvca.ca
Finances: *Annual Operating Budget:* Greater than $5 Million; *Funding Sources:* Province; Fundraising; Municipalities
Staff: 65 staff member(s)
Membership: 30 municipalities
Publications:
•Watershed Briefs
Type: Newsletter
Profile: Newsletter for municipal councillors

Rideau Valley Field Naturalists (RVFN)
PO Box 474, Perth ON K7H 3G1
rvfn.colmar176.ca
Overview: A small local organization founded in 1983
Mission: To promote the enjoyment of nature through environmental appreciation & conservation; To encourage the wise use & conservation of natural resources; to promote environmental protection; *Member of:* Federation of Ontario Naturalists; World Wildlife Federation; Canadian Nature Federation
Chief Officer(s):
Murray Hunt, Treasurer, 613-264-9273
mkhunt@ripnet.com
Finances: *Annual Operating Budget:* Less than $50,000; *Funding Sources:* Membership fees
Staff: 12 volunteer(s)
Membership: 96; *Fees:* $5 student; $20 individual; $30 family/institution; *Committees:* Flora & Fauna; Outings
Activities: Monthly meetings except July & August; mall displays; educational outings; bird identification; clinics; bird, mammal & amphibian monitoring; *Library:*

Rimbey Fish & Game Association
PO Box 634, Rimbey AB T0C 2J0
Tel: 403-843-3858
www.rimbeyfishandgame.com
Overview: A small local organization
Member of: Alberta Fish & Game Association
Chief Officer(s):
Daryl Hunt, President, 403-843-6466
Finances: *Annual Operating Budget:* Less than $50,000
Membership: 104; *Fees:* $29 family; $19 regular; $18 associate; $12 youth under 18
Activities: Fish & Game annual awards & trophies

Roads & Transportation Association of Canada *See* Transportation Association of Canada

Robert Sauvé Occupational Health & Safety Research Institute *Voir* Institut de recherche Robert-Sauvé en santé et en sécurité du travail

The Rocky Mountain Institute (RMI)
2317 Snowmass Creek Rd., Snowmass CO 81654 USA
Tel: 970-927-3851; *Fax:* 970-927-3420
e-mail: media@rmi.org
www.rmi.org
www.linkedin.com/company/rocky-mountain-institute
www.facebook.com/RockyMtnInst
twitter.com/RockyMtnInst
www.youtube.com/user/RockyMtnInstitute
Overview: A medium-sized national organization founded in 1982
Mission: To foster the efficient & sustainable use of resources as a path to global security; focuses on five program areas - energy, water, agriculture, economic renewal, security; stresses understanding the interconnections between resource issues, honoring people's integrity, seeking ideas that transcend ideology & harnessing the problem-solving power of free-market economics
Chief Officer(s):
Michael Potts, President & CEO
Marty Pickett, Executive Director & General Counsel
Finances: *Annual Operating Budget:* Greater than $5 Million; *Funding Sources:* Personal donations; grants
Staff: 45 staff member(s)
Membership: 23,000; *Fees:* $10
Activities: *Internships:* Yes; *Speaker Service:* Yes; *Library:* by appointment

Rocky Mountain Naturalists
PO Box 791, Cranbrook BC V1C 4J5

e-mail: scoutfir@shaw.ca
www.kootenaynaturalists.org/rocky/index.html
Overview: A small local charitable organization founded in 1985
Mission: To promote the enjoyment of nature through environmental appreciation & conservation; to encourage the wise use & conservation of natural resources & environmental protection; *Member of:* Federation of BC Naturalists
Chief Officer(s):
Mildred White, Director
Membership: 40; *Fees:* $20 single; $25 family
Activities: Field trips; study nights; conservation projects

Rose Society of Ontario *See* Canadian Rose Society

Royal Agricultural Winter Fair Association (RAWF) / Foire agricole royale d'hiver

The Ricoh Coliseum, 100 Princes' Blvd., Toronto ON M6K 3C3
Tel: 416-263-3400; *Fax:* 416-263-3488
e-mail: info@royalfair.org
www.royalfair.org
Also Known As: Royal Winter Fair
Overview: A medium-sized national charitable organization founded in 1922
Mission: To promote excellence in agricultural & equestrian activities through world class competition, exhibitions & education; *Member of:* Canadian Association of Fairs & Exhibitions
Chief Officer(s):
Bill Duron, CEO
Finances: *Annual Operating Budget:* Greater than $5 Million; *Funding Sources:* Sponsors; government; gate admissions; advertising
Staff: 12 staff member(s); 1000 volunteer(s)
Activities: *Internships:* Yes
Meetings/Conferences:
For more information see Trade Shows, Conferences and Seminars Chapter
2013 Royal Winter Agricultural Fair
November 2013 Toronto, ON

Royal Botanical Gardens (RBG) / Les jardins botaniques royaux

680 Plains Rd. West, Hamilton ON L7T 4H4
Tel: 905-527-1158; *Fax:* 905-577-0375
Toll-Free: 800-694-4769
e-mail: info@rbg.ca
www.rbg.ca
www.facebook.com/pages/Royal-Botanical-Gardens/140038459379746
twitter.com/RBGCanada
www.youtube.com/user/royalbotanicalgarden
Overview: A medium-sized local organization founded in 1932
Mission: To be recognized in Canada & throughout the world for its unique contribution to the collection, research, exhibition, & interpretation of the plant world & for the development of public understanding & appreciation of the relationship between the plant world, humanity, & the rest of nature; *Member of:* American Association of Botanical Gardens; Archives Association of Ontario; Canadian Museum Association; Museum Trustee Association
Chief Officer(s):
Mark C. Runciman, CEO
mrunciman@rbg.ca
Finances: *Annual Operating Budget:* Greater than $5 Million; *Funding Sources:* Ministry of Citizenship, Culture & Recreation
Staff: 37 staff member(s); 400 volunteer(s)
Membership: 7,500; *Fees:* $50 single; $70 dual; $25 youth; $750+ corporate
Activities: Over 150 programs a year for all ages including gardening, plant care, art, cooking, environmental awareness & wildlife; over 30 public festivals/events; RBG is open year-round & receives approx. 500,000 visitors annually; 5 garden areas: Arboretum, Laking Garden, Rock Garden, Hendrie Park, Mediterannean Greenhouse; *Speaker Service:* Yes

The Royal Canadian Geographical Society (RCGS) / La Société géographique royale du Canada

#200, 1155 Lola St., Ottawa ON K1K 4C1
Tel: 613-745-4629; *Fax:* 613-744-0947
Toll-Free: 800-267-0824
e-mail: rcgs@rcgs.org
www.rcgs.org
www.facebook.com/theRCGS
Overview: A large national organization founded in 1929
Mission: To impart a broader knowledge of Canada, including its environmental, economic, & social challenges, as well as it natural & cultural heritage
Chief Officer(s):
John Geiger, President
Beth Dye, Secretary
André Préfontaine, Executive Director
Finances: *Funding Sources:* Membership fees; Donations
Activities: Presenting education programs through the education committee, The Canadian Council for Geographic Education; Conducting research; *Speaker Service:* Yes
Awards:
•The Massey Medal (Award)
Awarded annually for outstanding achievement in the exploration, development, or description of the geography of Canada
•The Gold Medal (Award)
To recognize an achievement of one or more individuals in the field of geography, or a significant national or international event
•Geographic Literacy Award (Award)
To honour the contributions of a Canadian geography educator
•Research Grants (Grant)
Amount: Up to $3000 for individuals; Up to $5000 for groups
•The Martin Bergmann Medal (Award)
To recognizes achievement for "excellence in Arctic leadership and science."
Meetings/Conferences:
For more information see Trade Shows, Conferences and Seminars Chapter
The Royal Canadian Geographical Society 2013 Annual General Meeting & Annual Dinner of the College of Fellows
2013
Publications:
•Canadian Geographic
Type: Magazine; *Frequency:* Bimonthly; *ISSN:* 1182-3895
Profile: Subscription includes 4 issues of Canadian Geographic Travel
•géographica
Type: Magazine
Profile: The Royal Canadian Geographical Society's French publication
•Royal Canadian Geoographical Society Annual Report
Type: Yearbook; *Frequency:* Annually
Profile: Featuring the Society's audited financial statements

Royal City Field Naturalists

#903, 1219 Harwood St., Vancouver BC V6E 1S5
Tel: 604-609-0679
Overview: A small local organization
Mission: To promote the enjoyment of nature through environmental appreciation & conservation; to encourage wise use & conservation of natural resources & environmental protection; *Member of:* Federation of BC Naturalists
Chief Officer(s):
Gareth Llewellyn, Contact
gllew@telus.net
Membership: 12; *Fees:* $25

The Royal Society of Canada (RSC) / La Société royale du Canada

170 Waller St., Ottawa ON K1N 9B9
Tel: 613-991-6990; *Fax:* 613-991-6996
www.rsc.ca
Also Known As: Canadian Academy of the Sciences & Humanities
Overview: A medium-sized national charitable organization founded in 1882
Mission: To promote learning & research in the arts, humanities & sciences in Canada; in its role as a National Academy, to draw on the breadth of knowledge & expertise of its members to recognize & honour distinguished accomplishments; to advise on the state of scholarship & culture across Canada; to inform the public on noteworthy social, scientific & ethical questions of the day; it is organized into three academies covering the arts & humanities, the social sciences, & the natural & applied sciences
Environmental Activity: RSC established Canadian Global Change Program (CGCP) to ensure that global change research in Canada is cohesive, comprehensive & responsive to national needs & international initiatives; areas of attention include the Arctic, & critical zones
Chief Officer(s):
Darren Gilmour, Executive Director
Finances: *Funding Sources:* Membership dues; endowments; government; corporate
Staff: 5 staff member(s)
Membership: 2000 fellows; *Member Profile:* Fellows are elected by their peers on the basis of distinction in their field; *Committees:* Promotion of Women in Scholarship; Freedom of Scholarship
Activities: ; *Library:* Open to public
Awards:
•Miroslaw Romanowski Medal (Award)
Established in 1994; awarded every year in recognition of significant contributions to the resolution of scientific aspects of environmental problems or for important improvements to the quality of an eco-system in all aspects, terrestrial, atmospheric & aqueous brought about by scientific means. *Amount:* $3,000 & a medal *Contact:* Geneviève Gouin, Coordinator, 613/991-5760
•Eadie Medal (Award)
Established 1975; awarded annually in recognition of major contributions to any field in engineering or applied science with preference given to those having an impact on communications. *Amount:* $3,000 & a bronze medal *Contact:* Geneviève Gouin, Coordinator, 613/991-5760
•Bancroft Award (Award)
Established 1968; awarded every two years for publication, instruction & research in the earth sciences that have conspicuously contributed to public understanding & appreciation of the subject *Amount:* $2,500 & a presentation scroll *Contact:* Geneviève Gouin, Coordinator, 613/991-5760
•Willet G. Miller Medal (Award)
Established 1943; awarded every two years for outstanding research in any branch of the earth sciences *Contact:* Geneviève Gouin, Coordinator, 613/991-5760

The Rubber Association of Canada (RAC) / Association canadienne de l'industrie du caoutchouc

Plaza 4, #250, 2000 Argentia Rd., Mississauga ON L5N 1W1
Tel: 905-814-1714; *Fax:* 905-814-1085
e-mail: info@rubberassociation.ca
www.rubberassociation.ca
www.linkedin.com/company/the-rubber-association-of-canada
twitter.com/GTRadials
Overview: A large national organization founded in 1920
Mission: To upgrade & maintain good industry/government working relations; to explore ways of improving industry competitiveness & efficiency; To promote safety in members' products, in their use & in the workplace; To promote expansion & profitability of Canadian rubber manufacturing units; To enhance standing of Canadian rubber industry worldwide; To provide members with industry marketing statistics
Environmental Activity: Environment Committee to monitor provincial regulations, with particular emphasis on hazardous wastes
Chief Officer(s):
Glenn Maidment, President
glenn@rubberassociation.ca
Ralph Warner, Director, Operations
ralph@rubberassociation.ca
Antonia Issa, Communications Manager
Finances: *Annual Operating Budget:* $250,000-$500,000; *Funding Sources:* Membership dues
Staff: 4 staff member(s)
Membership: 24 corporate; *Fees:* Based on volume of product; *Member Profile:* Manufacturers of products made from rubber; suppliers; importers; *Committees:* Customs & Tariffs; General Rubber Products; Human Resources; Occupational Health & Safety; Workers' Compensation; Environment; Tire Statistical; Tire Technical; Scrap Tire
Activities: *Speaker Service:* Yes
Meetings/Conferences:
For more information see Trade Shows, Conferences and Seminars Chapter
The Rubber Association of Canada, 2013 Tire and Rubber Summit
June 2013 Niagara Falls, ON

Rubber Manufacturers Association (RMA)

#900, 1400 K St. NW, Washington DC 20005 USA
Tel: 202-682-4800
e-mail: info@rma.org
www.rma.org
Previous Name: The Scrap Tire Management Council
Overview: A small national organization founded in 1990
Mission: To advocate on behalf of the rubber products industry
Environmental Activity: Supporting programs to clean up scrap tire stockpiles to eliminate environmental threats; Promoting training of fire service personnel to deal with scrap tire fires
Chief Officer(s):
Charles A. Cannon, President/CEO
Membership: *Member Profile:* Tire group companies include tire manufacturers & retread & repair material suppliers; Elastomer Products Group companies include manufacturers of non-tire elastomer products & suppliers of raw materials & machinery

Activities: Producing publications on consumer tire information, the market, industry standards, government affairs, safety, scrap tire activities, & tire service professionals; *Awareness Events:* National Tire Safety Week, June
Meetings/Conferences:
For more information see Trade Shows, Conferences and Seminars Chapter
Rubber Recycling 2014 Biennial Symposium
2014
Publications:
•Rubber Manufacturers Association Member Directory
Type: Directory
Profile: RMA member company contact & product information

Ruiter Valley Land Trust (RVLT) / Fiducie foncière Vallée de Ruiter
PO Box 462, Mansonville QC J0E 1X0
www.ruitervalley.org
Overview: A small local charitable organization founded in 1987
Mission: To acquire & protect forest land; Affiliation(s): Nature Conservancy of Canada
Chief Officer(s):
Stansje Plantenga, President
Finances: *Annual Operating Budget:* $50,000-$100,000
Membership: 300; *Fees:* $25 individual; $40 family; $100 patron
Activities: *Speaker Service:* Yes

Rural Advancement Foundation International *See* ETC Group

Rural Municipal Administrators' Association of Saskatchewan (RMAA)
PO Box 130, Wilcox SK S0G 5E0
Tel: 306-732-2030; *Fax:* 306-732-4495
e-mail: rmaa@sasktel.net
www.rmaa.ca
Previous Name: Rural Municipal Secretary-Treasurers' Association of Saskatchewan
Overview: A medium-sized provincial organization founded in 1955
Mission: To address the needs of rural administrators in Saskatchewan; Affiliation(s): Saskatchewan Association of Rural Municipalities
Chief Officer(s):
Kevin Ritchie, Executive Director
rm129@sasktel.net
Don McCallum, President
rm439@sasktel.net
Tim Leurer, Vice-President
rm366@sasktel.net
Finances: *Funding Sources:* Membership fees; Sponsorships
Membership: *Member Profile:* Practising rural municipal administrators, assistant administrators, secretary-treasurers & assistant secretary-treasurers in Saskatchewan; Associate members include non-practising rural municipal administrators & secretary-treasurers; Honorary life members; *Committees:* Forms & Computer Programs; Curling; Salary Negotiations; Local Government Administration Program; Seminars / Workshops / Guest Speakers; Board of Examiners; Disciplinary; Municipal Employees' Pension Plan; Golfing; Executive & Finance; Wine & Cheese Reception; Convention Sponsors / Door Prizes; Rural Advisory to SAMA; Professional Development; Enhanced Benefits; Resolutions; Humanitarian Services; Board of Reference; Council Mediation; Career Promotion; RMAA Home Page; Workshop; Ex-Officio to S.A.R.M.
Activities: Coordinating the certification of rural municipal administrator in Saskatchewan; Providing professional development activities; Carrying out disciplinary measures regarding professional practice

Rural Municipal Secretary-Treasurers' Association of Saskatchewan *See* Rural Municipal Administrators' Association of Saskatchewan

Ruth's Daughters of Canada
71 Elm Grove Ave., Toronto ON M6K 2J2
Tel: 416-599-7937
www.ruthsdaughters.com
Also Known As: Daughters of Ruth
Overview: A small national organization
Mission: The Association offers support to women who are victims of domestic violence. Its chapters center around prayer, friendship & outreach, & also develops action plans to prevent violence against women.
Chief Officer(s):
Cheri DiNovo, Contact
Membership: *Member Profile:* Women of faith attending mosque, synagogue, church or temple
Activities: Annual national gathering

Safe Workplace Promotion Services Ontario *See* Workplace Safety & Prevention Services

Safety Services Manitoba (SSM)
#3, 1680 Notre Dame Ave., Winnipeg MB R3H 1H6
Tel: 204-949-1085; *Fax:* 204-949-2897
Toll-Free: 800-661-3321
e-mail: registrar@safetyservicesmanitoba.ca
www.safetyservicesmanitoba.ca
ca.linkedin.com/in/gotosafetyservicesmanitoba
www.facebook.com/SafetyServicesManitoba
twitter.com/SafetyServMB
Previous Name: Manitoba Safety Council
Overview: A medium-sized provincial licensing charitable organization founded in 1920
Mission: To prevent accidental injury or occupational illness in Manitoba by providing effective safety & health programs.
Chief Officer(s):
Judy Murphy, President & CEO
Finances: *Funding Sources:* Membership & course fees; fundraising
Staff: 10 staff member(s)
Membership: *Fees:* $500 partner; $750 leader; *Committees:* Executive; Motorcycle; Seat Belt; Operation Lifesaver; Road Safety Conference; OHS Conference
Activities: *Awareness Events:* Conference & AGM; Annual Golf Classic; Operation Red Nose
Meetings/Conferences:
For more information see Trade Shows, Conferences and Seminars Chapter
Safety Services Manitoba SAFE Work Conference 2014
January 2014 Winnipeg, MB

Safety Services New Brunswick (SSNB) / Services de Sécurité Nouveau-Brunswick
#204, 440 Wilsey Rd., Fredericton NB E3B 7G5
Tel: 506-458-8034; *Fax:* 506-444-0177
Toll-Free: 877-762-7233
e-mail: info@safetyservicesnb.ca
www.safetyservicesnb.ca
Previous Name: New Brunswick Safety Council Inc.
Overview: A small provincial charitable organization founded in 1967
Mission: To promote traffic, occupational & public safety issues & practices through safety training courses & programs, educational material, public information, safety campaigns & conferences.; *Member of:* National Safety Council; Affiliation(s): Canada Safety Council
Chief Officer(s):
Bill Walker, President & CEO, 506-444-0171
bill@safetyservicesnb.ca
Jim Arsenault, Director of OSH & Traffic Training, 506-444-0178
jim@safetyservicesnb.ca
Finances: *Annual Operating Budget:* $250,000-$500,000; *Funding Sources:* Safety training & workshop fees; membership fees; donations; grants
Staff: 8 staff member(s); 50 volunteer(s)
Membership: 200; *Fees:* Schedule available; *Committees:* Financial; Operation Lifesaver
Activities: *Speaker Service:* Yes

Safety Services Newfoundland and Labrador
1076 Topsail Rd., Mount Pearl NL A1N 5E7
Tel: 709-754-0210; *Fax:* 709-754-0010
e-mail: info@safetyservicesnl.ca
safetyservicesnl.ca
www.facebook.com/303428916390762
twitter.com/SafetyNL
Previous Name: Newfoundland & Labrador Safety Council
Overview: A medium-sized provincial organization
Mission: Safety Services Newfoundland Labrador is dedicated to the prevention of injuries and fatalities; represents all the major sectors of the province's industry, business, government departments, volunteer organizations and many individuals who have a personal interest in safety, both on and off the job.; Affiliation(s): Canada Safety Council

Safety Services Nova Scotia (SSNS)
Vantage Point 3, #3F, 110 Chain Lake Dr., Halifax NS B3S 1A9
Tel: 902-454-9621; *Fax:* 902-454-6027
www.safetyservicesns.com
Previous Name: Nova Scotia Safety Council; The Nova Scotia Highway Safety Council
Overview: A small provincial organization founded in 1958
Mission: The Safety Council develops & provides quality safety & health services, education & training programs to improve the quality of life of Nova Scotians.; Affiliation(s): Canada Safety Council
Chief Officer(s):
Jackie Norman, Executive Director, 902-454-9621 Ext. 223
norman@safetyservicesns.ca
Finances: *Funding Sources:* Membership; Courses; Provincial government
Membership: *Fees:* $250 associate; $500 corporate; *Member Profile:* Members include Nova Scotian businesses, government departments, charitable agencies, families, & hospital & police services.
Activities: Informing members of injury trends, new legislation, or anything that may affect the health & safety of members, their coworkers, family, & friends; *Library:*
Publications:
•Safety Lines
Type: Newsletter; *Frequency:* Quarterly

Saint John Naturalists' Club
PO Box 2071, Saint John NB E2L 3T5
saintjohnnaturalistsclub.org
Also Known As: sjnc
Overview: A small local organization founded in 1962
Affiliation(s): NatureNB (The New Brunswick Federation of Naturalists)
Chief Officer(s):
Charles Graves, President
president_at_saintjohnnaturalistsclub.org
Jan Riddell, Vice-President
Jeanne Finn-Allen, Secretary
Don MacPhail, Treasurer
Membership: *Fees:* $20 individuals; $25 families; *Member Profile:* Individuals interested in the conservation, study, & enjoyment of nature in New Brunswick; *Committees:* Program; Social; Greenlaw Mountain Hawk Watch (GMHW); Point Lepreau Bird Observatory (PLBO)
Activities: Hosting monthly meeting at the New Brunswick Museum; Planning field trips; Administering the Point Lepreau Bird Observatory project
Publications:
•Saint John Naturalists' Club Bulletin
Type: Newsletter
Profile: Information assembled by a different editor for each issue

Saint John SPCA Animal Rescue
295 Bayside Dr., Saint John NB E2J 1B1
Tel: 506-642-0920; *Fax:* 506-634-6101
www.spcaanimalrescue.com
www.facebook.com/Saint.John.SPCA.Animal.Rescue
twitter.com/SPCAAR
Overview: A small local charitable organization founded in 1913
Mission: To provide rescue, care, & temporary shelter to stray & unwanted animals in the Saint John area
Chief Officer(s):
Janet Foster, Executive Director
arlexec@nb.aibn.com
Melody McElman, President
Meredith Herny, Vice-President
Kevin Hoyt, Treasurer
Finances: *Funding Sources:* Donations; Fundraising; Sponsorships; Membership fees; Services
Membership: *Fees:* $25
Activities: Finding homes for animals; Educating residents of Saint John about humane treatment of animals, including information sessions at local schools; Providing humane euthanasia at owners' request; Conducting a seniors' program; Offering public tours; *Awareness Events:* Pets in the Park, including the Annual Dog Jog, July; "No Fleas" Flea Market; Be Kind To Animals Week, May
Publications:
•ARL [Animal Rescue League] Shelter Speak
Type: Newsletter; *Frequency:* 3-4 pa; *Price:* Free with League membership
Profile: Fundraising & donation updates & League information

St. John's Clean & Beautiful (SJCAB)
PO Box 908, 10 New Gower St., St. John's NL A1C 5M2
Tel: 709-570-0350; *Fax:* 709-754-3100
e-mail: sjcab@cleanandbeautiful.nf.ca
www.cleanandbeautiful.nf.ca
Overview: A small local organization founded in 1992

Mission: To inspire community pride & action in St. John's to lead to a clean community; Affiliation(s): Keep America Beautiful, Inc. (KAB)
Chief Officer(s):
Michelle Eagles, Chair
Activities: Increasing public awareness in the city's cleanliness; Encouraging community involvment; Promoting partnerships; Coordinating efforts for litter reduction; Planning beautification projects; Publishing brochures, such as the Litter Free Event Guide, the Graffiti Removal Guide, Are You Running a Dirty Business? & Beautiful Gardens & A Healthy Environment

St. John's Harbour ACAP ***See*** Northeast Avalon ACAP, Inc.

St. Lawrence Economic Development Council ***Voir*** Société de développement économique du Saint-Laurent

St Mary's River Association (SMRA)
PO Box 179, Sherbrooke NS B0J 3C0
Tel: 902-522-2099; *Fax:* 902-522-2241
e-mail: stmarysriver@ns.sympatico.ca
stmarysriverassociation.com
Overview: A small local charitable organization founded in 1979
Mission: To further in all ways possible the conservation, protection, propagation & perpetuation of the fishery in the St Mary's River & its tributaries in eastern Nova Scotia; to support & assist the efforts of the federal Department of Fisheries, the provincial Department of Fisheries, other government bodies & voluntary associations in any program to conserve & improve the fishery; to impress upon all concerned that the fresh & salt water fishery must be developed, harvested & protected in a spirit of cooperation, with each being dependent on the other for survival & each recognizing the need for conservation measures in this area; to work with the federal, provincial & municipal governments & the private sector in undertaking capital works programs which will enhance the fishery in the St Mary's River & tributaries; *Member of:* Atlantic Salmon Federation; Nova Scotia Salmon Association
Chief Officer(s):
Dale Archibald, President
Finances: *Annual Operating Budget:* $50,000-$100,000; *Funding Sources:* Private donations; industry donations; fundraising activities
Staff: 1 staff member(s)
Membership: 273; *Fees:* $20 regular; $50 contributing; $200 corporate; $5 junior; $500 gold; $300 silver; $100 bronze; *Member Profile:* Anglers; conservationists; business; *Committees:* Newsletter; Membership; River Projects; Fundraising; Interpretive Centre
Activities: River habitat improvement; operation of interpretive centre; fundraising; newsletter; community events; *Library:*

Salmon Arm Bay Nature Enhancement Society (SABNES)
PO Box 27, Salmon Arm BC V1E 4N2
Tel: 250-833-9717
www.sabnes.org
Overview: A small local organization founded in 1986
Mission: To assist the Wildlife Branch of the provincial government with the development & operation of their management plan for the Salmon Arm foreshore as a Nature Conservancy & viewing area; To develop, operate & promote a system of walkways, viewing areas & interpretive facilities for scientific, educational, environmental protection & public viewing purposes; & to promote environmental awareness & assist in projects meeting that goal in the Salmon Arm area.
Chief Officer(s):
Mike Saul, Treasurer
Finances: *Funding Sources:* Corporate sponsorship; Membership dues
Membership: *Fees:* $10 individual; $20 family; $50 sustaining individual; $100 sustaining family; $500 life membership; $50-2500 corporate membership

Salmon Preservation Association for the Waters of Newfoundland (SPAWN)
93 West St., Corner Brook NL A2H 2Y6
Tel: 709-634-3012; *Fax:* 709-634-4091
Toll-Free: 866-634-3012
e-mail: spawn@nf.aibn.com
www.spawn1.ca
Overview: A small local charitable organization founded in 1979
Member of: Salmonid Council of Newfoundland & Labrador; Affiliation(s): Atlantic Salmon Federation
Chief Officer(s):
John McCarthy, President
Finances: *Annual Operating Budget:* $50,000-$100,000; *Funding Sources:* Auctions
Staff: 1 staff member(s); 300 volunteer(s)
Membership: 300; *Fees:* $20 Canadian member; US$20 American member; US$25 outside North America; *Member Profile:* Conservationists; *Committees:* Enhancement; Enforcement; Habitat; Dinner/Auction; Magazine
Activities: Conservation projects; data collection; *Library:* by appointment

Salt Institute
Fairfax Plaza, #600, 700 North Fairfax St., Alexandria VA 22314-2040 USA
Tel: 703-549-4648; *Fax:* 703-548-2194
e-mail: info@saltinstitute.org
www.saltinstitute.org
Overview: A medium-sized national organization founded in 1914
Mission: The Institute advocates responsible salt use, enabling improved quality of water, healthy nutrition, & safe roadways.; Affiliation(s): Transportation Association of Canada
Chief Officer(s):
Lori Roman, President
lori@saltinstitute.org
Tammy Goodwin, Administrative Director
tammy@saltinstitute.org
Finances: *Annual Operating Budget:* $500,000-$1.5 Million; *Funding Sources:* Membership dues
Staff: 4 staff member(s)
Membership: 6 regular + 31 associate; *Fees:* Based on salt sales by company; *Member Profile:* Manufacturers, producers & sellers of sodium chloride; *Committees:* Highway; Safety & Environment
Activities: *Speaker Service:* Yes; *Library:* Open to public

Ottawa Office
Ottawa ON
Tel: 613-564-0534

Sarnia-Lambton Environmental Association
#111, 265 Front St. North, Sarnia ON N7T 7X1
Tel: 519-332-2010; *Fax:* 519-332-2015
www.sarniaenvironment.com
Previous Name: Lambton Industrial Society: An Environmental Co-operative
Overview: A small local organization founded in 1952
Mission: To be recognized by members, regulatory agencies & the community for excellence in promoting & fostering a healthy environment consistent with sustainable development
Chief Officer(s):
Dean Edwardson, General Manager
Finances: *Annual Operating Budget:* $500,000-$1.5 Million
Staff: 3 staff member(s); 50 volunteer(s)
Membership: 14 corporate + 2 associate; *Fees:* Variable; *Member Profile:* Industrial facilities operating in Lambton County; *Committees:* Technical; Air; Land; Water; Public Affairs
Activities: Environmental research; monitoring regional air & water quality; *Awareness Events:* EnviroFest, May; *Speaker Service:* Yes; *Library:* Open to public

Sarnia-Lambton Environmental Association (SLEA)
1489 London Rd., Sarnia ON N7S 1P6
Tel: 519-332-2010; *Fax:* 519-332-2015
www.sarniaenvironment.com
Overview: A small local organization founded in 1952
Mission: To monitor ambient environmental conditions to assess the impact of its members on the local environment's air, water and soil.
Chief Officer(s):
Dean Edwardson, General Manager
Membership: 20

Saskatchewan Anti-Tuberculosis League ***See*** Saskatchewan Lung Association

Saskatchewan Applied Science Technologists & Technicians (SASTT)
Parent Name: Canadian Council of Technicians & Technologists
363 Park St., Regina SK S4N 5B2
Tel: 306-721-6633; *Fax:* 306-721-0112
e-mail: info@sastt.ca
www.sastt.ca
Previous Name: Society of Engineering Technicians & Technologists of Saskatchewan (SETTS)
Overview: A medium-sized provincial licensing organization founded in 1965 overseen by Canadian Council of Technicians & Technologists
Mission: To regulate the professional conduct of applied science technologists & certified technicians in Saskatchewan, in order to protect the public
Chief Officer(s):
Jaime Britz, Executive Director & Registrar
Steve Oszust, President
Edward Worrall, 1st Vice-President
Kelly Ljunggren, 2nd Vice-President
Finances: *Funding Sources:* Membership fees
Membership: *Member Profile:* Individuals who have a recognized level of post-secondary academic & practical training in a specialized applied science or engineering technology field in Saskatchewan
Activities: Increasing the knowledge of applied science technologists & certified technicians; Raising awareness & understanding of applied science technologists & certified technicians; *Awareness Events:* Technology Week, November
Publications:
•Saskatchewan Applied Science Technologists & Technicians Salary Survey
Type: Survey; *Frequency:* Annually
Profile: Information distributed to all Saskatchewan Applied Science Technologists & Technicians members
•SASTT [Saskatchewan Applied Science Technologists & Technicians] Journal
Type: Journal; *Frequency:* Quarterly; *Accepts Advertising*
Profile: Technical articles, association news, & upcoming events

Saskatchewan Association of Agricultural Societies & Exhibitions (SAASE)
PO Box 31025, Regina SK S4R 8R6
Tel: 306-565-2121; *Fax:* 306-565-2079
e-mail: gduck.saase@sasktel.net
www.saase.ca
Overview: A medium-sized provincial organization founded in 1987
Mission: To provide the forum for exchange of ideas among Association members; to provide educational opportunities for members; to address relevant issues affecting members; to provide for district, board & provincial meetings of members; to promote fair & agricultural industry; to help promote & form new societies; to provide a liaison with the extension program of University of Saskatchewan; to assist governments & universities to reach their agricultural & educational objectives; *Member of:* Foundation for Animal Care Saskatchewan; International Association of Fairs & Exhibitions; Agriculture in the Classroom; Affiliation(s): Canadian Association of Fairs & Exhibitions
Chief Officer(s):
Glen Duck, Executive Director
Finances: *Annual Operating Budget:* $250,000-$500,000
Staff: 1 staff member(s)
Membership: 74 organizations

Saskatchewan Association of Landscape Architects (SALA)
#200, 642 Broadway Ave., Saskatoon SK S7N 1A9
www.sala.sk.ca
Overview: A small provincial organization founded in 1980
Mission: To promote, improve, & advance the profession of landscape architecture; To maintain standards of professional practice & conduct; *Member of:* Canadian Society of Landscape Architects
Chief Officer(s):
Trevor Tumach, President
trevor.tumach@aecom.ca
Membership: *Fees:* $430 full; $259.90 out-of-province; $100 associate and allied; $20 student; *Member Profile:* Landscape architects in Saskatchewan

Saskatchewan Association of Rural Municipalities (SARM)
2075 Hamilton St., Regina SK S4P 2E1
Tel: 306-757-3577; *Fax:* 306-565-2141
Toll-Free: 800-667-3604
e-mail: sarm@sarm.ca
www.sarm.ca
Overview: A medium-sized provincial organization founded in 1905
Mission: To represent & advocate for rural municipal government in Saskatchewan
Chief Officer(s):

Dale Harvey, Executive Director, 306-761-3721
dharvey@sarm.ca
David Marit, President
dmarit@sasktel.net
Membership: 296; *Member Profile:* Rural municipalities in Saskatchewan
Activities: Researching policies; Reviewing legislation; Providing employee benefits, municipal insurance, & fuel supply programs
Meetings/Conferences:
For more information see Trade Shows, Conferences and Seminars Chapter
Saskatchewan Association of Rural Municipalities 2013 Annual Convention
March 2013 Saskatoon, SK
Saskatchewan Association of Rural Municipalities 2013 Midterm Convention
November 2013 Regina, SK
Publications:
•Rural Councillor
Type: Magazine; *Frequency:* Bimonthly; *Accepts Advertising*
Profile: Issues facing rural Saskatchewan

Saskatchewan Camping Association (SCA)
Parent Name: Canadian Camping Association

3950 Castle Rd., Regina SK S4S 6A4
Tel: 306-586-4026; *Fax:* 306-790-8634
e-mail: info@saskcamping.ca
www.saskcamping.ca
Overview: A medium-sized provincial organization founded in 1974 overseen by Canadian Camping Association
Mission: To promote the development of quality organized camping in Saskatchewan; To act as the voice for leaders of organized camps throughout Saskatchewan
Environmental Activity: Partnering with the Canadian Camping Association & the Charitree foundation to provide trees for camps; Encouraging responsible use of the natural environment & its resources by campers
Chief Officer(s):
Donna Wilkinson, Executive Director, 306-586-4026
donnaw@sasktel.net
Finances: *Funding Sources:* Sask Lotteries Trust Fund
Membership: *Member Profile:* Camps in Saskatchewan
Activities: Engaging in advocacy activities; Facilitating the sharing of ideas among camp leaders; Providing education for camp leaders
Meetings/Conferences:
For more information see Trade Shows, Conferences and Seminars Chapter
Saskatchewan Camping Association 2013 Education Day
2013, SK
Saskatchewan Camping Association 2013 Annual General Meeting
April 2013 Saskatoon, SK
Saskatchewan Camping Association 2014 Annual General Meeting
2014, SK
Publications:
•Saskatchewan Directory of Camps
Type: Directory
Profile: Listings of camps that are members of the Saskatchewan Camping Association
•SCAN: The Saskatchewan Camping Association Newsletter
Type: Newsletter; *Accepts Advertising*; *Price:* Free with Saskatchewan Camping Association membership
Profile: News, issues, & articles of interest to the camping community of Saskatchewan

Saskatchewan Construction Safety Association Inc. (SCSA)

498 Henderson Dr., Regina SK S4N 6E3
Tel: 306-525-0175; *Fax:* 306-525-1542
Toll-Free: 800-817-2079
www.scsaonline.ca
Overview: A medium-sized provincial organization founded in 1995
Mission: To provide safety programs & servies to construction employers & employees in order to reduce human & financial loss associated with injuries in the construction industry
Chief Officer(s):
Bill Johnson, Executive Director
billj@scsaonline.ca
Dan Sherven, Manager, Operations
dans@scsaonline.ca
Kellie Lefebvre, Coordinator, Human Resources & Finance
kelliel@scsaonline.ca
Linda Rea-Rosseker, Coordinator, Publications & Communications
lindar@scsaonline.ca
Membership: *Fees:* $750 Supporter member; *Member Profile:* Saskatchewan companies with an active Workers' Compensation Board account within the construction rate group; Supporter members with accounts outside the construction rate group
Publications:
•Safety Advocate Newsletter
Type: Newsletter

Saskatchewan Eco-Network (SEN)
Parent Name: Canadian Environmental Network

#203, 115 - 2 Ave. North, Saskatoon SK S7K 2B1
Tel: 306-652-1275; *Fax:* 306-665-2128
e-mail: sen@link.ca
www.econet.sk.ca
Overview: A small provincial organization founded in 1980 overseen by Canadian Environmental Network
Mission: To provide educational activities to develop an awareness of conservation & enhancement of the environment; Affiliation(s): Canadian Environmental Network
Environmental Activity: Offering news & information on topics such as pesticides, global warming, endangered species, mining, water, organic agriculture, & The Great Sand Hills
Chief Officer(s):
Mike Finley, Chair
Lynn Hainsworth, Executive Director
Paddy Tutty, Administrator
Membership: *Member Profile:* Non-profit, non-governmental organizations in Saskatchewan concerned with environmental issues; *Committees:* Forests Working Group; Energy Working Group; Wilderness Protection Working Group; Biotechnology Working Group; Pesticides Working Group; Water Working Group
Activities: Promoting networking opportunities for members; Providing referrals for members, media, government personnel, & the public
Publications:
•Saskatchewan's Green Directory
Type: Directory
Profile: A project of the Saskatchewan Eco-Network, with assistance from the Saskatchewan Research Council & the Ministry of Environment, the directory presents information about green products forconsumers.
•SEN [Saskatchewan Eco-Network] Bulletin
Type: Newsletter; *Frequency:* Biweekly; *Price:* Free
Profile: News & events from across Saskatchewan

Saskatchewan Environmental Industry & Managers' Association (SEIMA)

2341 McIntyre St., Regina SK S4P 2s3
Tel: 306-543-1567; *Fax:* 306-543-1568
e-mail: info@seima.sk.ca
www.seima.sk.ca
www.facebook.com/group.php?gid=111586162187848
Previous Name: Saskatchewan Environmental Managers Association
Overview: A medium-sized provincial organization founded in 1994
Mission: To act as the voice of practitioners in Saskatchewan's environmental industry on environmental matters; To promote responsible environmental management in the province; To develop the environmental industry in Saskatchewan
Chief Officer(s):
Kathleen Livingston, Executive Director & COO
finnigan@westernheritage.ca
Jim Finnigan, President
finnigan@westernheritage.ca
Lawrence Pinter, Vice-President
lpinter@pinter.ca
Glen J. Weisbrod, Treasurer
glen.weisbrod@snclavalin.com
Cheryl Hender, Secretary
chender@innovationplace.com
Membership: 175; *Fees:* $25 students; Schedule, based upon number of employees for corporate & associate members; *Member Profile:* Environmental managers from various industries in Saskatchewan, such as agriculture, mining, & forestry; Companies in Saskatchewan's environmental industry; Suppliers to Saskatchewan's environmental industry; Students; Researchers; Consultants; Public policy developers
Activities: Engaging in advocacy activities; Liaising with governments; Providing access to current industry intelligence, such as environmental legislation & regulations, & potential opportunities; Offering professional development activities for Saskatchewan's environmental businesses & managers, such as seminars & conferences; Facilitating networking opportunities with industry colleagues, for the exchange of information & ideas; Presenting an Aboriginal Youth Career Fair; Conferences & trade shows; *Speaker Service:* Yes; *Library:*
Publications:
•Saskatchewan Environmental Industry & Managers' Association Member Directory & Buyer's Guide
Type: Directory; *Frequency:* Annually; *Price:* Free with membership in Saskatchewan Environmental Industry & Managers' Association
Profile: Information about Saskatchewan Environmental Industry & Managers' Association member businesses & their areas ofspecialization, to provide marketing support for its users throughout North American & Europe
•Saskatchewan Environmental Industry & Managers' Association Newsletter
Type: Nesletter

Saskatchewan Environmental Managers Association ***See*** Saskatchewan Environmental Industry & Managers' Association

Saskatchewan Environmental Society (SES)

PO Box 1372, #203, 115 - 2nd Ave. North, Saskatoon SK S7K 3N9
Tel: 306-665-1915; *Fax:* 306-665-2128
e-mail: info@environmentalsociety.ca
www.environmentalsociety.ca
Overview: A medium-sized provincial charitable organization founded in 1970
Mission: The Society works to maintain the integrity of Saskatchewan's forests, farmlands and natural prairie landscapes; protect the atmosphere, and promote energy conservation and the development of renewable energy resources; and build sustainable communities, responsible waste management, and enhanced water quality in the province's lakes and rivers.; *Member of:* Canadian Renewable Energy Alliance
Environmental Activity: Monitoring environmental issues; participating in multi-stakeholder task groups & environmental assessment processes; providing information services & educational material on environmental issues, such as books, videos, & teaching manuals
Chief Officer(s):
Allyson Brady, Executive Director
allysonb@environmentalsociety.ca
Peter Prebble, Director, Energy & Water Policy
prebble@sasktel.net
Jen Antony, Coordinator, Retire Your Ride
ryr@environmentalsociety.ca
Angie Bugg, Coordinator, Energy Conservation
angieb@environmentalsociety.ca
Greg Rooke, Coordinator, Pesticide Reduction
pesticidefree@environmentalsociety.ca
Alina Siegfried, Coordinator, Water Issues
water@environmentalsociety.ca
Finances: *Funding Sources:* Membership fees; Donations; Fundraising; Sponsorships
Membership: *Fees:* $20 / year; *Member Profile:* Persons concerned about the environment
Activities: Advocacy; policy development; educational projects; reports & fact sheets; *Speaker Service:* Yes; *Library:* Saskatchewan Environmental Society Resource Centre
Publications:
•Saskatchewan Environmental Society Newsletter
Type: Newsletter; *Frequency:* Bimonthly
Profile: Information about the society's involvement in environmental issues, plus upcoming events, for society members

Saskatchewan Forestry Association (SFA)
Parent Name: Canadian Forestry Association

#139, 1061 Central Ave., Prince Albert SK S6V 4V4
Tel: 306-763-2189; *Fax:* 306-763-6456
e-mail: info@whitebirch.ca
www.whitebirch.ca
Overview: A medium-sized provincial charitable organization founded in 1972 overseen by Canadian Forestry Association
Mission: To promote the wise use, protection, & management of forests, water, & wildlife in Saskatchewan; Affiliation(s): Canadian Forestry Association
Environmental Activity: Increasing public awareness of the management & protection of Saskatchewan's forests
Chief Officer(s):
Sindy Nicholson, President

Finances: *Funding Sources:* Membership fees; Donations; Sponsorships; Fundraising
Membership: *Fees:* Schedule available for corporations, based upon size; $15 students; $25 individuals; $35 families; *Member Profile:* Individuals, families, groups, & corporations who care about the future of Saskatchewan's forest resources
Activities: Delivering forest education materials & programming to schools & the public; Managing interpretive trails
Meetings/Conferences:
For more information see Trade Shows, Conferences and Seminars Chapter
Saskatchewan Forestry Association 2013 Annual General Meeting
2013, SK
Publications:
•TreeLines [a publication of the Saskatchewan Forestry Association]
Type: Newsletter; *Frequency:* Quarterly; *Editor:* Andrea Atkinson; *Price:* Free with membershipin the Saskatchewan Forestry Association
Profile: Information about association activities & forestry industry issues, as well as a "Teacher's Corner" for educators

Saskatchewan Ground Water Association (SGWA)
Parent Name: Canadian Ground Water Association
PO Box 9434, Saskatoon SK S7K 7E9
Tel: 306-244-7551; *Fax:* 306-343-0001
teksmarts.com/skgwa/home.html
Previous Name: Saskatchewan Water Well Association
Overview: A small provincial organization overseen by Canadian Ground Water Association
Mission: To act as the voice of the ground water industy throughout Saskatchewan; To promote the management of ground water throughout the province
Chief Officer(s):
Kathleen Watson, Contact
Activities: Providing education about ground water

Saskatchewan Herb & Spice Association
PO Box 18, Phippen SK S0K 3E0
Tel: 306-694-4622; *Fax:* 306-644-2182
e-mail: shsa@sasktel.net
www.saskherbspice.org
Overview: A small provincial organization
Mission: To support research, development & promotion of crops & products from yesterday & tomorrow for producers to processors to retails today
Chief Officer(s):
Connie Kehler, Executive Director
Membership: 300; *Fees:* $65 regular; $220 corporate; $540 corporate sponsorship
Activities: Member networking; annual member directory; public awareness; ongoing research of production & market promotion;

Saskatchewan Katahdin Sheep Association Inc. (SKSA)
Parent Name: Canadian Katahdin Sheep Association Inc.
PO Box 548, Quill Lake SK S0A 3E0
Tel: 306-383-2861
www.saskkatahdinsheep.com
Overview: A small provincial organization founded in 1993 overseen by Canadian Katahdin Sheep Association Inc.
Mission: To develop & advance the Katahdin sheep breed in Saskatchewan
Chief Officer(s):
Jean L'Arrivee, President, 306-769-8981, Fax: 306-769-8916
landjlarrivee@sasktel.net
Janette Mish, Vice-President, 306-429-2221, Fax: 306-429-2221
jmish@sasktel.net
Donna Schryver, Secretary, 306-383-2861
schryvers@sasktel.net
Donna Bruynooghe, Treasurer, 306-937-2041
dbruynooghe@highways.gov.sk.ca
Membership: 1-99;; *Fees:* $10 junior members, age 15 & under; $25 senior members; *Member Profile:* Owners of Canadian registered Katahdin sheep in Saskatchewan; *Committees:* Show & Sale; New Producer Liaison
Activities: Distributing breed information; Preparing displays for various shows throughout the province; Creating networking opportunities with other sheep producers; Providing education, such as on-farm seminars & hands-on-training sessions; Showing sheep at events such as the Canadian Western Agribition
Publications:
•News for Ewes
Type: Newsletter; *Frequency:* Quarterly; *Accepts Advertising*; *Editor:* Janette Mish
•Saskatchewan Katahdin Sheep Association Membership Directory
Type: Directory; *Price:* Free

Saskatchewan Land Surveyors' Association (SLSA)
Parent Name: Professional Surveyors Canada
#230, 408 Broad St., Regina SK S4R 1X3
Tel: 306-352-8999; *Fax:* 306-352-8366
e-mail: info@slsa.sk.ca
www.slsa.sk.ca
Overview: A small provincial licensing organization founded in 1910 overseen by Professional Surveyors Canada
Mission: To uphold the stewardship & standards of the legal survey profession in Saskatchewan; To regulate & govern members in the practice of professional land surveying & professional surveying; To ensure the competency of members; To administer the profession to protect the public
Chief Officer(s):
D.L. Gurnsey, President
A. Carl Shiels, Executive Director & Registrar
execdir@slsa.sk.ca
Ron J. Eichel, Vice-President
Membership: *Member Profile:* Registered members of the association, who are licensed to practice as Saskatchewan land surveyors in Saskatchewan, in accordance with the provisions of the Land Surveyors & Professional Surveyors Act of Saskatchewan
Activities: Providing continuing education to licensed members; Investigating complaints from the public
Publications:
•SLSA [Saskatchewan Land Surveyors' Association] Corner Post
Type: Newsletter; *Frequency:* Quarterly; *Accepts Advertising*; *Editor:* Doug A. Bouck, SLS
Profile: Articles about surveying, in addition to regular features, such as the president's message & council highlights

Saskatchewan Livestock Association (SLA)
Canada Center Building, Evraz Place, PO Box 3771, Regina SK S4P 3N8
Tel: 306-757-6133; *Fax:* 306-525-5852
e-mail: sla@accesscomm.ca
www.sasklivestock.com
Overview: A medium-sized provincial organization founded in 1075
Mission: To promote cooperation among the livestock organizations in Saskatchewan; To communicate opinions of livestock producers to government & other agencies; To encourage improvement in the production of livestock
Chief Officer(s):
Murray Andrew, Executive Director
Belinda Wagner, General Manager
Meetings/Conferences:
For more information see Trade Shows, Conferences and Seminars Chapter
Saskatchewan Beef Industry 2013 4th Annual Conference: Harvesting the Future
January 2013 Saskatoon, SK

Saskatchewan Lung Association
Parent Name: Canadian Lung Association
1231 - 8 St. East, Saskatoon SK S7H 0S5
Tel: 306-343-9511; *Fax:* 306-343-7007
Toll-Free: 888-566-5864
e-mail: info@sk.lung.ca
www.sk.lung.ca
Previous Name: Saskatchewan Anti-Tuberculosis League
Overview: A medium-sized provincial charitable organization founded in 1911 overseen by Canadian Lung Association
Mission: To improve respiratory health & overall quality of life; To advocate for support of education & research
Chief Officer(s):
Frank Scott, Chair
Helen Cotton, Vice-Chair
Brian Graham, President & Chief Executive Officer
Jan Haffner, Vice-President, Health Initiatives
Sharon Kremeniuk, Vice-President, Development
Jennifer Miller, Vice-President, Health Education
Leah Sullivan, Vice-President, Finance & Operations
Pat Smith, Treasurer
Finances: *Funding Sources:* Donations; Sponsorships; Fundraising
Membership: *Fees:* $25
Activities: Supporting & conducting research into respiratory health & disease; Providing educational programs; Offering the most current lung health information; Organizing sleep apnea support groups; Promoting the prevention of lung disease; Raising public awareness of the impact of respiratory diseases; Collaborating with other organizations to work toward lung health; *Awareness Events:* Breath of Spring Tulip Campaign; Loonies for Lungs
Publications:
•Breathworks: COPD Newsletter
Type: Newsletter
Profile: Educational articles plus notices of forthcoming support group meetings
•Lung Association of Saskatchewan Annual Report
Type: Yearbook; *Frequency:* Annually
•Nightly Nezzz Newsletter
Type: Newsletter; *Frequency:* Quarterly
Profile: Information for persons with sleep apnea & their families

Saskatchewan Medical Association (SMA)
Parent Name: Canadian Medical Association
#402, 321A - 21st St. East, Saskatoon SK S7K 0C1
Tel: 306-244-2196; *Fax:* 306-653-1631
Toll-Free: 800-667-3781
e-mail: sma@sma.sk.ca
www.sma.sk.ca
Overview: A medium-sized provincial organization founded in 1906 overseen by Canadian Medical Association
Mission: To represent physicians in Saskatchewan; To advance the professional, educational, & economic welfare of physicians in the province
Chief Officer(s):
George Miller
Martin Vogel, Executive Director
Ed Hobday, Administrative Director
Phillip Fourie, Treasurer
Membership: *Member Profile:* Saskatchewan physicians; *Committees:* Rural & Regional Practice; Continuing Medical Education Fund Advisory; Specialist Recruitment & Retention Fund; Information Technology; Membership Services; Medical Benevolent Society; Sports
Activities: Engaging in advocacy activities; Promoting quality health care in Saskatchewan; Acting as the bargaining agent for fee-for-service physicians; Providing information about health care issues in Saskatchewan; Supporting continuing professional learning; Managing funds to offer programs such as bursaries & educational grants; Supporting physician health, through programs such as the Saskatchewan Physician Support Program
Publications:
•SMA [Saskatchewan Medical Association] News
Type: Newsletter
Profile: Association issues & events

Saskatchewan Mining Association (SMA)
Parent Name: Mining Association of Canada
#1500, 2002 Victoria Ave., Regina SK S4P 0R7
Tel: 306-757-9505; *Fax:* 306-569-1085
e-mail: saskmining@sasktel.net
www.saskmining.ca
Overview: A small provincial organization founded in 1965 overseen by Mining Association of Canada
Mission: To ensure the safe & profitable development of mineral resources in Saskatchewan; To act as the voice of the mining industry throughout the province; To promote understanding of the development of mineral resources in Saskatchewan
Environmental Activity: Coordinating programs on issues such as health, safety, & environmental impact; Promoting environmental stewardship & sustainability in Saskatchewan's mining industry
Chief Officer(s):
Kelvin Dereski, President, 306-745-4200, Fax: 306-745-2100
Pamela Schwann, Executive Director, 306-757-9505, Fax: 306-569-1085
David Neuburger, 1st Vice-President, 306-956-6200, Fax: 306-956-6201
Stewart Brown, 2nd Vice-President, 306-257-3312, Fax: 306-257-4240
Tracey Irwin, Manager, Communications & Membership, 306-757-9505, Fax: 306-569-1085
Finances: *Funding Sources:* Membership fees
Membership: *Committees:* Safety; Public Awareness; Human Resources; Taxation; Environmental; Geotechnical
Activities: Liaising with both provincial & federal governments; Organizing research into matters such as industrial relations;

Cooperating with similar organizations; *Awareness Events:* Saskatchewan Mining Week, May

Saskatchewan Nursery Landscape Association (SNLA)
Parent Name: Canadian Nursery Landscape Association

c/o Landscape Alberta Nursery Trades Association, #200, 10331 - 178 St., Edmonton AB T5S 1R5
Tel: 780-489-1991; *Fax:* 780-444-2152
Toll-Free: 866-383-4711
e-mail: rebecca@canadanursery.com
www.snla.ca
Previous Name: Saskatchewan Nursery Trades Association
Overview: A medium-sized provincial organization overseen by Canadian Nursery Landscape Association
Finances: *Annual Operating Budget:* Less than $50,000
Membership: 70; *Fees:* Schedule available

Saskatchewan Nursery Trades Association *See* Saskatchewan Nursery Landscape Association

Saskatchewan Outdoor & Environmental Education Association (SOEEA)

26 Corkery Bay, Regina SK S4T 7K6
e-mail: soeea.sk@gmail.com
www.soeea.sk.ca
Overview: A small provincial organization founded in 1972
Mission: To encourage educators & people who participate in outdoor education to teach & practise environmental responsibility; Affiliation(s): North American Association for Environmental Education
Environmental Activity: Funding community or school groups to carry out environmental action projects for recreational or educational purposes; Supporting environmental education; Encouraging outdoor & environmental skills & practices
Chief Officer(s):
Jol Siemens, President
memyselfandjo@yahoo.ca
Kyle Lichtenwald, Vice-President
thekyleguy@gmail.com
Karen McIver, Director, Programs
karen.mciver@gmail.com
Mark Wilson, Treasurer
mark.wilson@rbe.sk.ca
Membership: *Committees:* Communications Working Goup; Decision Makers Working Group; Education Working Group; Partners Working Group; Public & Families Working Group
Activities: Developing & evaluating education activities; Providing professional development workshops; Partnering with related organizations; Facilitating networking opportunities;
Awards:
•B.M. Melanson Award (Award)
To be presented periodically to an individual who has made an outstanding contribution to outdoor & environmental education in Saskatchewan; candidates shall be active participants in outdoor & environmental education in Saskatchewan; candidates need not be a member of SOEEA *Contact:* Yvette Crane
Publications:
•Envisage [a publication of the Saskatchewan Outdoor & Environmental Education Association]
Type: Newsletter; *Frequency:* Quarterly
Profile: Articles on topics such as educational strategies & instructional methods
•Green Teacher

Saskatchewan Parks & Recreation Association (SPRA)
Parent Name: Canadian Parks & Recreation Association

#100, 1445 Park St., Regina SK S4N 4C5
Tel: 306-780-9231; *Fax:* 306-780-9257
Toll-Free: 800-563-2555
e-mail: office@spra.sk.ca
www.spra.sk.ca
Overview: A medium-sized provincial charitable organization founded in 1962 overseen by Canadian Parks & Recreation Association
Mission: To stimulate & advance parks, recreation & leisure activities, facilities, & programs in Saskatchewan
Finances: *Funding Sources:* Lottery ticket sales
Membership: 600 organizations; *Fees:* Schedule available
Activities: *Speaker Service:* Yes; *Library:* Resource Centre for Sport, Culture & Recreation; Open to public
Meetings/Conferences:
For more information see Trade Shows, Conferences and Seminars Chapter
Saskatchewan Parks & Recreation Association 2013 Spring Education & Training Symposium
April 2013 Humboldt, SK
Saskatchewan Parks & Recreation Association 2013 Scott Irving Memorial Golf Classic
June 2013 North Battleford, SK
Saskatchewan Parks & Recreation Association 2013 Conference & Annual General Meeting
October 2013 Swift Current, SK
Saskatchewan Parks & Recreation Association 2014 Conference & Annual General Meeting
October 2014
Saskatchewan Parks & Recreation Association 2015 Conference & Annual General Meeting
October 2015
Publications:
•DIRECTION [a publication of the Saskatchewan Parks & Recreation Association]
Type: Newsletter; *Accepts Advertising*; *Price:* Free with membership in the Saskatchewan Parks &Recreation Association
Profile: A newsmagazine with news, articles, stories, & funding opportunities

Saskatchewan Public Health Association Inc.
Parent Name: Canadian Public Health Association

PO Box 845, Regina SK S4P 3B1
e-mail: terry.gibson@saskatoonhealthregion.ca
Overview: A small provincial organization overseen by Canadian Public Health Association
Mission: To constitute a resource in Saskatchewan for the improvement & maintenance of health
Chief Officer(s):
Saqib Shahab, President
saqib.shahab@shr.sk.ca
Membership: 4 institutional; 124 individual; 4 student

Saskatchewan Safety Council

445 Hoffer Dr., Regina SK S4N 6E2
Tel: 306-757-3197; *Fax:* 306-569-1907
e-mail: ssc@sasksafety.org
sasksafety.org
Overview: A small provincial organization founded in 1955
Chief Officer(s):
Harley P. Toupin, CEO
htoupin@sasksafety.org
Dianne Wolbaum, Director, Operations
dwolbaum@sasksafety.org
Membership: *Fees:* Based on size of workplace

Saskatchewan Soil Conservation Association (SSCA)

PO Box 1360, Indian Head SK S0G 2K0
Tel: 306-695-4233; *Fax:* 306-695-4236
Toll-Free: 800-213-4287
e-mail: info@ssca.ca
www.ssca.ca
Overview: A small provincial charitable organization founded in 1987
Mission: To improve the land & environment; To increase public awareness of soil conservation; To promote conservation production systems to Saskatchewan producers
Environmental Activity: Offering soil conservation education programs, such as Project SOILS, a joint project with Agriculture in the Classroom; Promoting the use of agriculture soil sinks as part of Canada's greenhouse gas management strategy
Chief Officer(s):
Tim Nerbas, President
tnerbas@ssca.ca
Marilyn Martens, Office Manager, 306-695-4233
Finances: *Funding Sources:* Donations; Federal-Provincial sustainable agriculture programs
Membership: 800; *Member Profile:* Farmers in Saskatchewan
Activities: Sharing soil conservation information
Meetings/Conferences:
For more information see Trade Shows, Conferences and Seminars Chapter
Saskatchewan Soil Conservation Association 2013 25th Annual Conservation Agriculture Conference
January 2013 Saskatoon, SK
Saskatchewan Soil Conservation Association 2014 26th Annual Conservation Agriculture Conference
2014, SK
Publications:
•Direct Seeding Manual
Type: Manual
Profile: Developed & published with the Prairie Agricultural Machinery Institute for Saskatchewan growers
•Prairie Soils & Crops eJournal
Type: Journal
Profile: Peer-reviewed information from the Saskatchewan Soil Conservation Association, Agriculture & Agri-Food Canada, & the University of Saskatchewan for prairie producers & agrologists
•Prairie Steward
Type: Newsletter; *Frequency:* 3 pa
Profile: Association news & technical articles for Saskatchewan Soil Conservation Association members

Saskatchewan Stock Growers Association (SSGA)

Main Floor, Canada Centre Building, Evraz Place, PO Box 4752, Regina SK S4P 3Y4
Tel: 306-757-8523; *Fax:* 306-569-8799
e-mail: ssga@sasktel.net
www.skstockgrowers.com
Overview: A medium-sized provincial organization founded in 1913
Mission: To serve, protect, & advance the interests of the beef industry in Saskatchewan; To represent the cattle industry in Saskatchewan on the legislative front; *Member of:* Canadian Cattlemen's Association; Affiliation(s): Saskatchewan Prairie Conservation Action Plan (SK PCAP) Partnership
Environmental Activity: Providing information about stewardship
Chief Officer(s):
Chad MacPherson, General Manager
Calvin Knoss, President, 306-476-2512
cknoss@xplornet.com
Finances: *Funding Sources:* Membership fees
Membership: *Fees:* $105 / 1 year; $194.25 / 2 years; $262.50 / 3 years; $1050 / lifetime; *Member Profile:* Active members are individuals engaged in livestock production in Saskatchewan; Affiliate members are groups that are engaged in livestock marketing; Associate members have an interest in the industry
Activities: Providing education; Engaging in research; Advocating on behalf of the beef industry
Publications:
•Beef Business
Type: Magazine; *Frequency:* Bimonthly; *Accepts Advertising*; *Editor:* Jim Warren; *Price:* Included with SSGA membership
Profile: Industry news, markets & trade, features, analysis & opinion, science & productions, association news & reports, & stewardship

Saskatchewan Trade & Export Partnership Inc. (STEP)

PO Box 1787, #320, 1801 Hamilton St., Regina SK S4P 3C6
Tel: 306-933-6551; *Fax:* 306-933-6556
Toll-Free: 888-976-7875
e-mail: inquire@sasktrade.com
www.sasktrade.com
Overview: A medium-sized provincial organization founded in 1996
Mission: To work in partnership with Saskatchewan exporters & emerging exporters to maximize commercial success in global ventures; To deliver custom export solutions & market intelligence to member companies; To coordinate international development projects
Chief Officer(s):
Lionel LaBelle, President & Chief Executive Officer, 306-787-1550
Angela Krauss, Executive Director, Export Services, 306-787-3972
Brad Michnik, Executive Director, Trade Development, 306-933-6555
Pam Bartoshewski, Controller, 306-787-7946
Finances: *Funding Sources:* Private & public funding
Membership: 426; *Member Profile:* Saskatchewan exporters & companies providing services to exporters
Activities: Providing market intelligence, international finance solutions, export education, & marketing services; *Library:* Open to public
Publications:
•STEP Global Newsletter
Type: Newsletter; *Frequency:* Quarterly

Saskatchewan Trucking Association (STA)
Parent Name: Canadian Trucking Alliance

1335 Wallace St., Regina SK S4N 3Z5
Tel: 306-569-9696; *Fax:* 306-569-1008
Toll-Free: 800-563-7623

e-mail: ttoope@sasktrucking.com
www.sasktrucking.com
Overview: A medium-sized provincial licensing organization founded in 1937 overseen by Canadian Trucking Alliance
Mission: Helps the industry fight its battles in everything from deregulation to weights and measures. Represents the industry in discussions with government
Chief Officer(s):
Al Rosseker, Executive Director
arosseker@sasktrucking.com
Finances: *Annual Operating Budget:* $250,000-$500,000; *Funding Sources:* Membership fees; sponsorship of programs
Staff: 5 staff member(s)
Membership: 300; *Fees:* Schedule available
Activities: Truck Driver Roadeos

Saskatchewan Urban Municipalities Association (SUMA)

#200, 2222 - 13th Ave., Regina SK S4P 3M7
Tel: 306-525-3727; *Fax:* 306-525-4373
e-mail: suma@suma.org
www.suma.org
Overview: A medium-sized provincial organization founded in 1906
Mission: To work to enhance urban life in Saskatchewan, by providing administrative & consultative services to members, a forum for the discussion & resolution of current issues, & a negotiating vehicle for improvements in legislation, financing & programs. SUMA provides information & training for aldermen & mayors, and group benefits for its members; *Member of:* Federation of Canadian Municipalities
Chief Officer(s):
Laurent Mougeot, CEO
lmougeot@suma.org
Mark Cooper, Director, Policy & Communication
mcooper@suma.org
Gail Meyer, Manager, Member & Administrative Services
gmeyer@suma.org
Finances: *Funding Sources:* Membership fees
Staff: 13 staff member(s)
Membership: 465 municipalities; *Fees:* $175+; *Committees:* Protective Services; Environment; Sustainable Communities; Convention Planning; Resolutions; Transportation; Bylaw Review; Corporate Services
Activities: Group Benefits; Group Purchasing; *Rents Mailing List:* Yes
Meetings/Conferences:
For more information see Trade Shows, Conferences and Seminars Chapter
Saskatchewan Urban Municipalities Association (SUMA) 108th Annual Convention and Tradeshow 2013
February 2013 Saskatoon, SK
Saskatchewan Urban Municipalities Association (SUMA) 109th Annual Convention and Tradeshow 2014
February 2014 Regina, SK
Saskatchewan Urban Municipalities Association (SUMA) 110th Annual Convention and Tradeshow 2015
February 2015 Saskatoon, SK

Saskatchewan Waste Reduction Council (SWRC)

The Two-Twenty, #208, 220 - 20th St. West, Saskatoon SK S7M 0W9
Tel: 306-931-3242; *Fax:* 306-955-5852
e-mail: info@saskwastereduction.ca
www.saskwastereduction.ca
Overview: A medium-sized provincial charitable organization founded in 1991
Mission: To lead in addressing the underlying causes of waste by identifying opportunities, creating connections & promoting solutions.
Environmental Activity: Providing waste reduction information; Offering an online listing of recycling programs in Saskatchewan; Training for composting
Chief Officer(s):
Joanne Fedyk, Executive Director
joanne@saskwastereduction.ca
Martha Hollinger, Contact, Member Services & Administration
martha@saskwastereduction.ca
Membership: 150; *Fees:* Schedule available
Activities: *Awareness Events:* Waste Reduction Week; *Speaker Service:* Yes
Meetings/Conferences:
For more information see Trade Shows, Conferences and Seminars Chapter
Saskatchewan Waste Reduction Council Spring 2013 Waste Minimization ReForum
April 2013 Saskatoon, SK
Publications:
•SWRC Report
Frequency: a.

Saskatchewan Water Well Association ***See*** Saskatchewan Ground Water Association

Saskatchewan Wildlife Federation (SWF)
Parent Name: Canadian Wildlife Federation

9 Lancaster Rd., Moose Jaw SK S6J 1M8
Tel: 306-692-8812; *Fax:* 306-692-4370
Toll-Free: 877-793-9453
e-mail: sask.wildlife@sasktel.net
www.swf.sk.ca
www.facebook.com/pages/Saskatchewan-Wildlife-Federation/178255362147
Overview: A medium-sized provincial charitable organization founded in 1929 overseen by Canadian Wildlife Federation
Mission: To promote the wise use & management of natural resources in Saskatchewan
Environmental Activity: Encouraging hunting, fishing, & trapping in a responsible manner, in accordance with regulations; Maintaining conservation policies; Providing conservation education; Working with governments on projects such as stream enhancement & fish stocking
Chief Officer(s):
Darrell Crabbe, Executive Director
dcrabbe.swf@sasktel.net
Ray Wild, President, 306-731-2718
Marilee Herone, Manager, Office
mheron.swf@sasktel.net
Maureen Horrocks, Coordinator, Communications
maureenhorrocks@gmail.com
Jim Kroshus, Coordinator, Habitat Trust Land
jkroshus.swf@sasktel.net
Adam Matichuk, Coordinator, Fisheries Project
amatichuk.swf@sasktel.net
JeanAnne Prysliak, Coordinator, Education Program
jprysliak.swf@sasktel.net
Finances: *Funding Sources:* Membership fees; Donations; Fundraising
Membership: 30,000+
Activities: Advocating on behalf of members; *Awareness Events:* Great Canadian Shoreline Cleanup, September
Meetings/Conferences:
For more information see Trade Shows, Conferences and Seminars Chapter
Saskatchewan Wildlife Federation 2013 84th Annual Convention
February 2013 Saskatoon, SK
Publications:
•Outdoor Edge [a publication of the Saskatchewan Wildlife Federation]
Type: Magazine; *Price:* Free with Saskatchewan Wildlife Federation membership

Saskatoon Wildlife Federation

PO Box 32041, Saskatoon SK S7S 1N8
Tel: 306-242-1666; *Fax:* 306-933-0617
www.saskatoonwildlifefederation.com
Overview: A small local organization founded in 1931
Mission: Saskatoon Wildlife Federation is a non-profit organization committed to providing a clean welcoming enviroment for individuals who enjoy hunting, fishing and various other outdoor sports. The organization works closely with Ducks Unlimited and other groups to preserve wetlands and other wildspaces for habitat.; *Member of:* Saskatchewan Wildlife Federation
Membership: 1,800+; *Fees:* $50

Sault Naturalists

PO Box 21035, 306 Northern Ave. East, Sault Ste Marie ON P6B 6H3
e-mail: carrie@ginou.ca
soonats.pbworks.com
Overview: A small local organization
Mission: To promote the enjoyment of nature through environmental appreciation & conservation; to encourage wise use & conservation of natural resources; *Member of:* Federation of Ontario Naturalists; Affiliation(s): Canadian Nature Federation
Chief Officer(s):
Don Hall, President, 705-248-1834
Finances: *Annual Operating Budget:* Less than $50,000
Staff: 30 volunteer(s)
Membership: *Fees:* $20 individual; $25 family; $10 student

SauveTerre ***See*** Earthsave Canada

Save Ontario Shipwrecks (SOS)

PO Box 2389, Blenheim ON N0P 1A0
Tel: 519-676-4110; *Fax:* 519-676-7058
e-mail: rjequip@on.aibn.com
www.saveontarioshipwrecks.on.ca
www.facebook.com/group.php?gid=68638569592
Overview: A small provincial organization founded in 1981
Mission: To promote & preserve Ontario's marine heritage; *Member of:* Canadian Maritime Heritage Federation; Affiliation(s): Underwater Council
Chief Officer(s):
Michael Hill, President, 613-767-7446
Jonathan Ferguson, Secretary
jonathanferguson@hotmail.com
Finances: *Annual Operating Budget:* Less than $50,000
Membership: 350-400; *Fees:* $25 individual; $40 family/institution; $250 corporate; *Committees:* Data Base; Forum; Education; Membership; Promotion

Science Alberta Foundation

#260, 3512 - 33 St. NW, Calgary AB T2L 2A6
Tel: 403-220-0077; *Fax:* 403-284-4132
e-mail: info@sciencealberta.org
www.sciencealberta.org
twitter.com/sciencealberta
Overview: A medium-sized provincial organization founded in 1990
Mission: To increase science literacy by creating innovative programs for all Albertans
Chief Officer(s):
Arlene Ponting, CEO
Jill Maryniuk, Manager, Marketing & Communications
Finances: *Funding Sources:* Provincial government; private donations
Activities: Science-in-a-Crate; science festivals

Science Atlantic / Science Atlantique

PO Box 15000, 1390 Le Marchant St., Halifax NS B3H 4R2
Tel: 902-494-3421
e-mail: admin@scienceatlantic.ca
www.scienceatlantic.ca
twitter.com/scienceatlantic
Previous Name: Atlantic Provinces Council on the Sciences; Atlantic Provinces Inter-University Committee on the Sciences
Overview: A medium-sized local organization founded in 1962
Mission: To advance science & technology through education & public awareness & the promotion of scientific literacy education & research throughout the region
Chief Officer(s):
Rob Raeside, Chair
rob.raeside@acadiau.ca
Lois Whitehead, Executive Director
lois.whitehead@scienceatlantic.ca
Finances: *Annual Operating Budget:* $100,000-$250,000; *Funding Sources:* Membership dues
Staff: 2 staff member(s); 150 volunteer(s)
Membership: 18; *Committees:* Aquaculture & Fisheries; Biology; Chemistry; Computer Science; Earth Science; Environment; Mathematics & Statistics; Physics & Astronomy; Psychology; Animal Care; Research Working Group
Activities: Student conferences in nine disciplines; speaker tours by notable scientists; awards for outstanding undergraduate research
Meetings/Conferences:
For more information see Trade Shows, Conferences and Seminars Chapter
Science Atlantic's ChemCon 2013
May 2013 St. John's, NL

Science Atlantique ***See*** Science Atlantic

The Scrap Tire Management Council ***See*** Rubber Manufacturers Association

Sea Shepherd Conservation Society (SSCS)

PO Box 48446, Vancouver BC V7X 1A2
Tel: 604-688-7325
e-mail: canada@seashepherd.org
www.seashepherd.org
www.facebook.com/seashepherdconservationsociety
Overview: A medium-sized national organization founded in 1977
Mission: Investigates & documents violations of international laws, regulations & treaties protecting marine wildlife species; involved with the enforcement of these laws when there is no

enforcement by national governments or international regulatory organizations
Chief Officer(s):
Paul Watson, Founder & President
Finances: *Annual Operating Budget:* $500,000-$1.5 Million
Membership: 30,000; *Fees:* $25
Activities: Volunteers work as crew members aboard our ships to investigate & document any violations of international laws, treaties or regulations against marine wildlife & then enforce those laws; *Speaker Service:* Yes

Sea Shepherd Conservation Society - USA (SSCS)
PO Box 2616, Friday Harbor WA 98250 USA
Tel: 360-370-5650; *Fax:* 360-370-5651
e-mail: info@seashepherd.org
www.seashepherd.org
www.linkedin.com/company/590176?trk=tyah
www.facebook.com/seashepherdconservationsociety
twitter.com/seashepherd
www.youtube.com/seashepherd
Overview: A large international charitable organization founded in 1977
Mission: A direct action organization to protect dolphins, whales, seals & other marine life
Chief Officer(s):
Paul Watson, Founder & President
Carla Robinson, Administrative Director
Farley Mowat, Honorary Chair
Finances: *Annual Operating Budget:* $500,000-$1.5 Million; *Funding Sources:* Grants, public contributions
Staff: 5 staff member(s); 40 volunteer(s)
Membership: 30,000 worldwide; *Fees:* $25
Activities: Research, documentation & enforcement of international marine conservation law; *Rents Mailing List:* Yes; *Library:* Sea Shepherd Media Library
Publications:
•Sea Shepard Log
Type: Newsletter; *Frequency:* Annual
Profile: Contains educational information on marine issues, updates on current laws and legislation, and updates on Sea Shepherd programs and activities.

Seagull Foundation
PO Box 108, Pugwash NS B0K 1L0
Tel: 902-243-2416
Overview: A small local charitable organization
Mission: To protect significant wilderness areas; to support environmental education & conservation; to support Third World development projects; to support programs that create environmental awareness
Chief Officer(s):
Bonnie Bond, Chair
Finances: *Annual Operating Budget:* Less than $50,000
Staff: 1 staff member(s); 2 volunteer(s)

SeCan Association / Association SeCan
#400, 300 TErry Fox Dr., Kanata ON K2K 0E3
Tel: 613-592-8600; *Fax:* 613-592-9497
Toll-Free: 800-764-5487
e-mail: seed@secan.com
www.secan.com
Overview: A small national organization founded in 1976
Mission: As Canada's Seed Partner, SeCan actively seeks partnerships which promote profitability in Canadian agriculture. SeCan is the largest supplier of certified seed to Canadian farmers with more than 1,000 members from coast to coast engaged in seed production, processing and marketing. They are a private, not-for-profit, member corporation with the primary goal of accessing and promoting leading genetics.
Chief Officer(s):
Jeff Reid, General Manager
jreid@secan.com
Finances: *Annual Operating Budget:* $1.5 Million-$3 Million
Staff: 10 staff member(s)
Membership: 1,000; *Fees:* $525; *Committees:* Cereals, Oilseeds & Special Crops; Forage; Promotion; Liaison
Activities: ; *Library:*

Sechelt Marsh Protective Society ***See*** Sunshine Coast Natural History Society

Secrétariat des conférences intergouvernementales canadiennes ***See*** Canadian Intergovernmental Conference Secretariat

Sectorial Association - Transportation Equipment & Machinery Manufacturing ***Voir*** Association sectorielle - Fabrication d'équipement de transport et de machines

SEEDS Foundation
#400, 144 - 4th Ave. SW., Calgary AB T2P 3N4
Tel: 403-221-0835; *Fax:* 403-221-0876
Toll-Free: 800-661-8751
e-mail: seeds@telusplanet.net
www.seedsfoundation.ca
www.facebook.com/pages/SEEDS-Foundation/117021191648133
Also Known As: Society, Environment & Energy Development Studies Foundation
Overview: A medium-sized national charitable organization founded in 1976
Mission: To provide educational support materials & professional assistance to teachers in the area of energy, environment & sustainable development; To work toward the development of a society which understands & is committed to actions leading to wise stewardship of resources, resource use & the environment
Environmental Activity: Climate Change Program; The Green School Program; The Heat Challenge; May Bird Count Challenge
Chief Officer(s):
Diane Field, Executive Director, 403-221-0831
dfield@seedsfoundation.ca
Finances: *Annual Operating Budget:* $250,000-$500,000; *Funding Sources:* Donations (industry, business); government (federal/provincial, less than 5%); private foundations
Staff: 6 staff member(s); 19 volunteer(s)
Membership: 19; *Committees:* Education; Environment; Industry
Activities: Green School Program, environmental action program for elementary school students; Challenge Programs; Water & Clean Air; Writing & Bird challenges for elementary & junior high school students; Creating a Climate of Change Multimedia Program; Energy Literacy Series; Taking Action on Climate Change; *Awareness Events:* Green School Celebrations; Annual Bird Challenge; *Speaker Service:* Yes

Seeds of Diversity Canada (SoDC) / Semences du patrimoine Canada
PO Box 36, Stn. Q, Toronto ON M4T 2L7
Toll-Free: 866-509-7333
e-mail: mail@seeds.ca
www.seeds.ca
Also Known As: Heritage Seed Program
Overview: A medium-sized national organization founded in 1984
Mission: To search out & preserve rare & endangered varieties of vegetables, fruits, flowers, herbs & grains; Affiliation(s): Rare Breeds Canada; Canadian Organic Growers
Chief Officer(s):
Bob Wildfong, Executive Director
Finances: *Funding Sources:* Membership fees; grants
Staff: 2 staff member(s)
Membership: 1,700; *Fees:* $30 regular; $50 overseas; $25 fixed income
Activities: Canadian Tomato Project; Great Canadian Garlic Collection; Pollination Canada; *Awareness Events:* Seedy Saturdays & Seedy Sundays

Semences du patrimoine Canada ***See*** Seeds of Diversity Canada

Seniors for Nature Canoe Club (SFNCC)
PO Box 94051, Stn. Bedford Park, Toronto ON M4N 3R1
e-mail: info@sfncc.org
www.sfncc.org
Overview: A small local organization founded in 1985
Mission: To offer seniors the opportunity to canoe, camp, hike, ski & cycle; *Member of:* Federation of Ontario Naturalists
Chief Officer(s):
Paul Short, President
Finances: *Annual Operating Budget:* Less than $50,000; *Funding Sources:* Membership fees
Staff: 12 volunteer(s)
Membership: 135 senior; *Fees:* $35; *Member Profile:* Over 55 years of age; able to help transport & steer canoes & to swim; *Committees:* Program & Training; Purchasing & Inventory; Membership; Social; Publicity & Newsletter
Activities: Canoeing, hiking, skiing, biking, camping trips

Services de Sécurité Nouveau-Brunswick ***See*** Safety Services New Brunswick

Severn Sound Environmental Association (SSEA)
67 Fourth St., Midland ON L4R 3S9
Tel: 705-527-5166; *Fax:* 705-527-5167
www.severnsound.ca
Overview: A small local organization
Mission: To forge cooperative initiatives to address environmental issues by planning, designing, arranging funding and implementing environmental projects and promoting a sustainable Severn Sound community.
Environmental Activity: environmental monitoring
Chief Officer(s):
Keith Sherman, Executive Director
Membership: 9 municipalities

Shad Valley International
8 Young St. East, Waterloo ON N2J 2L3
Tel: 519-884-8844; *Fax:* 519-884-8191
e-mail: info@shad.ca
www.shad.ca
www.linkedin.com/groups?mostPopular=&gid=2101
www.facebook.com/ShadValley
twitter.com/shadvalley
www.youtube.com/ShadValleyOfficial
Also Known As: Shad Valley
Previous Name: Canadian Centre for Creative Technology
Overview: A medium-sized national charitable organization founded in 1981
Mission: To advance the scientific & technological capabilities of youth, integrated with the development of their entrepreneurial spirit; To collaborate with education, business & other communities, both domestic & international, to provide exceptional development opportunities
Chief Officer(s):
Barry Bisson, President
president@shad.ca
Wendy Zufelt-Baxter, Executive Director, Advancement
wendy@shad.ca
Mary Hamoodi, Director, Finance & Operations
maryh@shad.ca
Finances: *Annual Operating Budget:* $500,000-$1.5 Million
Staff: 8 staff member(s); 100 volunteer(s)
Membership: 13,000; *Fees:* $3,950
Activities: Shad Valley program involves 600+ outstanding senior high school students, some 200 corporate partners, & 12 Canadian universities each summer in an academic/co-op experience; *Speaker Service:* Yes

SHARE Agriculture Foundation
14110 Kennedy Rd., Caledon ON L7C 2G3
Tel: 905-838-0897; *Fax:* 905-838-0794
Toll-Free: 888- 33-7427
e-mail: info@shareagfoundation.org
www.shareagfoundation.org
www.facebook.com/119869878092172
Overview: A medium-sized international organization founded in 1976
Mission: To help improve the quality of life for agriculturally impoverished communities worldwide; SHARE stands for "Sending Help & Resources Everywhere."
Chief Officer(s):
Murray Brownridge, Chair
Les Frayne, Project Manager, Central America
Bob Thomas, Project Manager, South America
Finances: *Annual Operating Budget:* $500,000-$1.5 Million; *Funding Sources:* Canadian International Development Agency; donations
Membership: *Committees:* Communications; Fundraising; Finance; Human Resources
Publications:
•SHARE News [a publication of SHARE Agriculture Foundation]
Type: Newsletter

Sheet Metal & Air Conditioning Contractors' National Association (SMACNA)
PO Box 221230, 4201 Lafayette Center Dr., Chantilly VA 20153-1230 USA
Tel: 703-803-2980; *Fax:* 703-803-3732
e-mail: info@smacna.org
www.smacna.org
www.facebook.com/SMACNA
Overview: A large international organization founded in 1943
Finances: *Funding Sources:* Membership dues; Industry fund
Staff: 34 staff member(s)
Membership: 1,800
Meetings/Conferences:
For more information see Trade Shows, Conferences and

Seminars Chapter
Sheet Metal and Air Conditioning Contractors' National Association (SMACNA) 70th Annual Convention
October 2013 Maui, HI

Sheet Metal Contractors Association of Alberta (SMCAA)

#203, 2725 - 12th St. NE, Calgary AB T2E 7J2
Tel: 403-250-7040; *Fax:* 403-735-5910
Toll-Free: 888-265-6665
e-mail: wilma@smcaa.ca
www.smcaa.ca
Previous Name: Edmonton Association of Sheet Metal & Air Conditioning Contractors
Overview: A small local organization
Member of: Sheet Metal & Air Conditioning Contractors' National Association
Chief Officer(s):
Rod Ketcheson, Provincial President, 403-249-1475
Darcy Spicer, Treasurer
darcy@asmindustries.com
Wilma Agnew, Executive Director
Finances: *Funding Sources:* Membership
Staff: 1 staff member(s); 10+ volunteer(s)
Membership: 150+; *Fees:* Schedule available; *Committees:* Bylaw & Code of Ethics Review; Golf; Old-Timers; Programming
Activities: Providing educational programs; Preparing information about the profession for participation in career fairs; *Library:* SMACNA Manuals
Meetings/Conferences:
For more information see Trade Shows, Conferences and Seminars Chapter
2013 Sheet Metal Contractors Association of Alberta Provincial Conference
May 2013 Jasper, AB

Shipbuilding Association of Canada / Association de la construction navale du Canada

#1502, 222 Queen St., Ottawa ON K1P 5V9
Tel: 613-232-7127; *Fax:* 613-238-5519
Previous Name: Canadian Maritime Industries Association
Overview: A medium-sized national organization founded in 1995
Mission: Represents the interests of the Canadian shipbuilding, ship repair & associated marine equipment & services industries
Chief Officer(s):
Peter Cairns, President
David Reid, Chair
Finances: *Funding Sources:* Membership dues
Membership: 1-99;; *Fees:* Schedule available; *Member Profile:* Canadian organizations engaged in provision of services, products &/or facilities related to ship design, shipbuilding & ship repair, must be 65% Canadian content/owned; *Committees:* Technical; Finance; Personnel; International Marketing; Procurement Outlook; SAC/Government Working Groups
Activities: *Rents Mailing List:* Yes

Shuswap Naturalists

PO Box 1076, Salmon Arm BC V0E 2T0
Tel: 250-833-1098
e-mail: info@shuswapnaturalists.org
www.shuswapnaturalists.org
Overview: A small local charitable organization founded in 1971
Mission: To promote the enjoyment of nature through environmental appreciation & conservation; to encourage wise use & conservation of natural resources & environmental protection.; *Member of:* Federation of BC Naturalists
Chief Officer(s):
Ed McDoland, President
Membership: 32; *Fees:* $20 single; $30 family

Sierra Club

85 Second St., 2nd Fl., San Francisco CA 94105-3441 USA
Tel: 415-977-5500; *Fax:* 415-977-5797
e-mail: information@sierraclub.org
www.sierraclub.org
www.facebook.com/SierraClub
twitter.com/sierra_club
Overview: A large international organization founded in 1892
Mission: To promote conservation of the natural environment by influencing public policy decisions - legislative, administrative, legal & electoral; to explore, enjoy & protect the wild places of the earth; to practise & promote the responsible use of the earth's ecosystems & resources; to educate & enlist humanity to protect & restore the quality of the natural & human environment; to use all lawful means to carry out these objectives at the federal, state & local levels
Chief Officer(s):
Michael Brune, Executive Director
Robin Mann, President
Finances: *Annual Operating Budget:* $3 Million-$5 Million
Membership: 1,300,000; *Fees:* $15-$100
Activities: Conservation Programs (lobbying, expert testimony, grassroots activism, public education on major conservation campaigns); Sierra Book Clubs (nearly 600 titles published - 100 Bush St., 13th Fl., San Francisco, CA 94104 415/291-1600); Outings; *Awareness Events:* John Muir Day, April 21; *Library:* Open to public
Publications:
•Sierra
Type: Magazine

Sierra Club of Canada (SCC) / Sierre club du Canada

#412, 1 Nicholas St., Ottawa ON K1N 7B7
Tel: 613-241-4611; *Fax:* 613-241-2292
Toll-Free: 888-810-4204
e-mail: info@sierraclub.ca
www.sierraclub.ca
www.facebook.com/sierraclubcanada
twitter.com/SierraClubCan
www.youtube.com/sierraclubcanada
Overview: A medium-sized national charitable organization founded in 1992
Mission: To develop a diverse, well-trained grassroots network, working to protect the integrity of our global ecosystems; To focus on five overriding threats: loss of animal & plant species, deterioration of the planet's oceans & atmosphere, the ever-growing presence of toxic chemicals in all living things, destruction of our remaining wilderness, spiralling population growth & overconsumption; *Member of:* CANET; Green Budget Coalition; Canadian Renewable Energy Alliance; Affiliation(s): Common Front on the World Trade Organization
Chief Officer(s):
John Bennett, Executive Director
Anowara Baqi, CFO
Tania Beriau, Development Director
Daniel Spence, Director, Communications
Finances: *Annual Operating Budget:* $500,000-$1.5 Million; *Funding Sources:* Foundations; Governments; Individual donors
Staff: 20 staff member(s)
Membership: *Fees:* $50 regular; $25 student & senior/fixed income; $125 sustainer; $1,000 lifetime
Activities: Program Areas: Atmosphere & Energy; Health & Environment; Environmental Education; Protecting Biodiversity; Transition to a Sustainable Economy; *Internships:* Yes; *Rents Mailing List:* Yes
Publications:
•The RIO Report [a publication of the Sierra Club of Canada]
Type: Annual Report; *Frequency:* Annually
•SCAN - Sierra Club of Canada Activist News
Type: Newsletter

Atlantic Chapter
#533, 1657 Barrington St., Halifax NS B3J 2A1
Tel: 902-444-3113
e-mail: atlanticcanadachapter@sierraclub.ca
atlantic.sierraclub.ca
www.facebook.com/sierraatlanticcanada
twitter.com/SierraClubACC
www.youtube.com/sierraclubcanada
Chief Officer(s):
Gretchen Fitzgerald, Director, 902-444-3113
gretchenf@sierraclub.ca

British Columbia Chapter
#302, 733 Johnson St., Victoria BC V8W 3C7
Tel: 250-386-5255; *Fax:* 250-386-4453
e-mail: info@sierraclub.bc.ca
www.sierraclub.bc.ca
www.facebook.com/SierraClubBC
twitter.com/Sierra_BC
www.youtube.com/user/SierraClubofBC
Chief Officer(s):
George Heyman, Executive Director
george@sierraclub.bc.ca

Ontario Chapter
Evergreen Brickworks, #402, 550 Bayview Ave., Toronto ON M4W 3X8
Tel: 647-346-8744
e-mail: ontariochapter@sierraclub.on.ca
ontario.sierraclub.ca
Chief Officer(s):
Dan McDermott, Director

Prairie Chapter
6328 - 104 St., Edmonton AB T6H 2K9
Tel: 780-439-1160; *Fax:* 780-485-9640
e-mail: prairiechapter@sierraclub.ca
www.sierraclub.ca/prairie
www.facebook.com/groups/117941398216232
twitter.com/SCPrairie
www.youtube.com/user/sierraprairie?feature=mhum
Chief Officer(s):
Eriel Deranger, Chapter Director

Québec Chapter
1222, rue MacKay, Montréal QC H3G 2H4
Tél: 514-303-8668
Courriel: quebec@sierraclub.ca
quebec.sierraclub.ca
Chief Officer(s):
Claude Martel, Directeur
claudem@sierraclub.ca

Sierra Club of Eastern Canada ***See*** Sierra Club of Canada

Sierra Legal Defence Fund ***See*** Ecojustice Canada Society

Sierra Youth Coalition (SYC) / Coalition Jeunesse Sierra

Parent Name: Sierra Club of Canada
#406, 1 Nicholas St., Ottawa ON K1N 7B7
Tel: 613-241-1615; *Fax:* 613-241-2292
Toll-Free: 888-790-7393
e-mail: info@syc-cjs.org
www.syc-cjs.org
Overview: A medium-sized local organization overseen by Sierra Club of Canada
Mission: To empower young people to become active community leaders who contribute to making Canada a more sustainable society
Chief Officer(s):
Mark Hanlon, National Director
director@syc-cjs.org
Finances: *Funding Sources:* Donations; Membership dues
Membership: 80 colleges & universities; 50 high schools; *Fees:* $12; *Member Profile:* Sierra Club of Canada members 25 or under & students of any age

Sierre club du Canada ***See*** Sierra Club of Canada

Similkameen Naturalist Club

C5, Site 33, RR#1, Cawston BC V0X 1C0
Tel: 250-499-5404; *Fax:* 250-499-5379
e-mail: mariposaorgf@hotmail.com
Overview: A small local organization
Chief Officer(s):
Lee McFayden, Director

Similkameen Okanagan Organic Producers Association (SOOPA)

PO Box 577, Keremeos BC V0X 1N0
Tel: 250-499-5381; *Fax:* 250-499-5381
e-mail: soopa@nethop.net
www.soopa.ca
Overview: A small local organization founded in 1985
Mission: To set & maintain high standards of organic food production; to encourage growers to develop their horticultural skills; to educate consumers & encourage other farmers to begin to use sustainable farming methods; Affiliation(s): Certified Organic Associations of BC
Chief Officer(s):
Julie Hinton, Administrator
Guy Villecourt, President
Finances: *Annual Operating Budget:* Less than $50,000
Staff: 1 staff member(s); 15 volunteer(s)
Membership: 41 certified + 5 transitional + 7 associate; *Fees:* $200 certified & transitional depending on size of farm; $50 associate

Simon Fraser Public Interest Research Group (SFPIRG)

#TC326, Simon Fraser University, Burnaby BC V5A 1S6
Tel: 778-782-4360
e-mail: sfpirg@sfu.ca
www.sfpirg.ca
www.facebook.com/sfpirg
twitter.com/sfpirg
Also Known As: SFPIRG
Overview: A large local organization founded in 1981

Mission: To operate as a student funded & directed centre dedicated to environmental & social change; Affiliation(s): Simon Fraser University
Chief Officer(s):
Kalamity Hildebrandt, Coordinator, Research
arx@sfpirg.ca
Shahaa Kakar, Coordinator, Media & Outreach
outreach@sfpirg.ca
Craig Pavelich, Coordinator, Administrative & Resource
admin@sfpirg.ca
Finances: *Annual Operating Budget:* $100,000-$250,000; *Funding Sources:* Student fees
Staff: 3 staff member(s)
Membership: 30,000; *Fees:* Per semester: $3 full-time student; $1.50 part-time student; *Member Profile:* Students of Simon Fraser University, who support the centre through a small fee included in their tuition (students are free to opt out of this fee if they choose); *Committees:* Ancient Forests; Human Resources; Finance; Anti-Oppression; Grants
Activities: Forming Action Groups; research funding & grants; Action Research Exchange (ARX) program; *Internships:* Yes; *Library:* Social Justice Lending Library; Open to public

Skeena Valley Naturalists
1677 Lupine St., Terrace BC V8G 0G1
Tel: 250-798-2535
e-mail: weena@telus.net
Overview: A small local organization
Chief Officer(s):
Judy Chrysler, Director
Membership: 10; *Fees:* $15
Activities: Birdwatching; *Awareness Events:* Christmas Bird Count

Small Water Users Association of BC
4167 Highway 3A, Nelson BC V1L 6N1
Tel: 250-825-4308
e-mail: smallwaterusers@shaw.ca
www.smallwaterusers.com
Overview: A medium-sized provincial organization founded in 2003
Mission: The Small Water Users Association of BC is a new non-profit society dedicated to serving the interests of small water systems (1 to 300 connections) throughout British Columbia.
Chief Officer(s):
Denny Ross-Smith, Executive Director
Membership: 258; *Fees:* $35 basic fee (+$1 per connection); $90 affiliate

Smart Commute
c/o Metrolinx, #600, 20 Bay St., Toronto ON M5J 2W3
Tel: 416-874-5900; *Fax:* 416-869-1794
e-mail: info@smartcommute.ca
www.smartcommute.ca
www.linkedin.com/groups?home=&gid=2677721&trk=anet_ug_hm
www.facebook.com/pages/Smart-Commute/323016568512
twitter.com/SmartCommute
www.youtube.com/user/smartcommuteGTAH
Overview: A small local organization
Mission: To reduce the stress on our lives, roads & environment; to reduce traffic congestion & to take action on climate change through transportation efficiency
Chief Officer(s):
Aubrey Iwaniw, Acting Manager
Aubrey.Iwaniw@metrolinx.com
Finances: *Annual Operating Budget:* $500,000-$1.5 Million; *Funding Sources:* Transport Canada; Greater Toronto Area Municipalities
Membership: 100-499
Activities: *Awareness Events:* Bike to Work Day, May

Smoky Applied Research & Demonstration Association (SARDA)
Parent Name: Agricultural Research & Extension Council of Alberta
PO Box 90, 701 Main St., Falher AB T0H 1M0
Tel: 780-837-2900; *Fax:* 780-837-8223
e-mail: sarda@serbernet.com
www.areca.ab.ca/sardahome.html
twitter.com/SARDA6
Overview: A small local organization overseen by Agricultural Research & Extension Council of Alberta
Mission: To conduct agricultural research; *Member of:* Agricultural Research & Extension Council of Alberta
Chief Officer(s):
J.P. Pettyjohn, Manager
Shelleen Gerbig, Agrologist, AESA Program
shelleesarda@serbernet.com
Kabal Gill, Coordinator, Research Extension
gillsarda@serbernet.com
Membership: *Fees:* $50 individual; $100 corporate
Publications:
•Back Forty [a publication of the Smoky Applied Research & Demonstration Association]
Type: Newsletter

Social Ecology Research Group ***Voir*** Groupe de recherche en écologie sociale

Social Investment Organization (SIO)
184 Pearl St., 2nd Fl., Toronto ON M5H 1L5
Tel: 416-461-6042; *Fax:* 416-461-2481
www.socialinvestment.ca
Also Known As: Canadian Association for Socially Responsible Investment
Overview: A medium-sized national organization founded in 1989
Mission: To take a leadership role in coordinating the SRI agenda in Canada; to raise public awareness of SRI in Canada; to reach out to other groups interested in SRI; to provide information on SRI to our members & the public
Chief Officer(s):
Eugene Ellmen, Executive Director
Andrika Boshyk, Assistant Director
Finances: *Annual Operating Budget:* $250,000-$500,000
Staff: 2 staff member(s); 20 volunteer(s)
Membership: 450+; *Fees:* $5,000 associate; $1,500 supporting; $350 professional; *Member Profile:* Asset management companies; investment fund companies; financial advisors; investors
Activities: *Awareness Events:* SIO Conference; *Internships:* Yes; *Speaker Service:* Yes; *Rents Mailing List:* Yes

Societas Internationalis Limnologiae ***See*** International Society of Limnology

Société canadienne d'agroéconomie ***See*** Canadian Agricultural Economics Society

Société canadienne d'allergie et d'immunologie clinique ***See*** Canadian Society of Allergy & Clinical Immunology

Société canadienne de bioéthique ***See*** Canadian Bioethics Society

Société canadienne de biologie moléculaire ***See*** Canadian Society for Molecular Biology

Société canadienne de génie agroalimentaire et de bioingénierie ***See*** Canadian Society for Bioengineering

Société canadienne de génie biomédical inc. ***See*** Canadian Medical & Biological Engineering Society

Société canadienne de génie civil ***See*** Canadian Society for Civil Engineering

Société canadienne de génie mécanique ***See*** Canadian Society for Mechanical Engineering

Société canadienne de l'énergie du sol ***See*** Earth Energy Society of Canada

La société canadienne de l'espace ***See*** Canadian Space Society

Société canadienne de la santé et de la sécurité, inc. ***See*** Canadian Society of Safety Engineering, Inc.

Société canadienne de la santé internationale ***See*** Canadian Society for International Health

Société canadienne de la science du sol ***See*** Canadian Society of Soil Science

Société canadienne de météorologie et d'océanographie ***See*** Canadian Meteorological & Oceanographic Society

Société canadienne de physiologie ***See*** Canadian Physiological Society

Société canadienne de physiologie végétale ***See*** Canadian Society of Plant Physiologists

Société Canadienne de Phytopathologie ***See*** Canadian Phytopathological Society

Société canadienne de science animale ***Voir*** Canadian Society of Animal Science

Société canadienne de science horticole ***See*** Canadian Society for Horticultural Science

Société canadienne de télédétection ***See*** Canadian Remote Sensing Society

Société canadienne de zoologie ***See*** Canadian Society of Zoologists

Société canadienne des biologistes de l'environnement ***See*** Canadian Society of Environmental Biologists

Société canadienne des clinico-chimistes ***See*** Canadian Society of Clinical Chemists

La société canadienne des éleveurs de moutons ***See*** Canadian Sheep Breeders' Association

Société canadienne des microbiologistes ***See*** Canadian Society of Microbiologists

Société canadienne pour l'étude de l'éthique appliquée ***See*** Canadian Society for the Study of Practical Ethics

Société canadienne pour la conservation de la nature ***See*** The Nature Conservancy of Canada

Société Cousteau ***See*** The Cousteau Society

Société d'agriculture de Chicoutimi ***Voir*** Expo agricole de Chicoutimi

Société d'animation du Jardin et de l'Institut botanique ***Voir*** Les Amis du Jardin botanique de Montréal

Société d'entomologie du Québec (SEQ)
Insectarium de Montréal, 4581, rue Sherbrooke est, Montréal QC H1X 2B2
Courriel: registraire@seq.qc.ca
www.seq.qc.ca
www.facebook.com/groups/123516607707461
Aperçu: *Dimension:* petite; *Envergure:* provinciale; Organisme sans but lucratif; fondée en 1873
Mission: Promouvoir et soutenir l'intérêt et le développement de l'entomologie en matière de recherche, d'éducation et de conservation; Affiliation(s): Société d'entomologie du Canada
Membre(s) du bureau directeur:
Jade Savage, Président
presidence@seq.qc.ca
Finances: *Budget de fonctionnement annuel:* Moins de $50,000
Personnel: 15 bénévole(s)
Membre: 230 *Montant de la cotisation:* 40$; *Critères d'admissibilite:* Entomologiste

Société d'études socialistes ***See*** Society for Socialist Studies

Société d'Horticulture et d'Écologie de Prévost (SHEP)
CP 611, Prévost QC J0R 1T0
Tél: 450-224-9252
shep.qc.com
Aperçu: *Dimension:* petite; *Envergure:* locale
Affiliation(s): Fédération des Sociétés d'horticulture et d'écologie du Québec
Membre(s) du bureau directeur:
Florence Frigon, Présidente
Activités: Conférences; voyages horticoles; ateliers

La société de biophysique du Canada ***See*** Biophysical Society of Canada

Société de conservation de la Baie de l'Isle-Verte
CP 151, 371, rte 132 Est, L'Isle-Verte QC G0L 1K0
Tél: 418-898-4075
Courriel: scobiv@icrdl.net
Aperçu: *Dimension:* petite; *Envergure:* locale; Organisme sans but lucratif; fondée en 1984
Mission: Mise en valeur de la réserve national de faune, patrimoine culturel, historique et naturel de l'Isle-Vertex; gestion de trois centres d'interprétation
Membre(s) du bureau directeur:
Gerard Michaud
Finances: *Budget de fonctionnement annuel:* $100,000-$250,000; *Fonds:* Gouvernement fédéral
Personnel: 20 membre(s) du personnel; 3 bénévole(s)
Membre: 15 individu
Activités: Interprétation du marais salé, de la sauvagine et du baguage de la sauvagine; sentiers de randonnées pédestres;

Société de coopération pour le développement international (SOCODEVI)

#160, 850, av Ernest-Gagnon, Québec QC G1S 4S2
Tél: 418-683-7225; *Téléc:* 418-683-5229
Courriel: info@socodevi.org
www.socodevi.org
www.facebook.com/socodevi
twitter.com/socodevi
Aperçu: *Dimension:* moyenne; *Envergure:* internationale; Organisme sans but lucratif; fondée en 1985
Mission: Avec l'engagement de ses institutions membres, et par la mise en valeur de la formule coopérative ou d'autres formes associatives; contribue au développement durable des pays òu elle intervient en ayant pour objectif que les populations se prennent en charge
Membre(s) du bureau directeur:
Réjean Lantagne, Directeur général
r.lantagne@socodevi.org
Finances: *Budget de fonctionnement annuel:* Plus de $5 Million
Personnel: 200 membre(s) du personnel
Membre: 20 entreprises coopératives et mutualistes; *Critères d'admissibilite:* Coopératives et mutuelles
Activités: ; *Bibliothèque:* Bibliothèque publique

Société de développement économique du Saint-Laurent (SODES) / St. Lawrence Economic Development Council

271, rue de l'Estuaire, Québec QC G1K 8S8
Tél: 418-648-4572; *Téléc:* 418-648-4627
Courriel: sodes@st-laurent.org
www.st-laurent.org
Aperçu: *Dimension:* moyenne; *Envergure:* locale; Organisme sans but lucratif; fondée en 1985
Mission: Promouvoir le St-Laurent comme axe de développement; protéger les intérêts de la communauté maritime du St-Laurent et la représenter auprès des gouvernements; rassembler la communauté maritime du St-Laurent et mettre à sa disposition un forum d'échange et de concertation
Environmental Activity: Code d'éthique
Membre(s) du bureau directeur:
Nicole Trépanier, Président
nicole.trepanier@st-laurent.org
Finances: *Budget de fonctionnement annuel:* $100,000-$250,000
Personnel: 4 membre(s) du personnel
Membre: 80 *Montant de la cotisation:* Barème; *Comités:* Développement; Environnement; Réglementation; Tourisme; Assurances; Fiscalité municipale
Activités: Journée Maritime Québécoise; Prix du Saint-Laurent; *Stagiaires:* Oui; *Service de conférenciers:* Oui; *Bibliothèque:* Bibliothèque publique rendez-vous

Société de protection des plantes du Québec / Québec Society for the Protection of Plants

a/s trésorier, 2560, boul Hochelaga, Québec QC G1V 2J3
www.sppq.qc.ca
Aperçu: *Dimension:* petite; *Envergure:* provinciale; fondée en 1908
Mission: Vouée à la protection des plantes; regroupe des chercheurs universitaires et gouvernementaux, des agronomes, des biologistes, des ingénieurs forestiers, des technologistes, des étudiants, ainsi que toute personne intéressée à la protection des plantes.
Membre(s) du bureau directeur:
Danielle Bernier, Présidente
danielle.bernier@mapaq.gouv.qc.ca
Marie-Eve Bérubé, Secrétaire
me_berube@hotmail.com
Stéphan Pouleur, Trésorier
stephan.pouleur@agr.gc.ca
Membre: 100-499; *Montant de la cotisation:* 60$; 25$ étudiants/personnes retraitées; *Comités:* Promotion et recrutement; Bourses étudiantes; Futurs congrès; Présentation des nouveaux candidats; Nomenclature française des maladies des plantes du Canada; Phytoprotection

Société de toxicologie du Canada ***See*** Society of Toxicology of Canada

Société des canadiennes dans la science et la technologie ***See*** Society for Canadian Women in Science & Technology

Société des éleveurs de bovins canadiens ***See*** Canadian Cattle Breeders' Association

Société des énergie solaire et durable du Canada Inc. ***See*** Solar & Sustainable Energy Society of Canada Inc.

Société des établissements de plein air du Québec (SEPAQ)

Place de la Cité, Tour Cominar, #250, 2640 boul Laurier, Québec QC G1V 5L2
Tél: 418-890-6527; *Téléc:* 418-528-6025
Ligne sans frais: 800-665-6527
Courriel: inforeservation@sepaq.com
www.sepaq.com
Nom précédent: Société des parcs de sciences naturelles du Québec
Aperçu: *Dimension:* petite; *Envergure:* provinciale
Mission: La Sépaq est une société d'État qui a pour mandat d'administrer et de développer des territoires naturels et des équipements touristiques qui lui sont confiés en vertu de sa loi constitutive. Elle s'est donnée la mission d'assurer l'accessibilité, la mise en valeur et la protection de ces équipements publics pour le bénéfice de sa clientèle, des régions du Québec et des générations futures
Membre(s) du bureau directeur:
Yvan Bilodeau, Président-directeur général

Société des ingénieurs professionnels et associés ***See*** Society of Professional Engineers & Associates

Société des ornithologistes du Canada ***See*** Society of Canadian Ornithologists

Société des parcs de sciences naturelles du Québec ***Voir*** Société des établissements de plein air du Québec

Société des roses du Québec / Québec Rose Society

31, av Lorne, Saint-Lambert QC J4P 2G7
Tél: 450-653-9590
Courriel: mor-pol@sympatico.ca
www.rosesquebec.org
Aperçu: *Dimension:* petite; *Envergure:* provinciale
Mission: Étudier, promouvoir et encourager la culture des roses
Membre(s) du bureau directeur:
Diane Vigneault, Présidente
Membre: *Montant de la cotisation:* $25 individuel; 30$ couple

Société des techniciens et des technologues agréés du génie du Nouveau-Brunswick ***See*** New Brunswick Society of Certified Engineering Technicians & Technologists

La Société géographique royale du Canada ***See*** The Royal Canadian Geographical Society

Société internationale de biométéorolgy ***See*** International Society of Biometeorology

Société Internationale de Mécanique des Sols et de la Géotechnique ***See*** International Society for Soil Mechanics & Geotechnical Engineering

Société médicale du Nouveau-Brunswick ***See*** New Brunswick Medical Society

Société mondiale pour la protection des animaux ***See*** World Society for the Protection of Animals

Société nucléaire canadienne ***See*** Canadian Nuclear Society

Société ontarienne de gestion des déchets ***See*** Ontario Waste Management Association

La société ontarienne des professionelles et professionnels de la nutrition en santé publique ***See*** Ontario Society of Nutrition Professionals in Public Health

Société planétaire pour l'assainissement de l'énergie ***See*** Planetary Association for Clean Energy, Inc.

Société pour la nature et les parcs du Canada ***See*** Canadian Parks & Wilderness Society

Société pour la nature et les parcs du Canada, Section Québec ***Voir*** Canadian Parks & Wilderness Society

Société Provancher d'histoire naturelle du Canada (SPHNC) / Provancher Society of Natural History of Canada

1400 rue de l'Aéroport, Québec QC G2G 1G6
Tél: 418-554-8636; *Téléc:* 418-831-8744
Courriel: societe.provancher@gmail.com
www.provancher.qc.ca
www.facebook.com/groups/158959760781189
Aperçu: *Dimension:* petite; *Envergure:* provinciale; Organisme sans but lucratif; fondée en 1919
Mission: Société visant la protection de milieux naturels et l'éducation en sciences naturelles; *Membre de:* Reseau de milieux naturels protégés du Québec; Nature Québec; Institut Québécois de la Biodiversité
Environmental Activity: Protection et gestion de milieux naturels; Education du public
Membre(s) du bureau directeur:
Gilles Gaboury, Président
Eric-Yves Harvey, 1er Vice-Président
Louise Fortin, 2me Vice-Président
Michel Lepage, Secrétaire
André St-Hilaire, Trésorier
Elisabeth Bossert, Administratrice
Finances: *Budget de fonctionnement annuel:* $100,000-$250,000; *Fonds:* Cotisations des membres; dons; location de chalets
Personnel: 3 membre(s) du personnel; 25 bénévole(s)
Membre: 50 institutionnel; 1,500 individu; 30 associé *Montant de la cotisation:* 70$ corporatif; 35$ famille; 30$ individu; *Critères d'admissibilite:* Amant de la nature, scientifiques
Activités: Visites guidées; inventaires fauniques; conférences sur la nature; location de chalets (Ile aux Basques); *Evénements de sensibilisation:* Marais Léon-Provancher, oct.

Société québécoise de récupération et de recyclage

#200, 420, boul Charest est, Québec QC G1K 8M4
Tél: 418-643-0394; *Téléc:* 418-643-6507
Ligne sans frais: 800-807-0678
Courriel: info@recyc-quebec.gouv.qc.ca
www.recyc-quebec.gouv.qc.ca
Également appelé: RECYC-QUÉBEC
Aperçu: *Dimension:* moyenne; *Envergure:* provinciale; Organisme sans but lucratif; fondée en 1990
Mission: Promouvoir, développer et de favoriser la réduction, le réemploi, la récupération et le recyclage des contenants, d'emballages, de matières ou de produits ainsi que leur valorisation dans une perspective de conservation des ressources
Membre(s) du bureau directeur:
Ginette Bureau, Président-directeur général
Johanne Riverin, Vice-présidente, Communications, sensibilisation et éducation
Finances: *Budget de fonctionnement annuel:* Plus de $5 Million
Activités: Coordination des activités de mise en valeur; gestion intégrée des pneux hors d'usage; gestion de la consigne sur les contenants à remplissage unique de bière ou de boissons gazeuses; développement des marchés et technologies dans le domaine de la mise en valeur des matières résiduelles; R&D; information, sensibilisation et éducation; promotion des produits québécois à contenu recyclé; publication de répertoires, guides, études et fiches; campagne sur la récupération des contenants à remplissage unique consignés; *Evénements de sensibilisation:* Semaine québécoise de réduction des déchets; *Stagiaires:* Oui

Bureau à Montréal
141, av du Président-Kennedy, 8e étage, Montréal QC H2X 1Y4
Tél: 514-352-5002; *Téléc:* 514-873-6542
Ligne sans frais: 800-807-0678

Société québécoise de spéléologie (SQS)

CP 1000, Succ. M, 4545, av Pierre-de Coubertin, Montréal QC H1V 3R2
Tél: 514-252-3006; *Téléc:* 514-252-3201
Ligne sans frais: 800-338-6636
Courriel: info-sqs@speleo.qc.ca
www.speleo.qc.ca
Aperçu: *Dimension:* moyenne; *Envergure:* provinciale; Organisme sans but lucratif; fondée en 1970
Mission: La Société québécoise de spéléologie (SQS) a pour mission de favoriser le développement de la spéléologie ainsi que la préservation du milieu cavernicole et de son environnement. Organisme privé, sans but lucratif, la SQS est la fédération qui regroupe les spéléologues du Québec.; *Membre de:* Union internationale de spéléologie; Regroupement Loisir Québec
Membre(s) du bureau directeur:
Michel Cadieux, Directeur général
Finances: *Budget de fonctionnement annuel:* $100,000-$250,000
Personnel: 4 membre(s) du personnel; 200 bénévole(s)
Membre: 4 000 *Montant de la cotisation:* 35$ 1 an, 60$ 2 ans; 500$ à vie
Activités: *Stagiaires:* Oui; *Bibliothèque:* Centre de documentation

Société québécoise des hostas et des hémérocalles (SQHH)
4101 est, rue Sherbrooke, Montréal QC H1X 2B2
Tél: 514-868-3078
Courriel: sqhh-qhhs@live.ca
sites.google.com/site/hostaquebec
Aperçu: *Dimension:* petite; *Envergure:* provinciale
Membre(s) du bureau directeur:
Réjean Millette, Président
info@millettephotomedia.com
Membre: *Montant de la cotisation:* 39$ individu 43$ famille

Société québécoise du dahlia
11, rue Bellerose, Dollard-des-Ormeaux, QC QC H9G 2A7
Tél: 450-747-6521
Courriel: dahlia@videotron.qc.ca
www.sqdahlia.qc.ca
Aperçu: *Dimension:* petite; *Envergure:* locale; Organisme sans but lucratif; fondée en 1992
Mission: Regrouper les amateurs de dahlias et encourager la culture de cette plante; favoriser les échanges d'informations et de spécimens entre les membres; Affiliation(s): American Dahlia Society; Fédération des Sociétés d'horticulture et d'Écologie du Québec; Société Canadienne du Glaïeul
Membre(s) du bureau directeur:
François Lefebvre, Président
flefebvre@videotron.qc.ca
Finances: *Budget de fonctionnement annuel:* Moins de $50,000
Personnel: 9 membre(s) du personnel
Membre: 100-499; *Montant de la cotisation:* 20$; *Critères d'admissibilite:* Amateurs de dahlias et de beaux jardins
Activités: Expositions; conférences; salons annuels; *Service de conférenciers:* Oui

Société québécoise pour la défense des animaux (SQDA) / Québec Society for the Defense of Animals (QSDA)
Parent Name: Canadian Federation of Humane Societies
#102, 847, rue Cherrier, Montréal QC H2L 1H6
Tél: 514-524-1970
Courriel: info@sqda.org
www.sqda.org
Aperçu: *Dimension:* moyenne; *Envergure:* provinciale; Organisme sans but lucratif; fondée en 1976 surveillé par Canadian Federation of Humane Societies
Mission: Faire connaître et respecter le monde animal par tous les moyens possibles; obtenir une législation modifiée pour la protection de toute espèce; Combattre la destruction de notre faune; exposer l'aberration de l'élevage intensif; Contrôler l'expérimentation animale; Affiliation(s): The World Society for the Protection of Animals - England; The Royal Society for the Prevention of Cruelty to Animals - England; The Canadian Federation of Humane Societies; Société nationale pour la défense des animaux - France
Membre(s) du bureau directeur:
Ghislain A. Arsenault, Président
Membre: 500 *Montant de la cotisation:* 20$/an; 250$ bienfaiteur
Activités: *Evénements de sensibilisation:* Campagne annuelle de déménagement

La Société royale du Canada ***See*** The Royal Society of Canada

Société zoologique de Montréal ***See*** Zoological Society of Montréal

Society for Canadian Women in Science & Technology (SCWIST) / Société des canadiennes dans la science et la technologie
#471, 411 Dunsmuir St., Vancouver BC V6B 1X4
Tel: 604-893-8657; *Fax:* 604-893-8692
e-mail: scwist@sfu.ca
www.harbour.sfu.ca/scwist/
Overview: A small national charitable organization founded in 1981
Mission: To promote equal opportunities for women in scientific, technical & engineering careers; to educate public about careers in science & technology particularly to improve social attitudes on the stereotyping of careers in science; to assist educators by providing current information on careers & career training in sciences & scientific policies; Affiliation(s): BC Ministry of Advanced Education, Training & Technology; Industry, Science & Technology Canada; BC Ministry of Education; Canada Employment & Immigration Council; Secretary of State Canada, Women's Program; University of BC, Faculty of Science; Simon Fraser University; BC Institute of Technology; Capilano College; Vancouver School Board; Knowledge Network; Vancouver Foundation; Immigrant Women in Science Program; Douglas College
Chief Officer(s):
Elana Brief, President
Membership: 280; *Fees:* $60 professional; $20 student/retired/unemployed; *Member Profile:* Interest in promoting women in science & technology
Activities: 5-6 regular program meetings of various topics; collection of gender free science & mathematics examples of questions; Ms. Infinity & Hands On Math & Sciences held in May in community colleges & high schools throughout province; *Speaker Service:* Yes; *Library:* Resource Centre;

Society for Conservation Biology (SCB)
1017 O St. NW, Washington DC 20001-4229 USA
Tel: 202-234-4133; *Fax:* 703-995-4633
e-mail: information@conbio.org
www.conbio.org
Overview: A medium-sized international organization founded in 1985
Mission: To advance the scientific study of the phenomena that affect the maintenance, loss, & restoration of biological diversity; To promote the practice of conserving biological diversity
Environmental Activity: Disseminating scientific information & recommendations needed to conserve biological diversity
Chief Officer(s):
Colleen Cassady St. Clair, Canadian Board Member
cstclair@ualberta.ca
Pam Krannitz, Canadian Board Member
pam.krannitz@ec.gc.ca
Alan D. Thornhill, Executive Director
Membership: 10,000+; *Member Profile:* Persons from around the world, who are interested in the study & conservation of biological diversity, such as conservation workers, educators, government workers, resource managers, & students
Activities: Providing recommendations about policies to advance the conservation of biological diversity; Developing educational programs; Providing mentorship opportunities in the field of conservation; Facilitating networking with the professional community
Publications:
•Conservation
Type: Magazine; *Frequency:* Quarterly; *Accepts Advertising*; *Editor:* Kathryn A. Kohm
Profile: Conservation articles for members of the Society for Conservation Biology
•Conservation Biology
Type: Journal; *Frequency:* Bimonthly; *Editor:* Erica Fleishman; *ISSN:* 0888-8892
Profile: Information about conservation science for members of the Society for Conservation Biology
•Conservation Letters, A Journal of the Society for Conservation Biology
Type: Journal; *Editor:* Corey Bradshaw
Profile: Empirical, theoretical, & interdisciplinary research about the conservation of biological diversity worldwide
•SCB [Society for Conservation Biology] Newsletter
Type: Newsletter; *Frequency:* Quarterly; *Editor:* Sharon Collinge; *Price:* Free with membership in the Society for Conservation Biology

Society for Ecological Restoration International (SER)
#1, 285 West 18th St., Tucson AZ 85701 USA
Tel: 520-622-5485; *Fax:* 520-626-5485
www.ser.org
Overview: A medium-sized international organization founded in 1988
Mission: To promote ecological restoration as a means of sustaining the diversity of life; To reestablish an ecologically healthy relationship between nature & culture
Environmental Activity: Promoting ecological restoration around the world
Chief Officer(s):
Amanda Jorgenson, Executive Director
Sasha Alexander, Director, Programs
Levi Wickwire, Coordinator, GRN & Membership
Membership: 2,300 members from 37 countries; *Member Profile:* Individuals & organizations involved in ecologically-sensitive repair & the management of ecosystems, such as scientists, ecological consultants, planners, engineers, teachers, growers, & natural areas managers; *Committees:* Awards; Education & Training; Publications; Science & Policy
Activities: Raising public awareness of restoration; Facilitating communication among restorationists; Encouraging research; Providing input to discussions of public policy
Publications:
•Ecological Restoration
Type: Journal; *Frequency:* Quarterly; *Price:* Included with Society for Ecological Restoration International membership
Profile: Philosophical essays & summaries of current projects & techniques
•Restoration Ecology
Type: Journal; *Frequency:* Quarterly
Profile: Peer-reviewed scientific & technical research articles on topics of restoration & ecological principles
•Restore [a publication of the Society for Ecological Restoration International]
Type: Newsletter; *Frequency:* Weekly
Profile: Annotated links to news stories from around the globe
•Society for Ecological Restoration International Newsletter
Type: Newsletter; *Frequency:* Quarterly
Profile: Up-to-date information for members about the Society & it chapters

Society for Environmental Graphic Design (SEGD)
#400, 1000 Vermont Ave., NW, Washington DC 20005 USA
Tel: 202-638-5555; *Fax:* 202-638-0891
e-mail: segd@segd.org
www.segd.org
Overview: A medium-sized international organization
Chief Officer(s):
Leslie Gallery Dilworth, Chief Executive Officer, 202-638-5555
leslie@segd.org
Ann Makowski, Chief Operating Officer, 202-638-5555
Craig M. Berger, Director, Education & Professional Training, 202-638-5555
Membership: 1,600+; *Member Profile:* Individuals who work in the planning, design, fabrication, & implementation of communications in the built environment
Activities: Fostering research; Providing educational resources; Refining standards of practice; Collaborating across various design disciplines; Offering referrals to fabricators or designers; Providing networking opportunities
Publications:
•segdDESIGN: The International Journal of Environmental Graphic Design
Type: Journal; *Frequency:* Quarterly; *Accepts Advertising*; *Editor:* Pat Matson Knapp
Profile: Information about the people, research, technologies, materials, & resources that influence communications in the built environment
•Society for Environmental Graphic Design Membership Directory
Type: Directory

Society for Organic Urban Land Care
PO Box 8548, Victoria BC V8P 1L4
Tel: 250-386-7685
e-mail: info@organiclandcare.org
www.organiclandcare.org
Also Known As: SOUL
Overview: A small national organization
Mission: SOUL was formed in response to the growing need for ecologically responsible land care practices. Our mission is to promote and support organic practices in our communities through education, certification and standardization.
Chief Officer(s):
Lisa Atkins, President
Membership: 100; *Fees:* $30 public/professional; $250 supporting

Society for Socialist Studies (SSS) / Société d'études socialistes (SÉS)
c/o Kanchan Sarker, Sociology, Univ. of BC, Okanagan Campus, 3333 University Way, Kelowna BC V1V 1V7
Tel: 250-807-8707; *Fax:* 250-807-8001
e-mail: admin@socialiststudies.ca
socialiststudies.ca
www.facebook.com/SocietyForSocialistStudies
Overview: A small national charitable organization founded in 1967
Mission: The Society creates, fosters, & publishes, academic & scholarly research & analysis in Canada, with emphasis on socialist, feminist, anti-racist, & ecological points of view.; *Member of:* Humanities & Social Science Federation of Canada
Chief Officer(s):
Kanchan Sarker, President
kanchan.sarker@ubc.ca

Murray Cooke, Vice-President
mcooke@yorku.ca
Matthew Brett, Secretary & Moderator, E-mail List
David Huxtable, Treasurer
huxtable@uvic.ca
Finances: *Funding Sources:* Membership fees
Membership: 350; *Fees:* $60 regular; $30 student/low incomed; $100 Canadian institution; US$100 foreign institutions; *Member Profile:* Membership includesany person underwriting the Society's purpose.; *Committees:* Canadian Federation of Humanities and Social Sciences Congress Programme Committee; Journal Editorial Committee
Activities: Organizes conferences, seminars, & workshops; publishes educational material; advances public education
Publications:
•Socialist Studies: Journal of the Society for Socialist Studies
Type: Journal; *Editor:* Sandra Rollings-Magnusson

Society of Canadian Ornithologists (SCO) / Société des ornithologistes du Canada (SOC)

a/s Thérèse Beaudet, SCO Membership Secretary, 1281, ch des Lièges, St-Jean de l'Ile d'Orléans QC G0A 3W0
e-mail: beaudet.lamothe@sympatico.ca
www.sco-soc.ca
Overview: A medium-sized national charitable organization founded in 1983
Mission: To support research to understand & conserve Canadian birds; To represent Canadian ornithologists
Environmental Activity: Responding to requests for information about avian conservation issues; Encouraging the application of scientific bird studies to the field of conservation
Chief Officer(s):
Erica Nol, President
enol@trentu.ca
Joe Nocera, Vice-President
joe.nocera@ontario.ca
Thérèse Beaudet, Membership Secretary
beaudet.lamothe@sympatico.ca
Pierre Lamothe, Treasurer
beaudet.lamothe@sympatico.ca
Finances: *Funding Sources:* Membership fees; Donations
Membership: 357; *Fees:* $10 students; $25 regular members; $35 international members; $50 sustaining members; $500 life members; *Member Profile:* Amateur & professional ornithologists
Activities: Connecting with other professional ornithological societies; Disseminating information about the birds of Canada; Offering grants to study birds
Meetings/Conferences:
For more information see Trade Shows, Conferences and Seminars Chapter
Society of Canadian Ornithologists / Société des ornithologistes du Canada 2013 31st Annual Meeting
2013 Winnipeg, MB
Publications:
•Avian Conservation & Ecology
Type: Journal
Profile: Published by the Society of Canadian Ornithologists / Société des ornithologistes du Canada & Bird Studies Canada
•Biology & Conservation of Forest Birds
Editor: A.W, Diamond; D.N. Nettleship
Profile: A series of manuscripts from a Society of Canadian Ornithologists / Société des ornithologistes du Canada meeting
•Picoides: Bulletin of the Society of Canadian Ornithologists / Bulletin de la Société des Ornithologistes du Canada
Type: Newsletter; *Editor:* Rob Warnock
Profile: President, committee, & meeting reports, announcements, award news, research articles,essays, book reviews, bird surveys, & conservation information

Society of Chemical Industry - Canadian Section (SCI)

#550, 130 Slater St., Ottawa ON K1P 6E2
e-mail: scicanada@soci.org
www.soci.org
Overview: A small international organization founded in 1881
Mission: To encourage acquaintance & understanding among responsible individuals in the various fields of the industrial chemical process industries; to promote acquaintance & understanding between the chemical industry & the universities & governments; to encourage scientific education in universities by recognizing student achievements; to reward outstanding achievement in the Canadian chemical & allied industries & universities through awards & honorary lectureships; to promote communication between the members of the Canadian chemical & allied industries & those of other countries
Chief Officer(s):
Roger Hayward, Hon. Chair
Rosie Baston, Coorindator
scicanada@soci.org
Finances: *Annual Operating Budget:* Less than $50,000; *Funding Sources:* Membership fees; events
Staff: 12 volunteer(s)
Membership: 120 in Canada; *Fees:* $95
Activities: Sponsors Le Sueur Memorial Lectures & Purvis Memorial Lectures

Society of Engineering Technicians & Technologists of Saskatchewan (SETTS) ***See*** Saskatchewan Applied Science Technologists & Technicians

Society of Engineering Technologists of BC ***See*** Applied Science Technologists & Technicians of British Columbia

Society of Environmental Toxicology & Chemistry (SETAC)

SETAC Asia / Pacific, SETAC Latin America, & SETAC North America, 1010 - 12th Ave. North, Pensacola FL 32501-3370 USA
Tel: 850-469-1500; *Fax:* 850-469-9778
e-mail: setac@setac.org
www.setac.org
Overview: A small international organization founded in 1979
Mission: To develop principles & practices for the protection, enhancement, & management of sustainable environmental quality
Environmental Activity: Researching stressors in the environment; Providing education in the environmental sciences
Chief Officer(s):
Mike Mozur, Executive Director
mike.mozur@setac.org
Linda Fenner, Manager, Finance
linda.fenner@setac.org
Mimi Meredith, Manager, Publications
mimi.meredith@setac.org
Bruce Vigon, Manager, Scientific Affairs
bruce.vigon@setac.org
Membership: *Member Profile:* Individuals & institutions involved in environmental research, development, & education, as well as the management & regulation of natural resources; *Committees:* Awards & Fellowships; Development; Education; Endowment Fund; Finance; Long-range Planning; Meetings; Membership; Mentoring; Nominations; Regional Chapters; Short Courses; Student Activities; Student Council; Technical
Meetings/Conferences:
For more information see Trade Shows, Conferences and Seminars Chapter
Society of Environmental Toxicology & Chemistry North America 2013 34th Annual Meeting: Harmonizing Science Across Disciplines
November 2013 Nashville, TN
Publications:
•Environmental Toxicology & Chemistry
Type: Journal; *Editor:* C.H. Ward; *ISSN:* 0730-7268
•Integrated Environmental Assessment & Management
Type: Journal; *Editor:* Richard J. Wenning; *ISSN:* 1551-3777
•Society of Environmental Toxicology & Chemistry Annual Report
Type: Yearbook; *Frequency:* Annually

Society of Fire Protection Engineers (SFPE)

#620E, 7315 Wisconsin Ave., Bethesda MD 20814 USA
Tel: 301-718-2910; *Fax:* 301-718-2242
www.sfpe.org
www.facebook.com/careers.sfpe.org
twitter.com/SFPEAnnualMtg
Overview: A medium-sized international organization founded in 1950
Mission: To advance the practice & science of fire protection engineering & its allied fields; to maintain a high ethical standard among its members; to foster fire protection engineering education
Chief Officer(s):
Allan Freedman, Executive Director, 301-915-9723
Finances: *Annual Operating Budget:* $500,000-$1.5 Million
Staff: 6 staff member(s)
Membership: 4,500; *Fees:* US$195
Activities: *Rents Mailing List:* Yes

British Columbia Chapter
c/o Fire Protection, HRDC
Tel: 604-666-7399; *Fax:* 604-666-6206
www.sfpe.bc.ca
Chief Officer(s):
Rich Cheung, President, 604-591-4737, Fax: 604-591-2680
rwcheung@city.surrey.bc.ca

National Capital Region
1125 Colonel By Dr., Ottawa ON K1R 7X6
Tel: 613-520-2600
www.sfpe.org/Chapters/CanadaNCR.aspx
Chief Officer(s):
George Fawcett, President

Southern Ontario Chapter
Toronto ON
e-mail: info@sfpesoc.com
www.sfpesoc.com
Chief Officer(s):
Ed Koe, President
president@sfpesoc.com

St-Laurent Chapitre
Courriel: g.carrier@pgaexperts.com
Chief Officer(s):
Gilles Carrier, President

Society of Petroleum Engineers (SPE)

PO Box 833836, Richardson TX 75083-3868 USA
Tel: 972-952-9393; *Fax:* 972-952-9435
Toll-Free: 800-456-6863
e-mail: service@spe.org
www.spe.org
www.linkedin.com/groups?about=&gid=57660
www.facebook.com/spemembers
twitter.com/SPE_Events
www.youtube.com/user/2012SPE?feature=mhee
Overview: A large international organization founded in 1957
Mission: To collect, disseminate & exchange technical knowledge concerning the exploration, development & production of oil & gas resources & related technologies for the public benefit; provide opportunities for professionals to enhance their technical & professional competence
Chief Officer(s):
Mark A. Rubin, Executive Director
execdir@spe.org
Egbert Imomoh, President
president@spe.org
Finances: *Annual Operating Budget:* $3 Million-$5 Million
Staff: 87 staff member(s)
Membership: 79,000+ (active operations in some 50 countries); *Fees:* $10-$90; *Member Profile:* Managers, engineers, operating personnel & scientists engaged in the exploration, drilling & production sectors of the global oil & gas industry; *Committees:* Student Development; Global Training; Distinguished Lecturer; Membership; Forum Series Coordinating; DAA For PE Faculty; Education & Accreditation; Oil & Gas Reserves; Editorial Review; Twenty Five Year Club; TIG Coordinating; Research & Development; Young Professional Coordinating; SPE Energy Information; Sustainability; Robert Earll McConnell; Online Communities Advisory; Awards
Activities: *Internships:* Yes; *Speaker Service:* Yes; *Library:* Open to public
Publications:
•JPT [Journal of Petroleum Technology]
Type: Journal
•Oil Gas Facilities
Type: Magazine
•TWA [The Way Ahead]
Type: Magazine

Society of Professional Engineers & Associates (SPEA) / Société des ingénieurs professionnels et associés

#2, 2275 Speakman Dr., Mississauga ON L5K 1B1
Tel: 905-823-3606; *Fax:* 905-823-9602
www.spea.ca
Overview: A medium-sized national organization founded in 1974
Mission: To represent scientists, engineers, technologists, & tradespeople who work for Atomic Energy of Canada Limited (AECL) in Mississauga, Ontario & abroad
Chief Officer(s):
Ritu Luther, Office Administrator
Peter White, President
Val Aleyaseen, Chair, Membership
Vincent Tume, Secretary
Brian Girard, Treasurer
Membership: 900+ engineers & scientists + 300 technologists & tradespeople; *Member Profile:* Scientists, engineers,

technologists, & tradespeople who work for Atomic Energy of Canada Limited (AECL) in Mississauga, Ontario & abroad

Society of the Plastics Industry of Canada *See* Canadian Plastics Industry Association

Society of the Plastics Industry, Inc. (SPI)

#1000, 1667 K St. NW, Washington DC 20006 USA
Tel: 202-974-5200; *Fax:* 202-296-7005
www.plasticsindustry.org
www.facebook.com/pages/NPE/214402080959
twitter.com/SPI_4_Plastics
Overview: A large international organization founded in 1937
Mission: To be a world class trade association representing the entire plastics industry in a way that promotes the development of the plastics industry & enhances the public's understanding of its contributions while meeting the needs of society & providing value to its members
Chief Officer(s):
William R. Carteaux, President & CEO
Phyllis Hortie, Contact, Trade Shows & Conferences
Finances: *Annual Operating Budget:* Greater than $5 Million
Staff: 65 staff member(s)
Membership: 1,100; *Member Profile:* Members represent the entire plastics supply chain; *Committees:* Finance, Administration & Membership; Communications & Marketing Advisory; Equipment Statistics; Nominating; NPE Executive; Special Committees
Activities: Operates 12 divisions: Epoxy Resin Systems Task Group, Film & Bag Federation, Food, Drug & Cosmetic Packaging Materials, Fluropolymers, Machinery, Molders, Moldmakers, Organic Peroxide Producers Safety, Sheet Producers, Structural Plastics, Thermoforming Institute, Vinyl Formulators; *Library:* Plastics Data Source
Meetings/Conferences:
For more information see Trade Shows, Conferences and Seminars Chapter
Society of the Plastics Industry, Inc. Spring 2013 National Board Conference
April 2013 San Diego, CA

Society of Toxicology (SOT)

#300, 1821 Michael Faraday Dr., Reston VA 20190 USA
Tel: 703-438-3115; *Fax:* 703-438-3113
e-mail: sothq@toxicology.org
www.toxicology.org
Overview: A large international organization
Mission: To advance the science of toxicology; To promote the acquisition & utilization of knowledge in toxicology; To protect public health
Chief Officer(s):
Jon C. Cook, President
Rosibel Alvarenga, Contact, Membership & Customer Service, 703-438-3115 Ext. 1432
rosibel@toxicology.org
Betty Eidemiller, Contact, Teacher & Student Inquiries, 703-438-3115 Ext. 1430
bettye@toxicology.org
Martha Lindauer, Contact, Press & Media Inquiries, 703-438-3115 Ext. 1640
martha@toxicology.org
Membership: *Member Profile:* Scientists from academic institutions, government, & industry who practice toxicology
Meetings/Conferences:
For more information see Trade Shows, Conferences and Seminars Chapter
Society of Toxicology 52nd Annual Meeting & ToxExpo
March 2013 San Antonio, TX
Society of Toxicology 53rd Annual Meeting & ToxExpo
March 2014 Phoenix, AZ
Society of Toxicology 54th Annual Meeting & ToxExpo
March 2015 San Diego, CA
Society of Toxicology 55th Annual Meeting & ToxExpo
March 2016 New Orleans, LA
Society of Toxicology 56th Annual Meeting & ToxExpo
March 2017 Baltimore, MD
Publications:
•Communiqué [a publication of the Society of Toxicology]
Type: Newsletter; *Frequency:* Quarterly; *Accepts Advertising*
Profile: Society of Toxicology news; Member spotlight; Regional chapters, specialty sections, & special interest groups; Annual meeting; Science news
•Preliminary Program [a publication of the Society of Toxicology]
Accepts Advertising
Profile: Information about the annual meeting program, a registration form, & housing information
•Society of Toxicology Membership Directory
Accepts Advertising
Profile: Names, addresses, & e-mail addresses for more than 6,000 SOT members
•ToxExpo Directory
Accepts Advertising
•ToxSci Journal
Type: Journal

Society of Toxicology of Canada (STC) / Société de toxicologie du Canada

PO Box 55094, Montréal QC H3G 2W5
Tel: 514-697-9219; *Fax:* 514-697-9309
e-mail: stcsecretariat@mcgill.ca
www.stcweb.ca
Overview: A medium-sized national organization founded in 1964
Mission: To promote acquisition, facilitate dissemination & encourage utilization of knowledge in the science of toxicology; Affiliation(s): Canadian Federation of Biological Societies; International Union of Toxicology
Chief Officer(s):
Genevieve Bondy, President
Elise Boivin-Ford, Executive Secretary
Finances: *Funding Sources:* Membership fees
Staff: 1 staff member(s); 20 volunteer(s)
Membership: 400; *Fees:* $30-$100; *Member Profile:* Ordinary - qualified individual who has continuing professional interest in field of toxicology; associate - individual who has not satisfied requirement for ordinary membership; student - graduate student enrolled in postgraduate degree program with major emphasis on toxicology; *Committees:* Awards; Editorial/Newsletter; Education; Finance; Membership; Nominating; Science Policy; Scientific Program; Symposium; Web Site
Meetings/Conferences:
For more information see Trade Shows, Conferences and Seminars Chapter
The Society of Toxicology of Canada Annual Symposium 2013
December 2013 Ottawa, ON

Society Promoting Environmental Conservation (SPEC)

2150 Maple St., Vancouver BC V6J 3T3
Tel: 604-736-7732; *Fax:* 604-736-7115
e-mail: admin@spec.bc.ca
www.spec.bc.ca
Overview: A medium-sized provincial charitable organization founded in 1969
Mission: To address environmental issues in British Columbia, with a focus on urban communities in the Lower Mainland & the Georgia Basin; To encourage policies that lead to urban sustainability
Environmental Activity: Protecting land & water resources; Raising public awareness about environmental issues; Promoting sustainable urban transportation; Encouraging waste reduction; Promoting the use of renewable energy; Encouraging energy conservation
Chief Officer(s):
Joanna Robinson, President
Isle Sarady, Manager, Operations
admin@spec.bc.ca
Catriona Gordon, Coordinator, School Gardens Community
cagordon@telus.net
Alicia Embree, Secretary
aliciaembree@gmail.com
Jason Fast, Treasurer
jayfast@shaw.ca
Finances: *Funding Sources:* Donations
Activities: Advocating for food safety & security; Providing public education programs; Reducing the use of hazardous pesticides
Publications:
•SPECTRUM [a publication of the Society Promoting Environmental Conservation]
Type: Newsletter
Profile: Society Promoting Environmental Conservation activities, news releases, upcoming events, & articles

Soil & Water Conservation Society (SWCS)

945 SW Ankeny Rd., Ankeny IA 50023-9723 USA
Tel: 515-289-2331; *Fax:* 515-289-1227
e-mail: swcs@swcs.org
www.swcs.org
Overview: A large international organization founded in 1945
Mission: To promote the conservation of soil, water, & related resources; To promote an ethic that recognizes the interdependence of people & the environment
Chief Officer(s):
Jim Gulliford, Executive Director, 515-289-2331 Ext. 113, Fax: 515-289-1227
jim.gulliford@swcs.org
Jim Bruce, Representative, Canadian Policy, 613-731-5929
jpbruce@sympatico.ca
Dewayne Johnson, Director, Professional Development, 515-289-2331 Ext. 114, Fax: 515-289-1227
dewayne.johnson@swcs.org
Cammie Callen, Specialist, Membership Services, 515-289-2331 Ext. 118, Fax: 515-289-1227
memberservices@swcs.org
Membership: 5,000-14,999;; *Fees:* $220 Presidents Club; $145 leader; $90 conservationist; $30 student; *Member Profile:* Researchers; Administrators; Educators; Planners; Technicians; Legislators; Farmers & ranchers; Local conservation officials; Consultants; Students
Meetings/Conferences:
For more information see Trade Shows, Conferences and Seminars Chapter
Soil & Water Conservation Society 68th Annual International Conference
July 2013 Reno, NV
Publications:
•The Journal of Soil and Water Conservation (JSWC)
Type: Journal; *Frequency:* Bimonthly; *Editor:* Oksana Gieseman; *ISSN:* 0022-4561
Profile: A multidisciplinary journal of natural resource conservation research, practice, policy, and perspectives.

Soil Conservation Council of Canada (SCCC)

PO Box 998, Indian Head SK S0G 2K0
Tel: 306-972-7293; *Fax:* 306-695-3442
e-mail: info@soilcc.ca
www.soilcc.ca
Overview: A medium-sized national charitable organization founded in 1987
Mission: To act as the voice of soil conservation in Canada
Environmental Activity: Administering Canada's Agricultural Producers Addressing Environmental Issues (CAPAEI); Administering the Greenhouse Gas Mitigation Program for Canadian Agriculture (GHGMP), with three other national organizations
Chief Officer(s):
Glen Shaw, Executive Director, 306-972-7293
info@soilcc.ca
Don McCabe, President
Finances: *Funding Sources:* Corporations; Government
Membership: *Fees:* $35 individuals
Activities: Raising awareness about the causes of soil degradation; Presenting conservation issues to the government, private industry, producers, & the public; Delivering agriculture & environment programs for producers; Facilitating information exchange among researchers, government representatives, industry, & farmers; Partnering with similar organizations; *Awareness Events:* National Soil Conservation Week, April
Meetings/Conferences:
For more information see Trade Shows, Conferences and Seminars Chapter
Conservation Agriculture 2014 6th World Congress (hosted by Soil Conservation Council of Canada with Conservation Agriculture Systems Alliance)
June 2014 Winnipeg, MB
Publications:
•The Protector [a publication of the Soil Conservation Council of Canada]
Type: Newsletter
Profile: Up-to-date information about the Council's activities

Solar & Sustainable Energy Society of Canada Inc. (SESCI) / Societé des énergie solaire et durable du Canada Inc.

c/o Frederic Pouyot, #173, 207 Bank St., Ottawa ON k2P 2N2
Tel: 613-686-4474; *Fax:* 613-533-6550
e-mail: bruce@techonfoot.com
www.sesci.ca
Previous Name: Solar Energy Society of Canada Inc.
Overview: A medium-sized national charitable organization founded in 1974
Mission: To act as a voice for renewable energy in Canada; To increase the use of solar & sustainable energy in Canada; To support energy conservation; Affiliation(s): International Solar Energy Society (ISES)

Environmental Activity: Raising awareness of solar & sustainable energy in Canada; Encouraging improvements in solar energy applications
Chief Officer(s):
Frederic Pouyot, President
president@sesci.ca
Finances: *Annual Operating Budget:* $50,000-$100,000; *Funding Sources:* Membership fees; Donations
Membership: *Fees:* $20 students; $40 seniors; $100 regular members; $200 small organizations; $300 libraries; $500 medium organizations; $2000 large organizations
Activities: Presenting briefs & position papers to government departments in the environment, energy resource, & finance sectors; Liaising with other solar energy societies & environmental groups; Encouraging the exchange of information
Meetings/Conferences:
For more information see Trade Shows, Conferences and Seminars Chapter
Solar & Sustainable Energy Society of Canada Inc. 2013 Annual Conference
2013
Photovoltaics Industry 2013 6th Annual Workshop
2013
Publications:
•Canadian Renewable Energy Guide
Type: Guide
Profile: Comprehensive information about the use of renewables throughout Canada
•SOL [a publication of the Solar & Sustainable Energy Society of Canada Inc.]
Type: Newsletter; *Frequency:* Quarterly; *Price:* Free with Solar & Sustainable Energy Society of Canada Inc. membership
Profile: Developments in Canada's renewable energy industry, topical articles, & Solar & Sustainable Energy Society of Canada's forthcoming events &activities

---

Solar Energy Society of Canada Inc. ***See*** Solar & Sustainable Energy Society of Canada Inc.

Solid Waste Association of North America (SWANA)
#700, 1100 Wayne Ave., Silver Spring MD 20910 USA
Fax: 301-589-7068
Toll-Free: 800-467-9262
e-mail: info@swana.org
www.swana.org
www.linkedin.com/groups?home=&gid=45037
www.facebook.com/MySWANA
twitter.com/SWANA
Previous Name: Government Refuse Collection & Disposal Association
Overview: A medium-sized international organization founded in 1961
Mission: To serve individuals & communities responsible for the operation & management of solid waste management systems; To advance professional standards in the field through training programs, technical assistance, & education; *Member of:* International Solid Waste Association; Federation of Canadian Municipalities
Chief Officer(s):
John Skinner, Executive Director & CEO, 240-494-2254
Finances: *Annual Operating Budget:* $3 Million-$5 Million; *Funding Sources:* Membership dues; publications
Staff: 22 staff member(s)
Membership: 8,000; *Fees:* US$62 student; US$72 retired; US$183 public sector; US$243 small business; US$343 private sector; *Committees:* Technical; Recycling & Special Waste Management; Communication, Education & Marketing; Collection & Transfer; Landfill; Landfill Gas; Planning & Management; Waste-to-Energy
Activities: Technical divisions: collection & transfer, waste-to-energy, landfill gas management, landfill management, planning & management, special waste management; waste reduction, recycling & composting, communication, education & marketing; publications; trade shows & conferences; *Internships:* Yes; *Library:* Open to public

Atlantic Canada Chapter
#100, 137 Chainlake Dr., Halifax NS B3S 1V3
Fax: 902-450-2008
e-mail: info@atcanswana.org
www.atcanswana.org
Chief Officer(s):
Gus Green, President, 902-742-4451, Fax: 902-749-7638
gus@wastecheck.ca
Derrill Hynick, Executive Director & Service Provider, 902-445-3842
derrill.hynick@bellaliant.net
Sarah Devereaux, Treasurer, 902-450-4000
sdevereaux@dillon.ca

Northern Lights Chapter
PO Box 3317, Sherwood Park AB T8H 2T2
Tel: 780-496-5614; *Fax:* 866-698-8203
e-mail: info@swananorthernlights.org
www.swananorthernlights.org
Chief Officer(s):
Kelly Emke, Executive Director
kelly.emke@swananorthernlights.org
Sheri Praski, Executive Director, 306-227-8183
sheri.praski@swananorthernlights.org
Colin Joyal, President
colin.joyal@swananorthernlights.org
Sheila Reithmayer, Administrator, 780-496-5614
sheila.reithmayer@swananorthernlights.org
Darci Clark, Coordinator, Events & Marketing, 204-725-9234
darci.clark@swananorthernlights.org
Bud Latta, Treasurer
bud.latta@swananorthernlights.org

Ontario Chapter
PO Box 9, Hillsdale ON L0L 1V0
Tel: 705-835-3560; *Fax:* 705-835-6224
www.swanaon.org
Chief Officer(s):
John Lackie, Executive Director
j.lackie@sympatico.com

Pacific Chapter - BC & Yukon
PO Box 47007, #15, 555 West 12th Ave., Vancouver BC V5Z 3X0
Tel: 250-538-0110; *Fax:* 250-538-0120
Toll-Free: 800-648-2560
e-mail: info@swanabc.org
www.swanabc.org
Chief Officer(s):
Ralph Bischoff, Executive Director

Solidarité européenne pour une égale participation des peuples ***See*** European Solidarity Towards Equal Participation of People

---

Somenos Marsh Wildlife Society
PO Box 711, Duncan BC V9L 3Y1
Tel: 250-746-7030
e-mail: info@somenosmarsh.com
www.somenosmarsh.com
Overview: A small local organization
Mission: To preserve wetland habitat in Somenos Basin; to build wildlife viewing facilities; *Member of:* Cowichan Watershed Council; BC Environmental Network; Canadian Nature Federation
Chief Officer(s):
Paul Fletcher, President
Membership: 200; *Fees:* $20-$35

South Lake Simcoe Naturalists
PO Box 1044, Sutton West ON L0E 1R0
Tel: 416-722-8021
Overview: A small local organization founded in 1980
Mission: Conservation, education & recreation organization concerned with the study & experience of nature & the relationships between it & humans; *Member of:* Federation of Ontario Naturalists
Chief Officer(s):
Paul Harpley, President
Finances: *Annual Operating Budget:* Less than $50,000; *Funding Sources:* Federal & provincial governments; private
Membership: 100-499
Activities: Wildlife research; breeding bird census; South Lake Simcoe Wildlife Research Station (seasonal); lectures; outings; land use planning; *Internships:* Yes; *Speaker Service:* Yes

---

South Pacific Peoples Foundation ***See*** Pacific Peoples Partnership

---

South Peel Naturalists' Club (SPNC)
PO Box 69629, 109 Thomas St., Oakville ON L6J 7R4
Tel: 905-279-8807
e-mail: mail@spnc.ca
www.spnc.ca
Overview: A small local organization founded in 1952
Member of: Federation of Ontario Naturalists; Affiliation(s): Canadian Nature Federation
Chief Officer(s):
Don Morrison, President
Finances: *Annual Operating Budget:* Less than $50,000; *Funding Sources:* Membership fees; Donations
Staff: 35 volunteer(s)
Membership: 200+; *Fees:* $25 individual; $30 family; $15 student; $20 senior family; $15 senior individual

---

Southeast Environmental Association (SEA)
PO Box 1500, 41 Woods Islands Hill, Montague PE C0A 1R0
Tel: 902-838-3351; *Fax:* 902-838-0610
e-mail: sea@pei.aibn.com
www.seapei.ca
Overview: A medium-sized provincial organization founded in 1992
Mission: To protect, maintain, and enhance the ecology of south eastern Prince Edward Island for the environmental, social, and economic well being of area residents.
Chief Officer(s):
Sarah Jane Bell, Coordinator
Edgar Dewar, Chair

Southern Interior Local Government Association (SILGA)
c/o Alison Slater, 1996 Sheffield Way, Kamloops BC V2E 2M2
Tel: 250-374-3678; *Fax:* 250-374-3678
www.silga.ca
Previous Name: Okanagan Mainline Municipal Association; Okanagan Valley Municipal Association; Okanagan Valley Mayors & Reeves Association
Overview: A small local organization
Mission: To represent the municipalities & regional districts of the Okanagan Mainline area
Chief Officer(s):
Harry Kroeker, President
Marg Spina, First Vice-President
Tim Pennell, Second Vice-President
Alison Slater, Executive Director
alislater@shaw.ca
Membership: 36 municipalities; *Member Profile:* Elected officials from cities, towns, villages, districts, & regional districts in south central British Columbia
Activities: Working on water treatment standards issues; Organizing workshops for members; Liaising with the provincial & federal governments
Meetings/Conferences:
For more information see Trade Shows, Conferences and Seminars Chapter
Southern Interior Local Government Association 2013 Annual General Meeting & Convention
May 2013 Salmon Arm, BC

Southern Ontario Orchid Society
75 Ternhill Cres., North York ON M3C 2E4
Tel: 905-640-5643; *Fax:* 905-640-0696
e-mail: info@soos.ca
www.soos.ca
Overview: A small local organization
Chief Officer(s):
Yvonne Schreiber, President
president@soos.ca
Membership: *Fees:* $25

Southern Ontario Seismic Network (SOSN)
c/o University of Western Ontario, London ON N6A 5B7
Tel: 519-661-3605; *Fax:* 519-661-3198
www.gp.uwo.ca
Overview: A small local organization
Mission: To obtain information on the seismicity and seismic hazards of a region of southern Ontario in which a number of nuclear power facilities are located.; *Member of:* POLARIS Network; Canadian National Seismograph Network
Chief Officer(s):
R.F. Mereu, Administrator
rmereu@uwo.ca

Southwestern Nova Scotia Fish Packers Association ***See*** Nova Scotia Fish Packers Association

---

Specification Writers Association of Canada ***See*** Construction Specifications Canada

---

Spectroscopy Society of Canada ***See*** Canadian Society for Analytical Sciences & Spectroscopy

Stanley Park Ecology Society (SPES)
PO Box 5167, Vancouver BC V6B 4B2
Tel: 604-257-6908; *Fax:* 604-257-8378
e-mail: info@stanleyparkecology.ca
www.stanleyparkecology.ca
Overview: A small local organization founded in 1988
Mission: To encourage stewardship of our natural world through environmental education & action & by fostering awareness of the fragile balance that exists between urban populations & nature
Chief Officer(s):
Patricia Thomson, Executive Director
Membership: *Fees:* $20 individual; $15 senior/junior/volunteer; $40 family

Steel Recycling Institute (SRI)
680 Andersen Dr., Pittsburgh PA 15220 USA
Tel: 412-922-2772
www.recycle-steel.org
Overview: A medium-sized international organization founded in 1988
Mission: To promote the recycling of steel products
Environmental Activity: Providing education about the benefits of recycling steel; Working with both the private & public sectors to increase the volume of steel diverted from landfills
Chief Officer(s):
Bill Heenan, President
James Woods, Director, Public & Education Relations, 412-922-2772 Ext. 215

Stockholm Environment Institute (SEI)
Kräftriket 2B, Stockholm SE-106 91 Sweden
Tel: 46-8-674-7070
e-mail: info@sei-international.org
www.sei-international.org
Overview: A medium-sized international organization founded in 1988
Mission: International research institute focusing on local, regional & global environmental issues
Chief Officer(s):
Johan Kuylenstierna, Centre Director
johan.kuylenstiernaSE@sei-international.org
Finances: *Annual Operating Budget:* Greater than $5 Million; *Funding Sources:* Government; other sources in Sweden, UK, USA
Staff: 60 staff member(s); 2 volunteer(s)
Activities: *Internships:* Yes; *Speaker Service:* Yes; *Library:* by appointment

Strategic Leadership Forum, The Toronto Society for Strategic Management (SLF)
75 Dunkirk Rd., Toronto ON M4C 2M5
Tel: 416-574-1832; *Fax:* 647-436-3599
e-mail: membership@slftoronto.com
strategicleadershipforum.camp9.org
Previous Name: The Planning Forum
Overview: A medium-sized national organization founded in 1950
Mission: To provide our community of members with an independent & intellectually challenging forum that delivers practical insights & interactions on strategic management & leadership
Chief Officer(s):
Keith Beveridge, President
Debbie Powell, Manager, Administration
Finances: *Annual Operating Budget:* $100,000-$250,000; *Funding Sources:* Membership fees; program fees; sponsorship revenue
Staff: 1 staff member(s); 24 volunteer(s)
Membership: 500; *Fees:* $295 executive; $175 academic; $1,180 corporate; *Member Profile:* Managers, directors, vice-presidents
Activities: Meetings: breakfast, luncheon, half-day, full-day & evening

Strathcona Park Lodge & Outdoor Education Centre
PO Box 2160, Campbell River BC V9W 5C5
Tel: 250-286-3122; *Fax:* 250-286-6010
e-mail: info@strathcona.bc.ca
www.strathcona.bc.ca
Also Known As: Canadian Outdoor Leadership Training Centre Ltd.
Overview: A medium-sized local organization founded in 1959
Mission: To teach the wonder, spirit & worth of people & the natural world through outdoor pursuits; *Member of:* Outdoor Recreation Council of British Columbia; Affiliation(s): Sea Kayak Guides Alliance of BC; Tourism Association of Vancouver Island
Chief Officer(s):
Myrna Boulding, President
Jamie Boulding, Executive Director
Christine Clarke, Executive Director
Finances: *Annual Operating Budget:* $1.5 Million-$3 Million; *Funding Sources:* Private
Staff: 65 staff member(s)
Membership: 1-99
Activities: Kayaking; canoeing; sailing; ropes courses; rock climbing; mountaineering; hiking; backpacking; orienteering; wilderness ethics; survival; environmental education; *Library:* Open to public

Structural Pest Management Association of Alberta *See* Pest Management Association of Alberta

Structural Pest Management Association of British Columbia (SPMABC)
c/o Integrated Pest Supplies, #108, 360 Edworthy Way, New Westminster BC V3L 5T8
Tel: 604-520-9900; *Fax:* 604-522-5557
Toll-Free: 800-465-5511
e-mail: info@spmabc.com
www.spmabc.com
Overview: A small provincial organization
Member of: Canadian Pest Management Association
Chief Officer(s):
Larry Cross, President
Membership: 54; *Fees:* $295-$420

Structural Pest Management Association of Ontario (SPMAO)
#100E, 3800 Steeles Ave. West, Woodbridge ON L4L 4G9
Toll-Free: 800-461-6722
e-mail: info@spmao.ca
www.spmao.ca
Previous Name: Ontario Pest Control Association
Overview: A small provincial organization founded in 1950
Member of: Canadian Pest Management Association; National Pest Management Association (U.S.); Urban Pest Management Council of Canada
Chief Officer(s):
Ted Berdowski, President, 905-680-1830
Finances: *Annual Operating Budget:* Less than $50,000
Staff: 1 staff member(s); 11 volunteer(s)
Membership: 100; *Fees:* $325 active; $275 allied; $215 associate
Activities: Monthly meetings; annual conference; satellite meetings; *Library:* Open to public

Sudbury Rock & Lapidary Society (SRLS)
c/o 3171 Romeo St., Val Caron ON P3N 1G5
e-mail: mineral@isys.ca
www.ccfms.ca/Clubs/Sudbury
Overview: A small local organization founded in 1984
Mission: To promote rock, mineral, gem, & fossil collecting, & lapidary for both recreation & education; *Member of:* Central Canadian Federation of Mineralogical Societies
Chief Officer(s):
Roger Poulin, President, 705-897-6216
Ruth Debicki, Vice-President; Librarian
Ed Debicki, Secretary, 705-522-5140
ed.debicki@sympatico.ca
Gil Benoit, Treasurer
Membership: 85; *Fees:* $10 individual or family; *Member Profile:* Amateurs; Hobbyists; Professionals
Activities: Hosting monthly meetings from September to June; Offering courses in lapidary arts & silver smithing; Organizing field trips; *Awareness Events:* Annual Gem & Mineral Show, July; *Library:* Sudbury Rock & Lapidary Society Library
Publications:
•Nickel Basin Rockhound
Type: Newsletter; *Frequency:* 10 pa; *Number of Pages:* 10; *Editor:* Erv Mantler; *Price:* Free with Sudbury Rock & Lapidary Society membership
Profile: Information for Sudbury Rock & Lapidary Society members, published from Septemer to June

Summerhill Impact
30 Commercial Rd., Toronto ON M4G 1Z4
Tel: 416-922-2448; *Fax:* 416-922-1028
www.summerhillimpact.ca
www.linkedin.com/company/summerhill-group
www.facebook.com/SummerhillGroup
twitter.com/SummerhillTeam
www.youtube.com/summerhillgroup
Previous Name: Clean Air Foundation
Overview: A small national organization
Mission: To develop, implement, & manage public engagement programs & other strategic approaches that lead to measurable emission reductions, to improve air quality & protect the climate
Environmental Activity: Reducing emissions; Improving air quality
Chief Officer(s):
Corey Diamond, Managing Director
Activities: Offering Car Heaven, Mow Down Pollution, Keep Cool, Switch Out, Energy Smarts, & Cool Shops

Sunshine Coast Natural History Society (SCNHS)
PO Box 543, Sechelt BC V0N 3A0
Tel: 604-885-5539; *Fax:* 604-885-2904
e-mail: greenfieldtony@hotmail.com
sunshinecoastnature.blogspot.ca
Previous Name: Sechelt Marsh Protective Society
Overview: A small local organization founded in 1978
Member of: Federation of BC Naturalists
Finances: *Annual Operating Budget:* Less than $50,000; *Funding Sources:* Membership fees; municipal grant
Staff: 20 volunteer(s)
Membership: 120; *Fees:* $25
Activities: Monthly meetings; field trips; *Awareness Events:* Christmas Bird Count

Sustainable Buildings Canada (SBC) / Bâtiments Durables Canada
#1801, 18 Eastern Ave., lower level, Toronto ON M5A 1H5
Tel: 416-364-0050; *Fax:* 416-364-0606
e-mail: sbc@sbcanada.org
www.sbcanada.org
www.facebook.com/group.php?gid=118790911470730
twitter.com/SustBldgCan
Overview: A small national organization
Mission: To showcase to the world the Canadian cooperation that exists between the private sector & government, working together to implement innovative solutions to mitigate climate change, while serving the buildings industry
Chief Officer(s):
Lenard Hart, Chair
Michael Singleton, Executive Director

Sustainable Development Technology Canada (SDTC) / Technologies du développement durable Canada
#1850, 45 O'Connor St., Ottawa ON K1P 1A4
Tel: 613-234-6313; *Fax:* 613-234-0303
e-mail: info@sdtc.ca
www.sdtc.ca
twitter.com/SDTC_TDDC
Overview: A medium-sized national organization founded in 2001
Mission: To create a healthy environment & a high quality of life for Canadians; To identify & fund technologies with strong competitive & environmental potential
Environmental Activity: Supporting clean technology projects
Chief Officer(s):
Juergen Puetter, Chair
Vicky J. Sharpe, President & Chief Executive Officer
vj.sharpe@sdtc.ca
Rick Whittaker, Chief Technology Officer & Vice-President, Investments
Sailesh Thaker, Vice-President, Industry & Stakeholder Relations
Barry Wilson, Vice-President, Finance & Administration
David Minicola, Manager, Applications, 613-234-6313 Ext. 310
d.minicola@sdtc.ca
Patrice Breton, Director, Communications
p.breton@sdtc.ca
Finances: *Funding Sources:* Government of Canada
Membership: *Committees:* Corporate Governance; Human Resources; Project Review; Audit & Grant Investment
Publications:
•Sustainable Development Technology Canada Annual Report
Type: Yearbook; *Frequency:* Annually
•Sustainable Development Technology Canada Corporate Plan

Sustainable Forestry Initiative Inc.
#700, 900 - 17th St. NW, Washington DC 20006 USA
Tel: 202-596-3450; *Fax:* 202-596-3451
e-mail: info@sfiprogram.org
www.sfiprogram.org
twitter.com/sfiprogram
www.youtube.com/user/SFIProgram
Overview: A large international charitable organization founded in 1994

Mission: To promote sustainable forest management; To maintain & improve the sustainable forestry certification program
Environmental Activity: Empowering consumers to make responsible environmental choices by purchasing products from a certified forest or sourcing; Protecting forests, including water quality & habitat; Offering training related to the practice of responsible forestry
Chief Officer(s):
Robert A. (Bob) Luoto, Chair
Kathy Abusow, President & CEO, 613-722-8734
Kathy.abusow@sfiprogram.org
Rick Cantrell, Vice-President & COO, 864-653-7224
Rick.Cantrell@sfiprogram.org
Eli Weissman, Senior Director, Conservation Partnerships, 202-596-3452
Eli.Weissman@sfiprogram.org
Danny Karch, Director, Green Building, 450-242-1233
danny.karch@sfiprogram.org
Activities: Promoting research to improve forestry practices
Meetings/Conferences:
For more information see Trade Shows, Conferences and Seminars Chapter
Sustainable Forestry Initiative 2013 Annual Conference
September 2013 San Antonio, TX
Publications:
•Sustainable Forestry Initiative Newsletter
Type: Newsletter; *Frequency:* Bimonthly
Profile: Recent information about the SFI program, including conservation grants updates, new certifications, & program statistics

Sustainable Urban Development Association (SUDA)
2637 Council Ring Rd., Mississauga ON L5L 1S6
Tel: 416-400-0553
e-mail: mail@suda.ca
www.suda.ca
Overview: A medium-sized national organization
Mission: To foster a healthy natural environment by providing information about ways in which cities can become more efficient in the land, material, water and energy resources, and highly supportive of sustainable transportation.

Swift Current Agricultural & Exhibition Association
PO Box 146, 1700 - 17th Ave. SE, Swift Current SK S9H 3V5
Tel: 306-773-2944; *Fax:* 306-773-7015
e-mail: swiftcurrentex@sasktel.net
www.swiftcurrentex.com
Overview: A small provincial charitable organization founded in 1938
Mission: To facilitate education, entertainment, exhibitions & agricultural programs for the cultural & economic benefits of the community; *Member of:* Saskatchewan Association of Agricultural Societies & Exhibitions
Chief Officer(s):
Donna Sagin, General Manager
Stuart Smith, President
Finances: *Annual Operating Budget:* $500,000-$1.5 Million
Staff: 4 staff member(s); 500 volunteer(s)
Membership: 78; *Fees:* $5
Activities: Agricultural Fairs, Exhibitions, Livestock shows & sales, Trade shows

Swift Current Creek Watershed Stewards (SCCWS)
PO Box 1088, Swift Current SK S9H 3X3
Tel: 306-778-5007; *Fax:* 306-778-5020
e-mail: stewards@sccws.com
www.sccws.com
Overview: A small local organization
Mission: To enhance water quality and stream health of the Swift Current Creek Watershed by promoting awareness and understanding among water users.
Chief Officer(s):
Arlene Unvoas, Executive Director

Sydenham Field Naturalists (SFN)
PO Box 22008, Wallaceburg ON N8A 5G4
Overview: A small local charitable organization founded in 1985
Mission: To preserve wildlife, promote public interest, cooperate with others with similar interests, consider matters of environmental concern; *Member of:* Federation of Ontario Naturalists; Canadian Nature Federation; Carolinian Canada
Chief Officer(s):
Brett Groves, President
Finances: *Funding Sources:* Bingo profits; private donations; grants
Membership: 35-40; *Fees:* $15 single; $25 family
Activities: Field trips; planting of native shrubs/wildflowers; indoor meetings; wood lot acquisition

Syndicat canadien des communications, de l'énergie et du papier ***See*** Communications, Energy & Paperworkers Union of Canada

Syndicat national des cultivateurs ***See*** National Farmers Union

Syndicat national des cultivateurs ***See*** National Farmers Union

Syndicat national des cultivateurs ***See*** National Farmers Union

Syndicat national des cultivateurs ***See*** National Farmers Union

Syndicat national des cultivateurs ***See*** National Farmers Union

TD Friends of the Environment Foundation / Fondation des amis de l'environnement TD
TD Tower, 66 Wellington St., 17th Fl., Ottawa ON M5K 1A2
Toll-Free: 800-361-5333
e-mail: tdfef@td.com
www.fef.td.com
Previous Name: Friends of the Environment Foundation
Overview: A medium-sized national charitable organization founded in 1990
Mission: To protect & preserve the Canadian environment
Chief Officer(s):
Natasha Alleyne-Martin, Manager, National Programs, 416-308-5047
natasha.martin@td.com
Ellen Dungen, Regional Manager, Saskatchewan & Manitoba
ellen.dungen@td.com
Cathy Jowsey, Regional Manager, Northern & Eastern Ontario
cathy.jowsey@td.com
Mandip Kharod, Regional Manager, British Columbia, Alberta, Yukon, & Northwest Territories
mandip.kharod@td.com
Amelie Picher, Regional Manager, Québec
amelie.picher@td.com
Yvetter Scrivener, Regional Manager, Central & Southwestern Ontario
yvette.scrivener@td.com
Farzana Syed, Regional Manager, Greater Toronto Area, Surrounding Region, & Atlantic Provinces
farzana.syed@td.com
Finances: *Funding Sources:* Donations
Membership: 1,000+
Activities: *Speaker Service:* Yes

The technical society of the Canadian Nuclear Association (CNA) ***See*** Canadian Nuclear Society

TechnoCentre éolien / Wind Energy TechnoCentre
70, rue Bolduc, Gaspé QC G4X 1G2
Tél: 418-368-6162; *Téléc:* 418-368-4315
Courriel: info@eolien.qc.ca
www.eolien.qc.ca
twitter.com/TCEolien
Aperçu: *Dimension:* petite; *Envergure:* provinciale; fondée en 2000
Mission: Le TechnoCentre éolien a pour mission de contribuer au développement d'une filière industrielle éolienne québécoise, compétitive à l'échelle nord-américaine et internationale, tout en mettant en valeur la Gaspésie?Iles-de-la-Madeleine au cour de ce créneau émergeant de l'économie du Québec.
Membre(s) du bureau directeur:
Frédéric Côté, directeur général
fcote@eolien.qc.ca
Meetings/Conferences:
For more information see Trade Shows, Conferences and Seminars Chapter
7e Colloque de l'industrie éolienne québécoise / Québec's 7th Wind Energy Conference
June 2013 Matane, QC

Technologies du développement durable Canada ***See*** Sustainable Development Technology Canada

TechNova
Parent Name: Canadian Council of Technicians & Technologists
#A308, Cambridge 1, 202 Brownlow Ave., Dartmouth NS B3B 1T5
Tel: 902-463-3236; *Fax:* 902-465-7567
Toll-Free: 866-723-8867
e-mail: info@technova.ca
www.technova.ca
Also Known As: Society of Certified Engineering Technicians & Technologists of Nova Scotia
Overview: A medium-sized provincial licensing organization founded in 1967 overseen by Canadian Council of Technicians & Technologists
Mission: Certifying engineering & applied science technicians & technologists for the betterment of the public & the welfare of the environment
Chief Officer(s):
Louis LeBel, President
Finances: *Annual Operating Budget:* $100,000-$250,000; *Funding Sources:* Memberships
Staff: 1 staff member(s); 9 volunteer(s)
Membership: 1,500+; *Fees:* $150

Tellus Institute
11 Arlington St., Boston MA 02116-3411 USA
Tel: 617-266-5400; *Fax:* 617-266-8303
e-mail: info@tellus.org
www.tellus.org
Overview: A medium-sized international charitable organization founded in 1976
Mission: To conduct a diverse program of research, consulting, & communications; To address policy & planning issues in such areas as energy, water, waste, & land use for a sustainable world for future generations; *Member of:* Stockholm Environment Institute
Chief Officer(s):
Paul Raskin, President
praskin@tellus.org
David McAnulty, Administrative Director
dmac@tellus.org
Finances: *Funding Sources:* Government agencies; Foundations; Non-governmental organizations
Staff: 2 volunteer(s)
Activities: Conducting research; Analyzing problems & evaluating options for technological & institutional change

Temiskaming Environmental Action Committee (TEAC)
PO Box 541, New Liskeard ON P0J 1P0
Tel: 705-678-2404; *Fax:* 705-647-7511
Overview: A small local organization
Mission: To raise public awareness of environmental issues; Affiliation(s): Northwatch; Public Concern Temiskaming; Ontario Environmental Network
Membership: 1-99
Activities: *Speaker Service:* Yes

Thames Region Ecological Association (TREA)
1017 Western Rd., London ON N6G 1G5
Tel: 519-672-5991; *Fax:* 519-645-0981
e-mail: trea@wwdc.com
www.trea.ca
Overview: A small local charitable organization founded in 1986
Mission: Committed to educating ourselves & the community towards development of an ecologically responsible & sustainable future through awareness, reflection, caring & action; *Member of:* Grosvenor Lodge Resource Centre for Heritage & Environment; Affiliation(s): Urban League of London; London Composts
Finances: *Annual Operating Budget:* Less than $50,000; *Funding Sources:* Government; membership fees; Compost Day
Staff: 1 staff member(s); 40 volunteer(s)
Membership: 60 individual; *Fees:* $20 individual
Activities: TREATop; waste group; home cocmposting program; TREATalk, tree planting; pesticide group; London Bicycle Festival; *Speaker Service:* Yes

Thermal Environmental Comfort Association (TECA)
PO Box 73105, Stn. Evergreen RO, Surrey BC V3R 0J2
Tel: 604-594-5956; *Fax:* 604-594-5091
Toll-Free: 888-577-3818
e-mail: training@teca.ca
www.teca.ca
Overview: A large provincial organization
Mission: To offer the residential heating, cooling and ventilation industry up-to-date training courses and a collective voice in local and provincial issues.
Chief Officer(s):
Kim Savage, Executive Director, 604-596-0595
Gary Fabbro, President, 604-299-1353
Kathryn Kubossek, Administrator

Membership: 298; *Fees:* $185-$350; $100 associate

Thermal Insulation Association of Alberta

#400, 1040 - 7 Ave. SW, Calgary AB T2P 3G9
Tel: 403-244-4487; *Fax:* 403-244-2340
e-mail: info@tiaa.cc
www.tiaa.cc
Overview: A small provincial organization
Mission: To improve & elevate the technical & general knowledge of the mechanical insulation industry in Alberta, promoting excellence in manufacture, application, & installation of all insulation products & materials; *Member of:* Thermal Insulation Association of Canada
Chief Officer(s):
Mark Travors, Provincial President
Meetings/Conferences:
For more information see Trade Shows, Conferences and Seminars Chapter
Thermal Insulation Association of Alberta Annual General Meeting & Banquet 2013
May 2013 Red Deer, AB

Thunder Bay Field Naturalists (TBFN)

PO Box 10037, Thunder Bay ON P7B 6T6
Tel: 807-474-6007
www.tbfn.net
Overview: A small local charitable organization founded in 1933
Mission: To promote the enjoyment of nature through environmental appreciation & conservation; to encourage wise use & conservation of natural resources; to promote environmental protection; *Member of:* Federation of Ontario Naturalists; Affiliation(s): Thunder Cape Bird Observatory
Chief Officer(s):
Sue Bryan, Acting President
bryan@tbaytel.net
Rob Foster, Vice-President
rfoster@tbaytel.net
Finances: *Annual Operating Budget:* $50,000-$100,000; *Funding Sources:* Membership fees; donations; grants
Staff: 11 volunteer(s)
Membership: 200; *Fees:* $30 family; $25 single; $20 students/seniors; $350 life; *Member Profile:* Those interested in the study of nature & the environment; *Committees:* Nature Reserves; Bird Records; Peregrine Falcon Recovery; Bluebird Recovery
Activities: Adult & Junior Nature; oriented field trips; indoor lectures; *Speaker Service:* Yes

Timberline Trail & Nature Club

701 - 105th Ave., Dawson Creek BC V1G 2K5
Tel: 250-782-7680
Overview: A small local organization
Mission: To promote the enjoyment of nature through environmental appreciation & conservation; to encourage wise use & conservation of natural resources & environmental protection.; *Member of:* Federation of BC Naturalists

Tire Stewardship BC Association (TSBC)

PO Box 5366, 1627 Fort St., 4th Fl., Victoria BC V8R 6S4
Tel: 250-598-9112; *Fax:* 250-598-9119
Toll-Free: 866-759-0488
www.tirestewardshipbc.ca
Overview: A small provincial organization founded in 2006
Mission: The Tire Stewardship BC Association was founded by the Rubber Association of Canada, The Retail Council of Canada and the Western Canada Tire Dealers. In 2007 the New Car Dealers Association joined the Association. TSBC is governed by a Board that is made up of representatives from these four organizations
Chief Officer(s):
Don Blythe, Chair
Glenn Maidment, Secretary

Toronto Biotechnology Initiative (TBI) / L'Initiative torontoise de biotechnologie

#109, 1 Concorde Gate, Toronto ON M3C 3N5
Tel: 416-426-7293; *Fax:* 416-426-7280
e-mail: admin@ontbio.org
Overview: A small local organization founded in 1989
Mission: To further biotechnology in the Greater Toronto Area; to further TBI as a leading Canadian biotechnology organization; to further the Greater Toronto Area as a major international centre for biotechnology; Affiliation(s): Biotechnology Industry Organization; Council of Biotechnology Centres; BIOTECanada
Chief Officer(s):
Ali Ibrahimi, Manager, Communications & Membership
Finances: *Annual Operating Budget:* $50,000-$100,000; *Funding Sources:* Membership fees
Membership: 400; *Fees:* $200 regular; $100 student; *Committees:* Biofinance; Breakfast Meetings; Education; Membership; Public Interest Forum; Regulatory; Technology Transfer
Activities: Biofinance (events, awards dinner); Bioscan newsletter; community service award; education; entrepreunership program; international program; monthly meetings; public interest forum; regulatory affairs;

Toronto Entomologists Association (TEA)

c/o Chris Rickard, Treasurer, 16 Mount View Ct., Collingwood ON L9Y 5A9
e-mail: info@ontarioinsects.org
www.ontarioinsects.org
Overview: A small local charitable organization founded in 1969
Mission: To maintain an interest in the insects, particularly the butterflies & moths of Ontario; To record life histories, changes in distribution, unusual records, etc., of Ontario butterflies & moths; *Member of:* Federation of Ontario Naturalists
Chief Officer(s):
Glenn Richardson, President
glennr@personainternet.com
Finances: *Annual Operating Budget:* Less than $50,000; *Funding Sources:* Membership fees; donations
Membership: 170; *Fees:* $15 student; $25 individual; $30 family; *Member Profile:* Amateur insect enthusiasts; professionals
Activities: Butterfly counts

Toronto Environmental Alliance (TEA)

#201, 30 Duncan St., Toronto ON M5V 2C3
Tel: 416-596-0660; *Fax:* 416-596-0345
e-mail: tea@torontoenvironment.org
www.torontoenvironment.org
Overview: A small local organization
Mission: To bring together groups & individuals who share the common goal of making the communities of Greater Toronto area operate in an ecologically sustainable manner; *Member of:* Ontario Environmental Network
Chief Officer(s):
Franz Hartmann, Executive Director
Finances: *Annual Operating Budget:* $250,000-$500,000
Staff: 7 staff member(s); 200 volunteer(s)
Membership: 8,000; *Fees:* $25; *Committees:* Water; Climate Change; Waste; Smog; Transit
Activities: ; *Library:* Open to public by appointment

Toronto Field Naturalists (TFN)

#1519, 2 Carlton St., Toronto ON M5B 1J3
Tel: 416-593-2656
e-mail: office@torontofieldnaturalists.org
www.torontofieldnaturalists.org
www.facebook.com/TorontoFieldNaturalists
Overview: A medium-sized local charitable organization founded in 1923
Mission: To promote the enjoyment & preservation of nature; To raise public interest in natural history
Environmental Activity: Organizing stewardship work parties to clear trails & remove invasive species; Protecting & enhancing ravines, parks, & the waterfront in Toronto; Educating the public about nature
Chief Officer(s):
Bob Kortright, President
Walter Weary, Secretary-Treasurer
Finances: *Funding Sources:* Membership fees; Donations
Membership: *Fees:* $20 youth; $30 single seniors; $40 adults & senior families; $50 families
Activities: Partnering with organizations such as Ontario Nature, Toronto Green Community, Toronto Parks & Recreation, & the Toronto & Region Conservation Authority; Engaging in advocacy activities; Organizing monthly talks by experts on natural history topics
Meetings/Conferences:
For more information see Trade Shows, Conferences and Seminars Chapter
Toronto Field Naturalists 2013 Monthly Talks: The Flies We Despise: Reflections on the Wonderful World of Black Flies
November 2013 Toronto, ON
Toronto Field Naturalists 2013 Monthly Talks: The Don River
December 2013 Toronto, ON
Toronto Field Naturalists 2014 Monthly Talks: Planets Beyond Our Solar System: In Search of Other Earths
February 2014 Toronto, ON
Toronto Field Naturalists 2014 Monthly Talk: In the Eye of the Beholder: A Study of Beauty in the Natural World
March 2014 Toronto, ON
Toronto Field Naturalists 2014 Monthly Talk: The Reluctant Twitcher
April 2014 Toronto, ON
Toronto Field Naturalists 2014 Monthly Talk: Sand Dune Conservation
May 2014 Toronto, ON
Publications:
•Toronto Field Naturalist
Type: Newsletter; *Frequency:* 8 pa
Profile: Information about nature in Toronto, environmental issues, & the organization's upcoming activities

Toronto Ornithological Club (TOC)

Toronto ON
e-mail: info@torontobirding.ca
www.torontobirding.ca
Overview: A small local charitable organization founded in 1934
Mission: To afford opportunities for the meeting together of ornithologists at regular intervals for discussion; to facilitate cooperation in ornithological studies; to review & report on ornithological topics; to establish a liaison between members & visiting naturalists; *Member of:* Federation of Ontario Naturalists
Chief Officer(s):
Jeremy Hatt, Councillor, Membership
membership@torontobirding.ca
Finances: *Annual Operating Budget:* Less than $50,000
Membership: 150+; *Fees:* $25; *Committees:* Outings; Records; Editorial; Archives; Conservation
Activities: Bird outings; High Park hawk watch; fall field day;

Toronto Renewable Energy Co-operative (TREC)

#405, 401 Richmond St. W., Toronto ON M5V 3A8
Tel: 416-977-5093; *Fax:* 416-306-6476
Toll-Free: 866-560-9463
e-mail: info@trec.on.ca
www.trec.on.ca
twitter.com/TRECoop
Overview: A small local organization founded in 1998
Mission: A non-profit organization of citizens dedicated to renewable energy and energy conservation; *Member of:* Canadian Renewable Energy Alliance; Affiliation(s): Toronto District School Board; Ontario Trillium Foundation; Ontario Power Authority Conservation Fund; Toronto Atmospheric Fund; Community Power Fund; Ontario Sustainable Energy Ass'n
Chief Officer(s):
Judy Lipp, Executive Director
jlipp@trec.on.ca
Finances: *Funding Sources:* Donations
Activities: Community energy projects; interactive, hands-on education; Green City Bike Tours; Green Collar Career program; Our Power solar initiative; solar home tours; round table discussions; Bruce County wind energy co-operative project

Toronto Sheet Metal & Air Handling Group; Environmental Sheet Metal Association Toronto ***See*** Toronto Sheet Metal Contractors Association

Toronto Sheet Metal Contractors Association (TSMCA)

#26, 30 Wertheim Ct., Richmond Hill ON L4B 1B9
Tel: 905-886-9627; *Fax:* 905-886-9959
e-mail: shtmetal@bellnet.ca
www.tsmca.org
Previous Name: Toronto Sheet Metal & Air Handling Group; Environmental Sheet Metal Association Toronto
Overview: A medium-sized local organization
Member of: Ontario Sheet Metal & Air Handling Group
Chief Officer(s):
Jim Warner, President, 416-749-6031, Fax: 416-749-4673
jwarner@modernniagara.com
Finances: *Annual Operating Budget:* $250,000-$500,000; *Funding Sources:* Collective Agreement Assessment
Staff: 5 staff member(s)
Membership: 102 individual

Toronto Transportation Society (TTS)

PO Box 5187, Stn. A, Toronto ON M5W 1N5
www.torontotransportationsociety.org
Overview: A small local organization founded in 1973
Chief Officer(s):
Kevin Nichol, President
Richard Hooles, Vice-President
Robert Giles, Secretary
Robert Lubinski, Treasurer

Finances: *Funding Sources:* Membership fees
Membership: *Fees:* $25 CDN Canadians; $30 USD USA residents; $45 CDN international; *Member Profile:* Transportation enthusiasts with an interest in buses, streetcars, railways, & subways
Activities: Hosting monthly meetings; Organizing a Memorabilia Night, featuring an auction of transit collections; Arranging charters using unique transit vehicles
Publications:
•Transfer Points
Type: Newsletter; *Frequency:* 10 pa; *Editor:* Adam Zhelka; *Price:* Free with membership in the Toronto Transportation Society
Profile: Transportation related news, historic articles, photographs, & happenings in the Greater Toronto Area

Toronto Zoo

361A Old Finch Ave., Toronto ON M1B 5K7
Tel: 416-392-5929
www.torontozoo.com
www.facebook.com/TheTorontoZoo
Previous Name: Zoological Society of Metropolitan Toronto
Overview: A small local organization founded in 1969
Mission: To support the Toronto Zoo in its efforts to conserve species diversity through conservation, education, & research; Affiliation(s): Canadian Association of Zoos, Parks & Aquariums; American Association of Zoos, Parks & Aquariums; Canadian Centre for Philanthropy
Chief Officer(s):
Raymond Cho, Chair
John Tracogna, Chief Executive Officer
Finances: *Annual Operating Budget:* $500,000-$1.5 Million; *Funding Sources:* Grants; Events; Corporate; Memberships; Bequests
Staff: 5 staff member(s); 45 volunteer(s)
Membership: 20,000; *Fees:* Schedule available; *Committees:* Executive; Finance; Sponsorship
Activities: *Rents Mailing List:* Yes

Tourism Industry Association of New Brunswick Inc. (TIANB) / Association de l'industrie touristique du Nouveau-Brunswick inc. (AITNB)

#440, 500 Beaverbrook Ct., Fredericton NB E3B 5X4
Tel: 506-458-5646; *Fax:* 506-459-3634
Toll-Free: 800-668-5313
e-mail: info@tianb.com
www.tianb.com
www.facebook.com/pages/TIANB-AITNB/127475440600650?sk=wall&filter=12
twitter.com/tianb_aitnb
Previous Name: Hospitality New Brunswick
Overview: A medium-sized provincial organization founded in 1978
Mission: To act as the provincial tourism & hospitality organization of New Brunswick, existing to fulfill the needs of its membership, in cooperation with both private & public sector partners; committed to be a representative, industry driven organization which provides leadership & direction, making tourism & hospitality the leading & most viably sustainable industry in New Brunswick; *Member of:* Tourism Industry Association of Canada; Hotel Association of Canada; Canadian Tourism Human Resource Council; Provincial Territorial Tourism Industry Association
Environmental Activity: Sustainable Tourism Award
Chief Officer(s):
Réal Robichaud, Executive Director
Joanne Bérubé-Gagné, President
Finances: *Annual Operating Budget:* $500,000-$1.5 Million
Staff: 10 staff member(s); 22 volunteer(s)
Membership: 600; *Fees:* Schedule available; *Member Profile:* Businesses having anything to do with the tourism industry in New Brunswick; *Committees:* Tourism strategy; National HR product quality; Emerit certification
Activities: Annual golf tournament, Sept.; *Awareness Events:* Annual meeting & conference, May; Provincial Tourism Awareness Week, June; *Library:* Open to public

Toxics Watch Society of Alberta (TWS)

1-6328A - 104 St. NW, Edmonton AB T6H 2K9
Tel: 780-439-1912; *Fax:* 780-433-3792
www.toxwatch.ca
Overview: A small provincial organization founded in 1986
Mission: To promote reduction in the common use of toxic substances & zero discharge of toxic wastes; to ensure clean air & water & safe food for Albertans; to facilitate sustainable communities & environmental citizenship; *Member of:* Alberta Environmental Network; Canadian Environmental Network; Affiliation(s): Environmental Resource Centre; Tomorrow Foundation for a Sustainable Future
Chief Officer(s):
Conrad Nobert, President
Finances: *Annual Operating Budget:* Less than $50,000
Staff: 2 staff member(s); 7 volunteer(s)
Membership: 100; *Fees:* $10; *Committees:* Clear Air Strategic Alliance; AEN Steering; Beverage Container Management Board: Tire Recycling Management Board
Activities: Public Information Service; *Library:* Resource Library; Open to public

Trans Canada Trail Foundation (TCTF) / Fondation du sentier transcanadien

43, Westminster Ave. North, Montréal QC H4X 1Y8
Tel: 514-485-3959; *Fax:* 514-485-4541
Toll-Free: 800-465-3636
e-mail: info@tctrail.ca
www.tctrail.ca
Overview: A medium-sized national charitable organization founded in 1992
Mission: To promote & coordinate the planning, designing & building of a continuous, shared-use recreation trail that winds its way through every Province & Territory
Chief Officer(s):
Gail Urquhart, Vice President, Resource Development & Government Relations, 800-465-3636 Ext. 4359
gurquhart@tctrail.ca
Finances: *Annual Operating Budget:* $250,000-$500,000; *Funding Sources:* Public donations
Staff: 11 staff member(s); 1 volunteer(s)
Membership: 2,500; *Fees:* $75-150
Activities: Trail-building; trail locators & signage; guidebooks & maps

Trans Canada Yellowhead Highway Association (TCYHA)

#332, 10113 - 104 St., Edmonton AB T5J 1A1
Tel: 780-429-0444; *Fax:* 780-426-5078
www.yellowheadit.com
Previous Name: Yellowhead Highway Association
Overview: A small local organization founded in 1947
Mission: To improve highway infrastructure & promote tourism along the TransCanada/Yellowhead highway corridor
Chief Officer(s):
Irene Davidson-Fisher, CEO
Finances: *Annual Operating Budget:* $100,000-$250,000
Staff: 3 staff member(s); 1 volunteer(s)
Membership: 390; *Member Profile:* Municipal, commercial, & corporate organizations & individuals

Transport 2000 Canada *See* Transport Action Canada

Transport Action Canada

Bronson Centre, PO Box 858, Stn. B, #303, 211 Bronson Ave., Ottawa ON K1P 5P9
Tel: 613-594-3290; *Fax:* 613-594-3271
e-mail: info@transport-action.ca
www.transport-action.ca
Previous Name: Transport 2000 Canada
Overview: A medium-sized national charitable organization founded in 1976
Mission: National federation of environmental & consumer groups concerned about the importance of transportation on our environment & quality of life; to inform Canadians of the need for a coherent national transport policy which recognizes that conservation of resources must be a priority & that access to good public transportation is a right of all Canadians; to work for the improvement & greater use of bus & rail transportation in the interests of public safety, social equity & the protection of the environment; to press for the coordination of all transport services for the benefit of users; to demand more attention to the needs of pedestrians, cyclists & public transport users; to maximize the use of the energy-efficient rail & marine modes for the shipment of freight. PUBLICATIONS: National Transport Newsletter.; Affiliation(s): Transport 2000 International
Chief Officer(s):
David Jeanes, President
Justin Bur, VP East
Peter Lacey, VP West
Tony Turrittin, Secretary
Klaus Beltzner, Treasurer
Bert Titcomb, Manager
Finances: *Annual Operating Budget:* $50,000-$100,000; *Funding Sources:* Donations
Staff: 15 volunteer(s)
Membership: 1,500; *Fees:* $35 regular; $30 senior; $50 family; $75 affiliate non-profit; $170corporate
Activities: Research, public education & advocacy, representation of the consumer interests before federal, provincial, municipal public hearings & regulatory bodies, direction of consumer complaints to public carriers; *Speaker Service:* Yes; *Library:* Open to public

Transportation Association of Canada (TAC) / Association des transports du Canada (ATC)

2323 St. Laurent Blvd., Ottawa ON K1G 4J8
Tel: 613-736-1350; *Fax:* 613-736-1395
e-mail: secretariat@tac-atc.ca
www.tac-atc.ca
Previous Name: Roads & Transportation Association of Canada
Overview: A large national organization founded in 1970
Mission: To promote the provision of safe, efficient, effective & environmentally sustainable transportation services in support of Canada's social & economic goals; To act as a neutral forum for the discussion of transportation issues & matters; to act as a technical focus in the highway transportation area
Chief Officer(s):
Michel Gravel, Executive Director
mgravel@tac-atc.ca
Guylaine Brousseau, Manager, Finance & Administration
gbrousseau@tac-atc.ca
Sarah Wells, Director, Technical Programs
swells@tac-atc.ca
Erica Andersen, Director, Communications & Member Services
eandersen@tac-atc.ca
John Law, President
Joseph K. Lam, Vice-President
Alex Turnbull, Treasurer
Finances: *Annual Operating Budget:* Greater than $5 Million
Staff: 30 staff member(s); 500 volunteer(s)
Membership: 550 corporate; *Fees:* Schedule available; *Committees:* Technical & Research; Editing & Publications; Rules of the Road; Project; Technical Steering; Asphalts Advisory; Operations; Pavements; Structures; Aviation; Conference Technical Program; Geometric Design; Goods Movement; Soils & Materials; Traffic; Transit Planning; Technology
Activities: ; *Library:* Technical Information Centre; by appointment

Tree Canada Foundation / Arbres Canada

#402, 222 Somerset St. West, Ottawa ON K2P 2G3
Tel: 613-567-5545; *Fax:* 613-567-5270
Toll-Free: 877-666-1444
e-mail: tcf@treecanada.ca
www.treecanada.ca
www.facebook.com/group.php?gid=172923782752077
twitter.com/TreeCanada
Overview: A small national organization founded in 1992
Mission: To provide education, technical support, resources & financial support through working partnerships to encourage Canadians to plant & care for trees in our urban & rural environment in an effort to help reduce the harmful effects of carbon dioxide emissions
Chief Officer(s):
Michael Rosen, President
mrosen@treecanada.ca
Finances: *Annual Operating Budget:* $1.5 Million-$3 Million
Staff: 8 staff member(s); 1300 volunteer(s)
Activities: *Speaker Service:* Yes
Awards:
•Awards (Grant)
National tree-planting & tree-care program designed to offset the problem of global warming; provides technical advice & financial assistance to qualifying partners for certain planting costs & for buying trees; partners are expected to contribute cash &/or in-kind services *Eligibility:* Groups interested in tree-planting programs

Trees Winnipeg

1539 Waverley St., Winnipeg MB R3T 4V7
Tel: 204-832-7188; *Fax:* 204-986-4050
e-mail: office@treeswinnipeg.org
www.savetheelms.mb.ca
Previous Name: Coalition to Save the Elms
Overview: A medium-sized local charitable organization founded in 1992
Mission: To protect, preserve, & promote the urban forest & environment
Chief Officer(s):
Gerry Engel, President

Kerienne La France, Executive Director
Richard Westwood, Secretary-Treasurer
Finances: *Funding Sources:* Donations
Membership: 10,000; *Fees:* $25 preferred; $15 regular/renewal
Activities: Providing public workshops; Organizing a treebanding program; *Awareness Events:* Arbor Day, June; Adopt-a-Tree Program; *Speaker Service:* Yes
Publications:
•Manitoba Elm Survival Guide
Type: Guide
•Tree Owner's Manual
Type: Manual
•The Urban Forester
Type: Newsletter; *Frequency:* Quarterly
Profile: Information for Tree Winnipeg supporters & interested parties

Trout Unlimited Canada (TUC)

PO Box 339, Stn. T, Calgary AB T2G 2H9
Tel: 403-221-8360; *Fax:* 403-221-8368
Toll-Free: 800-909-6040
e-mail: tuc@tucanada.org
www.tucanada.org
Overview: A small national charitable organization founded in 1972
Mission: To promote the conservation & wise use of trout & other coldwater fisheries & their watersheds, through the undertaking of habitat restoration & enhancement, research, management, & public education
Environmental Activity: Restoring habitats
Chief Officer(s):
Doug Cressman, CEO
Finances: *Annual Operating Budget:* $500,000-$1.5 Million
Staff: 10 staff member(s); 1000 volunteer(s)
Membership: 4,000; *Fees:* $30
Activities: Yellow Fish Road Program; *Library:* by appointment

Truck Loggers Association (TLA)

#725, 815 Hastings St. West, Vancouver BC V6C 1B4
Tel: 604-684-4291; *Fax:* 604-684-7134
e-mail: contact@tla.ca
www.tla.ca
Overview: A medium-sized provincial organization founded in 1942
Affiliation(s): Pacific Logging Congress
Chief Officer(s):
Dave Lewis, Executive Director
contact@tla.ca
Finances: *Annual Operating Budget:* $500,000-$1.5 Million
Staff: 5 staff member(s); 17 volunteer(s)
Membership: 600 institutional; *Member Profile:* TO give the independent loggers a collective voice in the changes taking place in society and the forest industry; To share information about newly developing logging machines, methods, and technology.

Tunnelling Association of Canada (TAC) / Association canadienne des tunnels

8828 Pigott Rd., Richmond ON V7A 2C4
Tel: 604-241-1297; *Fax:* 604-241-1399
e-mail: admin@tunnelcanada.ca
www.tunnelcanada.ca
Overview: A medium-sized national organization
Mission: To promote Canadian tunnelling & underground excavation technologies, & safe design, construction & maintenance; to facilitate information exchange; to represent the tunnelling community in matters of public & technical concern; to publish a Canadian registry of tunnels, underground excavations & similar works; *Member of:* Canadian Geotechnical Society
Chief Officer(s):
Derek Zoldy, Secretary-Treasurer
secretary@tunnelcanada.ca
Rick Staples, President
president@tunnelcanada.ca
Membership: 350 individual, student & corporate members; *Fees:* $50 individual; $15 student; $250 corporate

Underwater Archaeological Society of British Columbia (UASBC)

c/o Vancouver Maritime Museum, 1905 Ogden Ave., Vancouver BC V6J 1A3
Tel: 604-942-9908; *Fax:* 604-980-0358
e-mail: uasbc@uasbc.com
www.uasbc.com
Overview: A small provincial charitable organization founded in 1975
Mission: To promote the science of underwater archaeology; to conserve, preserve & protect the maritime heritage lying beneath our coastal & inland waters; *Member of:* Outdoor Recreation Council of British Columbia
Chief Officer(s):
Jacques Marc, President
David Stone, Executive Director
Finances: *Annual Operating Budget:* $50,000-$100,000; *Funding Sources:* Membership dues; government; corporate
Staff: 1 staff member(s); 150 volunteer(s)
Membership: 175; *Fees:* $35 single; $88 corporate; $40 family; $26 senior; $18 student; *Committees:* Explorations; Education; Conservation
Activities: Archaeological site surveys, heritage awareness promotion; operates 4 chapters in Vancouver, Victoria, Kootenay & Okanagan; *Speaker Service:* Yes; *Library:* Archives; by appointment

UNEP - World Conservation Monitoring Centre (UNEP-WCMC)

219 Huntingdon Rd., Cambridge CB3 0DL United Kingdom
Tel: 44-1223-277-314; *Fax:* 44-1223-277-136
e-mail: info@unep-wcmc.org
www.unep-wcmc.org/
Previous Name: World Conservation Monitoring Centre
Overview: A small international charitable organization founded in 1988
Mission: To provide information services on conservation & sustainable use of the world's living resources; to help others to develop information system on their own; Affiliation(s): United Nations Environment Programme
Chief Officer(s):
Jon Hutton, Director
Activities: ; *Library:* by appointment

Unifarm ***See*** Wild Rose Agricultural Producers

Union des cultivateurs franco-ontariens (UCFO)

2474 rue Champlain, Clarence Creek ON K0A 1N0
Tél: 613-488-2929; *Téléc:* 613-488-2541
Ligne sans frais: 877-425-8366
Courriel: info@ucfo.ca
www.ucfo.ca
www.facebook.com/UCFO.ca
Aperçu: *Dimension:* petite; *Envergure:* provinciale; Organisme sans but lucratif; fondée en 1929
Mission: Regrouper les franco-ontariens et les franco-ontariennes qui oeuvrent dans le secteur agricole; concerter pour la protection de nos droits; promouvoir nos intérêts; informer notre communauté; appuyer les institutions et groupements qui favorisent notre développement; développer notre sentiment et fierté; stimuler le développement social et économique des régions agricoles et rurales
Membre(s) du bureau directeur:
Pierre Bercier, Président
Simon Durand, Directeur général
sdurand@lavoieagricole.ca
Finances: *Budget de fonctionnement annuel:* $100,000-$250,000
Personnel: 7 membre(s) du personnel; 10 bénévole(s)
Membre: 300 *Montant de la cotisation:* 15$ membre régulier; 35$ membre auxiliaire; *Critères d'admissibilite:* Agriculteurs, agricultrices de l'Ontario
Activités: Programme de développement de leadership coopératif; formation agricole

Union des municipalités du Québec (UMQ)

#680, 680, rue Sherbrooke ouest, Montréal QC H3A 2M7
Tél: 514-282-7700; *Téléc:* 514-282-8893
Courriel: info@umq.qc.ca
www.umq.qc.ca
twitter.com/UMQuebec
Aperçu: *Dimension:* grande; *Envergure:* provinciale; Organisme sans but lucratif; fondée en 1919
Mission: Au bénéfice des citoyens, représenter les municipalités auprès du gouvernement et contribuer à l'efficience de gestion des municipalités.; *Membre de:* Fédération canadienne des municipalités; Affiliation(s): Conseil du patronat du Québec; Fédération canadienne des municipalités
Membre(s) du bureau directeur:
Pierre Prévost, Directeur général par intérim
Robert Coulombe, Président
r.coulombe@ville.maniwaki.qc.ca
Finances: *Budget de fonctionnement annuel:* $3 Million-$5 Million
Personnel: 35 membre(s) du personnel
Membre: 300 *Montant de la cotisation:* 0,46$ per capita; *Critères d'admissibilite:* Toutes les municipalités du Québec
Activités: Formation des élus et des gestionnaires municipaux; *Stagiaires:* Oui; *Service de conférenciers:* Oui; *Listes de destinataires:* Oui; *Bibliothèque:* Bibliothèque publique

Union des municipalités régionales de comté et des municipalités locales du Québec ***Voir*** Fédération Québécoise des Municipalités

Union des producteurs agricoles (UPA)
Parent Name: Canadian Federation of Agriculture

#100, 555, boul. Roland-Therrien, Longueuil QC J4H 3Y9
Tél: 450-679-0530
Courriel: upa@upa.qc.ca
www.upa.qc.ca
www.facebook.com/pageUPA
twitter.com/upaqc
www.youtube.com/user/upa1972
Aperçu: *Dimension:* grande; *Envergure:* provinciale; fondée en 1924 surveillé par Canadian Federation of Agriculture
Mission: Promouvoir, défendre et développer les intérêts professionnels, économiques, sociaux et moraux des producteurs agricoles et forestiers, sans distinction de race, de nationalité, de sexe, de langue et de croyance; *Membre de:* Fédération canadienne des producteurs de lait
Membre(s) du bureau directeur:
Marcel Groleau, Président
Finances: *Budget de fonctionnement annuel:* $3 Million-$5 Million
Membre: 43 000

Union géodésique et géophysique internationale ***See*** International Union of Geodesy & Geophysics

Union géographique internationale ***See*** International Geographic Union

Union géophysique canadienne ***See*** Canadian Geophysical Union

Union internationale de la science du sol ***See*** International Union of Soil Sciences

Union internationale des architectes (UIA) / International Union of Architects

33, av du Maine, Paris 75755 France
Tel: 33-1-45-24-36-88; *Fax:* 33-1-45-24-02-78
e-mail: uia@uia-architectes.org
www.uia-architectes.org/
www.facebook.com/161916773874971
Overview: A medium-sized international organization founded in 1948
Mission: To create among architects, ties based on friendship, understanding & mutual esteem; to enable them to confront their ideas & concepts, share their experiences, broaden their knowledge & learn from their differences in order to better fulfill their role in the improvement of Man's living conditions & environment
Environmental Activity: Declaration of Interdependence for a Sustainable Future, adopted June 1993, commits UIA members to place environmental & social sustainability at the core of practices & professional responsibilities
Chief Officer(s):
Jordi Farrando, General Secretary
Louise Cox, Présidente
Finances: *Annual Operating Budget:* $500,000-$1.5 Million
Staff: 7 staff member(s)
Membership: 124 member countries; *Member Profile:* National associations of architects
Activities: Work groups; congresses; seminars; competitions, etc.; *Rents Mailing List:* Yes

Union internationale des instituts de recherches forestières ***See*** International Union of Forest Research Organizations

Union internationale des sciences biologiques ***See*** International Union of Biological Sciences

Union of British Columbia Municipalities (UBCM)

#60, 10551 Shellbridge Way, Richmond BC V6X 2W9
Tel: 604-270-8226; *Fax:* 604-270-9116
www.ubcm.ca
twitter.com/UBCM
Overview: A medium-sized provincial organization founded in 1905
Mission: To provide a common voice for local government; *Member of:* Federation of Canadian Municipalities
Chief Officer(s):

Mary Sjostrom, President
Gary MacIsaac, Executive Director
gmacisaac@ubcm.ca
Marie Crawford, Associate Executive Director
mcrawford@ubcm.ca
Anna-Maria Wijesinghe, Manager, Member & Association Services
amwijesinghe@ubcm.ca
Finances: *Annual Operating Budget:* $500,000-$1.5 Million
Staff: 20 staff member(s)
Membership: 161 municipalities + 29 regional districts; *Committees:* Community Economic Development; Community Safety; Convention; Environment; First Nations; Healthy Communities; Presidents; Resolutions
Activities: *Awareness Events:* Local Government Awareness Week, May; *Speaker Service:* Yes; *Library:* Open to public
Meetings/Conferences:
For more information see Trade Shows, Conferences and Seminars Chapter
Union of British Columbia Municipalities 2013 Annual Convention
September 2013 Vancouver, BC
Union of British Columbia Municipalities 2014 Annual Convention
September 2014 Whistler, BC
Union of British Columbia Municipalities 2015 Annual Convention
September 2015 Vancouver, BC
Union of British Columbia Municipalities 2016 Annual Convention
September 2016 Penticton, BC
Union of British Columbia Municipalities 2017 Annual Convention
September 2017 Vancouver, BC
Union of British Columbia Municipalities 2018 Annual Convention
2018, BC
Union of British Columbia Municipalities 2019 Annual Convention
September 2019 Vancouver, BC

Union of Energy, Mines & Resources Employees *See* Natural Resources Union

Union of Nova Scotia Municipalities (UNSM)
#1106, 1809 Barrington St., Halifax NS B3J 3K8
Tel: 902-423-8331; *Fax:* 902-425-5592
e-mail: info@unsm.ca
www.unsm.ca
Overview: A medium-sized provincial organization founded in 1905
Mission: To research, promote & represent provincial interests of local government; *Member of:* Federation of Canadian Municipalities
Chief Officer(s):
Betty MacDonald, Executive Director
bmacdonald@unsm.ca
Judy Webber, Event Planner/Financal Officer
jwebber@unsm.ca
Finances: *Annual Operating Budget:* $250,000-$500,000; *Funding Sources:* Membership dues
Staff: 3 staff member(s); 20 volunteer(s)
Membership: 455 individual; *Member Profile:* Elected to municipal office
Activities: ; *Library:* by appointment

Union québécoise pour la conservation de la nature *Voir* Nature Québec

Union Saint Laurent Grands Lacs *See* Great Lakes United

United Nations Association in Canada (UNAC) / Association canadienne pour les Nations-Unies (ACNU)
#300, 309 Cooper St., Ottawa ON K2P 0G5
Tel: 613-232-5751; *Fax:* 613-563-2455
e-mail: info@unac.org
www.unac.org
Also Known As: UNA - Canada
Overview: A medium-sized international charitable organization founded in 1946
Mission: To study international problems & Canada's relationship to them as a member of the UN & its related agencies; To foster mutual understanding, goodwill & cooperation between the people of Canada & those of other countries, with the object of promoting peace & justice; To study possible courses of action in the field of international affairs; To work for support by the government & the people of Canada for desirable policies; To furnish information about & stimulate public interest in the UN & its various agencies which have been established for direct or indirect promotion of international order, justice & security; To foster national commitment to principles of multilateralism & international cooperation; Affiliation(s): World Federation of United Nations Associations
Chief Officer(s):
Kathryn White, Executive Director
Finances: *Annual Operating Budget:* $500,000-$1.5 Million; *Funding Sources:* Individual donations; corporate support; government grants
Staff: 12 staff member(s); 200 volunteer(s)
Membership: 100 corporate + 12,000 individual; *Fees:* Suggested minimum of $25
Activities: Projects include: Healthy Children, Healthy Communities; Model United Nations; United Nations Professional Placement Programme; *Awareness Events:* UN Day, Oct. 24; Canadian International Model United Nations Conference; *Library:* Resource Centre; Open to public

Calgary
PO Box 6593, Stn. D, Calgary AB T2Z 2M3
e-mail: unac.calgary@gmail.com
calgary.unac.org
www.facebook.com/group.php?gid=7390276814&ref=ts
Chief Officer(s):
Michael Gretton, President

Edmonton
c/o C. Mensah, Grant MacEwan College, 10700 - 104 Ave., Edmonton AB T5J 4S2
Tel: 780-432-6531; *Fax:* 780-497-5308
e-mail: edmonton.unac.org
www.edmonton.unac.org
www.facebook.com/unacedmonton
twitter.com/unacanadayeg

Greater Montréal Office
a/s #J-4350, Université du Québec à Montréal, CP 8888, Succ. Centre-Ville, Montréal QC H3C 3P8
Tél: 514-987-8743; *Téléc:* 514-987-0249
Courriel: acnu@uqam.ca
Chief Officer(s):
Michèle Bertrand, Présidente

Hamilton
173 Dundurn St. South, Hamilton ON L8P 4K5
Tel: 905-527-0470
e-mail: info@hamilton.unac.org
hamilton.unac.org
Chief Officer(s):
Brian Reid, President

Kootenay Region
PO Box 760, Grand Forks BC V0H 1H0
Tel: 250-442-8252; *Fax:* 250-442-3433

National Capital Region
#300, 309 Cooper St., Ottawa ON K2P 0G5
Tel: 613-232-5751; *Fax:* 613-563-2455
e-mail: info@ncrb.unac.org
ncrb.unac.org

Québec Office
c/o Institut Québécois des Hautes Études Internationales (IQHEI), #5458, Pavillon Charles-de-Koninck, Université Laval, Québec QC G1K 7P4
Courriel: infos@acnu-quebec.org
Chief Officer(s):
Daniel Atangana, Président

Quinte & District
221 Charles St., Belleville ON K8N 3M3
Tel: 613-966-3928; *Fax:* 613-966-3928
e-mail: globalperspectives@cogeco.ca
Chief Officer(s):
Aruna Alexander, President

Saguenay/Lac-St-Jean
a/s UQAC, Département des sciences humaines, 555, boul de l'Université, Chicoutimi QC G7H 2B1
Tél: 418-545-5011; *Téléc:* 418-545-5012
Courriel: jules_dufour@uqac.uquebec.ca
Chief Officer(s):
Jules Dufour, Président

St. John's
c/o Ian McMaster, 3 Ross Rd., Paradise NL A1A 1M2
e-mail: unacnl@yahoo.ca
Chief Officer(s):
Lesley Herridge, Contact

Saskatoon
c/o John Parry, President, Saskatoon SK
Tel: 306-664-3698
e-mail: johnparry@shaw.ca

Toronto Office
PO Box 26008, 2345 Yonge St., Toronto ON M4P 3E0
Tel: 416-467-4672
e-mail: info@to.unac.org
to.unac.org
Chief Officer(s):
Ali Khachan, President, 416-467-4672

Vancouver Office
2305-867 Hamilton St., Vancouver BC V6B 6B7
Tel: 604-732-0448; *Fax:* 604-736-8963
e-mail: unacvancouver@gmail.com
edmonton.unac.org
Chief Officer(s):
Chrystal Coleman, President
cc@chrystalcoleman.com

Victoria Office
c/o France Gilbert, #200, 535 Yates St., Victoria BC V8W 2Z6
Tel: 250-388-7350
e-mail: unac.victoria@gmail.com
Chief Officer(s):
Nora Curry, Contact

Winnipeg Office
c/o Univ. of Winnipeg Library, 515 Portage Ave., Winnipeg MB R3B 2E9
Tel: 204-586-0173; *Fax:* 204-783-8910
e-mail: unacwinnipeg@gmail.com
www.unacwinnipeg.ca

United Nations Conference on Trade & Development (UNCTAD) / Conférence des Nations Unies sur le commerce et le développement (CNUCED)
Palais des Nations, 8-14, av de la Paix, Geneva 10 1211 Switzerland
Tel: 41-22-917-1234; *Fax:* 41-22-917-0057
e-mail: info@unctad.org
www.unctad.org
twitter.com/unctad
www.youtube.com/user/UNCTADOnline
Overview: A large international organization founded in 1964
Mission: Fostering sustainable growth & development in developing countries & countries in transition through analytical & operational activities in the areas of trade & related development issues, such as finance, technology, investment, enterprise development, & environment
Chief Officer(s):
Supachai Panitchpakdi, Secretary General
sgo@unctad.org
Finances: *Annual Operating Budget:* Greater than $5 Million
Staff: 394 staff member(s)
Membership: 194 countries
Activities: Promotes & examines the participation of developing countries in international trade & investment; monitors the implementation of the UN Programme of Action for the Least Developed Countries (LDCs); analyzes trends in foreign direct investment & their impact on development; strengthens the service sector capacity in developing countries; promotes the integration of trade, environment & development; reduces commodity dependence through diversification & risk management; faciliates trade; *Internships:* Yes; *Speaker Service:* Yes; *Library:* Open to public

United Nations Development Programme (UNDP)
One United Nations Plaza, New York NY 10017 USA
Tel: 212-906-5000
e-mail: UNDP-newsroom@undp.org
www.undp.org
www.facebook.com/UNDP
twitter.com/undp
www.youtube.com/user/undp/featured
Overview: A medium-sized international organization
Mission: To help the United Nations become a powerful & cohesive force for sustainable human development; To focus its own resources on a series of objectives central to sustainable human development: democratic governance, poverty reduction, crisis prevention & recovery, energy & environment, information & communications technology & HIV/AIDS: To help developing

countries attract & use aid effectively; To promote the protection of human rights & the empowerment of women
Chief Officer(s):
Helen Clark, Administrator
Rekha Thapa, Secretary
William Warner, Senior Editor, 212-906-5389
Soohyun Kim, Specialist, Reports & Policy, 212-906-5151

United Nations Environment Programme (UNEP) / Programme des nations unies pour l'environnement
Regional Office for North America (RONA), #506, 900 - 17th St. NW, Washington DC 20006 USA
Tel: 202-785-0465; *Fax:* 202-785-2096
www.rona.unep.org
www.facebook.com/unep.org
twitter.com/unep
www.youtube.com/unepandyou
Overview: A large international organization founded in 1972
Mission: To provide leadership & encourage partnership in caring for the environment by inspiring, informing & enabling nations & peoples to improve their quality of life without compromising that of future generations; Affiliation(s): Canadian Committee for UNEP
Chief Officer(s):
Amy Fraenkel, Regional Director
Elisabeth Guilbaud-Cox, Senior Programme Officer & Head, Communications
Finances: *Annual Operating Budget:* Greater than $5 Million; *Funding Sources:* UN member countries; private sector
Staff: 20 staff member(s)
Activities: Development of environmental law; collection & dissemination of environmental data; assistance to developing countries; *Awareness Events:* World Environment Day, June 5; *Internships:* Yes; *Speaker Service:* Yes
Publications:
•Our Planet [a publication of the United Nations Environment Programme]
Type: Magazine
Profile: Topics regarding environmentally sustainable development
•Tunza [a publication of the United Nations Environment Programme]
Type: Magazine
Profile: Magazine aimed at youth
•The UNEP [United Nations Environment Program] Year Book
Type: Yearbook

United Nations Environment Programme - Multilateral Fund for the Implementation of the Montréal Protocol
#4100, 1000, de la Gauchetière ouest, Montréal QC H3B 4W5
Tel: 514-282-1122; *Fax:* 514-282-0068
e-mail: secretariat@unmfs.org
www.multilateralfund.org
Overview: A medium-sized international organization
Mission: To assist developing countries party to the Montréal Protocol whose annual per capita consumption & production of Ozone Depleting Substances (ODS) is less than 0.3 Kg to comply with the control measures of the Protocol
Chief Officer(s):
Javier Camago, Chair

United Nations Environment Programme - Secretariat of the Convention on Biological Diversity
#800, 413, rue St-Jacques, Montréal QC H2Y 1N9
Tel: 514-288-2220; *Fax:* 514-288-6588
e-mail: secretariat@biodiv.org
www.cbd.int
Overview: A medium-sized international organization
Mission: The Convention on Biological Diversity was inspired by the world community's growing commitment to sustainable development. It represents a dramatic step forward in the conservation of biological diversity, the sustainable use of its components, and the fair and equitable sharing of benefits arising from the use of genetic resources.
Chief Officer(s):
Ahmed Djoghlaf, Executive Secretary
ahmed.djoghlaf@cbd.int

United Nations Industrial Development Organization (UNIDO)
Vienna International Centre, PO Box 300, Wagramerstr. 5, Vienna A-1400 Austria
Tel: 43-1-26026-0; *Fax:* 43-1-269-2669
e-mail: unido@unido.org
www.unido.org
www.facebook.com/UNIDO.HQ
twitter.com/UNIDO
www.youtube.com/user/UNIDObeta
Overview: A large international organization founded in 1966
Mission: To relieve poverty by fostering productivity growth; to help developing countries & countries in transition in their fight against marginalization in the globalized world; to mobilize knowledge, skills, information & technology to promote productive employment, a competitive economy & a sound environment
Chief Officer(s):
Kandeh K. Yumkella, Director General
Finances: *Annual Operating Budget:* Greater than $5 Million; *Funding Sources:* Regular & operational budgets; special contributions for technical cooperation activities
Staff: 700 staff member(s)
Membership: 174 member states; *Fees:* Regular & operational budgets; Special contributions for technical cooperation activities; *Member Profile:* States ratifying the UNIDO Constitution; *Committees:* Governing Bodies: Director-General; Member States; General Conference; Industrial Development Board; Program & Budget Committee
Activities: Business Plan is to strengthen industrial capacities; cleaner & sustainable industrial development; focused on least developed countries, in particular Africa, on agro-based & industries & small & medium enterprises; *Awareness Events:* Africa Industrialization Day; *Internships:* Yes

Upper Thames River Conservation Authority
1424 Clarke Rd., London ON N5V 5B9
Tel: 519-451-2800; *Fax:* 519-451-1188
e-mail: infoline@thamesriver.on.ca
www.thamesriver.on.ca
www.facebook.com/UpperThamesRiverConservationAuthority
twitter.com/UTRCAMarketing
www.youtube.com/user/UTRCA
Previous Name: Upper Thames River Conservation Foundation
Overview: A small local organization founded in 1947
Mission: To establish and undertake, in the area in which it has jurisdiction, a program designed to further the conservation, restoration, development and management of natural resources other than gas, oil, coal and minerals
Chief Officer(s):
Jane Boyce, Chair
Ian Wilcox, General Manager/Sec.-Treas.
wilcoxi@thamesriver.on.ca

Upper Thames River Conservation Foundation ***See*** Upper Thames River Conservation Authority

The Uranium Institute ***See*** World Nuclear Association

Urban & Regional Information Systems Association (URISA)
#680, 701 Lee St., Des Plaines IL 60016 USA
Tel: 847-824-6300; *Fax:* 847-824-6363
e-mail: info@urisa.org
www.urisa.org
Overview: A small international organization founded in 1963
Mission: To support the effective application of information technology; to provide a means for the exchange of information among members & others; to develop members' skills & knowledge relating to information management technology & systems; provides ongoing educational programs about Geographic Information Systems (GIS) & automated information management within all levels of government & a wide cross-section of the private sector (GIS - computer based technology that captures, stores, analyzes & displays information about places on the earth's surface; more than 80 percent of all information used by local governments is geographically referenced; with GIS any location, any point on the map can become an index to cultural, economic, environmental, demographic & political information about that location)
Chief Officer(s):
Al Butler, President
Finances: *Annual Operating Budget:* $1.5 Million-$3 Million
Staff: 9 staff member(s)
Membership: 3,500; *Fees:* US$132; *Member Profile:* IT professionals in all levels of government

British Columbia Chapter
PO Box 608, #101, 1001 West Broadway, Vancouver BC V6H 4E4
e-mail: news@urisabc.org
www.urisabc.org
Chief Officer(s):
Dan Toncon, President, 604-436-6854
Dan.Tancon@metrovancouver.org
Drew Rifkin, Vice-President, 604-501-9985 Ext. 294
drew.rifkin@safe.com
Robert Schultz, Treasurer, 604-264-2238
treasurer@urisabc.org

URISA Alberta
PO Box 76137, 468 Southgate Shopping Centre NW, Edmonton AB T6H 4M6
Tel: 780-492-3318; *Fax:* 780-464-8116
www.urisab.org
Chief Officer(s):
Randy Williamson, President
president@urisab.org

URISA Ontario
15 Thornlea Rd., Thornhill ON L3T 1X2
Tel: 416-338-2219; *Fax:* 905-709-0764
e-mail: newmember@urisaoc.ca
www.urisaoc.ca
Chief Officer(s):
Sandra Crutcher, Executive Director
execdirector@urisaoc.ca

URISA Québec
CP 32255, Succ. Waverly, Montréal QC H3L 3X1
Tél: 514-382-3873; *Téléc:* 514-382-9534
www.agmq.qc.ca
Chief Officer(s):
Marc Bélair, President
mbelair@gazmetro.com
Gilles Boislard, Direction générale
gilles.boislard@videotron.ca
Jasmine Ratté, Service aux membres
jasmine.ratte@agmq.qc.ca

Urban Development Institute of Canada (UDI) / Institut de développement urbain du Canada
200-602 West Hastings St., Vancouver BC V6B 1P2
Tel: 604-669-9585; *Fax:* 604-689-8691
e-mail: info@udi.org
www.udi.bc.ca
www.facebook.com/UDIBC
twitter.com/udibc
www.youtube.com/UDIPacific
Overview: A large national organization
Mission: To promote wise, efficient & productive urban growth; To be an effective voice of the land development & property management industry at all levels of government; To serve as a forum for the exchange of knowledge, experience & research on land use planning & development
Chief Officer(s):
Anne McMullin, President & CEO
Jeff Fisher, Vice President
jfisher@udi.org
Finances: *Annual Operating Budget:* $500,000-$1.5 Million; *Funding Sources:* Membership dues
Staff: 10 staff member(s)
Membership: 1,500 corporations; *Fees:* Schedule available; *Committees:* Tax & Legal; Planning; Housing Affordability; Environmental; Transportation & Infrastructure; News & Events
Activities: *Speaker Service:* Yes; *Library:* by appointment

Urban Municipal Administrators' Association of Saskatchewan (UMAAS)
PO Box 603, Hudson Bay SK S0E 0Y0
Tel: 306-865-2825; *Fax:* 306-865-2800
e-mail: umaas@sasktel.net
www.umaas.ca
Overview: A medium-sized provincial organization founded in 1974
Chief Officer(s):
Richard Dolezsar, Executive Director
Finances: *Annual Operating Budget:* Less than $50,000; *Funding Sources:* Membership; convention; donations
Membership: 350+; *Fees:* Schedule available; *Member Profile:* Local government administration certificate; employment in urban municipal government in Saskatchewan; *Committees:* Education; Discipline; Advisory; Administration; Convention

Urban Pest Management Council of Canada / Conseil canadien de la lutte antiparasitaire en milieu urbain
#627, 21 Four Seasons Pl., Toronto ON M9B 6J8
Tel: 416-622-9771; *Fax:* 416-622-6764
www.urbanpestmanagement.ca

Overview: A medium-sized national organization
Mission: The Urban Pest Management Council of Canada represents the manufacturers, formulators, distributors and allied associations of specialty pest management products, for the consumer or professional markets used in turf, ornamental, pest management, forestry, aquatic, vegetation management and other non-food/fibre applications
Chief Officer(s):
Pierre Petelle, Contact, 613-230-9811 Ext. 3222

U.S. Green Building Council

#500, 2101 L Street NW, Washington DC 20037 USA
Tel: 202-742-3792
Toll-Free: 800-795-1747
e-mail: leedinfo@usgbc.org
www.usgbc.org
Overview: A medium-sized national organization
Mission: To promote buildings that are environmentally responsible, profitable & healthy places to live & work
Chief Officer(s):
S. Richard Fedrizzi, President & CEO
Scot Horst, Senior Vice-President LEED
Judith Webb, Senior Vice-President, Marketing & Communications
Membership: 15,000+; *Fees:* Schedule available; *Committees:* Executive; Finance; Governance
Activities: Promotes LEED, Leadership in Energy & Environmental Design, green building rating system, a voluntary consensus-based national standard for developing high-performance, sustainable buildings

USC Canada

#705, 56 Sparks St., Ottawa ON K1P 5B1
Tel: 613-234-6827; *Fax:* 613-234-6842
Toll-Free: 800-565-6872
e-mail: info@usc-canada.org
usc-canada.org
www.facebook.com/pages/USC-Canada-Seeds-of-Survival/78368904729
twitter.com/usccanada
www.flickr.com/photos/usc-canada
Overview: A large national charitable organization
Mission: USC Canada promotes vibrant family farms, strong rural communities, and healthy ecosystems around the world. With engaged Canadians and partners in Africa, Asia, and Latin America, they support programs, training, and policies that strengthen biodiversity, food sovereignty, and the rights of those at the heart of resilient food systems - women, indigenous peoples, and small-scale farmers.
Chief Officer(s):
Susan Walsh, Executive Director

Utility Contractors Association of Ontario, Inc. (UCA)

PO Box 762, Oakville ON L6K 0A9
Tel: 905-847-7305; *Fax:* 905-412-0339
www.uca.on.ca
Overview: A medium-sized provincial organization founded in 1968
Mission: To negotiate & administer collective agreements with operating engineers & labourers in Ontario's utility sector
Chief Officer(s):
Rene Beaudry, President
Barry Brown, Executive Director
Glen Hansen, Treasurer
Membership: 10 contractor members + 34 associate (supplier) members
Activities: Organizing networking events; Recognizing exellence in safety through the presentation of awards
Meetings/Conferences:
For more information see Trade Shows, Conferences and Seminars Chapter
Utility Contractors Association of Ontario 2013 Annual Convention
July 2013 Minett, ON
Utility Contractors Association of Ontario 2014 Annual Convention
2014, ON
Publications:
•The Conduit [a publication of the Utility Contractors Association of Ontario]
Type: Newsletter; *Frequency:* Semiannually
Profile: Association news, action dates, & industry information

Uxbridge Conservation Association (UCA)

RR#3, Kirkfield ON K0M 2B0
Tel: 905-852-3044
Overview: A small local organization founded in 1987
Affiliation(s): Ontario Environment Network; Durham Environment Network
Chief Officer(s):
Dave Martin, Contact
Finances: *Annual Operating Budget:* Less than $50,000
Staff: 6 volunteer(s)
Membership: *Fees:* $10 student; $15 individual

Valhalla Wilderness Society (VWS)

PO Box 329, New Denver BC V0G 1S0
Tel: 250-358-2333; *Fax:* 250-358-2748
e-mail: info@vws.org
www.vws.org
Overview: A small local charitable organization founded in 1975
Mission: To raise awareness of environmental issues such as wildlife conservation & the protection of forests
Environmental Activity: Engaging in provincial, national, & international environmental projects
Finances: *Funding Sources:* Donations
Membership: *Fees:* $10
Activities: Participating in advocacy activities; Working with scientists & researchers, such as forest ecologists, wildlife biologists, botanists, & hydrologists; Providing information about environmental issues; Working with Aboriginal people on issues of environmental & social justice
Publications:
•Valhalla Wilderness Society Year-End Newsletter
Type: Newsletter; *Frequency:* Annually; *Price:* Free with membership in the Valhalla Wilderness Society
Profile: A report to members about the society's campaigns & activities

The Van Horne Institute for International Transportation & Regulatory Affairs

#620 Earth Sciences Bldg., 2500 University Dr. NW, Calgary AB T2N 1N4
Tel: 403-220-8455; *Fax:* 403-282-4663
e-mail: vanhorne@ucalgary.ca
www.vanhorne.info/
Overview: A small international organization founded in 1991
Mission: To contribute to public policy development & education in the areas of transportation & regulated industries. PUBLICATIONS: On-Trac.; Affiliation(s): University of Calgary; University of Alberta; Southern Alberta Institute of Technology
Chief Officer(s):
Peter C. Wallis, President & CEO
Sarah Ingram, Programs Manager
ingrams@ucalgary.ca
Carla Frede, Webmaster
Mel Belich, Chairman
Finances: *Annual Operating Budget:* Less than $50,000; *Funding Sources:* Private sector
Staff: 4 staff member(s)
Membership: 60; *Member Profile:* Government; industry; education; *Committees:* Centre for Transportation; Centre for Regulatory Affairs; Centre for Innovation & Communication
Activities: Transporation research & education; programs to assist in improving the efficiency & equity of transportation & regulated industries; *Speaker Service:* Yes; *Rents Mailing List:* Yes; *Library:* Open to public

Vancouver Botanical Gardens Association ***See*** VanDusen Botanical Garden Association

Vancouver Electric Vehicle Association (VEVA)

PO Box 3456, 349 West Georgia St., Vancouver BC V6B 3Y4
e-mail: info@veva.bc.ca
www.veva.bc.ca
www.linkedin.com/groups?home=&gid=4741516
www.facebook.com/vancouverelectricvehicleassociation
twitter.com/vevabc
www.youtube.com/user/VEVAEVTV/
Overview: A small local organization founded in 1987
Mission: To promote the development of clean alternative transportation with a focus on electric vehicles
Chief Officer(s):
Bruce Stout, President
pres@veva.dhs.org
Robert Shaw, Treasurer
treasurer@veva.dhs.org
Membership: *Fees:* $25; $10 students

Vancouver Natural History Society ***See*** Nature Vancouver

Vancouver Regional Construction Association (VRCA)

3636 - 4th Ave. East, Vancouver BC V5M 1M3
Tel: 604-294-3766; *Fax:* 604-298-9472
www.vrca.bc.ca
Previous Name: Amalgamated Construction Association of British Columbia
Overview: A medium-sized provincial organization founded in 1965
Mission: To promote construction investment & efficiency in the BC construction industry; to represent all sectors of the industry to government & the public; *Member of:* British Columbia Construction Association; Affiliation(s): Canadian Construction Association
Chief Officer(s):
Keith Sashaw, President
Finances: *Annual Operating Budget:* $500,000-$1.5 Million; *Funding Sources:* Membership dues; sale of documents
Staff: 9 staff member(s); 50 volunteer(s)
Membership: 650 organizations; *Fees:* Schedule available; *Committees:* Membership; Arbitration; Education; Special Events; Awards; Life Member; Standard Practices
Activities: ; *Library:* Open to public

VanDusen Botanical Garden Association (VBGA)

5251 Oak St., Vancouver BC V6M 4H1
Tel: 604-257-8666
e-mail: volunteer@vandusen.org
www.vandusengarden.org
www.facebook.com/210746535227
Previous Name: Vancouver Botanical Gardens Association
Overview: A small local charitable organization founded in 1965
Mission: To support & promote VanDusen Gardens as an outstanding botanical garden; to act as a source & focus of excellence in botanical/horticultural plant conservation & education; to enhance & perpetuate the Garden as a place of beauty, pleasure & inspiration for all; Affiliation(s): American Association of Botanical Gardens & Arboretums
Chief Officer(s):
Harry Jongerden, Garden Director
harry.jongerden@vancouver.ca
Judy Aird, Volunteer Director
volunteer@vandusen.org
Nancy Wong, Director, Public Relations
media@vandusen.org
Finances: *Annual Operating Budget:* $500,000-$1.5 Million; *Funding Sources:* Membership fees; private donations; special events
Staff: 18 staff member(s); 1200 volunteer(s)
Membership: 9,000; *Fees:* Schedule available
Activities: ; *Library:* VanDusen Library
Publications:
•The Bulletin [a publication of the VanDusen Botanical Garden Association]
Type: Newsletter; *Frequency:* Quarterly

Vanscoy & District Agricultural Society

PO Box 35, Vanscoy SK S0L 3J0
Tel: 306-493-2388; *Fax:* 306-956-3136
e-mail: vanscoyag@gmail.com
www.vanscoyanddistrictagsociety.ca
Overview: A small local organization founded in 1983
Mission: To improve agriculture & the quality of life in the community by educating members & the community; To provide a community forum for discussion of agricultural issues; to encourage the conservation of natural resources; *Member of:* Saskatchewan Association of Agricultural Societies & Exhibitions
Chief Officer(s):
Shelley Sowter, Administrator
Quinten Odnokon, President
Finances: *Funding Sources:* Saskatchewan lotteries; fundraising
Staff: 100 volunteer(s)
Membership: 200; *Fees:* $1
Activities: Rodeo; Taste of RM; Perennial Exchange; fair

Vegetable & Potato Producers' Association of Nova Scotia ***See*** Horticulture Nova Scotia

Vegetable Growers' Association of Manitoba (VGAM)

PO Box 894, Portage la Prairie MB R1N 3C4
Tel: 204-857-4581; *Fax:* 204-239-0260
e-mail: vgamveggies@hotmail.com
www.vgam.ca
Overview: A small provincial organization founded in 1953

Mission: To support Manitoba's vegetable growers; *Member of:* Canadian Horticultural Council
Chief Officer(s):
Todd Giffin, President
Finances: *Funding Sources:* Membership fees
Activities: Providing information to assist members;

Vermilion Forks Field Naturalists

e-mail: princetonartscouncilbc@gmail.com
www.princetonarts.ca/Vermilion_Forks_Field_Naturalists.html
Overview: A small local organization
Chief Officer(s):
Cathie Yingling, President, 250-295-4802
cathieyingling@gmail.com
Ken Heuser, Vice-President, 250-295-7647
Joan Kelly, Secretary, 250-295-7743
Linda Neumann, Treasurer, 250-295-7013
Membership: 84; *Fees:* $25

Victoria Lapidary & Mineral Society (VLMS)

PO Box 5114, Stn. B, Victoria BC V8R 6N3
e-mail: vlms@vlms.ca
www.islandnet.com/~vlms
Overview: A small local organization
Affiliation(s): British Columbia Lapidary Society; Gem & Mineral Federation of Canada
Chief Officer(s):
Gilles Lebrun, Contact, Field Trips, 250-382-6119
Finances: *Funding Sources:* Annual auction of used equipment & lapidary material
Membership: 100; *Fees:* $25 individuals; $35 couples; $40 families; *Member Profile:* Individuals with an interest in rocks, crystals, minerals, lapidary arts, or earth sciences in Victoria, British Columbia
Activities: Providing lapidary & silversmithing courses; Hosting monthly meetings with guest speakers; Planning field trips; *Awareness Events:* Rock & Gem Show; *Library:* Victoria Lapidary & Mineral Society Library
Publications:
•Victoria Lapidary & Mineral Society Newsletter
Type: Newsletter; *Price:* Free, if e-mailed; $15 for mailing
Profile: Information for VLMS members

Victoria Natural History Society

PO Box 5220, Stn. B, Victoria BC V8R 6N4
Tel: 250-479-2054
www.vicnhs.bc.ca/
Overview: A small local organization founded in 1944
Mission: To stimulate active interest in natural history; to study & protect flora & fauna & their habitats; *Member of:* Federation of BC Naturalists; Affiliation(s): Canadian Nature Federation
Chief Officer(s):
Darren Copley, President
Finances: *Annual Operating Budget:* Less than $50,000; *Funding Sources:* Membership fees
Staff: 200 volunteer(s)
Membership: 750; *Fees:* $30 Regular; $35 Family
Activities: Christmas Bird Count; *Speaker Service:* Yes; *Library:* Open to public

Victoria Orchid Society

1199 Tattersall Dr., Victoria BC V8P 1Y8
www.victoriaorchidsociety.ca
www.facebook.com/groups/103631859679933/members/
Overview: A small local organization
Chief Officer(s):
Ingrid Ostrander, President
ifl@telus.net
Membership: 153; *Fees:* $15 single; $20 family

The Vinyl Institute (VI)

#390, 1737 King St., Alexandria VA 22314 USA
Tel: 571-970-3400; *Fax:* 571-970-3271
www.vinylinfo.org
twitter.com/VinylinDesign
www.youtube.com/user/vinylinstitute
Overview: A small local organization founded in 1982
Mission: Clearinghouse for information about vinyl's environmental performance
Chief Officer(s):
Richard M. Doyle, President, 571-970-3372
ddoyle@vinylinfo.org

Voyageur Trail Association (VTA)

PO Box 20040, 150 Churchill Blvd., Sault Ste Marie ON P6A 6W3
Tel: 705-253-5353; *Fax:* 705-779-1111
Toll-Free: 877-393-4003
e-mail: info@voyageurtrail.ca
www.voyageurtrail.ca
www.facebook.com/voyageurtrailassociation
Overview: A small local charitable organization founded in 1974
Mission: The Voyageur Trail Association remains today as a trail building and maintenance organization to a trail building-and-hiking organization with several public outings held throughout the year in various clubs; *Member of:* Hike Ontario; Affiliation(s): National Trail; Trans Canada Trail
Chief Officer(s):
Gail Andrew, Treasurer
Finances: *Annual Operating Budget:* Less than $50,000; *Funding Sources:* Membership fees & donations
Staff: 200 volunteer(s)
Membership: 200; *Fees:* $30 family; $25 adult; $10 student
Activities: Trail follows the clear waters of North Channel to the cold granite coast of Lake Superior (640 km completed; 470+ km planned);

Vulcan & District Fish & Game Club

PO Box 301, Vulcan AB T0L 2B0
Tel: 403-485-6744
Overview: A small local organization
Member of: Alberta Fish & Game Association
Chief Officer(s):
Doug McIntyre, Treasurer

The W. Garfield Weston Foundation

c/o George Weston Ltd., #2001, 22 St. Clair Ave. East, Toronto ON M4T 2S3
Tel: 416-922-2500; *Fax:* 416-967-7949
e-mail: info@westonfoundation.org
www.westonfoundation.org
Overview: A medium-sized national organization
Mission: Focuses on education (through a scholarship & bursary program), conservation (via habitat conservation projects through national organizations only), & trustee-initiated grants (for which applications are not accepted)
Chief Officer(s):
Susan Cohen, Executive Director

Warmer Bulletin - Residua Ltd.

Yellow Cottage, Draughton, Skipton, North Yorkshire BD23 6EA United Kingdom
Tel: 44-0-1756-711-363; *Fax:* 44-0-1756-711-360
e-mail: info@resourcesnotwaste.org
www.resourcesnotwaste.org
Previous Name: Warmer Campaign (World Action for Recycling Materials & Energy from Rubbish)
Overview: A medium-sized international charitable organization founded in 1984
Mission: To collect & disseminate information on household waste, its minimization, reuse, recycling & energy from waste
Chief Officer(s):
Steve Read, Chair
Membership: 2,000; *Fees:* Depends on location & status
Activities: ; *Library:* Open to public by appointment

Warmer Campaign (World Action for Recycling Materials & Energy from Rubbish) *See* Warmer Bulletin - Residua Ltd.

Waswanipi Cree Model Forest

3 Rte 113, Waswanipi QC J0Y 3C0
Tel: 819-753-2900; *Fax:* 819-753-2904
Overview: A small local organization
Member of: Canadian Model Forest Network
Chief Officer(s):
Rhonda Oblin, General Manager

Water Environment Association of Ontario (WEAO)

PO Box 176, Milton ON L9T 4N9
Tel: 416-410-6933; *Fax:* 416-410-1626
e-mail: julie.vincent@weao.org
www.weao.org
Previous Name: Pollution Control Association of Ontario
Overview: A medium-sized provincial organization founded in 1971
Mission: To advance the water environment industry; To promote sound public policy; *Member of:* Water Environment Federation (WEF); Affiliation(s): Canadian Water & Wastewater Association
Environmental Activity: Promoting the water environment industry; Participating in environmental policy discussions
Chief Officer(s):
Catherine Jefferson, Executive Director, 416-410-6933 Ext. 2, Fax: 416-657-7006
catherine.jefferson@weao.org
Julie A. Vincent, Executive Administrator, 416-410-6933 Ext. 1, Fax: 416-410-1626
julie.vincent@weao.org
Anne Baliva, Admin. Assistant, 416-410-6933 Ext. 1, Fax: 416-410-1626
anne.baliva@weao.org.com
John Presta, Treasurer
john.presta@region.durham.on.ca
Finances: *Funding Sources:* Membership fees; Sponsorships
Staff: 3 staff member(s); 150 volunteer(s)
Membership: 1,400; *Member Profile:* Technical & professional individuals committed to the preservation & enhancement of Ontario's water environment, such as scientists, operators, engineers, & students; Employees of consulting firms, industries, equipment manufacturers, municipalities, colleges & universities, & provincial & federal government agencies; *Committees:* Asset Management; Communications; Conference; Environmental, Health, Safety & Security; Government Affairs; New Professionals; Operations Challenge; Promotions & Events Planning; Public Education; Residuals & Biosolids; Water for People - Canada; Wastewater Collection Systems; Wastewater Treatment & Technology
Activities: Delivering services to members; Providing a forum for members to interact for educational & professional advancement; Increasing public understanding; Promoting careers in the water environment industry; *Library:*
Meetings/Conferences:
For more information see Trade Shows, Conferences and Seminars Chapter
Water Environment Association of Ontario 2013 Nutrient Removal Seminar
February 2013 Milton, ON
Water Environment Association of Ontario 2013 42nd Annual Technical Symposium & Exhibition
April 2013 Toronto, ON
Water Environment Association of Ontario 2013 Annual Golf Tournament
September 2013 Newmarket, ON
Water Environment Association of Ontario 2013 Collection Systems Seminar
October 2013 Milton, ON
Water Environment Association of Ontario 2013 Residuals & Biosolids Seminar
November 2013 Burlington, ON
Water Environment Association of Ontario 2015 44th Annual Technical Symposium & Exhibition
April 2015 Toronto, ON
Water Environment Association of Ontario 2014 43rd Annual Technical Symposium & Exhibition
April 2014 London, ON
Publications:
•INFLUENTS [a publication of the Water Environment Association of Ontario]
Type: Magazine; *Frequency:* Quarterly; *Accepts Advertising*; *Editor:* Cole Kelman
Profile: Features on current issues, educational articles, project profiles, people in the news, committee reports, events, & marketplacedevelopments

Water Environment Federation (WEF)

601 Wythe St., Alexandria VA 22314-1994 USA
Tel: 703-684-2400; *Fax:* 703-684-2492
Toll-Free: 800-666-0206
e-mail: comments@wef.org
www.wef.org
www.facebook.com/WaterEnvironmentFederation
twitter.com/WEForg
Previous Name: Federation of Sewage Works Associations; Federation of Sewage & Industrial Wastes Associations; Water Pollution Control Federation
Overview: A large international organization founded in 1928
Mission: To ensure clean water for the protection of public health; To advance the water profession
Environmental Activity: Working for a sustainable water environment
Chief Officer(s):
Cordell Samuels, President
Jeff Eger, Executive Director, 703-684-2430
jeger@wef.org
Linda Kelly, Director, Communications, 703-684-2448
lkelly@wef.org

Membership: 36,000 individuals + 75 affiliated associations; *Member Profile:* Water quality professionals from around the globe; *Committees:* Air Quality & Odor Control; Audit; Automation & Info Tech; Awards & recognitions; Collection Systems; Constitution & Bylaws; Disinfection & Public Health; Government Affairs; Groundwater; Industrial Wastewater; International Coordination; Laboratory Practices; Literature Review; Manufacturers & Representatives; Membership; Municipal Wastewater Treatment Design; Nominating; Operations Challenge; Plant Operations & Maintenance; Professional Development; Program; Public Communication & Outreach; Research & Innovation; Residuals & Biosolids; and others...
Activities: Providing water quality information; offering networking opportunities; online Knowledge Center for members; *Library:* WEF Knowledge Center; Open to public
Meetings/Conferences:
For more information see Trade Shows, Conferences and Seminars Chapter
Water Environment Federation 2013 Water Arabia
February 2013 Al-Khobar
Water Environment Federation 2013 Residuals & Biosolids Conference: Emerging Opportunities for Sustainable Resource Recovery
May 2013 Nashville, TN
Water Environment Federation 2013 Energy & Water: Integrated Solutions for Advancing Technology & Management
May 2013 Nashville, TN
Water Environment Federation 2013 Collection Systems: Gold Nuggets of Knowledge
June 2013 Sacramento, CA
Water Environment Federation WEFTEC 2013: 86th Annual Water Environment Federation Technical Exhibition & Conference
October 2013 Chicago, IL
Water Environment Federation WEFTEC 2014: 87th Annual Water Environment Federation Technical Exhibition & Conference
September 2014 New Orleans, LA
Water Environment Federation and American Water Works Association (AWWA) The Utility Management Conference 2014
February 2014 Savannah, GA
Water Environment Federation Residuals and Biosolids 2014: Sustainability Made Simple: Facilitating Resource Recovery
May 2014 Austin, TX
Water Environment Federation WEFTEC 2015: 88th Annual Water Environment Federation Technical Exhibition & Conference
September 2015 Chicago, IL
Water Environment Federation WEFTEC 2016: 89th Annual Water Environment Federation Technical Exhibition & Conference
September 2016 New Orleans, LA
Publications:
•Water Environment & Technology [a publication of the Water Environment Federation]
Type: Magazine; *Accepts Advertising*; *Editor:* Melissa Jackson
Profile: Information for water professionals such as regulatory & legislative impacts, technologies, solutions, & professionaldevelopment activities
•Water Environment Laboratory Solutions [a publication of the Water Environment Federation]
Type: Newsletter; *Editor:* Steve Spicer (sspicer@wef.org)
Profile: Contents include equipment use, sample tracking, quality control, analytical methods, &certification
•Water Environment Regulation Watch [a publication of the Water Environment Federation]
Type: Newsletter; *Frequency:* Monthly
Profile: Reports of federal government actions related to water quality
•Water Environment Research [a publication of the Water Environment Federation]
Type: Journal; *Frequency:* Monthly; *Editor:* Anthony Krizel; *Price:* $100 (print only) withWater Environment Federation membership
Profile: Peer-reviewed research papers related to pollution control, water quality, & management
•WEF [Water Environment Federation] Highlights
Type: Newsletter; *Editor:* Jennifer Fulcher (jfulcher&wef.org)
Profile: Water Environment Federation activities & information for members
•World Water [a publication of the Water Environment Federation]
Type: Magazine
Profile: An international magazine focussing on water issues, such as groundwater, wastewater, sludge, desalination, & treatment
•World Water: Water Reuse & Desalination [a publication of the Water Environment Federation]
Type: Magazinr; *Frequency:* Monthly
Profile: Technical, scientific, policy, public health & financial aspects to water reuse & desalination

The Waterbird Society
c/o ONSA, #680, 5400 Bosque Blvd., Waco TX 76710-4446 USA
www.waterbirds.org
Previous Name: Colonial Waterbird Society
Overview: A small international organization founded in 1976
Mission: To study & conserve all aquatic birds; Affiliation(s): Ornithological Council; American Bird Conservancy
Environmental Activity: Protecting waterbird habitats; Contributing to the management of stressed populations of aquatic birds
Chief Officer(s):
D.V. Chip Weseloh, President
Chip.Weseloh@ec.gc.ca
Katharine Parsons, Vice-President
parsonsk@manomet.org
Clay Green, Secretary
claygreen@txstate.edu
Christine Custer, Treasurer
christine_custer@usgs.gov
Finances: *Funding Sources:* Membership dues
Membership: *Fees:* $40 students; $50 regular members; $55 families; $900 lifetimes members (Fees include copies of the paper journal); *Member Profile:* Persons interested in studying & monitoring aquatic birds; *Committees:* Archives; Membership; Nominations; Bylaws; International Awards; Finance & Investment; Resolutions; Student Awards; Research Grants; Distinguished Service Awards; Scientific Program; Conservation; Publications; Future Meetings
Activities: Facilitating communication among persons who study waterbirds;
Meetings/Conferences:
For more information see Trade Shows, Conferences and Seminars Chapter
37th Annual Meeting of the Waterbird Society
September 2013 Wilhelmshaven
Publications:
•Waterbirds
Type: Journal; *Frequency:* 3 pa; *Editor:* Dr. Robert W. Elner
Profile: Papers about biology, conservation, & techniques for study of the world's waterbirds, such as wading birds, seabirds, waterfowl, & shorebirds

WaterCan / Eau Vive
321 Chapel St., Ottawa ON K1N 7Z2
Tel: 613-230-5182; *Fax:* 613-230-0712
Toll-Free: 800-370-5658
e-mail: info@watercan.com
www.watercan.com
www.facebook.com/watercan
twitter.com/WaterCanCharity
www.youtube.com/Watercancontest
Overview: A small international charitable organization founded in 1987
Mission: To support integrated water supply, sanitation, & hygiene promotion projects that assist rural communities & the urban poor in Africa; *Member of:* Canadian Water Resources Association; Canadian Water & Wastewater Association
Chief Officer(s):
George Yap, Executive Director
Bonnie Kirkwood, Administrative Assistant
Erinn Steringa, Coordinator, Communications & Development
George Yap, Program Director
Amyn Hyder Ali, Financial Officer
Finances: *Annual Operating Budget:* $500,000-$1.5 Million; *Funding Sources:* Direct mail; special events; corporate donations; private donations; government grants; foundations
Staff: 7 staff member(s); 200 volunteer(s)
Membership: 1-99
Activities: Partnerships with local/indigenous organizations; technical training; knowledge networks in the international water & sanitation sector; education activities to raise awareness on the health & development benefits of clean water in the developing world; *Awareness Events:* World Water Day, March 22; *Library:* Open to public by appointment

Waterloo Regional Heritage Foundation (WRHF)
Regional Admin. Building, PO Box 9051, Stn. C, 150 Frederick St., 2nd Fl., Kitchener ON N2J 4J3
Tel: 519-575-4493; *Fax:* 519-575-4481
e-mail: wrhf@regionofwaterloo.ca
www.wrhf.org
Overview: A small local organization founded in 1973
Mission: To act as funding & support umbrella for organizations throughout the Region of Waterloo to preserve its heritage; *Member of:* Heritage Canada
Chief Officer(s):
Sandy Rung, Chair
Mike Grivicic, Administrative Contact
gmike@region.waterloo.on.ca
Finances: *Annual Operating Budget:* $100,000-$250,000; *Funding Sources:* Regional Municipality of Waterloo
Staff: 2 staff member(s)
Membership: 18; *Committees:* Allocations & Finance; Awards; Communications
Activities: *Awareness Events:* Heritage Day
Awards:
•Regional Award for Heritage Research (Scholarship)
For M.A. or Ph.D. student, resident of, or registered at a university in, the Waterloo region

Waterton Natural History Association (WNHA)
PO Box 145, Waterton Park AB T0K 2M0
Tel: 403-859-2624; *Fax:* 403-859-2624
www.wnha.ca
Overview: A small local charitable organization founded in 1983
Mission: To further the understanding & appropriate use of Waterton Lakes National Park; to provide & publish materials relevant to Waterton/Glacier International Peace Park; *Member of:* Canadian Parks Partnership; Alberta Museums Association; Alberta Historical Society; Canadian Booksellers Association
Chief Officer(s):
Gina Sydenham, Chair
Finances: *Annual Operating Budget:* $50,000-$100,000; *Funding Sources:* Fund-raising
Staff: 10 staff member(s); 20 volunteer(s)
Membership: 395; *Fees:* $20 individual lifetime; $25 family lifetime
Activities: Museum upgrade

Weed Science Society of America (WSSA)
PO Box 7050, Lawrence KS 66044-8897 USA
Fax: 785-843-1274
Toll-Free: 800-627-0629
e-mail: wssa@allenpress.com
www.wssa.net
Overview: A small national organization
Mission: To protect the environment through the use of safe & efficient weed control practices; to facilitate the exchange of information about weeds & their control; to enhance professionalism among scientists in teaching, extension & research
Chief Officer(s):
Joyce Lancaster, Executive Secretary

West Central Forage Association (WCFA)
Parent Name: Agricultural Research & Extension Council of Alberta
PO Box 360, #1, 5013 - 50 Ave., Evansburg AB T0E 0T0
Tel: 780-727-4447; *Fax:* 780-727-4424
Toll-Free: 866-725-4447
www.areca.ab.ca/wcfahome.html
www.facebook.com/103583293026991
Overview: A small local organization founded in 1978 overseen by Agricultural Research & Extension Council of Alberta
Mission: To share knowledge, conduct applied research & extension activities, & demonstrate new agricultural technology & production practices; *Member of:* Agricultural Research & Extension Council of Alberta
Chief Officer(s):
Bob Kidd, President
Carla Amonson, Manager
manager@westcentralforage.com
Membership: *Fees:* $20
Publications:
•Forage Views [a publication of the West Central Forage Association]
Type: Newsletter; *Frequency:* Monthly

West Coast Environmental Law (WCEL)
#200, 2006 West 10th Ave., Vancouver BC V6J 2B3
Tel: 604-684-7378; *Fax:* 604-684-1312
Toll-Free: 800-330-9235

e-mail: admin@wcel.org
www.wcel.org
www.facebook.com/WCELaw; twitter.com/WCELaw
Overview: A medium-sized local charitable organization founded in 1974
Mission: To safeguard the environment through law; To help British Columbians access legal assistance to protect the environment
Environmental Activity: Promoting environmental law reform in British Columbia; Establishing environmental legislative initiatives; Working with other environmental organizations; Providing financial aid grants through the Environmental Dispute Resolution Fund
Chief Officer(s):
Jessica Clogg, Executive Director & Senior Counsel, 604-601-2501
jessica_clogg@wcel.org
Lucy Hough, Director, Development, 604-601-2509
lucy_hough@wcel.org
Todd Monge, Manager, Environmental Dispute Resolution Fund & Communications, 604-601-2503
todd_monge@wcel.org
Finances: *Funding Sources:* Law Foundation of British Columbia & other foundations; Independent donations
Staff: 8 staff member(s)
Activities: Publishing policy papers; Offering legal advice; *Library:* West Coast Environmental Law; Open to public
Meetings/Conferences:
For more information see Trade Shows, Conferences and Seminars Chapter
West Coast Environmental Law 2013 Annual General Meeting
September 2013
West Coast Environmental Law 2014 Annual General Meeting
September 2014
Publications:
•Legal e-Brief
Type: Newsletter; *Frequency:* Monthly
Profile: Information about topical environmental law issues, plus explanations of new & existing laws & policies
•West Coast Environmental Law Annual Report
Type: Yearbook; *Frequency:* Annually

West Elgin Nature Club
PO Box 7, West Lorne ON N0L 2P0
Tel: 519-768-2691
www.naturallyelgin.org
Overview: A small local organization
Member of: Federation of Ontario Naturalists
Chief Officer(s):
Joan Neil, Contact
Membership: *Fees:* $8 individual; $10 family

West Kootenay Naturalists Association
1054 Bridgeview Cres., Castlegar BC V1N 4L1
Tel: 250-304-6840
e-mail: bhancock@shaw.ca
www.columbiariver.ca/wkna
Overview: A small local organization founded in 1973
Mission: To promote the enjoyment of nature through environmental appreciation & conservation; to encourage wise use & conservation of natural resources & environmental protection.; *Member of:* Federation of BC Naturalists; Affiliation(s): Creston Valley Wildlife Management Area
Chief Officer(s):
Brent Hancock, President
Finances: *Annual Operating Budget:* Less than $50,000; *Funding Sources:* Donations; membership fees
Membership: 65; *Fees:* $27 single; $42 family; *Committees:* Program; Banquet; Website; Area Reps; Water Use Planning; Conservation; Nominating; Bird Count
Activities: Botany & ornithology hikes; scenic hikes, skiing/snow shoeing; trail maintenance; bird counts; Violin Lake Conservation Project; educational presentations; Waldie Island Heron Project; *Awareness Events:* Rivers Day; National Wildlife Week; Mel DeAnna Trail Cleanup; Parks Day

Western Canada Tire Dealers Association (WCTD)
948 Jim Common Dr. North, Sherwood Park AB T8H 1Y3
Tel: 780-449-1130; *Fax:* 780-449-1284
e-mail: wctd2@telus.net
www.wctd.ca
Overview: A medium-sized local organization founded in 1962
Mission: To establish standards of excellence for members; To promote a professional image in the industry; To act as a unified voice in dealings with government agencies & equipment distributors; To inform members of advancements in products & services
Chief Officer(s):
Paul Newton, President, 306-244-9512, Fax: 306-244-9516
Paul_Newton@SWTire.com
Matt Matlock, Executive Director, 780-449-1130, Fax: 780-449-1284
wctd2@telus.net
Membership: 950+; *Fees:* $100; *Member Profile:* Independent tire dealers & retreaders from the Yukon, Northwest Territories, British Columbia, Alberta, Saskatchewan, Manitoba, & western Ontario; Manufacturers; Distributors; Exporters; Dealer support services
Activities: Maintaining standards of excellence for tire dealers; Providing a forum for members to discuss issues within the industry; Assisting members to develop beneficial business plans; Representing members on scrap tire boards across western Canada; Offering the Tire Certification Training Program to train employees, plus seminars on various subjects
Publications:
•Tracker
Type: Newsletter; *Frequency:* 5 pa; *Accepts Advertising*
Profile: Informative stories, guest editorials from industry leaders, & special reports on issues, for small to medium-sized enterprises throughout western Canada

Western Canada Water (WCWWA)
PO Box 1708, 126 - 3rd Ave. West, Cochrane AB T4C 1B6
Tel: 403-709-0064; *Fax:* 403-709-0068
Toll-Free: 877-283-2003
e-mail: member@wcwwa.ca
www.wcwwa.ca
Overview: A medium-sized local organization founded in 1948
Mission: To advance support for water professionals throughout western Canada; Affiliation(s): Alberta Water & Wastewater Operator Association (AWWOA); Manitoba Water & Wastewater Association (MWWA); Municipal Service & Suppliers Association (MSSA); Northern Territories Water & Waste Association (NTWWA); Saskatchewan Water & Wastewater Association (SWWA); Western Canada Water Environment Association (WCWEA)
Environmental Activity: Providing water conservation strategies
Chief Officer(s):
Audrey Arisman, Executive Director, 403-709-0064, Fax: 403-709-0068
aarisman@wcwwa.ca
Membership: 4,000; *Committees:* Alberta Provincial Council; Saskatchewan Provincial Council; Manitoba Provincial Council; Joint Operators; Conference Planning; Editorial
Activities: Offering education & training
Meetings/Conferences:
For more information see Trade Shows, Conferences and Seminars Chapter
Western Canada Water 2013 65th Annual Conference & Exhibition: Liquid Assets
September 2013 Edmonton, AB
Western Canada Water 2014 66th Annual Conference & Exhibition
September 2014 Regina, SK
Western Canada Water 2015 67th Annual Conference & Exhibition
September 2015 Winnipeg, MB
Western Canada Water 2016 68th Annual Conference & Exhibition
2016 Calgary, AB
Western Canada Water 2017 69th Annual Conference & Exhibition
2017
Publications:
•Western Canada Water
Type: Magazine; *Frequency:* Quarterly; *Accepts Advertising*; *Editor:* Terry Ross (terry@kelman.ca); *ISSN:* 1483-7730; *Price:* Free with Western Canada Water membership
Profile: Theme issues, plus regular departments such as the president's message, the calendar of events, going green, news from the field, the minister's forum, & a newproduct showcase
•Western Canada Water Member Newsletter
Type: Newsletter
Profile: Membership information & news about forthcoming events

Western Canada Wilderness Committee (WCWC)
PO Box 2205, Station Terminal, Vancouver BC V6B 3W2
Tel: 604-683-8220; *Fax:* 604-683-8229
Toll-Free: 800-661-9453
e-mail: info@wildernesscommittee.org
www.wildernesscommittee.org
www.facebook.com/wildernesscommittee
twitter.com/wildernews
Also Known As: Wilderness Committee
Overview: A large international charitable organization founded in 1980
Mission: To work for the protection of Canadian & the Earth's wilderness through research & education; to promote the principles which achieve ecologically sustainable communities
Chief Officer(s):
Beth Clarke, Director, Development & Program
Gwen Barlee, Director, Policy
Joe Foy, Director, National Campaign
Finances: *Annual Operating Budget:* $1.5 Million-$3 Million; *Funding Sources:* Donations; membership dues; merchandise sales; grants
Staff: 25 staff member(s); 300 volunteer(s)
Membership: 26,000; *Fees:* $35 individual (Canada); $50 international/family
Activities: Research; education; slide shows; events; trailbuilding; speaking tours; conferences; media relations; *Speaker Service:* Yes; *Library:* by appointment

Manitoba Field Office
#3, 303 Portage Ave., Winnipeg MB R3B 2B4
Tel: 204-942-9292; *Fax:* 204-949-1527
e-mail: contactmb@wildernesscommittee.org
wildernesscommittee.org/manitoba
www.facebook.com/WildernessCommitteeManitoba
twitter.com/WilderNewsMB
Chief Officer(s):
Eric Reder, Campaign Director

Toronto Office
#209, 425 Queen St. West, Toronto ON M5V 2A5
Tel: 416-849-6520

Vancouver Island - Mid-Island Office
PO Box 442, Qualicum Beach BC V3W 2B5
Tel: 250-752-6585
www.cathedragrovecanyon.com
Chief Officer(s):
Annette Tanner, Contact

Victoria Office & Outreach Centre
#202, 3 Fan Tan Alley, Victoria BC V8W 3G9
Tel: 250-388-9292; *Fax:* 250-388-9223
e-mail: vi_info@wildernesscommittee.org
wildernesscommittee.org/victoria
www.facebook.com/groups/vi.wildernesscommittee

Western Canadian Shippers' Coalition (WCSC)
31 Centennial Pkwy., Delta BC V4L 2C3
Tel: 604-943-8984; *Fax:* 604-943-8936
e-mail: contact@westshippers.com
www.westshippers.com
twitter.com/Westshippers
www.youtube.com/user/Rhobot?feature=mhee
Overview: A medium-sized provincial organization
Chief Officer(s):
Ian May, Chair
Membership: *Member Profile:* Companies & associations involved in the transportation industry in western Canada

Western Employers Labour Relations Association
#203, 27126 Fraser Hwy., Langley BC V4W 3P6
Tel: 604-857-5540; *Fax:* 604-857-5547
www.welra.com
Previous Name: Metal Industries Association
Overview: A medium-sized local organization founded in 1967
Mission: Employee relations services for both union & non-union employers
Chief Officer(s):
Jim Halliday, Director, Labour Relations, 604-218-0891
jimhalliday@shaw.ca

Western Fertilizer & Chemical Dealers Association *See* Canadian Association of Agri-Retailers

Western Newfoundland Model Forest *See* Model Forest of Newfoundland & Labrador

Western Red Cedar Lumber Association (WRCLA)
Pender Place 1, #1501, 700 West Pender St., Vancouver BC V6C 1G8
Tel: 604-684-0266; *Fax:* 604-687-4930
Toll-Free: 866-778-9096

e-mail: wrcla@wrcla.org
www.wrcla.org
www.facebook.com/RealCedar
twitter.com/RealCedar
www.youtube.com/user/WRCLA
Overview: A small local organization founded in 1954
Mission: Trade association representing quality producers of Western Red Cedar lumber products in BC & the Pacific Northwest states; members are dedicated to producing quality siding, decking, paneling, outdoor & other specialty cedar products
Chief Officer(s):
Peter Lang, General Manager
Membership: 22; *Fees:* Based on shipments; *Member Profile:* Producers of Western Red cedar

Western Retail Lumber Association (WRLA)

Western Retail Lumber Association Inc., #1004, 213 Notre Dame Ave., Winnipeg MB R3B 1N3
Tel: 204-957-1077; *Fax:* 204-947-5195
Toll-Free: 800-661-0253
e-mail: wrla@wrla.org
www.wrla.org
Overview: A medium-sized local organization founded in 1890
Mission: To serve & promote needs & common interests of lumber, building materials & hard goods industry on the Prairies
Chief Officer(s):
Gary Hamilton, Executive Director
Dwight Dixon, President
Membership: *Fees:* Schedule available
Meetings/Conferences:
For more information see Trade Shows, Conferences and Seminars Chapter
Western Retail Lumber Association 2013 Prairie Showcase Buying Show & Convention
January 2013 Saskatoon, SK
Western Retail Lumber Association 2014 Prairie Showcase Buying Show & Convention
January 2014 Saskatoon, SK
Western Retail Lumber Association 2015 Prairie Showcase Buying Show & Convention
January 2015 Calgary, AB
Western Retail Lumber Association 2016 Prairie Showcase Buying Show & Convention
January 2016 Calgary, AB
Western Retail Lumber Association 2017 Prairie Showcase Buying Show & Convention
January 2017 Calgary, AB
Publications:
•The YardStick [a publication of the Western Retail Lumber Association]
Type: Magazine; *Frequency:* 6 pa

Western Silvicultural Contractors' Association (WSCA)

#720, 999 West Broadway, Vancouver BC V5Z 1K5
Tel: 604-736-8660; *Fax:* 604-738-4080
e-mail: info@wsca.ca
www.wsca.ca
Overview: A medium-sized local organization founded in 1980
Mission: Dedicated to improving working conditions, quality of life and safety for all silviculture workers.
Chief Officer(s):
John Betts, Executive Director
Finances: *Annual Operating Budget:* $50,000-$100,000
Staff: 2 staff member(s); 15 volunteer(s)
Membership: 75; *Fees:* Schedule available; *Member Profile:* Silvicultural contractors

Western Transportation Advisory Council (WESTAC)

#1140, 800 Pender St. West, Vancouver BC V6C 2V6
Tel: 604-687-8691; *Fax:* 604-687-8751
e-mail: infoservices@westac.com
www.westac.com
Overview: A small local organization founded in 1973
Mission: To advance Western Canadian economy through the improvement of the region's transportation system.
Chief Officer(s):
Lisa Baratta, Director, Strategy
Ruth Sol, President
Marcella Szel, Chairman (Executive Committee)
Lois Jackson, Chairman of the Board
Finances: *Annual Operating Budget:* $500,000-$1.5 Million; *Funding Sources:* Membership fees; project fees; professional services fees
Staff: 4 staff member(s)
Membership: 52 corporate; *Fees:* Revenue-related scale; *Member Profile:* Carriers; shippers; ports & terminals; labour unions; government
Activities: ; *Library:* by appointment

Weyburn Agricultural Society

PO Box 699, Weyburn SK S4H 2K8
Tel: 306-842-4052; *Fax:* 306-842-1469
e-mail: agsociety@accesscomm.ca
www.weyburnagsociety.com
Overview: A small local charitable organization founded in 1908
Mission: To promote agriculture; to act as a liaison between the rural & urban population; To promote education on agriculture-related subjects; *Member of:* Saskatchewan Association of Agricultural Societies & Exhibitions; Affiliation(s): Western Canada Fairs; Canadian Association of Exhibitions
Chief Officer(s):
Treva Tollefson, President
Finances: *Annual Operating Budget:* $50,000-$100,000
Staff: 1 staff member(s); 250 volunteer(s)
Membership: 36 senior/lifetime; 120 individual; *Fees:* Schedule available; *Member Profile:* Interest in agriculture; *Committees:* Attractions; Commercial; Hospitality; Gates; Horse; Cattle; 4H Youth; 4H Calf; Publicity
Activities: *Awareness Events:* Weyburn Agricultural Society Fair, July; Weyburn Rodeo, Aug.; *Library:* Open to public

Weyburn Wildlife Federation

415 - 3 Ave. NW, Weyburn SK S4H 1R2
Tel: 306-842-7658
Overview: A small local organization
Member of: Saskatchewan Wildlife Federation

Whitecourt Fish & Game Association

PO Box 3, Whitecourt AB T7S 1N3
www.wfga.ca
Overview: A small local licensing charitable organization
Member of: Alberta Fish & Game Association; Affiliation(s): Alberta Bow Hunting Association
Chief Officer(s):
Rick Fetch, President
president@wfga.ca
Ron Brown, Vice-President
vicepresident@wfga.ca
Finances: *Annual Operating Budget:* Less than $50,000
Membership: 100; *Fees:* $25 regular; $15 associate; $35 family; $25 range passes
Activities: Archery & gun ranges; hunter education; 3D archery shoots; birdhouse building

Whole Village

20725 Shaws Creek Rd., Caledon ON L7K 1L7
Tel: 519-941-1099
e-mail: info@wholevillage.org
www.wholevillage.org
www.facebook.com/group.php?gid=6413163738
twitter.com/WholeVillageEco
www.youtube.com/watch?v=SUzdnR6dqwM&feature=plcp
Overview: A small local organization founded in 1996
Mission: To create an example of sustainable living; *Member of:* Ecovillage Network of Canada; Canadian Cohousing Network; Canadian Organic Growers; Affiliation(s): National Farmers Union; Ecological Farm Association of Ontario
Finances: *Annual Operating Budget:* $100,000-$250,000; *Funding Sources:* Membership fees; member loans; grants
Staff: 55 volunteer(s)
Membership: 25; *Fees:* $10/month or $120/year; *Committees:* Legal/Financial; Communications; Education; Farm; Community Dynamics
Activities: Sustainable agriculture; green construction; community development; *Internships:* Yes; *Speaker Service:* Yes

Wild Bird Care Centre (WBCC)

PO Box 11159, Nepean ON K2H 7T9
Tel: 613-828-2849
e-mail: mojo@wildbirdcarecentre.org
www.wildbirdcarecentre.org
Overview: A medium-sized national organization founded in 1981
Mission: To assess, treat, and rehabilitate sick, orphaned, or injured wild birds before releasing them back to the wild.
Chief Officer(s):
Kathy Nihei, Founder
Membership: *Fees:* $25 single; $40 family; $15 student/senior; $50 school; $100 business; $1000+ corporate/patron

Wild Rose Agricultural Producers

#102, 115 Portage Close, Sherwood Park AB T8H 2R5
Tel: 780-416-6530; *Fax:* 780-416-6531
Toll-Free: 888-616-6530
e-mail: info@wrap.ab.ca
www.wrap.ab.ca
Previous Name: Unifarm
Overview: A medium-sized provincial organization founded in 1996
Mission: To represent its members at the regional, provincial & national level for the benefit of agriculture; to create an atmosphere of cooperation & communication to ensure that areas of common concern among all producers are dealt with to the benefit of agriculture as a whole
Chief Officer(s):
Rod Scarlett, Executive Director
Finances: *Annual Operating Budget:* $100,000-$250,000
Membership: 1,000 individuals; *Fees:* $140 producer; $65 associate

Wilderness Canoe Association (WCA)

PO Box 91068, 2901 Bayview Ave., Toronto ON M2K 2Y6
Tel: 416-223-4646
e-mail: info@wildernesscanoe.ca
www.wildernesscanoe.ca/WCA_home
Overview: A small local organization founded in 1973
Mission: Organization of individuals interested in wilderness travel, mainly by canoe, kayak, and backpacking and, in winter, by skis and snowshoes; *Member of:* Federation of Ontario Naturalists
Environmental Activity: Wilderness preservation
Chief Officer(s):
David Young, Chair
chair@wildernesscanoe.ca
Finances: *Annual Operating Budget:* Less than $50,000
Membership: 750; *Fees:* $35 single; $45 family
Activities: Winter pool training sessions; Paddle the Don River; year-round outings; *Awareness Events:* Wine & Cheese, Nov.; Paddlers' Club Night, Feb.
Publications:
•Nastawgan Journal [a publication of the Wilderness Canoe Association]
Type: Journal; *Frequency:* Quarterly; *Editor:* Aleks Gusev

Wilderness Tourism Association (WTA)

PO Box 423, Cumberland BC V0R 1S0
Tel: 250-336-2862; *Fax:* 250-336-2861
e-mail: admin@wilderness-tourism.bc.ca
www.wilderness-tourism.bc.ca
Overview: A small local organization founded in 1999
Mission: To protect a land base for the wilderness tourism industry
Chief Officer(s):
Brian Gunn, President
Evan Loveless, Executive Director
Sam Purin, Director, Membership & Development
Jim DeHart, Secretary
Gilles Valade, Treasurer
Finances: *Funding Sources:* Membership fees; Donations
Membership: 100-499;; *Fees:* Schedule available; *Member Profile:* Wilderness tourism operators in British Columbia, such as businesses & community DMOs; Educational institutions; Industry suppliers
Activities: Engaging in advocacy activities; Providing education
Meetings/Conferences:
For more information see Trade Shows, Conferences and Seminars Chapter
Wilderness Tourism Association 2013 Summit & Annual General Meeting
2013

Wildlife Foundation of Manitoba; Fort Whyte Centre for Environmental Education ***See*** **FortWhyte Alive**

Wildlife Habitat Canada (WHC) / Habitat faunique Canada (HFC)

#310, 1740 Courtwood Cres., Ottawa ON K2C 2B5
Tel: 613-722-2090; *Fax:* 613-722-3318
Toll-Free: 800-669-7919
e-mail: reception@whc.org
www.whc.org
www.facebook.com/pages/Wildlife-Habitat-Canada/124492716000
Overview: A medium-sized national organization founded in 1984
Mission: To promote the conservation, restoration & enhancement of wildlife habitat to retain diversity, distribution &

abundance of wildlife; To provide a funding mechanism for the conservation, restoration & enhancement of wildlife habitat in Canada; To foster coordination & leadership in the conservation, restoration & enhancement of wildlife habitat in Canada
Chief Officer(s):
Len Ugarenko, President
lugarenko@whc.org
Finances: *Funding Sources:* Donations
Activities: *Awareness Events:* National Wildlife Week; *Rents Mailing List:* Yes

Wildlife Haven Rehabilitation Centre

PO Box 49, Glenlea MB R0G 0S0
Tel: 204-883-2122; *Fax:* 204-883-2582
www.mwro.mb.ca
Previous Name: Manitoba Wildlife Rehabilitation Organization
Overview: A small provincial charitable organization founded in 1984
Mission: To maintain & preserve the province's wildlife; to receive & professionally handle injured & orphaned native wildlife; to promote public education in wildlife conservation & appreciation; to establish & maintain a Wildlife Rehabilitation Centre; to stimulate & conduct applied noninvasive research; to record data & preserve materials pertaining to rehabilitation & captive breeding of endangered species; *Member of:* International Wildlife Rehabilitation Council
Finances: *Annual Operating Budget:* $50,000-$100,000
Staff: 3 staff member(s); 40 volunteer(s)
Membership: 550; *Fees:* $50 family; $30 individual; *Member Profile:* Individuals with an appreciation for wildlife & nature; all ages; *Committees:* Education; Fundraising; Relocation
Activities: Education; rehabilitation; *Internships:* Yes; *Speaker Service:* Yes

Wildlife Preservation Canada (WPC) / Conservation de la faune au Canada

RR#5, 5420 Hwy. 6 North, Guelph ON N1H 6J2
Tel: 519-836-9314; *Fax:* 519-836-8840
Toll-Free: 800-956-6608
e-mail: admin@wildlifepreservation.ca
www.wildlifepreservation.ca
www.facebook.com/group.php?gid=141989432535249
Previous Name: Wildlife Preservation Trust Canada
Overview: A medium-sized national charitable organization founded in 1985
Mission: To save endangered animal species from extinction in Canada & internationally
Environmental Activity: Engaging in focused species conservation, such as the Burrowing Owl, the Eastern Loggerhead Shrike, the Spiny Softshell Turtle, the Swift Fox, & the Vancouver Island Marmot in Canada; Partnering with other conservation organizations
Chief Officer(s):
Elaine Williams, Executive Director
H. Alec B. Monro, President
Jessica Steiner, Recovery Biologist
Ellen Reinhart, Contact, Member & Donor Relations
Activities: Providing training & outreach programs; Administering conservation grants
Publications:
•Home on the Range [a publication of Wildlife Preservation Canada]
Type: Newsletter
Profile: Updates on the Eastern Loggerhead Shrike recovery program
•On the Edge [a publication of Wildlife Preservation Canada]
Type: Newsletter; *Frequency:* 3 pa
Profile: Information about recovery & conservation efforts of Wildlife Preservation Canada
•Wildlife Preservation Canada Annual Report
Type: Yearbook; *Frequency:* Annually
Profile: Financial highlights & donation information

Wildlife Preservation Trust Canada *See* Wildlife Preservation Canada

Wildlife Rescue Association of British Columbia (WRA)

5216 Glencarin Dr., Burnaby BC V5B 3C1
Tel: 604-526-2747; *Fax:* 604-524-2890; *Crisis Hot-Line: 604-526-7275*
e-mail: info@wildliferescue.ca
www.wildliferescue.ca
www.facebook.com/group.php?gid=335147280556
Previous Name: Lower Mainland Wildlife Rescue Association
Overview: A medium-sized provincial charitable organization founded in 1979
Mission: To rehabilitate wildlife; To promote the welfare of wild animals in the urban environment
Environmental Activity: Caring for injured, orphaned, & pollution-damaged wild animals; Creating a wildlife habitat garden
Chief Officer(s):
Glenn J. Boyle, Executive Director
glenn@wildliferescue.ca
Craig Fisher, President
Sheila Gardiner, Administrator
sheila@wildliferescue.ca
Joanne Petrini, Vice-President
Linda Bakker, Coordinator, Volunteers
linda@wildliferescue.ca
Allan Dorff, Treasurer
Krystal Brennan, Coordinator, Education
krystal@wildliferescue.ca
Yolanda Brooks, Coordinator, Communications
yolanda@wildliferescue.ca
Lani Sheldon, Team Leader, Wildlife Rehabilitation
lani@wildliferescue.ca
Crystal Simmons, Liaison, Care Centre
crystal@wildliferescue.ca
Membership: *Fees:* $15 students & seniors; $25 individuals; $35 families; $250 businesses & life memberships
Activities: Providing education & outreach services
Publications:
•To the Rescue [a publication of the Wildlife Rescue Association of British Columbia]
Type: Newsletter; *Frequency:* 3 pa; *Accepts Advertising*; *Editor:* Yolanda Brooks
Profile: Educational information, success stories, care centre news, forthcoming events, donation information, campaigns, & avolunteer update from the association

Williams Lake Field Naturalists

1305A Borland Rd., Williams Lake BC V2G 5K5
Tel: 250-392-7680
e-mail: muskratexpress@midbc.com
www.williamslakefieldnaturalists.ca
Overview: A small local charitable organization
Mission: To promote the enjoyment of nature through environmental appreciation, education & conservation; To encourage wise use & conservation of natural resources & environmental protection; To administer the Scout Island Nature Centre in Williams Lake; *Member of:* Federation of BC Naturalists
Chief Officer(s):
Fred McMechan, President
Membership: *Fees:* $22 individual; $27 family
Activities: ; *Library:* Open to public

Willow Beach Field Naturalists (WBFN)

PO Box 421, Port Hope ON L1A 3W4
willowbeachfieldnaturalists.org
Overview: A small local charitable organization founded in 1953
Mission: To protect & enhance the natural heritage of Northumberland County & surrounding areas; to develop knowledge of our natural heritage; to record & share this knowledge; to encourage the preservation, renewal & enhancement of our natural heritage; *Member of:* Ontario Nature
Environmental Activity: Habitat preservation
Finances: *Annual Operating Budget:* Less than $50,000; *Funding Sources:* Membership fees; donations
Membership: 200; *Fees:* $25 individual; $35 family; *Member Profile:* Interest in all aspects of nature & conservation
Activities: Monthly meetings; outings; bird counts; breeding bird atlas
Publications:
•The Curlew [a publication of the Willow Beach Field Naturalists]
Type: Newsletter

Wind Energy TechnoCentre *Voir* TechnoCentre éolien

Windfall Ecology Centre

93A Industrial Pkwy. South, Aurora ON L4G 3V5
Toll-Free: 866-280-4431
e-mail: info@windfallcentre.ca
www.windfallcentre.ca
Overview: A medium-sized provincial organization founded in 1998
Mission: Windfall Ecology Centre is a community-based, non-profit organization dedicated to education and advocacy in the areas of energy conservation, renewable energy production, water protection and leadership development.; *Member of:* Canadian Renewable Energy Alliance; Green Communities Canada; Ontario Sustainable Energy Association; Climate Action Network; Ontario Environment Network; Affiliation(s): David Suzuki Foundation; Halton Recycling; Katimavik; Kortright Centre for Conservation; Lake Simcoe & Region Conservation Authority
Chief Officer(s):
Brent Kopperson, Executive Director
Activities: Programs for youth; First Nations joint projects; Well Aware and other water protection programs; Safe Routes to School, and ecoDriver; projects in wind energy, solar energy, and geothermal energy; Windfall Home Energy Assessment program; *Awareness Events:* Windfall Ecology Festival, June; Annual Trash Fashion Show; *Internships:* Yes
Meetings/Conferences:
For more information see Trade Shows, Conferences and Seminars Chapter
Windfall Ecology Centre Drive Electric Conference
June 2013 Aurora, ON
12th Annual Windfall Ecology Festival
June 2013 Newmarket, ON
13th Annual Windfall Ecology Festival
2014, ON

The Women & Environments Education & Development Foundation *See* Women's Healthy Environments Network

Women's Environment & Development Organization (WEDO)

355 Lexington Ave., 3rd Fl., New York NY 10017 USA
Tel: 212-973-0325; *Fax:* 212-973-0335
www.wedo.org
www.facebook.com/WEDOworldwide
twitter.com/wedo_worldwide
www.youtube.com/wedoworldwide;
www.flickr.com/photos/wedoworldwide
Overview: A medium-sized international organization founded in 1989
Mission: To empower women to be equal & active decision makers in environment & development matters
Chief Officer(s):
Monique Essed Fernandes, Chair
Activities: Monitor Implementation (focuses on specific recommendations for women); Outreach & Leadership (to help women become policy makers as well as policy monitors); Education & Communications; *Internships:* Yes

Women's Healthy Environments Network

#400, 215 Spadina Ave., Toronto ON M5T 2C7
Tel: 416-928-0880; *Fax:* 416-644-0116
e-mail: office@womenshealthyenvironments.ca
www.womenshealthyenvironments.ca
Also Known As: WHEN Foundation
Previous Name: The Women & Environments Education & Development Foundation
Overview: A medium-sized national charitable organization founded in 1987
Mission: To provide a forum for communication; to conduct research on issues relating to women in their environments of planning, health, ecology, workplace design, community development & urban & rural sociology & economy; Affiliation(s): National Action Committee on the Status of Women
Finances: *Funding Sources:* Government; corporate; private foundations
Staff: 1 staff member(s)
Membership: *Fees:* $20 individual; $30 institution
Activities: *Speaker Service:* Yes; *Library:* WEED Resource Centre

Wood Buffalo Environmental Association (WBEA)

#100, 330 Thickwood Blvd., Fort McMurray AB T9K 1Y1
Tel: 780-799-4420
e-mail: info@wbea.org
www.wbea.org
Overview: A small local organization
Mission: To provide state of the art air monitoring system that meets the needs of residents and stakeholders in the Wood Buffalo Region.
Chief Officer(s):
Carna MacEachern, Executive Director
Ann Dort-MacLean, President
Membership: 28 corporate

Wood Energy Technology Transfer Inc. (WETT)

#7, 296 Jarvis St., Toronto ON M5B 2C5
Tel: 416-968-7718; *Fax:* 416-968-6818
Toll-Free: 888-358-9388
e-mail: WETT@funnel.ca
www.wettinc.ca

Overview: A medium-sized national organization founded in 1993
Mission: To promote the safe & effective use of wood burning systems, WETT maintains a training program designed to confirm & recognize the knowledge & skills of practising wood energy professionals; to provide training to new people entering the industry; to provide training to non-industry professionals such as inspectors; to provide training to specialty audiences such as volunteer firefighters & carpenters in remote communities
Chief Officer(s):
Anthony Laycock, Executive Director
Finances: *Annual Operating Budget:* $100,000-$250,000; *Funding Sources:* Membership dues; member services
Staff: 2 staff member(s)
Membership: 1,400; *Fees:* $40-$75
Activities: Administers Wood Energy Technical Training Program for providers, installers, inspectors & cleaners of wood heat services

Wood Manufacturing Council (WMC) / Conseil des fabricants de bois (CFB)
#1016, 130 Albert St., Ottawa ON K1P 5G4
Tel: 613-567-5511; *Fax:* 613-567-5411
e-mail: wmc@wmc-cfb.ca
www.wmc-cfb.ca
Overview: A medium-sized national organization
Mission: To plan, develop & implement human resources strategies that support the long-term growth & competitiveness of Canada's advanced wood products manufacturing industry & meet the developmental needs of its workforce
Chief Officer(s):
Gary Williams, Chairman/President
Finances: *Funding Sources:* Federal government

Wood Preservation Canada (WPC) / Préservation du bois Canada
#202, 2141 Thurston Dr., Ottawa ON K1G 6C9
Tel: 613-737-4337; *Fax:* 613-247-0540
e-mail: info@woodpreservation.ca
www.woodpreservation.ca
Previous Name: Canadian Institute of Treated Wood
Overview: A medium-sized national organization founded in 1955
Mission: To represent, support & promote the treated wood industry in Canada
Environmental Activity: Producing safe, quality products in an environmentally sound manner; Promoting responsible stewardship of resources; Conserving forests through pressure treating
Chief Officer(s):
Henry Walthert, Executive Director

Woodstock Field Naturalists
PO Box 20037, Stn. Woodstock Centre, Woodstock ON N4S 8X8
e-mail: woodstockfnc@gmail.com
www.execulink.com/~wfnc
Overview: A small local organization founded in 1934
Mission: To promote the enjoyment of nature; to learn about natural history; To promote preservation of the environment through active participation in conservation projects; *Member of:* Federation of Ontario Naturalists
Chief Officer(s):
Roger Boyd, President
rogeboyd@oxford.net
Membership: *Fees:* $20 individual; $25 family

Workplace Safety & Prevention Services (WSPS)
Centre for Health & Safety Innovation, 5110 Creekbank Rd., Mississauga ON L4W 0A1
Tel: 905-614-1400; *Fax:* 905-614-1414
Toll-Free: 877-494-9777
e-mail: customercare@wsps.ca
www.wsps.ca
Previous Name: Safe Workplace Promotion Services Ontario
Merged from: Industrial Accident Prevention Association; Ontario Service Safety Alliance; Farm Safety Association
Overview: A large provincial organization founded in 2010
Mission: WSPS is a not-for-profit organization with a mandate to meet the health & safety needs of businesses in the agricultural, manufacturing & service industries. It provides programs, products & services for the prevention of injury & illness.; Affiliation(s): Amalgamated Industry Groups - Ceramics & Stone Accident Prevention Association; Chemical Industries Accident Prevention Association; Food Products Accident Prevention Association; Grain, Feed & Fertilizer Accident Prevention Association; Leather, Rubber & Tanners Accident Prevention Association; Metal Trades Accident Prevention Association; Printing Trades Accident Prevention Association; Textile & Allied Industries Accident Prevention Association; Woodworkers' Accident Prevention Association; High Tech; Offices & Related Services
Chief Officer(s):
Elizabeth Mills, CEO
Finances: *Funding Sources:* Ministry of Labour, WSIB employer premiums
Membership: 154,000 employers
Activities: ; *Library:* Information Centre; Open to public by appointment
Publications:
•HSO Network Magazine
Type: Magazine; *Frequency:* q.; *Price:* Free to members
Profile: Updates on health & safety resources, special events & product promotions
•Network News
Type: Newsletter; *Frequency:* monthly; *Price:* Free to members
Profile: Occupational health & safety news; notices & alerts on products, services & events

World Agroforestry Centre
PO Box 30677, United Nations Ave., Gigiri, Nairobi 00100 Kenya
Tel: 254 20 7224000; *Fax:* 254 20 7224001
e-mail: worldagroforestry@cgiar.org
www.worldagroforestry.org
www.facebook.com/worldagroforestry
twitter.com/ICRAF
www.youtube.com/user/WorldAgroforestry
Previous Name: International Centre for Research in Agroforestry (ICRAF)
Overview: A large international organization founded in 1977
Mission: To improve human welfare by alleviating poverty, increasing cash income, improving food & nutritional security, & enhancing environmental resilience in the tropics; To conduct strategic & applied research, in partnership with national agricultural systems, for more sustainable & productive land use. Programmes in Africa, India, Sri Lanka, Bangladesh, Indonesia, the Philippines, Viet Nam, Thailand, China, Brazil & Peru.; *Member of:* Consultative Group on International Agricultural Research
Chief Officer(s):
Eric Tollens, Chair
Tony Simons, Director General
Finances: *Annual Operating Budget:* Greater than $5 Million; *Funding Sources:* Donations; foundations
Staff: 402 staff member(s)
Activities: *Awareness Events:* Field Days; *Rents Mailing List:* Yes; *Library:* ICRAF Library; by appointment

World Aquaculture Society (WAS)
143 J.M. Parker Coliseum, LSU, Baton Rouge LA 70803-0001 USA
Tel: 225-578-3137; *Fax:* 225-578-3493
e-mail: carolm@was.org
www.was.org
Previous Name: World Mariculture Society
Overview: A medium-sized international organization founded in 1970
Mission: To secure, evaluate, promote & distribute educational, scientific & technological advancement of aquaculture & mariculture throughout the world; Affiliation(s): Aquaculture Association of Canada; European Acquaculture Association; Asian Fisheries Society; KOSFAS; Aquaculture Association of South Africa; Sociedad Brasileira de Aciculture; Indonesian Aquaculture Society; Society of Aquaculture Professionals (India); Malaysian Fisheries Society; Egyptian Aquaculture Society; Spanish Aquaculture Association; Aquaculture Without Frontiers; IAFI
Chief Officer(s):
Lorenzo Juarez, President
lorenzojuarez@yahoo.com
Membership: 3,000+ direct & affiliated; *Fees:* $65 individual; $255 corporate; $45 student; sustaining $105

World Association for World Federation *See* World Federalist Movement

World Association of Industrial & Technological Research Organizations (WAITRO)
c/o SIRIM Berhad, 1 Persiaran Dato'Menteri, PO Box 7035, Section 2, Shah Alam 40911 Malaysia
Tel: 603-544-6635; *Fax:* 603-554- 673
e-mail: info@waitro.sirim.my
www.waitro.org
Overview: A small international organization founded in 1970
Mission: To be the leading global network of research & technological organizations through collaboration & knowledge sharing for sustainable development; encourage & facilitate transfer of research results & technical know-how; promote exchange of experience in research & technology management; enhance capabilities in management of research & technological organizations; identify & promote fields of research suitable for international collaboration, new opportunities & markets; promote technological research & capability building in developing countries; Affiliation(s): Research & Productivity Council; Centre de recherche industrielle du Québec; International Development Research Centre; Canadian International Development Agency; BC Research
Chief Officer(s):
Dieter R. Fuchs, President
dieter.fuchs@zv.fraunhofer.de
David Grier, 1st Vice-President
grier@src.sk.ca
Nirmala M. Pieris, 2nd Vice-President
nirmala@iti.lk
Rohani Hashim, Secretary General
rohani_hashim@sirim.my
Suriati Mokhtar, Deputy Secretary-General
suriati@sirim.my
Membership: 200; *Fees:* Based on country's GNI, according to the World Bank; *Member Profile:* Technical membership - laboratories & other organizations actively engaged in industrial & technological research & development; sustaining membership - bodies active in encouraging & promoting technological research & assisting the Association with financial support or by otherwise advancing its aims

World Blue Chain for the Protection of Animals & Nature / La Chaine bleue mondiale
Avenue de Visé 39, Brussels B-1170 Belgium
Tel: 32-2-673-5230; *Fax:* 32-2-672-0947
e-mail: contact@bwk-cbm.be
www.bwk-cbm.be
Also Known As: Blauwe Wereldketen
Overview: A medium-sized international organization founded in 1962
Mission: Protection of animals by inspections, propaganda & cultural education; *Member of:* World Society for Protection of Animals
Chief Officer(s):
Bernard Guillaume, President
Robert Elsen, Secretary
Finances: *Annual Operating Budget:* $250,000-$500,000
Staff: 9 staff member(s); 250 volunteer(s)
Membership: 35,000 individual; *Fees:* 7.50, 12.50, 30.00 euros
Activities: ; *Library:* Open to public by appointment

World Business Council for Sustainable Development (WBCSD)
4, ch de Conches, Geneva 1231 Switzerland
Tel: 41-22-839-3100; *Fax:* 41-22-839-3131
e-mail: info@wbcsd.org
www.wbcsd.ch
Overview: A small international organization
Mission: To provide business leadership as a catalyst for change toward sustainable development; to promote the role of eco-efficiency, innovation & corporate social responsibility; Affiliation(s): The EXCEL Partnership (Canada)
Chief Officer(s):
James E. Rogers, Chairman, President & CEO
Markus Akermann, CEO
Membership: 170 companies in 35 countries

World Citizen Foundation (WCF)
#905, 211 East 43rd St., New York NY 10017 USA
www.worldcitizen.org
Previous Name: World Citizens Assembly
Overview: A large international organization founded in 1975
Mission: To raise awareness in the general public around the world to the need for world citizenship & the global rule of law as the foundation of a future World Democracy to legitimately enforce basic human rights & solve common global problems
Chief Officer(s):
Troy Davis, President
Finances: *Annual Operating Budget:* Less than $50,000; *Funding Sources:* Fundraising
Activities: School of Democracy Project

World Citizens Assembly *See* World Citizen Foundation

World Coal Institute (WCI)
Heddon House, 5th Fl., #149, 151 Regent St., London W1B 4JD United Kingdom
Tel: 44 (0) 20 7851 0052; *Fax:* 44 (0) 20 7851 0061
e-mail: info@worldcoal.org
www.worldcoal.org
twitter.com/WorldCoal
www.youtube.com/worldcoal
Overview: A small international organization founded in 1985
Mission: To promote the use of coal as an economic & environmentally sound energy source; to provide a voice for coal in international debates on energy & the environment; to improve public awareness of the merits & importance of coal as the single largest source of fuel for the generation of electricity; to ensure that decision makers, & public opinion generally, are fully informed on the advances in modern clean coal technology; to widen understanding of the vital role that metallurgical coal fulfills in the worldwide production of steel; to support other sectors of the worldwide coal industry
Chief Officer(s):
Milton Catelin, Chief Executive
Christine Copley, Senior Manager
Zhang Xiwu, Chair
Finances: *Annual Operating Budget:* $500,000-$1.5 Million
Staff: 4 staff member(s)
Membership: 20; *Committees:* Executive; Standing
Activities: ; *Library:*

World Conservation Monitoring Centre *See* UNEP - World Conservation Monitoring Centre

The World Conservation Union; International Union for Conservation of Nature & Natural Resources *See* International Union for Conservation of Nature

World Energy Council (WEC) / Conseil Mondial de l'Energie (CME)
Regency House, 1-4 Warwick St., 5th Fl., London W1B 5LT United Kingdom
Tel: 44-20-7734-5996; *Fax:* 44-20-7734-5926
e-mail: info@worldenergy.org
www.worldenergy.org
Overview: A small international organization founded in 1923
Mission: To promote the sustainable supply & use of energy for the greatest benefit of all
Chief Officer(s):
Pierre Gadonneix, Chair
Finances: *Annual Operating Budget:* $3 Million-$5 Million
Staff: 14 staff member(s)
Membership: 92 member countries; *Fees:* Variable; *Member Profile:* Commercial; government; non-government
Activities: Energy; energy conservation; *Library:* Information Services; by appointment
Meetings/Conferences:
For more information see Trade Shows, Conferences and Seminars Chapter
World Energy 2013 22nd Congress
2013 Daegu City,

World Energy Council - Canadian Member Committee *See* Energy Council of Canada

World Federalist Movement (WFM) / Mouvement féderalist mondial
708 Third Ave., 24th Fl., New York NY 10017 USA
Tel: 212-599-1320; *Fax:* 212-599-1332
e-mail: info@wfm.org
www.wfm.org
Previous Name: World Association for World Federation
Overview: A medium-sized international organization founded in 1947
Mission: An international citizens movement working for justice, peace & sustainable prosperity; calls for an end to the rule of force through a world governed by law, based on strengthened & democratized world institutions; Affiliation(s): World Federalists of Canada
Chief Officer(s):
William R. Pace, Executive Director
Finances: *Annual Operating Budget:* $100,000-$250,000
Membership: 39 affiliated organizations
Activities: Conferences; seminars; policy research; publishing of papers & monographs; lobbying; *Library:*

World Federation of Ukrainian Engineering Societies (WFUES)
27 Newell Ct., Toronto ON M9A 4T9
Tel: 416-235-2610; *Fax:* 416-240-9095
e-mail: jgk@the-wire.com
Overview: A medium-sized international organization founded in 1973
Mission: To maintain Ukrainian engineering tradition & culture; To publish Ukrainian engineering news; To organize conferences & seminars on technical subjects; To exchange information on technology & facilitate technology transfer
Environmental Activity: Provides information on environmental matters
Chief Officer(s):
J.G. Kurys, President
Finances: *Annual Operating Budget:* Less than $50,000; *Funding Sources:* Membership fees
Staff: 6 volunteer(s)
Membership: 5,000 individuals; *Fees:* Schedule available; *Member Profile:* Licensed professional engineer in respective country; *Committees:* Environmental; Educational; Social Events
Activities: *Speaker Service:* Yes

World Fuel Cell Council
Franfurter Strasse 10-14, Eschborn D-65760 Germany
e-mail: info@fuelcellworld.org
www.fuelcellworld.org
Overview: A medium-sized international organization founded in 1991
Mission: To promote the most rapid commercialization of this benign technology worldwide
Membership: *Member Profile:* Companies involved in the development & use of a variety of fuel cell technologies for both stationary & mobile applications

World Future Society (WFS)
#450, 7910 Woodmont Ave., Bethesda MD 20814-3032 USA
Tel: 301-656-8274; *Fax:* 301-951-0394
Toll-Free: 800-989-8274
e-mail: info@wfs.org
www.wfs.org
www.facebook.com/146987498680054
twitter.com/WorldFutureSoc
Overview: A medium-sized international organization founded in 1966
Mission: The nonpartisan scientific & educational association serves as a clearinghouse for ideas about the future, including forecasts, recommendations, & alternative scenarios.
Chief Officer(s):
Timothy C. Mack, President
Kenneth W. Harris, Secretary
Kenneth W. Hunter, Treasurer
Finances: *Funding Sources:* Membership fees
Membership: 25,000 in over 80 countries; *Fees:* $49; *Member Profile:* Persons who would like to know more about what the future will hold, including sociologists, scientists, corporate planners, educators, students, & retirees
Activities: *Speaker Service:* Yes
Publications:
•Future Survey
Frequency: Monthly; *Editor:* Michael Marien; *Price:* $109 individuals; $165 institutions
Profile: Abstract of books, articles, & reports about the future
•Future Times
•Futures Research Quarterly
Type: Journal; *Frequency:* Quarterly; *Editor:* Timothy Mack; *Price:* $85 individuals; $110 institutions
Profile: Refereed journal with articles, news items, reprints of classic papers, & reviews of selected new books or reports for those professionals involved with the theory, methodology,practice, & use of futures research
•Futurist Update
Type: Newsletter; *Frequency:* Monthly; *Editor:* Cindy Wagner
Profile: News & previews from the Society
•The Futurist
Type: Magazine; *Frequency:* Bimonthly; *Accepts Advertising*; *Editor:* Cindy Wagner; *Price:* $49
Profile: Feature articles, news briefs, & book reviews

World Health Organization (WHO) / Organisation mondiale de la santé (OMS)
20, avenue Appia, 27, Geneva CH-1211 Switzerland
Tel: 41-22-791-21-11; *Fax:* 41-22-791-31-11
e-mail: info@who.int
www.who.int
www.linkedin.com/company/world-health-organization
www.facebook.com/WorldHealthOrganization
twitter.com/WHONEWS
Overview: A large international organization founded in 1948
Mission: To attain for all peoples the highest possible level of health
Chief Officer(s):
Joy St. John, Chairman, Executive Board
Margaret Chan, Director General
Membership: 194 member states
Activities: Global strategy to achieve optimal health for all peoples of the world is based on the primary health care approach, involving the following components: education concerning prevailing health problems, proper food supply & nutrition, safe water & sanitation, maternal & child health, immunization against major infectious diseases, prevention & control of local diseases, appropriate treatment of common diseases & injuries, provision of essential drugs; *Awareness Events:* World Health Day, April 7; World No-Tobacco Day, May 31; World AIDS Day, Dec. 1; World TB (Tuberculosis) Day, March
Publications:
•International Classification of Diseases [a publication of the World Health Organization]
Profile: A diagnostic tool for epidemiology, health management & clinical purposes
•International Health Regulations [a publication of the World Health Organization]
Profile: Rules to enhance national, regional & global public health security
•The International Pharmacopoeia [a publication of the World Health Organization]
Profile: To harmonize global quality specifications for selected pharmaceutical products, excipients & dosage forms
•International Travel & Health [a publication of the World Health Organization]
Type: Report
Profile: Information on health risks for travellers
•The World Health Report [a publication of the World Health Organization]
Type: Report
Profile: An expert assessment of global health
•World Health Statistics [a publication of the World Health Organization]
Type: Report
Profile: Recent health statistics for member states

World Mariculture Society *See* World Aquaculture Society

World Meteorological Organization (WMO) / Organisation météorologique mondiale (OMM)
Information & Public Affairs, PO Box 2300, 7 bis, av de la Paix, Geneva 2, Geneva CH-1211 Switzerland
Tel: 41-22-730-8111; *Fax:* 41-22-730-8181
e-mail: cpa@wmo.int
www.wmo.int
Overview: A medium-sized international organization founded in 1950
Mission: Coordinates global scientific activity to allow prompt & accurate weather information & other services for public, private & commercial use; contributes to the safety of life & property, the socio-economic development of nations & the protection of the environment; disaster mitigation & reduction
Chief Officer(s):
Alexander I. Bedritsky, President
Ali Mohammad Noorian, 1st Vice-President
Tyrone W. Sutherland, 2nd Vice-President
Antonio Divino Moura, 3rd Vice-President
Finances: *Annual Operating Budget:* Greater than $5 Million; *Funding Sources:* Member governments
Staff: 246 staff member(s)
Membership: 187 governments; *Fees:* Assessed contributions; *Committees:* WMO Congress; Executive Council; Regional Associations; Technical
Activities: World Weather Watch; World Climate; Atmospheric Research & Environment; Applications of Meteorology; Hydrology & Water Resources; Education & Training; Technical Cooperation; Regional; *Library:* WMO Technical Library; Open to public
Meetings/Conferences:
For more information see Trade Shows, Conferences and Seminars Chapter
Arctic Observing Summit 2013
April 2013 Vancouver, BC

World Nuclear Association (WNA)
Carlton House, 22A St. James's Sq., London SW1Y 4JH United Kingdom

Tel: 44-20-7451-1520; *Fax:* 44-20-7839-1501
e-mail: wna@world-nuclear.org
www.world-nuclear.org
Previous Name: The Uranium Institute
Overview: A medium-sized international charitable organization founded in 1975
Mission: To promote the use of nuclear energy for peaceful purposes; to provide a forum for research & debate on economic & political issues affecting the nuclear industry; to play a central role in the collection, analysis & communication of information on all aspects of the industry & related subjects
Chief Officer(s):
John B. Ritch, Director General
Andy White, Chairman
Ralf Güldner, Vice-Chairman
Finances: *Annual Operating Budget:* $1.5 Million-$3 Million
Staff: 17 staff member(s)
Membership: 120; *Fees:* Schedule available; *Member Profile:* Uranium producers, electrical utilities, fuel processing, handling & trading companies, government organizations
Activities: ; *Library:* by appointment

World Organization of Building Officials (WOBO)

155 Bearspaw Meadows, Calgary AB T3L 2M3
Tel: 403-239-2889; *Fax:* 403-547-4546
e-mail: channan@telus.net
www.nfpa.org/wobo/index.html
Overview: A medium-sized international organization founded in 1984
Mission: To improve the quality of life & resource optimization internationally, through the development, exchange & application of knowledge & experience, affecting the health, safety, welfare & usefulness of the built environment; To promote safeguards from potential hazards & to recommend solutions for preventing fire risks in existing buildings or buildings under construction; To promote the concept of standardizing construction training, materials, equipment & appliances; To promote the unification of legislation pertaining to the administration & enforcement of codes & standards; To update the development of technology; *Member of:* Habitat International Coalition; Affiliation(s): Special conservative status with Economic & Social Council of the United Nations & the United Nations Industrial Development Organization
Chief Officer(s):
Omkar Nath Channan, Founding President & Governor
Finances: *Annual Operating Budget:* $50,000-$100,000; *Funding Sources:* Membership fees
Membership: 600; *Fees:* US$35 individuals; US$175 group
Activities: *Internships:* Yes; *Speaker Service:* Yes; *Rents Mailing List:* Yes

World Packaging Organization (WPO)

c/o STFI-Packforsk, PO Box 5604, Stockholm S-11486 Sweden
Tel: 46-8-676-7000; *Fax:* 46-8-411-5518
e-mail: carl.olsmats@stfi.se
www.worldpackaging.org
Overview: A medium-sized international organization founded in 1968
Mission: The World Packaging Organisation is a non-profit, non-governmental, international federation of national packaging institutes, regional packaging federations and other interested parties including individuals, corporations and trade associations
Chief Officer(s):
Carl Olsmats, General Secretary
carl.olsmats@stfi.se
Keith Pearson, President
glacier@tiscali.co.za
Membership: *Fees:* 300 Euros

World Petroleum Congress (WPC) / Congrès mondiaux du pétrole

#1, 1 Duchess St., 4th Fl., London W1W 6AN United Kingdom
Tel: 44-20-7637-4958
e-mail: info@world-petroleum.org
www.world-petroleum.org
Overview: A medium-sized international organization founded in 1933
Mission: To help the oil industry in the development of petroleum resources & the use of petroleum products for the benefit of mankind; to promote petroleum science & technology; to encourage the application of scientific advances & the transfer of technology; Affiliation(s): IEA; OPEN; United Nations
Chief Officer(s):
Pierce Riemer, Director General
pierce@world-petroleum.org
Randy Gossen, President
Finances: *Funding Sources:* Membership dues; royalties; levy on registration
Staff: 4 staff member(s)
Membership: 57 countries; *Fees:* Schedule available; *Member Profile:* Major oil producing & consuming nations of the world; each country has a National Committee made up of representatives of the oil industry, academic & research institutions, & government departments; *Committees:* Permanent Council; Executive Board; Scientific Program; Congress Arrangements; Environmental Affairs; Development

World Resources Institute (WRI)

#800, 10 G St. NE, Washington DC 20002 USA
Tel: 202-729-7600; *Fax:* 202-729-7610
e-mail: rspeight@wri.org
www.wri.org
Overview: A small international organization founded in 1982
Mission: To generate accurate information about global resources & environmental conditions, analyze emerging issues & develop creative responses to both problems & opportunities; to bring the insights of scientific research, economic analysis & practical experience to political, business & other leaders around the world by publishing books, reports & papers
Chief Officer(s):
Jonathan Lash, President
jlash@wri.org
Manish Bapna, Exec. Vice-President & Managing Dir
mbapna@wri.org
Steve Barker, CFO & Vice-President, Finance & Administration
sbarker@wri.org
Activities: Policy studies to present accurate infromation about global resources & environmental conditions, analysis of emerging issues & development of creative yet workable policy responses; in developing countries, provides field services & technical support for governments & nongovernmental organizations that are working to ensure the sustainability of natural resources; *Internships:* Yes; *Library:* Open to public by appointment

World Safety Organization (WSO)

WSO World Management Centre, PO Box 518, 106 West Young Ave., #F, Warrensburg MO 64093 USA
Tel: 660-747-3132; *Fax:* 660-747-2647
e-mail: info@worldsafety.org
www.worldsafety.org
Overview: A medium-sized international organization founded in 1875
Mission: To protect people, property, resources & the environment & to internationalize occupational & environmental safety through exchange of knowledge, programs, etc.; *Member of:* Consultative Status Category II (non-governmental) with Economic & Social Council of the United Nations
Chief Officer(s):
Vlado Senkovich, President/Director General
Edward E. Hogue, Vice-President
Lon S. McDaniel, CEO
Finances: *Annual Operating Budget:* $250,000-$500,000
Staff: 4 staff member(s)
Membership: 12,000; *Fees:* $55 associate; $80 affiliate; $35 student; $185 institution; $1,000 corporate; *Member Profile:* Open to all individuals & entities involved in the safety & accident prevention field; *Committees:* Transportation Safety; Construction Safety; Environmental Safety & Health; Occupational Safety & Health; Conference Organizing; Awards; Ethics; Membership Development; Certification Board
Activities: World Safety & Accident Prevention Congress (every 2-6 years); World Safety & Accident Prevention Educational Conference (annually); professional development courses & seminars; *Library:*

World Society for Ekistics (WSE)

24, Strat. Syndesmou St., Athens 106 73 Greece
Tel: 30-210-3623-216; *Fax:* 30-210-3629-337
e-mail: ekistics@otenet.gr
www.ekistics.org
Overview: A small international organization founded in 1965
Mission: To advance the science of ekistics (human settlements) by drawing on the research & experience of professionals in such fields as architecture, engineering, ekistics, regional & city planning & sociology
Chief Officer(s):
Suzanne Keller, President
Panayis Psomopoulos, Secretary General/Treasurer
Finances: *Annual Operating Budget:* Less than $50,000; *Funding Sources:* Membership dues; grants
Staff: 5 volunteer(s)
Membership: 200; *Fees:* $40
Activities: Human settlements

World Society for the Protection of Animals (WSPA) / Société mondiale pour la protection des animaux

#960, 90 Eglinton Ave. East, Toronto ON M4P 2Y3
Tel: 416-369-0044; *Fax:* 416-369-0147
Toll-Free: 800-363-9772
e-mail: wspa@wspa.ca
www.wspa.ca
www.facebook.com/group.php?gid=143249880633
www.twitter.com/wspacanada
www.youtube.com/wspacanada
Overview: A large international charitable organization founded in 1953
Mission: To promote effective means for the prevention of cruelty to, & relief of suffering of animals in any part of the world; 15 offices worldwide
Chief Officer(s):
Peter Davies, Director General
Finances: *Annual Operating Budget:* $1.5 Million-$3 Million; *Funding Sources:* General public
Staff: 9 staff member(s); 20 volunteer(s)
Membership: 900 member organizations in 150 countries; *Fees:* $25
Publications:
•WSPA News
Type: Newsletter; *Frequency:* Biannually

World Wildlife Fund - Canada (WWF-Canada) / Fonds mondial pour la nature

#410, 245 Eglinton Ave. East, Toronto ON M4P 3J1
Tel: 416-489-8800; *Fax:* 416-489-3611
Toll-Free: 800-267-2632
e-mail: ca-panda@wwfcanada.org
www.wwf.ca
www.facebook.com/WWFCanada
twitter.com/wwfcanada
www.youtube.com/wwfcanada
Overview: A large international charitable organization founded in 1967
Mission: To conserve wild animals, plants & habitats for their own sake & the long-term benefit of people; to protect the diversity of life on earth; to stop, & eventually reverse, the accelerating degradation of our planet's natural environment, & to help build a future in which humans live in harmony with nature; Affiliation(s): World Wide Fund for Nature (International)
Environmental Activity: Protecting wildlife & wild places in Canada & Latin America
Chief Officer(s):
Roger Dickhout, Chair
Monte Hummel, President Emeritus
Darcy Dobell, Vice-President, Pacific Conservation
Arlin Hackman, Chief Conservation Officer & Vice-President, Conservation
Sara Oates, CFO & Vice-President, Finance & Administration
Robert Rangeley, Vice-President, Atlantic Region
Christina Topp, Vice-President, Marketing & Communications
Finances: *Annual Operating Budget:* Greater than $5 Million; *Funding Sources:* Individuals; corporate donations; government; foundations
Staff: 80 staff member(s)
Membership: 64,000; *Fees:* Donation of $26 or more; *Committees:* Management
Activities: Endangered Species Recovery Fund; Marine, Forests & Trade Biodiversity; Arctic; *Awareness Events:* National Sweater Day, Feb.; Earth Hour, March; CN Tower Climb, April; *Rents Mailing List:* Yes
Awards:
•Endangered Species Recovery Fund (Grant)
Sponsors high-priority conservation projects to assist the recovery of endangered wildlife & their natural habitats. This program is under review *Eligibility:* Must be affiliated with a non-governmental organization or non-profit body with a mandate for conservation *Deadline:* January
Publications:
•World Wildlife Fund - Canada E-Newsletter
Type: Newsletter

Halifax
Duke Tower, #1202, 5251 Duke St., Halifax NS B3J 1P3
Tel: 902-482-1105; *Fax:* 902-487-1107

Inuvik
PO Box 1019, 191 Mackenzie Rd., 2nd Fl., Inuvik NT X0E 0T0
Tel: 867-777-5343

Iqaluit
Bldg. 959A, PO Box 1750, Iqaluit NU X0A 0H0
Tel: 867-979-7298; *Fax:* 867-979-7109

Montréal
#340, 50, rue Ste-Catherine ouest, Montréal QC H2X 3V4
Tél: 514-394-1106

Ottawa
#400, 30 Metcalfe St., Ottawa ON K1P 5L4
Tel: 613-232-8706; *Fax:* 613-232-4181

Prince Rupert
PO Box 362, #3, 437 - 3rd Ave. West, Prince Rupert PE V8J 3P9
Tel: 250-624-3705; *Fax:* 250-624-3725
e-mail: pacificmarine@wwfcanada.org

St. John's
TD Place, #305, 140 Water St., St. John's NL A1C 6H6
Tel: 709-722-9453; *Fax:* 709-726-0931

Vancouver
#1588, 409 Granville St., Vancouver BC V6T 1T2
Tel: 604-678-5152; *Fax:* 604-678-5155

World Wildlife Fund - USA (WWF-USA) / Fonds mondial pour la nature

PO Box 97180, 1250 - 24 St. NW, Washington DC 20090-7180 USA
Tel: 202-293-4800; *Fax:* 202-293-9211
Toll-Free: 800-960-0993
e-mail: PIResponse@worldwildlife.org
www.worldwildlife.org
www.facebook.com/worldwildlifefund
twitter.com/world_wildlife
www.youtube.com/wwfus
Overview: A large international organization founded in 1961
Mission: The largest private US organization working worldwide to conserve nature; to preserve the diversity & abundance of life on Earth & the health of ecological systems by protecting natural areas & wild populations of plants & animals, including endangered species; to promote sustainable approaches to the use of renewable natural resources; to promote more efficient use of resources & energy & the maximum reduction of pollution; committed to reversing the degradation of natural environment & to building a future in which human needs are met in harmony with nature; strives to determine how best to manage individual species & habitats & to obtain critical data for setting conservation priorities; Affiliation(s): WWF has national organizations, national associates & representatives in nearly 40 countries across five continents; affiliation with international WWF network headquarters in Gland, Switzerland
Chief Officer(s):
Carter S. Roberts, President
Neville Isdell, Chair
Finances: *Funding Sources:* Contributions from members; grants from foundations, corporations & government agencies
Membership: 1,000,000+; *Fees:* $25-$500
Activities: Golden Lion Tarmarin Project, Brazil; Hol Chan Marine Reserve, Belize; involved in over 50 projects involving protection of tropical rainforests; Osborn Center works to make the wise management & efficient use of renewable resources a more central element in the economic development plans of developing nations; conducts field work & policy research to promote sustainable & efficient approaches to community development in the US; *Library:* Open to public

World Wildlife Fund for Nature ***See*** WWF International

Worldwatch Institute

#800, 1776 Massachusetts Ave. NW, Washington DC 20036-1904 USA
Tel: 202-452-1999; *Fax:* 202-296-7365
e-mail: worldwatch@worldwatch.org
www.worldwatch.org
www.facebook.com/WorldwatchInst
twitter.com/WorldwatchInst
www.youtube.com/user/WorldwatchInst;
flickr.com/photos/worldwatchag
Overview: A medium-sized international charitable organization founded in 1974
Mission: Research organization that works for an environmentally sustainable & socially just society; provides compelling, accessible fact-based analysis of critical global issues; informs people about the interaction between nature, people & economies; focuses on the underlying causes & practical solutions to the world's problems
Chief Officer(s):
Robert Engelman, President
rengelman@worldwatch.org
Finances: *Annual Operating Budget:* $3 Million-$5 Million
Staff: 30 staff member(s)
Activities: *Internships:* Yes; *Rents Mailing List:* Yes; *Library:* Open to public

WWF International (WWF)

Avenue du Mont-Blanc, Gland CH-1196 Switzerland
Tel: 41-22-364-9111; *Fax:* 41-22-364-8836
wwf.panda.org
www.linkedin.com/groups/WWF-44458
www.facebook.com/WWF
twitter.com/wwf
www.youtube.com/wwf
Also Known As: World Wide Fund for Nature
Previous Name: World Wildlife Fund for Nature
Overview: A large international charitable organization founded in 1961
Mission: To stop the degradation of the planet's natural environment & to build a future in which humans live in harmony with nature by conserving the world's biological diversity, ensuring that the use of renewable & natural resources is sustainable, promoting the reduction of pollution & wasteful consumption; Affiliation(s): The World Conservation Union; International Council for Bird Protection; International Waterfowl Research Bureau; Charles Darwin Foundation
Chief Officer(s):
Yolanda Kakabadse, President
James P. Leape, Director General
Finances: *Annual Operating Budget:* Greater than $5 Million; *Funding Sources:* Individuals & general donations; legacies & bequests; corporate subscriptions & donations
Staff: 3800 staff member(s)
Membership: 4.7 million; *Fees:* Schedule available
Activities: Six international environmental issues: Climate Change, Endangered Seas, Forests, Fresh Water Programmes, Species, Toxics; sponsors educational & training programs for park & wildlife managers, ecologists & teachers; *Internships:* Yes

WWOOF Canada (WWOOF Canada)

4429 Carlson Rd., Nelson BC V1L 6X3
Tel: 250-354-4417
e-mail: wwoofcan@shaw.ca
www.wwoof.ca
Also Known As: Willing Workers on Organic Farms, World Wide Opportunities on Organic Farms
Overview: A small national organization founded in 1985
Mission: WWOOF Aims to get firsthand experience of organic farming & gardening and to lend a helping hand wherever needed; *Member of:* WWOOF International Federation
Finances: *Annual Operating Budget:* Less than $50,000
Staff: 1 staff member(s); 2000 volunteer(s)
Membership: 20,000; *Fees:* $45
Activities: WWOOFing is a cultural exchange & a helping exchange; *Internships:* Yes

Yellowhead Highway Association ***See*** Trans Canada Yellowhead Highway Association

York Rose & Garden Society ***See*** Greater Toronto Rose & Garden Society

Youth Challenge International (YCI)

PO Box 1205, #313, 555 Richmond St. West, Toronto ON M5V 3B1
Tel: 416-504-3370; *Fax:* 416-504-3376
Toll-Free: 877-504-3370
e-mail: generalinfo@yci.net
www.yci.org
www.facebook.com/yci.org
twitter.com/youthchallenge
www.youtube.com/profile?user=YCICanada
Overview: A small international charitable organization founded in 1989
Mission: To promote young people's active, responsible & continuing participation in the issues of local & global development; to promote & support the establishment of a YCI global network, with partners in developed & developing regions of the world; to foster increased international cooperation between individuals, communities, service organizations, governments & agencies by focusing expertise & materials upon locally indentified problems in developing regions
Chief Officer(s):
Stephen Brown, Chair & President
Bryan Cox, Executive Director
Finances: *Annual Operating Budget:* $500,000-$1.5 Million; *Funding Sources:* Private sources; foundations; government
Staff: 13 staff member(s); 200 volunteer(s)
Membership: 100-499; *Committees:* Social Justice; Global Development Education
Activities: Challenger Programme offers youth an opportunity for personal development through four challenges - selection, preparation, field project & returning home; a 10-week field programme followed by the transformation of skills into civic action in their home communities

Yukon Chamber of Mines (YCM)

3151B - 3rd Ave., Whitehorse YT Y1A 1G1
Tel: 867-667-2090; *Fax:* 867-668-7127
e-mail: info@yukonminers.ca
www.yukonminers.ca
Overview: A medium-sized provincial organization founded in 1959
Mission: To provides services to members, with a focus on the mining industry; To promote responsible exploration & sustainable mining practices; Affiliation(s): Mining Association of Canada
Chief Officer(s):
Mark Ayranto, President
Hugh Kitchen, Vice President
Finances: *Funding Sources:* Membership fees; Government funding
Membership: 350; *Fees:* $50 individual; $120-$6000 other
Activities: ; *Library:* Open to public
Meetings/Conferences:
For more information see Trade Shows, Conferences and Seminars Chapter
Yukon Chamber of Mines 2013 41st Annual Yukon Geoscience Forum & Trade Show
November 2013 Whitehorse, YT
Yukon Chamber of Mines 2014 42nd Annual Yukon Geoscience Forum & Trade Show
2014

Yukon Conservation Society (YCS)

302 Hawkins St., Whitehorse YT Y1A 1X6
Tel: 867-668-5678; *Fax:* 867-668-6637
e-mail: ycs@ycs.yk.ca
www.yukonconservation.org
Overview: A small provincial charitable organization founded in 1968
Mission: To pursue ecosystem well-being throughout the Yukon & beyond
Environmental Activity: Developing an educational website (climatechangenorth.ca), with partners in Yukon, the Northwest Territories, & Nunavut, for students from kindergarten to grade 12; Offering Leave No Trace Awareness workshops & trainer courses for outdoor enthusiasts
Chief Officer(s):
Karen Baltgailis, Executive Director
Georgia Greetham, Coordinator, Office
Sue Kemmett, Coordinator, Forestry
Anne Middler, Coordinator, Energy
Lewis Rifkind, Coordinator, Mining
Finances: *Funding Sources:* Membership fees; Donations
Membership: 400; *Fees:* $10 students; $25 individuals & corporate or business memberships; $40 families; *Committees:* Personnel Standing Committee; Executive Standing Committee; Finance Standing Committee; Membership / Fundraising Standing Committee; Energy & Climate Change Working Group; Forestry Working Group; Habitat & Wildlife Working Group; Mining Working Group; Whitehorse Area Issues Working Group
Activities: Influencing environmental policy in the North; Providing environmental educational programs; Raising environmental awareness & the realization that human well-being is dependent upon fully functioning healthy ecosystems; *Library:* Yukon Conservation Society Library; Open to public by appointment
Meetings/Conferences:
For more information see Trade Shows, Conferences and Seminars Chapter
Yukon Conservation Society 2013 Annual General Meeting
2013, YK
Publications:
•Walk Softly
Type: Newsletter; *Frequency:* Quarterly; *Editor:* Georgia Greetham; *Price:* Free with Yukon Conservation Society membership; $25 non-members
Profile: Information about current & upcoming issues & events

Yukon Fish & Game Association (YFGA)
Parent Name: Canadian Wildlife Federation

509 Strickland St., Whitehorse YT Y1A 2K5
Tel: 867-667-4263; *Fax:* 867-667-4237
www.yukonfga.ca
Overview: A medium-sized provincial organization founded in 1945 overseen by Canadian Wildlife Federation
Mission: To ensure the long-term management of fish, wildlife, & outdoor recreational resources in the Yukon; To improve wildlife habitat
Environmental Activity: Promoting conservation & habitat protection; Participating in the Wolf Creek salmon release, the fish stocking of Pothole Lakes, & the Turn In Poachers & Polluters (TIPS) program; Raising awareness of the dangers of air, water, & land pollution
Chief Officer(s):
Paul Jacobs, President
Gord Zealand, Executive Director
yfgaexdir@klondiker.com
Jillian Mclellan, Office Administrator
yfga@klondiker.com
Finances: *Funding Sources:* Membership fees; Donations; Sponsorships
Membership: *Fees:* $30 singles; $35 families; $500 corporate & lifetime membership
Activities: Providing hunter education & ethics development; Promoting proper catch & release; Meeting with government regarding fish & wildlife issues; Promoting sportsmanship; Managing the Whitehorse Rapids fish ladder & tourist facility; Overseeing the operation of a salmon hatchery
Meetings/Conferences:
For more information see Trade Shows, Conferences and Seminars Chapter
Yukon Fish & Game Association 2013 Annual General Meeting
January 2013 Whitehorse, YT
Yukon Fish & Game Association 2013 Annual Banquet, Awards & Dance
January 2013 Whitehorse, YT
Publications:
•Outdoor Edge [a publication of the Yukon Fish & Game Association]
Type: Newsletter; *Frequency:* Bimonthly; *Accepts Advertising*; *Price:* Free with Yukon Fish & Game Association membership
Profile: A publication sent to more than 450 households in the Yukon & throughout Canada

Yukon Green Party
Parent Name: Green Party of Canada

PO Box 31603, Whitehorse YT Y1A 6L2
Tel: 867-633-6334; *Fax:* 867-633-3392
e-mail: yukongreenparty@gmail.com
www.yukongreenparty.ca
Overview: A small provincial organization overseen by Green Party of Canada
Membership: *Fees:* $5

Yukon Public Legal Education Association (YPLEA)

PO Box 2799, Yukon College, Whitehorse YT Y1A 5K4
Tel: 867-668-5297
Toll-Free: 866-667-4305
www.yplea.com
Overview: A medium-sized provincial organization founded in 1984
Mission: To provide free legal information to Yukoners & promote greater accessibility to the legal system
Finances: *Annual Operating Budget:* $50,000-$100,000
Staff: 2 staff member(s); 7 volunteer(s)
Membership: *Fees:* $10
Activities: *Speaker Service:* Yes; *Library:*

Yukon Territory Environmental Network
Parent Name: Canadian Environmental Network

302 Hawkins St., Whitehorse YT Y1A 1X6
Tel: 867-668-5678; *Fax:* 867-668-6637
e-mail: yukonenvironet@gmail.com
Previous Name: Nornet-Yukon
Overview: A small provincial organization overseen by Canadian Environmental Network
Chief Officer(s):
Susan Davis, Coordinator

Yukon Tourism Education Council (YTEC)

#C, 202 Strickland St., Whitehorse YT Y1A 2J8
Tel: 867-667-4733; *Fax:* 867-667-2688
e-mail: yukontec@internorth.com
www.yukontec.com
Overview: A small provincial organization
Mission: To foster industry led development of a professional tourism workforce
Chief Officer(s):
Darlene Doerksen, Chief Executive Officer
Activities: Providing education & training
Publications:
•Yukon Tourism Education Council Newsletter
Type: Newsletter; *Frequency:* Monthly

Zero Population Growth ***See*** Population Connection

ZOOCHECK Canada Inc.

788 1/2 O'Connor Dr., Toronto ON M4B 2S6
Tel: 416-285-1744
e-mail: zoocheck@zoocheck.com
www.zoocheck.com
www.facebook.com/pages/Zoocheck/118864269587
Overview: A small national charitable organization founded in 1984
Mission: Zoocheck works to improve wildlife protection in Canada and to end the abuse, neglect and exploitation of individual wild animals through: investigation & research; public education & awareness campaigns; capacity building initiatives; legal programs; legislative actions.
Finances: *Funding Sources:* Donations
Activities: *Speaker Service:* Yes; *Rents Mailing List:* Yes

Zoological Society of Manitoba ***See*** Assiniboine Park Conservancy

Zoological Society of Metropolitan Toronto ***See*** Toronto Zoo

Zoological Society of Montréal / Société zoologique de Montréal

#525, 117, rue Ste-Catherine ouest, Montréal QC H3B 1H9
Tel: 514-845-8317
e-mail: contact@zoologicalsocietymtl.org
www.zoologicalsocietymtl.org
Overview: A small local organization founded in 1964
Mission: To promote & develop interest in & knowledge of wildlife; To encourage the study of biology & nature sciences; To encourage the protection of wildlife
Finances: *Funding Sources:* Fundrasing, donations, member dues
Membership: 500; *Fees:* $35 individual; $55 family
Activities: Field trips; monthly meetings; *Speaker Service:* Yes

Educational Programs

Academy College
2 University Dr., Corner Brook NL A2H 5G4
Tel: 709-637-2100; *Fax:* 709-637-2123
Toll-Free: 800-561-8000
www.academycanada.com

Natural Resources
Mission: The two year Natural Resources Academy Canada diploma program will prepare students to work in the exciting fields of wildlife, forestry, fisheries, enforcement and environmental consulting.

Acadia University
15 University Ave., Wolfville NS B4P 2R6
Tel: 902-542-2201
www2.acadiau.ca

Environmental & Sustainability Studies
Faculty of Arts, 12 University Ave., Wolfville NS B4P 2R6 Canada
Mission: The Environmental and Sustainability Studies (ESS) Major develops environmental leaders, managers, and professionals who are critical and insightful thinkers as well as creative problem solvers skilled in leading transformational change toward a more sustainable and just society.

Recreation Management & Community Development
Faculty of Professional Studies, 550 Main St., Wolfville NS B4P 2R6 Canada
Tel: 902-585-1307; *Fax:* 902-585-1702
rec.acadiau.ca
Mission: The Recreation Management and Community Development Program at Acadia University develops professional leaders who are critical and insightful thinkers as well as creative problem solvers. They are committed to promoting healthy, socially responsible, and environmentally sustainable lifestyles and communities in a broad range of human service organizations.

Environmental Geoscience
Dept of Earth & Environmental Science, 12 University Ave., Wolfville NS B4P 2R6 Canada
Tel: 902-585-1208; *Fax:* 902-585-1816
e-mail: ees@acadiau.ca
ees.acadiau.ca
Mission: The program is designed to prepare graduates for the requirements needed for professional registration as a Professional or Environmental Geoscientist in Nova Scotia. The program is offered at the undergraduate and graduate levels.

Environmental Science
Dept of Earth & Environmental Science, 12 University Ave., Wolfville NS B4P 2R6 Canada
Tel: 902-585-1208; *Fax:* 902-585-1816
e-mail: ees@acadiau.ca
ees.acadiau.ca
Mission: A four-year program available at both a BSc and BSc (Honours) level. Focus areas include: land use management; natural resource management; sustainable development; environmental health; ecology; conservation biology; and environmental geology/terrain analysis.

Algonquin College
1 College Way, Pembroke ON K8A 0C8
Tel: 613-735-4700; *Fax:* 613-735-4739
www2.algonquincollege.com

Environmental Technician
Mission: Students taking the Environmental Technician Program at Algonquin College gain the skills needed for entry-level practitioners within the environmental sciences sector.

Forestry Technician
www2.algonquincollege.com/pembroke/program/forestry-technician
Mission: This two-year Ontario College Diploma program delivered in a compressed format over 47 weeks is the most practical and field-oriented Forestry Technician program in Ontario. Students spend approximately 30 percent of the program duration outdoors in a diversity of landscapes including Algonquin Park, the Petawawa Research Forest, County forests, Crown lands and private woodlots.

Arctic College
Nunatta Campus, NU
Tel: 867-979-7222
Toll-Free: 866-979-7222
www.arcticcollege.ca

Environmental Technology Program
Nunavut Research Institute, Bldg. 959, PO Box 1720, Iqaluit NU X0A 0H0
Mission: The Environmental Technology Program is a two-year diploma program that incorporates classroom and practical lab and field experiences to develop student skills.

Aurora College
PO Box 1008, 87 Gwich'in Rd., Inuvik NT X0E 0T0
Tel: 867-777-7800; *Fax:* 867-777-2850
Toll-Free: 866-287-2655
www.auroracollege.nt.ca

Environment & Natural Resources Technology Access
Thebacha Campus, PO Box 600, 50 Conibear Cres., Fort Smith NT X0E 0P0
Tel: 867-872-7500; *Fax:* 867-872-4511
Toll-Free: 866-266-4966
Mission: This program is designed to prepare students to meet the academic admission requirements for Aurora College's Environment and Natural Resources Technology Program (ENRTP).

Environmental Monitoring Training
Mission: The five-week Environmental Monitoring Training Program provides students with the foundation, knowledge and skills to participate in environmental monitoring activities. The program is concentrated on students who are interested in working in the environmental sector and require pre-technician level training on environmental concepts and measures.

Environment and Natural Resources Technology Program
Mission: The Aurora College Environment and Natural Resources Technology Program (ENRTP) can prepare you for a great career working as a resource officer, an environmental technician or as an environmental manager. Courses cover wildlife management, environmental assessment, applied technology such as Geographic Information Systems, resource conservation and much more. ENRTP includes field camps with plenty of hands-on learning opportunities.

Bishop's University
2600 College St., Sherbrooke QC J1M 1Z7
Tel: 819-822-9600; *Fax:* 819-822-9661
www.ubishops.ca

Environmental Science
www.ubishops.ca/academic-programs/natural-sciences
Mission: The purpose of this programme is to provide students with knowledge inc hemical and physical aspects of the environment (atmosphere, energy, thermodynamics, fluid dynamics, etc.) with the goal of understanding global phenomena such as climate change, pollution, environmental impact, and resource management in a quantitative, physical science-based approach.

Biology
www.ubishops.ca/academic-programs/natural-sciences/biology
Mission: The biology programs at Bishop's University provide a broad foundation in the field of biology and prepares students for many opportunities. The options available include graduate studies in biological or life science, and professional studies in veterinary medicine, the allied health sciences, forestry, wildlife biology and many other areas. A degree in biology also prepares students for direct employment in the biotechnology sector, environmental biology, or the allied health fields.

Environmental Studies & Geography
Mission: A degree in Environmental Studies and Geography has a major focus on human-environment interaction, and provides students with a broad discipline which analyzes the distribution and interrelationships of physical and human phenomena on the earth. It combines subject matter and methodologies from the natural and social sciences.

Brandon University
270 - 18th St., Brandon MB R7A 6A9
Tel: 204-728-9520; *Fax:* 204-726-4573
www.brandonu.ca

Environmental Science Program
e-mail: science@brandonu.ca
www.brandonu.ca/environmental-science
Mission: Environmental Science is the interdisciplinary study of the environment, its functioning and its relationship to human activities. It encompasses many of the traditional science disciplines, but uses these in the study of terrestrial, aquatic and atmospheric systems and their interactions.

British Columbia Institute of Technology (BCIT)
3700 Willingdon Ave., Burnaby BC V5G 3H2
Tel: 604-434-5734
Toll-Free: 866-434-1610
www.bcit.ca

Sustainable Energy Management
www.bcit.ca/study/programs/5070adcert
Mission: The Sustainable Energy Management Advanced Certificate (SEMAC) program is a partnership between BC Hydro and BCIT, with initial funding support from the Natural Resources Canada - Office of Energy Efficiency. The program is designed to support employment opportunities in the emerging field of sustainable energy management, with focus on the energy demands of commercial, institutional, industrial and community facilities.

Chemical & Environmental Technology
www.bcit.ca/study/programs/537adiplt
Mission: The Chemical and Environmental Technology diploma program offers the student a broad background in technology and skills that can be applied to many industries. Near the end of their first year in the program, students will choose one of two options: Analytical Science or Process Engineering.

Fish, Wildlife & Recreation (FWR)
Mission: Part of the School of Construction and the Environment, FWR covers the management of fish, wildlife, and wild land recreation and includes habitat ecology, environmental inventory techniques, and environmental law with respect to these resources. Renewable Resources DIP

Sustainable Resource Management (SRM)
Mission: Provides a broad range of resource management skills for work in urban and rural settings, focusing on safety, field and academic training. There are 2 tracks in SRM: Forest Management and Environmental and Community Planning. SRM, FM or ECP, Part-time Diploma of Technology; Natural Resources Certificate (NRC)

Environmental Engineering Technology
www.bcit.ca/study/programs/8060btech
Mission: Designed to provide the additional skills and knowledge that engineering and science graduates require to successfully work on environmental assignments such as site remediation, site audits, waste treatments facilities, wastewater management, hydrogeology, residuals management, solid waste management, industrial air pollution, and recycling projects. Full- or Part-time Bachelor of Technology.

Ecological Restoration
Mission: A scientific discipline that has emerged due to the increasing need to restore damaged ecosystems; graduates leave with a strong foundation in the methods available to restore a broad range of ecosystems that have been impacted by human influences. The program combines classroom and field activities for a more complete education. Full- or Part-time Bachelor of Technology.

Environmental Health
Mission: The position of Public Health Inspector/Environmental Health Officer (PHI/EHO) is vital and this program aims to prepare students to enter the field as effective members of the multidisciplinary health team. Graduates will be able to recognize, evalulate and manage environmental factors that will impact that impact on human health, including long-range planning and environmental pollution situations, inspection and monitoring techniques. Full-time Bachelor of Technology

Geographic Information Systems (GIS)
Mission: Cirriculum combines theory and practice and covers GIS principles, training in software, technical issues, remote sensing, digital mapping, and management issues, and includes a work experience requirements. Full- or Part-time Advanced Diploma

Geomatics Engineering Technology
www.bcit.ca/study/programs/749cdiplt
Mission: This degree program offers two stream options: Surveying/Mapping, and GIS. The first will appeal to Geomatics Engineering technologists pursuing accreditation or otherwise developing their careers. The latter will teach professionals and students how to integrate GIS technology into their professions. Degrees: Bachelor of Technology (Surveying/Mapping); Geomatics DIP (Field Surveying or Digital Mapping).

Brock University
500 Glenridge Ave., St Catharines ON L2S 3A1
Tel: 905-688-5550
www.brocku.ca

Tourism & Environment Program
Faculty of Social Sciences
Mission: This program examines the key principles of sustainability, and applies them to environmental and tourism issues in a practical way. The Department of Tourism and Environment at Brock University combines knowledge of environmental issues and sustainability with an in-depth understanding of tourism in all its forms.

Camosun College
3100 Foul Bay Rd., Victoria BC V8P 5J2
Tel: 250-370-3000
camosun.ca

Environmental Technology Program
Mission: Gain academic expertise combined with hands-on laboratory and field skills to be ready to enter the work force as a Technologist. Students learn a range of skills and knowledge in such areas as: GIS map-reading, aquatic monitoring, soil classification, air quality, environmental impact assessments, sustainable resource and waste management, and horticulture and biodiversity. This program has a block transfer to the BSc in Environmental Science program at Royal Roads University. Paid work experience is also available with private and public sector employers: Institute of Ocean Science, Dept of National Defence, BC Hydro, First Nations organizations, numerous federal and provincial ministries and departments such as Forestry, Fisheries, Parks, and Water Management, and various municipalities and regional districts. Degree: DIP.

Cape Breton University
PO Box 5300, 1250 Grand Lake Rd., Sydney NS B1P 6L2
Tel: 902-539-5300; *Fax:* 902-562-0119
Toll-Free: 888-959-9995
www.cbu.ca

Engineering Technology-Environmental Studies
Mission: This Bachelor degree program combines theoretical principles with hand-on experience related to the understanding of biological, chemical, geological, and engineering principles applied to the environment. Emphasis is placed on assessment of air quality, water and soil, sustainable development, and management of waste products and pollutants.

Carleton University
1125 Colonel By Dr., Ottawa ON K1S 5B6
Tel: 613-520-2600; *Fax:* 613-520-7858
e-mail: info@carleton.ca
www.carleton.ca

Architectural Conservation and Sustainability Engineering
Mission: Carleton's program in Architectural Conservation and Sustainability Engineering teaches students to approach the design and retrofit of new and existing buildings with sustainability as the primary objective, which includes considering the life cycle costs and impacts of the materials selected, energy needs and consumption, and the effective reuse and adaptation of existing structures. Students in the program, working closely with Carleton's architecture students, have the option of following a Structural stream or an Environmental stream after their second year.

Environmental Engineering
Mission: The goal of environmental engineering is to offer sustainable and green solutions to many of the issues and challenges facing our society, and to provide a clean and healthy environment for us and our ecosystem. Environmental engineers use engineering and science principles to design innovative treatment technologies that help to minimize our environmental footprint, prevent pollution, reduce greenhouse gas emissions, improve air quality, ensure drinking water safety, and achieve environmental sustainability.

Environmental Sciences
Mission: The Environmental Science program at Carleton offers a four-year Bachelor of Science Honours program as well as a four-year BSc Major program. The programs are structured to provide the kind of thorough grounding in the sciences that you will need if your ambition is to help solve complex environmental problems.

Sustainable and Renewable Energy Engineering
Mission: This program provides analytical and hands-on skills for designing, building, operating and enhancing sustainable energy systems that combine energy generation, distribution and utilization in an environmentally responsible and economically beneficial manner. Two streams are offered: Smart Technologies for Power Generation and Distribution, and Efficient Energy Generation and Conversion.

Sustainable Energy Engineering & Policy
Mission: The Master's program in Sustainable Energy provides advanced training in the area of sustainable energy. Its objective is to prepare students for employment related to sustainable energy in government, business, or the civil society sector, and/or to serve as a foundation for further graduate education at the doctoral level. The program involves learning across two distinct disciplines - engineering and public policy.

Environmental Studies
Mission: The environmental studies program at Carleton University supports the education and preparation of informed, skilled individuals to participate in the resolution of environmental conflicts and in the larger environmental debates critical to our future. Participation in environmental decision-making and intervention may focus on conservation, management of natural systems, development of institutional frameworks, public participation, communication, environmental education or research.

Technology, Society, Environmental Studies
2240 Herzberg Laboratories, 1125 Colonel By Dr., Ottawa ON K1S 5B6 Canada
Tel: 613-520-4461; *Fax:* 613-520-3422
tse.carleton.ca
Mission: Covers a wide range of topics from technology in ancient societies to contemporary issues in risk, innovation, forecasting, information technology, environmental sustainability, product life cycle analysis, energy use and the philosophy of technology.

Centennial College
PO Box 631, Stn. A, Toronto ON M1K 5E9
Tel: 416-289-5300
Toll-Free: 800-268-4419
e-mail: success@centennialcollege.ca
www.centennialcollege.ca

Environmental Technician
Morningside Campus, 755 Morningside Ave., Toronto ON M1C 5J9
Tel: 416-289-5000
Toll-Free: 800-268-4419
e-mail: enviro@centennialcollege.ca
www.centennialcollege.ca
Mission: Students will gain practical training in the three foundation disciplines of biology, chemistry and civil engineering that teaches students to understand and manage complex environmental problems.

Environmental Technology
Mission: Students will learn to function effectively with the tools and equipment used in microbiology, ecological field sampling, analytical chemistry, hazardous material management, surveying and municipal engineering, AutoCAD drawing and Geographic Information Systems (GIS) mapping.

La Cité collégiale
801, promenade de l'Aviation, Ottawa ON K1K 4R3
Tel: 613-742-2483
Toll-Free: 800-267-2483
www.lacitec.on.ca

Pratiques en environnement forestier
Mission: Le programme forme des travailleurs en environnement forestier aptes à exercer de nombreuses fonctions reliées à la protection, à l'aménagement et à la gestion des forêts.

Techniques d'aménagement de la faune
Mission: Le programme forme des techniciens polyvalents aptes à exercer de multiples fonctions reliées à l'exploitation, à l'aménagement et à la protection de la faune aquatique et terrestre.

Techniques en environnement forestier
Mission: Dans le cadre du programme, l'étudiant fait l'étude de l'aménagement durable des forêts, de l'environnement, de l'aménagement des espaces verts en milieu urbain et des règlements de conservation existants.

Technologie en environnement forestier et faunique
Mission: Apprenez à identifier diverses espèces animales et végétales, à inventorier leurs populations, à traiter de la question de leur survie et à mener des recherches sur ces mêmes populations dans le cadre d'études d'impact qui serviront entre autres à éduquer les divers intervenants du domaine des sciences forestières et fauniques.

Techniques de l'environnement
Mission: Le programme permet aux étudiants d'acquérir d'importantes connaissances scientifiques et techniques requises pour travailler sur des projets d'évaluation, d'assainissement et de protection de l'environnement.

Technologie de l'environnement
Mission: e programme permet aux étudiants d'acquérir d'importantes connaissances scientifiques et techniques requises pour travailler sur des projets d'évaluation, d'assainissement et de protection de l'environnement.

Collège Boréal
21, boul Lasalle, Sudbury ON P3A 6B1
Tel: 705-560-6673
Toll-Free: 800-361-6673
e-mail: info@collegeboreal.ca
www.collegeboreal.ca

Forestry and Wildlife Management Technician
Mission: This two-year program trains the student to work as a technician in various fields relating to the management of natural resources.

Fish and Wildlife Management Technologist
Mission: This three-year program prepares students in monitoring compliance with federal and provincial regulations designed to protect fish, wildlife, and other natural resources.

Forest Technologist
Mission: In this specialization program, the student learns to work in forestry industries, related provincial and federal government departments, consulting firms and other forestry-related industries or establishments, or even to be self-employed.

Environmental Chemistry Technician
Mission: In this program, the student conducts chemical experiments, tests, and analyses using devices and equipments that are commonly employed in the fields of in chemical engineering, research, and industrial chemistry.

College of New Caledonia
3300 - 22nd Ave., Prince George BC V2N 1P8
Tel: 250-562-2131
Toll-Free: 800-371-8111

e-mail: askcnc@cnc.bc.ca
www.cnc.bc.ca

Forest Industry Safety Training
Lakes District Campus, PO Box 5000, Burns Lake BC V0J 1E0
Tel: 250-692-1715; *Fax:* 250-692-1750
Toll-Free: 866-692-1943
e-mail: lksdist@cnc.bc.ca
cnc.bc.ca/CNC_Programs/FIST.htm
Mission: Prepares students for careers in Fire Suppression, First Aid, Log Scaling and Grading, and Chainsaw Safety.

Natural Resources and Environmental Technology
3300 - 22nd Ave., Prince George BC V2N 1P8
Tel: 250-562-2131
Toll-Free: 800-371-8111
cnc.bc.ca/CNC_Programs/NRETech.htm
Mission: Students in this program will learn the practical skills of data collecting. summarizing and analyzing, reporting results, and implementing and enforcing environmental standards.

College of the North Atlantic
PO Box 822, Corner Brook NL A2H 6H6
Tel: 709-637-8530; *Fax:* 709-634-2126
www.cna.nl.ca

Forest Resources Technician
Mission: This two-year technical program provides graduates with the capacity of making a meaningful contribution to the expanded requirement for ecosystem-based technology within this changing environment. The program places great emphasis on experiential field-based activities.

Fish & Wildlife Technician
Mission: The two-year Fish and Wildlife Technician program is designed to enable students with a specific interest in fish and wildlife to participate in studies directed towards their career goals.

Northern Natural Resources Technician
Happy Valley-Goose Bay Campus, PO Box 1720, Stn. B, Happy Valley-Goose Bay NL A0P 1E0
Tel: 709-896-6300; *Fax:* 709-896-3733
Mission: The Northern Natural Resources Technician program is designed to produce competent technicians for various wildlife, forestry and fisheries agencies with major emphasis on working in northern ecosystems.

College of the Rockies
PO Box 8500, 2700 College Way, Cranbrook BC V1C 5L7
Tel: 250-489-2751; *Fax:* 250-489-1790
Toll-Free: 877-489-2687
www.cotr.bc.ca

Environmental Sciences
555 McKenzie St., Kimberley BC V1A 2C1 Canada
Tel: 250-427-7116; *Fax:* 250-427-3034
www.cotr.bc.ca/university/cotr_web.asp?IDNumber=160
Mission: The Associate of Science degree provides the student with the first two years of study towards a Bachelor of Science degree. The ASc, Environmental Studies, offers students an opportunity for cross-disciplinary studies in their areas of interest, particularly those that relate to the local and global environment.

Concordia University
1455 de Maisonneuve Blvd. W, Montreal QC H3G 1M8
Tel: 514-848-2424
www.concordia.ca

Environmental Science
Mission: The program provides students with excellent training for careers in the environment by providing a multidisciplinary approach to questions related to life on the Earth, degradation caused by pollution and disturbance, the sustainability of resource use, and the endangerment of species and natural systems.

Urban Studies & Urban Planning
Mission: This multidisciplinary program is designed to introduce students to the processes of planned change in urban environments. Urban Studies provides a core of urban-planning courses involving field studies, planning projects, and the acquisition of technical skills. Complementary courses in Sociology, Political Science, Economics and Geography provide the necessary approaches and understanding from which to consider complex urban development.

Environmental Geography
Mission: The program allows greater concentration on the biogeophysical environment, while maintaining a strong grounding in human interventions, policy and management.

Concordia University College of Alberta
7128 Ada Blvd., Edmonton AB T5B 4E4
Tel: 780-479-8481; *Fax:* 780-477-1033
Toll-Free: 866-479-5200
e-mail: info@concordia.ab.ca
concordia.ab.ca

Environmental Science
Mission: Environmental Science is an exciting and relatively new field which explores environmental principles and the interaction of humans and the environment. As a student in the Environmental Science program, you will investigate the effect of human activities on the environment and ways by which we all can become environmentally responsible citizens.

Confederation College
PO Box 398, 1450 Nakina Dr., Thunder Bay ON P7C 4W1
Tel: 807-475-6110
www.confederationc.on.ca

Forest Ecosystem Management Technician
Mission: In the two-year Forest Ecosystem Management Technician (Co-op) program, you will acquire the theoretical knowledge and technical skills needed to work effectively in the forest and environmental sectors.

Environmental Technician
Mission: This multi-faceted, two-year program is delivered in the middle of northwestern Ontario's beautiful Boreal Forest. It trains students to effectively manage natural and man-made environments, and how to communicate and work cooperatively with those from other sectors and disciplines.

Dalhousie University
Halifax NS B3H 4R2
Tel: 902-494-2211
www.dal.ca

Aquaculture
Faculty of Agriculture, PO Box 550, Truro NS B2N 5E3
Tel: 902-893-6600
www.dal.ca/academics/programs/undergraduate/aquaculture.html
Mission: In this four-year program, studdents will be exposed to a range of subjects related to fish production and aquatic ecosystems. Studies include both food production and environmental conservation.

Integrated Environmental Management
www.dal.ca/faculty/agriculture.html
Mission: The program offers training in green science and technology. It's founded on four educational pillars: bio-resources, precision agriculture, renewable energy and waste management. While studying at our Agricultural Campus in Truro, NS, students will gain the skills and experience to create immediate sustainable solutions and address our national and global resource management and food production needs.

Ocean Sciences
oceanography.dal.ca
Mission: The Ocean Sciences program offers a complete undergraduate major, as well as undergraduate training in a double major or combined honours degree with Marine Biology, Chemistry, Earth Sciences, Mathematics, Statistics, Environmental Science, and Physics and Atmospheric Science. This program focuses on the impact of pollution and the effects of marine resource exploitation and climate change.

Management & Globalization
www.dal.ca/academics/programs/undergraduate/management.html
Mission: The Bachelor of Management provides an innovative and interdisciplinary program that combines information management, environmental resource management, public administration and business.

Environmental Sciences
www.dal.ca/faculty/agriculture/environmental-sciences.html
Mission: The Environmental Science program encourages students to explore the environment from scientific perspectives-as well as the political, cultural, ethical, and historical angles. Studies focus on climate change, biodiversity, energy and the economy.

Environmental Design Studies
architectureandplanning.dal.ca
Mission: The Bachelor of Environmental Design Studies is a two-year program entered after two years of university studies in other subjects. Students learn to design environmentally-friendly buildings, architects shape and influences in our world.

Sustainability Leadership Certificate
College of Sustainability, PO Box 15000, #1401, 1459 LeMerchant St., Halifax NS B3H 3P8 Canada
Tel: 902-494-4581; *Fax:* 902-494-8923
www.dal.ca/faculty/sustainability/programs/slc.html
Mission: The Sustainability Leadership Certificate offers students the opportunity to: actively participate in an exploration of personal and group leadership; be inspired to take effective sustainability actions; develop agency and gain competencies and practical tools to lead change; demonstrate leadership to increase sustainability in their world and environment; and gain skills to inspire, motivate and build capacity in others to take action for sustainability.

Environment, Sustainability and Society (ESS)
www.dal.ca/faculty/sustainability/programs/ess.html
Mission: ESS classes are based on principles of academic collaboration, leading students to understand the complex real world of sustainability problems from a variety of perspectives and conceptual frameworks. The structure of the ESS program allows students to pursue the academic field of choice, anything from theatre to biology to business, and combine it with a major in ESS.

Environmental Engineering
Tel: 902-494-2963; *Fax:* 902-492-0011
biologicalengineering.dal.ca
Mission: Students learn various approaches to environment-based design, waste management, water and soil quality, energy conservation and renewables, and air quality.

School for Resource and Environmental Studies (SRES)
Kenneth C. Rowe Mgmt Bldg., #5010, 6100 University Ave., Halifax NS B3H 3J5 Canada
Tel: 902-494-3632; *Fax:* 902-494-3728
e-mail: sres@dal.ca
sres.management.dal.ca
Mission: The school offers two graduate programs in environmental management, science and policy. The first is a Master of Environmental Studies (MES), which is a two-year program that includes both course work and a thesis. The second is a Master of Resource and Environmental Management (MREM), which is a 16-month program that includes course work and an internship. Both programs emphasize interactions between social and natural sciences needed for resolving the complex environmental and resource management problems.

Marine & Environmental Law Programme (MELP)
Schulich School of Law, 6061 University Ave., Halifax NS B3H 4H9 Canada
Tel: 902-494-1988; *Fax:* 902-494-1316
e-mail: melp@dal.ca
www.dal.ca/faculty/law/melaw/programs.html
Mission: This certificate programme provides LL.B. and post graduate students (LL.M. and Doctoral) with extensive academic course offerings in the fields of Marine Law and Enironmental Law, taught from domestic and international perspectives.

Environmental Sciences
www.dal.ca/faculty/agriculture/environmental-sciences.html
Mission: The Environmental Science program allows students to pursue studies in the following range of specialty subject areas: Environmental Biology, Environmental Chemistry, Environmental Economics, Environmental Soil Science, Waste Management, and Pest Management. The Bio-Environmental Engineering Centre (BEEC) is frequently used as a research and demonstration facility.

Sustainable Resources & the Environment
Faculty of Management, PO Box 15000, Halifax NS B3H 4R2 Canada

Tel: 902-494-2582; *Fax:* 902-494-1195
bmgmt.management.dal.ca/Program_Details/sre/
Mission: This 4-year Bachelor of Management program allows students to learn how to manage natural resources (e.g. minerals, forests) and ecosystems (e.g. parks, protected areas) for a balance of public and private values. The program draws from business, environmental studies, information management, and public administration.

Agriculture (Graduate)
www.dal.ca/faculty/agriculture.html
Mission: The Master of Science in agriculture is offered at the Agricultural Campus, Truro NS, the only institution in the Atlantic Region with the faculty and facilities capable of providing such a program of study. This program is designed to provide a foundation for studies at the doctoral level and for professional careers in research and development, teaching, industry and extension.

Douglas College
700 Royal Ave., New Westminster BC V3M 5Z5
Tel: 604-527-5400
www.douglas.bc.ca

Environmental Studies
Mission: Associate of Arts Degree with an emphasis on Environmental Studies consists of a series of university transfer courses for the student interested in Earth functions and systems, the environment and global climate change, humans interaction with Earth, or the fields of park and urban planning, environmental consultation, and environmental education.

Earth Science
1250 Pinetree Way, Coquitlam BC V3M 5Z5 Canada
Tel: 604-527-6500; *Fax:* 604-527-5095
www.douglas.bc.ca/programs/earth-environmental-sciences.html
Mission: Study the materials, processes and history of our plant, including natural resources, natural hazards, rocks, minerals, fossils, and environmental issues, and learn how we explore for natural resources and about global clmiate change as a recurring phenomenon. 2-year Diploma.

Environmental Science
Mission: Study the interactions among Earth's fundamental systems: Lithosphere, Biosphere, Atmosphere, Hydrosphere; Explore the mechanisms of global change and the impact of human activites; Examine the nature of science. 2-year Diploma.

Durham College
2000 Simcoe St. North, Oshawa ON L1H 7K4
Tel: 905-721-2000
www.durhamcollege.ca

Energy Management & Sustainable Building Technology
Whitby Campus, 1610 Champlain Ave., Whitby ON L1N 6A7
Tel: L1N-905-7213
www.durhamcollege.ca
Mission: This program offers the opportunity to learn how to integrate a variety of technologies to quantify energy efficiency and conservation within commercial and institutional buildings through the application of energy management, business principles and clean energy technologies.

Environmental Technology
Mission: This program focuses on the chemical and biological sciences as they relate to environmental pollution. An emphasis is placed on ground and surface water quality, soil and waste management and recycling in urban and industrial settings.

Renewable Emergy Technician
Mission: This program prepares students to perform energy audits on new and existing homes and assist with site analysis and the installation and assembly of solar energy panels, geothermal heat pump systems and wind turbines.

Water Quality Technician
www.durhamcollege.ca/programs/water-quality-technician
Mission: The Water Quality Technician program is designed to provide you with training in water and wastewater treatment, water distribution, wastewater collection and environmental monitoring.

École de technologie supérieure
1100, rue Notre-Dame ouest, Montréal QC H3C 1K3
Tel: 514-396-8800
www.etsmtl.ca

Génie de l'environnement
Mission: Ce programme vise des objectifs de formation continue. Il s'adresse aux ingénieurs et aux professionnels désirant acquérir des connaissances avancées en génie de l'environnement et développer les habiletés et aptitudes nécessaires pour identifier les besoins en technologie dans une entreprise donnée et procéder au transfert de technologie dans l'industrie.

First Nations University of Canada
1 First Nations Way, Regina SK S4S 7K2
Tel: 306-790-5950; *Fax:* 306-790-5999
Toll-Free: 800-267-6303
www.fnuniv.ca

National First Nations Environmental Contaminants Program (NFNECP)
www.fnuniv.ca/programs/programs-dip/environmental-science
Mission: The National First Nations Environmental Contaminants Program (NFNECP) is a collaborative program between the First Nations University of Canada, the Assembly of First Nations and Health Canada that supports the research of potential environmental and health impacts from environmental chemicals in First Nations Communities.

Resource and Environmental Studies
Mission: The program is a collaborative degree program beginning with two years at SIAST Woodland Campus (Diploma in Resource and Environmental Law) and then a transfer for two more years at First Nations University of Canada. Students will learn indigenous perspectives in the areas of conservation, the environment, and natural resource issues.

Environmental Health and Science
Mission: This four year program leads to a BASc in Environmental Health and Science. It emphasizes First Nations traditions and culture while equipping graduates with the skills and knowledge necessary to address environmental health and science problem areas.

Fleming College
599 Brealey Dr., Peterborough ON K9J 7B1
Tel: 705-749-5530; *Fax:* 705-749-5507
Toll-Free: 866-353-6464
e-mail: info@flemingc.on.ca
flemingcollege.ca

Conservation & Environmental Law Enforcement
Frost Campus, 200 Albert St. South, Lindsay ON K9V 5E6
Tel: 705-749-5514; *Fax:* 705-749-5507
Toll-Free: 866-353-6464
Mission: Conservation and Environmental Law Enforcement is about regulating the use of natural resources, and accountability for activities that have an adverse effect on the environment.

Environmental Technician
flemingcollege.ca/programs/environmental-technician
Mission: Students are well-prepared to monitor and improve the natural environment with access to environmental training facilities and a biological water treatment system.

Environmental Visual Communication
Royal Ontario Museum, 100 Queen's Park, Toronto ON M5S 2C6
Tel: 705-749-5514; *Fax:* 705-749-5507
Toll-Free: 866-353-6464
e-mail: admissions@flemingc.on.ca
flemingcollege.ca/programs/environmental-visual-communication
Mission: The Environmental Visual Communication program is designed to fill a recognized void of individuals who possess a blend of environmental science skills and the ability to effectively communicate to a variety of audiences. The program takes place at the Royal Ontario Museum (ROM) in downtown Toronto.

Fish & Wildlife Technician
flemingcollege.ca/programs/fish-and-wildlife-technician
Mission: This program prepares students for positions like fish and wildlife technician/technologist, interpreter at fish and wildlife reserves, fishing/hunting guides, and wetlands inventory technicians.

Forestry Technician
flemingcollege.ca/programs/forestry-technician
Mission: This two-year Forestry Technician program will give students the skills to work effectively in natural resources management - from identifying trees to working with high-tech computers.

Urban Forestry Technician
flemingcollege.ca/programs/urban-forestry-technician-co-op
Mission: Urban forestry focuses on the care, protection and maintenance of trees, forests and green spaces in towns and cities.

Georgian College
One Georgian Dr., Barrie ON L4M 3X9
Tel: 705-728-1968; *Fax:* 705-722-5122
e-mail: Inquire@GeorgianCollege.ca
www.georgiancollege.ca

Environmental Technician
Mission: Environmental Technician graduates are trained as entry-level practitioners in the use of environmental sampling, monitoring and testing equipment and information technology tools and will be familiar with standard operating procedures for conducting environmental projects.

Environmental Technology
Mission: Environmental Technology graduates have advanced skills in the use of environmental sampling, monitoring and testing equipment; data analysis; and information technology tools. They are familiar with applying the principles of ecosystem-based management for sustainability and have the ability to manage environmental projects from planning through to implementation and maintenance.

Grande Prairie Regional College (GPRC)
10726 - 106 Ave., Grande Prairie AB T8V 4C4
Tel: 780-539-2911; *Fax:* 780-539-2832
Toll-Free: 888-539-4772
www.gprc.ab.ca

Environmental and Conservation Science
www.gprc.ab.ca/programs/viewcatalog.1.100.672.html
Mission: The five areas of specialization within the Environmental and Conservation Sciences program are conservation biology; environmental economics and policy; land reclamation; human dimensions of environmental management and wildlife and rangeland resources management.

Forestry
www.gprc.ab.ca/programs/viewcatalog.1.100.673.html
Mission: The Forestry specialization develops graduates who appreciate the need to manage forested areas with concern for all resources and who have the capability and knowledge to manage forested areas as integrated ecological entities.

Holland College
140 Weymouth St., Charlottetown PE C1A 4Z1
Tel: 902-629-4217; *Fax:* 902-629-4239
Toll-Free: 800-446-5265
e-mail: info@hollandcollege.com
www.hollandcollege.com

Environmental Applied Science Technology
Mission: The Environmental Applied Science Technology Program educates and trains Environmental Technicians to have the skills and knowledge to manage and enhance the sustainability of the environment.

Wildlife Conservation Technician
Mission: The Wildlife Conservation Technology program trains learners as wildlife technicians to work in the field of fish and wildlife conservation.

Institut national de la recherche scientifique
490, rue de la Couronne, Québec QC G1K 9A9
Tel: 418-654-2501
www.inrs.ca

Sciences de l'eau
Courriel: info@ete.inrs.ca
www.ete.inrs.ca
Mission: Ce programme propose aux diplômés de 1er cycle en sciences et génie un approfondissement des connaissances multidisciplinaires nécessaires à l'étude des problématiques environnementales reliées à l'eau. Les chercheurs du Centre possèdent une vaste expertise en

sciences de l'eau allant de la gestion par bassin versant jusqu'au traitement des eaux usées.

Sciences de la terre
Mission: Ce programme propose aux étudiants de 1er cycle en sciences de la terre d'acquérir des connaissances plus poussées dans un domaine particulier, de s'initier à la recherche scientifique et de se préparer adéquatement à la pratique professionnelle de la géologie ou du génie géologique. Les chercheurs du Centre possèdent une vaste expertise des ressources en eau souterraine, minières et pétrolières, ainsi que de l'ensemble des disciplines géologiques.

Institute for Resources, Environment & Sustainability (IRES) at the University of British Columbia (UBC)
429 - 2202 Main Hall, Vancouver BC V6T 1Z4 Canada
Tel: 604-822-7725; *Fax:* 604-822-9250
www.ires.ubc.ca

Resource Management & Environmental Studies (RMES)
Mission: An interdisciplinary Graduate program tailored to the goals of the student, and focused on research across a wide range of environmental concerns including: land management, environmental assessment, fisheries management, water resource management, agroforestry, and science and policy. Degrees: MSc, MA; PhD; Certificate program in Watershed Management.

Keyano College
8115 Franklin Ave., Fort McMurray AB T9H 2H7
Tel: 780-791-4800
Toll-Free: 800-251-1408
keyano.ca

Environmental Technology
8115 Franklin Ave., Fort McMurray AB T9H 2H7
Tel: 780-791-4800
Toll-Free: 800-251-1408
keyano.ca
Mission: The Environmental Technology program focuses on the environmental issues, problems and solutions that are associated with natural resources. The program is a two-year diploma which develops the skills required for environmental positions with industry and government.

King's University College
266 Epworth Ave., London ON N6A 2M3
Tel: 519-433-3491
Toll-Free: 800-265-4406
e-mail: kings@uwo.ca
www.kings.uwo.ca

Environmental Studies
9125 - 50 St., Edmonton AB T6B 2H3 Canada
Tel: 780-465-3500; *Fax:* 780-465-3534
Toll-Free: 800-661-8582
e-mail: general-info@kingsu.ca
www.kingsu.ca/faculties/interdisciplinary-studies
Mission: A study of the environment that involves many disciplines. Examines the relationship between human activities and the natural world, covers many traditional science subjects in the investigation of terrestrial (earth), aquatic (water), and atmospheric (air) systems and their interactions.

Kwantlen Polytechnic University
12666 - 72nd Ave., Surrey BC V3W 2M8
Tel: 604-599-2000
www.kwantlen.ca

Environmental Protection
Faculty of Science & Horticulture
Tel: 902-494-4581; *Fax:* 902-494-8923
e-mail: science@kwantlen.ca
www.kwantlen.ca/science/environment.html
Mission: Kwantlen's Environmental Protection Technology (EPT) Program is a two-year diploma program that prepares the graduate for technical work in the environmental field. Courses and two paid Co-op work terms give the student practical knowledge and experience in environmental protection technology, impact assessment, waste minimization and management, air and water pollution monitoring and control, and contaminated site investigations. The program also provides the student with a foundation in Biology, Ecology, Toxicology and Environmental Legislation.

Applied Science - Sustainable Agriculture
Faculty of Science & Horticulture, Kwantlen Polytechnic University, 12666 - 72nd Ave., Surrey BC V3W 2M8 Canada
Tel: 902-494-4581; *Fax:* 902-494-8923
e-mail: science@kwantlen.ca
kwantlen.ca/degrees/sustainable-agriculture.html
Mission: The Bachelor of Applied Science in Sustainable Agriculture degree is unique to North America and is distinguished from other agriculture degree programs by providing a broad scope of study related to sustainable food production as an integral and fundamentally critical element of sustainable human existence.

Kwantlen Polytechnic University

Horticulture Science - Urban Ecosystems
Faculty of Science & Horticulture, Kwantlen Polytechnic University, 12666 - 72nd Ave., Surrey BC V3W 2M8 Canada
Tel: 902-494-4581; *Fax:* 902-494-8923
e-mail: science@kwantlen.ca
kwantlen.ca/calendar/2012-13/science-hort/urbanecosystems-deg
Mission: The new Bachelor of Horticulture Science program is an interdisciplinary program that combines horticulture, business, mathematics, biology, and chemistry. Students will combine the science and practice of in horticulture to resolve community, industry, or research related problems.

Lakehead University
955 Oliver Rd., Thunder Bay ON P7B 5E1
Tel: 807-343-8110
e-mail: tbay@lakehead.ca
www.lakeheadu.ca

Environmental Management
Mission: This program builds expertise in the areas of wildlife habitat management, water/forest interactions, carbon management, climate change mitigation, natural resources policy, geographical information systems or First Nations forestry.

Environmental Studies
Mission: Three interdisciplinary programs (Biology, Geography, Earth Sciences) are offered at Lakehead that contain a common core of environmental studies plus courses required for an honours degree in each of the three disciplines.

Forestry
Mission: Students will be prepared to tackle the modern issues natural resource managers face. Lakehead University's HBScF programs are nationally accredited by the Canadian Forestry Accreditation Board (CFAB), providing graduates with the academic credentials to become a Registered Professional Forester anywhere in Canada. Masters and Doctoral programs are also available in Forestry.

Resource & Environmental Science
Mission: Students will learn to understand and evaluate how economic activity impacts the environment, combining the academic intensity of an economics degree with the scientific depth and breadth of an environmental science degree.

Water Resource Science
Mission: The Water Resource Science program will provide you with the skills and knowledge to work on water-related issues while armed with a firm scientific background. Training and expertise is taught necessary to work for both the private sector and government in areas related to environmental monitoring, remediation, and water supply and contamination.

Environmental Sustainability
500 University Ave., Orilla ON L3V 0B9 Canada
Mission: Orillia's HBASc in Environmental Sustainability has been designed to produce environmentally conscious and responsible citizens with excellent communication skills and problem solving abilities. Graduates will be trained to meet the growing demands of interdisciplinary environmental practitioners and to pursue graduate studies in a variety of disciplines related to Environmental Sustainability.

Environmental Studies (MES) in Nature-Based Recreation and Tourism
Mission: The Master of Environmental Studies (MES) in Nature-Based Recreation and Tourism with the School of Outdoor Recreation, Parks, and Tourism (ORPT) is an interdisciplinary degree that has its roots in social sciences such as leisure studies, human geography, sociology, psychology, and anthropology as well as in the professional areas of tourism, community development, resource management, parks and protected areas, and forestry.

Environmental Studies (MES) in Northern Environments & Cultures
Mission: This is a Masters interdisciplinary program offered jointly by the Departments of Anthropology and Geography, designed to train graduates to investigate, understand and appreciate issues peculiar to northern environments and cultures.

Langara College
100 West 49th Ave., Vancouver BC V5Y 2Z6
Tel: 604-323-5511; *Fax:* 604-323-5555
www.langara.bc.ca

Environmental Studies
Tel: 604-323-5908
Mission: Gain an awareness, knowledge, skills, experience, and environmental understanding in this interdisciplinary liberal arts program. The program draws from four critical areas of study - biology, chemistry, english, and georgaphy - as well as specific environmental courses. Degree: AA

Laurentian University / Université Laurentienne
935 Ramsey Lake Rd., Sudbury ON P3E 2C6
Tel: 705-675-1151
Toll-Free: 800-461-4030
www.laurentian.ca

Environmental Studies
Faculty of Social Sciences & Humanities
Toll-Free: 800-263-4188
Mission: The program offers an interdisciplinary education on environmental issues, with a particular emphasis on development and ethical issues in a location characterized by diversity and variability.

Environmental Science
Faculty of Science & Engineering
Mission: Students will understand the nature and impact that humans have on the habitat, on both a local and much wider scale. Set in the context of Northern Ontario, the program addresses challenges on land and aquatic ecosystems, while it aims to integrate the historical importance of the region's resource industry.

Loyalist College
PO Box 4200, 376 Wallbridge-Loyalist Rd., Belleville ON K8N 5B9
Tel: 613-969-1913; *Fax:* 613-962-1376
Toll-Free: 888-569-2547
www.loyalistcollege.com

Environmental Technician/Technologist
Mission: Students learn to sample natural environments, analyze environmental contaminants, and also gain an understanding of the underlying social systems that contribute to pollutants in water, soil and air.

Maritime College of Forest Technology (MCFT)
1350 Regent St., Fredericton NB E3C 2G6
Tel: 506-458-0199; *Fax:* 506-458-0679
mcft.ca

Advanced Diploma in Forest and Fish & Wildlife Technology
mcft.ca/en/explore/program
Mission: This program is only avaiable to students who have completed MCFT's Diploma in Forest Technology. Advanced Diploma students will be subject to both Forest Technology courses and the designated Fish & Wildlife courses including both summer and winter field camps.

Forest Technology Program
Mission: This program takes place over two years and includes a paid summer work term between year one and two. Each year the college accepts 60 new students. MCFT specializes in natural resource education which includes fish & wildlife.

McGill University
845 Sherbrook St. West, Montreal QC H3A 0G4
Tel: 514-398-4455
www.mcgill.ca

Agricultural & Environmental Sciences
Faculty of Agricultural & Environmental Sciences, 21111 Lakeshore Rd., Montreal QC H9X 3V9 Canada

Tel: 514-398-7707; *Fax:* 514-398-7766
www.mcgill.ca/macdonald/prospective/degrees/bscagenvsc
Mission: Bachelor of Science degree with specializtions available in Life Sciences, Environmental Biololgy, Agro-Environmental Sciences, International Agriculture and Food Systems, Agriculture Economics, and Environment.

Sustainability, Science & Society
Department of Geography
www.geog.mcgill.ca/SSS/
Mission: The SSS program is an "Interfaculty" program between the Arts and Sciences, offered in close partnership between Geography and the McGill School of Environment, and involving other departments at McGill.

Environment
3534 University St., Montreal QC H9X 3V9 Canada
Tel: 514-398-7707; *Fax:* 514-398-7766
www.mcgill.ca/mse
Mission: This major has two components: Core & Domain. The Core exposes students to a variety of approaches, perspectives and world views to give an understanding of the complexity and conflicts that underlie most environmental problems. The Domain is the area of specialization the student chooses and is immersed in cutting-edge interdisciplinary fields to provide expertise. Degrees: BA; BSc; BA&Sc.

Environmental Biology
Mission: A vibrant learning experience in the providing students extensive field training in the diversity, biology, convservations and ecology of a broad range of organisms, from plants and animals to microbes. Students will study ecosystems, species, and the adaptation, to name a few. BSc.

McMaster Univeristy
1200 Main St. West, Hamilton ON L8S 4L8
Tel: 905-525-9140
www.mcmaster.ca

Environmental & Earth Science
School of Geography and Earth Sciences, 1280 Main St. West, Hamilton ON L8S 4L8 Canada
future.mcmaster.ca/programs/enviro-earth
Mission: The Environmental and Earth Sciences program focuses on issues of environmental resources, as well as air, water, soil and the mineral and organic resources of the earth.

Memorial University of Newfoundland
PO Box 4200, St. John's NL A1C 5S7
Tel: 709-864-8000; *Fax:* 709-864-3514
www.mun.ca

Environmental Science
Dean of Science Office, St. John's NL A1B 3X7 Canada
Tel: 709-864-8154; *Fax:* 709-864-3316
www.mun.ca/science/graduate/interdisciplinary/envs/
Mission: The Environmental Science Program is an interdisciplinary graduate program offered by the Faculty of Science on the St. John's campus of Memorial University of Newfoundland. It is distinct from, but complementary to, two graduate programs in Memorial's Faculty of Engineering and Applied Science, namely Environmental Systems Engineering and Management and Environmental Engineering.iplines.

Earth Sciences
www.mun.ca/become/graduate/programs/easc.php
Mission: The Earth Sciences Department offers both MSc and PhD degrees in Geology and Geophysics. All graduate degrees require a research-based thesis. In addition to graduate research projects in these areas, the department also participates actively in multidisciplinary MSc programs in Environmental Science and Computational Science. These programs are initiatives of the Faculty of Science, and offer thesis-based degrees as well as course-only degrees.

Marine Environmental
PO Box PO Box 4920, St. John's NL A1C 5R3 Canada
Tel: 709-778-0454; *Fax:* 709-778-0346
Toll-Free: 800-563-5799
www.mi.mun.ca/programsandcourses/programs/marineenvironmental
Mission: With a Diploma of Technology in Marine Environmental Technology, you will be able to develop environmentally sound projects and work to prevent and create responses to marine pollution or degradation. You will go from lakes to rivers and coastal zones to the fragile offshore. You will be responsible for protecting the marine environment and developing solutions to manage marine resources.

Integrated Coastal and Ocean Management
Mission: This advanced diploma program focuses on the bio-ecological, socio-economic, cultural and technological elements of coastal zone development and management. It will prepare students for a career related to planning and management of coastal and ocean activities or coastal zone development.

Mohawk College
PO Box 2034, Hamilton ON L8N 3T2
Tel: 905-575-1212
www.mohawkcollege.ca

Energy Systems Engineering Technician - Clean and Renewable Energy
Mission: This two-year diploma program gives students the opportunity to develop theoretical and practical understanding of clean and renewable energy technologies and systems and their application in small-scale residential and commercial environments.

Environmental Technician
Mission: Students in the Environmental Technician program will learn the fundamentals of solid waste, water and wastewater treatment.

Mount Allison University
62 York St., Sackville NS E4L 1E2
Tel: 506-364-2269; *Fax:* 506-364-2272
www.mta.ca

Environmental Science
Faculty of Science, 144 Main St., Sackville NB E4L 1A7 Canada
Tel: 506-364-2390
www.mta.ca/faculty/socsci/geograph/sciencebsc.htm
Mission: The Environmental Science degree has been developed for students who have a strong interest in science and a concern for the environment. Students can complete a Major or Honours. The program is an interdisciplinary, science-intensive program, requiring comprehensive study of the sciences and mathematics.

Mount Royal University
4825 Mount Royal Gate SW, Calgary AB T3E 6K6
Tel: 403-440-6111
www.mtroyal.ca

Environmental Science
Mission: This four-year program deals with preventing pollution and promoting the efficient and appropriate use of energy, materials and natural resources. This encourages industries to establish sustainable systems that can help protect the environment, as well as improve the corporate bottom line.

Niagara College
300 Woodlawn Rd., Welland ON L3C 7L3
Tel: 905-735-2211; *Fax:* 905-736-6000
www.niagaracollege.ca

Environmental Technician - Field and Laboratory
Niagara on the Lake Campus, 135 Taylor Rd., Niagara-on-the-Lake ON L0S 1J0
Tel: 905-641-2252; *Fax:* 905-736-6000
Mission: Hands-on training that will allow students to help protect our water, air and land.

Renewable Energies Technician
Welland Campus
Mission: Students will learn to use and integrate renewable energy as a preferred energy source.

Ecosystem Restoration
Mission: This Graduate program gives students a competitive advantage in the environmental labour market including conservation authorities; municipal, provincial and federal government agencies; NGOs; engineering and consulting firms.

Environmental Management & Assessment
Mission: This program will equip students with specialized skills that can be applied to business, industry, government, consultants and environmental associations.

Nicola Valley Institute of Technology (NVIT)
4155 Belshaw St., Merritt BC V1K 1R1
Tel: 250-378-3300; *Fax:* 250-378-3332
Toll-Free: 877-682-3300
e-mail: nfo@nvit.bc.ca
www.nvit.ca

Enviromental Resource Technology
www.nvit.ca/environmentalresourcestechnology.htm
Mission: The new Environmental Resources Technology program ensures graduates are well rounded in natural resource sectors including forestry, fishery enhancement, environmental assessment, mining and grassland ecology. This generalist approach gives students various career paths they can travel within the natural resources sector.

Nipissing University
PO Box 5002, 100 College Dr., North Bay ON P1B 8L7
Tel: 705-474-3450; *Fax:* 705-474-1947
Toll-Free: 877-688-5507
e-mail: nuinfo@nipissingu.ca
www.nipissingu.ca

Environmental Sciences/Studies
Mission: Nipissing University's new MES/MESc program offers students degrees in either Master of Environmental Studies or Master of Environmental Sciences. Both programs offer the training and development of graduates capable of contributing to the study of the environment and environmental issues and to the environmental problem solving of the future.

Northern College of Applied Arts & Technology
140 Government Rd., Kirkland Lake ON P2N 3L8
Tel: 705-567-9291; *Fax:* 705-568-8186
www.northernc.on.ca

Environmental Technician - Water and Wastewater Systems Operations
www.northernc.on.ca/environmental-technician
Mission: This compressed (three years into two-years), co-op diploma program prepares students with a strong combination of theory and practical systems operator experience needed to work as water and wastewater treatment operators under Ontario's stringent standards.

Natural Resources Technician
www.northernc.on.ca/cd-nrt
Mission: This program allows students to work on environmental solutions, inventory and decision making for fish and wildlife, forestry, ecotourism, environmental assessment, and environomental remediation activities.

Northwest Community College
5331 McConnell Ave., Terrace BC V8G 4X2
Tel: 250-635-6511; *Fax:* 250-638-5432
Toll-Free: 877-277-2288
www.nwcc.bc.ca

Coastal Eco-Adventure Tourism
www.nwcc.bc.ca/Programs/Technical/Overview.cfm?Program=CEAT
Mission: The Coastal Eco-Adventure Tourism program is designed to address the growing demand for trained tourism professionals and to give students the opportunity to promote environmental stewardship as they create enriching adventures for travellers.

Applied Coastal Ecology
e-mail: ace@nwcc.bc.ca
universitycredit.nwcc.bc.ca/Transfer/Overview.cfm?Program=ACE
Mission: Applied Coastal Ecology is an applied biology and ecology program. It combines the practical technical skills and academic theory needed for careers in coastal ecosystem protection and restoration.

Applied Earth & Environment Studies
universitycredit.nwcc.bc.ca/Transfer/Overview.cfm?Program=EES
Mission: The Applied Earth and Environmental Studies Certificate-with Geostudies or Geosciences options-is a one-year program that emphasizes the practical application of earth and environmental studies.

Okanagan College
1000 K.L.O. Rd., Kelowna BC V1Y 4X8
Tel: 250-762-5445
www.okanagan.bc.ca

Environmental Studies
Mission: he Diploma in Environmental Studies offers an interdisciplinary opportunity to understand the physical principles governing the environment and the social and cultural aspects that influence human behaviour towards the environment.

Green Building Design & Construction
Mission: This 360-hour certificate program gives students the skills and hands on experience to design and create building envelopes with a sustainable focus on the main functions of the design and construction of the building envelope, including solar and thermal control, moisture control, indoor air quality, acoustics, aesthetics, construction waste management and cost effectiveness.

Water Engineering Technology
Mission: This Program is a unique blend of traditional chemical and civil engineering technology combined with innovative water-focused environmental studies. The goals of the program are to educate, train and equip students so they are able to play a leading role in the water industry - both in Canada and internationally - to monitor, assess and protect both public health and water in the environment.

Olds College
4500 - 50th St., Olds AB T4H 1R6
Tel: 403-556-8281; *Fax:* 403-556-4711
Toll-Free: 800-661-6537
e-mail: info@oldscollege.ca
www.oldscollege.ca

Environmental Horticulture
www.oldscollege.ca/programs/Horticulture/landscape.htm
Mission: An Environmental Horticulture diploma will give students the technical and business training you need as well as a credential that is recognized and respected in the horticulture industry.

Land & Water Resources Program
www.oldscollege.ca/programs/LandWater
Mission: Program offers training in environmentally sustainable management of rural land. It involves the study of soil, water, plants, ecosystems and environmental sciences with applications to the workplace.

Portage College
PO Box 417, 9531 - 94 Ave., Lac La Biche AB T0A 2C0
Toll-Free: 866-623-5551
www.portagecollege.ca

Natural Resources
PO Box 417, 9531 - 94 Ave., Lac La Biche AB T0A 2C0
Toll-Free: 866-623-5551
www.portagecollege.ca
Mission: This program blends theory and applied science skills that are valuable to forestry, oil/gas/mining exploration, utilities sectors, municipalities, parks.

Queen's University
99 University Ave., Kingston ON K7L 3N6
www.queensu.ca

Environmental Science
School of Environmental Science, #3134, Bioscience Complex, Kingston ON K7L 3N6 Canada
Tel: 613-533-6602; *Fax:* 613-533-6090
e-mail: envst@queensu.ca
www.queensu.ca/ensc
Mission: This multidisciplinary program in Environmental Science which provides solid grounding in the natural and physical sciences, while recognizing the human and cultural dimensions of the issues.

Environmental Studies Program
School of Environmental Science
www.queensu.ca/ensc/index.html
Mission: An interdisciplinary undergraduate and graduate training that integrates the concepts of environmental toxicology and chemistry, ecosystems, human health, environmental policy and management, as well as the importance of social, cultural, and economic systems into the overarching theme of sustainability.

Quest University Canada
3200 University Blvd., Squamish BC V8B 0N8
Tel: 604-898-8000; *Fax:* 604-815-0829
Toll-Free: 888-783-7808
e-mail: info@questu.ca
www.questu.ca

Life and the Natural Environment: The Life Sciences
Mission: After completing the Foundation Program at Quest University Canada, students can choose to complete their independent concentration program in the Life and the Natural Environment program. With a concentration in Ecology, students can take courses that include Forest Environments, Aquatic Ecosystems, and Environmental Chemistry.

Red Deer College (RDC)
PO Box 5005, 100 College Blvd., Red Deer AB T4N 5H5
Tel: 403-342-3300; *Fax:* 403-340-8940
e-mail: inquire@rdc.ab.ca
www.rdc.ab.ca

Environmental Earth Sciences
Mission: This program trains students for careers in urban and housing project planning, parks and recreation planning, energy and natural resources planning, and planning commissions.

Environmental Science
Mission: This degrees give students the scientific skills essential to problem solving and skills that can immediately be applied to the workplace. The program produces graduates who are capable decision makers on issues of environmental concern in government or industry. Students are employed in a range of environmental jobs.

Environmental Management
Mission: This degrees give students the scientific skills essential to problem solving and skills that can immediately be applied to the workplace. The program produces graduates who are capable decision makers on issues of environmental concern in government or industry. Students are employed in a range of environmental jobs.

Forest Business Management
Mission: BSc Forest Business Management is intended to prepare students for careers as professional foresters and is for individuals planning careers focusing on forest practices, but who also demand specialized knowledge in business management practices. The Forest Business Management program prepares students for careers as Registered Professional Foresters. Graduates may immediately apply to the Alberta Registered Professional Foresters Association to complete the registration process.

Forestry
Mission: A growing interest in forest management, resource management, and preservation of the natural ecology means an increasing number of jobs in the field of Forestry.

Environmental & Conservation Sciences Program
Mission: This program is for students interested in the natural world, its management, conservation and ecological perspectives. The program emphasizes integrating natural science, management, and social science as related to environmental issues. It also offers students courses and team projects that integrate both biophysical and socioeconomic aspects of the environment in cooperation with practicing professionals and experts.

Redeemer University College
777 Garner Rd. East, Ancaster ON L9K 1J4
Tel: 905-648-2131; *Fax:* 905-648-2134
Toll-Free: 877-779-0913
www.redeemer.ca

Environmental Studies Program
www.redeemer.ca/academics/departments/environmental
Mission: Teaches about the impact of humans on the environment and how we can live in ways that reduce our negative impact. As an environmental studies student, you will develop a comprehensive approach to environmental issues, addressing Biblical, ethical, economic political social and scientific aspects.

Royal Roads University
2005 Sooke Rd., Victoria BC V9B 5Y2
Tel: 250-391-2511; *Fax:* 250-391-2500
www.royalroads.ca

Sustainable Community Development
Mission: This six-month, interdisciplinary Graduate Certificate in Sustainable Community Development will enhance students leadership skills, and impart the essential economic, social, environmental, and cultural knowledge and skills needed to develop sustainable communities.

Environmental Science
Mission: The Bachelor of Science in Environmental Science (BSc-ES) program complements your existing knowledge in environmental science with courses in environmental management, economics, law, community relations, communications skills and sustainable development. This program will help you gain the problem solving skills necessary to assume leadership positions in business and government.

Environmental Practice
Mission: The online Master of Arts in Environmental Practice degree prepares students to advance their career and to contribute positively to finding solutions for environmental problems. The master's degree in Environmental Practice is available as a Master of Arts (MA) in Environmental Practice and as a Master of Science (MSc) in Environmental Practice.

Environmental Management
Mission: The Master of Environment and Management (MEM) program is a graduate degree of interdisciplinary study in either the Master of Arts (MA) or Master of Science (MSc) designed to enhance strategic decision making in the environmental field. The program emphasizes teamwork and focuses on technical, policy, and system and sustainability issues to prepare students to become environmental professionals who are effective leaders and managers.

Environmental Management
Mission: The BSc in Environmental Management is an integrated, interdisciplinary program that provides the skills, knowledge and tools to identify and assess the qualitative, scientific, and technical components of environmental issues. Students will acquire and apply relevant skills and knowledge in the fields of environmental ecology, atmospheric and ocean sciences, geomorphology, soil sciences, environmental hydrology and remediation.

Environmental Education & Communication
Mission: The MA in Environmental Education and Communication is for those interested in developing social systems that align with the natural living systems we depend on. Degrees: ENVEDCO-MA; ENVEDCO-CERT; ENVEDCO-DIP

Ryerson University
350 Victoria St., Toronto ON M5B 2K3
www.ryerson.ca

Environmental & Urban Sustainability
Faculty of Arts
www.ryerson.ca/eus/
Mission: The program in Environment and Urban Sustainability is designed for students interested in environmental and conservation issues. Students learn to evaluate effects of development on urban settlements and to assess and facilitate conservation and the development of sustainable responses. The program integrates the social sciences, natural sciences, and applied disciplines as related to environmental and sustainability issues.

Environmental Applied Science and Management
Yeates School of Graduate Studies
www.ryerson.ca/graduate/programs/ensciman/
Mission: Ryerson University offers a PhD and a Master's degree in Environmental Applied Science and Management. These multidisciplinary programs are for graduate students seeking advanced study in a professionally-based environmental program that provides research in a broad variety of environmental fields.

Saint Mary's University (SMU)
923 Robie St., Halifax NS B3H 3C3
Tel: 902-420-5400
www.smu.ca

Environmental Sciences
Faculty of Science, Calgary AB T2X 1Z4 Canada
e-mail: envs@smu.ca
www.smu.ca/academic/science/envstud/welcome.html
Mission: The Saint Mary's University Environmental Science Program is a rigorous science undergraduate program using an interdisciplinary approach to learning. Our goal is to provide students with the academic preparation to allow them to contribute positively to an environmentally sound future.

Environmental Studies
Faculty of Environment
www.smu.ca/academic/science/envstud/
Mission: The program offers a concentration, major, Honours and minor. The program combines core sciences with management, social sciences and humanities and leads to a Bachelor of Science in Environmental Studies.

St. Francis Xavier University (STFX)

PO Box 5000, 5005 Chapel Sq., Antigonish NS B2G 2W5
Tel: 902-867-2219; *Fax:* 902-867-2329
e-mail: admit@stfx.ca
www.stfx.ca

Aquatic Resources
J. Bruce Brown Hall 335F
Tel: 902-867-3905; *Fax:* 902-867-2389
e-mail: aqua_res@stfx.ca
www.sites.stfx.ca/aquatic_resources
Mission: This interdisciplinary studies program focuses on water, environment and sustainability. Located in a community nestled along Canada's rugged Atlantic coastline, this program provides hands-on learning that explores water (freshwater and marine) resources, aquatic life, climate change, policy, and the complexities of human-ecosystem interactions.

Environmental Sciences
#2052, 1 West St., Antigonish NS B2G 2W5 Canada
Tel: 902-867-5109; *Fax:* 902-867-2414
e-mail: igreen@stfx.ca
sites.stfx.ca/environmental_sciences
Mission: The Environmental Sciences program offers Honours and advanced majors in four different concentrations-biology, chemistry, biochemistry, and climate/water. Each concentration offers an integrated approach to understanding the interaction of biological, chemical and physical systems and processes in the environment.

St. Lawrence College

2 St. Lawrence Dr., Cornwall ON K6H 4Z1
Tel: 613-933-6080; *Fax:* 613-937-1523
www.stlawrencecollege.ca

Enivronmental Technician
Cornwall Campus, 2 St. Lawrence Dr., Cornwall ON K6H 4Z1
Tel: 613-933-6080; *Fax:* 613-937-1523
www.stlawrencecollege.ca
Mission: The Environmental Technician program provides a background in water and air quality, water management, occupational health and safety, and environmental assessment.

Saskatchewan Institute of Applied Science & Technology (SIAST)

#400, 119 - 4th Ave. South, Saskatoon SK S7K 5X2
Tel: 306-933-7331
gosiast.com

Environmental Engineering Technology
Palliser Campus, PO Box 1420, 600 Saskatchewan St., Moose Jaw SK S6H 4R4
Tel: 306-691-8200
gosiast.com
Mission: This Diploma program provides knowledge and skill development in applying the principles of science and engineering to traditional engineering practices.

Forest Ecosystem Technology
Woodland Campus, PO Box 3003, 1100 - 15th St. East, Prince Albert SK S6V 6G1
Tel: 306-765-1500
gosiast.com
Mission: This Diploma program provides the knowledge, skills and extensive field training needed to ensure success in meeting the challenges of ecosystem based forest management and protection in Saskatchewan.

Integrated Resource Management
Woodland Campus
Mission: This Diploma program provides knowledge and skill development in a variety of disciplines in the natural resource sector. These include enforcing regulations, collecting and analyzing data, monitoring resource use and public relations.

Resource and Environmental Law
Woodland Campus
gosiast.com
Mission: This specialized program streams graduates into the field of conservation and environmental law enforcement.

Vocational Forestry
Mission: This is an applied certificate program offered through work-based training. It is offered in Conventional Harvesting and Mechanical Harvesting.

Sault College

443 Northern Ave., Sault Ste Marie ON P6B 4J3
Tel: 705-759-2554
Toll-Free: 800-461-2260
e-mail: studentrecruitment@saultcollege.ca
www.saultcollege.ca

Environmental Technician - Water
Mission: The Environmental Technician - Water program prepares students to gain practical knowledge of water systems to work in the water industry.

Fish & Wildlife Conservation Technician
Mission: The two-year Fish and Wildlife Conservation Technician program provides the graduate with a broad background in natural resources and specialized skills in the fish and wildlife field.

Forest Conservation Technician
Mission: This program prepares graduates with a wide range of skills necessary to contribute to environmentally sound management of forest ecosystems.

Natural Environment Technician - Conservation & Management
Mission: In this program, students will study the natural environment and learn to understand how ecosystem components interact together.

Natural Environment Technologist - Conservation & Management
Mission: This advanced diploma expands on courses taken as part of two year natural resource/natural environment technician curriculum. It is geared towards those individuals looking to integrate conventional resource management techniques with new emerging disciplines such as Field Investigative Techniques, advanced GIS, Energy Site Development and Invasive Species Management.

Natural Resource/Environmental Law - Inspection & Enforcement
Mission: This graduate certificate program will prepare students to enter the profession of natural resource and/ or environmental law compliance monitoring and enforcement as inspectors, investigators, enforcement officers, conservation officers, and private industry/corporate environmental officers.

Selkirk College

301 Frank Beinder Way, Castlegar BC V1N 4L3
Fax: 250-365-6568
Toll-Free: 888-953-1133
selkirk.ca

Forest Technology
selkirk.ca/program/forest-technology
Mission: Selkirk's Forestry program is known throughout the country for exellence in forest technology education, emphasizing an ecological approach to forest land management and achievement of proficeiency is advanced technology. Subjects of study include applied ecology, planning, regeneration, inventory, hydrology, habitat and forest protection, GIS and GPS technologies. 2-year Diploma

Renewable Energy
selkirk.ca/program/renewable-energy
Mission: A new program of study designed to prepare students to enter the work force in with knowledge of some of the diverse technologies in the renweable energies field. 1-year Certificate.

Integrated Environmental Planning
selkirk.ca/program/iep
Mission: A nationally accredited program designed to prepare students to meet growing needs for technologists capable of assisting in all areas of environmental assessment and monitoring. Graduates are trained in GIS data entry and spacial analysis using Arc GIS and other software, environmental chemistry, ecology, hydrology, communication, economics and planning, in addition to a number of other areas of study pursued in the classroom, laboratory, and field. 2-year Diploma

Recreation, Fish and Wildlife
selkirk.ca/program/rfw
Mission: A nationally accredited program, the focus of which is to provide relevant learning experience for individuals seeking careers in parks, forest recreation, fish and wildlife management, conservation or commercial recreation. The emphasis of the program is in the growing field of recreation and tourism, and fish and wildlife management i the working forest and protected areas. 2-year Diploma

Geographic Information Systems (GIS)
selkirk.ca/program/gis
Mission: GIS training at Selkirk prepares individuals to be trained geospatial experts int he environmental plannign, business, industry, and resource sectors. Real world projects enable students to gain expertise in GIS, GIS remote sensing, Internet mapping,technology, database management applications, GPS, 3D visualization and a variety of related software applications. Degrees: Adv. DIP; BGIS.

Seneca College of Applied Arts & Technology

Newnham Campus, 1750 Finch Ave. East, Toronto ON M2J 2X5
Tel: 416-491-5050
Toll-Free: 800-361-6673
www.senecac.on.ca

Energy Management - Built Environment
www.senecac.on.ca/fulltime/EMB.html
Mission: Energy Management - Built Environment is an eight-month program of intensive environmental training in building systems and energy management.

Environmental Technician - Sampling and Monitoring
www.senecac.on.ca/fulltime/ESM.html
Mission: Environmental Technician - Sampling and Monitoring (ESM) is an intensive 16-month diploma program geared to individuals with an interest in environmental sampling, monitoring, data collection and analysis.

Environmental Technician
www.senecac.on.ca/fulltime/ETM.html
Mission: This program focuses on environmental technology, water resources and applied sciences, engineering and problem solving abilities, and public and communications skills.

Environmental Technology
www.senecac.on.ca/fulltime/EMT.html
Mission: Studies focus on environmental technology, water resources and applied sciences, engineering and problem-solving abilities, and public and communications skills.

Green Business Management
www.senecac.on.ca/fulltime/GBM.html
Mission: Students will learn management skills needed to help an organization implement environmental sustainability into its bottom-line.

Environmental Landscape Management
King Campus, 13990 Dufferin St., King City ON L7B 1B3
Tel: 416-491-5050
Toll-Free: 800-361-6673
www.senecac.on.ca/fulltime/EVLC.html
Mission: The EVLC program curriculum offers a link between the study of ecology with the more traditional type of landscaping and horticulture programs.

Sheridan College

PO Box 2500, Stn. Lakeshore West, Oakville ON L6K 0E1
Tel: 905-845-9430
e-mail: infosheridan@sheridaninstitute.ca
www.sheridancollege.ca

Environmental Control
Faculty of Applied Science & Technology
Mission: An Environmental Control graduate certificate from Sheridan offers quick entry into this rapidly expanding field for graduates from a traditional science, engineering or technology discipline.

Environmental Technician
Faculty of Applied Science & Technology
Mission: Sheridan's Environmental Technician Program emphasizes chemistry and practical lab work.

Simon Fraser University

8888 University Dr., Burnaby BC V5A 1S6
Tel: 778-782-3111
www.sfu.ca

Environmental Chemistry
Faculty of Chemistry
Tel: 778-782-4659; *Fax:* 778-782-4968
students.sfu.ca/programs/environmental-chemistry.html
Mission: This PhD program provides an opportunity for pursuing high-level research and interdisciplinary edutcation in natural resources and environmental management. Coursework and research supervision are available over a wide range of natural and social sciences.

Environmental Science
Faculty of Environment
Tel: 778-782-8787; *Fax:* 778-782-8788
e-mail: fenv-info@sfu.ca
www.sfu.ca/evsc.html
Mission: The Environmental Science Program is an interdisciplinary program that fosters critical thinking about our natural surroundings and educates students to understand and use science to resolve environmental issues.

Development & Sustainability
www.sfu.ca/devsprogram.html
Mission: The Development and Sustainability Program examines the problems in, processes involved with, and the prospects for the transformation of human, natural, and material resources in various contexts and at various levels of social interaction, from the local, national, and regional to the international/global level.

Resource Management
e-mail: reminfo@sfu.ca
www.rem.sfu.ca/programs/mrm
Mission: This Masters program is designed for recent graduates from a range of discplines and for individuals with experience in private or public organizations in dealing with natural resources and the environment. Provides understanding of the strategies and techniques of natural resource and environmental planning and management, biological, social, physical, economic and institutional implications of resouce decisions. REM Students have the option of completing the Resource and Environmental Planning Program, as well. Accredited and recognized by the CIP and PIBC, the advantages of this degree course include the option of membership in the CIP and the PIBC, improved employment prospects, participation in conferences and workshops, and access to professional development programs. Degrees: MSc MRM (Planning)

Resource & Environmental Management
TASC I #8405, 8888 University Dr., Burnaby BC V5A 1S6 Canada
Tel: 778-782-4659; *Fax:* 778-782-4968
e-mail: reminfo@sfu.ca
www.rem.sfu.ca
Mission: This PhD program provides an opportunity for pursuing high-level research and interdisciplinary edutcation in natural resources and environmental management. Coursework and research supervision are available over a wide range of natural and social sciences.

Sir Wilfred Grenfell College
20 University Dr., Corner Brook NL A2H 5G4
Tel: 709-637-6200
Toll-Free: 888-637-6269
e-mail: info@grenfell.mun.ca
www.swgc.mun.ca

Environmental Science
1 University Dr., Corner Brook NL A2H 6P9 Canada
Tel: 709-637-6200
www.swgc.mun.ca/social-science/environmental-studies
Mission: The Bachelor of Science in Environmental Science degree is interdisciplinary, combining aspects of all of the natural sciences, specifically as they contribute to a greater awareness and understanding of the environment. The program provides a broad education and includes courses designed to enhance the student's appreciation of the scientific, social, cultural and political issues that impinge on the environment.

Environmental Studies
Mission: The aim of the Bachelor of Arts in Environmental Studies program is to encourage students to critically examine and develop a broad yet integrated understanding of environmental issues, problems, and possible solutions.

Sustainable Resource Management
www.swgc.mun.ca/social-science/resource-management
Mission: The Sustainable Resource Management (SRM) Program is a new Bachelor of Resource Management degree (BRM) that bridges scientific concerns about natural resources with policy development and management. The program aims to produce a different type of resource manager, graduates who have an understanding of ethics, as well as the many ecological, sociological and economic factors. The program acknowledges the goals of sustainable development while simultaneously recognizing the move from the more traditional concept of resource management towards a broader management approach.

Thompson River University
900 McGill Rd., Kamloops BC V2C 0C8
Tel: 250-828-5000; *Fax:* 250-828-5086
www.tru.ca

Forestry Transfer
PO Box 3010, 900 McGill Rd., Kamloops BC V2C 5N3 Canada
Tel: 205-371-5530
www.tru.ca/science/programs
Mission: TRU offers the first general year of Forestry and the second year of Forest Resource Management, Forest Science, Natural Resource Conservation, and Forest Operations. The first two years are designed to prepare students for entry to the Faculty of Forestry UBC's four-year degree programs of undergraduate study in five areas of forestry: Forest Resource Management, Forest Operations, Forest Science, Wood Science and Industry, and Natural Resource Conservation.

Environmental Science
www.tru.ca/science/programs/msces.html
Mission: The TRU MSc in Environmental Science is an interdisciplinary research program designed to produce graduates who have a broad range of skills and knowledge that they can apply in an integrative and innovative approach in the field. MSc.

Environmental Sciences Seminar Series
www.tru.ca/science/programs/msces/mscseminar.html
Mission: Environmental Sciences is a broad filed that attempts to understand and solve environmental problems, integrating the diversity of elements involved, including: biology, natural resources sciences, geography, politics, history, philosophy, geology, tourism, sociology, education, physics, chemistry, mathematics,and economics. Most seminars are Thursdays from 3:30 to 4:30 unless otherwise indicated.

Natural Resource Sciences
www.tru.ca/science/programs/nrs.html
Mission: By understanding the scientific, economis, and social basis of natural resource issues, graduates will be able to effectively interface between diverse interest groups, all having a stake in how our terrestrial and aquatic resources are managed. Students will learn technical skills, social investment in the field, and economic factors, work in research settings, and have the option of applying to the Honours program. Degrees: BSc. Forestry Transfer program option also available with UNBC or UBC.

Trent University
1600 West Bank Dr., Peterborough ON K9J 7B8
Tel: 705-748-1011
Toll-Free: 855-698-7368
www.trentu.ca

Conservation Biology
2140 East Bank Dr., Peterborough ON K9J 7B8 Canada
Tel: 705-748-1011; *Fax:* 705-748-1569
www.trentu.ca/biology
Mission: The Department of Biology study life from its most elementary building blocks (molecules and cells) to its largest expressions (populations, communities, and global ecosystems).

Ecological Restoration
www.trentu.ca/ecologicalrestoration
Mission: Ecological Restoration is an emerging discipline that focuses on assisting the recovery of degraded, damaged or destroyed ecosystems at specific project sites. This new, collaborative program developed by Trent University and Fleming College provides a bold and innovative solution to this challenge.

Indigenous Environmental Studies
www.trentu.ca/ies
Mission: IES is a collaboration between the Department of Indigenous Studies (INDG) and the Environmental and Resource Science/Studies Program (ERS), and is designed to give students the necessary skills and knowledge to work in the growing field of Indigenous environmental issues. The IES program is unique in Canada and brings together principles of both Indigenous knowledge and western science. Instruction in these two approaches will provide students with the necessary skills and critical thinking abilities that they can begin to use in addressing the complex environmental problems facing both Indigenous and non-Indigenous communities around the world today.

Sustainable Agriculture and Food Systems
www.trentu.ca/agriculture
Mission: The Sustainable Agriculture and Food Systems Program examines each of the links between farm and table, and their implications for people, the economy, and the planet. Students will learn about the challenges and benefits of producing and distributing healthy, affordable food in sustainable ways.

Environmental and Resource Studies Program
e-mail: ers@trentu.ca
www.trentu.ca/ers
Mission: This program examines the issues of water pollution, climate change, revegetation of industrial sites, environmental law and policy, modeling health effets of toxins, the challenge of global forces, community-level natural resource stewardship, and renewable energy alternatives.

Trinity Western University
PO Box 1409, 7600 Glover Rd., Langley BC V2Y 1Y1
Tel: 604-888-7511
twu.ca

Environmental Studies
wwu.ca/academics/interdisciplinary/environment
Mission: Students will gain practical environmental experience working at one of TWU's Eco-Study Areas, and real-world perspective through the multidisciplinary courses. Offers a number of ES streams, including: natural systems and resources; biochemical studies; physical and analytical studies; environmental management and planning Degrees: BA; BSc

Ecology
www.twu.ca/academics/science/biology/programs
Mission: Through the Biology department at TWU, students work in research areas, developing occupational skills in Ecology. With off-campus field courses available in Washington State, Hawaii, Florida, India and Africa. Degree: BSc

Université de Montréal
PO Box 6128, Stn. Centre-Ville, Montréal QC H3C 3J7
Tel: 514-343-6111
www.umontreal.ca

Sciences appliquées - Conservation de l'environnement bâti

Géographie Environnementale
geographie.umontreal.ca
Mission: Le programme est à la jonction des sciences naturelles et des sciences sociales. C'est une excellente formation de base en géographie humaine et physique, centrée sur le thème de l'environnement et du développement durable. Une large place à l'apprentissage des méthodes et des outils géographiques de pointe utilisés sur le marché du travail: systèmes d'information géographique, modélisation environnementale, télédétection etphoto-interprétation.

Université du Québec à Chicoutimi
555, boul de l'université, Chicoutimi QC G7H 2B1
Tel: 418-545-5011; *Fax:* 418-545-5012
Toll-Free: 800-463-9880
www.uqac.ca

Sciences de l'environnement
programmes.uqac.ca/4139
Mission: Le Certificat ou mineure en sciences de l'environnement a pour but de donner une formation scientifique de base à ceux qui sont confrontés avec les problèmes actuels de l'environnement dans leur milieu de travail ou à toute personne qui s'intéresse à ce domaine particulier.

Université du Québec à Montréal

PO Box 8888, Stn. Centre-Ville, Montréal QC H3C 3P8
Tel: 514-987-3000
www.uqam.ca

Design de l'environnement

Courriel: prog.bacc.designenvironnement@uqam.ca
www.designuqam.com/premier-cycle/design-environnement.aspx
Mission: Le programme offre une formation fondamentale en design pour ceux qui désirent travailler à l'amélioration du cadre de vie des individus et des groupes formant notre société. Il prépare l'étudiant aux domaines du design industriel et du design des objets, au design des espaces intérieurs et extérieurs et au design architectural et urbain. La perspective du développement durable et de ses enjeux sociaux y est abordée d'un point de vue multiple.

Éducation, environnement et citoyenneté

Courriel: ere@uqam.ca
www.ere.uqam.ca
Mission: La formation est axée sur le développement de compétences permettant de mieux concevoir, animer et gérer des projets d'éducation et de formation relatives à l'environnement dans différents milieux d'intervention : à l'école, en milieu communautaire, en entreprise, dans les médias, les parcs, les musées, les centres d'interprétation, en contexte de coopération internationale, etc.

Sciences de l'environnement

Courriel: prog.scta@uqam.ca
scta.uqam.ca/programmes.html
Mission: Ce certificat vise à donner un enseignement en environnement relié plus particulièrement aux aspects relevant des sciences physiques.

Ressources énergétiques durables

Courriel: prog.scta@uqam.ca
scta.uqam.ca/programmes.html
Mission: Ce certificat s'adresse aux personnes qui s'intéressent aux problématiques énergétiques et environnementales; en particulier aux questions des bâtiments sains et de la maîtrise de l'énergie (efficacité énergétique, économie d'énergie et protection de l'environnement et de la santé humaine dans une perspective d'autonomie locale et d'usage de technologies ®appropriées au milieu.).

Université du Québec à Rimouski

PO Box 3300, Stn. A, 300 Allée des Ursulines, Rimouski QC
Tel: 418-723-1986
www.uqar.ca

Chimie de l'Environnement et des bioressources

www.uqar.ca/programmes/description/7077
Mission: Le programme de baccalauréat en chimie de l'environnement démontrer la place fondamentale qu'occupe la chimie dans l'étude et la solution des problèmes environnementaux.

Gestion de la faune et de ses habitats

www.uqar.ca/programmes/description/3721
Mission: Le programme de la maîtrise en gestion de la faune et de ses habitats vise à former des scientifiques possédant une vision globale et interdisciplinaire du domaine de la gestion de la faune et de ses habitats et capables de réaliser des recherches dans ce domaine, de manière à agrandir le champ d'application en vue d'une amélioration de la conservation et l'exploitation des ressources.

Sciences de l'environnement

www.uqar.ca/programmes/description/3669
Mission: Ce programme, de type scientifique, vise au développement et à l'intégration des connaissances dans cinq champs multidisciplinaires de spécialisation en sciences de l'environnement, regroupés sous le thème intégrateur de l'analyse de la dynamique des relations environnementales.

Nordicity

www.uqar.ca/english/nordicity
Mission: The Nordicity program at The University of Quebec at Rimouski offers degrees in the following programs: Biology, Wildlife Management, Wildlife Management & Habitats, and Environmental Studies.

Marine Science

www.uqar.ca/english/marine-science
Mission: The Marine Science program at The University of Quebec at Rimouski offers a Master's Degree in Oceanography which is aimed at training scientists to adopt a comprehensive, multidisciplinary approach to the study of ocean phenomena. The program also offers a PhD in Oceanography which focuses on training independent researchers on the cutting edge of their field.

Université du Québec à Trois-Rivières

3351, boul des Forges, Trois-Rivières QC G9A 5H7
Tel: 819-376-5011
www.uqtr.ca

Sciences de l'environnement

Courriel: crmultiservice@uqtr.ca
www.uqtr.uquebec.ca
Mission: Le programme vise à former des scientifiques aptes à traiter de l'environnement dans le but d'apporter des solutions à des problèmes environnementaux. L'approche préconisée pour l'atteinte de cet objectif consiste en l'apprentissage de connaissances et méthodes propres aux sciences naturelles telles qu'appliquées au domaine de l'environnement.

Université du Québec en Abitibi-Témiscamingue

445, boul de l'Université, Rouyn-Noranda QC J9X 5E4
Tel: 819-762-0971; *Fax:* 819-797-4727
Toll-Free: 877-870-8728
e-mail: information@uqat.ca
www.uqat.ca

Sciences de l'Environnement

www.uqat.ca/doctoratenv/?menu=prog
Mission: Ce programme a pour objectif de former des scientifiques capables de dépasser les frontières disciplinaires, en établissant des ponts avec d'autres disciplines des sciences de l'environnement, et conscients des interdépendances dynamiques en environnement.

Gestion durable des écosystèmes forestiers

www.uqat.ca/programmes/irf/?lang=fr&menu=mat-eco
Mission: Un programme bénéficiant de l'expertise du corps professoral de trois universités : l'UQAM, l'UQO et l'UQAT.

Université Laval

2325, rue de l'Université, Québec QC G1V 0A6
Tel: 418-656-2131
Toll-Free: 877-785-2825
www2.ulaval.ca

Aménagement et environnement forestiers

Courriel: info@ffgg.ulaval.ca
www.ffgg.ulaval.ca
Mission: Ce baccalauréat vous permettra de participer à l'aménagement durable de la forêt, à la gestion, à la protection de l'environnement, à la mise en valeur des habitats fauniques, à la régénération et à l'amélioration de la forêt.

Intégré en environnements naturels et aménagés

Courriel: info@ffgg.ulaval.ca
www.ffgg.ulaval.ca
Mission: Ce baccalauréat vise à former des professionnels de l'environnement et, plus particulièrement, de la conservation et de la gestion durable des écosystèmes.

Chimie - Environnement

Courriel: fsg@fsg.ulaval.ca
www.chm.ulaval.ca
Mission: Ce baccalauréat vous permettra d'assimiler les concepts, les méthodes et les principes sur lesquels s'appuient la chimie et la chimie de l'environnement.

University College of the North (UCN)

436 - 7th St. East, The Pas MB
Tel: 204-627-8500
Toll-Free: 866-627-8500
www.ucn.ca

Natural Resources Management Technolgy

436 - 7th St. East, The Pas MB
Tel: 204-627-8500
Toll-Free: 866-627-8500
www.ucn.ca
Mission: This two-year diploma program is designed to train the student for a wide range of employment opportunities in the field of natural resources management.

University of Alberta

116 St. and 85 Ave., Edmonton AB T6G 2R3
www.ualberta.ca

Forestry

Faculty of Agriculture, Life & Environmental Sciences, Edmonton AB T6G 2E3 Canada
www.ales.ualberta.ca
Mission: The BSc in Forestry develops graduates who appreciate the need to manage forested areas with due concern for all resources and who have the capability and knowledge to manage forested areas as integrated ecological entities. It focuses primarily on forest management, the protection, manipulation, and use of the forest resource while ensuring that sustainability and other social and cultural needs are met.

Forest Business Management

Mission: The Forest Business Management degree prepares students for designation as a Registered Professional Forester and is for individuals planning careers focusing on forest practices, but who also seek specialized knowledge in business management practices. The program is fully accredited by the Canadian Forestry Accreditation Board.

Environmental Studies

Mission: The Faculty of Agricultural, Life and Environmental Sciences and the Faculty of Arts have worked together to develop this degree which will educate students in the scientific, cultural, economic, moral, political and social dimensions of environmental issues. As the subject matter transcends the boundaries of any single discipline or faculty, this degree is offered through a collaborative program that draws on the Faculties of Native Studies and Science.

Agriculture

Mission: The program explores environmentally sustainable approaches to manage land used for the production of food, clothing, fuel and other consumer products.

Environmental & Conservation Sciences

Mission: The program develops solutions for environmental issues such as climate change, land and water use as well as biodiversity; explores how interactions between science, society and the economy influence environmental management decisions; participates in local and international environmental field school opportunities to develop hands-on skills; and applies knowledge and skills while completing a fourth-year project-based capstone course that examines issues faced by industry, government and environmental organizations. Majors include: Conservation Biology, Environmental Economics and Policy, Human Dimensions of Environmental Management, Land Reclamation, and Wildlife and Rangeland Resources Management.

Environmental Earth Sciences

Dept of Earth & Atmospheric Sciences, Edmonton AB T6G 2E3 Canada
Tel: 780-492-3265; *Fax:* 780-492-2030
easweb.eas.ualberta.ca/page/Environmental_Earth_Sciences
Mission: Environmental Earth science is the study of interactions between humans and Earth's natural environment. You will study the influence of human activities on the local and global environment as well as how human actions are shaped and controlled by the geologic and geomorphic processes occurring around us.

University of British Columbia (UBC)

2329 West Mall, Vancouver BC V6T 1Z4
Tel: 604-822-2211
www.ubc.ca

Environmental Engineering

Faculty of Applied Science (Engineering), Vancouver BC V6T 1Z4 Canada
Tel: 604-822-3482; *Fax:* 604-822-9106
you.ubc.ca/ubc/program.do?from=faculty&programID=61
Mission: The Environmental Engineering program is based on a unique collaboration between UNBC and UBC. The program starts with a two-year foundation in mathematics, basic sciences, and environmental sciences from UNBC. The third and fourth years offer training in engineering fundamentals, engineering analysis, and engineering design, through courses in Civil Engineering and Chemical & Biological Engineering at UBC.

Geography - Environment & Sustainability

Faculty of Arts, Vancouver BC V6T 1Z4 Canada
www.geog.ubc.ca/undergraduate/environment_sustainability.html
Mission: The Environment and Sustainability Program offers an integrated understanding of physical, ecological,

economic, socio-cultural and political systems, as they shape the world in which we live and influence the future of life on planet earth.

Earth & Environmental Sciences
Irving K. Barber School of Arts and Sciences, 3333 University Way, Kelowna BC V1V 1V7 Canada
Tel: 250-807-9597; *Fax:* 250-807-8001
www.ubc.ca/okanagan/eesc/undergrad/program/earth.html
Mission: This multi-disciplinary B.Sc. program provides an education reflecting the direction of modern Earth and Environmental Science programs in Canada and elsewhere. It is intended to prepare students to meet the knowledge requirements for professional designation according to the guidelines of the Canadian Council of Professional Geoscientists (CCPG).

Environmental Chemistry
chem.ok.ubc.ca/undergrad/program/enviro.html
Mission: This program provides students with a core education in the four important areas of chemistry: analytical, inorganic, organic, and physical chemistry, with specialization in environmental chemistry.

Freshwater Science
www.ubc.ca/okanagan/eesc/undergrad/program/fresh.html
Mission: This program prepares students for careers related to inland aquatic ecosystems. It is for science students and graduates of the Water Quality Technology Environmental Monitoring Laddering option at the new Okanagan College.

Food and the Environment
Faculty of Land & Food Systems, 2357 Main Mall, Vancouver BC V6T 1Z4 Canada
Tel: 604-822-1219; *Fax:* 604-822-6394
www.landfood.ubc.ca/undergraduate/applied-biology-majors
Mission: This major brings together agricultural sciences, ecology, and environmental thought to provide the background to issues surrounding the management of land and water to produce food, other agricultural products, and ecological services.

Atmospheric Science
6399 Stores Rd., Vancouver BC V6T 1Z4 Canada
Tel: 604-822-2713; *Fax:* 604-822-6088
www.eos.ubc.ca/academic/atsc
Mission: UBC offers degrees in the study of Atmospheric Science, including the following research areas: micrometeorology, weather, air pollution and atmospheric chemistry, climate, biometeorology, and geophysical fluid dynamics. Degrees: PhD; MSc; BSc.

Earth & Ocean Sciences
www.eos.ubc.ca
Mission: The Earth & Ocean Sciences Department (EOS) at UBC is one of the largest and most diverse of its kind in the world. This BSc with an Honours option is a flexible degree program that encompasses a broad spectrum of disciplines, with focus upon specializations such as geophysics, oceanography, environmental geology, or atmospheric sciences.

Environmental Sciences
www.ensc.ubc.ca
Mission: Designed to give students a broad perspective on the environment, the program concentrates on understanding the major environmental issues facing human societies with a cross-disciplinary approach. Degrees: BSc; BSc Honours.

Geological Engineering
www.geoeng.ubc.ca
Mission: This program is intended for students interested in the applications of earth sciences principals to engineering problems, and allows the student to base their studies either in the EOS Departments or Applied Science such as Civil or Mining Engineering. The program is highly interdisciplinary and draws upon courses labs, and faculty members from the departments of EOS, Civil and Mining Engineering, Forestry, Geography, and others. Degrees: PhD; MASc; MA Eng.

Environmental Design Program (ENDS)
370 - 2357 Main Mall, Vancouver BC V6T 1Z4 Canada
Tel: 604-822-9616; *Fax:* 604-822-2184
www.sala.ubc.ca/programs/environmental-design
Mission: The program focuses on themes emphasizing analysis and representation, history and theory, technology and practice, all anchored by a Core Studio Design cusrriculum. At the heart of the ENDS program is the goal of developing students into a constituency aware of the real challenges and opportunities in forming space and designing with the land who finds common ground first as a community, considering its central focus issues relevant to contemporary society. Their designs will be critically engaged and imaginiatively considered, engendering social and ecological rediscovery. Degree: BSc ENDS

Forest Sciences
2045 - 2424 Main Mall, Vancouver BC V6T 1Z4 Canada
Tel: 604-822-3482; *Fax:* 604-822-9106
e-mail: frm.recept@ubc.ca
www.forestry.ubc.ca
Mission: The Bachelor of Science in Forestry program focuses on the specific principles related to the growth and development of forest organisms, and the ecology of plant and animal communities.

Natural Resources Conservation
e-mail: frm.recept@ubc.ca
www.forestry.ubc.ca
Mission: The Bachelor of Science in Natural Resources Conservation program provides students with skills and knowledge to meet the challenges of maintaining healthy ecosystems and protecting natural environments in an era of changing climate.

Forest Operations Program
e-mail: frm.recept@ubc.ca
www.forestry.ubc.ca
Mission: The Bachelor of Science in Forestry, Forest Operations program focuses on preparing students for plannig and implementing complex harvesting operations that maximize exonomic returns and minimize environmental impact. The program is based on biological, physical and social sciences.

Forest Resources Management
e-mail: frm.recept@ubc.ca
www.forestry.ubc.ca
Mission: The Bachelor of Science in Forestry, Forest Resources Management program teaches students how to integrate the use of a wide variety of natural resources including range, recreation, timber, water and wildlife.

University of Calgary
2500 University Dr. NW, Calgary AB T2N 1N4
www.ucalgary.ca

Applied & Environmental Geology
Faculty of Science
Tel: 403-220-5841
geoscience.ucalgary.ca/EnvironmentalGeology
Mission: Environmental and engineering geology, and hydrogeology, the study of groundwater and the contaminants borne in it, have assumed much greater importance in the last few decades, and this program specifically addresses these disciplines. More emphasis is placed on near-surface and engineering applications of geology and on groundwater and applied geochemistry, than in the conventional geology program. This program is appropriate for students who have a strong background in math, chemistry and physics.

Energy Management
Haskayne School of Business
Tel: 403-220-6593
haskayne.ucalgary.ca/programs/bcomm/concentrations/enmg
Mission: The Energy Management program provides students with basic concepts, principles, and information for managing energy operations. This program prepares students for successful careers in the energy sector and related government and service sectors through courses in energy development. This concentration will provide business graduates with a competitive edge for developing careers in the energy sector.

Environmental Design
Faculty of Environmental Design
Tel: 403-220-6601
evds.ucalgary.ca/content/phd-environmental-design
Mission: The Faculty of Environmental Design emphasizes the importance of design, planning and management, in human interaction among the built and natural environments. Research emphasizes the development of leading-edge theory and the improvement of professional practice. Masters and PhD programs available.

Environmental Science Program
Faculty of Science
Tel: 403-220-8367; *Fax:* 403-210-8126
e-mail: ensc@ucalgary.ca
www.ucalgary.ca/ensc
Mission: Emphasizes a multi-disciplinary approach to understanding environmental issues facing society. It is a Collaborative Program administered jointly by the Faculties of Science and Social Sciences. It is designed to be a small program, with some 40 students a year, where hands-on experience is central. The program launched in 1996 and has more than 300 graduates.

Earth Science Program
Faculty of Arts
Tel: 403-220-8929; *Fax:* 403-282-6561
e-mail: earthsci@ucalgary.ca
www.ucalgary.ca/earthsci
Mission: Provides students with a mutli-disciplinary approach to studying the Earth. Students in this program are provided with a strong foundation in archaeology, geography, geology, and geophysics. Majors are exposed to extensive field and laboratory experiences. The program has a problem-solving focus with the following themes: climate and hydrology, biosphere interactions, global processes and change, earth science techniques.

Geomatics Engineering
Schulich School of Engineering
e-mail: geomatics@geomatics.ucalgary.ca
www.geomatics.ucalgary.ca
Mission: Geomatics Engineering is an emerging information technology in the 21st Century. Geomatics deals with the acquisition, modeling, analysis and management of spatial data and includes exciting applications such as positioning by satellites, remote sensing, land surveying, and geospatial information management. Geomatics is one of the fastest growing information sciences in Canada and throughout the World.

University of Guelph
50 Stone Rd. East, Guelph ON N1G 2W1
Tel: 519-824-4120
www.uoguelph.ca

Environmental Sciences
School of Environmental Sciences
www.uoguelph.ca/ses
Mission: This program uses the interdisciplinary expertise needed to deal with the environmental problems facing our world now and those we will face in the future. Balance scientifically grounded solutions with an understanding of the social and economic consequences of environmental change.

Bio-Resource Management
Ontario Agricultural College
www.uoguelph.ca/oac
Mission: The Bachelor of Bio-Resource Management (BBRM) is a degree program designed for students looking for career-oriented training focused on renewable resources, with majors in Environmental Management or Equine Management. This four-year, interdisciplinary program combines advanced studies in science, technology and business management with hands-on training in bio-resource management and stewardship.

University of Lethbridge
4401 University Dr., Lethbridge AB T1K 3M4
Tel: 403-329-2111
www.uleth.ca

Environmental Science Program
Faculty of Arts & Science
Tel: 403-332-4040; *Fax:* 403-332-4039
www.uleth.ca/artsci/environmental-science
Mission: The Environmental Science program will provide students with the natural and physical science background needed to understand a multitude of environmental systems, as well as the broad perspective required to appreciate the role of humanity in global environmental change.

University of Manitoba
66 Chancellors Circle, Winnipeg MB R3T 2N2
Toll-Free: 800-432-1960
umanitoba.ca

Environmental Design
Faculty of Architecture, 424 University Centre, Winnipeg MB R3T 2N2 Canada
Tel: 204-474-7252
umanitoba.ca/student/admissions/programs/environmental-design
Mission: The Bachelor of Environmental Design program is envisioned as a strong multidisciplinary undergraduate degree in its own right and provides a solid base of design education for students intending to pursue careers and/or graduate studies in a wide variety of disciplines. e degree and a Bachelor of Environmental Studies degree.

Environmental Science
Faculty of Environment, Earth & Resources
umanitoba.ca/student/admissions/programs/environmental-science
Mission: Environmental Science examines the physical, chemical, and biological components of the Earth's environment, its diverse systems, and the complex ways in which they interact.

Environmental Studies
Faculty of Environment, Earth & Resources
umanitoba.ca/student/admissions/programs/environmental-studies
Mission: The Environmental Studies Program uses not only scientific approaches but also traditional knowledge, and in doing so broadens the ways in which the environment is viewed.

Natural Resources Management
Faculty of Environment, Earth & Resources
Tel: 204-474-7252
www.umanitoba.ca/institutes/natural_resources
Mission: The Master of Natural Resources Management is an interdisciplinary, and thesis- and course-based program with courses in a wide variety of courses, such as ecology, human dimensions of natural resources management, conservation biology, quantitative or qualitative analyses, law, economic dimensions of natural resources management, policy, environmental impact assessments and more.

Environment & Geography
Department of Environment and Geography, 70A Dysart Rd., Winnipeg MB R3T 2N2 Canada
Tel: 204-474-7252
umanitoba.ca/faculties/environment/departments/geography
Mission: The Master of Science Environment & Geography is the appropriate science-stream graduate program option for those interested in furthering their academic training in the areas of environmental sciences, including physical geography.

University of Northern British Columbia (UNBC)

3333 University Way, Prince George BC V2N 4Z9
Tel: 250-960-5555
e-mail: unbc4u@unbc.ca
www.unbc.ca

Ecosystem Science & Management
www.unbc.ca/ecosystem-science-management
Mission: Houses faculty with interests in all aspects of ecosystem function, from cellular and molecular scale to the role of humans in modifying these ecosystems. The interdisciplinary nature of the ESM reflects the interwoven interests of faculty and the necessity of incorporating diverse perspectives in ecosystem management, from natural science to social science. Accredited by the Canadian Forestry Accreditation Board. Cooperative education options, and research opportunities abound. Degrees: BSc: Biology, NRM - Forest Ecology & Management, Wildlife and Fisheries, Environmental Studies; MA, MSc, MNRES or PhD in Natural Resources & Environmental Studies; additional masters and doctoral level interdisciplinary programs.

Environmental Studies
www.unbc.ca/environmental-studies
Mission: The program offers a selection of emphases from social science and humanities perspectives to Global Environmental Change. This is a BA program.

Environmental Science & Engineering
www.unbc.ca/environmental-science
Mission: The Environmental Science focus is designed to train scientists who will understand how the environment functions, and how to mitigate effects on the environments when functions and processes are disrupted. The Engineering focus teaches students to be aware of the need to integrate environmental and economic factors in providing environmental analysis and engineering design across a range of disciplines. Degrees: BSc Environmental Science; BASc Environmental Engineering; MSc NRES Environmental Science; MNRES Natural Resources & Environmental Studies; PhD Natural Resources & Environmental Studies

Natural Resource and Environmental Studies Graduate Program
www.unbc.ca/nres-graduate-program
Mission: Primarily concerned with "People and The Environment", with streams in Geography, Environmental Studies, Tourism, Biology, Environmental Science, Forestry, and Recreational Resource Management. Working with research partners from the local to the international levels. Degrees: Phd NRES, MA NRES, MSc NRES

University of Northern British Columbia (UNBC) & University of British Columbia (UBC)

Environmental Engineering (Joint Program)
2360 East Mall, Vancouver BC V6T 1Z3 Canada
Tel: 604-827-3415; *Fax:* 604-822-6003
e-mail: info@enve.ubc.ca
www.unbc.ca/environmental-engineering
Mission: A joint degree program offered by UBC and UNBC capitalizes on each university's strengths in sciences and engineering, and is the only Environmental Engineering program in the province. The first two-years are spent building the science foundation at UNBC, and the third and fourth will be spent building your engineering skills UBC. Then a final term at UNBC focusing on practical environmental engineering design problems. Degrees: BASc; upon graduation, eligible for registration as Professional Engineers (P.Eng.) with the Canadian Engineering Accreditation Board and the Association of P.Eng. & Geoscientists of BC.

University of Ontario Institute of Technology (UOIT)

2000 Simcoe St. Morth, Oshawa ON L1H 7K4
Tel: 905-721-8668
www.uoit.ca

Energy & the Environment
Mission: This program is designed to meet a rapidly increasing demand for graduates with the knowledge and skills required to help Canada and the world deal with the growing consumption of energy, by developing novel and economical means of generating and harvesting energy with minimum impact on the environment, and in the immediate future by meeting the terms of the Kyoto agreement; HBA

University of Ottawa

75 Laurier Ave. East, Ottawa ON K1N 6N5
Tel: 613-562-5700; *Fax:* 613-562-5323
Toll-Free: 877-868-8292
e-mail: uOttawaInfo@uOttawa.ca
www.uottawa.ca

Chemical & Environmental Toxicology
#181, Marion Hall, Ottawa ON K1N 6N5 Canada
Tel: 613-562-5800; *Fax:* 613-562-5192
e-mail: gradsci@uOttawa.ca
www.chemistry.uottawa.ca/students/current_grad.html
Mission: The University of Ottawa and Carleton University offer a joint collaborative program leading to a master of science or a PhD degree with specialization in chemical and environmental toxicology.

Environmental Engineering
Ottawa-Carleton Institute for Environmental Engineering, 161 Louis-Pasteur, Colonel By Hall, Ottawa ON K1N 6N5 Canada
e-mail: engineering.graduateadmissions@uottawa.ca
www.ociene.ca
Mission: The Ottawa-Carleton Institute of Environmental Engineering (OCIEE) combines the teaching and research strengths of the Department of Civil Engineering and the Department of Chemical Engineering at the University of Ottawa with that of the Departments of Civil and Environmental Engineering at Carleton University. The Institute offers graduate programs leading to the degrees of Master of Applied Science (MASc), Master of Engineering (MEng) and Doctor of Philosophy (PhD) in Environmental Engineering.

Environmental Sciences Program
#201, Marion Hall, Ottawa ON K1N 6N5 Canada
Tel: 613-562-5800; *Fax:* 613-562-5192
e-mail: evs@uottawa.ca
www.environmental.uottawa.ca
Mission: The EVS program is the study of natural systems, of resource use and development, of the migration of contaminants in the environment and of their impace on the ecosystem as a whole. The three streams of specialization are: Conservation and biodiversity, Global change, and Environmental geochemistry and ecotoxicology.

University of Prince Edward Island

550 University Ave., Charlottetown PE C1A 4P3
home.upei.ca

Environmental Studies
Faculty of Arts
Tel: 902-620-5066
e-mail: enviro@upei.ca
www.upei.ca/programsandcourses/environmental-studies
Mission: The environmental studies program aims to equip students with the knowledge to understand the environmental connections across academic fields, to critically analyze complex environmental issues, and to propose sound options toward sustainable solutions.

Wildlife Conservation
Faculty of Science
Tel: 902-566-0301; *Fax:* 902-566-0740
www.upei.ca/programsandcourses/bachelor-wildlife-conservation
Mission: The Bachelor of Wildlife Conservation program combines the practical, theoretical and analytical strengths of courses provided by accredited NAWTA (North American Wildlife Technology Association) colleges with courses from the University of Prince Edward Island, for students interested in obtaining rigorous training in wildlife conservation.

University of Regina

3737 Wascana Pkwy., Regina SK S4S 0A2
Tel: 306-585-4111
www.uregina.ca

Environmental Health & Science
Faculty of Science
www.uregina.ca/science
Mission: The program is a partnership between the department of science in the First Nations University of Canada and the Faculty of Engineering and Applied Science. The study of environmental health and science seeks to understand and address environmental health issues such as pollution, waste management and environmental issues facing First Nations people. Students will use analytical and problem solving skills to assess different types of health risks and will learn to develop and administer policies, programs and projects.

Environmental Studies
Faculty of Arts
e-mail: arts.studentservices@uregina.ca
www.uregina.ca/arts/environmental-studies
Mission: The Bachelor of Arts (BA) in Environmental Studies is an interdisciplinary program that studies the natural environment as informed through the diverse perspectives of the social sciences, natural sciences and the humanities. Students will look critically at environmental issues, while developing practical skills and understanding to contribute to future change.

Environmental Biology
Faculty of Science
www.uregina.ca/science
Mission: The Environmental Biology enables students to explore contemporary environmental issues and learn how to monitor, assess and manage the use of natural resources, apply mapping and remote sensing techniques and conduct research.

Environmental Systems Engineering
Faculty of Engineering and Applied Science
Tel: 306-585-4734; *Fax:* 306-585-4855
e-mail: engg@uregina.ca
www.urengineering.ca/programs/environmental-systems
Mission: A four-year program that teaches the application of Systems Engineering principles to environmental problems associated with water resources, transportation, industrial development and waste management. Students design and manage environmental/transportation systems and conduct environmental impact and remediation studies.

University of Saskatchewan

105 Administration Place, Saskatoon SK S7N 5B5
Tel: 306-966-4343
www.usask.ca

Environmental Science
College of Agriculture and Bioresources, 51 Campus Dr., Saskatoon SK S7N 5A8 Canada
Tel: 306-966-6825; *Fax:* 306-966-6881
explore.usask.ca/programs/colleges/agbio/environmentalscience
Mission: The environmental science program at the U of S explores the relationships between environmental constraints and sustainable development. An emphasis is placed on the challenges faced in Canada, including the impact of climate change, agriculture, forestry, and oil and gas exploration on the environment.

Environmental Earth Sciences
College of Arts and Science
Fax: 306-966-6881
explore.usask.ca/programs/colleges/arts_and_science
Mission: The interdisciplinary program in Environmental Earth Sciences is offered jointly though the departments of Geography, Geological Sciences, and Soil Science. It explores the relationships-both modern and ancient-among the solid Earth, the atmosphere, the oceans, and the biosphere. Its primary emphasis is on the physical sciences, rather than the biological sciences.

Environmental Biology
College of Arts and Science
Tel: 306-966-6825; *Fax:* 306-966-6881
explore.usask.ca/programs/colleges/arts_and_science
Mission: This interdisciplinary program examines ecosystems, focussing on how living organisms interact with their environment. A major in Environmental Biology will accommodate many student interests and aspirations, including a career in environmental science or as preparation for more advanced study.

Environment & Society
College of Arts and Science
Tel: 306-966-6825; *Fax:* 306-966-6881
explore.usask.ca/programs/colleges/arts_and_science
Mission: The Environment and Society program prepares students for employment or further study in a broad range of areas related to the environment. Through exposure to diverse perspectives, students will develop an understanding of environmental science, resource management, environmental philosophy, policy, and environmental studies.

Regional & Urban Planning
College of Arts and Science
Tel: 306-966-6825; *Fax:* 306-966-6881
explore.usask.ca/programs/colleges/arts_and_science
Mission: The Regional and Urban Planning program is a professional program, accredited by the Canadian Institute of Planners and Association of Professional Community Planners of Saskatchewan. Planners are place makers and community builders whose work can also include community land-use planning that maximizes travel mode choices, access to homes, work, retail, social and community services, and contributes to climate change solutions, energy conservation, protecting water supplies, and caring for natural areas.

Environmental Engineering
57 Campus Dr, #1B95 College of Eng.
Tel: 306-966-7827; *Fax:* 306-966-5407
e-mail: biomedical.engineering@usask.ca
www.engr.usask.ca/departments/environmental/
Mission: Offers a Bachelor of Engineering four-year degree. Multidisciplinary training includes a variety of engineering disciplines including: geological engineering, agriculture and bioresource engineering, chemical engineering, and civil engineering.

Soil Science
College of Agriculture and Bioresources
explore.usask.ca/programs/colleges/agbio/soilscience
Mission: Soil science draws from biology, ecology, geography, geology and a variety of other natural and life sciences. The soil science program at the University of Saskatchewan provides students with an in-depth understanding of the physical, biological and chemical processes that occur in soil and the role soil plays in plant production and environmental management.

Renewable Resource Management
College of Agriculture and Bioresources
Tel: 306-966-4056; *Fax:* 306-966-8894
e-mail: ag.bio@usask.ca
explore.usask.ca/programs/colleges/agbio
Mission: The BSc in Renewable Resource Management is an applied science degree that focuses on the study of water and biological resources and the management of land. Careers in this sector will include helping to protect the environment and ecosystems from industrial damage, determining how to make some of our industries sustainable, or helping to produce food.

Applied Plant Ecology
College of Agriculture and Bioresources
Tel: 306-966-5855; *Fax:* 306-966-5015
agbio.usask.ca
Mission: The Bachelor of Science in Agriculture provides students with a sound basis in the natural and social sciences and a broad knowledge of agriculture, agri-food systems, and the role of agriculture in both the Great Plains and global contexts. Graduates will be prepared to address major agricultural issues and challenges, including: resource use consistent with sustainable production of food, feed, fibre and fuel; production, processing and marketing of high quality food and non-food products; research; development and implementation of innovative and efficient production, processing and marketing systems.

Graduate Programs at School of Environment & Sustainability
Kirk Hall, #323, 117 Science Place, Saskatoon SK S7N 5C8 Canada
Tel: 306-966-1985; *Fax:* 306-966-2298
e-mail: sens.info@usask.ca
www.usask.ca/sens
Mission: Graduate programs offered by the School of Environment and Sustainability are designed to prepare a new generation of skilled professionals, researchers and academics to address the challenges facing the environment, both locally and globally. The Master of Sustainable Environmental Management, Master of Environment and Sustainability, and Doctor of Philosophy in Environment and Sustainability programs are interdisciplinary in nature and practical in their focus.

University of Toronto

27 King's College Circle, Toronto ON M5S 1A1
Tel: 416-978-2011
www.utoronto.ca

Environemnt & Science
School of the Environment, 33 Willcocks St., Toronto ON M5S 3E8 Canada
Tel: 416-946-8100; *Fax:* 416-978-3884
e-mail: environment@utoronto.ca
www.environment.utoronto.ca
Mission: The School's B.Sc. core program is a multidisciplinary program with a strong science focus which students must combine with another undergraduate science program in order to earn a BSc degree.

Environemntal Studies
School of the Environment
Tel: 416-946-8100; *Fax:* 416-978-3884
e-mail: environment@utoronto.ca
www.environment.utoronto.ca
Mission: The School's B.A. core program is an interdisciplinary program intended for students interested in studying and working in an environmental area, primarily within the social sciences or humanities.

Environemnt and Health
School of the Environment
Tel: 416-946-8100; *Fax:* 416-978-3884
e-mail: environment@utoronto.ca
www.environment.utoronto.ca
Mission: This program is designed to provide a basic understanding of behaviour of the planet Earth, the workings of the human body, and the relationship between the two.

Environemntal Chemistry
School of the Environment
Tel: 416-946-8100; *Fax:* 416-978-3884
e-mail: environment@utoronto.ca
www.environment.utoronto.ca
Mission: This program brings the basic science orientation of Environment and Science to a fundamental background in Chemistry as applied to understanding the chemical impacts of humankind's activities on the soil, water, and air.

Environemntal Geoscience
School of the Environment
Tel: 416-946-8100; *Fax:* 416-978-3884
e-mail: environment@utoronto.ca
www.environment.utoronto.ca
Mission: This program focuses on physical, chemical and biological events that have occurred over the past 4.5 billion years, including the present influences of humans as agents of geological change.

Environemnt and Toxicology
School of the Environment
Tel: 416-946-8100; *Fax:* 416-978-3884
e-mail: environment@utoronto.ca
www.environment.utoronto.ca
Mission: This program brings the basic science orientation of Environment and Science together with the examination of the adverse effects of chemicals to human beings and ecosystems.

Forestry Conservation
Faculty of Forestry
Tel: 416-978-5751
www.forestry.utoronto.ca
Mission: The Masters of Forest Conservation (MFC) program will enable students to make a difference by entering into professions responsible for the policies and practices that have a profound impact on all living organisms and on the sustainability of human social and economic systems - work that is crucial to society and the planet's health, prosperity and happiness.

Forest Conservation Science
Faculty of Forestry
Tel: 416-978-5751
www.forestry.utoronto.ca
Mission: This undergraduate program focuses on forest biology and ecology with electives in life and physical sciences.

Forest Conservation Arts
Faculty of Forestry
Tel: 416-978-5751
www.forestry.utoronto.ca
Mission: This undergraduate program focuses on community forest management, forest policy and economics, and forest product trade with electives in social sciences.

Forest Biomaterials Science
Faculty of Forestry
Tel: 416-978-5751
www.forestry.utoronto.ca
Mission: This undergraduate program focuses on fundamental knowledge of wood structure, properties and attributes, as well as lifecycle analysis, alternative energy strategies, and innovative product development.

University of Toronto - Mississauga

Enivornmental Management
3359 Mississauga Rd. North, Missisauga ON L5L 1C6 Canada
Tel: 905-569-4455
www.utm.utoronto.ca
Mission: The Environmental Management program at UTM focuses on the environment, society and public policy. HBA

Environmental Science
Mission: The Environmental Science program at UTM focusses on research development skills. HBSc

University of Toronto - Scarborough

Environmental Science
1265 Military Trail, Toronto ON M1C 1A4 Canada
Tel: 416-287-8872
www.utsc.utoronto.ca/~physsci/e
Mission: The Environmental Science program at UTS gives options for students to research and train in areas including Biology, Chemistry, Geoscience, and Physics.

University of Victoria (UVic)

3800 Finnerty Rd., Victoria BC V8P 5C2
Tel: 250-721-7211; *Fax:* 250-721-7212
www.uvic.ca

Restoration of Natural Systems
Division of Continuing Studies, PO Box 1700, Stn. CSC, Victoria BC V8W 2Y2 Canada
Tel: 250-721-8463; *Fax:* 250-721-8774
www.uvcs.uvic.ca/sustainability/programs
Mission: The Restoration of Natural Systems program is an accredited program created to disseminate information about the emerging field of environmental restoration and to provide practical background knowledge, training, and skill development for those working in areas related to the restoration of natural systems.

Environmental Studies Co-operative Education Program
Faculty of Social Sciences, PO Box 1700, Stn. CSC, Victoria BC V8W 2Y2 Canada
Tel: 250-721-8463; *Fax:* 250-721-8774
Mission: The Faculty of Social Sciences Co-operative Education Programs are year-round programs that formally integrate an education in the social sciences with relevant work experience. Students will complete a minimum of three, normally four, work terms of employment in appropriate fields of business, industry, government, social services and the professions.

Earth and Ocean Science Graduate Program
School of Earth and Ocean Science (SEOS), Petch 168, 3800 Finnerty Rd., Victoria BC V8P 5C2 Canada
Tel: 250-472-5133; *Fax:* 250-721-6200
e-mail: eosc@uvic.ca
www.seos.uvic.ca
Mission: Graduate Program at the School of Earth and Ocean Science (SEOS), research areas include a strong focus on earth system science with special studies in marine geology and geophysics, paleoceanography, tectonics, atmospheric modelling, air-sea interaction, biological oceanography, and various other areas. Degrees: PhD; MSc.

Environmental Studies
School of Environmental Studies, 2800 Finnerty Rd., Victoria BC V8W 3R4 Canada
Tel: 250-721-7354; *Fax:* 250-721-8985
e-mail: ses@uvic.ca
web.uvic.ca/enweb
Mission: Graduate Program at the School of Environmental Studies offers 3 core, interdisciplinary research areas in Ecological Restoration, Ethnoecology and Political Ecology. Degrees: MA; MSc in Environmental Studies.

Earth and Ocean Science Combined Major Programs - Undergraduate
School of Earth and Ocean Science (SEOS)
Mission: These Earth Science Programs require a core of Earth Science studies and corequisit studies in the partner science(s). BSc Degrees: Earth Sciences; Combined Major & Honours in Physics and Earth Sciences (Geophysics); Combined Major & Honours in Physics and Ocean Sciences (Ocean-Atmosphere Dynamics); Combined Major & Honours in Chemistry and Earth & Ocean Sciences; Combined Major & Honours in Physical Geograohy and Earth & Ocean Sciences; Combined Major & Honours in Biology and Earth & Ocean Sciences; Minor in Ocean Sciences.

University of Waterloo
200 University Ave. West, Waterloo ON N2L 3G1
Tel: 519-888-4567
uwaterloo.ca

Geography & Environmental Management
uwaterloo.ca/geography-environmental-management
Mission: Geography and Environmental Management students will draw upon science, social studies, and computer technology to understand our changing world.

Environment and Business
School of Environment, Enterprise & Development
uwaterloo.ca/school-environment-enterprise-development
Mission: The Environment and Business (B.E.S.) program produces knowledgeable and experienced graduates-people who can integrate the tools of business and sustainability and who have experience gained through paid co-op work terms. Program also offered in Graduate studies.

Environmental Studies in Sustainable Management
School of Environment, Enterprise & Development
Mission: The new one-year Sustainability Management graduate program launching in Fall 2013 is committed to providing future environmental leaders with the research skills, management tools, strategies and processes required to realize sustainable outcomes within business, government and third sector organizations.

Environment & Resource Studies
Faculty of Environment
uwaterloo.ca/environment
Mission: The Environment and Resource Studies (ERS) program is for students looking to study on the basis of their interest and the needs of society.

Climate Change
Faculty of Environment
uwaterloo.ca/environment/climate-change
Mission: Based in the Department of Geography and Environmental Management, the Master of Climate Change (MCC) program aims to provide a unique educational experience to students interested in the various emerging career paths in climate change science and policy and management.

Sustainability Management
Faculty of Environment
uwaterloo.ca/environment/sustainability-management
Mission: The new Masters of Sustainability Management program (Master of Environmental Studies (MES) Sustainability Management) of The University of Waterloo's School of Environment, Enterprise and Development (SEED) launching in Fall 2013 is committed to provide future leaders with the research skills, management tools, strategies and processes required to realize sustainable outcomes within business, government and third sector organizations.

Environmental Science
Dept. of Earth & Environmental Sciences
uwaterloo.ca/earth-environmental-sciences
Mission: This program provides a basic quantitative background in science and mathematics, while offering students greater opportunity to select courses in a wide range of environment-related subject areas, such as chemistry, ecology, microbiology, geography and hydrogeology.

University of Western Ontario
1151 Richmond St., London ON N6A 3K7
Tel: 519-661-2111
www.uwo.ca

Environmental Science
Centre for Environment & Sustainability, 109 Western Science Centre, London ON N6A 5B7 Canada
www.uwo.ca/enviro/undergraduate/UgradScience.html
Mission: Environmental Science at Western is a discipline within the Faculty of Science and not a Department. Students completing Environmental Science modules will earn a Bachelor of Science in Environmental Science. The Environmental Science programs are offered through the Centre for Environment and Sustainability.

Green Process Engineering
Faculty of Engineering, #2097, Spencer Engineering Bldg., London ON N6A 5B7 Canada
www.eng.uwo.ca/undergraduate/programs/GreenProcess.htm l
Mission: The curriculum integrates the fundamental principles of chemical engineering to design commercial products and processes that are safe, economical and environmentally friendly by reducing waste generation. The program also explores alternative sources of energy with reduced carbon emissions.

Civil & Environmental Engineering
Faculty of Engineering, 1151 Richmond St., London ON N6A 5B7 Canada
Tel: 519-850-2943; *Fax:* 519-661-3942
e-mail: civilgrad@uwo.ca
www.eng.uwo.ca/gradstudies/degree_options_MEng_CEE.ht m
Mission: The Department of Civil and Environmental Engineering (CEE) at Western University offers a professional coursework Master of Engineering (MEng) degree program in several diverse areas, with distinguished faculty expertise in each area. Areas of study include Environmental and Water Resources, Geotechnical and Geoenvironmental, Response to Natural Disaster Mitigation, Structural and Infrastructural, and Wind Engineering and Environmental Fluid Mechanics.

Environment & Sustainability
Centre for Environment & Sustainability
Tel: 519-661-2111
e-mail: sustainability@uwo.ca
sustainability.uwo.ca/index.html
Mission: Students can pursue a Masterís degree in Environment and Sustainability (MES). Incorporating both a consulting program and a co-op placement into the academic learning, the MES develops the intellectual and practical skills students need to advance environmental and sustainability issues in the scientific, industrial, business and policy sectors.

University of Windsor
401 Sunset Ave., Windsor ON N9B 3P4
Tel: 519-253-3000
www.uwindsor.ca

Environmental Engineering
Faculty of Arts & Sciences
www.uwindsor.ca/civil
Mission: The program in Environmental Engineering is built upon a broad base of science and mathematics combined with an emphasis on engineering principles and design.

Environmental Science
Faculty of Arts & Sciences
www.uwindsor.ca/science
Mission: This undergraduate program provides a background in all aspects of environmental science to prepare students for a wide variety of careers. Masters and Doctoral programs also available.

Environmental Studies
Centre for Inter-Faculty Programs
e-mail: envirostu@uwindsor.ca
web4.uwindsor.ca/units/environmentalStudies/main.nsf
Mission: The Environmental Studies program introduces students to the social, cultural, economic, political, legal and ethical factors affecting human interaction with the environment.

University of Winnipeg
515 Portage Ave., Winnipeg MB R3B 2E9
Tel: 204-786-7811
www.uwinnipeg.ca

Bioscience, Technolgy & Public Policy
Faculty of Science, 599 Portage Ave., Winnipeg MB R3B 2G3 Canada
www.uwinnipeg.ca/index/grad-studies-ms-btpp
Mission: This graduate program will give students advanced training in the Life Sciences in fields ranging from Genomics and Bioinformatics to Natural Resource Management. This program meets growing local, national and international demands in both the health and environmental sciences.

Applied Environmental Studies
e-mail: welcome@uwinnipeg.ca
www.uwinnipeg.ca/index/grad-studies-ms-btpp
Mission: This program is offered jointly between the Univeristy of Winnipeg and Red River College.

Environmental Studies
Dept. of Environmental Studies & Sciences
envstudies.uwinnipeg.ca
Mission: Environmental Studies is an interdisciplinary program that takes an holistic approach to the environment. Following the general principles of sustainability, the BA programs offer an integrated understanding of the environment, acknowledging human impact, and providing a framework to develop future solutions to environmental problems within two distinct streams: Issues in Sustainability and Urban Policy and the Environment. The BSc programs provide four options to choose from: Forest Ecology, Forest Policy and Management, Chemistry, and Global Environmental Systems.

Vancouver Island University
900 Fifth St., Nanaimo BC V9R 5S5
Tel: 250-753-3245
Toll-Free: 888-920-2221
e-mail: info@viu.ca
www.viu.ca

Energy Management
100 Fifth St., Nanaimo BC V9R 5S5 Canada
Tel: 250-740-6160; *Fax:* 250-740-6452
www.viu.ca/energymanagement
Mission: Energy conservation projects designed to improve on existing systems on campus, and reduce energy consumption.

Forest Resources Technology
Tel: 250-753-3245; *Fax:* 250-740-6556
www.viu.ca/forestry
Mission: This program provides technical training required for starting a career in most fields of forest technology, with emphasis on the recognition and appreciation of all major values of the forest including timber, recreation, wildlife, range, fish, water, and aesthetics. Bridge programs to UBC Bachelor programs are available, as is the opportunity to take the first two years of the UBC program at VIU. 2-year Technology Diploma

Resource Management Officer Technology
viu.ca/rmo
Mission: This program is designed to prepare students for careers related to the protection and management of Canada's fisheries, wildlife, and parks resources. RMOT students work first-hand with natural resource law enforcement agencies and are supported by an Advisory Committee made up of members of Federal Dept of Fisheries & Oceans, Provincial Ministry of Environment, BC Parks, Parks Canada, Environment Canada, and from resource users groups. 2-year Diploma.

Natural Resource Protection
Mission: The program builds on the existing 2-year RMOT dimploma for a BSc of Natural Resource Protection, for career opportunities in conservation and protection. In addition to advanced courses in natural resource management and law enforcement, there will be a four-month field practicum in the fall of the fourth yearduring which students will be able to choose an off-campus field placement in enforcement or resource management.

Natural Resources Extension Program
e-mail: nrep@viu.ca
www.viu.ca/nrep
Mission: The NREP is one of Canada's leading providers of applied, community-based natural resources professional development training. A series of 1-3 or 15-25 day certification programs are available in these areas: Aquatic, Environemntal Monitoring, Erosion & Sediment Control, Riparian, Fisheries, Aboriginal Environmental Tech, Fisheries Field Tech, Essential Fisheries Field Skills, Environmental Professional; and a 2-year Diploma program in First Nation Fisheries Technologist (FNFTDP).

Forest Resource Management-Transfer Program
viu.ca/forestry
Mission: VIU offers the equivalent of the first two years of the UBC Science in Forestry (BSF) degree program with direct tranfer into the 3rd year at UBC. (See listing under Forestry Resource Management)

Wilfrid Laurier University
75 University Ave. West, Waterloo ON N2L 3C5
Tel: 519-884-1970; *Fax:* 519-886-9351
www.wlu.ca

Environmental Studies
Faculty of Arts
www.wlu.ca/page.php?grp_id=65&p=1356
Mission: Students are exposed to all themes of geography and the environment in their first year and take required courses in all the main areas in their second year. In third and fourth years, students can specialize and develop advanced skills in research methods and techniques.

York University
4700 Keele St., Toronto ON M3J 1P3
Tel: 416-736-2100
www.yorku.ca

Environmental Biology
Glendon Campus, York Hall 162, 2275 Bayview Ave., Toronto ON M4N 3M6 Canada
Tel: 416-487-6732; *Fax:* 416-487-6851
futurestudents.yorku.ca/program/environmental-biology
Mission: This program focuses on the biology of environmental issues, integrating ecological theory and practice to predict, quantify, and address the impact of stressors such as habitat loss, pollutants, climate change, resource harvesting and invasive species on living systems.

Environmental Science
Glendon Campus, York Hall
Tel: 416-487-6732; *Fax:* 416-487-6851
futurestudents.yorku.ca/program/environmental-science
Mission: Environmental Science at York includes a compulsory Research Design & Field Study course that gets you out using the equipment of the profession. This involves a long weekend at Algonquin Park at The Frost Centre working on a project.

Environmental Studies
Glendon Campus, York Hall
futurestudents.yorku.ca/program/environmental_studies
Mission: The Faculty of Environmental Studies provides a unique educational experience in an expanding field of study, research and employment. After completing a common first year, students focus on one of four concentrations: Environmental Management: Policy, Resources and Conservation; Urban & Regional Environments: Analysis, Planning and Design; Environmental Politics: Development, Globalization and Justice; and Environment and Culture: Philosophy, Arts, Technology and Education.

Sustainable Energy
Glendon Campus, York Hall
Tel: 416-487-6732; *Fax:* 416-487-6851
futurestudents.yorku.ca/program/certificates/sustainable-ener gy
Mission: This certificate, open to student in the Faculty of Environmental Studies, encompasses the policy, economic, technological and managerial aspects of sustainable energy and provides students with applied skills in the field.

Urban Sustainability
Glendon Campus, York Hall
futurestudents.yorku.ca/program/urban_sustainability
Mission: Graduates of the program receive a Bachelor in Environmental Studies (BES) from York University and a Civil Engineering Technology Diploma from Seneca College of Applied Arts & Technology. Completion of the joint program will prepare you for work in the planning, design and construction of major infrastructure and services including roads, tunnels, bridges, water supplies, buildings and new communities.

Environmental and Health Studies Program
Glendon Campus, York Hall
e-mail: mds@glendon.yorku.ca
futurestudents.yorku.ca/program/environmental-health-studie s
Mission: A focused yet comprehensive analysis of issues in the fields of environment and health. This program will give you the opportunity to obtain a solid grasp of the bio-medical and environmental sciences within the broader context of a liberal arts education. Provides a chance to explore a variety of health-related issues, and your degree will help you understand the historical roots of contemporary environmental and bio-medical controversies.

Yukon College
PO Box 2799, 500 College Dr., Whitehorse YT Y1A 5K4
Tel: 867-668-8800
Toll-Free: 800-661-0504
www.yukoncollege.yk.ca

Environmental & Conservation Sciences
School of Science
Tel: 867-668-8760; *Fax:* 867-668-5210
Mission: In collaboration with the University of Alberta, Yukon College offers years 3 and 4 of a Bachelor of Science (BSc) degree in Environmental and Conservation Sciences (ENCS), with a curriculum that integrates natural and social sciences as related to issues such as wildlife conservation, land use, energy and global climate change.

Water and Wastewater Operator Program
School of Science
Tel: 867-668-8760; *Fax:* 867-668-5210
www.yukoncollege.yk.ca/programs/view/wwop
Mission: Work with our world's most precious resource - water. Courses in this area are geared to address rapid industry changes and provide upgrading to those already employed as water and wastewater operators, or those seeking to enter the field.

Renewable Resources Management
School of Science
Tel: 867-668-8760; *Fax:* 867-668-5210
www.yukoncollege.yk.ca/programs/view/rrmt
Mission: A two-year diploma program designed for those seeking immediate employment in the field of renewable resources or for those looking for practical training before moving on to a university.

Northern Outdoor Environmental Studies
School Of Liberal Arts
Tel: 867-668-8770; *Fax:* 867-668-8805
www.yukoncollege.yk.ca/programs/view/nes
Mission: A two-year diploma program that examines a variety of environment issues of northern concern including: resource depletion, wilderness fragmentation, pollution and global climate changes, and loss of biodiversity. Students may transfer to degree programs at other Canadian and American institutions.

Foundations & Grants

International

Foundation for Environmental Conservation (FEC)
1148 Moiry, Switzerland
Fax: 41-21-8666-6616
e-mail: envcons@ncl.ac.uk
URL: www.ncl.ac.uk/icef
Description: To undertake, in cooperation with appropriate individuals, organizations & other groups, all possible activities to further environmental conservation global sustainability.

Foundation for International Environmental Law & Development (FIELD)
3 Endsleigh St., London WC1H 0DD United Kingdom
Tel: 44-20-7872-7200; *Fax:* 44-20-7388-2826
e-mail: field.org@field.org.uk
URL: www.field.org.uk
Description: FIELD is a group of public international lawyers committed to helping vulnerable countries, communities and campaigners negotiate for fairer international environmental laws.

Alberta

Alberta Conservation Association (ACA)
#101, 9 Chippewa Rd., Sherwood Park AB T8A 6J7 Canada
Tel: 780-410-1999; *Fax:* 780-464-0141
e-mail: info@ab-conservation.com
URL: www.ab-conservation.com
Description: Formed in 1997, Alberta Conservation Association (ACA) is a not-for-profit, registered charity largely funded by Alberta's hunters and anglers through licence levies, and a growing number of corporate partners. Annually, ACA directs more than $10 million towards conservation efforts, delivering a wide variety of projects, programs and services across the province. Key conservation programs include Wildlife, Fisheries, Land Management and Communications (Grants in Biodiversity Program, Grant Eligible Conservation Fund, ACA Chair in Fisheries and Wildlife at the University of Alberta).

Alberta Ecotrust Foundation
1020 - 1202 Centre St. SE, Calgary AB T2G 5A5 Canada
Tel: 403-209-2245; *Fax:* 403-209-2086
Toll-Free: 800-465-2147
URL: www.albertaecotrust.com
Description: Conceived in 1991, Alberta Ecotrust is a unique partnership between the corporate sector and the environmental community. Together, they invest in the people and projects that help to make Alberta a stronger, more sustainable place to live, work and play. They achieve this goal through three main programs: environmental grant making, capacity building, and community collaboration. Together, we fund non-profit environmental projects, strengthen the ability of the voluntary sector to affect positive environmental change, and promote the environment as the foundation of a healthy community.

Alberta Lottery Fund
50 Corriveau Ave., St. Albert AB T8N 3T5 Canada
Fax: 780-447-8903
Toll-Free: 800-642-3855
URL: http://albertalotteryfund.ca
Description: The Alberta Lottery Fund is made up of the government's share of net revenues from VLTs, slot machines and ticket lotteries. These revenues total more than $1.5 billion each year, and are used to support thousands of volunteer, public and community-based initiatives annually. Revenues from the Alberta Lottery Fund are allocated to 13 specific ministries, including the Ministry of Environment.

Alberta Real Estate Foundation
#301-1240 Kensington Rd. NW, Calgary AB T2N 3P7 Canada
Tel: 403-228-4786; *Fax:* 403-229-1572
Toll-Free: 800-520-2485
e-mail: questions@aref.ab.ca
URL: www.aref.ab.ca
Description: The Alberta Real Estate Foundation supports real estate initiatives which benefit the industry and the people of Alberta. The Land Stewardship & Environment area of interest is to enable Albertans to understand and respond to changing land use patterns, growth pressures, air and water management issues and to enhance the ecological quality of their communities.

Alberta Sport, Recreation, Parks & Wildlife Foundation (ASRPWF)
Standard Life Centre, #901, 10405 Jasper Ave., Edmonton AB T5J 4R7
Tel: 780-415-1167
URL: www.tpr.alberta.ca/asrpwf
Description: The Alberta Sport, Recreation, Parks & Wildlife Foundation works to enhance sport, recreation, park, wildlife & conservation opportunities in Alberta. Financial support to organizations, to work towards a healthy population, economy, & natural environment, is provided through grants. The Park & Wildlife Ventures program provides funds to promote conservation in Alberta & to purchase lands which are ecologically sensitive, important to wildlife, or bordering other conservation lands.

Alpine Club Environment Fund
PO Box 8040, Indian Flats Rd., Canmore AB T1W 2T8 Canada
Tel: 403-678-3200; *Fax:* 403-678-3224
e-mail: info@AlpineClubofCanada.ca
URL: www.alpineclubofcanada.ca/grants/environment.html
Description: The purpose of the Fund is to provide support that contributes to the protection and preservation of mountain and climbing environments, including the preservation of alpine flora and fauna in their natural habitat.

Calgary Foundation
#700, 999 - 8th St. SW, Calgary AB T2R 1J5
Tel: 403-802-7700; *Fax:* 403-802-7701
e-mail: grants@thecalgaryfoundation.org
URL: www.thecalgaryfoundation.org
Overview: A organization founded in 1955
Description: The Calgary Foundation provides grants to support organizations in the following areas: arts & heritage, education, environment, health, human Services, & neighbourhoods. Projects must be in Calgary, or benefit the residents of Calgary & area.

Canada-Alberta Municipal Rural Infrastructure Fund (CAMRIF)
Twin Atria 1, 4999 - 98th Ave., 2nd Fl., Edmonton AB T6B 2X3 Canada
Tel: 780-422-1151; *Fax:* 780-427-5505
Toll-Free: 800-396-0214
e-mail: camrif@gov.ab.ca
URL: www.camrif.ca
Description: The Fund supports projects that enhance & renew public infrastructure, improve the quality of the environment, protect health & safety, support long-term economic growth, & develop sustainable communities in the smaller urban centres & rural municipalities of Alberta.

Carthy Foundation
PO Box 2554, Stn. M, Calgary AB T2P 2M7 Canada
Tel: 403-231-7922; *Fax:* 403-231-7959
URL: www.carthyfoundation.org
Description: Carthy Foundation, based in Calgary, Alberta, is a private foundation established in 1965. Carthy Foundation has two granting programs: Youth: Initiatives will have a primary focus on youth development or youth problem prevention; Environment: Initiatives will focus on market-based mechanisms, or urban ecology and ecological design.

City of Edmonton
Energy Management Revolving Fund
Century Place, 9803 - 102A Ave., 2nd Fl., Edmonton AB T5J 3A3 Canada
Tel: 780-496-2791; *Fax:* 780-496-5657
e-mail: env@edmonton.ca
URL: www.edmonton.ca/environmental/programs/
Description: The fund, established in 1995, provides support to energy efficiency projects such as upgrades to lighting, heating, cooling & ventilation systems, & envelope upgrades. The amount borrowed against the fund is repaid over a period of up to 8 years.

Edmonton Space & Science Foundation (ESSF)
11211 - 142 St., Edmonton AB T5M 4A1 Canada
Tel: 780-452-9100; *Fax:* 780-455-5882
e-mail: info@telusworldofscienceedmonton.com
URL: www.telusworldofscience.com/edmonton
Description: To inspire & motivate people to learn about & contribute to science & technology advances that strengthen themselves, their family & community.

Lethbridge Community Foundation
Professional Bldg., 404 - 8th St. South, Lethbridge AB T1J 2J7
Tel: 403-328-5297; *Fax:* 403-328-6061
e-mail: office@lethbridgecommunityfoundation.ca
URL: www.lethbridgecommunityfoundation.org
Overview: A organization founded in 1966
Description: The Lethbridge Community Foundation provides grants, to local non-profit organizations, in the following fields of interest: arts & culture, community service, education, environment, health, history, & recreation.; *Member of:* Community Foundations of Canada

Max Bell Foundation
#380, 1201 - 5th St. S.W., Calgary AB T2R 0Y6 Canada
Tel: 403-215-7310; *Fax:* 403-215-7319
URL: www.maxbell.org
Description: Max Bell Foundation is a Canadian independent grantmaking foundation that pursues its mission and strategic priority by supporting Canadian registered charities with project grants and internship/fellowship grants. The Foundation seeks to support environment initiatives that align with our mission and granting guidelines. We are interested in supporting projects that understand and take account of the social and economic contexts in which environmental concerns emerge as public policy and practice.

Science Alberta Foundation
#260, 3512 - 33 St. NW, Calgary AB T2L 2A6 Canada
Tel: 403-220-0077; *Fax:* 403-284-4132
e-mail: info@sciencealberta.org
URL: www.sciencealberta.org
Description: Science Alberta Foundation is a non-profit organization committed to increasing science literacy and awareness. They develop engaging resources that bring science to life for Albertans of all ages, in every corner of the province. Science Alberta Foundation collaborates with educators, parents, community leaders and scientists to develop programs, such as Science-In-A-Crate and Festivals of Science that showcase the importance science plays in our everyday lives.

SEEDS Foundation
#400, 144 - 4th Ave. SW., Calgary AB T2P 3N4 Canada
Tel: 403-221-0831; *Fax:* 403-221-0888
Toll-Free: 800-661-8751
e-mail: seeds@telusplanet.net
URL: www.seedsfoundation.ca
Also Known As: Society, Environment & Energy Development Studies Foundation
Description: To provide educational support materials & professional assistance to teachers in the area of energy, environment & sustainable development; to work toward the development of a society which understands & is committed to actions leading to wise stewardship of resources, resource use & the environment.

Shell Environmental Fund
PO Box 100, Stn. M, Calgary AB T2P 2H5 Canada
Tel: 403-691-2071; *Fax:* 403-269-8031
e-mail: admin-sef@shell.com
URL: www.shell.ca
Description: The Shell Environmental Fund (SEF) provides financial support for grass roots, action-oriented projects that improve and protect the Canadian environment.

Suncor Energy Foundation
PO Box 38, 112 - 4 Ave. SW, Calgary AB T2P 2V5 Canada
Tel: 403-269-8775
e-mail: sef@suncor.com
URL: www.suncor.com/default.aspx?cid=239&lang=1
Description: The Suncor Energy Foundation is a private, non-profit, charitable foundation established by Suncor Energy Inc. in 1998 to receive Suncor's contributions and support registered Canadian charitable organizations. The Foundation complements other forms of community investments by Suncor, such as product or in-kind contributions, sponsorships, and

employee giving and volunteer efforts. Funded entirely by Suncor, the Foundation's funding priorities are educational, environmental and community-based initiatives that are aligned with Suncor's key operating communities. The Foundation seeks unique opportunities to enhance the quality of life in those communities and to add value through effective collaborations.

British Columbia

African Wildlife Foundation (AWF)
#120, 1400 Sixteenth St. NW, Washington DC 20036 USA
Tel: 202-939-3333; *Fax:* 202-939-3332
Toll-Free: 888-494-5354
e-mail: africanwildlife@awf.org
URL: www.awf.org
Description: To promote conservation of Africa's wildlife & natural resources; to promote belief that the survival of African wildlife lies in a working knowledge of the relationship between man, his economics & his environment; to promote, establish & support grassroots & institutional programs in conservation education, wildlife management & training, & management of threatened conservation areas; to manage projects aimed at saving endangered species (eg. the African Elephant, Mountain Gorilla, Rhinoceros).

The Avian Preservation Foundation (APF)
PO Box 123, Chemainus BC V0R 1K0 Canada
Tel: 250-246-4803; *Fax:* 250-246-4912
e-mail: exec@aacc.ca
URL: www.aacc.ca
Description: To support recognized expert aviculturists who are endeavouring to breed rare & endangered avian species; to establish a Canadian breeding centre for rare & endangered avian species; to establish a monitoring body for captive avian stocks in Canada through surveys & computer software; to create & maintain a breeding program throughout Canada for avian species currently listed as endangered; to create a captive preservation program for rare & endangered species within zoos, bird parks & sanctuaries where re-introduction into the natural habitat is not possible or practical.

British Columbia Agriculture Council (BCAC)
#140, 32160 South Fraser Way, Abbotsford BC V2T 1W5
URL: www.bcac.bc.ca
Overview: A organization founded in 1997
Description: The Agriculture Environment Initiatives, of the British Columbia Agriculture Council, feature assistance to resolve environmental & wildlife issues related to agriculture in the province.

British Columbia Agriculture Council (AEWF)
Agriculture Environment & Wildlife Fund
1473 Water St., Kelowna BC V1Y 1J6
Tel: 250-763-9790; *Fax:* 250-762-2997
URL: www.bcac.bc.ca
Description: In order to advance the environmental sustainability of the agricultural industry in British Columbia, the Agriculture Environment & Wildlife Fund assists the agricultural sector to resolve environmental issues.

British Columbia Agriculture Council (AESI)
Agriculture Environment Stewardship Initiative
1473 Water St., Kelowna BC V1Y 1J6
Tel: 250-763-9790
Overview: A organization founded in 2001
Description: The Agriculture Environment Stewardship Initiative funds projects to resolve environmental & wildlife issues within British Columbia's agricultural sector. Applications for this funding are submitted or supported by farming organizations.

British Columbia Agriculture Council (BC EFP)
Canada - British Columbia Environmental Farm Plan Program
c/o Agricultural Research & Development Corporation, #140, 32160 South Fraser Way, Abbotsford BC V2T 1W5
Toll-Free: 866-522-3447
e-mail: reg@ardcorp.ca
URL: www.bcac.bc.ca/EFP_pages/about_us/index.html
Overview: A organization founded in 2003
Description: The British Columbia Agriculture Council is the delivery agent of the Canada - British Columbia Environmental Farm Plan Program, in partnership with Agriculture & Agri-food Canada & the British Columbia Ministry of Agriculture & Lands. The Program is designed to provide funding to enhance the stewardship practices of British Columbia's farms & ranches.

British Columbia Conservation Foundation (BCCF)
#206, 17564 - 56A Ave., Surrey BC V3S 1G3 Canada
Tel: 604-576-1433; *Fax:* 604-576-1482
e-mail: bccfho@bccf.com
URL: www.bccf.com
Description: The British Columbia Conservation Foundation (BCCF) was founded and incorporated under the Society Act of British Columbia in 1969, by the Directors of the BC Wildlife Federation, to contribute significantly to the perpetuation and expansion of fish and wildlife populations through the efficient implementation of projects in the field. They are a federally registered charity dedicated to the conservation and stewardship of British Columbia's ecosystems and species.

British Columbia Hydro Bridge Coastal Restoration Program (BCRP)
#E16, 6911 Southpoint Dr., Burnaby BC V3N 4X8
Tel: 604-528-8136
e-mail: bcrp@bchydro.com
URL: www.bchydro.com/bcrp
Overview: A organization founded in 1999
Description: British Columbia Hydro's Bridge Coastal Restoration Program aims to restore fish & wildlife resources impacted by hydroelectric facilities in the Bridge Coastal Generation Area. Projects funded by the program must involve restoration, conseravation, or research.

The ChariTREE Foundation
PO Box CL-58, Bowen Island BC V0N 1G0 Canada
Tel: 604-947-6803
Toll-Free: 888-947-6803
e-mail: info@charitree.ca
URL: http://charitree.ca
Description: The ChariTREE Foundation (TCF) is Canada's kid's environmental learning charity. TCF is a registered Canadian environmental charity established to help the planet by creating and supporting tree planting projects that benefit kids.

Coastal Ecosystems Research Foundation
General Delivery, Dawson's Landing BC V0N 1M0 Canada
Tel: 44-0-7745-730873; *Fax:* 815-327-0173
e-mail: info@cerf.bc.ca
URL: www.cerf.bc.ca
Description: To fund ecological research through eco-tourism.

Comox Valley Community Foundation
PO Box 3126, #201J, 2435 Mansfield Dr., Courtenay BC V9N 5N4
Tel: 250-338-8444
e-mail: cvcf@shawcable.com
URL: www.cvcfoundation.org
Description: The Comox Valley Community Foundation Board provides grants for projects in the following fields: arts & culture, education & youth, environment, health & welfare, & seniors. Projects must benefit British Columbia's Comox Valley region. Recipients have included the Comox Valley Naturalists Society, the Comox Valley Project Watershed Society, & Conservancy Hornby Island.

David Suzuki Foundation (DSF)
#219, 2211 - 4th Ave. West, Vancouver BC V6K 4S2 Canada
Tel: 604-732-4228; *Fax:* 604-732-0752
Toll-Free: 800-453-1533
e-mail: contact@davidsuzuki.org
URL: www.davidsuzuki.org
Description: To seek out & commission the best, most up-to-date research to help reveal ways we can live in balance with nature; to support the implementation of ecologically sustainable models - from local projects, such as habitat restoration, to international initiatives, such as better frameworks for economic decisions; to ensure the solutions developed through research & application to reach the widest possible audience, & help mobilize broadly supported change; to urge decision makers to adopt policies which encourage & guide individuals & businesses, so their daily decisions reflect the need to act within nature's constraints.

Endswell Foundation
200-163 W. Hastings St., Vancouver BC V6B 1H5 Canada
Tel: 604-844-7448; *Fax:* 604-844-7441
e-mail: endswell@renewalpartners.com
URL: www.renewalpartners.com
Description: The Endswell Foundation is an independent registered charity, operating under the Renewal group of organizations. Endswell has played a role in many initiatives, large and small, that have helped to preserve BC's wildernesses. Over the past 15 years the Endswell Foundation made over 700 grants totalling over $20 million dollars.

Environmental Health Foundation of Canada (EHFC)
Stn. #720, 999 West Broadway Ave., Vancouver BC V5Z 1K5 Canada
URL: www.ehfc.ca
Description: The research & educational arm of the Canadian Institute of Public Health Inspectors; Dedicated to advancing environmental health in Canada through thedevelopment & implementation of education & research initiatives.

Fish & Wildlife Compensation Program (FWCP)
#103, 333 Victoria St., Nelson BC V1L 4K3
Tel: 250-352-6874; *Fax:* 250-352-6178
e-mail: info@fwcp.ca
URL: www.fwcp.ca
Overview: A organization founded in 1995
Description: The Fish & Wildlife Compensation Program's mission is to offset the impacts of hydro dams in the Columbia Basin. Funds are invested in fish & wildlife projects. Many of the funded projects focus upon species-at-risk. Examples of funding include lake restoration programs, habitat restoration, species monitoring, & land acquisition for conservation purposes.

The GLOBE Foundation of Canada
World Trade Centre, #578, 999 Canada Pl., Vancouver BC V6C 3E1 Canada
Tel: 604-775-7300; *Fax:* 604-666-8123
Toll-Free: 800-274-6097
e-mail: info@globe.ca
URL: www.globe.ca
Description: The not-for-profit organization strives to find practical business-oriented solutions to environmental problems. It helps companies & individuals realize the value of economically viable environmental business opportunities.

Harmony Foundation of Canada
PO Box 50022, #15, 1594 Fairfield Rd., Victoria BC V8S 1G1 Canada
Tel: 250-380-3001; *Fax:* 250-380-0887
e-mail: harmony@islandnet.com
URL: www.harmonyfdn.ca
Description: To encourage development which is socially & environmentally sustainable; To strive towards ecological stability, long-term prosperity, & social harmony.

Investment Agriculture Foundation of British Columbia
PO Box 8248, 808 Douglas St., 3rd Fl., Victoria BC V8W 3R9
Tel: 250-356-1662; *Fax:* 250-953-5162
e-mail: info@iafbc.ca; funding@iafbc.ca
URL: www.iafbc.ca
Description: The Investment Agriculture Foundation of British Columbia provides assistance to the agricultural & food processing industries of British Columbia. The following are areas which qualify for funding: plant industries; animal industries; processing industries; environmental issues; & other issues, such as the livestock waste tissue initiative, the agri-tourism initiative, & the aboriginal agriculture initiative. Examples of environmental funding programs are environmental farm planning & the agriculture, environment & wildlife fund.

Lifeforce Foundation
PO Box 3117, Vancouver BC V6B 3X6 Canada
Tel: 604-649-5258
e-mail: lifeforcesociety@hotmail.com
URL: www.lifeforcefoundation.org
Description: Dedicated to raising public awareness of the interrelationship of human, animal & environmental problems; to urge society to address & solve problems by taking into consideration the long-term effects on all parts of the ecosystem.

Marmot Recovery Foundation
PO Box 2332, Stn. A, Nanaimo BC V94 6X6 Canada
Tel: 250-753-8080; *Fax:* 250-753-8070
Toll-Free: 877-462-7668
e-mail: marmot@islandnet.com
URL: www.marmots.org
Description: To manage the recovery effort for one of North America's most endangered mammals: the Vancouver Island marmot (Marmota vancouverensis).

Mountain Equipment Co-op (Environment Fund Grants)
149 West 4th Ave., Vancouver BC V5Y 4A6 Canada
Toll-Free: 866-632-3863
e-mail: community@mec.ca
URL: www.mec.ca
Description: The Mountain Equipment Co-op (MEC) wants to ensure that the environments of those outdoor areas that have

important wilderness or recreational value are preserved. To this end, MEC has established a program to support the projects of Canadian-based environmental and conservation groups who deal with issues affecting the environment. MEC will financially support activities, projects, research, and education concerned with environmental conservation and wilderness protection. Categories of projects supported are environmental research projects; studentships (research or advocacy proojects under the direction of a supervisor); advocacy and education projects that aadvance conservation and environmental causes; projects that facilitate public accesss to or recreational use of areas having significant recreational or wilderness value to MEC members; and land aquisitions for conservation.

Nanaimo Community Foundation (NCF)
#106, 619 Comox Rd., Nanaimo BC V9R 5V8
e-mail: administrator@nanaimocommunityfoundation.com
URL: www.nanaimocommunityfoundation.com
Overview: A organization founded in 1982
Description: The Nanaimo Community Foundation supports programs in the following categories: arts, culture & recreation; children & youth; community infrastructure & environment; education; health care; & seniors & housing. Grants are available to non-profit societies in British Columbia, which are also federally registered charities. Projects must take place in the County of Nanaimo.

Okanagan Water Basin Board (OBWB)
1450 KLO Rd., Kelowna BC V1W 3Z4 Canada
Tel: 250-469-6271; *Fax:* 250-762-7011
e-mail: info@obwb.ca
URL: www.obwb.ca
Description: The Okanagan Basin Water Board (OBWB) was instituted in 1970 through a collaboration of the three Okanagan regional districts to provide leadership on water issues that span the entire valley - recognizing the need to work together to protect our common resources. The purpose of the OBWB is to provide leadership to protect and enhance quality of life in the Okanagan Basin through sustainable water resource management.

Pacific Salmon Foundation
#300 - 1682 West 7th Ave., Vancouver BC V6J 4S6 Canada
Tel: 604-664-7664; *Fax:* 604-664-7665
e-mail: salmon@psf.ca
URL: www.psf.ca
Description: PSF continues to raise funds and direct funding to grassroots, volunteer and community driven projects focused on the conservation and recovery of Pacific salmon. PSF supports research and science, then integrates this knowledge into program plans at the community and watershed level. PSF works with First Nations, private companies, educational institutions, non-profit groups, all levels of government, and commercial and recreational anglers to bring salmon back to our streams.

Real Estate Foundation of British Columbia
Marine Bldg., #570, 355 Burrard St., 5th Fl., Vancouver BC V6C 2G8
Tel: 604-688-6800; *Fax:* 604-688-3669
Toll-Free: 866-912-6800
e-mail: askme@realestatefoundation.com
URL: www.realestatefoundation.com
Overview: A organization founded in 1985
Description: To benefit the people of British Columbia, the Real Estate Foundation of British Columbia supports sustainable real estate & land use practices. Non-profit organizations, such as the BC Ground Water Association, are recipients of project funding & endowment grants.

T. Buck Suzuki Environmental Foundation
#100 - 326 12th St., New Westminster BC V3M 4H6 Canada
Tel: 604-519-3635; *Fax:* 604-524-6944
e-mail: tbsef@bucksuzuki.org
URL: www.bucksuzuki.org
Description: The T. Buck Suzuki Foundation works to ensure that fish bearing marshes, streams, rivers, lakes are not polluted, dammed, diverted, wasted or degraded. The Foundation was set up in 1981 by the United Fishermen and Allied Workers' Union.

Tides Canada Foundation
400-163 Hastings St. West, Vancouver BC V6B 1H5 Canada
Tel: 604-647-6611; *Fax:* 866-780-6611
e-mail: info@tidescanada.org
URL: http://tidescanada.org
Description: Tides Canada provides innovative philanthropic, financial and project management services for change makers - philanthropists, foundations, activists, and civil organizations.

Turner Foundation, Inc.
133 Luckie St. NW, 2nd Fl., Atlanta GA 30303 USA
Tel: 404-681-9900; *Fax:* 404-681-0172
URL: www.turnerfoundation.org
Description: The objective for this grant program is the protection of rivers, lakes, wetlands, aquifers, oceans, and other water systems from contamination, degradation, and other abuses. The Turner Foundation invests in select national and priority state level efforts to conserve wildlife and habitat. Internationally, the Turner Foundation supports wildlife and habitat conservation in the Russian Far East (specifically salmon conservation) and along the central coast of British Columbia.

Vancouver City Savings Credit Union
The Vancity enviroFund
PO Box 2120, Stn. Terminal, Vancouver BC V6B 5R8 Canada
Toll-Free: 888-826-2489
URL: www.vancity.com/MyCommunity/; www.vancity.com/grants/
Description: The Fund was established to support community initiatives that address local environmental concerns. The Fund has supported organizations such as The Bowen Island Conservancy, The Centre for Sustainable Food Systems at UBC Farm, & The Delta Farmland & Wildlife Trust. See the website for grant guidelines & criteria.

Vancouver City Savings Credit Union
Climate Change Solutions Program
PO Box 2120, Stn. Terminal, Vancouver BC V6B 5R8 Canada
Toll-Free: 888-826-2489
URL: www.vancity.com/MyCommunity/OurVision/ActingOnClimateChange
Description: The Climate Change Solutions program is focused on curbing climate change by taking action as an organization "where we live", and supporting our members and community to do the same. They accomplish this by: reducing our organizational environmental impact by reducing our emissions from energy use, paper use, and employee travel; helping members to reduce their impact by offering unique products to our members; supporting community groups who are also taking action, by investing in community and industry leaders working towards solutions (e.g., Green Building Grants, investment in micro-hydro projects and green buildings); and advocating for development and advancement of public policy solutions to climate change.

Vancouver Foundation
Harbour Centre, PO Box 12132, #1200, 555 West Hastings St., Vancouver BC V6B 4N6
Tel: 604-688-2204; *Fax:* 604-688-4170
e-mail: info@vancouverfoundation.ca
URL: www.vancouverfoundation.bc.ca
Overview: A organization founded in 1943
Description: The Vancouver Foundation supports charities & innovative projects in British Columbia. The Foundation funds the following areas: animal welfare; arts & culture; children, youth, & families; education; environment; health & social development; health & medical research; youth homelessness; & youth philanthropy.; *Member of:* Community Foundations of Canada

Victoria Foundation
#109, 645 Fort St., Victoria BC V8W 1G2
Tel: 250-381-5532; *Fax:* 250-480-1129
e-mail: info@victoriafoundation.bc.ca
URL: www.victoriafoundation.bc.ca
Overview: A organization founded in 1936
Description: The Victoria Foundation's funds support local registered charities in the following fields: arts, culture, & heritage, community services, education, environment, & health & recreation. Examples of organizations which have received grants include the Federation of BC Naturalists & the SeaChange Marine Conservation Society.

West Coast Environmental Law Research Foundation (WCEL)
200 - 2006 West 10th Ave., Vancouver BC V6J 2B3 Canada
Tel: 604-684-7378; *Fax:* 604-684-1312
Toll-Free: 800-330-9235
e-mail: admin@wcel.org
URL: www.wcel.org
Description: To provide summary legal advice to anyone in British Columbia with environmental concerns; to protect & enhance the environment of British Columbia; to foster public participation in environmental decision making; to provide legal aid for citizens with environmental concerns; to undertake law review & law reform projects, legal research & education, community legal outreach; & to operate an archival & on-line law library.

The William & Flora Hewlett Foundation
2121 Sand Hill Rd., Menlo Park CA 94025 USA
Tel: 650-234-4500; *Fax:* 650-234-4501
URL: www.hewlett.org
Description: The William and Flora Hewlett Foundation provides assistance to organizations working on environmental issues primarily in the North American West, specifically Montana, Wyoming, Colorado, New Mexico, Arizona, Nevada, Utah, Idaho, Washington, Oregon, California, Alaska, and Hawaii, as well as the western provinces of Canada and the northern states of Mexico bordering the United States. The principle objectives of the Environment program are to assist communities and organizations throughout the West to manage the development of natural resources and to redirect or absorb increases in population growth in ways that are sustainable and that respect the special qualities of the western landscape.

Manitoba

Canadian Shield Foundation
#401, 250 Wellington Cres., Winnipeg MB R3M 0B3 Canada
Tel: 204-989-7580; *Fax:* 204-989-7581
e-mail: canadianshieldfoundation@shaw.ca
Description: The Foundation's stated purpose is to promote ecology in the Canadian Shield. Funding interests may include education, science, environment and conservation.

Manitoba Hydro
Forest Enhancement Program
PO Box 815, Stn. Main, Winnipeg MB R3C 2P4 Canada
Tel: 204-474-3311
e-mail: publicaffairs@hydro.mb.ca
URL: www.hydro.mb.ca
Description: The program funds projects that enhance & sustain the forest environment in Manitoba. Projects which address climate change impacts are of special interest. Project categories: tree planting, forest education projects, projects which are innovative in perspective & may deal with issues such as sustainability, forest protection, urban forestry, etc.

Manitoba Hydro
Environmental Partnership Fund
PO Box 815, Stn. Main, Winnipeg MB R3C 2P4 Canada
Tel: 204-474-3311
e-mail: publicaffairs@hydro.mb.ca
URL: www.hydro.mb.ca
Description: The fund provides support to education relating to sustainable development. Applicants open to educators, education institutions, NGOs, & not-for-profit community organizations.

The Murphy Foundation Incorporated
#919, 167 Lombard Ave., Winnipeg MB R3B 0V3 Canada
Tel: 204-942-5281; *Fax:* 204-957-5866
Description: Provides funds for projects in the areas of wildlife habitat, wildfowl habitat, & medical education & research.

Renewable Natural Resources Foundation (RNRF)
5430 Grosvenor Lane, Bethesda MD 20814-2142 USA
Tel: 301-493-9101; *Fax:* 301-493-6148
e-mail: info@rnrf.org
URL: www.rnrf.org
Description: To advance sciences & public education in renewable natural resources; to promote the application of sound, scientific practices in managing & conserving renewable natural resources; to foster coordination & cooperation among professional, scientific & educational organizations having leadership responsibilities for renewable natural resources; to develop a Renewable Natural Resources Center.

Sustainable Development Innovations Fund (SDIF)
160-123 Main St., Winnipeg MB R3C 1A5 Canada
Tel: 204-945-8443; *Fax:* 204-945-1211
Toll-Free: 800-282-8069
e-mail: pollupreve@gov.mb.ca
URL: www.gov.mb.ca/conservation/pollutionprevention/sdif

Description: The Sustainable Development Innovations Fund (SDIF) is a $3.4 million Fund, which was created in October 1989 to provide financial assistance towards development, implementation and promotion of environmental innovation and sustainable development projects. The SDIF provides support to research studies, demonstration of new technology, community enhancement and educational projects, which further the sustainability of Manitoba's economy, human health and social well-being, and help to protect Manitoba's environment. The Fund encourages the creation of sustainable communities and helps them meet their needs by providing grant funding to projects that demonstrate: Partnerships between groups and individuals; Pride in the community; Concern for the environment.

The Thomas Sill Foundation Inc.

115 Plymouth St., Winnipeg MB R2X 2T3 Canada
Tel: 204-947-3782; *Fax:* 204-956-4702
URL: www.thomassillfoundation.com
Description: The Thomas Sill Foundation exists to provide encouragement and financial assistance to qualifying organizations operating in Manitoba that are working to advance the quality of life in the province, including the Lake Winnipeg Project.

Winnipeg Foundation

#1350, One Lombard Pl., Winnipeg MB R3B 0X3
Tel: 204-944-9474; *Fax:* 204-942-2987
Toll-Free: 877-974-3631
e-mail: info@wpgfdn.org
URL: www.wpgfdn.org
Overview: A organization founded in 1921
Description: To benefit the community, The Winnipeg Foundation provides grants to local non-profit organizations in the following fields of interest: arts & culture, community service, education & employment, environment, health, heritage, & recreation. An example of a project supported by the Foundation is the Downtown Greenspaces Strategy in Winnipeg.; *Member of:* Community Foundations of Canada

New Brunswick

ACAP Saint John (ACAPSJ)

PO Box 6878, Stn. A, 76 Germain St., Saint John NB E2L 4S4 Canada
Tel: 506-652-2227; *Fax:* 506-633-2184
e-mail: acapsj@rogers.com
URL: www.acapsj.com
Overview: A organization founded in 1991
Description: ACAP Saint John is a community-based non-profit organization under Environment Canada's Atlantic Coastal Action Program, one of 16 such organizations. ACAP Saint John is decidated to promoting and funding local environmental projects. ACAP Saint John encourages local involvement from all areas of the Saint John community, from industry to academia to all levels of government.

Conservation Council of New Brunswick (CCNB)

180 St. John St., Fredericton NB E3B 4A9 Canada
Tel: 506-458-8747; *Fax:* 506-458-1047
URL: http://conservationcouncil.ca
Overview: A organization founded in 1969
Description: The Conservation Council of New Brunswick is a member-based organization dedicated to promoting environmental issues and solutions. The Council advocates solutions through education, research, and grassroots action.

Greater Saint John Community Foundation

Brunswick Square, PO Box 20061, 40 King St., Saint John NB E2L 5B2 Canada
Tel: 506-672-8880; *Fax:* 506-672-8881
e-mail: sjfoundation@nb.aibn.com
URL: www.saint-john-foundation.nb.ca
Description: Established in 1976, this is an independent charity serving as a trustee of gifts. Incorporated environmental groups, convservation authorities & universities within a radius of 50km of Saint John, NB, may apply. Projects which improve the quality of life for the community are considered.

Miramichi River Environmental Assessment Committee (MREAC)

PO Box 85, 21 Cove Rd., Miramichi NB E1V 3M2 Canada
Tel: 506-778-8591; *Fax:* 506-773-9755
e-mail: mreac@nb.aibn.com
URL: www.mreac.org
Overview: A organization founded in 1989
Description: The Miramichi River Environmental Assessment Committee (MREAC) is a community based organization dedicated to the environmental improvement of the Miramichi River ecosystem established in 1989. In 1993, the MREAC joined Environment Canada's Atlantic Coastal Action Program (ACAP). MREAC focuses on science based research and other environmental projects to protect and manage the Miramichi River watershed.

Nature Trust of New Brunswick / Fondation pour la protection des sites naturels du Nouveau-Brunswick

PO Box 603, Stn. A, 404 Queen St., 3rd Fl., Fredericton NB E3B 5A6 Canada
Tel: 506-457-2398; *Fax:* 506-450-2137
e-mail: ntnb@nbnet.nb.ca
URL: www.naturetrust.nb.ca
Description: The Nature Trust of New Brunswick is a charitable land trust dedicated to the preservation and conservation of New Brunswick's natural landscape. The goals of the trust are to identify, classify, protect, and preserve natural areas in New Brunswick, and to foster awareness and appreciation of natural heritage.

New Brunswick Environmental Network (NBEN) / Réseau environnemental du Nouveau-Brunswick (RENB)

#432, 236 St. George St., Moncton NB E1C 1W1 Canada
Tel: 506-855-4114; *Fax:* 506-433-6111
e-mail: nben@nben.ca
URL: www.nben.ca
Overview: A organization founded in 1991
Description: The New Brunswick Environmental Network (NBEN) is a network of over 70 non-profit environmental organizations. The goal of the Network is to facilitate communication and cooperation between these organizations and government and industry to promote growth of environmental activities and projects in New Brunswick.

New Brunswick Environmental Trust Fund

Marysville Place, PO Box 6000, Fredericton NB E3B 5H1 Canada
Tel: 506-444-2654; *Fax:* 506-444-2734
URL: www.gnb.ca/0009/index-e.asp
Description: The Fund provides assistance for action-oriented projects with tangible, measurable results, aimed at protecting, preserving and enhancing the Province's natural environment.

New Brunswick Wildlife Trust Fund

PO Box 30030, Fredericton NB E3B 0H8 Canada
Tel: 506-453-6655; *Fax:* 506-462-5054
e-mail: wildcoun@nbnet.nb.ca
URL: www.nbwtf.ca
Description: The New Brunswick Wildlife Trust Fund has been established to fund a range of programs for the enhancement of New Brunswick's wildlife, fish and their habitats. The main source of revenue is from a conservation fee on hunters, anglers, and fur harvesters licences. Other conservation-supporting New Brunswickers can contribute by purchasing the special Conservation licence plates or by becoming an "Supporter". Money was also received from Maritime Road Development Corporation to compensate for environmental impacts on watercourses.

Newfoundland and Labrador

Labrador Southeast Coastal Action Program Inc. (LSCAP)

PO Box 189, 3 Penney's Lane, Port Hope Simpson NL A0K 4E0 Canada
Tel: 709-960-1010; *Fax:* 709-960-1012
e-mail: lscap@nf.aibn.com
URL: www.lscap.ca
Description: The Labrador Southeast Coastal Action Program (LSCAP) was established in 2006, and is a part of Environment Canada's Atlantic Coastal Action Program. The LSCAP is a non-profit organization dedicated to conducting and supporting environmental efforts in the area.

Quidi Vidi Rennie's River Development Foundation (QVRRDF)

Nagle's Place, PO Box 5, St. John's NL A1B 2Z2 Canada
Tel: 709-754-3474; *Fax:* 709-754-5947
e-mail: info@fluvarium.ca
URL: www.fluvarium.ca
Description: To promote responsible environmental stewardship; to raise awareness of the nature of freshwater systems; to provide leadership in urban watershed management; to operate The Fluvarium as a public centre for environmental education.

Northwest Territories

The Weeden Foundation

747 Third Ave., 34th Fl., New York NY 10017 USA
Tel: 212-888-1672; *Fax:* 212-888-1354
e-mail: weedenfdn@weedenfdn.org
URL: www.weedenfdn.org
Description: The foundation embraces the protection of biodiversity as its main priority. The foundation is particularly interested in new and innovative efforts that help to develop sustainable models for conservation action. Projects that serve as catalysts inducing others to lend support receive priority consideration. Foundation habitat protection grants have concentrated on the Pacific Northwest, that is Northern California, Oregon, and Washington, and up into British Columbia and Southeast Alaska. This reflects a longstanding interest in coastal temperate forests, which also extends into the Southern Hemisphere of the Americas. In addition, some grants have been awarded to projects in the intermountain west, notably the northern Rockies.

Nova Scotia

Atlantic Canada Sustainability Initiative (ACSI)

c/o School of Recreation Management & Kinesiology, Acadia University, 550 Main St., Wolfville NS B4P 2R6 Canada
Tel: 902-585-1160; *Fax:* 902-585-1702
e-mail: coordinator@atlanticsustainability.ca
URL: www.atlanticsustainability.ca
Description: The Atlantic Canada Sustainability Initiative (ACSI) is a collaborative project designed to promote and encourage sustainability in Atlantic Canada. It was developed by a network of municipalities, businesses and NGOs in Atlantic Canada in order to better understand the challenges and opportunities of sustainability and to promote sustainability initiatives.

Bay of Fundy Ecosystem Project (BOFEP)

Acadia University, PO Box 115, 23 Westwood Ave., Wolfville NS B4P 2R6 Canada
Tel: 902-585-1113; *Fax:* 902-585-1054
e-mail: secretariat@bofep.org
URL: www.bofep.org
Overview: A organization founded in 1995
Description: The Bay of Fundy Ecosystem Partnership is a collaboration of individuals and groups that seek the well-being of the Bay of Fundy by promoting the integrity, vitality, biodiversity and productivity of the Bay of Fundy Ecosystem, and the social well-being and economic sustainability of its coastal communities and facilitating communication and co-operation among individuals and organizations interested in understanding, sustainably using and conserving the resources, habitats and ecological processes of the Bay of Fundy.

Bluenose Coastal Action Foundation (BCAF)

PO Box 10, 493 Main St., Mahone Nay NS B0J 2E0 Canada
URL: www.coastalaction.org
Overview: A organization founded in 1993
Description: The Bluenose Coastal Action Foundation (BCAF) was established in 1993 to develop action plans to restore human-impacted coastal environments in Lunenburg County Nova Scotia with sustainable use as the goal. The Foundation seeks to facilitate the necessary actions to protect and enhance coastal areas and watersheds through research, education and action.

Centre for Rural Sustainability (CRS)

c/o School of Kinesiology, Acadia University, 550 Main St., Wolfville NS B4P 2R6 Canada
Tel: 902-585-1123; *Fax:* 902-585-1702
e-mail: info@ruralsustainability.org
URL: www.ruralsustainability.org
Description: The Centre for Rural Sustainability is a non-profit organization that works with grassroots groups, educators, youth, and community leaders to promote the growth of sustainable communities and economies in rural Nova Scotia. Services provided include consultation and fundraising assistance.

Clean Annapolis River Project (CARP)

PO Box 395, 151 Victoria St., Annapolis Royal NS B0S 1A0 Canada
Tel: 902-532-7533; *Fax:* 902-532-3038
Toll-Free: 888-547-4344

e-mail: carp@annapolisriver.ca
URL: www.annapolisriver.ca
Overview: A organization founded in 1990
Description: The Clean Annapolis River Project (CARP) is a charitable, community-owned corporation created to work with the community and interested organizations to foster the conservation, restoration and sustainable use of the freshwater and marine ecosystems of Southwestern Nova Scotia's Annapolis River and its watershed. Since 1990 CARP has developed several projects that address pertinent environmental issues in the Annapolis River watershed. These projects range from environmental monitoring to public education to habitat restoration to home assessment.

Clean Nova Scotia
126 Portland St., Dartmouth NS B2Y 1H8 Canada
Tel: 902-420-3474; *Fax:* 902-424-5334
e-mail: cns@clean.ns.ca
URL: www.clean.ns.ca
Overview: A organization founded in 1988
Description: Clean Nova Scotia is a not-for-profit organization founded in 1988, with the mandate to work with individuals, government, business, and communities to improve the environment of Nova Scotia. Clean Nova Scotia is focused on achieving specific goals, such as reduction of fossil fuel use, education, waste reduction, resource conservation and protection, and clean air.

Nova Forest Alliance (NFA)
285 George St., Stewiacke NS B0N 2J0 Canada
Tel: 902-639-2921; *Fax:* 902-639-2981
e-mail: info@novaforestalliance.com
URL: www.novaforestalliance.com
Description: The Nova Forest Alliance (NFA) is a partnership of environmentalists, researcgers, academic institutions, industry, and government agencies committed to finding sustainable forest management solutions in Nova Scotia. The Alliance works on collaborative research and the promotion of sustainable resource management programs to help maintain the ecological integrity of the province.

Nova Scotia. Dept. of Natural Resources
Nova Scotia Habitat Conservation Fund
Wildlife Div., Nova Scotia Dept. of Natural Resources, 136 Exhibition St., Kentville NS B4N 4E5 Canada
Tel: 902-679-6091; *Fax:* 902-679-6176
e-mail: habfund@gov.ns.ca
URL: www.gov.ns.ca/natr/wildlife/habfund/
Description: The Fund assists with projects that protect & enhance wildlife habitats. Priority activities are delineated under the four key objectives of Enhancement, Acquisition, Research, & Education.

Nova Scotia Environmental Network (NSEN)
55 Willowbend Ct., Halifax NS B3M 3L3 Canada
Tel: 902-454-6846; *Fax:* 902-454-6841
e-mail: nsen@cen-rce.org
URL: www.nsen.ca
Overview: A organization founded in 1991
Description: The Nova Scotia Environmental Network (NSEN) is a non-profit organization dedicated to connecting environmental and health organizations to enhance environmental and sustainability projects in Nova Scotia. The NSEN's goal is to provide support for its members by facilitating information exchange and action plans.

Sable Island Preservation Trust (SIPT)
PO Box 622, #310, 1657 Barrington St., Halifax NS B3J 2R7 Canada
Tel: 902-425-7225; *Fax:* 902-425-4793
Toll-Free: 877-707-7225
URL: www.sabletrust.ns.ca
Description: Sable Island Preservation Trust is a non-profit organization established in 1997 to help preserve and protect the Sable Island ecosystem. The Trust's goal is to promote and conduct scientific research, monitoring, andconservation programs which will ensure the long-term stability and viability of Sable Island.

Seagull Foundation
PO Box 108, Pugwash NS B0K 1L0 Canada
Tel: 902-243-2416
Description: To protect significant wilderness areas; to support environmental education & conservation; to support Third World development projects; to support programs that create environmental awareness.

Ontario

Agricultural Institute of Canada Foundation (AICF)
#900, 280 Albert St., Ottawa ON K1P 5G8 Canada
Tel: 613-232-9459; *Fax:* 613-594-5190
Toll-Free: 888-277-7980
e-mail: office@aic.ca
URL: www.aic.ca
Description: Enhancing agriculture & the role it plays in providing Canadians with a safe, affordable, nutritious food supply; supporting activities by universities that improve students' knowledge and understanding of the agricultural industry and its importance to the economy and the environment.

Animal Welfare Foundation of Canada (AWF)
#343, 300 Earl Grey Dr., Ottawa ON K2T AC1 Canada
e-mail: info@awfc.ca
URL: www.awfc.ca
Description: The Animal Welfare Foundation of Canada is a registered charity, supported by donors and administered by a volunteer Board of Directors. The Foundation seeks to improve the quality of life for animals in this country. Since the 1960s the Foundation, an independent watchdog organization, has been at the forefront of issues of humane care of animals in Canada.

Ausable Bayfield Conservation Foundation
71108 Morrison Line, RR#3, Exeter ON N0M 1S5 Canada
Tel: 519-235-2610; *Fax:* 519-235-1963
Toll-Free: 888-286-2610
e-mail: info@abca.on.ca
URL: www.abca.on.ca
Description: Raising funds for conservation, preservation & protection of the natural landscapes of the Ausable River, Bayfield River & Packhill Creek watersheds.

Canada Foundation for Innovation
#450, 230 Queen St., Ottawa ON K1P 5E4 Canada
Tel: 613-947-6496; *Fax:* 613-943-0923
e-mail: info@innovation.ca
URL: www.innovation.ca
Description: The Foundation is an independent corporation, created by the Government of Canada, with a mandate to fund research infrastructure, with particular reference to the research efforts of Canadian universities & colleges, research hospitals, & non-profit research organizations.

Canadian Foundation for Climate and Atmospheric Sciences (CFCAS)
#901, 350 Sparks St., Ottawa ON K1R 7S8 Canada
Tel: 613-238-2223; *Fax:* 613-238-2227
e-mail: bellerive@cfcas.org
URL: www.cfcas.org
Description: The Canadian Foundation for Climate and Atmospheric Sciences provides focused support for excellent university-based research on weather and climate.

Canadian Institutes of Health Research (CIHR)
160 Elgin St., 9th Fl., 4809A, Ottawa ON K1A 0W9 Canada
Tel: 613-941-2672; *Fax:* 613-954-1800
Toll-Free: 888-603-4178
e-mail: info@cihr-irsc.gc.ca
URL: www.cihr-irsc.gc.ca
Description: Established in 2000, CIHR is the agency responsible for funding health research in Canada. Research focusing on environmental impacts on health is just one of many areas the Institute may consider for support.

Canadian Ornamental Plant Foundation (COPF)
5A - #218, 975 McKeown Ave., North Bay ON P1B 9P2 Canada
Tel: 705-495-2563; *Fax:* 705-495-1449
Toll-Free: 800-265-1629
e-mail: info@copf.org
URL: www.copf.org
Description: To encourage new plant development by strengthening relations between growers & breeders for the benefit of the horticulture industry.

Catherine Donnelly Foundation
10 Montcrest Blvd., Toronto ON M4K 1J7 Canada
Tel: 416-461-2996; *Fax:* 416-465-4193
e-mail: info@catherinedonnellyfoundation.org
URL: www.catherinedonnellyfoundation.org
Description: Environmental Enhancement Initiatives: The Foundation will consider applications that advance inter-religious/cultural cooperation on ecological issues; promote public engagement in environmental education and advocacy; advance community based environmental research; advocate ecologically sustainable communities that demonstrate ecological integrity. The Foundation will support groups, projects and initiatives that: Advance a religious/spiritual experience of the earth that leads to healing action for the earth; Promote environmental education that supports broad based public engagement and advocacy; Advocate, build and model sustainable communities that demonstrate ecological integrity; Advance practical and community based environmental research.

Clean Air Foundation
#201, 1216 Yonge St., Toronto ON M4T 1W1 Canada
Tel: 416-922-9038; *Fax:* 416-922-1028
URL: www.cleanairfoundation.org
Description: Dedicated to developing, implementing & managing public engagement programs & other strategic approaches that lead to measurable emission reductions, to improve air quality & protect the climate.

Conservation Foundation
5 Shoreham Dr., Toronto ON M3N 1S4 Canada
Tel: 416-667-6279; *Fax:* 416-667-6275
e-mail: fdn@trca.on.ca
URL: www.trca.on.ca
Description: A leader in the acquisition & management of 13,150 hectares of regional greenspace & watershed conservation lands through its support of watershed management, reforestation, wildlife habitats, public access & recreation, historic sites & environmental rehabilitation of natural spaces.

Conservation Halton Foundation
2596 Britannia Rd., RR#2, Milton ON L9T 2X6 Canada
Tel: 905-336-1158; *Fax:* 905-336-7014
e-mail: admin@hrca.on.ca
URL: www.conservationhalton.on.ca
Description: To raise funds for Conservation Halton projects & programs that protect & enhance the natural environment.

Credit Valley Conservation Foundation
1255 Old Derry Rd. West, Mississauga ON L5N 6R4 Canada
Tel: 905-670-1615; *Fax:* 905-670-2210
Toll-Free: 800-668-5557
e-mail: cvc@creditvalleycons.com
URL: www.creditvalleycons.com
Description: To raise funds & awareness in support of Credit Valley Conservation's goal of an environmentally healthy river for economically & socially healthy communities.

Donner Canadian Foundation
8 Prince Arthur Ave., 3rd Fl., Toronto ON M5R 1A9 Canada
Tel: 416-920-6400; *Fax:* 416-920-5577
e-mail: gosney@donner.ca
URL: www.donnerfoundation.org
Description: The Donner Canadian Foundation was established in 1950 by William H. Donner. In the mid-1960s, the Foundation began to focus on specific program interests, among these, research on public policy. The Donner family chose Canada's centennial year, 1967, to embark on a course of professional grantmaking that has contributed well over $100 million to more than 1,000 projects across Canada and around the world. In addition to ongoing funding of public policy research, the Foundation supports environmental, international development, and social service projects.

Energy Probe Research Foundation (EPRF)
225 Brunswick Ave., Toronto ON M5S 2M6 Canada
Tel: 416-964-9223; *Fax:* 416-964-8239
e-mail: webadmin@eprf.ca
URL: www.eprf.ca
Description: To educate Canadians about the benefits of conservation & renewable energy; to help Canada secure long-term energy self-sufficiency in the shortest possible time with the fewest disruptive effects & with the greatest societal, environmental & economic benefits; to provide business, government & the public with information on energy & energy-related issues; to help Canada contribute to global harmony & prosperity; recipient of the 1990 Lieutenant Governor's Conservation Award, the first time that an environmental organization has been so honoured; divisions include Energy Probe, Probe International, Environment Probe, Margaret Laurence Fund, Consumer Policy Institute, Environmental Bureau of Investigations, Urban Renaissance Institute.

Evergreen
Common Grounds
355 Adelaide St. West, 5th Fl., Toronto ON M5V 1S2 Canada

Tel: 416-596-1495; *Fax:* 416-596-1443
e-mail: info@evergreen.ca
URL: www.evergreen.ca
Description: Common Grounds provides grants to community groups doing environmental stewardship work. This is a national service which helps to protect natural & cultural landscapes, protect spaces for recreation & education, & restore areas that have been damaged. Offices in Toronto, Montréal & Vancouver.

Federation of Canadian Municipalities (FCM)
Green Municipal Fund
24 Clarence St., Ottawa ON K1N 5P3 Canada
Tel: 613-907-6357; *Fax:* 613-244-1515
e-mail: gmf@fcm.ca
URL: www.sustainablecommunities.fcm.ca
Description: FCM's Green Municipal Fund provides financial resources (grants & loans) & services to Canadian municipal governments for the purpose of improving environmental performance & reducing greenhouse gas emissions.

Friends of the Greenbelt Foundation
#201, 68 Scollard St., Toronto ON M5R 1G2 Canada
Tel: 416-960-0001; *Fax:* 416-960-0030
e-mail: info@ourgreenbelt.ca
URL: www.greenbelt.ca
Description: The Friends of the Greenbelt Foundation is a not-for-profit organization. The Foundation was created to help foster our Greenbelt's living countryside by nurturing and supporting activities that preserve its environmental and agricultural integrity.

George Cedric Metcalf Charitable Foundation
174 Ave. Rd., Toronto ON M5R 2J1 Canada
Tel: 416-926-0366; *Fax:* 416-926-0370
e-mail: info@metcalffoundation.com
URL: www.metcalffoundation.com
Description: The Metcalf Environment Program seeks to strengthen and enhance the effectiveness of people and organizations working together to ensure the ecological health and integrity of Southern Ontario's natural and working lands.

Grand River Conservation Foundation
400 Clyde Rd., Cambridge ON N1R 5W6 Canada
Tel: 519-621-2761; *Fax:* 519-621-4844
Toll-Free: 877-294-7263
e-mail: foundation@grandriver.ca
URL: www.grandriver.ca
Description: To provide leadership & support within the community of the Valley of the Grand River for the protection, conservation, responsible use & management of its natural resources, in response to the needs & wishes & for the ongoing enjoyment of its residents, as well as of the broader community of our province & country.

Helen McCrea Peacock Foundation
#1603, 33 Bloor St. East, Toronto ON M4W 3H1 Canada
Tel: 416-921-2035
e-mail: ngodkewitsch@tcf.ca
URL: www.tcf.ca/Default.aspx?tabid=136
Description: The Helen McCrea Peacock Foundation supports environmental organizations whose work and initiatives have a positive impact on the environment with a focus on remediation. The Foundation will fund: Registered Canadian charitable organizations & Environmental initiatives carried out within the Province of Ontario.

Jack Miner Migratory Bird Foundation, Inc.
PO Box 39, Kingsville ON N9Y 2E8 Canada
Tel: 519-733-4034
Toll-Free: 877-289-8328
e-mail: info@jackminer.com
URL: www.jackminer.com
Description: The sanctuary provides food, shelter & protection to migratory water fowl, tags birds & tracks migration patterns.

Lake Simcoe Region Conservation Foundation
PO Box 282, 120 Bayview Pkwy., Newmarket ON L3Y 4X1 Canada
Tel: 905-967-0112; *Fax:* 905-964-1265
Toll-Free: 800-465-0437
e-mail: foundation@lsrca.on.ca
URL: www.lsrca.on.ca/Foundation/index.html
Description: The Lake Simcoe Conservation Foundation (LSCF) invests in projects designed to protect and restore Lake Simcoe. Working in partnership with the Lake Simcoe Region Conservation Authority (LSRCA), watershed municipalities and other partners, they enable vital work to be done that maintains the natural environment, and in many places return the land and the rivers and the streams to a natural state.

Live Green Toronto
Eco-Roof Incentive Program
Toronto Environment Office, City of Toronto, 100 Queen St. W., East Tower, 21st Fl., Toronto ON M5H 2N2 Canada
e-mail: mygreenquestion@toronto.ca; teo@toronto.ca
URL: www.toronto.ca/livegreen/; www.toronto.ca/teo/
Description: Established in 2009, the incentive program promotes the use of green & cool roofs on Toronto's commercial, industrial & institutional buildings. Downloadable application form available on the website. Rebates & refunds for other energy saving practices also available.

The McLean Foundation
#1008, 2 St. Clair Ave. West, Toronto ON M4V 1L5 Canada
Tel: 416-964-6802; *Fax:* 416-964-2804
e-mail: mcleanfoundation.ca
URL: http://mcleanfoundation.ca
Description: The foundation makes grants in a wide range of areas, including arts, conservation, education, health and welfare. It maintains a flexible policy, with particular emphasis on projects showing promise of general social benefit but which may initially lack broad public appeal. In the 63 years of its existence, The McLean Foundation has received net investment income of $36,097,636 and has paid out a total of $37,946,157.

Natural Resources Canada
EcoENERGY Retrofit Incentive
580 Booth St., Ottawa ON K1A 0E4 Canada
Tel: 613-944-4506; *Fax:* 613-992-3161
e-mail: Chantal.Brouillard@NRCan-RNCan.gc.ca
URL: www.ecoaction.gc.ca/ecoenergy-ecoenergie/index-eng.cfm
Description: The ecoENERGY Retrofit - Homes program will provide homeowners with grants of up to $5,000 to offset the cost of making energy-efficiency improvements. Grants apply to a range of measures that reduce energy consumption and provide for a cleaner environment, from increasing insulation to upgrading windows and doors. To qualify, homeowners must first have a pre-retrofit energy evaluation by a certified evaluator and a post evaluation following the renovations. Funds are available for a limited time (to March 31, 2011) and are subject to availability.

The Neptis Foundation
501 - 1240 Bay St., Toronto ON M5R 2A7 Canada
Tel: 416-972-9199; *Fax:* 416-972-9198
URL: www.neptis.org
Description: The Neptis Foundation conducts and publishes nonpartisan research on the past, present and future of urban regions. An independent, privately-capitalized, charitable foundation, Neptis contributes timely, reliable knowledge and analysis on regional urban development to support informed public decisions and foster understanding of regional issues.

Niagara Peninsula Conservation Foundation (NPCF)
250 Thorold Rd. West, 3rd Fl., Welland ON L3C 3W2 Canada
Tel: 905-788-3135; *Fax:* 905-788-1121
e-mail: mcdougal@conservation-niagara.on.ca
URL: www.conservation-niagara.on.ca
Description: To assist the Niagara Peninsula Conservation Authority in the cultivation & advancement of conservation by actively seeking support for conservation projects & programs through fundraising efforts & by serving as the custodian for these donations & gifts.

Oak Ridges Moraine Foundation (ORMF)
The Gate House, 13990 Dufferin St. North, King City ON L7B 1B3 Canada
Tel: 905-833-5733; *Fax:* 905-833-8379
e-mail: support@ormf.com
URL: www.moraineforlife.org
Description: To date the Foundation has distributed $11.5 million in grants. Working closely with ORM partners, they have leveraged $25.3 million in partner funding, resulting in nearly $37 million in 145 new conservation and protection projects on the Moraine.

Ontario. Ministry of Energy & Infrastructure (OSTHI)
Ontario Solar Thermal Heating Incentive Program
Hearst Block, 900 Bay St., 4th Flo., Toronto ON M7A 2E1 Canada
Toll-Free: 888-668-4636
Description: The program supports the installation of solar thermal heating equipment. Applicants must be an industrial, commerical or institutional entity to be considered. Application forms available on the Ministry website.

Ontario. Ministry of Energy & Infrastructure
Hearst Block, 900 Bay St., 4th Fl., Toronto ON M7A 2E1 Canada

The Ontario Trillium Foundation
45 Charles St. East, 5th Fl., Toronto ON M4Y 1S2 Canada
Tel: 416-963-4927; *Fax:* 416-963-8781
Toll-Free: 800-263-2887
e-mail: trillium@trilliumfoundation.org
URL: www.trilliumfoundation.org
Description: The Ontario Trillium Foundation is an agency of the Government of Ontario. The Ontario Trillium Foundation distributes its funding to charities and not-for-profits through two granting programs: Community and Province-Wide. Within those programs, funding is allocated in four sectors: Arts and Culture, Environment, Sports and Recreation, and Human and Social Services.

The Pollution Probe Foundation (PPF)
#402, 625 Church St., Toronto ON M4Y 2G1 Canada
Tel: 416-926-1907; *Fax:* 416-926-1601
e-mail: pprobe@pollutionprobe.org
URL: www.pollutionprobe.org
Description: A registered Canadian charity which seeks to define environmental problems through research; to promote understanding through education & to press for practical solutions through advocacy. The organization is non-partison & works collaboratively with government agencies, other non-profit organizations, & private business to engage key issues & find solutions. Offices in Toronto & Ottawa.

Quetico Foundation
#1260, 390 Bay St., Toronto ON M5E 1G6 Canada
Tel: 416-941-9388; *Fax:* 416-941-9236
e-mail: office@queticofoundation.org
URL: www.queticofoundation.org
Description: To preserve wilderness areas of Ontario for recreation & scientific use.

Richard Ivey Foundation
#400, 11 Church St., Toronto ON M5E 1W1 Canada
Tel: 416-867-9229; *Fax:* 416-601-1689
e-mail: info@ivey.org
URL: www.ivey.org
Description: To pursue & support excellence by making grants that will improve the well-being of Canadians. Today, the Conserving Canada's Forests Program provides critical support for environmental sustainability across the country.

The Salamander Foundation
#1201, 180 Bloor St. West, Toronto ON M5S 2V6 Canada
Tel: 416-972-9200; *Fax:* 416-972-9203
e-mail: info@salamanderfoundation.org
URL: www.salamanderfoundation.org
Description: The Salamander Foundation currently has two areas of interest: Arts and Culture, and the Environment. The Foundation seeks to promote continuity and discovery in the arts and in culture, and to recognize the forms, functions and interactions of natural systems in the environment.

TD Friends of the Environment Foundation
#1100, 45 O'connor St., Ottawa ON K1P 1A4 Canada
Tel: 613-782-1196; *Fax:* 613-783-6319
Toll-Free: 800-361-5333
e-mail: tdfef@td.com
URL: www.td.com/fef
Description: The TD Friends of the Environment Foundation (TD FEF) is a national organization with a grassroots focus that funds local projects dedicated to preserving the environment. They work with Canadians who are committed to protecting the environment in their own community and across the country. Since 1990, the TD Friends of the Environment Foundation has provided more than $47 million to support over 17,500 grassroots environmental projects in communities across Canada. And every year TD Bank Financial Group contributes an additional $1 million to TD FEF.

Temagami Community Foundation
PO Box 338, Temagami ON P0H 2H0 Canada
Tel: 705-569-3737
e-mail: temafoun@onlink.net
URL: www.temagamifoundation.ca
Description: The Temagami Community Foundation is a public Canadian Charitable Foundation. Grants are available for sustainable development & environmental initiatives.

Toronto Atmospheric Fund
75 Elizabeth St., Toronto ON M5G 1P4 Canada
Tel: 416-392-0271; *Fax:* 416-338-0616
e-mail: taf@toronto.ca
URL: www.toronto.ca/taf
Description: Toronto City Council established the Toronto Atmospheric Fund (TAF) in 1991 to finance Toronto-based initiatives that combat global climate change and improve air quality. TAF provides grants and loans and undertakes special projects to advance its mandate. Working with all sectors of the community, and with city departments and agencies, TAF leverages its resources to develop innovative local actions that lead to significant emission reduction results. On an annual basis, TAF has approximately $1.2 million available for grants and special projects. Up to $8 million in financing is currently available for mandate-related loans.

Toronto Parks & Trees Foundation
#123, 157 Adelaide St. W., Toronto ON M5H 4E7 Canada
Tel: 416-397-5178; *Fax:* 416-392-3355
e-mail: parksandtrees@toronto.ca
URL: www.torontoparksandtrees.org
Description: The Foundation coordinates with City of Toronto Parks, Forestry & Recreation to indentify areas of need with regard to the city's parks & public spaces.It raises funds to support park beautification.

T.R. Meighen Family Foundation
#200, 12 Birch Ave., Toronto ON M4V 1C8 Canada
Tel: 416-413-1999; *Fax:* 416-413-0015
e-mail: info@meighen.ca
URL: www.meighen.ca
Description: The T.R. Meighen Family Foundation is a private charitable foundation that was established by letters patent in April 1969 with a gift from the founder, Mr. Theodore Roosevelt Meighen. Over the past 37 years the foundation has granted over 15 million dollars to various projects. Most of this support has been directed to community based activities in the fields of education, health, social welfare, cultural and environmental conservation.

Transport Canada
Moving on Sustainable Transportation Program
Place de Ville, Tower C, 18th Fl., 330 Sparks St., Ottawa ON K1A 0N5 Canada
Tel: 613-998-6607; *Fax:* 613-949-3874
e-mail: MOST-SRTD@tc.gc.ca
URL: www.tc.gc.ca/programs/environment/MOST/menu.htm
Description: Transport Canada has established the Moving On Sustainable Transportation (MOST) Program to support projects that produce the kinds of education, awareness and analytical tools we need if we are to make sustainable transportation a reality. The MOST Program will provide funding to help support projects that will: Stimulate the development of innovative tools, approaches and practices for increasing the sustainability of Canada's transportation system and the use of sustainable modes of transportation; Realize quantifiable environmental and sustainable development results on Transport Canada's sustainable development priorities; and Provide Canadians with practical information, tools and opportunities for better incorporating sustainable transportation options into their daily lives.

Transport Canada
330 Sparks St., Ottawa ON K1A 0N5 Canada

Tree Canada Foundation (TCF)
#402, 222 Somerset St. West, Ottawa ON K2P 2G3 Canada
Tel: 613-567-5545; *Fax:* 613-567-5270
Toll-Free: 877-666-1444
e-mail: tcf@treecanada.ca
URL: www.treecanada.ca
Description: To provide education, technical support, resources & financial support through working partnerships to encourage Canadians to plant & care for trees in our urban & rural environment in an effort to help reduce the harmful effects of carbon dioxide emissions.

Trees Ontario
50 Million Tree Program
#701, 200 Consumers Rd., Toronto ON M2J 4R4 Canada
Tel: 416-646-1193; *Fax:* 416-493-4608
Toll-Free: 877-646-1193
e-mail: info@treesontario.on.ca
URL: www.treesontario.ca
Description: A program introduced in 2007 by the Ontario Government to fund the planting of 50 million trees across the province by 2020, as part of its commitment to reduce greenhouse gas effects, fight climate change & "green" the province.

Trees Ontario
#701, 200 Consumers Rd., Toronto ON M2J 4R4 Canada

Unilever Canada Foundation
#1500, 160 Bloor St. East, Toronto ON M4W 3R2 Canada
Tel: 416-964-1857; *Fax:* 416-963-5197
URL: www.unilever.ca/ourvalues/environmentandsociety/UC_Foundation
Description: Founded as a registered charity in 1995 - The Unilever Canada Foundation donates approximately 1% of Unilever Canada's pre-tax profit towards its community initiatives. Unilever Canada's community vitality initiative focuses mainly on the two areas that we feel are most significant to Canada and its people; - helping the healthy development of children between the ages of 0-5 and the environment - by protecting rivers, lakes and wetlands.

The W. Garfield Weston Foundation
c/o George Weston Ltd., #2001, 22 St. Clair Ave. East, Toronto ON M4T 2S3 Canada
Tel: 416-922-2500; *Fax:* 416-967-7949
e-mail: info@westonfoundation.org
URL: www.westonfoundation.org
Description: Focuses on education (through a scholarship & bursary program), conservation (via habitat conservation projects through national organizations only), & trustee-initiated grants (for which applications are not accepted).

Walter & Duncan Gordon Foundation
#400, 11 Church St., Toronto ON M5E 1W1 Canada
Tel: 416-601-4776; *Fax:* 416-601-1689
e-mail: gordon@gordonfn.org
URL: www.gordonfn.org
Description: The Walter & Duncan Gordon Foundation is dedicated to the development of sound and innovative public policies, founded on those values fundamental to Canadians, and designed to foster the continuing evolution of a dynamic and independent Canada. They believe that human development needs must be met in a way that recognizes the imperative to protect the environment.

Prince Edward Island

Bedeque Bay Environmental Management Association (BBEMA)
PO Box 8310, Emerald PE C0B 1M0 Canada
Tel: 902-886-3211
URL: www.bbema.ca
Overview: A organization founded in 1992
Description: The Bedeque Bay Environmental Management Association (BBEMA) is a not-for-profit charitable organization originally established in 1992 as an Atlantic Coastal Action Program site under Environment Canada. The BBEMA's goal is to provide sustainable environmental opportunities to the citizens of the area through planning, education, partnerships, and projects. The BBEMA focuses on soil erosion, water quality, natural habitat conservation, climate change, and public awareness projects and actitvies.

Environmental Coalition of Prince Edward Island (ECO-PEI)
126 Richmond St., Charlottetown PE C1A 1H9 Canada
Tel: 902-566-4696; *Fax:* 902-566-4037
e-mail: energy@ecopei.ca
URL: www.ecopei.ca
Overview: A organization founded in 1988
Description: The Environmental Coalition of Prince Edward Island (ECO-PEI) is a community based action group formed in 1988. ECO-PEI's goal is to work in partnership to understand and improve the Island environment. Projects supported by ECO-PEI include research into renewable energy and energy efficiency and natural resource conservation.

Island Nature Trust
PO Box 265, Charlottetown PE C1A 7K4 Canada
Tel: 902-566-9150; *Fax:* 902-628-6331
e-mail: intrust@eastlink.ca
URL: www.islandnaturetrust.ca
Overview: A organization founded in 1979
Description: The Island Nature Trust is a non-government, not-for-profit organization dedicated to protection and management of Natural Areas on Prince Edward Island. The Trust conducts and supports projects including land aquisition and protection, habitat restoration and management, conservation, and education.

Prince Edward Island. Dept. of Environment, Energy & Forestry
Greening Spaces Program
J. Frank Gaudet Tree Nursery, PO Box 2000, Charlottetown PE C1A 7N8 Canada
Tel: 902-368-4800; *Fax:* 902-368-4806
e-mail: greeningspaces@gov.pe.ca
URL: www.gov.pe.ca
Description: Funds tree planting projects, provides quality native tree & shrub seedlings, education materials, & technical advice. Communities, schools & volunteer interest groups are invited to submit proposals for projects.

Prince Edward Island. Dept. of Environment, Energy & Forestry
Environment Futures Program
J. Frank Gaudet Tree Nursery, PO Box 2000, Charlottetown PE C1A 7N8 Canada
Tel: 902-368-5000; *Fax:* 902-368-5830
URL: www.gov.pe.ca
Description: A summer program that trains high school & university students to do environmental protection work in their regions. Organizations may apply to have student work teams provide labour for their environmental projects. Projects such as enhancement of fish & wildlife habitat, soil erosion control, protecting & enhancing natural areas, & solid waste management/clean-up are suggested, but other projects that provide demonstrable environmental benefit to the community, & offer educational & work experience to students will be considered for funding.

Québec

The Aboriginal Funds for Species at Risk
Gatineau QC K1A 0H3 Canada
URL: www.recovery.gc.ca/afsar-faep/
Description: Established in 2004, AFSR recognizes the role Aboriginal people play in wildlife conservation & is comprised of 2 funds: the Aboriginal Capacity Building Fund, & the Aboriginal Critical Habitat Protection Fund. The aim of the funds is to help Aboriginal communities & organizations build capacity to enable participation in the conservation & recovery of protected species & species at risk, & to protect & recover the critical habitat of species at risk on Aboriginal lands. Regional offices across Canada - please consult the website for complete contact details.

Canadian Wildlife Service
Habitat Stewardship Program
351 boul St-Joseph, Gatineau QC K1A 0H3 Canada
Tel: 819-997-1301; *Fax:* 819-953-7177
URL: www.cws-scf.ec.gc.ca/hsp-pih
Description: As part of Canada's national strategy for the protection of species at risk, the federal government established the Habitat Stewardship Program (HSP) for Species at Risk. The HSP became operational in 2000-2001 and allocates up to $10 million per year to projects that conserve and protect species at risk and their habitats. The overall goal of the HSP is to "contribute to the recovery of endangered, threatened, and other species at risk, and to prevent other species from becoming a conservation concern, by engaging Canadians from all walks of life in conservation actions to benefit wildlife."

Canadian Wildlife Service
Interdepartmental Recovery Fund
351 boul St-Joseph, 4e étage, Gatineau QC K1A 0H3 Canada
Tel: 819-997-4325; *Fax:* 819-956-5993
URL: www.sararegistry.gc.ca/involved/funding/irf_fir/default_e.cfm
Description: As part of the National Strategy for the Protection of Species at Risk, the federal government has established the Interdepartmental Recovery Fund (IRF) for federal departments and departmental corporations. The IRF became operational in the 2002-2003 fiscal year. The IRF provides funding to federal departments and departmental corporations for implementing recovery activities for species designated by the Committee on the Status of Endangered Wildlife in Canada (COSEWIC) as nationally extirpated, endangered or threatened that are on federal lands or under federal jurisdiction. IRF also supports surveys of endangered, threatened and extirpated species on federal lands. As such, it supports federal organizations in their efforts to meet the requirements of the Species At Risk Act. This program also fosters partnerships among federal organizations

and with other organizations interested in the recovery of species at risk.

Canadian Wildlife Service
351 St-Joseph Blvd., Gatineau QC K1A 0H3 Canada

Commission for Environmental Cooperation (CEC)
393, rue St-Jacques Ouest, Montréal QC H2Y 1N9 Canada
Tel: 514-350-4300; *Fax:* 514-350-4314
e-mail: info@cec.org
URL: www.cec.org
Description: The Commission for Environmental Cooperation (CEC) is an international organization created by Canada, Mexico and the United States under the North American Agreement on Environmental Cooperation (NAAEC). The CEC was established to address regional environmental concerns, help prevent potential trade and environmental conflicts, and to promote the effective enforcement of environmental law. The Agreement complements the environmental provisions of the North American Free Trade Agreement (NAFTA).

The EJLB Foundation
#1050, 1350 rue Sherbrooke ouest, Montréal QC H3G 1J1 Canada
Tel: 514-843-4080
URL: www.ejlb.qc.ca
Description: The EJLB Foundation has two main areas of interest: Mental health and support to community organizations providing assistance to persons suffering from mental illness; Protection of the environment, mainly through the acquisition and preservation, throughout Canada, of natural areas of ecological significance or of importance to the urban landscape. The Foundation also provides support, on a case by case basis, for a variety of other concrete environmental endeavours.

Fondation Hydro-Québec pour l'environnement
740, rue Notre-Dame Ouest, 8e étage, Montréal QC H3C 3X6 Canada
Tel: 514-289-5384; *Fax:* 514-289-2079
e-mail: fondation-environnement@hydro.qc.ca
URL: www.hydroquebec.com/fondation-environnement
Description: The Fondation Hydro-Québec pour l'environnement is a nonprofit organization whose mission is to help Québec communities develop a sense of ownership of their environment, enjoy it responsibly and pass on their natural heritage to future generations. The Foundation funds tangible initiatives that have positive environmental and social impacts and that serve the interests of local communities throughout Québec. It partners with local organizations on projects designed to: protect, restore and enhance natural habitats, and educate target audiences about local environmental issues.

Fonds d'action québécois pour le développement durable (FAQDD)
#200, 840, rue Raoul-Jobin, Québec QC G1N 1S7 Canada
Tel: 418-692-5888; *Fax:* 418-692-1148
e-mail: infos@faqdd.qc.ca
URL: www.faqdd.qc.ca
Description: Sponsored by the Government of Québec, the fund provides assistance to projects that emphasize behavioural changes that lead to positive steps towards sustainable development improvement. Projects., which may focus on air, water, soil, biodiversity, health, etc., must be collaborative in nature (between non-profit & business partners, for example).

Fonds d'action québécois pour le développement durable (FAQDD)
#200, 840, rue Raoul-Jobin, Québec QC G1N 1S7 Canada
Tel: 418-692-5888; *Fax:* 418-692-1148
e-mail: infos@faqdd.qc.ca
URL: www.faqdd.qc.ca
Description: Créé en mars 2000, le Fonds d'action québécois pour le développement durable (FAQDD) est un organisme à but non lucratif qui offre des programmes d'aide financière destinés à soutenir l'intégration du développement durable au cour des comportements des Québécoises et des Québécois. Pour la réalisation de sa mission, le FAQDD s'est vu confié une enveloppe budgétaire de 51 millions de dollars du gouvernement du Québec.

Jour de la Terre Québec
Fonds Écomunicipalité IGA
#504, 460, rue Sainte-Catherine Ouest, Montréal QC H3B 1A7 Canada
Tel: 514-728-0116
Toll-Free: 800-424-8758
e-mail: fonds@jourdelaterre.org
URL: www.jourdelaterre.org
Description: The fund, jointly sponsored by Jour de la Terre Québec & IGA, was established to provide Québec organizations & municipalities funding for sustainable development projects. Projects should focus on environmental conservation, protection, and reclamation, or recycling/reuse, & should outline practical strategies & solutions.

Jour de la Terre Québec
#504, 460, rue Sainte-Catherine Ouest, Montréal QC H3B 1A7 Canada

Québec-Labrador Foundation (Canada) Inc.
#901, 505 boul. René Lévesque Ouest, Montréal QC H2Z 1Y7 Canada
Tel: 514-395-6020; *Fax:* 514-395-4505
e-mail: montreal@qlf.org
URL: www.qlf.org
Description: To promote local leadership & assist in improvement of human conditions in northern New England, Eastern Québec, & Canadian Atlantic provinces; to conserve cultural heritage & natural resources of region; to conduct scientific research; to enrich educational experience of Canadian & US students.

Saskatchewan

Communities of Tomorrow
Innovation Place, #250, 10 Research Dr., Regina SK S4S 7J7 Canada
Tel: 306-522-6699; *Fax:* 306-522-6695
e-mail: info@communitiesoftomorrow.ca
URL: www.communitiesoftomorrow.ca
Description: Communities of Tomorrow brings together into a non-profit corporation The City of Regina, The University of Regina, The Saskatchewan Ministry of Enterprise & Innovation, Western Economic Diversification Canada, & the National Research Council. The role of the corporation is to build partnerships that create sustainable communities in Saskatchewan, with a view to addressing such areas as transportation, water, sewer, & waste systems, & developing innovative solutions to infrastructure challenges in municipalities.

The Kongsgaard-Goldman Foundation
#602, 1932 First Ave., Seattle WA 98101 USA
Tel: 206-448-1874; *Fax:* 206-448-1973
e-mail: kgf@kongsgaard-goldman.org
URL: www.kongsgaard-goldman.org
Description: The Kongsgaard-Goldman Foundation is a small, private foundation formed in 1988. The Foundation provides support to a wide range of nonprofit organizations in the Pacific Northwest (Washington, Oregon, Idaho, Alaska, Montana and British Columbia, Canada). Within the program areas of human rights, civic development, environmental protection, and arts and humanities, the Foundation favors projects reflecting a deep and broad level of citizen participation and leadership. Our priority is to help fund the building of grassroots organizations with the power to change their communities and improve their lives.

Yukon Territory

Laidlaw Foundation
#2000, 365 Bloor St. East, Toronto on M4W 3L4 Canada
Tel: 416-964-3614; *Fax:* 416-975-1428
e-mail: mail@laidlawfdn.org
URL: www.laidlawfdn.org
Description: The Foundation's current work promotes positive youth development through inclusive youth engagement in the arts, environment and in community. It recognizes that all young people need the unconditional support of significant adults in their lives and need multiple opportunities to locate an individual talent and the resources necessary to develop that talent.

Alberta

Calgary

Bennett Jones LLP - Calgary
#4500, Bankers Hall East Tower, 855 - 2nd St. SW, Calgary, AB T2P 4K7
Tel: 403-298-3100; *Fax:* 403-265-7219
www.bennettjones.ca
twitter.com/BennettJonesLaw
Profile: 9 Offices, 362 Lawyers, Founded in: 1922
Environmental Lawyers:
Sean R. Assié, Environmental; Oil & Gas; Regulatory
403-298-3083
assies@bennettjones.com
Lawrence D. Ator, Construction
403-298-3148
atorl@bennettjones.com
Darryl J. Barber, Q.C., Partner, Construction; Public Infrastructure Projects
403-298-3001
barberd@bennettjones.com
Robert P. Bodnar, Mining; Oil & Gas
403-298-3380
bodnarr@bennettjones.com
Robert T. Booth, Q.C., Partner, Construction; Electricity; Mining; Oil & Gas; Public Infrastructure Projects
403-298-3252
boothb@bennettjones.ca
Scott H.D. Bower, Partner, Energy Litigation; Research
403-298-3301
bowers@bennettjones.ca
Denise D. Bright, Partner, Oil & Gas; Public Infrastructure Projects
403-298-4468
brightd@bennettjones.ca
Drew C. Broughton, Oil & Gas
403-298-8140
broughtona@bennettjones.com
Marie H. Buchinski, Partner, Electricity; Environemtal; Oil & Gas; Regulatory; Renewable Energy & Fuels
403-298-8136
buchinskim@bennettjones.ca
John F. Cordeau, Q.C., Partner, Oil & Gas
403-298-3267
cordeauj@bennettjones.ca
John N. Craig, Partner, Construction; Energy Litigation
403-298-3463
craigj@bennettjones.ca
James A. D'Andrea, Partner, Oil & Gas
403-298-3271
dandreaj@bennettjones.ca
Marianne (Chuck) Davies, Electricity; Environmental; Regulatory
403-298-4474
daviesc@bennettjones.com
Kelsey J. Drozdowski, Construction; Environmental
403-298-3323
drozdowskik@bennettjones.ca
Nicholas P. Fader, Partner, Oil & Gas
403-298-3474
fadern@bennettjones.ca
Paul M. Farion, Partner, Electricity
403-298-3610
farionp@bennettjones.ca
Anthony L. Friend, Q.C., Partner, Energy Litigation; Oil & Gas
403-298-3182
frienda@bennettjones.ca
Andrea L. Froese, Partner, Energy Litigation; Environmental; Oil & Gas
403-298-3698
froesea@bennettjones.com
Daniel T. Gallagher, Q.C., Partner, Construction; Energy Litigation
403-298-3232
gallagherd@bennettjones.ca
Brad Gilmour, Partner, Climate Change & Emissions Testing; Electricity; Environmental Law; Oil & Gas; Regulatory; Renewable Energy & Fuels
403-298-3382
gilmourb@bennettjones.ca
Laurie A. Goldbach, Partner, Energy Litigation
403-298-3614
goldbachl@bennettjones.ca
Alison J. Gray, Construction; Energy Litigation
403-298-2063
graya@bennettjones.ca
Donald E. Greenfield, Partner, Climate Change & Emissions Trading; Electricity; Oil & Gas
403-298-3248
greenfieldd@bennettjones.ca
Nicholas M. Gretener, Partner, Regulatory; Electricity; Oil & Gas
403-298-3405
gretenern@bennettjones.ca
April D. Grosse, Partner, Energy Litigation
403-298-4442
grossea@bennettjones.ca
Lyle G. Guard, Climate Change & Emissions Trading; Construction
403-298-2068
guardl@bennettjones.com
Tracy L. Hall, Construction; Electricity; Oil & Gas
403-298-3431
hallt@bennettjones.com
Kristos J. Iatridis, Construction
403-298-3285
iatridisk@bennettjones.com
Karen L. Illsey, Partner, Electricity; Environmental; Oil & Gas; Regulatory Law
403-298-3318
illseyk@bennettjones.com
Brenda J. Johnson, Health Law; Research
403-298-3641
johnsonb@bennettjones.ca
Kimberly M. Kapesi-Miller, Construction; Oil & Gas
403-298-8162
millerk@bennettjones.com
H. Martin Kay, Q.C., Counsel, Electricity; Oil & Gas; Research
403-298-3180
kaym@bennettjones.ca
Loyola G. Keough, Partner, Regulatory; Environmental; Oil & Gas; Electricity; renewable Energy & Fuels
403-298-3429
keoughl@bennettjones.ca
Krishna P. Koul, Oil & Gas
403-298-7973
koulk@bennettjones.com
Lev Kramar, Oil & Gas
403-298-3116
kramarl@bennettjones.com
Russell J. Kruger, Energy Litigation; Research
403-298-3487
krugerr@bennettjones.com
Justin R. Lambert, Energy Litigation
403-298-3046
lambertj@bennettjones.com
Margaret G. Lemay, Partner, Oil & Gas
403-298-3122
lemaym@bennettjones.ca
David M. Lennox, Partner, Electricity; Oil & Gas
403-298-3124
lennoxd@bennettjones.ca
Kenneth T. Lenz, Partner, Energy Litigation
403-298-3317
lenzk@bennettjones.ca
Laurel Lui, Energy Litigation
403-298-3121
luil@bennettjones.com
David J. Macaulay, Partner, Construction; Electricity; Oil & Gas; Renewable Energy & Fuels
403-298-3479
macaulayd@bennettjones.ca
Patrick T. Maguire, Partner, Climate Change & Emissions Testing; Construction; Electricity; Oil & Gas
403-298-3184
maguirep@bennettjones.ca
Steven L. Major, Partner, Construction; Oil & Gas; Health Law
403-298-3643
majors@bennettjones.ca
Thomas W. McInerney, Partner, Climate Change & Emissions Trading; Construction; Electricity
400-298-4484
mcinerneyt@bennettjones.ca
David R. McKinnon, Energy Litigation
403-298-3495
mckinnond@bennettjones.com
Duncan M. McPherson, Environmental; Oil & Gas; Renewable Energy & Fuels
403-298-3255
mcphersond@bennettjones.com
E. Bruce Mellett, Partner, Construction; Energy Litigation
403-298-3319
mellettb@bennettjones.ca
Kristin J. Millar, Environmental; Regulatory
403-298-3249
millark@bennettjones.com
Angus B. Mitchell, Partner, Construction; Electricity; Oil & Gas
403-298-3023
mitchella@bennettjones.ca
Munaf Mohamed, Partner, Energy Litigation
403-298-4456
mohamedm@bennettjones.com
Shawn M. Munro, Partner, Environmental; Regulatory Law
403-298-3481
munros@bennettjones.ca
Michael D. Mysak, Partner, Construction
403-298-8143
mysakm@bennettjones.ca
Daron K. Naffin, Partner, Electricity; Environmental; Oil & Gas; Regulatory; Renewable Energy & Fuels
403-298-3668
naffind@bennettjones.ca
Bradley G. Nemetz, Q.C., Partner, Construction
403-298-3194
nemetzb@bennettjones.ca
Chelsea L. Nickles, Climate Change & Emissions Trading; Electricity; Renewable Energy & Fuels
403-298-3371
nicklesc@bennettjones.com
William S. Osler, Partner, Oil & Gas
406-298-3426
oslerw@bennettjones.ca
Darrell R. Peterson, Partner, Oil & Gas
403-298-3316
petersond@bennettjones.ca
Jean-Pierre Pham, Partner, Construction; Environmental; Oil & Gas
403-298-4462
phamj@bennettjones.ca
Mark S. Powell, Partner, Electricity; Oil & Gas
403-298-3365
powellm@bennettjones.ca
Valerie R. Prather, Partner, Energy Litigation; Health Law
403-298-3486
pratherv@bennettjones.ca
Cairns E. Price, Electricity; Environmental Law; Oil & Gas; Regulatory
403-298-8154
pricec@bennettjones.com
Brian P. Reid, Construction; Energy Litigation
403-298-3146
reidb@bennettjones.com
Tariq Remtulla, Oil & Gas
403-298-3022
remtullat@bennettjones.com
D. Alan Ross, Oil & Gas
403-298-3354
rossa@bennettjones.ca
Jason D. Roth, Partner, Construction; Oil & Gas
403-298-2070
rothj@bennettjones.com
Jeremy A.J. Russell, Oil & Gas
403-298-3151
russellj@bennettjones.com
Kieran F. Ryan, Oil & Gas
403-298-3187
ryank@bennettjones.com
Lenard M. Sali, Q.C., Partner, Energy Litigation
403-298-3469
sali@bennettjones.ca

Allison M. Sears, Regulatory
403-298-3681
searsa@bennettjones.com
Deirdre A. Sheehan, Partner, Environmental; Regulatory Law
403-298-3090
sheehand@bennettjones.ca
Christopher D. Simard, Partner, Energy Litigation
403-298-4485
simardc@bennettjones.ca
Christopher R. Skelton, Partner, Oil & Gas; Public Infrastructure Projects
403-298-3309
skeltonc@bennettjones.ca
Lawrence E. Smith, Q.C., Partner, Regulatory Law; Environmental; Transportation Law
403-298-3315
smithl@bennettjones.ca
Perry Spitznagel, Q.C., Vice-Chair & Managing Partner, Oil & Gas
403-298-3153
spitznagelp@bennettjones.ca
Grant N. Stapon, Q.C., Partner, Energy Litigation
403-298-3204
stapong@bennettjones.ca
Michael P. Theroux, Partner, Energy Litigation; Health Law
403-298-4438
therouxm@bennettjones.ca
Jon C. Truswell, Partner, Oil & Gas
403-298-3097
truswellj@bennettjones.ca
George M. Vlavianos, Partner, Construction; Energy Litigation
403-298-3608
vlavianosg@bennettjones.ca
Vivek T.A. Warrier, Partner, Construction; Electricity; Oil & Gas
403-298-3040
warrierv@bennettjones.ca
R. Blake Williams, Environmental; Oil & Gas; Regulatory
403-298-4483
williamsb@bennettjones.com
Blair C. Yorke-Slader, Q.C., Partner, Energy Litigation
403-298-3291
yorkesladerb@bennettjones.ca
Yun Zhu, Oil & Gas
403-298-3420
zhuy@bennettjones.com

Bishop & McKenzie LLP

#1700, 530 - 8th Ave. SW, Calgary, AB T2P 3S8
Tel: 403-237-5550; *Fax:* 403-263-3423
www.bishopmckenzie.com
Anthony L. Dekens, Associate, Construction Law; Employment Law
a.dekens@bishopmckenzie.com
Kerry Lynn Okita, Associate, Employment Law
k.okita@bishopmckenzie.com

Borden Ladner Gervais LLP - Calgary

#1900, Centennial Place, East Tower, 520 - 3rd Ave. SW, Calgary, AB T2P 0R3
Tel: 403-232-9500; *Fax:* 403-266-1395
info@blg.com
www.blg.com
Profile: 114 Lawyers
Environmental Lawyers:

Brownlee LLP - Calgary

#2000, Watermark Tower, 530 - 8th Ave. SW, Calgary, AB T2P 3S8
Tel: 403-232-8300; *Fax:* 403-232-8408
Toll-Free: 877-232-8303
contactus@brownleelaw.com
www.brownleelaw.com
Profile:
Brownlee LLP is a mid-sized regional law firm. Its main office is in Edmonton. Lawyers at the Calgary office have expertise in envrionmental law, municipal & public sector law, planning & development, & oil & gas law.
The Brownlee LLP environmental team assists clients in the following areas: defence of municipalities, land use planning, environmental due diligence, compliance with environmental & safety legislation, implementation of environmental management systems, waste management, water rights, & environmental spills.
In the energy sector, lawyers have worked on behalf of royalty owners, government entities, producers, & oil & gas companies across Alberta & western Canada. Lawyers advise on due diligence, exploration & development contracts, construction & plant operating agreements.
Environmental Lawyers:
Kelley L. Fiske-Nielsen, Associate, Environmental Law; Administrative Law; Municipal & Public Sector Law; Planning & Development
403-260-1464
kfiske.nielsen@brownleelaw.com
Mark Henderson, Associate, Municipal & Public Sector Law
403-260-1479
mhenderson@brownleelaw.com
Derek J. King, Partner, Environmental Law; Municipal & Public Sector Law; Planning & Development
403-260-1472
dking@brownleelaw.com
Marlena (Marny) Paul, Municipal & Public Sector Law; Administrative Law
403-260-5314
mpaul@brownleelaw.com
Glen B. Scott, QC, Partner, Infrastructure & Utilities; Municipal Law; Oil & Gas; Planning & Development
403-260-5302
gscott@brownleelaw.com
Paul S. Taylor, Associate, Planning & Development; Construction; Labour & Employment
403-260-5312
ptaylor@brownleelaw.com

Burnet, Duckworth & Palmer LLP

#2400, 525 - 8th Ave. SW, Calgary, AB T2P 1G1
Tel: 403-260-0100; *Fax:* 403-260-0332
counsel@bdplaw.com
www.bdplaw.com
Profile: 1 Office, 145 Lawyers, Founded in: 1905
Legal services in the commercial area relate to the following: oil & gas acquisitions & divestitures; public & private energy financing; major energy projects; exploration & development business structures; the formulation of energy policy; & legislation relating to federal & provincial petroleum & natural gas lands. Environmental lawyers offer clients comprehensive legal services encompassing virtually every aspect of regulatory environmental law & occupational health & safety issues.
Environmental Lawyers:
R. Bruce Allford, Partner, Energy
403-260-0247
rba@bdplaw.com
Brandon Barnes, Regulatory Energy
403-260-0130
jbb@bdplaw.com
Paul A. Beke, Occupational Health & Safety
R. Bruce Brander, Energy & Non-Energy Developments (Regulatory)
403-260-0165
rbb@bdplaw.com
Harry S. Campbell, Q.C., Senior Partner; Chair, Energy
403-260-0281
hsc@bdplaw
Barry R. Crump, Partner, Energy
403-260-0352
brc@bdplaw.com
John H. Cuthbertson, Partner, Energy
403-260-0305
jhc@bdplaw
Michael J. Donaldson, Partner, Energy
403-260-0228
mjd@bdplaw
John C. Goetz, Energy
David R. Haigh, Q.C., Partner, Occupational Health & Safety
403-260-0135
drh@bdplaw.com
Mark T. Houston, Partner, Energy, Climate Change
403-260-0375
mta@bdplaw
Cal D. Johnson, Q.C., Partner, Energy
403-260-0203
cdj@bdplaw.com
Jonathan M. Liteplo, Regulatory Energy; Water & Drainage Regulatory
403-260-0310
jml@bdplaw.com
John E. Lowe, Partner, Regulatory Energy & Telecommunications
403-260-0257
jel@bdplaw.com
Daniel J. McDonald, Q.C., Partner, Energy
403-260-5724
djm@bdplaw.com
Douglas A. McGillivray, Partner, Energy
403-260-0349
dam@bdplaw.com
Keith F. Miller, Partner, Energy & Non-Energy Development (Regulatory)
403-260-0153
kfm@bdplaw.com
Douglas G. Mills, Partner, Energy, Occupational Health & Safety
403-260-0226
dgm@bdplaw
J. Stuart Money, Energy
Melissa Moulton Tennison, Occupational Health & Safety
James D. Murphy, Occupational Health & Safety
Doug Nishimura, Partner, Energy
403-260-0269
dsn@bdplaw.com
Louise Novinger Grant, Partner, Energy
403-260-0163
lng@bdplaw
Arnold Olyan, Energy
403-260-0249
aho@bdplaw.com
Patricia E. Olyslager, Occupational Health & Safety
Alan T. Pettie, Partner, Energy
403-260-0127
atp@bdplaw.com
Rory G. Polson, Partner, Energy
403-260-0223
rgp@bdplaw.com
Kathy L. Pybus, Partner, Energy
403-260-0196
klp@bdplaw.com
Alicia K. Quesnel, Partner, Energy
403-260-0233
akq@bdplaw.com
Patricia Quinton-Campbell, Partner, Regulatory; Energy
403-260-0308
pqc@bdplaw.com
Jeff Sharpe, Partner, Occupational Health & Safety
403-260-0176
jes@bdplaw.com
Richard F. Steele, Partner, Energy
403-260-0151
rfs@bdplaw.com
David H. Strand, Partner, Energy
403-260-0259
dhs@bdplaw.com
John K. Taylor, Partner, Energy, Climate Change
403-260-0386
jkt@bdplaw.com
Allan R. Twa, Q.C., Partner, Energy
403-260-0221
art@bdplaw.com
W.H. Winters, Partner, Climate Change
403-260-0248
whw@bdplaw.com
Jody L. Wivcharuk, Partner, Energy
403-260-0129
jlw@bdplaw.com
Shannon L. Wray, Partner, Energy
403-260-0245
slw@bdplaw.com
Carolyn A. Wright, Energy

Carscallen LLP

#1500, 407 - 2 St. SW, Calgary, AB T2P 2Y3
Tel: 403-262-3775; *Fax:* 403-262-2952
info@carscallen.com
www.carscallen.com
Profile: 1 Office, 0 Lawyers,
Areas of practice at the independent Alberta law firm include construction law & oil & gas legal services.
Environmental Lawyers:
Glenn C. Blackett, Partner, Oil & Gas; Construction Law
403-298-8474
Blackett@Carscallen.com
Stanley Carscallen, Q.C., Partner, Oil & Gas
403-298-8451
Carscallen@Carscallen.com
Catherine A. Crang, Partner, Oil & Gas
403-298-8467
Crang@Carscallen.com

Donald C. Edie, Q.C., Counsel, Oil & Gas
403-298-8455
edie@carscallen.com
Allan L. Holme, Partner, Oil & Gas
403-298-8445
holme@carscallen.com
John A. MacIver, Partner, Construction Law
403-298-8452
maciver@carscallen.com
Michael B. Niven, Q.C., Partner, Oil & Gas
403-298-8464
niven@carscallen.com
Suzanne M. Porteous, Counsel, Oil & Gas
403-298-9288
porteous@carscallen.com
David L. Sevalrud, ICD.D., Partner, Oil & Gas
403-298-9290
Sevalrud@Carscallen.com
George Tai, Partner, Oil & Gas
403-298-9283
tai@carscallen.com
Leslie J. Weekes, Partner, Oil & Gas
403-298-8456
weekes@carscallen.com
Michael J. Whiting, Partner, Construction Law
403-298-8473
whiting@carscallen.com

D'Arcy & Deacon LLP - Calgary

#300, Notre Dame Place, 255 - 17th Ave. SW, Calgary, AB T2S 2T8
Tel: 403-266-5376; *Fax:* 403-266-5396
inquiries@darcydeacon.com
www.darcydeacon.com
Profile: 3 Lawyers,
The main office for D'Arcy & Deacon LLP is located in Winnipeg, Manitoba. At the Calgary branch office, lawyers are available with expertise in environmental, agricultural, regulatory, Aboriginal, municipal, & construction law.
D'Arcy & Deacon lawyers have represented government departments, municipalities, & corporations on environmental issues such as contaminated sites, oil & gas projects, air & water regulation, & permits & approvals.
Environmental Lawyers:
Bruce Corenblum, Associate, Construction; Municipal Law
bcorenblum@darcydeacon.com
Orvel L. Currie, Partner, Environmental Law; Municipal Law; Agricultural Law; Administrative & Regulatory Law; Aboriginal Law
ocurrie@darcydeacon.com

Davis LLP - Calgary

#1000, Livingston Place, 250 - 2nd St. SW, Calgary, AB T2P 0C1
Tel: 403-296-4470; *Fax:* 403-296-4474
www.davis.ca
Profile: 39 Lawyers,
The Environmental Law Group consists of a team of lawyers with extensive experience in advising clients in all aspects of environmental law. Experience ranges from providing clients with an understanding of the ever-changing regulatory landscape, to acting on civil litigation & in the defence of environmental prosecutions.
Environmental Lawyers:
Derrick K. Auch, Mining law; Energy & utilities
403-698-8714
dauch@davis.ca
James Bancroft, Q.C., Environmental law
403-698-8764
jbancroft@davis.ca
Timothy P. Chick, Environmental law; Mining law
403-698-8710
tchick@davis.ca
Terence Dalgleish, Q.C., Energy & utilities
403-698-8740
tdalgleish@davis.ca
Robert Donald, Aviation & transportation law
403-698-8788
rdonald@davis.ca
Roy H. Hudson, Climate change law; Mining law
403-698-8708
rhusdon@davis.ca
Daniel E. Kenney, Energy & utilities; Mining law
403-698-8704
dkenney@davis.ca
Andrew Lloyd, Aviation & transportation law
403-698-8786
alloyd@davis.ca
Catherine McKendry, Mining law
403-698-8789
cmckendry@davis.ca
Robert Perrin, Environmental law; Energy & utilities
403-698-8751
rperrin@davis.ca
Dana Schindelka, Environmental law; Energy & utilities; Municipal law
403-698-8705
dschindelka@davis.ca
Robert A. Seidel, Q.C., National Managing Partner, Climate change law; Environmental law; Forestry law
780-429-6814
rseidel@davis.ca
David J. Stratton, Q.C., Forestry law
403-296-4470
dstratton@davis.ca
Brian D. West, Life sciences
403-698-8762
bwest@davis.ca
Trevor Wong-Chor, Managing Partner, Energy & utilities
403-698-8711
twong-chor@davis.ca
Brian Yaworski, Q.C., Energy & utilities; Mining law; Climate change law
403-698-8746
byaworski@davis.ca

Dentons Canada LLP - Calgary

Bankers Court, 850 - 2nd St. SW, 15th Fl., Calgary, AB T2P 0R8
Tel: 403-268-7000; *Fax:* 403-268-3100
www.dentons.com
Profile: 106 Lawyers,
The firm offers expertise in Energy Law; Oil & Gas Industry Matters (including heavy oil, oil sands, liquified natural gas, pipeline projects, project finance, ligitation, mergers & acquisitions; & restructuring & insolvency); & Environmental Law
Environmental Lawyers:
Douglas J. Black, Q.C., Energy & Natural Resources Law
403-268-6879
doug.black@dentons.com
Tamela J. Coates, Environmental Law
403-268-6860
tamela.coates@dentons.com
Douglas E. Crowther, Energy & Natural Resources; Environmental Law; Power
403-268-6821
douglas.crowther@dentons.com
Laura K. Estep, Energy & Natural Resources
403-268-6308
laura.estep@dentons.com
William G. Gilliland, Energy & Natural Resources; Mining
william.gilliland@dentons.com
Michael A. Hurst, Energy & Natural Resources Law
michael.hurst@dentons.com
Matthew R. Lindsay, Managing Partner (Calgary), Energy Law; Oil & Gas Industry; Construction Industry
403-268-3037
matt.lindsay@dentons.com
Alexander G. MacWilliam, Environmental Law; Energy & Natural Resources; Transportation
403-268-7090
alex.macwilliam@dentons.com
Robert J. McKinnon, Energy & Natural Resources
403-268-7191
robert.mckinnon@dentons.com
Allan L. McLarty, Q.C., Energy & Natural Resources; Power; Mining
allan.mclarty@dentons.com
Richard A. Neufeld, Environmental Law; Energy & Natural Resources; Mining; Aboriginal Law
403-268-7023
richard.neufeld@dentons.com
Robert W. Poffenroth, Q.C., Energy & Natural Resources
robert.pottenroth@dentons.com
Bernie J. Roth, Environmental Law; Energy & Natural Resources
403-268-6888
bernard.roth@dentons.com
Scott W. Sangster, Energy & Natural Resources Law
403-268-7286
scott.sangster@dentons.com
Robert J. Simpson, Construction
robert.simpson@dentons.com
B.A.R. Smith, Q.C., Energy & Natural Resources
quincy.smith@dentons.com
Gordon L. Tarnowsky, Energy & Natural Resources
gordon.tarnowsky@dentons.com
E. David D. Tavender, Q.C., Energy & Natural Resources
403-268-7010
david.tavender@dentons.com
Heather L. Treacy, Aboriginal Law
Lowell A. Westersund, Q.C.
lowell.westersund@dentons.com
Laura J. Zurowski, Health
403-268-7048
laura.zurowski@dentons.com

Fasken Martineau - Calgary

#3400, First Canadian Centre, 350 - 7th Ave. SW, Calgary, AB T2P 3N9
Tel: 403-261-5350; *Fax:* 403-261-5351
Toll-Free: 877-336-5350
calgary@fasken.com
www.fasken.com/en/calgary
Profile: 28 Lawyers, Founded in: 2003
Fasken Martineau's Calgary office focueses on the energy & natural resources sector, Aboriginal law, construction, & infrastructure. The office has a range of clients from individuals to global companies.
Environmental Lawyers:
Niall Armstrong, Counsel, Energy
narmstrong@fasken.com
Michael Black, Partner, Energy
mblack@fasken.com
David Both, Associate, Environmental Law; Energy; Climate Change
dboth@fasken.com
A.W. (Sandy) Carpenter, Partner, Aboriginal Law; Energy; Environmental Law
scarpenter@fasken.com
Peter Feldberg, Partner, Aboriginal Law; Regulation of Utilities; Infrastructure Development
pfeldberg@fasken.com
Thomas Ferguson, Counsel, Construction
tferguson@fasken.com
Brenden Hunter, Associate, Aboriginal Law; Environmental Law; Regulatory Matters
bhunter@fasken.com
Alex Kotkas, Partner, Environmental Law
akotkas@fasken.com
Jonathan Liteplo, Partner, Environmental Law; Energy; Utilities
jliteplo@fasken.com
R. Greg Powers, QC, Partner, Oil & Gas; Corporate Social Responsibility Law
gpowers@fasken.com
Gulu Punia, Partner, Aboriginal Law
gpunia@fasken.com
Jennifer M. Shepherd, Associate, Occupational Health & Safety
jshepherd@fasken.com
Dean J. Watt, Associate, Environmental Law; Energy; Regulatory Law
djwatt@fasken.com.com
Michael J.G. Wright, Associate, Corporate Social Responsibility Law
miwright@fasken.com

Field LLP - Calgary

#400, 604 - 1st St. SW, Calgary, AB T2P 1M7
Tel: 403-260-8500; *Fax:* 403-264-7084
Toll-Free: 877-260-6515
www.fieldlaw.com
Profile: 49 Lawyers,
Energy & natural resource clients from both private & public companies are provided with legal advice from Field Law's Calgary office. Issues addressed include environmental & regulatory matters, due diligence reviews, & negotiation of contracts & agreements.
Environmental Lawyers:
Nancy Bains, Associate, Labour & Employment
nbains@fieldlaw.com
Laura Buckingham, Associate, Occupational Health & Safety
lbuckingham@fieldlaw.com
Erika Carrasco, Associate, Construction
ecarrasco@fieldlaw.com
Michael Casey, QC, Counsel, Construction
mcasey@fieldlaw.com
Justin Denis, Partner, Municipal Law
jdenis@fieldlaw.com

Dan Downe, QC, Partner, Health Industry Services
ddowne@fieldlaw.com
Steve Eichler, Partner, Occupational Health & Safety
seichler@fieldlaw.com
Christin Elawny, Associate, Labour & Employment
celawny@fieldlaw.com
Dylan Esch, Associate, Municipal Law
desch@fieldlaw.com
Joel Fairbrother, Associate, Labour & Employment
jfairbrother@fieldlaw.com
Neil Kathol, Partner, CleanTech & Clean Energy
nkathol@fieldlaw.com
Todd Kathol, Partner, Construction; Health Industry Services
tkathol@fieldlaw.com
Ian MacDonald, QC, Partner, Construction
imacdonald@fieldlaw.com
L. Frank Molnar, Partner, Labour & Employment
fmolnar@fieldlaw.com
Kelly Nicholson, Partner, Labour & Employment; Administrative Law
knicholson@fieldlaw.com
Doreen Saunderson, Managing Partner, Municipal Law; Health Industry Services; Alternative Dispute Resolution
dsaunderson@fieldlaw.com
Richard Stobbe, Associate, CleanTech & Clean Energy
rstobbe@fieldlaw.com
Andrew Wilkinson, Associate, Construction Law
awilkinson@fieldlaw.com
Jean C. van der Lee, Partner, Construction
jvanderlee@fieldlaw.com

Fleming LLP, Barristers & Solicitors
#900, 926 - 5th Ave. SW, Calgary, AB T2P 0N7
Tel: 403-266-5550; *Fax:* 403-265-6910
Toll-Free: 877-566-5550
www.flemingllp.com
Profile: 1 Office, 10 Lawyers, Founded in: 1921

Gowling Lafleur Henderson LLP - Calgary
#1400, Scotia Centre, 700 - 2nd St. SW, Calgary, AB T2P 4V5
Tel: 403-298-1000; *Fax:* 403-263-9193
Profile: 118 Lawyers, Founded in: 1972
Services include legal advice in the following areas: Corporate Transactions; Real Estate; Brownfields; Litigation & Advocacy; Environmental Assessments; Climate Change; Toxic Substances; Waste Management; First Nations/Aboriginal Rights; Water & Wastewater Treatement & Management; Transportation of Dangerous Goods; Emergency Response; International Development; & Environmental Law Training
Environmental Lawyers:
John N. Iredale, Q.C., Natural Resources Law; Oil & Gas; Energy; Infrastructure
403-298-1850
john.iredale@gowlings.com
James H. Smellie, Energy; Environmental Law; Regulatory
403-298-1816
james.smellie@gowlings.com

Heenan Blaikie LLP - Calgary
#1900, 215 - 9th Ave. SW, Calgary, AB T2P 1K3
Tel: 403-232-8223; *Fax:* 403-234-7987
www.heenanblaikie.com
Profile: 28 Lawyers
Environmental Lawyers:
Cynthia Amsterdam, Partner, Energy & Resources Litigation; Health; Construction Litigation
403-261-3469
camsterdam@heenan.ca
Robb D. Beeman, Partner, Energy & Resources Litigation
403-261-3452
rbeeman@heenan.ca
Brian Bidyk, Partner, Energy; Natural Resources; Climate, Cleantech & Sustainability
403-781-3389
bbidyk@heenan.ca
Michael J. Black, Energy & Natural Resources
403-261-3467
mblack@heenan.ca
David Elder, Energy
403-261-3464
delder@heenan.ca
Jillian Frank, Occupational Health & Safety
403-232-8223
jfrank@heenan.ca
Caireen E. Hanert, Partner, Energy & Resources Litigation; Construction Litigation
403-234-1262
chanert@heenan.ca
James R. Maclean, Energy; Natural Resources
403-261-3462
jmaclean@heenan.ca
Dawn Mains, Trade-mark Agent, Energy
403-261-3463
dmains@heenan.ca
Christopher B. Manderville, Partner, Natural Resources
403-234-1258
cmanderville@heenan.ca
Adrienne A. O'Reilly, Natural Resources
403-234-1259
aoreilly@heenan.ca
James Pasieka, Partner, Energy; Natural Resources
403-781-3382
jpasieka@heenan.ca
Christopher R. Peng, Partner, Energy
403-261-5232
cpeng@heenan.ca
Umesh (Mason) Shan, Energy
403-261-5514
mshan@heenan.ca
E. Mitchell Shier, Counsel, Energy; Environmental Law; Natural Resources
403-781-3394
mshier@heenan.ca
Edward A. Wooldridge, Partner, Energy
403-261-3454
ewooldridge@heena.ca

Lawson Lundell LLP - Calgary
#3700, Bow Valley Square 2, 205 - 5th Ave. SW, Calgary, AB T2P 2V7
Tel: 403-269-6900; *Fax:* 403-269-9494
calgary@lawsonlundell.com
www.lawsonlundell.com
Profile: 8 Lawyers, Founded in: 1997
Environmental Law Group serves clients in industries such as oil & gas, hydroelectric power generation, forest harvesting, pulp & paper, aquaculture, transporation, & real estate development. Services related to environmental law include environmental assessments, inspetions envrionmental audits, environmental compliance, regulatory requirements, applications for licences, site remediation requirements, spill reporting, & defence of environmental prosecutions.
Environmental Lawyers:
Trevor Ference, Associate, Aboriginal Law; Energy Law; Environmental Law; Public Utility & Regulatory Law
403-218-7527
tference@lawsonlundell.com
Michelle Forrieter, Associate, Aboriginal Law; Energy Law; Environmental Law; Public Utility & Regulatory Law
403-218-7536
mforrieter@lawsonlundell.com
JoAnn P. Jamieson, Partner, Aboriginal Law; Climate Change; Energy; Administrative, Constitutional & Public Law; Environmental Law; Mining; Project Permitting; Public Utility & Regulatory Law; Regulatory Compliance
403-218-7514
jjamieson@lawsonlundell.com
Jonathan (Jay) D. Lalach, Partner, Oil & Gas; Energy
403-218-7539
jlalach@lawsonlundell.com
Randy Madsen, Partner, Energy; Oil & Gas
403-218-7544
rmadsen@lawsonlundell.com
Lewis L. Manning, Partner, Energy Law; Public Utility & Regulatory Law; Administrative, Constitutional, & Public Law
403-782-9458
lmanning@lawsonlundell.com
Paul Negenman, Partner, Energy Law; Oil & Gas
403-218-7542
pnegenman@lawsonlundell.com
John M. Olynyk, Partner, Aboriginal Law; Energy Law; Environmental Law; Climate Change
403-781-9472
jolynyk@lawsonlundell.com
Jason Paton, Partner, Energy Law; Oil & Gas
403-218-7543
jpaton@lawsonlundell.com
Bernadita Tamura-O'Connor, Counsel, Energy Law; Oil & Gas
403-218-7545
btamuraoconnor@lawsonlundell.com

Machida Mack Shewchuk Meagher LLP
#1300, 707 - 7th Ave. SW, Calgary, AB T2P 3H6
Tel: 403-221-8333; *Fax:* 403-221-8339
nmachida@mmsmlawyers.com
Profile: 1 Office, 6 Lawyers, Founded in: 1989
Environmental Lawyers:
N.K. Machida, Oil & Gas; Waste; Regulatory

MacPherson Leslie & Tyerman LLP - Calgary
#1600, Centennial Place, 520 - 3rd Ave. SW, Calgary, AB T2P 0R3
Tel: 403-693-4300; *Fax:* 403-508-4349
www.mlt.com
Profile: 21 Lawyers, Founded in: 1920
MLT provides advice on environmental compliance & successor liability, & environmental risks of mergers & acquisitions. It has developed environmental due diligence systems & policies, including environmental audit programs. Experience includes advising during the planning phases of major industrial & mining projects, site decommissioning, transferring assets between parties, & moving hazardous products.

McCaffery Mudry Pritchard LLP, Barristers & Solicitors
#2200, 736 - 6 Ave. SW, Calgary, AB T2P 3T7
Tel: 403-260-1400; *Fax:* 403-260-1444
postmaster@mccafferylaw.ca
www.mccafferylaw.ca
Profile: 1 Office, 0 Lawyers, Founded in: 1922
Areas of practice include administrative law & environmental litigation.
Environmental Lawyers:
Gordon M. Bradley, Civil Litigation
403-260-1436
GBradley@mccafferylaw.ca
T. Thomas Mudry, Managing Partner
403-260-1422
TMudry@mccafferylaw.ca
J. Prescott Pritchard, Managing Partner
403-260-1418
SPritchard@mccafferylaw.ca

McCarthy Tétrault LLP - Calgary
#3300, 421 - 7th Ave. SW, Calgary, AB T2P 4K9
Tel: 403-260-3500; *Fax:* 403-260-3501
info@mccarthy.ca
www.mccarthy.ca
Profile: 7 Offices, 64 Lawyers,
Biotechnology; Energy; Environmental; Municipal
Environmental Lawyers:
Lisa M. Asbreuk, Environmental; Oil & Gas; Power
403-260-3538
lasbreuk@mccarthy.ca
Don Davies, Oil & Gas; Energy
403-260-3681
ddavies@mccarthy.ca
Robert N. DePoe, Oil & Gas; Energy
403-260-3702
rdepoe@mccarthy.ca
Derek S. Flaman, Natural Resources; Energy
403-206-5559
dflaman@mccarthy.ca
Michael Ford, Energy; Oil & Gas
403-260-3619
mford@mccarthy.ca
Terrance M. Hughes, Energy; Oil & Gas
403-260-3663
thughes@mccarthy.ca
Thomas F. Isaac, Aboriginal; Environmental; Mining; Oil & Gas
403-260-3708
tisaac@mccarthy.ca
Owen A. Johnson, Mining; Oil & Gas
403-260-3655
ojohnson@mccarthy.ca
Robert D. McCue, Energy; Oil & Gas
403-260-3568
rmccue@mccarthy.ca
Donald J. McLeod, Environmental
403-260-3748
dmcleod@mccarthy.ca
Debra Poon, Counsel, Mining; Oil & Gas
403-260-3743
dpoon@mccarthy.ca
William H. Smith, Q.C., Biotech/Life Sciences
403-260-3653
wsmith@mccarthy.ca

John B. Zaozirny, Q.C., Natural Resources & Energy
403-260-3613
jbzaozir@mccarthy.ca

McLennan Ross LLP - Calgary
#1600, Stock Exchange Tower, 300 - 5th Ave. SW, Calgary, AB T2P 3C4
Tel: 403-543-9120; *Fax:* 403-543-9150
Toll-Free: 888-543-9120
info@mross.com
www.mross.com
www.linkedin.com/company/mclennan-ross-llp
Profile: 3 Offices, 20 Lawyers, Founded in: 1903
Energy, Environmental & Regulatory; Labour & Employment; Occupational Health & Safety; Construction; Health Law; Municipal
Environmental Lawyers:
Evan W. Dixon, Associate, Energy; Environmental & regulatory
403-303-9103
edixon@mross.com
John J.P. Donihee, Partner, Energy; Environmental & regulatory; Northern practice group
403-303-2955
jdonihee@mross.com
Gavin S. Fitch, Partner, Energy; Environmental & regulatory; Northern practice group
403-303-9120
gfitch@mross.com
James P. Flanagan, Partner, Construction
403-303-9102
jflanagan@mross.com
James L. Lebo, Q.C., Partner, Construction
403-303-9111
jlebo@mross.com
Alexis N. Moulton, Partner, Health; Northern practice group
403-444-4081
amoulton@mross.com

McMillan LLP - Calgary
#1900, 736 - 6th Avenue S.W., Calgary, AB T2P 3T7
Tel: 403-531-4700; *Fax:* 403-531-4720
info@mcmillan.ca
www.mcmillan.ca
Profile: 16 Lawyers, Founded in: 1951
Environmental Lawyers:
Alain Breault, Litigation; Environmental Law
514-987-5037
alain.breault@mcmbm.com
Earl S. Cohen, Real Estate; Environmental Law
514-987-5045
earl.cohen@mcmbm.com
Céline Tessier
514-987-5032
celine.tessier@mcmbm.com

Merchant Law Group LLP - Calgary
#400, Deerfoot 17 Bldg., 2710 - 17th Ave. SE, Calgary, AB T2A 0P6
Tel: 403-225-7777; *Fax:* 403-273-9411
Toll-Free: 866-225-7777
merchant@merchantlaw.com
www.merchantlaw.com
Profile: 14 Lawyers
Environmental Lawyers:
Ronald E. Kampitsch, Energy Conservation; Health

Miles, Davison LLP
#1600, Bow Valley Square II, 205 - 5th Ave. SW, Calgary, AB T2P 2V7
Tel: 403-298-0333; *Fax:* 403-263-6840
thefirm@milesdavison.com
www.milesdavison.com
Profile: 1 Office, 24 Lawyers, Founded in: 2001
Environmental Lawyers:
Jason J. Irwin, Alternative Energy
403-298-0336
jirwin@milesdavison.com

Miller Thomson LLP - Calgary
#3000, 700 - 9th Ave. SW, Calgary, AB T2P 3V4
Tel: 403-298-2400; *Fax:* 403-262-0007
Toll-Free: 888-298-2400
calgary@millerthomson.com
www.millerthomson.com
Profile: 46 Lawyers, Founded in: 1987
Energy; Municipal & Planning; Oil & Gas; Construction; Forestry
Environmental Lawyers:
Gerald D. Chipeur, Q.C., Partner, Environmental Law; Aboriginal Law; Health Law
403-298-2434
gchipeur@millerthomson.com
Kathleen J. Kendrick, Associate, Environmental Law; Construction Law
403-298-2455
kkendrick@millerthomson.com
Jeffrey N. Thom, Q.C., Associate Counsel, Oil & Gas
403-298-2436
jthom@millerthomson.com

Osler, Hoskin & Harcourt LLP - Calgary
#2500, TransCanada Tower, 450 - 1st St. SW, Calgary, AB T2P 5H1
Tel: 403-260-7000; *Fax:* 403-260-7024
counsel@osler.com
www.osler.com
Profile: 52 Lawyers
Environmental Lawyers:
Robert Ashcroft, Energy
403-260-7087
rashcroft@osler.com
Simon C. Baines, Partner, Energy
403-260-7010
sbaines@osler.com
Donald Boykiw, Partner, Energy
403-260-7084
dboykiw@osler.com
Janice Buckingham, Partner, Energy
403-260-7006
jbuckingham@osler.com
Lorne Carson, Partner, Energy
403-260-7083
lcarson@osler.com
Shawn Denstedt, Q.C., Partner, Climate Change & Emissions Trading; Energy; Environmental, Regulatory & Aboriginal
403-260-7088
sdenstedt@osler.com
Robert Desbarats, Q.C., Partner, Energy
403-260-7015
rdesbarats@osler.com
Neil Herle, Energy; Environmental Financing
403-260-7072
nherle@osler.com
Josef Hocher, Partner, Energy
403-260-7066
jhocher@osler.com
Matthew Keen, Climate Change & Emissions Trading; Environmental, Regulatory & Aboriginal; Litigation
403-260-7005
mkeen@osler.com
Cheryl Kelly, Energy; Environmental Financing
403-260-7039
ckelly@osler.com
Maureen Killoran, Managing Partner, Energy; Environmental, Regulatory & Aboriginal; Litigation
403-260-7003
mkilloran@osler.com
Daina Kvisle, Energy
403-260-7086
dkvisle@osler.com
Gordon Nettleton, Partner, Climate Change & Emissions Trading; Energy; Environmental, Regulatory & Aboriginal; Litigation
403-260-7047
gnettleton@osler.com
Terri-Lee V. Oleniuk, Climate Change & Emissions Trading; Energy; Environmental, Regulatory & Aboriginal; Litigation
403-260-7034
toleniuk@osler.com
Paula Olexiuk, Partner, Construction; Energy
403-260-7080
polexiuk@osler.com
R.J. Jack Thrasher, Q.C., Partner, Energy
403-260-7019
jthrasher@osler.com
Frank Turner, Partner, Energy; Mining
403-260-7017
fturner@osler.com
Dylan Vandervecht, Energy
403-260-7069
dvandervecht@osler.com

Parlee McLaws LLP
#3400, Suncor Energy Centre, 150 - 6th Ave. SW, Calgary, AB T2P 3Y7
Tel: 403-294-7000; *Fax:* 403-265-8263
lawyers@parlee.com
www.parlee.com
Profile: 2 Offices, 82 Lawyers, Founded in: 1883
Aboriginal; Natural Resources
Environmental Lawyers:
Terry R. Davis, Partner, Environmental Law; Aboriginal Law
403-294-7091
tdavis@parlee.com
Shannon L. Kelley, Natural Resources
403-294-3456
skelley@parlee.com
Heidi L. Meldrum, Natural Resources
403-294-7098
hmeldrum@parlee.com
Nancy M. Penner, Counsel, Natural Resources
403-294-7011
npenner@parlee.com
Jayne R. Roberts, Occupational Health & Safety
403-294-7053
jroberts@parlee.com

Scott Venturo LLP
#203, Eau Claire Market, 200 Barclay Parade SW, Calgary, AB T2P 4R5
Tel: 403-261-9043; *Fax:* 403-265-4632
Toll-Free: 877-505-5651
www.scottventuro.com
Profile: 1 Office, 22 Lawyers, Founded in: 1986
Environmental Lawyers:
Colin D. McKinnon, Construction Litigation
403-231-8213
c.mckinnon@scottventuro.com
Janet E. Russell, Partner, Environmental Law; Aboriginal Law
403-231-8235
j.russell@scottventuro.com
Richard C. Tanner, Construction Litigation
403-231-8258
r.tanner@scottventuro.com

Stikeman Elliott LLP - Calgary
#4300, Bankers Hall West, 888 - 3rd St. SW, Calgary, AB T2P 5C5
Tel: 403-266-9000; *Fax:* 403-266-9034
www.stikeman.com
Profile: 36 Lawyers, Founded in: 1992
Energy law
Environmental Lawyers:
Harold K. Andersen, Partner, Emissions Trading & Climate Change; Energy
403-266-9063
handersen@stikeman.com
Glenn Cameron, Partner, Renewable Energy
403-266-9011
gcameron@stikeman.com
Mark A. Christensen, Environmental
403-266-9087
mchristensen@stikeman.com
Leland P. Corbett, Partner, Energy
403-266-9046
lcorbett@stikeman.com
Luigi A. Cusano, Partner, Environmental; Renewable Energy
403-266-9097
lcusano@stikeman.com
Evan Dickinson, Energy, Environmental & Regulatory Law
403-266-9074
edickinson@stikeman.com
Bradley B. Grant, Partner, Emissions Trading & Climate Change; Energy
403-266-9008
bgrant@stikeman.com
Benjamin Hudson, Emissions Trading & Climate Change
403-266-9049
bhudson@stikeman.com
April Kosten, Energy
403-266-9010
akosten@stikeman.com
Lisa A. McDowell, Partner, Energy; Mining
403-266-9099
lmcdowell@stikeman.com
Lisa A. McDowell, Partner, Energy; Mining
403-266-9099
lmcdowell@stikeman.com

Michael Mestinsek, Partner, Construction Litigation; Environmental Litigation
403-266-9078
mmestinsek@stikeman.com
Stuart M. Olley, Partner, Energy; Mining
403-266-9057
solley@stikeman.com
L. Greg Plater, Partner, Construction Litigation; Environmental; Forestry & Forest Products
403-266-9051
gplater@stikeman.com
Douglas Richardson, Partner, Emissions Trading & Climate Change
403-266-9048
drichardson@stikeman.com
Chris S. Scherman, Energy
403-781-9176
cscherman@stikeman.com
Matthew Synnott, Emissions Trading & Climate Change; Environmental; Renewable Energy
403-266-9028
msynnott@stikeman.com
David M. Wood, Partner, Energy; Environmental
403-266-9068
dwood@stikeman.com

Stones Carbert Waite Wells LLP
#2000, Encor Place, 645 - 7th Ave. SW, Calgary, AB T2P 4G8
Tel: 403-263-5656; *Fax:* 403-263-5553
info@scwlawyers.com
www.scwlawyers.com
Profile: 1 Office, 14 Lawyers
Environmental Lawyers:
Blair R. Carbert, Founding Partner, Health Law
403-705-3304
carbert@scwlawyers.com
Kelly P. Colborne, Health Law; Construction Litigation
403-705-3337
colborne@scwlawyers.com
Michelle L. Colley, Health
403-705-3309
colley@scwlawyers.com
Roxanne M. Davis, Construction Litigation; Health Law
403-705-3335
davis@scwlawyers.com
Bradley S. Dobbin, Construction Litigation
403-705-3330
dobbin@scwlawyers.com
Bryan L. Gallant, Health Law
403-705-3310
gallant@scwlawyers.com
Melissa A. Rico, Health Law
403-705-3308
rico@scwlawyers.com
Michael A. Waite, Partner, Health Law; Energy Litigation; Construction Litigation
403-705-3307
waite@scwlawyers.com
Gregory S. Wells, Q.C., Construction Litigation; Environmental Litigation
403-705-3328
wells@scwlawyers.com

Torys LLP - Calgary
Eighth Avenue Place East, 525 - 8th Ave. SW, 46th Fl., Calgary, AB T2P 1G1
Tel: 403-776-3700; *Fax:* 403-776-3800
www.torys.com
Profile: 17 Lawyers, Founded in: 2011

Walsh Wilkins Creighton LLP
#2800, 801 - 6 Ave. SW, Calgary, AB T2P 4A3
Tel: 403-267-8400; *Fax:* 403-264-9400
mail@wwclawyers.com
www.wwclawyers.com
Profile: 3 Offices, 18 Lawyers
Environmental Lawyers:
Raymond G. Hunt, Construction Law
403-267-8410
rhunt@wwclawyers.com

Warren Tettensor Amantea LLP
1413 - 2nd St. SW, Calgary, AB T2R 0W7
Tel: 403-228-7007; *Fax:* 403-244-1948
info@warren.ab.ca
www.warren.ab.ca
Profile: 1 Office, 12 Lawyers, Founded in: 1969
Environmental Lawyers:
Joseph B. Amantea, Partner, Construction Law
403-228-8374
amantea@warren.ab.ca
Tara L. Petersen, Partner, Construction Litigation
403-228-8383
petersen@warren.ab.ca

Wilson Laycraft
#1601, 333 - 11th Ave. SW, Calgary, AB T2R 1L9
Tel: 403-290-1601; *Fax:* 403-290-0828
reception@wilcraft.com
www.wilcraft.com
Profile: 1 Office, 10 Lawyers, Founded in: 1985
Environmental Lawyers:
Brian K. Dell, Construction Law
403-441-2098
bdell@wilcraft.com
Ronald S. Girvitz, Oil & Gas; Occupational Health & Safety
403-441-2099
ronsg@wilcraft.com
James B. Laycraft, Q.C., Founding Partner, Oil & Gas Litigation
403-441-2095
jamesbl@wilcraft.com

Wolch, Hursh, deWit & Watts
#1500, 633 - 6 Ave. SW, Calgary, AB T2P 2Y5
Tel: 403-265-6500; *Fax:* 403-263-1111
hersh@wolch.com; lhursh@shawcable.com; wtdewit@shawcable.com
Profile: 1 Office, 4 Lawyers, Founded in: 1995
Defending against environmental prosecutions

Edmonton

Ackroyd LLP Barristers & Solicitors
#1500, First Edmonton Place, 10665 Jasper Ave., Edmonton, AB T5J 3S9
Tel: 780-423-8905; *Fax:* 780-423-8946
info@ackroydlaw.com
www.ackroydlaw.com
Profile: Founded in: 1950
The firm's specialties include environmental, employment & Aboriginal law.
Environmental Lawyers:
Amy Abbott, Associate, Health
aabbott@ackroydlaw.com
James E. Cregan, Q.C., Partner, Land development
jcregan@ackroydlaw.com
Karine De Champlain, Associate, First Nations
kdechamplain@ackroydlaw.com
Penny Frederiksen, Partner, Employment law
pfred@ackroydlaw.com
Allyson F. Jeffs, Associate, Environment Law; First Nation Law; Employment Law
ajeffs@ackroydlaw.com
J. Trina Kondro, Partner, Employment Law; First Nations Law; Metis Law
tkondro@ackroydlaw.com
John P. Kudrinko, Managing Partner, Aboriginal Law; Employment
jkudrinko@ackroydlaw.com
Garry Laboucan, Partner, First Nations Law; Metis Law
glaboucan@ackroydlaw.com
Ian F. McDougall, Associate, Utilities
imcdougall@ackroydlaw.com
William L. McElhanney, Partner, Aboriginal Law; Surface Rights; Energy, Transmission & other Regulatory Matters
bmcelhanney@ackroydlaw.com
Neil Reddekopp, Associate, First Nations; Metis Communities
nreddekopp@ackroydlaw.com
Dennis B. Roth, Partner, Oil & Gas Law
droth@ackroydlaw.com
Richard C. Secord, Partner, Environmental Law; Aboriginal Law
rsecord@ackroydlaw.com
Jerome N. Slavik, Partner, Environmental Law; First Nations Law

Bishop & McKenzie LLP
#2500, Bell Tower, 10104 - 103 Ave., 25th Fl., Edmonton, AB T5J 1V3
Tel: 780-426-5550; *Fax:* 780-426-1305
edmonton@bishopmckenzie.com
www.bishopmckenzie.com
Profile: 2 Offices, Founded in: 1903
Legal services are available in the areas of construction & employment law.
Environmental Lawyers:
Jeffrey B. Champion, Q.C., Employment Law
j.champion@bishopmckenzie.com
Jose A. Delgado, Construction Law
j.delgado@bishopmckenzie.com
Robert A. Farmer, Partner, Construction Law
r.farmer@bishopmckenzie.com
Nigel J. Forster, Construction Law; Employment Law
n.forster@bishopmckenzie.com
Tara L. Hamelin, Partner, Employment Law
t.hamelin@bishopmckenzie.com
Patty P. Ko, Associate, Employment Law
p.ko@bishopmckenzie.com
Lora H. Lee, Associate, Employment Law
l.lee@bishopmckenzie.com
Jerritt R. Pawlyk, Partner, Construction Law
j.pawlyk@bishopmckenzie.com
Carmen L. Plante, Partner, Employment Law
c.plante@bishopmckenzie.com
W. Ben Russell, Counsel, Construction Law
b.russell@bishopmckenzie.com
J. Philip Warner, Q.C., Senior Partner, Employment Law; Construction Law
p.warner@bishopmckenzie.com

Brownlee LLP - Edmonton
#2200, Commerce Place, 10155 - 102 St., Edmonton, AB T5J 4G8
Tel: 780-497-4800; *Fax:* 780-424-3254
Toll-Free: 800-661-9069
contactus@brownleelaw.com
www.brownleelaw.com
Profile: 2 Offices, 44 Lawyers,
Brownlee LLP is a full service law firm, with a broad background & depth in almost all legal disciplines. While the overall practice of the firm can be described as general, within its membership the individual lawyers are each engaged in a variety of particular areas including, but not limited to, environmental law, municipal law, planning & development, utility regulation, & oil & gas law.
Environmental Lawyers:
Jenelle R. Butler, Associate, Labour & Employment
780-497-4838
jbutler@brownleelaw.com
Shad A. Chapman, Partner, Aboriginal Law; Administrative Law; Construction; Environmental Law; Labour & Employment
780-497-4840
schapman@brownleelaw.com
George (Joe) F. Chivers, Partner, Construction
780-497-4862
jchivers@brownleelaw.com
Steven T. Connors, Partner, Municipal & Public Sector Law; Occupational Health & Safety; Administrative Law
780-497-4842
sconnors@brownleelaw.com
Michael T. Coombs, Associate, Construction
780-497-4833
mcoombs@brownleelaw.com
Sean F.J. Curran, Associate, Aboriginal Law
780-497-4844
scurran@brownleelaw.com
Alison R. Espetveidt, Associate, Municipal Law; Planning & Development
780-497-4837
aespetveidt@brownleelaw.com
Ryan R. Ewasiuk, Partner, Construction; Labour & Employment
780-497-4850
rewasiuk@brownleelaw.com
Colin R. Fetter, Partner, Municipal & Public Sector; Labour & Employment
780-497-4867
cfetter@brownleelaw.com
Peter G. Gilchrist, Associate, Construction
pgilchrist@brownleelaw.com
Jeneane S. Grundberg, Partner, Municipal & Public Sector Law; Planning & Development; Administrative Law
780-497-4812
jgrundberg@brownleelaw.com
Alifeyah Gulamhusein, Associate, Municipal Law; Administrative Law
780-497-4829
agulamhusein@brownleelaw.com
Kristjana E. Kellgren, Associate, Municipal Law; Utility Regulation; Administrative Law

780-497-4890
kkellgren@brownleelaw.com
Alvin R. Kosak, Partner, Municipal & Public Sector Law; Administrative Law
780-497-4882
akosak@brownleelaw.com
Galan T. Lund, Partner, Construction; Administrative Law
780-497-4887
glund@brownleelaw.com
Havelock B. Madill, QC, Counsel, Construction
780-497-4898
hmadill@brownleelaw.com
Thomas D. Marriott, Managing Partner, Utility Regulation; Municipal Law; Administrative Law
780-497-4868
tmarriott@brownleelaw.com
John C. McDonnell, Partner, Infrastructure; Utilities; Municipal Law
780-497-4801
jmcdonnell@brownleelaw.com
Travis D. McKay, Associate, Municipal Law; Planning & Development; Administrative Law
780-497-4807
tmckay@brownleelaw.com
Raymond (Guy) G. Miki, Partner, Municipal Law; Construction; Infrastructure & Utilities; Planning & Development
780-497-4821
gmiki@brownleelaw.com
Bradley J. Nattrass, Associate, Municipal & Public Sector Law; Labour & Employment
780-497-4873
bnattrass@brownleelaw.com
Ronald R. Nelson, Partner, Municipal & Public Sector Law; Construction
780-497-4851
rnelson@brownleelaw.com
Daniel R. Peskett, Partner, Construction
780-497-4875
dpeskett@brownleelaw.com
Adina Preda, Associate, Municipal & Public Sector Law
780-497-4894
apreda@brownleelaw.com
Tore M. Purdy, Q.C., Associate, Municipal & Public Sector Law
780-497-4830
tpurdy@brownleelaw.com
Raymond C. Purdy, QC, Partner, Oil & Gas; Utility Regulation
780-497-4879
rpurdy@brownleelaw.com
Lorne I. Randa, Associate, Municipal & Public Sector Law; Utility Regulation; Planning & Development; Administrative Law
780-497-4832
lranda@brownleelaw.com
Jill L.A. Sheward, Associate, Municipal Law; Planning & Development
780-497-4835
jsheward@brownleelaw.com
Barry A. Sjolie, QC, Partner, Municipal & Public Sector Law; Planning & Development; Administrative Law; Construction Law; Infrastructure; Utilities; Utility Regulation; Labour & Employment
780-497-4818
bsjolie@brownleelaw.com
Jordan W. Smith, Associate, Municipal Law
780-497-4815
jsmith@brownleelaw.com
Michael S. Solowan, Associate, Municipal & Public Sector Law; Administrative Law
780-497-4893
msolowan@brownleelaw.com
Paul V. Stocco, Partner, Construction
780-497-4884
pstocco@brownleelaw.com
Jillian Swainson, Associate, Municipal Law
780-497-4802
jswainson@brownleelaw.com
Rodd C. Thorkelsson, Partner, Municipal & Public Sector Law; Infrastructure; Utilities
780-497-4843
rthorkelsson@brownleelaw.com
Christopher M. Young, Associate, Construction
780-497-4865
cyoung@brownleelaw.com

Davis LLP - Edmonton

#1201, Scotia Tower 2, 10060 Jasper Ave., Edmonton, AB T5J 4E5
Tel: 780-426-5330; *Fax:* 780-428-1066
www.davis.ca
Profile: 26 Lawyers,
Aboriginal; Municipal; Energy; Environment; Forestry; Mining
Environmental Lawyers:
Wendy-Anne Berkenbosch, Environmental Law
780-409-6810
wberkenbosch@davis.ca
Jennifer L. Cleall, Environmental law; Climate change law
780-429-6838
jcleall@davis.ca
Jonathan Cummings, Environmental law; Climate change law
780-637-4535
jcummings@davis.ca
Rachel J. Hamilton, Managing Partner, Climate change law; Energy & utilities
780-429-6633
rhamilton@davis.ca
Priscilla E.S.J. Kennedy, Environmental law
780-429-6830
pkennedy@davis.ca
Denis Lefebvre, Aboriginal law
780-637-4502
dlefebvre@davis.ca
Colin G.W. Lipsett, Energy & utilities; Environmental law; Municipal law
780-429-6821
clipsett@davis.ca
Brock A.F. Roe, Aboriginal law
780-429-6825
broe@davis.ca
Craig D. Rose, R.P.F., Environmental law; Forestry law; Climate change law
780-429-6807
crose@davis.ca
Avery Saunders, Construction law
780-429-6841
asaunders@davis.ca
Robert A. Seidel, Q.C., National Managing Partner, Environmental law; Forestry law; Climate change law; Municipal law; Energy & utilities; Projects, infrastructure, & P3
780-429-6814
rseidel@davis.ca
Josh Stachniak, Climate change law
780-429-6805
jstachniak@davis.ca
David J. Stratton, Q.C., Forestry Law; Projects, infrastructure, & P3
780-429-6804
dstratton@davis.ca
Robert B. White, Q.C., Environmental law
780-429-6803
rwhite@davis.ca
Donald J. Wilson, Q.C., Environmental law
780-429-6817
dwilson@davis.ca

Dentons Canada LLP - Edmonton

#2900, Manulife Place, 10180 - 101 St., Edmonton, AB T5J 3V5
Tel: 780-423-7100; *Fax:* 780-423-7276
www.dentons.com
Profile: 83 Lawyers,
FMC Edmonton serves the energy, engineering, forest products, technology, & transportation industries in the city
Environmental Lawyers:
Shauna Finlay, Administrative; Environmental; Occupational Health & Safety
780-423-7392
shauna.finlay@dentons.com
Gordon A. Salembier, Q.C., Energy & Natural Resources
780-423-7232
gordon.salembien@dentons.com
Terry J. Williams, Aboriginal Law
780-423-7366
terry.williams@dentons.com
Barry Zalmanowitz, Q.C., Energy & Natural Resources; Competition Law
780-423-7344
barry.zalmanowitz@dentons.com

Duncan Craig LLP - Edmonton

#2800, Scotia Place, 10060 Jasper Ave., Edmonton, AB T5J 3V9
Tel: 780-428-6036; *Fax:* 780-428-9683
Toll-Free: 800-782-9409
edmonton@dcllp.com
www.dcllp.com
ca.linkedin.com/company/duncan-&-craig-llp?trk=ppro_cprof
Profile: 3 Offices, 50 Lawyers, Founded in: 1894
The Alberta based law firm serves local, national, & international clients. Duncan & Craig LLP offers legal services related to agribusiness, surface rights, & construction law.
Environmental Lawyers:
Stewart G. Baker, QC, Counsel, Construction
780-441-4393
sbaker@dcllp.com
Darren R. Bieganek, Q.C., Managing Partner, Agribusiness
780-441-4386
dbieganek@dcllp.com
George E. Bowker, QC, Counsel, Construction
780-409-4407
gbowker@dcllp.com
Heather Gallant, Associate, Agribusiness
780-441-4379
hgallant@dcllp.com
John A. Kosolowski, Partner, Agribusiness; Surface Rights; First Nations Business
780-441-4307
jkoslowski@dcllp.com
Bryan A. Kwan, Associate, Construction
780-409-4420
brkwan@dcllp.com
Philip J. Renaud, QC, Partner, First Nations
780-441-4334
pjrenaud@dcllp.com
David C. Romaniuk, Partner, Surface Rights
780-441-4319
dcromaniuk@dcllp.com
Ronald T. Smith, Partner, Construction
780-409-2655
rsmith@dcllp.com
Tara Szott, Associate, Construction
780-441-4320
tszott@dcllp.com

Emery Jamieson LLP

#1700, 10235 - 101st St. NW, Edmonton, AB T5J 3G1
Tel: 780-426-5220; *Fax:* 780-420-6277
Toll-Free: 866-212-5220
general@emeryjamieson.com
www.emeryjamieson.com
Profile: 1 Office, Founded in: 1893
Emery Jamieson's practice areas include administrative law & municipal law. The firm's work includes appearances before administrative tribunals, such as the Energy Resources Conservation Board, the Natural Resources Conservation Board, the Municipal Government Board, the Energy Utilities Board, & the Subdivision & Development Appeal Board.
Environmental Lawyers:
Janet Alexander-Smith, Employment & Labour
780-426-5220
jasmith@emeryjamieson.com
Sydney A. Bercov, Q.C., Municipal Law
780-426-5220
sabercov@emeryjamieson.com
Richard B. Drewry, Q.C., Administrative Law; Construction Law; Employment & Labour
780-426-5220
rdrewry@emeryjamieson.com
Robert Feraco, Construction Law; Employment & Labour
780-970-6285
rferaco@emeryjamieson.com
Kember Handzic, Construction Law
780-426-5220
khandzic@emeryjamieson.com
Kate L. Hurlburt, Construction Law
780-426-5220
khurlburt@emeryjamieson.com
Brent W. Mielke, Construction Law; Employment & Labour
780-426-5220
bmielke@emeryjamieson.com
Rex M. Nielsen, Q.C., Municipal Law
780-426-5220
rnielsen@emeryjamieson.com
Colin D. Ouellette, Employment & Labour
780-426-5220
couellette@emeryjamieson.com
W. Paul Sharek, Q.C., Construction Law
780-426-5220
psharek@emeryjamieson.com

Stuart J. Weatherill, Employment & Labour
780-426-5220
sweatherill@emeryjamieson.com
Hugh Willis, Municipal Law
780-426-5220
hwillis@emeryjamieson.com

Environmental Law Centre (ELC)

#800, 10025 - 106 St., Edmonton, AB T5J 1G4
Tel: 780-424-5099; *Fax:* 780-424-5133
Toll-Free: 800-661-4238
elc@elc.ab.ca
www.elc.ab.ca
Profile: 1 Office, 4 Lawyers, Founded in: 1982

Field LLP - Edmonton

#2000, Oxford Tower, 10235 - 101st St., Edmonton, AB T5J 3G1
Tel: 780-423-3003; *Fax:* 780-428-9329
Toll-Free: 800-222-6479
www.fieldlaw.com
www.facebook.com/fieldlaw, twitter.com/#!/FieldLaw, www.linkedin.com/companies/field-law
Profile: 3 Offices, 116 Lawyers, Founded in: 1915
Energy & Natural Resource Law; Environmental Law; Municipal Law
Environmental Lawyers:
Daniel P. Carroll, Managing Partner, First Nations
780-423-7614
dcarroll@fieldlaw.com
Derek A. Cranna, First Nations; Occupational Health & Safety
780-423-7665
dcranna@fieldlaw.com
Dale Cunningham, First Nations
780-423-7610
dcunningham@fieldlaw.com
P. Jon Faulds, Q.C., First Nations
780-423-7625
jfaulds@fieldlaw.com
Donald K. Neeland, Energy & Natural Resources
780-423-7660
dneeland@fieldlaw.com

Kirwin LLP

#200, 10339 - 124 St., Edmonton, AB T5N 3W1
Tel: 780-448-7401; *Fax:* 780-453-3281
www.kirwinllp.com
Profile: 1 Office, 7 Lawyers, Founded in: 1987
Lawyers at Kirwin LLP handle environmental law issues involving environmental assessments, contaminated lands, environmental approvals, land development, & environmental civil litigation. The firm works with landowners, professional engineers, advocates, & regulators.
Environmental Lawyers:
Mark M. Kirwin, Environmental Law

McLennan Ross LLP - Edmonton

#600, West Chambers, 12220 Stony Plain Rd., Edmonton, AB T5N 3Y4
Tel: 780-482-9200; *Fax:* 780-482-9100
Toll-Free: 800-567-9200
info@mross.com
www.mross.com
Profile: 3 Offices, Founded in: 1903
McLennan Ross' energy, environmental, & regulatory practice group has expertise in the following areas: environmental assessments; permitting, licensing, & other regulatory authorizations; defence of regulatory prosecutions; utilities & mining; contaminated sites; northern practice; & Aboriginal issues.
Environmental Lawyers:
Daniel R. Bokenfohr, Partner, Occupational Health & Safety; Labour & Employment; Construction
780-482-9118
dbokenfohr@mross.com
Douglas J. Boyer, Partner, Municipal; Construction; Labour & Employment
780-482-9282
dboyer@mross.com
Stuart W. Chambers, Partner, Energy; Environmental; Regulatory; Construction; Occupational Health & Safety
780-482-9113
schambers@mross.com
Corbin D. Devlin, Partner, Energy; Environmental; Regulatory; Construction; Northern
780-482-9261
cdevlin@mross.com
Anthony C. Espejo, Associate, Occupational Health & Safety
780-482-9124
aespejo@mross.com
Douglas I. Evanchuk, Partner, Energy; Environmental; Regulatory; Construction
780-482-9106
devanchuk@mross.com
Dani V. Fialkov, Partner, Construction
780-482-9286
dfialkov@mross.com
Kenneth W. Fitz, Partner, Health; Construction
780-482-9231
kfitz@mross.com
Douglas J. Forer, Partner, Construction
780-482-9246
dforer@mross.com
Laurie A. Fumagalli, Associate, Construction
780-482-9228
lfumagalli@mross.com
Kathleen Garbutt, Associate, Occupational Health & Safety
780-482-9131
kgarbutt@mross.com
Vicki L. Giles, Partner, Construction; Labour & Employment
780-482-9123
vgiles@mross.com
Teresa R. Haykowsky, Partner, Labour & Employment, Northern Practice
780-482-9247
thaykowsky@mross.com
Raymond D. Hupfer, Partner, Construction
780-482-9249
rhupfer@mross.com
William R. Johnston, Associate, Construction; Health; Occupational Health & Safety; Labour & Employment
780-482-9155
wjohnston@mross.com
Samantha C. Kernahan, Associate, Construction
780-482-9144
skernahan@mross.com
Ronald M. Kruhlak, QC, Partner, Energy; Environmental & Regulatory; Construction
780-482-9226
rkruhlak@mross.com
Christopher J. Lane, Partner, Health; Construction; Labour & Employment
780-482-9238
clane@mross.com
James C. Lingwood, QC, Associate, Municipal; Occupational Health & Safety; Labour & Employment
780-482-9237
jlingwood@mross.com
Stephen J. Livingstone, Managing Partner, Construction
780-482-9242
slivingstone@mross.com
Roderick A. McLennan, QC, Partner, Construction
780-482-9201
rmclennan@mross.com
Hugh J.D. McPhail, QC, Partner, Construction; Labour & Employment
780-482-9212
hmcphail@mross.com
Robert D. Muller, Associate, Construction
780-482-9317
rmuller@mross.com
David G. Myrol, Partner, Occupational Health & Safety; Energy; Environmental & Regulatory; Construction; Labour & Employment
780-482-9290
dmyrol@mross.com
Sean D. Parker, Associate, Energy; Environmental & Regulatory; Construction
780-482-9309
sparker@mross.com
Janet M. Patterson, Associate, Construction; Health
780-482-9314
jpatterson@mross.com
Denise M. Prokopiuk, Partner, Health; Construction
780-482-9205
dprokopiuk@mross.com
Jessica Proudfoot, Associate, Envrionmental & Regulatory; Energy
780-482-9209
jproudfoot@mross.com
David J. Ross, QC, Partner, Construction; Labour & Employment
780-482-9202
dross@mross.com
Jonathan P. Rossall, QC, Partner, Health; Municipal, Northern Practice
780-482-9216
jrossall@mross.com
William S. Rosser, Partner, Construction
780-482-9222
brosser@mross.com
Gerhard J. Seifner, Partner, Occupational Health & Safety; Labour & Employment; Construction
780-482-9230
gseifner@mross.com
Lisa K. Semenchuk, Associate, Energy; Environmental & Regulatory; Construction, Northern Practice
780-482-9110
lsemenchuk@mross.com
Peter P. Taschuk, QC, Partner, Energy; Environmental & Regulatory; Occupational Health & Safety
780-482-9203
ptaschuk@mross.com
Yolanda S. Van Wachem, Associate, Health
780-482-9225
yvanwachem@mross.com

Merchant Law Group LLP - Edmonton

#310, Kingsway Garden Mall NW, Edmonton, AB T5G 3A6
Tel: 780-474-7777; *Fax:* 780-474-4064
Toll-Free: 866-225-7777
merchant@merchantlaw.com; edmonton@merchantlaw.com
www.merchantlaw.com
Profile: 10 Lawyers
Environmental Lawyers:
Ronald E. Kampitsch, Energy Conservation; Health

Miller Thomson LLP - Edmonton

#2700, Commerce Place, 10155 - 102nd St., Edmonton, AB T5J 4G8
Tel: 780-429-1751; *Fax:* 780-424-5866
Toll-Free: 800-215-1016
edmonton@millerthomson.com
www.millerthomson.com
Profile: 49 Lawyers, Founded in: 1953
Aboriginal Law; Energy Law; Environmental Law; Municipal & Planning; Oil & Gas; Mining; Construction Law; Forestry
Environmental Lawyers:
Debra Curcio Lister, Partner
780-429-9763
dcurciolister@millerthomson.com

Parlee McLaws LLP

#1500, Manulife Place, 10180 - 101 St., Edmonton, AB T5J 4K1
Tel: 780-423-8500; *Fax:* 780-423-2870
lawyers@parlee.com
www.parlee.com
Profile: 52 Lawyers, Founded in: 1883
Aboriginal; Natural Resources
Environmental Lawyers:
Terrence A. Cockrall, Q.C., Counsel, Natural Resources
780-423-8634
tcockrall@parlee.com
Jeremy H.H. Hockin, Partner, Natural Resources
780-423-8532
jhockin@parlee.com
Robert P. James, Partner, Occupational Health & Safety
780-423-8554
rjames@parlee.com

Reynolds Mirth Richards & Farmer LLP

#3200, Manulife Pl., 10180 - 101 St., Edmonton, AB T5J 3W8
Tel: 780-425-9510; *Fax:* 780-429-3044
Toll-Free: 800-661-7673
mail@rmrf.com
www.rmrf.com
Profile: 1 Office, Founded in: 1915
Reynolds Mirth Richards & Farmer has lawyers with expertise in Aboriginal, construction, health, & municipal law.
The firm provides advice to First Nations & Metis Settlement throughout Alberta in matters such as environmental protection, land issues, & resource development.
In the area of construction law, lawyers handle issues related to occupational health & safety issues & the environment. Envrionmental matters are also addressed in relation to health law.
The firm's lawyers also act as general legal counsel to water services commissions, sewage commissions, solid waste authorities, villages, towns, counties, & municipal districts. Reynolds Mirth Richards & Farmer lawyers have appeared before tribunals such as the Municipal Government Board, the

Environmental Appeal Board, the Natural Resources Conservation Board, Development Appeal Boards, & the Labour Relations Board.
Environmental Lawyers:
William W. Barclay, Partner, Municipal Law; Planning Law; Construction Law
780-497-3379
wbarclay@rmrf.com
Kelsey L. Becker Brookes, Partner, Municipal Law; Employment Law; Aboriginal Law
780-497-3304
kbeckerbrookes@rmrf.com
Shelly K. Chamaschuk, Municipal Law
780-497-3364
schamaschuk@rmrf.com
Allan Farmer, QC, Partner, Municipal Law; Administrative Law
780-497-3360
afarmer@rmrf.com
Julie Gagnon, Partner, Aboriginal Law; Health Law
780-497-3320
jgagnon@rmrf.com
William H. Hurlburt, QC, Counsel, Municipal Law; Utility regulation
780-425-9510
mail@rmrf.com
John Paul Janssens, Partner, Construction Law
780-497-3389
jpjanssens@rmrf.com
Cherisse N. Killick-Dzenick, Partner, Municipal Law; Administrative Law; Construction Law; Health Law
780-497-3372
ckillick@rmrf.com
Fred Kozak, QC, Partner, Health Law
780-497-3358
fkozak@rmrf.com
F. Albert X. Lavergne, Partner, Municipal Law; Occupational Health & Safety Law; Energy resources; Construction Law
780-497-3310
alavergne@rmrf.com
Victor L. Lirette, Managing Partner, Land development; Construction
780-497-3383
vlirette@rmrf.com
Donald C.I. Lucky, Partner, Construction Law
780-497-3354
dlucky@rmrf.com
Tim Mavko, Partner, Construction Law
780-497-3331
tmavko@rmrf.com
Sheila C. McNaughtan, QC, Partner, Municipal Law; Planning & development; Administrative Law
780-497-3362
smcnaughtan@rmrf.com
E. (Sonny) Mirth, QC, Partner, Property development; Health Law
780-497-3346
emirth@rmrf.com
Denis R. Noël, QC, Counsel, Construction Law; Administrative Law; Aboriginal Law; Health Law
780-497-3366
dnoel@rmrf.com
Atul Omkar, Partner, Construction Law
780-497-3368
aomkar@rmrf.com
Nick Parker, Partner, Municipal Law; Regulatory Law; Construction Law
780-497-3342
nparker@rmrf.com
Marco S. Poretti, Partner, Aboriginal Law
780-497-3325
mporetti@rmrf.com
Francis C.R. Price, QC, Partner, Oil & gas surface rights; Construction Law; Health Law
780-497-3388
fprice@rmrf.com
Aisling Ryan, Associate, Municipal Law
780-497-3315
aeryan@rmrf.com
Todd A. Shipley, Partner, Municipal Law; Construction Law
780-497-3339
tshipley@rmrf.com
Jeremy D. Taitinger, Partner, Construction Law
780-497-3317
jtaitinger@rmrf.com
Sean Ward, Partner, Municipal Law
780-497-3334
sward@rmrf.com
Matthew A. Woodley, Municipal Law; Health Law
780-497-3307
mwoodley@rmrf.com
Daina Young, Associate, Municipal Law
780-497-3309
dyoung@rmrf.com
Carol Zukiwski, Partner, Municipal Law
780-497-3350
czukiwski@rmrf.com

Sharek Logan & van Leenen LLP
#701, Tower 2, Scotia Place, 10060 Jasper Ave. NW, Edmonton, AB T5J 3R8
Tel: 780-413-3100; *Fax:* 780-413-3152
www.sharekco.com
Profile: 1 Office, 8 Lawyers

Fairview

Kay McVey Smith & Carlstrom LLP - Fairview
10316 - 110 St., Fairview, AB T0H 1L0
Tel: 780-835-4100; *Fax:* 780-835-4171
Toll-Free: 888-531-7771
info@mylawteam.ca
www.mylawteam.ca

Grande Prairie

Kay McVey Smith & Carlstrom LLP - Grande Prairie
#600, Windsor Ct., 9835 - 101st Ave., Grande Prairie, AB T8V 5V4
Tel: 780-532-7771; *Fax:* 780-532-1158
Toll-Free: 888-531-7771
info@mylawteam.ca
www.mylawteam.ca
Profile: 4 Offices, 12 Lawyers, Founded in: 1923
Kay McVey Smith & Carlstrom has four offices throughout the Peace Country area of Alberta. Lawyers are experienced in the practice of municipal law & construction law.
Environmental Lawyers:
Jennifer Laverick, Surface Rights
jennifer@mylawteam.ca
Owen A. Lewis, Managing Partner, Municipal / Administrative Law
owen@mylawteam.ca

Lethbridge

MacLachlan McNab Hembroff LLP
1003 - 4th Ave. South, Lethbridge, AB T1J 0P7
Tel: 403-381-4966; *Fax:* 403-329-9300
mmh@mmhlawyers.com
www.mmhlawyers.com
Profile: 3 Offices, 7 Lawyers,
The firm provides legal assistance in matters related to irrigation & water resources.
Environmental Lawyers:
Thomas B. MacLachlan
maclachlan@mmhlawyers.com

Sexsmith

Kay McVey Smith & Carlstrom LLP - Sexsmith
Sexsmith Insurance Bldg., 9910 - 100 St., Sexsmith, AB T0H 3C0
Tel: 780-568-3044; *Fax:* 780-532-1158
Toll-Free: 888-551-7771
info@mylawteam.ca
www.mylawteam.ca

Spirit River

Kay McVey Smith & Carlstrom LLP - Spirit River
Listhaeghe Bldg., P.O. Box 486, Spirit River, AB T0H 3G0
Tel: 780-864-3999; *Fax:* 780-532-1158
Toll-Free: 888-531-7771
info@mylawteam.ca
www.mylawteam.ca

British Columbia

Ashcroft

Morelli Chertkow LLP, Lawyers - Ashcroft
401 Railway Ave., Ashcroft, BC V0K 1A0
Tel: 250-453-2320; *Fax:* 250-453-2622
info@morellichertkow.com
www.morellichertkow.com

Campbell River

Shook, Wickham, Bishop & Field
906 Island Hwy., Campbell River, BC V9W 2C3
Tel: 250-287-8355; *Fax:* 250-287-8112
info@crlawyers.ca
www.crlawyers.ca
Profile: 1 Office, 9 Lawyers, Founded in: 1975
Environmental Lawyers:
Daniel A.J. Wickham, Partner, Forestry & Logging Law
250-287-8355
wickham@crlawyers.ca

Chilliwack

Waterstone Law Group LLP
#201, 45793 Luckakuck Way, Chilliwack, BC V2R 5S3
Tel: 604-824-7777; *Fax:* 604-824-7770
Toll-Free: 800-677-8772
info@waterstonelaw.com
www.waterstonelaw.com
Profile: 2 Offices, 9 Lawyers, Founded in: 1994
Environmental Lawyers:

Duncan

Ramsay Lampman Rhodes
130 Trans Canada Hwy., Duncan, BC V9L 3P7
Tel: 250-746-8800; *Toll-Free:* 800-263-3321
info@rlr-law.com
www.rlr-law.com

Kamloops

Fulton & Company LLP, Lawyers & Trade-Mark Agents
#300, 350 Lansdowne St., Kamloops, BC V2C 1Y1
Tel: 250-372-5542; *Fax:* 250-851-2300
law@fultonco.com
www.fultonco.com
Profile: 1 Office, 28 Lawyers, Founded in: 1885

Morelli Chertkow LLP, Lawyers - Kamloops
#300, 180 Seymour St., Kamloops, BC V2C 2E3
Tel: 250-374-3344; *Fax:* 250-374-1144
Toll-Free: 888-374-3350
info@morellichertkow.com
www.morellichertkow.com
www.facebook.com/MorelliChertkow
Profile: 4 Offices, 12 Lawyers, Founded in: 1911
Lawyers at Morelli Chertkow LLP provide legal services related to employment issues.
Environmental Lawyers:
K.F. Church, Associate, Employment Law
250-374-3344 ext. 248
kchurch@morellichertkow.com
Elizabeth A, Harris, Partner, Employment Law
250-374-3344 ext. 225
eharris@morellichertkow.com
John M. Hogg, QC, Partner, Employment Law
250-374-3344 ext. 205
jhogg@morellichertkow.com
Heather E. Johnston, Associate, Employment Law
250-374-3344 ext. 212
hjohnston@morellichertkow.com
Rachel R. Lammers, Associate, Employment Law
250-374-3344 ext. 241
rlammers@morellichertkow.com
Leigh Pedersen, Partner, Employment Law
250-374-3344 ext. 255
lpedersen@morellichertkow.com
Karen N. Schymon, Associate, Employment Law
250-374-3344 ext. 202
kschymon@morellichertkow.com

Kelowna

Farris, Vaughan, Wills & Murphy LLP - Kelowna
#800, 1708 Dolphin Ave., Kelowna, BC V1Y 9S4
Tel: 250-861-5332; *Fax:* 250-861-8772
info@farris.com
www.farris.com
Profile: 12 Lawyers

Pushor Mitchell LLP, Lawyers & Trade-Mark Agents
1665 Ellis St., 3rd Fl., Kelowna, BC V1Y 2B3
Tel: 250-762-2108; *Fax:* 250-762-9115
Toll-Free: 800-558-1155
lawyers@pushormitchell.com
www.pushormitchell.com
Profile: 1 Office, 31 Lawyers, Founded in: 1973
Environmental Lawyers:
Leona V. Baxter, Maritime law
baxter@pushormitchell.com

Langley

Lindsay Kenney LLP - Langley
#400, 20033 - 64th Ave., Langley, BC V2Y 1M9
Tel: 604-534-5114; *Fax:* 604-534-5927
Toll-Free: 866-687-1323
info@lklaw.ca
www.lklaw.ca
Profile: 16 Lawyers
Environmental Lawyers:
Trevor S. Fowler, Partner, Construction Law & Litigation
tfowler@lklaw.ca

Waterstone Law Group LLP
#304, 20338 - 65th Ave., Langley, BC V2Y 2X3
Tel: 604-533-2300; *Fax:* 604-533-2387
Toll-Free: 800-880-1667
info@waterstonelaw.com
www.waterstonelaw.com
Profile: 2 Offices, 0 Lawyers, Founded in: 1994
Areas of practice include employment law, farm transactions, * equine issues.
Environmental Lawyers:
Shelley J. Henshawe, Partner, Equine Issues
604-533-2300 ext. 111
shenshaw@waterstonelaw.com

Merritt

Morelli Chertkow LLP, Lawyers - Merritt
1988 Quilchena Ave., Merritt, BC V1K 1B8
Tel: 250-378-4218; *Fax:* 250-378-4997
info@morellichertkow.com
www.morellichertkow.com

Nanaimo

Ramsay Lampman Rhodes
111 Wallace St., Nanaimo, BC V9R 5B2
Tel: 250-754-3321; *Fax:* 250-754-1148
Toll-Free: 800-263-3321
info@rlr-law.com
www.rlr-law.com
Profile: 2 Offices, 16 Lawyers
Environmental Lawyers:
Peter C.P Behie, Q.C., Partner, Construction Law; Aboriginal & First Nations Law
pbehie@rlr-law.com
Derek Jonson, Partner, Construction Law
djonson@rlr-law.com
Jonathan W. Lampman, Counsel, Forestry Law; Land Use & Regulation
jlampman@rlr-law.com
Jennifer Millbank, Construction Law
jmillbank@rlr-law.com

North Vancouver

Ratcliff & Company LLP
#500, East Tower, 221 West Esplanade, North Vancouver, BC V7M 3J3
Tel: 604-988-5201; *Fax:* 604-988-1452
admin@ratcliff.com
www.ratcliff.com
Profile: 1 Office, 27 Lawyers, Founded in: 1950
The firm has developed a broad & comprehensive practice that now includes general Aboriginal litigation, Aboriginal & treaty rights, land claims & treaty negotiations, reserve-related claims, Aboriginal governance, employment issues, fisheries & forestry matters
Environmental Lawyers:
Kate Blomfield, Environmental Law; First Nations
Michelle M. Ellison, Environmental Law; Aboriginal Law
Lesley A. Giroday, Environmental Law; Forestry Land Use & Issues; First Nations
Stephanie A. Kearns, Environmental Law; Aboriginal Law
Matthew F. Kirchner, Partner, Environmental Law; Forestry Land Use & Issues; First Nations
Greg J. McDade, Q.C., Managing Partner, Environment; Forestry; First Nations
John R. Rich, Partner, Environment; Land & Resource Use; First Nations
Melinda J. Skeels, Environmental Law; Aboriginal Law
James P. Tate, Partner, Forestry Land Use & Issues; Aboriginal Law

Qualicum Beach

Marshall & Lamperson
CP 879, 710 Memorial Ave., Qualicum Beach, BC V9K 1T2
Tel: 250-752-5615; *Fax:* 250-752-2055
doug@qualicumlaw.ca
Profile: 1 Office, 2 Lawyers, Founded in: 1996

Richmond

Kahn Zack Ehrlich Lithwick
#270, 10711 Cambie Rd., Richmond, BC V6X 3G5
Tel: 604-270-9571; *Fax:* 604-270-8282
Toll-Free: 888-529-6368
general@kzellaw.com
www.kzellaw.com
Profile: 1 Office, 10 Lawyers, Founded in: 1973
The firm offers full service, in areas including construction.
Environmental Lawyers:
Marvin Lithwick, Partner, Construction
604-232-7204
lithwick@kzellaw.com

Vancouver

Alexander Holburn Beaudin & Lang, LLP
#2700, P.O. Box 10057, 700 West Georgia St., Vancouver, BC V7Y 1B8
Tel: 604-484-1700; *Fax:* 604-484-9700
Toll-Free: 877-688-1351
info@ahbl.ca
www.ahbl.ca
www.facebook.com/pages/Alexander-Holburn-Beaudin-Lang-LLP/310808898998791,
www.linkedin.com/company/alexander-holburn-beaudin-lang-llp
Profile: 1 Office, 72 Lawyers, Founded in: 1973
Works with industrial clients in the natural resource sector including mining, forestry and energy companies, corporate clients and their in-house counsel, engineers and environmental consultants, financial service providers, hospitals, insurers and individuals who need help dealing with an environmental issue or dispute.
Environmental Lawyers:
Greg J. Allen, Local government
604-484-1775
Rebecca Beatch, Construction & engineering
604-484-1737
rbeatch@ahbl.ca
Gordon A. Buck, Construction & engineering
604-484-1755
Megan Chorloton, Q.C., Local government
604-484-1766
mchorloton@ahbl.ca
Patrick S. Cleary, Construction & engineering
604-484-1741
pcleary@ahbl.ca
Todd R. Davies, Transportation law
604-484-1799
Bruno De Vita, Local government
604-484-1709
Michael A. Dery, Transportation law
604-484-1742
James A. Dowler, Environmental law; Local government
604-484-1706
jdowler@ahbl.ca
Ahmad Erfan, Transportation law
604-484-1778
aerfan@ahbl.ca
Fritz C. Gaerdes, Transportation law
604-484-1769
David A. Garner, Managing Partner, Environmental law; Health law; Construction & engineering
604-484-1708
David A. Gooderham, Local government
604-484-1788
dgooderham@ahbl.ca
D. John Goundrey, Environmental law; Health law; Transportation law; Local government
604-484-1710
jgoundrey@ahbl.ca
Christopher E. Hirst, Construction & engineering; Environmental law; Local government
604-484-1712
Dianna S. Hwang, Local government
604-484-1744
F. Stuart Lang, Health law
604-484-1770
slang@ahbl.ca
Andrew S. MacKay, Health law
604-484-1715
amackay@ahbl.ca
David F. McEwen, Q.C., Transportation law
604-484-1748
dmcewen@ahbl.ca
David T. McKnight, Local government
604-484-1716
dmcknight@ahbl.ca
Gary M. Nijman, Environmental law; Transportation law
604-484-1719
gnijman@ahbl.ca
Robert W. Pakrul, Health law; Transportation law
604-484-1720
rpakrul@ahbl.ca
Darryl G. Pankratz, Transportation law
604-484-1721
dpankratz@ahbl.ca
Jeremy M. Poole, Local government
604-484-1722
jpoole@ahbl.ca
Renee D. Ritchot, Transportation law
604-484-1703
Lawrence (Lanny) N. Robinson, Local government
604-484-1752
Michael V. Roche, Environmental law; Health law; Transportation law
604-484-1724
mroche@ahbl.ca
Dana L. Romanick, Environmental law
604-484-1753
dromanick@ahbl.ca
R. Patrick Saul, Transportation law
604-484-1728
psaul@ahbl.ca
Douglas G. Schmitt, Environmental law; Transportation law
604-484-1754
dschmitt@ahbl.ca
Emily A. Stock, Construction & engineering
604-484-1756
Sharon M. Urquhart, Environmental law; Transportation law
604-484-1757
Eileen E. Vanderburgh, Health law; Local government
604-484-1732
David B. Wende, Construction & engineering
604-484-1795
dwende@ahbl.ca

Baker & Baker
808 Nelson St., 17th Fl., Vancouver, BC V6Z 2H2
Tel: 604-642-0107; *Fax:* 604-681-3504
info@bakerbaker.ca
www.bakerbaker.ca
Profile: 1 Office, 3 Lawyers, Founded in: 1986

Barbeau, Evans & Goldstein, Barristers & Solicitors
#280, Park Place, 666 Burrard St., Vancouver, BC V6C 2X8
Tel: 604-688-4900; *Fax:* 604-688-0649
info@beg-law.com
www.beg-law.com

Profile: 1 Office, 4 Lawyers, Founded in: 1965
Land owners, contractors, engineers, & project managers are served by Barbeau, Evans & Goldstein lawyers who specialize in all aspects of construction law.
Environmental Lawyers:
Garth M. Evans, Real Estate Development; Constructions Law; Environmental Law
garth@beg-law.com

Bernard & Partners
#1500, 570 Granville St., Vancouver, BC V6C 3P1
Tel: 604-681-1700; *Fax:* 604-681-1788
tuytel@bernardpartners.com
www.bernardpartners.com
Profile: 1 Office, 15 Lawyers, Founded in: 2002
Bernard & Partners is a Vancouver based law firm, which provides legal services in both a commercial & litigation context. The goal of the firm is to provide innovative & cost-effective solutions to each client's legal needs. Lawyers at Bernard & Partners focus their efforts in a number of practice areas, including the following: Environmental law; Fisheries; Occupational health & safety; Employment law; Admiralty & maritime; Corporate, commercial & real estate; Business relocation, including immigration; Insurance defence (personal injury, disability, medical malpractice, products liability); & Litigation, including mediation & arbitration. Bernard & Partners has a wide range of experience in commercial transactions in the marine & fisheries community, international shipping, transportation, & in a variety of leading British Columbia industries. The firm's maritime litigation practice includes representation of shipowners & charterers, both local & foreign, all the major P&I Clubs, as well as a broad range of domestic & international underwriters. Lawyers at the firm are actively involved as members & directors of a number of organizations, including the following: the Canadian Maritime Law Association; the Vancouver Maritime Arbitrators Association; the Vancouver Maritime Museum; the Chamber of Shipping of British Columbia; & the International Sailors' Society Canada.
Environmental Lawyers:
Neo J. Tuytel
604-661-0614

Borden Ladner Gervais LLP - Vancouver
#1200, Waterfront Centre, P.O. Box 48600, 200 Burrard St., Vancouver, BC V7X 1T2
Tel: 604-687-5744; *Fax:* 604-687-1415
info@blg.com
www.blg.com
Profile: 136 Lawyers, Founded in: 1911
Energy; Forestry & Mining; Municipal; Oil & Gas; Environmental
Environmental Lawyers:

Boughton Law Corporation
#700, P.O. Box 49290, 595 Burrard St., Vancouver, BC V7X 1S8
Tel: 604-687-6789; *Fax:* 604-683-5317
lawyers@boughton.ca
www.boughton.ca
Profile: 2 Offices, 50 Lawyers, Founded in: 1949
Environmental Lawyers:
John Mostowich
604-647-4113
jmostowich@boughton.ca

Burns Fitzpatrick Rogers & Schwartz LLP, Barristers & Solicitors
#1400, 510 Burrard St., Vancouver, BC V6C 3A8
Tel: 604-685-0121; *Fax:* 604-685-2104
bfrs@bfrs.ca
www.bfrs.ca
Profile: 1 Office, 9 Lawyers,
Lawyers at the BFRS firm have experience in construction law, real property, employment law, & administrative law.
Environmental Lawyers:
J. Christopher Chan, Real Property Development
604-685-0121 ext. 315
John E. Rogers, Real Estate Development
604-685-0121 ext. 319

Clark Wilson LLP
#800, 885 Georgia St. West, Vancouver, BC V6C 3H1
Tel: 604-687-5700; *Fax:* 604-687-6314
agb@cwilson.com
www.cwilson.com
twitter.com/ClarkWilsonLLP
Profile: 1 Office, 79 Lawyers, Founded in: 1911
Environmental Lawyers:
Allyson L. Baker, Construction
604-891-7732
alb@cwilson.com
R. Glen Boswall, Construction
604-643-3125
rgb@cwilson.com
Matthew Both
604-643-3141
msb@cwilson.com
Warren G. Brazier, Carbon pricing; Carbon trading; Export market development
604-891-7762
wgb@cwilson.com
Nicole M. Byres, Energy; Municipal
604-643-3173
nmb@cwilson.com
Darren T. Donnelly, Municipal
604-643-3115
dtd@cwilson.com
Jonathan L.S. Hodes, Environmental; Construction
604-643-3168
jlh@cwilson.com
William D. Holder, Municipal; Clean-up litigation; Construction
604-643-3169
wdh@cwilson.com
Samantha Ip, Construction
604-643-3172
ssi@cwilson.com
R. Brock Johnston, Energy
604-643-3116
rbj@cwilson.com
Amy A. Mortimore, Construction
604-643-3177
aam@cwilson.com
Derek J. Mullan, Q.C., Construction
604-643-3162
djm@cwilson.com
D. Lawrence Munn, Energy
604-643-3160
lm@cwilson.com
Roy A. Nieuwenburg, Environmental & Construction Law; Expropriation; Energy; Municipal
604-643-3112
ran@cwilson.com
Aaron B. Singer, Environmental Law
604-643-3108
abs@cwilson.com

Davis LLP - Vancouver
#2800, Park Place, 666 Burrard St., Vancouver, BC V6C 2Z7
Tel: 604-687-9444; *Fax:* 604-687-1612
www.davis.ca
www.facebook.com/pages/Davis-LLP/223962770329, twitter.com/DavisLLP, www.linkedin.com/company/davis-llp
Profile: 8 Offices, 243 Lawyers, Founded in: 1892
As a full-service law firm, Davis LLP provides a comprehensive range of legal services to clients around the world, through offices across Canada & in Japan. The firm has 88 partners worldwide, & 134 other lawyers around the world. Business can be conducted in English, French, Japanese, Spanish, Mandarin, Cantonese, Korean, German, Italian, Dutch, Estonian, & Polish. Established in Vancouver in 1892, the firm has more than 240 lawyers working in integrated practice groups that focus on client service & specialization. Davis strives to help clients achieve their business objectives & resolve business problems quickly & effectively. The firm is strong in all the traditional areas of legal practice, & also offers the knowledge base of a broad array of innovative practice groups & integrated specialties, such as projects, infrastructure & P3, & climate change / renewable energy. Across the firm, lawyers continuously cultivate commercial & government relationships to both facilitate the conduct of business & to identify new business opportunities for clients. Davis & its lawyers are recognized as leaders in numerous domestic & international ratings publications.
Environmental Lawyers:
Robert T. Banno, Partner, Mining Law
604-643-2903
rbanno@davis.ca
Donald R.M. Bell, Partner, Mining
604-643-2949
dbell@davis.ca
Douglas B. Buchanan, Q.C., Partner, Energy & Utilities
604-643-2907
dbuchanan@davis.ca
Andrew J.G. Burton, Partner, Energy & Utilities
604-643-2962
aburton@davis.ca
D. Ross Clark, Q.C., Senior Partner, Environmental
604-643-2911
drclark@davis.ca
Donald R. Collie, Partner, Mining
604-643-6472
dcollie@davis.ca
Dean L. Dalke, Energy & Utilities; Municipal; Regulatory & Administrative
604-643-6369
ddalke@davis.ca
Warren H. Downs, Partner, Environmental; Construction; Forestry; Energy & Utilities
604-643-2916
whdowns@davis.ca
W. Ross Ellison, Q.C., Senior Partner, Municipal; Regulatory
604-643-2918
rellison@davis.ca
Shawn Hatch, Forestry
604-643-2969
shatch@davis.ca
Jason K. Herbert, Partner, Energy & Utilities; Employment & Labour; Regulatory & Administrative
604-643-2928
jherbert@davis.ca
Brian F. Hiebert, Managing Partner, Energy & Utilities; Forestry; Mining; Environmental; Climate change
604-643-2917
bhiebert@davis.ca
Jeffrey D. Horswill, Climate Change; Regulatory & Administrative
604-643-6357
jhorswill@davis.ca
Danielle R. Jarvis, Climate Change
604-643-2950
djarvis@davis.ca
Rolf N. Kaplun, Partner, Forestry; Energy & Utilities
604-643-2933
rkaplun@davis.ca
P. John Landry, Partner, Energy & Utilities; Regulatory
604-643-2935
pjl@davis.ca
Garry E.P. Mancell, R.P.F., Partner, Forestry; Environmental; Energy & Utilities
604-643-2977
garry_mancell@davis.ca
Elizabeth Mayer, Construction
604-643-6438
emayer@davis.ca
Brent A. Meckling, Partner, Environmental; Forestry; Construction
604-643-6405
bmeckling@davis.ca
Cynthia A. Millar, Partner, Regulatory & Administrative
604-643-2996
camillar@davis.ca
Stuart B. Morrow, Senior Partner, Mining; Energy & Utilities
604-643-2948
sbmorrow@davis.ca
David R. Reid, Partner, Mining
604-643-6428
drreid@davis.ca
Dale G. Sanderson, Q.C., Senior Partner, Energy & Utilities; Regulatory & Administrative; Construction
604-643-6330
dsanderson@davis.ca
Mark A. Schmidt, Managing Partner, Forestry
604-643-6401
mschmidt@davis.ca
Blair M. Shaw, Partner, Construction
604-643-2987
bmshaw@davis.ca
Douglas G. Shields, Partner, Mining
604-643-2998
dshields@davis.ca
Franco E. Trasolini, Construction; Municipal
604-643-2964
ftrasolini@davis.ca
Simon R. Wells, Partner, Environmental; Municipal; Forestry; Regulatory & Administrative
604-643-6460
simon_wells@davis.ca

Dentons Canada LLP - Vancouver
250 Howe St., 20th Fl., Vancouver, BC V6C 3R8

Tel: 604-687-4460; *Fax:* 604-683-5214
www.dentons.com
Profile: 62 Lawyers, Founded in: 1980
The firm provides legal services in the areas of Energy Law, & Mining Law
Environmental Lawyers:
Brian E. Abraham, Environmental; Securities & Mining Law
604-443-7134
brian.abraham@dentons.com
Waldemar Braul, Environmental Law, Aboriginal Law
604-443-7148
wally.braul@dentons.com
Colin J. McIver, Environmental Law; Energy & Natural Resources; Mining
604-443-7128
colin.mciver@dentons.com

Donovan & Company

73 Water St., 6th Fl., Vancouver, BC V6B 1A1
Tel: 604-688-4272; *Fax:* 604-688-4282
allan_donovan@aboriginal-law.com
www.aboriginal-law.com
Profile: 1 Office, 9 Lawyers, Founded in: 1996
Donovan & Company is a law firm in Vancouver, British Columbia that practices exclusively in the area of aboriginal law.

DuMoulin Boskovich LLP

#1800, Manulife Place, Box 52, 1095 West Pender St., Vancouver, BC V6E 2M6
Tel: 604-669-5500; *Fax:* 604-688-8491
Toll-Free: 800-288-9893
info@dubo.com
www.dubo.com
www.linkedin.com/company/2293070?trk=tyah
Profile: 1 Office, 16 Lawyers, Founded in: 1972
The partnership of DuMoulin Boskovich LLP is built upon the practice areas of fisheries law, real estate, corporate governance and litigation, all of which have been infused with environmental concerns, regulations and practices
Environmental Lawyers:
Joseph A. Boskovich, Fishing & Maritime
604-669-5500 ext. 214
joe@dubo.com

Edwards, Kenny & Bray LLP

#1900, The Grosvenor Bldg., 1040 West Georgia St., Vancouver, BC V6E 4H3
Tel: 604-689-1811; *Fax:* 604-689-5177
inquiry@ekb.com
www.ekb.com
Profile: 1 Office, 27 Lawyers, Founded in: 1965
Provides advice & representation in relation to matters such as: waste management, contaminated lands, pollution control, assisting in formulating & implementing compliance strategies, environmental due diligence for corporate transactions, remediation projects, etc.
Environmental Lawyers:
A. Thomas Clarke, Partner, Hazardous Waste Management
604-661-1025
tclarke@ekb.com
Douglas K. Harrison, Associate Counsel, Environmental Audits; General Advice; Asbestos
604-661-1081
dharrison@ekb.com
Geoffrey M. Sherrott, Partner
604-661-1060
gsherrott@ekb.com

Farris, Vaughan, Wills & Murphy LLP

P.O. Box 10026, 700 West Georgia St., 25th Floor, Vancouver, BC V7Y 1B3
Tel: 604-684-9151; *Fax:* 604-661-9349
Toll-Free: 877-684-9151
info@farris.com
www.farris.com
Profile: 3 Offices, 95 Lawyers, Founded in: 1903
Environmental Lawyers:
Robert S. Anderson
604-661-9372
randerson@farris.com
Brian R. Canfield
604-661-9362
bcanfield@farris.com
Ron A. Chin
604-661-9333
rchin@farris.com
Scott A. Dawson
604-661-9354
sdawson@farris.com
Robert J. McDonell
604-661-9371
rmcdonell@farris.com
J. Kenneth McEwan, Q.C.
604-661-9356
kmcewan@farris.com

Fasken Martineau - Vancouver

#2900, 550 Burrard St., Vancouver, BC V6C 0A3
Tel: 604-631-3131; *Fax:* 604-631-3232
Toll-Free: 866-635-3131
vancouver@fasken.com
www.fasken.com
www.linkedin.com/company/163768?trk=tyah
Profile: 135 Lawyers, Founded in: 1889
Environmental Services: Environmental, Energy & Natural Resource Law
Environmental Lawyers:
Ron Ezekiel
604-631-4708
rezekiel@van.fasken.com
Heidi Granger
604-631-4790
hgranger@van.fasken.com
Robert M. Lonergan
604-631-4718
rlonergan@van.fasken.com
Larry J. Nelson
604-631-4726
lnelson@van.fasken.com
Kevin O'Callaghan
604-631-4839
kocallaghan@van.fasken.com
Michelle Pockey
604-631-4825
mpockey@van.fasken.com
Darrell W. Podowski
604-631-3229
dpodowski@van.fasken.com
Dennis Ryan
604-631-4872
dryan@van.fasken.com
William Westeringh, Q.C., Managing Partner, Vancouver, Product Liability; Aviation; Mining; Insurance and Commercial Litigation
604-631-4728
wwesteringh@fasken.com
Paul C. Wilson
604-631-4728
pwilson@van.fasken.com

Ganapathi & Company

#302, 1224 Hamilton St., Vancouver, BC V6B 2S8
Tel: 604-689-9222; *Fax:* 604-689-4888
Toll-Free: 866-689-9222
info@ganapathico.com
www.ganapathico.com
Profile: 1 Office, 2 Lawyers, Founded in: 1975
Ganapathi & Company practises environmental law & fisheries law. Environmental services include the integration of environmental & ecological factors into planning & decision-making processes. Work related to the fisheries includes marine habitat protection, hatchery law, & fisheries offences.
Environmental Lawyers:
Michael Galambos
Nathan Ganapathi

Gowling Lafleur Henderson LLP - Vancouver

#2300, Bentall V, 550 Burrard St., Vancouver, BC V6C 2B5
Tel: 604-683-6498; *Fax:* 604-683-3558
Profile: 66 Lawyers
Environmental Lawyers:
K. Alan Blair, Environmental Law; Occupational Health & Safety; Regulatory & Compliance; Government Affairs; Mining Industry; Oil & Gas Industry; Chemical Industry; Manufacturing Industries
604-891-2288
alan.blair@gowlings.com
G. Henry Ellis, Energy Law; Infrastructure; Power Production & Distribution; Hydro Projects; Biomass Projects; Licensing; Regulatory & Compliance
604-891-2250
henry.ellis@gowlings.com
Martin L. Palleson, Environmental Law; Aboriginal Law; Natural Resources Law
604-443-7622
martin.palleson@gowlings.com
Donald J. Weaver, Energy Law; Infrastructure Industry; Mining Industry; Energy Distribution Industry; Forestry Industry
604-891-2731
don.weaver@gowlings.com

Heenan Blaikie LLP - Vancouver

#2200, 1055 West Hastings St., Vancouver, BC V6E 2E9
Tel: 604-669-0011; *Fax:* 604-669-5101
www.heenanblaikie.com
Profile: 49 Lawyers, Founded in: 1973
Environmental Lawyers:
Susan Arnold, Partner, Occupational Health & Safety
604-891-1151
sarnold@heenan.ca
Dean Crawford, Partner, Health
604-891-1162
dcrawford@heenan.ca
H. David Edinger, Partner, Construction Litigation
604-891-1158
hedinger@heenan.ca
Jillian Frank, Occupational Health & Safety
604-891-1160
jfrank@heenan.ca
Peter A. Gall, Q.C., Partner, Occupational Health & Safety
604-891-1152
pgall@heenan.ca
Jonathan D. Greenberg, Counsel, Energy
604-891-1153
jgreenberg@heenan.ca
Jay Hayden, Partner, Energy; Climate, Cleantech & Sustainability
604-891-1167
jhayden@heenan.ca
John A. Legge, Partner, Construction Litigation; Energy & Resources Litigation
604-891-1187
jlegge@heenan.ca
T. Murray Rankin, Q.C., Partner, Environmental Law; Aboriginal law; Natural Resources
250-381-1010
mrankin@heenan.ca
Tobin Robbins, Partner, Transportation
604-891-1194
trobbins@heenan.ca
Richard Shrieves, Partner, Natural Resources; Construction; Aboriginal Law
604-891-1169
rshrieves@heenan.ca
Catherine Wade, Partner, Mining
604-891-1165
cwade@heenan.ca

Hume, Forrest C., Law Corporation

#700, 1080 Howe St., Vancouver, BC V6Z 2T1
Tel: 604-488-1499; *Fax:* 604-488-1489
fchume@humelawcorp.com
Profile: 1 Office, 1 Lawyers, Founded in: 1999

Hunter Litigation Chambers

#2100, 1040 West Georgia St., Vancouver, BC V6E 4H1
Tel: 604-891-2400; *Fax:* 604-647-4554
www.litigationchambers.com
Profile: 1 Office, 19 Lawyers, Founded in: 2006

Hutchins Caron & Associates

#400, 601 West Broadway, Office 5, Vancouver, BC V5Z 4C2
Tel: 604-871-4327; *Fax:* 604-871-4336
admin@hutchinslegal.ca
www.hutchinslegal.ca
Profile: The firm is engaged in the practice of Aboriginal law, including resource management & development & environmental protection.

Lawson Lundell LLP - Vancouver

#1600, Cathedral Place, 925 West Georgia St., Vancouver, BC V6C 3L2
Tel: 604-685-3456; *Fax:* 604-669-1620
genmail@lawsonlundell.com
www.lawsonlundell.com
twitter.com/LawsonLundell,
www.linkedin.com/companies/lawson-lundell-llp

Profile: 3 Offices, 116 Lawyers, Founded in: 1886
Environmental Law Group is regularly involved in corporate transactions & environmental litigation, including dispute resolution, regulatory defense matters, environmental assessments, toxic torts, permit appeals, administrative actions & regulatory inspections & investigations; other environmental areas: energy law; forestry; mining; oil & gas; aboriginal law
Environmental Lawyers:
Khaled S. Abdel-Barr, B.Comm., J.D., LL.B., Partner, Mining & Natural Resources Law
604-631-9233
kabdel-barr@lawsonlundell.com
Brad Armstrong, QC, B.A.,M.Sc.,LL.B., Partner, Aboriginal Law; Climate Change; Environmental Law & Prosecutions; Project Permitting; Regulatory Compliance
604-631-9126
barmstrong@lawsonlundell.com
Chris G. Baldwin, B.A., J.D., Partner, Mining & Natural Resources Law; Aboriginal Law
604-631-9151
cbaldwin@lawsonlundell.com
Keith Bergner, B.A., LL.B., Partner, Aboriginal Law; Energy Law; Environmental Law; Project Permitting; Public Utility & Regulatory; Regulatory Compliance
604-631-9119
kbergner@lawsonlundell.com
Kinji C. Bourchier, B.A., LL.B., Partner, Environmental Law & Prosecutions
604-631-9267
kbourchier@lawsonlundell.com
Amy J. Carruthers, Partner, Climate Change; Energy
604-631-6711
acarruthers@lawsonlundell.com
Gordon R. Chambers, B.Comm., LL.B., Partner, Mining & Natural Resources Law
604-631-9191
grchambers@lawsonlundell.com
Randall C. Chatwin, Mining
604-631-6799
rchatwin@lawsonlundell.com
Jeff Christian, B.A.Sc., LL.B., Partner, Energy Law; Public Utility & Regulatory
604-631-9115
jchristian@lawsonlundell.com
Lauren E. Cook, Environmental Prosecutions
604-631-9111
lcook@lawsonlundell.com
Gordon M. Craig, B.A., LL.B., Partner, Energy Law; Climate Change; Public Utility & Regulatory
604-631-9155
gcraig@lawsonlundell.com
Laura E. Duke, Environment; Aboriginal Law
604-631-9129
lduke@lawsonlundell.com
William M. Everett, Q.C., B.A., LL.B., Partner, Environmental Litigation
604-631-9171
wmeverett@lawsonlundell.com
Brian D. Fulton, B.A., LL.B., Partner, Energy Law
604-631-9185
bfulton@lawsonlundell.com
Christopher R.C. Funt, Energy Law; Envvironment; Aboriginal Law
604-631-9272
cfunt@lawsonlundell.com
Sara J. Gregory, Environmental Prosecutions
604-631-6785
sgregory@lawsonlundell.com
Marianna Jasper, Energy; Environment; Aboriginal Law
604-631-9242
mjasper@lawsonlundell.com
Christine J. Kowbel, Climate Change; Environment; Aboriginal Law
604-631-6762
ckowbel@lawsonlundell.com
Michael L. Lee, BSc.,B.A.,M.A.,LL.B., Partner, Mining & Natural Resources Law
604-631-9139
mlee@lawsonlundell.com
Jennifer S. Nyland, Environment; Energy
604-631-9287
jnyland@lawsonlundell.com
Clifford G. Proudfoot, LL.B., LL.M., Partner, Aboriginal Law; Environmental Law & Prosecutions; Regulatory Compliance
604-631-9217
cproudfoot@lawsonlundell.com
Chris W. Sanderson, Q.C., B.A., LL.B., Partner, Energy Law; Public Utility & Regulatory
604-631-9183
csanderson@lawsonlundell.com
Jerrold W. Schramm, B.Comm., LL.B., Partner, Mining & Natural Resources Law; Energy Law
604-631-9131
jschramm@lawsonlundell.com
Ron A. Skolrood, B.A., LL.B., LL.M., Partner, Aboriginal Law
604-631-9134
rskolrood@lawsonlundell.com
Ian D. Webb, B.Sc., LL.B., Partner, Energy Law; Public Utility & Regulatory
604-631-9117
iwebb@lawsonlundell.com

Lesperance Mendes

#410, 900 Howe St., Vancouver, BC V6Z 2M4
Tel: 604-685-3567; *Fax:* 604-685-7505
kmw@lmlaw.ca
www.lmlaw.ca
Profile: 1 Office, 7 Lawyers, Founded in: 1997
Environmental law

Lindsay Kenney LLP - Vancouver

#1800, 401 West Georgia St., Vancouver, BC V6B 5A1
Tel: 604-687-1323; *Fax:* 604-687-2347
Toll-Free: 866-687-1323
info@lklaw.ca
www.lklaw.ca
Profile: 2 Offices, 35 Lawyers, Founded in: 1980
Environmental Lawyers:
Paul Backhouse, Construction Law & Litigation
604-484-3058
pbackhouse@lklaw.ca
Melissa Bryden, Construction Law & Litigation
604-484-3052
mbryden@lklaw.ca
Jesse Halperin, Construction Law & Litigation
604-484-3080
jhalperin@lklaw.ca
Richard B. Lindsay, Q.C., Founding Partner, Energy; Construction Law & Litigation
604-484-3067
rlindsay@lklaw.ca
Christopher D. Martin, Construction Law & Litigation
604-484-3085
cmartin@lklaw.ca
Greg S. Miller, Partner, Construction Law & Litigation
604-484-3070
gmiller@lklaw.ca
Carmen Tham, Construction Law & Litigation
604-484-3056
ctham@lklaw.ca

MacKenzie Fujisawa LLP

#1600, 1095 West Pender St., Vancouver, BC V6E 2M6
Tel: 604-689-3281; *Fax:* 604-685-6494
lawyers@maclaw.bc.ca
www.mackenziefujisawa.com
Profile: 1 Office, 20 Lawyers, Founded in: 1963
Environment Issues; Real Property Transactions; Waste Management Litigation; Environmental Criminal Defence
Environmental Lawyers:
William A. Ferguson, Aboriginal
604-687-3216
wferguson@maclaw.bc.ca
Christopher Harvey, Q.C., Marine; Aviation; Environmental; National Resources
604-443-1202
charvey@maclaw.bc.ca
Kenneth V. Krohman, Environment Issues; Real Property Transactions
604-443-1208
kkrohman@maclaw.bc.ca
Brian C. Poston, Maritime; Aviation
604-443-1213
bposton@maclaw.bc.ca
Christopher J. Watson, Aboriginal; Fisheries
604-443-1235
cwatson@maclaw.bc.ca
Robert V. Wickett, Waste Management Litigation; Environmental Criminal Defence
604-443-1242
rwickett@maclaw.bc.ca
Robert H. Wynick, Environmental Issues; Real Property Transactions
604-443-1209
rwynick@maclaw.bc.ca

McCarthy Tétrault LLP - Vancouver

#1300, Pacific Centre, CP 10424, 777 Dunsmuir St., Vancouver, BC V7Y 1K2
Tel: 604-643-7100; *Fax:* 604-643-7900
info@mccarthy.ca
www.mccarthy.ca
Profile: 7 Offices, 97 Lawyers, Founded in: 1960
Biotechnology; Energy; Environmental; Municipal
Environmental Lawyers:
Sam Adkins, Aboriginal; Mining
604-643-7984
sadkins@mccarthy.ca
Nicholas R. Hughes, Aboriginal; Environmental; Civil Litigation
604-643-7106
rhughes@mccarthy.ca
Thomas F. Isaac, Aboriginal; Environmental; Oil & Gas; Mining; Power
604-643-5987
tisaac@mccarthy.ca
Peter H. Kenward, Municipal Planning; Land Development & Planning; Envorinmental
604-643-7962
pkenward@mccarthy.ca
D. Anthony Knox, Aboriginal Law; Mining Law
604-643-7916
tknox@mccarthy.ca
Robert J. Miller, Aboriginal; Energy; Environmental; Mining
604-643-5897
rmiller@mccarthy.ca
Warren B. Milman, Environmental
604-643-7104
wmilman@mccarthy.ca
Linda G. Parker, Municipal Planning; Environmental Law
604-643-7909
lparker@mccarthy.ca
Robin M. Sirett, Energy; Oil & Gas
604-643-7911
rsirett@mccarthy.ca
James A. Titerle, Natural Resources; Environmental
604-643-7949
jtiterle@mccarthy.ca

McCullough O'Connor Irwin LLP

#2610, Oceanic Plaza, 1066 West Hastings St., Vancouver, BC V6E 3X1
Tel: 604-687-7077; *Fax:* 604-687-7099
moimail@moisolicitors.com
www.moisolicitors.com
Profile: 1 Office, 14 Lawyers, Founded in: 1994

McMillan LLP - Vancouver

#1500, Royal Centre, CP 11117, 1055 West Georgia St., Vancouver, BC V6E 4N7
Tel: 604-689-9111; *Fax:* 604-685-7084
info@mcmillan.ca
www.mcmillan.ca
Profile: 91 Lawyers, Founded in: 1926
Environmental Lawyers:
Desmond Balakrishnan, Mining & natural resources
Cheri Bocking, Mining & natural resources
Peter Botz, Forestry; Mining & natural resources
Corin Bowman, Environmental law; Energy; Emissions; Power generation; Utilities
Casper Bych, Mining & natural resources
Damon Chisholm, Mining & natural resources
Keith E. Clark, Environmental law; Energy; Emissions; Power generation; Utilities; Forestry; Mining & natural resources
David J. Cowan, Mining & natural resources
Thomas J. Deutsch, Mining & natural resources
Daniel D. Dex, Mining & natural resources
Claire E. Ellett, Environmental litigation; Administrative law
G. Barry Finlayson, Mining & natural resources
Gary C. Floyd, Mining & natural resources
Karl E. Gustafson, Q.C., Managing Partner, Environmental law; Energy; Power generation; Utilities; Emissions; Forestry; Mining & natural resources; Transportation & logistics (marine, aviation, & rail)
604-691-7427
karl.gustafson@mcmillan.ca
Linda J. Hogg, Mining & natural resources
Cory Kent, Mining & natural resources

Anthony H.S. Knight, Mining & natural resources
Sandra M. Knowler, Forestry; Mining & natural resources; Transportation & logistics (marine, aviation, & rail)
Christine Man, Mining & natural resources
Christine Mingie, Forestry; Mining & natural resources
John D. Morrison, Mining & natural resources
jmorrison@lmls.com
James R. Munro, Mining & natural resources
Mark Neighbor, Mining & natural resources
Sean O'Neill, Mining & natural resources
Siobhan O'Sullivan, Transportation & logistics (marine, aviation, & rail)
Herbert I. Ono, Mining & natural resources
Laurel M. Petryk, Mining & natural resources
Darrell W. Podowski, Mining & natural resources
David J. Ross, Forestry; Mining & natural resources
Amandeep Sandhu, Forestry
Jeremy Shelford, Forestry
Tom Theodorakis, Forestry; Transportation & logistics (marine, aviation, & rail)
François E.J. Tougas, Forestry; Mining & natural resources; Transportation & logistics (marine, aviation, & rail)
604-691-7425
francois.tougas@mcmillan.ca
R. Michael Tourigny, Forestry; Mining & natural resources
Ningyan (Sandy) Wang, Forestry; Mining & natural resources
Stephen D. Wortley, Forestry; Mining & natural resources
Joan M. Young, Administrative law
Bernhard Zinkhofer, Mining & natural resources
Louis J. Zivot, Transportation & logistics (marine, aviation, & rail)

Miller Thomson LLP - Vancouver

#1000, Robson Ct., 840 Howe St., Vancouver, BC V6Z 2M1
Tel: 604-687-2242; *Fax:* 604-643-1200
Toll-Free: 800-794-6866
vancouver@millerthomson.com
www.millerthomson.com
Profile: 61 Lawyers, Founded in: 2000
Aboriginal; Energy; Municipal & Planning; Oil & Gas; Construction; Forestry
Environmental Lawyers:
Wendy A. Baker, Q.C., Partner, Environmental Law; Construction Litigation; Aboriginal Law
604-643-1285
wbaker@millerthomson.com
Charles W. Bois, Partner, CleanTech; Environmental Law; Natural Resources; Renewable Energy; Aboriginal Law; Construction
604-643-1224
cbois@millerthomson.com
Tony Crossman, Partner, Envirnomental Law; CleanTech; Aboriginal Law; Energy
604-643-1244
tcrossman@millerthomson.com
Sarah D. Hansen, Partner, Energy; CleanTech; Forestry; Environmental; Aboriginal Rights
604-643-1273
shansen@millerthomson.com
Oleh W. Ilnyckyj, Partner, Health
604-643-1247
oilnyckyj@millerthomson.ca
Daniel L. Kiselbach, Partner, Environment Law
604-643-1263
dkiselbach@millerthomson.com
Amyn F. Lalji, Partner, Environmental Law; Mining; Aboriginal Law
604-643-1201
alalji@millerthomson.com
Peter J.G. McArthur, Partner, Mining; Natural Resources
604-643-1219
pmcarthur@millerthomson.ca
Paul A. McDonnell, Partner, Construction Litigation
604-643-1235
pmcdonnell@millerthomson.com
Ryan W. Morasiewicz, Health
604-643-1202
rmorasiewicz@millerthomson.com
Matthew M. Morawski, Construction Litigation
604-643-1213
mmorawski@millerthomson.com
Owen D. Pawson, Partner, Construction Litigation
604-643-1254
opawson@millerthomson.ca
Michael J. Percival, Partner, Construction Litigation
604-643-1230
mpercival@millerthomson.ca
David Rice, Counsel, Energy; Forestry
604-643-1209
drice@millerthomson.com
Darrell W. Roberts, Q.C., Counsel, Construction Litigation
604-643-1280
droberts@millerthomson.ca
Stephen R. Ross, Partner, Construction Litigation; Forestry
604-643-1205
sross@millerthomson.com
Gregory C. Smith, Partner, Mining
604-643-1258
gsmith@millerthomson.ca
Donald J. Sorochan, Q.C., Partner, Construction Litigation
604-643-1214
dsorodhan@millerthomson.com
Karen L. Weslowski, Partner, Construction Litigation
604-643-1290
kweslowski@millerthomson.com

Richards Buell Sutton LLP

#700, 401 West Georgia St., Vancouver, BC V6B 5A1
Tel: 604-682-3664; *Fax:* 604-688-3830
info@rbs.ca
www.rbs.ca
Profile: 1 Office, 37 Lawyers, Founded in: 1871
Environmental Lawyers:
Michael P. Shane, Partner, Environmental Waste Management
604-661-9223
mshane@rbs.ca

Rosenberg & Rosenberg

671D Market Hill, Vancouver, BC V5Z 4B5
Tel: 604-879-4505; *Fax:* 604-879-4934
reception@rosenberglaw.ca
www.rosenberglaw.ca
Profile: 1 Office, 4 Lawyers, Founded in: 1980
Lawyers at Rosenberg & Rosenberg have expertise in First Nations law, engineering, & construction.
Environmental Lawyers:
Paul S. Rosenberg, Engineering; Construction
David M. Rosenberg, QC, First Nations Law

Singleton Urquhart LLP

#1200, 925 Georgia St. West, Vancouver, BC V6C 3L2
Tel: 604-682-7474; *Fax:* 604-682-1283
su@singleton.com
www.singleton.com
Profile: 1 Office, 35 Lawyers, Founded in: 1986
Environmental Lawyers:
Daniel Barber, Construction
dbarber@singleton.com
Scott Brearley, Construction
sbrearley@singleton.com
Derek A. Brindle, Q.C., Counsel, Construction
dbrindle@singleton.com
Barbara Cornish, Partner, Construction
bcornish@singleton.com
Mitch Dermer, Construction
mdermer@singleton.com
Jennifer Frahm, Construction; Environmental Law
jfrahm@singleton.com
Jeffrey A. Hand, Partner, Construction
jhand@singleton.com
Robert A. Hodgins, Partner, Construction
rhodgins@singleton.com
Roger E. Holland, Partner, Construction
rholland@singleton.com
Ian C. Jones, Environmental Law
ijones@singleton.com
Steven L. Lesiuk, Environmental Law
slesiuk@singleton.com
Melissa Nagelbach, Construction
mnagelbach@singleton.com
Cornel Peana, Construction
cpeana@singleton.com
Michael Peraya, Construction
mperaya@singleton.com
David G. Perry, Partner, Environmental Law
dperry@singleton.com
Elizabeth (Betsy) Segal, Construction
esegal@singleton.com
Michael D. Shirreff, Construction
asherriff@singleton.com
John R. Singleton, Q.C., Partner, Environmental Law; Construction
jsingleton@singleton.com
Mark C. Stacey, Partner, Construction
mstacey@singleton.com
Wei Kiat Sun, Construction
wsun@singleton.com
Mark S. Thompson, Partner, Construction
mthompson@singleton.com
Glenn A. Urquhart, Q.C., Counsel, Construction
gurquhart@singleton.com

Stikeman Elliott LLP - Vancouver

#1700, 666 Burrard St., Vancouver, BC V6C 2X8
Tel: 604-631-1300; *Fax:* 604-681-1825
Toll-Free: 866-631-1300
www.stikeman.com
Profile: 36 Lawyers, Founded in: 1988
Environmental Lawyers:
Amyn M. Abdula, Pharmaceuticals, Biotechnology & Life Sciences; Energy; Forestry & Forest Products
604-631-1322
aabdula@stikeman.com
Michael S. Allen, Partner, Renewable Energy; Forestry & Forest Products; Mining
604-631-1346
mallen@stikeman.com
John F. Anderson, Partner, Forestry & Forest Products; Mining
604-631-1307
janderson@stikeman.com
Jonathan S. Drance, Partner, Emissions Trading & Climate Change; Forestry & Forest Products
604-631-1361
jdrance@stikeman.com
Annette E.F. Dueck, Mining
604-631-1315
adueck@stikeman.com
Ross A. MacDonald, Managing Partner, Construction Litigation; Environmental Law
604-631-1367
rmacdonald@stikeman.com
Neville J. McClure, Partner, Mining
604-631-1324
nmcclure@stikeman.com
Jonathan M. McLean, Senior Counsel, Construction Litigation; Environmental Litigation
604-631-1347
jmclean@stikeman.com
John E. Stark, Partner, Pharmaceuticals, Biotechnology & Life Sciences; Construction Litigation; Forestry & Forest Products; Mining
604-631-1395
jstark@stikeman.com
Jamie Templeton, Energy; Emissions Trading & Climate Change
604-631-1441
jtempleton@stikeman.com

Young, Anderson

#1616, Nelson Square, CP 12147, 808 Nelson St., Vancouver, BC V6Z 2H2
Tel: 604-689-7400; *Fax:* 604-689-3444
Toll-Free: 800-665-3540
reception@younganderson.ca
www.younganderson.ca
Profile: 2 Offices, 19 Lawyers, Founded in: 1982
Environmental Lawyers:
Bill Buholzer, Municipal
Reece Harding, Litigation
Sukhbir Manhas, Litigation
Barry Williamson, Litigation
Raymond E. Young, Municipal

Vernon

Nixon Wenger

3201 - 30 Ave., 4th Fl., Vernon, BC V1T 2C6
Tel: 250-542-5353; *Fax:* 250-542-7273
Toll-Free: 800-243-5353
nw@nixonwenger.com
www.nixonwenger.com
Profile: 1 Office, 19 Lawyers, Municipal Law & Land Development

Victoria

Cook Roberts LLP

1175 Douglas St., 7th Fl., Victoria, BC V8W 2E1

Tel: 250-385-1411; *Fax:* 250-413-3300
lawmark@cookroberts.bc.ca
www.cookroberts.bc.ca
Profile: 1 Office, 20 Lawyers, Founded in: 1970
Environmental Assessments & Review; Pollution & Contamination Claims & Defense; Environmental Prosecution & Defense; Aboriginal Law Issues
Environmental Lawyers:
Robert C. Freedman, Aboriginal Litigation & Treaty Rights
250-385-1411
rfreedman@cookroberts.bc.ca
Robert J.M. Janes, Aboriginal Litigation
250-385-1411
rjanes@cookroberts.bc.ca
Dominique A. Nouvet, Aboriginal Litigation & Treaty Rights
250-385-1411
dnouvet@cookroberts.bc.ca

Crease Harman & Company
#800, 1070 Douglas St., Victoria, BC V8W 2S8
Tel: 250-388-5421; *Fax:* 250-388-4294
creaseharman@creaseharman.com
www.creaseharman.com
Profile: 1 Office, 14 Lawyers, Founded in: 1879
Offers comprehensive advice in relation to all forms of municipal law; provides legal advice & representation in relation to all aspects of environmental law, including regulatory issues
Environmental Lawyers:
Bruce Hallsor, Municipal Law; Environmental Law
hallsor@creaseharman.com
Peter W. Klassen, Municipal Law
pwklassen@creaseharman.com

Farris, Vaughan, Wills & Murphy LLP - Victoria
#1100, 1175 Douglas St., Victoria, BC V8W 2E1
Tel: 250-382-1100; *Fax:* 250-405-1984
info@farris.com
www.farris.com
Profile: 3 Lawyers

Heenan Blaikie LLP - Victoria
1005 Langley, 3rd Fl., Victoria, BC V8W 1L6
Tel: 250-381-9321; *Fax:* 250-381-7023
www.heenanblaikie.com
Profile: 4 Lawyers, Founded in: 1973
Environmental Lawyers:
Lawrence Alexander, Environmental Law; Natural Resources; Energy
250-220-4342
lalexander@heenan.ca
Susan P. Arnold, Partner, Occupational Health & Safety
250-381-9321
sarnold@heenan.ca
Peter A. Gall, Q.C., Partner, Occupational Health & Safety
250-381-9321
pgalld@heenan.ca
Jay Hayden, Partner, Energy; Climate, Cleantech & Sustainability
250-381-9321
jhayden@heenan.ca
T. Murray Rankin, Q.C., Partner, Environmental Law; Aboriginal Law; Natural Resources
250-381-9321
mrankin@heenan.ca
Richard Shrieves, Partner, Aboriginal Law; Natural Resources
250-381-9321
rshrieves@heenan.ca

Merchant Law Group LLP - Victoria
Stn. ., 531 Quadra St., Victoria, BC V8V 3S4
Tel: 250-385-7777; *Fax:* 250-478-9943
Toll-Free: 866-765-7777
merchant@merchantlaw.com
Profile: 2 Lawyers
Environmental Lawyers:
Darren G. Williams, Energy

Moore-Stewart, Robert
#616, 620 View St., Victoria, BC V8W 1J6
Tel: 250-380-1887; *Fax:* 250-380-9134
rmoorest@telus.net
Profile: 1 Office, 1 Lawyers,
Defence lawyer for environmental activists & others involved in injunctions & related civil litigation
Environmental Lawyers:
Robert Moore-Stewart, Anti-Nuclear; Anti-Oldgrowth Logging
rmoorest@direct.ca

Woodward & Company
844 Courtney St., 2nd Fl., Victoria, BC V8W 1C4
Tel: 250-383-2356; *Fax:* 250-380-6560
reception@woodwardandcompany.com
www.woodwardandcompany.com
Profile: 1 Office, 14 Lawyers, Founded in: 1980
Largest Aboriginal law specialty firm in Canada

Williams Lake

Morelli Chertkow LLP, Lawyers - Williams Lake
#161A, 351 Hodgson Rd., Williams Lake, BC V2G 3P7
Tel: 250-398-7326; *Fax:* 250-398-7327
info@morellichertkow.com
www.morellichertkow.com
Profile: Morelli Chertkow LLP's head office is situated in Kamloops BC.

Manitoba

Brandon

Paterson Patterson Wyman & Abel
#1, Carriage House, 1040 Princess Ave., Brandon, MB R7A 0P8
Tel: 204-727-2424; *Fax:* 204-728-4670
patersons@mts.net
www.patersons.ca
Profile: 3 Offices, 0 Lawyers, Founded in: 1977
Environmental Lawyers:
Robert L. Patterson, Partner, Municipal law; Planning law

Gladstone

Thompson Dorfman Sweatman LLP - Gladstone
Foxon Agencies Building, 24 Dennis St. West, Gladstone, MB R0J 0T0
Tel: 204-385-2775; *Fax:* 204-385-2662
tds@tdslaw.com
www.tdslaw.com

MacGregor

Thompson Dorfman Sweatman LLP - MacGregor
78 Hampton St. East, MacGregor, MB R0H 0R0
Tel: 204-685-2192; *Fax:* 204-685-2341
tds@tdslaw.com
www.tdslaw.com

Portage la Prairie

Thompson Dorfman Sweatman LLP - Portage la Prairie
316 Saskatchewan Ave. East, Portage la Prairie, MB R1N 3C4
Tel: 204-857-7851; *Fax:* 204-857-3335
tds@tdslaw.com
www.tdslaw.com

Steinbach

Thompson Dorfman Sweatman LLP - Steinbach
#100, 250 Main St., Steinbach, MB R5G 1Y8
Tel: 204-934-2563; *Fax:* 204-934-0563
tds@tdslaw.com
www.tdslaw.com

Winkler

Thompson Dorfman Sweatman LLP - Winkler
915 Navigator Dr., Winkler, MB R6W 4B1
Tel: 204-509-9048; *Fax:* 204-934-0537
tds@tdslaw.com
www.tdslaw.com

Winnipeg

Aikins, MacAulay & Thorvaldson LLP
#30th Floor, 360 Main St., Winnipeg, MB R3C 4G1
Tel: 204-957-0050; *Fax:* 204-957-0840
amt@aikins.com
www.aikins.com
Profile: 1 Office, 97 Lawyers, Founded in: 1879
Work includes the environmental aspects of land use planning and property development, natural resource projects and all associated licensing assessments and regulatory processes, environmental planning and risk management, and strategic management; corporate transactional work.
Environmental Lawyers:
Theodor E. Bock, Aboriginal Law
204-957-4673
reb@aikins.com
Aaron J. Bowler, Environmental Law; Aboriginal Law; Municipal
204-957-4892
ajb@aikins.com
John R. Braun, Aboriginal Law
204-957-4672
jrb@aikins.com
Charles L. Chappell, Environmental Law; Municipal
204-957-4638
clc@aikins.com
Thomas P. Dooley, Environmental Law
204-957-4628
tpd@aikins.com
James A. Ferguson, Aboriginal Law
204-957-4696
jaf@aikins.com
James E. Foran, Q.C., Transportation
204-957-4613
jef@aikins.com
Allan F. Foran, Environmental Law; Transportation
204-957-4664
aff@aikins.com
Robert T. Gabor, Q.C., Environmental Law; Transportation
204-957-4642
rtg@aikins.com
Betty A. Johnstone, Aboriginal Law
204-957-4650
baj@aikins.com
Adam L. Levene, Aboriginal Law
204-957-4632
all@aikins.com
Colin R. MacArthur, Q.C., Municipal Law
204-957-4627
crm@aikins.com
A.J. (Telly) Mercury, Q.C., Municipal Law
204-957-4610
ajm@aikins.com
Herbert J. Peters, Aboriginal Law
204-957-4634
hjp@aikins.com
Michelle R. Redekopp, Transportation
204-957-4698
mrr@aikins.com
Barbara M. Shields, Aboriginal Law
204-957-4615
bms@aikins.com
Rod E. Stephenson, Q.C., Environmental Law
204-957-4635
res@aikins.com
Lucia M. Stuhldreier, Transportation
204-957-4676
lms@aikins.com
G. Bruce Taylor, Environmental Law; Aboriginal Law
204-957-4669
gbt@aikins.com
Nigel J. Thompson, Environmental Law; Aboriginal Law
204-957-4659
njt@aikins.com
Robert L. Tyler, Environmental Law; Municipal
204-957-4630
rlt@aikins.com
Joel A. Weinstein, Q.C., Aboriginal Law
204-957-4631
jaw@aikins.com

Antymniuk & Antymniuk
#11, 1500 Dakota St., Winnipeg, MB R2N 3Y7
Tel: 204-254-3511; *Fax:* 204-257-5139
Profile: 1 Office, 3 Lawyers

Campbell Marr
10 Donald St., Winnipeg, MB R3C 1L5
Tel: 204-942-3311; *Fax:* 204-943-7997
dimarr@campbellmarr.com
www.campbellmarr.com
Profile: 1 Office, 13 Lawyers, Founded in: 1990
Environmental Lawyers:
Anders Bruun, Agricultural Law
204-942-3311
abruun@campbellmarr.com

Law Firms

Kenton Fast, Agricultural Law
204-942-3311
klfast@campbellmarr.com
Roger B. King, Q.C.
204-942-3311
rking@campbellmarr.com
Douglas J. MacKenzie, Aboriginal Law
204-942-3311
djmack@campbellmarr.com
Garth P. Reimer, Agricultural Law
204-942-3311
greimer@campbellmarr.com

D'Arcy & Deacon LLP - Winnipeg

2200 One Lombard Pl., Winnipeg, MB R3B 0X7
Tel: 204-942-2271; *Fax:* 204-943-4242
inquiries@darcydeacon.com
www.darcydeacon.com
Profile: 2 Offices, 46 Lawyers, Founded in: 1878
D'Arcy & Deacon lawyers have represented individuals & corporations on matters related to environmental issues. Advice is offered with respect to potential environmental liability issues & environmental disclosure.
Environmental Lawyers:
Paul W. Barsy, Associate, Aboriginal Law; Agricultural Law; Municipal Law
pbarsy@darcydeacon.com
Luke R. Bernas, Associate, Labour & Employment
lbernas@darcydeacon.com
Harold (Sonny) Cochrane, Partner, Aboriginal Law
hcochrane@darcydeacon.com
Deryk W. Coward, Partner, Administrative & Regulatory Law; Labour & Employment
dcoward@darcydeacon.com
John E. Deacon, QC, Associate, Municipal Law; Administrative & Regulatory Law
jdeacon@darcydeacon.com
Kenneth A. Filkow, QC, Partner, Administrative & Rgulatory Law
kfilkow@darcydeacon.com
Michael G. Finlayson, Partner, Construction
mfinlayson@darcydeacon.com
R. Christopher H. Fultz, Associate, Aboriginal Law
cfultz@darcydeacon.com
Jonathan L. Goldenberg, Partner, Agriculture; Pharmaceutical
jgoldenberg@darcydeacon.com
Robert J. Graham, Associate, Labour & Employment
rgraham@darcydeacon.com
Roger D. Gripp, Partner, Municipal Law; Administrative & Regulatory Law; Transporation
rgripp@darcydeacon.com
R. Ivan Holloway, Partner, Construction; Administrative & Regulatory Law; Labour & Employment
jholloway@darcydeacon.com
Harold K. Irving, QC, Associate, Administrative & Regulatory Law; Labour & Employment; Transporation
hirving@darcydeacon.com
Greg A. Johnson, Partner, Aboriginal Law
gjohnson@darcydeacon.com
Brenda A. Johnston, Partner, Aboriginal Law; Labour & Employment
bjohnson@darcydeacon.com
Krista Klassen, Associate, Labour & Employment Law
kklassen@darcydeacon.com
Ken G. Mandzuik, Associate, Administrative & Regulatory Law
kmandzuik@darcydeacon.com
Andrew Marshall, Associate, Aboriginal Law
amarshall@darcydeacon.com
D. Tomas Masi, Associate, Labour & Employment
tmasi@darcydeacon.com
Tracy A. McMahon, Associate, Administrative & Regulatory Law
tmcmahon@darcydeacon.com
Brian J. Meronek, QC, Municipal Law; Aboriginal Law; Administrative & Regulatory Law; Environmental Law; Labour & Employment; Oil & Gas; Energy Regulation
bmeronek@darcydeacon.com
Vanessa Mulhern, Associate
vmulhern@darcydeacon.com
Lindsay M. Mulholland, Associate, Labour & Employment
lmulholland@darcydeacon.com
Kenneth J. Muys, Associate, Administrative & Regulatory Law; Labour & Employment
kmuys@darcydeacon.com
Bradley D. Regehr, Associate, Aboriginal Law; Environmental Law; Administrative & Regulatory Law
bregehr@darcydeacon.com
Michael D. Richards, Partner, Construction; Administrative & Regulatory Law; Agricultural Law; Labour & Employment
mrichards@darcydeacon.com
Uzma A. Saeed, Associate, Aboriginal Law; Administrative & Regulatory Law; Construction; Labour & Employment
usaeed@darcydeacon.com
Kris M. Saxberg, Partner, Administrative & Regulatory Law; Labour & Employment
ksaxberg@darcydeacon.com
Shawn C. Scarcello, Associate, Aboriginal Law; Administrative & Regulatory Law; Construction; Labour & Employment; Municipal
sscarcello@darcydeacon.com
Ian B. Scarth, Associate, Municipal Law
iscarth@darcydeacon.com
Gordon C. Steeves, Associate, Municipal Law; Administrative & Regulatory Law; Labour & Employment
gsteeves@darcydeacon.com
Grant A. Stefanson, Associate, Aboriginal Law; Administrative & Regulatory Law; Labour & Employment
gstefanson@darcydeacon.com
John C. Stewart, Partner, Agricultural Law
jstewart@darcydeacon.com
Michael D. Werier, Partner, Administrative & Regulatory Law; Health Law; Labour & Employment
mwerier@darcydeacon.com
Michael Willcock, Partner, Health; Municipal Law
mwillcock@darcydeacon.com
Jennifer S. Winter, Associate, Municipal Law; Labour & Employment
jwinter@darcydeacon.com
Russell G. Wookey, Associate, Construction; Administrative & Regulatory Law
rwookey@darcydeacon.com
Darcie C. Yale, Partner, Administrative & Regulatory Law; Labour & Employment
dyale@darcydeacon.com

Hook & Smith

#201, 3111 Portage Ave., Winnipeg, MB R3K 0W4
Tel: 204-885-4520; *Fax:* 204-837-9846
general@hookandsmith.com
www.hookandsmith.petrasite.com
Profile: 1 Office, Founded in: 1984
The firm offers services related to transporation law.
Environmental Lawyers:
Winston F. Smith, QC, Transporation
wsmith@hookandsmith.com

Pitblado LLP

#2500, Commodity Exchange Tower, 360 Main St., Winnipeg, MB R3C 4H6
Tel: 204-956-0560; *Fax:* 204-957-0227
firm@pitblado.com
www.pitblado.com
twitter.com/PitbladoLaw, www.linkedin.com/company/1049203
Profile: 1 Office, 61 Lawyers, Founded in: 1882
Environmental Lawyers:
Jeff A. Baigrie, Agriculture; Construction Law
204-956-3558
Joseph D. Barnsley, Aviation; Transportation
204-956-3522
Mark R. Beard, Environmental Due Diligence
204-956-3510
beard@pba-law.com
Tracey L. Epp, Health Law
204-956-3557
William S. Gardner, Health & Medical
204-956-3560
Richard J. Handlon, Recontamination & Damage; Medical Law; Construction Law
204-956-3556
Bruce H. King, Agriculture
204-956-3541
Jack R. London, Q.C., Counsel, Aboriginal Law; Construction law
204-956-3500
Howard P. Nerman, Aboriginal Issues
204-956-3530
nerman@pba-law.com
David G. Newman, Aboriginal Law
204-956-3521
David B.N. Ramsay, Construction Law
204-956-3529
Bryan P. Schwartz, Associate Counsel, Aboriginal Law
204-474-6142
Thomas W. Turner, Construction Law
204-956-3516

Pullan Kammerloch Frohlinger

#300, 240 Kennedy St., Winnipeg, MB R3C 1T1
Tel: 204-956-0490; *Fax:* 204-947-3747
www.pkflawyers.com
Profile: 5 Offices, 10 Lawyers, Founded in: 1924
Legal experts are available in the disciplines of First Nations law, mining & natural resource law, northern economic development, construction law, development, municipal law, & administrative law. New developments in legislation & policy related to these legal areas are monitored constantly to keep clients informed.
Environmental Lawyers:
Kevin Bolt, Construction & Real Estate Development; First Nations Law; Municipal Law
Vincent J. Bueti, Construction & Real Estate Development
Thomas G. Frohlinger, Construction & Real Estate Development; Mining & Natural Resource Law; Northern Economic Development
Gordon Morris Pullan, QC, Construction & Real Estate Development
Gary Michael Sarcida, Construction Litigation; Administrative Law
Harvey James Slobodzian, Construction; Municipal Litigation; Administrative Law
Amanda Verhaeghe, Construction & Development

Thompson Dorfman Sweatman LLP - Winnipeg

#2200, CanWest Global Place, 201 Portage Ave., Winnipeg, MB R3B 3L3
Tel: 204-957-1930; *Fax:* 204-934-0570
tds@tdslaw.com
www.tdslaw.com
www.facebook.com/tdslaw, www.twitter.com/tdslaw, www.linkedin.com/company/thompson-dorfman-sweatman-llp
Profile: 6 Offices, 75 Lawyers, Founded in: 1887
Natural Resource Management/Aboriginal Land Use; Land Claims; Urban Aboriginal Issues; Contaminated Sites; Environmental Issues in Commercial Acquisitions; Sustainable Development
Environmental Lawyers:
Richard H.G. Adams, Construction
204-934-2439
rhga@tdslaw.com
Robert J.M. Adkins, Aboriginal; Construction; Environmental & Sustainable Development; Municipal; Natural Resources & Energy
204-934-2483
rjma@tdslaw.com
Glen W. Agar, Natural Resources & Energy
204-934-2590
gwa@tdslaw.com
G.V. Brickman, Q.C., Natural Resources & Energy
204-934-2428
gvb@tdslaw.com
William J. Burnett, Q.C., Aboriginal; Construction; Natural Resources & Energy
204-934-2487
wjb@tdslaw.com
Karen L. Clearwater, Environmental & Sustainable Development
204-934-2362
klc@tdslaw.com
Kara L. Crawford, Aboriginal; Environmental & Sustainable Development; Municipal; Natural Resources & Energy
204-934-2346
kc@tdslaw.com
James G. Edmond, Construction; Environmental & Sustainable Development
204-934-2450
jge@tdslaw.com
Douglas J. Forbes, Environmental; Construction
204-934-2426
djf@tdslaw.com
Monina A.P. Glowacki, Construction
204-934-2380
mapg@tsdlaw.com
Maria L. Grande, Construction
204-934-2573
mlg@tdslaw.com
Antoine F. Hacault, Municipal
204-934-2513
afh@tdslaw.com
M. Lynne Harrison, Aboriginal; Construction; Natural Resources & Energy

204-934-2506
mlh@tdslaw.com
Jamie A. Kagan, Construction
204-934-2309
jk@tdslaw.com
Keith D. LaBossiere, Construction
204-934-2587
tdl@tdslaw.com
Sarantos Mattheos, Construction; Municipal
204-964-2518
sm@tdslaw.com
Ross A. McFayden, Municipal
204-934-2378
ram@tdslaw.com
Kathleen C. Murphy, Aboriginal; Environmental & Sustainable Development; Municipal; Natural Resources & Energy
204-934-2567
kcm@tdslaw.com
Ross A.L. Nugent, Q.C., Municipal
204-934-2431
raln@tdslaw.com
E. William Olson, Q.C., Construction
204-934-2534
ewo@tdslaw.com
Chrys Pappas, Q.C., Municipal
204-934-2452
cp@tdslaw.com
Sacha R. Paul, Aboriginal; Environmental & Sustainable Development; Natural Resources & Energy
204-934-2571
srp@tdslaw.com
Walter L. Ritchie, Q.C., Construction
204-934-2422
wlr@tdslaw.com
Sheryl A. Rosenberg, Environmental & Sustainable Development; Natural Resources & Energy
204-934-2312
sar@tdslaw.com
Arthur J. Stacey, Construction
204-934-2537
ajs@tdslaw.com
John D. Stefaniuk, Environmental & Sustainable Development; Municipal; Natural Resources & Energy
204-934-2597
jds@tdslaw.com
Lisa J. Stiver, Environmental & Sustainable Development; Municipal
204-934-2375
ljs@tdslaw.com
B. Douglas Tait, Municipal
204-934-2440
bdt@tdslaw.com
Gregory J. Tallon, Construction
204-934-2478
gjt@tdslaw.com
Andrew L. Thompson, Municipal
204-934-2358
alt@tdslaw.com
Lynda K. Troup, Municipal
204-934-2337
lkt@tdslaw.com
Cheryl A. Walker, Municipal
204-934-2369
caw@tdslaw.com
Jonathan M. Woolley, Construction; Environmental & Sustainable Development
204-934-2367
jmw@tdslaw.com

New Brunswick

Fredericton

Cox & Palmer - Fredericton
#400, Phoenix Square, P.O. Box 310, Stn. A, 371 Queen St., Fredericton, NB E3B 4Y9
Tel: 506-453-7771; *Fax:* 506-453-9600
fredericton@coxandpalmer.com
www.coxandpalmerlaw.com
Profile: 25 Lawyers,
The Fredericton office of Cox & Palmer provides counsel on a range of municipal, envrionmental, & construction matters. Municipal issues may involve planning, land development, waste management, & public utilities.
Environmental Lawyers:
Michael E. Bowlin, Partner, Environmental Law
506-453-9675
mbowlin@coxandpalmer.com
Ryan P. Burgoyne, Associate, Municipal Law; Environmental Law
506-453-9647
rburgoyne@coxandpalmer.com
Jamie Eddy, Managing Partner, Labour & Employment
506-462-4751
jeddy@coxandpalmer.com
Philippe M. Frenette, Associate, Construction
506-453-9650
pfrenette@coxandpalmer.com
Trisha E.M. Gallant-LeBlanc, Partner, Labour & Employment
506-462-4764
tgallant-leblanc@coxandpalmer.com
David T. Hashey, QC, Partner, Fisheries & Marine; Natural Resources & Energy
506-453-9672
dhashey@coxandpalmer.com
Bruce D. Hatfield, QC, Associate, Municipal Law
506-453-9674
bhatfield@coxandpalmer.com

McInnes Cooper - Fredericton
#600, Barker House, P.O. Box 610, Stn. A, 570 Queen St., Fredericton, NB E3B 5A6
Tel: 506-458-8572; *Fax:* 506-458-9903
mcftn@mcinnescooper.com
www.mcinnescooper.com
Profile: 22 Lawyers
Environmental Lawyers:
Leonard T. Hoyt, Q.C., Energy; Renewable Energy
506-458-1622
len.hoyt@mcinnescooper.com
Alan T. Rockwell, Energy; Municipal & Land Use Planning
506-458-1547
alan.rockwell@mcinnescooper.com
David Duncan Young, Construction Industry
506-458-1623
david.young@mcinnescooper.com

Pink Larkin
#210, 1133 Regent St., Fredericton, NB E3B 3Z2
Tel: 506-458-1989; *Fax:* 506-458-1127
www.pinklarkin.com
Profile: 2 Offices, 4 Lawyers,
Firm services include occupational health & safety, municipal law, & environmental law.

Stewart McKelvey - Fredericton
#600, Frederick Square, P.O. Box 730, 77 Westmorland St., Fredericton, NB E3B 5B4
Tel: 506-458-1970; *Fax:* 506-444-8974
fredericton@stewartmckelvey.com
www.stewartmckelvey.com
Profile: 13 Lawyers
Environmental Lawyers:
Clarence L. Bennett, Occupational Health & Safety; Construction Law
506-444-8978
cbennett@smss.com
Hugh J. Cameron, Partner, Construction Law
506-443-0120
hcameron@smss.com
J.E. Britt Dysart, Partner, Construction Law
506-443-0153
bdysart@smss.com
Gérard V. La Forest, C.C., Q.C., Counsel, Environmental Law
506-443-0135
glaforest@smss.com
J. Gordon Petrie, Q.C., Partner, Construction Law
506-443-0150
gpetrie@smss.com
Richard G. Petrie, Partner, Energy & Natural Resources; Environmental Law; Forestry; Occupational Health & Safety
506-443-0155
rpetrie@smss.com
Nicholas N. Russon, Construction Law
506-443-0128
nrusson@smss.com

Moncton

Cox & Palmer - Moncton
#500, Blue Cross Centre, 644 Main St., Moncton, NB E1C 1E2
Tel: 506-856-9800; *Fax:* 506-856-8150
moncton@coxandpalmer.com
www.coxandpalmerlaw.com
Profile: 17 Lawyers,
Lawyers at the Moncton location have expertise in environmental law, energy & natural resources, fisheries & marine law, construction law, & municipal law.
Examples of services include representation in hearings related to resource development projects, advice on environmental assessment & regulation, mineral & hydrocarbon rights, & land development, & compliance services for the energy & fishing industries.
Environmental Lawyers:
George L. Cooper, Managing Partner, Energy & Natural Resources
506-863-0793
gcooper@coxandpalmer.com
Richard E. DeBow, QC, Counsel, Construction
506-859-1240
rdebow@coxandpalmer.com
Blair C. Fraser, Partner, Environmental Law
506-863-1142
bfraser@coxandpalmer.com
George H. LeBlanc, Partner, Municipal Law; Labour & Employment
506-382-4529
gleblanc@coxandpalmer.com
Jon Lutes, Associate, Construction; Labour & Employment
506-852-9425
jlutes@coxandpalmer.com
Caitlin Mahoney, Associate, Administrative Law
506-852-9431
cmahoney@coxandpalmer.com
Christian E. Michaud, Partner, Fisheries & Marine Law; Administrative Law; Construction
506-863-1131
cmichaud@coxandpalmer.com
Talia C. Profit, Municipal Law; Health Law
506-859-1727
tprofit@coxandpalmer.com

Stewart McKelvey - Moncton
#601, Blue Cross Centre, P.O. Box 28051, 644 Main St., Moncton, NB E1C 9N4
Tel: 506-853-1970; *Fax:* 506-858-8454
moncton@stewartmckelvey.com
www.stewartmckelvey.com
Profile: 17 Lawyers,
Stewart McKelvey's head office is located in Halifax, Nova Scotia. Environmental, property development, marine, energy, & health legal services are provided from the Moncton office.
Environmental Lawyers:
Micheline Doiron, Associate, Environmental Law; Property Development
506-853-1963
Robert Dysart, Partner, Construction Law; Health
506-383-2230
Luc Elslinger, Office Partner, Property Development
506-383-2232
Karine LeBlanc, Associate, Labour & Employment Law
506-383-2222
Charles LeBlond, Q.C., Construction Law; Health; Workers' Compensation
506-853-1976
Sacha Morisset, Occupational Health & Safety; Labour & Employment
506-853-1942
André G. Richard, Q.C., Occupational Health & Safety; Labour & Employment
506-853-1962
Jennifer Ronalds, Associate, Labour & Employment
506-853-1979
Christopher Stewart, Partner, Energy & Natural Resources; Labour & Employment; Energy (Electricity Regulatory & Oil & Gas Regulatory); Marine Law
506-383-2224

Riverview

Wilbur & Wilbur
706B Coverdale Rd., Riverview, NB E1B 3L1
Tel: 506-387-7715; *Fax:* 506-387-5875
swilbur@wilburandwilbur.com
www.wilburandwilbur.com
Profile: 1 Office, 2 Lawyers, Founded in: 1987
Environmental Lawyers:

Stephen P. Wilbur
swilbur@wilburandwilbur.com

Saint John

Cox & Palmer - Saint John

#1500, Brunswick Square, P.O. Box 1324, Stn. Main, 1 Germain St., Saint John, NB E2L 4H8
Tel: 506-632-8900; *Fax:* 506-632-8809
saintjohn@coxandpalmer.com
www.coxandpalmerlaw.com
Profile: 18 Lawyers,
One area of law practised by lawyers at the Saint John location is emergy & natural resources law. The following are examples of services: advising on environmental assessments, regulations, & compliance; negotiating cogeneration projects; representing clients in hearings & selection processes related to resource development projects; & working on development agreements.
Environmental Lawyers:
Rebecca M. Atkinson, Associate, Environmental Law; Municipal Law
506-633-2783
ratkinson@coxandpalmer.com
Raymond F. Glennie, QC, Partner, Municipal Law; Energy & Natural Resources
506-633-2713
rglennie@coxandpalmer.com
Edward W. Keyes, Partner, Construction
506-633-2706
ekeyes@coxandpalmer.com
John D. Laidlaw, QC, Partner, Municipal Law
506-633-2710
jlaidlaw@coxandpalmer.com
Franklin O. Leger, QC, Counsel, Municipal Law
506-633-2712
fleger@coxandpalmer.com
Jane E. MacEachern, Associate, Construction
506-633-2777
jmaceachern@coxandpalmer.com
James R. McConnell, Associate, Construction
506-633-2767
jmcconnell@coxandpalmer.com
Joshua J.B. McElman, Managing Partner, Shipbuilding
506-633-2708
jmcelman@coxandpalmer.com
James K. O'Connell, QC, Partner, Environmental Law; Labour & Employment
506-633-2723
joconnell@coxandpalmer.com
Howard A. Spalding, QC, Partner, Environmental Law; Municipal Law; Construction; Transportation
506-633-4215
hspalding@coxandpalmer.com
William H. Teed, QC, Partner, Energy & Natural Resources
506-633-2718
wteed@coxandpalmer.com
Deirdre L. Wade, QC, Partner, Health Law; Construction; Environmental Law; Administrative Law; Labour & Employment
506-633-4205
dwade@coxandpalmer.com
Charles D. Whelly, QC, Partner, Environmental Law; Municipal Law; Construction; Labour & Employment
506-633-2720
cwhelly@coxandpalmer.com

Gilbert McGloan Gillis

P.O. Box 7174, 22 King St., Saint John, NB E2L 1G3
Tel: 506-634-3600; *Fax:* 506-634-3612
Toll-Free: 888-246-4529
gmg@gmglaw.com
www.gmglaw.com
Profile: 1 Office, 7 Lawyers, Founded in: 1929
Practice areas include admiralty law & real property law. Gilbert McGloan Gillis represents a diversity of clients, including fishers, seamen, shipping enterprises, aquaculture businesses, land purchasers, land developers, & land owners.
Environmental Lawyers:
R. Gary Faloon, QC, Associate, Construction Law
rgfaloon@gmglaw.com
Rodney J. Gillis, QC, Partner, Real Property
rjgillis@gmglaw.com
Scott N. Larson, Associate, Health Law
slarson@gmglaw.com
Claire B.N. Porter, Associate, Real Property
cbporter@gmglaw.com
David N. Rogers, Partner, Fisheries / Admiralty Law; Construction Law
dnrogers@gmglaw.com
Andrew J. Valeri, Associate, Real Property
avaleri@gmglaw.com

Gorman Nason Lawyers

P.O. Box 7286, Stn. A, 121 Germain St., Saint John, NB E2L 4S6
Tel: 506-634-8600; *Fax:* 506-634-8685
info@GormanNason.com
www.gormannason.com
Profile: 1 Office, 10 Lawyers,
Areas of practice include municipal, property, & construction law.
Environmental Lawyers:
John Bujold
506-636-7323
jebujold@gormannason.com
Raymond P. Gorman, Q.C.
Frank P. Hamm
506-636-7331
fph@gormannason.com
Caroline J. Higgins
Timothy M. Hopkins
506-636-7333
tmh@gormannason.com
Cheryl G. Johnson
506-636-7320
cgj@gormannason.com
John J. MacGillivray
506-636-7326
jjm@gormannason.com
H. David McLellan
John M. McNair
Ralph D. Poley
506-636-7329
rdp@gormannason.com
Derek J. Weaver
506-636-7330
derek.weaver@gormannason.com
Frederick A. Welsford
506-636-7325
faw@gormannason.com

Stewart McKelvey - Saint John

#1000, Brunswick House, P.O. Box 7289, Stn. A, 44 Chipman Hill, Saint John, NB E2L 4S6
Tel: 506-632-1970; *Fax:* 506-652-1989
saint-john@stewartmckelvey.com
www.stewartmckelvey.com
Profile: 32 Lawyers
Environmental Lawyers:
William B. Goss, Q.C., Partner, Occupational Health & Safety
506-632-4515
wgoss@smss.com
Gregory S. Harding, Partner, Energy & Natural Resources; Construction Law
506-634-6417
gharding@smss.com
J. Paul M. Harquail, Partner, Environmental Law; Marine Law; Occupational Health & Safety
506-632-8313
pharquail@smss.com
Catherine A. Lahey, Managing Partner, Environmental Law; Occupational Health & Safety
506-632-8307
clahey@smss.com
James F. LeMesurier, Partner, Occupational Health & Safety
506-632-2776
jlemesurier@smss.com
Neal L.D. Leard, Partner, Energy & Natural Resources; Construction Law
506-634-6416
nleard@smss.com
Kenneth B. McCullogh, Q.C., Partner, Construction Law; Marine Law
506-632-2781
kmccullogh@smss.com
E. Neil McKelvey, Q.C., Counsel, Construction Law; Marine Law
506-632-2770
nmckelvey@smss.com
Gerald S. McMackin, Q.C., Partner, Energy & Natural Resources; Health
506-632-2768
gmcmackin@smss.com
Darrell J. Stephenson, Partner, Energy & Natural Resources; Marine Law
506-632-2790
dstephenson@smss.com
Robert G. Vincent, Q.C., Partner, Environmental Law; Energy & Natural Resources; Occupational Health & Safety
506-632-2780
rvincent@smss.com
Misty R. Watson, Construction Law
506-632-8317
mwatson@smss.com

St. Stephen

McInnes Cooper - St. Stephen

46 Milltown Blvd., St. Stephen, NB E3L 1G3
Tel: 506-466-2338; *Fax:* 506-466-0160
mcsjn@mcinnescooper.com
www.mcinnescooper.com

Newfoundland & Labrador

Corner Brook

Poole Althouse, Barristers & Solicitors

Western Trust Bldg., P.O. Box 812, 49 - 51 Park St., Corner Brook, NL A2H 6H7
Tel: 709-634-3136; *Fax:* 709-634-8247
Toll-Free: 877-634-3136
info@pa-law.ca
www.poolealthouse.ca
Profile: 1 Office, 10 Lawyers, Founded in: 1956
Environmental Lawyers:
George L. Murphy, Q.C., Partner, Municipal law
709-637-6428
gmurphy@pa-law.ca
Dean A. Porter, Partner, Administrative law; Municipal law
709-634-3136
dporter@pa-law.ca
Cillian D. Sheahan, Partner, Municipal law
709-637-6426
csheahan@pa-law.ca

St. John's

Benson Myles

#900, Atlantic Place, P.O. Box 1538, 215 Water St., St. John's, NL A1C 5N8
Tel: 709-579-2081; *Fax:* 709-579-2647
info@bensonmyles.com
www.bensonmyles.com
Profile: 1 Office, 21 Lawyers
Environmental Lawyers:
Benjamin J. Kavanagh, Oil & Gas; Mining
709-570-7252
bkavanagh@bensonmyles.com
R. Wayne Myles, Q.C., Mining, Oil & Gas, Transportation
709-570-7232
wmyles@bensonmyles.com
Geoffrey L. Spencer, Transportation
709-570-7263
gspencer@bensonmyles.com

Cox & Palmer - St. John's

#1000, Scotia Centre, 235 Water St., St. John's, NL A1C 1B6
Tel: 709-738-7800; *Fax:* 709-738-7999
stjohns@coxandpalmer.com
www.coxandpalmerlaw.com
twitter.com/CoxandPalmer
Profile: 10 Offices, 171 Lawyers,
Cox & Palmer lawyers at the Newfoundland location specialize in environmental law, energy & natural resource law, & fisheries & marine law. Regulatory & commercial advice & legal representation are available to off-shore oil & gas projects, exploration, production, & pipe laying companies, fisheries, the marine transportation industry, & governments.
Environmental Lawyers:
Megan Alexander, Associate, Municipal Law; Construction
709-570-5339
malexander@coxandpalmer.com
Gregory M. Anthony, Partner, Energy & Natural Resources; Administrative Law; Labour & Employment

709-570-5532
ganthony@coxandpalmer.com
Erin Best, Associate, Health Law; Construction
709-570-5579
ebest@coxandpalmer.com
William T. Cahill, Associate, Fisheries & Marine; Energy & Natural Resources
709-570-5577
wcahill@coxandpalmer.com
Sandra R. Chaytor, QC, Partner, Environmental Law; Health Law; Energy & Natural Resources
709-570-5329
schaytor@coxandpalmer.com
F. Richard Gosse, Partner, Construction; Shipbuilding; Municipal Law
709-570-5330
rgosse@coxandpalmer.com
Stephanie Hickman, Partner, Natural Resources & Energy; Construction
709-570-5536
shickman@coxandpalmer.com
Terri C. Higdon, Associate, Health Law
709-570-5573
thigdon@coxandpalmer.com
John J. Hogan, Associate, Energy & Natural Resources
709-570-5340
jhogan@coxandpalmer.com
Shawn M. Kavanagh, Partner, Energy & Natural Resources
709-570-5524
skavanagh@coxandpalmer.com
Daniel Kutcher, Associate, Environmental Law; Adminstrative Law
709-570-5521
dkutcher@coxandpalmer.com
Alexander (Sandy) MacDonald, QC, Managing Partner, Construction; Energy & Natural Resources
709-570-5512
amacdonald@coxandpalmer.com
Stephen J. May, Partner, Environmental Law; Administrative Law
709-570-5528
smay@coxandpalmer.com
Paul M. McDonald, Partner, Health Law
709-570-5328
pmcdonald@coxandpalmer.com
Wayne Myles, QC, Counsel
709-570-5510
wmyles@coxandpalmer.com
Glen L.C. Noel, Partner, Construction
709-570-5534
gnoel@coxandpalmer.com
Darren D. O'Keefe, Associate, Construction
709-570-5509
dokeefe@coxandpalmer.com
Christopher J. Payne, Associate
709-570-5327
cpayne@coxandpalmer.com
Christopher J. Peddigrew, Partner, Construction; Administrative Law
709-570-5338
cpeddigrew@coxandpalmer.com
D. Richard Robbins, Partner, Natural Resources & Energy
709-570-5325
rrobbins@coxandpalmer.com
Griffith D. Roberts, Partner, Energy & Natural Resources
709-570-5336
groberts@coxandpalmer.com
Mark A. Russell, Associate, Energy & Natural Resources
709-570-5575
mrussell@coxandpalmer.com
Peter D. Shea, Partner, Municipal Law; Health Law; Environmental Law
709-570-5334
pshea@coxandpalmer.com
Randall W. Smith, Partner, Fisheries & Marine; Municipal Law
709-570-5326
rsmith@coxandpalmer.com
J. Alex Templeton, Associate, Environmental Law; Energy & Natural Resources
709-570-5560
atempleton@coxandpalmer.com
Clyde K. Wells, QC, Counsel, Construction; Energy & Natural Resources
709-570-5526
ckwells@coxandpalmer.com
Douglas Wright, Associate, Fisheries & Marine
709-520-5544
dwright@coxandpalmer.com

Martin Whalen Hennebury Stamp

P.O. Box 5910, 15 Church Hill, St. John's, NL A1C 5X4
Tel: 709-754-1400; *Fax:* 709-754-0915
info@mwhslaw.com
www.mwhslaw.com
Profile: 1 Office, 11 Lawyers,
Fisheries & Marine; Oil & Gas

McInnes Cooper - St. John's

P.O. Box 5939, 10 Fort William Place, 5th Fl., St. John's, NL A1C 5X4
Tel: 709-722-8735; *Fax:* 709-722-1763
mcsjs@mcinnescooper.com
www.mcinnescooper.com
Profile: 24 Lawyers, Founded in: 1859
Environmental Lawyers:
O. Noel Clarke, Q.C., Energy and Natural Resources
709-724-8232
noel.clarke@mcinnescooper.com
Dennis N. Clarke, Energy; Environmental Law; Waste Management
709-724-8282
dennis.clarke@mcinnescooper.com
Gregory J. Connors, Natural Resources
709-724-8264
greg.connors@mcinnescooper.com
Michael J. Crosbie, Construction Industry; Municipal
709-724-8242
michael.crosbie@mcinnescooper.com
J. David B. Eaton, Q.C., Construction Industry
709-724-8262
david.eaton@mcinnescooper.com
John M. Green, Q.C., Natural Resources
709-724-8238
john.green@mcinnescooper.com
Deborah L.J. Hutchings, Energy; Environmental Law; Maritime Law
709-724-8254
deborah.hutchings@mcinnescooper.com
John V. O'Dea, Construction Industry
709-724-8261
john.odea@mcinnescooper.com
Jacqueline A.M. Penney, Energy & Natural Resources
709-724-8239
jackie.penney@mcinnescooper.com
Douglas B. Skinner, Maritime Law
709-724-8249
doug.skinner@mcinnescooper.com
James L. Thistle, Q.C., Construction Industry; Energy; Environmental Law; Natural Resources
709-724-8247
jim.thistle@mcinnescooper.com
Caroline C. Watton, Natural Resources Law
709-724-8251
caroline.watton@mcinnescooper.com

Ottenheimer Baker

Baine Johnson Centre, P.O. Box 5457, 10 Fort William Pl., St. John's, NL A1C 5W4
Tel: 709-722-7584; *Fax:* 709-722-9210
info@ottenheimerbaker.com
www.ottenheimerbaker.com
Profile: 1 Office, 19 Lawyers, Founded in: 1972
Environmental Lawyers:
Robert B. Andrews, Q.C., Partner, Construction Law
709-570-7331
randrews@ottenheimerbaker.com
Mark R. Andrews, Partner, Natural Resources; Oil & Gas Law; Mining Law
709-570-7341
mandrews@ottenheimerbaker.com
John A. Baker, Q.C., Founding Partner, Natural Resources; Oil & Gas Law; Mining Law
709-570-7305
jbaker@ottenheimerbaker.com
William C. Boyd, Managing Partner, Maritime Law; Fisheries
709-570-7306
wboyd@ottenheimerbaker.com
Gregory W. Dickie, Q.C., Partner, Oil & Gas Law
709-570-7307
gdickie@ottenheimerbaker.com
John W. Lavers, Partner, Maritime Law; Fisheries; Aboriginal Law
709-570-7324
jlavers@ottenheimerbaker.com
Raelene L. Lee, Partner, Construction; Occupational Health & Safety
709-570-7322
rlee@ottenheimerbaker.com
Rosalie E. McGrath, Partner, Natural Resources; Oil & Gas Law; Maritime & Fisheries
709-570-7344
rmcgrath@ottenheimerbaker.com
Beth M.W. McGrath, Natural Resources; Oil & Gas Law; Mining Law
709-570-7342
bmcgrath@ottenheimerbaker.com
Geoffrey K. Penney, Partner, Maritime & Fisheries
709-570-7312
gpenney@ottenheimerbaker.com
Neil F. Pittman, Partner, Natural Resources; Oil & Gas Law
709-570-7358
npittman@ottenheimerbaker.com
Daniel W. Simmons, Partner, Construction Law
709-570-7328
dsimmons@ottenheimerbaker.com
Wayne F. Spracklin, Q.C., Partner, Maritime Law; Fisheries
709-570-7321
wspracklin@ottenheimerbaker.com
Sheri H. Wicks, Partner, Construction Law; Aboriginal Law
709-570-7360
swicks@ottenheimerbaker.com

Stewart McKelvey - St. John's

#1100, Cabot Place, P.O. Box 5038, 100 New Gower St., St. John's, NL A1C 5V3
Tel: 709-722-4270; *Fax:* 709-722-4565
st-johns@stewartmckelvey.com
www.stewartmckelvey.com
Profile: 31 Lawyers
Environmental Lawyers:
Daniel M. Boone, Managing Partner, Health
709-570-8879
dboone@smss.com
Geoffrey E.J. Brown, Q.C., Partner, Environmental Law; Construction Law
709-570-8845
gbrown@smss.com
Paul L. Coxworthy, Partner, Energy & Natural Resources; Health
709-570-8830
pcoxworthy@smss.com
Gerry R. Fleming, Partner, Construction Law
709-570-8836
gfleming@smss.com
Janet L. Grant, Health
709-570-5794
jgrant@smss.com
Bruce C. Grant, Q.C., Partner, Energy & Natural Resources; Construction Law
709-570-8882
bgrant@smss.com
Neil L. Jacobs, Partner, Health
709-570-8888
njacobs@smss.com
Jennifer E. Lundrigan, Environmental Law; Marine Law
709-570-8823
jlundrigan@smss.com
Gregory A.C. Moores, Partner, Environmental Law; Energy & Natural Resources; Construction Law
709-570-5797
gmoores@smss.com
Stephen F. Penney, Partner, Construction Law; Occupational Health & Safety
709-570-8881
spenney@smss.com
Twila E. Reid, Partner, Occupational Health & Safety
709-570-8828
treid@smss.com
Dennis J. Ryan, Partner, Energy & Natural Resources
709-570-8824
dryan@smss.com
Maureen E. Ryan, Partner, Energy & Natural Resources
709-570-8880
mryan@smss.com
Steven A. Scruton, Energy & Natural Resources; Marine Law; Aboriginal Law

709-570-8837
sscruton@smss.com
Colm St. Roch Seviour, Partner, Mining; Energy & Natural Resources; Environmental Law; Forestry; Construction Law
709-570-8847
cseviour@smss.com
Harold M. Smith, Q.C., Partner, Energy & Natural Resources; Occupational Health & Safety
709-570-8895
hsmith@smss.com
Tauna M. Staniland, Energy & Natural Resources
709-570-8842
tstaniland@smss.com
Cecily Y. Strickland, Partner, Environmental Law; Energy & Natural Resources; Occupational Health & Safety
709-570-8826
cstrickland@smss.com
Ruth E. Trask, Environmental Law
709-570-8893
rtrask@smss.com
Ian C. Wallace, Partner, Occupational Health & Safety
709-570-8839
iwallace@smss.com
Kimberley A. Walsh, Partner, Energy & Natural Resources; Marine Law
709-570-8834
kwalsh@smss.com
Rodney J. Zdebiak, Partner, Energy & Natural Resources
709-570-8841
rzdebiak@smss.com

Northwest Territories

Yellowknife

Davis LLP - Yellowknife
#802, Northwest Tower, 5201 - 50th Ave., Yellowknife, NT X1A 3S9
Tel: 867-669-8400; *Fax:* 867-669-8420
www.davis.ca
Profile: 1 Lawyers,
Aboriginal; Mining; Oil & Gas
Environmental Lawyers:
Cynthia J. Levy, Managing Partner, Municipal law
867-669-9402
clevy@davis.ca

Field LLP - Yellowknife
#601, 4920 - 52 St., Yellowknife, NT X1A 3T1
Tel: 867-920-4542; *Fax:* 867-873-4790
Toll-Free: 800-753-1294
www.fieldlaw.com
Profile: 4 Lawyers, Founded in: 2001
Field Law was created in 2001, when Field Atkinson Perraton merged with Williams & Company. Practice areas at the Yellowknife office include Metis & First Nations law, labour & employment law, & northern law.
Environmental Lawyers:
Dale Cunningham, Partner, Metis & First Nations; Administrative
867-669-8470
dcunningham@fieldlaw.com
Magnolia Unka, Associate, Northern; Metis & First Nations
867-669-8474
munka@fieldlaw.com
Jack Williams, Partner, Metis & First Nations; Labour & Employment
867-669-8471
jwilliams@fieldlaw.com

Lawson Lundell LLP - Yellowknife
#200, P.O. Box 818, 4915 - 48 St., Yellowknife, NT X1A 2N6
Tel: 867-669-5500; *Fax:* 867-920-2206
Toll-Free: 888-465-7608
www.lawsonlundell.com
Profile: 4 Lawyers, Founded in: 2002
Environmental Lawyers:
Paul N.K. Smith, Partner, Environmental; Occupational Health & Safety; Mining; Energy; Natural Resources
867-669-5532
psmith@lawsonlundell.com

McLennan Ross LLP - Yellowknife
#1001, Precambrian Bldg., 4920 - 52nd St., Yellowknife, NT X1A 3T1
Tel: 867-766-7677; *Fax:* 867-766-7678
Toll-Free: 888-836-6684
info@mross.com
www.mross.com
Profile: 3 Lawyers,
Areas of practice in the Northwest Territories include municipal law, construction law, & labour & employment law.
Environmental Lawyers:
Edward W. Gullberg, Partner, Municipal Law; Construction Law
867-766-7680
egullberg@mross.com
Glenn D. Tait, Partner, Municipal; Labour & Employment
867-766-7676
gtait@mross.com

Nova Scotia

Berwick

Stewart & Turner
P.O. Box 208, 196 Cottage St., Berwick, NS B0P 1E0
Tel: 902-538-3123; *Fax:* 902-538-7933
stewart.turner@ns.sympatico.ca
Profile: 1 Office, 2 Lawyers
Environmental Lawyers:
Robert C. Stewart
Greg J. Turner

Dartmouth

Burton Ronald W. Lawyers
169 Main St., Dartmouth, NS B2X 1S1
Tel: 902-434-4492; *Fax:* 902-434-5485
burtonl@ns.sympatico.ca
Profile: 1 Lawyers
Environmental Lawyers:

Elmsdale

Burchell MacDougall Lawyers - Elmsdale
#205, MacMillan Centre, 550 Highway #2, Elmsdale, NS B2S 1A3
Tel: 902-883-1067; *Fax:* 902-883-4902
Toll-Free: 800-552-1451
elmsdale@burchellmacdougall.com
www.burchellmacdougall.com
Profile: 3 Lawyers,
Employment law is practised at the Halifax location.

Halifax

Boyne Clarke LLP
#600, P.O. Box 876, Stn. Darmouth Main, 99 Wyse Rd., Halifax, NS B2Y 3Z5
Tel: 902-469-9500; *Fax:* 902-463-7500
Toll-Free: 866-339-3400
info@boyneclarke.ca
www.boyneclarke.ca
Profile: 1 Office, 0 Lawyers, Founded in: 1972
The firm provides services in the following languages: English, French, Czech, Filipino, German, Slovak, & Spanish. Lawyers are available who practise environmental law, employment & labour law, health law, oil & gas law, & government relations.
Environmental Lawyers:
Ian D. Brown, Associate, Labour & Employment Law
ibrown@boyneclarke.ca
Allen A. Campbell, Environmental Law
acampbell@boyneclarke.ca
Brian P. Casey, Associate, Environmental Law
bcasey@boyneclarke.ca
David G. Coles, Q.C., Partner, Business Litigation - Construction Law
dcoles@boyneclarke.ca
James D. MacNeil, Managing Partner, Environmental Law; Construction Law
jmacneil@boyneclarke.ca
Robert L. Miedema, Partner, Environmental Law
rmiedema@boyneclarke.ca
Claire E. Milton, Q.C., Labour & Employment Law
cmilton@boyneclarke.ca
Gordon F. Proudfoot, Q.C., Environmental Law
gproudfoot@boyneclarke.ca
Kathryn A. Raymond, Health Law & Policy; Labour Relations; Workplace Investigations
kraymond@boyneclarke.ca
Joshua J. Santimaw, Partner, Environmental Law
jsantimaw@boyneclarke.ca
John A. Young, Q.C., Firm Chair, Oil & Gas Law; Government Relations; Health Law
jyoung@boyneclarke.ca

Burchell MacDougall Lawyers - Halifax
#210, Clayton Professional Centre, 255 Lacewood Dr., Halifax, NS B3M 4G2
Tel: 902-445-5511; *Fax:* 902-443-2600
Toll-Free: 800-552-1451
halifax@burchellmacdougall.com
www.burchellmacdougall.com
Profile: 4 Lawyers,
Employment law is practised at the Halifax location.
Environmental Lawyers:
Megan Roberts, Associate, Employment Law
902-445-4810
mroberts@burchellmacdougall.com

Burchells LLP
#1800, 1801 Hollis St., Halifax, NS B3J 3N4
Tel: 902-423-6361; *Fax:* 902-420-9326
firm@burchells.ca
www.burchells.ca
Profile: 1 Office, 23 Lawyers, Founded in: 1912
Burchells LLP assists individuals, not-for-profit organizations, businesses, governments, & Aboriginal peoples with issues related to environmental law. Legal advice is available in the following areas: licensing & permitting; regulatory compliance & approvals; environmental due diligence in property transactions; land use planning; environmental assessments; renewable energy; natural resources; land conservation; species at risk; oil spills; contaminated property; & environmental impacts on Aboriginal peoples.
Environmental Lawyers:
David A. Cameron, Labour & Employment Law
902-428-8390
dcameron@burchells.ca
D. Bruce Clarke, QC, Aboriginal Law
902-423-6361 ext. 313
bclarke@burchells.ca
Jason Cooke, Transporation Law; Labour & Employment Law
902-422-5374
jcooke@burchells.ca
Stuart C.B. Gilby, Aboriginal Law
902-423-6361 ext. 330
sgilby@burchells.ca
Kelly L. Greenwood, Environmental Law
902-428-8391
kgreenwood@burchells.ca
Alan G. Hayman, QC, Construction
902-442-8311
ahayman@burchells.ca
Wayne Howatt, Construction Law
902-442-8329
whowatt@burchells.ca
David Hutt, Transportation Law; Labour & Employment Law
902-442-8373
dhutt@burchells.ca
Naiomi W. Metallic, Aboriginal Law; Labour & Employment Law
902-428-8344
nmetallic@burchells.ca
Denny L. Pickup, Aboriginal Law
902-422-5378
dpickup@burchells.ca
Tiffany Robertson, Administrative Law; Labour & Employment Law
902-423-6361 ext. 320
trobertson@burchells.ca
Betony Rowland, Aboriginal Law; Environmental Law
902-423-6361
browland@burchells.ca
Derek A. Simon, Aboriginal Law; Environmental Law
902-423-8363
dsimon@burchells.ca
Ann E. Smith, QC, Labour & Employment Law
902-442-8367
asmith@burchells.ca
R. Paul Thorne, Environmental Law
902-428-8377
pthorne@burchells.ca
Cory J. Withrow, Aboriginal Law; Construction Law; Labour & Employment Law
902-442-8386
cwithrow@burchells.ca

Cox & Palmer - Halifax
#1100, Purdy's Wharf, Tower One, P.O. Box 2380, Stn. Central, 1959 Upper Water St., Halifax, NS B3J 3E5
Tel: 902-421-6262; *Fax:* 902-421-3130
halifax@coxandpalmer.com
www.coxandpalmerlaw.com
Profile: 56 Lawyers,
In 2011, Irving Shipbuilding Inc., of Halifax Nova Scotia, was awarded a combat package under Canada's National Shipbuilding Procurement Strategy. Lawyers at the Halifax location of Cox & Palmer have expertise in legal services related to shipbuilding, transportation, & maritime law to assist clients involved in the National Shipbuilding Procurement Strategy.
Environmental Lawyers:
Sharon L. Avery, Associate, Health Law
902-491-4114
savery@coxandpalmer.com
Ian B. Bilek, Partner, Environmental Law; Energy & Natural Resources; Construction
902-491-4127
ibilek@coxandpalmer.com
Alison J. Bird, Associate, Labour & Employment
902-491-4138
abird@coxandpalmer.com
D. Kevin Burke, Partner, Transportation Law; Fisheries & Marine; Administrative Law
902-491-4202
kburke@coxandpalmer.com
Joseph F. Burke, Partner, Environmental Law
902-491-4123
jburke@coxandpalmer.com
Jocelyn M. Campbell, QC, Partner, Construction; Municipal Law; Administrative Law
902-491-4210
jmcampbell@coxandpalmer.com
Daniel M. Campbell, QC, Partner, Health Law
902-491-4105
dmcampbell@coxandpalmer.com
Anthony L. Chapman, QC, Partner, Environmental Law
902-491-4106
achapman@coxandpalmer.com
Thomas P. Donovan, QC, Partner, Construction; Health Law; Shipbuilding; Administrative Law
902-491-4213
tdonovan@coxandpalmer.com
Brian W. Downie, QC, Partner, Health Law
902-491-4206
bdownie@coxandpalmer.com
Ashley P. Dunn, Associate, Health Law
902-491-4457
adunn@coxandpalmer.com
Michael E. Dunphy, QC, Partner, Environmental Law; Municipal Law; Construction; Administrative Law
902-491-4205
mdunphy@coxandpalmer.com
Jeffrey P. Flinn, Associate, Construction
902-491-4233
jflinn@coxandpalmer.com
Jennifer Forster, Partner, Construction
902-491-4107
jforster@coxandpalmer.com
Daniel F. Gallivan, QC, Partner, Energy & Natural Resources
902-491-4126
dgallivan@coxandpalmer.com
Joseph Herschorn, Associate, Construction; Health Law
902-491-4116
jherschorn@coxandpalmer.com
Daniel W. Ingersoll, QC, Partner, Municipal Law; Labour & Employment; Administrative Law
902-491-4211
ingersoll@coxandpalmer.com
John A. Keith, Partner, Municipal Law
902-491-4217
jkeith@coxandpalmer.com
Michelle M. Kelly, Partner, Construction
902-491-4465
mkelly@coxandpalmer.com
Kevin Latimer, QC, Managing Partner, Municipal Law; Labour & Employment; Administrative Law
902-491-4212
klatimer@coxandpalmer.com
Peter LeCain, Associate, Shipbuilding; Municipal Law
902-491-4132
plecain@coxandpalmer.com
Gavin D.F. MacDonald, Partner, Fisheries & Marine
902-491-4464
gmacdonald@coxandpalmer.com
Loretta M. Manning, Partner, Health Law
902-491-4125
lmanning@coxandpalmer.com
J. Craig McCrea, QC, Partner, Fisheries & Marine; Energy & Natural Resources
902-491-4120
cmccrea@coxandpalmer.com
Richard W. Norman, Associate, Construction; Energy & Natural Resources; Municipal Law Administrative Law
902-491-4128
rnorman@coxandpalmer.com
Joey D. Palov, Partner, Environmental Law
902-491-4201
jpalov@coxandpalmer.com
Terry L. Roane, QC, Counsel, Construction; Adminstrative Law; Labour & Employment
902-491-4112
troane@coxandpalmer.com
Peter C. Rumscheidt, Partner, Construction; Labour & Employment
902-491-4144
prumscheidt@coxandpalmer.com
Michael S. Ryan, QC, Counsel, Fisheries & Marine; Construction; Administrative Law
902-491-4221
mryan@coxandpalmer.com
Jillian B. Strugnell, Associate, Health Law
902-491-4214
jstrugnell@coxandpalmer.com
Jack K. Townsend, Associate, Health Law; Municipal Law; Administrative Law
902-491-4141
jktownsend@coxandpalmer.com
Peter T. Zed, Associate, Shipbuilding
902-491-4157
pzed@coxandpalmer.com
Ezra B. van Gelder, Associate, Construction Law; Administrative Law
902-491-4239
evangelder@coxandpalmer.com

MacInnis, Kenneth Associates
#340, 1801 Hollis St., Halifax, NS B3J 3N4
Tel: 902-421-1817; *Fax:* 902-423-8504
Profile: 1 Office, 3 Lawyers

McInnes Cooper - Halifax
Purdy's Wharf Tower II, P.O. Box 730, 1300-1969 Upper Water St., Halifax, NS B3J 2V1
Tel: 902-425-6500; *Fax:* 902-425-6350
mchfx@mcinnescooper.com
www.mcinnescooper.com
Profile: 111 Lawyers,
Aboriginal Law; Energy Law; Environmental Law; Maritime Law; Municipal & Land Use Planning
Environmental Lawyers:
Michelle C. Awad, Energy; Construction
902-444-8509
michelle.awad@mcinnescooper.com
Robert G. Belliveau, Q.C., Environmental Law
902-444-8513
robert.belliveau@mcinnescooper.com
David Demirkan, Maritime Law; Municipal & Land Use Planning
902-424-1388
david.demirkan@mcinnescooper.com
Kevin D. Gibson, Construction
902-444-8539
kevin.gibson@mcinnescooper.com
David A. Graves, Construction
902-424-1330
david.graves@mcinnescooper.com
Thomas E. Hart, Aboriginal Law; Environmental Law; Maritime Law
902-424-1329
tom.hart@mcinnescooper.com
Sarah M. Kirby, Maritime Law
John Kulik, Construction
902-424-1339
john.kulik@mcinnescooper.com
Douglas Lutz, Energy
902-424-1352
doug.lutz@mcinnescooper.com
George W. MacDonald, Q.C., Construction
902-424-1365
george.macdonald@mcinnescooper.com
Aidan J. Meade, Construction; Energy
Harvey L. Morrison, Aboriginal Law; Construction; Environmental Law
Christopher C. Robinson, Q.C., Construction; Energy
902-424-1325
chris.robinson@mcinnescooper.com
Wylie Spicer, Q.C., Energy; Maritime Law
902-424-1366
wylie.spicer@mcinnescooper.com

Patterson Law
P.O. Box 1068, 10 Church St., Truro, NS B2N 5B9
Tel: 902-897-2000; *Fax:* 902-893-3071
Toll-Free: 888-897-2001
contactus@pattersonlaw.ca
www.pattersonlaw.ca
Profile: 2 Offices, 31 Lawyers

Patterson Law
1718 Argyle St., 5th Fl., Halifax, NS B3J 3N6
Tel: 902-405-8000; *Fax:* 902-405-8001
Toll-Free: 888-897-2001
contactus@pattersonlaw.ca
www.pattersonlaw.ca
Profile: 2 Offices, Founded in: 1928
Lawyers at Patterson Law have expertise in the following areas of law: Aboriginal, administrative, agricultural, construction, forestry, health, & municipal. Examples of issues addressed include natural resources harvesting rights, compliance with environmental laws & regulations, conservation easements, development planning, & land use regulations.

Patterson Law
1718 Argyle Street, 5th Floor, Halifax, NS B3J 3N6
Tel: 902-405-8000; *Fax:* 902-405-8001
Toll-Free: 888-897-2001
contactus@pattersonlaw.ca
www.pattersonlaw.ca
Profile: 2 Offices, 31 Lawyers
Environmental Lawyers:
Lloyd I. Berliner, QC, Labour & Employment
lberliner@pattersonlaw.ca
J. Ronald Creighton, QC, Aboriginal Law; Forestry
rcreighton@pattersonlaw.ca
Margot J. Ferguson, Health Law
mferguson@pattersonlaw.ca
Jane M. Gourley-Davis, Agriculture; Municipal Law
jgourleydavis@pattersonlaw.ca
Jennifer J. Hamilton Upham, Agriculture
jupham@pattersonlaw.ca
Joel D. Henderson, Forestry
jhenderson@pattersonlaw.ca
Jeffrey R. Hunt, Construction; Labour & Employment
jhunt@pattersonlaw.ca
Dennis J. James, Aboriginal Law; Administrative Law; Labour & Employment; Municipal Law
djames@pattersonlaw.ca
Sandra L. McCulloch, Municipal Law
smcculloch@pattersonlaw.ca
Robert L. Mellish, Agriculture; Construction
rmellish@pattersonlaw.ca
L. Martina Munden, Construction; Health Law; Labour & Employment
mmunden@pattersonlaw.ca
Robert M. Purdy, QC, Health Law
rpurdy@pattersonlaw.ca
George L. White, QC, Agriculture; Forestry
gwhite@pattersonlaw.ca

Ritch Durnford, Lawyers
#1200, CIBC Bldg., 1809 Barrington St., Halifax, NS B3J 3K8
Tel: 902-429-3400; *Fax:* 902-422-4713
info@ritchdurnford.com; library@ritchdurnford.com
www.ritchdurnford.com
Profile: 1 Office, 16 Lawyers, Founded in: 1948
Areas of practice include municipal law & litigation of admiralty, environmental & marine claims.
Environmental Lawyers:
Lisa Richards, Municipal Law
lisa.richards@ritchdunford.com
Matthew G. Williams, Maritime Law
matthew.williams@ritchdurnford.com

Stewart McKelvey - Halifax
#900, Purdy's Wharf Tower One, P.O. Box 997, Stn. Central, 1959 Upper Water St., Halifax, NS B3J 2X2
Tel: 902-420-3200; *Fax:* 902-420-1417
halifax@stewartmckelvey.com
www.stewartmckelvey.com
twitter.com/SM_Law, www.linkedin.com/company/85897
Profile: 6 Offices, 221 Lawyers, Founded in: 1867
Energy; Oil & Gas; Renewable Energy; Electric; Natural Resources & Environmental (Aquaculture, Forestry & Mining)
Environmental Lawyers:
T. Arthur Barry, Q.C., General Counsel, Construction
902-420-3364
abarry@stewartmckelvey.com
Christa M. Brothers, Partner, Construction Law
902-420-3331
cbrothers@stewartmckelvey.com
Lydia S. Bugden, Partner, Energy & Natural Resources
902-420-3372
lbugden@stewartmckelvey.com
Tyana R. Caplan, Health
902-420-3356
tcaplan@stewartmckelvey.com
James M. Dickson, Partner, Energy & Natural Resources
902-420-3308
jdickson@stewartmckelvey.com
Meinhard Doelle, Counsel, Energy & Natural Resources; Environmental
902-420-3352
mdoelle@stewartmckelvey.com
Andrew Fraser, Partner, Construction Law
902-420-3390
afraser@stewartmckelvey.com
Robert G. Grant, Q.C., Partner, Energy & Natural Resources; Environmental; Public Hearings; Defence of Prosecutions; Environmental Liability
902-420-3328
rgrant@stewartmckelvey.com
David G. Henley, Partner, Marine Law; Energy & Natural Resources; Environmental; Construction
902-420-3381
dhenley@stewartmckelvey.com
D. Geoffrey Machum, Partner, Construction
902-420-3330
gmachum@stewartmckelvey.com
Carman G. McCormick, Q.C., Partner, Health
902-420-3318
cmccormick@stewartmckelvey.com
John S. McFarlane, Q.C., Partner, Environmental
902-420-3315
jmcfarlane@stewartmckelvey.com
Andrew J. McFarlane, Partner, Environmental
902-420-3315
jmcfarlane@stewartmckelvey.com
David A. Miller, Q.C., Partner, Construction
902-420-3319
dmiller@stewartmckelvey.com
William Moreira, Partner, Marine Law; Energy & Natural Resources; Construction Law
902-420-3346
wmoreira@stewartmckelvey.com
Colin D. Piercey, Partner, Energy & Natural Resources; Environmental; Construction
902-420-3345
cpiercey@stewartmckelvey.com
Nancy G. Rubin, Partner, Energy & Natural Resources; Environmental
902-420-3337
nrubin@stewartmckelvey.com
William L. (Mick) Ryan, Q.C., Partner, Construction
902-420-3316
wryan@stewartmckelvey.com
Richard F. Southcott, Regional Managing Partner, Marine Law; Environmental; Energy & Natural Resources
902-420-3304
rsouthcott@stewartmckelvey.com

Wickwire Holm
#2100, P.O. Box 1054, 1801 Hollis St., Halifax, NS B3J 2X6
Tel: 902-429-4111; *Fax:* 902-429-8215
Toll-Free: 866-429-4111
wh@wickwireholm.com
www.wickwireholm.com
www.facebook.com/pages/Wickwire-Holm/281421025262399, www.facebook.com/pages/Wickwire-Holm/281421025262399
Profile: 3 Offices,
Wickwire Holm provides legal services related to environmental issues to power generation companies, resource-based companies, oil & gas companies, property developers, financial organizations, governments & First Nations. Education & guidance is available in the areas of regulatory & public hearings, land use planning, environmental assessments & approvals, due diligence, & occupational health & safety.
Environmental Lawyers:
Selina Bath, Associate, Construction; Labour & Employment
902-482-7030
sbath@wickwireholm.com
James P. Boudreau, Partner, Construction; Labour & Employment
902-482-7006
jboudreau@wickwireholm.com
Marc Dunning, Associate, Energy & the Environment; Construction; Labour & Employment; Advocacy & Dispute Resolution
902-482-7017
mdunning@wickwireholm.com
Sean Foreman, Partner, Energy & the Environment; Advocacy & Dispute Resolution
902-482-7020
sforeman@wickwireholm.com
Brian Hebert, Partner, Aboriginal Law; Energy & the Environment
902-429-7707
bhebert@wickwireholm.com
Noella Martin, QC, Partner, Labour & Employment
902-482-7013
nmartin@wickwireholm.com
Daniel Pink, Associate, Labour & Employment
902-482-7009
dpink@wickwireholm.com
Geoffrey Saunders, Partner, Energy & the Environment; Construction
902-482-7005
gsaunders@wickwireholm.com
Dillon Trider, Associate, Construction; Labour & Employment
902-482-7002
dtrider@wickwireholm.com
Aaron Ward, Associate, Energy & the Environment; Construction; Labour & Employment; Advocacy & Dispute Resolution
902-482-7010
award@wickwireholm.com

Kentville

Muttarts Law Firm
P.O. Box 515, 20 Cornwallis St., Kentville, NS B4N 3X3
Tel: 902-678-2157; *Fax:* 902-678-9455
lcrowell@muttartslaw.ca
www.muttartslaw.ca
Profile: 1 Office, 6 Lawyers, Founded in: 1968

Truro

Burchell MacDougall Lawyers - Truro
P.O. Box 1128, 710 Prince St., Truro, NS B2N 5H1
Tel: 902-895-1561; *Fax:* 902-895-7709
Toll-Free: 800-565-1200
truro@burchellmacdougall.com
www.burchellmacdougall.com
www.facebook.com/burmaclawyers, twitter.com/burmaclawyers, www.linkedin.com/company/burchell-macdougall-lawyers
Profile: 4 Offices, 27 Lawyers
Environmental Lawyers:
Michael A. Maddalena, Farm & Resources Group

Patterson Law
P.O. Box 1068, 10 Church St., Truro, NS B2N 5B9
Tel: 902-897-2000; *Fax:* 902-893-3071
Toll-Free: 888-897-2001
contactus@pattersonlaw.ca
www.pattersonlaw.ca

Wolfville

Burchell MacDougall Lawyers - Wolfville
29 Elm Ave., Wolfville, NS B4P 2A1
Tel: 902-542-4543; *Fax:* 902-542-5474
Toll-Free: 800-329-0121
wolfville@burchellmacdougall.com
www.burchellmacdougall.com
Profile: 2 Lawyers,
Lawyers at the Wolfville location offer services in the areas of agricultural law & environmental litigation.
Environmental Lawyers:
Michael R. Brooker, Q.C., Managing Partner, Environmental Litigation
902-542-4068
mbrooker@burchellmacdougall.com
Daniel L. Oulton, Partner, Agricultural Law
902-542-4071
doulton@burchellmacdougall.com

Ontario

Renick, Jim Law Office
23 Talbot St. North, ON N8M 1A5
Tel: 519-776-9020; *Fax:* 519-776-9027
info@jamesrenick.com
www.jamesrenick.com
Profile: 1 Office, 1 Lawyers,
Environmental law services to municipal & corporate business clients
Environmental Lawyers:
J. James Renick, Environmental; Municipal

Alexandria

Nelligan O'Brien Payne
139 Main St. South, Alexandria, ON K0C 1A0
Tel: 613-525-2396; *Fax:* 613-525-2752
Toll-Free: 888-565-9912
info@nelligan.ca
www.nelligan.ca
Profile: 4 Offices, 46 Lawyers

Barrie

HGR Graham Partners LLP - Barrie
#107, 190 Cundles Rd. East, Barrie, ON L4M 4S5
Tel: 705-737-1811; *Fax:* 705-737-5390
info@hgrgp.ca
www.hgr.ca
Profile: Founded in: 1975
Lawyers at the Barrie office of HGR Graham Partners are available to advise & represent municipalities on issues & transactions related to land use planning & development & municipal services.
Environmental Lawyers:
Tracy Arkell, Land Development; Municipal Law
tarkell@hgrgp.ca
Rob Bigioni, Construction Law
rbigioni@hgrgp.ca
Ellen Brohm, Environmental Law; Municipal Law
ebrohm@hgrgp.ca
George Cameron, Land Development
gcameron@hgrgp.ca
E. Marshall Green, Municipal Law; Land Development
mgreen@hgrgp.ca
Peter Krysiak, Municipal Law; Planning Law; Land Development
pkrysiak@hgrgp.ca
Bola Ogunmefun, Land Development; Municipal Law
bogunmefun@hgrgp.ca
Paul Rabinovitch, Land Development; Municipal Law
prabinovitch@hgrgp.ca
Tom C. Tsakopoulos, Municipal Law; Land Development; Construction Law
ttsakopoulos@hgrgp.ca

Belleville

Templeman Menninga LLP
#200, P.O. Box 234, 205 Dundas St. East, Belleville, ON K8N 5A2
Tel: 613-966-2620; *Fax:* 613-966-2866
info@tmlegal.com
www.tmlegal.ca
Profile: 4 Offices, 24 Lawyers, Founded in: 1981
Representation at Environmental Assessment Board and Environmental Appeal Board Hearings; Environmental Law and Remediation; Appeals before the Ontario Municipal Board, regarding Official Plans, Zoning Bylaws, Subdivisions, etc.; Subdivision, Site Plan, Condominium and other Development
Environmental Lawyers:

David W. DeMille, Environmental Law
613-966-2620
dwd@tmlegal.ca
Stephen Ellsworth, Environmental Law
se@tmlegal.ca
Wayne Fairbrother, Partner, Municipal; Landfill Site Management; Environmental Assessment
dwf@tmlegal.ca
Jeffrey D. Paine, Water Resources; Environment
jp@tmlegal.ca

Brampton

Lawrence, Lawrence, Stevenson LLP

43 Queen St. West, Brampton, ON L6Y 1L9
Tel: 905-451-3040; *Fax:* 905-451-5058
www.lawrences.com
Profile: 1 Office, 0 Lawyers, Founded in: 1924
The Brampton law firm consists of more than 40 lawyers. Individuals, businesses, & institutions are served. Environmental law & land development & municiapl law are some practice areas.
Environmental Lawyers:
Anthony E. Bak, Environmental Law; Land Development & Municipal Law
905-452-6875
Karie Ann Benham, Employment Law
Damien M.E. Buntsma, Labour Law
905-452-6876
Chris Markou, Land Development & Municipal Law
905-452-6887
Heather M. Picken, Land Development & Municipal Law
905-452-6891
lls@lawrences.com
Edwin G. Upenieks, Land Development & Municipal Law
905-452-6873

Brantford

Waterous, Holden, Amey, Hitchon LLP

P.O. Box 1510, 20 Wellington St., Brantford, ON N3T 5V6
Tel: 519-759-6220; *Fax:* 519-759-8360
law@waterousholden.com
www.waterousholden.com
Profile: 3 Offices, 19 Lawyers, Founded in: 1921
Environmental Lawyers:
David Clement, Municipal law
Pat Corless, Municipal law
Jay Hitchon, Municipal law
Steven Portelli, Municipal law

Burlington

SimpsonWigle LAW LLP

#501, Sims Square Bldg., 390 Brant St., Burlington, ON L7R 4J4
Tel: 905-639-1052; *Fax:* 905-333-3960
Toll-Free: 800-434-4414
info@simpsonwigle.com
www.simpsonwigle.com
Profile: 2 Offices, 27 Lawyers, Founded in: 1990
Environmental Lawyers:
Serena Lee, Mining; Health
lees@simpsonwigle.com
Derek A. Schmuck, Partner, Construction Law ext. 353
schmuckd@simpsonwigle.com

Carleton Place

Howard Ryan Kelford Knott & Dixon - Carleton Place

9 Emily St., Carleton Place, ON K7C 1R9
Tel: 613-253-9772; *Fax:* 613-253-0772
www.smithsfallslaw.ca

Embrun

Campbell & Sabourin LLP/SRL

#1, 165 Bay St., Embrun, ON K0A 1W1
Tel: 613-443-5683; *Fax:* 613-443-3285
info@campbellaw.on.ca
www.campbellaw.on.ca
Profile: 1 Office, 2 Lawyers
Environmental Lawyers:

Goderich

Donnelly & Murphy Lawyers

18 Court House Sq., Goderich, ON N7A 3Y7
Tel: 519-524-2154; *Fax:* 519-524-8550
Toll-Free: 800-332-7160
admin@dmlaw.on.ca
www.donnellymurphy.com
Profile: 2 Offices, 8 Lawyers, Founded in: 1930
Donnelly & Murphy serves the businesses & residents of southwestern Ontario. Municipal & planning law & labour & employment law are among the areas of law practised by lawyers at the firm.
Environmental Lawyers:
Sheryl Feagan, Labour & Employment Law
sfeagan@dmlaw.ca
Greg Stewart, Municipal & Planning Law; Labour & Employment Law
gstewart@dmlaw.ca

Hamilton

Lazier Hickey Langs O'Neal

25 Main St. West, 15th Fl., Hamilton, ON L8P 1H1
Tel: 905-525-3652; *Fax:* 905-525-6278
lawfirm@lazierhickey.com
www.lazierhickey.com
Profile: 1 Office, Founded in: 1863
The firm offers legal advice & representation related to residential, commercial, & institutional development projects. Clients include land owners, developers, engineers, & builders.
Environmental Lawyers:
Peter J. Sullivan, Partner, Construction Law; Employment Law
sullivanpj@lazierhickey.com
Karen C. Watters, Construction Law; Employment Law
kwatters@lazierhickey.com

Ross & McBride LLP

Commerce Place, P.O. Box 907, 1 King Street West, 10th Fl., Hamilton, ON L8N 3P6
Tel: 905-526-9800; *Fax:* 905-526-0732
contact@rossmcbride.com
www.rossmcbride.com
Profile: 1 Office, 37 Lawyers, Founded in: 1890
Environmental Lawyers:
Paul D. Paradis, Partner, Environmental Law
905-572-5811
paul.paradis@rossmcbride.com
Rick D. Simmons, Occupational Health & Safety
905-572-5833
rsimmons@rossmcbride.com

Scarfone Hawkins LLP

P.O. Box 926, Stn. Depot 1, 1 James St. South, 14th Fl., Hamilton, ON L8N 3P9
Tel: 905-523-1333; *Fax:* 905-523-5878
info@shlaw.ca
www.scarfonehawkinsllp.com
Profile: 1 Office, 19 Lawyers, Founded in: 1975
Environmental Lawyers:
Donald B. Hawkins, Construction Law
dhawkins@shlaw.ca
Catherine Buntain Jeske, Construction Law
cjeske@shlaw.ca
James W. Mahler, Construction Law
jmahler@shlaw.ca
Matthew G. Moloci, Construction Law
moloci@shlaw.ca
Krystyn Ordyniec, Construction Law
kordyniec@shlaw.ca
Frank Pignoli, Environmental Torts; Construction Law
fpignoli@shlaw.ca
James A. Scarfone, Environmental Litigation
scarfone@shlaw.ca
Joseph G. Speranzini, Construction Law
speranzini@shlaw.ca
Michael Stanton, Construction Law
mstanton@shlaw.ca
Jeffrey C. Teal, Construction Law; Health Law
jteal@shlaw.ca
David Thompson, Construction Law
thompson@shlaw.ca
Michael J. Valente, Construction Law
mvalente@shlaw.ca
Colleen Yamashita, Construction Law
cyamashita@shlaw.ca

SimpsonWigle LAW LLP

#200, 1 Hunter Street East, Hamilton, ON L8N 3R1
Tel: 905-528-8411; *Fax:* 905-528-9008
Toll-Free: 800-464-4414
info@simpsonwigle.com
www.simpsonwigle.com
Profile: 18 Lawyers, Founded in: 1986
Environmental Lawyers:
Timothy Bullock, Managing Partner, Construction Law ext. 354
bullockt@simpsonwigle.com
Brian J. Decaire, Construction Law ext. 337
decaireb@simpsonwigle.com
Catherine A. Olsiak, Health Law ext. 362
olsiakc@simpsonwigle.com
Derek A. Schmuck, Partner, Construction Law ext. 353
schmuck@simpsonwigle.com

Thoman Soule LLP, Lawyers

P.O. Box 187, Stn. LCD 1, 46 Jackson St. East, Hamilton, ON L8N 3C5
Tel: 905-529-8195; *Fax:* 905-529-7906
Toll-Free: 877-529-8195
info@thomansoule.com
www.thomansoule.com
Profile: 2 Offices, Founded in: 1930
Waste management, planning, & land use cases are handled at Thoman Soule LLP.
Environmental Lawyers:
Frederick E. Leitch, Environmental assessment advocacy (waste management cases); Municipal advocacy (planning & land use cases); Construction litigation
fleitch@thomansoule.com

Turkstra Mazza Associates

15 Bold St., Hamilton, ON L8P 1T3
Tel: 905-529-3476; *Fax:* 905-529-3663
Profile: 1 Office, 6 Lawyers, Founded in: 1977
Environmental Lawyers:
Herman Turkstra, Partner, Environmental Law
hturkstra@tmalaw.ca

Kingston

Cunningham, Swan, Carty, Little & Bonham LLP

#201, City Place II, 1473 John Counter Blvd., Kingston, ON K7M 8Z6
Tel: 613-544-0211; *Fax:* 613-542-9814
info@cswan.com
www.cswan.com
Profile: 1 Office, 24 Lawyers, Founded in: 1988
Municipal Law; Land Use Planning; Health Law; Development & Environmental Law
Environmental Lawyers:
Roy B. Conacher, Q.C., Planning & Development
613-544-7030
rconacher@cswan.com
Bob Little, Q.C., Municipal Law; Health Law
613-546-8070
rlittle@cswan.com
R.P. Tchegus, Planning & Development
613-546-8073
rtchegus@cswan.com
T.J. Wilkin, Planning & Development; Municipal Law
613-546-8074
twilkin@cswan.com

Hicks Morley Hamilton Stewart Storie LLP - Kingston

#310, 366 King St. East, Kingston, ON K7K 6Y3
Tel: 613-549-6353; *Fax:* 613-549-4068
www.hicksmorley.com
Profile: 4 Lawyers,
Environmental practice areas include occupational health, municipal law, & construction law.
Environmental Lawyers:
Kees Kort, Partner, Municipal Law; Healthcare; Employment Law
613-541-4001
kees-kort@hicksmorley.com
Vince M. Panetta, Partner, Municipal Law; Construction; Workplace Safety; Healthcare; Transportation
613-541-4003
vince-panetta@hicksmorley.com
Colin J. Youngman, Associate, Municipal Law; Construction; Healthcare; Occupational Health

613-541-4005
colin-youngman@hicksmorley.com

Nelligan O'Brien Payne
#202, The Woolen Mill, 4 Cataraqui St., Kingston, ON K7K 1Z7
Tel: 613-531-7905; *Fax:* 613-531-0857
Toll-Free: 888-565-9912
info@nelligan.ca
www.nelligan.ca
Profile: 4 Offices, 46 Lawyers
Environmental Lawyers:

Soloway, Wright LLP - Kingston
#510, 366 King St. East, Kingston, ON K7K 6Y3
Tel: 613-544-7334; *Fax:* 800-263-4213
Toll-Free: 800-263-4257
info@solowaywright.com
www.soloways.com

Kitchener

Cohen Highley LLP - Kitchener
#1002, 55 King St. West, Kitchener, ON N2G 4W1
Tel: 226-476-4444; *Fax:* 519-576-2830
www.cohenhighley.com
Profile: 3 Lawyers,
The main office of Cohen Highley LLP is located in London, Ontario. Clients in southwestern Ontario are also served through law offices in Kitchener & Sarnia. The law team at the Kitchener office offers representation in the area of municipal law.
Environmental Lawyers:
R. Tyler Hortie, Partner, Municipal Law
hortie@cohenhighley.com

Madorin, Snyder LLP
P.O. Box 1234, Stn. C, 55 King St. West, Kitchener, ON N2G 4G9
Tel: 519-744-4491; *Fax:* 519-741-8060
reception@kw-law.com
www.kw-law.com
Profile: 1 Office, 16 Lawyers, Founded in: 1954
Environmental Lawyers:
W.H.P. Madorin, Q.C., Managing Partner, Environmental law
pmadorin@kw-law.com
Leanne E. Way, Municipal law
lway@kw-law.com

London

Cohen Highley LLP - London
One London Pl., 255 Queens Ave., 11th Fl., London, ON N6A 5R8
Tel: 519-672-9330; *Fax:* 519-672-5960
www.cohenhighley.com
Profile: 3 Offices, 25 Lawyers, Founded in: 1974
Cohen Highley's Environmental Law Group provides legal advice & representation on a variety of environmental matters. Lawyers serve individuals, private industry, First Nation communities, & municipalities. The following services are provided: decommission of contaminated land; satisfying envrionmental assessment requirements; adoption of due diligence strategies; compliance with environmental protection legislation; implementaion of environmental policies & environmental management systems; & prevention of emergency spills.
Environmental Lawyers:
Gene P. Chiarello, Associate, Environmental Law; Energy Law; Labour & Employment
chiarello@cohenhighley.com
Frank Highley, Counsel, Construction Law
highley@cohenhighley.com
Joseph Hoffer, Partner, Municipal Law; Administrative Law
Kristin Ley, Partner, Municipal Law; Administrative Law
ley@cohenhighley.com
Laura M. McKeen, Associate, Municipal Law; Administrative Law
mckeen@cohenhighley.com
Paul G. Vogel, Partner, Energy Regulation; Environmental Law; Farm Regulation
vogel@cohenhighley.com

Hicks Morley Hamilton Stewart Storie LLP - London
#1608, 148 Fullerton St., London, ON N6A 5P3
Tel: 519-433-7515; *Fax:* 519-433-8827
www.hicksmorley.com
Profile: 5 Lawyers,
Environmental areas of practice include workplace safety & insurance.
Environmental Lawyers:

McKenzie Lake Lawyers
#1800, 140 Fullarton St., London, ON N6A 5P2
Tel: 519-672-5666; *Fax:* 519-672-2674
info@mckenzielake.com
www.mckenzielake.com
Profile: 1 Office, 42 Lawyers, Founded in: 1988
McKenzie Lake Lawyers LLP has expertise in the area of land development.
Environmental Lawyers:
Donald Bryant, Healthcare Law
519-672-5666 ext. 355
bryant@mckenzielake.com
Mavis Butkus, Administrative & Regulatory Law
519-672-5666 ext. 309
butkus@mckenzielake.com
Diane Chick, Healthcare Law
519-672-5666 ext. 363
chick@mckenzielake.com
Brian Daly, Aboriginal Law; Labour & Employment
519-672-5666 ext. 392
daly@mckenzielake.com
Kevin A. Egan, Administrative & Regulatory Law; Labour & Employment
519-672-5666 ext. 315
egan@mckenzielake.com
Sean Flaherty, Aboriginal Law
519-672-5666 ext. 335
flaherty@mckenzielake.com
Steve Gibson, Administrative Law; Municipal Law; Regulatory Prosecution & Defence Proceedings
519-672-5666 ext. 310
gibson@mckenzielake.com
Mort Glanville, QC, Land Development
519-672-5666 ext. 338
glanville@mckenzielake.com
Christopher A. Lewis, Oil & Gas & Energy Law
519-672-5666 ext. 352
lewis@mckenzielake.com
Sarah Low, Aboriginal Law; Labour & Employment
519-672-5666 ext. 293
low@mckenzielake.com
Stuart Mackay, Administrative & Regulatory Law; Labour & Employment
519-672-5666 ext. 326
mackay@mckenzielake.com
Erin McDermid, Administrative & Regulatory Law; Labour & Employment
519-672-5666 ext. 387
mcdermid@mckenzielake.com
Richard McLaren, Administrative & Regulatory Law; Labour & Employment
519-672-5666 ext. 366
mclaren@mckenzielake.com
John McNair, Administrative & Regulatory Law; Labour & Employment
519-672-5666 ext. 378
mcnair@mckenzielake.com
David Nash, Healthcare Law; Administrative & Regulatory Law; Aboriginal Law; Labour & Employment
519-672-5666 ext. 347
nash@mckenzielake.com
Russell M. Raikes, Aboriginal Law; Labour & Employment
519-672-5666 ext. 342
raikes@mckenzielake.com
Erin Rankin Nash, Administrative & Regulatory Law; Healthcare Law; Labour & Employment
519-672-5666 ext. 317
rankinnash@mckenzielake.com
Julie Zamprogna Ballès, Administrative & Regulatory Law; Healthcare Law
519-672-5666 ext. 300
zamprogna@mckenzielake.com

Patton Cormier & Associates
#1512, 140 Fullarton St., London, ON N6A 5P2
Tel: 519-432-8282; *Fax:* 519-432-7285
www.pattoncormier.ca
Profile: 1 Office, 4 Lawyers,
Municipal law is practised.
Environmental Lawyers:
Elizabeth K. Cormier
ecormier@pattoncormier.ca
Analee J.M. Ferreira
aferreira@pattoncormier.ca
Alan R. Patton
apatton@pattoncormier.ca

Siskind LLP - London
P.O. Box 2520, 680 Waterloo St., London, ON N6A 3V8
Tel: 519-672-2121; *Fax:* 519-672-6065
Toll-Free: 877-672-2121
info@siskinds.com
www.siskinds.com
www.facebook.com/siskinds, twitter.com/SiskindsLLP
Profile: 4 Offices, 100 Lawyers, Founded in: 1933
Defend, prosecute under the Environmental Protection Act; expertise in Building Code Act applications involving environmental issues, obtaining waste related approvals & providing advice on maintaining compliance & handling waste disposal issues for industrial & municipal clients
Environmental Lawyers:
Paula Lombardi
519-660-7850
paula.lombardi@siskinds.com
Andrew Wright
519-660-7751
andrew.wright@siskinds.com

Markham

Miller Thomson LLP - Markham
#600, 60 Columbia Way, Markham, ON L3R 0C9
Tel: 905-415-6700; *Fax:* 905-415-6777
Toll-Free: 866-348-2432
markham@millerthomson.com
www.millerthomson.com
Profile: 11 Lawyers, Founded in: 1957
Aboriginal Law; Energy Law; Municipal & Planning; Oil & Gas; Construction; Forestry
Environmental Lawyers:
Roderick M. McLeod, Q.C., Environmental Law; Policy
905-415-6707
rmcleod@millerthomson.com
J. Bruce McMeekin, Municipal; Environmental Law; Regulations
905-415-6791
bmcmeekin@millerthomson.com
John R. Tidball, Environmental Law; Waste Management
905-415-6710
jtidball@millerthomson.com

Midland

HGR Graham Partners LLP - Midland
518 Yonge St., Midland, ON L4R 2C5
Tel: 705-526-2231; *Fax:* 705-526-0313
info@hgrgp.ca
www.hgrgp.ca
Profile: 5 Offices, 29 Lawyers, Founded in: 2012
In 2012, Hacker Gignac Rice LLP, with offices in Midland, Penetanguishene, Orillia, & Wasaga Beach, merged with Graham Partners LLP of Barrie Ontario.
Lawyers are available at the Midland office who specialize in matters related to municipal law, land use planning, & land development. Clients have been represented before tribunals such as the Environmental Review Board & the Ontario Municipal Board.
Environmental Lawyers:
Ron Crane, Land Development
rcrane@hgrgp.ca
Paul Peterson, Environmental Issues; Municipal Planning; Land Development
ppeterson@hgrgp.ca
John Walker, Land Development; Municipal Law
jwalker@hgrgp.ca

Niagara Falls

Martin Sheppard Fraser LLP - Niagara Falls
P.O. Box 900, 4701 St. Clair Ave., 2nd Fl., Niagara Falls, ON L2E 6V7
Tel: 905-354-1611; *Fax:* 905-354-5540
Toll-Free: 800-263-2502
lawyers@martinshep.com
www.martinshep.com
Profile: 2 Offices, 13 Lawyers, Founded in: 1887
Environmental Lawyers:
Andrew J. Larmand, Health
larmand@martinshep.com

Oakville

O'Connor MacLeod Hanna LLP
700 Kerr St., Oakville, ON L6K 3W5
Tel: 905-842-8030; *Fax:* 905-842-2460
info@omh.ca
www.omh.ca
Profile: 1 Office, 21 Lawyers, Founded in: 1991
Advises & represents both public & private sector clients on a full range of Municipal, Environmental & Administrative Law issues
Environmental Lawyers:
Danny Chou, Municipal; Administration
905-842-8030 ext. 3352
taylor@omh.ca
Owen Duguid, Municipal; Administration
905-842-8030 ext. 3352
taylor@omh.ca
Andrew C. Knox, Q.C., Municipal & Land Development
905-849-5010
knox@omh.ca
James McAskill, Municipal & Land Use
905-842-8030 ext. 3304
mcaskill@omh.ca
Carolyn McCarney, Municipal; Administration
905-842-8030 ext. 3352
taylor@omh.ca
Melanie Peters, Municipal; Administration
905-842-8030 ext. 3352
taylor@omh.ca
Blair S. Taylor, Municipal; Administration
905-842-8030 ext. 3352
taylor@omh.ca
Karen Trzaska, Municipal; Administration
905-842-8030 ext. 3352
taylor@omh.ca
Harold R. Watson, Municipal; Land Use
905-849-5016
watson@omh.ca
Kenneth W. Watts, Construction
905-842-8030 ext. 3361
watts@omh.ca

Orillia

Russell, Christie LLP
P.O. Box 158, 505 Memorial Ave., Orillia, ON L3V 6J3
Tel: 705-325-1326; *Fax:* 705-327-1811
rcmkw@russellchristie.com
Profile: 1 Office, 7 Lawyers,
Issues related to municipal law are handled.
Environmental Lawyers:
Douglas S. Christie, Partner, Municipal Law
dchristie@russellchristie.com
William S. Koughan, Partner, Municipal Law
bkoughan@russellchristie.com
Michael M. Miller, Partner, Municipal Law
mmiller@russellchristie.com
W.D (Rusty) Russell, QC, Counsel, Municipal Law
wdrussell@russellchristie.com
Michael F. Sirdevan, Municipal Law
msirdevan@russellchristie.com
Edward B. Veldboom, Partner, Municipal Law
eveldboom@russellchristie.com
David M. Winnitoy, Partner, Municipal Law
dwinnitoy@russellchristie.com

Ottawa

Beament Green
979 Wellington St. West, Ottawa, ON K1Y 2X7
Tel: 613-241-3400; *Fax:* 613-241-8555
info@beament.com
www.beament.com
Profile: 1 Office, 7 Lawyers,
Beament Green specializes in environmental law & employment law.
Environmental Lawyers:
Cheryl Gerhardt McLuckie, Environmental Law; Construction Law
cgerhardt@beament.com
Tia Hazra, Employment Law
thazra@beament.com
Michael S. Hebert, Environmental Law
mhebert@beament.com
Jeffrey Meleras, Worker's Safety Insurance Board matters
jmeleras@beament.com
Sig Pantazis, Environmental Law
spantazis@beament.com
John Read, Employment Law
jread@beament.com

Borden Ladner Gervais LLP - Ottawa
#1100, World Exchange Plaza, 100 Queen St., Ottawa, ON K1P 1J9
Tel: 613-237-5160; *Fax:* 613-230-8842
info@blg.com
www.blg.com
Profile: 91 Lawyers,
The environmental law group at Borden Ladner Gervais provides service to clients in the areas of environmental compliance, climate change, transactional work, & civil & regulatory disputes.
Environmental Lawyers:
Emma Blanchard, Environmental Law; Municipal & Land Use Planning Law
eblanchard@blg.com
Janet Bradley, Partner, Environmental Law; Municipal Law; Planning Law; Land Development Law; Construction Law
bradley@blg.com
Noëlle Caloren, Labour & Employment Law
ncaloren@blg.com
Kirsten Crain, Partner, Health Sector Litigation
kcrain@blg.com
Marc Jolicoeur, Regional Managing Partner, Forestry Law; Health Sector Services
mjolicoeur@blg.com
Gar Knutson, P.C., Government Relations
gknutson@blg.com
Gerry Stobo, Construction Law
gstobo@blg.com

Brazeau Seller LLP
#750, 55 Metcalfe St., Ottawa, ON K1P 6L5
Tel: 613-237-4000; *Fax:* 613-237-4001
www.brazeauseller.com
Profile: 1 Office, 17 Lawyers, Founded in: 1989

Dentons Canada LLP - Ottawa
#1420, 99 Bank St., Ottawa, ON K1P 1H4
Tel: 613-783-9611; *Fax:* 613-783-9690
www.dentons.com
Profile: 25 Lawyers
Environmental Lawyers:
John F. Blakney, Environmental Law; Transportation; Health
613-783-9602
john.blakney@dentons.com
Susan H. Brown, Environmental Law
613-783-9658
susan.brown@dentons.com
Philip M. Rimer, Aboriginal Law; Infrastructure & Construction Matters; Property Development; Land Use Planning
613-783-9634
philip.rimer@dentons.com

Donald R. Good & Associates
#207, 43 Roydon Pl., Ottawa, ON K2E 1A3
Tel: 613-228-9676; *Fax:* 613-228-7404
farmlaw@on.aibn.com
Profile: 3 Lawyers, Founded in: 1981
The practice specializes in agricultural legal matters.
Environmental Lawyers:
Kurtis R. Andrews, Environmental Law; Agricultural Law
kandrews@farm-law.ca
Donald R. Good, Environmental Law; Agricultural Law
Lisa A. Lemieux, Environmental Law; Agricultural Law
llemieux@farm-law.ca

Fasken Martineau - Ottawa
#1300, 55 Metcalfe St., Ottawa, ON K1P 6L5
Tel: 613-236-3882; *Fax:* 613-230-6423
ottawa@fasken.com
www.fasken.com
Profile: 19 Lawyers, Founded in: 2007

Heenan Blaikie LLP - Ottawa
#300, 55 Metcalfe St., Ottawa, ON K1P 6L5
Tel: 613-236-1668; *Fax:* 613-236-9632
www.heenanblaikie.com
Profile: 28 Lawyers
Environmental Lawyers:
Justin Bertrand, Construction Litigation
613-236-1627
jbertrand@heenan.ca
Pierre Champagne, Partner, Construction Litigation
613-236-4859
pchampagne@heenan.ca
Benoit M. Duchesne, Partner, Construction Litigation; Aboriginal Law
613-236-1946
bduchesne@heenan.ca
Justin R. Fogarty, Counsel, Construction
613-236-1668
jfogarty@heenan.ca
Louis-Pierre Grégoire, Construction Litigation
613-236-1751
lpgregoire@heenan.ca
Kevin D. MacNeill, Partner, Occupational Health & Safety
613-236-1668
kmacneill@heenan.ca
Peter Mantas, Partner, Environmental Law
613-237-1733
pmantas@heenan.ca
Dan Palayew, Partner, Occupational Health & Safety
613-236-6970
dpalayew@heenan.ca
Jeff Saikaley, Construction Litigation
613-236-1629
jsaikaley@heenan.ca
Marc Sauvé, Construction Litigation
613-236-6945
msauve@heenan.ca
Julie Thibault, Occupational Health & Safety
613-236-2161
juthibault@heenan.ca
Ivan G. Whitehall, Q.C., Counsel, Construction Litigation; Aboriginal Law
613-236-1696
iwhitehall@heenan.ca

Hicks Morley Hamilton Stewart Storie LLP - Ottawa
#2000, 150 Metcalfe St., Ottawa, ON K2P 1P1
Tel: 613-234-0386; *Fax:* 613-234-0418
www.hicksmorley.com
Profile: 8 Lawyers,
Environmental practice areas include energy law, occupational health, workpace safety, healthcare, municipal law, & construction law.
Environmental Lawyers:
Leanne N. Fisher, Associate, Municipal Law; Employment Law
613-369-2106
leanne-fisher@hicksmorley.com
Andrew J. McCreary, Partner, Employment Law; Municipal Law; Construction Law
613-369-2104
andrew-mccreary@hicksmorley.com
Siobhan O'Brien, Associate, Occupational Health; Workplace Safety & Insurance; Healthcare; Municipal Law; Construction Law; Energy; Transporation
613-369-2111
siobhan-obrien@hicksmorley.com
Lynn Thomson, Partner, Employment Law; Municipal Law; Healthcare
613-369-2102
lynn-thomson@hicksmorley.com
George G. Vuicic, Partner, Construction Law; Occupational Health; Workplace Safety; Healthcare; Mining & Resources; Municipal Law
613-369-2103
george-vuicic@hicksmorley.com
Cheryl Waram, Associate, Energy; Occupational Health; Workplace Safety; Healthcare; Municipal Law; Construction Law
613-369-2120
cheryl-waram@hicksmorley.com

Lavery, de Billy - Ottawa
#1810, 360 Albert St., Ottawa, ON K1R 7X7
Tel: 613-594-4936; *Fax:* 613-594-8783
info@lavery.ca
www.lavery.ca
Profile: 5 Lawyers, Founded in: 1913
Environmental Lawyers:
Jacques Y. Desjardins, Partner, Construction & Surety Law
613-560-2522
jdesjardins@lavery.ca

Mélanie Vadeboncoeur, Construction & Surety Law
613-560-2528
mvadeboncoeur@lavery.ca

McMillan LLP - Ottawa

#300, 50 O'Connor St., Ottawa, ON K1P 6L2
Tel: 613-232-7171; *Fax:* 613-231-3191
info@mcmillan.ca
www.mcmillan.ca
Profile: 29 Lawyers, Founded in: 1984
Lang Michener LLP assists organizations with legal issues related to the environment & energy, through its Environment, Energy & Emissions Trading Group. The lawyers at Lang Michener also provide legal advice to the aviation, rail, & marine industries, the Canadian & international mining & natural resource industry & to the forestry & paper products industry.
Environmental Lawyers:
David Debenham, Environmental law
C.J. Michael Flavell, Q.C., Forestry; Transportation & logistics (marine, aviation, & rail)
John G.M. Hooper, Q.C., Health care & life sciences
Marie-France Major, Mining & natural resources
Martin G. Masse, Forestry
Eugene Meehan, Q.C., Forestry; Transportation & logistics (marine, aviation, & rail)
Terry W. Peterman, Mining & natural resources

Nelligan O'Brien Payne

#1500, 50 O'Connor St., Ottawa, ON K1P 6L2
Tel: 613-238-8080; *Fax:* 613-238-2098
Toll-Free: 888-565-9912
info@nelligan.ca
www.nelligan.ca
Profile: 4 Offices, 46 Lawyers
Environmental Lawyers:
Deborah A. Bellinger, Environmental Law
debbie.bellinger@nelligan.ca
Geoffrey Cantello, Municipal law
geoffrey.cantello@nelligan.ca
Colin Dubeau, Municipal law
colin.dubeau@nelligan.ca
Suzanne M. Farag, Municipal law
suzanne.farag@nelligan.ca
John Nelligan, Q.C., LSM, D.U., Municipal law
john.nelligan@nelligan.ca
Allan R. O'Brien, Municipal law
allan.obrien@nelligan.ca
David R. Shelly, Municipal law
david.shelly@nelligan.ca

Perley-Robertson, Hill & McDougall LLP / s.r.l.

#1400, Constitution Square, 340 Albert St., Ottawa, ON K1R 0A5
Tel: 613-238-2022; *Fax:* 613-238-8775
Toll-Free: 800-268-8292
lawyers@perlaw.ca
www.perlaw.ca
Profile: 1 Office, 51 Lawyers, Founded in: 1971
The large, independent law firm in the National Capital Region has lawyers with expertise in land development & construction law. Legal advice is available to land developers & builders on issues related to municipal law, environmental regulations, & contracts.
Environmental Lawyers:
Lynda A. Bordeleau, Head of Police Law Group, Labour & Employment; Administrative Tribunals
613-566-2847
lbordeleau@perlaw.ca
Owen Bourns, Associate, Employment & Labour; Administrative Truibunals
613-566-2823
obourns@perlaw.ca
Paul D'Angelo, Partner, Construction Law
613-566-2808
pdangelo@perlaw.ca
Joël M. Dubois, Partner, Labour & Employment; Administrative Tribunals
613-566-2815
jdubois@perlaw.ca
Jean-Marc Eddie, Partner, Labour & Employment; Administrative Tribunals
613-566-2841
jmeddie@perlaw.ca
David H. Hill, QC, Partner, Employment; Administrative Tribunals
613-566-2800
dhill@perlaw.ca
Robert P. Kinghan, Partner, Construction Law
613-566-2848
rkinghan@perlaw.ca
Andrew J.F. Lenz, Partner, Employment; Administrative Tribunals
613-566-2842
alenz@perlaw.ca
Barry Leon, Head International Arbitration, Employment; Administrative Tribunals
613-566-2843
bleon@perlaw.ca
Keith A. MacLaren, Construction Law
Thomas A. McDougall, QC, Founding Partner, Employment & Labour; Administrative Tribunals
613-566-2830
tmcdougall@perlaw.ca
David Migicovsky, Head, Litigation Group, Employment & Labour; Administrative Tribunals
613-566-2833
dmigicovsky@perlaw.ca
Joshua P. Moon, Partner, Land Development
613-566-2801
jmoon@perlaw.ca
Christopher P. Morris, Associate, Employment; Administrative Tribunals
613-566-2802
cmorris@perlaw.ca
Karin Pagé, Associate, Employment & Labour; Administrative Tribunals
613-566-2860
kpage@perlaw.ca
Emily S. Rahn, Associate, Employment & Labour; Administrative Tribunals
613-566-2859
erahn@perlaw.ca
Charles Saikaley, Partner, Construction Law; Land Development
613-566-2836
csaikaley@perlaw.ca
Gregory Sanders, Head, Tax Law Group
613-566-2846
gsanders@perlaw.ca
Greg Sim, Head, Real Estate Group, Construction Law; Land Development
Margaret Truesdale, Research Director, Labour & Employment; Administrative Tribunals
613-566-2820
mtruesdale@perlaw.ca

Rick & Associates

#109, 591 March Rd., Ottawa, ON K2K 2M5
Tel: 613-592-0088; *Fax:* 613-592-3322
info@rickassociates.com
www.rickassociates.com
Profile: 2 Offices, 3 Lawyers, Founded in: 1993
A second office is located at 359 Ottawa St., Almonte, ON, 613-256-3480.
Environmental Lawyers:
W. John Rick, Managing Partner, Environmental Law
jrick@rickassociates.com

Riopelle Griener Professional Corporation

2888 St. Joseph Blvd., Ottawa, ON K1C 1G7
Tel: 613-834-4800; *Fax:* 613-834-4828
Toll-Free: 877-834-4855
www.rglaw.ca
Profile: 2 Offices, 2 Lawyers, Founded in: 2005
Environmental Lawyers:
Robert M. Riopelle, Municipal law; Administrative law
613-834-4800
robert@rglaw.ca

Soloway, Wright LLP - Ottawa

#900, 427 Laurier Ave. West, Ottawa, ON K1R 7Y2
Tel: 613-236-0111; *Fax:* 613-238-8507
Toll-Free: 800-207-5880
info@solowaywright.com
www.soloways.com
Profile: 2 Offices, 27 Lawyers, Founded in: 1945
Soloway, Wright LLP serves clients in eastern Ontario. Lawyers are available with expertise in the area of municipal law. The firm offers advice & assistance to clients, such as planners, land developers, engineers, & architects, in matters of land use & development. Soloway, Wright LLP lawyers have appeared regularly before municipal councils, committees, & tribunals, the Ontario Municipal Board, as well as Ontario Courts for municipal, planning, & expropriation matters.
Environmental Lawyers:
Alan K. Cohen, Planning Law; Development Law; Municipal Law
613-782-3217
cohena@solowaywright.com
January L. Cohen, Planning Law; Development Law; Municipal Law
613-782-3216
cohenj@solowaywright.com
Abraham Feinstein, QC, Land Development
613-782-3218
feinstea@solowaywright.com
Peter Hagen, Environmental Issues; Construction Issues
613-782-3228
hagenp@solowaywright.com
Douglas B. Kelly, Municipal Law; Planning & Development Law
613-782-3215
kellyd@solowaywright.com
Paull N. Leamen, Municipal Litigation; Construction Litigation
613-782-3233
leamenp@solowaywright.com
Elizabeth A. Maiden, Municipal Law; Land Development
613-782-3230
emaiden@solowaywright.com
Ursula Melinz, Municipal Law; Development & Planning Law
613-782-3214
melinzu@solowaywright.com
Stephen R. Polowin, Land Development
613-782-3219
polowins@solowaywright.com
Alan M. Riddell, Labour & Employment Law
613-782-3235
riddella@solowaywright.com
Brian Roach, Land Development
613-782-3226
roachb@solowaywright.com
Tara M. Sweeney, Health Law
613-782-3234
sweeneyt@solowaywright.com

Stikeman Elliott LLP - Ottawa

#1600, 50 O'Connor St., Ottawa, ON K1P 6L2
Tel: 613-234-4555; *Fax:* 613-230-8877
Toll-Free: 877-776-2263
www.stikeman.com
Profile: 13 Lawyers, Founded in: 1981
Environmental Lawyers:
Susan M. Hutton, Partner, Pharmaceuticals, Biotechnology & Life Sciences; Construction Litigation; Energy; Forestry & Forest Products; Mining
613-566-0530
shutton@stikeman.com
T. Gregory Kane, Q.C., Partner, Renewable Energy
613-566-0524
gkane@stikeman.com
Stuart C. McCormack, Managing Partner, Pharmaceuticals, Biotechnology & Life Sciences
613-566-0526
smccormack@stikeman.com
Nicholas P. McHaffie, Partner, Environmental Litigation; Pharmaceuticals, Biotechnology & Life Sciences
613-566-0546
nmchaffie@stikeman.com

Perth

Anderson Foss

10 Market Sq., Perth, ON K7H 1V7
Tel: 613-267-9898; *Fax:* 613-267-2741
www.andersonfoss.ca
Profile: 1 Office, 2 Lawyers,
Municipal law is practised.
Environmental Lawyers:
Mary Foss, B.A., J.D., Municipal Law
mary@andersonfoss.ca

Peterborough

LLF Lawyers LLP

P.O. Box 1146, 332 Aylmer St. North, Peterborough, ON K9J 7H4
Tel: 705-742-1674; *Fax:* 705-742-4677
info@llf.ca
www.llf.ca

Profile: 2 Offices, 16 Lawyers,
In 2012, the law practices of Howell Fleming & LLF Lawyers combined. The firm provides legal services related to land development & health. Clients include individuals, organizations, businesses, & institutions.
Environmental Lawyers:
Jim Baird, Associate, Land Use Planning; Municipal Law
705-745-1361 ext. 344
jbaird@llf.ca
Melinda Booth, Associate, Municipal Law; Planning
705-742-1674 ext. 248
mbooth@llf.ca
Robert E. Pakenham, Counsel, Municipal Law; Land Use Planning; Administrative Law
705-745-1361 ext. 306
bpakenham@llf.ca
Chris Russell, Associate, Construction Litigation & liens; Employment Law
705-742-1674 ext. 220
crussell@llf.ca
Emily Whetung MacInnes, Associate, Aboriginal Law; Development matters
705-742-1674 ext. 258
ewhetung@llf.ca
Tammy Williams, Partner, Employment Law
705-742-1674 ext. 242
twilliams@llf.ca

Whetung Law Office, Barristers & Solicitors, Notarie Public
P.O. Box 29, 521 George St. North, Peterborough, ON K9J 6Y5
Tel: 705-743-6470; *Fax:* 705-743-3128
info@whetunglaw.com
www.whetunglaw.com
Profile: 1 Office, 1 Lawyers, Founded in: 1949
The firm focuses on reap property law.
Environmental Lawyers:
Linda Willcox Whetung, First Nations issues; Real Property Development
linda@whetunglaw.com

Sarnia

Cohen Highley LLP - Sarnia
1350 L'Heritage Dr., Sarnia, ON N7S 6H8
Tel: 519-344-2020; *Fax:* 519-672-5960
www.cohenhighley.com

Sault Ste. Marie

Wishart Law Firm LLP
#500, 390 Bay St., Sault Ste. Marie, ON P6A 1X2
Tel: 705-949-6700; *Fax:* 705-949-2465
wishart@wishartlaw.com
www.wishartlaw.com
Profile: 5 Lawyers,
Wishart Law Firm's environmental law services include ensuring environmental compliance & due diligence, defending environmental charges, handling occupational health & safety issues; & advising municipalities.
Environmental Lawyers:
Gordon P. Acton, Senior Business Partner
Orlando M. Rosa, Managing Partner, Envrionmental Law; Municipal Law

Simcoe

Cline Backus Nightingale McArthur
P.O. Box 528, 39 Colborne St. North, Simcoe, ON N3Y 4N5
Tel: 519-426-6763; *Fax:* 519-426-2055
cbnmlaw@kwic.com
www.clinebackus.com
Profile: 1 Office, 8 Lawyers, Founded in: 1963
Practice areas include municipal planning & agriculture & farming. The firm's lawyers provide representation before the Ontario Municipal Board & Committees of Council. Cline Backus Nightingale McArthur has a great number of clients in the agriculture & farming sectors. Lawyers handle issues related to land development & municipal planning & tobacco & ginseng.
Environmental Lawyers:
Thomas A. Cline, QC, Municipal Law; Land Use Planning; Environmental Municipal Assessment
cline@clinebackus.com
R. Paul Hosack, Employment Law
hosack@clinebackus.com

Smiths Falls

Howard Ryan Kelford Knott & Dixon - Smiths Falls
2 Main St. East, Smiths Falls, ON K7A 1A2
Tel: 613-283-6772; *Fax:* 613-283-8840
Toll-Free: 888-852-5175
reception@smithsfallslaw.ca
www.smithsfallslaw.ca
Profile: 2 Offices, 5 Lawyers, Founded in: 1976
The firm is engaged in the practice of municipal law.
Environmental Lawyers:
Paul Howard, Land Development; Municipal Law
phoward@smithsfallslaw.ca
Shane Kelford, Municipal Law; Labour & Employment
skelford@smithsfallslaw.ca

St Catharines

Chown, Cairns LLP
#900, P.O. Box 760, 80 King St., St Catharines, ON L2R 6Y8
Tel: 905-346-0775; *Fax:* 905-688-0015
lawyers@chowlaw.com
www.chownlaw.com
Profile: 1 Office, 16 Lawyers,
Lawyers at Chown, Cairns LLP provide representation on behalf of businesses & individuals of the Niagara Peninsula in matters involving land development & construction.
Environmental Lawyers:
Nicholas F. Ferguson, Land Development; Construction
nfferguson@chownlaw.com
Harry Korosis, Land Development; Construction
hkorosis@chownlaw.com
John E. Mirynech, Land Development
jemirynech@chownlaw.com
Peter D. Nicholson, Land Development
pnicholson@chownlaw.com
Glenn G. Parker, Land Development
ggparker@chownlaw.com
John C. Willey, Land Development
jcwilley@chownlaw.com

Daniel & Partners LLP
P.O. Box 24022, 39 Queen St., St Catharines, ON L2R 7P7
Tel: 905-688-9411; *Fax:* 905-688-5747
Toll-Free: 800-263-3650
www.niagaralaw.ca
Profile: 1 Office, 10 Lawyers, Founded in: 1922
Daniel & Partners provides legal services in the areas of municipal law, planning law, land develpment & use, & employment law. Lawyers appear regularly before municipal councils & administrative tribunals, such as the Ontario Municipal Board, the Environmental Review Tribunal, the Conservation Review Board, & the Niagara Escarpment Commission. The Niagara region firm serves personal, corporate, & municipal clients.
Environmental Lawyers:
Brandon M. Boone, Planning & Development; Land Use
Donald C. DeLorenzo, Municipal Law; Employment Law
Robert Di Lallo, Municipal Law
Sarah J. Draper, Municipal Law; Employment Law
Terrence H. Hill, Municipal Law; Administrative Law
Callum Shedden, Planning & Development; Land Use; Municipal Law; Administrative Law
905-688-9411
sheddenc@niagaralaw.ca

Heelis, Williams, Little & Almas LLP, Barristers & Solicitors
P.O. Box 1056, 14 Church St., St Catharines, ON L2R 7A3
Tel: 905-687-8200; *Fax:* 905-684-4844
www.14churchstlawoffice.com
Profile: 1 Office, 4 Lawyers, Founded in: 1976
The law firm serves land owners, developers, engineers, architects, & builders, throughout Ontario's Niagara Peninsula, in all matters related to construction law.
Environmental Lawyers:
William (Bill) E. Heelis, Construction Law; Employment & Labour
bheelis@14churchstlawoffice.com

Sudbury

Weaver, Simmons LLP
#400, 233 Brady Street, Sudbury, ON P3B 4H5
Tel: 705-674-6421; *Fax:* 705-674-9948
thefirm@weaversimmons.com
www.weaversimmons.com
Profile: 34 Lawyers, Founded in: 1931
Environmental Lawyers:
Peter Archambault, Municipal Law
705-671-3292
pjarchambault@weaversimmons.com
R. Martin Bayer, Aboriginal Law
705-671-3286
rmbayer@weaversimmons.com
Harold P. Beaudry, Q.C., Counsel, Transportation
705-671-3270
hpbeaudry@weaversimmons.com
Jack Braithwaite, Counsel
705-671-3288
jbraithwaite@weaversimmons.com
Geoff Jeffery, Occupational Health & Safety
705-671-3269
gjeffery@weaversimmons.com
P. Berk Keaney
705-671-3296
pbkeaney@weaversimmons.com
Andrew M. Little, Natural Resources Law; Mining
705-671-3291
amlittle@weaversimmons.com
Steve S. Moutsatsos, Occupational Health & Safety; Aboriginal Law; Natural Resources Law; Mining
705-671-3290
ssmoutsatsos@weaversimmons.com
James C. Simmons, Q.C.
705-671-3299
jcsimmons@weaversimmons.com
Daniel C. Sirois, Occupational Health & Safety
705-671-3287
dcsirois@weaversimmons.com

Thornhill

Burlew, Edward L.
16 John St., Thornhill, ON L3T 1X8
Tel: 905-882-2422; *Fax:* 905-882-2431
Toll-Free: 888-486-5677
Profile: 1 Office, 1 Lawyers, Founded in: 1979

Thunder Bay

Erickson & Partners, Barristers, Solicitors, Notaries
291 Court St. South, Thunder Bay, ON P7B 2Y1
Tel: 807-345-1213; *Fax:* 807-345-2526
Toll-Free: 800-465-3912
www.erickson-law.com
Profile: 2 Offices, 10 Lawyers,
The firm handles matters related to Aboriginal law, construction, health & medical law, & employment & labour.
Environmental Lawyers:
Nicole Crowe, First Nations Lands & Resources
ncrowe@erickson-law.com
Robert C. Edwards, Labour & Employment; First Nations; Administrative; Environmental Law
bedwards@erickson-law.com
John W. Erickson, QC, Aboriginal Law; Construction Law; Employment Law
Theodore L. Scollie, Corporate & Commercial Law; Aboriginal / First Nations Law; Labour & Employment Law
Holly Walbourne, Labour & Employment

Weiler, Maloney, Nelson
#201, 1001 William St., Thunder Bay, ON P7B 6M1
Tel: 807-623-1111; *Fax:* 807-623-4947
Toll-Free: 866-934-5377
weilers@wmnlaw.com
www.weilers.ca
Profile: 1 Office, 14 Lawyers,
The Thunder Bay law firm works to resolve problems for clients in areas involving mining, forestry, energy, transporation, construction, & health care.
In the area of natural resources law, Weiler, Maloney, Nelson lawyers have advised clients such as FIrst Natuion, exploration, development, & operating compnaies, & engineers. Issues handled include environmental requirements, environmental prosecutions, mine development & operation, & site rehabilitation & remediation.
Environmental Lawyers:

Brian A. Babcock, Partner, Municipal Law
bbabcock@wmnlaw.com
Frederick J.W. Bickford, Partner, Labour & Employment; Administrative Law
fbickfor@wmnlaw.com
John A. Cyr, Partner, Mining & Exploration
jcyr@wmnlaw.com
Ross Judge, Counsel, Municipal Law; Mining & Exploration
rjudge@wmnlaw.com
Jennifer Lohuis, Associate, Municipal Law
jlohuis@wmnlaw.com
Nick Melchiorre, Partner, Mining Law
nmelchio@wmnlaw.com
Mark Mikulasik, Associate, Natural Resources Law; Environmental Law; Mining Law; Administrative Law
mmikulas@wmnlaw.com
Garth O'Neill, Partner, Employment & Labour
goneill@wmnlaw.com
Fhara Pottinger, Associate, Employment Law; Administrative Law
fpotting@wmnlaw.com
Bradley A. Smith, Partner, Aboriginal Law; Employment Law; Administrative Law
basmith@wmnlaw.com

Timmins

Riopelle Griener Professional Corporation
#202, 85 Pine St. South, Timmins, ON P4N 2K1
Tel: 705-264-9591; *Fax:* 705-264-1393
Toll-Free: 866-624-1614
www.rglaw.ca
http://www.facebook.com/#!/RiopelleGriener
Profile: 2 Offices, 8 Lawyers, Founded in: 2005
Environmental Lawyers:
Joshua Bond, Municipal law; Administrative law
705-264-9591
josh@rglaw.ca
Gordon G. Conley, Municipal law; Administrative law
705-264-9591
gordon@rglaw.ca

Toronto

Aird & Berlis LLP
#1800, Brookfield Place, CP 754, 181 Bay St., Toronto, ON M5J 2T9
Tel: 416-863-1500; *Fax:* 416-863-1515
www.airdberlis.com
www.facebook.com/pages/Aird-Berlis/116517495028459, twitter.com/AirdBerlis, www.linkedin.com/company/aird-&-berlis-llp
Profile: 1 Office, 137 Lawyers, Founded in: 1919
Legal services in the areas of Energy Law, Environmental Law, Municipal Law & Land Use Planning.
Environmental Lawyers:
Fred D. Cass, Energy Law; Regulatory & Compliance; Electricity Industry; Oil & Gas Industry
416-865-7742
fcassl@airdberlis.com
Ron Clark, Energy Law; Electricity Industry
416-865-7701
rclark@airdberlis.com
Ken Clark, Energy Law
416-865-4736
kclark@airdberlis.com
Thomas A. Fenton, Energy Law; Natural Resources Law
416-865-4631
tfenton@airdberlis.com
Patricia A. Foran, Municipal & Land Use Planning
416-865-3425
pforan@airdberlis.com
Donald B. Johnston, Natural Resources Practice; Renewable Fuel Industry
416-865-3072
djohnston@airdberlis.com
Leo F. Longo, Senior Partner, Municipal & Land Use Planning
416-865-7778
llongo@airdberlis.com
Dennis M. O'Leary, Energy Law; Environmental Law; Transportation Law; Regulatory & Compliance; Electricity Industry; Landfills & Waste Facilities Matters; Environmental Assessment Matters; Transport of Dangerous Goods Matters
416-865-4711
doleary@airdberlis.com
Scott Stoll, Energy Law; Environmental Law; First Nations Practice; Infrastructure Practice; Electricity Industry; Natural Gas Industry; Regulatory & Compliance; Environmental Assessment Matters; Land Remediation Matters
416-865-4703
sstoll@airdberlis.com

Baker & McKenzie LLP
#2100, Brookfield Place, P.O. Box 874, 181 Bay St., Toronto, ON M5J 2T3
Tel: 416-863-1221; *Fax:* 416-863-6275
www.bakermckenzie.com
Profile: 73 Offices, 51 Lawyers, Founded in: 1962
Advising on the restoration of contaminated properties; compliance with environmental laws; the development of training requirements & procedure when handling hazardous substances; officer & director liability; corporate/commercial transactions with environmental implications; environmental litigation matters; ISO 14001 registration & certification; branches in 30 foreign countries
Environmental Lawyers:
Jonathan Cocker
416-865-6968
jonathan.d.cocker@bakernet.com

Birchall Northey
533 College Street, Toronto, ON M6G 1A8
Tel: 416-860-1212; *Fax:* 416-860-1827
admin@birchallnorthey.com
www.birchallnorthey.com
Profile: 2 Offices, 2 Lawyers, Founded in: 1997
Environmental Lawyers:
Paul Pelzer
Michael Pohorecky, Partner

Blaney McMurtry LLP
#1500, 2 Queen St. East, Toronto, ON M5C 3G5
Tel: 416-593-1221; *Fax:* 416-593-5437
info@blaney.com
www.blaney.com
www.facebook.com/note.php?note_id=108702482506316#!/pages/Blaney-McMurtry-L, twitter.com/blaneymcmurtry, www.linkedin.com/company/blaney-mcmurtry-llp
Profile: 1 Office, 132 Lawyers, Founded in: 1954
Environmental Law; Architectural, Construction, and Engineering Services; Health Law; Mining; Life Sciences
Environmental Lawyers:
Timothy P. Alexander, Construction; Engineering Services
416-593-3900
talexander@blaney.com
Geza R. Banfai, Construction; Engineering Services
416-593-3904
gbanfai@blaney.com
Joanna Carroll, Construction; Engineering Services
416-593-3911
jcarroll@blaney.com
Dominic T. Clarke, Aboriginal
416-593-3968
dclarke@blaney.com
Chris Ellis, Construction; Engineering Services
416-593-3954
cellis@blaney.com
Elizabeth J. Forster, Construction; Engineering Services
416-593-3919
eforster@blaney.com
Jeffery L. Freelan, Municipal; Environmental
416-593-3921
jfreelan@blaney.com
Louis-Pierre Gregoire, Construction; Engineering Services
416-593-3941
lgregoir@blaney.com
Andrew J. Heal, Construction; Engineering Services; Municipal; Environmental
416-593-3934
aheal@blaney.com
Michele A. Hecke, Construction; Engineering Services
416-593-3935
mhecke@blaney.com
Roger Horst, Aboriginal
416-593-3938
rhorst@blaney.com
Steven P. Jeffery, Municipal; Environmental
416-593-3939
sjeffery@blaney.com
Chad Kopach, Construction; Engineering Services
416-593-2985
ckopach@blaney.com
Tanya Litzenberger, Construction; Engineering Services
416-593-2954
tlitzenberger@blaney.com
William R. McMurtry, Q.C., Aboriginal
416-593-3948
bmcmurtry@blaney.com
Robert Muir, Construction; Engineering Services
416-593-3951
rmuir@blaney.com
Robert J. Potts, Aboriginal
416-593-3952
bpotts@blaney.com
Maria Scarfo
mscarfo@blaney.com
Robert C. Taylor, Construction; Engineering Services
416-593-2957
rtaylor@blaney.com
Brett J. Tkatch, Municipal; Environmental
416-593-3969
btkatch@blaney.com
David S. Wilson, Construction; Engineering Services; Municipal; Environmental
416-593-3970
dwilson@blaney.com
Roderick S.W. Winsor
rwinsor@blaney.com

Borden Ladner Gervais LLP - Toronto
Scotia Plaza, 40 King St. West, 44th Fl., Toronto, ON M5H 3Y4
Tel: 416-367-6000; *Fax:* 416-367-6749
Toll-Free: 855-660-6003
info@blg.com
www.blg.com
www.facebook.com/BordenLadnerGervaisLLP, twitter.com/blglaw, www.linkedin.com/company/BLGLaw
Profile: 6 Offices, 765 Lawyers, Founded in: 1936
Covers the areas of Environmental Law, Energy, Health Law, Construction and Engineering, Maritime Law and Infrastructure in a variety of industries.

Cassels Brock & Blackwell LLP
#2100, Scotia Plaza, 40 King St. West, Toronto, ON M5H 3C2
Tel: 416-869-5300; *Fax:* 416-360-8877
www.casselsbrock.com
twitter.com/casselsbrock
Profile: 2 Offices, 209 Lawyers, Founded in: 1888
Environmental Lawyers:
Chad Accursi, Partner, Mining
416-860-2937
caccursi@casselsbrock.com
Jason Arbuck, Partner, Renewable Energy & Clean Technology
416-860-6889
jarbuck@casselsbrock.com
James Ayres, Partner, Municipal, Planning & Environmental; Land Development; Renewable Energy & Clean Technology
416-869-5967
jayres@casselsbrock.com
Joan Beck, Partner, Mining
416-860-6754
jbeck@casselsbrock.com
Bruce C. Bell, Partner, Mining
416-869-5737
bbell@casselsbrock.com
Eva Bellissimo, Partner, Mining
416-860-2959
ebellissimo@casselsbrock.com
Mark Bennett, Partner, Mining
416-869-5407
mbennett@casselsbrock.com
Andre Boivin, Partner, Mining
416-860-6580
aboivin@casselsbrock.com
David Budd, Partner, Renewable Energy & Clean Technology
416-869-5392
dbudd@casselsbrock.com
Jason K.S. Bullen, Partner, Renewable Energy & Clean Technology
416-860-2953
jbullen@casselsbrock.com
Jennifer Campbell, Partner, Mining
416-860-6462
jcampbell@casselsbrock.com

Noble Chummar, Partner, Energy & Utilities; Infrastructure; Renewable Energy & Clean Technology
416-869-5454
nchummar@casselsbrock.com
Lindsay Clements, Partner, Mining
416-869-5491
lclements@casselsbrock.com
John H. Craig, Partner, Mining
416-869-5756
jcraig@casselsbrock.com
Brian P. Dominique, Partner, Energy & Utilities; Mining; Renewable Energy & Clean Technology
416-869-5434
bdominique@casselsbrock.com
Stuart English, Partner, Renewable Energy & Clean Technology
416-869-5223
senglish@casselsbrock.com
Norman Findlay, Partner, Mining
416-869-5212
nfindlay@casselsbrock.com
Andrea Fitzgerald, Partner, Mining
416-860-6525
afitzgerald@casselsbrock.com
Jonathan Fleisher, Partner, Renewable Energy & Clean Technology
416-860-6596
jfleisher@casselsbrock.com
Jay Goldman, Partner, Mining
416-860-6474
jgoldman@casselsbrock.com
Erik Goldsilver, Partner, Energy & Utilities; Mining; Renewable Energy & Clean Technology
416-860-2901
egoldsilver@casselsbrock.com
Colin Ground, Partner, Renewable Energy & Clean Technology
416-860-6742
cground@casselsbrock.com
Arthur Hamilton, Partner, Energy & Utilities
416-869-6574
ahamilton@casselsbrock.com
Lawrence L. Herman, Partner, Renewable Energy & Clean Technology
416-869-5983
lherman@casselsbrock.com
Gregory Hogan, Partner, Mining
416-860-6554
ghogan@casselsbrock.com
Tom Kapsales, Partner, Land Development; Renewable Energy & Clean Technology
416-869-5786
tkapsales@casselsbrock.com
Jay King, Partner, Mining; Renewable Energy & Clean Technology
416-869-5480
jking@casselsbrock.com
Brian Koscak, Partner, Renewable Energy & Clean Technology
416-869-2955
bkoscak@casselsbrock.com
Tom Koutoulakis, Partner, Mining
416-869-5311
tkoutoulakis@casselsbrock.com
M. Janine Kovach, Partner, Construction; Land Development
416-869-5714
jkovach@casselsbrock.com
Ralph E. Lean, Q.C., Partner, Energy & Utilities; Infrastructure
416-869-5703
rlean@casselsbrock.com
Signe Leisk, Partner, Land Development; Municipal, Planning & Environmental
416-869-5411
sleisk@casselsbrock.com
Bruce T. McNeely, Partner, Energy & Utilities; Clean Technology
416-869-5399
bmcneely@casselsbrock.com
Cathy L. Mercer, Partner, Mining
416-869-5772
cmercer@casselsbrock.com
Marc Mercier, Partner, Energy & Utilities; Infrastructure; Renewable Energy & Clean Technology
416-869-5770
mmercier@casselsbrock.com
Cameron Mingay, Partner, Mining
416-860-6615
cmingay@casselsbrock.com
Stephen Morrison, Partner, Construction; Land Development; Infrastructure
416-860-6624
smorrison@casselsbrock.com
Paul Muchnik, Partner, Land Development
416-869-5975
pmuchnik@casselsbrock.com
Andrew M. Reback, Partner, Renewable Energy & Clean Technology
416-860-2980
areback@casselsbrock.com
David A. Redmond, Partner, Land Development
416-869-5382
dredmond@casselsbrock.com
Jeffrey Roy, Partner, Mining
416-860-6616
jroy@casselsbrock.com
Paul M. Stein, Partner, Mining
416-869-5487
pstein@casselsbrock.com
France M. Tenaille, Partner, Mining
416-869-5318
ftenaille@casselsbrock.com
Jennifer Traub, Partner, Mining
416-860-6526
jtraub@casselsbrock.com
John Vettese, Partner, Mining
416-869-5336
jvettese@casselsbrock.com
Ann L. Watterworth, Partner, Mining
416-869-5484
awatterworth@casselsbrock.com
Mark I. Young, Partner, Mining
416-869-5380
myoung@casselsbrock.com

Conway Davis Gryski

#601, 130 Adelaide St. West, Toronto, ON M5H 3P5
Tel: 416-214-4554; *Fax:* 416-214-9915
Toll-Free: 877-559-4554
contactus@cdglaw.net
www.conwaydavisgryski.com
Profile: 1 Office, 6 Lawyers, Founded in: 1996
Conway Davis Gryski practises in the area of municipal assessment. Work is restricted to municipalities & assessing authorities.
Environmental Lawyers:
Carl Davis, Municipal Law
416-214-5793
davis@cdglaw.net
Chester Gryski, Municipal Law
416-214-0988
gryski@cdglaw.net
Karey Lunau, Managing Partner, Municipal Law
416-214-2882
lunau@cdglaw.net
Don Mitchell, Municipal Law
416-214-0976
mitchell@cdglaw.net
Frank Shea, Municipal Law
416-214-2885
shea@cdglaw.net
Melissa E. VanBerkum, Municipal Law
416-214-9925
vanberkum@cdglaw.net

Davies Howe Partners LLP

99 Spadina Ave., 5th Fl., Toronto, ON M5V 3P8
Tel: 416-977-7088; *Fax:* 416-977-8931
info@davieshowe.com
www.davieshowe.com
Profile: 1 Office, 18 Lawyers,
Lawyers at Davies Howe Partners specialize in land use & development, energy & regulatory matters, & employment & labour law. The firm serves businesses from small entrepreneurs to major Canadian & international corporation.
Environmental Lawyers:
John M. Alati, Land Use; Environmental Law; Energy
416-977-7088
johna@davieshowe.com
Isaiah Banach, Land Use Planning; Municipal Law; Development Law
416-977-7088
isaiahb@davieshowe.com
Kimberly L. Beckman, Land Use Planning; Land Development
416-977-7088
kimb@davieshowe.com
Jeffrey L. Davies, Land Development; Planning; Water & Sewer Capacity Allocation
416-977-7088
jeffd@davieshowe.com
Mark R. Flowers, Municipal Law; Land Use Planning; Development Law
416-977-7088
markf@davieshowe.com
Raj Kehar, Land Use Planning; Municipal Law; Development Law
416-977-7088
Jason Lewis, Land Use Planning; Municipal Law; Development Law
416-977-7088
Meaghan McDermid, Land Use Planning; Municipal Law; Development Law
416-977-7088
Michael Melling, Land Use Planning & Development
416-977-7088
michaelm@davieshowe.com
Tanya Nayler, Land Use Planning; Municipal Law; Development Law
416-977-7088
Aaron I. Platt, Land Use Planning; Development Law
416-977-7088
aaronp@davieshowe.com
Susan Rosenthal, Land Use Planning & Development
416-977-7088
susanr@davieshowe.com
Katarzyna Sliwa, Land Use Planning & Development
416-977-7088
katarzynas@davieshowe.com
Daniel H. Steinberg, Land Use Planning; Development Law
416-977-7088
daniels@davieshowe.com

Davies Ward Phillips & Vineberg LLP

155 Wellington St. West, Toronto, ON M5V 3J7
Tel: 416-863-0900; *Fax:* 416-863-0871
www.dwpv.com
twitter.com/_Davies_
Profile: 3 Offices, 246 Lawyers, Founded in: 1961
Environmental Lawyers:
William M. Ainley, Senior Partner, Energy Law; Mining Law
416-863-5509
wainley@dwpv.com
Lisa C. Damiani, Partner, Mining Law
416-367-6905
ldamiani@dwpv.com
Richard Fridman, Partner, Mining Law
416-367-7483
rfridman@dwpv.com
Jennifer Grossklaus, Partner, Mining Law
416-367-7438
jgrossklaus@dwpv.com
Peter Hong, Partner, Energy Law
416-863-5557
phong@dwpv.com
Ian R. McBride, Partner, Energy Law; Mining Law
416-863-5530
imcbride@dwpv.com
Ian R. McBride, Partner, Energy Law; Mining Law
416-863-5530
imcbride@dwpv.com
Vincent A. Mercier, Energy Law
416-863-5579
vmercier@dwpv.com
J. Alexander Moore, Partner, Energy Law
416-863-5570
amoore@dwpv.com
Robert S. Murphy, Partner, Mining Law
416-863-5537
rmurphy@dwpv.com
Patricia L. Olasker, Partner, Mining Law
416-863-5551
polasker@dwpv.com
Alexandria J. Pike, Partner, Energy Law; Environmental Law; Mining Industry; Chemical Industry; Pulp & Paper Industry; Manufacturing Industry; Oil & Gas Industry; Hydroelectric Power Industry; Renewable Energy Industry; Nuclear Industry
416-367-6989
apike@dwpv.com
Sarah V. Powell, Partner, Environmental Law; Energy Law; Environmental Assessments & Approvals
416-367-6931
spowell@dwpv.com

Law Firms

James R. Reid, Partner, Emergy Law
416-367-6974
jreid@dwpv.com
Philippe C. Rousseau, Partner, Energy Law
416-863-5589
prousseau@dwpv.com
Philippe C. Rousseau, Partner, Energy Law; Renewable Energy Industry; Solar Power Industry; Hydroelectric Power Industry; Nuclear Power Industry; Wind Power Industry; Oil & Gas Industry; Remediation Industry
416-863-5589
prousseau@dwpv.com
Jason Saltzman, Partner, Mining Law
416-863-5518
jsaltzman@dwpv.com
Arthur Shiff, Partner, Energy Law
416-863-5513
ashiff@dwpv.com
Melanie A. Shishler, Partner, Mining Law
416-863-5510
mshishler@dwpv.com
Lori K. Sullivan, Partner, Energy Law; Mining Law
416-863-5556
lsullivan@dwpv.com
Kevin J. Thomson, Senior Partner, Mining Law
416-863-5590
kthomson@dwpv.com
Nicholas C. Williams, Partner, Energy Law
416-863-5559
nwilliams@dwpv.com

Davis LLP - Toronto

#6000, 1 First Canadian Place, P.O. Box 367, 100 King St. West, Toronto, ON M5X 1E2
Tel: 416-365-3500; *Fax:* 416-365-7886
www.davis.ca
Profile: 49 Lawyers
Environmental Lawyers:
Alexis Alyea, Environmental law; Municipal law
416-369-5262
aalyea@davis.ca
Chris Barnett, Municipal law; Environmental law
416-365-3502
cbarnett@davis.ca
Donald R.M. Bell, Mining law; Projects, infrastructure, & P3
416-369-5265
dbell@davis.ca
Laura K. Bisset, Environmental law; Municipal law
416-941-5400
lbisset@davis.ca
Robert N. Black, Environmental law
416-365-3405
rblack@davis.ca
Douglas Buchanan, Q.C., Energy & utilities; Projects, infrastructure, & P3
416-365-3507
dbuchanan@davis.ca
Andrew J.G. Burton, Energy & utilities; Projects, infrastructure, & P3
416-365-3520
aburton@davis.ca
Tudor Carsten, Environmental law
416-365-3505
tcarsten@davis.ca
David I. Crocker, Energy & utilities; Environmental law; Forestry law; Mining law; Municipal law; Health law; Aviation & transportation law; Climate change law; Aboriginal law; Municipal law
416-941-5415
dcrocker@davis.ca
Lana J. Finney, Environmental law; Municipal law
416-941-5409
lfinney@davis.ca
Kelly Friedman, Energy & utilities
416-369-5263
kfriedman@davis.ca
Lee-Ann Gibbs
416-365-3522
lgibbs@davis.ca
Lindsay Krauss
416-941-5393
lkrauss@davis.ca
Andrew Lord, Climate change law; Energy & utilities
416-369-5264
alord@davis.ca
Mitchell Mostyn, Energy & utilities; Projects, infrastructure, & P3
416-369-5254
mmostyn@davis.ca
Richard R. Neville, Environmental law
416-365-3526
rneville@davis.ca
Amy Pressman, Environmental law
416-369-5293
apressman@davis.ca
David dos Reis, Environmental law; environmental disputes, environmental contamination
416-365-3420
ddosreis@davis.ca

Dentons Canada LLP - Toronto

#400, Toronto-Dominion Centre, 77 King St. West, Toronto, ON M5K 0A1
Tel: 416-863-4511; *Fax:* 416-863-4592
www.dentons.com
twitter.com/dentons, www.linkedin.com/company/Dentons
Profile: 6 Offices, 536 Lawyers,
In the environmental law area, the firm provides services in Energy Law, including CleanTech, Climate Change, Electricity Industry, Oil & Gas Industry, Renewable Energy Industry; Environmental Law; Forest Products Industry; Natural Resources & Infrastructure; Mining Industry; and Land Use Planning/Property Development
Environmental Lawyers:
Abbas Ali Khan, Partner, Alternative Energy Industry; Mining Industry
416-863-4398
abbas.alikhan@dentons.com
Vivek Bakshi, Partner, Energy Law; Natural Resources Law & Project Finance; Infrastructure Industry; Oil & Gas Industry; Electricity Industry; CleanTech; Climate Change Matters; Renewable Energy Matters
416-863-4658
vivek.bakshi@dentons.com
Patrick J. Devine, Partner, Land Use Planning; Property Development
416-863-4515
patrick.devine@dentons.com
Don Macintosh, Partner, Energy Industry; Climate Change; CleanTech; Oil & Gas Industry; Renewable Energy Industry; Transportation Industry
416-361-2330
don.macintosh@dentons.com
David McCutcheon, Partner, Environmental Law; Aboriginal Law; Pulp & Paper Industry; Mining Industry
416-863-4538
david.mccutcheon@dentons.com
Helen Newland, Partner, Energy Law; Energy Project Development; Utilities Regulatory
416-863-4471
helen.newland@dentons.com
Jason Park, Partner, Land Use Planning; Property Development; Municipal Law
416-863-4786
jason.park@dentons.com
Andrew E. Salem, Partner, Land Use Planning; Property Development; Planning & Development Approvals; Municipal Law; Government Affairs; Energy Industry; Conservation Industry
416-863-4728
andrew.salem@dentons.com
Marina E. Sampson, Partner, Environmental Law & Litigation; Energy Law & Litigation; Renewable Energy Industry
416-863-4783
marina.sampson@dentons.com
Michael Schafler, Partner, Energy Law; Renewable Energy Industry; Oil & Gas Industry; Mining Industry; Forestry Industry; Litigation & Dispute Resolution; Class Actions
416-863-4457
michael.schafler@dentons.com
Paul D. Shantz, Counsel, Environmental Law; Land Use Planning; Property Development; Environmental Assessments
416-863-4768
paul.shantz@dentons.com

Eccleston LLP

#4020, Toronto-Dominion Centre, 66 Wellington St. West, Toronto, ON M5K 1J3
Tel: 416-504-2722; *Fax:* 416-504-2686
info@ecclestonllp.com
www.ecclestonllp.com
Profile: 1 Office, 4 Lawyers, Founded in: 1994
Eccleston LLP specializes in construction law. Lawyers represent clients in the construction field such as landowners, architects, engineers, material suppliers, & contactors.
Environmental Lawyers:
Sonia Cordeiro, Construction Law
jquigg@ecclestonllp.com
Matthew Mostyn, Construction Law
mmostyn@ecclestonllp.com
Janice L. Quigg, Construction Law
jquigg@ecclestonllp.com

Fasken Martineau - Toronto

#2400, Bay Adelaide Centre, P.O. Box 20, 333 Bay St., Toronto, ON M5H 2T6
Tel: 416-366-8381; *Fax:* 416-364-7813
Toll-Free: 800-268-8424
toronto@fasken.com
www.fasken.com
www.facebook.com/group.php?gid=154446131283771, twitter.com/faskenmartineau, www.linkedin.com/company/fasken-martineau-dumoulin
Profile: 9 Offices, 712 Lawyers, Founded in: 1863
Environmental Services: Environmental, Energy & Natural Resource Law
Environmental Lawyers:
Peter Ascherl, Partner, Environmental Law
416-868-3499
pascherl@fasken.com
W. Thomas Barlow, Partner, Infrastructure; Municipal Law; Transportation; Construction
416-868-3403
tbarlow@fasken.com
Steve Blimkie, Partner, Mining
416-868-4416
sblimkie@fasken.com
Michael Bourassa, Partner, Mining
416-865-5455
mbourassa@fasken.com
Daniel Brock, Partner, Health
416-865-4513
dbrock@fasken.com
John A. Campion, Senior Partner, Municipal Law; Transportation; Mining
416-865-4357
jcampion@fasken.com
Andrea L. Centa, Partner, Mining
416-868-3348
acenta@fasken.com
Rosalind H. Cooper, Partner, Environmental Law
416-865-5127
rcooper@fasken.com
Robert W. Cosman, Partner, Health
416-865-4364
rcosman@fasken.com
John M. Elias, Partner, Mining
416-868-3334
jelias@fasken.com
Annie M. Finn, Partner, Forestry; Transportation
416-868-3418
afinn@fasken.com
Charles L.K. Higgins, Environmental
416-865-4392
chiggins@tor.fasken.com
Darrell Jarvis, Partner, Construction; Infrastructure
416-868-3530
djarvis@fasken.com
Charles Kazaz, Partner, Energy; Environmental; Climate Change; Regulatory; Aboriginal Law; Mining
416-868-3517
ckazaz@fasken.com
Brian C. Kelsall, Partner, Mining; Infrastructure
416-865-5493
bkelsall@fasken.com
Daniel R. Law, Partner, Environmental Law
416-868-3479
dlaw@fasken.com
Brian A. O'Byrne, Partner, Health
416-868-3347
bobyrne@fasken.com
Ella Plotkin, Partner, Mining; Infrastructure
416-865-4489
eplotkin@fasken.com
Tracy A. Pratt, Partner, Aboriginal Law; Mining
416-865-4429
tpratt@fasken.com

Gilbert Sharpe, Partner, Health; Infrastructure
416-868-3492
gsharpe@fasken.com
Mark Sills, Partner, Mining
416-865-5495
msills@fasken.com
Neil M. Smiley, Partner, Energy; Environmental; Climate Change; Regulatory; Mining; Transportation
416-865-5122
nsmiley@fasken.com
Richard J. Steinberg, Partner, Mining
416-865-5443
rsteinberg@fasken.com
Douglas V. Tingey
416-865-5126
dtingey@tor.fasken.com
John Turner, Partner, Mining
416-865-4380
jturner@fasken.com
Krisztián T¢th, Partner, Mining
416-865-5467
ktoth@fasken.com

Gardiner, Roberts LLP

#3100, Scotia Plaza, 40 King St. West, Toronto, ON M5H 3Y2
Tel: 416-865-6600; *Fax:* 416-865-6636
www.gardiner-roberts.com
Profile: 1 Office, 67 Lawyers
Environmental Lawyers:
Richard J. Hassard, Q.C., Counsel, Environmental
416-865-6682
rhassard@gardiner-roberts.com

Glaholt LLP

#800, 141 Adelaide St. West, Toronto, ON M5H 3L5
Tel: 416-368-8280; *Fax:* 416-368-3467
www.glaholt.com
twitter.com/GlaholtLLP
Profile: 1 Office, 13 Lawyers, Founded in: 1987
Glaholt LLP lawyers provide advocacy & advisory services to national & international clients in all aspects of construction law.
Environmental Lawyers:
Keith A. Bannon, Partner, Construction Litigation
416-368-8280 ext. 224
kb@glaholt.com
Brendan D. Bowles, Managing Partner, Construction Law
bb@glaholt.com
Adam Brody, Associate, Construction Litigation
adambrody@glaholt.com
Peter-Paul E. Du Vernet, Counsel, Construction
ped@glaholt.com
Duncan W. Glaholt, Partner, Construction Law; Construction Claims
dwg@glaholt.com
Harvey Kirsh, Counsel, Construction Law
hkirsh@glaholt.com
Andrea Lee, Partner, Construction Law; Civil Litigation
al@glaholt.com
John Margie, Partner, Construction
jm@glaholt.com
Damien McCotter, Associate, Infrastructure, Energy, & Resource Construction
dmccotter@glaholt.com
Charles Powell, Associate, Construction Litigation
cp@glaholt.com
Lawlor Rochester, Counsel, Construction Law; Engineering Litigation
lr@glaholt.com
Markus Rotterdam, Legal Researcher, Construction
mr@glaholt.com
Michael Valo, Associate, Construction; Infrastructure Projects
mvalo@glaholt.com

Goodmans LLP

#3400, Bay Adelaide Centre, 333 Bay St., Toronto, ON M5H 2S7
Tel: 416-979-2211; *Fax:* 416-979-1234
info@goodmans.ca
www.goodmans.ca
Profile: 2 Offices, 211 Lawyers, Founded in: 1917
The firm's environmental law practice is multidisciplinary in nature, with expertise in a diverse range of specialities including litigation, real estate law, municipal & planning matters, land development issues, regulatory & compliance requirements, and government affairs. Environmental law factors into all commercial transactions where environmental matters are a concern
Environmental Lawyers:

Gowling Lafleur Henderson LLP - Toronto

#1600, 1 First Canadian Place, 100 King St. West, Toronto, ON M5X 1G5
Tel: 416-862-7525; *Fax:* 416-862-7661
www.gowlings.com
twitter.com/gowlings
Profile: 10 Offices, 786 Lawyers, Founded in: 1887
Environmental law expertise in Climate Change, Energy, Infrastructure, Mining, & Technology
Environmental Lawyers:
Paul H. Harricks, Lead, Energy, Infra. & Miningu, Mergers and Acquisitions; Project Development; Consumer and Corporate Finance
416-369-7296
paul.harricks@gowlings.com

Heenan Blaikie LLP - Toronto

#2900, Bay Adelaide Centre, P.O. Box 2900, 333 Bay St., Toronto, ON M5H 2T4
Tel: 416-360-6336; *Fax:* 416-360-8425
www.heenanblaikie.com
Profile: 207 Lawyers, Founded in: 1973
Environmental Lawyers:
Ahab Abdel-Aziz, Partner, Environmental Law; Regulatory & Public Law; Energy & Resources Litigation
416-643-6929
aabdelaziz@heenan.ca
Samantha Ambrozy, Construction Litigation
416-360-3546
sambrozy@heenan.ca
Cynthia Amsterdam, Partner, Energy & Resources Litigation; Health; Construction Litigation
416-360-2880
camsterdam@heenan.ca
Brett Baker, Counsel, Energy; Natural Resources; Environmental Law
416-643-6939
bbaker@heenan.ca
Geza Banfai, Partner, Construction; Infrastructure & Construction Litigation
416-643-6968
gbanfai@heenan.ca
Matthew Benson, Environmental Law; Energy & Resources Litigation
416-643-6956
mbenson@heenan.ca
Henry Bertossi, Partner, Health
416-643-6862
hbertossi@heenan.ca
Brian W. Burkett, Senior Partner, Occupational Health & Safety
416-360-3529
bburkett@heenan.ca
David Carbonaro, Senior Partner, Mining
416-643-6836
dcarbonaro@heenan.ca
Simon Chester, Partner, Environmental Law
416-643-6905
schester@heenan.ca
Michael Davies, Partner, Construction
416-643-6807
mdavies@heenan.ca
Henry Y. Dinsdale, Partner, Occupational Health & Safety
416-360-3528
hdinsdale@heenan.ca
Cheryl A. Edwards, Partner, Occupational Health & Safety
416-360-2897
cedwards@heenan.ca
Andrew Elbaz, Energy; Natural Resources
416-643-6974
aelbaz@heenan.ca
Julia Falevich, Construction Litigation
416-643-6979
jfalevich@heenan.ca
Joanna Fine, Health
416-360-3599
jfine@heenan.ca
Allen H. Garson, Partner, Climate, Cleantech & Sustainability; Infrastructure
416-360-3533
agarson@heenan.ca
Margaret Gavins, Partner, Occupational Health & Safety
416-360-3557
mgavins@heenan.ca
Ian Godfrey, Partner, Construction Litigation
416-360-3551
igodfrey@heenan.ca
Jeffrey Goodman, Partner, Occupational Health & Safety
416-643-6824
jgoodman@heenan.ca
Jayashree Goswami, Construction Litigation; Condominium Law
416-643-6936
jgoswami@heenan.ca
Don Jack, Partner, Construction Litigation
416-643-6933
djack@heenan.ca
George J. Karayannides, Partner, Transportation
416-360-3521
georgek@heenan.ca
Adam Kardash, Partner, Health
416-360-3559
akardash@heenan.ca
Tony Kiru, Partner, Construction; Real Estate
416-360-3547
tkiru@heenan.ca
Kenneth David Kraft, Partner, Transportation
416-643-6822
kkraft@heenan.ca
Howard Krupat, Partner, Construction Litigation; Infrastructure
416-643-6969
hkrupat@heenan.ca
Tim Lawson, Partner, Occupational Health & Safety
416-360-3522
tlawson@heenan.ca
Corey MacKinnon, Natural Resources; Mining
416-643-6850
cmackinnon@heenan.ca
Kevin D. MacNeill, Partner, Occupational Health & Safety
416-360-2602
kmacneill@heenan.ca
Alejandro Manevich, Energy; Environmental Law
416-643-6944
amanevich@heenan.ca
Gregs T. McGinnis, Partner, Construction
416-643-6957
gmcginnis@heenan.ca
James McVicar, Partner, Mining
416-643-6903
jmcvicar@heenan.ca
Lynn Mitchell, Partner, Environmental Law; Energy & Resources Litigation
416-643-6931
lmitchell@heenan.ca
Maureen Quinlan, Partner, Occupational Health & Safety
416-643-6812
mquinlan@heenan.ca
Wendy S. Reed, Counsel, Climate, Cleantech & Sustainability
416-360-3542
wreed@heenan.ca
Katrina Reyes, Environmental Law; Energy & Resources Litigation
416-643-6990
kreyes@heenan.ca
Bonnie Roberts Jones, Construction Litigation; Condominium Law
416-360-3567
brobertsjones@heenan.ca
L. David Roebuck, Partner, Environmental Law
416-643-6887
droebuck@heenan.ca
Kevin Rooney, Partner, Natural Resources; Mining
416-643-6899
krooney@heenan.ca
Rhonda R. Shirreff, Occupational Health & Safety
416-643-6858
rshirreff@heenan.ca
Gavin Sinclair, Partner, Energy
416-643-6963
gsinclair@heenan.ca
Kara Smith, Energy & Resources Litigation
416-643-6925
ksmith@heenan.ca
Jon S. Smithen, Environment Law
416-643-6918
jsmithen@heenan.ca
Michael Smyth, Partner, Occupational Health & Safety
416-360-2887
msmyth@heenan.ca

Steven Sokalsky, Energy; Environmental Law
416-643-6941
ssokalsky@heenan.ca
Jonathan Stainsby, Partner, Construction Litigation
416-360-3568
jstainsby@heenan.ca
Stephanie J. Sykes, Partner, Mining
416-643-6906
ssykes@heenan.ca
Shane Todd, Occupational Health & Safety
416-643-6958
stodd@heenan.ca
Verki Tunteng, Energy
416-643-6898
vtunteng@heenan.ca
Claire Vachon, Partner, Occupational Health & Safety
416-643-6803
cvachon@heenan.ca
Jackie VanDerMeulen, Occupational Health & Safety
416-643-6987
jvandermeulen@heenan.ca
Steve Vaughan, Partner, Energy & Resources Litigation; Natural Resources; Mining
416-643-6924
svaughan@heenan.ca
Joel Watson, Partner, Construction Litigation; Real Estate
416-643-6955
jwatson@heenan.ca
Julian Worsley, Partner, Health
416-643-6871
jworsley@heenan.ca

Hicks Morley Hamilton Stewart Storie LLP - Toronto

TD Centre, P.O. Box 371, 77 King St. West, 39th Fl., Toronto, ON M5K 1K8
Tel: 416-362-1011; *Fax:* 416-362-9680
www.hicksmorley.com
Profile: 5 Offices, 117 Lawyers,
Environmental practice areas include occupational health & workplace safety & insurance.
Environmental Lawyers:
Martin J. Addario, Partner, Healthcare; Mining/Resources; Petrochemical; Steel; Transportation/Automotive
416-864-7312
martin-addario@hicksmorley.com
Martin J. Addario, Partner, Healthcare; Mining/Resources; Petrochemical; Steel; Transportation/Automotive
416-864-7312
martin-addario@hicksmorley.com
John-Paul Alexandrowicz, Partner, Construction; Transportation/Automotive
416-864-7292
jpa@hicksmorley.com
Michelle A. Alton, Associate, Occupational Health
416-864-7238
michelle-alton@hicksmorley.com
Harvey A. Beresford, Q.C., Partner, Healthcare; Mining/Resources
416-864-7262
harvey-beresford@hicksmorley.com
Kathryn J. Bird, Associate, Healthcare; Occupational Health; Mining/Resources; Construction; Energy; Petrochemical; Transportation/Automotive
416-864-7353
kathryn-bird@hicksmorley.com
David W. Brady, Partner, Occupational Health; Healthcare; Mining/Resources; Steel; Transportation/Automotive
416-864-7310
david-brady@hicksmorley.com
John E. Brooks, Partner, Healthcare
416-864-7226
john-brooks@hicksmorley.com
John J. Bruce, Partner, Construction; Healthcare; Occupational Health; Mining/Resources; Petrochemical; Transportation/Automotive
416-864-7285
john-bruce@hicksmorley.com
Donna M. D'Andrea, Partner, Occupational Health; Steel; Mining/Resources; Transportation/Automotive
416-864-7275
donna-dandrea@hicksmorley.com
John C. Field, Partner, Occupational Health; Mining/Resources; Steel; Petrochemical; Transportation/Automotive
416-864-7301
john-field@hicksmorley.com
Allyson M. Fischer, Partner, Mining/Resources; Petrochemical; Transportation/Automotive
416-864-7216
allyson-fischer@hicksmorley.com
Daniel B. Fogel, Partner, Construction; Steel; Transportation/Automotive
416-864-7349
daniel-fogel@hicksmorley.com
Stephen F. Gleave, Partner, Mining/Resources; Petrochemical; Transportation/Automotive
416-864-7208
stephen-gleave@hicksmorley.com
Michael A. Hines, Partner, Steel
416-864-7248
michael-hines@hicksmorley.com
Amanda J. Hunter, Partner, Transportation/Automotive
416-864-7265
amanda-hunter@hicksmorley.com
Elisha C. Jamieson, Associate, Transportation/Automotive
416-864-7344
elisha-jamieson@hicksmorley.com
Wallace M. Kenny, Partner, Mining/Resources; Steel; Transportation/Automotive
416-864-7306
wallace-kenny@hicksmorley.com
Mireille Khoraych, Associate, Occupational Health; Steel; Transportation/Automotive
416-864-7356
mireille-khoraych@hicksmorley.com
Elizabeth Kosmidis, Associate, Construction; Occupational Health
416-864-7246
elizabeth-kosmidis@hicksmorley.com
William L. LeMay, Partner, Construction; Mining/Resources; Transportation/Automotive
416-864-7276
william-lemay@hicksmorley.com
Robert W. Little, Partner, Occupational Health; Transportation/Automotive; Mining/Resources; Petrochemical; Steel
416-864-7332
robert-little@hicksmorley.com
Jason E. Mandlowitz, VP, Consulting Services, Occupational Health
416-864-7278
jason-mandlowitz@hicksmorley.com
M. Patrick Moran, Partner, Construction; Transportation/Automotive; Mining/Resources; Petrochemical; Steel; Occupational Health
416-864-7308
patrick-moran@hicksmorley.com
Simon E. Mortimer, Partner, Transportation/Automotive; Mining/Resources; Steel
416-864-7311
simon-mortimer@hicksmorley.com
Tom Moutsatsos, Partner, Energy
416-864-7293
tom-moutsatsos@hicksmorley.com
Patty G. Murray, Partner, Transportation/Automotive; Steel; Healthcare
416-864-7307
patty-murray@hicksmorley.com
Susan L. Nickerson, Partner, Transportation/Automotive; Mining/Resources
416-864-7257
susan-nickerson@hicksmorley.com
Leola W. Pon, Associate, Occupational Health
416-864-7294
leola-pon@hicksmorley.com
Gregory J. Power, Associate, Construction
416-864-7240
gregory-power@hicksmorley.com
Lauri A. Reesor, Associate, Mining/Resources
416-864-7288
lauri-reesor@hicksmorley.com
Christopher G. Riggs, Q.C., Partner, Steel
416-864-7322
christopher-riggs@hicksmorley.com
M. David Ross, Associate, Construction; Occupational Health; Transportation/Automotive; Mining/Resources; Petrochemical; Steel; Energy
416-864-7438
david-ross@hicksmorley.com
John W. Saunders, Partner, Transportation/Automotive; Mining/Resources; Steel; Occupational Health
416-864-7247
john-saunders@hicksmorley.com
Stephen J. Shamie, Managing Partner, Steel
416-864-7304
stephen-shamie@hicksmorley.com
Scott G. Thompson, Partner, Construction; Transportation/Automotive; Mining/Resources; Petrochemical; Steel; Occupational Health
416-864-7283
scott-thompson@hicksmorley.com
Andrew N. Zabrovsky, Associate, Transportation/Automotive; Occupational Health
416-864-7536
andrew-zabrovsky@hicksmorley.com
Nadine S. Zacks, Associate, Occupational Health; Construction; Transportation/Automotive
416-864-7484
nadine-zacks@hicksmorley.com

Hodgson Russ LLP

#2309, P.O. Box 30, 150 King St. West, Toronto, ON M5H 1J9
Tel: 416-595-5100; *Fax:* 416-595-5021
info@hodgsonruss.com
www.hodgsonruss.com
twitter.com/HodgsonRuss,
www.linkedin.com/company/hodgson-russ-llp
Profile: 6 Offices, 3 Lawyers

Hughes, Amys LLP

#200, 48 Yonge St., Toronto, ON M5E 1G6
Tel: 416-367-1608; *Fax:* 416-367-8821
Toll-Free: 800-565-1713
info@hughesamys.com
www.hughesamys.com
Profile: 2 Offices, 28 Lawyers, Founded in: 1918
Environmental Lawyers:
Michael S. Teitelbaum, Partner, Environmental Law
416-367-1608 ext. 257
mteitelbaum@hughesamys.com
Wendell S. Wigle, Q.C., Senior Partner, Environmental Litigation
416-367-1608 ext. 235
wwigle@hughesamys.com

Lax O'Sullivan Scott Lisus LLP

#2750, 145 King St. West, Toronto, ON M5H 1J8
Tel: 416-598-1744; *Fax:* 416-598-3730
www.counsel-toronto.com
Profile: 1 Office, 20 Lawyers, Founded in: 1997

Levy, Alan D.

75 Robert St., Toronto, ON M5S 2K4
Tel: 416-929-8282; *Fax:* 416-929-9895
Profile: 1 Office, 1 Lawyers,
Areas of practice include environmental law, municipal law, alternative dispute resolution, & mediation.
Environmental Lawyers:
Alan D. Levy, Environmental Law; Municipal Law
alan@alanlevy.ca

Loopstra Nixon LLP Barristers & Solicitors

#600, Woodbine Place, 135 Queens Plate Dr., Toronto, ON M9W 6V7
Tel: 416-746-4710; *Fax:* 416-746-8319
www.loopstranixon.com
Profile: 1 Office, 23 Lawyers, Founded in: 1973
Loopstra Nixon's Municipal & Land Use Planning lawyers appear regularly before municipal authorities, provincial municipal boards, & other public agencies.
Environmental Lawyers:
Quinto M. Annibale, Land Use Planning & Development Law; Municipal Law
qannibale@loonix.com
Michael J. Calich, Municipal Liability
mcalich@loonix.com
Alison Carr, Municipal Law; Labour & Employment
acarr@loonix.com
Danette Cashman, Municipal Law
dcashman@loonix.com
Daron L. Earthy, Municipal Law; Construction
dearthy@loonix.com
Steven C. Ferri, Land Use Planning & Development Law; Municipal Law
sferri@loonix.com
W. Mark Fryer, Occupational Health & Safety
mfryer@loonix.com
Scott E. Hamilton, Municipal Law
shamilton@loonix.com

Andy C. Jairam, Municipal Law; Construction Law
ajairam@loonix.com
J. Mark Joblin, Municipal Law; Land Use Planning & Development Law
dearthy@loonix.com
Charles M.K. (Chuck) Loopstra, QC, Environmental Law; Construction; Municipal Law; Land Use Planning & Development
cloopstra@loonix.com
Malcolm J. MacLeod, Municipal Liability Litigation; Construction Litigation
mmacleod@loonix.com
Michael B. McWilliams, Municipal Litigation; Construction
mmcwilliams@loonix.com
Reg D. Theriault, Property Development; Real Estate
rtheriault@loonix.com

Mattson, Mark O.

17 Fenwood Heights, Toronto, ON M1M 2V6
Tel: 416-265-6548;
Profile: 1 Office, 1 Lawyers

McCarthy Tétrault LLP - Toronto

#5300, Toronto-Dominion Bank Tower, Box 48, Toronto, ON M5K 1E6
Tel: 416-362-1812; *Fax:* 416-868-0673
Toll-Free: 877-244-7711
info@mccarthy.ca
www.mccarthy.ca
Profile: 6 Offices, 608 Lawyers, Founded in: 1855
Biotechnology; Energy; Environmental; Municipal
Environmental Lawyers:
Gordon D. Baird, Partner, Power
416-601-7892
gbaird@mccarthy.ca
John Boscariol, Partner, Energy; Infrastructure; Mining
416-601-7835
jboscari@mccarthy.ca
Andrew Collingwood, Partner, Infrastructure; Real Property Development
416-601-7519
acollingwood@mccarthy.ca
Abraham Costin, Partner, Municipal Planning; Infrastructure; Real Property Development
416-601-7762
acostin@mccarthy.ca
John C. Currie, Partner, Municipal Planning; Infrastructure; Real Property Development
416-601-8154
jcurrie@mccarthy.ca
John A.R. Dawson, Partner, Municipal Planning; Real Property Development
416-601-8300
jdawson@mccarthy.ca
Stephen Furlan, Partner, Infrastructure
416-601-7708
sfurlan@mccarthy.ca
Tzen-Yi Goh, Partner, Real Property Development
416-601-8189
tgoh@mccarthy.ca
Danny C. Grandilli, Partner, Municipal Planning; Infrastructure; Real Property Development
416-601-7597
dgrandil@mccarthy.ca
Shanon O.N. Grauer, Partner, Health
416-601-7664
sgrauer@mccarthy.ca
Brian C. Graves, Partner, Mining
416-601-8153
bgraves@mccarthy.ca
Bram J. Green, Partner, Municipal Planning; Infrastructure; Real Property Development
416-601-8429
bgreen@mccarthy.ca
Douglas Hamilton, Partner, Environmental; Litigation
416-601-7642
dhamilton@mccarthy.ca
Joel Heard, Partner, Energy; Infrastructure
416-601-7925
jheard@mccarthy.ca
Thomas Isaac, Partner, Aboriginal Law; Environmental; Litigation; Mining; Oil & Gas; Power
416-601-7598
tisaac@mccarthy.ca
David A.N. Lever, Partner, Clean Technology; Energy; Infrastructure; Oil & Gas; Power
416-601-7655
dlever@mccarthy.ca
Gary M. Litwack, Partner, Mining
416-601-7591
glitwack@mccarthy.ca
Cynthia MacDougall, Partner, Municipal Planning; Real Property Development
416-601-7634
cmacdoug@mccarthy.ca
William McCullough, Partner, Municipal Planning; Infrastructure; Real Property Development
416-601-7646
bmccullo@mccarthy.ca
Richard Miner, Partner, Mining
416-601-7910
rminer@mccarthy.ca
Suzanne Murphy, Clean Technology; Energy; Power
416-601-8278
smurphy@mccarthy.ca
Jamie Orzech, Partner, Municipal Planning; Infrastructure; Real Property Development
416-601-7723
jorzech@mccarthy.ca
W. Ian Palm, Partner, Clean Technology; Power
416-601-7832
ipalm@mccarthy.ca
Tara L. Piurko, Partner, Municipal Planning; Real Property Development
416-601-7675
tpiurko@mccarthy.ca
Peter D. Quinn, Partner, Municipal Planning; Infrastructure
416-601-7668
pquinn@mccarthy.ca
Joanna Rosengarten, Counsel, Environmental
jrosengarten@mccarthy.ca
Fred Rubinoff, Partner, Municipal Planning; Infrastructure; Real Property Development
416-601-7824
frubinof@mccarthy.ca
Phillip L. Sanford, Partner, Municipal Planning; Real Property Development
416-601-7680
psanford@mccarthy.ca
Gordon Sato, Partner, Municipal Planning; Infrastructure; Real Property Development
416-601-7682
gsato@mccarthy.ca
Joel M. Scoler, Partner, Power
416-601-7864
jscoler@mccarthy.ca
Jonathan D. See, Partner, Municipal Planning; Infrastructure; Real Property Development
416-601-7560
jsee@mccarthy.ca
Godyne Sibay, Partner, Municipal Planning; Infrastructure; Real Property Development
416-601-7748
gsibay@mccarthy.ca
Awanish Sinha, Partner, Infrastructure
416-601-8030
asinha@mccarthy.ca
Cheryl L. Slusarchuk, Partner, Clean Technology
416-601-7986
cslusarchuk@mccarthy.ca
Shea T. Small, Partner, Mining
416-601-8425
ssmall@mccarthy.ca
Barry B. Sookman, Partner, Clean Technology
416-601-7949
bsookman@mccarthy.ca
Brenda C. Swick, Partner, Clean Technology; Energy; Environmental; Mining; Power
416-601-7545
bswick@mccarthy.ca
Christopher J. Tanzola, Partner, Municipal Planning
416-601-7855
ctanzola@mccarthy.ca
Brad Teichman, Partner, Municipal Planning
416-601-7681
bteichma@mccarthy.ca
Douglas R. Thomson, Partner, Environmental; Litigation
416-601-7512
dthomson@mccarthy.ca
Alysha Valenti, Partner, Real Property Development
416-601-7716
avalenti@mccarthy.ca
Philip H.G. Walker, Q.C., Partner, Real Property Development
416-601-7989
phwalker@mccarthy.ca
Michael Weizman, Partner, Clean Technology; Power
416-601-7793
mweizman@mccarthy.ca
Henry Wiercinski, Partner, Clean Technology; Infrastructure
416-601-7842
hwiercin@mccarthy.ca
Gordon Willcocks, Partner, Municipal Planning; Infrastructure; Real Property Development
416-601-7818
gwillcocks@mccarthy.ca

McMillan LLP - Toronto

#4400, Brookfield Place, 181 Bay St., Toronto, ON M5J 2T3
Tel: 416-865-7000; *Fax:* 416-865-7048
Toll-Free: 888-622-4624
info@mcmillan.ca
www.mcmillan.ca
Profile: 6 Offices, 376 Lawyers, Founded in: 1903
Environmental Lawyers:
Chris Bennett, Partner, Electricity; Energy
416-865-7858
chris.bennett@mcmillan.ca
Michael Burns, Partner, Natural Resources
416-865-7261
michael.burns@mcmillan.ca
A.Neil Campbell, Partner, Electricity; Energy
416-865-7025
neil.campbell@mcmillan.ca
Hilary E. Clarke, Partner, Electricity
416-865-7289
hilary.clarke@mcmillan.ca
Carmen Diges, Partner, Natural Resources; Aboriginal Law; Environmental
416-865-7925
carmen.diges@mcmillan.ca
David R. Dunlop, Partner, Health; Mining
416-865-7175
david.dunlop@mcmillan.ca
Sean Farrell, Partner, Electricity; Energy; Natural Resources
416-865-7910
sean.farrell@mcmillan.ca
Michael Friedman, Partner, Natural Resources
416-865-7914
michael.friedman@mcmillan.ca
Chris N. Germanakos, Partner, Energy
416-865-7865
chris.germanakos@mcmillan.ca
Glenn Grenier, Partner, Construction
416-307-4005
glenn.grenier@mcmillan.ca
W. Brad Hanna, Partner, Environmental; Health
416-865-7276
brad.hanna@mcmillan.ca
William Hearn, Partner, Construction
416-865-7240
bill.hearn@mcmillan.ca
Luigi Macchione, Partner, Electricity; Energy
416-865-7116
luigi.macchione@mcmillan.ca
Robert K. McDermott, Partner, Electricity; Energy; Natural Resources
416-865-7085
robert.mcdermott@mcmillan.ca
Greg McIlwain, Partner, Mining; Natural Resources
416-307-4169
greg.mcilwain@mcmillan.ca
Bruce A. McKenna, Partner, Mining; Natural Resources; Construction
416-307-4112
bruce.mckenna@mcmillan.ca
Brent McPherson, Partner, Mining; Natural Resources; Construction
416-307-4103
brent.mcpherson@mcmillan.ca
Bruce McWilliam, Partner, Electricity; Energy
416-865-7214
bruce.mcwilliam@mcmillan.ca
Todd A. Miller, Partner, Electricity; Energy; Emissions Trading & Climate Change
416-865-7058
todd.miller@mcmillan.ca
Timothy John Murphy, Partner, Aboriginal Law; Construction; Electricity; Emissions Trading & Climate Change; Energy;

Law Firms

Health
416-865-7908
tim.murphy@mcmillan.ca
Frank Palmay, Partner, Mining; Natural Resources
416-307-4037
frank.palmay@mcmillan.ca
Mike Richmond, Partner, Energy; Electricity; Renewables; Oil & Gas; Utilities; Projects; Government Affairs
416-865-7832
mike.richmond@mcmillan.ca
Catherine A. Roberts, Partner, Health
416-865-7202
catherine.roberts@mcmillan.ca
William A. Rowlands, Partner, Mining; Natural Resources
416-307-4065
william.rowlands@mcmillan.ca
Graham W.S. Scott, Q.C., Senior Partner, Health
416-865-7247
graham.scott@mcmillan.ca
William J.V. Sheridan, Partner, Mining; Natural Resources
416-307-4060
william.sheridan@mcmillan.ca
Hellen L. Siwanowicz, Partner, Mining; Natural Resources
416-307-4032
hellen.siwanowicz@mcmillan.ca
David E. Thring, Partner, Environment; Energy; Emissions Trading & Climate Change
416-307-4028
david.thring@mcmillan.ca
George Waggott, Partner, Forestry & Paper Products; Health; Mining; Natural Resources
416-307-4221
george.waggott@mcmillan.ca
Lydia Wakulowsky, Partner, Health
416-865-7066
lydia.wakulowsky@mcmillan.ca
R. Nairn Waterman, Partner, Construction; Mining; Natural Resources; Health
416-307-4024
nairn.waterman@mcmillan.ca
Michael P. Whitcombe, Senior Partner, Health
416-865-7126
michael.whitcombe@mcmillan.ca
Robert Wisner, Partner, Natural Resources
416-865-7127
robert.wisner@mcmillan.ca
David M.W. Young, Partner, Environment; Energy; Emissions Trading & Climate Change
416-307-4118
david.young@mcmillan.ca

Miller Thomson LLP - Toronto
#5800, Scotia Plaza, P.O. Box 1011, 40 King St. West, Toronto, ON M5H 3S1
Tel: 416-595-8500; *Fax:* 416-595-8695
Toll-Free: 888-762-5559
toronto@millerthomson.com
www.millerthomson.com
twitter.com/millerthomson,
www.linkedin.com/company/Miller-Thomson-LLP
Profile: 11 Office, 499 Lawyers, Founded in: 1957
Miller Thomson's Environmental Law Group lawyers are legal planners, negotiators and advocates. Many have experience as professional engineers, regulators, prosecutors and policy makers. Our lawyers have cultivated a thorough knowledge of government processes and regulators and continue to maintain excellent relationships with existing personnel. Owing to the size and expertise of our Group and the relationships our lawyers havewith a wide variety of environmental consultants, our partners delegate internally and out-source to consultants and paralegals to the client's advantage. Thus, we are always able to offer cost-effective and timely legal advice.
Environmental Lawyers:
Elizabeth K. Ackman, Partner, Environmental
416-595-8161
eackman@millerthomson.com
Gita Anand, Partner, Municipal Services
416-595-8542
ganand@millerthomson.com
Nancy M. Avison, Associate Counsel, Land Development
416-422-1711
navison@millerthomson.com
Drazen F. Bulat, Partner, Construction; Infrastructure
416-595-8613
dbulat@millerthomson.com
Bryan J. Buttigieg, Partner, Environmental; CleanTech; Workplace Safety; Regulatory Enforcement
416-595-8172
bbuttigieg@millerthomson.com
William Cortis, Partner, Electricity
416-595-2109
wcortis@millerthomson.com
Barbara R.C. Doherty, Senior Partner, CleanTech
416-595-8621
bdoherty@millerthomson.com
Robert L. Falby, Partner, Environmental
416-595-8173
rfalby@millerthomson.com
Tamara Farber, Partner, Environmental; CleanTech; Regulatory
416-595-8520
tfarber@millerthomson.com
Peter K. Foulds, Partner, Construction; Infrastructure
416-596-2112
pfoulds@millerthomson.com
Kathryn M. Frelick, Partner, Health; Administrative Law
416-595-2979
kfrelick@millerthomson.com
Leonard A. Gangbar, Partner, Land Development
416-595-8199
lgangbar@millerthomson.com
Eugene J.A. Gierczak, P. Eng., Partner, Municipal Services
416-596-2132
egierczak@millerthomson.com
Sandra A. Gogal, Partner, Aboriginal Law; Environmental; Litigation
416-595-8574
sgogal@millerthomson.com
Patrick Greco, Partner, Construction; Infrastructure
416-595-2982
pgreco@millerthomson.com
Jay M. Hoffman, Partner, Mining
416-595-8508
jhoffman@millerthomson.com
David Judson, Partner, Mining
416-595-8664
djudson@millerthomson.com
Karima Kanani, Partner, Health
416-595-7908
kkanani@millerthomson.com
Perry Katz, Partner, Land Development
416-595-7918
pkatz@millerthomson.com
Kate Lazier, Partner, Municipal Services
416-595-8197
klazier@millerthomson.com
Joshua Liswood, Partner, Health
416-595-8525
jliswood@millerthomson.com
J. Fraser Mann, Partner, Municipal Services
416-595-8195
fmann@millerthomson.com
Max Maréchaux, Partner, Municipal Services
416-595-8522
mmarechaux@millerthomson.com
Susan Adam Metzler, Partner, Oil & Gas
416-595-8178
smetzler@millerthomson.com
Michael J. Pace, Partner, Electricity
416-595-8533
mpace@millerthomson.com
William (Bill) M. Pigott, Partner, Construction; Infrastructure; Health
416-595-8179
wpigott@millerthomson.com
Andrew J. Roman, Partner, Electricity; Municipal Services; Administrative Law
416-595-8604
aroman@millerthomson.com
Daniel A. Rothberg, Partner, Mining
416-595-8632
drothberg@millerthomson.com
Charles J. Schwartz, Q.C., Partner, Land Development
416-595-7904
cschwartz@millerthomson.com
Shane Smith, Partner, Health
416-595-8166
ssmith@millerthomson.com
Robert M. Stewart, Partner, CleanTech
416-595-2963
rstewart@millerthomson.com
Elisabeth Symons, Partner, Municipal Services
416-595-8575
esymons@millerthomson.com
Thomas R. Whitby, Partner, Construction; Infrastructure
416-595-8561
twhitby@millerthomson.com
Alexandra L. White, Associate, Environmental Litigation
416-595-8667
awhite@millerthomson.com
Michael J. Wren, Partner, Land Development
416-595-8184
mwren@millerthomson.ca

Norton Rose Fulbright Canada LLP - Toronto - Dominion Centre
#2300, Toronto-Dominion Centre, TD South Tower, P.O. Box 128, 79 Wellington St. West, Toronto, ON M5K 1H1
Tel: 416-360-8511; *Fax:* 416-360-8277
toronto@nortonrosefulbright.com
www.nortonrosefulbright.com/ca
Profile: 190 Lawyers

Norton Rose Fulbright Canada LLP - Calgary
#3700, 400 - 3rd Ave. SW, Calgary, AB T2P 4H2
Tel: 403-267-8222; *Fax:* 403-264-5973
calgary@nortonrosefulbright.com
www.nortonrosefulbright.com/ca
Profile: 154 Lawyers,
Environmental risk management, counsel, assistance in all forms of transactional matters, representation & litigation

Norton Rose Fulbright Canada LLP - Ottawa
#1500, 45 O'Connor Street, Ottawa, ON K1P 1A4
Tel: 613-780-8661; *Fax:* 613-230-5459
ottawa@nortonrosefulbright.com
www.nortonrosefulbright.com/ca
Profile: 35 Lawyers,
Environmental risk management, counsel, assistance in all forms of transactional matters, representation & litigation

Norton Rose Fulbright Canada LLP - Québec
#1500, Complexe Jules-Dallaire/Tour Norton Rose, 2828 boulevard Laurier, Québec, QC G1V 0B9
Tél: 418-640-5000; *Téléc:* 418-640-1500
quebec@nortonrosefulbright.com
www.nortonrosefulbright.com/ca
Profile: 41 Lawyers,
Environmental risk management, counsel, assistance in all forms of transactional matters, representation & litigation

Norton Rose Fulbright Canada LLP - Toronto - Royal Bank Plaza
#3800, Royal Bank Plaza South Tower, P.O. Box 84, 200 Bay St., Toronto, ON M5J 2Z4
Tel: 416-216-4000; *Fax:* 416-216-3930
toronto@nortonrosefulbright.com
www.nortonrosefulbright.com/ca
Profile: 190 Lawyers,
Environmental risk management, counsel, assistance in all forms of transactional matters, representation & litigation
Environmental Lawyers:
Leeora Avrahami, Occupational Health & Safety
416-216-4843
lavrahami@ogilvyrenault.com
David Badurina, Life Sciences; Microbiology
416-216-1904
dbadurina@ogilvyrenault.com
David J. Bannon, Partner, Occupational Health & Safety
416-216-3907
dbannon@ogilvyrenault.com
John Beauchamp, Environment; Energy
416-216-1927
jbeauchamp@ogilvyrenault.com
Penny S. Bonner, Senior Partner, Life Sciences; Bioethics; Natural Health Products; Biotechnology
416-216-6629
pbonner@ogilvyrenault.com
Andrea Brewer, Mining & Resources
416-216-1917
abrewer@ogilvyrenault.com
James R. Cade, Senior Partner, Cleantech; Life Sciences
416-216-4840
jcade@ogilvyrenault.com
Richard J. Charney, Senior Partner, Occupational Health & Safety; Mining & Resources

416-216-1867
rcharney@ogilvyrenault.com
Jung-Kay Chiu, Partner, Cleantech; Life Sciences; Genetics; Molecular Biology; Biotechnology
416-216-2994
jchiu@ogilvyrenault.com
Mark A. Convery, Senior Partner, Cleantech
416-216-4803
mconvery@ogilvyrenault.com
Rebecca Crane, Cleantech; Life Sciences; Pharmaceutical Industry
416-216-1886
rcrane@ogilvyrenault.com
Pierre R. Dagenais, Partner, Mining & Resources
416-216-1857
pdagenais@ogilvyrenault.com
Jill Daley, Life Sciences; Natural Healthcare
416-216-1930
jdaley@ogilvyrenault.com
Jeremy J. Devereux, Partner, Mining Law; Natural Resources
416-216-4073
jdevereux@ogilvyrenault.com
Paul J. Field, Partner, Cleantech; Mining & Resources
416-216-3903
pfield@ogilvyrenault.com
Paul Fitzgerald, Partner, Mining & Resources
416-216-3941
pfitzgerald@ogilvyrenault.com
Andrew Fleming, Senior Partner, Mining & Resources
416-216-4007
afleming@ogilvyrenault.com
Brian W. Gray, Senior Partner, Cleantech; Life Sciences
416-216-1905
bgray@ogilvyrenault.com
Andrew Grossman, Partner, Cleantech; Energy; Mining & Resources
416-216-2312
agrossman@ogilvyrenault.com
Jeremy Grushcow, Partner, Cleantech; Life Sciences
416-216-2301
jgrushcow@ogilvyrenault.com
James A. Hodgson, Senior Partner, Construction Litigation
416-216-2989
jhodgson@ogilvyrenault.com
Sanjay Joshi, Partner, Energy; Mining & Resources
416-216-3984
sjoshi@ogilvyrenault.com
Richard J. King, Partner, Environmental Law; Energy Law; Aboriginal Law; Cleantech
416-216-2311
rking@ogilvyrenault.com
Jay A. Lefton, Senior Partner, Cleantech; Life Sciences
416-216-4018
jlefton@ogilvyrenault.com
Suzana A. Lobo, Cleantech
416-216-2990
slobo@ogilvyrenault.com
Madeleine L.S. Loewenberg, Occupational Health & Safety
416-216-3932
mloewenberg@ogilvyrenault.com
Alan Mark, Senior Partner, Energy
416-216-4865
amark@ogilvyrenault.com
Jason C. Markwell, Partner, Life Sciences
416-216-2977
jmarkwell@ogilvyrenault.com
Michael G. McFadden, Partner, Occupational Health & Safety
416-216-3973
mmcfadden@ogilvyrenault.com
Peter S. Newell, Senior Partner, Cleantech; Mining & Resources
416-216-2963
pnewell@ogilvyrenault.com
Sandra Nissan, Partner, Cleantech; Mining & Resources
416-216-3965
snissan@ogilvyrenault.com
James Padwick, Cleantech; Energy; Environmental Law
416-216-1912
jpadwick@ogilvyrenault.com
Robert L. Percival, Partner, Cleantech
416-216-4075
rpercival@ogilvyrenault.com
Aditya Rebbapragada, Mining & Resources
416-216-2975
arebbapragada@ogilvyrenault.com
Heidi Reinhart, Mining & Resources
416-216-2979
hreinhart@ogilvyrenault.com
Mark Sajewycz, Partner, Cleantech; Mining & Resources
416-216-1924
msajewycz@ogilvyrenault.com
Yursa Siddiquee, Partner, Mining & Resources; Health Sciences; Energy
416-216-4062
ysiddiquee@ogilvyrenault.com
C. Nicole Sigouin, Partner, Cleantech; Mining & Resources
416-216-3929
nsigouin@ogilvyrenault.com
Cathy Singer, Partner, Mining & Resources
416-216-4053
csinger@ogilvyrenault.com
Walied Soliman, Partner, Cleantech; Mining & Resources
416-216-4820
wsoliman@ogilvyrenault.com
Pierre L. Soulard, Partner, Mining & Resources
416-216-4806
psoulard@ogilvyrenault.com
Ned A. Steinman, Partner, Construction; Mining & Resources; Real Estate
416-216-3915
nsteinman@ogilvyrenault.com
Richard S. Sutin, Senior Partner, Cleantech; Life Sciences; Mining & Resources
416-216-4821
rsutin@ogilvyrenault.com
Derrick C. Tay, Senior Partner, Environmental Law
416-216-4832
tday@ogilvyrenault.com
Michael Torrance, Mining & Resources; Health
416-216-1908
mtorrance@ogilvyrenault.com
John B. West, Senior Partner, Occupational Health & Safety
416-216-3976
jwest@ogilvyrenault.com
Anna Wilkinson, Cleantech; Life Sciences
416-216-3975
awilkinson@ogilvyrenault.com
Jordan D. Winch, Partner, Occupational Health & Safety
416-216-4788
jwinch@ogilvyrenault.com

Olthuis Kleer Townshend LLP

229 College St., 3rd Fl., Toronto, ON M5T 1R4
Tel: 416-981-9330; *Fax:* 416-981-9350
tmckenna@oktlaw.com (General Inquiries)
www.oktlaw.com
Profile: 1 Office, 1 Lawyers,
Specializing in Aboriginal & Environmental law

Osler, Hoskin & Harcourt LLP - Toronto

#4600, One First Canadian Place, P.O. Box 50, 100 King Street West, Toronto, ON M5X 1B8
Tel: 416-362-2111; *Fax:* 416-862-6666
counsel@osler.com
www.osler.com
Profile: 5 Offices, 445 Lawyers,
Climate Change and Emissions Trading; Environmental, Regulatory and Aboriginal Law
Environmental Lawyers:
Mark Austin, Partner, Health; Life Sciences
416-862-6524
maustin@osler.com
Jason Ball, Health
416-862-5963
jball@osler.com
Chad Bayne, Partner, Mining
416-862-4708
cbayne@osler.com
D. Robert Beaumont, Partner, Construction
416-862-5861
rbeaumont@osler.com
Michael H.D. Bowman, Partner, Environmental, Regulatory & Aboriginal; Litigation
416-862-6834
mbowman@osler.com
James R. Brown, Mining
416-862-6647
jbrown@osler.com
John B. (Jack) Cook, Partner, Climate Change & Emissions Trading; Environmental, Regulatory & Aboriginal; Litigation
416-862-4896
jcook@osler.com
Raj Dhaliwal, Construction; Energy; Renewable Energy & Environmental Financing
416-862-6816
rdhaliwal@osler.com
Tobor Emakpor, Partner, Construction
416-862-4268
temakpor@osler.com
Jennifer Fairfax, Construction; Environmental, Regulatory & Aboriginal; Litigation
416-862-5998
jfairfax@osler.com
Jeremy Fraiberg, Partner, Mining
416-862-6505
jfraiberg@osler.com
Roger Gillott, Partner, Construction
416-862-6818
rgillott@osler.com
Brian Gray, Mining
416-862-4862
bgray@osler.com
David Hanick, Partner, Mining
416-862-5979
dhanick@osler.com
Judith E. Harris, Senior Partner, Health
416-862-4609
jharris@osler.com
Simon Hodgett, Partner, Health
416-862-6819
shodgett@osler.com
Paul Ivanoff, Partner, Construction
416-862-4223
pivanoff@osler.com
Ken Jennings, Energy; Construction
416-862-4935
kjennings@osler.com
Jennifer Kelly, Construction
416-862-4720
jkelly@osler.com
C.W. Daniel Kirby, Partner, Climate Change & Emissions Trading; Environmental, Regulatory & Aboriginal; Litigation
416-862-6661
dkirby@osler.com
Harvey Kirsh, Senior Partner, Construction
416-862-6844
hkirsh@osler.com
Paul J. Morassutti, Partner, Environmental, Regulatory & Aboriginal
416-862-6806
pmorassutti@osler.com
Jeffrey Murray, Energy
416-862-4250
jmurray@osler.com
Jay Nathwani, Construction
416-862-5885
jnathwani@osler.com
Christopher Portner, Partner, Energy
416-862-6412
cportner@osler.com
Jacob A. Sadikman, Climate Change & Emissions Trading; Renewable Energy & Environmental Financing
416-862-4931
jsadikman@osler.com
Rocco M. Sebastiano, Partner, Energy
416-862-5859
rsebastiano@osler.com
Elliot A. Smith, Construction; Energy
416-862-6435
esmith@osler.com
Steve Suarez, Partner, Mining
416-862-5905
ssuarez@osler.com
Paula Trattner, Partner, Health
416-862-6495
ptrattner@osler.com
David Vernon, Mining
416-862-5966
dvernon@osler.com
Michael Watts, Partner, Health
416-862-6605
mwatts@osler.com
Andrew Wong, Partner, Construction; Energy
416-862-6564
anwong@osler.com

Richard Wong, Partner, Construction; Energy
416-862-6467
rwong@osler.com

Paterson, MacDougall LLP, Barristers, Solicitors
#900, P.O. Box 100, 1 Queen St. East, Toronto, ON M5C 2W5
Tel: 416-366-9607; *Fax:* 416-366-3743
bmacdoug@pmlaw.com
www.pmlaw.com
Profile: 1 Office, 13 Lawyers,
The law firm provides representation in commercial, litigation & environmental marine matters. Clients include the following: ship owners, stevedores, agents, marina operators, & protection & indemnity associations.
Environmental Lawyers:
Matthew A. Biderman, Marine law
mbiderman@pmlaw.com
Clay Hunter, Marine law
chunter@pmlaw.com
Peter F.M. Jones, Marine law
pfmjones@pmlaw.com
Carol E. McCall, Marine law
cmccall@pmlaw.com

Poch, Harry Environmental Lawyer
20 Beaverhall Dr., Toronto, ON M2L 2C7
Tel: 416-444-7971; *Fax:* 416-444-8971
harrypoch@rogers.com
Profile: 1 Office, 1 Lawyers, Founded in: 1979

Saxe, Dianne
248 Russell Hill Rd., Toronto, ON M4V 2T2
Tel: 416-962-5882; *Fax:* 416-962-8817
admin@envirolaw.com
www.envirolaw.com
http://www.linkedin.com/in/envirolaw
Profile: 2 Offices, 3 Lawyers, Founded in: 1991
Toronto Environmental Lawyer of the Year
Environmental Lawyers:
R.G. Inglis
ginglis@lip.on.ca

Shibley Righton LLP
#700, 250 University Ave., Toronto, ON M5H 3E5
Tel: 416-214-5200; *Fax:* 416-214-5400
Toll-Free: 877-214-5200
torontoinfo@shibleyrighton.com
www.shibleyrighton.com
Profile: 2 Offices, 32 Lawyers, Founded in: 1964
Areas of practice at Shibley Righton LLP, Barristers & Solicitors include municipal & planning law & energy law.
Environmental Lawyers:
John Bell, Municipal & planning law
416-214-5212
john.bell@shibleyrighton.com

Stikeman Elliott LLP - Toronto
#5300, Commerce Court West, 199 Bay St., Toronto, ON M5L 1B9
Tel: 416-869-5500; *Fax:* 416-947-0866
Toll-Free: 973-550-0263
www.stikeman.com
Profile: 219 Lawyers

Stringer LLP
#1100, 110 Yonge St., Toronto, ON M5C 1T4
Tel: 416-862-1616; *Fax:* 416-363-7358
Toll-Free: 866-821-7306
info@stringerllp.com
www.stringerllp.com
Profile: 1 Office, 6 Lawyers,
Stringer LLP advises employers from the public & private sectors in occupational health & safety matters.
Environmental Lawyers:
Ryan J. Conlin, Partner, Occupational Health & Safety
rconlin@stringerllp.com
Jeffrey D.A. Murray, Partner, Labour & Employment (construction, healthcare, & public sectors)
jmurray@stringerllp.com
Jeremy D. Schwartz, Partner, Health & Safety Due Diligence
jschwartz@stringerllp.com
Allison L. Taylor, Counsel, Employment Law
ataylor@stringerllp.com
Jessica A.N. Young, Employment & Labour Law
jyoung@stringerllp.com
Landon P. Young, Managing Partner, Occupational Health & Safety
lyoung@stringerllp.com

Thomson, Rogers
#3100, 390 Bay St., Toronto, ON M5H 1W2
Tel: 416-868-3100; *Fax:* 416-868-3134
Toll-Free: 888-223-0448
info@thomsonrogers.com
www.thomsonrogers.com
Profile: 1 Office, 33 Lawyers, Founded in: 1936
The firm provides legal services in the areas of Environmental Law, and Expropriations Law
Environmental Lawyers:
Roger T. Beaman, Municipal & Environmental Law Practice; Municipal Law; Environmental Law; Planning Law; Expropriations Law
416-868-3157
rbeaman@thomsonrogers.com
Alstair H. A. Burton, Environmental Law; Environmental Approvals; Municipal Law; Land Use Planning; Expropriations Law
416-868-3113
aburton@thomsonrogers.com
Stephen J. D'Agostino, Environmental Law; Environmental Assessments & Approvals; Municipal Law; Planning Law; Landfill Matters; Expropriations Law; Telecommunications Networks Matters; Electric Generating Facilities Permitting
416-868-3126
sdagostino@thomsonrogers.com
Jeffrey J. Wilker, Environmental Law; Municipal Law; Land Use Litigation; Planning Law; Expropriations Law
416-868-3118
jwilker@thomsonrogers.com

Torys LLP - Toronto
#3000, Toronto-Dominion Centre, P.O. Box 270, 79 Wellington St. West, Toronto, ON M5K 1N2
Tel: 416-865-0040; *Fax:* 416-865-7380
www.torys.com
www.facebook.com/TorysLLP, twitter.com/torysllp, www.linkedin.com/company/torys-llp
Profile: 3 Offices, 272 Lawyers, Founded in: 1941
Environmental Lawyers:
David P. Chernos, Environmental Law & Litigation
416-865-8246
dchernos@torys.com
David A. Dell, Infrastructure & Energy; Power Project Development & Finance; Construction Law
416-865-8100
ddell@torys.com
Daniel A. Ford, Infrastructure & Energy; Wind Energy Industry
416-865-7372
dford@torys.com
Michael J. Fortier, Environmental Law; Aboriginal Law; Climate Change & Emissions Trading; Chemical Industry; Energy Industry; Manufacturing Industry; Mining Industry; Water & Wastewaster Industry; Regulatory & Compliance
416-865-8147
mfortier@torys.com
Sabrina A. Gherbaz, Infrastructure & Energy; Climate Change & Emissions Trading; Energy Project Development & Finance
416-865-8179
sgherbaz@torys.com
Valerie Helbronner, Infrastructure & Energy; Renewable Energy Project Development & Finance; Wind Energy Projects; Solar Energy Projects; Biomass Energy Projects; Hydro Project Development; Aboriginal Law; Regulatory & Compliance
416-865-7516
vhelbronner@torys.com
Krista F. Hill, Infrastructure & Energy; Energy Law; Natural Resources Law
416-865-7953
khill@torys.com
Patricia D. S. (Trisha) Jackson, Environmental Law & Litigation; Energy Law & Litigation
416-865-7323
tjackson@torys.com
Charles Keizer, Infrastructure & Energy; Energy Law; Regulatory & Compliance; Project Development & Finance; Power Generation Industry; Renewable Energy Industry
416-865-7512
ckeizer@torys.com
Scott Kraag, Renewable Energy Project Development & Finance; Infrastructure Development & Finance; Mining Industry
416-865-7980
skraag@torys.com
Alison Lacy, Energy Project Development & Finance; Electricity Industry; Mining Industry; Natural Resources Industry
416-865-7503
alacy@torys.com
Tara A. Mackay, Infrastructure & Energy; Public Infrastructure Projects; Project Development & Finance
416-865-7528
tmackay@torys.com
Dennis E. Mahony, Environmental Law; Climate Change & Emissions Trading; Infrastructure & Energy; Pulp & Paper Industry; Mining Industry; Chemical Industry; Water & Wastewater Industry; Manufacturing Industry; Regulatory & Compliance
416-865-8214
dmahony@torys.com
Michael T. Pickersgill, Climate Change & Emissions Trading; Mining & Metals Industry
416-865-8180
mpickersgill@torys.com
James D. Scarlett, Mining & Metals
416-865-8199
jscarlett@torys.com
Philip D. A. Symmonds, Partner, Energy & Infrastructure; Energy Project Development & Finance; Solar Energy Industry; Nuclear Energy Industry; Hydroelectric Power Industry; Mining & Metals Industry
416-865-8219
psymmonds@torys.com
John J. Tobin, Energy Project Development & Finance; Climate Change Matters; Wind Energy Industry; Solar Energy Industry; Hydroelectric Power Industry
416-865-7999
jtobin@torys.com
Jonathan B. Weisz, Energy & Infrastructure; Mining Industry; Energy Project Development & Finance; Climate Change & Emissions Trading
416-865-8157
jweisz@torys.com

WeirFoulds LLP
#1600, Exchange Tower, P.O. Box 480, 130 King St. West, Toronto, ON M5X 1J5
Tel: 416-365-1110; *Fax:* 416-365-1876
firm@weirfoulds.com
www.weirfoulds.com
Profile: 1 Office, 78 Lawyers, Founded in: 1860
Environmental Lawyers:
J.M. Buhlman
416-947-5070
jbuhlman@weirfoulds.com
J.G. Cowan
416-947-5007
jcowan@weirfoulds.com
S.G. Foran
416-947-5019
sforan@weirfoulds.com
S.A. Metcalfe
416-947-5084
smetcalfe@weirfoulds.com
W.A.D. Millar
416-947-5021
dmillar@weirfoulds.com
R.B. Warren
416-947-5075
rwarren@weirfoulds.com

William M. Sharpe Barrister & Solicitor
#307, 40 Wynford Dr., Toronto, ON M3C 1J5
Tel: 416-482-5321; *Fax:* 416-322-2083
wmsharpe@shippinglaw.ca
www.yachtsales.com/sharpe
Profile: 1 Office, 3 Lawyers, Founded in: 1990
Deals with marine transportation law.

Willms & Shier Environmental Lawyers LLP
#900, 4 King St. West, Toronto, ON M5H 1B6
Tel: 416-863-0711; *Fax:* 416-863-1938
info@willmsshier.com
www.willmsshier.com
www.linkedin.com/company/willms-&-shier-environmental-lawyers-llp
Profile: 1 Office, 13 Lawyers, Founded in: 1975
Willms & Shier Environmental Lawyers LLP guides companies & municipalities to environmental due diligence in managing

industrial operations, contaminated land clean-up, transactions, & lawsuits.
Clients are represented in civil litigation trials & at regulatory tribunal hearings. The firm defends clients from prosecutions, & helps them to obtain apporvals for air emissions, water discharges, & waste management & disposal.
The following are the firm's practice areas: Aboriginal law; clean technology; energy law; environmental litigation; government policy & law; natural resource law; approvals & compliance; contaminated land & Brownfields; environmental law for municipalities; environmental management; land use planning & development; & regulatory orders & prosecutions.
Approvals & compliance work by the firm is as follows: air, noise & vibration emissions; drinking water & source protection; environmental assessment; industrial pollution control; pesticides & new substances notification; waste management; & wastewater treatment.
Environmental Lawyers:
Juli Abouchar, Partner, Environmental Law; Environmental regulatory matters; Government policy & law; Aboriginal Law; Energy Law
416-862-4836
jabouchar@willmsshier.com
Charles Birchall, Partner, Environmental Law; Energy Law; Aboriginal Law; Litigation
613-761-2424
cbirchall@willmsshier.com
Cherie Brant, Partner, Energy Law; Aboriginal Law
416-862-4829
cbrant@willmsshier.com
Matthew Gardner, Associate, Environmental Law; Energy Law; Litigation
416-862-4825
mgardner@willmsshier.com
John Georgakopoulos, Partner, Environmental Law
416-862-4826
jgeorgakopoulos@willmsshier.com
Katherine Koostachin, Associate, Aboriginal Law
416-862-4823
kkoostachin@willmsshier.com
Marc McAree, Partner, Environmental Law; Litigation
416-862-4820
mmcaree@willmsshier.com
Carl McKay, Associate, Energy Law; Aboriginal Law
416-862-4831
cmckay@willmsshier.com
P. Douglas Petrie, Counsel, Environmental Law
416-862-4835
dpetrie@willmsshier.com
Donna Shier, Partner, Environmental Law
416-862-4822
dshier@willmsshier.com
Jacquelyn Stevens, Associate, Environmental Law; Litigation; Energy Law; Aboriginal Law
416-862-4828
jstevens@willmsshier.com
Joanna Vince, Associate, Aboriginal Law; Environmental Law; Energy Law
416-862-4830
jvince@willmsshier.com
John Willms, Partner, Environmental Law
416-862-4821
jwillms@willmsshier.com

Woolgar VanWiechen Ketcheson Ducoffe LLP
#401, 70 The Esplanade, Toronto, ON M5E 1R2
Tel: 416-867-1666; *Fax:* 416-867-1434
www.woolvan.com
Profile: 1 Office, 9 Lawyers

Vancouver

Cassels Brock & Blackwell LLP
#2200, HSBC Building, 885 West Georgia St., Vancouver, ON V6C 3E8
Tel: 604-691-6100; *Fax:* 604-691-6120
Profile: 5 Lawyers

Vankleek Hill

Nelligan O'Brien Payne
P.O. Box 190, 86 High St., Vankleek Hill, ON K0B 1R0
Tel: 613-678-2490; *Fax:* 613-678-3762
Toll-Free: 888-565-9912
info@nelligan.ca
www.nelligan.ca
Profile: 4 Offices, 46 Lawyers

Vaughan

Bratty & Partners, LLP Barristers & Solicitors
#200, 7501 Keele St., Vaughan, ON L4K 1Y2
Tel: 905-760-2600; *Fax:* 905-760-2900
info@bratty.com
www.bratty.com
Profile: 1 Office, 15 Lawyers,
The planning & municipal law section at Bratty & Partners LLP handles land acquisition, planning, & development matters. Lawyers have experience in issues related to environmental law. They have appeared before the Ontario Municipal Board, municipal councils, & other administrative tribunals.
Environmental Lawyers:
Daniel P. Botelho, Land Development
dbotelho@bratty.com
Michael N. Durisin, Land Development
mdurisin@bratty.com
Caterina Facciolo, Land Use Planning & Government Compliance
cfacciolo@bratty.com
Brian B. Finer, Land Development
bfiner@bratty.com
Barry A. Horosko, Municipal Law; Land Development
bhorosko@bratty.com
Paul Merrick, Land Acquisition & Development
pmerrick@bratty.com
Helen A. Mihailidi, Land Development
hmihailidi@bratty.com
Larry R. Trifon, Land Development
ltrifon@bratty.com
Michael C. Volpatti, Land Development
mvolpatti@bratty.com
Herbert L. Wisebrod, QC, Land Development
hwisebrod@bratty.com

Walkerton

Magwood, Van De Vyvere, Thompson, & Grove-McClement LLP
P.O. Box 880, 215 Durham St., Walkerton, ON N0G 2V0
Tel: 519-881-3230; *Fax:* 519-881-3595
wmvt@bmts.com
Profile: 1 Office, 4 Lawyers, Founded in: 1957
Environmental Lawyers:
Tammy W. Grove-McClement, Municipal Law
George C. Magwood, Municipal Law

Waterloo

Miller Thomson LLP - Waterloo
#300, Accelerator Bldg., 295 Hagey Blvd., Waterloo, ON N2L 6R5
Tel: 519-579-3660; *Fax:* 519-743-2540
Toll-Free: 866-658-0091
waterloo@millerthomson.com
www.millerthomson.com
Profile: 41 Lawyers, Founded in: 1876
Aboriginal Law; Energy Law; Municipal & Planning; Oil & Gas; Construction; Forestry
Environmental Lawyers:
F. Stephen Finch, Q.C.
519-593-3210
sfinch@millerthomson.com
Gregory P. Hanmer, Environmental; Health
519-593-3233
ghanmer@millerthomson.com
Robin-Lee Norris
519-780-4638
morris@millerthomson.com
Richard J. Trafford
519- -
rtrafford@millerthomson.com

Windsor

Bartlet & Richardes LLP
#1000, Canada Bldg., 374 Ouellette Ave., Windsor, ON N9A 1A9
Tel: 519-253-7461; *Fax:* 519-253-2321
mail@bartlet.com
www.bartlet.com
Profile: 1 Office, 13 Lawyers, Founded in: 1887
Environmental Lawyers:
D. Stephen Jovanovic, Construction Law

Shibley Righton LLP
#301, 2510 Ouellette Ave., Windsor, ON N8X 1L4
Tel: 519-969-9844; *Fax:* 519-969-8045
Toll-Free: 866-422-7988
Profile: 2 Offices, 0 Lawyers

Sutts, Strosberg LLP
#600, Westcourt Place, 251 Goyeau St., Windsor, ON N9A 6V4
Tel: 519-258-9333; *Fax:* 519-186-6613
www.strosbergco.com
Profile: 1 Office, 20 Lawyers, Founded in: 1958
Environmental Law: Counseling & Audits, Crisis Management, Pollution & Contamination, Transactions, Land Development
Environmental Lawyers:
James K. Ball, Construction & Development; Environmental; Land Development
Werner H. Keller, Environmental
519-561-6233
werner_h_keller@strosbergco.com
David L. Robins, Environmental
Clifford N. Sutts, Q.C., Construction & Development; Environmental; Land Development
519-561-6229
cnsutts@strosbergco.com

Prince Edward Island

Alberton

Cox & Palmer - Alberton
P.O. Box 40, 334 Church St., Alberton, PE C0B 1B0
Tel: 902-853-3313; *Fax:* 902-853-3753
alberton@coxandpalmer.com
www.coxandpalmerlaw.com
Profile: 1 Lawyers,
Part of one of the largest full-service law firms in Atlantic Canada, the Alberton office of Cox & Palmer serves both individuals & businesses.
Environmental Lawyers:
Mary Lynn Kane, QC, Managing Partner, Health Law
902-629-3904
mkane@coxandpalmer.com

Charlottetown

Campbell Lea Barristers & Solicitors
P.O. Box 429, 15 Queen St., Charlottetown, PE C1A 7K7
Tel: 902-566-3400; *Fax:* 902-566-9266
office@campbelllea.com
www.campbelllea.com
Profile: 1 Office, 9 Lawyers,
The full-service independent law firm provides services in the areas of public law & labour & employment.
Environmental Lawyers:
D. Brandon Forbes, Partner, Fisheries Law
bforbes@campbelllea.com
Kenneth L. Godfrey, Partner, Public Law
klgodfrey@campbelllea.com
Paul D. Michael, Q.C., Partner, Public Law; Employment & Labour Law
pmichael@campbelllea.com

Cox & Palmer - Charlottetown
#600, 97 Queen St., Charlottetown, PE C1A 4A9
Tel: 902-628-1033; *Fax:* 902-566-2639
charlottetown@coxandpalmer.com
www.coxandpalmerlaw.com
Profile: 12 Lawyers,
Envrionmental legal services include advising clients during envrionmental assessments & representing clients in prosecutions under environmental protection legislation.
Environmental Lawyers:
Bria Brown, Associate, Muncipal Law
902-629-3936
bbrown@coxandpalmer.com
Karen A. Campbell, QC, Municipal Law; Administrative Law; Labour & Employment
902-629-3911
kcampbell@coxandpalmer.com
David W. Hooley, QC, Partner, Environmental Law; Municipal Law; Administrative Law; Construction; Labour & Employment

902-629-3903
dhooley@coxandpalmer.com
Mary Lynn Kane, QC, Managing Partner, Health Law
902-629-3904
mkane@coxandpalmer.com
Wendy E. Reid, QC, Municipal Law
902-629-3907
wreid@coxandpalmer.com
Pamela J. Williams, QC, Shipbuilding; Administrative
902-629-3916
pwilliams@coxandpalmer.com

Matheson & Murray
#202, 119 Queen St., Charlottetown, PE C1A 4B3
Tel: 902-894-7051; *Fax:* 902-368-3762
info@mathesonandmurray.com
www.mathesonandmurray.com
Profile: 1 Office, 9 Lawyers, Founded in: 1981
Lawyers at Matheson & Murray have expertise in the areas of environmental law & labour & employment law.
Environmental Lawyers:
Sophie MacDonald, Labour & Employment
902-368-7823
smacdonald@mathesonandmurray.com
Randy MacDonald, Labour & Employment Law
902-368-7816
rbmacdonald@mathesonandmurray.com
M. Lynn Murray, Q.C., Environmental Law; Labour & Employment
902-368-7821
lmurray@mathesonandmurray.com
Michael Ramsay, Labour & Employment Law
902-368-7822
mramsay@mathesonandmurray.com
Kerri Lynn Seward Carpenter, Environmental Law
902-368-7826
kseward@mathesonandmurray.com

Montague

Cox & Palmer - Montague
P.O. Box 516, 4A Riverside Dr., Montague, PE C0A 1R0
Tel: 902-838-1033; *Fax:* 902-838-3440
montague@coxandpalmer.com
www.coxandpalmerlaw.com
Profile: 2 Lawyers,
Municipalities, companies, & individuals are represented.
Environmental Lawyers:
Mary Lynn Kane, QC, Managing Partner, Health Law
902-629-3904
mkane@coxandpalmer.com

Morell

Cox & Palmer - Morell
29 Park St., Morell, PE C0A 1S0
Tel: 902-961-9300;
www.coxandpalmerlaw.com
Mary Lynn Kane, QC, Managing Partner, Health Law
902-629-3904
mkane@coxandpalmer.com

Summerside

Cox & Palmer - Summerside
82 Summer St., Summerside, PE C1N 3H9
Tel: 902-888-1033; *Fax:* 902-436-7131
summerside@coxandpalmer.com
www.coxandpalmerlaw.com
Profile: 3 Lawyers,
Legal representation is provided to the fishing & domestic & international marine transportation industries. Environmental & commercial matters in a marine context are handled.
Environmental Lawyers:
J. Andrew D. Campbell, Partner, Fisheries & Marine
902-888-4566
adcampbell@coxandpalmer.com
Mary Lynn Kane, Managing Partner, Health Law
902-629-3904
mkane@coxandpalmer.com
Jeffrey H. Leard, Partner, Construction
902-888-4570
jleard@coxandpalmer.com
Krista J. MacKay, Partner, Municipal Law; Labour & Employment
902-888-4568
kristamackay@coxandpalmer.com

McInnes Cooper - Summerside
494 Granville St., Summerside, PE C1N 4K4
Tel: 902-436-4851; *Fax:* 902-436-5063
mcsse@mcinnescooper.com
www.mcinnescooper.com
Profile: 7 Lawyers

Québec

Alma

Cain Lamarre Casgrain Wells - Alma
#03, Complexe Jacques-Gagnon, 100, rue St-Joseph sud, Alma, QC G8B 7A6
Tél: 418-669-4580; *Téléc:* 418-669-0088
info@clcw.ca
www.clcw.qc.ca
Profile: 4 Lawyers
Environmental Lawyers:
Denis Bonneville, Santé
denis.bonneville@clcw.ca
Martine Tremblay, Droit de l'environnement
martine.tremblay@clcw.ca

Amos

Cain Lamarre Casgrain Wells - Amos
#201, 101, 1re av est, Amos, QC J9T 1H4
Tél: 819-727-4153; *Téléc:* 819-727-9769
info@clcw.ca
www.clcw.qc.ca
Profile: 2 Lawyers
Environmental Lawyers:
Marianne Gagnon-Bourget, Santé
marianne.gagnon.bourget@clcw.ca

Amqui

Cain Lamarre Casgrain Wells - Amqui
20, rue Desbiens, Amqui, QC G5J 3P1
Tél: 418-629-3302; *Téléc:* 418-629-3333
info@clcw.ca
www.clcw.qc.ca
Profile: 1 Lawyers
Environmental Lawyers:
François Bérubé, Associé, Droit de la construction
francois.berube@clcw.ca

Chicoutimi

Cain Lamarre Casgrain Wells - Saguenay
#600, CP 5420, 255, rue Racine est, Chicoutimi, QC G7H 6J6
Tél: 418-545-4580; *Téléc:* 418-549-9590
info@clcw.ca
www.clcw.qc.ca
Profile: 31 Lawyers
Environmental Lawyers:
Jean-Sébastien Bergeron, Droit de l'environnement
jean.sebastien.bergeron@clcw.ca
Richard Bergeron, Associé, Droit de la construction
richard.bergeron@clcw.ca
Karine Boies, Droit de l'environnement
karine.boies@clcw.ca
François Bouchard, Associé, Droit de l'environnement
francois.bouchard@clcw.ca
Raynald Brassard, Santé
raynald.brassard@clcw.ca
Louis Coulombe, Associé, Droit de la construction
louis.coulombe@clcw.ca
Jean-François Delisle, Droit de l'environnement
jean.francois.delisle@clcw.ca
Chantal Lavallée, Associée, Santé
chantal.lavallee@clcw.ca
Marie-Claude Néron, Santé
marie.claude.neron@clcw.ca
Annie Tremblay, Santé; Droit de la construction
annie.tremblay@clcw.ca
Dominic Tremblay, Droit de l'environnement
dominic.tremblay@clcw.ca
Guy Wells, Associé, Santé
guy.wells@clcw.ca

Drummondville

Cain Lamarre Casgrain Wells - Drummondville
#201, 330, rue Cormier, Drummondville, QC J2C 8B3
Tél: 819-477-2544; *Téléc:* 819-477-4343
info@clcw.ca
www.clcw.qc.ca
Profile: 10 Lawyers
Environmental Lawyers:
Marc Boisselle, Associé directeur régional, Droit de la construction
marc.boisselle@clcw.ca
Jean-François Brouillard, Associé, Litige de la construction
jean.francois.brouillard@clcw.ca
Maurice Laplante, Environnement
maurice.laplante@clcw.ca

Gatineau

Beaudry, Bertrand, s.e.n.c.r.l.
#107, 160, boul de l'Hôpital, Gatineau, QC J8T 8J1
Tel: 819-770-4880; *Fax:* 819-595-4979
www.beaudry-bertrand.com
Profile: 1 Office, Founded in: 1929
Legal services are available in the areas of environmental & planning, municipal, & labour & employment law.
Environmental Lawyers:
Joan Archer-Cournoyer, Municipal Law
819-770-4880
jacournoyer@beaudry-bertrand.com
Guy Bélanger, Municipal Law
gbelanger@beaudry-bertrand.com
Darquise Jolicoeur, Partner, Environmental cases
djolicoeur@beaudry-bertrand.com
Joelle Mauraises, Municipal Law
jmaurais@beaudry-bertrand.com
Pierre McMartin, Construction Law
pmcmartin@beaudry-bertrand.com

Joliette

Bélanger, Sauvé
#101, 574, rue Saint-Viateur, Joliette, QC J6E 3B6
Tel: 450-755-3081; *Fax:* 450-755-6721
info@belangersauve.com
www.belangersauve.com
Profile: 4 Offices, 73 Lawyers, Founded in: 1967
Environmental Lawyers:
Denis Beaupré, Environmental Law; Land Use and Development
450-755-3011
dbeaupre@belangersauve.com
Yves Chaîné, Environmental Law
450-755-3011
ychaine@belangersuave.com

Lac-Mégantic

Monty Coulombe s.e.n.c. - Lac-Mégantic
5109, rue Frontenac, Lac-Mégantic, QC G6B 1H2
Tel: 819-583-3833; *Fax:* 819-583-5673
www.montycoulombe.com
Robert Giguère, Environmental Law; Municipal Law; Construction Law; Labour & Employment
819-583-3833
rgiguere@axion.ca
Marie-Éve Maillé, Environmental Law; Municipal Law
819-583-3833
memaille@axion.ca

Montréal

Bélanger, Sauvé
#1700, 1, Place Ville Marie, Montréal, QC H3B 2C1
Tel: 514-878-3081; *Fax:* 514-878-3053
info@belangersauve.com
www.belangersauve.com
Profile: 4 Offices, 73 Lawyers, Founded in: 1967
Environmental Lawyers:
Sylvain Bélair
sbelair@belangersauve.com
Michel Cantin
514-878-3089
mcantin@belangersauve.com

Yvon Denault
514-878-3089
ydenault@belangersauve.com
Alain-Claude Desforges
acdesforges@belangersauve.com
Marc Lalonde
514-878-3089
mlalonde@belangersauve.com
Marc Lapierrière
514-878-3089
Diane Larose
514-878-3089
dlarose@belangersauve.com
Pierre LePage
514-878-3089
plepage@belangersauve.com
Pierre B. Paquin
514-878-3089
pbpaquin@belangersauve.com

Borden Ladner Gervais LLP - Montréal
#900, 1000, rue de La Gauchetière ouest, Montréal, QC H3B 5H4
Tel: 514-879-1212; *Fax:* 514-954-1905
info@blg.com
www.blg.com
Profile: 123 Lawyers

Cain Lamarre Casgrain Wells - Montréal
#2780, 630, boul René-Lévesque ouest, Montréal, QC H3B 1S6
Tél: 514-393-4580; *Téléc:* 514-393-9590
info@clcw.ca
www.clcw.qc.ca
Profile: 30 Lawyers
Environmental Lawyers:
François Lamarre, Droit de la construction
francois.lamarre@clcw.ca
Mario Proulx, Droit de la construction
mario.proulx@clcw.ca
Sylvain Toupin, Santé et sécurité du travail
sylvain.toupin@clcw.ca
André Tremblay, Droit de la santé
andre.tremblay@clcw.ca
Marie-Josée Trudeau, Environnement; Agroalimentaire
marie.josee.trudeau@clcw.ca

Daigneault, avocats inc.
#400, Place D'Youville, 353, rue Saint-Nicolas, Montréal, QC H2Y 2P1
Tél: 514-985-2929; *Téléc:* 514-985-0595
Ligne sans frais: 888-228-5834
enviro@daigneaultinc.com
www.daigneaultinc.com
Profile: 1 Office, 4 Lawyers, Founded in: 2001
The firm specializes in environmental, resource, & land-use law.

Davies Ward Phillips & Vineberg S.E.N.C.R.L., s.r.l.
1501, av McGill College, 26e étage, Montréal, QC H3A 3N9
Tél: 514-841-6400; *Téléc:* 514-841-6499
Ligne sans frais: 888-841-6400
www.dwpv.com
Profile: 85 Lawyers,
Environmental Law; Environmental Transactions; Energy Law; Energy Transactions; Regulatory & Compliance; Climate Change & Emission Trading; Contaminated Sites; Natural Resources Projects; Renewable Energy Industry; Oil & Gas Industry; Hydroelectric Industry; Nuclear Industry

Davis LLP - Montréal
#1400, 1501, av McGill College, Montréal, QC H3A 3M8
Tél: 514-392-1991; *Téléc:* 514-392-1999
www.davis.ca
Profile: 10 Lawyers
Environmental Lawyers:
Julien Archambault, Municipal law
514-392-8446
jarchambault@davis.ca
Peter Riddell, Environmental law; mining, energy and utilities
514-392-8413
priddell@davis.ca
David W. Rothschild, Environmental law
514-392-8401
drothschild@davis.ca

Dentons Canada LLP - Montreal
#3900, 1, Place Ville-Marie, Montréal, QC H3B 4M7
Tel: 514-878-8800; *Fax:* 514-866-2241
www.dentons.com
Profile: 90 Lawyers,
The firm provides legal services in the areas of Construction & Infrastructure Law; Forest Products; Hydroelectric Energy; Mining Law; & Natural Resources Law
Environmental Lawyers:
Jean Bazin, Q.C., Environmental & Natural Resources; Aboriginal Law; Energy; Business Strategies
514-878-8804
jean.bazin@dentons.com
Alexandre Boileau, Construction
514-878-5836
alexandre.boileau@dentons.com
Michel A. Brunet, Construction
514-878-8832
michel.brunet@dentons.com
Mathilde Carrière, Energy; Construction
514-878-5823
mathilde.carriere@dentons.com
Marie-Hélène Dufour, Construction
514-878-5876
m-h.dufour@dentons.com
Jean-Pierre Dépelteau, Energy, Construction
514-878-8814
j-p.depelteau@dentons.com
Jean Groleau, Construction
514-878-8851
jean.groleau@dentons.com
Mélanie Jacques, Construction
514-878-5869
melanie.jacques@dentons.com
Gentiane Joyal, Environment & Natural Resources
514-878-5826
gentiane.joyal@dentons.com
Serge Lalonde, Energy; Litigation; Construction
514-878-5815
serge.lalonde@dentons.com
John F. Lemieux, Aboriginal Law
514-878-8811
john.lemieux@dentons.com
Stephen Lloyd, Aboriginal Law
514-878-5831
stephen.lloyd@dentons.com
Nicolas Roy, Energy
514-878-5861
nicolas.roy@dentons.com
Gil Rémillard, Counsel, Environment & Natural Resources; Litigation
514-878-8864
gil.remillard@dentons.com
Charles R. Spector, Energy, Municipal
514-878-8847
charles.spector@dentons.com
Jean-François Vézina, Construction
514-878-8885
j-f.vezina@dentons.com
Margaret Weltrowska, Construction
514-878-5841
margaret.weltrowska@dentons.com

Fasken Martineau - Montréal
#3700, Tour de la Bourse, CP 242, 800, place Victoria, Montréal, QC H4Z 1E9
Tel: 514-397-7400; *Fax:* 514-397-7600
Toll-Free: 800-361-6266
montreal@fasken.com
www.fasken.com
Profile: 175 Lawyers, Founded in: 1907
Environmental Lawyers:
Marie-Claude Bellemare
514-397-7571
mbellemare@mtl.fasken.com
Luc Bourbonnais, Energy, Environmental and Regulatory
514-397-4356
lbourbonnais@mtl.fasken.com
Florence Dagicour, Environmental Law; Climate change; Nuclear Law
514-397-5236
fdagicour@mtl.fasken.com
André Durocher, Partner, Environmental Law; Municipal Law; Pharmaceutical Law; Aboriginal Law
514-397-7495
adurocher@mtl.fasken.com
Gaël C. Gravenor, Energy, Environmental & Regulatory
514-397-7524
ggravenor@mtl.fasken.com
Shelley L. Kath
514-397-5236
skath@mtl.fasken.com
Charles Kazaz, Environmental Law; Waste Management; Mining
514-397-4348
ckazaz@tor.fasken.com
Pierre B. Meunier, Environmental Law; Energy Regulatory Law
514-397-4380
pmeunier@mtl.fasken.com
André Turmel, Energy and Climate Change Law
514-397-5141
aturmel@mtl.fasken.com

Gowling Lafleur Henderson S.E.N.C.R.L./LLP
#3700, 1, Place Ville Marie, 37e étage, Montréal, QC H3B 3P4
Tel: 514-878-9641; *Fax:* 514-878-1450
Profile: 88 Lawyers,
Environmental Law; Energy Law; Aboriginal Law; Climate Change; Infrastructure; Regulatory & Compliance
Environmental Lawyers:
Denis Blanchette, Aboriginal Law; Environmental Law
514-392-9445
denis.blanchette@gowlings.com
Douglas W. Clarke, Climate Change; Greenhouse Gas Emissions Regulatory; Carbon Finance; Technology Industry & CleanTech; Wind Farm Project Finance
514-392-9518
douglas.clarke@gowlings.com
Jean-Sébastien Clément, Aboriginal Law; Natural Resources Law; Forestry related Legal Matters; Environmental Law; Class Actions; Government Affairs
514-392-9567
jean-sebastien.clement@gowlings.com
François Dandonneau, Aboriginal Law; First Nations & Hydro-Québec Matters
514-392-9503
francois.dandonneau@gowlings.com
Paul R. Granda, Environmental Law; Regulatory & Compliance; Brownfield Redevelopment; Environmental Management Systems; Waste Management Industry; Oil Industry; Mining Industry; Chemical Industry; Forestry Industry; Professional Liability
514-392-9598
paul.granda@gowlings.com
John Hurley, Aboriginal Law; Environmental Law; Energy Law; Infrastructure; Regulatory; Government Affairs; Natural Resources Law; Power Project Matters
514-392-9431
john.hurley@gowlings.com
Pierre Legault, Energy Law; Electricity & Power Generation Matters; Power Transmission Agreements; Regulatory
514-392-9599
pierre.legault@gowlings.com
Emmanuel Manolakis, Biomass Conversion; Biotechnology; Alternative Fuels
514-392-9592
emmanuel.manolakis@gowlings.com
Charles-Antoine Robitaille, Infrastructure; Energy Law; Energy Projects; Construction Law; Natural Resources Industry
514-392-9584
charlesantoine.robitaille@gowlings.com

Heenan Blaikie LLP - Montréal
#2500, 1250, boul René-Lévesque ouest, Montréal, QC H3B 4Y1
Tel: 514-846-1212; *Fax:* 514-846-3427
www.heenanblaikie.com
www.twitter.com/heenanblaikie,
www.linkedin.com/company/heenan-blaikie
Profile: 10 Offices, 565 Lawyers, Founded in: 1973
Environmental Lawyers:
Marcel M.A. Aubut, Partner, Construction; Energy
514-846-2326
maubut@heenan.ca
Poupak Bahamin, Partner, Natural Resources; Mining
514-846-2377
pbahamin@heenan.ca
Geneviève Beaudin, Occupational Health & Safety
514-846-2393
gbeaudin@heenan.ca
Marie-Claude Bellemare, Partner, Environmental Law; Energy; Natural Resources

514-846-7224
mcbellemare@heenan.ca
Max R. Bernard, Partner, Construction; Real estate
514-846-2216
mbernard@heenan.ca
Peter M. Blaikie, Founding Partner, Construction
514-846-2328
pblaikie@heenan.ca
Robert Bonhomme, National Co-managing Partner, Occupational Health & Safety
514-846-2260
rbonhomme@heenan.ca
Jacques Bouchard Jr., Partner, Mining
514-846-2252
jbouchard@heenan.ca
Amélie Bélisle, Occupational Health & Safety
514-846-2224
abelisle@heenan.ca
Jean E. Clerk, Partner, Transportation
514-846-2262
jclerk@heenan.ca
Magali Cournoyer-Proulx, Partner, Health
514-846-2292
mproulx@heenan.ca
Marie Cousineau, Occupational Health & Safety
514-846-2346
mcousineau@heenan.ca
Christophe De Koster, Partner, Energy; Not-For-Profit Organizations
514-846-4760
cdekoster@heenan.ca
Ilan Dunsky, Partner, Energy; Natural Resources; Transportation
514-846-4763
idunsky@heenan.ca
Marie-Christine Frenette, Energy
514-846-2334
mcfrenette@heenan.ca
Simon Gagné, Partner, Health
514-846-2277
simon@heenan.ca
Eva Gazurek, Natural Resources; Mining
514-846-2322
egazurek@heenan.ca
Joel Goldberg, Partner, Environmental Law; Construction
514-846-2310
jgoldberg@heenan.ca
Lucie Guimond, Partner, Occupational Health & Safety
514-846-2304
lguimond@heenan.ca
Marie-Josée Hogue, Partner, Health
514-846-2201
mhogue@heenan.ca
Tibor Holländer, Partner, Health
514-846-2384
thollander@heenan.ca
Véronique Iezzoni, Partner, Health
514-846-2230
viezzoni@heenan.ca
David Joanisse, Partner, Construction Litigation
514-846-2261
djoanisse@heenan.ca
Pierre-Marc Johnson, Counsel, Environmental Issues; Health
514-846-2200
pjohnson@heenan.ca
Manon Jolicoeur, Partner, Construction
514-846-2220
mjolicoeur@heenan.ca
Kosta Kostic, Partner, Mining
514-846-2395
kkostic@heenan.ca
Simon Labarge, Occupational Health & Safety
514-846-7248
slaberge@heenan.ca
Pierre Langlois, Partner, Environmental Law; Natural Resources; Mining
514-846-7234
planglois@heenan.ca
Marie-Christine Lauzone, Occupational Health & Safety
514-846-2290
mlauzon@heenan.ca
Francine Legault, Partner, Occupational Health & Safety
514-846-2348
flegault@heenan.ca
Eric M. Levy, Partner, Mining
514-846-2256
elevy@heenan.ca
Eric Maldoff, Partner, Health; Aboriginal Law
514-846-2249
emaldoff@heenan.ca
Bruce McNiven, Partner, Health
514-846-2244
bmcniven@heenan.ca
Patrick A. Molinari, Health
514-846-2343
pmolinari@heenan.ca
Gary D.D. Morrison, Partner, Construction
514-846-2268
gmorrison@heenan.ca
Dominique Ménard, Partner, Construction Litigation
514-846-2238
domenard@heenan.ca
Alexandre Panneton, Construction Litigation
514-846-2246
apanneton@heenan.ca
Claude Paquet, Partner, Environmental Law
514-846-2378
cpaquet@heenan.ca
Rhéaume Perreault, Partner, Health; Occupational Health & Safety
514-846-2306
rperreaul@heenan.ca
Sylvain Poirier, Partner, Health
514-846-2273
spoirier@heenan.ca
Michel Poirier, Partner, Land Use; Environmental Law; Municipal Law
514-846-2295
mpoirier@heenan.ca
Normand Quesnel, Partner, Construction
514-846-2217
nquesnel@heenan.ca
Karen M. Rogers, Partner, Construction Litigation; Real Estate
514-846-2210
krogers@heenan.ca.ca
Mélanie Sauriol, Occupational Health & Safety
514-846-2281
msauriol@heenan.ca
Sarah-Anne Savoie, Health
514-846-7055
sasavoie@heenan.ca
Lampros Stougiannos, Energy
514-846-6882
lstougiannos@heenan.ca
Chantal Sylvestre, Partner, Energy; Real Estate
514-846-2344
csylvestr@heenan.ca
Charles Olivier Thibault, Health
514-846-2276
cothibeault@heenan.ca
Philippe Tremblay, Partner, Construction Litigation
514-846-2237
ptremblay@heenan.ca
Stephan H. Trihey, Partner, Construction Litigation
514-846-7228
strihey@heenan.ca
Yves Turgeon, Partner, Natural Resources; Construction
514-846-2818
yturgeon@heenan.ca
Virginie Vigeant, Occupational Health & Safety
514-846-2285
vvigeant@heenan.ca
Neil Wiener, Partner, Mining
514-846-2208
nwiener@heenan.ca
Jeremy Wisniewski, Construction Litigation
514-846-2274
jwisniewski@heenan.ca

Hutchins Caron & Associés

#700, 485 rue McGill, Montréal, QC H2Y 2H4
Tel: 514-849-2403; *Fax:* 514-849-4907
Toll-Free: 877-849-2403
admin@hutchinslegal.ca
www.hutchinslegal.ca
Profile: 2 Offices, 5 Lawyers,
Le cabinet possède près de trente années d'expérience, notamment dans les domaines du droit autochtone et du droit de l'environnement.
Environmental Lawyers:
Monique Caron, Droit autochtone; Droit de l'environnement
mcaron@hutchinslegal.ca
Julie Corry, Droit autochtone; Droit de l'environnement
jcorry@hutchinslegal.ca
Lysane Cree, Droit autochtone; Droit de l'environnement
lcree@hutchinslegal.ca
Peter W. Hutchins, Associé, Droit de l'environnement; Droit autochtone
phutchins@hutchinslegal.ca
David Kalmakoff, Droit autochtone; Droit de l'environnement
dkalmakoff@hutchinslegal.ca

Joli-Coeur Lacasse Avocats - Montréal

#900, 2001, av McGill College, Montréal, QC H3A 1G1
Tel: 514-871-2800; *Fax:* 514-871-3933
infos@jolicoeurlacasse.com
www.jolicoeurlacasse.com
Profile: 32 Lawyers,
Joli-Coeur Lacasse's main office is located in Québec. At the Montréal office, legal advice & representation are available in the areas of Aboriginal, municipal, construction, & health law.
Environmental Lawyers:
Hugo Beaulieu, Construction
hugo.beaulieu@jolicoeurlacasse.com
Josée Brière, Construction Law
josee.briere@jolicoeurlacasse.com
Marie-Josée Corriveau, Municipal Law
marie-josee.corriveau@jolicoeurlacasse.com
Jean-François Demers, Construction Law
jean-francois.demers@jolicoeurlacasse.com
Daniel L'Africain, Construction Law
daniel.lafricain@jolicoeurlacasse.com
Manon Lavoie, Aboriginal Law; Administrative Law
manon.lavoie@jolicoeurlacasse.com
Miriam Morissette, Health Law
miriam.morissette@jolicoeurlacasse.com
Jean-François Nadon
jean-francois.nadon@jolicoeurlacasse.com

Lamarre Perron Lambert Vincent

#200, 480, boul St-Laurent, Montréal, QC H2Y 3Y7
Tél: 514-798-1515; *Téléc:* 514-798-5599
info@lplv.com
www.lplv.com
Profile: 1 Office, 6 Lawyers, Founded in: 2003
Lamarre Perron Lambert Vincent was created when Roy Perron Lambert merged with Lamarre Trépanier Vincent in 2003. Lawyers have experience & expertise in labour law, including ocuupational health & safety.
Environmental Lawyers:
Chantal Labelle, Construction Law
514-798-1814
c.labelle@lplv.com
Paul Lamarre, Partner, Construction
514-798-1918
p.lamarre@lplv.com
Jean-Martin Lambert, Partner, Occupational Health & Safety
514-798-1588
jm.lambert@lplv.com

Langlois Kronström Desjardins

1002, rue Sherbrooke ouest, 28e étage, Montréal, QC H3A 3L6
Tel: 514-842-9512; *Fax:* 514-845-6573
Toll-Free: 888-650-7001
info@lkd.ca
www.langloiskronstromdesjardins.com
Profile: 33 Lawyers
Environmental Lawyers:
Serge Amar, Associé, Droit de la construction; Santé
514-282-7828
serge.amar@lkd.ca
Gerry Apostolatos, Associé, Droit de la construction
514-282-7831
gerry.apostolatos@lkd.ca
Martine Bergeron, Santé
514-282-7836
martine.bergeron@lkd.ca
Yann Bernard, Associé, Santé & sécurité au travail
514-282-7838
yann.bernard@lkd.ca
Annie Bourgeois, Santé & sécurité au travail
514-282-7834
annie.bourgeois@lkd.ca
Louise Boutin, Associée, Santé; Droit de la construction
514-282-7833
louise.boutin@lkd.ca

Stefan Chripounoff, Énergie & ressources naturelles
514-282-7807
stefan.chripounoff@lkd.ca
Catherine Galardo, Santé
514-282-7810
catherine.galardo@lkd.ca
Pierre Galardo, Associé, Santé; Urbanisme
514-282-7819
pierre.galardo@lkd.ca
Céline Garneau, Associée, Droit de la construction
514-282-7818
celine.garneau@lkd.ca
Alexander Herman, Santé
514-282-7801
alexander.herman@lkd.ca
Tina Hobday, Associée, Énergie & ressources naturelles
514-282-7816
tina.hobday@lkd.ca
Michel Huart, Énergie & ressources naturelles; Environment
514-282-7829
michel.huart@lkd.ca
Dimitri Maniatis, Associé, Énergie & ressources naturelles
514-282-7832
dimitri.maniatis@lkd.ca
Marie-Geneviève Masson, Associée, Santé
514-282-7821
marie-genevieve.masson@lkd.ca
René Paquette, Associé, Santé & sécurité au travail
514-282-7826
rene.paquette@lkd.ca
Marc-André Sansregret, Associé, Droit de la construction
514-282-7839
marc-andre.sansregret@lkd.ca
Rébecca St-Pierre, Santé
514-282-7824
rebecca.st-pierre@lkd.ca

Lapointe Rosenstein Marchand Melançon

#1400, 1250, boul René-Lévesque ouest, Montréal, QC H3B 5E9
Tel: 514-925-6300; *Fax:* 514-925-9001
Toll-Free: 800-728-6228
www.lrmm.com
Profile: 1 Office, 70 Lawyers, Founded in: 1966
Environmental Lawyers:
Frédéric Blanchette, Associé, Droit de la construction
514-925-6375
frederic.blanchette@lrmm.com
Louis P. Brien, Associé, Droit de la construction
514-925-6348
louis.brien@lrmm.com
Jeanne Fortin, Associée, Droit de l'énergie
514-925-6311
jeanne.fortin@lrmm.com
Guillaume Hébert, Associé, Droit de la construction
514-925-6378
guillaume.hebert@lrmm.com
Paul A. Melançon, Associé, Droit de la construction
514-925-6308
paul.melancon@lrmm.com
Michel G. Ménard, Associé, Droit de la construction
514-925-6328
michel.menard@lrmm.com
Bertrand Paiement, Associé, Droit de la construction
514-925-6309
bertrand.paiement@lrmm.com
Mark M. Rosenstein, Associé, Droit de l'énergie
514-925-6335
mark.rosenstein@lrmm.com
André Rousseau, Associé, Droit de la construction
514-925-6389
andre.rousseau@lrmm.com
Stéphane Roy, Associé, Droit de la construction; Droit de l'énergie
514-925-6349
stephane.roy@lrmm.com
Michel Tourangeau, Associé, Droit de la construction
514-925-6317
michel.tourangeau@lrmm.com
Ruth Veilleux, Associée, Droit de la construction
514-925-6329
ruth.veilleux@lrmm.com

Lavery, de Billy - Montréal

#4000, 1, Place Ville-Marie, Montréal, QC H3B 4M4
Tel: 514-871-1522; *Fax:* 514-871-8977
info@lavery.ca
www.lavery.ca
facebook.com/LaverydeBilly, twitter.com/LaverydeBilly, www.linkedin.com/company/797440?trk=tyah
Profile: 3 Offices, 169 Lawyers, Founded in: 1913
Environmental Lawyers:
Pierre-L. Baribeau, Health Law
514-877-2965
pbaribeau@lavery.ca
Loïc Berdnikoff, Health Law
514-877-2981
lberdnikoff@lavery.ca
Yvan Biron, Environmental, Energy & Natural Resources Law
514-877-2910
ybiron@lavery.ca
Michel Blouin, Mining Law
514-877-3041
mblouin@lavery.ca
Monique Brassard, Health Law
514-877-2942
mbrassard@lavery.ca
Anne Bélanger, Health Law
514-877-3091
abelanger@lavery.ca
Marie-Claude Cantin, Partner, Construction & Surety Law
514-877-3006
mccantin@lavery.ca
Louis Charette, Partner, Transportation Law
514-877-2946
lcharette@lavery.ca
Melanie Chartrand, Mining Law
514-878-5663
mchartrand@lavery.ca
Daniel Alain Dagenais, Partner, Construction & Surety Law; Mining Law
514-877-2924
dadagenais@lavery.ca
Marc Dagenais, Partner, Environmental, Energy & Natural Resources Law; Mining Law
514-877-2995
mdagenais@lavery.ca
Pierre Denis, Partner, Mining Law
514-877-2908
pdenis@lavery.ca
Raymond Doray, Partner, Health Law
514-877-2913
rdoray@lavery.ca
Geneviève Fournier, Mining Law
514-877-3055
gfournier@lavery.ca
Philippe Frère, Partner, Aboriginal Law
514-877-2978
pfrere@lavery.ca
Marie-Andrée Gagnon, Health Law
514-877-3011
magagnon@lavery.ca
Nicolas Gagnon, Partner, Construction & Surety Law
514-877-3046
ngagnon@lavery.ca
Jocelyne Gagné, Partner, Construction & Surety Law
514-878-5542
jgagne@lavery.ca
Julie Grondin, Construction & Surety Law
514-877-2957
jgrondin@lavery.ca
Benjamin David Gross, Partner, Mining Law
514-877-2983
bgross@lavery.ca
Jean Hébert, Partner, Construction & Surety Law
514-877-2926
jhebert@lavery.ca
Maude Lafortune-Bélair, Health Law
514-877-3077
mlafortunebelair@lavery.ca
Jean-François Lepage, Partner, Health Law
514-877-2970
jflepage@lavery.ca
Jean-Philippe Lincourt, Transportation Law; Environmental Law
514-877-2922
jplincourt@lavery.ca
Anne-Marie Lévesque, Health Law
514-877-2944
amlevesque@lavery.ca
Zeïneb Mellouli, Environmental, Energy & Natural Resources Law
514-877-3056
zmellouli@lavery.ca
Véronique Morin, Health Law
514-877-3082
vmorin@lavery.ca
Philip Nolan, Partner, Mining Law
514-877-2914
pnolan@lavery.ca
Jacques Nols, Partner, Health Law
514-877-2932
jnols@lavery.ca
Frédéric Pagé, Environmental, Energy & Natural Resources Law; Mining Law; Aboriginal Law
514-877-3095
fpage@lavery.ca
Jacques Perron, Partner, Transportation Law
514-877-2905
jperron@lavery.ca
Martin Pichette, Partner, Construction & Surety Law; Transportation Law
514-877-3032
mpichette@lavery.ca
Sophie Prégent, Environmental, Energy & Natural Resources Law; Aboriginal Law
514-877-2948
spregent@lavery.ca
Mathieu Quenneville, Environmental, Energy & Natural Resources Law; Aboriginal Law
514-877-3087
mquenneville@lavery.ca
Patrice Racicot, Partner, Construction & Surety Law
514-878-5567
pracicot@lavery.ca
Dina Raphaël, Partner, Construction & Surety Law
514-877-3013
draphael@lavery.ca
Carl M. Ravinsky, Partner, Mining Law
514-878-5594
cravinsky@lavery.ca
Michel Servant, Partner, Mining Law
514-877-2915
mservant@lavery.ca
Virginie Simard, Health Law
514-877-2931
vsimard@lavery.ca
Dominique Vallières, Construction & Surety Law
514-877-2917
dvallieres@lavery.ca
Emil Vidrascu, Partner, Construction & Surety Law
514-877-3007
evidrascu@lavery.ca
Luc Villiard, Partner, Construction & Surety Law
514-877-2951
lvilliard@lavery.ca
Sébastien Vézina, Partner, Mining Law
514-877-2964
svezina@lavery.ca
Michel Yergeau, Partner, Environmental, Energy & Natural Resources Law; Aboriginal Law
514-877-2911
myergeau@lavery.ca
Philippe d'Etcheverry, Construction & Surety Law
514-877-2996
pdetcheverry@lavery.ca

McCarthy Tétrault LLP - Montréal

#2500, 1000, rue de la Gauchetière ouest, Montréal, QC H3B 0A2
Tel: 514-397-4100; *Fax:* 514-875-6246
Toll-Free: 877-397-4100
info@mccarthy.ca
www.mccarthy.ca
Profile: 7 Offices, 142 Lawyers, Founded in: 1855
Biotechnology; Energy; Environmental; Municipal
Environmental Lawyers:
Julie Belley Perron, Environmental Law
514-397-5451
jbperron@mccarthy.ca
Ann M. Bigué, Energy; Aboriginal Rights; Environmental Assessment
514-397-4127
abigue@mccarthy.ca
Martin Boodman, Environmental Litigation
514-397-4117
mboodman@mccarthy.ca

Andrée-Claude Bérubé, Environmental Law; Environmental Aspects of Financial Transactions; Energy
514-397-5476
acberube@mccarthy.ca
Michel Gagné, General Counsel; Litigation
514-397-4204
mgagne@mccarthy.ca
Mira Gauvin, Environmental Law
514-397-4134
mgauvin@mccarthy.ca
Mira Gauvin, Environmental Law
514-397-4134
mgauvin@mccarthy.ca
François Grondin, Litigation; Business Transactions; Environmental Litigation
514-397-4283
fgrondin@mccarthy.ca
Jérémie-Nicolas Moisan, Environmental Litigation
514-397-7854
jnmoisan@mccarthy.ca
Ann-Marie Sheahan, Environmental Law; Climate Change; Mining; Oil & Gas
514-397-4212
amsheahan@mccarthy.ca
Chantal C. Tremblay, Environmental Litigation
514-397-4231
cctremblay@mccarthy.ca
Cindy Vaillancourt, Environmental Law
514-397-4177
cvaillancourt@mccarthy.ca

McMillan S.E.N.C.R.L., s.r.l. - Montréal

#2700, 1000, rue Sherbrooke ouest, Montréal, QC H3A 3G4
Tél: 514-987-5000; *Téléc:* 514-987-1213
info@mcmillan.ca
www.mcmillan.ca
Profile: 36 Lawyers, Founded in: 1951

Miller Thomson LLP - Montréal

#3700, 1000, rue de la Gauchetière ouest, Montréal, QC H3B 4W5
Tél: 514-875-5210; *Téléc:* 514-875-4308
Ligne sans frais: 888-875-5210
info@millerthomsonpouliot.com
www.millerthomson.com
Profile: 59 Lawyers, Founded in: 1952
Environmental Lawyers:
Lonnie Brodkin-Schneider, Associée, Santé
514-871-5449
lbschneider@millerthomsonpouliot.com
Christian J. Brossard, Associé, Litige construction
514-871-5407
cjbrossard@millerthomsonpouliot.com
Normand D'Amour, Associé, Litige construction
514-871-5487
ndamour@millerthomsonpouliot.com
Benoît Gascon, Associé, Industrie minière
514-871-5490
bgascon@millerthomsonpouliot.com
Adina-Cristina Georgescu, Environnement; Technologies vertes; Santé; Énergie et ressources naturelles
514-871-5494
acgeorgescu@millerthomsonpouliot.com
Luc Gratton, Associé, Technologies vertes; Production d'énergie
514-871-5482
lgratton@millerthomsonpouliot.com
Antonio Iacovelli, Litige construction
514-841-5483
aiacovelli@millerthomsonpouliot.com
Frank Mariage, Associé, Industrie minière
514-871-5446
mariage@millerthomsonpouliot.com
J. Brent Muir, Associé, Industrie minière
514-871-5478
bmuir@millerthomsonpouliot.com
Marc Pothier, Associé, Industrie minière
514-871-5442
mpothier@millerthomsonpouliot.com
Louis-Michel Tremblay, Associé, Litige construction
514-871-5421
lmtremblay@millerthomsonpouliot.com
Mathieu Turcotte, Associé, Litige construction
514-871-5492
mturcotte@millerthonsonpouliot.com

Norton Rose Fulbright Canada LLP - Montréal

#2500, 1 Place Ville Marie, Montréal, QC H3B 1R1
Tél: 514-847-4747; *Téléc:* 514-286-5474
montreal@nortonrosefulbright.com
www.nortonrosefulbright.com/ca
twitter.com/NLegal_CA,
www.linkedin.com/company/nortonrosefulbright
Profile: 6 Offices, 585 Lawyers, Founded in: 1879
Environmental risk management, counsel, assistance in all forms of transactional matters, representation & litigation
Environmental Lawyers:
Jean R. Allard, Senior Partner, Infrastructure, Mining & Commodities
514-847-4400
jean.allard@nortonrosefulbright.com
R. Luc Beaulieu, Senior Partner, Infrastructure, Mining & Commodities
514-847-4428
luc.beaulieu@nortonrosefulbright.com
Dominic C. Belley, Partner, Energy; Infrastructure, Mining & Commodities
514-847-4318
dominic.belley@nortonrose.com
Jean G. Bertrand, Managing Partner, Aboriginal Law; Energy; Infrastructure, Mining & Commodities; Transportation; Administrative Law; Litigation
514-847-4401
jean.bertrand@nortonrosefulbright.com
Gregory B. Bordan, Partner, Construction & Engineering; Environment Safety & Planning; Litigation
514-847-4423
gregory.bordan@nortonrose.com
Robert G. Borduas, Partner, Mining & Resources; Infrastructure; Transportation; Energy
514-847-4524
robert.borduas@nortonrose.com
Danièle Boutet, Senior Partner, Energy; Infrastructure, Mining & Commodities; Transportation
514-847-4527
daniele.boutet@nortonrosefulbright.com
Jean-Philippe Brunet, Partner, Mining & Resources
514-847-4856
jeanphilippe.brunet@nortonrose.com
Michel G. Carle, Senior Partner, Infrastructure, Mining & Commodities; Transportation
514-847-4501
michel.carle@nortonrose.com
Jules Charette, Senior Partner, Energy; Infrastructure, Mining & Commodities
514-847-4450
jules.charette@nortonrose.com
Derek G. Chiasson, Partner, Infrastructure, Mining & Commodities
514-847-6114
derek.chiasson@nortonrose.com
Alexandra Daoud, Partner, Energy; Infrastructure, Mining & Commodities; Transportation
514-847-4333
alexandra.daoud@nortonrose.com
Thomas R.M. Davis, Partner, Energy; Infrastructure, Mining & Commodities; Nuclear
514-847-4857
thomas.davis@nortonrose.com
Richard L. Desgagnés, Partner, Energy; Infrastructure, Mining & Commodities; Transporation; PortsRoads; Shipping
514-847-4431
richard.desgagnes@nortonrose.com
Stephen L. Drymer, Partner, Climate Change; Energy; Infrastructure, Mining & Commodities; Oil & Gas
514-847-4606
stephen.drymer@nortonrose.com
Éric Dunberry, Partner, Construction & Engineering; Energy; Environment Safety & Planning; Mining; Nucelar
514-847-4492
eric.dunberry@nortonrose.com
Claudia Déry, Partner, Construction & Engineering
514-847-4607
claudia.dery@nortonrose.com
François Fontaine, Senior Partner, Climate Change; Environment Safety & Planning; Mining
514-847-4413
francois.fontaine@nortonrose.com
L. Yves Fortier, C.C., Q.C., Senior Partner, Energy; Infrastructure, Mining & Commodities
514-847-4740
yves.fortier@nortonrose.com
Denis Gascon, Partner, Infrastructure, Mining & Commodities; Transportation
514-847-4435
denis.gascon@nortonrose.com
Lukasz Granosik, Partner, Environment Safety & Planning; Infrastructure, Mining & Commodities
514-847-4996
lukasz.granosik@nortonrose.com
William Hesler, Q.C., Senior Partner, Construction & Engineering; Environment Safety & Planning
514-847-4510
william.hesler@nortonrose.com
Marie-Christine Hivon, Partner, Construction & Engineering; Energy; Environment Safety & Planning; Nuclear; Transportation
514-847-4805
marie-christine.hivon@nortonrose.com
Azim Hussain, Partner, Construction, Engineering & Infrastructure; Transportation
514-847-4827
azim.hussain@nortonrose.com
Pierre Hébert, Senior Partner, Energy; Infrastructure, Mining & Commodities
514-847-4474
pierre.hebert@nortonrose.com
Marie-Hélène Jetté, Partner, Environment Safety & Planning
514-847-4650
marie-helene.jette@nortonrose.com
Olivier F. Kott, Senior Partner, Construction & Engineering; Environment Safety & Planning; Energy
514-847-4445
olivier.kott@nortonrose.com
Amar Leclair-Ghosh, Partner, Energy; Infrastructure, Mining & Commodities
514-847-4612
amar.leclair-ghosh@nortonrose.com
Serge Levy, Partner, Infrastructure
514-847-6037
serge.levy@nortonrose.com
Miguel F. Manzano, Partner, Energy; Infrastructure, Miing & Commodities
514-847-4813
miguel.manzano@nortonrose.com
Catherine Martel, Partner, Environment Safety & Planning; Energy; Infrastructure, Mining & Commodities; Transportation
514-847-4987
catherine.martel@nortonrose.com
Jean-François Michaud, Partner, Construction & Engineering
514-847-4722
jean-francois.michaud@nortonrose.com
Brian Mulroney, P.C., C.C., LL.D., Senior Partner, Energy; Infrastructure, Mining & Commodities
514-847-4779
brian.mulroney@nortonrose.com
Sophie Perreault, Partner, Climate Change; Energy; Environment Safety & Planning
514-847-4810
sophie.perreault@nortonrose.com
Jean Piette, Senior Partner, Climate Change; Commodities; Energy; Mining & Resources; Nuclear
514-847-4584
jean.piette@nortonrose.com
Paul S. Prosterman, Partner, Environment Safety & Planning
514-847-4481
paul.prosterman@nortonrose.com
Bernard P. Quinn, Partner, Construction & Engineering; Energy; Mining; Infrastructure, Mining & Commodities
514-847-4518
bernard.quinn@nortonrose.com
Paul Raymond, Partner, Mining & Resources; Transportation
514-847-4479
paul.raymond@nortonrose.com
Jean-Charles René, Partner, Environment Safety & Planning
514-847-4609
jean-charles.rene@nortonrose.com
Sylvie Rodrigue, Partner, Environment Safety & Planning; Transportation
514-847-4559
sylvie.rodrigue@nortonrose.com
Michel G. Sylvestre, Senior Partner, Climate Change; Construction & Engineering; Environment Safety & Planning; Transportation
514-847-4460
michel.sylvestre@nortonrose.com
Martin Thériault, Partner, Energy; Infrastructure, Mining & Commodities; Transportation

514-847-4940
martin.theriault@nortonrose.com
Gilles Touchette, Senior Partner, Infrastructure, Mining & Commodities; Energy; Transportation
514-847-4532
gilles.touchette@nortonrose.com
Marc A. Tremblay, Partner, Energy; Transportation
514-847-4896
marc.tremblay@nortonrose.com
Marc Tremblay, Partner, Energy; Transportation
514-847-4896
marc.tremblay@nortonrose.com
Martin J. Valasek, Partner, CleanTech; Energy; Infrastructure, Mining & Commodities
514-847-4818
martin.valasek@nortonrose.com
Peter J. Wiazowski, Partner, Energy; Infrastructure, Mining & Commodities; Transportation
514-847-6047
peter.wiazowski@nortonrose.com

Osler, Hoskin & Harcourt S.E.N.C.R.L./LLP
#2100, 1000, rue de la Gauchetière ouest, Montréal, QC H3B 4W5
Tel: 514-904-8100; *Fax:* 514-904-8101
counsel@osler.com
www.osler.com
Profile: 66 Lawyers
Environmental Lawyers:
Nathalie Beauregard, Partner, Renewable Energy & Environmental Financing; Life Sciences
514-904-8121
nbeauregard@osler.com
Guy Lord, Partner, Life Sciences
514-904-8124
glord@osler.com
Karen Shaw, Life Sciences
514-904-5391
kshaw@osler.com

Robinson Sheppard Shapiro LLP
#4600, 800, Place Victoria, Montréal, QC H4Z 1H6
Tel: 514-878-2631; *Fax:* 514-878-1865
info@rsslex.com
www.rsslex.com
Profile: 2 Offices, 71 Lawyers, Founded in: 1921
Bureau de Quebec: #209, 686 Grande-Allée est, Québec, QC, G1R 2K5, 418-907-9445
Environmental Lawyers:
Jean Denis Boucher, Associé, Santé et sécurité au travail
514-393-4047
jdboucher@rsslex.com
Jacques Bélanger, Santé et sécurité au travail
514-393-4018
jbelanger@rsslex.com
France Dulude, Associée, Droit de la construction
514-393-4029
fdulude@rsslex.com
Jean-Marc Fortier, Associé, Ressources naturelles (minier)
514-393-7400
jmfortier@rsslex.com
Theodore Goloff, Associé, Santé et sécurité au travail
514-393-4007
tgoloff@rsslex.com
Marc Prévost, Associé, Droit de la construction
514-393-7453
mprevost@rsslex.com
Philippe-André Tessier, Associé, Santé et sécurité au travail
514-393-7454
patessier@rsslex.com

Stikeman Elliott LLP - Montréal
1155, boul René-Lévesque ouest, 40th Fl., Montréal, QC H3B 3V2
Tel: 514-397-3000; *Fax:* 514-397-3222
www.stikeman.com
Profile: 8 Offices, 491 Lawyers, Founded in: 1952
Environmental Lawyers:
Lev Alexeev, Droit minier; Énergie
514-397-2416
lalexeev@stikeman.com
Marc B. Barbeau, Associé, Foresterie et produits forestiers
514-397-3212
mbarbeau@stikeman.com
Bruno Barrette, Associé, Pharmaceutiques, biotechnologie et sciences de la vie
514-397-3297
bbarrette@stikeman.com
Marie-Andrée Beaudry, Associée, Énergie
514-397-3663
mabeaudry@stikeman.com
Olivier Boulva, Énergie
514-397-6488
oboulva@stikeman.com
Louis P. Bélanger, Associé, Litige en environnement
514-397-3078
lbelanger@stikeman.com
Jean Carrier, Associé, Droit de l'environnement; Droit minier; Énergie; Foresterie et produits forestiers
514-397-3101
jcarrier@stikeman.com
Edward B. Claxton, Associé, Pharmaceutiques, biotechnologie et sciences de la vie
514-397-3364
eclaxton@stikeman.com
Peter J. Cullen, Associé, Énergie
514-397-3135
pcullen@stikeman.com
Pierre-Paul Daunais, Litige en construction
514-397-2428
ppdaunais@stikeman.com
Marie-Claude David, Droit de l'environnement
514-397-3298
mcdavid@stikeman.com
Michel Décary, c.r., Associé, Litige en construction
514-397-3099
mdecary@stikeman.com
Myriam Fortin, Droit de l'environnement; Énergie; Droit minier
514-397-3270
mfortin@stikeman.com
Patrick Girard, Associé, Énergie; Litige en construction; Litige en environnement
514-397-3657
pgirard@stikeman.com
Kevin Kyte, Associé, Foresterie et produits forestiers; Pharmaceutiques, biotechnologie et sciences de la vie
514-397-3346
kkyte@stikeman.com
Pierre-Yves Leduc, Associé, Pharmaceutiques, biotechnologie et sciences de la vie
514-397-3696
pyleduc@stikeman.com
Christine Legé, Énergie
514-397-6465
clege@stikeman.com
Valérie Mac-Seing, Associée, Droit de la construction
514-397-2425
vmacseing@stikeman.com
Yves Martineau, Associé, Litige en construction
514-397-3380
ymartineau@stikeman.com
David Massé, Droit minier
514-397-3685
dmasse@stikeman.com
Nathalie Mercier-Filteau, Litige en construction
514-397-3691
nmercierfilteau@stikeman.com
Éric Mongeau, Associé, Droit de la construction; Énergie
514-397-3043
emongeau@stikeman.com
Bertrand P. Ménard, Associé, Droit de la construction; Énergie
514-397-3147
bmenard@stikeman.com
Charles Nadeau, Associé, Litige en construction
514-397-3388
cnadeau@stikeman.com
François H. Ouimet, Associé, Droit de la construction
514-397-3057
fouimet@stikeman.com
Frédéric Pierrestiger, Associé, Litige en construction
514-397-3278
fpierrestiger@stikeman.com
Erik Richer La Flèche, Associé, Énergie renouvelable; Droit de la construction; Droit minier
514-397-3109
ericherlafleche@stikeman.com
Steeve Robitaille, Associé, Foresterie et produits forestiers
514-397-3024
srobitaille@stikeman.com
Richard J. Rusk, Associé, Litige en environnement
514-397-3268
rrusk@stikeman.com
Sébastien Thomas, Droit de la construction
514-397-3336
sthomas@stikeman.com
claire Zikovsky, Associée, Énergie
514-397-3340
czikovsky@stikeman.com
Alix d'Anglejan-Chatillon, Associée, Échange de droits d'émission et changements climatiques
514-397-3240
adanglejan@stikeman.com

Torys LLP - Montréal
#1919, 1 Place Ville Marie, Montréal, QC H3B 2C3
Tel: 514-868-5600; *Fax:* 514-868-5700
www.torysmontreal.com
Profile: Founded in: 2013

Plessisville

Cain Lamarre Casgrain Wells - Plessisville
2014, rue Saint-Calixte, Plessisville, QC G6L 1R9
Tél: 819-362-6699; *Téléc:* 819-362-2121
info@clcw.ca
www.clcw.qc.ca
Profile: 1 Lawyers

Québec

Cain Lamarre Casgrain Wells - Québec
#440, 580, Grande Allée est, Québec, QC G1R 2K2
Tél: 418-522-4580; *Téléc:* 418-529-9590
info@clcw.ca
www.clcw.qc.ca
Profile: 35 Lawyers
Environmental Lawyers:
Mélanie Boivin, Droit de la santé
melanie.boivin@clcw.ca
Anne-Marie Béchard, Santé et sécurité du travail
anne.marie.bechard@clcw.ca
Pierre Caouette, Santé et sécurité du travail
pierre.caouette@clcw.ca
Hélène Carrier, Droit de la santé
helene.carrier@clcw.ca
Geneviève Carrier, Santé et sécurité du travail
genevieve.carrier@clcw.ca
Hubert Crépault, Droit minier
hubert.crepault@clcw.ca
Normand Drolet, Associé, Santé et sécurité du travail
normand.drolet@clcw.ca
Raymond Gouge, Santé et sécurité au travail
raymond.gouge@clcw.ca
Marie-Douce Huard, Droit de la construction
marie.douce.huard@clcw.ca
Karl Jessop, Associé, Santé et sécurité du travail
karl.jessop@clcw.ca
Dominique Pelletier-Giroux, Droit de la santé
dominique.pelletier.giroux@clcw.ca
Simon Rainville, Droit de la construction
simon.rainville@clcw.ca

Fasken Martineau - Québec
#800, 140, Grande Allée est, Québec, QC G1R 5M8
Tel: 418-640-2000; *Fax:* 418-647-2455
Toll-Free: 800-463-2827
quebec@fasken.com
www.fasken.com
Profile: 41 Lawyers, Founded in: 1983
Environmental Services: Environmental, Energy & Natural Resource Law
Environmental Lawyers:
Jean M. Gagné, Mining; Forestry
418-640-2010
jgagne@qc.fasken.com
Martin R. Gagné, Mining; Forestry
418-640-2001
mrgagne@qc.fasken.com
Annick Gilbert, Municipal Law
agilbert@qc.fasken.com
Ianny Xénopoulos, Mining; Forestry
418-640-2020
ixenopoulos@qc.fasken.com

Grondin, Poudrier, Bernier
#900, 500, Grande Allée est, Québec, QC G1R 2J7
Tél: 418-683-3000; *Téléc:* 418-683-8784
Ligne sans frais: 800-463-5172

gpb@grondinpoudrier.com
www.grondinpoudrier.com
Profile: 2 Offices, 36 Lawyers, Founded in: 1948
Environmental Lawyers:
Denis Bradet, Droit de la santé et de la sécurite du travail
dbradet@grondinpoudrier.com
Marie-José Côté, Droit de la construction
mjcote@grondinpoudrier.com
Marc Delâge, Environnement, Droit du transport
mdelage@grondinpoudrier.com
Marie-Christine Dufour, Droit de la santé et de la sécurité du travail
mcdufour@grondinpoudrier.com
Marc Hurtubise, Droit de la santé et de la sécurité du travail
mhurtubise@grondinpoudrier.com
Jean Morin, Construction
jmorin@grondinpoudier.com
Bruno Néron, Droit de la santé et de la sécurité du travail
bneron@grondinpoudrier.com
Pierre Ouellet, Construction
pouellet@grondinpoudrier.com
Gilles Reny, Droit minier
greny@grondinpoudrier.com
John White, Droit de la construction
jwhite@grondinpoudrier.com

Heenan Blaikie S.E.N.C.R.L./SRL - Québec
#600, 900, boul René-Lévesque est, Québec, QC G1R 2B5
Tel: 418-524-5131; *Fax:* 418-524-1717
www.heenanblaikie.com
Profile: 37 Lawyers, Founded in: 1973
Environmental Lawyers:
Marcel Aubut, Q.C., Partner, Energy; Construction; Aboriginal Law
418-529-4254
maubut@heenan.ca
Pierre Beaulieu, Partner, Construction
418-649-5464
pbeaulieu@heenan.ca
Pierre C. Bellavance, Partner, Environmental Law; Health
418-649-5476
pbellavance@heenan.ca
Anik Bernatchez, Construction
418-649-5467
abernatchez@heenan.ca
David F. Blair, Partner, Transportation
418-649-5483
dblair@heenan.ca
Louis Carrière, Partner, Construction Litigation
418-649-5465
lcarriere@heenan.ca
Nicolas Croteau, Construction
418-649-5477
ncroteau@heenan.ca
Louis-Antoine Côté, Occupational Health & Safety
418-649-5067
lcote@heenan.ca
Jean-François Dolbec, Partner, Occupational Health & Safety
418-649-5645
jfdolbec@heenan.ca
Christian Drolet, Partner, Occupational Health & Safety
418-649-5480
cdrolet@heenan.ca
Olivier Hébert, Construction Litigation; Health
418-649-5026
ohebert@heenan.ca
Isabelle L'Écuyer, Health
418-649-5080
ilecuyer@heenan.ca
Annie-Claude Labrecque, Construction Litigation
418-649-5472
alabrecque@heenan.ca
Isabelle Landry, Environmental Law; Energy
418-649-5479
ilandry@heenan.ca
Pierre Larrivée, Partner, Construction Litigation; Health
418-649-5532
plarrivee@heenan.ca
André Lepage, Partner, Occupational Health & Safety
418-649-5487
alepage@heenan.ca
Samuel Massicotte, Construction Litigation
418-649-5474
smassicotte@heenan.ca
Pierre-Étienne Morand, Occupational Health & Safety
418-649-5339
pemorand@heenan.ca
Pierre-Olivier Ménard Dumas, Transportation
418-649-5073
podumas@heenan.ca
Pierre Picard, Construction
418-649-5466
ppicard@heenan.ca
Gilles Rancourt, Occupational Health & Safety
418-649-5493
grancourt@heenan.ca
Simon Ruel, Health
418-649-5131
sruel@heenan.ca
Mario Welsh, Partner, Construction Litigation
418-649-5473
mwelsh@heenan.ca

Joli-Coeur Lacasse Avocats - Québec
#600, 1134, Grande-Allée ouest, Québec, QC G1S 1E5
Tél: 418-681-7007; *Téléc:* 418-681-7100
infos@jolicoeurlacasse.com
www.jolicoeurlacasse.com
Profile: 3 Offices, 59 Lawyers,
The firm provides services in the areas of environmental, municipal, construction, planning, & transportation law.
Environmental Lawyers:
Amélie Asselin, Labour Safety
amelie.asselin@jolicoeurlacasse.com
André Asselin, Labour & Employment
andre.asselin@jolicoeurlacasse.com
François Barbeau, Labour & Employment
francois.barbeau@jolicoeurlacasse.com
Alexandre Brousseau, Construction Law
alexandre.brousseau@jolicoeurlacasse.com
Jacques Cantin, Construction Law
jacques.cantin@jolicoeurlacasse.com
Lise Côté, Municipal Law; Labour Law; Administrative Law
lise.cote@jolicoeurlacasse.com
MArie-José Côté, Construction Law
marie-jose.cote@jolicoeurlacasse.com
Pierre Gagnon, Construction Law
pierre.gagnon@jolicoeurlacasse.com
Vincent Gingras, Municipal Law; Environmental Law; Agricultural Law
vincent.gingras@hotmail.com
Guy Godreau, Environmental Law; Municipal Law; Land Use Planning; Urban Planning; Administrative Law
guy.godreau@jolicoeurlacasse.com
André Joli-Coeur, Administrative Law; Transportation; Aboriginal Law; Environmental Law
andre.joli-coeur@jolicoeurlacasse.com
Antoine La Rue, Municipal Law
antoine.larue@jolicoeurlacasse.com
Alphonse Lacasse, Labour & Employment; Administrative Law
alphonse.lacasse@jolicoeurlacasse.com
Nelson Larrivée, Construction Law
nelson.larrivee@jolicoeurlacasse.com
Raymond Mainguy, Municipal Law
raymond.mainguy@jolicoeurlacasse.com
Louis Masson, Administrative Law
louis.masson@jolicoeurlacasse.com
Andréanne Maurice, Construction Law
andreanne.maurice@jolicoeurlacasse.com
Jean Morin, Construction Law
jean.morin@jolicoeurlacasse.com
Philippe Morisset, Construction
philippe.morisset@jolicoeurlacasse.com
Charles Morisset, Construction Law
charles.morisset@jolicoeurlacasse.com
Michel Paradis, Administrative Law; Transporation Law
michel.paradis@jolicoeurlacasse.com
Paul Routhier, Transporation Law
paul.routhier@jolicoeurlacasse.com
Stéphan Samson, Construction Law
stephan.samson@jolicoeurlacasse.com
Lyne Thériault, Labour & Employment
lyne.theriault@jolicoeurlacasse.com
Nathalie Vaillant, Emvironmental Law
nathalie.vaillant@jolicoeurlacasse.com

Langlois Kronström Desjardins
Complexe Jules-Dallaire, T3, 2820, boul. Laurier, 13e étage, Québec, QC G1V 0C1
Tel: 418-650-7000; *Fax:* 418-650-7075
Toll-Free: 888-650-7001
info@lkd.ca
www.langloiskronstromdesjardins.com
Profile: 2 Offices, 81 Lawyers

Lavery, de Billy - Québec
#500, 925, Grande Allée ouest, Québec, QC G1S 1C1
Tel: 418-688-5000; *Fax:* 418-688-3458
Toll-Free: 800-463-4002
info@lavery.ca
www.lavery.ca
Profile: 22 Lawyers, Founded in: 1913
Environmental Lawyers:
Pierre Beaudoin, Partner, Health Law; Transportation Law
418-266-3068
pbeaudoin@lavery.ca
Daniel Bouchard, Partner, Environmental, Energy & Natural Resources Law
418-266-3055
dbouchard@lavery.ca
Jules Brière, Partner, Health Law; Aboriginal Law
418-266-3093
jbriere@lavery.ca
Marie-Eve Clavet, Health Law
418-266-3067
meclavet@lavery.ca
Olga Farman, Health Law
418-266-3052
ofarman@lavery.ca
Hélène Gauvin, Health Law
418-266-3053
hgauvin@lavery.ca
Claude Lacroix, Partner, Construction & Surety Law
418-266-3063
clacroix@lavery.ca
Denis Michaud, Environmental, Energy & Natural Resources Law
418-266-3058
dmichaud@lavery.ca
Louis Rochette, Partner, Health Law; Life Sciences
418-266-3077
lrochette@lavery.ca

McCarthy Tétrault LLP - Québec
Le Complexe St-Amable, 1150, rue de Claire-Fontaine, 7e étage, Québec, QC G1R 5G4
Tel: 418-521-3000; *Fax:* 418-521-3099
Toll-Free: 877-244-7711
info@mccarthy.ca
www.mccarthy.ca
Profile: 7 Offices, 25 Lawyers
Environmental Lawyers:
Pierre Boivin, Mining; Energy
418-521-3012
piboivin@mccarthy.ca
Philippe Boivin, Biotech/Life Sciences
418-521-3014
pboivin@mccarthy.ca
Anastassia Chtaneva, Energy & Infrastructure financing
418-521-3054
achtaneva@mccarthy.ca
Marc N. Dorion, Q.C., Energy
418-521-3007
mdorion@mccarthy.ca
Pauline Motard, Energy Law
418-521-3055
pmotard@mccarthy.ca

Morency Société d'Avocats - Québec
#400, 3075, ch des Quatre-Bourgeois, Québec, QC G1W 4X5
Tél: 418-651-9900; *Téléc:* 418-651-5184
avocats@morencyavocats.com
www.morencyavocats.com
www.facebook.com/pages/Morency-Soci%C3%A9t%C3%A9-dAvocats/218984404818137?s, twitter.com/morencyavocats, ca.linkedin.com/pub/avocats-morency/3a/2b7/300
Profile: 4 Offices, 58 Lawyers, Founded in: 1969
Environmental Lawyers:
Philippe Asselin, Municipal Law
passelin@morencyavocats.com
Sandra Bilodeau, Municipal; Environmental Law
sbilodeau@morencyavocats.com
Martin Bouffard, Municipal Law
mbouffard@morencyavocats.com

Jean-Claude Girard, Municipal Law
jcgirard@morencyavocats.com
Bertrand Gobeil, Municipal
bgobeil@morencyavocats.com
Dennis Pakenham, Municipal Law
dpakenham@morencyavocats.com
Jacques Tremblay, Land Use Management; Municipal Law
jtremblay@morencyavocats.com
Charles A. Veilleux, Municipal
cveilleux@morencyavocats.com

Tremblay Bois Mignault Lemay S.E.N.C.R.L.
#200, 1195, av Lavigerie, Québec, QC G1V 4N3
Tél: 418-658-9966; *Téléc:* 418-658-6100
avocats@tremblaybois.qc.ca
www.tremblaybois.qc.ca
Profile: 1 Office, 31 Lawyers,
Practice areas include envionmental, municipal, & construction law.
Environmental Lawyers:
Myriam Asselin, Environmental; Municipal
masselin@tremblaybois.qc.ca
Patrick Beauchemin, Environmental; Municipal
pbeauchemin@tremblaybois.qc.ca
Yves Boudreault, Environmental; Municipal; Construction
yboudreault@tremblaybois.qc.ca
Gabriel Chassé, Environmental; Municipal
gchasse@tremblaybois.qc.ca
Pierre Giroux, Construction
pgiroux@tremblaybois.qc.ca
Claude Jean, Environmental; Municipal
cjean@tremblaybois.qc.ca
Michel Langlais, Construction
mlanglais@tremblaybois.qc.ca
Pierre Laurin, Environmental; Municipal
plaurin@tremblaybois.qc.ca
Marc Lemaire, Construction Law
mlemaire@tremblaybois.qc.ca
André Lemay, Environmental; Municipal
alemay@tremblaybois.qc.ca
Mireille Lemay, Environmental; Municipal; Construction; Agricultural Zoning
mlemay@tremblaybois.qc.ca
Caroline Pelchat, Environmental; Municipal
cpelchat@tremblaybois.qc.ca
Richard Talbot, Construction
rtalbot@tremblaybois.qc.ca

Rimouski

Cain Lamarre Casgrain Wells - Rimouski
#400, Edifice Trust General, CP 580, 2, boul St-Germain est, Rimouski, QC G5L 7C6
Tél: 418-723-3302; *Téléc:* 418-722-6939
info@clcw.ca
www.clcw.qc.ca
Profile: 9 Lawyers
Environmental Lawyers:
Yvan Bujold, Associé, Droit de la santé
yvan.bujold@clcw.ca

Rivière-du-Loup

Cain Lamarre Casgrain Wells - Rivière-du-Loup
#201, CP 1104, 299, rue Lafontaine, Rivière-du-Loup, QC G5R 4C3
Tél: 418-860-4580; *Téléc:* 418-860-4588
info@clcw.ca
www.clcw.qc.ca
Profile: 6 Lawyers

Moreau Avocats inc.
CP 487, 12, rue de la Cour, Rivière-du-Loup, QC G5R 3Z1
Tél: 418-862-3565; *Téléc:* 418-862-4408
Profile: 1 Office, 6 Lawyers, Founded in: 1969
Practice areas include municipal & construction law.
Environmental Lawyers:
Gilles Moreau, Municipal Law; Construction Law
gmoreau@moreauavocats.com
Denis Rioux, Construction
drioux@moreauavocats.com

Saint-Hyacinthe

Sylvestre & Associés Avocats S.E.N.C.
#236, 1600, rue Girouard ouest, Saint-Hyacinthe, QC J2S 2Z8
Tél: 450-773-8445; *Téléc:* 450-773-2112
etude@avocatssylvestre.ca
www.avocatssylvestre.ca
Profile: 1 Office, 16 Lawyers,
The law firms serves individuals, businesspeople, & large corporations in areas such as construction law, agricultural law, & municipal law.
Environmental Lawyers:
Diana Baltazar, Construction Law; Occupational Health & Safety
dbaltazar@avocatssylvestre.ca
Jean-Pierre Boileau, Municipal Law
jpboileau@avocatssylvestre.ca
Maryse Dubé, Corporate Law (agricultural & manufacturing sectors)
mdube@avocatssylvestre.ca
Isabelle Labranche, Construction Law
ilabranche@avocatssylvestre.ca
Philippe Laverdière, Construction Law
plaverdiere@avocatssylvestre.ca
Rodolphe Maruca, Construction
rmaruca@avocatssylvestre.ca
Frédéric Sylvestre, Agricultural Law; Envrionmental Law; Municipal Law Labour Law; Administrative Law
fsylvestre@avocatssylvestre.ca

Saint-Jérôme

Lalonde Geraghty Riendeau Lapierre Avocats
44, rue De Martigny ouest, Saint-Jérôme, QC J7Z 2E9
Tél: 450-436-8022; *Téléc:* 450-436-5185
info@lgrl.ca
www.lgrl.ca
Profile: 1 Office, 10 Lawyers,
Services include advice in the areas of municipal law & construction law.
Environmental Lawyers:
Dennis Geraghty, Construction; Municipal Law
dgeraghty@lgrl.ca
Denis Lapierre, Construction; Administrative Law
dlapierre@lgrl.ca
Benoit Morissette, Construction
bmorissette@lgrl.ca
Geneviève Raymond, Construction
graymond@lgrl.ca

Sainte-Marie

Sylvain Parent Gobeil Simard S.E.N.C.R.L.
225, av du College, Sainte-Marie, QC G6E 3X9
Tél: 418-387-2727; *Téléc:* 418-387-7070
spgs@globetrotter.net
www.spgs.ca
Profile: 1 Office, Founded in: 1970
Legal advice is available in the areas of agricultural, environmental, municipal, & construction law.
Environmental Lawyers:
Isabelle Bourgeois
418-390-1329
bourgeois.isabelle@globetrotter.net
Isabelle Fortier
418-386-1501
fortier.isabelle@globetrotter.net
Michaël Laplante
418-386-1501
laplante.michael@globetrotter.net
Jean-Guy Parent
418-386-1500
parent.jeanguy@globetrotter.net
Patrice Simard
418-386-1502
simard.patrice@globetrotter.net

Sept-Iles

Cain Lamarre Casgrain Wells - Sept-Iles
1, rue de Mingan, Sept-Iles, QC G4R 4L8
Tél: 418-962-6572; *Téléc:* 418-968-8576
info@clcw.ca
www.clcw.qc.ca
Profile: 6 Lawyers
Environmental Lawyers:
Marc Brouillette, Associé, Droit de la santé
marc.brouillette@clcw.ca
Julie Lapointe, Droit de la santé
julie.lapointe@clcw.ca
Mélanie Trudeau, Droit de la santé; Affaires autochtones
melanie.trudeau@clcw.ca

Sherbrooke

Cain Lamarre Casgrain Wells - Sherbrooke
#100, 195, rue Belvédère nord, Sherbrooke, QC J1H 4A7
Tél: 819-780-1515; *Téléc:* 819-780-1341
info@clcw.ca
www.clcw.qc.ca
Profile: 6 Lawyers

Delorme, LeBel, Bureau, Savoie
#100, 2355, rue King ouest, Sherbrooke, QC J1J 2G6
Tél: 819-566-6222; *Téléc:* 819-566-4221
dlb@dlbavocats.com
www.dlbavocats.com
Profile: 1 Office, 11 Lawyers,
Delorme, LeBel, Bureau, Savoie advises, assists & represents clients in the areas of environmental law & municipal law. The firm also handles issues related to occupational health & safety.
Environmental Lawyers:
Paul Bureau, Municipal Law; Administrative Law
pbureau@dlbavocats.com
Hugo Champoux, Construction Law; Labour & Employment
hchampoux@dlbavocats.com
Isabelle Cloutier, Construction Law; Municipal Law
icloutier@dlbavocats.com
Richard Delorme, Labour & Employment
rdelorme@dlbavocats.com
Elise Longpré, Labour & Employment; Administrative Law
elongpre@dlbavocats.com
Charles Michaud, Health & Safety
cmichaud@dlbavocats.com
Matthew Prince, Health & Safety; Municipal Law
mprince@dlbavocats.com
Marc Savoie, Labour Law
msavoie@dlbavocats.com
Josée Thibault, Health & Safety; Construction Law
jthibault@dlbavocats.com

Heenan Blaikie S.E.N.C.R.L/SRL - Sherbrooke
#210, 455, rue King ouest, Sherbrooke, QC J1H 6E9
Tel: 819-346-5058; *Fax:* 819-346-5007
www.heenanblaikie.com
Profile: 20 Lawyers, Founded in: 1973
Environmental Lawyers:
Geneviève Chamberland, Health
819-346-2562
gchamberland@heenan.ca
Simon Delisle-Beaulieu, Occupational Health & Safety
819-346-2103
sdelisle@heenan.ca
Danielle Gauthier, Partner, Occupational Health & Safety
819-346-8073
dgauthier@heenan.ca
Cheryl Gilbert, Health
819-346-2207
cgilbert@heenan.ca
Jean-François Pagé, Partner, Occupational Health & Safety
819-346-7999
jfpage@heenan.ca
Sébastien Pierre-Roy, Construction Litigation; Health
819-346-7928
spierreroy@heenan.ca
Hubert Pépin, Partner, Construction
819-346-0638
hpepin@heenan.ca
Claude Villeneuve, Partner, Occupational Health & Safety
819-346-4117
cvilleneuve@heenan.ca
Yanick Vlasak, Partner, Construction Litigation
819-346-3720
yvlasak@heenan.ca

Monty Coulombe s.e.n.c. - Sherbrooke
#200, 234, rue Dufferin, Sherbrooke, QC J1H 4M2
Tel: 819-566-4466; *Fax:* 819-565-2891
legal@montycoulombe.com
www.montycoulombe.com
Profile: 20 Lawyers, Founded in: 1978
Monty Coulombe provides services in the following areas of law:

environmental, municipal, construction, & labour & employment. The firm's clients include private corporations, health & education institutions, & municipalities.
Environmental Lawyers:
Guy Achim, Municipal Law; Environmental Law; Construction
819-566-4466 ext. 500
achim.guy@montycoulombe.com
Martin Brunet, Municipal Law; Environmental Law; Lavour & Employment
819-566-4466 ext. 710
brunet.martin@montycoulombe.com
Tiffany Dorais, Construction Law
819-566-4466 ext. 690
dorais.tiffany@montycoulombe.com
André Fournier, Environmental Law; Municipal Law; Labour & Employment
819-566-4466 ext. 560
fournier.andre@montycoulombe.com
Charles Gaulin, Construction; Labour & Employment
819-566-4466 ext. 525
gaulin.charles@montycoulombe.com
Karine L'Heureux, Construction; Labour & Employment
819-566-4466 ext. 605
lheureux.karine@montycoulombe.com
Jean-Guy Marchesseault, Environmental Law; Municipal Law; Labour & Employment
819-566-4466 ext. 600
marchesseault.jean-guy@montycoulombe.com
Richard McLernon, Environmental Law; Municipal Law; Labour & Employment
819-566-4466 ext. 650
mclernon.richard@montycoulombe.com
Mélanie Pelletier, Environmental Law; Municipal Law; Construction Law
819-566-4466 ext. 570
pelletier.melanie@montycoulombe.com
Dominique Pelletier-Giroux, Construction Law; Labour & Employment
819-566-4466 ext. 580
p-giroux.dominique@montycoulombe.com
Stéphane Reynolds, Environmental Law; Municipal Law; Construction Law; Labour & Employment
819-566-4466 ext. 590
reynolds.stephane@montycoulombe.com
Roland Veilleux, Municipal Law; Environmental Law
819-566-4466 ext. 640
veilleux.roland@montycoulombe.com
Marie-Claude Veilleux, Municipal Law; Environmental Law
819-566-4466 ext. 530
veilleux.marie-claude@montycoulombe.com

Trois-Rivières

Heenan Blaikie S.E.N.C.R.L/SRL - Trois-Rivières
#360, 1500, rue Royale, Trois-Rivières, QC G9A 6E6
Tel: 819-373-7000; *Fax:* 819-373-0943
www.heenanblaikie.com
Profile: 10 Lawyers, Founded in: 1973
Environmental Lawyers:
Jean Boulet, Partner, Occupational Health & Safety
819-373-4370
jboulet@heenan.ca
Marc-André Germain, Occupational Health & Safety
819-373-5543
magermain@heenan.ca
Marie-Josée Hétu, Partner, Occupational Health & Safety
819-373-4274
mhetu@heenan.ca
Myriam Lavallée, Occupational Health & Safety
819-373-0339
mlavallee@heenan.ca

Hénaire, Louis
983, rue Hart, Trois-Rivières, QC G9A 4S3
Tél: 819-379-3355; *Téléc:* 819-379-1227
Profile: 1 Office, 1 Lawyers, Founded in: 1982
Environmental Lawyers:
Louis Hénaire

Joli-Coeur Lacasse Avocats - Trois-Rivières
#450, 1500, rue Royale, Trois-Rivières, QC G9A 6E6
Tel: 819-379-4331; *Fax:* 819-379-3624
infos@jolicoeurlacasse.com
www.jolicoeurlacasse.com
Profile: 6 Lawyers,
The head office of Joli-Coeur Lacasse Avocats is located in Québec. Areas of law practised from the Trois-Rivières office include health care, construction, & labour & employment.
Environmental Lawyers:
Éric Beauchesne, Construction Law
eric.beauchesne@jolicoeurlacasse.com
Richard-Alexandre Grenier, Labour & Employment; Construction Law
richard-alexandre.grenier@jolicoeurlacasse.com
Véronique Néron, Health Care
veronique.neron@jolicoeurlacasse.com

Val-d'Or

Cain Lamarre Casgrain Wells - Val-d'Or
#202, 855, 3e av, Val-d'Or, QC J9P 1T2
Tél: 819-825-4153; *Téléc:* 819-825-9769
info@clcw.ca
www.clcw.qc.ca
www.facebook.com/pages/Cain-Lamarre-Casgrain-Wells-SENCRL-Avocats-Recruteme, twitter.com/Cain_Lamarre, www.linkedin.com/company/cain-lamarre-casgrain-wells
Profile: 16 Offices, 158 Lawyers, Founded in: 1999
Environmental Lawyers:
Robert-André Adam, Associé, Santé
robert.andre.adam@clcw.ca
Alexandre Cimon, Santé et Sécurité
alexandre.cimon@clcw.ca
Stéphanie Lachance, Santé; Affaires autochtones
stephanie.lachance@clcw.ca
Pascal Porlier, Droit de la construction; Affaires autochtones
pascal.porlier@clcw.ca

Saskatchewan

Estevan

McDougall Gauley - Estevan
#300, Wicklow Centre, 1133 - 4th St., Estevan, SK S4A 0W6
Tel: 306-634-6334; *Fax:* 306-634-3852
www.mcdougallgauley.com
Profile: 2 Lawyers
Environmental Lawyers:
Barry D. Bridges, Oil & Gas, Natural Resources & Energy Law
bbridges@mcdougallgauley.com
Chad W. Jesse, Oil & Gas, Natural Resources & Energy Law
cjesse@mcdougallgauley.com

Prince Albert

Abrametz & Eggum
#101, 88 - 13th St. East, Prince Albert, SK S6V 1C6
Tel: 306-763-7441; *Fax:* 306-764-2882
Profile: 1 Office,
Issues related to municipal law are handled.
Environmental Lawyers:
Peter V. Abrametz
petervabrametz@inet2000.com
Krista Eggum
klleggum@inet2000.com

Cherkewich, Ronald, Legal Services
#202, 1000 - 1st Ave. East, Prince Albert, SK S6V 2A7
Tel: 306-764-1537; *Fax:* 306-763-0505
Profile: 1 Office, Founded in: 1969

Regina

Kanuka Thuringer LLP, Barristers & Solicitors
#1400, 2500 Victoria Ave., Regina, SK S4P 3X2
Tel: 306-525-7200; *Fax:* 306-359-0590
firm@ktllp.ca
www.kanukathuringer.com
Profile: 2 Offices, 25 Lawyers, Founded in: 1955
Kanuka Thuringer LLP is an established Saskatchewan law firm. It is based in Regina & Swift Current, but the firm regularly provides services to clients throughout the province. The cliente is varied, including local, national, international corporations, individuals, non-profit organizations, entrepreneurs, & small businesses. Kanuka Thuringer LLP has a diverse practice, but it is likely best known for providing business advice & dispute resolution in its signature practice areas of business law, energy & natural resources, financial services, construction, family law, & transportation.
Environmental Lawyers:
Keith D. Boyd, Q.C., Oil & Gas; Land & natural resources; Surface rights
306-525-7203
kboyd@kanukathuringer.com
Murray W. Douglas, Commercial litigation (energy industry)
306-525-7227
mdouglas@kanukathuringer.com
James S. Ehmann, Q.C., Oil & gas litigation
306-525-7225
jehmann@kanukathuringer.com
Paul J. Harasen, Employment & labour law; Construction law
306-525-7230
pharasen@kanukathuringer.com
Carrie G. Ho, Natural resources; Environmental law
306-525-7237
cho@kanukathuringer.com
Keith D. Kilback, Managing Partner, Transportation; Commercial litigation (Oil & gas, construction)
306-525-7229
kkilback@kanukathuringer.com
T. Micheal McDougall, Oil & Gas; Water regulation; Environmental law
306-525-7211
mmcdougall@kanukathuringer.com
Ronald M. Warsaba, Oil & gas
306-525-7207
rwarsaba@kanukathuringer.com

MacPherson Leslie & Tyerman LLP - Regina
#1500, Hill Centre I, 1874 Scarth St., Regina, SK S4P 4E9
Tel: 306-347-8000; *Fax:* 306-352-5250
www.mlt.com
Profile: 4 Offices, 121 Lawyers, Founded in: 1920
Agribusiness; Aboriginal Law; Natural Resources Law
Environmental Lawyers:
Leonard D. Andrychuk, Q.C., Partner, Construction; Environmental; First Nations
306-347-8440
landrychuk@mlt.com
Randy U. Brunet, Partner, Health Care
306-347-8415
rbrunet@mlt.com
Brianna Demofsky, Health
306-347-8459
bdemofsky@mlt.com
John A. Dipple, Partner, Energy; Construction
306-347-8414
jdipple@mlt.com
Deron A. Kuski, Partner, Construction
306-347-8404
dkuski@mlt.com
Harold H. MacKay, Q.C., O.C., Counsel, Natural Resources Law
306-347-8417
hmackay@mlt.com
Robert B. Pletch, Q.C., Chairman, Mining & Natural Resources
306-347-8416
rpletch@mlt.com
Hilary Stedwill, Construction; Environment
306-347-8486
hstedwill@mlt.com
Bradley N. Vance, Counsel, Health
306-347-8604
bvance@mlt.com
Donald K. Wilson, Q.C., Managing Partner, Mining & Natural Resources
306-347-8437
dwilson@mlt.com
Erin Wolff, Health
306-347-8449
ewolff@mlt.com

McDougall Gauley - Regina
1500 - 1881 Scarth St., Regina, SK S4P 4K9
Tel: 306-757-1641; *Fax:* 306-359-0785
www.mcdougallgauley.com
Profile: 4 Offices, 75 Lawyers, Founded in: 1891
Diligence issues, environmental permits, matters relative to site clean-up and remediation, as well as litigation involving environmental matters.
Environmental Lawyers:
Darren W. Carlson, Oil & Gas, Natural Resources & Energy Law
306-565-5194
dcarlson@mcdougallgauley.com
Terence G. Graf, Q.C., Healthcare Law
306-565-5106
tgraf@mcdougallgauley.com

Neil N. Karkut, Oil & Gas, Natural Resources & Energy Law
306-565-5193
nkarkut@mcdougallgauley.com
G. Brett Ledingham, Oil & Gas, Natural Resources & Energy Law
306-565-5151
bledingham@mcdougallgauley.com
Michael W. Milani, Q.C., Oil & Gas, Natural Resources & Energy Law
306-565-5117
mmilani@mcdougallgauley.com
Dan G. Morris, Oil & Gas, Natural Resources & Energy Law
306-565-5181
dmorris@mcdougallgauley.com
Kenneth A. Ready, Q.C., Healthcare Law
306-565-5125
kready@mcdougallgauley.com
Murray R. Sawatzky, Q.C., Construction Law; Environmental Law
306-565-5141
msawatzky@mcdougallgauley.com
Angela Stolz, Environmental Law
306-565-5113
astolz@mcdougallgauley.com

Saskatoon

MacPherson Leslie & Tyerman LLP - Saskatoon

#1500, Saskatoon Square, 410 - 22nd St. East, Saskatoon, SK S7K 5T6
Tel: 306-975-7100; *Fax:* 306-975-7145
www.mlt.com
Profile: 37 Lawyers
Environmental Lawyers:
John Agioritis, Environment
306-975-7143
jagioritis@mlt.com
Danny R. Anderson, Partner, Energy; Mining & Natural Resources
306-975-7133
danderson@mlt.com
Naheed Bardai, Partner, Construction
306-975-7115
nbardai@mlt.com
Kelly Caruk, Mining & Natural Resources
306-975-7129
kcaruk@mlt.com
Lynn E. Hnatick, Partner, Mining & Natural Resources
306-975-7104
lhnatick@mlt.com
Rangi G. Jeerakathil, Partner, Energy; Environment; First Nations
306-975-7107
rjeerakathil@mlt.com
Josh Lommer, Mining & Natural Resources
306-975-7139
jlommer@mlt.com
R. Neil MacKay, Q.C., Partner, Mining & Natural Resources
306-975-7124
nmackay@mlt.com
Brent Robinson, Mining & Natural Resources
306-956-6965
brobinson@mlt.com
Ryan Rodier, Energy; Environment; First Nations
306-975-7113
rrodier@mlt.com
Leah A. Schatz, Partner, Health
306-975-7144
lschatz@mlt.com
Tyler Wake, Mining & Natural Resources
306-975-7134
twake@mlt.com
Chris A. Woodland, Partner, Construction
306-975-7128
cwoodland@mlt.com
Penny L. Yeager, Energy; Mining & Natural Resources
306-975-7131
pyeager@mlt.com

McDougall Gauley - Saskatoon

P.O. Box 638, 701 Broadway Ave., Saskatoon, SK S7K 3L7
Tel: 306-653-1212; *Fax:* 306-652-1323
www.mcdougallgauley.com
Profile: 37 Lawyers
Environmental Lawyers:
Christopher C. Boychuk, Q.C., Construction Law; Health Law
306-665-5456
cboychuk@mcdougallgauley.com
Chantelle C. Eisner, Healthcare Law
306-665-5424
ceisner@mcdougallgauley.com
David (Tom) E. Gauley, Q.C., Healthcare Law
306-665-5422
tgauley@mcdougallgauley.com
Chad M. Haaf, Oil & Gas, Natural Resources & Energy Law
306-665-5494
chaaf@mcdougallgauley.com
Derek D. Hoffman, Oil & Gas, Natural Resources & Energy Law
306-665-5477
dhoffman@mcdougallgauley.com
Lindsay M. Jones, Environmental Law
306-665-5436
ljones@mcdougallgauley.com
Brad S. Mitchell, Natural Resource Law; Environmental Law
306-665-5449
bmitchell@mcdougallgauley.com
William A. Nickel, Oil & Gas, Natural Resources & Energy Law
306-665-5448
bnickel@mcdougallgauley.com
Dusty L. Robinson, Oil & Gas, Natural Resources & Energy Law
306-665-5446
drobinson@mcdougallgauley.com
William J. Shaw, Oil & Gas, Natural Resources & Energy Law
306-665-5426
bshaw@mcdougallgauley.com

Merchant Law Group LLP - Saskatoon

#501, 224 - 4th Ave. South, Saskatoon, SK S7K 5M5
Tel: 306-653-7777; *Fax:* 306-975-1983
Toll-Free: 866-567-7777
merchant@merchantlaw.com
www.merchantlaw.com
Profile: 7 Lawyers
Environmental Lawyers:

Robertson Stromberg LLP

#600, Canada Building, 105 - 21st St. East, Saskatoon, SK S7K 0B3
Tel: 306-652-7575; *Fax:* 306-652-2445
Toll-Free: 800-667-0070
www.rslaw.com
www.facebook.com/Robertsonstromberg, twitter.com/RSLLP, www.linkedin.com/company/robertson-stromberg-llp
Profile: 1 Office, 27 Lawyers, Founded in: 1918
Environmental Lawyers:
Misty Alexandre, Partner, Construction Law
306-933-1352
m.alexandre@rslaw.com
Melvin Gerspacher, Managing Partner, Natural Resources
306-933-1324
m.gerspacher@rslaw.com
Bill D. Preston, Q.C., Construction Law
306-933-1388
b.preston@thinkrsplaw.com
Leslie W. Prosser, Q.C., Managing Partner, Natural Resources
306-933-1302
l.prosser@thinkrsplaw.com
Reynold A. Robertson, Q.C., Construction Law
306-933-1348
r.robertson@thinkrsplaw.com
Kenneth K.E. Ziegler, Forestry; Aboriginal Law
306-933-1314
k.ziegler@thinkrsplaw.com

Scott Phelps & Mason Barristers & Solicitors

#400, 135 - 21st St. East, Saskatoon, SK S7K 0B4
Tel: 306-244-2201; *Fax:* 306-244-2420
barristers@spmlaw.ca
www.spmlaw.ca
Profile: 1 Office, 6 Lawyers,
Clients are served throughout Saskatchewan & western Canada.
Environmental Lawyers:
Andrew M. Mason, Labour & Human Resources Law; Administrative Law
a.mason@spmlaw.ca
Gordon Phelps, Real Property Law
g.phelps@spmlaw.ca

Wallace Meschishnick Clackson Zawada

#901, 119 - 4th Ave. South, Saskatoon, SK S7K 5X2
Tel: 306-933-0004; *Fax:* 306-933-2006
info@wmcz.com
www.wmcz.com
Profile: 1 Office, 16 Lawyers

Swift Current

Kanuka Thuringer LLP, Barristers & Solicitors

El Wood Bldg., 350 Cheadle St. West, Swift Current, SK S9H 4G3
Tel: 306-773-4800; *Fax:* 306-773-0040
firm@ktllp.ca
www.kanukathuringer.com
Profile: 2 Offices, 4 Lawyers,
Kanuka Thuringer LLP is an established Saskatchewan law firm. It is based in Regina & Swift Current, but the firm regularly provides services to clients throughout the province. The cliente is varied, including local, national, international corporations, individuals, non-profit organizations, entrepreneurs, & small businesses. Kanuka Thuringer LLP has a diverse practice, but it is likely best known for providing business advice & dispute resolution in its signature practice areas of business law, energy & natural resources, financial services, construction, family law, & transportation.
Environmental Lawyers:
Andrea V. Argue, Agriculture
306-773-4865
aargue@kanukathuringer.com

Weyburn

Nimegeers Schuck Wormsbecker Bobbitt

P.O. Box 8, 319 Souris Ave. NE, Weyburn, SK S4H 2J8
Tel: 306-842-4654; *Fax:* 306-842-0522
law@nswb.com
www.nswb.com
www.facebook.com/pages/NSWB-Law-Firm/195047653897186
Profile: 1 Office, 3 Lawyers, Founded in: 1967
The NSWB Law Firm provides legal services in southern Saskatchewan in the areas of farm law & oil & gas law.
Environmental Lawyers:
Thomas A. Schuck, Oil & Gas Law

Yukon Territory

Whitehorse

Austring, Fendrick & Fairman

3081 Third Ave., Whitehorse, YT Y1A 4Z7
Tel: 867-668-4405; *Fax:* 867-668-3710
info@lawyukon.com
www.lawyukon.com
Profile: 1 Office, 7 Lawyers, Founded in: 1973
Legal services are offered to a variety of clients inside & outside the Yukon Territory. Advice is available in the areas of mining & employment.
Environmental Lawyers:
Bhreagh Dabbs, Associate, Employment Law; Administrative Law
bdabbs@lawyukon.com
Gregory A. Fekete, Partner, Mining
gf@lawyukon.com

Davis LLP - Whitehorse

#201, 4109 - 4th Ave., Whitehorse, YT Y1A 1H6
Tel: 867-393-5100; *Fax:* 867-667-2669
www.davis.ca
Profile: 3 Lawyers,
Specialized practice areas include Aboriginal and Environmental law.
Environmental Lawyers:
Peter Sandiford, Environmental law; Mining law; Aboriginal law
867-393-5112
psandiford@davis.ca

Libraries & Resource Centres

Alberta

Athabasca: Athabasca University Library
1 University Dr.
Athabasca, AB T9S 3A3
800-788-9041 ext: 6254
Fax: 780-675-6477
e-mail: library@athabascau.ca
URL: library.athabascau.ca
National Library Symbol: AEAU
Consortia Membership: The Alberta Library; Canadian Research Knowledge Network (CRKN); Council of Prairie & Pacific University Libraries (COPPUL); Health Knowledge Network (HKN); Alberta Video Co-Acquisition Consortium
Founded in: 1970
Hours: M-F 8:30-4:30
Acquisitions Budget: $250,000 - $499,999
For Print: $50,000 - $99,999
For Electronic: $250,000 - $499,999
Special Collections: Byrne Collection; The Reverend Edward Checkland Collection (Distance Education); University archives
Subjects covered: Distance Education, Women's Studies
Services:
Internet Access
Inter-Library Loan (ILL)
Digital Reference Centre for distance learners
Microform Equipment: Reader
Steve Schafer, Director, Library Services
steves@athabascau.ca
Burke Mortimer, Sr. Reference Librarian & Circulation Supervisor
burkem@athabascau.ca
Douglas Kariel, Head, Technical Services & Systems
Judy Stady, Supervisor, Interlibrary Loan
Elaine Magusin, Reference Services Librarian
Tony Tin, Electronic Resources Librarian
Lorraine Hirning, Serials Technician

Brooks: Brooks Campus Library
200 Horticultural Rd. East
Brooks, AB T1A 3Y6
Mailing Address: 299 College Dr. SE
Medicine Hat, AB T1A 3Y6
403-362-1690
Fax: 403-362-8926
866-282-8394
e-mail: blibrary@mhc.ab.ca
reference@mhc.ab.ca
illo@mhc.ab.ca
URL: www.mhc.ab.ca/Library.aspx
Founded in: 1979
Hours: M-Th 8:00-8:00; F 8:00-4:00
Note: Address all correspondence to main library
Services:
Internet Access
Inter-Library Loan (ILL)
Personnel: *Summary:* 3 Total; 3 Technical(s)
Keith Walker, Director, Library Services
kwalker@mhc.ab.ca
403-504-3539
Reni Smith, Administrative Assistant
lsmith@mhc.ab.ca
403-504-3541

Calgary: Alberta Children's Hospital Knowledge Centre
#A2-908, 2888 Shaganappi Trail NW
Calgary, AB T3B 6A8
Mailing Address: 2888 Shaganappi Trail NW
Calgary, AB T3B 6A8
403-943-7077
Fax: 403-955-2799
e-mail: achinfo@ucalgary.ca
National Library Symbol: ACACH
No public access
Hours: M-F 8:00-4:00
Acquisitions Budget: $25,000 - $49,999
Subjects covered: Child Health Care
Services:
Inter-Library Loan (ILL) for a fee of $5
Personnel: *Summary:* 2 Total; 2 Technical(s); 5 Volunteer(s)
Spencer Stevens, Information Specialist
sstevens@ucalgary.ca
403-955-2723

Calgary: Alberta Speleological Society Library
#1606-924 - 14th Ave. SW
Calgary, AB T2R 0N7
Mailing Address: c/o Andrea Corlett
Calgary, AB T2R 0N7
e-mail: info@caving.ab.ca
URL: www.caving.ab.ca
Founded in: 1968
Hours: by appointment only
Special Collections: Reports, books, & periodicals pertaining to cave & karst explorations, science, & conservation
Subjects covered: Caves; Conservation

Calgary: Alberta Wilderness Resource Centre Library
455 - 12th St., NW
Calgary, AB T2P 2E1
Mailing Address: PO Box 6398, Stn D
Calgary, AB T2P 2E1
403-283-2025
Fax: 403-270-2743
866-313-0713
e-mail: awa@shaw.ca
URL: www.albertawilderness.ca
Hours: by appointment only
Acquisitions Budget: $25,000 - $49,999
Subjects covered: Wilderness, Land Use, Forestry, Wildlife, Natural Resources, Conservation, National Parks, Environment, Protected Areas, Rivers
Services:
Internet Access
Personnel: *Summary:* 1 Total; 1 Professional(s)
Christyann Olson, Director
awa.ed@shaw.ca

Calgary: AMEC Inc. Information Resource Centre
#900, 801 - 6th Ave. SW
Calgary, AB T2P 3W3
403-298-4170
Fax: 403-298-4125
URL: www.amec.com
National Library Symbol: ACME
Hours: 7:30-5:00 by appointment only
Acquisitions Budget: $25,000 - $49,999
Subjects covered: Energy, Environment, Physical Science, Engineering, Technology, Natural Resources
Services:
Inter-Library Loan (ILL)
Personnel: *Summary:* 1 Total; 1 Professional(s); 1 Technical(s)
Anne Marie Gazsi, Library Technician
Joanna Becker, Head, Technical Services
Carol Ann Ruaro, Document Control/Library
carolann.ruaro@amec.com

Calgary: Anadarko Canada Corp. Library
425 - 1st St. SW
Calgary, AB T2P 4V4
Mailing Address: PO Box 2595, Stn M
Calgary, AB T2P 4V4
403-231-0539
Fax: 403-231-0356
e-mail: robert_mclauchlin@anadarko.com
National Library Symbol: ACNER
No public access
Hours: M-F 7:00-4:00
Subjects covered: Oil & Gas, Geology, Geophysics
Services:
Inter-Library Loan (ILL)
Personnel: *Summary:* 2 Total; 1 Professional(s); 1 Technical(s)
Robert McLauchlin, Supervisor
Jean Pearson, Contact
jean_pearson@anadarko.com

Calgary: Bennett Jones Law Library
2500 University Dr. NW
Calgary, AB T2N 1N4
403-220-3727
Fax: 403-282-3000
e-mail: lawlib@ucalgary.ca
lawill@ucalgary.ca
URL: library.ucalgary.ca/branches/lawlibrary
National Library Symbol: ACUL
Founded in: 1976
Hours: M-Th 8:00am-10:00pm; F 8:00-6:00; Sa 10:00-6:00; Su 10:00-8:00
Subjects covered: Law
Services:
Inter-Library Loan (ILL)
Microform Equipment: Reader
Personnel: *Summary:* 2 Professional(s); 5 Technical(s)

Calgary: Calgary Earth Sciences Library
3303 - 33rd St. NW, 2nd Fl.
Calgary, AB T2L 2A7
403-292-7165
Fax: 403-292-5377
e-mail: calgary.ref@nrcan.gc.ca
National Library Symbol: ACSP
Founded in: 1967
Hours: M-Th 8:00-12:00, 12:45-4:00; F 8:00-12:00, 12:45-3:15
Acquisitions Budget: $100,000 - $249,999
For Print: $50,000 - $99,999
For Electronic: 0-$9,999
Note: Limited online searching. Formerly the Institute of Sedimentary & Petroleum Geology. Photocopying: .25/pg, .10/pg for students. Memberships: $50/yr.
Subjects covered: Geological Sciences; Petroleum & Coal Geology; Paleontology; Micropaleontology; Stratigraphy; Structural Geology; Sedimentary Geology; Geochemistry; Geology of the Western Canadian Sedimentary Basin & the Arctic
Services:
Inter-Library Loan (ILL)
Memberships
Microform Equipment: Reader
Personnel: *Summary:* 3 Total; 2 Professional(s); 1 Technical(s)
Edward Hau, Manager
Edward.Hau@NRCan-RNCan.gc.ca

Calgary: Calgary Library
#700, 840 - 7th Ave. SW
Calgary, AB T2P 3G2
403-920-3101
Fax: 403-266-5730
No public access
Hours: Tu-Th 8:30-4:00
Acquisitions Budget: 0-$9,999
For Print: 0-$9,999
For Electronic: 0-$9,999
Subjects covered: Power engineering, Water resouces engineering, Hydrocarbon engineering, Tranportation engineering
Personnel: *Summary:* 1 Professional(s)
Anneliese Dalmoro, Information Research Specialist
adalmoro@hatch.ca

Calgary: Calgary Library & Information Centre
3608 - 33rd St. NW
Calgary, AB T2L 2A6
403-210-5292
Fax: 403-210-5380
e-mail: calgary_library@albertainnovates.ca
National Library Symbol: ACRS
Consortia Membership: NEOS Library Consortium
Hours: M-F 8:15-12:00, 1:00-4:30 by appointment only
Special Collections: Heavy Oil Recovery
Subjects covered: Artificial Intelligence, Industrial Engineering, Advanced Manufacturing Technologies
Services:
Inter-Library Loan (ILL)
Personnel: *Summary:* 1 Total; 1 Professional(s)

Guy Trott, Library Manager
guy.trott@albertainnovates.ca

Calgary: Calgary Zoological Society
Calgary Zoo, Botanical Garden, & Prehistoric Park
1300 Zoo Rd. NE
Calgary, AB T2E 7V6
403-232-9300
Fax: 403-237-7582
800-588-9993
e-mail: comments@calgaryzoo.ab.ca
guestrelations@calgaryzoo.ab.ca
URL: www.calgaryzoo.org
Hours: M-F by appointment only
Acquisitions Budget: 0-$9,999
Subjects covered: Zoology; Horticulture; Animal Husbandry
Deanna Snell, Registrar

Calgary: Canadian Association of Oilwell Drilling Contractors Library
#800, 540 - 5 Ave. SW
Calgary, AB T2P 0M2
403-264-4311
Fax: 403-263-3796
e-mail: info@caodc.ca
publications@caodc.ca
URL: www.caodc.ca
Founded in: 1949
Subjects covered: Oilwells; Drilling

Calgary: Canadian Centre For Energy Information Library
#1600, 800 - 6th Ave. SW
Calgary, AB T2P 3G3
403-263-7722
Fax: 403-237-6286
877-606-4636
e-mail: infoservices@centreforenergy.com
URL: www.centreforenergy.com
No public access
Founded in: 1975
Subjects covered: Petroleum, Natural Gas, Sour Gas, Crude Oil, Canadian Energy
Personnel: *Summary:* 1 Total; 4 Professional(s); 1 Technical(s);

Calgary: Canadian Institute of Resources Law Library
#3353, Murray Fraser Hall, University of Calgary
2500 University Dr. NW
Calgary, AB T2N 1N4
403-220-3200
Fax: 403-282-6182
e-mail: cirl@ucalgary.ca
URL: www.cirl.ca
Profile: A leading, national centre of expertise on legal & policy issues relating to Canada's natural resources. Since its establishment, it has pursued a 3-fold mandate of research, education & publication; it initiates projects & responds to requests from the public & private sectors, & from non-governmental organizations
Founded in: 1979
Hours: M-F by appointment only
Acquisitions Budget: For Print: 0-$9,999
For Electronic: 0-$9,999
Note: The Canadian Institute of Resources Law (CIRL) is a leading national centre of expertise on legal & policy issues relating to Canada's natural resources, with a mandate to undertake research, publication & educational programmes. A non-profit organization, CIRL maintains a small library serving lawyers, government & industry personnel & law students
Subjects covered: Energy Regulation & Policy; Environmental Law & Policy; Aboriginal Law, Water Law & Policy; Forestry Law & Policy; Mining Law & Policy
Personnel: *Summary:* 6 Professional(s)
Allan Ingelson, Executive Director
allan.ingelson@ucalgary.ca
Sue Parsons, Information Resources Officer
sue.parsons@ucalgary.ca

Calgary: Canadian Pacific Railway Business Information Services/Centre d'info-affaires
#500, 401 - 9th Ave. SW
Calgary, AB T2P 4Z4
Fax: 403-205-9013
888-333-8111
URL: www.cpr.ca
National Library Symbol: ACCPR
Founded in: 1972
Hours: by appointment only
Subjects covered: Transportation, Industry, Business
Services:
Inter-Library Loan (ILL)
Personnel: *Summary:* 5 Total; 3 Professional(s)
Carole Lacourte, Head, Business Intelligence & Archives

Calgary: Cancer Care Knowledge Centres
TBCC Knowledge Centre
1331 - 29 St. NW, #CC116
Calgary, AB T2V 1P9
Mailing Address: 7007 - 14 St. SW
Calgary, AB T2V 1P9
403-521-3765
e-mail: tbccinfo@ucalgary.ca
Hours: M-F 8:00-4:00
Services:
Internet Access
Inter-Library Loan (ILL)
Marcus Vaska, Librarian
mmvaska@ucalgary.ca
403-521-3765

Calgary: Chevron Canada Resources Library
500 - 5th Ave. SW
Calgary, AB T2P 0L7
403-234-5000
Fax: 403-234-5947
URL: www.chevron.ca
www.chevron.com
No public access
Founded in: 1954
Subjects covered: Physical Sciences, Engineering, Technology, Natural Resources, Earth Sciences

Calgary: Devon Energy Corporation (Canada) Corporate Library
#2000, 400 - 3rd Ave. SW
Calgary, AB T2P 4H2
403-232-5581
Fax: 403-213-8099
National Library Symbol: ACH
No public access
Hours: M-F 8:00-12:00, 1:00-5:00
Acquisitions Budget: $250,000 - $499,999
For Print: $100,000 - $249,999
For Electronic: $250,000 - $499,999
Special Collections: GSC Publications
Subjects covered: Energy, Mineral Resources, Oil & Gas, Engineering.
Services:
Remote Access
Internet Access
Access to Subscription Databases
Inter-Library Loan (ILL)
Personnel: *Summary:* 3 Total; 1 Professional(s); 2 Other employees
Mariela Parra, Corporate Librarian
mariela.parra@devoncanada.com
403-232-5581

Calgary: DeVry Institute of Technology Calgary Library
2700 - 3rd Ave. SE
Calgary, AB T2A 7W4
403-235-3450
Fax: 403-207-6227
800-363-5558
URL: www.devry.ca/student_library.html
No public access
Hours: M, W, F 8:00-6:00; Tu-Th 8:00-5:00
Acquisitions Budget: $10,000 - $24,999
Subjects covered: Business, Electronics, Computer, General Education
Services:
Remote Access
Internet Access
Access to Subscription Databases
Inter-Library Loan (ILL)

Suzzette Campbell, Library Assistant
406-207-3100

Calgary: Doucette Library of Teaching Resources
370 Education Block, 2500 University Dr. NW
Calgary, AB T2N 1N4
403-220-5637
Fax: 403-220-8211
URL: www.educ1.ucalgary.ca/doucette/index.shtml
Profile: Education
Hours: M-F 8:30-16:30
Special Collections: Alberta curriculum documents, curriculum resource materials, professional support materials, children's literature, French language materials, audiovisual resources, historical collection, thesis collection.
Subjects covered: Education

Barbara Brydges, Director
brydges@ucalgary.ca
403-220-6295

Calgary: EnCana Corporation Information Centre
150 - 9 Ave., SW
Calgary, AB T2P 2S5
403-645-7645
Fax: 403-645-7649
URL: www.encana.com
National Library Symbol: ACPP
No public access
Hours: M-F 7:30-5:00
Acquisitions Budget: $250,000 - $499,999
Subjects covered: Energy; Oil & Gas
Services:
Access to Subscription Databases
Personnel: *Summary:* 4 Total; 4 Technical(s)
Jeanne Kimber, Group Leader, Information Centre
Alicia Hawkings, Information Analyst
alicia.hawkings@encana.com
403-645-3085
Pat Bolander, Information Technician
pat.bolander@encana.com
403-645-7641
Barb Miller, Information Technician
barb.miller@encana.com
403-645-6642

Calgary: Energy Resources Conservation Board (ERCB) Library
640 - 5th Ave. SW
Calgary, AB T2P 3G4
403-297-8242
Fax: 403-297-3517
e-mail: library@ercb.ca
infoservices@ercb.ca
URL: www.ercb.ca
National Library Symbol: ACER
Founded in: 1956
Hours: M-F 12:00-4:00
Acquisitions Budget: $50,000 - $99,999
Special Collections: EUB publications & decisions
Subjects covered: Energy, Natural Resources, Conservation
Services:
Internet Access for a fee
Inter-Library Loan (ILL)
Microform Equipment: Reader
Personnel: *Summary:* 3 Total; 1 Professional(s); 3 Technical(s); 1 Other employees
Angela Burns, Librarian
angela.burns@ercb.ca
403-297-3515

Calgary: Gallagher Library of Geology & Geophysics
#180, Earth Science Bldg., 2500 University Dr. NW
Calgary, AB T2N 1N4
403-220-6042
Fax: 403-282-6075
e-mail: gallagher.library@ucalgary.ca
URL: library.ucalary.ca/branches/gallagherlibrary
Founded in: 1974
Hours: M-Th 8:30am-9:00pm; F 8:30-4:30; Sa 12:00-4:00
Acquisitions Budget: $50,000 - $99,999
Subjects covered: Energy, Natural Resources, Physical Sciences, Earth Sciences, Mineral Resources, Sedimentary & Petroleum Geology, Geophysics

Services:
Internet Access
Access to Subscription Databases
Inter-Library Loan (ILL)
Personnel: *Summary:* 3 Total; 1 Professional(s); 2 Other employees
Claudette Cloutier, Manager
ccloutie@ucalgary.ca
403-220-3447
Regina Shedd, Reference Specialist
Patricia Johnson, Reference Specialist
Sandy Blazina, Document Delivery Specialist

Calgary: Health Information Network Calgary University of Calgary Health Sciences Library

#1450, 3330 Hospital Dr. NW
Calgary, AB T2N 1N4
Mailing Address: 3330 Hospital Dr. NW
Calgary, AB T2N 1N4
403-220-6855
e-mail: hslibr@ucalgary.ca
hslcirc@ucalgary.ca
URL: hinc.ucalgary.ca
National Library Symbol: ACUM
Consortia Membership: Canadian Virtual Health Library (CVHL)
Hours: M-Th 8:00am-10:00pm; F 8:00-6:00; Sa 10:00-6:00; Su 12:00-8:00
Subjects covered: Nursing, Physical Therapy, Psychiatry, Psychology, Occupational Therapy, Patient Education, Consumer Health, Social Work, Pastoral Care & Health Care Administration
Services:
Internet Access
Inter-Library Loan (ILL)
Personnel: *Summary:* 2 Total; 2 Technical(s)
Taryn Lenders, Manager
tlenders@ucalgary.ca
403-220-5573

Calgary: Health Sciences Library

Health Sciences Centre
3330 Hospital Dr. NW
Calgary, AB T2N 4N1
403-220-6857
Fax: 403-282-7992
e-mail: hslibr@ucalgary.ca
hslcirc@ucalgary.ca
URL: library.ucalgary.ca/hsl
National Library Symbol: ACUM
Consortia Membership: Canadian Virtual Health Library (CVHL)
Founded in: 1972
Hours: M-Th 8:00am-10:00pm; F 8:00-6:00; Sa 10:00-6:00; Su 12:00-8:00
Acquisitions Budget: $1,000,000 plus
Special Collections: Family Medicine, History of Medicine
Subjects covered: Medicine, Health Sciences, Nursing
Services:
Internet Access
Access to Subscription Databases
Inter-Library Loan (ILL) for a fee
Microform Equipment: Computer; Reader
Personnel: *Summary:* 16 Total; 4 Professional(s); 11 Technical(s)
Christine Hayward, Interim Director
hayward@ucalgary.ca
403-220-6858
Lorraine Toews, Head, Public Services
ltoews@ucalgary.ca
403-220-3750
Helen Lee Robertson, Liaison/Document Delivery
roberthl@ucalgary.ca
403-220-3736
Lorraine Baker, ILL Assistant

Calgary: Husky Energy Inc. Corporate Library

707 - 8th Ave. SW
Calgary, AB T2P 3G7
Mailing Address: PO Box 6525, Station D
Calgary, AB T2P 3G7
403-298-6111
Fax: 403-298-7464
URL: www.huskyenergy.com
No public access
Founded in: 1975
Hours: 8:00-5:00
Subjects covered: Earth Sciences, Petroleum, Engineering, Technology, Business, Management
Services:
Inter-Library Loan (ILL)
Personnel: *Summary:* 3 Total; 1 Professional(s); 1 Technical(s)

Calgary: Imperial Oil Resources Limited Research Centre

3535 Research Rd. NW
Calgary, AB T2L 2K8
403-284-7417
Fax: 403-284-7589
e-mail: contact.imperial@esso.ca
National Library Symbol: ACIPRD
No public access
Acquisitions Budget: $25,000 - $49,999
Subjects covered: Petroleum Engineering, Ice Engineering, Soil Mechanics, Oil Spill, Corrosion
Personnel: *Summary:* 1 Total; 1 Professional(s)

Calgary: Imperial Oil Resources Limited Information Centre

237 - 4th Ave. SW
Calgary, AB T2P 0H6
403-237-4520
Fax: 403-237-3728
e-mail: contact.imperial@esso.ca
National Library Symbol: ACI
No public access
Subjects covered: Energy
Services:
Inter-Library Loan (ILL)
Personnel: *Summary:* 4 Total; 3 Professional(s); 1 Technical(s)

Calgary: Information Centre (Calgary)

Government of Alberta, Justice, Office of the Chief Medical Examiner
4070 Bowness Rd. NW
Calgary, AB T3B 3R7
Mailing Address: 4070 Bowness Rd. NW
Calgary, AB T3B 3R7
403-297-8123
Fax: 403-297-3429
National Library Symbol: ACCME
No public access
Hours: Staff available W 8:30-3:30 only
Acquisitions Budget: 0-$9,999
For Print: 0-$9,999
For Electronic: 0-$9,999
Subjects covered: Forensic Medicine, Toxicology, Bereavement, Death Investigation
Services:
Inter-Library Loan (ILL)
Personnel: *Summary:* 1 Professional(s)
Karen McManus, Librarian
karen.mcmanus@gov.ab.ca

Calgary: Jacobs Canada Inc. Library

PO Box 5244, Stn A
Calgary, AB T2H 2N7
403-258-6527
e-mail: carol.seebruch@jacobs.com
No public access
Founded in: 1978
Hours: M-F
Acquisitions Budget: $50,000 - $99,999
Subjects covered: Physical Sciences, Engineering, Technology
Services:
Inter-Library Loan (ILL)
Microform Equipment: Reader
Personnel: *Summary:* 1 Total; 1 Professional(s)
Carol A. Seebruch, Information Resources Coordinator
carol.seebruch@jacobs.com

Calgary: Mount Royal University Library

4825 Mount Royal Gate SW
Calgary, AB T3E 6K6
403-440-6140
Fax: 403-440-6758
URL: library.mtroyal.ca
National Library Symbol: ACMR
Consortia Membership: The Alberta Library; Council of Prairie & Pacific University Libraries (COPPUL); Canadian Research Knowledge Network (CRKN)
Founded in: 1911
Hours: M-Th 7:45am-10:00pm; F 7:45M-8:00pm; Sa-Su 10:00-8:00
Acquisitions Budget: $500,000 - $999,999
For Print: $500,000 - $999,999
For Electronic: $100,000 - $249,999
Note: The library is an affiliate member of the Council of Prairie and Pacific University Libraries (COPPUL).
Special Collections: Canadian Public Relations Society
Subjects covered: Applied Degrees
Services:
Internet Access
Inter-Library Loan (ILL)
Microform Equipment: Reader
Personnel: *Summary:* 41 Total; 9 Professional(s); 36 Technical(s);
Carol Shepstone, Director of Library Services
403-440-6134
Pearl Herscovitch, Chairperson
403-440-6022
Katharine Barrette, Collections Librarian
403-440-6022
Francine May, Coordinator, Technical Services
403-440-6128
Geoff Owens, Coordinator, Media
403-440-7737
Michelle Sinotte, Coordinator, Information Services
403-440-5683

Calgary: National Energy Board / L'Office national de l'energie Library

444 - 7th Ave. SW
Calgary, AB T2P 0X8
403-299-3561
Fax: 403-292-5503
800-899-1265
TDD: 8006321663
e-mail: library@neb-one.gc.ca
bibliotheque@neb-one.gc.ca
URL: www.neb-one.gc.ca
Profile: Provides a range of services including consultation of regulatory documents, copies of NEB publications, referrals to other sources of information
National Library Symbol: ACNEB
Consortia Membership: Federal Libraries Consortium (FLC)
Founded in: 1959
Hours: M-F 9:00-4:00
Acquisitions Budget: $250,000 - $499,999
Note: Public cannot borrow materials directly, but can order them through inter-library loans
Special Collections: Statutes, federal regulations, books, annual reports; directories, encyclopediae, industry-related indexes; journals, newspapers; half of collection is directly related to NEB hearings
Subjects covered: Energy, Natural Resources
Services:
Internet Access
Inter-Library Loan (ILL)
Photocopies at no charge
Personnel: *Summary:* 5 Total; 1 Professional(s); 3 Technical(s); 1 Other employees
Shelley Watt, Group Leader
403-299-3571

Calgary: Nexen Inc. Library

801 - 7th Ave. SW
Calgary, AB T2P 3P7
403-699-5425
Fax: 403-232-1826
e-mail: marlene_robertson@nexeninc.com
National Library Symbol: ACCOP
No public access
Founded in: 1978
Hours: M-F
Acquisitions Budget: $50,000 - $99,999
Subjects covered: Oil & Gas, Business
Services:
Inter-Library Loan (ILL)
Personnel: *Summary:* 3 Total; 1 Professional(s); 2 Technical(s)

Marlene Robertson, Librarian
marlene_robertson@nexeninc.com
Louise Dickson, Library Technician
louise_dickson@nexeninc.com

Calgary: NOVA Chemicals Corporation
1000 - 7th Ave. SW
Calgary, AB T2P 5C6
Mailing Address: PO Box 2518
Calgary, AB T2P 5C6
403-750-3600
Fax: 403-291-3208
URL: www.novachem.com
National Library Symbol: ACNH
No public access
Hours: M-F
Subjects covered: Plastics, Petrochemicals, Polymers, Fluid Dynamics
Services:
Inter-Library Loan (ILL)
Microform Equipment: Reader

Calgary: Peter Lougheed Knowledge Centre
#0634, 3500 - 26 Ave. NE
Calgary, AB T1Y 6J4
403-943-4737
Fax: 403-219-3559
e-mail: plcinfo@ucalgary.ca
National Library Symbol: ACPLC
Hours: M-F 8:00-4:00
Note: Health Connection (Consumer Health Library)
Subjects covered: Medicine, Nursing, Health Sciences
Services:
Inter-Library Loan (ILL)
Kathryn Ranjit, Librarian
kathryn.ranjit@ucalgary.ca
403-943-4736
Tuyet Lam, Information Specialist
tlam@ucalgary.ca
403-943-4074

Calgary: Rockyview General Hospital Knowledge Centre
#4EE11, 7007 - 14 St. SW
Calgary, AB T2V 1P9
Mailing Address: 7007 - 14 St. SW
Calgary, AB T2V 1P9
403-943-3373
Fax: 403-943-3486
e-mail: rghinfo@ucalgary.ca
National Library Symbol: ACRVH
Hours: M-F 8:00-4:00
Acquisitions Budget: $50,000 - $99,999
Note: Health Connection (Consumer Health Library)
Special Collections: Health Connection (Consumer Health)
Subjects covered: Medicine, Nursing, Allied Health, Consumer Health
Services:
Internet Access
Inter-Library Loan (ILL) for a fee of $3 per article
Personnel: *Summary:* 1 Professional(s); 9 Technical(s); 5 Volunteer(s)
Christie Hurrell, Libararian
christie.hurrell@ucalgary.ca
403-943-3488
Melanie Belliveau, Information Services
mbellive@ucalgary.ca
403-943-3483

Calgary: Shell Canada Limited Calgary Research Centre Technical Library
3655 - 36th St. NW
Calgary, AB T2P 1Y8
403-384-6500
800-661-1600
e-mail: questions@Shell.com
URL: www.shell.ca
National Library Symbol: ACSCL
No public access
Founded in: 1983
Hours: M-F
Subjects covered: Engineering; Analytical Chemistry; Oil Sands; Refining

Calgary: South Health Campus Knowledge Centre
Wellness Centre, 1st Fl.
4448 Front St. SE
Calgary, AB T3M 1M4
403-956-3930
e-mail: shcinfo@ucalgary.ca
Services:
Internet Access
Inter-Library Loan (ILL)
Elizabeth Atken, Librarian
eaitken@ucalgary.ca
403-956-3921

Calgary: Southern Alberta Institute of Technology Library
1301 - 16th Ave. NW
Calgary, AB T2M 0L4
403-284-8616
Fax: 403-284-8619
Other contact info: Text: 403-805-2436
e-mail: library.intercampus@sait.ca
URL: library.sait.ca
National Library Symbol: ACSA
Consortia Membership: The Alberta Library
Founded in: 1916
Hours: Sept.-May: M-Th 7:30am-11:00pm; F 7:30-5:00; Sa, Su 10:00-5:00. June-Aug.: M-Th 8:00-6:30; F 8:00-5:00
Acquisitions Budget: $250,000 - $499,999
For Print: $100,000 - $249,999
For Electronic: $100,000 - $249,999
Note: The library is an affiliate member of the Council of Prairie and Pacific University Libraries (COPPUL).
Special Collections: Standards, Statistics Canada, SAIT Archives
Subjects covered: Communications, Technology, Physical Sciences, Engineering, Economics, Medicine, Nursing, Health Sciences, Business, Media, Allied Health
Services:
Internet Access
Access to Subscription Databases
Inter-Library Loan (ILL) for a fee
Fee Based Research
Microform Equipment: Computer; Reader
Personnel: *Summary:* 22 Total; 5 Professional(s); 10 Technical(s); 7 Other employees
Susan Brayford, Manager, Library Operations
susan.brayford@sait.ca
403-210-4477
Dave Weber, Liaison Librarian
dave.weber@sait.ca
403-284-8476
Anne Marie DeGroot, Liaison Librarian
annemarie.degroot@sait.ca
403-284-8431

Calgary: Sproule Associates Limited Library
#900, North Tower, Sunlife Plaza, 140 - 4th Ave. SW
Calgary, AB T2P 3N3
403-294-5500
Fax: 403-294-5590
877-777-6135
e-mail: info@sproule.com
URL: www.sproule.com
No public access
Hours: M-F 8:00-4:30
Subjects covered: Physical Sciences, Engineering, Technology
Rita Loughlin, Records/Information Manager

Calgary: Suncor Inc. Library
150 - 6 Ave. SW
Calgary, AB T2P 3E3
Mailing Address: PO Box 2844
Calgary, AB T2P 3E3
403-269-8000
Fax: 403-296-3030
e-mail: bzinter@suncor.com
No public access
Hours: M-F
Subjects covered: Oil & Gas, Petroleum, Geology, Petroleum Engineering, Business
Services:
Inter-Library Loan (ILL)
Personnel: *Summary:* 1 Total; 1 Professional(s)
Barbara Zinter, Communications Researcher
bzinter@suncor.com
403-269-8128

Calgary: Talisman Energy Inc. Information Resource Centre
#2000, 888 - 3rd St. SW
Calgary, AB T2P 5C5
403-237-1429
Fax: 403-231-2823
e-mail: irc@talisman-energy.com
National Library Symbol: ACBPE
No public access
Subjects covered: Physical Sciences, Engineering, Technology, Energy, Natural Resources
Personnel: *Summary:* 5 Total; 2 Professional(s); 3 Technical(s)
Cathy Ross, Coordinator, Information Resources
cross@talisman-energy.com
403-237-1040

Calgary: TransAlta Corporation Library
110 - 12th Ave. SW
Calgary, AB T2P 2M1
Mailing Address: PO Box 1900, Stn. M
Calgary, AB T2P 2M1
403-267-7110
e-mail: customers@transalta.com
URL: www.transalta.com
Hours: M-F by appointment only
Subjects covered: Energy; Environment

Calgary: TransCanada Corporation Document Library
450 - 1st St. SW
Calgary, AB T2P 5H1
403-920-2000
Fax: 403-920-2200
800-661-3805
URL: www.transcanada.com
National Library Symbol: ACTRPL
Founded in: 1957
Special Collections: Reports; Publications; Archives; Videos
Subjects covered: Energy; Engineering; Natural Gas

Calgary: University of Calgary Libraries & Cultural Resources
410 University Crt. NW
Calgary, AB T2N 1N4
403-220-8895
Fax: 403-282-6024
e-mail: libinfo@ucalgary.ca
illacu@isis.lib.ucalgary.ca
URL: library.ucalgary.ca
National Library Symbol: ACU
Consortia Membership: The Alberta Library; Canadian Research Knowledge Network (CRKN); Council of Prairie & Pacific University Libraries (COPPUL); Health Knowledge Network (HKN); Health Information Network
Founded in: 1966
Hours: M-Th 7:30am-10:45pm; F 7:30am-7:45pm; Sa 10:00-5:45; Su 10:00-10:45
Acquisitions Budget: $1,000,000 plus
For Print: $1,000,000 plus
For Electronic: $1,000,000 plus
Services:
Remote Access
Internet Access
Access to Subscription Databases
Inter-Library Loan (ILL)
Fee Based Research
Microform Equipment: Computer; Reader
Personnel: *Summary:* 221 Total; 43 Professional(s); 5 Technical(s); 173 Other employees
H. Thomas Hickerson, University Librarian
Peggy White, Interim Associate University Librarian, Client Services
pwhite@ucalgary.ca
403-220-3611
Helen Clarke, Associate Vice Provost, Collections & Technical Services
hclarke@ucalgary.ca
403-220-3755
Terry Reilly, Director, Archives & Special Collections
reilly@ucalgary.ca

Mary Westell, Assoc. University Librarian, Info. Technology & Scholarly Publishing
westell@ucalgary.ca
403-220-3764
Mary McConnell, Associate University Librarian, Planning & Administration
mmconne@ucalgary.ca
403-220-3725

Calgary: Women's Health Knowledge Centre
#185, 1441 - 29th St. NW
Calgary, AB T2N 4J8
403-944-2267
Fax: 403-944-4772
e-mail: whkcinfo@ucalgary.ca
Hours: M, W, F 8:00-4:00; Tu, Th 8:00-8:00
Services:
Internet Access
Inter-Library Loan (ILL)
Julie Alati-it, Information Specialist
jjsalati@ucalgary.ca
403-944-2267

Camrose: Augustana Campus Library
Classroom Bldg.
4901 - 46th Ave.
Camrose, AB T4V 2R3
780-679-1156
Fax: 780-679-1594
Other contact info: Phone, ILL: 780-679-1593
e-mail: augustana.library@ualberta.ca
augustana.reference@ualberta.ca
National Library Symbol: ACAL
Consortia Membership: NEOS Library Consortium
Founded in: 1911
Hours: M-Th 8:30-10:00; F 8:30-4:00; Sa 10:00-5:00; Su 2:00-10:00 by appointment only
Note: Augustana Faculty was formerly known as Augustana University College.
Services:
Inter-Library Loan (ILL)
Microform Equipment: Reader
Personnel: *Summary:* 10 Total; 3 Professional(s); 1 Technical(s); 5 Other employees;
Nancy Goebell, Head Librarian
nancy.goebel@ualberta.ca

Cold Lake: Aerospace Engineering Test Establishment Technical Reference Library/Bibliothèque de référence technique
Canadian Forces Base
Cold Lake, AB T9M 2C6
Mailing Address: PO Box 6550, Stn Forces
Cold Lake, AB T9M 2C6
780-840-8000 ext: 8062
Fax: 780-840-7381
URL: www.rcaf-arc.forces.gc.ca/4w-4e/units-unites
National Library Symbol: AMECFA
Hours: M-F 7:30-4:00 by appointment only
Note: Physical location: Louis St Laurent Bldg., 555, boul de la Carrière, 1e étage, Gatineau QC
Subjects covered: Materials from former Maritime & Land Technical libraries & Ammunition library
Services:
Microform Equipment: Computer; Reader

Devon: Devon Library & Information Centre
#A129, 1 Oil Patch Dr.
Devon, AB T9G 1A8
780-987-8773
Fax: 780-987-8778
e-mail: devon_library@albertainnovates.ca
National Library Symbol: ADCR
Consortia Membership: NEOS Library Consortium
Hours: M-F 8:15-12:00
Note: While a collection remains on-site, this library is no longer staffed & is not open to the public; please direct all inquiries to the Mill Woods branch.
Subjects covered: Coal & Hydrocarbon Processing, Chemistry & Chemical Engineering, Oil Sands/Heavy Oil Upgrading, Catalysis
Lucy Heintz, Circulation/Serials
lucy.heintz@albertainnovates.ca
780-450-5064

Drayton Valley: The Pembina Institute for Appropriate Development Library
PO Box 7558
Drayton Valley, AB T7A 1S7
780-542-6272
Fax: 780-542-6464
URL: www.pembina.org
Subjects covered: Environment

Drumheller: Royal Tyrrell Museum of Palaeontology Library
Hwy. 838, Midland Provincial Park
Drumheller, AB T0J 0Y0
Mailing Address: PO Box 7500
Drumheller, AB T0J 0Y0
403-823-7707 ext: 6213
Fax: 403-823-7131
888-440-4240
Other contact info: 310-0000 & ask for 823-7707 (in Alberta)
e-mail: tyrrell.library@gov.ab.ca
URL: www.tyrrellmuseum.com
National Library Symbol: ADTMP
Founded in: 1982
Hours: M-F 8:15-4:30 by appointment only
Acquisitions Budget: $50,000 - $99,999
Special Collections: Tyrrell Museum Archives, 20,000 slides & photographs, field notes
Subjects covered: Life Sciences, Palaeontology, Geology, Natural History
Services:
Inter-Library Loan (ILL)
Fee Based Research
Microform Equipment: Computer; Reader
Personnel: *Summary:* 1 Total; 1 Professional(s)

Edmonton: Acuren Inc. Library
7450 - 18th St.
Edmonton, AB T6P 1N8
780-440-2131
Fax: 780-440-1167
800-663-9729
URL: www.acuren.com
Hours: M-F 8:00-5:00 by appointment only
Acquisitions Budget: $25,000 - $49,999
Subjects covered: Physical Sciences, Engineering, Technology
Services:
Inter-Library Loan (ILL)
Susan Lim, Library Clerk

Edmonton: AECOM
17007 - 107th Ave.
Edmonton, AB T5S 1G3
780-486-7000
Fax: 780-486-7070
URL: www.aecom.com
No public access
Acquisitions Budget: $25,000 - $49,999
Subjects covered: Physical Sciences, Engineering, Technology
Services:
Inter-Library Loan (ILL)

Edmonton: Alberta Government Library (Administration), Service Alberta
South Tower, Capital Health Centre
10030 - 107 St., 3rd Fl.
Edmonton, AB T5J 3E4
780-427-7272
Fax: 780-422-3980
e-mail: library.107st@gov.ab.ca
National Library Symbol: AEHSD
Consortia Membership: NEOS Library Consortium; The Alberta Library; Canadian Virtual Health Library (CVHL)
Founded in: 2000
Hours: M-F 8:15-4:30
Acquisitions Budget: For Print: $250,000 - $499,999
Subjects covered: Government
Linda Scott, Manager, Library Services
linda.r.scott@gov.ab.ca
780-415-8344

Edmonton: Alberta Hospital Edmonton Library
Bldg. 9
#33, 17480 Fort Rd. SW
Edmonton, AB T5J 2J7
Mailing Address: PO Box 307
Edmonton, AB T5J 2J7
780-342-5268
Fax: 780-342-5608
e-mail: AHELibrary@albertahealthservices.ca
National Library Symbol: AEAH
Consortia Membership: NEOS Library Consortium; Canadian Virtual Health Library (CVHL)
Founded in: 1955
Hours: M-F 8:00-4:15
Acquisitions Budget: $25,000 - $49,999; Serves mental health staff & patients.
Subjects covered: Mental health
Services:
Inter-Library Loan (ILL)
Personnel: *Summary:* 1 Total; 1 Technical(s)
Eileen Cardy, Library Technician
Eileen.Cardy@albertahealthservices.ca

Edmonton: Alberta Innovates - Technology Futures Mill Woods Library
250 Karl Clark Rd.
Edmonton, AB T6N 1E4
780-450-5229
Fax: 780-450-8996
e-mail: millwoods_library@albertainnovates.ca
URL: www.albertatechfutures.ca; www.albertainnovates.ca
National Library Symbol: AER
Consortia Membership: NEOS Library Consortium
Hours: M-F: 8:15-12:00, 1:00-4:30
Subjects covered: Advanced Materials & Processes, Biotechnology, Environmental Research & Engineering, Forestry Research, Industrial Engineering, Manufacturing Technologies, Pharmaceuticals, Pulp & Paper, Heavy Oil / Oil Sands
Services:
Inter-Library Loan (ILL)
Personnel: *Summary:* 7 Total; 1 Professional(s); 2 Technical(s)
Renee Morrissey, Reference Librarian
renee.morrissey@albertainnovates.ca
780-450-5022

Edmonton: Alberta Justice, Office of the Chief Medical Examiner Information Centre (Edmonton)
7007 - 116th St. NW
Edmonton, AB T6H 5R8
780-427-4987
Fax: 780-422-1265
URL: justice.alberta.ca
National Library Symbol: AEOCME
No public access
Founded in: 1981
Hours: W 8:00-4:00
Acquisitions Budget: 0-$9,999
Subjects covered: Pathology, Forensic Medicine, Toxicology, Bereavement, Death Investigation
Services:
Inter-Library Loan (ILL)
Personnel: *Summary:* 1 Total; 1 Professional(s)
Natalie LaFleur, Librarian
natalie.lafleur@gov.ab.ca

Edmonton: Alberta Land Surveyors' Association ALSA Library
#1000, 10020 - 101 A Ave.
Edmonton, AB T5J 3G2
780-429-8805
Fax: 780-429-3374
800-665-2572
e-mail: info@alsa.ab.ca
URL: www.alsa.ab.ca
Founded in: 1910
Special Collections: Technical reports
Subjects covered: Surveying; Mapping; Geomatics
Brian Munday, Executive Director
munday@alsa.ab.ca
Sharon Armstrong, Executive Assistant
armstrong@alsa.ab.ca
Dawn Phelan, Information Services Administrator
phelan@alsa.ab.ca

Edmonton: Cameron Science & Technology Library
1-50 Cameron Library, University of Alberta
Edmonton, AB T6G 2J8

780-492-8440
Fax: 780-492-2721
e-mail: sciref@library.ualberta.ca
Consortia Membership: NEOS Library Consortium
Founded in: 1964
Hours: M-Th 8:00-10:00; F 8:00-6:00; Sa 11:00-10:00; Su 11:00-6:00
Acquisitions Budget: $500,000 - $999,999
Note: Comprises the main Science & Technology Library, the Canadian Circumpolar Library, the Mathematics Library, the Physical Sciences Library, & the William C. Wonders Map Collection. Member of NEOS, COPPUL & TAL
Subjects covered: Science, Engineering, Home Economics, Agriculture, Forestry, Northern
Services:
Internet Access
Inter-Library Loan (ILL)
Microform Equipment: Computer; Reader
Personnel: *Summary:* 41 Total; 9 Professional(s); 32 Technical(s); 3 Volunteer(s)
Margaret Law, Associate Director Libraries
margaret.law@ualberta.ca
Susan Moysa, Reference Coordinator
susan.moysa@ualberta.ca
780-492-7907
Sandy Campbell, Collection Coordinator
sandy.campbell@ualberta.ca
780-492-7915

Edmonton: Canadian Circumpolar Collection
Cameron Library, University of Alberta
Edmonton, AB T6G 2E9
780-492-7915
Fax: 780-492-2721
National Library Symbol: AEUB
Founded in: 1961
Hours: M-Th 8:00-8:00; F 8:00-5:00; Sa, Su 11:00-5:00
Note: Formerly: Boreal Institute for Northern Studies Library. Member of NEOS, COPPUL & The Alberta Library
Special Collections: Theses, Expeditions
Subjects covered: Area oriented - all subjects Arctic, Canadian North, other cold regions; Canadian native materials
Services:
Inter-Library Loan (ILL)

Edmonton: Concordia University College of Alberta Arnold Guebert Memorial Library
7128 Ada Blvd.
Edmonton, AB T5B 4E4
780-479-9338
Fax: 780-471-6796
866-479-5200
e-mail: library@concordia.ab.ca
URL: library.concordia.ab.ca
National Library Symbol: AEC
Consortia Membership: Canadian Research Knowledge Network (CRKN); Council of Prairie & Pacific University Libraries (COPPUL); NEOS Library Consortium; The Alberta Library
Founded in: 1926
Hours: Sept-Apr: M-Th 8:00-9:00; F 8:00-5:00; Sa 11:00-5:00; Su 1:00-9:00. May-Aug: M-F 8:00-5:00.
Acquisitions Budget: $250,000 - $499,999
Subjects covered: Undergraduate, Religion, Math, Philosophy, Psychology, Chemistry, English, Biology, Environmental Sciences, History, After-Degree in Education, After-Degree in Environmental Health, Information Systems Security, Career Development, Music
Services:
Remote Access
Internet Access
Access to Subscription Databases
Inter-Library Loan (ILL)
Microform Equipment: Computer; Reader
Personnel: *Summary:* 12 Total; 3 Professional(s); 7 Technical(s); 2 Other employees
Dan Mirau, Library Director
dan.mirau@concordia.ab.ca
780-479-9334
Dana Ouellette, Information Services Librarian
dana.ouellette@concordia.ab.ca
780-479-9293
Anna Spencer, Librarian, Bibliographic Services & Acquisitions
anna.spencer@concordia.ab.ca
780-479-9333
Karen Hildebrandt, Access Services Coordinator
karen.hildebrandt@concordia.ab.ca
780-479-9336
Lynette Toews-Neufeldt, Information Services Coordinator & Campus Copyright Officer
lynette.toews-neufeldt@concordia.ab.ca
780-479-9339

Edmonton: Covenant Health Grey Nuns Community Hospital Health Sciences Library
#0634, 1100 Youville Dr. West
Edmonton, AB T6L 5X8
780-735-7300
Fax: 780-735-7202
e-mail: GNHLibrary@covenanthealth.ca
CovenantLibrary@covenanthealth.ca
URL: www.covenanthealth.ca
National Library Symbol: AEGNH
Consortia Membership: NEOS Library Consortium; Canadian Virtual Health Library (CVHL)
Hours: M-F 7:30-3:45
Acquisitions Budget: $250,000 - $499,999
Subjects covered: Medicine, Health Sciences, Nursing
Services:
Remote Access
Inter-Library Loan (ILL) for a fee of $6
Fee Based Research
Personnel: *Summary:* 6 Total; 1 Professional(s); 2 Technical(s); 2 Other employees
Sharna Polard, Manager, Learning Resources

Edmonton: Dept. of Resource Economics & Environmental Sociology REES Library
#515, General Services Bldg.
Edmonton, AB T6G 2H1
780-492-0815
Fax: 780-492-0268
URL: www.rees.ualberta.ca
Founded in: 1976
Hours: M-F 9:30-12:00, 12:30-4:00
Acquisitions Budget: $10,000 - $24,999
For Print: $10,000 - $24,999
For Electronic: 0-$9,999
Subjects covered: Agricultural Economics, Forest Economics, Rural Sociology, Agribusiness, Environmental Economics, Environmental Sociology
Personnel: *Summary:* 1 Total; 1 Technical(s)

Edmonton: Edmonton Planning & Development Dept. Library
10250 - 101 St., 6th Fl.
Edmonton, AB T5J 3P4
780-496-6165
Fax: 780-401-7069
Founded in: 1970
Hours: M-F 8:30-12:00, 1:00-4:30 by appointment only
Acquisitions Budget: $25,000 - $49,999
For Print: $25,000 - $49,999
For Electronic: 0-$9,999
Special Collections: Land Use Planning, Urban Design
Subjects covered: Housing, Planning & Public Works, Local Government, City Planning, Transportation Planning, Historic Preservation, Downtown & Neighbourhood Planning
Services:
Inter-Library Loan (ILL)
Fee Based Research
Personnel: *Summary:* 2 Total; 2 Professional(s)
Katherina Hui, Librarian
katherina.hui@edmonton.ca

Edmonton: EPCOR Research Services
#2000, 10423 - 101 St. NW
Edmonton, AB T5H 0E8
780-412-3414
URL: www.epcor.ca
National Library Symbol: AEEP
No public access
Subjects covered: Engineering, Technology, Physical Sciences, Electronics, Computer Data
Services:
Inter-Library Loan (ILL)
Personnel: *Summary:* 1 Technical(s)
Aileen Fung, Research Services Coordinator

Edmonton: Faculty of Native Studies Native Studies Reading Room
#2-31 Pembina Hall
Edmonton, AB T6G 2H8
780-492-2991
Fax: 780-492-0527
e-mail: nativestudies@ualberta.ca
URL: www.ualberta.ca/nativestudies
Subjects covered: Native Studies
Personnel: *Summary:* 1 Total; 1 Other employees

Edmonton: Grant MacEwan University City Centre Campus Library
10700 - 104 Ave.
Edmonton, AB T5J 2P2
Mailing Address: PO Box 1796
Edmonton, AB T5J 2P2
780-497-5850
e-mail: info@macewan.ca
URL: library.macewan.ca
National Library Symbol: AEGMCT
Consortia Membership: The Alberta Library; Health Knowledge Network (HKN); NEOS Library Consortium; Council of Prairie & Pacific University Libraries (COPPUL)
Founded in: 1971
Hours: Winter: M-Th 7:30-11:00; F 7:30-9:00; Sa, Su 10:00-6:00
Acquisitions Budget: $500,000 - $999,999
Note: The library is an affiliate member of the Council of Prairie & Pacific University Libraries (COPPUL).
Subjects covered: Arts, Fine Arts, Business, Science, Nursing, Social Services
Services:
Internet Access
Inter-Library Loan (ILL)
Access to online catalogue & databases
Microform Equipment: Computer; Reader
Personnel: *Summary:* 43 Total; 9 Professional(s); 35 Other employees
Jane Duffy, Dean of Libraries
780-497-5849
Glenna Helm, Manager, Library Administration
780-497-5893
Jill Day, Manager, Cataloguing and Acquisitions
dayj@macewan.ca
780-497-5867
Gordon Bertrand, Coordinator, Library Technology
bertrandg@macewan.ca
780-497-5778
Nick Ursulak, Acting Manager, Borrower Services
780-497-5853

Edmonton: Hemisphere Engineering Inc Library
10950 - 119th St.
Edmonton, AB T5H 3P5
780-452-1800
Fax: 780-453-5205
URL: hemisphere-eng.com
No public access
Founded in: 1958
Acquisitions Budget: $25,000 - $49,999
Subjects covered: Physical Sciences, Engineering, Technology

Edmonton: John Alexander Weir Memorial Law Library
2nd Fl., Law Centre, University of Alberta
Edmonton, AB T6G 2H5
780-492-3371
Fax: 780-492-7546
e-mail: lawref@library.ualberta.ca
National Library Symbol: AEUL
Consortia Membership: NEOS Library Consortium
Hours: M-Th 8:00am-10:00pm; F 8:00-6:00; Sa 11:00-6:00; Su 11:00-10:00
Acquisitions Budget: $500,000 - $999,999
Subjects covered: Anglo-American Law (mainly coverage strong in countries that use the common law system); Constitutional Law; Environment Law; Health Law; Human Rights; Aboriginal Law
Services:
Microform Equipment: Computer; Reader
Personnel: *Summary:* 7 Total; 1 Professional(s); 6 Other employees
Grant Kayler, Librarian
grant.kyler@ualberta.ca
780-492-3305

Wanda Quoika-Stanka, Acting Librarian
wanda.quoika-stanka@ualberta.ca
780-492-1448
Shelley Brown, Circulation/Reserve
shelley.brown@ualberta.ca
780-492-1445

Edmonton: John W. Scott Health Sciences Library
#2K3.28 Walter C. Mackenzie Health Sciences Centre
University of Alberta
Edmonton, AB T6G 2R7
780-492-3899
Fax: 780-492-6960
e-mail: jwsinfo@library.ualberta.ca
Consortia Membership: NEOS Library Consortium; Canadian Virtual Health Library (CVHL)
Hours: Fall/Winter: M-Th 8:0012:00 (midnight); F 8:00am-10:00pm; Sa, Su 11:00-10:00. Spring/Summer: 8:00am-9:00pm; F 8:00-6:00' Sa, Su 11:00-6:00
Acquisitions Budget: $500,000 - $999,999
Note: Research Librarian a joint appointment with Alberta Heritage Foundation for Medical Research
Subjects covered: Medicine, Health Sciences; Disease
Services:
Internet Access
Inter-Library Loan (ILL)
Document delivery
Microform Equipment: Computer; Reader
Personnel: *Summary:* 16 Total; 8 Professional(s); 12 Technical(s)
Marlene Dorgan, Head, Health Sciences Libraries
780-492-7945
Iris Richardson, Head, Circulation
780-492-7954
Linda Seale, Head, Information Services
780-492-7943
Jerry Kubina, Head, Interlibrary Loans
780-492-5154

Edmonton: J.P. Das Developmental Disabilities Centre Library
#6-102, Education Bldg. North
Edmonton, AB T6G 2G5
780-492-4505
Fax: 780-492-1318
URL: dascentre.educ.ualberta.ca
No public access

Edmonton: King's University College Simona Maaskant Library
9125 - 50 St.
Edmonton, AB T6B 2H3
780-465-8304
Fax: 780-465-3534
e-mail: library@kingsu.ca
URL: www.kingsu.ca
National Library Symbol: AEKC
Consortia Membership: Canadian Research Knowledge Network (CRKN); Council of Prairie & Pacific University Libraries (COPPUL); Health Knowledge Network (HKN); NEOS Library Consortium; The Alberta Library
Founded in: 1979
Hours: Sept.-April: M-Th 7:45am-9:00pm; F 7:45-5:00; Sa 10:00-5:00. May-Aug.: M-F 8:00-4:00
Acquisitions Budget: $100,000 - $249,999
For Print: $100,000 - $249,999
For Electronic: $25,000 - $49,999
Special Collections: Dutch language collection
Services:
Remote Access
Internet Access
Access to Subscription Databases
Inter-Library Loan (ILL)
Selected internet resources available from an Internet Resources page
Microform Equipment: Computer; Reader
Personnel: *Summary:* 7 Total; 2 Professional(s); 2 Technical(s); 3 Other employees
G. Marcille Frederick, Director of Library Services
marcille.frederick@kingsu.ca
780-465-3500 ext. 8053
Karna Antoniw, Reference Librarian
karna.antoniw@kingsu.ca
780-465-3500 ext. 8052
Katherine Jenkins, Contact, Technical Services/Acquisitions & Cataloguing
katherine.jenkins@kingsu.ca
780-465-3500 ext. 8051
Merlene Staatz, Contact, Technical Services, Serials, Interlibrary Loans
merlene.staatz@kingsu.ca
780-564-3500 ext. 8054
Hyacinth Barrett, Contact, Circulation Services
hyacinth.barrett@kingsu.ca
780-465-3500 ext. 8016

Edmonton: Library (Edmonton)
#200, 9636 - 51st Ave.
Edmonton, AB T6E 6A5
780-438-1460
Fax: 780-437-7125
No public access
Subjects covered: Environmental & Geotechnical Engineering
Personnel: *Summary:* 1 Total; 1 Professional(s)

Edmonton: Millard Health Clinical Library
131 Airport Rd.
Edmonton, AB T5G 0W6
780-498-3221
Fax: 780-498-7858
888-498-9902
URL: www.millardhealth.com
Consortia Membership: Health Knowledge Network (HKN)
No public access
Founded in: 1995
Hours: M-Th 7:00-5:00, F 7:00-4:30
Acquisitions Budget: $25,000 - $49,999
Subjects covered: Rehabilitation, Disability, Psychosocial & Medical Issues
Services:
Internet Access
Personnel: *Summary:* 4 Total; 1 Technical(s); 3 Other employees
Roger Salus, Library Technician
roger.salus@millardhealth.com

Edmonton: Misericordia Community Hospital Weinlos Library
#INW-32, 16940 - 87th Ave.
Edmonton, AB T5R 4H5
780-930-2708
Fax: 780-930-2909
e-mail: MISLibrary@covenanthealth.ca
National Library Symbol: AEMH
Consortia Membership: NEOS Library Consortium; Canadian Virtual Health Library (CVHL)
Founded in: 1971
Hours: M-F 7:30-3:45
Acquisitions Budget: $50,000 - $99,999
Subjects covered: Medicine, Nursing, Health Sciences
Services:
Remote Access
Inter-Library Loan (ILL)
Personnel: *Summary:* 3 Total; 1 Professional(s); 1 Technical(s); 1 Other employees;
Sharna Polard, Manager, Library Services
sharna.polard@covenanthealth.ca
780-735-7251
Tara Boizard, Library Technician
tara.boizard@covenanthealth.ca
780-735-9303

Edmonton: NorQuest College Library
Learner Centre, Downtown Campus, 10215 - 108th St., 5th Fl.
Edmonton, AB T5J 1L6
Mailing Address: Main Building, Downtown Campus, 10215 - 108th St., 5th Fl.
Edmonton, AB T5J 1L6
780-644-6070
Fax: 780-644-6082
Other contact info: Computer Assistance, Phone: 780-644-6085
e-mail: library@norquest.ca
URL: library.norquest.ca
National Library Symbol: AECV
Consortia Membership: The Alberta Library
Founded in: 1970
Hours: M-Th 7:30am-8:00pm; F 7:30-5:00; Sa 12:00-4:00
Acquisitions Budget: $50,000 - $99,999
Subjects covered: Education; English as a Second Language; Literacy; Vocational Training; Skills Training
Services:
Internet Access
Access to Subscription Databases
Inter-Library Loan (ILL)
Personnel: *Summary:* 11 Total; 1 Professional(s); 6 Technical(s); 4 Other employees

Edmonton: Northern Alberta Institute of Technology McNally Library
#3000, 11762 - 106 St. NW
Edmonton, AB T5G 2R1
780-471-8844
Fax: 780-471-8813
877-222-1722
e-mail: illo@nait.ab.ca
URL: www.nait.ca
National Library Symbol: AENA
Consortia Membership: The Alberta Library; Health Knowledge Network (HKN)
Founded in: 1963
Hours: M-F 7:45-5:00; W 7:45-8:00; Sa 12:00-5:00
Acquisitions Budget: $250,000 - $499,999
Subjects covered: Business, Physical & Health Sciences, Engineering, Trades, Computers, Technology
Services:
Remote Access
Internet Access
Inter-Library Loan (ILL)
Microform Equipment: Computer; Reader
Helga Kinnaird, Manager, Technology & Curriculum Innovation Operations
helgak@nait.ab.ca
780-471-8712
Harriet Arnold, Coordinator, Information Research & Instruction
harrieta@nait.ab.ca
780-471-8796
Liz Pegoraro, Coordinator, Information Support
lizp@nait.ca
Wayne Hofman, Coordinator, LR Computer Services
whofman@nait.ab.ca

Edmonton: Northern Forestry Centre Edmonton Library
#M052, 5320 - 122nd St.
Edmonton, AB T6H 3S5
780-435-7324
Fax: 780-435-7359
Other contact info: Alternate Fax: 780-435-7356
National Library Symbol: AEF
Founded in: 1948
Hours: M-F 8:00-4:00
Acquisitions Budget: $50,000 - $99,999
Special Collections: Trees, Insects, Diseases of Trees, Hydrology, Forest Influences, Biomass, Depository for all Canadian Forest Service publications, selection of U.S. & foreign forestry-related publications, Woodlot Extension Library, ENFOR Publications
Subjects covered: Natural Resources, Conservation, Environment, Forest Entomology, Plant Pathology, Forest Influences, Climate Change, Hydrology, Silviculture, Economics, Forest Fire Research, Socio-Economic Research
Services:
Inter-Library Loan (ILL)
Microform Equipment: Computer; Reader
Personnel: *Summary:* 2 Total; 1 Professional(s); 1 Technical(s)
Denise Leroy, Manager, Library Services
Denise.Leroy@NRCan-RNCan.gc.ca

Edmonton: Prairie & Northern Region - Edmonton Library - Environment Canada
#200, 4999 - 98th Ave.
Edmonton, AB T6B 2X3
780-951-8817
Fax: 780-951-8819
e-mail: librarybiblio.edmonton@ec.gc.ca
National Library Symbol: AEECW
Hours: M-F 1:00-4:00
Acquisitions Budget: $25,000 - $49,999
Subjects covered: Environment
Services:
Inter-Library Loan (ILL)
Personnel: *Summary:* 2 Total; 1 Professional(s); 1 Technical(s)
Terri Fraser, Head, Regional Library & Records Services
780-951-8818

***Edmonton:* South Campus Library**
7319 - 29 Ave.
Edmonton, AB T6K 2P1
780-497-4054
877-497-4267
Other contact info: Reference: 780-497-4055 (4052)
e-mail: info@macewan.ca
URL: library.macewan.ca/south
National Library Symbol: AEGMMW
Consortia Membership: NEOS Library Consortium
Founded in: 1971
Hours: Winter: M-Th 7:45am-8:00pm; F 7:45-5:30; Sa 11:00-4:00
Acquisitions Budget: $50,000 - $99,999
For Print: $50,000 - $99,999
For Electronic: $10,000 - $24,999
Subjects covered: Massage Therapy, Social Work, Child & Youth Care, Rehabilitation Practitioner, Police & Security Corrections, Mental Health, Management, Accounting
Services:
Remote Access
Internet Access
Inter-Library Loan (ILL)
Laser printing
Microform Equipment: Computer; Reader
Personnel: *Summary:* 5 Total; 1 Professional(s); 4 Technical(s)
Melinda Spears, Campus Librarian
780-497-3353
Marge Gray, Reference Library Technician
graym@macewan.ca
780-497-4052
Judy Nelson, Librarian
780-633-4055

***Edmonton:* Syncrude Canada Ltd. Research Library**
9421 - 17th Ave. SW
Edmonton, AB T6N 1H4
780-970-6800
Fax: 780-970-6805
National Library Symbol: AESC
No public access
Founded in: 1964
Acquisitions Budget: $50,000 - $99,999
For Print: $50,000 - $99,999
For Electronic: 0-$9,999
Subjects covered: Oil Sands, Engineering, Chemistry, Chemical Engineering, Metallurgy, Petroleum Refining, Reclamation, Tailings, Engineering Mechanics & Materials, Geology, Fluid Mechanics, Physical & Analytical Chemistry
Services:
Microform Equipment: Reader
Personnel: *Summary:* 1 Technical(s)

***Edmonton:* University of Alberta Cameron Library - Library Administration Department**
#1-50 Cameron Library, University of Alberta
Edmonton, AB T6G 2J8
780-492-8440
Fax: 780-492-2721
URL: www.library.ualberta.ca
Consortia Membership: The Alberta Library; Canadian Research Knowledge Network (CRKN); Council of Prairie & Pacific University Libraries (COPPUL); Health Knowledge Network (HKN); NEOS Library Consortium
Founded in: 1909
Hours: M-Th 8:00-7:00; F 8:00-5:00; Sa, Su 11:00-6:00
Services:
Inter-Library Loan (ILL) for a fee
Fee Based Research
Microform Equipment: Computer; Reader
Personnel: *Summary:* 1 Total; 1 Professional(s)
Karen Adams, Director, Library Services & Information Resources
karen.adams@ualberta.ca
780-492-6491
Tina James, Associate Director, Facilities & Administration
Kathleen DeLong, Associate Director, Finance & Human Resources

***Edmonton:* Westmount Campus Branch Library**
#218, 11140 - 131 St.
Edmonton, AB T5M 1C1
780-644-6709
e-mail: library@norquest.ca
URL: library.norquest.ca
Hours: M-Th 8:00-3:00
Special Collections: English as a Second Language collection
Services:
Internet Access
Connie Vogler, Library Technician

***Edmonton:* William C. Wonders Map Collection**
University of Alberta, Cameron Library, Main Fl.
Edmonton, AB T6G 2J8
780-492-2728
Fax: 780-492-2721
URL: maps.library.ualberta.ca
National Library Symbol: AEUM
Founded in: 1966
Hours: M-Th 8:00-8:00; F 8:00-5:00; Sa, Su 11:00-5:00
Acquisitions Budget: $10,000 - $24,999
Note: Member of NEOS Consortium
Special Collections: Western & Northern Canada; Austro-Hungary & Central Europe; UK
Subjects covered: Worldwide Topographic & Thematic Maps
Services:
Internet Access
Inter-Library Loan (ILL)
Microform Equipment: Reader
Personnel: *Summary:* 2 Total; 1 Professional(s); 1 Technical(s)
Virginia Pow, Map Librarian
virginia.pow@ualberta.ca

***Edmonton:* Workers' Compensation Board of Alberta Library**
9912 - 107 St.
Edmonton, AB T5J 2S5
Mailing Address: PO Box 2415
Edmonton, AB T5J 2S5
780-498-3999
866-922-9221
Other contact info: TTY: 780-498-7895
URL: www.wcb.ab.ca
No public access
Subjects covered: Medical; Rehabilitation; Occupational Health & Safety; Sports Medicine

***Fort McMurray:* Keyano College Library & Media Services**
8115 Franklin Ave.
Fort McMurray, AB T9H 2H7
780-791-4917
Fax: 780-791-4935
e-mail: circulation.services@keyano.ca
URL: www.keyano.ca/library
National Library Symbol: AFMK
Consortia Membership: The Alberta Library; NEOS Library Consortium
Founded in: 1965
Hours: M-Th 8:30am-9:00pm; F 8:30-4:30; Sa-Su 12:00-4:00
Acquisitions Budget: $50,000 - $99,999
For Print: $50,000 - $99,999
For Electronic: $25,000 - $49,999
Services:
Internet Access
Access to Subscription Databases
Personnel: *Summary:* 9 Total; 2 Professional(s); 2 Technical(s); 5 Other employees
John Burgess, Director, Library
john.burgess@keyano.ca
780-791-8927
Corinne Hope, Access Services Coordinator
corinne.hope@keyano.ca
780-791-8910
Evelyn Graham, Serials Technician
evelyn.graham@keyano.ca
780-791-4916
Kimberly Kerr, Information Librarian
kimberly.kerr@keyano.ca
780-791-8911
Audrey Oake, Circulation Clerk
audrey.oake@keyano.ca
780-791-4917

***Fort McMurray:* Northern Lights Regional Health Centre Health Information Access & Disclosure**
7 Hospital St.
Fort McMurray, AB T9H 1P2
780-791-6171
Fax: 780-791-6167
No public access
Founded in: 1981
Acquisitions Budget: $25,000 - $49,999
Note: Information released only on written request; access provided to individuals, other service providers, lawyers, or any other authorized party according to the Health Information Act.
Subjects covered: Health Sciences, Medicine, Hospital Administration, Nursing
Services:
Inter-Library Loan (ILL)
Personnel: *Summary:* 1 Professional(s)
Barb Di Persio, Director HR
hdipersio@nlhr.ca
780-791-6176
JoAnne Weigelt, Clerk
jweigelt@nlhr.ca

***Grande Prairie:* Grande Prairie Regional College Library & Media Services**
10726 - 106th Ave.
Grande Prairie, AB T8V 4C4
780-539-2939
Fax: 780-539-2832
888-539-4772
e-mail: library@gprc.ab.ca
URL: www.gprc.ab.ca/departments/library/
National Library Symbol: AGPC
Consortia Membership: The Alberta Library; Health Knowledge Network (HKN); NEOS Library Consortium
Founded in: 1966
Hours: Fall & Winter: M-Th 8:00am-9:00pm; F 8:00-6:00; Sa, Su 12:00-6:00; Spring & Summer: M-F 8:30-4:30
Acquisitions Budget: For Print: $100,000 - $249,999
Special Collections: Statistics Canada publications, Government publications, Curriculum items, Juvenile collection, Test & Careers Special Collection
Subjects covered: Arts, Humanities, Science & Technology, Technical
Services:
Remote Access
Internet Access
Access to Subscription Databases
Inter-Library Loan (ILL)
Microform Equipment: Computer; Reader
Personnel: *Summary:* 17 Total; 2 Professional(s); 15 Technical(s)
Jennifer Thomas, Chair
jthomas@gprc.ab.ca
780-539-2772
Ann Gish, Access Services Librarian
agish@gprc.ab.ca

***Grande Prairie:* Queen Elizabeth II Hospital Regional Library**
10409 - 98th St.
Grande Prairie, AB T8V 2E8
Mailing Address: Bag 2600
Grande Prairie, AB T8V 2E8
780-538-7124
Fax: 780-538-7507
Founded in: 1984
Hours: M-F 8:00-4:15
Acquisitions Budget: $25,000 - $49,999
Note: Library Databases: Microcat & Ultraplus
Subjects covered: Health Science, Medicine, Nursing
Services:
Inter-Library Loan (ILL)
Personnel: *Summary:* 2 Total; 1 Technical(s); 1 Other employees; 1 Volunteer(s)

***Grouard:* Northern Lakes College Grouard Campus Library**
PO Bag 3000
Grouard, AB T0G 1C0
780-751-3275
Fax: 780-751-3376
e-mail: library@northernlakescollege.ca
URL: www.northernlakescollege.ca

National Library Symbol: AGVC
Founded in: 1975
Hours: M-Th 8:15-7:00; F 8:15-4:30
Acquisitions Budget: $100,000 - $249,999
For Print: $100,000 - $249,999
For Electronic: $50,000 - $99,999
Special Collections: First Nations Collection
Subjects covered: Vocational Training, Education
Services:
Remote Access
Internet Access
Access to Subscription Databases
Inter-Library Loan (ILL)
Microform Equipment: Computer; Reader
Personnel: *Summary:* 1 Professional(s); 4 Technical(s)
Shirley Anderson, Library Technician
andersons@northernlakescollege.ca
780-751-3273

Kirriemuir: Prairie Association for Water Management
Library
PO Box 721
Kirriemuir, AB T0C 1R0
403-854-2509
URL: www.pawm.ca
Subjects covered: Environment

Lac La Biche: Portage College
Library
9531 - 94 Ave.
Lac La Biche, AB T0A 2C0
Mailing Address: PO Box 417
Lac La Biche, AB T0A 2C0
780-623-5650
Fax: 780-623-5656
866-623-5551
e-mail: library@portagecollege.ca
URL: www.portagecollege.ca/Library.htm
moodle.portagecollege.ca
National Library Symbol: ALLBVC
Consortia Membership: The Alberta Library
Founded in: 1987
Hours: M-Th 8:00am-9:00pm; F 8:00-4:30; Sa 1:00-4:00; Su 1:00-7:00; Summer: M-F 8:00am-4:30
Acquisitions Budget: $50,000 - $99,999
For Print: $50,000 - $99,999
For Electronic: 0-$9,999
Subjects covered: Upgrading, Vocational Training, Native Studies, Community Social Work, Emergency Medical Technician, University Studies
Services:
Remote Access
Internet Access for a fee
Inter-Library Loan (ILL)
Personnel: *Summary:* 7 Total; 2 Professional(s); 1 Technical(s); 4 Other employees
Barb Palmer, Manager, Library Services
780-623-5653
Terry Donovan, Public Services Librarian
terry.donovan@portagecollege.ca
780-623-5755
Marcia Holmes, Technical Services Technician
marcia.holmes@portagecollege.ca
780-623-5632
Janice Bryks, Acquisitions Assistant
janice.bryks@portagecollege.ca
780-623-5654
Reno Larocque, Serials Assistant
reno.larocque@portagecollege.ca
780-623-3501
Michele Norton, Circulation Assistant
michele.norton@portagecollege.ca
780-623-5655

Lacombe: Canadian University College
Library
5410 Ramona Ave.
Lacombe, AB T4L 2B7
403-782-3381
Fax: 866-930-4928
e-mail: library@cauc.ca
URL: www.cauc.ca/Library
National Library Symbol: ACHCU
Consortia Membership: NEOS Library Consortium; The Alberta Library
Founded in: 1907
Hours: Fall/Winter: M-Th 8:00am-10:30pm; F 8:00-3:00; Su 1:00-10:30; Summer: M-Th 8:30-9:30; F 8:30-5:00; Su 1:00-9:30; Breaks M-Th 1:00-4:00
Acquisitions Budget: $50,000 - $99,999
For Print: $50,000 - $99,999
For Electronic: $10,000 - $24,999
Note: Database access available.
Special Collections: Seventh-Day Adventist Church
Subjects covered: Humanities, Social Science, Science, Religion
Services:
Remote Access
Internet Access
Access to Subscription Databases
Inter-Library Loan (ILL) for a fee of $10.00 outside Alberta
Microform Equipment: Reader
Personnel: *Summary:* 15 Total; 2 Professional(s); 1 Technical(s); 12 Other employees
Sheila Clark, Library Director, Public Services
sclark@cauc.ca
403-782-3381 ext. 4102
Kieren Bailey, Assistant Librarian, Technical Services/Systems
kbailey@cauc.ca
403-782-3381 ext. 4105
Wilmer Tenerife, Library Technician
wtenerif@cauc.ca
403-782-3381 ext. 4104

Lacombe: Lacombe Research Centre
Canadian Agriculture Library - Lacombe
6000 C&E Trail
Lacombe, AB T4L 1W1
403-782-8136
Fax: 403-782-6120
National Library Symbol: ALAAG
Founded in: 1984
Hours: Tu-Th 9:00-4:00
Acquisitions Budget: $25,000 - $49,999
Subjects covered: Agriculture, Food, Food Safety, Meat Research
Services:
Inter-Library Loan (ILL)
Personnel: *Summary:* 1 Total; 1 Professional(s)
Kathryn Moore, Head Librarian
kathy.moore@agr.gc.ca

Lethbridge: Lethbridge Community College
Buchanan Library
3000 College Dr. South
Lethbridge, AB T1K 1L6
403-320-3352
Fax: 403-320-1461
800-572-0103
URL: www.lethbridgecollege.ca
Social Media: buchananlibraryonebookblog.blogspot.ca
National Library Symbol: ALC
Consortia Membership: The Alberta Library
Founded in: 1957
Hours: M-Th 7:30am-9:45pm; F 7:30-4:45; Sa 10:00-6:30; Su 10:00-6:30; Serves student, staff and faculty of the college.
Subjects covered: Agriculture, Criminal Justice, Physical Sciences, Engineering Technologies, Environmental Sciences, Health & Human Services
Services:
Remote Access
Internet Access
Access to Subscription Databases
Inter-Library Loan (ILL)
Email for LCC students, CD products
Personnel: *Summary:* 2 Professional(s); 25 Other employees
Fiona Dyer, Manager, Library Services
fiona.dyer@lethbridgecollege.ab.ca

Lethbridge: Lethbridge Research Centre
Canadian Agriculture Library - Lethbridge
5403 - 1st Ave. South
Lethbridge, AB T1J 4B1
Mailing Address: PO Box 3000
Lethbridge, AB T1J 4B1
403-317-3310
Fax: 403-382-3156
National Library Symbol: ALAG
Founded in: 1950
Hours: M-F 8:00-12:00, 1:00-4:00 by appointment only
Subjects covered: Agriculture, Crop Entomology, Animal & Crop Science, Soils
Services:
Inter-Library Loan (ILL) for a fee
Personnel: *Summary:* 2 Total; 1 Professional(s); 1 Technical(s)
Karen Mah, Head Librarian
karen.mah@agr.gc.ca

Lethbridge: University of Lethbridge
Library
4401 University Dr.
Lethbridge, AB T1K 3M4
403-329-2265
Fax: 403-329-2234
e-mail: gsd.library@uleth.ca
URL: www.uleth.ca/lib/
National Library Symbol: ALU
Consortia Membership: The Alberta Libary; Canadian Research Knowledge Network (CRKN); Council of Prairie & Pacific University Libraries (COPPUL); Health Knowledge Network (HKN); Alberta Video Co-Acquisition Consortium
Founded in: 1967
Hours: M-Su
Acquisitions Budget: $1,000,000 plus
For Print: $500,000 - $999,999
For Electronic: $500,000 - $999,999
Special Collections: Canadiana (Woodworth) Collection
Services:
Remote Access
Internet Access
Access to Subscription Databases
Inter-Library Loan (ILL)
Microform Equipment: Computer; Reader
Personnel: *Summary:* 53 Total; 15 Professional(s); 32 Technical(s); 6 Other employees
Marinus Swanepoel, University Librarian
librarian@uleth.ca
Donna Seyed Mahmoud, Associate University Librarian
libadmin@uleth.ca
403-329-2031
Bill Glaister, Coordinator of Faculty of Education Curriculum Lab
bill.glaister@uleth.ca
403-329-2715

Medicine Hat: Medicine Hat College
Library
299 College Dr. SE
Medicine Hat, AB T1A 3Y6
403-529-3867
Fax: 403-504-3634
866-282-8394
e-mail: reference@mhc.ab.ca
illo@mhc.ab.ca
circulation@mhc.ab.ca
URL: www.mhc.ab.ca/Library.aspx
National Library Symbol: AMMC
Consortia Membership: The Alberta Library
Founded in: 1965
Hours: M-Th 7:30-10:00; F 7:30-6:00; Sa 9:00-5:00; Su 1:00-8:00
Acquisitions Budget: $250,000 - $499,999
For Print: $100,000 - $249,999
For Electronic: $50,000 - $99,999
Note: Ariel: 192.139.34.241
Subjects covered: Undergraduate College Prep
Services:
Internet Access
Inter-Library Loan (ILL)
Microform Equipment: Computer; Reader
Personnel: *Summary:* 8 Total; 3 Professional(s); 15 Technical(s)
Keith Walker, Director, Library Services
kwalker@mhc.ab.ca
403-504-3539
Vacant , Librarian, Information & Technology
Barb Banasch, Supervisor, Circulation & AV
bbansch@mhc.ab.ca
403-529-3866
Terry Lagran, Technician, Acquisitions & Information
tlagran@mhc.ab.ca
403-529-3871

Olds: Olds College
Library
4500 - 50th St.
Olds, AB T4H 1R6

403-556-4600
Fax: 403-556-4705
e-mail: library@oldscollege.ca
libraryill@oldscollege.ca
URL: www.oldscollege.ca/library
National Library Symbol: AOAC
Consortia Membership: The Alberta Library; NEOS Library Consortium
Founded in: 1913
Hours: School Term: M-Th 7:45am-10:00pm; Sa 11:00-5:00; Su 10:00-10:00. Summer: hours vary
Acquisitions Budget: $100,000 - $249,999
Subjects covered: Agriculture, Horticulture, Animal Science, Land Science, Business, Agricultural Mechanics
Services:
Internet Access
Inter-Library Loan (ILL)
Microform Equipment: Computer; Reader
Personnel: *Summary:* 7 Total; 1 Professional(s); 6 Technical(s);

Robin Minion, Director, Library Services
rminion@oldscollege.ca
403-556-4602
Scott Mckay, Head of Technical Services
smckay@oldscollge.ca
403-556-4604
Connie Clark, Head of Acquisitions
cclark2@oldscollege.ca
403-556-4603

Red Deer: Red Deer College Library

100 College Blvd.
Red Deer, AB T4N 5H5
Mailing Address: PO Box 5005
Red Deer, AB T4N 5H5
403-342-3344
Fax: 403-346-8500
e-mail: rdclibrary@gmail.com
URL: www.rdc.ab.ca/library
National Library Symbol: ARDC
Consortia Membership: The Alberta Library; Health Knowledge Network (HKN); NEOS Library Consortium
Founded in: 1965
Hours: M-Su
Acquisitions Budget: $250,000 - $499,999
Note: The library is an affiliate member of the Council of Prairie and Pacific University Libraries (COPPUL).
Special Collections: Alberta K-12 curriculum
Subjects covered: University transfer, Degree completion, Certificate/Diploma, Apprenticeship/Trades
Services:
Remote Access
Internet Access
Inter-Library Loan (ILL)
Microform Equipment: Reader
Personnel: *Summary:* 7 Total; 3 Professional(s); 3 Technical(s)
Alice McNair, Dean, Learning Resources
403-342-3306
Maureen Toews, Librarian
maureen.toews@rdc.ab.ca
403-342-3351
Kristine Plastow, Librarian
kristine.plastow@rdc.ab.ca
403-342-3578
Leslie Beattie, Librarian
leslie.beattie@rdc.ab.ca
403-342-3352
Charlene Jones, Program & Service Manager
charlene.jones@rdc.ab.ca
403-342-3547

Slave Lake: Slave Lake Campus Library

1201 Main St. SE
Slave Lake, AB T0G 2A3
780-849-8670
Fax: 780-849-8688
533-652-3456
National Library Symbol: ASAV
Consortia Membership: The Alberta Library
Founded in: 1975
Hours: M-W 8:15-4:30, 6:00-9:00; T-F 8:15-4:30. Evening hours take place from Oct.-June only.
Acquisitions Budget: $50,000 - $99,999
For Print: $50,000 - $99,999
For Electronic: $50,000 - $99,999
Special Collections: Native Peoples
Subjects covered: Education; Upgrading; Social Work
Services:
Remote Access
Internet Access
Access to Subscription Databases
Inter-Library Loan (ILL)
Microform Equipment: Reader
Deborah Kendze, Director, Library Services
kendzed@northernlakescollege.ca
780-849-8671
Susan Oxford, Assistant Director, Library Services
oxfords@northernlakescollege.ca
780-849-8672

Stettler: Buffalo Lake Naturalists Club

PO Box 1802
Stettler, AB T0C 2L0
403-742-4800
e-mail: BuffaloLakeNC@gmail.com
URL: www.naturealberta.ca/clubs/buffalo-lake-naturalists-club
No public access
Subjects covered: Conservation
Claudia Cameron, Contact
clipskic@rttinc.com

Vegreville: Vegreville Knowledge Centre

76th St. & Hwy. 16A
Vegreville, AB T9C 1T4
Mailing Address: PO Bag 4000
Vegreville, AB T9C 1T4
780-632-8417
Fax: 780-632-8300
-310-0000
e-mail: veg_library@albertainnovates.ca
National Library Symbol: AVEE
Consortia Membership: NEOS Library Consortium
Founded in: 1979
Hours: M-F 8:15-4:30
Acquisitions Budget: $50,000 - $99,999
For Print: 0-$9,999
For Electronic: $50,000 - $99,999
Subjects covered: Veterinary Sciences, Plant Science, Environmental Chemistry, Air, Water & Waste Management, Environmental Toxicology & Enhancement, Wildlife Ecology, Aquatic Biology, Forestry & Soils
Services:
Internet Access
Access to Subscription Databases
Inter-Library Loan (ILL)
Fee Based Research
Microform Equipment: Computer; Reader
Personnel: *Summary:* 2 Total; 1 Technical(s); 1 Other employees
Audrey Lyons, Acquisitions/Cataloguing
audrey.lyons@albertainnovates.ca
Melanie Thibault, Interlibrary Loans
melanie.thibault@albertainnovates.ca
780-632-8419

Vermilion: Lakeland College Vermilion Campus Library

5707 College Dr.
Vermilion, AB T9X 1K5
780-853-8463
Fax: 780-853-8662
URL: www.lakelandcollege.ca/library
National Library Symbol: AUC
Consortia Membership: The Alberta Library; NEOS Library Consortium
Founded in: 1913
Hours: M-Th 8:15am-10:00pm; F 8:15-4:30; Sa, Su 1:00-5:00
Acquisitions Budget: $50,000 - $99,999
Subjects covered: Agriculture, Environment, Interior Design, Early Childhood Education, Trades, Business
Services:
Remote Access
Internet Access
Access to Subscription Databases
Inter-Library Loan (ILL)
Personnel: *Summary:* 8 Total; 2 Professional(s); 2 Technical(s); 4 Other employees
Angela Wilm, Chair, Academic Services
angela.wilm@lakelandcollege.ca
780-853-8532
Wanjiku Kaai, Librarian, Public Services
wanjiku.kaai@lakelandcollege.ca
780-853-8731

Wetaskiwin: Alberta Community Development Reynolds-Alberta Museum Library

6426 - 40 Ave.
Wetaskiwin, AB T9A 2G1
Mailing Address: PO Box 6360
Wetaskiwin, AB T9A 2G1
780-361-1351
Fax: 780-361-1239
800-661-4726
e-mail: reynoldsalbertamuseum@gov.ab.ca
URL: www.reynoldsalbertamuseum.com
National Library Symbol: AWRAM
Founded in: 1992
Hours: Sept-May: T-Su 10:00-5:00; May-July: M-Su 10:00-5:00; July-Sept M-Su 10:00-6:00
Acquisitions Budget: 0-$9,999
Note: Located 2 kms west of Wetaskiwin on Hwy. 13.
Special Collections: Library collection of Canada's Aviation Hall of Fame available through request of Hall of Fame curator.
Subjects covered: Transportation, Agriculture, Industry, Technology, Aviation
Services:
Inter-Library Loan (ILL)
Microform Equipment: Reader
Personnel: *Summary:* 2 Total; 1 Professional(s); 1 Other employees; 3 Volunteer(s)
Randy Kvill, Curator, Agriculture & Documentary Collections
randy.kvill@gov.ab.ca
780-361-1351 ext. 254/2

British Columbia

Abbotsford: Pacific Region Regional Health Centre Library

33344 King Rd.
Abbotsford, BC V2S 4P4
Mailing Address: PO Box 3000
Abbotsford, BC V2S 4P4
604-870-7700
National Library Symbol: BARP
No public access
Hours: M-F
Acquisitions Budget: $25,000 - $49,999
Subjects covered: Psychology, Psychiatry, Health
Services:
Inter-Library Loan (ILL)
Personnel: *Summary:* 1 Total; 1 Technical(s)

Abbotsford: University of the Fraser Valley Library

33844 King Rd.
Abbotsford, BC V2S 7M8
604-854-4545
Fax: 604-853-8055
URL: www.ufv.ca/library.htm
National Library Symbol: BCLF
Consortia Membership: Canadian Research Knowledge Network (CRKN); Council of Prairie & Pacific University Libraries (COPPUL); British Columbia Electronic Library Network (BC ELN); Electronic Health Library of BC (e-HLbc)
Founded in: 1974
Acquisitions Budget: $500,000 - $999,999
Special Collections: Fraser Valley Heritage Collection
Subjects covered: University & Community College Level Subject Areas
Kim Isaac, University Librarian
kim.isaac@ufv.ca
604-864-4696
Patti Wilson, Collections Librarian
patti.wilson@ufv.ca
604-504-7441 ext. 4277
June Reedman, Technician in Charge, Acquisitions
june.reedman@ufv.ca
604-864-4651

Burnaby: British Columbia Housing Records & Information Centre

#1701, 4555 Kingsway
Burnaby, BC V5H 4V8
604-433-1711
Fax: 604-439-4722

e-mail: webeditor@bchousing.org
URL: www.bchousing.org
National Library Symbol: NFCBF
No public access
Founded in: 1985
Acquisitions Budget: $25,000 - $49,999
Subjects covered: Social Housing, Urban Planning, Social Policy, Statistics, Construction, Property Management
Personnel: *Summary:* 55 Total
Lorna Balderstone, Library/Records Clerk
lbalders@bchmc.bc.ca
604-439-4750 ext. 369

Burnaby: British Columbia Hydro Corporate Research & Information Services
6911 Southpoint Dr.
Burnaby, BC V3N 4X8
604-528-3008
Fax: 604-528-3137
URL: www.bchydro.com
National Library Symbol: BVAH
No public access
Hours: M-F 8:00-4:30
Special Collections: A/V Collection
Subjects covered: Physical Sciences, Electric Utilities, Energy & Mineral Resources, Standards & Specifications, Engineering
Personnel: *Summary:* 6 Total; 1 Professional(s); 3 Technical(s)
Patricia Crawford, Head of Library

Burnaby: British Columbia Institute of Technology Library Services
3700 Willingdon Ave.
Burnaby, BC V5G 3H2
604-432-8371
Fax: 604-430-5443
URL: www.lib.bcit.ca
National Library Symbol: BBIT
Consortia Membership: British Columbia Electronic Library Network (BC ELN); Electronic Health Library of BC (e-HLbc)
Founded in: 1965
Hours: M-Th 7:30am-10:30pm; F 7:30-5:00; Sa, Su 9:00-5:00
Acquisitions Budget: $500,000 - $999,999
For Print: $250,000 - $499,999
For Electronic: $250,000 - $499,999
Note: The library is an affiliate member of the Council of Prairie and Pacific University Libraries (COPPUL).
Special Collections: International Maritime Organ1zation, Standards, Aircraft Technical Reports, BCIT Archives
Subjects covered: Health Sciences, Business, Transportation, Aviation, Marine Engineering, Computer Studies
Services:
Remote Access
Inter-Library Loan (ILL)
Microform Equipment: Reader
Personnel: *Summary:* 34 Total; 10 Professional(s); 1 Technical(s); 23 Other employees
David Pepper, Director, Library Services
david_pepper@bcit.ca
604-432-8360
Bill Nadiger, Librarian, Transportation
bill_nadiger@bcit.ca
604-453-4042
Patricia Cumming, Librarian, Electronics; Marketing Coordinator
patricia_cumming@bcit.ca
604-453-4064
Merilee MacKinnon, Librarian, Construction Trades & Technologies; Reference Coordinator
merilee_mackinnon@bcit.ca
604-432-8647
Kathleen Dutchak, Services & Systems Librarian
kathleen_dutchak@bcit.ca
604-453-4041

Burnaby: Burnaby Hospital H.H.W. Brooke Memorial Library
3935 Kincaid St.
Burnaby, BC V5G 2X6
604-412-6255
Fax: 604-412-6177
Hours: M-F 8:00-4:00 by appointment only
Acquisitions Budget: $25,000 - $49,999
Note: Part of Fraser Health Authority
Subjects covered: Medicine; Nursing
Services:
Internet Access
Access to Subscription Databases
Inter-Library Loan (ILL)
Personnel: *Summary:* 1 Professional(s)

Burnaby: Library (Burnaby)
#500, 4260 Still Creek Dr.
Burnaby, BC V5C 6C6
604-296-4200
Fax: 604-298-5253
No public access
Hours: M-F
Acquisitions Budget: $25,000 - $49,999
Special Collections: Environmental Waste Management, Mining, Rock Mechanics, Hydrogeology
Subjects covered: Engineering, Environment, Mining, Geotechnical
Services:
Inter-Library Loan (ILL)
Personnel: *Summary:* 1 Total; 1 Professional(s)
Tomi Inkinen, Library Technician
tinkinen@golder.com

Burnaby: Metro Vancouver (formerly Greater Vancouver Regional District) Harry Lash Library
4330 Kingsway, Main Fl.
Burnaby, BC V5H 4G8
604-432-6335
Fax: 604-432-6445
e-mail: library@metrovancouver.org
URL:
www.metrovancouver.org/about/catalogue/Pages/default.aspx
National Library Symbol: BBGV
Founded in: 1970
Hours: M-F 8:00-4:30
Acquisitions Budget: $25,000 - $49,999
Note: Annette Dignan & Thora Gislason jobshare position of Librarian.
Special Collections: Collection of GVRD reports; publications relevant to GVRD & municipal functions & operations
Subjects covered: Regional & Urban Development, Planning & Public Policy, Housing, Parks & Outdoor Recreation, Sewage & Solid Waste Disposal, Drinking Water Supply, Air Quality & Source Control, Urban Transit
Services:
Remote Access
Inter-Library Loan (ILL)
Personnel: *Summary:* 3 Total; 2 Professional(s); 1 Technical(s)
Annette Dignan, Librarian
annette.dignan@metrovancouver.org
Thora Gislason, Librarian
Janice Dudas, Library Technician

Burnaby: Science Library
#400, 4595 Canada Way
Burnaby, BC V5G 4P2
Mailing Address: 3155 Willingdon Green
Burnaby, BC V5G 4P2
604-666-3147
Fax: 604-666-3149
e-mail: elizabeth_hardacre@hc-sc.gc.ca
National Library Symbol: BVANH
No public access
Hours: M-F 8:00-4:00
Acquisitions Budget: $25,000 - $49,999
Subjects covered: Microbiology, Analytical Chemistry, Food Science & Technology, Analysis & Regulation, Drug Manufacturing, Cosmetics Regulation
Elizabeth Hardacre, Librarian
elizabeth_hardacre@hc-sc.gc.ca

Burnaby: Simon Fraser University W.A.C. Bennett Library
8888 University Dr.
Burnaby, BC V5A 1S6
778-782-4084
URL: www.lib.sfu.ca
National Library Symbol: BVAS
Consortia Membership: Canadian Research Knowledge Network (CRKN); Council of Prairie & Pacific University Libraries (COPPUL); BC Libraries Cooperative; British Columbia Electronic Library Network (BC ELN); Electronic Health Library of BC (e-HLbc)
Founded in: 1965
Hours: M-Th 8:00am-11:45pm; F 8:00-8:00; Sa, Su 10:00-10:00
Acquisitions Budget: $1,000,000 plus
Special Collections: Contemporary Literature, Post-War Avant-Garde Poetry, Wordsworth Collection, Editorial Cartoons
Subjects covered: Humanities, Sciences, Social Sciences, Business, Education
Services:
Remote Access
Internet Access
Access to Subscription Databases
Inter-Library Loan (ILL)
Microform Equipment: Reader
Personnel: *Summary:* 147 Total; 43 Professional(s); 5 Technical(s); 100 Other employees
Chuck Eckman, Dean of Library Services
ceckman@sfu.ca
778-782-3265
Todd Mundle, Associate University Librarian
tmundle@sfu.ca
778-782-3263
Elaine Fairey, Associate University Librarian
efairey@sfu.ca
778-782-3252
Brian Owen, Associate University Librarian
brian_owen@sfu.ca
778-782-7095

Campbell River: Campbell River Campus Library
1685 South Dogwood St.
Campbell River, BC V9W 8C1
250-923-9785
Fax: 250-923-9786
e-mail: diane.newman@nic.bc.ca
URL: library.nic.bc.ca
National Library Symbol: BCOMN
No public access
Hours: M-Th 8:00-7:30; F 8:00-4:00
Acquisitions Budget: For Print: $25,000 - $49,999; Students & staff
Services:
Remote Access
Inter-Library Loan (ILL)
Microform Equipment: Reader
Personnel: *Summary:* 2 Technical(s)
Jana Allingham, Library Assistant
jana.allingham@nic.bc.ca
Kerry Strain, Library Assistant
kerry.strain@nic.bc.ca
250-923-9785

Campbell River: Strathcona Park Lodge & Outdoor Education Centre
41040 Gold River Hwy.
Campbell River, BC V9W 5C5
Mailing Address: PO Box 2160
Campbell River, BC V9W 5C5
250-286-3122
Fax: 250-286-6010
e-mail: info@strathcona.bc.ca
URL: www.strathcona.bc.ca
Social Media: www.youtube.com/user/strathconaparklodge
www.facebook.com/StrathconaParkLodge
twitter.com/strathconapark
No public access
Founded in: 1959
Hours: Winter: M-Su 8:00-5:00. Summer: M-Su 8:00-8:00
Note: Library is for use by residents & guests of the lodge & by students of Canadian Outdoor Leadership Training (C.O.L.T.)
Subjects covered: Outdoor education; Wilderness leadership; Survival skills
Jim Miller, Director, Canadian Outdoor Leadership Training

Castlegar: Selkirk College Library
301 Frank Beinder Way
Castlegar, BC V1N 4L3
250-365-1229
Fax: 250-365-7259
888-953-1133
e-mail: bcs@selkirk.ca
URL: library.selkirk.bc.ca
National Library Symbol: BCS
Consortia Membership: British Columbia Electronic Library Network (BC ELN); Electronic Health Library of BC (e-HLbc)
Founded in: 1966
Hours: M, F 8:30-5:00; Tu-Th 7:30-7:00; Sa, Su 12:00-4:00
Acquisitions Budget: $50,000 - $99,999

For Print: $50,000 - $99,999
For Electronic: $10,000 - $24,999
Special Collections: West Kootenay Collection; Doukhobor Collection
Services:
Remote Access
Internet Access
Access to Subscription Databases
Inter-Library Loan (ILL)
Microform Equipment: Computer; Reader
Personnel: *Summary:* 9 Total; 2 Professional(s); 1 Technical(s); 6 Other employees
Gregg Currie, College Librarian
250-365-1263
Danielle Cossarini, Librarian
Sian Landis, Librarian

Chilliwack: Chilliwack Campus Library
45190 Caen Ave.
Chilliwack, BC V2R 0N3
604-795-2824
Fax: 604-792-8550
National Library Symbol: BCLF
Founded in: 1974
Hours: M-Th 8:00am-9:00pm; F 8:00-4:30; Sa 10:00-4:00
Services:
Internet Access
Access to Subscription Databases
Microform Equipment: Computer; Reader
Personnel: *Summary:* 3 Technical(s)

Courtenay: North Island College Library Comox Valley Campus
2300 Ryan Rd.
Courtenay, BC V9N 8N6
250-334-5037
Fax: 250-334-5291
e-mail: guenther@nic.bc.ca
URL: library.nic.bc.ca
National Library Symbol: BCOMN
Consortia Membership: British Columbia Electronic Library Network (BC ELN); Electronic Health Library of BC (e-HLbc)
Founded in: 1991
Hours: M-Th 8:00-7:30; F 8:00-4:00
Acquisitions Budget: $25,000 - $49,999
Subjects covered: Social & General Sciences, Humanities, Art
Services:
Internet Access
Access to Subscription Databases
Inter-Library Loan (ILL)
Personnel: *Summary:* 4 Total; 2 Professional(s); 2 Technical(s)
Mary Ann Guenther, Coordinator, Library Services
guenther@nic.bc.ca
250-334-5001
Amanda Pitchford, Collections/Reference Librarian
amanda.pitchford@nic.bc.ca
250-334-5097
Hélène Wickins, Library Assistant
wickins@nic.bc.ca

Cranbrook: College of the Rockies Learning Resources Centre
2700 College Way
Cranbrook, BC V1C 5L7
Mailing Address: PO Box 8500
Cranbrook, BC V1C 5L7
250-489-8294
Fax: 250-489-8256
e-mail: library@cotr.bc.ca
URL: library.cotr.bc.ca
National Library Symbol: BCREK
Consortia Membership: BC Libraries Cooperative; British Columbia Electronic Library Network (BC ELN); Electronic Health Library of BC (e-HLbc)
Founded in: 1975
Hours: M-Th 7:45-9:30; Fr 7:45-5:00; Sa 10:00-4:00; Su 12:00-4:00
Acquisitions Budget: For Print: $25,000 - $49,999
Services:
Internet Access
Access to Subscription Databases
Inter-Library Loan (ILL)
Microform Equipment: Reader
Personnel: *Summary:* 6 Total; 1 Professional(s); 5 Technical(s)
Shahida Rashid, Manager, College Library Services
srashid@cotr.bc.ca
250-489-8293
Susan Fleming, Library Technician (Website, Library Software & Serials)
fleming@cotr.bc.ca
250-489-8291 ext. 3291
Lynn Hughes, Library Technician (Copyright)
hughes@cotr.bc.ca
250-489-2751 ext. 3407
Maureen Davidson, Library Technician (Cataloguing & Acquisitions)
davidson@cotr.bc.ca
250-489-8288 ext. 3288

Creston: Creston Campus Library
301 - 16th Ave.
Creston, BC V0B 1G0
Mailing Address: PO Box 1978
Creston, BC V0B 1G0
250-428-5332
Fax: 250-428-4314
866-740-2687
e-mail: creston@cotr.bc.ca
URL: www.cotr.bc.ca/creston

Dawson Creek: Northern Lights College Dawson Creek Library
11401 - 8th St.
Dawson Creek, BC V1G 4G2
250-784-7533 ext: 7533
Fax: 250-784-7567
866-463-6652
e-mail: dc-lib@nlc.bc.ca
URL: nlc.bc.ca/services/library.aspx
National Library Symbol: BDCNL
Consortia Membership: British Columbia Electronic Library Network (BC ELN); Electronic Health Library of BC (e-HLbc)
Hours: M-Th 8:30-8:00; F 8:30-4:30; Sa 1:00-5:00
Services:
Remote Access
Internet Access
Inter-Library Loan (ILL)
Bibliographic instruction; Group study room; TV/VCR room; TeleSensory magnifier unit; Computer lab
Janet Beavers, Librarian
Bev Weidman, Library Services Assistant

Delta: Econotech Services Ltd. Library
852 Derwent Way
Delta, BC V3M 5R1
604-526-4221
Fax: 604-526-1898
800-463-5700
e-mail: info@econotech.com
URL: www.econotech.com
No public access
Founded in: 1972
Hours: M-F 8:00-4:30
Subjects covered: Industry, Pulp & Paper

Duncan: Cowichan Campus Library
2011 University Way
Duncan, BC V9L 0C7
250-746-3517
Fax: 250-746-3531
e-mail: cowlibrary@viu.ca
National Library Symbol: BNM
Founded in: 1989
Hours: M-Th 8:00am-9:00pm; F 8:00-4:00; Sa 12:00-4:00
Acquisitions Budget: $25,000 - $49,999
Services:
Internet Access
Access to Subscription Databases
Inter-Library Loan (ILL)
Microform Equipment: Reader
Personnel: *Summary:* 7 Total; 1 Professional(s); 3 Technical(s); 2 Other employees
Eileen Edmunds, Liaison Librarian & Regional Campus Coordinator
eileen.edmunds@viu.ca
250-740-6330 ext. 2272

Fort Nelson: Fort Nelson Campus Library
5201 Simpson Trail
Fort Nelson, BC V0C 1R0
250-774-4640 ext: 4640
Fax: 250-774-2750
866-463-6652
e-mail: fn-lib@nlc.bc.ca
National Library Symbol: BDCNL
Hours: M-Th 7:30-6:00; F 8:30-4:30
Acquisitions Budget: For Print: 0-$9,999
For Electronic: 0-$9,999
Subjects covered: History, Computer, Psychology
Services:
Remote Access
Internet Access
Inter-Library Loan (ILL)
Rachel Thompson, Library Assistant

Fort St. John: Fort St. John Campus Library
9820 - 120 St.
Fort St. John, BC V1J 6K1
Mailing Address: PO Box 1000
Fort St. John, BC V1J 6K1
250-787-6213 ext: 6213
Fax: 250-785-1294
866-463-6652
e-mail: fsj-lib@nlc.bc.ca
National Library Symbol: BDCNL
Founded in: 1977
Hours: M-Th 8:30-8:00; F 8:30-4:30; Sa 12:00-4:00
Acquisitions Budget: $25,000 - $49,999
Services:
Remote Access
Internet Access
Access to Subscription Databases
Inter-Library Loan (ILL) for a fee of Free to students; $5.50 for community users
Microform Equipment: Reader
Personnel: *Summary:* 3 Total; 1 Professional(s); 2 Technical(s)
Dawna Turcotte, Campus Librarian
dturcotte@nlc.bc.ca
250-787-6213
Tricia Hotchkiss, Library Services Assistant

Hazelton: Hazelton Campus Library
4815 Swannell Dr.
Hazelton, BC V8G 4X2
Mailing Address: 5331 McConnell Ave.
Terrace, BC V8G 4X2
250-842-5291
Fax: 250-842-5813
877-277-2288
e-mail: library@nwcc.bc.ca
ill@nwcc.bc.ca
URL: library.nwcc.bc.ca
Regional System: North Coast Library Federation
Consortia Membership: British Columbia Electronic Library Network (BC ELN); Electronic Health Library of BC (e-HLbc)
Hours: M-F 8:00-4:00
Services:
Internet Access
Inter-Library Loan (ILL)

Houston: Houston Campus Library
3221 - 14th St. West
Houston, BC V8G 4X2
Mailing Address: 5331 McConnell Ave.
Terrace, BC V8G 4X2
250-845-7266
Fax: 250-845-5629
877-277-2288
e-mail: library@nwcc.bc.ca
ill@nwcc.bc.ca
URL: library.nwcc.bc.ca
Regional System: North Coast Library Federation
Consortia Membership: British Columbia Electronic Library Network (BC ELN); Electronic Health Library of BC (e-HLbc)
Hours: M-F 9:00-12:00, 12:45-4:00
Services:
Internet Access
Inter-Library Loan (ILL)

Kamloops: Entomological Society of British Columbia
c/o Dr. L. Maclauchlan, Treasurer
441 Columbia St.
Kamloops, BC V2C 2T3
250-828-4179
Fax: 250-828-4442
e-mail: EntSocBC@gmail.com
Founded in: 1902
Hours: by appointment only
Subjects covered: Entomological serials from around the world

Kamloops: Interior Health Authority Royal Inland Hospital Library
Royal Inland Hospital
311 Columbia St.
Kamloops, BC V2C 2T1
Mailing Address: 311 Columbia St.
Kamloops, BC V2C 2T1
250-314-2234
Fax: 250-314-2189
e-mail: tcslibrary@interiorhealth.ca
URL: www.interiorhealth.ca
National Library Symbol: BCCRAL
Consortia Membership: Electronic Health Library of BC (e-HLbc)
No public access
Acquisitions Budget: $50,000 - $99,999
For Print: $10,000 - $24,999
For Electronic: $50,000 - $99,999
Note: Library provides resources & information services to Hospital personnel
Subjects covered: Medicine, Nursing, Health Science
Services:
Inter-Library Loan (ILL)
Personnel: *Summary:* 2 Total; 1 Professional(s); 1 Technical(s)
Lisa Gysel, Librarian
Paula Hardy, Library Technician
250-314-2342

Kamloops: Thompson Rivers University Kamloops Campus Library
900 McGill Rd.
Kamloops, BC V2C 0C8
250-828-5300
Fax: 250-828-5313
URL: www.tru.ca/library
National Library Symbol: BKCC
Consortia Membership: Canadian Research Knowledge Network (CRKN); Council of Prairie & Pacific University Libraries (COPPUL); British Columbia Electronic Library Network (BC ELN); Electronic Health Library of BC (e-HLbc)
Founded in: 1970
Hours: M-Th 8:00am-9:00pm; F 8:00-5:00; Sa 9:00-5:00; Su 12:00-8:00
Note: British Columbia Open University & University College of the Cariboo have merged to create Thompson Rivers University
Services:
Inter-Library Loan (ILL)
Microform Equipment: Reader
Personnel: *Summary:* 23 Total
Kathy Gaynor, Interim University Library Director
kgaynor@tru.ca
250-828-5305
Penny Haggarty, Collections Librarian
phaggarty@tru.ca
250-828-5303
Larry McCallum, Web Services Librarian
lmccallum@tru.ca
250-377-6055
Christina Nilsen, Borrower & Data Services Librarian
cnilsen@tru.ca
250-852-7287
Elizabeth Rennie, Instruction & Outreach Librarian
erennie@tru.ca
250-371-5775
Brenda Smith, Distance & Document Delivery Librarian
brsmith@tru.ca
250-828-5098

Kelowna: Okanagan College Library
1000 KLO Rd.
Kelowna, BC V1Y 4X8
250-762-5445
Fax: 250-862-5609
URL: www.okanagan.bc.ca/library
National Library Symbol: BKOC
Consortia Membership: BC Libraries Cooperative; British Columbia Electronic Library Network (BC ELN); Electronic Health Library of BC (e-HLbc)
Hours: Sept.-April: M-Th 8:00am-10:00pm; F 8:00-6:00; Sa 9:00-5:00; Su 9:00-5:00
Acquisitions Budget: $500,000 - $999,999
Note: The library is an affiliate member of the Council of Prairie & Pacific University Libraries (COPPUL).
Services:
Remote Access
Internet Access
Inter-Library Loan (ILL)
Ross Tyner, Director, Library Services
rhtyner@okanagan.bc.ca
250-762-5445 ext. 4665
Gilbert Bede, Librarian, Systems & Acquisitions
gbede@okanagan.bc.ca
250-762-5445 ext. 4751
Eva Engman, Librarian, Collections & Cataloguing
eengman@okanagan.bc.ca
250-762-5445 ext. 4490
Jasmine McGee, Contact
jmcgee@okanagan.bc.ca

Kitimat: Kitimat Campus Library
606 Mountainview Square
Kitimat, BC V8G 4X2
Mailing Address: 5331 McConnell Ave.
Terrace, BC V8G 4X2
250-632-4766
Fax: 250-632-5069
877-277-2288
e-mail: library@nwcc.bc.ca
ill@nwcc.bc.ca
URL: library.nwcc.bc.ca
Regional System: North Coast Library Federation
Consortia Membership: British Columbia Electronic Library Network (BC ELN); Electronic Health Library of BC (e-HLbc)
Hours: M-Th 9:00-12:00
Services:
Internet Access
Inter-Library Loan (ILL)

Langley: Langley Campus Library
20901 Langley By-Pass
Langley, BC V3A 2M8
Mailing Address: 12666 - 72nd Ave.
Surrey, BC V3A 2M8
604-599-3204
Fax: 604-599-3202
National Library Symbol: BSKC
Hours: M-Th 7:45am-9:00pm; F 7:45-5:00; Sa 10:00-4:00
Subjects covered: Horticulture, Music
Services:
Internet Access
Inter-Library Loan (ILL)
Microform Equipment: Computer; Reader
Personnel: *Summary:* 9 Total; 3 Professional(s); 6 Other employees

Langley: Trinity Western University Norma Marion Alloway Library
7600 Glover Rd.
Langley, BC V2Y 1Y1
604-513-2023
Fax: 604-513-2063
e-mail: library@twu.ca
ill@twu.ca
URL: www.twu.ca/library
National Library Symbol: BLTW
Consortia Membership: Canadian Research Knowledge Network (CRKN); Council of Prairie & Pacific University Libraries (COPPUL); British Columbia Electronic Library Network (BC ELN); Electronic Health Library of BC (e-HLbc)
Founded in: 1962
Hours: M-Th 7:45am-11:00pm; F 7:45-6:00; Sa 10:00-6:00; Su 1:30-5:00
Acquisitions Budget: $50,000 - $99,999
For Print: $50,000 - $99,999
For Electronic: $50,000 - $99,999
Note: Associated Canadian Theological Schools library has integrated with Trinity Western University
Special Collections: Robert N. Thompson Collection, University Archives, Mel Smith Papers
Subjects covered: Arts, Liberal Arts, Sciences, Nursing, Business, Religious Studies
Services:
Remote Access
Internet Access for a fee of $60/yr
Inter-Library Loan (ILL)
Microform Equipment: Computer; Reader
Personnel: *Summary:* 15 Total; 7 Professional(s); 10 Technical(s)
Ted Goshulak, University Librarian
Ron Braid, Head, Reference
Suzana Maunaga, Head, Cataloguing
Stan Olson, Head, Acquisitions & Systems
Bill Badke, Head, Theology
Sylvia Stopforth, Head, Archives
stopfort@twu.ca

Merritt: Nicola Valley Institute of Technology - Merritt Campus Library
4155 Belshaw St.
Merritt, BC V1K 1R1
250-378-3302
Fax: 250-378-3332
877-682-3300
e-mail: info@nvit.bc.ca
sgarcia@nvit.bc.ca
URL: www.nvit.bc.ca/library/index.htm
National Library Symbol: BMNVI
Consortia Membership: BC Libraries Cooperative; British Columbia Electronic Library Network (BC ELN); Electronic Health Library of BC (e-HLbc)
Founded in: 1979
Hours: Sept.-April: M-Th 8:30-8:30; F 8:30-4:30; Sa 12:00-6:00; Su 12:00-4:00. May-Aug.: M-F 8:30-4:30.
Acquisitions Budget: $25,000 - $49,999
For Print: $25,000 - $49,999
For Electronic: $10,000 - $24,999
Note: Member of BC Electronic Library Network
Subjects covered: First Nations; Social Work; Forestry; Natural Resource Technologies; Academic & Indigenous Studies; Aboriginal Community Economic Development
Services:
Remote Access
Internet Access
Inter-Library Loan (ILL) for a fee
Current awareness service; Computer lab; Instructional equipment & mobile computer loans
Linda Epps, Librarian
lepps@nvit.bc.ca
250-378-3303
Sherry Garcia, Library Coordinator
lgarcia@nvit.bc.ca
250-378-3302

Merritt: Vancouver Campus Library
#200, 4355 Mathissi Place
Merritt, BC V5G 4S8
604-602-3405
877-682-3300
National Library Symbol: BBNVI
Founded in: 1979
Hours: Sept.-April: M-F 8:30-4:30
Acquisitions Budget: $25,000 - $49,999
For Print: $25,000 - $49,999
For Electronic: $10,000 - $24,999
Services:
Remote Access
Internet Access
Inter-Library Loan (ILL) for a fee
Emily Smith, Library Technician
esmith@nvit.bc.ca

Mission: Mission Campus at Heritage Park Centre Library
#D129, 33700 Prentis Ave.
Mission, BC V2V 7B1
Mailing Address: PO Box 1000
Mission, BC V2V 7B1
604-557-7609
Fax: 604-826-0681

National Library Symbol: BCLF
Hours: M-Th 8:30-7:00
Services:
Internet Access
Access to Subscription Databases
Microform Equipment: Computer; Reader
Personnel: *Summary:* 1 Technical(s)

Nanaimo: Vancouver Island University Library
900 - 5th St.
Nanaimo, BC V9R 5S5
250-740-6330
Fax: 250-740-6333
e-mail: library@viu.ca
reference@viu.ca
ill@viu.ca
URL: www.viu.ca/library
National Library Symbol: BNM
Consortia Membership: Canadian Research Knowledge Network (CRKN); Council of Prairie & Pacific University Libraries (COPPUL); British Columbia Electronic Library Network (BC ELN)
Founded in: 1969
Hours: M-Th 7:00am-11:00pm; F 7:00-6:00; Sa, Su 10:00-6:00
Acquisitions Budget: $500,000 - $999,999
Note: Formerly known as Malaspina College
Subjects covered: Physical Sciences, Health & Human Sciences, History, Canadian History, First Nations, Business, Arts, Education
Services:
Remote Access
Internet Access
Access to Subscription Databases
Inter-Library Loan (ILL)
Microform Equipment: Computer; Reader
Personnel: *Summary:* 33 Total; 9 Professional(s); 26 Technical(s)
Bob Foley, Library Director
bob.foley@viu.ca
250-740-6332
Jennifer Brownlow, Liaison Librarian
jennifer.brownlow@viu.ca
250-740-6335
Daniel Sifton, Coordinator, Automation & Technical Services
daniel.sifton@viu.ca
250-740-6330 ext. 2444
Faith Takishita, Coordinator, Special Collections & Archives
faith.takishita@viu.ca
250-740-6330 ext. 2268

Nelson: Chamber of Mines of Eastern British Columbia Library of Government Geological Reports
215 Hall St.
Nelson, BC V1L 5X4
250-352-5242
e-mail: chamberofmines@netidea.com
URL: www.cmebc.com
Founded in: 1925
Hours: M-F 10:00-4:00
Acquisitions Budget: $25,000 - $49,999
Subjects covered: Historical data on mines of BC; technical data on mining operations; area maps; geological & geochemical data
Services:
Internet Access for a fee of $2/15 minutes min.

Nelson: Silver King Campus Library
2001 Silver King Rd.
Nelson, BC V1L 1C8
250-354-3249 ext: 249
Fax: 250-352-3180
886-301-6601
National Library Symbol: BCS
Founded in: 1966
Hours: M, W, Th, 8:20-12:30; Tu 8:20-4:00
Acquisitions Budget: $50,000 - $99,999
Personnel: *Summary:* 9 Total; 1 Technical(s)
Anne Verkerk, Library & Bookshop Contact

New Westminster: Douglas College Library
700 Royal Ave.
New Westminster, BC V3L 5B2
Mailing Address: PO Box 2503
New Westminster, BC V3L 5B2
604-527-5568
e-mail: infodesk@douglascollege.ca
URL: library.douglas.bc.ca
National Library Symbol: BNWD
Consortia Membership: British Columbia Electronic Library Network (BC ELN); Electronic Health Library of BC (e-HLbc)
Founded in: 1969
Hours: Fall & Winter: M-Th 8:00am-9pm; F 8:00-5:00; Sa 9:00-5:00. Summer: M, F 8:00-4:30; Tu-Th 8:00am-9:00pm
Acquisitions Budget: $250,000 - $499,999
Note: The library is an affiliate member of the Council of Prairie and Pacific University Libraries (COPPUL).
Subjects covered: Arts, Sciences, Business, Nursing, Community, Social, Family, Environmental Science, Theatre
Services:
Access to Subscription Databases
Inter-Library Loan (ILL)
Personnel: *Summary:* 45 Total; 16 Professional(s); 27 Technical(s); 2 Other employees
Debbie Schachter, Director
schachterd@douglascollege.ca
604-527-5182
Shelley Waldie, Assistant
waldies@groupwise.douglas.bc.ca
604-527-5180
Mary Matthews, Reference Services Librarian
matthewsm@groupwise.douglas.bc.ca
604-527-5438
Debra Flewelling, Emerging Technologies Librarian
flewellingd@groupwise.douglas.bc.ca
604-527-5190
Gretchen Goertz, Technical Services & Systems Librarian
goertzg@groupwise.douglas.bc.ca
604-527-5259
Dianne Hewitt, Web Development Librarian
hewittd@groupwise.douglas.bc.ca
604-527-5181
Susan Ashcroft, Collections Librarian
ashcrofts@groupwise.douglas.bc.ca
604-527-5189
Patti Romanko, Instructional Services Librarian
romankop@groupwise.douglas.bc.ca
604-527-5183
Christian Guillou, Electronic Resources Librarian
guillouc@groupwise.douglas.bc.ca
604-527-5184
Sandra Hochstein, Information Literacy Librarian
hochsteins@douglascollege.ca
604-527-5181
Szabi Stikker, Educational Technology
stikkers@douglas.bc.ca
604-527-5168

New Westminster: Justice Institute of British Columbia Library
715 McBride Blvd.
New Westminster, BC V3L 5T4
604-528-5599
Fax: 604-528-5593
TDD: 6045285656
e-mail: library@jibc.ca
URL: www.jibc.ca/library
Profile: Provides services to faculty & students enrolled incertificate, diploma & degree programs
National Library Symbol: BVAJI
Consortia Membership: British Columbia Electronic Library Network (BC ELN); Electronic Health Library of BC (e-HLbc)
Founded in: 1978
Hours: Sept.-Apr.: M-Th 8:00-8:00; F 8:00-5:00; Sa 9:00-4:00. May-Aug.: M-Th 8:00-5:00
Acquisitions Budget: $50,000 - $99,999
For Print: $25,000 - $49,999
For Electronic: $25,000 - $49,999
Note: Service to police officers, fire fighters, Court Services Branch personnel, Corrections Branch employees, paramedics, search & rescue volunteers, emergency management volunteers, emergency social services volunteers, family justice counsellors, & MCFD Youth Justice personnel
Special Collections: Justice & public safety topics; search & rescue; emergency management; criminology; corrections; forensic science; family violence; conflict resolution; policing
Subjects covered: Police Science, Fire Science, Emergency Medicine, Criminology, Penology, Corrections, Management, Adult Education, Disaster Planning, Search & Rescue
Services:
Remote Access
Internet Access
Inter-Library Loan (ILL)
Personnel: *Summary:* 6 Total; 4 Professional(s); 2 Technical(s)
April Haddad, Institute Librarian
ahaddad@jibc.ca
604-528-5594
Christine Babec, Reference Librarian
cbabec@jibc.ca
604-528-5595
Christine-Louise Dujmovich, Librarian, Reference & Electronic Resources
cdujmovich@jibc.ca
604-528-5597
Marjory Jardine, Librarian, Reference & Instruction
mjardine@jibc.ca
604-528-5592

New Westminster: Royal Columbian Hospital Medical Library
330 East Columbia St.
New Westminster, BC V3L 3W7
604-520-4281
Fax: 604-520-4755
e-mail: feedback@fraserhealth.ca
URL: www.fraserhealth.ca
National Library Symbol: BNWRC
No public access
Hours: M-F
Acquisitions Budget: $50,000 - $99,999
Note: Part of Fraser Health Authority
Subjects covered: Medicine, Hospital Administration, Health Sciences, Nursing
Services:
Inter-Library Loan (ILL)
Personnel: *Summary:* 3 Total; 1 Professional(s); 2 Technical(s)
Brooke Ballantyne Scott, Librarian
brooke.scott@fraserhealth.ca
Allison Lambert, Library Technician
allison.lambert@fraserhealth.ca

North Vancouver: Capilano University Library
2055 Purcell Way
North Vancouver, BC V7J 3H5
604-984-4944
Fax: 604-984-1728
e-mail: library@capilanou.ca
capill@capilanou.ca
media@capilanou.ca
URL: www.capilanou.ca/library/Library2
Social Media: www.youtube.com/user/CapilanoUniversity
www.facebook.com/capilanou
National Library Symbol: BVAC
Consortia Membership: British Columbia Electronic Library Network (BC ELN); Electronic Health Library of BC (e-HLbc)
Founded in: 1968
Hours: M-Th 8:00am-9:30pm; F 8:00-4:30; Sa, Su 1:00-5:00
Acquisitions Budget: $100,000 - $249,999
For Print: $100,000 - $249,999
For Electronic: $50,000 - $99,999
Special Collections: Jazz Music, Music Therapy, Tourism, General Undergraduate
Subjects covered: Arts, Sciences, Career, Vocational, Technical, Asian Pacific Business, Environmental, Paralegal Materials, Music, Film Studies, theatre
Services:
Remote Access
Internet Access
Access to Subscription Databases
Inter-Library Loan (ILL)
Microform Equipment: Computer; Reader
Personnel: *Summary:* 25 Total; 6 Professional(s); 19 Technical(s)
Grace Makarewicz, University Librarian
gracemakarewicz@capilanou.ca
604-986-1911 ext. 3660
Sidney Myers, Technical Services Librarian
smyers@capilanou.ca
604-986-1911 ext. 2129
Karin Hall, Collections Development Librarian
khall@capilanou.ca
604-984-1911 ext. 2164

Leanna Jantzi, Electronic Resources Librarian
leannajantzi@capilanou.ca
604-986-1911 ext. 2111
George Villavicencio, Systems Librarian
gvillavi@capilanou.ca
604-986-1911 ext. 2143
David Lambert, Reference Services Librarian
dlambert@capilanou.ca
604-986-1911 ext. 2108

North Vancouver: Marine Campus Library
265 West Esplanade
North Vancouver, BC V7M 1A5
604-453-4107
Fax: 604-980-0827
Hours: M-F 8:00-12:00, 1:00-4:00; Sa, Su 1:00-2:00
Subjects covered: Marine Engineering, Nautical Subjects, Safety, Shipping, Care & Transportation of Hazardous Materials (Hazmat), Seamanship
Services:
Access to Subscription Databases
Personnel: *Summary:* 2 Total; 1 Professional(s); 1 Technical(s)
Bill Nadiger, Reference Librarian
bill_nadiger@bcit.ca
604-453-4118
Jennifer Hunter, Library Assistant
jennifer_hunter@bcit.ca

Penticton: Penticton Campus Library
583 Duncan Ave. West
Penticton, BC V2A 8E1
250-490-3951
Fax: 250-490-3954
Hours: M-Th 7:45am-9:00pm; F 7:45-5:00; Sa 8:30-4:30; Su 12:00-4:00
Services:
Inter-Library Loan (ILL)

Port Alberni: Port Alberni Regional Campus Library
3699 Roger St.
Port Alberni, BC V9Y 8E3
250-724-8733
Fax: 250-724-8780
e-mail: sherry.kropninski@nic.bc.ca
URL: library.nic.bc.ca
National Library Symbol: BCPNI
Founded in: 1992
Hours: Sept.-April: M-Th 8:30-6:00; F 8:30-4:30. May-June: M-F 8:30-4:30
Acquisitions Budget: For Print: $25,000 - $49,999
For Electronic: $10,000 - $24,999
Note: Public access limited to use of books & materials in library, OPAC station but not the student computers.
Services:
Remote Access
Internet Access
Access to Subscription Databases
Inter-Library Loan (ILL)
Personnel: *Summary:* 4 Total; 2 Technical(s); 2 Other employees
Mary Anne Guenther, Coordinator, Library Services
250-334-5001
Sherry Kropninski, Library Technician
sherry.kropninski@nic.bc.ca
250-724-8733
Hannah Leprette, Library Assistant
hannah.leprette@nic.bc.ca
250-724-8760

Port Hardy: Port Hardy Centre
9300 Trustee Rd.
Port Hardy, BC V0N 2P0
Mailing Address: PO Box 901
Port Hardy, BC V0N 2P0
250-949-2863
Fax: 250-949-2617
866-332-1113
e-mail: reference@nic.bc.ca
URL: library.nic.bc.ca
Hours: Hours vary. Please contact the campus library.
Services:
Internet Access
Inter-Library Loan (ILL)
Personnel: *Summary:* 1 Total; 1 Other employees

Powell River: Powell River Campus Library
#100, 7085 Nootka St.
Powell River, BC V8A 3C6
604-485-8044
Fax: 604-485-2459
e-mail: prlibrary@viu.ca
reference@viu.ca
URL: www.pr.viu.ca
National Library Symbol: BNM
Founded in: 1978
Special Collections: Databases; Journals; CDs; Videos
Services:
Remote Access
Internet Access
Access to Subscription Databases
Inter-Library Loan (ILL)
Providing library instruction
Eileen Edmunds, Liaison Librarian & Regional Campus Coordinator
eileen.edmunds@viu.ca

Prince George: College of New Caledonia Library
3330 - 22nd Ave.
Prince George, BC V2N 1P8
250-561-5811
Fax: 250-561-5845
800-371-8111
e-mail: cnclibrary@cnc.bc.ca
URL: www.cnc.bc.ca/Exploring/Services/Library.htm
National Library Symbol: BPGC
Consortia Membership: British Columbia Electronic Library Network (BC ELN); Electronic Health Library of BC (e-HLbc)
Founded in: 1969
Hours: Fall/Winter: M-W 8:00am-10:00pm, Th-F 8:00am-8:00pm, Sa-Su 12:00-5:00; Summer: M-F 9:00-5:00, Sa 12:00-5:00 (May only)
Acquisitions Budget: $50,000 - $99,999
For Print: $50,000 - $99,999
For Electronic: $25,000 - $49,999
Subjects covered: Arts, Humanities, Science, Technologies
Services:
Remote Access
Internet Access
Inter-Library Loan (ILL)
Personnel: *Summary:* 16 Total; 5 Professional(s); 11 Technical(s)
Kathy Plett, Library Director
plett@cnc.bc.ca
Jennifer Sauvé, Public Services Librarian & Coordinator
sauvej@cnc.bc.ca
Brenda Yee, Technical Services Librarian
yee@cnc.bc.ca
Terry Hounsell, Director, Acquisitions/Accounts
hounsellt1@cnc.bc.ca

Prince George: University of Northern British Columbia
Geoffrey R. Weller Library
3333 University Way
Prince George, BC V2N 4Z9
250-960-6613
Fax: 250-960-6610
888-440-3440
Other contact info: Reference: 250-960-6475; ILL: 250-960-6460
URL: library.unbc.ca
Social Media: www.youtube.com/user/WellerLibrary
www.facebook.com/170324924795
twitter.com/unbc_library
National Library Symbol: BPGVB
Consortia Membership: Canadian Research Knowledge Network (CRKN); Council of Prairie & Pacific University Libraries (COPPUL); British Columbia Electronic Library Network (BC ELN); Electronic Health Library of BC (e-HLbc)
Hours: M-Th 8:00am-11:00pm; F 8:00am-9:00pm; Sa 10:00-6:00; Su 10:00-9:00
Acquisitions Budget: $1,000,000 plus
For Print: $250,000 - $499,999
For Electronic: $500,000 - $999,999
Special Collections: Northern British Columbia Archives & Special Collections: focus is historical exploration, early surveying, travel literature, First Nations, ethnology, culture, industry & resource management; Rare book collection; Education resources relevant to the B.C. curriculum; Maps; Information repository on oil & gas exploration
Subjects covered: Natural Resource Management, First Nations Studies, Environmental Studies, Resource Recreation & Tourism
Services:
Remote Access
Internet Access
Inter-Library Loan (ILL) for a fee of free (students, faculty, staff); $2/request (alumni); $10/request (comm
Curriculum lab; Special equipment for patrons with disabilities; Audio/visual equipment
Microform Equipment: Computer; Reader
Personnel: *Summary:* 34 Total; 9 Professional(s); 25 Technical(s)
Gohar Ashoughian, University Librarian
gashough@unbc.ca
250-960-6612
Heather Empey, Acquisitions, Collections & Information Resources Librarian
empeyh@unbc.ca
250-960-6468
Ramona Rose, Head, Archives/Special Collections
roserm@unbc.ca
250-960-6603
Eleanor Annis, Catalogue Librarian
eleanora@unbc.ca
250-960-6617
Gail Curry, Data, Map & Government Information Librarian
curryg@unbc.ca
250-960-6607
Nancy E. Black, Manager, Access & Information Services
blackn@unbc.ca
250-960-6473
Trina Fyfe, Northern Health Sciences Librarian
fyfet@unbc.ca
250-960-5195
James MacDonald, Digital Initiatives Librarian
macdonaj@unbc.ca
250-960-6601

Richmond: Aerospace Technology Campus Library
3800 Cessna Dr.
Richmond, BC V7B 0A1
604-419-3708
Fax: 604-207-8437
Hours: M-F 7:30-7:00
Note: Card must be purchased to borrow material, $50/year
Special Collections: Aircraft Maintenance; Aviation; Avionics
Services:
Internet Access
Bill Nadiger, Reference Librarian
bill_nadiger@bcit.ca
604-419-3739
Lori Pederson, Library Assistant
lori_pederson@bcit.ca

Richmond: MacDonald Dettwiler & Associates Ltd. Library
13800 Commerce Pkwy.
Richmond, BC V6V 2J3
604-278-3411
Fax: 604-231-2768
888-780-6444
e-mail: info@mdacorporation.com
URL: www.mda.ca
No public access
Founded in: 1980
Special Collections: Remote Sensing Collection
Subjects covered: Science, Technology, High Technology, Electronics Engineering
Services:
Microform Equipment: Reader
Personnel: *Summary:* 1 Professional(s)
Julie Jarvis, Librarian

Richmond: Richmond Campus Library
8771 Lansdowne Rd.
Richmond, BC V3W 2M8
Mailing Address: 12666 - 72nd Ave.
Surrey, BC V3W 2M8
604-599-3111
Fax: 604-599-2532
National Library Symbol: BSKC
Founded in: 1981
Hours: M-Th 7:45am-9:00pm; F 7:45-5:00; Sa 10:00-4:00

Special Collections: Videos
Subjects covered: Fashion Design, Environmental Protection Technology, Journalism, Public Relations, University transfer courses, applied BA degree courses
Services:
Internet Access
Inter-Library Loan (ILL)
Microform Equipment: Computer; Reader
Personnel: *Summary:* 17 Total; 5 Professional(s); 12 Other employees

Richmond: Triton Environmental Consultants Ltd. Library
8971 Beckwith Rd.
Richmond, BC V6X 1V4
604-279-2093
Fax: 604-279-2047
e-mail: ameeder@triton-env.com
info@triton-env.com
URL: www.triton-env.com
National Library Symbol: BVAEN
No public access
Founded in: 1980
Subjects covered: Environment, Fisheries, Engineering, Hydrology
Services:
Inter-Library Loan (ILL)
Personnel: *Summary:* 1 Professional(s)
Anneli Meeder, Librarian
ameeder@triton-env.com

Richmond: Union of British Columbia Municipalities Library
#60, 10551 Shellbridge Way
Richmond, BC V6X 2W9
604-270-8226
Fax: 604-270-9116
URL: www.civicnet.bc.ca
Founded in: 1905
Hours: M-F 8:30-4:30 by appointment only
Acquisitions Budget: 0-$9,999
For Print: 0-$9,999
For Electronic: 0-$9,999; BC local governments
Special Collections: Extensive, unorganized (as yet) archives of BC local government history
Subjects covered: Local Government, Legislation, Statistcs, History
Services:
Inter-Library Loan (ILL)
Personnel: *Summary:* 1 Total; 1 Professional(s)
Reiko Tagami, Information & Resolutions Coordinator
rtagami@ubcm.ca
604-270-8226 ext. 115

Salmon Arm: Salmon Arm Campus Library
2552 10 Ave. NE (TCH)
Salmon Arm, BC V1E 2S4
250-804-8851
Fax: 250-804-8852
National Library Symbol: BCSA
Hours: M-Th 8:00am-9:00pm; F 8:00-4:30; Sa 8:30-4:00; Su 12:00-4:00. May-Mid-Jun M-F 8:30-4:00
Special Collections: Deakin Collection of Children's Literature
Services:
Remote Access
Internet Access
Inter-Library Loan (ILL)
Adult Academic and Career Preparation; adult foundational programs; Adult Special Eduication (ESL) and Vocational Programs; LPN; Early childhood education; Home support
Personnel: *Summary:* 5 Total
Taryn Schmid, Campus Librarian
tschmid@okanagan.bc.ca

Sidney: Institute of Ocean Sciences Library
9860 West Saanich Rd.
Sidney, BC V8L 4B2
Mailing Address: PO Box 6000
Sidney, BC V8L 4B2
250-363-6392
Fax: 250-363-6749
e-mail: paclibraryios@dfo-mpo.gc.ca
URL: www.pac.dfo-mpo.gc.ca
National Library Symbol: BVIEM
Founded in: 1970
Hours: M-F 8:30-4:30 by appointment only
Special Collections: Published & unpublished books, journals & literature to support the research of the Institue & Natural Resources Canada's Pacific Geoscience Centre; Collections focus on oceanography, hydrography, ocean research, environmental science, geology, geophysics, seismology & earthquake studies
Subjects covered: Ocean Studies; Life Sciences; Earth Sciences; Geology
Services:
Inter-Library Loan (ILL)
Personnel: *Summary:* 1 Total
Pamela G. Wilkins, Librarian

Summerland: Canadian Agriculture Library - Summerland
4200 Hwy. 97
Summerland, BC V0H 1Z0
Mailing Address: PO Box 5000
Summerland, BC V0H 1Z0
250-494-2100
Fax: 250-494-0755
National Library Symbol: BSUAG
Founded in: 1951
Hours: 8:30-4:00 by appointment only
Acquisitions Budget: For Print: 0-$9,999
Note: Restricted service to the public because of staffing limits. On-site use of the collection. For ILL contact the Canadian Agriculture Library-Ottawa. See listing.
Subjects covered: Food Processing, Orchard Diseases & Pests, Biotechnology, Tree Fruit, Biological Control, Viticulture
Personnel: *Summary:* 1 Total; 1 Professional(s)
Lynne Boyd, Head Librarian
lynne.boyd@agr.gc.ca

Surrey: Fraser Valley Real Estate Board Academic Library (Surrey)
#250, 13450 - 102nd Ave.
Surrey, BC V3T 0A3
778-782-7411
Fax: 778-782-7420
Other contact info: Reference: 778-782-7414
e-mail: lib-surrey@sfu.ca
URL: www.lib.sfu.ca/surrey
Hours: M, T, Th 9:00-6:00; W 9:00-9:00; F 9:00-6:00
Natialie Gick, Acting Campus Librarian
ngick@sfu.ca
778-782-3266

Surrey: Kwantlen Polytechnic University Coast Capital Savings Library (Surrey)
12666 - 72nd Ave.
Surrey, BC V3W 2M8
604-599-2103
Fax: 604-599-2106
URL: www.kwantlen.ca/library
National Library Symbol: BSKC
Consortia Membership: Council of Prairie & Pacific University Libraries (COPPUL); Canadian Research Knowledge Network (CRKN); British Columbia Electronic Library Network (BC ELN); Electronic Health Library of BC (e-HLbc)
Founded in: 1981
Hours: M-Th 7:45am-9:00pm; F 7:45-5:00; Sa 10:00-4:00
Acquisitions Budget: $500,000 - $999,999; Students + faculty & staff
Note: The library is an affiliate member of the Council of Prairie and Pacific University Libraries (COPPUL).
Subjects covered: Music, Horticulture, Fashion Design, Interior Design, Nursing, Business, University Transfer Courses, Trades, Applied Skills BA Degree Programs
Services:
Internet Access
Access to Subscription Databases
Inter-Library Loan (ILL)
Audiovisual services
Microform Equipment: Computer; Reader
Personnel: *Summary:* 40 Total; 15 Professional(s); 3 Technical(s); 27 Other employees
Todd Mundle, University Librarian
todd.mundle@kwantlen.ca
604-599-2090
Celia Brinkerhoff, Public Services Librarian
celia.brinkerhoff@kwantlen.ca
604-599-3235
Linda Woodcock, Technical Services & Public Services Librarian
linda.woodcock@kwantlen.ca
604-599-2450
Caroline Daniels, Systems, Web & ILL Librarian
caroline.daniels@kwantlen.ca
604-599-3036
Colleen Van de Voort, Circulation/AV Librarian
colleen.vandevoort@kwantlen.ca
604-599-2090
Jan Penhorwood, Public Services Librarian
jan.penhorwood@kwantlen.ca
604-599-3236
Margaret Brown, Serials & Government Publications Librarian
margaret.brown@kwantlen.ca
604-599-2087
Linda Rogers, Collection Development Librarian
linda.rogers@kwantlen.ca
604-599-2942
Sigrid Kargut, AV Collection Librarian & Chair, Faculty Library
sigrid.kargut@kwantlen.ca
604-599-2378
Denise Dale, Reference Services Coordinator & Archives
denise.dale@kwantlen.ca
604-599-2999
Chris Burns, Research Support & Data Librarian
chris.burns@kwantlen.ca
604-599-3198
Lisa Hubick, Public Relations Librarian
lisa.hubick@kwantlen.ca
604-599-3404

Surrey: Powertech Labs Inc. Library
12388 - 88th Ave.
Surrey, BC V3W 7R7
604-590-7500
Fax: 604-590-6611
URL: www.powertechlabs.com
www.powertechlabs.com/knowledge-centre
No public access
Founded in: 1980
Hours: Tu-Th 8:30-4:30
Acquisitions Budget: 0-$9,999
For Print: 0-$9,999
For Electronic: 0-$9,999
Note: The online Knowledge Centre provides access to case studies, technical papers, standards bodies/associations, patents, & videos
Special Collections: Canadian Electrical Association reports; EPRI reports
Subjects covered: Energy, Technology, Electrical & Chemical Research, Power Engineering Materials, Engineering & Applied Chemistry
Services:
Inter-Library Loan (ILL)
Personnel: *Summary:* 1 Total; 1 Technical(s)
Elizabeth Irwin, Library Assistant
elizabeth.irwin@powertechlabs.com

Surrey: Surrey Memorial Hospital Library Services
13750 - 96th Ave.
Surrey, BC V3V 1Z2
604-585-5666 ext: 2467
Fax: 604-588-3320
e-mail: feedback@fraserhealth.ca
URL: www.fraserhealth.ca
Consortia Membership: Health Libraries Association of BC, Electronic Health Library of BC
Founded in: 1987
Hours: M-F 9:00-5:00 by appointment only
Acquisitions Budget: $25,000 - $49,999
For Print: $10,000 - $24,999
For Electronic: $25,000 - $49,999; Hospital staff, affiliated physicians, students
Note: Part of Fraser Health Authority; Member of Health Libraries Association of B.C.; Docline for ILL
Subjects covered: Clinical Medicine, Nursing, Allied Health Management
Services:
Inter-Library Loan (ILL)
Personnel: *Summary:* 5 Total; 1 Professional(s); 4 Technical(s); 2 Volunteer(s)
Linda Howard, Librarian
linda.howard@fraserhealth.ca

Anita Thompson, Library Technician
anita.thompson@fraserhealth.ca

Terrace: Northwest Community College Library Terrace Campus Library

5331 McConnell Ave.
Terrace, BC V8G 4X2
250-638-5407
Fax: 250-635-1594
877-277-2288
e-mail: library@nwcc.bc.ca
ill@nwcc.bc.ca
URL: library.nwcc.bc.ca
National Library Symbol: BTENW
Regional System: North Coast Library Federation
Consortia Membership: British Columbia Electronic Library Network (BC ELN); Electronic Health Library of BC (e-HLbc)
Founded in: 1977
Hours: M-Th 8:00am-9:00pm; F 8:00-5:00; Sa, Su 1:00-5:00
Acquisitions Budget: $50,000 - $99,999
For Print: $50,000 - $99,999
For Electronic: $10,000 - $24,999
Special Collections: BC Northwest Archives, Children's Books, Literacy Collection, Government Documents, Forestry
Subjects covered: Trades, Social Services, Natural Resources, University 1st & 2nd year Arts & Science, Cook Training, Business Administration, Adult Upgrading, Early Childhood Education, Wilderness Guiding, Eco-Tourism, Applied Computers
Services:
Internet Access
Access to Subscription Databases
Inter-Library Loan (ILL) for a fee of Free to staff & students; $10 community
Microform Equipment: Reader
Personnel: *Summary:* 7 Total; 2 Professional(s); 3 Technical(s); 2 Other employees
Tim MacDonald, College Librarian
tmacdonald@nwcc.bc.ca
250-638-5407
Michele Cook, Eastern Region Librarian
mcook@nwcc.bc.ca
250-847-4461 ext. 5836

Terrace: Prince Rupert Campus Library

353 - 5th St.
Terrace, BC V8G 4X2
Mailing Address: 5331 McConnell Ave.
Terrace, BC V8G 4X2
250-624-6054
Fax: 250-624-2572
877-277-2288
e-mail: library@nwcc.bc.ca
ill@nwcc.bc.ca
URL: library.nwcc.bc.ca
Regional System: North Coast Library Federation
Consortia Membership: British Columbia Electronic Library Network (BC ELN); Electronic Health Library of BC (e-HLbc)
Hours: M-Th 8:30-8:30; F 8:30-4:30
Services:
Internet Access
Inter-Library Loan (ILL)

Terrace: Smithers Campus Library

3966 - 2nd Ave.
Terrace, BC V8G 4X2
Mailing Address: 5331 McConnell Ave.
Terrace, BC V8G 4X2
250-847-4461
Fax: 250-847-8046
877-277-2288
e-mail: library@nwcc.bc.ca
ill@nwcc.bc.ca
URL: library.nwcc.bc.ca
Regional System: North Coast Library Federation
Consortia Membership: British Columbia Electronic Library Network (BC ELN); Electronic Health Library of BC (e-HLbc)
Hours: M-Th 9:00-1:30, 2:00-4:00
Services:
Internet Access
Inter-Library Loan (ILL)

Trail: Teck Metals Ltd. Research Centre

PO Box 2000
Trail, BC V1R 4S4
250-364-4432
Fax: 250-364-4400
e-mail: art@teck.com
URL: www.teck.com
National Library Symbol: BTC
No public access
Founded in: 1925
Hours: M-F
Acquisitions Budget: $50,000 - $99,999
Special Collections: Chemical & Metallurgical Abstracts, Metals Abstracts, Engineering Index, U.S. Patent Office Gazette
Subjects covered: Physical Sciences, Engineering, Technology, Chemicals, Metallurgy
Personnel: *Summary:* 1 Professional(s); 1 Technical(s)
Fran Noone, Information Specialist

Vancouver: Association for Mineral Exploration British Columbia Charles S. Ney Library

#800, 889 West Pender St.
Vancouver, BC V6C 3B2
604-689-5271
Fax: 604-681-2363
e-mail: info@amebc.ca
URL: www.amebc.ca/resources-and-publications/library.aspx
Founded in: 1912
Hours: M-F 8:30-4:00
Acquisitions Budget: 0-$9,999
For Print: 0-$9,999
For Electronic: 0-$9,999; Members & general public
Subjects covered: Mineral Exploration, Mining
Services:
Internet Access
Jonathan Buchanan, Director, Communications & Public Affairs
jbuchanan@amebc.ca
604-630-3923

Vancouver: Biomedical Branch Library

Gordon & Leslie Diamond Health Centre
2775 Laurel St., 2nd Fl.
Vancouver, BC V5Z 1M9
Mailing Address: 2775 Laurel St., 2nd Fl.
Vancouver, BC V5Z 1M9
604-875-4505
Fax: 604-875-4689
URL: www.library.ubc.ca/bmb
www.library.ubc.ca/life
Consortia Membership: Electronic Health Library of BC (e-HLbc)
Hours: M-Th 8:00am-10:00pm; F 8:00-8:00; Sa 10:00-8:00; Su 10:00-10:00
Note: Off-campus branch
Subjects covered: Health Sciences, Clinical Medicine
Personnel: *Summary:* 4 Total; 1 Professional(s); 3 Other employees
Dean Giustini, Reference Librarian
dean.giustini@ubc.ca
604-875-4505

Vancouver: British Columbia Utilities Commission Resource Library

900 Howe St., 6th Fl.
Vancouver, BC V6Z 2N3
Mailing Address: PO Box 250
Vancouver, BC V6Z 2N3
604-660-4700
Fax: 604-660-1102
800-663-1385
e-mail: Commission.Secretary@bcuc.com
URL: www.bcuc.com
Founded in: 1973
Hours: M-F
Acquisitions Budget: $25,000 - $49,999
Note: Resources and archives also vailable online.
Special Collections: BCUC Hearings (transcripts & exhibits)
Subjects covered: Economics, Regulation, Housing, Planning & Public Works, Government, Architecture, Law, Law Enforcement, Public Utilities, Income Tax, Municipal Government, Provincial Statutes & Legislation, Canadian Statutes
Alison Cormack, Information Services Officer

Vancouver: Broadway Campus Library

#A2014, 1155 East Broadway
Vancouver, BC V5T 4V5
604-871-7326
Fax: 604-871-7446
TDD: 6048717325
National Library Symbol: BVAVCC
Founded in: 1965
Hours: M-Th 8:00-8:00; F 8:00-4:00
Acquisitions Budget: $100,000 - $249,999
For Print: $100,000 - $249,999
For Electronic: $50,000 - $99,999
Note: Computer loans & Internet access for students, faculty & staff only
Special Collections: Special Education, Braille Collection, Talking Books, Literacy, English as a Second Language, Career Resources
Subjects covered: Adult Basic Education, Automotive Trades, Business, Culinary Arts, Education, Health & Dental, Hospitality, Humanities, Music, Sciences, Technology
Services:
Remote Access
Internet Access
Access to Subscription Databases
Inter-Library Loan (ILL)
Group & quiet study facilities; audiovisual materials & equipment; scanning, printing & photocopying; library tours & research classes; homework help & tutoring; services & adaptive technologies for users who are deaf or hard of hearing, or with print disabilities; services for distance learners
Microform Equipment: Computer; Reader
Personnel: *Summary:* 30 Total; 11 Professional(s); 19 Technical(s)

Vancouver: EarthSave Canada Library

349 West Georgia St.
Vancouver, BC V6B 3W2
Mailing Address: PO Box 2213
Vancouver, BC V6B 3W2
604-731-5885
e-mail: office@earthsave.ca
URL: www.earthsave.bc.ca
Acquisitions Budget: 0-$9,999
For Print: 0-$9,999
For Electronic: 0-$9,999
Note: Lending for Earthsave members
Special Collections: Library carries over 500 books, magazines, videos, DVDs, & audio cassettes covering health, nutrition, animal ethics, environmentalism, & vegetarian cooking
Subjects covered: Health; Ecology; Ethics
Services:
Providing education on how diet affects health & the planet
Carolyn Mill, Office Manager

Vancouver: Ecojustice Canada Library

#214, 131 Water St.
Vancouver, QC V6B 4M3
604-685-5618
Fax: 604-685-7813
800-926-7744
e-mail: info@ecojustice.ca
URL: www.ecojustice.ca
Profile: Dedicated to using law to protect & restore Canada's environment; part of the environment protection movement; provides free legal expertise; offices in Vancouver, Toronto, Ottawa & Alberta
Founded in: 1990
Hours: by appointment only
Acquisitions Budget: 0-$9,999
For Print: 0-$9,999
For Electronic: 0-$9,999
Note: A non-profit environmental law organization
Subjects covered: Law, Environment
Devon Page, Executive Director
dpage@ecojustice.ca
Carol McDonald, Director of Admin. & Human Resources
cmcdonald@ecojustice.ca

Vancouver: FP Innovations Forintek Division Vancouver Library

2665 East Mall
Vancouver, BC V6T 1W5
604-224-3221 ext: 668
Fax: 604-222-5690
e-mail: info@fpinnovations.ca
URL: www.fpinnovations.ca

National Library Symbol: BVAFP
No public access
Founded in: 1927
Hours: M-F
Subjects covered: Forest Products Research, Sawmilling, Timber Engineering, Wood Preservation, Wood Chemistry, Wood Science, Secondary/Value Wood Processing
Services:
Inter-Library Loan (ILL)
Personnel: *Summary:* 2 Total; 1 Professional(s); 1 Technical(s)
Barbara Holder, Librarian

Vancouver: FPInnovations - Paprican Division, Vancouver Research Library

3800 Wesbrook Mall
Vancouver, BC V6S 2L9
604-222-3200
Fax: 604-222-3207
URL: www.paprican.ca
National Library Symbol: BVAPPR
No public access
Founded in: 1986
Hours: M-F 8:30-4:30
Subjects covered: Pulp & Paper Science & Technology, Forest Products
Services:
Inter-Library Loan (ILL)
Personnel: *Summary:* 1 Total; 1 Professional(s)
Judy Mackenzie, Librarian
jmackenzie@paprican.ca

Vancouver: Geoscience Research Library / Bibliothèque de recherches géoscientifiques GSC Pacific (Vancouver)/CGC de la division du Pacifique (Vancouver)

625 Robson St., 15th Fl.
Vancouver, BC V6B 5J3
604-666-1147
Fax: 604-666-7186
e-mail: libvan@nrcan.gc.ca
National Library Symbol: BVAG
Founded in: 1973
Hours: M-F 8:30-4:30
Acquisitions Budget: $100,000 - $249,999
For Print: $100,000 - $249,999
For Electronic: $50,000 - $99,999
Special Collections: British Columbia Energy, Mines & Petroleum Resources publications, US Bureau of Mines publications, Energy Mines & Resources Canada publications, theses on the Canadian Cordillera, Natural Resources Canada publications, Environment Canada, USGS, Geological Survey of Canada
Subjects covered: Earth Sciences, Geoscience with special emphasis on North American Cordillera & Pacific margin, Micropaleontology, World wide earth sciences journals
Services:
Remote Access
Internet Access
Access to Subscription Databases
Inter-Library Loan (ILL)
Personnel: *Summary:* 2 Total; 1 Professional(s); 1 Technical(s); 1 Volunteer(s)
Diane Thompson, Manager
Diane.Thompson@NRCan-RNCan.gc.ca

Vancouver: Klohn Crippen Berger Ltd. Library

#500, 2955 Virtual Way
Vancouver, BC V5M 4X6
604-669-3800
Fax: 604-669-3835
e-mail: geotechnical@klohn.com
info@klohn.com
URL: www.klohn.com
National Library Symbol: BRKL
Hours: M-F by appointment only
Acquisitions Budget: $10,000 - $24,999
For Print: $10,000 - $24,999
For Electronic: 0-$9,999
Subjects covered: Soil Mechanics, Civil & Environmental Engineering, Community Development
Services:
Inter-Library Loan (ILL) for a fee of shipping
Personnel: *Summary:* 2 Total; 1 Professional(s); 1 Other employees
Kim Feltham, Library & Records Coordinator
kfeltham@klohn.com
604-251-8435

Vancouver: Langara College Library

100 West 49th Ave.
Vancouver, BC V5Y 2Z6
604-323-5384
Fax: 604-323-5512
e-mail: ill@langara.bc.ca
URL: www.langara.bc.ca/library
National Library Symbol: BVAVCL
Consortia Membership: British Columbia Electronic Library Network (BC ELN); Electronic Health Library of BC (e-HLbc)
Founded in: 1970
Hours: M-Th 8:00am-9:00pm; F 8:00-6:00; Sa-Su 10:00-5:00; Summer Term: M-Th 8:00am-7:30pm; F 8:00-5:00
Acquisitions Budget: $100,000 - $249,999
For Print: $50,000 - $99,999
For Electronic: $50,000 - $99,999
Subjects covered: Academic & careers program
Services:
Remote Access
Internet Access
Access to Subscription Databases
Inter-Library Loan (ILL) for a fee of $5
Microform Equipment: Reader
Personnel: *Summary:* 27 Total; 9 Professional(s); 18 Technical(s);
Grace Makarewicz, Director, Library Services
gmakarewicz@langara.bc.ca
604-323-5460
Vivian Feng, Coordinator, Reference & Instructional Services
vfeng@langara.bc.ca
604-323-5346
Patricia Cia, Coordinator, Technical Services & Library Systems
pcia@langara.bc.ca
604-323-5243
Joyce Wong, Department Chair
joyce.wong@langara.bc.ca
604-323-5047
Alison Curtis, Coordinator, Collection Development
acurtis@langara.bc.ca
604-323-5465

Vancouver: Library (Vancouver)

#900, 1281 West Georgia St.
Vancouver, BC V6E 3J7
604-684-4384
Fax: 604-684-5124
No public access
Founded in: 1957
Subjects covered: Physical Sciences, Maps, Geology, Soil Mechanics, Rock Mechanics. Comprehensive collections on geological hazards, including landslides, avalanches, earthquakes, ground subsidence & erosion. Other collections on BC soils, highways, harbours & terrain.
Personnel: *Summary:* 1 Total; 1 Professional(s); 2 Volunteer(s)

Vancouver: Pacific & Yukon Region - Vancouver Library - Environment Canada

#201, 401 Burrard St.
Vancouver, BC V6C 3S5
604-666-5914
Fax: 604-666-1788
Other contact info: 604-666-1794
e-mail: nvan.library@ec.gc.ca
URL: www.ec.gc.ca/default.asp?lang=en&n=b047b5b1-1
National Library Symbol: BVAEP
Founded in: 1973
Hours: M-F by appointment only
Services:
Inter-Library Loan (ILL)
Microform Equipment: Computer; Reader
Personnel: *Summary:* 1 Total; 1 Professional(s)
Andrew Fabro, Chief Librarian
andrew.fabro@ec.gc.ca

Vancouver: Pacific Salmon Commission Library

#600, 1155 Robson St.
Vancouver, BC V6E 1B5
604-684-8081
Fax: 604-666-8707
e-mail: tarita@psc.org
library@psc.org
URL: www.psc.org
National Library Symbol: BVAPSC
Hours: M-F 8:00-4:00 by appointment only
Acquisitions Budget: 0-$9,999
For Print: 0-$9,999
For Electronic: 0-$9,999
Subjects covered: Fishery Management, Ichthyology, Salmon Biology
Personnel: *Summary:* 1 Professional(s)
Teri Tarita, Librarian
tarita@psc.org

Vancouver: St Paul's Health Sciences Library

Providence Building, level 1, 1081 Burrard St.
Vancouver, BC V6Z 1Y6
604-806-8425
Fax: 604-806-8013
e-mail: stpauls.library@ubc.ca
URL: www.library.ubc.ca/stpauls/
www.library.ubc.ca/life
Consortia Membership: Electronic Health Library of BC (e-HLbc)
Founded in: 1950
Hours: M-Th 8:00am-9:00pm; F 8:00-5:00; Sa 12:00-5:00
Acquisitions Budget: $50,000 - $99,999
Note: Off-campus branch
Subjects covered: Health Sciences, Clinical Medicine
Services:
Remote Access
Internet Access
Access to Subscription Databases
Inter-Library Loan (ILL)
Personnel: *Summary:* 3 Total; 1 Professional(s); 2 Other employees
Barbara Saint, Reference Librarian
bsaint@interchange.ubc.ca
604-682-2344 ext. 62090

Vancouver: Samuel & Frances Belzberg Library

515 West Hastings St.
Vancouver, BC V6B 5K3
604-291-5050
Fax: 604-291-5052
e-mail: libask@sfu.ca
URL: www.lib.sfu.ca/belzberg
Hours: M-Th 10:00-9:00; F 10:00-7:00; Sa 10:00-5:00
Subjects covered: Economics, Industry, Business, Finance, Banking Industry, Gerontology
Karen Marotz, Head Librarian
marotz@sfu.ca
778-782-5054

Vancouver: Teck Resources Corporate Library

#3300, 550 Burrard St.
Vancouver, BC V6C 0B3
604-699-4000
Fax: 604-699-4711
e-mail: keith.low@teck.com
URL: www.teck.com
National Library Symbol: BVATE
Hours: M-F by appointment only
Special Collections: Company annual reports; government publications; geology materials; mining engineering
Subjects covered: Geology, Mining & Exploration, Environment, Economics
Services:
Inter-Library Loan (ILL)
Personnel: *Summary:* 4 Total; 2 Professional(s); 1 Technical(s)
Suzanne McBeath, Librarian
suzanne.mcbeath@teck.com

Vancouver: University of British Columbia Library

1961 East Mall
Vancouver, BC V6T 1Z1
604-822-6375
Fax: 604-822-3893
URL: www.library.ubc.ca
Social Media: www.flickr.com/photos/ubclibrary
www.facebook.com/UBCLibrary
twitter.com/ubclibrary
National Library Symbol: BVAU
Consortia Membership: Canadian Research Knowledge Network (CRKN); Council of Prairie & Pacific University Libraries

(COPPUL); BC Libraries Cooperative; British Columbia Electronic Library Network (BC ELN)
Founded in: 1915
Hours: M-Su
Acquisitions Budget: $1,000,000 plus
For Print: $1,000,000 plus
For Electronic: $1,000,000 plus; Students, faculty & staff
Special Collections: Pacific Northwest History, Canadiana, English 19th Century Literature (Colbeck), History of Cartography, Cartographic Archives, Early Japanese Maps (Bean), English & American Children's Literature from 18th Century to 1930's, University Archives, UBC Theses, History of Medicine & Science, Oriental Collection including The P'u-pan Collection, Harry Hawthorne Angling Collection, Literature (Colbeck), Canadiana Maps (Rogers-Tucker), The Chung Collection, The H.C.S. Stravinsky Collection
Services:
Remote Access
Internet Access
Access to Subscription Databases
Inter-Library Loan (ILL)
Microform Equipment: Computer; Reader
Personnel: *Summary:* 310 Total; 73 Professional(s); 201 Technical(s); 36 Other employees
Ingrid Parent, University Librarian
ingrid.parent@ubc.ca
Melody Burton, Deputy University Librarian
melody.burton@ubc.ca
Lea Starr, Associate University Librarian, Research Services
lea.starr@ubc.ca
604-822-2826
Rue Ramirez, Associate University Librarian, Library Systems & IT
rue.ramirez@ubc.ca
604-822-5241
Jo Anne Newyear-Ramirez, Assist. University Librarian, Collections & Scholarly Communication
joanne.newyear-ramirez@ubc.ca
604-822-2740

Vancouver: Vancouver Aquarium Marine Science Centre
Robin Best Library
845 Avison Way
Vancouver, BC V6B 3E2
Mailing Address: PO Box 3232
Vancouver, BC V6B 3E2
604-659-3404
Fax: 604-659-3515
Other contact info: Info-line: 604-659-3474
e-mail: library@vanaqua.org
URL: www.vanaqua.org
No public access
Hours: Library is not open to the public, but will answer questions via e-mail.
Special Collections: Archives, Photographs
Subjects covered: Contains over 5,000 books & periodicals on the following topics: Tropical Fish; Freshwater & Marine Fish; Marine Mammals; Reptiles; Amphibians; Birds
Services:
Inter-Library Loan (ILL)
Personnel: *Summary:* 1 Professional(s); 1 Volunteer(s)
Ann Dreolini, Manager, Information Services

Vancouver: Vancouver Coastal Health Authority Library
520 West 6th Ave.
Vancouver, BC V5Z 1A1
604-730-7656
Fax: 604-730-7660
e-mail: VCHLibraryServices@vch.ca
URL: www.vch.ca/libraryservices/index.htm
Consortia Membership: Electronic Health Library of BC (e-HLbc)
No public access
Founded in: 1979
Hours: M-F 8:30-5:00
Note: Public use of library on-site only. Library supports & trains volunteers to staff community health centre-based health information centres. Volunteer health finders provide access to health information using electronic & print resources, provides referral services to health agencies & health care providers.
Subjects covered: Long Term Care, Health Education, Community Health Services, Public Health
Services:
Inter-Library Loan (ILL) for a fee of reciprical
Personnel: *Summary:* 2 Total; 1 Professional(s); 1 Technical(s)
Patricia Young, Librarian
Pat.Young@vch.ca
604-730-7653
Marjory Jardine, Librarian
Marjory.Jardine@vch.ca
604-730-7652
Paula Ludwig, Library Technician
Paula.Ludwig@vch.ca
604-730-7656

Vancouver: Vancouver Community College Downtown Campus Library
#242, 250 West Pender St
Vancouver, BC V6B 1S9
604-443-8339
Fax: 604-443-8588
866-565-7819
TDD: 6048718549
e-mail: libraryhelp@vcc.ca
URL: library.vcc.ca
www.vcc.ca/learning-support/library.cfm
National Library Symbol: BVAVCC
Consortia Membership: British Columbia Electronic Library Network (BC ELN); Electronic Health Library of BC (e-HLbc)
Founded in: 1965
Acquisitions Budget: $100,000 - $249,999
For Print: $50,000 - $99,999
For Electronic: $50,000 - $99,999; Students
Special Collections: Collections in support of all VCC programs
Subjects covered: Humanities, Social Sciences, Applied Sciences, English as a Second Language, Tourism, Business, Hospitality, Pacific Rim, Food, Culinary Arts, Education, Health (including Nursing, Dental Technology, Dental Hygiene, Denturists, Lab Assistants), Trades training & Computer Technologists
Services:
Inter-Library Loan (ILL)
Public Services, Reference Services & Information Literacy, Technical Services, Library Systems, Circulation & ILL, Acquisitions, Collections, Cataloguing
Personnel: *Summary:* 33 Total; 9 Professional(s); 24 Technical(s)
Tim Atkinson, Director, Library & Learning Resources
tatkinson@vcc.caa
604-871-7000 ext. 7007
Virgina Adams, Dept Head, Library Public Services
vadams@vcc.ca
604-871-7319
Shirley Lew, Coordinator, Library Systems & Technical Services
slew@vcc.ca
604-871-7000 ext. 8519

Vancouver: Vancouver Museum Library & Resource Centre
1100 Chestnut St.
Vancouver, BC V6J 3J9
604-736-4431
Fax: 604-736-5417
No public access
Founded in: 1968
Subjects covered: Ethnology, Museology, Art, Culture, History, Asian Studies, Natural History, Anthropology, Archaeology, Museum Conservation
Personnel: *Summary:* 1 Other employees
Lynn Maranda, Curator of Anthropology
lmaranda@vanmuseum.bc.ca
604-730-5318

Vancouver: VanDusen Gardens Library
5251 Oak St.
Vancouver, BC V6M 4H1
604-257-8668
Fax: 604-266-4236
e-mail: library@vandusen.org
URL: www.city.vancouver.bc.ca
Founded in: 1977
Hours: Sept-June: T-F 10:00-3:00, W evenings 7:00-9:00, Su 1:00-4:00, July-Aug T-F 10:00-3:00
Acquisitions Budget: For Print: 0-$9,999
Personnel: *Summary:* 1 Total; 1 Professional(s); 12 Volunteer(s)
Marina Princz, Librarian

Vancouver: West Coast Environmental Law Library
#200, 2006 West 10th Ave.
Vancouver, BC V6J 2B3
604-684-7378
Fax: 604-684-1312
800-330-9235
e-mail: admin@wcel.org
URL: www.wcel.org
Founded in: 1974
Special Collections: Aboriginal law; Energy; Environmental assessment; Climate change; Forest & land use; Green communities
Subjects covered: Environmental law
Jessica Clogg, Executive Director & Senior Counsel
jessica_clogg@wcel.org
604-601-2501

Vancouver: Woodward Library
2198 Health Sciences Mall
Vancouver, BC V6T 1Z3
604-822-4440
Fax: 604-822-5596
Other contact info: Reference: 604-822-3295
e-mail: scieng.library@ubc.ca
URL: www.library.ubc.ca/woodward
scieng.library.ubc.ca
National Library Symbol: BVAUW
Consortia Membership: Electronic Health Library of BC (e-HLbc)
Founded in: 1950
Hours: M-Th 8:00am-11:00pm; F 8:00-6:00; Sa 10:00-6:00; Su 12:00-6:00
Special Collections: History of Life Sciences collection; Various records relating to Canadian, British & European scientists
Subjects covered: Health Sciences, Clinical Medicine, Biology
Services:
Inter-Library Loan (ILL)
Personnel: *Summary:* 23 Total
Kathryn Hornby, Head
kathryn.hornby@ubc.ca
604-822-4970
Aletela Greenwood, Acting Head, Woodward Library and Hospital Branch Libraries
aleteia.greenwood@ubc.ca
604-822-0689

Vernon: Vernon Campus Library
7000 College Way
Vernon, BC V1B 2N5
250-545-7291 ext: 2247
Fax: 250-503-3277
Hours: M-Th 7:30am-9:00pm; F 7:30-4:30; Sa 8:30-4:00, Su 12:00-4:00
Margaret Hodgins, Campus Librarian
mhodgins@okanagan.bc.ca

Victoria: British Columbia Ferry Services Inc. Library
#500, 1321 Blanshard St.
Victoria, BC V8W 0B7
250-978-1241
Fax: 250-978-1501
URL: www.bcferries.com
National Library Symbol: BVIFC
Hours: M-F 8:30-4:00
Special Collections: Clippings, Archive, Corporate Records
Subjects covered: Marine Engineering, Shipping
Services:
Inter-Library Loan (ILL)
Personnel: *Summary:* 1 Total; 1 Professional(s)
Terrell Les Strange, Corporate Records Manager
terrell.lesstrange@bcferries.com

Victoria: British Columbia Health & Human Services Library
1515 Blanshard St., 1st Fl.
Victoria, BC V8W 3C8
250-952-2196
Fax: 250-952-2180
e-mail: hlth.library@gov.bc.ca
URL: www.healthservices.gov.bc.ca/library
National Library Symbol: BVIHE
Founded in: 1978
Hours: M-F 8:30-4:30 by appointment only

Note: Provides library services to Ministry of Health Services & Ministry of Children & Family Development
Subjects covered: Public Health, Medicine, Nursing, Health Sciences, Community Mental Health Services, Family Health, Communicable Disease Control, Epidemiology, Health Administration, Dentistry, Nutrition, Resource Allocation, Health Economics, Child Welfare, Child Abuse & Neglect, Child Protection, Adoption, Family Issues, Social Work, Counselling, Employment Research, Labour, Market, Poverty, Public Welfare, Social Policy, Welfare Reform, Training
Services:
Inter-Library Loan (ILL)
Personnel: *Summary:* 8 Total; 3 Professional(s); 3 Technical(s); 2 Other employees
Antje Helmuth, Head Librarian
Antje.Helmuth@gov.bc.ca

Victoria: British Columbia Ministry of Environment James T. Fyles Library
1810 Blanshard St.
Victoria, BC V8W 9N3
Mailing Address: PO Box 9321, Stn. Prov Govt
Victoria, BC V8W 9N3
250-952-0660
Fax: 250-952-0581
e-mail: jennifer.lu@gov.bc.ca
National Library Symbol: BVIM
Founded in: 1896
Hours: Tu-Th 10:30-4:00 by appointment only
Special Collections: Tourism BC reports; BC Mines bulletins; Assessment reports; Property Geological Survey of Canada Collection; US Geological Survey; BC & Canadian company annual reports
Personnel: *Summary:* 2 Total

Victoria: Camosun College Lansdowne Library
Alan Batey Library Media Centre
3100 Foul Bay Rd.
Victoria, BC V8P 5J2
Mailing Address: 3100 Foul Bay Rd.
Victoria, BC V8P 5J2
250-370-3619
Fax: 250-370-3624
Other contact info: Information desk/Research assistance: 250-370-3622
e-mail: library@camosun.bc.ca
ill@camosun.bc.ca
URL: camosun.bc.ca/services/library
National Library Symbol: BVIC
Consortia Membership: British Columbia Electronic Library Network (BC ELN); Electronic Health Library of BC (e-HLbc)
Founded in: 1971
Hours: M-Th 9:00-9:00; F 9:00-5:00; Sa 10:00-6:00; Su 2:00-6:00
Acquisitions Budget: $100,000 - $249,999
For Print: $100,000 - $249,999
For Electronic: $25,000 - $49,999
Note: Library hours are subject to change in spring and summer sessions.
Special Collections: Native studies, Criminology
Services:
Remote Access
Internet Access
Inter-Library Loan (ILL)
Microform Equipment: Reader
Personnel: *Summary:* 18 Total; 5 Professional(s); 2 Technical(s); 11 Other employees
Nancy Henwood, Chair, Library Services & Media Librarian
henwood@camosun.bc.ca
250-370-3611
Sybil Harrison, College Librarian
harrisons@camosun.bc.ca
250-370-3604

Victoria: Diana M. Priestly Law Library
1 McGill Rd.
Victoria, BC V8W 3B1
Mailing Address: PO Box 2300, Stn CSC
Victoria, BC V8W 3B1
250-721-8562
Fax: 250-472-4174
e-mail: lawlib@uvic.ca
URL: library.law.uvic.ca
National Library Symbol: BVIVL
Founded in: 1974
Hours: M-F 8:30-6:00; Sa, Su 9:00-5:00
Acquisitions Budget: $500,000 - $999,999
Subjects covered: Law
Services:
Internet Access
Inter-Library Loan (ILL)
Microform Equipment: Computer; Reader
Personnel: *Summary:* 13 Total; 4 Professional(s); 9 Technical(s)
Neil A. Campbell, Law Librarian & Associate Professor
neilcam@uvic.ca
Caron Rollins, Associate Law Librarian
crollins@uvic.ca
250-721-8566
Serena Ableson, Assistant Law Librarian, Akitsiraq Law School
sableson@uvic.ca
250-721-8564
Irene Godfrey, Supervisor
irenegod@uvic.ca
250-721-8568
Richard McCue, Systems Administrator
rmccue@uvic.ca
250-472-4716

Victoria: Interurban Campus Library
Campus Centre
4461 Interurban Rd., 3rd Fl.
Victoria, BC V9E 2C1
250-370-3828
Fax: 250-370-4640
Other contact info: Information desk/Research assistance: 250-370-4630
e-mail: library@camosun.bc.ca
ill@camosun.bc.ca
URL: camosun.ca/services/library
Hours: M-W 8:00-8:00; Th 8:00-6:00; F 8:00-4:00
Note: Library hours are subject to change in spring and summer sessions.
Services:
Inter-Library Loan (ILL)
Library research classes
Microform Equipment: Reader
Personnel: *Summary:* 5 Total; 1 Professional(s); 1 Technical(s); 3 Other employees
Debbie Webb, Access Services Supervisor
250-370-4531
Susan Bagstad, Reference Technician
250-370-4532

Victoria: Map Library
McPherson Library
Victoria, BC V8W 3H5
Mailing Address: PO Box 1800, Stn CSC
Victoria, BC V8W 3H5
250-721-7356
Fax: 250-721-8235
e-mail: maps@uvic.ca
URL: dirserv.uvic.ca
National Library Symbol: BVIV
Hours: Winter: M-Th 9:00-9:00; F 9:00-5:00; Sa, Su 1:00-5:00. Summer: M-F 9:00-5:00
Acquisitions Budget: $25,000 - $49,999
Special Collections: Maps & Air Photos of Southern Vancouver Island
Subjects covered: Maps, Air Photos, Geography, Earth Sciences
Services:
Remote Access
Internet Access
Microform Equipment: Reader
Personnel: *Summary:* 1 Total; 2 Technical(s)
Lori Sugden, Map Curator
lsugden@uvic.ca
250-721-7356

Victoria: Pacific Forestry Centre Library
506 West Burnside Rd.
Victoria, BC V8Z 1M5
250-363-0680
Fax: 250-363-6035
National Library Symbol: BVIF
No public access
Founded in: 1960
Hours: M-F 9:00-4:00
Note: Member of Council of Canadian Forest Services Network
Special Collections: Depository for all Canadian Forestry Service publications, selection of other foreign forestry publications; Entomological Society of British Columbia Library Collection
Subjects covered: Natural Resources, Conservation, Environment, Forest Entomology, Plant Pathology, Silviculture, Forest Research, Remote Sensing
Services:
Inter-Library Loan (ILL)
Personnel: *Summary:* 2 Total; 1 Professional(s); 1 Technical(s); 2 Volunteer(s)
Alice Solyma, Manager
Alice.Solyma@NRCan-RNCan.gc.ca

Victoria: Pearson College UWC Library
650 Pearson College Dr.
Victoria, BC V9C 4H7
250-391-2411
URL: www.pearsoncollege.ca
Profile: Pearson College UWC is a pre-university school for students from different countries.
National Library Symbol: BVILBP
Founded in: 1974
Hours: by appointment only
Services:
Remote Access
Internet Access
Inter-Library Loan (ILL)
Sherry Crowther, Librarian

Victoria: Royal Roads University Library
2005 Sooke Rd.
Victoria, BC V9B 5Y2
250-391-2575
Fax: 250-391-2594
e-mail: reflib@royalroads.ca
rruill@royalroads.ca
URL: library.royalroads.ca
rrulibrarylowdown.blogspot.ca
National Library Symbol: BRC
Consortia Membership: Canadian Research Knowledge Network (CRKN); Council of Prairie & Pacific University Libraries (COPPUL); British Columbia Electronic Library Network (BC ELN); Electronic Health Library of BC (e-HLbc)
Founded in: 1995
Hours: M-Th 8:30am-10:00pm; F 8:30-6:00; Sa 10:00-6:00; Su 10:00-8:00
Acquisitions Budget: $250,000 - $499,999
Note: Member of ELN; COPPUL.
Subjects covered: Environment, Business, Management, Leadership, Conflict Analysis
Services:
Internet Access
Inter-Library Loan (ILL) for a fee
Information literacy instruction, Reference, Reserve
Microform Equipment: Computer; Reader
Personnel: *Summary:* 13 Total; 5 Professional(s); 4 Technical(s); 4 Other employees
Rosie Croft, University Librarian
rosie.croft@royalroads.ca
250-391-2699
Moriah Whitley, Library Office Assistant, Technical Services
moriah.whitley@royalroads.ca
250-391-2600 ext. 4322

Victoria: Thurber Group Library
#100, 436 West Saanich Rd.
Victoria, BC V8Z 3E9
250-727-2201
Fax: 250-727-3710
e-mail: victoria-manager@thurber.ca
URL: www.thurber.ca
National Library Symbol: BVIT
No public access
Hours: M-F
Acquisitions Budget: 0-$9,999
For Print: 0-$9,999
For Electronic: 0-$9,999
Special Collections: Aerial Photographs, Maps, Standards & Test Procedures
Subjects covered: Physical Sciences, Maps, Geology, Geotechnical & Environmental Engineering

Services:
Internet Access
Inter-Library Loan (ILL)
Fee Based Research
Personnel: *Summary:* 1 Technical(s)
Stephen Bean, Victoria Office Contact

Victoria: University of Victoria Libraries University Librarian's Office
PO Box 1800
Victoria, BC V8W 3H5
250-721-6673
e-mail: summon@UVic Libraries
URL: gateway.uvic.ca
Consortia Membership: Canadian Research Knowledge Network (CRKN); Council of Prairie & Pacific University Libraries (COPPUL); British Columbia Electronic Library Network (BC ELN); Electronic Health Library of BC (e-HLbc)
Founded in: 1963
Acquisitions Budget: For Print: $1,000,000 plus
For Electronic: $1,000,000 plus
Services:
Internet Access
Inter-Library Loan (ILL)
Microform Equipment: Computer; Reader
Personnel: *Summary:* 141 Total; 41 Professional(s); 64 Technical(s); 36 Other employees
Marnie Swanson, University Librarian
mswanson@uvic.ca
250-721-8211
Joanne Henning, Associate University Librarian, Reference & Collections
jhenning@uvic.ca
250-721-8268
Ken Cooley, Associate University Librarian, IT & Technical Services
kcooley@uvic.ca
250-721-6088
Neil Campbell, Associate University Librarian, Law
saquila@uvic.ca
250-721-8238
Shailoo Bedi, Head, Access Services
sbedi@uvic.ca
250-721-8226

Victoria: University of Victoria School of Health Information Science Library
Health Information Science, U. of Victoria
#A202, 3800 Finnerty Rd.
Victoria, BC V8W 3P5
Mailing Address: PO Box 3050, Stn. CSC
Victoria, BC V8W 3P5
250-721-8575
Fax: 250-472-4751
e-mail: his@uvic.ca
URL: www.uvic.ca/hsd/hinf
Abdul Roudsari, Director
abdul@uvic.ca
250-721-8576

Williams Lake: Williams Lake Campus Library
1250 Western Ave.
Williams Lake, BC V2G 1H7
250-392-8030
Fax: 250-392-8116
National Library Symbol: BWLCC
Hours: M-Th 8:30-8:00; F 8:30-4:00
Shane Neifer, Williams Lake Campus Library Contact
sneifer@tru.ca
250-828-5098

Manitoba

Brandon: Assiniboine Community College Library
1430 Victoria Ave. East
Brandon, MB R7A 2A9
204-725-8727
Fax: 204-725-8740
800-862-6307
e-mail: library@assiniboine.net
URL: public.assiniboine.net/CurrentStudents/Library.aspx
National Library Symbol: MBAC
Consortia Membership: Manitoba Library Consortium Inc.
Founded in: 1965
Hours: M-Th 8:00-7:30; F 8:00-4:30
Acquisitions Budget: $50,000 - $99,999
Note: Students & Alumni have access to internet, general public does not
Subjects covered: Trades, Business, Agriculture, Nursing, Technology
Services:
Remote Access
Internet Access
Inter-Library Loan (ILL)
Microform Equipment: Reader
Personnel: *Summary:* 7 Total; 1 Professional(s); 2 Technical(s); 4 Other employees
Susan Gatin, Manager
gatins@Assiniboine.net
204-725-8700 ext. 6637

Brandon: Brandon Regional Health Centre Health Resource Centre
150 McTavish Ave. East
Brandon, MB R7A 2B3
204-578-4080
Fax: 204-578-4984
e-mail: library@brandonrha.mb.ca
URL: www.brandonrha.mb.ca/en/Health_Resource_Centre
National Library Symbol: MBGH
Founded in: 1950
Hours: M-F 8:00-4:30
Acquisitions Budget: $50,000 - $99,999
Note: Member of Manitoba Health Libraries Association
Subjects covered: Medical, Nursing, Allied Health, Consumer Health, Hospital Administration
Services:
Internet Access
Access to Subscription Databases
Inter-Library Loan (ILL)
Personnel: *Summary:* 4 Total; 2 Technical(s); 2 Other employees
Wendy Wareham, Manager, Health Resource Centre

Brandon: Brandon Research Centre Canadian Agriculture Library - Brandon
#93, 2701 Grand Valley Rd., RR#3
Brandon, MB R7A 5Y3
Mailing Address: PO Box 1000A
Brandon, MB R7A 5Y3
204-726-7650 ext: 247
Fax: 204-728-3858
National Library Symbol: MBAG
Founded in: 1884
Hours: M-F 8:00-4:30
Subjects covered: Land Resource Management, Beef Cattle Production & Barley Breeding
Services:
Inter-Library Loan (ILL) for a fee
Personnel: *Summary:* 2 Total; 1 Professional(s); 1 Technical(s)
Carol Enns, Head Librarian
carol.enns@agr.gc.ca

Brandon: Brandon University John E. Robbins Library
270 - 18th St.
Brandon, MB R7A 6A9
204-727-9646
Fax: 204-726-1072
URL: www.brandonu.ca/library
National Library Symbol: MBC
Consortia Membership: Canadian Research Knowledge Network (CRKN); Council of Prairie & Pacific University Libraries (COPPUL); Manitoba Library Consortium Inc.
Founded in: 1899
Hours: M-Th 8:30am-10:00pm; F 8:30-5:00; Sa 1:00-6:00; Su 1:00-8:00
Acquisitions Budget: $500,000 - $999,999
For Print: $500,000 - $999,999
For Electronic: $100,000 - $249,999
Note: University Archives is part of the library. Archives Fax: 204-726-1072
Special Collections: Great Plains Collection; 20th Century Literature by Native North American Authors; Music Scores, Audiotapes, CDs, Videos; Historical Collection of Jazz Recordings; Manitoba Pool Elevators Collection; Photo Collection of the Manitoba Provincial Exhibition (Royal Winter Fair); Brandon Sun Collection
Services:
Internet Access
Inter-Library Loan (ILL) for a fee
Microform Equipment: Computer; Reader
Personnel: *Summary:* 21 Total; 5 Professional(s); 16 Technical(s)
Karen H. Anderson, Library Assistant
andersonk@brandonu.ca
204-727-9643
Donna Andersen, Library Assistant
andersen@brandonu.ca
204-727-9646
Christy Henry, Archives Contact
Henryc@Brandonu.ca
204-727-9634

Churchill: Churchill Northern Studies Centre Library
PO Box 610
Churchill, MB R0B 0E0
204-675-2307
Fax: 204-675-2139
e-mail: cnsc@churchillscience.ca
URL: www.churchillscience.ca
Founded in: 1976
Hours: M-F 9:00-5:00 by appointment only
Acquisitions Budget: $25,000 - $49,999
Subjects covered: Native Peoples & Northern Affairs, Physical Sciences, Maps
Services:
Internet Access
Michael Goodyear, Executive Director

Hamiota: Hamiota District Health Centre Library
177 Birch Ave. East
Hamiota, MB R0M 0T0
204-764-2412 ext: 327
Fax: 204-764-2049
Founded in: 1974
Hours: M-Su
Acquisitions Budget: $25,000 - $49,999
Subjects covered: Medical, Nursing, Allied Consumer Health
Personnel: *Summary:* 1 Professional(s)

Portage la Prairie: Food Development Centre Library
810 Phillips St.
Portage la Prairie, MB R1N 3J9
204-239-3150
Fax: 204-239-3180
800-870-1044
URL: www.gov.mb.ca/agriculture/fdc
National Library Symbol: MPCFP
Founded in: 1978
Hours: M-F 8:30-4:30 by appointment only
Acquisitions Budget: $25,000 - $49,999
For Print: $25,000 - $49,999
Note: Special operating agency of Manitoba Agriculture, Food & Rural Initiatives
Subjects covered: Agriculture, Food Science, Analytical Chemistry, Food Microbiology, Food Product Development, HACCP, Nutritional Information, Canadian & American Food Legislation, Nutraceuticals & Functional Foods, Economic Development, Government Information
Services:
Internet Access
Inter-Library Loan (ILL) for a fee of $5
Fee Based Research
Personnel: *Summary:* 1 Total; 1 Technical(s);

Steinbach: Red River Apiarists' Association
c/o 216 Loewen Blvd.
Steinbach, MB R5G 0E5
Mailing Address: 216 Loewen Blvd.
Steinbach, MB R5G 0E5
204-326-3763
URL: www.beekeepingmanitoba.com
No public access
Founded in: 1963
Subjects covered: Honey Production, Entomology (Bees), Pollination
Ron Rudiak, Secretary
manbeekr@mts.net
204-326-3763

Stonewall: Ducks Unlimited Canada Institute for Wetland & Waterfowl Research Library
1 Mallard Bay, Hwy. 220
Stonewall, MB R0C 2Z0
Mailing Address: PO Box 1160
Stonewall, MB R0C 2Z0
204-467-3276
Fax: 204-467-9028
800-665-3825
e-mail: library@ducks.ca
URL: www.ducks.ca/conserve/research/library
National Library Symbol: MWDU
Founded in: 1998
Hours: M-F 8:30-4:30 by appointment only
Acquisitions Budget: $25,000 - $49,999
For Print: 0-$9,999
For Electronic: $10,000 - $24,999
Special Collections: Extensive wetland & waterfowl research collection
Subjects covered: Wetland Ecology & Management, Land Use, Environment, Waterfowl Ecology
Services:
Inter-Library Loan (ILL)
Personnel: *Summary:* 1 Total; 1 Professional(s)
Ian Glass, Librarian
i_glass@ducks.ca

The Pas: University College of the North Libraries Library
The Pas Campus, 436 - 7th St. East
The Pas, MB R9A 1M7
204-627-8561
Fax: 204-623-4597
866-627-8500
e-mail: library@ucn.ca
URL: www.ucn.ca/ics/library
National Library Symbol: MTPK
Consortia Membership: Manitoba Library Consortium Inc.
Founded in: 1966
Hours: M-Th 8:00am-10:00pm; F 8:00-5:00; Su 5:00-9:00
Special Collections: Periodicals & newspapers; Government publications; Pamphlets; Films; DVDs; CDs; Kits; Slides; Filmstrips; Microfilm; Microfiche; Microcomputer software; Technical reports
Subjects covered: Aboriginal studies; Business & Economics; Construction; Education; Environment; Energy; Geography; History; Law; Mining; Nursing; Social sciences
Services:
Internet Access
Access to Subscription Databases
Microform Equipment: Computer; Reader
Stan Gardner, Dean, Library & Instructional Services
sgardner@ucn.ca
Heather Smith, Librarian
hsmith@ucn.ca
Meaghan Buchanan, Archivist
mbuchanan@ucn.ca

Winnipeg: Architecture & Fine Arts Library
#206, Russell Bldg.
84 Curry Pl.
Winnipeg, MB R3T 2N2
204-474-9216
Fax: 204-474-7539
Other contact info: Slide Collection, Phone: 204-474-6440
Profile: Supporting the research & teaching needs of the Faculty of Architecture, the Library contains the largest collection of resources on art, design & planning in Manitoba
National Library Symbol: MWUAF
Founded in: 1916
Hours: M-F 8:30-4:30
Acquisitions Budget: $50,000 - $99,999
Special Collections: Monographs, serials, videos & DVDs, CDROMs; Architectural Drawings; Building File; Vertical Files
Subjects covered: Fine Arts, Architecture, City Planning, Interior Design, Landscape Architecture
Services:
Remote Access
Internet Access
Access to Subscription Databases
Inter-Library Loan (ILL)
Personnel: *Summary:* 9 Total; 2 Professional(s); 7 Technical(s)
Mary Lochhead, Head Librarian
mary_lochhead@umanitoba.ca
204-474-9217
Eleanor Reimer, Supervisor
eleanor_reimer@umanitoba.ca
204-474-6567
Liv Valmstead, Reference Librarian
liv_valmstead@umanitoba.ca
204-474-8447

Winnipeg: Canadian Agriculture Library - Winnipeg
195 Dafoe Rd.
Winnipeg, MB R3T 2M9
204-983-0755
Fax: 204-983-4604
Hours: by appointment only
Sean O'Hara, Head Librarian
sean.ohara@agr.gc.ca

Winnipeg: Canadian Grain Commission / Commission canadienne des grains Library
#600, 303 Main St.
Winnipeg, MB R3C 3G8
204-983-0878
Fax: 204-983-6098
e-mail: library@grainscanada.gc.ca
URL: www.grainscanada.gc.ca
National Library Symbol: MWGR
Consortia Membership: Federal Libraries Consortium (FLC)
Founded in: 1913
Hours: M-F 8:00-4:30 by appointment only
Acquisitions Budget: $50,000 - $99,999
For Print: $50,000 - $99,999
For Electronic: $10,000 - $24,999
Special Collections: Canadian International Grains Institute: Lecture series 1973-2002.
Subjects covered: Grain Handling & Transportation; Grain Quality; Cereal Science; Oilseed Science
Services:
Internet Access
Inter-Library Loan (ILL) for a fee of Federal libraries: Free. Other libraries: $10/articles; $15/books
Personnel: *Summary:* 2 Total; 1 Professional(s); 1 Technical(s)
Sean O'Hara, Librarian
sohara@grainscanada.gc.ca

Winnipeg: Collège universitaire de St-Boniface Bibliothèque Alfred-Monnin
200, av de la Cathédrale
Winnipeg, MB R2H 0H7
204-235-4403
Téléc: 204-237-3240
Couriel: biblio@ustboniface.mb.ca
URL: www2.ustboniface.ca/cusb/biblio
Sigle: MSC
Membre d'un consortium: Manitoba Library Consortium Inc.
Fondée en: 1818
Heures: L-J 8h-21h30; V 8h-16h30; S 10h-17h; D 13h-17havec rendez-vous seulement
Budget d'acquisitions: $100,000 - $249,999
Population desservie: 0
Collections spécialisées: Maurice Constantin-Weyer, études canadiennes, études féminines, histoire des francophones de l'Ouest, auteurs francophones de l'Ouest
Sujets: Administration, anglais, allemand, anthropologie, biologie, chimie, comptabilité, ééconomie, éducation, espagnol, français, géographie, histoire, informatique, marketing, mathématiques, philosophie, physique, politique, psychologie, religion, sociologie, soins de santé, statistiques, traduction
Services:
Accès public à l'internet
Prêts entre bibliothèques(PEB) frais
Lecteur/reproduction de microformes: Ordinateur; Lecteurs
Personnel: *Sommaire:* 12 Total; 2 Professionnel(s); 3 Technicien(s); 7 Autre(s) employé(s)
Louise Ayotte-Zaretski, Directrice
layottez@ustboniface.mb.ca
204-237-1818 ext. 331
Daniel Beaulieu, Bibliothécaire de référence
dbeaulieu@ustboniface.mb.ca
204-237-1818 ext. 308
Carole Pelchat, Archiviste, Gestionnaire de documents
cpelchat@ustboniface.mb.ca
204-237-1818 ext. 398
Alice Gilbert-Collet, Bibliotechnicienne, Acquisitions
acollet@ustboniface.mb.ca
204-237-1818 ext. 362
Diane Johnson, Bibliotechnicienne, Traitement, catalogage, sys. info.
djohnson@ustboniface.mb.ca
204-237-1818 ext. 340
Brigitte L'Heureux, Bibliotechnicienne, Référence et service du prêt
blheureux@ustboniface.mb.ca
204-237-1818 ext. 213
Joanne Pelletier, Bibliotechnicienne, Service du prêt entre bibliothèques
jpelletier@ustboniface.mb.ca
204-237-1818 ext. 332
Thérèse Tinguely, Aide-bibliothécaire
ttinguel@ustboniface.mb.ca
204-235-4403

Winnipeg: Concordia Hospital Library
1095 Concordia Ave.
Winnipeg, MB R2K 3S8
204-661-7163
Fax: 204-661-7282
e-mail: chlibrary@umanitoba.ca
URL: libguides.lib.umanitoba.ca/concordia
National Library Symbol: MWCH
Founded in: 1975
Hours: M-F 8:30-4:30
Note: A branch of the University of Manitoba Neil John Maclean Health Sciences library
Subjects covered: Medicine, Nursing, Allied Health, Patient Care
Personnel: *Summary:* 2 Total; 1 Professional(s); 1 Technical(s)
Melissa Raynard, Hospital Librarian
204-661-7440

Winnipeg: Conservation & Environment Library
#160, 123 Main St.
Winnipeg, MB R3C 1A5
204-945-7126
Fax: 204-948-2357
Other contact info: 204-945-7125
URL: www.gov.mb.ca/conservation/library/
National Library Symbol: MWECW
MWEEP
MWEAE
Consortia Membership: Manitoba Library Consortium Inc.
Hours: M-F 8:00-4:30
Special Collections: Climatology, Weather Services
Subjects covered: Climatology, Weather Services
Personnel: *Summary:* 2 Total; 2 Professional(s)
Wendy Barber, Coordinator of Library Services
Wendy.Barber@gov.mb.ca
204-945-7126
Marvyl Ginter, Library Technician
Marvyl.Ginter@gov.mb.ca
204-945-7125

Winnipeg: Donald W. Craik Engineering Library
#E3-361 Engineering Bldg.
Winnipeg, MB R3T 2N2
204-474-6360
Fax: 204-474-7520
URL: www.umanitoba.ca/libraries/units/engineering
Hours: M-F 8:30-4:30
Subjects covered: Physical Sciences, Engineering, Technology
Services:
Inter-Library Loan (ILL)
Microform Equipment: Computer; Reader
Personnel: *Summary:* 7 Total; 2 Professional(s); 4 Technical(s); 1 Other employees
Norma Godavari, Head
norma_godavari@umanitoba.ca
204-474-9445

Winnipeg: E.K. Williams Law Library
#401, Robson Hall, 224 Dysart Rd.
Winnipeg, MB R3T 2N2
204-474-9995
Fax: 204-474-7582
e-mail: lawill@cc.umanitoba.ca
URL: www.umanitoba.ca/libraries/units/law/
National Library Symbol: MWUL
Founded in: 1922
Hours: M-Th 8:30-10:00; F 8:30-6:00; Sa, Su 1:00-5:00
Acquisitions Budget: $100,000 - $249,999
Special Collections: Aboriginal Justice, International Trade,

Manitoba Legislation
Subjects covered: Law
Services:
Inter-Library Loan (ILL)
Microform Equipment: Computer; Reader
Personnel: *Summary:* 11 Total; 3 Professional(s); 8 Technical(s)
John Eaton, Head Librarian
john_eaton@umanitoba.ca
204-474-9996
Muriel St. John, Reference Librarian
muriel_stjohn@umanitoba.ca
204-474-6372
Ariana Sirko, Technical Services Librarian
ariana_sirko@umanitoba.ca
204-474-6371

Winnipeg: Elizabeth Dafoe Library
University of Manitoba, 25 Chancellors Circle
Winnipeg, MB R3T 2N2
204-474-9844
e-mail: dafref@ms.umanitoba.ca
URL: umanitoba.ca/libraries/units/dafoe/
National Library Symbol: MWU
Founded in: 1876
Hours: M-Su
Acquisitions Budget: $500,000 - $999,999
For Print: $500,000 - $999,999
Special Collections: Icelandic Collection, Slavic Collection, Archives & Special Collections
Subjects covered: Arts, Humanities, Culture, Nursing, Social Work, Human Ecology, Social Sciences, Education, Physical Education, Recreation Studies, Environment
Services:
Internet Access
Inter-Library Loan (ILL)
Microform Equipment: Computer; Reader
Personnel: *Summary:* 38 Total; 13 Professional(s); 25 Technical(s)
Nicole Michaud-Oystryk, Head
Nicole_Michaud-Oystryk@umanitoba.ca
204-474-9211

Winnipeg: Industrial Technology Centre Library & Technical Information
#200, 78 Innovation Dr.
Winnipeg, MB R3T 6C2
204-480-0336
Fax: 204-480-0345
e-mail: library@itc.mb.ca
URL: www.itc.mb.ca/online_library.php
National Library Symbol: MWMRC
Consortia Membership: Manitoba Library Consortium Inc.
Founded in: 1981
Hours: M-F 8:30-4:30
Subjects covered: Engineering, Technology, Industry, Manufacturing, Industry Standards
Services:
Internet Access
Inter-Library Loan (ILL) for a fee of reciprocal
Fee Based Research
Personnel: *Summary:* 1 Total; 1 Professional(s)
Betty Dearth, Librarian
bdearth@itc.mb.ca

Winnipeg: Institute of Urban Studies Library
599 Portage Ave., 3rd Fl.
Winnipeg, MB R3B 2G3
204-982-1145
Fax: 204-943-4695
e-mail: ius@uwinnipeg.ca
URL: ius.uwinnipeg.ca/library
Founded in: 1985
Hours: M-F 8:30-4:30
Acquisitions Budget: $25,000 - $49,999
Note: Loans to students, faculty & alumni of the Universities of Winnipeg & Manitoba, Red River College & Canadian Mennonite University
Special Collections: Winnipeg Core Area Initiative Partial Collection, Children & Youth in the Urban Environment, City of Winnipeg ACT Review
Subjects covered: Housing, Urban Ecology, Architecture, Urban Geography, Urban Sociology, Native Peoples, Public Administration, Urban History, Sustainable Development, Revitalization, Community Development, Urban Planning
Services:
Remote Access
Inter-Library Loan (ILL)
Michael Dudley, Research Associate
m.dudley@uwinnipeg.ca
204-982-1145

Winnipeg: International Institute for Sustainable Development / Institut international du développement durable Library
161 Portage Ave. East, 6th Fl.
Winnipeg, MB R3B 0Y4
204-958-7724
Fax: 204-958-7710
e-mail: library@iisd.ca
URL: www.iisd.org/ic
www.iisd.org/generata
Founded in: 1993
Hours: M-F 8:30-4:30 by appointment only
Acquisitions Budget: $50,000 - $99,999
Subjects covered: Journals; Monographs; Documents relating to sustainable development, trade, UN negotiations, sustainable livelihoods, ecological economics, Agenda 21, environmental policy, agriculture, climate change
Services:
Remote Access
Internet Access
Personnel: *Summary:* 4 Total; 1 Professional(s); 1 Technical(s)
Marlene Roy, Research and Learning Resources
mroy@iisd.ca
204-958-7724
Janice Gair, Director, Human Resources & Administration
jgair@iisb.ca
204-958-7708
Stacy Matwick, Information Centre Assistant
smatwick@iisd.ca
204-956-7755
Karin Clegg, Information Centre Assistant
kclegg@iisd.ca

Winnipeg: Manitoba Dept. of Science, Technology, Energy & Mines Mineral Resources Library
#360, 1395 Ellice Ave.
Winnipeg, MB R3G 3P2
204-945-6569
Fax: 204-945-8427
800-223-5215
e-mail: minesinfo@gov.mb.ca
URL: www.gov.mb.ca/stem/mrd/info/library/index.html
National Library Symbol: MWEMM
Consortia Membership: Manitoba Library Consortium Inc.
Founded in: 1975
Hours: M-F 8:30-4:30
Acquisitions Budget: For Print: 0-$9,999
For Electronic: 0-$9,999
Note: Resources may be used in-house, or through another library via interlibrary loan
Special Collections: Manitoba Geological Survey Reports & Maps, Geological Survey of Canada Publications; Government Publications, Journals, Video/Audio
Subjects covered: Geology, Mining, Petroleum
Services:
Remote Access
Internet Access
Inter-Library Loan (ILL)
GEOREF, Canadian MineSCAN and access to other databases; fact sheets; Bibliography of Rockhounding; photocopying
Personnel: *Summary:* 2 Total; 1 Professional(s); 1 Technical(s)
Lori Janower, Library Services Coordinator
Lori.Janower@gov.mb.ca

Winnipeg: Manitoba Eco-Network Inc. / Réseau écologique du Manitoba Alice Chambers Memorial Library
#3, 303 Portage Ave.
Winnipeg, MB R3B 1E7
204-947-6511
Fax: 866-237-3130
e-mail: library@mbeconetwork.org
info@mbeconetwork.org
URL: www.mbeconetwork.org
Hours: M-F 9:00-4:00
Acquisitions Budget: 0-$9,999
For Print: 0-$9,999
For Electronic: 0-$9,999
Special Collections: Public Registry items
Subjects covered: Environment; Sustainable Development; Climate Change
Services:
Inter-Library Loan (ILL)
Wynne Haaksma, Contact, Library
204-947-6511

Winnipeg: Manitoba Hydro Library
360 Portage Ave.
Winnipeg, MB R3C 2P4
Mailing Address: PO Box 815
Winnipeg, MB R3C 2P4
204-360-3019
Fax: 204-360-6104
e-mail: docdel@hydro.mb.ca
URL: www.hydro.mb.ca
National Library Symbol: MWH
Hours: M-F 8:00-4:30 by appointment only
Acquisitions Budget: $250,000 - $499,999
Subjects covered: Engineering, Electrical, Public Utilities
Services:
Inter-Library Loan (ILL)
Personnel: *Summary:* 6 Total; 2 Professional(s); 4 Technical(s)
Rhona Lapierre, Corporate Librarian
rlapierre@hydro.mb.ca
Angie Vaccaro, Reference Librarian
avaccaro@hydro.mb.ca
204-360-3945
Paulette Mazur, Cataloguing Technician
pmazur@hydro.mb.ca
204-474-3019

Winnipeg: Manitoba Museum Information Services
190 Rupert Ave.
Winnipeg, MB R3B 0N2
204-988-0662
Fax: 204-942-3679
e-mail: info@manitobamuseum.ca
URL: www.manitobamuseum.ca
National Library Symbol: MWMM
Consortia Membership: Manitoba Library Consortium Inc.
Founded in: 1970
Hours: M-F 8:30-4:30 by appointment only
Acquisitions Budget: $25,000 - $49,999
Special Collections: Oral history tapes collection
Subjects covered: Canadian, Natural, Human History, Physical Science, Ethnology, Applied Art, Astronomy, Museology
Services:
Inter-Library Loan (ILL)
Microform Equipment: Reader
Personnel: *Summary:* 2 Total; 1 Professional(s)
Cindi Steffan, Manager, Information Services
csteffan@manitobamuseum.ca

Winnipeg: MFL Occupational Health Centre Resource Centre
#102, 275 Broadway
Winnipeg, MB R3C 4M6
204-949-0811
Fax: 204-956-0848
888-843-1229
e-mail: mflohc@mflohc.mb.ca
URL:
www.mflohc.mb.ca/mflohc_folder/information_&_resources.html
National Library Symbol: MWMFL
Founded in: 1983
Hours: M-F 9:00-5:00
Note: Internat access to OPAC. Library holdings are for use on site only. Library does not lend out.
Subjects covered: Occupational Health, Labour, Social Affairs
Services:
Internet Access
Inter-Library Loan (ILL)
Personnel: *Summary:* 1 Total; 1 Technical(s)
Tiffany Pau, Library Coordinator
204-949-7909

Winnipeg: Misericordia Health Centre Sister St. Odilon Library
691 Wolseley Ave., 1st Fl.
Winnipeg, MB R3C 1A2

Mailing Address: 99 Cornish Ave.
Winnipeg, MB R3C 1A2
204-788-8109
Fax: 204-889-4174
888-315-9257
e-mail: library@miseri.winnipeg.mb.ca
mhclibrary@umanitoba.ca
URL: www.misericordia.mb.ca
umanitoba.ca/libraries/units/health/misericordia/
Profile: The Sister St. Odilon Library is a branch of the Neil John Maclean Health Sciences Library. It is a resource to the health care providers of the Misericordia Health Care facility.
National Library Symbol: MWMG
Founded in: 1974
Hours: M-F 8:30-4:30
Acquisitions Budget: $25,000 - $49,999
Subjects covered: Medicine, Nursing, Health Sciences, Opthamology
Services:
Remote Access
Access to Subscription Databases
Inter-Library Loan (ILL)
Personnel: *Summary:* 1 Professional(s); 2 Volunteer(s)
Laurie Blanchard, Hospital Librarian
Kathy Finlayson, Library Assistant

Winnipeg: National Energy Conservation Association Library
400-283 Bannatyne Ave.
Winnipeg, MB R3B 3B2
204-956-5888
Fax: 204-956-5819
800-263-5974
e-mail: neca@neca.ca
URL: www.neca.ca
Founded in: 1983
Subjects covered: Energy Conservation, Construction, Quality Assurance
Ryan Dalgleish, Manager
Laverne Dalgleish, CEO

Winnipeg: Nature Manitoba Library
#401, 63 Albert St.
Winnipeg, MB R3B 1G4
204-943-9029
Fax: 204-943-9029
e-mail: mns@escape.ca
URL: www.manitobanature.ca
No public access
Founded in: 1920
Subjects covered: Wildlife, Environment, Natural History, Conservation
Debbie Friesen, Office Administrator
Jenny Gates, Editor, The Bulletin

Winnipeg: Neil John Maclean Health Sciences Library
Brodie Centre
727 McDermot Ave., 200 Level
Winnipeg, MB R3E 0W3
Mailing Address: 770 Bannatyne Ave.
Winnipeg, MB R3E 0W3
204-789-3464
Fax: 204-789-3923
e-mail: healthlibrary@umanitoba.ca
njmcirc@ms.umanitoba.ca
URL: libguides.lib.umanitoba.ca/njmhsl
National Library Symbol: MWM
Founded in: 1928
Hours: M-F 8:00am-11:00pm; Sa 9:00am-11:00pm; Su 10:00-9:00. Reference Services: M-Th 9:00-9:00; Sa 9:00-5:00; Su 1:00-5:00. Reference hours may vary.
Acquisitions Budget: $500,000 - $999,999
Note: The Medical Library, Neilson Dental Library & Health Sciences Centre Library merged to form the Neil John Maclean Health Sciences Library
Special Collections: History of Medicine, Aboriginal Health, Archives of the Faculty of Medicine
Subjects covered: Medical Instruction, Consumer Health Information, Outreach, Aboriginal Health, Nursing, Allied Health, Dentistry, Dental Hygiene, Medical Rehabilitation, Hospital Administration, Medicine
Services:
Internet Access
Access to Subscription Databases
Inter-Library Loan (ILL)
e-journal Access
Personnel: *Summary:* 31 Total; 11 Professional(s); 20 Other employees
Ada Ducas, Head Librarian
ada_ducas@umanitoba.ca
204-789-3821

Winnipeg: Red River College Notre Dame Campus Library
2055 Notre Dame Ave.
Winnipeg, MB R3H 0J9
204-632-2233
Fax: 204-697-4791
e-mail: library@rrc.ca
circndc@rrc.ca
illmwrr@rrc.ca
URL: library.rrc.ca
National Library Symbol: MWRR
Consortia Membership: Manitoba Library Consortium Inc.
Founded in: 1963
Hours: M-Th 7:45-9:00; F 7:45-4:40; Sa 8:30-4:00
Acquisitions Budget: $250,000 - $499,999
Subjects covered: Business, Health Sciences, Engineering Technologies, Education, Child Care, Hospitality, Multimedia Technology, Graphic Arts
Services:
Remote Access
Internet Access
Access to Subscription Databases
Inter-Library Loan (ILL)
Microform Equipment: Reader
Personnel: *Summary:* 33 Total; 4 Professional(s); 19 Technical(s); 10 Other employees
Patricia Burt, Library Director
204-632-2382
Norman Beattie, Coordinator, Reference
mbeattie@rrcc.mb.ca
204-632-2470
Carlos Wong-Martinez, Coordinator, Technical Services & Systems
204-632-3761
Phyllis Barich, Coordinator, Off Campus & Media Services
pbarich@ppc.mb.ca
204-632-3761

Winnipeg: Resource Conservation Manitoba Resource Library
303 Portage Ave., 3rd Fl.
Winnipeg, MB R3B 2B4
204-925-3777
Fax: 204-942-4207
URL: www.resourceconservation.mb.ca
Founded in: 1985
Hours: M-F 9:00-5:00
Note: A non-profit, non-governmental environmental education group; Resource library is operated jointly with the Manitoba Eco-Network
Subjects covered: Environment

Winnipeg: St Boniface General Hospital Carolyn Sifton-Helene Fuld Library/Bibliothèque Carolyn Sifton-Helene Fuld
409 Tache Ave.
Winnipeg, MB R2H 2A6
204-237-2807
Fax: 204-235-3339
e-mail: sbghlibrary@umanitoba.ca
URL: libguides.lib.umanitoba.ca/sbh
National Library Symbol: MWSBM
Founded in: 1994
Hours: M-F 8:30-4:30
Acquisitions Budget: $50,000 - $99,999
Note: Satellite operation of the Neil John MacLean Health Sciences Library, University of Manitoba
Subjects covered: Medicine, Nursing
Services:
Inter-Library Loan (ILL)
DOCLINE
Personnel: *Summary:* 26 Total; 1 Professional(s); 3 Technical(s); 1 Volunteer(s)
Carol Cooke, Acting Hospital Librarian
carol_cooke@umanitoba.ca
204-789-3840

Winnipeg: Sciences & Technology Library
#211, Machray Hall
Winnipeg, MB R3T 2N2
204-474-8171
Fax: 204-474-7627
e-mail: sci_ref@umanitoba.ca
URL: libguides.lib.umanitoba.ca/science_library
Hours: M-Su
Acquisitions Budget: $500,000 - $999,999
Note: Most of the Agriculture & Engineering circulating collections are now located in the Sciences & Technology Library
Subjects covered: Life Sciences, Physical Sciences, Technology, Mathematics, Computer Science, Statistics, Science, Pharmacy, Agriculture, Food Sciences, Engineering
Services:
Inter-Library Loan (ILL)
Personnel: *Summary:* 5 Total; 5 Professional(s)
Vera Keown, Head Librarian
vera_keown@umanitoba.ca
204-474-8302

Winnipeg: Seven Oaks General Hospital Library
2300 McPhillips St.
Winnipeg, MB R2V 3M3
204-632-3124
Fax: 204-694-8240
e-mail: soghlibrary@umanitoba.ca
URL: sogh.ca/hospital-services/library
libguides.lib.umanitoba.ca/sogh
National Library Symbol: MWSOGH
Founded in: 1981
Hours: M-F 8:30-4:30
Acquisitions Budget: $25,000 - $49,999
Note: Satellite operation of Neil John MacLean Health Sciences Library, University of Manitoba
Subjects covered: Health, Nursing, Medicine
Services:
Internet Access
Inter-Library Loan (ILL)
Document Delivery
Personnel: *Summary:* 2 Total; 1 Professional(s); 1 Technical(s)
Kerry Macdonald, Hospital Librarian
kerry.macdonald@ad.umanitoba.ca
Stefania Zimarino, Library Assistant
stefania.zimarino@ad.umanitoba.ca

Winnipeg: University of Manitoba Libraries Director's Office
Elizabeth Dafoe Library, University of Manitoba
#156, 25 Chancellor's Circle
Winnipeg, MB R3T 2N2
204-474-9881
Fax: 204-474-7583
e-mail: illdaf@cc.umanitoba.ca
URL: www.umanitoba.ca/libraries/
National Library Symbol: MWU
Consortia Membership: Canadian Research Knowledge Network (CRKN); Council of Prairie & Pacific University Libraries (COPPUL); Manitoba Library Consortium Inc.; Health Knowledge Network (HKN)
Founded in: 1885
Acquisitions Budget: $1,000,000 plus
For Print: $1,000,000 plus
Services:
Internet Access
Inter-Library Loan (ILL)
Microform Equipment: Computer; Reader
Personnel: *Summary:* 55 Professional(s); 150 Other employees
Karen Adams, Director of Libraries
Donna Breyfogle, Associate Director, Collections
Vacant , Head, Technical Services
Lynne Partington, Head, Bibliographic Control
Pat Nicholls, Head, Systems

Winnipeg: University of Winnipeg Library
515 Portage Ave.
Winnipeg, MB R3B 2E9
204-786-9808
Fax: 204-783-8910
888-393-1830
e-mail: infoedge@uwinnipeg.ca
ill@uwinnipeg.ca
URL: library.uwinnipeg.ca

National Library Symbol: MWUC
Consortia Membership: Canadian Research Knowledge Network (CRKN); Council of Prairie & Pacific University Libraries (COPPUL); Manitoba Library Consortium Inc.
Founded in: 1871
Hours: M-F 8:00am-10:45pm; Sa, Su 11:00-5:45
Acquisitions Budget: $1,000,000 plus
For Print: $500,000 - $999,999
For Electronic: $500,000 - $999,999; Full-time students
Special Collections: University of Winnipeg Archives; United Church Conference of Manitoba & Northwestern Ontario Archives; William Wanka Collection; Drache Law Library; East European Genealogical Society Inc. Collection; Edith & Margaret Graham Picture Book Collection; George H. Reavis Reading Collection
Subjects covered: Liberal Arts
Services:
Remote Access
Internet Access
Access to Subscription Databases
Inter-Library Loan (ILL)
Fee Based Research
Personnel: *Summary:* 55 Total; 8 Professional(s); 33 Technical(s); 4 Other employees
Linda Dietrick, Acting University Librarian
l.dietrick@uwinnipeg.ca
Linwood DeLong, Collections Coordinator
linwood.delong@uwinnipeg.ca
204-786-9124
Christine Hoeppner, Digital Resources & Aquisitions Coordinator
c.hoeppner@uwinnipeg.ca
204-786-9813
Gabrielle Prefontaine, University Archivist/FIPPA Coordinator
g.prefontaine@uwinnipeg.ca
204-786-9914
Pat Duguay, Library Administration/Admin. Assistant
p.duguay@uwinnipeg.ca
204-786-9801

Winnipeg: Victoria General Hospital (Winnipeg) Library
2340 Pembina Hwy.
Winnipeg, MB R3T 2E8
204-477-3307
Fax: 204-269-7936
e-mail: info@vgh.mb.ca
URL: www.vgh.mb.ca
libguides.lib.umanitoba.ca/victoria
Hours: M-F by appointment only
Services:
Internet Access
Access to Subscription Databases
Inter-Library Loan (ILL) for a fee of $10
Personnel: *Summary:* 1 Professional(s); 1 Technical(s)
Lisa Demczuk, Hospital Librarian
lisa_demczuk@umanitoba.ca
204-477-3284

Winnipeg: William R. Newman Library
#236 Agriculture Bldg., University of Manitoba
66 Dafoe Rd.
Winnipeg, MB R3T 2N2
204-474-8382
Fax: 204-474-7527
e-mail: eleanor_reimer@umanitoba.ca
URL: umanitoba.ca/libraries/units/agriculture
Founded in: 1997
Hours: M-F 8:30-4:30
Subjects covered: Agriculture
Services:
Remote Access
Internet Access
Personnel: *Summary:* 2 Total; 1 Professional(s); 1 Technical(s)
Mora Gregg, Head of Library
mora_gregg@umanitoba.ca
204-474-6334

Winnipeg: Yellowquill College Library
480 Madison St.
Winnipeg, MB R3J 1J1
204-953-2800
Fax: 204-953-2810
e-mail: administration@yellowquill.org
URL: yellowquill.org
Founded in: 1984
Hours: M-F 8:30-4:30
Subjects covered: First nations, education
Mary Fagnan, Contact

New Brunswick

Bathurst: Bathurst Campus / Campus de Bathurst Library/Bibliothèque
725 College St.
Bathurst, NB E2A 3Z2
Mailing Address: PO Box 266
Bathurst, NB E2A 3Z2
506-546-4176
Fax: 506-546-2829
e-mail: info@mcft.ca
URL: www.mcft.ca
No public access
Founded in: 1980
Hours: 8:30am-10:00pm
Acquisitions Budget: For Print: 0-$9,999
Subjects covered: Forestry, Natural Resources, Environment, Conservation
Personnel: *Summary:* 3 Total; 1 Professional(s); 2 Technical(s)
Claude Chiasson, Associate Director
cchiasson@mcft.ca

Bathurst: Vitalité Health Network / Réseau de sante vitalité Library Services
#600, 275 Main St.
Bathurst, NB E2A 1A9
888-472-2220
URL: www.santevitalitehealth.ca
No public access
Subjects covered: Health Sciences, Medicine, Hospital Administration
Aline Johanns, Vice-President, HR (responsible for health care library services)

Edmundston: Campus d'Edmundston Bibliothèque Rhéa-Larose
165, boul. Hébert
Edmundston, NB E3V 2S8
506-737-5058
Téléc: 506-737-5373
Couriel: glefranc@umce.ca
URL: www.umoncton.ca/umce-bibliotheque
Sigle: NBESLM
Fondée en: 1970
Heures: L-J 8h30-21h; V 8h30-17h; S, D 12h-17h3
Budget d'acquisitions: $50,000 - $99,999
Population desservie: 0
Collections spécialisées: Plus de 75,000 volumes; livres rares; archives locales; publications gouvernementales
Sujets: Sylviculture, sciences humaines, administration, sciences infirmières; littérature, histoire, sciences
Services:
Accès public à l'internet
Prêts entre bibliothèques(PEB)
Aide à la recherche; locaux; ordinateurs, portables, imprimantes; réserve académique; Centre de documentation & d'études madawaskayennes
Personnel: *Sommaire:* 8 Total; 1 Professionnel(s); 2 Technicien(s); 5 Autre(s) employé(s)
Guy Lefrançois, Bibliothécaire/Directeur
glefranc@umce.ca
506-737-5266
Claire Charest Knoetze, Technicienne en documentation
cknoetze@umce.ca
506-737-5247
Dany Marquis, Technicienne en documentation
dmarquis@umce.ca
506-737-5265
Johanne Albert, Secrétaire
jalbert@umce.ca
506-737-5058

Fredericton: ADI Group Library
1133 Regent St.
Fredericton, NB E3B 4Y2
506-452-9000
Fax: 506-451-7451
e-mail: adigroup@adi.ca
dee@adi.ca
Hours: M-F by appointment only
Special Collections: CSA Standards; NFPA Codes; Statutes of New Brunswick
Subjects covered: Physical Sciences, Engineering, Technology, Housing, Planning, Public Works, Local Government, Architecture, Geography
Personnel: *Summary:* 1 Total; 1 Technical(s)
Debra E. Edmondson, Librarian
dee@adi.ca

Fredericton: Agricultural Alliance of New Brunswick / Alliance agricole du N.-B.
#303, 259 Brunswick St.
Fredericton, NB E3B 1G8
506-452-8101
Fax: 506-452-1085
e-mail: alliance@fermeNBfarm.ca
URL: www.fermeNBfarm.ca
Hours: M-F
Subjects covered: Agriculture
Gerry Gartner, Chief Operations Officer

Fredericton: Canadian Forest Service / Service canadien des forêts Atlantic Forestry Centre
#1-112, 1350 Regent St. South
Fredericton, NB E3B 5P7
Mailing Address: PO Box 4000
Fredericton, NB E3B 5P7
506-452-3541
Fax: 506-452-3525
National Library Symbol: NBFE
Founded in: 1911
Hours: M-F 8:30-4:30 by appointment only
Note: Member of Council of Canadian Forest Service Libraries. Library serves the Atlantic Region
Special Collections: Canadian Forestry Service, USFS & Atlantic Provinces Government Publications
Subjects covered: Forestry, Genetics, Biodiversity, Botany, Entomology, Agriculture, Ecology, Sustainable Development
Services:
Inter-Library Loan (ILL)
Microform Equipment: Reader
Personnel: *Summary:* 2 Total; 1 Professional(s); 1 Technical(s)
Emmanuel Bayo Aregbesola, Manager
EmmanuelBayo.Aregbesola@NRCan-RNCan.gc.ca

Fredericton: Conservation Council of New Brunswick Environmental Resource Centre
180 St. John St.
Fredericton, NB E3B 4A9
506-458-8747
Fax: 506-458-1047
e-mail: info@conservationcouncil.ca
URL: www.conservationcouncil.ca
Hours: M-F 9:00-5:00
Subjects covered: Environment, Energy
Krista Morrissey, Executive Director

Fredericton: Dr. Everett Chalmers Regional Hospital Health Sciences Library
700 Priestman St.
Fredericton, NB E3B 5N5
Mailing Address: PO Box 9000
Fredericton, NB E3B 5N5
506-452-5432
Fax: 506-452-5585
e-mail: library.services@rvh.nb.ca
URL: www.rhvlibrary.nb.ca
National Library Symbol: NBFDEC
Founded in: 1976
Hours: Sept.-May: M-F 8:00-6:00; June-Aug.: M-F 8:00-4:30
Note: Member of Maritime Health Libraries Association/Canadian Health Libraries Association. Public may access Patient Library collection.
Special Collections: Classics of Medicine Series
Subjects covered: Medicine, Nursing, Health Sciences, Consumer Health
Services:
Internet Access
Inter-Library Loan (ILL)
Fee Based Research
Personnel: *Summary:* 2 Total; 1 Professional(s); 1 Technical(s); 1 Volunteer(s)

Paul Clark, Librarian
Paul.Clark@rvh.nb.ca
506-450-7308

Fredericton: Engineering Library
15 Dineen Dr.
Fredericton, NB E3B 5H5
Mailing Address: PO Box 7500
Fredericton, NB E3B 5H5
506-453-4747
Fax: 506-453-4829
e-mail: englib@unb.ca
URL: www.lib.unb.ca/engineering/
National Library Symbol: NBFU
Founded in: 1968
Hours: M-Su. Hours vary throughout the academic year
Acquisitions Budget: $50,000 - $99,999
Note: ILL supplemented by cooperative Document Delivery process, providing 7 day access for books & periodicals from other libraries
Special Collections: Engineering (all branches); Computer Science; Technical Reports; Standards; Engineering & Computer Science Theses
Subjects covered: Engineering, Technology, Computer Science
Services:
Remote Access
Internet Access
Access to Subscription Databases
Inter-Library Loan (ILL)
Quiet study space & group meeting rooms; laptop loans
Microform Equipment: Reader
Personnel: *Summary:* 8 Total; 1 Professional(s); 7 Technical(s)
Steve Lelievre, Head Librarian
lelievre@unb.ca
506-452-6039

Fredericton: Gerard V. La Forest Law Library
41 Dineen Dr., University of New Brunswick
Fredericton, NB E3B 6C9
Mailing Address: Bag Sevice 44999
Fredericton, NB E3B 6C9
506-453-4734
Fax: 506-451-6948
e-mail: lawlib@unb.ca
URL: www.unbf.ca/law/library
National Library Symbol: NBFUL
Founded in: 1892
Hours: M-Th 8:00am-11:00pm; F 8:00-5:00; Sa 10:00-6:00; Su 12:00-11:00. Hours may vary throughout the academic year
Acquisitions Budget: $250,000 - $499,999
For Print: $100,000 - $249,999
For Electronic: $50,000 - $99,999
Note: Public access to internet where licences permit, for law related use only
Special Collections: Beaverbrook Law Collection; Gordon Fairweather Collection in Human Rights; Immigration & Refugee Law; digital collections include the Allan Legere Digital Archive; texts & treatises; Canadian and international law reports; government documents; statutes & regulations; periodicals; dissertations; law exams
Subjects covered: Law, Law Enforcement, Administration of Justice
Services:
Remote Access
Internet Access
Access to Subscription Databases
Inter-Library Loan (ILL)
Study rooms & equipment for persons with special needs; laptop loans; public access computers; quiet study space & group meeting areas
Microform Equipment: Computer; Reader
Personnel: *Summary:* 10 Total; 3 Professional(s); 4 Technical(s); 3 Other employees
Janet Moss, Head Law Librarian
jmoss@unb.ca
506-447-3266
Catherine Cotter, Reference & Instruction Librarian
cacotter@unb.ca
506-447-3265
Yolande Gagnon, Senior Library Assistant, Circulation & Serials Management
gagnon@unb.ca
506-458-7979

Fredericton: Maritime College of Forest Technology / Collège de technologie forestière des Maritimes Library
1350 Regent St.
Fredericton, NB E3C 2G6
506-458-0199
Fax: 506-458-0652
e-mail: info@mcft.ca
URL: www.mcft.ca
Founded in: 1950
Hours: Tu, Th 6:00-9:00 by appointment only
Acquisitions Budget: 0-$9,999
Subjects covered: Forestry, Wildlife, Environment, Conservation
Personnel: *Summary:* 1 Total; 1 Professional(s)
Philip Hughes, Instructor/Librarian
phughes@mcft.ca
506-485-0199

Fredericton: New Brunswick Dept. of Environment / Ministère de l'Environnement Library
20 McGloin St.
Fredericton, NB E3B 5H1
Mailing Address: PO Box 6000
Fredericton, NB E3B 5H1
506-453-2566
Fax: 506-453-3676
e-mail: gail.darby@gnb.ca
URL: www.gnb.ca/0009/index-e.asp
National Library Symbol: NBFME
Founded in: 1970
Hours: M-F by appointment only
Note: Please call for an appointment
Special Collections: Technical reports of the Department
Subjects covered: Environment, Conservation, Pesticides, Environmental Impact Assessment, Water Quality, Pollution, Local Government
Gail Darby, Librarian
gail.darby@gnb.ca

Fredericton: Potato Research Centre / Centre de recherches sur la pomme de terre Canadian Agriculture Library/Bibliothèque canadienne de l'agriculture - Fredericton
850 Lincoln Rd.
Fredericton, NB E3B 4Z7
Mailing Address: PO Box 20280
Fredericton, NB E3B 4Z7
506-452-4810
Fax: 506-452-3316
National Library Symbol: NBFAG
Founded in: 1952
Hours: M-F 8:30-5:00 by appointment only
Acquisitions Budget: For Print: $25,000 - $49,999
Special Collections: Potatoes; Agriculture Canada publications
Subjects covered: Agriculture, Food, Potatoes, Soil Science
Services:
Inter-Library Loan (ILL) for a fee
Personnel: *Summary:* 1 Total; 1 Professional(s)
André Gionet, Head Librarian
andre.gionet@agr.gc.ca

Fredericton: Science & Forestry Library
4 Bailey Dr.
Fredericton, NB E3B 5H5
Mailing Address: PO Box 7500
Fredericton, NB E3B 5H5
506-453-4601
Fax: 506-453-3518
e-mail: scilib@unb.ca
URL: www.lib.unb.ca/science/
Founded in: 1976
Hours: M-Su. Hours vary throughout the academic year by appointment only
Special Collections: FORF (Forestry related pamphlet/report collection); GEOSCAN (NB Mineral Exploration Assessment Reports on microfiche)
Subjects covered: Physical Sciences, Engineering, Technology, Maps, Environment, Life Sciences, Medicine, Chemistry, Forestry, Earth Sciences
Services:
Remote Access
Internet Access
Inter-Library Loan (ILL)
Microform Equipment: Computer; Reader
Personnel: *Summary:* 8 Total; 2 Professional(s); 6 Technical(s)
Francesca Holyoke, Head Librarian
holyoke@unb.ca
506-453-4965

Fredericton: University of New Brunswick Harriet Irving Library
5 Macaulay Lane
Fredericton, NB E3B 5H5
Mailing Address: PO Box 7500
Fredericton, NB E3B 5H5
506-453-4740
Fax: 506-453-4595
e-mail: library@unb.ca
URL: www.lib.unb.ca
National Library Symbol: NBFU
Consortia Membership: Canadian Research Knowledge Network (CRKN); Council of Atlantic University Libraries (CAUL)
Founded in: 1967
Hours: M-Su. Hours vary throughout the academic year
Acquisitions Budget: $1,000,000 plus
For Print: $1,000,000 plus
For Electronic: $1,000,000 plus
Note: The library is an affiliate member of the Council of Prairie and Pacific University Libraries (COPPUL).
Special Collections: Canadian Literature; Eileen Wallace Children's Literature Collection; Loyalist Collection
Subjects covered: Arts, Humanities, Physical Sciences, Engineering, Technology, Forestry, Tourism, Social Sciences
Services:
Remote Access
Internet Access
Access to Subscription Databases
Inter-Library Loan (ILL)
Fee Based Research
Electronic Text Centre; Digitization; Scanning; Photocopying & Printing; Access for persons with disabilities; Document Delivery
Microform Equipment: Computer; Reader
Personnel: *Summary:* 20 Professional(s)
John Teskey, Director of Libraries
jteskey@unb.ca
506-458-7582
Jocelyne Thompson, Associate Director, Collections Services
jlt@unb.ca
506-458-7053
Lesley Balcom, Associate Director, Learning & Research Services
lbalcom@unb.ca
506-458-7056

Miramichi: Miramichi Campus Library
80 University Ave.
Miramichi, NB E1N 3W4
Mailing Address: PO Box 1053
Miramichi, NB E1N 3W4
506-778-6484
Fax: 506-778-6001
e-mail: nbcc.miramichi@nbcc.ca
National Library Symbol: NBCCC
Founded in: 1985
Hours: M-F
Acquisitions Budget: $50,000 - $99,999
Subjects covered: Computers, Social Sciences, Law, Environment, Educational Technology
Services:
Inter-Library Loan (ILL)
Microform Equipment: Reader
Personnel: *Summary:* 1 Total; 1 Professional(s)

Moncton: Horizon Health Network Library Services
135 MacBeath Ave.
Moncton, NB E1C 6Z8
506-857-5447
Fax: 506-857-5785
URL: www.horizonnb.ca
Founded in: 1963
Hours: M-F 9:00-4:00 by appointment only
Acquisitions Budget: $50,000 - $99,999
For Print: $50,000 - $99,999
For Electronic: $50,000 - $99,999
Subjects covered: Health Sciences
Services:
Remote Access

Internet Access
Inter-Library Loan (ILL)
Personnel: *Summary:* 1 Professional(s); 3 Technical(s)
Lori W. Léger, M.Sc., MLIS, Manager of Library Services

Moncton: New Brunswick Community College / Collège communautaire du Nouveau-Brunswick Moncton Campus, Library

1234 Mountain Rd.
Moncton, NB E1C 8H9
506-856-2229
Fax: 506-856-3288
888-664-1477
e-mail: student.services@nbcc.ca
URL: www.nbcc.ca
National Library Symbol: NBECC
Founded in: 1987
Hours: L-V 8h15-16h30
Acquisitions Budget: 0-$9,999
For Print: 0-$9,999
For Electronic: 0-$9,999
Special Collections: Génie civil; hôtellerie; techniques de bureau
Subjects covered: Arts, sciences humaines, culture, alimentation, génie, technologie, cuisine avancée, construction, hôtellerie, restauration, télécommunications, informatique, tourisme, santé, techniques de bureau
Services:
Internet Access
Inter-Library Loan (ILL)
Microform Equipment: Reader
Personnel: *Summary:* 2 Total; 1 Professional(s); 1 Other employees
Elizabeth Crawford, Librarian
elizabeth.crawford@nbcc.ca

Moncton: Université de Moncton Bibliothèque Champlain

18, av. Antonine-Maillet
Moncton, NB E1A 3E9
506-858-4012
Téléc: 506-858-4086
Couriel: bichamp@umoncton.ca
bcref@umoncton.ca
pretcham@umoncton.ca
URL: www.umoncton.ca/umcm-bibliotheque-champlain\
Profile: Adresse civique: 415, av. de l'Université
Sigle: NBMOU
Membre d'un consortium: Canadian Research Knowledge Network (CRKN); Council of Atlantic University Libraries (CAUL)
Fondée en: 1965
Heures: L-J 8h30-22h30; V 8h30-20h; S 12h-18h; D 13h-22h30
Budget d'acquisitions: $1,000,000 plus
Matériel imprimé: $500,000 - $999,999
Matériel électronique: $250,000 - $499,999
Population desservie: 0
Collections spécialisées: Acadiana; collection du centres d'études acadiennes
Sujets: Génie; musique; nutrition; arts; humanités; sciences physiques
Services:
Accèss distance aux bases de donn
Accès public à l'internet
Réseau en ligne
Prêts entre bibliothèques(PEB)
Aide à la recherche; aide à la rédaction; locaux & casiers; réserve académique; services pour personnes ayant un handicap visuel
Lecteur/reproduction de microformes: Lecteurs
Personnel: *Sommaire:* 35 Total; 8 Professionnel(s); 7 Technicien(s); 20 Autre(s) employé(s)
Alain Roberge, Bibliothécaire en chef
alain.roberge@umoncton.ca
506-858-4073
Héctor Alvarez, Chef des services publics
hector.alvarez@umoncton.ca
506-858-4911
Victoria Volkanova, Chef du service des systèmes informatisés
victoria.volkanova@umoncton.ca
506-858-4458

Sackville: Canadian Wildlife Service Atlantic Region Library

17 Waterfowl Lane
Sackville, NB E4L 1G6
506-364-5019
Fax: 506-364-5062
URL: www.ec.gc.ca
National Library Symbol: NBSACW
Hours: M-F 8:30-12:00, 1:00-4:30
Acquisitions Budget: 0-$9,999
For Print: 0-$9,999
For Electronic: 0-$9,999
Note: Library is staffed from 8:30 to noon.
Subjects covered: Environment, Air/Water Pollution, Hazardous Substances, Climate
Services:
Internet Access
Access to Subscription Databases
Inter-Library Loan (ILL)
Microform Equipment: Reader
Personnel: *Summary:* 1 Total; 1 Professional(s)
Andrew Fabro, Head Librarian
andrew.fabro@ec.gc.ca
Adele Cohen, Librarian
adele.cohen@ec.gc.ca
604-666-1794

Sackville: Mount Allison University Ralph Pickard Bell Library

49 York St.
Sackville, NB E4L 1C6
506-364-2567
Fax: 506-364-2617
e-mail: circ@mta.ca
infodesk@mta.ca
URL: www.mta.ca/library
National Library Symbol: NBSAM
Consortia Membership: Canadian Research Knowledge Network (CRKN); Council of Atlantic University Libraries (CAUL)
Founded in: 1862
Hours: M-Su
Acquisitions Budget: $500,000 - $999,999
Special Collections: Winthrop Pickard Bell Collection of Acadiana
Subjects covered: Liberal Arts
Services:
Inter-Library Loan (ILL)
Microform Equipment: Computer; Reader
Personnel: *Summary:* 29 Total; 8 Professional(s); 21 Technical(s)
Bruno Gnassi, University Librarian

Saint John: New Brunswick Museum Archives & Research Library

277 Douglas Ave.
Saint John, NB E2K 1E5
506-643-2322
Fax: 506-643-2360
888-268-9595
e-mail: archives@nbm-mnb.ca
URL: www.nbm-mnb.ca
National Library Symbol: NBSM
Hours: Tu-F 10:00-4:30
Acquisitions Budget: $25,000 - $49,999
Note: No access to subscription database through website.
Special Collections: Records & papers dealing with the economic, social, legal, military, relgious & political areas of life in New Brunswick, with a particular focus on the 19th century; fine & decorative arts; Webster Canadiana Library; Ganong Library (history & cartography of New Brunswick)
Subjects covered: Natural Sciences, Fine & Decorative Arts, New Brunswick History, Shipping, Archives
Services:
Remote Access
Internet Access
Access to Subscription Databases
Inter-Library Loan (ILL)
Personnel: *Summary:* 3 Total
Felicity Osepchook, Head
felicity.osepchook@nbm-mnb.ca
506-643-2324

Saint John: Saint John Campus Library L.R. Fulton Library & Audiovisual Centre

950 Grandview Ave.
Saint John, NB E2L 3V1
506-658-6726
Fax: 506-658-6792
800-416-4080
e-mail: studentservices.nbccsj@nbcc.ca
Founded in: 1962
Hours: M-F 8:15-4:30
Acquisitions Budget: $25,000 - $49,999
Subjects covered: Trades & Technology
Services:
Inter-Library Loan (ILL)
Personnel: *Summary:* 3 Total; 1 Professional(s); 2 Other employees

Saint John: St Joseph's Hospital (Saint John) Patient Library

130 Bayard Dr.
Saint John, NB E2L 3L6
506-632-5555
Fax: 506-632-5551
URL: www.horizonnb.ca
Subjects covered: Health

Saint John: Ward Chipman Library Saint John Campus

100 Tucker Park Rd.
Saint John, NB E2L 4L5
Mailing Address: PO Box 5050
Saint John, NB E2L 4L5
506-648-5700
Fax: 506-648-5701
URL: www.lib.unb.ca/wcl/
National Library Symbol: NBSU
Founded in: 1965
Hours: M-Su. Hours may vary throughout the academic year
Acquisitions Budget: $250,000 - $499,999
Special Collections: Science Fiction & Fantasy Collection, Governors-General of Canada Collection, Beat Generation, Marine Biology
Services:
Remote Access
Internet Access
Inter-Library Loan (ILL)
Microform Equipment: Reader
Personnel: *Summary:* 19 Total; 8 Professional(s); 11 Technical(s)
Terry Nikkel, Director, Information Services & Systems
tnikkel@unb.ca
506-648-5700
Linda Hansen, Electronic Services Librarian
lhansen@unb.ca
Janet Fraser, Bibliographic & Collection Services Librarian
jdfraser@unb.ca
506-648-5996

Shippagan: Campus de Shippagan Bibliothèque

218, boul. J.-D.-Gauthier
Shippagan, NB E8S 1P6
506-336-3420
Téléc: 506-336-3434
800-363-8336
Couriel: biblioweb@umcs.ca
URL: www.umoncton.ca/umcs-bibliotheque
Sigle: NBSCU
Heures: L-J 8h30-22h45; V 8h30-19h45; S 10h-17h; D 13h-21h
Budget d'acquisitions: $50,000 - $99,999
Population desservie: 0
Collections spécialisées: Près de 40,000 volumes; 325 titres de périodiques; 3,000 publications gouvernementales; livres rares; collections spécialisées en gestion de l'information & en pêche; collection de la Bibliothèque du CCNB de Bathurst; publications officielles
Services:
Accèss distance aux bases de donn
Accès public à l'internet
Réseau en ligne
Prêts entre bibliothèques(PEB)
Formation documentaire; réserve; salles de séminaire; laboratoire informatique; salle multimédia
Lecteur/reproduction de microformes: Ordinateur; Lecteurs
Personnel: *Sommaire:* 14 Total; 1 Professionnel(s); 3 Technicien(s); 10 Autre(s) employé(s)
Hélène McLaughlin, Directrice de la bibliothèque
mchelene@umcs.ca
506-336-3418
Cédric Landry, Conseiller en documentation
cedric.landry@umcs.ca
506-333-486

Marie-Josée Diotte, Responsable, Service du prêt
mjdiotte@umcs.ca
506-336-3420

St. Andrews: St. Andrews Campus Library

99 Augustus St.
St. Andrews, NB E5B 2E9
506-529-5070
Fax: 506-529-5009
e-mail: webinquiries@nbcc.ca
National Library Symbol: NBSTAC
Founded in: 1987
Hours: M-Th 8:15am-9:00pm; F 8:15-4:30
Acquisitions Budget: $25,000 - $49,999
Subjects covered: Tourism & Travel, Economics, Boat Building, Business Education, Heating, Air Conditioning & Refrigeration, Hospitality, Hotel Management
Services:
Internet Access
Inter-Library Loan (ILL)
Personnel: *Summary:* 1 Total
Mary Doon, Librarian
mary.doon@nbcc.ca

Woodstock: Woodstock Campus Library

100 Broadway St.
Woodstock, NB E7M 5C5
506-325-4877
Fax: 506-328-8426
e-mail: nbccwd-studentservice@nbcc.ca
National Library Symbol: NBWC
Founded in: 1984
Acquisitions Budget: 0-$9,999
Subjects covered: Agriculture, Arts, Economics, Communications, Mass Media, Business, Journalism, Photography, Carpentry, Secretarial Studies, Graphic Arts, Technology, Video Production
Services:
Internet Access
Inter-Library Loan (ILL)
Personnel: *Summary:* 1 Technical(s)
Sandra Harris, Librarian
sandra.harris@nbcc.ca

Newfoundland & Labrador

Bonavista: Bonavista Campus Learning Resource Centre

#A110, 301 Confederation Dr.
Bonavista, NL A0C 1B0
Mailing Address: PO Box 670
Bonavista, NL A0C 1B0
709-468-1716
Fax: 709-468-2004
Founded in: 1994
Hours: M-F 8:30-11:45, 12:15-4:00. Hours may vary during the academic year
Subjects covered: Adult Basic Education, Trades/Occupations, Natural Resources, Office Administration
Services:
Remote Access
Internet Access
Inter-Library Loan (ILL)
Personnel: *Summary:* 1 Technical(s)
Tracy Mouland, Library Technician
tracy.mouland@cna.nl.ca

Burin Bay Arm: Burin Campus Library

105 Main St.
Burin Bay Arm, NL A0E 1G0
Mailing Address: PO Box 370
Burin Bay Arm, NL A0E 1G0
709-891-5622
Fax: 709-891-2256
Hours: M-F 8:30-4:00
Special Collections: Social Justice Special Edition (Fredette/Matthews); The Days Special Collection (Labrador Reflections); French Language course materials; Maps
Subjects covered: Social Sciences, Business, Applied Arts, Technology
Services:
Remote Access
Internet Access
Access to Subscription Databases
Inter-Library Loan (ILL)
Orientation sessions; individual and group study facilities; computers; audiovisual equipment; scanner
Personnel: *Summary:* 1 Total; 1 Other employees
Sandra Shallow, Library Technician
sandra.shallow@cna.nl.ca

Carbonear: Carbonear Campus Library

#127, 4 Pike's Lane
Carbonear, NL A1Y 1B5
Mailing Address: PO Box 60
Carbonear, NL A1Y 1B5
709-596-8925
Fax: 709-596-2688
Hours: M-F 8:30-5:00
Acquisitions Budget: 0-$9,999
For Print: 0-$9,999
For Electronic: 0-$9,999
Special Collections: Newfoundland Literature Collection
Subjects covered: Adult Education, Carpentry, Engineering Technology
Services:
Remote Access
Internet Access
Inter-Library Loan (ILL)
Quiet study space; personal computers
Personnel: *Summary:* 1 Professional(s); 1 Technical(s)
Stephen Nolan, Librarian
stephen.nolan@cna.nl.ca
Brenda Peach, Library Technician
brenda.peach@cna.nl.ca
709-596-8940

Clarenville: Clarenville Campus Learning Resource Centre

#229, 69 Pleasant St.
Clarenville, NL A5A 1V9
709-466-6940
Fax: 709-466-2771
Hours: M-F 8:30-4:00
Subjects covered: Business, Trades/Occupations, Engineering Technology
Services:
Remote Access
Internet Access
Inter-Library Loan (ILL)
Personnel: *Summary:* 1 Professional(s)
Joanne Deluney, Librarian
joanne.deluney@cna.nl.ca

Conception Bay South: Seal Cove Campus Library

#215, 1670 Conception Bay Hwy.
Conception Bay South, NL A1X 5C7
Mailing Address: PO Box 19003, Stn Seal Cove
Conception Bay South, NL A1X 5C7
709-744-6829
Fax: 709-744-3929
e-mail: libs@cna.nl.ca
National Library Symbol: NFSCS
Founded in: 1992
Hours: M-F 8:30-4:30
Acquisitions Budget: 0-$9,999
For Print: 0-$9,999
For Electronic: 0-$9,999
Special Collections: Newfoundland Collection
Subjects covered: Electrical, Oil Burner Mechanic, Commercial Cooking, Power Line Technician, Industrial Instrumentation, Petroleum Industry Training, Construction Technician, Adult Basic Education
Services:
Internet Access
Access to Subscription Databases
Inter-Library Loan (ILL)
Orientation sessions & tours; computers for research; office productivity tools; printing; audiovisual resource room; facilities for quiet individual & group study
Personnel: *Summary:* 2 Total; 1 Professional(s); 1 Other employees
Brent Slade, Librarian
brent.slade@cna.nl.ca
Bernadette Woodford, Library Clerk
bernadette.woodford@cna.nl.ca

Corner Brook: Corner Brook Campus Library

141 O'Connell Dr.
Corner Brook, NL A2H 6H6
Mailing Address: PO Box 822
Corner Brook, NL A2H 6H6
709-637-8528
Fax: 709-634-2126
e-mail: libcb@cna.nl.ca
National Library Symbol: NFCBFT
Hours: M-W 8:00-5:00, 6:00-9:00; Th, F 8:00-4:30; Su 1:00-5:00, 6:00-9:00. Hours may vary during the academic year
Acquisitions Budget: $25,000 - $49,999
Subjects covered: Adult Basic Education, Adventure Tourism & Outdoor Recreation, Business, Industrial Technologies & Trades, Early Childhood Education, English as a Second Language, Fish & Wildlife, Forestry, Office Administration
Services:
Remote Access
Inter-Library Loan (ILL)
Group & individual study facilities; audiovisual room; computer access; photocopying
Personnel: *Summary:* 3 Total; 1 Professional(s); 2 Technical(s)
Marian Burnett, Librarian
marian.burnett@cna.nl.ca
709-637-8587

Corner Brook: Newfoundland & Labrador Dept. of Forest Resources & Agrifood Forestry Resources Library

Fortis Bldg., 2nd Fl.
4 Herald Ave.
Corner Brook, NL A2H 6J8
Mailing Address: PO Box 2006
Corner Brook, NL A2H 6J8
709-637-2307
Fax: 709-637-2403
URL: www.nr.gov.nl.ca.nr.forestry/library
National Library Symbol: NFCBF
Founded in: 1984
Hours: M-F by appointment only
Acquisitions Budget: $25,000 - $49,999
Special Collections: Newfoundland Forestry
Subjects covered: Natural Resources, Land Use, Environment; Forestry
Services:
Inter-Library Loan (ILL)
Personnel: *Summary:* 1 Total; 1 Professional(s)
Bruce Boland, Librarian
bboland@gov.nl.ca

Corner Brook: Sir Wilfred Grenfell College Ferriss Hodgett Library

University Dr.
Corner Brook, NL A2H 6P9
709-637-6236
Fax: 709-637-6273
e-mail: library@swgc.mun.ca
URL: www.library.mun.ca/swgc
National Library Symbol: NFSCF
Founded in: 1964
Hours: M,Th,F 8:00-5:00; T,W 8:00-8:00
Acquisitions Budget: $50,000 - $99,999
Services:
Internet Access
Access to Subscription Databases
Inter-Library Loan (ILL)
Microform Equipment: Reader
Personnel: *Summary:* 6 Total; 1 Professional(s); 5 Technical(s)
Elizabeth Behrens, Associate University Librarian
ebehrens@swgc.mun.ca
709-637-6236 ext. 6120

Corner Brook: Western Health Care Corporation Health Sciences Library

PO Box 2005
Corner Brook, NL A2H 6J7
709-637-5000 ext: 5218
Fax: 709-637-5453
e-mail: library@healthwest.nf.ca
URL: www.healthwest.nf.ca
National Library Symbol: NFCBW
Services:
Internet Access
Inter-Library Loan (ILL) for a fee of $5
Personnel: *Summary:* 4 Total; 2 Professional(s); 1 Technical(s)
Kimberly Hancock, Director, Library Services
khanco@healthwest.nf.ca
709-637-5395

Gander: Gander Campus Library & Career Exploration Centre
1 Magee Rd.
Gander, NL A1V 1W8
Mailing Address: PO Box 395
Gander, NL A1V 1W8
709-651-4815
Fax: 709-651-4854
e-mail: karen.rowe@cna.nl.ca
libga@cna.nl.ca
Founded in: 1993
Hours: M-Th 8:00-12:00, 12:30-4:00; F 8:00-1:00
Note: Career Exploration Centre provides job search resources & a job board
Special Collections: Adult Basic Education textbook collection; literature & literary biographies; history; sociology; videos
Subjects covered: Industrial Trades, Automotive, Aircraft Technology, Hairstyling
Services:
Remote Access
Internet Access
Access to Subscription Databases
Inter-Library Loan (ILL)
Photocopying; laminating
Personnel: *Summary:* 1 Professional(s)
Karen Rowe, Librarian/Website Administrator
karen.rowe@cna.nl.ca
709-651-4815

Gander: Newfoundland & Labrador Department of Health & Community Services
Literature Depot (Central Printed Resource Location)
125 Trans Canada Hwy.
Gander, NL A1V 1P7
Fax: 709-651-1100
URL: www.health.gov.nl.ca/health/index.html
National Library Symbol: NFSHCS
Founded in: 1995
Hours: Winter: M-F 8:45-4:30. Summer: 8:45-4:00 by appointment only
Subjects covered: Social Work, Income Support, Health Policy
Services:
Internet Access
Inter-Library Loan (ILL)

Grand Falls-Windsor: Central Newfoundland Regional Health Centre
Regional Resource Centre
50 Union St.
Grand Falls-Windsor, NL A2A 2E1
709-292-2500
URL: www.centralhealth.nl.ca
Hours: M-F by appointment only
Acquisitions Budget: $25,000 - $49,999
Note: Member of Central West Health Care Board Library Services
Subjects covered: Medical, Para-Medical, Allied Health
Services:
Inter-Library Loan (ILL)
Personnel: *Summary:* 1 Total; 1 Technical(s)
Kelly Adams, Chief Operating Officer
kelly.adams@centralhealth.nl.ca

Grand Falls-Windsor: Grand Falls-Windsor Campus Library
#113, 5 Cromer Ave.
Grand Falls-Windsor, NL A2A 1X3
Mailing Address: PO Box 19003
Grand Falls-Windsor, NL A2A 1X3
709-292-5637
Fax: 709-489-5765
e-mail: libgf@cna.nl.ca
Hours: M, F 8:30-5:00; Tu-Th 8:30am-9:30pm; Sa 9:00-4:00. Hours may vary during the academic year
Subjects covered: Business, Office Administration
Services:
Remote Access
Internet Access
Inter-Library Loan (ILL)
Library is wheelchair accessible; orientation sessions; photocopying
Personnel: *Summary:* 3 Total; 1 Professional(s); 2 Technical(s)
John Whelan, Librarian III
john.whelan@cna.nl.ca

Labrador City: Labrador West Campus
Raymond J. Condon Memorial Library & Learning Resource Centre
#177, 1600 Nichols-Adam Hwy.
Labrador City, NL A2V 0B8
709-944-6862
Fax: 709-944-5413
e-mail: liblw@cna.nl.ca
Founded in: 1990
Hours: M-Th 8:00-8:00; F 8:00-4:30. Spring & Summer: M-F 8:30-4:30
Acquisitions Budget: $10,000 - $24,999
Special Collections: Newfoundland Collection; maps; videos; material supporting courses, particularly in technology, science, mining
Subjects covered: Engineering Technology, Industrial Trades, Mining Technology
Services:
Remote Access
Internet Access for a fee
Access to Subscription Databases
Inter-Library Loan (ILL)
Personnel: *Summary:* 3 Total; 1 Professional(s); 2 Technical(s);
Roxanne Sutton, Librarian
709-944-5765
Kyle Eades, Library Technician

Placentia: Placentia Campus Learning Resource Centre
1 Roosevelt Ave.
Placentia, NL A0B 2Y0
Mailing Address: PO Box 190
Placentia, NL A0B 2Y0
709-227-6264
Fax: 709-227-7185
Founded in: 1993
Hours: M, W 8:00-4:00, 6:00-9:00; Tu, Th 8:00-7:00; F 8:00-4:00. Hours may vary during the academic year
Subjects covered: Adult Basic Education; Heavy Equipment Operator, Machinist, Millwright, Welder programs
Services:
Internet Access
Inter-Library Loan (ILL)
Personnel: *Summary:* 1 Total
Linda Reddigan, Librarian
linda.reddigan@cna.nl.ca

Port aux Basques: Port aux Basques Campus Library
59 Grand Bay Rd.
Port aux Basques, NL A0M 1C0
Mailing Address: PO Box 760
Port aux Basques, NL A0M 1C0
709-695-3343
Fax: 709-695-2963
e-mail: libpab@cna.nl.ca
Founded in: 1963
Hours: M-F 8:30-4:30
Subjects covered: Non-Destructive Testing, Cabinet Making, Business, Office Administration
Services:
Remote Access
Internet Access
Inter-Library Loan (ILL)
Personnel: *Summary:* 1 Technical(s)
Pamela Hardy, Library Technician II
pamela.hardy@cna.nl.ca

St Anthony: St Anthony Campus Library
PO Box 550
St Anthony, NL A0K 4S0
709-454-3559
Fax: 709-454-8808
e-mail: nina.woodward@cna.nl.ca
Hours: M, W 9:30-3:30; Tu 12:30-3:30; Th 9:30-3:00
Services:
Internet Access
Inter-Library Loan (ILL)
Personnel: *Summary:* 1 Total; 1 Other employees
Nina Woodward, Librarian
nina.woodward@cna.nl.ca
709-454-3559

St. John's: Canada-Newfoundland Offshore Petroleum Board
Library
TD Place, #500, 140 Water St.
St. John's, NL A1C 6H6
709-778-1400
Fax: 709-778-1473
e-mail: information@cnlopb.nl.ca
URL: www.cnlopb.nl.ca
Founded in: 1986
Hours: M-F
Acquisitions Budget: $25,000 - $49,999
Subjects covered: Offshore Petroleum Engineering
Services:
Microform Equipment: Reader
Debra Downing, Contact
Sheila Duff, Technical Files Clerk
709-778-1423

St. John's: Centre for Newfoundland Studies Library
Queen Elizabeth II Library, Memorial University
St. John's, NL A1B 3Y1
709-737-7475
Fax: 709-737-2153
e-mail: cnsqeii@mun.ca
URL: www.library.mun.ca/qeii/cns/cns_main.php
National Library Symbol: NFSM
Founded in: 1965
Hours: M-Th 8:30am-5:45pm; F 8:30-4:45; Sa 10:00-4:45
Acquisitions Budget: $50,000 - $99,999
Note: Member of Atlantic Scholarly Information Network
Subjects covered: Newfoundland, Labrador, Social Sciences, Sciences, Humanities, Arts
Services:
Remote Access
Internet Access
Access to Subscription Databases
Inter-Library Loan (ILL)
Microform Equipment: Computer; Reader
Personnel: *Summary:* 15 Total; 3 Professional(s); 12 Technical(s)
Joan Ritcey, Head
jritcey@mun.ca
Colleen Field, Assistant Head
Bert Riggs, Archivist

St. John's: Fisheries & Marine Institute
Dr. C.R. Barrett Library
155 Ridge Rd.
St. John's, NL A1C 5R3
Mailing Address: PO Box 4920
St. John's, NL A1C 5R3
709-778-0662
Fax: 709-778-0316
e-mail: barrett@mi.mun.ca
URL: www.library.mun.ca/mi/
National Library Symbol: NFSCF
Founded in: 1964
Hours: M-Th 8:00-8:45; F 8:30-5:00; Sa, Su 10:00-5:00
Acquisitions Budget: $50,000 - $99,999
Note: Publications accessible through internet: info.library.mun.ca/marine.htm. The C.R. Barrett Library shares a joint-service library with the Ridge Road Campus of the College of the North Atlantic
Special Collections: Collection includes audio visual materials, ship drawings
Subjects covered: Engineering, Technology, Fisheries, Naval Architecture, Marine Engineering, Food Technology, Marine Emergency Duties, Nautical Science, Electronics, Marine Environment
Services:
Internet Access
Access to Subscription Databases
Inter-Library Loan (ILL)
Microform Equipment: Reader
Personnel: *Summary:* 6 Total; 1 Professional(s); 5 Technical(s)
Catherine Lawton, Librarian
catherine.lawton@mi.mun.ca
709-778-0662

St. John's: Health Sciences Library
Memorial University of Newfoundland
300 Prince Philip Dr.
St. John's, NL A1B 3V6
Mailing Address: 300 Prince Philip Dr., Memorial Univesity of

Newfoundland
St. John's, NL A1B 3V6
709-777-6672
Fax: 709-777-6866
e-mail: hslinfo@mun.ca
URL: www.library.mun.ca/hsl
National Library Symbol: NFSMM
Founded in: 1969
Hours: M-Th 8:00am-11:30pm; F 8:00-6:00; Sa 10:00-5:30; Su 12:00-8:30
Acquisitions Budget: $1,000,000 plus
For Print: $250,000 - $499,999
For Electronic: $500,000 - $999,999
Special Collections: History of Medicine Collection
Subjects covered: Medicine, Health Sciences, Pharmacy, Nursing
Services:
Remote Access
Internet Access
Access to Subscription Databases
Inter-Library Loan (ILL) for a fee of $2.50/article
Microform Equipment: Computer; Reader
Personnel: *Summary:* 24 Total; 7 Professional(s); 17 Technical(s)
George Beckett, Associate University Librarian, Health Sciences
georger@mun.ca
709-777-6670
Linda Barnett, Head of Public Services
lbarnett@mun.ca
709-777-6676

St. John's: Memorial University of Newfoundland Queen Elizabeth II Library

234 Elizabeth Ave.
St. John's, NL A1B 3Y1
709-864-7428
Fax: 709-864-2153
e-mail: qe2ill@mun.ca
URL: www.library.mun.ca
National Library Symbol: NFSM
Consortia Membership: Canadian Research Knowledge Network (CRKN); Council of Atlantic University Libraries (CAUL); Atlantic Health Knowledge Partnership (AHKP)
Founded in: 1925
Hours: M-Th 8:00am-9:45pm; F 8:00-4:45; Sa 10:00-4:45; Su 2:00-8:45
Acquisitions Budget: $500,000 - $999,999
Note: The library is an affiliate member of the Council of Prairie and Pacific University Libraries (COPPUL). Archive holdings are held at the Queen Elizabeth II library.
Special Collections: Centre for Newfoundland Studies
Services:
Internet Access
Access to Subscription Databases
Inter-Library Loan (ILL)
Microform Equipment: Computer; Reader
Personnel: *Summary:* 127 Total; 28 Professional(s); 99 Other employees
Richard H. Ellis, University Librarian
rhellis@mun.ca
709-737-7428
Karen Lippold, Head of Information Services
klippold@mun.ca
Slavko Manojlovich, Assistant to Librarian, Systems & Planning
slavko@mun.ca
Patrick Warner, Head, Lending Services Division
pwarner@mun.ca
709-737-3189

St. John's: Newfoundland & Labrador Department of Natural Resources Geoscience Publications & Information Section

50 Elizabeth Ave.
St. John's, NL A1B 4J6
Mailing Address: PO Box 8700
St. John's, NL A1B 4J6
709-729-1311
Fax: 709-729-4491
e-mail: pub@gov.nl.ca
URL: www.nr.gov.nl.ca
National Library Symbol: NFSMEM
Hours: M-F
Acquisitions Budget: $25,000 - $49,999
Special Collections: Company Reports; Geoscience of Newfoundland; Labrador & Offshore East
Subjects covered: Minerals; Mineral Industry; Earth Sciences
Services:
Internet Access
Access to Subscription Databases
Inter-Library Loan (ILL)
Microform Equipment: Reader
Personnel: *Summary:* 2 Total; 1 Professional(s); 2 Technical(s)
Sean O'Brien, Senior Geologist
seanobrien@gov.nl.ca
709-729-2775
Paula Bowdridge, Library Technician
paulabowdridge@gov.nl.ca
709-729-1311
Randy Meehan, Information Officer, Publications Sales
randymeehan@gov.nl.ca
709-729-6928
Cindy Saunders, Indexing Geologist
cindysaunders@gov.nl.ca
709-729-6280

St. John's: Newfoundland & Labrador Dept. of Innovation, Trade & Rural Development Information

Confederation Bldg.
St. John's, NL A1B 4J6
Mailing Address: PO Box 8700
St. John's, NL A1B 4J6
709-729-7000
Fax: 709-729-0654
e-mail: IBRD@gov.nl.ca.ca
URL: www.intrd.gov.nl.ca/intrd/
Hours: M-F 8:30-4:30
Subjects covered: Industry, Trade, Technology
Services:
Microform Equipment: Reader

St. John's: Newfoundland & Labrador Hydro

Hydro Place, 500 Columbus Dr.
St. John's, NL A1B 4K7
Mailing Address: PO Box 12400
St. John's, NL A1B 4K7
709-737-1400
Fax: 709-737-1800
888-737-1296
e-mail: hydro@nlh.nl.ca
customerservices@nlh.nl.ca
URL: www.nlh.nl.ca
No public access
Hours: M-F
Subjects covered: Legal; Energy; Engineering; Environment
Services:
Inter-Library Loan (ILL)

St. John's: Newfoundland Ocean Industries Association Library

#602, Atlantic Pl., 215 Water St.
St. John's, NL A1C 6C9
Mailing Address: PO Box 44
St. John's, NL A1C 6C9
709-758-6610
Fax: 709-758-6611
URL: www.noia.ca
National Library Symbol: NFSOI
Founded in: 1977
Hours: M-F 9:00-5:00 by appointment only
Acquisitions Budget: $25,000 - $49,999
Subjects covered: Natural Resources, Environment, Life Sciences, Ocean Industries, Marine, Fisheries, Oil & Gas
Services:
Inter-Library Loan (ILL)
Personnel: *Summary:* 12 Total; 9 Professional(s); 1 Technical(s); 2 Other employees

St. John's: NRC Information Centre - St John's / Centre d'information CNRC, St John's Institute for Ocean Technology

1 Kerwin Pl.
St. John's, NL A1B 3T5
Mailing Address: PO Box 12093
St. John's, NL A1B 3T5
709-772-2468
Fax: 709-772-3670
e-mail: nic.stjohns@nrc-cnrc.gc.ca
URL: cisti-icist.nrc-cnrc.gc.ca/eng/locations/cisti/stjohns.html
National Library Symbol: NFSNM
Founded in: 1985
Hours: M-F 8:30-4:30
Acquisitions Budget: $25,000 - $49,999
Note: ILL done via OON.
Special Collections: Reports of the Institute for Marine Dynamics
Subjects covered: Naval Architecture, Offshore Structures, Ice, Computational Hydrodynamics
Services:
Internet Access
Inter-Library Loan (ILL)
Fee Based Research
Personnel: *Summary:* 3 Total; 2 Professional(s); 1 Technical(s)
Jennifer Mersereau, Client Services Officer
jennifer.mersereau@nrc-cnrc.gc.ca
709-772-2468

St. John's: Prince Philip Drive Campus Library

1 Prince Philip Dr.
St. John's, NL A1C 5P7
Mailing Address: PO Box 1693
St. John's, NL A1C 5P7
709-758-7274
Fax: 709-758-7231
Other contact info: Reference Service: 709-758-7448
e-mail: LibPP@cna.nl.ca
Founded in: 1965
Hours: M-W 8:00-5:00, 6:00-9:00; Th, F 8:00-4:30. Hours may vary during the acadmic year
Acquisitions Budget: $50,000 - $99,999
Subjects covered: Adult Basic Education, Automotive, Business, Diagnostic Ultrasonograhy, Early Childhood Education, English as a Second Language, Food Service & Nutrition, Hospitality, Graphic Design, Medical & paramedical sciences, Office Administration, Textile Studies
Services:
Remote Access
Internet Access
Access to Subscription Databases
Inter-Library Loan (ILL)
Audio Visual Centre; Career Centre; group & individual study facilities; computers, printers, transparency maker
Personnel: *Summary:* 5 Total; 1 Professional(s); 3 Technical(s); 1 Other employees
Sandra Hallett, Librarian
sandra.hallett@cna.nl.ca

St. John's: St John's Department of Planning Department of Planning

10 New Gower St.
St. John's, NL A1C 5M2
Mailing Address: PO Box 908
St. John's, NL A1C 5M2
709-576-8285
Fax: 709-576-8625
e-mail: planning@stjohns.ca
URL: www.stjohns.ca
Founded in: 1980
Hours: M-F 9:00-4:30 by appointment only
Subjects covered: Housing; Planning & Public Works; Local Government; Population Statistics; Land Use; Zoning
Services:
Fee Based Research

Stephenville: College of the North Atlantic Bay St. George Campus Learning Resource Centres

432 Massachusetts Dr.
Stephenville, NL A2N 2Z6
Mailing Address: PO Box 5400
Stephenville, NL A2N 2Z6
709-643-7762
Fax: 709-643-7786
URL: www.cna.nl.ca/library-services
Founded in: 1977
Hours: D.S.B Flowlow Bldg LRC: M-Th 8:00-8:00; F 8:00-4:00; Sa 2:00-6:00; Su 6:00-9:00. Other LRC's: M-F 8:00-4:00. Hours may vary during the academic year
Acquisitions Budget: $25,000 - $49,999
Note: Westviking College, Eastern College, Cabot College of Applied Arts, Technology & Continuing Education, & Central Newfoundland Regional College merged to create the College of the North Atlantic. The Bay St. George Campus includes the D.S.B. Fowlow Bldg Learning Resource Centre and the L.A. Bown LRC, located at 423 Massachusetts Dr. in Stephenville, and the Martin Gallant Bldg LRC located at 15 Washington Dr. in Stephenville Crossing. For information on Library Services available to the Ridge Road Campus, please see the entry for

the Dr. C.R. Barrett Library, listed under Memorial University of Newfoundland
Special Collections: College of the North Atlantic Folklore & Language Archives; Newfoundland Collection
Subjects covered: Hospitality, Visual Arts, Film & Video Production, Music Industry/Production, Recording Arts, Journalism, Business Administration, Industrial Trades, Multimedia
Services:
Remote Access
Internet Access
Access to Subscription Databases
Inter-Library Loan (ILL)
Computer lab with networked computers, scanners, laser printers; photocopiers
Microform Equipment: Reader
Personnel: *Summary:* 4 Total; 1 Professional(s); 3 Technical(s)
Lisa Marshall, College Librarian, D.S.B. Fowlow Bldg.
lisa.marshall@cna.nl.ca
Barbara King, Library Technician, D.S.B. Fowlow Bldg.
barb.king@cna.nl.ca
709-643-7752
Theresa Hynes, Library Technician, Martin Gallant Bldg.
theresa.hynes@cna.nl.ca
709-643-5704
Cathy Ash, Library Technician, L.A. Bown Bldg.
cathy.ash@cna.nl.ca
709-643-7787

Twillingate: Notre Dame Bay Memorial Health Centre Library
Twillingate, NL A0G 4M0
709-884-2131
URL:
www.centralhealth.nl.ca/notre-dame-bay-memorial-health-centre
Founded in: 1924
Hours: M, F 8:00-11:45 by appointment only
Subjects covered: Health Sciences, Medicine, Nursing
Services:
Internet Access
Inter-Library Loan (ILL)
Personnel: *Summary:* 1 Technical(s)

Northwest Territories

Fort Smith: Aurora College Thebacha Campus Library
50 Conibear St.
Fort Smith, NT X0E 0P0
Mailing Address: PO Bag Service 2
Fort Smith, NT X0E 0P0
867-872-7549
Fax: 867-872-4511
e-mail: tclibrary@auroracollege.nt.ca
URL:
www.auroracollege.nt.ca/_live/pages/wpPages/LibrariesThebacha.aspx
National Library Symbol: NWFST
Founded in: 1983
Hours: M-F 8:30am-9:00pm; Sa 1:00-5:00; Su 1:00-9:00
Acquisitions Budget: $250,000 - $499,999
Subjects covered: All subjects with emphasis on Native Peoples & Northern Affairs
Services:
Remote Access
Internet Access
Access to Subscription Databases
Inter-Library Loan (ILL)
Microform Equipment: Reader
Personnel: *Summary:* 3 Total; 1 Professional(s); 1 Technical(s); 1 Other employees
Alexandra Hook, Librarian
ahook@auroracollege.nt.ca
867-872-7544
Margo Harney, Library Technician
867-872-7549

Inuvik: Aurora College. Aurora Research Institute Inuvik Research Centre Library
191 Mackenzie Rd.
Inuvik, NT X0E 0T0
Mailing Address: PO Box 1450
Inuvik, NT X0E 0T0
867-777-3298 ext: 28
Fax: 867-777-4264
e-mail: irc_library@gov.nt.ca
URL: www.nwtresearch.com
National Library Symbol: NWII
Consortia Membership: NWT Libraries
Hours: M-F 8:30-12:00, 1:00-5:00
Acquisitions Budget: 0-$9,999
For Print: 0-$9,999
For Electronic: 0-$9,999
Special Collections: Northern rare books, maps, airphotos
Subjects covered: Arctic Research, Arctic Life Sciences, Arctic Earth Sciences, Arctic Social Sciences
Services:
Internet Access
Access to Subscription Databases
Inter-Library Loan (ILL)
Microform Equipment: Reader
Andrew Applejohn, Institute Director
867-777-3298

Yellowknife: Canadian Forces Northern Area Headquarters Library
PO Box 6666, Stn Main
Yellowknife, NT X1A 2R3
867-873-0700 ext: 805
Fax: 867-873-0708
e-mail: labonte.jk@forces.gc.ca
National Library Symbol: NWYND
Founded in: 1972
Hours: M-F 9:00-12:00, 1:00-4:00 by appointment only
Acquisitions Budget: $25,000 - $49,999
Subjects covered: Physical Sciences, Engineering, Technology, Northern Culture & History, Communications - subjects as applicable to military operations in the Canadian North
Services:
Internet Access
Personnel: *Summary:* 1 Total; 1 Technical(s)
Kevin Rowe, Librarian

Yellowknife: ENR-ITI Shared Services Departmental Library Library
#600, 5102 - 50th Ave.
Yellowknife, NT X1A 3S8
867-920-8606
Fax: 867-873-0293
e-mail: enriti_library@gov.nt.ca
URL: www.enr.gov.nt.ca/_live/pages/wpPages/ENR_library.aspx
207.67.203.75/G92011/OPAC/Index.aspx
National Library Symbol: NWYRR
Founded in: 1980
Hours: M-F 8:30-12:00, 1:00-5:00 by appointment only
Acquisitions Budget: $25,000 - $49,999
Note: Serves staff of the Department of Environment & Natural Resources and the Department of Industry, Tourism & Investment
Subjects covered: Environment, Natural Resources, Wildlife, Minerals, Parks, Tourism, Oil & Gas, Economic Development
Services:
Inter-Library Loan (ILL)
Microform Equipment: Reader
Personnel: *Summary:* 2 Total; 1 Professional(s); 1 Technical(s); 1 Other employees
Ainsley Zock, Manager, Information Services
ainsley_zock@gov.nt.ca
867-920-8606
Aingeal Stone, Information Coordinator
aingeal_stone@gov.nt.ca
867-920-8606

Yellowknife: Northwest Territories Legislative Assembly Legislative Library of the Northwest Territories
Legislative Assembly Bldg.
Yellowknife, NT X1A 2L9
Mailing Address: PO Box 1320
Yellowknife, NT X1A 2L9
867-669-2203
Fax: 867-873-0207
e-mail: leglib@gov.nt.ca
URL:
www.assembly.gov.nt.ca/_live/pages/wpPages/Library.aspx
National Library Symbol: NWYGI
Hours: M-F 8:30-5:00
Acquisitions Budget: $25,000 - $49,999
Special Collections: NWT Government Documents
Subjects covered: Native Peoples & Northern Affairs, Natural Resources, Environment, Politics, Public Administration
Services:
Internet Access
Access to Subscription Databases
Inter-Library Loan (ILL)
Microform Equipment: Reader
Personnel: *Summary:* 3 Total; 2 Professional(s); 1 Technical(s)
Vera Raschke, Legislative Librarian
867-669-2203

Yellowknife: Northwest Territories Public Works & Services Records Management
Stuart M. Hodgson Building, Box 1320
Yellowknife, NT X1A 2L9
Mailing Address: PO Box 1320, Stuart M. Hodgson Building
Yellowknife, NT X1A 2L9
867-920-6451
Fax: 867-873-0226
URL: www.pws.gov.nt.ca
National Library Symbol: NWYPW
Founded in: 1985
Subjects covered: Petroleum Products; Water Systems; Community Fuel Provision
Services:
Internet Access
Steve Hagerman, Records Manager
Steve_Hagerman@gov.nt.ca
867-873-7446
Tracey Belton, Senior Records Analyst
Tracey_Belton@gov.nt.ca
867-920-3009
Clara Allen, Petroleum Products & Records Administrator
Clara_Allen@gov.nt.ca
867-777-7216

Yellowknife: Prairie & Northern Region - Yellowknife Library - Environment Canada
5019 - 52 St., 4th Fl.
Yellowknife, NT X1A 2P7
867-669-4717
Fax: 867-873-8185
e-mail: librarybiblio.yellowknife@ec.gc.ca
National Library Symbol: NWYECW
Hours: M-F 8:30-3:00 by appointment only
Acquisitions Budget: 0-$9,999
Subjects covered: Conservation, Natural Resources, Environmental Impact Analysis, Land Use, Pollution, Meteorology, Climatology, Hydrology, Water Management & Resources, Environmental Protection, Air Quality, Severe Weather & Environmental Emergencies
Services:
Inter-Library Loan (ILL)
Microform Equipment: Reader
Personnel: *Summary:* 1 Total; 1 Professional(s)

Yellowknife: Workers' Compensation Board Northwest Territories Kathi Mackay Memorial Library
5022 - 49th St., 5th Fl.
Yellowknife, NT X1A 2R3
Mailing Address: PO Box 8888
Yellowknife, NT X1A 2R3
867-920-3888
Fax: 867-873-4596
800-661-0792
URL:
www.wscc.nt.ca/YourWSCC/Resources/Pages/Library.aspx
Founded in: 1986
Hours: M-F 8:30-5:00
Acquisitions Budget: $25,000 - $49,999
Services:
Inter-Library Loan (ILL)
Personnel: *Summary:* 2 Total; 1 Professional(s); 1 Other employees

Nova Scotia

Sydney: Beaton Institute
1250 Grand Lake Rd.
Sydney, NS B1P 6L2
Mailing Address: PO Box 5300
Sydney, NS B1P 6L2
902-563-1329
Fax: 902-562-8899

e-mail: beaton@cbu.ca
URL: www.cbu.ca/beaton
Founded in: 1954
Hours: Tu, Th, F 9:00-4:00; W 9:00-7:00; Sa 9:00-12:00 once/month
Acquisitions Budget: $10,000 - $24,999
For Print: 0-$9,999
For Electronic: 0-$9,999
Special Collections: Manuscripts, maps, tapes, photos, books, newspapers & pamphlets pertaining to culture & history of Cape Breton Island
Subjects covered: History, Culture, Maps, Genealogy
Services:
Internet Access
Fee Based Research
Microform Equipment: Reader
Personnel: *Summary:* 5 Total; 2 Professional(s); 3 Technical(s)
Jane Arnold, Archivist
jane_arnold@cbu.ca
902-563-1690
Catherine Arseneau, Manager
catherine_arseneau@cbu.ca
902-563-1326
Gerardette Brown, Secretary
gerardette_brown@cbu.ca
902-563-1327

Antigonish: Coady International Institute Marie Michael Library

St. Francis-Xavier University
Antigonish, NS B2G 2W5
Mailing Address: PO Box 5000
Antigonish, NS B2G 2W5
902-867-3964
Fax: 902-867-3907
e-mail: cirving@stfx.ca
URL: www.coady.stfx.ca/library
National Library Symbol: NSASF
Consortia Membership: Novanet
Founded in: 1959
Hours: M-F 9:00-5:00
Acquisitions Budget: $10,000 - $24,999
For Print: $10,000 - $24,999
For Electronic: 0-$9,999
Special Collections: Antigonish Movement, St Francis Xavier University Extension
Subjects covered: Cooperatives, International Development, Adult Education, Women in Development, Environment, Peacebuilding, Advocacy, Health
Services:
Remote Access
Internet Access
Inter-Library Loan (ILL)
Personnel: *Summary:* 2 Total; 1 Professional(s); 1 Technical(s);
Catherine Irving, Librarian

Antigonish: St Francis-Xavier University Angus L. Macdonald Library

PO Box 5000
Antigonish, NS B2G 2W5
902-867-2228
Fax: 902-867-5153
e-mail: illoan@stfx.ca
circdesk@stfx.ca
URL: library.stfx.ca
National Library Symbol: NSAS
Consortia Membership: Canadian Research Knowledge Network (CRKN); Council of Atlantic University Libraries (CAUL); Novanet; Atlantic Health Knowledge Partnership (AHKP)
Founded in: 1853
Hours: M-Su
Acquisitions Budget: $50,000 - $99,999
Note: Member of CAUL, Council of Atlantic University Librarians, Atlantic Provinces Library Association
Special Collections: Celtic collections
Services:
Inter-Library Loan (ILL)
Microform Equipment: Computer; Reader
Personnel: *Summary:* 39 Total; 9 Professional(s); 23 Technical(s); 7 Other employees
Lynne Murphy, University Librarian
lmurphy@stfx.ca
902-867-2267
Elaine MacLean, Collection Librarian
emaclean@stfx.ca
902-867-3670
Glenna Quinn, Reference & Research Services Librarian
gquinn@stfx.ca
902-867-3866
Susan Cameron, Special Collections Librarian
scameron@stfx.ca
902-867-5328
Rita Campbell, Special Projects Librarian
rcampbel@stfx.ca
902-867-5218

Church Point: Université Sainte-Anne Bibliothèque Louis-R.-Comeau

1695, rte 1
Church Point, NS B0W 1M0
Adresse postale: CP 40
Church Point, NS B0W 1M0
902-769-2114
Téléc: 902-769-2930
Couriel: acquisitions@usainteanne.ca
comptoir@usainteanne.ca
pebill@usainteanne.ca
URL: www.usainteanne.ca/bibliotheque
Sigle: NSCS
Membre d'un consortium: Canadian Research Knowledge Network (CRKN); Council of Atlantic University Libraries (CAUL); Novanet
Fondée en: 1890
Heures: D'automne-Hiver: L-J 9h-22h; V 9h-16h30, 18h-21h; S 13h-16h30; D 13h-16h30, 18h-22h30; Printemps L-J 9h-16h30, 18h-21h; V 9h-16h30, Sa-V Fermé
Budget d'acquisitions: $100,000 - $249,999
Matériel imprimé: $50,000 - $99,999
Matériel électronique: $25,000 - $49,999
Population desservie: 0
Collections spécialisées: Collection Centre acadien
Services:
Accèss distance aux bases de donn
Accès public à l'internet
Réseau en ligne
Prêts entre bibliothèques(PEB)
Lecteur/reproduction de microformes: Ordinateur; Lecteurs
Personnel: *Sommaire:* 5 Total; 2 Professionnel(s); 3 Autre(s) employé(s)
Pamela Maher, Directrice
pamela.maher@usainteanne.ca
902-769-2114 ext. 7161
Cécile Pothier-Comeau, Bibliothécaire
cecile.pothiercomeau@usaintanne.ca
902-769-2114 ext. 7162
Corinne Arsenault, PEB
corinne.arsenault@usainteanne.ca
902-769-2114 ext. 7163
Janice Comeau, Comptoir de prêt
janice.comeau@usainteanne.ca
902-769-2114 ext. 7158
Réjeanne LeBlanc-Comeau, Acquisitions
rejeanne.leblanccomeau@usainteanne.ca
902-769-2114 ext. 7170

Dartmouth: Akerley Campus Library

21 Woodlawn Rd.
Dartmouth, NS B2W 2R7
902-491-4968
Fax: 902-491-2012
e-mail: library.akerley@nscc.ca
URL: www.library.nscc.ca
National Library Symbol: NSDRV
Consortia Membership: Novanet
Founded in: 1989
Hours: M-F 8:00-4:00
Personnel: *Summary:* 3 Total; 1 Professional(s); 2 Technical(s)
Ann Roman, Librarian
ann.roman@nscc.ca

Dartmouth: Atlantic Region Library

Queen Square, 45 Alderney Dr., 5th Fl.
Dartmouth, NS B2Y 2N6
902-426-7232
Fax: 902-426-6143
e-mail: librarybiblio.dartmouth@ec.gc.ca
National Library Symbol: NSDE
Founded in: 1981
Hours: M-F 7:00-3:30 by appointment only
Acquisitions Budget: $50,000 - $99,999
Subjects covered: Environment
Services:
Inter-Library Loan (ILL)
Microform Equipment: Reader
Personnel: *Summary:* 1 Professional(s); 1 Technical(s)
Jean Sealy, Librarian
jean.sealy@ec.gc.ca

Dartmouth: Atlantic Regional Library

#1625, 1505 Barrington St.
Dartmouth, NS B3J 3Y6
902-426-6694
Fax: 902-426-6676
National Library Symbol: NSHHW
Hours: M-F 8:00-4:00
Special Collections: Food Science
Subjects covered: Health Sciences

Dartmouth: Bedford Institute of Oceanography / Institut océanographique de Bedford Library

Holland Bldg.
1 Challenger Dr., 4th Fl.
Dartmouth, NS B2Y 4A2
Mailing Address: PO Box 1006
Dartmouth, NS B2Y 4A2
902-426-6266
Fax: 902-496-1544
e-mail: Dartmouth.Library-Bibliotheque@dfo-mpo.gc.ca
National Library Symbol: NSDB
Founded in: 1962
Hours: M-F 8:00-4:30
Acquisitions Budget: $250,000 - $499,999
Subjects covered: Environmental Assessment; Oceanography; Marine Sciences
Services:
Internet Access
Inter-Library Loan (ILL)
Microform Equipment: Computer; Reader
Personnel: *Summary:* 10 Total; 4 Professional(s); 6 Technical(s)
Lori Collins, Head of Information Services
Marilynn J. Rudi, Archivist/Librarian
Marilynn.Rudi@dfo-mpo.gc.ca

Dartmouth: Clean Nova Scotia Resource Centre

126 Portland St.
Dartmouth, NS B2Y 1H8
902-420-3474
Fax: 902-424-5334
888-380-5008
e-mail: cns@clean.ns.ca
URL: www.clean.ns.ca
Founded in: 1987
Special Collections: Information on topics including climate change & energy, solid waste, health & the environment & water
Subjects covered: Magazines, journals & publications on environmental topics including litter, marine debris, recycling & waste reduction, climate change

---

Dartmouth: Defence R & D Canada - Atlantic Library

9 Grove St.
Dartmouth, NS B2Y 3Z7
Mailing Address: PO Box 1012
Dartmouth, NS B2Y 3Z7
902-426-3100 ext: 135
Fax: 902-426-9654
e-mail: iris.ouellette@drdc-rddc.gc.ca
atl.library@drdc-rddc.gc.ca
National Library Symbol: NSHN
No public access
Hours: M-F 8:00-4:00
Acquisitions Budget: $100,000 - $249,999
For Print: $25,000 - $49,999
For Electronic: $50,000 - $99,999
Subjects covered: Engineering, Physical Sciences, Acoustics
Services:
Inter-Library Loan (ILL)
Microform Equipment: Reader
Personnel: *Summary:* 2 Total; 1 Technical(s); 1 Other employees

Iris Ouellett, Library Manager
iris.ouellette@drdc-rddc.gc.ca
902-426-3100 ext. 135
Mary Gillis, Circulation Clerk
mary.gillis@drdc-rddc.gc.ca
902-426-3100 ext. 108

Halifax: Capital Health
Health Sciences Library, Halifax Infirmary Site
#2201, 1796 Summer St.
Halifax, NS B3H 3A6
Mailing Address: 1796 Summer St.
Halifax, NS B3H 3A6
902-473-4287
Fax: 902-473-7168
e-mail: cdhalib@cdha.nshealth.ca
URL: www.cdha.nshealth.ca
National Library Symbol: NSHQ
Consortia Membership: Atlantic Health Knowledge Partnership (AHKP)
Founded in: 1996
Hours: M-F 8:30-4:30
Acquisitions Budget: $500,000 - $999,999
For Print: $50,000 - $99,999
For Electronic: $250,000 - $499,999
Subjects covered: Health Sciences
Services:
Remote Access
Internet Access
Inter-Library Loan (ILL)
Personnel: *Summary:* 5 Total; 1 Professional(s); 3 Technical(s); 1 Other employees; 1 Volunteer(s)
Penny Logan, Manager, Library Services
penny.logan@cdha.nshealth.ca
902-473-4383

Halifax: Dalhousie University Libraries
Killam Memorial Library
6225 University Ave.
Halifax, NS B3H 4R2
Mailing Address: PO Box 15000
Halifax, NS B3H 4R2
902-494-3601
Fax: 902-494-2062
Other contact info: Reference: 902-494-3611
URL: libraries.dal.ca
Social Media: www.youtube.com/user/DalhousieLibraries
www.facebook.com/36011919042
twitter.com/DalLibraries
National Library Symbol: NSHD
Consortia Membership: Canadian Research Knowledge Network (CRKN); Council of Atlantic University Libraries (CAUL); Novanet; Atlantic Health Knowledge Partnership (AHKP)
Founded in: 1968
Hours: M-F 8:00am-12:00am; Sa 10:00-6:00; Su 10:00am-12:00am
Acquisitions Budget: $1,000,000 plus
For Print: $500,000 - $999,999
For Electronic: $1,000,000 plus
Note: The library is an affiliate member of the Council of Prairie and Pacific University Libraries (COPPUL).
Special Collections: Kipling Collection, Morse Collection, J.J. Stewart Collection, Canadian Small Press Collection, Bacon Collection, Cockerell Collection, Canadiana
Subjects covered: Science, Social Sciences & Humanities
Services:
Internet Access
Inter-Library Loan (ILL)
Microform Equipment: Computer; Reader
Personnel: *Summary:* 75 Total; 20 Professional(s); 55 Technical(s);
Donna Bourne-Tyson, University Librarian
donna.bourne-tyson@dal.ca
902-494-3601
Sharon Longard, Reference
902-494-1101
Geoffrey Brown, Technical Services
902-494-2826

Halifax: Halifax Office
Knowledge & Research Program
Ralston Bldg.
Halifax, NS B3J 2T5
Hours: M-F 8:00-4:00 by appointment only
Special Collections: Taxation, Customs, Excise, Law Reports & Statutes
Subjects covered: Taxation, Law, Accounting, Government, Management
Services:
Access to Subscription Databases
Inter-Library Loan (ILL)
Fee Based Research
Microform Equipment: Reader
Hilary Carr, Assistant Director, Knowledge & Research Program
450-926-7509
Craig Dutton, Library Technician
902-426-1983

Halifax: Institute of Technology Campus
Library
5685 Leeds St.
Halifax, NS B3K 2T3
902-491-4694
Fax: 902-491-2015
e-mail: library.institute@nscc.ca
URL: www.library.nscc.ca
National Library Symbol: NSHTI
Consortia Membership: Novanet
Founded in: 1972
Hours: M-F 8:00-4:00
Personnel: *Summary:* 2 Total; 1 Professional(s); 1 Technical(s)
Nola Brennan, Librarian
nola.brennan@nscc.ca

Halifax: Legal Information Society of Nova Scotia
5523B Young St.
Halifax, NS B3K 1Z7
902-454-2198
Fax: 902-455-3105
800-665-9779
e-mail: lisns@legalinfo.org
URL: www.legalinfo.org
No public access
Founded in: 1982
Acquisitions Budget: 0-$9,999
For Print: 0-$9,999
Subjects covered: Law
Maria Franks, Executive Director
Wendy Turner, Manager, Legal Information Services

Halifax: Nova Scotia Community College
Library Services - Administration
5685 Leeds St.
Halifax, NS B3K 2T3
Mailing Address: PO Box 1153
Halifax, NS B3K 2T3
902-491-6772
Fax: 902-491-2178
e-mail: andrea.stewart@nscc.ca
URL: www.library.nscc.ca
Consortia Membership: Council of Atlantic University Libraries (CAUL); Novanet
Acquisitions Budget: $250,000 - $499,999
Personnel: *Summary:* 5 Total; 3 Professional(s); 2 Technical(s)
Andrea Stewart, Director, Library Services
andrea.stewart@nscc.ca
902-491-6772
Debbie Costelo, Public Services Librarian
debbie.costelo@nscc.ca
902-491-1031
Denise Parrott, Technical Services Librarian
denise.parrott@nscc.ca
902-893-5306

Halifax: Nova Scotia Dept. of Natural Resources
Library
1701 Hollis, 3rd Fl.
Halifax, NS B3J 2T9
Mailing Address: PO Box 698
Halifax, NS B3J 2T9
902-424-8633
Fax: 902-424-7735
e-mail: nsdnrlib@gov.ns.ca
lenfestl@gov.ns.ca
URL: www.gov.ns.ca/natr/library
National Library Symbol: NSHDOM
Founded in: 1962
Hours: M-F 8:30-4:00
Acquisitions Budget: 0-$9,999
For Print: 0-$9,999
For Electronic: 0-$9,999
Special Collections: Nova Scotia Department of Mines Reports, Geological Survey of Canada Publications, Historical Aerial Photography (1931-1955), Historical Maps (A.F. Church), Crown Land Grants
Subjects covered: Mineral Resources, Mines, Mineral Development, Forestry, Parks & Recreation, Wildlife, GIS, Integrated Resource Management, Land Use
Services:
Remote Access
Internet Access
Access to Subscription Databases
Inter-Library Loan (ILL)
Online catalogue with other NS government libraries on Multilis; Web version available via web page
Microform Equipment: Computer; Reader
Personnel: *Summary:* 2 Total; 1 Professional(s); 1 Technical(s);
Tracy Lenfesty, Head librarian
lenfestl@gov.ns.ca
902-424-1290
Janelle Brenton, Library Staff
brentonjl@gov.ns.ca

Halifax: Nova Scotia Dept. of Transportation & Infrastructure Renewal
Library
1672 Granville St.
Halifax, NS B3J 2N2
Mailing Address: PO Box 186
Halifax, NS B3J 2N2
902-424-0532
Fax: 902-424-0532
e-mail: tpwpaff@gov.ns.ca
URL: www.gov.ns.ca/tran
Hours: Open to public by appointment only by appointment only
Acquisitions Budget: $25,000 - $49,999
Subjects covered: Transportation, Engineering, Public Works
Services:
Inter-Library Loan (ILL)
Personnel: *Summary:* 1 Total; 1 Professional(s)

Halifax: Nova Scotia Environment & Labour
Library
5151 Terminal Rd., 5th Fl.
Halifax, NS B3J 2T8
Mailing Address: PO Box 697
Halifax, NS B3J 2T8
902-424-8474
Fax: 902-424-6925
e-mail: enlalibr@gov.ns.ca
National Library Symbol: NSDEL
Founded in: 1977
Hours: M-F 2:00-4:00 by appointment only
Acquisitions Budget: $50,000 - $99,999
Note: Participate in Provincial Interdepartmental
Special Collections: Occupational Health & Safety Video Collection; Uranium Exploration & Mining Collection; Environmental Impact & Assessment Collection; Nova Scotia Reports; Collective Agreements; Grievance Arbitrations; Workers' Compensation Appeals Tribunal/Workers' Compensation Board-Internal Appeals Decisions; Labour Standards Tribunal Decisions; Labour Relations Board/Construction Industry Panel Decisions; Industry Standards (ie. CSA, ASME, ANSI)
Subjects covered: Environment, Pollution Prevention, Air & Water Pollution, Solid Waste Management, Labour Law, Occupational Health & Safety
Services:
Internet Access
Access to Subscription Databases
Inter-Library Loan (ILL)
Fee Based Research
Microform Equipment: Computer; Reader
Personnel: *Summary:* 3 Total; 1 Professional(s); 1 Technical(s)
Natalie MacPherson, Information Resources Manager
enlalibr@gov.ns.ca
902-424-8474
Joanne Babin, Library Assistant
enlalibr@gov.ns.ca

Halifax: NRC Information Centre - Halifax
Institute for Marine Biosciences
1411 Oxford St.
Halifax, NS B3H 3Z1
902-426-8250
Fax: 902-426-4900
e-mail: nic.halifax@nrc-cnrc.gc.ca

Bernadette.Kennedy@nrc.gc.ca
URL: cisti-icist.nrc-cnrc.gc.ca
Hours: M-F 8:30-5:00
Acquisitions Budget: $50,000 - $99,999
Note: Fee for services
Subjects covered: Aquaculture Production/Aquaculture Nutrition; Natural Toxins; Shellfish; Aquatic Animal Health; Mass Spectrometry Techologies; Natural Products; Proteomics; Biochemistry & Functional Genomics
Services:
Internet Access
Access to Subscription Databases
Inter-Library Loan (ILL)
Personnel: *Summary:* 2 Total; 1 Professional(s); 1 Technical(s)
Donna Curtis, Head
Anna Backman, Client Services Officer

Halifax: Saint Mary's University Patrick Power Library

923 Robie St.
Halifax, NS B3H 3C3
902-420-5534
Fax: 902-420-5561
e-mail: research@smu.ca
ill@smu.ca
access@smu.ca
URL: www.smu.ca/administration/library
National Library Symbol: NSHS
Consortia Membership: Canadian Research Knowledge Network (CRKN); Council of Atlantic University Libraries (CAUL); Novanet
Founded in: 1802
Hours: M-F 8:15am-11:00pm; Sa 11:00-2:00; Su 1:00-11:00
Acquisitions Budget: $500,000 - $999,999
Special Collections: Irish Studies
Subjects covered: Education, Business, Arts, Science
Services:
Remote Access
Internet Access
Inter-Library Loan (ILL)
Microform Equipment: Computer; Reader
Personnel: *Summary:* 45 Total; 9 Professional(s); 1 Technical(s); 35 Other employees
Marie DeYoung, University Librarian
marie.deyoung@smu.ca
902-420-5532
Douglas Vaisey, Librarian, Reference & Research
douglas.vaisey@smu.ca
902-420-5540
Peter Webster, Associate University Librarian
peter.webster@smu.ca
902-420-5507
Joyce Thomson, Digital Librarian
joyce.thomson@smu.ca
902-420-5549
Heather Sanderson, Librarian, Information Literacy
heather.sanderson@smu.ca
902-420-5541

Halifax: Sexton Design & Technology Library

1360 Barrington St.
Halifax, NS B3H 4R2
Mailing Address: PO Box 15000
Halifax, NS B3H 4R2
902-494-3285
Fax: 902-494-6089
Other contact info: Reference: 902-494-3965
URL: sexton.library.dal.ca
National Library Symbol: NSHT
Consortia Membership: Novanet
Hours: M-Th 8:00am-12:00am; F 8:00am-9:00pm; Sa 9:00am-9:00pm; Su 10:00am-12:00am
Note: Part of Novanet.
Special Collections: Electronic Books; Journals, Images; Patents; Standards; Technical Reports; Theses
Subjects covered: Engineering (civil, electrical, computer, mathematical, industrial, biological, environmental, chemical, oil & gas, mechanical, materials, mining); Technology; Planning; Architecture
Services:
Internet Access
Inter-Library Loan (ILL)
Fee Based Research
Document delivery, Electronic reading room, Research service & instruction
Helen Powell, Design & Technology Librarian
helen.powell@dal.ca
902-494-3285
Sarah Jane Dooley, Reference & Liaison Librarian/Promotion & Outreach Coordinator
902-494-3428
Allison Fulford, Assistant Design & Technology Librarian
902-494-3255

Halifax: W.K. Kellogg Health Sciences Library

Sir Charles Tupper Bldg., Dalhousie University
5850 College St.
Halifax, NS B3H 4R2
Mailing Address: PO Box 15000
Halifax, NS B3H 4R2
902-494-2458
Fax: 902-494-3798
Other contact info: Reference: 902-494-2482; Circulation: 902-494-2479
National Library Symbol: NSHDM
Consortia Membership: Novanet
Founded in: 1879
Hours: M-Th 7:30-11:00; F 7:30-7:00; Sa 10:00-6:00; Su 11:00-11:00. Summer: M-F 8:00-5:00
Acquisitions Budget: $100,000 - $249,999
Special Collections: Dr Charles Cogswell's Medical Library, 1864
Subjects covered: Medicine, Dentistry, Health Services Administration, Human Communication Disorders, Nursing, Occupational Therapy, Pharmacy, Physiotherapy, Kinesiology
Services:
Remote Access
Internet Access
Access to Subscription Databases
Inter-Library Loan (ILL)
Personnel: *Summary:* 24 Total; 6 Professional(s); 18 Technical(s)
Patrick Ellis, Health Sciences Librarian
902-494-1669
Judith Coughlan-Lambly, Technical Services Librarian
902-494-3741
Nadine Day-Boutilier, Circulation/Document Delivery/Reference Librarian
902-494-2479
Ann Barrett, Administration
902-494-1649

Kentville: Canadian Agriculture Library - Kentville / Bibliothèque canadienne de l'agriculture - Kentville

32 Main St.
Kentville, NS B4N 1J5
902-679-5508
Fax: 902-679-2311
National Library Symbol: NSKR
Founded in: 1952
Hours: M-F
Acquisitions Budget: $50,000 - $99,999
Subjects covered: Agriculture, Food
Services:
Inter-Library Loan (ILL)
Microform Equipment: Reader
Personnel: *Summary:* 2 Total; 1 Professional(s); 1 Technical(s)
Seana Collins, Head Librarian
seana.collins@agr.gc.ca

Kentville: Kingstec Campus Library

236 Belcher St.
Kentville, NS B4N 0A6
902-679-7380
Fax: 902-679-5187
e-mail: library.kinstec@nscc.ca
URL: www.library.nscc.ca
National Library Symbol: NSKKR
Consortia Membership: Novanet
Founded in: 1965
Hours: M-F 8:00-5:00
Personnel: *Summary:* 2 Total; 1 Professional(s); 1 Technical(s)
Lana Kamennof-Sine, Librarian
lana.kamennof-sine@nscc.ca

Port Hawkesbury: Strait Area Campus Library

226 Reeves St.
Port Hawkesbury, NS B9A 2A2
902-625-4364
Fax: 902-625-0193
e-mail: library.straitarea@nscc.ca
URL: www.library.nscc.ca
National Library Symbol: NSPHS
Consortia Membership: Novanet
Hours: M-F 8:00-4:00
Personnel: *Summary:* 2 Total; 1 Professional(s); 1 Technical(s)
Lana MacLean, Librarian
lana.maclean@nscc.ca

Sydney: Cape Breton District Health Authority Health Sciences Library

1482 George St.
Sydney, NS B1P 1P3
902-567-8000
Fax: 902-567-7878
URL: www.cbdha.nshealth.ca
National Library Symbol: NSSCBH
Consortia Membership: Atlantic Health Knowledge Partnership (AHKP)
Hours: M-F 8:30-4:30 by appointment only
Acquisitions Budget: For Print: $25,000 - $49,999
For Electronic: $10,000 - $24,999
Note: Sydney Community Hospital, Sydney City Hospital & Cape Breton Mental Health Hospital have closed & have merged into one facility, Cape Breton Healthcare Complex
Subjects covered: Medical, Psychiatry, Pediatrics, Obstetrics & Gynecology, Nursing, Allied Health, Oncology, Mental Health
Services:
Remote Access
Inter-Library Loan (ILL)
Personnel: *Summary:* 2 Total; 1 Professional(s); 1 Technical(s); 1 Other employees
Ken Garland, IT & Health Information
garlandk@cbdha.nshealth.ca
902-567-7796

Sydney: Cape Breton University Library

1250 Grand Lake Rd.
Sydney, NS B1P 6L2
Mailing Address: PO Box 5300
Sydney, NS B1P 6L2
902-563-1320
Fax: 902-563-1177
888-959-9995
Other contact info: Reference Desk: 902-563-1387
e-mail: library_infoservices@cbu.ca
URL: www.cbu.ca/library
National Library Symbol: NSSX
Consortia Membership: Canadian Research Knowledge Network (CRKN); Council of Atlantic University Libraries (CAUL); Novanet; Atlantic Health Knowledge Partnership (AHKP)
Founded in: 1951
Hours: M-Th 8:30-10:00; F 8:30-5:00; Sa 11:00-4:00; Su 12:00-9:00
Acquisitions Budget: $50,000 - $99,999
For Print: $50,000 - $99,999
For Electronic: $50,000 - $99,999
Note: Hours may vary depending upon time of year.
Special Collections: National Film Board Collection; Audio Collection; Bras d'or Institute Resource Center; Dr. Thomas Joseph Khattar Collection; Scottish Collection; Centre for International Studies
Services:
Remote Access
Internet Access
Inter-Library Loan (ILL)
Services include library instruction, reserve service & information & alerting services for faculty
Microform Equipment: Computer; Reader
Personnel: *Summary:* 17 Total; 6 Professional(s); 11 Technical(s)
Robert Campbell, Director, Library Services
robert_campbell@cbu.ca
Debbie MacInnis, Head of Circulation
debbie_macinnis@cbu.ca
902-563-1674
Cathy Chisholm, Information Services Librarian
cathy_chisholm@cbu.ca
902-563-1993
Mary Dobson, Technical Services Librarian
mary_dobson@cbu.ca
902-563-1231

Laura Syms, Business & Data Services Librarian
laura_syms@cbu.ca
902-563-1994
Nick Sobol, Library Technician, Serials
nick_sobol@cbu.ca
902-563-1320

Truro: Nova Scotia Agricultural College MacRae Library

135 College Rd.
Truro, NS B2N 5E3
Mailing Address: PO Box 550
Truro, NS B2N 5E3
902-893-6669
Fax: 902-895-0934
e-mail: library@nsac.ca
URL: www.nsac.ca/library
National Library Symbol: NSTA
Consortia Membership: Canadian Research Knowledge Network (CRKN); Novanet
Founded in: 1905
Hours: Academic Term: M-Th 8:30am-10:30pm; F 8:30-5:00; Sa 10:00-5:00; Su 10:00am-10:30pm; Summer: M-F 8:30-4:30
Acquisitions Budget: $250,000 - $499,999
For Print: $100,000 - $249,999
For Electronic: $100,000 - $249,999
Special Collections: Agricola Collection
Subjects covered: Agriculture & Food, Agricultural Chemistry, Environmental Sciences, Agricultural Engineering, Aquaculture, Plant & Animal Sciences
Services:
Remote Access
Internet Access
Access to Subscription Databases
Inter-Library Loan (ILL)
Document delivery, Information Commons (42 PCs)
Microform Equipment: Reader
Personnel: *Summary:* 6 Total; 1 Professional(s); 2 Technical(s); 3 Other employees
Bonnie R. Waddell, Chief Librarian
902-893-6670
Janelle Brenton, Cataloguer
jbrenton@nsac.ca
902-893-4593
Verna Mingo, Head, Acquisitions/Serials
vmingo@nsac.ca
902-893-4581
Sherree Miller, Circulation Assistant
smiller@nsac.ca
902-893-4576
Cindy Stevens, Tech Services Assistant
cstevens@nsac.ca
902-893-4583

Truro: Truro Campus Library

36 Arthur St.
Truro, NS B2N 1X5
902-893-5326
Fax: 902-895-5322
e-mail: library.truro@nscc.ca
URL: www.library.nscc.ca
National Library Symbol: NSTT
Consortia Membership: Novanet
Hours: M-F 8:00-4:30
Personnel: *Summary:* 2 Total; 1 Professional(s); 1 Technical(s)
Charmaine Borden, Librarian
charmaine.borden@nscc.ca

Wolfville: Acadia University Vaughan Memorial Library

50 Acadia St.
Wolfville, NS B4P 2R6
Mailing Address: PO Box 4
Wolfville, NS B4P 2R6
902-585-1249
Fax: 902-585-1748
e-mail: libweb@acadiau.ca
ref-desk@acadiau.ca
access-circ@acadiau.ca
URL: library.acadiau.ca
National Library Symbol: NSWA
Consortia Membership: Canadian Research Knowledge Network (CRKN); Council of Atlantic University Libraries (CAUL)
Founded in: 1838
Hours: M-Su
Special Collections: George Nowlan Collection; J.D. Logan Collection; Marshall Saunders Collection; Zeman Collection; Kirkconnell Collection; William Inglis Morse Collection; Eric R. Dennis Collection of Canadiana; Atlantic Baptist Historical Collection; Hannah Maria Norris Armstrong Fonds
Subjects covered: Liberal Arts, Humanities, Pure & Applied Sciences, Theology
Services:
Internet Access
Inter-Library Loan (ILL)
Microform Equipment: Reader
Personnel: *Summary:* 37 Total; 8 Professional(s); 29 Other employees
Sara Lochhead, University Librarian
sara.lochhead@acadiau.ca
902-585-1510
Ann Hennigar, Circulation Librarian
902-585-1115
Melissa Kendrick, Acquisitions
melissa.kendrick@acadiau.ca
902-585-1634

Yarmouth: South West Health Information Resources & Library Services

60 Vancouver St.
Yarmouth, NS B5A 2P5
902-742-3541
Fax: 902-742-0369
URL: www.swndha.nshealth.ca
National Library Symbol: NSYR
Consortia Membership: Atlantic Health Knowledge Partnership (AHKP)
Founded in: 1998
Note: Self services, may borrow with local public library borrowers card through agreement with public library. No service to public, no access to networks but public may borrow with public library card. Provides library services to the following hospitals: Annapolis Community Health Centre (Annapolis); Western Kings Memorial Hospital (Berwick); Digby General Hospital (Digby); Soldiers Memorial Hospital (Middleton); South Shore Regional Hospital (Bridgewater); Queens General Hospital (Liverpool); Fishermens Memorial Hospital (Lunenburg); Roseway Hospital (Shelburne); Valley Regional Hospital (Kentville); Eastern Kings Hospital (Wolfville); Yarmouth Regional Regional Hospital (Yarmouth)
Subjects covered: Health Sciences, Nursing, Medicine
Services:
Internet Access
Document Delivery, information retrieval, user education & acquisition
Personnel: *Summary:* 3 Total; 1 Professional(s); 2 Technical(s); 6 Volunteer(s)

Nunavut

Igloolik: Nunavut Research Institute Igloolik Research Centre Library

PO Box 210
Igloolik, NU X0A 0L0
867-934-2069
URL: www.nri.nu.ca
Founded in: 1975
Hours: by appointment only
Acquisitions Budget: $25,000 - $49,999
Special Collections: Inuit oral history & traditional knowledge
Subjects covered: Northern science & technology

Iqaluit: Nunavut Arctic College Nunatta Campus Library

Tunnganaqsarvik Building, Main Campus, 1st Fl.
Iqaluit, NU X0A 0H0
Mailing Address: PO Box 600
Iqaluit, NU X0A 0H0
867-979-7220
Fax: 867-979-7102
e-mail: librarian@arcticcollege.ca
URL: www.arcticcollege.ca/en/library
National Library Symbol: NUINAC
Founded in: 1988
Hours: M, W, F 8:45-12:00, 1:00-4:45; Tu, Th 8:45-12:00, 1:00-4:45, 6:00-8:00; Sa 1:00-5:00
Note: The College also maintains the Kivalliq Campus Library (Rankin Inlet) & the Kitikkmeot Campus Library (Cambridge Bay), each staffed by a library assistant on a part-time basis throughout the school year
Special Collections: Inuktitut materials collection; Northern resources collection; Rare books; Taylor & Pilot collections on archaeology & Arctic exploration
Subjects covered: Adult Basic Education; Carpentry; Environmental Technology; Language & Culture; Jewellery & Metalwork; Management Studies; Office Administration; Teacher Education; Industrial Trades; Early Childhood Education; Nursing
Services:
Internet Access
Inter-Library Loan (ILL) for a fee
Table of Contents service; Library tours & orientation sessions; Public access computers; Printing; Photocopying
Personnel: *Summary:* 1 Professional(s); 1 Technical(s)

Iqaluit: Nunavut Dept. of Environment Resource Centre

PO Box 1000, Stn 1310
Iqaluit, NU X0A 0H0
867-975-7722
Fax: 867-975-7742
e-mail: nuisd@gov.nu.ca
librarian@nwmb.com
URL: www.nwrcc.ca
National Library Symbol: NUISD
Founded in: 1999
Hours: M-F 8:30-5:00
Acquisitions Budget: 0-$9,999
For Print: 0-$9,999
For Electronic: 0-$9,999
Subjects covered: Wildlife; Environmental Protection; Economic Development; Resource Management
Services:
Inter-Library Loan (ILL)
Carolyn Mallory, Resource Centre Coordinator
867-975-7722

Ontario

Alfred: Collège d'Alfred University of Guelph, Bibliothèque

31, rue St-Paul
Alfred, ON K0B 1A0
Mailing Address: CP 580
Alfred, ON K0B 1A0
613-679-2218
URL: www.alfredc.uoguelph.ca
National Library Symbol: OAMAC
Founded in: 1981
Hours: Sept.-Avr.: L-V 8h30-16h30, 17h30-20h30; Mai-Août: L-V 8h30-12h, 13h-16h.
Acquisitions Budget: $10,000 - $24,999
Note: Bilingue
Subjects covered: Agriculture; Physiologie; Alimentation; Éducation; Développement international; Francophonie; Soins vétérinaires; Environnement
Services:
Remote Access
Internet Access
Inter-Library Loan (ILL)
Fee Based Research
Microform Equipment: Computer; Reader
Personnel: *Summary:* 1 Professional(s); 1 Technical(s)
Lyne Gagne-Lalonde, Library Associate

Atikokan: John B. Ridley Research Library

Quetico Park Information Pavilion, Lower Level, Quetico Park
Atikokan, ON P0T 1C0
807-929-2571 ext: 224
Fax: 807-929-2123
URL: catalogue.legacyforest.ca
National Library Symbol: OATR
Founded in: 1986
Hours: Mid May-mid Sept.: 8:00-4:15. Book appointment during off season
Acquisitions Budget: 0-$9,999
Special Collections: Quetico Park Archives; Oral History; Slide & Photograph Collection
Subjects covered: Natural History; Wilderness; Quetico-Superior Area
Services:
Inter-Library Loan (ILL)
Andrea Allison, Librarian
andrea.allison@mnr.gov.on.ca
807-929-2571 ext. 224

Barrie: Georgian College of Applied Arts & Technology
Library Commons
1 Georgian Dr.
Barrie, ON L4M 3X9
705-722-5139
Fax: 705-722-1508
877-890-8477
e-mail: library@georgiancollege.ca
URL: library.georgianc.on.ca
National Library Symbol: OBAGC
Consortia Membership: Ontario Colleges Library Service
Founded in: 1967
Hours: M-Th 7:45am-11:00pm; F 7:45-5:00; Sa 10:00-5:00; Su 1:00-8:00
Acquisitions Budget: $50,000 - $99,999
For Electronic: $50,000 - $99,999
Special Collections: Culture, Economics, Health Sciences, Engineering, Technology, Hospitality & Tourism
Subjects covered: Arts, Humanities, Culture, Economics, Health Sciences, Engineering, Technology, Hospitality & Tourism
Services:
Remote Access
Internet Access
Access to Subscription Databases
Inter-Library Loan (ILL)
Microform Equipment: Computer; Reader
Personnel: *Summary:* 25 Total; 8 Professional(s); 3 Technical(s); 14 Other employees
Katherine Wallis, Director, Learning Resource Centres
kwallis@georgianc.on.ca
705-728-1968 ext. 1684
Pat Whyte, Operations Manager
pat.whyte@georgiancollege.ca
705-728-1968 ext. 1199
Karen Halliday, Health Sciences and Community Studies Librarian
khalliday@georgianc.on.ca
705-728-1968 ext. 1753
Joanne Fowlie, Business and Management Studies Librarian
jfowlie@georgianc.on.ca
705-728-1968 ext. 1305
Kimberly Thomas, Science, Technology and Social Science Librarian
kthomas@georgianc.on.ca
705-728-1968 ext. 1847
Carol McNabb, Head, Technical Services
cmcnabb@georgianc.on.ca
708-728-1968 ext. 1679

Belleville: Loyalist College of Applied Arts & Technology
The Parrott Centre
376 Wallbridge-Loyalist Rd.
Belleville, ON K8N 5B9
Mailing Address: PO Box 4200
Belleville, ON K8N 5B9
613-969-1913 ext: 2249
Fax: 613-969-5183
888-569-2547
e-mail: library@loyalistc.on.ca
URL: www.loyalistlibrary.com
National Library Symbol: OBEL
Consortia Membership: Ontario Colleges Library Service
Founded in: 1968
Hours: M-Th 8:00am-9:00pm; F 8:00-4:30; Sa 9:00-4:00; Su 12:00-4:00. Summer: M-Th 8:00-4:30; F 8:00-12:00
Acquisitions Budget: $50,000 - $99,999
For Print: $50,000 - $99,999
For Electronic: $25,000 - $49,999
Note: Remote access to online databases for staff & students only
Special Collections: Lorraine Monk Photography Collection; John Peterson Photography Collection
Subjects covered: Law & Security, Nursing, Media, Human Studies, Business, Technology
Services:
Remote Access
Internet Access
Access to Subscription Databases
Inter-Library Loan (ILL)
Microform Equipment: Computer; Reader
Personnel: *Summary:* 10 Total; 1 Professional(s); 7 Technical(s); 2 Other employees
Ross Danaher, Director, Educational Resources
rdanaher@loyalistc.on.ca
613-969-1913 ext. 2339
Connie McDonald, Library Technician, Information
cmcdonal@loyalistc.on.ca
613-969-1913 ext. 2317
Lynn McCracken, Library Technician, Information/ILL
lmccrack@loyalistc.on.ca
613-969-1913 ext. 2175
Danielle Emon, Library Technician, Technical Services
emon@loyalistc.on.ca
613-969-1913 ext. 2183
Dayle Gorsline, Library Technician, Acquisitions & Electronic Resources
dgorsline@loyalistc.on.ca
613-969-1913 ext. 2216
Julie Rivers, Research Analyst
jrivers@loyalistc.on.ca
613-969-1913 ext. 2363

Brampton: Davis Campus
Library Services
#B212, 7899 McLaughlin Rd.
Brampton, ON L6V 1G6
Mailing Address: PO Box 7500
Brampton, ON L6V 1G6
905-459-7533 ext: 4338
Fax: 905-874-4346
e-mail: researchhelp.davis@sheridanc.on.ca
National Library Symbol: OBRASC
Hours: Sept.-June: M-Th 8:30am-11:00pm; F 9:00-5:00; Sa-Su 11:00-4:00. July-Aug.: M-F 8:30-4:30; Sa-Su 11:00-4:00
Acquisitions Budget: $50,000 - $99,999
Services:
Internet Access
Access to Subscription Databases
Inter-Library Loan (ILL) for a fee of as charged
Research
Microform Equipment: Computer; Reader
Personnel: *Summary:* 4 Total; 1 Professional(s); 2 Technical(s); 1 Other employees
Marian Traynor, Manager, Library Service
marian.traynor@sheridanc.on.ca

Brantford: Brantford Campus
Library Resource Centre
411 Elgin St.
Brantford, ON N3T 5V2
519-758-6019
Fax: 519-758-6008
Other contact info: 519-758-6020 (Information Desk)
URL: brain.mohawkcollege.ca
Hours: M-F 8:30-4:30
Services:
Remote Access
Internet Access
Inter-Library Loan (ILL)
Personnel: *Summary:* 6 Total; 1 Professional(s); 4 Technical(s)
Christine Chiasson, Digital Services Technican
christine.chiasson@mohawkcollege.ca
519-759-7200 ext. 6020

Brockville: Brockville Campus
Library
2288 Parkdale Ave.
Brockville, ON K6V 5X3
613-345-0556 ext: 3104
Fax: 613-345-0660
National Library Symbol: OBSL
Founded in: 1972
Hours: M-F 8:00-4:00
Acquisitions Budget: 0-$9,999
Note: Member of Ontario College & University Libraries Association
Subjects covered: Business, Law & Security, Nursing, Music Theatre, Pre-service Firefighter
Services:
Internet Access
Access to Subscription Databases
Inter-Library Loan (ILL) for a fee of Shipping cost
Fee Based Research
Microform Equipment: Computer; Reader
Personnel: *Summary:* 1 Total; 1 Technical(s)
Carrie Lanigan, Librarian
CLanigan@sl.on.ca

Burlington: Canada Centre for Inland Waters Library
867 Lakeshore Rd.
Burlington, ON L7R 4A6
Mailing Address: PO Box 5050
Burlington, ON L7R 4A6
905-336-4982
Fax: 905-338-4428
e-mail: librarybiblio.burlington@ec.gc.ca
National Library Symbol: OBUC
Founded in: 1968
Hours: by appointment only
Special Collections: AES Training Branch Archives; MSC Archives; WMO publications; Audio-visual materials; Journal collection; Microfiche reports; Observational weather data; Weather resources for children; Maps & atlases; Pamphlets; Great Lakes Remedial Action Plan reports; Ontario Region Canadian Wildlife Service reports
Subjects covered: Meteorology, Climatology, Atmospheric Research
Services:
Inter-Library Loan (ILL)
Personnel: *Summary:* 1 Professional(s); 2 Technical(s)

Burlington: Royal Botanical Gardens
Library
680 Plains Rd. West
Burlington, ON L8N 3H8
Mailing Address: PO Box 399
Hamilton, ON L8N 3H8
905-527-1158 ext: 531
Fax: 905-577-0375
905-825-5040
e-mail: info@rbg.ca
URL: www.rbg.ca
National Library Symbol: OHRB
No public access
Founded in: 1947
Acquisitions Budget: 0-$9,999
Note: Please email or phone in advance to make an appointment for reference service.
Special Collections: Nursery & seed trade catalogue collection; information on cultivar breeding & selection & introductions of Canadian origin
Subjects covered: Botany, Floristics, Ornamental Horticulture, Gardening, Landscape Design
Personnel: *Summary:* 8 Volunteer(s)
Mark Runciman, CEO
David Galbraith, Head, Scientific Development

Cambridge: Cambridge Campus
Learning Resource Centre
#A1109, 850 Fountain St. South
Cambridge, ON N3H 0A8
Mailing Address: 850 Fountain St. South
Cambridge, ON N3H 0A8
519-748-5220 ext: 4526
e-mail: lrccamb@conestogac.on.ca
Hours: M, W 8:00-7:30; Tu, Th, F 8:00-4:30
Services:
Remote Access
Inter-Library Loan (ILL) for a fee
Microform Equipment: Computer; Reader

Cambridge: School of Architecture
Musagetes Architecture Library
7 Melville St. South
Cambridge, ON N1S 2H4
519-888-4567 ext: 27602
Fax: 519-622-3525
e-mail: architecture@uwaterloo.ca
URL: www.lib.uwaterloo.ca/musagetes/index.html
National Library Symbol: OWTU
Founded in: 2004
Hours: M-F 8:30-4:30
Subjects covered: Architecture Books, Journals; Rare Books; Product Catalogues
Services:
Inter-Library Loan (ILL)
Circulation, course reserves, reference & library instruction
Michele Laing, Branch Head
mlaing@library.uwaterloo.ca
519-888-4567 ext. 7620

Chalk River: Atomic Energy of Canada Ltd. Library
Chalk River Nuclear Laboratories
Chalk River, N K0J 1J0
613-584-3311 ext: 43900
e-mail: librarycr@aecl.ca
URL: www.aecl.ca
Profile: Documents available on request.
National Library Symbol: OCKA
Founded in: 1945
Hours: M-F by appointment only
Special Collections: National depository for literature on Nuclear Science & Technology, Extensive collection on all aspects of peaceful uses of nuclear science & atomic energy
Subjects covered: Nuclear Energy, Nuclear Engineering, Environmental Protection, Metallurgy, Material Sciences
Services:
Inter-Library Loan (ILL)
Microform Equipment: Computer; Reader
Personnel: *Summary:* 5 Total; 1 Professional(s); 8 Technical(s)
Monica Lim, Section Head, AECL Library Services
limm@aecl.ca
613-584-3311 ext. 4626
Linda Crawford, Supervisor, CRL Library
crawfordl@aecl.ca
613-484-3311 ext. 4632

Chatham: Chatham-Kent Health Alliance Medical Library
80 Grand Ave. West
Chatham, ON N7M 5L9
Mailing Address: PO Box 2030
Chatham, ON N7M 5L9
519-352-6400
URL: ckha.on.ca
National Library Symbol: OCHAH
Consortia Membership: Western Ontario Health Knowledge Network
Founded in: 1980
Hours: M-F 8:00-4:00 by appointment only
Note: The library is a member of SOHLIN & OHLA. Open to the public by appointment only
Subjects covered: Medicine, Nursing, Health Sciences
Services:
Inter-Library Loan (ILL)
Personnel: *Summary:* 1 Total; 1 Volunteer(s)
Margaret Campbell, Librarian
519-352-6401 ext. 6420

Chatham: Thames Campus Library
1001 Grand Ave. West
Chatham, ON N7M 5W4
519-354-9100 ext: 3287
Fax: 519-354-6941
URL: www.stclaircollege.ca
Hours: M-Th 7:30am-9:00pm; F 7:30am-4:00pm; Sa 9:00-3:00; Students & staff of Thames Campus
Subjects covered: Business; Social services; Nursing; Security
Services:
Remote Access
Internet Access
Access to Subscription Databases
Inter-Library Loan (ILL)
Jeanette Giroux, Contact
519-354-9100 ext. 3287
Cheryl Smith, Contact
519-354-9100 ext. 3273

Chatham: Union Gas Ltd., a Spectra Energy Company Information Resource Centre
50 Keil Dr. North
Chatham, ON N7M 5M1
Mailing Address: PO Box 2001
Chatham, ON N7M 5M1
519-352-3100 ext: 2595
Fax: 519-436-5320
URL: www.uniongas.com
No public access
Hours: 8:00-4:30
Subjects covered: Energy
Jane Perry, Librarian

Cornwall: Cornwall Campus Library
2 St Lawrence Dr.
Cornwall, ON K6H 4Z1
613-933-6080 ext: 2701
Fax: 613-937-1523
National Library Symbol: OCSL
Founded in: 1967
Hours: M, W 8:30-2:00; Tu, Th 8:30-5:00
Acquisitions Budget: $10,000 - $24,999
Subjects covered: Business, Technology, Literature, Applied Arts, Science, Social Sciences
Services:
Inter-Library Loan (ILL)
Personnel: *Summary:* 3 Total; 1 Professional(s); 1 Technical(s)
Alison Adams, Librarian
AAdams@sl.on.ca

Deseronto: Ontario Trails Council Library
PO Box 500
Deseronto, ON K0K 1X0
877-668-7245
e-mail: ontrails@gmail.com
URL: www.ontariotrails.on.ca
Founded in: 1992
Hours: Sept.-April
Subjects covered: Trails
Personnel: *Summary:* 2 Volunteer(s)
Patrick Connor, Executive Director
execdir@ontariotrails.on.ca

Gatineau: Canadian Museum of Nature / Musée canadien de la nature Library & Archives
1740, ch Pink
Gatineau, ON K1P 6P4
Mailing Address: PO Box 3443, Stn D
Ottawa, ON K1P 6P4
613-364-4042
Fax: 613-364-4026
e-mail: cmnlib@mus-nature.ca
URL: nature.ca/en/research-collections/library-archives
National Library Symbol: OONMNS
Consortia Membership: Federal Libraries Consortium (FLC)
Founded in: 1842
Hours: M-F 8:30-4:30
Acquisitions Budget: $50,000 - $99,999
For Print: $50,000 - $99,999
For Electronic: 0-$9,999
Special Collections: Rare Books; Photo Collection; Nature Art Collection, Archives
Subjects covered: Natural Sciences, Botany, Invertebrate & Vertebrate Zoology, Mineral Sciences, Paleobiology, Natural History, Biodiversity
Services:
Inter-Library Loan (ILL)
Microform Equipment: Reader
Personnel: *Summary:* 4 Total; 2 Professional(s); 2 Technical(s); 1 Volunteer(s)
Chantal Dussault, Head, Archives, Records & Library
cdussault@mus-nature.ca
613-364-4047

Gloucester Rd.: Engineering Branch Library
1901 Research Rd.
Gloucester Rd., ON K1A 1K8
613-990-0884
Fax: 613-998-5572
e-mail: rita.pascolo@tsb.gc.ca
National Library Symbol: OOTSE
Hours: Tu, Th 8:00-4:30, appointment required. by appointment only
Acquisitions Budget: 0-$9,999
For Print: 0-$9,999
For Electronic: 0-$9,999
Subjects covered: Engineering
Services:
Inter-Library Loan (ILL)
Personnel: *Summary:* 1 Total; 1 Technical(s)
Rita Pascolo, Library Technician
rita.pascolo@tsb.gc.ca

Guelph: Farm & Food Care Ontario
#106, 100 Stone Rd. West
Guelph, ON N1G 5L3
519-837-1326
e-mail: info@farmfoodcare.org
URL: www.farmfoodcare.org
Social Media: www.youtube.com/user/FarmandFoodCare
www.facebook.com/FarmFoodCare
twitter.com/farmfoodcare
Profile: Farm & Food Care was created in 2012, with the amalgamation of Ontario Farm Animal Council (OFAC) & Agricultural Groups Concerned about Resources & the Environment (AGCare).
Founded in: 2012
Subjects covered: Farm Animals; Food
Crystal Mackay, Executive Director

Guelph: Farm Safety Association Inc.
#101, 75 Farquhar St.
Guelph, ON N1H 3N4
519-823-5600
Fax: 519-823-8880
800-361-8855
e-mail: info@farmsafety.ca
URL: www.farmsafety.ca
Special Collections: Farm health & safety educational videos
Subjects covered: Agriculture
Dean Anderson, General Manager & Chief Operating Officer
Zeenat Bhojani, Specialist, Informaton Technology
Tammie Karsten, Coordinator, Marketing

Guelph: Food Research Program Canadian Agriculture Library - Guelph
93 Stone Rd. West
Guelph, ON N1G 5C9
519-780-8042
Fax: 519-829-2600
Hours: by appointment only
Francesco Lai, Head Librarian
laif@agr.gc.ca

Guelph: Homewood Health Centre Library
150 Delhi St.
Guelph, ON N1E 6K9
519-824-1010
Fax: 519-824-1827
URL: www.homewood.org
Consortia Membership: WWD Health Library Netowrk, CHLA, OHLA, OLA
Founded in: 1979
Hours: M-Su 9:00am-9:00pm by appointment only
Acquisitions Budget: $25,000 - $49,999
For Print: $10,000 - $24,999
For Electronic: $50,000 - $99,999
Special Collections: Collection includes pamphlets, consumer health information, fiction, magazines, newspaper, reference material, large-print books; talking books; music. The staff library includes clinical text books; professional journals; e-journals; college/university catalogues; hospital archives; quick reference; EbscoHost full text databases.
Subjects covered: Substance abuse; Psychiatry; Consumer health; Eating disorders
Services:
Remote Access
Internet Access
Access to Subscription Databases
Inter-Library Loan (ILL)
Personnel: *Summary:* 2 Total; 1 Professional(s); 1 Other employees; 52 Volunteer(s)
Joyce Pharoah, Coordinator of Library
pharjoyc@homewood.org
Jayne Harley, Library Assistant
harljayn@homewood.org

Guelph: University of Guelph McLaughlin Library
50 Stone Rd. East
Guelph, ON N1G 2W1
519-824-4120 ext: 53617
Fax: 519-824-6931
e-mail: mridley@uoguelph.ca
URL: www.lib.uoguelph.ca
National Library Symbol: OGU
Consortia Membership: Canadian Research Knowledge Network (CRKN); Ontario Council of University Libraries

(OCUL); TriUniversity Group of Libraries (TUG)
Founded in: 1964
Hours: M-F 8:00-10:00; Sa, Su 11:00-6:00
Acquisitions Budget: $500,000 - $999,999
Special Collections: Theatre Archives, George Bernard Shaw Collection, Scottish Collection, L.M. Montgomery Collection, Agiculture, Ontario History, Travel in Ontario
Subjects covered: Arts, Humanities, Social Sciences, Sciences including Agribusiness, Agriculture, Family Studies, Hotel & Food Administration, Landscape Architecture, Regional History, Travel, Veterinary Medicine
Services:
Inter-Library Loan (ILL)
Microform Equipment: Computer; Reader
Personnel: *Summary:* 137 Total
Michael Ridley, Chief Librarian
mridley@uoguelph.ca

Haileybury: Haileybury Campus Library Resource Centre

640 Latchford St.
Haileybury, ON P0J 1K0
Mailing Address: PO Box 2060
Haileybury, ON P0J 1K0
705-672-3376 ext: 8806
Fax: 705-672-5404
e-mail: libraryh@northern.on.ca
morissetteb@northern.on.ca
National Library Symbol: OHAINC
Founded in: 1912
Hours: M, F 8:00-4:00; Tu-Th 8:00-7:00. Summer M-F 8:00-1:00, 2:00-4:00
Acquisitions Budget: $10,000 - $24,999
For Print: $10,000 - $24,999
For Electronic: 0-$9,999
Special Collections: Maps
Subjects covered: Mining, Geology, Natural Resources, Veterinary Sciences & Applied Arts, Social Work, Business, Instrumental, Social Sciences
Services:
Remote Access
Internet Access
Inter-Library Loan (ILL)
Personnel: *Summary:* 1 Total; 1 Professional(s)
Brenda Morissette, Library Technician
morissetteb@northern.on.ca
705-672-3376 ext. 8806

Hamilton: Canadian Institute for NDE

135 Fennell Ave. West
Hamilton, ON L8N 3T2
905-387-1655
Fax: 905-574-6080
800-964-9488
e-mail: info@cinde.ca
URL: www.cinde.ca
Founded in: 1976
Subjects covered: Nondestructive Testing
Larry Cote, President, Chief Executive Officer, & Journal Contact
905-387-1655 ext. 225
Sharon Bond, Manager, Training
956-387-1655 ext. 222

Hamilton: Dofasco Inc. Library Resource Centre

1330 Burlington St. East
Hamilton, ON L8N 3J5
Mailing Address: PO Box 2460
Hamilton, ON L8N 3J5
905-548-7200 ext: 6223
Fax: 905-548-4630
URL: www.dofasco.ca
No public access
Founded in: 1961
Subjects covered: Steel Industry, Management, Ironmaking, Steelmaking, Coal, Coke, Finishing Processes

Hamilton: H. G. Thode Library of Science & Engineering

McMaster University
1280 Main St. West
Hamilton, ON L8S 4P5
Mailing Address: 1280 Main St. West
Hamilton, ON L8S 4P5
905-525-9140 ext: 22000
e-mail: library@mcmaster.ca
URL: library.mcmaster.ca/about/thode
Founded in: 1978
Special Collections: Periodicals; Government publications; Technical reports
Subjects covered: Science; Engineering
Services:
Remote Access
Internet Access
Microform Equipment: Reader
Jill Bedford, Contact, Library Services
bedford@mcmaster.ca
Linda Cardwell, Contact, Library Services
cardwell@mcmaster.ca
Hope Li, Contact, Library Services
lihope@mcmaster.ca
Susan Ryan, Contact, Library Services
ryansu@mcmaster.ca
Dorothy Sage, Contact, Library Services
sage@mcmaster.ca
Lynn Sorowka, Contact, Library Services
sorowka@mcmaster.ca
Julie Willson, Contact, Library Services
willsonj@mcmaster.ca

Hamilton: Hamilton Health Sciences General Medical Library

286 Victoria Ave. North
Hamilton, ON L8L 5G4
905-527-4322 ext: 44287
Fax: 905-577-1453
e-mail: libraryg@hhsc.ca
URL: www.hhsc.ca
www.hamiltonhealthsciences.ca/library
Founded in: 1931
Hours: by appointment only
Acquisitions Budget: $250,000 - $499,999
For Print: $100,000 - $249,999
For Electronic: $100,000 - $249,999
Subjects covered: Medicine, Health Sciences
Personnel: *Summary:* 4 Total; 1 Professional(s); 3 Technical(s)

Hamilton: Health Sciences Library

1280 Main St. West
Hamilton, ON L8S 4K1
905-525-9140 ext: 22327
Fax: 905-528-3733
e-mail: hslib@mcmaster.ca
URL: hsl.mcmaster.ca
National Library Symbol: OHMB
Consortia Membership: Consortium of Ontario Academic Health Libraries (COAHL)
Founded in: 1969
Hours: M-Th 8:00-11:30; F 8:00-10:00; Sa 10:00-7:00; Su 10:00-11:00
Acquisitions Budget: $500,000 - $999,999
Note: Also part of Hamilton Health Sciences Corp. Member of Hamilton & District Health Library Network.
Special Collections: History of Medicine (Canadian, World Wars), Archives
Subjects covered: Biomedical Sciences, Clinical Health Sciences, Medicine & Medical Specialities, Nursing, Occupational Therapy & Physiotherapy, Midwifery
Services:
Inter-Library Loan (ILL)
Personnel: *Summary:* 33 Total; 7 Professional(s); 5 Technical(s); 21 Other employees
Liz Bayley, Director
bayleyl@mcmaster.ca
905-525-9140 ext. 22545
Jennifer McKinnell, Head of Public Services
mckinn@mcmaster.ca
Andrea McLelland, Head, Collections & Technical Services
mclell@mcmaster.ca

Hamilton: Innis Library

Kenneth Tayor Hall, McMaster University
#108, 1280 Main St. West
Hamilton, ON L8S 4M4
905-525-9140 ext: 22081
e-mail: library@mcmaster.ca
URL: library.mcmaster.ca/about/innis
Founded in: 1974
Special Collections: Resources to support the academic & research interests of the DeGroote School of Business; McMaster Business Working Papers; McMaster World Congress audiotapes; Newspapers; Business magazines & e-Journals; Databases
Subjects covered: Business; Management; Industrial relations; Marketing; Information science; Finance
Services:
Internet Access
Access to Subscription Databases
Inter-Library Loan (ILL)
Pat Collins, Contact, Library Services
collinp@mcmaster.ca
Ann Pearce, Contact, Library Services
apearce@mcmaster.ca
Ines Perkovic, Contact, Library Services
perkovic@mcmaster.ca
Margit Wessner, Contact, Library Services
wessner@mcmaster.ca

Hamilton: Juravinski Hospital Library

711 Concession St.
Hamilton, ON L8V 1C3
905-527-4322 ext: 42579
Fax: 905-389-5247
e-mail: libraryjh@hhsc.ca
Subjects covered: Medicine, Health Sciences

Hamilton: McMaster University McMaster University Library

1280 Main St. West
Hamilton, ON L8S 4L8
905-525-9140 ext: 24359
Fax: 905-524-9850
URL: library.mcmaster.ca
Social Media: www.youtube.com/maclibraries
www.facebook.com/maclibraries
twitter.com/maclibraries
National Library Symbol: OHM
Consortia Membership: Canadian Research Knowledge Network (CRKN); Ontario Council of University Libraries (OCUL)
Founded in: 1887
Acquisitions Budget: $1,000,000 plus
For Print: $1,000,000 plus
For Electronic: $1,000,000 plus
Special Collections: Bertrand Russell Archives, Eighteenth Century British & European Imprints, Canadian Archives (Social History, Labour Studies), Pacifism, Maps
Subjects covered: Business, Engineering, Humanities, Sciences, Social Sciences
Services:
Inter-Library Loan (ILL)
Microform Equipment: Computer
Personnel: *Summary:* 115 Total; 27 Professional(s); 88 Other employees
Vivian Lewis, Acting University Librarian
lewisvm@mcmaster.ca
905-525-9140 ext. 23883
Anne Pottier, Associate University Librarian, Library Services
pottier@mcmaster.ca
905-525-9140 ext. 22410
Dale Askey, Associate University Librarian, Library & Learning Technologies
askeyd@mcmaster.ca
905-525-9140 ext. 21880
Marelene Mastragostino, Administrator
mastrag@mcmaster.ca
905-525-9140 ext. 24355

Hamilton: Mills Memorial Library

McMaster University
1280 Main St. West
Hamilton, ON L8S 4L6
Mailing Address: 1280 Main St. West
Hamilton, ON L8S 4L6
905-525-9140 ext: 22077
e-mail: library@mcmaster.ca
URL: library.mcmaster.ca/about/mills
Founded in: 1951
Special Collections: Print & digital resources in the subjects areas of the humanities & social sciences; Lloyd Reeds Map Collection; Government publications; Music; Archives
Subjects covered: Humanities; Social Science
Sylvia Dion, Contact, Library Services
dions@mcmaster.ca
Denise Johnson, Contact, Library Services
dmjohso@mcmaster.ca

Erin Joyce, Contact, Library Services
joyceec@mcmaster.ca
Mila Khayutin, Contact, Library Services
khayuti@mcmaster.ca
Tamara Monster, Contact, Library Services
tmonste@mcmaster.ca
Debbie Trebych, Contact, Library Services
trebych@mcmaster.ca
Barbara Zingel, Contact, Library Services
zingelb@mcmaster.ca

Hamilton: Minerals & Metals Information Centre
#116, 183 Longwood Rd. South, 1st Fl.
Hamilton, ON L8P 0A5
905-645-0651
Fax: 905-645-0850
National Library Symbol: OHNR
Hours: M-F 8:30-4:30
Subjects covered: Materials Science; metallurgy, advanced materials, pipelines, corrosion, and non-destructive tests.
Services:
Inter-Library Loan (ILL)
Alana Pollock, Manager
Alana.Pollock@NRCan-RNCan.gc.ca

Hamilton: Mohawk College of Applied Arts & Technology Library
135 Fennell Ave. West
Hamilton, ON L8N 3T2
Mailing Address: Mohawk College, PO Box 2034
Hamilton, ON L8N 3T2
905-575-2077
Fax: 905-575-2011
Other contact info: Reference: 905-575-2274
e-mail: braintogo@mohawkcollege.ca
URL: brain.mohawkcollege.ca/BRAIN/
Social Media: librarybrainblog.wordpress.com
www.facebook.com/pages/Mohawk-College-Library/294972783642
twitter.com/mohawklibrary
National Library Symbol: OHMC
Consortia Membership: Ontario Colleges Library Service
Founded in: 1966
Hours: M-F 7:00-10:00; Sa, Su 8:30-4:30
Subjects covered: Industry, Nursing, Health Technology, Apprentice Trades, Physical Sciences, Technology
Services:
Remote Access
Internet Access
Access to Subscription Databases
Inter-Library Loan (ILL)
Microform Equipment: Reader
Personnel: *Summary:* 31 Total; 5 Professional(s); 18 Technical(s); 8 Other employees
Jo-Anne Westerby, Dean, College Librarian
joanne.westerby@mohawkcollege.ca
905-575-2079
Anna Johnston, Acting Associate Dean: Libraries & Learning
anna.johnston@mohawkcollege.ca
905-575-2737

Hamilton: Mohawk-McMaster Institute for Applied Health Sciences Library Resource Centre/IAHS
1400 Main St. West
Hamilton, ON L8N 3T2
Mailing Address: PO Box 2034
Hamilton, ON L8N 3T2
905-540-4247 ext: 26835
Fax: 905-528-5307
National Library Symbol: OHMCHC
Founded in: 1978
Hours: M-Th 8:30am-7:00pm; F 8:30-4:30; Sa 11:00-3:00
Acquisitions Budget: $25,000 - $49,999
Special Collections: Nursing, Radiography, Ultrasound, Occupational Therapy, Physical Therapy, Pharmacy, Medical Laboratory Technology
Subjects covered: Nursing & Allied Health
Services:
Internet Access
Inter-Library Loan (ILL) for a fee
Personnel: *Summary:* 5 Total; 1 Professional(s); 3 Technical(s); 1 Other employees
Maureen Price, Campus Librarian
maureen.price@mohawkcollege.ca
905-575-1212 ext. 4024

Hamilton: St Joseph's Hospital (Hamilton) Sherman Library, Charlton Campus
Juravinski Innovation Tower, #2305 2nd Floor
50 Charlton Ave. East
Hamilton, ON L8N 4A6
Mailing Address: 50 Charlton Ave. East
Hamilton, ON L8N 4A6
905-522-1155 ext: 3410
Fax: 905-540-6504
e-mail: library@stjosham.on.ca
URL: www.stjosham.on.ca
Social Media: www.youtube.com/Stjoesfoundation
www.linkedin.com/company/st.-joseph's-healthcare-hamilton
twitter.com/STJOESHAMILTON
Founded in: 1964
Hours: M, W, F 8:00-6:00; T, Th 8:00am-8:00pm; Sa 1:00-4:00 (Open on Saturdays Sept.-April only). by appointment only
Acquisitions Budget: $25,000 - $49,999
Note: Member of Hamilton Health Library Network.
Subjects covered: Medicine, Health Sciences
Services:
Inter-Library Loan (ILL)
Microform Equipment: Reader
Personnel: *Summary:* 4 Total; 1 Professional(s); 1 Technical(s); 2 Other employees
Jean Maragno, Manager, Library Services
marag@mcmaster.ca
Lois Cottrell, Library Technician

Hamilton: U.S. Steel Canada Corporate R & D Information Centre
386 Wilcox St.
Hamilton, ON L8N 3T1
Mailing Address: PO Box 2030
Hamilton, ON L8N 3T1
905-528-2511 ext: 2076
Fax: 905-308-7002
800-263-9305
e-mail: InfoCanada@uss.com
URL: www.ussteelcanada.com/ussca/index.aspx
National Library Symbol: OHSCC
Hours: M-F by appointment only
Subjects covered: Steel Industry Research & Development
Services:
Inter-Library Loan (ILL)
Microform Equipment: Computer; Reader
Personnel: *Summary:* 1 Total; 1 Technical(s)
Carol Cernile, Research Library Technician

Hearst: Université de Hearst Bibliothèque Maurice Saulnier
60, 9e rue
Hearst, ON P0L 1N0
Adresse postale: CP 580
Hearst, ON P0L 1N0
705-372-1781 ext: 235
Téléc: 705-362-7518
URL: www.uhearst.ca/services/bibliotheque
Sigle: OHCU
Fondée en: 1953
Heures: L-J 8h30-16h30, 18h30-21h; V 8h30-16h
Budget d'acquisitions: $25,000 - $49,999
Population desservie: 0
Annotation: Affilié à l'Université Laurentienne
Johanne Morin-Corbeil, Bibliothécaire responsable
Diane Gaulin, Responsable, Services techniques

Kanata: BMT Fleet Technology Limited Resources
311 Legget Dr.
Kanata, ON K2K 1Z8
613-592-2830
Fax: 613-592-4950
e-mail: fleet@fleetech.com
URL: www.fleetech.com
No public access
Special Collections: Technical papers, newsletters, & online documents in the following areas: marine; municipal engineering; maintenance & integrity management; training; inspection & quality assurance; welding engineering & technology; & software
Subjects covered: Technology
S. Nicholson, Contact

Kemptville: Kemptville College University of Guelph, Purvis Library
830 Prescott St.
Kemptville, ON K0G 1J0
Mailing Address: PO Bag 2003
Kemptville, ON K0G 1J0
613-258-8336 ext: 634
Fax: 613-258-8294
e-mail: kcampus@kemptvillec.uoguelph.ca
URL: www.kemptvillec.uoguelph.ca/library2/mission.htm
National Library Symbol: OKEMC
Founded in: 1969
Hours: M-F, Su
Subjects covered: Food Service, Agriculture, Equine, Horticulture & Related Areas
Services:
Inter-Library Loan (ILL)
Debra Simpson, Library Associate

King City: King Campus
13990 Dufferin St.
King City, ON L7B 1B3
905-833-3333 ext: 55108
Fax: 905-833-1106
Hours: M-Th 7:30-7:30; F 7:30-5:00
Cynthia McKeich, Manager
cynthia.mckeich@senecacollege.ca
416-491-5050 ext. 55105

Kingston: Bracken Health Sciences Library
Botterell Hall, Queen's University
20 Stuart St.
Kingston, ON K7L 3N6
613-533-3176
Fax: 613-533-6892
877-209-5641
e-mail: bracken.library@queensu.ca
okqh@post.queensu.ca
bracken.circdesk@queensu.ca
URL: library.queensu.ca/webmed
National Library Symbol: OKQH
Consortia Membership: Consortium of Ontario Academic Health Libraries (COAHL)
Founded in: 1854
Hours: M-F 8:00am-11:00pm; Sa 10:00-8:00; Su 10:00-10:00
Acquisitions Budget: $1,000,000 plus
For Print: $250,000 - $499,999
For Electronic: $1,000,000 plus
Subjects covered: Medicine, Nursing, Health Sciences, Life Sciences, Rehab Therapy
Services:
Internet Access
Inter-Library Loan (ILL) for a fee
Remote access to online databases & full-text resources-restricted to Queen's users
Microform Equipment: Reader
Personnel: *Summary:* 16 Total; 8 Professional(s); 11 Technical(s)
Suzanne Maranda, Head
marandas@queensu.ca
613-533-6000 ext. 74522
Brett Waytuck, Head, Public Services & Education
brett.waytuck@queensu.ca
613-533-6000 ext. 77694
Anne Smithers, Head, Technical & Document Services
smithers@post.queensu.ca
613-533-6000 ext. 74530
Sandra Halliday, Librarian, Public Services/Circulation Supervisor
halliday@post.queensu.ca
613-533-6000 ext. 77568
Paola Durando, Librarian, Public Services
paola.durando@queensu.ca
613-533-6000 ext. 74733
Gillian Griffith, Librarian, Outreach Services
gillian.griffith@queensu.ca
613-533-6000 ext. 78136
Elizabeth MacDonald-Pratt, Co-ordinator, Circulation & Reserve
pratte@post.queensu.ca
613-533-2510
Darlene Lake, Co-ordinator, Document Services
ddl@post.queensu.ca
613-533-3039
Trish Morgan, Library Systems Support
morgant@post.queensu.ca
613-533-6000 ext. 74527

Amanda Ross, Librarian, Outreach Services
amanda.ross-white@queensu.ca
613-533-6000 ext. 78136
Sarah Wickett, Health Informatics Librarian
wickets@post.queens.ca
613-533-6000 ext. 77078

Kingston: Engineering & Science Library

Douglas Library, Queen's University
93 University Ave.
Kingston, ON K7L 5C4
613-533-6981
Fax: 613-533-2584
866-267-7407
e-mail: engsci@queensu.ca
engsci.circdesk@queensu.ca
racer.stauffer@queensu.ca
URL: library.queensu.ca/webeng
National Library Symbol: OKQENG
Founded in: 1997
Hours: M-Su
Acquisitions Budget: $500,000 - $999,999
Note: Geological Sciences Reading Room, Miller Hall
613/533-6000 ext. 7822
Subjects covered: Pure & Applied Science
Services:
Remote Access
Internet Access
Access to Subscription Databases
Inter-Library Loan (ILL)
Microform Equipment: Computer; Reader
Personnel: *Summary:* 18 Total; 5 Professional(s); 10 Technical(s); 3 Other employees
Laurie Scott, Acting Head
laurie.scott@queensu.ca
613-533-6000 ext. 77694

Kingston: Maps, Data & Government Information Centre (MADGIC)

Joseph S. Stauffer Library, Lower Level
Kingston, ON K7L 5C4
Mailing Address: Documents Unit, Queen's University Library
Kingston, ON K7L 5C4
613-533-6314
Fax: 613-533-6401
e-mail: madgic@queensu.ca
URL: library.queensu.ca/webdoc
National Library Symbol: OKQ
Founded in: 1847
Hours: M-Su
Acquisitions Budget: $100,000 - $249,999
For Print: $100,000 - $249,999
Note: Unit includes Government Documents, Map & Air Photos Collection & Social Science Data Centre
Special Collections: Pre-Confederation & League of Nations material, Survey Data, Historical Cartography
Subjects covered: Economics, Statistics, Politics, History, Geography
Services:
Internet Access
Personnel: *Summary:* 6 Total; 3 Professional(s); 3 Technical(s)
Jeffrey Moon, Head, Maps, Data & Government Information Centre
moonj@queensu.ca
Sheila Johnson, Public Services Librarian
johnsons@queensu.ca
Susan Greaves, GIS/Map Librarian
greaves@post.queensu.ca

Kingston: Massey Library (Science & Engineering) / Bibliothèque des sciences et du génie

c/o Sawyer Bldg., #3083, 11 General Crerar Cres.
Kingston, ON K7K 7B4
Mailing Address: c/o PO Box 17000, Stn Forces
Kingston, ON K7K 7B4
613-541-6000 ext: 6330
e-mail: okr@rmc.ca
URL: www.rmc.ca/lib-bib/sg-gt/nse-sgn-eng.asp
National Library Symbol: OKRS
Founded in: 1977
Hours: M-Th 8:30-9:00; F 8:30-5:00; Sa 1:00-5:00; Su 1:00-8:00
Acquisitions Budget: $500,000 - $999,999
Subjects covered: Engineering; Mathematics; Computer Science; Physics; Chemistry; Environmental Science; Military Science & Technology; Nuclear Science; Oceanography; Space Science
Services:
Internet Access
Access to Subscription Databases
Inter-Library Loan (ILL)
Personnel: *Summary:* 1 Professional(s); 1 Technical(s); 2 Other employees
Clarinda Olsen, Head, Science/Engineering Library, ILL & Reference
clarinda.olsen@rmc.ca
613-541-6000 ext. 6079
Carroll Balkham, Contact, Circulation & Journals
carroll.balkham@rmc.ca
613-541-6000 ext. 6312

Kingston: Novelis Inc. Novelis Global Technology Centre, Technical Information Centre

945 Princess St.
Kingston, ON K7L 5L9
Mailing Address: PO Box 8400
Kingston, ON K7L 5L9
613-541-2400
Fax: 613-541-2134
URL: www.novelis.com
National Library Symbol: OKA
Founded in: 1946
Hours: by appointment only
Acquisitions Budget: $50,000 - $99,999
Special Collections: Patents
Subjects covered: Aluminum production, Fabrication, Alloys
Services:
Remote Access
Internet Access
Access to Subscription Databases
Personnel: *Summary:* 3 Total; 1 Professional(s); 2 Technical(s);

Brian Chenoweth, Manager

Kingston: Queen's University Stauffer Humanities & Social Sciences Library

101 Union St., Queen's University
Kingston, ON K7L 5C4
613-533-2519
Fax: 613-533-6362
URL: library.queensu.ca/stauffer
National Library Symbol: OKQ
Consortia Membership: Canadian Research Knowledge Network (CRKN); Ontario Council of University Libraries (OCUL)
Hours: M-Th 8:00am-11:00pm; F 8:00-8:00; Sa 10:00-8:00; Su 10:00am-11:00pm
Special Collections: Edith & Lorne Pierce Collection of Canadiana; Buchan Collection; McNicol Collection; Dated Collection; Rare Books; 18th Century British Pamphlets
Services:
Internet Access
Inter-Library Loan (ILL)
Microform Equipment: Computer; Reader
Personnel: *Summary:* 180 Total; 180 Other employees
Martha Whitehead, University Librarian
martha.whitehead@queensu.ca
613-533-2516
Cory Laverty, Acting Head, Reference
Wayne Jones, Head, Technical Services
Dianne Cook, Collection Development Librarian
cookdc@post.queensu.ca
613-533-2523
Mary Mason, Associate Librarian
masonm@post.queensu.ca
613-533-2516
Barbara Teatero, Associate Librarian
teaterob@post.queensu.ca

Kingston: Research & Business Development Library

461 Front Rd.
Kingston, ON K7L 5A5
Mailing Address: PO Box 5000
Kingston, ON K7L 5A5
613-548-5000
Fax: 613-548-5240
No public access
Founded in: 1955
Subjects covered: Engineering, Physical Sciences, Technology, Polymers

Kingston: Royal Military College of Canada / Collège militaire royal du Canada Massey Library

7 Prom Valour Dr.
Kingston, ON K7K 7B4
Mailing Address: PO Box 17000, Stn Forces
Kingston, ON K7K 7B4
613-541-6000 ext: 6330
Fax: 613-542-5055
e-mail: okr@rmc.ca
URL: www.rmc.ca/lib-bib
National Library Symbol: OKR
Consortia Membership: Canadian Research Knowledge Network (CRKN); Ontario Council of University Libraries (OCUL)
Founded in: 1876
Hours: M-Th 8:30-9:00; F 8:30-5:00; Sa 1:00-5:00; Su 1:00-8:00
Acquisitions Budget: $500,000 - $999,999
Special Collections: Military Studies; Leadership Library Collection
Subjects covered: Science, Engineering, Humanities, Social Science, Military Studies
Services:
Inter-Library Loan (ILL)
Microform Equipment: Reader
Personnel: *Summary:* 15 Total; 5 Professional(s); 3 Technical(s); 6 Other employees
Sarah Toomey, Chief Librarian
toomey-s@rmc.ca
613-541-6000 ext. 6229
Ginette Matheson, Head, Acquisitions
Ginette.Matheson@rmc.ca
613-541-6000 ext. 6305

Kingston: St Lawrence College of Applied Arts & Technology Library

100 Portsmouth Ave.
Kingston, ON K7L 5A6
Mailing Address: PO Box 6000
Kingston, ON K7L 5A6
613-544-5400 ext: 1705
Fax: 613-545-3914
URL: slcconnect.sl.on.ca/Library
National Library Symbol: OKSL
Consortia Membership: Ontario Colleges Library Service
Founded in: 1967
Hours: M-Th 8:00-9:00; F 8:00-4:00; Sa 12:00-4:00
Acquisitions Budget: $50,000 - $99,999
Subjects covered: Business, Technology, Health Sciences
Services:
Internet Access
Inter-Library Loan (ILL)
Microform Equipment: Computer; Reader
Personnel: *Summary:* 5 Total; 1 Professional(s); 4 Technical(s)
Jill Baker, Librarian
jillbaker@sl.on.ca

Kingston: William R. Lederman Law Library

Macdonald Hall, Queen's University
128 Union St.
Kingston, ON K7L 3N6
613-533-2842
Fax: 613-533-2594
URL: library.queensu.ca/law/
Hours: M-Th 8:30-10:00; F 8:30-5:00; Sa 10:00-5:00; Su 10:00-10:00
Subjects covered: Canadian Law, Quebec Civil Law, International Law
Services:
Inter-Library Loan (ILL)
Personnel: *Summary:* 3 Professional(s); 7 Technical(s)
Amy Kaufman, Head, Law Library
kaufman@queensu.ca
613-533-2465
Leslie Taylor, Reference/Technical Services Librarian
leslie.taylor@queensu.ca

Kirkland Lake: Kirkland Lake Campus Library

140 Government Rd. East
Kirkland Lake, ON P2N 3L8
705-567-9291 ext: 3712 or 3700
Fax: 705-567-3350
e-mail: libraryk@northern.on.ca
URL: www.northernc.on.ca/lrckirklandlake

National Library Symbol: OKLNC
Hours: M-Thu 8:00-9:00; F 8:00-6:00; Sa-Su 10:00-3:00
Acquisitions Budget: $25,000 - $49,999
Subjects covered: Business, Technology, Social Science
Services:
Inter-Library Loan (ILL)
Personnel: *Summary:* 2 Total; 1 Technical(s)

Kitchener: Conestoga College Institute of Technology & Advanced Learning Learning Resource Centre

299 Doon Valley Dr.
B Wing, #2B18
Kitchener, ON N2G 4M4
519-748-5220 ext: 3361
Fax: 519-748-3538
e-mail: lrcinfo@conestogac.on.ca
lrccirc@conestogac.on.ca
lrcdocd@conestogac.on.ca
URL: www.conestogac.on.ca/lrc/
National Library Symbol: OKITC
Consortia Membership: Ontario Colleges Library Service
Founded in: 1967
Hours: M-Th 7:30am-7:30pm; F 7:30-5:00; Sa-Su 1:00-4:00
Subjects covered: Engineering Technology, Health Sciences, Business, Genereal & Applied Arts
Services:
Remote Access
Inter-Library Loan (ILL) for a fee
Microform Equipment: Computer; Reader
Personnel: *Summary:* 17 Total; 2 Professional(s); 12 Technical(s); 3 Other employees
Linda Schneider, Director
lschneider@conestogac.on.ca

Leamington: Point Pelee National Park Library

RR#1, 407 Monarch Lane
Leamington, ON N8H 3V4
519-322-2365
Fax: 519-322-1277
888-773-888
TDD: 8667876221
e-mail: pelee.info@pc.gc.ca
URL: www.pc.gc.ca/pn-np/on/pelee/index.aspx
Founded in: 1918
Hours: by appointment only
Special Collections: Mammal/bird study skins, Insect collections, Archaeological collection
Subjects covered: Ecosystem related, Park history

Lindsay: Frost Campus, School of Environmental & Natural Resources Sciences Learning Resources & Support Services

200 Albert St. South
Lindsay, ON K9V 5E6
Mailing Address: PO Box 8000
Lindsay, ON K9V 5E6
705-878-9319
Fax: 705-878-9312
e-mail: info@flemingc.on.ca
URL: flemingcollege.ca/campus/frost-campus
National Library Symbol: OLISF
Founded in: 1967
Hours: M-Th 7:45-4:30; F 7:45-4:00
Special Collections: Natural Resources, Maps, Terrain & Water, Fish & Wildlife, Cartography, Geographic Information Systems Technology, Geology, Forestry, Ecosystem Management, Drilling & Blasting, Heavy Equipment
Services:
Inter-Library Loan (ILL)
Personnel: *Summary:* 4 Total; 4 Technical(s)

London: Allyn & Betty Taylor Library

Natural Sciences Centre, University of Western Ontario
#1, 1151 Richmond St.
London, ON N6A 5B7
519-661-3168 ext: 83168
e-mail: taylib@uwo.ca
National Library Symbol: OLUM
Consortia Membership: Consortium of Ontario Academic Health Libraries (COAHL); Western Ontario Health Knowledge Network
Founded in: 1878
Note: Houses all materials from the old Engineering Library
Subjects covered: Medicine, Health Sciences, Life Sciences, Technology, Dentistry, Nursing, Pure Sciences, Engineering-Civil, Chemical, Electrical, Material, Mechanical, Computer
Services:
Inter-Library Loan (ILL)
Computer printing
Microform Equipment: Reader
Personnel: *Summary:* 27 Total; 11 Professional(s); 17 Other employees
Eeva Munoz, Assistant University Librarian, Allyn & Betty Taylor Library
ekmunoz@uwo.ca
519-679-2111 ext. 86362
Harriet Rykse, Research & Instructional Services
hrykse@uwo.ca
Joan Kammerer, Resource Support Services
kammerer@uwo.ca

London: Canadian Agriculture Library - London

1391 Sandford St.
London, ON N5V 4T3
519-457-1470 ext: 263
Fax: 519-457-3997
Hours: by appointment only
Dorothy Drew, Head Librarian
drewd@agr.gc.ca

London: Department of Geography Map & Data Centre, University of Western Ontario

#1051, Social Science Centre, University of Western Ontario
London, ON N6A 5C2
519-661-3424
Fax: 519-661-3493
URL: geography.uwo.ca/maplibrary
National Library Symbol: OLUG
Founded in: 1966
Hours: Sept.-April: M-F 8:30-4:30; May-Aug.: M-F 9:30-4:30.
Acquisitions Budget: 0-$9,999
For Print: 0-$9,999
For Electronic: 0-$9,999
Special Collections: Canadiana; Great Lakes; Fire Insurance Plans
Subjects covered: Maps; Geography; Transportation; Cartography; Hydrology; Topography; Urban Studies
Services:
Remote Access
Internet Access
Inter-Library Loan (ILL)
Scanner; GIS workstation
Personnel: *Summary:* 6 Total; 1 Professional(s); 1 Technical(s); 4 Other employees; 1 Volunteer(s)
Vince Gray, Data Librarian
519-661-2111 ext. 85044
Elizabeth Hill, Data Librarian
519-661-2111 ext. 85049
Cheryl Woods, Data Librarian
519-661-2111 ext. 85005

London: Fanshawe College Library & Media Services

#L1003, 1001 Fanshawe College Blvd.
P.O. Box 7005
London, ON N5Y 5R6
Mailing Address: PO Box 7005
London, ON N5Y 5R6
519-452-4240
Fax: 519-452-4473
e-mail: infodesk@fanshawec.ca
eguthrie@fanshawec.on.ca
URL: www.fanshawec.libguides.com/fanshawelibrary
Social Media: pinterest.com/fanshawelibrary
www.facebook.com/fanshawelibrary
twitter.com/fanshawelibrary
National Library Symbol: OLFC
Consortia Membership: Ontario Colleges Library Service
Hours: M-Su 8:00am-9:45pm
Acquisitions Budget: $50,000 - $99,999
Special Collections: Statistics Canada Collection
Subjects covered: Economics, Health Sciences, Engineering, Technology, Health Technology, Business
Services:
Internet Access
Access to Subscription Databases
Inter-Library Loan (ILL)
Microform Equipment: Reader
Personnel: *Summary:* 16 Total; 4 Professional(s); 13 Technical(s)
Martie Grof-Iannelli, Manager, Library & Media Services
mgrof-iannelli@fanshawec.on.ca
519-452-4240 ext. 4351
Megan Anderson, Librarian, Data, Access & Media
manderson@fanshawec.ca
519-452-4240 ext. 4349
Linda Crosby, Librarian, Systems & Technical Services
lcrosby@fanshawec.ca
519-452-4142
Martha Joyce, Liasion and Instruction Librarian
mjoyce@fanshawec.ca
519-452-4430 ext. 4556

London: John & Dotsa Bitove Family Law Library

Josephine Spencer Niblett Bldg., University of Western Ontario
1151 Richmond St.
London, ON N6A 3K7
519-661-2111 ext: 88273
Fax: 519-661-2012
Other contact info: 519-661-2111, ext 88274
e-mail: lawlib@uwo.ca
National Library Symbol: OLUL
Founded in: 1959
Hours: M-Su
Special Collections: Law; Canadian legislation and law reports, the principal British and American legal sources, European and international materials
Subjects covered: Law
Personnel: *Summary:* 7 Total; 4 Professional(s); 3 Other employees
John Sadler, Director
jsadler@uwo.ca
519-661-2111 ext. 88271
Marianne Welch, Reference/Collections Librarian
mwelch@uwo.ca
Elizabeth Bruton, Reference/Electronic Services Librarian
ebruton@uwo.ca
Deb Grey, Reference Librarian
djgrey@uwo.ca

London: London Health Sciences Centre Health Sciences Library

800 Commissioners Rd. East
London, ON N6A 5W9
519-685-8300 ext: 52042
URL: www.wohkn.ca/lhsclibrary
National Library Symbol: OLWT
Consortia Membership: Western Ontario Health Knowledge Network
Hours: M-F 8:00-4:00
Acquisitions Budget: $100,000 - $249,999
Note: Site libraries located at University Campus, South Street Site, Victoria Campus, & London Regional Cancer Program
Subjects covered: Medicine, Nursing, Health Sciences
Services:
Inter-Library Loan (ILL) for a fee
Personnel: *Summary:* 9 Total; 2 Professional(s); 7 Technical(s)
Karla VanKessel, Manager
karla.vankessel@lhsc.on.ca
519-685-8500 ext. 75934

London: Ontario Petroleum Institute Inc. Ontario Oil, Gas & Salt Resources Library

669 Exeter Rd.
London, ON N6E 1L3
519-686-2772
Fax: 519-686-7225
URL: www.ogsrlibrary.com
Founded in: 1998
Hours: M-F 8:00-4:30
Note: Service fees based on labour time, reproduction cost & a Member/Non-member structure
Special Collections: Information on over 20,000 wells
Subjects covered: Subsurface geology; Petroleum; Salt; Underground hydrocarbon storage resources of Ontario
Services:
On-site use of microscopes; Roller tables; Client workroom for viewing samples
Richard Ostrowski, Manager
Jordan Clark, Technician
Joe Van Overberghe, Trustee

London: St Joseph's Health Care, London Robert M. McFarlane Library
268 Grosvenor St.
London, ON N6A 4V2
Mailing Address: PO Box 5777
London, ON N6A 4V2
519-646-6000 ext: 64439
Fax: 519-646-6228
e-mail: stjoseph_library@sjhc.london.on.ca
URL: www.sjhc.london.on.ca
National Library Symbol: OLSJ
Consortia Membership: Western Ontario Health Knowledge Network
No public access
Founded in: 1966
Hours: M-F 8:30-5:00
Acquisitions Budget: $50,000 - $99,999
Note: Member of London Area Health Libraries Association
Subjects covered: Medicine, Health Sciences
Services:
Inter-Library Loan (ILL)
Personnel: *Summary:* 2 Total; 1 Professional(s); 1 Technical(s); 1 Volunteer(s)
Brad Dishan, Medical Librarian
brad.dishan@sjhc.london.on.ca
519-646-6100 ext. 65727
Ellen Apps, Library Assistant
519-646-6100 ext. 64439

London: 3M Canada Company Corporate Library & Information Services
1840 Oxford St. East
London, ON N6A 4T1
Mailing Address: PO Box 5757
London, ON N6A 4T1
519-451-2500 ext: 2486
Fax: 519-452-6253
URL: www.3M.com
National Library Symbol: OLTMC
No public access
Founded in: 1979
Hours: M-F, 7:00-4:30
Acquisitions Budget: $25,000 - $49,999
Subjects covered: Adhesives, Polymers, Plastics
Services:
Inter-Library Loan (ILL)
Microform Equipment: Computer; Reader
Personnel: *Summary:* 2 Total
Cheryl Stephenson, Senior Information Specialist
cstephenson@mmm.com

London: Western University Libraries
Western University
1151 Richmond St.
London, ON N6A 3K7
519-661-2111 ext: 84796
URL: www.lib.uwo.ca
Social Media: pinterest.com/westernubuslib
www.facebook.com/westernlibraries
twitter.com/westernlibs
National Library Symbol: OLU
Consortia Membership: Canadian Research Knowledge Network (CRKN); Ontario Council of University Libraries (OCUL)
Founded in: 1882
Acquisitions Budget: $500,000 - $999,999
Personnel: *Summary:* 176 Total; 75 Professional(s); 101 Other employees
Joyce C. Garnett, University Librarian
jgarnett@uwo.ca
Karen Marshall, Director, Library
karen.marshall@uwo.ca
Lorraine Busby, Associate University Librarian, Information Resources
lbusby@uwo.ca
Penny Westmacott, Director, Library Information Technology Services
pwestmac@uwo.ca
Wendy Kennedy, Associate University Librarian, Information Services
wkennedy@uwo.ca
Joe Vandeloo, Assistant University Librarian, Administrative Services
vandeloo@uwo.ca
Robin Keirstead, University Archivist
rkeirste@uwo.ca

Manotick: Rideau Valley Conservation Authority LandOwner Resource Centre
3889 Rideau Valley Dr.
Manotick, ON K4M 1A5
Mailing Address: PO Box 599
Manotick, ON K4M 1A5
613-692-3571 ext: 1128
Fax: 613-692-0831
800-267-3504
e-mail: info@lrconline.com
URL: www.lrconline.com
Founded in: 1993
Hours: M-F 8:30-4:30
Acquisitions Budget: $25,000 - $49,999
Subjects covered: Agriculture; Forestry; Wildlife; Water; Soil; Land Management
Personnel: *Summary:* 2 Professional(s)

Markham: IBM Canada Ltd. Research Information Centre
3600 Steeles Ave., #E-F2/270
Markham, ON L3R 9Z7
905-316-2507
Fax: 905-316-2535
e-mail: askibm@ca.ibm.com
URL: www.ibm.com/ca
No public access
Founded in: 1983
Hours: M-F
Subjects covered: Information Technology, Market Analysis, Sales, Canadian Business
Services:
Internet Access
Personnel: *Summary:* 1 Total; 1 Professional(s)
Anne Wharton, Coordinator

Markham: Markham Campus
8 The Seneca Way
Markham, ON L3R 5Y1
416-491-5050 ext: 7521
Fax: 905-477-8980
Hours: M-Th 8:00-8:00; F 8:00-5:00
Joy Muller, Manager, Teaching, Learning & Copyright Services
joy.muller@senecacollege.ca
416-491-5050 ext. 77524

Midland: Midland Campus Library
649 Prospect Blvd.
Midland, ON L4R 4L3
705-526-3666 ext: 3716
Hours: M-Th 8:30-6:30; F 8:30-4:00
Services:
Remote Access
Internet Access
Access to Subscription Databases
Inter-Library Loan (ILL)
Video & DVD booking; Library orientations; Research assistance; Photocopying & Printing
Vikram Singh Chandel, Contact
Vikram.Chandel@GeorgianCollege.ca

Mississauga: Canadian Centre for Pollution Prevention / Centre canadien pour la prévention de la pollution
c/o The Bloom Centre for Sustainability (BLOOM)
#201A, 2070 Hadwen Rd.
Mississauga, ON L5K 2C9
Mailing Address: c/o OCETA, #201A, 2070 Hadwen Rd.
Mississauga, ON L5K 2C9
905-822-4133 ext: 247
Fax: 905-822-3558
800-667-9790
e-mail: info@c2p2online.com
URL: www.c2p2online.com
Hours: M-F
Subjects covered: Manuals, subject files, videos, periodicals, clearinghouse items relating to pollution prevention.
Fred Granek, Chief Operating Officer

Mississauga: Credit Valley Hospital Dr. Keith G. MacDonald Health Sciences Library
2200 Eglinton Ave. West
Mississauga, ON L5M 2N1
905-813-2411
Fax: 905-813-4294
URL: www.cvh.on.ca/library/index.php
National Library Symbol: OMCVH
Consortia Membership: Health Science Information Consortium of Toronto
Founded in: 1985
Hours: M-F 9:00-5:00
Acquisitions Budget: $50,000 - $99,999
For Print: $50,000 - $99,999
For Electronic: $25,000 - $49,999
Note: Member of the University of Toronto Libraries.
Special Collections: Consumer health collection
Subjects covered: Medicine; Nursing; Health Sciences; Allied Health; Public Health
Services:
Remote Access
Internet Access
Personnel: *Summary:* 2 Professional(s); 3 Volunteer(s)
Penka Stoyanova, Health Sciences Librarian
pstoyanova@cvh.on.ca

Mississauga: E.I. duPont Canada Company Central Library
7070 Mississauga Rd.
Mississauga, ON L5M 2H3
Mailing Address: PO Box 2200
Mississauga, ON L5M 2H3
905-821-5782
Fax: 905-821-5519
URL: www2.dupont.com/DuPont_Home/en_CA/index
National Library Symbol: OMDC
No public access
Founded in: 1954
Hours: M-F
Acquisitions Budget: $50,000 - $99,999
Subjects covered: Business, Finance, Industry, Physical Sciences, Engineering, Technology, Intellectual Property, Corporate Law, Management
Personnel: *Summary:* 1 Technical(s)
Caren Larner, Librarian

Mississauga: Golder Associates Ltd. Library (Mississauga)
2390 Argentia Rd.
Mississauga, ON L5N 5Z7
905-567-4444
Fax: 905-567-6561
e-mail: smcfarland@golder.com
URL: www.golder.com
No public access
Founded in: 1960
Acquisitions Budget: $25,000 - $49,999
Subjects covered: Physical Sciences, Engineering, Technology, Geology, Hydrogeology, Rock & Soil Mechanics
Personnel: *Summary:* 1 Total; 1 Professional(s)
Mira Wrezel, Librarian
mwrezel@golder.com

Mississauga: Hatch Information Research Centre
2800 Speakman Dr.
Mississauga, ON L5K 2R7
905-855-7600
Fax: 905-855-8270
e-mail: infocentre@hatch.ca
hatch@hatch.ca
URL: www.hatch.ca
Profile: Hatch supplies engineering, project & construction management services, process & business consulting services to the mining, metallurgical & infrastructure industries
National Library Symbol: OTHA
Founded in: 1955
Hours: by appointment only
Acquisitions Budget: $50,000 - $99,999
Subjects covered: Physical Sciences, Engineering, Technology, Metallurgy
Services:
Internet Access
Access to Subscription Databases
Inter-Library Loan (ILL)
Fee Based Research
Microform Equipment: Reader
Personnel: *Summary:* 2 Total; 1 Professional(s); 1 Other employees
Ljiljana Radman, Library Technician

Mississauga: Industrial Accident Prevention Association
Information Centre
#300, 5110 Creekbank Rd.
Mississauga, ON L4W 0A1
905-614-4272 ext: 2298
Fax: 905-614-1414
800-406-4272
e-mail: infocentre@iapa.ca
URL: www.iapa.ca/resources/information_centre.asp
National Library Symbol: OTIAP
Founded in: 1977
Hours: M-F 9:00-4:00 by appointment only
Subjects covered: Industrial Hygiene, Occupational Safety & Health, Ergonomics
Services:
Internet Access
Personnel: *Summary:* 2 Total; 1 Professional(s); 1 Technical(s)

Mississauga: Infrastructure Health & Safety Association
Video Library
#400, 5110 Creekbank Rd.
Mississauga, ON L4W 0A1
905-625-0100
Fax: 905-625-8998
800-263-5024
e-mail: info@ihsa.ca
URL: www.ihsa.ca
Subjects covered: Transportation, Health & Safety

Mississauga: Intertek CanTox
Resources
#308, 2233 Argentia Rd.
Mississauga, ON L5N 2X7
905-542-2900
Fax: 905-542-1011
e-mail: info@cantox.com
URL: www.cantox.com
National Library Symbol: OOAKC
No public access
Founded in: 1989
Subjects covered: Toxicology
Services:
Inter-Library Loan (ILL)

Mississauga: Ontario Safety League / Ligue de sécurité du Ontario
#212, 2595 Skymark Ave.
Mississauga, ON L4W 4L5
905-625-0556
Fax: 905-625-0677
e-mail: info@osl.org
URL: www.ontariosafetyleague.com
No public access
Founded in: 1913
Hours: M-F 8:30-4:30
Subjects covered: Road safety
Personnel: *Summary:* 1 Professional(s)

Mississauga: Peel Public Health
Health Library, Office of the MOH
7120 Hurontario St.
Mississauga, ON L5M 2C2
Mailing Address: PO Box 667, RPO Streetsville
Mississauga, ON L5M 2C2
905-789-1604
e-mail: Peelhealthlibrary@peelregion.ca
URL: www.peelregion.ca/health/library
National Library Symbol: OBRPHL
Consortia Membership: Health Science Information Consortium of Toronto
Hours: M-F 8:30-4:30 by appointment only
Subjects covered: Public Health, Nursing, Medicine, Health Sciences, Public Health Policy
Services:

Rebecca Strange, Librarian Specialist
rebecca.strange@peelregion.ca

Mississauga: Trillium Health Centre - Mississauga Site
L.G. Brayley Health Sciences Library
100 Queensway West
Mississauga, ON L5B 1B8
905-848-7511
URL: www.trilliumhealthcentre.org
Consortia Membership: Health Science Information Consortium of Toronto
Founded in: 1981
Hours: M-F 8:30-4:30
Acquisitions Budget: $25,000 - $49,999
Note: Mississauga Hospital & Queensway Hospital amalgamated to create Trillium Health Centre
Subjects covered: Medicine, Health Sciences, Nursing
Services:
Inter-Library Loan (ILL)
Personnel: *Summary:* 1 Total; 1 Professional(s); 6 Volunteer(s)
Christina Woodward, Manager
cwoodward@thc.on.ca

Mississauga: University of Toronto at Mississauga Library
#2109A South Bldg., 3359 Mississauga Rd. North
Mississauga, ON L5L 1C6
905-828-5236
Fax: 905-569-4320
URL: library.utm.utoronto.ca
Social Media: www.youtube.com/user/utmlibrary101
www.facebook.com/UTMLibrary
twitter.com/UTMlibrary
Founded in: 1967
Hours: M-Th open 24 hours; F 8:00am-11:00pm; Sa 10:00-9:00; Su 1:00pm onwards Hours vary depending on the time of year.
Acquisitions Budget: $1,000,000 plus
Special Collections: Forensic Science, Infant Studies, Government Documents (partial depository), Biotechnology
Subjects covered: Arts & Science
Services:
Internet Access
Access to Subscription Databases
Inter-Library Loan (ILL)
Microform Equipment: Computer; Reader
Personnel: *Summary:* 38 Total; 13 Professional(s); 25 Technical(s)
Mary Ann Mavrinac, Chief Librarian
maryann.mavrinac@utoronto.ca
905-828-5235
Ian Whyte, Deputy Chief Librarian
ian.whyte@utoronto.ca
905-828-5332
Shelley Hawrychuk, Collection Development Librarian
shelley.hawrychuk@utoronto.ca
905-569-4365
Nga Foster, Assistant to the Chief Librarian
nga.foster@utoronto.ca
905-569-4923
Sheril Hook, Coordinator of Instructional Services
shook@utm.utoronto.ca
905-828-3885

Mississauga: Vale Canada Limited
Information Services
2060 Flavelle Blvd.
Mississauga, ON L5K 1Z9
905-403-2448
Fax: 905-403-2401
National Library Symbol: OMIN
No public access
Founded in: 1966
Hours: M-F 8:30-5:00
Acquisitions Budget: $25,000 - $49,999
Subjects covered: Metallurgy, Research & Development
Services:
Inter-Library Loan (ILL)
Personnel: *Summary:* 2 Total; 1 Professional(s); 1 Technical(s)
Diane Baksa
diane.baksa@vale.com

Mississauga: Xerox Research Centre of Canada
XRCC Library
2660 Speakman Dr.
Mississauga, ON L5K 2L1
905-823-7091 ext: 302
Fax: 905-822-7022
e-mail: xrcc.library@xrcc.xeroxlabs.com
National Library Symbol: OMX
Founded in: 1974
Hours: M-F 8:30-5:00 by appointment only
Services:
Inter-Library Loan (ILL)
Personnel: *Summary:* 2 Total; 1 Professional(s); 1 Technical(s)
Carolyne Sidey, Manager
carolyne.sidey@xrcc.xeroxlabs.com

Niagara Falls: Hatch Ltd.
Information Resource Centre
#500, 4342 Queen St.
Niagara Falls, ON L2E 7J7
905-374-5200 ext: 5247
Fax: 905-374-1157
URL: www.hatch.ca
National Library Symbol: ONFA
No public access
Founded in: 1959
Acquisitions Budget: $50,000 - $99,999
Subjects covered: Engineering, Technology
Personnel: *Summary:* 1 Total; 1 Professional(s)
Marion D'Amboise, Librarian
mdamboise@hatch.ca

Niagara Falls: Niagara Parks Botanical Gardens School of Horticulture
C.H. Henning Library
2565 Niagara Parkway
Niagara Falls, ON L2E 6T2
Mailing Address: PO Box 150
Niagara Falls, ON L2E 6T2
905-356-8554 ext: 226
Fax: 905-356-5488
e-mail: sohlib@niagaraparks.com
schoolofhorticulture@niagaraparks.com
National Library Symbol: ONFNP
Founded in: 1965
Hours: M-F 8:00-4:30 by appointment only
Note: Public access reference only
Special Collections: Archives
Subjects covered: Horticulture, Botany, Landscape Architecture, Soil Science, Entomology, Plant Pathology
Personnel: *Summary:* 1 Total; 1 Technical(s)
Ruth Stoner, Librarian

North Bay: Commerce Court Educational Resources
#W101, 60 Commerce Ct.
North Bay, ON P1B 8K9
Mailing Address: PO Box 5001
North Bay, ON P1B 8K9
705-474-7600 ext: 5614
Fax: 705-472-7169
URL: www.eclibrary.ca
Hours: M-Th 8:00-4:30; F 8:00-4:00
Services:
Remote Access
Internet Access
Inter-Library Loan (ILL)
Diane Newman, Circulation Clerk
705-474-7600 ext. 5614
Joanne Boissonneault, Library Clerk
705-474-7600 ext. 5617

North Bay: Nippissing University & Canadore College of Applie Arts & Technology Libraries
Education Centre Library
100 College Dr.
North Bay, ON P1B 8L7
705-474-3450 ext: 4221
Fax: 705-497-1455
800-655-5154
e-mail: info@eclibrary.ca
URL: www.eclibrary.ca
National Library Symbol: ONBEC
Consortia Membership: Ontario Colleges Library Service
Founded in: 1972
Hours: M-Sa
Acquisitions Budget: $1,000,000 plus
For Print: $100,000 - $249,999
For Electronic: $250,000 - $499,999
Note: Serves Nipissing University & Canadore College
Special Collections: Statistics Canada partial depository
Services:
Remote Access
Internet Access
Access to Subscription Databases
Inter-Library Loan (ILL) for a fee
Personnel: *Summary:* 26 Total; 5 Professional(s); 14 Technical(s); 7 Other employees

Paula Cardozo, Librarian
705-474-3450 ext. 4765
Laura Sinclair, Librarian
705-474-3450 ext. 4444/

North Bay: Workplace Safety North
Occupational Health & Safety Resources
690 McKeown Ave.
North Bay, ON P1B 9P1
Mailing Address: PO Box 2050, Stn. Main
North Bay, ON P1B 9P1
705-474-7233
Fax: 705-472-5800
888-730-7821
e-mail: info@workplacesafetynorth.ca
URL: www.healthandsafetyontario.ca/WSN
Profile: Workplace Safety North was formed in 2010, when the following safety associations amalgamated: Mines & Aggregates Safety & Health Association, Ontario Forestry Safe Workplace Association, & Pulp & Paper Health & Safety Association.
Founded in: 2010
Subjects covered: Health & Safety
Candys Ballanger-Michaud, Chief Executive Officer

Oakville: Halton Healthcare Services Corporation
Health Sciences Library
327 Reynolds St.
Oakville, ON L6J 3L7
905-845-2571 ext: 6746
Fax: 905-338-4632
URL: www.haltonhealthcare.com
National Library Symbol: OMDH
ONCKOT
Consortia Membership: Health Science Information Consortium of Toronto
Hours: M-F 9:00-5:00
Acquisitions Budget: $50,000 - $99,999
For Print: $50,000 - $99,999
For Electronic: $25,000 - $49,999
Services:
Internet Access
Personnel: *Summary:* 2 Professional(s); 3 Volunteer(s)
Jeanna Hough, Contact
JHOUGH@haltonhealthcare.on.ca

Oakville: Pollutech Group of Companies Inc.
768 Westgate Rd.
Oakville, ON L6L 5N2
905-847-0065
Fax: 905-847-3840
e-mail: info@pollutechgroup.com
URL: www.pollutechgroup.com
Subjects covered: Environment
Personnel: *Summary:* 9 Total; 9 Professional(s);

Oakville: Sheridan College Institute of Technology & Advanced Learning
Library Services
1430 Trafalgar Rd.
Oakville, ON L6H 2L1
905-845-9430 ext: 2480
Fax: 905-815-4123
URL: www.sheridancollege.ca/services/library/library.htm
National Library Symbol: OOAKSC
Consortia Membership: Ontario Colleges Library Service
Founded in: 1967
Hours: M-Th 8:30am-9:00pm; F 8:30-4:30; Sa, Su 11:00-3:00
Acquisitions Budget: $50,000 - $99,999
Services:
Access to Subscription Databases
Inter-Library Loan (ILL)
Microform Equipment: Reader
Personnel: *Summary:* 4 Total; 1 Professional(s); 2 Technical(s); 1 Other employees
Joan Sweeney Marsh, Manager, Library Services
joan.sweeneymarsh@sheridanc.on.ca

Oakville: Trafalgar Campus Library
1430 Trafalgar Rd.
Oakville, ON L6H 6W4
905-845-9430 ext: 2482
Fax: 905-815-4123
National Library Symbol: OOAKSC
Founded in: 1967
Hours: M-Th 8:30am-10:00pm; F 8:30-4:30; Sa-Su 11:00-4:00
Acquisitions Budget: $50,000 - $99,999
Subjects covered: Arts, Animation, Ceramics, Glass, Photography, Textiles, Wood, Sculpture, Illustration, Business, Early Childhood Education, Corrections
Services:
Remote Access
Inter-Library Loan (ILL)
Microform Equipment: Computer; Reader
Personnel: *Summary:* 6 Total; 1 Professional(s); 3 Technical(s); 2 Other employees
Janet Fear, Reference
janet.fear@sheridanc.on.ca
905-845-9430 ext. 2484

Oil Springs: Oil Museum of Canada
2324 Kelly Rd.
Oil Springs, ON N0N 1P0
Mailing Address: PO Box 16
Oil Springs, ON N0N 1P0
519-834-2840
Fax: 519-834-2840
e-mail: oil.museum@county-lambton.on.ca
URL: www.lclmg.org/lclmg/Default.aspx?tabid=114
Hours: May-Oct.: M-Su 10:00-5:00. Nov.-April: M-F 10:00-5:00
Subjects covered: Materials relating to petroleum & the petroleum industry in Canada
Personnel: *Summary:* 1 Total; 1 Professional(s)
Connie Bell, Manager
connie.bell@county-lambton.on.ca

Orangeville: Orangeville Campus
Alder Street Library
Recreation Centre, 275 Alder St.
Orangeville, ON L9W 5H6
Mailing Address: 275 Alder St.
Orangeville, ON L9W 5H6
416-675-6622 ext: 5909
Fax: 416-252-0918
Hours: Closed April 30-Sept. 3
Services:
Internet Access
Inter-Library Loan (ILL)
Microform Equipment: Computer; Reader
Personnel: *Summary:* 7 Total; 2 Professional(s); 3 Technical(s); 2 Other employees

Orillia: Orillia Campus
Library
825 Memorial Ave.
Orillia, ON L3V 6S2
705-325-3050 ext: 3050
Fax: 705-329-3107
National Library Symbol: OORIGC
Founded in: 1967
Hours: Winter: M-Th 7:45am-8:00pm; F 7:45-4:30; Sa 12:00-4:00. Summer: M-F 8:30-4:30
Services:
Internet Access
Access to Subscription Databases
Inter-Library Loan (ILL)
Laser printing; Tours; Orientations; Video bookings; Student learning centres
Microform Equipment: Computer; Reader
Personnel: *Summary:* 5 Total; 1 Professional(s); 3 Technical(s); 1 Other employees
Jen Booth, Emerging Technologies Librarian
jen.booth@GeorgianCollege.ca
705-325-2740 ext. 3543
Jana Bickell, Library Technician, Videos/DVD Booking
705-325-2740 ext. 3052

Orillia: Orillia Library
500 University Ave.
Orillia, ON L3V 0B9
705-330-4008 ext: 2250
e-mail: orlib@lakeheadu.ca
URL: library.lakeheadu.ca/orillia
new-library.lakeheadu.ca:8080/orillia.php
National Library Symbol: OPAL
Founded in: 2006
Acquisitions Budget: $25,000 - $49,999
Subjects covered: Humanities; Social Sciences; Sciences
Services:
Remote Access
Internet Access
Access to Subscription Databases
Inter-Library Loan (ILL)
Reference workshops; Labtops; Headphones; White board markets; Group study rooms; Printing
Personnel: *Summary:* 4 Total; 1 Professional(s); 3 Technical(s); 1 Other employees
Chris Tomasini, Librarian, Orillia Campus
ctomasin@lakeheadu.ca
705-330-4008 ext. 2260
Kim Vallée, Senior Library Technician
kavallee@lakeheadu.ca
705-330-4008 ext. 2261

Oshawa: Durham College
Oshawa Campus Library Resource Centre
50 Founders Dr.
Oshawa, ON L1H 7L7
Mailing Address: PO Box 385
Oshawa, ON L1H 7L7
905-721-2000 ext: 2390
Fax: 905-721-3029
Other contact info: 905-721-3082 (Circulation)
e-mail: library@durhamcollege.ca
reference@durhamcollege.ca
URL: www.durhamcollege.ca
Social Media: www.youtube.com/durhamcollege
www.facebook.com/durhamcollege
twitter.com/durhamcollege
National Library Symbol: OOSHD
Consortia Membership: Ontario Colleges Library Service
Founded in: 1968
Hours: M-Th 8:00am-12:00am; F 8:00am-9:00pm; Sa, Su 10:00-6:00
Acquisitions Budget: $100,000 - $249,999
Note: Member of Durham Region Information Network (DRIN). Staff & student access for internet, Cd-roms & databases on & off campus. Public access on campus only.
Subjects covered: Health Sciences, Science & Technology, Design & Communication Arts, Business, Justice Studies, Manufacturing, Computers
Services:
Remote Access
Access to Subscription Databases
Inter-Library Loan (ILL)
Microform Equipment: Reader
Personnel: *Summary:* 25 Total
Pamela Drayson, Chief Librarian
905-721-2000 ext. 2348
Gabor Feuer, Manager, IT
905-721-2000 ext. 2974
Karin Downie, Access Service Manager
karin.downie@dc-uoit.ca
905-721-3111 ext. 2967

Ottawa: Agriculture & Agri-Food Canada / Agriculture et Agroalimentaire Canada
Canadian Agriculture Library/Bibliothèque canadienne de l'agriculture
1341 Baseline Rd.
Ottawa, ON K1A 0C5
613-759-1000
Fax: 613-773-1499
TDD: 6137597470
e-mail: CAL-BCA-ref@agr.gc.ca
URL: www.agr.gc.ca
agriculture.canadiana.ca
National Library Symbol: OOAG
Consortia Membership: Federal Libraries Consortium (FLC)
Founded in: 1910
Hours: M-F 8:30-4:30
Acquisitions Budget: $1,000,000 plus
Note: 21 information centres located in research stations across the country
Special Collections: More than one million volumes, including 4,000 current subscriptions & numerous special collections; FAO; Statistics Canada; digital collection showcasing the Department of Agriculture's history
Subjects covered: Agriculture; Horticulture; Dairying; Entomology; Pesticides; Plant Diseases; Soil Science; Veterinary Medicine
Services:
Remote Access
Internet Access
Access to Subscription Databases
Inter-Library Loan (ILL)
Microform Equipment: Reader
Personnel: *Summary:* 30 Professional(s); 6 Technical(s); 27 Other employees

Ingrit Monasterios, Acting Director
ingrit.monasterios@agr.gc.ca
613-773-2230
Chantal Marcoux, Asst. Director, Information Services
chantal.marcoux@agr.gc.ca
613-773-2254
Alison Ball, Assistant Director, Library Infrastructure Services
alison.ball@agr.gc.ca
613-773-1479

Ottawa: Algonquin College of Applied Arts & Technology / Collège Algonquin des Arts appliqués et de la Technologie
Woodroffe Campus, Learning Resource Centre

#C205, 1385 Woodroffe Ave.
Ottawa, ON K2G 1V8
613-727-4723 ext: 5834
Fax: 613-727-7642
e-mail: lrc@algonquincollege.com
URL: www.algonquincollege.com/lrc/
National Library Symbol: OOAC
Consortia Membership: Ontario Colleges Library Service; Capital Smart Library
Founded in: 1967
Hours: Winter: M-Th 7:30am-9:00pm; F 7:30-5:00; Sa 11:00-4:00
Acquisitions Budget: $100,000 - $249,999
For Print: $100,000 - $249,999
For Electronic: $100,000 - $249,999
Note: Hours vary throughout year
Special Collections: Statistics Canada publications; Selective depository for government publications
Subjects covered: Business; Technology; Trades; Health Sciences; Applied Arts
Services:
Remote Access
Internet Access
Inter-Library Loan (ILL)
Personnel: *Summary:* 15 Total; 2 Professional(s); 12 Technical(s); 1 Other employees
Tim Thornton, Acting Manager
thorntt@algonquincollege.com
613-727-4723 ext. 5062
Brenda Mahoney, Librarian, Coordinator Instruction
mahoneb@algonquincollege.com
Maureen Sheppard, Librarian, Coordinator Selection
sheppam@algonquincollege.com

Ottawa: Bibliothèque des sciences de la santé
Health Sciences Library

#1020, 451 Smyth Rd.
Ottawa, ON K1H 8M5
613-562-5407
Fax: 613-562-5401
e-mail: refrgn@uottawa.ca
illpebhs@uottawa.ca
URL: www.biblio.uottawa.ca/health
National Library Symbol: OOUH
Consortia Membership: Consortium of Ontario Academic Health Libraries (COAHL)
Founded in: 1984
Hours: M-Th 8:15am-10:30pm; F 8:15-8:00; Sept.-May: Sa, Su 9:00-7:00
Acquisitions Budget: $500,000 - $999,999
Note: Bibliothèque bilingue.
Subjects covered: Physiotherapy, Medicine, Nursing, Occupational Therapy, Audiology, Speech Pathology
Services:
Internet Access
Inter-Library Loan (ILL) for a fee
SDI (fee)
Personnel: *Summary:* 9 Total; 3 Professional(s); 1 Technical(s); 5 Other employees;
Lee-Anne Ufholz, Director
Lee-Anne.Ufholz@uOttawa.ca
613-562-5418
Karine Fournier, Head, Reference
613-562-5800 ext. 8517

Ottawa: Branch Library

415 Legget Dr.
Ottawa, ON K2K 2B2
Mailing Address: PO Box 13330
Ottawa, ON K2K 2B2
613-592-6500
Fax: 613-592-7427
National Library Symbol: OKCM
No public access
Founded in: 1984
Subjects covered: Engineering

Ottawa: Brian Dickson Law Library / Bibliothèque de droit Brian-Dickson

Fauteux Hall
57 Louis-Pasteur Pvt.
Ottawa, ON K1N 6N5
Adresse postale: 57 Louis-Pasteur Pvt.
Ottawa, ON K1N 6N5
613-562-5812
Couriel: droitlaw@uottawa.ca
Sigle: OOUD
Fondée en: 1973
Heures: L-D
Budget d'acquisitions: $1,000,000 plus
Population desservie: 0
Sujets: Droit
Services:
Prêts entre bibliothèques(PEB)
Lecteur/reproduction de microformes: Lecteurs
Personnel: *Sommaire:* 4 Professionnel(s); 2 Technicien(s); 14 Autre(s) employé(s)
Margo Jeske, Directrice
margo.jeske@uottawa.ca

Ottawa: Canada Department of National Defence & the Canadian Forces / Ministère de la défense nationale et des forces canadiennes
Library

Major-General George R. Pearkes Building, National Defence Headquarters
101 Colonel By Dr.
Ottawa, ON K1A 0K2
Mailing Address: National Defence Headquarters, 101 Colonel By Dr.
Ottawa, ON K1A 0K2
613-995-2534
Fax: 613-992-4739
TDD: 8004679877
Other contact info: Library Phone: 613-996-0843
e-mail: LibraryNDHQ@forces.gc.ca
URL: www.cfsuo.forces.gc.ca/adm/lib-bib
www.forces.gc.ca
National Library Symbol: OOND
Consortia Membership: Federal Libraries Consortium (FLC)
No public access
Founded in: 1903
Hours: M-F
Subjects covered: Defence, Military Administration, History especially Canadian Military History
Services:
Inter-Library Loan (ILL)

Ottawa: Canada Mortgage & Housing Corporation / Société canadienne d'hypothèques et de logement
Canadian Housing Information Centre/Centre canadien de documentation sur l'habitation

#C1-200, 700 Montreal Rd.
Ottawa, ON K1A 0P7
613-748-2367
Fax: 613-748-4069
800-668-2642
e-mail: chic@cmhc-schl.gc.ca
URL: www.cmhc-schl.gc.ca/en/corp/li
National Library Symbol: OOCM
Consortia Membership: Federal Libraries Consortium (FLC); Capital Smart Library
Founded in: 1979
Hours: M-F 9:00-4:00
Note: CMHC Library serves consumers, builders, developers, academics & industry decision-makers; online catalogue
Special Collections: Historical material; Corporation research reports; Images; Audiovisual materials; Photo Library
Subjects covered: Community development & planning; Housing; Management; Finance & economics; Public policy; Public administration
Services:
Remote Access
Access to Subscription Databases
Inter-Library Loan (ILL)
Microform Equipment: Computer; Reader
Olis Colp, Senior Cataloguer & Systems Librarian
613-748-2300 ext. 3442

Ottawa: Canada Revenue Agency / Agence du revenu du Canada
Research & Knowledge Program/Programme du savoir et de la recherche

Place de Ville, Tower A, Concourse Level
320 Queen St.
Ottawa, ON K1A 0L5
613-957-9194
Fax: 613-957-9514
URL: www.cra-arc.gc.ca
National Library Symbol: OONR
Consortia Membership: Federal Libraries Consortium (FLC)
Founded in: 1942
Hours: M-F 8:00-4:00 by appointment only
Acquisitions Budget: $100,000 - $249,999
For Print: $100,000 - $249,999
For Electronic: $10,000 - $24,999
Special Collections: Taxation, Customs, Excise, Law Reports & Statutes
Subjects covered: Taxation, Law, Accounting, Government, Management
Services:
Access to Subscription Databases
Inter-Library Loan (ILL)
Fee Based Research
Microform Equipment: Reader
Personnel: *Summary:* 12 Total; 3 Professional(s); 3 Technical(s); 6 Other employees
Barbara Kaye, Manager
Althea Sproule, Librarian
613-941-3978

Ottawa: Canada Science & Technology Museum / Musée des sciences et de la technologie du Canada
Library & Information Services

1867 St Laurent Blvd.
Ottawa, ON K1G 5A3
Mailing Address: PO Box 9724, Stn T
Ottawa, ON K1G 5A3
613-991-2982
Fax: 613-990-3636
e-mail: library@technomuses.ca
URL:
www.sciencetech.technomuses.ca/english/about/library.cfm
Social Media: www.flickr.com/photos/cstmweb
www.facebook.com/group.php?gid=53267368995
www.linkedin.com/company/canada-science-and-technology-museum
twitter.com/SciTechMuseum
National Library Symbol: OONMS
Consortia Membership: Capital Smart Library
Founded in: 1967
Hours: M-F 8:30-12:00, 1:00-4:00. Appointments are recommended but not necessary by appointment only
Acquisitions Budget: $25,000 - $49,999
Note: Also listing for Canada Aviation Museum. Horizon Library System (Dynix inc.) Youtube: www.youtube.com/user/cstmweb
Special Collections: Bicycling; Trade Literature; Railway Photographs & Railway Engineering Drawings; CN (Canadian National) Photo Collection; Archives
Subjects covered: Agricultural, Industrial & Space Technology; Graphic Arts; Communications; Energy; Physical Sciences; Transportation
Services:
Internet Access
Inter-Library Loan (ILL)
Photograph & engineering drawing reproduction
Microform Equipment: Computer; Reader
Personnel: *Summary:* 6 Total; 1 Professional(s); 4 Technical(s);
David McGee, Manager
dmcgee@technomuses.ca
613-991-4975
Sylvie Bertrand, Reader's Services Assistant
library@technomuses.ca
613-991-2982
Joyce Hay, Acquisitions Coordinator
jhay@technomuses.ca
613-991-5701

Ottawa: Canadian Forces Health Services Group Headquarters / Quartier général du Groupe des Services de Santé des Forces canadiennes
Medical Library

1745 Alta Vista Dr.
Ottawa, ON K1A 0K6

613-945-6517
Fax: 613-998-8093
National Library Symbol: OONDM
Founded in: 1961
Hours: M-F 8:30-4:30 by appointment only
Acquisitions Budget: $25,000 - $49,999
Subjects covered: Medicine, Health Sciences
Services:
Inter-Library Loan (ILL)
Personnel: *Summary:* 1 Professional(s); 1 Volunteer(s)

Ottawa: Canadian Institute for Scientific & Technical Information (CISTI) / Institut canadien de l'information scientifique et technique (ICIST)

Bldg. M-55, National Research Council
1200 Montreal Rd.
Ottawa, ON K1A 0S2
613-993-1600
Fax: 613-952-9112
800-668-1222
URL: cisti-icist.nrc-cnrc.gc.ca
National Library Symbol: ON
Consortia Membership: Federal Libraries Consortium (FLC)
No public access
Founded in: 1924
Hours: M-F 8:30-4:30
Acquisitions Budget: $1,000,000 plus
For Print: $500,000 - $999,999
For Electronic: $500,000 - $999,999; Serves BRI employees.
Note: Library staff is available during regular hours. Library is open to BRI employees 24 hours.
Special Collections: Rare Book Collection; Scientific Technical and Medical Translations
Subjects covered: Science, Technology, Engineering, Medicine
Services:
Remote Access
Internet Access
Access to Subscription Databases
Document delivery, Online catalogue, Tables of contents, Reference
Personnel: *Summary:* 250 Total; 132 Professional(s); 118 Other employees
Bernard Dumouchel, Director General
bernard.dumouchel@nrc-CNRC.GC.CA
613-993-2341
François Dubé, Director, Technology & Research Services
613-993-3234
Suzanne Bureau, Director, Collection & Metadata Services
613-993-9029
Michael Ireland, Acting Director, Information Access & Delivery
Cameron Macdonald, Director, Publishing (NRC Research Press)
613-993-1931
Michel Gauthieu, Director, NRC Information Services
613-993-3969
Pam Bjornson, Director, Business Affairs
613-993-9637
Lucie Molgat, Director, Csi Project Managment Office
613-991-2462

Ottawa: Canadian Institute of Biotechnology Library

#600, 1 Nicholas St.
Ottawa, ON K1N 7B7
613-230-5585
Fax: 613-563-8850
e-mail: info@biotech.ca
URL: www.biotech.ca
Founded in: 1998
Note: Information packages available to the public.
Subjects covered: Biotechnology
Services:
Canadian & international resources; Newsletters
Cate McCready, Vice-President, External Affairs
613-230-5585 ext. 230

Ottawa: Canadian Institute of Geomatics / Association canadienne des sciences géomatiques Archives

#100D, 900 Dynes Rd.
Ottawa, ON K2C 3L6
613-224-9851
Fax: 613-224-9577
URL: www.cig-acsg.ca
Founded in: 1922
Hours: M-F
Acquisitions Budget: 0-$9,999
For Print: 0-$9,999
For Electronic: 0-$9,999
Special Collections: CIG archives of 116 years, including technical writing & photos on surveying & mapping subjects
Subjects covered: Surveying; Photogeomatry; Remote Sensing; GIS GPS
Carol E. Railer, Manager, Production & Advertising for Geomatica
editgeo@magma.ca

Ottawa: Canadian Nuclear Safety Commission Library

280 Slater St., 2nd Fl.
Ottawa, ON K1P 1C2
Mailing Address: PO Box 1046, Stn B
Ottawa, ON K1P 1C2
613-943-1538
Fax: 613-995-5086
e-mail: library-bibliotheque@cnsc-ccsn.gc.ca
illpeb@cnsc-ccsn.gc.ca
URL: www.nuclearsafety.gc.ca
National Library Symbol: OOAECB
Consortia Membership: Federal Libraries Consortium (FLC)
Hours: M-F 8:00-5:00
Acquisitions Budget: $100,000 - $249,999
Subjects covered: Nuclear Science & Technology, Radiation Protection, Radioactive Waste Management, Nonproliferation
Services:
Inter-Library Loan (ILL)
Personnel: *Summary:* 4 Total; 2 Professional(s); 2 Technical(s)
Frank Rautenkranz, Librarian
frank.rautenkranz@cnsc-ccsn.gc.ca
613-996-2060
Carole Blais, Reference & Collections Officer
613-995-1359

Ottawa: Canadian Organic Growers Inc. Library

39 McArthur Ave., Level 1-3
Ottawa, ON K1L 8L7
613-216-0741
Fax: 613-236-0743
888-375-7383
e-mail: library@cog.ca
URL: www.cog.ca/our-services/library
Acquisitions Budget: 0-$9,999
For Print: 0-$9,999
For Electronic: 0-$9,999
Subjects covered: Agriculture, Bees, Biodynamics, Botany, Conservation, Crops, Economics, Energy, Farming, Forestry, Fruit, Gardening, Greenhouse, Health, Herbs, Livestock, Market Gardening, Marketing, Permaculture, Pest Management, Seeds, Soil, Sustainability, Vegetables, and Weeds.
Services:
Access to Subscription Databases
Personnel: *Summary:* 1 Volunteer(s)
Kristine Swaren, Librarian

Ottawa: Canadian Wildlife Federation Resource Library

350 Michael Cowpland Dr.
Ottawa, ON K2M 2W1
613-599-9594
Fax: 613-599-4428
800-563-9453
e-mail: info@cwf-fcf.org
URL: www.cwf-fcf.org
Subjects covered: Wildlife; Habitat conservation; Research; Advocacy

Ottawa: Carleton University Maxwell MacOdrum Library

1125 Colonel By Dr.
Ottawa, ON K1S 5B6
613-520-2735
Fax: 613-520-2750
URL: www.library.carleton.ca
National Library Symbol: OOCC
Consortia Membership: Canadian Research Knowledge Network (CRKN); Ontario Council of University Libraries (OCUL)
Founded in: 1942
Hours: M-F 8:00am-2:00am; Sa-Su 10:00am-2:00am
Acquisitions Budget: $1,000,000 plus
For Print: $1,000,000 plus
For Electronic: $1,000,000 plus
Note: Limited access to walk-in users for internet & database access. Print copies from microfilm available. There is a $5 fee for photocopying (ILL). Remote access to online databases to members of the University only.
Special Collections: Batchinsky Collection (Ukrainian politics, 19th-20th century) Canadian, British & American small-press poetry, Canadian Institute of Historical Microreproductions (CIHM), French Revolution, Novosti Press Agency Photograph Files, William Blake (Trianon Press), Archival Materials-records of the library & other material relating to the University; The CBC Newsworld Collection; Extensive collection of maps, atlases, cartographic references & data. Carleton University Library has Canadian dissemination rights for the following data collections: Canadian Gallup polls, POLLARA polls, & the International Social Survey Project, I.C.A. Barbara Petchenik Children's Map Competition Archive.
Subjects covered: Humanities, Social Sciences, Architecture, Industrial Design, Journalism & Mass Communication, Public Administration, Science & Engineering, Canadian Federal & Provincial Government Documents & Publications of International Agencies, International Affairs
Services:
Remote Access
Inter-Library Loan (ILL) for a fee of $5 for photocopying articles
Microform Equipment: Computer; Reader
Personnel: *Summary:* 104 Total; 25 Professional(s); 74 Technical(s); 6 Other employees
Margaret Haines, University Librarian
margaret_haines@carleton.ca
613-520-2600 ext. 8260
Pat Moore, Associate University Librarian & Head, Systems
pat_moore@carleton.ca
613-520-2600 ext. 2745
Susan Jackson, Head, Maps, Data & Government Information Centre (MADGIC)
susan_jackson@carleton.ca
613-520-2600 ext. 8946
Colleen Neely, Head, Technical Services
colleen_neely@carleton.ca
613-520-2600 ext. 8140
Janice Scammell, Head, Reference Services
janice_scammell@carleton.ca
613-520-2600 ext. 2017

Ottawa: La Cité Collégiale Centre de documentation

801, promenade de l'Aviation
Ottawa, ON K1K 4R3
613-742-2493 ext: 2077
Téléc: 613-742-2498
Couriel: bibliotheque@lacitec.on.ca
pebill@lacitec.on.ca
URL: www.lacitec.on.ca/webdoc
Sigle: OOCCO
Membre d'un consortium: Ontario Colleges Library Service; Capital Smart Library
Fondée en: 1990
Heures: Hiver: L-J 7h45-20h; V 7h45-17h; D 12h-16h. Été: L-V 7h45-16h
Budget d'acquisitions: $50,000 - $99,999
Population desservie: 0
Sujets: Sciences humaines et santé, communication et média, technologie, commerce
Services:
Accèss distance aux bases de donn
Accès public à l'internet
Réseau en ligne
Prêts entre bibliothèques(PEB)
Personnel: *Sommaire:* 5 Total; 1 Professionnel(s); 4 Technicien(s); 2 Autre(s) employé(s)
Marie Robertson, Directrice
marober@lacitec.on.ca
613-742-2493 ext. 2168
Michael Rouzier, Bibliothécaire
mrouzi@lacitec.on.ca
613-742-2493 ext. 2563
Hélène Ratté, Bibliotechnicienne
hratte@lacitec.on.ca
613-742-2493 ext. 2082
Lyne Charron, Responsable, PEB
lcharr@lacitec.on.ca
613-742-2493 ext. 2078
Jocelyne Agnew, Bibliotechnicienne
jagnew@lacitec.on.ca
613-742-2493 ext. 2838

Fernande Renaud, Responsable, Périodiques
frenau@lacitec.on.ca
613-742-2493 ext. 2844

Ottawa: Civic Campus
Medical Library
#D1, 1053 Carling Ave.
Ottawa, ON K1Y 4E9
613-798-5555 ext: 14450
Fax: 613-761-5292
e-mail: libraryservices@ottawahospital.on.ca
National Library Symbol: OOOCH
No public access
Founded in: 1960
Hours: M-F 7:30-5:00; Serves staff of the hospital.
Special Collections: Consumer Health Information
Subjects covered: Medicine, Nursing, Health Sciences, Allied Health Sciences
Services:
Internet Access
Inter-Library Loan (ILL)
Microform Equipment: Reader
Personnel: *Summary:* 6 Total; 2 Professional(s); 2 Technical(s)
Debbie Ayotte, Librarian
dayotte@toh.on.ca
613-737-7700 ext. 15122
Alexandra Davis, Librarian
adavis@toh.on.ca
613-737-7700 ext. 14459
Roxanne Hart, Librarian
ddoughty@toh.on.ca
613-737-7700 ext. 17545
Diane Doughty, Library Technician
ddoughty@toh.on.ca
613-737-7700 ext. 14450

Ottawa: DBM6/LSTL Building
Material Group Technical Resource Centre
101 Colonel By Dr.
Ottawa, ON K1A 0K2
613-997-9574
Fax: 819-997-7135
National Library Symbol: OOLSTL
No public access
Hours: M-F
Subjects covered: Law, Law Enforcement
Services:
Inter-Library Loan (ILL)

Ottawa: Eastern Cereal & Oilseed Research Centre Library
960 Carling Ave.
Ottawa, ON K1A 0C6
Mailing Address: KW Neatby Bldg., Central Experimental Farm, 960 Carling Ave.
Ottawa, ON K1A 0C6
613-759-1807
Fax: 613-759-1924
National Library Symbol: OOAGE
Hours: by appointment only
Acquisitions Budget: $50,000 - $99,999
Subjects covered: Life Sciences, Entomology, Taxonomy, Botany, Crop Sciences, Soil Sciences
Services:
Microform Equipment: Reader
Personnel: *Summary:* 2 Total; 1 Professional(s); 1 Technical(s)
Patricia Madaire, Head Librarian
patricia.madaire@agr.gc.ca

Ottawa: Entomological Society of Ontario
c/o Vista Centre, 1830 Bank St.
Ottawa, ON K1V 1A3
Mailing Address: PO Box 83025
Ottawa, ON K1V 1A3
URL: www.entsocont.com
Subjects covered: Insects
Michelle Locke, Chair, Public Education Committee

Ottawa: Explosives & Energy Technology Infomration Centre
Bells Corners Complex, Bldg. 3A
1 Haanel Dr.
Ottawa, ON K1A 0G1
613-996-1114
Fax: 613-947-2792
No public access
Hours: M-F 8:30-4:30
Subjects covered: Biotechnology, biomass conversion and utilization technologies, CO2 capture and storage, hydrogen production, hydrogen storage, hydrogen utilization, fuel cells, decentralized energy production, renewable energy technologies, cleaner fossil fuels.
Services:
Inter-Library Loan (ILL)
Microform Equipment: Reader
Personnel: *Summary:* 2 Total; 1 Professional(s); 1 Technical(s)
Linda Hall, Manager, Library Services
Linda.Hall@NRCan-RNCan.gc.ca
613-996-1114

Ottawa: Faculty of Social Sciences Library
#FSS2010, 120 University
Ottawa, ON K1N 6N5
613-562-5800 ext: 6783
e-mail: socialsciences@uOttawa.ca
Founded in: 2013
Hours: M-F 7:30am-10:00pm
Subjects covered: Social Sciences
Services:
Inter-Library Loan (ILL)
Andrée Côté, Librarian
acote@uottawa.ca

Ottawa: Fisheries & Oceans Canada / Pêches et océans Canada
Library Policy & Services/Services et politiques de bibliothèque
200 Kent St., #7E244
Ottawa, ON K1A 0E6
613-993-2950
Fax: 613-990-4901
e-mail: oofi@dfo-mpo.gc.ca
oofiillpeb@dfo-mpo.gc.ca
URL: www.dfo-mpo.gc.ca
waves-vagues.dfo-mpo.gc.ca/waves-vagues
National Library Symbol: OOFI
Consortia Membership: Federal Libraries Consortium (FLC)
Founded in: 1979
Hours: M-F 8:00-4:00
Acquisitions Budget: $250,000 - $499,999
For Print: $50,000 - $99,999
For Electronic: $250,000 - $499,999
Subjects covered: Fisheries; Aquatic Sciences; Nautical Sciences
Services:
Inter-Library Loan (ILL)
Microform Equipment: Computer; Reader
Personnel: *Summary:* 7 Total; 3 Professional(s); 3 Technical(s); 1 Other employees
Anna R. Fiander, Manager, Regional Libraries
fiandera@mar.dfo-mpo.gc.ca
902-426-3675
Jacqueline Lalande, Systems Librarian
lalandej@dfo-mpo.gc.ca
Darlene Tan, Reference Librarian
tand@dfo-mpo.gc.ca

Ottawa: Geographic, Statistical & Government Information Centre
Morisset Hall, 65 University Private
Ottawa, ON K1N 6N5
613-562-5211
e-mail: gsg@uottawa.ca
URL: www.biblio.uottawa.ca
Hours: L-D
Acquisitions Budget: $25,000 - $49,999
Special Collections: Geographical & statistical software; Cartographic resources, such as thematic, national, provincial, international, topographic, & historical maps; Gazetteers; Government documents, such as data from Statistics Canada, & publications from municipal, provincial, & federal governments; Aerial photographs; GIS manuals
Subjects covered: Geography; Cartography; Statistics; Government
Services:
Internet Access
Inter-Library Loan (ILL)
Facility tours
Microform Equipment: Computer; Reader
Personnel: *Summary:* 3 Total; 1 Professional(s); 2 Technical(s)
Talia Chung, Head, Geographic, Statistical, & Government Information Centre
tchun3@uottawa.ca
Erin Forward, Librarian, GIS & Geography
eforward@uottawa.ca
Susan Mowers, Librarian, Data
smowers@uottawa.ca
Téa Rokolj, Librarian, Government Information
trokolj@uottawa.ca
Pierre Leblanc, Specialist, Cartographic & GIS Support
pierre.leblanc@uottawa.ca
Caroline Desrochers, Analyst, Cartographic Metadata
caroline.desrochers@uottawa.ca

Ottawa: Geomatics, Maps & Special Collections Library / Bibliothèque de géomatique, cartes et collections spéciales
#180, 615 Booth St.
Ottawa, ON K1A 0E9
613-996-3919
Fax: 613-943-8742
National Library Symbol: OOG
Hours: M-F 10:00-12:00, 1:00-3:00
Acquisitions Budget: $25,000 - $49,999
Note: This library is a division of Geomatics Canada, which is also a branch of Natural Resources Canada
Special Collections: Earth sciences maps; photo & video collections; books pertaining to Canadian geography & related fields; Circle of Nations Book Collection; Sir William Logan Collection; National Air Photo Library
Subjects covered: Physical Sciences, Maps
Services:
Remote Access
Internet Access
Personnel: *Summary:* 3 Technical(s)
George Duimovich, Manager

Ottawa: Health Canada / Santé Canada
Departmental Library/Bibliothèque ministérielle
Tunney's Pasture
200 Eglantine Driveway
Ottawa, ON K1A 0K9
Mailing Address: Postal Locator 1902B
Ottawa, ON K1A 0K9
613-957-1545
Fax: 613-957-0292
e-mail: HCLibrary_BibliothequeSC@hc-sc.gc.ca
URL: www.hc-sc.gc.ca
National Library Symbol: OONHHS
Consortia Membership: Federal Libraries Consortium (FLC)
Founded in: 1992
Hours: M-F 8:30-4:30 by appointment only
Acquisitions Budget: $50,000 - $99,999
Special Collections: WHO Depository
Subjects covered: Health, Health Policy, Health Services, Health Promotion, Health Economics, Mental Health, Native Health, Population Health
Services:
Internet Access
Inter-Library Loan (ILL)
Microform Equipment: Computer; Reader
Personnel: *Summary:* 13 Total; 2 Professional(s); 9 Technical(s)
Marty Lovelock, Chief Librarian
Marty_Lovelock@hc-sc.gc.ca
613-957-1547
Jean King, Head, Acquisitions Unit
jean_king@hc-sc.gc.ca

Ottawa: Health Canada, Health Products & Food Branch
Science Library Network/Réseau des bibliothèques scientifiques
Banting Research Centre, Tunney's Pasture
251 Sir Frederick Banting Driveway
Ottawa, ON K1A 0k9
613-957-0885
e-mail: merle_mcconnell@hc-sc.gc.ca
National Library Symbol: OONHBR
Subjects covered: Health Sciences, Medicine, Pharmacology
Merle McConnell, Chief
Elizabeth Geehan, Head, Technical Services
Lyn Gamble, Head, Systems

Ottawa: HECS Library / Bibliothèque DSESC
269 Laurier Ave. West, 4th Fl.
Ottawa, ON K1A 0K9
613-957-1725
Fax: 613-941-8583
e-mail: hecs_library@hc-sc.gc.ca
Profile: The HECS (Healthy Environments and Consumer Safety) Branch helps Canadians maintain & improve their health by promoting healthy & safe living, working & recreational environments, by reducing the harm caused by tobacco, alcohol & other substances, environmental contaminants & unsafe consumer & industrial products
National Library Symbol: OONHH
Founded in: 1973
Hours: M-F 8:30-4:00
Note: Part of the Health Canada Science Library Network. Clients served: Healthy Environments & Consumer Safety Branch. Resources & services in English & French
Special Collections: Radiation Protection Library, Product Safety Library
Subjects covered: Exposure Levels, Environmental Health, Industrial Toxicology, Radiation Protection, Chemical Toxicology, Pesticides, Occupational Health, Hazardous Substances, Drinking Water Quality, Product Safety, Tobacco Control, Controlled Substances, Air Quality
Services:
Internet Access
Inter-Library Loan (ILL)
Microform Equipment: Reader
Personnel: *Summary:* 2 Professional(s); 1 Technical(s)
Kathryn Jackson, Manager

Ottawa: Institute for Research in Construction / Institut de recherche en construction Information Service Library/Internet Services
National Research Council
1200 Montreal Rd.
Ottawa, ON K1A 0R6
613-993-2466
Fax: 613-952-7671
e-mail: irc.library@nrc-cnrc.gc.ca
URL: irc.nrc-cnrc.gc.ca
National Library Symbol: OONBR
Founded in: 1952
Hours: M-F 8:15-4:30
Acquisitions Budget: $50,000 - $99,999
Subjects covered: Physical Sciences, Engineering, Technology, Construction, Construction Science & Technology, Fire Science, Construction Materials & Structures, Building Performance
Services:
Inter-Library Loan (ILL)
Personnel: *Summary:* 3 Total; 2 Professional(s); 1 Technical(s)
Mike Culhane, Head, Library & Internet Services
mike.culhane@nrc-cnrc.gc.ca
613-993-3774

Ottawa: International Joint Commission Records Management
Canadian Section Office, 234 Laurier Ave. West, 22nd Fl.
Ottawa, ON K1P 6K6
613-995-2984
Fax: 613-993-5583
URL: www.ijc.org
Subjects covered: Lake & river systems; Canada - United States of America border; Water pollution; Air pollution; Water quality in the Great Lakes
Services:
Reports & studies published by the International Joint Commission are available free of charge
John Yee, Chief Information Manager
yeej@ottawa.ijc.org
Jeff Laberge, Officer, Records Management
labergej@ottawa.ijc.org

Ottawa: Management Library
Desmarais Hall
#2141, 55 Laurier Ave. East
Ottawa, ON K1N 6N5
613-562-5800 ext: 6783
e-mail: management.library@uottawa.ca
Hours: M-Th 9:00-9:00; F 9:00-8:00; Sa 1:00-6:00; Su 1:00-5:00
Subjects covered: Business
Services:
Inter-Library Loan (ILL)

Ottawa: Minerals & Materials Sciences Information Centre / Centre d'information sur les sciences des minéraux et métaux
555 Booth St.
Ottawa, ON K1A 0G1
Mailing Address: PO Box 4000
Ottawa, ON K1A 0G1
613-943-8773
Fax: 613-995-8730
National Library Symbol: OOM
No public access
Founded in: 1907
Hours: M-F 8:30-4:30
Acquisitions Budget: $50,000 - $99,999
Special Collections: Scientific & technical literature in the fields of mining, minerals, & metals
Subjects covered: Metallurgy, Energy Technology, Materials Science Mining
Services:
Inter-Library Loan (ILL)
Microform Equipment: Computer; Reader
Personnel: *Summary:* 11 Total; 5 Professional(s); 3 Technical(s); 3 Other employees
George Duimovich, Manager

Ottawa: Natural Resources Canada Library / Bibliothèque Ressources naturelles Canada
#A5-2, 580 Booth St., 2nd Fl.
Ottawa, ON K1A 0E4
613-996-3919
Fax: 613-943-8742
TDD: 6139964397
e-mail: nrcanlibrary@nrcan.gc.ca
URL: www.nrcan.gc.ca/library/home
Profile: Specialized libraries for forestry, energy, earth sciences, minerals & metals, management & economics. Locations across Canada
Consortia Membership: Federal Libraries Consortium (FLC)
Founded in: 1846
Hours: M-F 8:30-4:30
Acquisitions Budget: $250,000 - $499,999
Special Collections: Early Exploration Collection; Science of Geology Collection, Map Archival Collection; Photo collection (1842-present); Polunin Arctic exploration/history collection; Minproc, Mintec
Subjects covered: Earth Sciences, Geology, Geomatics, Biotechnology, renewable energy, climate change, hydrology, forestry, botany, entomology, physics, chemisty
Services:
Inter-Library Loan (ILL)
Microform Equipment: Reader
Personnel: *Summary:* 21 Total; 9 Professional(s); 10 Technical(s); 2 Other employees
Margaret Ahearn, Head Librarian
Margaret.Ahearn@NRCan-RNCan.gc.ca

Ottawa: Nature Canada Library
#300, 75 Albert St.
Ottawa, ON K1P 6A4
613-562-3447
Fax: 613-562-3371
800-267-4088
e-mail: info@naturecanada.ca
URL: www.naturecanada.ca
Founded in: 1939
Special Collections: Back issues of Nature Canada, published by CNF
Subjects covered: Educational materials about Canadian wild species & natural habitats

Ottawa: Ottawa Hospital / Hôpital d'Ottawa General Campus Medical Library
#M1404, 501 Smyth Rd.
Ottawa, ON K1H 8L6
613-737-8899 ext: 78530
Fax: 613-737-8521
e-mail: libraryservices@ottawahospital.on.ca
URL: www.ottawahospital.on.ca
Social Media: www.youtube.com/user/TheOttawaHospital
www.facebook.com/OttawaHospital
twitter.com/OttawaHospital
National Library Symbol: OOHG
No public access
Founded in: 1946
Hours: M-F 7:30-5:00
Acquisitions Budget: $250,000 - $499,999; Serves staff of the hospital.
Note: Amalgamation of the Civic Hospital, the General Hospital & the Ottawa Regional Cancer Centre Libraries
Special Collections: Sexual abuse; Special cancer collection
Subjects covered: Medicine, Nursing, Allied Health
Services:
Internet Access
Access to Subscription Databases
Inter-Library Loan (ILL) for a fee
Fee Based Research
Personnel: *Summary:* 13 Total; 6 Professional(s); 6 Technical(s); 1 Other employees; 1 Volunteer(s)
Margaret Quirie, Director, Library Services
mquirie@ottawahospital.on.ca
Shelley Ferrell, Librarian
mquirie@ottawahospital.on.ca
613-737-8899 ext. 74823
Michelle Purcell, Librarian
mpurcell@toh.on.ca
613-737-8899 ext. 72811
Risa Shorr, Librarian
rshorr@toh.on.ca
613-737-8899 ext. 78501
Johanne Gohier, Library Technician
jgohier@toh.on.ca
613-737-8899 ext. 78530
Josee Skuce, Library Technician
jrskuce@toh.on.ca
613-737-8899 ext. 78530

Ottawa: Peace & Environment Resource Centre
174 First Ave.
Ottawa, ON K1S 5B1
Mailing Address: PO Box 4075, Stn. E
Ottawa, ON K1S 5B1
613-230-4590
e-mail: info@perc.ca
perc@perc.ca
editor@perc.ca
URL: www.perc.ca
Hours: W-F 12:00-6:00; Sa 10:00-4:00
Special Collections: Video, audiotape & CD collection; News clippings
Subjects covered: Environment

Ottawa: Policy, Management & Economics Information Centre / Centre d'information sur les politique, gestion et économie
580 Booth St.
Ottawa, ON K1A 0E4
Mailing Address: PO Box 4000
Ottawa, ON K1A 0E4
613-996-8282
Fax: 613-992-7211
Hours: M-F 8:30-4:30 by appointment only
Acquisitions Budget: $50,000 - $99,999
Special Collections: Canadian policy & economics literature in the fields of forestry, energy, minerals, & metals
Subjects covered: Legislation, Policies, Management, Human Resources & Career Development, Energy, Minerals
Personnel: *Summary:* 14 Total; 6 Professional(s); 5 Technical(s); 3 Other employees
George Duimovich, Manager

Ottawa: Public Works & Government Services Canada / Travaux Publics et Services Gouvernmentaux Canada Publishing & Depository Services
350 Albert St., 5th Fl.
Ottawa, QC K1A 0S5
613-941-5995
Fax: 613-954-5779
800-635-7943
e-mail: dsp-spd@pwgsc.gc.ca
URL: publications.gc.ca
No public access
Services:
Remote Access
Inter-Library Loan (ILL)
Joanne Joanisse, Acting Director, Publishing & Depository Services
joanne.joanisse@tpsgc-pwgsc.gc.ca
613-996-3049

Ottawa: Science & Engineering Directorate
Science & Engineering Library
79 Bentley Ave.
Ottawa, ON K1A 0L8
Fax: 613-952-7825
e-mail: sed-dsi.library@cbsa.gc.ca
National Library Symbol: OOSTI
No public access
Founded in: 1974
Hours: M-F 8:00-4:00
Acquisitions Budget: $25,000 - $49,999
For Print: $25,000 - $49,999
For Electronic: $25,000 - $49,999
Subjects covered: Physical Sciences, Engineering, Technology
Services:
Inter-Library Loan (ILL)
Microform Equipment: Computer; Reader
Personnel: *Summary:* 1 Total; 1 Professional(s)

Ottawa: Sir F.G. Banting Research Centre / Centre de recherches Sir F.G. Banting
Library/Bibliothèque
120 Parkdale Ave.
Ottawa, ON K1A 0L2
613-957-1022
Fax: 613-941-6957
e-mail: banting_library@hc-sc.gc.ca
National Library Symbol: OONHBR
Hours: M-F 8:30-4:30 by appointment only
Note: Inter-library loan & photocopying are limited/restricted; Part of the Science Library Network.
Subjects covered: Medical Devices, Nutrition, Pharmacology, Toxicology, Natural Health Products
Services:
Inter-Library Loan (ILL)
Personnel: *Summary:* 7 Total; 2 Professional(s); 4 Technical(s)
Terry Chernis, Manager
terry_chernis@hc-sc.gc.ca
613-957-1025

Ottawa: S.L. Ross Environmental Research Ltd.
Library
#200, 1140 Morrison Dr.
Ottawa, ON K2H 8S9
613-232-1564
Fax: 613-232-6660
e-mail: info@slross.com
URL: www.slross.com
No public access
Founded in: 1981
Acquisitions Budget: $25,000 - $49,999
Subjects covered: Oil Spill Research, Spill Risk Assessment, Environmental Impact

Ottawa: Transportation Association of Canada / Association des transports du Canada
Transportation Information Service
2323 St-Laurent Blvd.
Ottawa, ON K1G 4J8
613-736-1350
Fax: 613-736-1395
e-mail: tis@tac-atc.ca
URL: www.tac-atc.ca/english/resourcecentre/library
National Library Symbol: OORTA
Acquisitions Budget: $25,000 - $49,999
Note: Canadian Surface Transportation Research (online database); Library catalogue accessible on web site
Special Collections: Deposit Collections of Exchange Agreements with the American Association of State Highway & Transportation Officials, Australian Road Research Board, & the US Transportation Research Board
Subjects covered: Ground Transportation; Roads
Services:
Inter-Library Loan (ILL) for a fee of $25
Fee Based Research
Personnel: *Summary:* 3 Total; 1 Professional(s)
Glenn Cole, Manager, Technical Information Programs

Ottawa: University of Ottawa / Université d'Ottawa
Morisset Library / Bibliothèque Morisset
Morisset Hall
65 University Private
Ottawa, ON K1N 6N5
613-562-5213
Other contact info: Loans: 613-562-5212
e-mail: referenc@uottawa.ca
URL: www.biblio.uottawa.ca
National Library Symbol: OOU
Consortia Membership: Canadian Research Knowledge Network (CRKN); Ontario Council of University Libraries (OCUL); Capital Smart Library
Founded in: 1848
Hours: M-F 8:00-8:00; Sa 10:00-4:30
Note: The Morrisset Library is open 24 hours a day during exam periods.
Special Collections: e-Books; eJournals; Government publications; Databases
Subjects covered: Arts; Sciences
Services:
Internet Access
Access to Subscription Databases
Inter-Library Loan (ILL)
Research guides; Workshops; Tours
Microform Equipment: Computer; Reader
Leslie Weir, University Librarian
lweir@uottawa.ca

Owen Sound: Owen Sound Campus
Library
1450 - 8th St. East
Owen Sound, ON N4K 5R4
519-376-2034 ext: 2034
Fax: 519-376-5395
877-890-8477
National Library Symbol: OOWGC
Founded in: 1971
Hours: M, W, F 8:00-4:30; Tu, Th 8:00-7:00
Services:
Remote Access
Internet Access
Access to Subscription Databases
Inter-Library Loan (ILL)
Video & DVD booking; Library orientations; Research assistance; Photocopying & Printing
Jo-ann O'Connor, Library Technician
Jo-ann.O'Connor@GeorgianCollege.ca
Sherri Pringle, Library Technician
Sherri.Pringle@GeorgianCollege.ca
Dale Van-Dyk, Contact, Customer Service

Pembroke: Pembrook Campus
Learning Resource Centre
#145, 1 College Way
Pembroke, ON K8A 0C8
613-735-4700 ext: 2707
Fax: 613-735-8801
e-mail: illpemb@algonquincollege.com
URL: www.algonquincollege.com/lrc
National Library Symbol: OPEMAC
Founded in: 1967
Hours: M-Th 8:00-8:00; F 8:00-5:00; Sa 12:00-4:00
Acquisitions Budget: 0-$9,999
Subjects covered: Health Sciences, Forestry, Office Administration, Early Childhood Education, Outdoor Adventure
Services:
Microform Equipment: Reader
Personnel: *Summary:* 4 Total; 1 Professional(s); 2 Technical(s)
Mythili Kaneshalingam, Interim Librarian, Coordinator
kaneshm@algonquincollege.com
613-735-4707 ext. 2779

Perth: Perth Campus
Learning Resource Centre
#117, 7 Craig St.
Perth, ON K7H 1X7
613-267-2859 ext: 5644
Fax: 613-267-3950
e-mail: illpert@algonquincollege.com
National Library Symbol: OPAC
Hours: M-Th 8:00-8:00; F 8:00-5:00
Acquisitions Budget: $25,000 - $49,999
For Print: 0-$9,999
For Electronic: $25,000 - $49,999; College community + public
Special Collections: Lanark County Historical Collection, Heritage
Subjects covered: Carpentry, Architecture, Trades, Health Sciences
Services:
Remote Access
Inter-Library Loan (ILL)
Fee Based Research
Microform Equipment: Computer; Reader
Ann McPhail, Operational Head & Library Technician
macphaa@algonquincollege.com
613-267-2859 ext. 5607

Peterborough: Fleming College
Sutherland Campus Learning Resource Centre
599 Brealey Dr.
Peterborough, ON K9J 7B1
705-749-5516
URL: www.flemingcollege.ca
National Library Symbol: OPETSF
Consortia Membership: Ontario Colleges Library Service
Founded in: 1967
Hours: M-Th 7:30-7:30; F 7:30-4:00; Sa, Su 12:30-4:30
Special Collections: Periodicals; Audiovisual materials; e-Books; Electronic databases
Subjects covered: Art; Psychology; Marketing; Sociology; Recreation; Nursing; Manufacturing; Law Enforcement; Electronics; Merchandising; Business
Services:
Remote Access
Internet Access
Access to Subscription Databases
Inter-Library Loan (ILL)
Library orientation
Microform Equipment: Reader

Peterborough: Kawartha World Issues Centre
#B101, Environmental Sciences Building, East Bank
Trent University
Peterborough, ON K9J 7A2
Mailing Address: PO Box 895
Peterborough, ON K9J 7A2
705-748-1680
Fax: 705-748-1681
e-mail: info@kwic.info
URL: www.kwic.info
Social Media: www.youtube.com/user/KWICpeterborough/feed
www.facebook.com/KWICPeterborough
twitter.com/KWICnews
Subjects covered: Environment; Ecology; Militarism; Community developmentl Indigenous peoples; Women's issues; Foreign aid; Africa; Asia; Latin America; Middle East; Media
Julie Cosgrove, Coordinator

Peterborough: Ontario Federation of Anglers & Hunters
Library
4601 Guthrie Dr.
Peterborough, ON K9J 8L5
Mailing Address: PO Box 2800
Peterborough, ON K9J 8L5
705-748-6324
Fax: 705-748-9577
e-mail: ofah@ofah.org
URL: www.ofah.org
Social Media: www.youtube.com/OFAHCommunications
www.facebook.com/group.php?gid=127166042780
twitter.com/ofah
Hours: M-F 9:00-5:00 by appointment only
Subjects covered: Fishing; Hunting; Natural Resources

Peterborough: Ontario Ministry of Natural Resources / Ontario Ministère des Richesses naturelles
Library Services
300 Water St.
Peterborough, ON K9J 8M5
Mailing Address: PO Box 7000
Peterborough, ON K9J 8M5
705-755-1888
Fax: 705-755-1882
e-mail: mnr.library@ontario.ca
National Library Symbol: OTLF
Founded in: 1972
Hours: M-F by appointment only
Acquisitions Budget: $50,000 - $99,999
Special Collections: MNR publications
Subjects covered: Natural Resources, Conservation, Forestry, Fisheries, Wildlife, Water, Parks, Ecology, Land, Sustainable Development, GIS
Services:
Inter-Library Loan (ILL)
Research

Personnel: *Summary:* 3 Total
Heath Finley, Senior Librarian
heath.finley@ontario.ca

Peterborough: Trent University Thomas J. Bata Library
1600 Westbank Dr.
Peterborough, ON K9J 7B8
705-748-1011 ext: 7416
Fax: 705-748-1126
e-mail: robertclarke@trentu.ca
URL: www.trentu.ca/library/
National Library Symbol: OPET
Consortia Membership: Canadian Research Knowledge Network (CRKN); Ontario Council of University Libraries (OCUL)
Founded in: 1963
Hours: M-Th 8:00am-11:00pm; F 8:00-8:00; Sa 11:00-8:00; Su 11:00-11:00
Acquisitions Budget: $1,000,000 plus
For Print: $250,000 - $499,999
For Electronic: $500,000 - $999,999
Special Collections: Trent Collection, A.J.M. Smith Collection of Canadian Poetry, Floyd Chalmers Collection, G.M. Douglas Arctic Collection
Subjects covered: History, Native Studies, Canadiana
Services:
Remote Access
Internet Access
Access to Subscription Databases
Inter-Library Loan (ILL)
Microform Equipment: Computer; Reader
Personnel: *Summary:* 40 Total; 10 Professional(s); 30 Other employees
Robert Clarke, University Librarian
robertclarke@trentu.ca
705-748-1011 ext. 7957
Jean Luyben, Liaison Librarian
jluyben@trentu.ca
705-748-1011 ext. 7481
Marisa Scigliano, Technical Services Librarian
mscigliano@trentu.ca
705-748-1101 ext. 7643
Barbara Znamirowski, Government Publications, Maps & Lab
bznamirowski@trentu.ca
Ken Field, Access Services Librarian
kfield@trentu.ca
Goro Ripley, Systems Librarian
gripley@trentu.ca
705-748-1011

Port Rowan: David Winton Bell Memorial Library
115 Front St.
Port Rowan, ON N0E 1M0
Mailing Address: PO Box 160
Port Rowan, ON N0E 1M0
888-448-2473
e-mail: info@longpointwaterfowl.org
URL:
longpointwaterfowl.org/research-and-education-centre/library
National Library Symbol: MDW
Founded in: 1952
Hours: M-F by appointment only
Note: Long Point Waterfowl is currently preparing an online database of the libary's holdings
Special Collections: Rare book collection on waterfowl
Subjects covered: Conservation, Natural resources, Environment, Ornithology
Services:
Inter-Library Loan (ILL)

Richmond Hill: Canadian Bottled Water Association / Fédération canadienne des embouteilleurs d'eau
#203-1, 70 East Beaver Creek Rd.
Richmond Hill, ON L4B 3B2
905-886-6928
Fax: 905-886-9531
e-mail: info@cbwa.ca
URL: www.cbwa.ca
Founded in: 1992
Hours: M-F 9:00-5:00 by appointment only
Subjects covered: Tap; Well & Bottled Water; Technology; Environment

Ridgetown: Ridgetown Campus University of Guelph, Library
120 Main St. East
Ridgetown, ON N0P 2C0
519-674-1500 ext: 63540
Fax: 519-674-1539
e-mail: library@ridgetownc.uoguelph.ca
URL: www.ridgetownc.uoguelph.ca/library
National Library Symbol: ORRCAT
Regional System: Tri Universities Group (TUG)
Consortia Membership: University of Guelph
Founded in: 1952
Hours: Academic year: M-Th 8:30am-9pm; F 8:30-4:30; Sa 1:00-4:00; Students + Staff
Note: Library serves the university community & certificate & diploma students
Special Collections: Soil Maps, Agricultural Statistics, Archives of Ridgetown College
Subjects covered: Agriculture, Horticulture, Veterinary Technology, Crop Science, Soil Science, Farm Business, Management, Livestock Production, Landscaping, Ornamental Horticulture
Services:
Remote Access
Internet Access
Inter-Library Loan (ILL)
Microform Equipment: Reader
Personnel: *Summary:* 1 Professional(s); 1 Technical(s)
Chantal Phillips, Head Librarian
cphillip@ridgetownc.uoguelph.ca
519-674-1500 ext. 63521

Sarnia: Imperial Oil Resources Limited Research Department Information Resources
453 Christina St.
Sarnia, ON N7T 8C8
Mailing Address: PO Box 3022
Sarnia, ON N7T 8C8
519-339-2617
Fax: 519-339-4436
e-mail: contact.imperial@esso.ca
National Library Symbol: OSI
No public access
Founded in: 1928
Hours: M-F 8:00-4:30
Special Collections: Chemical Abstracts, API Abstracts, US Chemical Patents, Canadian Patents
Subjects covered: Chemistry, Petrochemicals
Services:
Internet Access
Inter-Library Loan (ILL)
Microform Equipment: Computer; Reader
Personnel: *Summary:* 2 Total; 1 Professional(s)
Nancy Bourque, Information Specialist

Sarnia: Lambton College of Applied Arts & Technology Library Resource Centre
1457 London Rd.
Sarnia, ON N7S 6K4
519-542-7751 ext: 2441
e-mail: diane@lambton.on.ca
URL: platinum.lambton.on.ca/lrc/
www.lambton.on.ca/blogs
Social Media: www.youtube.com/user/LambtonCollegeSarnia
www.facebook.com/lambtoncollege.ca
www.linkedin.com/company/443242
twitter.com/lambtoncollege
National Library Symbol: OSLC
Consortia Membership: Ontario Colleges Library Service
Founded in: 1967
Hours: M-F 8:30-4:30
Services:
Remote Access
Internet Access
Inter-Library Loan (ILL)
Photocopying; printing; fax; scanners
Personnel: *Summary:* 8 Total
Tim Pearce, Director
Tim.Pearce@lambtoncollege.ca
519-542-7751 ext. 3224

Sarnia: Lanxess Inc. Information Center
1265 Vidal St.
Sarnia, ON N7T 7M2
Mailing Address: PO Box 3001
Sarnia, ON N7T 7M2
519-337-8251 ext: 5711
National Library Symbol: OSP
Founded in: 1942
Hours: M-F by appointment only
Subjects covered: Rubber, Polymer Science, Chemistry, Chemical Engineering
Services:
Inter-Library Loan (ILL)
Microform Equipment: Reader
Personnel: *Summary:* 4 Total; 2 Professional(s); 1 Technical(s)
Tina Demars, Information Specialist

Sarnia: Sarnia-Lambton Environmental Association Lending Library
1489 London Rd.
Sarnia, ON N7S 1P6
519-332-2010
Fax: 519-332-2015
e-mail: admin@slea.ca
URL: www.sarniaenvironment.com
Hours: M-F 8:30-4:30
Special Collections: Enviroscan newsletter, with environmental initiatives of member companies

Sault Ste Marie: Algoma University Arthur A. Wishart Library
1520 Queen St. East
Sault Ste Marie, ON P6A 2G4
705-949-2101
Fax: 705-949-6583
e-mail: library@algomau.ca
circulation@algomau.ca
inter-library.loan@algomau.ca
URL: www.algomau.ca/wishart-library
Social Media: www.youtube.com/user/WishartLibrary/feed
www.facebook.com/211329768894092
twitter.com/wishartlibrary
National Library Symbol: OSTMA
Consortia Membership: Canadian Research Knowledge Network (CRKN); Ontario Council of University Libraries (OCUL)
Founded in: 1967
Hours: Fall/Winter: M-Th 8:30am-10:30pm; F 8:30-4:30; Sa-Su 12:00-5:00; Spring: M-Th 8:30-8:00; F 8:30-4:30; Su 12:00-5:00; Summer: M-F 8:30-4:30; Sa-Su Closed
Acquisitions Budget: $100,000 - $249,999
For Print: $50,000 - $99,999
For Electronic: $50,000 - $99,999; Students & community users
Note: Affiliated with Laurentian University
Special Collections: Government Publications (partial depository), Archival material
Subjects covered: Social Sciences, Humanities, Sciences
Services:
Internet Access
Access to Subscription Databases
Inter-Library Loan (ILL)
Microform Equipment: Reader
Personnel: *Summary:* 12 Total; 1 Professional(s); 5 Technical(s); 6 Other employees
Ken Hernden, University Librarian
ken.hernden@algomau.ca
705-949-2301 ext. 4612
Anne Beaupré, University Librarian
anne.beaupre@algomau.ca
705-949-2301 ext. 4610

Sault Ste Marie: Clean North Environmental Resource Room
736A Queen St. East
Sault Ste Marie, ON P6A 2A9
705-945-1573
e-mail: info@cleannorth.org
URL: www.cleannorth.org
Founded in: 1989
Hours: by appointment only
Special Collections: Government documents; Scientific papers; Magazines; A/V media; Curriculum materials
Subjects covered: Environment
Suzanne Hanna, Secretary

Sault Ste Marie: Great Lakes Forestry Centre Ontario Region Library
1219 Queen St. East
Sault Ste Marie, ON P6A 2E5

705-541-5597
Fax: 705-541-5700
National Library Symbol: OSTMF
Founded in: 1949
Hours: M-F 8:30-4:30 by appointment only
Acquisitions Budget: $50,000 - $99,999
Subjects covered: Natural Resources, Conservation, Environment, Forestry, Entomology
Services:
Inter-Library Loan (ILL)
Personnel: *Summary:* 1 Professional(s); 1 Technical(s)
Nancy Jean Dukes, Manager

Sault Ste Marie: Sault Area Hospital Health Sciences Library

750 Great Northern Rd.
Sault Ste Marie, ON P6B 0A8
705-759-3434 ext: 4368
Fax: 705-759-3847
e-mail: aslettk@sah.on.ca
URL: www.sah.on.ca
National Library Symbol: OSTMPH
Founded in: 1979
Hours: M-F 9:00-4:00 by appointment only
Acquisitions Budget: $25,000 - $49,999; Staff, public
Subjects covered: Medicine, Nursing, Allied Health, Health Administration
Services:
Remote Access
Internet Access
Access to Subscription Databases
Inter-Library Loan (ILL) for a fee of Free to staff; $5 for public
Database training
Personnel: *Summary:* 2 Total; 1 Professional(s); 1 Technical(s)
Kimberley Aslett, Head, Library
aslettk@sah.on.ca
705-759-3434 ext. 4368

Sault Ste Marie: Sault College Ron Doyle Library

443 Northern Ave.
Sault Ste Marie, ON P6A 5L3
Mailing Address: PO Box 60
Sault Ste Marie, ON P6A 5L3
705-759-2554 ext: 2711
Fax: 705-759-1319
e-mail: library@saultcollege.ca
URL: www.saultcollegelibrary.ca
National Library Symbol: OSTMSC
Consortia Membership: Ontario Colleges Library Service
Hours: Academic year: M-Th 8:00-8:00; F 8:00-4:30; Sa 12:00-5:00; Su 11:00-9:00. Spring & Summer hours: M-F, 8:30-4:00/4:30, depending on the time of year.
Acquisitions Budget: $50,000 - $99,999
For Print: $25,000 - $49,999
For Electronic: $25,000 - $49,999
Subjects covered: Health Sciences, Technology, Business, Natural Resources, Native, Environmental Studies, Nursing, Aviation
Services:
Remote Access
Internet Access for a fee of $5
Inter-Library Loan (ILL)
Microform Equipment: Reader
Personnel: *Summary:* 6 Total; 1 Professional(s); 5 Technical(s)
Jason Bird, Director
sue.morin@saultc.on.ca
Sue Morin, Library Technician
sue.morin@saultc.on.ca
705-848-2285

Simcoe: James N. Allan Campus Library & Media Services Branch

634 Ireland Rd.
Simcoe, ON N3Y 4K8
Mailing Address: PO Box 10
Simcoe, ON N3Y 4K8
519-426-8260
Fax: 519-428-3112
Founded in: 1978
Services:
Internet Access
Inter-Library Loan (ILL)
Donna Gates, Campus Chair
dgates@fanshawec.ca
519-426-8260

St Catharines: Brock University James A. Gibson Library

500 Glenridge Ave.
St Catharines, ON L2S 3A1
905-688-5550
Fax: 905-988-5490
e-mail: mgrove@brocku.ca
ostcb@brocku.ca
URL: www.brocku.ca/library
National Library Symbol: OSTCB
Consortia Membership: Canadian Research Knowledge Network (CRKN); Ontario Council of University Libraries (OCUL)
Founded in: 1964
Hours: Reference M-Th 8:30-7:00; Fr 8:30-5:00
Acquisitions Budget: $1,000,000 plus
For Print: $500,000 - $999,999
For Electronic: $1,000,000 plus
Special Collections: Niagara Regional Collection
Subjects covered: Humanities, Social Sciences, Science, Business, Education, Applied Health Sciences
Services:
Inter-Library Loan (ILL)
Reference, Copying, Instruction
Microform Equipment: Computer; Reader
Personnel: *Summary:* 73 Total; 19 Professional(s); 54 Technical(s);
Margaret Grove, University Librarian
mgrove@brocku.ca
905-688-5550 ext. 3226
Debbie Kalvee, Associate University Librarian, Services
dkalvee@brocku.ca
905-688-5550 ext. 3198
Barbara McDonald, Associate University Librarian, Collections & Liaison Services
bmcdonald@brocku.ca
905-688-5550 ext. 3949
Ian Gordon, Head, Circulation Services
igordon@brock.ca
905-688-5550 ext. 3727
Laurie Morrison, Head, Liaison Services
lmorrisonbrocku.ca
905-688-5550 ext. 5281
Jonathan Younker, Head, Library Systems & Technologies
jyounker@brocku.ca
905-688-5550 ext. 4899

St Catharines: Ontario Ministry of Transportation Library

301 St Paul St.
St Catharines, ON L2R 7R4
905-704-2065
Fax: 905-704-2005
e-mail: library@mto.gov.on.ca
URL: www.mto.gov.on.ca/english/transrd/index.html
National Library Symbol: OTDT
No public access
Founded in: 1960
Hours: M-F 8:00-4:00
Acquisitions Budget: For Print: 0-$9,999
Note: ILL service only
Special Collections: TRB publications, Ontario roads studies
Subjects covered: Engineering, Technology, Transportation, Highway Engineering Material published by the Ministry
Personnel: *Summary:* 2 Total; 1 Professional(s); 1 Technical(s)
June E. Wilson, Information Broker
june.wilson@mto.gov.on.ca
A. Julia Manning, Reference
julia.manning@mto.gov.on.ca
Patricia Bartel, Library Staff
patricia.bartel@mto.gov.on.ca

St Catharines: University Map Library

Mackenzie Chown Complex
#C306, 500 Glenridge Ave.
St Catharines, ON L2S 3A1
Mailing Address: 500 Glenridge Ave.
St Catharines, ON L2S 3A1
905-688-5550 ext: 3468
Fax: 905-682-9020
e-mail: maplib@brocku.ca
URL: www.brocku.ca/library/collections/maplibrary
National Library Symbol: OSTCB
Hours: (Mid-Sept to April) M-Th 8:30-7:00; Fr 8:30-4:30; Sa&Su closed. (April-Sept) M-F 8:30-4:30; Sa&Su closed.
Acquisitions Budget: $25,000 - $49,999
Special Collections: Historical Niagara Region, Welland Canals
Subjects covered: Geology, Airphotos, Digital Geographic Data, Topography
Personnel: *Summary:* 2 Total; 1 Professional(s); 1 Other employees
Colleen Beard, Map Librarian
cbeard@brocku.ca

Stoney Creek: Stoney Creek Campus Library Resource Centre

481 Barton St. East
Stoney Creek, ON L8E 2L7
905-575-2504
Fax: 905-575-2549
e-mail: sandra.arklie@MohawkCollege.ca
Founded in: 1971
Hours: M-Th 8:30-7:00; F 8:30-4:00
Acquisitions Budget: $25,000 - $49,999
Subjects covered: Apprenticeship/Trades
Services:
Inter-Library Loan (ILL)
Personnel: *Summary:* 3 Professional(s)
Sandra Arklie, Library Supervisor
sandra.arklie@MohawkCollege.ca
905-575-1212 ext. 5038

Sudbury: Cambrian College of Applied Arts & Technology Library

#3021, 1400 Barrydowne Rd.
Sudbury, ON P3A 3V8
Mailing Address: 1400 Barrydowne Rd.
Sudbury, ON P3A 3V8
705-524-7333
Fax: 705-566-6163
e-mail: library@cambriancollege.ca
URL: www.cambriancollege.ca/departments/library
National Library Symbol: OSUC
Consortia Membership: Ontario Colleges Library Service
Founded in: 1968
Hours: M-Th 8:00-8:00; F 8:00-5:00; Sa-Su 11:00-4:00
Acquisitions Budget: $50,000 - $99,999
Special Collections: College Art Collection
Subjects covered: Technology, Health Sciences, Social Sciences, Native Studies
Services:
Remote Access
Inter-Library Loan (ILL)
Personnel: *Summary:* 6 Total; 6 Technical(s);
France Quirion, Registrar/Director, Student Affairs
france.quirion@cambriancollege.ca
705-566-8101 ext. 7542

Sudbury: Laurentian University / Université Laurentienne J.N. Desmarais Library/Bibliothèque J.N. Desmarais

935 Ramsey Lake Rd.
Sudbury, ON P3E 2C6
705-675-4803
Fax: 705-675-4877
800-461-4030
e-mail: library@laurentian.ca
reference@laurentian.ca
URL: www.laurentian.ca/library
National Library Symbol: OSUL
Consortia Membership: Canadian Research Knowledge Network (CRKN); Ontario Council of University Libraries (OCUL)
Founded in: 1960
Hours: Sept.-April: M-Th 8:00am-11:00pm; F 8:00-8:00; Sa-Su 10:00-8:00
Acquisitions Budget: $1,000,000 plus
For Print: $250,000 - $499,999
For Electronic: $1,000,000 plus
Special Collections: Collection Franco-Ontarienne, Northeastern Ontario Collection, Mining Environment
Subjects covered: Humanities, Professional School, Sciences, Social Sciences
Services:
Remote Access
Internet Access for a fee of $.07 if printing/copy
Access to Subscription Databases
Inter-Library Loan (ILL) for a fee
Microform Equipment: Computer; Reader
Personnel: *Summary:* 47 Total; 11 Professional(s); 6 Technical(s); 30 Other employees

Lionel Bonin, Director of Library
lbonin@laurentian.ca
705-675-4841
Ron Slater, Chair, Information & Instruction
rslater@laurentian.ca
705-675-1151 ext. 3329
Hélène Anselmo, Supervisor of Processing
hanselmo@laurentian.ca
705-675-1151 ext. 3311
Lise Séguin, Supervisor of Circulation
lseguin@laurentian.ca
705-675-1151 ext. 3336
Dan Scott, Systems Librarian
dscott@laurentian.ca
705-675-1151 ext. 3315
Sylvie Lafortune, Coordinator of ILL & Cataloguing
slafortune@laurentian.ca
705-675-1151 ext. 3318

Sudbury: Northern Ontario School of Medicine Health Sciences Library, East (Laurentian) Campus

Laurentian University
#MS120, 935 Ramsey Lake Rd.
Sudbury, ON P3E 2C6
705-662-7282
Fax: 705-662-7269
e-mail: askthelibrary@nosm.ca
URL: www.nosm.ca/about_us/library
Profile: The Northern Ontario School of Medicine serves as the faculty of medicine for Laurentian University in Sudbury & Lakehead University in Thunder Bay, Ontario.
National Library Symbol: OSULN
Consortia Membership: Consortium of Ontario Academic Health Libraries (COAHL)
Hours: Sept.-April: M-Th 8:00am-10:00pm; F 8:00-4:30; Sa, Su 10:00-6:00. May-Aug.: M-F 8:00-4:30; Students, faculty, & staff members of Lakehead or Laurentian University
Note: The Health Sciences Library is a member of the following organizations: Association of Academic Health Sciences Libraries (AAHSL); Association of American Medical Colleges (AAMC); Canadian Health Libraries Association (CHLA); Committee on Libraries of the Association of Faculties of Medicine of Canada (AFMC); & the Medical Library Association (MLA).
Special Collections: e-Books; e-Journals; Databases
Subjects covered: Medicine
Services:
Remote Access
Internet Access
Access to Subscription Databases
Inter-Library Loan (ILL)
Tutorials & guides; Research support

Sudbury: Ontario Ministry of Northern Development & Mines
John B. Gammon Geoscience Library

Willet Green Miller Centre, 933 Ramsey Lake Rd.
Sudbury, ON P3E 6B5
705-670-5614
Fax: 705-670-5770
888-415-9845
e-mail: mines.library.ndm@ontario.ca
URL: www.mndm.gov.on.ca
National Library Symbol: OTDM
Hours: 8:30-5:00
Note: Library of the Ontario Geological Survey
Special Collections: Theses on Geology & Mining of Ontario, Geological & Geophysical Maps
Subjects covered: Geology, Mineral Resources, Mining, Mineral Economics
Services:
Internet Access
Microform Equipment: Reader
Personnel: *Summary:* 2 Total; 1 Professional(s); 1 Other employees
Johanne Roux-Guindon, Library Technician
johanne.roux-guindon@ontario.ca

Sudbury: University of Sudbury / Université de Sudbury
Library

935 Ramsey Lake Rd.
Sudbury, ON P3E 2C6
705-673-5661 ext: 216
Fax: 705-673-4912
e-mail: biblio@usudbury.ca
URL: usudbury.ca/index.php/en/library
Profile: A bilingual, tri-cultural (English, French, & Indigenous) undergraduate library serving Laurentian University
National Library Symbol: OSUU
Founded in: 1913
Hours: M-We 9:00-7:30; Th-F 9:00-4:30
Acquisitions Budget: $25,000 - $49,999; Students, staff & faculty
Note: Federated with Laurentian University
Special Collections: Luc Lacourciere; Fr. Chester Warenda; rare books; Jesuit Collection
Subjects covered: Religion, Philosophy, Native People & Northern Affairs, History, Folklore
Services:
Remote Access
Internet Access
Inter-Library Loan (ILL)
Personnel: *Summary:* 4 Total
Paul Laverdure, Director, Library & Archives
plaverdure@usudbury.ca

Thorndale: Ecologistics Research Services Library

21599 Cherry Hill Rd.
Thorndale, ON N0M 2P0
519-461-1167
Fax: 519-461-1151
e-mail: info@ecologistics.com
URL: www.ecologistics.com
No public access
Brian Kerr, President & Project Manager
Sarah Neals-Bolinger, Research Technician, Compliance Manager, & Archivist

Thunder Bay: Confederation College of Applied Arts & Technology
Paterson Library Commons

1450 Nakina Dr.
Thunder Bay, ON P7C 4W1
Mailing Address: PO Box 398
Thunder Bay, ON P7C 4W1
807-475-6219
Fax: 807-622-3258
e-mail: library@confederationc.on.ca
URL: www.confederationc.on.ca/library
National Library Symbol: OTBCC
Consortia Membership: Ontario Colleges Library Service
Founded in: 1967
Hours: Fall & Winter: M-Th 8:00am-9:00pm; F 8:00-4:30; Sa 12:00-5:00; Su 12:00-9:00. Summer: M-F 8:30-4:30
Acquisitions Budget: $100,000 - $249,999
For Print: $100,000 - $249,999
For Electronic: $25,000 - $49,999
Special Collections: Womens' Issues, Learning Disabilities, International Business, Entrepreneurship, Print, A/V & CD-ROM circulating resources, foreign films
Subjects covered: Aboriginal Studies, Applied Arts, Health Sciences, Business, Technology
Services:
Remote Access
Internet Access
Access to Subscription Databases
Inter-Library Loan (ILL) for a fee of $5
Microform Equipment: Computer; Reader
Personnel: *Summary:* 7 Total; 1 Professional(s); 5 Technical(s); 1 Other employees
Marshall Erickson, Director, Teaching & Learning Resources
mericks2@confederationc.on.ca
807-475-6419

Thunder Bay: Lakehead University
Chancellor Paterson Library

955 Oliver Rd.
Thunder Bay, ON P7B 5E1
807-343-8205
Fax: 807-343-8007
e-mail: webcom@lakeheadu.ca
URL: library.lakeheadu.ca
National Library Symbol: OPAL
Consortia Membership: Canadian Research Knowledge Network (CRKN); Ontario Council of University Libraries (OCUL)
Founded in: 1965
Hours: M-Th 8:00-11:30; Sa 10:00-9:00; Su 11:00-9:00
Acquisitions Budget: $1,000,000 plus
Services:
Remote Access
Internet Access
Inter-Library Loan (ILL)
Microform Equipment: Computer; Reader
Personnel: *Summary:* 22 Total; 10 Professional(s); 12 Technical(s)
Anne Deighton, University Librarian
anne.deighton@lakeheadu.ca
807-343-8205

Thunder Bay: Northern Ontario School of Medicine Dr. Serafina Penny Petrone Health Sciences Library, West (Lakehead) Campus

Lakehead University
#MS2007, 955 Oliver Rd.
Thunder Bay, ON P7B 5E1
807-766-7375
Fax: 807-766-7361
e-mail: askthelibrary@nosm.ca
URL: www.nosm.ca/about_us/library
Profile: The Northern Ontario School of Medicine serves as the faculty of medicine for Lakehead University in Thunder Bay & Laurentian University in Sudbury in Ontario.
National Library Symbol: OTBNOM
Consortia Membership: Consortium of Ontario Academic Health Libraries (COAHL)
Hours: Sept.-April: M-Th 8:00am-10:00pm; F 8:00-4:30; Sa, Su 10:00-6:00. May-Aug.: M-F 8:00-4:30; Students, faculty, & staff members of Lakehead or Laurentian University
Note: The Health Sciences Library is a member of the following organizations: Association of Academic Health Sciences Libraries (AAHSL); Association of American Medical Colleges (AAMC); Canadian Health Libraries Association (CHLA); Committee on Libraries of the Association of Faculties of Medicine of Canada (AFMC); & the Medical Library Association (MLA).
Special Collections: Databases; e-Books; e-Journals
Subjects covered: Medicine
Services:
Remote Access
Internet Access
Access to Subscription Databases
Inter-Library Loan (ILL)
Research support; Guides & tutorials
Melissa Helwig, Health Sciences Librarian
melissa.helwig@nosm.ca
807-766-7458
Cyndy MacKenzie, Health Sciences Librarian
cyndy.mackenzie@nosm.ca
807-766-7413
Donna Brown, Library Technician
donna.brown@nosm.ca
807-766-7376

Timmins: Northern College of Applied Arts & Technology
Porcupine Campus, Library Resource Centre

PO Box 3211
Timmins, ON P4N 8R6
705-235-7150
Fax: 705-235-7279
e-mail: libraryp@northern.on.ca
URL: www.northernc.on.ca
National Library Symbol: OSPNC
Consortia Membership: Ontario Colleges Library Service
Hours: M-Th 8:00-8:00; F 8:00-7:00; Sa, Su 10:00-3:00
Acquisitions Budget: $25,000 - $49,999
Special Collections: Maps, Toy Library
Subjects covered: Technology, Applied Arts, Fine Arts, Business Administration, Health
Services:
Internet Access
Access to Subscription Databases
Inter-Library Loan (ILL)
Personnel: *Summary:* 6 Total; 2 Technical(s); 4 Other employees
Marie Leigh Sheppard, Library Technician
sheppardm@northern.on.ca
Christine Dorval, Library Technician

Toronto: A.D. Allen Chemistry Library

Lash Miller Chemical Laboratories
#480, 80 St George St.
Toronto, ON M5S 1A5

416-978-3587
Fax: 416-946-8059
e-mail: pmeindl@chem.utoronto.ca
URL: www.chem.utoronto.ca/facilities/chemlib
National Library Symbol: OTUC
Hours: M-F 9:00-5:00. Summer: 9:00-4:30
Subjects covered: Chemistry
Services:
Inter-Library Loan (ILL) for a fee
Personnel: *Summary:* 2 Professional(s); 1 Technical(s)
Diane Dearborn, Librarian

Toronto: Allergy/Asthma Information Association Information & Resource Centre
#118, 295 The West Mall
Toronto, ON L4H 3H9
416-621-4571
Fax: 416-621-5034
800-611-7011
e-mail: admin@aaia.ca
URL: www.aaia.ca
Founded in: 1964
Hours: M-F 9:00-4:30
Note: Anaphylaxis reference kit
Special Collections: Wide range of allergy-related information letters, newsletter with information & tips; restaurant warning cards, allergy alert buttons, anaphylaxis education package.
Subjects covered: Allergy, Asthma, Anaphylaxis
Services:
Internet Access

Toronto: Association of Municipalities of Ontario Information Services
#801, 200 University Ave.
Toronto, ON M5H 3C6
416-971-9856 ext: 322
Fax: 416-971-6191
877-426-6527
e-mail: amo@amo.on.ca
URL: www.amo.on.ca
Founded in: 1991
Hours: M-F by appointment only
Acquisitions Budget: $25,000 - $49,999
Subjects covered: Municipal government
Services:
Internet Access
Access to Subscription Databases
Personnel: *Summary:* 2 Total; 2 Professional(s)
Snezana Vukelic, Manager, Information Services
svukelic@amo.on.ca
416-971-9856 ext. 322
Julia Shiu, Information Analyst & Researcher
jshiu@amo.on.ca
416-971-9856 ext. 321

Toronto: Birchmount Campus Health Information Resource Centre/Glenn Gould Memorial Library
3030 Birchmount Rd.
Toronto, ON M1W 3W3
416-495-2437
Fax: 416-495-2562
e-mail: librarygen@tsh.to
National Library Symbol: OSSG
ONCVSG
No public access
Hours: M-F 8:30-4:30
Services:
Inter-Library Loan (ILL)
Tonya Mahar, Manager
tmahar@tsh.to
Lucinda Rajaselvan, Librarian
lrajaselvan@tsh.to

Toronto: Bora Laskin Law Library
Flavelle House
78 Queen's Park Cres.
Toronto, ON M5S 2C5
416-978-1073
Fax: 416-978-8396
URL: library.law.utoronto.ca
bllreference.wordpress.com
National Library Symbol: OTUL
Founded in: 1956
Hours: M-Th 8:30am-11:00pm; F 8:30-8:00; Sa, Su 10:00-8:00; hours vary in Summer
Acquisitions Budget: $500,000 - $999,999
Note: Library is wheelchair accessible
Special Collections: 285,000 volumes of primary legal material; 650 scholarly legal periodicals; online resources including Quicklaw, Westlaw, Lexis-Nexis, Westlaw; collection supports the Faculty of Law curriculum and faculty research interests
Subjects covered: Law, Law Enforcement
Services:
Remote Access
Internet Access
Inter-Library Loan (ILL) for a fee
Fee Based Research
Reference service; reading areas & group study rooms; computer laboratory
Microform Equipment: Computer; Reader
Personnel: *Summary:* 11 Total; 5 Professional(s); 4 Technical(s); 2 Other employees
John Papadopoulos, Chief Librarian
john.papadopoulos@utoronto.ca
416-978-4290
Susan Barker, Digital Services & Reference Librarian
susan.barker@utoronto.ca
416-978-5799
Kathryn Roberts, Coordinator, Collection Services
k.roberts@utoronto.ca
416-978-6195
Humayun Rashid, Reference Librarian & Cataloguer
humayn.rashid@utoronto.ca
416-978-4209
Sooin Kim, Faculty Services Librarian
sooin.kim@utoronto.ca
416-946-5923
Anna Szot-Sacawa, Circulation Coordinator
anna.szot.sacawa@utoronto.ca
416-978-5924

Toronto: Canadian Centre for German & European Studies Resource Centre
York Research Tower, 7th Fl.
Toronto, ON M3J 1P3
416-736-2100 ext: 40089
Fax: 416-650-8069
e-mail: ccges@yorku.ca
URL: ccges.apps01.yorku.ca/wp
Hours: M-F 9:00-04:30
Note: Functions jointly with a Centre at the University of Montreal.
Special Collections: German-language periodicals and newspapers
Subjects covered: German
Services:
Access to Subscription Databases
Christina Kraenzle, Director
kraenzle@yorku.ca

Toronto: Canadian Sugar Institute Nutrition Information Service, Scientific Library
WaterPark Pl., #620, 10 Bay St.
Toronto, ON M5J 2R8
416-368-8091
Fax: 416-368-6426
e-mail: info@sugar.ca
URL: www.sugar.ca
No public access
Founded in: 1987
Special Collections: Consumer & professional research & resources
Subjects covered: Sugar; Carbohydrates & health; Nutrition
Personnel: *Summary:* 4 Total; 1 Professional(s); 1 Technical(s)

Toronto: Canadian Urban Transit Association Library
#1401, 55 York St.
Toronto, ON M5J 1R7
416-365-9800
Fax: 416-365-1295
e-mail: techservices@cutaactu.ca
URL: www.cutaactu.ca
No public access
Founded in: 1978
Acquisitions Budget: 0-$9,999
Note: Services restricted to members only
Subjects covered: Urban Transit Policy, Operations, Planning, Marketing, & Technology
Services:
Access to Subscription Databases
Personnel: *Summary:* 20 Professional(s)
Christopher Norris, Manager of Technical Services
norris@cutaactu.ca
416-365-9800 ext. 109
Ilja Green, Technical Services Assistant
techservices@cutaactu.ca
416-365-9800 ext. 113

Toronto: Canadian Water Quality Association / Association canadienne pour la qualité de l'eau
#330, 295 The West Mall
Toronto, ON M9C 4Z4
416-695-3068
Fax: 416-695-2945
URL: www.cwqa.com
Subjects covered: Statistical information & other educational materials related to the water quality industry

Toronto: Career Centre Reference Library
McLaughlin College
#202, 4700 Keele St.
Toronto, ON M3J 1P3
416-736-5351
Fax: 416-736-5684
e-mail: career@yorku.ca
URL: www.yorku.ca/careers/services/resourcearea.htm
Hours: M-Th 9:00-4:00; F 10:00-4:00
Subjects covered: Career planning, occupational research, job search, building work experience, working abroad and education
Stephen Anderson, Contact

Toronto: Casa Loma Campus Library
#330C, 160 Kendal Ave.
Toronto, ON M5T 2T8
Mailing Address: PO Box 1015, Stn B
Toronto, ON M5T 2T8
416-415-5000 ext: 4634
Fax: 416-415-4765
TDD: 8775155559
e-mail: llc@georgebrown.ca
National Library Symbol: OTGBC
Founded in: 1968
Hours: M-F 7:30am-10:00pm; Sa 10:00-6:00; Su 10:00-5:00
Acquisitions Budget: $100,000 - $249,999
Special Collections: Jewellery, Ontarion Instititue of Quantity Surveyors
Subjects covered: Dental Assisting, Hygiene & Technology; Electrical & Electronics Engineering Technology; Information Technology; Fitness Management; Theatre Arts, Jewellery Arts & Gemmology; Fashion Management & Arts; Building Technology; Micro-Electronics; English as a Second Language; Mechanical & Manufacturing Technology; Architectural Technology
Services:
Remote Access
Inter-Library Loan (ILL)
Personnel: *Summary:* 8 Total; 4 Professional(s); 4 Technical(s)
Bill McAskill, Librarian
bmcaskil@georgebrown.ca

Toronto: Casa Loma ESL Resource Centre
#315, 1 Dartnell Ave.
Toronto, ON M5R 3A3
416-415-5000 ext: 4950
Hours: M-Th 11:00-4:00; F 12:00-4:00
Bill McAskill, Librarian
bmcaskil@georgebrown.ca
416-415-5000 ext. 3702

Toronto: C.D. Howe Institute Library
#300, 67 Yonge St.
Toronto, ON M5E 1J8
416-865-1904
Fax: 416-865-1866
e-mail: cdhowe@cdhowe.org
library@cdhowe.org
URL: www.cdhowe.org
National Library Symbol: OTCDH
Founded in: 1973
Hours: M-W 8:00-5:00 by appointment only
Acquisitions Budget: $10,000 - $24,999
For Print: $10,000 - $24,999

Special Collections: Federal & provincial government documents, especially budget material
Subjects covered: Economics, Energy, Industry, Labour, International Trade, Industrial Relations, Public Policy
Services:
Inter-Library Loan (ILL)
Personnel: *Summary:* 1 Total; 1 Professional(s)
Alyson Henry, Library & Information Services Coordinator
AHenry@cdhowe.org

Toronto: Centennial College Learning & Resource Centres

PO Box 631, Stn A
Toronto, ON M1K 5E9
416-289-5000 ext: 2601
Fax: 416-289-5228
e-mail: illocen@centennialcollege.ca
URL: library.centennialcollege.ca
National Library Symbol: OTARC
Consortia Membership: Ontario Colleges Library Service
Founded in: 1966
Hours: M-Th 8:00am-7:00pm; F 8:00-4:00; Sa 11:00-3:00 (hours may vary according to campus & time of year)
Acquisitions Budget: $250,000 - $499,999
For Print: $250,000 - $499,999
For Electronic: $100,000 - $249,999; Students, faculty & public
Note: Branches: Ashtonbee, Centre for Creative Communications, Progress, HP Science & Technology Centre, mailing address for all as above
Special Collections: John & Molly Pollock Holocaust Collection
Subjects covered: Business, Physical Sciences, Automotive, Health Sciences, Applied Arts, Humanities, Engineering, Technology, Economics, Aviation, Transportation
Services:
Remote Access
Internet Access
Inter-Library Loan (ILL)
Microform Equipment: Reader
Personnel: *Summary:* 30 Total; 5 Professional(s); 23 Technical(s); 2 Other employees
Gladys Watson, Director, Learning & Resource Centres
gwatson@centennialcollege.ca
416-289-5000 ext. 2601
Jan Tallon, Manager, Learning Centres & LRC Operations
jtallon@centennialcollege.ca
416-289-5000 ext. 2602
Dmitry Nikiforov, Acting Manager, Systems & Media
dnikiforov@centennialcollege.ca
416-289-5000 ext. 2612

Toronto: Centre for International & Security Studies R.B. Byers Memorial Research Library

York Research Tower, 6th Fl.
4700 Keele St.
Toronto, ON M3J 1P3
416-736-5156
Fax: 416-650-8069
e-mail: yciss@yorku.ca
URL: yciss.info.yorku.ca/publications/library
Hours: M-F 10:00-4:00
Subjects covered: Canadian defence policy; security studies; arms control and disarmament; regional security; conflict management
David Mutimer, Contact

Toronto: Centre for Refugee Studies Resource Centre

York Research Tower, 6th Fl.
4700 Keele St.
Toronto, ON M3J 1P3
416-736-2100 ext: 30391
URL: crs.yorku.ca
Hours: M-F 10:00-4:00
Special Collections: International legal instruments on refugees, government documents, scholarly papers, bibliographic citations
Subjects covered: Refugee Rights; Human Rights
Services:
Access to Subscription Databases
Michele Millard, Coordinator
mmillard@yorku.ca

Toronto: Centre for Research in Work & Society Resource Centre

York Research Tower, 6th Fl.
4700 Keele St.
Toronto, ON M3J 1P3
416-736-5612
Fax: 416-736-5916
e-mail: crws@yorku.ca
URL: www.yorku.ca/crws
Hours: By appointment only.
Special Collections: Queen's labour journals
Subjects covered: Work, Unions, Arbitration

Toronto: Centre for Research on Latin America & the Carribbean Documentation Centre

York Research Tower, 8th Fl.
4700 Keele St.
Toronto, ON M3J 1P3
416-736-5237
Fax: 416-736-5688
e-mail: cerlac@yorku.ca
URL: www.yorku.ca/cerlac
Founded in: 1978
Hours: M-F 9:00-4:00
Note: Half of the material is in Spanish.
Special Collections: Documents from the UN's Economic Commission for Latin America and the Caribbean
Subjects covered: Canadian-Latin American/Caribbean relations

Toronto: Centre for Women & Trans People - Ontario Public Interest Research Group Dr. Chun Resource Library

University of Toronto
#100, 563 Spadina Ave.
Toronto, ON M5S 2J7
416-978-8201
Fax: 416-978-1078
e-mail: resourcelibrary@riseup.net
womens.centre@utoronto.ca
cwpt@utoronto.ca
URL:
womenscentre.sa.utoronto.ca/programming/resource-library
Hours: Tu-Th 12:000-6:00; Community members & University of Toronto students
Note: Downtown Women's Centre resources is at this location
Services:
Internet Access
Personnel: *Summary:* 1 Total;
Vashti Persad, Administrative Coordinaor

Toronto: CH2M Hill Canada Limited Library

255 Consumers Rd.
Toronto, ON M2J 5B6
416-499-9000 ext: 305
Fax: 416-499-4687
URL: www.ch2m.com
National Library Symbol: OTGS
No public access
Founded in: 1984
Hours: M-F 8:00-4:00
Acquisitions Budget: $25,000 - $49,999
Subjects covered: Physical Sciences, Engineering, Technology
Services:
Inter-Library Loan (ILL)
Microform Equipment: Computer; Reader
Personnel: *Summary:* 1 Professional(s)
Dianne Sawh, Librarian
dsawh@ch2m.com

Toronto: Connexions Information Sharing Services Library

#305, 489 College St.
Toronto, ON M6G 1A5
416-964-1511
Fax: 416-964-8763
e-mail: connexions@connexions.org
URL: www.connexions.org
Founded in: 1976
Hours: by appointment only
Acquisitions Budget: $25,000 - $49,999
Special Collections: Alternative Press
Subjects covered: Social Criticism, Activism, Environment
Personnel: *Summary:* 2 Total; 1 Professional(s); 1 Technical(s); 6 Volunteer(s)
Ulli Diemer, Head
Chris Defreitas, Head of Technical Services

Toronto: CSA International Information Centre

178 Rexdale Blvd.
Toronto, ON M9W 1R3
416-747-4000
800-463-6727
Other contact info: Publications Phone: 416-747-4044; Fax: 416-747-2510
e-mail: info@csa-international.org
sales@csagroup.org
URL: www.csa-international.org
National Library Symbol: OTCSA
Founded in: 1970
Hours: M-F 9:00-4:00
Note: Publications can be bought through the group's online store
Special Collections: Standards Collections; some collections are comprehensive
Subjects covered: Product testing & certification
Personnel: *Summary:* 4 Total

Toronto: Energy Probe Research Foundation

225 Brunswick Ave.
Toronto, ON M5S 2M6
416-964-9223
Fax: 416-964-8239
URL: www.eprf.ca
Founded in: 1980
Subjects covered: Energy
Patricia Adams, President

Toronto: Engineering & Computer Science Library

University of Toronto
#2402, 10 King's College Rd.
Toronto, ON M5S 1A5
416-978-6494
Fax: 416-971-2091
e-mail: engineering.library@utoronto.ca
URL: engineering.library.utoronto.ca
National Library Symbol: OTUE
Founded in: 1974
Hours: M-Th 8:30am-10:30pm; F 8:30-6:00; Sa 9:00-5:00; Su 1:00-6:00
Subjects covered: Engineering, Applied Science, Computer Science
Services:
Remote Access
Internet Access
Access to Subscription Databases
Inter-Library Loan (ILL) for a fee
Personnel: *Summary:* 10 Total; 3 Professional(s); 6 Technical(s)
Jiabin Wang, Head of Library
jiabin.wang@utoronto.ca
416-946-5966
Neil Allen, Ciculation Supervisor
neil.allen@utoronto.ca
416-978-7681
Cristina Sewerin, Instruction & Reference Librarian
cris.sewerin@utoronto.ca
416-946-4020

Toronto: Environment Canada Library, Downsview / Environnement Canada bibliothèque, Downsview

4905 Dufferin St.
Toronto, ON M3H 5T4
416-739-5702
Fax: 416-739-4212
e-mail: librarybiblio.downsview@ec.gc.ca
URL: ec.gc.ca/bd-dl
National Library Symbol: OTM
Founded in: 1871
Hours: M-F 8:30-4:30
Subjects covered: Environment, Natural Resources, Conservation
Services:
Inter-Library Loan (ILL)
Microform Equipment: Computer; Reader
Maria Latyszewskyj, Head, Library Services
416-739-4828

Toronto: Environmental Commissioner of Ontario Resource Centre Library
#605, 1075 Bay St.
Toronto, ON M5S 2B1
416-325-0363
Fax: 416-325-3370
Other contact info: Media Inquiries, Phone: 416-325-3371
URL: www.eco.on.ca
Social Media: www.youtube.com/user/EcoComms
www.facebook.com/OntarioEnvironmentalCommissioner
twitter.com/Ont_ECO
National Library Symbol: OTECO
Founded in: 1995
Hours: M-F 9:30-5:00
Acquisitions Budget: $10,000 - $24,999
Special Collections: Federal and provincial government publications and reports; Corporate and government annual reports; Environmental legislation and policy literature; Environmental periodicals and reference works; Environmental management literature
Subjects covered: Environmental policy & law; Environmental Bill of Rights information; Environmental reports by Ontario ministries
Services:
Internet Access
Personnel: *Summary:* 1 Total; 1 Professional(s)
Carrie Cauz, Resource Centre Coordinator
Yazmin Shroff, Public Information / Outreach Officer

Toronto: E.W. Bickle Centre for Complex Continuing Care Library Services
130 Dunn Ave., #N234
Toronto, ON M5G 2A2
416-597-3422 ext: 2512
Hours: Tu
Subjects covered: Neurorehabilitation
Services:
Inter-Library Loan (ILL)
Holly Phillips, Library Contact
phillips.holly@torontorehab.on.ca

Toronto: Federation of Ontario Naturalists Ontario Nature Resources
#201, 366 Adelaide St. W
Toronto, ON M5V 1R9
416-444-8419
Fax: 416-444-9866
800-440-2366
URL: www.ontarionature.org
Subjects covered: Natural History (focus on Ontario), Environmental Education, Conservation
Services:
'Teaching Naturally' resources in English & some in French

Toronto: Geographic Resource Centre
#S403, Ross Bldg.
4700 Keele St.
Toronto, ON M3J 1P3
416-736-5086
e-mail: lapsgrc@yorku.ca
URL: www.yorku.ca/laps/geog/grc/index.html
Hours: M-F 9:00-1:00, 2:00-5:00; Geography faculty and students
Special Collections: 10,000 maps; geographic journals, DVDs, and atlases; Geological Survey of Canada Reports; Census of Canada; variety of tree and plant identification manuals; Aerial Photographs; Historical Road Maps; Slides of Southern Ontario, Canada, USA and other parts of the World Slides
Subjects covered: Geography

Toronto: George Brown College of Applied Arts & Technology Educational Resources
PO Box 1015, Stn B
Toronto, ON M5T 2T9
416-415-5000 ext: 2676
Fax: 416-415-2698
e-mail: askgbclibrary@georgebrown.ca
URL: library.georgebrown.ca
National Library Symbol: OTGBC
Consortia Membership: Ontario Colleges Library Service
Founded in: 1968
Acquisitions Budget: $50,000 - $99,999
Special Collections: Sommelier Wine Collection-St. James, OIQS-Ontario Institute of Quantity Surveyors-Casa Loma, Jewellery Arts-Casa Loma
Subjects covered: Arts, Medicine, Nursing, Health Sciences, Economics, Industry, Physical Sciences, Engineering, Applied Arts, Technology, Hospitality Services, Fashion, Social Sciences
Services:
Internet Access
Access to Subscription Databases
Inter-Library Loan (ILL)
Personnel: *Summary:* 22 Total; 4 Professional(s); 10 Technical(s); 10 Other employees
John L. Hardy, Director, Educational Resources
jhardy@gbrownc.on.ca
416-415-5000 ext. 2676

Toronto: Gerstein Science Information Centre
9 King's College Circle
Toronto, ON M5S 1A5
Mailing Address: 9 King's College Circle
Toronto, ON M5S 1A5
416-978-2280
Fax: 416-971-2848
e-mail: ask.gerstein@utoronto.ca
URL: gerstein.library.utoronto.ca
National Library Symbol: OTUH
Consortia Membership: Health Science Information Consortium of Toronto
Hours: M-Su
Note: Pharmacy Library has closed & the collection integrated with Gerstein.
Special Collections: Technical reports, Microfiche, Landmarks of Science
Subjects covered: Health Sciences, Physical & Applied Sciences, Biological Sciences
Services:
Internet Access
Inter-Library Loan (ILL)
Microform Equipment: Computer; Reader
Personnel: *Summary:* 45 Total; 10 Professional(s); 35 Technical(s)
Sandra Langlands, Director
s.langlands.melvin@utoronto.ca
416-978-6370
Bonnie Horne, Librarian, Resource Sharing & Access Services Unit Coordinator
b.horne@utoronto.ca
416-978-5329

Toronto: Harriet Tubman Resource Centre
314 York Lanes
Toronto, ON M3J 1P3
416-736-2100 ext: 44561
URL: tubman.info.yorku.ca/resource-centre
Hours: M 10:00-3:30; Tu 10:00-2:00; W, Th 10:00-4:30
Subjects covered: African Diaspora
Services:
Microform Equipment: Computer
Diana Lee, Librarian
dianelee@yorku.ca

Toronto: H.H. Angus & Associates Limited Consulting Engineers Library
1127 Leslie St.
Toronto, ON M3C 2J6
416-443-8200
Fax: 416-443-8290
866-955-8201
e-mail: info@hhangus.com
URL: www.hhangus.com
National Library Symbol: OTHHA
No public access
Subjects covered: Mechanical & Electrical Engineering Consulting
Services:
Remote Access
Internet Access
Access to Subscription Databases
Personnel: *Summary:* 3 Total; 1 Professional(s); 2 Technical(s)
Wendy Scott, Library & Resources Manager

Toronto: H.H. Mu Far Eastern Library
100 Queen's Park Cres.
Toronto, ON M5S 2C6
416-586-5718
Fax: 416-586-5877
e-mail: fe.library@rom.on.ca
National Library Symbol: OTRMF
Hours: M-F 1:00-5:00
Subjects covered: Ornithology, Asian Art & Archaeology; Egypt
Services:
Internet Access
Inter-Library Loan (ILL)
Jack Howard, Librarian
jackh@rom.on.ca
Kangmei Wang, Library Technician
kang-mei@rom.on.ca

Toronto: Hospital for Sick Children Hospital Library
555 University Ave.
Toronto, ON M5G 1X8
416-813-6693
Fax: 416-813-7523
e-mail: hsclink@sickkids.ca
URL: www.sickkids.ca/Learning/HospitalLibrary
National Library Symbol: OTHSC
Consortia Membership: Health Science Information Consortium of Toronto
Founded in: 1919
Hours: M-Th 8:00-8:00; F 8:00-6:00; Su 11:00-6:00 by appointment only
Acquisitions Budget: $50,000 - $99,999
Subjects covered: Pediatrics
Services:
Remote Access
Access to Subscription Databases
Inter-Library Loan (ILL) for a fee of $5/non-profit; $10/profit
Personnel: *Summary:* 8 Total; 3 Professional(s); 6 Technical(s)
Elizabeth Uleryk, Director
elizabeth.uleryk@sickkids.ca
416-813-6695
Tamsin Adams-Webber, Librarian
thomasin.adams-webber@sickkids.ca

Toronto: Humber College Institute of Technology & Advanced Learning North Campus Library
NX Bldg.
205 Humber College Blvd.
Toronto, ON M9W 5L7
Mailing Address: 205 Humber College Blvd.
Toronto, ON M9W 5L7
416-675-5079
Fax: 416-675-7439
Other contact info: Reference: 416-675-6622, ext.4421
URL: www.library.humber.ca
Consortia Membership: Ontario Colleges Library Service
Founded in: 1967
Hours: Sept.-April: M-Th 7:45am-9:00pm; F 7:45-6:00; Sa 8:45-3:00; Su 12:00-5:00. May-June: M-Th 8:30-7:30; F 8:30-4:30; Sa 8:45-3:00. July-Aug.: M-Th 8:30-6
Special Collections: AV equipment & software; Record & CD collection
Subjects covered: Arts & Science; Business; Technology; Health Sciences; Media Studies
Services:
Internet Access
Microform Equipment: Computer; Reader
Personnel: *Summary:* 6 Total; 6 Professional(s)
Lynne Bentley, Director
lynne.bentley@humber.ca
416-675-6622 ext. 4574
Mark Bryant, Reference & Information Literacy Librarian
mark.bryant@humber.ca
416-675-6222 ext. 4170
Maureen Hyland, Collections Development & Technical Services Librarian
maureen.hyland@humber.ca
416-675-6622 ext. 4501
Nancy Pierobon, Health Sciences Librarian
Dawne Hoogkamer, Library Technician, Government Documents/Statistics Canada
Marlene Beck, Library Technician, Interlibrary Loans & Special Needs
marlene.beck@humber.ca
Jennifer Rayment, Library Technician, Periodicals
Lisa DiBarbora, Virtual Services Librarian
lisa.dibarbora@humer.ca
416-675-6622 ext. 4170
Gina Matesic, Guelph-Humber Librarian
gina.matesic@humber.ca
416-675-6622 ext. 6090

Toronto: IBI Group
Library
230 Richmond St. West, 5th Fl.
Toronto, ON M5V 1V6
416-596-1930
Fax: 416-596-0644
URL: www.ibigroup.com
National Library Symbol: OTIBI
No public access
Founded in: 1974
Subjects covered: Engineering
Services:
Internet Access
Jennifer Osther, Librarian
josther@ibigroup.com
416-596-1930 ext. 1300

Toronto: Imperial Oil Resources Limited Products Division, Engineering & Petroleum Information Centre
#4104, 90 Wynford Dr.
Toronto, ON M3C 1K5
416-441-7858
Fax: 416-441-7926
e-mail: contact.imperial@esso.ca
No public access
Founded in: 1982
Hours: M-W 8:00-4:30
Acquisitions Budget: $25,000 - $49,999
Subjects covered: Physical Sciences, Engineering, Technology, Natural Resources
Personnel: *Summary:* 1 Total; 1 Professional(s)

Toronto: Intergovernmental Committee on Urban & Regional Research (ICURR) / Comité intergouvernemental de recherches urbaines et régionales (CIRUR)
Library
#210, 40 Wynford Dr.
Toronto, ON M3C 1J5
647-345-7004
Fax: 647-345-6991
e-mail: icurrlib@icurr.org
URL: www.muniscope.ca/library
National Library Symbol: OTICU
Founded in: 1967
Hours: M-F 8:30-5:00 by appointment only
Acquisitions Budget: $25,000 - $49,999
Note: Online catalogue access. Also called Muniscope Information & Networking.
Special Collections: Municipal Bylaws
Subjects covered: Local Government; Urban Regional Planning; Environment; Municipal Issues
Services:
Internet Access
Fee Based Research
Personnel: *Summary:* 3 Total; 2 Professional(s); 1 Other employees
Mark Rose, Information Services Manager
mrose@icurr.org
647-345-7004
Katherine d'Entremont, Director
kdentremont@icurr.org
647-345-6454

Toronto: John H. Daniels Faculty of Architecture, Landscape & Design
Shore & Moffat Library
230 College St., 2nd Fl.
Toronto, ON M5T 1R2
416-978-2649
Fax: 416-971-2094
e-mail: library@daniels.utoronto.ca
URL: www.daniels.utoronto.ca/library
National Library Symbol: OTUSA
Founded in: 1998
Hours: M-Th 9:00-9:00; F 9:00-7:00; Sa 12:00-5:00. Hours may vary throughout the academic year
Acquisitions Budget: $25,000 - $49,999
Note: Loans are restricted to users with University of Toronto library cards.
Subjects covered: Architecture, Landscape Architecture, Design, Urban Studies
Services:
Remote Access
Internet Access
Access to Subscription Databases
Inter-Library Loan (ILL)
Personnel: *Summary:* 4 Total; 1 Professional(s); 2 Technical(s); 1 Other employees
Irene Puchalski, Librarian (on leave 2012-2013)
irene.puchalski@utoronto.ca
416-978-6787
Effie Patelos, Acting Librarian
effie.patelos@daniels.utoronto.ca
416-978-6787

Toronto: Laboratories Library
81 Resources Rd.
Toronto, ON M9P 3T1
416-235-5935
Fax: 416-235-6196
Consortia Membership: Health Science Information Consortium of Toronto
Hours: M-F 8:00-4:00 by appointment only
Gabrielle Gaedecke, Library Technician
gabrielle.gaedecke@oahpp.ca

Toronto: Lakeshore Campus
Library
#B202, 3199 Lakeshore Blvd. West
Toronto, ON M8V 1K8
416-675-6622 ext: 3247
Fax: 416-252-0918
Other contact info: Reference: 416-675-6622 ext. 3351
Founded in: 1975
Hours: Sept.-April: M-Th 7:45am-9:00pm; F 7:45-4:30; Sa 10:00-3:00; Su 12:00-5:00. May-June: M-Th 8:30-6:30; F 8:30-4:30. July-Aug.: M-F 8:30-4:30
Special Collections: Statistics Canada, Company report collections
Subjects covered: Child Care, Business, Microcomputer Training, Law Enforcement, Theatre, Music, Social Services
Services:
Internet Access
Inter-Library Loan (ILL)
Media Centre (audiovisual equipment, records, screening room)
Microform Equipment: Computer; Reader
Personnel: *Summary:* 7 Total; 2 Professional(s); 3 Technical(s); 2 Other employees
Janet Hollingsworth, Library Coordinator
janet.hollingsworth@humber.ca
416-675-6622 ext. 3250
Alexandra Ross, Liaison Librarian
alexandra.ross@humber.ca
416-675-6622 ext. 3143
Karen Reece, Sr. Library Technician, Technical Services & Scheduling
karen.reece@humber.ca
416-675-6622 ext. 3208
Valerie Walton, Library Technician, Reference, Periodicals, & Government Documents
valerie.walton@humber.ca
416-675-6622 ext. 3146
Liz Crim, Library Clerk, Circulation & Student Assistants
liz.crim@humber.ca
416-675-6622 ext. 3142

Toronto: LaMarch Centre for Child & Youth Research
Michael Smith Resource Centre
5022 TEL Bldg., 5th Fl.
Toronto, ON M3J 1P3
416-736-5528
Fax: 416-736-5647
e-mail: lamarsh@yorku.ca
URL: www.yorku.ca/lamarsh
Hours: M-F 9:00-4:30
Subjects covered: Health, Education, Relationships and development of infants, children, adolescents, emerging adults and families everywhere
Services:
Microform Equipment: Computer

Toronto: Lyndhurst Centre
Library Services
#208, 520 Sutherland Dr.
Toronto, ON M5G 2A2
416-597-3422 ext: 6136
Hours: M-F afternoons
Subjects covered: Spinal Cord
Services:
Inter-Library Loan (ILL)
Maureen Pakosh, Library Contact
pakosh.maureen@torontorehab.on.ca

Toronto: Map & Data Library
Robarts Library
130 St. George St., 5th Fl.
Toronto, ON M5S 1A5
Mailing Address: 130 St. George St., 5th Fl.
Toronto, ON M5S 1A5
416-978-5589
e-mail: gis.maps@utoronto.ca
URL: mdl.library.utoronto.ca
maplib.blogspot.ca
National Library Symbol: OTUM
Founded in: 1996
Hours: M-F 11:00-5:00
Acquisitions Budget: $50,000 - $99,999
Special Collections: Atlases; Toronto maps & aerial photos; Canada maps; rare maps; general topography; thematic world maps; GIS data; Data Library Service Collection: Computer-readable numeric & textual research files, primarily in the social sciences & humanities; Map Library Collection: includes maps & atlases providing world wide coverage on a large range of subjects
Services:
Internet Access
Inter-Library Loan (ILL) for a fee
Microform Equipment: Reader
Personnel: *Summary:* 10 Total; 5 Professional(s); 6 Technical(s)
Berenica Vejvoda, Data Librarian
berenica.vejvoda.utoronto.ca
Marcel Fortin, GIS & Map Librarian
marcel.fortin@utoronto.ca

Toronto: Map Library
#102, Scott Library, 4700 Keele St.
Toronto, ON M3J 1P3
416-736-2100 ext: 33353
Fax: 416-736-5838
Founded in: 1970
Hours: M-Th 10:00-9:00; F 10:00-5:00; Sa, Su 12:00-5:00
Acquisitions Budget: $25,000 - $49,999
Special Collections: Maps, Air Photos; Atlases; Geospatial data
Subjects covered: Maps of Toronto, Southern Ontario, Canada, United States, West Indies
Personnel: *Summary:* 3 Total; 1 Professional(s); 2 Technical(s)
Rosa Orlandini, Map Librarian
rorlan@yorku.ca
Mary McDowell, Map Library Assistant
marymc@yorku.ca
Janet Howarth, Reference Assistant
howarth@yorku.ca

Toronto: Marion Powell Women's Health Information Centre
#916, 76 Grenville St.
Toronto, ON M5S 1B2
416-323-6045 ext: 4076
Fax: 416-323-6122
e-mail: askus.whic@wchospital.ca
Services:
Inter-Library Loan (ILL)

Toronto: Medical Reform Group of Ontario
Resource Centre
PO Box 40074, RPO Marlee
Toronto, ON M6B 4K4
416-787-5246
Fax: 416-352-1454
e-mail: medicalreform@sympatico.ca
URL: www.medicalreformgroup.ca
Founded in: 1979
Hours: by appointment only
Acquisitions Budget: $25,000 - $49,999
Note: Resource Centre consists of association archives
Subjects covered: Health Reform

Toronto: The Michener Institute for Applied Health Sciences
Learning Resource Centre
222 St Patrick St., 2nd Fl.
Toronto, ON M5T 1V4

416-596-3123 ext: 3123
Fax: 416-596-3137
800-387-9066
e-mail: lrc@michener.ca
URL: www.michener.ca/lrc
National Library Symbol: OTTIM
No public access
Founded in: 1972
Hours: M-Th 8:00am-9:00pm; F 8:00-5:00; Sa-Su 9:00-5:00
Acquisitions Budget: $50,000 - $99,999
For Print: $50,000 - $99,999
For Electronic: $10,000 - $24,999
Services:
Inter-Library Loan (ILL)
Personnel: *Summary:* 3 Total; 1 Professional(s); 2 Technical(s)
Winnie Ho, Library Assistant
who@michener.ca
416-596-3101 ext. 3464

Toronto: Miss Margaret Robins Archives
76 Grenville St., Basement
Toronto, ON M5S 1B2
416-323-6400 ext: 4076
Fax: 416-323-6122
e-mail: wch.archives@wchospital.ca
Hours: M-Th, and every other F 9:00-4:00 by appointment only
Special Collections: Photographs; historical records; Academic papers
Services:
Inter-Library Loan (ILL)

Toronto: Mount Sinai Hospital
Sidney Liswood Library
#18-234, 600 University Ave.
Toronto, ON M5G 1X5
416-586-4800 ext: 4614
Fax: 416-586-4998
e-mail: library@mtsinai.on.ca
URL: www.mountsinai.on.ca/education/library
National Library Symbol: OTMS
Consortia Membership: Health Science Information Consortium of Toronto
Founded in: 1990
Hours: M-F 8:30-5:00 by appointment only
Acquisitions Budget: $250,000 - $499,999
Subjects covered: Medicine, Nursing, Health Sciences; Maternal, Fetal & Newborn Health Sciences; Surgical Oncology; Musculoskeletal Disease; Gastrointestinal Disease; and Molecular; Sub-Specialty Medicine
Services:
Internet Access
Inter-Library Loan (ILL)
Personnel: *Summary:* 5 Total; 2 Professional(s); 3 Technical(s)
Sandra Kendall, Director, Library Services
416-586-4800 ext. 4614

Toronto: Nickel Institute
Brookfield Pl., #2700, 161 Bay St.
Toronto, ON M5J 2S1
416-591-7999
e-mail: ni_toronto@nickelinstitute.org
URL: www.nickelinstitute.org
No public access

Toronto: Noranda Earth Sciences Library
5 Bancroft Ave., 2nd Fl.
Toronto, ON M5S 1A5
416-978-3024
Fax: 416-971-2101
e-mail: earth.sciences@utoronto.ca
URL: earth.library.utoronto.ca
National Library Symbol: OTUNE
Hours: M-Th 9:00-9:00; F 9:00-5:00; Sa 9:00-5:00
Special Collections: University of Toronto Dissertations in Botany, Geology, Forestry; Environmental Grey Literature Collection
Subjects covered: Botany, Forestry, Geology
Services:
Remote Access
Internet Access
Access to Subscription Databases
Personnel: *Summary:* 10 Total; 1 Professional(s); 2 Technical(s); 6 Other employees
Eric James, Reference Specialist
eric.james@utoronto.ca
416-978-6673
Lynn Barrett, Access Services Generalist
lynn.barrett@utoronto.ca
416-978-3024

Toronto: Office of the Fire Marshal
Fire Sciences Library & Audio-Visual Resource Centre
5775 Yonge St., 7th Fl.
Toronto, ON M2M 4J1
416-325-3121
Fax: 416-325-3213
e-mail: firesciences.information@ofm.ca
URL: www.ofm.gov.on.ca/en/Library
National Library Symbol: OTFM
Consortia Membership: Ontario Government Libraries Council (OGLC)
Founded in: 1962
Hours: M-F 8:30-4:15
Acquisitions Budget: $25,000 - $49,999
Note: Under the auspices of Ontario. Ministry of Community Safety & Correctional Services
Special Collections: Collection of ULC standards, CSA standards, NFPA codes, Building & fire codes
Subjects covered: Physical Sciences, Engineering, Technology, Fire Prevention, Fighting, Investigation, & Management, Hazardous Materials, Health & Safety, Building Construction, Arson, Fire Codes, Risk Management, Emergency Response, Juvenile Fire Setters
Services:
Internet Access
Inter-Library Loan (ILL)
Microform Equipment: Reader
Personnel: *Summary:* 1 Total
Martha Murphy, Librarian
martha.murphy@jus.gov.on.ca
416-325-3235

Toronto: Ontario Energy Board / Commission d'énergie de l'Ontario
Publications
2300 Yonge St.
Toronto, ON M4P 1E4
Mailing Address: PO Box 2319
Toronto, ON M4P 1E4
416-481-1967
Fax: 416-440-7656
888-632-6273
Other contact info: OEB Consumer Relations Centre: 1-877-632-2727
e-mail: BoardSec@ontarioenergyboard.ca
URL: www.ontarioenergyboard.ca
National Library Symbol: OTOEB
Founded in: 1982
Hours: M-F by appointment only
Acquisitions Budget: $25,000 - $49,999
Note: Under auspices of Ministry of Energy, Science & Technology
Special Collections: OEB & NEB transcripts & decisions (selected), Provincial & State boards/commissions (selected), Environmental materials, Annual Reports, Public Utilities Reports Digests 1934-, Public Utilities Fortnightly 1960-
Subjects covered: Utilities, Energy Resources & Regulation
Services:
Inter-Library Loan (ILL)
Lina Buccilli, Librarian
lina.buccilli@ontarioenergyboard.ca

Toronto: Ontario Ministry of Economic Development & Innovation
Communications & Public Affairs Branch, Heart Block
900 Bay St., 8th Fl.
Toronto, ON M7A 2E1
416-325-6666
Fax: 416-325-6688
866-668-4249
e-mail: info@edt.gov.on.ca
URL: www.ontario.ca/economy
Social Media: www.youtube.com/MEDTOntario
www.facebook.com/ontarioinnovation
416-325-4402Onteconomy
No public access
Founded in: 1994
Hours: M-F 8:30-4:30
Acquisitions Budget: For Print: 0-$9,999
For Electronic: $10,000 - $24,999
Subjects covered: Business; Economic Development; Industry; Enterprise; Trade; Investment
Personnel: *Summary:* 1 Total; 1 Professional(s)
Dino Rocca, Director, Communiations & Public Affairs
dino.rocca@ontario.ca

Toronto: Ontario Ministry of Environment
40 St. Clair Ave. West, 11th Fl.
Toronto, ON M4V 1M2
416-314-5017
Fax: 705-755-1599
URL: www.ene.gov.on.ca/environment
National Library Symbol: OTENL
Founded in: 1964
Hours: by appointment only
Subjects covered: Environmental Studies
Services:
Microform Equipment: Computer; Reader
Robert Hollis, Chief Information Officer
robert.hollis@ontario.ca

Toronto: Ontario Ministry of Health & Long-Term Care
Health Services Information & Information Technology
56 Wellesley St. West, 10th Fl.
Toronto, ON M5S 2S3
416-314-4243
Fax: 416-314-0289
URL: www.health.gov.on.ca
Social Media: www.youtube.com/user/ontariomohltc
www.facebook.com/group.php?gid=217753654940869
twitter.com/ONThealth
No public access
Founded in: 1963
Hours: M-F
Acquisitions Budget: $50,000 - $99,999
For Print: $25,000 - $49,999
For Electronic: 0-$9,999
Subjects covered: Microbiology; Infectious Diseases
Services:
Internet Access
Personnel: *Summary:* 1 Total; 1 Technical(s)
Lorelle Taylor, Chief Information Officer
416-314-1279

Toronto: Ontario Ministry of Municipal Affairs & Housing
InfoLink - Library & Information Centre
777 Bay St., 3rd Fl.
Toronto, ON M5G 2E5
416-585-7333
Fax: 416-585-7122
e-mail: infolink@mah.gov.on.ca
National Library Symbol: OTOH
No public access
Founded in: 1968
Hours: M-F 9:00-5:00
Subjects covered: Housing, Public Works, Local Government, Architecture, Planning, Geography, Low Income Housing, Housing Management, Conservation, Municipal Finance
Services:
Inter-Library Loan (ILL)
Fee Based Research
Personnel: *Summary:* 2 Total; 2 Professional(s)
Florence Lam, Information Specialist
Sarah Nichols, Information Specialist

Toronto: Ontario Power Generation
Business Information Centre
#H17 G10, 700 University Ave.
Toronto, ON M5G 1X6
416-592-2715
Fax: 416-592-7532
e-mail: library@opg.com
No public access
Hours: M-F 8:00-4:00
Acquisitions Budget: $500,000 - $999,999
Subjects covered: Energy
Personnel: *Summary:* 13 Total; 5 Professional(s); 3 Technical(s)
Nancy Fish, Manager, Library

Toronto: Ontario Science Centre Library
770 Don Mills Rd.
Toronto, ON M3C 1T3
416-696-3149
Fax: 416-696-3157
e-mail: vhatten@osc.on.ca
URL: www.ontariosciencecentre.ca
National Library Symbol: OTST
Founded in: 1966
Hours: M-F 8:45-5:00 by appointment only
Acquisitions Budget: $25,000 - $49,999
Special Collections: Exhibit slides, Audio-Visual
Subjects covered: General Sciences, Technology, Museum & Exhibit Design, Applied Arts, Museology
Services:
Inter-Library Loan (ILL)
Personnel: *Summary:* 1 Total; 1 Professional(s)
Valerie Hatten, Librarian

Toronto: Osgoode Hall Law School Law Library
4700 Keele St.
Toronto, ON M3J 1P3
416-736-5206
Fax: 416-736-5298
e-mail: lawref@osgoode.yorku.ca
National Library Symbol: OTYL
Hours: M-Th 8:00-10:00; F 8:00-5:00; Sa, Su 10:00-6:00
Special Collections: Canadian legal material published through 1900; U.K. material published through 1860 plus early trials published through 1900; Canadian & U.K. manuscripts; broadsides mainly from England; Osgoodiana Law
Subjects covered: Law
Services:
Inter-Library Loan (ILL)
Microform Equipment: Computer; Reader

Toronto: Petro Jacyk Central & East European Resource Centre
#3008, 130 St George St.
Toronto, ON M5S 1A5
416-978-0588
URL: pjrc.library.utoronto.ca
Special Collections: H. Gordon Skilling's collection on the political development of Czechoslovakia; Jazz Section of the Czechoslovak Union of Musicians collection; 1919 diary by Dmitrii Dmitrievich Litovchenko
Subjects covered: Eastern Europe
Services:
Internet Access
Ksenya Kiebuzinski, Head, PJRC & Slavic Resources Coordinator
ksenya.kiebuzinski@utoronto.ca

Toronto: Physics Library
#211C, 60 St. George St.
Toronto, ON M5S 1A7
416-978-5188
Fax: 416-978-5919
e-mail: library@physics.utoronto.ca
URL: www.physics.utoronto.ca/physics-at-uoft/library
National Library Symbol: OTUP
No public access
Hours: M-F 9:00-5:00
Special Collections: Physics abstracts, 1969 to present online, pre-1969 paper copy; U of T Physics theses/dissertations
Subjects covered: Math, Physics, Atmospheric Sciences, Geophysics
Services:
Inter-Library Loan (ILL)
Personnel: *Summary:* 2 Total; 1 Professional(s); 1 Technical(s)
Dylanne Dearborn, Physics Librarian
dearborn@physics.utoronto.ca

Toronto: Prospectors & Developers Association of Canada
135 King St. East
Toronto, ON M5C 1G6
416-362-1969
Fax: 416-362-0101
e-mail: info@pdac.ca
URL: www.pdac.ca
Subjects covered: Mines; Minerals; Industry

Toronto: Public Health Ontario Health Ontario Library
#300, 480 University Ave.
Toronto, ON M5G 1V2
647-250-7242
e-mail: library@oahpp.ca
URL: www.oahpp.ca/resources/library.html
Consortia Membership: Health Science Information Consortium of Toronto
Hours: by appointment only
Beata Pach, Manager, Library Services
beata.pach@oahpp.ca

Toronto: Qualitative Research & Resource Centre
#N141, Ross Bldg.
4700 Keele St.
Toronto, ON M3J 1P3
416-736-5014
e-mail: qrrc@yorku.ca
URL: www.yorku.ca/laps/soci/qrrc/index.html
Hours: M-Th 9:00-4:30
Subjects covered: Focus groups, longitudinal research, narrative inquiry, natural observation, group interviews
Services:
Microform Equipment: Computer

Toronto: Radiation Safety Institute of Canada Resource Library
#607, 1120 Finch Ave. West
Toronto, ON M3J 3H7
416-650-9090
Fax: 416-650-9920
800-263-5803
e-mail: info@radiationsafety.ca
URL: www.radiationsafety.ca
Founded in: 1980
Hours: M-F 9:00-4:00
Acquisitions Budget: 0-$9,999
Subjects covered: Radiation

Toronto: The Resource Library for the Environment and the Law / L'Association canadienne du droit de l'environnement Library
#301, 130 Spadina Ave.
Toronto, ON M5V 2L4
416-960-2284
Fax: 416-960-9392
URL: www.cela.ca/library
www.ecolawinfo.org
Founded in: 1993
Hours: M-F 9:00-5:00
Acquisitions Budget: $10,000 - $24,999
For Print: $10,000 - $24,999
Note: Phone for current public access hours
Subjects covered: Environmental Law, Pollution, Pollution Control, Resource Management, Environmental Health, Land Use Planning, Trade, Water
Services:
Internet Access
Personnel: *Summary:* 7 Total; 1 Professional(s); 2 Volunteer(s)
Sarah Miller, Coordinator and Researcher
millers@lao.on.ca

Toronto: Retirement Planning Centre
#101, Central Square
4700 Keele St.
Toronto, ON M3J 1P3
416-736-2100 ext: 66228
e-mail: retire@yorku.ca
URL: www.yorku.ca/retire/index.htm
Hours: M-F 8:30-4:30
Subjects covered: Retirement, Aging, Housing, Pensions
Services:
Microform Equipment: Computer
Catherine Federico, Coordinator

Toronto: Royal Ontario Museum / Musée royal de l'Ontario Library & Archives
100 Queen's Park Cres.
Toronto, ON M5S 2C6
416-586-5595
Fax: 416-586-5519
e-mail: info@rom.on.ca
library@rom.on.ca
URL:
www.rom.on.ca/en/collections-research/rom-library-archives
National Library Symbol: OTRM
Founded in: 1961
Hours: M-F 10:00-5:00
Acquisitions Budget: $500,000 - $999,999
For Print: $100,000 - $249,999
For Electronic: 0-$9,999
Note: Under the auspices of the Ministry of Culture. Closed stacks. Collection is non-circulating, however materials may be borrowed by ROM staff, University of Toronto faculty, and University of Toronto students enrolled in the Museum Studies Program. Consult the University of Toronto catalogue for holdings. Public may access the Library & Archives for reference use only
Special Collections: Main Library & Archives houses the Archives of the Royal Ontario Museum, as well as the J.H. Fleming Collection of books relating to ornithology; Rare Book Collection; H.H. Mu Far Eastern Library, the premier library in Canada devoted to the arts of the Orient; Textiles Collection; Canadian Collections
Subjects covered: Archaeology, Botany, Canadiana, Decorative Arts, Geology, Minerology, Museology, Ethnology, Palaeontology, Zoology, Textiles & Costume, Asian Art & Archaeology, Egyptology
Services:
Remote Access
Internet Access
Access to Subscription Databases
Inter-Library Loan (ILL) for a fee of $20
Scanning
Microform Equipment: Reader
Personnel: *Summary:* 4 Total; 2 Volunteer(s)
Arthur Smith, Head, Library & Archives
arthurs@rom.on.ca
416-586-5740

Toronto: Rumsey Centre - Cardiac Library Services
#224, 345 Rumsey Rd.
Toronto, ON M5G 2A2
416-597-3422 ext: 5224
Hours: M-F mornings
Subjects covered: Cardiac
Services:
Inter-Library Loan (ILL)
Maureen Pakosh, Library Contact
pakosh.maureen@torontorehab.on.ca

Toronto: Rumsey Centre - Neurorehabilitation Library Services
#150, 345 Rumsey Rd.
Toronto, ON M5G 2A2
416-597-3422 ext: 5338
Hours: M-F mornings
Subjects covered: Neurorehabilitation
Services:
Inter-Library Loan (ILL)
Maureen Pakosh, Library Contact
pakosh.maureen@torontorehab.on.ca

Toronto: R.V. Anderson Associates Limited Library
#400, 2001 Sheppard Ave. East
Toronto, ON M2J 4Z8
416-497-8600 ext: 212
Fax: 416-497-0342
e-mail: tzimmer@rvanderson.com
toronto@rvanderson.com
URL: www.rvanderson.com
National Library Symbol: OWAA
No public access
Founded in: 1948
Hours: M-F 9:00-5:00
Note: Extensive engineering journals collection
Subjects covered: Environmental & Civil Engineering, Telecommunications Engineering, Architecture
Services:
Inter-Library Loan (ILL)
Personnel: *Summary:* 3 Total; 2 Professional(s); 1 Technical(s)
Terri Zimmer, Librarian
tzimmer@randerson.com
416-497-8600 ext. 212
Leah Swift, Researcher
lswift@randerson.com
416-497-8600 ext. 212

Liane Wilson, Content Administrator
lwilson@randerson.com
416-497-8600 ext. 212

Toronto: Ryerson University Library & Archives

350 Victoria St.
Toronto, ON M5B 2K3
416-979-5055
Fax: 416-979-5215
Other contact info: Archives: 416-979-5000, ext. 7027
e-mail: refdesk@ryerson.ca
racer@ryerson.ca
archives@ryerson.ca
URL: www.ryerson.ca/library
www.ryerson.ca/archives
National Library Symbol: OTR
Consortia Membership: Canadian Research Knowledge Network (CRKN); Ontario Council of University Libraries (OCUL)
Founded in: 1947
Hours: M-F 8:00am-12:00am; Sa, Su 10:00am-12:00am
Acquisitions Budget: $1,000,000 plus
For Print: $1,000,000 plus
For Electronic: $1,000,000 plus
Special Collections: Collection dates from 1783 to present day and focuses on Ryerson University and its predecessor institutions, including items such as year books, photographs, film, sound recordings, manuals, newspapers, etc.
Subjects covered: Applied Arts, Engineering, Business, Community Services, Social Science, Communication & Design
Services:
Remote Access
Internet Access
Access to Subscription Databases
Inter-Library Loan (ILL)
Microform Equipment: Computer; Reader
Personnel: *Summary:* 81 Total; 23 Professional(s); 58 Other employees
Madeleine Lefebvre, Chief Librarian
mjlefebv@ryerson.ca
416-979-5142
Jane Schmidt, Collections Team Manager
jschmidt@ryerson.ca
416-979-5146
Susan Patrick, Head, Special Collections & Archives
spatrick@ryerson.ca
416-979-6897

Toronto: St James Library/Learning Commons

#121, 200 King St. East
Toronto, ON M5A 3W8
Mailing Address: 200 King St. East
Toronto, ON M5A 3W8
416-415-5000 ext: 2173
Fax: 416-415-2698
TDD: 8775155559
e-mail: llc@georgebrown.ca
Founded in: 1976
Hours: M-F 7:30-10:00; Sa 10:00-6:00; Su 10:00-5:00 by appointment only
Special Collections: Canadian Guild of Sommeliers, Ontario Hostelry
Subjects covered: Hospitality, Nursing, Business, Graphic Arts, Community Services
Services:
Inter-Library Loan (ILL)
Personnel: *Summary:* 6 Total; 1 Professional(s); 5 Technical(s)

Toronto: St Michael's Hospital Health Sciences Library

East Bldg., Li Ka Shing International Healthcare Education Centre
209 Victoria St., 3rd Fl.
Toronto, ON M5B 1T8
416-864-5059
Fax: 416-864-5296
e-mail: hslibrary@smh.ca
URL: www.stmichaelshospital.com/learn/library.php
National Library Symbol: OTSM
Consortia Membership: Health Science Information Consortium of Toronto
No public access
Hours: M-F 9:00-5:00; Hospital employees, staff, current patients and their families and authorized students & volunteers
Subjects covered: Health Sciences, Medicine
Personnel: *Summary:* 6 Professional(s); 3 Technical(s)
Pat Richards, Team Leader
RICHARDSP@smh.ca

Toronto: The Scarborough Hospital - General Campus Health Information Resource Centre

3050 Lawrence Ave. East
Toronto, ON M1P 2V5
416-431-8114
Fax: 416-431-8232
e-mail: librarygen@tsh.to
URL: tsh.to
National Library Symbol: OSGH
Consortia Membership: Health Science Information Consortium of Toronto
No public access
Hours: M-F 8:30-4:30
Subjects covered: Medicine & Allied Health
Services:
Inter-Library Loan (ILL) for a fee of $12
Personnel: *Summary:* 2 Total; 1 Professional(s); 1 Technical(s); 3 Volunteer(s)
Fatimah Ahmed, Manager, Health Information Resource Centre
fahmed@tsh.to
Judy Ng, Library Technician
jung@tsh.to
416-431-8200 ext. 6593

Toronto: The Scarborough Hospital - Grace Campus Library

3030 Birchmount Rd.
Toronto, ON M1W 3W3
416-495-2437
Fax: 416-495-2562
e-mail: fahmed@tsh.to
URL: www.library.tsh.to
Hours: M-F 8:30-4:30
Subjects covered: Health Sciences, Medicine, Hospital Administration
Fatimah Ahmed, Librarian
fahmed@tsh.to

Toronto: Seneca College of Applied Arts & Technology Newnham Campus

1750 Finch Ave. East
Toronto, ON M2J 2X5
416-491-5050 ext: 2099
e-mail: askthelibrary@senecacollege.ca
ill@senecacollege.ca
URL: library.senecacollege.ca
National Library Symbol: OTSC
Consortia Membership: Ontario Colleges Library Service
Founded in: 1967
Hours: M-Th 8:00am-11:00pm; F 8:00-10:00; Sa 8:30-5:00; Su 9:00-5:00
Acquisitions Budget: $500,000 - $999,999
Note: Newnham Campus Learning Commons located here
Subjects covered: Applied Arts, Technology, Business, General Education
Services:
Internet Access
Access to Subscription Databases
Inter-Library Loan (ILL)
Personnel: *Summary:* 71 Total; 15 Professional(s); 32 Technical(s); 24 Other employees
Tanis Fink, Chief Librarian & Director
tanis.fink@senecacollege.ca
416-491-5050 ext. 22096

Toronto: Seneca@York Campus

70 The Pond Rd.
Toronto, ON M3J 3M6
416-491-5050 ext: 3055
Fax: 416-736-1163
Hours: M-F 8:00-10:30; Sa, Su 9:00-5:00
Joy Muller, Manager, Teaching, Learning & Copyright Services
joy.muller@senecacollege.ca
416-491-5050 ext. 33042

Toronto: Sound & Moving Image Library

#125, Scott Library, 4700 Keele St.
Toronto, ON M3J 1P3
416-736-5508 ext: 55508
Fax: 416-736-5838
Hours: M-Th 9:00-9:00; F 9:00-8:00; Sa, Su 12:00-5:00
Special Collections: Video and sound recordings collections; 20th century western art, jazz, folk, rock, electroacoustic and world music; documentary and feature films; Jazz ProgramREsource Collection
Subjects covered: Music, Film, Art
Kathryn Elder, Head Librarian
kelder@yorku.ca
Rob van der Bliek, Music Librarian
bliek@yorku.ca

Toronto: Steacie Science and Engineering Library

4700 Keele St.
Toronto, ON M3J 1P3
416-736-5639
Fax: 416-736-5452
e-mail: steacref@yorku.ca
Founded in: 1966
Hours: M-Th 8:00-11:00; F 8:00-5:00; Sa 10:00-6:00; Su 12:00-8:00
Acquisitions Budget: $500,000 - $999,999
Subjects covered: Life Sciences, Physical Sciences, Technology, Biological Sciences, Chemistry, Physics, Terrestrial & Space Sciences, Mathematics, Applied Computational Mathematics, Computer Science, Engineering
Services:
Internet Access
Inter-Library Loan (ILL)
Microform Equipment: Reader
Personnel: *Summary:* 9 Total; 3 Professional(s); 7 Technical(s)
Ilo-Katryn Maimets, Head Librarian
ilo@yorku.ca
Leila Fernadez, Science Librarian
leilaf@yorku.ca

Toronto: Sunnybrook Health Sciences Centre R. Ian MacDonald Library

Sunnybrook Campus
2075 Bayview Ave.
Toronto, ON M4N 3M5
Mailing Address: 2075 Bayview Ave.
Toronto, ON M4N 3M5
416-480-6100
Fax: 416-480-6848
e-mail: ILL@sunnybrook.ca
URL: sunnybrook.ca/content/?page=Care_Serv_Lib
National Library Symbol: OTSMC
Consortia Membership: Health Science Information Consortium of Toronto
Founded in: 1968
Hours: M-F 9:00-5:00; Sa 1:00-5:00
Acquisitions Budget: $50,000 - $99,999
Subjects covered: Medicine, Nursing, Health Sciences
Services:
Remote Access
Internet Access
Access to Subscription Databases
Personnel: *Summary:* 7 Total; 2 Professional(s); 3 Technical(s); 2 Other employees

Toronto: Surrey Place Centre The Joseph M. Berg Library & Resources Centre

2 Surrey Place
Toronto, ON M5S 2C2
416-925-5141 ext: 277
Fax: 416-923-8476
URL: www.surreyplace.on.ca/Pages/Library.aspx
National Library Symbol: OTSU
Consortia Membership: Health Science Information Consortium of Toronto
Hours: M-F 9:00-5:00
Marika Korossy, Librarian
marika.korossy@surreyplace.on.ca

Toronto: Toronto Botanical Garden Weston Family Library

777 Lawrence Ave. East
Toronto, ON M3C 1P2
416-397-1343
Fax: 416-397-1354
e-mail: librarydesk@torontobotanicalgarden.ca
URL: torontobotanicalgarden.ca/learn/weston-family-library
Social Media: Instagr.am/TBG_Canada
www.facebook.com/pages/toronto-botanical-garden/1403595493 34415

www.linkedin.com/TorontoBotanicalGardens
twitter.com/TBG_Canada
National Library Symbol: OTBG
Founded in: 1959
Hours: M-Sa 10:00-5:00; Su 12:00-4:00
Acquisitions Budget: $10,000 - $24,999
For Print: $10,000 - $24,999
For Electronic: 0-$9,999
Special Collections: Historical Collection, Children's Collection, Orchid Collection, Multimedia Collection, Herb Collection, Green Roof Collection
Subjects covered: Horticulture, Floral Arts, Landscape Architecure, Botany
Services:
Internet Access
Access to Subscription Databases
Public computer workstation for free internet access
Personnel: *Summary:* 1 Total; 1 Professional(s); 25 Volunteer(s)
Zack Osborne, Head Librarian
librarian@torontobotanicalgarden.ca
416-397-1375

Toronto: Toronto City Planning Information Resource Centre

Toronto City Hall, 12th Fl. E., 100 Queen St. West
Toronto, ON M5H 2N2
416-392-7501
Fax: 416-392-1330
URL: www.toronto.ca/planning
Hours: by appointment only
Subjects covered: Building, Construction & Design, Codes & Standards, Urban Planning with emphasis on Toronto
Services:
Inter-Library Loan (ILL)
Personnel: *Summary:* 2 Total; 1 Professional(s)
Gregg Lintern, Director
416-392-0427

Toronto: Toronto East General Hospital Health Sciences Library

825 Coxwell Ave.
Toronto, ON M4C 3E7
416-469-6580
Fax: 416-469-6106
e-mail: library@tegh.on.ca
URL: www.tegh.on.ca
National Library Symbol: OTEG
Consortia Membership: Health Science Information Consortium of Toronto
Founded in: 1960
Hours: M-F 8:00-4:00 by appointment only
Personnel: *Summary:* 2 Total; 1 Professional(s)

Toronto: Toronto General Hospital Health Sciences Library

Eaton North Wing
#1-418, 200 Elizabeth St.
Toronto, ON M5G 2C4
416-340-3429
Fax: 416-340-4384
Other contact info: Public Access: 416-340-3429
Founded in: 1964
Hours: M-F 8:30am-8:00pm; Sa 10:00-5:00 by appointment only
Acquisitions Budget: $500,000 - $999,999
Services:
Internet Access
Inter-Library Loan (ILL) for a fee
Personnel: *Summary:* 20 Total; 9 Professional(s); 11 Technical(s); 3 Volunteer(s)

Toronto: Toronto Public Health Library

277 Victoria St., 6th Fl.
Toronto, ON M5B 1W2
416-338-7865
Fax: 416-338-0049
e-mail: hlibrary@toronto.ca
URL: www.toronto.ca/health
Consortia Membership: Health Science Information Consortium of Toronto
Hours: M-F 8:30-4:30 by appointment only
Acquisitions Budget: $50,000 - $99,999
For Print: $10,000 - $24,999
For Electronic: $50,000 - $99,999
Subjects covered: Public Health, Nursing, Medicine, Health Sciences, Public Health Policy
Personnel: *Summary:* 4 Total; 3 Professional(s); 1 Other employees
Bruce Gardham, Senior Librarian
bgardha@toronto.ca
416-338-8284

Toronto: Toronto Rehabilitation Institute University Centre Library Services

#306, 550 University Ave.
Toronto, ON M5G 2A2
416-597-3422 ext: 3050
e-mail: libraryall@torontorehab.on.ca
URL: www.torontorehab.com
Consortia Membership: Health Science Information Consortium of Toronto
Hours: M-F 9:00-5:00
Acquisitions Budget: $50,000 - $99,999
Services:
Inter-Library Loan (ILL) for a fee of $10
Personnel: *Summary:* 7 Total; 3 Professional(s); 3 Technical(s)
Marcia Winterbottom, Acting Manager
winterbottom.marcia@torontorehab.on.ca
Doris Extavour, Librarian
extavour.doris@torontorehab.on.ca
Holly Phillips, Librarian
phillips.holly@torontorehab.on.ca

Toronto: Toronto Western Hospital R.C. Laird Health Sciences Library

Fell Pavilion
#5-505, 399 Bathurst St.
Toronto, ON M5T 2S8
416-603-5750
Fax: 416-603-5326
Other contact info: Public Access: 416-340-3429
No public access
Founded in: 1961
Hours: M-F 8:30-7:00
Subjects covered: Medicine, Nursing, Health Sciences
Services:
Inter-Library Loan (ILL)

Toronto: Toronto Zoo

361A Old Finch Ave.
Toronto, ON M1B 5K7
416-392-5929
Other contact info: Conservation & Research, Phone: 416-392-5962
e-mail: conservation_info@torontozoo.ca
URL: www.torontozoo.com
Founded in: 1994
Hours: M-F 8:30-4:00 by appointment only
Acquisitions Budget: 0-$9,999
For Print: 0-$9,999
For Electronic: 0-$9,999
Services:
Access to Subscription Databases
Personnel: *Summary:* 1 Total; 1 Professional(s)

Toronto: University Health Network Princess Margaret Hospital/Ontario Cancer Institute - Health Sciences Library

610 University Ave., 5th Fl.
Toronto, ON M5G 2M9
416-946-4482
Fax: 416-946-2084
Other contact info: Public Access: 416-340-3429
e-mail: uhnlibraries@uhn.on.ca
URL: www.uhn.ca/Education/library_services.asp
Consortia Membership: Health Science Information Consortium of Toronto
No public access
Hours: M-F 8:30-7:00
Subjects covered: Health Sciences, Oncology, Molecular Biology, Medical Biophysics, Cancer Nursing
Services:
Inter-Library Loan (ILL)
Bogusia Trojan, Director, Library Services
boguslawa.trojan@uhn.on.ca

Toronto: University of Toronto Libraries

130 St George St.
Toronto, ON M5S 1A5
416-978-8450
Fax: 416-978-7653
e-mail: library.info@utoronto.ca
URL: www.library.utoronto.ca
National Library Symbol: UTL
Consortia Membership: Canadian Research Knowledge Network (CRKN); Ontario Council of University Libraries (OCUL)
Founded in: 1892
Hours: M-F 8:30am-12:00am; Sa 9:00am-10:00pm; Su 1:00-10:00pm
Acquisitions Budget: $500,000 - $999,999
Services:
Internet Access
Access to Subscription Databases
Inter-Library Loan (ILL)
Fee Based Research
Microform Equipment: Reader
Larry Alford, Chief Librarian
larry.alford@utoronto.ca
416-978-2292
Alastair Boyd, Head, Cataloguing
416-978-8934
Caitlin Tillman, Head, Collection Development
416-978-3856
Peter Clinton, Director, Information Technology Services
416-978-7649

Toronto: University of Toronto, Innis College Innis Library

2 Sussex Ave., 2nd Fl.
Toronto, ON M5S 1J5
416-978-4497
Fax: 416-946-0168
URL: www.utoronto.ca/innis/library
Founded in: 1974
Hours: M-Th 9:30-6:00; F 9:30-5:00
Acquisitions Budget: $25,000 - $49,999
Special Collections: Cinema Collection
Subjects covered: Cinema Studies, Environmental Studies, Urban Studies
Services:
Internet Access
Inter-Library Loan (ILL)
Personnel: *Summary:* 1 Technical(s); 6 Other employees
Leonard Ferstman, Librarian
l.ferstman@utoronto.ca

Toronto: University of Toronto, Massey College Robertson Davies Library

4 Devonshire Pl.
Toronto, ON M5S 2E1
416-978-2893
Fax: 416-978-1759
e-mail: library@masseycollege.ca
URL: www.masseycollege.ca/library
National Library Symbol: OTMC
Founded in: 1963
Hours: M-F 10:00-5:00
Acquisitions Budget: For Print: $25,000 - $49,999
Special Collections: Frederick Hagan Collection of Private Press Books
Subjects covered: History of the Book, printing, papermaking, bookbinding, palaeography, calligraphy, type design, book collecting, bibliography; papers of Carl Dair; editions and translations of Robertson Davies
Services:
Internet Access
Personnel: *Summary:* 2 Total; 2 Professional(s)
P.J. MacDougall, Librarian

Toronto: University of Toronto, Scarborough Library

1265 Military Trail
Toronto, ON M1C 1A4
416-287-7508
Fax: 416-287-7507
e-mail: askalibrarian@utsc.utoronto.ca
circulation@utsc.utoronto.ca
URL: utsc.library.utoronto.ca
Founded in: 1964
Hours: M-Su, library hours vary throughout the year; please check website
Acquisitions Budget: $100,000 - $249,999
Note: Public access to resources is limited. Extensive electronic & print collections

Special Collections: Maps; Slides; CDs; DVDs; Videos; Digital Images
Services:
Remote Access
Internet Access
Access to Subscription Databases
Inter-Library Loan (ILL)
Microform Equipment: Computer; Reader
Personnel: *Summary:* 20 Total; 7 Professional(s); 13 Technical(s)
Victoria Owen, Head Librarian
owen@utsc.utoronto.ca
416-287-7519
Chad Crichton, Coordinator, Reference, Research & Instruction
ccrichton@utsc.utoronto.ca
416-287-7492
Catherine Devion, Coordinator, Circulation & Access
devion@utsc.utoronto.ca
416-287-7485
Patricia LaCivita, Coordinator, Collections & Information Management
lacivita@utsc.utoronto.ca
416-287-7484
Sarah Fedko, Coordinator, Campus Information Literacy
sfedko@utsc.utoronto.ca
416-208-2708

Toronto: Vale Inco Records & Information Management
South Tower, Royal Bank Plaza
#1600, 200 Bay St.
Toronto, ON M5J 2K2
Mailing Address: PO Box 70
Toronto, ON M5J 2K2
416-361-7511
Fax: 416-361-7781
e-mail: valebasemetals@vale.com
No public access
Acquisitions Budget: $50,000 - $99,999
Special Collections: Annual Reports, Maps
Subjects covered: Economics, Industry, Energy, Natural Resources, Business, Banking, Taxation, Finance, Investment, Mining & Mining Processes, Geology, Mineral Economics
Services:
Inter-Library Loan (ILL)
Personnel: *Summary:* 4 Total; 1 Professional(s); 1 Technical(s)
Jeanette Bleskie, Manager, Records & Information Technology

Toronto: Walker, Nott, Dragicevic Associates Limited Library
#701, 90 Eglinton Ave. East
Toronto, ON M4P 2Y3
416-968-3511
Fax: 416-960-0172
e-mail: admin@wndplan.com
URL: www.wndplan.com
No public access
Founded in: 1988
Acquisitions Budget: $25,000 - $49,999
Services:
Remote Access
Access to Subscription Databases
Personnel: *Summary:* 2 Total; 1 Professional(s); 1 Other employees
Jutta Szep, Librarian

Toronto: Waterfront Regeneration Trust E-Library
#308, 372 Richmond St. West
Toronto, ON M5V 1X6
416-943-8080
Fax: 416-943-8068
e-mail: info@wrtrust.com
URL: www.waterfronttrail.org/library.html
Hours: by appointment only
Subjects covered: Waterfront planning & development; Shoreline management; Transportation; Environment; Tourism; Recreation
Services:
Internet Access
Marlaine Koehler, Executive Director

Toronto: Watts, Griffis & McOuat Limited Library
#400, 8 King St. East
Toronto, ON M5C 1B5
416-364-6244
Fax: 416-864-1675
e-mail: info@wgm.ca
URL: www.wgm.on.ca
Founded in: 1971
Hours: by appointment only
Acquisitions Budget: $25,000 - $49,999
Subjects covered: Energy, Mineral Resources, Mining, Geology
Personnel: *Summary:* 1 Total; 1 Professional(s)

Toronto: Women's College Hospital Health Sciences Library
76 Grenville St.
Toronto, ON M5S 1B2
416-323-6078
Fax: 416-323-6122
URL: www.womenscollegehospital.ca
Consortia Membership: Health Science Information Consortium of Toronto
No public access
Founded in: 1955
Hours: M, Tu, Th, F 9:00-5:00
Special Collections: Hospital Archives
Subjects covered: Obstetrics, Gynecology, High Risk Pregnancy, Dermatology, Diabetes, Internal Medicine, Nursing
Services:
Inter-Library Loan (ILL)
Personnel: *Summary:* 4 Total
Mary Anne Howse, Manager, Library Services
Maryanne.howse@wchospital.ca
Jane Sauder, Library Technician
Grazyna Wiercinska, Library Technician

Toronto: York International Resource Library
#244, York Lanes
4700 Keele St.
Toronto, ON M3J 1P3
416-736-5177
e-mail: yiinfo@yorku.ca
URL: international.yorku.ca
Hours: M-F 8:30-4:30
Subjects covered: Study Abroad, Travel
Services:
Microform Equipment: Computer

Toronto: York University Glendon College Campus Leslie Frost Library/Bibliothèque Leslie Frost
2275 Bayview Ave.
Toronto, ON M4N 3M6
416-487-6726
Fax: 416-487-6705
URL: www.library.yorku.ca
National Library Symbol: OTY
Founded in: 1960
Hours: M-Th 8:30-6:30; F 9:30-4:30; Sa 11:00-6:00
Acquisitions Budget: $100,000 - $249,999
For Print: $50,000 - $99,999
For Electronic: $100,000 - $249,999
Note: Part of York University Libraries
Special Collections: 30% of collection in French, emphasis on dictionaries for translation
Subjects covered: Humanities, Social Sciences, Natural Science, Liberal Arts, International Relations, Translation
Services:
Inter-Library Loan (ILL)
Microform Equipment: Computer; Reader
Personnel: *Summary:* 6 Total; 3 Professional(s); 3 Technical(s)
Sarah Coysh, Head Librarian
scoysh@yorku.ca
Julianna Drexler, Reference Librarian
drexler@yorku.ca

Toronto: York University Libraries Scott Library
4700 Keele St.
Toronto, ON M3J 1P3
416-736-5601
Fax: 416-736-5451
e-mail: scottref@yorku.ca
ereport@yorku.ca (e-Resources)
circinfo@yorku.ca
URL: www.library.yorku.ca
National Library Symbol: OTY
Consortia Membership: Canadian Research Knowledge Network (CRKN); Ontario Council of University Libraries (OCUL)
Founded in: 1971
Hours: M-Th 8:00-11:00; F 8:00-8:00; Sa 12:00-6:00; Su 12:00-8:00
Acquisitions Budget: $500,000 - $999,999
Note: Scott Library houses the Archives and Special Collections, the Map Library, and the Sound and Moving Image Library (SMIL).
Special Collections: Archives & Special Collections; Social Sciences & Humanities collections; microtexts, maps, audiovisual formats, archival papers, government documents
Services:
Internet Access
Access to Subscription Databases
Inter-Library Loan (ILL)
Microform Equipment: Computer; Reader
Personnel: *Summary:* 175 Total; 53 Professional(s); 121 Technical(s)
Cynthia Archer, University Librarian
carcher@yorku.ca
John Dupuis, Acting Associate University Librarian, Informtion Services
jdupuis@yorku.ca
Catherine Davidson, Associate University Librarian, Collections
cdavidson@yorku.ca
Robert Thompson, Director, Library Computing Services
rthompson@yorku.ca
Nancy Hall, Head, Monograph Acquisitions
nhall@yorku.ca
Elif Aytek Gurses, Manager, Acquisitions & York University Libraries
egurses@yorku.ca

Uxbridge: Nuclear Awareness Project Library
34 Church St.
Uxbridge, ON L9P 1M6
Mailing Address: PO Box 104
Uxbridge, ON L9P 1M6
905-852-0571
Fax: 905-852-0571
Founded in: 1980
Hours: by appointment only
Acquisitions Budget: $25,000 - $49,999
Note: Hours vary, call for appointment
Subjects covered: Energy Issues, Nuclear Issues
Personnel: *Summary:* 2 Volunteer(s)
David H. Martin, Research Director

Val Caron: Sudbury Rock & Lapidary Society Library
c/o 3171 Romeo St.
Val Caron, ON P3N 1G5
URL: www.ccfms.ca/clubs/Sudbury
No public access
Founded in: 1987
Acquisitions Budget: 0-$9,999
For Print: 0-$9,999
For Electronic: 0-$9,999
Note: Library available only to members of the Sudbury Rock & Lapidary Society; Library housed at Naughton Community Centre
Special Collections: Mineralogical Record; Back issues of Lapidary Journal
Subjects covered: Rocks; Minerals; Gems; Fossils; Lapidary Arts
Personnel: *Summary:* 1 Volunteer(s)
Ruth Debicki, Vice-President & Librarian
Ed Debicki, Secretary
ed.debicki@sympatico.ca
705-522-5140

Vineland: Southern Crop Protection & Food Research Centre Canadian Agriculture Library - Vineland
4902 Victoria Ave. North
Vineland, ON L0R 2E0
Mailing Address: PO Box 6000
Vineland Station, ON L0R 2E0
905-562-4113 ext: 212
Fax: 905-562-4335
National Library Symbol: OVAGR
Hours: M-Th by appointment only
Acquisitions Budget: $25,000 - $49,999
Subjects covered: Plant Protection & Pathology, Entomology, Nematology
Services:
Inter-Library Loan (ILL)

Personnel: *Summary:* 1 Professional(s)
Sheridan L. Alder, Head Librarian
sheridan.alder@agr.gc.ca

Waterloo: Dana Porter Library
200 University Ave. West
Waterloo, ON N2L 3G1
519-888-4567 ext: 32282
Fax: 519-888-4320
URL: www.lib.uwaterloo.ca
Hours: M-F 8:00am-11:00pm; Sa, Su 11:00-11:00
Subjects covered: Arts & Humanities, Social Sciences, Environmental Studies
Services:
Internet Access
Access to Subscription Databases
Inter-Library Loan (ILL)
Microform Equipment: Computer; Reader
Mark Haslett, University Librarian
mhaslett@library.uwaterloo.ca

Waterloo: Davis Centre Library
200 University Ave. West
Waterloo, ON N2L 3G1
519-888-4567 ext: 37469
Fax: 519-888-4311
URL: www.lib.uwaterloo.ca
Hours: M-F 8:00am-12:00am; Sa, Su 11:00am-12:00am
Subjects covered: Engineering, Mathematics, Applied Health Sciences, Sciences
Services:
Internet Access
Access to Subscription Databases
Inter-Library Loan (ILL)
Microform Equipment: Computer; Reader
Jennifer Haas, Department Head, Information Services & Resources, Davis Library
j2haas@library.uwaterloo.ca

Waterloo: University Map Library
Geospatial Centre
#328, 200 University Ave. West
Waterloo, ON N2L 3G1
519-888-4567 ext: 32795
Fax: 519-888-4320
e-mail: LibraryUMDref@library.uwaterloo.ca
URL: www.lib.uwaterloo.ca/locations/umd/index.html
National Library Symbol: OWTU
Founded in: 1966
Hours: M-F 8:30-4:30
Subjects covered: Maps, Atlases, Aerial Photographs, Geospatial Data
Services:
Photocopying, Scanning, CD/DVD burning, Geospatial Data Service (Data Delivery & Instruction); Cartographic Reference; Circulation & Course Reserves; Library Instruction; ILL for maps
Richard Hugh Pinnell, Manager, University Map Library & Branch Library Services
rhpinnel@library.uwaterloo.ca
519-888-4567 ext. 33412

Waterloo: University of Waterloo Administrative Offices
200 University Ave. West
Waterloo, ON N2L 3G1
519-888-4883
Other contact info: ILL Fax: 519/888-4323
URL: www.lib.uwaterloo.ca/
National Library Symbol: OWTU
Consortia Membership: Canadian Research Knowledge Network (CRKN); Ontario Council of University Libraries (OCUL); TriUniversity Group of Libraries (TUG)
Founded in: 1957
Acquisitions Budget: $100,000 - $249,999
For Print: $100,000 - $249,999
For Electronic: $250,000 - $499,999; Faculty, students + staff
Note: The University of Waterloo Library is in five locations: Dana Porter Library, Davis Centre Library, University Map Library, Musagetes Architecture Library & Optometry Learning Resource Centre. Online catalogue: Endeavor Voyager System
Services:
Remote Access
Internet Access
Access to Subscription Databases
Inter-Library Loan (ILL)
Microform Equipment: Computer; Reader
Personnel: *Summary:* 136 Total; 37 Professional(s); 2 Technical(s); 97 Other employees
Mark Haslett, University Librarian
mhaslett@library.uwaterloo.ca
519-888-4567 ext. 3568
Sharon Lamont, Director, Organizational Services
sljlamon@library.uwaterloo.ca
519-888-4567 ext. 33519
Allan Bell, Associate University Librarian, Information Technology Services
abell@library.uwaterloo.ca
519-888-4567 ext. 38215
Wish Leonard, Manager, Circulation Services, Resource Sharing
aleonard@library.uwaterloo.ca
519-888-4567 ext. 35430

Waterloo: Wilfrid Laurier University Library
75 University Ave. West
Waterloo, ON N2L 3C5
519-884-0710 ext: 3246
Fax: 519-884-3209
e-mail: rmacneil@wlu.ca
URL: library.wlu.ca
National Library Symbol: OWTL
Consortia Membership: Canadian Research Knowledge Network (CRKN); Ontario Council of University Libraries (OCUL); TriUniversity Group of Libraries (TUG)
Founded in: 1960
Hours: M-F 8:30am-10:00pm; Sa, Su 11:00-10:00
Acquisitions Budget: $1,000,000 plus
For Print: $1,000,000 plus
For Electronic: $1,000,000 plus
Services:
Internet Access
Access to Subscription Databases
Inter-Library Loan (ILL)
Microform Equipment: Reader
Personnel: *Summary:* 54 Total; 15 Professional(s); 2 Technical(s); 37 Other employees
Sharon Brown, University Librarian
519-884-0710 ext. 3380
Diane Peters, Acting Head of Reference
dpeters@wlu.ca
519-884-0710 ext. 3419
Brooke Skelton, Head of Cataloguing
Joanne Oud, Collections & Acquistions Dept. Head
joud@wlu.ca
519-884-0710 ext. 2073
Vera Fesnak, Head of Access Services
Linda Cracknell, Head, Acquisitions & Serials
Don Hamilton, Information Technology Manager
Joan Mitchell, Archives Librarian

Welland: Niagara College Libraries & Learning Commons
Lewis Library, Welland Campus
300 Woodlawn Rd.
Welland, ON L3C 7L3
905-735-2211 ext: 7767
Fax: 905-736-6021
e-mail: library@niagaracollege.ca
URL: www.niagaracollege.ca/library
National Library Symbol: OWEN
Consortia Membership: Ontario Colleges Library Service
Founded in: 1967
Hours: Winter: M-Th 8:00-8:00; F 8:00-5:00; Su 1:00-5:00. Summer: M-f 8:30-4:30
Acquisitions Budget: $250,000 - $499,999
For Print: $25,000 - $49,999
For Electronic: $100,000 - $249,999
Subjects covered: Health Studies, Applied Arts, Technology, Business, Community Services
Services:
Remote Access
Internet Access
Access to Subscription Databases
Inter-Library Loan (ILL)
Microform Equipment: Reader
Personnel: *Summary:* 10 Total; 2 Professional(s); 8 Technical(s)
Karen McGrath, Manager, Library Services
kmcgrath@niagaracollege.ca
905-735-2211 ext. 7799
Gordana Vietz, Library Services/Systems Coordinator
gvitez@niagaracollege.ca
905-735-2211 ext. 7404

Whitby: Durham College
Whitby Campus Library Resource Centre
1610 Champlain Ave.
Whitby, ON L1H 7L7
Mailing Address: PO Box 385
Oshawa, ON L1H 7L7
905-721-2000 ext: 4218
Fax: 905-721-3029
Hours: M-Th 8:00am-12:00am; F 8:00am-9:00pm; Sa, Su 10:00-6:00
Acquisitions Budget: $100,000 - $249,999
Services:
Remote Access
Inter-Library Loan (ILL)
Caren Bosyj, Library Technician

Windsor: Great Lakes Regional Office Reference Resources
100 Ouellette Ave., 8th Fl.
Windsor, ON N9A 6T3
519-257-6733
Fax: 519-257-6740
URL: www.ijc.org
Subjects covered: Great Lakes environment
Services:
Great Lakes Water Quality Biennial Reports & other IJC reports produced under the Great Lakes Water Quality Agreement are available to the public free of charge
John Nevin, Public Information Officer
nevinj@windsor.ijc.org
Mae Carter, Reference Resource Specialist
carterm@windsor.ijc.org

Windsor: Paul Martin Law Library
401 Sunset Ave.
Windsor, ON N9B 3P4
519-253-4232 ext: 2977
e-mail: lawcirc@uwindsor.ca
URL: www.uwindsor.ca/lawlibrary/
National Library Symbol: OWAL
Hours: M-F
Acquisitions Budget: $500,000 - $999,999
Subjects covered: Law
Services:
Inter-Library Loan (ILL)
Microform Equipment: Reader
Personnel: *Summary:* 11 Total; 2 Professional(s); 9 Technical(s)
Paul Murphy, Director
murphy6@uwindsor.ca
519-253-3000 ext. 2972
Annette Demers, Reference Librarian
ademers@uwindsor.ca
519-253-3000 ext. 2976

Windsor: St Clair College of Applied Arts & Technology - Main Campus
Library Resource Centre
#252, 2000 Talbot Rd. West
Windsor, ON N9A 6S4
Mailing Address: 2000 Talbot Rd. West
Windsor, ON N9A 6S4
519-972-2739
Fax: 519-972-2757
e-mail: library@stclaircollege.ca
gturnbull@stclaircollege.ca
URL: www.stclaircollege.ca/studentservices/library
National Library Symbol: OWSC
Consortia Membership: Ontario Colleges Library Service
Founded in: 1967
Hours: Sept-April: M-Th 7:45am-10:00pm; F 7:45-6:00; Sa 9:00-5:00. May-Aug: M-Th 7:45am-9:00pm; F 7:45-4:30
Acquisitions Budget: $50,000 - $99,999
Services:
Internet Access
Access to Subscription Databases
Inter-Library Loan (ILL)
Personnel: *Summary:* 8 Total; 8 Technical(s)
Joan Oliver, Library Technician
joliver@stclairecollege.ca
519-972-2727 ext. 4692

***Windsor:* University of Windsor**
Leddy Library
401 Sunset Ave.
Windsor, ON N9B 3P4
519-253-3000 ext: 3161
Fax: 519-971-3638
e-mail: gebbett@uwindsor.ca
URL: www.uwindsor.ca/library
National Library Symbol: OWA
Consortia Membership: Canadian Research Knowledge Network (CRKN); Ontario Council of University Libraries (OCUL)
Founded in: 1960
Hours: M-Th 8:00am-2:00am, F 8:00am-11:00pm; Sa 10:00am-11:00pm; Su 10:00am-2:00am
Acquisitions Budget: $500,000 - $999,999; Serves the university community & general public
Note: Systems Information: Endeavor; ILS: Voyager, ScholarsPortal; Member of Ontario Council of University Libraries Consortia (OCUL)
Special Collections: Material on Essex, Kent & Lambton County, Great Lakes
Subjects covered: Arts, Social Science, Humanities, Science, Engineering, Business, Education, Law
Services:
Remote Access
Internet Access
Access to Subscription Databases
Inter-Library Loan (ILL)
Microform Equipment: Reader
Personnel: *Summary:* 25 Professional(s); 52 Technical(s)
Gwendolyn Ebbett, University Librarian
gebbett@uwindsor.ca
519-253-3000 ext. 3161
Joan Dalton, Associate University Librarian
jdalton@uwindsor.ca
519-253-3000 ext. 3212
Cathy Maskell, Associate University Librarian
cmaskel@uwindsor.ca
519-253-3000 ext. 3206
Art Rhyno, Head, Systems Department
arhyno@uwindsor.ca
519-253-3000 ext. 3163
Peter Zimmerman, Head, Information Services Department
pzimmerman@uwindsor.ca
519-253-3000 ext. 3178

***Windsor:* Windsor Regional Hospital - Metropolitan Campus**
Library
1995 Lens Ave.
Windsor, ON N8W 1L9
519-254-5577
e-mail: library@wrh.on.ca
URL: www.wrh.on.ca
No public access
Hours: M-F
Mary Ellen Bechard, Coordinator, Library Services

***Woodstock:* Woodstock Campus**
Resource Centre
369 Finkle St.
Woodstock, ON N4V 1A3
519-421-0144
Fax: 519-539-3870
Hours: M-F 8:30-4:30
Acquisitions Budget: $25,000 - $49,999
Subjects covered: Business, Computer, Nursing, Social Sciences
Services:
Inter-Library Loan (ILL)
Personnel: *Summary:* 1 Total; 1 Technical(s)
Judith Bell, Support Services
jbell@fanshawec.ca
519-421-0144 ext. 225

Prince Edward Island

***Charlottetown:* Holland College**
Charlottetown Centre Library
140 Weymouth St.
Charlottetown, PE C1A 4Z1
902-566-9558
Fax: 902-566-9522
e-mail: library@hollandcollege.com
URL: www.hollandcollege.com/library
National Library Symbol: PCHC
Founded in: 1969
Hours: M,Tu,Th 8:30-7:00; W 8:30-9:00; F 8:30-5:00; Su 1:00-4:00
Acquisitions Budget: $25,000 - $49,999
Services:
Inter-Library Loan (ILL)
Microform Equipment: Reader
Personnel: *Summary:* 7 Total; 3 Professional(s); 4 Technical(s)
Patricia Doucette, Manager, Library Services
pmdoucette@hollandcollege.com
902-566-9350

***Charlottetown:* Prince Edward Island Dept. of Provincial Treasury**
Geomatics Library
11 Kent St.
Charlottetown, PE C1A 7N8
902-368-5178
Fax: 902-368-4399
Hours: M-F 8:30-5:00. Summer: M-F 8:00-4:00
Special Collections: Orthophotos
Subjects covered: Property mapping
Bill Burden, Librarian

***Charlottetown:* Prince Edward Island Food Technology Centre**
Information Services
101 Belvedere Ave.
Charlottetown, PE C1A 7N8
Mailing Address: PO Box 2000
Charlottetown, PE C1A 7N8
902-368-5548
Fax: 902-368-5549
877-368-5548
e-mail: biofoodtech@biofoodtech.ca
ftcweb@gov.pe.ca
URL: www.gov.pe.ca/ftc/
Founded in: 1987
Hours: M-F 8:30-4:00
Acquisitions Budget: $25,000 - $49,999
Subjects covered: Agriculture, Food, Technology, Food Research
Personnel: *Summary:* 2 Total; 2 Professional(s)
Kathy MacEwen, Information & Promotion Assistant
Jim Smith, Division Head, Technical Services/Research

***Charlottetown:* University of Prince Edward Island**
Robertson Library
550 University Ave.
Charlottetown, PE C1A 4P3
902-566-0583
Fax: 902-628-4305
e-mail: ill@upei.ca
reference@upei.ca
URL: www.upei.ca/library/
National Library Symbol: PCU
Consortia Membership: Canadian Research Knowledge Network (CRKN); Council of Atlantic University Libraries (CAUL)
Founded in: 1969
Hours: M-Th 8:00am-11:00pm; F 8:00-8:00;; Sa 10:00-5:00; Su 12:00-10:00
Acquisitions Budget: $500,000 - $999,999
Note: Provides all library services for the Atlantic Veterinary College.
Special Collections: Prince Edward Island Collection
Subjects covered: Humanities, Social Sciences, Science, Veterinary Medicine, Nursing, Education
Services:
Remote Access
Internet Access
Inter-Library Loan (ILL) for a fee of varies
Microform Equipment: Computer; Reader
Personnel: *Summary:* 26 Total; 7 Professional(s); 17 Technical(s); 2 Other employees;
Mark Leggott, University Librarian
mleggott@upei.ca
902-566-0460
Cathy Callaghan, Information Services Librarian
ccallaghan@upei.ca
506-566-0681

Québec

***Sherbrooke:* Old Library**
McGreer Hall
2600 College St.
Sherbrooke, QC J1M 0C8
Mailing Address: 2600 College St.
Sherbrooke, QC J1M 0C8
819-822-9600 ext: 2609
Profile: Serves as the consultation room for the University Archives and the Archives Service of the Eastern Townships Resource Centre, the special collection of books pertaining to the history of the Eastern Townships, Canada, and special volumes concerning Bishop's University.
Founded in: 1909
Hours: M-F 9:00-12:00, 1:00-4:30
Note: Archival material must be requested at least 24 hours prior to visit to allow for transfer of requested documents from storage to the Old Library.
Services:
Internet Access
Inter-Library Loan (ILL)
Microform Equipment: Computer; Reader
Anna Grant, Archivist
agrant@ubishops.ca

***Alma:* Collège d'Alma**
Bibliothèque
675, boul Auger ouest
Alma, QC G8B 2B7
418-668-2387 ext: 225
Téléc: 418-668-3806
Couriel: biblio@calma.qc.ca
URL: www.calma.qc.ca/bibliotheque
Sigle: QALC
Fondée en: 1971
Heures: L-J, 8h15-21h30; V 8h30-16h15; Été: L-J, 8h30-12h00, 13h00-16h00; V 8h30-12h00
Budget d'acquisitions: $25,000 - $49,999
Population desservie: 0
Sujets: Sciences humaines, musique, art et lettres, agriculture
Services:
Accès public à l'internet
Prêts entre bibliothèques(PEB)
Lecteur/reproduction de microformes: Ordinateur; Lecteurs
Personnel: *Sommaire:* 3 Total; 1 Professionnel(s); 2 Technicien(s); 2 Autre(s) employé(s)
Laïla Ferris, SMTE - Responsable
laila.ferris@calma.qc.ca
418-668-2387 ext. 225
Marie-Eve Renaud, Technicienne en documentation
marieeve.renaud@calma.qc.ca

***Baie-Comeau:* CÉGEP de Baie-Comeau**
Centre des ressources éducatives
537, boul Blanche
Baie-Comeau, QC G5C 2B2
418-589-5707 ext: 325
Téléc: 418-589-9842
800-463-2030
Couriel: biblio@cegep-baie-comeau.qc.ca
URL: www.cegep-baie-comeau.qc.ca/services-offerts.html
Sigle: QHAC
Fondée en: 1959
Heures: L-J 8h15-18h; V 8h15-16h
Budget d'acquisitions: $10,000 - $24,999
Population desservie: 0
Collections spécialisées: Faune et flore, éducation specialisée
Services:
Accès public à l'internet
Réseau en ligne
Prêts entre bibliothèques(PEB)
Lecteur/reproduction de microformes: Ordinateur; Lecteurs
Personnel: *Sommaire:* 2 Total; 2 Technicien(s); 3 Autre(s) employé(s)
Marie-Line Degagnier, Spécialiste en moyens techniques d'enseignement
mldegagnier@cegep-baie-comeau.qc.ca
Mélanie C. Foster, Technicienne en documentation
mfoster@cegep-baie-comeau.qc.ca

***Boucherville:* NRC Information Centre / Centre d'information du CNRC**
75, boul de Mortagne
Boucherville, QC J4B 6Y4

450-641-5132
Fax: 450-641-5133
e-mail: lmi-Info@cnrc-nrc.gc.ca
info@nrc-cnrc.gc.ca
URL: www.nrc-cnrc.gc.ca/eng/locations/cities/boucherville.html
National Library Symbol: QBOG
Founded in: 1979
Hours: M-F 8:00-4:00 (only with appointments) by appointment only
Acquisitions Budget: $50,000 - $99,999
For Print: $10,000 - $24,999
For Electronic: $50,000 - $99,999
Subjects covered: Plastics, Metals, Ceramics, Instrumentation
Services:
Internet Access
Personnel: *Summary:* 6 Total; 5 Professional(s); 1 Technical(s); 1 Volunteer(s)
Patrice Dupont, Information Specialist
Brigitte Paradis, Client Services Officer

Brossard: Gazoduc Trans Québec & Maritimes Inc. Centre de documentation
525, 6300, av Auteuil
Brossard, QC J4Z 3P2
450-462-5300
Téléc: 450-462-5388
888-810-8800
URL: www.gazoductqm.com/fr/index.html
Sigle: QMTQM
Fondée en: 1980
Heures:avec rendez-vous seulement
Budget d'acquisitions: $25,000 - $49,999
Population desservie: 0
Sujets: Gaz naturel, énergie, environnement
Services:
Prêts entre bibliothèques(PEB)
Lecteur/reproduction de microformes: Lecteurs
Chantale Dion, Documentaliste
cdion@gazoductqm.com
450-462-5335

Carleton: Campus de Carleton-sur-mer Bibliothèque
776, boul Perron
Carleton, QC G0C 1J0
418-364-3341 ext: 8704
Téléc: 418-364-7938
URL: biblioceccarleton.blogspot.ca
Fondée en: 1989
Heures: L-V 8h-16h45
Budget d'acquisitions: Matériel imprimé: $10,000 - $24,999
Matériel électronique: $100,000 - $249,999
Population desservie: 0
Sujets: Éducation collégiale
Services:
Accèss distance aux bases de donn
Accès public à l'internet
Réseau en ligne
Prêts entre bibliothèques(PEB) frais de 2$
Frais de recherche
Lecteur/reproduction de microformes: Lecteurs
Personnel: *Sommaire:* 3 Total; 1 Technicien(s); 2 Autre(s) employé(s)
Madeleine Tremblay, Documentaliste
mtremblay@cgaspesie.qc.ca
Diane Leblanc, Agente de bureau
dleblanc@cgaspesie.qc.ca

Chicoutimi: CÉGEP de Chicoutimi Centre des médias
534, rue Jacques-Cartier est
Chicoutimi, QC G7H 1Z6
418-549-9520 ext: 345
Téléc: 418-549-1315
URL: www.cegep-chicoutimi.qc.ca
Fondée en: 1968
Heures: L-J 8h-21h; V 8h-16h
Budget d'acquisitions: $50,000 - $99,999
Population desservie: 0
Sujets: Arts, humanités, pilotage, techniques de la santé
Services:
Accèss distance aux bases de donn
Accès public à l'internet
Prêts entre bibliothèques(PEB) frais
Lecteur/reproduction de microformes: Lecteurs
Personnel: *Sommaire:* 13 Total; 2 Professionnel(s); 3 Technicien(s); 5 Autre(s) employé(s)
Louis Gaudreau, Coordonnateur, Conseiller en documentation
lgaudrea@cegep-chicoutimi.qc.ca
418-549-9520 ext. 345
Annie Gagnon, Responsable, Périodiques
annie.gagnon@cegep-chicoutimi.qc.ca
418-549-9520 ext. 342
Johanne Gauthier, Responsable, Acquisition
jogauth@cegep-chicoutimi.qc.ca
418-549-9520 ext. 335
France Houde, Responsable, Comptoir du prêt
fhoude@cegep-chicoutimi.qc.ca
418-549-9520 ext. 333
Céline Roussel, Responsable, Catalogage et classification
croussel@cegep-chicoutimi.qc.ca
418-549-9520 ext. 364

Chicoutimi: Université du Québec à Chicoutimi Bibliothèque Paul-Emile Boulet
555, boul de l'Université
Chicoutimi, QC G7H 2B1
418-545-5011 ext: 5630
Téléc: 418-693-5896
Couriel: directionbib@uqac.ca
URL: bibliotheque.uqac.ca
Social Media: www.youtube.com/user/bibliouqac
www.facebook.com/BiblioUQAC
twitter.com/BiblioUQAC
Sigle: QCU
Membre d'un consortium: Canadian Research Knowledge Network (CRKN); Conférence des recteurs et des principaux des universités du Québec (CREPUQ)
Fondée en: 1969
Heures: L-J 7h30-22h30; V 7h30-20h30; Sa 9h-17h; D 12h-17h
Budget d'acquisitions: $500,000 - $999,999
Population desservie: 0
Collections spécialisées: Génétique des populations; études régionales et moyen-nord
Sujets: Éducation, arts, sciences humaines, histoire, économie, sciences physiques, littérature, sciences sociales, sciences économiques, administration, sciences pures
Services:
Accès public à l'internet
Prêts entre bibliothèques(PEB)
Lecteur/reproduction de microformes: Ordinateur; Lecteurs
Personnel: *Sommaire:* 37 Total; 9 Professionnel(s); 12 Technicien(s); 16 Autre(s) employé(s)
Johanne Belley, Directrice
johanne1_belley@uqac.ca
418-545-5011 ext. 5631
Lino Tremblay, Bibliothécaire des systèmes et des ressources électroniques
lino_tremblay@uqac.ca
418-454-5011 ext. 2358

Chomedey: Boehringer Ingelheim (Canada) Ltd. Library
2100, rue Cunard
Chomedey, QC H7S 2G5
450-682-4640 ext: 210
Fax: 450-682-4939
e-mail: info@lav.boehringer-ingelheim.com
URL: www.boehringer-ingelheim.ca
National Library Symbol: QMBIM
No public access
Founded in: 1984
Acquisitions Budget: $25,000 - $49,999
For Print: $25,000 - $49,999
Subjects covered: Virologie
Services:
Inter-Library Loan (ILL)
Personnel: *Summary:* 3 Total; 2 Professional(s); 1 Technical(s)
Sandra Honsinger, Library Technician
Hélène Gagnon, Specialist, Scientific Information
Christine Martens, Specialist, Scientific Information

Drummondville: CÉGEP de Drummondville Bibliothèque
960, rue St-Georges
Drummondville, QC J2C 6A2
819-478-4671
Téléc: 819-474-6859
URL: www.cdrummond.qc.ca
Sigle: QDCE
Fondée en: 1969
Heures: L-Me 8h-21h; J 8h-19h; V 1h-17h; Sa 12h-16h
Budget d'acquisitions: $25,000 - $49,999
Population desservie: 0
Sujets: Arts, lettres et langues, sciences humaines, éducation physique, mathématiques, philosophie, sciences de la nature, techniques professionnelles: technologie de l'estimation et de l'évaluation immobilière, techniques administratives, musique, technologie musicale, techniques de bureau, électrotechnique, techniques de l'informatique, soins infirmiers, génie mécanique
Services:
Accès public à l'internet
Prêts entre bibliothèques(PEB)
Personnel: *Sommaire:* 13 Total; 1 Professionnel(s); 4 Technicien(s); 4 Autre(s) employé(s)
Martin Dubé, Conseiller pédagogique en bibliothéconomie
dubem@cdrummond.qc.ca
819-478-4671 ext. 4700
Johanne Boisvert, Technicienne en documentation, Service des périodiques
boisverj@cdrummond.qc.ca
819-478-4671 ext. 4703
Lucille Gagnon, Technicienne en informatique, Atelier multimédia et production
gagnonl@cdrummond.qc.ca
819-478-4671 ext. 4704
Nicole Landry, Technicienne en documentation, Services techniques
landryn@cdrummond.qc.ca
819-478-4671 ext. 4702
Rachelle Leblanc, Technicienne en documentation, Service des documents audiovisuels
leblancr@cdrummond.qc.ca
819-478-4671 ext. 4705
Line Martel, Agente de bureau, Service de prêts
martell@cdrummond.qc.ca
819-478-4671 ext. 4707
Anny Leroux, Secrétaire
lerouxa@cdrummond.qc.ca
819-478-4671 ext. 4701

Gaspé: CÉGEP de la Gaspésie et des Iles Centre des études collégiales - Gaspé Bibliothèque
96, rue Jacques-Cartier
Gaspé, QC G4X 2S8
418-368-2201
Téléc: 418-368-7003
URL: www.cgaspesie.qc.ca
bibliothequecegepgaspe.blogspot.ca
Sigle: QGC
Fondée en: 1968
Heures: L-J 8h-17h; V 8h-16h
Budget d'acquisitions: $25,000 - $49,999
Matériel imprimé: $25,000 - $49,999
Matériel électronique: 0-$9,999
Population desservie: 0
Services:
Accès public à l'internet frais de 3 $/h
Réseau en ligne
Prêts entre bibliothèques(PEB)
Personnel: *Sommaire:* 2 Total; 1 Technicien(s)
Elsa Moulin, Technicienne en documentation

Gaspé: Merinov centre d'innovation de l'aquaculture et des pêches du Québec Centre de documentation
#205, 96, montée Sandy Beach
Gaspé, QC G0C 1R0
Adresse postale: CP 1070
Gaspé, QC G0C 1R0
418-368-7629
Téléc: 418-360-8514
Couriel: gaspedoc@mapaq.gouv.qc.ca
URL: www.merinov.ca
Sigle: QGAP
Fondée en: 1951
Heures: L-V 8h30-12h, 13h-16h30
Budget d'acquisitions: $25,000 - $49,999
Population desservie: 0
Sujets: Pêche commerciale, biologie poisson, transformation et mise en marché, développement de nouveau produits, aquaculture
Services:
Accès public à l'internet
Prêts entre bibliothèques(PEB)
Lecteur/reproduction de microformes: Ordinateur; Lecteurs

Personnel: *Sommaire:* 3 Total; 1 Professionnel(s); 1 Technicien(s); 5 Autre(s) employé(s);

Gatineau: Campus Félix-Leclerc

820, boul La Gappe
Gatineau, QC J8T 7T7
819-770-4012
Téléc: 819-243-9007
Fermée au public
Budget d'acquisitions: Matériel imprimé: $100,000 - $249,999
Population desservie: 0
Personnel: *Sommaire:* 1 Professionnel(s); 1 Technicien(s); 1 Autre(s) employé(s)
Diane Gravelle, Agente de bureau
diane.gravelle@cegepoutaouais.qc.ca

Gatineau: Canadian Heritage / Patrimoine Canadien Knowledge Centre & Library Services

#15-2-B, 15 Eddy St., 2nd Fl.
Gatineau, QC K1A 0M5
819-997-2155
Fax: 819-953-8007
866-811-0055
TDD: 8889973123
URL: www.pch.gc.ca
National Library Symbol: OOSS
Consortia Membership: Federal Libraries Consortium (FLC)
Founded in: 1993
Hours: M-F 8:00-4:30 by appointment only
Acquisitions Budget: $100,000 - $249,999
Subjects covered: Cultural industries & institutions; Arts; Multiculturalism; Active citizenship & civic participation; Canadian identity; Official languages; Amateur sport; National parks; Canadian history & historical sites; Canadian content; Culture online
Services:
Internet Access
Access to Subscription Databases
Inter-Library Loan (ILL)
Reference; Research; Borrowing; Accessible technology for the disabled; Multimedia services; Training & conference facilities
Microform Equipment: Computer; Reader
Personnel: *Summary:* 8 Total; 7 Professional(s); 1 Technical(s)
Debbie Laplante, Head, Information Management
613-998-3721
Finbarr Healy, Client Services Librarian
finbarr.healy@pch.gc.ca
613-998-3721

Gatineau: Canadian Transportation Agency / Office des transports du Canada Library

15 Eddy St.
Gatineau, QC K1A 0N9
819-997-7160
Fax: 819-953-9815
888-222-2592
e-mail: cta.library@cta-otc.gc.ca
National Library Symbol: OOTT
Hours: M-F 9:00-4:00 by appointment only
Acquisitions Budget: $50,000 - $99,999
Subjects covered: Transportation, Legal
Services:
Inter-Library Loan (ILL)
Personnel: *Summary:* 2 Total; 1 Professional(s); 1 Technical(s)
Alison Hale, Librarian, Library Services
819-953-0482

Gatineau: CÉGEP de l'Outaouais Campus Gabrielle-Roy/Bibliothèque

333, boul Cité-des-Jeunes
Gatineau, QC J8Y 6M4
819-770-4012 ext: 2343
Téléc: 819-770-1629
Couriel: bibliotheque@cegepoutaouais.qc.ca
URL: biblio.cegepoutaouais.qc.ca
bibcegepoutaouais.blogspot.ca
Sigle: QHC
Fermée au public
Fondée en: 1970
Heures: L-V
Budget d'acquisitions: $100,000 - $249,999
Matériel imprimé: $100,000 - $249,999
Matériel électronique: 0-$9,999
Population desservie: 0
Collections spécialisées: Collection de l'Outaouais
Sujets: Collection Encyclopédique
Services:
Accèss distance aux bases de donn
Accès public à l'internet
Prêts entre bibliothèques(PEB)
Frais de recherche
Lecteur/reproduction de microformes: Ordinateur; Lecteurs
Personnel: *Sommaire:* 10 Total; 1 Professionnel(s); 3 Technicien(s); 4 Autre(s) employé(s)
Catherine Stassin, Responsable, Bibliothèque
catherine.stassin@cegepoutaouais.qc.ca
819-770-4012 ext. 2343
Monique Moyneur, Responsable, Acquisitions
mmoyneur@cegepoutaouais.qc.ca
819-770-4012 ext. 3241
Mireille Baron, Secrétaire
mireille.baron@cegepoutaouais.qc.ca
819-770-4012 ext. 2342

Gatineau: Centre de santé et de services sociaux de Gatineau, Hôpital de Hull Les ressources informationnelles

116, boul Lionel-Emond
Gatineau, QC J8Y 1W7
819-966-6200
Couriel: www.csssgatineau.qc.ca
Sigle: QHSC
Heures: L-V
Population desservie: 0
Sujets: Médecine
Services:
Prêts entre bibliothèques(PEB)
Personnel: *Sommaire:* 1 Technicien(s)

Gatineau: Environment Canada / Environnement Canada Departmental Library/Bibliothèque du ministère

Place Vincent Massey
351 St Joseph Blvd., 2nd Fl.
Gatineau, QC K1A 0H3
Mailing Address: 351 St Joseph Blvd., 2nd Fl.
Gatineau, QC K1A 0H3
819-997-1767
Fax: 819-997-5349
e-mail: librarybiblio.gatineau@ec.gc.ca
URL: www.ec.gc.ca
National Library Symbol: OOFF
Consortia Membership: Federal Libraries Consortium (FLC)
Founded in: 1973
Hours: M-F 8:30-4:30
Note: Microform facilites
Subjects covered: Global Warming, Biodiversity, Chemicals of Environmental Concern, Conservation, Sustainable Development, Pollution, Ozone Depletion, Water Resources, Pollution Prevention, Wildlife Management, Environmental Impact Analysis, Climatology & Meteorology
Services:
Internet Access
Inter-Library Loan (ILL)
Personnel: *Summary:* 11 Total; 4 Professional(s); 3 Technical(s); 2 Other employees;
Christine McCutcheon, Chief, Library Services
905-336-4530

Gatineau: Heritage College / Collège Héritage Library

325, boul Cité des Jeunes
Gatineau, QC J8Y 6T3
819-778-2270 ext: 1470
Fax: 819-778-7364
e-mail: libraryservices@cegep-heritage.qc.ca
URL:
www.cegep-heritage.qc.ca/Institution/Services/LibraryServices
National Library Symbol: QHCH
Founded in: 1972
Hours: M-Th 7:45-5:00; F 7:45-4:30
Acquisitions Budget: $25,000 - $49,999
For Print: $25,000 - $49,999
For Electronic: $10,000 - $24,999
Subjects covered: General Academic, Nursing, Computer Science, Early Childhood
Services:
Remote Access
Internet Access
Access to Subscription Databases
Inter-Library Loan (ILL)
Microform Equipment: Computer; Reader
Personnel: *Summary:* 4 Total; 1 Professional(s); 2 Technical(s); 2 Other employees
Natalie Meggison, Librarian
nmeggison@cegep-heritage.qc.ca
819-778-2270 ext. 1570

Granby: CÉGEP de Granby Bibliothèque

235, rue Saint-Jacques
Granby, QC J2G 9H7
Adresse postale: CP 7000
Granby, QC J2G 9H7
450-372-6614 ext: 1205
Téléc: 450-372-6565
URL: www.cegepgranby.qc.ca/biblio-web
Fondée en: 1966
Heures: L-J 7h45-17h30; V 7h45-16h15. Salle McLuhan: L-V 7h45-22h; S, D 8h-16h
Population desservie: 0
Sujets: Arts et lettres, sciences humaines, culture, médecine, soins infirmiers, sciences de la santé, sciences pures, tourisme, production manufacturière, électronique industrielle, tech. administratives, bureautique, informatique
Services:
Accès public à l'internet
Prêts entre bibliothèques(PEB)
Lecteur/reproduction de microformes: Ordinateur; Lecteurs
Daniel Marquis, Bibliothécaire professionnel
dmarquis@cegepgranby.qc.ca
Élise Laplante, Technicienne en documentation
elaplante@cegepgranby.qc.ca

Grande-Rivière: École des pêches et de l'aquaculture du Québec Bibliothèque

167, Grande Allée ouest
Grande-Rivière, QC G0C 1V0
Adresse postale: CP 220
Grande-Rivière, QC G0C 1V0
418-385-2241
Téléc: 418-385-2888
855-385-2241
Couriel: biblio-epaq@cegepgim.ca
URL: www.epaq.qc.ca/index.php/bibliotheque
Sigle: QGCSP
Heures: L-V 7h45-11h45, 13h-16h
Budget d'acquisitions: $25,000 - $49,999
Population desservie: 0
Collections spécialisées: Pêche; aquaculture; transformation des produits marins; biologie marine; mécanique marin; navigation
Sujets: Pêche maritime, aquaculture, transformation produits marins, navigation maritime
Services:
Accès public à l'internet
Prêts entre bibliothèques(PEB)
Frais de recherche
Lecteur/reproduction de microformes: Lecteurs
Personnel: *Sommaire:* 1 Total
Daniel Larochelle, Responsable de la bibliothèque
dlarochelle@cegepgim.ca
418-385-2241 ext. 4111

Joliette: CÉGEP Régional de Lanaudière à Joliette Bibliothèque

20, rue St-Charles
Joliette, QC J6E 4T1
450-759-1661
Téléc: 450-759-7120
Couriel: Bibliotheque.Joliette@collanaud.qc.ca
URL: biblio-joliette.collanaud.qc.ca
Heures: L-V
Budget d'acquisitions: $50,000 - $99,999
Population desservie: 0
Services:
Accèss distance aux bases de donn
Accès public à l'internet frais de 30$/an
Réseau en ligne
Prêts entre bibliothèques(PEB)
Personnel: *Sommaire:* 4 Total; 1 Professionnel(s); 3 Autre(s) employé(s)
Marie-Carole McKenzie, Directrice Adjointe
marie.carole.mckenzie@collanaud.qc.ca
450-759-1661 ext. 1134

***Jonquière:* CÉGEP de Jonquière**
Centre des ressources éducatives (diffusion)
2505, rue St-Hubert
Jonquière, QC G7X 7W2
418-547-2191 ext: 266
Téléc: 418-547-0917
URL: cegepjonquiere.ca/bibliotheque
Fondée en: 1967
Heures: L-J 8h-21h; V 8h-17h; S 13h-17h
Budget d'acquisitions: $100,000 - $249,999
Matériel imprimé: $100,000 - $249,999
Matériel électronique: $10,000 - $24,999
Population desservie: 0
Collections spécialisées: Bibliothèque de la Pléiade, livres anciens
Sujets: Arts et lettres, sciences humaines, sciences administratives, sciences
Services:
Accès public à l'internet
Prêts entre bibliothèques(PEB)
Lecteur/reproduction de microformes: Ordinateur; Lecteurs
Personnel: *Sommaire:* 14 Total; 1 Professionnel(s); 5 Technicien(s); 7 Autre(s) employé(s)
Mathieu Arsenault, Technicienne en audio-visuel
mathieu.arseneault@cjonquiere.qc.ca
Gervaise Aubin, Technicienne en documentation
gervaise.aubin@cjonquiere.qc.ca
Nancy Compartino, Technicienne en documentation
nancy.compartino@cjonquiere.qc.ca
Hélène Jeannotte, Conseillère pédagogique
helene.jeannotte@cjonquiere.qc.ca
Fabienne Simard, Technicienne en documentation
fabienne.simard@cjonquiere.qc.ca

***Jonquière:* Rio Tinto Alcan**
Centre de recherche et de développement Arvida (CRDA)
1955, boul Mellon
Jonquière, QC G7S 4K8
Adresse postale: CP 1250
Jonquière, QC G7S 4K8
418-699-6585 ext: 2817
Téléc: 418-699-3996
URL: www.riotintoalcan.com
Sigle: QAA
Fermée au public
Fondée en: 1946
Budget d'acquisitions: $50,000 - $99,999
Population desservie: 0
Sujets: Industrie de l'aluminium
Services:
Accès public à l'internet
Prêts entre bibliothèques(PEB)
Personnel: *Sommaire:* 3 Total; 1 Professionnel(s); 2 Technicien(s)

***Kirkland:* Merck Canada Inc.**
Research Library
16711 Transcanada Hwy.
Kirkland, QC H9H 3L1
514-428-8600
Fax: 514-428-8535
800-567-2594
URL: www.merckfrosst.ca
National Library Symbol: QMCF
Founded in: 1937
Hours: by appointment only
Acquisitions Budget: $500,000 - $999,999
Note: Access by appointment based on need to access.
Subjects covered: Medicine, Pharmacy, Pharmacology, Biology, Genetics, Chemistry, Molecular Biology, Biochemistry, Microbiology
Services:
Inter-Library Loan (ILL)
Document delivery, Reference
Microform Equipment: Computer; Reader
Personnel: *Summary:* 7 Total; 7 Other employees
Josée Schepper, Manager
Mary-Lynn Gaal, Research Librarian

***Kirkland:* Pfizer Canada, Inc.**
Library & Information Services
17300 Transcanada Hwy.
Kirkland, QC H9J 2M5
514-693-4159
Fax: 514-426-7558
e-mail: sharon.pipon@pfizer.com
URL: www.pfizer.ca
National Library Symbol: QKPC
No public access
Founded in: 1980
Hours: M-F 8:00-5:00
Acquisitions Budget: $50,000 - $99,999
Subjects covered: Medicine, Nursing, Health Sciences, Pharmacology, Biomedicine
Personnel: *Summary:* 2 Professional(s); 1 Technical(s)
Sharon Pipon, Manager
sharon.pipon@pfizer.com
514-693-4159

***L'Étang-du-Nord:* Campus des Iles-de-la-Madeleine**
Bibliothèque
15, ch de la Piscine
L'Étang-du-Nord, QC G4T 3X4
418-986-5187 ext: 6233
Téléc: 418-986-6788
URL: www.bibliothequedesiles.org
Sigle: QIMC
Heures: L 8h-17h; Ma, J 8h-20h; V 8h-16h30
Budget d'acquisitions: $10,000 - $24,999
Matériel imprimé: $10,000 - $24,999
Matériel électronique: 0-$9,999
Population desservie: 0
Services:
Accès public à l'internet
Réseau en ligne
Prêts entre bibliothèques(PEB)
Personnel: *Sommaire:* 2 Total; 1 Technicien(s); 1 Autre(s) employé(s)
Lionel Boudreau, Responsable, bibliothèque
lboudreau@cegepgim.ca
Veronique Chevarie, Agente de bureau
vchevarie@cegepgim.ca
Isabelle Vigneau, Agente de bureau
ivigneau@cegepgim.ca

***La Pocatière:* CÉGEP de la Pocatière**
Bibliothèque François-Hertel
140, 4e av
La Pocatière, QC G0R 1Z0
418-856-1525
Téléc: 418-856-4589
Couriel: information@cegeplapocatiere.qc.ca
URL: www.cegeplapocatiere.qc.ca
Fondée en: 1978
Heures: L-Me 7h50-21h; J 7h50-18h; V 7h50-16h30
Budget d'acquisitions: $25,000 - $49,999
Population desservie: 0
Collections spécialisées: Collection complète des oeuvres de François Hertel.
Services:
Accès public à l'internet
Prêts entre bibliothèques(PEB)
Personnel: *Sommaire:* 1 Professionnel(s); 2 Technicien(s); 4 Autre(s) employé(s)
Jean-Louis Demers, Bibliothécaire en chef
jldemers@cglapocatiere.qc.ca
418-856-1525 ext. 2228
Marthe Bergeron, Responsable, Référence et periodiques
Jocelyne Dubé, technicienne en documentation

***La Pocatière:* Institut de technologie agro-alimentaire de la Pocatière**
Centre de documentation
401, rue Poiré
La Pocatière, QC G0R 1Z0
418-856-1110 ext: 258
Téléc: 418-856-1719
URL: www.ita.qc.ca/fr/lapocatiere/Pages/lapocatiere.aspx
Sigle: QPES
Fondée en: 1859
Heures: L-V 7h30-17h; L-J 18h-21h
Budget d'acquisitions: $25,000 - $49,999
Population desservie: 0
Sujets: Agriculture, alimentation, environnement, biologie, économie, entomologie, faune, sylviculture, ornithologie, zootechnie, pédologie, génie rural
Services:
Prêts entre bibliothèques(PEB)
Lecteur/reproduction de microformes: Lecteurs
Personnel: *Sommaire:* 2 Total; 1 Professionnel(s); 2 Technicien(s); 1 Autre(s) employé(s)
Pierre Duncan, Professionnel
pduncan@agr.gouv.qc.ca
418-856-1110 ext. 258
Dominique Therriault, Technicienne agricole
dominique.therriault@agr.gouv.qc.ca
418-856-1110 ext. 279
Agathe Plante, Agente de secrétariat
agathe.plante@agr.gouv.qc.ca
418-856-1110 ext. 257

***Lasalle:* CÉGEP d'André-Laurendeau**
Carrefour de l'information et des médias
1111, rue Lapierre
Lasalle, QC H8N 2J4
514-364-3320 ext: 147
Téléc: 514-364-2627
Couriel: bibliotheque@claurendeau.qc.ca
URL: www.claurendeau.qc.ca
Sigle: QLSC
Heures: L-J 7h30-20h; V 7h30-17h
Budget d'acquisitions: $50,000 - $99,999
Population desservie: 0
Services:
Accès public à l'internet
Prêts entre bibliothèques(PEB)
Personnel: *Sommaire:* 7 Total; 1 Professionnel(s); 3 Technicien(s); 3 Autre(s) employé(s)
Ginette Leclair, Directrice, Ressources matérielles

***Laval:* Centre de santé et de services sociaux de Laval**
Bibliothèque de CSSS de Laval
1755, boul René-Laënnec
Laval, QC H7M 3L9
450-975-5493
Téléc: 450-975-5572
Couriel: biblio.csssl@ssss.gouv.qc.ca
URL: catalogue.cssslaval.qc.ca
bibliocsssl.wordpress.com
Sigle: QLACS
Fondée en: 1978
Heures: L-V 8h-16h30
Budget d'acquisitions: $25,000 - $49,999
Population desservie: 0
Annotation: Membre de l'Association des Bibliothèques de la Santé affiliées à l'Université de Montréal (ABSAUM)
Sujets: Sciences de la santé
Services:
Prêts entre bibliothèques(PEB)
Personnel: *Sommaire:* 2 Total; 1 Professionnel(s); 1 Technicien(s)
France Pontbriand, Bibliothécaire
fpontbriand.csssl@ssss.gouv.qc.ca
450-668-1010 ext. 23215
Robyn Maler, Centre de documentation pour les personnes atteintes de cancer
rmaler.csssl@ssss.gouv.qc.ca
450-668-1010 ext. 23984

***Laval:* Collège Montmorency**
Centre des ressources didactiques
475, boul de l'Avenir
Laval, QC H7N 5H9
450-975-6100
Téléc: 450-975-6496
URL: biblio.cmontmorency.qc.ca
Fondée en: 1969
Heures: L-J 8h-21h; V 8h-18h
Budget d'acquisitions: $100,000 - $249,999
Population desservie: 0
Collections spécialisées: Informatique, électronique
Sujets: Éducation, architecture, soins infirmiers, réadaptation, muséologie, tourisme
Services:
Accèss distance aux bases de donn
Prêts entre bibliothèques(PEB) frais
Lecteur/reproduction de microformes: Lecteurs
Personnel: *Sommaire:* 8 Total; 1 Professionnel(s); 6 Technicien(s); 1 Autre(s) employé(s)
Dominique Alaire, Responsable
adjress@cmontmorency.qc.ca

***Laval:* INRS - Institut Armand-Frappier**
Bibliothèque
531, boul des Prairies Laval-des-Rapides
Laval, QC H7V 1B7

450-687-5010 ext: 4265
Téléc: 418-654-2660
Couriel: sdis@adm.inrs.ca
info@iaf.inrs.ca
URL: sdis.inrs.ca
Sigle: QMIM
Heures: L-V 9h-17havec rendez-vous seulement
Budget d'acquisitions: $250,000 - $499,999
Population desservie: 0
Sujets: Microbiologie, virologie, epidémiologie, immunologie, médecine comparée, sciences alimentaires
Services:
Accès public à l'internet
Réseau en ligne
Prêts entre bibliothèques(PEB) frais
Frais de recherche
Personnel: *Sommaire:* 3 Total; 1 Professionnel(s); 1 Technicien(s); 1 Autre(s) employé(s)
Michel Courcelles, Bibliothécaire
michel.courcelles@iaf.inrs.ca
Diane Sauvé, Bibliothécaire

Longueuil: **Collège Édouard-Montpetit Centre des ressources documentaires**
945, ch de Chambly
Longueuil, QC J4H 3M6
450-679-2631 ext: 6047
Couriel: bibliolong@college-em.qc.ca
URL: blogues.college-em.qc.ca/bibli
Fondée en: 1967
Heures: L-J 8h-20h; V 8h-16h30; S 9h-13h. Modification de cet horaire entre les sessions
Budget d'acquisitions: $50,000 - $99,999
Matériel imprimé: $50,000 - $99,999
Matériel électronique: $10,000 - $24,999
Population desservie: 0
Collections spécialisées: Dentisterie, électrotechnique, optique, aérotechnique
Sujets: Santé, sciences sociales, techniques physiques, aérotechnique, sciences humaines, cinéma
Services:
Accès public à l'internet
Réseau en ligne
Prêts entre bibliothèques(PEB) frais de 10$
Lecteur/reproduction de microformes: Lecteurs
Personnel: *Sommaire:* 17 Total; 2 Professionnel(s); 6 Technicien(s); 9 Autre(s) employé(s)
Louis-Marie Dussault, Directrice
Michelle Chartier, Responsable, services techniques

Longueuil: **Quebec Regional Library**
1001, boul St-Laurent ouest
Longueuil, QC J4K 1C7
450-646-1353 ext: 222
Fax: 450-928-4102
National Library Symbol: QMNHH
Hours: M-F by appointment only
Acquisitions Budget: $25,000 - $49,999
Special Collections: Food Technology, Analytical Chemistry, Analysis & Regulation, Drug Manufacturing, Cosmetics Regulation, Microbiology
Personnel: *Summary:* 1 Total; 1 Technical(s)
Chantal Boileau, Librarian
chantal_boileau@hc-sc.gc.ca
450-646-1353 ext. 369

Lévis: **CÉGEP de Lévis-Lauzon Services des ressources didactiques**
205, rue Mgr Bourget
Lévis, QC G6V 6Z9
418-833-5110
Téléc: 418-833-7323
Couriel: paule.drouin@clevislauzon.qc.ca
sylvie.dube@clevislauzon.qc.ca
URL: www.clevislauzon.qc.ca/biblio
Social Media: vimeo.com/channels/165827
www.facebook.com/groups/107568799263796
twitter.com/Biblio_CLL
Fondée en: 1969
Heures: L-J 7h45-21h; V 7h45-18h; Sa 10h-16havec rendez-vous seulement
Budget d'acquisitions: Matériel imprimé: $100,000 - $249,999
Matériel électronique: 0-$9,999
Population desservie: 0
Sujets: Sciences, électronique, biotechnologie, technologie, soins infirmiers, arts
Services:
Accès public à l'internet
Prêts entre bibliothèques(PEB) frais
Lecteur/reproduction de microformes: Lecteurs
Personnel: *Sommaire:* 9 Total; 1 Professionnel(s); 5 Technicien(s); 3 Autre(s) employé(s)
Paule Drouin, SMTE-Bibliothécaire
paule.drouin@clevislauzon.qc.ca
418-833-5110 ext. 3404
Sylvie Dubé, Référence-PEB
sylvie.dube@clevislauzon.qc.ca
418-833-5110 ext. 3409

Matane: **CÉGEP de Matane Bibliothèque Lucien-Lelièvre**
616, av St-Rédempteur
Matane, QC G4W 1L1
418-562-1240 ext: 2141
Téléc: 418-566-2115
Couriel: bibliotheque@cgmatane.qc.ca
URL: www.cegep-matane.qc.ca
Sigle: PMATC
Heures: L-J 8h-20h, V 8h-17h
Budget d'acquisitions: $25,000 - $49,999
Population desservie: 0
Sujets: Tourisme, agriculture, aménagement, photographie
Services:
Accès public à l'internet
Prêts entre bibliothèques(PEB)
Personnel: *Sommaire:* 3 Total; 1 Professionnel(s); 1 Technicien(s); 1 Autre(s) employé(s)
Jano Asatoury, Cadre services technologiques

Mirabel: **Bell Helicopter Textron Canada Limited Library**
12800, rue de l'Avenir
Mirabel, QC J7J 1R4
450-437-3400
URL: www.bellhelicopter.com
National Library Symbol: QSTTB
No public access
Founded in: 1986
Acquisitions Budget: $25,000 - $49,999
Special Collections: BHTC Technical Reports & Manuals, Helicopter History
Subjects covered: Engineering, Technology, Transportation, Aerodynamics, Fluid Mechanics, Applied Mechanics, Aircraft (design, component fatigue, structures, weight control), Avionics, Dynamics, Electrical Engineering, Helicopter Flight Technology, Metallurgy, Metals, Plastics, Powerplant Design, Airworthiness, Safety, Vehicle Design, Helicopter Flight Technology
Services:
Internet Access
Inter-Library Loan (ILL)
Personnel: *Summary:* 1 Technical(s)

Montréal: **Bibliothèque centrale**
Pavillon Hubert-Aquin, local A-M100
400, rue St-Catherine est
Montréal, QC H3C 3P3
Adresse postale: CP 8889, Succ Centre-ville
Montréal, QC H3C 3P3
514-987-6114
Téléc: 514-987-4213
URL: www.bibliotheques.uqam.ca/centrale
Sigle: QMUQ
Heures: L-V 9h-22h; S, D 12h-17h
Budget d'acquisitions: $500,000 - $999,999
Population desservie: 0
Sujets: Sciences humaines, lettres, langues et communications, sciences de la gestion
Services:
Accès public à l'internet
Réseau en ligne
Prêts entre bibliothèques(PEB)
Lecteur/reproduction de microformes: Lecteurs
Personnel: *Sommaire:* 50 Total; 13 Professionnel(s); 10 Technicien(s); 25 Autre(s) employé(s)
Stephen Park, Directeur
park.stephen@uqam.ca
514-987-3000 ext. 4353
Benoît Kelly, Bibliothécaire
kelly.benoit@uqam.ca
514-987-3000 ext. 4343
Hélène Bussière, Bibliothécaire
bussiere.helene@uqam.ca
514-987-3000 ext. 6648
Marjolaine Fortin, Bibliothécaire
fortin.marjolaine@uqam.ca
514-987-3000 ext. 4363
Madeleine Hébert-Erban, Bibliothécaire
hebert-erban.madeleine@uqam.ca
514-987-3000 ext. 4323
Guy Courtemanche, Bibliothécaire
courtemanche.guy@uqam.ca
514-987-3000 ext. 3813
Pierrette Richèr, Bibliothécaire
richer.pierrette@uqam.ca
514-987-3000 ext. 7724
Sylvie St-Pierre, Bibliothécaire
st-pierre.sylive@uqam.ca
514-987-3000 ext. 7866
Christine Médaille, Bibliothécaire
medaille.christine@uqam.ca
514-987-3000 ext. 4332

Montréal: **Bibliothèque d'aménagement**
#1162, 2940, ch de la Côte-Ste-Catherine
Montréal, QC H3C 3J7
Adresse postale: CP 6128, Succ Centre-ville
Montréal, QC H3C 3J7
514-343-7177
Téléc: 514-343-6457
Couriel: biblios@bib.umontreal.ca
pebqmu@bib.umontreal.ca
URL: www.bib.umontreal.ca
Heures: L-J 8h30-21h; V 8h30-17H; S, D 12h-17h
Budget d'acquisitions: $100,000 - $249,999
Population desservie: 0
Sujets: Architecture, architecture de paysage, urbanisme, design industriel, histoire des jardins
Personnel: *Sommaire:* 10 Total; 2 Professionnel(s); 3 Technicien(s); 5 Autre(s) employé(s)
Lyne Bélanger, Chef de bibliothèque
lyne.belanger@umontreal.ca
514-343-6111 ext. 4700
Ginette-Denyse Melançon-Bolduc, Responsable, Référence
ginette-denyse.melancon.bolduc@umontreal.ca
514-343-6111 ext. 2740

Montréal: **Bibliothèque de botanique - L'Institut de recherche en biologie végétale**
#E-328, 4101, rue Sherbrooke est
Montréal, QC H1X 2B2
514-343-6612
Téléc: 514-343-6457
Couriel: biblios@bib.umontreal.ca
pebqmu@bib.umontreal.ca
URL: www.bib.umontreal.ca
Heures: L-V 9h-17h
Budget d'acquisitions: $25,000 - $49,999
Population desservie: 0
Collections spécialisées: Fonds Marie-Victorin (Herbier)
Sujets: Botanique, biologie végétale, biotechnologie des plantes, floristique, génétique, morphologie végétale, biologie moléculaire
Services:
Prêts entre bibliothèques(PEB)
Personnel: *Sommaire:* 2 Total; 1 Technicien(s)
Hélène Tardif, Bibliothécaire
helene.tardif@umontreal.ca
514-343-6111 ext. 1702
Marie-Claude Dumont, Technicienne en documentation
marie.claude.dumon@umontreal.ca
514-343-6111 ext. 82353

Montréal: **Bibliothèque de chimie**
#H-715, Pavillon Roger-Gaudry, 2900, boul Édouard-Montpetit
Montréal, QC H3C 3J7
Adresse postale: CP 6128, Succ Centre-ville
Montréal, QC H3C 3J7
514-343-6459
Téléc: 514-343-5878
Couriel: biblios@bib.umontreal.ca
pebqmu@bib.umontreal.ca
URL: www.bib.umontreal.ca
Heures: L-J 9h-21h; V 9h-17h; S 11h-17h
Budget d'acquisitions: $250,000 - $499,999
Population desservie: 0

Sujets: Chimie analytique, chimie organique et inorganique, chimie physique, chimie théorique, biochimie, chimie des protéines, spectrométrie, polymères
Personnel: *Sommaire:* 6 Total; 2 Professionnel(s); 1 Technicien(s); 3 Autre(s) employé(s)
Maryna Beaulieu, Chef de bibliothèque
maryna.beaulieu@umontreal.ca
514-343-6111 ext. 26778
Malivahn Sananikone, Bibnliothécaire
malivanh.sananikone@umontreal.ca
514-343-6111 ext. 3571

Montréal: Bibliothèque de didacthèque

Pavillion Marie-Victorin, 90, av. Vincent d'Indy, #A-128
Montréal, QC H3C 3J7
Adresse postale: CP 6128, Succursale Centre-ville
Montréal, QC H3C 3J7
514-343-6195
Téléc: 514-343-6457
URL: www.bib.umontreal.ca/DI/
Fondée en: 1976
Heures: L, Me 8h30-20h; Ma, J, V 8h30-17h; S 11h-17h
Population desservie: 0
Collections spécialisées: Matériel didactique, publications officielles, ouvrages de pédagogie, littérature jeunesse, accessoires didactiques, jeux éducatifs, audiovisuel, périodiques, logiciels éducatifs, matériel d'évaluation, dossiers de press,club vidéo.
Sujets: Ressources didactiques regroupant tous les documents disponibles en milieu scolaire pour les ordres d'enseignement préscolaire, primaire et secondaire.
Laurence Rajotte, Chef de bibliothèque
laurence.rajotte@utoronto.ca
514-343-6111 ext. 1707
Dalie Matton, Bibliothécaire, Référence, dévelopment des collections, formation
dalie.matton@utoronto.ca
514-343-6111 ext. 1746

Montréal: Bibliothèque de droit / Law Library

Pavillon Maximilien-Caron
3101, ch de la tour, 4e étage
Montréal, QC H3C 3J7
Adresse postale: CP 6128, Succ Centre-ville
Montréal, QC H3C 3J7
514-343-7095
Téléc: 514-343-5928
Couriel: biblios@bib.umontreal.ca
URL: www.bib.umontreal.ca
Heures: L-J 8h30-20h; V 8h30-17h; D 10h-19h
Budget d'acquisitions: $500,000 - $999,999
Population desservie: 0
Sujets: Droit, justice
Services:
Accès public à l'internet
Personnel: *Sommaire:* 18 Total; 5 Professionnel(s); 4 Technicien(s); 9 Autre(s) employé(s)
Michèle Leroux, Bibliothécaire
michele.leroux@umontreal.ca
514-343-6111 ext. 4317
Luc Marceau, Bibliothécaire
luc.marceau@umontreal.ca
514-343-6111 ext. 4310
Stéphanie Pham-Dang, Bibliothécaire
stephanie.pham-dang@umontreal.ca
514-343-6111 ext. 4308
Julia Smocot, Bibliothécaire
julia.smocot@umontreal.ca
514-343-6111 ext. 4319

Montréal: Bibliothèque de géographie

339,520, ch Côte Ste-Catherine
Montréal, QC H3C 3J7
Adresse postale: CP 6128, Succ Centre-ville
Montréal, QC H3C 3J7
514-343-8063
Téléc: 514-343-8008
Couriel: biblios@bib.umontreal.ca
maryna.beaulieu@umontreal.ca
URL: www.bib.umontreal.ca/GP/
Heures: L-J 9h-20h; V 9h-16h30
Budget d'acquisitions: $25,000 - $49,999
Population desservie: 0; Étudiants, professeurs, chercheurs
Annotation: Service de formation documentaire
Sujets: Géographie physique, géographie humaine, cartographie et télédétection, géographie économique, géographie sociale, géographie des populations, géographie urbaine, géographie médicale
Services:
Accèss distance aux bases de donn
Accès public à l'internet
Réseau en ligne
Prêts entre bibliothèques(PEB)
Personnel: *Sommaire:* 7 Total; 1 Professionnel(s); 1 Technicien(s); 5 Autre(s) employé(s)
Claire Dubois, Directrice
claire.dubois@umontreal.ca
514-343-6111 ext. 5965
Sophie Labelle, Technicienne en documentation
sophie.labelle@umontreal.ca
514-343-6111 ext. 8063
Anne Hakier, Bibliothécaire
anne.hakier@umontreal.ca
514-343-8038
Lucy Caetano, Commis
lucy.caetano@umontreal.ca
514-343-6111 ext. 8063

Montréal: Bibliothèque de physique

#H-825, Pavillon Roger-Gaudry, 2900, boul Édouard-Montpetit
Montréal, QC H3C 3J7
Adresse postale: CP 6128, Succ Centre-ville
Montréal, QC H3C 3J7
514-343-6613
Téléc: 514-343-5698
Couriel: biblios@bib.umontreal.ca
pebqmu@bib.umontreal.ca
URL: www.bib.umontreal.ca
Heures: L-J 9h-21h; V 9h-17h; S 11h-17h
Budget d'acquisitions: $250,000 - $499,999
Population desservie: 0
Sujets: Physique, astronomie, astrophysique, biophysique
Personnel: *Sommaire:* 3 Total; 1 Professionnel(s); 1 Technicien(s); 2 Autre(s) employé(s)
Maryna Beaulieu, Chef de bibliothèque
maryna.baulieu@umontreal.ca
Luce Brazeau, Bibliothécaire
luce.brazeau@umontreal.ca
514-343-6111 ext. 3570

Montréal: Bibliothèque des sciences

#KI-R100. 145, av du Président-Kennedy
Montréal, QC H3C 3P3
Adresse postale: CP 8889, Succ Centre-Ville
Montréal, QC H3C 3P3
514-987-6164
Téléc: 514-987-6821
URL: www.bibliotheques.uqam.ca/sciences
Sigle: QHUDS
Fondée en: 1974
Heures: L, Ma 8h30-22h; Me-V 8h30-20h; S 10h-17havec rendez-vous seulement
Budget d'acquisitions: $500,000 - $999,999
Population desservie: 0
Sujets: Sciences pures et appliquées
Services:
Prêts entre bibliothèques(PEB)
Lecteur/reproduction de microformes: Ordinateur; Lecteurs
Marcel Simoneau, Directeur
simoneau.marcel@uqam.ca
514-987-3000 ext. 3570
Mychelle Boulet, Bibliothécaire
boulet.mychelle@uqam.ca
514-987-3000 ext. 3247
Karim Debbah, Bibliothécaire
karim.debbah@uqam.ca
514-987-3000 ext. 3403
Sylvie Goulet, Bibliothécaire
goulet.sylvie@uqam.ca
514-987-3000 ext. 3401
Camil David, Technicien en documentation
david.camil@uqam.ca
514-987-3000 ext. 7924
Denise Fortin-Carrière, Technicienne en documentation
fortin-carriere.denis@uqam.ca
514-987-3000 ext. 3402

Montréal: Bibliothèque des sciences de la santé

#L-623, Pavillon Roger-Gaudry, 2900, boul Édouard-Montpetit
Montréal, QC H3C 3J7
Adresse postale: CP 6128, Succ Centre-ville
Montréal, QC H3C 3J7
514-343-7664
Téléc: 514-343-2350
Couriel: biblios@bib.umontreal.ca
pebqmum@bib.umontreal.ca
URL: www.bib.umontreal.ca
Sigle: QMUM
Fondée en: 1975
Heures: L,M,M,V 8h30-17h; J 8h30-21h
Budget d'acquisitions: $500,000 - $999,999
Population desservie: 0
Sujets: Médecine, pharmacologie, médecine dentaire
Services:
Accès public à l'internet
Prêts entre bibliothèques(PEB)
Personnel: *Sommaire:* 25 Total; 6 Professionnel(s); 8 Technicien(s); 13 Autre(s) employé(s)
Monique St-Jean, Directrice
monique.st-jean@umontreal.ca
514-343-7810
Sylvie Desbiens, Chef, Dév. collections/référence
sylvie.desbiens@umontreal.ca
514-343-6111 ext. 3583
Marie-Josée Leboeuf, Chef de service, Prêt et traitement des collections
marie.josee.leboeuf@umontreal.ca
514-343-6111 ext. 3576

Montréal: Bibliothèque des sciences juridiques

Pavillion Hubert-Aquin, local A-2100
400, rue St-Catherine est
Montréal, QC H3C 3P3
Adresse postale: CP 8889, Succ Centre-ville
Montréal, QC H3C 3P3
514-987-6184
Téléc: 514-987-4392
Sigle: MUQ
Heures: L, Ma 8h30-22h; Me-V 8h30-20h; S 10h-17h
Budget d'acquisitions: $50,000 - $99,999
Population desservie: 0
Sujets: Traités, recueils de lois, monographies, périodiques, ouvrages de référence sur le droit
Personnel: *Sommaire:* 3 Professionnel(s); 1 Technicien(s); 5 Autre(s) employé(s)
Lucie Rebelo, Directrice
rebelo.lucie@uqam.ca
514-987-3000 ext. 4301
Sylvie Girouard, Bibliothécaire
girouard.sylvie@uqam.ca
514-987-3000 ext. 3681
Jean St-Amant, Bibliothécaire
st-amant.jean@uqam.ca
514-987-3000 ext. 4312
Pierre-Luc Brosseau, Technicienne en documentation
brosseau.pierre-luc@uqam.ca
514-987-3000 ext. 3183

Montréal: Bibliothèque paramédicale

#2120, 2375, ch Côte Ste Catherine
Montréal, QC H3C 3J7
Adresse postale: CP 6128, Succ Centre-ville
Montréal, QC H3C 3J7
514-343-6180
Téléc: 514-343-6457
Couriel: biblios@bib.umontreal.ca
denise.diamond@umontreal.ca
URL: www.bib.umontreal.ca/SA/param.htm
Sigle: QMUP
Fondée en: 1967
Heures: L-M 8h-22h; J-V 8h-17h; S 10h-17h
Budget d'acquisitions: $250,000 - $499,999
Population desservie: 0
Sujets: Nutrition, réadaptation, sciences infirmières, ortho-audio, administration de la santé, médecine sociale et préventive, médecine du travail, diététique, technologies alimentaires, santé et sécurité au travail, toxicologie
Services:
Accès public à l'internet
Prêts entre bibliothèques(PEB)
Frais de recherche
Lecteur/reproduction de microformes: Ordinateur; Lecteurs
Personnel: *Sommaire:* 9 Total; 4 Professionnel(s); 3 Technicien(s); 8 Autre(s) employé(s)

Denise Diamond, Chef de bibliothèque
denise.diamond@umontreal.ca
514-343-6111 ext. 1848
Siv Kham Cao, Bibliothécaire
siv.kham.chao@umontreal.ca
514-343-6111 ext. 1846
Myrian Grondin, Bibliothécaire
myrian.grondin@umontreal.ca
514-343-6111 ext. 2515
Louise Paradis, Bibliothécaire
514-343-6111 ext. 1845

Montréal: Bombardier Inc./Canadair Aerospace & Defence Groups Technical Information Centre

800, boul René-Lévesque ouest
Montréal, QC H3B 1Y8
514-861-9481
Other contact info: Operator, Phone: 514-855-5001
URL: www.bombardier.com
No public access
Founded in: 1947
Hours: M-F
Special Collections: NASA Reports; NACA Reports; ESDU's; AIAA; SAE; IEEE
Subjects covered: Aerospace Engineering; Electrical & Mechanical Engineering; Chemistry; Physics; Materials Science; Management; Computer Science; Finance & Customer Support; Human Resources & Legal
Services:
Microform Equipment: Computer; Reader
Personnel: *Summary:* 9 Total; 2 Professional(s); 6 Technical(s); 1 Other employees

Montréal: CÉGEP de Marie-Victorin Bibliothèque

7000, rue Marie Victorin
Montréal, QC H1G 2J6
514-325-0150 ext: 2311
Téléc: 514-328-3830
URL: pedagogie.collegemv.qc.ca/bibliotheque
Fermée au public
Fondée en: 1962
Heures: L-V 8h-17h
Population desservie: 0
Annotation: Matériathèque (centre documentation des techniques en services de garde); Salles de travail de groupe; Appareils audiovisuels
Collections spécialisées: 80,000 livres; 150 abonnements périodiques
Services:
Accès public à l'internet
Prêts entre bibliothèques(PEB)
Lecteur/reproduction de microformes: Lecteurs
Personnel: *Sommaire:* 4 Total; 3 Professionnel(s); 1 Technicien(s)
Pierre Duchesneau, Coordonnateur des ressources didactiques et documentaires
pierre.duchesneau@collegemv.qc.ca
Pierre Bélanger, Technicien en documentation
Nicole Bélanger-Cadieux, Responsable, acquisitions

Montréal: CÉGEP du Vieux-Montréal Bibliothèque

255, rue Ontario est
Montréal, QC H2X 1X6
514-982-3437 ext: 2219
Téléc: 514-982-3448
Couriel: gestionnairew3@cvm.qc.ca
cjolicoeur@cvm.qc.ca
URL: www.cvm.qc.ca/bibliotheque/Pages/index.aspx
Heures: L-J 8h-21h; V 8h-17havec rendez-vous seulement
Budget d'acquisitions: Matériel imprimé: $50,000 - $99,999
Matériel électronique: $10,000 - $24,999
Population desservie: 0
Collections spécialisées: Métiers d'art
Sujets: Sciences humaines et techniques
Personnel: *Sommaire:* 6 Total; 1 Professionnel(s); 5 Technicien(s); 5 Bénévole(s)
Catherine Jolicoeur, Bibliothécaire responsable
cjolicoeur@cvm.qc.ca
514-982-3437 ext. 2210

Montréal: Centre de documentation (Succursale Montréal)

35, rue de Port-Royal est, 4e étage
Montréal, QC H3L 3T1
514-864-1666
Téléc: 514-864-3332
Couriel: doc-qmtra@mtq.gouv.qc.ca
Sigle: QMTRA
Fondée en: 1978
Heures: L-V 8h30-12h, 13h-16h30
Budget d'acquisitions: $10,000 - $24,999
Matériel imprimé: 0-$9,999
Matériel électronique: 0-$9,999
Population desservie: 0
Collections spécialisées: Transports Québec, Transports Canada, Transportation Research Board
Sujets: Transports urbains et publiques, urbanisme, environnement
Services:
Accès public à l'internet
Prêts entre bibliothèques(PEB)
Lecteur/reproduction de microformes: Lecteurs
Personnel: *Sommaire:* 3 Total; 1 Professionnel(s); 2 Technicien(s);

Montréal: Centre hospitalier de l'Université de Montréal Hôpital Notre-Dame Centre de documentation

1560, rue Sherbrooke est
Montréal, QC H2L 4M1
514-890-8000 ext: 26862
Sigle: QMHND
Heures: L-V 8h-17h
Budget d'acquisitions: $250,000 - $499,999
Population desservie: 0
Annotation: Affiliée à L'Association des bibliothèques de la santé affiliées à l'Université de Montréal (ABSAUM).
Sujets: Sciences de la santé
Services:
Prêts entre bibliothèques(PEB) frais
Personnel: *Sommaire:* 1 Professionnel(s); 3 Technicien(s); 2 Autre(s) employé(s)

Montréal: Centre hospitalier de l'Université de Montréal Hôpital Saint-Luc Centre de documentation

1058, rue St-Denis
Montréal, QC H2X 3J4
514-890-8000 ext: 35867
Fax: 514-412-7317
National Library Symbol: QMHSL
Founded in: 1945
Hours: L-V 8h-18h. A partir du 2 mai: L-V 8h-17h; S 9h-12h, 13h-17h; D 11h-17
Note: Membre de l'Association des bibliothèques de la santé affiliées à l'Université de Montréal (ABSAUM)
Special Collections: Hépatologie, médecine interne
Subjects covered: Sciences de la santé, médecine
Services:
Inter-Library Loan (ILL)
Personnel: *Summary:* 3 Total; 1 Professional(s); 2 Technical(s); 1 Volunteer(s)

Montréal: Centre hospitalier de l'Université de Montréal Hôtel-Dieu Centre de documentation, Audiovidéothèque

3840, rue St-Urbain
Montréal, QC H2W 1T8
514-890-8000 ext: 14355
Téléc: 514-412-7194
Couriel: biblio.hdm.chum@sssss.gouv.qc.ca
Sigle: QMCHUM
Fermée au public
Fondée en: 1947
Heures: L-V 8h-16h30
Budget d'acquisitions: $50,000 - $99,999
Population desservie: 0
Annotation: Affilié à l'Association des bibliothèques de la santé affiliées à l'Université de Montréal (ABSAUM)
Sujets: Médecine, soins infirmiers, sciences de la santé
Services:
Accès public à l'internet
Prêts entre bibliothèques(PEB) frais de 7$
Personnel: *Sommaire:* 4 Total; 1 Professionnel(s); 3 Technicien(s)
André Allard, Responsable
Andre.Allard.Chum@ssss.gouv.qc.ca
514-890-8000 ext. 14355
Diane St-Aubin, Bibliothécaire
diane.st-aubin.chum@ssss.gouv.qc.ca

Montréal: Collège André-Grasset Bibliothèque

1001, boul Crémazie est
Montréal, QC H2M 1M3
514-381-4293
Téléc: 514-381-7421
URL: www.grasset.qc.ca/Bibliotheque/Bibliotheque-7.php
Heures:avec rendez-vous seulement
Budget d'acquisitions: Matériel imprimé: $10,000 - $24,999
Matériel électronique: 0-$9,999
Population desservie: 0
Sujets: Enseignement
Services:
Réseau en ligne
Prêts entre bibliothèques(PEB) frais de 10$
Personnel: *Sommaire:* 6 Total; 1 Professionnel(s); 3 Technicien(s); 2 Autre(s) employé(s)

Montréal: Collège d'Ahuntsic Bibliothèque Laurent-Michel-Vacher

9155, rue Saint-Hubert
Montréal, QC H2M 1Y8
514-389-5921
866-389-5921
URL: ww2.collegeahuntsic.qc.ca/webbibli
Sigle: QMDCA
Heures: L-J 8h-19h30; V 8h-17h; S 12h30-16h30
Population desservie: 0
Services:
Accès public à l'internet
Réseau en ligne
Prêts entre bibliothèques(PEB)
Personnel: *Sommaire:* 12 Total; 1 Professionnel(s); 4 Technicien(s); 7 Autre(s) employé(s)

Montréal: Collège de Maisonneuve Bibliothèque

3800, rue Sherbrooke est
Montréal, QC H1X 2A2
514-254-7131
Téléc: 514-254-9741
Couriel: biblio@cmaisonneuve.qc.ca
communic@cmaisonneuve.qc.ca
URL: www.cmaisonneuve.qc.ca/etudiant-actuel/bibliotheque
Heures: L-J 8h-21h; V 8h-16h30
Budget d'acquisitions: $100,000 - $249,999
Population desservie: 0
Sujets: Bibliothèque académique de niveau collégial
Services:
Accès public à l'internet
Réseau en ligne
Prêts entre bibliothèques(PEB)
Lecteur/reproduction de microformes: Ordinateur; Lecteurs
Personnel: *Sommaire:* 17 Total; 2 Professionnel(s); 2 Technicien(s); 13 Autre(s) employé(s)

Montréal: Collège de Rosemont Bibliothèque

6400, 16e av
Montréal, QC H1X 2S9
514-376-1620 ext: 265
Téléc: 514-376-1440
URL: www.crosemont.qc.ca/services-etudiants/bibliotheque
www.biblioweb.info/crosemont/index.html
Fondée en: 1968
Heures: L-Me 8h-21h; J 8h-18h; V 8h-16h30
Budget d'acquisitions: $25,000 - $49,999
Population desservie: 0
Collections spécialisées: Acupuncture, laboratoire médical, thanatologie
Services:
Prêts entre bibliothèques(PEB)
Personnel: *Sommaire:* 1 Professionnel(s); 3 Technicien(s); 3 Autre(s) employé(s)
Josée Corriveau, Conseillère pédagogique
jcorriveau@crosemont.qc.ca

Montréal: Collège Français
Bibliothèque
185, rue Fairmount ouest
Montréal, QC H2T 2M6
514-495-2581
Téléc: 514-271-2823
URL: www.collegefrancais.ca
Heures: L-V 8h30-17h30avec rendez-vous seulement
Population desservie: 0
Personnel: *Sommaire:* 2 Total; 1 Professionnel(s); 1 Autre(s) employé(s)

Montréal: Collège Jean-de-Brébeuf
Bibliothèque du cours collégial
5625, av Decelles
Montréal, QC H3T 1W4
514-342-9342 ext: 5346
Téléc: 514-342-1558
Couriel: bibliocol@brebeuf.qc.ca
URL: www.brebeuf.qc.ca/collegial/bibliotheque
Fondée en: 1957
Heures: L-J 8h-17h45; V 8h-16h
Budget d'acquisitions: $50,000 - $99,999
Population desservie: 0
Services:
Réseau en ligne
Prêts entre bibliothèques(PEB)
Lecteur/reproduction de microformes: Lecteurs
Personnel: *Sommaire:* 2 Professionnel(s); 2 Technicien(s); 3 Autre(s) employé(s)
Violaine Fortier, Responsable
violaine.fortier@brebeuf.qc.ca
514-342-9342 ext. 5374
Philippe Garneau, Bibliothécaire - Archiviste
archives@brebeuf.qc.ca
514-342-9342 ext. 5133
Noëlline Charron, Technicienne en documentation
noelline.charron@brebeuf.qc.ca
514-342-9342 ext. 5346

Montréal: Collège Lasalle
Centre de documentation
#4100, 2000, rue Sainte-Catherine ouest
Montréal, QC H3H 2T2
514-939-2006 ext: 4503
Fax: 514-939-7292
800-363-3541
URL: www.collegelasalle.com
Founded in: 1959
Hours: L-J 7h30-20h; V 7h30-18h
Acquisitions Budget: $50,000 - $99,999
Subjects covered: Mode; tourisme; hôtellerie; gestion
Services:
Internet Access
Access to Subscription Databases
Personnel: *Summary:* 5 Total; 1 Professional(s); 2 Technical(s); 1 Other employees

Montréal: Collège O'Sullivan / O'Sullivan College
Bibliothèque
1191, rue de la Montagne
Montréal, QC H3G 1Z2
514-866-4622
Fax: 514-866-0668
800-621-8055
URL: www.osullivan.edu
No public access
Hours: M-Thu 8:30-6:00; F 8:30-5:00
Acquisitions Budget: $25,000 - $49,999
Subjects covered: Business Administration, Paralegal, Computer Science, Office Systems Technology
Services:
Internet Access
Personnel: *Summary:* 1 Total; 1 Professional(s); 2 Volunteer(s)

Montréal: Collège St-Jean-Vianney
Bibliothèque
#A-222, 12630, boul Gouin est
Montréal, QC H1C 1B9
Adresse postale: 12630, boul Gouin est
Montréal, QC H1C 1B9
514-648-3821
Téléc: 514-648-8401
URL: www.st-jean-vianney.qc.ca
Heures: L-V 7h30-16h
Population desservie: 0
Personnel: *Sommaire:* 1 Professionnel(s); 1 Autre(s) employé(s)

Montréal: Comité national de recherche sur le logement
Centre de documentation Marie-Morin
#5100, 303, rue Notre-Dame est
Montréal, QC H2Y 3Y8
514-872-4119
Sigle: QMURB
Fermée au public
Fondée en: 1988
Heures: L-V
Budget d'acquisitions: $25,000 - $49,999
Population desservie: 0
Sujets: Urbanisme; Aménagement; Patrimoine; Architecture; Gestion municipale
Ginette Dugas, Librarian
ginettedugas@ville.montreal.qc.ca
514-872-4119

Montréal: Commission de la santé et de la securité du travail
Centre de documentation (Montréal)
1199, rue de Bleury, 4e étage
Montréal, QC H3C 4E2
Adresse postale: CP 6067, Succ Centre-ville
Montréal, QC H3C 4E2
514-906-3760
Téléc: 514-906-3820
888-873-3160
URL: centredoc.csst.qc.ca
Sigle: QMCSST
Fondée en: 1980
Heures: L-V 8h30-16h30
Population desservie: 0
Collections spécialisées: Cis/Bit Sur CD-ROM, Rapports d'enquête d'accident accessibles en ligne
Sujets: Travail, droit, médecine, sciences de la santé, médecine du travail, hygiène industrielle, toxicologie, droit du travail, droit de la santé et de la sécurité au travail
Services:
Accès public à l'internet
Personnel: *Sommaire:* 15 Total; 8 Professionnel(s); 3 Technicien(s); 4 Autre(s) employé(s)
Johanne Lauzon, Bibliothécaire & Chef d'équipe

Montréal: Concordia University Libraries / Bibliothèques de l'Université Concordia
1400, boul de Maisonneuve ouest
Montréal, QC H3G 2V8
Mailing Address: 1455, boul de Maisonneuve ouest
Montréal, QC H3G 2V8
514-848-2424 ext: 7777
Fax: 514-848-2882
e-mail: libadmin@alcor.concordia.ca
lib-colombo@concordia.ca
lib-Circulation@concordia.ca
URL: www.library.concordia.ca
clues.concordia.ca
National Library Symbol: QML
Consortia Membership: Canadian Research Knowledge Network (CRKN); Conférence des recteurs et des principaux des universités du Québec (CREPUQ)
Founded in: 1974
Hours: Vanier: open 24 hours; Webster: open 24 hours: Summer M-Th 8:30 am-10:00 pm, Fr 8:30 am-9:00 pm, Sa-Su 10:00 am-9:00 pm
Acquisitions Budget: $1,000,000 plus
Special Collections: Held at Vanier Library: Irving Layton Collection; Azrieli Collection; Masonic Collection; Rudnyckyj Collection; Gay & Lesbian Literature Collection; James Card Cinema Collection; Belloc Collection; McGee Collection; Peter Desbarats Collection; Antique Maps; René Balcer Archives; first edition Christopher Fry work; Adrien Arcans Collection; Collins Political Cartoon Collection; Concordia University Performance Recordings Collection; Jonassohn Genocide Collection
Subjects covered: Arts, Humanities, Physical Sciences, Life Sciences, Economics, Commerce, Administration, Social Sciences, Visual Arts, Culture, Engineering, Biological Sciences, Performing Arts, Recreation, Exercise Science, Leisure Studies, Communication Studies
Services:
Remote Access
Internet Access
Access to Subscription Databases
Inter-Library Loan (ILL)
Microform Equipment: Computer; Reader
Personnel: *Summary:* 142 Total; 42 Professional(s); 100 Other employees
Gerald Beasley, University Librarian
Gerald.Beasley@concordia.ca
514-848-2424 ext. 7695
Jean Marc Edwards, Associate University Librarian, Information Systems/Technology
Jean-Marc.Edwards@concordia.ca
514-848-2424 ext. 7732
Cynthia Holt, Associate University Librarian, Collection Services
cynthia.holt@concordia.ca
514-848-2424 ext. 5255
David Thirlwall, Associate University Librarian, Library Personnel
David.Thirlwall@concordia.ca
514-848-2424 ext. 7693

Montréal: Dawson College
Library
3040, rue Sherbrooke ouest
Montréal, QC H3Z 1A4
514-931-8731
e-mail: libreference@dawsoncollege.qc.ca
filmservices@dawsoncollege.qc.ca
URL: dolls.dawsoncollege.qc.ca
Founded in: 1988
Hours: Winter: M-Th 8:00-7:30; F 8:00-5:00. Summer: M-Th 12:00-7:00
Special Collections: Audio & video tapes; CD-Roms; Audio CDs
Subjects covered: Social, political & physical science; Mathematics; Fine Arts & Music; Medicine; Agriculture; Technology; Law; Education; History; Geography; Philosophy
Services:
Internet Access
Access to Subscription Databases
Inter-Library Loan (ILL)
Group study rooms
Microform Equipment: Computer; Reader
Carolyn Gilmore, Coordinator
imcgilmore@dawsoncollege.qc.ca
Anne Scott, Librarian, Cataloguing, Acquisitions & Library Systems
ascott@dawsoncollege.qc.ca
Margaret Black, Librarian, Cataloguing & Interlibrary Loans
mblack@dawsoncollege.qc.ca
Donna Harris, Support Librarian, Acquisitions
dharris@dawsoncollege.qc.ca

Montréal: École polytechnique de Montréal
Bibliothèque
2900, boul Édouard-Montpetit
Montréal, QC H3C 3A7
Adresse postale: CP 6079, Succ Centre-ville
Montréal, QC H3C 3A7
514-340-4666
Téléc: 514-340-4026
Couriel: biblio@polymtl.ca
URL: www.polymtl.ca/biblio
Sigle: QMEP
Membre d'un consortium: Canadian Research Knowledge Network (CRKN); Conférence des recteurs et des principaux des universités du Québec (CREPUQ)
Fondée en: 1873
Heures: L-S
Budget d'acquisitions: $500,000 - $999,999
Population desservie: 0
Annotation: Membre de CREPUQ (Conférence des recteurs et des principaux des universités du Québec).
Collections spécialisées: Normes techniques
Sujets: Génie, science et technologie
Services:
Accès public à l'internet
Réseau en ligne
Prêts entre bibliothèques(PEB)
Lecteur/reproduction de microformes: Ordinateur; Lecteurs
Personnel: *Sommaire:* 37 Total; 14 Professionnel(s); 16 Technicien(s); 7 Autre(s) employé(s)
Sylvain Meunier, Directeur
sylvain.meunier@polymtl.ca
514-340-4711 ext. 4652
Marie-Hélène Dupuis, Conseillère principale, développement des services
marie-helene.dupuis@polymtl.ca
514-340-4711 ext. 4213

Marc Hiller, Conseiller principal, développement des collections
marc.hiller@polymtl.ca
514-340-4711 ext. 5214
Greg Whitney, Chef, Services techniques et systèmes informatisés
greg.whitney@polymtl.ca
514-340-4711 ext. 4641

Montréal: Georges P. Vanier Library
Loyola Campus
7141, rue Sherbrooke ouest
Montréal, QC H4B 1R6
514-848-2424 ext: 7766
Fax: 514-848-2804
National Library Symbol: QML
Founded in: 1916
Hours: Academic year: Open 24 hours. Summer: M-Th 8:30 am - 10:00 pm; F 8:30 am-9:00 pm; Sa, Su 10:00 am-9:00 pm.
Services:
Internet Access
Inter-Library Loan (ILL)
Microform Equipment: Computer; Reader
Personnel: *Summary:* 27 Total
Dubravka Kapa, Director
Dubravka.Kapa@concordia.ca
514-848-2424 ext. 7721
Annie Murray, Digital & Special Collections Librarian
Annie.Murray@concordia.ca
514-848-2424 ext. 7774

Montréal: HEC Montréal
Bibliothèque Myrian et J.-Robert Ouimet
3000, ch Côte-Sainte-Catherine
Montréal, QC H3T 2A7
514-340-6220
Téléc: 514-340-5639
Couriel: biblio.info@hec.ca
peb.qmbe@hec.ca
URL: www.hec.ca/biblio
Sigle: QMHE
Membre d'un consortium: Canadian Research Knowledge Network (CRKN); Conférence des recteurs et des principaux des universités du Québec (CREPUQ)
Fondée en: 1907
Heures: L-J 8h-22h; V 8h-21h; S 9h-17h; D 9h-17h.
Budget d'acquisitions: $500,000 - $999,999
Population desservie: 0
Annotation: Auparavant l'École des hautes études commerciales de Montréal
Collections spécialisées: Banques de données; périodiques électroniques; livres électroniques; ressources dans toutes les disciplines de la gestion
Sujets: Économie, industrie, administration
Services:
Prêts entre bibliothèques(PEB)
Maureen Clapperton, Directrice
maureen.clapperton@hec.ca
Sylvain Champagne, Directeur, Services à la clientèle
sylvain.champagne@hec.ca
Bernard Bizimana, Directeur, Services techniques & informatisés
bernard.bizimana@hec.ca

Montréal: Héritage Montréal
Bibliothèque
#0500, 100, rue Sherbrooke est
Montréal, QC H2X 1C3
514-286-2662
Fax: 514-286-1661
URL: www.heritagemontreal.org
Subjects covered: Livres; Rapports d'études, monographies; Périodiques et dossiers internes de documentation sur l'histoire de l'architecture de la ville de Montréal et de l'Amérique du Nord, sur la renovation, sur l'urbanisme (conservation)

Montréal: Hydro-Québec
Bibliothèque
800, boul de Maisonneuve est
Montréal, QC H2L 4P5
Adresse postale: 855, rue Ste-Catherine
Montréal, QC H2L 4P5
514-840-5939
Téléc: 514-840-5044
URL: www.hydroquebec.com
Sigle: QMH
Fermée au public
Fondée en: 1962
Heures: L-V
Population desservie: 0
Sujets: Énergie, génie civil, génie électrique, information et documentation, normes, télécommunications
Services:
Prêts entre bibliothèques(PEB) frais de 10$
Lecteur/reproduction de microformes: Ordinateur; Lecteurs
Personnel: *Sommaire:* 6 Total; 4 Professionnel(s); 2 Autre(s) employé(s)
Marc Archambault, Chef entreposage et exploitation des fonds documentaires
archambault.marc@hydro.qc.ca
514-289-5551 ext. 4472

Montréal: Institut Teccart Inc.
Bibliothèque
3030, rue Hochelaga
Montréal, QC H1W 1G2
514-526-2501
Téléc: 514-526-9192
866-832-2278
URL: www.teccart.qc.ca
Fondée en: 1945
Heures: L-S
Budget d'acquisitions: $25,000 - $49,999
Population desservie: 0
Sujets: Sciences physiques, génie, technologie, électronique
Personnel: *Sommaire:* 1 Total; 1 Professionnel(s)

Montréal: Institute for the Study of International Development
Library
3460, rue McTavish
Montréal, QC H3A 1X9
514-398-3507
Fax: 514-398-8432
e-mail: info.isid@mcgill.ca
URL: www.mcgill.ca/isid/publications/library
Hours: M-F 9:30-5:00 by appointment only
Acquisitions Budget: 0-$9,999
Note: By appointment only.
Special Collections: International development materials
Subjects covered: Politics, Environment
Services:
Inter-Library Loan (ILL)
Personnel: *Summary:* 1 Professional(s)
Iain Blair, Administrative Officer
iain.blair@mcgill.ca

Montréal: International Civil Aviation Organization / Organisation de l'aviation civile internationale
Web, Library & Archives Section
999, rue Université
Montréal, QC H3C 5H7
514-954-8207
Fax: 514-954-6077
e-mail: library@icao.int
URL: www.icao.int
National Library Symbol: QMIC
Founded in: 1946
Hours: M-F 9:00-5:00 by appointment only
Special Collections: International Civil Aviation Organization, United Nations, & specialized agencies publications, serials, & monographs
Subjects covered: Air transportation; Civil aviation; Air law; Aviation medicine; Meteorology; Communications
Services:
Inter-Library Loan (ILL)
Microform Equipment: Computer; Reader
Ghislaine Giroux, Web & Library Assistant
ggiroux@icao.int

Montréal: Investissement Québec
Centre de documentation
#1500, 600, rue de la Gauchetière ouest
Montréal, QC H3B 4L8
514-876-9290 ext: 1468
Téléc: 514-395-8055
URL: www.investquebec.com
Fermée au public
Fondée en: 1978
Population desservie: 0
Sujets: Capital de développement aux entreprises dans les secteurs de chimie, pétrochmie, mines, métaux, industries, foresterie, énergie, environnement, santé, technologie, agroalimentaire
Personnel: *Sommaire:* 2 Total; 1 Professionnel(s)
Marie-France Dubuc, Directrice, Information stratégique

Montréal: Jardin Botanique de Montréal
Bibliothèque
4101, rue Sherbrooke est
Montréal, QC H1X 2B2
514-872-1824
Fax: 514-872-5167
e-mail: jardin_botanique@ville.montreal.qc.ca
URL: www2.ville.montreal.qc.ca/jardin/en/biblio/biblio.htm
National Library Symbol: QMJB
Founded in: 1950
Hours: L-V 9h-16h30; S 9h12h; 13h-16h30
Note: Ouverte au public, sans rendez-vous, pour consultation sur place
Special Collections: Phytopathologie, écologie végétale; botanique économique, entomologie
Subjects covered: Botanique, horticulture, aménagement paysagé
Services:
Inter-Library Loan (ILL)
Personnel: *Summary:* 6 Total; 1 Professional(s); 2 Technical(s); 3 Other employees
Céline Arseneault, Botaniste/bibliothécaire
carseneault@ville.montreal.qc.ca
Guy Frenette, Bibliotechnicien
guy-frenette@ville.montreal.qc.ca

Montréal: KSH Solutions Inc. (KSH)
Library
#1600, 3400, de Maisonneuve ouest
Montréal, QC H3Z 3B8
514-932-4611
Fax: 514-932-9700
URL: www.ksh.ca
National Library Symbol: QMSHE
No public access
Founded in: 1976
Hours: M-F
Acquisitions Budget: 0-$9,999
Note: Library is open part-time.
Subjects covered: Engineering; Forestry; Energy
Services:
Inter-Library Loan (ILL)
Personnel: *Summary:* 1 Total; 1 Professional(s)
Dorothy Ozolins, Librarian
514-932-4611

Montréal: Life Sciences Library
McIntyre Medical Bldg,
3655, Promenade Sir William Osler
Montréal, QC H3G 1Y6
Mailing Address: 3655, Promenade Sir William Osler
Montréal, QC H3G 1Y6
514-398-4475 ext: 9185
Fax: 514-398-3890
e-mail: lsl.library@mcgill.ca
lslcirc.library@mcgill.ca
National Library Symbol: QMMM
Founded in: 1823
Hours: Jan.-May: M-Th 9:00am-10:00pm; F 9:00-5:00; Su 12:00-8:00
Acquisitions Budget: $500,000 - $999,999
Subjects covered: Medicine, Health Sciences, Surgery, Dentistry, Physical & Occupational Therapy, Nursing, Communication Disorders
Services:
Access to Subscription Databases
Inter-Library Loan (ILL)
Microform Equipment: Computer; Reader
Personnel: *Summary:* 20 Total; 6 Professional(s); 1 Technical(s); 14 Other employees
Susan Murray, Head, Life Sciences Library
susan.murray@mcgill.ca
514-398-4475 ext. 9855
Vacant , Library Supervisor
Rachel Demoskoff, Sr. Library Clerk, Circulation
rachel.demoskoff@mcgill.ca
514-398-4475 ext. 9220

Montréal: Marianopolis College
Library
4873 Westmount Ave.
Montréal, QC H3Y 1X9

514-931-8792
Fax: 514-931-8790
URL: www.marianopolis.edu/library
Founded in: 1908
Hours: M-F 7:30-6:00
Amy MacLean, Coordinator, Library Services
a.maclean@marianopolis.edu

Montréal: McGill University Library

McLennan Library Building, 3459, rue McTavish
Montréal, QC H3A 0C9
514-398-4677
Fax: 514-398-7356
e-mail: doadmin.library@mcgill.ca
URL: www.mcgill.ca/library
Consortia Membership: Canadian Research Knowledge Network (CRKN); Conférence des recteurs et des principaux des universités du Québec (CREPUQ)
Special Collections: e-Journals; e-Books; CDs & audiocassettes; DVDs & videocassettes; Microforms
Services:
Remote Access
Internet Access
Access to Subscription Databases
Inter-Library Loan (ILL)
Offering workshops & tours; Printing & copying; Computer workstations; Group study rooms
Microform Equipment: Computer; Reader
C. Colleen Cook, PhD, Trenholme Dean of Libraries
director.libraries@mcgill.ca
Bruna Ceccolini, Assistant to the Trenholme Dean of Libraries
doadmin.library@mcgill.ca
Merika Ramundo, Officer, Communications
merika.ramundo@mcgill.ca

Montréal: Montréal General Hospital / L'Hôpital général de Montréal Medical Library

#E6-157, 1650, av Cedar
Montréal, QC H3G 1A4
514-934-1934 ext: 43056
Fax: 514-934-8250
e-mail: library.mgh@muhc.mcgill.ca
URL: www.mghlib.mcgill.ca
National Library Symbol: QMGH
Founded in: 1955
Hours: M-F 8:00-5:00
Acquisitions Budget: $50,000 - $99,999
Note: Associated with McGill University
Subjects covered: Medicine, Health Sciences
Services:
Inter-Library Loan (ILL)
Personnel: *Summary:* 4 Total; 1 Professional(s); 2 Technical(s)
Elizabeth Lamont, Chief Librarian
elizabeth.lamont@muhc.mcgill.ca
514-934-1934 ext. 35293

Montréal: Nahum Gelber Law Library / Nahum Gelber Bibliothèque de droit

3660, rue Peel
Montréal, QC H3A 1W9
514-398-4715 ext: 171
Fax: 514-398-3585
e-mail: law.library@mcgill.ca
lawcirc.library@mcgill.ca
National Library Symbol: QMML
Founded in: 1890
Hours: M-F open 24 hours; Sa-Su 8:00am-midnight
Acquisitions Budget: $500,000 - $999,999
Special Collections: Wainwright Antiquarian French Law collection; John Peters Humphrey United Nations collection
Subjects covered: Law
Services:
Inter-Library Loan (ILL)
Microform Equipment: Computer; Reader
Personnel: *Summary:* 17 Total; 5 Professional(s); 9 Technical(s)
Daniel Boyer, Head Librarian
daniel.boyer@mcgill.ca
514-398-4715 ext. 156
Mary Lourenço, Library Supervisor
mary.lourenco@mcgill.ca
514-398-4715 ext. 166

Montréal: NRC Information Centre - Montréal / Centre d'information du CNRC Montréal

6100, av Royalmount
Montréal, QC H4P 2R2
514-496-6117
Fax: 514-496-7885
URL: cisti-icist.nrc-cnrc.gc.ca/nis/montreal_e.shtml
National Library Symbol: QMNB
Founded in: 1985
Hours: M-F 8:30-12:00, 1:00-4:30 by appointment only
Acquisitions Budget: $50,000 - $99,999
For Print: $25,000 - $49,999
For Electronic: $25,000 - $49,999
Subjects covered: Biotechnology, Bioengineering, Genetic Engineering, Environment, Bioprocess
Personnel: *Summary:* 3 Total; 2 Professional(s); 1 Technical(s)
Eveline Landa, Head
eveline.landa@cnrc-nrc.gc.ca
514-496-4254

Montréal: Office des personnes handicapées de Québec Centre de documentation

#15.600, 500, boul René-Lévesque ouest
Montréal, QC H2Z 1W7
866-680-1930
Fax: 514-873-9706
800-567-1465
TDD: 8005671477
e-mail: documentation@ophq.gouv.qc.ca
URL: www.ophq.gouv.qc.ca/documentation-et-publications
National Library Symbol: QDOPH
Founded in: 1979
Hours: L-V 8h30-12h, 13h-16h30
Acquisitions Budget: $25,000 - $49,999
Subjects covered: Sciences de la santé, affaires sociales, personnes handicapées, intégration sociale, déficience, adaptation/réadaptation, santé publique, promotion des droits, travail, éducation
Services:
Internet Access
Inter-Library Loan (ILL)
Personnel: *Summary:* 2 Total; 2 Professional(s); 1 Technical(s)

Montréal: Perkin Elmer Optoelectronics

#600, 1744, rue William
Montréal, QC H3J 1R4
514-937-9949
Fax: 514-937-0777
800-293-4501
URL: www.perkinelmer.com
National Library Symbol: QVGEC
No public access
Founded in: 1989
Hours: M-F 8:10-4:20
Special Collections: RCA Review; Company Documents; Engineering Lab Notebooks
Subjects covered: Physical Sciences; Engineering; Technology; Electronics; Marketing; Metallurgy; Metals; Optics; Physics
Services:
Inter-Library Loan (ILL)
Current awareness
Microform Equipment: Computer

Montréal: Québec Ministère de la sécurité publique Laboratoire de sciences judiciaires et de médecine légale

Édifice Wilfrid Derome, 1701, rue Parthenais, 12e étage
Montréal, QC H2K 3S7
514-873-3301
Téléc: 514-864-7752
URL: www.securitepublique.gouv.qc.ca
Sigle: QMJLP
Fondée en: 1968
Heures: L-Vavec rendez-vous seulement
Population desservie: 0
Annotation: Collection: environ 6 000 monographies et environ 310 périodiques
Collections spécialisées: Collection du Dr. Wilfrid Derome
Sujets: Médecine légale; Chimie judiciaire; Balistique; Expertise de documents; Toxicologie; Explosifs; Génétique légale; Imageriel; Biologie légale; Anthropologie légale
Services:
Prêts entre bibliothèques(PEB)
Consultation sur rendez-vous

Montréal: R. Howard Webster Library

Sir George Williams Campus
1455, boul de Maisonneuve ouest
Montréal, QC H3G 1M8
Mailing Address: 1455, boul de Maisonneuve ouest
Montréal, QC H3G 1M8
514-848-2424 ext: 7777
Fax: 514-848-2882
National Library Symbol: QMG
Founded in: 1926
Hours: Academic year open 24 hours: Summer M-Th 8:30 am-10:00 pm, Fr 8:30 am-9:00 pm, Sa-Su 10:00 am-9:00 pm
Services:
Internet Access
Inter-Library Loan (ILL)
Microform Equipment: Computer; Reader
Guylaine Beaudry, Director
Guylaine.Beaudry@concordia.ca
514-848-2424 ext. 7699

Montréal: Royal Victoria Hospital Medical Library

Rm H4.01, 687, av des Pins ouest
Montréal, QC H3A 1A1
Mailing Address: 687, av des Pins ouest
Montréal, QC H3A 1A1
514-934-1934 ext: 35290
Fax: 514-843-1483
e-mail: rvh.library@muhc.mcgill.ca
URL: muhclibraries.mcgill.ca
National Library Symbol: QMRV
Founded in: 1924
Hours: M-F 9:00-6:00
Subjects covered: Medicine, Nursing, Cardiology, Surgery, Emergency Medicine, Transplantation
Services:
Inter-Library Loan (ILL)
Personnel: *Summary:* 3 Total; 2 Professional(s); 2 Technical(s)
Elizabeth Lamont, Chief Librarian
elizabeth.lamont@muhc.mcgill.ca
514-934-1934 ext. 35293
Robyn Maler, Librarian
514-934-1934 ext. 35290
Vincent Caetano, Documentation Technician
vincent.caetano@muhc.mcgill.ca
514-934-1934 ext. 35290
George Mallari-Lee, Documentation Technician
george.mallari-lee@muhc.mcgill.ca
514-934-1934 ext. 35291

Montréal: Schulich Library of Science & Engineering

Macdonald-Stewart Library Bldg.
809, rue Sherbrooke ouest
Montréal, QC H3A 2K6
Mailing Address: 809, rue Sherbrooke ouest
Montréal, QC H3A 2K6
514-398-4769
Fax: 514-398-3903
e-mail: schulich.library@mcgill.ca
schulichloans.library@mcgill.ca
National Library Symbol: QMME
Founded in: 1982
Hours: Jan.-Mar.: M-F open 24 hours; Sa 8:00-midnight; Su open 24 hours from 8:00am
Special Collections: Books & journals in the physical sciences & engineering subject areas; e-Journals; Databases
Subjects covered: Physical Sciences; Engineering; Technology; Computer Science
Services:
Internet Access
Access to Subscription Databases
Inter-Library Loan (ILL)
Printing, copying, & scanning; Workshops; Tours
Microform Equipment: Computer; Reader
Louis Houle, Associate Director, Client Services, Sciences, Health, & Engineering
louis.houle@mcgill.ca
Giovanna Badia, Liaison Librarian, Chemical Engineering & Earth & Planetary Sciences
giovanna.badia@mcgill.ca
April Colosimo, Liaison Librarian, Chemistry, Mathematices, Statistics, & Physics
april.colosimo@mcgill.ca
Tara Mawhinney, Liaison Librarian, Atmospheric & Oceanic Science, Civil Engineering

Jennifer Zhao, Liaison Librarian, Electrical & Computer Engineering & Geography
jennifer.zhao@mcgill.ca

Montréal: Secretariat of the Convention on Biological Diversity

#800, 413, rue St-Jacques
Montréal, QC H2Y 1N9
514-288-2220
Fax: 514-288-6588
e-mail: secretariat@cbd.int
URL: www.cbd.int
Hours: M-F
Subjects covered: Biosafety
Ulrika Nilsson, Associate Public Information Officer, Biosafety
ulrika.nilsson@cbd.int.int
514-287-8720

Montréal: Sir Mortimer B. Davis Jewish General Hospital / Hôpital général juif Health Sciences Library

#A-200, 3755, côte Ste-Catherine
Montréal, QC H3T 1E2
514-340-8222 ext: 5927
Fax: 514-340-7552
e-mail: library.jgh@mail.mcgill.ca
URL: www.jgh.ca/bss
National Library Symbol: QMJG
Founded in: 1950
Hours: M-Th 8:30-5:00; F 8:30-4:30
Acquisitions Budget: $250,000 - $499,999
Note: Member of McGill Affiliated Health Sciences Library Consortium & McGill Medical & Health Libraries Association
Special Collections: General medical; Judaica & Medical Ethics
Subjects covered: Medicine, Nursing, Health Sciences, Allied Health, Patient Care
Services:
Internet Access
Inter-Library Loan (ILL) for a fee of $3 +
Personnel: *Summary:* 4 Total; 1 Professional(s); 4 Technical(s)
Arlene Greenberg, Chief Medical Librarian
arlene.greenberg@mail.mcgill.ca
514-340-8222 ext. 5930
Liz Breier, Library Technician
liz.breier@mail.mcgill.ca
514-340-8222

Montréal: SNC-Lavalin inc. Bibliothèque principale

455, boul René-Lévesque ouest
Montréal, QC H2Z 1Z3
514-393-1000
Téléc: 514-866-0795
URL: www.snclavalin.com
Sigle: QMSNC
Fermée au public
Fondée en: 1911
Heures: L-V
Population desservie: 0
Sujets: Génie, technologie, énergie, affaires, environnement, mines et métallurgie
Services:
Prêts entre bibliothèques(PEB)
Personnel: *Sommaire:* 3 Total; 1 Professionnel(s); 2 Technicien(s)

Montréal: Société québécoise de spéléologie Centre de documentation

4545, av Pierre-de-Coubertin
Montréal, QC H1V 3R2
Adresse postale: CP 1000, Succ M
Montréal, QC H1V 3R2
514-252-3006
Téléc: 514-252-3201
800-338-6636
Couriel: info-sqs@speleo.qc.ca
URL: www.speleo.qc.ca
Fermée au public
Fondée en: 1970
Population desservie: 0
Sujets: Spéléologie
Personnel: *Sommaire:* 1 Professionnel(s); 3 Technicien(s); 200 Bénévole(s)

Montréal: Succursale de Montréal Service de documentation et d'information en habitation

500, boul René-Lévesque ouest, 5e étage
Montréal, QC H2Z 1W7
514-873-8775 ext: 3081
URL: www.habitation.gouv.qc.ca
Sigle: QQSHQ
Fondée en: 1988
Heures:avec rendez-vous seulement
Population desservie: 0
Sujets: Construction; Architecture
Services:
Accès public à l'internet
Prêts entre bibliothèques(PEB)

Montréal: Université de Montréal Direction générale des bibliothèques

#3, 2910, boul Édouard-Montpetit
Montréal, QC H3C 3J7
Adresse postale: CP 6128, Succ Centre-ville
Montréal, QC H3C 3J7
514-343-6905
Téléc: 514-343-6457
Couriel: biblios@bib.umontreal.ca
pebqmu@bib.umontreal.ca
URL: www.bib.umontreal.ca
Sigle: QMU
Membre d'un consortium: Canadian Research Knowledge Network (CRKN); Conférence des recteurs et des principaux des universités du Québec (CREPUQ)
Fermée au public
Budget d'acquisitions: $1,000,000 plus
Population desservie: 0
Services:
Numérisation de documents originaux individuels
Personnel: *Sommaire:* 22 Total; 2 Professionnel(s); 6 Technicien(s); 7 Autre(s) employé(s)
Richard Dumont, Directeur général
richard.dumont@umontreal.ca
514-343-6905
Julie Cardinal, Directrice, Traitement et accès aux documents
julie.cardinal@umontreal.ca
514-343-7687
Michel Gaudreault, Directeur administratif
michel.gaudreault@umontreal.ca
514-343-6111 ext. 8733
Céline Amnotte, Directrice, Développement collections et acquisitions
celine.amnotte@umontreal.ca
514-343-7653
Martin Sévigny, Directeur, Bureau systèmes
martin.sevingny@umontreal.ca
415-343-2080

Montréal: Université du Québec à Montréal Direction des bibliothèques

Pavillon Hubert-Aquin
400, rue St-Catherine est
Montréal, QC H3C 3P3
Adresse postale: CP 8889, Succ Centre-Ville
Montréal, QC H3C 3P3
514-987-6114
Téléc: 514-987-3542
Couriel: bibliotheques@uqam.ca
URL: www.bibliotheques.uqam.ca
Sigle: QMUQ
Membre d'un consortium: Canadian Research Knowledge Network (CRKN); Conférence des recteurs et des principaux des universités du Québec (CREPUQ)
Fondée en: 1969
Heures: Sept.-mai: L-V 8h30-22h; S 11h-17h; D 12h-17h. Mai-juin: L-M 8h30-22h; M, J, V 8h30-18h; S 12h-17h. Juillet-août: L-J 9h-17h
Budget d'acquisitions: $1,000,000 plus
Matériel imprimé: $1,000,000 plus
Matériel électronique: $1,000,000 plus
Population desservie: 0
Collections spécialisées: Audiovidéothèque, cartothèque, livres rares, testothèque, didactèque, microthèque, diapothèque
Sujets: Sciences sociales et humaines, droit, arts, technologies, musique, lettres, éducation, sciences, lettres, communication
Services:
Accèss distance aux bases de donn
Accès public à l'internet
Réseau en ligne
Prêts entre bibliothèques(PEB)
Lecteur/reproduction de microformes: Ordinateur; Lecteurs
Personnel: *Sommaire:* 45 Professionnel(s); 122 Technicien(s); 1 Autre(s) employé(s)
Lynda Gadoury, Directrice des bibliothèques
gadoury.lynda@uqam.ca
514-987-3000 ext. 3160
Stephen Park, Directeur, Bibliothèque centrale
park.stephen@uqam.ca
514-987-3000 ext. 4353
Claire Boisvert, Directrice, Services techniques
boisvert.claire@uqam.ca
514-987-8351
Pierre Roberge, Directeur, Services des technologies de l'information
roberge.pierre@uqam.ca
514-987-3000 ext. 3163
Anne Bourgeois, Directrice, Bibliothèque sciences de l'éducation
bourgeois.anne@uqam.ca
514-987-3000 ext. 3884
Lynda Gadoury, Directrice, Bibliothèque des arts et musique (par intérim)
gadoury.lynda@uqam.ca
514-987-3000 ext. 3160
Lucie Rebelo, Directeur, Bibliothèque sciences juridiques
rebelo.lucie@uqam.ca
514-987-3000 ext. 4301
Mohammed Harti, Directeur, Bibliothèque des sciences
harti.mohammed@uqam.ca
514-987-3000 ext. 3570

Montréal: Université du Québec École de technologie supérieure Bibliothèque de l'ÉTS

1100, rue Notre-Dame ouest
Montréal, QC H3C 1K3
514-396-8960
Téléc: 514-396-8633
Couriel: bibref@etsmtl.ca
biblio@etsmtl.ca
URL: www.etsmtl.ca/biblio
Social Media: www.youtube.com/user/etsmtl
www.facebook.com/bibliothequeets
twitter.com/BiblioETS
Sigle: QMUQET
Membre d'un consortium: Canadian Research Knowledge Network (CRKN); Conférence des recteurs et des principaux des universités du Québec (CREPUQ)
Fondée en: 1974
Heures: L-V 8h30-22h; S, D 11h-18h
Budget d'acquisitions: $500,000 - $999,999
Population desservie: 0
Sujets: Génie; Technologie; Construction; Génie mécanique; Génie électrique; Génie civil; Production automatisée; Génie logiciel
Services:
Accèss distance aux bases de donn
Accès public à l'internet
Réseau en ligne
Prêts entre bibliothèques(PEB) frais
Lecteur/reproduction de microformes: Ordinateur; Lecteurs
Personnel: *Sommaire:* 19 Total; 7 Professionnel(s); 6 Technicien(s); 5 Autre(s) employé(s)
Guy Gosselin, Directeur, service de la bibliothèque
guy.gosselin@etsmtl.ca
514-396-8946
Gaston Fournier, Personne-ressource, génie logiciel
gaston.fournier@etsmtl.ca
514-396-8633
Vicky Gagnon-Mountzouris, Personne-ressource, endnote, formation
vicky.gagnon@etsmtl.ca
514-396-8800 ext. 7200
Diane Girard, Personne-ressource, génie de la production automatisée
diane.girard@etsmtl.ca
514-396-8800 ext. 7742
Édith Healy, Personne-ressource, génie de la construction
edith.healy@etsmtl.ca
514-396-8800 ext. 7583
Denis Levasseur, Personne-ressource, accès hors campus (dépannage), site web
denis.levasseur@etsmtl.ca
514-396-8800 ext. 8881

Paul Marchand, Personne-ressource, génie électrique
paul.marchand@etsmtl.ca
514-396-8800 ext. 7523

Montréal: Walter Hitschfeld Geographic Information Centre
Burnside Hall
805, rue Sherbrooke ouest, 5e étage
Montréal, QC H3A 0B9
514-398-7438
Fax: 514-398-3903
e-mail: gic.library@mcgill.ca
gicsupport@mcgill.ca
URL: gic.geog.mcgill.ca
National Library Symbol: QMMG
Founded in: 1945
Hours: Jan.-March: M-F 8:00am-9:00pm; Sa-Su 10:00-6:00
Special Collections: Geospatial information in print & digital form; Paper map collection, featuring atlases, aerial photography, & monographs; Journals about Geographic Information Systems & cartography
Subjects covered: Cartography; Geographic Information Systems
Services:
Inter-Library Loan (ILL)
Workshops; Tours; Printing, copying, & scanning
Pablo Arroyo, Director
Deena Yanofsky, Coordinator & Liaison Librarian, Maps & Geospatial Data
deena.yanofsky@mcgill.ca

Outremont: Collège Stanislas inc Bibliothèque
780, boul Dollard
Outremont, QC H2V 3G5
514-273-9521
Téléc: 514-273-3409
Couriel: cdi@stanislas.qc.ca
URL: www.stanislas.qc.ca
Fermée au public
Population desservie: 0
Personnel: *Sommaire:* 1 Professionnel(s); 2 Technicien(s)

Pointe-Claire: FPInnovations Information Resources
580, boul Saint-Jean
Pointe-Claire, QC H9R 3J9
514-694-1140
Fax: 514-694-4351
URL: www.feric.ca
National Library Symbol: QMFER
Founded in: 1976
Hours: M-F 9:00-5:00 by appointment only
Special Collections: Canadian & US patent collection on mechanization of wood harvesting & silviculture (last 10 years)
Subjects covered: Forestry, Forest Engineering, Wood Transportation, Natural Resources
Services:
Internet Access
Inter-Library Loan (ILL)
Personnel: *Summary:* 3 Total; 1 Professional(s); 1 Technical(s); 1 Other employees
Martine Brebeau, Head, Information Resources
Margaret Jeanvoine, Library Clerk
margaret-j@mtl.feric.ca

Pointe-Claire: FPInnovations Library
570, boul St-Jean
Pointe-Claire, QC H9R 3J9
514-630-4101 ext: 4626
Fax: 514-630-4134
e-mail: library@fpinnovations.ca
info@fpinnovations.ca
publications@fpinnovations.ca
URL: www.fpinnovations.ca
National Library Symbol: QMPP
Founded in: 1929
Subjects covered: Engineering, Technology, Environment, Pulp and Paper, Chemistry, Physics, Environmental & Physical Sciences, Measurements & Standards
Personnel: *Summary:* 5 Total; 2 Professional(s); 2 Technical(s)

Québec: Bibliothèque des sciences humaines et sociales
Pavillon Jean-Charles-Bonenfant
2345 allée des bibliothèques
Québec, QC G1K 7P4
418-656-3344
Couriel: peb_qqla@bibl.ulaval.ca
URL: www.bibl.ulaval.ca
Sigle: QQLA
Heures: 30 avri - 15 juin: L-V 8h-21h, 18 juin-31 août: L-V 8h-19h
Budget d'acquisitions: $1,000,000 plus
Population desservie: 0
Sujets: Droit, arts, sciences humaines, sciences sociales
Services:
Accèss distance aux bases de donn
Accès public à l'internet
Réseau en ligne
Prêts entre bibliothèques(PEB)
service de finances, bureau de regestraire, services ressources humaines, division des affaires juridiques, division des archives, bureau des affaires prefessorales et du personal enseighnant et de recherche (BAPPER), currier et messagerie, division des diplomes et des publications officielles, bureau du secretaire general
Lecteur/reproduction de microformes: Ordinateur; Lecteurs
Personnel: *Sommaire:* 93 Total; 24 Professionnel(s); 16 Technicien(s); 47 Autre(s) employé(s)
Loubna Ghaouti, Chef, Bibliothèque des sciences humaines et sociales
loubna.ghaouti@bibl.ulaval.ca
418-656-2131 ext. 5196
Chantal St-Louis, Chef, services-conseils en ressources documentaires
chantal.st-louis@bibl.ulaval.ca
418-656-2131 ext. 7986
Sarah Samson, Secteur de la circulation
sarah.samson@bibl.ulaval.ca
418-656-2131 ext. 7934
Françoise Sorieul, Secteur des collections spéciales
francoise.sorieul@bibl.ulaval.ca
418-656-2131 ext. 3227
Pierre Carrier, Secteur de la consultation
pierre.carrier@bibl@ulaval.ca
418-656-2131 ext. 3224

Québec: Campus de Charlesbourg Centre des médias
Local 2511, 7600, 3e av est
Québec, QC G1H 7L4
418-647-6600 ext: 3653
Téléc: 418-624-3698
Couriel: bibliotheques@climoilou.qc.ca
URL: www.climoilou.qc.ca
Fondée en: 1991
Heures: L-J 7H45-20h30; V 7h45-17h
Budget d'acquisitions: $25,000 - $49,999
Population desservie: 0
Services:
Prêts entre bibliothèques(PEB)
Lecteur/reproduction de microformes: Ordinateur; Lecteurs
Personnel: *Sommaire:* 2 Total; 1 Technicien(s); 3 Autre(s) employé(s)
Marc Julien, Responsable
marc.julien@climoilou.qc.ca
418-647-6600 ext. 3713

Québec: CÉGEP de Sainte-Foy Centre des médias
2410, ch Ste-Foy
Québec, QC G1V 1T3
418-659-6600 ext: 3603
Téléc: 418-659-4563
URL: biblio.cegep-ste-foy.qc.ca
Fondée en: 1980
Heures: Sessions régulières: L-J 8h30-21h; V 7h30-18h30; Sa-D 12h-16h.
Budget d'acquisitions: $50,000 - $99,999
Population desservie: 0
Annotation: Services: Salles de lecture et de travail
Services:
Accèss distance aux bases de donn
Accès public à l'internet
Réseau en ligne
Prêts entre bibliothèques(PEB)
Personnel: *Sommaire:* 1 Professionnel(s); 5 Technicien(s); 7 Autre(s) employé(s)
Francine Piché, Coordonnatrice, service des ressources documentaires
francine.piche@cegep-ste-foy.qc.ca
418-659-6600 ext. 3603
Michelle Ribière, Bibliothécaire
michelle.ribiere@cegep-ste-foy.qc.ca
418-659-6600 ext. 3864

Québec: CÉGEP Limoilou Bibliothèque
Local 2114, 1300, 8e av
Québec, QC G1J 5L5
718-647-6600
Téléc: 418-647-6793
URL: www.climoilou.qc.ca
Fondée en: 1967
Heures: L-J 7h50-21h30; V 7h50-17h
Budget d'acquisitions: $50,000 - $99,999
Population desservie: 0
Collections spécialisées: Collection Pierre George Roy, Collection Gabriel Garcia Marquez
Services:
Accès public à l'internet
Réseau en ligne
Prêts entre bibliothèques(PEB)
Personnel: *Sommaire:* 5 Total; 1 Professionnel(s); 4 Technicien(s)
Alexandra Lavallée, Responsable
alexandra.lavallee@climoilou.qc.ca
418-647-6600 ext. 6884
Marie-Claude Beaudry, Technicienne en documentation, ILL
marie-claude.beaudry@climoilou.ca
418-647-6600 ext. 3653

Québec: Centre de documentation (Succursale Bois-Fontaine)
930, ch Sainte-Foy, 6e étage
Québec, QC G1S 4X9
418-643-2256
Téléc: 418-643-0345
Couriel: doc-qtrd@mtq.gouv.qc.ca
Sigle: QTRD
Heures: L-V 8h30-12h, 13h-16h30
Population desservie: 0
Collections spécialisées: Publications du Transportation Research Board
Sujets: Construction et entretien des routes, ponts, viaducs; transport; environnement
Services:
Accès public à l'internet
Prêts entre bibliothèques(PEB)
Personnel: *Sommaire:* 3 Total; 1 Technicien(s)

Québec: Centre de recherche industrielle du Québec Centre de documentation
333, rue Franquet
Québec, QC G1P 4C7
418-659-1550
Téléc: 418-652-2225
800-667-2386
Couriel: infocriq@criq.qc.ca
URL: www.criq.qc.ca
Sigle: QSFCR
Fermée au public
Fondée en: 1971
Budget d'acquisitions: $50,000 - $99,999
Population desservie: 0
Collections spécialisées: Normes: CSA, ASTM, ULC, CGA, BNQ, ONGC, AFNOR, ISO
Sujets: Normes, sciences et technologie, industrie, information et documentation, métallurgie, biotechnologie, R8D
Personnel: *Sommaire:* 1 Total; 1 Technicien(s);
Huguette Beaumont, Technicienne en documentation
huguette.beaumont@criq.qc.ca

Québec: CHUQ-CHUL Bibliothèque AstraZeneca des sciences de la santé
#RC-315, 2705, boul Laurier
Québec, QC G1V 4G2
418-525-4444 ext: 17157
Téléc: 418-654-2143
URL: www.chuq.qc.ca/fr/les_services/bibliotheque/
Sigle: QQLACH
Fondée en: 1968

Heures: L-V 8h30-16h30
Budget d'acquisitions: $50,000 - $99,999
Population desservie: 0
Annotation: Groupe Biblio-Santé de la Région du Québec. Fax, Lizette Germain: 416/525-4170
Sujets: Santé, pédiatrie, opthalmologie, psychiatrie, rhumatologie
Services:
Accès public à l'internet
Prêts entre bibliothèques(PEB)
Personnel: *Sommaire:* 3 Total; 1 Professionnel(s); 2 Technicien(s)
Lizette Germain, Bibliothécaire
418-525-4444 ext. 52414
Denise Morin, Bibliotechnicienne
Patricia Chamberland, Bibliotechnicienne

Québec: Collège Mérici
Bibliothèque
755, Grande Allée ouest
Québec, QC G1S 1C1
418-683-2104 ext: 2213
Téléc: 418-682-8938
800-208-1463
Couriel: information@merici.ca
URL: www.college-merici.qc.ca
Profile: Merici College is a private co-educational college-level institution dispensing a variety of pre-university & professional programs with an annual student enrolment of about 1 200. Founded by the sisters of the Ursuline Order, Merici College has remained faithful to a long tradition of excellence while constantly adjusting to the changing educational needs of its students
Sigle: QQCM
Fondée en: 1930
Heures: L-J 8h-20h; V 8h-17h
Budget d'acquisitions: $25,000 - $49,999
Population desservie: 0
Collections spécialisées: Natural Science, Social Science, Multimedia Design, Creative Advertising, Orthotics and Prosthetics, Special Education, Tourism, Hotel Management, Restaurant Management
Sujets: Sciences, sciences humaines, arts et lettres, communication visuelle, multimédia, dessin animé, orthèses et prothèses orthopédiques, administration, tourisme, hôtellerie, services alimentaires et restauration, loisirs, enseignement, recherche sociale, enquête, sondage, éducation spécialisée
Services:
Accès public à l'internet
Réseau en ligne
Prêts entre bibliothèques(PEB)
Personnel: *Sommaire:* 6 Total; 1 Professionnel(s); 1 Technicien(s); 4 Autre(s) employé(s)
Maryse Messely, Responsable, Bibliothèque
mmessely@college-merici.qc.ca
418-683-1591 ext. 2213
France Simard-Pageau, Technicienne, documentation
fpageau@college-merici.qc.ca
418-683-1591 ext. 2251

Québec: Commission de toponymie du Québec, Bibliothèque (Library)
Bibliothèque
750, boul Charest est
Québec, QC G1K 9K4
418-643-4575
Téléc: 418-528-1373
Couriel: qqolf@oqlf.gouv.qc.ca
URL: www.toponymie.gouv.qc.ca/ct/nos-services/bibliotheque
Sigle: QQCT
Fondée en: 1977
Heures: L-V 8h30-12h, 13h-16h30avec rendez-vous seulement
Budget d'acquisitions: 0-$9,999
Matériel imprimé: 0-$9,999
Matériel électronique: 0-$9,999
Population desservie: 0
Collections spécialisées: Monographies paroissiales; répertoires géographiques; rapports géologiques
Sujets: Toponymie, linguistique, géographie, histoire
Services:
Prêts entre bibliothèques(PEB)
Personnel: *Sommaire:* 1 Technicien(s)
Frederic Gagnon, Bibliothécaire
frederic.gagnon@oqlf.gouv.qc.ca

Québec: Donald-Petzel Memorial Library
790, av Nérée-Tremblay
Québec, QC G1V 4K2
418-656-6921 ext: 230
Fax: 418-656-6925
e-mail: circulation@slc.qc.ca
reference@slc.qc.ca
URL: www.slc.qc.ca/library
National Library Symbol: QSTFCR
Founded in: 1958
Hours: M-Th 8:00-7:00; F 8:00-4:00
Acquisitions Budget: $25,000 - $49,999
For Print: $10,000 - $24,999
For Electronic: 0-$9,999
Subjects covered: Pre-University, Business
Services:
Remote Access
Internet Access
Access to Subscription Databases
Inter-Library Loan (ILL)
Microform Equipment: Computer; Reader
Personnel: *Summary:* 3 Total; 1 Professional(s); 1 Technical(s); 1 Other employees
Chelsea Baker, Librarian
cbaker@slc.qc.ca
Linda Belanger, Library Secretary

Québec: DRDC Valcartier
Bibliothèque / Library
2459, boul Pie-XI nord
Québec, QC G3J 1X5
418-844-4000 ext: 4244
Téléc: 418-844-4635
Couriel: info-valcartier@drdc-rddc.gc.ca
URL: www.drdc-rddc.gc.ca
Sigle: QQC
Fondée en: 1945
Heures: L-Vavec rendez-vous seulement
Population desservie: 0
Collections spécialisées: Jane's Military Specifications
Sujets: Technologie; Génie; Armement; électro-optique
Services:
Prêts entre bibliothèques(PEB)

Québec: Eastern Division Library/Bibliothèque de la division de l'est
319, rue Franquet
Québec, QC G1P 4R4
418-659-2647
Fax: 418-659-2922
e-mail: info@fpinnovations.ca
National Library Symbol: QSFF
No public access
Founded in: 1912
Hours: M-F
Acquisitions Budget: $50,000 - $99,999
Special Collections: Standards
Subjects covered: Solid wood products technology, Forest products, Value-Added wood products, Building systems, Composite products technology
Services:
Inter-Library Loan (ILL)
Personnel: *Summary:* 2 Total; 1 Professional(s); 1 Technical(s)
Odile Fleury, Documentaliste

Québec: INRS - Université du Québec, CGC - Québec
Bibliothèque
#1400, 490, de la Couronne
Québec, QC G1K 9A9
418-654-2577
Fax: 418-654-2660
e-mail: sdis@adm.inrs.ca
peb-qsfig@uquebec.ca
URL: sdis.inrs.ca
National Library Symbol: QSFIG
Consortia Membership: CREPUQ; SDIS; NRCanLibrary
Founded in: 1970
Hours: M-F 8:00-12:00, 1:00-4:00
Acquisitions Budget: $50,000 - $99,999
For Print: $25,000 - $49,999
For Electronic: $50,000 - $99,999
Subjects covered: Earth Sciences, Water Sciences, Environmental Sciences
Services:
Remote Access
Internet Access
Access to Subscription Databases
Inter-Library Loan (ILL)
Reference
Microform Equipment: Reader
Personnel: *Summary:* 6 Total; 1 Professional(s); 2 Technical(s); 3 Other employees
Jean-Daniel Bourgault, Head Librarian
jean-daniel.bourgault@ete.inrs.ca
418-654-2667
Anne Robitaille, Technician
418-654-2588
Chantal Paquin, Technician
418-654-3727

Québec: Institut de l'Énergie et de l'environnement de la francophonie
Bibliothèque
56, rue St-Pierre, 3e étage
Québec, QC G1K 4A1
418-692-5727
Téléc: 418-692-5644
Couriel: iepf@francophonie.org
URL: www.iepf.org
Heures: L-V 9h-17h
Budget d'acquisitions: Matériel imprimé: 0-$9,999
Population desservie: 0
Sujets: Énergie, Environnement
Personnel: *Sommaire:* 1 Total; 1 Professionnel(s)
Louis-Noël Jail, Chef du service, Information et documentation
Pauline Malenfant, Assistante
p.malenfant@iepf.org
418-692-5727 ext. 247
Jacinthe Potvin, Assistante
j.potvin@iepf.org
418-692-5727 ext. 227

Québec: Laurentian Forestry Centre / Centre de foresterie des Laurentides
1055, rue du P.E.P.S.
Québec, QC G1V 4C7
Mailing Address: CP 10380, Succ. Ste-Foy
Québec, QC G1V 4C7
418-648-4850
Fax: 418-648-3433
National Library Symbol: QQMF
Founded in: 1954
Hours: L-V 8h-16h
Acquisitions Budget: $50,000 - $99,999
For Print: $50,000 - $99,999
For Electronic: $25,000 - $49,999
Subjects covered: Foresterie, entomologie, biologie, mycologie, biotechnologie, génétique des plantes
Services:
Remote Access
Internet Access
Inter-Library Loan (ILL)
Personnel: *Summary:* 2 Total; 1 Professional(s); 1 Technical(s)
Deirdre Moore, Manager
Deirdre.Moore@RNCan-NRCan.gc.ca

Québec: Parc Aquarium du Québec
Centre de documentation
1675, av des Hôtels
Québec, QC G1W 4S3
418-659-5264
Téléc: 418-646-9238
866-659-5264
Couriel: aquarium@sepaq.com
URL: www.sepaq.com/aquarium
Sigle: QQZ
Fermée au public
Fondée en: 1972
Heures: L-V 9h-16h
Budget d'acquisitions: 0-$9,999
Population desservie: 0
Annotation: Formerly known as Société des parcs de sciences naturelles du Québec.
Sujets: Biologie
Services:
Prêts entre bibliothèques(PEB)
Stéphane Masson, Coordonateur scientifique
masson.stephane@sepaq.com

***Québec:* Québec Ministère de l'agriculture, des pêcheries et de l'alimentation**
Bibliothèque
200, ch Ste-Foy
Québec, QC G1R 4X6
418-380-2140
Téléc: 418-380-2172
866-822-2140
Couriel: bibli200@mapaq.gouv.qc.ca
bib_peb@mapaq.gouv.qc.ca
URL: www.mapaq.gouv.qc.ca
Sigle: QQAG
Fondée en: 1943
Heures: L-V 8h30-12h, 13h-16h30
Budget d'acquisitions: $25,000 - $49,999
Population desservie: 0
Annotation: Téléréférence réservé aux employés(es) du ministère.
Collections spécialisées: Publications du Mapaq
Sujets: Agriculture, alimentation
Services:
Prêts entre bibliothèques(PEB)
Personnel: *Sommaire:* 6 Total; 1 Professionnel(s); 4 Technicien(s); 1 Autre(s) employé(s)
Michel Lévesque, Chef de service
michel.levesque@mapaq.gouv.qc.ca
Anne Lafond, Technicienne en documentation
418-380-2100 ext. 3516
Line Gauvin, Technicienne en documentation
418-380-2100 ext. 3509
Guylaine Hazen, Technicienne en documentation
Suzy LaForest, Technicienne en documentation

***Québec:* Québec Ministère de la santé et des services sociaux**
Centre de documentation
1075, ch Sainte-Foy, 5e étage
Québec, QC G1S 2M1
418-266-7007
Téléc: 418-266-7024
Couriel: peb.servdoc@msss.gouv.qc.ca
URL: www.msss.gouv.qc.ca/documentation/centrededoc.php
Sigle: QQIAS
Fondée en: 1983
Heures: L-V 8h30-12h, 13h-16h30
Budget d'acquisitions: $50,000 - $99,999
Population desservie: 0
Collections spécialisées: 30 000 livres; 400 titres de périodiques ainsi que des documents audiovisuels (DVD, CD et vidéocassettes)
Sujets: Services sociaux, santé, santé mentale, personnes agées, la famille, jeunes, personnes handicapées, toxicomanie
Services:
Accès public à l'internet
Prêts entre bibliothèques(PEB) frais de Réciprocité
Lecteur/reproduction de microformes: Lecteurs
Personnel: *Sommaire:* 13 Total
Claude Lamarre, Chef du service des ressources documentaires
claude.lamarre@msss.gouv.qc.ca
418-266-7005

***Québec:* Québec Ministère des affaires municipales, Régions et Occupation du territoire**
Centre de documentation
10, rue Pierre-Olivier-Chauveau, Sous-sol, aile Chauveau
Québec, QC G1R 4J3
418-691-2018
Couriel: centre.doc@mamrot.gouv.qc.ca
URL: www.mamrot.gouv.qc.ca/publications
Sigle: QQAM
Fondée en: 1979
Heures: 8h30-12h, 13h-16h30
Budget d'acquisitions: $25,000 - $49,999
Matériel imprimé: $10,000 - $24,999
Matériel électronique: 0-$9,999
Population desservie: 0
Sujets: Affaires municipales; Administration municipale; Aménagement; Cartographie; Démographie; Droit et législation municipale; Finances municipales; Urbanisme
Services:
Prêts entre bibliothèques(PEB)
Personnel: *Sommaire:* 1 Technicien(s)

***Québec:* Québec Ministère des ressources naturelles et de la faune**
Bibliothèque
D-316, 5700, 4e av ouest
Québec, QC G1H 6R1
418-627-8686
Téléc: 418-644-1124
Couriel: bibliotheque@mrnf.gouv.qc.ca
Sigle: QQFO
Membre d'un consortium: Réseau informatisé des bibliothèques gouvernementales
Fondée en: 1994
Heures: L-V 8h30-12h, 13h-16h30
Budget d'acquisitions: $100,000 - $249,999
Matériel imprimé: $25,000 - $49,999
Matériel électronique: $100,000 - $249,999
Population desservie: 0
Collections spécialisées: US Geology Survey; Commission géologique du Canada; Service géologique du Québec; The US Bureau of Mines; Documents des Services canadiens des forêts; US Department of Agriculture; Forestry Commission United Kingdom; Rapports annuels depuis le 19e siècle; DP, DPV, MB; US Bureau of Mines; Service canadien des forêts; Forestry Commission UK, DP, DPV, MS
Sujets: Forêts, sylviculture, énergie, mines, terres, géologie, faune, information foncière
Services:
Accès public à l'internet
Prêts entre bibliothèques(PEB)
Lecteur/reproduction de microformes: Ordinateur; Lecteurs
Personnel: *Sommaire:* 13 Total; 2 Professionnel(s); 8 Technicien(s); 3 Autre(s) employé(s)
Pierrette Labbé, Technicienne en documentation
pierrette.labbe@mrnf.gouv.qc.ca
418-627-8686 ext. 3594
Lynda Racine, Technicienne en documentation
Lynda.Racine@mrnf.gouv.qc.ca
418-627-8686 ext. 3597
Carmel Blanchard, Technicienne en administration
Carmel.Blanchard@mrnf.gouv.qc.ca
418-627-8686 ext. 3457
Sylvie Laliberté, Technicienne en documentation
sylvie.laliberte@mrnf.gouv.qc.ca
418-627-8686 ext. 3664

***Québec:* Québec Ministère des transports**
Centre de documentation (Succursale Centre)
700, boul René-Lévesque est, 21e étage
Québec, QC G1R 5H1
418-643-3578
Téléc: 418-646-2343
Couriel: doc-qtr@mtq.gouv.qc.ca
URL: www.mtq.gouv.qc.ca
Sigle: QTR
Fondée en: 1978
Heures: L-V 8h30-12h, 13h-16h30
Population desservie: 0
Collections spécialisées: Transport Québec, Transports Canada, Transportation Research Board (E-U), Conférence européenne des ministres des transports, Institut national de recherche sur les transports et leur sécurité (France)
Sujets: Transports, énergie, environnement, génie, technologie, aménagement de territoire, urbanisme
Services:
Accès public à l'internet
Prêts entre bibliothèques(PEB)
Personnel: *Sommaire:* 15 Total; 4 Professionnel(s); 10 Technicien(s); 3 Autre(s) employé(s)

***Québec:* Québec Ministère du développement économique, de l'innovation et de l'exportation**
Bibliothèque
710, Place d'Youville, 2e étage
Québec, QC G1R 4Y4
418-691-5972
Téléc: 418-643-8936
Sigle: QQIC
Fondée en: 1957
Heures: L-V 8h30-12h, 13h-16h30avec rendez-vous seulement
Budget d'acquisitions: $50,000 - $99,999
Matériel imprimé: $25,000 - $49,999
Matériel électronique: $25,000 - $49,999
Population desservie: 0
Annotation: Accès à Internet, aux cédéroms et bases de données pour employés du ministère; Membre du Réseau Informatisé des Bibliothèques Gouvernementales
Sujets: Économie, industrie, commerce, coopération, relations industrielles, technologie, PME, commerce international
Services:
Prêts entre bibliothèques(PEB)
Personnel: *Sommaire:* 5 Total; 1 Professionnel(s); 1 Technicien(s); 1 Autre(s) employé(s)
Nicole Nadeau, Responsable
nicole.nadeau@mdeie.gouv.qc.ca
418-691-5698 ext. 4181
Aline Labreque, Bibliotechnicienne
aline.labrecque@mdeie.gouv.qc.ca
418-691-5698 ext. 4145

***Québec:* Région du Québec**
1141, route de l'Église
Québec, QC G1J 0C3
Mailing Address: CP 10100
Québec, QC G1J 0C3
418-649-6546
Fax: 418-648-7166
800-668-6767
e-mail: librarybiblio.quebec@ec.gc.ca
URL: www.ec.gc.ca
National Library Symbol: QQE
Services:
Inter-Library Loan (ILL)
Microform Equipment: Computer; Reader

***Québec:* Société d'habitation du Québec**
Service de documentation et d'information en habitation
1054, rue Louis-Alexandre Taschereau, 3e étage
Québec, QC G1R 5E7
418-643-4035 ext: 1374
URL: www.habitation.gouv.qc.ca
Sigle: QMSHQ
Fondée en: 1987
Heures: L-V
Budget d'acquisitions: 0
Population desservie: 0
Sujets: Construction; Architecture
Services:
Accès public à l'internet
Prêts entre bibliothèques(PEB)

***Québec:* Télé-Université**
Service de la Bibliotech à distance
455, rue du Parvis
Québec, QC G1K 9H6
418-657-2747 ext: 5397
Téléc: 418-657-2094
800-463-4728
Couriel: assdoc@teluq.ca
URL: www.biblio.teluq.ca
Sigle: QQUQT
Membre d'un consortium: Canadian Research Knowledge Network (CRKN)
Fondée en: 1978
Heures: L-V 8h30-12h, 13h-16h30avec rendez-vous seulement
Budget d'acquisitions: $50,000 - $99,999
Population desservie: 0
Collections spécialisées: Enseignement supérieurl; communication organisationnelle
Sujets: Éducation enseignement à distance; Technologie éducative; Éducation des adultes
Services:
Accèss distance aux bases de donn
Accès public à l'internet
Réseau en ligne
Prêts entre bibliothèques(PEB) frais de selon réciprocité
Frais de recherche
Lecteur/reproduction de microformes: Ordinateur; Lecteurs
Personnel: *Sommaire:* 5 Total
Dominique Avoine, Coodonnateur
dominique.avoine@teluq.ca

***Québec:* Union québécoise pour la conservation de la nature / Québec Union for Nature Conservation**
Bibliothèque
#207, 870, av De Salaberry
Québec, QC G1R 2T9
418-648-2104
Téléc: 418-648-0991
Couriel: conservons@naturequebec.org
URL: www.naturequebec.org

Heures:avec rendez-vous seulement
Population desservie: 0
Sujets: Conservation
Christian Simard, Directeur général
christian.simard@naturequebec.org

Québec: Université du Québec Institut national de la recherche scientifique, INRS-Service de documentation et d'information spécialisées

490, rue de la Couronne
Québec, QC G1K 9A9
418-654-2577
Téléc: 418-654-2660
877-326-5762
Couriel: sdis@adm.inrs.ca
URL: sdis.inrs.ca
Sigle: QSFIG
Fondée en: 1970
Heures: L-V 8h30-16h30
Budget d'acquisitions: $250,000 - $499,999
Matériel imprimé: $25,000 - $49,999
Matériel électronique: $100,000 - $249,999
Population desservie: 0
Sujets: Espace régional, espace urbain/métropolitain, espace micro-urbain, science et technologie
Services:
Accèss distance aux bases de donn
Accès public à l'internet
Prêts entre bibliothèques(PEB)
Personnel: *Sommaire:* 3 Total; 1 Professionnel(s); 1 Technicien(s); 1 Autre(s) employé(s)
Marie-Eve Dugas, Bibliothécaire
marie-eve.dugas@ucs.inrs.ca
514-499-4098
Ginette Casavant, Technicienne
ginette_casavant@ucs.inrs.ca
514-499-4017
Linda Joly, Commis bibliothèque
linda_joly@ucs.inrs.ca
514-499-8265

Québec: Université du Québec Institut national de la recherche scientifique, INRS-ETE Service de documentation et d'information spécialisées

2800, rue Einstein
Québec, QC G1V 4C7
Adresse postale: CP 7500
Québec, QC G1V 4C7
418-654-2577
Téléc: 418-654-2600
Couriel: peb_qquie@uquebec.ca
URL: sdis.inrs.ca
Sigle: QQUIE
Membre d'un consortium: Canadian Research Knowledge Network (CRKN); Conférence des recteurs et des principaux des universités du Québec (CREPUQ)
Fondée en: 1970
Heures: L-V
Budget d'acquisitions: $25,000 - $49,999
Population desservie: 0
Sujets: Environnement, biologie, environnement aquatique, hydrologie, assainissement, gestion et administration de l'eau
Services:
Accès public à l'internet
Prêts entre bibliothèques(PEB)
Lecteur/reproduction de microformes: Lecteurs
Personnel: *Sommaire:* 3 Total; 2 Professionnel(s); 2 Technicien(s)
Sophie Renaud, Responsable
sophie_renaud@inrs-ete.uquebec.ca
418-654-2649
Jean-Daniel Bourgault, Bibliothécaire
bourgajd@inrs-ete.uquebec.ca
418-654-2663
Chantal Paquin, Technicienne
paquinch@inrs-ete.uquebec.ca
418-654-2577
Anne Robitaille, Responsable des acquisitions
anne.robitaille@inrs-ete.uquebec.ca
418-654-3724

Québec: Université Laval Bibliothèque

Pavillon Jean-Charles-Bonenfant
2345, allée des Bibliothèques
Québec, QC G1V 0A6
418-656-3344
Autres numéros: Information (recording): 418-656-2317
Couriel: bibl@bibl.ulaval.ca
URL: www.bibl.ulaval.ca
Sigle: QQLA
Membre d'un consortium: Canadian Research Knowledge Network (CRKN); Conférence des recteurs et des principaux des universités du Québec (CREPUQ)
Fondée en: 1852
Heures: 30 Avril - 15 Juin: L-V 8h-21h, 18 Juin - 31 aout: L-V 8h-19h
Budget d'acquisitions: $1,000,000 plus
Population desservie: 0
Sujets: Sciences humaines et sociales, sciences pures et appliquées, sciences de la santé, droit
Services:
Accèss distance aux bases de donn
Accès public à l'internet
Réseau en ligne
Prêts entre bibliothèques(PEB)
Lecteur/reproduction de microformes: Ordinateur; Lecteurs
Personnel: *Sommaire:* 213 Total; 60 Professionnel(s); 59 Technicien(s); 100 Autre(s) employé(s)
Loubna Ghaouti, Directrice
loubna.ghaouti@bibl.ulaval.ca
418-656-2131 ext. 3451
Louise Allard, Chef, Division du Traitement des fonds documentaires
louise.allard@bibl.ulaval.ca
418-656-2131 ext. 2888
Chantal Vézina, Secteur des acquisitions
chantal.vezina@bibl.ulaval.ca
418-656-2131 ext. 5991
Marcel Plourde, Secteur du catalogage
marcel.plourde@bibl.ulaval.ca
418-656-2131 ext. 6313
Jo-Anne Bélair, Secteur du répertoire de vedettes-matière
jo-anne.belair@bibl.ulaval.ca
418-656-2131 ext. 2871
Louise Pelletier, Pilote du système Unicorn
louise.pelletier@bibl.ulaval.ca
418-656-3131 ext. 13997
Guy Teasdale, Directeur, Bibliothèques numérique et technologies de l'information
guy.teasdale@bibl.ulaval.ca
418-656-2131 ext. 3918
Martine Lemieux, Secteur du soutien informatique
martine.lemieux@bibl.ulaval.ca
418-656-2131 ext. 4672
Rida Benjelloun, Secteur recherche et développements numériques
rida.benjelloun@bibl.ulaval.ca
418-656-2131 ext. 2090

Rigaud: Collège Bourget / Bourget College Bibliothèque

65, rue Saint-Pierre
Rigaud, QC J0P 1P0
450-451-0815
Téléc: 450-451-4171
Couriel: biblio@collegebourget.qc.ca
URL: www.collegebourget.qc.ca
Sigle: QRCB
Fondée en: 1850
Heures: 8h15-16h15avec rendez-vous seulement
Budget d'acquisitions: $25,000 - $49,999
Population desservie: 0
Sujets: Culture générale, sciences, langues
Services:
Réseau en ligne
Personnel: *Sommaire:* 3 Total

Rimouski: CÉGEP de Rimouski Bibliothèque Gilles-Vigneault

60, rue de l'Évêché ouest
Rimouski, QC G5L 4H6
418-723-1880
Téléc: 418-724-4961
URL: www.cegep-rimouski.qc.ca/biblio
Sigle: ORIC
Heures: L-J 8h-19h; V 8h-17h
Budget d'acquisitions: $50,000 - $99,999
Population desservie: 0
Collections spécialisées: Laurentiana du Séminaire de Rimouski
Services:
Accès public à l'internet
Réseau en ligne
Prêts entre bibliothèques(PEB)
Lecteur/reproduction de microformes: Lecteurs
Personnel: *Sommaire:* 9 Total; 2 Professionnel(s); 5 Technicien(s); 3 Autre(s) employé(s)
Frederic Hardel, Responsable, Services aux usagers
418-723-1880 ext. 2192
Ginette Michaud, Responsable, Services techniques
418-723-1880 ext. 2194

Rimouski: Institut maritime du Québec Bibliothèque

53, rue St-Germain ouest
Rimouski, QC G5L 4B4
418-724-2822
Téléc: 418-724-0606
URL: www.imq.qc.ca/bibliotheque/accueil-bibliotheque.php
Fondée en: 1976
Heures: L-V 8h-17h
Budget d'acquisitions: $25,000 - $49,999
Population desservie: 0
Sujets: Architecture navale, navigation, mécanique de marine, plongée professionnelle, logistique du transport, droit maritime, électronique du maritime
Services:
Accès public à l'internet
Prêts entre bibliothèques(PEB)
Personnel: *Sommaire:* 2 Total; 1 Technicien(s); 1 Autre(s) employé(s)
Nadine Leblanc, Technicienne en documentation
nleblanc@imq.qc.ca
418-724-2822 ext. 4203
Jeannine Tremblay, Agente de bureau
mbiblio@imq.qc.ca
418-724-2822 ext. 4204

Rimouski: Le siège social du CSSS de Rimouski-Neigette, Hôpital régional - Rimouski Centre de documentation

150, av Rouleau
Rimouski, QC G5L 5T1
418-724-3000 ext: 11
Téléc: 418-724-8632
URL: www.chrr.qc.ca
Sigle: QRCH
Heures: L-V
Budget d'acquisitions: $50,000 - $99,999
Population desservie: 0
Sujets: Médecine, soins infirmiers
Services:
Accès public à l'internet
Personnel: *Sommaire:* 1 Technicien(s)

Rimouski: Université du Québec à Rimouski Bibliothèque

#J200, 300, Allée des Ursulines
Rimouski, QC G5L 3A1
418-724-1470
Téléc: 418-724-1621
800-511-3382
Couriel: bibliotheque@uqar.qc.ca
URL: biblio.uqar.qc.ca
Sigle: QRU
Membre d'un consortium: Canadian Research Knowledge Network (CRKN); Conférence des recteurs et des principaux des universités du Québec (CREPUQ)
Fondée en: 1969
Heures: L-V 8h30-22h30; Sa-D 12h-17h
Budget d'acquisitions: $1,000,000 plus
Matériel imprimé: $100,000 - $249,999
Matériel électronique: $250,000 - $499,999
Population desservie: 0
Collections spécialisées: Développement régional, Est du Québec
Sujets: Biologie, environnement, océanographie, développement régional, pêcherie
Services:
Accès public à l'internet
Réseau en ligne

Prêts entre bibliothèques(PEB)
Lecteur/reproduction de microformes: Ordinateur; Lecteurs
Personnel: *Sommaire:* 25 Total; 7 Professionnel(s); 5 Technicien(s); 13 Autre(s) employé(s)
Denis Boisvert, Directeur
denis_boisvert@uquar.qc.ca
418-724-1470
Josée Pelletier, Coordonnatrice, serv. d'accès information/documention
josee_pelletier@uqar.ca
418-724-1476
Jacques St-Laurent, Commis specialisé en approvisionnements
jacques_st-laurent@uqar.qc.ca
418-723-1986 ext. 1500
Bruno Langlois, Responsable, Analyste information
burno_langlois@uqar.qc.ca
418-723-1986 ext. 1479

***Rivière-du-Loup:* CÉGEP de Rivière-du-Loup**
Centre des ressources didactiques
80, rue Frontenac
Rivière-du-Loup, QC G5R 1R1
418-862-6903
Téléc: 418-862-4959
URL: www.cegep-rdl.qc.ca
bibliotheque.cegep-rdl.qc.ca
Sigle: QRLC
Fondée en: 1969
Heures: L, Me 8h30-21h; Ma, J 8h30-18h; V 8h30-15h30
Budget d'acquisitions: $25,000 - $49,999
Population desservie: 0
Collections spécialisées: Arts, loisirs, techniques en services de garde
Services:
Accès public à l'internet
Prêts entre bibliothèques(PEB)
Personnel: *Sommaire:* 6 Total; 1 Professionnel(s); 2 Technicien(s); 2 Autre(s) employé(s)
Joanne Laforest, Responsable du centre de ressources didactiques
joalaf@cegep-rdl.qc.ca
418-862-6903 ext. 2238
Marie Bourbeau, Technicienne aux acquisitions et au traitement de la documentation
mbourbeau@cegep-rdl.qc.ca
418-862-6903 ext. 2325
Diane Ouellet, Technicienne à la référence, aux périodiques et au PEB
diaoue@cegep-rdl.qc.ca
418-862-6903 ext. 2326

***Rivière-du-Loup:* Centre hospitalier régional du Grand-Portage**
Les ressources informationnelles
75, rue St-Henri
Rivière-du-Loup, QC G5R 2A4
418-868-1000
Téléc: 418-868-1032
URL: www.csssriviereduloup.qc.ca
Heures: L-J
Population desservie: 0
Sujets: Médecine; Chirurgie
Daniel Pigeon, Chef des ressources informationnelles
418-868-1010 ext. 2262

***Rouyn-Noranda:* CÉGEP de l'Abitibi-Témiscamingue**
Bibliothèque
425, boul du Collège
Rouyn-Noranda, QC J9X 5M5
Adresse postale: CP 8000
Rouyn-Noranda, QC J9X 5M5
819-762-0931 ext: 1234
Téléc: 819-762-2071
866-234-3728
Couriel: aide.bibliotheque@uqat.ca
URL: bibliotheque.uqat.ca
Sigle: QRCN
Fondée en: 1951
Heures: L-J 8h-21h45; V 8h-20h45; Sa-D 12h-16h15. Library hours vary depending on the campus.
Budget d'acquisitions: $50,000 - $99,999
Matériel imprimé: $50,000 - $99,999
Matériel électronique: 0-$9,999
Population desservie: 0
Collections spécialisées: Collection de Louis-Edmond Hamelin, Collection de la Baie James, Collection Marcel de Grandpré, Collection en éducation nordique, centre de documentation régionale
Sujets: Éducation, administration, profession d'infirmier, psychologie, génie, foresterie, mines, sociologie
Services:
Accèss distance aux bases de donn
Accès public à l'internet
Réseau en ligne
Prêts entre bibliothèques(PEB)
Lecteur/reproduction de microformes: Lecteurs
Personnel: *Sommaire:* 14 Total; 1 Professionnel(s); 4 Technicien(s); 9 Autre(s) employé(s)
François de la Chevrotière, Directeur
francois.delachevrotiere@uqat.ca
819-762-0931 ext. 1216
David Fournier-Viger, Bibliothécaire et référence
david.fournier-viger@uqat.ca
Lucie Laprise, Responsable, acquisitions/périodique
lucie.laprise@uqat.ca

***Rouyn-Noranda:* Université du Québec en Abitibi-Témiscamingue**
Bibliothèque
425, boul de l'Université
Rouyn-Noranda, QC J9X 5M5
Adresse postale: CP 8000
Rouyn-Noranda, QC J9X 5M5
819-762-0931 ext: 1234
Téléc: 819-762-2071
866-234-3728
Couriel: aide.bibliotheque@uqat.ca
URL: www.uqat.ca/bibliotheque/
Sigle: QRUQR
Membre d'un consortium: Canadian Research Knowledge Network (CRKN); Conférence des recteurs et des principaux des universités du Québec (CREPUQ)
Fondée en: 1970
Heures: L-J 8h-21h45; V 8h-20h45; Sa-D 12h-16h15avec rendez-vous seulement
Budget d'acquisitions: $100,000 - $249,999
Matériel imprimé: $50,000 - $99,999
Matériel électronique: $50,000 - $99,999
Population desservie: 0
Collections spécialisées: Collection en éducation nordique; centre de documention régionale
Sujets: Administration, sciences infirmières, génie, psychologie, mines, foresterie, gestion, sciences appliquées, sciences sociales, éducation, santé
Services:
Accèss distance aux bases de donn
Accès public à l'internet
Réseau en ligne
Prêts entre bibliothèques(PEB)
Lecteur/reproduction de microformes: Lecteurs
Personnel: *Sommaire:* 20 Total
Luc Sigouin, Directeur
Luc.Sigouin@uqat.ca
Thérèse Cyr, Responsable, Didacthèque
Therese.Cyr@uqat.ca
Liette Leclerc, Responsable, Traitement documentaire
liette.leclerc@uqat.ca
Manon Lapointe, Service du prêt
Manon.Lapointe@uqat.ca
Suzanne Daigle, Responsable, Publications gouvernementales
Suzanne.Daigle@uqat.ca
Lucie Laprise, Responsable, Acquisition et périodique
Lucie.Laprise@uqat.ca
Gisèle Neas, Responsable, Audiovidéothèque
Gisele.Neas@uqat.ca
David Fournier-Viger, Conseiller en documentation
david.fournier-viger@uqat.ca

***Saint-Augustin-de-Desmaures:* Campus Notre-Dame-de-Foy**
Bibliothèque Jean-Paul-Desbiens
5000, rue Clément-Lockquell
Saint-Augustin-de-Desmaures, QC G3A 1B3
418-872-8242 ext: 618
Téléc: 418-872-3448
800-463-8041
Couriel: biblio@cndf.qc.ca
URL: www.cndf.qc.ca
Fermée au public
Fondée en: 1965
Heures: Ma 14h-21h; Me-V 16h-21h; Sa 10h-16h
Budget d'acquisitions: $25,000 - $49,999
Matériel imprimé: $25,000 - $49,999
Matériel électronique: $10,000 - $24,999
Population desservie: 0
Sujets: Éducation, enseignement
Services:
Accès public à l'internet
Réseau en ligne
Prêts entre bibliothèques(PEB)
Personnel: *Sommaire:* 5 Total; 3 Technicien(s); 2 Autre(s) employé(s)
François Casabon, Directeur du service
casabonf@cndf.qc.ca
418-872-8242 ext. 243
Andrée Lajoie, Technicienne en documentation
lajoiea@cndf.qc.ca
418-872-8242 ext. 293
Claude Roy, Directeur, Études
roy.claude@cndf.qc.ca
418-872-8242 ext. 109
Josée Gaudreau, Technicienne en documentation
gaudreauj@cndf.qc.ca
418-872-8242 ext. 229
Serge Gingras, Technicien en audiovisuel
gingrass@cndf.qc.ca
418-872-8242 ext. 368

***Saint-Félicien:* CÉGEP de Saint-Félicien**
Centre de documentation
1105, boul Hamel
Saint-Félicien, QC G8K 2R8
Adresse postale: CP 7300
Saint-Félicien, QC G8K 2R8
418-679-5412 ext: 284
Téléc: 418-679-1040
Couriel: biblio@cstfelicien.qc.ca
URL: www.cegepstfe.ca/fr/centre_documentation
Social Media: bibliocstfelicien.wordpress.com
www.facebook.com/149971531714060
Fondée en: 1971
Heures: L-J 8h-20h; V 8h-17h
Budget d'acquisitions: $10,000 - $24,999
Population desservie: 0
Services:
Prêts entre bibliothèques(PEB)
Personnel: *Sommaire:* 3 Total; 1 Professionnel(s); 2 Technicien(s)
Sylvie Dallaire, Conseiller pédagogique
sdallaire@cstfelicien.qc.ca
418-679-5412 ext. 206
Diane Bernier, Technicienne, Référence, catalogage, et PEB
dbernier@cstfelicien.qc.ca
418-679-5412 ext. 226
Nathalie Desmeules, Secrétaire
418-679-5412 ext. 284

***Saint-Georges:* CÉGEP de Beauce-Appalaches**
Bibliothèque Jean-Marie Derouin
1055, 116ième Rue
Saint-Georges, QC G5Y 3G1
418-228-8896
Téléc: 418-228-0562
Couriel: info@cegepba.qc.ca
URL: www.cegepba.qc.ca
Heures: L-V 8h-17h30, 18h30-21h30avec rendez-vous seulement
Population desservie: 0
Collections spécialisées: Collection Que sais-je?, dépôts de publications gouvernementales provinciales et fédérales
Sujets: Sciences humaines; soins infirmiers; sciences de la nature; mathématiques; informatique, génie-civil et techniques de production manufacturiers; techniques administratives; techniques de l'imprimerie et services de garde; arts et lettres; langues; éducation spécialisée
Services:
Prêts entre bibliothèques(PEB)
Lecteur/reproduction de microformes: Lecteurs
Personnel: *Sommaire:* 1 Professionnel(s); 2 Technicien(s); 2 Autre(s) employé(s)

***Saint-Honoré-de-Chicoutimi:* Centre québécois de formation aéronautique**
Bibliothèque
1, rue de l'Aéroport
Saint-Honoré-de-Chicoutimi, QC G0V 1L0
418-673-3421 ext: 314
Téléc: 418-673-3950

Couriel: cqfa@cegep-chicoutimi.qc.ca
URL: www.cqfa.ca
Heures:avec rendez-vous seulement
Population desservie: 0
Annotation: Bilingue
Sujets: L'aéronautique
Pierre Laberge, Bibliothécaire
plaberge@cqfa.ca

Saint-Hubert: École nationale d'aérotechnique Bibliothèque
5555, Place de la Savane
Saint-Hubert, QC J3Y 8Y9
450-678-3561 ext: 4551
Couriel: biblioena@college-em.qc.ca
URL: blogues.college-em.qc.ca/bibli
Sigle: QSTHUC
Fondée en: 1964
Heures: L-V 8h-17h30
Budget d'acquisitions: $50,000 - $99,999
Population desservie: 0
Collections spécialisées: Périodiques en aérospatial
Sujets: Aérotechnique; Aéronautique; Aérospatiale
Services:
Accès public à l'internet
Prêts entre bibliothèques(PEB)
Personnel: *Sommaire:* 5 Total; 1 Professionnel(s); 1 Technicien(s); 3 Autre(s) employé(s)
Lise Chaillez, Bibliothécaire
Stephane Baillie, Technicienne en documentation

Saint-Hyacinthe: CÉGEP de Saint-Hyacinthe Centre des ressources didactiques
3000, av Boullé
Saint-Hyacinthe, QC J2S 1H9
450-773-6800
Téléc: 450-773-9971
URL: www.biblios.saint-hyacinthe.qc.ca
Fondée en: 1968
Heures: L-V
Budget d'acquisitions: $25,000 - $49,999
Population desservie: 0
Sujets: Arts, sciences humaines, culture
Services:
Prêts entre bibliothèques(PEB)
Lecteur/reproduction de microformes: Lecteurs
Personnel: *Sommaire:* 1 Professionnel(s); 1 Technicien(s); 4 Autre(s) employé(s)
Marc Leclerc, Coordonnateur
Sylviane Houle, Bibliothécaire

Saint-Hyacinthe: Centre de recherche et de développement sur les aliments / Food Research & Development Centre Bibliothèque canadienne de l'agriculture/Canadian Agriculture Library - Saint-Hyacinthe
3600, boul Casavant ouest
Saint-Hyacinthe, QC J2S 8E3
450-768-3247
Fax: 450-773-8461
National Library Symbol: QSHAG
Hours: L-V 8h30-17h
Acquisitions Budget: $50,000 - $99,999
Subjects covered: Agriculture, Engineering, Resource Conservation
Services:
Inter-Library Loan (ILL) for a fee of 12$
Microform Equipment: Reader
Personnel: *Summary:* 2 Professional(s); 3 Technical(s); 1 Other employees
Pierre Di Campo, Head Librarian
pierre.dicampo@agr.gc.ca
Hélène Simard-Vermette, Library Techician
helene.simard-vermette@agr.gc.ca

Saint-Hyacinthe: Centre de santé et de services sociaux Richelieu-Yamaska Bibliothèque Roméo-Germain
2750, boul Laframboise
Saint-Hyacinthe, QC J2S 4Y8
450-771-3333 ext: 3242
Téléc: 450-771-3304
Couriel: peb.csssry@rrsss16.gouv.qc.ca
URL: www.santemonteregie.qc.ca/richelieu-yamaska
Sigle: QSTHC
Heures: L-V 8h30-16h30 (vendredi fermée de 11h30 à 12h30)avec rendez-vous seulement
Budget d'acquisitions: $50,000 - $99,999
Population desservie: 0
Sujets: Sciences médicales, administration hospitalière
Services:
Accès public à l'internet
Prêts entre bibliothèques(PEB) frais de 5$ ou Gratuité réciproque
Frais de recherche
Personnel: *Sommaire:* 1 Total; 1 Technicien(s);
Alain Déry, Technicien en documentation
alain.dery@rrsss16.gouv.qc.ca

Saint-Hyacinthe: Institut de technologie agro-alimentaire de Saint-Hyacinthe Centre de documentation
3230, rue Sicotte
Saint-Hyacinthe, QC J2S 7B3
Adresse postale: CP 70
Saint-Hyacinthe, QC J2S 7B3
450-778-6504 ext: 6277
Téléc: 450-778-6536
Couriel: ita.st.hyacinthe@mapaq.gouv.qc.ca
URL: www.ita.qc.ca
Sigle: QSTHTA
Fondée en: 1963
Heures: L-V
Budget d'acquisitions: $25,000 - $49,999
Matériel imprimé: $10,000 - $24,999
Matériel électronique: $10,000 - $24,999
Population desservie: 0
Sujets: Agriculture, Botanique, Alimentation
Services:
Accès public à l'internet
Prêts entre bibliothèques(PEB)
Lecteur/reproduction de microformes: Lecteurs
Personnel: *Sommaire:* 1 Professionnel(s); 3 Autre(s) employé(s)
Karine Lévesque, Contact
karine.levesque@mapaq.gouv.qc.ca

Saint-Jean-sur-Richelieu: CÉGEP St-Jean-sur-Richelieu Bibliothèque
#E-120, 30 boul de Séminaire
Saint-Jean-sur-Richelieu, QC J3B 7B1
Adresse postale: CP 1018
Saint-Jean-sur-Richelieu, QC J3B 7B1
450-347-5301 ext: 2283
Téléc: 450-347-3329
Couriel: bibliotheque@cstjean.qc.ca
URL: www.cstjean.qc.ca/bibliotheque
Fondée en: 1962
Heures: L-J 8h-20h30; V 8h-16h; S, D 12h-16h
Budget d'acquisitions: Matériel imprimé: $50,000 - $99,999
Population desservie: 0
Annotation: Catalogue disponible sur Internet: regard.cstjean.qc.ca; Heures d'ouverture prolongées suite à un protocole d'entente avec la ville de St-Jean-sur-Richelieu; Abonnement gratuit pour les citoyens de St-Jean-sur-Richelieu
Sujets: Histoire québécoise, littérature québécoise, arts
Services:
Accès public à l'internet frais
Réseau en ligne
Prêts entre bibliothèques(PEB) frais
Personnel: *Sommaire:* 1 Professionnel(s); 2 Technicien(s); 3 Autre(s) employé(s)
Jean-Louis Demers, Responsable
jean-louis.demers@cstjean.qc.ca
450-347-5301 ext. 2161
Christine Bergeron, Technicienne en documentation
christine.bergeron@cstjean.qc.ca
450-347-5301 ext. 2680
Lucie Bouret, Technicienne en documentation
lucie.bouret@cstjean.qc.ca
450-347-5301 ext. 2280
Johanne Lorion, Technicienne en documentation
johanne.lorion@cstjean.qc.ca
450-347-5301 ext. 2284
Danielle Gauthier, Secrétaire & acquisitions
danielle.gauthier@cstjean.qc.ca
450-347-5301 ext. 2333
Manon Benoit, Agente de bureau, Comptoir de prêt
manon.benoit@cstjean.qc.ca
450-347-5301 ext. 2552
Carole Leblanc, Agente de bureau, Comptoir de prêt
carole.leblanc@cstjean.qc.ca
450-347-5301 ext. 2549

Saint-Jean-sur-Richelieu: Centre de recherche et de développement en horticulture / Horticulture Research & Development Centre Bibliothèque canadienne de l'agriculture/Canadian Agriculture Library - Saint-Jean-sur-Richelieu
430, boul Gouin
Saint-Jean-sur-Richelieu, QC J3B 6Z8
450-515-2065
Téléc: 450-346-7740
Sigle: QSTJAG
Heures: L-V 8h-16havec rendez-vous seulement
Budget d'acquisitions: $25,000 - $49,999
Population desservie: 0
Collections spécialisées: Horticulture ornementale, culture tropicale
Sujets: Cultures fruitières, génie et sol, cultures maraîchères, protection des plantes, agriculture
Services:
Prêts entre bibliothèques(PEB) frais
Lecteur/reproduction de microformes: Ordinateur
Personnel: *Sommaire:* 2 Total; 1 Professionnel(s)
Lise Lavallée, Adjointe, Bibliothèque
lise.lavallee@agr.gc.ca

Saint-Jean-sur-Richelieu: Rheinmetall Canada Inc. Information Centre / Centre d'information
225, boul du Séminaire sud
Saint-Jean-sur-Richelieu, QC J3B 8E9
450-358-2000
Fax: 450-358-1744
e-mail: info@rheinmetall.ca
URL: www.rheinmetall.ca
No public access
Founded in: 1987
Acquisitions Budget: $50,000 - $99,999
Subjects covered: Engineering
Diane Roy, Coordinator, Documentation

Saint-Jérôme: CÉGEP de St-Jérôme Bibliothèque
455, rue Fournier
Saint-Jérôme, QC J7Z 4V2
450-436-1580 ext: 150
Téléc: 450-436-1756
Couriel: biblio@cstj.qc.ca
URL: www.cegep-st-jerome.qc.ca
Sigle: QSTJEC
Fondée en: 1970
Heures: L-J 8h-20h; V 8h-17h
Budget d'acquisitions: $50,000 - $99,999
Matériel imprimé: $25,000 - $49,999
Matériel électronique: 0-$9,999
Population desservie: 0; 3,000 régulier; 4,000 formation continue
Annotation: Fédération des CEGEPS-RESDOC
Collections spécialisées: Dépositaire des publications du gouvernement du Canada
Sujets: Éducation
Services:
Accès public à l'internet
Réseau en ligne
Prêts entre bibliothèques(PEB)
Lecteur/reproduction de microformes: Ordinateur; Lecteurs
Personnel: *Sommaire:* 10 Total; 2 Professionnel(s); 4 Technicien(s); 4 Autre(s) employé(s)
Raymonde Trudel, Bibliothécaire responsable
rtrudel@cstj.qc.ca
450-436-1580 ext. 5615
Solange Beaulieu, Responsible, Prêt
sbeaulieu@cstj.qc.ca
450-436-1580 ext. 5613
Carole Laflamme, Responsible, Achats, commandes, et PEB
calaflam@cstj.qc.ca
450-436-1580 ext. 5618
Richard Laforge, Responsable, Audiovidéothèque
rlaforge@cstj.qc.ca
450-436-1580 ext. 5611
Isabelle Sauvé, Responsable, Classification et catalogage
isauve@cstj.qc.ca
450-436-1580 ext. 5617

***Saint-Lambert:* Champlain College Saint-Lambert George Wallace Library**
900 Riverside Dr.
Saint-Lambert, QC J4P 3P2
450-672-7360
Fax: 450-672-9299
URL: www.champlainonline.com/student-zone/library
National Library Symbol: QSLCR
Founded in: 1975
Hours: M-Th 8:00-5:00; F 8:00-4:00
Acquisitions Budget: $25,000 - $49,999
For Print: $10,000 - $24,999
For Electronic: $10,000 - $24,999
Services:
Remote Access
Internet Access
Access to Subscription Databases
Inter-Library Loan (ILL)
Microform Equipment: Computer; Reader
Personnel: *Summary:* 7 Total; 2 Professional(s); 4 Technical(s); 1 Other employees
Nicole Haché, Library Coordinator
nhache@champlaincollege.qc.ca
450-672-7360 ext. 200
Dale Huston, Reference Librarian
huston@champlaincollege.qc.ca
450-672-7360 ext. 345
Sabrina Burke, Library Technician
450-672-7360 ext. 221

***Saint-Laurent:* Abbott Laboratories Limited Library**
8401, rte Transcanadienne
Saint-Laurent, QC H3C 3K6
Mailing Address: CP 6150
Montréal, QC H3C 3K6
514-832-7000
Fax: 514-832-7800
Other contact info: 800-361-7852
URL: www.abbott.ca
National Library Symbol: QMALL
No public access
Founded in: 1931
Hours: Tu-Th 8:30-4:30
Acquisitions Budget: $50,000 - $99,999
Special Collections: Business, Management
Subjects covered: Medicine, Pharmacology, Toxicology, Nutrition
Services:
Inter-Library Loan (ILL)
Personnel: *Summary:* 1 Professional(s)
Georgette Vincze, Librarian
514-832-7734

***Saint-Laurent:* CÉGEP de Saint-Laurent Centre des ressources didactiques**
625, av St-Croix
Saint-Laurent, QC H4L 3X7
514-747-6521 ext: 7424
Téléc: 514-748-1249
URL: www.cegep-st-laurent.qc.ca/bibliotheque
Heures: L-J 8h-18h15; V 8h-16h15
Budget d'acquisitions: $50,000 - $99,999
Population desservie: 0
Services:
Prêts entre bibliothèques(PEB)
Lecteur/reproduction de microformes: Lecteurs
Personnel: *Sommaire:* 7 Total; 2 Professionnel(s); 2 Technicien(s); 3 Autre(s) employé(s)
Guy Gibeau, Adjoint au directeur des études
ggibeau@cegep-st-laurent.qc.ca
514-747-6521 ext. 7277
Mathieu Cormier, Adjoint au directeur des études
mcormier@cegep-st-laurent.qc.ca
514-747-6521 ext. 7218
Grant Forrest, Responsable, Référence
gforrest@cegep-st-laurent.qc.ca
514-747-6521 ext. 7212
Yolande Felx, SMTE
yfelx@cegep-st-laurent.qc.ca
514-747-6521 ext. 7211
Johanne Desjardins, Technicienne en documentation
jdesjardins@cegep-st-laurent.qc.ca
514-747-6521 ext. 7209

***Saint-Laurent:* CMC Electronics Inc. Library**
600, boul Dr Frederik Philips
Saint-Laurent, QC H4M 2S9
514-748-3148
Fax: 514-748-3100
URL: www.esterline.com
National Library Symbol: QMCM
No public access
Founded in: 1952
Hours: M-F 8:00-4:00
Acquisitions Budget: $25,000 - $49,999
Subjects covered: Electronics, Aeronautics, Communications
Services:
Internet Access
Inter-Library Loan (ILL)
Personnel: *Summary:* 1 Professional(s)

***Sainte-Anne-de-Bellevue:* Macdonald Campus Library**
Barton Bldg.
21111 Lakeshore Rd.
Sainte-Anne-de-Bellevue, QC H9X 3V9
Mailing Address: 21111 Lakeshore Rd.
Sainte-Anne-de-Bellevue, QC H9X 3V9
514-398-7881
Fax: 514-398-7960
e-mail: macdonald.library@mcgill.ca
macdcirc.library@mcgill.ca
National Library Symbol: QMAC
Founded in: 1907
Hours: Jan-May: M-Th 9:00am-10:00pm; F 9:00-6:00; Sa-Su 10:00-6:00
Acquisitions Budget: $250,000 - $499,999
Special Collections: Lyman Entomology Collection
Subjects covered: Agriculture, Human Nutrition & Dietetics, Environment, Animal Science, Bioresource Engineering, Environmental Science, Biotechnology, Food Science, Plant Science, Soil Science, Parasitology
Services:
Internet Access
Inter-Library Loan (ILL)
Microform Equipment: Computer; Reader
Personnel: *Summary:* 8 Total; 2 Professional(s); 6 Other employees
Natalie Waters, Head Librarian
natalie.waters@mcgill.ca
514-398-7876
Anne McMahon, Librarian, Serials, Processing, & ILL
anne.mcmahon@mcgill.ca
514-398-4400 ext. 7576

***Sainte-Anne-de-Bellevue:* MDA Space Library/Information Resource Centre/Bibliothèque/Centre de ressources d'information**
21025, rte Trans Canada
Sainte-Anne-de-Bellevue, QC H9X 3R2
514-457-2150 ext: 3259
Fax: 514-425-3048
National Library Symbol: QSTAS
No public access
Hours: M-F
Subjects covered: Space, Electronics, Materials, Business
Services:
Inter-Library Loan (ILL)
Personnel: *Summary:* 1 Total; 1 Professional(s)
Margaret Gross, Manager
margaret.gross@mdacorporation.com

***Sainte-Foy:* Centre de recherche et de développement sur les sols et les grandes cultures / Soils and Crops Research & Development Centre Bibliothèque canadienne de l'agriculture/Canadian Agriculture Library - Sainte-Foy**
2560, boul Hochelaga
Sainte-Foy, QC G1V 2J3
418-210-5035
Téléc: 418-648-2402
Sigle: QSFAG
Fondée en: 1970
Heures: 9h-13h, 13h30-16havec rendez-vous seulement
Population desservie: 0
Sujets: Agriculture, Céréales, Plantes Fourragères, Biologie Moléculaire, Sols
Services:
Prêts entre bibliothèques(PEB)
Caroline Hudon, Library Assistant
caroline.hudon@agr.gc.ca

***Sainte-Thérèse:* Collège Lionel-Groulx Bibliothèque**
100, rue Duquet
Sainte-Thérèse, QC J7E 3G6
450-430-3120 ext: 2286
Téléc: 450-971-2891
Couriel: peb@clg.gc.ca
URL: www.clg.qc.ca/bibliotheque/accueil-et-horaire/index
Heures: L-J 8h-22h; V 8h-18h
Budget d'acquisitions: $50,000 - $99,999
Population desservie: 0
Collections spécialisées: Partitions musicales, collections patrimoniales
Services:
Accès public à l'internet
Prêts entre bibliothèques(PEB)
Lecteur/reproduction de microformes: Lecteurs
Personnel: *Sommaire:* 9 Total
Benoît Archambault, Directeur adjoint aux études
benoit.archambault@clg.gc.ca
Josiane Sauvè, SMTE
josiane.suve@clg.qc.ca
Renee Locas, Technicienne en documentation
renee.locas@clg.qc.ca

***Sept-Iles:* CÉGEP de Sept-Iles Bibliothèque**
175, de la Vérendrye
Sept-Iles, QC G4R 5B7
418-962-9848
Téléc: 418-962-2458
Couriel: communications@cegep-sept-iles.qc.ca
URL: www.cegep-sept-iles.qc.ca
Fondée en: 1980
Heures: L-V 8h-17h; L, Me 19h-22h. Hors session: L-V 8h-17h
Budget d'acquisitions: $25,000 - $49,999
Population desservie: 0
Collections spécialisées: Documentation pour l'histoire et l'économie de la Côte-Nord
Sujets: Économie, industrie, médecine, sciences de la santé, technologie, technique de bureau, électronique, informatique
Services:
Accès public à l'internet
Réseau en ligne
Prêts entre bibliothèques(PEB)
Lecteur/reproduction de microformes: Lecteurs
Personnel: *Sommaire:* 2 Total; 1 Professionnel(s); 1 Technicien(s)
Maryse Gallant
maryse.gallant@cegep-sept-iles.qc.ca
418-962-9848 ext. 296
Nancy Malenfant
nancy.malenfant@cegep-sept-iles.qc.ca
418-962-9848 ext. 211

***Shawinigan:* Collège Shawinigan Bibliothèque**
2263, av du Collège
Shawinigan, QC G9N 6V8
Adresse postale: CP 610
Shawinigan, QC G9N 6V8
819-539-6401 ext: 2287
Téléc: 819-539-8819
Couriel: comptoir@collegeshawinigan.qc.ca
URL: www.collegeshawinigan.ca/bibliotheque-services-offerts
Sigle: QSHC
Fondée en: 1969
Heures: L-J 8h-19h30; V 8h15-16h30
Budget d'acquisitions: $50,000 - $99,999
Population desservie: 0
Services:
Prêts entre bibliothèques(PEB)
Lecteur/reproduction de microformes: Lecteurs
Personnel: *Sommaire:* 6 Total; 1 Professionnel(s); 2 Technicien(s); 3 Autre(s) employé(s)
Catherine Patry, Spécialiste, Moyen et techniques d'enseignement
cpatry@collegeshawinigan.qc.ca
819-593-6401 ext. 2219

Céline Bourque, Technicienne en documentation
cbourque@collegeshawinigan.qc.ca
819-539-6401 ext. 2288
Renée Pouliot, Technicienne en documentation
rpouliot@collegeshawinigan.qc.ca
819-539-6401 ext. 2218

Sherbrooke: Bibliothèque de droit et publications gouvernementales

2500, boul de l'Université
Sherbrooke, QC J1K 2R1
819-821-7519
Téléc: 819-821-7551
866-506-2433
Couriel: pretdr@usherbrooke.ca
URL: www.usherbrooke.ca/biblio/
Sigle: QSHERUD
Fondée en: 1961
Heures: L-J 8h30-19h; V 8h30-17h
Budget d'acquisitions: $250,000 - $499,999
Population desservie: 0
Collections spécialisées: Droit; publications gouvernementales
Sujets: Droit, droit de la santé, droit fiscal
Services:
Accès public à l'internet
Réseau en ligne
Prêts entre bibliothèques(PEB) frais de 12$
Lecteur/reproduction de microformes: Ordinateur; Lecteurs
Personnel: *Sommaire:* 9 Total; 4 Professionnel(s); 4 Technicien(s); 1 Autre(s) employé(s)
Claire Lecompte, Bibliothécaire responsable
claire.lecompte@usherbrooke.ca
819-821-8000 ext. 2433

Sherbrooke: Bibliothèque de musique

2500 boul. Université
Sherbrooke, QC J1K 2R1
819-821-8201
Téléc: 819-821-7635
866-506-2433
Couriel: comptoir.musique@usherbrooke.ca
URL: www.usherbrooke.ca/biblio/nous-joindre/musique/
Heures: L-V 8h30-16h30
Population desservie: 0
Personnel: *Sommaire:* 7 Total; 2 Professionnel(s); 3 Technicien(s); 2 Autre(s) employé(s)
Sylvie Bareil, Responsable
sylvie.bareil@usherbrooke.ca
819-821-8201

Sherbrooke: Bibliothèque des sciences de la santé

3001, 12e av nord
Sherbrooke, QC J1H 5N4
819-564-5296
Téléc: 819-820-6817
866-325-2433
Couriel: bsante@courrier.usherb.ca
bibliotheque.sante@USherbrooke.ca
URL: www.usherbrooke.ca/biblio/
Sigle: QSHERC
Heures: L-V 8h-21h; S 11h-17h; D 13h-17h
Budget d'acquisitions: $500,000 - $999,999
Population desservie: 0
Annotation: Ariel: 132.210.164.21
Sujets: Sciences de la santé, sciences infirmières
Services:
Prêts entre bibliothèques(PEB)
Personnel: *Sommaire:* 7 Total; 2 Professionnel(s); 3 Technicien(s); 3 Autre(s) employé(s)
Marthe Brideau, Directrice
marthe.brideau@usherbrooke.ca
819-821-8000 ext. 75297
Mireille Lapierre, Bibliothécaire
mireille.lapierre@usherbrooke.ca
819-821-8000 ext. 75298

Sherbrooke: Bibliothèque des sciences et de génie

Pavillon Marie-Victorin, Université de Sherbrooke
2500, boul de l'Université
Sherbrooke, QC J1K 2R1
Adresse postale: Université de Sherbrooke
Sherbrooke, QC J1K 2R1
819-821-7099
Téléc: 819-821-7245
866-506-2433
Couriel: pretsci@usherbrooke.ca
URL: www.usherbrooke.ca/biblio/
Sigle: QSHERUS
Fondée en: 1960
Heures: L-J 8h30-23h; V 8h30-21h; Sa, D 9h-17h
Budget d'acquisitions: $500,000 - $999,999
Population desservie: 0
Sujets: Biologie, chimie, mathématiques, informatique, sciences physiques, génie civil, génie chimique, génie électronique, génie mécanique, génie informatique
Services:
Accès public à l'internet
Réseau en ligne
Prêts entre bibliothèques(PEB)
Lecteur/reproduction de microformes: Lecteurs
Personnel: *Sommaire:* 10 Total; 2 Professionnel(s); 2 Technicien(s); 5 Autre(s) employé(s)
Pierre Adant, Responsable
pierre.adant@usherbrooke.ca
819-821-8000 ext. 63598
Hélène Bernier, Bibliothécaire
helene.bernier@usherbrooke.ca
819-821-8000 ext. 62584

Sherbrooke: Bishop's University John Bassett Memorial Library

2600 College St.
Sherbrooke, QC J1M 0C8
819-822-9600 ext: 2605
Fax: 819-822-9644
e-mail: ill@ubishops.ca
URL: www.ubishops.ca/library
National Library Symbol: QLB
Consortia Membership: Canadian Research Knowledge Network (CRKN); Conférence des recteurs et des principaux des universités du Québec (CREPUQ)
Founded in: 1843
Hours: Academic year: M-F 8:00am-12:00am; Sa, Su 11:00am-12:00am
Acquisitions Budget: $500,000 - $999,999
For Print: $500,000 - $999,999
For Electronic: $250,000 - $499,999
Special Collections: Archives of Bishop's University; Eastern Twp Archives; Archives of Church of England in Diocese of Quebec from year 1759 to the present; Map collection; Hon. C. Gordon McKinnon Collection of Canadiana; Bélanger-Gardner Collection;
Subjects covered: Humanities, Business, Social Sciences, Sciences
Services:
Remote Access
Internet Access
Access to Subscription Databases
Inter-Library Loan (ILL)
Microform Equipment: Computer; Reader
Personnel: *Summary:* 21 Total; 7 Professional(s); 7 Technical(s); 15 Other employees
Bruno Gnassi, University Librarian
bgnassi@ubishops.ca
819-822-9600 ext. 2483
Gary McCormick, Reference Librarian
gmccormi@ubishops.ca
819-822-9600 ext. 2608
Lorraine Smith, Acquisitions
lsmith@ubishops.ca
819-822-9600 ext. 2283

Sherbrooke: Canadian Agriculture Library - Sherbrooke

2000 College St.
Sherbrooke, QC J1M 0C8
819-565-9174 ext: 204
Fax: 819-564-5507
Hours: by appointment only
Diane Roy, Library Assistant
diane.royfontaine@agr.gc.ca

Sherbrooke: Cartothèque Jean-Marie Roy

A8-122, boul Université de Sherbrooke
Sherbrooke, QC J1K 2R1
Adresse postale: Université de Sherbrooke
Sherbrooke, QC J1K 2R1
819-821-7560
866-506-2433
Couriel: cartotheque-biblio@listes.usherbrooke.ca
URL:
usherbrooke.ca/biblio/nous-joindre/cartotheque-jean-marie-roy
Heures: L, V 8h15-17h; Ma-J 8h15-20h30; S 13h-17h
Budget d'acquisitions: $25,000 - $49,999
Matériel imprimé: $25,000 - $49,999
Population desservie: 0
Collections spécialisées: 80 000 photographie aériennes, orthophotographies, images satellitaires, données géospaciales, cartes, atlas
Sujets: Géographie physique, géomatique, cartographie, environnement, télédétection
Services:
Prêts entre bibliothèques(PEB)
Référence; accès électronique réservé à la communauté universitaire
Personnel: *Sommaire:* 3 Total; 1 Professionnel(s); 2 Technicien(s)
Lucie Gendron, Directrice
lucie.gendron@usherbrooke.ca
819-821-8000 ext. 63870

Sherbrooke: CÉGEP de Sherbrooke Centre des médias

475, rue du Cégep
Sherbrooke, QC J1E 4K1
819-564-6350 ext: 5231
Téléc: 819-564-4025
URL: cegepsherbrooke.qc.ca
Sigle: QSHERE
Fondée en: 1967
Heures: L-J 8h-21h45; V 8h-16h45
Budget d'acquisitions: $100,000 - $249,999
Matériel imprimé: $50,000 - $99,999
Matériel électronique: $10,000 - $24,999
Population desservie: 0
Sujets: Sciences, lettres et arts; Sciences de la nature; Sciences humaines; Sciences informatiques et mathématiques; Musique; Arts et Lettres; Danse; Arts plastiques; Histoire et civilisation
Services:
Accèss distance aux bases de donn
Accès public à l'internet
Réseau en ligne
Prêts entre bibliothèques(PEB)
Lecteur/reproduction de microformes: Lecteurs
Personnel: *Sommaire:* 11 Total; 1 Professionnel(s); 3 Technicien(s); 7 Autre(s) employé(s)
Francine Pelletier, Bibliothécaire
francine.peletier@cegepsherbrooke.qc.ca
819-564-6350 ext. 5233
Louise Marceau, Technicienne en documentation
louise.marceau@cegepsherbrooke.qc.ca
819-564-6350 ext. 5238

Sherbrooke: Centre hospitalier universitaire de Sherbrooke Hôtel-Dieu Bibliothèque

#1110, 580, rue Bowen sud
Sherbrooke, QC J1G 2E8
819-346-1110 ext: 21126
Téléc: 819-822-6745
URL: pole.usherbrooke.ca/fr/biblio/chus.html
Sigle: QSHERHD
Fermée au public
Heures: L-V 8h00-16h00
Budget d'acquisitions: $50,000 - $99,999
Population desservie: 0
Sujets: Médecine
Services:
Prêts entre bibliothèques(PEB)
Gilberte Poirier, Responsable

Sherbrooke: CHUS Hôtel-Dieu Bibliothèque médicale

#1110, 580, rue Bowen sud
Sherbrooke, QC J1G 2E8
Adresse postale: 580, rue Bowen sud
Sherbrooke, QC J1G 2E8
819-346-1110 ext: 21126
Téléc: 819-822-6745
Couriel: chushd@videotron.ca
URL:
www.chus.qc.ca/fr/volet-academique-ruis/bibliotheque-medicale/
Heures: L-V 8h-16havec rendez-vous seulement
Budget d'acquisitions: $50,000 - $99,999
Population desservie: 0
Annotation: Association des services de documentation en

santé de l'Estrie
Sujets: Médecine, soins infirmiers, tech médicale, administration
Services:
Prêts entre bibliothèques(PEB)
Personnel: *Sommaire:* 2 Total; 1 Professionnel(s); 1 Technicien(s)
Gilberte Poirier, Responsable
Gilbertepoirier.chus@ssss.gouv.qc.ca

Sherbrooke: Université de Sherbrooke Services des bibliothèques
Cité Universitaire
Sherbrooke, QC J1K 2R1
819-821-7550
Téléc: 819-821-7935
866-506-2433
URL: www.usherbrooke.ca/biblio/
Social Media: www.youtube.com/bibliosusherbrooke
www.facebook.com/BibliothequesUdeS
twitter.com/BiblioUdeS
Sigle: QSHERU
Membre d'un consortium: Canadian Research Knowledge Network (CRKN); Conférence des recteurs et des principaux des universités du Québec (CREPUQ)
Fondée en: 1964
Heures: L-J 8h30-23h; V 8h30-21h; S 9h-17h; D 11h- 17h
Budget d'acquisitions: $1,000,000 plus
Matériel imprimé: $1,000,000 plus
Matériel électronique: $1,000,000 plus
Population desservie: 0
Annotation: Accès à distance aux bases de données en ligne uniquement pour l'univ. de Sherbrooke
Services:
Accèss distance aux bases de donn
Accès public à l'internet
Réseau en ligne
Prêts entre bibliothèques(PEB) frais de 2 $
Lecteur/reproduction de microformes: Ordinateur; Lecteurs
Personnel: *Sommaire:* 75 Total; 23 Professionnel(s); 36 Technicien(s); 17 Autre(s) employé(s)
Sylvie Belzile, Directrice
sylvie.belzile@usherbrooke.ca
819-821-7550
France Paul, Responsable, Services techniques
france.paul@usherbrooke.ca
Pierre Adant, Responsable, Bibliothèque sciences et génie
pierre.adant@usherbrooke.ca
819-821-8000 ext. 3598
Diane Quirion, Responsable, Bibliothèque sciences humaines
diane.quirion@usherbrooke.ca
819-821-8000 ext. 3553
Karine Couture, Responsable, Bibliothèque droit et publications gouvernementales
karine.couture@usherbrooke.ca
819-821-8000 ext. 1096
Marthe Brideau, Responsable, Bibliothèque sciences de la santé
marthe.brideau@usherbooke.ca
819-564-5297

Sorel-Tracy: CÉGEP de Sorel-Tracy Bibliothèque Roland-Gaudreau
3000, boul de Tracy
Sorel-Tracy, QC J3R 5B9
450-742-6651 ext: 2703
Téléc: 450-742-1136
Couriel: bibliocomptoir@cegepst.qc.ca
URL: www.cegepst.qc.ca/biblio
Fondée en: 1969
Heures: 15 août-31 mai: L-J 7h45-17h; V 7h45-16h. 1er juin-12 août: L-V 8h-16h
Budget d'acquisitions: $25,000 - $49,999
Population desservie: 0
Services:
Accès public à l'internet
Réseau en ligne
Prêts entre bibliothèques(PEB)
Lecteur/reproduction de microformes: Ordinateur; Lecteurs
Personnel: *Sommaire:* 3 Total; 1 Professionnel(s); 2 Technicien(s); 3 Autre(s) employé(s)
Suzie Roy, Bibliothécaire
450-742-6651 ext. 2707

Sorel-Tracy: Rio Tinto Fer et Titane inc Bibliothèque
1625, rte Marie-Victorin
Sorel-Tracy, QC J3R 1M6
450-746-3000
Téléc: 450-746-4438
Couriel: rtft.info@riotinto.com
URL: www.rtft.com
Sigle: QSOCS
Fermée au public
Fondée en: 1950
Heures: J-V
Budget d'acquisitions: $25,000 - $49,999
Population desservie: 0
Collections spécialisées: Brevets
Sujets: Sciences physiques, génie, technologie
Personnel: *Sommaire:* 1 Total; 1 Professionnel(s);
Marc Duval, Bibliothécaire consultant
marc.duval@marc.duval@riotinto.com

Trois-Rivières: CÉGEP de Trois-Rivières Centre documentaire Louis-Martel
3500, rue de Courval
Trois-Rivières, QC G9A 5E6
Adresse postale: CP 97
Trois-Rivières, QC G9A 5E6
819-376-1721 ext: 2608
Téléc: 819-693-3844
Couriel: bibliotheque@cegeptr.qc.ca
comptoir.biblio@cegeptr.qc.ca
URL: bibliotheque.cegeptr.qc.ca/accueil
Sigle: QTCE
Fondée en: 1968
Heures: L-J 8h-20h; V 8h-17h
Budget d'acquisitions: $50,000 - $99,999
Matériel imprimé: $25,000 - $49,999
Matériel électronique: $25,000 - $49,999
Population desservie: 0
Annotation: Membre de l'Association pour l'avancement des sciences et des techniques de la documentation; Fédération des CEGEPS
Sujets: Éducation, enseignement général, sciences humaines pures et appliquées, littérature, philosophie, pédagogie
Services:
Accès public à l'internet
Réseau en ligne
Prêts entre bibliothèques(PEB)
Recherche
Lecteur/reproduction de microformes: Lecteurs
Personnel: *Sommaire:* 14 Total; 3 Professionnel(s); 4 Technicien(s); 7 Autre(s) employé(s)
Lucie Hamel, Directrice
lucie.hamel@cegeptr.qc.ca
819-376-1721 ext. 2609
Danièle Baillargeon, Bibliothécaire
daniele.baillargeon@cegeptr.qc.ca
819-376-1721 ext. 2609
Roger Charland, Bibliothécaire
roger.charland@cegeptr.qc.ca
819-376-1721 ext. 2603
Solange Coulombe, Technicienne en documentation
solange.coulombe@cegeptr.qc.ca
819-376-1721 ext. 2605

Trois-Rivières: Collège Laflèche Centre des ressources didactiques
1687, boul du Carmel
Trois-Rivières, QC G8Z 3R8
819-375-7346
Téléc: 819-375-7347
Couriel: cecile.baril@clafleche.qc.ca
URL: www.clafleche.qc.ca
intranet.clafleche.qc.ca
Sigle: QTCL
Fondée en: 1969
Heures: L-Me 7h45-18h; J, V 7h45-17havec rendez-vous seulement
Budget d'acquisitions: $25,000 - $49,999
Matériel imprimé: $10,000 - $24,999
Matériel électronique: $10,000 - $24,999
Population desservie: 0
Services:
Accès public à l'internet
Prêts entre bibliothèques(PEB)
Personnel: *Sommaire:* 3 Total; 2 Technicien(s); 1 Autre(s) employé(s)
Cécile Baril, Agente de bureau
cecile.baril@clafleche.qc.ca

Trois-Rivières: Matériauthèque
3500, rue de Courval
Trois-Rivières, QC G9A 5E6
Adresse postale: CP 97
Trois-Rivières, QC G9A 5E6
819-376-1721 ext: 2134
Téléc: 819-693-8023
Couriel: materiautheque@cegeptr.qc.ca
URL: cstp.cegeptr.qc.ca/biblio/services/materiautheque
Fondée en: 1978
Heures: L-J 8h-18h, V 8h-17havec rendez-vous seulement
Budget d'acquisitions: 0-$9,999
Matériel imprimé: 0-$9,999
Matériel électronique: 0-$9,999
Population desservie: 0
Sujets: Architecture, design d'intérieur, électrotechnique, méchanique du bâtiment
Services:
Accès public à l'internet
Personnel: *Sommaire:* 2 Total; 2 Technicien(s)
Karine Robichaud, Technicienne en documentation
karine.robichaud@cegeptr.qc.ca
Danielle Dufresne, Agente de bureau
danielle.dufresne@cegeptr.qc.ca

Trois-Rivières: Université du Québec à Trois-Rivières Service de la bibliothèque
3351, boul des Forges
Trois-Rivières, QC G9A 5H7
Adresse postale: CP 500
Trois-Rivières, QC G9A 5H7
819-376-5005
Téléc: 819-376-5144
800-365-0922
URL: www.uqtr.ca/biblio/
Sigle: QTU
Membre d'un consortium: Canadian Research Knowledge Network (CRKN); Conférence des recteurs et des principaux des universités du Québec (CREPUQ)
Fondée en: 1969
Heures: L-J 8h-22h45; V 8h-21h15; S, D 9h30-16h45
Budget d'acquisitions: $500,000 - $999,999
Population desservie: 0
Collections spécialisées: Biophysique, pâtes et papiers, études québécoises, psychologie
Sujets: Arts, sciences humaines, économie, sciences, génie, technologie, biologie, administration, chimie, éducation, arts et lettres, sciences pures, sciences appliquées
Services:
Accès public à l'internet
Réseau en ligne
Prêts entre bibliothèques(PEB)
Lecteur/reproduction de microformes: Ordinateur; Lecteurs
Personnel: *Sommaire:* 22 Total
Étienne Audet, Directeur adjoint - Services techniques et informatisés
Etienne.Audet@uqtr.ca
Éve-Marie Houyoux, Directrice adjointe - gestion du prêt et des collections
Eve-Marie.Houyoux@uqtr.ca
Benoit Séguin, Directeur du Service de la bibliothèque
benoit_seguin@uqtr.uquebec.ca

Varennes: Energy Technology Library / Bibliothèque sur le technologie de énergie
1615, boul Lionel-Boulet
Varennes, QC J3X 1S6
Mailing Address: CP 4800
Varennes, QC J3X 1S6
450-652-3210
Fax: 450-652-5177
National Library Symbol: QVNR
Founded in: 1992
Hours: M-F 8:00-4:30 by appointment only
Acquisitions Budget: $25,000 - $49,999
Subjects covered: Energy & Environment, Wastewater, Natural Gas, Photovoltaics
Services:
Internet Access
Inter-Library Loan (ILL)
Scientific & technical documents pertaining to energy efficiency & renewable energy research
Personnel: *Summary:* 1 Technical(s)
Marie-Josée Neveu, Manager
Marie-Josee.Neveu@RNCan-NRCan.gc.ca

Victoriaville: CÉGEP de Victoriaville Centre de documentation
475, rue Notre Dame est
Victoriaville, QC G6P 4B3
819-758-6401 ext: 2486
Téléc: 819-758-2729
URL: www.cgpvicto.qc.ca
Sigle: QVC
Fondée en: 1968
Heures: L-V
Budget d'acquisitions: $25,000 - $49,999
Population desservie: 0
Collections spécialisées: École du meuble et du bois ouvré
Services:
Accès public à l'internet
Réseau en ligne
Prêts entre bibliothèques(PEB)
Personnel: *Sommaire:* 4 Total; 1 Technicien(s); 3 Autre(s) employé(s)
Lousie Grondines, Spécialiste en moyens et techniques d'enseignement
grondines.louise@cgpvicto.qc.ca
819-758-6401 ext. 2486

Île-Perrot: Quebec Young Farmers' 4H Association
41 Grand Blvd.
Île-Perrot, QC J7V 4W3
514-453-1731
Fax: 514-453-7017
e-mail: office@quebec4h.com
Founded in: 1969
Hours: 9:00-12:00, 1:00-5:00
Subjects covered: Agriculture, Food, Life Sciences
Tammy Oswick-Kearney, Provincial Coordinator
tammy@qfaqyf.org

Saskatchewan

Humboldt: Prairie Agricultural Machinery Institute Resource Library
2215 - 8th Ave.
Humboldt, SK S0K 2A0
Mailing Address: PO Box 1150
Humboldt, SK S0K 2A0
306-682-2555 ext: 243
Fax: 306-682-5080
800-567-7264
e-mail: humboldt@pami.ca
URL: pami.ca/resources
National Library Symbol: SHPA
Consortia Membership: Saskatchewan Multitype Library Board
Founded in: 1974
Hours: M-F 9:00-12:00, 1:00-5:00
Special Collections: Farm equipment testing collection, Standards, OECD/Nebraska tractor tests
Subjects covered: Agricultural Machinery, Engineering, Agriculture
Services:
Inter-Library Loan (ILL)

Moose Jaw: Five Hills Health Region Resource Centre
455 Fairford St. East
Moose Jaw, SK S6H 1H3
306-694-0374
Fax: 306-694-0270
e-mail: inquiries@fhhr.ca
medlib@fhhr.ca
URL: www.fhhr.ca
Founded in: 1963
Hours: M, Tu, Th 8:00-12:00 by appointment only
Subjects covered: Medicine, Health Sciences, Nursing
Personnel: *Summary:* 2 Volunteer(s)

Moose Jaw: Saskatchewan Watershed Authority Library
111 Fairford St. East
Moose Jaw, SK S6H 7X9
306-694-3900
Fax: 306-694-3465
e-mail: comm@swa.ca
URL: www.swa.ca
Founded in: 1986
Hours: M-F by appointment only
Acquisitions Budget: $25,000 - $49,999
Subjects covered: Water Resources, Water Management
Services:
Inter-Library Loan (ILL)
Arlene Adam, Executive Assistant
arlene.adam@swa.ca
306-694-3989

Moose Jaw: SIAST Palliser Campus Palliser Library
600 Saskatchewan St. West
Moose Jaw, SK S6H 4R4
Mailing Address: PO Box 1420
Moose Jaw, SK S6H 4R4
306-691-8233
Fax: 306-694-3427
866-460-4430
Other contact info: Reference Desk, Phone: 306-691-8228
e-mail: libpal@siast.sk.ca
URL: libraries.gosiast.com
National Library Symbol: SMJT
Consortia Membership: Saskatchewan Multitype Library Board
Founded in: 1960
Hours: M-Th 8:00am-9:00pm; F 8:00-5:00; Sa, Su 1:00-5:00
Acquisitions Budget: $50,000 - $99,999
Subjects covered: Economics; Engineering; Technology; Industrial Arts; Business
Services:
Internet Access
Access to Subscription Databases
Inter-Library Loan (ILL)
Microform Equipment: Computer; Reader
Personnel: *Summary:* 4 Total; 2 Professional(s); 2 Technical(s); 2 Other employees
Beverley Brooks, Program Head & Technical Services Librarian
brooks@siast.sk.ca
306-691-8227
Jennifer Shrubsole, Librarian, Collection Development
shrubsolej@siast.sk.ca
306-691-8229

Prince Albert: Prince Albert Campus Library
1301 Central Ave.
Prince Albert, SK S6V 4W1
306-765-3333
800-267-6303
URL: www.fnuniv.ca/index.php/library-2/library-northern-main
Hours: Fall & Winter: M 8:30-4:30; Tu-Th 8:30-8:00; F 8:30-4:30. Summer: M-F 8:30-4:10
Note: Affiliated with the University of Regina; interlibrary loan available through the university
Special Collections: Monographs, periodicals, newspapers, & AV materials relating to the Indigenous people of North, South & Central America
Subjects covered: Indigenous Studies, Nursing
Services:
Internet Access
Access to Subscription Databases
Inter-Library Loan (ILL)
Nursing material
Glenda Goertzen, Library Technician
ggoertzen@fnuniv.ca
306-765-3333 ext. 7425
Kim Horner, Library Technician
khorner@fnuniv.ca
306-765-3333 ext. 7430

Prince Albert: Prince Albert Model Forest Association Inc. Library
#139, 1061 Central Ave.
Prince Albert, SK S6V 7G3
306-922-1944
Fax: 306-763-6456
URL: www.pamodelforest.sk.ca
Founded in: 1992
Hours: M-F 8:00-5:00
Note: Some publications available on website.
Subjects covered: Forest ecosystem, silviculture & biodiversity research reports

Regina: Canadian Agriculture Library - Regina
FCC Tower, Fl. 6
1800 Hamilton St.
Regina, SK S4P 4L2
Mailing Address: 1800 Hamilton St.
Regina, SK S4P 4L2
306-780-3855
Fax: 306-780-5018
National Library Symbol: SRRE
Founded in: 1969
Hours: M-F 8:00-4:00
Subjects covered: Agriculture, Resource Conservation
Personnel: *Summary:* 3 Total; 1 Professional(s); 1 Technical(s); 1 Other employees
Barb Senkow, Library Technician
barb.senkow@agr.gc.ca

Regina: First Nations University of Canada Library
1 First Nations Way
Regina, SK S4S 7K2
306-790-5950 ext: 3429
Fax: 306-790-5990
800-267-6303
URL: www.fnuniv.ca/index.php/library-2
National Library Symbol: SRIFC
Founded in: 1977
Hours: Fall & Winter: M-Th 8:00-8:10; F 8:00-4:10; Sa, Su 11:30-4:30. Summer: M-F 8:00-4:10
Acquisitions Budget: $50,000 - $99,999
For Print: $50,000 - $99,999
For Electronic: $10,000 - $24,999
Note: Affiliated with University of Regina; interlibrary loan available through the University
Special Collections: Eleanor Brass collection; Stewart Raby collection; Indian History Film Project; Microfilm/fiche collections; Special collection (rare material relating to Indigenous peoples)
Subjects covered: Arts, Culture, Education, Humanities, Communications, Indigenous Studies, Indian Art, Indian Education, First Nations History, Indian Languages, Linguistics & Literature, Social Work, Administration & Management
Services:
Remote Access
Internet Access
Inter-Library Loan (ILL)
Microform Equipment: Computer; Reader
Personnel: *Summary:* 15 Total; 3 Professional(s); 5 Technical(s); 7 Other employees
Phyllis G. Lerat, Head Librarian
plerat@fnuniv.ca
306-790-5950 ext. 3425
Belle Young, Library Technician
byoung@fnuniv.ca
306-790-5950 ext. 3427

Regina: Gabriel Dumont Institute of Native Studies & Applied Research Library
College West, University of Regina
#218, 3737 Wascana Pkwy.
Regina, SK S4S 0A2
306-347-4124
Fax: 306-565-0809
Other contact info: Borrowing Desk: 306-347-4117
e-mail: marilyn.belhumeur@uregina.ca
URL: www.gdins.org/library
gdi.voyager.uregina.ca
Consortia Membership: Saskatchewan Multitype Library Board
Founded in: 1980
Special Collections: Rare history collection; Native studies; Archives
Subjects covered: Métis history & culture
Services:
Internet Access
Computer lab; Computer lab
Personnel: *Summary:* 2 Total; 1 Professional(s); 1 Technical(s)

Regina: Regina Qu'Appelle Health Region - Wascana Rehabilitation Centre Health Sciences Library
1440 14th Ave.
Regina, SK S4P 0W5
306-766-4142
e-mail: library@rqhealth.ca
URL: www.rqhealth.ca/inside/hlthy_live_learn/library_page.shtml
Profile: Provides reference & research services, and extends borrowing privileges to RQHR staff & physicians, and students of medicine. Public may use the library during specified hours
National Library Symbol: SRSH
Hours: M-F 8:30-4:30
Acquisitions Budget: $25,000 - $49,999

Note: Online resources restricted to RQHR staff & physicians
Subjects covered: Rehabilitation
Services:
Remote Access
Internet Access
Inter-Library Loan (ILL) for a fee of $5
Current awareness, document delivery, photocopying
Microform Equipment: Reader
Personnel: *Summary:* 1 Total; 1 Technical(s)
Joan Harmsworth Dow, Library Technician
library@rqhealth.ca
306-766-5441

Regina: Regina Qu'Appelle Health Region Library Services - Regina General Hospital Health Sciences Library

1440 - 14th Ave.
Regina, SK S4P 0W5
306-766-4142
Fax: 306-766-3839
e-mail: library@rqhealth.ca
URL: www.rqhealth.ca/inside/hlthy_live_learn/library_page.shtml
Profile: Provides reference & research services, and extends borrowing privileges to RQHR staff & physicians, and students of medicine. Public may use the library during specified hours
National Library Symbol: SRG
Consortia Membership: Saskatchewan Multitype Library Board
Hours: M-F 8:00-4:30
Note: Online resources restricted to RQHR staff & physicians
Special Collections: RQHR Archives houses student records from Regina General Hospital School of Nursing
Subjects covered: Medicine, Nursing, Health Sciences
Services:
Remote Access
Internet Access
Inter-Library Loan (ILL)
Current awareness, document delivery, photocopying; library orientation & instruction
Microform Equipment: Computer; Reader
Personnel: *Summary:* 9 Total; 4 Professional(s); 4 Technical(s); 1 Other employees

Regina: Saskatchewan Environment Information Management / Geomatics

3211 Albert St., 3rd Fl.
Regina, SK S4S 5W6
306-787-3482
Fax: 306-787-3913
e-mail: Centre.Inquiry@gov.sk.ca
URL: www.environment.gov.sk.ca
National Library Symbol: SPAE
Founded in: 1974
Hours: M-F
Acquisitions Budget: For Print: $10,000 - $24,999
Special Collections: Department Annual Reports; Department Technical Reports; Saskatchewan Aerial Photos
Subjects covered: Forestry; Agroforestry; Ecology
Services:
Internet Access
Access to Subscription Databases
Inter-Library Loan (ILL)
Personnel: *Summary:* 1 Professional(s); 1 Technical(s)
Ginny Nisbet, Director, Information Management / Geomatics
306-787-2913

Regina: Saskatchewan Highways & Infrastructure Resource Centre

1855 Victoria Ave., 11th Fl.
Regina, SK S4P 3V5
306-787-2099
Fax: 306-787-8700
URL: www.highways.gov.sk.ca
National Library Symbol: SRHP
Founded in: 1973
Special Collections: Ministry manuals
Subjects covered: Transportation; Civil Engineering; Construction

Regina: Saskatchewan Institute of Applied Science & Technology Wascana Library

c/o Wascana Campus, 4500 Wascana Pkwy.
Regina, SK S4P 3S7
Mailing Address: PO Box 7150, Wascana Campus
Regina, SK S4P 3S7
306-775-7408
Fax: 306-798-0560
866-460-4430
Other contact info: Reference Information, Phone: 306-775-7401
e-mail: wascanalibrary@siast.sk.ca
URL: libraries.gosiast.com
Consortia Membership: Saskatchewan Multitype Library Board; Health Knowledge Network (HKN); Saskatchewan Health Information Resources Partnership (SHIRP)
No public access
Note: The library is an affiliate member of the Council of Prairie & Pacific University Libraries (COPPUL).
Heather West, Academic Director, Library & Testing Services
west@siast.sk.ca
306-775-7710
Robin Canham, Librarian, Services Assessment
canhamr@siast.sk.ca
306-775-7409
Rian Misfeldt, Librarian, Marketing
misfeldt@siast.sk.ca
306-775-7413
Juliet Nielsen, Librarian, Distance Education
nielsenju@siast.sk.ca
306-775-7412
Val Younge, Librarian, Emergent Technologies
youngev@siast.sk.ca
306-775-7411

Regina: SaskPower Corporation Operations Support Library

2901 Powerhouse Dr.
Regina, SK S4N 0A1
306-566-3333
Fax: 306-566-3348
e-mail: twrighteastley@saskpower.com
National Library Symbol: SRPCRD
Hours: M-F 8:00-4:30 by appointment only
Acquisitions Budget: $50,000 - $99,999
Special Collections: Periodicals, Research Reports, Standards
Subjects covered: Electricity, Energy
Services:
Inter-Library Loan (ILL)
Teresa Wright Eastley, Librarian
twrighteastley@saskpower.com

Regina: SaskTel Corporate Resource Centre

2121 Saskatchewan Dr., 12th Fl.
Regina, SK S4P 3Y2
306-777-2899
Fax: 306-359-9022
URL: www.sasktel.sk.com
National Library Symbol: SRST
No public access
Founded in: 1980
Hours: M-F 8:00-5:00
Acquisitions Budget: $50,000 - $99,999
Subjects covered: Telecommunications, Business, Management, Computing, Engineering
Services:
Inter-Library Loan (ILL)
Personnel: *Summary:* 2 Total; 1 Professional(s); 1 Other employees;
Colleen McMahon, Manager, Competitive Intelligence
306-777-1333
Charlene Kramer, Librarian
charlene.kramer@sasktel.sk.ca

Regina: Technical Library

#220, 6 Research Dr.
Regina, SK S4S 7J7
306-787-1881
Fax: 306-787-8811
National Library Symbol: SRRCP
Founded in: 1981
Hours: M-F 8:00-12:00, 1:00-4:30
Note: Photocopying Fee: $8/item; Microform copy Fee: $8/item
Special Collections: SPE (Society of Petroleum Engineers) microfilm collections
Subjects covered: Petroleum Engineering, Enhanced Recovery, Reservoir & Chemical Engineering, Analytical Chemistry
Services:
Access to Subscription Databases
Inter-Library Loan (ILL) for a fee of $10
Microform Equipment: Computer; Reader
Personnel: *Summary:* 1 Professional(s)
Nadine Zerr, Library Officer
zerr@src.sk.ca

Regina: University of Regina Dr. John Archer Library

3737 Wascana Pkwy.
Regina, SK S4S 0A2
306-585-4295
Fax: 306-585-4878
e-mail: Library.Admin.Office@uregina.ca
illsru@uregina.ca
URL: www.uregina.ca/library/
National Library Symbol: SRU
Consortia Membership: Canadian Research Knowledge Network (CRKN); Council of Prairie & Pacific University Libraries (COPPUL); Saskatchewan Multitype Library Board
Founded in: 1934
Hours: M-Th different times throughout the year
Acquisitions Budget: $1,000,000 plus
For Print: $1,000,000 plus
For Electronic: $1,000,000 plus
Special Collections: Canadian Plains, Local History, Aboriginal Peoples
Subjects covered: Arts, Humanities, Culture, Education, Science, Engineering, Social Work, Social Sciences
Services:
Remote Access
Access to Subscription Databases
Inter-Library Loan (ILL)
Microform Equipment: Computer; Reader
Personnel: *Summary:* 64 Total; 22 Professional(s); 2 Technical(s); 40 Other employees
William Sgrazzutti, University Librarian
william.sgrazzutti@uregina.ca
306-585-4132
Peter Resch, Associate University Librarian Planning and Assessment
peter.resch@uregina.ca
306-585-5107
Carol MacDonald, Associate University Librarian Systems and Information Technology
carol.macdonald@uregina.ca
306-585-4015
Colleen Murphy, Associate University Librarian Academic Liaison and User Services
colleen.murphy@uregina.ca
306-585-4028

Saskatoon: Ag-West Bio Inc.

#101, 111 Research Dr.
Saskatoon, SK S7N 3R2
306-975-1939
Fax: 306-975-1966
e-mail: agwest@agwest.sk.ca
URL: www.agwest.sk.ca
Founded in: 1989
Subjects covered: Science & Technology; Bio Product & Bio Processes; Health & Nutrition; Biotechnology; Business; Finance
Jackie Robin, Director, Communications
jackie.robin@agwest.sk.ca

Saskatoon: Cameco Corporation Library

2121 - 11th St. West
Saskatoon, SK S7M 1J3
306-956-6399
Fax: 306-956-6201
URL: www.cameco.com
National Library Symbol: SSMD
Founded in: 1962
Hours: by appointment only
Acquisitions Budget: $25,000 - $49,999
Subjects covered: Earth Sciences, Engineering, Mining, Environment, Nuclear Sciences
Personnel: *Summary:* 1 Professional(s); 1 Technical(s)
Phyllis Moen-Nijssen, Library Technician

Saskatoon: Canadian Agriculture Library - Saskatoon Western Region

107 Science Pl.
Saskatoon, SK S7N 0X2
306-956-7222
Fax: 306-956-7247
Other contact info: Alternate phone: 306-956-7223

National Library Symbol: SSAGR
Founded in: 1957
Hours: M-F 8:00-4:30 by appointment only
Acquisitions Budget: 0-$9,999
For Print: 0-$9,999
For Electronic: 0-$9,999
Subjects covered: Agriculture, Physical Sciences, Agronomy, Entomology, Crop Breeding & Protection, Biotechnology
Services:
Inter-Library Loan (ILL)
Personnel: *Summary:* 1 Professional(s); 1 Technical(s);
Joan Martin, Chief, Information Services, Western Region
joan.martin@agr.gc.ca
Kelly Dawson, Library Assistant
kelly.dawson@agr.gc.ca

Saskatoon: Engineering Library
#1B08, Engineering Bldg., 57 Campus Dr.
Saskatoon, SK S7N 5A9
306-966-5976
e-mail: victor.wiebe@usask.ca
URL: library.usask.ca/engin/
Hours: M-F 8:30am-4:30pm
Subjects covered: Engineering, Computer Science
Services:
Internet Access
Personnel: *Summary:* 1 Professional(s); 5 Technical(s)
Victor G. Wiebe, Engineering Librarian
victor.wiebe@usask.ca
306-966-5978

Saskatoon: Environment Canada Library Saskatoon / Bibliotheque d'Environnement Canada à Saskatoon
11 Innovation Blvd.
Saskatoon, SK S7N 3H5
306-975-4069
Fax: 306-975-5513
e-mail: librarybiblio.saskatoonec@ec.gc.ca
URL:
www.ec.gc.ca/scitech/default.asp?lang=En&n=44EEFEB3-1#nhrc
Profile: The library serves Environment Canada employees & members of the public interested in environmental research
National Library Symbol: SSEH
Founded in: 1986
Hours: M-F 8:30-4:00
Acquisitions Budget: $50,000 - $99,999
Note: The National Hydrology Research Centre (NHRC) library closed & merged with this branch of Environment Canada's library system.
Special Collections: Ornithology; hydrology; meteorology; general biology
Services:
Inter-Library Loan (ILL)
Microform Equipment: Reader
Personnel: *Summary:* 1 Total; 1 Professional(s)
Warren Wulf, Librarian, Information Management
warren.wulf@ec.gc.ca

Saskatoon: Health Sciences Library
#B205 Health Sciences Bldg., 107 Wiggins Rd.
Saskatoon, SK S7N 5E5
306-966-5991
Fax: 306-966-5918
e-mail: uaskhsl@library.usask.ca
URL: library.usask.ca/hsl
National Library Symbol: SSUM
Consortia Membership: Saskatchewan Health Information Resources Partnership (SHIRP)
Hours: M-Th 8:00am-10:00pm; F 8:00-6:00; Sa 10:00-6:00; Su 12:00-8:00
Acquisitions Budget: $500,000 - $999,999
Special Collections: Baltzan Medical Canadiana, Brodie History of Medicine
Subjects covered: Medicine, Dentistry, Nursing, Physiotherapy, Biochemistry, Microbiology, Pharmacology, Physiology, Pharmacy, Nutrition
Services:
Internet Access
Access to Subscription Databases
Inter-Library Loan (ILL) for a fee of varies
Fee Based Research
Personnel: *Summary:* 14 Total; 4 Professional(s); 7 Technical(s); 3 Other employees
Janet Bangma, Head Librarian
janet.bangma@usask.ca

Saskatoon: Law Library
#8, 15 Campus Dr., Ground Fl.
Saskatoon, SK S7N 5A6
306-966-6053
Fax: 306-966-6162
e-mail: Ken.Whiteway@usask.ca
lawill@sklib.usask.ca
URL: library.usask.ca/law/
National Library Symbol: SSUL
Founded in: 1912
Hours: by appointment only
Subjects covered: Law
Services:
Inter-Library Loan (ILL)
Microform Equipment: Reader
Personnel: *Summary:* 3 Professional(s)
Kenneth Whiteway, Law Librarian
Ken.Whiteway@usask.ca
306-966-6032
Mary Tastad, Reference Librarian
tastad@duke.usask.ca
306-966-6020
Greg Wurzer, Reference Librarian
Bryan Fredrickson, Head, Acquisitions
fredrickson@sklib.usask.ca

Saskatoon: Natural Sciences Library
#180 Geology Bldg., 114 Science Pl.
Saskatoon, SK S7N 5E2
306-966-6047
Fax: 306-966-1911
e-mail: nsmail@library.usask.ca
URL: library.usask.ca/nsl/
Hours: M-F 8:30am-4:30pm
Subjects covered: Physics, Chemistry, Biology, Computer Science, Maps
Services:
Inter-Library Loan (ILL)
Microform Equipment: Reader
Personnel: *Summary:* 7 Total; 2 Professional(s); 5 Technical(s);
Jane Lamothe, Head, Natural Sciences Library
jane.lamothe@usask.ca
306-966-6049

Saskatoon: NRC Information Centre - Saskatoon
110 Gymnasium Pl.
Saskatoon, SK S7N 0W9
306-975-5256
Fax: 306-975-6144
Other contact info: 306-975-5602
e-mail: nic.saskatoon@nrc-cnrc.gc.ca
URL: cisti-icist.nrc-cnrc.gc.ca/eng/locations/cisti/saskatoon.html
Founded in: 1948
Hours: M-F 8:30-4:30 by appointment only
Acquisitions Budget: $25,000 - $49,999
Subjects covered: Plant Biotechnology, Plant Molecular Biology, Plant Genetics
Services:
Internet Access
Inter-Library Loan (ILL) for a fee
Microform Equipment: Reader
Personnel: *Summary:* 2 Total; 1 Professional(s); 1 Technical(s)
Dianne Pammett, Information Specialist/Head
dianne.pammett@nrc-cnrc.gc.ca
Henry Chou, Client Services Officer
henry.chou@nrc-cnrc.gc.ca
306-975-5602

Saskatoon: POS Bio-sciences Information Services
118 Veterinary Rd.
Saskatoon, SK S7N 2R4
306-978-2811
Fax: 306-975-3766
800-230-2751
URL: www.pos.ca
Profile: The organization is involved in confidential contract research, toll processing & analytical services, and specializes in the extraction and purification of bio-based materials
National Library Symbol: SSPP
Consortia Membership: Saskatchewan Multitype Library Board
Founded in: 1977
Hours: M-F 8:00-4:00, by appointment by appointment only
Acquisitions Budget: $10,000 - $24,999
Note: Information services in support of the corporation's research and other activities
Subjects covered: Agriculture & food
Services:
Inter-Library Loan (ILL)
Fee Based Research
Personnel: *Summary:* 2 Total; 1 Professional(s); 1 Technical(s)
Aleksandra Hankey, Librarian
ahankey@pos.ca
306-978-2811

Saskatoon: Potash Corporation of Saskatchewan Inc.
Library Services
#500, 122 - 1st Ave. South
Saskatoon, SK S7K 7G3
306-933-8501
Fax: 306-652-2699
800-667-0403
URL: www.potashcorp.com
National Library Symbol: SSPCT
Founded in: 1979
Hours: M-F by appointment only
Special Collections: PCS Historical File
Subjects covered: Agriculture, Mining, Process Engineering, Environment, Marketing, Fertilizer, Business
Services:
Inter-Library Loan (ILL)
Microform Equipment: Reader
Personnel: *Summary:* 1 Total
Marybelle White, Library Coordinator

Saskatoon: Prairie Region
Regional Psychiatric Centre, Library
2313 Hanselman Pl.
Saskatoon, SK S7K 3X5
Mailing Address: PO Box 9223
Saskatoon, SK S7K 3X5
306-975-4850
Fax: 306-975-5186
e-mail: johnsonaa@csc-scc.gc.ca
URL: www.csc-scc.gc.ca/text/region/nat-fac-dir-eng.shtml#p1
National Library Symbol: SSRP
No public access
Founded in: 1978
Hours: M-F 8:00-4:00
Acquisitions Budget: $25,000 - $49,999
Note: Combined patient/staff library
Subjects covered: Forensic Psychiatry, Health Sciences, Medicine, Nursing, Psychiatry, Psychology, Psychiatric Nursing
Adrian Johnson, Librarian
johnsonaa@csc-scc.gc.ca
306-975-5442

Saskatoon: St. Paul's Hospital
Medical Library
1702 - 20th St. West
Saskatoon, SK S7M 0Z9
306-655-5224
Fax: 306-655-5209
e-mail: library@saskatoonhealthregion.ca
URL: libguides.saskatoonhealthregion.ca/medlib
No public access
Hours: M-F 7:30-4:00
Subjects covered: Medicine, Nursing, Health Sciences
Services:
Inter-Library Loan (ILL)
Personnel: *Summary:* 1 Technical(s)

Saskatoon: Saskatchewan Environmental Society
220 - 20 St. West
Saskatoon, SK S7K 3N9
Mailing Address: PO Box 1372
Saskatoon, SK S7K 3N9
306-665-1915
Fax: 306-665-2128
e-mail: info@environmentalsociety.ca
communications@environmentalsociety.ca
URL: www.environmentalsociety.ca
Founded in: 1988
Hours: M-F 9:00-5:00
Subjects covered: Nuclear energy; Water pollution; Energy efficient housing; Sustainable development; Community action; World watch papers & magazines; Environmental issues
Pam Belcher, Resource Worker

Saskatoon: Saskatchewan Research Council Information Services

#125, 15 Innovation Blvd.
Saskatoon, SK S7N 2X8
306-933-5489
Fax: 306-933-7446
e-mail: library@src.sk.ca
URL: www.src.sk.ca
National Library Symbol: SSR
Consortia Membership: Saskatchewan Multitype Library Board
No public access
Founded in: 1947
Acquisitions Budget: $25,000 - $49,999
Special Collections: SRC publications in the fields of agriculture, biotechnology, alternative energy, environment, mining
Subjects covered: Engineering, Technology, Physical Sciences, Business, Agriculture, Geology
Services:
Internet Access
Inter-Library Loan (ILL) for a fee
Personnel: *Summary:* 1 Total; 1 Professional(s)
Laurier L. Schramm, President & CEO

Saskatoon: Saskatoon Campus Library

#226, 230 - 20th St. East
Saskatoon, SK S7K 0A6
306-931-1800
Fax: 306-931-1847
800-267-6303
URL: www.fnuniv.ca/index.php/library-2/library-saskatoon-main
Founded in: 1985
Hours: Fall & Winter: M-Th 8:30-6:00; F 8:30-4:30. Summer: M-F 8:30-4:30
Acquisitions Budget: $50,000 - $99,999
Note: Affiliated with the University of Regina; interlibrary loan available through the university
Special Collections: Office of the Treaty Commissioner Collection
Subjects covered: Aboriginal Social Work, Indigenous Studies, Business Administration
Services:
Internet Access
Access to Subscription Databases
Inter-Library Loan (ILL)
Research
Microform Equipment: Computer; Reader
Personnel: *Summary:* 8 Total; 2 Professional(s); 2 Technical(s); 4 Other employees
Hongru Liu, Library Technician
hliu@fnuniv.ca
306-931-1800 ext. 5425

Saskatoon: Saskatoon City Hospital Medical Library

#1923, 701 Queen St.
Saskatoon, SK S7K 0M7
Mailing Address: 701 Queen St.
Saskatoon, SK S7K 0M7
306-655-8228
Fax: 306-655-8614
e-mail: library@saskatoonhealthregion.ca
URL: libguides.saskatoonhealthregion.ca/medlib
National Library Symbol: SSCH
No public access
Hours: M-F 7:30-4:00
Subjects covered: Medicine, Nursing, Health Sciences
Services:
Internet Access
Inter-Library Loan (ILL)
Personnel: *Summary:* 4 Total
Shirley Blanchette, Library Technician
blanchettes@sdh.sk.ca

Saskatoon: Saskatoon Health Region Health Records

Privacy & Compliance, Saskatoon Health Region, Saskatoon City Hospital
701 Queen St., Level 1
Saskatoon, SK S7K 0M7
306-655-7677
Fax: 306-655-8727
URL: www.saskatoonhealthregion.ca
Consortia Membership: Saskatchewan Health Information Resources Partnership (SHIRP)
Subjects covered: Health Sciences; Public Health

Saskatoon: SIAST Kelsey Campus Kelsey Library

1130 Idylwyld Dr. North
Saskatoon, SK S7K 3R5
Mailing Address: PO Box 1520
Saskatoon, SK S7K 3R5
306-659-4040
Fax: 306-964-1222
866-460-4430
e-mail: kelseylibrary@siast.sk.ca
URL: libraries.gosiast.com
National Library Symbol: SSSI
Consortia Membership: Saskatchewan Multitype Library Board
Founded in: 1963
Hours: M-Th 7:30-9:00; F 7:30-5:00; Sa, Su 10:00-5:00
Subjects covered: Health Sciences; Nursing; Trades & Technologies; Personal & Community Services; Adult Basic Education; Extension Services
Services:
Remote Access
Internet Access
Inter-Library Loan (ILL)
Microform Equipment: Reader
Fabian Harrison, Program Head & Training Librarian
harrisonf@siast.sk.ca
306-659-4240
Kelly Burke, Librarian, Borrower Services
burkek@siast.sk.ca
306-659-4241
Mike Sainsbury, Librarian, Information Literacy
sainsburym@siast.sk.ca
306-659-4774
Kristin Schoonover, Librarian, Archives & Digitization
schoonover@siast.sk.ca
306-659-4425

Saskatoon: SIAST Kelsey Campus Kelsey Avenue West Centre

450 Ave. West North
Saskatoon, SK S7K 3R5
Mailing Address: PO Box 1520
Saskatoon, SK S7K 3R5
306-659-4929
Fax: 306-964-1222
866-460-4430
e-mail: kelseylibrary@siast.sk.ca
URL: libraries.gosiast.com
Consortia Membership: Saskatchewan Multitype Library Board
Robert D. O'Neil, Coordinator, Library Services

Saskatoon: University of Saskatchewan Murray Library

Main Library, Murray Bldg.,#156, 3 Campus Dr.
Saskatoon, SK S7N 5A4
306-966-5927
Fax: 306-966-5932
TDD: 3069665921
e-mail: frank.winter@usask.ca
URL: library.usask.ca
National Library Symbol: SSU
Consortia Membership: Canadian Research Knowledge Network (CRKN); Council of Prairie & Pacific University Libraries (COPPUL); Health Knowledge Network (HKN); Saskatchewan Multitype Library Board
Founded in: 1912
Hours: M-Su
Acquisitions Budget: $1,000,000 plus
For Print: $1,000,000 plus
For Electronic: $1,000,000 plus
Special Collections: Adam Shortt Library of Western Canadiana
Services:
Internet Access
Inter-Library Loan (ILL)
Personnel: *Summary:* 147 Total; 41 Professional(s); 94 Technical(s); 12 Other employees
Vicki Williamson, Dean
vicki.williamson@usask.ca
306-966-5927
Ken Ladd, Associate Dean
ken.ladd@usask.ca
306-966-5946
David Fox, Head, Information Technology Services & Technical Services
david.fox@usask.ca
306-966-6031
Linda Fritz, Head, Research Services
linda.fritz@usask.ca
306-966-6003
Carol Shepstone, Head, Access Services
carol.shepstone@usask.ca
306-966-5960

Saskatoon: Western Development Museum George Shepherd Library

2935 Melville St
Saskatoon, SK S7J 5A6
306-934-1400
Fax: 306-934-4467
800-363-6345
e-mail: info@wdm.ca
URL: www.wdm.ca
Social Media: www.youtube.com/user/SKWDM
www.facebook.com/skwdm?ref=ts
twitter.com/SaskWDM
Founded in: 1972
Hours: M-F 8:30-4:30
Acquisitions Budget: 0-$9,999
Warren Clubb, Exhibits Curator
wclubb@wdm.ca
306-934-1400
Juanelle Finlay, Library Technician
jfinlay@wdm.ca
306-934-1400

Swift Current: Semi-Arid Prairie Agricultural Research Centre Canadian Agriculture Library - Swift Current

PO Box 1030
Swift Current, SK S9H 3X2
306-778-7260
Fax: 306-778-3188
National Library Symbol: SSCAG
Founded in: 1921
Hours: M-F 8:00-4:30 by appointment only
Subjects covered: Cereal & Forage Production, Agrometeorology, Soil Science
Services:
Inter-Library Loan (ILL)
Microform Equipment: Computer; Reader
Personnel: *Summary:* 1 Professional(s); 1 Other employees
Aidan Beaubier, Head Librarian
aidan.beaubier@agr.gc.ca
Kathryn H. Olson, Library Assistant
kathie.olson@agr.gc.ca

Yukon Territory

Whitehorse: Pacific & Yukon Region - Whitehorse Library - Environment Canada

91782 route Alaska
Whitehorse, YT Y1A 5X7
Mailing Address: 91782 Alaska Hwy.
Whitehorse, YT Y1A 5X7
867-667-3407
Fax: 867-667-7962
e-mail: librarybiblio.whitehorse@ec.gc.ca
National Library Symbol: YWEEP
Founded in: 1978
Hours: Tu 8:30-2:30 by appointment only
Services:
Inter-Library Loan (ILL)
Microform Equipment: Reader

Whitehorse: Yukon Chamber of Mines

3151B Third Ave.
Whitehorse, YT Y1A 1G1
867-667-2090
Fax: 867-668-7127
e-mail: info@yukonminers.ca
URL: www.yukonminers.ca
Hours: M-F by appointment only
Acquisitions Budget: $25,000 - $49,999
Subjects covered: Mining; Minerals; Mining History
Services:
Internet Access
Personnel: *Summary:* 1 Total; 1 Other employees
Michael Kokiw, Executive Director
info@yukonminers.ca
867-667-2090

Whitehorse: Yukon College Library

500 College Dr.
Whitehorse, YT Y1A 5K4
Mailing Address: PO Box 2799
Whitehorse, YT Y1A 5K4
867-668-8870
Fax: 867-668-8808
URL: library.yukoncollege.yk.ca
National Library Symbol: YWC
Consortia Membership: British Columbia Electronic Library Network (BC ELN); Electronic Health Library of BC (e-HLbc)
Founded in: 1983
Hours: M-Th 10:00-9:00; F-Sa 11:00-5:00; Su 10:00-9:00
Acquisitions Budget: $50,000 - $99,999
Subjects covered: Native Peoples & Northern Affairs
Services:
Internet Access
Access to Subscription Databases
Inter-Library Loan (ILL)
Microform Equipment: Computer; Reader
Personnel: *Summary:* 11 Total; 3 Professional(s); 3 Technical(s); 5 Other employees
Robert Sutherland, Manager, Library, Archives & Record Management
rsuther@yukoncollege.yk.ca
867-668-8888
Aline Goncalves, Reference Librarian
agoncalves@yukoncollege.yk.ca
867-668-8727
Derek Yap, Cataloguing Librarian
dyap@yukoncollege.yk.ca
867-668-8769

Whitehorse: Yukon Conservation Society Library

302 Hawkins St.
Whitehorse, YT Y1A 1X6
867-668-5678
Fax: 867-668-6637
e-mail: ycs@ycs.yk.ca
URL: www.yukonconservation.org/ycs_library.htm
Founded in: 1968
Hours: M-F 10:00-2:00
Acquisitions Budget: $25,000 - $49,999
Services:
Internet Access
Personnel: *Summary:* 2 Professional(s)
Georgia Greetham, Office Coordinator

Whitehorse: Yukon Department of Energy, Mines & Resources Library

#335, 300 Main St.
Whitehorse, YT Y1A 2C6
Mailing Address: PO Box 2703 (K-335)
Whitehorse, YT Y1A 2C6
867-667-3111
Fax: 867-456-3888
e-mail: emrlibrary@gov.yk.ca
URL: www.emr.gov.yk.ca/library
National Library Symbol: YWED
Founded in: 1978
Hours: M-F 8:30-4:30
Acquisitions Budget: $25,000 - $49,999
Services:
Internet Access for a fee
Inter-Library Loan (ILL)
Personnel: *Summary:* 4 Total
Aimee Ellis, Head, Library Services
aimee.ellis@gov.yk.ca
867-667-3108
Anna Pearson, Research & Systems Librarian
anna.pearson@gov.yk.ca
867-456-3903
Margaret Donnelly, Research & Client Services Librarian
margaret.donnelly@gov.yk.ca
867-667-5818
Pam Walden, Aerial Photograph & Serials Technician
pam.walden@gov.yk.ca
867-456-3968

Whitehorse: Yukon Department of Environment Environment Yukon Library

PO Box 2703
Whitehorse, YT Y1A 2C6
867-667-3029
Fax: 867-393-6219
800-661-0408
URL: www.env.gov.yk.ca/mapspublications/library.php
National Library Symbol: YWRR
Founded in: 1983
Hours: M-Th 8:30-12:00, 1:00-5:00 by appointment only
Acquisitions Budget: $10,000 - $24,999
For Print: $10,000 - $24,999
For Electronic: 0-$9,999
Subjects covered: Natural History, Biology, Zoology, Wildlife Conservation & Management & Environmental Issues
Services:
Internet Access
Inter-Library Loan (ILL) for a fee
Personnel: *Summary:* 1 Technical(s)
Vicki McCollum, Librarian
vicki.mccollum@gov.yk.ca

Whitehorse: Yukon Energy Solutions Centre Library

206A Lowe St. 1st Fl.
Whitehorse, YT Y1A 1W6
867-393-7063
Fax: 867-393-7061
e-mail: energy@gov.yk.ca
URL: www.energy.gov.yk.ca
Founded in: 2001
Hours: M-F 8:00-5:00
Special Collections: Energy related publications
Subjects covered: Energy, Climate Change, Renewable Resources
Cathy Cottrell, Sr. Energy Efficiency Advisor
cathy.cottrell@nrgsc.yk.ca
867-393-7148

Whitehorse: Yukon Workers' Compensation Health & Safety Board Library

401 Strickland St.
Whitehorse, YT Y1A 5N8
867-667-5645
Fax: 867-393-6279
800-661-0443
e-mail: worksafe@gov.yk.ca
URL: www.wcb.yk.ca
Profile: A DVD library containing workplace health & safety videos.
Hours: 9:00-4:30
Acquisitions Budget: $500,000 - $999,999
Services:
Internet Access
Access to Subscription Databases
Linda Powers, Contact
linda.powers@gov.yk.ca

Non-government Publications

Alternatives Journal: Canadian Environmental Ideas & Action
c/o Faculty of Environmental Studies, University of Waterloo, 200 University Ave. West, Waterloo, ON N2L 3G1
519-888-4442, Fax: 519-746-0292, 866-437-2587
infoalternativesjournal.ca
www.alternativesjournal.ca
Circulation: 4,500 Frequency: 6 times a year; ISSN: 1205-7398
A theme-based publication dedicated to illustrating the relationships between the environment and social justice, politics and the economy. It looks at the challenges and issues related to the interaction of humanity and the environment, and the responses to those issues.
Tara Flynn, Executive Editor

The Atlantic Salmon Journal
Atlantic Salmon Federation, PO Box 5200, St Andrews, NB E5B 3S8
506-529-1033, Fax: 506-529-4438
tiffinic@nb.aibn.com
www.asf.ca
Circulation: 11,000 Frequency: 4 times a year
This magazine is the world's oldest publication regarding conservation-minded salmon angling, covering issues related to fly-fishing for Atlantic salmon and the over-all protection of the species.
Martin Silverstone, Editor

Between the Issues
Ecology Action Centre 2705 Fern Lane Halifax, Nova Scotia B3K 4L3
902-429-2202, Fax: 902-405-3716
info@ecologyaction.ca
www.ecologyaction.ca
Circulation: 3,500 Frequency: 3 times a year
Published by the Ecological Action Centre, the magazine provides updates on the activities of the centre, as well as information on environmental practices from around the world.

Canadian Environmental Protection
#201, 2323 Boundary Rd., Vancouver, BC V5M 4V8
604-291-9900, Fax: 604-291-1906
ebaum@baumpub.com
www.baumpub.com
Circulation: 20,000 Frequency: 8 times a year
This publication is one of Canada's most popular environmental trade publications, with four marketplace issues, an internet version and industry supplements. Some issues this magazine covers are bio-fuels, specialty gasses and air pollution.

Canadian Geographic
PO Box: 923 Main #200, 1155 Lola St. Ottawa, ON K1K 4C1
613-745-4629, Fax: 613-744-0947
editorial@canadiangeographic.ca
www.canadiangeographic.ca
Circulation: 222,000 Frequency: 6 times a year; ISSN: 0706-2168
Publication aims to promote Canada both to Canadians and around the world. It looks at issues relating to the nature and wildlife within Canada, and what can be done to preserve the natural Canadian landscape.
John L. Thomson, CEO & Publisher
Rick Boychuk, Editor

Canadian Journal of Environmental Education
Faculty of Education, Lakehead University, 955 Oliver Rd, Thunder Bay, ON P7B 5E1
cjee@lakeheadu.ca
cjee.lakeheadu.ca
Frequency: Annually; ISSN: 1205-5352
The journal's goal is to progress the scholarly pursuit of environmental education, by provoking thought and discussion through its articles. The journal receives online submissions from a variety of authors, and publishes a range of written work, such as essays, case studies, reports and reviews.
Bob Jickling, Editor
Connie Russell, Editor

Canadian Wildlife
350 Michael Cowpland Dr., Kanata, ON K2M 2W1
613-599-9594, Fax: 613-599-4428, 800-563-9453
info@cwf-fcf.org
www.cwf-fcf.org
Frequency: 6 times a year
Aimed at both teenagers and adults, this magazine covers issues relating to Canadian and international wildlife, and reports on the work of the Canadian Wildlife Federation.

Corporate Knights
#207, 147 Spadina Ave., Toronto, ON M5V 2L7
416-203-4674, Fax: 416-946-1770
inquiries@corporateknights.com
corporateknights.com
Circulation: 125,000 Frequency: 4 times a year
This magazine promotes clean capitalism, which is defined as having social, economical and environmental costs and benefits factor into the price of an item. They believe that by taking these costs into account, the economy will become an improved market.

EcoWeek.ca
#800, 12 Concorde Pl., Toronto, ON M3C 4J2
416-442-5600, Fax: 416-510-5133
dorchard@ecolog.com
www.ecoweek.ca
Frequency: Weekly
Formally EcoLog Week, this publication aims to show its readers how to live a green lifestyle, as well keeping the public up-to-date on environmental issues of the day, including the environmental regulatory programs, new developments in waste-treatment, and how to get involved with local environmentalist organizations.
Lidia Lubka, Editor

EcoCompliance.ca
#800, 12 Concorde Place, Toronto, ON M3C 4J2
416-422-5600, Fax: 416-510-5148, 888-702-1111
llubka@ecolog.com
www.ecocompliance.ca
Frequency: Monthly
A monthly national newsletter that examines the developments and amendments in Canadian environmental law. It gives its readers commentary on new legislation, proposed environmental bills, changing environmental legislation, and all other issues affecting enviromental law policies in Canada.
Lidia Lubka, Associate Publisher

Ecoforestry
Ecoforestry Institute Society, PO Box 5070 B, Victoria, BC V8R 6N3
250-595-0655
journal@ecoforestry.ca
ecoforestry.ca
Frequency: Quarterly
Journal looks at issues relating to the forestry industry using a low-impact approach to forest management. Its goal is to increase public awareness of ecoforestry by working with community organizations, offering workshops to the public and providing information.

EnviroLine
PO Box 77042 Chinatown, 4905 - 23 Ave. NW, Calgary, AB T2G 5J8
403-263-3272, Fax: 403-263-3280
enviroline@shaw.ca; enviroca@cadvision.com
www.envirolinenews.ca
Circulation: 500 Frequency: 20 times a year
Provides Western Canadian resource industries with reviews of important and up-to-date environmental issues.
Mark Lowey, Managing Editor

EnviroZine
70 Crémazie St., 7th Fl., Gatineau, QC K1A 0H3
819-997-2800, Fax: 819-994-1412, 800-668-6767
enviroinfo@ec.gc.ca
www.ec.gc.ca/envirozine
Circulation: Available online only Frequency: Monthly ISSN: English ed. ISSN 1499-1411; French ed. 1499-142X
This webzine covers a wide range of environmental issues that are of importance to Canadians. It provides information in several categories, such as Air, Climate Change, Environmental Action, Nature and Wildlife, Pollution, Science & Technology, Water, and Weather, and attracts readers from 58 countries.

Environmental Reviews
M-55, 1200 Montreal Rd., Ottawa, ON K1A 0R6
613-993-9101, Fax: 613-952-9907, 877-672-2672
pubs@nrc-cnrc.gc.ca; info@nrc-cnrc.gc.ca
pubs.nrc-cnrc.gc.ca
Circulation: 300 Frequency: Annually ISSN: 1208-6053
Publication presents reviews on a range of environmental issues and topics, emphasizing the effects humans have on natural and manmade ecosystems. Topics investigated in this publication include climate change, air and marine pollution, erosion and agroforestry.
Bruce P. Dancik, Editor
Bushra Waheed, Managing Editor
Cameron Macdonald, Director

Environmental Science & Engineering Magazine
#30, 220 Industrial Parkway South, Aurora, ON L4G 3V6
905-727-4666, Fax: 905-841-7271
sandra@esemag.com
www.esemag.com
Circulation: 19,000 Frequency: 6 times a year
This publicationis the largest documentary magazine in Canada and has articles on various environmental issues, including air pollution, water filtration, hazerdous waste, alternative energy, greenhouse gasses, among others.

Geoscience Canada
Geological Association of Canada, c/o Department of Earth Sciences, Room ER4063, Alexander Murray Building, Memorial University of Newfoundland, St. John's, NL A1B 3X5
709-864-7660; Fax: 709-864-2532
gac@mun.ca
www.gac.ca
Frequency: Quarterly; ISSN: 1911-4850
The purpose of the journal, published by the Geological Association of Canada, is to inform Canadians of local and international geological events that are of interest to them. The publication comprises articles, reports and papers.
Reginald A. Wilson, Editor

Green Living Magazine
Green Living Enterprises, 66 the Esplanade, Toronto, ON M5E 1A6
416-360-0044, 416-362-2387
info@green-living.ca
www.greenlivingmagazine.ca
Circulation: 150,000 Frequency: Quarterly
Green Living Magazine attempts to promote living a green lifestyle to its readers by providing information about organics, health, the environment and eco-consumer products. They support sustainable and healthy living and publicizing the green message.
Laurie Simmonds, Publisher

Green Solutions Magazine
P.O. Box 65001, RPO Chester, Toronto, ON M4K 3Z2
info@greensolutionsmag.com
www.greensolutionsmag.com
Frequency: 12 times a year
An online publication that provides information and solutions which are designed to help corporations and individuals create and maintain healthier environmental practices. It strives to help readers realize what can be done in order to improve the environment for the future.

HazMat Magazine
80 Valleybrook Drive, Toronto, ON M3B 2S9
416-510-6798, Fax: 416-510-5133, 800-268-7742
www.hazmatmag.com
Frequency: Quarterly
This magazine provides you with in-depth analysis of current issues related to environmental performance, emergency response, safety and water management. It is available in print or digital form.
Brad O'Brien, Publisher
bobrien@hazmatmag.com

Journal of Environmental Engineering and Science
M-55, 1200 Montreal Rd., Ottawa, ON K1A 0R6
613-993-9084, Fax: 613-952-7656, 800-668-1222
pubs@nrc-cnrc.gc.ca
pubs.nrc-cnrc.gc.ca

Frequency: 6 times a year ISSN: 1496-256X
This publication provides a forum for the discussion of environmental engineering and science research. Topics this journal explores include environmental engineering, physical and analytical sciences, life sciences related to environmental issues, health sciences, and oceanography.

La Maison du 21e siècle
2955, lac Lucerne, Sainte-Adèle, QC J8B 3K9
450-228-1555, Fax: 450-228-1555
info@21esiecle.qc.ca
www.21esiecle.qc.ca
Fréquence: 4 fois par an
Ce magazine encourage ses lecteurs à nourrir les maisons écologiques. Éditant depuis 1994, *La Maison du 21e siècle* se concentre sur l'efficacité énergétique de ménage et les matériaux qui sont plus respectueuses de l'environnement.
André Fauteux, Éditeur

Natural Life
Life Media, #52, B2-125 The Queensway Toronto, ON M8Y 1H6
416-260-0303, 800-215-9574
generalstore@LifeMedia.ca
www.life.ca
Circulation: 35,000 Frequency: 6 times a year; ISSN 0701-8002
This independently owned magazine has an international focus on providing intelligent and in-depth practical information on issues such as healthy cooking, organic gardening, sustainable homes, natural parenting, wellness and natural healing, eco-leisure and eco-travel and sustainable business.
Wendy Priesnitz, Editor
Rolf Priesnitz, Publisher

Nature Canada
c/o Nature Canada, #900, 84 Albert St., Ottawa, ON K1P 6A4
613-562-3447, Fax: 613-562-3371, 800-267-4088
info@naturecanada.ca
naturecanada.ca
Circulation: 26,400 Frequency: 4 times a year; ISSN: 0374-9894
The mission of this magazine is to protect nature, its diversity and the processes that sustain it, and does this by providing information regarding several environmental topics including bird conservation, wilderness protection, endangered species and national parks. The publication supports community-based efforts to protect wildlife; encourages the development of an effective network of parks and protected areas across Canada; and promoting biodiversity in Canada and abroad.

ON Nature
Federation of Ontario Naturalists, #612, 214 King St. West, Toronto, ON M5H 3S6
416-444-8419, Fax: 416-444-9866, 800-440-2366
onnature@ontarionature.org
Circulation: 14,500 Frequency: 4 times a year; ISSN: 0227-793X
ON Nature attempts to bring its readers closer to nature by providing information about Ontario's natural areas and wildlife, and by providing insight into current environmental issues. Magazine features articles by nature specialists, colour photography, information regarding wilderness travel and up-to-date news on conservation battles.
Caroline Schultz, Executive Director
Victoria Foote, Editor

Québec Oiseaux
1251, rue Rachel est, Montréal, QC H2S 2J9
514-521-8356, Fax: 514-521-5711
quebecoiseaux@aqgo.qc.ca
www.quebecoiseaux.qc.ca
Tirage: 7 928 Fréquence: 4 fois par an
Québec Oiseaux fournit ses lecteurs avec des informations sur le sujet des oiseaux et l'observation des oiseaux au Québec. Aussi, il présente des conseils et des livres qui peuvent aider promouvoir l'activité de l'observation des oiseaux.
Michel Préville, Rédacteur-en-chef

Recycling Canada
PO Box 378, Campbellford, ON K0L 1L0
705-653-1112, Fax: 705-653-1113
dbp@personainternet.com
Mark Sabourin, Publisher & Editor

Recycling Product News
#201, 2323 Boundary Rd., Vancouver, BC V5M 4V8
604-291-9900, Fax: 604-291-1906
ebaum@baumpub.com
www.baumpub.com
Circulation: 18,000 Frequency: 8 times a year
Publication focuses on products, technologies services and industry news in recycling and waste management, ranging from composting to scrap metal.
Engelbert J. Baum, Publisher
Keith Barker, Editor

ReNew Canada: The Infrastructure Magazine
218 Adelaide St. West, 3rd Floor, Toronto, ON M5H 1W7
416-444-5842, Fax: 416-444-1176, 877-663-6866
renewcanada.net
Circulation: 30,000 Frequency: Bi-monthly
A national magazine that profiles the design, construction, financing models, management methods and leading-edge technologies behind infrastructure in Canada.
Mira Shenker, Editor

Shared Vision
#301, 873 Beatty St., Vancouver, BC V6B 2M6
604-731-1050
Circulation: 42,000 Frequency: 12 times a year
This publication attempts to help its readers live healthy, happy lives while creating and maintaining a sustainable society. The magazine features information on topics including green living, natural wellness, and organic food.
Rebecca Edhraim, Publisher

Solid Waste & Recycling
#800, 12 Concorde Place, Toronto, ON M3C 4J2
416-510-6798, Fax: 416-510-5133, 800-268-7742
bobrien@solidwastemag.com
www.solidwastemag.com
Circulation: 9,426 Frequency: 6 times a year
This publication dicusses all issues and topics pertaining to recyling and waste management.

The Sustainable Times
1225 Prospect Bay Rd., Prospect Village, NS B3T 2A6
902-850-2510
times@chebucto.ns.ca
www.sustainabletimes.ca
Circulation: Online only
A webzine that discusses and publicizes global issues including environmetalism, the Third World, and Fair Trade. The webzine is published by CUSO, which works for sustainable developtment in places such as Africa, Asia, Latin America and the Caribbean.
Sean Kelly, Editor

Vecteur Environnement
#220, 911, rue Jean-Talon est, Montréal, QC H2R 1V5
514-270-7110, Fax: 514-270-7154
info@reseau-environnement.com
www.reseau-environnement.co m
Tirage: 4 000 Fréquence: 5 fois par an; français
Revue de l'industrie, des sciences et techniques de l'environnement du Québec; publiée par RÉSEAU environnement
Martine Boivin, Rédactrice-en-chef

Voir Vert
1500, boul. Jules-Poitras, bur. 200, Ville Saint-Laurent, QC, H4N 1X7
514-339-2267
info@voirvert.ca
www.voirvert.ca
Tirage: 21 000 Fréquence: 4 fois par an
Voir Vert est une publication qui se concentre sur le sujet de la durabilité au Québec. Il fournit des informations aux sujets des méthodes de construction et de conception viables.
Anik Girard, Éditeur

Water Canada
218 Adelaide St. West, 3rd Floor, Toronto, ON M5H 1W7
416-444-5842, Fax: 416-444-1176, 877-663-6866
watercanada.net
Circulation: 15,000 Frequency: Bi-monthly
Todd Latham, Publisher, todd@watercanada.net
Water Canada discusses water quality and stewardship in Canada. It holds news and information on drinking water, residential and commercial water treatment, source water protection and conservation, wastewater treatment, stormwater management, water resource management, technology advancement, policy and governance, business and investment, and waterworks infrastrcture.

Watershed Sentinel
PO Box 1270, Comox, BC V9M 7Z8
250-339-6117
editor@watershedsentinel.ca
www.watershedsentinel.ca
Circulation: 5,000 Frequency: 6 times a year
This West Coast based publication focuses on how humanity affect the environment around them, by looking at issues such as logging and fishing practices and air and water pollution. It covers both bioregional and global perspectives on topics such as the environment, health and sustainability.
Delores Broten, Publisher & Editor

Women & Environments International Magazine
HNES Building, room 234, York University, 4700 Keele St., Toronto, ON M3J 1P3
416-736-2100, Fax: 416-736-5679
weimag@yorku.ca
www.weimag.com
Circulation: 2,000 Frequency: 2 times a year
Publication examines the relationships between women and the environment from a feminist perspective. It provides a forum for academic research and theory, professional practice and community experience and covers topics such as ecology and environmental activism, community development, childcare, and urban and rural agriculture.
Prabha Khosla
Reggie Modlich

Government Distribution Centres

The following offices may be contacted for copies of federal/provincial legislation.

Canada

Communications Canada
The documents comprising the Consolidated Statutes & Regulations are reproduced in HTML only & are not available in PDF. Documents can be reproduced in accordance with the Reproduction of Federal Law Order.
For federal statutes & regulations see: laws-lois.justice.gc.ca/

Alberta

Queen's Printer
Edmonton BookstoreFifth Floor, Park Plaza10611 - 98 AvenueEdmonton AB T5K 2P7; 780-427-4952; Fax: 780-452-0668; Toll Free: 800-310-0000; Email: qp@gov.ab.ca; URL: www.qp.gov.ab.ca/
For provincial statutes & regulations see: www.qp.gov.ab.ca/catalogue/display/cfm?page_id=40
The monthly e-Bookmark newsletter is produced by the Alberta Queen's Printer to keep customers informed of changes toAlberta's laws, as well as new and updated products andservices via email. To subscribe, send an email or fax as listed above, including your email address.

British Columbia

British Columbia
Crown Publications, Inc.106 Ontario St.Victoria, BC, V8V 1M9; 250-386-4636; Fax: 250-386-0221; Email: crown@crownpub.bc.ca; URL: www.crownpub.bc.ca
Crown Bookstore 514 Government St.Victoria BC V8L 2L7; 250-356-6778; Fax: 250-356-0404; URL: crownpub.bc.ca/
For provincial statutes & regulations see: www.leg.bc.ca

Manitoba

Statutory Publications
20-200 Vaughan St. Winnipeg MB R3C 1T5; 204-945-3101; Toll free Manitoba only: 1-800-321-1203; Fax: 204-945-7172; Email: statpub@gov.mb.ca; URL: www.gov.mb.ca/queensprinter
For provincial statutes & regulations see URL above.

New Brunswick

Queen's Printer
#117, 670 King St.Fredericton NB E3B 5H1; 506-453-2520; Fax: 506-457-7899; Email: queens.printer@gnb.ca; URL: www.gnb.ca/0062/acts/index-e.asp
For provincial statutes see URL above.

Newfoundland & Labrador

Queen's Printer
Office of the Queen's Printer Dept. of Government Services Ground Floor, Confederation Building, East Block PO Box 8700 St. John's NF A1B 4J6; 709-729-3649; URL: www.gs.gov.nl.ca/printer/index.html
For provincial statutes & regulations see: www.assembly.nl.ca

Northwest Territories

Northwest Territories
Consolidations of statutes & regulations can be viewed in either PDF or WordPerfect. See: www.justice.gov.nt.ca/legislation/searchleg®.shtml

Nova Scotia

Government Publications
PO Box 637 Halifax NS, B3J 2T3; 902-424-5200; Fax: 902-424-0516; Toll free within Nova Scotia: 800-670-4357; URL: www.gov.ns.ca/snsmr/publications/
For provincial statutes & regulations see:www.gov.ns.ca/legislature/legc//index.htm

Nunavut

Law Library
Nunavut Justice Centre, Building 510; PO Box 297 Iqaluit NU X0A 0H0; 867-975-6134; Fax: 867-975-6380; Email: courtlibrary@gov.nu.ca; URL: www.nucj.ca/library/library..htm
For territorial statutes & regulations see URL above.

Ontario

Publications Ontario
50 Grosvenor St.Toronto ON M7A 1N8416-326-5300Toll free in Ontario: 800-668-9938; Fax: 613-566-2234; Toll free in Ontario: 800-268-7095; URL: www.publications.serviceontario.ca/ecom
For provincial statutes & regulations see: www.e-laws.gov.on.ca/

Prince Edward Island

Queen's Printer & Document Publishing Centre
Island Information Service PO Box 2000 Charlottetown PE C1A 7N8; 902-368-4000; Email: island@gov.pe.ca; URL: www.gov.pe.ca/publications/index.php3
For provincial statutes & regulations see: www.gov.pe.ca/law/index.php3

Québec

Les Publications du Québec
1000, route de l'Église, 5e étage Québec, QC G1V 3V9; 418-643-5150 Toll free in Québec: 800-463-2100; Email: publicationsduquebec@spq.gouv.qc.ca; URL: www.publicationsduquebec.gouv.qc.ca
For provincial statutes & regulations see URL above.

Saskatchewan

Queen's Printer
#B19, 3085 Albert St. Regina SK S4S 0B1; 306-787-6894; Toll Free in Saskatchewan: 800-226-7302; Fax: 306-798-0835; Email: qprinter@gov.sk.ca; URL: www.qp.gov.sk.ca/
For provincial statutes & regulations see URL above.

Yukon

Queen's Printer Subscriptions
Box 2703Whitehorse YK Y1A 2C6; 867-667-8573; Fax: 867-393-6210; Email: queens.printer@gov.yk.ca; URL: www.hpw.gov.yk.ca/selling/legissubs.html
For territorial statutes & regulations see: www.justice.gov.yk.ca/legislation/index.html

Research Centres

Acadia University (ACER)
Acadia Centre for Estuarine Research
War Memorial House, PO Box 115, 23 Westwood Ave., Wolfville NS B4P 2R6 Canada
Tel: 902-585-1113; *Fax:* 902-585-1054
science.acadiau.ca/cer
Overview: A organization founded in 1985
Mission: Research facility with a focus on estuaries and nearshore coastal waters. The Centre is focused primarily in the Bay of Fundy, Gulf of Maine, and Georges Bank, as well as various international projects through Acadia University. Projects include environmental impact studies, sediment and soil erosion studies, and research of wildlife activities.

Acadia University (AIAE)
The Arthur Irving Academy for the Environment
Acadia University, PO Box 90, 52 University Dr., Wolfville NS B4P 2R6 Canada
Tel: 902-585-1311; *Fax:* 902-585-1055
e-mail: academy@acadiau.ca
aiae.acadiau.ca
Mission: Centre for interdisciplinary scholarship, education, and environmental advocacy. The centre focuses on sustainability and funding of research projects in the field of environmental sustainability

Acadia University
K.C. Irving Environmental Science Centre
Acadia University, PO Box 48, 32 University Ave., Wolfville NS B4P 2R6 Canada
Tel: 902-585-5242; *Fax:* 902-585-1034
kcirvingcentre.acadiau.ca
Mission: The K.C. Irving Environmental Science Centre opened in 2002 at Acadia University. The Centre is intended for the study of the natural environment, concentrating on the ecology of the native flora of the Acadia Forest Region of northeastern North America. The Centre functions as both a research and teaching facility with classrooms, labs, and conference capabilities. The Centre is also home to the six-acre Harriet Irving Botanical Gardens which features a collection of native plants including rare and endangered species.

Acadia University
Centre for Wildlife & Conservation Biology
Dept. of Biology, Acadia University, Wolfville NS B4P 2R6 Canada
Tel: 902-585-1870; *Fax:* 902-585-1059
www.acadiau.ca/~smockfor
Overview: A organization founded in 1992
Mission: The Centre for Wildlife and Conservation Biology (CWCB) aims to integtate research and education to promote the importance of biodiversity stewardship. The Centre works in conjutction with the Biology Department of Acadia University, focusing on research in protected areas management, forestry and wildlife, and species at risk.

Acadia University
Morton Centre
Heckman's Island, Lunenburg NS Canada
ees.acadiau.ca/morton.html
Overview: A organization founded in 1995
Mission: The centre is currently focusing on collecting baseline data using Environment Canada's protocol Ecological Monitoring and Assessment Network (EMAN). The following five focus research areas will branch out from there: Social Ecology, Earth Systems, Biodiversity & Ecosystems, Environmental Conditions Monitoring, and Applied Sustainability. In the future the centre will develop methods to share knowledge with the Acadia University faculty and the general public within the county and island.

Alberta Biodiversity Monitoring Institute
Vegreville
ABMI Monitoring Centre, Alberta Research Council, PO Box 4000, Vegreville AB T9C 1T4
Tel: 780-632-8356; *Fax:* 780-632-8379

Alberta Sulphur Research Ltd. (ASRL)
Center for Applied Catalysis & Industrial Sulfur Chemistry, #6, 3535 Research Rd. NW, University Research Centre, Calgary AB T2L 2K8
Tel: 403-220-5346; *Fax:* 403-284-2054
e-mail: asrinfo@ucalgary.ca
www.chem.ucalgary.ca/asr
Overview: A organization founded in 1964
Mission: The non-profit sulfur research organization focuses upon the following areas of research: the environmental aspects of gas & sulfur industries, the handling & transportation of elemental sulfur, the recovery of sour natural gas, & Claus plant operations.

Alberta Water Research Institute (AWRI)
Manulife Place, #2410, 10180 - 101 St., Edmonton AB T5J 3S4
Tel: 780-701-5406; *Fax:* 780-420-0018
Overview: A organization founded in 2007
Mission: Administered through the Alberta Ingenuity Fund, the Alberta Water Research Institute coordinates research to support Alberta's water strategy. The provincial water strategy contains goals such as healthy aquatic ecosystems, a safe & secure drinking water supply, & a reliable water supply for a sustainable economy. The Institute's activity areas include strategic research programs, joint tesearch collaboration, strategic opportunity studies, technology development & commercialization, & education & outreach.

Alex Fraser Research Forest (AFRF)
72 South 7th Ave., Williams Lake BC V2G 4N5
Tel: 250-392-2207; *Fax:* 250-398-5708
afrf.forestry.ubc.ca
Overview: A organization founded in 1987
Mission: Part of the Faculty of Forestry at the University of British Columbia, the Alex Fraser Research Forest has conducted more than 200 research projects in the Gavin Lake block & the Knife Creek block. The region provides a demonstration of integrated resource management, involving forestry, cattle, wildlife, & tourism.

Aleza Lake Research Forest Society (ALRF)
3333 University Way, Prince George BC V2N 4Z9
Tel: 250-960-6339; *Fax:* 250-960-6498
alrf.unbc.ca
Mission: The university-based, multidisciplinary, outdoor research facility studies the ecosystem & resource management of the wet sub-boreal spruce biogeoclimatic zone. Areas of research include environmental monitoring in small forest tenures, biological diversity, climate change, & partial cut harvest systems.

Aquaculture Collaborative Research and Development Program (ACRDP)
#@12E239, 200 Kent St., Ottawa ON K1A 0E6 Canada
Tel: 613-998-2904; *Fax:* 613-991-1378
e-mail: ACRDP-PCRDA@dfo-mpo.gc.ca
www.dfo-mpo.gc.ca/science/enviro/aquaculture/acrdp-pcrda
Mission: The Aquaculture Collaborative Research and Development Program (ACRDP) is an initiative of the Department of Fisheries and Oceans to increase the level of collaborative research. The ACRDP seeks to increase research in optimizing fish production, optimizing fish health, and optimizing environmental sustainability.

Athabasca University (ARBRI)
Athabasca River Basin Research Institute
Athabasca University, 1 University Dr., Athabasca AB T9S 3A3 Canada
arbri.athabascau.ca
Mission: An interdisciplinary research centre that studies the Athabasca River Basin and its people from a broad range of perspectives.

Atlantic Environmental Sciences Network
e-mail: aesn-info@ec.gc.ca
aesn-rsea.ca
Mission: The Atlantic Environmental Sciences Network (AESN) was established to facilitate in cooperative environmental research and training with the goal of creating environmentally sustainable economic development in Atlantic Canada. The AESN focuses on six major areas of research: Biodiversity, watersheds, environmental and human health, climate change, environmental engineering and waste management, and marine life/national capital valuation.

Atlantic Forestry Centre (AFC)
Corner Brook Office
PO Box 960, 26 University Dr., Corner Brook NB A2H 6J3 Canada
Tel: 709-637-4900; *Fax:* 709-637-4910

Atlantic Forestry Centre (AFC)
PO Box 4000, 1350 Regent St. South, Fredericton NB E3B 5P7 Canada
Tel: 506-452-3500; *Fax:* 506-452-3525
e-mail: afcinquiries@nrcan.gc.ca
cfs.nrcan.gc.ca/regions/afc
Mission: The Atlantic Forestry Centre (AFC) is a research facility under National Resources Canada based out of Fredericton, New Brunswick and Corner Brook, Newfoundland. The AFC conducts research projects in biodiversity, effects of air pollution and climate change, forest health, pest management, genetics, and risk analyses to advance forest ecosystem sustainability.

Atlantic Laboratory for Environmental Testing (ESC)
Morton Ave. & University Ave., Moncton NB E1A 6S8 Canada
Tel: 506-851-2622; *Fax:* 506-851-6608
www.ec.gc.ca/inre-nwri/Default.asp?lang=En&n=9DC31CC7-1
Mission: The Atlantic Region Environmental Science Centre is based out of the Université de Moncton Campus. The Centre conducts research in a variety of areas including the toxicity of pesticides and nonylphenol, studies on amphibians, studies on sand shrimp, and other areas. The Centre houses a chemistry laboratory that focuses on pesticides, oil analysis, and toxicology testing.

Bamfield Marine Sciences Centre (BMSC)
100 Pachena Rd., Bamfield BC V0R 1B0
Tel: 250-728-3301; *Fax:* 250-728-3452
e-mail: info@bms.bc.ca
www.bms.bc.ca
Overview: A organization founded in 1972
Mission: Established by the Western Canadian Universities Marine Sciences Society, the research & training facility supports coastal & marine research.

Bedford Institute of Oceanography (BIO)
PO Box 1006, 1 Challenger Dr., Dartmouth NS B2Y 4A2 Canada
e-mail: WebmasterBIO-IOB@dfo-mpo.gc.ca
www.bio.gc.ca
Overview: A organization founded in 1962
Mission: The Bedford Institute of Oceanography (BIO) is Canada's largest centre for ocean research, established in 1962. BIO performs targeted research through the Canadian Department of Fisheries and Oceans, the Geological Survey of Canada, the Department of National Defence, and Environment Canada. The research done at BIO ranges from navigational charts, fisheries studies, and offshore resource studies.

Biometeorology & Soil Physics Group of The University of British Columbia (BIOMET)
Faculty of Land & Food Systems, Univeristy of British Columbia, #266B, 2357 Main Mall, Vancouver BC V6T 1Z4
www.landfood.ubc.ca/biomet/index.htm
Mission: The University of British Columbia's Biometeorology & Soil Physics Group is engaged in the monitoring of carbon dioxide, water & energy exchanges between the atmosphere & forests. The Group focuses upon the effects of climate variability & disturbance on carbon sequestration. Some projects are as follows: CO2, H2O, & energy exchange between Douglas-fir west-coast temperate forests & the atmosphere; & the impact of mountain pine beetles on CO2, H2O, & energy exchange between northern lodgepole pine forests & the atmosphere.

The Bloom Centre for Sustainability
#101A, 2070 Hadwen Rd., Mississauga ON L5K 2C9 Canada
Tel: 905-822-4133
e-mail: BLOOM@bloomcentre.com
www.bloomcentre.com
Also Known As: BLOOM
Previous Name: Ontario Centre for Environmental Technology Advancement
Mission: Brings together public and private sector interests to drive change, and implement sustainability initiatives that deliver economic, environmental and social benefit.

Brandon University (RDI)
Rural Development Institute
McMaster Hall Complex, Brandon University, 270 - 18th St., Lower Concourse, Brandon MB R7A 6A9
Tel: 204-571-8515; *Fax:* 204-725-0364
e-mail: rdi@brandonu.ca
www.brandonu.ca/rdi
Overview: A organization founded in 1989
Mission: The not-for-profit research & development organization conducts multi-disciplinary academic & applied research on rural issues. Topics of research include environmental & agro-economic issues, rural / northern health & well-being, rural adaptation & change, & policy & program research & development.

British Columbia Environmental & Occupational Health Research Network (BCEOHRN)
c/o Henry Harder, Associate Professor, University of Northern BC, 3333 University Way, Prince George BC V2N 4Z9
Tel: 250-960-6506; *Fax:* 250-960-5744
www.bceohrn.ca
Overview: A organization founded in 2005
Mission: The BC Environmental & Occupational Health Research Network facilitates interdisciplinary research in the area of occupational & environmental health.

Brock University (ESRC)
Environmental Sustainability Research Centre
Brock University, 500 Glenridge Ave., St Catharines ON L2S 3A1 Canada
e-mail: ESRC@brocku.ca
brocku.ca/environmental-sustainability-research-centre
Mission: The purpose of the Environmental Sustainability Research Centre is to pursue innovative and interdisciplinary research concerning the environment, sustainability and social-ecological resilience.

Calgary Zoo
Centre for Conservation Research
c/o Calgary Zoo, 1300 Zoo Rd. NE, Calgary BC T2E 7V6 Canada
Tel: 403-232-9300
Toll-Free: 800-588-9993
e-mail: research@calgaryzoo.ab.ca
www.calgaryzoo.ab.ca/content/view/25/40/
Overview: A organization founded in 1999
Mission: The Centre for Conservation Research was established to develop conservation initiatives and to protect and restore endangered species and their ecosystems - both nationally and internationally.

Canadian Cooperative Wildlife Health Centre (CCWHC)
Atlantic Region
Atlantic Veterinary College, 550 University Ave., Charlottetown PE C1A 4P3 Canada
Tel: 902-628-4314; *Fax:* 902-566-0871
atlantic.ccwhc.ca
Mission: The Canadian Cooperative Wildlife Health Centre (CCWHC) is a cooperative effort encompassing all five Canadian Veterinary Colleges. The Cooperative seeks to apply veterinary medical sciences to the field of wildlife conservation and management in Canada. Additionally, the Cooperative is dedicated to developing knowledge of wildlife health and disease through research and education. Recent projects of the Atlantic branch include studies of raccoons and skunks in maritime provinces, beached whale recovery, and studies on birds in the Maritime region.

Canadian Energy Research Institute (CERI)
#150, 3512 - 33rd St. NW, Calgary AB T2L 2A6
Tel: 403-282-1231; *Fax:* 403-284-4181
e-mail: info@ceri.ca
www.ceri.ca
Overview: A organization founded in 1975
Mission: An independent, non-profit research organization, the Canadian Energy Research Institute is engaged in the study of energy economics & related environmental issues. Environmental issues involve production, transportation, & consumption. Research teams operate within the areas of oil, natural gas, electricity, & energy / environment. An example of research includes oil sands supply & carbon costs & the impact of low GHG intensity methods for oil sands development.

Canmet Energy Technology Centre (CETC)
Ottawa Research Centre, Natural Resources Canada, 1 Haanel Dr., Ottawa ON K1A 1M1
Toll-Free: 855-879-1211; *TTY:* 613-996-4397
www.canmetenergy-canmetenergie.nrcan-rncan.gc.ca
Overview: A organization founded in 1996
Mission: Natural Resources Canada's Canmet Energy is engaged in the research of clean energy & the development of clean energy technology. The energy research centre works to develop & deploy clean energy technologies in order to reduce air & greenhouse gas emissions & to improve the health of Canadians.

Canmet Energy Technology Centre (CETC - Devon)
Devon
Devon Research Centre, #202A, 1 Oil Patch Dr., Devon AB T9G 1A8
Tel: 780-987-8682; *Fax:* 780-987-5349
Mission: The Canmet Energy Technology Centre in Devon focuses on oil sands & heavy oil, in the development of cleaner fossil fuels & related technologies.

Canmet Energy Technology Centre (CETC - Varennes)
Varennes
Varennes Research Centre, CP 4800, 11615, boul Lionel-Boulet, Varennes QC J3X 1S6
Mission: The Canmet Energy Technology Centre in Varennes manages the RETScreen International Clean Energy Decision Support Centre. The Varennes Research Centre also directs programs in renewables, buildings & communities, & industrial processes. Examples of research projects are as follows: photovoltaic systems in buildings & stand-alone photovoltaic systems, integration of decentralized energy resources, industrial systems optimization, intelligent buildings, efficient refrigeration applications, & recommissioning.

Cape Breton University
Verschuren Centre for Sustainability in Energy & the Environment
Cape Breton University, PO Box 5300, 1250 Grand Lake Rd., Sydney NS B1P 6L2 Canada
Tel: 902-563-1292; *Fax:* 902-563-1360
www.cbu.ca/verschuren-centre
Mission: Cape Breton University's Verschuren Centre for Sustainability in Energy and the Environment was established to find innovative and sustainable solutions to energy and environmental issues.

Carleton University (CSERC)
Carleton Sustainable Energy Research Centre
River Bldg., Carleton University, #5142, 1125 Ccolonel By Dr., Ottawa ON K1S 5B6
www5.carleton.ca/cserc
Mission: SEC supports research into leading-edge policies and engineering technology. The research centre is integrating the work in sustainable energy by the Faculty of Engineering and Design and the Faculty of Public Administration, together with other faculties in the sciences, social sciences, economics and business.

Carleton University (CRUISE)
Carleton Research Unit on Innovation, Science & Environment
Carleton University, 1125 Ccolonel By Dr., Ottawa ON K1S 5B6
www6.carleton.ca/cruise
Mission: CRUISE is Carleton University's major initiative in the field of innovation, science and environmental policy and research. It is a leading example of Carleton's effort to focus on its areas of strength in science, sustainable development, energy and environmental policy.

C-Core Innovative Engineering Solutions
Captain Robert A. Bartlett Bldg., Morrisey Rd., St. John's NL A1B 3X5 Canada
Tel: 709-737-8354; *Fax:* 709-737-4706
e-mail: info@c-core.ca
www.c-core.ca
Overview: A organization founded in 1975
Mission: C-Core provides engineering services worldwide with a focus on solutions for the Energy industry. Specific areas of expertise include issues encountered in offshore oil and gas production, mining, pulp and paper, and gas transmission, with a focus on assessing and mitigating risk from ice environments.

Centre de recherche industrielle du Québec (CRIQ) / Quebec Centre for Industrial Research
1201 boul Crémazie Est, Montréal QC H2M 0A6 Canada
Tél: 514-383-1550; *Téléc:* 514-383-3250
Ligne sans frais: 800-667-4570
Courriel: infocriq@criq.qc.ca
Mission: While a major emphasis of research is on industrial equipment & productivity, eco-efficiency & innovation through sustainable industrial practices are an important focus. Among a number of projects, a study of recycling & reclamation of composite waste material is being developed.

Centre for Applied Science in Ontario Protected Areas (CASIOPA)
c/o Faculty of Environment, University of Waterloo, Waterloo ON N2L 3G1 Canada
Tel: 519-888-4567
e-mail: casiopa@uwaterloo.ca
casiopa.mediamouse.ca
Previous Name: The Parks Research Forum of Ontario
Overview: A organization founded in 2009
Mission: The Centre for Applied Science In Ontario Protected Areas (CASIOPA) provides state of the science workshops and networking for all those interested in protected areas with increased emphasis for solutions based on social, natural, and physical science for best practices in all types of protected areas.

Centre for Aquaculture & Environmental Research (CAER)
4160 Marine Dr., West Vancouver BC V7V 1N6
Tel: 604-666-7453; *Fax:* 604-666-3497
Mission: A collaborative effort between the federal Department of Fisheries & Oceans & the University of British Columbia, the Centre for Aquaculture & Environmental Research specializes in aquaculture & coastal research. The Centre's research into sustainable aquaculture & marine ecosystems concentrates on the following main topics: salmon migration physiology & ecology; coastal habitat issues; biotechnology & genomics; & aquatic animal nutrition.

Centre for Global Studies (PCIC)
Victoria - Pacific Climate Impacts Consortium
University House 1, PO Box 3060, Stn. CSC, Victoria BC V8W 3R4
Tel: 250-721-6236; *Fax:* 250-721-7217
e-mail: climate@uvic.ca
www.pacificclimate.org
Overview: A organization founded in 2005
Mission: A division of the University of Victoria's Centre for Global Studies, the Pacific Climate Impacts Consortium delivers climate system information, with a focus upon North America's Pacific Northwest. The Consortium works toward adaptation & the reduction of vulnerability to climate change, climate variability, & extreme weather events. The Pacific Climate Impacts Consortium studies sectors which face impacts of climate change, such as water resources, forestry, biodiversity, agriculture, & health.

Centre for Natural Hazard Research (CNHR)
Technical & Sciences Complex, Dept. of Earth Sciences, Simon Fraser U., 8888 University Dr., Burnaby BC V5A 1S6
Tel: 778-782-4924; *Fax:* 778-782-4198
www.sfu.ca/cnhr
Mission: Simon Fraser University's Centre for Natural Hazard Research is engaged in the physical & social scientific research of geophysical processes, such as climate change, landslides, floods, snow avalanches, volcanism, earthquakes, & tsunamis. In the area of climate change, for example, the Centre studies how some natural disasters, such as floods & landslides, occur more often due to global warming. Research, into land use planning, critical infrastructure, hazardous waste, & emergency planning, leads to sustained improvements to the environment & society through policy-making.

Centre for Ocean Model Development for Applications (COMDA)
Bedford Institute of Oceanography, PO Box 1006, Dartmouth NS Canada
Tel: 902-426-8232
www.dfo-mpo.gc.ca/science/coe-cde/comda-cmoa/index-eng.html
Mission: The Centre for Ocean Model Development for Applications (COMDA) was established to provide national leadership, coordination and advice in areas of ocean model development through the Department of Fisheries and Oceans. Research projects include the Canadian Network of Operational Oceanography Systems, the Canadian Operational Network for Coupled Environmental Prediction Systems, and the Canada-Newfoundland Operational Ocean Forecasting System.

Centre for Offshore Oil and Gas Environmental Research (COOGER)
Bedford Institute of Oceanography, PO Box 1006, Dartmouth NS B2Y 4A2 Canada
Tel: 902-426-1440
www.dfo-mpo.gc.ca/science/coe-cde/cooger-crepge/index-eng.htm
Mission: Fisheries and Oceans Canada established the Centre for Offshore Oil and Gas Environmental Research (COOGER) to coordinate the department's nation-wide research into the environmental and oceanographic impacts of offshore petroleum exploration, production and transportation.

Centre géoscientifique de Québec
c/o CGC-Québec & INRS Eau Terre Environnement, 490, rue de la Couronne, Québec QC G1K 9A9 Canada
Tél: 418-654-2604; *Téléc:* 418-654-2615
www.cgq-qgc.ca
Mission: The focus of research is on socio-economic issues as they relate to aspects of environmental geoscience (climate change, environmental geodynamics, remediation of contaminated sites, etc.), regional geology, & georesources (groundwater, minerals, fossil fuels). The Centre is the result of a partnership between government & academia.

Concordia University (CIWESS)
Concordia Institute for Water, Energy and Sustainable Systems
Faculty of Engineering & Computer Science, Concordia University, 1455 de Maisonneuve Blvd. West, Montreal QC H3G 1M8 Canada
Tel: 514-848-2424
www.encs.concordia.ca/research/ciwess
Overview: A organization founded in 2012
Mission: The Concordia Institute for Water, Energy and Sustainable Systems (CIWESS) trains students to be at the forefront of sustainable development practices. It promotes research into new systems, technologies and solutions for water, energy and resource conservation.

Craighead Institute
#B2D, 201 South Wallace Ave., Bozeman MT 59715 Canada
Tel: 406-585-8705; *Fax:* 406-585-8705
e-mail: info@craigheadinstitute.org
www.craigheadresearch.org
Previous Name: Craighead Environmental Research Institute
Overview: A organization founded in 1964
Mission: Craighead Institute is an applied science and research organization with a long history of designing and managing innovative research projects in support of conservation in the Northern Rockies and around the world. Their is to maintain healthy populations of native plants, wildlife and people as part of sustainable, functioning ecosystems. Craighead Institute has also been active in guiding conservation policy and management, developing wildlife habitat suitability and connectivity models, and completing large-scale conservation area designs for regions in the United States, Canada, and Tibet.

Cultus Lake Salmon Research Laboratory
4222 Columbia Valley Hwy., Cultus Lake BC V2R 5B6
Tel: 604-824-4700
Mission: The Cultus Lake Salmon Research Laboratory conducts research on factors which affect the freshwater life-cycle stages of Pacific salmon. The Fisheries & Oceans Canada research facility consists of many laboratories, such as the radioisotope laboratory & the inorganic chemistry laboratory. Cultus Lake Salmon Research Laboratory also features artificial streams & ponds, plus an experimental hatchery.

Dalhousie University
Christmas Tree Research Centre
Faculty Of Agriculture, Dalhousie University, PO Box 550, Halifax NS B2N 53E Canada
Mission: The Atlantic Christmas Tree Research Centre (CRC) aims to enhance Atlantic Canada's knowledge-based bio-economy through the development of science-driven innovative technologies and products for increasing the sustainability of Atlantic Canada's Christmas tree and greenery industry.

Dalhousie University
Eco-Efficiency Centre
Dalhousie University, 5269 Morris St., Halifax NS B3J 1B6 Canada
Tel: 902-461-6704
e-mail: eecentre@dal.ca
eco-efficiency.management.dal.ca/index.htm
Overview: A organization founded in 1998
Mission: Dalhousie University's Eco-Efficiency Centre is a non-profit environmental management centre supporting small- and medium-sized enterprises in Nova Scotia.

Dalhousie University (MELAW)
Marine & Environmental Law Institute
Schulich School of Law, 6061 University Ave., Halifax NS B3H 4R2 Canada
Tel: 902-494-1988; *Fax:* 902-494-4227
e-mail: melaw@dal.ca
www.dal.ca/law/MELAW
Overview: A organization founded in 1974
Mission: The Marine & Environmental Law Institute (MELAW) is internationally recognized for excellence in marine and environmental law teaching and research.

Dalhousie University (CMEP)
Centre for Marine Environmental Prediction
c/o Dalhousie University, Halifax NS B3H 3J5 Canada
www.cmep.ca
Overview: A organization founded in 1998
Mission: The Centre for Marine Environmental Prediction (CMEP) was founded with the mission of researching marine environmental changes for the improvement of forecasting technologies and public education. The Centre is based out of Dalhousie University, and has projects focused on flooding forecasts and risk assessment, as well as ongoing research in the North Atlantic Basin and Scotian Shelf.

Dalhousie University
Centre for Water Resources Studies
PO Box 1000, Office D-514, 1360 Barrington St., Halifax NS B3J 2X4 Canada
Tel: 902-494-6070; *Fax:* 902-494-3105
e-mail: water@dal.ca
centreforwaterresourcesstudies.dal.ca
Overview: A organization founded in 1981
Mission: The Centre for Water Resources Studies (CWRS) was established at Dalhousie University to apply the research resources of the University to water resource concerns in Atlantic Canada. The Centre conducts research in sewage disposal, technology for water supply, watershed acidification, water and wastewater treatment, and international development. The Centre also has research panels on sewage disposal, drinking water quality, erosion and sediment control, and rain water cisterns.

Dalhousie University
Aquatron Laboratory
Life Sciences Centre, 1355 Oxford St., Halifax NS B3H 4R2 Canada
Tel: 902-494-3874; *Fax:* 902-494-3877
e-mail: aquatron@dal.ca
aquatron.dal.ca
Mission: The Aquatron Laboratory is an aquatic research facility at Dalhousie University. The facility houses a 684,000 litre pool tank, a 117,000 litre tower tank, a behavioural observation tank, and 18 independent wet labs. Research conducted at the Aquatron Laboratory ranges from aquaculture to wildlife studies to marine fisheries.

Dalhousie University (DREAMS)
Dalhousie Research in Energy, Advanced Materials & Sustainability
Institute for Research in Materials, Dalhousie University, PO Box 15000, 6414 Coburg Rd., Halifax NS B3H 4R2 Canada
Tel: 902-494-1904; *Fax:* 902-494-8016
e-mail: DREAMS@dal.ca
dreams.irm.dal.ca
Mission: The purpose of DREAMS is to train a cohort of research scholars in Chemistry, Physics and Mechanical Engineering) at Dalhousie University who will address important aspects of energy production/storage and sustainability. DREAMS research scholars play a pivotal role in renewable energy production and storage, as well as the sustainable production of environmentally acceptable or re-usable materials.

East Coast Ecosystems Research Organization
PO Box 36, Freeport NS B0V 1B0 Canada
Toll-Free: 888-854-4440
Mission: East Coast Ecosystems Research Organization is a charitable organization dedicated to education and research about natural processes and human involvement in nature. Since 1986, East Coast Ecosystems has been conducting research in collaboration with the New England Aquarium in the Bay of Fundy and on the Southern Scotian Shelf to study the seasonal distribution, abundance, and behavior of the endangered North Atlantic right whale. The Organization's goal is to compile the scientific evidence and foster the public support to encourage the federal government to develop sound practices of ocean management to ensure the recovery and the survival of the North Atlantic right whale.

Eastern Canada Soil and Water Conservation Centre (CCSE) / Centre de conservation des sols et de l'eau de l'est du Canada
160 Rue Réservoir, Grand Falls NB E3Y 3W3 Canada
Tel: 506-475-4040; *Fax:* 506-475-4030
e-mail: ccse-swcc@umce.ca
www.ccse-swcc.nb.ca
Mission: The Eastern Canada Soil and Water Conservation Centre is a non-governmental organization affiliated with Université de Moncton, Campus d'Edmundston. The Centre is dedicated to the promotion of sustainable natural resource management for the agriculture industry in Eastern Canada. The Centre specializes in soil and water conservation, environmental planning, sustainable development, climate change and greenhouse gas emissions, and studies of production systems.

Eastern Scotian Shelf Integrated Management Initiative (ESSIM)
Bedford Institute of Oceanography, PO Box 1006, Dartmouth NS B2Y 4A2 Canada
Tel: 902-426-9900; *Fax:* 902-426-3855
www.dfo-mpo.gc.ca/oceans/publications/essim-giepne-eng.asp
Mission: The Eastern Scotian Shelf Integrated Management (ESSIM) Initiative is a collaborative ocean management and planning process led by Fisheries and Oceans Canada (DFO) under Canada's Oceans Act. The goal of the Initiative is to develop and implement an Integrated Ocean Management Plan for the region. The Initiative's primary objectives are collaborative governance, sustainable use, and healthy ecosystems, and collaborates with government, aboriginal groups, ocean industry, conservation groups, communities, and University researchers.

Edmonton Waste Management Centre of Excellence (EWMCE)
Solid Waste Research & Development Facility, #310, 13111 Meridian St., Edmonton AB T6S 1G9
Tel: 780-496-7316; *Fax:* 780-944-5709
e-mail: ewmce@edmonton.ca
www.ewmce.com
Overview: A organization founded in 2003
Mission: The Edmonton Waste Management Centre of Excellence is engaged in the following activities related to waste management & environmental practices: research, technology development, & training. Research takes place in the following areas: solid waste, wastewater, & energy from waste. The Centre of Excellence strives to develop sustainable solutions for both local & global applications.

Edmonton Waste Management Centre of Excellence
Clover Bar Solid Waste Research & Development
#310, 13111 Meridian St., Edmonton AB T6S 1G9
Tel: 780-496-7316; *Fax:* 780-944-5709

Edmonton Waste Management Centre of Excellence
Gold Bar Wastewater Research & Training Centre
EPCOR's Gold Bar Wastewater Treatment Plant, 10977 - 50th St., Edmonton AB T6A 2E9
Tel: 780-969-8421; *Fax:* 780-969-8777

Environment Canada (CRIACC)
Centre de Ressources en Impacts et Adaptation au Climat et à ses Changements
Place Bonaventure, Portail Nord-Est, #7810, 800, rue de la Gauchetière ouest, Montréal QC H5A 1L9 Canada
Téléc: 514-282-2264
Courriel: climat.quebec@ec.qc.ca
www.climat-quebec.qc.ca
Également appelé: Climat-Québec
Mission: Provides reports & resources on the impacts of climate change in Québec.

Environment Canada (CCCMA)
Canadian Centre for Climate Modelling & Analysis
Bob Wright Centre, University Of Victoria, PO Box 1700, Stn. CSC, Victoria BC V8W 2Y2 Canada
www.ec.gc.ca/ccmac-cccma

Mission: CCCMA is a division of the Climate Research Branch of Environment Canada. The Centre is engaged in research on atmospheric climate modelling, sea-ice modelling, climate variability & predictability, the carbon cycle, & other climate issues.

Environment Canada (CCCSN)

Canadian Climate Change Scenarios Network
AIRD, Atmospheric Sci. & Tech. Directorate, Sci. & Tech. Branch, 4905 Dufferin St., Toronto ON M3H 5T4 Canada
Fax: 416-739-4297
www.cccsn.ec.gc.ca
Overview: A organization founded in 2005
Mission: Supported by the Adaptation and Impacts Research Division (AIRD), CCCSN is a national network that supports research into the impacts of climate change, provides technical assistance for downscaling & impacts & adaptation research, & offers training in the use of research tools developed by AIRD. Offices in each region of Canada.

Environment Canada

Meteorological Service of Canada. Atmospheric Science & Technology Directorate. Climate Research Branch
4905 Dufferin St., Toronto ON M3H 5T4 Canada
Tel: 416-739-4249; *Fax:* 416-739-5700
www.msc-smc.ec.gc.ca
Mission: The Branch is engaged in research into cold-climate processes in the climate system, with a focus on energy & water cycles, land surface process modelling, development & validation of climate processes in hydrological & atmospheric models, climate/cryosphere interactions & processes; remote sensing of climate variables, & assessment of errors in in-situ measurements & their compatibility over time. Climate monitoring, analysis & prediction, & climate system modelling are two important goals/activities.

Environment Canada

Meteorological Service of Canada. Atmospheric Science & Technology Directorate. Meteorological Research Branch
2121, rte Transcanadienne, Dorval QC H9P 1J3 Canada
Tel: 514-421-5020; *Fax:* 514-421-4679
www.msc-smc.ec.gc.ca
Mission: The Branch is engaged in meteorological research, with a focus on remote sensing, severe weather, atmospheric processes, & weather prediction. The goal of research is to provide the science required to improve weather predicting. The Branch is comprised of a Data Assimilation & Satellite Meteorology division, a Numerical Prediction Research division, & a Cloud Physics Research division.

Environment Canada

Meteorological Service of Canada. Atmospheric Science & Technology Directorate. Air Quality Research Branch
4905 Dufferin St., Toronto ON M3H 5T4 Canada
Tel: 416-739-4613; *Fax:* 416-739-4224
www.msc-smc.ec.gc.ca
Mission: The Branch brings together the largest group of atmospheric specialists in Canada, studying the chemistry & physics of the atmosphere as it pertains to acid rain, as well as aspects of air pollution such as acid deposition & oxidants, hazardous air pollutants, particulate matter, stratospheric ozone depletion, & greenhouse gases buildup. Activities include modelling, systematic measurements, & process research. The Branch is comprised of a Modelling & Integration division, a Measurements & Analysis division, a Processes Research division, & an Experimental Studies division.

Environment Canada (AIRG)

Adaptation & Impacts Research Group
4905 Dufferin St., Toronto ON M3H 5T4 Canada
Tel: 416-739-4271; *Fax:* 416-739-4297
www.environment.uwaterloo.ca/research/aird/
Overview: A organization founded in 1994
Mission: The Adaptation and Impacts Research Section (AIRS) is part of the Climate Research Division of the Atmospheric Science and Technology Directorate (ASTD), within the Science and Technology Branch of Environment Canada. They focus on the field of climate change research.
Affliation(s): University of Waterloo

Environment Canada (ESTC)

Environmental Protection Service. Science & Technology Branch. Environmental Science & Technology Centre
335 River Rd., Ottawa ON K1A 0H3 Canada
Tel: 613-991-5633; *Fax:* 613-998-0004
e-mail: enviroinfo@ec.gc.ca
www.etc-cte.ec.gc.ca/etchome_e.html
Mission: The Centre collaborates with the private, public & academic sectors to provide research which focusses on science & technology for environmental protection. Specifically, the Centre researches & provides new knowledge in the areas of pollution measurement, prevention, control & remediation of both air pollution & hazardous materials or oil spills, & provides the relevant sampling & analytical expertise for these areas. The Centre is comprised of 5 divisions: Analysis & Air Quality, Biological Methods, Emergencies Science & Technologies, Emissions Research & Measurement, & Green Technologies.

Fanshawe College (CSEE)

Centre for Sustainable Energy & Evironments
Fanshawe College, London Campus, #T3010, 1001 Fanshawe College Blvd, London ON N5Y 5R6 Canada
e-mail: research@fanshawec.ca
www.fanshawec.ca/services/research
Mission: The Centre for Sustainable Energy & Environments (CSEE) is a virtual, applied research centre at Fanshawe College. CSEE brings together academics, entrepreneurial, technical and business expertise to help companies innovate in the fields of renewable energy, energy management technologies, integration, sustainable buildings/construction, alternative transportation and other green technologies. CSEE offers a broad range of project development and R&D services to business clients.

Fisheries & Oceans Canada

Maurice Lamontagne Institute (MLI)
CP 1000, 850, route de la Mer, Mont-Joli QC G5H 3Z4 Canada
Tél: 418-775-0500; *Téléc:* 418-775-0730
Courriel: info@dfo-mpo.gc.ca
www.qc.dfo-mpo.gc.ca
Aperçu: ; fondée en 1987
Mission: The Institute is mandated to provide the Canadian government with a scientific basis for the conservation of living marine resources, the protection of the marine environment, & safe maritime navigation. Research into fisheries, marine mammals, oceanography, & habitats of the Estuary & Gulf of St. Lawrence & Northern Québec is carried out, as is environmental monitoring & assessment.

Fishermen & Scientists Research Society (FSRS)

PO Box 25125, Halifax NS B3M 4H4 Canada
www.fsrs.ns.ca
Mission: The Fishermen and Scientists Research Society (FSRS) is a non-profit organization that seeks to develop a network of fishermen and scientists concerned with the long-term sustainability of the fishing industry in Atlantic Canada. The FSRS's research projects include studies on fish habitats, fish diet studies, tagging projects, ecosystem studies, and reproduction studies.

Fleming College (CAWT)

Centre for Alternative Wastewater Treatment
School of Environmental and Natural Resource Sciences, Frost Campus, 200 Albert St. South, Lindsay ON K9V 5E6 Canada
e-mail: cawt@flemingc.on.ca
cawt.ca
Mission: The CAWT conducts research in the areas of water and wastewater treatment science and communicates results in high quality publications. The Centre continues to expand research capacity and productivity over time.

Freshwater Institute Science Laboratory (FWI)

501 University Cres., Winnipeg MB R3T 2N6
Tel: 204-983-5000
Mission: Fisheries & Oceans Canada's Freshwater Institute Science Laboratory in Winnipeg is the the regional headquarters of the Central & Arctic Region. The research facility features a solar warehouse, an ozone waste treatment facility, & a water treatment facility. Research activities are conducted in the key areas of freshwater & marine fisheries, & aquatic biology. Programs are carried out in freshwater science, oceans management, Arctic research, fisheries management, & fish habitat management.

Genuine Progress Index for Atlantic Canada / Indice de progrès véritable - Atlantique

535 Indian Point Rd., Glen Haven NS B3Z 2T5 Canada
Tel: 902-823-1944; *Fax:* 902-826-7088
e-mail: info@gpiatlantic.org
www.gpiatlantic.org
Also Known As: GPI Atlantic
Overview: A organization founded in 1997
Mission: GPI Atlantic is an independent, non-profit research and education organization dedicated to the development of the Genuine Progress Index (GPI), a means of measuring social, economic, and environmental assets for use in future planning and sustainability. The GPI measures time use, living standards, natural capital, human impact on the environment, and social capital and is an alternative to the Gross Domestic Product (GDP) measurement system.

Geological Survey of Canada (GSC)

Atlantic
Bedford Institute of Oceanography, PO Box 1006, 1 Challenger Dr., Dartmouth NS B2Y 4A2 Canada
Tel: 902-426-3225; *Fax:* 902-426-1466
e-mail: info-dartmouth@gsc.nrcan.gc.ca
Mission: The Geological Survey of Canada Atlantic (GSC) is Canada's principal marine geoscience facility, a branch of the Canadian Department of Natural Resources. The GSC Atlantic conducts research in marine and petroleum geology, geophysics, marine geoscience, geochemistry, and geotechnology. Research projects are split into two streams: the Marine Environmental Geoscience Subdivision, which studies the environmental impact of development and processes, and the Marine Resources Geoscience Subdivision, which studies the geology of the region to evaluate its oil and gas potential.

Global Institute for Food Security

University of Saskatchewan, Saskatoon SK S7N 5A2 Canada
www.globalinstituteforfoodsecurity.org
Mission: The Global Institute for Food Security builds on Saskatchewan's existing strengths and expertise to lead in the discovery, development and commercialization of new and innovative knowledge and technologies to sustainably meet the escalating global demand for food.
Affliation(s): University of Saskatchewan; Potash Corp.; Government of Saskatchewan

Great Lakes Environmental Research Laboratory (GLERL)

4840 S. State Rd., Ann Arbor MI 48108-9719 USA
Tel: 734-741-2235; *Fax:* 734-741-2055
e-mail: www.glerl@noaa.gov
www.glerl.noaa.gov
Overview: A organization founded in 1974
Mission: The Research Laboratory is under the aegis of the U.S. National Oceanic and Atmospheric Administration & is mandated to conduct high quality research & provide leadership on issues concerning the Great Lakes & marine coastal environments. The focus of research is on the physical environment of the Great Lakes, water quality & quantity, human health, fish recruitment & productivity, & invasive species affecting the Lakes. GLERL collaborates with Canadian scientists & with institutions such as Environment Canada, Fisheries & Oceans Canada, the Canadian Ice Service & the Canadian Hydrographic Service, & conducts research in the Canadian waters of the Lakes as well as in Canada's inland lakes.

Great Lakes Forestry Centre (GLFC)

1219 Queen St. East, Sault Ste Marie ON P6A 2E5 Canada
Tel: 705-949-9461; *Fax:* 705-541-5700
cfs.nrcan.gc.ca/centres/glfc
Mission: The centre is home to Canada's Insect Production and Quarantine Laboratories, a one-of-a-kind research facility that employs clean-room technology and allows scientists to study alien invasive insects. The GLFC has a worldwide reputation for scientific excellence and is a world leader in forest research.

Great Lakes Research Consortium (GLRC)

College of Environmental Science & Forestry, SUNY, 1 Forestry Dr., 253 Baker Labs, Syracuse NY 13210 USA
Tel: 315-470-6720; *Fax:* 315-470-6970
e-mail: glrc@esf.edu
www.esf.edu/glrc/
Mission: GLRC is comprised of 18 New York universities & 9 Canadian affiliates (McMaster University, Brock University, University of Ottawa, University of Toronto, University of Guelph, University of Waterloo, University of Windsor, Queens University, & Ryerson University). The focus is on collaborative research & education on aspects of Great Lakes ecology, environmental concerns, & issues such as Great Lakes security.

The Consortium hosts an annual conference, develops & delivers seminars, & publishes research.

Guelph Turfgrass Institute & Environmental Research Centre

G.M. Frost Research and Information Centre, 328 Victoria Rd. South, Guelph ON N1H 6H8 Canada
Tel: 519-824-4120
e-mail: info@guelphturfgrass.ca
www.guelphturfgrass.ca
Overview: A organization founded in 1987
Mission: The Institute has a mandate to conduct research on turfgrass, provide extension services & professional development to members of the Ontario turfgrass industry, & to foster interest in turfgrass science as both a program of study & career choice for students. Research at the Institute continues the University of Guelph's recognized expertise in turfgrass science & focuses on environmental aspects such as pesticide use, evaluation of grass species, seed varieties & seeding methods, fertility & management programs, & the biological & cultural control of diseases & weeds. Staff at the Institute provide consulting & diagnostic services, publish factsheets & research reports, provide public demonstration project assistance, & expert testimony. Meeting facilities are available. The G.M. Frost Research & Information Centre is located on site.

Gulf Fisheries Centre (GFC)

PO Box 5030, Moncton NB E1C 9B6 Canada
Tel: 506-851-6206; *Fax:* 506-851-2378
www.glf.dfo-mpo.gc.ca/e0008111
Mission: The Gulf Fisheries Centre is a research facility of the Canada Department of Fisheries and Oceans based in New Brunswick. The Centre focuses on research in aquaculture and environmental sciences, fisheries sciences and aquatic resources, and oceans and habitat projects. Specific research areas include studies of indigenous species, stock assessment and population biology, and studies on the ecosystems of the Gulf of St. Lawrence. The Gulf Fisheries Centre has one of only two laboratories in Canada that specialize in shellfish health.

Hakai Beach Institute

PO Box 309, Heriot Bay BC V0P 1H0 Canada
e-mail: welcome@hakai.org
hakai.org
Mission: The Hakai Beach Institute engages in research in three areas: in-house long term ecological research (LTER) program, called Changing Landscape; Research by partners that directly complements Changing Landscape; and other related research on the Central Coast, such as that conducted via the Hakai Network and other vehicles.

Health Canada

Environmental Health Research Division
Jeanne Mance Bldg., Tunney's Pasture, Ottawa ON K1A 0K9 Canada
Tel: 613-957-2991; *Fax:* 613-941-5366
e-mail: info@hc-sc.gc.ca
www.hc-sc.gc.ca
Mission: In concert with the Assembly of First Nations, First Nations & Inuit Health Branch, & the Dept. of Indian Affairs & Northern Development, the Division conducts, coordinates & funds contaminants-related research; coordinates the replacement or upgrading of diesel-fuel tanks & the remediation of fuel oil contaminated sites on First Nations reserves across Canada; provides lab services supporting the research; & coordinates & manages First Nations & Inuit Health Branch drinking water-related research & analysis of First Nations drinking water quality data.

Health Canada

Environmental Health, Science & Research Bureau
Jeanne Mance Bldg., Tunney's Pasture, Ottawa ON K1A 0K9 Canada
e-mail: info@hc-sc.gc.ca
www.hc-sc.gc.ca
Mission: The Bureau's mandate is to reduce the negative impacts of environmental exposures on the health of Canadians through research, surveillance, monitoring, epidemiological investigations & emergency planning. It generates data in support of regulatory programs & interprets & formulates it so that it is useful to policy makers, conducts studies to investigate the effects of contaminants on human health, identifies vulnerable populations as well as potential hazards, provides expert advice, develops more effective testing & research tools for hazard identification, & provides chemical emergency preparedness & response capacity through the Safe Environment Programme.

Huntsman Marine Science Centre (HSMC)

1 Lower Campus Rd., St. Andrews NB E5B 2L7 Canada
Tel: 506-529-1200; *Fax:* 506-529-1212
e-mail: huntsman@huntsmanmarine.ca
www.huntsmanmarine.ca
Overview: A organization founded in 1970
Mission: The Huntsman Marine Science Centre (HSMC) was established in 1970 through a consortium of 20 Universities and various Government departments. The HSMC is dedicated to research and education in the field of marine science for the benefit of both the private and public sector. One of it's key research projects is the banding of birds to study the impact of habitat changes on indigenous bird species. The HSMC also operates a public aquarium in addition to research facilities.

Huntsman Marine Science Centre

Atlantic Reference Centre
1 Lower Campus Rd., St. Andrews NB E5B 2L7 Canada
Tel: 506-529-1203; *Fax:* 506-529-1212
e-mail: arc@mar.dfo-mpo.gc.ca
www.huntsmanmarine.ca/subcontents.php?id=18&sid=27
Overview: A organization founded in 1984
Mission: The Huntsman Marine Science Centre and Fisheries and Ocean Canada (DFO) created the Atlantic Reference Centre (ARC) to archive samples of Canadian Atlantic marine life collected by research surveys and as a source of taxonomic information. The ARC and DFO collaborate on marine biodiversity research and planning. Services provided by the ARC include sample processing, specimen identification, and research services for government, academic, private, and public organizations.

Institute for Energy, Environment and Sustainable Communities (CC-IEESC)

China-Canada Institute for Energy, Environment and Sustainable Communities
University of Regina, Regina SK S4S 0A2 Canada
Tel: 306-337-3359; *Fax:* 306-585-4855
e-mail: ieesc@env.uregina.ca
env.uregina.ca/ieesc/ccieesr.aspx
Mission: The China-Canada Institute for Energy, Environment and Sustainability Research (CC-IEESR) was established to provide much needed research in energy and environmental studies related to social responsibility, climate change and adaptation. Teaching and research related to pollution mitigation, clean energy, greenhouse gas emission reductions, climate change and environmental modeling. These joint research and teaching collaborations place both universities in a unique role to help power industries develop solutions to energy, environment and climate change challenges.
Affliation(s): North China Electric Power University

Institute for Environmental Learning

BC Canada
e-mail: info@eco-learning.org
www.eco-learning.org
Overview: A organization founded in 2010
Mission: The Institute for Environmental Learning is a collaborative of researchers and practitioners committed to high quality environmental and sustainability learning in British Columbia. The Institute supports community-based research on best practices for environmental and sustainability education in both the formal and informal education sectors.

Institute for Environmental Monitoring and Research (IEMR)

PO Box 1859, Stn. B, 114 Hamilton River Rd., Happy Valley-Goose Bay NL A0P 1E0 Canada
Tel: 709-896-3266; *Fax:* 709-896-3076
e-mail: iemr@iemr.org
www.iemr.org
Mission: The Institute for Environmental Monitoring and Research was established in 1995 at the recommendation of an independent Environmental Assessment panel to review the ecological effects of flight training conducted at Canadian Forcesd Base Goose Bay. The IEMR specifically conducts research into indigenous wildlife, contaminants, and ecosystem impacts related to low-level flights in the Labrador area.

Institute for Sustainable Energy, Environment, & Economy (EESG)

Calgary - ISEEE Energy & Environmental Systems Group
Earth Sciences Bldg., University of Calgary, #602, 2500 University Dr. NW, Calgary AB T2N 1N4
Tel: 403-220-8872; *Fax:* 403-210-3894
e-mail: eespinfo@ucalgary.ca
Mission: The Energy & Environmental Systems Group at the University of Calgary researches problems that arise from the interaction of energy systems with the environment. The Group's research is interdisciplinary & policy-relevant. Examples of research include the life cycle assessment of oil sands technologies project & the development of materials to improve the conversion of solar energy into electrical energy.

Institute of Ocean Sciences (IOS)

PO Box 6000, 9860 West Saanich Rd., Sidney BC V8L 4B2
Tel: 250-363-6517
Mission: Affiliated with Fisheries & Oceans Canada, the scientific facility is engaged in research on the coastal waters of the following regions: British Columbia, the western Canadian Arctic, the Northeastern Pacific Ocean, & the navigable fresh waters east to the Alberta border. The Institute of Ocean Sciences contributes to the restoration & management of coastal ecosystems.

John Prince Research Forest (JPRF)

c/o S. Grainger, Ecosystem Science/Mgmt. Program, U. of Northern BC, #8-313, 3333 University Way, Prince George BC V2N 4Z9
Tel: 250-648-3322
researchforest.unbc.ca/jprf/jprf.htm
Overview: A organization founded in 1999
Mission: Located in north central British Columbia, the John Prince Research Forest is jointly managed by the University of Northern British Columbia & the Tl'azt'en First Nation. Interdisciplinary research is conducted. Examples of research include a bat ecology study, forest health & bark beetle infestation treatment methods, & leave-tree survival & wind damage after partial cutting in the upland SBS forests.

Kahiltna Research Group

#108 125A, 1030 Denman St., Vancouver BC V6G 1R8
www.kahiltna.org
Mission: The Vancouver location of the Kahiltna Research Group is a branch of the group at California State University Long Beach. In British Columbia, the Kahiltna Research Group is associated with the Centre for Wildlife Ecology at Simon Fraser University. The Group is engaged in research of ecological topics, with a focus on marine ecology. An example of research is the migration of shorebirds. The Kahiltna Research Group provides information to government, agencies, & non-profit organization to assit the ecologically related work.

Lakehead University (BRI)

Biorefining Research Initiative
1294 Balmoral St. Bldg., #3001D, 955 Oliver Rd., Thunder Bay ON P7B 5E1 Canada
Tel: 807-343-8844; *Fax:* 807-343-8240
lubri.lakeheadu.ca
Overview: A organization founded in 2007
Mission: The BRI is engaged in research into biorefining, an important alternative to the refining of fossil oil, with an emphasis on developing new technologies, solutions & products. Specifically, the research will focus on bioconversion: the conversion of cellulose in forest biomass into biofuels (ethanol, methane), other bio-based chemicals & bioenergy; chemical conversion: production of chemicals from forest biomass by thermochemical processes; & forest microbiota: chemicals, including pharmaceuticals, enzymes & microbial agents for bioremediation.

Lakehead University (ATRC)

Aquatic Toxicity Research Centre
Centennial Bldg., Lakehead University, #0018, 955 Oliver Rd., Thunder Bay ON P7B 5E1 Canada
Tel: 807-343-8179; *Fax:* 807-343-8023
lucas.lakeheadu.ca/atrc/
Mission: The Centre is engaged in regulatory testing-monitoring of the effects of effluents on aquatic organisms from pulp & paper mills, mines & related industrial discharges in Northwestern Ontario. Testing services, which includes acute testing with rainbow trout & water fleas, are available to industry & government. The Centre is a member of the Lakehead University Centre for Analytical Services (LUCAS).

Lakehead University

Environmental Laboratory
#CB3022, Centennial Bldg., Lakehead University, 955 Oliver Rd., Thunder Bay ON P7B 5E1 Canada
Tel: 807-343-8368; *Fax:* 807-346-7796
lucas.lakeheadu.ca/luel/
Mission: The Laboratory, a member of the Lakehead University Centre for Analytical Services (LUCAS), provides chemical

analysis of soils, foliage, water, & wastewater, & supports research & teaching at Lakehead University.

Lakehead University (FoReST)
Forest Resources & Soils Testing Laboratory
Lakehead University, 955 Oliver Rd., Thunder Bay ON P7B 5E1 Canada
Tel: 807-343-8639
e-mail: forestlab@lakeheadu.ca
lucas.lakeheadu.ca/forest/
Mission: The Lab, a member of the Lakehead University Centre for Analytical Services (LUCAS), provides reliable testing of soils, vegetation & nutrients. It collaborates with business, industry & researchers to enhance entrepreneurial activity & encourages & supports research in Northern Ontario.

Lakehead University (LUNE)
Lakehead University Nutrient Ecology Laboratory
Lakehead University, 955 Oliver Rd., Thunder Bay ON P7B 5E1 Canada
Tel: 807-343-8110; *Fax:* 807-343-8023
lucas.lakeheadu.ca/lune/
Overview: A organization founded in 2003
Mission: The Laboratory supports water quality research in lakes, streams & wetlands in Northwestern Ontario, & offers hands-on training to University students with an interest in freshwater ecosystems. The Lab is a member of the Lakehead University Centre for Analytical Services (LUCAS).

Lakehead University (LUCAS)
Lakehead University Centre for Analytical Services
#0001A, 1294 Balmoral Bldg., Lakehead University, 955 Oliver Rd., Thunder Bay ON P7B 5E1 Canada
Tel: 807-343-8110; *Fax:* 807-343-8023
lucas.lakeheadu.ca
Mission: The Centre brings together internationally recognized scientists & research teams, & supports research & training.

Laurentian Forestry Centre (LFC)
PO Box 10380, Stn. Sainte-Foy, 1055 du P.E.P.S., Québec QC G1V 4C7 Canada
Tel: 418-648-3335; *Fax:* 418-648-5849
cfs.nrcan.gc.ca/centres/lfc
Mission: the Laurentian Forestry Centre (LFC) is involved in the acquisition and dissemination of forest knowledge. Staff use state-of the art infrastructure, including molecular biology, remote sensing, geomatics and modelling labs, to conduct research in areas such as climate change, forest ecology, forest pest biology, ecogenomics and forest ecosystem dynamics and productivity. LFC also has a collection of insects and fungi, an experimental station in Valcartier, an arboretum, greenhouses, and several experimental plots across Quebec.

Laurentian University (CFEU)
Cooperative Freshwater Ecology Unit
Vale Living with Lakes Centre, Laurentian University, 935 Ramsay Lake Rd., Sudbury ON P3E 2C6 Canada
Tel: 705-671-1151; *Fax:* 705-671-3857
e-mail: livingwithlakes@laurentian.ca
www3.laurentian.ca/livingwithlakes
Overview: A organization founded in 1989
Mission: The Co-op Unit was formed in partnership with the Ontario Ministries of Natural Resources, & Environment, & it collaborates also with Vale Inco, Xstrata Nickel, the City of Sudbury & other universities & research agencies. The research focus is on restoration ecology of acid & metal damaged waters in Northeastern Ontario, & issues such as climate change, invasive species, urban development, trace contaminants, aquaculture, loss of biodiversity & the general health of aquatic ecosystems. In addition to the research program, the Unit provides water monitoring & reporting services, & supports education, teaching & training. The Living with Lakes Centre will form the hub of activities in the future.

Laurentian University
Elliot Lake Research Field Station
Willet Green Miller Center, #A-5030, 935 Ramsey Lake Rd., Sudbury ON P3E 2C6 Canada
Tel: 705-675-1151; *Fax:* 705-675-4838
www.elrfs.org
Mission: The Field Station houses the Analytical Services Laboratory, which supports research into the effects of low-level radioactivity, resulting from uranium mine waste tailings, on the environment. Services include lab testing for a range of inorganic & radionuclide substances such as soil, manure, plant & animal tissue, effluent, & environmental monitoring & research.

Macleod Institute
#223, 20 Coachway Rd. SW, Calgary AB T3H 1E6
Tel: 403-240-2573; *Fax:* 403-246-1852
e-mail: macleod@macleodinstitute.com
www.macleodinstitute.com
Overview: A organization founded in 1995
Mission: An independent organization, affiliated with the University of Calgary, the Macleod Institute is engaged in environmental management, performance benchmarking, policy & program development, business process transformation, & program evaluations. In the area of environmental management, the Institute delivers climate change strategies, guides to environmental practices, risk communication plans, micro-power distributed energy options, & environmental performance measures.

Maritime College of Forest Technology (HJFFC)
Hugh John Flemming Forestry Centre
1350 Regent St., Fredericton NB E3C 2G6 Canada
Tel: 506-458-0653; *Fax:* 506-458-0652
www.mcft.ca
Mission: Works with forest technologists for service with private, industrial or public (government) forestry or natural resource organizations.

McGill University (ASCC)
Avian Science and Conservation Centre
Macdonald Campus, McGill University, 21,111 Lakeshore Rd., Ste-Anne-de-Bellevue QC H9X 3V9 Canada
Tel: 514-398-7760; *Fax:* 514-398-7990
ascc.mcgill.ca
Overview: A organization founded in 1973
Mission: The centre's purpose is to foster a greater understanding of the biology, conservation, and management of birds through a multipurpose program of research and education. Major areas of Research research include behaviour, ecology, nutrition, toxicology, reproductive physiology, and parasitology of captive and wild birds, as well as captive breeding and management of endangered species.

McGill University
Brace Centre for Water Resources Management
MacDonald Campus, McGill University, Stewart Park Three, 21111 Lakeshore Rd., Ste. Anne de Bellevue QC H9X 3V9 Canada
Tel: 514-398-7833; *Fax:* 514-398-7767
e-mail: brace@mcgill.ca
www.mcgill.ca/brace
Mission: The Brace Centre for Water Resources Management brings together staff from several McGill faculties, to undertake research, teaching, specialized training, and policy and strategic studies in water resources management, both in Canada and internationally.

McGill University (GEC3)
Global Environmental & Climate Change Centre
Department of Geography, McGill University, 805 Sherbrooke St. West, Montréal QC H3A 2K6 Canada
Tel: 514-398-3759; *Fax:* 514-398-1381
www.geog.mcgill.ca/gec3
Mission: The Global Environmental and Climate Change Centre (GEC3) is a cross-disciplinary, multi-university research centre bringing together more than 40 researchers from six Quebec universities (McGill University, Université de Montréal, Université du Québec à Montréal, Université de Sherbrooke, Université Laval, Université du Québec à Rimouski) to study processes, modelling and impact of environmental and climate change.

McGill University (CINE)
Centre for Indigenous Peoples' Nutrition and Environment
Macdonald Campus, McGill University, 21,111 Lakeshore Rd., Ste-Anne-de-Bellevue QC H9X 3V9 Canada
Tel: 514-398-7757; *Fax:* 514-398-1020
e-mail: cine@cine.mcgill.ca
www.mcgill.ca/cine
Mission: This Centre was created at McGill University in response to a need expressed by Aboriginal peoples for participatory research and education to address concerns about the integrity of their traditional food systems. Deterioration in the environment has adverse impacts on the health and lifestyles of indigenous peoples, in particular health and nutrition as derived from food and food traditions. CINE is a university-based endeavour to assist indigenous peoples in dealing with their concerns related to traditional food systems, nutrition and the environment.

McMaster University (MIEH)
McMaster Institute of Environment & Health
Burke Science Bldg., #333, 1280 Main St. West, Hamilton ON L8S 4K1 Canada
Tel: 905-525-9140; *Fax:* 905-524-2400
www.mcmaster.ca/mieh/
Overview: A organization founded in 1996
Mission: MIEH facilitates collaborative, interdisciplinary research into the complex relationships between human health & the environment. The Institute communicates its findings to policy & decision makers, the general public & other stakeholders & offers expertise & consultation on environmental health issues, particularly to the City of Hamilton. It also cooperates with local boards of education, the Hamilton Industrial Environmental Association, local citizen groups, as well as all levels of government. The Institute supports & encourages education & study at all levels.

Memorial University of Newfoundland (MI)
Marine Institute
Office of Research and Development, PO Box 4920, 155 Ridge Rd., St. John's NL A1C 5R3 Canada
Tel: 709-778-0200; *Fax:* 709-778-0346
Toll-Free: 800-563-5799
www.mi.mun.ca
Mission: Multidisciplinary research institute with research centres focusing on Aquaculture and Seafood Development, Sustainable Aquatic Resources, Marine Simulation, and Ocean Technology, as well as projects in conjunction with the international branch of the Marine Institute (MI International)

Memorial University of Newfoundland (MII)
Marine Institute International
Marine Institute - Memorial University, PO Box 4920, St. John's NL A1C 5R3 Canada
Tel: 709-778-0484; *Fax:* 709-778-0371
e-mail: miintl@mi.mun.ca
www.mi.mun.ca/mi_international
Mission: International research institute based out of Memorial University's Marine Institute. Over 85 marine research projects have been carried out through MI International in over 35 countries. Areas of research include fisheries resource management, marine environment, food safety, aquaculture, and others.

Memorial University of Newfoundland (CURRA)
Community - University Research for Recovery Alliance
Memorial University of Newfoundland, St. John's NL A1C 5S7 Canada
Tel: 709-737-7244; *Fax:* 709-737-7530
www.curra.ca
Mission: Five-year research program based in Memorial University dedicated to developing strategies for the recovery of fish stocks and fishery communities by examining a variety of topics in social, economic and environmental areas.

Memorial University of Newfoundland (CEE)
Centre of Environmental Excellence
c/o Sir Wilfred Grenfell College, 10 University Dr., Corner Brook NL A2H 6P9 Canada
www.ceenl.ca
Mission: The Newfoundland Centre of Environmental Excellence (CEE) is a research institute based in Western Newfoundland. The CEE is focused on environmental research in the field of sustainability and economic growth. The CEE focuses on Sustainable Forestry, Sustainable Tourism, and Sustainable Municipal and Rural Infrastructure ad key areas of research and development projects.

Memorial University of Newfoundland
Institute for Biodiversity, Ecosystem Science & Sustainability
c/o Sir Wilfred Grenfell College, University Drive, Corner Brook NL A2H 6P9 Canada
Tel: 709-639-7590; *Fax:* 709-639-7591
e-mail: ibes@swgc.mun.ca
www.ibes.swgc.mun.ca
Mission: The Institute for Biodiversity, Ecosystem Science & Sustainability (IBES) is a research initiative within Memorial University's Sir Wilfred Grenfell College and the Newfoundland & Labrador Department of Environment and Conservation. The IBES broadly focuses on research in the fields of natural resource conservation, management, and sustainability and specifically in sustainable development, ecosystems ecology, climate change, population ecology, fisheries & aquaculture science, natural resource management, and urban planning and design.

Memorial University of Newfoundland

Fisheries Conservation Group
Marine Institute - Memorial University, PO Box 4920, St. John's NL A1C 5R3 Canada
Tel: 709-778-0318; *Fax:* 709-778-0669
fishcons.mi.mun.ca
Overview: A organization founded in 1996
Mission: The Fisheries Conservation Group is a research group created at the Fisheries and Marine Institute of Memorial University to develop an independent fisheries research and training program with a focus on the fisheries ecosystems of the Northwest Atlantic. The Group focuses on researching groundfish stocks in Atlantic Canada, the ecology of commercial fisheries, and collaboration with fishers and industry.

Memorial University of Newfoundland

Ocean Sciences Centre
Memorial University of Newfoundland, St. John's NL A1C 5S7 Canada
Tel: 709-737-3708; *Fax:* 709-737-3220
www.mun.ca/osc
Mission: The Ocean Sciences Centre (OSC) is a cold ocean research facility operated in conjunction with Memorial University. The Centre houses laboratories where research is conducted on the North Atlantic fishery industry, aquaculture, oceanography, ecology, behavior and physiology. The Centre also performs research on a variety of organisms; from bacteria to mammals.

Memorial University of Newfoundland

Bonne Bay Marine Station
PO Box 69, Norris Point NL A0K 3V0 Canada
Tel: 709-458-2550; *Fax:* 709-458-2605
www.bonnebay.mun.ca
Mission: The Bonne Bay Marine Station is a research and teaching facility operated by Memorial University and the Gros Morne Co-operating Association. The Station provides services for research in marine ecosystems. Research projects and areas include aquaculture, marine ecology/biology, habitat sensitivity, ecology of indigenous species, oceanography, and ocean dynamics.

Memorial University of Newfoundland (CASD)

Centre for Aquaculture and Seafood Development
Fisheries and Marine Institute of Memorial University of Newfoundland, PO Box 4920, St. John's NL A1C 5R3 Canada
Tel: 709-778-0532; *Fax:* 709-778-0532
e-mail: casd@mi.mun.ca
www.mi.mun.ca/departments/centreforaquacultureandseafoo ddevelopme
Mission: The Centre for Aquaculture and Seafood Development (CASD) carries out research in collaboration with industry partners. The Facility houses numerous state-of-the-art research and training facilities, including a sea water system designed for temperature-controlled flow-through and water circulation, as well as hatcheries, 15 silos ranging in size from 1000 litres to 12,000 litres, and outdoor cages. The Facility's research is focused largely on fish species and biodiversity.

Memorial University of Newfoundland (CCFI)

Canadian Centre for Fisheries Innovation
PO Box 4920, St. John's NL A1C 5R3 Canada
Tel: 709-778-0517; *Fax:* 709-778-0516
e-mail: ccfi@mi.mun.ca
www.ccfi.ca
Mission: The Canadian Centre for Fisheries Innovation (CCFI) is a non-profit organization owned by Memorial University of Newfoundland and funded by Atlantic Innovation Fund. The Centre provides the tools of scientific research and technology to the fishing industry. The Centre focuses research on aquaculture, harvesting, processing, biotechnology, and resource sustainability.

Memorial University of Newfoundland (TERRA)

The Earth Resources Research and Analysis Facility
Department of Earth Sciences, 300 Prince Philip Dr., St. John's NL A1B 3X5 Canada
Tel: 709-864-8142; *Fax:* 709-864-7437
www.mun.ca/research/resources/creait/physical-sci/terra
Mission: TERRA provides chemical and physical analyses utilizing a large variety of instrumentations, including ICP-MS, XRF, XRD, Microprobe, radiogenic isotope, stable isotope, gamma detector, multisensor core logger and CT scanner instruments.

Mount Allison University

Coastal Wetlands Institute
Department of Geography, 65 York St., Sackville NB E4L 1E4 Canada
Tel: 506-364-2428; *Fax:* 506-364-2625
www.mta.ca/research/macwi
Mission: Research facility at Mount Allison University focused on the study of coastal wetlands at the biological, chemical, and physical level. The Institute seeks to promote and conduct research on the scientific, social, and economic aspects of coastal wetlands while enhancing understanding of coastal wetlands in eastern Canada.

Mount Royal University

Miistakis Institute for the Rockies
Mount Royal University, #U271, 4825 Mount Royal Gate SW, Calgary AB T3E 6K6
Tel: 403-440-8444; *Fax:* 403-440-8446
e-mail: institute@rockies.ca
www.rockies.ca
Overview: A organization founded in 1995
Mission: A non-profit corporation, affiliated with the University of Calgary, the Miistakis Institute for the Rockies' area of concern is the Crown of the Continent, which is an international ecosystem with the Waterton-Glacier International Peace Park at its core. The Crown of the Continent covers areas of Alberta, British Columbia, & Montana. The Institute engages in research programs that reflect conservation issues in the region. Examples of programs include a literature eeview of golf course impacts on wildlife; spatial analysis of residential expansion in the Crown of the Continent ecosystem; & recreation & wildlife in the Rockies of southwestern Alberta.

Mushkegowuk Environmental Research Centre (MERC)

36 Birch St. South, Timmins ON P4N 2A5 Canada
Tel: 705-268-1123; *Fax:* 705-268-3282
e-mail: csutherland@vianet.ca
www.merc.ontera.net
Overview: A organization founded in 2005
Mission: The Mushkegowuk Environmental Research Centre (MERC) is a First Nation owned independent agency that undertakes and coordinates research relating to the environmental and natural resources with a focus on the Western James Bay basin in Ontario.

National Hydrology Research Centre (NHRC)

11 Innovation Blvd., Saskatoon SK S7N 3H5
Overview: A organization founded in 1986
Mission: A centre of the National Water Research Institute, the National Hydrology Research Centre focuses upon water-related issues of public concern to sustain freshwater ecosystems & natural resources. The Centre monitors stream & river levels throughout Canada.

National Water Research Institute (NWRI)

PO Box 5050, 867 Lakeshore Rd., Burlington ON L7R 4A6 Canada
Tel: 905-336-4625; *Fax:* 905-336-6444
www.ec.gc.ca/inre-nwri/default.asp?lang=En&n=7CE9E3AC-1
Mission: Canada's preeminent freshwater research facility. With partners in the Canadian and international science communities, NWRI conducts a comprehensive program of ecosystem-based research and development in the aquatic sciences.
Affiliation(s): Water Science and Technology Directorate (WSTD); National Water Quality Monitoring Office

North Pacific Marine Science Organization (PICES)

c/o Institute of Ocean Sciences, PO Box 6000, 9860 West Saanich Rd., Sidney BC V8L 4B2
Tel: 250-363-6366; *Fax:* 250-363-6827
e-mail: secretariat@PICES.int
www.pices.int
Overview: A organization founded in 1992
Mission: The intergovernmental scientific organization coordinates marine research in the North Pacific & its surrounding seas. The following countries are members of the North Pacific Marine Science Organization: Canada, the United States of America, the Russian Federation, the People's Republic of China, Japan, & the Republic of Korea.

Northern Forestry Centre (NoFC)

5320 - 122nd St., Edmonton AB T6H 3S5
Tel: 780-435-7210; *Fax:* 780-435-7359
e-mail: webmaster@nofc.cfs.nrcan.gc.ca
cfs.nrcan.gc.ca/centres/nofc
Mission: The Canadian Forest Service centre carries out research in areas such as biodivesity, climate change, ecology & ecosystems, forest & landscape management, & silviculture & regeneration. Examples of research projects are as follows: climate change impacts on the productivity & health of aspen; fire & forest dynamics under climate change scenarios; reconstruction of natural fire regimes; impacts of fire & harvesting on soils & site productivity; & human dimensions of biodiversity conservation in the Foothills Model Forest.

Northwest Atlantic Fisheries Centre (NAFC)

PO Box 5667, St. John's NL A1C 5X1 Canada
Tel: 709-772-4355; *Fax:* 709-772-6100
Mission: The Northwest Atlantic Fisheries Centre is a research facility used through the Canadian Department of Fisheries and Oceans. The Centre conducts research in a variety of fields related to the fisheries industry, including habitat research and assessment, oceanography, environmental and habitat management, aquaculture, ecology and population dynamics, parasitology, and toxicology.

Nova Scotia Department of Natural Resources

Renewable Resources Branch
Founders Square, PO Box 698, 1701 Hollis St., Halifax NS B3J 3M8 Canada
www.gov.ns.ca/natr/thedepartment/renewable.asp
Mission: The Renewable Resources Branch of Natural Resources Nova Scotia provides policy, planning and program development in the area of management and conservation of forests, parks, and wildlife resources in Nova Scotia. The Branch coordinates research and development projects aimed at improving resource management and sustainability goals.

Oil Sands Tailing Research Facility (OSTRF)

c/o Devon Research Centre, One Oil Patch Dr., Devon AB T9G 1A8
www.ostrf.com
Mission: The Oil Sands Tailings Research Facility was established to provide research to develop environmentally superior tailings disposal options. To improve tailings management in the oil sands industry, the Facility works with the Canadian Oil Sands Network for Research & Development Extraction Research Group. Examples of research projects include water treatment options & their application to oil sands operations for recycling & safe discharge, & advanced treatment of oil sands tailings water.

Ontario Rural Wastewater Centre (ORWC)

Baxter
c/o Rideau Valley Conservation Authority, 3889 Rideau Valley Dr., Manotick ON K4M 1A5 Canada
Tel: 613-692-3571; *Fax:* 613-692-0831
e-mail: rosalind.kee@rvca.ca

Ontario Rural Wastewater Centre (ORWC)

Campus d'Alfred
Campus d'Alfred, University of Guelph, 31 St. Paul St., Alfred ON K0B 1A0 Canada
Tel: 613-679-2218; *Fax:* 613-679-2420
e-mail: ckinsley@alfredc.uoguelph.ca

Ouranos

Tour Ouest, 19e étage, 550, rue Sherbrooke ouest, Montréal QC H3A 1B9 Canada
Tél: 514-282-6464; *Téléc:* 514-282-7131
Courriel: webmestre@ouranos.ca
www.ouranos.ca
Mission: Ouranos is a non-profit consortium of 400 scientists & others doing research in the areas of climate science & adaptation to climate change. The focus is on developing new knowledge on climate change & its socioeconomic & environmental impacts, with a view to providing solid information to decision & policy makers.

Pacific Biological Station (PBS)

3190 Hammond Bay Rd., Nanaimo BC V9T 6N7
Tel: 250-756-7000; *Fax:* 250-756-7053
Overview: A organization founded in 1908
Mission: As a research facility of Fisheries & Oceans Canada, the fisheries research centre concentrates its studies on the following waters: British Columbia's coastal waters, the Western Arctic, the Northeast Pacific Ocean, & the navigable waters east to the Manitoba, Saskatchewan border. The Pacific Biological Station's research contributes to the following areas: stock assessment, fish productivity, habitat, ocean science, & marine environment.

Pacific Environmental Science Centre (PESC)
2645 Dollarton Hwy., North Vancouver BC V7H 1V2
Tel: 604-903-4444; *Fax:* 604-903-4408
Mission: A federal laboratory of Environment Canada, The Pacific Environmental Science Centre is engaged in testing the quality of water, sediments, soil, & biota. The testing contributes to research in environmental protection, shellfish water quality, emergency response, & environmental quality monitoring. The Centre partners with Health Canada, BC Environment, Fisheries & Oceans Canada, Transport Canada, & the University of Victoria. Its clients include municipal & territorial governments & First Nations.

Pacific Forestry Centre (PFC)
506 West Burnside Rd., Victoria BC V8Z 1M5
Tel: 250-363-0600; *Fax:* 250-363-0775
e-mail: webmaster@pfc.cfs.nrcan.gc.ca
cfs.nrcan.gc.ca/centres/pfc
Mission: The Canadian Forest Service centre conducts research in the following areas: biodiversity, ecology & ecosystems, entomology, & forest & landscape management. Examples or research projects in the Pacific Region are as follows: stand development following mountain pine beetle outbreaks in south-central British Columbia; application of Landsat Satellite Imagery to monitor land-cover changes at the Athabasca Oil Sands; & investigating the effectiveness of mountain pine beetle mitigation strategies.

Pacific Geoscience Centre
PO Box 6000, 9860 West Saanich Rd., Sidney BC V8L 4B2
Tel: 250-363-6500; *Fax:* 250-363-6565
Also Known As: Geological Survey of Canada Pacific (Sidney)
Mission: The Pacific Geoscience Centre conducts research in the following areas: Marine Geoscience, to study the the coastal marine environment; Earthquakes Canada; & Geodynamics, to investigate the movement of the Earth's crust. An example of one of the Centre's projects is the Georgia Basin Geohazards Initiative, to provide research to aid in environmental & resource management decision making.

Pacific Wildlife Research Centre (PWRC)
5421 Robertson Rd., Delta BC V4K 3N2
Tel: 604-940-4700; *Fax:* 604-946-7022
Mission: The mission of the Pacific Wildlife Research Centre is the management & protection of wildlife, endangered species, & migratory birds & their habitats. The Centre also strives to maintain biological diversity.

Petroleum Research Newfoundland & Labrador (PRNL)
Bbaine Johnston Centre, #802, 10 Fort William Place, St. John's NL A1C 1K4 Canada
Tel: 709-738-7916; *Fax:* 709-738-7922
pr-ac.ca
Mission: Petroleum Research is a federally-incorporated, not-for-profit organization that funds and facilitates collaborative research and development (R&D) on behalf of Newfoundland and Labrador's offshore oil and gas industry.

Pipeline Engineering Center
c/o Dr. R. Hugo, Department of Mechanical & Manufacturing Engineering, 2500 University Dr. NW, Schulich School of Engineering, U. of Calgary, Calgary AB T2N 1N4
Tel: 403-220-5770
schulich.ucalgary.ca/PEC
Mission: The Pipeline Engineering Center is engaged in the maintenance & management of pipelines, the development of new pipeline technologies, & project management. Some areas of research include improvements in pipeline safety & environmental control, hydrogen & carbon dioxide transmission, & new coatings synthesis.

Prairie & Northern Laboratory for Environmental Testing (PNLET)
Northern Forestry Centre, NRCan, 5320 - 122 St., Edmonton AB T6H 3S5
Tel: 780-435-7335; *Fax:* 780-435-7268
Mission: The Prairie & Northern Laboratory for Environmental Testing consists of an ecotoxicology laboratory & chemistry laboratories. Examples of specialization include sediment studies for the Water Survey of Canada's National Sediment Program, ozone depleting substances, & phosphate in detergent guidelines related to the Fisheries Act. Its work supports the Canadian Environmental Protection Act & the Fisheries Act, as well as other federal government departments & prairie provincial governments.

Prairie Northern Wildlife Research Centre
Canadian Wildlife Service, 115 Perimeter Rd., Saskatoon SK S7N 0X4
Tel: 306-975-4087; *Fax:* 306-975-4089
Overview: A organization founded in 1966
Mission: Affiliated with Environment Canada, the Prairie Northern Wildlife Research Centre is involved in research related to prairie & northern wildlife ecology & conservation. Examples of research include the impacts of forestry upon birds, & the effects of pesticides on wildlife. The Centre also focuses upon migratory birds & their habitat, such as prairie waterfowl, songbirds, shorebirds, & Arctic-nesting geese.

Québec Ministère du Développement durable, de l'Environnement et des Parcs
Centre d'expertise hydrique
Édifice Marie-Guyart, Aile René-Lévesque, 1er étage, 675, boul René-Lévesque est, Québec QC G1R 5V7 Canada
Tél: 418-521-3866; *Téléc:* 418-643-6900
Courriel: cehq@mddep.gouv.qc.ca
www.cehq.gouv.qc.ca
Aperçu: ; fondée en 2001
Mission: Le Centre d'expertise hydrique du Québec (CEHQ) est une unité administrative du ministère du Développement durable, de l'Environnement, de la Faune et des Parcs (MDDEFP). Conformément à la Convention de performance et d'imputabilité (CPI) conclue en avril 2001 avec le ministre de l'Environnement, il forme une agence, laquelle relève de la Direction générale de l'expertise hydrique, de l'analyse et des évaluations environnementales. Il évolue constamment pour rester à la fine pointe des connaissances et du savoir-faire dans les domaines des barrages, du régime hydrique et du domaine hydrique de l'État.

Queen's University
Queen's Institute for Energy & Power Electronics Research
Walter Light Hall, Queen's University, 19 Union St., Kingston ON K7L 3N6 Canada
www.queensu.ca/epower
Also Known As: ePOWER
Overview: A organization founded in 2011
Mission: The Queen's Centre for Energy and Power Electronics Research (ePOWER) fosters collaboration among academic and industrial researchers to advance fundamental energy and power electronics research, to develop a broad range of commercially competitive and environmentally friendly technologies, and to train the next generation of innovators.

Queen's University (QIEEP)
Queen's Institute for Energy and Environmental Policy
Policy Studies Bldg., Queen's University, #137, 138 Union St., Kingston ON K7L 3N6 Canada
Tel: 613-533-6000; *Fax:* 613-533-6875
www.queensu.ca/qieep/
Mission: The Institute aims to produce recommendations on energy & environmental policy that is of use to governments & the public. It assists with information gathering & securing research-related funding, & seeks general funding as well. A multi-disciplinary approach that results in high quality, timely & relevant research is a focus.

Queen's University
GeoEngineering Centre
#101, Ellis Hall, Queen's University, Kingston ON K7L 3N6 Canada
Tel: 613-533-6370; *Fax:* 613-533-2128
e-mail: info@geoeng.ca
www.geoeng.ca
Overview: A organization founded in 2001
Mission: A collaborative venture, the Centre brings together researchers from engineering departments at Queen's University & Royal Military College to develop knowledge & innovative solutions in the areas of geotechnical, geohydrological, geochemical & geosynthetics engineering. Specific research & project areas include groundwater & remediation; soil mechanics; geoenvironmental concerns such as soil & water pollution, solid waste management; geomechanics; geosynthetics (the effects of polymeric & other types of material as they contact soil or rock); & geochemistry.

Réseau de recherche en santé environnementale (RRSE) / Environmental Health Research Network (EHRN)
Institut national de la recherche scientifique, 531, boul des Prairies, Laval QC H7V 1B7 Canada
Courriel: rrse@uquebec.ca
www.rrse.ca
Mission: Le RRSE, financé par le Fonds de recherche du Québec - Santé (FRQS), regroupe virtuellement tous les chercheurs universitaires du Québec qui ouvrent dans le domaine de la santé environnementale. La recherche en santé environnementale, qui est de nature préventive, vise à caractériser l'impact des contaminants chimiques et physiques de l'environnement comme déterminants de la santé.

Royal Roads University (CLE)
Centre for Livelihoods and Ecology
2005 Sooks Rd., Victoria BC V9B 5Y2 Canada
Tel: 250-391-2600; *Fax:* 250-391-2563
e-mail: cle@royalroads.ca
cle.royalroads.ca
Mission: The Centre for Livelihoods and Ecology (CLE) conducts strategic and applied research to encourage the wise use of natural resources as a way to diversify and sustain rural communities.

Ryerson University (CSFS)
Centre for Studies in Food Security
KHS 348 C, Ryerson University, 350 Victoria St., Toronto ON M5B 2K3 Canada
Fax: 416-979-5204
www.ryerson.ca/foodsecurity
Overview: A organization founded in 1994
Mission: The Centre for Studies in Food Security promotes food security through research, dissemination, education, community action and professional practice. They take an interdisciplinary and systemic approach to the social justice, environmental sustainability, health and socio-cultural aspects of food security.

Ryerson University (CUE)
Centre for Urban Energy
Ryerson University, 147 Dalhousie St., Toronto ON M5B 2K3 Canada
Tel: 416-979-5000
e-mail: info@cue.ryerson.ca
www.cue.ryerson.ca
Mission: The Centre for Urban Energy collaborates with academic, public- and private-sector organizations, and CUE researchers to light the way in developing and commercializing innovative solutions to urban energy issues. Research areas include Renewable Energy, Smart Building & Net-Zero Homes, Efficiency, Conservation & Demand Management, Energy Storage, and Environmental, Social & Economic Impacts.
Affliation(s): Hydro One, Ontario Power Authority, Toronto Hydro

St. Andrews Biological Station (SABS)
531 Brandy Cove Rd., St. Andrews NB E5B 2L9 Canada
Tel: 506-529-8854; *Fax:* 506-529-5862
e-mail: XMARSABS@mar.dfo-mpo.gc.ca
www.mar.dfo-mpo.gc.ca/sabs
Mission: The St. Andrews Biological Station (SABS) was established in 1908 and carries out research via Fisheries and Oceans Canada. SABS performs studies in Aquaculture and Biological Interactions, Coastal Ocean Research, Population Ecology, and other areas.

St. Francis Xavier University (CASI)
Climate & Atmospheric Sciences Institute
Physical Sciences Complex, St. Francis Xavier University, PO Box 5000, 1 West St., Antigonish NS B2G 2W5 Canada
Tel: 902-867-5416; *Fax:* 902-867-2414
e-mail: climate@stfx.ca
climate.stfx.ca
Overview: A organization founded in 2004
Mission: The Climate & Atmospheric Sciences Institute (CASI) is a multidisciplinary research institute whose primary objective is to facilitate and promote the advancement of fundamental research in areas of Climate, Atmospheric, and some aspects of Environmental Sciences, with a strong emphasis on post graduate student training through research.

St. Francis Xavier University
Centre for Applied Petroleum Sciences
St. Francis Xavier University, PO Box 5000, Antigonish NS B2G 2W5 Canada
Tel: 902-867-2396; *Fax:* 902-867-2414
sites.stfx.ca/caps
Mission: Multidisciplinary research institute working in areas related to the oil and gas industry with researchers from Dalhousie, Lakehead, Guelph, and other Canadian Universities.

Current research projects include biofilms, colloids, and high-performance computing.

St. Francis Xavier University
St. Georges Bay Ecosystem Project
c/o St. Francis Xavier University, PO Box 5000, Antigonish NS B2G 2W5 Canada
people.stfx.ca/rsg/gbayesp
Mission: Interdisciplinary and collaborative research project working towards improved marine resource management, focused on researching the marine and human ecology of St. Georges Bay.

St. Francis Xavier University
Marine Ecology Lab
Department of Biology, Saint Francis Xavier University, 2320 Notre Dame Ave., Antigonish NS B2G 2W5 Canada
Tel: 902-867-5289; *Fax:* 902-867-2389
www.marineecologylab.com
Mission: The Marine Ecology Lab at St. Francis Xavier University is focused on research of the ecology of marine rocky shores. Research projects include species diversity, environmental stress, ecosystem biodiversity, species interactions, and ecological theory.

St. Mary's University
Maritimes Centre for Green Chemistry
Department of Chemistry, 923 Robie St., Halifax NS B3H 3C3 Canada
Tel: 902-496-8104
www.smu.ca/institutes/mcgc/welcome.html
Overview: A organization founded in 2010
Mission: The main purpose of the centre is to advance basic and applied research in the area of Green Chemistry that will in turn contribute to the application of chemical products and processes that use benign substances, reduce waste and energy consumption and make the most efficient use of non-renewable resources, offers industry a clean sustainable alternative to traditional chemical and manufacturing processes.

St. Mary's University
Community Based Environmental Monitoring Network
Department of Geography, Burke Building, #204A, 923 Robie St., Halifax NS B3H 3C3 Canada
Tel: 902-491-6243; *Fax:* 902-496-8213
e-mail: environmental.network@smu.ca
www.envnetwork.smu.ca
Mission: Environmental monitoring research network. The network is geared towards public participation and transparency in environmental monitoring systems and cooperation among organizations committed to environmental stewardship. The network also offers equipment and facilities at Saint Mary's University for environmental organizations. Projects include the monitoring of water and air quality.

St. Mary's University
Coastal CURA
c/o St. Mary's University, 923 Robie St., Halifax NS B3H 3C3 Canada
Tel: 902-420-5003; *Fax:* 902-496-8101
e-mail: coastalcura@smu.ca
www.coastalcura.ca
Mission: Five-year research project that consists of eight Maritime-based partners including Universities, First Nations partners, and Community organizations. The goal of the project is to implement a community-based governance of coastal resources. Research projects include local ecosystem research, ocean resource management, and fisheries.

St. Mary's University
Maritime Provinces Spatial Analysis Research Centre
c/o St. Mary's University, 923 Robie St., Halifax NS B3H 3C3 Canada
Tel: 902-420-5472
husky1.smu.ca/~dvanproo/Research_MP_SpARC.html
Also Known As: MP_SpARC
Overview: A organization founded in 2003
Mission: The Maritime Provinces Spatial Analysis Research Centre (MP_SpARC) is a computer-based, cross-discipline unit dedicated to spatial analysis using geomatics technologies. The purpose of the unit is to provide the necessary infrastructure and geomatics software to support research within the Maritime Provinces.

St. Mary's University (CEAR)
Centre for Environmental Analysis and Remediation
Science Building, St. Mary's University, #501, 923 Robie St., Halifax NS B3H 3C3 Canada
Tel: 902-496-8798; *Fax:* 902-420-5261
e-mail: cear@smu.ca
www.smu.ca/academic/fgsr/cear/welcome.html
Overview: A organization founded in 2000
Mission: Established as a research facility at St. Mary's University. The laboratory specializes in chemical analysis in the areas of chromatography, mass spectrometry and element analysis technologies. These technologies can be used for the separation and purification of compounds, structural and identification of organic compounds, identification of unknown substances, and quantification of elements and compounds.

St. Mary's University
Gorsebrook Research Institute
5960 Inglis St., Halifax NS B3H 1K8 Canada
Tel: 902-420-5668; *Fax:* 902-496-8135
e-mail: gorsebrook@smu.ca
www.smu.ca/administration/gorsebrook/north.html
Mission: The Office of Aboriginal and Northern Research was established at St. Mary's University through the Gorsebrook Research Institute in 2006. The Office maintains a collaboration between the Innu First Nation and Environment Canada. The Office works with both First Nation and Government researchers to develop First Nation solutions to ecological issues in the area.

Simon Fraser University
Centre for Coastal Science and Management
Lifelong Learning, Continuing Studies, #WMC 1356, 8888 University Dr., Burnaby BC V5A 1S6 Canada
www.sfu.ca/coastal.html
Mission: The Centre for Coastal Science and Management focuses on coastal and marine ecosystems, and resource conservation and sustainability through collaborative research projects and community engagement at local, national and international levels.

Simon Fraser University (E2O)
Earth2Ocean Group
Dept. of Biological Sciences, Simon Fraser University, #B6220, 8888 University Dr., Burnaby BC V5A 1S6 Canada
Tel: 778-782-4659; *Fax:* 778-782-4968
e-mail: e2o@sfu.ca
www.sfu.ca/biology/earth2ocean/Earth2Ocean
Overview: A organization founded in 2010
Mission: The E2O Group was formed to tackle global environmental problems through interdisciplinary collaborative science. Studies of aquatic ecology and conservation range from tropical reef ecosystems to the rivers and wetlands of Alaska.

Simon Fraser University (CRMI)
Cooperative Resource Management Institute
c/o School of Resource & Environment Management, 8888 University Dr., Burnaby BC V5A 1S6
Tel: 778-782-3074; *Fax:* 778-782-4968
www.rem.sfu.ca/crmi
Overview: A organization founded in 1998
Mission: Fisheries & Oceans Canada's SAFE Division, at Simon Fraser University, carries out research activities in the following areas related to salmonids: incubation, rearing, feeding behaviour, migration, & their habitat. Research is conducted in coastal & interior British Columbia, & the Yukon. Examples of the SAFE Division's research projects are as follows: the impacts of energy generation on adult salmon migration; & the effects of timber harvesting on fish habitat.

Simon Fraser University (CSCD)
Centre for Sustainable Community Development
c/o Faculty of Environment, Simon Fraser University, #tASC2 8800, 8888 University Dr., Burnaby BC V5A 1S6
Tel: 778-782-8787; *Fax:* 778-782-8788
e-mail: scdadmin@sfu.ca
www.sfu.ca/cscd

Overview: A organization founded in 1989
Mission: Simon Fraser University's Centre for Sustainable Community Development conducts research to support the sustainable development of communities. Research considers the relationship between economic factors & the natural environment, health, housing, education, & the arts.

Simon Fraser University (CWE)
Centre for Wildlife Ecology
Department of Biological Sciences, Simon Fraser University, 8888 University Dr., Burnaby BC V5A 1S6
Tel: 778-782-5958; *Fax:* 778-782-3496
www.sfu.ca/biology/wildberg
Mission: A collaboration between Simon Fraser University & the Canadian Wildlife Service, the Centre for Wildlife Ecology conducts research in wildlife ecology. Research aids in meeting conservation challenges. Examples of research include Triangle Island seabird research, landbird ecology, avian reproduction & environmental change, & the sustainable shellfish aquaculture initiative.

Simon Fraser University (EBERG)
Evolutionary & Behavioural Ecology Research Group
Department of Biological Sciences, Simon Fraser University, 8888 University Dr., Burnaby BC V5A 1S6
www.sfu.ca/biology/berg
Overview: A organization founded in 1989
Mission: Simon Fraser University's Evolutionary & Behavioural Ecology Research Group studies behaviours of organisms, such as plants, insects, fish, birds, & mammals, & their relationship with the environment. An example of research is behaviour & conservation biology, in association with Simon Fraser University's Centre for Wildlife Ecology.

Sustainable Forest Management Network (SFMN) / Réseau de gestion durable des forêts
#3-03, Civil Engineering Bldg., University of Alberta, Edmonton AB T6G 2G7
Tel: 780-492-6659; *Fax:* 780-492-8160
e-mail: info@sfmnetwork.ca
www.sfmnetwork.ca
Overview: A organization founded in 1995
Mission: The non-profit Canadian research group is engaged in conducting interdisciplinary, university-based research related to sustainable forest management. The following are examples of research projects: climate change vulnerability & adaptation for forest management in Canada; eEcological & economic trade-off analysis of conservation strategies for woodland caribou; & evaluation of the potential effect of insect outbreaks on sustainable forest management.

Tree Ring Lab
c/o Dr. K.J. Lewis, College of Science & Management, U. of Northern BC, #LABB 212, 3333 University Way, Prince George BC V2N 4Z9
www.unbc.ca/dendrolab
Mission: Examples of research conducted by the University of Northern British Columbia's Tree Ring Lab are as follows: change in Douglas fir sensitivity to climate variation in British Columbia; the influence of disturbance agents on mature spruce-subalpine fir forests in central British Columbia; & wood decay & degradation in lodgepole pine killed by mountain pine beetles.

Trent University
Trent Water Quality Centre
Dept. of Physics & Astronomy & Chemistry, Trent University, 1600 West Bank Dr., Peterborough ON K9J 7B8 Canada
Tel: 705-748-1011; *Fax:* 705-750-2786
e-mail: waterqualitycentre@trentu.ca
www.trentu.ca/wqc
Mission: Specializes in method development and the application of new and innovative techniques for measuirng isotopes and trace amounts of organic and inorganic contaminants in water.

Trent University
Trent Centre for Biomaterials Research Program and Laboratory
Dept. of Physics & Astronomy & Chemistry, Trent University, 1600 West Bank Dr., Peterborough ON K9J 7B8 Canada
Tel: 705-748-1011; *Fax:* 705-750-2786
www.trentu.ca/biomaterials
Mission: Research in the Trent Centre for Biomaterials Research is focussed on the utilization of vegetable oils (soybean, canola, flax, corn, jatropha, palm, etc.) for the synthesis of functional polymers (for use as intelligent coatings, biomedical delivery systems and other specialized polymers), lubricants, greases and waxes, nano-matrices for the delivery of bioactive compounds and fertilizers, and crystallized networks of lipids for use as healthy food materials.

Trent University
James McLean Oliver Ecological Centre
Trent University, 1481 Mill Line Rd., Bobcaygeon ON K0M 1A0 Canada
Tel: 705-731-0183
www.trentu.ca/olivercentre
Mission: The Centre is being developed as a residential field station for teaching and for long-term ecological research.

Trent University
Institute for Watershed Science
Trent University, Symons Campus, Sicence Complex Bldg., #204, 1600 West Bank Dr., Peterborough ON K9J 7B8 Canada
Tel: 705-748-1011; *Fax:* 705-748-1022
Toll-Free: 888-739-8885
www.trentu.ca/iws

Overview: A organization founded in 1998
Mission: The Institute aims to further the understanding of physical and ecological processes governing watershed function and to transfer this knowledge to support resource management decision-making.
Affliation(s): Ontario Ministry of Natural Resources; Sir Sandford Fleming College

Trent University
Centre for Environmental Modelling and Chemistry
Trent University, 1600 West Bank Dr., Peterborough ON K9J 7B8 Canada
www.trentu.ca/academic/aminss/envmodel

Overview: A organization founded in 1995
Mission: The Centre's goal is to understand and predict quantitatively the pathways of contaminant transport and the resulting exposure, often through the use of computer programs which simulate or model the chemicals' behaviour.

Université de Moncton
Southern Gulf of St. Lawrence Coalition on Sustainability / Coalition pour la viabilité du sud du Golfe du Saint-Laurent
047B Pavillion Irêne Léger, Université de Moncton, Campus de Shippagan, 218, boul J.-D.-Gauthier, Shippagan NB E8S 1P6 Canada
Tel: 506-336-9005; *Fax:* 506-336-9006
e-mail: coord@coalition-sgsl.ca
www.coalition-sgsl.ca
Mission: The Southern Gulf of St. Lawrence Coalition on Sustainability is a non-profit organization seeking to promote an environmentally, economically, and socially sustainable Southern Gulf of St. Lawrence. The Coalition seeks to promote awareness and education on sustainability issues by supporting community initiattives, monitoring progress, as well as working with local science and research organizations. The Coalition's Science, Research & Habitat working group seeks to establish indicators for project monitoring and evaluation.

Université de Moncton
Coastal Zones Research Institute Inc. (CZRI) / Institut de recherche sur les zones côtières inc. (IRZC)
Université de Moncton, Campus de Shippagan, 232B, ave de l'Eglise, Shippagan NB E8S 1J2 Canada
Tel: 506-336-6600; *Fax:* 506-336-6601
e-mail: info@irzc.umcs.ca
www.irzc.umcs.ca
Mission: The Coastal Zones Research Institute Inc. (CZRI) is a private non-profit institution affiliated with the Université de Moncton and established in 2002. The Institute promotes a multidisciplinary approach that focuses on three main areas of research: aquaculture, fishery and marine products, and peat and peatlands. The Institute also conducts research on the sustainable development of coastal zones.

Université du Québec
Institut national de la recherche scientifique - Centre-Eau Terre Environnement
490, rue de la Couronne, Québec QC G1K 9A9 Canada
Tél: 418-654-2524; *Téléc:* 418-654-2600
Ligne sans frais: 877-326-5762
Courriel: info@ete.inrs.ca
ete.inrs.ca
Mission: A university research group dedicated to higher research into water & earth resources, with a focus on sustainable development issues, conservation & effective resource management. Issues such as environmental risk factors, pollution/contamination, climate change, remediation solutions are current research areas.

Université du Québec à Montréal
Centre d'étude de la forêt
CP 8888, Succ. Centre-ville, Montréal QC H3C 3P8 Canada
Tél: 514-987-3000; *Téléc:* 514-987-4647
www.cef-cfr.ca
Mission: The Centre for Forest Research brings together researchers from across universities in Québec in a collaborative endeavour to provide research into forest ecosystems, forest management & silviculture. The focus is on integrating scientific knowledge with an innovative approach in order to more effectively & sustainably manage forests in the province.

Université du Québec à Montréal
Institut des sciences de l'environnement
CP 8888, Succ. Centre-ville, Montréal QC H3C 3P8 Canada
Tél: 514-987-4717; *Téléc:* 514-987-4718
Courriel: ise@uqam.ca
www.ise.uqam.ca
Mission: Brings together students, faculty & researchers in a collaborative, interdisciplinary research endeavour, with a focus on environment & human health, urban ecosystems, forest & water management, & climate change & its effects on the environment.

Université du Québec à Montréal (ESCER)
Centre pour l'étude et la simulation du climat à l'échelle régionale
CP 8888, Succ. Centre-ville, Montréal QC H3C 3P8 Canada
Tél: 514-987-3000; *Téléc:* 514-987-6853
www.escer.uqam.ca
Mission: Le Centre de recherche ESCER, unique en son genre, vise le développement d'outils prévisionnels performants qui serviront à de nombreux organismes concernés par les changements climatiques.

Université du Québec à Montréal (MDCR)
Réseau canadien en modélisation et diagnostics du climat régional
Centre ESCER, CP 8888, Succ. Centre-ville, Montréal QC H3C 3P8 Canada
Tél: 514-987-3000; *Téléc:* 514-987-6853
www.mrcc.uqam.ca
Mission: Développer un nouveau modèle régional du climat à haute résolution pour l'évaluation climatique régionale, grâce à des techniques diagnostiques appropriées pour analyser les grands ensembles d'informations climatiques haute résolution.

University of Alberta
Canadian Centre for Clean Coal/Carbon and Mineral Processing Technologies (C5MPT)
University of Alberta, ECERF Bldg., 9107 - 116th St., 7th Fl., Edmonton AB T6G 2V4
Tel: 780-492-1375; *Fax:* 780-492-2881
e-mail: cfivempt@ualberta.ca
www.ualberta.ca/CMENG/c5mpt
Mission: The Canadian Centre for Clean Coal/Carbon and Mineral processing Technologies (C5MPT) is a research and education centre that supports sustainable and responsible energy and mineral development. It is part of the University of Alberta's Faculty of Engineering and is housed within the Department of Chemical and Materials Engineering. Research addresses three aligned themes:imization of the surface footprint in the mining process, & the reduction of the amount of energy used in upgrading bitumen.

University of Alberta (CEFM)
Centre for Enhanced Forest Management
Department of Renewable Resources, University of Alberta, #442, Earth Sciences Bldg., Edmonton AB T6G 2E3
www.cefm.rr.ualberta.ca
Mission: The Centre for Enhanced Forest Management at the University of Alberta is engaged in research to contribute to the sustainable management & productivity of northern forests. The Centre works to develop & test forestry practices that will enhance wood production & values such as biodiversity, watershed, wildlife, & recreation. Areas of research are as follows: forest soils; silviculture & reclamation; forest management & protection; forest genetics & tree improvement; & growth & yield.

University of Alberta (ERSC)
Environmental Research & Studies Centre
University of Alberta, #3-23, Business Bldg., Edmonton AB T6G 2R6
Tel: 780-492-5825; *Fax:* 780-492-3325
e-mail: ersc@ualberta.ca
www.ualberta.ca/~ersc/ERSC1.html
Overview: A organization founded in 1990
Mission: The Environmental Research & Studies Centre promotes interdisciplinary, inter-university, & international environmental research.

University of Alberta (COSI)
Centre for Oil Sands Innovation
University of Alberta, ECERF Bldg., 9107 - 116th St., 7th Fl., Edmonton AB T6G 2V4
Tel: 780-492-8811; *Fax:* 780-492-9952
e-mail: cosiexec@ualberta.ca
www.engineering.ualberta.ca/COSI.cfm
Mission: The Imperial Oil-Alberta Ingenuity Centre for Oil Sands Innovation at the University of Alberta strives to improve oil sand operations. The Centre works to develop technology in oil sands mining, extraction, & upgrading, for cleaner & less expensive oil sands operations. Examples of the Centre's projects include the reduction of the amount of water used in oil sands extraction, the minimization of the surface footprint in the mining process, & the reduction of the amount of energy used in upgrading bitumen.

University of Alberta (CEOS)
Center for Earth Observation Sciences
Department of Earth & Atmospheric Sciences, University of Alberta, #1-26 Earth Sciences Bldg., Edmonton AB T6G 2E3
Tel: 780-492-9870; *Fax:* 780-492-2030
e-mail: ceos@ualberta.ca
www.ceos.ualberta.ca
Mission: The University of Alberta Center for Earth Observation Sciences is a multi-disciplinary research network, which monitors environmental changes & resource management, & formulates sustainable development policies. Examples of monitoring activities include changes in biodiversity, the effects of forest fires, & snow cover & land ice.

University of Alberta
Alberta Centre for Surface Engineering & Science (ACSES)
University of Alberta, #607, Chemical & Materials Engineering Bldg., Edmonton AB T6G 2G6
Tel: 780-492-1246; *Fax:* 780-492-1250
www.ualberta.ca/ACSES
Mission: The Alberta Centre for Surface Engineering & Science of the University of Alberta is involved in research related to corrosion & wear, natural resource extraction, & microfabrication. An application of research is the development of methods to reduce waste produced in oil sands extraction.

University of Alberta (CIMS)
Centre for Intelligent Mining Systems
Department of Computing Science, University of Alberta, #351, Computer Science Centre, Edmonton AB T6G 2E1
Tel: 780-492-6365
e-mail: cims@cs.ualberta.ca
www.cs.ualberta.ca/~cims
Mission: The Centre for Intelligent Mining Systems is engaged in exploratory research in intelligent systems for the oil sands mining industry. Research is conducted to develop intelligent systems technology to improve the surface mining process, by minimizing the environmental footprint & increasing efficiencies.

University of Alberta (CABREE)
Centre for Applied Business Research in Energy & the Environment
c/o Richard Dixon, University of Alberta, 3-23, School of Business, Edmonton AB T6G 2R6
www.business.ualberta.ca/cabree
Mission: The independent research centre provides applied economic analysis to affect public policy. The Centre for Applied Business Research in Energy & the Environment focuses upon the following research areas: climate change issues, electricity restructuring, & energy markets.

University of Alberta (ABMI)
Alberta Biodiversity Monitoring Institute
University of Alberta, #405CW, Biological Sciences Building, Edmonton AB T6G 2E9
Tel: 780-248-1592; *Fax:* 780-492-7635
e-mail: abmiinfo@ualberta.ca
www.abmi.ca
Mission: The Alberta Biodiversity Monitoring Institute facilitates environmental management, by monitoring ecosystems, species, & habitats in Alberta. The Institute's research on the state of Alberta's biodiversity is used to support decision-making related to natural resources.

University of Alberta (CBEEDAC)
Canadian Building Energy End-Use Data & Analysis Centre
Department of Economics, University of Alberta, #8-14 Tory Bldg., Edmonton AB T6G 2H4
Tel: 780-492-4134; *Fax:* 780-492-3300
e-mail: cbeedac@ualberta.ca
www.ualberta.ca/~cbeedac

Mission: The Canadian Building Energy End-Use Data & Analysis Centre is engaged in the provision of building energy data. The data is used by the Canadian residential, commercial, & institutional sectors.

University of Alberta (CCI)
Canadian Circumpolar Institute
University of Alberta, #1-37, Pembina Hall, Edmonton AB T6G 2H8
Tel: 780-492-4512; *Fax:* 780-492-1153
e-mail: ccinst@gpu.srv.ualberta.ca
www.uofaweb.ualberta.ca/polar
Mission: The interdisciplinary centre conducts research to contribute to the development of sustainable communities & to increase understanding of northern Canada, the Arctic, & Antarctica. Examples of research include climate change in the Arctic, rivers & lakes, & wildlife habitats under stress.

University of Alberta (AGC)
Alberta Glycomics Centre
Dept. of Chemistry, University Of Alberta, Edmonton AB T6G 2G2
Tel: 780-492-4794; *Fax:* 780-492-7705
www.glycomicscentre.ca

Overview: A organization founded in 2004
Mission: The Alberta Glycomics Centre spans a multidisciplinary array of biological processes and technologies specific to carbohydrate research. The fields of chemistry, biology, medicine, and engineering are dynamically integrated as experts in areas such as carbohydrate synthesis, proteincarbohydrate interactions, glycoengineering, drug discovery, vaccine development, mass spectrometry, and X-ray crystallography work together to explore carbohydrate science.

University of British Columbia (AFRICAD)
Africa Forests Research Initiative on Conservation & Development
c/o Faculty of Forestry, University of British Columbia, #2900, 2424 Main Mall, Vancouver BC V6T 1Z4
e-mail: africad.info@ubc.ca
www.africad.ubc.ca
Mission: AFRICAD is a conservation-oriented research initiative located within the Faculty of Forestry at the University of British Columbia. They work in Africa's forested regions on applied research that addresses poverty alleviation, sustainable livelihoods, social equity, and conflicts over forest resources.

University of British Columbia (CAS)
Centre for Alpine Studies
c/o Faculty of Forestry, University of British Columbia, #3041, 2424 Main Mall, Vancouver BC V6T 1Z4
web.forestry.ubc.ca/alpine
Mission: The Centre for Alpine Studies serves to coordinate scientific research conducted on alpine ecosystems.
Affiliation(s): Centre for Applied Conservation Research

University of British Columbia (CFCG)
Centre for Forest Conservation Genetics
Forest Science Centre, University of British Columbia, 2424 Main Mall, 3rd Fl., Vancouver BC V6T 1Z4
www.genetics.forestry.ubc.ca/cfcg
Overview: A organization founded in 2000
Mission: Centre for Forest Conservation Genetics develops strategies to meet gene conservation goals.

University of British Columbia (AERL)
Aquatic Ecosystems Research Laboratory
Fisheries Centre, University of British Columbia, #230, 2202 Main Mall, Vancouver BC V6T 1Z4
Tel: 604-822-2731; *Fax:* 604-822-8934
e-mail: office@fisheries.ubc.ca
www.fisheries.ubc.ca
Mission: The Aquatic Ecosystems Research Laboratory is engaged in multidisciplinary research, which focuses upon conserving aquatic life, restoring fisheries, & rebuilding ecosystems. The Fisheries Centre consists of the following research units: Sea Around Us, to assess the impacts of fisheries; Fisheries Economics Research Unit; Back to the Future, to study the restoration of aquatic ecosystems & sustainable fishing; Project Seahorse, to advance marine conservation; Marine Mammal Research Unit; Quantitative Modeling Group, to develop mathematical models to assist biologists & resource managers; & Aboriginal Fisheries, to find how the First Nations of BC could contribute their knowledge towards fisheries conservation & management.

University of British Columbia (FRE Group)
Food & Resource Economics Group
Faculty of Land & Food Systems, University of British Columbia, #329, 2357 Main Mall, Vancouver BC V6T 1Z4
Tel: 604-822-1219; *Fax:* 604-822-2184
www.landfood.ubc.ca/fre

Mission: The University of British Columbia Group researches policy & economic issues related to food markets, renewable natural resources, & the environmnent. In the area of natural resource economics, examples of research include biodiversity & wildlife habitat. Examples of research within the area of environmental economics are ground water contamination & climate change.

University of British Columbia
Soil Water Environmental Group
Faculty of Land & Food Systems, University of British Columbia, #227, 2357 Main Mall, Vancouver BC V6T 1Z4
Tel: 604-822-6360
www.landfood.ubc.ca/swal
Mission: The University of British Columbia Group is involved in the research of human & natural processes which affect land & water resources. Examples of the Soil - Water Environmental Group's research are as follows: climate & land use changes on water resources, non-point source pollution, & land use impacts on water & soil quality.

University of British Columbia
Biodiversity Research Centre
University of British Columbia, #112, 2212 Main Mall, Vancouver BC V6T 1Z4
Tel: 604-822-0862; *Fax:* 604-827-5350
e-mail: biodiversity.centre@ubc.ca
www.zoology.ubc.ca/biodiversity
Mission: The Biodiversity Research Centre seeks to understand & conserve the diversity of life. Biological diversity is researched, from genes to ecosystems. Examples of the Centre's projects are as follows: conservation biology, fisheries management, & population & community ecology.

University of British Columbia (CERC)
Clean Energy Research Centre
University of British Columbia, 2360 East Mall, Vancouver BC V6T 1Z3
Tel: 604-827-4768
e-mail: info@cerc.ubc.ca
www.cerc.ubc.ca
Mission: The University of British Columbia's Clean Energy Centre strives to reduce the environmental impact of energy use, by investigating technologies which will provide sustainable energy. Examples of research projects are as follows: reducing energy loss from coking & fouling; biomass storage, handling & processing; hydrogen generation; & clean burning engines.

University of British Columbia
Norman B. Keevil Institute of Mining Engineering
University of British Columbia, 6350 Stores Rd., 5th fl., Vancouver BC V6T 1Z4
Tel: 604-822-2540; *Fax:* 604-822-5599
e-mail: info@mining.ubc.ca
www.mining.ubc.ca
Mission: The University of British Columbia's NBK Institute of Mining Engineering conducts research which promotes sustainability & improved working processes in the mining industry. Research projects range from mine safety to environmental issues. Examples of research are as follows: environmental research in minerals, metals, & materials; environmental services; & remote-monitoring systems for environmental protection.

University of British Columbia (CERM3)
Centre for Environmental Research in Minerals, Metals, & Materials
Norman B. Keevil Institute of Mining Engineering, University of BC, 6350 Stores Rd., Vancouver BC V6T 1Z4
Tel: 604-822-6217; *Fax:* 604-822-5599
e-mail: cerm3dir@mining.ubc.ca
www.cerm3.mining.ubc.ca
Overview: A organization founded in 2000
Mission: The Centre for Environmental Research in Minerals, Metals, & Materials works to understand & solve environmental problems caused by mining activity. The Centre is comprised of the following research facilities: The Environmental Quality Laboratory; The Mine Health & Safety Laboratory; The Bioremediation & Reclamation Laboratory; The Energy & Mining Laboratory; The Mine Automation & Environmental Simulation Laboratory; & The Environmental Technology Laboratory.

University of British Columbia
Liu Institute for Global Issues
The University of British Columbia, 6476 Marine Dr. NW, Vancouver BC V6T 1Z2
Fax: 604-822-6966
e-mail: liu.institute@ubc.ca
www.ligi.ubc.ca
Overview: A organization founded in 2000
Mission: The Liu Institute for Global Issues is engaged in interdisciplinary, policy-relevant research in the following areas: the environment, peace & security, development, justice, & health. Examples of environmental projects are as follows: Climate Science, Equity & Development: The Role of International Institutions in Capacity Building for Climate Change; Risks & Benefits of Nanotechnology; & Risk, Regulation & Controversy: Agricultural Biotechnology in Developing Countries.

University of British Columbia (CMPE)
Centre for Metallurgical Process Engineering
The University of British Columbia, #309, 6350 Stores Rd., Vancouver BC V6T 1Z4
www.cmpe.ubc.ca
Mission: The interdisciplinary research centre at the University of British Columbia is engaged in the development of advanced metallurgical processes & products. Researchers work to develop metallurgical processing technologies & practices which focus upon improved sustainability & efficiency.

University of British Columbia
Pulp & Paper Centre
The University of British Columbia, 2385 East Mall, Vancouver BC V6T 1Z4
Tel: 604-822-8560; *Fax:* 604-822-8563
e-mail: ppc-info@ppc.ubc.ca
www.ppc.ubc.ca
Mission: The Pulp & Paper Centre hosts collaborative research programs between the Pulp & Paper Research Institute of Canada (Paprican) & the University of British Columbia. Examples of environmental research include waste water & solids treatment, air emissions, life cycle assessment, & fouling & condensates.

University of British Columbia (IRES)
Institute for Resources, Environment & Sustainability
Aquatic Ecosystem Research Laboratory, University of British Columbia, #429, 2202 Main Mall, Vancouver BC V6T 1Z4
Tel: 604-822-7725; *Fax:* 604-822-9250
www.ires.ubc.ca
Mission: The interdisciplinary research institute at the University of British Columbia studies environmental & sustainability issues in order to foster sustainable futures. Research is conducted in the following areas: local & global environmental change; water, ecosystems & communities; & energy, technology, health, & society. The Institute for Resources, Environment & Sustainability carries out its research by working with governmental organizations, NGOs, local enterprises & international businesses.

University of Calgary (CEERE)
Centre for Environmental Engineering Research & Education
Schulich School of Engineering, University of Calgary, 2500 University Dr. NW, Calgary AB T2N 1N4
Tel: 403-220-2881
e-mail: ceere@ucalgary.ca
www.eng.ucalgary.ca/CEERE
Mission: The following are some research projects conducted by the Centre for Environmental Engineering Research & Education at the University of Calgary: Nanotechnology for the environment; Industrial & hazardous waste management technology; Sustainable landfills; Air pollution assessment & control technologies; Energy sector contaminated site remediation; Renewable energy; & Clean air & clean water technology.

University of Calgary (ISEEE)
Institute for Sustainable Energy, Environment, & Economy
Earth Sciences Bldg., University of Calgary, #1040, 2500 University Dr. NW, Calgary AB T2N 1N4
Tel: 403-210-9776; *Fax:* 403-220-2400
e-mail: info@iseee.ca
www.iseee.ca

Overview: A organization founded in 2003
Mission: The Institute for Sustainable Energy, Environment, & Economy is engaged in the development & implementation of energy & environment related initiatives at the University of Calgary. Interdisciplinary research is conducted at the Institute for the advancement of sustainable energy, the environment, & the economy. Areas of focus include energy & environment systems & modelling, applied geoscience, alternative energy, hydrocarbon recovery & upgrading, & business, legal & policy aspects of energy & the environment.

University of Calgary (BGS)
Biogeoscience Institute
Biosciences Bldg., University of Calgary, #186, 2500 University Dr. NW, Calgary AB T2N 1N4
Tel: 403-220-5355; *Fax:* 403-673-3671
www.bgs.ucalgary.ca

Mission: The Biogeoscience Institute focuses research studies in the Canadian Rockies & surrounding areas, in order to increase understanding of ecosystem processes in the region. Field stations are located in the Kananakis Valley & the Sheep River Provincial Park. Examples of research projects include hot trees & melting snow in the Rockies, collapse & recovery of recreational fisheries, & altitudinal gradients of stable isotopes in lee-slope precipitation in the Canadian Rocky Mountains. Research is used to affect environmental & natural resource policies.

University of Calgary (IRIS)
International Resource Industries & Sustainability Centre
Scurfield Hall, Haskayne School of Business, University of Calgary, 2500 University Dr. NW, Calgary AB T2N 1N4
Tel: 403-220-5685
haskayne.ucalgary.ca/research/research-centres/IRIS
Mission: The International Resource Industries & Sustainability Centre is engaged in interdisciplinary sustainability research of resource-based industry management practices & their impacts on environmental & social issues. Examples of research include the management of limited water resources, & the development & implementation of successful climate change mitigation & adaptation strategies.

University of Calgary (AINA)
Arctic Institute of North America
University of Calgary, 2500 University Dr. NW, Calgary AB T2N 1N4
Tel: 403-220-7515; *Fax:* 403-282-4609
e-mail: arctic@ucalgary.ca
www.arctic.ucalgary.ca
Overview: A organization founded in 1945
Mission: A multi-disciplinary research institute of the University of Calgary, the Arctic Institute of North America aims to advance the study of the North American & circumpolar Arctic region. The Institute provides information about the region's environmental, physical, & social conditions. Examples of research projects are as follows: the Beaufort Sea project for climate change - impact & adaptation to climate change for fish & marine mammals in the Canadian Beaufort Sea; wildlife, environment, & resource management, & the role of traditional & local knowledge; & human ecology & the impact of chemical pollutants on Arctic communities.

University of Guelph (USEDC)
Urban System Environmental Design Centre
c/o School of Engineering, University of Guelph, Guelph ON N1G 2W1 Canada
Tel: 519-824-4120; *Fax:* 519-836-0227
www.soe.uoguelph.ca/webfiles/used
Mission: The Centre aims to minimize the environmental impact of urban settings in an integrated manner, provide the setting for advancing environmental design engineering education and capabilities, and to reduce the environmental impact of urban communities in an integrated manner.

University of Guelph (ORWC)
Ontario Rural Wastewater Centre
c/o School of Engineering, University of Guelph, Guelph ON N1G 2W1 Canada
Tel: 519-824-4120; *Fax:* 519-836-0227
www.orwc.uoguelph.ca
Mission: The Centre promotes environmentally sustainable development of rural and unsewered areas through the effective use of wastewater treatment and dispersal technologies.

University of Guelph
Canadian Pollination Initiative
c/o School of Environmental Sciences, University of Guelph, Guelph ON N1G 2W1 Canada
Tel: 519-824-4120; *Fax:* 519-837-0442
e-mail: canpolin@uoguelph.ca
www.uoguelph.ca/canpolin
Also Known As: CANPOLIN
Mission: NSERC-CANPOLIN is a five-year NSERC Strategic Network that is addressing the growing problem of pollinator decline in agricultural and natural ecosystems in Canada.

University of Guelph (BDDC)
Bioproducts Discovery & Development Centre
Crop Science Bldg., Dept. of Plant Agriculture, 50 Stone Rd. East, Guelph ON N1E 2W1 Canada
Tel: 519-824-4120; *Fax:* 519-763-8933
www.bioproductscentre.com
Mission: The Bioproducts Discovery and Development Centre (BDDC) is an interdisciplinary centre where plant biologists, chemists and engineers converge to investigate and commercialize biomaterials. BDDC combines distinct areas of study including genetics, molecular biology, agronomy, materials engineering to produce leading edge research and innovative materials and chemicals derived from renewable resources.

University of Guelph (AARS)
Alma Aquaculture Research Station
6957 Eighth Line West, RR #1, Elora ON N0B 1S0 Canada
Tel: 519-669-5411; *Fax:* 519-669-5412
e-mail: aars2@hsfx.ca
www.aps.uoguelph.ca/~aquacentre/aars/aars.html
Overview: A organization founded in 1993
Mission: The Alma Aquaculture Research Station (AARS) is a state-of-the-art aquaculture research and development facility providing up-scale systems for aquaculture researchers at the University of Guelph and other institutions

University of Guelph (CNTC)
Canadian Network of Toxicology Centres
University of Guelph, Bovey Bldg., 2nd Fl., Gordon St., Guelph ON N1G 2W1 Canada
Tel: 519-824-4120; *Fax:* 519-837-3861
www.uoguelph.ca/ses/content/canadian-network-toxicology-centres
Overview: A organization founded in 1988
Mission: The Canadian Network of Toxicology Centres (CNTC) is a national network of collaborating researchers from academia and government. The Network conducts environmental health-related research along well articulated and planned themes of interdisciplinary research. Implicit in the CNTC approach is a commitment to joint, interactive efforts, centralized planning, project accountability for both intellectual and financial objectives, and regular reporting of research progress beyond the usual publication in scientific journals.

University of Guelph (GIE)
Guelph Institute for the Environment
University of Guelph, Guelph ON N1G 2W1 Canada
Tel: 519-824-4120
e-mail: gie@uoguelph.ca
gie.uoguelph.ca
Overview: A organization founded in 2007
Mission: The Institute, a unit of the Faculty of Environmental Science with a mandate to utilize the University of Guelph's recognized expertise on environmental issues & to foster opportunities for dialogue with government agencies on environmental challenges such as water resources management, waste management, heavy metal pollution, & climate change. The focus is on facilitating communication among researchers, government, & the wider community, with a view to enhancing problem solving & policy making. GIE hosts meetings, conferences & workshops on the issues, bringing together experts from on & off campus, & encourages student involvement with environmental policy & research.

University of Guelph (AC)
The Aquaculture Centre
Dept. of Animal & Poultry Science, University of Guelph, 491 Gordon St., Guelph ON N1G 2W1 Canada
Tel: 519-824-4120; *Fax:* 519-837-8867
e-mail: aquacntr@uoguelph.ca
www.aps.uoguelph.ca/~aquacentre/aquacentre/aquacentre.html
Overview: A organization founded in 1990
Mission: The Aquaculture Centre coordinates research, extension & educational activities & liaises with other provincial & national aquaculture institutions to facilitate information & technology transfer to the private sector. Services include troubleshooting a range of non-diagnostic problems faced by commercial farmers, & providing information & training. The Centre's staff also contribute to industry & government committees looking into issues such as pathogen control, fish health legislation, policy development regarding waste management, species for culture, pharmaceutical usage, product quality control, performance measures, & educational/training programs in aquaculture. While assisting with technology transfer, The Centre also acts as an advocate for balanced, sustainable development of the aquaculture industry in Ontario & in Canada.

University of Guelph (CESRF)
Controlled Environment Systems Research Facility
Ontario Agricultural College, Guelph ON N1G 2W1 Canada
Tel: 519-824-4120; *Fax:* 519-837-0442
e-mail: info@ces.uoguelph.ca
www.ces.uoguelph.ca
Mission: CESRF is engaged in whole plant research, & provides a controlled environment for the measurement of plant growth, gas exchange, volatile organic compound evolution, & nutrient remediation. The facility is comprised of 24 sealed environment chambers, with several variable pressure plant growth hypobaric chambers capable of sustaining a vacuum. The facility is useful to a diverse clientele, including those doing research into plant physiology, growth & production, in the aerospace, chemical, plant production & academic fields, to name a few. Facility staff offer expertise in plant physiology, environment analysis & sensor technology. CESRF's Space & Advanced Life Support Agriculture program contributes to the efforts of plant research at the Canadian Space Agency. In addition, a biofiltration lab utilizing plant-microbe interactions from green plants is used to investigate potential solutions to air quality problems.

University of Guelph (BIO)
Biodiversity Institute of Ontario
University of Guelph, 50 Stone Rd. East, Guelph ON N1G 2W1 Canada
Tel: 519-824-4120; *Fax:* 519-824-5703
www.biodiversity.ca
Overview: A organization founded in 2007
Mission: The Biodiversity Institute of Ontario takes a multidisciplinary approach to research into species identity, genetic variation, ecological roles & ecosystem processes, with a view to answering pressing concerns such as endangered species, particulary in S. Ontario. The Institute is comprised of 4 main research divisions: the Canadian Centre for DNA Barcoding (first organization of its kind in the world - see www.barcodeoflife.org); Experimental Ecosystems (oversees the Limnotron, a controlled environment facility & the world's largest aquatic mesocosm facility); the OAC Herbarium, engaging in plant barcoding research (see www.uoguelph.ca/foibis/); & the OAC Insect Collection, an important heritage collection for North American species. Digital education programs for students & the general public are another important focus (see the links to Canada's Aquatic Environment, & Canada's Polar Life).

University of Guelph (CLAWS)
Centre for Land and Water Stewardship
Richards Bldg., University of Guelph, 50 Stone Rd. East, Guelph ON N1G 2W1 Canada
Tel: 519-824-4120; *Fax:* 519-767-1686
e-mail: claws@uoguelph.ca
www.uoguelph.ca/~claws/
Overview: A organization founded in 1986
Mission: The Centre evolved from the former Centre for Soil & Water Conservation is engaged in research into sustainable use of land & water resources. Agricultural practices, nutrient management, water quality, conservation of natural areas, & stewardship policies & programs are a focus. Recent research has concentrated on areas such as manure management practices & their effect on water quality, modeling of on-farm nitrogen use, land trusts & their role in conservation, reforestation in S. Ontario, & conservation planning for rural landowners.

University of New Brunswick (NBCCRC)
New Brunswick Climate Change Research Collaborative
Faculty of Forestry & Environmental Management, PO Box 4400, 28 Dineen Dr., Fredericton NB E3B 5A3 Canada
Tel: 506-453-4923; *Fax:* 506-453-3538
www.unb.ca/fredericton/forestry/research/nbccrc/index.html
Mission: The New Brunswick Climate Change Research Collaborative (NBCCRC) at the University of New Brunswick aims to increase the capacity of New Brunswick communities to

effectively respond to climatic change over the short and long term.

University of New Brunswick (WSTC)

Wood Science & Technolgy Centre
Hugh John Fleming Forestry Centre, 1350 Regent St., Fredericton NB E3C 2G6 Canada
Tel: 506-453-4507; *Fax:* 506-453-3574
e-mail: woodsci@unb.ca
www.unb.ca/fredericton/forestry/wstc

Overview: A organization founded in 1988
Mission: The University of New Brunswick's Wood Science and Technology Centre (WSTC) is a centre of excellence dedicated to research, development, education and technical support for the wood products industry.

University of New Brunswick (CBEC)

Canadian BioEnergy Centre
Hugh John Flemming Forestry Centre, 1350 Regent St., Fredericton NB E3C 2G6 Canada
Tel: 506-453-4507; *Fax:* 506-453-3574
e-mail: woodsci@unb.ca
www.unb.ca/fredericton/forestry/wstc/cbec

Mission: The Canadian BioEnergy Centre (CBEC) is a centre of excellence dedicated to providing technological support to the bioenergy sector in Canada and beyond.

University of New Brunswick (CRI)

Canadian Rivers Institute
#202, IUC Forestry Bldg., Univeristy of New Brunswick Fredericton, PO Box 4400, Fredericton NB E3B 5A3 Canada
Tel: 506-453-4770
www.unb.ca/research/institutes/cri

Mission: Research institute specializing in aquatic science. The CRI is focused primarily on water resources conservation, protection, restoration, and sustainable use.

University of New Brunswick (NBCFWRU)

New Brunswick Cooperative Fish & Wildlife Unit
Faculty of Forestry and Environmental Management, PO Box 44555, Fredericton NB E3B 6C2 Canada
Tel: 506-453-4929; *Fax:* 506-453-3538
www.unb.ca/nbcfwru/NBCFWRU.html

Overview: A organization founded in 1989
Mission: Cooperative research project focused on fish and wildlife resource information, including specific studies on wildlife, with a focus on enhancing conservation efforts.

University of New Brunswick

Greater Fundy Ecosystem Project
PO Box 4400, Fredericton NB E3B 5A3 Canada
www.unbf.ca/forestry/centers/fundy

Mission: Research centre focused on providing research, monitoring, and scientific support for conservation and sustainability efforts in New Brunswick.

University of New Brunswick

Groundwater Studies Group
Department of Civil Engineering, PO Box 4400, Fredericton NB E3B 5A3 Canada
www.unb.ca/fredericton/engineering/depts/civil/research

Mission: Research organization based out of the University of New Brunswick focused primarily on water resources management. The group works on technical, manegerial, and environmental aspects of these issues including hydrogeology, groundwater quality, and contamination.

University of New Brunswick

Forest Watershed Research Centre
PO Box 4400, Fredericton NB E3B 5A3 Canada
watershed.for.unb.ca

Mission: Research centre through the Faculty of Forestry and Environmental Management at the University of New Brunswick. The centre focuses on sustainable forest management projects including water quality testing, hydrology modeling, trail and route optimization, and soil studies.

University of New Brunswick

Centre for Coastal Studies & Aquaculture
PO Box 5050, 100 Tucker Park Rd., Saint John NB E2L 4L5 Canada
Tel: 506-648-5605; *Fax:* 506-648-5650
e-mail: coastal@unbsj.ca

Overview: A organization founded in 1985
Mission: The Centre for Coastal Studies and Aquaculture at the Saint John Campus of the University of New Brunswick. The Centre performs multidisciplinary research projects in the field of coastal studies and aquaculture primarily in the Bay of Fundy. The University conducts both in-house research at it's laboratory and library facilities and offshore research on the Mary-O vessel.

University of Northern British Columbia (PICS)

Pacific Institute for Climate Solutions
c/o Kyle Abe, University of Northern British Columbia, #7-232, Main Agora, Prince George BC V2N 4Z9
Tel: 250-396-0678
www.unbc.ca/pacific-institute-for-climate-solutions

Overview: A organization founded in 2008
Mission: The Pacific Institute for Climate Solutions (PICS) develops innovative climate change solutions with a focus on low-carbon economies. The Institute researchs, monitors, and assesses the potential impacts of climate change and assesses, develops and promotes viable mitigation and adaptation options to better inform climate change policies and actions.

University of Northern British Columbia (LERG)

Landscape Ecology Research Group
University of Northern British Columbia, PO Box 28, Likely BC V0L 1N0

Mission: The Landscape Ecology Research Group is closely affiliated with the Quesnel River Research Centre. Research is focused on diverse geographic areas made up of various ecosystems such as forests, grasslands, and lakes to human-dominated environments including agricultural and urban settings.

University of Northern British Columbia (EFL)

I.K Barber Enhanced Forestry Laboratory
Bldg. 12, University of Northern British Columbia, #11-103, 3333 University Way, Prince George BC V2N 4Z9
Tel: 250-960-6498
www.unbc.ca/efl

Overview: A organization founded in 2000
Mission: The Enhanced Forestry Lab at the University of Northern British Columbia conducts controlled environmental research.

University of Northern British Columbia (NRESI)

Natural Resources & Environmental Studies Institute
University of Northern British Columbia, 3333 University Way, Prince George BC V2N 4Z9
Tel: 250-960-5825; *Fax:* 250-960-5539
e-mail: nresi@unbc.ca
www.unbc.ca/nres/institute_overview.html

Mission: The University of Northern British Columbia's Natural Resources & Environmental Studies Institute promotes interdisciplinary research related to natural resource systems & human uses of the environment. The Institute focuses upon northern regions. Areas of research include ecological patterns & processes, earth systems & dynamics, & societal structures & values. Examples of research include habitat effects on behaviour & reproduction in forest generalist birds, the rehabilitation of petroleum wellsites, & the Prince George sustainable landscaping initiative.

University of Northern British Columbia (QRCC)

Dr. Max Blouw Quesnel River Research Centre
University of Northern British Columbia, PO Box 28, Likely BC V0L 1N0
www.unbc.ca/qrrc

Also Known As: Quesnel River Research Centre
Mission: The University of Northern British Columbia's Quesnel River Research Centre is engaged in research projects on the Quesnel River. Examples of research projects are as follows: northern hydrometeorological processes & their impacts; factors related to spawning site locations in interior Fraser coho salmon; & the effect of landscape disturbance, from factors such as forestry, agriculture, & mining, & climate change, on the behaviour of water, sediment & chemicals in the environment.

University of Ottawa (CELGS)

Centre for Environmental Law and Global Sustainability
Fauteux Hall, University of Ottawa, 57 Louis Pasteur St., Ottawa ON K1N 6N5 Canada
Tel: 613-562-5794; *Fax:* 613-562-5124
www.commonlaw.uottawa.ca/celgs

Mission: The Centre for Environmental Law and Global Sustainability is the University of Ottawa's forum for research, teaching, discussion and advocacy related to environmental law.

University of Ottawa (CAREG)

Center for Advanced Research in Environmental Genomics
Dept. of Biology, University of Ottawa, 20 Marie Curie St., Ottawa ON K1N 6N5 Canada
Tel: 613-562-5800; *Fax:* 613-562-5486
www.careg.uottawa.ca

Overview: A organization founded in 2000
Mission: CAREG is a group of researchers in environmental biology, fish physiology, & molecular evolution but has evolved to include researchers outside the Dept. of Biology. The research focuses on the effects of enviromental stressors on genome function & expression, with a view to developing solutions to problems of environmental biology.

University of Ottawa

Centre for Research on Environmental Microbiology (CREM) / centre De recherche En microbiologie environmentale (CRME)
University of Ottawa, 451 Smyth Rd., Rm. 4119, Ottawa ON K1H 8M5 Canada
Tel: 613-562-5800; *Fax:* 613-562-5452
e-mail: crem@uottawa.ca
www.medicine.uottawa.ca/crem/

Mission: CREM's research endeavours are focused on how human pathogens get into the environment & survive there; the environmental factors affecting pathogen survival & transport & the potential for human exposure; how the spread of infections may be interrupted through the application of environmental control measures to water, air, food, waste, etc. Specific interests include the treatment & disinfection of drinking water, the microbiological quality of potable & recreational waters, food safety, survival & transport of pathogens in wastewater & soil, biomedical waste management & monitoring, & other areas.

University of Ottawa (IE)

Institute of the Environment
555 King Edward Ave., Ottawa ON K1N 6N5 Canada
Tel: 613-562-5800; *Fax:* 613-562-5873
e-mail: info@ie.uOttawa.ca
www.ie.uottawa.ca

Overview: A organization founded in 1989
Mission: The Institute is mandated to facilitate interdisciplinary research on the environment, both on & off campus, & to identify & encourage new areas of environmental research & educational endeavour. Current research foci include biodiversity conservation, impacts of climate change, freshwater conservation, environmental assessment, toxicants & ecosystem health, & Aboriginal community health.

University of Ottawa

Sustainable Prosperity Research and Policy Network
555 King Edward Ave., Ottawa ON K1N 6N5 Canada
Tel: 613-562-5800
e-mail: info@sustainableprosperity.ca
www.sustainableprosperity.ca

Overview: A organization founded in 2007
Mission: The Network brings together leaders from academia & business to facilitate dialogue, generate innovative ideas, & produce research & policy tools to help build a productive Canadian economy while taking strong account of sustainability. The Network's perspective is that market forces can be used to enhance & work FOR (not against) the environment, & can provide incentive to individual consumers & businesses to lower their environmental footprint.

University of Regina (IEESC)

Institute for Energy, Environment and Sustainable Communities
University of Regina, Regina SK S4S 0A2 Canada
Tel: 306-337-3359; *Fax:* 306-585-4855
e-mail: ieesc@env.uregina.ca
env.uregina.ca/ieesc

Mission: The Institute for Energy, Environment and Sustainable Communities of the University of Regina is a research and demonstration institute that integrates energy, environment and sustainability research expertise and undertakes thematic research to address the impacts and challenges of climate change.

University of Regina (PARC)

Prairie Adaptation Research Collaborative
University of Regina, #120, 2 Research Dr., Regina SK S4S 7H9 Canada
Tel: 306-337-2300; *Fax:* 306-337-2301
e-mail: alberta@parc.ca; sask@parc.ca; manitoba@parc.ca
www.parc.ca

Mission: The Prairie Adaptation Research Collaborative is a partnership of the governments of Canada, Alberta, Saskatchewan and Manitoba mandated to pursue climate change impacts and adaptation research in the Prairie Provinces.

University of Regina

Canadian Plains Research Center
Research Park, University of Regina, 3737 Wascana Pkwy., Regina SK S4S 0A2
Tel: 306-585-4758; *Fax:* 306-585-4699
Toll-Free: 866-874-2257
e-mail: canadian.plains@uregina.ca
www.cprc.ca
Overview: A organization founded in 1973
Mission: The research institute at the University of Regina is engaged in the interdisciplinary study of issues relevant to Canadian prairie life. Examples of research projects are as follows: rural community water conservation, & institutional adaptations to climate change.
Affliation(s): Brandon University; Canadian Council on Ecological Areas; Prairie Adaptation Research Collaborative; Saskatchewan Institute for Public Policy; University of Alberta; University of Calgary; University of Lethbridge; University of Saskatchewan; University of Manitoba; University of Winnipeg

University of Regina (EQAL)

Environmental Quality Analysis Laboratory
265 Laboratory Building, Regina SK S4S 0A2 Canada
Tel: 306-585-4890; *Fax:* 306-337-2410
www.uregina.ca/science/eqal/
Mission: A non-profit research and analysis laboratory that provides advanced analytical and data interpretation services primarily in the fields of environmental science. The lab is available for University of Regina research projects as well as other academic units and non-academic institutions.

University of Saskatchewan (CCHSA)

Canadian Centre for Health & Safety in Agriculture
Royal University Hospital, University of Saskatchewan, PO Box 120, Stn. Royal University Hospital, #3608, 103 Hospital Dr., Wing 3E, Saskatoon SK S7N 0W8
Tel: 306-966-8286; *Fax:* 306-966-8799
e-mail: canadian.centre@usask.ca
www.cchsa-ccssma.usask.ca
Overview: A organization founded in 2006
Mission: The Canadian Centre for Health & Safety in Agriculture focuses upon public health issues related to the agricultural rural ecosystem. Examples of research projects are as follows: cross-Canada study of pesticides & health; grainhandlers, genetic polymorphisms, & respiratory health; & prairie ecosystem study.

University of Saskatchewan

Centre for Northern Agroforestry & Afforestation
c/o Ken Van Rees, Dept. Of Soil Science, University of Saskatchewan, 51 Campus Dr., Saskatoon SK S7N 5A8
Tel: 306-966-6853; *Fax:* 306-966-6881
www.saskagroforestry.ca
Mission: The Centre for Northern Agroforestry & Afforestation strives to advance the sustainable agroforestry industry. Agroforestry research focuses upon shelterbelts, silvopastures, & riparian buffer zones. Afforestation research involves plantation production of fast-growing hardwood & softwood species. A willow research program was implemented to study willow production for biomass energy. Scientific research by the Centre contributes to a growing economy & a healthier environment.

University of Saskatchewan (CCWHC)

Canadian Cooperative Wildlife Health Centre
University of Saskatchewan, 52 Campus Dr., Saskatoon SK S7N 5B4 Canada
Tel: 306-966-5099; *Fax:* 306-966-7387
e-mail: headquarters@ccwhc.ca
www.ccwhc.ca
Mission: The CCWHC is an organization encompassing Canada's veterinary colleges. Its purpose is to apply the veterinary medical sciences to wildlife conservation and management in Canada. The organization is also dedicated to developing and using knowledge of wildlife health and disease to improve human health and the health of domestic animals.
Affliation(s): University of Calgary; University of Prince Edward Island; Université de Montréal; University of Guelph

University of Saskatchewan

Indigenous Land Management Institute (ILMI)
51 Campus Dr., Saskatoon SK S7N 5A8 Canada
Tel: 306-966-6474; *Fax:* 306-966-4353
e-mail: lmi.info@usask.ca
ilmi.usask.ca
Mission: The ILMI was established to respond to the need of Aboriginal Peoples to gain access to research-based information that can be used in making informed land management decisions. Aboriginal peoples are assuming a greater role in the management and administration of land and resources. The institute brings together teaching, research, outreach and engagement activities in the area of indigenous land and resource management under one unit. Themes include Environmental Sustainability and Governance of Land.

University of Toronto

Program on Water Issues (POW)
Munk School of Global Affairs, University of Toronto, #258, 1 Devonshire Place, Toronto ON M5S 3K7 Canada
Tel: 416-946-8919
e-mail: powi@utoronto.ca
powi.ca
Overview: A organization founded in 2001
Mission: The Program On Water Issues provides the public with analysis, information, and opinion on a range of important and emerging water issues.

University of Toronto

Ecohydrology Research Group
Dept. of Geography, University Of Toronto Mississauga, 3359 Mississauga Rd. North, Mississauga ON L5L 1C6 Canada
Tel: 905-569-4649; *Fax:* 905-828-5273
geog.utm.utoronto.ca/branfireun/Branfireun/Branfireun_Home.html
Mission: The Group does research projects on wetlands and mercury cycling from the Canadian sub-arctic to the sub-tropics of Mexico.

University of Toronto (JGI)

The Jane Goodall Institute of Canada
Earth Sciences Bldg., University of Toronto, #1046/1047A, 5 Bancroft Ave., Toronto ON M5S 1C1 Canada
Tel: 416-978-3711; *Fax:* 416-978-3713
Toll-Free: 888-882-4467
e-mail: info@janegoodall.ca
www.janegoodall.ca
Mission: JGI Canada is one of 23 offices of the Institute located around the world. Its mission is to support wildlife research, education & conservation. Research continues to focus on Dr. Goodall's groundbreaking work on chimpanzee behaviour, as well as the environmental & human impacts on chimpanzee habitat & species wellbeing. The Institute's Roots & Shoots education program supports environmental & humanitarian education & projects, with an emphasis on a community-centred approach. The University of Toronto's Centre for Environment is a key partner.

University of Toronto

Diamond Environmental Research Group
45 St. George St., Toronto ON M5S 3G3 Canada
Tel: 416-978-1586; *Fax:* 416-946-5992
faculty.geog.utoronto.ca/mdiamond/
Mission: The Research Group focuses on the dynamics of organic & inorganic contaminants in lakes, urban areas, aquatic food-webs & indoor environments. Mathematical modelling, analytical chemistry, & lab & field studies in the areas of aquatic systems (air, water, sediment), & multimedia movement (air, water, soil, sediment, vegetation & impervious surfaces) are activities of interest. The Group collaborates with the provincial Ministry of Environment, Environment Canada & the City of Toronto.

University of Toronto (CGCS)

Centre for Global Change Science
Dept. of Physics, University of Toronto, 60 St. George St., Toronto ON M5S 1A7 Canada
Tel: 416-978-2933; *Fax:* 416-978-8905
www.cgcs.utoronto.ca
Mission: The Centre's focus is on research into climate models & dynamics, atmospheric chemistry & global change, global change & the biosphere & hydrosphere/cryosphere, & global change & space-based remote sounding.

University of Toronto

Centre for Biocomposites & Biomaterials Processing
Fac. of Forestry, University of Toronto, 33 Willcocks St., Toronto ON M5S 3B3 Canada
Tel: 416-946-3191; *Fax:* 416-978-3834
www.forestry.utoronto.ca/research/bbp/
Mission: The Centre focuses on research into engineered wood & natural fibre composite materials, with an emphasis on engineering principles, & physico-chemical & biological phenomena involved in designing sustainable engineered products from wood residues & agro-fibers.

University of Toronto (SOCAAR)

Southern Ontario Centre for Atmospheric Aerosol Research
University of Toronto, 200 College St., Toronto ON M5S 3E5 Canada
www.socaar.utoronto.ca
Mission: The Centre is engaged in collaborative, interdisciplinary research into air quality, specifically on how aerosols impact the environment & human health. SOCAAR brings together researchers from the medical field, engineering, & atmospheric chemistry, & partners with government & industry.
Affliation(s): The Canadian Aerosol Research Network

University of Toronto

Sustainability Office
University of Toronto, 255 McCaul St., 4th Fl., Toronto ON M5T 1W7 Canada
Tel: 416-978-6792
e-mail: sustainability@utoronto.ca
sustainability.utoronto.ca
Overview: A organization founded in 2004
Mission: The Office is mandated to address sustainability issues on campus; to facilitate student, faculty & staff environmental stewardship; to develop & implement energy & resource conservation projects; to establish baselines & targets, & monitor progress; to develop & integrate University policies to increase energy & resource conservation efforts; & to develop networks & partnerships with external organizations with similar aims.

University of Victoria (CCCma)

Canadian Centre for Climate Modelling & Analysis
Ocean, Earth & Atmospheric Sciences Bldg., University of Victoria, PO Box 3065, Stn. CSC, #203A, 3800 Finnerty Rd., 2nd Fl., Victoria BC V8W 3V6
Tel: 250-363-8228; *Fax:* 250-363-8247
e-mail: cccma_info@ec.gc.ca
www.cccma.ec.gc.ca
Mission: A division of the Climate Research Branch of Environment Canada, the Canadian Centre for Climate Modelling & Analysis conducts research in the following main areas: sea-ice modelling, coupled & atmospheric climate modelling, the carbon cycle, & climate variability & predictability.

University of Victoria (W-CIRC) / Centre de Recherche sur les Eaux et d'Impacts du Climat (CREIC)

Water & Climate Impacts Research Centre
Social Sciences & Mathematics Bldg., University of Victoria, PO Box 3060, Stn. CSC, 3800 Finnerty Rd., Victoria BC V8W 3R4
w-circ.uvic.ca
Overview: A organization founded in 2002
Mission: Created as a result of an agreement between the University of Victoria & Environment Canada's National Water Research Institute, the Water & Climate Impacts Research Centre's studies include the hydrologic & ecological impacts of atmospheric change & variability. Research focuses upon the following areas: groundwater systems, lake heat & energy budgets of lakes, floods & droughts, river & lake ice, aquatic ecology, alpine & reservoir water supplies, & forest hydrology.

University of Victoria

Centre for Forest Biology
University of Victoria, PO Box 3020, Stn. CSC, Victoria BC V8W 3N5
Tel: 250-721-7119; *Fax:* 250-721-6611
e-mail: forbiol@uvic.ca
web.uvic.ca/~forbiol
Mission: The University of Victoria's Centre for Forest Biology carries out research related to the adaptation of trees & their interactions with the environment, with an emphasis upon forest regeneration & forest biotechnology. Examples of research include plant-pest interactions, carbon sequestration by forests & soils, water relations & gas exchange, & plant stress physiology.

University of Victoria (CFGS)

Centre for Global Studies
University of Victoria, PO Box 1700, Stn. CSC, Victoria BC V8W 2Y2
Tel: 250-472-4990; *Fax:* 250-472-4830
e-mail: cfgs@uvic.ca
www.globalcentres.org
Overview: A organization founded in 1998
Mission: The Centre for Global Studies studies issues such as the environment, sustainable development, international

governance & finance, & security. Examples of research projects include low carbon, building capacity to manage aquaculture in Thailand, & climate change adaptation & mitigation.

University of Victoria

NEPTUNE Canada

Ttechnology Eenterprise Ffacility, University of Victoria, PO Box 1700, Stn. CSC, #155, 2300 McKenzie Ave., Victoria BC V8W 2Y2
Tel: 250-472-5400; *Fax:* 250-472-5370
e-mail: neptune@uvic.ca
www.neptunecanada.com

Mission: NEPTUNE Canada gathers live data from a rich constellation of instruments deployed in a broad spectrum of undersea environments. Scientists work in a wide range of disciplines including underwaterwater volcanic processes, earthquakes and tsunamis, climate change, fish stocks, marine ecosystems, and much more.

University of Victoria (IESVic)

Institute for Integrated Energy Systems

University of Victoria, PO Box 3055, Stn. CSC, Victoria BC V8W 3P6
Tel: 250-721-6295; *Fax:* 250-721-6323
e-mail: iesvic-request@iesvic.uvic.ca
www.iesvic.uvic.ca

Overview: A organization founded in 1989

Mission: The University of Victoria's Institute for Integrated Energy Systems studies sustainable energy systems. Areas of research include hydrogen technology, fuel cell science & technology, energy systems analysis & economics, & sustainable energy systems integration. Its research leads to the development of technologies for the adoption of sustainable, clean energy.

University of Waterloo (CCIN)

The Canadian Cryospheric Information Network

c/o Dept. of Geography, University of Waterloo, 200 University Ave. West, Waterloo ON N2L 3G1 Canada
Tel: 519-888-4567; *Fax:* 519-888-6768
e-mail: pdc@uwaterloo.ca
www.ccin.ca

Mission: The Canadian Cryospheric Information Network (CCIN) was developed in the mid-1990's to provide the data and information management infrastructure for the Canadian cryospheric community. The main objective of the CCIN is to enhance awareness and access to Canadian cryospheric information and related data. CCIN and ArcticNet are the founding partners of the Polar Data Catalogue (PDC), which has been developed as a metadata "Discovery Portal" and data repository for Arctic and Antarctic researchers.

Affliation(s): British Antarctic Survey; Norwegian Meteorological Institute; US National Snow and Ice Data Center; Interdisciplinary Centre on Climate Change

University of Waterloo (WSC)

Waterloo Summit Centre for the Environment

University of Waterloo, 87 Forbes Hill Dr., Huntsville ON P1H 0B6 Canada
Tel: 705-571-0259
uwaterloo.ca/waterloo-summit-centre

Mission: The Waterloo Summit Centre for the Environment is a year-round research and teaching centre. Part of the University of Waterloo, the university is establishing the Centre as a high-profile research centre for ecology, climate change, tourism, land-use planning, and local economic development.

University of Waterloo (WPGG)

Water Policy & Governance Group

c/o Dept. of Environment and Resource Studies, Uni of Waterloo, 200 University Ave. West, Waterloo ON N2L 3G1 Canada
Tel: 519-888-4567; *Fax:* 519-746-2031
www.wpgg.ca

Mission: The Water Policy and Governance Group is a multi-university, collaborative research team based at the University of Waterloo. The group's focus is water governance and water policy, emphasizing Canadian experiences. Major themes in research programs include collaborative water governance, water security, source water protection, water allocation, and adaptation to climate change.

University of Waterloo (ERA)

Centre for Ecosystem Resilience & Adaptation

c/o Dr. Stephen Murphy, Dept. of Environment and Resource Studies, Waterloo ON N2L 3G1 Canada
Tel: 519-888-4567; *Fax:* 519-746-2031
www.era.uwaterloo.ca

Mission: To address this growing crisis and to ensure a healthy environment for future generations, researchers in the Centre for Ecosystem Resilience and Adaptation (ERA) at the University of Waterloo are working to repair damaged ecosystems, conserve rare habitats, and protect species-at-risk.

University Of Waterloo (CWN)

Canadian Water Network

University Of Waterloo, 200 University Ave. West, Waterloo ON N2L 3G1 Canada
Tel: 519-888-4567; *Fax:* 519-883-7574
e-mail: info@cwn-rce.ca
www.cwn-rce.ca

Mission: The Canadian Water Network (CWN) was created as one of Canada's Networks of Centres of Excellence (NCE), to build a network that develops opportunities related to the provision of safe, clean water. In collaboration with universities, government and industry, the CWN has developed a variety of scientific projects and initiatives that address key water-related issues facing Canadians while embracing strong multidisciplinary and multi-sectoral partnerships.

University of Waterloo

Ecological Restoration Group

Fac. of Environment, University of Waterloo, 200 University Ave. West, Waterloo ON N2L 3G1 Canada
Tel: 519-888-4567; *Fax:* 519-746-2031

Mission: The Group conducts research, teaches, & promotes community involvement in ecological restoration, rehabilitation & management. Projects have included the Quetico Provincial Park Resource Survey; gravel pit rehabilitation at the Stanley Park Optimist Natural Area in Kitchener, ON; a marsh restoration project in Iraq; & rehabilitation of industrial land for Cytec Canada Inc. Facilities include GIS (Geographic Information Systems) & remote sensing labs, an ecology lab, natural gardens & reserves, & the RS Dorney Ecology Garden which features native species. The Group works closely with the Quetico Foundation, the Nature Conservancy of Canada, the Cruickston Charitable Research Reserive, the Heritage Resources Centre, Hydro One, the University of Guelph, & municipalites, conservation authorities & corporations.

University of Waterloo (IC3)

Interdisciplinary Centre on Climate Change

University of Waterloo, 200 University Ave. West, Waterloo ON N2L 3G1 Canada
Tel: 519-888-4567
www.environment.uwaterloo.ca/research/ic3/

Mission: The Centre aims to contribute to the science of climate change & its impacts on human life. Using leading edge systems, technologies & numerical modeling, researchers from diverse disciplines (Environment, Engineering, Mathematics, Sciences) focus on various spatial & temporal scales in their work. Core research themes include atmospheric science, cryospheric science, human dimensions of climate change, observing systems & modeling, & water, ecosystems, & biogeochemical cycling. The Centre also provides education & outreach to the public, particularly to high school & undergraduate students, & liaises with government & industry as appropriate. For information on cryospheric research, consult The Canadian Cryosphere Information Network, as well as the link to the State of the Canadian Cryosphere page at www.ccin.ca.

University of Waterloo

Ecohydrology Research Group

Centre for Environmental & Information Technology, #EIT1006, 200 University Ave. West, Waterloo ON N2L 3G1 Canada
Tel: 519-888-4567
e-mail: ecohydrology@uwaterloo.ca
uwaterloo.ca/ecohydrology

Mission: The Group is engaged in collaborative research projects on wetlands & mercury cycling, with a focus on the peatlands of the Hudson Bay lowlands, mercury cycling in Ontario watersheds, & hydrology & biogeochemistry of small watersheds in Western Mexico.

University of Windsor (GLIER)

Great Lakes Institute for Environmental Research

c/o London Life Great Lakes Environmental Research Centre, 2990 Riverside Dr. East, Windsor ON N9C 1A2 Canada
Tel: 519-253-3000; *Fax:* 519-971-3616
e-mail: glier@uwindsor.ca
www.uwindsor.ca/glier

Mission: The Great Lakes Institute for Environmental Research (GLIER) is multidisciplinary with faculty and collaborators from many disciplines, including biology, geology, chemistry, engineering, marine biology, molecular biology, genetics and ecology.

University of Windsor (LEMN)

Lake Erie Millenium Network

c/o Dept. of Biol. Sci./GLIER, University of Windsor, Windsor ON N9B 3P4 Canada
Tel: 519-253-3000; *Fax:* 519-971-3609
www.lemn.org

Overview: A organization founded in 1998

Mission: The Network was formed at the University of Windsor, the National Water Research Institute (Burlington, ON), the F.T. Stone Lab at Ohio State University, & the U.S. E.P.A at Grosse Ile, MI, in order to coordinate research into the ecological challenges & concerns regarding Lake Erie. It endeavours to summarize the current environmental status of the Lake; document the research & management needs of users & agencies; develop a framework for a research network to ensure a coordinated effort in the collection & dissemination of data that will address the research & management needs.

University of Winnipeg (C-FIR)

Centre for Forest Interdisciplinary Research

c/o Department of Geography, University of Winnipeg, #5L13, 515 Portage Ave., Winnipeg MB R3B 2E9
Tel: 204-786-9435
www.cfir.uwinnipeg.ca

Mission: The research centre at the University of Winnipeg conducts interdisciplinary research in the following areas: forest ecosystems, forestry, the human uses of forests, & forest values. Examples of research projects have included forest growth response to climate change, the influence of long term insecticide spraying on forest structure, & climate & fire relationships in the central & eastern boreal forest.

Vancouver Island University

Deep Bay Marine Field Station

370 Crome Point Rd., Bowser BC V0R 1G0 Canada
Tel: 250-740-6611
e-mail: deepbay@viu.ca
www.viu.ca/deepbay

Mission: The Deep Bay Marine Field Station supports both pure and applied coastal and marine research activities related to: sustainable shellfish aquaculture development; preservation of coastal ecosystems; and inter-disciplinary projects involving local communities.

Vancouver Island University (CCH)

Centre for Coastal Health

900 Fifth St., Nanaimo BC V9R 5S5 Canada
centreforcoastalhealth.ca

Mission: The Centre for Coastal Health (CCH) is an independent, non-profit organization whose mission is to identify and understand the interactions of human, animal and environmental health.

Vancouver Island University (ICR)

Institute for Coastal Research

100 Fifth St., Nanaimo BC V9R 5S5 Canada
www.viu.ca/icr

Mission: The Institute for Coastal Research at Vancouver Island University is made up of a team of people working to further understanding of the cultural, economic, environmental and social dynamics of the B.C. coast through collaborative research, creative exploration, dialogue, engagement and education.

Vancouver Island University (AERL)

Applied Environmental Research Laboratories

100 Fifth St., Nanaimo BC V9R 5S5 Canada
web.viu.ca/aerl

Mission: The AERL conducts pure and applied research in the environmental sciences and supports the training of highly qualified personnel in environmental chemical analysis.

Wilfrid Laurier University

Cold Regions Research Centre

Alumni Hall, Wilfrid Laurier University, #AH231, 75 University Ave. West, Waterloo ON N2L 3C5 Canada
Tel: 519-884-0710; *Fax:* 519-725-1342
info.wlu.ca/~wwwgeog/ColdRegions4/

Overview: A organization founded in 1988

Mission: The Centre's research focus is on Arctic & mountain glaciology, hydrology, geochemistry, resource management, parks planning, & other aspects of Cold Regions. The approach is collaborative & interdisciplinary.

Wilfrid Laurier University (IWS)

Laurier Institute for Water Science

Office of Research Services, Wilfrid Laurier University, 75 University Ave. West, Waterloo ON N2L 3C5 Canada
Tel: 519-884-0710; *Fax:* 519-884-7670
www.wlu.ca/homepage.php?grp_id=2586

Mission: The Institute is engaged in collaborative, multidisciplinary research in the areas of hydrological sciences, ecological & biogeochemcial sciences, & public policy & management. The focus is on the effects of climate change on water resources, sustainability of healthy aquatic & coastal ecosystems, & development of policy & regulations relating to water use.

York University (CAC)

Centre for Atmospheric Chemistry

006 Steacie Science and Engineering Bldg., 136 Campus Walk, 4700 Keele St., Toronto ON M3J 1P3 Canada
Tel: 416-736-5410; *Fax:* 416-736-5411
e-mail: cac@yorku.ca
www.cac.yorku.ca

Overview: A organization founded in 1985

Mission: The Centre for Atmospheric Chemistry (CAC) is comprised of York scientists working within the Department of Chemistry and the Department of Earth and Space Science and Engineering. The centre's research includes laboratory, field and computer imulation studies that further our fundamental understanding of chemical processes in the atmosphere. Issues of interest include urban and regional oxidation, aerosol formation, stratospheric ozone, acid precipitation, airborne toxic chemicals, global atmospheric change and arctic pollution.

York University (IRIS)

Institute for Research & Innovation in Sustainability

347 York Lanes, York University, 4700 Keele St., Toronto ON M3J 1P3 Canada
Tel: 416-736-2100; *Fax:* 416-736-5837
e-mail: irisinfo@yorku.ca
www.yorku.ca/irisinfo/

Overview: A organization founded in 2004

Mission: IRIS is a university-wide, interdisciplinary institute with a focus on collaborative research into the environmental, scientific, economic, social & cultural aspects of sustainability. Past research projects have included an inventory of York University's trees, & a study & recommendations to the Government of the NWT on a strategy for monitoring invasive species. Among other endeavours, current research will focus on food sustainability at York University, a study of white-tailed deer in London, ON, & an assessment of invasive species in Ontario.

Yukon College

Yukon Research Centre

Yukon College, 500 College Dr., Whitehorse YT Y1A 5K4 Canada
Tel: 867-668-8772; *Fax:* 867-456-8672
www.yukoncollege.yk.ca/research

Mission: The institute was conceived as a northern centre to promote, coordinate and perform research activities that complement the college's goal of pursuing excellence in all areas of Yukon and Northern Studies. It provides research services and support to the college and other organizations.

Government Listings

ABORIGINAL AFFAIRS

Aboriginal Affairs & Northern Development Canada, 10 Wellington St., North Tower, Gatineau, QC K1A 0H4
819-997-0380, Fax: 866-817-3977, 800-567-9604, infopubs@aadnc-aandc.gc.ca

Canadian Heritage, 15 Eddy St., Gatineau, QC K1A 0M5
819-997-0055, 866-811-0055, info@pch.gc.ca

Canadian Northern Economic Development Agency, Ottawa, ON K1A 0H4
Fax: 866-817-3977, 800-567-9604, InfoNorth-InfoNord@CanNor.gc.ca

Manitoba

Manitoba Aboriginal & Northern Affairs, Legislative Bldg, 344-450 Broadway, Winnipeg, MB R3C 0V8
204-945-3719, Fax: 204-945-8374, anaweb@gov.mb.ca

Northwest Territories

Northwest Territories Department of Aboriginal Affairs & Intergovernmental Relations, 4910 - 52nd St., PO Box 1320, Yellowknife, NT X1A 2L9
867-873-7143, Fax: 867-873-0233, 877-838-8194, nancy_gardiner@gov.nt.ca

Nunavut

Nunavut Territory Department of Culture, Language, Elders & Youth, PO Box 1000 800,Iqaluit, NU X0A 0H0
867-975-5500, Fax: 867-975-5504, 866-934-2035

Saskatchewan

Saskatchewan Government Relations, 1855 Victoria Ave., Regina, SK S4P 3T2
306-787-8885

ACTS & REGULATIONS

Office of the Administrator of the Ship-source Oil Pollution Fund, #830, 180 Kent St., Ottawa, ON K1A 0N5
613-991-1726, Fax: 613-990-5423

Newfoundland & Labrador

Newfoundland & Labrador Department of Transportation & Works, Confederation Bldg., West Block, 6th Fl., PO Box 8700, St. John's, NL A1B 4J6
709-729-3679, Fax: 709-729-4285, twminister@gov.nl.ca

Nova Scotia

Nova Scotia Department of Service Nova Scotia & Municipal Relations, 1505 Barrington St., PO Box 216, Halifax, NS B3J 3K5
902-424-5200, Fax: 902-424-0581, 800-670-4357, askus@gov.ns.ca

AGRICULTURE

See Also: Land Resources

Agriculture & Agri-Food Canada, 1341 Baseline Rd., Ottawa, ON K1A 0C5
613-773-1000, Fax: 613-773-1081, 855-773-0241, info@agr.gc.ca

Farm Products Council of Canada, Building 59, Central Experimental Farm, 960 Carling Ave., Ottawa, ON K1A 0C6
613-759-1555, Fax: 613-759-1566, fpcc-cpac@agr.gc.ca

Alberta

Agricultural Products Marketing Council, JG O'Donoghue Bldg., 7000 - 113 St., 3rd Fl., Edmonton, AB T6H 5T6
780-427-2164, Fax: 780-422-9690

Alberta Agriculture & Rural Development, JG O'Donoghue Bldg., #100A, 7000 - 113th St., Edmonton, AB T6H 5T6
780-427-2727, -310-3276, duke@gov.ab.ca

British Columbia

British Columbia Ministry of Agriculture, PO Box 9120 Prov Govt,Victoria, BC V8W 9E2
250-387-5121

Manitoba

Agricultural Societies, 1129 Queens Ave., Brandon, MB R7A 1L9
204-726-6195, Fax: 204-726-6260

Manitoba Agriculture, Food & Rural Initiatives, Legislative Bldg., 165-450 Broadway, Winnipeg, MB R3C 0V8
204-945-3722, Fax: 204-945-3470, minagr@leg.gov.mb.ca

Food Development Centre, 810 Phillips St., PO Box 1240, Portage la Prairie, MB R1N 3J9
204-239-3150, Fax: 204-239-3180, 800-870-1044

New Brunswick

New Brunswick Department of Agriculture, Aquaculture & Fisheries, Agricultural Research Station (Experimental Farm), PO Box 6000, Fredericton, NB E3B 5H1
506-453-2666, Fax: 506-453-7170, DAAF-MAAP@gnb.ca

Newfoundland & Labrador

Agrifoods Development Branch, Provincial Agriculture Bldg., Brookfield Rd., PO Box 8700, St. John's, NL A1B 4J6
709-729-6588, Fax: 709-729-2674

Northwest Territories

Northwest Territories Department of Environment & Natural Resources, PO Box 1320, Yellowknife, NT X1A 2L9

Nova Scotia

Nova Scotia Department of Agriculture, 1741 Brunswick St., 3rd Fl., PO Box 2223, Halifax, NS B3J 3C4
902-424-4560, Fax: 902-424-4671

Ontario

Ontario Ministry of Agriculture, Food & Rural Affairs, Ontario Government Bldg., 1 Stone Rd. West, Guelph, ON N1G 4Y2
519-826-3100, 888-466-2372

Ontario Ministry of Rural Affairs, c/o Ministry of Agriculture & Food, 1 Stone Rd. West, Guelph, ON N1G 4Y2
519-826-3100, Fax: 519-826-4335, 888-466-2372, about.omafra@ontario.ca

Prince Edward Island

Prince Edward Island Department of Agriculture & Forestry, Jones Bldg., 11 Kent St., PO Box 2000, Charlottetown, PE C1A 7N8
902-368-4880, Fax: 902-368-4857

Quebec

Ministère de l'Agriculture, des Pêcheries et de l'Alimentation, 200, ch Sainte-Foy, Québec, QC G1R 4X6
418-380-2110, 888-222-6272

Saskatchewan

Saskatchewan Agriculture, Walter Scott Bldg., 3085 Albert St., Regina, SK S4S 0B1
866-457-2377, aginfo@gov.sk.ca

AGRICULTURE & FOOD

Agriculture & Agri-Food Canada, 1341 Baseline Rd., Ottawa, ON K1A 0C5
613-773-1000, Fax: 613-773-1081, 855-773-0241, info@agr.gc.ca

Market & Industry Services Branch, Tower 5, 1341 Baseline Rd., Ottawa, ON K1A 0C5
613-759-1000, Fax: 613-773-1711

Science & Technology Branch, Tower 5, 1341 Baseline Rd., Ottawa, ON K1A 0C5
613-759-1000, Fax: 613-773-1866

Strategic Policy Branch, Tower 7, 1341 Baseline Rd., Ottawa, ON K1A 0C5
613-759-1000, Fax: 613-773-2111,

Alberta

Agricultural Products Marketing Council, JG O'Donoghue Bldg., 7000 - 113 St., 3rd Fl., Edmonton, AB T6H 5T6
780-427-2164, Fax: 780-422-9690

Alberta Agriculture & Rural Development, JG O'Donoghue Bldg., #100A, 7000 - 113th St., Edmonton, AB T6H 5T6
780-427-2727, -310-3276, duke@gov.ab.ca

Alberta Livestock & Meat Agency, Ellwood Office Park South, #101, 1003 Ellwood Rd. SW, Edmonton, AB T6X 0B3
780-638-1699, Fax: 780-638-6495, info@almaltd.ca

Irrigation Council, Provincial Bldg., 200 - 5 Ave. South, 3rd Fl., Lethbridge, AB T1J 4L1
403-381-5176, Fax: 403-382-4406

British Columbia

Agricultural Land Commission, #133, 4940 Canada Way, Burnaby, BC V5G 4K6
604-660-7000, Fax: 604-660-7033, ALCBurnaby@Victoria1.gov.bc.ca

British Columbia Ministry of Agriculture, PO Box 9120 Prov Govt,Victoria, BC V8W 9E2
250-387-5121

Manitoba

Agricultural Societies, 1129 Queens Ave., Brandon, MB R7A 1L9
204-726-6195, Fax: 204-726-6260

Manitoba Agriculture, Food & Rural Initiatives, Legislative Bldg., 165-450 Broadway, Winnipeg, MB R3C 0V8
204-945-3722, Fax: 204-945-3470, minagr@leg.gov.mb.ca

Farm Lands Ownership Board, #812, Norquay Bldg., 401 York Ave., Winnipeg, MB R3C 0P8
204-945-3149, Fax: 204-945-1489, 800-282-8069

Farm Machinery & Equipment Board, Norquay Bldg., #812, 401 York Ave., Winnipeg, MB R3C 0P8
204-945-3856, Fax: 204-948-2844

Manitoba Agricultural Services Corporation, #100, 1525 First St. South, Brandon, MB R7A 7A1
204-726-6850, Fax: 204-726-6849, mailbox@masc.mb.ca

New Brunswick

New Brunswick Farm Products Commission, c/o Department of Agriculture, Aquaculture & Fisheries, PO Box 6000, Fredericton, NB E3B 5H1
506-453-3647, Fax: 506-444-5969

Newfoundland & Labrador

Agrifoods Development Branch, Provincial Agriculture Bldg., Brookfield Rd., PO Box 8700, St. John's, NL A1B 4J6
709-729-6588, Fax: 709-729-2674

Newfoundland & Labrador Department of Natural Resources, Natural Resources Bldg., 50 Elizabeth Ave., 7th Fl., PO Box 8700, St. John's, NL A1B 4J6
709-729-2920, Fax: 709-729-0059

Soil, Plant & Feed Laboratory, 308 Brookfield Rd., PO Box 8700, St. John's, NL A1B 4J6
709-729-6738, Fax: 709-729-6734

Nova Scotia

Nova Scotia Department of Agriculture, 1741 Brunswick St., 3rd Fl., PO Box 2223, Halifax, NS B3J 3C4
902-424-4560, Fax: 902-424-4671

Ontario

Agricorp, 1 Stone Rd. West, 3rd Fl., PO Box 3660 Central, Guelph, ON N1H 8M4
Fax: 519-826-4118, 888-247-4999, contact@agricorp.com

Agricultural Research Institute of Ontario, 1 Stone Rd. West, 2nd Fl., Guelph, ON N1G 4Y2
519-826-4554, 888-466-2372, research.omafra@ontario.ca

Agriculture, Food & Rural Affairs Tribunal & Board of Negotiation, 1 Stone Rd. West, 2nd Fl., Guelph, ON N1G 4Y2
519-826-3433, Fax: 519-826-4232, 888-466-2372, appeals.tribunal@omafra.gov.on.ca

Ontario Ministry of Agriculture, Food & Rural Affairs, Ontario Government Bldg., 1 Stone Rd. West, Guelph, ON N1G 4Y2
519-826-3100, 888-466-2372

Ontario Ministry of Rural Affairs, c/o Ministry of Agriculture & Food, 1 Stone Rd. West, Guelph, ON N1G 4Y2
519-826-3100, Fax: 519-826-4335, 888-466-2372, about.omafra@ontario.ca

Prince Edward Island

Agricultural Insurance Corporation, 29 Indigo Cres., PO Box 1600, Charlottetown, PE C1A 7N3
902-368-4842, Fax: 902-368-6677

Prince Edward Island Department of Agriculture & Forestry, Jones Bldg., 11 Kent St., PO Box 2000, Charlottetown, PE C1A 7N8
902-368-4880, Fax: 902-368-4857

Agriculture Policy & Regulatory Division, Jones Bldg., 11 Kent St., 5th Fl., Charlottetown, PE C1A 7N8

BIO|FOOD|TECH, 101 Belvedere Ave., PO Box 2000, Charlottetown, PE C1A 7N8
902-368-5548, Fax: 902-368-5549, 877-368-5548, biofoodtech@biofoodtech.ca

Quebec

Ministère de l'Agriculture, des Pêcheries et de l'Alimentation, 200, ch Sainte-Foy, Québec, QC G1R 4X6
418-380-2110, 888-222-6272

Commission de protection du territoire agricole du Québec, 200, ch Ste-Foy, 2e étage, Québec, QC G1R 4X6
418-643-3314, Fax: 418-643-2261, 800-667-5294, info@cptaq.gouv.qc.ca

Régie des marchés agricoles et alimentaires du Québec, 201, boul Crémazie est, 5e étage, Montréal, QC H2M 1L3
514-873-4024, Fax: 514-873-3984

Saskatchewan

Saskatchewan Agriculture, Walter Scott Bldg., 3085 Albert St., Regina, SK S4S 0B1
866-457-2377, aginfo@gov.sk.ca

Saskatchewan Crop Insurance Corporation, 484 Prince William Dr., PO Box 3000, Melville, SK S0A 2P0
306-728-7200, Fax: 306-728-7202, 888-935-0000, customer.service@scic.gov.sk.ca

Yukon Territory

Yukon Environment, PO Box 2703, Whitehorse, YT Y1A 2C6
867-667-5652, Fax: 867-393-7197, environment.yukon@gov.yk.ca

AIR POLLUTION

See Also: Environment

Environmental Stewardship Branch, 351 boul St-Joseph, Gatineau, QC K1A 0H3
819-997-1575, Fax: 819-953-9452

International Joint Commission, 234 Laurier Ave. West, 22nd Fl., Ottawa, ON K1P 6K6
613-947-1420, Fax: 613-993-5583, beckhoffb@ottawa.ijc.org

Alberta

Clean Energy Division, Centre West Building, 10035 - 108 St., 8th Fl., Edmonton, AB T5J 3E1

Alberta Environment & Sustainable Resource Development, Oxbridge Place, 9820 - 106 St., Main Fl., Edmonton, AB T5K 2J6
780-427-2700, Fax: 780-422-4086, -310-0000, env.infocent@gov.ab.ca; srd.infocent@gov.ab.ca

British Columbia

British Columbia Ministry of Environment, PO Box 9339 Prov Govt,Victoria, BC V8W 9M1
250-387-1161, Fax: 250-387-5669, envmail@gov.bc.ca

Manitoba

Manitoba Conservation & Water Stewardship, 200 Saulteaux Cres., Winnipeg, MB R3J 3W3
800-214-6497, mws@gov.mb.ca

New Brunswick

Community Planning & Environmental Protection Division, Marysville Place, PO Box 6000, Fredericton, NB E3B 5H1
506-444-5119, Fax: 506-457-7333, elg/egl-info@gnb.ca

New Brunswick Department of Environment & Local Government, Marysville Place, PO Box 6000, Fredericton, NB E3B 5H1
506-453-2690, Fax: 506-457-4994, elg/egl-info@gnb.ca

New Brunswick Department of Natural Resources, Hugh John Flemming Forestry Centre, PO Box 6000, Fredericton, NB E3B 5H1
506-453-3826, Fax: 506-444-4367, dnrweb@gnb.ca

Partnerships & Innovation Division, Marysville Place, PO Box 6000, Fredericton, NB E3B 5H1
506-453-2862, Fax: 506-453-2265, elg/egl-info@gnb.ca

Newfoundland & Labrador

Newfoundland & Labrador Department of Environment & Conservation, Confederation Bldg., West Block, 4th Fl., PO Box 8700, St. John's, NL A1B 4J6
709-729-2664, Fax: 709-729-6639, 800-563-6181, envcinquires@gov.nl.ca

Springdale, 200 Main St., Springdale, NL A0J 1T0
709-673-4218, Fax: 709-673-4232,

Northwest Territories

Northwest Territories Department of Environment & Natural Resources, PO Box 1320, Yellowknife, NT X1A 2L9

Nova Scotia

Nova Scotia Department of Environment, Terminal Bldg., 5151 Terminal Rd., 5th Fl., PO Box 697, Halifax, NS B3J 2T8
902-424-3600, Fax: 902-424-0503, 877-936-8476

Nunavut

Nunavut Territory Department of Environment, PO Box 1000 1300,Iqaluit, NU X0A 0H0
867-975-7700, Fax: 867-975-7742, environment@gov.nu.ca

Ontario

Ontario Ministry of Environment, 135 St. Clair Ave. West, Toronto, ON M4V 1P5
416-325-4000, Fax: 416-325-3159, 800-565-4923, picemail.moe@ontario.ca

Integrated Environmental Policy Division, 77 Wellesley St. West, 11th Fl., Toronto, ON M7A 2T5
416-314-6338, Fax: 416-314-6346

Prince Edward Island

Prince Edward Island Department of Environment, Labour & Justice, Shaw Bldg. South, 95 Rochford St., 4th Fl., PO Box 2000, Charlottetown, PE C1A 7N8
902-368-6410, Fax: 902-368-6488

Quebec

Ministère du Développement durable, de l'Environnement, de la Faune, et des Parcs, Édifice Marie-Guyart, 675, boul René-Lévesque est, 29e étage, Québec, QC G1R 5V7
418-521-3911, Fax: 418-643-4143, 800-561-1616, info@mddep.gouv.qc.ca

Saskatchewan

Saskatchewan Environment, 3211 Albert St., 2nd Fl., Regina, SK S4S 5W6
306-787-2584, Fax: 306-787-9544, 800-567-4224, Centre.Inquiry@gov.sk.ca

Yukon Territory

Yukon Environment, PO Box 2703, Whitehorse, YT Y1A 2C6
867-667-5652, Fax: 867-393-7197, environment.yukon@gov.yk.ca

AIRPORTS & AVIATION

See Also: Transportation

Canadian Air Transport Security Authority, 99 Bank St., 13th Fl., Ottawa, ON K1P 6B9
Fax: 613-990-1295, 888-294-2202

Transport Canada, Place de Ville, 330 Sparks St., Tower C, Ottawa, ON K1A 0N5
613-990-2309, Fax: 613-954-4731, 866-995-9737

Transportation Appeal Tribunal of Canada, #1201, 333 Laurier Ave. West, 12th Fl., Ottawa, ON K1A 0N5
613-990-6906, Fax: 613-990-9153, info@tatc.gc.ca

Newfoundland & Labrador

Newfoundland & Labrador Department of Transportation & Works, Confederation Bldg., West Block, 6th Fl., PO Box 8700, St. John's, NL A1B 4J6
709-729-3679, Fax: 709-729-4285, twminister@gov.nl.ca

Northwest Territories

Northwest Territories Department of Transportation, Lahm Ridge Bldg., 4501 50 Ave., PO Box 1320, Yellowknife, NT X1A 2L9
867-920-3460, Fax: 867-873-0363

Nunavut

Nunavut Territory Department of Community & Government Services, W.G. Brown Bldg., 4th Fl., PO Box 1000 700,Iqaluit, NU X0A 0H0
867-975-5400, Fax: 867-975-5305

Ontario

Ontario Ministry of Transportation, Ferguson Block, 77 Wellesley St. West, 3rd Fl., Toronto, ON M7A 1Z8
416-235-4686, Fax: 905-704-2001, 800-268-4686

Saskatchewan

Saskatchewan Highways & Infrastructure, Victoria Tower, 1855 Victoria Ave., Regina, SK S4P 3T2
306-787-4800, communications@highways.gov.sk.ca

Yukon Territory

Yukon Highways & Public Works, PO Box 2703, Whitehorse, YT Y1A 2C6
867-393-7193, Fax: 867-393-6218, 800-661-0408, hpw-info@gov.yk.ca

APPRENTICESHIP PROGRAMS

Canadian Council of Directors of Apprenticeship, 140 Promenade du Portage, 5th Fl, Phase IV, Gatineau, QC K1A 0J9
819-953-7443, Fax: 819-994-0202, redseal-sceaurouge@hrsdc-rhdcc.gc.ca

Alberta

Community, Learner & Industry Connections Division, Phipps-McKinnon Bldg., 10020 - 101A Ave., 5th Fl., Edmonton, AB T5J 3G2

Alberta Enterprise & Advanced Education, Legislature Bldg., #324, 10800 - 97 Ave., Edmonton, AB T5K 2B6
780-422-5400, -310-0000

New Brunswick

New Brunswick Department of Post-Secondary Education, Training & Labour, Chestnut Complex, PO Box 6000, Fredericton, NB E3B 5H1
506-453-2597, Fax: 506-453-3618, dpetlinfo@gnb.ca

Northwest Territories

Northwest Territories Apprenticeship, Trade & Occupations Certification Board, PO Box 1320, Yellowknife, NT X1A 2L9
867-873-7357, Fax: 867-873-0200

Prince Edward Island

SkillsPEI, Atlantic Technology Centre, #212, 90 University Ave., Charlottetown, PE C1A 4K9
902-368-6290, Fax: 902-368-6340, 877-491-4766

Quebec

Conseil consultatif du travail et de la main d'oeuvre, #17.100, 500, boul René-Lévesque ouest, Montréal, QC H2Z 1W7
514-873-2880, Fax: 514-873-1129, cctm@cctm.gouv.qc.ca

ARCTIC & NORTHERN AFFAIRS

Aboriginal Affairs & Northern Development Canada, 10 Wellington St., North Tower, Gatineau, QC K1A 0H4
819-997-0380, Fax: 866-817-3977, 800-567-9604, infopubs@aadnc-aandc.gc.ca

Canadian Polar Commission, Constitution Square, #1710, 360 Albert St., Ottawa, ON K1R 7X7
613-943-8605, Fax: 613-943-8607, 888-765-2701, mail@polarcom.gc.ca

Polar Continental Shelf Program, #487, 615 Booth St., Ottawa, ON K1A 0E4
613-947-1650, Fax: 613-947-1611, pcsp@nrcan-rncan.gc.ca

British Columbia

Northern Development Initiative Trust, #301, 1268 Fifth Ave., Prince George, BC V2L 3L2
250-561-2525, Fax: 250-561-2563, info@northerndevelopment.bc.ca

Manitoba

Manitoba Aboriginal & Northern Affairs, Legislative Bldg, 344-450 Broadway, Winnipeg, MB R3C 0V8
204-945-3719, Fax: 204-945-8374, anaweb@gov.mb.ca

Northwest Territories

Northwest Territories Department of Environment & Natural Resources, PO Box 1320, Yellowknife, NT X1A 2L9

Nunavut

Nunavut Territory Department of Executive & Intergovernmental Affairs, 1084 Aeroplex bldg., PO Box 1000 200,Iqaluit, NU X0A 0H0
867-975-6000, Fax: 867-975-6099

Ontario

Ontario Ministry of Northern Development & Mines, 159 Cedar St., Sudbury, ON P3E 6A5
705-670-5755, Fax: 705-670-5818, 888-415-9845

Northern Development Division, Roberta Bondar Place, #200, 70 Foster Dr., Sault Ste Marie, ON P6A 6V8
705-945-5900, Fax: 705-945-5931, 800-461-2287

Yukon Territory

Yukon Economic Development, PO Box 2703, Whitehorse, YT Y1A 2C6
867-393-7191, Fax: 867-393-6412, 800-661-0408, ecdev@gov.yk.ca

ARTS & CULTURE

Canada Science & Technology Museum Corporation, PO Box 9724 T,Ottawa, ON K1G 5A3
613-991-6090, Fax: 613-990-3636, info@technomuses.ca

Canadian Heritage, 15 Eddy St., Gatineau, QC K1A 0M5
819-997-0055, 866-811-0055, info@pch.gc.ca

Canadian Museum of Nature, PO Box 3443 D,Ottawa, ON K1P 6P4
613-566-4700, Fax: 613-364-4021, 800-263-4433

Parks Canada, 25 Eddy St., Gatineau, QC K1A 0M5
613-860-1251, 888-773-8888, information@pc.gc.ca

British Columbia

British Columbia Film Commission, #201, 865 Hornby St., Vancouver, BC V6Z 2G3
604-660-2732, Fax: 604-660-4790, info@bcfilmcommission.com

Islands Trust, #200, 1627 Fort St., Victoria, BC V8R 1H8
250-405-5151, Fax: 250-405-5155,
information@islandstrust.bc.ca
Provincial Capital Commission, 613 Pandora Ave., Victoria, BC V8W 1N8
250-953-8800, Fax: 250-386-1303, info.pcc@bcpcc.com

Manitoba

Communications Services Manitoba, 155 Carlton St., 10th Fl., Winnipeg, MB R3C 3H8
204-945-3765, Fax: 204-948-2147
Manitoba Culture, Heritage & Tourism, Legislative Building, #118, 450 Broadway Ave., Winnipeg, MB R3C 0V8
204-945-3729, Fax: 204-945-5223, mincht@leg.gov.mb.ca
Heritage Grants Advisory Council, 213 Notre Dame Ave., 3rd Fl., Winnipeg, MB R3B 1N3
204-945-2213, Fax: 204-948-2086
Le Centre Culturel franco-manitobain/Franco-Manitoban Cultural Centre, 340, boul Provencher, St Boniface, MB R2H 0G7
204-233-8972, Fax: 204-233-3324, ccfm@ccfm.mb.ca
Manitoba Arts Council, #525, 93 Lombard Ave., Winnipeg, MB R3B 3B1
204-945-2237, Fax: 204-945-5925, 866-994-2787,
info@artscouncil.mb.ca
Manitoba Centennial Centre Corporation, 555 Main St., Winnipeg, MB R3B 1C3
204-956-1360, Fax: 204-944-1390, inquiries@mbccc.ca
Manitoba Film Classification Board, #216, 301 Weston St., Winnipeg, MB R3E 3H4
204-945-8962, Fax: 204-945-0890, 866-612-2399,
MFCB@gov.mb.ca
Manitoba Heritage Council, 213 Notre Dame Ave., Main Fl., Winnipeg, MB R3B 1N3
204-945-2118, Fax: 204-948-2384, hrb@gov.mb.ca
Manitoba Museum, 190 Rupert Ave., Winnipeg, MB R3B 0N2
204-956-2830, Fax: 204-942-3679,
info@manitobamuseum.mb.ca
Multiculturalism Secretariat, 213 Notre Dame Ave., 9th Fl., Winnipeg, MB R3B 1N3
204-945-5632, multisec@gov.mb.ca

New Brunswick

New Brunswick Arts Board, 61 Carleton St., Fredericton, NB E3B 3T2
506-444-4444, Fax: 506-444-5543, 866-460-2787

Northwest Territories

Northwest Territories Department of Education, Culture & Employment, PO Box 1320, Yellowknife, NT X1A 2L9
867-669-2399, Fax: 867-873-0431, 866-606-5627
NWT Arts Council, PO Box 1320 Main, Yellowknife, NT X1A 2L9
867-920-6370, Fax: 867-873-0205,
boris_atamanenko@gov.nt.ca

Nova Scotia

Culture Division, #601, 1800 Argyle St., PO Box 456, Halifax, NS B3J 2R5
902-424-4510, Fax: 902-424-0710, culture@gov.ns.ca

Nunavut

Nunavut Territory Department of Culture, Language, Elders & Youth, PO Box 1000 800,Iqaluit, NU X0A 0H0
867-975-5500, Fax: 867-975-5504, 866-934-2035

Ontario

Ontario Heritage Trust, 10 Adelaide St. East, Toronto, ON M5C 1J3
416-325-5000, Fax: 416-325-5071
Ontario Library Service - North, 334 Regent St., Sudbury, ON P3C 4E2
705-675-6467, Fax: 705-675-2285, 800-461-6348
Ontario Media Development Corporation, South Tower, #501, 175 Bloor St. East, Toronto, ON M4W 3R8
416-314-6858, Fax: 416-314-6876, reception@omdc.on.ca
Ontario Northland, 555 Oak St. East, North Bay, ON P1B 8L3
705-472-4500, Fax: 705-476-5598, 800-363-7512,
info@ontarionorthland.ca; pr@ontarionorthland.ca
Ontario Place Corporation, 955 Lake Shore Blvd. West, Toronto, ON M6K 3B9
416-314-9900, Fax: 416-314-9989, 866-663-4386
Ontario Tourism Marketing Partnership Corporation, #900, 10 Dundas St. East, Toronto, ON M7A 2A1
416-212-0757, Fax: 416-325-6004, 800-668-2746
Ontario Trillium Foundation, 800 Bay St., 5th Fl., Toronto, ON M5S 3A9
416-963-4927, Fax: 416-963-8781, 800-263-2887, otf@otf.ca
Ottawa Convention Centre, 55 Colonel By Dr., Ottawa, ON K1N 9J2
613-563-1984, Fax: 613-563-7646, 800-450-0077,
info@ottawaconventioncentre.com
Royal Ontario Museum, 100 Queen's Park Cres., Toronto, ON M5S 2C6
416-586-5549, Fax: 416-586-5685, info@rom.on.ca
Southern Ontario Library Service, #902, 111 Peter St., Toronto, ON M5V 2H1
416-961-1669, Fax: 416-961-5122, 800-387-5765
Ontario Ministry of Tourism, Culture & Sport, Hearst Block, 900 Bay St., 9th Fl., Toronto, ON M7A 2E1
416-326-9326, Fax: 416-314-7854, 888-997-9015

Prince Edward Island

Prince Edward Island Department of Community Services & Seniors, Jones Bldg., 11 Kent St., 2nd Fl., PO Box 2000, Charlottetown, PE C1A 7N8
902-620-3777, Fax: 902-894-0242, 866-594-3777

Quebec

Commission des biens culturels du Québec, Bloc A-RC, 225, Grande Allée est, Québec, QC G1R 5G5
418-643-8378, Fax: 418-643-8591, info@cbcq.gouv.qc.ca
Ministère de la Culture et Communications, 225, Grande Allée est, Québec, QC G1R 5G5
888-380-8882

Saskatchewan

Conexus Arts Centre, 200A Lakeshore Dr., Regina, SK S4S 7L3
306-565-4500, 800-667-8497,
cac.admin@conexusartscentre.ca
Provincial Capital Commission, 4607 Dewdney Ave., Regina, SK S4T 1B7
306-787-9261

Yukon Territory

Yukon Tourism & Culture, 100 Hanson St., Whitehorse, YT Y1A 2C6
867-667-5036, Fax: 867-667-3546,

ASSESSMENT

Newfoundland & Labrador

Municipal Assessment Agency Inc., 75 O'Leary Ave., St. John's, NL A1B 2C9
709-724-1532, 877-777-2807, info@maa.ca

AUDITORS-GENERAL

Auditor General of Canada, 240 Sparks St., Ottawa, ON K1A 0G6
613-995-3708, Fax: 613-957-0474, 888-761-5953,
communications@oag-bvg.gc.ca; infomedia@oag-bvg.gc.ca

AUTOMOBILE INSURANCE

See Also: Insurance (Life, Fire Property)

Quebec

Société de l'assurance automobile du Québec, 333, boul Jean-Lesage, CP 19600 Terminus, Québec, QC G1K 8J6
418-643-7620, Fax: 418-644-0339, 800-361-7620,
courrier@saaq.gouv.qc.ca

BANKING & FINANCIAL INSTITUTIONS

Business Development Bank of Canada, #400, 5, Place Ville-Marie, Montréal, QC H3B 5E7
514-283-5904, Fax: 514-283-5626, 877-232-2269
Finance Canada, L'esplanade Laurier, 140 O'Connor St., Ottawa, ON K1A 0G5
613-992-1573, Fax: 613-943-0938, finpub@fin.gc.ca

Newfoundland & Labrador

Credit Union Deposit Guarantee Corporation, PO Box 340, Marystown, NL A0E 2M0
709-279-0170, Fax: 709-279-0177, 877-279-0170

Nunavut

Nunavut Business Credit Corporation, Parnaivak Bldg., #100, PO Box 2548, Iqaluit, NU X0A 0H0
867-975-7891, Fax: 867-975-7897, 800-758-0038,
credit@nbcc.nu.ca

Yukon Territory

Yukon Finance, PO Box 2703, Whitehorse, YT Y1A 2C6
867-667-5343, Fax: 867-393-6217, fininfo@gov.yk.ca

BILINGUALISM

Canadian Heritage, 15 Eddy St., Gatineau, QC K1A 0M5
819-997-0055, 866-811-0055, info@pch.gc.ca

Manitoba

Le Centre Culturel franco-manitobain/Franco-Manitoban Cultural Centre, 340, boul Provencher, St Boniface, MB R2H 0G7
204-233-8972, Fax: 204-233-3324, ccfm@ccfm.mb.ca

Nunavut

Nunavut Territory Department of Culture, Language, Elders & Youth, PO Box 1000 800,Iqaluit, NU X0A 0H0
867-975-5500, Fax: 867-975-5504, 866-934-2035

BIOTECHNOLOGY

National Research Council Industrial Partnership Facility, c/o Montréal (av Royalmount) Research Facilities, 6100, av Royalmount, Montréal, QC H4P 2R2
514-496-6100

BOARDS OF REVIEW

Canadian Nuclear Safety Commission, 280 Slater St., PO Box 1046 B,Ottawa, ON K1P 5S9
613-995-5894, Fax: 613-995-5086, 800-668-5284
Committee on the Status of Endangered Wildlife in Canada, c/o Canadian Wildlife Service, 351 St. Joseph Blvd, 4th Fl., Gatineau, QC K1A 0H3
819-953-3215, Fax: 819-994-3684,
cosewic/cosepac@ec.gc.ca
Mackenzie Valley Environmental Impact Review Board, 200 Scotia Centre, #5102, 50th Ave., PO Box 938, Yellowknife, NT X1A 2N7
867-766-7050, Fax: 867-766-7074, 866-912-3472
Merchant Seamen Compensation Board, Secretary, Merchant Seamen Compensation Board, Phase II, Place du Portage, 10th Fl., Ottawa, ON K1A 0J2
819-953-8001, Fax: 819-994-5368
National Energy Board, 444 - 7 Ave. SW, Calgary, AB T2P 0X8
403-292-4800, Fax: 403-292-5503, 800-899-1265,
info@neb-one.gc.ca
Nunavut Impact Review Board, PO Box 1360, Cambridge Bay, NU X0B 0C0
867-983-4600, Fax: 867-983-2594, 866-233-3033,
info@nirb.ca
Nunavut Water Board, PO Box 119, Gjoa Haven, NU X0B 1J0
867-360-6338, Fax: 867-360-6369
Porcupine Caribou Management Board, PO Box 31723, Whitehorse, YT Y1A 6L3
867-633-4780, Fax: 867-393-3904, pcmb@taiga.net

Northwest Territories

Territorial Board of Revision, #400, 5201 - 50th Ave., PO Box 1320, Yellowknife, NT X1A 2L9
867-873-7125, Fax: 867-873-0609

Ontario

Animal Care Review Board, 77 Grenville St., 8th Fl., Toronto, ON M5S 1B3
416-314-5336, Fax: 416-314-5559, acrb.info@ontario.ca;
acrb.registrar@ontario.ca
Medical Eligibility Committee, 370 Select Dr., PO Box 168, Kingston, ON K7M 8T4
613-536-3058
Ontario Review Board, 151 Bloor St. West, 10th Fl., Toronto, ON M5S 2T5
416-327-8866, Fax: 416-327-8867, orb@ontario.ca

Quebec

Bureau d'audiences publiques sur l'environnement, Édifice Lomer-Gouin, #2.10, 575, rue Saint-Amable, Québec, QC G1R 6A6
418-643-7447, Fax: 418-643-9474, 800-463-4732,
communication@bape.gouv.qc.ca

BOATS

See: Leisure Craft & Vehicle Regulations
Office of the Administrator of the Ship-source Oil Pollution Fund, #830, 180 Kent St., Ottawa, ON K1A 0N5
613-991-1726, Fax: 613-990-5423,

BROADCASTING

Alberta

Alberta Public Affairs Bureau, Park Plaza, 10611 - 98 Ave., 6th Fl., Edmonton, AB T5K 2P7
780-427-2754, Fax: 780-422-4168, -310-0000

British Columbia

Knowledge Network Corporation, 4355 Mathissi Pl., Burnaby, BC V5G 4S8
604-431-3222, Fax: 604-431-3387, 877-456-6988, info@knowledge.ca; hr@knowledge.ca (employment information)

BUSINESS & FINANCE

Atlantic Canada Opportunities Agency, Blue Cross Centre, 644 Main St., 3rd Fl., PO Box 6051, Moncton, NB E1C 9J8
506-851-2271, Fax: 506-851-7403, 800-561-7862, information@acoa-apeca.gc.ca

Auditor General of Canada, 240 Sparks St., Ottawa, ON K1A 0G6
613-995-3708, Fax: 613-957-0474, 888-761-5953, communications@oag-bvg.gc.ca; infomedia@oag-bvg.gc.ca

Business Development Bank of Canada, #400, 5, Place Ville-Marie, Montréal, QC H3B 5E7
514-283-5904, Fax: 514-283-5626, 877-232-2269

Canada Business Network, 235 Queen St., Ottawa, ON K1A 0H5
888-576-4444

Canada Economic Development for Québec Regions, Édifice Dominion Square, #900, 1255, rue Peel, Montréal, QC H3B 2T9
514-283-6412, Fax: 514-283-3302, 866-385-6412

Canada Mortgage & Housing Corporation, 700 Montreal Rd., Ottawa, ON K1A 0P7
613-748-2000, Fax: 613-748-2098, 800-668-2642, chic@cmhc-schl.gc.ca

Canada Revenue Agency, 875 Heron Rd., Ottawa, ON K1A 0L5
800-267-6999

Canada Savings Bonds, #900, 110 Yonge St., Toronto, ON M5C 1T4
416-952-1252, Fax: 416-952-1270, 800-575-5151, csb@csb.gc.ca

Canadian Commercial Corporation, 50 O'Connor St., 11th Fl., Ottawa, ON K1A 0S6
613-996-0034, Fax: 613-995-2121, 800-748-8191

Canadian International Development Agency, 200, Promenade du Portage, Gatineau, QC K1A 0G4
819-997-5456, Fax: 819-953-6088, 800-230-6349, info@acdi-cida.gc.ca

Competition Bureau Canada, Place du Portage, Phase I, 50 Victoria St., Ottawa, ON K1A 0C9
819-997-4282, Fax: 819-997-0324, 800-348-5358

Competition Tribunal, Thomas D'Arcy McGee Bldg., #600, 90 Sparks St., Ottawa, ON K1P 5B4
613-957-3172, Fax: 613-957-3170, tribunal@ct-tc.gc.ca

Electronic Commerce Branch, 300 Slater St., Ottawa, ON K1A 0C8
613-954-5031, Fax: 613-954-2340, 800-328-6189

Enterprise Cape Breton Corporation, 70 Crescent St., PO Box 1750, Sydney, NS B1P 6T7
902-564-3600, Fax: 902-564-3825, 800-705-3926, information@ecbc-secb.gc.ca

Export Development Canada, 151 Slater St., Ottawa, ON K1A 1K3
613-598-2500, Fax: 613-598-3811, 800-267-8510

Finance Canada, L'esplanade Laurier, 140 O'Connor St., Ottawa, ON K1A 0G5
613-992-1573, Fax: 613-943-0938, finpub@fin.gc.ca

Financial Transactions & Reports Analysis Centre of Canada, 234 Laurier Ave. West, 24th Fl., Ottawa, ON K1P 1H7
Fax: 613-943-7931, 866-346-8722, guidelines-lignesdirectrices@fintrac-canafe.gc.ca

Foreign Affairs & International Trade Canada, Enquiries Service, 125 Sussex Dr., Ottawa, ON K1A 0G2
613-944-4000, Fax: 613-996-9709, 800-267-8376, enqserv@international.gc.ca; travel@international.gc.ca

Industry Canada, C.D. Howe Building, 235 Queen St., Ottawa, ON K1A 0H5
613-954-5031, Fax: 613-954-2340, 800-328-6189, info@ic.gc.ca

National Round Table on the Environment & Economy, #200, 344 Slater St., Ottawa, ON K1R 7Y3
613-992-7189, Fax: 613-992-7385, info@nrtee-trnee.ca

Public Sector Pension Investment Board, #200, 440 Laurier Ave. West, Ottawa, ON K1R 7X6
613-782-3095, Fax: 613-782-6864, info@investpsp.ca

Statistics Canada, R.H. Coats Bldg., Tunney's Pasture, 150 Tunney's Pasture Driveway, Ottawa, ON K1A 0T6
613-951-8116, Fax: 877-287-4369, 800-263-1136, infostats@statcan.ca

Treasury Board of Canada, 140 O'Connor St., Ottawa, ON K1A 0R5
613-957-2400, Fax: 613-941-4000, 877-636-0656

Western Economic Diversification Canada, Canada Place, #1500, 9700 Jasper Ave. NW, Edmonton, AB T5J 4H7
780-495-4164, Fax: 780-495-4557, 888-338-9378

Alberta

Agricultural Products Marketing Council, JG O'Donoghue Bldg., 7000 - 113 St., 3rd Fl., Edmonton, AB T6H 5T6
780-427-2164, Fax: 780-422-9690

Financial & Corporate Services Division, Telus Plaza NT, 10025 Jasper Ave., 19th Fl., Edmonton, AB T5J 1S6

Intergovernmental Relations, Commerce Place, 10155 - 102 St., 12th Fl., Edmonton, AB T5J 4G8
780-427-6543, Fax: 780-427-0939

British Columbia

Provincial Capital Commission, 613 Pandora Ave., Victoria, BC V8W 1N8
250-953-8800, Fax: 250-386-1303, info.pcc@bcpcc.com

Timber Export Advisory Committee, PO Box 9514 Prov Govt, Victoria, BC V8W 9C2
250-387-8916, Fax: 250-387-5050

Manitoba

Communities Economic Development Fund, 15 Moak CRes., Thompson, MB R8N 2B8
204-778-4138, Fax: 204-778-4313, 800-561-4315

Manitoba Entrepreneurship, Training & Trade, #1000, 259 Portage Ave, Winnipeg, MB R3B 3P4
204-945-2475, Fax: 204-945-3977, minctt@leg.gov.mb.ca

Heritage Grants Advisory Council, 213 Notre Dame Ave., 3rd Fl., Winnipeg, MB R3B 1N3
204-945-2213, Fax: 204-948-2086

Manitoba Local Government, #301, 450 Broadway Ave., Winnipeg, MB R3C 0V8
Fax: 204-945-1383, mnia@leg.gov.mb.ca

Manitoba Agricultural Services Corporation, #100, 1525 First St. South, Brandon, MB R7A 7A1
204-726-6850, Fax: 204-726-6849, mailbox@masc.mb.ca

Manitoba Round Table for Sustainable Development, #160, 123 Main St., Winnipeg, MB R3C 1A5
204-945-1869, Fax: 204-948-2357, mrtsd@gov.mb.ca

New Brunswick

New Brunswick Farm Products Commission, c/o Department of Agriculture, Aquaculture & Fisheries, PO Box 6000, Fredericton, NB E3B 5H1
506-453-3647, Fax: 506-444-5969

Regional Development Corporation, RDC Bldg., 836 Churchill Row, PO Box 428, Fredericton, NB E3B 5R4
506-453-2277, Fax: 506-453-7988

Newfoundland & Labrador

Credit Union Deposit Guarantee Corporation, PO Box 340, Marystown, NL A0E 2M0
709-279-0170, Fax: 709-279-0177, 877-279-0170

Northwest Territories

Northwest Territories Department of Public Works & Services, PO Box 1320, Yellowknife, NT X1A 2L9

Ontario

Advertising Review Board, Macdonald Block, #M2-56, 900 Bay St., 2nd Fl., Toronto, ON M7A 1N3
416-327-2183, Fax: 416-327-2179

Agriculture, Food & Rural Affairs Tribunal & Board of Negotiation, 1 Stone Rd. West, 2nd Fl., Guelph, ON N1G 4Y2
519-826-3433, Fax: 519-826-4232, 888-466-2372, appeals.tribunal@omafra.gov.on.ca

Ontario Ministry of Consumer Services, Mowat Block, 900 Bay St., 6th Fl., Toronto, ON M7A 1L2
416-327-8300, Fax: 416-326-1947, 866-665-0662, infomcs@ontario.ca; consumer@ontario.ca

Ontario Ministry of Economic Development, Trade & Employment, Hearst Block, 900 Bay St., 8th Fl., Toronto, ON M7A 2E1
416-325-6666, Fax: 416-325-6688, 866-668-4249, info@edt.gov.on.ca

Ontario Ministry of Government Services, Ferguson Block, 77 Wellesley St. West, 8th Fl., Toronto, ON M7A 1N3
416-326-8555, 800-268-1142

Grain Financial Protection Board, 1 Stone Rd. West, 1st Fl. Northeast, PO Box 3660 Central, Guelph, ON N1H 8M4
519-826-3949, Fax: 519-826-3367,

Licence Appeal Tribunal, #530, 20 Dundas St. West, Toronto, ON M5G 2C2
416-314-4260, Fax: 416-314-4270, 800-255-2214

Livestock Financial Protection Board, 1 Stone Rd. West, 5th Fl. Northwest, Guelph, ON N1G 4Y2
519-826-3886, Fax: 519-826-4375, 888-466-2372

Metro Toronto Convention Centre Corporation, 255 Front St. West, Toronto, ON M5V 2W6
416-585-8120, Fax: 416-585-8198, info@mtccc.com; sales@mtccc.com

Normal Farm Practices Protection Board, 1 Stone Rd. West, 3rd Fl., Guelph, ON N1G 4Y2
519-826-4047, Fax: 519-826-3259, 877-424-1300, ag.info.omafra@ontario.ca

Ontario Farm Products Marketing Commission, 1 Stone Rd. West, 5th Fl. Southwest, Guelph, ON N1G 4Y2
519-826-4220, Fax: 519-826-3400

Ontario Food Terminal Board, 165 The Queensway, Toronto, ON M8Y 1H8
416-259-5479, Fax: 416-259-4303, oftboard@interlog.com

Ontario Place Corporation, 955 Lake Shore Blvd. West, Toronto, ON M6K 3B9
416-314-9900, Fax: 416-314-9989, 866-663-4386

Ottawa Convention Centre, 55 Colonel By Dr., Ottawa, ON K1N 9J2
613-563-1984, Fax: 613-563-7646, 800-450-0077, info@ottawaconventioncentre.com

Pay Equity Commission, #300, 180 Dundas St. West, Toronto, ON M7A 2S6
416-314-1896, Fax: 416-314-8741, 800-387-8813

Prince Edward Island

Agricultural Insurance Corporation, 29 Indigo Cres., PO Box 1600, Charlottetown, PE C1A 7N3
902-368-4842, Fax: 902-368-6677

Charlottetown Area Development Corporation, 4 Pownal St., PO Box 786, Charlottetown, PE C1A 7L9
902-892-5341, Fax: 902-368-1935

Prince Edward Island Department of Innovation & Advanced Learning, Shaw Bldg., 105 Rochford St., 5th Fl., PO Box 2000, Charlottetown, PE C1A 7N8
902-368-4240, Fax: 902-368-4242

Prince Edward Island Lending Agency, Homburg Financial Tower, 98 Fitzroy St., 2nd Fl., Charlottetown, PE C1A 1R7
902-368-6200, Fax: 902-368-6201

Quebec

Fonds de la recherche en santé du Québec, #800, 500, rue Sherbrooke ouest, Montréal, QC H3A 3C6
514-873-2114, Fax: 514-873-8768

Innovatech Québec, #410, 888, rue St-Jean, Québec, QC G1R 5H6
418-528-9770, Fax: 418-528-9783, 866-605-1676

Société du Centre des congrès de Québec, 1000, boul René-Lévesque est, Québec, QC G1R 5T8
418-644-4000, Fax: 418-644-6455, 888-679-4000

Saskatchewan

Energy & Resources, #300, 2103 - 11th Ave., Regina, SK S4P 3Z8
306-787-2528

Saskatchewan Crop Insurance Corporation, 484 Prince William Dr., PO Box 3000, Melville, SK S0A 2P0
306-728-7200, Fax: 306-728-7202, 888-935-0000, customer.service@scic.gov.sk.ca

Yukon Territory

Yukon Finance, PO Box 2703, Whitehorse, YT Y1A 2C6
867-667-5343, Fax: 867-393-6217, fininfo@gov.yk.ca

Yukon Lottery Commission, 312 Wood St., Whitehorse, YT Y1A 2E6
867-633-7890, Fax: 867-668-7561, lotteriesyukon@gov.yk.ca

BUSINESS DEVELOPMENT

See Also: Industry; Science & Technology

Atlantic Canada Opportunities Agency, Blue Cross Centre, 644 Main St., 3rd Fl., PO Box 6051, Moncton, NB E1C 9J8
506-851-2271, Fax: 506-851-7403, 800-561-7862, information@acoa-apeca.gc.ca

Business Development Bank of Canada, #400, 5, Place Ville-Marie, Montréal, QC H3B 5E7
514-283-5904, Fax: 514-283-5626, 877-232-2269

Canada Business Network, 235 Queen St., Ottawa, ON K1A 0H5
888-576-4444

Canada Economic Development for Québec Regions, Édifice Dominion Square, #900, 1255, rue Peel, Montréal, QC H3B

2T9
514-283-6412, Fax: 514-283-3302, 866-385-6412
Canadian Northern Economic Development Agency, Ottawa, ON K1A 0H4
Fax: 866-817-3977, 800-567-9604, InfoNorth-InfoNord@CanNor.gc.ca
Enterprise Cape Breton Corporation, 70 Crescent St., PO Box 1750, Sydney, NS B1P 6T7
902-564-3600, Fax: 902-564-3825, 800-705-3926, information@ecbc-secb.gc.ca
Export Development Canada, 151 Slater St., Ottawa, ON K1A 1K3
613-598-2500, Fax: 613-598-3811, 800-267-8510
Federal Economic Development Agency for Southern Ontario, 101 Frederick St., 4th Fl., Kitchener, ON N2H 6R2
Fax: 519-571-5750, 866-593-5505
Industry Canada, C.D. Howe Building, 235 Queen St., Ottawa, ON K1A 0H5
613-954-5031, Fax: 613-954-2340, 800-328-6189, info@ic.gc.ca
Market & Industry Services Branch, Tower 5, 1341 Baseline Rd., Ottawa, ON K1A 0C5
613-759-1000, Fax: 613-773-1711
Western Economic Diversification Canada, Canada Place, #1500, 9700 Jasper Ave. NW, Edmonton, AB T5J 4H7
780-495-4164, Fax: 780-495-4557, 888-338-9378

British Columbia
British Columbia Ministry of Jobs, Tourism, & Skills Training (& Responsible for Labour), PO Box 9071 Prov Govt,Victoria, BC V8W 9E2
EnquiryBC@gov.bc.ca; GCPE.JTI.Media.Requests@gov.bc.ca
Northern Development Initiative Trust, #301, 1268 Fifth Ave., Prince George, BC V2L 3L2
250-561-2525, Fax: 250-561-2563, info@northerndevelopment.bc.ca

Manitoba
Manitoba Entrepreneurship, Training & Trade, #1000, 259 Portage Ave, Winnipeg, MB R3B 3P4
204-945-2475, Fax: 204-945-3977, minctt@leg.gov.mb.ca

New Brunswick
Regional Development Corporation, RDC Bldg., 836 Churchill Row, PO Box 428, Fredericton, NB E3B 5R4
506-453-2277, Fax: 506-453-7988

Northwest Territories
Northwest Territories Department of Industry, Tourism & Investment, PO Box 1320, Yellowknife, NT X1A 2L9
Fax: 867-873-0306, info@iti.ca

Nunavut
Nunavut Territory Department of Economic Development & Transportation, Bldg. 1104 A, Inuksugait Plaza, PO Box 1000 1500,Iqaluit, NU X0A 0H0
867-975-7800, Fax: 867-975-7870, 888-975-5999, edt@gov.nu.ca

Ontario
Ontario Ministry of Consumer Services, Mowat Block, 900 Bay St., 6th Fl., Toronto, ON M7A 1L2
416-327-8300, Fax: 416-326-1947, 866-665-0662, infomcs@ontario.ca; consumer@ontario.ca
Ontario Ministry of Economic Development, Trade & Employment, Hearst Block, 900 Bay St., 8th Fl., Toronto, ON M7A 2E1
416-325-6666, Fax: 416-325-6688, 866-668-4249, info@edt.gov.on.ca
Northern Development Division, Roberta Bondar Place, #200, 70 Foster Dr., Sault Ste Marie, ON P6A 6V8
705-945-5900, Fax: 705-945-5931, 800-461-2287

Prince Edward Island
Charlottetown Area Development Corporation, 4 Pownal St., PO Box 786, Charlottetown, PE C1A 7L9
902-892-5341, Fax: 902-368-1935
Prince Edward Island Department of Innovation & Advanced Learning, Shaw Bldg., 105 Rochford St., 5th Fl., PO Box 2000, Charlottetown, PE C1A 7N8
902-368-4240, Fax: 902-368-4242
Innovation PEI, 94 Euston St., PO Box 910, Charlottetown, PE C1A 7L9
902-368-6300, Fax: 902-368-6301, 800-563-3734, innovation@gov.pe.ca
Prince Edward Island Lending Agency, Homburg Financial Tower, 98 Fitzroy St., 2nd Fl., Charlottetown, PE C1A 1R7
902-368-6200, Fax: 902-368-6201

Quebec
Ministère du Développement économique, de l'Innovation et de l'Exportation, 710, place D'Youville, 3e étage, Québec, QC G1R 4Y4
418-691-5950, Fax: 418-644-0118, 866-680-1884

Saskatchewan
Energy & Resources, #300, 2103 - 11th Ave., Regina, SK S4P 3Z8
306-787-2528,
Enterprise Saskatchewan, #200, 3085 Albert St., Regina, SK S4S 0B1
306-787-4484, Fax: 306-798-0629, invest@gov.sk.ca

Yukon Territory
Yukon Development Corporation, #2 Miles Canyon Rd., PO Box 5920, Whitehorse, YT Y1A 6S7
867-393-5337, Fax: 867-393-5401
Yukon Economic Development, PO Box 2703, Whitehorse, YT Y1A 2C6
867-393-7191, Fax: 867-393-6412, 800-661-0408, ecdev@gov.yk.ca

BUSINESS REGULATIONS

Canada Revenue Agency, 875 Heron Rd., Ottawa, ON K1A 0L5
800-267-6999
Industry Canada, C.D. Howe Building, 235 Queen St., Ottawa, ON K1A 0H5
613-954-5031, Fax: 613-954-2340, 800-328-6189, info@ic.gc.ca

Alberta
Strategic Planning & Financial Services, Commerce Place, 10155 - 102 St., 13th Fl., Edmonton, AB T5J 4G8
780-422-8545

CANADIANS & SOCIETY

Aboriginal Affairs & Northern Development Canada, 10 Wellington St., North Tower, Gatineau, QC K1A 0H4
819-997-0380, Fax: 866-817-3977, 800-567-9604, infopubs@aadnc-aandc.gc.ca
Beverly & Qamanirjuaq Caribou Management Board, Secretariat, PO Box 629, Stonewall, MB R0C 2Z0
204-467-2438, caribounews@arctic-caribou.com
Canadian Heritage, 15 Eddy St., Gatineau, QC K1A 0M5
819-997-0055, 866-811-0055, info@pch.gc.ca
First Nations Tax Commission, #321, 345 Yellowhead Hwy, Kamloops, BC V2H 1H1
250-828-9857, Fax: 250-828-9858, mailkamloops@fntc.ca
Foreign Affairs & International Trade Canada, Enquiries Service, 125 Sussex Dr., Ottawa, ON K1A 0G2
613-944-4000, Fax: 613-996-9709, 800-267-8376, enqserv@international.gc.ca; travel@international.gc.ca
Government of Canada, c/o Canada Enquiry Centre, Service Canada, Ottawa, ON K1A 0J9
613-941-1827, 800-622-6232, canadasite@canada.gc.ca
Historic Sites & Monuments Board of Canada, Terrasses de la Chaudière, 25 Eddy St., Gatineau, QC K1A 0M5
Fax: 819-934-1115, 855-283-8730, hsmbc-clmhc@pc.gc.ca
Human Resources & Skills Development Canada, 140 Promenade du Portage, Gatineau, QC K1A 0J9
National Battlefields Commission, 390, av de Bernières, Québec, QC G1R 2L7
418-648-3506, Fax: 418-648-3638, information@ccbn-nbc.gc.ca
National Capital Commission, #202, 40 Elgin St., Ottawa, ON K1P 1C7
613-239-5000, Fax: 613-239-5063, 800-465-1867, info@ncc-ccn.ca; contracts-contrats@ncc-ccn.ca (Contracting)
National Round Table on the Environment & Economy, #200, 344 Slater St., Ottawa, ON K1R 7Y3
613-992-7189, Fax: 613-992-7385, info@nrtee-trnee.ca
Nunavut Impact Review Board, PO Box 1360, Cambridge Bay, NU X0B 0C0
867-983-4600, Fax: 867-983-2594, 866-233-3033, info@nirb.ca
Nunavut Planning Commission, PO Box 2101, Cambridge Bay, NU X0B 0C0
867-983-4625, Fax: 867-983-4626
Nunavut Water Board, PO Box 119, Gjoa Haven, NU X0B 1J0
867-360-6338, Fax: 867-360-6369
Office of the Public Sector Integrity Commissioner of Canada, 60 Queen St., 7th Fl., Ottawa, ON K1P 5Y7
613-941-6400, Fax: 613-941-6535
Porcupine Caribou Management Board, PO Box 31723, Whitehorse, YT Y1A 6L3
867-633-4780, Fax: 867-393-3904, pcmb@taiga.net

Alberta
Alberta Sport, Recreation, Parks, & Wildlife Foundation, Standard Life Centre, #903, 10405 Jasper Ave., 9th Fl., Edmonton, AB T5J 4R7
780-415-1167, Fax: 780-415-0308, -310-0000
Alberta Health, PO Box 1360 Main,Edmonton, AB T5J 2N3
780-427-7164, Fax: 780-427-1171, -310-0000
Labour Relations Board, Labour Building, 10808 - 99 Ave., 5th Fl., Edmonton, AB T5K 0G5
780-422-5926, Fax: 780-422-0970, 800-463-2572, alrbinfo@lab.gov.ab.ca
Premier's Council on the Status of Persons with Disabilities, HSBC Building, 10055 - 106 St., 11th Fl., Edmonton, AB T5J 1G3
780-422-1095, 800-272-8841, pcspd@gov.ab.ca
Seniors Advisory Council for Alberta, Standard Life Centre, #600, 10405 Jasper Ave., 6th Fl., Edmonton, AB T5J 4R7
780-422-2321, Fax: 780-422-8762, -310-0000, saca@gov.ab.ca
Alberta Tourism, Parks, & Recreation, Communications Branch, Commerce Place, 10155 - 102 St., 6th Fl., Edmonton, AB T5J 4L6
780-644-5589, TPR.Communications@gov.ab.ca

British Columbia
British Columbia Ministry of Community, Sport, & Cultural Development, PO Box 9490 Prov Govt,Victoria, BC V8W 9N7
Local Government, PO Box 9490 Prov Govt,Victoria, BC V8W 9N7
250-356-6575, Fax: 250-387-7973

Manitoba
Manitoba Aboriginal & Northern Affairs, Legislative Bldg, 344-450 Broadway, Winnipeg, MB R3C OV8
204-945-3719, Fax: 204-945-8374, anaweb@gov.mb.ca
Communications Services Manitoba, 155 Carlton St., 10th Fl., Winnipeg, MB R3C 3H8
204-945-3765, Fax: 204-948-2147
Communities Economic Development Fund, 15 Moak CRes., Thompson, MB R8N 2B8
204-778-4138, Fax: 204-778-4313, 800-561-4315
Manitoba Culture, Heritage & Tourism, Legislative Building, #118, 450 Broadway Ave., Winnipeg, MB R3C 0V8
204-945-3729, Fax: 204-945-5223, mincht@leg.gov.mb.ca
Heritage Grants Advisory Council, 213 Notre Dame Ave., 3rd Fl., Winnipeg, MB R3B 1N3
204-945-2213, Fax: 204-948-2086
Le Centre Culturel franco-manitobain/Franco-Manitoban Cultural Centre, 340, boul Provencher, St Boniface, MB R2H 0G7
204-233-8972, Fax: 204-233-3324, ccfm@ccfm.mb.ca
Manitoba Centennial Centre Corporation, 555 Main St., Winnipeg, MB R3B 1C3
204-956-1360, Fax: 204-944-1390, inquiries@mbccc.ca
Manitoba Film Classification Board, #216, 301 Weston St., Winnipeg, MB R3E 3H4
204-945-8962, Fax: 204-945-0890, 866-612-2399, MFCB@gov.mb.ca
Manitoba Heritage Council, 213 Notre Dame Ave., Main Fl., Winnipeg, MB R3B 1N3
204-945-2118, Fax: 204-948-2384, hrb@gov.mb.ca
Multiculturalism Secretariat, 213 Notre Dame Ave., 9th Fl., Winnipeg, MB R3B 1N3
204-945-5632, multisec@gov.mb.ca
Public Health & Primary Health Care, 300 Carlton St., 2nd Floor, Winnipeg, MB R3B 3M9

New Brunswick
New Brunswick Department of Health, PO Box 5100, Fredericton, NB E3B 5G8
506-457-4800, Fax: 506-453-5243, dh-ms@dh-ms.ca
Regional Development Corporation, RDC Bldg., 836 Churchill Row, PO Box 428, Fredericton, NB E3B 5R4
506-453-2277, Fax: 506-453-7988

Newfoundland & Labrador
C.A. Pippy Park Commission, Mount Scio House, 15 Mount Scio Rd., St. John's, NL A1B 3T2
709-737-3655, Fax: 709-737-3303, info@pippypark.com

Northwest Territories
Northwest Territories Department of Aboriginal Affairs & Intergovernmental Relations, 4910 - 52nd St., PO Box 1320, Yellowknife, NT X1A 2L9

867-873-7143, Fax: 867-873-0233, 877-838-8194, nancy_gardiner@gov.nt.ca
Northwest Territories Department of Municipal & Community Affairs, PO Box 1320, Yellowknife, NT X1A 2L9
867-873-7118, Fax: 867-873-0309

Nova Scotia
Nova Scotia Department of Service Nova Scotia & Municipal Relations, 1505 Barrington St., PO Box 216, Halifax, NS B3J 3K5
902-424-5200, Fax: 902-424-0581, 800-670-4357, askus@gov.ns.ca

Ontario
Ontario Ministry of Government Services, Ferguson Block, 77 Wellesley St. West, 8th Fl., Toronto, ON M7A 1N3
416-326-8555, 800-268-1142
Ontario Heritage Trust, 10 Adelaide St. East, Toronto, ON M5C 1J3
416-325-5000, Fax: 416-325-5071
Ontario Northland, 555 Oak St. East, North Bay, ON P1B 8L3
705-472-4500, Fax: 705-476-5598, 800-363-7512, info@ontarionorthland.ca; pr@ontarionorthland.ca
Royal Ontario Museum, 100 Queen's Park Cres., Toronto, ON M5S 2C6
416-586-5549, Fax: 416-586-5685, info@rom.on.ca
Ontario Ministry of Rural Affairs, c/o Ministry of Agriculture & Food, 1 Stone Rd. West, Guelph, ON N1G 4Y2
519-826-3100, Fax: 519-826-4335, 888-466-2372, about.omafra@ontario.ca

Prince Edward Island
Prince Edward Island Department of Community Services & Seniors, Jones Bldg., 11 Kent St., 2nd Fl., PO Box 2000, Charlottetown, PE C1A 7N8
902-620-3777, Fax: 902-894-0242, 866-594-3777

Quebec
Commission des biens culturels du Québec, Bloc A-RC, 225, Grande Allée est, Québec, QC G1R 5G5
418-643-8378, Fax: 418-643-8591, info@cbcq.gouv.qc.ca
Ministère de la Culture et Communications, 225, Grande Allée est, Québec, QC G1R 5G5
888-380-8882
Fonds québécois de la recherche sur la société et la culture, #470, 140, Grande Allée est, Québec, QC G1R 5M8
418-643-7582, Fax: 418-644-5248, frq.sc@frq.gouv.qc.ca
Office des personnes handicapées du Québec, 309, rue Brock, Drummondville, QC J2B 1C5
Fax: 819-475-8753, 800-567-1465, aide@ophq.gouv.qc.ca
Ministère de la Santé et des Services sociaux, Direction des communications, 1075, ch Sainte-Foy, 16e étage, Québec, QC G1S 2M1
418-643-9395, Fax: 418-643-4768, regisseur.web@msss.gouv.qc.ca

Yukon Territory
Yukon Community Services, PO Box 2703, Whitehorse, YT Y1A 2C6
867-667-5811, Fax: 867-393-6295, 800-661-0408, inquiry@gov.yk.ca
Yukon Health & Social Services, PO Box 2703, Whitehorse, YT Y1A 2C6
867-667-3673, Fax: 867-667-3096, hss@gov.yk.ca

CAREER PLANNING

New Brunswick
Labour & Planning Division, Chestnut Complex, PO Box 6000, Fredericton, NB E3B 5H1
506-453-8202, Fax: 506-453-3038, dpetlinfo@gnb.ca

CENSORSHIP (MEDIA)

Manitoba
Manitoba Film Classification Board, #216, 301 Weston St., Winnipeg, MB R3E 3H4
204-945-8962, Fax: 204-945-0890, 866-612-2399, MFCB@gov.mb.ca

Nunavut
Nunavut Territory Department of Community & Government Services, W.G. Brown Bldg., 4th Fl., PO Box 1000 700,Iqaluit, NU X0A 0H0
867-975-5400, Fax: 867-975-5305

CHILD WELFARE

See Also: Day Care Services

Alberta
Office of the Child & Youth Advocate, Peace Hills Trust Tower, #805, 10011 - 109 St., Edmonton, AB T5J 3S8
780-422-6056, Fax: 780-644-8833, 800-661-3446

Northwest Territories
Northwest Territories Department of Health & Social Services, Centre Square Tower, PO Box 1320, Yellowknife, NT X1A 2L9
Fax: 867-873-0266

Nunavut
Nunavut Territory Department of Health & Social Services, PO Box 1000 1000,Iqaluit, NU X0A 0H0
867-975-5766, Fax: 867-975-5705, 800-661-0833

CLIMATE & WEATHER

Canadian Hurricane Centre, 45 Alderney Dr., 16th Fl., Dartmouth, NS B2Y 2N6
902-426-7231, Fax: 902-426-6348, 15th.reception@ec.gc.ca
Canadian Space Agency, John H. Chapman Space Centre, 6767, rte de l'Aéroport, Saint-Hubert, QC J3Y 8Y9
450-926-4800, Fax: 450-926-4352, promo@asc-csa.gc.ca

CLIMATE CHANGE

Climate Change Impacts & Adaptation Division, 601, rue Booth, Ottawa, ON K1A 0E8
613-992-8302, Fax: 613-947-0126, adaptation@nrcan.gc.ca

Newfoundland & Labrador
Springdale, 200 Main St., Springdale, NL A0J 1T0
709-673-4218, Fax: 709-673-4232

Quebec
Ministère du Développement durable, de l'Environnement, de la Faune, et des Parcs, Édifice Marie-Guyart, 675, boul René-Lévesque est, 29e étage, Québec, QC G1R 5V7
418-521-3911, Fax: 418-643-4143, 800-561-1616, info@mddep.gouv.qc.ca

COAL

See Also: Energy

Alberta
Energy Resources Conservation Board, #1000, 250 - 5 Ave. SW, Calgary, AB T2P 0R4
403-297-8311, Fax: 403-297-7336, 855-297-8311, inquiries@ercb.ca; infoservices@ercb.ca; ADR@ercb.ca

Ontario
Ontario Power Generation, 700 University Ave., Toronto, ON M5G 1X6
416-592-2555, 877-592-2555, webmaster@opg.com

Saskatchewan
Saskatchewan Power Corporation (SaskPower), 2025 Victoria Ave., Regina, SK S4P 0S1
306-566-3306, Fax: 800-757-6937, 888-757-6937,

COMMUNICATIONS

See: Telecommunications
Communications Research Centre Canada, 3701 Carling Ave., PO Box 11490 H, Ottawa, ON K2H 8S2
613-991-3313, Fax: 613-998-5355, info@crc.gc.ca

Alberta
Alberta Public Affairs Bureau, Park Plaza, 10611 - 98 Ave., 6th Fl., Edmonton, AB T5K 2P7
780-427-2754, Fax: 780-422-4168, -310-0000

Manitoba
Communications Services Manitoba, 155 Carlton St., 10th Fl., Winnipeg, MB R3C 3H8
204-945-3765, Fax: 204-948-2147

New Brunswick
Northern Development Division, Harbourview Place, #400, 275 Main St., Bathurst, NB E2A 1A9
506-547-2227, Fax: 506-547-2269

Ontario
Ontario Library Service - North, 334 Regent St., Sudbury, ON P3C 4E2
705-675-6467, Fax: 705-675-2285, 800-461-6348

Quebec
Ministère de la Culture et Communications, 225, Grande Allée est, Québec, QC G1R 5G5
888-380-8882

Saskatchewan
Communications, 1919 Saskatchewan Dr., 4th Fl., Regina, SK S4P 4H2
306-787-0346, Fax: 306-798-0033

COMMUNITY & MUNICIPAL DEVELOPMENT

Atlantic Canada Opportunities Agency, Blue Cross Centre, 644 Main St., 3rd Fl., PO Box 6051, Moncton, NB E1C 9J8
506-851-2271, Fax: 506-851-7403, 800-561-7862, information@acoa-apeca.gc.ca
Canada Economic Development for Québec Regions, Édifice Dominion Square, #900, 1255, rue Peel, Montréal, QC H3B 2T9
514-283-6412, Fax: 514-283-3302, 866-385-6412
Canadian Northern Economic Development Agency, Ottawa, ON K1A 0H4
Fax: 866-817-3977, 800-567-9604, InfoNorth-InfoNord@CanNor.gc.ca
Federal Economic Development Agency for Southern Ontario, 101 Frederick St., 4th Fl., Kitchener, ON N2H 6R2
Fax: 519-571-5750, 866-593-5505
Western Economic Diversification Canada, Canada Place, #1500, 9700 Jasper Ave. NW, Edmonton, AB T5J 4H7
780-495-4164, Fax: 780-495-4557, 888-338-9378

Alberta
Alberta Tourism, Parks, & Recreation, Communications Branch, Commerce Place, 10155 - 102 St., 6th Fl., Edmonton, AB T5J 4L6
780-644-5589, TPR.Communications@gov.ab.ca

British Columbia
Local Government, PO Box 9490 Prov Govt,Victoria, BC V8W 9N7
250-356-6575, Fax: 250-387-7973

Manitoba
Manitoba Aboriginal & Northern Affairs, Legislative Bldg, 344-450 Broadway, Winnipeg, MB R3C OV8
204-945-3719, Fax: 204-945-8374, anaweb@gov.mb.ca
Provincial-Municipal Support Services, #508, 800 Portage Ave., Winnipeg, MB R3G 0N4

New Brunswick
Regional Development Corporation, RDC Bldg., 836 Churchill Row, PO Box 428, Fredericton, NB E3B 5R4
506-453-2277, Fax: 506-453-7988

Newfoundland & Labrador
Newfoundland & Labrador Department of Health & Community Services, West Block, Confederation Bldg., PO Box 8700, St. John's, NL A1B 4J6
709-729-4984, healthinfo@gov.nl.ca

Northwest Territories
Northwest Territories Department of Municipal & Community Affairs, PO Box 1320, Yellowknife, NT X1A 2L9
867-873-7118, Fax: 867-873-0309

Nova Scotia
Nova Scotia Department of Service Nova Scotia & Municipal Relations, 1505 Barrington St., PO Box 216, Halifax, NS B3J 3K5
902-424-5200, Fax: 902-424-0581, 800-670-4357, askus@gov.ns.ca

Nunavut
Nunavut Territory Department of Community & Government Services, W.G. Brown Bldg., 4th Fl., PO Box 1000 700,Iqaluit, NU X0A 0H0
867-975-5400, Fax: 867-975-5305

Ontario
Ontario Ministry of Municipal Affairs & Housing, College Park, 777 Bay St., 17th Fl., Toronto, ON M5G 2E5
416-585-7041, Fax: 416-585-6470, 866-220-2290, mininfo.mah@ontario.ca

Prince Edward Island
SkillsPEI, Atlantic Technology Centre, #212, 90 University Ave., Charlottetown, PE C1A 4K9
902-368-6290, Fax: 902-368-6340, 877-491-4766

Quebec
Ministère des Affaires municipales, des Régions et de l'Occupation du territoire, Aile Chaveau, 10, rue Pierre-Olivier-Chauveau, 3e étage, Québec, QC G1R 4J3
418-691-2019, Fax: 418-643-7385, communications@mamrot.gouv.qc.ca

Ministère du Développement économique, de l'Innovation et de l'Exportation, 710, place D'Youville, 3e étage, Québec, QC G1R 4Y4
418-691-5950, Fax: 418-644-0118, 866-680-1884

Saskatchewan

Enterprise Saskatchewan, #200, 3085 Albert St., Regina, SK S4S 0B1
306-787-4484, Fax: 306-798-0629, invest@gov.sk.ca

Saskatchewan Government Relations, 1855 Victoria Ave., Regina, SK S4P 3T2
306-787-8885

COMMUNITY FINANCING

Atlantic Canada Opportunities Agency, Blue Cross Centre, 644 Main St., 3rd Fl., PO Box 6051, Moncton, NB E1C 9J8
506-851-2271, Fax: 506-851-7403, 800-561-7862, information@acoa-apeca.gc.ca

Business Development Bank of Canada, #400, 5, Place Ville-Marie, Montréal, QC H3B 5E7
514-283-5904, Fax: 514-283-5626, 877-232-2269

Canada Economic Development for Québec Regions, Édifice Dominion Square, #900, 1255, rue Peel, Montréal, QC H3B 2T9
514-283-6412, Fax: 514-283-3302, 866-385-6412

Canada Savings Bonds, #900, 110 Yonge St., Toronto, ON M5C 1T4
416-952-1252, Fax: 416-952-1270, 800-575-5151, csb@csb.gc.ca

Finance Canada, L'esplanade Laurier, 140 O'Connor St., Ottawa, ON K1A 0G5
613-992-1573, Fax: 613-943-0938, finpub@fin.gc.ca

Western Economic Diversification Canada, Canada Place, #1500, 9700 Jasper Ave. NW, Edmonton, AB T5J 4H7
780-495-4164, Fax: 780-495-4557, 888-338-9378

Manitoba

Communities Economic Development Fund, 15 Moak CRes., Thompson, MB R8N 2B8
204-778-4138, Fax: 204-778-4313, 800-561-4315,

Provincial-Municipal Support Services, #508, 800 Portage Ave., Winnipeg, MB R3G 0N4

Nova Scotia

Nova Scotia Municipal Finance Corporation, Maritime Centre, 1505 Barrington St., 10th Fl. South, PO Box 850 M, Halifax, NS B3J 2V2
902-424-4590, Fax: 902-424-0525

Prince Edward Island

SkillsPEI, Atlantic Technology Centre, #212, 90 University Ave., Charlottetown, PE C1A 4K9
902-368-6290, Fax: 902-368-6340, 877-491-4766

Quebec

Ministère des Affaires municipales, des Régions et de l'Occupation du territoire, Aile Chaveau, 10, rue Pierre-Olivier-Chauveau, 3e étage, Québec, QC G1R 4J3
418-691-2019, Fax: 418-643-7385, communications@mamrot.gouv.qc.ca

Yukon Territory

Yukon Economic Development, PO Box 2703, Whitehorse, YT Y1A 2C6
867-393-7191, Fax: 867-393-6412, 800-661-0408, ecdev@gov.yk.ca

COMMUNITY SERVICES

Alberta

Alberta Tourism, Parks, & Recreation, Communications Branch, Commerce Place, 10155 - 102 St., 6th Fl., Edmonton, AB T5J 4L6
780-644-5589, TPR.Communications@gov.ab.ca

British Columbia

British Columbia Ministry of Community, Sport, & Cultural Development, PO Box 9490 Prov Govt,Victoria, BC V8W 9N7

Manitoba

Local Government Development Division, 59 Elizabeth Dr., PO Box 33, Thompson, MB R8N 1X4
204-677-6794, Fax: 204-677-6525

Newfoundland & Labrador

Newfoundland & Labrador Department of Health & Community Services, West Block, Confederation Bldg., PO Box 8700, St. John's, NL A1B 4J6
709-729-4984, healthinfo@gov.nl.ca

Northwest Territories

Northwest Territories Department of Municipal & Community Affairs, PO Box 1320, Yellowknife, NT X1A 2L9
867-873-7118, Fax: 867-873-0309

Nunavut

Nunavut Territory Department of Community & Government Services, W.G. Brown Bldg., 4th Fl., PO Box 1000 700,Iqaluit, NU X0A 0H0
867-975-5400, Fax: 867-975-5305

Prince Edward Island

Prince Edward Island Department of Community Services & Seniors, Jones Bldg., 11 Kent St., 2nd Fl., PO Box 2000, Charlottetown, PE C1A 7N8
902-620-3777, Fax: 902-894-0242, 866-594-3777

Yukon Territory

Yukon Community Services, PO Box 2703, Whitehorse, YT Y1A 2C6
867-667-5811, Fax: 867-393-6295, 800-661-0408, inquiry@gov.yk.ca

CONSERVATION & ECOLOGY

See Also: Heritage Resources; Natural Resources

Canadian Heritage, 15 Eddy St., Gatineau, QC K1A 0M5
819-997-0055, 866-811-0055, info@pch.gc.ca

Canadian Polar Commission, Constitution Square, #1710, 360 Albert St., Ottawa, ON K1R 7X7
613-943-8605, Fax: 613-943-8607, 888-765-2701, mail@polarcom.gc.ca

Canadian Wildlife Service, 351, boul St-Joseph, Gatineau, QC K1A 0H3
819-997-1301, Fax: 819-953-7177

Commission for Environmental Cooperation, Secretariat, #200, 393, rue St-Jacques ouest, Montréal, QC H2Y 1N9
514-350-4300, Fax: 514-350-4314, info@cec.org

Environment Canada, 10 Wellington St., Gatineau, QC K1A 0H3
819-997-2800, Fax: 819-994-1412, 800-668-6767, enviroinfo@ec.gc.ca

Fisheries Resource Conservation Council, PO Box 2001 D, Ottawa, ON K1P 5W3
613-998-0433, Fax: 613-998-1146, info@frcc-ccrh.ca

Natural Resources Canada, 580 Booth St., Ottawa, ON K1A 0E4
613-995-0947, Fax: 613-992-7211

North American Bird Conservation Initiative, Canadian Wildlife Service, 351, boul St-Joseph, 3e étage, Gatineau, QC K1A 0H3
819-994-0512, Fax: 819-994-4445, nabci@ec.gc.ca

North American Waterfowl Management Plan, NAWCC (Canada) Secretariat, Place Vincent Massey, 351 St. Joseph Blvd., 7th Fl., Gatineau, QC K1A 0H3
819-934-6034, Fax: 819-934-6017, nawmp@ec.gc.ca

Parks Canada, 25 Eddy St., Gatineau, QC K1A 0M5
613-860-1251, 888-773-8888, information@pc.gc.ca

Alberta

Alberta Environmental Appeals Board, Peace Hills Trust Tower, #306, 10011 - 109 St., Edmonton, AB T5J 3S8
780-427-6207, Fax: 780-427-4693

Alberta Used Oil Management Association, Empire Building, #1008, 10080 Jasper Ave., Edmonton, AB T5J 1V9
780-414-1510, Fax: 780-414-1519, 866-414-1510, reception@usedoilrecycling.ca

Arctic Goose, c/o Prairie & Northern Region, CWS, #200, 4999 - 98 Ave., Edmonton, AB T6B 2X3
780-951-8652, Fax: 780-495-2615, agjv@ec.gc.ca

Beverage Container Management Board, #750, 10707 - 100 Ave., Edmonton, AB T5J 3M1
780-424-3193, Fax: 780-428-4620, 888-424-7671

Alberta Environment & Sustainable Resource Development, Oxbridge Place, 9820 - 106 St., Main Fl., Edmonton, AB T5K 2J6
780-427-2700, Fax: 780-422-4086, -310-0000, env.infocent@gov.ab.ca; srd.infocent@gov.ab.ca

Forestry Division, Petroleum Plaza ST, 9915 - 108 St. 11th Fl., Edmonton, AB T5K 2G8

Land Use Secretariat, Centre West Building, 10035 - 108 St., Edmonton, AB T5J 3E1
780-644-7972, Fax: 780-644-1034, luf@gov.ab.ca

Natural Resources Conservation Board, Sterling Place, 9940 - 106 St., Edmonton, AB T5K 2N2
780-422-1977, Fax: 780-427-0607, 866-383-6722, info@nrcb.gov.ab.ca

Prairie Habitat, c/o Prairie & Northern Region, CWS, #200, 4999 - 98 Ave., Edmonton, AB T6B 2X3
780-951-8652, phjv@ec.gc.ca

Special Areas Board, Special Areas Board Administration, 212 - 2nd Ave. West, PO Box 820, Hanna, AB T0J 1P0
403-854-5600, Fax: 403-854-5527, specarea@telus.net

British Columbia

British Columbia Assessment Authority, #400, 3450 Uptown Blvd., Victoria, BC V8Z 0B9
250-595-6211, Fax: 250-595-6222, info@bcassessment.ca

British Columbia Ministry of Environment, PO Box 9339 Prov Govt,Victoria, BC V8W 9M1
250-387-1161, Fax: 250-387-5669, envmail@gov.bc.ca

Environmental Stewardship Division, PO Box 9339 Prov Govt,Victoria, BC V8W 9M1
250-356-0121, Fax: 250-387-5669

Forest Practices Board, 1675 Douglas St., 3rd Fl., PO Box 9905 Prov Govt, Victoria, BC V8W 9R1
250-213-4700, Fax: 250-213-4725, 800-994-5899, fpboard@gov.bc.ca

North Area, 1011 - 4 Ave., 5th Fl., Prince George, BC V2L 3H9
250-565-6100

Pacific Coast, c/o Environment Canada, Canadian Wildlife Service, #201, 401 Burrard St., Vancouver, BC V6C 3S5
604-940-4703

Manitoba

Clean Environment Commission, #305, 155 Carlton St., Winnipeg, MB R3C 3H8
204-945-0594, Fax: 204-945-0090

Manitoba Conservation & Water Stewardship, 200 Saulteaux Cres., Winnipeg, MB R3J 3W3
800-214-6497, mws@gov.mb.ca

Ecological Reserves Advisory Committee, c/o Manitoba Conservation, Parks & Natural Areas Branch, 200 Saulteaux Cres., Winnipeg, MB R3J 3W3
204-945-4148, Fax: 204-945-0012

Manitoba Conservation Districts Commission, Secretariat c/o Planning & Coordination Branch, 123 Main St., PO Box 20000, Neepawa, MB R0J 1H0
204-476-7033, Fax: 204-476-7539

New Brunswick

New Brunswick Department of Environment & Local Government, Marysville Place, PO Box 6000, Fredericton, NB E3B 5H1
506-453-2690, Fax: 506-457-4994, elg/egl-info@gnb.ca

Newfoundland & Labrador

Newfoundland & Labrador Department of Environment & Conservation, Confederation Bldg., West Block, 4th Fl., PO Box 8700, St. John's, NL A1B 4J6
709-729-2664, Fax: 709-729-6639, 800-563-6181, envcinquires@gov.nl.ca

Northwest Territories

Northwest Territories Department of Environment & Natural Resources, PO Box 1320, Yellowknife, NT X1A 2L9

Nova Scotia

Nova Scotia Department of Natural Resources, Founder's Square, 1701 Hollis St., 3rd Fl., PO Box 698, Halifax, NS B3J 2T9
902-424-5935, Fax: 902-424-0594, 800-565-2224

Black Duck, Environment Canada, Canadian Wildlife Service, 335 River Rd., Ottawa, ON K1A 0H3
613-949-8254

Eastern Habitat, c/o Environment Canada, Canadian Wildlife Service, 335 River Rd., Ottawa, ON K1A 0H3
613-949-8264

Ontario Ministry of Environment, 135 St. Clair Ave. West, Toronto, ON M4V 1P5
416-325-4000, Fax: 416-325-3159, 800-565-4923, picemail.moe@ontario.ca

Integrated Environmental Policy Division, 77 Wellesley St. West, 11th Fl., Toronto, ON M7A 2T5
416-314-6338, Fax: 416-314-6346

Ontario Ministry of Natural Resources, 300 Water St., PO Box 7000, Peterborough, ON K9J 8M5
705-755-2000, Fax: 705-755-1677, 800-667-1940, mnr.nric.mnr@ontario.ca

Niagara Escarpment Commission, 232 Guelph St., Georgetown, ON L7G 4B1
905-877-5191, Fax: 905-873-7452

Prince Edward Island

Prince Edward Island Department of Environment, Labour & Justice, Shaw Bldg. South, 95 Rochford St., 4th Fl., PO Box 2000, Charlottetown, PE C1A 7N8
902-368-6410, Fax: 902-368-6488

Environmental Advisory Council, 11 Kent St., 4th Fl., PO Box 2000, Charlottetown, PE C1A 7N8

Quebec

Comité consultatif de l'environnement Kativik, CP 930, Kuujjuaq, QC J0M 1C0
819-964-2961, Fax: 819-964-0694, keac-ccek@krg.ca

Ministère du Développement durable, de l'Environnement, de la Faune, et des Parcs, Édifice Marie-Guyart, 675, boul René-Lévesque est, 29e étage, Québec, QC G1R 5V7
418-521-3911, Fax: 418-643-4143, 800-561-1616, info@mddep.gouv.qc.ca

Fondation de la faune du Québec, Place Iberville II, #420, 1175, av Lavigerie, Québec, QC G1V 4P1
418-644-7926, Fax: 418-643-7655, 877-639-0742, ffq@fondationdelafaune.qc.ca

Société de développement de la Baie James, 110, boul Matagami, CP 970, Matagami, QC J0Y 2A0
819-739-4717, Fax: 819-739-4329, mat@sdbj.gouv.qc.ca

Société québécoise de récupération et de recyclage, #200, 420, boul Charest est, Québec, QC G1K 8M4
418-643-0394, Fax: 418-643-6507, 866-523-8290, info@recyc-quebec.gouv.qc.ca

Saskatchewan

Saskatchewan Assessment Management Agency, #200, 2201 - 11th Ave., Regina, SK S4P 0J8
306-924-8000, Fax: 306-924-8070, 800-667-7262, info.request@sama.sk.ca

Saskatchewan Conservation Data Centre, 3211 Albert St., Regina, SK S4S 5W6
306-787-9038, Fax: 306-787-9544

Saskatchewan Environment, 3211 Albert St., 2nd Fl., Regina, SK S4S 5W6
306-787-2584, Fax: 306-787-9544, 800-567-4224, Centre.Inquiry@gov.sk.ca

Saskatchewan Watershed Authority, 111 Fairford St. East, Moose Jaw, SK S6H 7X9
306-694-3900, Fax: 306-694-3944, comm@swa.ca

Wascana Centre Authority, 2900 Wascana Dr., PO Box 7111, Regina, SK S4P 3S7
306-522-3661, Fax: 306-565-2742, wca@wascana.ca

Yukon Territory

Alsek Renewable Resource Council, PO Box 2077, Haines Junction, YT Y0B 1L0
867-634-2524, Fax: 867-634-2527

Carmacks Renewable Resource Council, PO Box 122, Carmacks, YT Y0B 1C0
867-863-6838, Fax: 867-863-6429, carmacksrrc@northwestel.net

Dawson District Renewable Resource Council, PO Box 1380, Dawson City, YT Y0B 1G0
867-993-6976, Fax: 867-993-6093, dawsonrrc@northwestel.net

Yukon Environment, PO Box 2703, Whitehorse, YT Y1A 2C6
867-667-5652, Fax: 867-393-7197, environment.yukon@gov.yk.ca

Mayo District Renewable Resources Council, PO Box 249, Mayo, YT Y0B 1M0
867-996-2942, Fax: 867-996-2948, mayorrc@yknet.yk.ca

North Yukon Renewable Resources Council, PO Box 80, Old Crow, YT Y0B 1N0
867-966-3034, Fax: 867-966-3036, vgrrc@yknet.yk.ca

Selkirk Renewable Resources Council, PO Box 32, Pelly Crossing, YT Y0B 1P0
867-537-3937, Fax: 867-537-3939, selkirkrrc@yknet.yk.ca

Teslin Renewable Resource Council, PO Box 186, Teslin, YT Y0A 1B0
867-390-2323, Fax: 867-390-2919, teslinrrc@northwestel.net

Yukon Land Use Planning Council, #201, 307 Jarvis St., Whitehorse, YT Y1A 2H3
867-667-7397, Fax: 867-667-4624, ylupc@planyukon.ca

CONSTRUCTION

Canada Mortgage & Housing Corporation, 700 Montreal Rd., Ottawa, ON K1A 0P7
613-748-2000, Fax: 613-748-2098, 800-668-2642, chic@cmhc-schl.gc.ca

Defence Construction Canada, Constitution Square, 350 Albert St., 19th Fl., Ottawa, ON K1A 0K3
613-998-9548, Fax: 613-998-1061, 800-514-3555, info@dcc-cdc.gc.ca

Infrastructure Canada, 180 Kent St., Ottawa, ON K1P 0B6
613-948-1148, 877-250-7154, info@infc.gc.ca

Alberta

Alberta Infrastructure, Infrastructure Building, 6950 - 113 St., Edmonton, AB T6H 5V7
780-415-0507, Fax: 780-427-2187, -310-0000, Infra.Contact.Us.m@gov.ab.ca

Newfoundland & Labrador

Newfoundland & Labrador Department of Transportation & Works, Confederation Bldg., West Block, 6th Fl., PO Box 8700, St. John's, NL A1B 4J6
709-729-3679, Fax: 709-729-4285, twminister@gov.nl.ca

Northwest Territories

Asset Management Division, Stuart M. Hodgson Bldg., 5009 - 49th St., 3rd Fl., Yellowknife, NT X1A 2L9

Nunavut

Nunavut Territory Department of Community & Government Services, W.G. Brown Bldg., 4th Fl., PO Box 1000 700,Iqaluit, NU X0A 0H0
867-975-5400, Fax: 867-975-5305

Ontario

Building Code Commission, 777 Bay St., 2nd Fl., Toronto, ON M5G 2E5
416-585-6666, Fax: 416-585-7531, codeinfo@ontario.ca

Building Materials Evaluation Commission, 777 Bay St., 2nd Fl., Toronto, ON M5G 2E5
416-585-4234, Fax: 416-585-7531

Quebec

Commission de la construction du Québec, 8485, av Christophe-Colomb, Montréal, QC H2M 0A7
888-842-8282

Régie du bâtiment du Québec, 545, boul Crémazie est, 4e étage, Montréal, QC H2M 2V2
514-873-0976, Fax: 514-864-2903, 800-361-0761, crc@rbq.gouv.qc.ca

CONSUMER PROTECTION

See Also: Public Safety

Nova Scotia

Nova Scotia Department of Service Nova Scotia & Municipal Relations, 1505 Barrington St., PO Box 216, Halifax, NS B3J 3K5
902-424-5200, Fax: 902-424-0581, 800-670-4357, askus@gov.ns.ca

Nunavut

Nunavut Territory Department of Community & Government Services, W.G. Brown Bldg., 4th Fl., PO Box 1000 700,Iqaluit, NU X0A 0H0
867-975-5400, Fax: 867-975-5305

Yukon Territory

Consumer Services & Information Development, Berska Bldg., 2nd Fl., 307 Black St., Whitehorse, YT
Fax: 867-393-6943

CORONERS

Quebec

Bureau du coroner, Édifice le Delta 2, #390, 2875, boul Laurier, Québec, QC G1V 5B1
418-643-1845, Fax: 418-643-6174, 866-312-7051, clientele.coroner@msp.gouv.qc.ca

CORRECTIONAL SERVICES

Saskatchewan

Saskatchewan Corrections & Policing, 1874 Scarth St., Regina, SK S4P 4B3
306-787-7872, communicationsCPSP@gov.sk.ca

CULTURE & HERITAGE

See: Arts & Culture

Aboriginal Affairs & Northern Development Canada, 10 Wellington St., North Tower, Gatineau, QC K1A 0H4
819-997-0380, Fax: 866-817-3977, 800-567-9604, infopubs@aadnc-aandc.gc.ca

Canadian Heritage, 15 Eddy St., Gatineau, QC K1A 0M5
819-997-0055, 866-811-0055, info@pch.gc.ca

Historic Sites & Monuments Board of Canada, Terrasses de la Chaudière, 25 Eddy St., Gatineau, QC K1A 0M5
Fax: 819-934-1115, 855-283-8730, hsmbc-clmhc@pc.gc.ca

Alberta

Alberta Sport, Recreation, Parks, & Wildlife Foundation, Standard Life Centre, #903, 10405 Jasper Ave., 9th Fl., Edmonton, AB T5J 4R7
780-415-1167, Fax: 780-415-0308, -310-0000

Alberta International & Intergovernmental Relations, Commerce Place, 10155 - 102 St., 12th Fl., Edmonton, AB T5J 4G8
780-422-1510, -310-0000

British Columbia

British Columbia Ministry of Community, Sport, & Cultural Development, PO Box 9490 Prov Govt,Victoria, BC V8W 9N7

Manitoba

Manitoba Culture, Heritage & Tourism, Legislative Building, #118, 450 Broadway Ave., Winnipeg, MB R3C 0V8
204-945-3729, Fax: 204-945-5223, mincht@leg.gov.mb.ca

Manitoba Heritage Council, 213 Notre Dame Ave., Main Fl., Winnipeg, MB R3B 1N3
204-945-2118, Fax: 204-948-2384, hrb@gov.mb.ca

New Brunswick

New Brunswick Department of Tourism, Heritage & Culture, Centennial Building, PO Box 6000, Fredericton, NB E3B 5H1
506-444-5205, Fax: 506-457-4984, taponlinedirectory@gnb.ca

Northwest Territories

Northwest Territories Department of Aboriginal Affairs & Intergovernmental Relations, 4910 - 52nd St., PO Box 1320, Yellowknife, NT X1A 2L9
867-873-7143, Fax: 867-873-0233, 877-838-8194, nancy_gardiner@gov.nt.ca

Northwest Territories Department of Education, Culture & Employment, PO Box 1320, Yellowknife, NT X1A 2L9
867-669-2399, Fax: 867-873-0431, 866-606-5627

Nova Scotia

Culture Division, #601, 1800 Argyle St., PO Box 456, Halifax, NS B3J 2R5
902-424-4510, Fax: 902-424-0710, culture@gov.ns.ca

Ontario

Ontario Trillium Foundation, 800 Bay St., 5th Fl., Toronto, ON M5S 3A9
416-963-4927, Fax: 416-963-8781, 800-263-2887, otf@otf.ca

Prince Edward Island

Housing, Seniors & Corporate Support, Jones Bldg., 11 Kent St., 2nd Fl., PO Box 2000, Charlottetown, PE C1A 7N8
Fax: 902-894-0242

Saskatchewan

Cultural Planning & Development, 1919 Saskatchewan Dr., 2nd Fl., Regina, SK S4P 4H2
306-787-5877, Fax: 306-798-3177

Provincial Capital Commission, 4607 Dewdney Ave., Regina, SK S4T 1B7
306-787-9261

Saskatchewan Parks, Culture, & Sport, 1919 Saskatchewan Dr., 4th Fl., Regina, SK S4P 4H2
306-787-5729, Fax: 306-798-0033, 800-205-7070, info@tpcs.gov.sk.ca

Wascana Centre Authority, 2900 Wascana Dr., PO Box 7111, Regina, SK S4P 3S7
306-522-3661, Fax: 306-565-2742, wca@wascana.ca

CUSTOMS

Canada Border Services Agency, Headquarters, 191 Laurier Ave. West, Ottawa, ON K1A 0L8
800-461-9999, Contact@cbsa.gc.ca; communications@ps.gc.ca (Public Safety)

DAIRY INDUSTRY

Manitoba

Manitoba Milk Prices Review Commission, c/o Boards, Commissions & Legislation Branch, #812, 401 York Ave., Winnipeg, MB R3C 0P8
204-945-3854, Fax: 204-948-2844

Prince Edward Island

Prince Edward Island Department of Agriculture & Forestry, Jones Bldg., 11 Kent St., PO Box 2000, Charlottetown, PE C1A 7N8
902-368-4880, Fax: 902-368-4857,

DANGEROUS GOODS & HAZARDOUS MATERIALS

See Also: Occupational Safety; Waste Management

Hazardous Materials Information Review Commission, 427 Laurier Ave. West, 7th Fl., Ottawa, ON K1A 1M3
613-993-4331, Fax: 613-993-4686, hmirc-ccrmd@hc-sc.gc.ca

British Columbia
British Columbia Ministry of Transportation & Infrastructure, PO Box 9850 Prov Govt,Victoria, BC V8W 9T5
250-387-3198, Fax: 250-356-7706

Newfoundland & Labrador
Government Services Branch, PO Box 8700, St. John's, NL A1B 4J6

Northwest Territories
Northwest Territories Department of Transportation, Lahm Ridge Bldg., 4501 50 Ave., PO Box 1320, Yellowknife, NT X1A 2L9
867-920-3460, Fax: 867-873-0363

Nova Scotia
Nova Scotia Department of Transportation & Infrastructure Renewal, Johnston Bldg., 1672 Granville St., 2nd Fl., PO Box 186, Halifax, NS B3J 2N2
902-424-2297, Fax: 902-424-0532, tpwpaff@gov.ns.ca

Ontario
Ontario Ministry of Transportation, Ferguson Block, 77 Wellesley St. West, 3rd Fl., Toronto, ON M7A 1Z8
416-235-4686, Fax: 905-704-2001, 800-268-4686

Prince Edward Island
Prince Edward Island Department of Transportation & Infrastructure Renewal, Jones Bldg., 11 Kent St., 3rd Fl., PO Box 2000, Charlottetown, PE C1A 7N8
902-368-5100, Fax: 902-368-5395

Quebec
Ministère du Développement durable, de l'Environnement, de la Faune, et des Parcs, Édifice Marie-Guyart, 675, boul René-Lévesque est, 29e étage, Québec, QC G1R 5V7
418-521-3911, Fax: 418-643-4143, 800-561-1616, info@mddep.gouv.qc.ca

Saskatchewan
Saskatchewan Highways & Infrastructure, Victoria Tower, 1855 Victoria Ave., Regina, SK S4P 3T2
306-787-4800, communications@highways.gov.sk.ca

Yukon Territory
Yukon Highways & Public Works, PO Box 2703, Whitehorse, YT Y1A 2C6
867-393-7193, Fax: 867-393-6218, 800-661-0408, hpw-info@gov.yk.ca

DEBT MANAGEMENT
Finance Canada, L'esplanade Laurier, 140 O'Connor St., Ottawa, ON K1A 0G5
613-992-1573, Fax: 613-943-0938, finpub@fin.gc.ca

DEFENCE
See Also: Emergency Response; Public Safety
Defence Construction Canada, Constitution Square, 350 Albert St., 19th Fl., Ottawa, ON K1A 0K3
613-998-9548, Fax: 613-998-1061, 800-514-3555, info@dcc-cdc.gc.ca
Department of National Defence & the Canadian Forces, National Defence HQ, Major-General George R. Pearkes Bldg., 101 Colonel By Dr., Ottawa, ON K1A 0K2
613-995-2534, Fax: 613-992-4739, DNDRecruitment-RecrutementMDN@forces.gc.ca (Civilian Careers)
Military Police Complaints Commission, 270 Albert St., 10th Fl., Ottawa, ON K1P 5G8
613-947-5625, Fax: 613-947-5713, 800-632-0566, commission@mpcc-cppm.gc.ca

DISABLED PERSONS SERVICES
Transportation Development Centre, Tour Ouest, Complexe Guy-Favreau, 800, boul René-Lévesque ouest, 6e étage, Montréal, QC H3B 1X9
514-283-0000, Fax: 514-283-7158, tdccdt@tc.gc.ca

Alberta
Persons with Developmental Disabilities Community Boards, c/o PDD Program Branch, Peace Hills Trust Tower, 10011 - 109 St., 4th Fl., Edmonton, AB T5J 3S8
780-427-1177, Fax: 780-427-1220, 800-310-0000, PDDinfo@gov.ab.ca
Premier's Council on the Status of Persons with Disabilities, HSBC Building, 10055 - 106 St., 11th Fl., Edmonton, AB T5J 1G3
780-422-1095, 800-272-8841, pcspd@gov.ab.ca

Nunavut
Nunavut Territory Department of Culture, Language, Elders & Youth, PO Box 1000 800,Iqaluit, NU X0A 0H0
867-975-5500, Fax: 867-975-5504, 866-934-2035

Quebec
Office des personnes handicapées du Québec, 309, rue Brock, Drummondville, QC J2B 1C5
Fax: 819-475-8753, 800-567-1465, aide@ophq.gouv.qc.ca

DISCRIMINATION & EMPLOYMENT EQUITY
Office of the Public Sector Integrity Commissioner of Canada, 60 Queen St., 7th Fl., Ottawa, ON K1P 5Y7
613-941-6400, Fax: 613-941-6535

Alberta
Labour Relations Board, Labour Building, 10808 - 99 Ave., 5th Fl., Edmonton, AB T5K 0G5
780-422-5926, Fax: 780-422-0970, 800-463-2572, alrbinfo@lab.gov.ab.ca

Quebec
Commission de l'équité salariale, 200, ch Ste-Foy, 4e étage, Québec, QC G1R 6A1
418-528-8765, Fax: 418-528-6999, 888-528-8765, equite.salariale@ces.gouv.qc.ca

DRIVERS' LICENCES

Alberta
Strategic Planning & Financial Services, Commerce Place, 10155 - 102 St., 13th Fl., Edmonton, AB T5J 4G8
780-422-8545

British Columbia
British Columbia Ministry of Transportation & Infrastructure, PO Box 9850 Prov Govt,Victoria, BC V8W 9T5
250-387-3198, Fax: 250-356-7706

Manitoba
Manitoba Infrastructure & Transportation, Legislative Building, #203, 450 Broadway Ave., Winnipeg, MB R3C 0V8
204-945-3723, Fax: 204-945-7610,

Ontario
Licence Appeal Tribunal, #530, 20 Dundas St. West, Toronto, ON M5G 2C2
416-314-4260, Fax: 416-314-4270, 800-255-2214
Ontario Ministry of Transportation, Ferguson Block, 77 Wellesley St. West, 3rd Fl., Toronto, ON M7A 1Z8
416-235-4686, Fax: 905-704-2001, 800-268-4686

Prince Edward Island
Prince Edward Island Department of Transportation & Infrastructure Renewal, Jones Bldg., 11 Kent St., 3rd Fl., PO Box 2000, Charlottetown, PE C1A 7N8
902-368-5100, Fax: 902-368-5395

Quebec
Société de l'assurance automobile du Québec, 333, boul Jean-Lesage, CP 19600 Terminus, Québec, QC G1K 8J6
418-643-7620, Fax: 418-644-0339, 800-361-7620, courrier@saaq.gouv.qc.ca

Yukon Territory
Driver Control Board, 2130 Second Ave., 3rd Fl., PO Box 2703, Whitehorse, YT Y1A 2C6
867-667-5111, Fax: 867-667-3609, dcb@gov.yk.ca

DRUGS & ALCOHOL
See Also: Liquor Control

Alberta
Alberta Health Services, Corporate Office, North Tower, Seventh Street Plaza, 10030 - 107th St. NW, 14th Fl., Edmonton, AB T5J 3E4
780-342-2000, Fax: 780-342-2060, 888-342-2471, ahsb.admin@albertahealthservices.ca

British Columbia
British Columbia Ministry of Health, 1515 Blanshard St., Victoria, BC V8W 3C8
800-663-7100, hlth.health@gov.bc.ca

Quebec
Modernisation des centres hospitaliers universitaires de Montréal, CHUM, CUSM, CHU Sainte-Justine, #10.049, 2021, rue Union, Montréal, QC H3A 2S9
514-864-9883, Fax: 514-873-7362, info.construction3chu@msss.gouv.qc.ca
Ministère de la Santé et des Services sociaux, Direction des communications, 1075, ch Sainte-Foy, 16e étage, Québec, QC G1S 2M1
418-643-9395, Fax: 418-643-4768, regisseur.web@msss.gouv.qc.ca

ECONOMIC DEVELOPMENT
See: Business Development
Federal Economic Development Agency for Southern Ontario, 101 Frederick St., 4th Fl., Kitchener, ON N2H 6R2
Fax: 519-571-5750, 866-593-5505

Manitoba
Invest NB, HSBC Place, PO Box 6000, Fredericton, NB E3B 5H1

Ontario
Ontario Ministry of Research & Innovation, Hearst Block, 900 Bay St., 8th Fl., Toronto, ON M7A 2E1
416-325-6666, Fax: 416-325-6688, 866-668-4249, info@edt.gov.on.ca
Ontario Ministry of Rural Affairs, c/o Ministry of Agriculture & Food, 1 Stone Rd. West, Guelph, ON N1G 4Y2
519-826-3100, Fax: 519-826-4335, 888-466-2372, about.omafra@ontario.ca

Prince Edward Island
Innovation PEI, 94 Euston St., PO Box 910, Charlottetown, PE C1A 7L9
902-368-6300, Fax: 902-368-6301, 800-563-3734, innovation@gov.pe.ca
Summerside Regional Development Corporation Ltd., 268 Water St., Summerside, PE C1N 1B6
902-436-2246, Fax: 902-436-9269

EDUCATION
Canadian Council of Directors of Apprenticeship, 140 Promenade du Portage, 5th Fl, Phase IV, Gatineau, QC K1A 0J9
819-953-7443, Fax: 819-994-0202, redseal-sceaurouge@hrsdc-rhdcc.gc.ca

Alberta
Alberta Apprenticeship & Industry Training Board, Commerce Place, 10155 - 102nd St., 10th Fl., Edmonton, AB T5J 4L5
780-427-8765, Fax: 780-422-7376, -310-0000
Alberta Council on Admissions & Transfer, Commerce Place, 10155 - 102 St., 11th Fl., Edmonton, AB T5J 4L5
780-422-9021, Fax: 780-422-3688, -310-0000, acat@gov.ab.ca
Alberta Enterprise Corporation Board, Alberta Enterprise Corporation, #1100, 10830 Jasper Ave., Edmonton, AB T5J 2B3
780-392-3901
Alberta Innovates - Technology Futures, 250 Karl Clark Rd., Edmonton, AB T6N 1E4
780-450-5111, Fax: 780-450-5333, referral@albertainnovates.ca
Campus Alberta Quality Council, Commerce Place, 10155 - 102 St., 11th Fl., Edmonton, AB T5J 4L5
780-427-8921, Fax: 780-427-4185, caqc@gov.ab.ca
Community, Learner & Industry Connections Division, Phipps-McKinnon Bldg., 10020 - 101A Ave., 5th Fl., Edmonton, AB T5J 3G2
Alberta Enterprise & Advanced Education, Legislature Bldg., #324, 10800 - 97 Ave., Edmonton, AB T5K 2B6
780-422-5400, -310-0000

British Columbia
Leading Edge Endowment Fund Board, 1188 West Georgia St., 9th Fl., Vancouver, BC V6E 4A2
604-438-3220, contact@leefbc.ca

Manitoba
Manitoba Education, Research & Learning Information Networks, #100 - 135 Innovation Dr., University of Manitoba, Winnipeg, MB R3T 6A8
204-474-7800, Fax: 204-474-7830, 800-430-6404

New Brunswick
New Brunswick Department of Post-Secondary Education, Training & Labour, Chestnut Complex, PO Box 6000, Fredericton, NB E3B 5H1
506-453-2597, Fax: 506-453-3618, dpetlinfo@gnb.ca

Northwest Territories
Aurora Research Institute, 191 MacKenzie Rd., PO Box 1450, Inuvik, NT X0E 0T0

867-777-3298, Fax: 867-777-4264, webmaster@nwtresearch.com
Northwest Territories Department of Education, Culture & Employment, PO Box 1320, Yellowknife, NT X1A 2L9
867-669-2399, Fax: 867-873-0431, 866-606-5627

Ontario
Academic & Experience Requirements Committee of the Association of Ontario Land Surveyors, 1043 McNicoll Ave., Toronto, ON M1W 3W6
416-491-9020, Fax: 416-491-2576
College of Veterinarians of Ontario, 2106 Gordon St., Guelph, ON N1L 1G6
519-824-5600, Fax: 519-824-6497, 800-424-2856, inquiries@cvo.org

Saskatchewan
Saskatchewan Research Council, #125, 15 Innovation Blvd., Saskatoon, SK S7N 2X8
306-933-5400, Fax: 306-933-7446, info@src.sk.ca

EDUCATION & TRAINING
Human Resources & Skills Development Canada, 140 Promenade du Portage, Gatineau, QC K1A 0J9

Alberta
Alberta Human Services, Office of the Minister, Legislature Building, #224, 10800 - 97 Ave., Edmonton, AB T5K 2B6
780-644-5135, 866-644-5135

British Columbia
British Columbia Ministry of Citizens' Services, PO Box 9594 Prov Govt,Victoria, BC V8W 9E2
250-952-7623, Fax: 250-952-7628, 800-663-7867, EnquiryBC@gov.bc.ca

New Brunswick
New Brunswick Department of Post-Secondary Education, Training & Labour, Chestnut Complex, PO Box 6000, Fredericton, NB E3B 5H1
506-453-2597, Fax: 506-453-3618, dpetlinfo@gnb.ca

Northwest Territories
Northwest Territories Department of Education, Culture & Employment, PO Box 1320, Yellowknife, NT X1A 2L9
867-669-2399, Fax: 867-873-0431, 866-606-5627

Ontario
Ontario Ministry of Labour, 400 University Ave., 14th Fl., Toronto, ON M7A 1T7
416-326-7160, 800-531-5551

EMERGENCY MEASURES
Environment Canada, 10 Wellington St., Gatineau, QC K1A 0H3
819-997-2800, Fax: 819-994-1412, 800-668-6767, enviroinfo@ec.gc.ca
National Search & Rescue Secretariat, #400, 275 Slater St., Ottawa, ON K1A 0K2
613-992-0054, Fax: 613-996-3746, 800-727-9414, inquiry@nss.gc.ca

Alberta
Alberta Environment & Sustainable Resource Development, Oxbridge Place, 9820 - 106 St., Main Fl., Edmonton, AB T5K 2J6
780-427-2700, Fax: 780-422-4086, -310-0000, env.infocent@gov.ab.ca; srd.infocent@gov.ab.ca

Manitoba
Emergency Measures Organization, 405 Broadway Ave., 15th Floor, Winnipeg, MB R3C 3L6
204-945-4772, Fax: 204-945-4929, 888-267-8298, emo@gov.mb.ca

Nova Scotia
Nova Scotia Emergency Management Office, PO Box 2581, Halifax, NS B3J 3N5
902-424-5620, Fax: 902-424-5376, 866-424-5620, emo@gov.ns.ca

Nunavut
Nunavut Emergency Management, PO Box 1000 700,Iqaluit, NU X0A 0H0
867-975-5403, Fax: 867-979-4221, 800-693-1666

Yukon Territory
Emergency Measures Organization, Combined Services Bldg., 2nd Fl., 60 Norseman Rd, Airport, Whitehorse, YT Y1A 2C6
867-667-5220, Fax: 867-393-6266, 800-661-0408, emo.yukon@gov.yk.ca

EMPLOYMENT
Alberta
Alberta Human Services, Office of the Minister, Legislature Building, #224, 10800 - 97 Ave., Edmonton, AB T5K 2B6
780-644-5135, 866-644-5135

Manitoba
Manitoba Immigration & Multiculturalism, Legislative Building, 317, 450 Broadway Ave., Winnipeg, MB R3C 0V8
204-945-4079, Fax: 204-945-8312, minlab@leg.gov.mb.ca

Quebec
Ministère du Travail, 200, ch Sainte-Foy, 5e étage, Québec, QC G1R 5S1
418-644-4545, Fax: 418-528-0559, 800-643-4817

EMPLOYMENT EQUITY
See: Discrimination & Employment Equity
Office of the Public Sector Integrity Commissioner of Canada, 60 Queen St., 7th Fl., Ottawa, ON K1P 5Y7
613-941-6400, Fax: 613-941-6535

EMPLOYMENT INSURANCE
Canada Employment Insurance Commission, 140, Promenade du Portage, Phase IV, Gatineau, QC K1A 0J9
800-206-7218

Saskatchewan
Saskatchewan Labour Relations & Workplace Safety, #300, 1870 Albert St., Regina, SK S4P 4W1
306-787-7404, webmaster@lab.gov.sk.ca

ENERGY
See Also: Natural Resources
Canadian Nuclear Safety Commission, 280 Slater St., PO Box 1046 B,Ottawa, ON K1P 5S9
613-995-5894, Fax: 613-995-5086, 800-668-5284
CANMET Energy Technology Centre-Devon, 1 Oil Patch Dr., #A202, PO Box 1280, Devon, AB T9G 1A8
780-987-8614, Fax: 780-987-8690, hamza@nrcan.gc.ca
CANMET Energy Technology Centre-Ottawa, 1 Haanel Dr., Nepean, ON K1A 1M1
613-996-8201, Fax: 613-995-9584
CANMET Energy Technology Centre-Varennes, 1615, boul Lionel-Boulet, CP 4800, Varennes, QC J3X 1S6
450-652-4621, Fax: 450-652-0999, 800-322-8122, canmetenergy.nrcan.gc.ca
Chalk River Laboratories, NRC Canadian Neutron Beam Centre, Building 459, Station 18, Chalk River, ON K0J 1J0
613-584-8293, 800-364-6989
Indian Oil & Gas Canada, #100, 9911 Chiila Blvd., Tsuu T'ina (Sarcee), AB T2W 6H6
403-292-5625, Fax: 403-292-5618, ContactIOGC@inac-ainc.gc.ca
National Energy Board, 444 - 7 Ave. SW, Calgary, AB T2P 0X8
403-292-4800, Fax: 403-292-5503, 800-899-1265, info@neb-one.gc.ca
National Research Council Waste Biotreatability Facility, c/o National Research Council, 1200 Montreal Rd., Ottawa, ON K1A 0R6
Office of Energy Research & Development, 580 Booth St., 14th Fl., Ottawa, ON K1A 0E4
613-947-1421, Fax: 613-995-6146

Alberta
Energy Resources Conservation Board, #1000, 250 - 5 Ave. SW, Calgary, AB T2P 0R4
403-297-8311, Fax: 403-297-7336, 855-297-8311, inquiries@ercb.ca; infoservices@ercb.ca; ADR@ercb.ca
Alberta Energy, North Petroleum Plaza, 9945 - 108 St., Edmonton, AB T5K 2G6
780-427-8050, Fax: 780-422-0698, -310-0000, Library.Energy@gov.ab.ca

British Columbia
British Columbia Hydro, 6911 Southpoint Dr., Burnaby, BC V3N 4X8
604-224-9376, 800-224-9376
British Columbia Utilities Commission, 900 Howe St., 6th Fl., PO Box 250, Vancouver, BC V6Z 2N3
604-660-4700, Fax: 604-660-1102, 800-663-1385, commission.secretary@bcuc.com
British Columbia Ministry of Energy, Mines, & Natural Gas (& Responsible for Housing), PO Box 9053 Prov Govt,Victoria, BC V8W 9E2
Oil & Gas Commission, #100, 10003 - 110 Ave., Fort St John, BC V1J 6M7
250-794-5200, Fax: 250-794-5375
Powerex Corp., #1400, 666 Burrard St., Vancouver, BC V6C 2X8
604-891-5000, Fax: 604-891-6060, 800-220-4907, Brian.Moghadam@powerex.com
Powertech Labs Inc., 12388 - 88 Ave., Surrey, BC V8W 7R7
604-590-7500, Fax: 604-590-6611

Manitoba
Manitoba Hydro, 360 Portage Ave., PO Box 815 Main,Winnipeg, MB R3C 2P4
204-474-3311, publicaffairs@hydro.mb.ca

New Brunswick
New Brunswick Department of Energy & Mines, Brunswick Square, #100M, 1 Germain St., Saint John, NB E2L 4V1
506-658-3180, Fax: 506-643-2919, DOEweb@gnb.ca
Lands, Minerals & Petroleum Division, Hugh John Flemming Forestry Centre, PO Box 6000, Fredericton, NB E3B 5H1
506-453-2684, Fax: 506-453-2930, dnrweb@gnb.ca
New Brunswick Department of Natural Resources, Hugh John Flemming Forestry Centre, PO Box 6000, Fredericton, NB E3B 5H1
506-453-3826, Fax: 506-444-4367, dnrweb@gnb.ca

Newfoundland & Labrador
Canada-Newfoundland & Labrador Offshore Petroleum Board, TD Place, 140 Water St., 5th Fl., St. John's, NL A1C 6H6
709-778-1400, Fax: 709-778-1473, information@cnlopb.nl.ca
Churchill Falls (Labrador) Corporation Limited, Hydro Place, 500 Columbus Dr., PO Box 12500, St. John's, NL A1B 4K7
709-737-1859, Fax: 709-737-1816
Newfoundland & Labrador Hydro, Hydro Place, 500 Columbus Dr., PO Box 12400, St. John's, NL A1B 4K7
709-737-1400, Fax: 709-737-1800, 888-737-1296, hydro@nlh.nl.ca
Nalcor Energy, 500 Columbus Dr., St. John's, NL A1E 2B2
709-737-1400, Fax: 709-737-1800
Newfoundland & Labrador Board of Commissioners of Public Utilities, Prince Charles Bldg., #E-210, 120 Torbay Rd., PO Box 21040, St. John's, NL A1A 5B2
709-726-8600, Fax: 709-726-9604, 866-782-0006, ito@pub.nf.ca
Twin Falls Power Corporation, PO Box 12500, St. John's, NL A1B 3T5

Northwest Territories
Northwest Territories Department of Environment & Natural Resources, PO Box 1320, Yellowknife, NT X1A 2L9
Petroleum Products Division, Stuart M. Hodgson, 5009 - 49th St., 1st Fl., Yellowknife, NT X1A 2L9
867-920-3447, Fax: 867-873-0100
Northwest Territories Power Corporation, 4 Capital Dr., Hay River, NT X0E 1G2
867-874-5200, Fax: 867-874-5251, info@ntpc.com

Nova Scotia
Nova Scotia Department of Energy, Bank of Montreal Bldg., #400, 5151 George St., PO Box 2664, Halifax, NS B3J 3P7
902-424-4575, Fax: 902-424-0528, energyinfo@gov.ns.ca
Nova Scotia Utility & Review Board, Summit Place, 1601 Lower Water St., 3rd Fl., PO Box 1692 M,Halifax, NS B3J 3S3
902-424-4448, Fax: 902-424-3919, uarb.board@gov.ns.ca

Ontario
Ontario Ministry of Energy, Hearst Block, 900 Bay St., 4th Fl., Toronto, ON M7A 2E1
416-327-6758, Fax: 416-325-8440, 888-668-4636, write2us@ontario.ca
Ontario Ministry of Environment, 135 St. Clair Ave. West, Toronto, ON M4V 1P5
416-325-4000, Fax: 416-325-3159, 800-565-4923, picemail.moe@ontario.ca
Hydro One Inc., North Tower, 483 Bay St., 15th Fl., Toronto, ON M5G 2P5
416-345-5000, Fax: 905-944-3251, 877-955-1155, customercommunications@hydroone.com
Independent Electricity System Operator, PO Box 4474 A,Toronto, ON M5W 4E5
905-403-6900, Fax: 905-403-6921, 888-448-7777, customer.relations@ieso.ca
Ontario Energy Board, #2700, 2300 Yonge St., Toronto, ON M4P 1E4
416-481-1967, Fax: 416-440-7656, 888-632-6273
Ontario Power Authority, #1600, 120 Adelaide St. West, Toronto, ON M5H 1T1

416-967-7474, Fax: 416-967-1947, 800-797-9604, info@powerauthority.on.ca
Ontario Power Generation, 700 University Ave., Toronto, ON M5G 1X6
416-592-2555, 877-592-2555, webmaster@opg.com

Prince Edward Island
Prince Edward Island Department of Environment, Labour & Justice, Shaw Bldg. South, 95 Rochford St., 4th Fl., PO Box 2000, Charlottetown, PE C1A 7N8
902-368-6410, Fax: 902-368-6488
Prince Edward Island Energy Corporation, Jones Bldg., 11 Kent St., 4th Fl., PO Box 2000, Charlottetown, PE C1A 7N8

Quebec
Agence de l'efficacité énergétique, #B406, 5700, 4e av ouest, Québec, QC G1H 6R1
418-627-6379, Fax: 418-643-5828, 877-727-6655, efficaciteenergetique@mrn.gouv.qc.ca
Hydro-Québec, 75, boul René-Lévesque ouest, Montréal, QC H2Z 1A4
514-289-2211
Régie de l'énergie, Tour de la Bourse, #2.55, 800, Place Victoria, Montréal, QC H4Z 1A2
514-873-2452, Fax: 514-873-2070, 888-873-2452, secretariat@regie-energie.qc.ca; greffe@regie-energie.qc.ca
Société d'énergie de la Baie-James, 888, de Maisonneuve est, 6e étage, Montréal, QC H2L 5B2
514-286-2020

Saskatchewan
Energy & Resources, #300, 2103 - 11th Ave., Regina, SK S4P 3Z8
306-787-2528
Saskatchewan Power Corporation (SaskPower), 2025 Victoria Ave., Regina, SK S4P 0S1
306-566-3306, Fax: 800-757-6937, 888-757-6937
SaskEnergy Incorporated, 1777 Victoria Ave., Regina, SK S4P 4K5
306-777-9225, 800-567-8899

Yukon Territory
Energy Solutions Centre, 206A Lowe St., 1st Fl., Whitehorse, YT Y1A 1W6
867-393-7063, Fax: 867-393-7061, esc@gov.yk.ca
Yukon Energy, Mines & Resources, PO Box 2703, Whitehorse, YT Y1A 2C6
867-667-3130, Fax: 867-456-3965, 800-661-0408, emr@gov.yk.ca
Yukon Energy Corporation, 2 Miles Canyon Rd., PO Box 5920, Whitehorse, YT Y1A 6S7
867-393-5300, 866-926-3749, communications@yukonenergy.ca

ENGINEERING & CONSULTING
Canadian Environmental Assessment Agency, Place Bell Canada, 160 Elgin St., 22nd Fl., Ottawa, ON K1A 0H3
613-957-0700, Fax: 613-957-0862, 866-582-1884, info@ceaa-acee.gc.ca
Defence Construction Canada, Constitution Square, 350 Albert St., 19th Fl., Ottawa, ON K1A 0K3
613-998-9548, Fax: 613-998-1061, 800-514-3555, info@dcc-cdc.gc.ca
Natural Sciences & Engineering Research Council of Canada, Constitution Square, Tower II, 350 Albert St., Ottawa, ON K1A 1H5
613-995-4273, Fax: 613-943-1624, marie-josee.duval@nserc-crsng.gc.ca

British Columbia
Transportation Policy & Programs Department, PO Box 9850 Prov Govt,Victoria, BC V8W 9T5
250-387-5062, Fax: 250-387-6431

Manitoba
Manitoba Infrastructure & Transportation, Legislative Building, #203, 450 Broadway Ave., Winnipeg, MB R3C 0V8
204-945-3723, Fax: 204-945-7610

Northwest Territories
Highways & Marine, 4510 - 50 Ave., 2nd fl., PO Box 1320, Yellowknife, NT X1A 2L9
867-920-8771, Fax: 867-873-0288

Saskatchewan
Saskatchewan Highways & Infrastructure, Victoria Tower, 1855 Victoria Ave., Regina, SK S4P 3T2
306-787-4800, communications@highways.gov.sk.ca

ENVIRONMENT
Commissioner of the Environment & Sustainable Development, 240 Sparks St., Ottawa, ON K1A 0G6
613-995-3708, Fax: 613-957-0474, petitions@oag-bvg.gc.ca
Environment Canada, 10 Wellington St., Gatineau, QC K1A 0H3
819-997-2800, Fax: 819-994-1412, 800-668-6767, enviroinfo@ec.gc.ca
National Laboratory for Environmental Testing, Environment Canada, 867 Lakeshore Rd., PO Box 5050, Burlington, ON L7R 4A6
905-336-4563, Fax: 905-336-6404
National Round Table on the Environment & Economy, #200, 344 Slater St., Ottawa, ON K1R 7Y3
613-992-7189, Fax: 613-992-7385, info@nrtee-trnee.ca

Alberta
Alberta Environment & Sustainable Resource Development, Oxbridge Place, 9820 - 106 St., Main Fl., Edmonton, AB T5K 2J6
780-427-2700, Fax: 780-422-4086, -310-0000, env.infocent@gov.ab.ca; srd.infocent@gov.ab.ca

British Columbia
British Columbia Ministry of Environment, PO Box 9339 Prov Govt,Victoria, BC V8W 9M1
250-387-1161, Fax: 250-387-5669, envmail@gov.bc.ca

Manitoba
Manitoba Conservation & Water Stewardship, 200 Saulteaux Cres., Winnipeg, MB R3J 3W3
800-214-6497, mws@gov.mb.ca

New Brunswick
New Brunswick Department of Environment & Local Government, Marysville Place, PO Box 6000, Fredericton, NB E3B 5H1
506-453-2690, Fax: 506-457-4994, elg/egl-info@gnb.ca

Newfoundland & Labrador
Newfoundland & Labrador Department of Environment & Conservation, Confederation Bldg., West Block, 4th Fl., PO Box 8700, St. John's, NL A1B 4J6
709-729-2664, Fax: 709-729-6639, 800-563-6181, envcinquires@gov.nl.ca

Northwest Territories
Northwest Territories Department of Environment & Natural Resources, PO Box 1320, Yellowknife, NT X1A 2L9

Nova Scotia
Nova Scotia Department of Environment, Terminal Bldg., 5151 Terminal Rd., 5th Fl., PO Box 697, Halifax, NS B3J 2T8
902-424-3600, Fax: 902-424-0503, 877-936-8476

Nunavut
Nunavut Territory Department of Environment, PO Box 1000 1300,Iqaluit, NU X0A 0H0
867-975-7700, Fax: 867-975-7742, environment@gov.nu.ca

Ontario
Ontario Ministry of Environment, 135 St. Clair Ave. West, Toronto, ON M4V 1P5
416-325-4000, Fax: 416-325-3159, 800-565-4923, picemail.moe@ontario.ca
Environmental Commissioner of Ontario, #605, 1075 Bay St., Toronto, ON M5S 2B1
416-325-3377, Fax: 416-325-3370, 800-701-6454, commissioner@eco.on.ca

Prince Edward Island
Prince Edward Island Department of Environment, Labour & Justice, Shaw Bldg. South, 95 Rochford St., 4th Fl., PO Box 2000, Charlottetown, PE C1A 7N8
902-368-6410, Fax: 902-368-6488

Quebec
Bureau d'audiences publiques sur l'environnement, Édifice Lomer-Gouin, #2.10, 575, rue Saint-Amable, Québec, QC G1R 6A6
418-643-7447, Fax: 418-643-9474, 800-463-4732, communication@bape.gouv.qc.ca
Ministère du Développement durable, de l'Environnement, de la Faune, et des Parcs, Édifice Marie-Guyart, 675, boul René-Lévesque est, 29e étage, Québec, QC G1R 5V7
418-521-3911, Fax: 418-643-4143, 800-561-1616, info@mddep.gouv.qc.ca

Saskatchewan
Saskatchewan Environment, 3211 Albert St., 2nd Fl., Regina, SK S4S 5W6
306-787-2584, Fax: 306-787-9544, 800-567-4224, Centre.Inquiry@gov.sk.ca

ENVIRONMENT DEPARTMENTS/MINISTRIES
Environment Canada, 10 Wellington St., Gatineau, QC K1A 0H3
819-997-2800, Fax: 819-994-1412, 800-668-6767, enviroinfo@ec.gc.ca

Alberta
Alberta Environment & Sustainable Resource Development, Oxbridge Place, 9820 - 106 St., Main Fl., Edmonton, AB T5K 2J6
780-427-2700, Fax: 780-422-4086, -310-0000, env.infocent@gov.ab.ca; srd.infocent@gov.ab.ca

British Columbia
British Columbia Ministry of Environment, PO Box 9339 Prov Govt,Victoria, BC V8W 9M1
250-387-1161, Fax: 250-387-5669, envmail@gov.bc.ca

Manitoba
Manitoba Conservation & Water Stewardship, 200 Saulteaux Cres., Winnipeg, MB R3J 3W3
800-214-6497, mws@gov.mb.ca

New Brunswick
New Brunswick Department of Environment & Local Government, Marysville Place, PO Box 6000, Fredericton, NB E3B 5H1
506-453-2690, Fax: 506-457-4994, elg/egl-info@gnb.ca

Newfoundland & Labrador
Newfoundland & Labrador Department of Environment & Conservation, Confederation Bldg., West Block, 4th Fl., PO Box 8700, St. John's, NL A1B 4J6
709-729-2664, Fax: 709-729-6639, 800-563-6181, envcinquires@gov.nl.ca

Northwest Territories
Northwest Territories Department of Environment & Natural Resources, PO Box 1320, Yellowknife, NT X1A 2L9

Nova Scotia
Nova Scotia Department of Environment, Terminal Bldg., 5151 Terminal Rd., 5th Fl., PO Box 697, Halifax, NS B3J 2T8
902-424-3600, Fax: 902-424-0503, 877-936-8476

Nunavut
Nunavut Territory Department of Environment, PO Box 1000 1300,Iqaluit, NU X0A 0H0
867-975-7700, Fax: 867-975-7742, environment@gov.nu.ca

Ontario
Ontario Ministry of Environment, 135 St. Clair Ave. West, Toronto, ON M4V 1P5
416-325-4000, Fax: 416-325-3159, 800-565-4923, picemail.moe@ontario.ca

Prince Edward Island
Prince Edward Island Department of Environment, Labour & Justice, Shaw Bldg. South, 95 Rochford St., 4th Fl., PO Box 2000, Charlottetown, PE C1A 7N8
902-368-6410, Fax: 902-368-6488

Quebec
Ministère du Développement durable, de l'Environnement, de la Faune, et des Parcs, Édifice Marie-Guyart, 675, boul René-Lévesque est, 29e étage, Québec, QC G1R 5V7
418-521-3911, Fax: 418-643-4143, 800-561-1616, info@mddep.gouv.qc.ca

Saskatchewan
Saskatchewan Environment, 3211 Albert St., 2nd Fl., Regina, SK S4S 5W6
306-787-2584, Fax: 306-787-9544, 800-567-4224, Centre.Inquiry@gov.sk.ca

Yukon Territory
Yukon Environment, PO Box 2703, Whitehorse, YT Y1A 2C6
867-667-5652, Fax: 867-393-7197, environment.yukon@gov.yk.ca

ENVIRONMENTAL ASSESSMENT
Canadian Environmental Assessment Agency, Place Bell Canada, 160 Elgin St., 22nd Fl., Ottawa, ON K1A 0H3
613-957-0700, Fax: 613-957-0862, 866-582-1884, info@ceaa-acee.gc.ca
National Laboratory for Environmental Testing, Environment Canada, 867 Lakeshore Rd., PO Box 5050, Burlington, ON L7R 4A6
905-336-4563, Fax: 905-336-6404

New Brunswick
Community Planning & Environmental Protection Division, Marysville Place, PO Box 6000, Fredericton, NB E3B 5H1
506-444-5119, Fax: 506-457-7333, elg/egl-info@gnb.ca

Newfoundland & Labrador
Port aux Basques, Provincial Bldg., Main St., PO Box 478, Port Aux Basques, NL A0M 1C0
709-695-2835, Fax: 709-695-2393

Prince Edward Island
Land & Environment Division, Jones Bldg., 11 Kent St., 3rd Fl., PO Box 2000, Charlottetown, PE C1A 7N8
902-368-5221, Fax: 902-368-5395

EROSION CONTROL

Science & Technology Branch, Tower 5, 1341 Baseline Rd., Ottawa, ON K1A 0C5
613-759-1000, Fax: 613-773-1866

Prince Edward Island
Agriculture Policy & Regulatory Division, Jones Bldg., 11 Kent St., 5th Fl., Charlottetown, PE C1A 7N8

Quebec
Commission de protection du territoire agricole du Québec, 200, ch Ste-Foy, 2e étage, Québec, QC G1R 4X6
418-643-3314, Fax: 418-643-2261, 800-667-5294, info@cptaq.gouv.qc.ca

Saskatchewan
Saskatchewan Agriculture, Walter Scott Bldg., 3085 Albert St., Regina, SK S4S 0B1
866-457-2377, aginfo@gov.sk.ca

EXPORT DEVELOPMENT

Business Development Bank of Canada, #400, 5, Place Ville-Marie, Montréal, QC H3B 5E7
514-283-5904, Fax: 514-283-5626, 877-232-2269

Canadian Trade Commissioner Service, c/o Foreign Affairs & International Trade, 125 Sussex Dr., Ottawa, ON K1A 0G2
613-944-9991, Fax: 613-996-9709, 888-306-9991, enqserv@international.gc.ca

Export Development Canada, 151 Slater St., Ottawa, ON K1A 1K3
613-598-2500, Fax: 613-598-3811, 800-267-8510

Industry Canada, C.D. Howe Building, 235 Queen St., Ottawa, ON K1A 0H5
613-954-5031, Fax: 613-954-2340, 800-328-6189, info@ic.gc.ca

Western Economic Diversification Canada, Canada Place, #1500, 9700 Jasper Ave. NW, Edmonton, AB T5J 4H7
780-495-4164, Fax: 780-495-4557, 888-338-9378

New Brunswick
Northern Development Division, Harbourview Place, #400, 275 Main St., Bathurst, NB E2A 1A9
506-547-2227, Fax: 506-547-2269

Ontario
Ontario Ministry of Economic Development, Trade & Employment, Hearst Block, 900 Bay St., 8th Fl., Toronto, ON M7A 2E1
416-325-6666, Fax: 416-325-6688, 866-668-4249, info@edt.gov.on.ca

Saskatchewan
Energy & Resources, #300, 2103 - 11th Ave., Regina, SK S4P 3Z8
306-787-2528

EXPROPRIATION

Department of National Defence & the Canadian Forces, National Defence HQ, Major-General George R. Pearkes Bldg., 101 Colonel By Dr., Ottawa, ON K1A 0K2
613-995-2534, Fax: 613-992-4739, DNDRecruitment-RecrutementMDN@forces.gc.ca (Civilian Careers)

Alberta
Land Compensation Board, 1229 - 91 St. SW, Edmonton, AB T6X 1E9
srb.lcb@gov.ab.ca

Manitoba
Manitoba Land Value Appraisal Commission, #1144, 363 Broadway, Winnipeg, MB R3C 3N9
204-945-5455, Fax: 204-948-2235

Quebec
Ministère des Transports, 700, boul René-Lévesque est, 28e étage, Québec, QC G1R 5H1
418-643-6980, Fax: 418-643-2033, 888-355-0511, communications@mtq.gouv.qc.ca

FAMILY BENEFITS

See Also: Income Security; Social Services

Northwest Territories
Northwest Territories Department of Education, Culture & Employment, PO Box 1320, Yellowknife, NT X1A 2L9
867-669-2399, Fax: 867-873-0431, 866-606-5627

FEDERAL-PROVINCIAL AFFAIRS

Alberta
Alberta International & Intergovernmental Relations, Commerce Place, 10155 - 102 St., 12th Fl., Edmonton, AB T5J 4G8
780-422-1510, -310-0000

Northwest Territories
Northwest Territories Department of Aboriginal Affairs & Intergovernmental Relations, 4910 - 52nd St., PO Box 1320, Yellowknife, NT X1A 2L9
867-873-7143, Fax: 867-873-0233, 877-838-8194, nancy_gardiner@gov.nt.ca

Nova Scotia
Nova Scotia Department of Intergovernmental Affairs, Duke Tower, 5251 Duke St., 5th Fl., PO Box 1617, Halifax, NS B3J 2Y3
Fax: 902-424-0728, iga@gov.ns.ca

Nunavut
Nunavut Territory Department of Executive & Intergovernmental Affairs, 1084 Aeroplex bldg., PO Box 1000 200,Iqaluit, NU X0A 0H0
867-975-6000, Fax: 867-975-6099

FILM PRODUCTION & COLLECTIONS

British Columbia
British Columbia Film Commission, #201, 865 Hornby St., Vancouver, BC V6Z 2G3
604-660-2732, Fax: 604-660-4790, info@bcfilmcommission.com

Manitoba
Manitoba Film & Music, #410, 93 Lombard Ave., Winnipeg, MB R3B 3B1
204-947-2040, Fax: 204-956-5261, info@mbfilmmusic.ca

Ontario
Ontario Media Development Corporation, South Tower, #501, 175 Bloor St. East, Toronto, ON M4W 3R8
416-314-6858, Fax: 416-314-6876, reception@omdc.on.ca

FINANCE

See Also: Banking & Financial Institutions

Finance Canada, L'esplanade Laurier, 140 O'Connor St., Ottawa, ON K1A 0G5
613-992-1573, Fax: 613-943-0938, finpub@fin.gc.ca

Prince Edward Island
Prince Edward Island Department of Finance, Energy & Municipal Affairs, Shaw Bldg., 95 Rochford St. South, 2nd Fl., PO Box 2000, Charlottetown, PE C1A 7N8
902-368-4000, Fax: 902-368-5544

Yukon Territory
Yukon Finance, PO Box 2703, Whitehorse, YT Y1A 2C6
867-667-5343, Fax: 867-393-6217, fininfo@gov.yk.ca

FINANCING & LOANS

See Also: Investment

Business Development Bank of Canada, #400, 5, Place Ville-Marie, Montréal, QC H3B 5E7
514-283-5904, Fax: 514-283-5626, 877-232-2269

Canada Mortgage & Housing Corporation, 700 Montreal Rd., Ottawa, ON K1A 0P7
613-748-2000, Fax: 613-748-2098, 800-668-2642, chic@cmhc-schl.gc.ca

Manitoba
Manitoba Agricultural Services Corporation, #100, 1525 First St. South, Brandon, MB R7A 7A1
204-726-6850, Fax: 204-726-6849, mailbox@masc.mb.ca

Northwest Territories
Northwest Territories Department of Industry, Tourism & Investment, PO Box 1320, Yellowknife, NT X1A 2L9
Fax: 867-873-0306, info@iti.ca

Nova Scotia
Nova Scotia Farm Loan Board, PO Box 550, Truro, NS B2N 5E3
902-893-6506, Fax: 902-895-7693, flb@gov.ns.ca

Nunavut
Nunavut Business Credit Corporation, Parnaivak Bldg., #100, PO Box 2548, Iqaluit, NU X0A 0H0
867-975-7891, Fax: 867-975-7897, 800-758-0038, credit@nbcc.nu.ca

Ontario
Ontario Ministry of Rural Affairs, c/o Ministry of Agriculture & Food, 1 Stone Rd. West, Guelph, ON N1G 4Y2
519-826-3100, Fax: 519-826-4335, 888-466-2372, about.omafra@ontario.ca

Prince Edward Island
Prince Edward Island Lending Agency, Homburg Financial Tower, 98 Fitzroy St., 2nd Fl., Charlottetown, PE C1A 1R7
902-368-6200, Fax: 902-368-6201

Quebec
La financière agricole de Québec, 1400, boul de la Rive-Sud, Saint-Romuald, QC G6W 8K7
418-838-5602, Fax: 418-833-3871, 800-749-3646, financiereagricole@fadq.qc.ca

Yukon Territory
Yukon Economic Development, PO Box 2703, Whitehorse, YT Y1A 2C6
867-393-7191, Fax: 867-393-6412, 800-661-0408, ecdev@gov.yk.ca

FIRE PREVENTION

National Research Council Fire Resistance & Performance of Structures Testing Facilities, c/o National Research Council, 1200 Montreal Rd., Ottawa, ON K1A 0R6
construction@nrc-cnrc.gc.ca

British Columbia
Emergency Management BC, PO Box 9223 Prov Govt,Victoria, BC V8W 9J1
250-953-4002, Fax: 250-953-4081, BC.CorSer@gov.bc.ca (Coroner); OFC@gov.bc.ca (Fire Commissioner)

Newfoundland & Labrador
Eastern Waste Management Commission, #3, 255 Majors Path, St. John's, NL A1A 0L5
709-579-7960, Fax: 709-579-5392, info@easternwaste.ca

Northwest Territories
Northwest Territories Department of Municipal & Community Affairs, PO Box 1320, Yellowknife, NT X1A 2L9
867-873-7118, Fax: 867-873-0309

Nunavut
Nunavut Emergency Management, PO Box 1000 700,Iqaluit, NU X0A 0H0
867-975-5403, Fax: 867-979-4221, 800-693-1666

Ontario
Fire Safety Commission, Place Nouveau Bldg., 5775 Yonge St., 7th Fl., Toronto, ON M2M 4J1
416-325-3100, Fax: 416-314-1217

Quebec
Commissariat des incendies, 455, rue Dupont, Québec, QC G1K 6N2
418-529-5706, Fax: 418-529-9922

Yukon Territory
Fire Marshal's Office, 91790 Alaska Hwy., Whitehorse, YT Y1A 5X7
867-667-5811, Fax: 867-667-3165, inquiry@gov.yk.ca

FISHERIES

Fisheries & Oceans Canada, 200 Kent St., Ottawa, ON K1A 0E6
613-993-0999, Fax: 613-990-1866, info@dfo-mpo.gc.ca

Fisheries Resource Conservation Council, PO Box 2001 D, Ottawa, ON K1P 5W3
613-998-0433, Fax: 613-998-1146, info@frcc-ccrh.ca

Gulf Fisheries Centre, 343, av Université, 5th Fl., Moncton, NB E1C 9B6
506-851-6227, Fax: 506-851-2435, info@dfo-mpo.gc.ca

British Columbia

British Columbia Ministry of Agriculture, PO Box 9120 Prov Govt,Victoria, BC V8W 9E2
250-387-5121

New Brunswick

New Brunswick Department of Agriculture, Aquaculture & Fisheries, Agricultural Research Station (Experimental Farm), PO Box 6000, Fredericton, NB E3B 5H1
506-453-2666, Fax: 506-453-7170, DAAF-MAAP@gnb.ca

Newfoundland & Labrador

Newfoundland & Labrador Department of Fisheries & Aquaculture, Petten Bldg., 30 Strawberry Marsh Rd., PO Box 8700, St. John's, NL A1B 4J6
709-729-3723, Fax: 709-729-6082, fisheries@gov.nl.ca

Northwest Territories

Northwest Territories Department of Environment & Natural Resources, PO Box 1320, Yellowknife, NT X1A 2L9

Nova Scotia

Fisheries & Aquaculture Loan Board, 1741 Brunswick St., 3rd Fl., PO Box 2223, Halifax, NS B3J 3C4
902-424-0318, Fax: 902-424-3502

Nova Scotia Department of Fisheries & Aquaculture, 1741 Brunswick St., 3rd Fl., PO Box 2223, Halifax, NS B3J 3C4
902-424-4560, Fax: 902-424-4671

Ontario

Ontario Fish & Wildlife Heritage Commission, Robinson Pl., 300 Water St., PO Box 7000, Peterborough, ON K9J 8M5
705-755-1905, Fax: 705-755-1900

Prince Edward Island

Prince Edward Island Department of Agriculture & Forestry, Jones Bldg., 11 Kent St., PO Box 2000, Charlottetown, PE C1A 7N8
902-368-4880, Fax: 902-368-4857

FISHERIES & WILDLIFE

Beverly & Qamanirjuaq Caribou Management Board, Secretariat, PO Box 629, Stonewall, MB R0C 2Z0
204-467-2438, caribounews@arctic-caribou.com

Canadian Wildlife Service, 351, boul St-Joseph, Gatineau, QC K1A 0H3
819-997-1301, Fax: 819-953-7177

Committee on the Status of Endangered Wildlife in Canada, c/o Canadian Wildlife Service, 351 St. Joseph Blvd, 4th Fl., Gatineau, QC K1A 0H3
819-953-3215, Fax: 819-994-3684, cosewic/cosepac@ec.gc.ca

Fisheries & Oceans Canada, 200 Kent St., Ottawa, ON K1A 0E6
613-993-0999, Fax: 613-990-1866, info@dfo-mpo.gc.ca

Natural Resources Canada, 580 Booth St., Ottawa, ON K1A 0E4
613-995-0947, Fax: 613-992-7211

North American Bird Conservation Initiative, Canadian Wildlife Service, 351, boul St-Joseph, 3e étage, Gatineau, QC K1A 0H3
819-994-0512, Fax: 819-994-4445, nabci@ec.gc.ca

North American Waterfowl Management Plan, NAWCC (Canada) Secretariat, Place Vincent Massey, 351 St. Joseph Blvd., 7th Fl., Gatineau, QC K1A 0H3
819-934-6034, Fax: 819-934-6017, nawmp@ec.gc.ca

Porcupine Caribou Management Board, PO Box 31723, Whitehorse, YT Y1A 6L3
867-633-4780, Fax: 867-393-3904, pcmb@taiga.net

Arctic Goose, c/o Prairie & Northern Region, CWS, #200, 4999 - 98 Ave., Edmonton, AB T6B 2X3
780-951-8652, Fax: 780-495-2615, agjv@ec.gc.ca

Alberta Environment & Sustainable Resource Development, Oxbridge Place, 9820 - 106 St., Main Fl., Edmonton, AB T5K 2J6
780-427-2700, Fax: 780-422-4086, -310-0000, env.infocent@gov.ab.ca; srd.infocent@gov.ab.ca

Prairie Habitat, c/o Prairie & Northern Region, CWS, #200, 4999 - 98 Ave., Edmonton, AB T6B 2X3
780-951-8652, phjv@ec.gc.ca

British Columbia

British Columbia Ministry of Environment, PO Box 9339 Prov Govt,Victoria, BC V8W 9M1
250-387-1161, Fax: 250-387-5669, envmail@gov.bc.ca

Pacific Coast, c/o Environment Canada, Canadian Wildlife Service, #201, 401 Burrard St., Vancouver, BC V6C 3S5
604-940-4703

Manitoba

Endangered Species Advisory Committee, 200 Saulteaux Cres., PO Box 24, Winnipeg, MB R3J 3W3
204-945-7465, Fax: 204-945-3077

Manitoba Habitat Heritage Corporation, #200, 1555 St. James St., Winnipeg, MB R3H 1B5
204-784-4350, Fax: 204-784-7359, mhhc@mhhc.mb.ca

New Brunswick

New Brunswick Department of Agriculture, Aquaculture & Fisheries, Agricultural Research Station (Experimental Farm), PO Box 6000, Fredericton, NB E3B 5H1
506-453-2666, Fax: 506-453-7170, DAAF-MAAP@gnb.ca

Newfoundland & Labrador

Newfoundland & Labrador Department of Fisheries & Aquaculture, Petten Bldg., 30 Strawberry Marsh Rd., PO Box 8700, St. John's, NL A1B 4J6
709-729-3723, Fax: 709-729-6082, fisheries@gov.nl.ca

Northwest Territories

Northwest Territories Department of Environment & Natural Resources, PO Box 1320, Yellowknife, NT X1A 2L9

Nova Scotia

Nova Scotia Department of Natural Resources, Founder's Square, 1701 Hollis St., 3rd Fl., PO Box 698, Halifax, NS B3J 2T9
902-424-5935, Fax: 902-424-0594, 800-565-2224

Black Duck, Environment Canada, Canadian Wildlife Service, 335 River Rd., Ottawa, ON K1A 0H3
613-949-8254

Eastern Habitat, c/o Environment Canada, Canadian Wildlife Service, 335 River Rd., Ottawa, ON K1A 0H3
613-949-8264

Ontario Ministry of Natural Resources, 300 Water St., PO Box 7000, Peterborough, ON K9J 8M5
705-755-2000, Fax: 705-755-1677, 800-667-1940, mnr.nric.mnr@ontario.ca

Prince Edward Island

Prince Edward Island Department of Environment, Labour & Justice, Shaw Bldg. South, 95 Rochford St., 4th Fl., PO Box 2000, Charlottetown, PE C1A 7N8
902-368-6410, Fax: 902-368-6488

Quebec

Ministère de l'Agriculture, des Pêcheries et de l'Alimentation, 200, ch Sainte-Foy, Québec, QC G1R 4X6
418-380-2110, 888-222-6272

Yukon Territory

Yukon Environment, PO Box 2703, Whitehorse, YT Y1A 2C6
867-667-5652, Fax: 867-393-7197, environment.yukon@gov.yk.ca

Yukon Fish & Wildlife Management Board, 106 Main St., 2nd Fl., Whitehorse, YT Y1A 5P7
867-667-3754, Fax: 867-393-6947, officemanager@yfwmb.ca

FOOD

See: Agriculture; Nutrition

Prince Edward Island

BIO|FOOD|TECH, 101 Belvedere Ave., PO Box 2000, Charlottetown, PE C1A 7N8
902-368-5548, Fax: 902-368-5549, 877-368-5548, biofoodtech@biofoodtech.ca

FOREST RESOURCES

Alberta

Alberta Innovates - Bio Solutions, Phipps McKinnon Bldg., 10020 - 101A Ave., Edmonton, AB T5J 3G2
780-427-1956, Fax: 780-427-3252, 877-828-0444, bio@albertainnovates.ca

Forestry Division, Petroleum Plaza ST, 9915 - 108 St. 11th Fl., Edmonton, AB T5K 2G8

British Columbia

British Columbia Ministry of Forests, Lands & Natural Resource Operations, PO Box 9352 Prov Govt,Victoria, BC V8W 9M1
250-387-4809, 877-855-3222, FLNRO.MediaRequests@gov.bc.ca

Northwest Territories

Forest Management Division, PO Box 7, Fort Smith, NT X0E 0P0
Fax: 867-874-2077, forestmanagement.enr.gov.nt/

Nova Scotia

NS Primary Forest Products Marketing Board, #804, 45 Alderney Dr., Dartmouth, NS B2Y 2N6
902-424-7598, Fax: 902-424-6965

Nunavut

Nunavut Territory Department of Environment, PO Box 1000 1300,Iqaluit, NU X0A 0H0
867-975-7700, Fax: 867-975-7742, environment@gov.nu.ca

Ontario

Algonquin Forestry Authority - Huntsville, 222 Main St. West, Huntsville, ON P1H 1Y1
705-789-9647, Fax: 705-789-3353, info@algonquinforestry.on.ca

Algonquin Forestry Authority - Pembroke, Victoria Centre, 84 Isabella St., 2nd Fl., Pembroke, ON K8A 5S5
613-735-0173, Fax: 613-735-4192, info@algonquinforestry.on.ca

Policy Division, #6540, 99 Wellesley St. West, Toronto, ON M7A 1W3
Fax: 416-314-1994, 800-667-1940

Quebec

Forêt Québec, 880, ch Ste-Foy, #RC 120, Québec, QC G1S 4X4
418-627-8652, Fax: 418-528-1278, foretquebec@mrnf.gouv.qc.ca

Yukon Territory

Yukon Energy, Mines & Resources, PO Box 2703, Whitehorse, YT Y1A 2C6
867-667-3130, Fax: 867-456-3965, 800-661-0408, emr@gov.yk.ca

Yukon Environment, PO Box 2703, Whitehorse, YT Y1A 2C6
867-667-5652, Fax: 867-393-7197, environment.yukon@gov.yk.ca

FORESTRY & PAPER

Natural Resources Canada, 580 Booth St., Ottawa, ON K1A 0E4
613-995-0947, Fax: 613-992-7211

Alberta

Alberta Innovates - Bio Solutions, Phipps McKinnon Bldg., 10020 - 101A Ave., Edmonton, AB T5J 3G2
780-427-1956, Fax: 780-427-3252, 877-828-0444, bio@albertainnovates.ca

Forestry Division, Petroleum Plaza ST, 9915 - 108 St. 11th Fl., Edmonton, AB T5K 2G8

British Columbia

Forest Practices Board, 1675 Douglas St., 3rd Fl., PO Box 9905 Prov Govt, Victoria, BC V8W 9R1
250-213-4700, Fax: 250-213-4725, 800-994-5899, fpboard@gov.bc.ca

British Columbia Ministry of Forests, Lands & Natural Resource Operations, PO Box 9352 Prov Govt,Victoria, BC V8W 9M1
250-387-4809, 877-855-3222, FLNRO.MediaRequests@gov.bc.ca

Timber Export Advisory Committee, PO Box 9514 Prov Govt, Victoria, BC V8W 9C2
250-387-8916, Fax: 250-387-5050

Newfoundland & Labrador

Newfoundland & Labrador Department of Natural Resources, Natural Resources Bldg., 50 Elizabeth Ave., 7th Fl., PO Box 8700, St. John's, NL A1B 4J6
709-729-2920, Fax: 709-729-0059

Nova Scotia

Nova Scotia Department of Natural Resources, Founder's Square, 1701 Hollis St., 3rd Fl., PO Box 698, Halifax, NS B3J 2T9
902-424-5935, Fax: 902-424-0594, 800-565-2224

Ontario

Algonquin Forestry Authority - Huntsville, 222 Main St. West, Huntsville, ON P1H 1Y1
705-789-9647, Fax: 705-789-3353, info@algonquinforestry.on.ca

Algonquin Forestry Authority - Pembroke, Victoria Centre, 84 Isabella St., 2nd Fl., Pembroke, ON K8A 5S5
613-735-0173, Fax: 613-735-4192, info@algonquinforestry.on.ca

Ontario Ministry of Natural Resources, 300 Water St., PO Box 7000, Peterborough, ON K9J 8M5
705-755-2000, Fax: 705-755-1677, 800-667-1940, mnr.nric.mnr@ontario.ca

Quebec
Ministère du Développement durable, de l'Environnement, de la Faune, et des Parcs, Édifice Marie-Guyart, 675, boul René-Lévesque est, 29e étage, Québec, QC G1R 5V7
418-521-3911, Fax: 418-643-4143, 800-561-1616, info@mddep.gouv.qc.ca

Saskatchewan
Saskatchewan Environment, 3211 Albert St., 2nd Fl., Regina, SK S4S 5W6
306-787-2584, Fax: 306-787-9544, 800-567-4224, Centre.Inquiry@gov.sk.ca

Yukon Territory
Yukon Environment, PO Box 2703, Whitehorse, YT Y1A 2C6
867-667-5652, Fax: 867-393-7197, environment.yukon@gov.yk.ca

GEOLOGICAL SERVICES
Geological Survey of Canada, 601 Booth St., Ottawa, ON K1A 0E8
613-996-3919, Fax: 613-943-8742, esic@nrcan.gc.ca
Mapping Services Branch - Geomatics Canada, 615 Booth St., Ottawa, ON K1A 0E9
613-995-4945, Fax: 613-995-8737

Alberta
Energy Resources Conservation Board, #1000, 250 - 5 Ave. SW, Calgary, AB T2P 0R4
403-297-8311, Fax: 403-297-7336, 855-297-8311, inquiries@ercb.ca; infoservices@ercb.ca; ADR@ercb.ca

British Columbia
British Columbia Ministry of Energy, Mines, & Natural Gas (& Responsible for Housing), PO Box 9053 Prov Govt,Victoria, BC V8W 9E2

Northwest Territories
Northwest Territories Geoscience Office, 4601 B - 52 Ave., PO Box 1500, Yellowknife, NT X1A 2R3
867-669-2636, Fax: 867-669-2725, ntgo@gov.nt.ca

Nova Scotia
Geomatics Centre, 160 Willow St., Amherst, NS B4H 3W5
902-667-7231, Fax: 902-667-6008, 800-798-0706, geoinfo@gov.ns.ca

Ontario
Ontario Geological Survey, Willet Green Miller Centre, 933 Ramsey Lake Rd., Level B6, Sudbury, ON P3E 6B5
705-670-5758, Fax: 705-670-5818, 888-415-9845

GOVERNMENT
Aboriginal Affairs & Northern Development Canada, 10 Wellington St., North Tower, Gatineau, QC K1A 0H4
819-997-0380, Fax: 866-817-3977, 800-567-9604, infopubs@aadnc-aandc.gc.ca
Auditor General of Canada, 240 Sparks St., Ottawa, ON K1A 0G6
613-995-3708, Fax: 613-957-0474, 888-761-5953, communications@oag-bvg.gc.ca; infomedia@oag-bvg.gc.ca
Business Development Bank of Canada, #400, 5, Place Ville-Marie, Montréal, QC H3B 5E7
514-283-5904, Fax: 514-283-5626, 877-232-2269
Canada Economic Development for Québec Regions, Édifice Dominion Square, #900, 1255, rue Peel, Montréal, QC H3B 2T9
514-283-6412, Fax: 514-283-3302, 866-385-6412
Canada Revenue Agency, 875 Heron Rd., Ottawa, ON K1A 0L5
800-267-6999
Canadian Nuclear Safety Commission, 280 Slater St., PO Box 1046 B,Ottawa, ON K1P 5S9
613-995-5894, Fax: 613-995-5086, 800-668-5284
Defence Construction Canada, Constitution Square, 350 Albert St., 19th Fl., Ottawa, ON K1A 0K3
613-998-9548, Fax: 613-998-1061, 800-514-3555, info@dcc-cdc.gc.ca
Department of National Defence & the Canadian Forces, National Defence HQ, Major-General George R. Pearkes Bldg., 101 Colonel By Dr., Ottawa, ON K1A 0K2
613-995-2534, Fax: 613-992-4739, DNDRecruitment-RecrutementMDN@forces.gc.ca (Civilian Careers)
Finance Canada, L'esplanade Laurier, 140 O'Connor St., Ottawa, ON K1A 0G5
613-992-1573, Fax: 613-943-0938, finpub@fin.gc.ca
First Nations Tax Commission, #321, 345 Yellowhead Hwy, Kamloops, BC V2H 1H1
250-828-9857, Fax: 250-828-9858, mailkamloops@fntc.ca
Foreign Affairs & International Trade Canada, Enquiries Service, 125 Sussex Dr., Ottawa, ON K1A 0G2
613-944-4000, Fax: 613-996-9709, 800-267-8376, enqserv@international.gc.ca; travel@international.gc.ca
Government of Canada, c/o Canada Enquiry Centre, Service Canada, Ottawa, ON K1A 0J9
613-941-1827, 800-622-6232, canadasite@canada.gc.ca
Industry Canada, C.D. Howe Building, 235 Queen St., Ottawa, ON K1A 0H5
613-954-5031, Fax: 613-954-2340, 800-328-6189, info@ic.gc.ca
International Development Research Centre, 150 Kent St., PO Box 8500, Ottawa, ON K1G 3H9
613-236-6163, Fax: 613-238-7230, info@idrc.ca
Nunavut Impact Review Board, PO Box 1360, Cambridge Bay, NU X0B 0C0
867-983-4600, Fax: 867-983-2594, 866-233-3033, info@nirb.ca
Nunavut Planning Commission, PO Box 2101, Cambridge Bay, NU X0B 0C0
867-983-4625, Fax: 867-983-4626
Public Works & Government Services Canada, Place du Portage, Phase III, 11, rue Laurier, Ottawa, ON K1A 0S5
questions@tpsgc-pwgsc.gc.ca
Statistics Canada, R.H. Coats Bldg., Tunney's Pasture, 150 Tunney's Pasture Driveway, Ottawa, ON K1A 0T6
613-951-8116, Fax: 877-287-4369, 800-263-1136, infostats@statcan.ca
Treasury Board of Canada, 140 O'Connor St., Ottawa, ON K1A 0R5
613-957-2400, Fax: 613-941-4000, 877-636-0656

Alberta
Alberta Apprenticeship & Industry Training Board, Commerce Place, 10155 - 102nd St., 10th Fl., Edmonton, AB T5J 4L5
780-427-8765, Fax: 780-422-7376, -310-0000
Government of Alberta, PO Box 1333, Edmonton, AB T5J 2N2
780-427-2711, Fax: 780-422-2852, -310-0000
Alberta Infrastructure, Infrastructure Building, 6950 - 113 St., Edmonton, AB T6H 5V7
780-415-0507, Fax: 780-427-2187, -310-0000, Infra.Contact.Us.m@gov.ab.ca
Alberta International & Intergovernmental Relations, Commerce Place, 10155 - 102 St., 12th Fl., Edmonton, AB T5J 4G8
780-422-1510, -310-0000
Alberta Municipal Affairs, Communications Branch, Commerce Place, 10155 - 102 St., 18th Fl., Edmonton, AB T5J 4L4
780-427-2732, Fax: 780-422-1419, comments@gov.ab.ca
Alberta Public Affairs Bureau, Park Plaza, 10611 - 98 Ave., 6th Fl., Edmonton, AB T5K 2P7
780-427-2754, Fax: 780-422-4168, -310-0000
Special Areas Board, Special Areas Board Administration, 212 - 2nd Ave. West, PO Box 820, Hanna, AB T0J 1P0
403-854-5600, Fax: 403-854-5527, specarea@telus.net

British Columbia
Agricultural Land Commission, #133, 4940 Canada Way, Burnaby, BC V5G 4K6
604-660-7000, Fax: 604-660-7033, ALCBurnaby@Victoria1.gov.bc.ca
British Columbia Assessment Authority, #400, 3450 Uptown Blvd., Victoria, BC V8Z 0B9
250-595-6211, Fax: 250-595-6222, info@bcassessment.ca
British Columbia Pavilion Corporation (PavCo), #850, 999 West Hastings St., PO Box 16, Vancouver, BC V6C 2W2
604-482-2200, Fax: 604-681-9017, info@bcpavco.com
British Columbia Utilities Commission, 900 Howe St., 6th Fl., PO Box 250, Vancouver, BC V6Z 2N3
604-660-4700, Fax: 604-660-1102, 800-663-1385, commission.secretary@bcuc.com
Government of British Columbia, Parliament Bldgs., Victoria, BC V8V 1X4
250-387-6121, 800-663-7867

Manitoba
Board of Electrical Examiners, #500, 401 York Ave, Winnipeg, MB R3C 0P8
204-945-3507, terry.rieger@gov.mb.ca
Government of Manitoba, Legislative Building, Rm. 237, Winnipeg, MB R3C 0V8
204-945-3636, Fax: 204-948-2507, clerkla@leg.gov.mb.ca
Local Government Development Division, 59 Elizabeth Dr., PO Box 33, Thompson, MB R8N 1X4
204-677-6794, Fax: 204-677-6525
Manitoba Local Government, #301, 450 Broadway Ave., Winnipeg, MB R3C 0V8
Fax: 204-945-1383, mnia@leg.gov.mb.ca
Manitoba Land Value Appraisal Commission, #1144, 363 Broadway, Winnipeg, MB R3C 3N9
204-945-5455, Fax: 204-948-2235
Manitoba Municipal Board, #1144, 363 Broadway, Winnipeg, MB R3C 3N9
204-945-2941, Fax: 204-948-2235
Provincial-Municipal Support Services, #508, 800 Portage Ave., Winnipeg, MB R3G 0N4

New Brunswick
Government of New Brunswick, PO Box 6000, Fredericton, NB E3B 5H1

Newfoundland & Labrador
Government of Newfoundland & Labrador, Confederation Bldg., St. John's, NL A1B 4J6
info@gov.nl.ca
Newfoundland & Labrador Department of Municipal Affairs, West Block, Main Fl., Confederation Bldg., PO Box 8700, St. John's, NL A1B 4J6
709-729-3046, Fax: 709-729-0943, mainfo@gov.nl.ca
Newfoundland & Labrador Department of Service NL, PO Box 8700, St. John's, NL A1B 4J6
709-729-4834, servicenlinfo@gov.nl.ca

Northwest Territories
Northwest Territories Department of Aboriginal Affairs & Intergovernmental Relations, 4910 - 52nd St., PO Box 1320, Yellowknife, NT X1A 2L9
867-873-7143, Fax: 867-873-0233, 877-838-8194, nancy_gardiner@gov.nt.ca
Government of the Northwest Territories, PO Box 1320, Yellowknife, NT X1A 2L9
Northwest Territories Department of Public Works & Services, PO Box 1320, Yellowknife, NT X1A 2L9

Nova Scotia
Crown Land Information Management Centre, Founders Square, #501, 1701 Hollis St., PO Box 698, Halifax, NS B3J 2T9
902-424-3171
Government of Nova Scotia, Province House, 1726 Hollis St., Halifax, NS B3J 2T3
Nova Scotia Department of Service Nova Scotia & Municipal Relations, 1505 Barrington St., PO Box 216, Halifax, NS B3J 3K5
902-424-5200, Fax: 902-424-0581, 800-670-4357, askus@gov.ns.ca
Nova Scotia Utility & Review Board, Summit Place, 1601 Lower Water St., 3rd Fl., PO Box 1692 M,Halifax, NS B3J 3S3
902-424-4448, Fax: 902-424-3919, uarb.board@gov.ns.ca

Nunavut
Nunavut Territory Department of Community & Government Services, W.G. Brown Bldg., 4th Fl., PO Box 1000 700,Iqaluit, NU X0A 0H0
867-975-5400, Fax: 867-975-5305
Nunavut Territory Department of Culture, Language, Elders & Youth, PO Box 1000 800,Iqaluit, NU X0A 0H0
867-975-5500, Fax: 867-975-5504, 866-934-2035
Nunavut Emergency Management, PO Box 1000 700,Iqaluit, NU X0A 0H0
867-975-5403, Fax: 867-979-4221, 800-693-1666
Nunavut Territory Department of Environment, PO Box 1000 1300,Iqaluit, NU X0A 0H0
867-975-7700, Fax: 867-975-7742, environment@gov.nu.ca
Nunavut Territory Department of Executive & Intergovernmental Affairs, 1084 Aeroplex bldg., PO Box 1000 200,Iqaluit, NU X0A 0H0
867-975-6000, Fax: 867-975-6099
Government of Nunavut, PO Box 1200, Iqaluit, NU X0A 0H0
867-975-6000, 877-212-6438, info@gov.nu.ca
Nunavut Territory Department of Health & Social Services, PO Box 1000 1000,Iqaluit, NU X0A 0H0
867-975-5766, Fax: 867-975-5705, 800-661-0833

Ontario
Cancer Care Ontario, 620 University Ave., 15th Fl., Toronto, ON M5G 2L7
416-971-9800, Fax: 416-971-6888
Government of Ontario, Queen's Park, Toronto, ON M7A 1A2
416-326-1234, 800-267-8097
Ontario Ministry of Municipal Affairs & Housing, College Park, 777 Bay St., 17th Fl., Toronto, ON M5G 2E5
416-585-7041, Fax: 416-585-6470, 866-220-2290, mininfo.mah@ontario.ca

Ontario Mental Health Foundation, 441 Jarvis St., 2nd Fl., Toronto, ON M4Y 2G8
416-920-7721, Fax: 416-920-0026, grants@omhf.on.ca

Ontario Northland, 555 Oak St. East, North Bay, ON P1B 8L3
705-472-4500, Fax: 705-476-5598, 800-363-7512, info@ontarionorthland.ca; pr@ontarionorthland.ca

Ontario Pension Board, Sun Life Bldg., #2200, 200 King St. West, Toronto, ON M5H 3X6
416-364-8558, Fax: 416-364-7578, 800-668-6203, clientservice@opb.ca

Prince Edward Island

Government of Prince Edward Island, Island Information Service, PO Box 2000, Charlottetown, PE C1A 7N8
902-368-4000, island@gov.pe.ca

Quebec

Ministère des Affaires municipales, des Régions et de l'Occupation du territoire, Aile Chaveau, 10, rue Pierre-Olivier-Chauveau, 3e étage, Québec, QC G1R 4J3
418-691-2019, Fax: 418-643-7385, communications@mamrot.gouv.qc.ca

Bureau du coroner, Édifice le Delta 2, #390, 2875, boul Laurier, Québec, QC G1V 5B1
418-643-1845, Fax: 418-643-6174, 866-312-7051, clientele.coroner@msp.gouv.qc.ca

Centre de recherche industrielle du Québec, 333, rue Franquet, Québec, QC G1P 4C7
418-659-1550, 800-667-2386, infocriq@criq.qc.ca

Comité de déontologie policière, Tour du Saint-Laurent, #A-200, 2525, boul Laurier, 2e étage, Québec, QC G1V 4Z6
418-646-1936, Fax: 418-528-0987, comite.deontologie@msp.gouv.qc.ca

Commissaire à la déontologie policière, #1-40, 1200, rte de l'Église, Québec, QC G1V 4Y9
418-643-7897, Fax: 418-528-9473, 877-237-7897, deontologie-policiere.quebec@msp.gouv.qc.ca

Commissariat des incendies, 455, rue Dupont, Québec, QC G1K 6N2
418-529-5706, Fax: 418-529-9922

Commission québecoise des libérations conditionnelles, #1.32A, 300, boul Jean-Lesage, Québec, QC G1K 8K6
418-646-8300, Fax: 418-643-7217, cqlc@msp.gouv.qc.ca

Direction générale de la Sûreté du Québec, 1701, rue Parthenais, Montréal, QC H2K 3S7
514-598-4141, Fax: 514-598-4242

Ministère du Développement économique, de l'Innovation et de l'Exportation, 710, place D'Youville, 3e étage, Québec, QC G1R 4Y4
418-691-5950, Fax: 418-644-0118, 866-680-1884

Gouvernement du Québec, Hôtel du Parlement, 1045, rue des Parlementaires, Québec, QC G1A 1A3
418-643-7239, Fax: 418-646-4271, 866-337-8837

Ministère des Ressources naturelles, 880, ch Sainte-Foy, Québec, QC G1S 4X4
418-627-8600, Fax: 418-644-6513, 866-248-6936, services.clientele@mrnf.gouv.qc.ca

Régie des alcools, des courses et des jeux, 560, boul Charest est, Québec, QC G1K 3J3
418-643-7667, Fax: 418-643-5971, 800-363-0320

École nationale de police du Québec, 350, rue Marguerite-d'Youville, Nicolet, QC J3T 1X4
819-293-8631, Fax: 819-293-8630, courriel@enpq.qc.ca

Saskatchewan

Government of Saskatchewan, Regina, SK S4S 0B3

Yukon Territory

Government of the Yukon Territory, PO Box 2703, Whitehorse, YT Y1A 2C6
867-667-5811, 800-661-0408

GOVERNMENT (GENERAL INFORMATION)

Aboriginal Affairs & Northern Development Canada, 10 Wellington St., North Tower, Gatineau, QC K1A 0H4
819-997-0380, Fax: 866-817-3977, 800-567-9604, infopubs@aadnc-aandc.gc.ca

Auditor General of Canada, 240 Sparks St., Ottawa, ON K1A 0G6
613-995-3708, Fax: 613-957-0474, 888-761-5953, communications@oag-bvg.gc.ca; infomedia@oag-bvg.gc.ca

Canada Business Network, 235 Queen St., Ottawa, ON K1A 0H5
888-576-4444

Department of National Defence & the Canadian Forces, National Defence HQ, Major-General George R. Pearkes Bldg., 101 Colonel By Dr., Ottawa, ON K1A 0K2
613-995-2534, Fax: 613-992-4739, DNDRecruitment-RecrutementMDN@forces.gc.ca (Civilian Careers)

Environment Canada, 10 Wellington St., Gatineau, QC K1A 0H3
819-997-2800, Fax: 819-994-1412, 800-668-6767, enviroinfo@ec.gc.ca

Fisheries & Oceans Canada, 200 Kent St., Ottawa, ON K1A 0E6
613-993-0999, Fax: 613-990-1866, info@dfo-mpo.gc.ca

Foreign Affairs & International Trade Canada, Enquiries Service, 125 Sussex Dr., Ottawa, ON K1A 0G2
613-944-4000, Fax: 613-996-9709, 800-267-8376, enqserv@international.gc.ca; travel@international.gc.ca

Health Canada, Tunney's Pasture, Ottawa, ON K1A 0K9
613-957-2991, Fax: 613-941-5366, 866-225-0709, info@hc-sc.gc.ca

Human Resources & Skills Development Canada, 140 Promenade du Portage, Gatineau, QC K1A 0J9

Industry Canada, C.D. Howe Building, 235 Queen St., Ottawa, ON K1A 0H5
613-954-5031, Fax: 613-954-2340, 800-328-6189, info@ic.gc.ca

Service Canada, 140, Promenade du Portage, Gatineau, QC K1A 0J9
Fax: 613-941-1827, 800-622-6232

Statistics Canada, R.H. Coats Bldg., Tunney's Pasture, 150 Tunney's Pasture Driveway, Ottawa, ON K1A 0T6
613-951-8116, Fax: 877-287-4369, 800-263-1136, infostats@statcan.ca

Transport Canada, Place de Ville, 330 Sparks St., Tower C, Ottawa, ON K1A 0N5
613-990-2309, Fax: 613-954-4731, 866-995-9737

Treasury Board of Canada, 140 O'Connor St., Ottawa, ON K1A 0R5
613-957-2400, Fax: 613-941-4000, 877-636-0656

Alberta

Alberta Public Affairs Bureau, Park Plaza, 10611 - 98 Ave., 6th Fl., Edmonton, AB T5K 2P7
780-427-2754, Fax: 780-422-4168, -310-0000

Service Alberta, Government of Alberta, PO Box 1333, Edmonton, AB T5J 2N2
780-427-4088, -310-0000, service.alberta@gov.ab.ca

Newfoundland & Labrador

Newfoundland & Labrador Department of Service NL, PO Box 8700, St. John's, NL A1B 4J6
709-729-4834, servicenlinfo@gov.nl.ca

Nova Scotia

Nova Scotia Department of Service Nova Scotia & Municipal Relations, 1505 Barrington St., PO Box 216, Halifax, NS B3J 3K5
902-424-5200, Fax: 902-424-0581, 800-670-4357, askus@gov.ns.ca

Nunavut

Nunavut Territory Department of Executive & Intergovernmental Affairs, 1084 Aeroplex bldg., PO Box 1000 200,Iqaluit, NU X0A 0H0
867-975-6000, Fax: 867-975-6099,

Quebec

Services Québec, Bureau de la qualité, 800, place D'Youville, 20e étage, Québec, QC G1R 3P4
418-644-4545, 877-644-4545

GRANTS & SUBSIDIES

See Also: Student Aid

Atlantic Canada Opportunities Agency, Blue Cross Centre, 644 Main St., 3rd Fl., PO Box 6051, Moncton, NB E1C 9J8
506-851-2271, Fax: 506-851-7403, 800-561-7862, information@acoa-apeca.gc.ca

Business Development Bank of Canada, #400, 5, Place Ville-Marie, Montréal, QC H3B 5E7
514-283-5904, Fax: 514-283-5626, 877-232-2269

Canada Economic Development for Québec Regions, Édifice Dominion Square, #900, 1255, rue Peel, Montréal, QC H3B 2T9
514-283-6412, Fax: 514-283-3302, 866-385-6412

Canada Mortgage & Housing Corporation, 700 Montreal Rd., Ottawa, ON K1A 0P7
613-748-2000, Fax: 613-748-2098, 800-668-2642, chic@cmhc-schl.gc.ca

Canadian Institutes of Health Research, 160 Elgin St., 9th Fl., Ottawa, ON K1A 0W9
613-941-2672, Fax: 613-954-1800, 888-603-4178, info@cihr-irsc.gc.ca

International Development Research Centre, 150 Kent St., PO Box 8500, Ottawa, ON K1G 3H9
613-236-6163, Fax: 613-238-7230, info@idrc.ca

Natural Sciences & Engineering Research Council of Canada, Constitution Square, Tower II, 350 Albert St., Ottawa, ON K1A 1H5
613-995-4273, Fax: 613-943-1624, marie-josee.duval@nserc-crsng.gc.ca

Western Economic Diversification Canada, Canada Place, #1500, 9700 Jasper Ave. NW, Edmonton, AB T5J 4H7
780-495-4164, Fax: 780-495-4557, 888-338-9378

Alberta

Local Government Services Division, Commerce Place, 10155 - 102 St., 17th Fl., Edmonton, AB T5J 4L4

Saskatchewan

Energy & Resources, #300, 2103 - 11th Ave., Regina, SK S4P 3Z8
306-787-2528

HAZARDOUS MATERIALS

Hazardous Materials Information Review Commission, 427 Laurier Ave. West, 7th Fl., Ottawa, ON K1A 1M3
613-993-4331, Fax: 613-993-4686, hmirc-ccrmd@hc-sc.gc.ca

Low-Level Radioactive Waste Management Office, #200, 1900 City Park Dr., Ottawa, ON K1J 1A3
613-998-9442, Fax: 613-952-0760, 800-377-5995, info@llrwmo.org

Manitoba

Emergency Measures Organization, 405 Broadway Ave., 15th Floor, Winnipeg, MB R3C 3L6
204-945-4772, Fax: 204-945-4929, 888-267-8298, emo@gov.mb.ca

Ontario

Ontario Ministry of Environment, 135 St. Clair Ave. West, Toronto, ON M4V 1P5
416-325-4000, Fax: 416-325-3159, 800-565-4923, picemail.moe@ontario.ca

Pesticides Advisory Committee, 135 St. Clair Ave. West, 15th Fl., Toronto, ON M4V 1P5
416-314-9230, Fax: 416-314-9237

HEALTH

Canadian Centre for Occupational Health & Safety, 135 Hunter St. East, Hamilton, ON L8N 1M5
905-572-2981, Fax: 905-572-2206, 800-668-4284

Canadian Food Inspection Agency, 1400 Merivale Rd., Ottawa, ON K1A 0Y9
613-225-2342, Fax: 613-228-6601, 800-442-2342

Hazardous Materials Information Review Commission, 427 Laurier Ave. West, 7th Fl., Ottawa, ON K1A 1M3
613-993-4331, Fax: 613-993-4686, hmirc-ccrmd@hc-sc.gc.ca

Health Canada, Tunney's Pasture, Ottawa, ON K1A 0K9
613-957-2991, Fax: 613-941-5366, 866-225-0709, info@hc-sc.gc.ca

National Research Council Medical Device Facilities, Boucherville Research Facilities, 75, boul de Mortagne, Boucherville, QC J4B 6Y4
450-641-5100

National Research Council Single Domain Antibody Facility, c/o National Research Council, 1200 Montreal Rd., Ottawa, ON K1A 0R6

National Research Council Zebrafish Screening Facility, c/o National Research Council, 1200 Montreal Rd., Ottawa, ON K1A 0R6

Public Health Agency of Canada, 130 Colonnade Rd., Ottawa, ON K1A 0K9

Alberta

Alberta Health Services, Corporate Office, North Tower, Seventh Street Plaza, 10030 - 107th St. NW, 14th Fl., Edmonton, AB T5J 3E4
780-342-2000, Fax: 780-342-2060, 888-342-2471, ahsb.admin@albertahealthservices.ca

Financial & Corporate Services Division, Telus Plaza NT, 10025 Jasper Ave., 19th Fl., Edmonton, AB T5J 1S6

Health Quality Council of Alberta, #210, 811 - 14 St. NW, Calgary, AB T2N 2A4
403-297-8162, Fax: 403-297-8258, info@hqca.ca

Health Workforce Division, Telus Plaza NT, 10025 Jasper Ave., 10th Fl., Edmonton, AB T5J 1S6

Alberta Health, PO Box 1360 Main,Edmonton, AB T5J 2N3
780-427-7164, Fax: 780-427-1171, -310-0000
Occupational Health & Safety Council, Labour Building, 10808 - 99 Ave., 9th Fl., Edmonton, AB T5K 0G5
780-415-8690, 866-415-8690
Office of the Chief Medical Officer of Health, Telus Plaza NT, 10025 Jasper Ave., 24th Fl., Edmonton, AB T5J 1S6
780-427-5263
Premier's Council on the Status of Persons with Disabilities, HSBC Building, 10055 - 106 St., 11th Fl., Edmonton, AB T5J 1G3
780-422-1095, 800-272-8841, pcspd@gov.ab.ca
Seniors Advisory Council for Alberta, Standard Life Centre, #600, 10405 Jasper Ave., 6th Fl., Edmonton, AB T5J 4R7
780-422-2321, Fax: 780-422-8762, -310-0000, saca@gov.ab.ca

British Columbia

British Columbia Ministry of Health, 1515 Blanshard St., Victoria, BC V8W 3C8
800-663-7100, hlth.health@gov.bc.ca

Manitoba

Addictions Foundation of Manitoba, 1031 Portage Ave., Winnipeg, MB R3G 0R8
204-944-6200, Fax: 204-786-7768, library@afm.mb.ca
Manitoba Health, #100, 300 Carlton St., Winnipeg, MB R3B 3M9
204-786-7191, minhlt@leg.gov.mb.ca
Manitoba Drug Standards & Therapeutics Committee, #1014, 300 Carlton St., Winnipeg, MB R3B 3M9
204-786-7317, Fax: 204-942-2030
Public Health & Primary Health Care, 300 Carlton St., 2nd Floor, Winnipeg, MB R3B 3M9

New Brunswick

Addiction, Mental Health, Primary Health Care & Extra Mural Services Division, HSBC Place, 520 King St., 5th Fl., PO Box 5100, Fredericton, NB E3B 5G8
506-457-4800, Fax: 506-453-5243, Health.Sante@gnb.ca
Communications Branch, HSBC Place, 520 King St., 5th Fl., PO Box 5100, Fredericton, NB E3B 6G3
506-457-2356, Fax: 506-444-4697, Health.Sante@gnb.ca
New Brunswick Department of Health, PO Box 5100, Fredericton, NB E3B 5G8
506-457-4800, Fax: 506-453-5243, dh-ms@dh-ms.ca
New Brunswick Department of Tourism, Heritage & Culture, Centennial Building, PO Box 6000, Fredericton, NB E3B 5H1
506-444-5205, Fax: 506-457-4984, taponlinedirectory@gnb.ca
Workplace Health, Safety & Compensation Commission of New Brunswick, 1 Portland St., PO Box 160, Saint John, NB E2L 3X9
506-632-2200, 800-222-9775, communications@ws-ts.nb.ca

Newfoundland & Labrador

Newfoundland & Labrador Department of Health & Community Services, West Block, Confederation Bldg., PO Box 8700, St. John's, NL A1B 4J6
709-729-4984, healthinfo@gov.nl.ca
Newfoundland & Labrador Health Boards Association, Beothuck Bldg., 20 Crosbie Pl., 2nd Fl., St. John's, NL A1B 3Y8
709-364-7701, Fax: 709-364-6460

Northwest Territories

Northwest Territories Department of Health & Social Services, Centre Square Tower, PO Box 1320, Yellowknife, NT X1A 2L9
Fax: 867-873-0266

Nunavut

Nunavut Territory Department of Culture, Language, Elders & Youth, PO Box 1000 800,Iqaluit, NU X0A 0H0
867-975-5500, Fax: 867-975-5504, 866-934-2035
Nunavut Territory Department of Health & Social Services, PO Box 1000 1000,Iqaluit, NU X0A 0H0
867-975-5766, Fax: 867-975-5705, 800-661-0833

Ontario

Cancer Care Ontario, 620 University Ave., 15th Fl., Toronto, ON M5G 2L7
416-971-9800, Fax: 416-971-6888
Consent & Capacity Board, 151 Bloor St. West, 10th Fl., Toronto, ON M5S 2T5
416-327-4142, Fax: 416-924-8873, 866-777-7391
Ontario Ministry of Health & Long-Term Care, Hepburn Block, 80 Grosvenor St., 10th Fl, Toronto, ON M7A 2C4
416-327-4327, 800-268-1153
Health Boards Secretariat, 151 Bloor St. West, 9th Fl., Toronto, ON M5S 2T5
416-327-8512, Fax: 416-327-8524, 866-282-2179
Medical Eligibility Committee, 370 Select Dr., PO Box 168, Kingston, ON K7M 8T4
613-536-3058
Ontario Mental Health Foundation, 441 Jarvis St., 2nd Fl., Toronto, ON M4Y 2G8
416-920-7721, Fax: 416-920-0026, grants@omhf.on.ca
Ontario Review Board, 151 Bloor St. West, 10th Fl., Toronto, ON M5S 2T5
416-327-8866, Fax: 416-327-8867, orb@ontario.ca
Pesticides Advisory Committee, 135 St. Clair Ave. West, 15th Fl., Toronto, ON M4V 1P5
416-314-9230, Fax: 416-314-9237
Trillium Gift of Life Network, #900, 522 University Ave., Toronto, ON M5G 1W7
416-363-4001, Fax: 416-363-4002, 800-263-2833

Prince Edward Island

BIO|FOOD|TECH, 101 Belvedere Ave., PO Box 2000, Charlottetown, PE C1A 7N8
902-368-5548, Fax: 902-368-5549, 877-368-5548, biofoodtech@biofoodtech.ca
Prince Edward Island Department of Health & Wellness, 105 Rochford St. North, 4th Fl., PO Box 2000, Charlottetown, PE C1A 7N8
902-368-6414, Fax: 902-368-4121
Health PEI, PO Box 2000, Charlottetown, PE C1A 7N8
902-368-6130, Fax: 902-368-6136, healthinput@gov.pe.ca

Quebec

Bureau du coroner, Édifice le Delta 2, #390, 2875, boul Laurier, Québec, QC G1V 5B1
418-643-1845, Fax: 418-643-6174, 866-312-7051, clientele.coroner@msp.gouv.qc.ca
Commissaire à la santé et du bien-être, #700, 1020, rte de l'Église, Québec, QC G1V 3V9
418-643-3040, Fax: 418-644-0654, csbe@csbe.gouv.qc.ca
Corporation d'hébergement du Québec, 2535, boul Laurier, 5e étage, Québec, QC G1V 4M3
418-644-3600, Fax: 418-644-3609, 877-747-9911, clientele.sante@siq.gouv.qc.ca
Fonds de la recherche en santé du Québec, #800, 500, rue Sherbrooke ouest, Montréal, QC H3A 3C6
514-873-2114, Fax: 514-873-8768
Institut national d'excellence en santé et en services sociaux, #10.083, 2021, av Union, Montréal, QC H3A 2S9
514-873-2563, Fax: 514-873-1369, inesss@inesss.qc.ca
Institut national de santé publique du Québec, 945, av Wolfe, Québec, QC G1V 5B3
418-650-5115, Fax: 418-646-9328, info@inspq.qc.ca
Modernisation des centres hospitaliers universitaires de Montréal, CHUM, CUSM, CHU Sainte-Justine, #10.049, 2021, rue Union, Montréal, QC H3A 2S9
514-864-9883, Fax: 514-873-7362, info.construction3chu@msss.gouv.qc.ca
Régie de l'assurance maladie du Québec, 1125, Grande Allée ouest, Québec, QC G1S 1E7
418-646-4636, 800-561-9749
Commission de la santé et de la sécurité du travail du Québec, 425, rue du Pont, CP 4900 Terminus,Québec, QC G1K 7S6
Fax: 418-266-4015, 866-302-2778
Ministère de la Santé et des Services sociaux, Direction des communications, 1075, ch Sainte-Foy, 16e étage, Québec, QC G1S 2M1
418-643-9395, Fax: 418-643-4768, regisseur.web@msss.gouv.qc.ca
Secrétariat à l'accès aux services en langue anglaise et aux communautés ethnoculturelles, #840, 2021, av Union, Montréal, QC H3A 2S9
514-873-5163, Fax: 514-873-9876
Urgences-santé Québec, 3232, rue Bélanger, Montréal, QC H1Y 3H5
514-723-5600, info@urgences-sante.qc.ca

Saskatchewan

Health Quality Council, 241, 111 Research Dr., Saskatoon, SK S7N 3R2
306-668-8810, Fax: 306-668-8820, info@hqc.sk.ca
Saskatchewan Health, T.C. Douglas Bldg., 3475 Albert St., Regina, SK S4S 6X6
306-787-0146, 800-667-7766, info@health.gov.sk.ca

Yukon Territory

Yukon Health & Social Services, PO Box 2703, Whitehorse, YT Y1A 2C6
867-667-3673, Fax: 867-667-3096, hss@gov.yk.ca

HEALTH & SAFETY

Canadian Centre for Occupational Health & Safety, 135 Hunter St. East, Hamilton, ON L8N 1M5
905-572-2981, Fax: 905-572-2206, 800-668-4284
Canadian Coast Guard, Centennial Towers, #6S018, 200 Kent St., Ottawa, ON K1A 0E6
613-993-0999, Fax: 613-990-1866, info@dfo-mpo.gc.ca
Canadian Environmental Assessment Agency, Place Bell Canada, 160 Elgin St., 22nd Fl., Ottawa, ON K1A 0H3
613-957-0700, Fax: 613-957-0862, 866-582-1884, info@ceaa-acee.gc.ca
Canadian Food Inspection Agency, 1400 Merivale Rd., Ottawa, ON K1A 0Y9
613-225-2342, Fax: 613-228-6601, 800-442-2342
Department of National Defence & the Canadian Forces, National Defence HQ, Major-General George R. Pearkes Bldg., 101 Colonel By Dr., Ottawa, ON K1A 0K2
613-995-2534, Fax: 613-992-4739, DNDRecruitment-RecrutementMDN@forces.gc.ca (Civilian Careers)
Hazardous Materials Information Review Commission, 427 Laurier Ave. West, 7th Fl., Ottawa, ON K1A 1M3
613-993-4331, Fax: 613-993-4686, hmirc-ccrmd@hc-sc.gc.ca
Health Canada, Tunney's Pasture, Ottawa, ON K1A 0K9
613-957-2991, Fax: 613-941-5366, 866-225-0709, info@hc-sc.gc.ca
Human Resources & Skills Development Canada, 140 Promenade du Portage, Gatineau, QC K1A 0J9
Transportation Safety Board of Canada, 200 Promenade du Portage, 4th Fl., Ottawa, ON K1A 1K8
819-994-3741, Fax: 819-997-2239, 800-387-3557

Alberta

Alberta Health, PO Box 1360 Main,Edmonton, AB T5J 2N3
780-427-7164, Fax: 780-427-1171, -310-0000
Alberta Human Services, Office of the Minister, Legislature Building, #224, 10800 - 97 Ave., Edmonton, AB T5K 2B6
780-644-5135, 866-644-5135
Occupational Health & Safety Council, Labour Building, 10808 - 99 Ave., 9th Fl., Edmonton, AB T5K 0G5
780-415-8690, 866-415-8690
Transportation Safety Board, North Office, Twin Atria Building, 4999 - 98 Ave., Main Fl., Edmonton, AB T6B 2X3
780-427-7178, Fax: 780-422-9739, -310-0000
Workers' Compensation Board, 9912 - 107 St., Edmonton, AB T5J 2S5
780-498-3999, Fax: 780-427-5863, 866-922-9221

British Columbia

British Columbia Ministry of Citizens' Services, PO Box 9594 Prov Govt,Victoria, BC V8W 9E2
250-952-7623, Fax: 250-952-7628, 800-663-7867, EnquiryBC@gov.bc.ca
British Columbia Ministry of Health, 1515 Blanshard St., Victoria, BC V8W 3C8
800-663-7100, hlth.health@gov.bc.ca
Workers' Compensation Board of British Columbia, PO Box 5350 Terminal,Vancouver, BC V6B 5L5
604-276-3100, Fax: 604-276-3247, 888-621-7233

Manitoba

Advisory Council on Workplace Safety & Health (SAFE Work), #200, 401 York Ave., Winnipeg, MB R3C 0P8
204-945-3446, Fax: 204-945-4556
Emergency Measures Organization, 405 Broadway Ave., 15th Floor, Winnipeg, MB R3C 3L6
204-945-4772, Fax: 204-945-4929, 888-267-8298, emo@gov.mb.ca
Manitoba Health, #100, 300 Carlton St., Winnipeg, MB R3B 3M9
204-786-7191, minhlt@leg.gov.mb.ca
Manitoba Immigration & Multiculturalism, Legislative Building, 317, 450 Broadway Ave., Winnipeg, MB R3C 0V8
204-945-4079, Fax: 204-945-8312, minlab@leg.gov.mb.ca

New Brunswick

New Brunswick Department of Health, PO Box 5100, Fredericton, NB E3B 5G8
506-457-4800, Fax: 506-453-5243, dh-ms@dh-ms.ca
New Brunswick Department of Post-Secondary Education, Training & Labour, Chestnut Complex, PO Box 6000,

Fredericton, NB E3B 5H1
506-453-2597, Fax: 506-453-3618, dpetlinfo@gnb.ca
Workplace Health, Safety & Compensation Commission of New Brunswick, 1 Portland St., PO Box 160, Saint John, NB E2L 3X9
506-632-2200, 800-222-9775, communications@ws-ts.nb.ca

Newfoundland & Labrador
Newfoundland & Labrador Department of Environment & Conservation, Confederation Bldg., West Block, 4th Fl., PO Box 8700, St. John's, NL A1B 4J6
709-729-2664, Fax: 709-729-6639, 800-563-6181, envcinquires@gov.nl.ca
Newfoundland & Labrador Department of Health & Community Services, West Block, Confederation Bldg., PO Box 8700, St. John's, NL A1B 4J6
709-729-4984, healthinfo@gov.nl.ca
Newfoundland & Labrador Workplace Health, Safety & Compensation Commission, 146 - 148 Forest Rd., PO Box 9000, St. John's, NL A1A 3B8
709-778-1000, Fax: 709-738-1714, 800-563-9000, general.inquiries@whscc.nl.ca

Northwest Territories
Northwest Territories Department of Health & Social Services, Centre Square Tower, PO Box 1320, Yellowknife, NT X1A 2L9
Fax: 867-873-0266
Northwest Territories & Nunavut Workers' Safety & Compensation Commission, Centre Square Tower, 5022 - 49th St., 5th Fl., PO Box 8888, Yellowknife, NT X1A 2R3
867-920-3888, Fax: 867-873-4596, 800-661-0792

Nova Scotia
Nova Scotia Emergency Management Office, PO Box 2581, Halifax, NS B3J 3N5
902-424-5620, Fax: 902-424-5376, 866-424-5620, emo@gov.ns.ca

Ontario
Ontario Ministry of Government Services, Ferguson Block, 77 Wellesley St. West, 8th Fl., Toronto, ON M7A 1N3
416-326-8555, 800-268-1142
Ontario Ministry of Health & Long-Term Care, Hepburn Block, 80 Grosvenor St., 10th Fl, Toronto, ON M7A 2C4
416-327-4327, 800-268-1153
Ontario Ministry of Labour, 400 University Ave., 14th Fl., Toronto, ON M7A 1T7
416-326-7160, 800-531-5551
Road User Safety Division, Bldg A, #191, 1201 Wilson Ave., Downsview, ON M3M 1J8
416-235-2999, Fax: 416-235-4153

Prince Edward Island
Prince Edward Island Department of Health & Wellness, 105 Rochford St. North, 4th Fl., PO Box 2000, Charlottetown, PE C1A 7N8
902-368-6414, Fax: 902-368-4121
Prince Edward Island Workers Compensation Board, 14 Weymouth St., PO Box 757, Charlottetown, PE C1A 7L7
902-368-5680, Fax: 902-368-5696, 800-237-5049

Quebec
Commission de la santé et de la sécurité du travail du Québec, 425, rue du Pont, CP 4900 Terminus,Québec, QC G1K 7S6
Fax: 418-266-4015, 866-302-2778
Ministère de la Santé et des Services sociaux, Direction des communications, 1075, ch Sainte-Foy, 16e étage, Québec, QC G1S 2M1
418-643-9395, Fax: 418-643-4768, regisseur.web@msss.gouv.qc.ca
Ministère de la Sécurité publique, Tour des Laurentides, 2525, boul Laurier, 5e étage, Québec, QC G1V 2L2
418-643-2112, Fax: 418-646-6168, 866-644-6826
Ministère du Travail, 200, ch Sainte-Foy, 5e étage, Québec, QC G1R 5S1
418-644-4545, Fax: 418-528-0559, 800-643-4817

Saskatchewan
Saskatchewan Health, T.C. Douglas Bldg., 3475 Albert St., Regina, SK S4S 6X6
306-787-0146, 800-667-7766, info@health.gov.sk.ca
Saskatchewan Labour Relations & Workplace Safety, #300, 1870 Albert St., Regina, SK S4P 4W1
306-787-7404, webmaster@lab.gov.sk.ca

Yukon Territory
Emergency Measures Organization, Combined Services Bldg., 2nd Fl., 60 Norseman Rd, Airport, Whitehorse, YT Y1A 2C6
867-667-5220, Fax: 867-393-6266, 800-661-0408, emo.yukon@gov.yk.ca
Yukon Health & Social Services, PO Box 2703, Whitehorse, YT Y1A 2C6
867-667-3673, Fax: 867-667-3096, hss@gov.yk.ca
Yukon Workers' Compensation Health & Safety Board, 401 Strickland St., Whitehorse, YT Y1A 5N8
867-667-5645, Fax: 867-393-6279, 800-661-0443, worksafe@gov.yk.ca

HEALTH CARE INSURANCE

Health Canada, Tunney's Pasture, Ottawa, ON K1A 0K9
613-957-2991, Fax: 613-941-5366, 866-225-0709, info@hc-sc.gc.ca

Alberta
Health Workforce Division, Telus Plaza NT, 10025 Jasper Ave., 10th Fl., Edmonton, AB T5J 1S6

British Columbia
Medical Services Commission, 1515 Blanshard St., 3rd Fl., Victoria, BC V8W 3C8
250-952-3073, Fax: 250-952-3131

Newfoundland & Labrador
Newfoundland & Labrador Department of Health & Community Services, West Block, Confederation Bldg., PO Box 8700, St. John's, NL A1B 4J6
709-729-4984, healthinfo@gov.nl.ca

Northwest Territories
Northwest Territories Department of Health & Social Services, Centre Square Tower, PO Box 1320, Yellowknife, NT X1A 2L9
Fax: 867-873-0266

Nunavut
Nunavut Territory Department of Health & Social Services, PO Box 1000 1000,Iqaluit, NU X0A 0H0
867-975-5766, Fax: 867-975-5705, 800-661-0833

Prince Edward Island
Prince Edward Island Department of Health & Wellness, 105 Rochford St. North, 4th Fl., PO Box 2000, Charlottetown, PE C1A 7N8
902-368-6414, Fax: 902-368-4121

Quebec
Régie de l'assurance maladie du Québec, 1125, Grande Allée ouest, Québec, QC G1S 1E7
418-646-4636, 800-561-9749

HEALTH SERVICES

See Also: Health Care Insurance; Occupational Safety
Canadian Centre for Occupational Health & Safety, 135 Hunter St. East, Hamilton, ON L8N 1M5
905-572-2981, Fax: 905-572-2206, 800-668-4284
Canadian Institutes of Health Research, 160 Elgin St., 9th Fl., Ottawa, ON K1A 0W9
613-941-2672, Fax: 613-954-1800, 888-603-4178, info@cihr-irsc.gc.ca
Health Canada, Tunney's Pasture, Ottawa, ON K1A 0K9
613-957-2991, Fax: 613-941-5366, 866-225-0709, info@hc-sc.gc.ca

Alberta
Alberta Health, PO Box 1360 Main,Edmonton, AB T5J 2N3
780-427-7164, Fax: 780-427-1171, -310-0000

British Columbia
British Columbia Ministry of Health, 1515 Blanshard St., Victoria, BC V8W 3C8
800-663-7100, hlth.health@gov.bc.ca
Medical Services Commission, 1515 Blanshard St., 3rd Fl., Victoria, BC V8W 3C8
250-952-3073, Fax: 250-952-3131

Manitoba
Manitoba Health, #100, 300 Carlton St., Winnipeg, MB R3B 3M9
204-786-7191, minhlt@leg.gov.mb.ca
Manitoba Healthy Child Office, 332 Bannatyne Ave., 3rd Fl., Winnipeg, MB R3A 0E2
204-945-2266, 888-848-0140, healthychild@gov.mb.ca
Manitoba Health Appeal Board, #4011, 300 Carlton St., Winnipeg, MB R3B 3M9
204-788-6704, Fax: 204-948-2024, 866-744-3257

New Brunswick
New Brunswick Department of Health, PO Box 5100, Fredericton, NB E3B 5G8
506-457-4800, Fax: 506-453-5243, dh-ms@dh-ms.ca

Newfoundland & Labrador
Newfoundland & Labrador Department of Health & Community Services, West Block, Confederation Bldg., PO Box 8700, St. John's, NL A1B 4J6
709-729-4984, healthinfo@gov.nl.ca

Northwest Territories
Northwest Territories Department of Health & Social Services, Centre Square Tower, PO Box 1320, Yellowknife, NT X1A 2L9
Fax: 867-873-0266

Nunavut
Nunavut Territory Department of Health & Social Services, PO Box 1000 1000,Iqaluit, NU X0A 0H0
867-975-5766, Fax: 867-975-5705, 800-661-0833

Prince Edward Island
Prince Edward Island Department of Health & Wellness, 105 Rochford St. North, 4th Fl., PO Box 2000, Charlottetown, PE C1A 7N8
902-368-6414, Fax: 902-368-4121
Health PEI, PO Box 2000, Charlottetown, PE C1A 7N8
902-368-6130, Fax: 902-368-6136, healthinput@gov.pe.ca

Quebec
Institut national de santé publique du Québec, 945, av Wolfe, Québec, QC G1V 5B3
418-650-5115, Fax: 418-646-9328, info@inspq.qc.ca
Ministère de la Santé et des Services sociaux, Direction des communications, 1075, ch Sainte-Foy, 16e étage, Québec, QC G1S 2M1
418-643-9395, Fax: 418-643-4768, regisseur.web@msss.gouv.qc.ca

Saskatchewan
Saskatchewan Health, T.C. Douglas Bldg., 3475 Albert St., Regina, SK S4S 6X6
306-787-0146, 800-667-7766, info@health.gov.sk.ca

HERITAGE RESOURCES

See Also: Land Resources; Parks
Canadian Heritage, 15 Eddy St., Gatineau, QC K1A 0M5
819-997-0055, 866-811-0055, info@pch.gc.ca
Parks Canada, 25 Eddy St., Gatineau, QC K1A 0M5
613-860-1251, 888-773-8888, information@pc.gc.ca

Manitoba
Manitoba Culture, Heritage & Tourism, Legislative Building, #118, 450 Broadway Ave., Winnipeg, MB R3C 0V8
204-945-3729, Fax: 204-945-5223, mincht@leg.gov.mb.ca
Heritage Grants Advisory Council, 213 Notre Dame Ave., 3rd Fl., Winnipeg, MB R3B 1N3
204-945-2213, Fax: 204-948-2086
Manitoba Heritage Council, 213 Notre Dame Ave., Main Fl., Winnipeg, MB R3B 1N3
204-945-2118, Fax: 204-948-2384, hrb@gov.mb.ca

Nova Scotia
Heritage Division, 1747 Summer St., Halifax, NS B3H 3A6
902-424-7344, Fax: 902-424-0560, 800-632-1114, heritage@gov.ns.ca

Nunavut
Nunavut Territory Department of Culture, Language, Elders & Youth, PO Box 1000 800,Iqaluit, NU X0A 0H0
867-975-5500, Fax: 867-975-5504, 866-934-2035

Ontario
Conservation Review Board, #1500, 655 Bay St., Toronto, ON M5G 1E5
416-212-6349, Fax: 416-326-6209, conservation.review.board@ontario.ca
Ontario Heritage Trust, 10 Adelaide St. East, Toronto, ON M5C 1J3
416-325-5000, Fax: 416-325-5071

Prince Edward Island
Child & Family Services, Jones Bldg., 11 Kent St., 2nd Fl., PO Box 2000, Charlottetown, PE C1A 7N8
902-368-5294

Quebec
Commission des biens culturels du Québec, Bloc A-RC, 225, Grande Allée est, Québec, QC G1R 5G5
418-643-8378, Fax: 418-643-8591, info@cbcq.gouv.qc.ca

Saskatchewan
Provincial Capital Commission, 4607 Dewdney Ave., Regina, SK S4T 1B7
306-787-9261

Yukon Territory
Yukon Tourism & Culture, 100 Hanson St., Whitehorse, YT Y1A 2C6
867-667-5036, Fax: 867-667-3546

HISTORY & ARCHIVES

Alberta
Recreation & Sport Development Division, Standard Life Centre, 10405 Jasper Ave., 9th Fl., Edmonton, AB T5J 4R7

Nova Scotia
Culture Division, #601, 1800 Argyle St., PO Box 456, Halifax, NS B3J 2R5
902-424-4510, Fax: 902-424-0710, culture@gov.ns.ca

HOSPITALS
See Also: Health Care Insurance

Alberta
Alberta Health, PO Box 1360 Main,Edmonton, AB T5J 2N3
780-427-7164, Fax: 780-427-1171, -310-0000,

British Columbia
British Columbia Ministry of Health, 1515 Blanshard St., Victoria, BC V8W 3C8
800-663-7100, hlth.health@gov.bc.ca

Hospital Appeal Board, 747 Fort St., 4th Fl., PO Box 9425 Prov Govt, Victoria, BC V8W 9V1
250-387-3464, Fax: 250-356-9923, 800-663-7867, hab@gov.bc.ca

Northwest Territories
Northwest Territories Department of Health & Social Services, Centre Square Tower, PO Box 1320, Yellowknife, NT X1A 2L9
Fax: 867-873-0266

Nunavut
Nunavut Territory Department of Health & Social Services, PO Box 1000 1000,Iqaluit, NU X0A 0H0
867-975-5766, Fax: 867-975-5705, 800-661-0833

Prince Edward Island
Prince Edward Island Department of Health & Wellness, 105 Rochford St. North, 4th Fl., PO Box 2000, Charlottetown, PE C1A 7N8
902-368-6414, Fax: 902-368-4121

Quebec
Ministère de la Santé et des Services sociaux, Direction des communications, 1075, ch Sainte-Foy, 16e étage, Québec, QC G1S 2M1
418-643-9395, Fax: 418-643-4768, regisseur.web@msss.gouv.qc.ca

HOUSING
Canada Mortgage & Housing Corporation, 700 Montreal Rd., Ottawa, ON K1A 0P7
613-748-2000, Fax: 613-748-2098, 800-668-2642, chic@cmhc-schl.gc.ca

Canadian Centre for Housing Technology, c/o National Research Council Canada, Building M-20, 1200 Montreal Rd., Ottawa, ON K1A 0R6
construction@nrc-cnrc.gc.ca

British Columbia
Local Government, PO Box 9490 Prov Govt,Victoria, BC V8W 9N7
250-356-6575, Fax: 250-387-7973

Newfoundland & Labrador
Newfoundland & Labrador Housing Corporation, Sir Brian Dunfield Bldg., 2 Canada Dr., PO Box 220, St. John's, NL A1C 5J2
709-724-3000, Fax: 709-724-3250

Nova Scotia
Nova Scotia Department of Service Nova Scotia & Municipal Relations, 1505 Barrington St., PO Box 216, Halifax, NS B3J 3K5
902-424-5200, Fax: 902-424-0581, 800-670-4357, askus@gov.ns.ca

Nunavut
Nunavut Territory Department of Community & Government Services, W.G. Brown Bldg., 4th Fl., PO Box 1000 700,Iqaluit, NU X0A 0H0
867-975-5400, Fax: 867-975-5305

HYDRO, ELECTRIC POWER
National Energy Board, 444 - 7 Ave. SW, Calgary, AB T2P 0X8
403-292-4800, Fax: 403-292-5503, 800-899-1265, info@neb-one.gc.ca

Alberta
Energy Resources Conservation Board, #1000, 250 - 5 Ave. SW, Calgary, AB T2P 0R4
403-297-8311, Fax: 403-297-7336, 855-297-8311, inquiries@ercb.ca; infoservices@ercb.ca; ADR@ercb.ca

British Columbia
British Columbia Hydro, 6911 Southpoint Dr., Burnaby, BC V3N 4X8
604-224-9376, 800-224-9376

Powertech Labs Inc., 12388 - 88 Ave., Surrey, BC V8W 7R7
604-590-7500, Fax: 604-590-6611

Manitoba
Manitoba Hydro, 360 Portage Ave., PO Box 815 Main,Winnipeg, MB R3C 2P4
204-474-3311, publicaffairs@hydro.mb.ca

Newfoundland & Labrador
Churchill Falls (Labrador) Corporation Limited, Hydro Place, 500 Columbus Dr., PO Box 12500, St. John's, NL A1B 4K7
709-737-1859, Fax: 709-737-1816

Newfoundland & Labrador Hydro, Hydro Place, 500 Columbus Dr., PO Box 12400, St. John's, NL A1B 4K7
709-737-1400, Fax: 709-737-1800, 888-737-1296, hydro@nlh.nl.ca

Nalcor Energy, 500 Columbus Dr., St. John's, NL A1E 2B2
709-737-1400, Fax: 709-737-1800

Twin Falls Power Corporation, PO Box 12500, St. John's, NL A1B 3T5

Northwest Territories
Northwest Territories Power Corporation, 4 Capital Dr., Hay River, NT X0E 1G2
867-874-5200, Fax: 867-874-5251, info@ntpc.com

Nova Scotia
Nova Scotia Utility & Review Board, Summit Place, 1601 Lower Water St., 3rd Fl., PO Box 1692 M,Halifax, NS B3J 3S3
902-424-4448, Fax: 902-424-3919, uarb.board@gov.ns.ca

Ontario
Hydro One Inc., North Tower, 483 Bay St., 15th Fl., Toronto, ON M5G 2P5
416-345-5000, Fax: 905-944-3251, 877-955-1155, customercommunications@hydroone.com

Independent Electricity System Operator, PO Box 4474 A,Toronto, ON M5W 4E5
905-403-6900, Fax: 905-403-6921, 888-448-7777, customer.relations@ieso.ca

Ontario Power Authority, #1600, 120 Adelaide St. West, Toronto, ON M5H 1T1
416-967-7474, Fax: 416-967-1947, 800-797-9604, info@powerauthority.on.ca

Ontario Power Generation, 700 University Ave., Toronto, ON M5G 1X6
416-592-2555, 877-592-2555, webmaster@opg.com

Quebec
Hydro-Québec, 75, boul René-Lévesque ouest, Montréal, QC H2Z 1A4
514-289-2211

Société d'énergie de la Baie-James, 888, de Maisonneuve est, 6e étage, Montréal, QC H2L 5B2
514-286-2020

Saskatchewan
Saskatchewan Power Corporation (SaskPower), 2025 Victoria Ave., Regina, SK S4P 0S1
306-566-3306, Fax: 800-757-6937, 888-757-6937

Yukon Territory
Yukon Energy Corporation, 2 Miles Canyon Rd., PO Box 5920, Whitehorse, YT Y1A 6S7
867-393-5300, 866-926-3749, communications@yukonenergy.ca

IMMIGRATION
See Also: Citizenship

Prince Edward Island
Island Investment Development Inc., 94 Euston St., 2nd Fl., Charlottetown, PE C1A 7M8
902-620-3628, Fax: 902-368-5886, peinominee@gov.pe.ca

IMPORTS
See Also: Trade

Canada Border Services Agency, Headquarters, 191 Laurier Ave. West, Ottawa, ON K1A 0L8
800-461-9999, Contact@cbsa.gc.ca; communications@ps.gc.ca (Public Safety)

INCOME SECURITY
See Also: Social Services

Yukon Territory
Yukon Health & Social Services, PO Box 2703, Whitehorse, YT Y1A 2C6
867-667-3673, Fax: 867-667-3096, hss@gov.yk.ca

INCORPORATION OF COMPANIES & ASSOCIATIONS

Alberta
Strategic Planning & Financial Services, Commerce Place, 10155 - 102 St., 13th Fl., Edmonton, AB T5J 4G8
780-422-8545

Yukon Territory
Yukon Community Services, PO Box 2703, Whitehorse, YT Y1A 2C6
867-667-5811, Fax: 867-393-6295, 800-661-0408, inquiry@gov.yk.ca

INDUSTRY
See Also: Business Development

Agriculture & Agri-Food Canada, 1341 Baseline Rd., Ottawa, ON K1A 0C5
613-773-1000, Fax: 613-773-1081, 855-773-0241, info@agr.gc.ca

Atlantic Canada Opportunities Agency, Blue Cross Centre, 644 Main St., 3rd Fl., PO Box 6051, Moncton, NB E1C 9J8
506-851-2271, Fax: 506-851-7403, 800-561-7862, information@acoa-apeca.gc.ca

Canada Mortgage & Housing Corporation, 700 Montreal Rd., Ottawa, ON K1A 0P7
613-748-2000, Fax: 613-748-2098, 800-668-2642, chic@cmhc-schl.gc.ca

Canadian Food Inspection Agency, 1400 Merivale Rd., Ottawa, ON K1A 0Y9
613-225-2342, Fax: 613-228-6601, 800-442-2342

Canadian International Development Agency, 200, Promenade du Portage, Gatineau, QC K1A 0G4
819-997-5456, Fax: 819-953-6088, 800-230-6349, info@acdi-cida.gc.ca

Canadian Nuclear Safety Commission, 280 Slater St., PO Box 1046 B,Ottawa, ON K1P 5S9
613-995-5894, Fax: 613-995-5086, 800-668-5284

Canadian Space Agency, John H. Chapman Space Centre, 6767, rte de l'Aéroport, Saint-Hubert, QC J3Y 8Y9
450-926-4800, Fax: 450-926-4352, promo@asc-csa.gc.ca

Canadian Tourism Commission, #1400, 1055 Dunsmuir St., PO Box 49230, Vancouver, BC V7X 1L2
604-638-8300

Communications Research Centre Canada, 3701 Carling Ave., PO Box 11490 H, Ottawa, ON K2H 8S2
613-991-3313, Fax: 613-998-5355, info@crc.gc.ca

Competition Bureau Canada, Place du Portage, Phase I, 50 Victoria St., Ottawa, ON K1A 0C9
819-997-4282, Fax: 819-997-0324, 800-348-5358

Competition Tribunal, Thomas D'Arcy McGee Bldg., #600, 90 Sparks St., Ottawa, ON K1P 5B4
613-957-3172, Fax: 613-957-3170, tribunal@ct-tc.gc.ca

Defence Construction Canada, Constitution Square, 350 Albert St., 19th Fl., Ottawa, ON K1A 0K3
613-998-9548, Fax: 613-998-1061, 800-514-3555, info@dcc-cdc.gc.ca

Enterprise Cape Breton Corporation, 70 Crescent St., PO Box 1750, Sydney, NS B1P 6T7
902-564-3600, Fax: 902-564-3825, 800-705-3926, information@ecbc-secb.gc.ca

Export Development Canada, 151 Slater St., Ottawa, ON K1A 1K3
613-598-2500, Fax: 613-598-3811, 800-267-8510

Farm Products Council of Canada, Building 59, Central Experimental Farm, 960 Carling Ave., Ottawa, ON K1A 0C6
613-759-1555, Fax: 613-759-1566, fpcc-cpac@agr.gc.ca
Fisheries & Oceans Canada, 200 Kent St., Ottawa, ON K1A 0E6
613-993-0999, Fax: 613-990-1866, info@dfo-mpo.gc.ca
Foreign Affairs & International Trade Canada, Enquiries Service, 125 Sussex Dr., Ottawa, ON K1A 0G2
613-944-4000, Fax: 613-996-9709, 800-267-8376, enqserv@international.gc.ca; travel@international.gc.ca
Hazardous Materials Information Review Commission, 427 Laurier Ave. West, 7th Fl., Ottawa, ON K1A 1M3
613-993-4331, Fax: 613-993-4686, hmirc-ccrmd@hc-sc.gc.ca

Indian Oil & Gas Canada, #100, 9911 Chiila Blvd., Tsuu T'ina (Sarcee), AB T2W 6H6
403-292-5625, Fax: 403-292-5618, ContactIOGC@inac-ainc.gc.ca
Industry Canada, C.D. Howe Building, 235 Queen St., Ottawa, ON K1A 0H5
613-954-5031, Fax: 613-954-2340, 800-328-6189, info@ic.gc.ca
National Energy Board, 444 - 7 Ave. SW, Calgary, AB T2P 0X8
403-292-4800, Fax: 403-292-5503, 800-899-1265, info@neb-one.gc.ca
National Research Council Canada, Building M-58, 1200 Montreal Rd., Ottawa, ON K1A 0R6
613-993-9101, Fax: 613-952-9907, 877-672-2672, info@nrc-cnrc.ca; media@nrc-cnrc.gc.ca
National Round Table on the Environment & Economy, #200, 344 Slater St., Ottawa, ON K1R 7Y3
613-992-7189, Fax: 613-992-7385, info@nrtee-trnee.ca
Natural Resources Canada, 580 Booth St., Ottawa, ON K1A 0E4
613-995-0947, Fax: 613-992-7211
Natural Sciences & Engineering Research Council of Canada, Constitution Square, Tower II, 350 Albert St., Ottawa, ON K1A 1H5
613-995-4273, Fax: 613-943-1624, marie-josee.duval@nserc-crsng.gc.ca
Standards Council of Canada, #200, 270 Albert St., Ottawa, ON K1P 6N7
613-238-3222, Fax: 613-569-7808, info@scc.ca
Western Economic Diversification Canada, Canada Place, #1500, 9700 Jasper Ave. NW, Edmonton, AB T5J 4H7
780-495-4164, Fax: 780-495-4557, 888-338-9378

Alberta

Alberta Agriculture & Rural Development, JG O'Donoghue Bldg., #100A, 7000 - 113th St., Edmonton, AB T6H 5T6
780-427-2727, -310-3276, duke@gov.ab.ca
Alberta Grains Council, JG O'Donoghue Bldg., 7000 - 113 St., 3rd Fl., Edmonton, AB T6H 5T6
780-427-7329, Fax: 780-422-9690
Alberta Innovates - Energy & Environmental Solutions, AMEC Place, #2540, 801 - 6th Ave. SW, Calgary, AB T2P 3W2
403-297-7089, ees@albertainnovates.ca
Alberta Livestock & Meat Agency, Ellwood Office Park South, #101, 1003 Ellwood Rd. SW, Edmonton, AB T6X 0B3
780-638-1699, Fax: 780-638-6495, info@almaltd.ca
Community, Learner & Industry Connections Division, Phipps-McKinnon Bldg., 10020 - 101A Ave., 5th Fl., Edmonton, AB T5J 3G2
Energy Resources Conservation Board, #1000, 250 - 5 Ave. SW, Calgary, AB T2P 0R4
403-297-8311, Fax: 403-297-7336, 855-297-8311, inquiries@ercb.ca; infoservices@ercb.ca; ADR@ercb.ca
Alberta Energy, North Petroleum Plaza, 9945 - 108 St., Edmonton, AB T5K 2G6
780-427-8050, Fax: 780-422-0698, -310-0000, Library.Energy@gov.ab.ca
Alberta Environment & Sustainable Resource Development, Oxbridge Place, 9820 - 106 St., Main Fl., Edmonton, AB T5K 2J6
780-427-2700, Fax: 780-422-4086, -310-0000, env.infocent@gov.ab.ca; srd.infocent@gov.ab.ca
Intergovernmental Relations, Commerce Place, 10155 - 102 St., 12th Fl., Edmonton, AB T5J 4G8
780-427-6543, Fax: 780-427-0939
Land Compensation Board, 1229 - 91 St. SW, Edmonton, AB T6X 1E9
srb.lcb@gov.ab.ca

British Columbia

Agricultural Land Commission, #133, 4940 Canada Way, Burnaby, BC V5G 4K6
604-660-7000, Fax: 604-660-7033, ALCBurnaby@Victoria1.gov.bc.ca
British Columbia Ministry of Agriculture, PO Box 9120 Prov Govt,Victoria, BC V8W 9E2
250-387-5121
British Columbia Farm Industry Review Board, 780 Blanshard St., PO Box 9129 Prov Govt, Victoria, BC V8W 9B5
250-356-8945, Fax: 250-356-5131, firb@gov.bc.ca
British Columbia Hydro, 6911 Southpoint Dr., Burnaby, BC V3N 4X8
604-224-9376, 800-224-9376,
British Columbia Utilities Commission, 900 Howe St., 6th Fl., PO Box 250, Vancouver, BC V6Z 2N3
604-660-4700, Fax: 604-660-1102, 800-663-1385, commission.secretary@bcuc.com
British Columbia Ministry of Citizens' Services, PO Box 9594 Prov Govt,Victoria, BC V8W 9E2
250-952-7623, Fax: 250-952-7628, 800-663-7867, EnquiryBC@gov.bc.ca
British Columbia Ministry of Energy, Mines, & Natural Gas (& Responsible for Housing), PO Box 9053 Prov Govt,Victoria, BC V8W 9E2
Forest Practices Board, 1675 Douglas St., 3rd Fl., PO Box 9905 Prov Govt, Victoria, BC V8W 9R1
250-213-4700, Fax: 250-213-4725, 800-994-5899, fpboard@gov.bc.ca
British Columbia Ministry of Forests, Lands & Natural Resource Operations, PO Box 9352 Prov Govt,Victoria, BC V8W 9M1
250-387-4809, 877-855-3222, FLNRO.MediaRequests@gov.bc.ca
British Columbia Ministry of Jobs, Tourism, & Skills Training (& Responsible for Labour), PO Box 9071 Prov Govt,Victoria, BC V8W 9E2
EnquiryBC@gov.bc.ca; GCPE.JTI.Media.Requests@gov.bc.ca
Oil & Gas Commission, #100, 10003 - 110 Ave., Fort St John, BC V1J 6M7
250-794-5200, Fax: 250-794-5375

Manitoba

Manitoba Aboriginal & Northern Affairs, Legislative Bldg, 344-450 Broadway, Winnipeg, MB R3C 0V8
204-945-3719, Fax: 204-945-8374, anaweb@gov.mb.ca
Advisory Council on Workplace Safety & Health (SAFE Work), #200, 401 York Ave., Winnipeg, MB R3C 0P8
204-945-3446, Fax: 204-945-4556
Agricultural Societies, 1129 Queens Ave., Brandon, MB R7A 1L9
204-726-6195, Fax: 204-726-6260
Manitoba Agriculture, Food & Rural Initiatives, Legislative Bldg., 165-450 Broadway, Winnipeg, MB R3C 0V8
204-945-3722, Fax: 204-945-3470, minagr@leg.gov.mb.ca
Manitoba Entrepreneurship, Training & Trade, #1000, 259 Portage Ave, Winnipeg, MB R3B 3P4
204-945-2475, Fax: 204-945-3977, minctt@leg.gov.mb.ca
Farm Lands Ownership Board, #812, Norquay Bldg., 401 York Ave., Winnipeg, MB R3C 0P8
204-945-3149, Fax: 204-945-1489, 800-282-8069
Farm Machinery & Equipment Board, Norquay Bldg., #812, 401 York Ave., Winnipeg, MB R3C 0P8
204-945-3856, Fax: 204-948-2844
Manitoba Hydro, 360 Portage Ave., PO Box 815 Main,Winnipeg, MB R3C 2P4
204-474-3311, publicaffairs@hydro.mb.ca
Manitoba Immigration & Multiculturalism, Legislative Building, 317, 450 Broadway Ave., Winnipeg, MB R3C 0V8
204-945-4079, Fax: 204-945-8312, minlab@leg.gov.mb.ca
Manitoba Agricultural Services Corporation, #100, 1525 First St. South, Brandon, MB R7A 7A1
204-726-6850, Fax: 204-726-6849, mailbox@masc.mb.ca
Manitoba Habitat Heritage Corporation, #200, 1555 St. James St., Winnipeg, MB R3H 1B5
204-784-4350, Fax: 204-784-7359, mhhc@mhhc.mb.ca
Taxicab Board, #200, 301 Weston St., Winnipeg, MB R3E 3H4
204-945-8919, Fax: 204-948-2315, Joan.Wilson@gov.mb.ca
Tourism Secretariat, 155 Carlton St., 7th Fl., Winnipeg, MB R3C 3H8
800-665-0040
Manitoba Workers' Compensation Board, 333 Broadway Ave., Winnipeg, MB R3C 4W3
204-954-4321, Fax: 204-954-4999, 800-362-3340, wcb@wcb.mb.ca

New Brunswick

New Brunswick Department of Agriculture, Aquaculture & Fisheries, Agricultural Research Station (Experimental Farm), PO Box 6000, Fredericton, NB E3B 5H1
506-453-2666, Fax: 506-453-7170, DAAF-MAAP@gnb.ca
New Brunswick Department of Environment & Local Government, Marysville Place, PO Box 6000, Fredericton, NB E3B 5H1
506-453-2690, Fax: 506-457-4994, elg/egl-info@gnb.ca
New Brunswick Department of Natural Resources, Hugh John Flemming Forestry Centre, PO Box 6000, Fredericton, NB E3B 5H1
506-453-3826, Fax: 506-444-4367, dnrweb@gnb.ca
New Brunswick Farm Products Commission, c/o Department of Agriculture, Aquaculture & Fisheries, PO Box 6000, Fredericton, NB E3B 5H1
506-453-3647, Fax: 506-444-5969
Regional Development Corporation, RDC Bldg., 836 Churchill Row, PO Box 428, Fredericton, NB E3B 5R4
506-453-2277, Fax: 506-453-7988
New Brunswick Research & Productivity Council, 921 College Hill Rd., Fredericton, NB E3B 6Z9
506-452-1212, Fax: 506-452-1395, info@rpc.ca
Workplace Health, Safety & Compensation Commission of New Brunswick, 1 Portland St., PO Box 160, Saint John, NB E2L 3X9
506-632-2200, 800-222-9775, communications@ws-ts.nb.ca

Newfoundland & Labrador

Newfoundland & Labrador Department of Fisheries & Aquaculture, Petten Bldg., 30 Strawberry Marsh Rd., PO Box 8700, St. John's, NL A1B 4J6
709-729-3723, Fax: 709-729-6082, fisheries@gov.nl.ca
Newfoundland & Labrador Housing Corporation, Sir Brian Dunfield Bldg., 2 Canada Dr., PO Box 220, St. John's, NL A1C 5J2
709-724-3000, Fax: 709-724-3250
Newfoundland & Labrador Hydro, Hydro Place, 500 Columbus Dr., PO Box 12400, St. John's, NL A1B 4K7
709-737-1400, Fax: 709-737-1800, 888-737-1296, hydro@nlh.nl.ca
Nalcor Energy, 500 Columbus Dr., St. John's, NL A1E 2B2
709-737-1400, Fax: 709-737-1800
Newfoundland & Labrador Department of Natural Resources, Natural Resources Bldg., 50 Elizabeth Ave., 7th Fl., PO Box 8700, St. John's, NL A1B 4J6
709-729-2920, Fax: 709-729-0059
Professional Fish Harvesters Certification Board, 368 Hamilton Ave., PO Box 8541, St. John's, NL A1B 3P2
709-722-8170, Fax: 709-722-8201, pfh@pfhcb.com
Newfoundland & Labrador Board of Commissioners of Public Utilities, Prince Charles Bldg., #E-210, 120 Torbay Rd., PO Box 21040, St. John's, NL A1A 5B2
709-726-8600, Fax: 709-726-9604, 866-782-0006, ito@pub.nf.ca

Northwest Territories

Northwest Territories Department of Environment & Natural Resources, PO Box 1320, Yellowknife, NT X1A 2L9
Highways & Marine, 4510 - 50 Ave., 2nd fl., PO Box 1320, Yellowknife, NT X1A 2L9
867-920-8771, Fax: 867-873-0288
Northwest Territories Department of Industry, Tourism & Investment, PO Box 1320, Yellowknife, NT X1A 2L9
Fax: 867-873-0306, info@iti.ca
Northwest Territories Power Corporation, 4 Capital Dr., Hay River, NT X0E 1G2
867-874-5200, Fax: 867-874-5251, info@ntpc.com

Nova Scotia

Nova Scotia Department of Agriculture, 1741 Brunswick St., 3rd Fl., PO Box 2223, Halifax, NS B3J 3C4
902-424-4560, Fax: 902-424-4671
Nova Scotia Department of Natural Resources, Founder's Square, 1701 Hollis St., 3rd Fl., PO Box 698, Halifax, NS B3J 2T9
902-424-5935, Fax: 902-424-0594, 800-565-2224
Nova Scotia Farm Loan Board, PO Box 550, Truro, NS B2N 5E3
902-893-6506, Fax: 902-895-7693, flb@gov.ns.ca
Nova Scotia Utility & Review Board, Summit Place, 1601 Lower Water St., 3rd Fl., PO Box 1692 M,Halifax, NS B3J 3S3
902-424-4448, Fax: 902-424-3919, uarb.board@gov.ns.ca

Nunavut

Nunavut Territory Department of Economic Development & Transportation, Bldg. 1104 A, Inuksugait Plaza, PO Box 1000 1500,Iqaluit, NU X0A 0H0
867-975-7800, Fax: 867-975-7870, 888-975-5999, edt@gov.nu.ca

Ontario

Agricorp, 1 Stone Rd. West, 3rd Fl., PO Box 3660 Central, Guelph, ON N1H 8M4
Fax: 519-826-4118, 888-247-4999, contact@agricorp.com

Agricultural Research Institute of Ontario, 1 Stone Rd. West, 2nd Fl., Guelph, ON N1G 4Y2
519-826-4554, 888-466-2372, research.omafra@ontario.ca

Ontario Ministry of Agriculture, Food & Rural Affairs, Ontario Government Bldg., 1 Stone Rd. West, Guelph, ON N1G 4Y2
519-826-3100, 888-466-2372

Building Code Commission, 777 Bay St., 2nd Fl., Toronto, ON M5G 2E5
416-585-6666, Fax: 416-585-7531, codeinfo@ontario.ca

Building Materials Evaluation Commission, 777 Bay St., 2nd Fl., Toronto, ON M5G 2E5
416-585-4234, Fax: 416-585-7531

Ontario Ministry of Consumer Services, Mowat Block, 900 Bay St., 6th Fl., Toronto, ON M7A 1L2
416-327-8300, Fax: 416-326-1947, 866-665-0662, infomcs@ontario.ca; consumer@ontario.ca

Ontario Ministry of Economic Development, Trade & Employment, Hearst Block, 900 Bay St., 8th Fl., Toronto, ON M7A 2E1
416-325-6666, Fax: 416-325-6688, 866-668-4249, info@edt.gov.on.ca

Ontario Ministry of Environment, 135 St. Clair Ave. West, Toronto, ON M4V 1P5
416-325-4000, Fax: 416-325-3159, 800-565-4923, picemail.moe@ontario.ca

Environmental Commissioner of Ontario, #605, 1075 Bay St., Toronto, ON M5S 2B1
416-325-3377, Fax: 416-325-3370, 800-701-6454, commissioner@eco.on.ca

Environmental Sciences & Standards Division, 135 St. Clair Ave. West, 14th Fl., Toronto, ON M4V 1P5
Fax: 416-314-6358

Ontario Ministry of Government Services, Ferguson Block, 77 Wellesley St. West, 8th Fl., Toronto, ON M7A 1N3
416-326-8555, 800-268-1142,

Hydro One Inc., North Tower, 483 Bay St., 15th Fl., Toronto, ON M5G 2P5
416-345-5000, Fax: 905-944-3251, 877-955-1155, customercommunications@hydroone.com

Independent Electricity System Operator, PO Box 4474 A,Toronto, ON M5W 4E5
905-403-6900, Fax: 905-403-6921, 888-448-7777, customer.relations@ieso.ca

Ontario Ministry of Labour, 400 University Ave., 14th Fl., Toronto, ON M7A 1T7
416-326-7160, 800-531-5551

Ontario Ministry of Municipal Affairs & Housing, College Park, 777 Bay St., 17th Fl., Toronto, ON M5G 2E5
416-585-7041, Fax: 416-585-6470, 866-220-2290, mininfo.mah@ontario.ca

Ontario Ministry of Natural Resources, 300 Water St., PO Box 7000, Peterborough, ON K9J 8M5
705-755-2000, Fax: 705-755-1677, 800-667-1940, mnr.nric.mnr@ontario.ca

Ontario Ministry of Northern Development & Mines, 159 Cedar St., Sudbury, ON P3E 6A5
705-670-5755, Fax: 705-670-5818, 888-415-9845

Office of the Employer Advisor, #704, 151 Bloor St. West., Toronto, ON M5S 1S4
416-327-0020, Fax: 416-327-0726, 800-387-0774

Ontario Media Development Corporation, South Tower, #501, 175 Bloor St. East, Toronto, ON M4W 3R8
416-314-6858, Fax: 416-314-6876, reception@omdc.on.ca

Ontario Power Generation, 700 University Ave., Toronto, ON M5G 1X6
416-592-2555, 877-592-2555, webmaster@opg.com

Ontario Ministry of Rural Affairs, c/o Ministry of Agriculture & Food, 1 Stone Rd. West, Guelph, ON N1G 4Y2
519-826-3100, Fax: 519-826-4335, 888-466-2372, about.omafra@ontario.ca

Ontario Ministry of Tourism, Culture & Sport, Hearst Block, 900 Bay St., 9th Fl., Toronto, ON M7A 2E1
416-326-9326, Fax: 416-314-7854, 888-997-9015

Workplace Safety & Insurance Board, 200 Front St. West, Ground Fl., Toronto, ON M5V 3J1
416-344-1000, Fax: 416-344-4684, 800-387-0750, wsibcomm@wsib.on.ca; prevention@wsib.on.ca (training programs)

Prince Edward Island

Advisory Council on the Status of Women, Sherwood Business Centre, 161 St. Peter's Rd., Main Level, PO Box 2000, Charlottetown, PE C1A 7N8
902-368-4510, Fax: 902-368-3269, peistatusofwomen@eastlink.ca; info@peistatusofwomen.ca

Agricultural Insurance Corporation, 29 Indigo Cres., PO Box 1600, Charlottetown, PE C1A 7N3
902-368-4842, Fax: 902-368-6677

Prince Edward Island Department of Agriculture & Forestry, Jones Bldg., 11 Kent St., PO Box 2000, Charlottetown, PE C1A 7N8
902-368-4880, Fax: 902-368-4857

Anne of Green Gables Licensing Authority Inc., 94 Euston St., PO Box 910, Charlottetown, PE C1A 7L9
902-569-7787, Fax: 902-368-6301, kobaker@gov.pe.ca; aggla@bellnet.ca

BIO|FOOD|TECH, 101 Belvedere Ave., PO Box 2000, Charlottetown, PE C1A 7N8
902-368-5548, Fax: 902-368-5549, 877-368-5548, biofoodtech@biofoodtech.ca

Charlottetown Area Development Corporation, 4 Pownal St., PO Box 786, Charlottetown, PE C1A 7L9
902-892-5341, Fax: 902-368-1935

Grain Elevators Corporation, 7 Gerald McCarville Dr., PO Box 250, Kensington, PE C0B 1M0
902-836-8935, Fax: 902-836-8926

Housing, Seniors & Corporate Support, Jones Bldg., 11 Kent St., 2nd Fl., PO Box 2000, Charlottetown, PE C1A 7N8
Fax: 902-894-0242

Prince Edward Island Department of Innovation & Advanced Learning, Shaw Bldg., 105 Rochford St., 5th Fl., PO Box 2000, Charlottetown, PE C1A 7N8
902-368-4240, Fax: 902-368-4242

Innovation PEI, 94 Euston St., PO Box 910, Charlottetown, PE C1A 7L9
902-368-6300, Fax: 902-368-6301, 800-563-3734, innovation@gov.pe.ca

Prince Edward Island Workers Compensation Board, 14 Weymouth St., PO Box 757, Charlottetown, PE C1A 7L7
902-368-5680, Fax: 902-368-5696, 800-237-5049

SkillsPEI, Atlantic Technology Centre, #212, 90 University Ave., Charlottetown, PE C1A 4K9
902-368-6290, Fax: 902-368-6340, 877-491-4766

Prince Edward Island Department of Transportation & Infrastructure Renewal, Jones Bldg., 11 Kent St., 3rd Fl., PO Box 2000, Charlottetown, PE C1A 7N8
902-368-5100, Fax: 902-368-5395

Quebec

Agence de l'efficacité énergétique, #B406, 5700, 4e av ouest, Québec, QC G1H 6R1
418-627-6379, Fax: 418-643-5828, 877-727-6655, efficaciteenergetique@mrn.gouv.qc.ca

Ministère de l'Agriculture, des Pêcheries et de l'Alimentation, 200, ch Sainte-Foy, Québec, QC G1R 4X6
418-380-2110, 888-222-6272

Centre de recherche industrielle du Québec, 333, rue Franquet, Québec, QC G1P 4C7
418-659-1550, 800-667-2386, infocriq@criq.qc.ca

Comité conjoint de chasse, de pêche et de piégeage, #C220, 383 rue Saint-Jacques, Montréal, QC H2Y 1N9
514-284-2151, Fax: 514-284-0039, infohftcc@cccpp-hftcc.com

Commission de protection du territoire agricole du Québec, 200, ch Ste-Foy, 2e étage, Québec, QC G1R 4X6
418-643-3314, Fax: 418-643-2261, 800-667-5294, info@cptaq.gouv.qc.ca

Conseil consultatif du travail et de la main d'oeuvre, #17.100, 500, boul René-Lévesque ouest, Montréal, QC H2Z 1W7
514-873-2880, Fax: 514-873-1129, cctm@cctm.gouv.qc.ca

Ministère de la Culture et Communications, 225, Grande Allée est, Québec, QC G1R 5G5
888-380-8882

Ministère du Développement durable, de l'Environnement, de la Faune, et des Parcs, Édifice Marie-Guyart, 675, boul René-Lévesque est, 29e étage, Québec, QC G1R 5V7
418-521-3911, Fax: 418-643-4143, 800-561-1616, info@mddep.gouv.qc.ca

Ministère du Développement économique, de l'Innovation et de l'Exportation, 710, place D'Youville, 3e étage, Québec, QC G1R 4Y4
418-691-5950, Fax: 418-644-0118, 866-680-1884

Hydro-Québec, 75, boul René-Lévesque ouest, Montréal, QC H2Z 1A4
514-289-2211

Innovatech Québec, #410, 888, rue St-Jean, Québec, QC G1R 5H6
418-528-9770, Fax: 418-528-9783, 866-605-1676

La financière agricole de Québec, 1400, boul de la Rive-Sud, Saint-Romuald, QC G6W 8K7
418-838-5602, Fax: 418-833-3871, 800-749-3646, financiereagricole@fadq.qc.ca

Régie des marchés agricoles et alimentaires du Québec, 201, boul Crémazie est, 5e étage, Montréal, QC H2M 1L3
514-873-4024, Fax: 514-873-3984

Régie du bâtiment du Québec, 545, boul Crémazie est, 4e étage, Montréal, QC H2M 2V2
514-873-0976, Fax: 514-864-2903, 800-361-0761, crc@rbq.gouv.qc.ca

Société québécoise de récupération et de recyclage, #200, 420, boul Charest est, Québec, QC G1K 8M4
418-643-0394, Fax: 418-643-6507, 866-523-8290, info@recyc-quebec.gouv.qc.ca

Ministère du Tourisme, #400, 900, boul René-Lévesque est, Québec, QC G1R 2B5
418-643-5959, Fax: 418-646-8723, 800-482-2433

Saskatchewan

Agri-Food Council, #302, 3085 Albert St., Regina, SK S4S 0B1
306-787-5978, Fax: 306-787-5134, corey.ruud@gov.sk.ca

Energy & Resources, #300, 2103 - 11th Ave., Regina, SK S4P 3Z8
306-787-2528

Farm Stress Unit, #125, 3085 Albert St., Regina, SK S4S 0B1
306-787-5196, Fax: 306-798-3042, 800-667-4442

Labour Relations Board, #1600, 1920 Broad St., Regina, SK S4P 3V2
306-787-2406, Fax: 306-787-2664

Prairie Agricultural Machinery Institute, Hwy 5 West, PO Box 1150, Humboldt, SK S0K 2A0
306-682-2555, Fax: 306-682-5080, 800-567-7264, humboldt@pami.ca

Saskatchewan Agriculture, Walter Scott Bldg., 3085 Albert St., Regina, SK S4S 0B1
866-457-2377, aginfo@gov.sk.ca

Saskatchewan Crop Insurance Corporation, 484 Prince William Dr., PO Box 3000, Melville, SK S0A 2P0
306-728-7200, Fax: 306-728-7202, 888-935-0000, customer.service@scic.gov.sk.ca

Saskatchewan Environment, 3211 Albert St., 2nd Fl., Regina, SK S4S 5W6
306-787-2584, Fax: 306-787-9544, 800-567-4224, Centre.Inquiry@gov.sk.ca

Saskatchewan Lands Appeal Board, #202, 3085 Albert St., Regina, SK S4S 0B1
306-787-4693, Fax: 306-787-1315, Donald.Brooks@gov.sk.ca

Saskatchewan Power Corporation (SaskPower), 2025 Victoria Ave., Regina, SK S4P 0S1
306-566-3306, Fax: 800-757-6937, 888-757-6937

Saskatchewan Water Corporation (SaskWater), #200, 111 Fairford St. East, Moose Jaw, SK S6H 1C8
Fax: 306-694-3207, 888-230-1111, comm@saskwater.com; customerservice@saskwater.com

Saskatchewan Workers' Compensation Board, #200, 1881 Scarth St., Regina, SK S4P 4L1
306-787-4370, Fax: 306-787-4311, 800-667-7590, internet_clientsvc@wcbsask.com

SaskEnergy Incorporated, 1777 Victoria Ave., Regina, SK S4P 4K5
306-777-9225, 800-567-8899

Yukon Territory

Yukon Development Corporation, #2 Miles Canyon Rd., PO Box 5920, Whitehorse, YT Y1A 6S7
867-393-5337, Fax: 867-393-5401

Yukon Economic Development, PO Box 2703, Whitehorse, YT Y1A 2C6
867-393-7191, Fax: 867-393-6412, 800-661-0408, ecdev@gov.yk.ca

Yukon Environment, PO Box 2703, Whitehorse, YT Y1A 2C6
867-667-5652, Fax: 867-393-7197, environment.yukon@gov.yk.ca

Parks, PO Box 2703 V-4, Whitehorse, YT Y1A 2C6
867-667-5648, Fax: 867-393-6223, 800-661-0408, yukon.parks@gov.yk.ca

Yukon Tourism & Culture, 100 Hanson St., Whitehorse, YT Y1A 2C6
867-667-5036, Fax: 867-667-3546

INDUSTRY & TRADE

Atlantic Canada Opportunities Agency, Blue Cross Centre, 644 Main St., 3rd Fl., PO Box 6051, Moncton, NB E1C 9J8

506-851-2271, Fax: 506-851-7403, 800-561-7862, information@acoa-apeca.gc.ca
Business Development Bank of Canada, #400, 5, Place Ville-Marie, Montréal, QC H3B 5E7
514-283-5904, Fax: 514-283-5626, 877-232-2269
Defence Construction Canada, Constitution Square, 350 Albert St., 19th Fl., Ottawa, ON K1A 0K3
613-998-9548, Fax: 613-998-1061, 800-514-3555, info@dcc-cdc.gc.ca
Export Development Canada, 151 Slater St., Ottawa, ON K1A 1K3
613-598-2500, Fax: 613-598-3811, 800-267-8510
Foreign Affairs & International Trade Canada, Enquiries Service, 125 Sussex Dr., Ottawa, ON K1A 0G2
613-944-4000, Fax: 613-996-9709, 800-267-8376, enqserv@international.gc.ca; travel@international.gc.ca
Industry Canada, C.D. Howe Building, 235 Queen St., Ottawa, ON K1A 0H5
613-954-5031, Fax: 613-954-2340, 800-328-6189, info@ic.gc.ca
Market & Industry Services Branch, Tower 5, 1341 Baseline Rd., Ottawa, ON K1A 0C5
613-759-1000, Fax: 613-773-1711
Standards Council of Canada, #200, 270 Albert St., Ottawa, ON K1P 6N7
613-238-3222, Fax: 613-569-7808, info@scc.ca
Western Economic Diversification Canada, Canada Place, #1500, 9700 Jasper Ave. NW, Edmonton, AB T5J 4H7
780-495-4164, Fax: 780-495-4557, 888-338-9378

British Columbia

Timber Export Advisory Committee, PO Box 9514 Prov Govt, Victoria, BC V8W 9C2
250-387-8916, Fax: 250-387-5050

Manitoba

Manitoba Entrepreneurship, Training & Trade, #1000, 259 Portage Ave, Winnipeg, MB R3B 3P4
204-945-2475, Fax: 204-945-3977, minctt@leg.gov.mb.ca

New Brunswick

Regional Development Corporation, RDC Bldg., 836 Churchill Row, PO Box 428, Fredericton, NB E3B 5R4
506-453-2277, Fax: 506-453-7988

Northwest Territories

Northwest Territories Department of Environment & Natural Resources, PO Box 1320, Yellowknife, NT X1A 2L9

Nova Scotia

Nova Scotia Department of Agriculture, 1741 Brunswick St., 3rd Fl., PO Box 2223, Halifax, NS B3J 3C4
902-424-4560, Fax: 902-424-4671
Workers' Compensation Board of Nova Scotia, 5668 South St., PO Box 1150, Halifax, NS B3J 2Y2
902-491-8999, Fax: 902-491-8002, 800-870-3331, info@wcb.gov.ns.ca

Ontario

Ontario Ministry of Economic Development, Trade & Employment, Hearst Block, 900 Bay St., 8th Fl., Toronto, ON M7A 2E1
416-325-6666, Fax: 416-325-6688, 866-668-4249, info@edt.gov.on.ca
Ontario Ministry of Northern Development & Mines, 159 Cedar St., Sudbury, ON P3E 6A5
705-670-5755, Fax: 705-670-5818, 888-415-9845

Prince Edward Island

Prince Edward Island Department of Innovation & Advanced Learning, Shaw Bldg., 105 Rochford St., 5th Fl., PO Box 2000, Charlottetown, PE C1A 7N8
902-368-4240, Fax: 902-368-4242

Quebec

Commission des lésions professionnelles, #700, 900, Place d'Youville, Québec, QC G1R 3P7
418-644-7777, Fax: 418-644-6443, 800-463-1591
Innovatech Québec, #410, 888, rue St-Jean, Québec, QC G1R 5H6
418-528-9770, Fax: 418-528-9783, 866-605-1676

Saskatchewan

Energy & Resources, #300, 2103 - 11th Ave., Regina, SK S4P 3Z8
306-787-2528

Yukon Territory

Yukon Development Corporation, #2 Miles Canyon Rd., PO Box 5920, Whitehorse, YT Y1A 6S7
867-393-5337, Fax: 867-393-5401

INFORMATION RESOURCES

Industry Canada, C.D. Howe Building, 235 Queen St., Ottawa, ON K1A 0H5
613-954-5031, Fax: 613-954-2340, 800-328-6189, info@ic.gc.ca
Mapping Services Branch - Geomatics Canada, 615 Booth St., Ottawa, ON K1A 0E9
613-995-4945, Fax: 613-995-8737
National Research Council Canada - Canada Institute for Scientific & Technical Information, Building M-55, 1200 Montreal Rd., Ottawa, ON K1A 0R6
613-998-8544, Fax: 613-993-7619, 800-668-1222
Public Works & Government Services Canada, Place du Portage, Phase III, 11, rue Laurier, Ottawa, ON K1A 0S5
questions@tpsgc-pwgsc.gc.ca
Statistics Canada, R.H. Coats Bldg., Tunney's Pasture, 150 Tunney's Pasture Driveway, Ottawa, ON K1A 0T6
613-951-8116, Fax: 877-287-4369, 800-263-1136, infostats@statcan.ca

Nova Scotia

Geomatics Centre, 160 Willow St., Amherst, NS B4H 3W5
902-667-7231, Fax: 902-667-6008, 800-798-0706, geoinfo@gov.ns.ca

Ontario

Ontario Geographic Names Board, Robinson Place, 300 Water St., 2nd Fl., PO Box 7000, Peterborough, ON K9J 8M5
705-755-2132
Science & Information Resources Division, Roberta Bondar Pl., #400, 70 Foster Dr., Sault Ste Marie, ON P6A 6V5
705-755-2000, Fax: 705-755-2802, 800-667-1940

Saskatchewan

Saskatchewan Conservation Data Centre, 3211 Albert St., Regina, SK S4S 5W6
306-787-9038, Fax: 306-787-9544

INSURANCE (LIFE, FIRE, PROPERTY)

See Also: Automobile Insurance; Health Care Insurance

Manitoba

Manitoba Agricultural Services Corporation, #100, 1525 First St. South, Brandon, MB R7A 7A1
204-726-6850, Fax: 204-726-6849, mailbox@masc.mb.ca

Prince Edward Island

Agricultural Insurance Corporation, 29 Indigo Cres., PO Box 1600, Charlottetown, PE C1A 7N3
902-368-4842, Fax: 902-368-6677

Saskatchewan

Saskatchewan Crop Insurance Corporation, 484 Prince William Dr., PO Box 3000, Melville, SK S0A 2P0
306-728-7200, Fax: 306-728-7202, 888-935-0000, customer.service@scic.gov.sk.ca

INTERNATIONAL AFFAIRS

See Also: Trade
Canadian International Development Agency, 200, Promenade du Portage, Gatineau, QC K1A 0G4
819-997-5456, Fax: 819-953-6088, 800-230-6349, info@acdi-cida.gc.ca
Department of National Defence & the Canadian Forces, National Defence HQ, Major-General George R. Pearkes Bldg., 101 Colonel By Dr., Ottawa, ON K1A 0K2
613-995-2534, Fax: 613-992-4739, DNDRecruitment-RecrutementMDN@forces.gc.ca (Civilian Careers)
Foreign Affairs & International Trade Canada, Enquiries Service, 125 Sussex Dr., Ottawa, ON K1A 0G2
613-944-4000, Fax: 613-996-9709, 800-267-8376, enqserv@international.gc.ca; travel@international.gc.ca
International Development Research Centre, 150 Kent St., PO Box 8500, Ottawa, ON K1G 3H9
613-236-6163, Fax: 613-238-7230, info@idrc.ca

Alberta

Alberta International & Intergovernmental Relations, Commerce Place, 10155 - 102 St., 12th Fl., Edmonton, AB T5J 4G8
780-422-1510, -310-0000

Manitoba

Manitoba Local Government, #301, 450 Broadway Ave., Winnipeg, MB R3C 0V8
Fax: 204-945-1383, mnia@leg.gov.mb.ca

INTERNATIONAL AID

Canadian International Development Agency, 200, Promenade du Portage, Gatineau, QC K1A 0G4
819-997-5456, Fax: 819-953-6088, 800-230-6349, info@acdi-cida.gc.ca
International Development Research Centre, 150 Kent St., PO Box 8500, Ottawa, ON K1G 3H9
613-236-6163, Fax: 613-238-7230, info@idrc.ca

INUIT

See: Aboriginal Affairs
Canadian Northern Economic Development Agency, Ottawa, ON K1A 0H4
Fax: 866-817-3977, 800-567-9604, InfoNorth-InfoNord@CanNor.gc.ca

INVESTMENT

See Also: Business Development; Industry
Canada Economic Development for Québec Regions, Édifice Dominion Square, #900, 1255, rue Peel, Montréal, QC H3B 2T9
514-283-6412, Fax: 514-283-3302, 866-385-6412
Canada Savings Bonds, #900, 110 Yonge St., Toronto, ON M5C 1T4
416-952-1252, Fax: 416-952-1270, 800-575-5151, csb@csb.gc.ca
Canadian Northern Economic Development Agency, Ottawa, ON K1A 0H4
Fax: 866-817-3977, 800-567-9604, InfoNorth-InfoNord@CanNor.gc.ca
Federal Economic Development Agency for Southern Ontario, 101 Frederick St., 4th Fl., Kitchener, ON N2H 6R2
Fax: 519-571-5750, 866-593-5505
Finance Canada, L'esplanade Laurier, 140 O'Connor St., Ottawa, ON K1A 0G5
613-992-1573, Fax: 613-943-0938, finpub@fin.gc.ca
Industry Canada, C.D. Howe Building, 235 Queen St., Ottawa, ON K1A 0H5
613-954-5031, Fax: 613-954-2340, 800-328-6189, info@ic.gc.ca
Public Sector Pension Investment Board, #200, 440 Laurier Ave. West, Ottawa, ON K1R 7X6
613-782-3095, Fax: 613-782-6864, info@investpsp.ca

Alberta

Intergovernmental Relations, Commerce Place, 10155 - 102 St., 12th Fl., Edmonton, AB T5J 4G8
780-427-6543, Fax: 780-427-0939

British Columbia

Forestry Innovation Investment Ltd., #1200, 1130 West Pender St., Vancouver, BC V6E 4A4
604-685-7507, Fax: 604-685-5373, info@bcfii.ca

Northwest Territories

Northwest Territories Department of Industry, Tourism & Investment, PO Box 1320, Yellowknife, NT X1A 2L9
Fax: 867-873-0306, info@iti.ca

Prince Edward Island

Charlottetown Area Development Corporation, 4 Pownal St., PO Box 786, Charlottetown, PE C1A 7L9
902-892-5341, Fax: 902-368-1935
Prince Edward Island Lending Agency, Homburg Financial Tower, 98 Fitzroy St., 2nd Fl., Charlottetown, PE C1A 1R7
902-368-6200, Fax: 902-368-6201

LABOUR

Canadian Council of Directors of Apprenticeship, 140 Promenade du Portage, 5th Fl, Phase IV, Gatineau, QC K1A 0J9
819-953-7443, Fax: 819-994-0202, redseal-sceaurouge@hrsdc-rhdcc.gc.ca
Human Resources & Skills Development Canada, 140 Promenade du Portage, Gatineau, QC K1A 0J9
Merchant Seamen Compensation Board, Secretary, Merchant Seamen Compensation Board, Phase II, Place du Portage, 10th Fl., Ottawa, ON K1A 0J2
819-953-8001, Fax: 819-994-5368
Public Service Labour Relations Board, CD Howe Building, 240 Sparks St., 6th Fl., PO Box 1525 B, Ottawa, ON K1P 5V2

613-990-1800, Fax: 613-990-1849, 866-931-3454, mail.courrier@pslrb-crtfp.gc.ca

Alberta

Alberta Apprenticeship & Industry Training Board, Commerce Place, 10155 - 102nd St., 10th Fl., Edmonton, AB T5J 4L5
780-427-8765, Fax: 780-422-7376, -310-0000

Community, Learner & Industry Connections Division, Phipps-McKinnon Bldg., 10020 - 101A Ave., 5th Fl., Edmonton, AB T5J 3G2

Health Quality Council of Alberta, #210, 811 - 14 St. NW, Calgary, AB T2N 2A4
403-297-8162, Fax: 403-297-8258, info@hqca.ca

Alberta Human Services, Office of the Minister, Legislature Building, #224, 10800 - 97 Ave., Edmonton, AB T5K 2B6
780-644-5135, 866-644-5135

Labour Relations Board, Labour Building, 10808 - 99 Ave., 5th Fl., Edmonton, AB T5K 0G5
780-422-5926, Fax: 780-422-0970, 800-463-2572, alrbinfo@lab.gov.ab.ca

Occupational Health & Safety Council, Labour Building, 10808 - 99 Ave., 9th Fl., Edmonton, AB T5K 0G5
780-415-8690, 866-415-8690

British Columbia

British Columbia Labour Relations Board, Oceanic Plaza, #600, 1066 West Hastings St., Vancouver, BC V6E 3X1
604-660-1300, Fax: 604-660-1892, information@lrb.bc.ca

British Columbia Ministry of Citizens' Services, PO Box 9594 Prov Govt,Victoria, BC V8W 9E2
250-952-7623, Fax: 250-952-7628, 800-663-7867, EnquiryBC@gov.bc.ca

Employment Standards Tribunal, Oceanic Plaza, #650, 1066 West Hastings St., Vancouver, BC V6E 3X1
604-775-3512, Fax: 604-775-3372, registrar@bcest.bc.ca

Workers' Compensation Appeal Tribunal, #150, 4600 Jacombs Rd., Richmond, BC V6V 3B1
604-664-7800, Fax: 604-664-7898, 800-663-2782

Workers' Compensation Board of British Columbia, PO Box 5350 Terminal,Vancouver, BC V6B 5L5
604-276-3100, Fax: 604-276-3247, 888-621-7233

Manitoba

Advisory Council on Workplace Safety & Health (SAFE Work), #200, 401 York Ave., Winnipeg, MB R3C 0P8
204-945-3446, Fax: 204-945-4556,

Board of Electrical Examiners, #500, 401 York Ave, Winnipeg, MB R3C 0P8
204-945-3507, terry.rieger@gov.mb.ca

Manitoba Immigration & Multiculturalism, Legislative Building, 317, 450 Broadway Ave., Winnipeg, MB R3C 0V8
204-945-4079, Fax: 204-945-8312, minlab@leg.gov.mb.ca

Manitoba Workers' Compensation Board, 333 Broadway Ave., Winnipeg, MB R3C 4W3
204-954-4321, Fax: 204-954-4999, 800-362-3340, wcb@wcb.mb.ca

New Brunswick

Labour & Planning Division, Chestnut Complex, PO Box 6000, Fredericton, NB E3B 5H1
506-453-8202, Fax: 506-453-3038, dpetlinfo@gnb.ca

New Brunswick Department of Post-Secondary Education, Training & Labour, Chestnut Complex, PO Box 6000, Fredericton, NB E3B 5H1
506-453-2597, Fax: 506-453-3618, dpetlinfo@gnb.ca

Workplace Health, Safety & Compensation Commission of New Brunswick, 1 Portland St., PO Box 160, Saint John, NB E2L 3X9
506-632-2200, 800-222-9775, communications@ws-ts.nb.ca

Newfoundland & Labrador

Newfoundland & Labrador Workplace Health, Safety & Compensation Commission, 146 - 148 Forest Rd., PO Box 9000, St. John's, NL A1A 3B8
709-778-1000, Fax: 709-738-1714, 800-563-9000, general.inquiries@whscc.nl.ca

Northwest Territories

Northwest Territories Department of Education, Culture & Employment, PO Box 1320, Yellowknife, NT X1A 2L9
867-669-2399, Fax: 867-873-0431, 866-606-5627

Northwest Territories Apprenticeship, Trade & Occupations Certification Board, PO Box 1320, Yellowknife, NT X1A 2L9
867-873-7357, Fax: 867-873-0200

Northwest Territories & Nunavut Workers' Safety & Compensation Commission, Centre Square Tower, 5022 - 49th St., 5th Fl., PO Box 8888, Yellowknife, NT X1A 2R3
867-920-3888, Fax: 867-873-4596, 800-661-0792

Nova Scotia

Workers' Compensation Board of Nova Scotia, 5668 South St., PO Box 1150, Halifax, NS B3J 2Y2
902-491-8999, Fax: 902-491-8002, 800-870-3331, info@wcb.gov.ns.ca

Ontario

Ontario Ministry of Labour, 400 University Ave., 14th Fl., Toronto, ON M7A 1T7
416-326-7160, 800-531-5551

Office of the Employer Advisor, #704, 151 Bloor St. West., Toronto, ON M5S 1S4
416-327-0020, Fax: 416-327-0726, 800-387-0774

Office of the Worker Advisor, #1300, 123 Edward St., Toronto, ON M5G 1E2
416-325-8570, Fax: 416-325-4830, 800-435-8980

Ontario Labour Relations Board, 505 University Ave., 2nd Fl., Toronto, ON M5G 2P1
416-326-7500, Fax: 416-326-7531, 877-339-3335

Operations Division, 400 University Ave., 14th Fl., Toronto, ON M7A 1T7
416-326-7606, Fax: 416-212-4455

Pay Equity Commission, #300, 180 Dundas St. West, Toronto, ON M7A 2S6
416-314-1896, Fax: 416-314-8741, 800-387-8813

Workplace Safety & Insurance Board, 200 Front St. West, Ground Fl., Toronto, ON M5V 3J1
416-344-1000, Fax: 416-344-4684, 800-387-0750, wsibcomm@wsib.on.ca; prevention@wsib.on.ca (training programs)

Prince Edward Island

Advisory Council on the Status of Women, Sherwood Business Centre, 161 St. Peter's Rd., Main Level, PO Box 2000, Charlottetown, PE C1A 7N8
902-368-4510, Fax: 902-368-3269, peistatusofwomen@eastlink.ca; info@peistatusofwomen.ca

Prince Edward Island Workers Compensation Board, 14 Weymouth St., PO Box 757, Charlottetown, PE C1A 7L7
902-368-5680, Fax: 902-368-5696, 800-237-5049

Workers Compensation Appeal Tribunal, 161 St. Peters Rd., 1st Fl., PO Box 2000, Charlottetown, PE C1A 7N8

Quebec

Commission de l'équité salariale, 200, ch Ste-Foy, 4e étage, Québec, QC G1R 6A1
418-528-8765, Fax: 418-528-6999, 888-528-8765, equite.salariale@ces.gouv.qc.ca

Commission de la construction du Québec, 8485, av Christophe-Colomb, Montréal, QC H2M 0A7
888-842-8282

Commission des lésions professionnelles, #700, 900, Place d'Youville, Québec, QC G1R 3P7
418-644-7777, Fax: 418-644-6443, 800-463-1591

Commission des normes du travail, Hall Est, 400, boul Jean-Lesage, 7e étage, Québec, QC G1K 8W1
514-873-7061, 800-265-1414

Commission des relations du travail, 900, boul René-Lévesque est, 5e étage, Québec, QC G1R 6C9
418-643-3208, Fax: 418-643-8946, 866-864-3646, crtm@crt.gouv.qc.ca

Conseil consultatif du travail et de la main d'oeuvre, #17.100, 500, boul René-Lévesque ouest, Montréal, QC H2Z 1W7
514-873-2880, Fax: 514-873-1129, cctm@cctm.gouv.qc.ca

Régie du bâtiment du Québec, 545, boul Crémazie est, 4e étage, Montréal, QC H2M 2V2
514-873-0976, Fax: 514-864-2903, 800-361-0761, crc@rbq.gouv.qc.ca

Commission de la santé et de la sécurité du travail du Québec, 425, rue du Pont, CP 4900 Terminus,Québec, QC G1K 7S6
Fax: 418-266-4015, 866-302-2778

Ministère du Travail, 200, ch Sainte-Foy, 5e étage, Québec, QC G1R 5S1
418-644-4545, Fax: 418-528-0559, 800-643-4817

Saskatchewan

Labour Relations Board, #1600, 1920 Broad St., Regina, SK S4P 3V2
306-787-2406, Fax: 306-787-2664

Minimum Wage Board, #400, 1870 Albert St., Regina, SK S4P 4W1

Office of the Worker's Advocate, #300, 1870 Albert St., Regina, SK S4P 4W1
306-787-2456, Fax: 306-787-0249, 877-787-2456

Saskatchewan Labour Relations & Workplace Safety, #300, 1870 Albert St., Regina, SK S4P 4W1
306-787-7404, webmaster@lab.gov.sk.ca

Saskatchewan Workers' Compensation Board, #200, 1881 Scarth St., Regina, SK S4P 4L1
306-787-4370, Fax: 306-787-4311, 800-667-7590, internet_clientsvc@wcbsask.com

Yukon Territory

Yukon Workers' Compensation Health & Safety Board, 401 Strickland St., Whitehorse, YT Y1A 5N8
867-667-5645, Fax: 867-393-6279, 800-661-0443, worksafe@gov.yk.ca

LAND RESOURCES

See Also: Agriculture; Forest Resources; Parks

Natural Resources Canada, 580 Booth St., Ottawa, ON K1A 0E4
613-995-0947, Fax: 613-992-7211

Parks Canada, 25 Eddy St., Gatineau, QC K1A 0M5
613-860-1251, 888-773-8888, information@pc.gc.ca

Alberta

Land Use Secretariat, Centre West Building, 10035 - 108 St., Edmonton, AB T5J 3E1
780-644-7972, Fax: 780-644-1034, luf@gov.ab.ca

Special Areas Board, Special Areas Board Administration, 212 - 2nd Ave. West, PO Box 820, Hanna, AB T0J 1P0
403-854-5600, Fax: 403-854-5527, specarea@telus.net

British Columbia

Strategic Industry Partnerships Division, PO Box 9120 Prov Govt,Victoria, BC V8W 9B4
250-356-1122, Fax: 250-356-7279

Manitoba

Farm Lands Ownership Board, #812, Norquay Bldg., 401 York Ave., Winnipeg, MB R3C 0P8
204-945-3149, Fax: 204-945-1489, 800-282-8069

Manitoba Conservation Districts Commission, Secretariat c/o Planning & Coordination Branch, 123 Main St., PO Box 20000, Neepawa, MB R0J 1H0
204-476-7033, Fax: 204-476-7539

Manitoba Land Value Appraisal Commission, #1144, 363 Broadway, Winnipeg, MB R3C 3N9
204-945-5455, Fax: 204-948-2235

Northwest Territories

Northwest Territories Department of Environment & Natural Resources, PO Box 1320, Yellowknife, NT X1A 2L9

Northwest Territories Department of Municipal & Community Affairs, PO Box 1320, Yellowknife, NT X1A 2L9
867-873-7118, Fax: 867-873-0309,

Nunavut

Nunavut Territory Department of Environment, PO Box 1000 1300,Iqaluit, NU X0A 0H0
867-975-7700, Fax: 867-975-7742, environment@gov.nu.ca

Prince Edward Island

Prince Edward Island Department of Environment, Labour & Justice, Shaw Bldg. South, 95 Rochford St., 4th Fl., PO Box 2000, Charlottetown, PE C1A 7N8
902-368-6410, Fax: 902-368-6488

Quebec

Commission de protection du territoire agricole du Québec, 200, ch Ste-Foy, 2e étage, Québec, QC G1R 4X6
418-643-3314, Fax: 418-643-2261, 800-667-5294, info@cptaq.gouv.qc.ca

Foncier Québec, 5700, 4e av ouest, Québec, QC G1H 6R1
418-643-3582, Fax: 418-528-8721, 866-226-0977, assistance.clientele@mrnf.registrefoncier.gouv.qc.ca

Territoire, #A313, 5700, 4e av ouest, Québec, QC G1H 6R1
418-627-6256, Fax: 418-528-2075

Saskatchewan

Saskatchewan Lands Appeal Board, #202, 3085 Albert St., Regina, SK S4S 0B1
306-787-4693, Fax: 306-787-1315, Donald.Brooks@gov.sk.ca

Yukon Territory

Yukon Land Use Planning Council, #201, 307 Jarvis St., Whitehorse, YT Y1A 2H3
867-667-7397, Fax: 867-667-4624, ylupc@planyukon.ca

LAND TITLES

See Also: Real Estate

British Columbia

British Columbia Assessment Authority, #400, 3450 Uptown Blvd., Victoria, BC V8Z 0B9
250-595-6211, Fax: 250-595-6222, info@bcassessment.ca

LANDLORD & TENANT REGULATIONS

Prince Edward Island

Prince Edward Island Regulatory & Appeals Commission, National Bank Tower, #501, 134 Kent St., PO Box 577, Charlottetown, PE C1A 7L1
902-892-3501, Fax: 902-566-4076, 800-501-6268, info@irac.pe.ca

LANDS & SOILS

Aboriginal Affairs & Northern Development Canada, 10 Wellington St., North Tower, Gatineau, QC K1A 0H4
819-997-0380, Fax: 866-817-3977, 800-567-9604, infopubs@aadnc-aandc.gc.ca

Agriculture & Agri-Food Canada, 1341 Baseline Rd., Ottawa, ON K1A 0C5
613-773-1000, Fax: 613-773-1081, 855-773-0241, info@agr.gc.ca

Canada Centre for Remote Sensing - Geomatics Canada, 588 Booth St., Ottawa, ON K1A 0Y7
613-995-0947, Fax: 613-947-1382

Natural Resources Canada, 580 Booth St., Ottawa, ON K1A 0E4
613-995-0947, Fax: 613-992-7211

Alberta

Irrigation Council, Provincial Bldg., 200 - 5 Ave. South, 3rd Fl., Lethbridge, AB T1J 4L1
403-381-5176, Fax: 403-382-4406

Land Compensation Board, 1229 - 91 St. SW, Edmonton, AB T6X 1E9
srb.lcb@gov.ab.ca

British Columbia

British Columbia Ministry of Environment, PO Box 9339 Prov Govt,Victoria, BC V8W 9M1
250-387-1161, Fax: 250-387-5669, envmail@gov.bc.ca

Forest Practices Board, 1675 Douglas St., 3rd Fl., PO Box 9905 Prov Govt, Victoria, BC V8W 9R1
250-213-4700, Fax: 250-213-4725, 800-994-5899, fpboard@gov.bc.ca

Timber Export Advisory Committee, PO Box 9514 Prov Govt, Victoria, BC V8W 9C2
250-387-8916, Fax: 250-387-5050

New Brunswick

New Brunswick Department of Environment & Local Government, Marysville Place, PO Box 6000, Fredericton, NB E3B 5H1
506-453-2690, Fax: 506-457-4994, elg/egl-info@gnb.ca

New Brunswick Department of Natural Resources, Hugh John Flemming Forestry Centre, PO Box 6000, Fredericton, NB E3B 5H1
506-453-3826, Fax: 506-444-4367, dnrweb@gnb.ca

Newfoundland & Labrador

Newfoundland & Labrador Department of Service NL, PO Box 8700, St. John's, NL A1B 4J6
709-729-4834, servicenlinfo@gov.nl.ca

Soil, Plant & Feed Laboratory, 308 Brookfield Rd., PO Box 8700, St. John's, NL A1B 4J6
709-729-6738, Fax: 709-729-6734

Northwest Territories

Northwest Territories Department of Environment & Natural Resources, PO Box 1320, Yellowknife, NT X1A 2L9

Nova Scotia

Nova Scotia Department of Natural Resources, Founder's Square, 1701 Hollis St., 3rd Fl., PO Box 698, Halifax, NS B3J 2T9
902-424-5935, Fax: 902-424-0594, 800-565-2224

Prince Edward Island

Prince Edward Island Department of Environment, Labour & Justice, Shaw Bldg. South, 95 Rochford St., 4th Fl., PO Box 2000, Charlottetown, PE C1A 7N8
902-368-6410, Fax: 902-368-6488

Quebec

Ministère du Développement durable, de l'Environnement, de la Faune, et des Parcs, Édifice Marie-Guyart, 675, boul René-Lévesque est, 29e étage, Québec, QC G1R 5V7
418-521-3911, Fax: 418-643-4143, 800-561-1616, info@mddep.gouv.qc.ca

Territoire, #A313, 5700, 4e av ouest, Québec, QC G1H 6R1
418-627-6256, Fax: 418-528-2075

Saskatchewan

Saskatchewan Assessment Management Agency, #200, 2201 - 11th Ave., Regina, SK S4P 0J8
306-924-8000, Fax: 306-924-8070, 800-667-7262, info.request@sama.sk.ca

Yukon Territory

Carmacks Renewable Resource Council, PO Box 122, Carmacks, YT Y0B 1C0
867-863-6838, Fax: 867-863-6429, carmacksrrc@northwestel.net

Yukon Environment, PO Box 2703, Whitehorse, YT Y1A 2C6
867-667-5652, Fax: 867-393-7197, environment.yukon@gov.yk.ca

Selkirk Renewable Resources Council, PO Box 32, Pelly Crossing, YT Y0B 1P0
867-537-3937, Fax: 867-537-3939, selkirkrrc@yknet.yk.ca

Yukon Land Use Planning Council, #201, 307 Jarvis St., Whitehorse, YT Y1A 2H3
867-667-7397, Fax: 867-667-4624, ylupc@planyukon.ca

LAW & JUSTICE

Auditor General of Canada, 240 Sparks St., Ottawa, ON K1A 0G6
613-995-3708, Fax: 613-957-0474, 888-761-5953, communications@oag-bvg.gc.ca; infomedia@oag-bvg.gc.ca

Financial Transactions & Reports Analysis Centre of Canada, 234 Laurier Ave. West, 24th Fl., Ottawa, ON K1P 1H7
Fax: 613-943-7931, 866-346-8722, guidelines-lignesdirectrices@fintrac-canafe.gc.ca

International Joint Commission, 234 Laurier Ave. West, 22nd Fl., Ottawa, ON K1P 6K6
613-947-1420, Fax: 613-993-5583, beckhoffb@ottawa.ijc.org

Military Police Complaints Commission, 270 Albert St., 10th Fl., Ottawa, ON K1P 5G8
613-947-5625, Fax: 613-947-5713, 800-632-0566, commission@mpcc-cppm.gc.ca

Transportation Appeal Tribunal of Canada, #1201, 333 Laurier Ave. West, 12th Fl., Ottawa, ON K1A 0N5
613-990-6906, Fax: 613-990-9153, info@tatc.gc.ca

Transportation Safety Board of Canada, 200 Promenade du Portage, 4th Fl., Ottawa, ON K1A 1K8
819-994-3741, Fax: 819-997-2239, 800-387-3557

Alberta

Land Compensation Board, 1229 - 91 St. SW, Edmonton, AB T6X 1E9
srb.lcb@gov.ab.ca

Manitoba

Advisory Council on Workplace Safety & Health (SAFE Work), #200, 401 York Ave., Winnipeg, MB R3C 0P8
204-945-3446, Fax: 204-945-4556

Health Information Privacy Committee, #4043, 300 Carlton St., Winnipeg, MB R3B 3M9

Highway Traffic Board/Motor Transport Board, #200, 301 Weston St., Winnipeg, MB R3E 3H4
204-945-8912, Fax: 204-783-6529

License Suspension Appeal Board/Medical Review Committee, #200, 301 Weston St., Winnipeg, MB R3E 3H4
204-945-7350, Fax: 204-948-2682

Manitoba Film Classification Board, #216, 301 Weston St., Winnipeg, MB R3E 3H4
204-945-8962, Fax: 204-945-0890, 866-612-2399, MFCB@gov.mb.ca

Manitoba Land Value Appraisal Commission, #1144, 363 Broadway, Winnipeg, MB R3C 3N9
204-945-5455, Fax: 204-948-2235

Manitoba Workers' Compensation Board, 333 Broadway Ave., Winnipeg, MB R3C 4W3
204-954-4321, Fax: 204-954-4999, 800-362-3340, wcb@wcb.mb.ca

New Brunswick

New Brunswick Department of Public Safety, 364 Argyle St., PO Box 6000, Fredericton, NB E3B 5H1
506-453-3992, Fax: 506-453-3870, DPS-MSP.Information@gnb.ca

Workplace Health, Safety & Compensation Commission of New Brunswick, 1 Portland St., PO Box 160, Saint John, NB E2L 3X9
506-632-2200, 800-222-9775, communications@ws-ts.nb.ca

Northwest Territories

Assessment Appeal Tribunal of the Northwest Territories, #400, 5201 - 50th Ave., PO Box 1320, Yellowknife, NT X1A 2L9
867-873-7125, Fax: 867-873-0609

Territorial Board of Revision, #400, 5201 - 50th Ave., PO Box 1320, Yellowknife, NT X1A 2L9
867-873-7125, Fax: 867-873-0609

Northwest Territories & Nunavut Workers' Safety & Compensation Commission, Centre Square Tower, 5022 - 49th St., 5th Fl., PO Box 8888, Yellowknife, NT X1A 2R3
867-920-3888, Fax: 867-873-4596, 800-661-0792

Nova Scotia

Workers' Compensation Board of Nova Scotia, 5668 South St., PO Box 1150, Halifax, NS B3J 2Y2
902-491-8999, Fax: 902-491-8002, 800-870-3331, info@wcb.gov.ns.ca

Ontario

Association of Ontario Land Surveyors, 1043 McNicoll Ave., Toronto, ON M1W 3W6
416-491-9020, Fax: 416-491-2576, 800-268-0718

Ontario Ministry of Community Safety & Correctional Services, George Drew Bldg., 25 Grosvenor St., 18th Fl., Toronto, ON M7A 1Y6
416-326-5000, Fax: 416-326-0498, 866-517-0571, mcscs.feedback@ontario.ca

Environmental Sciences & Standards Division, 135 St. Clair Ave. West, 14th Fl., Toronto, ON M4V 1P5
Fax: 416-314-6358

Licence Appeal Tribunal, #530, 20 Dundas St. West, Toronto, ON M5G 2C2
416-314-4260, Fax: 416-314-4270, 800-255-2214

Ontario Civilian Police Commission, #605, 250 Dundas St. West, Toronto, ON M7A 2T3
416-314-3004, Fax: 416-314-0198, 888-515-5005

Ontario Labour Relations Board, 505 University Ave., 2nd Fl., Toronto, ON M5G 2P1
416-326-7500, Fax: 416-326-7531, 877-339-3335

Ontario Parole Board, #1803, 415 Yonge St., Toronto, ON M5B 2E7
416-325-4480, Fax: 416-325-4485, 888-579-2888

Ontario Police Arbitration Commission, George Drew Bldg., 25 Grosvenor St., 1st Fl., Toronto, ON M7A 1Y6
416-314-3520, Fax: 416-314-3522

Ontario Review Board, 151 Bloor St. West, 10th Fl., Toronto, ON M5S 2T5
416-327-8866, Fax: 416-327-8867, orb@ontario.ca

OPSEU Pension Trust, #1200, 1 Adelaide St. East, Toronto, ON M5C 3A7
416-681-6161, Fax: 416-681-6175, 800-637-0024

Road User Safety Division, Bldg A, #191, 1201 Wilson Ave., Downsview, ON M3M 1J8
416-235-2999, Fax: 416-235-4153

Workplace Safety & Insurance Board, 200 Front St. West, Ground Fl., Toronto, ON M5V 3J1
416-344-1000, Fax: 416-344-4684, 800-387-0750, wsibcomm@wsib.on.ca; prevention@wsib.on.ca (training programs)

Prince Edward Island

Advisory Council on the Status of Women, Sherwood Business Centre, 161 St. Peter's Rd., Main Level, PO Box 2000, Charlottetown, PE C1A 7N8
902-368-4510, Fax: 902-368-3269, peistatusofwomen@eastlink.ca; info@peistatusofwomen.ca

Housing, Seniors & Corporate Support, Jones Bldg., 11 Kent St., 2nd Fl., PO Box 2000, Charlottetown, PE C1A 7N8
Fax: 902-894-0242

Prince Edward Island Workers Compensation Board, 14 Weymouth St., PO Box 757, Charlottetown, PE C1A 7L7
902-368-5680, Fax: 902-368-5696, 800-237-5049

Prince Edward Island Regulatory & Appeals Commission, National Bank Tower, #501, 134 Kent St., PO Box 577, Charlottetown, PE C1A 7L1
902-892-3501, Fax: 902-566-4076, 800-501-6268, info@irac.pe.ca

Workers Compensation Appeal Tribunal, 161 St. Peters Rd., 1st Fl., PO Box 2000, Charlottetown, PE C1A 7N8

Quebec

Bureau du coroner, Édifice le Delta 2, #390, 2875, boul Laurier, Québec, QC G1V 5B1
418-643-1845, Fax: 418-643-6174, 866-312-7051, clientele.coroner@msp.gouv.qc.ca

Comité de déontologie policière, Tour du Saint-Laurent, #A-200, 2525, boul Laurier, 2e étage, Québec, QC G1V 4Z6
418-646-1936, Fax: 418-528-0987, comite.deontologie@msp.gouv.qc.ca

Commissaire à la déontologie policière, #1-40, 1200, rte de l'Église, Québec, QC G1V 4Y9

418-643-7897, Fax: 418-528-9473, 877-237-7897, deontologie-policiere.quebec@msp.gouv.qc.ca
Commissariat des incendies, 455, rue Dupont, Québec, QC G1K 6N2
418-529-5706, Fax: 418-529-9922
Commission des lésions professionnelles, #700, 900, Place d'Youville, Québec, QC G1R 3P7
418-644-7777, Fax: 418-644-6443, 800-463-1591
Commission québecoise des libérations conditionnelles, #1.32A, 300, boul Jean-Lesage, Québec, QC G1K 8K6
418-646-8300, Fax: 418-643-7217, cqlc@msp.gouv.qc.ca
Direction générale de la Sûreté du Québec, 1701, rue Parthenais, Montréal, QC H2K 3S7
514-598-4141, Fax: 514-598-4242
Régie des alcools, des courses et des jeux, 560, boul Charest est, Québec, QC G1K 3J3
418-643-7667, Fax: 418-643-5971, 800-363-0320
Ministère de la Sécurité publique, Tour des Laurentides, 2525, boul Laurier, 5e étage, Québec, QC G1V 2L2
418-643-2112, Fax: 418-646-6168, 866-644-6826
École nationale de police du Québec, 350, rue Marguerite-d'Youville, Nicolet, QC J3T 1X4
819-293-8631, Fax: 819-293-8630, courriel@enpq.qc.ca

Saskatchewan
Agricultural Implements Board, #202, 3085 Albert St., Regina, SK S4S 0B1
306-787-4693, Fax: 306-787-1315
Saskatchewan Workers' Compensation Board, #200, 1881 Scarth St., Regina, SK S4P 4L1
306-787-4370, Fax: 306-787-4311, 800-667-7590, internet_clientsvc@wcbsask.com

Yukon Territory
Driver Control Board, 2130 Second Ave., 3rd Fl., PO Box 2703, Whitehorse, YT Y1A 2C6
867-667-5111, Fax: 867-667-3609, dcb@gov.yk.ca
Yukon Workers' Compensation Health & Safety Board, 401 Strickland St., Whitehorse, YT Y1A 5N8
867-667-5645, Fax: 867-393-6279, 800-661-0443, worksafe@gov.yk.ca

LEGAL & REGULATORY

Canadian Coast Guard, Centennial Towers, #6S018, 200 Kent St., Ottawa, ON K1A 0E6
613-993-0999, Fax: 613-990-1866, info@dfo-mpo.gc.ca
Commission for Environmental Cooperation, Secretariat, #200, 393, rue St-Jacques ouest, Montréal, QC H2Y 1N9
514-350-4300, Fax: 514-350-4314, info@cec.org
Office of the Public Sector Integrity Commissioner of Canada, 60 Queen St., 7th Fl., Ottawa, ON K1P 5Y7
613-941-6400, Fax: 613-941-6535
Public Servants Disclosure Protection Tribunal, #512, 90 Sparks St., Ottawa, ON K1P 5B4
613-943-8310, Fax: 613-943-8325, tribunal@psdpt-tpfd.gc.ca
Standards Council of Canada, #200, 270 Albert St., Ottawa, ON K1P 6N7
613-238-3222, Fax: 613-569-7808, info@scc.ca
Standards Council of Canada, #200, 270 Albert Street, Ottawa, ON K1P 6N7
613-238-3222, Fax: 613-569-7808, info@scc.ca

New Brunswick
Community Planning & Environmental Protection Division, Marysville Place, PO Box 6000, Fredericton, NB E3B 5H1
506-444-5119, Fax: 506-457-7333, elg/egl-info@gnb.ca

Northwest Territories
Assessment Appeal Tribunal of the Northwest Territories, #400, 5201 - 50th Ave., PO Box 1320, Yellowknife, NT X1A 2L9
867-873-7125, Fax: 867-873-0609

Nova Scotia
Workers' Compensation Board of Nova Scotia, 5668 South St., PO Box 1150, Halifax, NS B3J 2Y2
902-491-8999, Fax: 902-491-8002, 800-870-3331, info@wcb.gov.ns.ca

Ontario
Ontario Ministry of Community Safety & Correctional Services, George Drew Bldg., 25 Grosvenor St., 18th Fl., Toronto, ON M7A 1Y6
416-326-5000, Fax: 416-326-0498, 866-517-0571, mcscs.feedback@ontario.ca
Environmental Commissioner of Ontario, #605, 1075 Bay St., Toronto, ON M5S 2B1
416-325-3377, Fax: 416-325-3370, 800-701-6454, commissioner@eco.on.ca

Road User Safety Division, Bldg A, #191, 1201 Wilson Ave., Downsview, ON M3M 1J8
416-235-2999, Fax: 416-235-4153

Prince Edward Island
Prince Edward Island Regulatory & Appeals Commission, National Bank Tower, #501, 134 Kent St., PO Box 577, Charlottetown, PE C1A 7L1
902-892-3501, Fax: 902-566-4076, 800-501-6268, info@irac.pe.ca

LEISURE CRAFT & VEHICLE REGULATIONS

Alberta
Strategic Planning & Financial Services, Commerce Place, 10155 - 102 St., 13th Fl., Edmonton, AB T5J 4G8
780-422-8545

Nova Scotia
Nova Scotia Department of Transportation & Infrastructure Renewal, Johnston Bldg., 1672 Granville St., 2nd Fl., PO Box 186, Halifax, NS B3J 2N2
902-424-2297, Fax: 902-424-0532, tpwpaff@gov.ns.ca

Ontario
Ontario Ministry of Transportation, Ferguson Block, 77 Wellesley St. West, 3rd Fl., Toronto, ON M7A 1Z8
416-235-4686, Fax: 905-704-2001, 800-268-4686

Quebec
Ministère des Transports, 700, boul René-Lévesque est, 28e étage, Québec, QC G1R 5H1
418-643-6980, Fax: 418-643-2033, 888-355-0511, communications@mtq.gouv.qc.ca

LIBRARIES

National Research Council Canada - Canada Institute for Scientific & Technical Information, Building M-55, 1200 Montreal Rd., Ottawa, ON K1A 0R6
613-998-8544, Fax: 613-993-7619, 800-668-1222

Nunavut
Nunavut Territory Department of Culture, Language, Elders & Youth, PO Box 1000 800,Iqaluit, NU X0A 0H0
867-975-5500, Fax: 867-975-5504, 866-934-2035

Ontario
Ontario Library Service - North, 334 Regent St., Sudbury, ON P3C 4E2
705-675-6467, Fax: 705-675-2285, 800-461-6348
Southern Ontario Library Service, #902, 111 Peter St., Toronto, ON M5V 2H1
416-961-1669, Fax: 416-961-5122, 800-387-5765

LIQUOR CONTROL

See Also: Drugs & Alcohol

Quebec
Régie des alcools, des courses et des jeux, 560, boul Charest est, Québec, QC G1K 3J3
418-643-7667, Fax: 418-643-5971, 800-363-0320

LOTTERIES & GAMING

British Columbia
British Columbia Lottery Corporation, 74 West Seymour St., Kamloops, BC V2C 1E2
250-828-5500, Fax: 250-828-5631, 866-815-0222

Manitoba
Manitoba Gaming Control Commission, #800, 215 Garry St., Winnipeg, MB R3C 3P3
204-954-9400, Fax: 204-954-9450, 800-782-0363, information@mgcc.mb.ca

Newfoundland & Labrador
Newfoundland & Labrador Department of Service NL, PO Box 8700, St. John's, NL A1B 4J6
709-729-4834, servicenlinfo@gov.nl.ca

Nunavut
Nunavut Territory Department of Community & Government Services, W.G. Brown Bldg., 4th Fl., PO Box 1000 700,Iqaluit, NU X0A 0H0
867-975-5400, Fax: 867-975-5305

Quebec
Régie des alcools, des courses et des jeux, 560, boul Charest est, Québec, QC G1K 3J3
418-643-7667, Fax: 418-643-5971, 800-363-0320

Yukon Territory
Yukon Lottery Commission, 312 Wood St., Whitehorse, YT Y1A 2E6
867-633-7890, Fax: 867-668-7561, lotteriesyukon@gov.yk.ca

MAPS, CHARTS & AERIAL PHOTOGRAPHS

Canada Centre for Remote Sensing - Geomatics Canada, 588 Booth St., Ottawa, ON K1A 0Y7
613-995-0947, Fax: 613-947-1382
Mapping Services Branch - Geomatics Canada, 615 Booth St., Ottawa, ON K1A 0E9
613-995-4945, Fax: 613-995-8737

Nova Scotia
Geomatics Centre, 160 Willow St., Amherst, NS B4H 3W5
902-667-7231, Fax: 902-667-6008, 800-798-0706, geoinfo@gov.ns.ca

Ontario
Association of Ontario Land Surveyors, 1043 McNicoll Ave., Toronto, ON M1W 3W6
416-491-9020, Fax: 416-491-2576, 800-268-0718

MARINE SCIENCES

National Research Council Marine Performance Evaluation & Testing Facilities, c/o National Research Council, 1200 Montreal Rd., Ottawa, ON K1A 0R6

MINERALS & MINING

Alberta
Resource Development Policy Division, Petroleum Plaza NT, 9945 - 108 St., Edmonton, AB T5K 2G6

British Columbia
Mines & Mineral Resources, PO Box 9319 Prov Govt,Victoria, BC V8W 9N3

Manitoba
Mining Board, #360, 1395 Ellice Ave., Winnipeg, MB R3G 3P2
204-489-0018

New Brunswick
Lands, Minerals & Petroleum Division, Hugh John Flemming Forestry Centre, PO Box 6000, Fredericton, NB E3B 5H1
506-453-2684, Fax: 506-453-2930, dnrweb@gnb.ca

Northwest Territories
Northwest Territories Department of Industry, Tourism & Investment, PO Box 1320, Yellowknife, NT X1A 2L9
Fax: 867-873-0306, info@iti.ca

Nova Scotia
Nova Scotia Department of Energy, Bank of Montreal Bldg., #400, 5151 George St., PO Box 2664, Halifax, NS B3J 3P7
902-424-4575, Fax: 902-424-0528, energyinfo@gov.ns.ca

Nunavut
Nunavut Territory Department of Environment, PO Box 1000 1300,Iqaluit, NU X0A 0H0
867-975-7700, Fax: 867-975-7742, environment@gov.nu.ca

Ontario
Mines & Minerals Division, Willet Green Miller Centre, 933 Ramsey Lake Rd., Sudbury, ON P3E 6B5
705-670-5755, Fax: 705-670-5818, 888-415-9845

Quebec
Mines, Centre de service des Mines, 1685, boul Wilfrid Hamel ouest, 1er étage, Québec, QC G1N 3Y7
418-627-6278, Fax: 418-644-8960, 800-363-7233, service.mines@mrnf.gouv.qc.ca
Énergie, #B401, 5700, 4e av ouest, Québec, QC G1H 6R1
418-627-6377, Fax: 418-643-0701

Saskatchewan
Energy & Resources, #300, 2103 - 11th Ave., Regina, SK S4P 3Z8
306-787-2528

Yukon Territory
Yukon Energy, Mines & Resources, PO Box 2703, Whitehorse, YT Y1A 2C6
867-667-3130, Fax: 867-456-3965, 800-661-0408, emr@gov.yk.ca

MINES & MINERALS

CANMET Mineral Technology Branch, 555 Booth St., Ottawa, ON K1A 0G1

Alberta

Alberta Sport, Recreation, Parks, & Wildlife Foundation, Standard Life Centre, #903, 10405 Jasper Ave., 9th Fl., Edmonton, AB T5J 4R7
780-415-1167, Fax: 780-415-0308, -310-0000

Resource Development Policy Division, Petroleum Plaza NT, 9945 - 108 St., Edmonton, AB T5K 2G6

British Columbia

British Columbia Ministry of Energy, Mines, & Natural Gas (& Responsible for Housing), PO Box 9053 Prov Govt,Victoria, BC V8W 9E2

Manitoba

Mining Board, #360, 1395 Ellice Ave., Winnipeg, MB R3G 3P2
204-489-0018

New Brunswick

Lands, Minerals & Petroleum Division, Hugh John Flemming Forestry Centre, PO Box 6000, Fredericton, NB E3B 5H1
506-453-2684, Fax: 506-453-2930, dnrweb@gnb.ca

Northwest Territories

Northwest Territories Department of Environment & Natural Resources, PO Box 1320, Yellowknife, NT X1A 2L9

Ontario

Mines & Minerals Division, Willet Green Miller Centre, 933 Ramsey Lake Rd., Sudbury, ON P3E 6B5
705-670-5755, Fax: 705-670-5818, 888-415-9845

Ontario Ministry of Northern Development & Mines, 159 Cedar St., Sudbury, ON P3E 6A5
705-670-5755, Fax: 705-670-5818, 888-415-9845

Quebec

Mines, Centre de service des Mines, 1685, boul Wilfrid Hamel ouest, 1er étage, Québec, QC G1N 3Y7
418-627-6278, Fax: 418-644-8960, 800-363-7233, service.mines@mrnf.gouv.qc.ca

MINIMUM WAGES

See Also: Labour

British Columbia

British Columbia Ministry of Citizens' Services, PO Box 9594 Prov Govt,Victoria, BC V8W 9E2
250-952-7623, Fax: 250-952-7628, 800-663-7867, EnquiryBC@gov.bc.ca

Quebec

Commission des normes du travail, Hall Est, 400, boul Jean-Lesage, 7e étage, Québec, QC G1K 8W1
514-873-7061, 800-265-1414

Saskatchewan

Minimum Wage Board, #400, 1870 Albert St., Regina, SK S4P 4W1

MULTICULTURALISM

British Columbia

Multicultural Advisory Council of BC, Multiculturalism & Inclusive Communities Office, 605 Robson St., 5th Fl., Vancouver, BC V6B 5J3
604-660-2203, Fax: 604-775-0670

Manitoba

Manitoba Ethnocultural Advisory & Advocacy Council, 215 Notre Dame Ave. 4th Fl., Winnipeg, MB R3B 1N3
204-945-2339, Fax: 204-948-2323, 800-665-8332, meaac@gov.mb.ca

Multiculturalism Secretariat, 213 Notre Dame Ave., 9th Fl., Winnipeg, MB R3B 1N3
204-945-5632, multisec@gov.mb.ca

Northwest Territories

Northwest Territories Department of Education, Culture & Employment, PO Box 1320, Yellowknife, NT X1A 2L9
867-669-2399, Fax: 867-873-0431, 866-606-5627

Quebec

Ministère de la Culture et Communications, 225, Grande Allée est, Québec, QC G1R 5G5
888-380-8882

MUNICIPAL & RURAL AFFAIRS

Aboriginal Affairs & Northern Development Canada, 10 Wellington St., North Tower, Gatineau, QC K1A 0H4
819-997-0380, Fax: 866-817-3977, 800-567-9604, infopubs@aadnc-aandc.gc.ca

Canada Economic Development for Québec Regions, Édifice Dominion Square, #900, 1255, rue Peel, Montréal, QC H3B 2T9
514-283-6412, Fax: 514-283-3302, 866-385-6412

Canada Mortgage & Housing Corporation, 700 Montreal Rd., Ottawa, ON K1A 0P7
613-748-2000, Fax: 613-748-2098, 800-668-2642, chic@cmhc-schl.gc.ca

Mackenzie Valley Environmental Impact Review Board, 200 Scotia Centre, #5102, 50th Ave., PO Box 938, Yellowknife, NT X1A 2N7
867-766-7050, Fax: 867-766-7074, 866-912-3472

Nunavut Impact Review Board, PO Box 1360, Cambridge Bay, NU X0B 0C0
867-983-4600, Fax: 867-983-2594, 866-233-3033, info@nirb.ca

Nunavut Planning Commission, PO Box 2101, Cambridge Bay, NU X0B 0C0
867-983-4625, Fax: 867-983-4626

Alberta

Alberta Agriculture & Rural Development, JG O'Donoghue Bldg., #100A, 7000 - 113th St., Edmonton, AB T6H 5T6
780-427-2727, -310-3276, duke@gov.ab.ca

Alberta Municipal Affairs, Communications Branch, Commerce Place, 10155 - 102 St., 18th Fl., Edmonton, AB T5J 4L4
780-427-2732, Fax: 780-422-1419, comments@gov.ab.ca

Municipal Government Board, Commerce Place, 10155 - 102 St., 15th Fl., Edmonton, AB T5J 4L4
780-427-4864, Fax: 780-427-0986, -310-0000, mgbmail@gov.ab.ca

Alberta Tourism, Parks, & Recreation, Communications Branch, Commerce Place, 10155 - 102 St., 6th Fl., Edmonton, AB T5J 4L6
780-644-5589, TPR.Communications@gov.ab.ca

British Columbia

Local Government, PO Box 9490 Prov Govt,Victoria, BC V8W 9N7
250-356-6575, Fax: 250-387-7973

Manitoba

Manitoba Aboriginal & Northern Affairs, Legislative Bldg, 344-450 Broadway, Winnipeg, MB R3C OV8
204-945-3719, Fax: 204-945-8374, anaweb@gov.mb.ca

Manitoba Local Government, #301, 450 Broadway Ave., Winnipeg, MB R3C 0V8
Fax: 204-945-1383, mnia@leg.gov.mb.ca

Manitoba Municipal Board, #1144, 363 Broadway, Winnipeg, MB R3C 3N9
204-945-2941, Fax: 204-948-2235

New Brunswick

New Brunswick Department of Health, PO Box 5100, Fredericton, NB E3B 5G8
506-457-4800, Fax: 506-453-5243, dh-ms@dh-ms.ca

Regional Development Corporation, RDC Bldg., 836 Churchill Row, PO Box 428, Fredericton, NB E3B 5R4
506-453-2277, Fax: 506-453-7988

Newfoundland & Labrador

Newfoundland & Labrador Department of Health & Community Services, West Block, Confederation Bldg., PO Box 8700, St. John's, NL A1B 4J6
709-729-4984, healthinfo@gov.nl.ca

Newfoundland & Labrador Department of Municipal Affairs, West Block, Main Fl., Confederation Bldg., PO Box 8700, St. John's, NL A1B 4J6
709-729-3046, Fax: 709-729-0943, mainfo@gov.nl.ca

Municipal Assessment Agency Inc., 75 O'Leary Ave., St. John's, NL A1B 2C9
709-724-1532, 877-777-2807, info@maa.ca

Northwest Territories

Northwest Territories Department of Municipal & Community Affairs, PO Box 1320, Yellowknife, NT X1A 2L9
867-873-7118, Fax: 867-873-0309

Nova Scotia

Nova Scotia Department of Service Nova Scotia & Municipal Relations, 1505 Barrington St., PO Box 216, Halifax, NS B3J 3K5
902-424-5200, Fax: 902-424-0581, 800-670-4357, askus@gov.ns.ca

Nova Scotia Department of Transportation & Infrastructure Renewal, Johnston Bldg., 1672 Granville St., 2nd Fl., PO Box 186, Halifax, NS B3J 2N2
902-424-2297, Fax: 902-424-0532, tpwpaff@gov.ns.ca

Ontario

Ontario Ministry of Agriculture, Food & Rural Affairs, Ontario Government Bldg., 1 Stone Rd. West, Guelph, ON N1G 4Y2
519-826-3100, 888-466-2372

Ontario Ministry of Municipal Affairs & Housing, College Park, 777 Bay St., 17th Fl., Toronto, ON M5G 2E5
416-585-7041, Fax: 416-585-6470, 866-220-2290, mininfo.mah@ontario.ca

Ontario Ministry of Northern Development & Mines, 159 Cedar St., Sudbury, ON P3E 6A5
705-670-5755, Fax: 705-670-5818, 888-415-9845

Northern Development Division, Roberta Bondar Place, #200, 70 Foster Dr., Sault Ste Marie, ON P6A 6V8
705-945-5900, Fax: 705-945-5931, 800-461-2287

Prince Edward Island

Prince Edward Island Department of Transportation & Infrastructure Renewal, Jones Bldg., 11 Kent St., 3rd Fl., PO Box 2000, Charlottetown, PE C1A 7N8
902-368-5100, Fax: 902-368-5395

Quebec

Ministère des Affaires municipales, des Régions et de l'Occupation du territoire, Aile Chaveau, 10, rue Pierre-Olivier-Chauveau, 3e étage, Québec, QC G1R 4J3
418-691-2019, Fax: 418-643-7385, communications@mamrot.gouv.qc.ca

Comité consultatif de l'environnement Kativik, CP 930, Kuujjuaq, QC J0M 1C0
819-964-2961, Fax: 819-964-0694, keac-ccek@krg.ca

Ministère du Développement économique, de l'Innovation et de l'Exportation, 710, place D'Youville, 3e étage, Québec, QC G1R 4Y4
418-691-5950, Fax: 418-644-0118, 866-680-1884

Saskatchewan

Saskatchewan Government Relations, 1855 Victoria Ave., Regina, SK S4P 3T2
306-787-8885,

Yukon Territory

Yukon Community Services, PO Box 2703, Whitehorse, YT Y1A 2C6
867-667-5811, Fax: 867-393-6295, 800-661-0408, inquiry@gov.yk.ca

MUNICIPAL AFFAIRS

Alberta

Alberta Municipal Affairs, Communications Branch, Commerce Place, 10155 - 102 St., 18th Fl., Edmonton, AB T5J 4L4
780-427-2732, Fax: 780-422-1419, comments@gov.ab.ca

British Columbia

Local Government, PO Box 9490 Prov Govt,Victoria, BC V8W 9N7
250-356-6575, Fax: 250-387-7973

Manitoba

Manitoba Aboriginal & Northern Affairs, Legislative Bldg, 344-450 Broadway, Winnipeg, MB R3C OV8
204-945-3719, Fax: 204-945-8374, anaweb@gov.mb.ca

Local Government Development Division, 59 Elizabeth Dr., PO Box 33, Thompson, MB R8N 1X4
204-677-6794, Fax: 204-677-6525

Manitoba Local Government, #301, 450 Broadway Ave., Winnipeg, MB R3C 0V8
Fax: 204-945-1383, mnia@leg.gov.mb.ca

Manitoba Municipal Board, #1144, 363 Broadway, Winnipeg, MB R3C 3N9
204-945-2941, Fax: 204-948-2235

Provincial-Municipal Support Services, #508, 800 Portage Ave., Winnipeg, MB R3G 0N4

New Brunswick

Regional Development Corporation, RDC Bldg., 836 Churchill Row, PO Box 428, Fredericton, NB E3B 5R4
506-453-2277, Fax: 506-453-7988

Newfoundland & Labrador

Newfoundland & Labrador Department of Municipal Affairs, West Block, Main Fl., Confederation Bldg., PO Box 8700, St. John's, NL A1B 4J6
709-729-3046, Fax: 709-729-0943, mainfo@gov.nl.ca

Municipal Assessment Agency Inc., 75 O'Leary Ave., St. John's, NL A1B 2C9
709-724-1532, 877-777-2807, info@maa.ca

Northwest Territories
Northwest Territories Department of Municipal & Community Affairs, PO Box 1320, Yellowknife, NT X1A 2L9
867-873-7118, Fax: 867-873-0309

Nova Scotia
Nova Scotia Municipal Finance Corporation, Maritime Centre, 1505 Barrington St., 10th Fl. South, PO Box 850 M, Halifax, NS B3J 2V2
902-424-4590, Fax: 902-424-0525
Nova Scotia Department of Service Nova Scotia & Municipal Relations, 1505 Barrington St., PO Box 216, Halifax, NS B3J 3K5
902-424-5200, Fax: 902-424-0581, 800-670-4357, askus@gov.ns.ca

Nunavut
Nunavut Territory Department of Community & Government Services, W.G. Brown Bldg., 4th Fl., PO Box 1000 700,Iqaluit, NU X0A 0H0
867-975-5400, Fax: 867-975-5305

Ontario
Ontario Ministry of Municipal Affairs & Housing, College Park, 777 Bay St., 17th Fl., Toronto, ON M5G 2E5
416-585-7041, Fax: 416-585-6470, 866-220-2290, mininfo.mah@ontario.ca

Prince Edward Island
Prince Edward Island Department of Community Services & Seniors, Jones Bldg., 11 Kent St., 2nd Fl., PO Box 2000, Charlottetown, PE C1A 7N8
902-620-3777, Fax: 902-894-0242, 866-594-3777
Prince Edward Island Department of Finance, Energy & Municipal Affairs, Shaw Bldg., 95 Rochford St. South, 2nd Fl., PO Box 2000, Charlottetown, PE C1A 7N8
902-368-4000, Fax: 902-368-5544

Quebec
Ministère des Affaires municipales, des Régions et de l'Occupation du territoire, Aile Chaveau, 10, rue Pierre-Olivier-Chauveau, 3e étage, Québec, QC G1R 4J3
418-691-2019, Fax: 418-643-7385, communications@mamrot.gouv.qc.ca

MUSEUMS

Canada Science & Technology Museum Corporation, PO Box 9724 T,Ottawa, ON K1G 5A3
613-991-6090, Fax: 613-990-3636, info@technomuses.ca
Canadian Heritage, 15 Eddy St., Gatineau, QC K1A 0M5
819-997-0055, 866-811-0055, info@pch.gc.ca
Canadian Museum of Nature, PO Box 3443 D,Ottawa, ON K1P 6P4
613-566-4700, Fax: 613-364-4021, 800-263-4433

Alberta
Recreation & Sport Development Division, Standard Life Centre, 10405 Jasper Ave., 9th Fl., Edmonton, AB T5J 4R7

British Columbia
Royal BC Museum Corporation, 675 Belleville St., Victoria, BC V8W 9W2
250-356-7226, Fax: 250-387-5674, 888-447-7977, reception@royalbcmuseum.bc.ca

Manitoba
Manitoba Museum, 190 Rupert Ave., Winnipeg, MB R3B 0N2
204-956-2830, Fax: 204-942-3679, info@manitobamuseum.mb.ca

Newfoundland & Labrador
Newfoundland & Labrador Department of Fisheries & Aquaculture, Petten Bldg., 30 Strawberry Marsh Rd., PO Box 8700, St. John's, NL A1B 4J6
709-729-3723, Fax: 709-729-6082, fisheries@gov.nl.ca

Nova Scotia
Culture Division, #601, 1800 Argyle St., PO Box 456, Halifax, NS B3J 2R5
902-424-4510, Fax: 902-424-0710, culture@gov.ns.ca

Ontario
Royal Ontario Museum, 100 Queen's Park Cres., Toronto, ON M5S 2C6
416-586-5549, Fax: 416-586-5685, info@rom.on.ca

Quebec
Ministère de la Culture et Communications, 225, Grande Allée est, Québec, QC G1R 5G5
888-380-8882

Saskatchewan
Western Development Museum, Curatorial Centre, 2935 Melville St,, Saskatoon, SK S7J 5A6
306-934-1400, Fax: 306-934-4467, 800-363-6345, info@wdm.ca; curatorial@wdm.ca

Yukon Territory
Yukon Tourism & Culture, 100 Hanson St., Whitehorse, YT Y1A 2C6
867-667-5036, Fax: 867-667-3546

NATIVE AFFAIRS

See: Aboriginal Affairs
Canadian Northern Economic Development Agency, Ottawa, ON K1A 0H4
Fax: 866-817-3977, 800-567-9604, InfoNorth-InfoNord@CanNor.gc.ca

NATIVE PEOPLES & NORTHERN AFFAIRS

Canadian Northern Economic Development Agency, Ottawa, ON K1A 0H4
Fax: 866-817-3977, 800-567-9604, InfoNorth-InfoNord@CanNor.gc.ca

British Columbia
North Area, 1011 - 4 Ave., 5th Fl., Prince George, BC V2L 3H9
250-565-6100

Yukon Territory
Yukon Development Corporation, #2 Miles Canyon Rd., PO Box 5920, Whitehorse, YT Y1A 6S7
867-393-5337, Fax: 867-393-5401
Yukon Land Use Planning Council, #201, 307 Jarvis St., Whitehorse, YT Y1A 2H3
867-667-7397, Fax: 867-667-4624, ylupc@planyukon.ca

NATURAL RESOURCES

Canadian Museum of Nature, PO Box 3443 D,Ottawa, ON K1P 6P4
613-566-4700, Fax: 613-364-4021, 800-263-4433
Natural Resources Canada, 580 Booth St., Ottawa, ON K1A 0E4
613-995-0947, Fax: 613-992-7211

Alberta
Fish & Wildlife Division, Petroleum Plaza ST, 9915 - 108 St., 11th Fl., Edmonton, AB T5K 2G8
Natural Resources Conservation Board, Sterling Place, 9940 - 106 St., Edmonton, AB T5K 2N2
780-422-1977, Fax: 780-427-0607, 866-383-6722, info@nrcb.gov.ab.ca

British Columbia
British Columbia Ministry of Energy, Mines, & Natural Gas (& Responsible for Housing), PO Box 9053 Prov Govt,Victoria, BC V8W 9E2
British Columbia Ministry of Environment, PO Box 9339 Prov Govt,Victoria, BC V8W 9M1
250-387-1161, Fax: 250-387-5669, envmail@gov.bc.ca
British Columbia Ministry of Forests, Lands & Natural Resource Operations, PO Box 9352 Prov Govt,Victoria, BC V8W 9M1
250-387-4809, 877-855-3222, FLNRO.MediaRequests@gov.bc.ca

Manitoba
Manitoba Conservation & Water Stewardship, 200 Saulteaux Cres., Winnipeg, MB R3J 3W3
800-214-6497, mws@gov.mb.ca
Manitoba Conservation Districts Commission, Secretariat c/o Planning & Coordination Branch, 123 Main St., PO Box 20000, Neepawa, MB R0J 1H0
204-476-7033, Fax: 204-476-7539

New Brunswick
New Brunswick Department of Natural Resources, Hugh John Flemming Forestry Centre, PO Box 6000, Fredericton, NB E3B 5H1
506-453-3826, Fax: 506-444-4367, dnrweb@gnb.ca

Newfoundland & Labrador
Newfoundland & Labrador Department of Natural Resources, Natural Resources Bldg., 50 Elizabeth Ave., 7th Fl., PO Box 8700, St. John's, NL A1B 4J6
709-729-2920, Fax: 709-729-0059

Northwest Territories
Northwest Territories Department of Environment & Natural Resources, PO Box 1320, Yellowknife, NT X1A 2L9

Nova Scotia
Nova Scotia Department of Natural Resources, Founder's Square, 1701 Hollis St., 3rd Fl., PO Box 698, Halifax, NS B3J 2T9
902-424-5935, Fax: 902-424-0594, 800-565-2224

Nunavut
Nunavut Territory Department of Environment, PO Box 1000 1300,Iqaluit, NU X0A 0H0
867-975-7700, Fax: 867-975-7742, environment@gov.nu.ca

Ontario
Ontario Ministry of Natural Resources, 300 Water St., PO Box 7000, Peterborough, ON K9J 8M5
705-755-2000, Fax: 705-755-1677, 800-667-1940, mnr.nric.mnr@ontario.ca
Ontario Ministry of Northern Development & Mines, 159 Cedar St., Sudbury, ON P3E 6A5
705-670-5755, Fax: 705-670-5818, 888-415-9845

Prince Edward Island
Prince Edward Island Department of Agriculture & Forestry, Jones Bldg., 11 Kent St., PO Box 2000, Charlottetown, PE C1A 7N8
902-368-4880, Fax: 902-368-4857
Prince Edward Island Department of Environment, Labour & Justice, Shaw Bldg. South, 95 Rochford St., 4th Fl., PO Box 2000, Charlottetown, PE C1A 7N8
902-368-6410, Fax: 902-368-6488

Quebec
Ministère du Développement durable, de l'Environnement, de la Faune, et des Parcs, Édifice Marie-Guyart, 675, boul René-Lévesque est, 29e étage, Québec, QC G1R 5V7
418-521-3911, Fax: 418-643-4143, 800-561-1616, info@mddep.gouv.qc.ca
Ministère des Ressources naturelles, 880, ch Sainte-Foy, Québec, QC G1S 4X4
418-627-8600, Fax: 418-644-6513, 866-248-6936, services.clientele@mrnf.gouv.qc.ca

Saskatchewan
Energy & Resources, #300, 2103 - 11th Ave., Regina, SK S4P 3Z8
306-787-2528
Saskatchewan Environment, 3211 Albert St., 2nd Fl., Regina, SK S4S 5W6
306-787-2584, Fax: 306-787-9544, 800-567-4224, Centre.Inquiry@gov.sk.ca
Wascana Centre Authority, 2900 Wascana Dr., PO Box 7111, Regina, SK S4P 3S7
306-522-3661, Fax: 306-565-2742, wca@wascana.ca

Yukon Territory
Yukon Energy, Mines & Resources, PO Box 2703, Whitehorse, YT Y1A 2C6
867-667-3130, Fax: 867-456-3965, 800-661-0408, emr@gov.yk.ca
Yukon Environment, PO Box 2703, Whitehorse, YT Y1A 2C6
867-667-5652, Fax: 867-393-7197, environment.yukon@gov.yk.ca

NUCLEAR ENERGY

Canadian Nuclear Safety Commission, 280 Slater St., PO Box 1046 B,Ottawa, ON K1P 5S9
613-995-5894, Fax: 613-995-5086, 800-668-5284

Alberta
Alberta Energy, North Petroleum Plaza, 9945 - 108 St., Edmonton, AB T5K 2G6
780-427-8050, Fax: 780-422-0698, -310-0000, Library.Energy@gov.ab.ca

Ontario
Ontario Power Generation, 700 University Ave., Toronto, ON M5G 1X6
416-592-2555, 877-592-2555, webmaster@opg.com

Quebec
Hydro-Québec, 75, boul René-Lévesque ouest, Montréal, QC H2Z 1A4
514-289-2211,

NUTRITION

Science & Technology Branch, Tower 5, 1341 Baseline Rd., Ottawa, ON K1A 0C5
613-759-1000, Fax: 613-773-1866

Alberta
Health Workforce Division, Telus Plaza NT, 10025 Jasper Ave., 10th Fl., Edmonton, AB T5J 1S6

Manitoba
Manitoba Healthy Child Office, 332 Bannatyne Ave., 3rd Fl., Winnipeg, MB R3A 0E2
204-945-2266, 888-848-0140, healthychild@gov.mb.ca
Public Health & Primary Health Care, 300 Carlton St., 2nd Floor, Winnipeg, MB R3B 3M9

New Brunswick
Communications Branch, HSBC Place, 520 King St., 5th Fl., PO Box 5100, Fredericton, NB E3B 6G3
506-457-2356, Fax: 506-444-4697, Health.Sante@gnb.ca

Newfoundland & Labrador
Newfoundland & Labrador Department of Health & Community Services, West Block, Confederation Bldg., PO Box 8700, St. John's, NL A1B 4J6
709-729-4984, healthinfo@gov.nl.ca

Northwest Territories
Northwest Territories Department of Health & Social Services, Centre Square Tower, PO Box 1320, Yellowknife, NT X1A 2L9
Fax: 867-873-0266

Nunavut
Nunavut Territory Department of Health & Social Services, PO Box 1000 1000,Iqaluit, NU X0A 0H0
867-975-5766, Fax: 867-975-5705, 800-661-0833

Ontario
Ontario Ministry of Health & Long-Term Care, Hepburn Block, 80 Grosvenor St., 10th Fl, Toronto, ON M7A 2C4
416-327-4327, 800-268-1153

Prince Edward Island
Prince Edward Island Department of Health & Wellness, 105 Rochford St. North, 4th Fl., PO Box 2000, Charlottetown, PE C1A 7N8
902-368-6414, Fax: 902-368-4121

Quebec
Ministère de la Santé et des Services sociaux, Direction des communications, 1075, ch Sainte-Foy, 16e étage, Québec, QC G1S 2M1
418-643-9395, Fax: 418-643-4768, regisseur.web@msss.gouv.qc.ca

Saskatchewan
Saskatchewan Health, T.C. Douglas Bldg., 3475 Albert St., Regina, SK S4S 6X6
306-787-0146, 800-667-7766, info@health.gov.sk.ca

OCCUPATIONAL SAFETY

See Also: Dangerous Goods & Hazardous Materials
Canadian Centre for Occupational Health & Safety, 135 Hunter St. East, Hamilton, ON L8N 1M5
905-572-2981, Fax: 905-572-2206, 800-668-4284

Alberta
Occupational Health & Safety Council, Labour Building, 10808 - 99 Ave., 9th Fl., Edmonton, AB T5K 0G5
780-415-8690, 866-415-8690
Workplace Standards Division, Labour Building, 10808 - 99 Ave., 9th Fl., Edmonton, AB T5K 0G5
780-644-1500, Fax: 780-422-0014

British Columbia
British Columbia Ministry of Citizens' Services, PO Box 9594 Prov Govt,Victoria, BC V8W 9E2
250-952-7623, Fax: 250-952-7628, 800-663-7867, EnquiryBC@gov.bc.ca
Workers' Compensation Board of British Columbia, PO Box 5350 Terminal,Vancouver, BC V6B 5L5
604-276-3100, Fax: 604-276-3247, 888-621-7233

Manitoba
Advisory Council on Workplace Safety & Health (SAFE Work), #200, 401 York Ave., Winnipeg, MB R3C 0P8
204-945-3446, Fax: 204-945-4556

New Brunswick
Workplace Health, Safety & Compensation Commission of New Brunswick, 1 Portland St., PO Box 160, Saint John, NB E2L 3X9
506-632-2200, 800-222-9775, communications@ws-ts.nb.ca

Newfoundland & Labrador
Occupational Health & Safety Branch, PO Box 8700, St. John's, NL A1B 4J6
Newfoundland & Labrador Workplace Health, Safety & Compensation Commission, 146 - 148 Forest Rd., PO Box 9000, St. John's, NL A1A 3B8
709-778-1000, Fax: 709-738-1714, 800-563-9000, general.inquiries@whscc.nl.ca

Northwest Territories
Northwest Territories & Nunavut Workers' Safety & Compensation Commission, Centre Square Tower, 5022 - 49th St., 5th Fl., PO Box 8888, Yellowknife, NT X1A 2R3
867-920-3888, Fax: 867-873-4596, 800-661-0792

Nova Scotia
Workers' Compensation Board of Nova Scotia, 5668 South St., PO Box 1150, Halifax, NS B3J 2Y2
902-491-8999, Fax: 902-491-8002, 800-870-3331, info@wcb.gov.ns.ca

Ontario
Workplace Safety & Insurance Board, 200 Front St. West, Ground Fl., Toronto, ON M5V 3J1
416-344-1000, Fax: 416-344-4684, 800-387-0750, wsibcomm@wsib.on.ca; prevention@wsib.on.ca (training programs)

Prince Edward Island
Prince Edward Island Workers Compensation Board, 14 Weymouth St., PO Box 757, Charlottetown, PE C1A 7L7
902-368-5680, Fax: 902-368-5696, 800-237-5049

Quebec
Commission des lésions professionnelles, #700, 900, Place d'Youville, Québec, QC G1R 3P7
418-644-7777, Fax: 418-644-6443, 800-463-1591
Commission de la santé et de la sécurité du travail du Québec, 425, rue du Pont, CP 4900 Terminus,Québec, QC G1K 7S6
Fax: 418-266-4015, 866-302-2778

Saskatchewan
Office of the Worker's Advocate, #300, 1870 Albert St., Regina, SK S4P 4W1
306-787-2456, Fax: 306-787-0249, 877-787-2456
Saskatchewan Workers' Compensation Board, #200, 1881 Scarth St., Regina, SK S4P 4L1
306-787-4370, Fax: 306-787-4311, 800-667-7590, internet_clientsvc@wcbsask.com

Yukon Territory
Yukon Workers' Compensation Health & Safety Board, 401 Strickland St., Whitehorse, YT Y1A 5N8
867-667-5645, Fax: 867-393-6279, 800-661-0443, worksafe@gov.yk.ca

OCCUPATIONAL TRAINING

Alberta
Community, Learner & Industry Connections Division, Phipps-McKinnon Bldg., 10020 - 101A Ave., 5th Fl., Edmonton, AB T5J 3G2

British Columbia
British Columbia Ministry of Citizens' Services, PO Box 9594 Prov Govt,Victoria, BC V8W 9E2
250-952-7623, Fax: 250-952-7628, 800-663-7867, EnquiryBC@gov.bc.ca

New Brunswick
New Brunswick Department of Post-Secondary Education, Training & Labour, Chestnut Complex, PO Box 6000, Fredericton, NB E3B 5H1
506-453-2597, Fax: 506-453-3618, dpetlinfo@gnb.ca

Quebec
École nationale de police du Québec, 350, rue Marguerite-d'Youville, Nicolet, QC J3T 1X4
819-293-8631, Fax: 819-293-8630, courriel@enpq.qc.ca
École nationale des pompiers du Québec, #3.08, 2800, boul Saint-Martin ouest, Laval, QC H7T 2S9
450-680-6800, Fax: 450-680-6818, 866-680-3677

OCEANOGRAPHY

Bayfield Institute, 867 Lakeshore Rd., PO Box 5050, Burlington, ON L7R 4A6
905-336-6240
Bedford Institute of Oceanography, 1 Challenger Dr., PO Box 1006, Dartmouth, NS B2Y 4A2
902-426-3492, Fax: 902-426-8484, WebmasterBIO-IOB@dfo-mpo.gc.ca
Fisheries & Oceans Canada, 200 Kent St., Ottawa, ON K1A 0E6
613-993-0999, Fax: 613-990-1866, info@dfo-mpo.gc.ca
Institut Maurice-Lamontagne, 850, rte de le Mer, CP 1000, Mont-Joli, QC G5H 3Z4
418-775-0500, Fax: 418-775-0730
Institute of Ocean Sciences, 9860 West Saanich Rd., PO Box 6000, Sidney, BC V8L 4B2
250-363-6517, Fax: 250-363-6390
National Research Council Ocean Technology Enterprise Centre, PO Box 12093, St. John's, NL A1B 3T5
709-772-2469, 877-672-2672

OIL & NATURAL GAS RESOURCES

See Also: Energy; Natural Resources
Indian Oil & Gas Canada, #100, 9911 Chiila Blvd., Tsuu T'ina (Sarcee), AB T2W 6H6
403-292-5625, Fax: 403-292-5618, ContactIOGC@inac-ainc.gc.ca
National Energy Board, 444 - 7 Ave. SW, Calgary, AB T2P 0X8
403-292-4800, Fax: 403-292-5503, 800-899-1265, info@neb-one.gc.ca

Alberta
Energy Resources Conservation Board, #1000, 250 - 5 Ave. SW, Calgary, AB T2P 0R4
403-297-8311, Fax: 403-297-7336, 855-297-8311, inquiries@ercb.ca; infoservices@ercb.ca; ADR@ercb.ca
Alberta Energy, North Petroleum Plaza, 9945 - 108 St., Edmonton, AB T5K 2G6
780-427-8050, Fax: 780-422-0698, -310-0000, Library.Energy@gov.ab.ca

British Columbia
British Columbia Utilities Commission, 900 Howe St., 6th Fl., PO Box 250, Vancouver, BC V6Z 2N3
604-660-4700, Fax: 604-660-1102, 800-663-1385, commission.secretary@bcuc.com
British Columbia Ministry of Energy, Mines, & Natural Gas (& Responsible for Housing), PO Box 9053 Prov Govt,Victoria, BC V8W 9E2
Oil & Gas Commission, #100, 10003 - 110 Ave., Fort St John, BC V1J 6M7
250-794-5200, Fax: 250-794-5375

Manitoba
Surface Rights Board, #360, 1395 Ellice Ave., Winnipeg, MB R3G 3P2
204-945-0731, Fax: 204-948-2578, 800-282-8069

New Brunswick
Lands, Minerals & Petroleum Division, Hugh John Flemming Forestry Centre, PO Box 6000, Fredericton, NB E3B 5H1
506-453-2684, Fax: 506-453-2930, dnrweb@gnb.ca

Newfoundland & Labrador
Canada-Newfoundland & Labrador Offshore Petroleum Board, TD Place, 140 Water St., 5th Fl., St. John's, NL A1C 6H6
709-778-1400, Fax: 709-778-1473, information@cnlopb.nl.ca

Northwest Territories
Petroleum Products Division, Stuart M. Hodgson, 5009 - 49th St., 1st Fl., Yellowknife, NT X1A 2L9
867-920-3447, Fax: 867-873-0100

Nova Scotia
Nova Scotia Utility & Review Board, Summit Place, 1601 Lower Water St., 3rd Fl., PO Box 1692 M,Halifax, NS B3J 3S3
902-424-4448, Fax: 902-424-3919, uarb.board@gov.ns.ca

Nunavut
Nunavut Territory Department of Environment, PO Box 1000 1300,Iqaluit, NU X0A 0H0
867-975-7700, Fax: 867-975-7742, environment@gov.nu.ca

Ontario
Ontario Ministry of Natural Resources, 300 Water St., PO Box 7000, Peterborough, ON K9J 8M5
705-755-2000, Fax: 705-755-1677, 800-667-1940, mnr.nric.mnr@ontario.ca

Saskatchewan
SaskEnergy Incorporated, 1777 Victoria Ave., Regina, SK S4P 4K5
306-777-9225, 800-567-8899

Yukon Territory
Oil & Gas Mineral Resources, #300, 211 Main St., Whitehorse, YT Y1A 2B2
867-667-5087, Fax: 867-393-6262, oilandgas@gov.yk.ca

OIL SPILLS
Canadian Coast Guard, Centennial Towers, #6S018, 200 Kent St., Ottawa, ON K1A 0E6
613-993-0999, Fax: 613-990-1866, info@dfo-mpo.gc.ca
Office of the Administrator of the Ship-source Oil Pollution Fund, #830, 180 Kent St., Ottawa, ON K1A 0N5
613-991-1726, Fax: 613-990-5423

Newfoundland & Labrador
Canada-Newfoundland & Labrador Offshore Petroleum Board, TD Place, 140 Water St., 5th Fl., St. John's, NL A1C 6H6
709-778-1400, Fax: 709-778-1473, information@cnlopb.nl.ca

PARKS
See Also: Land Resources

Saskatchewan
Saskatchewan Parks, Culture, & Sport, 1919 Saskatchewan Dr., 4th Fl., Regina, SK S4P 4H2
306-787-5729, Fax: 306-798-0033, 800-205-7070, info@tpcs.gov.sk.ca

PARKS & RECREATION
Auyuittuq National Park of Canada, PO Box 353, Pangnirtung, NU X0A 0R0
867-473-2500, Fax: 867-473-8612, nunavut.info@pc.gc.ca
Canadian Heritage, 15 Eddy St., Gatineau, QC K1A 0M5
819-997-0055, 866-811-0055, info@pch.gc.ca
Historic Sites & Monuments Board of Canada, Terrasses de la Chaudière, 25 Eddy St., Gatineau, QC K1A 0M5
Fax: 819-934-1115, 855-283-8730, hsmbc-clmhc@pc.gc.ca
Parks Canada, 25 Eddy St., Gatineau, QC K1A 0M5
613-860-1251, 888-773-8888, information@pc.gc.ca

Alberta
Alberta Sport, Recreation, Parks, & Wildlife Foundation, Standard Life Centre, #903, 10405 Jasper Ave., 9th Fl., Edmonton, AB T5J 4R7
780-415-1167, Fax: 780-415-0308, -310-0000
Parks Division, Oxbridge Place, 9820 - 106 St., 2nd Fl., Edmonton, AB T5K 2J6
780-427-3582, Fax: 780-427-5980, 866-427-3582
Special Areas Board, Special Areas Board Administration, 212 - 2nd Ave. West, PO Box 820, Hanna, AB T0J 1P0
403-854-5600, Fax: 403-854-5527, specarea@telus.net

British Columbia
British Columbia Ministry of Environment, PO Box 9339 Prov Govt,Victoria, BC V8W 9M1
250-387-1161, Fax: 250-387-5669, envmail@gov.bc.ca

Manitoba
Ecological Reserves Advisory Committee, c/o Manitoba Conservation, Parks & Natural Areas Branch, 200 Saulteaux Cres., Winnipeg, MB R3J 3W3
204-945-4148, Fax: 204-945-0012
Manitoba Entrepreneurship, Training & Trade, #1000, 259 Portage Ave, Winnipeg, MB R3B 3P4
204-945-2475, Fax: 204-945-3977, minctt@leg.gov.mb.ca

New Brunswick
New Brunswick Department of Tourism, Heritage & Culture, Centennial Building, PO Box 6000, Fredericton, NB E3B 5H1
506-444-5205, Fax: 506-457-4984, taponlinedirectory@gnb.ca

Northwest Territories
Northwest Territories Department of Environment & Natural Resources, PO Box 1320, Yellowknife, NT X1A 2L9

Nunavut
Nunavut Territory Department of Environment, PO Box 1000 1300,Iqaluit, NU X0A 0H0
867-975-7700, Fax: 867-975-7742, environment@gov.nu.ca

Ontario
Ontario Ministry of Economic Development, Trade & Employment, Hearst Block, 900 Bay St., 8th Fl., Toronto, ON M7A 2E1
416-325-6666, Fax: 416-325-6688, 866-668-4249, info@edt.gov.on.ca

Prince Edward Island
Prince Edward Island Department of Innovation & Advanced Learning, Shaw Bldg., 105 Rochford St., 5th Fl., PO Box 2000, Charlottetown, PE C1A 7N8
902-368-4240, Fax: 902-368-4242

Quebec
Ministère du Développement durable, de l'Environnement, de la Faune, et des Parcs, Édifice Marie-Guyart, 675, boul René-Lévesque est, 29e étage, Québec, QC G1R 5V7
418-521-3911, Fax: 418-643-4143, 800-561-1616, info@mddep.gouv.qc.ca
Société des établissements en plein air du Québec, Place de la Cité, Tour Cominar, #250, 2640, boul Laurier, 2e étage, Québec, QC G1V 5C2
418-890-6527, Fax: 418-528-6025, 800-665-6527, inforeservation@sepaq.com

Saskatchewan
Saskatchewan Parks, Culture, & Sport, 1919 Saskatchewan Dr., 4th Fl., Regina, SK S4P 4H2
306-787-5729, Fax: 306-798-0033, 800-205-7070, info@tpcs.gov.sk.ca

Yukon Territory
Parks, PO Box 2703 V-4, Whitehorse, YT Y1A 2C6
867-667-5648, Fax: 867-393-6223, 800-661-0408, yukon.parks@gov.yk.ca
Yukon Tourism & Culture, 100 Hanson St., Whitehorse, YT Y1A 2C6
867-667-5036, Fax: 867-667-3546

PAROLE BOARDS
See Also: Correctional Services

New Brunswick
New Brunswick Department of Public Safety, 364 Argyle St., PO Box 6000, Fredericton, NB E3B 5H1
506-453-3992, Fax: 506-453-3870, DPS-MSP.Information@gnb.ca

Ontario
Ontario Parole Board, #1803, 415 Yonge St., Toronto, ON M5B 2E7
416-325-4480, Fax: 416-325-4485, 888-579-2888

Quebec
Commission québecoise des libérations conditionnelles, #1.32A, 300, boul Jean-Lesage, Québec, QC G1K 8K6
418-646-8300, Fax: 418-643-7217, cqlc@msp.gouv.qc.ca

PAY EQUITY
Human Resources & Skills Development Canada, 140 Promenade du Portage, Gatineau, QC K1A 0J9

British Columbia
British Columbia Ministry of Citizens' Services, PO Box 9594 Prov Govt,Victoria, BC V8W 9E2
250-952-7623, Fax: 250-952-7628, 800-663-7867, EnquiryBC@gov.bc.ca
Employment Standards Tribunal, Oceanic Plaza, #650, 1066 West Hastings St., Vancouver, BC V6E 3X1
604-775-3512, Fax: 604-775-3372, registrar@bcest.bc.ca

Ontario
Pay Equity Commission, #300, 180 Dundas St. West, Toronto, ON M7A 2S6
416-314-1896, Fax: 416-314-8741, 800-387-8813

Prince Edward Island
Workers Compensation Appeal Tribunal, 161 St. Peters Rd., 1st Fl., PO Box 2000, Charlottetown, PE C1A 7N8

Quebec
Commission de l'équité salariale, 200, ch Ste-Foy, 4e étage, Québec, QC G1R 6A1
418-528-8765, Fax: 418-528-6999, 888-528-8765, equite.salariale@ces.gouv.qc.ca

PENSIONS
Finance Canada, L'esplanade Laurier, 140 O'Connor St., Ottawa, ON K1A 0G5
613-992-1573, Fax: 613-943-0938, finpub@fin.gc.ca
Office of the Commissioner of Review Tribunals, PO Box 8250 T, Ottawa, ON K1G 5S5
613-954-1313, Fax: 613-946-1588, 800-363-0076, info@ocrt-bctr.gc.ca
Pension Appeals Board, PO Box 8567 T, Ottawa, ON K1G 3H9
613-995-0612, Fax: 613-995-6834, 888-640-8001, info@pab-cap.gc.ca
Public Sector Pension Investment Board, #200, 440 Laurier Ave. West, Ottawa, ON K1R 7X6
613-782-3095, Fax: 613-782-6864, info@investpsp.ca

Ontario
Ontario Pension Board, Sun Life Bldg., #2200, 200 King St. West, Toronto, ON M5H 3X6
416-364-8558, Fax: 416-364-7578, 800-668-6203, clientservice@opb.ca
OPSEU Pension Trust, #1200, 1 Adelaide St. East, Toronto, ON M5C 3A7
416-681-6161, Fax: 416-681-6175, 800-637-0024,

PERFORMING ARTS
See: Arts & Culture

Saskatchewan
Conexus Arts Centre, 200A Lakeshore Dr., Regina, SK S4S 7L3
306-565-4500, 800-667-8497, cac.admin@conexusartscentre.ca

PESTICIDES, HERBICIDES
Pest Management Regulatory Agency, 2720 Riverside Dr., Ottawa, ON K1A 0K9
613-736-3401, Fax: 613-736-3798
Programs Branch, Tower 7, 1341 Baseline Rd., Ottawa, ON K1A 0C5
613-759-1000, Fax: 613-773-2121

New Brunswick
Community Planning & Environmental Protection Division, Marysville Place, PO Box 6000, Fredericton, NB E3B 5H1
506-444-5119, Fax: 506-457-7333, elg/egl-info@gnb.ca

Newfoundland & Labrador
Port aux Basques, Provincial Bldg., Main St., PO Box 478, Port Aux Basques, NL A0M 1C0
709-695-2835, Fax: 709-695-2393

Ontario
Pesticides Advisory Committee, 135 St. Clair Ave. West, 15th Fl., Toronto, ON M4V 1P5
416-314-9230, Fax: 416-314-9237

PIPELINES
National Energy Board, 444 - 7 Ave. SW, Calgary, AB T2P 0X8
403-292-4800, Fax: 403-292-5503, 800-899-1265, info@neb-one.gc.ca

Alberta
Energy Resources Conservation Board, #1000, 250 - 5 Ave. SW, Calgary, AB T2P 0R4
403-297-8311, Fax: 403-297-7336, 855-297-8311, inquiries@ercb.ca; infoservices@ercb.ca; ADR@ercb.ca
Alberta Energy, North Petroleum Plaza, 9945 - 108 St., Edmonton, AB T5K 2G6
780-427-8050, Fax: 780-422-0698, -310-0000, Library.Energy@gov.ab.ca

British Columbia
British Columbia Hydro, 6911 Southpoint Dr., Burnaby, BC V3N 4X8
604-224-9376, 800-224-9376

New Brunswick
Lands, Minerals & Petroleum Division, Hugh John Flemming Forestry Centre, PO Box 6000, Fredericton, NB E3B 5H1
506-453-2684, Fax: 506-453-2930, dnrweb@gnb.ca

Northwest Territories
Northwest Territories Department of Environment & Natural Resources, PO Box 1320, Yellowknife, NT X1A 2L9

Nova Scotia
Nova Scotia Department of Energy, Bank of Montreal Bldg., #400, 5151 George St., PO Box 2664, Halifax, NS B3J 3P7
902-424-4575, Fax: 902-424-0528, energyinfo@gov.ns.ca
Nova Scotia Utility & Review Board, Summit Place, 1601 Lower Water St., 3rd Fl., PO Box 1692 M,Halifax, NS B3J 3S3
902-424-4448, Fax: 902-424-3919, uarb.board@gov.ns.ca

Saskatchewan
SaskEnergy Incorporated, 1777 Victoria Ave., Regina, SK S4P 4K5
306-777-9225, 800-567-8899

POLICING SERVICES

Manitoba
Health Information Privacy Committee, #4043, 300 Carlton St., Winnipeg, MB R3B 3M9

Quebec
Direction générale de la Sûreté du Québec, 1701, rue Parthenais, Montréal, QC H2K 3S7
514-598-4141, Fax: 514-598-4242

POLITICS & SOCIETY

Auditor General of Canada, 240 Sparks St., Ottawa, ON K1A 0G6
613-995-3708, Fax: 613-957-0474, 888-761-5953, communications@oag-bvg.gc.ca; infomedia@oag-bvg.gc.ca
Canadian International Development Agency, 200, Promenade du Portage, Gatineau, QC K1A 0G4
819-997-5456, Fax: 819-953-6088, 800-230-6349, info@acdi-cida.gc.ca
Commission for Environmental Cooperation, Secretariat, #200, 393, rue St-Jacques ouest, Montréal, QC H2Y 1N9
514-350-4300, Fax: 514-350-4314, info@cec.org
Department of National Defence & the Canadian Forces, National Defence HQ, Major-General George R. Pearkes Bldg., 101 Colonel By Dr., Ottawa, ON K1A 0K2
613-995-2534, Fax: 613-992-4739, DNDRecruitment-RecrutementMDN@forces.gc.ca (Civilian Careers)
Finance Canada, L'esplanade Laurier, 140 O'Connor St., Ottawa, ON K1A 0G5
613-992-1573, Fax: 613-943-0938, finpub@fin.gc.ca
Foreign Affairs & International Trade Canada, Enquiries Service, 125 Sussex Dr., Ottawa, ON K1A 0G2
613-944-4000, Fax: 613-996-9709, 800-267-8376, enqserv@international.gc.ca; travel@international.gc.ca
International Development Research Centre, 150 Kent St., PO Box 8500, Ottawa, ON K1G 3H9
613-236-6163, Fax: 613-238-7230, info@idrc.ca
International Joint Commission, 234 Laurier Ave. West, 22nd Fl., Ottawa, ON K1P 6K6
613-947-1420, Fax: 613-993-5583, beckhoffb@ottawa.ijc.org
National Capital Commission, #202, 40 Elgin St., Ottawa, ON K1P 1C7
613-239-5000, Fax: 613-239-5063, 800-465-1867, info@ncc-ccn.ca; contracts-contrats@ncc-ccn.ca (Contracting)
National Round Table on the Environment & Economy, #200, 344 Slater St., Ottawa, ON K1R 7Y3
613-992-7189, Fax: 613-992-7385, info@nrtee-trnee.ca
Public Works & Government Services Canada, Place du Portage, Phase III, 11, rue Laurier, Ottawa, ON K1A 0S5
questions@tpsgc-pwgsc.gc.ca
Strategic Policy Branch, Tower 7, 1341 Baseline Rd., Ottawa, ON K1A 0C5
613-759-1000, Fax: 613-773-2111

Alberta
Alberta International & Intergovernmental Relations, Commerce Place, 10155 - 102 St., 12th Fl., Edmonton, AB T5J 4G8
780-422-1510, -310-0000
Alberta Public Affairs Bureau, Park Plaza, 10611 - 98 Ave., 6th Fl., Edmonton, AB T5K 2P7
780-427-2754, Fax: 780-422-4168, -310-0000

British Columbia
British Columbia Ministry of Community, Sport, & Cultural Development, PO Box 9490 Prov Govt,Victoria, BC V8W 9N7

Manitoba
Manitoba Round Table for Sustainable Development, #160, 123 Main St., Winnipeg, MB R3C 1A5
204-945-1869, Fax: 204-948-2357, mrtsd@gov.mb.ca

Newfoundland & Labrador
Government Services Branch, PO Box 8700, St. John's, NL A1B 4J6
Newfoundland & Labrador Department of Service NL, PO Box 8700, St. John's, NL A1B 4J6
709-729-4834, servicenlinfo@gov.nl.ca
Newfoundland & Labrador Department of Transportation & Works, Confederation Bldg., West Block, 6th Fl., PO Box 8700, St. John's, NL A1B 4J6
709-729-3679, Fax: 709-729-4285, twminister@gov.nl.ca

Northwest Territories
Northwest Territories Department of Aboriginal Affairs & Intergovernmental Relations, 4910 - 52nd St., PO Box 1320, Yellowknife, NT X1A 2L9
867-873-7143, Fax: 867-873-0233, 877-838-8194, nancy_gardiner@gov.nt.ca
Northwest Territories Department of Public Works & Services, PO Box 1320, Yellowknife, NT X1A 2L9

Nova Scotia
Nova Scotia Emergency Management Office, PO Box 2581, Halifax, NS B3J 3N5
902-424-5620, Fax: 902-424-5376, 866-424-5620, emo@gov.ns.ca

Ontario
Environmental Commissioner of Ontario, #605, 1075 Bay St., Toronto, ON M5S 2B1
416-325-3377, Fax: 416-325-3370, 800-701-6454, commissioner@eco.on.ca

Prince Edward Island
Prince Edward Island Department of Health & Wellness, 105 Rochford St. North, 4th Fl., PO Box 2000, Charlottetown, PE C1A 7N8
902-368-6414, Fax: 902-368-4121

Yukon Territory
Emergency Measures Organization, Combined Services Bldg., 2nd Fl., 60 Norseman Rd, Airport, Whitehorse, YT Y1A 2C6
867-667-5220, Fax: 867-393-6266, 800-661-0408, emo.yukon@gov.yk.ca

POLLUTION

See: Air Pollution; Water Resources
Office of the Administrator of the Ship-source Oil Pollution Fund, #830, 180 Kent St., Ottawa, ON K1A 0N5
613-991-1726, Fax: 613-990-5423

POPULATION

See Also: Statistics
Statistics Canada, R.H. Coats Bldg., Tunney's Pasture, 150 Tunney's Pasture Driveway, Ottawa, ON K1A 0T6
613-951-8116, Fax: 877-287-4369, 800-263-1136, infostats@statcan.ca

Nunavut
Nunavut Territory Department of Executive & Intergovernmental Affairs, 1084 Aeroplex bldg., PO Box 1000 200,Iqaluit, NU X0A 0H0
867-975-6000, Fax: 867-975-6099

PROPERTY ASSESSMENT

British Columbia
British Columbia Assessment Authority, #400, 3450 Uptown Blvd., Victoria, BC V8Z 0B9
250-595-6211, Fax: 250-595-6222, info@bcassessment.ca

New Brunswick
Assessment & Plannning Appeal Board, City Centre, PO Box 6000, Fredericton, NB E3B 5H1
506-453-2126, Fax: 506-444-4881, lg/gl-info@gnb.ca

Newfoundland & Labrador
Newfoundland & Labrador Department of Municipal Affairs, West Block, Main Fl., Confederation Bldg., PO Box 8700, St. John's, NL A1B 4J6
709-729-3046, Fax: 709-729-0943, mainfo@gov.nl.ca

Northwest Territories
Assessment Appeal Tribunal of the Northwest Territories, #400, 5201 - 50th Ave., PO Box 1320, Yellowknife, NT X1A 2L9
867-873-7125, Fax: 867-873-0609

Prince Edward Island
Prince Edward Island Regulatory & Appeals Commission, National Bank Tower, #501, 134 Kent St., PO Box 577, Charlottetown, PE C1A 7L1
902-892-3501, Fax: 902-566-4076, 800-501-6268, info@irac.pe.ca

Saskatchewan
Saskatchewan Assessment Management Agency, #200, 2201 - 11th Ave., Regina, SK S4P 0J8
306-924-8000, Fax: 306-924-8070, 800-667-7262, info.request@sama.sk.ca

PUBLIC SAFETY

See Also: Occupational Safety
Canadian Coast Guard, Centennial Towers, #6S018, 200 Kent St., Ottawa, ON K1A 0E6
613-993-0999, Fax: 613-990-1866, info@dfo-mpo.gc.ca
Canadian Transportation Agency, Les Terrasses de la Chaudière, 15, rue Eddy, Gatineau, QC J8X 4B3
Fax: 819-997-6727, 888-222-2592, info@otc-cta.gc.ca
Communications Security Establishment, 1500 Bronson Ave., PO Box 9703 Terminal, Ottawa, ON K1A OK2
613-991-7600, Fax: 613-991-8514
Department of National Defence & the Canadian Forces, National Defence HQ, Major-General George R. Pearkes Bldg., 101 Colonel By Dr., Ottawa, ON K1A 0K2
613-995-2534, Fax: 613-992-4739, DNDRecruitment-RecrutementMDN@forces.gc.ca (Civilian Careers)
Office of the Communications Security Establishment Commissioner, PO Box 1984 B, Ottawa, ON K1P 5R5
613-992-3044

New Brunswick
New Brunswick Department of Public Safety, 364 Argyle St., PO Box 6000, Fredericton, NB E3B 5H1
506-453-3992, Fax: 506-453-3870, DPS-MSP.Information@gnb.ca

Quebec
Ministère de la Sécurité publique, Tour des Laurentides, 2525, boul Laurier, 5e étage, Québec, QC G1V 2L2
418-643-2112, Fax: 418-646-6168, 866-644-6826

Saskatchewan
Saskatchewan Corrections & Policing, 1874 Scarth St., Regina, SK S4P 4B3
306-787-7872, communicationsCPSP@gov.sk.ca

PUBLIC SERVICES

Canadian Centre for Occupational Health & Safety, 135 Hunter St. East, Hamilton, ON L8N 1M5
905-572-2981, Fax: 905-572-2206, 800-668-4284
Canadian Coast Guard, Centennial Towers, #6S018, 200 Kent St., Ottawa, ON K1A 0E6
613-993-0999, Fax: 613-990-1866, info@dfo-mpo.gc.ca
Department of National Defence & the Canadian Forces, National Defence HQ, Major-General George R. Pearkes Bldg., 101 Colonel By Dr., Ottawa, ON K1A 0K2
613-995-2534, Fax: 613-992-4739, DNDRecruitment-RecrutementMDN@forces.gc.ca (Civilian Careers)
Human Resources & Skills Development Canada, 140 Promenade du Portage, Gatineau, QC K1A 0J9
MERX, PO Box 11684 Centre-ville,Montreal, QC H3C 6H4
613-727-4900, Fax: 888-235-5800, 800-964-6379, merx@merx.com
Military Police Complaints Commission, 270 Albert St., 10th Fl., Ottawa, ON K1P 5G8
613-947-5625, Fax: 613-947-5713, 800-632-0566, commission@mpcc-cppm.gc.ca
National Capital Commission, #202, 40 Elgin St., Ottawa, ON K1P 1C7
613-239-5000, Fax: 613-239-5063, 800-465-1867, info@ncc-ccn.ca; contracts-contrats@ncc-ccn.ca (Contracting)
National Search & Rescue Secretariat, #400, 275 Slater St., Ottawa, ON K1A 0K2
613-992-0054, Fax: 613-996-3746, 800-727-9414, inquiry@nss.gc.ca
Public Works & Government Services Canada, Place du Portage, Phase III, 11, rue Laurier, Ottawa, ON K1A 0S5
questions@tpsgc-pwgsc.gc.ca

Alberta
Alberta Health Services, Corporate Office, North Tower, Seventh Street Plaza, 10030 - 107th St. NW, 14th Fl., Edmonton, AB T5J 3E4
780-342-2000, Fax: 780-342-2060, 888-342-2471, ahsb.admin@albertahealthservices.ca
Energy Resources Conservation Board, #1000, 250 - 5 Ave. SW, Calgary, AB T2P 0R4
403-297-8311, Fax: 403-297-7336, 855-297-8311, inquiries@ercb.ca; infoservices@ercb.ca; ADR@ercb.ca
Health Workforce Division, Telus Plaza NT, 10025 Jasper Ave., 10th Fl., Edmonton, AB T5J 1S6
Alberta Infrastructure, Infrastructure Building, 6950 - 113 St., Edmonton, AB T6H 5V7
780-415-0507, Fax: 780-427-2187, -310-0000, Infra.Contact.Us.m@gov.ab.ca
Labour Relations Board, Labour Building, 10808 - 99 Ave., 5th Fl., Edmonton, AB T5K 0G5
780-422-5926, Fax: 780-422-0970, 800-463-2572, alrbinfo@lab.gov.ab.ca
Alberta Municipal Affairs, Communications Branch, Commerce Place, 10155 - 102 St., 18th Fl., Edmonton, AB T5J 4L4
780-427-2732, Fax: 780-422-1419, comments@gov.ab.ca

Municipal Government Board, Commerce Place, 10155 - 102 St., 15th Fl., Edmonton, AB T5J 4L4
780-427-4864, Fax: 780-427-0986, -310-0000, mgbmail@gov.ab.ca

Alberta Tourism, Parks, & Recreation, Communications Branch, Commerce Place, 10155 - 102 St., 6th Fl., Edmonton, AB T5J 4L6
780-644-5589, TPR.Communications@gov.ab.ca

British Columbia

British Columbia Assessment Authority, #400, 3450 Uptown Blvd., Victoria, BC V8Z 0B9
250-595-6211, Fax: 250-595-6222, info@bcassessment.ca

British Columbia Transit, 520 Gorge Rd. East, Victoria, BC V8W 2P3
250-385-2551, Fax: 250-995-5639

Local Government, PO Box 9490 Prov Govt,Victoria, BC V8W 9N7
250-356-6575, Fax: 250-387-7973

Manitoba

Advisory Council on Workplace Safety & Health (SAFE Work), #200, 401 York Ave., Winnipeg, MB R3C 0P8
204-945-3446, Fax: 204-945-4556

Manitoba Culture, Heritage & Tourism, Legislative Building, #118, 450 Broadway Ave., Winnipeg, MB R3C 0V8
204-945-3729, Fax: 204-945-5223, mincht@leg.gov.mb.ca

Emergency Measures Organization, 405 Broadway Ave., 15th Floor, Winnipeg, MB R3C 3L6
204-945-4772, Fax: 204-945-4929, 888-267-8298, emo@gov.mb.ca

Health Information Privacy Committee, #4043, 300 Carlton St., Winnipeg, MB R3B 3M9

Manitoba Health, #100, 300 Carlton St., Winnipeg, MB R3B 3M9
204-786-7191, minhlt@leg.gov.mb.ca

Manitoba Hydro, 360 Portage Ave., PO Box 815 Main,Winnipeg, MB R3C 2P4
204-474-3311, publicaffairs@hydro.mb.ca

Manitoba Immigration & Multiculturalism, Legislative Building, 317, 450 Broadway Ave., Winnipeg, MB R3C 0V8
204-945-4079, Fax: 204-945-8312, minlab@leg.gov.mb.ca

Manitoba Infrastructure & Transportation, Legislative Building, #203, 450 Broadway Ave., Winnipeg, MB R3C 0V8
204-945-3723, Fax: 204-945-7610

Local Government Development Division, 59 Elizabeth Dr., PO Box 33, Thompson, MB R8N 1X4
204-677-6794, Fax: 204-677-6525

Manitoba Film Classification Board, #216, 301 Weston St., Winnipeg, MB R3E 3H4
204-945-8962, Fax: 204-945-0890, 866-612-2399, MFCB@gov.mb.ca

Manitoba Land Value Appraisal Commission, #1144, 363 Broadway, Winnipeg, MB R3C 3N9
204-945-5455, Fax: 204-948-2235

Provincial-Municipal Support Services, #508, 800 Portage Ave., Winnipeg, MB R3G 0N4

Public Health & Primary Health Care, 300 Carlton St., 2nd Floor, Winnipeg, MB R3B 3M9

Manitoba Workers' Compensation Board, 333 Broadway Ave., Winnipeg, MB R3C 4W3
204-954-4321, Fax: 204-954-4999, 800-362-3340, wcb@wcb.mb.ca

New Brunswick

Communications Branch, HSBC Place, 520 King St., 5th Fl., PO Box 5100, Fredericton, NB E3B 6G3
506-457-2356, Fax: 506-444-4697, Health.Sante@gnb.ca

New Brunswick Department of Health, PO Box 5100, Fredericton, NB E3B 5G8
506-457-4800, Fax: 506-453-5243, dh-ms@dh-ms.ca

New Brunswick Department of Post-Secondary Education, Training & Labour, Chestnut Complex, PO Box 6000, Fredericton, NB E3B 5H1
506-453-2597, Fax: 506-453-3618, dpetlinfo@gnb.ca

Newfoundland & Labrador

C.A. Pippy Park Commission, Mount Scio House, 15 Mount Scio Rd., St. John's, NL A1B 3T2
709-737-3655, Fax: 709-737-3303, info@pippypark.com

Eastern Waste Management Commission, #3, 255 Majors Path, St. John's, NL A1A 0L5
709-579-7960, Fax: 709-579-5392, info@easternwaste.ca

Newfoundland & Labrador Department of Municipal Affairs, West Block, Main Fl., Confederation Bldg., PO Box 8700, St. John's, NL A1B 4J6
709-729-3046, Fax: 709-729-0943, mainfo@gov.nl.ca

Newfoundland & Labrador Department of Service NL, PO Box 8700, St. John's, NL A1B 4J6
709-729-4834, servicenlinfo@gov.nl.ca

Newfoundland & Labrador Department of Transportation & Works, Confederation Bldg., West Block, 6th Fl., PO Box 8700, St. John's, NL A1B 4J6
709-729-3679, Fax: 709-729-4285, twminister@gov.nl.ca

Northwest Territories

Northwest Territories Department of Health & Social Services, Centre Square Tower, PO Box 1320, Yellowknife, NT X1A 2L9
Fax: 867-873-0266

Northwest Territories Department of Municipal & Community Affairs, PO Box 1320, Yellowknife, NT X1A 2L9
867-873-7118, Fax: 867-873-0309

Northwest Territories Power Corporation, 4 Capital Dr., Hay River, NT X0E 1G2
867-874-5200, Fax: 867-874-5251, info@ntpc.com

Northwest Territories Department of Public Works & Services, PO Box 1320, Yellowknife, NT X1A 2L9

Northwest Territories Water Board, 125 Mackenzie Rd., PO Box 2531, Yellowknife, NT X0E 0T0
867-678-2942, Fax: 867-678-2943, info@nwtwb.com

Nova Scotia

Nova Scotia Emergency Management Office, PO Box 2581, Halifax, NS B3J 3N5
902-424-5620, Fax: 902-424-5376, 866-424-5620, emo@gov.ns.ca

Nova Scotia Department of Transportation & Infrastructure Renewal, Johnston Bldg., 1672 Granville St., 2nd Fl., PO Box 186, Halifax, NS B3J 2N2
902-424-2297, Fax: 902-424-0532, tpwpaff@gov.ns.ca

Nunavut

Nunavut Territory Department of Community & Government Services, W.G. Brown Bldg., 4th Fl., PO Box 1000 700,Iqaluit, NU X0A 0H0
867-975-5400, Fax: 867-975-5305

Nunavut Emergency Management, PO Box 1000 700,Iqaluit, NU X0A 0H0
867-975-5403, Fax: 867-979-4221, 800-693-1666

Nunavut Territory Department of Health & Social Services, PO Box 1000 1000,Iqaluit, NU X0A 0H0
867-975-5766, Fax: 867-975-5705, 800-661-0833

Ontario

Advertising Review Board, Macdonald Block, #M2-56, 900 Bay St., 2nd Fl., Toronto, ON M7A 1N3
416-327-2183, Fax: 416-327-2179

Ontario Ministry of Community Safety & Correctional Services, George Drew Bldg., 25 Grosvenor St., 18th Fl., Toronto, ON M7A 1Y6
416-326-5000, Fax: 416-326-0498, 866-517-0571, mcscs.feedback@ontario.ca

Fire Safety Commission, Place Nouveau Bldg., 5775 Yonge St., 7th Fl., Toronto, ON M2M 4J1
416-325-3100, Fax: 416-314-1217

Hydro One Inc., North Tower, 483 Bay St., 15th Fl., Toronto, ON M5G 2P5
416-345-5000, Fax: 905-944-3251, 877-955-1155, customercommunications@hydroone.com

Independent Electricity System Operator, PO Box 4474 A,Toronto, ON M5W 4E5
905-403-6900, Fax: 905-403-6921, 888-448-7777, customer.relations@ieso.ca

Ontario Ministry of Municipal Affairs & Housing, College Park, 777 Bay St., 17th Fl., Toronto, ON M5G 2E5
416-585-7041, Fax: 416-585-6470, 866-220-2290, mininfo.mah@ontario.ca

Office of the Employer Advisor, #704, 151 Bloor St. West., Toronto, ON M5S 1S4
416-327-0020, Fax: 416-327-0726, 800-387-0774

Office of the Worker Advisor, #1300, 123 Edward St., Toronto, ON M5G 1E2
416-325-8570, Fax: 416-325-4830, 800-435-8980

Ontario Pension Board, Sun Life Bldg., #2200, 200 King St. West, Toronto, ON M5H 3X6
416-364-8558, Fax: 416-364-7578, 800-668-6203, clientservice@opb.ca

Ontario Power Generation, 700 University Ave., Toronto, ON M5G 1X6
416-592-2555, 877-592-2555, webmaster@opg.com

Southern Ontario Library Service, #902, 111 Peter St., Toronto, ON M5V 2H1
416-961-1669, Fax: 416-961-5122, 800-387-5765

Ontario Ministry of Transportation, Ferguson Block, 77 Wellesley St. West, 3rd Fl., Toronto, ON M7A 1Z8
416-235-4686, Fax: 905-704-2001, 800-268-4686

Prince Edward Island

Prince Edward Island Department of Community Services & Seniors, Jones Bldg., 11 Kent St., 2nd Fl., PO Box 2000, Charlottetown, PE C1A 7N8
902-620-3777, Fax: 902-894-0242, 866-594-3777

Prince Edward Island Department of Health & Wellness, 105 Rochford St. North, 4th Fl., PO Box 2000, Charlottetown, PE C1A 7N8
902-368-6414, Fax: 902-368-4121

Housing, Seniors & Corporate Support, Jones Bldg., 11 Kent St., 2nd Fl., PO Box 2000, Charlottetown, PE C1A 7N8
Fax: 902-894-0242

Island Waste Management Corporation, 110 Watts Ave., Charlottetown, PE C1E 2C1
902-894-0330, Fax: 902-894-0331, 888-280-8111, info@iwmc.pe.ca

SkillsPEI, Atlantic Technology Centre, #212, 90 University Ave., Charlottetown, PE C1A 4K9
902-368-6290, Fax: 902-368-6340, 877-491-4766

Quebec

Ministère des Affaires municipales, des Régions et de l'Occupation du territoire, Aile Chaveau, 10, rue Pierre-Olivier-Chauveau, 3e étage, Québec, QC G1R 4J3
418-691-2019, Fax: 418-643-7385, communications@mamrot.gouv.qc.ca

Commissariat des incendies, 455, rue Dupont, Québec, QC G1K 6N2
418-529-5706, Fax: 418-529-9922

Hydro-Québec, 75, boul René-Lévesque ouest, Montréal, QC H2Z 1A4
514-289-2211

Modernisation des centres hospitaliers universitaires de Montréal, CHUM, CUSM, CHU Sainte-Justine, #10.049, 2021, rue Union, Montréal, QC H3A 2S9
514-864-9883, Fax: 514-873-7362, info.construction3chu@msss.gouv.qc.ca

Office des personnes handicapées du Québec, 309, rue Brock, Drummondville, QC J2B 1C5
Fax: 819-475-8753, 800-567-1465, aide@ophq.gouv.qc.ca

Régie de l'assurance maladie du Québec, 1125, Grande Allée ouest, Québec, QC G1S 1E7
418-646-4636, 800-561-9749

Ministère de la Santé et des Services sociaux, Direction des communications, 1075, ch Sainte-Foy, 16e étage, Québec, QC G1S 2M1
418-643-9395, Fax: 418-643-4768, regisseur.web@msss.gouv.qc.ca

Société de l'assurance automobile du Québec, 333, boul Jean-Lesage, CP 19600 Terminus, Québec, QC G1K 8J6
418-643-7620, Fax: 418-644-0339, 800-361-7620, courrier@saaq.gouv.qc.ca

Société du Palais des congrès de Montréal, 159, rue Saint-Antoine ouest, 9é étage, Montréal, QC H2Z 1H2
514-871-8122, Fax: 514-871-9389, 800-268-8122, info@congresmtl.com

Ministère de la Sécurité publique, Tour des Laurentides, 2525, boul Laurier, 5e étage, Québec, QC G1V 2L2
418-643-2112, Fax: 418-646-6168, 866-644-6826

Urgences-santé Québec, 3232, rue Bélanger, Montréal, QC H1Y 3H5
514-723-5600, info@urgences-sante.qc.ca

École nationale des pompiers du Québec, #3.08, 2800, boul Saint-Martin ouest, Laval, QC H7T 2S9
450-680-6800, Fax: 450-680-6818, 866-680-3677

Saskatchewan

Saskatchewan Assessment Management Agency, #200, 2201 - 11th Ave., Regina, SK S4P 0J8
306-924-8000, Fax: 306-924-8070, 800-667-7262, info.request@sama.sk.ca

Saskatchewan Power Corporation (SaskPower), 2025 Victoria Ave., Regina, SK S4P 0S1
306-566-3306, Fax: 800-757-6937, 888-757-6937

Saskatchewan Water Corporation (SaskWater), #200, 111 Fairford St. East, Moose Jaw, SK S6H 1C8
Fax: 306-694-3207, 888-230-1111, comm@saskwater.com; customerservice@saskwater.com

SaskEnergy Incorporated, 1777 Victoria Ave., Regina, SK S4P 4K5
306-777-9225, 800-567-8899

Yukon Territory
Yukon Community Services, PO Box 2703, Whitehorse, YT Y1A 2C6
867-667-5811, Fax: 867-393-6295, 800-661-0408, inquiry@gov.yk.ca
Emergency Measures Organization, Combined Services Bldg., 2nd Fl., 60 Norseman Rd, Airport, Whitehorse, YT Y1A 2C6
867-667-5220, Fax: 867-393-6266, 800-661-0408, emo.yukon@gov.yk.ca
Yukon Health & Social Services, PO Box 2703, Whitehorse, YT Y1A 2C6
867-667-3673, Fax: 867-667-3096, hss@gov.yk.ca

PUBLIC UTILITIES

Alberta
Energy Resources Conservation Board, #1000, 250 - 5 Ave. SW, Calgary, AB T2P 0R4
403-297-8311, Fax: 403-297-7336, 855-297-8311, inquiries@ercb.ca; infoservices@ercb.ca; ADR@ercb.ca

British Columbia
British Columbia Hydro, 6911 Southpoint Dr., Burnaby, BC V3N 4X8
604-224-9376, 800-224-9376
British Columbia Utilities Commission, 900 Howe St., 6th Fl., PO Box 250, Vancouver, BC V6Z 2N3
604-660-4700, Fax: 604-660-1102, 800-663-1385, commission.secretary@bcuc.com

Manitoba
Manitoba Hydro, 360 Portage Ave., PO Box 815 Main,Winnipeg, MB R3C 2P4
204-474-3311, publicaffairs@hydro.mb.ca

Newfoundland & Labrador
Churchill Falls (Labrador) Corporation Limited, Hydro Place, 500 Columbus Dr., PO Box 12500, St. John's, NL A1B 4K7
709-737-1859, Fax: 709-737-1816
Newfoundland & Labrador Hydro, Hydro Place, 500 Columbus Dr., PO Box 12400, St. John's, NL A1B 4K7
709-737-1400, Fax: 709-737-1800, 888-737-1296, hydro@nlh.nl.ca
Nalcor Energy, 500 Columbus Dr., St. John's, NL A1E 2B2
709-737-1400, Fax: 709-737-1800
Newfoundland & Labrador Board of Commissioners of Public Utilities, Prince Charles Bldg., #E-210, 120 Torbay Rd., PO Box 21040, St. John's, NL A1A 5B2
709-726-8600, Fax: 709-726-9604, 866-782-0006, ito@pub.nf.ca

Northwest Territories
Northwest Territories Power Corporation, 4 Capital Dr., Hay River, NT X0E 1G2
867-874-5200, Fax: 867-874-5251, info@ntpc.com
Northwest Territories Water Board, 125 Mackenzie Rd., PO Box 2531, Yellowknife, NT X0E 0T0
867-678-2942, Fax: 867-678-2943, info@nwtwb.com

Nova Scotia
Nova Scotia Utility & Review Board, Summit Place, 1601 Lower Water St., 3rd Fl., PO Box 1692 M,Halifax, NS B3J 3S3
902-424-4448, Fax: 902-424-3919, uarb.board@gov.ns.ca

Ontario
Hydro One Inc., North Tower, 483 Bay St., 15th Fl., Toronto, ON M5G 2P5
416-345-5000, Fax: 905-944-3251, 877-955-1155, customercommunications@hydroone.com
Independent Electricity System Operator, PO Box 4474 A,Toronto, ON M5W 4E5
905-403-6900, Fax: 905-403-6921, 888-448-7777, customer.relations@ieso.ca
Ontario Power Generation, 700 University Ave., Toronto, ON M5G 1X6
416-592-2555, 877-592-2555, webmaster@opg.com

Prince Edward Island
Prince Edward Island Regulatory & Appeals Commission, National Bank Tower, #501, 134 Kent St., PO Box 577, Charlottetown, PE C1A 7L1
902-892-3501, Fax: 902-566-4076, 800-501-6268, info@irac.pe.ca

Quebec
Hydro-Québec, 75, boul René-Lévesque ouest, Montréal, QC H2Z 1A4
514-289-2211
Régie de l'énergie, Tour de la Bourse, #2.55, 800, Place Victoria, Montréal, QC H4Z 1A2
514-873-2452, Fax: 514-873-2070, 888-873-2452, secretariat@regie-energie.qc.ca; greffe@regie-energie.qc.ca

Saskatchewan
Saskatchewan Power Corporation (SaskPower), 2025 Victoria Ave., Regina, SK S4P 0S1
306-566-3306, Fax: 800-757-6937, 888-757-6937
Saskatchewan Water Corporation (SaskWater), #200, 111 Fairford St. East, Moose Jaw, SK S6H 1C8
Fax: 306-694-3207, 888-230-1111, comm@saskwater.com; customerservice@saskwater.com
SaskEnergy Incorporated, 1777 Victoria Ave., Regina, SK S4P 4K5
306-777-9225, 800-567-8899

Yukon Territory
Yukon Energy Corporation, 2 Miles Canyon Rd., PO Box 5920, Whitehorse, YT Y1A 6S7
867-393-5300, 866-926-3749, communications@yukonenergy.ca

PUBLIC WORKS

Public Works & Government Services Canada, Place du Portage, Phase III, 11, rue Laurier, Ottawa, ON K1A 0S5
questions@tpsgc-pwgsc.gc.ca

Alberta
Alberta Infrastructure, Infrastructure Building, 6950 - 113 St., Edmonton, AB T6H 5V7
780-415-0507, Fax: 780-427-2187, -310-0000, Infra.Contact.Us.m@gov.ab.ca

British Columbia
British Columbia Ministry of Citizens' Services, PO Box 9594 Prov Govt,Victoria, BC V8W 9E2
250-952-7623, Fax: 250-952-7628, 800-663-7867, EnquiryBC@gov.bc.ca

Manitoba
Manitoba Infrastructure & Transportation, Legislative Building, #203, 450 Broadway Ave., Winnipeg, MB R3C 0V8
204-945-3723, Fax: 204-945-7610

Newfoundland & Labrador
Newfoundland & Labrador Department of Transportation & Works, Confederation Bldg., West Block, 6th Fl., PO Box 8700, St. John's, NL A1B 4J6
709-729-3679, Fax: 709-729-4285, twminister@gov.nl.ca

Northwest Territories
Northwest Territories Department of Public Works & Services, PO Box 1320, Yellowknife, NT X1A 2L9

Nova Scotia
Nova Scotia Department of Transportation & Infrastructure Renewal, Johnston Bldg., 1672 Granville St., 2nd Fl., PO Box 186, Halifax, NS B3J 2N2
902-424-2297, Fax: 902-424-0532, tpwpaff@gov.ns.ca

Nunavut
Nunavut Territory Department of Community & Government Services, W.G. Brown Bldg., 4th Fl., PO Box 1000 700,Iqaluit, NU X0A 0H0
867-975-5400, Fax: 867-975-5305

Prince Edward Island
Prince Edward Island Department of Transportation & Infrastructure Renewal, Jones Bldg., 11 Kent St., 3rd Fl., PO Box 2000, Charlottetown, PE C1A 7N8
902-368-5100, Fax: 902-368-5395

Yukon Territory
Yukon Highways & Public Works, PO Box 2703, Whitehorse, YT Y1A 2C6
867-393-7193, Fax: 867-393-6218, 800-661-0408, hpw-info@gov.yk.ca

PUBLICATIONS

Public Works & Government Services Canada, Place du Portage, Phase III, 11, rue Laurier, Ottawa, ON K1A 0S5
questions@tpsgc-pwgsc.gc.ca

Nova Scotia
Nova Scotia Department of Service Nova Scotia & Municipal Relations, 1505 Barrington St., PO Box 216, Halifax, NS B3J 3K5
902-424-5200, Fax: 902-424-0581, 800-670-4357, askus@gov.ns.ca

Quebec
Ministère de la Culture et Communications, 225, Grande Allée est, Québec, QC G1R 5G5
888-380-8882

Yukon Territory
Yukon Highways & Public Works, PO Box 2703, Whitehorse, YT Y1A 2C6
867-393-7193, Fax: 867-393-6218, 800-661-0408, hpw-info@gov.yk.ca

PURCHASING

MERX, PO Box 11684 Centre-ville,Montreal, QC H3C 6H4
613-727-4900, Fax: 888-235-5800, 800-964-6379, merx@merx.com

Alberta
Alberta Infrastructure, Infrastructure Building, 6950 - 113 St., Edmonton, AB T6H 5V7
780-415-0507, Fax: 780-427-2187, -310-0000, Infra.Contact.Us.m@gov.ab.ca

British Columbia
British Columbia Ministry of Citizens' Services, PO Box 9594 Prov Govt,Victoria, BC V8W 9E2
250-952-7623, Fax: 250-952-7628, 800-663-7867, EnquiryBC@gov.bc.ca

Newfoundland & Labrador
Government Purchasing Agency, 30 Strawberry Marsh Rd., St. John's, NL A1B 4R4
709-729-3348, Fax: 709-729-5817, tenders@gov.nl.ca
Newfoundland & Labrador Department of Service NL, PO Box 8700, St. John's, NL A1B 4J6
709-729-4834, servicenlinfo@gov.nl.ca

Northwest Territories
Northwest Territories Department of Public Works & Services, PO Box 1320, Yellowknife, NT X1A 2L9

Nunavut
Nunavut Territory Department of Community & Government Services, W.G. Brown Bldg., 4th Fl., PO Box 1000 700,Iqaluit, NU X0A 0H0
867-975-5400, Fax: 867-975-5305

Prince Edward Island
Prince Edward Island Department of Transportation & Infrastructure Renewal, Jones Bldg., 11 Kent St., 3rd Fl., PO Box 2000, Charlottetown, PE C1A 7N8
902-368-5100, Fax: 902-368-5395,

RAIL TRANSPORTATION

See Also: Transportation
Transportation Safety Board of Canada, 200 Promenade du Portage, 4th Fl., Ottawa, ON K1A 1K8
819-994-3741, Fax: 819-997-2239, 800-387-3557
VIA Rail Canada Inc., #500, 3, Place Ville-Marie, Montréal, QC H3B 2C9
514-871-6000, Fax: 514-871-6104, 888-842-7245

Manitoba
Manitoba Infrastructure & Transportation, Legislative Building, #203, 450 Broadway Ave., Winnipeg, MB R3C 0V8
204-945-3723, Fax: 204-945-7610

New Brunswick
New Brunswick Department of Transportation & Infrastructure, Kings Place, PO Box 6000, Fredericton, NB E3B 5H1
506-453-3939, Fax: 506-453-2900, Transportation.Web@gnb.ca

Newfoundland & Labrador
Newfoundland & Labrador Department of Transportation & Works, Confederation Bldg., West Block, 6th Fl., PO Box 8700, St. John's, NL A1B 4J6
709-729-3679, Fax: 709-729-4285, twminister@gov.nl.ca

Nova Scotia
Nova Scotia Department of Transportation & Infrastructure Renewal, Johnston Bldg., 1672 Granville St., 2nd Fl., PO Box 186, Halifax, NS B3J 2N2
902-424-2297, Fax: 902-424-0532, tpwpaff@gov.ns.ca

Ontario
Metrolinx, #600, 20 Bay St., Toronto, ON M5J 2W3
416-874-5900, Fax: 416-869-1755

Quebec
Société du port ferroviaire Baie-Comeau-Hauterive, 18, rte Maritime, Baie-Comeau, QC G4Z 2L6

418-296-6785, Fax: 418-296-2377, societeduport@globetrotter.net
Ministère des Transports, 700, boul René-Lévesque est, 28e étage, Québec, QC G1R 5H1
418-643-6980, Fax: 418-643-2033, 888-355-0511, communications@mtq.gouv.qc.ca

Saskatchewan
Saskatchewan Highways & Infrastructure, Victoria Tower, 1855 Victoria Ave., Regina, SK S4P 3T2
306-787-4800, communications@highways.gov.sk.ca

REAL ESTATE

See Also: Land Titles
Canada Mortgage & Housing Corporation, 700 Montreal Rd., Ottawa, ON K1A 0P7
613-748-2000, Fax: 613-748-2098, 800-668-2642, chic@cmhc-schl.gc.ca

Alberta
Strategic Planning & Financial Services, Commerce Place, 10155 - 102 St., 13th Fl., Edmonton, AB T5J 4G8
780-422-8545

Nova Scotia
Nova Scotia Department of Service Nova Scotia & Municipal Relations, 1505 Barrington St., PO Box 216, Halifax, NS B3J 3K5
902-424-5200, Fax: 902-424-0581, 800-670-4357, askus@gov.ns.ca

RECREATION

See Also: Tourism & Tourist Information
Canadian Heritage, 15 Eddy St., Gatineau, QC K1A 0M5
819-997-0055, 866-811-0055, info@pch.gc.ca
Canadian Tourism Commission, #1400, 1055 Dunsmuir St., PO Box 49230, Vancouver, BC V7X 1L2
604-638-8300
National Battlefields Commission, 390, av de Bernières, Québec, QC G1R 2L7
418-648-3506, Fax: 418-648-3638, information@ccbn-nbc.gc.ca
Parks Canada, 25 Eddy St., Gatineau, QC K1A 0M5
613-860-1251, 888-773-8888, information@pc.gc.ca

Alberta
Alberta Sport, Recreation, Parks, & Wildlife Foundation, Standard Life Centre, #903, 10405 Jasper Ave., 9th Fl., Edmonton, AB T5J 4R7
780-415-1167, Fax: 780-415-0308, -310-0000

British Columbia
British Columbia Lottery Corporation, 74 West Seymour St., Kamloops, BC V2C 1E2
250-828-5500, Fax: 250-828-5631, 866-815-0222

Manitoba
Manitoba Entrepreneurship, Training & Trade, #1000, 259 Portage Ave, Winnipeg, MB R3B 3P4
204-945-2475, Fax: 204-945-3977, minctt@leg.gov.mb.ca
Manitoba Horse Racing Commission, c/o Boards, Commissions & Legislation Branch, #812, 401 York Ave., Winnipeg, MB R3C 0P8
204-945-4495, Fax: 204-948-2844
Tourism Secretariat, 155 Carlton St., 7th Fl., Winnipeg, MB R3C 3H8
800-665-0040

New Brunswick
New Brunswick Department of Tourism, Heritage & Culture, Centennial Building, PO Box 6000, Fredericton, NB E3B 5H1
506-444-5205, Fax: 506-457-4984, taponlinedirectory@gnb.ca

Newfoundland & Labrador
C.A. Pippy Park Commission, Mount Scio House, 15 Mount Scio Rd., St. John's, NL A1B 3T2
709-737-3655, Fax: 709-737-3303, info@pippypark.com

Ontario
Ontario Ministry of Economic Development, Trade & Employment, Hearst Block, 900 Bay St., 8th Fl., Toronto, ON M7A 2E1
416-325-6666, Fax: 416-325-6688, 866-668-4249, info@edt.gov.on.ca
Metro Toronto Convention Centre Corporation, 255 Front St. West, Toronto, ON M5V 2W6
416-585-8120, Fax: 416-585-8198, info@mtccc.com; sales@mtccc.com
Niagara Parks Commission, Oak Hall Administration Bldg., 7400 Portage Rd. South, PO Box 150, Niagara Falls, ON L2E 6T2
905-356-2241, Fax: 905-354-6041, 877-642-7275, corporateinfo@niagaraparks.com
Ontario Place Corporation, 955 Lake Shore Blvd. West, Toronto, ON M6K 3B9
416-314-9900, Fax: 416-314-9989, 866-663-4386
Ottawa Convention Centre, 55 Colonel By Dr., Ottawa, ON K1N 9J2
613-563-1984, Fax: 613-563-7646, 800-450-0077, info@ottawaconventioncentre.com
St. Lawrence Parks Commission, 13740 County Rd. 2, Morrisburg, ON K0C 1X0
613-543-3704, Fax: 613-543-2847, 800-437-2233, getaway@parks.on.ca
Ontario Ministry of Tourism, Culture & Sport, Hearst Block, 900 Bay St., 9th Fl., Toronto, ON M7A 2E1
416-326-9326, Fax: 416-314-7854, 888-997-9015

Prince Edward Island
Prince Edward Island Department of Community Services & Seniors, Jones Bldg., 11 Kent St., 2nd Fl., PO Box 2000, Charlottetown, PE C1A 7N8
902-620-3777, Fax: 902-894-0242, 866-594-3777
Prince Edward Island Department of Innovation & Advanced Learning, Shaw Bldg., 105 Rochford St., 5th Fl., PO Box 2000, Charlottetown, PE C1A 7N8
902-368-4240, Fax: 902-368-4242

Quebec
Comité conjoint de chasse, de pêche et de piégeage, #C220, 383 rue Saint-Jacques, Montréal, QC H2Y 1N9
514-284-2151, Fax: 514-284-0039, infohftcc@cccpp-hftcc.com
Régie des alcools, des courses et des jeux, 560, boul Charest est, Québec, QC G1K 3J3
418-643-7667, Fax: 418-643-5971, 800-363-0320
Société des établissements en plein air du Québec, Place de la Cité, Tour Cominar, #250, 2640, boul Laurier, 2e étage, Québec, QC G1V 5C2
418-890-6527, Fax: 418-528-6025, 800-665-6527, inforeservation@sepaq.com

Saskatchewan
Sport, Recreation, & Stewardship, 1919 Saskatchewan Dr., 9th Fl., Regina, SK S4P 4H2
306-787-7451, Fax: 306-787-0069
Wascana Centre Authority, 2900 Wascana Dr., PO Box 7111, Regina, SK S4P 3S7
306-522-3661, Fax: 306-565-2742, wca@wascana.ca

Yukon Territory
Parks, PO Box 2703 V-4, Whitehorse, YT Y1A 2C6
867-667-5648, Fax: 867-393-6223, 800-661-0408, yukon.parks@gov.yk.ca
Yukon Tourism & Culture, 100 Hanson St., Whitehorse, YT Y1A 2C6
867-667-5036, Fax: 867-667-3546
Yukon Lottery Commission, 312 Wood St., Whitehorse, YT Y1A 2E6
867-633-7890, Fax: 867-668-7561, lotteriesyukon@gov.yk.ca

RECYCLING

Alberta
Alberta Recycling Management Authority, Scotia Tower 1, #1310, 10060 Jasper Ave., PO Box 189, Edmonton, AB T5J 2J1
780-990-1111, Fax: 780-990-1122, 888-999-8762, info@albertarecycling.ca

Newfoundland & Labrador
Multi-Materials Stewardship Board, PO Box 8131 A, St. John's, NL A1B 3M9
709-753-0948, Fax: 709-753-0974, 800-901-6672, inquiries@mmsb.nl.ca

RESEARCH

Ontario
Ontario Ministry of Research & Innovation, Hearst Block, 900 Bay St., 8th Fl., Toronto, ON M7A 2E1
416-325-6666, Fax: 416-325-6688, 866-668-4249, info@edt.gov.on.ca

RESEARCH & DEVELOPMENT

Bayfield Institute, 867 Lakeshore Rd., PO Box 5050, Burlington, ON L7R 4A6
905-336-6240
Bedford Institute of Oceanography, 1 Challenger Dr., PO Box 1006, Dartmouth, NS B2Y 4A2
902-426-3492, Fax: 902-426-8484, WebmasterBIO-IOB@dfo-mpo.gc.ca
Canada Centre for Remote Sensing - Geomatics Canada, 588 Booth St., Ottawa, ON K1A 0Y7
613-995-0947, Fax: 613-947-1382
Canadian Centre for Housing Technology, c/o National Research Council Canada, Building M-20, 1200 Montreal Rd., Ottawa, ON K1A 0R6
construction@nrc-cnrc.gc.ca
Canadian Hydrographic Service, 615 Booth St., Ottawa, ON K1A 0E6
613-998-4931, Fax: 613-998-1217, chsinfo@dfo-mpo.gc.ca
Canadian Ice Service, 373 Sussex Dr., Block E, 3rd Fl., Ottawa, ON K1A 0H3
613-996-4489, 800-767-2885, cis-scg.client@ec.gc.ca
Canadian Space Agency, John H. Chapman Space Centre, 6767, rte de l'Aéroport, Saint-Hubert, QC J3Y 8Y9
450-926-4800, Fax: 450-926-4352, promo@asc-csa.gc.ca
CANMET Energy Technology Centre-Varennes, 1615, boul Lionel-Boulet, CP 4800, Varennes, QC J3X 1S6
450-652-4621, Fax: 450-652-0999, 800-322-8122, canmetenergy.nrcan.gc.ca
Chalk River Laboratories, NRC Canadian Neutron Beam Centre, Building 459, Station 18, Chalk River, ON K0J 1J0
613-584-8293, 800-364-6989
Fisheries Resource Conservation Council, PO Box 2001 D, Ottawa, ON K1P 5W3
613-998-0433, Fax: 613-998-1146, info@frcc-ccrh.ca
Freshwater Institute Science Laboratory, 501 University Cres., Winnipeg, MB R3T 2N6
204-983-5000, Fax: 204-983-6285
Institut Maurice-Lamontagne, 850, rte de le Mer, CP 1000, Mont-Joli, QC G5H 3Z4
418-775-0500, Fax: 418-775-0730
Institute of Ocean Sciences, 9860 West Saanich Rd., PO Box 6000, Sidney, BC V8L 4B2
250-363-6517, Fax: 250-363-6390
National Research Council Aerospace Manufacturing Technologies Centre, Campus Université de Montréal, 5145, av Decelles, Montréal, QC H3T 2B2
National Research Council Anaerobic Bioprocessing Pilot Plant, c/o Montréal (av Royalmount) Research Facilities, 6100, av Royalmount, Montréal, QC H4P 2R2
National Research Council Animal Cell Pilot Plant, c/o Montréal (av Royalmount) Research Facilities, 6100, av Royalmount, Montréal, QC H4P 2R2
National Research Council Canada, Building M-58, 1200 Montreal Rd., Ottawa, ON K1A 0R6
613-993-9101, Fax: 613-952-9907, 877-672-2672, info@nrc-cnrc.ca; media@nrc-cnrc.gc.ca
National Research Council Canada - Industrial Research Assistance Program, 1200 Montreal Rd., Ottawa, ON K1A 0R6
Fax: 613-952-1086, 877-994-4727, publicinquiries.irap-pari@nrc-cnrc.gc.ca
National Research Council Canadian Photonics Fabrication Centre, c/o National Research Council Canada, Building M-50, 1200 Montral Rd., Ottawa, ON K1A 0R6
National Research Council Fire Resistance & Performance of Structures Testing Facilities, c/o National Research Council, 1200 Montreal Rd., Ottawa, ON K1A 0R6
construction@nrc-cnrc.gc.ca
National Research Council Hydraulics Laboratories, c/o National Research Council, 1200 Montreal Rd., Ottawa, ON K1A OR6
877-672-2672
National Research Council Indoor Environment Testing Facilities, c/o National Research Council, 1200 Montreal Rd., Ottawa, ON K1A 0R6
construction@nrc-cnrc.gc.ca
National Research Council Industrial Partnership Facility, c/o Montréal (av Royalmount) Research Facilities, 6100, av Royalmount, Montréal, QC H4P 2R2
514-496-6100
National Research Council Marine Performance Evaluation & Testing Facilities, c/o National Research Council, 1200 Montreal Rd., Ottawa, ON K1A 0R6
National Research Council Medical Device Facilities, Boucherville Research Facilities, 75, boul de Mortagne,

Boucherville, QC J4B 6Y4
450-641-5100
National Research Council Ocean Technology Enterprise Centre, PO Box 12093, St. John's, NL A1B 3T5
709-772-2469, 877-672-2672
National Research Council Performance Assessment of Civil Infrastructure & Related Structures Research Facilities, Water Quality Testing Facility, Research Innovation Centre, #508, 3737 Wascana Pkwy., Regina, SK S4S 0A2
306-780-3208, construction@nrc-cnrc.gc.ca
National Research Council Single Domain Antibody Facility, c/o National Research Council, 1200 Montreal Rd., Ottawa, ON K1A 0R6
National Research Council Surface Transportation Research Facilities, Ottawa Uplands Research Facilities, 2320 Lester Rd., Ottawa, ON K1V 1S2
613-998-9639, Fax: 613-957-0831, inquiries.ST@nrc-cnrc.gc.ca
National Research Council SWCNT (Single-Wall Carbon Nanotubes) Technology Accelerator Centre, Montreal Road Campus, National Research Council, 1200 Montreal Rd., Ottawa, ON K1A 0R6
613-993-9101
National Research Council Waste Biotreatability Facility, c/o National Research Council, 1200 Montreal Rd., Ottawa, ON K1A 0R6
National Research Council Wind Tunnel Testing Facilities, c/o National Research Council, 1200 Montreal Rd., Ottawa, ON K1A 0R6
National Research Council Zebrafish Screening Facility, c/o National Research Council, 1200 Montreal Rd., Ottawa, ON K1A 0R6
Natural Sciences & Engineering Research Council of Canada, Constitution Square, Tower II, 350 Albert St., Ottawa, ON K1A 1H5
613-995-4273, Fax: 613-943-1624, marie-josee.duval@nserc-crsng.gc.ca
Office of Energy Research & Development, 580 Booth St., 14th Fl., Ottawa, ON K1A 0E4
613-947-1421, Fax: 613-995-6146,
Pacific Biological Station, 3190 Hammond Bay Rd., Nanaimo, BC V9T 6N7
250-756-7000, Fax: 250-756-7053
Polar Continental Shelf Program, #487, 615 Booth St., Ottawa, ON K1A 0E4
613-947-1650, Fax: 613-947-1611, pcsp@nrcan-rncan.gc.ca
Safe Environments Programme, Environmental Health Centre, Bldg. 8, 120 Parkdale Ave., Ottawa, ON K1A 0K9
613-954-0291, Fax: 613-952-2206
Science & Technology Branch, Tower 5, 1341 Baseline Rd., Ottawa, ON K1A 0C5
613-759-1000, Fax: 613-773-1866
St. Andrews Biological Station, 531 Brandy Cove Rd., St Andrews, NB E5B 2L9
506-529-8854, Fax: 506-529-5862, XMARSABS@mar.dfo-mpo.gc.ca
Transportation Development Centre, Tour Ouest, Complexe Guy-Favreau, 800, boul René-Lévesque ouest, 6e étage, Montréal, QC H3B 1X9
514-283-0000, Fax: 514-283-7158, tdccdt@tc.gc.ca

Alberta

Alberta Innovates - Energy & Environmental Solutions, AMEC Place, #2540, 801 - 6th Ave. SW, Calgary, AB T2P 3W2
403-297-7089, ees@albertainnovates.ca

British Columbia

Powertech Labs Inc., 12388 - 88 Ave., Surrey, BC V8W 7R7
604-590-7500, Fax: 604-590-6611

New Brunswick

New Brunswick Research & Productivity Council, 921 College Hill Rd., Fredericton, NB E3B 6Z9
506-452-1212, Fax: 506-452-1395, info@rpc.ca

Northwest Territories

Aurora Research Institute, 191 MacKenzie Rd., PO Box 1450, Inuvik, NT X0E 0T0
867-777-3298, Fax: 867-777-4264, webmaster@nwtresearch.com

Ontario

Ontario Ministry of Research & Innovation, Hearst Block, 900 Bay St., 8th Fl., Toronto, ON M7A 2E1
416-325-6666, Fax: 416-325-6688, 866-668-4249, info@edt.gov.on.ca

Science & Information Resources Division, Roberta Bondar Pl., #400, 70 Foster Dr., Sault Ste Marie, ON P6A 6V5
705-755-2000, Fax: 705-755-2802, 800-667-1940

Prince Edward Island

Agricultural Insurance Corporation, 29 Indigo Cres., PO Box 1600, Charlottetown, PE C1A 7N3
902-368-4842, Fax: 902-368-6677
BIO|FOOD|TECH, 101 Belvedere Ave., PO Box 2000, Charlottetown, PE C1A 7N8
902-368-5548, Fax: 902-368-5549, 877-368-5548, biofoodtech@biofoodtech.ca

Quebec

Centre de recherche industrielle du Québec, 333, rue Franquet, Québec, QC G1P 4C7
418-659-1550, 800-667-2386, infocriq@criq.qc.ca
Fonds de la recherche en santé du Québec, #800, 500, rue Sherbrooke ouest, Montréal, QC H3A 3C6
514-873-2114, Fax: 514-873-8768
Fonds québécois de la recherche sur la nature et les technologies, #450, 140, Grande Allée est, Québec, QC G1R 5M8
418-643-8560, Fax: 418-643-1451, info.nt@frq.gouv.qc.ca
Innovatech Québec, #410, 888, rue St-Jean, Québec, QC G1R 5H6
418-528-9770, Fax: 418-528-9783, 866-605-1676

Saskatchewan

Saskatchewan Power Corporation (SaskPower), 2025 Victoria Ave., Regina, SK S4P 0S1
306-566-3306, Fax: 800-757-6937, 888-757-6937
Saskatchewan Research Council, #125, 15 Innovation Blvd., Saskatoon, SK S7N 2X8
306-933-5400, Fax: 306-933-7446, info@src.sk.ca

RESOURCE DEVELOPMENT

See: Natural Resources

Ontario

Ontario Ministry of Rural Affairs, c/o Ministry of Agriculture & Food, 1 Stone Rd. West, Guelph, ON N1G 4Y2
519-826-3100, Fax: 519-826-4335, 888-466-2372, about.omafra@ontario.ca

ROUND TABLES

National Round Table on the Environment & Economy, #200, 344 Slater St., Ottawa, ON K1R 7Y3
613-992-7189, Fax: 613-992-7385, info@nrtee-trnee.ca

Manitoba

Manitoba Round Table for Sustainable Development, #160, 123 Main St., Winnipeg, MB R3C 1A5
204-945-1869, Fax: 204-948-2357, mrtsd@gov.mb.ca

SCIENCE & NATURE

Aboriginal Affairs & Northern Development Canada, 10 Wellington St., North Tower, Gatineau, QC K1A 0H4
819-997-0380, Fax: 866-817-3977, 800-567-9604, infopubs@aadnc-aandc.gc.ca
Agriculture & Agri-Food Canada, 1341 Baseline Rd., Ottawa, ON K1A 0C5
613-773-1000, Fax: 613-773-1081, 855-773-0241, info@agr.gc.ca
Beverly & Qamanirjuaq Caribou Management Board, Secretariat, PO Box 629, Stonewall, MB R0C 2Z0
204-467-2438, caribounews@arctic-caribou.com
Canada Centre for Remote Sensing - Geomatics Canada, 588 Booth St., Ottawa, ON K1A 0Y7
613-995-0947, Fax: 613-947-1382
Canadian Institutes of Health Research, 160 Elgin St., 9th Fl., Ottawa, ON K1A 0W9
613-941-2672, Fax: 613-954-1800, 888-603-4178, info@cihr-irsc.gc.ca
Canadian Nuclear Safety Commission, 280 Slater St., PO Box 1046 B,Ottawa, ON K1P 5S9
613-995-5894, Fax: 613-995-5086, 800-668-5284
Canadian Polar Commission, Constitution Square, #1710, 360 Albert St., Ottawa, ON K1R 7X7
613-943-8605, Fax: 613-943-8607, 888-765-2701, mail@polarcom.gc.ca
Canadian Space Agency, John H. Chapman Space Centre, 6767, rte de l'Aéroport, Saint-Hubert, QC J3Y 8Y9
450-926-4800, Fax: 450-926-4352, promo@asc-csa.gc.ca
Commission for Environmental Cooperation, Secretariat, #200, 393, rue St-Jacques ouest, Montréal, QC H2Y 1N9
514-350-4300, Fax: 514-350-4314, info@cec.org

Committee on the Status of Endangered Wildlife in Canada, c/o Canadian Wildlife Service, 351 St. Joseph Blvd, 4th Fl., Gatineau, QC K1A 0H3
819-953-3215, Fax: 819-994-3684, cosewic/cosepac@ec.gc.ca
Ecosystems & Fisheries Management, 200 Kent St., Ottawa, ON K1A 0E6
Electronic Commerce Branch, 300 Slater St., Ottawa, ON K1A 0C8
613-954-5031, Fax: 613-954-2340, 800-328-6189
Environment Canada, 10 Wellington St., Gatineau, QC K1A 0H3
819-997-2800, Fax: 819-994-1412, 800-668-6767, enviroinfo@ec.gc.ca
Fisheries & Oceans Canada, 200 Kent St., Ottawa, ON K1A 0E6
613-993-0999, Fax: 613-990-1866, info@dfo-mpo.gc.ca
Fisheries Resource Conservation Council, PO Box 2001 D, Ottawa, ON K1P 5W3
613-998-0433, Fax: 613-998-1146, info@frcc-ccrh.ca
Geological Survey of Canada, 601 Booth St., Ottawa, ON K1A 0E8
613-996-3919, Fax: 613-943-8742, esic@nrcan.gc.ca
Hazardous Materials Information Review Commission, 427 Laurier Ave. West, 7th Fl., Ottawa, ON K1A 1M3
613-993-4331, Fax: 613-993-4686, hmirc-ccrmd@hc-sc.gc.ca

Indian Oil & Gas Canada, #100, 9911 Chiila Blvd., Tsuu T'ina (Sarcee), AB T2W 6H6
403-292-5625, Fax: 403-292-5618, ContactIOGC@inac-ainc.gc.ca
International Development Research Centre, 150 Kent St., PO Box 8500, Ottawa, ON K1G 3H9
613-236-6163, Fax: 613-238-7230, info@idrc.ca
Mackenzie Valley Environmental Impact Review Board, 200 Scotia Centre, #5102, 50th Ave., PO Box 938, Yellowknife, NT X1A 2N7
867-766-7050, Fax: 867-766-7074, 866-912-3472,
National Energy Board, 444 - 7 Ave. SW, Calgary, AB T2P 0X8
403-292-4800, Fax: 403-292-5503, 800-899-1265, info@neb-one.gc.ca
National Research Council Animal Cell Pilot Plant, c/o Montréal (av Royalmount) Research Facilities, 6100, av Royalmount, Montréal, QC H4P 2R2
National Research Council Canada, Building M-58, 1200 Montreal Rd., Ottawa, ON K1A 0R6
613-993-9101, Fax: 613-952-9907, 877-672-2672, info@nrc-cnrc.ca; media@nrc-cnrc.gc.ca
National Round Table on the Environment & Economy, #200, 344 Slater St., Ottawa, ON K1R 7Y3
613-992-7189, Fax: 613-992-7385, info@nrtee-trnee.ca
Natural Resources Canada, 580 Booth St., Ottawa, ON K1A 0E4
613-995-0947, Fax: 613-992-7211
Natural Sciences & Engineering Research Council of Canada, Constitution Square, Tower II, 350 Albert St., Ottawa, ON K1A 1H5
613-995-4273, Fax: 613-943-1624, marie-josee.duval@nserc-crsng.gc.ca
North American Bird Conservation Initiative, Canadian Wildlife Service, 351, boul St-Joseph, 3e étage, Gatineau, QC K1A 0H3
819-994-0512, Fax: 819-994-4445, nabci@ec.gc.ca
North American Waterfowl Management Plan, NAWCC (Canada) Secretariat, Place Vincent Massey, 351 St. Joseph Blvd., 7th Fl., Gatineau, QC K1A 0H3
819-934-6034, Fax: 819-934-6017, nawmp@ec.gc.ca
Nunavut Impact Review Board, PO Box 1360, Cambridge Bay, NU X0B 0C0
867-983-4600, Fax: 867-983-2594, 866-233-3033, info@nirb.ca
Nunavut Water Board, PO Box 119, Gjoa Haven, NU X0B 1J0
867-360-6338, Fax: 867-360-6369
Pest Management Regulatory Agency, 2720 Riverside Dr., Ottawa, ON K1A 0K9
613-736-3401, Fax: 613-736-3798
Polar Continental Shelf Program, #487, 615 Booth St., Ottawa, ON K1A 0E4
613-947-1650, Fax: 613-947-1611, pcsp@nrcan-rncan.gc.ca
Porcupine Caribou Management Board, PO Box 31723, Whitehorse, YT Y1A 6L3
867-633-4780, Fax: 867-393-3904, pcmb@taiga.net
Program Policy, 200 Kent St., Ottawa, ON K1A 0E6

Alberta

Access Advisory Council, Sterling Place, 9940 - 106 St., 4th Fl., Edmonton, AB
780-644-3183

Alberta Agriculture & Rural Development, JG O'Donoghue Bldg., #100A, 7000 - 113th St., Edmonton, AB T6H 5T6
780-427-2727, -310-3276, duke@gov.ab.ca

Alberta Environmental Appeals Board, Peace Hills Trust Tower, #306, 10011 - 109 St., Edmonton, AB T5J 3S8
780-427-6207, Fax: 780-427-4693

Alberta Innovates - Energy & Environmental Solutions, AMEC Place, #2540, 801 - 6th Ave. SW, Calgary, AB T2P 3W2
403-297-7089, ees@albertainnovates.ca

Alberta Innovates - Health Solutions, #1500, 10104 - 103 Ave., Edmonton, AB T5J 4A7
780-423-5727, Fax: 780-429-3509, 877-423-5727, health@albertainnovates.ca

Alberta Livestock & Meat Agency, Ellwood Office Park South, #101, 1003 Ellwood Rd. SW, Edmonton, AB T6X 0B3
780-638-1699, Fax: 780-638-6495, info@almaltd.ca

Alberta Recycling Management Authority, Scotia Tower 1, #1310, 10060 Jasper Ave., PO Box 189, Edmonton, AB T5J 2J1
780-990-1111, Fax: 780-990-1122, 888-999-8762, info@albertarecycling.ca

Alberta Research & Innvoation Authority, Phipps-McKinnon Bldg., #500, 101A Ave., Edmonton, AB T5J 3G2
780-427-1488, Fax: 780-427-0979, aria@albertainnovates.ca

Alberta Sport, Recreation, Parks, & Wildlife Foundation, Standard Life Centre, #903, 10405 Jasper Ave., 9th Fl., Edmonton, AB T5J 4R7
780-415-1167, Fax: 780-415-0308, -310-0000

Alberta Used Oil Management Association, Empire Building, #1008, 10080 Jasper Ave., Edmonton, AB T5J 1V9
780-414-1510, Fax: 780-414-1519, 866-414-1510, reception@usedoilrecycling.ca

Beverage Container Management Board, #750, 10707 - 100 Ave., Edmonton, AB T5J 3M1
780-424-3193, Fax: 780-428-4620, 888-424-7671

Alberta Energy, North Petroleum Plaza, 9945 - 108 St., Edmonton, AB T5K 2G6
780-427-8050, Fax: 780-422-0698, -310-0000, Library.Energy@gov.ab.ca

Alberta Environment & Sustainable Resource Development, Oxbridge Place, 9820 - 106 St., Main Fl., Edmonton, AB T5K 2J6
780-427-2700, Fax: 780-422-4086, -310-0000, env.infocent@gov.ab.ca; srd.infocent@gov.ab.ca

Irrigation Council, Provincial Bldg., 200 - 5 Ave. South, 3rd Fl., Lethbridge, AB T1J 4L1
403-381-5176, Fax: 403-382-4406

Land Compensation Board, 1229 - 91 St. SW, Edmonton, AB T6X 1E9
srb.lcb@gov.ab.ca

Natural Resources Conservation Board, Sterling Place, 9940 - 106 St., Edmonton, AB T5K 2N2
780-422-1977, Fax: 780-427-0607, 866-383-6722, info@nrcb.gov.ab.ca

Special Areas Board, Special Areas Board Administration, 212 - 2nd Ave. West, PO Box 820, Hanna, AB T0J 1P0
403-854-5600, Fax: 403-854-5527, specarea@telus.net

British Columbia

Agricultural Land Commission, #133, 4940 Canada Way, Burnaby, BC V5G 4K6
604-660-7000, Fax: 604-660-7033, ALCBurnaby@Victoria1.gov.bc.ca

British Columbia Ministry of Agriculture, PO Box 9120 Prov Govt,Victoria, BC V8W 9E2
250-387-5121

British Columbia Farm Industry Review Board, 780 Blanshard St., PO Box 9129 Prov Govt, Victoria, BC V8W 9B5
250-356-8945, Fax: 250-356-5131, firb@gov.bc.ca

Emergency Management BC, PO Box 9223 Prov Govt,Victoria, BC V8W 9J1
250-953-4002, Fax: 250-953-4081, BC.CorSer@gov.bc.ca (Coroner); OFC@gov.bc.ca (Fire Commissioner)

British Columbia Ministry of Energy, Mines, & Natural Gas (& Responsible for Housing), PO Box 9053 Prov Govt,Victoria, BC V8W 9E2

British Columbia Ministry of Environment, PO Box 9339 Prov Govt,Victoria, BC V8W 9M1
250-387-1161, Fax: 250-387-5669, envmail@gov.bc.ca

Environmental Protection Division, PO Box 9339, Victoria, BC V8W 9M1
250-387-1288, Fax: 250-387-5669

Environmental Stewardship Division, PO Box 9339 Prov Govt,Victoria, BC V8W 9M1
250-356-0121, Fax: 250-387-5669

Forest Practices Board, 1675 Douglas St., 3rd Fl., PO Box 9905 Prov Govt, Victoria, BC V8W 9R1
250-213-4700, Fax: 250-213-4725, 800-994-5899, fpboard@gov.bc.ca

Forestry Innovation Investment Ltd., #1200, 1130 West Pender St., Vancouver, BC V6E 4A4
604-685-7507, Fax: 604-685-5373, info@bcfii.ca

British Columbia Ministry of Forests, Lands & Natural Resource Operations, PO Box 9352 Prov Govt,Victoria, BC V8W 9M1
250-387-4809, 877-855-3222, FLNRO.MediaRequests@gov.bc.ca

Islands Trust, #200, 1627 Fort St., Victoria, BC V8R 1H8
250-405-5151, Fax: 250-405-5155, information@islandstrust.bc.ca

Oil & Gas Commission, #100, 10003 - 110 Ave., Fort St John, BC V1J 6M7
250-794-5200, Fax: 250-794-5375

Timber Export Advisory Committee, PO Box 9514 Prov Govt, Victoria, BC V8W 9C2
250-387-8916, Fax: 250-387-5050

Manitoba

Manitoba Aboriginal & Northern Affairs, Legislative Bldg, 344-450 Broadway, Winnipeg, MB R3C OV8
204-945-3719, Fax: 204-945-8374, anaweb@gov.mb.ca

Agricultural Societies, 1129 Queens Ave., Brandon, MB R7A 1L9
204-726-6195, Fax: 204-726-6260

Manitoba Agriculture, Food & Rural Initiatives, Legislative Bldg., 165-450 Broadway, Winnipeg, MB R3C 0V8
204-945-3722, Fax: 204-945-3470, minagr@leg.gov.mb.ca

Clean Environment Commission, #305, 155 Carlton St., Winnipeg, MB R3C 3H8
204-945-0594, Fax: 204-945-0090

Manitoba Conservation & Water Stewardship, 200 Saulteaux Cres., Winnipeg, MB R3J 3W3
800-214-6497, mws@gov.mb.ca

Ecological Reserves Advisory Committee, c/o Manitoba Conservation, Parks & Natural Areas Branch, 200 Saulteaux Cres., Winnipeg, MB R3J 3W3
204-945-4148, Fax: 204-945-0012

Endangered Species Advisory Committee, 200 Saulteaux Cres., PO Box 24, Winnipeg, MB R3J 3W3
204-945-7465, Fax: 204-945-3077

Farm Lands Ownership Board, #812, Norquay Bldg., 401 York Ave., Winnipeg, MB R3C 0P8
204-945-3149, Fax: 204-945-1489, 800-282-8069

Farm Machinery & Equipment Board, Norquay Bldg., #812, 401 York Ave., Winnipeg, MB R3C 0P8
204-945-3856, Fax: 204-948-2844

Manitoba Hydro, 360 Portage Ave., PO Box 815 Main,Winnipeg, MB R3C 2P4
204-474-3311, publicaffairs@hydro.mb.ca

Local Government Development Division, 59 Elizabeth Dr., PO Box 33, Thompson, MB R8N 1X4
204-677-6794, Fax: 204-677-6525

Manitoba Habitat Heritage Corporation, #200, 1555 St. James St., Winnipeg, MB R3H 1B5
204-784-4350, Fax: 204-784-7359, mhhc@mhhc.mb.ca

New Brunswick

New Brunswick Department of Agriculture, Aquaculture & Fisheries, Agricultural Research Station (Experimental Farm), PO Box 6000, Fredericton, NB E3B 5H1
506-453-2666, Fax: 506-453-7170, DAAF-MAAP@gnb.ca

New Brunswick Department of Environment & Local Government, Marysville Place, PO Box 6000, Fredericton, NB E3B 5H1
506-453-2690, Fax: 506-457-4994, elg/egl-info@gnb.ca

New Brunswick Department of Natural Resources, Hugh John Flemming Forestry Centre, PO Box 6000, Fredericton, NB E3B 5H1
506-453-3826, Fax: 506-444-4367, dnrweb@gnb.ca

New Brunswick Farm Products Commission, c/o Department of Agriculture, Aquaculture & Fisheries, PO Box 6000, Fredericton, NB E3B 5H1
506-453-3647, Fax: 506-444-5969

Northern Development Division, Harbourview Place, #400, 275 Main St., Bathurst, NB E2A 1A9
506-547-2227, Fax: 506-547-2269

Renewable Resources, Hugh John Flemming Forestry Centre, Suite 310, Fl 3rd, PO Box 6000, Fredericton, NB E3B 5H1
506-453-2684, Fax: 506-453-2684, dnrweb@gnb.ca

New Brunswick Research & Productivity Council, 921 College Hill Rd., Fredericton, NB E3B 6Z9
506-452-1212, Fax: 506-452-1395, info@rpc.ca

Newfoundland & Labrador

C.A. Pippy Park Commission, Mount Scio House, 15 Mount Scio Rd., St. John's, NL A1B 3T2
709-737-3655, Fax: 709-737-3303, info@pippypark.com

Newfoundland & Labrador Department of Environment & Conservation, Confederation Bldg., West Block, 4th Fl., PO Box 8700, St. John's, NL A1B 4J6
709-729-2664, Fax: 709-729-6639, 800-563-6181, envcinquires@gov.nl.ca

Newfoundland & Labrador Department of Fisheries & Aquaculture, Petten Bldg., 30 Strawberry Marsh Rd., PO Box 8700, St. John's, NL A1B 4J6
709-729-3723, Fax: 709-729-6082, fisheries@gov.nl.ca

Newfoundland & Labrador Department of Natural Resources, Natural Resources Bldg., 50 Elizabeth Ave., 7th Fl., PO Box 8700, St. John's, NL A1B 4J6
709-729-2920, Fax: 709-729-0059

Professional Fish Harvesters Certification Board, 368 Hamilton Ave., PO Box 8541, St. John's, NL A1B 3P2
709-722-8170, Fax: 709-722-8201, pfh@pfhcb.com

Northwest Territories

Aurora Research Institute, 191 MacKenzie Rd., PO Box 1450, Inuvik, NT X0E 0T0
867-777-3298, Fax: 867-777-4264, webmaster@nwtresearch.com

Northwest Territories Department of Environment & Natural Resources, PO Box 1320, Yellowknife, NT X1A 2L9

Nova Scotia

Nova Scotia Department of Agriculture, 1741 Brunswick St., 3rd Fl., PO Box 2223, Halifax, NS B3J 3C4
902-424-4560, Fax: 902-424-4671

Crown Land Information Management Centre, Founders Square, #501, 1701 Hollis St., PO Box 698, Halifax, NS B3J 2T9
902-424-3171

Geomatics Centre, 160 Willow St., Amherst, NS B4H 3W5
902-667-7231, Fax: 902-667-6008, 800-798-0706, geoinfo@gov.ns.ca

Nova Scotia Department of Natural Resources, Founder's Square, 1701 Hollis St., 3rd Fl., PO Box 698, Halifax, NS B3J 2T9
902-424-5935, Fax: 902-424-0594, 800-565-2224

Nova Scotia Farm Loan Board, PO Box 550, Truro, NS B2N 5E3
902-893-6506, Fax: 902-895-7693, flb@gov.ns.ca

Nunavut

Nunavut Territory Department of Environment, PO Box 1000 1300,Iqaluit, NU X0A 0H0
867-975-7700, Fax: 867-975-7742, environment@gov.nu.ca

Ontario

Advisory Council on Drinking Water Quality & Testing Standards, 40 St. Clair Ave. West, 3rd Fl., Toronto, ON M4V 1M2
416-212-7779, Fax: 416-212-7595

Ontario Ministry of Agriculture, Food & Rural Affairs, Ontario Government Bldg., 1 Stone Rd. West, Guelph, ON N1G 4Y2
519-826-3100, 888-466-2372

Algonquin Forestry Authority - Huntsville, 222 Main St. West, Huntsville, ON P1H 1Y1
705-789-9647, Fax: 705-789-3353, info@algonquinforestry.on.ca

Algonquin Forestry Authority - Pembroke, Victoria Centre, 84 Isabella St., 2nd Fl., Pembroke, ON K8A 5S5
613-735-0173, Fax: 613-735-4192, info@algonquinforestry.on.ca

Animal Care Review Board, 77 Grenville St., 8th Fl., Toronto, ON M5S 1B3
416-314-5336, Fax: 416-314-5559, acrb.info@ontario.ca; acrb.registrar@ontario.ca

Association of Ontario Land Surveyors, 1043 McNicoll Ave., Toronto, ON M1W 3W6
416-491-9020, Fax: 416-491-2576, 800-268-0718

Cancer Care Ontario, 620 University Ave., 15th Fl., Toronto, ON M5G 2L7
416-971-9800, Fax: 416-971-6888

Conservation Review Board, #1500, 655 Bay St., Toronto, ON M5G 1E5
416-212-6349, Fax: 416-326-6209, conservation.review.board@ontario.ca

Ontario Ministry of Environment, 135 St. Clair Ave. West, Toronto, ON M4V 1P5
416-325-4000, Fax: 416-325-3159, 800-565-4923, picemail.moe@ontario.ca

Environmental Commissioner of Ontario, #605, 1075 Bay St., Toronto, ON M5S 2B1
416-325-3377, Fax: 416-325-3370, 800-701-6454, commissioner@eco.on.ca

Environmental Sciences & Standards Division, 135 St. Clair Ave. West, 14th Fl., Toronto, ON M4V 1P5
Fax: 416-314-6358

Lake of the Woods Control Board, c/o Executive Engineer, Ottawa, ON K1A 0H3
Fax: 819-953-4666, 800-661-5922, secretariat@lwcb.ca

Livestock Medicines Advisory Committee, 1 Stone Rd. West, 3rd Fl. Northeast, Guelph, ON N1G 4Y2
519-826-4110, Fax: 519-826-3254, ag.info.omafra@ontario.ca

Mines & Minerals Division, Willet Green Miller Centre, 933 Ramsey Lake Rd., Sudbury, ON P3E 6B5
705-670-5755, Fax: 705-670-5818, 888-415-9845

Ontario Ministry of Natural Resources, 300 Water St., PO Box 7000, Peterborough, ON K9J 8M5
705-755-2000, Fax: 705-755-1677, 800-667-1940, mnr.nric.mnr@ontario.ca

Niagara Parks Commission, Oak Hall Administration Bldg., 7400 Portage Rd. South, PO Box 150, Niagara Falls, ON L2E 6T2
905-356-2241, Fax: 905-354-6041, 877-642-7275, corporateinfo@niagaraparks.com

Ontario Ministry of Northern Development & Mines, 159 Cedar St., Sudbury, ON P3E 6A5
705-670-5755, Fax: 705-670-5818, 888-415-9845

Ontario Clean Water Agency, 1 Yonge St., 17th Fl., Toronto, ON M5E 1E5
416-314-5600, Fax: 416-314-8300, 800-667-6292

Ontario Fish & Wildlife Heritage Commission, Robinson Pl., 300 Water St., PO Box 7000, Peterborough, ON K9J 8M5
705-755-1905, Fax: 705-755-1900

Ontario Geographic Names Board, Robinson Place, 300 Water St., 2nd Fl., PO Box 7000, Peterborough, ON K9J 8M5
705-755-2132

Ontario Moose & Bear Allocation Advisory Committee, PO Box 964, Sioux Lookout, ON P8T 1B3
807-737-2615, Fax: 807-737-4173

Ontario Science Centre, 770 Don Mills Rd., Toronto, ON M3C 1T3
416-696-1000, Fax: 416-696-3166, 888-696-1110

Pesticides Advisory Committee, 135 St. Clair Ave. West, 15th Fl., Toronto, ON M4V 1P5
416-314-9230, Fax: 416-314-9237

Provincial Services Division, #6540, 99 Wellesley St. West, Toronto, ON M7A 1W3
416-326-9504

Rabies Advisory Committee, DNA Bldg, Trent University, 2140 East Bank Dr., Peterborough, ON K9J 7B8
705-755-2273

Royal Botanical Gardens, 680 Plains Rd. West, Burlington, ON L7T 4H4
905-527-1158, Fax: 905-577-0375, 800-694-4769, info@rbg.ca; auxiliary@rbg.ca

Science & Information Resources Division, Roberta Bondar Pl., #400, 70 Foster Dr., Sault Ste Marie, ON P6A 6V5
705-755-2000, Fax: 705-755-2802, 800-667-1940

Science North, 100 Ramsey Lake Rd., Sudbury, ON P3E 5S9
705-522-3701, Fax: 705-522-4954, 800-461-4898, contactus@sciencenorth.ca

Shibogama Interim Planning Board, PO Box 105, Wunnumin, ON P0V 2Z0
807-442-2559, Fax: 807-442-2627

St. Lawrence Parks Commission, 13740 County Rd. 2, Morrisburg, ON K0C 1X0
613-543-3704, Fax: 613-543-2847, 800-437-2233, getaway@parks.on.ca

Windigo Interim Planning Board, PO Box 299, Sioux Lookout, ON P8T 1A3
807-737-1585, Fax: 807-737-3133

Prince Edward Island

Agricultural Insurance Corporation, 29 Indigo Cres., PO Box 1600, Charlottetown, PE C1A 7N3
902-368-4842, Fax: 902-368-6677

Prince Edward Island Department of Agriculture & Forestry, Jones Bldg., 11 Kent St., PO Box 2000, Charlottetown, PE C1A 7N8
902-368-4880, Fax: 902-368-4857

Grain Elevators Corporation, 7 Gerald McCarville Dr., PO Box 250, Kensington, PE C0B 1M0
902-836-8935, Fax: 902-836-8926

Prince Edward Island Energy Corporation, Jones Bldg., 11 Kent St., 4th Fl., PO Box 2000, Charlottetown, PE C1A 7N8

Quebec

Ministère de l'Agriculture, des Pêcheries et de l'Alimentation, 200, ch Sainte-Foy, Québec, QC G1R 4X6
418-380-2110, 888-222-6272,

Bureau d'audiences publiques sur l'environnement, Édifice Lomer-Gouin, #2.10, 575, rue Saint-Amable, Québec, QC G1R 6A6
418-643-7447, Fax: 418-643-9474, 800-463-4732, communication@bape.gouv.qc.ca

Comité consultatif de l'environnement Kativik, CP 930, Kuujjuaq, QC J0M 1C0
819-964-2961, Fax: 819-964-0694, keac-ccek@krg.ca

Fondation de la faune du Québec, Place Iberville II, #420, 1175, av Lavigerie, Québec, QC G1V 4P1
418-644-7926, Fax: 418-643-7655, 877-639-0742, ffq@fondationdelafaune.qc.ca

Fonds québécois de la recherche sur la nature et les technologies, #450, 140, Grande Allée est, Québec, QC G1R 5M8
418-643-8560, Fax: 418-643-1451, info.nt@frq.gouv.qc.ca

Ottawa River Regulation Planning Board, 351, boul St Joseph, Gatineau, QC J8Y 3Z5
613-994-7079, 800-778-1246, secretariat@ottawariver.ca

Ministère des Ressources naturelles, 880, ch Sainte-Foy, Québec, QC G1S 4X4
418-627-8600, Fax: 418-644-6513, 866-248-6936, services.clientele@mrnf.gouv.qc.ca

Régie de l'énergie, Tour de la Bourse, #2.55, 800, Place Victoria, Montréal, QC H4Z 1A2
514-873-2452, Fax: 514-873-2070, 888-873-2452, secretariat@regie-energie.qc.ca; greffe@regie-energie.qc.ca

Société de développement de la Baie James, 110, boul Matagami, CP 970, Matagami, QC J0Y 2A0
819-739-4717, Fax: 819-739-4329, mat@sdbj.gouv.qc.ca

Saskatchewan

Agri-Food Council, #302, 3085 Albert St., Regina, SK S4S 0B1
306-787-5978, Fax: 306-787-5134, corey.ruud@gov.sk.ca

Agricultural Implements Board, #202, 3085 Albert St., Regina, SK S4S 0B1
306-787-4693, Fax: 306-787-1315

Enterprise Saskatchewan, #200, 3085 Albert St., Regina, SK S4S 0B1
306-787-4484, Fax: 306-798-0629, invest@gov.sk.ca

Farm Stress Unit, #125, 3085 Albert St., Regina, SK S4S 0B1
306-787-5196, Fax: 306-798-3042, 800-667-4442

Health Quality Council, 241, 111 Research Dr., Saskatoon, SK S7N 3R2
306-668-8810, Fax: 306-668-8820, info@hqc.sk.ca

Prairie Agricultural Machinery Institute, Hwy 5 West, PO Box 1150, Humboldt, SK S0K 2A0
306-682-2555, Fax: 306-682-5080, 800-567-7264, humboldt@pami.ca

Saskatchewan Agriculture, Walter Scott Bldg., 3085 Albert St., Regina, SK S4S 0B1
866-457-2377, aginfo@gov.sk.ca

Saskatchewan Conservation Data Centre, 3211 Albert St., Regina, SK S4S 5W6
306-787-9038, Fax: 306-787-9544

Saskatchewan Crop Insurance Corporation, 484 Prince William Dr., PO Box 3000, Melville, SK S0A 2P0
306-728-7200, Fax: 306-728-7202, 888-935-0000, customer.service@scic.gov.sk.ca

Saskatchewan Environment, 3211 Albert St., 2nd Fl., Regina, SK S4S 5W6
306-787-2584, Fax: 306-787-9544, 800-567-4224, Centre.Inquiry@gov.sk.ca

Saskatchewan Lands Appeal Board, #202, 3085 Albert St., Regina, SK S4S 0B1
306-787-4693, Fax: 306-787-1315, Donald.Brooks@gov.sk.ca

Saskatchewan Research Council, #125, 15 Innovation Blvd., Saskatoon, SK S7N 2X8
306-933-5400, Fax: 306-933-7446, info@src.sk.ca

Yukon Territory

Alsek Renewable Resource Council, PO Box 2077, Haines Junction, YT Y0B 1L0
867-634-2524, Fax: 867-634-2527

Carmacks Renewable Resource Council, PO Box 122, Carmacks, YT Y0B 1C0
867-863-6838, Fax: 867-863-6429, carmacksrrc@northwestel.net

Dawson District Renewable Resource Council, PO Box 1380, Dawson City, YT Y0B 1G0
867-993-6976, Fax: 867-993-6093, dawsonrrc@northwestel.net

Yukon Development Corporation, #2 Miles Canyon Rd., PO Box 5920, Whitehorse, YT Y1A 6S7
867-393-5337, Fax: 867-393-5401

Yukon Environment, PO Box 2703, Whitehorse, YT Y1A 2C6
867-667-5652, Fax: 867-393-7197, environment.yukon@gov.yk.ca

Mayo District Renewable Resources Council, PO Box 249, Mayo, YT Y0B 1M0
867-996-2942, Fax: 867-996-2948, mayorrc@yknet.yk.ca

North Yukon Renewable Resources Council, PO Box 80, Old Crow, YT Y0B 1N0
867-966-3034, Fax: 867-966-3036, vgrrc@yknet.yk.ca

Parks, PO Box 2703 V-4, Whitehorse, YT Y1A 2C6
867-667-5648, Fax: 867-393-6223, 800-661-0408, yukon.parks@gov.yk.ca

Selkirk Renewable Resources Council, PO Box 32, Pelly Crossing, YT Y0B 1P0
867-537-3937, Fax: 867-537-3939, selkirkrrc@yknet.yk.ca

Teslin Renewable Resource Council, PO Box 186, Teslin, YT Y0A 1B0
867-390-2323, Fax: 867-390-2919, teslinrrc@northwestel.net

Yukon Fish & Wildlife Management Board, 106 Main St., 2nd Fl., Whitehorse, YT Y1A 5P7
867-667-3754, Fax: 867-393-6947, officemanager@yfwmb.ca

Yukon Land Use Planning Council, #201, 307 Jarvis St., Whitehorse, YT Y1A 2H3
867-667-7397, Fax: 867-667-4624, ylupc@planyukon.ca

SCIENCE & TECHNOLOGY

See Also: Business Development

Bedford Institute of Oceanography, 1 Challenger Dr., PO Box 1006, Dartmouth, NS B2Y 4A2
902-426-3492, Fax: 902-426-8484, WebmasterBIO-IOB@dfo-mpo.gc.ca

Canada Centre for Remote Sensing - Geomatics Canada, 588 Booth St., Ottawa, ON K1A 0Y7
613-995-0947, Fax: 613-947-1382

Canada Science & Technology Museum Corporation, PO Box 9724 T,Ottawa, ON K1G 5A3
613-991-6090, Fax: 613-990-3636, info@technomuses.ca

Canadian Centre for Housing Technology, c/o National Research Council Canada, Building M-20, 1200 Montreal Rd., Ottawa, ON K1A 0R6
construction@nrc-cnrc.gc.ca

Canadian Food Inspection Agency, 1400 Merivale Rd., Ottawa, ON K1A 0Y9
613-225-2342, Fax: 613-228-6601, 800-442-2342

Canadian Institutes of Health Research, 160 Elgin St., 9th Fl., Ottawa, ON K1A 0W9
613-941-2672, Fax: 613-954-1800, 888-603-4178, info@cihr-irsc.gc.ca

Canadian Space Agency, John H. Chapman Space Centre, 6767, rte de l'Aéroport, Saint-Hubert, QC J3Y 8Y9
450-926-4800, Fax: 450-926-4352, promo@asc-csa.gc.ca

CANMET Energy Technology Centre-Devon, 1 Oil Patch Dr., #A202, PO Box 1280, Devon, AB T9G 1A8
780-987-8614, Fax: 780-987-8690, hamza@nrcan.gc.ca

Chalk River Laboratories, NRC Canadian Neutron Beam Centre, Building 459, Station 18, Chalk River, ON K0J 1J0
613-584-8293, 800-364-6989

Freshwater Institute Science Laboratory, 501 University Cres., Winnipeg, MB R3T 2N6
204-983-5000, Fax: 204-983-6285

Institut Maurice-Lamontagne, 850, rte de le Mer, CP 1000, Mont-Joli, QC G5H 3Z4
418-775-0500, Fax: 418-775-0730

Institute of Ocean Sciences, 9860 West Saanich Rd., PO Box 6000, Sidney, BC V8L 4B2
250-363-6517, Fax: 250-363-6390

International Development Research Centre, 150 Kent St., PO Box 8500, Ottawa, ON K1G 3H9
613-236-6163, Fax: 613-238-7230, info@idrc.ca

National Research Council Aerospace Manufacturing Technologies Centre, Campus Université de Montréal, 5145, av Decelles, Montréal, QC H3T 2B2

National Research Council Anaerobic Bioprocessing Pilot Plant, c/o Montréal (av Royalmount) Research Facilities, 6100, av Royalmount, Montréal, QC H4P 2R2

National Research Council Canada, Building M-58, 1200 Montreal Rd., Ottawa, ON K1A 0R6
613-993-9101, Fax: 613-952-9907, 877-672-2672, info@nrc-cnrc.ca; media@nrc-cnrc.gc.ca

National Research Council Canada - Canada Institute for Scientific & Technical Information, Building M-55, 1200 Montreal Rd., Ottawa, ON K1A 0R6
613-998-8544, Fax: 613-993-7619, 800-668-1222

National Research Council Canadian Photonics Fabrication Centre, c/o National Research Council Canada, Building M-50, 1200 Montral Rd., Ottawa, ON K1A 0R6

National Research Council Hydraulics Laboratories, c/o National Research Council, 1200 Montreal Rd., Ottawa, ON K1A OR6
877-672-2672

Natural Sciences & Engineering Research Council of Canada, Constitution Square, Tower II, 350 Albert St., Ottawa, ON K1A 1H5
613-995-4273, Fax: 613-943-1624, marie-josee.duval@nserc-crsng.gc.ca

Office of Energy Research & Development, 580 Booth St., 14th Fl., Ottawa, ON K1A 0E4
613-947-1421, Fax: 613-995-6146

Pacific Biological Station, 3190 Hammond Bay Rd., Nanaimo, BC V9T 6N7
250-756-7000, Fax: 250-756-7053

Polar Continental Shelf Program, #487, 615 Booth St., Ottawa, ON K1A 0E4
613-947-1650, Fax: 613-947-1611, pcsp@nrcan-rncan.gc.ca

Program Policy, 200 Kent St., Ottawa, ON K1A 0E6

Safe Environments Programme, Environmental Health Centre, Bldg. 8, 120 Parkdale Ave., Ottawa, ON K1A 0K9
613-954-0291, Fax: 613-952-2206,

St. Andrews Biological Station, 531 Brandy Cove Rd., St Andrews, NB E5B 2L9
506-529-8854, Fax: 506-529-5862, XMARSABS@mar.dfo-mpo.gc.ca

Transportation Development Centre, Tour Ouest, Complexe Guy-Favreau, 800, boul René-Lévesque ouest, 6e étage, Montréal, QC H3B 1X9
514-283-0000, Fax: 514-283-7158, tdccdt@tc.gc.ca

Alberta

Alberta Innovates - Energy & Environmental Solutions, AMEC Place, #2540, 801 - 6th Ave. SW, Calgary, AB T2P 3W2
403-297-7089, ees@albertainnovates.ca

British Columbia

Leading Edge Endowment Fund Board, 1188 West Georgia St., 9th Fl., Vancouver, BC V6E 4A2
604-438-3220, contact@leefbc.ca

Powertech Labs Inc., 12388 - 88 Ave., Surrey, BC V8W 7R7
604-590-7500, Fax: 604-590-6611

Manitoba

Industrial Technology Centre, #200, 78 Innovation Dr., Winnipeg, MB R3T 6C2
204-480-3333, Fax: 204-480-0345, tech@itc.mb.ca

Manitoba Education, Research & Learning Information Networks, #100 - 135 Innovation Dr., University of Manitoba, Winnipeg, MB R3T 6A8
204-474-7800, Fax: 204-474-7830, 800-430-6404

New Brunswick

Northern Development Division, Harbourview Place, #400, 275 Main St., Bathurst, NB E2A 1A9
506-547-2227, Fax: 506-547-2269

Partnerships & Innovation Division, Marysville Place, PO Box 6000, Fredericton, NB E3B 5H1
506-453-2862, Fax: 506-453-2265, elg/egl-info@gnb.ca

New Brunswick Research & Productivity Council, 921 College Hill Rd., Fredericton, NB E3B 6Z9
506-452-1212, Fax: 506-452-1395, info@rpc.ca

Newfoundland & Labrador

Soil, Plant & Feed Laboratory, 308 Brookfield Rd., PO Box 8700, St. John's, NL A1B 4J6
709-729-6738, Fax: 709-729-6734

Northwest Territories

Aurora Research Institute, 191 MacKenzie Rd., PO Box 1450, Inuvik, NT X0E 0T0
867-777-3298, Fax: 867-777-4264, webmaster@nwtresearch.com

Ontario

Environmental Sciences & Standards Division, 135 St. Clair Ave. West, 14th Fl., Toronto, ON M4V 1P5
Fax: 416-314-6358

Ontario Science Centre, 770 Don Mills Rd., Toronto, ON M3C 1T3
416-696-1000, Fax: 416-696-3166, 888-696-1110

Science North, 100 Ramsey Lake Rd., Sudbury, ON P3E 5S9
705-522-3701, Fax: 705-522-4954, 800-461-4898, contactus@sciencenorth.ca

Prince Edward Island

Prince Edward Island Department of Environment, Labour & Justice, Shaw Bldg. South, 95 Rochford St., 4th Fl., PO Box 2000, Charlottetown, PE C1A 7N8
902-368-6410, Fax: 902-368-6488

Quebec

Centre de recherche industrielle du Québec, 333, rue Franquet, Québec, QC G1P 4C7
418-659-1550, 800-667-2386, infocriq@criq.qc.ca

Fonds québécois de la recherche sur la nature et les technologies, #450, 140, Grande Allée est, Québec, QC G1R 5M8
418-643-8560, Fax: 418-643-1451, info.nt@frq.gouv.qc.ca

Saskatchewan

Saskatchewan Research Council, #125, 15 Innovation Blvd., Saskatoon, SK S7N 2X8
306-933-5400, Fax: 306-933-7446, info@src.sk.ca

Yukon Territory

Yukon Energy, Mines & Resources, PO Box 2703, Whitehorse, YT Y1A 2C6
867-667-3130, Fax: 867-456-3965, 800-661-0408, emr@gov.yk.ca

SENIOR CITIZENS SERVICES

Office of the Commissioner of Review Tribunals, PO Box 8250 T, Ottawa, ON K1G 5S5
613-954-1313, Fax: 613-946-1588, 800-363-0076, info@ocrt-bctr.gc.ca

Alberta

Seniors Advisory Council for Alberta, Standard Life Centre, #600, 10405 Jasper Ave., 6th Fl., Edmonton, AB T5J 4R7
780-422-2321, Fax: 780-422-8762, -310-0000, saca@gov.ab.ca

Nunavut

Nunavut Territory Department of Culture, Language, Elders & Youth, PO Box 1000 800,Iqaluit, NU X0A 0H0
867-975-5500, Fax: 867-975-5504, 866-934-2035

Quebec

Ministère de la Santé et des Services sociaux, Direction des communications, 1075, ch Sainte-Foy, 16e étage, Québec, QC G1S 2M1
418-643-9395, Fax: 418-643-4768, regisseur.web@msss.gouv.qc.ca

Yukon Territory

Yukon Health & Social Services, PO Box 2703, Whitehorse, YT Y1A 2C6
867-667-3673, Fax: 867-667-3096, hss@gov.yk.ca

SEXUALLY TRANSMITTED DISEASE CONTROL

See Also: AIDS

Prince Edward Island

Prince Edward Island Department of Health & Wellness, 105 Rochford St. North, 4th Fl., PO Box 2000, Charlottetown, PE C1A 7N8
902-368-6414, Fax: 902-368-4121

SOCIAL AFFAIRS

Ontario

Ontario Trillium Foundation, 800 Bay St., 5th Fl., Toronto, ON M5S 3A9
416-963-4927, Fax: 416-963-8781, 800-263-2887, otf@otf.ca

SOCIAL SERVICES

See Also: Community Services

British Columbia

British Columbia Ministry of Community, Sport, & Cultural Development, PO Box 9490 Prov Govt,Victoria, BC V8W 9N7

Northwest Territories

Northwest Territories Department of Health & Social Services, Centre Square Tower, PO Box 1320, Yellowknife, NT X1A 2L9
Fax: 867-873-0266

Nunavut

Nunavut Territory Department of Health & Social Services, PO Box 1000 1000,Iqaluit, NU X0A 0H0
867-975-5766, Fax: 867-975-5705, 800-661-0833,

Quebec

Ministère de la Santé et des Services sociaux, Direction des communications, 1075, ch Sainte-Foy, 16e étage, Québec, QC G1S 2M1
418-643-9395, Fax: 418-643-4768, regisseur.web@msss.gouv.qc.ca

SOIL RESOURCES

Soils & Crops Research & Development Centre, 2560, boul Hochelaga, Québec, QC G1V 2J3
418-657-7980, Fax: 418-648-2402

Newfoundland & Labrador

Soil, Plant & Feed Laboratory, 308 Brookfield Rd., PO Box 8700, St. John's, NL A1B 4J6
709-729-6738, Fax: 709-729-6734

Nova Scotia

Resource Stewardship Division, PO Box 550, Truro, NS B2N 5E3

Quebec

Commission de protection du territoire agricole du Québec, 200, ch Ste-Foy, 2e étage, Québec, QC G1R 4X6
418-643-3314, Fax: 418-643-2261, 800-667-5294, info@cptaq.gouv.qc.ca

SOLICITORS GENERAL

Ontario

Ontario Ministry of Community Safety & Correctional Services, George Drew Bldg., 25 Grosvenor St., 18th Fl., Toronto, ON M7A 1Y6
416-326-5000, Fax: 416-326-0498, 866-517-0571, mcscs.feedback@ontario.ca

Quebec

Ministère de la Sécurité publique, Tour des Laurentides, 2525, boul Laurier, 5e étage, Québec, QC G1V 2L2
418-643-2112, Fax: 418-646-6168, 866-644-6826

SPACE & ASTRONOMY

Canada Science & Technology Museum Corporation, PO Box 9724 T,Ottawa, ON K1G 5A3
613-991-6090, Fax: 613-990-3636, info@technomuses.ca

Canadian Space Agency, John H. Chapman Space Centre, 6767, rte de l'Aéroport, Saint-Hubert, QC J3Y 8Y9
450-926-4800, Fax: 450-926-4352, promo@asc-csa.gc.ca

SPORTS

See: Recreation

New Brunswick

New Brunswick Department of Tourism, Heritage & Culture, Centennial Building, PO Box 6000, Fredericton, NB E3B 5H1
506-444-5205, Fax: 506-457-4984, taponlinedirectory@gnb.ca

Saskatchewan

Saskatchewan Parks, Culture, & Sport, 1919 Saskatchewan Dr., 4th Fl., Regina, SK S4P 4H2
306-787-5729, Fax: 306-798-0033, 800-205-7070, info@tpcs.gov.sk.ca

Sport, Recreation, & Stewardship, 1919 Saskatchewan Dr., 9th Fl., Regina, SK S4P 4H2
306-787-7451, Fax: 306-787-0069

STANDARDS

Standards Council of Canada, #200, 270 Albert St., Ottawa, ON K1P 6N7
613-238-3222, Fax: 613-569-7808, info@scc.ca

STATISTICS

See Also: Vital Statistics

Statistics Canada, R.H. Coats Bldg., Tunney's Pasture, 150 Tunney's Pasture Driveway, Ottawa, ON K1A 0T6
613-951-8116, Fax: 877-287-4369, 800-263-1136, infostats@statcan.ca

Nunavut

Nunavut Territory Department of Executive & Intergovernmental Affairs, 1084 Aeroplex bldg., PO Box 1000 200,Iqaluit, NU X0A 0H0
867-975-6000, Fax: 867-975-6099

Prince Edward Island
Prince Edward Island Department of Health & Wellness, 105 Rochford St. North, 4th Fl., PO Box 2000, Charlottetown, PE C1A 7N8
902-368-6414, Fax: 902-368-4121

STATISTICS (ENVIRONMENTAL)
Statistics Canada, R.H. Coats Bldg., Tunney's Pasture, 150 Tunney's Pasture Driveway, Ottawa, ON K1A 0T6
613-951-8116, Fax: 877-287-4369, 800-263-1136, infostats@statcan.ca

SUSTAINABLE DEVELOPMENT
Commissioner of the Environment & Sustainable Development, 240 Sparks St., Ottawa, ON K1A 0G6
613-995-3708, Fax: 613-957-0474, petitions@oag-bvg.gc.ca

Manitoba
Manitoba Round Table for Sustainable Development, #160, 123 Main St., Winnipeg, MB R3C 1A5
204-945-1869, Fax: 204-948-2357, mrtsd@gov.mb.ca

Quebec
Ministère du Développement durable, de l'Environnement, de la Faune, et des Parcs, Édifice Marie-Guyart, 675, boul René-Lévesque est, 29e étage, Québec, QC G1R 5V7
418-521-3911, Fax: 418-643-4143, 800-561-1616, info@mddep.gouv.qc.ca

TAXATION
See Also: Sales Tax
Canada Revenue Agency, 875 Heron Rd., Ottawa, ON K1A 0L5
800-267-6999
First Nations Tax Commission, #321, 345 Yellowhead Hwy, Kamloops, BC V2H 1H1
250-828-9857, Fax: 250-828-9858, mailkamloops@fntc.ca

TELECOMMUNICATIONS
See Also: Broadcasting
Communications Research Centre Canada, 3701 Carling Ave., PO Box 11490 H, Ottawa, ON K2H 8S2
613-991-3313, Fax: 613-998-5355, info@crc.gc.ca

Prince Edward Island
Prince Edward Island Department of Innovation & Advanced Learning, Shaw Bldg., 105 Rochford St., 5th Fl., PO Box 2000, Charlottetown, PE C1A 7N8
902-368-4240, Fax: 902-368-4242

Quebec
Ministère de la Culture et Communications, 225, Grande Allée est, Québec, QC G1R 5G5
888-380-8882

TOURISM & TOURIST INFORMATION
Canadian Tourism Commission, #1400, 1055 Dunsmuir St., PO Box 49230, Vancouver, BC V7X 1L2
604-638-8300
Parks Canada, 25 Eddy St., Gatineau, QC K1A 0M5
613-860-1251, 888-773-8888, information@pc.gc.ca

British Columbia
Tourism British Columbia, 1803 Douglas St., 3rd Fl., Victoria, BC V8W 9W5
250-356-6363, research@tourismbc.com; superhost@tourismbc.com

Manitoba
Tourism Secretariat, 155 Carlton St., 7th Fl., Winnipeg, MB R3C 3H8
800-665-0040

New Brunswick
New Brunswick Department of Tourism, Heritage & Culture, Centennial Building, PO Box 6000, Fredericton, NB E3B 5H1
506-444-5205, Fax: 506-457-4984, taponlinedirectory@gnb.ca

Northwest Territories
Northwest Territories Department of Industry, Tourism & Investment, PO Box 1320, Yellowknife, NT X1A 2L9
Fax: 867-873-0306, info@iti.ca

Ontario
Tourism Policy & Development Division, Hearst Block, 900 Bay St., 10th Fl., Toronto, ON M7A 2E1
416-326-9326, Fax: 416-325-6985
Ontario Ministry of Tourism, Culture & Sport, Hearst Block, 900 Bay St., 9th Fl., Toronto, ON M7A 2E1
416-326-9326, Fax: 416-314-7854, 888-997-9015

Prince Edward Island
Charlottetown Civic Centre Management Inc., 46 Kensington Rd., Charlottetown, PE C1A 5H7
902-629-6600, Fax: 902-629-6650

Quebec
Société des établissements en plein air du Québec, Place de la Cité, Tour Cominar, #250, 2640, boul Laurier, 2e étage, Québec, QC G1V 5C2
418-890-6527, Fax: 418-528-6025, 800-665-6527, inforeservation@sepaq.com
Ministère du Tourisme, #400, 900, boul René-Lévesque est, Québec, QC G1R 2B5
418-643-5959, Fax: 418-646-8723, 800-482-2433

Saskatchewan
Tourism Initiatives, 1919 Saskatchewan Dr., 2nd Fl., Regina, SK S4P 4H2
306-787-8985, Fax: 306-798-3177

Yukon Territory
Yukon Tourism & Culture, 100 Hanson St., Whitehorse, YT Y1A 2C6
867-667-5036, Fax: 867-667-3546

TRADE
See Also: Business Development; Imports
Business Development Bank of Canada, #400, 5, Place Ville-Marie, Montréal, QC H3B 5E7
514-283-5904, Fax: 514-283-5626, 877-232-2269
Canadian Commercial Corporation, 50 O'Connor St., 11th Fl., Ottawa, ON K1A 0S6
613-996-0034, Fax: 613-995-2121, 800-748-8191
Commission for Environmental Cooperation, Secretariat, #200, 393, rue St-Jacques ouest, Montréal, QC H2Y 1N9
514-350-4300, Fax: 514-350-4314, info@cec.org
Export Development Canada, 151 Slater St., Ottawa, ON K1A 1K3
613-598-2500, Fax: 613-598-3811, 800-267-8510
Market & Industry Services Branch, Tower 5, 1341 Baseline Rd., Ottawa, ON K1A 0C5
613-759-1000, Fax: 613-773-1711

Alberta
Intergovernmental Relations, Commerce Place, 10155 - 102 St., 12th Fl., Edmonton, AB T5J 4G8
780-427-6543, Fax: 780-427-0939

Manitoba
Manitoba Entrepreneurship, Training & Trade, #1000, 259 Portage Ave, Winnipeg, MB R3B 3P4
204-945-2475, Fax: 204-945-3977, minctt@leg.gov.mb.ca

Prince Edward Island
Prince Edward Island Department of Innovation & Advanced Learning, Shaw Bldg., 105 Rochford St., 5th Fl., PO Box 2000, Charlottetown, PE C1A 7N8
902-368-4240, Fax: 902-368-4242

Quebec
Ministère du Développement économique, de l'Innovation et de l'Exportation, 710, place D'Youville, 3e étage, Québec, QC G1R 4Y4 418-691-5950, Fax: 418-644-0118, 866-680-1884

Yukon Territory
Yukon Economic Development, PO Box 2703, Whitehorse, YT Y1A 2C6
867-393-7191, Fax: 867-393-6412, 800-661-0408, ecdev@gov.yk.ca

TRADE - MEXICAN
Vancouver, 4250 Westbrook Mall, Vancouver, BC V6T 1W5
604-221-3035

TRADE - UNITED STATES
Chicoutimi, 501, boul Université est, Chicoutimi, QC G7H 8C3
Montréal, 6100, av Royalmount, Montréal, QC H4P 2R2
514-496-6117
Penticton, Observatory, Herzberg Institute of Astrophysics, 717 White Lake Rd., PO Box 248, Kaleden, BC VOH 1K0
250-497-2311, Fax: 250-497-2355
St. John's, 1 Kerwin Pl., St. John's, NL A1B 3T5
709-772-2468,

TRADE-MARKS
See: Patents & Copyright

Prince Edward Island
Anne of Green Gables Licensing Authority Inc., 94 Euston St., PO Box 910, Charlottetown, PE C1A 7L9
902-569-7787, Fax: 902-368-6301, kobaker@gov.pe.ca; aggla@bellnet.ca

TRAINING, ENVIRONMENTAL

Alberta
Community, Learner & Industry Connections Division, Phipps-McKinnon Bldg., 10020 - 101A Ave., 5th Fl., Edmonton, AB T5J 3G2

TRANSPORTATION
Canadian Air Transport Security Authority, 99 Bank St., 13th Fl., Ottawa, ON K1P 6B9
Fax: 613-990-1295, 888-294-2202
Canadian Coast Guard, Centennial Towers, #6S018, 200 Kent St., Ottawa, ON K1A 0E6
613-993-0999, Fax: 613-990-1866, info@dfo-mpo.gc.ca
Canadian Transportation Agency, Les Terrasses de la Chaudière, 15, rue Eddy, Gatineau, QC J8X 4B3
Fax: 819-997-6727, 888-222-2592, info@otc-cta.gc.ca
Federal Bridge Corporation Limited, #1210, 55 Metcalfe St., Ottawa, ON K1P 6L5
613-993-6880, Fax: 613-993-6945, info@federalbridge.ca
Marine Atlantic Inc., Corporate Office, Baine Johnston Centre, #302, 10 Fort William Pl., St. John's, NL A1C 1K4
800-897-2797, customer_relations@marine-atlantic.ca; marketing@marine-atlantic.ca
Transport Canada, Place de Ville, 330 Sparks St., Tower C, Ottawa, ON K1A 0N5
613-990-2309, Fax: 613-954-4731, 866-995-9737
Transportation Appeal Tribunal of Canada, #1201, 333 Laurier Ave. West, 12th Fl., Ottawa, ON K1A 0N5
613-990-6906, Fax: 613-990-9153, info@tatc.gc.ca
Transportation Development Centre, Tour Ouest, Complexe Guy-Favreau, 800, boul René-Lévesque ouest, 6e étage, Montréal, QC H3B 1X9
514-283-0000, Fax: 514-283-7158, tdccdt@tc.gc.ca
Transportation Safety Board of Canada, 200 Promenade du Portage, 4th Fl., Ottawa, ON K1A 1K8
819-994-3741, Fax: 819-997-2239, 800-387-3557
VIA Rail Canada Inc., #500, 3, Place Ville-Marie, Montréal, QC H3B 2C9
514-871-6000, Fax: 514-871-6104, 888-842-7245

Alberta
Alberta Infrastructure, Infrastructure Building, 6950 - 113 St., Edmonton, AB T6H 5V7
780-415-0507, Fax: 780-427-2187, -310-0000, Infra.Contact.Us.m@gov.ab.ca
Transportation & Civil Engineering Division, Twin Atria Building, 4999 - 98 Ave., 2nd Fl., Edmonton, AB T6B 2X3
780-422-2184, Fax: 780-415-1268
Transportation Safety Board, North Office, Twin Atria Building, 4999 - 98 Ave., Main Fl., Edmonton, AB T6B 2X3
780-427-7178, Fax: 780-422-9739, -310-0000
Transportation Safety Services Division, Twin Atria Building, 4999 - 98 Ave., Main Fl., Edmonton, AB T6B 2X3
780-427-8901, Fax: 780-415-0782, 800-666-5036

British Columbia
British Columbia Transit, 520 Gorge Rd. East, Victoria, BC V8W 2P3
250-385-2551, Fax: 250-995-5639
Passenger Transportation Board, #202, 940 Blanshard St., PO Box 9850 Prov Govt, Victoria, BC V8W 9T5
250-953-3777, Fax: 250-953-3788, ptboard@gov.bc.ca
British Columbia Ministry of Transportation & Infrastructure, PO Box 9850 Prov Govt,Victoria, BC V8W 9T5
250-387-3198, Fax: 250-356-7706
Transportation Policy & Programs Department, PO Box 9850 Prov Govt,Victoria, BC V8W 9T5
250-387-5062, Fax: 250-387-6431

Manitoba
Highway Traffic Board/Motor Transport Board, #200, 301 Weston St., Winnipeg, MB R3E 3H4
204-945-8912, Fax: 204-783-6529
Manitoba Infrastructure & Transportation, Legislative Building, #203, 450 Broadway Ave., Winnipeg, MB R3C 0V8
204-945-3723, Fax: 204-945-7610

License Suspension Appeal Board/Medical Review Committee, #200, 301 Weston St., Winnipeg, MB R3E 3H4
204-945-7350, Fax: 204-948-2682
Taxicab Board, #200, 301 Weston St., Winnipeg, MB R3E 3H4
204-945-8919, Fax: 204-948-2315, Joan.Wilson@gov.mb.ca

New Brunswick
New Brunswick Department of Transportation & Infrastructure, Kings Place, PO Box 6000, Fredericton, NB E3B 5H1
506-453-3939, Fax: 506-453-2900, Transportation.Web@gnb.ca
Vehicle Management Agency, Vehicle Management Center, PO Box 6000, Fredericton, NB E3B 5H1
506-453-3939, Fax: 506-453-3628, Transportation.Web@gnb.ca

Newfoundland & Labrador
Newfoundland & Labrador Department of Transportation & Works, Confederation Bldg., West Block, 6th Fl., PO Box 8700, St. John's, NL A1B 4J6
709-729-3679, Fax: 709-729-4285, twminister@gov.nl.ca

Northwest Territories
Highways & Marine, 4510 - 50 Ave., 2nd fl., PO Box 1320, Yellowknife, NT X1A 2L9
867-920-8771, Fax: 867-873-0288
Northwest Territories Department of Transportation, Lahm Ridge Bldg., 4501 50 Ave., PO Box 1320, Yellowknife, NT X1A 2L9
867-920-3460, Fax: 867-873-0363

Nova Scotia
Nova Scotia Department of Transportation & Infrastructure Renewal, Johnston Bldg., 1672 Granville St., 2nd Fl., PO Box 186, Halifax, NS B3J 2N2
902-424-2297, Fax: 902-424-0532, tpwpaff@gov.ns.ca

Nunavut
Nunavut Territory Department of Community & Government Services, W.G. Brown Bldg., 4th Fl., PO Box 1000 700,Iqaluit, NU X0A 0H0 867-975-5400, Fax: 867-975-5305
Nunavut Territory Department of Economic Development & Transportation, Bldg. 1104 A, Inuksugait Plaza, PO Box 1000 1500,Iqaluit, NU X0A 0H0
867-975-7800, Fax: 867-975-7870, 888-975-5999, edt@gov.nu.ca

Ontario
Licence Appeal Tribunal, #530, 20 Dundas St. West, Toronto, ON M5G 2C2
416-314-4260, Fax: 416-314-4270, 800-255-2214
Metrolinx, #600, 20 Bay St., Toronto, ON M5J 2W3
416-874-5900, Fax: 416-869-1755
Ontario Highway Transport Board, 151 Bloor St. West, 10th Fl., Toronto, ON M5S 2T5
416-326-6732, Fax: 416-326-6738, ohtb@mto.gov.on.ca
Owen Sound Transportation Company Ltd., 717875, Hwy. 6, Owen Sound, ON N4K 5N7
519-376-8740, 800-265-3163
Road User Safety Division, Bldg A, #191, 1201 Wilson Ave., Downsview, ON M3M 1J8
416-235-2999, Fax: 416-235-4153
Ontario Ministry of Transportation, Ferguson Block, 77 Wellesley St. West, 3rd Fl., Toronto, ON M7A 1Z8
416-235-4686, Fax: 905-704-2001, 800-268-4686

Prince Edward Island
Prince Edward Island Department of Transportation & Infrastructure Renewal, Jones Bldg., 11 Kent St., 3rd Fl., PO Box 2000, Charlottetown, PE C1A 7N8
902-368-5100, Fax: 902-368-5395

Quebec
Abitibi-Témiscamingue, 80, av Québec, Rouyn-Noranda, QC J9X 6R1
819-763-3271, Fax: 819-763-3493, dat@mtq.gouv.qc.ca
Bas-Saint-Laurent—Gaspésie—Îles-de-la-Madeleine, #101, 92, 2e rue ouest, Rimouski, QC G5L 8E6
418-727-3674, Fax: 418-727-3673, dtbgi@mtq.gouv.qc.ca
Capitale-Nationale, 475, boul de l'Atrium, 2e étage, Québec, QC G1H 7H9
418-643-1911, Fax: 418-646-0003, dcnat@mtq.gouv.qc.ca
Chaudière-Appalaches, 1156, boul de la Rive-Sud, Saint-Romuald, QC G6W 5M6
418-839-5581, Fax: 418-834-7338, dtca@mtq.gouv.qc.ca
Commission des transports du Québec, 200, ch Sainte-Foy, 7e étage, Québec, QC G1R 5V5
Fax: 418-644-8034, 888-461-2433
Côte-Nord, #110, 625, boul Laflèche, Baie-Comeau, QC G5C 1C5
418-295-4765, Fax: 418-295-4766, cotenord@mtq.gouv.qc.ca
Est-de-la-Montérégie, 201, place Charles-Lemoyne, 5e étage, Longueuil, QC J4K 2T5
450-677-3413, Fax: 450-442-1317, dtem@mtq.gouv.qc.ca
Estrie, #2.02, 200, rue Belvédère nord, Sherbrooke, QC J1H 4A9
819-820-3280, Fax: 819-820-3118, dte@mtq.gouv.qc.ca
Laurentides-Lanaudière, 222, rue Saint-Georges, 2e étage, Saint-Jérôme, QC J7Z 4Z9
450-569-3057, Fax: 450-569-3072, dll@mtq.gouv.qc.ca
Laval-Mille-Îles, 1725, boul Le Corbusier, Laval, QC H7S 2K7
450-680-6330, Fax: 450-973-4959, dtlmi@mtq.gouv.qc.ca
Mauricie—Centre-du-Québec, 100, rue Laviolette, 4e étage, Trois-Rivières, QC G9A 5S9
819-371-6896, Fax: 819-371-6136, dmcq@mtq.gouv.qc.ca
Ouest-de-la-Montérégie, #200, 180, boul d'Anjou, Châteauguay, QC J6K 1C4
450-698-3400, Fax: 450-698-3452, dtom@mtq.gouv.qc.ca
Outaouais, #5.110, 170, rue de l'Hôtel-de-Ville, Gatineau, QC J8X 4C2
819-772-3849, Fax: 819-772-3338, dto@mtq.gouv.qc.ca
Saguenay—Lac-Saint-Jean—Chibougamau, 3950, boul Harvey, Jonquière, QC G7X 8L6
418-695-7916, Fax: 418-695-7926, dt.slsjc@mtq.gouv.qc.ca
Société de l'assurance automobile du Québec, 333, boul Jean-Lesage, CP 19600 Terminus, Québec, QC G1K 8J6
418-643-7620, Fax: 418-644-0339, 800-361-7620, courrier@saaq.gouv.qc.ca
Société des traversiers du Québec, 250, rue Saint-Paul, Québec, QC G1K 9K9
418-643-2019, Fax: 418-643-7308, stq@traversiers.gouv.qc.ca
Société du port ferroviaire Baie-Comeau-Hauterive, 18, rte Maritime, Baie-Comeau, QC G4Z 2L6
418-296-6785, Fax: 418-296-2377, societeduport@globetrotter.net
Ministère des Transports, 700, boul René-Lévesque est, 28e étage, Québec, QC G1R 5H1
418-643-6980, Fax: 418-643-2033, 888-355-0511, communications@mtq.gouv.qc.ca
Île-de-Montréal, 500, boul René-Lévesque ouest, 12e étage, CP 5, Montréal, QC H2Z 1W7
514-873-7781, Fax: 514-864-3867, dtim@mtq.gouv.qc.ca

Saskatchewan
Saskatchewan Highway Traffic Board, 1550 Saskatchewan Dr., Regina, SK S4P 0E4
306-775-6674, contactus@highwaytrafficboard.sk.ca
Saskatchewan Highways & Infrastructure, Victoria Tower, 1855 Victoria Ave., Regina, SK S4P 3T2
306-787-4800, communications@highways.gov.sk.ca

Yukon Territory
Yukon Community Services, PO Box 2703, Whitehorse, YT Y1A 2C6 867-667-5811, Fax: 867-393-6295, 800-661-0408, inquiry@gov.yk.ca
Driver Control Board, 2130 Second Ave., 3rd Fl., PO Box 2703, Whitehorse, YT Y1A 2C6
867-667-5111, Fax: 867-667-3609, dcb@gov.yk.ca
Yukon Highways & Public Works, PO Box 2703, Whitehorse, YT Y1A 2C6 867-393-7193, Fax: 867-393-6218, 800-661-0408, hpw-info@gov.yk.ca

TRANSPORTATION

National Research Council Surface Transportation Research Facilities, Ottawa Uplands Research Facilities, 2320 Lester Rd., Ottawa, ON K1V 1S2 613-998-9639, Fax: 613-957-0831, inquiries.ST@nrc-cnrc.gc.ca

TRANSPORTATION OF DANGEROUS GOODS

Nova Scotia
Nova Scotia Department of Transportation & Infrastructure Renewal, Johnston Bldg., 1672 Granville St., 2nd Fl., PO Box 186, Halifax, NS B3J 2N2
902-424-2297, Fax: 902-424-0532, tpwpaff@gov.ns.ca

Ontario
Road User Safety Division, Bldg A, #191, 1201 Wilson Ave., Downsview, ON M3M 1J8
416-235-2999, Fax: 416-235-4153

Prince Edward Island
Prince Edward Island Department of Transportation & Infrastructure Renewal, Jones Bldg., 11 Kent St., 3rd Fl., PO Box 2000, Charlottetown, PE C1A 7N8
902-368-5100, Fax: 902-368-5395

Saskatchewan
Saskatchewan Highways & Infrastructure, Victoria Tower, 1855 Victoria Ave., Regina, SK S4P 3T2
306-787-4800, communications@highways.gov.sk.ca

TRAPPING & FUR INDUSTRY

Ontario
Ontario Moose & Bear Allocation Advisory Committee, PO Box 964, Sioux Lookout, ON P8T 1B3
807-737-2615, Fax: 807-737-4173

Quebec
Comité conjoint de chasse, de pêche et de piégeage, #C220, 383 rue Saint-Jacques, Montréal, QC H2Y 1N9
514-284-2151, Fax: 514-284-0039, infohftcc@cccpp-hftcc.com

Saskatchewan
Saskatchewan Environment, 3211 Albert St., 2nd Fl., Regina, SK S4S 5W6
306-787-2584, Fax: 306-787-9544, 800-567-4224, Centre.Inquiry@gov.sk.ca

TREASURY SERVICES

See Also: Finance
Treasury Board of Canada, 140 O'Connor St., Ottawa, ON K1A 0R5 613-957-2400, Fax: 613-941-4000, 877-636-0656

URBAN RENEWAL & DESIGN

See Also: Municipal Affairs

Alberta
Local Government Services Division, Commerce Place, 10155 - 102 St., 17th Fl., Edmonton, AB T5J 4L4

Newfoundland & Labrador
Newfoundland & Labrador Housing Corporation, Sir Brian Dunfield Bldg., 2 Canada Dr., PO Box 220, St. John's, NL A1C 5J2 709-724-3000, Fax: 709-724-3250

Northwest Territories
Northwest Territories Department of Municipal & Community Affairs, PO Box 1320, Yellowknife, NT X1A 2L9
867-873-7118, Fax: 867-873-0309,

Ontario
Ontario Ministry of Municipal Affairs & Housing, College Park, 777 Bay St., 17th Fl., Toronto, ON M5G 2E5
416-585-7041, Fax: 416-585-6470, 866-220-2290, mininfo.mah@ontario.ca

Prince Edward Island
SkillsPEI, Atlantic Technology Centre, #212, 90 University Ave., Charlottetown, PE C1A 4K9
902-368-6290, Fax: 902-368-6340, 877-491-4766

VITAL STATISTICS

Prince Edward Island
Prince Edward Island Department of Health & Wellness, 105 Rochford St. North, 4th Fl., PO Box 2000, Charlottetown, PE C1A 7N8
902-368-6414, Fax: 902-368-4121

WASTE & GARBAGE

Low-Level Radioactive Waste Management Office, #200, 1900 City Park Dr., Ottawa, ON K1J 1A3
613-998-9442, Fax: 613-952-0760, 800-377-5995, info@llrwmo.org

Newfoundland & Labrador
Newfoundland & Labrador Department of Municipal Affairs, West Block, Main Fl., Confederation Bldg., PO Box 8700, St. John's, NL A1B 4J6
709-729-3046, Fax: 709-729-0943, mainfo@gov.nl.ca
Newfoundland & Labrador Department of Service NL, PO Box 8700, St. John's, NL A1B 4J6
709-729-4834, servicenlinfo@gov.nl.ca

Ontario
Ontario Ministry of Environment, 135 St. Clair Ave. West, Toronto, ON M4V 1P5
416-325-4000, Fax: 416-325-3159, 800-565-4923, picemail.moe@ontario.ca

Quebec

Bureau d'audiences publiques sur l'environnement, Édifice Lomer-Gouin, #2.10, 575, rue Saint-Amable, Québec, QC G1R 6A6
418-643-7447, Fax: 418-643-9474, 800-463-4732, communication@bape.gouv.qc.ca

Société québécoise de récupération et de recyclage, #200, 420, boul Charest est, Québec, QC G1K 8M4
418-643-0394, Fax: 418-643-6507, 866-523-8290, info@recyc-quebec.gouv.qc.ca

WASTE MANAGEMENT

See Also: Dangerous Goods & Hazardous Materials

National Research Council Waste Biotreatability Facility, c/o National Research Council, 1200 Montreal Rd., Ottawa, ON K1A 0R6

Alberta

Alberta Recycling Management Authority, Scotia Tower 1, #1310, 10060 Jasper Ave., PO Box 189, Edmonton, AB T5J 2J1
780-990-1111, Fax: 780-990-1122, 888-999-8762, info@albertarecycling.ca

Alberta Used Oil Management Association, Empire Building, #1008, 10080 Jasper Ave., Edmonton, AB T5J 1V9
780-414-1510, Fax: 780-414-1519, 866-414-1510, reception@usedoilrecycling.ca

Beverage Container Management Board, #750, 10707 - 100 Ave., Edmonton, AB T5J 3M1
780-424-3193, Fax: 780-428-4620, 888-424-7671

Alberta Environment & Sustainable Resource Development, Oxbridge Place, 9820 - 106 St., Main Fl., Edmonton, AB T5K 2J6
780-427-2700, Fax: 780-422-4086, -310-0000, env.infocent@gov.ab.ca; srd.infocent@gov.ab.ca

Newfoundland & Labrador

Multi-Materials Stewardship Board, PO Box 8131 A, St. John's, NL A1B 3M9
709-753-0948, Fax: 709-753-0974, 800-901-6672, inquiries@mmsb.nl.ca

Northwest Territories

Northwest Territories Department of Municipal & Community Affairs, PO Box 1320, Yellowknife, NT X1A 2L9
867-873-7118, Fax: 867-873-0309

Ontario

Integrated Environmental Policy Division, 77 Wellesley St. West, 11th Fl., Toronto, ON M7A 2T5
416-314-6338, Fax: 416-314-6346

Prince Edward Island

Island Waste Management Corporation, 110 Watts Ave., Charlottetown, PE C1E 2C1
902-894-0330, Fax: 902-894-0331, 888-280-8111, info@iwmc.pe.ca

Quebec

Société québécoise de récupération et de recyclage, #200, 420, boul Charest est, Québec, QC G1K 8M4
418-643-0394, Fax: 418-643-6507, 866-523-8290, info@recyc-quebec.gouv.qc.ca

Saskatchewan

Saskatchewan Environment, 3211 Albert St., 2nd Fl., Regina, SK S4S 5W6
306-787-2584, Fax: 306-787-9544, 800-567-4224, Centre.Inquiry@gov.sk.ca

Yukon Territory

Yukon Environment, PO Box 2703, Whitehorse, YT Y1A 2C6
867-667-5652, Fax: 867-393-7197, environment.yukon@gov.yk.ca

WATER & WASTEWATER

Bedford Institute of Oceanography, 1 Challenger Dr., PO Box 1006, Dartmouth, NS B2Y 4A2
902-426-3492, Fax: 902-426-8484, WebmasterBIO-IOB@dfo-mpo.gc.ca

Canadian Hydrographic Service, 615 Booth St., Ottawa, ON K1A 0E6
613-998-4931, Fax: 613-998-1217, chsinfo@dfo-mpo.gc.ca

Environment Canada, 10 Wellington St., Gatineau, QC K1A 0H3
819-997-2800, Fax: 819-994-1412, 800-668-6767, enviroinfo@ec.gc.ca

Fisheries & Oceans Canada, 200 Kent St., Ottawa, ON K1A 0E6
613-993-0999, Fax: 613-990-1866, info@dfo-mpo.gc.ca

Freshwater Institute Science Laboratory, 501 University Cres., Winnipeg, MB R3T 2N6
204-983-5000, Fax: 204-983-6285

Institut Maurice-Lamontagne, 850, rte de le Mer, CP 1000, Mont-Joli, QC G5H 3Z4
418-775-0500, Fax: 418-775-0730

Institute of Ocean Sciences, 9860 West Saanich Rd., PO Box 6000, Sidney, BC V8L 4B2
250-363-6517, Fax: 250-363-6390

National Research Council Performance Assessment of Civil Infrastructure & Related Structures Research Facilities, Water Quality Testing Facility, Research Innovation Centre, #508, 3737 Wascana Pkwy., Regina, SK S4S 0A2
306-780-3208, construction@nrc-cnrc.gc.ca

Nunavut Water Board, PO Box 119, Gjoa Haven, NU X0B 1J0
867-360-6338, Fax: 867-360-6369

Alberta

Alberta Environment & Sustainable Resource Development, Oxbridge Place, 9820 - 106 St., Main Fl., Edmonton, AB T5K 2J6
780-427-2700, Fax: 780-422-4086, -310-0000, env.infocent@gov.ab.ca; srd.infocent@gov.ab.ca

Irrigation Council, Provincial Bldg., 200 - 5 Ave. South, 3rd Fl., Lethbridge, AB T1J 4L1
403-381-5176, Fax: 403-382-4406

British Columbia

British Columbia Utilities Commission, 900 Howe St., 6th Fl., PO Box 250, Vancouver, BC V6Z 2N3
604-660-4700, Fax: 604-660-1102, 800-663-1385, commission.secretary@bcuc.com

British Columbia Ministry of Environment, PO Box 9339 Prov Govt,Victoria, BC V8W 9M1
250-387-1161, Fax: 250-387-5669, envmail@gov.bc.ca

Manitoba

Manitoba Conservation & Water Stewardship, 200 Saulteaux Cres., Winnipeg, MB R3J 3W3
800-214-6497, mws@gov.mb.ca

Manitoba Water Council, 200 Saulteaux Cres., PO Box 27, Winnipeg, MB R3J 3W3
water.council@gov.mb.ca

New Brunswick

New Brunswick Department of Environment & Local Government, Marysville Place, PO Box 6000, Fredericton, NB E3B 5H1
506-453-2690, Fax: 506-457-4994, elg/egl-info@gnb.ca

New Brunswick Department of Natural Resources, Hugh John Flemming Forestry Centre, PO Box 6000, Fredericton, NB E3B 5H1
506-453-3826, Fax: 506-444-4367, dnrweb@gnb.ca

Newfoundland & Labrador

Newfoundland & Labrador Department of Environment & Conservation, Confederation Bldg., West Block, 4th Fl., PO Box 8700, St. John's, NL A1B 4J6
709-729-2664, Fax: 709-729-6639, 800-563-6181, envcinquires@gov.nl.ca

Newfoundland & Labrador Board of Commissioners of Public Utilities, Prince Charles Bldg., #E-210, 120 Torbay Rd., PO Box 21040, St. John's, NL A1A 5B2
709-726-8600, Fax: 709-726-9604, 866-782-0006, ito@pub.nf.ca

Northwest Territories

Northwest Territories Department of Environment & Natural Resources, PO Box 1320, Yellowknife, NT X1A 2L9

Northwest Territories Water Board, 125 Mackenzie Rd., PO Box 2531, Yellowknife, NT X0E 0T0
867-678-2942, Fax: 867-678-2943, info@nwtwb.com

Nova Scotia

Nova Scotia Department of Natural Resources, Founder's Square, 1701 Hollis St., 3rd Fl., PO Box 698, Halifax, NS B3J 2T9
902-424-5935, Fax: 902-424-0594, 800-565-2224

Nova Scotia Utility & Review Board, Summit Place, 1601 Lower Water St., 3rd Fl., PO Box 1692 M,Halifax, NS B3J 3S3
902-424-4448, Fax: 902-424-3919, uarb.board@gov.ns.ca

Ontario

Ontario Ministry of Environment, 135 St. Clair Ave. West, Toronto, ON M4V 1P5
416-325-4000, Fax: 416-325-3159, 800-565-4923, picemail.moe@ontario.ca

Lake of the Woods Control Board, c/o Executive Engineer, Ottawa, ON K1A 0H3
Fax: 819-953-4666, 800-661-5922, secretariat@lwcb.ca

Ontario Ministry of Natural Resources, 300 Water St., PO Box 7000, Peterborough, ON K9J 8M5
705-755-2000, Fax: 705-755-1677, 800-667-1940, mnr.nric.mnr@ontario.ca

Ontario Clean Water Agency, 1 Yonge St., 17th Fl., Toronto, ON M5E 1E5
416-314-5600, Fax: 416-314-8300, 800-667-6292

Walkerton Clean Water Centre, 20 Ontario Rd., PO Box 160, Walkerton, ON N0G 2V0
519-881-2003, Fax: 519-881-4947, 866-515-0550, inquiry@wcwc.ca

Prince Edward Island

Prince Edward Island Department of Environment, Labour & Justice, Shaw Bldg. South, 95 Rochford St., 4th Fl., PO Box 2000, Charlottetown, PE C1A 7N8902-368-6410, Fax: 902-368-6488

Quebec

Ministère du Développement durable, de l'Environnement, de la Faune, et des Parcs, Édifice Marie-Guyart, 675, boul René-Lévesque est, 29e étage, Québec, QC G1R 5V7
418-521-3911, Fax: 418-643-4143, 800-561-1616, info@mddep.gouv.qc.ca

Saskatchewan

Saskatchewan Environment, 3211 Albert St., 2nd Fl., Regina, SK S4S 5W6
306-787-2584, Fax: 306-787-9544, 800-567-4224, Centre.Inquiry@gov.sk.ca

Saskatchewan Water Corporation (SaskWater), #200, 111 Fairford St. East, Moose Jaw, SK S6H 1C8
Fax: 306-694-3207, 888-230-1111, comm@saskwater.com; customerservice@saskwater.com

Saskatchewan Watershed Authority, 111 Fairford St. East, Moose Jaw, SK S6H 7X9
306-694-3900, Fax: 306-694-3944, comm@swa.ca

Yukon Territory

Yukon Environment, PO Box 2703, Whitehorse, YT Y1A 2C6
867-667-5652, Fax: 867-393-7197, environment.yukon@gov.yk.ca

WATER RESOURCES

See Also: Oceanography

Environmental Stewardship Branch, 351 boul St-Joseph, Gatineau, QC K1A 0H3
819-997-1575, Fax: 819-953-9452

Freshwater Institute Science Laboratory, 501 University Cres., Winnipeg, MB R3T 2N6
204-983-5000, Fax: 204-983-6285

International Joint Commission, 234 Laurier Ave. West, 22nd Fl., Ottawa, ON K1P 6K6
613-947-1420, Fax: 613-993-5583, beckhoffb@ottawa.ijc.org

National Water Research Institute, 867 Lakeshore Rd., PO Box 5050, Burlington, ON L7R 4A6
905-336-4625, Fax: 905-336-6444, nwriscience.liaison@ec.gc.ca

Nunavut Water Board, PO Box 119, Gjoa Haven, NU X0B 1J0
867-360-6338, Fax: 867-360-6369

Water Science & Technology, 867 Lakeshore Rd., PO Box 5050, Burlington, ON L7R 4A6 905-336-4625, Fax: 905-336-6444

Alberta

Alberta Environment & Sustainable Resource Development, Oxbridge Place, 9820 - 106 St., Main Fl., Edmonton, AB T5K 2J6 780-427-2700, Fax: 780-422-4086, -310-0000, env.infocent@gov.ab.ca; srd.infocent@gov.ab.ca

Monitoring & Science Division, Petroleum Plaza ST, 9915 - 108 St., 10th Fl., Edmonton, AB T5K 2G8

British Columbia

Environmental Protection Division, PO Box 9339, Victoria, BC V8W 9M1 250-387-1288, Fax: 250-387-5669

Water Stewardship Division, PO Box 9339 Prov Govt,Victoria, BC V8W 9M1
Fax: 250-387-6003

Manitoba

Manitoba Water Council, 200 Saulteaux Cres., PO Box 27, Winnipeg, MB R3J 3W3
water.council@gov.mb.ca

New Brunswick

Community Planning & Environmental Protection Division, Marysville Place, PO Box 6000, Fredericton, NB E3B 5H1
506-444-5119, Fax: 506-457-7333, elg/egl-info@gnb.ca

New Brunswick Department of Environment & Local Government, Marysville Place, PO Box 6000, Fredericton, NB E3B 5H1
506-453-2690, Fax: 506-457-4994, elg/egl-info@gnb.ca

Partnerships & Innovation Division, Marysville Place, PO Box 6000, Fredericton, NB E3B 5H1
506-453-2862, Fax: 506-453-2265, elg/egl-info@gnb.ca

Northwest Territories

Asset Management Division, Stuart M. Hodgson Bldg., 5009 - 49th St., 3rd Fl., Yellowknife, NT X1A 2L9

Northwest Territories Water Board, 125 Mackenzie Rd., PO Box 2531, Yellowknife, NT X0E 0T0
867-678-2942, Fax: 867-678-2943, info@nwtwb.com

Nova Scotia

Nova Scotia Department of Agriculture, 1741 Brunswick St., 3rd Fl., PO Box 2223, Halifax, NS B3J 3C4
902-424-4560, Fax: 902-424-4671

Nunavut

Nunavut Territory Department of Health & Social Services, PO Box 1000 1000,Iqaluit, NU X0A 0H0
867-975-5766, Fax: 867-975-5705, 800-661-0833

Ontario

Advisory Council on Drinking Water Quality & Testing Standards, 40 St. Clair Ave. West, 3rd Fl., Toronto, ON M4V 1M2 416-212-7779, Fax: 416-212-7595,

Drinking Water Management Division, 135 St. Clair Ave. West, 14th Fl., Toronto, ON M4V 1P5
416-314-4475, Fax: 416-314-6935

Integrated Environmental Policy Division, 77 Wellesley St. West, 11th Fl., Toronto, ON M7A 2T5
416-314-6338, Fax: 416-314-6346

Ontario Clean Water Agency, 1 Yonge St., 17th Fl., Toronto, ON M5E 1E5
416-314-5600, Fax: 416-314-8300, 800-667-6292

Walkerton Clean Water Centre, 20 Ontario Rd., PO Box 160, Walkerton, ON N0G 2V0
519-881-2003, Fax: 519-881-4947, 866-515-0550, inquiry@wcwc.ca

Prince Edward Island

Energy & Minerals Division, Jones Bldg., 4th Fl., PO Box 2000, Charlottetown, PE C1A 7N8
902-894-0288, Fax: 902-894-0290

Quebec

Ministère du Développement durable, de l'Environnement, de la Faune, et des Parcs, Édifice Marie-Guyart, 675, boul René-Lévesque est, 29e étage, Québec, QC G1R 5V7
418-521-3911, Fax: 418-643-4143, 800-561-1616, info@mddep.gouv.qc.ca

Saskatchewan

Environmental Protection & Audit Division, 3211 Albert St., 5th Fl., Regina, SK S4S 5W6 306-787-2947

Saskatchewan Environment, 3211 Albert St., 2nd Fl., Regina, SK S4S 5W6
306-787-2584, Fax: 306-787-9544, 800-567-4224, Centre.Inquiry@gov.sk.ca

Saskatchewan Water Corporation (SaskWater), #200, 111 Fairford St. East, Moose Jaw, SK S6H 1C8
Fax: 306-694-3207, 888-230-1111, comm@saskwater.com; customerservice@saskwater.com

Saskatchewan Watershed Authority, 111 Fairford St. East, Moose Jaw, SK S6H 7X9
306-694-3900, Fax: 306-694-3944, comm@swa.ca

Yukon Territory

Yukon Environment, PO Box 2703, Whitehorse, YT Y1A 2C6
867-667-5652, Fax: 867-393-7197, environment.yukon@gov.yk.ca

WEATHER

National Research Council Wind Tunnel Testing Facilities, c/o National Research Council, 1200 Montreal Rd., Ottawa, ON K1A 0R6

WEIGHTS & MEASURES

Standards Council of Canada, #200, 270 Albert St., Ottawa, ON K1P 6N7 613-238-3222, Fax: 613-569-7808, info@scc.ca

WILDLIFE RESOURCES

Canadian Wildlife Service, 351, boul St-Joseph, Gatineau, QC K1A 0H3 819-997-1301, Fax: 819-953-7177

Committee on the Status of Endangered Wildlife in Canada, c/o Canadian Wildlife Service, 351 St. Joseph Blvd, 4th Fl., Gatineau, QC K1A 0H3
819-953-3215, Fax: 819-994-3684, cosewic/cosepac@ec.gc.ca

North American Bird Conservation Initiative, Canadian Wildlife Service, 351, boul St-Joseph, 3e étage, Gatineau, QC K1A 0H3
819-994-0512, Fax: 819-994-4445, nabci@ec.gc.ca

North American Waterfowl Management Plan, NAWCC (Canada) Secretariat, Place Vincent Massey, 351 St. Joseph Blvd., 7th Fl., Gatineau, QC K1A 0H3
819-934-6034, Fax: 819-934-6017, nawmp@ec.gc.ca

Alberta

Alberta Sport, Recreation, Parks, & Wildlife Foundation, Standard Life Centre, #903, 10405 Jasper Ave., 9th Fl., Edmonton, AB T5J 4R7
780-415-1167, Fax: 780-415-0308, -310-0000

Fish & Wildlife Division, Petroleum Plaza ST, 9915 - 108 St., 11th Fl., Edmonton, AB T5K 2G8

British Columbia

Environmental Stewardship Division, PO Box 9339 Prov Govt,Victoria, BC V8W 9M1
250-356-0121, Fax: 250-387-5669

Manitoba

Endangered Species Advisory Committee, 200 Saulteaux Cres., PO Box 24, Winnipeg, MB R3J 3W3
204-945-7465, Fax: 204-945-3077

Nunavut

Nunavut Territory Department of Environment, PO Box 1000 1300,Iqaluit, NU X0A 0H0
867-975-7700, Fax: 867-975-7742, environment@gov.nu.ca

Ontario

Ontario Ministry of Environment, 135 St. Clair Ave. West, Toronto, ON M4V 1P5
416-325-4000, Fax: 416-325-3159, 800-565-4923, picemail.moe@ontario.ca

Ontario Fish & Wildlife Heritage Commission, Robinson Pl., 300 Water St., PO Box 7000, Peterborough, ON K9J 8M5
705-755-1905, Fax: 705-755-1900

Quebec

Fondation de la faune du Québec, Place Iberville II, #420, 1175, av Lavigerie, Québec, QC G1V 4P1
418-644-7926, Fax: 418-643-7655, 877-639-0742, ffq@fondationdelafaune.qc.ca

Ministère des Ressources naturelles, 880, ch Sainte-Foy, Québec, QC G1S 4X4
418-627-8600, Fax: 418-644-6513, 866-248-6936, services.clientele@mrnf.gouv.qc.ca

WOMEN'S ISSUES

See Also: Pay Equity

Alberta

Alberta Tourism, Parks, & Recreation, Communications Branch, Commerce Place, 10155 - 102 St., 6th Fl., Edmonton, AB T5J 4L6 780-644-5589, TPR.Communications@gov.ab.ca

Nunavut

Nunavut Territory Department of Culture, Language, Elders & Youth, PO Box 1000 800,Iqaluit, NU X0A 0H0
867-975-5500, Fax: 867-975-5504, 866-934-2035

WORKERS' COMPENSATION

Merchant Seamen Compensation Board, Secretary, Merchant Seamen Compensation Board, Phase II, Place du Portage, 10th Fl., Ottawa, ON K1A 0J2
819-953-8001, Fax: 819-994-5368

Alberta

Appeals Commission for Alberta Workers' Compensation, Energy Square Building, #901, 10109 - 106th St., Edmonton, AB T5J 3L7 780-412-8700, Fax: 780-412-8701, webmaster1@appealscommission.ab.ca

British Columbia

Workers' Compensation Appeal Tribunal, #150, 4600 Jacombs Rd., Richmond, BC V6V 3B1
604-664-7800, Fax: 604-664-7898, 800-663-2782

Workers' Compensation Board of British Columbia, PO Box 5350 Terminal,Vancouver, BC V6B 5L5
604-276-3100, Fax: 604-276-3247, 888-621-7233,

Manitoba

Manitoba Workers' Compensation Board, 333 Broadway Ave., Winnipeg, MB R3C 4W3
204-954-4321, Fax: 204-954-4999, 800-362-3340, wcb@wcb.mb.ca

New Brunswick

Workplace Health, Safety & Compensation Commission of New Brunswick, 1 Portland St., PO Box 160, Saint John, NB E2L 3X9
506-632-2200, 800-222-9775, communications@ws-ts.nb.ca

Newfoundland & Labrador

Newfoundland & Labrador Workplace Health, Safety & Compensation Commission, 146 - 148 Forest Rd., PO Box 9000, St. John's, NL A1A 3B8
709-778-1000, Fax: 709-738-1714, 800-563-9000, general.inquiries@whscc.nl.ca

Northwest Territories

Northwest Territories & Nunavut Workers' Safety & Compensation Commission, Centre Square Tower, 5022 - 49th St., 5th Fl., PO Box 8888, Yellowknife, NT X1A 2R3
867-920-3888, Fax: 867-873-4596, 800-661-0792

Nova Scotia

Workers' Compensation Board of Nova Scotia, 5668 South St., PO Box 1150, Halifax, NS B3J 2Y2
902-491-8999, Fax: 902-491-8002, 800-870-3331, info@wcb.gov.ns.ca

Ontario

Workplace Safety & Insurance Board, 200 Front St. West, Ground Fl., Toronto, ON M5V 3J1
416-344-1000, Fax: 416-344-4684, 800-387-0750, wsibcomm@wsib.on.ca; prevention@wsib.on.ca (training programs)

Prince Edward Island

Prince Edward Island Workers Compensation Board, 14 Weymouth St., PO Box 757, Charlottetown, PE C1A 7L7
902-368-5680, Fax: 902-368-5696, 800-237-5049

Quebec

Commission des lésions professionnelles, #700, 900, Place d'Youville, Québec, QC G1R 3P7
418-644-7777, Fax: 418-644-6443, 800-463-1591

Commission de la santé et de la sécurité du travail du Québec, 425, rue du Pont, CP 4900 Terminus,Québec, QC G1K 7S6
Fax: 418-266-4015, 866-302-2778

Saskatchewan

Saskatchewan Workers' Compensation Board, #200, 1881 Scarth St., Regina, SK S4P 4L1
306-787-4370, Fax: 306-787-4311, 800-667-7590, internet_clientsvc@wcbsask.com

Yukon Territory

Yukon Workers' Compensation Health & Safety Board, 401 Strickland St., Whitehorse, YT Y1A 5N8
867-667-5645, Fax: 867-393-6279, 800-661-0443, worksafe@gov.yk.ca

YOUTH SERVICES

Federal Economic Development Agency for Southern Ontario, 101 Frederick St., 4th Fl., Kitchener, ON N2H 6R2
Fax: 519-571-5750, 866-593-5505

Alberta

Office of the Child & Youth Advocate, Peace Hills Trust Tower, #805, 10011 - 109 St., Edmonton, AB T5J 3S8
780-422-6056, Fax: 780-644-8833, 800-661-3446

Nunavut

Nunavut Territory Department of Culture, Language, Elders & Youth, PO Box 1000 800,Iqaluit, NU X0A 0H0
867-975-5500, Fax: 867-975-5504, 866-934-2035

Quebec

Ministère de la Santé et des Services sociaux, Direction des communications, 1075, ch Sainte-Foy, 16e étage, Québec, QC G1S 2M1 418-643-9395, Fax: 418-643-4768, regisseur.web@msss.gouv.qc.ca

ZONING

Alberta

Local Government Services Division, Commerce Place, 10155 - 102 St., 17th Fl., Edmonton, AB T5J 4L4

British Columbia

British Columbia Ministry of Community, Sport, & Cultural Development, PO Box 9490 Prov Govt,Victoria, BC V8W 9N7

Manitoba

Manitoba Municipal Board, #1144, 363 Broadway, Winnipeg, MB R3C 3N9 204-945-2941, Fax: 204-948-2235

Government Acts & Regulations

Federal Legislation

Environment Canada/Environnement Canada
Antarctic Environmental Protection Act
Canada Emission Reduction Incentives Agency Act
Canada Water Act
Canada Wildlife Act
  Administration, Management & Control of Certain Public Lands
  Wildlife Area Regulations
Canadian Environment Week Act
Canadian Environmental Assessment Act
  Canada Port Authority Environmental Assessment Regulations
  Comprehensive Study List Regulation
  Exclusion List Regulation
  Federal Authorities Regulations
  Inclusion List Regulation
  Law List Regulation
  Projects Outside Canada Environmental Assessment Regulations
Canadian Environmental Protection Act
  Alberta Equivalency Order
  Asbestos Mines & Mills Release Regulations
  Benzene in Gasoline Regulations
  Chlor-Alkali, Mercury Release Regulations
  Chlorobiphenyls Regulations
  Contaminated Fuel Regulations
  Disposal at Sea Regulations
  Environmental Emergency Regulations
  Export Control List of Notification Regulations
  Export & Import of Hazardous Wastes Regulations
  Export of Substances under the Rotterdam Convention Regulations
  Federal Halocarbon Regulations
  Federal Mobile PCB Treatment & Destruction Regulations
  Federal Registration of Storage Tank Systems for Petroleum Products & Allied Petroleum Products on Federal Lands or Aboriginal Lands Regulations
  Fuels Information Regulations, No. 1
  Gasoline & Gasoline Blend Dispensing Flow Rate Regulations
  Gasoline Regulations
  Interprovincial Movement of Hazardous Waste Regulations
  List of Hazardous Waste Authorities
  List of Toxic Substances Authorities
  Masked Name Regulations
  New Substances Fees Regulations
  New Substances Notification Regulations
  Off-Road Small Spark-Ignition Engine Emission Regulations
  On-Road Vehicle & Engine Emission Regulations
  Ozone Depleting Substances Regulations
  PCB Waste Export Regulations
  Persistence & Bioaccumulation Regulations
  Phosphorus Concentration Regulations
  Prohibition of Certain Toxic Substances
  Pulp & Paper Mill Defoamer & Wood Chip Regulations
  Pulp & Paper Mill Effluent Chlorinated Dioxins & Furans Regulations
  Regulations respecting Applications for Permits for Disposal at Sea
  Rules for Procedures for Boards of Review
  Secondary Lead Smelter Release Regulations
  Solvent Degreasing Regulations
  Sulphur in Diesel Fuel Regulations
  Sulphur in Gasoline Regulations
  Storage of PCB Material Regulations
  Tetrachloroethylene (Use in Dry Cleaning & Reporting Requirements) Regulations
  Tributyltetradeclyphosphonium Chloride Regulations
  Vinyl Chloride Release Regulations
Convention on International Trade in Endangered Species of Wild Fauna & Flora
Department of the Environment Act
  Kemano Completion Project Guidelines Order
International River Improvements Act
Lac Seul Conservation Act, 1928
Lake of the Woods Control Board Act
Manganese-Based Fuel Additives Act
Migratory Birds Convention Act, 1994
  Migratory Bird Regulations
  Migratory Bird Sanctuary Regulations
National Wildlife Week Act
Species at Risk Act
Weather Modification Information Act
Wild Animal & Plant Protection & Regulation of International & Interprovincial Trade Act

Acts Administered in Part by Environment Canada
James Bay & Northern Québec Native Claims Settlement Act
Resources & Technical Surveys Act (jointly with Natural Resources/Fisheries & Oceans)

Environment Canada Related Acts & Regulations
Agricultural & Rural Development Act (jointly with Industry)
Alternative Fuels Act & Regulations (jointly with Treasury Board)
Canada Marine Act (jointly with Transport)
Canada Oil & Gas Operations Act (jointly with Indian & Northern Affairs/Natural Resources)
  Canada Oil & Gas Certificate of Fitness Regulations
  Canada Oil & Gas Drilling Regulations
  Canada Oil & Gas Geophysical Operations Regulations
  Canada Oil & Gas Operations Regulations
  Canada Oil & Gas Production & Conservation Regulations
Canada Petroleum Resources Act (jointly with Indian Affairs & Northern Development/Natural Resouces)
  Environmental Studies Research Fund Regions Regulations
Canadian Transportation Accident Investigation & Safety Board Act (jointly with Privy Council)
Transportation Safety Board Regulations
Food & Drugs Act (jointly with Agriculture & Agri-Foods/Industry)
Mackenzie Valley Resource Management Act (jointly with Indian & Northern Affairs)
National Energy Board Act (jointly with Natural Resources/Transport Canada)
  Electricity Regulations
  Oil & Gas Regulations
  Onshore Pipeline Regulations
  Rules of Practice & Procedure
National Round Table on the Environment & the Economy Act (jointly with Environment)
Northern Pipeline Act (jointly with Natural Resources)
  Northern Pipeline Socio-Economic & Environmental Terms & Conditions (jointly with Northern BC, Southern BC, AB, SK & Swift River Portion in BC)
Oceans Act (jointly with Fisheries & Oceans)

Agriculture & Agri-Food Canada/Agriculture et Agro-alimentaire Canada
Agricultural Marketing Programs Act
Agricultural Products Marketing Act
Canada Agricultural Products Act
Canada Grain Act
Canadian Food Inspection Agency Act (CFIA)
Consumer Packaging & Labelling Act (jointly with Industry)
Department of Agriculture & Agri-Food Act
Experimental Farm Stations Act
Prairie Farm Rehabilitation Act

Canada Revenue Agency/Agence du revenu du Canada
Customs & Excise Offshore Application Act

Canadian Food Inspection Agency/Agence canadienne d'inspection des aliments
Canada Agricultural Products Act
Canadian Food Inspection Agency Act
Feeds Act
Fertilizers Act
Fish Inspection Act
Health of Animals Act
Meat Inspection Act
Plant Breeders' Rights Act
Plant Protection Act
Seeds Act

Acts Administered in Part by the Canadian Food Inspection Agency
Consumer Packaging & Labelling Act
Food & Drugs Act

Canadian Heritage/Patrimoine canadien
Cultural Property Export & Import Act
Department of Canadian Heritage Act
Fitness & Amateur Sport Act (jointly with Health)
Historic Sites & Monuments Act
Library & Archives of Canada Act
Museums Act
National Sports of Canada Act
Physical Activity & Sport Act (jointly with Health)

Citizenship & Immigration Canada/Citoyenneté et Immigration Canada
Canadian Multiculturalism Act

Fisheries & Oceans Canada/Pêches et Océans Canada
Canada Shipping Act, 2001 (jointly with Transport)
  Air Pollution Regulations
  Dangerous Chemicals & Noxious Liquid Substances Regulations
  Garbage Pollution Prevention Regulations
  Great Lakes Sewage Pollution Prevention Regulations
  Non-Pleasure Craft Sewage Pollution Prevention Regulations
  Oil Pollution Prevention Regulations
  Pleasure Craft Sewage Pollution Prevention Regulations
  Pollutant Discharge Reporting Regulations
  Pollutant Substances Regulations
  Ship-Source Oil Pollution Fund Regulations
Coastal Fisheries Protection Act
Department of Fisheries & Oceans Act
Fisheries Act
  Aboriginal Communal Fishing Licences Regulations
  Alberta Fishery Regulations, 1998
  Alice Arm Tailings Deposit Regulations
  Atlantic Fishery Regulations
  British Columbia Gravel Removal Order
  British Columbia Logging Order
  British Columbia Sport Fishing Regulations
  Fish Health Protection Regulations
  Fish Toxicant Regulations
  Fishery (General) Regulations
  Foreign Vessel Fishing Regulations
  Management of Contaminated Fisheries Regulations
  Manitoba Fishery Regulations
  Marine Mammal Regulations
  Maritime Provinces Fishery Regulations
  Newfoundland & Labrador Fishery Regulations
  Northwest Territories Fishery Regulations
  Ontario Fishery Regulations
  Pacific Fishery Management Area Regulations
  Pacific Fishery Regulations
  Potato Processing Plant Liquid Effluent Regulations
  Provincial Regulations
  Pulp & Paper Effluent Regulations
  Quebec Fishery Regulations
  Saskatchewan Fishery Regulations
  Yukon Territory Fishery Regulations
Fisheries Development Act
Fisheries Improvement Loans Act
  Fisheries & Oceans Canada Orders
Fishing & Recreational Harbours Act
Freshwater Fish Marketing Act
Oceans Act
  Basic Head Marine Protected Area Regulations
  Confederation Bridge Area Provincial (PEI) Laws Application Regulations
  Eastport Marine Protected Area Regulations
  Endeavour Hydrothermal Vents Marine Protected Areas Regulations
  Fishing Zones of Canada (Zones 1, 2 & 3) Order
  Fishing Zones of Canada (Zones 4 & 5) Order
  Fishing Zones of Canada (Zone 6) Order
  Gilbert Bay Marine Protected Area Regulations
  Gully Marine Protected Area Regulations
  Territorial Sea Geographical Coordinates (Area 7) Order
  Territorial Sea Geographical Coordinated Order

Foreign Affairs & International Trade Canada/Affaires étrangères et Commerce international Canada
Canada-Chile Free Trade Agreement
  Implementation Act
Comprehensive Nuclear Test-Ban Treaty Implementation Act
Department of Foreign Affairs & International Trade Act
Export Development Act
Export & Import Permits Act
Food & Agriculture Organization of the United Nations Act
International Boundary Waters Treaty Act
North American Free Trade Agreement Implementation Act
Rainy Lake Watershed Emergency Control Act
Roosevelt-Campobello International Park Commission Act
Skagit River Valley Treaty Implementation Act
United Nations Act

Health Canada/Santé Canada
Canada Health Act
Department of Health Act
Fitness & Amateur Sport Act (jointly with Heritage)
Food & Drugs Act (jointly with Agriculture)
Hazardous Materials Information Review Act (jointly with Human Resources & Skills Development)
  Appeal Board Procedures Regulations
  Hazardous Material Information Review Regulations
Hazardous Products Act
  Carbonated Beverage Glass Containers Regulations
  Consumer Chemicals & Containers Regulations
  Controlled Products Regulations
  Hazardous Products Regulations (Cellulose Insulation, Charcoal, Crocidolite Asbestos, Liquid Coating Materials, etc.)
  Ingredient Disclosure List
Pest Control Products Act, 2002 & Regulations
Pesticide Residue Compensation Act
Physical Activity & Sport Act (jointly with Heritage)
Quarantine Act, 2005
Radiation Emitting Devices Act
Tobacco Act

Human Resources & Social Development Canada/Ressources humaines et développement social Canada
Canada Labour Code
  Aviation Occupational Safety & Health Regulations
  Canada Occupational Health & Safety Regulations
  Coal Mines (CBDC) Occupational Safety & Health Regulations
  Coal Mining Safety Commission Regulations
  Marine Occupational Safety & Health Regulations
  Oil & Gas Occupational Safety & Health Regulations
  On Board Trains Occupational Safety & Health Regulations
Canadian Centre for Occupational Health & Safety Act
Non-smokers' Health Act (Transport Canada)

Indian & Northern Affairs Canada/Affaires indiennes et du Nord Canada
Arctic Waters Pollution Prevention Act (jointly with Transport/Natural Resources)
Department of Indian & Northern Affairs Development Act
Canada Lands Surveys Act (jointly with Natural Resources)
Canada Oil & Gas Operations Act (jointly with Natural Resources)
Canada Petroleum Resources Act (jointly with Natural Resources)
Canada - Yukon Oil & Gas Accord Implementation Act
Canadian Polar Commission Act
Claims Settlement (Alberta & Saskatchewan) Implementation Act
Fort Nelson Indian Reserve Minerals Revenue Sharing Act
Indian Act (jointly with Health)
Indian Lands Agreement Act
Indian Lands Settlement of Differences Act
  Indian Reserve Waste Disposal Regulations
  Territorial Land Titles Offices Regulations
Indian Oil & Gas Act
Land Titles Repeal Act
Mackenzie Valley Resource Management Act
Nelson House First Nation Flooded Land Act
Northern Canada Power Commission (Share Issuance & Sale Authorization) Act
Northern Canada Power Commission Yukon Assets Disposal Authorization Act
Northwest Territories Act
Northwest Territories Waters Act
Nunavut Act
Nunavut Waters & Nunavut Surface Rights Tribunal Act, 2002
Railway Belt Act
Railway Belt Water Act
Saskatchewan Natural Resources Act
Split Lake Cree First Nation Flooded Land Act
Territorial Lands Act
  Canada Mining Regulations
  Canada Oil & Gas Drilling & Production Regulations
  Canada Oil & Gas Land Regulations
  Crown Waiver Orders
  Government Employees Land Acquisition Orders
  Northwest Territories Mining Districts Order & Nunavut Mining District
  Oil & Gas Land Orders
  Orders Authorizing Acquisition of Interest in Certain Lands
  Orders Respecting Withdrawal from Disposal of Certain Lands
  Polar Bear Pass Withdrawal Order
  Reservations to Crown Waiver Orders
  Territorial Coal Regulations
  Territorial Dredging Regulations
  Territorial Land Use Regulations
  Territorial Lands Act Exclusion Orders
  Territorial Lands Regulations

Territorial Quarrying Regulations
Withdrawal of Certain Lands from Disposal Orders
Withdrawals of Disposal Orders
York Factory First Nation Flooded Land Act
Yukon Act
Yukon Environmental & Socio-Economic Assessment Act, 2003
Yukon Placer Mining Act
Yukon Quartz Mining Act
Yukon Waters Act

Industry Canada/Industrie Canada
Agricultural & Rural Development Act
Canadian Space Agency Act
Canadian Tourism Commission Act
Consumer Packaging & Labelling Act (jointly with Agriculture)
Corporations Returns Act
Department of Industry Act
Electricity & Gas Inspection Act
Industrial Design Act
National Research Council Act
Natural Sciences & Engineering Research Council Act
Standards Council of Canada Act
Timber Marking Act

Minister for the purposes of the Atlantic Canada Opportunities Agency Act
Cape Breton Development Corporation Act

National Defence (Canada)/Défense nationale
Emergencies Act

Natural Resources Canada/Ressources naturelles Canada
Canada Foundation for Sustainable Development Technology Act
Canada-Newfoundland Atlantic Accord Implementation Act
Canada-Newfoundland Oil & Gas Spills & Debris Liability Regulations
Newfoundland Offshore Area Oil & Gas Operations Regulations
Newfoundland Offshore Area Petroleum Diving Regulations
Newfoundland Offshore Area Petroleum Geophysical Operations Regulations
Newfoundland Offshore Area Petroleum Production & Conservation Regulations
Newfoundland Offshore Area Registration Regulations
Newfoundland Offshore Certificate of Fitness Regulations
Newfoundland Offshore Petroleum Drilling Regulations
Newfoundland Offshore Petroleum Installations Regulations
Canada-Nova Scotia Offshore Petroleum Resources Accord Implementation Act
Canada-Nova Scotia Oil & Gas Spills & Debris Liability Regulations
Nova Scotia Offshore Area Certificate of Fitness Regulations
Nova Scotia Offshore Area Petroleum Diving Regulations
Nova Scotia Offshore Area Petroleum Drilling Regulations
Nova Scotia Offshore Area Petroleum Geophysical Operations Regulations
Nova Scotia Offshore Area Petroleum Installations Regulations
Nova Scotia Offshore Area Petroleum Production & Conservation Regulations
Nova Scotia Resources (Ventures) Ltd. Drilling Assistance Regulations
Canada Oil & Gas Operations Act (Indian Affairs & Northern Development)
Canada Oil & Gas Certificate of Fitness Regulations
Canada Oil & Gas Diving Regulations
Canada Oil & Gas Drilling Regulations
Canada Oil & Gas Geophysical Operations Regulations
Canada Oil & Gas Installations Regulations
Canada Oil & Gas Operations Regulations
Canada Oil & Gas Production & Conservation Regulations
Nova Scotia Offshore Area Production & Conservation Regulations
Oil & Gas Spills & Debris Liability Regulations
Canadian Ownership & Control Determination Act
Co-operative Energy Act
Department of Natural Resources Act
Report on the State of Canada's Forests Regulations
Energy Administration Act
Energy Efficiency Act
Energy Monitoring Act
Energy Supplies Emergency Act
Explosives Act
Forestry Act
Gros Morne Forestry Timber Regulations
Timber Regulations
Hibernia Development Project Act
International Boundary Commission Act
National Energy Board Act (jointly with Transport)
National Energy Board Coast Recovery Regulations
National Energy Board Electricity Regulations
National Energy Board Export & Import Reporting Regulations
National Energy Board Pipeline Crossing Regulations, I & II
National Energy Board Processing Plant Regulations
National Energy Board Rules of Practice & Procedure
National Energy Board Substituted Service Regulations
Onshore Pipeline Regulations
Pipeline Arbitration Committee Procedure Rules
Power Line Crossing Regulations
Northern Pipeline Act
Uranium Mines (Ontario) Occupational Health & Safety Regulations
Nuclear Energy Act
Transport Packaging of Radioactive Materials Regulations
Uranium & Thorium Mining Regulations
Nuclear Energy Act
Nuclear Fuel Waste Act, 2002
Nuclear Liability Act
Nuclear Safety & Control Act
Canadian Nuclear Safety Commission Rules of Procedure
Class I Nuclear Facilities Regulations
Class II Nuclear Facilities & Prescribed Equipment Regulations
General Nuclear Safety & Control Regulations
Nuclear Non-Proliferation Import & Export Control Regulations
Nuclear Security Regulations
Nuclear Substances & Radiation Devices Regulations
Packaging & Transport of Nuclear Substances Regulations
Radiation Protection Regulations
Uranium Mines & Mills Regulations
Uranium Mines (Ontario) Occupational Health & Safety Regulations
Oil Substitution & Conservation Act

Administration of Acts with respect to Changes in Provincial Boundaries
Alberta Act
Alberta/BC Boundary Act, 1974
Alberta/NWT Boundary Act, 1958
British Columbia 1857, 1866
BC-Yukon-NWT Boundary Act, 1967
Keewatin Act
Manitoba Boundaries Extension Act, 1912
Manitoba-NWT Boundary Act, 1966
Manitoba/Saskatchewan Boundary Act, 1966
New Brunswick, 1851
Newfoundland, 1949
Northwest Territories, 1905
Nova Scotia, 1851
Nunavut, 1993
Ontario, 1889
Ontario Boundaries Extension Act, 1912
Ontario-Manitoba Boundary Act
Prince Edward Island, 1873
Energy Supplies Emergency Act
Québec Boundaries Extension Act, 1912
Saskatchewan, 1905
Saskatchewan/NWT Boundary Act, 1966
Yukon, 1898

Acts Administered in Part by Natural Resources Canada
Arctic Waters Pollution Prevention Act (jointly with Transport Canada/Indian & Northern Affairs)
Arctic Shipping Pollution Prevention Regulations
Arctic Waters Experimental Pollution Regulations
Arctic Waters Pollution Prevention Regulations
Order Exempting the United States Coast Guard Icebreaker "Healy" from the Application of the Arctic Shipping Pollution Prevention Regulations
Canada Lands Survey Act (jointly with Indian & Northern Affairs)
Canada Lands Surveys Examination Regulation
Canada-Newfoundland Oil & Gas Spills & Debris Liability Regulations
Land Survey Tariff Regulations
Newfoundland & Labrador Offshore Area Line Regulations
Newfoundland Offshore Area Oil & Gas Operations Regulations
Newfoundland Offshore Area Petroleum Diving Regulations
Newfoundland Offshore Area Petroleum Geophysical Operations Regulations
Newfoundland Offshore Area Petroleum Production & Conservation Regulations
Newfoundland Offshore Area Registration Regulations
Newfoundland Offshore Petroleum Drilling Regulations
Newfoundland Offshore Petroleum Installations Regulations
Newfoundland Offshore Petroleum Resource Revenue Fund Regulations
Nova Scotia Resources (Ventures) Limited Drilling Assistance Regulations
Shipping Safety Control Zones Order
Canada Petroleum Resources Act (jointly with Indian & Northern Affairs)
Environmental Studies Research Fund Regions Regulations
Frontier Lands Petroleum Royalty Regulations
Frontier Lands Registration Regulations

Lancaster Sound Designated Area Regulations
Orders Prohibiting the Issuance of Interests at Lapierre House Historic Site (Yukon) & Rampart House (Yukon)
National Energy Board Act (jointly with Transport Canada)
Resources & Technical Surveys Act (jointly with Fisheries & Oceans/Environment)

Privy Council Office/Bureau du Conseil privé
Anti-Personnel Mines Convention Implementation Act

Public Safety/Sécurité publique Canada
Emergency Preparedness Act

Public Works & Government Services Canada/Travaux publics et services gouvernementaux
Bridges Act
Expropriation Act
Federal District Commission to have acquired certain lands, An Act to Confirm the Authority of
Government Property Traffic Act (jointly with Transport)
Ottawa River, Act Respecting Certain Works
Public Works & Government Services Act

Transport Canada/Transports Canada
Aeronautics Act
Arctic Waters Pollution Prevention Act (jointly with Natural Resources/Indian Affairs & Northern Development)
Canada Marine Act
Canada Shipping Act, 2001 (jointly with Fisheries & Oceans)
Canada Transportation Act
Canadian Air Transport Security Authority Act
Department of Transport Act
Government Property Traffic Act (jointly with Public Works)
Marine Transportation Security Act
Motor Vehicle Fuel Consumption Standards Act
Motor Vehicle Safety Act
Motor Vehicle Transport Act, 1987
National Energy Board Act (jointly with Natural Resources)
Navigable Waters Protection Act
Pilotage Act
Railway Safety Act
Safe Containers Convention Act
Transportation Appeal Tribunal of Canada Act
Transportation of Dangerous Goods Act, 1992

Treasury Board of Canada/Conseil du Trésor du Canada
Alternative Fuels Act
Auditor General Act
Federal Real Property & Federal Immovables Act
Motor Vehicle Safety Act, 1993

Alberta Legislation

Alberta Environment
Climate Change & Emissions Management Act, 2003
Specified Gas Reporting Regulation
Drainage District Act, 2000
Energy Statutes Amendment Act
Environmental Protection & Enhancement (Clean-Up) Instructions Amendment Act, 2002, (Unproclaimed)
Environmental Protection & Enhancement Act (Community Development & Sustainable Resource Development)
Activities Designation Amendment Regulation
Activities Designation Regulation
Approvals & Registration Procedures Regulation
Beverage Container Recycling Regulation
Codes of Practice (Waterworks System Consisting Solely of a Water Distribution System; Asphalt Paving Plants; Compost Facilities; Landfills; Pesticides, etc.)
Conservation Easement Registration Regulation
Conservation & Reclamation Regulation
Designated Material Recycling & Management Regulation
Disclosure of Information Regulation
Electronics Designation Regulation
Emissions Trading Regulation
Environmental Appeal Board Regulation
Environmental Assessment Regulation
Environmental Assessment (Mandatory & Exempted Activities) Regulation
Environmental Protection & Enhancement (Miscellaneous) Regulation
Forest Resources Improvement Regulation
Lubricating Oil Material Environmental Handling Charge By-Law
Lubricating Oil Material Recycling & Management By-Law
Lubricating Oil Material Recycling Management Regulation
Mercury Emissions from Coal-fired Power Plants Regulation
Ozone-depleting Substances & Halocarbons Regulation
Pesticide (Ministerial) Regulation
Pesticide Sales, Handling, Use & Application Regulation
Potable Water Regulation
Release Reporting Regulation
Substance Release Regulation
Tire Designation Regulation
Waste Control Regulation
Wastewater & Storm Drainage Regulation
Wastewater & Storm Drainage (Ministerial) Regulation
Mines & Minerals Act (jointly with Energy/Sustainable Resource Development)
Natural Resources Conservation Board Act (jointly with Sustainable Resource Development)
Rules of Practice of the Natural Resources Conservation Board
North Red Deer Water Authorization Act
Stettler Regional Water Authorization Act
Water Act
Codes of Practice (Various) Regulations
Water Allocation Orders (Various) Regulation
Water (Ministerial) Regulation
Water (Offences & Penalities) Regulation
Wilderness Areas, Ecological Reserves & Natural Areas Amendment Act
Wilderness Areas, Ecological Reserves, Natural Areas & Heritage Rangelands Act

Alberta Agriculture, Food & Rural Development
Agricultural Operations Practices Act
Agricultural Pest Act
Pest & Nuisance Control Regulation
Agricultural Services Board Act
Alberta Wheats & Barley Test Market Act
Animal Keepers Act
Animal Protection Act
Federal-Provincial Farm Assistance Act
Fuel Tax Act
Fur Farms Act & Regulation
Gas Distribution Act
Irrigation Districts Act
Irrigation Forms Regulation
Irrigation Plebiscite Regulation
Irrigation Seepage Claims Exemption Regulation
Livestock Diseases Act
Destruction & Disposal of Dead Animals Regulation
Designated Communicable Diseases Regulation
Livestock Disease Control Regulation
Livestock Market & Assembly Station Regulation
Production Animal Medicine Regulation
Marketing of Agricultural Products Act
Rural Utilities Act
Soil Conservation Act
Weed Control Act
Seed Cleaning Plant Regulations
Weed Designation Regulations

Alberta Community Development
Alberta Sport, Recreation, Parks & Wildlife Foundation Act
Black Creek Heritage Rangeland Trails Act
Environmental Protection & Enhancement Act 35(d) to (f.4)
Historical Resources Act
Archaeological & Palaeontological Research Permit Regulation
Fort Mcleod Provincial Historic Area Establishment Regulation
Provincial Parks Act
Recreation Development Act
Wilderness Areas, Ecological Reserves & Natural Areas Act (amendment 2000-not yet proclaimed)
Willmore Wilderness Park Act

Alberta Energy
Alberta Energy & Utilities Board Act Security Management Regulation
Coal Conservation Act
Coal Sales Act
Electric Utilities Act
Flare Gas Generation Regulation
Independent Power & Small Power Regulation
Energy Resources Conservation Act
Freehold Mineral Rights Tax Act
Gas Resources Preservation Act
Gas Utilities Act
Hydro & Electric Energy Act
The Mineral Titles Redemption Act

Mines & Minerals Act
- Ammonite Shell Regulations
- CO2 Projects Royalty Credit Regulation
- Exploration Regulation
- Gas Processing Efficiency Assistance Regulation
- Innovative Energy Technologies Regulation
- Metallic & Industrial Minerals Exploration Regulation
- Metallic & Industrial Minerals Regulation
- Mineral Rights Compensation Regulation
- Oil Sands Tenure Regulation

Natural Gas Marketing Act
Oil & Gas Conservation Act
Oil Sands Conservation Act
Petroleum Marketing Act
Pipeline Act
Small Power Research & Development Act
Turner Valley Unit Operations Act
Water, Gas & Electric Companies Act

Alberta Government Services
Land Titles Act
Surveys Act, Section 5(1)(d) & (2)(b) (jointly with Alberta Sustainable Development)

Alberta Health & Wellness
Public Health Act
- Communicable Disease Regulation
- Nuisance & General Sanitation Regulations
- Regulated Matter Regulations

Smoke-free Places Act

Alberta Human Resources & Employment
Agrologists Act
Land Surveyors Act
Occupational Health & Safety Act
- Occupational Health & Safety Code
- Occupational Health & Safety Regulation

Radiation Protection Act & Regulations
Regulated Forestry Profession Act
Workers' Compensation Act

Alberta Infrastructure & Transportation
City Transportation Act
Dangerous Goods Transportation & Handling Act
Highways Development & Protection Act
Public Highways Development Act
Railway (Alberta) Act
Regional Airports Authorities Act
Water Act (jointly with Environment)
Water, Gas & Electric Companies Act (jointly with Energy)

Alberta Innovation & Science
Alberta Heritage Foundation for Medical Research Act
Alberta Science, Research & Technology Authority Act

Alberta Justice & Attorney General
Expropriation Act (jointly with Sustainable Resource Development)

Alberta Municipal Affairs
Disaster Services Act
- Disaster Recovery Regulation
- Government Emergency Planning Regulation

Municipal Government Act
- Waste Management Services, Water Services & Wastewater Commissions Regulations

Safety Codes Act

Alberta Sustainable Resource Development
Boundary Surveys Act
Environmental Protection & Enhancement Act (jointly with Environment)
Expropriation Act (sections 25 to 28 & 72)
Fisheries (Alberta) Act
Forest & Prairie Protection Act
Forest Reserves Act
Forests Act
Government Organization Act (jointly with Environment/Infrastructure)
Natural Resources Conservation Board Act (jointly with Environment)
Public Lands Act
Surface Rights Act
Surveys Act (jointly with Service Alberta)
Wildlife Act

British Columbia Legislation

Ministry of Environment
Ecological Reserve Act
- Application of Park Legislation to Ecological Reserves Regulation
- Ecological Reserve Regulations

Environmental Assessment Act
- Concurrent Approval Regulation
- Public Consultation Policy Regulation
- Regional District Definition Regulation
- Transition Regulation

Environmental Management Act (jointly with Attourney General/Forests, Lands & Natural Resource Operations)
- Agricultural Waste Control Regulation
- Antisapstain Chemical Waste Control Regulation
- Asphalt Plant Regulation
- Cleaner Gasoline Regulation
- Code of Practice for the Discharge of Produced Water from Coalbed Gas Operations
- Conservation Office Service Authority Regulation
- Contaminated Sites Regulation
- Environmental Appeal Board Procedure Regulation
- Environmental Data Quality Assurance Regulation
- Environmental Impact Assessment Regulation
- Finfish Aquaculture Waste Control Regulation
- Gasoline Vapour Control Regulation
- Hazardous Waste Regulation
- Land-based Fin Fish Waste Control Regulation
- Motor Vehicle Emissions Control Warranty Regulation
- Municipal Sewage Regulations
- Mushroom Composting Pollution Prevention Regulation
- Oil & Gas Waste Regulation
- Ootsa Lake Beehive Burner Regulation
- Open Burning Smoke Control Regulation
- Organic Matter Recycling Regulation
- Ozone Depleting Substances & Other Halocarbons Regulation
- Permit Fees Regulation
- Petroleum Storage & Distribution Facilities Storm Water Regulation
- Placer Mining Waste Control Regulation
- Post-Consumer Residual Stewardship Program Regulation
- Public Notification Regulation
- Pulp Mill & Pulp & Paper Mill Liquid Effluent Control Regulation
- Rebate of Waste Management Fee Regulation
- Recycling Regulation
- Solid Fuel Burning Domestic Appliance Regulation
- Spill Cost Recovery Regulation
- Spill Reporting Regulation
- Storage of Recyclable Material Regulation
- Sulphur Content of Fuel Regulation
- Waste Discharge Regulation
- Wood Residue Burner & Incinerator Regulation

Forest Land Reserve Act
Integrated Pest Management Act, 2003
Ministry of Environment Act
Okanagan River Boundaries Settlement Act
Park Act
Parks & Protected Areas Statutes Amendment Act, 2004
- Park & Recreation Area Regulation

Protected Areas of British Columbia Act
Sustainable Environment Fund Act
Wildlife Act (jointly with Forests, Lands & Natural Resource Operations)
- Angling & Scientific Collection Regulation
- Closed Areas Regulation
- Designation & Exemption Regulation
- Designation of Officers Regulation
- Freshwater Fish Regulation
- Habitat Conservation Trust Fund Regulation
- Hunter Safety Training Regulation
- Hunting Licensing Regulation
- Hunting Regulation
- Limited Entry Hunting Regulation
- Management Unit Regulation
- Motor Vehicle Prohibition Regulation
- Permit Regulation
- Public Access Prohibition Regulation
- Tofino Mudflats Wildlife Management Area Regulation
- Wildlife Act Commercial Activities Regulation
- Wildlife Act General Regulation
- Wildlife Management Areas Regulations

Wildlife Amendment Act

Ministry of Aboriginal Relations & Reconciliation

Indian Cut-off Lands Dispute
Treaty Commission Act

Ministry of Agriculture

Agri-Food Choice & Quality Act
  Organic Agricultural Products Certification Regulation
Agricultural Land Commission Act
Animal Disease Control Act
Columbia Basin Trust Act
Farm Practices Protection (Right to Farm) Act
Farming & Fishing Industries Development Act
Fisheries Act (jointly with Forests, Lands & Natural Resource Operations)
Food Products Standards Act
Fur Farm Act
Game Farm Act
Livestock Act
Livestock Protection Act
Ministry of Agriculture & Food Act
Natural Products Marketing (BC) Act
Pesticide Control Act
Plant Protection Act
Prevention of Cruelty to Animals Act
Range Act (jointly with Finance/Forests)
Veterinarians Act

Ministry of the Attorney General

Coastal Ferry Act (jointly with Transportation)
Expropriation Act
Forest & Range Practices Act (jointly with Finance/Forests)
Forest Practices Code of British Columbia Act (jointly with Finance/Forests)
Utilities Commission Act

Ministry of Community, Sport & Cultural Development

Arts Council Act
Assessment Act
Assessment Authority Act
Capital Commission Act
Capital Region Water Supply & Sooke Hills Protection
Community Charter Act
Islands Trust Act
Local Government Act (jointly with Agriculture/Energy & Mines)
Local Services Act
Museum Act
Recreational Facility Act

Ministry of Energy & Mines

BC Hydro Public Power Legacy & Heritage Contract Act
Clean Energy Act (jointly with Aboriginal Relations & Reconciliation)
Coal Act
Coalbed Gas Act, 2003
Columbia Basin Trust Act
Energy Efficiency Act
  Energy Efficiency Standards Regulation
Gas Utility Act
Geothermal Resources Act
Hydro & Power Authority Act
Hydro Power Measures Act
Mineral Land Tax Act (jointly with Finance)
Mineral Tax Act (jointly with Finance)
Mineral Tenure Act
Mines Act
  Mine Reclamation Fund Regulation
  Mines Regulation
  Workplace Hazardous Materials Information
  System Regulation (Mines)
Mining Right of Way Act
Mining Tax Act
Ministry of Energy & Mines Act
Oil & Gas Activities Act (jointly with Attorney General)
Petroleum & Natural Gas Act
Petroleum & Natural Gas (Vancouver Island Railway Lands) Act
Safety Authority Act
Safety Standards Act
Vancouver Island Natural Gas Pipeline Act
West Kootenay Power & Light Company, Ltd. Act

Ministry of Finance

Budget Measures Implementation Act
Financial Administration Act
Forest Act
Forest & Range Practices Act (jointly with Attorney General/Forests)
Forest Practices Code of British Columbia Act (jointly with Attorney General/Forests)
Forest Stand Management Fund Act (jointly with Forests)
Range Act (jointly with Agriculture/Forests)
Wildfire Act, 2004 (jointly with Forests)

Ministry of Forests, Lands & Natural Resource Operations

Boundary Act
Creston Valley Wildlife Act
  Discharge of Firearms Regulation
  Summit Creek Campground & Recreation Area
Dike Maintenance Act
Drainage, Ditch & Dike Act
Drinking Water Protection Act
  Ground Water Protection Regulations
Environment & Land Use Act
Fisheries Act
Fish Protection Act
  Riparian Areas Regulation
  Sensitive Streams Designation & Licensing Regulation
  Streamside Protection Regulation
Flood Hazard Statutes Amendment Act, 2003
Forest Act (jointly with Finance)
  Advertising, Deposits & Disposition Regulation
  Allowable Annual Cut Proportionate Reduction Regulation
  Annual Rent Regulation
  BC Timber Sales Business Areas Regulation
  BC Timber Sales Business Regulation
  Christmas Tree Regulation
  Community Forest Agreement Regulation
  Credit to Stumpage Regulation
  Cut Control Regulation
  Effective Director Regulation
  Forest Accounts Receivable Interest Regulation
  Forest Regions Regulation
  Free Use Permit Regulation
  Innovative Forestry Practices Regulation
  Interest Rate Under Various Statutes Regulation
  Log Salvage Regulation (Vancouver District)
  Manufactured Forest Products Regulation
  Minimum Stumpage Rate Regulation
  Performance Based Harvesting Regulation
  Scaling Regulation
  Special Forest Products Regulation
  Timber Definition Regulation
  Timber Harvesting Contract & Subcontract Regulation
  Timber Marketing & Transportation Regulation
  Woodlot Licence Regulation
Forest & Range Practices Act (jointly with Attorney General/Finance)
Forest Practices Code of British Columbia Act (jointly with Finance/Attorney General)
  Government Actions Regulation
  Provincial Forest Use Regulation
  Stillwater Pilot Project Regulation
Forest & Range Practises Act (jointly with Finance/Attorney General)
  Administrative Remedies Regulation
  Administrative Review & Appeal Procedure (Forest Practices) Regulation
  Forest Planning & Practices Regulation
  Forest Practices Board Regulation
  Forest Recreation Regulation
  Forest Service Road Use Regulation
  Fort St. John Pilot Project Regulation
  Invasive Plants Regulation
  Range Planning & Practices Regulation
  Security for Forest Practice Liabilities Regulation
  TFL 49 Pilot Project Regulation
  Woodlot Licence Planning & Practices Regulation
Forest Stand Management Fund Act (jointly with Finance)
  Forest Stand Management Fund Regulation
Foresters Act
Forestry Revitalization Act, 2003
Greenbelt Act
Heritage Conservation Act
Hunting & Fishing Heritage Act
Industrial Operation Compensation Act
Land Act
Land Survey Act
Land Surveyors Act
Land Title & Survey Authority Act

Libby Dam Reservoir Act
Manufactured Forest Products Regulation
Ministry of Forests Act
Motor Vehicle (All Terrain) Act
Muskwa-Kechika Management Area Act
Private Managed Forest Land Act
Protected Areas Forests Compensation Act
Railway Act (jointly with Transportation)
Range Act (jointly with Agriculture/Finance)
Skagit Environmental Enhancement Act
Water, Land & Air Protection Statutes Amendment Act, 2003
Water Act
Water Protection Act
  Groundwater Protection Regulations
Water Utility Act
Weed Control Act
Wildfire Act, 2004 (jointly with Finance)

Ministry of Health
Drinking Water Protection Act
Food Safety Act
Health Act
  Health Hazard Regulation
  Industrial Camps Health Regulations
  Sanitary Regulations
  Sewage Disposal Regulations
  Sewage System Regulation
  West Nile Virus Control Regulations
Health Emergency Act
  Health Emergency Regulation
Ministry of Health Act
Tobacco Damages & Health Care Costs Recovery Act
Tobacco Control Act

Ministry of Jobs, Tourism & Innovation
BC-Alcan Northern Development Fund Act
British Columbia Enterprise Corporation Act (jointly with Community)
Economic Development Act
Ministry of International Business & Immigration Act
Northern Development Initiative Trust Act
Tourism Act

Ministry of Labour, Citizens' Services & Open Government
Coastal Forest Industry Dispute Settlement Act
Employment Standards Act
Labour Relations Code
Ministry of Labour Act (except in relation to gas, electrical, elevating devices, boiler & pressure vessel safety)
Workers' Compensation Act

Ministry of Public Safety & Solicitor General
Commercial Transport Act (jointly with Transportation)
Emergency Communications Corporations Act
Emergency Program Act
  Compensation & Disaster Financial Assistance Regulation
  Emergency Program Management Regulation
  Local Authority Emergency Management Regulation
  Environment & Land Use Act (Sustainable Resource Management)
Fire Services Act
Flood Relief Act
Motor Vehicle Act (jointly with Transportation)

Ministry of Transportation & Infrastructure
Commercial Transport Act (jointly with Public Safety)
Coastal Ferry Act (jointly with Attorney General)
South Coast British Columbia Transportation Authority Act
Industrial Roads Act
Motor Vehicle Act (jointly with Public Safety)
  Emission Inspection Exemption Regulation
  Heavy Vehicle Diesel Emission Standards Regulation
  Inspection Standards (Safety & Repair) Regulation
Passenger Transportation Act
Railway Act (jointly with Forests)
Transport of Dangerous Goods Act
  Tunnel Transportation of Dangerous Commodities Regulation
Transportation Act

Manitoba Legislation

Manitoba Conservation
Contaminated Sites Remediation Act
Crown Lands Act
Dangerous Goods Handling & Transportation Act
  Anhydrous Ammonia Handling & Transport Regulations
  Classification for Products, Substances & Organisms Regulation
  Dangerous Goods Handling & Transportation Fees Regulation
  Dangerous Goods Handling & Transportation Regulation
  Environmental Accident Reporting Regulation
  Generator Registration & Carrier Licensing Regulation
  Manifest Regulation
  PCB Storage Site Regulation
  Special Waste (Shredder Residue) Regulation
  Storage & Handling of Petroleum Products & Allied Products Regulation
Ecological Reserves Act
  Ecological Reserves Designation Regulation
Endangered Species Act
Environment Act
  Burning of Crop Residue & Non-Crop Herbage Regulation
  Campgrounds Regulation
  Classes of Development Regulation
  Disposal of Whey Regulation
  Environment Act Fees Regulation
  Environmental Assessment Hearing Costs Recovery Regulation
  Incinerators Regulation
  Inco Ltd. & Hudson Bay Mining & Smelting Co., Ltd. Smelting Complex Regulation
  Joint Environmental Assessment Regulation
  Litter Regulation
  Livestock Manure & Mortalities Management Regulation
  Onsite Wastewater Management Systems Regulation
  Participant Assistance Regulation
  Peat Smoke Control Regulation
  Pesticides Regulation
  Rockwood Sensitive Area Regulation
  Waste Disposal Grounds Regulation
  Wastewater Management Systems Regulations
  Water & Wastewater Facility Operators Regulation
Forest Act
Forest Health & Protection Act & Regulations
High-Level Radioactive Waste Act
International Peace Garden Act
Manitoba Hazardous Waste Management Corporation Act
Manitoba Natural Resources Transfer Act
Manitoba Natural Resources Transfer Act, Amendment Act
Manitoba Natural Resources Transfer Act, Amendment Act, 1963
Ozone Depleting Substances Act
Provincial Parks Act
Plant Pests & Diseases Act
Polar Bear Protection Act, 2003
  Protection of Water Resources Regulation
  Sanitary Areas Regulation
  Water Supplies Regulation
  Water Works, Sewage & Sewage Disposal Regulations
Resource Tourism Operators Act
Surveys Act (Part II)
Sustainable Development Act
Waste Reduction & Prevention Act
  Multi-Material Stewardship (Interim Measures) Regulation
  Tire Stewardship Regulation
  Used Oil, Oil Filters & Containers Stewardship Regulation
Wildlife Act
  Designation of Wild Animals Regulation
  Designation of Wildlife Lands Regulation
  Threatened, Endangered & Extirpated Species Regulation
Wild Rice Act

Manitoba Aboriginal & Northern Affairs
Northern Affairs Act
Planning Act

Manitoba Agriculture, Food & Rural Initiatives
Animal Diseases Act
Crown Lands Act, (in part) Sections 6, 7, 10, 12(1), 14, 16, 17, 18, 21, 23, 24 to 28 both inclusive
Department of Agriculture, Food & Rural Initiatives Act
Farm Lands Ownership Act
Farm Practices Protection Act
Farm Products Marketing Act
Land Rehabilitation Act
Livestock Industry Diversification Act
Livestock & Livestock Products Act
Noxious Weeds Act
Pesticides & Fertilizers Control Act

Prescribed Spraying Equipment & Controlled Products
Plant Pests & Diseases Act
Wildlife Act, (in part) Section 89(e)

Manitoba Conservation
Sustainable Development Act

Manitoba Culture, Heritage & Tourism
Heritage Manitoba Act
Heritage Resources Act
Travel Manitoba Act

Manitoba Finance
Manitoba Hydro Act (responsibility of Hon. Rosann Wowchuk)

Manitoba Health
Public Health Act
Atmospheric Pollution Regulation
Collection & Disposal of Wastes Regulation
Fumigation & Pest Control Regulation
Protection of Water Sources Regulation
Sanitation Regulation
Water Supplies Regulation
Water Works, Sewerage & Sewage Disposal Regulation
X-Ray Safety Regulation

Manitoba Infrastructure & Transportation
Crown Lands Act
Drivers & Vehicles Act
Emergency Measures Act (responsibility of Hon. Steve Ashton)
Emergency 911 Public Safety Answering Point Act (responsibility of Hon. Steve Ashton)
Highway Traffic Act
Highways Protection Act
Highways & Transportation Act
Land Acquisition Act
Manitoba Floodway and East Side Road Authority Act
Manitoba Water Services Board Act
Off-Road Vehicles Act
Provincial Parks Act
Provincial Railways Act
Trans-Canada Highway Act
Wild Rice Act

Manitoba Innovation, Energy & Mines
Biofuels Act
Economic Innovation & Technology Council Act
Energy Act
Gas Allocation Act
Gas Pipe Line Act
Greater Winnipeg Gas Distribution Act (S.M. 1988-89, C.40)
Mines & Minerals Act
Mining & Metallurgy Compensation Act
Oil & Gas Act
Drilling & Production Regulation
Oil & Gas Production Tax Act

Manitoba Justice
Expropriation Act
Gaming Control Act (responsibility of Hon. David Walter)
Transboundary Pollution Reciprocal Act

Manitoba Labour & Immigration
Employment Standards Code
Fires Prevention & Emergency Response Act
Gas & Oil Burner Act
Steam & Pressure Plants Act
Workplace Safety & Health Act
Construction Industry Safety Regulation
Fibrosis & Silicosis Regulation
Forestry, Logging & Log Hauling Regulation
Hearing Conservation & Noise Control Regulation
Operation of Mines Regulation
Sanitary & Hygienic Welfare Regulation
Workplace Hazardous Materials Information System Regulation
Workplace Health Hazard Regulation
Workplace Safety & Health Committee Regulation
Workplace Safety Regulation
Minimum Wage & Working Conditions Regulation

Manitoba Local Government
Municipal Act
Municipal Assessment Act
Planning Act (in part)
Northern Manitoba Planning & Bylaws Regulation
Provincial Land Use Policies Regulation
Subdivision Regulation
Regional Waste Management Authorities Act

Manitoba Water Stewardship
Conservation Agreements Act
Conservation Agreement Forms Regulation
Eligible Conservation Agencies Regulation
Conservation Districts Act
Drinking Water Safety Act, 2004
Dyking Authority Act
Fisheries Act
Fishermen's Assistance & Polluter's Liability Act
Ground Water & Water Well Act
Well Drilling Regulation
Lake of the Woods Control Board Act
Manitoba Habitat Heritage Act
Manitoba Natural Resources Transfer Act
Natural Resources Agreement Act
Red River Floodway Act
Water Power Act
Water Protection Act
Water Resources Administration Act
Water Resources Conservation & Protection Act
Water Rights Act
Water Supply Commissions Act

New Brunswick Legislation

Department of the Environment/Environnement
Agricultural Land Protection & Development Act (in part)
Assessment & Planning Appeal Board Act (jointly with Local Government)
Beverage Containers Act
Clean Air Act
Administrative Penalties Regulation
Air Quality Regulation
Appeal Regulation
Ozone Depleting Substances Regulation
Clean Environment Act
Appeal Regulation
Environmental Impact Assessment Regulation
Petroleum Product Storage & Handling Regulation
New Brunswick Tire Stewardship Regulation
Public Participation Regulation
Regional Solid Waste Commissions Regulation
Used Oil Regulation
Water Quality Regulation
Clean Water Act
Appeal Regulation
Fees for Industrial Approvals
Potable Water Regulation
Protected Area Exemption Regulation
Protected Areas Order
Water Classification Regulation
Water Well Regulation
Watercourse & Wetland Alteration Regulation
Watershed Protected Area Designation Order
Wellfield Protected Area Designation Order
Community Planning Act
Environmental Trust Fund Act
Gas Distribution Act (in part)
Highway Act (Sections 58 to 62.1)
Mining Act (Subsection 68(2))
Pesticides Control Act
Pipeline Act (in part)
Topsoil Preservation Act

Department of Attorney General/Procureur général
Municipalities Act
Protected Natural Areas Act
Establishment of Protected Natural Areas Regulation
General Regulation, Protected Natural Areas Act

Department of Agriculture, Fisheries & Aquaculture/Agriculture, Pêches et Aquaculture
Agricultural Land Protection & Development Act
Agricultural Operation Practices Act
Aquaculture Act
Diseases of Animals Act

Fisheries & Aquaculture Development Act
Fish Processing Act
Fish & Wildlife Act (in part)
Inshore Fisheries Representation Act
Livestock Operations Act
Livestock Incentives Act
Marshland Reclamation Act
Natural Products Act
Plant Health Act
Potato Disease Eradication Act

Department of Business New Brunswick/Entreprises Nouveau-Brunswick
Economic Development Act

Department of Energy/Énergie
Electricity Act
Energy Efficiency Act
Energy Efficiency and Conservation Agency of New Brunswick Act
Gas Distribution Act, 1999
Petroleum Products Pricing Act
Pipeline Act, 2005

Department of Health/Santé
Clean Air (Paragraph 8(2a) & Subsection 4)
Clean Water Act (in part)
Motor Vehicle Act (in part)
Pesticides Control Act (in part)
Public Health Act
Smoke-Free Places Act, 2004

Department of Local Government/Gouvernements locaux
Assessment & Planning Appeal Board Act (jointly with Environment)
Control of Municipalities Act
Unsightly Premises Act

Department of Natural Resources/Ressources naturelles
An Act respecting Angling Lease Number 7
Bituminous Shale Act
Conservation Easements Act
Crown Grant Restrictions Act
Crown Lands & Forests Act
    Leasing Regulation
Endangered Species Act
Fish & Wildlife Act
Forest Fires Act
Forest Products Act
Grants Act
Kouchibougac National Park Act
Maritime Forestry Complex Coporation Act
Metallic Minerals Tax Act
Mining Act (in part)
National Parks Act
Natural Products Act (in part)
Off-Road Vehicle Act
Oil & Natural Gas Act
Ownership of Minerals Act
Parks Act
Protected Natural Areas Act, 2003
Quarriable Substances Act
Scalers Act
Territorial Divisions Act
Transportation of Primary Forest Products Act
Underground Storage Act

Department of Post-Secondary Education & Training/Éducation postsecondaire et Formation
Occupational Health & Safety Act
    Code of Practice for Working with Material Containing Asbestos
    Underground Mine Regulation
    Workplace Hazardous Materials Information System (WHMIS) Regulation
Silicosis Compensation Act
Workplace Health, Safety & Compensation Commission Act

New Brunswick Power Group of Companies/Énergie NB
Electric Power Act

Department of Public Safety/Sécurité publique
Boiler & Pressure Vessel Act
Elevators & Lifts Act
Emergency 911 Act
Emergency Measures Act
Fire Prevention Act
Motor Vehicle Act
Salvage Dealers Licensing Act
Transportation of Dangerous Goods Act

Service New Brunswick/Services Nouveau-Brunswick
Boundaries Confirmation Act
Land Titles Act
Surveys Act

Department of Supply & Services/Approvisionnement et services
Public Purchasing Act
Public Works Act

Department of Tourism & Parks/Tourisme et Parcs
Parks Act
Tourism Development Act, 2008 (unproclaimed)

Department of Transportation/Transports
Highway Act
Motor Carrier Act
New Brunswick Highway Corporation Act
New Brunswick Transportation Authority Act
Public Landings Act
Shortline Railways Act

Newfoundland & Labrador Legislation

Department of Environment & Conservation
Endangered Species Act
    Endangered Species Regulation
    Species Status Advisory Committee Regulations
Environmental Protection Act
    Air Pollution Control Regulations, 2004
    Environmental Assessment Regulations, 2003
    Gasoline Volatility Control Regulations, 2003
    Halocarbon Regulations
    Heating Oil Storage Tank System Regulations
    Ozone Depleting Substances Regulations, 2003
    Pesticides Control Regulations, 2003
    Storage & Handling of Gasoline & Associated Products Regulations, 2003
    Storage of PCB Waste Regulations, 2003
    Used Oil Control Regulations
    Waste Management Regulations, 2003
    Waste Material Disposal Areas Regulations
Geographical Name Act
Land Surveyors Act
Lands Act
National Parks Lands Act
Provincial Parks Act
Water Resources Act
    Environmental Control Water & Sewage Regulations
    Notices of Protected Water Supplies, Watershed Areas, Wellhead Protected Water Supplies
    Water Power Rental Regulations, 2003
    Well Drilling Regulations, 2003
Wild Life Act
    Wild Life Park Order
    Wild Life Park Regulations
    Wild Life Regulations
    Wild Life Reserve Regulations
Wilderness & Ecological Reserves Act

Department of Fisheries & Aquaculture
Aquaculture Act
Fish Inspection Act
Fish Processing Licensing Board Act
Fisheries Act
Fisheries Restructuring Act
Fishing Industry Collective Bargaining Act
Professional Fish Harvesters Act

Department of Government Services
Architects Act
Occupational Health & Safety Act
    Asbestos Abatement Regulations
    Asbestos Exposure Code Regulations
    Mines Safety of Workers Regulations
    Occupational Health & Safety Electrical & Fisheries Advisory Committees Regulations
    Occupational Health & Safety Regulations
    Workplace Hazardous Materials Information System (WHMIS) Regulations
Petroleum Products Act

Radiation Health & Safety Act

Acts Shared in Part with Other Ministries
Building Standards Act (Municipal Affairs)
Dangerous Goods Transportation Act (Justice)
Environmental Protection Act (Environment & Conservation)
Fire Prevention Act, 1991 (Municipal Affairs)
Health & Community Services Act (Health & Community Services)
Highway Traffic Act (Transportation & Works)
Motor Carrier Act (Transportation & Works)
Motorized Snow Vehicles & All-Terrain Vehicles Act (Natural Resources)
Tobacco Act (Federal) (Health & Community Services)
Urban & Rural Planning Act (Municipal Affairs)
Water Resources Act (Environment & Conservation)

Department of Health & Community Services
Food & Drug Act
Health & Community Services Act
  Public Health (Sanitation) Regulation
Smoke-Free Environment Act, 2005

Department of Innovation, Trade & Rural Development
Economic Diversification & Growth Enterprises (EDGE) Act
Research Council Act

Department of Municipal Affairs
Assessment Act, 2006
Building Standards Act
Emergency Services Act
Evacuated Communities Act
Fire Prevention Act, 1991
Municipalities Act, 1999
Regional Service Boards Act
St. John's Municipal Council Parks Act
Urban & Rural Planning Act, 2000

Department of Natural Resources
Animal Health & Protection Act
Canada-Newfoundland Atlantic Accord Implementation Act, 1986
  Canada-Newfoundland & Labrador Oil & Gas Spills & Debris Liability Newfoundland & Labrador Regulations
  Certificate of Fitness Newfoundland & Labrador Regulations
  Offshore Area Oil & Gas Operations Regulations
  Offshore Area Petroleum Geophysical
  Operations Newfoundland & Labrador Regulations
  Offshore Area Petroleum Production & Conservation Newfoundland & Labrador Regulations
  Offshore Petroleum Drilling Newfoundland & Labrador Regulations
  Offshore Petroleum Installations Newfoundland & Labrador Regulations
Electrical Power Control Act, 1994
Forest Protection Act
  Cutting of Timber Regulations
  Forest Fire Regulations
  Forest Management Districts Proclamation
Forestry Act
  Cutting of Timber Regulations
  Forest Fire Offence & Penalty Regulation
  Forest Fire Regulations
  Forest Fires Liability & Compensation Regulations
  Forest Land Management & Taxation Regulations
  Forest Management Districts Proclamation Regulations
  Mill Regulations
  Timber Royalty Regulations
  Timber Scaling Regulations
Heritage Animals Act
Hydro Corporation Act, 2007
Lower Churchill Development Act
Mineral Act
Mineral Holdings Impost Act
Mining Act
Motorized Snow Vehicles & All-Terrain Vehicles Act (jointly with Government Services)
Natural Products Marketing Act
Petroleum & Natural Gas Act
Plant Protection Act
  Seed Potato Regulations
Quarry Materials Act, 1998
Undeveloped Minerals Areas Act

Department of Tourism, Culture & Recreation
Colonial Buildings Act
Historic Resources Act
Tourist Establishments Act

Department of Transportation & Works
Expropriation Act
Local Road Boards Act
Motor Carrier Act
Pippy Park Commission Act
Rail Services Act
Transportation & Works Act

Northwest Territories Legislation

Department of Environment & Natural Resources
Environmental Protection Act
  Asphalt Paving Industry Emission Regulations
  Spill Contingency Planning & Reporting Regulations
  Used Oil & Waste Fuel Management Regulations
Environmental Rights Act
Forest Management Act
Forest Protection Act
Natural Resources Conservation Trust Act
Pesticide Act
Species at Risk (NWT) Act
Waste Reduction & Recovery Act
  Beverage Container Regulations
  Single-Use Retail Bag Regulations
Water Resources Agreement Act
Wildlife Act
  Big Game Hunting Regulations
  Birds of Prey Regulations
  Certification and Disposal of Wildlife Regulations
  Critical Wildlife Areas Regulations
  Dempster Highway Special Management Area Regulations
  Inuvialuit Settlement Region Hunters and Trappers Committees Regulations
  Nuisance Bison Control Regulations
  Sale of Wildlife Regulations
  Small Game Hunting Regulations
  Trapping Regulations
  Wildlife Business Regulations
  Wildlife Export Regulations
  Wildlife General Regulations
  Wildlife Licences and Permits Regulations
  Wildlife Management Barren-Ground Caribou Areas Regulations
  Wildlife Management Areas Regulations
  Wildlife Preserves Regulations
  Wildlife Regions Regulations
  Wildlife Sanctuaries Regulations

Department of Health & Social Services
Public Health Act
  Disease Surveillance Regulations
  Food Establishment Safety Regulations General Sanitation Exemption Regulations
  General Sanitation Regulations
  Public Pool Regulations
  Public Sewerage Systems Regulations
  Reportable Disease Control Regulations
  Tourist Accommodation Health Regulations
  Water Supply System Regulations

Department of Industry, Tourism & Investment
Agricultural Products Marketing Act
Co-operative Associations Act
Freshwater Fish Marketing Act
Herd and Fencing Act
Northwest Territories Business Development and Investment Corporation Act
Territorial Parks Act
Tourism Act

Department of Municipal & Community Affairs
Area Development Act
Cities, Towns & Villages Act
Civil Emergency Measures Act
Commissioner's Land Act
Fire Prevention Act
Hamlets Act
Planning Act
Property Assessment & Taxation Act
Settlements Act
Tåîchô Community Government Act

Department of Public Works & Services
Boilers & Pressure Vessels Act
Electrical Protection Act

Gas Protection Act
Public Utilities Act

Department of Transportation
All-Terrain Vehicles Act
Motor Vehicles Act
Public Airports Act
Public Highways Act
Transportation of Dangerous Goods Act
  Transportation of Dangerous Goods Regulations

Northwest Territories & Nunavut Workers' Compensation Board
Explosives Use Act
Mine Health & Safety Act
  Environmental Tobacco Smoke Worksite Regulations
Safety Act
  Asbestos Safety Regulations
  Work Site Hazardous Materials Information System Regulations
Workers' Compensation Act

Nova Scotia Legislation

Nova Scotia Environment
Anti-idling Act
Environment Act
  Activities Designation Regulations
  Air Quality Regulations
  Approvals Procedure Regulations
  Asbestos Waste Management Regulations
  Dangerous Goods Management Regulations
  Emergency Spill Regulations
  Environmental Assessment Regulations
  Environment Act & Regulations Fees Regulations
  Greenhouse Gas Emissions Regulations
  Motive Fuel & Fuel Oil Approval Regulations
  NS Environmental Assessment Boards Regulations
  NS Environmental Trust Regulations
  On-Site Services Advisory Board Regulations
  On-Site Sewage Disposal Systems Regulations
  Ozone Layer Protection Regulations
  PCB Management Regulations
  Pesticides Regulations
  Petroleum Management Regulations
  Solid Waste-Resource Management Regulations
  Sulphide Bearing Material Disposal Regulations
  Used Oil Regulations
  Water and Wastewater Facilities and Public Drinking Water Supplies Regulations
  Well Construction Regulations
Environmental Goals and Sustainable Prosperity Act
Non-essential Pesticides Control Act
Off Highway Vehicles Act
Water Resources Protection Act
Voluntary Carbon Emissions Offset Fund Act
Wilderness Area Protection Act

Department of Agriculture
Agriculture & Marketing Act
Agriculture Marshland Conservation Act
  Marsh Land Use Regulations: Bishop-Beckwith, Dentiballis, Dugau/ Ryerson, Grand Pré, Lower Truro, Masstown, St. Croix, Victoria Diamond Jubilee, Wellington
  Non-Agricultural Use Land Exemption Regulations
Animal Health & Protection Act
  Animal Health & Protection Regulations
Bee Industry Act
Dairy Industry Act
Farm Practices Act
Livestock Health Services Act
  Livestock Health Services Regulations
Meat Inspection Act
Natural Products Act
Potato Industry Act
Weed Control Act
Wildlife Act
  Game Farming Regulations (jointly with Natural Resources)

Department of Communities, Culture and Heritage
Heritage Property Act
Sherbrooke Restoration Commission Act

Department of Economic and Rural Development and Tourism
Cooperative Associations Act
Tourist Accommodations Act

Nova Scotia Emergency Management Office
Emergency 911 Act
Emergency Management Act

Department of Energy
Canada-Nova Scotia Offshore Petroleum Resources Accord Implementation (Nova Scotia) Act
  Nova Scotia Offshore Area Certificate of Fitness Regulations
  Nova Scotia Offshore Area Oil & Gas Spills & Debris Liability Regulations
  Nova Scotia Offshore Area Petroleum Diving Regulations
  Nova Scotia Offshore Area Petroleum Drilling & Production Regulations
  Nova Scotia Offshore Area Petroleum Geophysical Operations Regulations
  Nova Scotia Offshore Area Petroleum Installations Regulations
Electricity Act
Energy-Efficient Appliances Act
Energy Resources Conservation Act
  Gas Plant Facility Regulations
  Onshore Petroleum Geophysical Exploration Regulations
  Sable Offshore Energy Project Regulations
Gas Distribution Act
Petroleum Resources Act
  Onshore Petroleum Drilling Regulations
  Onshore Petroleum Geophysical Exploration Regulations
  Petroleum Resources Regulations
  Withdrawal of Petroleum Products from the Act Regulations
Petroleum Resources Removal Permit Act
Pipeline Act
  Gas Plant Facility Regulations
  Land Acquisition Regulations
  Pipeline Benefits Plan Regulations
  Pipeline Regulations
Underground Hydrocarbons Storage Act

Nova Scotia Fisheries & Aquaculture
Fisheries & Coastal Resources Act
Fisheries Organizations Support Act
Wildlife Act
  Fishing Regulations (jointly with Natural Resources)

Department of Health & Wellness
Health Act
Health Protection Act (jointly with Department of Agriculture)
Health Research Foundation Act
Medical Laboratory Technology Act
Safer Needles in Healthcare Workplaces Act
Smoke Free Places Act
Tobacco Access Act

Department of Labour & Advanced Education
Amusement Devices Safety Act
Apprenticeship and Trades Qualifications Act
Building Code Act
Electrical Installation and Inspection Act
Elevators and Lifts Act
Fire Safety Act
Labour Standards Code
Occupational Health and Safety Act
  Occupational Health & Safety Appeal Panel Regulations
  Occupational Safety General Regulations
  Underground Mining Regulations
  Workplace Hazardous Materials Information System Regulations
Technical Safety Act
Workers' Compensation Act

Department of Natural Resources
Beaches Act
Conservation Easements Act
Endangered Species Act
  Species At Risk List Regulations
Forests Act
  Christmas Tree Grading Regulations
  Christmas Tree Levy Regulations
  Dutch Elm Disease Regulations
  Forest Fire Protection Regulations
  Forest Sustainability Regulations
  Registration & Statistical Returns Regulations
  Timber Loan Board Regulations
  Wildlife Habitat & Watercourses Protection Regulations
Land Surveyors Act

Mineral Resources Act
Mines Act
Nova Scotia Federation of Anglers & Hunters Act
Off Highway Vehicles Act (jointly with Environment/Service Nova Scotia & Municipal Relations/Transportation & Infrastructure Renewal)
Primary Forest Products Marketing Act
Provincial Parks Act
Scalers Act
Trails Act
Wildlife Act
- Bear Harvesting Regulations
- Deer Farming and Marketing of Deer Products Regulations
- Deer Hunting Regulations
- Fishing Regulations (jointly with Fisheries & Aquaculture)
- Forfeiture of Seized Property Regulations
- Fur Buyers, Hide Dealers and Taxidermists Regulations
- Fur Harvesting Regulations
- Game Farming Regulations (jointly with Agriculture)
- General Wildlife Regulations
- Guide Regulations
- Hunter Education, Safety, and Training Regulations
- Licence and Permit Suspension Regulations
- Moose Hunting Regulations
- Pheasant Shooting Preserve Regulations
- Small Game Hunting Regulations

Department of Service Nova Scotia & Municipal Relations
Assessment Act
Land Registration Act
Motor Vehicle Act
Municipal Government Act
Off-Highway Vehicles Act (jointly with Environment/Natural Resources/Transportation & Infrastructure Renewal)
- Off-Highway Vehicles Designated Trails
- Off-Highway Vehicle Infrastructure Fund Regulations
- Off-Highway Vehicles Closed Courses Regulations
- Off-Highway Vehicles Designated Trails and Trail Permits Regulations
- Off-Highway Vehicles Fees Regulations
- Off-Highway Vehicles General Regulations
- Off-Highway Vehicles Safety and Training Regulations
- Off-Highway Vehicles Vulnerable Areas Licensing Regulations

Department of Economic & Rural Development & Tourism
Peggy's Cove Commission Act

Department of Communities, Culture & Heritage
Heritage Property Act
Schooner Bluenose Foundation Act Special Places Protection Act (Ecological Site Designations: Abraham Lake, Bornish Hill,
- Duncans Cove, Great Barren & Quinan Lakes, Indian Man Lake, MacFarlane Woods, Panuke Lake, Ponhook Lake,
- Quinns Meadow, River Inhabitants, Roman Valley, Spinneys Health, Sporting Lake, Tusket River, Washabuck River;
- Protected Site Designations: Certain lands at Debert, Colchester County, Fletcher Lake, Joggins Fossil Cliff, Parrsboro
- Fossil Site, Port Morien French Mine Site)

Department of Transportation & Infrastructure Renewal
Dangerous Goods Transportation Act
- Dangerous Goods Transportation Regulations

Ferries Act
Highway 104 Western Alignment Act
Motor Carrier Act
Motor Vehicle Act
Off-Highway Vehicles Act (jointly with Environment/Natural Resources/Service Nova Scotia & Municipal Relations)
Public Highways Act
Railways Act
Surplus Crown Property Disposal Act

Nova Scotia Utility & Review Board
Petroleum Products Pricing Act
Public Utilities Act
Utility & Review Board Act

Nunavut Territory Legislation

Department of Environment
Environmental Protection Act
- Asphalt Paving Industry Emission Regulations
- Spill Contingency Planning & Reporting

Environmental Rights Act
Flood Damage Reduction Agreements Act
Forest Management Act
- Forest Management Regulations

Forest Protection Act
Freshwater Fish Marketing Act
- Establishing Freshwater Fish Marketing Corporation Regulations

Herd & Fencing Act
Natural Resource Conservation Trust Act
Pesticides Act
Territorial Park Act
- Community Parks Order
- Historical Parks Order
- Territorial Parks Regulations

Travel & Tourism Act
- Outfitter Regulations
- Tourist Establishment Regulations

Water Resources Agreements Act
Wildlife Act
- Big Game Hunting Regulations
- Birds of Prey Regulations
- Certification & Disposal of Wildlife Regulations
- Critical Wildlife Areas Regulations
- Dempster Highway Special Management Area Regulations
- Nuisance Bison Control Regulations
- Polar Bear Defence Kill Regulations
- Sale of Wildlife Regulations
- Small Game Hunting Regulations
- Trapping Regulations
- Wildlife Business Regulations
- Wildlife Export Regulations
- Wildlife General Regulations
- Wildlife Licenses & Permits Regulations
- Wildlife Management Barren Ground Caribou Area Regulation
- Wildlife Management Grizzly Bear Area Regulations
- Wildlife Management Muskox Areas Regulations
- Wildlife Management Outfitter Area Regulations
- Wildlife Management Polar Bear Areas Regulations
- Wildlife Management Units Regulations
- Wildlife Management Wood Bison Area Regulations
- Wildlife Management Zones Regulations
- Wildlife Preserves Regulations
- Wildlife Regions Regulations
- Wildlife Sanctuaries Regulations

Department of Community & Government Services
Area Development Act
- Resolute Bay Development Area Regulations
- Strathcona Sound Development Area Regulations

Cities, Towns & Villages Act
- Iqaluit By-Law Exemption Order
- Town of Iqaluit Continuation Order

Commissioner's Land Act
- Commissioner's Airport Lands Regulations
- Commissioner's Land Regulations

Consumer Protection Act
Dog Act
Emergency Measures Act
Fire Prevention Act
- Fire Prevention Regulations
- Fireworks Regulations
- Propane Cylinder Storage

Gas Protection Act
Hamlets Act
Planning Act
Settlements Act
Safety Act

Department of Economic Development & Transportation
All-Terrain Vehicles Act
- All-Terrain Vehicles Regulations
- Special All-Terrain Vehicles Fees Regulations
- Special All-Terrain Vehicles Helmet Regulations

Economic Development Agreements Act
Motor Vehicles Act
- Carrier Fitness Regulations
- Exemption of Motor Vehicles Act Regulations
- Hours of Service Regulations
- Large Vehicle Control Regulations
- Motor Vehicle Equipment Regulations

School Bus Regulations
Seasonal Highway Regulations
Nunavut Development Corporation
Public Highways Act
Highway Designation & Classification Regulations
Highway Signs Regulations
Transportation of Dangerous Goods Act
Transportation of Dangerous Goods Regulations
Travel & Tourism Act
Guide Exemption Regulations
Outfitter Regulations
Tourist Establishment Regulations
Travel Development Area Regulations

Department of Executive & Intergovernmental Affairs
Nunavut Power Corporation Assets Transfer Confirmation Act
Public Utilities Act
Public Utilities Regulations

Department of Finance
Consolodation of Workers' Compensation Act
Explosives Use Act
Explosives Regulations
Mine Health & Safety Act
Mine Health & Safety Regulations
Safety Act
Asbestos Safety Regulations
Environmental Tobacco Smoke Work Site Regulations
General Safety Regulations
Safety Forms Regulations
Silica Sand Blasting Safety Regulations
Work Site Hazardous Materials Information System Regulations

Department of Health & Social Services
Boards of Management Dissolution Act
Disease Registries Act
Reportable Diseases Order
Public Health Act
Camp Sanitation Regulations
Communicable Diseases Regulations
General Sanitation Exemption Regulations
General Sanitation Regulations
Meat Inspection Regulations
Public Sewerage Systems Regulations
Public Water Supply Regulations
Tourist Accomodation Health Regulations
Tobacco Control Act

Ontario Legislation

Ministry of Environment
Environmental Assessment Act
Designations & Exemptions
Electricity Projects Regulation
Environmental Assessment General Regulations
Environmental Protection Act
Air Pollution - Local Air Quality Regulations
Airborne Contaminant Discharge Monitoring & Reporting Regulations
Boilers Regulation
Certificates of Approval Exemptions Air Regulation
Cessation of Coal Use - Atikokan, Lambton, Nanticoke and Thunder Bay Generating Stations Regulations
Classes of Contaminants Exemption Regulations
Classification & Exemption of Spills & Reporting of Discharges Regulations
Containers Regulation
Deep Well Disposal Regulation
Designation of Waste Regulation
Discharge of Sewage from Pleasure Boats Regulation
Disposable Containers for Milk Regulations
Disposable Paper Containers for Milk Regulations
Dry Cleaners Regulations
Effluent Monitoring & Effluent Limits Regulations (organic chemicals, inorganic chemicals, iron & steel manufacturers, electric power generation, petroleum sector, metal mining sector, industrial minerals sector, metal casting sector, pulp & paper sector)
Emissions Trading Regulation
Environmental Penalities Regulation
Ethanol in Gasoline
Exemption Regulations
Gasoline Volatility Regulation
General Waste Management Regulation
Greenhouse Gas Emissions Reporting Regulations
Ground Source Heat Pumps Regulation
Halon Fire Extinguishing Equipment Regulation
Hot Mix Asphalt Facilities Regulation
Industrial, Commercial & Institutional Source
Separation Programs Regulation
Industry Emissions - Nitrogen Oxides & Sulphur Dioxide
Lakeview Generating Station Regulations
Lambton Industry Meteorological Alert Regulation
Landfilling Sites Regulation
Marinas Regulation
Mobile PCB Destruction Facilities Regulation
Motor Vehicles Regulation
Municipal Sewage & Water & Roads Class Environmental Assessment Project Regulation
Municipalities, Secured Creditors, Receivers, Trustees in Bankruptcy & Fiduciaries, Pt.XV.2 of the Act Regulations, 2002
Ontario Power Generation Regulations
Ozone Depleting Substances & Other Halocarbons Regulation
Packaging Audits & Packaging Reduction Work Plans Regulation
Plasco Demonstration Project Regulation
Records of Site Condition, Pt.XV.1 of the Act Regulations, 2004
Recovery of Gasoline Vapour in Bulk Transfers Regulation
Recycling & Composting of Municipal Waste Regulation
Refillable Containers for Carbonated Soft Drink Regulation
Refrigerants Regulation
Renewable Energy Approvals Under Part V.0.1. of the Act Regulation
Solvents Regulation
Spill Prevention & Contingency Plans Regulation
Spills Regulation
Sulphur Content of Fuels Regulation
Transitional Provisions Relating to the Repeal of Pt.VIII of the Act Regulations
Waste Audits & Waste Reduction Workplans Regulation
Waste Disposal Sites & Waste Management Systems Subject to Approval Under or Exempt from the Environmental Assessment Act Regulations
Waste Management (PCBs) Regulation
Environmental Review Tribunal
Ministry of the Environment Act
Ontario Water Resources Act
Additional Charges Regulation
Charges for Industrial & Commercial Water Users Regulation
Environmental Penalties Regulation
Exemption - City of Detroit Regulation
Lake Simcoe Protection Regulation
Licensing of Sewage Works Operators Regulations
Municipal Sewage & Water & Roads Class Environmental Assessment Projects Regulation
Secured Creditors, Receivers, Trustees in Bankruptcy Regulations, 2002
Sewage Works Subject to Approval under the Environmental Assessment Act Regulations
Transitional Provisions Relating to the Repeal of Pt.VIII of the Environmental Protection Act Regulations
Water Taking Regulation
Wells Regulation
Pesticides Act
Safe Drinking Water Act, 2002
Certification of Drinking-Water System Operators & Water Quality Analysts
Compliance & Enforcement
Definitions of "Deficiency" & "Municipal Drinking-Water System" Regulations, 2003
Definitions of Words & Expressions Used the Act Regulations, 2003
Drinking-Water Systems Regulations, 2003
Drinking-Water Testing Services Regulations, 2003
Licensing of Municipal Drinking Water Systems Regulation
Ontario Drinking-Water Quality Standards Regulations, 2003
Schools, Private Schools & Day Nurseries Regulations, 2003
Sustainable Water & Sewage Systems Act, 2002 (not in Force)
Toxics Reduction Act
Waste Diversion Act, 2002
Blue Box Waste Regulations, 2002
Municipal Hazardous or Special Waste Regulation
Stewardship Ontario Regulation
Used Oil Material Regulations, 2003
Used Tires Regulations, 2003
Waste Electrical & Electronic Equipment

Ministry of Agriculture, Food & Rural Affairs
Agricorp Act
Agricultural Employees Protection Act 2002
Agricultural & Horticultural Organizations Act

Agricultural Research Institute of Ontario Act
  Agricultural Lands Regulations
Agricultural Tile Drainage Installation Act
Animals for Research Act
Dead Animal Disposal Act
Drainage Act
Farm Products Container Act
Farm Products Marketing Act
Farming & Food Production Protection Act
Food Safety & Quality Act, 2001
Livestock & Livestock Products Act
Meat Inspection Act (Ontario)
Ministry of Agriculture, Food & Rural Affairs Act
Nutrient Management Act, 2002
Plant Diseases Act
Tile Drainage Act
Weed Control Act

Ministry of Community Safety & Correctional Services
Emergency Management and Civil Protection Act
Fire Protection & Prevention Act, 1997

Ministry of Culture
AGO Act
Arts Council Act
George R. Gardiner Museum of Ceramic Art Act
Historical Parks Act
Hummingbird Performing Arts Centre Corporation Act
McMichael Canadian Art Collection Act
Metropolitan Toronto Convention Centre Act
Ontario Heritage Act
Ontario Place Corporation Act
Public Libraries Act
Royal Ontario Museum Act
St. Lawrence Parks Commission Act
Science North Act

Ministry of Economic Development & Trade
Ministry of Economic Development & Trade Act
Research Foundation Act

Ministry of Energy
Electricity Restructuring Act, 2004
Energy Efficiency Act
Green Energy Act
Ministry of Energy Act
Ontario Energy Board Act
Ontario Energy Board Amendment Act (Electricity Pricing), 2003
Toronto District Heating Corporation Act

Ministry of Government Services
Archives & Recordkeeping Act
Boundaries Act
Electricity Act
Land Registration Reform Act
Land Titles Act
Safety & Consumer Statutes Administration Act
Technical Standards & Safety Act, 2000

Ministry of Health & Long-Term Care
Excellent Care for All Act, 2010
Health Protection & Promotion Act
Health System Improvements Act, 2007
Ministry of Health & Long-Term Care Act
Tobacco Control Act, 1994

Ministry of Infrastructure
Places to Grow Act, 2005
  Growth Plan Areas Regulation

Ministry of Labour
Occupational Health & Safety Act
  Control of Exposure to Biological or Chemical Agents Regulations
  Designated Substance Regulations (Various)
  Farming Operations Regulation
  Oil & Gas - Offshore Regulation
  Workplace Hazardous Materials Information System (WHMIS) Regulations
Rights of Labour Act
Workplace Safety & Insurance Act

Ministry of Municipal Affairs & Housing
Greenbelt Act
Housing Development Act
Ministry of Municipal Affairs & Housing Act
Municipal Act
Municipal Water & Sewage Transfer Act
Oak Ridges Moraine Conservation Act
Oak Ridges Moraine Protection Act, 2001
  Oak Ridges Moraine Conservation Plan
Ontario Planning & Development Act
Planning Act
Public Utilities Act
Road Access Act
Shoreline Property Assistance Act
Snow Roads & Fences Act
Toronto Islands Residential Community Stewardship Act

Ministry of Natural Resources
Aggregate Resources Act
Algonquin Forestry Authority Act
Beds of Navigable Waters Act
Conservation Authorities Act
Conservation Land Act
  Conservation Bodies Land Regulation
Crown Forest Sustainability Act
Endangered Species Act
  Endangered Species Regulation
Fish Inspection Act
Fish & Wildlife Conservation Act
  Possession, Buying & Selling of Wildlife
  Wildlife in Captivity
  Wildlife Management Units
  Wildlife Schedules
Forest Fires Prevention Act
Forestry Act
Gas & Oil Leases Act
Heritage Hunting & Fishing Act, 2002
Indian Lands Act
Indian Lands Agreement Confirmation Act
Industrial & Mining Lands Compensation Act
Kawartha Highlands Signature Park Act
Lac Seul Conservation Act
Lake of the Woods Control Board Act
Lakes & Rivers Improvement Act
Manitoba-Ontario Lake St. Joseph Diversion Agreement Authorization Act
Migratory Birds Convention Act (Canada)
  Ontario Regulations
Mining Act
Ministry of Natural Resources Act
Niagara Escarpment Planning & Development Act
North Georgian Bay Recreational Reserve Act
Northern Ontario Heritage Fund Act
Northern Services Boards Act
Oil, Gas & Salt Resources Act
Ontario Geographic Names Board Act
Ontario Harbours Agreement Act
Ottawa River Water Powers Act
Professional Foresters Act
Provincial Parks & Conservation Reserves Act
  Conservation Reserves: General Provisions Regulation
  Designation & Classification of Provincial Parks Regulation
  Designation of Conservation Reserves Regulation
  Mechanized Travel in Wilderness Parks Regulation
  Provincial Parks: General Provisions Regulation
Public Lands Act
Surveys Act
Wild Rice Harvesting Act
Wilderness Areas Act

Ministry of Northern Development, Mines & Forestry
Mining Act
Ministry of Northern Development, Mines & Forestry Act
Ontario Northland Transportation Commission Act

Ministry of Transportation
Airports Act
Dangerous Goods Transportation Act
Highway Traffic Act
Ministry of Transportation Act
Motorized Snow Vehicles Act
Off-Road Vehicles Act
Ontario Highway Transport Board Act

Public Service Works on Highways Act
Public Transportation & Highway Improvement Act
Public Vehicles Act
Shortline Railways Act

Prince Edward Island Legislation

Department of Environment, Energy & Forestry
Agricultural Crop Rotation Act
Automobile Junk Yards Act
Beverage Containers Act
  General Regulations
  Recyclable Beverage Container Deposit Regulations
Boilers & Pressure Vessels Act
Electrical Inspection Act
Elevators & Lifts Act
Energy Corporation Act
Environmental Protection Act
  Air Quality Regulations
  Code for Plumbing Services Regulations
  Environmental Assessment Fees Regulation
  Environmental Records Review Regulations
  Drinking Water & Wastewater Facility Operating Regulations
  Excavation Pits Regulations
  Litter Control Regulation
  Materials Recycling Regulation
  Ozone Layer Protection Regulations
  Petroleum Hydrocarbon Remediation Regulations
  Petroleum Storage Tank Regulations
  Sewage Disposal Regulations
  Waste Resource Management Regulations
  Watercourse & Wetland Protection Regulations
  Water Well Regulations
Fisheries Act (related)
Forest Management Act
  Forest Renewal Program Regulations
  Provincial Forests Regulations
Mineral Resources Act
Natural Areas Protection Act
Oil & Natural Gas Act
  Oil & Gas Conservation Regulations
Pesticides Control Act
Power Engineers Act
Provincial Building Code Act
Public Forest Council Act
Renewable Energy Act
Unsightly Property Act
Wildlife Conservation Act
  Angling Regulations
  Fur Harvesting Regulations
  Ground Hemlock Regulations
  Hunting & Trapping Seasons Regulation
  Hunting Guide Regulations
  Snowshoe Hare Snaring Regulations
  Wildlife Conservation Fund Regulations
  Wildlife Management Areas Regulations

Department of Agriculture, Fisheries & Aquaculture
Agricultural Products Standards Act
Animal Health & Protection Act
Dairy Industry Act
Environmental Protection Act (in part)
Farm Machinery Dealers & Vendors Act
Farm Practices Act
Fire Prevention Act
Occupational Health & Safety Act
Plant Health Act
Weed Control Act

Department of Community Services, Seniors & Labour
Employment Standards Act

Department of Finance & Municipal Affairs
Environment Tax Act
Gasoline Tax Act

Department of Health
Health Services Act
Public Health Act
Smoke-Free Places Act

Department of Innovation & Advanced Learning
Area Industrial Commission Act

Department of Justice & Public Safety
Emergency 911 Act
Emergency Measures Act
Fire Prevention Act
Rural Community Fire Companies Act

Island Regulatory & Appeals Commission
Electric Power Act
Petroleum Products Act
Water & Sewerage Act

Department of Tourism & Culture
Fathers of Confederation Buildings Act
Heritage Places Protection Act
Lucy Maud Montgomery Foundation Act
Museum Act
National Park Act
Recreation Development Act
  Provincial Parks Regulations
Tourism Industry Act
Tourism PEI Act
Trails Act

Department of Transportation & Infrastructure Renewal
Dangerous Goods (Transportation) Act
Expropriation Act
Highway Traffic Act
Land Survey Act
Off Highway Vehicle Act
Public Works Act
Roads Act
  Closing of Roads Regulations
  Highway Access Regulations
  Public Utility Easement (Fees) Regulations
  Vehicle Weights & Dimensions Regulations

Prince Edward Island Workers Compensation Board
Occupational Health & Safety Act
Workers Compensation Act

Québec Legislation

Ministère du Développement durable, de l'Environnement et des Parcs/Sustainable Development, Environment & Parks
Loi portant restrictions à l'élevage de porcs/Act to Impose Restrictions on Pig Farming, 2002
Loi portant sur la délimitation de la ligne des hautes eaux du Fleuve Saint-Laurent sur le territoire de la municipalité régionale
  de comté de la Côte-de-Beaupré/An Act to delimit the high water mark of the St. Lawrence River in the territory of
  Municipalité régionale de comté de La Côte-de-Beaupré
Loi sur la conservation du patrimoine naturel/Natural Heritage Conservation Act
Loi sur la conservation et la mise en valeur de la faune/Act respecting the Conservation & Development of Wildlife (in part)
Loi sur la protection des arbres/Tree Protection Act
Loi sur la provocation artificielle de la pluie/Act respecting the artificial inducement of rain
Loi sur la qualité de l'environnement/Environment Quality Act
  Agricultural Operations Regulation, 2002
  Groundwater Catchment Regulation, 2002
  Land Protection & Rehabilitation Regulation, 2003
  Regulation respecting certain bodies for the protection of the environment and social milieu of the territory of James Bay and

Northern Québec
Regulation respecting Compensation for Municipal Services Provided to Recover & Reclaim Residual Materials
Regulation respecting Environmental Impact Assessments in Northeastern Québec
Regulation respecting Halocarbons
Regulation respecting Hazardous Materials
Regulation respecting Hot Mix Asphalt Plants
Regulation respecting Industrial Depollution Attestations
Regulation respecting Motor Vehicle Traffic in Certain Fragile Environments
Regulation respecting Ozone-Depleting Substances
Regulation respecting Permits & Certificates for the Sale & Use of Pesticides
Regulation respecting Pits & Quarries
Regulation respecting Prevention of Water
Pollution in Livestock Operations
Regulation respecting Public Swimming & Wading Pools
Regulation respecting Pulp & Paper Mills
Regulation respecting Sanitary Conditions in Industrial or other Camps
Regulation respecting Snow Elimination Sites
Regulation respecting Solid Waste
Regulation respecting the Application of the Environment Quality Act
Regulation respecting the Artificial Inducement of Rain
Regulation respecting the Burial of Contaminated Soils
Regulation respecting the environmental and social impact assessment and review procedure applicable to the territory of James Bay and Northern Québec
Regulation respecting the environmental impact assessment and review applicable to a part of the northeastern Québec region
Regulation respecting the Liquid Effluents of Petroleum Refineries
Regulation respecting the Quality of Drinking Water
Regulation respecting the Quality of the Atmosphere
Regulation respecting the Recovery & Reclamation of Discarded Paint Containers & Paints
Regulation respecting the Recovery & Reclamation of Used Oils, Oil or Fluid Containers & Used Filters
Regulation respecting threatened or vulnerable plant species and their habitats
Regulation respecting Used Tire Storage
Regulation Respecting Waste Water Disposal Systems for Isolated Dwellings
Regulation respecting the Water Property in the Domain of the State, 2003
Regulation respecting Waterworks & Sewer Services
Rules of internal management of the James Bay Advisory Committee on the Environment
Rules of internal management of the Kativik Environmental Advisory Committee
Loi sur la sécurité des barrages/Dam Safety Act
Loi sur la Société des établissements de plein air du Québec
Loi sur la Société québécoise de récupération et de recyclage
Loi sur la vente et la distribution de bière et de boissons gazeuses dans des contenants à remplissage unique/Act respecting the Sale & Distribution of Beer & Soft Drinks in Non-returnable Containers
Loi sur le développement durable
Loi sur le ministère du Développement durable, de l'Environnement et des Parcs
Loi sur le parc de la Mauricie et ses environs
Loi sur le Parc Forillon et des environs
Loi sur le parc marin du Saguenay-Saint-Laurent
Loi sur le régime des eaux/Watercourses Act
Loi sur les espèces menacées ou vulnérables/Act respecting Threatened or Vulnerable Species
Loi sur les pesticides/Pesticides Act
Pesticides Management Code, 2003
Loi sur les parcs
Loi visant la préservation des ressources en eau/Water Resources Preservation Act

Ministère des Affaires municipales et des Régions/Municipal Affairs
Code municipal du Québec
Loi concernant la réglementation municipale des édifices publics
Loi sur l'aménagement et l'urbanisme
Loi sur la Régie du logement
Loi sur la Société québécoise d'assainissement des eaux
Loi sur les abus préjudiciables à l'agriculture
Loi sur les cités et villes
Loi sur les conseils intermunicipaux de transport dans la région de Montréal
Loi sur les immeubles industriels municipaux
Loi sur les travaux municipaux

Ministère de l'Agriculture, des Pêcheries et de l'Alimentation/Agriculture, Fisheries & Food
Loi sur l'acquisition de terres agricoles par des non-résidants/An Act governing the acquisition of farm land by non-residents
Loi sur l'aquaculture commerciale/ An Act respecting commercial aquaculture
Loi sur l'assurance-récolte/Crop Insurance Act
Loi sur la commercialisation des produits marins/An Act respecting the marketing of marine products
Loi sur la conservation et la mise en valeur de la faune/An Act respecting the conservation & development of wildlife
Loi sur la prévention des maladies de la pomme de terre/An Act respecting prevention of disease in potatoes
Loi sur la protection sanitaire des animaux/Animal Health Protection Act
Loi sur le ministère de l'Agriculture, des Pêcheries et de l'Alimentation/An Act respecting the Ministère de l'Agriculture, des Pêcheries et de l'Alimentation
Loi sur les abus préjudiciables à l'agriculture/Agricultural Abuses Act
Loi sur les cités et villes/Cities & Towns Act (certaines sections)
Loi sur les terres agricoles du domaine de l'État/An Act respecting agricultural lands in the domain of the state

Ministère de la Culture et des Communications/Culture & Communications
Loi sur les musées nationaux

Ministère des Ressources naturelles et de la Faune/Natural Resources & Wildlife
Loi approuvant la convention de la Baie-James et du nord québécois/An Act approving the Agreement concerning James Bay and Northern Québec
Loi approuvant la convention du nord-est québécois/An Act approving the Northeastern Québec Agreement
Loi assurant la mise en oeuvre de l'entente concernant une nouvelle relation entre le gouvernement du Québec et les Cris du Québec/An Act to ensure the implementation of the Agreement Concerning a New Relationship Between the Government of Québec and the Crees of Québec
Loi concernant la construction par Hydro-Québec d'infrastructures et d'équipements par suite de la tempête de verglas survenue du 5 au 9 janvier 1998
Loi concernant les droits sur les mines/Mining Duties Act
Loi de 1994 sur la convention concernant les oiseaux migrateurs
Loi favorisant la réforme du cadastre québécois/An Act to promote the reform of the cadastre in Québec
Loi sur les forêts/Forest Act
Loi régissant les activités d'aménagement forestier de bénéficiaires de contrats d'approvisionnement et d'aménagement forestier pour les années 2000-2001 et 2001-2002
Loi sur Hydro-Québec/Hydro-Québec Act
Loi sur l'agence de l'efficacité énergétique/An Act respecting the Agence de l'efficacité énergétique
Loi sur l'efficacité énergétique d'appareils fonctionnant à l'électricité ou aux hydrocarbures/An Act respecting the energy efficiency of electrical or hydrocarbon-fuelled appliances
Loi sur la conservation et la mise en valeur de la faune/Act respecting the conservation and development of wildlife
Regulation respecting aquaculture and the sale of fish
Lands in the Domain of the State Designated for Development of Wildlife Resources Regulation
Regulation respecting hunting and fishing controlled
Regulation respecting the enforcement of certain legislative and regulatory provisions respecting the protection of the environment by wildlife protection officers
Regulation respecting wildlife habitats
Regulation respecting wildlife sanctuaries
Loi sur la division territoriale/Territorial Division Act
Loi sur la Régie de l'énergie/An Act respecting the Régie de l'énergie
Loi sur la société de développement autochtone de la Baie James/An Act respecting the James Bay Native Development Corporation
Loi sur la société Eeyou de la Baie-James/An Act respecting the James Bay Eeyou Corporation
Loi sur la société nationale de l'amiante/An Act respecting the Société nationale de l'amiante
Loi sur le cadastre/Cadastre Act
Loi sur le développement et l'organisation municipale de la région de la Baie-James/James Bay Region Development and Municipal Organization Act
Loi sur le ministère des ressources naturelles, de la faune et des parcs/An Act respecting the Ministère des Ressources naturelles, de la Faune et des Parcs
Loi sur le programme d'aide aux Inuits bénéficiaires de la convention de la Baie-James et du nord québécois pour leurs activités de chasse, de pêche et de piégeage/An Act respecting the support program for Inuit beneficiaries of the James Bay and Northern Québec agreement for their hunting, fishing and trapping activities
Loi sur le régime des eaux/Watercourses Act
Regulation respecting the water property in the domain of the State
Loi sur le régime des terres dans les territoires de la Baie-James et du Nouveau-Québec/An Act respecting the land regime in the James Bay and New Québec territories

Loi sur les arpentages/An Act respecting land survey
Loi sur les bureaux de la publicité des droits/An Act respecting registry offices
Loi sur les clubs de chasse et de pêche/Fish and Game Clubs Act
Loi sur les compagnies de flottage/ Timber-Driving Companies Act
Loi sur les droits de chasse et de pêche dans les territoires de la Baie James et du Nouveau-Québec/An Act respecting hunting and fishing rights in the James Bay and New Québec territories
Loi sur les espèces menacées ou vulnérables/An Act respecting threatened or vulnerable species
Loi sur les mines/Mining Act
Loi sur les Pêches
Loi sur les produits et les équipements pétroliers/An Act respecting petroleum products and equipment
Loi sur les systèmes municipaux et les systèmes privés d'électricité/An Act respecting municipal and private electric power systems
Loi sur les terres du domaine de l'état/An Act respecting the lands in the domain of the State
Loi sur les titres de propriété dans certains districts électoraux/An Act respecting land titles in certain electoral districts
Loi sur l'exportation de l'électricité/An Act respecting the exportation of electric power

Ministère de la Santé et des Services sociaux/Health & Social Services
Loi sur la protection de la santé publique/Public Health Protection Act
Loi sur la santé publique/Public Health Act
Loi sur le tabac/Tobacco Act

Ministère de la Sécurité publique/Public Security
Loi sur la sécurité civile/Civil Protection Act
Loi sur la sécurité incendie/Fire Safety Act
Loi sur le ministère de la Sécurité publique/An Act respecting the Ministère de la Sécurité publique
Loi sur les bombes lacrymogènes/Act respecting tear bombs
Loi sur les explosifs/An Act respecting explosives

Ministère des Transports/Transportation
Code de la sécurité routière/Highway Safety Code
Loi concernant les partenariats en matière d'infrastructures de transport/Act respecting transport infrastructure partnerships
Loi concernant les propriétaires et exploitants de véhicules lourds/Act respecting owners and operators of heavy vehicles
Loi modifiant la Loi sur les transports en matière de camionnage en vrac/Act to amend the Transport Act as regards bulk trucking
Loi sur l'expropriation/Expropriation Act
Loi sur la sécurité du transport terrestre guidé/Act to ensure safety in guided land transportation
Loi sur les chemins de fer/Railway Act
Loi sur les sociétés de transport en commun/Act respecting public transit authorities
Loi sur les véhicules hors route/Act respecting off-highway vehicles

Ministère du Travail/Labour
Loi sur les accidents du travail et les maladies professionnelles/Act respecting accidents at work & professional illness or sickness
Loi sur la santé et la sécurité du travail/Occupational Health & Safety Act

Saskatchewan Legislation

Saskatchewan Environment
Clean Air Act
  Clean Air Regulation
Conservation Easements Act
  Potash Refining Air Emissions Regulations
Ecological Reserves Act
  Assiniboine Slopes Provincial Ecological Reserves Regulations
  Buffalograss Ecological Reserve Regulations
  Provincial Ecological Reserves Regulation
  Qu'Appelle Coulee Provincial Ecological Reserves Regulations
  Representative Area Ecological Reserve Regulations
Environmental Assessment Act
Environmental Management & Protection Act, 2002
  Environmental Spill Control Regulations
  Halocarbon Control Regulations
  Hazardous Substances & Dangerous Goods Regulations
  Mineral Industry Environmental Protection Regulations
  Municipal Refuse Management Regulations
  Ozone-Depleting Substances Control Regulations
  PCB Waste Storage Regulations
  Reservoir Development Area Regulations
  Scrap Tire Management Regulations
  Used Oil Collection Regulations
  Waste Electronic Equipment Regulations
  Waste Paint Management Regulations
  Water Regulations
Fisheries Act
  Fisheries Regulations
Forest Resources Management Act
  Dutch Elm Disease Regulations
  Forest Resources Management Regulations
  Indian Treaty Obligations Regulations
  Surface Lease Agreement Regulations: Beaverlodge, Cigar Lake, Cluff Lake, Jolu Project, Key Lake, Konuto Project, McArthur River Operation, McClean Lake, Midwest Joint, Rabbit Lake
  Wild Rice Regulations
  Withdrawal of Land from Forests; Historical Interest Regulations
Grasslands National Park Act
Litter Control Act
Natural Resources Act
  Commercial Activities Regulations
  Commercial Fishing Production Incentive Regulations
  Outfitter & Guide Regulations, 1996
  Resource Protection & Development Services Regulations
  Park Land Reserve Regulations
  Parks Regulations
  Recreation Site Regulations, 1991
Parks Act
  Government Land Reserves Regulation
  Historic Sites Regulations
  Park Land Reserves Regulations
Prairie & Forest Fires Act, 1982
Provincial Lands Act
  Crown Resource Lands Regulations, 1989
  Provincial Lands Regulations
  Surface Rights Regulations (Grasslands Park, Komis Project, Parks Lake Uranium Mining, Seabee)
Regional Parks Act, 1979
Sale or Lease of Certain Lands Act
State of the Environment Report Act
Water Appeal Board Act
Water Regulations Act, 2002
Wildlife Act, 1998
  Captive Wildlife Regulations
  Dog Training Regulations
  Open Seasons Game Regulations
  Wild Species at Risk Regulations
  Wildlife Landowner Assistance Regulations, 1991
  Wildlife Management Zones & Special Areas Boundaries Regulations, 1990
  Wildlife Regulations, 1981
Wildlife Habitat Protection Act
  Treaty Land Entitlement Withdrawal Regulations
  Wildlife Habitat Lands Designation Regulations
  Wildlife Habitat Lands Disposition & Alteration Regulations

Saskatchewan Agriculture & Food
Agri-Food Act, 2004
Agri-Food Innovation Act
Animal Products Act
Department of Agriculture, Food & Rural Revitilization Act
Disease of Animal Act
Expropriation (Rehabilitation Projects) Act
Farming Communities Land Act
Irrigation Act
Line Fence Act
Pastures Act
Pest Control Act
  Bacterial Ring Rot Control Regulations
  Dutch Elm Disease Control Regulations
Pest Control Products (Saskatchewan) Act
Provincial Lands Act
Sale or Lease of Certain Lands Act
  Saskatchewan Wetland Conservation Corporation Land Regulation
Soil Drifting Control Act

Saskatchewan Health
Department of Health Act
Public Health Act, 1994
Tobacco Control Act

Saskatchewan Highways & Infrastructure
Dangerous Goods Transportation Act
Highways & Transportation Act, 1997
Railway Act

Saskatchewan Industry & Resources
Crown Minerals Act
Department of Energy & Mines Act
Ethanol Fuel Act, 2002
  Ethanol Fuel (General) Regulations
  Ethanol Fuel (Grant) Regulations
Mineral Resources Act
  Seismic Exploration Regulations
Oil & Gas Conservation Act
  Oil & Gas Conservation Regulations
Pipelines Act

Saskatchewan Labour Relations & Workplace Safety
Occupational Health & Safety Act, 1993 (Mines Regulation)
Occupational Health & Safety Regulations, 1996
Radiation Health & Safety Act, 1985
  Radiation Health & Safety Regulations
Worker's Compensation Act
  Worker's Compensation Act Exclusion Regulations
Worker's Compensation General Regulations, 1985

Saskatchewan Municipal Affairs
Border Areas Act
Cities Act
Department of Rural Development Act
Municipal Expropriation Act
Municipalities Act
Northern Municipalities Act, 2010
Planning & Development Act, 2007
Rural Development Act

Saskatchewan Watershed Authority
Conservation & Development Act
Saskatchewan Watershed Authority Act 2005
  Drainage Control Regulations
  Groundwater Regulations
  Reservoir Development Area Regulations
Water Power Act
Watershed Associations Act

SaskEnergy Incorporated
SaskEnergy Act

SaskWater
Saskatchewan Water Corporation Act, 2002

Yukon Territory Legislation

Yukon Environment
Animal Health Act, (jointly with Energy, Mines & Resources)
Environment Act
  Administrative Regulation
  Air Emissions Regulations
  Beverage Container Regulation
  Contaminated Sites Regulations
  Designated Materials
  Ozone Depleting Substances & Other
  Halocarbons Regulation
  Pesticides Regulations
  Recycling Fund Regulation
  Solid Waste Regulations
  Special Waste Regulations
  Spills Regulations
  Storage Tank Regulations
  Yukon Council on the Economy & the Environment Regulation
Environmental Assessment Act
  Activities Requiring Environmental Assessment (Inclusion List) Regulations
  Comprehensive Study List Regulation
  Coordination of Environmental Assessment Procedures & Requirement Regulations
  Exclusion List Regulation
  Law List Regulation
Mackenzie River Basin Agreement Act
Parks & Land Certainty Act
  Campground Regulations
  Coal River Springs Ecological Reserve
  Establish Ni'iinlii Njik (Fishing Branch) Ecological Reserve
  Establish Ni'iinlii Njik (Fishing Branch) Wilderness Preserve
  Herschel Island Nature Preserve
  Herschel Island Park Regulations
  Tombstone Territorial Park Regulations
  Waters Act, (jointly with Energy, Mines & Resources & the Executive Council Office)
    Waters Regulation
Wilderness Tourism Licensing Act
Wildlife Act
  Concession & Compensation Review Board Regulations
  Conservation Fund Regulations
  Game Farm Regulations
  Game Management Sub-zone Regulations
  Outfitting Concession Area Boundary Regulations
  Trapping Concession Area Boundary Regulations
  Trapping Regulations
  Wildlife Sanctuary Regulation
Yukon River Basin & Alsek River Basin Agreements Act

Yukon Community Services
Animal Protection Act (jointly with Energy, Mines & Resources)
Assessment & Taxation Act
Building Standards Act
Civil Emergency Measures Act
Fire Prevention Act
Forest Protection Act (jointly with Department of Energy, Mines & Resources
Gasoline Handling Act
Miner's Lien Act
Motor Vehicles Act (jointly with Highways & Public Works)
Municipal Act
Recreation Act

Yukon Energy, Mines & Resources
Agriculture Development Act
Animal Health Act, (jointly with Environment)
Area Development Act
Forest Protection Act, (jointly with Community Services)
Lands Act
Oil & Gas Act
  Oil & Gas Disposition Regulations
  Oil & Gas Drilling & Production Regulations
  Oil & Gas Geoscience & Exploration Regulations
  Oil & Gas Licence Administration Regulations
Placer Mining Act
Quartz Mining Act
Territorial Lands (Yukon) Act
Waters Act, (jointly with Environment & the Executive Council Office)

Yukon Health & Social Services
Public Health & Safety Act
  Regulations to Establish Butylnitrite as Regulated Matter
  Rubbish Disposal
  Sewage Disposal Systems Regulations

Yukon Highways & Public Works
Dangerous Goods Transportation Act
Highways Act
Motor Transport Act
Motor Vehicles Act (jointly with Community Services)

Yukon Tourism & Culture
Archives Act
Arts Act
Historical Resources Act
Scientists & Explorers Act

Yukon Workers' Compensation Health & Safety Board
Occupational Health & Safety Act
Worker's Compensation Act
  Workplace Hazardous Materials Information System (WHMIS) Regulations

Government of Canada

c/o Canada Enquiry Centre, Service Canada, Ottawa, ON K1A 0J9
Tel: 613-941-1827
Toll-Free: 800-622-6232
TTY: 800-926-9105
canadasite@canada.gc.ca
www.canada.gc.ca
All political authority in Canada is divided between the federal & provincial governments, according to the provisions of the Constitution Act, 1867. Local municipalities are a concern of the provinces, & derive their authority from Acts of provincial legislation. The Parliament of Canada consists of Her Majesty Queen Elizabeth II (represented in Canada by the Governor General, His Excellency the Right Honourable David Johnston), an Upper House called the Senate, & an elected House of Commons.

Aboriginal Affairs & Northern Development Canada (AANDC) / Affaires autochtones et Dévelopment du Nord Canada (AADNC)

10 Wellington St., North Tower, Gatineau, QC K1A 0H4
Tel: 819-997-0380
Fax: 866-817-3977
Toll-Free: 800-567-9604
TTY: 866-553-0554
infopubs@aadnc-aandc.gc.ca
www.aadnc-aandc.gc.ca
AANDC supports First Nations, Inuit & Métis people in their effort to develop healthy, sustainable communities & achieve their economic & social aspirations. This mandate is derived largely from the Department of Indian & Northern Development Act, the Indian Act, territorial acts & legal obligations arising from section 91(24) of the Constitution Act, 1867. The department administers over 50 statutes.
Acts Administered:
Canada - Yukon Oil & Gas Accord Implementation Act
Canada Lands Surveys Act (jointly Natural Resources)
Canada Mining Regulations
Canada Oil & Gas Drilling & Production Regulations
Canada Oil & Gas Land Regulations
Canada Oil & Gas Operations Act (jointly with Natural Resources)
Canada Petroleum Resources Act (jointly with Natural Resources)
Canadian Polar Commission Act
Claim Settlements (Alberta & Saskatchewan) Implementation Act
Crown Waiver Orders
Department of Indian & Northern Affairs Development Act
Fort Nelson Indian Reserve Minerals Revenue Sharing Act
Government Employees Land Acquisition Orders
Indian Act
Indian Lands Agreement (1986) Act
Indian Oil & Gas Act
Indian Reserve Waste Disposal Regulations
Land Titles Repeal Act
Mackenzie Valley Resource Management Act
Nelson House First Nation Flooded Land Act
Northern Canada Power Commission (Share Issuance & Sale Authorization) Act
Northern Canada Power Commission Yukon Assets Disposal Authorization Act
Northwest Territories Act
Northwest Territories Mining Districts Order & Nunavut Mining District
Northwest Territories Waters Act
Nunavut Act
Nunavut Waters & Nunavut Surface Rights Tribunal Act, 2002
Oil & Gas Land Orders
Orders Authorizing Acquisition of Interest in Certain Lands
Orders Respecting Withdrawal from Disposal of Certain Lands
Polar Bear Pass Withdrawal Order
Railway Belt Act
Railway Belt Water Act
Reservations to Crown Waiver Orders
Saskatchewan Natural Resources Act
Split Lake Cree First Nation Flooded Land Act
Territorial Coal Regulations
Territorial Dredging Regulations
Territorial Land Titles Offices Regulations
Territorial Land Use Regulations
Territorial Lands Act
Territorial Lands Act Exclusion Orders
Territorial Lands Regulations
Territorial Quarrying Regulations
Withdrawal of Certain Lands from Disposal Orders
Withdrawals of Disposal Orders
York Factory First Nation Flooded Land Act
Yukon Act
Yukon Environmental & Socio-Economic Assessment Act, 2003

Minister, Aboriginal Affairs & Northern Development, Hon. Bernard Valcourt, B.Sc.F.
Tel: 613-995-0581
Fax: 613-996-9736
Bernard.Valcourt@parl.gc.ca

Deputy Minister, Michael Wernick
Tel: 819-997-0133
Fax: 819-953-2251

Associate Deputy Minister, Colleen Swords
Tel: 819-934-0583
Fax: 819-953-2251

Associated Agencies, Boards & Commissions:
• Beverly & Qamanirjuaq Caribou Management Board
Secretariat
PO Box 629
Stonewall, MB R0C 2Z0
Tel: 204-467-2438
caribounews@arctic-caribou.com
www.arctic-caribou.com
Group of hunters, biologists & wildlife managers working together to conserve Canada's vast Beverly & Qamanirjuaq caribou herds for the welfare of traditional caribou-using communities in northern Manitoba, Saskatchewan, Northwest Territories & Nunavut.
Chair, Albert Thorassie
Tel: 204-684-2266
Fax: 204-684-2450
Vice-Chair, Operations, Daryll Hedman
Tel: 204-677-6643
Fax: 204-677-6359
dhedman@gov.mb.ca
Vice-Chair, Administration, Tim Trottier
Tel: 306-425-4237
Fax: 306-425-2580
ttrottier@serm.gov.sk.ca
Secretary-Treasurer, Ross Thompson
rossthompson@mymts.net
• First Nations Tax Commission (FNTC) / Commission de la fiscalité des premières nations (CFPN)
#321, 345 Yellowhead Hwy
Kamloops, BC V2H 1H1
Tel: 250-828-9857
Fax: 250-828-9858
mailkamloops@fntc.ca
www.fntc.ca
Other Communication: National Capital Region Email: mail@fntc.ca
The FNTC operates in the larger context of First Nation issues which goes beyond property tax. The FNTC is concerned with reducing the barriers to economic development on First Nation lands, increasing investor certainty, and enabling First Nations to be part of their regional economies. The FNTC is working to fill the institutional vacuum that has prevented First Nations from participating in the market economy and creating a national regulatory framework for First Nation tax systems that meets or beats the standards of provinces.
• Indian Oil & Gas Canada (IOGC) / Pétrole et gaz des Indiens du Canada
#100, 9911 Chiila Blvd.
Tsuu T'ina (Sarcee), AB T2W 6H6
Tel: 403-292-5625
Fax: 403-292-5618
ContactIOGC@inac-ainc.gc.ca
www.pgic-iogc.gc.ca
Indian Oil and Gas Canada (IOGC) is an organization committed to managing and regulating oil and gas resources on First Nation reserve lands. It is a special operating agency within Aboriginal Affairs & Northern Development Canada.
Chief Executive Officer & Executive Director, Strater Crowfoot
Tel: 403-292-5628
Fax: 403-292-4864
Director, Planning & Corporate Services, Brenda Cherniawsky
Tel: 403-292-5655
Director, Policy, John Dempsey
Tel: 403-292-5661
Fax: 403-292-4864
Director, Strategic Project, Bill Currie
Tel: 403-292-6023
Fax: 403-292-4864
Senior Advisor, Regulatory Development, Elaine Blais
Tel: 403-292-5873
• Mackenzie Valley Environmental Impact Review Board
200 Scotia Centre
#5102, 50th Ave.
PO Box 938
Yellowknife, NT X1A 2N7
Tel: 867-766-7050
Fax: 867-766-7074
Toll-free: 866-912-3472
www.reviewboard.ca
In 1998, the Mackenzie Valley Environmental Impact Review Board was established under the Mackenzie Valley Resources Management Act. The co-management Review Board is made up of members nominated by First Nations & federal & territorial governments. Board members represent the interests of all residents of the Mackenzie Valley.
Chair, Richard Edjericon
Tel: 867-766-7059
board@reviewboard.ca
Executive Director, Vern Christensen
Tel: 867-766-7055
vchristensen@reviewboard.ca
Acting Manager, Environmental Impact Assessment, Alan Ehrlich
Tel: 867-766-7056
aehrlich@reviewboard.ca
Head, Communications, Renita Jenkins
Tel: 867-766-7051
rjenkins@reviewboard.ca
Acting Finance & Administration Officer, Donna McLeod
Tel: 867-766-7054
dmcleod@reviewboard.ca
• Nunavut Impact Review Board
PO Box 1360
Cambridge Bay, NU X0B 0C0
Tel: 867-983-4600
Fax: 867-983-2594
Toll-free: 866-233-3033
info@nirb.ca
www.nirb.ca
An institution of the government established under the Nunavut Land Claims Agreement to conduct environmental & socio-economic assessments. The NIRB process involves participation by members of the community, Inuit organizations, the Government of Nunavut & the Government of Canada through the entire environmental assessment. Under the Canadian Environmental Assessment Act, the federal departments with specific responsibilities for the project must ensure that the requirements of the Act are met throughout the assessment process. This open process facilitates sound environmental stewardship & promotes economic & sustainable development.
Executive Director, Ryan Barry
Tel: 867-983-4608
rbarry@nirb.ca
• Nunavut Planning Commission
PO Box 2101
Cambridge Bay, NU X0B 0C0
Tel: 867-983-4625
Fax: 867-983-4626
www.nunavut.ca
Responsible for land use planning & environmental reporting & management in Nunavut.
Chair, Ron Roach

Executive Director, Sharon Ehaloak
sehaloak@npc.nunavut.ca
Director, Regional Planning, Brian Aglukark
Tel: 867-857-2242
Fax: 867-857-2243
aglukark@nunavut.ca
Director, Policy, Adrian Boyd
Tel: 867-873-2613
Fax: 867-873-2614
aboyd@nunavut.ca

• Nunavut Water Board
PO Box 119
Gjoa Haven, NU X0B 1J0
Tel: 867-360-6338
Fax: 867-360-6369
www.nunavutwaterboard.org
Responsible for the regulation, use & management of water in the Nunavut Settlement Area.
Executive Director, Dionne Filiatrault
Manager, Licensing, Phyllis Beaulieu

• Porcupine Caribou Management Board
PO Box 31723
Whitehorse, YT Y1A 6L3
Tel: 867-633-4780
Fax: 867-393-3904
pcmb@taiga.net
taiga.net/pcmb
Works to manage the Porcupine Caribou herd, one of the largest herds of migratory caribou in North America, & to protect & maintain its habitat.
Chair, Joe Tetlichi
Secretariat, Deana Lemke

• Truth & Reconciliation Commission of Canada
#1500, 360 Main St.
Winnipeg, MB R3C 3Z3
Tel: 204-984-5885
Fax: 204-984-5915
Toll-free: 888-872-5554
info@trc.ca
www.trc.ca
Other Communication: Inuit Sub-commission Phone, Ottawa: 613-992-8183; Yellowknife: 867-766-8494
The Commission was established as part of the Indian Residential Schools Settlement Agreement, to learn the truth about what happend in Canada's residential schools & report those findings to the Canadian public. The Commission's Ottawa office can be reached at the following address: 100 Sparks St., 4th Fl., Ottawa, ON K1P 5B7; Phone: 613-947-3649; Fax: 613-947-5794. The Commission's Yellowknife office can be reached at the following address: 5114 - 49th St., Yellowknife, NT X1A 1P7; Phone: 867-766-8491; Fax: 867-669-9082.
Chair, Hon. Murray Sinclair
Commissioner, Dr. Marie Wilson
Commissioner, Chief Wilton Littlechild

Lands & Economic Development / Terres et Développement économique
Fax: 819-953-0248
Manages land-related statutory duties under the Indian Act & duties related to transferring land management services to First Nations. The Environment Directorate maintains an Inventory of Contaminated Sites on reserve land & coordinates remediation planning; responsible for the design & implementation of the Indian & Inuit Affairs Program Environmental Stewardship Strategy Action Plan; development of First Nations capacity, tools & enabling legislation in order that First Nations undertake their own environmental protection initiatives; supports First Nation, Métis & Inuit communities in efforts to promote environmental stewardship in a manner that is consistent with the principles of sustainable development.
Assistant Deputy Minister, Sara Filbee
Tel: 819-997-0114
Fax: 819-953-0248
Director General, Lands & Environmental Management, Margaret Buist
Tel: 819-997-8883
Fax: 819-953-3201
Senior Director, Lands Modernization, Kris Johnson
Tel: 819-994-7311
Fax: 819-994-5697
Acting Director, First Nations Land Management Directorate, Isabelle Dupuis
Tel: 819-994-2210
Fax: 819-997-8522
Director, Lands & Environmental Operations Directorate, Marvin Hare
Tel: 819-997-9939
Fax: 819-953-1885
Director, Lands & Environmental Operational Policy, Jolene Head
Tel: 819-953-7024
Fax: 819-994-1667
Director, Resource Planning & Financial Services, Natasha Mozes
Tel: 819-997-0014
Fax: 819-994-2088
Director, Policy & Research Coordination Directorate, Gorazd Ruseski
Tel: 819-953-4903
Fax: 819-994-7223

Northern Affairs / Affaires du Nord
Tel: 819-994-0044
Fax: 819-953-6121
Supports northern political & economic development through the management of federal interests; promotes sustainable development of the North's natural resources & northern communities. Works toward the devolution of all province-like responsibilities to northern governments of NWT, Nunavut & the Yukon. Develops & coordinates policies & programs related to northern environment & conservation, like the federal Northern Affairs Program Sustainable Development Strategy, the cleanup of northern hazardous waste sites, climate change & interdepartmental liaison with key policy departments like Environment Canada. Northern Contaminants Program is managed by AANDC in partnership with the federal departments of Health, Environment & Fisheries & Oceans, the territorial governments, Aboriginal organizations & university researchers, & its aim is to work toward reducing & eliminating, where possible, contaminants in traditionally harvested foods. The Northern Information Network is designed to link users to information about the Yukon, the Northwest Territories & Nunavut for more effective decision-making in areas such as resource management & economic development. NIN supports various research initiatives about the North, including project impact assessme nts, sustainable development strategies, wildlife management planning, land use planning & emergency preparedness. NIN has a directory of geo-referenced databases, provides a forum for discussion & has information & research documents pertaining to the North.
Assistant Deputy Minister, Janet King
Tel: 819-953-3760
Fax: 819-953-6121
Director General, Northern Oil & Gas Branch, Mimi Fortier
Tel: 819-953-9393
Fax: 819-934-6375
Director General, Natural Resources & Environment Branch, Paula Isaak
Tel: 819-997-9381
Fax: 819-953-8766
Acting Director General, Northern Policy & Science Integration Branch, John Kozij
Tel: 819-997-9449
Fax: 819-997-0552
Director General, Devolution & Territorial Relations, Stephen Van Dine
Tel: 819-997-0223
Fax: 819-953-9323
Executive Director, IPY 2012 Conference Secretariat, Julie Boyer
Tel: 613-995-6575
Fax: 613-995-7038
Director, Strategic Management Directorate, Trevor Thibault
Tel: 819-934-9886
Fax: 819-934-9888
Scientific Advisor, Genevieve Carr
Tel: 819-953-3939
Fax: 819-934-6375
Director General, Financial Management & Strategic Services, Tony Richard
Tel: 819-997-9757
Fax: 819-994-0273

Office of the Administrator of the Ship-source Oil Pollution Fund (SOPF) / Administrateur de la Caisse d'indemnisation des dommages dus à la pollution par les hydrocarbures causée par les navires

#830, 180 Kent St., Ottawa, ON K1A 0N5
Tel: 613-991-1726
Fax: 613-990-5423
www.ssopfund.gc.ca
The Administrator oversees the Ship-source Oil Pollution Fund, which provides compensation for oil spills from ships, & handles all claims filed against it.
Administrator, Alfred H. Popp, Q.C.

Agriculture & Agri-Food Canada / Agriculture et Agro-alimentaire Canada

1341 Baseline Rd., Ottawa, ON K1A 0C5
Tel: 613-773-1000
Fax: 613-773-1081
Toll-Free: 855-773-0241
TTY: 613-773-2600
info@agr.gc.ca
www.agr.ca
Other Communication: Toll-Free Phone: AgriInvest & AgriStability, 1-866-367-8506; Agricultural Innovation Program, 1-877-246-4682; Prairie Shelterbelt Program, 1-866-766-2284
Agriculture & Agri-Food Canada is responsible for all matters related to agriculture. Examples of services provided by Agriculture & Agri-Food Canada include the following: research, development, & technology; policies & programs; the inspection & regulation of animals & plant-life forms; the coordination of rural development; the support of agricultural productivity & trade; the stabilization of farm incomes; & the provision of information. The goals of Agriculture & Agri-Food Canada are as follows: to achieve security of the food system; to ensure health of the environment; & to provide innovation for growth. Agriculture & Agri-Food Canada reports to Parliament & Canadians through the Minister of Agriculture & Agri-Food & the Minister for the Canadian Wheat Board.

Acts Administered:
Agricultural Products Marketing Act
Canadian Agricultural Loans Act
Department of Agriculture & Agri-Food Act
Farm Income Protection Act
Farm Products Agencies Act

Minister, Agriculture & Agri-Food; Minister, Canadian Wheat Board, Hon. Gerry Ritz
Tel: 613-773-1059
Fax: 613-773-1060
Ritz.G@parl.gc.ca

Minister, Minister of Industry, Minister of State (Agriculture), Hon. Christian Paradis
Tel: 613-773-1107
Fax: 613-773-1081
christian.paradis@agr.gc.ca

Associated Agencies, Boards & Commissions:

• Canada Agricultural Review Tribunal (CART) / Commission de révision agricole du Canada (CRAC)
Bldg. 60
Birch Dr.
Ottawa, ON K1A 0C6
Tel: 613-792-2087
Fax: 613-792-2088
infotribunal@cart-crac.gc.ca
www.cart-crac.gc.ca
The Tribunal provides independent oversight of the use of Administrative Monetary Penalties by federal agencies, with regards to agriculture & agri-food.
Chair & CEO, Donald Buckingham, LL.D., Dip. Int. Law (Cambridge), LL.B.
Tel: 613-792-2085
Fax: 613-792-2088

• Canadian Dairy Commission (CDC) / Commission canadienne du lait
See Entry Name Index for detailed listing.

• Canadian Food Inspection Agency (CFIA) / Agence canadienne d'inspection des aliments
See Entry Name Index for detailed listing.

• Canadian Grain Commission (CGC) / Commission canadienne des grains
See Entry Name Index for detailed listing.

• Canadian International Grains Institute / Institut international du Canada pour le grain
#1000, 303 Main St.
Winnipeg, MB R3C 3G7
Tel: 204-983-5344
Fax: 204-983-2642

cigi@cigi.ca
cigi.ca
Chief Executive Officer, Earl Geddes
Tel: 204-983-4980
egeddes@cigi.ca
Chief Financial Officer, Larry Nentwig
Tel: 204-983-3289
lnentwig@cigi.ca
Vice-President, Client Relations & Communications, Dave Burrows
Tel: 204-983-2032
dburrows@cigi.ca
Vice-President, Research & Innovation, Rex Newkirk, Ph.D.
Tel: 204-983-2031
rnewkirk@cigi.ca

• Canadian Pari-Mutuel Agency (CPMA) / Agence canadienne du pari mutuel (ACPM)
PO Box 5904 Merivale
Ottawa, ON K2C 3X7
Tel: 613-949-0735
Fax: 613-949-0750
Toll-free: 800-268-8835
cpmawebacpm@agr.gc.ca
www4.agr.gc.ca/AAFC-AAC/display-afficher.do?id=1204043533186&lang
Other Communication: Equine Drug Control Program, Phone: 613-949-0745; Fax: 613-949-1538

• Canadian Wheat Board (CWB) / Commission canadienne du blé
See Entry Name Index for detailed listing.

• Farm Credit Canada (FCC) / Financement agricole Canada
See Entry Name Index for detailed listing.

• Farm Products Council of Canada (FPCC) / Conseil des produits agricoles du Canada (CPAC)
Canada Bldg.
344 Slater St., 10th Fl.
Ottawa, ON K1R 7Y3
Tel: 613-995-6752
Fax: 613-995-2097
TTY: 613-943-3707
fpcc-cpac@agr.gc.ca
www.fpcc-cpac.gc.ca
Chair, Laurent Pellerin
Tel: 613-995-2298
Fax: 613-995-2097
laurent.pellerin@agr.gc.ca
Vice-Chair, Brent Montgomery

Agri-Environment Services Branch (AESB)
Tower 4, 1341 Baseline Rd., Ottawa, ON K1A 0C5
Tel: 613-759-1000
Fax: 613-773-1211
www4.agr.gc.ca/AAFC-AAC/display-afficher.do?id=1187362338955&lang
Other Communication: Agroforestry Development Centre, Phone: 1-866-766-2284, Fax: 306-695-2568; Canada-Manitoba Crop Diversification Centre, Phone: 204-834-6000, Fax: 204-834-3777
The Agri-Environment Services Branch integrates the following components: Prairie Farm Rehabilitation Administration; National Land & Water Information Service; & Agri-Environmental Policy Bureau. The mission of the branch is to deliver innovative environmental solutions to the agriculture & agri-food sector. Applied Technology Development Centres of the Agri-Environment Services Branch include the following: Agroforestry Development Centre (formerly known as the Prairie Farm Rehabilitation Administration); Canada-Saskatchewan Irrigation Diversification Centre; & the Canada-Manitoba Crop Diversification Centre.
Assistant Deputy Minister, Vacant
Director General, Agri-Environmental Knowledge, Innovation, & Technology Directorate, Vacant
Tel: 506-452-4802
Fax: 506-474-7533
850 Lincoln Rd.
PO Box 20280
Fredericton, NB E3B 4Z7
Chief, Land & Soil Resources, Michelle A. Harland
Tel: 204-259-4033
Fax: 204-259-4055
michelle.harland@agr.gc.ca
#200, 303 Main St.
Winnipeg, MB R3C 3G7
Acting Chief, Water & Bio Systems Engineering, Bruce B. Shewfelt
Tel: 204-822-7519
Fax: 204-822-7572
bruce.shewfelt@agr.gc.ca
101 Rte. 100
Morden, MB R6M 1Y5
Manager, Soil Quality & Management, John L. Fitzmaurice
Tel: 204-259-4016
Fax: 204-259-4055
john.fitzmaurice@agr.gc.ca
Site Supervisor, Canada-Manitoba Crop Diversification Centre, Brian Baron
Tel: 204-834-6010
Fax: 204-834-3777
brian.baron@agr.gc.ca
PO Box 309
Carberry, MB R0K 0H0
Potato Agronomist & Supervisor, Canada-Manitoba Crop Diversification Centre, Portage Site, Curtis Cavers
Tel: 204-857-4441
Fax: 204-857-4997
curtis.cavers@agr.gc.ca
370 River Rd.
Portage la Prairie, MB R1N 3V6
Senior Hydrogeologist, Water Quality & Geoenvironment Unit, Dr. Yefang Jiang
Tel: 902-370-1430
Fax: 902-370-1444
yefang.jiang@agr.gc.ca
Senior Soil Resource Specialist, Land & Soil Resources Unit, Alan J. Stewart
Tel: 780-495-5236
Fax: 780-495-4504
alan.stewart@agr.gc.ca
LUMDS Senior Land Resource Specialist, Landscape Integration Unit, Jason A. Vanrobaeys
Tel: 204-822-7580
Fax: 204-822-7572
jason.vanrobaeys@agr.gc.ca

Corporate Management Branch
Tower 4, 1341 Baseline Rd., Ottawa, ON K1A 0C5
Tel: 613-759-1000
Fax: 613-773-0911
Assistant Deputy Minister, Pierre Corriveau
Tel: 613-773-1330
Fax: 613-773-1233
pierre.corriveau@agr.gc.ca
Acting Executive Director, Canadian Pari-Mutuel Agency, Steve Suttie
Tel: 613-949-0726
Fax: 613-949-0750
steve.suttie@agr.gc.ca
#100, 1130 Morrison Dr., Room 121
PO Box 5904
Ottawa, ON K2C 3X7
Acting Director, Operations, Canadian Pari-Mutuel Agency, Sylvie Dubreuil
Tel: 613-949-0732
Fax: 613-949-0750
sylvie.dubreuil@agr.gc.ca
Director, Real Property & Building Operations, Michel Falardeau
Tel: 613-759-6107
Fax: 613-759-1576
michel.falardeau@agr.gc.ca
Director, Water Infrastructure Divison, Scott Roy
Tel: 306-780-8704
Fax: 306-780-6683
scott.roy@agr.gc.ca
Director, Environmental & Engineering Services, Louis Vallée
Tel: 613-773-0920
Fax: 613-773-0966
louis.vallee@agr.gc.ca
Assistant Director, Environmental & Engineering Services, Chris Keith
Tel: 613-759-6758
Fax: 613-759-7799
chris.keith@agr.gc.ca

Market & Industry Services Branch (MISB) / Direction générale des services à l'industrie et aux marchés
Tower 5, 1341 Baseline Rd., Ottawa, ON K1A 0C5
Tel: 613-759-1000
Fax: 613-773-1711
Other Communication: Government of Canada Export Services Information, Toll-Free Phone: 1-888-576-4444
The Market & Industry Services Branch of Agriculture & Agri-Food Canada oversees the following organizations: Bilateral Relations & Technical Trade Policy Directorate; Food Value Chain Bureau; International Markets Bureau; Market Access Secretariat; Negotiations & Multilateral Trade Policy Directorate; & the Operations Directorate. The Operations Directorate operates regional offices throughout Canada, which provide access to market & trade programs & services. Marketing & trade officers offer the following information: statistics by country & product; market access advice; investment opportunities; regulatory issues; export counselling; & news about promotional events.
Assistant Deputy Minister, Tina Namiesniowski
Tel: 613-773-1790
Fax: 613-773-1711
tina.namiesniowski@agr.gc.ca
Director General, Market Access Secretariat, Fred Gorrell
Tel: 613-773-1512
Fax: 613-773-0199
fred.gorrell@agr.gc.ca
Director General, Sector Development & Analysis Directorate, Susie Miller
Tel: 613-773-1750
Fax: 613-773-0300
susie.miller@agr.gc.ca
Director General, Trade Agreements & Negotiations, Frédéric Seppey
Tel: 613-773-0985
Fax: 613-773-1755
frederic.seppey@agr.gc.ca
Director General, Operations Directorate, Lisa Wellman-Patterson
Tel: 613-773-1503
Fax: 613-773-1500
lisa.wellman-patterson@agr.gc.ca
Executive Director, Strategic Trade Policy Division, Doug Forsyth
Tel: 613-773-2730
Fax: 613-773-1755
doug.forsyth@agr.gc.ca
Acting Executive Director, Canada Brand, Bruce Howard
Tel: 613-773-1571
Fax: 613-773-1585
bruce.howard@agr.gc.ca
Executive Director, Market Access Coordination, Donna Seymour
Tel: 613-773-0213
Fax: 613-773-1616
donna.seymour@agr.gc.ca
Acting Director, Trade Commissioner & Market Development Division, Sheila M. Barth
Tel: 613-773-2650
Fax: 613-773-2600
sheila.barth@agr.gc.ca
Director, Market Access Secretariat-Europe, Middle East & Africa Division, Denise J Climenhage
Tel: 613-773-1648
Fax: 613-773-1666
denise.climenhage@agr.gc.ca
Director, Americas Division, Nathalie Durand
Tel: 613-773-3491
Fax: 613-773-1616
nathalie.durand@agr.gc.ca
Director, Food Industry Division, Maurice Egan
Tel: 613-773-3154
Fax: 613-773-0200
maurice.egan@agr.gc.ca
Director, Operations & Emergency Management Division, Peter Gaudet
Tel: 613-773-1511
Fax: 613-773-1500
peter.gaudet@agr.gc.ca
Director, Horticulture & Cross Sectoral Division, Sheila Jones
Tel: 613-773-0171
Fax: 613-773-0299
sheila.jones@agr.gc.ca
Director, Grains & Oilseeds Division, Stephen Lavergne
Tel: 204-259-4145
Fax: 204-259-4170
steve.lavergne@agr.gc.ca
Director, Industry Engagement Division, Sylvie Millette LeDuc
Tel: 613-773-1740
Fax: 613-773-0200
sylvie.milletteleduc@agr.gc.ca
Director, International Policy & Coordination Division, Shelley Monlezun

Tel: 613-773-1930
Fax: 613-773-0199
shelley.monlezun@agr.gc.ca
Director, Animal Industry Division, John Ross
Tel: 613-773-0220
Fax: 613-773-0300
john.ross@agr.gc.ca
Director, Market Access Secretariat-Asia & Oceania Division, Alan Schlachter
Tel: 613-773-0862
Fax: 613-773-1616
alan.schlatcher@agr.gc.ca
Director, Food Regulatory Issues Division, Lynn Stewart
Tel: 613-773-0153
Fax: 613-773-0200
lynn.stewart@agr.gc.ca
Acting Director, Technical Trade Policy Division, Brent Wilson
Tel: 613-773-1651
Fax: 613-773-1616
brent.wilson@agr.gc.ca
Deputy Director, Trade Show Strategy & Delivery, Ben Berry
Tel: 613-773-1565
Fax: 613-773-1555
ben.berry@agr.gc.ca
Deputy Director, Canada Brand Integration, Rose McParland
Tel: 613-773-1692
Fax: 613-773-1555
rose.mcparland@agr.gc.ca
Deputy Director, Regional Coordination & Correspondence, Josy Parrotta-Marck
Tel: 613-773-1876
Fax: 613-773-1500
josy.parrotta-marck@agr.gc.ca
Associate Director, Global Analysis, Susan Winkelaar
Tel: 613-773-1526
Fax: 613-773-1555
susan.winkelaar@agr.gc.ca
Lead Negotiator, Regional Agreements, Trade Negotiations Division, Denis Landreville
Tel: 613-773-1761
Fax: 613-773-1755
denis.landreville@agr.gc.ca
Market & Industry Services Branch Regional Offices
Alberta & Territories Regional Office
#720, 9700 Jasper Ave., Edmonton, AB T5J 4G5
Tel: 780-495-4141
Fax: 780-495-3324
Regional Director, Rodney Dlugos
Tel: 780-495-5525
Fax: 780-495-3324
rodney.dlugos@agr.gc.ca
Deputy Director, Janet Dorey
Tel: 780-495-5526
Fax: 780-495-3324
janet.dorey@agr.gc.ca
Atlantic Regional Office
#405, 1791 Barrington St., PO Box 248Halifax, NS B3J 2N7
Tel: 902-426-3198
Fax: 902-426-3439
The Atlantic Regional Office in Halifax, Nova Scotia, is the headquarters for the following operations: New Brunswick Operations (Phone: 506-452-3706, Fax: 506-452-3509); Newfoundland & Labrador Operations (Phone: 709-772-4063, Fax: 709-772-4803); Nova Scotia Operations (Phone: 902-896-0332, Fax: 902-896-0100); & Prince Edward Island Operations (Phone: 902-566-7300, Fax: 902-566-7316).
Regional Director, Janet Steele
Tel: 902-426-7171
Fax: 902-426-3439
janet.steele@agr.gc.ca
Deputy Director, Prince Edward Island Operations, Heath Coles
Tel: 902-566-7305
Fax: 902-566-7316
heath.coles@agr.gc.ca
Deputy Director, New Brunswick Operations, Kevin Bulmer
Tel: 506-460-4351
Fax: 506-460-4345
kevin.bulmer@agr.gc.ca
Deputy Director, Nova Scotia Operations, Shelley Manning
Tel: 902-896-0098
Fax: 902-896-0100
shelley.manning@agr.gc.ca
Senior Marketing & Trade Officer, Newfoundland & Labrador Operations, Paul Rose
Tel: 709-772-5907
Fax: 709-772-4803
paul.rose@agr.gc.ca
British Columbia Regional Office
#420, 4321 Stillcreek Dr., Burnaby, BC V5C 6S7
Tel: 604-666-6344
Fax: 604-666-7235
Deputy Director, Michelle Soucie
Tel: 604-666-3054
Fax: 604-666-7235
michelle.soucie@agr.gc.ca
Ontario Regional Office
174 Stone Rd. West, Guelph, ON N1G 4S9
Tel: 519-837-9400
Fax: 519-837-9782
Acting Regional Director, Richard Séguin
Tel: 226-217-8056
Fax: 226-217-8187
richard.seguin@agr.gc.ca
Deputy Director, Fred Brandenburg
Tel: 226-217-8048
Fax: 226-217-8187
fred.brandenburg@agr.gc.ca
Deputy Director, Michael Metson
Tel: 226-217-8061
Fax: 226-217-8187
michael.metson@agr.gc.ca
Québec Regional Office
2001, rue Université, 7e étage, Montréal, QC H3A 3N2
Tel: 514-283-8888
Fax: 514-496-3966
Acting Regional Director, Scott Patterson
Tel: 514-315-6171
Fax: 514-496-3966
scott.patterson2@agr.gc.ca
Acting Deputy Director, Roger Riverin
Tel: 514-315-6183
Fax: 514-496-3966
roger.riverin@agr.gc.ca
Saskatchewan Regional Office
1800 Hamilton St., Regina, SK S4P 4K7
Tel: 306-780-5545
Fax: 306-780-7360
Regional Director, Dean L. Vey
Tel: 306-780-7065
Fax: 306-780-7360
dean.vey@agr.gc.ca
Deputy Director, Wendy Collinge
Tel: 306-780-5452
Fax: 306-780-7360
wendy.collinge@agr.gc.ca
Deputy Director, Markets & Trade, Gavin M. Conacher
Tel: 306-780-5216
Fax: 306-780-7360
gavin.conacher@agr.gc.ca
Deputy Director, Bob Nawolsky
Tel: 204-259-4068
Fax: 204-259-4055
bob.nawolsky@agr.gc.ca
Acting Deputy Director, Ron Wonneck
Tel: 204-259-4069
Fax: 204-259-4055
ron.wonneck@agr.gc.ca

Office of Audit & Evaluation
Tower 4, 1341 Baseline Rd., Ottawa, ON K1A 0C5
Tel: 613-759-1000
Fax: 613-773-0660
Agriculture & Agri-Food Canada's Office of Audit & Evaluation is responsible for the following services: evaluation; governance & review; & internal audit & assurance.

Programs Branch / Direction générale des programmes
Tower 7, 1341 Baseline Rd., Ottawa, ON K1A 0C5
Tel: 613-759-1000
Fax: 613-773-2121
The Farm Financial Programs Branch of Agriculture & Agri-Food Canada oversees the following organizations: Agriculture Transformation Programs Directorate; Business Risk Management Program Development; Centre of Program Excellence (COPE); Farm Income Programs Directorate; Finance & Renewal Programs Directorate; & Service Policy & Transformation Directorate.
Assistant Deputy Minister, Rita Moritz
Tel: 613-773-2815
Fax: 613-773-2121
rita.moritz@agr.gc.ca
Acting Director General, Farm Income Programs Directorate, Jocelyn Beaudette
Tel: 204-259-5800
Fax: 204-259-5888
jocelyn.beaudette@agr.gc.ca
Grain Exchange Bldg.
167 Lombard Ave., 10th Fl.
PO Box 6100
Winnipeg, MB R3C 4N3
Director General, Service & Program Excellence Directorate, Ray Edwards
Tel: 613-773-0612
Fax: 613-773-1911
ray.edwards@agr.gc.ca
Grain Exchange Bldg.
167 Lombard Ave., 10th Fl.
PO Box 6100
Winnipeg, MB R3C 4N3
Director General, Business Risk Management Programs Directorate, Rosser Lloyd
Tel: 613-773-2116
Fax: 613-773-2198
rosser.lloyd@agr.gc.ca
Acting Director General, Business Development & Competitiveness Directorate, Sean Malone
Tel: 613-773-2005
Fax: 613-773-2099
sean.malone@agr.gc.ca
Director General, Community Pastures Program, Alan Parkinson
Tel: 306-780-8808
Fax: 306-780-6533
alan.parkinson@agr.gc.ca
#408, 1800 Hamilton St.
Regina, SK S4P 4L2
Director General, Innovation Programs Directorate, Linda Parsons
Tel: 613-773-1900
Fax: 613-773-1911
linda.parsons@agr.gc.ca
Executive Director, Grants & Contributions Delivery Project (GCDP), Julie Leese
Tel: 613-773-2157
Fax: 613-773-2121
julie.leese@agr.gc.ca
Director, AgriMarketing, Lynne Guerrette
Tel: 613-773-0121
Fax: 613-773-2099
lynne.guerrette@agr.gc.ca
Director, Commercialization & Environmental Programs Division, Suzanne Keating
Tel: 613-773-2092
Fax: 613-773-2098
suzanne.keating@agr.gc.ca
Director, Centre of Program Excellence, Nathanael Olson, P.Ag.
Tel: 613-773-2074
Fax: 613-773-2098
nathanael.olson@agr.gc.ca
Director, Industry Development Division, Lynn Renaud
Tel: 613-773-1905
Fax: 613-773-1922
lynn.renaud@agr.gc.ca
Director, Financial Guarantee Programs Division, Adele Shaughnessy
Tel: 613-773-0656
Fax: 613-773-2020
adele.shaughnessy@agr.gc.ca
Assistant Director, Community Pastures Program, Rick Ashton
Tel: 306-523-6650
Fax: 306-780-5018
rick.ashton@agr.gc.ca
Assistant Director, Industry Development Division, Julie Grimard
Tel: 613-773-2108
Fax: 613-773-1922
julie.grimard@agr.gc.ca
Manager, Land Management Unit, Rick D. Gaube
Tel: 306-780-5154
Fax: 306-780-7166
rick.gaube@agr.gc.ca
Manager, Aboriginal & Environmental Programming, Michal Jacob-Fletcher
Tel: 613-773-3104
Fax: 613-773-2098
michal.jacob-fletcher@agr.gc.ca

Senior Administrative Officer, Branch Planning & Coordination Team, Suzie Da Costa
Tel: 613-773-2136
Fax: 613-773-2098
suzie.dacosta@agr.gc.ca

Science & Technology Branch / Direction générale des sciences et de la technologie
Tower 5, 1341 Baseline Rd., Ottawa, ON K1A 0C5
Tel: 613-759-1000
Fax: 613-773-1866
Agriculture & Agri-Food Canada's Research Branch consists of the following organizations: Innovation Directorate; International Scientific Cooperation Bureau; Land Resources; Science Centres Directorate, Science Partnerships Directorate; & Science Policy & Planning. Scientists from Agriculture & Agri-Food Canada work on projects to benefit the agricultural & agri-food sector at research centres located across Canada.
Assistant Deputy Minister, Dr. Siddika Mithani
Tel: 613-773-1860
Fax: 613-773-1866
siddika.mithani@agr.gc.ca
Associate Assistant Deputy Minister, Gilles Saindon, Ph.D.
Tel: 613-773-1840
Fax: 613-773-1844
gilles.saindon@agr.gc.ca
Director General, Cross-Sectoral Strategic Direction, Dr. Richard Butts
Tel: 506-460-4380
Fax: 506-460-4388
richard.butts@agr.gc.ca
Director General, Coastal Ecozone, Christiane Deslauriers, Ph.D.
Tel: 902-365-8514
Fax: 902-365-8455
christiane.deslauriers@agr.gc.ca
Director General, Cross-Sectoral Strategic Direction, Dr. Jespinder Komal
Tel: 613-773-1501
Fax: 613-773-1500
jaspinder.komal@agr.gc.ca
Director General, Prairie/Boreal Plain Ecozone, Stephen D. Morgan Jones
Tel: 403-317-2200
Fax: 403-317-2197
steve.morganjones@agr.gc.ca
Director, Science & Technology Quality Assurance & Programs, Dr. Ian D. Campbell
Tel: 613-773-1242
Fax: 613-773-1299
iand.campbell@agr.gc.ca
Director, Science Policy Integration, Steve Dunnigan
Tel: 613-773-1872
Fax: 613-773-1877
steve.dunnigan@agr.gc.ca
Director, Local Outreach Office - Ontario, Maxine S. Kingston
Tel: 226-217-8003
Fax: 226-217-8187
maxine.kingston@agr.gc.ca
174 Stone Rd. West
Guelph, ON N1G 4S9
Director, AgroClimate, Geomatics & Earth Observations Division, Sherman D. Nelson
Tel: 613-773-1297
Fax: 613-773-1299
sherman.nelson@agr.gc.ca
Director, Office of Intellectual Property & Commercialization, Anita Ploj
Tel: 613-773-1851
Fax: 613-773-0299
anita.ploj@agr.gc.ca
Director, Risk Management Office, Darren Ramlal
Tel: 204-984-5707
Fax: 204-984-0797
darren.ramlal@agr.gc.ca
Director, Pest Management Centre, Dr. Manjeet S. Sethi
Tel: 613-759-7431
Fax: 613-759-7490
manjeet.sethi@agr.gc.ca
Director, Local Outreach Office - Québec, Dr. Eric van Bochove
Tel: 418-648-3316
Fax: 418-648-7342
eric.vanbochove@agr.gc.ca
Assistant Director, Operations, Science Program Support, Jean-Pierre Charuest
Tel: 819-780-7105
Fax: 819-564-5507
jeanpierre.charuest@agr.gc.ca
Manager, Canadian Collection of Fungal Cultures, Biodiversity & Collections, Carolyn Babcock
Tel: 613-759-1772
Fax: 613-759-1927
carolyn.babcock@agr.gc.ca
Manager, Greenhouse Crops, Experimental Farms & Greenhouses, Guy Boulet
Tel: 450-515-2016
Fax: 450-346-7740
guy.boulet@agr.gc.ca
Manager, Water & Wastewater Technologies, Development, Larry A. Braul
Tel: 306-780-3214
Fax: 306-780-5998
larry.braul@agr.gc.ca
Manager, Pesticide Risk Reduction, Risk Reduction, Leslie Cass
Tel: 613-694-2438
Fax: 613-694-2525
leslie.cass@agr.gc.ca
Manager, Innovative Systems Engineering, Development, Graham P. Copithorn
Tel: 306-780-6654
Fax: 306-780-5018
graham.copithorn@agr.gc.ca
Manager, Watershed & Hydrological Engineering, Development, Stella Fedeniuk
Tel: 204-578-6637
Fax: 204-578-6677
stella.fedeniuk@agr.gc.ca
Manager, Soil Landscape Analysis & Application, Environmental Health, Xiaoyuan Geng
Tel: 613-759-1895
Fax: 613-759-1937
xiaoyuan.geng@agr.gc.ca
Manager, Soil Nutrient & Greenhouse Gas Management (West), Environmental Health, Dennis E. Haak
Tel: 604-796-1740
Fax: 604-796-0359
dennis.haak@agr.gc.ca
Manager, Irrigation & Drainage Engineering, Development, Dave A. Kiely
Tel: 780-495-6365
Fax: 780-495-4504
dave.kiely@agr.gc.ca
Manager, Science Planning & Reporting, Lorrie L. Marchand
Tel: 613-773-1880
Fax: 613-773-1877
lorrie.marchand@agr.gc.ca
Manager, Water Quality Impacts, Development, Sharon Reedyk
Tel: 780-495-5965
Fax: 780-495-4504
sharon.reedyk@agr.gc.ca
Manager, Groundwater, Development, Harry Rohde
Tel: 306-780-8142
Fax: 306-780-5018
harry.rohde@agr.gc.ca
Manager, Electron Microscopy & Imaging Labratory, Bioproducts & Bioprocesses, Michael M. Weis
Tel: 250-494-6410
Fax: 250-494-0755
michael.weis@agr.gc.ca
Research Centres

Agroforestry Development Centre
PO Box 940Indian Head, SK S0G 2K0
Tel: 306-695-2284
Fax: 306-695-2568
Manager, Agroforestry Development, Henry C. de Gooijer
Tel: 306-695-5102
Fax: 306-695-2568
henry.degooijer@agr.gc.ca
Research Manager, Bill R. Schroeder
Tel: 306-695-5126
Fax: 306-695-2568
bill.schroeder@agr.gc.ca

Atlantic Cool Climate Crop Research Centre
308 Brookfield Rd., PO Box 39088St. John's, NL A1E 5Y7
Tel: 709-772-4619
Fax: 709-772-6064
Director, Operations, Sandy Todd, PAg
Tel: 709-772-4606
Fax: 709-772-3820
sandy.todd@agr.gc.ca
Agricultural Systems Engineer, Environmental Health, Gary A. Bishop
Tel: 709-772-4170
Fax: 709-772-6064
gary.bishop@agr.gc.ca

Atlantic Food & Horticulture Research Centre
32 Main St., Kentville, NS B4N 1J5
Tel: 902-679-5333
Fax: 902-365-8477
Director, Operations, Dr. Mark Hodges, Ph.D.
Tel: 902-365-8500
Fax: 902-365-8477
mark.hodges@agr.gc.ca
Manager, Farm, Innovation & Renewal, David L. Bowlby
Tel: 902-679-5589
Fax: 902-670-0004
david.bowlby@agr.gc.ca

Brandon Research Centre
RR#3, PO Box 1000ABrandon, MB R7A 5Y3
Tel: 204-726-7650
Fax: 204-728-3858
Director, Operations, Byron Irvine, Ph.D.
Tel: 204-578-6539
Fax: 204-578-6528
byron.irvine@agr.gc.ca
Research Assistant, Clayton J. Jackson, P.Ag.
Tel: 204-578-6615
Fax: 204-578-6524
clayton.jackson@agr.gc.ca

Canada-Manitoba Crop Diversification Centre
PO Box 309Carberry, MB R0K 0H0
Tel: 204-834-6000
Fax: 204-834-3777

Canada-Saskatchewan Irrigation Diversification Centre
901 McKenzie St. South, PO Box 700Outlook, SK S0L 2N0
Tel: 306-867-5400
Fax: 306-867-9656
csidc@agr.gc.ca

Cereal Research Centre
195 Dafoe Rd., Winnipeg, MB R3T 2M9
Tel: 204-983-5533
Fax: 204-983-4604
Director, Operations, Dr. David Wall
Tel: 204-983-0099
Fax: 204-984-6333
david.wall@agr.gc.ca

Crops & Livestock Research Centre
440 University Ave., Charlottetown, PE C1A 4N6
Tel: 902-566-6800
Fax: 902-566-6821
The Crops & Livestock Research Centre (CLRC) in Charlottetown, Prince Edward Island is one of Agriculture and Agri-Food Canada's network of 19 research centres. The Centre's mandate is to develop scientific knowledge & new technologies in agriculture with the prime focus on Prince Edward Island & Atlantic Canada.
Director, Operations, Dr. Maria Rodriguez
Tel: 902-370-1420
Fax: 902-370-1444
maria.rodriguez@agr.gc.ca
Manager, Research Operations, Roddy C. Pratt
Tel: 902-672-6426
Fax: 902-672-6369
roddy.pratt@agr.gc.ca

Dairy & Swine Research & Development Centre
2000, rue College, CP 90 Succ Lennoxville, Sherbrooke, QC J1M 1Z3
Tél: 819-565-9171
Téléc: 819-564-5507
The Dairy & Swine Research & Development Centre oversees the operations of the Beef Research Farm in Kapuskasing, Ontario, as well as the Office of Intellectual Property & Commercialization in Sherbrooke, Québec.
Director, Operations, Dr. Alain Giguère
Tel: 819-780-7103
Fax: 819-564-5407
alain.giguere@agr.gc.ca
Director, Research & Development, Jacques Surprenant, PhD, MPA
Tel: 819-565-9174 ext: 101

Fax: 819-564-4974
jacques.surprenant@agr.gc.ca
Head Herdsman, Kapuskasing Beef Research Farm, Maurice Portelance
Tel: 705-335-6148
Fax: 705-337-6000
maurice.portelance@agr.gc.ca
Assistant Director, Operations, Science Program Support, Jean-Pierre Charuest
Tel: 819-780-7105
Fax: 819-564-5507
jeanpierre.charuest@agr.gc.ca

Eastern Cereal & Oilseed Research Centre
960 Carling Ave., Ottawa, ON K1A 0C6
Tel: 613-759-1858
Fax: 613-759-1970
Director, Research & Development, Michèle Marcotte, Ph.D., Eng.
Tel: 613-759-1525
Fax: 613-759-1970
michele.marcotte@agr.gc.ca
Director, Operations, Dr. Marc Savard
Tel: 613-759-1683
Fax: 613-759-1970
marc.savard@agr.gc.ca
Manager, Research Support, Ron Wheeler
Tel: 613-759-1544
Fax: 613-952-6438
ron.wheeler@agr.gc.ca

Food Research & Development Centre
3600, boul Casavant ouest, Saint-Hyacinthe, QC J2S 8E3
Tel: 450-773-1105
Fax: 450-773-8461
Director, Operations, Alain Houde
Tel: 450-768-3273
Fax: 450-773-8461
alain.houde@agr.gc.ca

Greenhouse & Processing Crops Research Centre
2585 Country Rd. 20, Harrow, ON N0R 1G0
Tel: 519-738-2251
Fax: 519-738-2929
Director, Operations, Dr. Ranjana Sharma
Tel: 519-738-1208
Fax: 519-738-2929
ranjana.sharma@agr.gc.ca
Director, Research & Development, Dr. Gary Whitfield
Tel: 519-738-1218
Fax: 519-738-3300
gary.whitfield@agr.gc.ca
Manager, Greenhouse, Environmental Health, Saeed Akhtar
Tel: 519-738-1212
Fax: 519-738-2929
saeed.akhtar@agr.gc.ca

Guelph Food Research Centre
93 Stone Rd. West, Guelph, ON N1G 5C9
Tel: 519-829-2400
Fax: 519-829-2600
Director, Research & Development, Gabriel Piette
Tel: 450-768-3304
Fax: 450-773-2888
gabriel.pietter@agr.gc.ca
Director, Operations, Dr. Punidadas Piyasena
Tel: 226-217-8109
Fax: 226-217-8183
puni.piyasena@agr.gc.ca

Horticulture Research & Development Centre
430, boul Gouin, Saint-Jean-sur-Richelieu, QC J3B 3E6
Tel: 450-346-4494
Fax: 450-346-7740
Director, Operations, Roger Chagnon
Tel: 450-515-2001
Fax: 450-346-7908
roger.chagnon@agr.gc.ca
Director, Research & Development, Dr. Jacques Suprenant
Tel: 819-565-9174 ext: 101
Fax: 450-346-7908
jacques.suprenant@agr.gc.ca
Manager, Greenhouse, Guy Boulet
Tel: 450-515-2016
Fax: 450-346-7740
guy.boulet@agr.gc.ca

Lacombe Research Centre
6000 C & E Trail, Lacombe, AB T4L 1W1
Tel: 403-782-8100
Fax: 403-782-6120
The Lacombe Research Centre is responsible for the operations of research farms in Beaverlodge & Fort Vermilion in Alberta.
Acting Director, Operations, Dr. Manuel Juarez Davila
Tel: 403-782-8118
Fax: 403-782-6120
manuel.juarez@agr.gc.ca
Director, Research & Development, Dr. Jeff Stewart
Tel: 403-317-2208
Fax: 403-317-2197
jeff.stewart@agr.gc.ca
Manager, Farm, Ken B. Grimson
Tel: 403-782-8139
Fax: 403-782-8186
ken.grimson@agr.gc.ca

Lethbridge Research Centre
5403 - 1st Ave. South, PO Box 3000Lethbridge, AB T1J 4B1
Tel: 403-327-4561
Fax: 403-382-3156
The Lethbridge Research Centre oversees the operations of the Onefour Research Substation, the Stavely Research Substation, & the Vauxhall Research Substation in Alberta.
Director, Operations, Brian Freeze, Ph.D.
Tel: 403-317-3445
Fax: 403-317-2211
brian.freeze@agr.gc.ca
Manager, Feed Mill, Dave Dancoisne
Tel: 403-317-3383
Fax: 403-382-3156
dave.dancoisne@agr.gc.ca
Manager, Stavely Research Substation Site, Albert J. Middleton
Tel: 403-549-2152
Fax: 403-549-3744
albert.middleton@agr.gc.ca
Manager, Vauxhall Research Substation Site, Jim Sukeroff
Tel: 403-654-2255
Fax: 403-654-4243
jim.sukeroff@agr.gc.ca
Manager, Onefour Research Substation Site, Ian Walker
Tel: 403-868-2364
Fax: 403-868-2489
ian.walker@agr.gc.ca
Director, Research & Development, Dr. Jeff Stewart
Tel: 403-317-2208
Fax: 403-317-2197
jeff.stewart@agr.gc.ca

Pacific Agri-Food Research Centre (PARC)
4200 Hwy. 97, PO Box 5000Summerland, BC V0H 1Z0
Tel: 250-494-7711
Fax: 250-494-6415
The Pacific Agri-Food Research Centre oversees the following organizations: the Agassiz Site, the Kamloops Range Research Unit, & the Summerland Site.
Director, Research & Development, Dr. Barry W. Grace, Ph.D.
Tel: 250-494-6412
Fax: 250-494-2122
barry.grace@agr.gc.ca
Director, Operations - Summerland Site, Kenna MacKenzie
Tel: 250-494-6358
Fax: 250-494-6415
kenna.mackenzie@agr.gc.ca
Director, Operations - Agassiz Site, Dr. Sankaran KrishnaRaj
Tel: 604-796-1709
Fax: 604-796-0359
sankaran.krishnaraj@agr.gc.ca
Facility Manager, Kamloops Range Research Unit, Larry Maio
Tel: 250-554-5227
Fax: 250-554-5229
larry.maio@agr.gc.ca

Potato Research Centre
850 Lincoln Rd., PO Box 20280Fredericton, NB E3B 4Z7
Tel: 506-452-3260
Fax: 506-460-4377
The Potato Research Centre is also responsible for the Senator Hervé J. Michaud Research Farm, located in Bouctouche, New Brunswick.
Director, Operations, Edward Hurley
Tel: 506-452-4845
Fax: 506-452-3212
edward.hurley@agr.gc.ca
Director, Research & Development, Claudel Lemieux, Ph.D.
Tel: 418-210-5003
Fax: 418-648-7231
claudel.lemieux@agr.gc.ca
Manager, Integrated Services, Senator Hervé J Michaud Research Farm, Louise Boucher
Tel: 506-743-1140
Fax: 506-743-8316
louise.boucher@agr.gc.ca
Manager, Farm, Larry McMillan
Tel: 506-452-4838
Fax: 506-452-3316
larry.mcmillan@agr.gc.ca

Saskatoon Research Centre
107 Science Pl., Saskatoon, SK S7N 0X2
Tel: 306-956-7200
Fax: 306-956-7247
Director, Research & Development, Dr. Paul McCaughey
Tel: 306-956-7211
Fax: 306-956-7248
paul.mccaughey@agr.gc.ca
Acting Director, Operations, Owen Olfert
Tel: 306-956-7288
Fax: 306-956-7248
owen.olfert@agr.gc.ca
Acting Director, Reserch & Development - South, Yves Plante
Tel: 306-956-2489
Fax: 306-956-7248
yves.plante@agr.gc.ca

Semiarid Prairie Agricultural Research Centre
PO Box 1030Swift Current, SK S9H 3X2
Tel: 306-778-7200
Fax: 306-778-3188
The Semiarid Prairie Agricultural Research Centre is responsible for the operations of research farms in Indian Head & Regina, Saskatchewan. As of May 2013, the Centre has assumed responsibility for the cattle research previously conducted in Lethbridge, AB.
Director, Research & Development, Ed Coulthard
Tel: 306-780-3915
Fax: 306-780-6533
ed.coulthard@agr.gc.ca
Director, Operations, Bruce McArthur
Tel: 306-778-7270
Fax: 306-778-3188
bruce.mcarthur@agr.gc.ca
Supervisor, Indian Head Research Farm, Darren Pollock
Tel: 306-695-5264
Fax: 306-695-3445
darren.pollock@agr.gc.ca

Soils & Crops Research & Development Centre
2560, boul Hochelaga, Québec, QC G1V 2J3
Tel: 418-657-7980
Fax: 418-648-2402
The Soils & Crops Research & Development Centre is also responsible for a research farm in Normandin, Québec.
Director, Research & Development, Claudel Lemieux
Tel: 418-210-5003
Fax: 418-648-7231
claudel.lemieux@agr.gc.ca
Director, Operations, Geneviève Levasseur
Tel: 418-210-5001
Fax: 418-648-7231
genevieve.levasseur@agr.gc.ca

Southern Crop Protection & Food Research Centre
1391 Sandford St., London, ON N5V 4T3
Tel: 519-457-1470
Fax: 519-457-3997
The Southern Crop Protection & Food Research Centre oversees the operations of research farms in Delhi & Vineland, Ontario, as well as an Office of Intellectual Property & Commercialization in London, Ontario.
Director, Research & Development, Gary Whitfield
Tel: 519-738-1218
Fax: 519-738-3300
gary.whitfield@agr.gc.ca
Director, Operations, Dr. Karl Volkmar
Tel: 519-457-1470 ext: 206
karl.volkmar@agr.gc.ca
Research Scientist, Vineland Research Farm, Antonet Svircev
Tel: 905-562-2018
Fax: 905-562-4335
antonet.svircev@agr.gc.ca

Supervisor, Farm Services, Delhi Research Farm, Albert Asztalos
Tel: 519-457-1470 ext: 299
Fax: 519-457-3997
albert.asztalos@agr.gc.ca

Strategic Policy Branch / Direction générale des politiques stratégiques
Tower 7, 1341 Baseline Rd., Ottawa, ON K1A 0C5
Tel: 613-759-1000
Fax: 613-773-2111
The Strategic Policy Branch of Agriculture & Agri-Food Canada includes the following organizations: Policy Development & Analysis Directorate; Policy, Planning, & Integration Directorate; & the Research & Analysis Directorate.
Assistant Deputy Minister, Greg Meredith
Tel: 613-773-2930
Fax: 613-773-2121
greg.meredith@agr.gc.ca
Acting Director General, Policy Development & Analysis Directorate, Anna Romano
Tel: 613-773-2128
Fax: 613-773-2111
anna.romano@agr.gc.ca
Director General, Research & Analysis Directorate, Greg Stain
Tel: 613-773-1207
Fax: 613-773-2444
greg.strain@agr.gc.ca
Director, Farm Economic Analysis Division, Fay Abizadeh
Tel: 613-773-2410
Fax: 613-773-2499
fay.abizadeh@agr.gc.ca
Director, Crop Sector Policy Division, Tom Askin
Tel: 204-984-7789
Fax: 204-983-5300
tom.askin@agr.gc.ca

Atlantic Canada Opportunities Agency (ACOA) / Agence de promotion économique du Canada atlantique (APECA)

Blue Cross Centre, 644 Main St., 3rd Fl., PO Box 6051Moncton, NB E1C 9J8
Tel: 506-851-2271
Fax: 506-851-7403
Toll-Free: 800-561-7862
TTY: 877-456-6500
information@acoa-apeca.gc.ca
www.acoa-apeca.gc.ca
Other Communication: Secure fax: 506-875-1301; Access to information / privacy: 506-851-6202
The role of the Atlantic Canada Opportunities Agency is the development of opportunities for economic growth in Atlantic Canada. The agency achieves its mission in the following ways: assisting businesses to become more innovative, productive, & competitive; promoting the strengths of Atlantic Canada; & helping communities to develop more diversified local economies.

Minister for the Atlantic Canada Opportunities Agency; Minister, National Revenue, Hon. Gail Shea
Tel: 613-992-9223
Fax: 613-992-1974
gail.shea@parl.gc.ca

Deputy Minister & President, Paul J. LeBlanc
Tel: 506-851-6128
Fax: 506-851-6295

Director, Energy, Environment Policy, & Coordination, Daniel McCarthy
Tel: 613-952-8216

Finance & Corporate Services / Finances et services corporatifs
Vice-President, Denise Frenette
Tel: 506-851-6438
Director General, Chief Information Officer Directorate, Marc Gagnon
Tel: 506-851-6511
Fax: 506-851-7403

Policy & Programs / Politiques et programmes
Senior Vice-President, Daryell Nowlan
Tel: 506-851-3805
Fax: 506-851-7403
Acting Director General, Community Development, Wade Aucoin
Tel: 506-851-2576
Acting Director General, Policy, Kent Estabrooks
Tel: 506-851-3070
Director General, Enterprise Development, Lucienne Godbout
Tel: 506-851-3806
Director General, Advocacy & Industrial Benefits, Madonna Kent
Tel: 613-952-7494
Fax: 613-995-1719
Director General, Trade & Investment, Michel Têtu
Tel: 506-851-6496
Fax: 506-851-7403
New Brunswick Regional Office
570 Queen St., 3rd Fl., PO Box 578Fredericton, NB E3B 5A6
Tel: 506-452-3184
Fax: 506-452-3285
Toll-Free: 800-561-4030
TTY: 877-456-6500
The New Brunswick Regional Office oversees operations at the following offices: Campbellton (Phone: 506-789-4735); Edmundston (Phone: 506-735-4236); Fundy Region (Phone: 506-636-4485); Miramichi (506-778-1909); Northeast (Phone: 506-548-7420); Northwest (Phone: 506-473-5556); Southeast (Phone: 506-851-6432); Southwest (506-452-3135); & Tracadie-Sheila (506-395-1025).
Vice-President, New Brunswick, Janet Gagnon
Tel: 506-452-3342
Executive Director, New Brunswick Federal Council, Raymond Gallant
Tel: 506-452-4986
Director, Business Programs, André Charron
Tel: 506-452-2413
Director, Communications, Patricia Field
Tel: 506-452-4287
Director, Financial Management Services, David Hubbard
Tel: 506-452-2423
Director, Policy, Advocacy, & Coordination, Gail Moser
Tel: 506-452-3155
Newfoundland & Labrador Regional Office
John Cabot Building, 10 Barter's Hill, 11th Fl., PO Box 1060 Stn. C, St. John's, NL A1C 5M5
Tel: 709-772-2751
Fax: 709-772-2712
Toll-Free: 800-668-1010
TTY: 877-456-6500
The Newfoundland & Labrador Regional Office oversees the following offices throughout the province: Clarenville (Phone: 709-466-5980); Corner Brook (Phone: 709-637-4477); Gander (Phone: 709-651-4457); Grand Bank (Phone: 709-832-2517); Grand Falls-Windsor (Phone: 709-489-6600); & Labrador (709-896-2648).
Nova Scotia Regional Office
#600, 1801 Hollis St., PO Box 2284 Stn. C, Halifax, NS B3J 3C8
Tel: 902-426-6743
Fax: 902-426-2054
Toll-Free: 800-565-1228
TTY: 877-456-6500
The Nova Scotia Regional Office of the Atlantic Canada Opportunities Agency oversees the following offices throughout Nova Scotia: Antigonish (Phone: 902-867-6075); Bridgewater (Phone: 902-541-5543); Church Point Office (Phone: 902-260-3590); Kentville (902-679-5356); Pictou (Phone: 902-755-3746); Truro (902-895-2743), & Yarmouth (Phone: 902-742-0809).
Vice-President, Nova Scotia (acting), Peter Hogan
Tel: 902-426-1288
Director General, Regional Operations, Peter Hogan
Tel: 902-426-1288
Director, Finance & Management Services, Nancy Ives
Tel: 902-426-5968
Director, Intergovernmental Affairs & Coordination, Lisa Muton
Tel: 902-426-4820
Director, Communications, Alexander Smith
Tel: 902-426-9417
Fax: 902-426-5843
Prince Edward Island Regional Office
Royal Bank Building, 100 Sydney St., 3rd Floor, PO Box 40Charlottetown, PE C1A 7K2
Tel: 902-566-7492
Fax: 902-566-7098
Toll-Free: 800-871-2596
TTY: 877-456-6500
The Prince Edward Island Regional Office oversees the Summerside District Office (Phone: 902-888-4145).
Vice-President, Prince Edward Island & Tourism, Patrick Dorsey
Tel: 902-368-0760
Director General, Enterprise Development & Policy, Wayne Hooper
Tel: 902-626-2877
Fax: 902-566-7098
Director General, Atlantic Tourism, Robert McCloskey
Tel: 902-626-2479
Fax: 902-566-7098
Executive Director, Prince Edward Island Federal Council, Catherine MacInnis
Tel: 902-368-0889
Fax: 902-566-7489
Director, Corporate Programs & Services, Lynne Beairsto
Tel: 902-566-7499
Director, Infrastructure Programs, Pat MacAulay
Tel: 902-626-2794
Director, Communicatons, Cindy Roy
Tel: 902-566-7569
Fax: 902-566-7098
Director, Trade & Business Programs, Douglas Smith
Tel: 902-368-0890
Ottawa Office
60 Queen St., 4th Fl., PO Box 1667 Stn. B, Ottawa, ON K1P 5R5
Tel: 613-954-2422
Fax: 613-954-0429

Enterprise Cape Breton Corporation (ECBC) / Société d'expansion du Cap-Breton
Silicon Island, 70 Crescent St., PO Box 1750Sydney, NS B1P 6T7
Tel: 902-564-3600
Fax: 902-564-3825
Toll-Free: 800-705-3926
information@ecbc-secb.gc.ca
www.ecbc-secb.gc.ca
As the principal federal organization for economic development on Cape Breton Island, ECBC focuses on the major issues affecting the economy of the area. In partnership with all levels of government, the private sector, & other community stakeholders, ECBC promotes & assists the financing & development of communities and industry with a view to creating sustainable wealth on Cape Breton Island. In addition to its own programs, ECBC is responsible for the delivery of ACOA's programs on Cape Breton Island.
Chair, Paul J. LeBlanc
Tel: 506-851-6128
Fax: 506-851-7403
Chief Executive Officer, John Lynn
Tel: 902-564-3508
Fax: 902-564-2760

Atomic Energy of Canada Limited (AECL) / Énergie atomique du Canada Ltée (EACL)

Head Office, Chalk River Laboratories, Chalk River, ON K0J 1J0
Tel: 613-584-3311
Toll-Free: 866-513-2325
librarycr@aecl.ca (library requests)
www.aecl.ca
Other Communication: Media Enquiries, Toll-Free Phone: 1-866-886-2325
Atomic Energy of Canada develops peaceful applications from nuclear technology. Services include research, design, engineering, waste management, & decommissioning.
The following offices & laboratories are part of Atomic Energy of Canada: Whiteshell Laboratories in Pinawa, Manitoba (204-753-2311); Low-Level Radioactive Waste Management in Ottawa, Ontario (613-998-9442); AECL Ottawa (613-237-3270); Port Hope Office & Laboratory in Port Hope, Ontario (905-885-9488); Port Hope Area Initiative (905-885-0291); & Centre for Nuclear Energy Research at the University of New Brunswick in Fredericton (506-453-5111).
President & Chief Executive Officer, Dr. Robert Walker

Senior Vice-President, Strategic Contracting, Allan A. Hawryluk

Senior Vice-President & General Manager, Jon Lundy

Chief Financial Officer & Vice-President, Steve Halpenny

Chief Nuclear Officer & Vice-President, Operations, Randy Lesco

Vice-President, General Counsel, & Corporate Secretary, Richard Fujarczuk

Vice-President, Research & Development, William Kupferschmidt

Vice-President, Decommissioning & Waste Management, Joan Miller

Chalk River Laboratories (CRL)
NRC Canadian Neutron Beam Centre, Building 459, Station 18, Chalk River, ON K0J 1J0
Tel: 613-584-8293
Toll-Free: 800-364-6989
Programs cover a wide range of topics associated with atomic power. Supports all aspects of nuclear technology & serves as a national laboratory in nuclear sciences. Developmental work is performed to demonstrate that low & intermediate level radioactive wastes arising from reactor operation can be immobilized in a stable form before disposal in a repository. The Fuel Packaging & Storage Project is underway to replace aging waste fuel storage containers, with 2013 as a completion date for the project.

Low-Level Radioactive Waste Management Office (LLRWMO) / Bureau de gestion des déchets radioactifs de faible activité
#200, 1900 City Park Dr., Ottawa, ON K1J 1A3
Tel: 613-998-9442
Fax: 613-952-0760
Toll-Free: 800-377-5995
info@llrwmo.org
www.llrwmo.org
Carries out the responsibilities of the federal government for low-level radioactive waste (LLRW) management in Canada.
Director, Robert L. Zelmer, P.Eng, RPP

Auditor General of Canada / Vérificateur général du Canada

240 Sparks St., Ottawa, ON K1A 0G6
Tel: 613-995-3708
Fax: 613-957-0474
Toll-Free: 888-761-5953
TTY: 613-954-8042
communications@oag-bvg.gc.ca; infomedia@oag-bvg.gc.ca
www.oag-bvg.gc.ca
Other Communication: Media Relations, Phone: 613-952-0213, ext. 6292; Publications, Toll-Free Phone: 1-888-761-5953; Work Opportunities, E-mail: emplo@oag-bvg.gc.ca
The Office of the Auditor General of Canada was established in 1878. Today, the head office in Ottawa & regional offices in Halifax, Montréal, Edmonton, & Vancouver employ approximately 650 employees. The Office of the Auditor General of Canada provides objective, fact-based information required by Parliament to hold the federal government accountable for its stewardship of public funds. An Officer of Parliament, the Auditor General of Canada is responsible for auditing the following organizations: federal government departments; federal government agencies; most Crown corporations; many federal organizations; the government of the Yukon; the government of the Northwest Territories; & the government of Nunavut. The Auditor General, Michael Ferguson, reports publicly to the House of Commons about matters he believes should be brought to the attention of the House of Commons. The report can include chapters on audits & studies, sustainable development strategies, & environmental petitions.

Auditor General, Michael Ferguson

Commissioner of the Environment & Sustainable Development / Commissaire à l'environnement et au développement durable
240 Sparks St., Ottawa, ON K1A 0G6
Tel: 613-995-3708
Fax: 613-957-0474
petitions@oag-bvg.gc.ca
www.oag-bvg.gc.ca
Commissioner, Environment & Sustainable Development, Scott Vaughan
Tel: 613-952-0213 ext: 640
Principal, Sustainable Development Strategies, Audits, & Studies, Andrew Ferguson
Tel: 613-952-0213 ext: 630
Principal, Sustainable Development Strategies, Audits, & Studies, James McKenzie
Tel: 613-952-0213 ext: 635
Principal, Sustainable Development Strategies, Audits, & Studies, Kimberly Leach
Tel: 613-952-0213 ext: 624
Principal, Sustainable Development Strategies, Audits, & Studies, Bruce Sloan
Tel: 613-952-0213 ext: 230
Principal, Heather McManaman
Tel: 902-426-7728
Director, Glenn Doucette
Tel: 902-426-2097
Director, Paul Kelly
Tel: 902-426-6512
Principal, René Béliveau
Tel: 514-283-8324
Director, Jean-Pierre Morin
Tel: 514-283-8136
Director, Tina Swiderski
Tel: 514-283-7793
Principal, Eric Hellsten
Tel: 604-666-7600

Business Development Bank of Canada (BDC) / Banque de développement du Canada (BDC)

#400, 5, Place Ville-Marie, Montréal, QC H3B 5E7
Tel: 514-283-5904
Fax: 514-283-5626
Toll-Free: 877-232-2269
www.bdc.ca
Other Communication: Toll-Free Fax 1-877-329-9232; Corporate Financing (Québec & Atlantic Regions), Fax: 514-283-8410
The Business Development Bank of Canada is a financial institution which is wholly owned by the Government of Canada. It was created by an Act of Parliament in 1944. The Bank is governed by an independent Board of Directors, & reports to the Minister of Industry. The mission of the Business Development Bank of Canada is to assist in the establishment & development of Canadian businesses in all industries. The Bank focuses its efforts on small & medium-sized enterprises. The following services are carried out by the Business Development Bank of Canada: consulting services; flexible financing, such as long term business financing & subordinate financing; & venture capital. Branches of the Business Development Bank of Canada are located throughout Canada. Smaller communities are served by satellite branches, consultants & travelling account managers.

Chair, John A. MacNaughton

President & Chief Executive Officer, Jean-René Halde

Executive Vice-President & Chief Financial Officer, Paul Buron

Executive Vice-President, Financing & Consulting, Edmée Métivier

Senior Vice President, Human Resources, Mary Karamanos

Alberta Branches
Calgary Area Branch
Barclay Centre, #110, 444 - 7 Ave. SW, Calgary, AB T2P 0X8
Tel: 403-292-5600
Fax: 403-292-6616
Other Communication: Subordinate Financing (Prairies & Northwest Territories), Phone: 403-292-5000, Fax: 403-292-5862
Calgary North Branch
#100, 1935 - 32 Ave. NE, Calgary, AB T2E 7C8
Tel: 403-292-5333
Fax: 403-292-6651
Calgary South Branch
#200, 6700 MacLeod Trail SE, Calgary, AB T2H 0L3
Tel: 403-292-8882
Fax: 403-292-4345
Edmonton Branch
#200, 10665 Jasper Ave., Edmonton, AB T5J 3S9
Tel: 780-495-2277
Fax: 780-495-6616
Edmonton South Branch
#201, 4628 Calgary Trail NW, Edmonton, AB T6H 6A1
Tel: 780-495-7200
Fax: 780-495-7198
Edmonton West Branch
236 Mayfield Common, Edmonton, AB T5P 4B3
Tel: 780-442-7312
Fax: 780-495-3102
Grande Prairie Branch
#203, 10625 West Side Dr., Grande Prairie, AB T8V 8E6
Tel: 780-532-8875
Fax: 780-539-5130
Lethbridge Branch
520 - 5th Ave. South, Lethbridge, AB T1J 0T8
Tel: 403-382-3000
Fax: 403-382-3162
Medicine Hat Branch
#101, 2248 - 13th Ave. SE, Medicine Hat, AB T1A 8G6
Tel: 403-527-2601
Fax: 403-528-6899
Office by appointment.
Red Deer Branch
#107, 4815 - 50th Ave., Red Deer, AB T4N 4A5
Tel: 403-340-4203
Fax: 403-340-4243
British Columbia Branches
Cranbrook Branch
205B Cranbrook St. North, Cranbrook, BC V1C 3R1
Tel: 250-417-2200
Fax: 250-417-2213
Fort St. John Branch
#7, 10230 - 100th St., Fort St. John, BC V1J 3Y9
Tel: 250-787-0622
Fax: 250-787-9423
Kamloops Branch
205 Victoria St., Kamloops, BC V2C 2A1
Tel: 250-851-4900
Fax: 250-851-4925
Kelowna Branch
313 Bernard Ave., Kelowna, BC V1Y 6N6
Tel: 250-470-4802
Fax: 250-470-4832
Langley Branch
#101B, 6424 - 200th St., Langley, BC V2Y 2T3
Tel: 604-532-5150
Fax: 604-532-5166
Nanaimo Branch
#500, 6581 Aulds Rd., Nanaimo, BC V9T 6J6
Tel: 250-390-5757
Fax: 250-390-5753
Nelson Branch
#1, 619B Front St., Nelson, BC V1L 4B6
Tel: 250-352-3837
Fax: 250-352-3809
North Vancouver Branch
#3, 221 West Esplanade, North Vancouver, BC V7M 3J3
Tel: 604-666-7703
Fax: 604-666-1957
Prince George Branch
#150, 177 Victoria St., Prince George, BC V2L 5R8
Tel: 250-561-5323
Fax: 250-561-5512
South Vancouver Branch
#101, 5811 Cooney Rd., Richmond, BC V6X 3M1
Tel: 604-666-7850
Fax: 604-666-1068
Surrey Branch
#160, 10362 King George Blvd., Surrey, BC V3T 2W5
Tel: 604-586-2400
Fax: 604-586-2430
Terrace Branch
3233 Emerson St., Terrace, BC V8G 5L2
Tel: 250-615-5300
Fax: 250-615-5320
Tri-Cities Branch
#370, 2755 Lougheed Highway, Port Coquitlam, BC V3B 5Y9
Tel: 604-927-1400
Fax: 604-927-1415
Vancouver Branch
One Bentall Centre, #2100, 505 Burrard St., PO Box 6Vancouver, BC V7X 1M6
Tel: 604-666-7850
Fax: 604-666-1068
Other Communication: Subordinate Financing (British Columbia & Yukon), Phone: 604-666-7875, Fax: 604-666-8482; Corporate Financing (Western Canada), Phone: 604-666-1068
Vernon Branch
#302, 3105 - 33rd St., Vernon, BC V1T 9P7
Tel: 250-260-5061
Fax: 250-260-5011
Victoria Branch
990 Fort St., Victoria, BC V8V 3K2

Tel: 250-363-0161
Fax: 250-363-8029

Manitoba Branches
Brandon Branch
#10, 940 Princess Ave., Brandon, MB R7A 0P6
Tel: 204-726-7570
Fax: 204-726-7555
Winnipeg Branch
#1100, 155 Carlton St., Winnipeg, MB R3C 3H8
Tel: 204-983-7900
Fax: 204-983-0870
Winnipeg West Branch
#200, 1655 Kenaston Blvd., Winnipeg, MB R3P 2M4
Tel: 204-983-6530
Fax: 204-983-6531

New Brunswick Branches
Bathurst Branch
#205, 275 Main St., Bathurst, NB E2A 1A9
Tel: 506-548-7360
Fax: 506-548-7381
Edmundston Branch
#407, 121, rue de l'Église, Edmundston, NB E3V 1J9
Tél: 506-739-8311
Téléc: 506-735-0019
Office by appointment.
Fredericton Branch
#504, 570 Queen St., PO Box 754Fredericton, NB E3B 5B4
Tel: 506-452-3030
Fax: 506-452-2416
Moncton Branch
766 Main St., Moncton, NB E1C 1E6
Tel: 506-851-6120
Fax: 506-851-6033
Saint John Branch
53 King St., Saint John, NB E2L 1G5
Tel: 506-636-4751
Fax: 506-636-3892

Newfoundland & Labrador Branches
Corner Brook Branch
4 Herald Ave., 1st Fl., Corner Brook, NL A2H 4B4
Tel: 709-637-4515
Fax: 709-637-4522
Grand Falls-Windsor Branch
42 High St., PO Box 744Grand Falls-Windsor, NL A2A 2M4
Tel: 709-489-2181
Fax: 709-489-6569
St. John's Branch
215 Water St., PO Box 520St. John's, NL A1C 5K4
Tel: 709-722-5505
Fax: 709-772-2516

Northwest Territories & Nunavut Branches
Yellowknife & Nunavut Branch
4912 - 49th St., Yellowknife, NT X1A 1P3
Tel: 867-873-3565
Fax: 867-873-3501

Nova Scotia Branches
Halifax Branch
#1400, 2000 Barrington St., Halifax, NS B3J 2Z7
Tel: 902-426-7850
Fax: 902-426-6783
Vice-President & Area Manager, Craig Levangie
Tel: 902-426-7865
craig.levangie@bdc.ca
Sydney Branch
#117, 275 Charlotte St., Sydney, NS B1P 1C6
Tel: 902-564-7700
Fax: 902-564-3975
Truro Branch
622 Prince St., PO Box 1378Truro, NS B2N 5N2
Tel: 902-895-6377
Fax: 902-893-7957
Yarmouth Branch
103 Water St., PO Box 98Yarmouth, NS B5A 4B1
Tel: 902-742-7119
Fax: 902-742-8180

Ontario Branches
Barrie Branch
#301, 151 Ferris Lane, PO Box 876Barrie, ON L4M 4Y6
Tel: 705-725-2533
Fax: 705-739-0467
Belleville Branch
284B Wallbridge-Loyalist Rd., Belleville, ON K8N 5B3
Tel: 613-969-4009
Fax: 613-969-4018
Office by appointment.
Brampton Branch
#100, 24 Queen St. East, Brampton, ON L6V 1A3
Tel: 905-450-9845
Fax: 905-450-7514
Brantford Branch
#10, 330 West St., Brantford, ON N3R 7V5
Tel: 519-751-3005
Fax: 519-751-3006
Office by appointment.
Burlington / Halton Branch
#401, 4145 North Service Rd., Burlington, ON L7L 6A3
Tel: 905-315-9230
Fax: 905-315-9243
Chatham Branch
62 Keil Dr. South, Chatham, ON N7M 3G8
Tel: 519-380-8886
Fax: 519-380-8850
Office by appointment.
Durham (Whitby) Branch
400 Dundas St. West, Whitby, ON L1N 2M7
Tel: 905-666-6694
Fax: 905-666-1059
Etobicoke Branch
#1001, 1243 Islington Ave., Toronto, ON M8X 1Y9
Tel: 416-954-2604
Fax: 416-954-2631
Other Communication: Subordinate Financing (Greater Toronto Area), Phone: 416-952-6291, Fax: 416-954-2630
Guelph Branch
#100, 120 Research Lane, Guelph, ON N1G 0B5
Tel: 519-826-2663
Fax: 519-826-2662
Hamilton Branch
#1900, 25 Main St. West, Hamilton, ON L8P 1H1
Tel: 905-572-2954
Fax: 905-572-4282
Kenora Branch
227 - 2nd St. South, Kenora, ON P9N 1G1
Tel: 807-467-3535
Fax: 807-467-3533
Kingston Branch
#201, 1000 Gardiners Rd., Kingston, ON K7P 3C4
Tel: 613-389-0999
Fax: 613-389-2543
Kitchener-Waterloo Branch
#110, 50 Queen St. North, Kitchener, ON N2H 6P4
Tel: 519-571-6676
Fax: 519-571-6685
London Branch
380 Wellington St., London, ON N6A 5B5
Tel: 519-645-4229
Fax: 519-645-5450
Other Communication: Subordinate Financing (Southwestern Ontario), Phone: 519-675-3114, Fax: 519-645-5989
Markham Branch
3130 Hwy. 7 East, Markham, ON L3R 5A1
Tel: 905-305-6867
Fax: 905-305-1969
Mississauga Branch
#100, 4310 Sherwoodtowne Blvd., Mississauga, ON L4Z 4C4
Tel: 905-566-6417
Fax: 905-566-6425
North Bay Branch
222 McIntyre St. West, North Bay, ON P1B 2Y8
Tel: 705-495-5700
Fax: 705-495-5707
North York Branch
#502, Islington Ave. West, North York, ON M3J 3H7
Tel: 416-736-3420
Fax: 416-736-3425
Ottawa Branch
55 Metcalfe St., Ground Fl., Ottawa, ON K1P 6L5
Tel: 613-995-0234
Fax: 613-995-9045
Other Communication: Subordinate Financing (Ottawa & Atlantic Regions), Phone: 613-995-4084, Fax: 613-943-9866
Ottawa West Branch
#100, 700 Silver Seven Rd., Kanata, ON K2V 1C3
Tel: 613-592-2968
Fax: 613-592-5053
Owen Sound Branch
173 - 8th St. East, Owen Sound, ON N4K 5N3
Tel: 519-371-5666
Fax: 519-371-1707
Office by appointment.
Peterborough Branch
340 George St. North, 4th Fl., PO Box 1419Peterborough, ON K9J 7H6
Tel: 705-750-4800
Fax: 705-750-4808
Sarnia Branch
1086 Modeland Rd., Sarnia, ON N7S 6L2
Tel: 519-383-1848
Fax: 519-383-1849
Office by appointment.
Sault Ste Marie Branch
153 Great Northern Rd., Sault Ste Marie, ON P6B 4Y9
Tel: 705-941-3030
Fax: 705-941-3040
Scarborough Branch
#112, 305 Milner Ave., Toronto, ON M1B 3V4
Tel: 416-954-0709
Fax: 416-954-0716
St Catharines Branch
#100, 39 Queen St., PO Box 1193St Catharines, ON L2R 7A7
Tel: 905-988-2874
Fax: 905-988-2890
Stratford Branch
516 Huron St., Stratford, ON N5A 5T7
Tel: 519-271-5650
Fax: 519-271-8472
Sudbury Branch
#10, 233 Brady St., Sudbury, ON P3B 4H5
Tel: 705-670-6482
Fax: 705-670-6387
Thunder Bay Branch
#102, 1136 Alloy Dr., Thunder Bay, ON P7B 6M9
Tel: 807-346-1780
Fax: 807-346-1790
Timmins Branch
#202, 85 Pine St. South, Timmins, ON P4N 2K1
Tel: 705-267-1246
Fax: 705-268-5437
Office by appointment.
Toronto Branch
#1200, 121 King St. West, Toronto, ON M5H 3T9
Tel: 416-973-0341
Fax: 416-954-5009
The King Street West branch offers corporate financing for the Greater Toronto Area.
Vaughan Branch
#600, 3901 Hwy. 7 West, Vaughan, ON L4L 8L5
Tel: 905-264-2100
Fax: 905-264-2122
Windsor Branch
#200, 2485 Ouellette Ave., Windsor, ON N8X 1L5
Tel: 519-257-6808
Fax: 519-257-6811

Prince Edward Island Branches
Charlottetown Branch
#230, 119 Kent St., PO Box 488Charlottetown, PE C1A 7L1
Tel: 902-566-7454
Fax: 902-566-7459

Québec Branches
Boucherville Branch
1570 Ampère St, Boucherville, QC J4B 7L4
Tél: 450-928-4120
Téléc: 450-928-4127
Brossard Branch
#200, 4255, boul Lapinière, Brossard, QC J4Z 0C7
Tel: 450-926-7220
Fax: 450-926-7221
Chaudière - Appalaches (Saint-Romuald) Regional Branch
#100, 1175, boul de la Rive sud, Saint-Romuald, QC G6W 5M6
Tel: 418-834-5144
Fax: 418-834-1855

Des Moulins - Lanaudière (Terrebonne) Regional Branch
2785, boul des Plateaux, Terrebonne, QC J6X 4J9
Tél: 450-964-8778
Téléc: 450-964-8773
Drummondville Branch
1010, boul René-Lévesque, Drummondville, QC J2C 5W4
Tél: 819-478-4951
Téléc: 819-478-5864
Gatineau Branch
#104, 259, boul St-Joseph, Gatineau, QC J8Y 6T1
Tél: 819-997-4434
Téléc: 819-997-4435
Granby Branch
#302, 155, rue St-Jacques, Granby, QC J2G 9A7
Tél: 450-372-5202
Téléc: 450-372-2423
Laval Branch
#100, 2525, Daniel-Johnson, Laval, QC H7T 1S9
Tél: 450-973-3727
Téléc: 450-973-6860
Montréal Branch
#12525, 5, Place Ville-Marie, Montréal, QC H3B 2G2
Tél: 514-496-7966
Téléc: 514-496-7974
Autres nombres: Subordinate Financing (Montréal), Phone: 514-496-0626, Fax: 514-496-1020; Subordinate Financing (North-Shore & South-Shore), Phone: 514-283-8265, Fax: 514-496-1020
Montreal East Branch
6347, rue Jean-Talon est, Saint-Léonard, QC H1S 3E7
Tél: 514-251-2818
Téléc: 514-251-2758
Pointe-Claire Branch
#110, 755, boul St-Jean, Pointe-Claire, QC H9R 5M9
Tel: 514-697-8014
Fax: 514-697-3160
Québec Branch
1134, Grande-Allée ouest, Québec, QC G1S 1E5
Tél: 418-648-3972
Téléc: 418-648-5525
Autres nombres: Subordinate Financing (Eastern Quebec), Phone: 418-648-5517, Fax: 418-649-6301
Québec North West Branch
#310, 1165, boul Lebourgneuf, Québec, QC G2K 2C9
Tel: 418-648-4740
Fax: 418-648-4745
Rimouski Branch
391, boul Jessop, Rimouski, QC G5L 1M9
Tél: 418-722-3300
Téléc: 418-722-3362
Rouyn-Noranda Branch
#301, 139, boul Québec, Rouyn-Noranda, QC J9X 6M8
Tél: 819-764-6701
Téléc: 819-764-5472
Saguenay / Lac St-Jean Branch
#210, 325 des Saguenéens St, Chicoutimi, QC G7H 6K9
Tél: 418-698-5599
Téléc: 418-698-5678
Saint-Jérôme Branch
#102, 55, rue Castonguay, Saint-Jérôme, QC J7Y 2H9
Tél: 450-432-7111
Téléc: 450-432-8366
Saint-Laurent Branch
#160, 3100, boul de la Côte-Vertu, Saint-Laurent, QC H4R 2J8
Tél: 514-496-7500
Téléc: 514-496-7510
Sherbrooke Branch
2532, rue King ouest, Sherbrooke, QC J1J 2E8
Tél: 819-564-5700
Téléc: 819-564-4276
Thérèse-de-Blainville (Boisbriand) Regional Branch
3000, rue Cours le Corbusier, Boisbriand, QC J7G 3E8
Tél: 450-420-4900
Téléc: 450-420-4904
Trois-Rivières Branch
#150, 1500, rue Royale, Trois-Rivières, QC G9A 6E6
Tél: 819-371-5215
Téléc: 819-371-5220
Vaudreuil-Soulanges
450, rue Aimé-Vincent, Vaudreuil-Dorion, QC J7V 5V5
Tél: 450-455-9370
Téléc: 450-455-8126
Office by appointment.

Saskatchewan Branches
Prince Albert Branch
#1, 1499 - 10th Ave. E, Prince Albert, SK S6V 7S6
Tel: 306-953-8599
Fax: 306-953-1343
Office by appointment.
Regina
#320, 2220 - 12th Ave., Regina, SK S4P 0M8
Tel: 306-780-6478
Fax: 306-780-7516
Saskatoon
135 - 21st St. East, Main Fl., Saskatoon, SK S7K 0B4
Tel: 306-975-4822
Fax: 306-975-5955

Yukon Branches
Whitehorse
#202, 204 Lambert St., Whitehorse, YT Y1A 1Z4
Tel: 867-633-7510
Fax: 867-667-4058

Canada Border Services Agency (CBSA) / Agence des services frontaliers du Canada (ASFC)

Headquarters, 191 Laurier Ave. West, Ottawa, ON K1A 0L8
Toll-Free: 800-461-9999
TTY: 866-335-3237
Contact@cbsa.gc.ca; communications@ps.gc.ca (Public Safety)
www.cbsa-asfc.gc.ca
Other Communication: Border Information Service, Service in French, Toll-Free Phone: 1-800-959-2036; Public Safety Canada, Phone: 613-944-4875, Toll-Free: 1-800-830-3118
Established in 2003, as a response to the need for increased border services, the Canada Border Services Agency ensures the security & prosperity of Canada. The agency is responsible for managing the access of people & goods to & from Canada. To carry out its mission, Canada Border Services Agency administers more than ninety pieces of legislation. Some of the agencies duties include the following: managing over 100 border crossings; offering services at points throughout Canada & internationally; operating detention centres across the nation; conducting marine operations at the ports of Prince Rupert, Vancouver, Montréal, & Halifax; managing postal services at major mail centres in Montréal, Toronto, & Vancouver; & forming part of more than twenty Integrated Border Enforcement Teams across Canada.

Acts Administered:
Agriculture & Agri-Food Administrative Monetary Penalties Act
Canada Agricultural Products Act
Canadian Environmental Protection Act, 1999
Citizenship Act
Coastal Fisheries Protection Act
Consumer Packaging & Labelling Act
Convention on International Trade in Endangered Species of Wild Fauna & Flora
Fertilizers Act
Hazardous Products Act
Pest Control Products Act
Transportation of Dangerous Goods Act, 1992
Wild Animals & Plant Protection & Regulation of International & Interprovincial Trade Act

Minister, Public Safety, Hon. Vic Toews
Tel: 613-992-3128
Fax: 613-995-1049
Toews.V@parl.gc.ca

President, Luc Portelance
Tel: 613-952-3200
Fax: 613-948-3177

Executive Vice-President, Malcolm Brown
Tel: 613-952-3200
Fax: 613-952-1851

Associate Vice-President, Martin Bolduc
Tel: 613-952-5269
Fax: 613-948-7130

Regional Director General, Niagara Region, Rick Comerford
Tel: 905-994-6000
Fax: 905-994-6010
Other Communications: Executive Assistant, Phone: 905-994-6002

Regional Director General, Windsor - St. Clair Region, Pete Diponio
Tel: 519-967-4010

Regional Director General, Pacific Region, Roslyn MacVicar
Tel: 604-666-0760
Other Communications: Executive Assistant, Phone: 604-666-3305

Canada Business Network / Réseau Entreprises Canada

235 Queen St., Ottawa, ON K1A 0H5
Toll-Free: 888-576-4444
TTY: 800-457-8466
www.canadabusiness.ca
twitter.com/CanadaBusiness
www.facebook.com/244892072221776
Canada Business provides a wide range of information on government services, programs & regulations to Canadian business people. The base framework is an organized network of centres across Canada, one in each province & territory. The network of Canada Business is expanding to include regional access partners in many other communities across Canada. The centres offer various products & services aimed at helping clients obtain quick, accurate & comprehensive business information. Each centre exists as a result of cooperative arrangements between federal & provincial governments, & the private sector in some cases. Administration & management of the CBSC varies depending on location between the following federal agencies: Western Economic Diversification (WD), Industry Canada, the Canada Economic Development for Quebec Regions (CEDQR) & the Atlantic Canada Opportunities Agency (ACOA). The Federal Business Information System (BIS) is a collection of information on business-related programs, services & selected regulations which are accessible through the CBSC & on the CBSC web site (www.cbsc.org). The Federal BIS acts as a single window for individuals or businesses to access relevant information from all federal departments

Senior Manager, Canada Business Network Operations, Laura Collier
Tel: 613-952-5888
Fax: 613-954-5463

Regional Offices
The Business Link Business Service Centre
10160 - 103th St. NW, Edmonton, AB T5J 1B1
Tel: 780-422-7722
Fax: 780-422-0055
Toll-Free: 888-576-4444
TTY: 800-457-8466
www.canadabusiness.ab.ca
Other Communication: Research Services Phone: 780-422-7780; Calgary Phone: 403-221-7800; Fax: 403-221-7817
twitter.com/BusinessLinkAB
www.facebook.com/BusinessLinkAB
Small Business BC
82 - 601 West Cordova St., Vancouver, BC V6B 1G1
Tel: 604-775-5525
Fax: 604-775-5520
Toll-Free: 800-667-2272
TTY: 800-457-8466
askus@smallbusinessbc.ca
www.smallbusinessbc.ca
Other Communication: Feedback E-mail: feedback@smallbusinessbc.ca
twitter.com/smallbusinessbc
www.facebook.com/smallbusinessbc
www.linkedin.com/groups/Small-Business-BC-2397794
Canada/Manitoba Business Service Centre
#250, 240 Graham Ave., PO Box 2609Winnipeg, MB R3C 0J7
Tel: 204-984-2272
Fax: 204-983-3852
Toll-Free: 888-576-4444
TTY: 800-457-8466
www.canadabusiness.mb.ca
twitter.com/CMBSCca
Canada/New Brunswick Business Service Centre
Barker House, #102, 570 Queen St., Fredericton, NB E3B 6Z6
Tel: 506-444-6140
Fax: 506-444-6172
Toll-Free: 888-576-4444
TTY: 800-457-8466

Canada/Newfoundland & Labrador Business Service Centre
John Cabot Bldg., 10 Barter's Hill, 11th Fl., St. John's, NL A1C 5M5
Tel: 709-772-6022
Fax: 709-772-6090
Toll-Free: 888-576-4444
TTY: 800-457-8466
Canada/NWT Business Service Centre
#701, 5201 - 50 Ave., Yellowknife, NT X1A 3S9
Tel: 876-873-7958
Fax: 876-873-7960
Toll-Free: 800-661-0599
TTY: 800-457-8466
Canada/Nova Scotia Business Service Centre (CNSBSC)
#700, 1801 Hollis St., Halifax, NS B3J 3C8
Tel: 902-426-8604
Toll-Free: 888-576-4444
TTY: 800-457-8466
Canada/Nunavut Business Service Centre
Inuksugait Plaza, PO Box 1000 Stn. 1198, Iqaluit, NU X0A 0H0
Tel: 867-975-7860
Fax: 867-975-7885
Toll-Free: 888-576-4444
TTY: 800-457-8466
Other Communication: Rankin Inlet, Phone: 867-645-8450, Fax: 867-645-8455; Cambridge Bay, Phone: 867-983-7383, Fax: 967-983-7380
Canada/Ontario Business Service Centre (COBSC)
151 Yonge St., 4rd Fl., Toronto, ON M5C 2W7
Toll-Free: 888-745-8888
TTY: 800-457-8466
www.cbo-eco.ca/en/locations.cfm
Other Communication: Canada Business Network, Toll-Free Phone: 1-888-576-4444
Canada/Prince Edward Island Business Service Centre (CPEIBSC)
100 Sydney St., 3rd Fl., PO Box 40Charlottetown, PE C1A 7K2
Tel: 902-368-0771
Toll-Free: 888-576-4444
TTY: 800-457-8466
info.cb.pei@acoa-apeca.gc.ca
Canada/Saskatchewan Business Service Centre (CSBSC)
#2, 345 - 3rd Ave. South, Saskatoon, SK S7K 1M6
Tel: 306-956-2323
Fax: 306-956-2328
Toll-Free: 888-576-4444
TTY: 800-457-8466
Canada/Yukon Business Service Centre
#101, 307 Jarvis St., Whitehorse, YT Y1A 2H3
Tel: 867-667-2000
Fax: 867-667-2001
Toll-Free: 888-576-4444
TTY: 800-457-8466
Info entrepreneurs
#W204, 380, rue St-Antoine ouest, local 6000, Montréal, QC H2Y 3X7
Tél: 514-496-4636
Téléc: 514-496-5934
Ligne sans frais: 888-576-4444
TTY: 800-457-8466
infoentrepreneurs.org
Autres nombres: Toll-Free Fax: 1-888-417-0442; Québec, Phone: 418-649-6116; Fax: 418-682-1144
twitter.com/chambremontreal
www.facebook.com/chambremontreal

Canada Economic Development for Québec Regions / Développement économique Canada pour les régions du Québec

Édifice Dominion Square, #900, 1255, rue Peel, Montréal, QC H3B 2T9
Tel: 514-283-6412
Fax: 514-283-3302
Toll-Free: 866-385-6412
www.dec-ced.gc.ca
Secondary Address: 165, rue Hôtel de Ville
Place du Portage, Phase IIPO Box 1110 B Sta.
Gatineau, QC J8X 3X5 Canada
Fax: 819-997-3340
Defines federal objectives relating to development opportunities & delivers business assistance programs for small- & medium-sized businesses in Qu,bec for innovation, entrepreneurial & market development purposes. Supports a series of programs for appropriate environmental initiatives in various regions of Québec. The agency fosters alliances among the various environmental industry stakeholders including small- & medium-sized enterprises & industrial associations. Goals include a strengthening of existing & new partnerships, & an improvement of access to government programs. The agency also provides a significant amount of support for research & development in areas of environmental technology, demonstration, marketing & transfer projects. Supports initiatives that contribute to making Montréal an industrial centre of excellence in the environment. Aids small- & medium-sized firms in gaining access to federal procurement process, & encourages training & education focusing on business management. Helps business develop export markets through cooperative efforts with Industry Canada & Foreign Affairs & International Trade Canada

Minister, Economic Development Agency of Canada for the Regions of Québec; Minister, Intergovernmental Affairs, Minister, Transport, Infrastructure, & Communities; President, Queen's Privy Council for Canada, Hon. Denis Lebel
Tel: 61- 99- 623
Fax: 613-996-6252
denis.lebel@parl.gc.ca

Deputy Minister & President, Guy Mc Kenzie
Tel: 514-283-4843
Fax: 514-283-7778
Abitibi-Témiscamingue
906, 5e av, Val-d'Or, QC J9P 1B9
Tel: 819-825-5260
Fax: 819-825-3245
Toll-Free: 800-567-6451
Bas St-Laurent
Édifice Trust général du Canada, #310, 2, rue Saint-Germain Est, Rimouski, QC G5L 8T7
Tel: 418-722-3282
Fax: 418-722-3285
Toll-Free: 800-463-9073
Regional Director, Pierre Roberge
Tel: 418-722-3255
Fax: 418-722-3285
Centre-du-Québec
#105, 1100 boul René-Lévesque, Drummondville, QC J2C 5W4
Tel: 819-478-4664
Fax: 819-478-4666
Toll-Free: 800-567-1418
Regional Director, Georges Arseneau
Tel: 819-478-4664
Fax: 819-478-4666
Estrie
Place Andrew Paton, #100, 202, rue Wellington nord, Sherbrooke, QC J1H 5C6
Tel: 819-564-5904
Fax: 819-564-5912
Toll-Free: 800-567-6084
Gaspésie—Iles-de-la-Madeleine
Place Jacques-Cartier, 120, rue de la Reine, 3e étage, Gaspé, QC G4X 2S1
Tel: 418-368-5870
Fax: 418-368-6256
Toll-Free: 866-368-0044
Regional Director, France Simard
Tel: 418-368-5879
Fax: 418-368-6256
Ile-de-Montréal
Édifice Dominion Square, #900, 1255, rue Peel, Montréal, QC H3B 2T9
Tel: 514-283-2500
Fax: 514-496-8310
Toll-Free: 800-322-4636
Laval - Laurentides - Lanaudière
#410, 2990, av Pierre-Péladeau, Laval, QC H7T 3B3
Tel: 450-973-6844
Fax: 450-973-6851
Toll-Free: 800-430-6844
Mauricie
Immeuble Bourg du Fleuve, #413, 25, rue des Forges, Trois-Rivières, QC G9A 2G4
Tel: 819-371-5182
Fax: 819-371-5186
Toll-Free: 800-567-8637
Montérégie
Place Agropur, #400, 101, boul Roland-Therrien, Longueuil, QC J4H 4B9
Tel: 450-928-4088
Fax: 450-928-4097
Toll-Free: 800-284-0335
Regional Director, Charles Lambert
Tel: 450-928-4088
Fax: 450-928-4097
Nord-du-Québec
Édifice Dominion Square, #900, 1255 rue Peel, Montréal, QC H3B 2T9
Tel: 514-283-8131
Fax: 514-283-3637
Toll-Free: 800-561-0633
Regional Director, Sophie Legendre
Tel: 514-283-8866
Fax: 514-283-3637
Outaouais
#202, 259 boul Saint-Joseph, Gatineau, QC J8Y 6T1
Tel: 819-994-7442
Fax: 819-994-7846
Toll-Free: 800-561-4353
Regional Director, Marc Boily
Tel: 819-994-7442
Fax: 819-994-7846
Other Communications: Administrative Assistant, Phone: 819-944-7442
Québec - Chaudière - Appalaches
Place Iberville IV, #030, 2954, boul Laurier, Québec, QC G1V 4T2
Tel: 418-648-4826
Fax: 418-648-7291
Toll-Free: 800-463-5204
Saguenay - Lac-Saint-Jean
#203, 100, rue Saint-Joseph sud, Alma, QC G8B 7A6
Tel: 418-668-3084
Fax: 418-668-7584
Toll-Free: 800-463-9808

Canada Mortgage & Housing Corporation (CMHC) / Société canadienne d'hypothèques et de logement (SCHL)

700 Montreal Rd., Ottawa, ON K1A 0P7
Tel: 613-748-2000
Fax: 613-748-2098
Toll-Free: 800-668-2642
TTY: 613-748-2447
chic@cmhc-schl.gc.ca
www.cmhc.ca; www.schl.ca
Other Communication: Canadian Housing Information Centre: 613-748-2367
CMHC works closely with a network of professional associations, groups & institutions concerned with regional planning & the residential sector. It prepares various research projects for the examination of relationships between urban areas, housing & sustainable development issues. Involved in numerous technical research projects addressing interrelationships between housing, energy & resource use. Through its research & information transfer function, CMHC will undertake initiatives such as identifying approaches & solutions that lead to more sustainable & healthy communities, examining barriers to potential development of brownfield sites. CMHC will focus on ways to reduce residential energy consumption in multiple-unit housing, educate consumers on energy-saving changes to homes. The Net Zero Healthy Healthy Housing Initiative combines passive solar, energy-efficient design, construction & appliances, integrated with renewable energy systems, to achieve net zero energy consumption on an annual basis, significantly reducing environmental impacts & GHG emissions. Twenty demonstration projects across Canada are underway.

Chair, Dino Chiesa

Canada Revenue Agency (CRA) / Agence du revenu du Canada

875 Heron Rd., Ottawa, ON K1A 0L5
Toll-Free: 800-267-6999
TTY: 800-665-0354
www.cra-arc.gc.ca
Other Communication: Individual Income Tax Enquiries: 1-800-959-8281; Telerefund: 1-800-959-1956; Business & Self-Employed Individuals: 1-800-959-5525; GST/HST Credit: 1-800-959-1953
The Canada Revenue Agency administers tax laws for the Canadian federal government & for most provincial & territorial governments. The Agency is also responisible for various social &

economic benefit & incentive programs, which are delivered through the tax system.
Acts Administered:
Customs & Excise Offshore Application Act

Minister, National Revenue; Minister for the Atlantic Canada Opportunities Agency, Hon. Gail Shea
Tel: 613-995-2960
Fax: 613-952-6608
Shea.G@parl.gc.ca

Commissioner & Chief Executive Officer, Linda Lizotte-MacPherson
Tel: 613-957-3688

Canada Science & Technology Museum Corporation (CSTM) / Musée des sciences et de la technologie du Canada (MSTC)

PO Box 9724 Stn. T, Ottawa, ON K1G 5A3
Tel: 613-991-6090
Fax: 613-990-3636
info@technomuses.ca
www.technomuses.ca
The Corporation is the only comprehensive science & technology collecting institution in Canada, & focuses on the following major subject areas: aviation, communications, manufacturing, natural resources, renewable resources including agriculture, scientific instrumentation, & transportation. The Corporation operates three Museums: the Canada Agriculture Museum, the Canada Aviation Museum & the Canada Science & Technology Museum.

President & Chief Executive Officer, Denise Amyot
Tel: 613-993-0775

Director General; Vice-President, Exhibitions, Canada Science & Technology Museum, Claude Faubert
Tel: 613-991-0372

Curator, Agriculture, Franz Klingender
Tel: 613-996-7822

Curator, Transportation, Sharon Babaian
Tel: 613-991-3029

Canadian Centre for Occupational Health & Safety (CCOHS) / Centre canadien d'hygiène et de sécurité au travail (CCHST)

135 Hunter St. East, Hamilton, ON L8N 1M5
Tel: 905-572-2981
Fax: 905-572-2206
Toll-Free: 800-668-4284
www.ccohs.ca
Provides occupational health & safety & environmental information in the form of publications, responses to inquiries & a computerized information service available in various formats. Topics include: environmental acts & regulations; occupational & environmental health data; toxic effects of chemical substances; transport of dangerous goods; chemical evaluation; hazardous substances; & domestic substances listed under the Canadian Environmental Protection Act; biological hazards; ergonomics

President & Chief Executive Officer, S. Len Hong
Tel: 905-572-2981 ext: 443

Vice-President, Dr. Patabendi K. Abeytunga
Tel: 905-572-2981 ext: 453

Controller, Bonnie Easterbrook
Tel: 905-572-2981 ext: 440

Manager, Inquiries & Client Services, Renzo Bertolini
Tel: 905-572-2981 ext: 447

Manager, Computer Systems & Services, David Brophy
Tel: 905-572-2981 ext: 449

Manager, Chemical Services, Lorraine Davison
Tel: 905-572-2981 ext: 446

Manager, General Health & Safety Services, Norma Gibson-MacDonald
Tel: 905-572-2981 ext: 452

Manager, Human Resources, Louise Henderson
Tel: 905-572-2981 ext: 440

Manager, Training & Education Services, Chris Moore
Tel: 905-572-2981 ext: 446

Manager, Communications, Eleanor Westwood
Tel: 905-572-2981 ext: 440

Canadian Commercial Corporation (CCC) / Corporation commerciale canadienne

50 O'Connor St., 11th Fl., Ottawa, ON K1A 0S6
Tel: 613-996-0034
Fax: 613-995-2121
Toll-Free: 800-748-8191
www.ccc.ca
A Crown Corporation mandated to facilitate international trade, particularly in government markets. CCC specializes in international procurement markets for Canadian companies & provides services to help them win, negotiate & manage export contracts. As prime contractor, CCC offers a government-to-government agreement that simplifies customer access to Canadian technology & expertise. CCC contracts have a government guarantee for performance.

Chair, Robert C. Kay

President & Chief Executive Officer, Marc Whittingham
Tel: 613-996-0042
Fax: 613-992-2134
Other Communications: Alternative Telephone: 613-996-0043

Vice-President, Business Development & Sales, Pierre Alarie
Tel: 613-943-0953
Fax: 613-995-2121

Vice-President, Strategy & Organizational Development, Mariette Fyfe-Fortin
Tel: 613-943-4360
Fax: 613-995-2121

Vice-President, Contract Management & Procurement, Jacques Greffe
Tel: 613-996-0161
Fax: 613-995-2121

Vice-President/Legal General Counsel & Corporate Secretary, Legal Services, Tamara Parschin-Rybkin, Q.C.
Tel: 613-992-4419
Fax: 613-947-3903

Vice-President/Chief Financial Officer, Risk & Finance, Martin Zablocki
Tel: 613-992-9638
Fax: 613-995-2121

Canadian Environmental Assessment Agency (CEAA) / Agence canadienne d'évaluation environnementale (ACEE)

Place Bell Canada, 160 Elgin St., 22nd Fl., Ottawa, ON K1A 0H3
Tel: 613-957-0700
Fax: 613-957-0862
Toll-Free: 866-582-1884
info@ceaa-acee.gc.ca
www.ceaa-acee.gc.ca
The Canadian Environmental Assessment Agency (CEAA) was established to administer the Canadian Environmental Assessment Act (the Act). The environmental assessment process identifies the environmental effects of proposed projects & measures to address those effects, in support of sustainable development. CEAA promotes environmental assessment as a tool to protect & sustain a healthy environment in harmony with a growing economy. The CEAA advocates high-quality environmental assessments by assisting federal departments & agencies with training & guidance & by investing in the research & development of best practices. CEAA provides administrative support to mediators & review panels & ensures that the public has opportunities to participate effectively in the environmental assessment process. Public participation strengthens the quality & credibility of environmental assessments by providing local & traditional knowledge, & insight into possible environmental effects. A publicly accessible master index of environmental assessments carried out by federal departments is available in the Canadian Environmental Assessment Registry (projects beginning before November 2003 are available in the Federal Environmental Assessment Index) located on the CEAA we b site. In addition, CEAA's participant funding program provides limited funds to ensure that interested individuals & groups have the opportunity to participate in mediations & panel reviews.
Accountable to the Minister of the Environment

President, Elaine Feldman
Tel: 613-948-2671
Fax: 613-948-2208
elaine.feldman@ceaa-acee.gc.ca

Vice-President, Policy Development, Helen Cutts
Tel: 613-948-2662
Fax: 613-957-0897
helen.cutts@ceaa-acee.gc.ca

Vice-President, Operations, Yves Leboeuf
Tel: 613-948-2665
Fax: 613-957-0935
yves.leboeuf@ceaa-acee.gc.ca

Executive Director, Project Reviews, Steve Burgess
Tel: 613-948-2663
Fax: 613-957-0941
steve.burgess@ceaa-acee.gc.ca

Director General, Corporate Services, Richard Gagné
Tel: 613-957-0467
Fax: 613-957-0946
richard.gagne@ceaa-acee.gc.ca

Director, Operational Support, Andrée Chevrier
Tel: 613-957-0641
Fax: 613-948-1354
andree.chevrier@ceaa-acee.gc.ca

Director, Communications, Charlene Gaudet
Tel: 613-957-0712
Fax: 613-957-0946
charlene.gaudet@ceaa-acee.gc.ca

Director, Legislative & Regulatory Affairs, John McCauley
Tel: 613-948-1785
Fax: 613-957-0897
john.mccauley@ceaa-acee.gc.ca

Director, Finance & Administration, Daniel Nadeau
Tel: 613-948-2677
Fax: 613-957-0862
daniel.nadeau@ceaa-acee.gc.ca

Director, Human Resources, Brigitte Schryer
Tel: 613-954-2201
Fax: 613-957-0858
brigitte.schryer@ceaa-acee.gc.ca

Senior Policy Analyst, Legislative & Regulatory Affairs, Natalie Deschamps
Tel: 613-957-0366
Fax: 613-857-0366
natalie.deschamps@ceaa-acee.gc.ca

General Counsel & Executive Director, Legal Services, Irene V. Gendron
Tel: 613-957-0735
Fax: 613-957-0942
Director, Margaret Fairbairn
Tel: 780-495-2236
Fax: 780-495-2876
margaret.fairbairn@ceaa-acee.gc.ca
Atlantic Region
#200, 1801 Hollis St., Halifax, NS B3J 3N4
Tel: 902-426-0564
Fax: 902-426-6550
Director, Mike Atkinson
Tel: 902-426-7496
Fax: 902-426-6550
mike.atkinson@ceaa-acee.gc.ca
Director, Louise Knox
Tel: 416-952-1575
Fax: 416-952-1573
louise.knox@ceaa-acee.gc.ca
Director, Lisa Walls
Tel: 604-666-6989

Fax: 604-666-6990
lisa.walls@ceaa-acee.gc.ca
Director, Daniel McNaughton
Tel: 204-984-2457
Fax: 204-983-7174
dan.mcnaughton@ceaa-acee.gc.ca
Director, François Boulanger
Tel: 418-649-6438
Fax: 418-649-6443
francois.boulanger@acee-ceaa.gc.ca

Canadian Food Inspection Agency (CFIA) / Agence canadienne d'inspection des aliments (ACIA)

1400 Merivale Rd., Ottawa, ON K1A 0Y9
Tel: 613-225-2342
Fax: 613-228-6601
Toll-Free: 800-442-2342
TTY: 800-465-7735
www.inspection.gc.ca
Other Communication: Atlantic Area, Phone: 506-851-7400; Ontario Area: 519-837-9400; Québec Area: 514-283-8888; Western Area: 403-292-4301
twitter.com/CFIA_food
The agency is responsible for all inspection services related to food safety, economic fraud, trade-related requirements, & animal & plant health programs.
Acts Administered:
Acts Administered in Part by the Canadian Food Inspection Agency
Canada Agricultural Products Act
Canadian Food Inspection Agency Act
Consumer Packaging & Labelling Act
Feeds Act
Fertilizers Act
Fish Inspection Act
Food & Drugs Act
Health of Animals Act
Meat Inspection Act
Plant Breeders' Rights Act
Plant Protection Act
Seeds Act

President, George Da Pont
Tel: 613-773-6000
Fax: 613-773-6060
George.DaPont@inspection.gc.ca

Executive Vice-President, Office of the President, Mary Komarynsky
Tel: 613-773-6500
Fax: 613-773-6060
Mary.Komarynsky@inspection.gc.ca

Chief Food Safety Officer, Dr. Martine Dubuc
Tel: 613-773-5763
Fax: 613-773-6060
martine.dubuc@inspection.gc.ca

Chief Veterinary Officer, Dr. Ian Alexander
Tel: 613-773-5763
Fax: 613-773-6060
ian.alexander@inspection.gc.ca

Vice-President, Operations, Stephen Baker
Tel: 613-773-5700
Fax: 613-773-5671
Stephen.Baker@inspection.gc.ca

Vice-President, Human Resources, Gérard Étienne
Tel: 613-773-5725
Fax: 613-773-5795
Gerard.Etienne@inspection.gc.ca

Vice-President, Policy & Programs, Neil Bouwer
Tel: 613-773-5734
Fax: 613-773-5791
Neil.Bouwer@inspection.gc.ca

Vice-President, Science, Vacant
Tel: 613-773-5722
Fax: 613-773-5797

Vice-President, Corporate Management, Peter Everson
Tel: 613-773-5759
Fax: 613-773-5792
Peter.Everson@inspection.gc.ca

Vice-President, Inspection Modernization, Cameron Prince
Tel: 613-773-7030
Fax: 613-773-5671
Cameron.Prince@inspection.gc.ca

Acting Vice-President, Information Management & Information Technology, Peter Bruce
Tel: 613-773-1395
Fax: 613-773-0676
Peter.Bruce@inspection.gc.ca

Vice-President, Public Affairs Branch, George W. Shaw
Tel: 613-773-5776
Fax: 613-773-5559
George.Shaw@inspection.gc.ca

Vice-President, Business Transformation, Bill Teeter
Tel: 613-221-3125
Fax: 613-221-3158
Bill.Teeter@inspection.gc.ca

Assoc. Vice-President, Integration & Management Services, Jim Butcher
Tel: 613-773-6298
Fax: 613-773-5791
Jim.Butcher@inspection.gc.ca

Executive Director, Strategic Communication, Laurel Herwig
Tel: 613-773-5501
Fax: 613-773-5618
Laurel.Herwig@inspection.gc.ca

Executive Director, Corporate Secretariat, Veronica McGuire
Tel: 613-773-5751
Fax: 613-773-5791
Veronica.McGuire@inspection.gc.ca

Executive Director, Audit, Evaluation & Risk Oversight, Brian Smithon
Tel: 613-773-5349
Fax: 613-773-5696
Brian.Smith@inspection.gc.ca

Director, Executive Support & Coordination, Aline Dimitri
Tel: 613-773-5542
Fax: 613-773-5606
Aline.Dimitri@inspection.gc.ca

Director, Corporate Planning & Reporting, Everett Ethier
Tel: 613-221-7571
Fax: 613-221-5270
Everett.Ethier@inspection.gc.ca
Atlantic
1081 Main St., 5th Fl., PO Box 6088Moncton, NB E1C 8R2
Tel: 506-851-7400
Fax: 506-851-2689
Executive Director, Nicole Bouchard-Steeves
Tel: 506-851-7670
Nicole.Bouchard-Steeves@inspection.gc.ca
Ontario
174 Stone Rd. West, Guelph, ON N1G 4S9
Tel: 519-837-9400
Fax: 519-837-9766
Executive Director, James D. Crawford
Tel: 519-837-5802
Fax: 519-837-9766
James.Crawford@inspection.gc.ca
Québec
#746-C, 2001, av Université, Montréal, QC H3A 3N2
Tel: 514-283-8888
Fax: 514-283-3143
Executive Director, Dr. Robert Charlebois, DVM
Tel: 514-283-3815 ext: 432
Fax: 514-496-4699
Robert.Charlebois@inspection.gc.ca
Western
1115- 57th Ave. NE, Calgary, AB T2E 9B2
Tel: 403-292-4301
Fax: 403-292-5707
Executive Director, Kathryn Emmett
Tel: 403-292-5717
Fax: 403-292-5707
Kathryn.Emmett@inspection.gc.ca

Canadian Heritage / Patrimoine canadien

15 Eddy St., Gatineau, QC K1A 0M5
Tel: 819-997-0055
Toll-Free: 866-811-0055
TTY: 888-997-3123
info@pch.gc.ca
www.pch.gc.ca
Canadian Heritage works to achieve a more cohesive & creative nation. Goals of the department are for Canadians to express & share their cultural experiences with others in their own country & globally & for Canadians to live in an inclusive society with intercultural understanding & citizen participation. Responsibilities are carried out by the following sectors: Citizenship & Heritage; Cultural Affairs; Sport, Major Events & Regions; & Strategic Policy, Planning & Corporate Affairs.
Acts Administered:
Cultural Property Export & Import Act
Department of Canadian Heritage Act
Fitness & Amateur Sport Act
Foreign Publishers Advertising Services Act
Library & Archives of Canada Act
Museums Act
National Sports of Canada Act
Physical Activity & Sport Act

Minister, Canadian Heritage & Official Languages, Hon. James Moore
Tel: 819-997-7788
Fax: 819-994-1267
james.moore@pch.gc.ca

Minister of State (Status of Women), Hon. Rona Ambrose
Tel: 819-956-4000
Fax: 613-995-1761
minister-ministre@swc-cfc.gc.ca

Minister of State (Sport), Hon. Bal Gosal
Tel: 819-934-1122
Fax: 819-953-8055
bal.gosal@pch.gc.ca

Deputy Minister, Daniel Jean
Tel: 819-994-1132
Fax: 819-997-0979
daniel.jean@pch.gc.ca

Director, Communications, Jessica Fletcher
Tel: 819-956-2169
Fax: 819-994-1267
Jessica.Fletcher@pch.gc.ca

Liaison & Agenda Officer, Associate Deputy Minister's Office, Joanne Courchesne
Tel: 819-997-1356
Fax: 819-997-2978
joanne.courchesne@pch.gc.ca

Associated Agencies, Boards & Commissions:

• **Canada Council for the Arts / Conseil des Arts du Canada**
See Entry Name Index for detailed listing.
• **Canada Science & Technology Museum Corporation / Musée des sciences et de la technologie du Canada**
See Entry Name Index for detailed listing.
• **Canadian Broadcasting Corporation (CBC) / Société Radio-Canada (SRC)**
See Entry Name Index for detailed listing.
• **Canadian Museum of Civilization (CMC) / Musée canadien des civilisations**
See Entry Name Index for detailed listing.
• **Canadian Museum of Nature (CMN) / Musée canadien de la nature (MCN)**
See Entry Name Index for detailed listing.
• **Canadian Museum of Civilization (CMC) / Musée canadien des civilisations**
See Entry Name Index for detailed listing.
• **Canadian Museum of Nature (CMN) / Musée canadien de la nature (MCN)**
See Entry Name Index for detailed listing.
• **Canadian Radio-television & Telecommunications Commission (CRTC) / Conseil de la radiodiffusion et des télécommunications canadiennes**
See Entry Name Index for detailed listing.
• **Library & Archives Canada**
See Entry Name Index for detailed listing.
• **National Arts Centre (NAC) / Centre national des Arts (CNA)**
See Entry Name Index for detailed listing.
• **National Battlefields Commission / Commission des champs de bataille nationaux**
See Entry Name Index for detailed listing.
• **National Film Board of Canada / Office national du film du Canada**
See Entry Name Index for detailed listing.
• **National Gallery of Canada / Musée des Beaux-Arts du Canada**
See Entry Name Index for detailed listing.
• **Public Service Commission of Canada / Commission de la fonction publique du Canada**
See Entry Name Index for detailed listing.
• **Status of Women Canada / Condition féminine Canada**
See Entry Name Index for detailed listing.
• **Telefilm Canada / Téléfilm Canada**
See Entry Name Index for detailed listing.

Citizenship & Heritage Sector / Citoyenneté et patrimoine
Assistant Deputy Minister, Tom Scrimger
Tel: 819-997-2832
Fax: 819-994-5032
tom.scrimger@pch.gc.ca
Director General, Canadian Heritage Information Network (CHIN), Gabrielle Blais
Tel: 819-997-0091
Fax: 819-994-9555
Gabrielle.Blais@pch.gc.ca
Director General, Canadian Conservation Institute & Chief Operating Officer, Jeanne E. Inch
Tel: 613-998-3721
Fax: 613-952-1431
jeanne.inch@pch.gc.ca
Director, Heritage Group, Pierre Derome
Tel: 819-956-5555
Fax: 819-934-3201
pierre.derome@pch.gc.ca
Director, Policy & Research, Yvan M. Déry
Tel: 819-994-2224
Fax: 819-994-3697
yvan.dery@pch.gc.ca

Canadian Institutes of Health Research (CIHR) / Instituts de recherche en santé du Canada (IRSC)

160 Elgin St., 9th Fl., Ottawa, ON K1A 0W9
Tel: 613-941-2672
Fax: 613-954-1800
Toll-Free: 888-603-4178
info@cihr-irsc.gc.ca
www.cihr-irsc.gc.ca
Promotes health research excellence in Canada through training & funding programs in basic, clinical, health systems & services, & population health research. Research is carried out in universities, in the health sciences faculties, affiliated hospitals & institutions & other faculties where research projects are highly relevant to human health. University-Industry programs create the opportunity for collaboration between Canadian companies & researchers conducting research in Canadian universities or affiliated institutions. Also manages the health-related Networks of Centres of Excellence.

President, Alain Beaudet
Tel: 613-954-1808

Executive Vice-President, Christine Fitzgerald
Tel: 613-957-6134

Vice-President, Knowledge Translation & Public Outreach, Ian Graham
Tel: 613-948-2318

Executive Director, Secretariat on Research Ethics, Susan Zimmerman
Tel: 613-947-7148

Director, PAN - Institute Affairs & Initiatives, Terry Campbell
Tel: 613-960-6211

Director, Ethics Office, Geneviève Dubois-Flynn
Tel: 613-954-1801

Director, Human Resources, Diane Massicotte
Tel: 613-957-8762

Director, Evaluations, Internal Audit & Risk Management, Martin Rubenstein
Tel: 613-941-3557

Director, Communications & Marketing, Karen Spierkel
Tel: 613-954-1812

Institute of Population & Public Health (IPPH) / Institut de la santé publique et des populations (ISPP)
#124, 1 Stewart St., Ottawa, ON K1N 6N5
ipph@cihr-irsc.gc.ca
www.cihr-irsc.gc.ca
One of 13 CIHR Institutes, IPPH focuses on the interactions (biological, social, cultural, environmental) that determine the health of individuals, communities & global populations. Research includes environment & health issues, such as radiation, contaminants, ecosystems & air quality.
Scientific Director, Nancy Edwards
Tel: 613-562-5800 ext: 841
nedwards@uottawa.ca

Canadian International Development Agency (CIDA) / Agence canadienne de développement international (ACDI)

200, Promenade du Portage, Gatineau, QC K1A 0G4
Tel: 819-997-5456
Fax: 819-953-6088
Toll-Free: 800-230-6349
TTY: 819-953-5023
info@acdi-cida.gc.ca
www.acdi-cida.gc.ca
Other Communication: Toll-Free TTY: 1-800-331-5018
Major agency responsible for delivering most of Canada's foreign aid. CIDA is committed to supporting sustainable development in developing countries to meet the needs of current & future generations. The mission statement demands that criteria of sustainability be integrated into each project undertaken by the Agency in order to improve the economic, social, cultural, ecological & political condition of the world's developing nations. Many of the projects CIDA supports are aimed directly at the environment. Projects include reforestation & watershed rehabilitation, small scale fishing development (to increase output & food), water projects (to improve health), increased food production, improved rural quality, & supply & generation of electricity. Various other projects help nations develop the legal & administrative framework needed to promote environmentally sustainable development.

Minister, International Cooperation, Hon. Julian Fantino, P.C., C.O.M., O. Ont.
Tel: 819-953-6238
Fax: 819-953-8525
julian.fantino@parl.gc.ca

Parliamentary Secretary to the Minister of International Cooperation, Lois Brown
Tel: 613-992-9310
Fax: 613-992-9407

Chief of Staff, Neil Desai
Tel: 819-953-6238

Executive Director & General Counsel, Legal Services Division, Winston Fogarty
Tel: 819-994-0809
Fax: 819-953-3771

Director, Policy, Idee Inyangudor
Tel: 819-953-6238
Fax: 819-953-8525

Director, Communications, Meagan Murdoch
Tel: 819-953-6238
Fax: 819-953-8525

Press Secretary, Daniel Bezalel Richardsen
Tel: 819-953-6238

Administrative Officer, Claudine Taillefer
Tel: 819-997-6912

Geographic Programs Branch (GPB) / Direction générale des programmes géographiques (DGPG)
Senior Vice-President, David Morrison
Tel: 819-997-1666
Director General, Planning, Operations & Specialists Directorate, Isabelle Bérard
Tel: 819-994-5961
Acting Regional Director General, Southern & Eastern Africa, Philip Baker
Tel: 819-997-1322
Regional Director General, Americas, Lise Filiatrault
Tel: 819-934-0301
Regional Director General, Europe, Middle East, Maghreb, Afghanistan & Pakistan, Bob Johnston
Tel: 819-994-2041
Acting Regional Director General, Asia, Jeff Nankivell
Tel: 819-953-5044
Acting Regional Director General, West & Central Africa, Susan Steffen
Tel: 819-997-0477

Multilateral & Global Programs Branch / Direction générale des programmes multilatéraux et mondiaux
Vice-President, Diane Jacovella
Tel: 819-997-7537
Fax: 819-953-5348
Director General, Strategic Planning, Integration & Management Directorate, Christine Campbell
Tel: 819-994-3945
Fax: 819-934-5269
Director General, International Humanitarian Assistance Directorate, Leslie Norton
Tel: 819-997-2750
Fax: 819-997-2637
Director General, Multilateral Development Institutions Directorate, Paul Samson
Tel: 819-994-3967
Director General, Global Initiatives Directorate, David Stevenson
Tel: 819-997-0919
Director, Health & Education Programming & Institutions Division, Pierre Blais
Tel: 819-934-8005
Director, Humanitarian Assistance Division, Stephen Salewicz
Tel: 819-934-1553
Fax: 819-997-2637
Manager, Global Environment & Climate Finance Unit, Michelle Kaminski
Tel: 819-934-8538

Office of the Chief Audit Executive (OCAE) / Bureau du dirigeant principal de la vérification (BDV)
Chief Audit Executive, Jean Goulet
Tel: 819-994-0714
Acting Director, Audit Operations Division, Jean-Marc Lafrenière
Tel: 819-994-0683

Partnerships with Canadians Branch (PWCB) / Direction générale des partenariats avec les Canadiens (DGPC)
Vice-President, Darren Schemmer
Tel: 819-997-6057
Fax: 819-997-0602

President's Office / Bureau de la présidente
Fax: 819-953-3352
President, Margaret Biggs
Tel: 819-997-7951
Fax: 819-953-3352
Senior Executive Vice-President, Greta Bossenmaier
Tel: 819-934-6553
Acting Vice-President, Business Modernization Initiative, Nadia Kostiuk
Tel: 819-997-1643
Director General, International Operations, Reid Sirrs
Tel: 819-956-3074

Canadian Museum of Nature (CMN) / Musée Canadien de la Nature (MCN)

PO Box 3443 Stn. D, Ottawa, ON K1P 6P4
Tel: 613-566-4700
Fax: 613-364-4021
Toll-Free: 800-263-4433
TTY: 613-566-4770
www.nature.ca
Other Communication: Toll-Free TTY: 1-866-600-8801
A diverse natural history collection encompassing some 10 million specimens, & thousands of species. Provides access to specimens & data for research & access to knowledge on biodiversity, biosystematics & the environment. Carries out research on management & care of collections & employs a staff of researchers working on national & international projects. Through public programs, CMN communicates knowledge & promotes understanding of science & nature to diverseaudiences. It includes permanent, special & travelling exhibits, curriculum-based & interpretive programs, & print, electronic, audiovisual & multimedia publications.

Canadian Centre for Biodiversity (CCB) / Centre canadien de la biodiversité
Canadian Museum of Nature
nature.ca
A repository for the understanding, interpretation & dissemination of knowledge on biodiversity & conservation issues. The Centre supports & participates in the activities of COSEWIC (Committee of the Status of Endangered Wildlife in Canada) & the Ecological Monitoring & Assessment Network (EMAN), the Working Group on Museums & Sustainable Communities. It is home to the Secretariat for the Canadian Committee for IUCN - the World Conservation Union. The Biological Survey acts as a clearing house & source of information on insects & related animals of general concern to biologists.
Chief, Anne Breau
Tel: 613-566-4795
Fax: 613-364-4022
abreau@mus-nature.ca
Environmental Specialist, Jean Lauriault
Tel: 613-566-4217
Fax: 613-364-4022
jlauriault@mus-nature.ca

Canadian Northern Economic Development Agency (CanNor) / Agence canadienne de développement économique du Nord

Ottawa, ON K1A 0H4
Fax: 866-817-3977
Toll-Free: 800-567-9604
TTY: 866-553-0554
InfoNorth-InfoNord@CanNor.gc.ca
www.cannor.gc.ca
Other Communication: NU Phone: 867-975-3734, E-mail: ecdevnunavut@cannor.gc.ca; NT Phone: 867-766-8327, E-mail: ecdevnwt@cannor.gc.ca; YT Phone: 867-667-3263, E-mail ytinfo@cannor.gc.ca
Inuksugait Plaza IIPO Box 40 Sta.
Iqaluit, NU X0A 0H0
CanNor was established in 2009 to promote growth & development in Northern Canada through economic development programs & collaboration between northern & southern partnerships. The agency also coordinates the activities of other federal departments in relation to northern project development through the Northern Projects Management Office (NPMO). Programs offered by the agency include: Strategic Investments in Northern Economic Development (SINED); Aboriginal Economic Development (AED); Northern Adult Basic Education Program (NABEP); Community Infrastructure Improvement Fund (CIIF); & promotion of official language minority communities.

Minister, Canadian Northern Economic Development Agency; Minister, Health; Minister for the Arctic Council, Hon. Leona Aglukkaq, P.C.
Tel: 613-992-2848
Fax: 613-996-9764
leona.aglukkaq@parl.gc.ca

Deputy Minister & President, Patrick Borbey
Tel: 613-947-0221
Fax: 613-947-0242

Northern Projects Management Office (NPMO) / Bureau de gestion des projets nordiques
Nova Plaza, 5019 - 52nd St., 3rd Fl., PO Box 1500Yellowknife, NT X1A 2R3
Tel: 867-920-6766
The NMPO provides the following services: issues management & advice for industry & communities; coordinating the participation of federal departments in the regulatory review process; providing transparency through publicly tracking the progress of projects.
Director General, Matthew Spence
Tel: 867-766-8439
Fax: 867-766-8469
Iqaluit
Allavvik Bldg., 1106 Inuksugait Plaza, PO Box 40Iqaluit, NU X0A 0H0
Acting Director General, Operations, Peter Rinaldi
Tel: 867-975-3721
Fax: 867-975-3724
Executive Director, Nunavut Federal Council, Hagar Idlout-Sudlovenick
Tel: 867-975-4771
Fax: 867-975-4773
Regional Director, Sylvie Renaud
Tel: 867-975-3737
Fax: 867-975-3740
Ottawa
400 Cooper St., 5th Fl., Ottawa, ON K1A 0H4
Chief Financial Officer & Director, Corporate Services, Yves Robineau
Tel: 613-992-5072
Fax: 613-995-9495
Vice-President, Policy, Planning, Communications & NPMO, Mitch Bloom
Tel: 613-995-9432
Fax: 613-995-9472
Whitehorse
#215, 305 Main St., Whitehorse, YT V1A 2B3
Regional Director, Michael Bloor
Tel: 867-667-3310
Fax: 867-667-3801
Yellowknife
Nova Plaza, 5019 - 52nd St., 3rd Fl., PO Box 1500Yellowknife, NT X1A 2R3
Executive Director, Northwest Territories Federal Council, Trevor Sinclair
Tel: 867-766-8451
Regional Director, Kevin Lewis
Tel: 867-766-8405
Fax: 867-766-8401

Canadian Nuclear Safety Commission (CNSC) / Commission canadienne de sûreté nucléaire (CCSN)

280 Slater St., PO Box 1046 Stn. B, Ottawa, ON K1P 5S9
Tel: 613-995-5894
Fax: 613-995-5086
Toll-Free: 800-668-5284
www.nuclearsafety.gc.ca
Federal agency which regulates activities involving nuclear energy & prescribed substances in the interests of health & safety for workers & the public. Areas covered under the AECB's licensing process include the nuclear fuel cycle (from mining to waste disposal), heavy water plants, research reactors & accelerators, & radioisotopes. Operations ensure that the use of nuclear energy in Canada does not pose undue risk to health, safety, security & the environment. The Research & Support Program (RSP) augments & extends the AECB's regulatory program beyond the capability of in-house resources. It produces pertinent & independent information that will assist the Board & its staff in making sound, timely & credible decisions on regulating nuclear facilities & materials. The nine sectors of the program include: safety of nuclear facilities; radioactive waste management; health physics; physical security; development of regulatory processes; & social services

President, Michael Binder
Tel: 613-992-8828
Fax: 613-995-5086

Executive Vice-President/Chief Regulatory Operations Officer, Ramzi Jammal
Tel: 613-947-8899
Fax: 613-995-5086
Other Communications: Executive Assistant, Phone: 613-947-8896

Vice-President/CSB & Chief Financial Officer, Corporate Services Branch, Michel Cavallin
Tel: 613-995-0104
Fax: 613-995-5086
Other Communications: Executive Assistant, Phone: 613-992-4543

Vice-President, Technical Support Branch, Terry Jamieson
Tel: 613-947-8931
Fax: 613-995-5086
Other Communications: Executive Assistant, Phone: 613-996-0260

Vice-President, Regulatory Affairs, Gordon White
Tel: 613-943-7662
Fax: 613-995-5086
Other Communications: Executive Assistant, Phone: 613-996-9505

Director General, Security & Safeguards, Raoul R. Awad
Tel: 613-992-2943
Fax: 613-995-5086

Director General, Strategic Planning, Jason K. Cameron
Tel: 613-947-3773
Fax: 613-995-5086

Director General, Finance & Administration, Stéphane Cyr
Tel: 613-995-8273
Fax: 613-995-5086

Director General, Regulatory Policy, Mark Dallaire
Tel: 613-947-3728
Fax: 613-995-5086

Director General, Nuclear Cycle & Facilities Regulation, Peter H. Elder
Tel: 613-943-8948
Fax: 613-995-5086

Director General, Assessment & Analysis, Gerry Frappier
Tel: 613-995-2031
Fax: 613-995-5086

Director General, Safety Management, Kathleen Heppell-Masys
Tel: 613-991-3220
Fax: 613-995-5086

Director General, Regulatory Improvement & Major Projects Management, Barclay Howden
Tel: 613-943-0179
Fax: 613-995-5086

Director General, Nuclear Substance Regulation, André Régimbald
Tel: 613-993-7699
Fax: 613-995-5086

Director General, Information Management & Technology, Hugh Robertson
Tel: 613-949-9498
Fax: 613-995-5086

Director General, Power Reactor Regulation, Greg Rzentkowski
Tel: 613-995-2655
Fax: 613-995-5086

Director General, Environmental & Radiation Protection & Assessment, Patsy Thompson
Tel: 613-947-3352
Fax: 613-995-5086

Canadian Polar Commission (CPC) / Commission canadienne des affaires polaires (CCAP)

Constitution Square, #1710, 360 Albert St., Ottawa, ON K1R 7X7
Tel: 613-943-8605
Fax: 613-943-8607
Toll-Free: 888-765-2701
mail@polarcom.gc.ca
www.polarcom.gc.ca
Mandated to enhance the public's awareness of polar regions & to foster both international & domestic liaison & cooperation in circumpolar research & technology development. One of the Commission's main objectives in the short term is focus on climate change & energy. Maintains the Canadian Polar Information System (CPIS) which, in addition to polar data & information, includes services such as the Polar Science Forum, Researcher's Directory, Researcher's Toolbox, & links to International Partners. In September 2005, the federal government announced it will provide $150 million in new funding over six years for International Polar Year 2007-2008, an international research program.

Chair, Bernard Funston

Executive Director, Steven Bigras
Tel: 613-943-8606
steven.bigras@polarcom.gc.ca

Manager, Information, John Bennett
Tel: 613-943-0716
Fax: 613-943-8607
john.bennett@polarcom.gc.ca

Senior Science Advisor, Jean-Marie Beaulieu
Tel: 613-947-9108
Fax: 613-943-8607
jean-marie.beaulieu@polarcom.gc.ca

Executive Secretary, Sandy Bianchini
Tel: 613-943-8605

Financial Analyst, Tom Egan
Tel: 613-943-0718
Fax: 613-943-8607

Polar Research Analyst, Laurie Buckland
laurie.buckland@polarcom.gc.ca

Canadian Space Agency (CSA) / Agence spatiale canadienne (ASC)

John H. Chapman Space Centre, 6767, rte de l'Aéroport, Saint-Hubert, QC J3Y 8Y9
Tel: 450-926-4800
Fax: 450-926-4352
promo@asc-csa.gc.ca
www.asc-csa.gc.ca
Other Communication: Client Services, Phone: 450-926-4351
Established in 1989, & responsible for coordinating all civil, space-related policies & programs on behalf of the Government of Canada. Scientific research & industrial development in earth observation, space science & exploration, satellite communications, & space awareness & learning. RADARSAT International (RSI) develops products & services demanded by world markets. RADARSAT-1, the first Canadian commercial Earth Observation (EO) satellite, is uniquely capable of responding to disasters around the world. The system can support the operational mapping & monitoring of natural disasters in four critical ways: prevention, preparedness, emergency response & recovery. Moreover, the development of the high performance RADARSAT-2 to be launched in 2007, will further enhance Canada's competitive position. RADARSAT-2 will offer improved quality of data images to meet the growing world demand of Earth observation information. The SCISAT satellite is used in ozone depletion research.

Minister, Industry; Minister Responsible, Canadian Space Agency, Hon. Christian Paradis
Tel: 613-995-9001
Fax: 613-992-0302
Minister.Industry@ic.gc.ca

President & Chief Astronaut, Steven MacLean
Tel: 450-926-4301
Fax: 450-926-4315

Vice-President, Chummer Farina
Tel: 613-998-5284
Fax: 613-990-4994

Chief Financial Officer, Marie-Claude Guerard
Tel: 450-926-4407
Fax: 450-926-4424

Chief Information Officer, Charles Ouellette
Tel: 450-926-4851

Chief, Management & Liaison Services, Agathe Jérôme
Tel: 613-991-3250
Fax: 613-990-4994

Chief, Human Resources Officer, Yves Saulnier
Tel: 450-926-4815
Fax: 450-926-5194

Chief of the Astronauts, Jean-Marc Comtois
Tel: 450-926-4755

Director General, Space Science, David Kendall
Tel: 450-926-4770
Fax: 450-926-4766

Director General, Space Exploration, Gilles Leclerc
Tel: 450-926-4606
Fax: 450-926-4323

Director General, Corporate Services, Benoît Marcotte
Tel: 450-926-4667
Fax: 450-926-4612

Director General, Space Utilization, Savi Sachdev
Tel: 450-926-4461
Fax: 450-926-6521

Canadian Transportation Agency (CTA) / Office des transports du Canada (OTC)

Les Terrasses de la Chaudière, 15, rue Eddy, Gatineau, QC J8X 4B3
Fax: 819-997-6727
Toll-Free: 888-222-2592
TTY: 800-669-5575
info@otc-cta.gc.ca
www.cta-otc.gc.ca
Responsible for the economic regulation of transportation in Canada. The agency requires that all applications for new railway lines, modifications to existing railway lines, disputed railway crossings at grade, grade separation, utility crossings & private crossings be accompanied by an environment impact assessment

Chair & Chief Executive Officer, Geoffrey C. Hare
Tel: 819-997-9233
Fax: 819-953-9979
geoffrey.hare@otc-cta.gc.ca

Vice-Chair, John Scott
Tel: 819-953-8915
Fax: 819-953-9979
john.scott@otc-cta.gc.ca

Director General, Industry Regulation & Determinations Branch, Ghislain Blanchard
Tel: 819-953-4657
Fax: 819-994-8807
ghislain.blanchard@otc-cta.gc.ca

Director General, Dispute Resolution Branch, Nina Frid
Tel: 819-953-5074
Fax: 819-953-5562
nina.frid@otc-cta.gc.ca

Director General, Corporate Management Branch, Arun Thangaraj
Tel: 819-997-6764
Fax: 819-953-9842

Senior Director, Regulatory Approvals & Compliance Directorate, Carole Girard
Tel: 819-997-8761
Fax: 819-953-5562
carole.girard@otc-cta.gc.ca

Director, Communications Directorate, Jacqueline Bannister
Tel: 819-953-7666
Fax: 819-953-8353
jacqueline.bannister@otc-cta.gc.ca

Director, Rail, Air & Marine Disputes Directorate, Joseph Dion
Tel: 819-953-0327
Fax: 819-953-8353
joseph.dion@otc-cta.gc.ca

Senior Counsel, Legal Services, Claude Jacques
Tel: 819-997-9323
Fax: 819-953-9269
claude.jacques@otc-cta.gc.ca

Minister, Citizenship, Immigration, & Multiculturalism, Hon. Jason Kenney
Tel: 613-992-2235
Fax: 613-992-1920
jason.kenney@parl.gc.ca

Defence Construction Canada (DCC) / Construction de Défense Canada (CDC)

Constitution Square, 350 Albert St., 19th Fl., Ottawa, ON K1A 0K3
Tel: 613-998-9548
Fax: 613-998-1061
Toll-Free: 800-514-3555
info@dcc-cdc.gc.ca
www.dcc-cdc.gc.ca
Federal government crown corporation responsible for the contracting & supervising of major military construction & maintenance projects required by National Defence. Services include construction, project management, environmental services & operational support services. DCC provides environmental science & environmental engineering services to help fulfill the Department of National Defence's sustainable development strategy, including: environmental impact & site assessment; environmental site remediation; environmental support for project & program management; sustainable development strategy support services; policy, compliance & advisory services; site decommissioning services; facility deconstruction & demolition; firing range decommissioning; waste management auditing & planning; waste reduction planning; landfill inventories & investigations; hazardous waste management; UST removals; training & education; ISO 14000 environmental management systems; environmental CIS applications; environmental checklists for property transactions & decommissioning; environmental monitoring & compliance auditing; designated substances inventories; environmental disclosures reporting; treatment & disposal facilities conceptual designs; environmental contrac ting & contract management; energy conservation. Projects include: the DEW (Distant Early Warning) Line cleanup, a dismantling of the DEW sites, scheduled for completion in 2012, & a major environmental project in the Canadian Arctic; green demolition at CFB Comox; biodiesel pilot program at 4 Wing Cold Lake, launched in 2005

President & Chief Executive Officer, James S. Paul
Tel: 613-998-9541
Fax: 613-998-1218

Senior Vice-President, Operations, Ron de Vries, P.Eng
Tel: 613-998-9543
Fax: 613-998-1218

Vice-President, Operations, Steve Irwin, P.Eng
Tel: 613-949-7721
Fax: 613-998-1218

Vice-President, Operations, Randy McGee, P.Eng., GSC
Tel: 613-949-0052
Fax: 613-998-1218

Vice-President, Corporate Services & CFO, Angelo Ottoni, C.A.
Tel: 613-998-1001

Director, Atlantic Region, Business Operations - Atlantic Region, Ross Welsman, P.Eng., PMP
Tel: 902-426-5640
Fax: 902-426-9655

#202, 1597 Bedford Hwy.
Bedford, NS B4A 1E7

Manager, Operations Coordination, Business Operations - Atlantic Region, George Theoharopoulos
Tel: 902-426-4040
Fax: 902-426-9655

Director, Ontario Region, Environmental Services - Ontario, John Graham, P.Eng., PMP
Tel: 613-384-1256 ext: 230
Fax: 613-384-7747
Howard Maitland Building
#205, 780 Midpark Dr.
Kingston, ON K7M 7P6

Manager, Environmental Services - Ontario, Dennis Katic
Tel: 613-384-1256 ext: 227
Fax: 613-384-7747

Director, Quebec Region, Environmental Services - Québec, Marc Lanteigne, P.Eng.
Tel: 514-496-2729
Fax: 514-283-8347
Village olympique Pyramide Ouest
#2700, 5199, rue Sherbrooke est
Montréal, QC H1T 3X2

Manager, Environmental Services - Québec, Alain Dufresne
Tel: 514-283-8165
Fax: 514-283-8347

Director, Western Region, Environmental Services - Western Region, Stephen G. Karpyshin, P.Eng.
Tel: 780-495-2555
Fax: 780-495-5959
#210, 13220 St. Albert Trail
Edmonton, AB T5L 4W1

Manager, Environmental Services - Western Region, Sabrina Rock
Tel: 780-495-3979
Fax: 780-495-5959

Director, Contract Services, Contract Services, Melinda Nycholat, P.Eng., PMP
Tel: 613-991-9313
Fax: 613-998-9547
Constitution Square
350 Albert St., 17th Fl.
Ottawa, ON K1A 0K3

Executive Administrative Assistant, Claire Péladeau
Tel: 613-991-3475
Fax: 613-998-1218

Environment Canada (EC) / Environnement Canada

10 Wellington St., Gatineau, QC K1A 0H3
Tel: 819-997-2800
Fax: 819-994-1412
Toll-Free: 800-668-6767
TTY: 819-994-0736
enviroinfo@ec.gc.ca
www.ec.gc.ca
Other Communication: Environmental Emergencies (24-hour): 819-997-3742; TTY: 819-994-0736
Fosters a national capacity for sustainable development in cooperation with other governments, departments of government & the private sector that will result in a safe & healthy environment & a sound & prosperous economy by: undertaking & promoting programs to augment understanding of the environment; supporting environmentally responsible public & private decision-making; warning Canadians of risks to & from the environment; engaging Canadians as partners in measurably beneficial action to conserve, protect & restore the integrity of Canada's environment for the benefit of present & future generations.
Acts Administered:
Acts Administered in Part by Environment Canada
Acts in which Environment Canada Provides Assistance
Administration, Management & Control of Certain Public Lands
Agricultural & Rural Development Act (Agriculture & Agri-Foods)
Air Pollution Regulations
Alberta Equivalency Order
Alternative Fuels Act & Regulations (Treasury Board)
Antarctic Environmental Protection Act
Arctic Shipping Pollution Prevention Regulations
Arctic Waters Pollution Prevention Act
Arctic Waters Pollution Prevention Regulations
Asbestos Mines & Mills Release Regulations
Atomic Energy Control Act
Auditor General Act (Treasury Board)
Benzene in Gasoline Regulations
Canada Agricultural Products Act
Canada Emission Reduction Incentives Agency Act
Canada Marine Act (Transport Canada)
Canada Oil & Gas Certificate of Fitness Regulations
Canada Oil & Gas Drilling Regulations
Canada Oil & Gas Geophysical Operations Regulations
Canada Oil & Gas Operations Act (Indian & Northern Affairs/Natural Resources)
Canada Oil & Gas Operations Regulations
Canada Oil & Gas Production & Conservation Regulations
Canada Petroleum Resources Act (Indian Affairs & Northern Development/Natural Resouces)
Canada Port Authority Environmental Assessment Regulations
Canada Shipping Act
Canada Water Act
Canada Wildlife Act
Canada-Chile Free Trade Agreement Implementation Act (International Trade)
Canada-Newfoundland Atlantic Accord Implementation Act
Canada-Nova Scotia Offshore Petroleum Resources Accord Implementation Act
Canadian Environment Week Act
Canadian Environmental Assessment Act
Canadian Environmental Protection Act
Canadian Transportation Accident Investigation & Safety Board Act (Privy Council)
Chlor-alkali Mercury Liquid Effluent Regulations
Chlor-Alkali, Mercury Release Regulations
Chlorobiphenyls Regulations
Clean Air Act
Comprehensive Study List Regulation
Contaminated Fuel Regulations
Controlled Products Regulations
Dangerous Chemicals & Noxious Liquid Substances Regulations
Department of the Environment Act
Disposal at Sea Regulations
Electricity Regulations
Emergency Preparedness Act (National Defence)
Energy Supplies Emergency Act (National Research)
Environment Canada Related Acts & Regulations
Environmental Emergency Regulations
Environmental Studies Research Fund Regions Regulations
Exclusion List Regulation
Export & Import of Hazardous Wastes Regulations
Export Control List of Notification Regulations
Export of Substances under the Rotterdam Convention Regulations
Federal Authorities Regulations
Federal Halocarbon Regulations
Federal Mobile PCB Treatment & Destruction Regulations
Federal Registration of Storage Tank Systems for Petroleum Products & Allied Petroleum Products on Federal Lands or Aboriginal Lands Regulations
Fisheries Act (Fisheries & Oceans)
Food & Drugs Act (Agriculture & Agri-Foods/Health Canada)
Fuels Information Regulations, No. 1
Garbage Pollution Prevention Regulations
Gasoline & Gasoline Blend Dispensing Flow Rate Regulations
Gasoline Regulations
Great Lakes Sewage Pollution Prevention Regulations
Hazardous Products Act (Health Canada)
Inclusion List Regulation
International Boundary Waters Treaty Act (Foreign Affairs)
International River Improvements Act
Interprovincial Movement of Hazardous Waste Regulations
James Bay & Northern Québec Native Claims Settlement Act
Kemano Completion Project Guidelines Order
Lac Seul Conservation Act
Lake of the Woods Control Board Act
Law List Regulation
List of Hazardous Waste Authorities
List of Toxic Substances Authorities
Mackenzie Valley Resource Management Act (Indian & Northern Affairs)
Manganese-Based Fuel Additives Act
Masked Name Regulations
Meat & Poultry Products Plant Liquid Effluent Regulations
Metal Mining Effluent Regulations
Migratory Bird Regulations
Migratory Bird Sanctuary Regulations
Migratory Birds Convention Act
Motor Vehicle Safety Act (Transport)
National Energy Board Act (Natural Resources/Transport Canada)
National Round Table on the Environment & the Economy Act (Prime Minister)
National Wildlife Week Act
New Substances Fees Regulations
New Substances Notification Regulations
Newfoundland Offshore Area Oil & Gas Operations Regulations
Newfoundland Offshore Area Petroleum Geophysical Operations Regulations
Newfoundland Offshore Area Petroleum Production & Conservation Regulations
Newfoundland Offshore Certificate of Fitness Regulations
Newfoundland Offshore Petroleum Drilling Regulations
Newfoundland Offshore Petroleum Installations Regulations
Non-Pleasure Craft Sewage Pollution Prevention Regulations
North American Free Trade Agreement Implementation Act
Northern Pipeline Act (Natural Resources)
Northern Pipeline Socio-Economic & Environmental Terms & Conditions (Northern BC, Southern BC, AB, SK & Swift River Portion in BC)
Nova Scotia Offshore Petroleum Drilling Regulations
Oceans Act (Fisheries & Oceans)
Off-Road Small Spark-Ignition Engine Emission Regulations
Oil & Gas Regulations
Oil Pollution Prevention Regulations
On-Road Vehicle & Engine Emission Regulations
Onshore Pipeline Regulations
Ozone Depleting Substances Regulations
PCB Waste Export Regulations
Persistence & Bioaccumulation Regulations
Pest Control Products Act & Regulations (Health Canada)
Petroleum Refinery Liquid Effluent Regulations
Phosphorus Concentration Regulations
Pleasure Craft Sewage Pollution Prevention Regulations
Pollutant Discharge Reporting Regulations
Pollutant Substances Regulations
Port Alberni Pulp & Paper Effluent Regulations
Potato Processing Plant Liquid Effluent Regulations
Prohibition of Certain Toxic Substances
Projects Outside Canada Environmental Assessment Regulations
Pulp & Paper Effluent Regulations
Pulp & Paper Mill Defoamer & Wood Chip Regulations
Pulp & Paper Mill Effluent Chlorinated Dioxins & Furans Regulations
Regulations respecting Applications for Permits for Disposal at Sea
Resources & Technical Surveys Act (Natural Resources/Fisheries & Oceans)
Rules for Procedures for Boards of Review
Rules of Practice & Procedure
Secondary Lead Smelter Release Regulations
Ship-Source Oil Pollution Fund Regulations
Solvent Degreasing Regulations
Species at Risk Act, 2002
Storage of PCB Material Regulations
Sulphur in Diesel Fuel Regulations
Sulphur in Gasoline Regulations
Tetrachloroethylene (Use in Dry Cleaning & Reporting Requirements) Regulations
Transport Packaging of Radioactive Materials Regulations
Transportation of Dangerous Goods Act & Regulations (Transport Canada)
Transportation Safety Board Regulations
Tributyltetradeclyphosphonium Chloride Regulations
Uranium & Thorium Mining Regulations
Vinyl Chloride Release Regulations
Weather Modification Information Act
Wild Animal & Plant Protection & Regulation of International & Interprovincial Trade Act
Wildlife Area Regulations

Minister, Environment, Hon. Peter Kent
Tel: 819-997-1441
Fax: 819-953-0279
minister@ec.gc.ca

Deputy Minister, Bob Hamilton

Tel: 819-997-4203
Fax: 819-953-6897

Associate Deputy Minister, Andrea Lyon
Tel: 819-997-4203
Fax: 819-953-6897

Executive Assistant Deputy Minister, Debra Tompkins-Caron
Tel: 819-994-5020

Director General, Corporate Secretariat, Pierre Bernier
Tel: 819-953-2743
Fax: 819-953-0749

Director, Values, Integrity & Disclosure, Claude M. Chartrand
Tel: 819-953-4605
Fax: 819-956-5585

Director, Parliamentary Affairs, Lori Dawe
Tel: 819-997-1441

Associated Agencies, Boards & Commissions:
• Committee on the Status of Endangered Wildlife in Canada (COSEWIC) / Comité sur la situation des espèces en péril au Canada
c/o Canadian Wildlife Service
351 St. Joseph Blvd, 4th Fl.
Gatineau, QC K1A 0H3
Tel: 819-953-3215
Fax: 819-994-3684
cosewic/cosepac@ec.gc.ca
www.cosewic.gc.ca
Other Communication: Species at Risk Act Public Registry: www.sararegistry.gc.ca
Committee of experts that assesses & designates which wild species are in some danger of disappearing from Canada. COSEWIC determines the national status of wild Canadian species, subspecies & separate populations suspected of being at risk. COSEWIC bases its decisions on the best up-to-date scientific information & Aboriginal traditional knowledge available. All native mammals, birds, reptiles, amphibians, fish, mollusks, lepidopterans (butterflies & moths), vascular plants, mosses & lichens are included in its current mandate. In its 2010 Annual report, COSEWIC's assessment results indicate there are 602 species in the risk category (extirpated, endangered, threatened or of special concern) & 13 species found to be extinct.
Chair, Dr. Marty L. Leonard
Tel: 902-494-2158
Fax: 902-494-3736
mleonard@dal.ca
• North American Waterfowl Management Plan (NAWMP) / Le plan nord-américain de gestion de la sauvagine
NAWCC (Canada) Secretariat, Place Vincent Massey
351 St. Joseph Blvd., 7th Fl.
Gatineau, QC K1A 0H3
Tel: 819-934-6034
Fax: 819-934-6017
nawmp@ec.gc.ca
www.nawmp.ca
The North American Waterfowl Management Plan is an international action plan to conserve migratory birds throughout the continent. The Plan's goal is to return waterfowl populations to their 1970's levels by conserving wetland & upland habitat. Canada & the United States signed the Plan in 1986 in reaction to critically low numbers of waterfowl. Mexico joined in 1994 making it a truly continental effort. The Plan is a partnership of federal, provincial/state & municipal governments, non-governmental organizations, private companies & many individuals, all working towards achieving better wetland habitat for the benefit of migratory birds, other wetland-associated species & people. The Plan's unique combination of biology, landscape conservation & partnerships comprise its exemplary conservation legacy. Plan projects are international in scope, but implemented at regional levels. These projects contribute to the protection of habitat & wildlife species across the North American landscape.
• North American Bird Conservation Initiative (NABCI)
Canadian Wildlife Service
351, boul St-Joseph, 3e étage
Gatineau, QC K1A 0H3
Tel: 819-994-0512
Fax: 819-994-4445
nabci@ec.gc.ca
www.nabci.net
The NABCI is a coordinated effort among Canada, the United States & Mexico to maintain the diversity & abundance of all North American birds. National coordination of this effort in Canada occurs through the NABCI Canada Council, chaired by the Asst. Deputy Minister of Environment Canada's Environmental Conservation Service. Council members include representatives from provincial governments, non-government organizations, four bird plans (waterfowl, landbirds, shorebirds, waterbirds), & habitat joint ventures. In Canada, the joint venture conservation projects has three habitat joint ventures (Pacific Coast, Prairie Habitat, Eastern Habitat) & three species (Arctic Goose, Black Duck, Sea Duck.)
Canadian Coordinator, Martin Damus
martin.damus@ec.gc.ca

Corporate Services Branch / Direction générale des services ministériels
Tel: 819-934-4151
Fax: 819-934-7975
Acting Assistant Deputy Minister, George Enei
Tel: 819-994-3634
Fax: 819-934-7975
Director General, Business Applications & Solutions Directorate, Denis Benoit
Tel: 819-934-1523
Acting Director General, Infrastructure Operations Directorate, Carl Girard
Tel: 819-934-4562
Fax: 819-994-4224
Director General, Major Projects & Supercomputing Directorate, Mike Minuk
Tel: 514-421-4765
Fax: 514-421-4703
Director, MSC Regional Operations Renewal, Susan Wild
Tel: 416-739-4799
Fax: 416-739-4999
4905 Dufferin St.
Toronto, ON M3H 5T4

Enforcement Branch / Direction générale de l'application de la loi
351 boul St-Joseph, Gatineau, QC K1A 0H3
Tel: 819-997-2019
Fax: 819-997-0086
The Branch is built around the principle of ensuring that companies & individuals comply with the pollution prevention & conservation goals of environmental & wildlife protection acts & regulations. Enforcement is delivered through the work of in-the-field enforcement officers across Canada working through the Environmental Enforcement Directorate & The Wildlife Enforcement Directorate. Their work is carried out in cooperation with other federal, provincial & territorial governments & with international organizations involved in enforcement such as the United States Fish & Wildlife Service, the United States Environmental Protection Agency & Interpol.
Chief Enforcement Officer, Gordon T. Owen
Tel: 819-997-2019
Fax: 819-997-0086
National Director, Environmental Enforcement, Manon Bombardier
Tel: 819-953-1523
Fax: 819-953-3459
National Director, Enforcement Services, Kim Hibbeln
Tel: 819-997-4712
Fax: 819-994-0724
National Director, Wildlife Enforcement, Sheldon Jordan
Tel: 819-956-1969
Fax: 819-997-0086
Acting Director, Strategic Policy, Planning & Coordination Directorate, Marc Sicard
Tel: 819-953-0331
Fax: 819-210-7398
Branch Administration Officer, Management Services, Suzanne Chevalier
Tel: 819-953-1173
Fax: 819-994-5836

Environmental Stewardship Branch / Direction générale de l'intendance environnementale
351 boul St-Joseph, Gatineau, QC K1A 0H3
Tel: 819-997-1575
Fax: 819-953-9452
Assessment & management of risk associated with domestic & international sources of pollution. The range of activity is broad, assessment of substances & practices that pose a risk to the environment, development & implementation of environmental protection measures including pollution prevention, regulations, permits & technology advancement & ensuring compliance with federal pollution & wildlife laws. These activities lead to improvements in environmental quality which helps to support the health of Canadians & their economic security.
Assistant Deputy Minister, Coleen Volk
Tel: 819-953-1711
Fax: 819-953-9452
Associate Assistant Deputy Minister, Mike Beale
Tel: 819-956-9500
Director General, Chemicals Sector, Margaret Kenny
Tel: 819-934-4960
Fax: 819-953-3213
Director General, Energy & Transportation, Steve McCauley
Tel: 819-997-1298
Fax: 819-953-9547
Director General, Public & Resources Sectors, Randall Meades
Tel: 819-934-4205
Director General, Strategic Priorities, Louise Métivier
Tel: 819-994-5022
Fax: 819-953-7941
Director General, Environmental Protection Operations, Sue Milburn-Hopwood
Tel: 819-934-5666
Fax: 819-934-6531
Director General, Legislative & Regulatory Affairs, John Moffet
Tel: 819-953-2833
Fax: 819-997-0449
Acting Director, Trading Regimes, Lynda Danquah
Tel: 819-956-4448
Fax: 819-953-5963
Director, Waste Reduction & Management, Timothy Gardiner
Tel: 819-934-1509
Fax: 819-997-3068
Director, Waste Reduction & Management, Timothy Gardiner
Tel: 819-934-1509
Fax: 819-997-3068
Acting Director, Outreach, Gwen C.B. Goodier
Tel: 819-953-6851
Fax: 819-997-3331
Director, Environmental Emergencies, Grant Hogg
Tel: 819-953-0607
Fax: 819-997-5029
Director, Air Emissions Priorities, Matt Jones
Tel: 819-994-5076
Fax: 819-953-7962
Director, Forestry, Agriculture & Aquaculture, Josée Lanctôt
Tel: 819-994-3504
Fax: 819-994-9848
Director, Biosphere, Jean Langlais
Tel: 514-283-2324
Fax: 514-240-5955
Director, Chemical Production, Bernard Madé
Tel: 819-994-4404
Fax: 819-994-5030
Director, Compliance Promotion & Analysis, Louise Power
Tel: 819-994-2335
Fax: 819-934-6217
Director, Products, Astrid Télasco
Tel: 819-953-0224
Fax: 819-953-3132
Director, Sustainable Water Management, Hermenegilde Twagiramungu
Tel: 819-934-1515
Fax: 819-953-7253
Senior Advisor, Regulatory Innovation & Management Systems, Julie Carrière
Tel: 819-997-3640

Canadian Wildlife Service (CWS) / Service canadien de la faune
351, boul St-Joseph, Gatineau, QC K1A 0H3
Tel: 819-997-1301
Fax: 819-953-7177
Other Communication: Ecological Gifts Program: www.ec.gc.ca/pde-egp
Director General, Virginia Poter
Tel: 819-994-1360
Fax: 819-953-7177
Executive Director, Habitat & Ecosystem Conservation, Robert McLean
Tel: 819-997-1303
Fax: 819-994-4445

Director, Wildlife Program Support Division, Caroline Ladanowski
Tel: 819-994-3432
Director, Conservation Service Delivery & Permitting, Mary Taylor
Tel: 819-953-9097
Fax: 819-953-6283
Director, Population Conservation & Management, Basile van Havre
Tel: 819-997-2957
Fax: 819-964-3684

Finance Branch / Direction générale des finances
Tel: 819-953-7026
Fax: 819-953-4064
Acting Assistant Deputy Minister, Carol Najm
Tel: 819-953-4736
Acting Director General, Corporate Management, Karen Turcotte
Tel: 819-953-5842
Acting Director General, Finance Directorate, Randy Larkin
Tel: 819-953-9569
Fax: 819-953-2459
Acting Director General, Integrated Enterprise Services, Cheryl Bertrand
Tel: 819-953-8911
Fax: 819-953-4064

Human Resources Branch / Direction générale des ressources humaines
Tel: 819-997-1847
Fax: 819-953-2757
Assistant Deputy Minister, Lynette Cox
Tel: 819-997-1847
Fax: 819-953-2757
Director General, National HR Services, Donna Richard
Tel: 819-934-7215
Fax: 819-953-2675
Acting Director General, Performance Measurement & Monitoring Business Systems, Donald Bilodeau
Tel: 819-994-0201
Director General, Human Resources Corporate Programs, Deirdre Keane
Tel: 819-953-0432
Fax: 819-953-6963
Director, Conflict Management, Julie Lalonde
Tel: 819-994-1185
Fax: 819-934-8030
Director, Executive Group Services & Management Development, Carole Lemay
Tel: 819-994-3447
Fax: 819-994-3346

International Affairs / Direction générale des affaires internationales
Tel: 819-997-4882
Fax: 819-953-5981
Assistant Deputy Minister, Dan McDougall
Tel: 819-934-6020
Fax: 819-953-9412
Director General, Americas, Dean Knudson
Tel: 819-994-1670
Fax: 819-997-0199
Director General, Climate Change International, Stephen de Boer
Tel: 819-953-6830
Fax: 819-953-9333
Director General, Multilateral & Bilateral Affairs, France Jacovella
Tel: 819-956-5263
Fax: 819-994-6227
Director, Partnerships Division, Darren Goetze
Tel: 819-953-9525
Fax: 819-953-9333

Legal Services / Services juridiques
Tel: 819-953-3680
Fax: 819-953-9110
Senior General Counsel & Executive Director, Legal Services, Kathleen Roussel
Tel: 819-953-8680
Fax: 819-953-9110
General Counsel & Director, Environment Canada Regulations, Peter Beaman
Tel: 819-994-6346
Fax: 819-953-9373

Meteorological Service of Canada (MSC) / Le service météorologique du Canada
Tel: 819-997-2696
Fax: 819-994-8841
The Meteorological Service of Canada monitors water quantities, provides information & conducts research on climate, atmospheric science, air quality, ice & other environmental issues.
Assistant Deputy Minister, David Grimes
Tel: 613-943-5585
Fax: 613-943-5737
Director General, Business Policy, Danielle Lacasse
Tel: 613-943-5532
Fax: 613-995-0389
Director General, Weather & Environmental Monitoring, Jim Abraham
Tel: 416-739-4965
Fax: 416-739-4261
Director General, Weather & Environmental Monitoring, Michel Jean
Tel: 514-421-4601
Fax: 514-421-7250
Director General, Weather & Environmental Prediction & Services, Diane E. Campbell
Tel: 613-947-9200
Fax: 613-943-6440

Science & Technology Branch / Direction générale des sciences et de la technologie
Tel: 819-994-4751
Fax: 819-997-1541
Assistant Deputy Minister, Karen L. Dodds
Tel: 819-934-6851
Director General, Atmospheric Science & Technology, Charles A. Lin
Tel: 416-739-4995
Fax: 416-739-4265
Director, Meteorological Research, Dr. Gilbert Brunet
Tel: 514-421-4617
Fax: 514-421-2106
Other Communications: Alternate Phone: 514-501-2265
Acting Director, Air Quality Research Division, Véronique Bouchet
Tel: 514-421-5020
Fax: 514-421-4679
Other Communications: Secure Phone: 416-739-4836
Director, Climate Research, Francis Zwiers
Tel: 416-739-4767
Fax: 416-739-5700
Acting Manager, Experimental Studies Section, Dr. Cathy Banic
Tel: 416-739-4613
Fax: 416-739-4224

Science & Risk Assessment Directorate / Direction générale de Science et évaluation des risques
351, boul St-Joseph, Gatineau, QC K1A 0H3
Tel: 819-953-1114
Fax: 819-953-5371
Acting Director General, David Morin
Tel: 819-953-3091
Fax: 819-953-7155
Director, Ecological Assessment Division, Robert Chenier
Tel: 819-953-1680
Fax: 819-953-4936
Director, Emerging Priorities, Nicole Davidson
Tel: 819-997-3253
Fax: 819-953-5371
Director, Program Integration, Karen Mailhiot
Tel: 819-953-0385
Fax: 819-953-9542
Acting Director, Pollutant Inventories & Reporting, Aïda Warah
Tel: 819-953-3588
Fax: 819-953-2341
Senior Science Advisor, Ecological Assessment, Mark A. Bonnell
Tel: 819-994-5845
Fax: 819-994-3120
Senior Administrative Officer, Directorate Operations Unit, Monique Bourassa
Tel: 819-953-9246
Fax: 819-953-3006
Executive Assistant, Program Development & Engagement, Chantal D. Dallaire
Tel: 819-997-1593
Fax: 819-953-4936
Executive Assistant, Louise Lesage
Tel: 819-953-6022
Fax: 819-953-5371

Science & Technology Strategies / Science et technologies, statégies
200, boul Sacré-Coeur, 11e étage, Gatineau, QC K1A 0H3
Tel: 905-336-4503
Director General, Javier A. Gracia-Garza, PhD
Tel: 819-953-3090
Fax: 819-953-9029
Director, Science & Technology Integration Division, Dr. Pierre-Yves Caux
Tel: 819-953-9364
Fax: 819-953-8924
Other Communications: Executive Assistant: 819-997-7914
Director, Science Policy Division, Eric Gagné
Tel: 819-994-5434
Fax: 819-953-0550
Director, Science & Technology Priorities & Planning, Donald Renaud
Tel: 819-956-9317
Fax: 819-953-5371
Senior Policy Analyst, Science & Technology Integration Division, Joanne Egan
Tel: 819-994-3053
Fax: 819-953-8924
Executive Assistant to the Director, Science & Technology Liaison, Mike Jamieson
Tel: 905-336-4675
Fax: 905-336-4420
Executive Assistant, Science & Technology Integration Division, Cheryl A. Devine
Tel: 819-997-7914
Fax: 819-953-8924
Executive Assistant, Farah Milord
Tel: 819-953-4388
Fax: 819-953-7177
Executive Assistant, Science & Technology Priorities & Planning, Roxana Orué, MA
Tel: 819-994-3542
Fax: 819-953-8924
Administrative Assistant, Science Policy Division, Jane-Ann Graham
Tel: 819-953-9610
Fax: 819-953-0550

Water Science & Technology / Science et technologie de l'eau
867 Lakeshore Rd., PO Box 5050Burlington, ON L7R 4A6
Tel: 905-336-4625
Fax: 905-336-6444
Director General, Dan Wicklum, PhD
Tel: 819-994-4533
Acting Director, Aquatic Ecosystem Impacts Research, Patricia Chambers, PhD
Tel: 905-336-4529
Fax: 905-336-6430
Other Communications: Executive Assistant: 905-336-4936
Director, Aquatic Ecosystem Management Research, John Lawrence, PhD
Tel: 905-336-4913
Fax: 905-336-6430
Director, Aquatic Ecosystem Protection Research, Andre J. Talbot, PhD
Tel: 514-283-2509
Fax: 514-283-1719
Director, Emergencies, Operational Analytical Laboratories & Research Support, Marc R. Bernier, MSc
Tel: 506-851-2622
Fax: 506-851-6608
Director, Water Quality Monitoring & Surveillance, Caroline Ladanowski
Tel: 819-994-3661
Fax: 514-283-1719
Executive Assistant to the Director General, Karie Petz
Tel: 905-336-4625
Fax: 905-336-6444

Wildlife & Landscape Science / Sciences de la faune et du paysage
Carleton University, Raven Rd., Ottawa, ON K1A 0H3
Tel: 613-998-0313
Fax: 613-998-0315

Director General, Kevin J. Cash, PhD
Tel: 613-998-0329
Fax: 613-998-0458
Director, Landscape Science & Technology, Ken Harris
Tel: 613-998-0331
Director, Ecotoxicology & Wildlife Health, Laird J. Shutt, PhD
Tel: 613-998-7379
Fax: 613-998-0458
Other Communications: Alternate Phone: 613-889-9085
Research Scientist, Wildlife Research, Ray T. Alisauskas, PhD
Tel: 306-975-4556
Fax: 306-975-4089
Wildlife Technician, Wildlife Research, Dana Kellett
Tel: 306-975-5509
Fax: 306-975-4089

Strategic Policy / Direction générale de la politique stratégique
Tel: 819-953-4818
Fax: 819-953-5981
Assistant Deputy Minister, Michael Keenan
Tel: 819-953-4818
Fax: 819-953-5981
Director General, Sustainability Directorate, Jan Dyer
Tel: 819-934-6028
Fax: 819-994-8864
Director General, Strategic Policy Directorate, Lawrence Hanson
Tel: 819-934-4149
Fax: 819-953-4679
Acting Director General, Intergovernmental & Stakeholder Relations Directorate, Nancy Roberts
Tel: 819-953-3353
Fax: 819-994-6787
Director General, Economic Analysis Directorate, Tony Young
Tel: 819-953-7624
Fax: 819-953-5916
Manager, Clean Air Agenda, Zella Osberg
Tel: 819-956-9231
Fax: 819-994-8864
Manager, ADM's Office, Juie Philippe
Tel: 819-953-2667
Fax: 819-953-5981
Senior Economist, Economic Research & Liaison, Judith Hamel
Tel: 819-934-6000
Fax: 819-635-7952
Correspondence Officer, Suzanne Beaudoin
Tel: 819-953-1494
Fax: 819-953-5981
Executive Assistant to the ADM, Anne Morin
Tel: 819-997-8382
Fax: 819-953-5981
Administrative Assistant, Ashley Russell
Tel: 819-934-0000
Fax: 819-953-5981

Environment Canada Regional Offices
Atlantic
Queen Sq., 45 Alderney Dr., Dartmouth, NS B2Y 2N6
Tel: 902-426-7231
Fax: 902-426-6348
TTY: 819-994-0736
15th.reception@ec.gc.ca
atlantic-web1.ns.ec.gc.ca/index_e.html
Acting Regional Director General, Jackie Olsen
Tel: 902-426-0628
Fax: 902-426-6348
Manager, Community Outreach, ATL Head - Integrated Ecosystem & Public Engagement Programs, Ted Jennex
Tel: 902-426-7696
Fax: 902-426-2062
Manager, Sustainable Communities & Ecosystems, ATL Head - Integrated Ecosystem & Public Engagement Programs, Larry P. Hildebrand
Tel: 902-426-2131
Fax: 902-426-6348
Manager, Strategic Analysis & Policy, David M. Kelly
Tel: 902-426-0739
Fax: 902-426-6348
Contact, Aboriginal Relations, Lindiwe Macdonald, MES
Tel: 902-426-8374
Fax: 902-426-6348
Contact, Intergovernmental Affairs, Adam Fancy
Tel: 902-426-8374
Senior Advisor, Policy & International Relations, Peter W. Johnson
Tel: 902-426-8374
Fax: 902-426-6348
Senior Advisor, Policy, Research & Economic Analysis, Lisa Fougere
Tel: 902-426-8879
Pacific & Yukon
201, 401 Burrard St., Vancouver, BC V6C 3S5
Tel: 604-664-9145
Fax: 604-664-9190
greenlane.pyr@ec.gc.ca
www.pyr.ec.gc.ca
Regional Director General, Paul Kluckner
Tel: 604-664-9145
Fax: 604-664-9190
Director, Strategic Integration Office, Kendall Woo
Tel: 604-664-9399
Fax: 604-713-9527
Manager, Aboriginal Affairs, Ian Macleod
Tel: 604-666-7419
Manager, Community Programs, Mary Pender
Tel: 604-713-9513
Fax: 604-713-9527
Manager, Intergovernmental & International Affairs, Lorraine Cameron
Tel: 604-713-9530
Fax: 604-713-9527
Manager, Water Management & Indicators, Gwyn Graham
Tel: 604-664-4052
Fax: 604-664-9126
Senior Policy Advisor, Sustainability Division, Anoma Patirana
Tel: 604-666-8107
Contact, Pacific Environment Centre Office, Marlene Elliot
Tel: 604-666-5958
Other Communications: Office Phone: 604-666-8425
Ontario
4905 Dufferin St., Toronto, ON M3H 5T4
Tel: 416-739-4826
Fax: 416-739-4776
enviroinfo.ontario@ec.gc.ca
www.on.ec.gc.ca
Acting Regional Director General, Michael Goffin
Tel: 416-739-4666
Fax: 416-739-4691
Acting Director, Great Lakes Division, Kevin Guerin
Tel: 416-514-2662
Manager, Areas of Concern, Great Lakes Division, Jon Gee
Tel: 416-739-4129
Fax: 416-739-4804
Manager, Environment Office, Jon Gee
Tel: 416-739-4129
Fax: 416-739-4804
Manager, Management & Reporting, John Marsden
Tel: 416-739-4759
Fax: 416-739-4804
Director, Strategic Integration & Partnerships, Sandra Weston
Tel: 416-739-4404
Community Program Officer, Strategic Integration & Partnerships, Kim Colavecchia
Tel: 416-739-4768
Fax: 416-739-4235
Acting Manager, Policy & Aboriginal Relations, Shaffina Kassam
Tel: 416-739-4714
Fax: 416-739-4804
Pacific & Yukon: Yukon Office
Canadian Wildlife Service, 91782 Alaska Hwy., Yellowknife, YT Y1A 5B7
Tel: 867-393-6700
Fax: 867-393-7970
Prairie & Northern
Twin Atria Bldg., #200, 4999 - 98 Ave., Edmonton, AB T6B 2X3
Tel: 780-951-8869
Fax: 780-495-3086
Acting Regional Director General, Mike Norton
Tel: 780-951-8869
Fax: 780-495-2758
Executive Director, Transboundary Waters Unit, Mike Renouf
Tel: 306-780-7004
Fax: 306-780-6810
Manager, Community Programs, Greg Stevens
Tel: 204-984-5297
Fax: 204-983-0964
Manager, Policy, Strategic Integration & Partnerships, Stacey Smythe
Tel: 780-951-8632
Fax: 780-495-4367
Executive Assistant, Strategic Integration & Partnerships, Barbara Kreider
Tel: 780-951-8728
Fax: 780-495-3086
Prairie & Northern: Manitoba Office
#150, 123 Main St., Winnipeg, MB R3C 4W2
Tel: 204-984-6203
Fax: 204-983-0964
Toll-Free: 800-263-0595
Québec
1141, rte de l'Église, 6e étage, CP 10100Québec, QC G1V 4H5
Tél: 418-648-4077
Téléc: 418-648-4613
Ligne sans frais: 800-463-4311
quebec.lavoieverte@ec.gc.ca
Regional Director General, Philippe Morel
Tel: 418-648-4077
Fax: 418-649-6213
Director, Strategic Integration & Partnerships, Marie-Josée Couture
Tel: 418-648-4619
Fax: 418-649-6213
Manager, Aboriginal & Corporative Affairs, Strategic Integration & Partnerships, Jean Picard
Tel: 418-648-5675
Fax: 418-649-6213
Regional Manager, Community Funding Programs, Strategic Integration & Partnerships, Manon Therriault
Tel: 418-648-3493
Fax: 418-649-6674
Manager, Coordination Office St Lawrence Plan, Strategic Integration & Partnerships, Anne Gauthier
Tel: 418-648-3178
Fax: 418-649-6213
Manager, Strategic Analysis & Policies, Strategic Integration & Partnerships, Jérôme Clément
Tel: 418-648-5933
Fax: 418-649-6213

Partners in Flight / Partenaires d'envol
c/o Canadian Wildlife Service, Ottawa, ON K1A 0H3
Tel: 819-953-4390
Fax: 819-994-4445
migratorybirds.oiseauxmigrateurs@ec.gc.ca
www.ec.gc.ca/mbc-com/default.asp?lang=En&n=7AEDFD2C-1
The goal of Partners in Flight - Canada (PIF) is to ensure the long-term viability of populations of native Canadian landbirds across their range of habitats. The Canadian Wildlife Service, with its mandate for migratory bird conservation, is working with partners to build a national landbird conservation program. Implementation of this goal will occur at national, regional & local levels. Work is overseen by the National Working Group & includes representatives from government & non-government conservation agencies & regional PIF programs & welcomes participation from industry, academia, & other interested stakeholders. Activities & products of the National Working Group support landbird conservation at international, national, regional & local levels. To date, these include the Framework for Landbird Conservation in Canada (provides context for a Canadian landbird conservation program) the Canadian Landbird Monitoring Strategy (highlights existing surveys & discusses how to fill gaps in our knowledge of landbird populations), the National Action Needs for Canadian Landbird Conservation (outlines priority research & monitoring needs for specific landbird species.) Regional & provincial/territorial landbird conservation efforts are undertaken inde pendently through conservation plans developed by partnerships. PIF encourages regional efforts to use Bird Conservation Regions as the geographic framework for conservation plans
Contact, Martin Damus

Energy & Transportation / Énergie et transports
Tel: 819-997-1298
Fax: 819-953-9547
Director General, Steve McCauley
Tel: 819-997-1298
Fax: 819-953-9547
Director, Electricity & Combustion, Caroline Blais
Tel: 819-994-6272
Fax: 819-994-9938
Executive Director, Oil, Gas & Alternative Energy, Margaret Meroni
Tel: 819-997-1221
Fax: 819-953-8903

Director, Transportation, Mark Cauchi
Tel: 819-994-3706
Fax: 819-953-7815

EcoAction
Queen Square, 16th Fl., 45 Alderley Dr., Dartmouth, NS B2Y 2N6
Tel: 902-426-8521
Fax: 902-426-0262
ecoaction@ec.gc.ca
www.ec.gc.ca/ecoaction
The EcoAction Community Funding Program provides financial support to community groups for projects that have measurable, positive impacts on the environment. Non-profit groups & organizations are eligible to apply to the Funding Program. EcoAction encourages projects that deal with climate change, clean water, nature & clean air.

Canadian Ice Service / Service canadien des glaces
373 Sussex Dr., Block E, 3rd Fl., Ottawa, ON K1A 0H3
Tel: 613-996-4489
Toll-Free: 800-767-2885
cis-scg.cient@ec.gc.ca
ice-glaces.ec.gc.ca
The Canadian Ice Service (CIS) is the leading authority for information about ice in Canada's navigable waters. CIS provides daily ice hazard bulletins & charts describing ice conditions in active navigable waters; an ice warning service for extreme ice events within ice-encumbered waters; daily iceberg bulletins & charts for Canadian waters south of 60 ree N; weekly ice analyses of active ice areas for strategic planning purposes; conducts ice reconnaissance with a specially instrumented Dash-7 aircraft, as well as by helicopter; maintains the Canadian Ice Service Archive for climatological purposes; contributes Canadian ice data to the World Data Center for Glaciology.
Director, Lina Assad
Tel: 613-996-4489

Canadian Hurricane Centre / Centre canadien de prévision d'ouragan
45 Alderney Dr., 16th Fl., Dartmouth, NS B2Y 2N6
Tel: 902-426-7231
Fax: 902-426-6348
15th.reception@ec.gc.ca
www.atl.ec.gc.ca/weather/hurricane/index_e.html
The CHC exists to advise Canadians on the threat of hurricanes & tropical storms. The Centre serves to provide guidance to weather centres in all regions potentially affected by one of these storms. The CHC gathers information on tropical & post-tropical cyclones, predicts their evolution, & assesses their potential impact on Canadian territory. The CHC's Area of Forecast Responsibility lies along the Canada-United States border & extends into Canadian waters to 200 nautical miles. The CHC makes presentations about hurricanes to schools, businesses, the media, & other governmental agencies & receives calls from the public for more information about hurricanes in Canada.

National Climate Data & Information Archive / Archives nationales d'information et de données climatologiques
Fax: 416-739-4446
climate.services@ec.gc.ca
www.climate.weatheroffice.ec.gc.ca/Welcome_e.html
The National Climate Data & Information Archive, operated & maintained by Environment Canada, contains official climate & weather observations for Canada. Climate elements, such as temperature, precipitation, relative humidity, atmospheric pressure, wind speed, wind direction, visability, cloud types, cloud heights & amounts, soil temperature, evaporation, solar radiation & sunshine as well as occurrences of thunderstorms, hail, fog or other weather phenomena are warehoused in a digital database. Access to selected portions of this data, as well as related products such as CD-ROMS & climate normals & averages are available on their website. Information regarding obtaining extremes, monthly summaries, microfilm, microfiche, paper documents & technical documents, is also available.

Science Horizons: Environment Canada's Youth Internship Program
351, boul St-Joseph, Gatineau, QC K1A 0H3
Fax: 819-956-5602
Toll-Free: 800-668-6767
science.horiz@ec.gc.ca
www.ec.gc.ca/sci_hor
Environment Canada's Science Horizons Program is a collaborative effort with Canadian universities, the private sector & NGOs which offers promising young scientists & post-secondary graduates hands-on experience working on environmental projects under the mentorship & coaching of experienced scientists & program managers. Approximately one hundred youth placements, lasting from 6 months to 1 year, are awarded annually across Canada.

Environmental Effects Monitoring Office (EEM) / Bureau national des études de suivi des effets sur l'environnement (ESEE)
4905 Dufferin St., Toronto, ON M3H 5T4
Tel: 416-739-4215
Fax: 416-739-4342
EEM-ESEE@ec.gc.ca
www.ec.gc.ca/eem
EEM provides national leadership for the regulated environmental effects monitoring (EEM) programs for the pulp & paper & metal mining sectors.
Regional Coordinator, Debbie Audet
eem.ontario@ec.gc.ca
Head, Metal Mining, Lise Trudel
Tel: 819-953-1527

National Guidelines & Standards Office (NGSO)
Environment Canada, 200 boul. Sacré-Coeur, Gatineau, QC K1A 0H3
Tel: 819-953-1550
ceqg-rcqe@ec.gc.ca
ceqg-rcqe.ccme.ca
The National Guidelines & Standards Office (NGSO) provides nationally approved, science-based measures of environmental quality including guidelines, standards, & objectives. The primary focus of the group is developing national guidelines for water, sediment & soil quality, & aquatic tissue residues. Guidelines are recommended numerical or narrative limits for a variety of substances & environmental quality characteristics (such as dissolved oxygen or pH), which, if exceeded, may impair the health of Canadian ecosystems. Guidelines are mandated federally under the Canadian Environmental Protection Act (CEPA) & nationally under various federal-provincial agreements (Canadian Council of Ministers of the Environment, Great Lakes Water Quality Agreement). In addition, the NGSO leads & supports various ecosystem management initiatives (with a focus on consultative, community-based, right-to-know approaches) cooperatively with the CCME, Environment Canada Regions & other federal departments. The NGSO's thrust is to develop & promote effective implementation of science-based guidelines, objectives & indicators to achieve ecosystem health & sustainable development.
Acting Manager, Doug Spry
Tel: 819-953-3206

National Hydrology Research Centre (NHRC) / Centre national de recherche en hydrologie (CNRH)
www.ec.gc.ca/inre-nwri
NHRC houses five groups: the western centre of the National Water Research Institute, the Water Quality Laboratory of the Environmental Protection Service, Prairie & Northern Region, which provides analytical services to support government & university research & monitoring programs in western Canada, the Climate Processes & Earth Observation Division, the Prairie & Northern Region, & the Saskatchewan Inspection Office of the Meteorological Service of Canada (MSC). These MSC groups monitor the state of Canada's climate, install, maintain & regularly inspect weather stations in Saskatchewan, & disseminates weather information & warnings of extreme weather events.

National Laboratory for Environmental Testing (NLET) / Laboratoire national des essais environnementaux
Environment Canada, 867 Lakeshore Rd., PO Box 5050Burlington, ON L7R 4A6
Tel: 905-336-4563
Fax: 905-336-6404
NLET delivers a range of specialized & accredited analytical laboratory services, including sample characterization, technical consulting, quality management & laboratory information management systems development, in support of Environment Canada monitoring, assessment & research programs across the country. This is accomplished at facilities located in Burlington, Ontario, & at the Regional Water Quality Laboratory in Saskatoon, Saskatchewan. The mission is to support the laboratory science needs of Environment Canada research & monitoring programs & to deliver quality management products & services through responsive, cost-effective laboratory services that meet international standards of quality. The role of NLET within Environment Canada is a national analytical support laboratory capable of providing Environment Canada program managers with standarized & fully accredited environmental analysis capability for a wide range of organic & inorganic chemicals, unique analytical capabilities used to deliver collaborative projects outside the normal boundaries of the QA framework & usually delivered through MOUs, & partnership-based applied research projects such as developing/adapting new methods. NLET consists of two operational laboratories, the associated enabling infrastructure & a quality assurance/management group.
Manager, Pat Falletta

National Water Research Institute (NWRI) / Centre canadien des eaux intérieures (CCIW)
867 Lakeshore Rd., PO Box 5050Burlington, ON L7R 4A6
Tel: 905-336-4625
Fax: 905-336-6444
nwriscience.liaison@ec.gc.ca
www.nwri.ca
The National Water Research Institute (NWRI) is Canada's largest freshwater research facility, with centres in Burlington, Ontario & Saskatoon, Saskatchewan. As part of the Environmental Conservation Service of Environment Canada, NWRI conducts research & development in the aquatic sciences, often in collaboration with Canadian & international science communities. NWRI generates scientific knowledge through ecosystem-based research to support the development of sound government policies & programs, public decision making, & early identification of environmental problems.

St. Lawrence Centre (SLC) / Centre Saint-Laurent
#105 McGill St., 7th Fl., Montréal, QC H2Y 2E7
quebec.csl@ec.gc.ca
www.qc.ec.gc.ca/csl/
SLC is the only federal research & development centre devoted entirely to the river ecosystem. SLC experts study the ecosystems of the St. Lawrence River & conduct research programs with the aim of better understanding how these ecosystems function & maintaining knowledge of the St. Lawrence River up to date. SLC is divided into four sections Environmental Chemistry, Environmental Biology, State of the St. Lawrence Environment & Information Management.

North American Waterfowl Management Plan (NAWMP) / Plan nord-américain de gestion de la sauvagine
NAWCC (Canada) Secretariat, Place Vincent Massey, 351 St. Joseph Blvd., 7th Fl., Gatineau, QC K1A 0H3
Tel: 819-934-6034
Fax: 819-934-6017
nawmp@ec.gc.ca
www.nawmp.ca
The North American Waterfowl Management Plan is an international action plan to conserve migratory birds throughout the continent. The Plan's goal is to return waterfowl populations to their 1970s levels by conserving wetland & upland habitat.

Joint Venture Coordinators

Arctic Goose
c/o Prairie & Northern Region, CWS, #200, 4999 - 98 Ave., Edmonton, AB T6B 2X3
Tel: 780-951-8652
Fax: 780-495-2615
agjv@ec.gc.ca
www.agjv.ca
Coordinator, Deanna Dixon

Black Duck
Environment Canada, Canadian Wildlife Service, 335 River Rd., Ottawa, ON K1A 0H3
Tel: 613-949-8254
www.blackduckjv.org
Coordinator, Brigitte Collins
brigitte.collins@ec.gc.ca

Eastern Habitat
c/o Environment Canada, Canadian Wildlife Service, 335 River Rd., Ottawa, ON K1A 0H3
Tel: 613-949-8264
www.ec.gc.ca/pch-hjv

Pacific Coast
c/o Environment Canada, Canadian Wildlife Service, #201, 401 Burrard St., Vancouver, BC V6C 3S5
Tel: 604-940-4703
www.pcjv.org
Coordinator, Tasha Sargent
tasha_sargent@pcjv.org

Prairie Habitat
c/o Prairie & Northern Region, CWS, #200, 4999 - 98 Ave., Edmonton, AB T6B 2X3
Tel: 780-951-8652
phjv@ec.gc.ca
phjv.ca
Coordinator, Deanna Dixon
deanna.dixon@ec.gc.ca

Commission for Environmental Cooperation (CEC) / Commission coopération environnementale

Secretariat, #200, 393, rue St-Jacques ouest, Montréal, QC H2Y 1N9
Tel: 514-350-4300
Fax: 514-350-4314
info@cec.org
www.cec.org
The Commission for Environmental Cooperation (CEC) is an international organization created by Canada, Mexico & the United States under the North American Agreement on Environmental Cooperation (NAAEC). The CEC was established to address regional environmental concerns, help prevent potential trade & environmental conflicts & to promote the effective enforcement of environmental law. The Agreement complements the environmental provisions of the North American Free Trade Agreement (NAFTA).

Executive Director, Evan Lloyd
Tel: 514-350-4303
melhadj@cec.org

Legal Officer, Submission on Enforcement Matters Unit, Paolo Solano
Tel: 514-350-4321
psolano@cec.org

Program Manager, Air Quality & PRTR, Orlando Cabrera-Rivera
Tel: 514-350-4323
ocabrera@cec.org

Program Manager, Chemicals Management, Ned T. Brooks
Tel: 514-350-4372
nbrooks@cec.org

Program Manager, Environmental Information, Karen Richardson
Tel: 514-350-4326
krichardson@cec.org

Program Manager, Environmental Law, Marco Antonio Heredia Fragoso
Tel: 514-350-4302
maheredia@cec.org

Council Secretary, Nathalie Daoust
Tel: 514-350-4310
ndaoust@cec.org

Environmental Protection Review Canada / Révision de la protection de l'environnement Canada

240 Sparks St., 1st Fl. West, Ottawa, ON K1A 1A1
Tel: 613-995-7599
Fax: 613-992-4918
eprc-rpec@eprc-rpec.gc.ca
www.eprc-rpec.gc.ca
Environmental Protection Review Canada is a group of expert adjudicators, entirely separate from Environment Canada, that conducts reviews of Environmental Protection Compliance Orders (EPCOs). Under the Canadian Environmental Protection Act, 1999 (CEPA, 1999), enforcement officers have the power to issue EPCOs to prevent a violation, to stop an on-going violation or to require that violations be corrected. Any person who has been issued an EPCO may ask for an independent review conducted by a Review Officer. Review Officers have the authority to confirm or cancel an EPCO. They may also amend, suspend, add or delete a term or condition of the Order. The decisions of Review Officers may be appealed to the Federal Court, Trial Division.

Chief Review Officer, Allan Pope
Tel: 613-997-4060
Fax: 613-992-4918

Review Officer, Louis LaPierre, Ph.D.
Tel: 506-863-2056
Fax: 506-863-2000
lapierl@umoncton.ca

Export Development Canada (EDC) / Exportation et développement Canada (SEE)

151 Slater St., Ottawa, ON K1A 1K3
Tel: 613-598-2500
Fax: 613-598-3811
Toll-Free: 800-267-8510
TTY: 866-574-0451
www.edc.ca
twitter.com/ExportDevCanada
www.facebook.com/ExportDevCanada
www.linkedin.com/company/export-development-canada
A financial services corporation assisting Canadian business to succeed in foreign markets. EDC provides a wide range of financial solutions to exporters across Canada & their customers around the world. The corporation's risk management services include: export-credit insurance protecting exporters against losses due to non-payment relating to commercial & political risks; & flexible medium- or long-term financing & guarantees. As a financially self-sustaining Crown corporation, EDC operates on commercial principles, charging fees & premiums for its products & interest on its loans. EDC is governed by a board of directors composed of representatives from both the private & public sectors, & reports to Parliament through the minister for international trade. An Environmental Review Directive is used to assess the environmental impacts of projects EDC is asked to support. EDC pursues an international multilateral consensus on environmental review practices so that all exporters are subject to the same rules. EDC has adopted & implemented the OECD Recommendation on Common Approaches on Environment & Officially Supported Export Credits. EDC has signed the UNEP Statement of Financial Institutions. Through the EnviroExport initiative, EDC helps Canadia n environmental exporters succeed internationally through financing products. Where EDC is considering providing financing support, political risk insurance or equity to the sponsor of a Category A project under the Environmental Review Directive, EDC will seek consent to inform the public on its website that it is considering support to such a project.

President & Chief Executive Officer, Vacant

Senior Vice-President & Chief Risk Officer, Enterprise Risk Management, Pierre Gignac
pierre.gignac@edc.ca
Vice-President, Western Region, Linda Morris
LMorris@edc.ca

Farm Products Council of Canada (FPCC) / Conseil des produits agricoles du Canada (CPAC)

Building 59, Central Experimental Farm, 960 Carling Ave., Ottawa, ON K1A 0C6
Tel: 613-759-1555
Fax: 613-759-1566
TTY: 613-759-1737
fpcc-cpac@agr.gc.ca
www.fpcc-cpac.gc.ca
In 1972, the Natioanl Farm Products Council was established by Parliament. The National Farm Products Council became known as the Farm Products Council of Canada in 2009.
The mission of the council is as follows: to oversee the national supply management agencies for poultry & eggs & the national promotion research agencies; to liaise with provincial governments interested in the work of the national agencies; to review operations of the national agencies to ensure they act in accordance with the *Farm Products Agencies Act*; to investigate complaints in relation to national agency decisions & to hold public hearings if necessary; to administer the *Agricultural Products Marketing Act* & to encourage effective marketing of farm products; & to advise the Minister on matters related to the national agencies.
The Council consists of at least three members & up to seven. Members of the Council are appointed by Cabinet.
Acts Administered:
Agricultural Products Marketing Act, 1949
Farm Products Marketing Agencies Act, 1972
Farm Products Marketing Agencies Act, 1972

Chair, Laurent Pellerin
Tel: 613-759-1265
Fax: 613-759-1566
laurent.pellerin@agr.gc.ca

Vice-Chair, Brent Montgomery

Executive Director, Claude Janelle
Tel: 613-759-1412
Fax: 613-759-1757
claude.janelle@agr.gc.ca

Council Secretary; Registrar, Nathalie Vanasse
Tel: 613-759-1562
Fax: 613-759-1505
nathalie.vanasse@agr.gc.ca

Director, Corporate & Regulatory Affairs, Marc Chamaillard
Tel: 613-759-1706
Fax: 613-759-1566
marc.chamaillard@agr.gc.ca

Manager, Policy Analysis, Hélène Devost
Tel: 613-759-1589
Fax: 613-759-1505
helene.devost@agr.gc.ca

Officer, Communications, Chantal Lafontaine
Tel: 613-759-1742
Fax: 613-759-1505
chantal.lafontaine@agr.gc.ca

Federal Economic Development Agency for Southern Ontario (FedDev Ontario) / Agence fédérale de développement économique pour le Sud de l'Ontario

101 Frederick St., 4th Fl., Kitchener, ON N2H 6R2
Fax: 519-571-5750
Toll-Free: 866-593-5505
www.feddevontario.gc.ca
twitter.com/FedDevOntario
FedDev Ontario was launched in 2009, & has the mandate to strengthen the economy in Southern Ontario. It accomplishes this through investment, job creation & programs. Examples of programs & initiatives are as follows: Applied Research & Commercialization Initiative; Building Canada Fund-Communities Component; Canada-Ontario Infrastructure Program; Canada-Ontario Municipal Rural Infrastructure Fund; Canada Strategic Infrastructure Fund; Community Adjustment Fund; Community Infrastructure Improvement Fund; Community Futures Program; Eastern Ontario Development Program; Economic Development Initiative; Graduate Enterprise Internship; Investing in Business Innovation; Municipal Rural Infrastructure Fund Top-Up; Ontario Potable Water Program; Prosperity Initiative; Recreational Infrastructure Canada Program in Ontario; Scientists & Engineers in Business; Southern Ontario Development Program; Technology Development Program; & Youth STEM.

Minister of State, Federal Economic Development Agency for Southern Ontario; Minister of State, Science & Technology, Hon. Dr. Gary Goodyear
Tel: 613-947-2956
Fax: 613-960-7724

Parliamentary Secretary, Pierre Poilievre
Tel: 519-571-5702
Fax: 519-571-5750
pierre.poilievre@parl.gc.ca

Deputy Minister & President, B.A. (Bruce) Archibald, Ph.D.
Tel: 519-571-5702
Fax: 519-571-5750

Chief Financial Officer, Linda Cousineau
Tel: 519-571-5753
Fax: 519-585-2893

Director General, Human Resources, Colleen Robinson
Tel: 519-571-5594
Fax: 519-571-6895

Director General, Communications, Alexandra Sutton
Tel: 519-571-5773
Fax: 519-585-2882

Business, Innovation & Community Development / Innovation, commerciale et développement communautaire

Vice-President, Clair Gartley
Tel: 519-571-5703
Fax: 519-571-5750
Director General, Innovation & Economic Development, Susan Anzolin
Tel: 519-585-2905
Fax: 519-571-5750
Director General, Infrastructure Operations, Natasha Kay Brenders
Tel: 416-952-4083
Fax: 416-954-6654

Policy, Partnerships & Performance Management / Politiques, partenariats et gestion de rendement
Vice-President, Jeff Moore
Tel: 613-941-2479
Fax: 613-954-6710
Ottawa
155 Queen St., 14th Fl., Ottawa, ON K1P 6L1
Fax: 613-952-9026
Toll-Free: 866-593-5505
Toronto
151 Yonge St., 3rd Fl., Toronto, ON M5C 2W7
Fax: 416-954-6654
Toll-Free: 866-593-5505
Peterborough
143 Simcoe St., Peterborough, ON K9H 0A3
Fax: 705-750-4827
Toll-Free: 866-593-5505

Finance Canada / Finances Canada

L'esplanade Laurier, 140 O'Connor St., Ottawa, ON K1A 0G5
Tel: 613-992-1573
Fax: 613-943-0938
TTY: 613-995-1455
finpub@fin.gc.ca
www.fin.gc.ca
Other Communication: Library Services: 613-995-5877
The Department of Finance Canada is responsible for providing the federal government with analysis & advice on financial & economic issues. It also monitors & researches the performance of the Canadian economy's major factors (output, growth, employment, income, price stability, monetary policy, & long-term change). Interacting with various other federal departments & agencies, the Department encourages coordination in all federal initiatives with an impact on the economy. Emphasis is placed on consulting with the public regarding policy directions & options.

Minister, Finance, Hon. James Michael (Jim) Flaherty, B.A., LL.B.
Tel: 613-992-6344
Fax: 513-992-8320
jim.flaherty@parl.gc.ca

Minister of State (Finance), Ted Menzies
Tel: 613-996-7861
Fax: 613-995-5176
ted.menzies@fin.gc.ca

Deputy Minister, Michael J. Horgan
Tel: 613-992-4925
Fax: 613-996-0830

Associate Deputy Minister & G-7 Deputy for Canada, Paul Rochon
Tel: 613-943-2314
Fax: 613-952-9569

Associate Deputy Minister, Louise Levonian
Tel: 613-996-1963
Fax: 613-952-9569

Assistant Deputy Minister, Denis Gauthier
Tel: 613-992-1527
Fax: 613-992-0387

Associated Agencies, Boards & Commissions:

• **Auditor General of Canada / Vérificateur Général du Canada**
See Entry Name Index for detailed listing.
• **Bank of Canada / Banque du Canada**
See Entry Name Index for detailed listing.
• **Canada Deposit Insurance Corporation / Société d'assurance-dépôts du Canada**
See Entry Name Index for detailed listing.
• **Canada Savings Bonds (CSB) / Obligations d'épargne du Canada (OEC)**
#900, 110 Yonge St.
Toronto, ON M5C 1T4
Tel: 416-952-1252
Fax: 416-952-1270
Toll-free: 800-575-5151
csb@csb.gc.ca
www.csb.gc.ca
• **Canada Revenue Agency / Agence du revenu du Canada**
See Entry Name Index for detailed listing.
• **Financial Consumer Agency of Canada / Agence de la consommation en matière financière du Canada**
See Entry Name Index for detailed listing.
• **Financial Transactions & Reports Analysis Centre of Canada (FINTRAC) / Centre d'analyse des opérations et déclarations financières du Canada (CANAFE)**
234 Laurier Ave. West, 24th Fl.
Ottawa, ON K1P 1H7
Fax: 613-943-7931
Toll-free: 866-346-8722
guidelines-lignesdirectrices@fintrac-canafe.gc.ca
www.fintrac.gc.ca
Created in 2000, FINTRAC is Canada's financial intelligence unit, a specialized agency created to collect, analyze & disclose financial information & intelligence on suspected money laundering & terrorist activities financing.
• **Office of the Superintendent of Financial Institutions / Bureau du surintendant des institutions financières Canada**
See Entry Name Index for detailed listing.

Sectoral Policy Analysis / Analyse des politiques sectorielles
Fax: 613-992-0387
www.fin.gc.ca/branches-directions/edcf-eng.asp#Sectoral
As part of the Economic Development & Corporate Finance Branch, Sectoral Policy Analysis advises the Minister on issues related to environment, resources, energy, transport, privatization, Crown corporations.

Tax Policy Branch / Direction de la politique de l'impôt
Assistant Deputy Minister, Nancy Horsman
Tel: 613-992-1630
Fax: 613-996-1630
Chief, Resource & Environmental Taxation, James Greene
Tel: 613-992-0960
Fax: 613-943-2486

Fisheries & Oceans Canada (DFO) / Pêches et Océans Canada (MPO)

200 Kent St., Ottawa, ON K1A 0E6
Tel: 613-993-0999
Fax: 613-990-1866
TTY: 800-465-7735
info@dfo-mpo.gc.ca
www.dfo-mpo.gc.ca
twitter.com/DFO_CCG_Quebec
The Department of Fisheries & Oceans (DFO), on behalf of the Government of Canada, is responsible for policies & programs in support of Canada's economic, ecological & scientific interests in the oceans & freshwater fish habitat; for the conservation & sustainable utilization of Canada's fisheries resources in marine & inland waters; & for safe, effective & environmentally sound marine services responsive to the needs of Canadians in a global economy. The Department's mandate is extremely broad & covers management & protection of the marine & fisheries resources inside the 200-mile exclusive economic zone; management & protection of freshwater fisheries resources; marine safety along the world's longest coastline; facilitation of marine transportation; protection of the marine environment; support to other federal government institutions & objectives, as the government's civilian marine service; & research to support government priorities such as climate change & biodiversity. Because of its broad mandate, DFO does not operate alone. Federal & provincial governments share jurisdiction in a number of areas related to the Department's mandate. A $28-million investment over two years for the first phase of the Oceans Action Plan was announced in Feb ruary, 2005. The Plan is designed to develop ocean resources while protecting marine ecosystems, through sustainable development, integrated management plans, & marine protected areas.

Acts Administered:
Aboriginal Communal Fishing Licences Regulations
Alberta Fishery Regulations, 1998
Alice Arm Tailings Deposit Regulations
Atlantic Fishery Regulations
Basic Head Marine Protected Area Regulations
British Columbia Gravel Removal Order
British Columbia Logging Order
British Columbia Sport Fishing Regulations
Canada Shipping Act
Coastal Fisheries Protection Act
Confederation Bridge Area Provincial (PEI) Laws Application Regulations
Department of Fisheries & Oceans Act
Eastport Marine Protected Area Regulations
Endeavour Hydrothermal Vents Marine Protected Areas Regulations
Fish Health Protection Regulations
Fish Toxicant Regulations
Fisheries & Oceans Canada Orders
Fisheries Act
Fisheries Development Act
Fisheries Improvement Loans Act
Fishery (General) Regulations
Fishing & Recreational Harbours Act
Fishing Zones of Canada (Zones 1, 2 & 3) Order
Fishing Zones of Canada (Zones 4 & 5) Order
Fishing Zones of Canada (Zone 6) Order
Foreign Vessel Fishing Regulations
Freshwater Fish Marketing Act
Gilbert Bay Marine Protected Area Regulations
Gully Marine Protected Area Regulations
Management of Contaminated Fisheries Regulations
Manitoba Fishery Regulations
Marine Mammal Regulations
Maritime Provinces Fishery Regulations
Navigable Waters Protection Act
Newfoundland & Labrador Fishery Regulations
Northwest Territories Fishery Regulations
Oceans Act
Ontario Fishery Regulations
Pacific Fishery Management Area Regulations
Pacific Fishery Regulations
Pleasure Craft Sewage Pollution Prevention Regulations
Potato Processing Plant Liquid Effluent Regulations
Provincial Regulations
Pulp & Paper Effluent Regulations
Quebec Fishery Regulations
Saskatchewan Fishery Regulations
Species at Risk Act
Territorial Sea Geographical Coordinates (Area 7) Order
Territorial Sea Geographical Coordinated Order
Yukon Territory Fishery Regulations

Minister, Fisheries & Oceans, Hon. Keith Ashfield
Tel: 613-992-3474
Fax: 613-992-1974
Min@dfo-mpo.gc.ca
Other Communications: Fisheries & Oceans, Phone: 613-992-3474

Deputy Minister, Matthew King
Tel: 613-993-2200
Fax: 613-993-2194

Parliamentary Secretary to the Minister of Fisheries & Oceans, Randy Kamp
Tel: 613-992-3474
Fax: 613-947-4615
Kamp.R@parl.gc.ca

Director General, Communications, Louise Girouard
Tel: 613-990-0219
Fax: 613-993-8277

Executive Director & Senior General Counsel, Legal Services Unit, Lynn Lovett
Tel: 613-993-0966

Chief of Staff to the Deputy Minister, Blair Hodgson
Tel: 613-993-9226

Fax: 613-993-2194
blair.hodgson@dfo-mpo.gc.ca

Associated Agencies, Boards & Commissions:
• Fisheries Resource Conservation Council (FRCC) / Le Conseil pour la conservation des ressources halieutiques (CCRH)
PO Box 2001 D
Ottawa, ON K1P 5W3
Tel: 613-998-0433
Fax: 613-998-1146
info@frcc-ccrh.ca
www.frcc.ca
Created in 1993 to form a partnership between scientific & academic expertise, & all sectors of the fishing industry. Council members make public recommendations to the Minister of Fisheries & Oceans on conservation measures for the Atlantic fishery.
Executive Director, Arthur Willett
Chair, Jean Guy d'Entremont
Tel: 613-998-0433
• Freshwater Fish Marketing Corporation / Office de commercialisation du poisson d'eau douce
See Entry Name Index for detailed listing.

Canadian Coast Guard (CCG) / Garde côtière canadienne
Centennial Towers, #6S018, 200 Kent St., Ottawa, ON K1A 0E6
Tel: 613-993-0999
Fax: 613-990-1866
TTY: 613-941-6517
info@dfo-mpo.gc.ca
www.ccg-gcc.gc.ca
The Canadian Coast Guard provides the following maritime programs & services: search & rescue; marine communications & traffic services, including radio communications & radio navigational aids services; marine navigation services, a program which establishes & maintains navigational aids to assist vessels in safe navigation; enrvironmental response program, which works to minimize impacts of marine pollution incidents & to provide humanitarian aid in disasters; aids to navigation, such as the Differential Global Positioning System (DGPS) & Notices to Mariners (NOTMAR); icebreaking services; & client relations & international affairs.
Commissioner, Marc Grégoire
Tel: 613-998-1571
Fax: 613-990-2780
Assistant Commissioner, Newfoundland & Labrador Region, John Butler
Tel: 709-772-5150
Fax: 709-772-4194
Assistant Commissioner, Quebec Region, Marc Demonceaux
Tel: 418-648-4535
Fax: 418-649-6066
Assistant Commissioner, Mario Pelletier
Tel: 613-991-6108
Fax: 613-993-5333
Assistant Commissioner, Canadian Coast Guard, Vija Poruks
Tel: 604-775-8810
Assistant Commissioner, Maritimes Region, Gary Sidock
Tel: 902-425-3907
Fax: 613-993-3421
Assistant Commissioner, Central & Arctic Region, Vacant
Tel: 519-383-1800
Fax: 519-383-1998
Assistant Commissioner, Pacific Region, Vacant
Deputy Commissioner, Operations, Jody Thomas
Tel: 613-998-1575
Director, Operational Restructuring, Neil O'Rourke
Tel: 613-998-8164
Fax: 613-993-5333
Deputy Commissioner, Vessel Procurement, Michel G. Vermette
Tel: 613-994-9220
Fax: 613-949-6816
Special Advisor to the Commissioner, David G. Faulkner
Tel: 613-993-1628
Fax: 613-993-5333
Director General, Operations, Wade Spurrell
Tel: 613-990-9172
Fax: 613-995-4700

Maritime Services Directorate / Direction générale des services maritimes
Fax: 613-991-4982
Director General, Jacqueline Gonçalves
Tel: 613-993-7728
Director, Maritime Safety Systems, Alex Li
Tel: 613-990-3115

Ecosystems & Fisheries Management / Gestion des écosystèmes et des pêches
200 Kent St., Ottawa, ON K1A 0E6
Responsible for the management & development of all federal fisheries & habitat in Canada. The division conserves, protects, develops & enhances fishery resources & habitats, encompassing the Atlantic & Pacific sectors, adjacent provinces, & the 200-mile offshore zone. Also manages Canadian parts of trans-boundary rivers.
Senior Assistant Deputy Minister, David Balfour
Tel: 613-990-9864
Director General, Ecosystem Management, Sharon Ashley
Tel: 613-990-0007
Acting Director General, Operations Integration, Jaime Caceres
Tel: 613-990-7556
Director General, Small Craft Harbours, Micheline Leduc
Tel: 613-990-8989
Director General, Conservation & Protection, Allan D. MacLean
Tel: 613-993-1414
Fax: 613-941-2718
Director General, Aboriginal Programs & Governance, David Millette
Tel: 613-990-7201
Director General, Conservation & Protection, Paul Steele
Tel: 613-998-9537
Executive Director, Aquaculture Operations Management Directorate, Eric Gilbert
Tel: 613-993-1884
Fax: 613-991-0212
Executive Director, Fisheries Modernization Initiative, Gus van Helvoort
Tel: 902-426-3625
Senior Director, Fisheries Protection Program, Christine Stoneman
Tel: 613-991-6355
Fax: 613-993-7493
Director, Conservation & Protection, Enforcement Policies & Standards, Jacinta Berthier
Tel: 902-426-2392
Fax: 902-426-8003
Director, Regional Oceans Operations, Mary Jean Comfort
Tel: 613-993-2401
Fax: 613-990-4810
Director, Regional Oceans Operations, Gail Faulkner
Tel: 613-993-2401
Director, Atlantic Integrated Commercial Fisheries Initiative, Kevin Fram
Tel: 613-993-3096
Fax: 613-993-7651
Director, Harbours Operations & Engineering, Donna Jean Kilpatrick
Tel: 613-991-6112
Director, Species at Risk Program Management, Susan Mojgani
Tel: 613-990-0280
Acting Director, Resource Management - National, Dawn Pearcey
Tel: 613-991-1955
Director, Pacific Integrated Commercial Fisheries Initiative, Julie Stewart
Tel: 613-990-8756
Fax: 613-993-7651
Director, Fisheries Protection Program, Richard Vermette
Tel: 613-991-1776
Fax: 613-993-7493
Director, Aboriginal Programs, Susan Waters
Tel: 613-949-7518
Fax: 613-993-7651
Director, Resource Management - Pacific, Arctic & Inland, Arthur Willett
Tel: 613-993-5045

Ecosystems & Oceans Science / Océans et science
200 Kent St., Ottawa, ON K1A 0E6
Services include: oceans sciences (ocean's physical properties, behaviour of organic & inorganic materials & their impact on fish & ecosystems, pollutants); regulation, enforcement & management of fisheries resources & habitat that are exploited for aboriginal, commercial & recreational purposes. The Marine Protected Areas Policy & the National Framework for Establishing & Managing Marine Protected Areas represents DFO's approach to establishing & maintaining MPOs in Canada.
Assistant Deputy Minister, Kevin Stringer
Tel: 613-993-5123
Fax: 613-990-5113
Director General, Ecosystem Science, David Gillis
Tel: 613-990-0271
Director General, Special Projects, Kathleen Fischer
Tel: 613-998-9003
Fax: 613-990-0313
Director General, Strategic & Regulatory Science, Wayne Moore
Tel: 613-990-0001
Fax: 613-990-0313
Director, Fish Population Science, Jean Landry
Tel: 613-993-0029
Fax: 613-991-1378
Director, Aquaculture Science Branch, Jay Parsons
Tel: 613-990-0278
Fax: 613-990-0313
Director, Environment & Biodiversity Science, Patrice Simon
Tel: 613-990-0289
Director, Biotechnology & Aquatic Animal Health Sciences, Stephen Stephen
Tel: 613-990-0292
Fax: 613-990-0313

Canadian Hydrographic Service (CHS) / Service hydrographique du Canada
615 Booth St., Ottawa, ON K1A 0E6
Tel: 613-998-4931
Fax: 613-998-1217
chsinfo@dfo-mpo.gc.ca
www.chs-shc.gc.ca/pub
Federal program which offers the following: conducts field studies & gathers hydrographic information on tides, water levels & currents; compiles & publishes navigational charts & manuals for Canadian & adjacent international waters; works with Natural Resources Canada to cooperatively map boundary waters.
Director General, Savithri Narayanan
Tel: 613-995-4413
Executive Director, Canada Meteorological & Oceanographic Society, Ian D. Rutherford
Tel: 613-990-0300
Fax: 613-990-1617
Director, Oceanography & Climate Branch, Helen Joseph
Tel: 613-990-6930
Fax: 613-990-6131
Multidisciplinary Hydrographer, Law of the Sea Project (UNCLOS), Joe P. Manning
Tel: 709-772-0450

Human Resources & Corporate Services / Services généraux
200 Kent St., Ottawa, ON K1A 0E6
Assistant Deputy Minister, Diane Orange
Tel: 613-993-8726
Fax: 613-993-3246
Chief Information Officer & Director General, Information Management & Technology Services, Filippo Gagliardi
Tel: 613-993-2051
Director, Office of Environmental Coordination, Brenda Morehouse
Tel: 613-991-6867
Director, Client Portfolio Management, Hélène Mousseau
Tel: 613-998-0235
Fax: 613-993-8930
Director, Infrastructure Operations (Networks/Telephony), Karl K. Primmer
Tel: 709-772-2111
Fax: 709-772-4567
Director, Real Property, Long Term Capital Management, Andrea Raper
Tel: 613-998-4315
Fax: 613-954-5674
Director, Corporate Compensation Branch, Diane Séguin-Guérette
Tel: 613-990-5860
Fax: 613-990-0035
Director, Human Resources Operations - National Capital Region, Cathryn Taubman
Tel: 613-991-0363
Fax: 613-990-5675
Director, Infrastructure/Operations (PC/RDI), Brad Tinney
Tel: 905-336-6260

Program Policy / Politiques relatives aux programmes
200 Kent St., Ottawa, ON K1A 0E6

Services provided by the science sector include the following: research & data gathering; provision of information & advice in the fields of fisheries sciences (fish, invertebrates, marine mammals & plants, & ecosystems), oceans sciences (ocean's physical properties, behaviour of organic & inorganic materials & their impact on fish & ecosystems, pollutants), & hydrography (bathymetric, tide & current systems); & regulation, enforcement & management of fisheries resources & habitat that are exploited for aboriginal, commercial & recreational purposes. The sector assesses major stocks of exploited species of anadromous & marine fish, invertebrates, mammals & plants in Canada's Atlantic, Pacific, Arctic & marine waters, as well as freshwater fish in the Yukon & Northwest Territories. Research is conducted in the following areas: the biology & population of fish stocks, in order to provide scientific information & advice to fishery managers; the effects of changes in the ocean environment on the recruitment & distribution of fish populations; & studies to improve the productivity of aquaculture.
Assistant Deputy Minister, Trevor Swerdfager
Tel: 613-949-4919
Fax: 613-990-2768
Director General, Aquaculture Management, Guy Beaupré
Tel: 613-991-4315
Director General, Fisheries & Aboriginal Policy, Nadia Bouffard
Tel: 613-998-3111
Acting Director General, Ecosystem Programs Policy, Steve Burgess
Tel: 613-998-9088
Fax: 613-993-5995
Director, Aquaculture Regulatory Policy, Sharon Ford
Tel: 613-990-1459
Fax: 613-993-8607
Director, Aboriginal Policy & Treaty, Robert Lamirande
Tel: 613-991-6979
Fax: 613-990-4111
Director, Oceans Policy & Planning, Camille Mageau
Tel: 613-991-1285
Fax: 613-990-4810
Director, Strategic Aboriginal Policy, Deborah Price
Tel: 613-990-9569
Fax: 613-990-4111
Director, Oceans & Species at Risk, Policies & Strategies, Gina Sinclair
Tel: 613-949-7524
Director, Certification & Sustainability Reporting, James Smith
Tel: 506-447-7193
Fax: 613-993-8607
Acting Director, Oceans & Species at Risk, Policies & Strategies, Darren Williams
Tel: 613-993-2287
Fax: 613-993-5995
Director, Habitat Program Policy Branch, Nicholas Winfield
Tel: 613-990-2574
Fax: 613-993-7493

Strategic Policy / Politiques
200 Kent St., Ottawa, ON K1A 0E6
Provides leadership in recommending, developing & monitoring policy frameworks that advance DFO's initiatives, support DFO programs, & are responsive to the changing needs of DFO clients. Provides strategic advice on departmental programs, develops long-term planning priorities for the department & coordinates cross-sectoral activities in support of government goals & departmental objectives.
Senior Assistant Deputy Minister, France Pégeot
Tel: 613-993-1808
Director General, Economic Analysis & Statistics, Robert Elliott
Tel: 613-993-8597
Director General, Strategic Policy & Priorities, Dilhari Fernando
Tel: 613-990-0287
Director General, Legislative & Intergovernmental Affairs, Jeff MacDonald
Tel: 613-991-6651
Fax: 613-990-2811
Director General, Executive Secretariat, Michael Olsen
Tel: 613-998-5012
Fax: 613-949-9022
Director General, International Affairs, Michael Pearson
Tel: 613-993-1908
Associate Director General, International Affairs, Sylvie Lapointe
Tel: 613-993-6853
Fax: 613-993-5995
Executive Director, Legislation & Regulatory Affairs, Bhagwant Sandhu
Tel: 613-998-8117
Director, Horizontal Policy & Priorities, Tim Angus
Tel: 613-993-1841
Fax: 613-993-5085
Director, Global Trade & Market Access, John Campbell
Tel: 613-990-3682
Fax: 613-993-5085
Director, Legislation & Regulatory Affairs, Tiffany Caron
Tel: 613-998-5571
Fax: 613-993-5204
Director, Intergovernmental Affairs, Katerina Daniel
Tel: 613-991-1273
Director, Atlantic & Americas Regional Affairs, Katerina Daniel
Tel: 613-991-1273
Director, Global Marine & Northern Affairs, Renée Sauvé
Tel: 613-991-6740
Acting Director, US & Asia/Pacific Regional Affairs, Allison Webb
Tel: 604-666-0920
Fax: 604-666-3295
Acting Executive Advisor to the Senior ADM, Tanya Dagenais
Tel: 613-993-0823
Fax: 613-993-6958
Central & Arctic
520 Exmouth St., Sarnia, ON N7T 8B1
Fax: 519-464-5128
Acting Regional Director General, David Burden
Tel: 519-383-1810
Fax: 519-464-5128
Gulf
Gulf Fisheries Centre, 343, av Université, PO Box 5030Moncton, NB E1C 9B6
Tel: 506-851-7751
Fax: 506-851-2224
Regional Director General, Morley B. Knight
Tel: 506-851-7750
Fax: 506-851-2224
Regional Director General, Serge Theriault
Tel: 506-851-7750
Fax: 506-851-2224
Maritimes
Marine House, 176 Portland St., Halifax, NS B2Y 4T3
Tel: 902-426-2581
Fax: 902-426-3479
Regional Director General, Faith G. Scattolon
Tel: 902-426-2581
Newfoundland & Labrador
Northwest Atlantic Fisheries Centre, 80 East White Hills, PO Box 5667St. John's, NL A1C 5X1
Tel: 709-772-4423
Fax: 709-772-6306
Regional Director General, Michael J. Alexander
Tel: 709-772-4417
Fax: 709-772-6306
Pacific
#200, 401 Burrard St., Vancouver, BC V6C 3S4
Fax: 604-666-8956
Regional Director General, Susan Farlinger
Tel: 604-666-6098
Regional Director General, Paul Sprout
Tel: 604-666-6098
Québec
104, rue Dalhousie, Québec, QC G1K 7Y7
Tél: 418-648-7747
Téléc: 418-648-4758
Regional Director General, Richard Nadeau
Tel: 418-648-4158
Fax: 418-648-4758

Bayfield Institute
867 Lakeshore Rd., PO Box 5050Burlington, ON L7R 4A6
Tel: 905-336-6240
www.dfo-mpo.gc.ca/regions/central/pub/bayfield/index-eng.htm
Comprises fisheries research, habitat management, hydrographic surveys & chart production & ships support. Together with the Freshwater Institute in Winnipeg, it provides the federal Fisheries & Oceans science programs for the Central & Arctic Region. Multiple partnerships with a variety of external stakeholders allow the Institute to be recognized internationally as a site of leading research in freshwater science.

Bedford Institute of Oceanography (BIO) / L'institut océanographique de Bedford
1 Challenger Dr., PO Box 1006Dartmouth, NS B2Y 4A2
Tel: 902-426-3492
Fax: 902-426-8484
WebmasterBIO-IOB@dfo-mpo.gc.ca
www.bio.gc.ca
Administered by Fisheries & Oceans, Bedford Institute of Oceanography (BIO) is Canada's largest centre for ocean research. Scientists, engineers & technicians primarily from Fisheries & Oceans, & Natural Resources Canada, (smaller components are from National Defense & Environment Canada) perform targeted research & provide advice on Atlantic marine environments. Programs include: fisheries research, ocean sciences & management, habitat ecology, marine chemistry, Canadian Hydrographic Service (producing navigation charts for the Atlantic & Arctic areas), marine environmental regional & resources geoscience, & seabird research & management. BIO based staff also conduct joint projects, such as sea floor mapping & exploration, & provide scientific response to marine environmental emergencies. Also located at Bedford is the Canadian Shark Research Laboratory & the Otolith Research Laboratory.
Regional Director, Science, Alain Vézina
Director, Natural Resources Canada - Geological Survey of Canada (Atlantic), Stephen Locke
Tel: 902-426-2730
Fax: 902-426-1466

Centre for Aquaculture & Environmental Research / Centre de recherche sur l'aquaculture et l'environnement
4160 Marine Dr., West Vancouver, BC V7V 1N6
Tel: 604-666-7453
Fax: 604-666-3497
The Center for Aquaculture & Environmental Research (CAER) is a specialized centre for aquaculture & coastal research co-founded by Fisheries & Oceans Canada & the University of British Columbia.
Regional Director, Science Branch, Laura Richards
Tel: 250-729-8369
Fax: 250-756-7053

Experimental Lakes Area (ELA) / Région des lacs expérimentaux
Kenora, ON
The Experimental Lakes Area, located on the Precambrian Shield of northwestern Ontario, consists of numerous lakes & watersheds that have been set aside by the Ontario & Canadian governments for the purpose of scientific research & whole-lake manipulation studies.
Contact, Mark Lyng
Tel: 204-983-5203

Freshwater Institute Science Laboratory / Laboratoire scientifique de l'Institut des eaux douces
501 University Cres., Winnipeg, MB R3T 2N6
Tel: 204-983-5000
Fax: 204-983-6285
www.dfo-mpo.gc.ca/regions/central/pub/fresh-douces/index-eng.htm
Main areas of research are: fish habitats; limnology emphasizing mechanisms & processes of biological production & decomposition in lakes; studies related to energy development use, acidification, radionuclide & heavy metal pollution. Arctic research emphasizes commercially important fish & marine mammals & associated ecosystems, & the effects of hydroelectric developments & toxic chemical pollution on aquatic ecosystems. The Institute supports a major field camp at the Experimental Lakes Area. Activities include freshwater & arctic science, science oceans initiative, fish habitat management, fisheries management, small craft harbours, corporate services, communications & regional senior management. The federal fish inspection program, recently transferred to the new Canadian Food Inspection Agency (CFIA), continues to operate out of the FWI.

Gulf Fisheries Centre / Centre de poissonerie du gulfe
343, av Université, 5th Fl., Moncton, NB E1C 9B6
Tél: 506-851-6227
Téléc: 506-851-2435
info@dfo-mpo.gc.ca
www.inter.dfo-mpo.gc.ca/e0008111
The Gulf Fisheries Centre contains the Mère Juliette Library, which is open to the general public. The library's collection contains 20,000 books & reports, 100 scientific journals, 10,000 microfiches & over a hundred videos.
Regional Director General, Serge Thériault
Tel: 506-851-7750
Fax: 506-851-2224

Institut Maurice-Lamontagne (IML) / Maurice Lamontagne Institute (MLI)
850, rte de le Mer, CP 1000Mont-Joli, QC G5H 3Z4
Tél: 418-775-0500
Téléc: 418-775-0730
www.qc.dfo-mpo.gc.ca/iml-mli/institut-institute/index-eng.asp

Provides extensive research on: fisheries, fish habitat, oceanography, hydrography; development of marine renewable resources in the fields of fisheries, ocean industry development, commercial shipping & recreational boating. Main area of focus centres on the Gulf of St. Lawrence & estuary, Saguenay Fjord, Canadian Arctic, & the James, Hudson & Ungava Bays. Also performs the following research: environmental chemistry research on the distribution, transport & fate of contaminants in sediments, water & the food chain; ecotoxicology research & field assessments for biomarkers, fish pathology & embryotoxicity; molecular toxicology research for biomarkers, fish reproduction & steroid hormones; bioremediation study on the microbial degradation of petroleum oil hydrocarbons & microbial bioassays. Projects include the temporal & spatial monitoring of organic & inorganic contaminants in fish, shellfish & sediments of the St. Lawrence gulf & estuary. Also studying the effects of pulp & paper effluents & mercury & municipal effluents on the reproduction of fish.
Regional Director, Regional Science Branch, Ariane Plourde
Tel: 418-775-0555

Institute of Ocean Sciences (IOS) / Institut des sciences de la mer (ISM)
9860 West Saanich Rd., PO Box 6000Sidney, BC V8L 4B2
Tel: 250-363-6517
Fax: 250-363-6390
Science divisions at IOS include: Canadian Hydrographic Service, Marine Environment & Habitat Science, Ocean Science & Productivity. Other departments & organizations at the IOS facility include: GSC Pacific - Sidney Pacific Geoscience Centre, Canadian Wildlife Service, Canadian Coast Guard, North Pacific Marine Science Organization (PICES).
Director, Canadian Hydrographic Service, Denis D'Amours
Tel: 250-363-6347
Manager, Ocean Sciences Directorate, Robin Brown
Tel: 250-363-6378

Pacific Biological Station (PBS) / La station de biologie du Pacifique
3190 Hammond Bay Rd., Nanaimo, BC V9T 6N7
Tel: 250-756-7000
Fax: 250-756-7053
Research at PBS responds to stock assessment, aquaculture, marine environment & habitat science, & ocean science & productivity priorities.
Regional Director, Science Branch, Dr. Laura Richards
Tel: 250-729-8369

Resolute Bay Laboratories / Laboratoires de Resolute Bay
Resolute Bay, NT
The Eastern Arctic field camp at Resolute Bay has been inactive for several years due to deteriorating conditions. However, with increasing interest in how global warming is affecting arctic marine conditions, the site, which includes a laboratory, warehouse & living quarters may be re-opened in the future.

St. Andrews Biological Station / La Station biologique de St. Andrews
531 Brandy Cove Rd., St Andrews, NB E5B 2L9
Tel: 506-529-8854
Fax: 506-529-5862
XMARSABS@mar.dfo-mpo.gc.ca
www.mar.dfo-mpo.gc.ca/sabs
Chemical & ecological studies on the interaction between oceanography & fisheries/aquaculture & the aquatic environment. Stock assessments & associated research on commercially important groundfish, pelagic finfish, invertebrate species in the Bay of Fundy & other areas of Atlantic Canada. Research in support of the existing salmon aquaculture industry & research on other species with potential for aquaculture in Atlantic Canada. Major environmental research projects include: risk assessment of organic chemicals to fisheries; biochemical indicators of health of aquatic animals; aquatic toxicity of marine phytotoxins; molluscan toxins, techniques & improvements; phytotoxin research; aquaculture ecology research; effectiveness of acid rain control programs; effects of aquaculture in the coastal environment.
Station Director & SABS Division Manager, Sharon McGladdery
Tel: 506-529-5916
Sharon.McGladdery@dfo-mpo.gc.ca

Sea Lamprey Control Centre / Centre de contôle de la lamproie de mer
1 Canal Dr., Sault Ste Marie, ON P6A 6W4
The Centre is a combined office, lab, warehouse, aquarium, & maintenance & chemical storage facility that houses Canada's Sea Lamprey Control program & the research lab of the Great Lakes Laboratory for Fisheries & Aquatic Sciences (GLLFAS). It is located on the grounds of the Sault Ste. Marie Canal National Historic Site.

Ecosystem Research Division (ERD) / Division de la recherche écosystémique (DRE)
www2.mar.dfo-mpo.gc.ca/science/ocean/sci/sci-e.html
Manager, Ecosystem Research, Glenn Harrison
Tel: 902-426-3879
glenn.harrison@dfo-mpo.gc.ca

Ocean Sciences
www2.mar.dfo-mpo.gc.ca/science/ocean/osd/osd-e.html
Manager, Ocean Sciences, Michel Mitchell
Tel: 902-426-8366
michel.mitchell@dfo-mpo.gc.ca

Integrated Science Data Management (ISDM) / Gestion des données scientifiques intégrées (GDSI)
Tel: 613-990-0265
Fax: 613-993-4658
service@meds-sdmm.dfo-mpo.gc.ca
www.meds-sdmm.dfo-mpo.gc.ca/isdm-gdsi/index-eng.html
Manages & archives ocean data collected by DFO or acquired through national or international programmes conducted in ocean areas adjacent to Canada; disseminates data, data products & services to the marine community. MEDS is a member of the International Oceanographic Data & Information Exchange, whose mission is to enhance marine research, exploitation & development by facilitating the exchange of oceanographic information between participating member countries.
Chief, Data Management & Client Services Division, Jean J. Gagnon
gagnonj@dfo-mpo.gc.ca
Senior Technical & Policy Advisor, J. Robert Keeley
keeley@meds-sdmm.dfo-mpo.gc.ca

Foreign Affairs & International Trade Canada (DFAIT) / Affaires étrangères et Commerce international Canada (MAECI)

Enquiries Service, 125 Sussex Dr., Ottawa, ON K1A 0G2
Tel: 613-944-4000
Fax: 613-996-9709
Toll-Free: 800-267-8376
TTY: 613-944-9136
enqserv@international.gc.ca; travel@international.gc.ca
www.international.gc.ca
Other Communication: Emergencies, Phone: 613-996-8885; Jules Léger Library: 613-992-6150; Canadian Foreign Service Institute: 819-994-6932; Media Relations Office: 613-995-1874
twitter.com/DFAIT_MAECI
www.youtube.com/user/dfaitmaeci
In 1909, the Canada Department of External Affairs was established. The department is now known as Foreign Affairs & International Trade Canada.
The mandate of Foreign Affairs & International Trade Canada includes the following responsibilities: to manage the nation's diplomatic & consular relations; to ensure that foreign policy advances national interests; to promote international trade; to strengthen trading arrangements; to increase free & fair market access at bilateral, regional, & global levels; & to work with partners to attain improved economic opportunity & enhanced security for Canadians at home & abroad.
The Department of Foreign Affairs & International Trade funds the following programs in Canada & throughout the world: Anti-Crime Capacity Building Program; Canada in La Francophonie; Canadian International Arctic Fund; Counter-Terrorism Capacity Building Program; Global Commerce Support Program (Invest Canada-Community Initiatives, Going Global Innovation, & Global Opportunities for Associations); Global Partnership Program; Global Peace and Security Fund (Global Peace & Security Program, Global Peace Operations Program, & Glyn Berry Program); International Education & Youth; International Science & Technology Partnerships Program ; Investment Cooperation Program; Permanent Secretariat of the UN Convention on Biological Diversity; United Nations Trust Fund on Indigenous Issues; & United Nations Voluntary Fund for Victims of Torture.
Foreign Affiars & International Trade Canada also offers travel reports & warnings, such as information about security, entry requirements, health condiotns, & local customs & laws (www.voyage.gc.ca/countries_pays/menu-eng.asp).

Minister, Foreign Affairs, Hon. John Baird
Tel: 613-996-0984
Fax: 613-996-9880
john.baird@parl.gc.ca
www.johnbaird.com
Social Media: twitter.com/JohnBairdOWN

Minister, International Trade; Minister, Asia-Pacific Gateway, Hon. Edward Fast, P.C., LL.B.
Tel: 613-995-0183
Fax: 613-996-9795
ed.fast@parl.gc.ca
www.edfast.ca
Social Media: www.facebook.com/EdFastMP

Parliamentary Secretary to the Minister, International Cooperation, Lois Brown
Tel: 613-992-9310
Fax: 613-992-9407
lois.brown@parl.gc.ca

Parliamentary Secretary to the Minister, Foreign Affairs, Bob Dechert
Tel: 613-995-7321
Fax: 613-992-6708
bob.dechert@parl.gc.ca

Parliamentary Secretary to the Minister, Fisheries & Oceans & for the Asia-Pacific Gateway, Randy Kamp, B.A.
Tel: 613-947-4613
Toll-free: 888-255-8140
Fax: 613-947-4615
randy.kamp@parl.gc.ca
www.randykamp.com
Social Media: twitter.com/RandyKamp_com, www.facebook.com/10029901492

Parliamentary Secretary to the Minister, International Trade, for the Atlantic Canada Opportunities Agency & for the Atlantic Gateway, Gerald Keddy, B.A.
Tel: 613-996-0877
Fax: 613-996-0878
keddyg@parl.gc.ca

Parliamentary Secretary to the Minister, Foreign Affairs, Deepak Obhrai
Tel: 613-947-4566
Fax: 613-947-4569
deepak.obhrai@parl.gc.ca
www.deepakobhrai.com
Social Media: twitter.com/deepakobhrai, www.facebook.com/DeepakObhrai

Ambassador of Religious Freedom, Andrew P.W. Bennett

Corporate Social Responsibiltiy Counsellor for the Extractive Sector, Marketa Evans
Tel: 416-973-2058
Fax: 416-973-2070
1 Front St.
Toronto, ON M5J 1A4

Associated Agencies, Boards & Commissions:
- **Canadian Commercial Corporation**
See Entry Name Index for detailed listing.
- **Export Development Canada**
See Entry Name Index for detailed listing.
- **International Development Research Centre**
See Entry Name Index for detailed listing.
- **International Joint Commission**
See Entry Name Index for detailed listing.
- **National Capital Commission**
See Entry Name Index for detailed listing.
- **North American Free Trade Agreement (NAFTA) Canadian Secretariat**
See Entry Name Index for detailed listing.

Office of the Minister, Foreign Affairs
The Minister of Foreign Affairs is responsible for Canada's foreign policy & issues related to external affairs. The Minister oversees the International Centre for Human Rights & Democratic Development, the International Development Research Centre, the International Joint Commission, & the National Capital Commission.
Minister, Foreign Affairs, Hon. John Baird
Tel: 613-996-0984
Fax: 613-996-9880
john.baird@parl.gc.ca; bairdj1@parl.gc.ca

www.johnbaird.com
Social Media: twitter.com/JohnBairdOWN
Chief of Staff, Garry Keller
Tel: 613-995-1851
Director, Communications; Deputy Chief of Staff, Chris Day
Tel: 613-995-1851
Director, Strategic Communications & New Media, Joseph Lavoie
Tel: 613-995-1851
Director, Regional Affairs, John Light
Tel: 613-995-1851
Director, Parliamentary Affairs & Issues Management, Katherine E. Locke
Tel: 613-995-1851
Press Secretary, Rick Roth
Tel: 613-995-1851

Office of the Minister, International Trade
Responsibilities of the Minister of Foreign Affairs include international trade & commerce. The Minister oversee the Canadian Commercial Corporation, Export Development Canada, & NAFTA - Canadian Secretariat.
Minister, International Trade; Minister, Asia-Pacific Gateway, Hon. Edward Fast, P.C., LL.B.
Tel: 613-995-0183
Fax: 613-996-9795
ed.fast@parl.gc.ca; faste@parl.gc.ca; ed@edfast.ca
Social Media: www.facebook.com/EdFastMP
Chief of Staff, Bill Hawkins
Tel: 613-992-7332
Director, Parliamentary Affairs & Issues Management, Christopher Green
Tel: 613-992-7332
Director, Policy & Stakeholder Relations, Lise-Ann Jackson
Tel: 613-992-7332
Director, Communications & Forward Planning, Adam Taylor
Tel: 613-992-7332
Manager, Forward Planning & Events, Rebecca Rogers
Tel: 613-992-7332
Press Secretary, Rudy Husny
Tel: 613-992-7332

Office of the Minister of State, Foreign Affairs (Americas & Consular Affairs)
Responsibilities of foreign affairs personnel include diplomatic & consular relations & the the administration of the Foreign Service & Canada's missions abroad.
Minister of State, Foreign Affairs (Americas & Consular Affairs), Hon. Diane Ablonczy, P.C., B.Ed., LL.B.
Tel: 613-996-2756
Fax: 613-992-2537
diane.ablonczy@parl.gc.ca
Social Media: twitter.com/dianeablonczymp
Chief of Staff, Stephen B. Snell
Tel: 613-944-5377
Senior Policy Advisor, Yves Gagnon
Tel: 613-992-6094
Senior Policy Advisor, Consular Affairs, Ashley McArthur
Tel: 613-944-2300
Departmental Advisor, Americas, Alan Wilde
Tel: 613-944-4993
Advisor, Parliamentary Affairs & Issues Management, Amanda Murphy
Tel: 613-996-2756

Office of the Deputy Minister, Foreign Affairs

Associate Deputy Minister / Sous-ministre délégué
Fax: 613-947-8497
Associate Deputy Minister, Peter M. Boehm
Tel: 613-944-2771
Chief of Protocol of Canada, Office of Protocol, Angela Bogdan
Tel: 613-992-2344

Afghanistan, Middle East, & Maghreb
Assistant Deputy Minister, Afghanistan, Middle East, & Maghreb, Gordon Venner
Tel: 613-943-3660
Director General, Middle East & Maghreb Bureau, Mark Bailey
Tel: 613-944-1144

Americas
Tel: 613-944-7877
Fax: 613-944-0561
Director General, North America Policy Bureau, Martial Pagé
Tel: 613-944-1966
Director General, North America Programs & Operations Bureau, Roxanne Dubé
Tel: 613-944-1286
Fax: 613-995-2603
Director General, Latin America & Caribbean Bureau, Neil Reeder
Tel: 613-996-8435
Fax: 613-944-0924

Consular, Security & Emergency Management Branch / Secteur des services consulaires, de la sécurité et de la gestion des urgences
Tel: 613-943-3797
Assistant Deputy Minister & Chief Security Officer, William Crosbie
Tel: 613-943-3770
Director General, Emergency Management Bureau, Robin Dubeau
Tel: 613-992-8448
Director General, Consular Operations Bureau, Barbara Richardson
Tel: 613-996-0639
Fax: 613-947-0366
Director General, Consular Policy & Advocacy Bureau, Marc Vidricaire
Tel: 613-943-3774
Fax: 613-947-0366
Director General, Security & Intelligence Bureau, Artur Wilczynski
Tel: 613-992-7400
Fax: 613-996-1724

Europe, Eurasia & Africa / Europe, Eurasie et Afrique
Tel: 613-996-7832
Fax: 613-944-1471
Assistant Deputy Minister, Jillian Stirk
Tel: 613-996-5095
Fax: 613-944-1471
Chief Negotiator, Canada-EU Political Framework, Vacant
Director General, Africa Bureau, Brenda Côté
Tel: 613-944-5990
Fax: 613-944-1199
Other Communications: Secure Fax: 613-944-1568
Director General, Europe & Eurasia Bureau, John Kur
Tel: 613-992-8333
Fax: 613-995-5772
Director General, Africa Bureau, Patricia Malikail
Tel: 613-995-1097
Fax: 613-944-7432
Other Communications: Secure Fax: 613-944-1568
Director General, North Asia, Graham Shantz
Tel: 613-995-1097
Fax: 613-944-2535
Other Communications: Secure Phone: 613-995-1097

Global Issues / Enjeux mondiaux
Assistant Deputy Minister, Vacant
Director General, International Organizations, Human Rights & Democracy Bureau, Sarah A. Fountain Smith
Tel: 613-944-0928
Director, Circumpolar Affairs, Sigrid Anna Johnson
Tel: 613-944-9173
Fax: 613-943-0606

International Security Branch & Political Director / Sécurité international et directeur politique
Assistant Deputy Minister & Political Director, Kerry Buck
Tel: 613-944-4228
Fax: 613-944-1180
Assistant Deputy Minister, Vacant
Director General, Strategic Policy, Policy Planning Bureau, Dan Costello
Tel: 613-944-3179

Office of the Deputy Minister, International Trade
Deputy Minister, International Trade, Simon Kennedy
Tel: 613-944-5000
Director, Office of the Deputy Director, International Trade, Owen Teo
Tel: 613-944-0358
Deputy Director, Office of the Deputy Minister, International Trade, Shalini Anand
Tel: 613-944-0357
Chief Air Negotiator & Director General, IP & Services Trade, Martin Loken
Tel: 613-944-1116
Fax: 613-996-1667
Assistant Deputy Minister & Chief Trade Commissioner, Peter McGovern
Tel: 613-944-2695
Fax: 613-944-2697
Director General, South, Southeast Asia & Oceania, Peter MacArthur
Tel: 613-992-6129
Fax: 613-996-5897
Director General, Office of the Chief Trade Commissioner, Louis Marcotte
Tel: 613-996-0550
Fax: 613-944-3473

International Business Development, Investment & Innovation / Développement du commerce international, investissement et innovation
Tel: 613-944-3178
Associate Assistant Deputy Minister, Grant Manuge
Tel: 613-944-0504
Fax: 613-944-3062
Director, Innovation, Science & Technology Divisionion, Kevin Fitzgibbons
Tel: 613-995-2224
Fax: 613-944-0111
Director, Cleantech, Infrastructure & Life Sciences Practices Division, Charles Larabie
Tel: 613-996-3490

Resources Management / Gestion des ressources
Tel: 613-944-2016
Fax: 613-943-2058
Director, Area Management Office - Trade Policy & Negotiations Branch, Svend Holm
Tel: 613-992-7021
Deputy Director & Area Management Advisor, Area Management Office - Investment, Innovation & Sectors, Kathy Couturier
Tel: 613-944-3210
Fax: 613-992-8727
Deputy Director, Area Management Office - Investment, Innovation & Sectors, Manon M. Plouffe
Tel: 613-944-0284
Fax: 613-943-2058

Trade Policy & Negotiations Branch / Secteur de la politique et des négociations commerciales
Tel: 613-996-5677
Fax: 613-996-1667
Assistant Deputy Minister, Ian Burney
Tel: 613-992-0293
Acting Director, Sanitary & Phytosanitary Measures Division, Josée De Menezes
Tel: 613-944-8980
Fax: 613-943-0346

Canadian Trade Commissioner Service / Service des délégués commerciaux du Canada
c/o Foreign Affairs & International Trade, 125 Sussex Dr., Ottawa, ON K1A 0G2
Tel: 613-944-9991
Fax: 613-996-9709
Toll-Free: 888-306-9991
enqserv@international.gc.ca
www.tradecommissioner.gc.ca
twitter.com/tcs_sdc
www.linkedin.com/groups?mostPopular=&gid=1808582
The Virtual Trade Commissioner (VTC) is a federal service that provides Canadian businesses with export assistance to increase overseas sales. VTC provides access to free services of the Canadian Trade Commissioner Service, with over 500 trade officers in 140 cities worldwide, information & services available through a personalized webpage, & access to international business leads from the International Business Opportunities Centre.
Director General, Trade Commissioner Service Operations & Trade Strategy Bureau, Judith St. George
Tel: 613-944-1678
Director, Investment Cooperation Program Division, Martin Jensen
Tel: 613-943-3938
Fax: 613-943-3919
Deputy Director, Investment Cooperation Program Division, Charles Tremblay
Tel: 613-996-6416

Spokesperson, Media Relations, Outreach & E-Communications Division, Caitlin Workman
Tel: 613-992-6490

International Business Opportunities Centre / Centre des occasions d'affaires internationales
Toll-Free: 877-232-2269
www.bdc.ca/en/dfait/financing/Pages/iboc.aspx
twitter.com/BDC_News
www.facebook.com/BDC.ca
www.linkedin.com/company/bdc
Operates an electronic trade leads system that is made available to companies registered through the Virtual Trade Commissioner. The service is free of charge & exclusive to Canadian companies.

International Trade Centres
Calgary
#400, 639 - 5 Ave. SW, Calgary, AB T2P 0M9
Fax: 403-292-4578
Toll-Free: 888-306-9991
Prairies.TCS-SDC@international.gc.ca
www.tradecommissioner.gc.ca/alta
Secondary Address: #300, 639 - 5 Ave. SW
Physical Address:
Calgary, AB Canada
Director & Senior Trade Commissioner, Patricia Elliott
patricia.elliott@international.gc.ca
Charlottetown
191 University Ave., Charlottetown, PE C1A 4L2
Fax: 902-566-6859
Toll-Free: 888-306-9991
Atlantic-Atlantique.TCS-SDC@international.gc.ca
www.tradeteampei.com
Other Communication: Alternate URL:
www.tradecommissioner.gc.ca/pei
Senior Trade Commissioner, Aerospace & Defence, Agricultural Technology & Equipment, Bio-Industries, Chemicals, Environmental Industries, Health Industries, Service Industries & Capital Projects, Bernard (Butch) Postma
bernard.postma@international.gc.ca
Edmonton
Canada Place, #725, 9700 Jasper Ave., Edmonton, AB T5J 4C3
Fax: 780-495-4507
Toll-Free: 888-306-9991
Prairies.TCS-SDC@international.gc.ca
www.tradecommisioner.gc.ca/alta
Trade Commissioner, Service Industries & Capital Projects, Sameena Qureshi
sameena.qureshi@international.gc.ca
Halifax
1791 Barrington St., 11th Fl., Halifax, NS B3J 3L1
Fax: 902-426-5218
Toll-Free: 888-306-9991
Atlantic-Atlantique.TCS-SDC@international.gc.ca
www.tradecommisioner.gc.ca/ns
Senior Trade Commissioner, Ocean Technologies, Christine Smith
christine.smith@international.gc.ca
Moncton
#104, 1045 Main St., Moncton, NB E1C 1H1
Tel: 506-453-3772
Fax: 506-453-3783
Toll-Free: 888-306-9991
Atlantic-Atlantique.TCS-SDC@international.gc.ca
www.ttnb.ca
Other Communication: Alternate Fax: 902-426-5218; Toll-Free Phone: 1-888-576-4444; URL: www.tradecommissioner.gc.ca/nb
Director, Atlantic Region, Economic & Trade Policy, Michelyne Paulin
michelyne.paulin@international.gc.ca
Senior Trade Commissioner, Information & Communications Technologies, Sarah Dionne
sarah.dionne@international.gc.ca
Montréal
Place Bonaventure, Portail Sud-Ouest, #8750, 800, rue de la Gauchetiere ouest, Montréal, QC H3B 2G2
Fax: 514-283-8794
Toll-Free: 888-306-9991
quebec.tcs-sdc@international.gc.ca
www.tradecommissioner.gc.ca/que
Director & Senior Trade Commissioner, Julie Insley
Tel: 514-283-3531
Fax: 514-283-8794
Acting Deputy Director & Trade Commissioner (InfoCentre), Michel Lamarre
Tel: 514-283-0435
Fax: 514-283-8794
Ottawa
55 Metcalfe St., Ottawa, ON K1P 6L5
Fax: 613-995-1720
Toll-Free: 888-306-9991
Ontario.TCS-SDC@international.gc.ca
www.tradecommissioner.gc.ca/ont
Trade Commissioner, Jane Rooney
Tel: 613-995-1708
Fax: 613-995-1708
Québec
Place Iberville IV, #030, 2954, boul Laurier, Québec, QC G1V 4T2
Fax: 418-648-7428
Toll-Free: 888-306-9991
quebec.tcs-sdc@international.gc.ca
www.tradecommissioner.gc.ca/que
Senior Trade Commissioner, Ocean Technologies, Joane Hallé
Tel: 418-648-7464
Fax: 418-648-7428
Regina
#600, 1945 Hamilton St., Regina, SK S4P 2C7
Fax: 306-780-8797
Toll-Free: 888-306-9991
Prairies.TCS-SDC@international.gc.ca
www.tradecommissioner.gc.ca/sask
Senior Trade Commissioner, Mona M. Taylor
mona.taylor@international.gc.ca
St. John's
John Cabot Bldg., 10 Barter's HIll, 10th Fl., PO Box 2009 Stn. C, St. John's, NL A1C 5R6
Fax: 709-772-2373
Toll-Free: 888-306-9991
Atlantic-Atlantique.TCS-SDC@international.gc.ca
www.tradecommissioner.gc.ca/nfldlab
Senior Trade Commissioner, Anthony McLevey
anthony.mclevey@international.gc.ca
Toronto
Yonge-Richmond Centre, 151 Yonge St., 4th Fl., Toronto, ON M5C 2W7
Fax: 416-973-8161
Toll-Free: 888-306-9991
Ontario.TCS-SDC@international.gc.ca
www.tradecommisioner.gc.ca/ont
Director & Senior Trade Commissioner, Jim Feir
Tel: 416-954-6326
Fax: 416-973-8161
Deputy Director & Trade Commissioner, Jeffrey Crossman
Tel: 416-973-5187
Vancouver
#2000, 300 West Georgia St., Vancouver, BC V6B 6E1
Fax: 604-666-0954
Toll-Free: 888-306-9991
pacific-pacifique.tcs-sdc@international.gc.ca
www.britishcolumbia.ca
Other Communication: Alternate URL:
www.tradecommissioner.gc.ca/bc
twitter.com/BCTradeInvest
www.linkedin.com/company/trade-&-invest-british-columbia
Regional Director & Senior Trade Commissioner, Alan Minz
Tel: 604-666-8888
Deputy Director & Trade Commissioner, Building Products, Forest Industries, Martin Barratt
Tel: 604-666-1445
Fax: 604-666-0954
Victoria
#100, 990 Fort St., Victoria, BC V8V 3K2
Fax: 250-363-0502
Toll-Free: 888-306-9991
pacific-pacifique.tcs-sdc@international.gc.ca
www.britishcolumbia.ca
Other Communication: Alternate URL:
www.tradecommissioner.gc.ca/bc
twitter.com/BCTradeInvest
www.linkedin.com/company/trade-&-invest-british-columbia
Trade Commissioner, Ocean Technologies, Marilyn Denton
Tel: 250-363-0575
Fax: 250-363-0502
Waterloo
#110, 50 Queen St. North, Kitchener, ON N2H 6P4
Fax: 519-571-6658
Toll-Free: 888-306-9991
Ontario.TCS-SDC@international.gc.ca
www.tradecommissioner.gc.ca/ont
Trade Commissioner, Robin McNabb
Ontario.TCS-SDC@international.gc.ca
Winnipeg
400 St. Mary Ave., 4th Fl., Winnipeg, MB R3C 4K5
Fax: 204-984-7082
Toll-Free: 888-306-9991
Prairies.TCS-SDC@international.gc.ca
www.gov.mb.ca/trade/index.html
Other Communication: Alternate URL:
www.tradecommissioner.gc.ca/man
Senior Trade Commissioner, Bio-Industries, Health Industries & Investment Promotion, Amanda McNaughton
amanda.mcnaughton@international.gc.ca

Health Canada / Santé Canada

Tunney's Pasture, Ottawa, ON K1A 0K9
Tel: 613-957-2991
Fax: 613-941-5366
Toll-Free: 866-225-0709
info@hc-sc.gc.ca
www.hc-sc.gc.ca
Other Communication: Office of the Access to Information: 613-954-8744
In partnership with provincial & territorial governments, Health Canada (HC) develops health policy, enforces health regulations, promotes disease prevention, & enhances healthy living for all Canadians. HC ensures that health services are available & accessible to First Nations & Inuit communities. It works closely with other federal departments, agencies & health stakeholders to reduce health & safety risks to Canadians. Through its Health Intelligence Network, HC works with other levels of government & the health care system in the surveillance, prevention, control & research of disease outbreaks across Canada & around the world. It also monitors health & safety risks related to the sale & use of drugs, food, chemicals, pesticides, medical devices & certain consumer products. HC negotiates agreements regarding hazardous materials in the workplace, performs medical assessments for pilots & air traffic controllers, & conducts environmental health assessments.
Acts Administered:
Appeal Board Procedures Regulations
Canada Health Act
Consumer Chemicals & Containers Regulations
Controlled Products Regulations
Department of Health Act
Fitness & Amateur Sport Act
Food & Drugs Act (Agriculture & Agri-Food Canada)
Hazardous Material Information Review Regulations
Hazardous Materials Information Review Act (Human Resources & Skills Development)
Hazardous Products Act
Hazardous Products Regulations (Cellulose Insulation, Charcoal, Crocidolite Asbestos, Liquid Coating Materials, etc.)
Ingredient Disclosure List
Pest Control Products Act, 2002
Pesticide Residue Compensation Act
Quarantine Act
Radiation Emitting Devices Act
Tobacco Act

Minister, Health, Hon. Leona Aglukkaq, P.C.
Tel: 613-957-0200
Fax: 613-952-1154
leona.aglukkaq@parl.gc.ca

Director, Policy, Leah Canning
Tel: 613-957-0200

Associated Agencies, Boards & Commissions:
• Canadian Institutes of Health Research / Instituts de recherche en santé du Canada
• Hazardous Materials Information Review Commission (HMIRC) / Conseil de contrôle des renseignements relatifs aux matières dangereuses
427 Laurier Ave. West, 7th Fl.
Ottawa, ON K1A 1M3
Tel: 613-993-4331
Fax: 613-993-4686
hmirc-ccrmd@hc-sc.gc.ca
www.hmirc-ccrmd.gc.ca
The HMIRC is an administrative agency charged with carrying out a multi-faceted mandate under the authority of the Hazardous Materials Information Review Act, & provincial & territorial occupational health & safety acts. The mandate includes: for-

mally registering claims for trade-secret exemptions & issuing registry numbers; adjudicating & issuing decisions on the validity of claims for exemption using prescribed regulatory criteria; making decisions on the compliance of material safety data sheets (MSDSs) & labels within the Workplace Hazardous Materials Information System (WHMIS) requirements; & convening independent, tripartite boards to hear appeals from claimants or affected parties on decisions & orders issued by HMIRC. Clients consist of a number of WHMIS stakeholders: suppliers & employers in the chemical industry who wish to protect their trade secrets from being disclosed on MSDSs or labels; employers who rely on supplier MSDS information to prepare their own workplace MSDSs & training programs; & labour organizations representing all workers who are exposed to these products.
President & Chief Executive Officer, Sharon Watts
Tel: 613-993-4472
Fax: 613-993-5016
Vice-President, Operations Branch, Kimberly Empey
Tel: 613-993-5015
Fax: 613-993-4686
Vice-President, Corporate Services & Adjudication Branch, Daniele Dionne
Tel: 613-941-2945
Fax: 613-993-5016
Officer, Client Services, Denis St-Amour
Tel: 613-993-4685
Fax: 613-993-4686
Manager, Policy Development, Jason Wood
Tel: 613-993-4429
Fax: 613-993-5016
Director, Screening Division, Vacant
Tel: 613-993-4873
Fax: 613-993-4686
Director, Material Safety Data Sheets Compliance Division, Colleen Dimock
Tel: 613-993-4711
Fax: 613-993-4686
colleen_dimock@hc-sc.gc.ca

• Pest Management Regulatory Agency (PMRA) / Agence de réglementation de la lutte antiparasitaire (ARLA)
2720 Riverside Dr.
Ottawa, ON K1A 0K9
Tel: 613-736-3401
Fax: 613-736-3798
www.hc-sc.gc.ca/cps-spc/pest/index-eng.php
Other Communication: Pesticides Information: 1-800-267-6315
The PMRA determines if proposed pesticides can be used safely when label directions are followed & will be effective for their intended use. If there is reasonable certainty from scientific evaluation that no harm to human health, future generations or the environment will result from exposure to or use of a pesticide, its registration for use in Canada will be approved. Once the pesticides are on the market, the PMRA monitors their use through a series of education, compliance & enforcement programs. Pesticides are also reviewed every fifteen years or sooner as new information is discovered & as science evolves. Companies are also required to report any incident they receive about their products, just as the public is encouraged to report any incidents to these companies or through the Incident Reporting Program. The PMRA administers the Pest Control Products Act on behalf of the Minister of Health.
Executive Director, Karen Dodds
Tel: 613-736-3708
Fax: 613-736-3707
Chief Registrar, Richard Aucoin
Tel: 613-736-3704
Director, Environmental Assessment Division, Karen Lloyd
Tel: 613-736-3715

• Public Health Agency of Canada / Agence de santé publique du Canada
130 Colonnade Rd.
Ottawa, ON K1A 0K9
www.phac-aspc.gc.ca
Other Communication: Alberta/NWT: 780-495-2754; Atlantic: 902-426-2700; BC/Yukon: 604-666-2729; Manitoba/Saskatchewan: 204-789-2000; Ontario/Nunavut: 416-973-0003; Quebec: 514-283-2858
Promotes & protects the health & safety of all Canadians. Its activities focus on preventing chronic diseases, including cancer & heart disease, preventing injuries, & responding to public health emergencies & infectious disease outbreaks.
Chief Public Health Officer, Dr. David Butler-Jones
Tel: 613-954-8524
Deputy Chief Public Health Officer, Health Promotion & Chronic Disease, Sylvie Stachenko
Tel: 613-946-3537
Fax: 613-941-1108
Deputy Chief Public Health Officer, Infectious Disease & Emergency Preparedness, Paul R. Gully
Tel: 613-954-9663
Deputy Chief Public Health Officer, Public Health Practice & Regional Operations, David Mowat
Tel: 613-957-7661
Deputy Minister, Glenda Yeates
Tel: 613-957-0212
Fax: 613-952-8422
glenda.yeates@hc-sc.gc.ca
Associate Deputy Minister, Associate Deputy Minister's Office, Anne-Marie Robinson
Tel: 613-954-5904
Fax: 613-952-8422
anne-marie.robinson@hc-sc.gc.ca
Director General, Associate Deputy Minister's Office, Sony Perron
Tel: 613-941-2567
sony.perron@hc-sc.gc.ca
Director, Operations, Danielle Dubois
Tel: 613-948-6420
danielle.dubois@hc-sc.gc.ca
Director, Associate Deputy Minister's Office, Robert Ianiro
Tel: 613-941-2526
robert.ianiro@hc-sc.gc.ca

First Nations & Inuit Health Branch (FNIHB) / Direction générale de la santé des Premières nations et des Inuits (DGSPNI)
Assists First Nations & Inuit communities & people to address health inequalities & diseases threats through health surveillance & population health interventions. Ensures the availability of, or access to, health services for First Nations & Inuit people. Devolves control & management of community-based health services to First Nations & Inuit communities & organizations. The Environmental Health Division addresses conditions in the environment that could affect the health of community members, such as drinking water quality, mould, food safety, facilities inspections, transportation of dangerous goods. The Environmental Research Division conducts, coordinates & funds contaminants-related research, coordinates the replacement or upgrading of diesel-fuel tanks & remediation of fuel oil-contaminated sites, lab services for testing of PCBs & mercury, drinking water-related research & testing.
Assistant Deputy Minister, Michel Roy
Tel: 613-957-7701
Fax: 613-957-1118
michel.roy@hc-sc.gc.ca
Senior Director General, Debbie L. Reid
Tel: 613-952-3135
Fax: 613-957-1118
debbie.l.reid@hc-sc.gc.ca
Director General, Strategic Policy, Planning & Analysis, Valerie Gideon
Tel: 613-957-3402
valerie.gideon@hc-sc.gc.ca
Acting Executive Director, Office of Nursing Services, Dorothy Laplante
Tel: 613-946-0442
Fax: 613-957-9986
dorothy.laplante@hc-sc.gc.ca
Executive Director, Office of Community Medicine, Dr. RoseMarie Ramsingh
Tel: 613-941-5358
Fax: 613-952-6407
rosemarie.ramsingh@hc-sc.gc.ca
Acting Director, Policy & Operations, Lori Brooks
Tel: 613-941-4400
lori.brooks@hc-sc.gc.ca
Director, Environmental Public Health, Primary Health Care & Public Health, Ivy Chan
Tel: 613-948-7773
Fax: 613-952-8639
ivy.chan@hc-sc.gc.ca
Director, Environmental Health Research, Primary Health Care & Public Health, Roy Kwiatkowski
Tel: 613-952-2828
Fax: 613-954-0692
roy.kwiatkowski@hc-sc.gc.ca
Director, Strategic Relations, Strategic Policy, Planning & Analysis, Paul McKinstry
Tel: 204-983-0989
Fax: 204-983-0079
paul.mckinstry@hc-sc.gc.ca
Director, Primary Health Care & Public Health, Shelagh Jane Woods
Tel: 613-941-1956
Fax: 613-941-8904
shelagh.jane.woods@hc-sc.gc.ca

Health Canada Regulations / Section de la réglementation
Fax: 613-954-4627
General Counsel & Director, Claude Lesage
Tel: 613-952-9645
Fax: 613-954-4627
claude.lesage@hc-sc.gc.ca
Senior Counsel, Wendy Gordon
Tel: 613-954-4761
Fax: 613-954-4627
wendy.gordon@hc-sc.gc.ca

Health Products & Food Branch (HPFB) / Direction générale des produits de santé et des aliments (DGPSA)
HPFB's mandate is to take an integrated apporach to the management of risks & benefits related to health products & food by minimizing health factors to Canadians while maximizing the safety provided by the regulatory system for health products & food; & to promote conditions that enable Canadians to make healthy choices & provide information so that they can make informed decisions about their health. The Environmental Impact Initiative develops strategy & policy in response to the Canadian Environmental Protection Act requirement that all new substances for use in Canada must be assessed for direct & indirect impact on human health & the environment.
Assistant Deputy Minister, Paul Glover
Tel: 613-957-1804
Fax: 613-957-3954
paul_glover@hc-sc.gc.ca

Healthy Environments & Consumer Safety (HECSB) / Direction générale, santé environnementale et sécurité des consommateurs (DGSESC)
The HECSB mission is to help Canadians to maintain & improve their health by promoting healthy & safe living, working & recreational environments & by reducing the harm caused by tobacco, alcohol, controlled substances, environmental contaminants, & unsafe consumer & industrial products.
Assistant Deputy Minister, Hilary Geller
Tel: 613-946-6701
Fax: 613-946-6666
hilary.geller@hc-sc.gc.ca
Director General, Consumer Product Safety, Athana Mentzelopoulos
Tel: 613-960-4725
Fax: 613-946-1100
athana.mentzelopoulos@hc-sc.gc.ca
Director General, Environmental & Radiation Health Sciences, Beth Pieterson
Tel: 613-954-3859
beth.pieterson@hc-sc.gc.ca
Director General, Controlled Substances & Tobacco, Cathy A. Sabiston
Tel: 613-941-1977
Fax: 613-946-6460
cathy.a.sabiston@hc-sc.gc.ca
Director, Planning & Administrative Services, Policy, Planning & Integration, Wendy Kiernan
Tel: 613-941-3137
Fax: 613-941-8632
wendy.kiernan@hc-sc.gc.ca
Director, Planning & Administrative Services, Safe Environments, Karen Lloyd
Tel: 613-954-0291
Fax: 613-952-2206
karen.lloyd@hc-sc.gc.ca
Director, Office of Controlled Substances, Johanne Beaulieu
Tel: 613-952-2177
Fax: 613-946-4224
johanne.beaulieu@hc-sc.gc.ca

Legal Services / Services juridiques
www.hc-sc.gc.ca/ahc-asc/branch-dirgen/ls-sj/index-eng.php

Pest Management Regulatory Agency (PMRA) / Agence de réglementation de la lutte antiparasitaire (ARLA)
The PMRA is responsible for pesticide regulation in Canada. Created in 1995, this branch of Health Canada consolidates the

resources & responsibilities for pest management regulation. Pesticides are stringently regulated in Canada to ensure they pose minimal risk to human health & the environment. Health Canada also promotes & verifies compliance with the Act & enforces situations of non compliance warranting action.
Executive Director, Richard Aucoin
Tel: 613-736-3701
Fax: 613-736-3707
richard.aucoin@hc-sc.gc.ca
Chief Registrar, Marion Law
Tel: 613-736-3704
Fax: 613-736-3707
marion.law@hc-sc.gc.ca
Director General, Health Evaluation, Dr. Peter Chan, PhD
Tel: 613-736-3510
Fax: 613-736-3909
peter.chan@hc-sc.gc.ca
Director General, Re-evaluation Management, Margherita Conti
Tel: 613-736-3485
Fax: 613-736-9840
margherita.conti@hc-sc.gc.ca
Director General, Policy, Communications & Regulatory Affairs, Trish MacQuarrie
Tel: 613-736-3660
Fax: 613-736-3659
trish.macquarrie@hc-sc.gc.ca
Director General, Environmental Assessment, Mary Mitchell
Tel: 613-736-3715
mary.mitchell@hc-sc.gc.ca
Director General, Compliance, Lab Services & Regional Operations, Dr. Martin Tomkin
Tel: 613-736-3484
Fax: 613-736-3540
martin.tomkin@hc-sc.gc.ca
Director General, Value & Sustainability Assessment, John Worgan
Tel: 613-736-3780
Fax: 613-736-3770
john.worgan@hc-sc.gc.ca
Director, Strategic Planning, Financial & Business Operations, Anne Lapierre
Tel: 613-736-3411
anne.lapierre@hc-sc.gc.ca

Public Affairs, Consultation & Communications (PACCB) / Direction générale des affaires publiques, de la consultation et des communications (DGAPCC)

The PACCB integrates national & regional perspectives into all of its policies & strategies, communications & consultation functions. The Branch plays a key role in delivering Health Canada's commitment to transparency. Through PACCB, Health Canada will continue to improve communications & the flow of information to & from stakeholders, clients, partners, media & the Canadian public.
Assistant Deputy Minister, Anne Lamar
Tel: 613-960-2176
Fax: 613-960-2183
anne.lamar@hc-sc.gc.ca
Director General, Marketing & Communications Services, Jane Hazel
Tel: 613-957-0215
Fax: 613-948-8092
jane.hazel@hc-sc.gc.ca
Director General, Strategic Communications, Charles Mojsej
Tel: 613-948-8916
Fax: 613-957-1729
charles.mojsej@hc-sc.gc.ca
Director General, Consultations, Planning & Coordination, Aruna Sadana
Tel: 613-960-6043
Fax: 613-960-6063
aruna.sadana@hc-sc.gc.ca

Regions & Programs Branch / Direction générale des régions et des programmes

Assistant Deputy Minister, Michel C. Doré
Tel: 613-941-8081
Fax: 613-948-0082
michel.c.dore@hc-sc.gc.ca
Acting Senior Director General, Programs, Debbie Beresford-Green
Tel: 613-952-3579
Fax: 613-941-7360
debbie.beresford-green@hc-sc.gc.ca
Director General, Emergency Preparedness & Occupational Health, Anthony Sangster
Tel: 613-957-7669
Fax: 613-954-5822
anthony.sangster@hc-sc.gc.ca
Director General, Branch Management Services, Nicholas Trudel
Tel: 613-954-0681
Fax: 613-941-7360
nicholas.trudel@hc-sc.gc.ca
Director, Colleen Ryan
Tel: 613-952-2074
Fax: 613-941-7360
colleen.ryan@hc-sc.gc.ca

Strategic Policy Branch (SPB) / Direction générale de la politique stratégique (DGPS)

The SPB plays a lead role in health policy, communications & consultations. The SPB's objective is to promote national coordination & development of a strong, shared knowledge base to address health & health care priorities for all Canadians. They also aim to facilitate successful health system adaptation to changes in technology, society, industry & the environment, such that Canadians will continue to be protected from health risks, have access to quality health care, & gain positive health benefits from information & innovation.
Assistant Deputy Minister, Abby Hoffman
Tel: 613-946-1791
Fax: 613-954-0336
abby.hoffman@hc-sc.gc.ca
Associate Assistant Deputy Minister, Michelle Kovacevic
Tel: 613-954-2645
michelle.kovacevic@hc-sc.gc.ca
Acting Director General, Health Care Policy, Gavin Brown
Tel: 613-957-8994
Fax: 613-648-4663
gavin.brown@hc-sc.gc.ca
Director General, Science Policy, Dr. Pierre Charest
Tel: 613-941-3003
Fax: 613-941-3007
pierre.charest@hc-sc.gc.ca
Director General, International Affairs, Bersabel Ephrem
Tel: 613-941-3335
Fax: 613-952-7417
bersabel.ephrem@hc-sc.gc.ca
Director General, Legislative & Regulatory Policy, Regi Mathew
Tel: 613-960-7353
regi.mathew@hc-sc.gc.ca
Director General, Applied Research & Analysis, Sylvain Paradis
Tel: 613-946-8030
sylvain.paradis@hc-sc.gc.ca
Executive Director, Office of Nursing Policy, Sandra MacDonald-Rencz
Tel: 613-941-4314
Fax: 613-946-3166
sandra.macdonald-rencz@hc-sc.gc.ca
Acting Executive Director, Office of Pharmaceuticals Management Strategies, Jean Pruneau
Tel: 613-941-8218
Fax: 613-941-5258
jean.pruneau@hc-sc.gc.ca
Director, Canada Health Act Division, Gigi Mandy
Tel: 613-954-8685
Fax: 613-952-8542
gigi.mandy@hc-sc.gc.ca
Acting Director, Federal/Provincial Relations, Noel Kivimaki
Tel: 613-946-8860
Fax: 613-954-3580
noel.kivimaki@hc-sc.gc.ca
Director, Policy Coordination & Planning, Phyllis Colvin
Tel: 613-957-3085
phyllis.colvin@hc-sc.gc.ca

Food Directorate / Direction des aliments

Tel: 613-957-0365
Fax: 613-941-5070
Research, analysis of risk & benefit & policy development regarding chemical & microbiological contaminants of food, food processes, genetically modified foods.

Safe Environments Programme

Environmental Health Centre, Bldg. 8, 120 Parkdale Ave., Ottawa, ON K1A 0K9
Tel: 613-954-0291
Fax: 613-952-2206
Investigates, monitors & assesses health risks in the work, home & natural environments. Areas investigated & regulated include: medical devices, chemicals & biotechnology products in the environment, drinking water, air quality, tobacco, hazardous products & toxic waste, as well as anything that emits radiation from natural & human sources. Aims to protect Canadians from health hazards associated with natural & man-made environments through assessment & investigation of the health effects of environmental pollutants & health hazards associated with radiation sources & hazardous products.

Workplace Hazardous Materials Information System (WHMIS)

Fax: 613-952-1994
www.hc-sc.gc.ca/ewh-semt/occup-travail/whmis-simdut/index_e.html
A nationwide hazard communication system providing information on hazardous materials used in the workplace. Key elements of the system are cautionary labelling on containers of hazardous materials, material safety data sheets (MSDSs) that contain more detailed information, & worker training. Suppliers must ensure that products are appropriately labelled & that MSDSs are provided to purchasers. Employers are required to make MSDSs available to their employees & provide workers with training on WHMIS & the safe use of hazardous materials. WHMIS supports the workers' right to know the hazards of the materials they use. WHMIS requirements are administered through federal & provincial coordinators.

Workplace Health & Public Safety

Vanguard Bldg., 171 Slater St., 9th Fl., Ottawa, ON K1A 0K9
corporate_whpsp@hc-sc.gc.ca
Workplace Health & Public Safety Programme (WHPSP) is responsible for helping Canadian private & public sector employers maintain & improve the health of their workers. WHPSP provides national leadership to develop health policy, best practices in the workplace, & enhance healthy living for all working Canadians.
Director General, Stéphane Hardy
Tel: 613-957-7669
Fax: 613-954-5822
stephane_hardy@hc-sc.gc.ca

Hazardous Materials Information Review Commission (HMIRC)

427 Laurier Ave. West, Ottawa, ON K1A 1M3
www.hmirc-ccrmd.gc.ca
The Hazardous Materials Information Review Commission works with the Ministry of Health to help safeguard the workers and trade secrets of Canada's chemical industry.

Human Resources & Skills Development Canada (HRSDC) / Ressources humaines et Développement des compétences Canada (RHDCC)

140 Promenade du Portage, Gatineau, QC K1A 0J9
www.hrsdc.gc.ca
Other Communication: Media enquiries: 819-994-5559
HRSDC works to build a competitive country & to support Canadians in making choices to live productively. The following are key responsibilities of the federal department: developing policies to assist Canadaians to use their talents, skills & resources to participate in learning, work, & their community; creating programs to support initiative to help citizens in life transitions; improving outcomes for people through services offered by Service Canada & other partners; & establishing a healthy work environment.

Acts Administered:
Aviation Occupational Safety & Health Regulations
Canada Labour Code
Canada Occupational Health & Safety Regulations
Canadian Centre for Occupational Health & Safety Act
Coal Mines (CBDC) Occupational Safety & Health Regulations
Coal Mining Safety Commission Regulations
Corporations & Labour Unions Returns Act
Marine Occupational Safety & Health Regulations
Non-smokers' Health Act (Transport Canada)
Oil & Gas Occupational Safety & Health Regulations
On Board Trains Occupational Safety & Health Regulations

Minister, Human Resources & Skills Development, Hon. Diane Finley, B.A., M.B.A.
Tel: 819-994-2482
Fax: 819-994-0448
diane.finley@hrsdc-rhdcc.gc.ca

Minister, Labour, Hon. Lisa Raitt
Tel: 819-953-5646

Fax: 819-994-5168
lisa.raitt@hrsdc-rhdcc.gc.ca

Minister of State (Seniors), Hon. Alice Wong
Tel: 613-995-2021
Fax: 819-995-2174

Deputy Minister, Labour, Hélène Gosselin
Tel: 819-934-3320
Fax: 819-934-7066
helene.gosselin@labour-travail.gc.ca

Deputy Minister, Human Resources & Skills Development Canada, Ian Shugart
Tel: 819-994-4514
Fax: 819-953-5603
ian.shugart@hrsdc-rhdcc.gc.ca

Chief Audit Executive, Vincent DaLuz
Tel: 819-953-0821
Fax: 819-953-0831
vincent.daluz@hrsdc-rhdcc.gc.ca

Associated Agencies, Boards & Commissions:

• Canada Employment Insurance Commission (CEIC) / Commission de l'assurance-emploi du Canada (CAEC)
140, Promenade du Portage, Phase IV
Gatineau, QC K1A 0J9
Toll-free: 800-206-7218
www.ei-ae.gc.ca
Manages the Employment Insurance Program.

• Canada Industrial Relations Board / Conseil canadien des relations industrielles
See Entry Name Index for detailed listing.

• Canadian Centre for Occupational Health & Safety / Centre canadien d'hygiène et de sécurité au travail
See Entry Name Index for detailed listing.

• Canadian Council of Directors of Apprenticeship / Conseil canadien des directeurs de l'apprentissage
140 Promenade du Portage, 5th Fl, Phase IV
Gatineau, QC K1A 0J9
Tel: 819-953-7443
Fax: 819-994-0202
redseal-sceaurouge@hrsdc-rhdcc.gc.ca
www.red-seal.ca
A national body responsible for the certification of skilled workers, in the regulated trade, under the Interprovincial Standards (Red Seal) Program. This program is designed to facilitate the mobility of workers employed in the apprenticeable occupations in Canada through the establishment of common standards for certification. The apprenticeship program is generally administered by provincial & territorial departments responsible for education, labour & training (under the direction of the provincial & territorial Director of Apprenticeship) with authority delegated from the legislation in each province & territory. Through the program, apprentices who have completed their training & certified journeymen are able to obtain a Red Seal endorsement on their Certificate of Qualification by successfully completing an Interprovincial Standards Examination. The program encourages standardization of provincial & territorial apprenticeship training & certification programs. The Red Seal allows qualified trade persons to practice the trade in any province or territory in Canada where the trade is designated without having to write further examinations.

• Merchant Seamen Compensation Board / Commission d'indemnisation des marins marchands du Canada
Secretary, Merchant Seamen Compensation Board
Phase II, Place du Portage, 10th Fl.
Ottawa, ON K1A 0J2
Tel: 819-953-8001
Fax: 819-994-5368
The Merchant Seamen Compensation Board consists of three members who are appointed by the Governor in Council pursuant to the Merchant Seamen Compensation Act . The Board reports to the federal Minister of Labour who has the overall responsibility for the Act. The Board hears & decides claims arising under the Act. The Act provides benefits to merchant seamen who are injured or disabled as a result of their work. Employers are liable to pay benefits awarded & the administrative expenses of the Board. They must maintain insurance against the risk of claims & report all accidents to the Board.

• Office of the Commissioner of Review Tribunals / Bureau du Commissaire des tribunaux de revision
PO Box 8250 T
Ottawa, ON K1G 5S5
Tel: 613-954-1313
Fax: 613-946-1588
Toll-free: 800-363-0076
info@ocrt-bctr.gc.ca
www.ocrt-bctr.gc.ca
Review Tribunals were created to provide a body independent from government to make determinations about eligibility for persons claiming CPP & OAS benefits that had previously been denied.

• Pension Appeals Board / Commission d'appel des pensions
PO Box 8567 T
Ottawa, ON K1G 3H9
Tel: 613-995-0612
Fax: 613-995-6834
Toll-free: 888-640-8001
info@pab-cap.gc.ca
www.pab-cap.gc.ca
The Pension Appeals Board is the final opportunity for appeal under the Canada Pension Plan. Responsible for the hearing of appeals which arise from the decisions of the Review Tribunals of the Office of the Commissioner.

Chief Financial Officer's Office / Bureau de l'agent principal des finances

---

Human Resources Services Branch / Direction générale des services des ressources humaines
Human Resources Services provides human resource services & technical expertise to HRSDC including succession planning, career development, orientation & training; compensation & benefits; classification & staffing; organizational renewal design & development; labour relations; occupational health & safety; & employment equity & official languages.

Income Security & Social Development Branch / Direction générale de la sécurité du revenu et du développement social
Income Security & Social Development is the focal point for social policy & programs designed to ensure that children, families, seniors, people with disabilities, the homeless & those at risk of homelessness, communities & others who are facing social challenges have the support, knowledge, & information they need to maintain their well-being & facilitate their participation in society.

Labour Program / Programme du travail
The Labour Program promotes safe, healthy, cooperative & productive workplaces. They develop, administer & enforce workplace legislation & regulations, such as the Canada Labour Code, which covers industrial relations, health & safety & employment standards, & the Employment Equity Act, which promotes workplace equality by removing the barriers faced by women, Aboriginal peoples, persons with disabilities & visible minorities while on the job. These laws cover federally regulated workers & employers.

Learning Branch / Apprentissage
The Learning branch helps Canadians attend college, university & trade schools by providing advice, loans, assistance, grants to students, by encouraging individuals & organizations to save for a child's post-secondary education, & by assisting children from low-income families through grants. It is responsible for programs & services related to learning, including student financial assistance, savings incentives for post-secondary education, & literacy.

Legal Services / Services juridiques
Legal Services provides legal services to support the core operations & key initiatives of HRSDC. The services provided include: legal advice on program statutes & policies administered by the Department, policy advice for developing policy & legislative or regulatory proposals, & representing the Department before boards, tribunals & courts.

Program Operations / Opérations des programmes
Program Operations handles the operation & coordination of the Grant & Contributions programs across the Department.

Public Affairs & Stakeholder Relations / Affaires publiques et Relations avec les intervenants
Public Affairs & Stakeholder Relations informs Canadians about HRSDC's mandate, policies & programs. It also supports departmental activities in engaging & communicating with stakeholders & citizens.

Service Canada
140, Promenade du Portage, Gatineau, QC K1A 0J9
Fax: 613-941-1827
Toll-Free: 800-622-6232
TTY: 800-926-9105
www.servicecanada.gc.ca
Other Communication: Media enquiries: 819-994-5559
twitter.com/ServiceCanada_E; twitter.com/servicecanada_f
Service Canada provides convenient access to a great range of Government of Canada programs & services. Service Canada Centres, as well as scheduled outreach sites, are located throughout Canada. The Service Canada web site & call centres are also available to assist Canadian citizens.
The following contact information is for frequently used programs:
Apprenticeship Grants: Toll-Free Phone 1-866-742-3644, TTY 1-800-255-4786;
Canada Pension Plan (CPP): Toll-Free Phone 1-800-277-9914, TTY 1-800-255-4786;
Employer Contact Centre: Toll-Free Phone 1-800-367-5693, TTY 1-855-881-9874;
Employment Insurance (EI): Toll-Free Phone 1-800-206-7218, TTY 1-800-529-3742;
Old Age Security (OAS): Toll-Free Phone 1-800-277-9914, TTY 1-800-255-4786;
Passports: Toll-Free Phone: 1-800-567-6868, TTY 1-866-255-7655;
Social Insurance Number (SIN): Toll-Free Phone: 1-800-206-7218;
Wage Earner Protection Program (WEPP): Toll-Free Phone 1-866-683-6516, TTY 1-800-926-9105.
Minister, Human Resources & Skills Development, Hon. Diane Finley
Tel: 613-996-4974
Fax: 613-996-9749
diane.finley@parl.gc.ca
www.dianefinley.ca
Senior Associate Deputy Minister, Human Resources & Skills Development; Chief Operating Officer, Service Canada, Karen Jackson
Tel: 819-994-4520
Fax: 819-934-5770
karen.jackson@hrsdc-rhdcc.gc.ca
Assistant Deputy Minister, Integrity Services, Louis Beauséjour
Tel: 819-953-2422
Fax: 819-934-9312
louis.beausejour@hrsdc-rhdcc.gc.ca
Assistant Deputy Minister, Citizen Services, Peter Simeoni
Tel: 613-957-4500
Fax: 613-960-2489
peter.simeoni@servicecanada.gc.ca
Assistant Deputy Minister, Processing & Payment Services, Paul Thompson
Tel: 613-954-5305
paul.thompson@servicecanada.gc.ca
Senior Executive Director, Citizen Services & Program Delivery - Ontario, William J. Woods
Tel: 416-954-7714
Fax: 416-954-7814
william.woods@servicecanada.gc.ca
Executive Director, Strategic Services Directorate - Québec, Ann Bonner
Tel: 514-982-2384 ext: 270
Fax: 514-283-1691
ann.bonner@servicecanada.gc.ca
Executive Director, Community Services - Western Canada & Territories, Hal M. Howie
Tel: 604-666-0123
Fax: 604-666-0086
hal.howie@servicecanada.gc.ca
Executive Director, Strategic & Communications Services - Atlantic, Jacques J. Laprise
Tel: 506-851-3240
Fax: 506-851-2572
jacques.j.laprise@servicecanada.gc.ca
Director General, Strategic Services Directorate, Lorri Biesenthal
Tel: 613-957-6384
lorri.biesenthal@servicecanada.gc.ca
Director General, Call Centre Directorate, Jacquie Manchevsky
Tel: 613-948-3730
Fax: 613-954-6400
jacquie.manchevsky@servicecanada.gc.ca
Director General, Benefits Processing, Ron Meighan
Tel: 613-946-0266
Fax: 613-954-6105
ron.meighan@servicecanada.gc.ca

Senior Director, Canada Pension Plan (CPP) & Old Age Security (OAS) Operations, George Markus
Tel: 613-957-3005
Fax: 613-957-3005
george.markus@servicecanada.gc.ca
Director, Strategic Communications & Employee Engagement, Services Management, Cheryl L. Meek
Tel: 819-934-5731
Fax: 819-934-1505
cheryl.meek@servicecanada.gc.ca

Alberta Service Canada Centres
Brooks
Cassils Plaza, 608 - 2 St. West, Brooks, AB T1R 1A8
Calgary - 4th Ave. SE
Calgary Centre Service Canada Centre, Harry Hays Building, #270, 220 - 4 Ave. SE, Calgary, AB T2G 4X3
Calgary - Crowchild Trail NW
Calgary North Service Canada Centre, One Executive Place, 1816 Crowchild Trail NW, Main Fl., Calgary, AB T2M 3Y7
Calgary - Fisher St. SE
Calgary South Service Canada Centre, Fisher Park Place II, #100, 6712 Fisher St. SE, Calgary, AB T2H 2A7
Calgary - Marlborough Way NE
Calgary East Service Canada Centre, #1502, 515 Marlborough Way NE, Calgary, AB T2A 7E7
Camrose
Federal Building, 4901 - 50 Ave., 2nd Fl., Camrose, AB T4V 0S2
Canmore
Building C, #113, 802 Bow Valley Trail, Canmore, AB T1W 1N6
Edmonton - 87th Ave. NW
Edmonton Meadowlark Service Canada, Meadowlark Shopping Ctr, #120, 15710 - 87th Ave. NW, Edmonton, AB T5R 5W9
Edmonton - 137th Ave. NW
Edmonton North Service Canada Centre, Northgate Centre, #2000, 9499 - 137th Ave. NW, Edmonton, AB T5E 5R8
Tel: 780-495-3904
Toll-Free: 800-622-6232
Edmonton - Jasper Ave.
Edmonton Canada Place Service Canada Centre, Canada Place, 9700 Jasper Ave., Main Fl., Edmonton, AB T5J 4C3
Edmonton - Millbourne Shopping Centre NW
Edmonton Millbourne Service Canada Centre, #148, Millbourne Shopping Centre NW, Edmonton, AB T6K 3L6
Edson
4905 - 4 Ave., Edson, AB T7E 1T5
Fort McMurray
#107, 8530 Manning Ave., Main Fl., Fort McMurray, AB T9H 5G2
Grande Prairie
Towne Centre Mall, #100, 9845 - 99 Ave., Grande Prairie, AB T8V 0R3
Lethbridge
Crowsnest Trail Plaza, 101, 920 - 2A Ave. North, Lethbridge, AB T1H 0E3
Medicine Hat
Northside Centre, 78 - 8 St. NW, Medicine Hat, AB T1A 6P1
Red Deer
#101, 4901 - 46th St., Red Deer, AB T4N 1N2
St Paul
4807 - 50 Ave., St Paul, AB T0A 3A0
Slave Lake
Sawridge Plaza, 100 Main St. South, Slave Lake, AB T0G 2A3
Service Canada Outreach Sites - Alberta

Toll-Free: 800-622-6232
TTY: 800-926-9105
The following places in Alberta are scheduled outreach sites for Service Canada:
Athabasca (Duniece Centre, 4810 - 50th St., 3rd Fl.);
Barrhead (6203 - 49 St.);
Blairmore (Provincial Building, 12501 - 20th Ave.);
Cold Lake (Cold Lake Public Library, 5513B - 48th Ave.);
Drayton Valley (5136 - 1 Ave., 2nd Fl.);
Drumheller (90 - 3rd Ave., 4th Fl.);
Falher (308 Main St.);
Grande Cache (4500 Pine Plaza);
High Level (Provincial Building, 10106 - 100 Ave.);
High Prairie (5226 - 53 Ave., 2nd Fl.);
Hinton (568 Carmichael Lane);
Hobbema (Maskwacis Health Centre);
Jasper (Château Jasper, 96 Geikie St.);
Lac La Biche (Provincial Building, 503 Beaver Hill Rd.);
Peace River (Valley Chrysler Building, 9603 - 90 Ave.);
Rocky Mountain House (4919 - 51st St.);
Stettler (4835 - 50 St.);
Taber (5324 - 48th Ave.);
Vegreville (5121 - 49 St.);
Wabasca-Desmarais (891 Mistassiniy Rd.);
Westlock (11304 - 99 St.);
Whitecourt (Midtown Mall, 5115 - 49th St.).

British Columbia Service Canada Centres
Abbotsford
100, 32525 Simon Ave., Abbotsford, BC V2T 6T6
Burnaby
#100, 3480 Gilmore Way, Burnaby, BC V5G 4Y1
Campbell River
#101, 950 Alder St., Campbell River, BC V9W 2P8
Chilliwack
#100, 9345 Main St., Chilliwack, BC V2P 4M3
Coquitlam
#100, 2963 Glen Dr., Coquitlam, BC V3B 2P7
Courtenay
Comox Valley Service Canada Centre, 130 - 19 St., Courtenay, BC V9N 8S1
Cranbrook
1113 Baker St., Cranbrook, BC V1C 1A7
Dawson Creek
#103, 1508 - 102 Ave., Dawson Creek, BC V1G 2E2
Duncan
Cowichan Service Canada Centre, 211 Jubilee St., Duncan, BC V9L 1W8
Kamloops
317 Seymour St., 1st Fl., Kamloops, BC V2C 2E8
Kelowna
#106, 471 Queensway, Kelowna, BC V1Y 6S5
Langley
#102, 8747 - 204 St., Langley, BC V1M 2Y5
Maple Ridge
Ridge Meadows Service Canada Centre, 22325 Loughheed Hwy., Maple Ridge, BC V2X 2T3
Nanaimo
#201, 60 Front St., Nanaimo, BC V9R 5H7
Nelson
Chahko Mika Mall, 1125 Lakeside Dr., Main Fl., Nelson, BC V1L 5Z3
New Westminster
#201, 620 Royal Ave., New Westminster, BC V3M 1J2
North Vancouver
North Shore Service Canada Centre, #100, 221 West Esplanade, North Vancouver, BC V7M 3N7
Penticton
#101, 386 Ellis St., Penticton, BC V2A 8C9
Port Alberni
4805 Mar St., #A, Port Alberni, BC V9Y 8J5
Powell River
7061 Duncan St., #A, Powell River, BC V8A 1W1
Prince George
1363 - 4 Ave., Prince George, BC V2L 3J6
Prince Rupert
#100, 215 - 3 St., Prince Rupert, BC V8J 3J9
Quesnel
283 Reid St. East, Quesnel, BC V2J 2M1
Richmond
#350, 5611 Cooney Rd., Richmond, BC V6X 3J6
Salmon Arm
191 Shuswap St. NW, 1st Fl., Salmon Arm, BC V1E 4P6
Smithers
1020 Murray St., Smithers, BC V0J 2N0
Squamish
1440 Winnipeg St., Squamish, BC V8B 0C3
Surrey - 104th Ave.
Surrey North Service Canada Centre, 13889 - 104 Ave., Surrey, BC V3T 1W8
Surrey - Hwy. 10
Surrey South Service Canada Centre, #103, 15295 Hwy. 10, Surrey, BC V3S 0X9
Terrace
4630 Lazelle Ave., Terrace, BC V8G 1S6
Trail
#101, 1101 Dewdney Ave., Trail, BC V1R 4T1
Vancouver - Broadway
Vancouver (West Broadway) Service Centre, 1263 West Broadway, Vancouver, BC V6H 1G7
Vancouver - Hastings St. West
Sinclair Centre Service Canada Centre, #125, 757 Hastings St. West, Vancouver, BC V6C 1A1
Vancouver - Kingsway
Vancouver East Service Canada Centre, 1420 Kingsway, Vancouver, BC V5N 2R5
Vanderhoof
189 Stewart St. East, RR#2, Vanderhoof, BC V0J 3A2
Vernon
3202 - 31st St., Vernon, BC V1T 2H3
Victoria - Douglas St.
1401 Douglas St., Victoria, BC V8W 2G2
Victoria - Jacklin Rd.
Victoria West Shore Service Canada Centre, 3179 Jacklin Rd., Victoria, BC V9B 3Y7
Williams Lake
79 - Fourth Ave. South, Williams Lake, BC V2G 1J6
Service Canada Outreach Sites - British Columbia

Toll-Free: 800-622-6232
TTY: 800-926-9105
The following places in British Columbia are scheduled outreach sites for Service Canada:
Alert Bay (Namgis Health Centre, 48 School Rd.);
Bella Bella (Heiltsuk Social Development Office);
Cache Creek (Village of Cache Creek Offices, 1389 Quartz Rd.);
Clearwater (Community Resource Centre for the North Thompson, 751 Clearwater Village Rd.);
Fort St John (10600 - 100th St.);
Hope (895 - 3rd Ave.);
Lytton (Village of Lytton Office, 380 Main St.);
Mackenzie (64 Centennial Dr.);
Masset (1666 Orr St.);
Merritt (Rail Yard Mall, 2194 Coutlee Ave.);
Port Hardy (8785 Gray St.);
Richmond - Multi-Language Extension Services in Cantonese & Mandarin (Immigrant Services Society, #150, 8400 Alexandra Rd.);
Sechelt (#102, 5710 Teredo St.);
Surrey - Multi-Language Extension Services in Punjabi (#205, 12725 - 80th Ave.);
Surrey - Multi-Language Extension Services in Punjabi (DiverseCity, #1107, 7330 - 137th St.);
Vancouver - Multi-Language Extension Services in Cantonese & Mandarin (MOSAIC, 1720 Grant St., Fl. 2);
Vancouver - Multi-Language Extension Services in Cantonese & Mandarin (SUCCESS, 28 West Pender St.);
Vancouver - Multi-Language Extension Services in Punjabi (Progressive Intercultural Community Services Society, 8153 M ain St.);
Whistler (Whistler Chamber of Commerce, #201, 4230 Gateway Dr.).

Manitoba Service Canada Centres
Brandon
Government of Canada Building, #100, 1039 Princess Ave., Brandon, MB R7A 4J5
Churchill
1 Mantayo Seepee Meskanow, Churchill, MB R0B 0E0
Dauphin
181 - 1st Ave. NE, Dauphin, MB R7N 1A6
Tel: 800-622-6232
Fax: 204-622-4045
Flin Flon
Government of Canada Building, 111 Main St., Flin Flon, MB R8A 1J9
Morden
Government of Canada Building, 158 Stephen St., Morden, MB R6M 1T3
Notre Dame de Lourdes
51 Rodgers St., Notre Dame de Lourdes, MB R0G 1M0
Portage la Prairie
Government of Canada Building, 1016 Saskatchewan Ave. East, Portage la Prairie, MB R1N 3V2
Saint Pierre Jolys
427 Sabourin St., Saint Pierre Jolys, MB R0A 1V0
Selkirk
51 Main St., Selkirk, MB R1A 1P9
Fax: 204-785-6222
Steinbach
Steinbach Place, 321 Main St., Main Fl., Steinbach, MB R5G 1Z2
Swan River
#1, 355 Kelsey Trail, Swan River, MB R0L 1Z0
The Pas
Uptown Mall, 333 Edwards Ave., PO Box 660The Pas, MB R9A 1K7

Thompson
60 Moak Cres., Thompson, MB R8N 2B7
Winnipeg - Henderson Hwy.
Winnipeg NE Service Canada Ctr., Kildonan Village Mall, 1122 Henderson Hwy., Winnipeg, MB R2G 1L1
Winnipeg - Portage Ave.
Winnipeg South-West Service Canada Centre, Westwood Centre, 3338 Portage Ave., Winnipeg, MB R3K 0Z1
Winnipeg - St. Mary's Rd.
Winnipeg St-Vital Service Canada Centre, 1001 St. Mary's Rd., Winnipeg, MB R2M 3S4
Winnipeg - York Ave.
Winnipeg Centre Service Canada Ctr., Stanley Knowles Bldg., 391 York Ave., Winnipeg, MB R3C 0P4
Service Canada Outreach Sites - Manitoba
Toll-Free: 800-622-6232
TTY: 800-926-9105
The following places in Manitoba are scheduled outreach sites for Service Canada:
Arborg (317 River Rd.);
Ashern (Fieldstone Ventures Education & Training Centre, 61 Main St.);
Beausejour (20 - 1st St. South);
Carberry (112 Main St.);
Carman (15 - 1st Ave. SW);
Deloraine (220 South Railway Ave. West);
Fisher Branch (23 Main St.);
Gillam (323 Railway Ave.);
Gimli (62 - 2nd Ave., 2nd Fl.);
Gladstone (MAFRI Gladstone GO Centre, 37 Morris Ave. North);
Killarney (318 Williams Ave.);
Lac du Bonnet (4 Park Ave.);
McCreary (436 - 2nd Ave.);
Minnedosa (Yellowhead Regional Employment Skills & Services, 133 Main St. South);
Morris (220 Main St. North);
Neepawa (290 Davidson St.);
Russell (IGA Mall, Main St. & Lawrence Ave.);
Saint-Georges (Allard Library, 104086 Hwy. #11);
Saint Laurent (Saint Laurent Recreation Cente, Lot 825, Hwy. #6);
Shoal Lake (438 Station St.);
Snow Lake (Snow Lake Family Resource Centre, 131 Balsam St.);
Sprague (East Borderland Primary Health Care Centre, Hwy. #12 & Rd. 308);
Stonewall (South Interlake Regional Library, 419 Main St.);
Teulon (19 Beach Rd.);
Virden (227 Wellington St. West);
Winnipeg (#100, 614 des Meurons St.);
Winnipegosis (Village of Winnipegosis Office, 130 - 2 nd St.)

New Brunswick Service Canada Centres
Bathurst
Nicolas Denys Building, 120 Harbourview Blvd., 1st Fl., Bathurst, NB E2A 7R2
Campbellton
Campbellton City Center Mall, #111, 157 Water St., Campbellton, NB E3N 3L4
Caraquet
Bellevue Place, 20E St. Pierre Blvd. West, Caraquet, NB E1W 1B6
Dalhousie
Darlington Mall, 110 Plaza Blvd., Dalhousie, NB E8C 2E2
Edmundston
Federal Building, 22 Emmerson St., Edmundston, NB E3V 1R8
Fredericton
Federal Building, 633 Queen St., Fredericton, NB E3B 1C3
Grand Falls / Grand-Sault
#100, 441 Madawaska Rd., Grand Falls, NB E3Y 1C6
Miramichi
Roach Building, 150 Pleasant St., Miramichi, NB E1V 1Y1
Moncton
Heritage Court, #310, 95 Foundry St., Moncton, NB E1C 5H7
Richibucto
Cartier Place, 25 Cartier Blvd., Richibucto, NB E4W 3W7
Sackville
East Main Plaza, 170 Main St., Sackville, NB E4L 4B4
Saint John
1 Agar Pl., 1st Fl., Saint John, NB E2L 5G4
Saint Quentin
193 Canada St., Saint-Quentin, NB E8A 1J8
St Stephen
Post Office Building, 93 Milltown Blvd., St Stephen, NB E3L 1G5
Shediac
Centre-Ville Mall, 342 Main St., Shediac, NB E4P 2E7
Shippagan
196A J.D. Gauthier Blvd., 1st Fl., Shippagan, NB E8S 1P2
Sussex
Mapleton Place, 10 Gateway St., Sussex, NB E4E 1T1
Tracadie-Sheila
Le Rond Point Shopping Center, #17, 3409 Principale St., Tracadie-Sheila, NB E1X 1C7
Woodstock
Post Office Building, 680 Main St., Woodstock, NB E7M 5Z9
Service Canada Outreach Sites - New Brunswick
Toll-Free: 800-622-6232
TTY: 800-926-9105
The following places in New Brunswick are scheduled outreach sites for Service Canada:
Baie-Sainte-Anne (5383 Rte. 117);
Doaktown (328 Main St.);
Florenceville-Bristol (#1, 8768 Main St.);
Grand Manan (North Head Grand Manan Business Center, 130 Rte. 776);
Minto (420 Pleasant Dr.);
Neguac (430 Principale St.);
Perth-Andover (588E East Riverside Dr.);
Rogersville (11117 Main St.);
Fredericton (Kchikhusis Complex, 150 Cliffe St., Fl. 3);
Tobique Narrows (Tobique Employment & Training Centre, 278 Main St.).

Newfoundland & Labrador Service Canada Centres
Channel-Port-aux-Basques
#4, 10 High St., Channel-Port-aux-Basques, NL A0M 1C0
Clarenville
Park Place, 50 Manitoba Dr., Clarenville, NL A5A 1K5
Corner Brook
Joseph R. Smallwood Building, 1 Regent Sq., Corner Brook, NL A2H 7K6
Gander
McCurdy Complex, 1 Markham Place, 3rd Fl., Gander, NL A1V 0A8
Grand Falls-Windsor
Bayley Building, #100, 4A Bayley St., Grand Falls, NL A2A 2T5
Happy Valley-Goose Bay
23 Broomfield St., Happy Valley-Goose Bay, NL A0P 1E0
Harbour Grace
Babb Building, 33-35 Harvey St., Harbour Grace, NL A0A 2M0
Labrador City
Labrador Mall, 500 Vanier Ave., Labrador City, NL A2V 2W7
Marystown
Jerrett Building, #130, 140 Ville Marie Dr., Marystown, NL A0E 2M0
Placentia
Dalfens Mall, 61 Blockhouse Rd., Placentia, NL A0B 2Y0
Rocky Harbour
Budgeon Building, 118 Pond Rd., Rocky Harbour, NL A0K 4N0
St. Anthony
Viking Mall, 1 Goose Cove Rd., St. Anthony, NL A0K 4S0
St. John's
Building 223, Pleasantville, 223 Churchill Ave., St. John's, NL A1A 1N3
Springdale
Wells Building, 130 Main St., RR#2, Springdale, NL A0J 1T0
Stephenville
133 Carolina Ave., Stephenville, NL A2N 2S5
Service Canada Outreach Sites - Newfoundland & Labrador
Toll-Free: 800-622-6232
TTY: 800-926-9105
The following places in Newfoundland & Labrador are scheduled outreach sites for Service Canada:
Baie Verte (Barker Building, 325 Hwy. #410);
Bonavista (Bonavista Campus, College of the North Atlantic, #A118, 301 Confederation Dr.);
Burgeo (142 Reach Rd.);
Forteau (32 Main St.);
Harbour Breton (Halfyard Building, #30, 42 Canada Dr.);
Mainland (School & Community Centre of Sainte-Anne, Rte. 463);
Newville (Development Association Building, Rte. 340);
Old Perlican (John Hoskins Community Centre, 575A Main St.);
Pollards Point (Main St.);
Port Saunders (Dobbin Building, 90 Main St.);
Ramea (21 Main St.);
Saint Alban's (St. Alban's Resource Centre, 3 Cormier Ave.);
Sheshatshiu (Innu Nation Building, Main Fl.);
Trepassey (Opportunities Complex, Main Hwy.);
Wesleyville (Employment Assistance Office, Cape Freels Development Association, 344 Main St.)

Northwest Territories Service Canada Centres
Fort Simpson
Federal Building, 9606 - 100th St., Fort Simpson, NT X0E 0N0
Fort Smith
Federal Building, 149 McDougal Rd., Fort Smith, NT X0E 0P0
Hay River
Federal Building, #204, 41 Capital Dr., Hay River, NT X0E 1G2
Inuvik
85 Kingmingya Rd., Inuvik, NT X0E 0T0
Yellowknife
Greenstone Building, 5101 - 50 Ave., Main Fl., Yellowknife, NT X1A 3Z4
Service Canada Outreach Sites - Northwest Territories
Toll-Free: 800-622-6232
TTY: 800-926-9105
The following places in the Northwest Territories are scheduled outreach sites for Service Canada:
Behchoko (Tli Cho Government Building);
Deline (Deline Charter Community Office);
Fort Liard (Deh Cho Health & Social Services);
Fort Providence (Zhati Koe Friendship Centre);
Fort Resolution (Deninu Ku'e First Nation Office);
Tuktoyaktuk (Tuktoyaktuk Community Corporation Office).

Nova Scotia Service Canada Centres
Amherst
#202, 26-28 Prince Arthur St., Amherst, NS B4H 1V6
Antigonish
Federal Building, 325 Main St., 2nd Fl., Antigonish, NS B2G 2C3
Bedford
Royal Bank Building, 1597 Bedford Hwy., 2nd Fl., Bedford, NS B4A 1E7
Bridgewater
Dawson B. Dauphinee Building, 77 Dufferin St., Bridgewater, NS B4V 9A2
Dartmouth
Belmont House, 33 Alderney Dr., 3rd Fl., Dartmouth, NS B2Y 2N4
Digby
98 Sydney St., Digby, NS B0V 1A0
Glace Bay
Senator's Place, #101, 633 Main St., Glace Bay, NS B1A 6J3
Guysborough
Chedabucto Centre, 9996 Hwy. #16, Guysborough, NS B0H 1N0
Halifax
Tower 2, Mumford Towers, 7001 Mumford Rd., Halifax, NS B3L 4R3
Inverness
15926 Central Ave., Inverness, NS B0E 1N0
Kentville
Federal Building, 495 Main St., 2nd Fl., Kentville, NS B4N 3W5
New Glasgow
340 East River Rd., New Glasgow, NS B2H 3P7
North Sydney
105 King St., Main Fl., North Sydney, NS B2A 3S1
Port Hawkesbury
Shediac Shopping Centre, #8, 811 Reeves St., Port Hawkesbury, NS B9A 2S4
Shelburne
Loyalist Plaza, 218 Water St., Shelburne, NS B0T 1W0
Sydney
Commerce Tower, 15 Dorchester St., 1st Fl., Sydney, NS B1P 5Y9
Truro
181 Willow St., Truro, NS B2N 4Z9
Windsor
80 Water St., Windsor, NS B0N 2T0
Yarmouth
Canada Post Office Building, 13 Willow St., 2nd Fl., Yarmouth, NS B5A 1T8
Service Canada Outreach Sites - Nova Scotia
Toll-Free: 800-622-6232
TTY: 800-926-910
The following places in Nova Scotia are scheduled outreach sites for Service Canada:
Church Point (Sainte-Anne University Campus, 1649 Rte. 1);
Sheet Harbour (Bluewater Building, 22756 Hwy. 7, 2nd Fl.).

Nunavut Service Canada Centres

Nunavut Service Canada Centres
Cambridge Bay
16 Mitik St., 1st Fl., PO Box 2010Cambridge Bay, NU X0B 0C0

Nunavut Service Canada Centres
Iqaluit
#306, Iqaluit House, Building 622, Main Fl., Queen Elizabeth Way, PO Box 639Iqaluit, NU X0A 0H0
Tel: 867-975-4700

Nunavut Service Canada Centres
Rankin Inlet
Rockland Building, PO Box 97Rankin Inlet, NU X0C 0G0

Ontario Service Canada Centres
Ajax
#200, 274 Mackenzie Ave., Ajax, ON L1S 2E9
Arnprior
Heritage Square, #1 & 2, 75 Elgin St. West, Arnprior, ON K7S 3T9
Bancroft
Fairway Plaza, 5 Fairway Blvd., Bancroft, ON K0L 1C0
Barrie
48 Owen St., 1st Fl., Barrie, ON L4M 3H1
Belleville
Business Building, 1 North Front St., 2nd Fl., Belleville, ON K8P 5G9
Bracebridge
Federal Bldg., 98 Manitoba St., 2nd Fl., Bracebridge, ON P1L 2B5
Brampton
Human Resources Development Canada, 18 Corporation Dr., Brampton, ON L6S 6B2
Brantford
58 Dalhousie St., 2nd Fl., Brantford, ON N3T 2J2
Brockville
Thomas Fuller Building, 14 Court House Ave., 1st Fl., Brockville, ON K6V 4T1
Burlington
#108E, 676 Appleby Line, Burlington, ON L7L 5Y1
Cambridge
#2C, 350 Conestoga Blvd., Cambridge, ON N1R 7L7
Carleton Place
46 Lansdowne Ave., Carleton Place, ON K7C 2T8
Chatham
Chatham-Kent Service Canada Centre, Federal Building, 120 Wellington St. West, Chatham, ON N7M 3P3
Cobourg
1005 Elgin St. West, Cobourg, ON K9A 5J4
Collingwood
44 Huronontario St., Collingwood, ON L9Y 2L6
Cornwall
#100, 111 Water St. East, Cornwall, ON K6H 6S2
Dryden
119 King St., Dryden, ON P8N 1C1
East Gwillimbury
Newmarket Service Canada Centre, #1, 18183 Yonge St. East, East Gwillimbury, ON L9N 0H9
Elliot Lake
Ministry, Training, Colleges & Universities, Employment Ctr, 50 Hillside Dr. North, Elliot Lake, ON P5A 1X4
Espanola
#2, 721 Centre St., Espanola, ON P5E 1T3
Fort Frances
301 Scott St., Fort Frances, ON P9A 1H1
Gananoque
5 Charles St. South, Gananoque, ON K7G 1V9
Georgetown
232 Guelph St., 1st Fl., Georgetown, ON L7G 4B1
Geraldton
208 Beamish Ave. West, Geraldton, ON P0T 1M0
Goderich
52 East St., Goderich, ON N7A 1N3
Guelph
259 Woodlawn Rd. West, #C, Guelph, ON N1H 8J1
Hamilton - Barton St. East
Hamilton East Service Canada Centre, Red Hill Creek Centre, 2255 Barton St. East, Hamilton, ON L8H 7T4
Hamilton - Upper James St.
Hamilton Main Service Canada Centre, 1550 Upper James St., 1st Fl., Hamilton, ON L9B 2L6
Hawkesbury
521 Main St. East, Hawkesbury, ON K6A 1B3
Kapuskasing
8 Queen St., Kapuskasing, ON P5N 1G7
Kenora
Kenora Market Square, #201, 308 - 2nd St. South, Kenora, ON P9N 1G4
Kingston
Frontenac Mall, 1300 Bath Rd., 1st Fl., Kingston, ON K7M 4X4
Kirkland Lake
Ontario Northlands Telecommunications Building, 10 Government Rd. East, Kirkland Lake, ON P2N 1A2
Kitchener
409 Weber St. West, Kitchener, ON N2H 4B1
Leamington
Leamington Mall, 215 Talbot St. East, Leamington, ON N8H 3X5
Lindsay
65 Kent St. West, Lindsay, ON K9V 2Y3
Listowel
210 Main St. East, Listowel, ON N4W 2B7
London
Dominion Public Building, 457 Richmond St., London, ON N6A 3E3
Malton
#5, 6877 Goreway Dr., Malton, ON L4V 1L9
Marathon
#105, 52 Peninsula Rd., Marathon, ON P0T 2E0
Markham
#14, 5051 Hwy. #7 East, Markham, ON L3R 1N3
Midland
Huronia Mall, 9225 Hwy. #93, RR#2, Midland, ON L4R 4K4
Milton
Trafalgar Square, 310 Main St. East, Milton, ON L9T 1P4
Mississauga - Dixie Rd.
Mississauga East Service Canada Centre, 2525 Dixie Rd., Mississauga, ON L4Y 2A1
Mississauga - Glen Erin Dr.
Mississauga West Service Canada Centre, 3085A Glen Erin Dr., Mississauga, ON L5L 1J3
Napanee
Murphy's Plaza, 2 Dairy Ave., Napanee, ON K7R 3T1
New Liskeard
280 Armstrong St. North, RR#3, New Liskeard, ON P0J 1P0
Niagara Falls
Customs Building, 5853 Peer St., Niagara Falls, ON L2G 1X4
North Bay
Canada Place, #102, 107 Shirreff Ave., North Bay, ON P1B 7K8
Oakville
#5B, 117 Cross Ave., Oakville, ON L6J 2W7
Orangeville
#102, 210 Broadway Ave., Orangeville, ON L9W 5G4
Orillia
#101, 50 Andrew St. South, Orillia, ON L3V 7T5
Oshawa
Midtown Mall, #6C, 200 John St. West, Oshawa, ON L1J 2B4
Ottawa - Carling Ave.
Ottawa West Service Canada Centre, Lincoln Fields Galleria, 2525 Carling Ave., 1st Fl., Ottawa, ON K2B 7Z2
Ottawa - Laurier Ave. West
Ottawa Government Service Centre, 110 Laurier Ave. West, Ottawa, ON K1P 1J1
Ottawa - Laurier Ave. West
Ottawa Centre Service Canada Centre, L'Esplanade Laurier, 300 Laurier Ave. West, 2nd Fl., Ottawa, ON K1A 0R3
Ottawa - Ogilvie Rd.
Ottawa East Service Canada Centre, Beacon Hill Shopping Ctr, 2339 Ogilvie Rd., Ottawa, ON K1J 8M6
Owen Sound
Heritage Place Shopping Centre, 1350 - 16 St. East, Owen Sound, ON N4K 6N7
Parry Sound
74 James St., 2nd Fl., Parry Sound, ON P2A 1T8
Pembroke
141 Lake St., Pembroke, ON K8A 5L8
Perth
The Factory, 40 Sunset Blvd., Perth, ON K7H 2Y4
Peterborough
219 George St. North, Peterborough, ON K9J 3G7
Picton
229 Main St., Picton, ON K0K 2T0
Prescott
292 Centre St., Prescott, ON K0E 1T0
Tel: 613-925-2808
Fax: 613-925-3846
ontario.inquiry@hrsdc-rhdcc.gc.ca
Renfrew
350 Raglan St. South, Renfrew, ON K7V 1R7
Richmond Hill
35 Beresford Dr., Richmond Hill, ON L4B 4M3
St Catherines
Henley Square Plaza, 395 Ontario St., #E & F, St Catharines, ON L2N 7N6
St Thomas
#34, 1010 Talbot St., St Thomas, ON N5P 4N2
Sarnia
529 Exmouth St., Sarnia, ON N7T 5P6
Sault Ste. Marie
22 Bay St., 1st Fl., Sault Ste. Marie, ON P6A 5S2
Simcoe
5 Queensway East, Simcoe, ON N3Y 5K2
Smiths Falls
#115, 91 Cornelia St. West, Smiths Falls, ON K7A 5L3
Stratford
#2, 61 Lorne Ave. East, Ground Fl., Stratford, ON N5A 6S4
Sudbury
Federal Building, 19 Lisgar St., Main Fl., Sudbury, ON P3E 3L4
Thunder Bay
975 Alloy Dr., Thunder Bay, ON P7B 5Z8
Tillsonburg
Livingston Centre, 96 Tillson Ave., Tillsonburg, ON N4G 3A1
Timmins
120 Cedar St. South, 1st Fl., Timmins, ON P4N 2G8
Toronto - Chesswood Dr.
Toronto North Service Canada Centre, 3737 Chesswood Dr., Toronto, ON M3J 2P6
Toronto - College St.
#100, 559 College St., Toronto, ON M6G 1A9
Toronto - Dundas St. West
Toronto Etobicoke Service Canada Centre, 5343 Dundas St. West, Toronto, ON M9B 6K6
Toronto - Gerrard St. East
Gerrard Square Mall, 1000 Gerrard St. East, #DD10/11, 2nd Fl., Toronto, ON M4M 1Z3
Toronto - Lawrence Ave. West
Lawrence Square, #103-105, 700 Lawrence Ave. West, Toronto, ON M6A 3B3
Toronto - Queen St. West
Toronto City Hall Service Canada Centre, City Hall, 100 Queen St. West, 1st Fl., Toronto, ON M5H 2N2
Toronto - St. Clair Ave. East
Toronto Centre Service Canada Ctr., Arthur Meighen Building, 25 St. Clair Ave. East, 1st Fl., Toronto, ON M4T 3A4
Toronto - Tapscott Rd.
Toronto Malvern Service Canada Ctr., Malvern Town Ctr. Mall, 31 Tapscott Rd., Toronto, ON M1B 4Y7
Toronto - Town Centre Ct.
Toronto Scarborough Service Canada Centre, Canada Centre, 200 Town Centre Ct., 1st Fl., Toronto, ON M1P 4X9
Toronto - Yonge St.
Toronto Willowdale Service Canada Ctr., Joseph Shepard Bldg, 4900 Yonge St., 1st Fl., Toronto, ON M2N 6B1
Trenton
50 Dundas St. West, Trenton, ON K8V 6R5
Walkerton
200 McNab St., Walkerton, ON N0G 2V0
Wallaceburg
Municipal Service Centre, 786 Dufferin Ave., 2nd Fl., Wallaceburg, ON N8A 2V3
Welland
250 Thorold Rd. West, Welland, ON L3C 3W2
Tel: 905-988-2700
Fax: 905-735-7036
Windsor
#103, 400 City Hall Sq. East, Windsor, ON N9A 7K6
Woodstock
#101, 959 Dundas St., Woodstock, ON N4S 1H2
Service Canada Outreach Sites - Ontario
Toll-Free: 800-622-6232
TTY: 800-926-9105
The following places in Ontario are scheduled outreach sites for Service Canada:
Alliston (49 Wellington St. West);
Amherstburg (179 Victoria St. South);
Ancaster (Ancaster Square, 300 Wilson St. East);
Atikokan (Atikokan Employment Centre, #206, 214 Main St. West);
Attawapiskat (Attawapiskat Development Corporation, 1001 Riverside Rd. West);
Aylmer (Aylmer Community Services, 25 Centre St.);
Bearskin Lake (Bearskin Lake Band Office);
Belle River (499 Notre Dame St.);
Big Trout Lake (Big Trout Lake Band Council Office);

Blind River (62 Queen Ave.);
Bolton (Caledon Community Services, 18 King St. East, Upper Fl.);
Bowmanville (132 Church St.);
Brampton (Community Door, 7700 Hurontario St.);
Cat Lake (Cat Lake First Nation Band Office;
Chapleau (Sudbury Manitoulin District Social Services Administration Board Office, 12 Birch St.);
Cochrane (143 Fourth Ave.);
Cornwall Island (CIA 111 Building);
Deer Lake (Deer Lake First Nation Band Office);
Dundas (Old Town Hall, 60 Main St., Main Fl.);
Dunnville (Dunnville Employment Centre, St. Leonard's Community Services, 208 Broad St. East);
Embrun (La Cité Collégiale, 993 Notre Dame St.);
Exeter (349 Main St. South);
Fenelon Falls (Fenelon Falls Branch, Kawartha L akes Public Library, 19 Market St.);
Fergus (552 Wellington County Rd. 18 West);
Flamborough (#117, 7 Innovation Dr.);
Flinton (3641 Flinton Rd.);
Forest (6247 Indian Lane, RR#2);
Fort Albany (Peetabeck Health Services);
Fort Erie (469 Central Ave.);
Fort Hope (Fort Hope Band Council Office);
Fort Severn (Fort Severn Band Council Office);
Gore Bay (35 Merideth St.);
Grimsby (63 Main St. West);
Haliburton (49 Maple Ave.);
Hamilton (71 Main St. West, 1st Fl.);
Havelock (13 Quebec St.);
Hearst (523 Hwy. 11 East);
Hudson (Lac Seul First Nation Band Office);
Huntsville (207 Main St. West);
Iroquois Falls (33 Ambridge Dr.);
Kasabonika (Kasabonika First Nations Band Council);
Kashechewan (13B Riverside Rd. West);
Keewaydin (Keewaywin First Nation Band Office);
Kemptville (#3 & 4, 125 Prescott St.);
Kenora (Dalles First Nation Band Office);
Keswick (90 Wexford Dr.);
Kincardine (727 Queen St.);
Kingfisher Lake (Kingfisher Lake Band Council Office);
Lansdowne House (Lansdowne House First Nation Band Office);
Madoc (20 Davidson St.);
Mindemoya (6020 Hwy. #542);
Monetville (Dokis Reserve Rd.);
Moose Factory (22 Jonathan Cheechoo Dr.);
Moosonee (34 Revillion Rd. North);
Muncey (300 East River Rd.);
Muskrat Dam (Muskrat Dam Band Council Office);
New Osnaburgh (Mishkeegogamang First Nation Band Office);
Nipigon (5 Wadsworth Dr., 1st Fl.);
North Spirit Lake (North Spirit Lake First Nation Band Office);
Petrolia (4200 P etrolia Line);
Pikangikum (Pikangikum Band Council Office);
Poplar Hill (Poplar Hill Band Council Office);
Port Colborne (92 Charlotte St.);
Port Perry (#3, 119 Perry St.);
Red Lake (227 Howey St.);
Sachigo Lake (Sachigo Band Council Office);
Sandy Lake (Sandy Lake Band Council Office);
Seaforth (138 Main St. South);
Shelburne (167 Centre St.);
Shoal Lake (Shoal Lake First Nation Band Office);
Sioux Lookout (80 Front St.);
Sioux Narrows (Northwest Angle First Nation Band Office);
Slate Falls (48 Lakeview Dr.);
Southwold (Oneida First Nation Administrative Building;
Strathroy (34 Frank St.);
Sturgeon Falls (109 Third St.)
Summer Beaver (Summer Beaver First Nation Band Office);
Terrace Bay (Hwy, #17 & Selkirk Ave.);
Tilbury (20 Queen St. North);
Thessalon (214 Main St.);
Toronto (220 Attwell Dr.);
Toronto (58 Cecil St.);
Toronto (55 John St.);
Toronto (779 The Queensway);
Toronto (605 Rogers Rd.);
Toronto (29 St. Dennis Dr.);
Toronto (2900 Warden Ave.);
Uxbridge (#201, 2 Campbell Dr.);
Vaughan (9100 Jane St.);
Wasaga Beach (30 Lewis St.);
Wawa (48 Mission Rd.);
Webequie (Webequie First Nation Band Council);
West Lorne (160 Main St.);
Wiarton (542 Berford St.);
Wikwemikong (19A Complex Dr.);
Wingham (152 Josephine St.);
Woodbridge (8401 Weston Rd.);
Wunnumin Lake (Wunnumin Lake First Nation Band Council Office)

Prince Edward Island Service Canada Centres
Charlottetown
Jean Canfield Government of Canada Building, 191 University Ave., 1st Fl., Charlottetown, PE C1A 4L2
Montague
491 Main St., Montague, PE C0A 1R0
O'Leary
371 Main St., O'Leary, PE C0B 1V0
Souris
Save Easy Mall, 173 Main St., 2nd Fl., Souris, PE C0A 2B0
Summerside
Government of Canada Building, 294 Church St., Summerside, PE C1N 0C1
Service Canada Outreach Sites - Prince Edward Island
Toll-Free: 800-622-6232
TTY: 800-926-9105
The following place in Prince Edward Island is a scheduled outreach site for Service Canada: 48 Mill Rd., Wellington, PE, C0B 2E0.

Québec Service Canada Centres
Alma
Complexe Jacques-Gagnon, #105, 100, rue St-Joseph sud, Alma, QC G8B 7A6
Amos
502, 4e rue est, Amos, QC J9T 2R9
Asbestos
#204, 309, rue Chassé, Asbestos, QC J1T 2B4
Baie-Comeau
Centre d'achats Laflèche, #204, 625, boul Laflèche ouest, Baie-Comeau, QC G5C 1C4
Bécancour
#200, 1580, boul de Port-Royal, 1e étage, Bécancour, QC G9H 1X6
Brossard
Centre de ressources humaines Canada, 2501, boul Lapinière,, 1e étage, Brossard, QC J4Z 3P1
Campbell's Bay
2, rue John, Campbell's Bay, QC J0X 1K0
Cap-aux-Meules
Centre de ressources humaines Canada, #200, 380, ch Principal, Cap-aux-Meules, QC G4T 1S2
Causapscal
8, rue Saint-Jacques nord, Causapscal, QC G0J 1J0
Chandler
#201, 75, boul René-Lévesque est, Chandler, QC G0C 1K0
Châteauguay
#101, 245, boul St-Jean Baptiste, Châteauguay, QC J6K 3C3
Chibougamau
623, 3e rue, Chibougamau, QC G8P 3A2
Chicoutimi
98, rue Racine est, Chicoutimi, QC G7H 1R1
Chisasibi
453, rue Wolverine, Chisasibi, QC J0M 1E0
Coaticook
#300, 14, rue Adams, Coaticook, QC J1A 1K3
Cote Saint-Luc
Côte-des-Neiges Service Canada Centre, Carré Décarie, #3015, 6900, boul Décarie, 3e étage, Cote-St-Luc, QC H3X 2T8
Cowansville
224, rue du Sud, 2e étage, Cowansville, QC J2K 2X4
Dolbeau -Mistassini
1400, rue des Érables, Dolbeau-Mistassini, QC G8L 2W7
Donnacona
#110, 100, rte 138, Donnacona, QC G3M 1B5
Drummondville
Édifice Surprenant, 1525, boul Saint-Joseph, Drummondville, QC J2C 2E9
Forestville
Centre Forestville, #800, 25, rte 138 est, Forestville, QC G0T 1E0
Gaspé
Édifice Frédérica-Giroux, 98, rue de la Reine, 1e étage, Gaspé, QC G4X 2V4
Gatineau - Bellehumeur
L'Atrium, #150, 85, rue Bellehumeur, Gatineau, QC J8T 8B7
Gatineau - MacLaren est
Buckingham (Gatineau) Service Canada Center, 101, rue MacLaren est, 2e étage, Gatineau, QC J8L 1J9
Gatineau - Saint-Joseph
Hull-Aylmer (Gatineau) Service Canada Centre, 920, boul Saint-Joseph, Gatineau, QC J8Z 1S9
Granby
82, rue Robinson sud, Granby, QC J2G 7L4
Joliette
Comlexe Joliette, #100, 46, rue Gauthier sud, Joliette, QC J6E 4J4
Jonquière
#102, 3750, boul du Royaume, Jonquière, QC G7X 0A4
Kuujjuaq
Nunavik Service Canada Center, 5207, ch de l'Aéroport, Kuujjuaq, QC J0M 1C0
La Malbaie
541, rue St-Étienne, La Malbaie, QC G5A 1J3
La Pocatière
Les Cours Painchaud, #103, 708, 4e av, La Pocatière, QC G0R 1Z0
La Sarre
Carrefour La Sarre Marketplace, #30, 255, 3e rue est, La Sarre, QC J9Z 3N7
La Tuque
Carrefour La Tuque Inc., 290, rue Saint-Joseph, La Tuque, QC G9X 3Z8
Lac Mégantic
#201, 5200, rue Frontenac, 2e étage, Lac-Mégantic, QC G6B 1H3
Laval
1041, boul des Laurentides, Laval, QC H7G 2W2
Lévis
Place Lévis, #175, 50, rte du Président-Kennedy, Lévis, QC G6V 6W8
Longueuil
#100, 1195, ch du Tremblay, Longueuil, QC J4N 1R4
Louiseville
507, rue Marcel, Louiseville, QC J5V 1N1
Magog
#100A, 1700, rue Sherbrooke, Magog, QC J1X 5B4
Maniwaki
Galeries Maniwaki, #220, 100, rue Principale sud, Maniwaki, QC J9E 3L4
Matane
Les Galeries du Vieux-Port, #220, 750, av du Phare ouest, Matane, QC G4W 3W8
Mont-Laurier
431, rue de la Madone, 1e étage, Mont-Laurier, QC J9L 1S1
Montmagny
37, av Sainte-Brigitte sud, Montmagny, QC G5V 2Y3
Montréal - Chauveau
Mercier (Montréal) Service Canada Centre, 5455, rue Chauveau, 1e étage, Montréal, QC H1N 1G8
Téléc: 514-255-0624
Montréal - Jarry est
Villeray (Montréal) Service Canada Centre, #300, 1415, rue Jarry est, 3e étage, Montréal, QC H2E 3B2
Montréal - Jean-Talon est
Saint-Léonard (Montréal) Service Canada Centre, #500, 6020, rue Jean-Talon est, Montréal, QC H1S 3B1
Montréal - Newman
Lasalle (Montréal) Service Canada Centre, 7655, boul Newman, Montréal, QC H8N 1X7
Montréal - René-Lévesque ouest
Montréal Downtown Service Canada Centre, Place Guy-Favreau, #034, 200, boul René-Lévesque ouest, Montréal, QC H2Z 1X4
Montréal - Sherbrooke est
Pointe-aux-Trembles (Montréal) Service Canada Centre, 13313, rue Sherbrooke est, Montréal, QC H1A 1C2
Montréal - Transcanadienne
Pointe-Claire (Montréal) Service Canada Centre, #100, 6500, aut Transcanadienne, 1e étage, Montréal, QC H9R 0A5
Montréal - Wellington
Verdun Service Canada Centre, 4110, rue Wellington, 2e étage, Montréal, QC H4G 1V7
New Richmond
Carrefour Baie-des-Chaleurs, 122, boul Perron ouest, 2e étage, New Richmond, QC G0C 2B0
Québec - Gare-du-Palais
Québec (Centre-Ville) Service Canada Centre, 330, rue de la Gare-du-Palais, Québec, QC G1K 3X2

Québec - Montmorency
La Cité-Limoilou Service Canada Centre, #101, 2500, boul Montmorency, Québec, QC G1J 5C7
Québec - Quatre-Bourgeois
Sainte-Foy (Québec) Service Canada Centre, #200, 3229, ch des Quatre-Bourgeois, 3e étage, Québec, QC G1W 0C1
Repentigny
Place Repentigny, #54, 155, rue Notre-Dame, Repentigny, QC J6A 7G5
Rimouski
Édifice Boisé Langevin, #102, 287, rue Pierre-Saindon, Rimouski, QC G5L 9A7
Rivière-du-Loup
298, boul Armand-Thériault, 2e étage, Rivière-du-Loup, QC G5R 4C2
Roberval
Plaza Roberval, #202, 755, boul Saint-Joseph, Roberval, QC G8H 2L4
Rouyn-Noranda
Édifice Réal-Caouette, #300, 151, av du Lac, Rouyn-Noranda, QC J9X 6C3
Saint-Eustache
250, boul Arthur-Sauvé, Saint-Eustache, QC J7R 2H9
Saint-Georges
Centre de ressources humaines Canada, 11400 - 1re av est, 2e étage, Saint-Georges, QC G5Y 7H2
Saint-Hyacinthe
Galeries St-Hyacinthe Shopping Mall, #2500, 3225, av Cusson, 2e étage, Saint-Hyacinthe, QC J2S 0H7
Saint-Jean-sur-Richelieu
#106, 320, boul du Séminaire nord, Saint-Jean-sur-Richelieu, QC J3B 5K9
Saint-Jérôme
#100, 339, boul Jean-Paul-Hogue, Saint-Jérôme, QC J7Z 7A5
Sainte-Agathe-des-Monts
118, rue Principale est, 2e étage, Sainte-Agathe-des-Monts, QC J8C 1L8
Sainte-Anne-des-Monts
230, 1ére av ouest, Sainte-Anne-des-Monts, QC G4V 1E2
Sainte-Thérèse
#110, 100, boul Ducharme, Sainte-Thérèse, QC J7E 1X2
Salaberry-de-Valleyfield
Valleyfield Service Canada Centre, #100, 73, rue Maden, Salaberry-de-Valleyfield, QC J6S 3V4
Senneterre
761 - 10e av, Senneterre, QC J0Y 2M0
Sept-Îles
701, boul Laure, 3e étage, Sept-Îles, QC G4R 1X8
Shawinigan
444 - 5e rue, Shawinigan, QC G9N 1E6
Sherbrooke
124, rue Wellington nord, Sherbrooke, QC J1H 5X8
Sorel-Tracy
101, rue Augusta, Sorel, QC J3P 1A8
Terrebonne
835, montée Masson, Terrebonne, QC J6W 2C7
Thetford Mines
#500, 350, boul Frontenac ouest, Thetford Mines, QC G6G 6N7
Trois-Rivières
#100, 1660, rue Royale, Trois-Rivières, QC G9A 4K3
Val-d'Or
400, av Centrale, Val-d'Or, QC J9P 1P3
Vaudreuil-Dorion
2555, rue Dutrisac, Vaudreuil-Dorion, QC J7V 7E6
Victoriaville
84, boul Labbé sud, Victoriaville, QC G6S 1K4
Ville-Marie
69B, rue Sainte-Anne, Ville-Marie, QC J9V 2B6
Service Canada Outreach Sites - Québec
Ligne sans frais: 800-622-6232
TTY: 800-926-9105
The following places in Québec are scheduled outreach sites for Service Canada:
L'Anse-Saint-Jean (La Petite École Community Centre, 239, rue St-Jean-Baptiste);
Baie-Saint-Paul (René-Richard Library, 9, rue Forget);
Belleterre (Saint-Andre School, 255, 3e av);
Cadillac (2, rue Dumont est);
Chapeau (120, rue King);
Chénéville (90A, rue Albert Ferland);
Dégelis (663, 6e rue ouest);
Fortierville (Fortierville Municipal Library, 198A, rue de la Fabrique);
Grande-Entrée (Auberge La Salicorne, 355, rte 199);
Grande-Vallée (1, rue du Vieux Pont);
Lac-Sainte-Marie (Lac-Ste-Marie City Hall, 106, ch Lac-Ste-Marie);
Lachute (Maison populaire d'Argenteuil, 335, rue Principale);
Lamarche (100, rue Principale);
Lebel-sur-Quévillon (107, rue Principal sud);
Les Escoumins (459, rte 138);
Lyster (2375, rue Bécancour);
Matagami (180, place du Commerce);
Matapédia (City Hall, 1, rue de l'Hôtel-de-ville);
Mont-Joli (1572, boul Jacque Cartier);
Mont-Louis (40, 7e rue est);
New Carisle (208, rue Gerard D. Levesque);
Normandin (Town Hall, 1048, rue Saint-Cyrille);
Notre-Dame-de-Montauban (421, rue Principal);
Notre-Dame-du-Laus (Municipal Library, 4, rue de l'Église);
Pohénégamook (1309, rue Principale);
Potton (The Re illy House, 302, rue Principale);
Port-Cartier (4C, boul des îles);
Rivière-Rouge (Municipal Library, 230, rue de L'Annonciation sud);
Sacré-Coeur (88, rue Principale nord);
Saint-Fabien-de-Panet (195, rue Bilodeau);
Saint-Michel-des-Saints (521, rue Brassard);
Saint-Pamphile (164, rue de l'Église ouest);
Taschereau (52, rue Morin);
Témiscaming (Le Centre, 20, rue Humphrey);
Weedon (Weedon Community Centre, #314, 209 rue des Érables).

Saskatchewan Service Canada Centres
Estevan
#10, 419 Kensington Ave., Estevan, SK S4A 2A1
La Ronge
1016 La Ronge Ave., La Ronge, SK S0J 1L0
Melfort
McKendry Plaza, 104 McKendry Ave. West, Melfort, SK S0E 1A0
Moose Jaw
Victoria Place, #501, 111 Fairford St. East, Moose Jaw, SK S6H 7X5
North Battleford
Territorial Place, #15, 9800 Territorial Dr., North Battleford, SK S9A 3N6
Prince Albert
1288 Central Ave., Prince Albert, SK S6V 4V8
Regina
Alvin Hamilton Building, 1783 Hamilton St., Regina, SK S4P 2B6
Saskatoon
Federal Building, 101 - 22 St. East, Saskatoon, SK S7K 0E1
Swift Current
Chinook Building, 250 Central Ave. North, Swift Current, SK S9H 0L2
Weyburn
City Centre Mall, 110 Souris Ave., Main Fl., Weyburn, SK S4H 2Z8
Yorkton
Imperial Plaza, 214 Smith St. East, Yorkton, SK S3N 3S6
Service Canada Outreach Sites - Saskatchewan
Toll-Free: 800-622-6232
TTY: 800-926-9105
The following places in Saskatchewan are scheduled outreach sites for Service Canada:
Assiniboia (313 Centre St.);
Beauval (Lavoie St.);
Black Lake (Black Lake First Nation Band Office);
Buffalo Narrows (#4, 1491 Pederson Ave.);
Carlyle (100 Main St.);
Clearwater River (Clearwater Dene Nation Band Office);
Davidson (204 Washington St.);
Debden (204 - 2nd Ave. East);
Domremy (Domremy Fransaskois Community Centre, 109 - 1st St. North);
Fond-du-Lac (Fond-du-Lac First Nation Band Office;
Gravelbourg (133 - 5th Ave. East);
Hudson Bay (501 Prince St.);
Humboldt (623 - 7th St.);
Ile-à-la-Crosse (Lajeunesse Ave.);
Kindersley (207 Main St.);
La Loche (La Loche Recreation Centre (Montgrand St.);
Maple Creek (114 Jasper St.);
Meadow Lake (Meadow Lake Tribal Council Main Office, 8155 Flying Dust First Nation);
Nipawin (233 Centre St.);
North Battleford (1371 - 103rd St.);
Ponteix (Royer Cultural Centre, 110 Railway Ave.);
Preeceville (27 Main St. North);
Regina (3115 - 5th Ave.);
St. Isidore-de-Bellevue (Bellevue Cultural Association, 716 Hwy. #225);
Shaunavon (23 - 4th Ave. West);
Stony Rapids (Transwest Air Terminal, 2nd Fl.);Uranium City (Northern Settlement of Uranium City Office, 205 Fredette Rd.);
Wo llaston Lake (Economic Development Office);
Wynyard (400A Ave. D West);
Zenon Park (Zenon Park Fransaskoise Association, 755 Main St.).

Yukon Service Canada Centres
Whitehorse
Elijah Smith Building, #125, 300 Main St., Whitehorse, YT Y1A 2B5

Skills & Employment / Direction générale des compétences et de l'emploi
Skills & Employment provides programs & initiatives that promote skills development, labour market participation & inclusiveness, as well as ensuring labour market efficiency. Specifically, these programs seek to address the employment & skills needs of those facing employment barriers, & contribute to life long learning & building a skilled inclusive labour force. Other programs that support an efficient labour market include the labour market integration of recent immigrants, the entry of temporary foreign workers, the mobility of workers across Canada & the dissemination of labour market information. This branch is also responsible for programs that provide temporary income support to eligible unemployed workers.

Strategic Policy & Research / Direction générale de la politique stratégique et de la recherche
Strategic Policy & Research leads on integrating human resources & social development issues in strategic policy, evaluation, & knowledge & research dissemination. It also leads on emerging & long-term policy development, corporate planning, & central agency, intergovernmental & international relations.
Service Canada Outreach Sites - Yukon
The following places in the Yukon are scheduled outreach sites for Service Canada:
Dawson City (Oak Hall, 1017 - 2nd Ave.);
Watson Lake (Yukon College Campus, Robert Campbell Hwy.).

Industry Canada / Industrie Canada

C.D. Howe Building, 235 Queen St., Ottawa, ON K1A 0H5
Tel: 613-954-5031
Fax: 613-954-2340
Toll-Free: 800-328-6189
TTY: 866-694-8389
info@ic.gc.ca
www.ic.gc.ca
The mission of Industry Canada is to help make Canadians more productive & competitive in a global, knowledge-based economy. The department's policies, programs & services assist in the creation of an economy that provides more & better-paying jobs for Canadians; supports stronger business growth through sustained improvements in productivity; & gives consumers, businesses & investors confidence that the marketplace is fair, efficient & competitive. To reach its clients, Industry Canada collaborates extensively with partners at all levels of government & the private sector.
Acts Administered:
Canadian Space Agency Act
Canadian Tourism Commission Act
Consumer Packaging & Labelling Act
Department of Industry Act
Industrial & Regional Development Act
Industrial Design Act
National Research Council Act
Natural Sciences & Engineering Research Council Act
Standards Council of Canada Act
Timber Marking Act

Minister, Industry; Minister, State (Agriculture), Hon. Christian Paradis
Tel: 613-995-9001
minister.industry@ic.gc.ca

Minister, State (Small Business & Tourism), Hon. Maxime Bernier
Tel: 613-943-6183
Fax: 613-990-4056

Minister of State, Science & Technology; Minister of State, Federal Economic Development Agency for Southern Ontario, Hon. Dr. Gary Goodyear
Tel: 613-947-2956
Fax: 613-943-7598
gary.goodyear@parl.gc.ca

Deputy Minister, John Knubley
Tel: 613-992-4292
Fax: 613-954-3272

Chief of Staff, Office of the Minister of Industry, Marc Vallières
Tel: 613-995-9001
Fax: 613-992-0302

Chief of Staff, Office of the Deputy Minister, Belinda White
Tel: 613-996-3408
Fax: 613-954-3272

Chief of Staff, Office of the Minister of State (Small Business & Tourism), Marc-André Plouffe
Tel: 613-943-6183
Fax: 613-990-4056

Chief of Staff, Office of the Minister of State (Science & Technology), Jeannie Smith
Tel: 613-947-2956
Fax: 613-943-7598

Acting Chief, Translation Bureau, Guylaine Boisvert
Tel: 613-996-7784
Fax: 613-952-7155

Senior General Counsel & Executive Director, Legal Services, David Dunbar
Tel: 613-952-2391
Fax: 613-954-5356

Associated Agencies, Boards & Commissions:
• Canadian Tourism Commission (CTC) / Commission canadienne du tourisme (CCT)
#1400, 1055 Dunsmuir St.
PO Box 49230
Vancouver, BC V7X 1L2
Tel: 604-638-8300
en-corporate.canada.travel
CTC is a unique partnership between tourism business & associations, provincial & territorial governments, & the Government of Canada. The CTC's Board of Directors is a decision-making body composed of 26 members with a wide variety of skills & knowledge, representing all regions of the country. The CTC's mission is to sustain a vibrant & profitable Canadian tourism industry.
• Communications Research Centre Canada (CRC) / Centre de recherches sur les communications
3701 Carling Ave.
PO Box 11490 H
Ottawa, ON K2H 8S2
Tel: 613-991-3313
Fax: 613-998-5355
info@crc.gc.ca
www.crc.gc.ca
Dedicated to advanced communications research & development for over 50 years. Key research areas include radio science, terrestrial wireless systems, satellite communications broadcasting & broadband network technologies. CRC has a long history of technology transfer. CRC operates an Innovation Centre, a technology incubator for small & medium-sized high-tech start-ups, which provides increased access to CRC's technologies, research expertise & unique laboratories & facilities.
• Competition Tribunal (CT) / Tribunal de la concurrence (TC)
Thomas D'Arcy McGee Bldg.
#600, 90 Sparks St.
Ottawa, ON K1P 5B4
Tel: 613-957-3172
Fax: 613-957-3170
tribunal@ct-tc.gc.ca
www.ct-tc.gc.ca
Hears & decides all applications made under Parts V11.1 & VIII of the Competition Act.
• Electronic Commerce Branch / Direction générale du commerce électronique
300 Slater St.
Ottawa, ON K1A 0C8
Tel: 613-954-5031
Fax: 613-954-2340
Toll-free: 800-328-6189
TTY: 866-694-8389
www.ic.gc.ca/eic/site/ecic-ceac.nsf/eng/home
Coordinates the development & implementation of a national electronic commerce strategy. It is responsible for both domestic & international aspects of electronic commerce. The Canadian Electronic Commerce Strategy was announced in September 1998. The Strategy, which was developed in collaboration with provincial & territorial governments, industry & consumer groups, among others, establishes a framework, goals, timetable, & implementation plan for electronic commerce domestically. The Strategy involves coordinating strategic elements that fall within the federal government's responsibilities, including the policy development areas of encryption & privacy.
• Enterprise Cape Breton Corporation (ECBC) / Société d'expansion du Cap-Breton
70 Crescent St.
PO Box 1750
Sydney, NS B1P 6T7
Tel: 902-564-3600
Fax: 902-564-3825
Toll-free: 800-705-3926
information@ecbc-secb.gc.ca
www.ecbc-secb.gc.ca
Crown corporation established pursuant to Part II of the Government Organization Act, Atlantic Canada, 1987, with a jurisdictional mandate which includes all of Cape Breton Island & a portion of mainland Nova Scotia in & around the Town of Mulgrave. The Corporation is charged with the responsibility for promoting & assisting the financing & development of industry in the region, providing employment outside the coal-producing sector & broadening the base of the local economy.
• Standards Council of Canada (SCC) / Conseil canadien des normes (CCN)
#200, 270 Albert Street
Ottawa, ON K1P 6N7
Tel: 613-238-3222
Fax: 613-569-7808
info@scc.ca
www.scc.ca
The Standards Council of Canada (SCC) works to promote the development & use of national & international standards and reports to Parliament through the Minister of Industry. It consists of 15 members and a staff of 90.
Interim Chair, W.A. Sam Shaw
Chief Executive Officer, John Walter
Tel: 613-238-3222 ext: 400
jwalter@scc.ca

Audit & Evaluation Branch (AEB) / Direction générale de la vérification et de l'évaluation (DGVE)
Tel: 613-943-7047
Fax: 613-995-8568
Director General, Audit & Evaluation, Susan Hart, CAE
Tel: 613-954-5084
Fax: 613-954-5070

Communications & Marketing Branch (CMB) / Direction générale des communications et du marketing (DGCM)
Director General, Brian Spurling
Tel: 613-947-2597
Fax: 613-954-6436
Senior Director, Public Affairs & Ministerial Services, Louise Baird
Tel: 613-943-4097
Fax: 613-954-6436
Senior Director, Digital Media & Marketing, Stephan Bélanger
Tel: 613-943-7081
Fax: 613-954-6436
Director, Advisory Services Group, Corinne Guénette
Tel: 613-943-2522
Fax: 613-954-6436
Acting Director, Operations & Corporate Communications, Naomi Sterling
Tel: 613-944-2967
Fax: 613-954-6436

Competition Bureau Canada / Bureau de la concurrence Canada
Place du Portage, Phase I, 50 Victoria St., Ottawa, ON K1A 0C9
Tel: 819-997-4282
Fax: 819-997-0324
Toll-Free: 800-348-5358
TTY: 800-642-3844
www.competitionbureau.gc.ca
The Competition Bureau is the organization responsible for the enforcement of the Competition Act, the Consumer Packaging & Labelling Act except as it relates to food, the Precious Metals Marking Act & the Textile Labelling Act. The Competition Bureau ensures compliance by the business community with legislation administered by the Bureau, & oversees the development of policy & dissemination of information aimed at ensuring optimal compliance levels.
Commissioner of Competition, John Pecman
Tel: 819-997-3304
Fax: 819-953-5013

Canadian Intellectual Property Office (CIPO) / Office de la propriété intellectuelle du Canada (OPIC)
Place du Portage I, #C-229, 50 Victoria St., Gatineau, QC K1A 0C9
Tel: 866-997-1936
Fax: 819-953-7620
TTY: 866-442-2476
cipo.contact@ic.gc.ca
www.cipo.ic.gc.ca
Other Communication: International calls: 819-934-0544
Commissioner, Patents; Registrar, Trademarks; Chief Executive Officer, Sylvain Laporte
Tel: 819-997-1057
Fax: 819-997-1890
Chief, Patent Branch - General Chemistry & Organic Division, David Campbell
Tel: 819-997-2928
Fax: 819-994-1989
Chief, Strategic & Corporate Planning, Policy, Planning, International Affairs & Research Office, Sara Ellis
Tel: 819-956-0527
Fax: 819-953-8998
Chief, Patent Branch - Mechanical Division, Lillo Giardina
Tel: 819-997-2179
Fax: 819-994-1989
Chief, Patent Branch - Biotechnology Division, Michael Gillen
Tel: 819-997-1263
Fax: 819-994-1989
Chief, Creative Services, Yoland Mallet
Tel: 819-994-9777
Fax: 819-934-9284
Chief, International Affairs, Policy, International Affairs & Research Office, Michel Patenaude
Tel: 819-956-9970
Fax: 819-953-8638
Chief, Patent Branch - Electrical Division, Nathalie Tremblay
Tel: 819-997-2198
Fax: 819-994-1989
Chief, Patent Administrative Policy, Classification & International Affairs Division, Scott Vasudev
Tel: 819-997-3055
Fax: 819-994-1989
Director General, Enterprise Solution Branch, Daniel Boulet
Tel: 819-953-3995
Fax: 819-953-5059
Director General, Trade-Marks branch, Lisa Power
Tel: 819-997-2423
Fax: 819-953-2476
Executive Director, Corporate Strategies & Services, Pierre Belisle
Tel: 819-994-2828
Fax: 819-997-1890

Industry Sector / Secteur de l'industrie
Tel: 613-954-3395
Fax: 613-941-1134
Industry Sector (IS) assists Canadian industry & businesses compete, expand & create jobs in the knowledge-based economy. IS contributes to Industry Canada's strategic objectives, trade, investment, innovation, connectedness & marketplace. It facilitates delivery of industrial, related policy analyses & strategies to promote global competitiveness of Canadian industry. IS provides a broad range of services, information resources, sector policies & strategies to support business growth. IS provides Canadian businesses with timely information products, business tools, research, strategic analyses, data & information resources.

Assistant Deputy Minister, Philip Jennings
Tel: 613-946-4448
Fax: 613-941-1134

Aerospace, Defence & Marine Branch / Aérospatiale, defense et la marine
Tel: 613-954-3786
Fax: 613-998-6703
Assistant Deputy Minister & Director General, Brian Gear
Tel: 613-941-8123
Fax: 613-998-6703
Executive Director, Industrial & Regional Benefit Directorate, Mary Gregory
Tel: 613-957-2651
Fax: 613-998-6703
Senior Director, Aerospace, André Bernier
Tel: 613-954-3166
Fax: 613-952-5822
Acting Director, Defence & Marine, Sharon Irwin
Tel: 613-954-3774
Fax: 613-998-6703
Director, F-35 Industrial Participation, Jeff Waring
Tel: 613-948-8008
Fax: 613-998-6703
Deputy Director, Industrial & Regional Benefit Directorate, Stephanie Batstone
Tel: 613-960-8793
Fax: 613-998-6703
Deputy Director, Marine, Delbert McBrine
Tel: 613-954-3167
Fax: 613-998-6703
Deputy Director, F-35 Industrial Participation, Craig Morris
Tel: 613-941-3469
Fax: 613-998-6703
Deputy Director, Commercial Aerospace, Alex Thompson
Tel: 613-946-7007
Fax: 613-998-6703
Senior Policy Advisor, Katie Durling
Tel: 613-960-9403
Fax: 613-998-6703

Automotive & Transportation Industries Branch / Direction générale des industries de l'automobile et des transports
Tel: 613-952-0441
Fax: 613-952-8088
Director General, Colette Downie
Tel: 613-954-2949
Fax: 613-952-8088
Senior Director, Planning & Programming Directorate, Charles Vincent
Tel: 613-952-0441
Fax: 613-952-8088
Director, Policy Research & Advice Directorate, Elaine Hood
Tel: 613-954-3762
Fax: 613-952-8088

Manufacturing & Life Sciences Branch / Industries de la fabrication et des sciences de la vie
Tel: 613-946-3144
Fax: 613-946-3144
Acting Director General & Director, Emerging Technologies Directorate, Tim Karlsson
Tel: 613-954-2991
Fax: 613-954-3107
Director, Resource Manufacturing Directorate, Patrick Hum
Tel: 613-954-2703
Fax: 613-954-3107
Director, Pharmaceutical Sector Directorate, Mark Schaan
Tel: 613-946-6726
Fax: 613-952-5822

Science & Innovation Sector / Secteur science et innovation
Tel: 613-995-9605
Fax: 613-995-2233
Assistant Deputy Minister, Robert Dunlop
Tel: 613-957-4392
Fax: 613-995-2233
Associate Assistant Deputy Minister, Mitch Davies
Tel: 613-960-1850
Fax: 613-995-2233
Director General, Policy Branch, Shannon Glenn
Tel: 613-949-4370
Fax: 613-996-7887
Acting Director General, Program Coordination Branch, Alison McDermott
Tel: 613-998-4417
Fax: 613-996-7887
Acting Director General, Policy Branch, Lisa Setlakwe
Tel: 613-949-4370
Fax: 613-996-7887
Executive Director, Science, Technology & Innovation Council Secretariat, Dianne Caldbick
Tel: 613-960-0145
Fax: 613-952-0459
Executive Director, Industrial Technologies Office, Karen Corkery
Tel: 613-941-6747
Fax: 613-954-5649
Executive Director, Knowledge Infrastructure Program, Science Partnerships Team, Karen Corkery
Tel: 613-960-9337
Fax: 613-960-7768
Acting Senior Director, Strategic Planning & Management Services, Michel Galipeau
Tel: 613-954-0710
Fax: 613-954-5649
Acting Senior Director, S&T Policy Advice Directorate, Marie-Hélène Légaré
Tel: 613-948-2270
Fax: 613-996-7887
Director, Science Partnerships Team & Knowledge Infrastructure Program, Tim F. Stupich
Tel: 613-941-0261
Fax: 613-996-7887
Director, Natural Science & Engineering Research Council (NSERC) Liaison, Melanie Vanstone
Tel: 613-960-5759
Fax: 613-996-7887

FedNor (Federal Economic Development Initiative in Northern Ontario) / FedNor (Initiative fédérale du développement économique dans le Nord de l'Ontario)
Minister, FedNor; President, Treasury Board, Hon. Tony Clement
Tel: 613-944-7740
Fax: 613-941-4553
tony.clement@parl.gc.ca
Director General, Aime Dimatteo
Tel: 705-671-0723
Fax: 705-670-6103
Sepcial Advisor to the Director General, Julie Vaillancourt
Tel: 705-670-6753
Fax: 705-670-6457

Small Business, Tourism & Marketplace Services / Services axés sur le marché, le tourisme et la petite entreprise
Tel: 613-995-9305
Fax: 613-941-1938
Assistant Deputy Minister, Marie-Josée Thivierge
Tel: 613-995-9605
Fax: 613-948-9088
Director General, Services to Business, Garima Dwivedi
Tel: 613-960-6488
Fax: 613-941-0253
Advisor to the ADM, Line Rudeen
Tel: 613-995-6288
Fax: 613-948-9088
Executive Assistant to the ADM, Rachelle Saumure
Tel: 613-995-6999
Fax: 613-948-9088

Chief Informatics Office / Bureau principal de l'informatique
Tel: 613-954-3570
Fax: 613-941-1938
Chief Informatics Officer, Rick Rinholm
Tel: 613-954-3574
Fax: 613-941-1938

Corporations Canada
365 Laurier Avenue West, Ottawa, ON K1A 0C8
Tel: 613-941-4550
Fax: 613-941-0601
Director General, Corporations Canada, Marcie Girouard
Tel: 613-954-3576
Fax: 613-941-5783
Director, Incorporation & Information Products & Services Directorate, Beate Schiffer-Graham
Tel: 613-941-8141
Fax: 613-941-5781
Director, Corporate Services, Christiane M. Gagnon
Tel: 613-941-1419
Fax: 613-941-5722
Director, Compliance & Policy Branch, Cheryl Ringor
Tel: 613-941-5756
Fax: 613-941-5781

Information Management Branch / Direction générale de la gestion de l'information
Tel: 613-954-3749
Fax: 613-990-4848
Acting Director General, Harvey Wong
Tel: 613-952-6368
Fax: 613-990-4848

Investment Review & Strategic Planning Branch / Direction générale de l'examen des investissements et de la planification stratégique
Tel: 613-954-1887
Fax: 613-996-2515
investcan.ic.gc.ca
Director General, Jenifer Aitken
Tel: 613-946-9108
Fax: 613-996-2515

Measurement Canada / Mesures Canada
151 Tunney's Pasture Driveway, Ottawa, ON K1A 0C9
Tel: 613-952-0652
Fax: 613-957-1265
mc.ic.gc.ca
President, Alan Johnston
Tel: 613-952-0655
Fax: 613-957-1265
Acting Vice-President, Engineering & Laboratory Services, Jean Lafortune
Tel: 613-952-0635
Fax: 613-952-1754
Vice-President, Innovative Services Directorate, Sonia Roussy
Tel: 613-952-4285
Fax: 613-952-1736
Vice-President, Program Development Directorate, Gilles Vinet
Tel: 613-941-8918
Fax: 613-952-1736

Office of the Superintendent of Bankruptcy / Bureau du surintendant des faillites
155 Queen St., Ottawa, ON K1A 0H5
Tel: 613-941-1000
Fax: 613-941-2862
osb-bsf.ic.gc.ca
Superintendent of Bankruptcy, Bill James
Tel: 613-941-2691
Fax: 613-946-9205
Deputy Superintendent, Patricia Alferez
Tel: 613-946-2157
Fax: 613-946-6367
Director General, Program Policy & Regulatory Affairs, Elisabeth Lang
Tel: 613-946-2166
Fax: 613-946-2168
Director General, Service Transformation, Vidya ShankarNarayan
Tel: 613-960-5767
Fax: 613-946-9205
Director General, Outreach Services, Ginette Trahan
Tel: 613-941-2854
Fax: 613-941-2862

Small Business / Direction générale de la petite entreprise
Tel: 613-954-5479
Fax: 613-946-1035
Director General, Éric Dagenais
Tel: 613-954-5489
Fax: 613-946-1035
Senior Director, Service Delivery & Partnerships, Dan Batista
Tel: 613-946-7302
Fax: 613-954-5463

Tourism Branch / Direction générale du tourisme
Director General, Ilona Rehberg
Tel: 613-946-1881
Fax: 613-960-5770

Infrastructure Canada

180 Kent St., Ottawa, ON K1P 0B6
Tel: 613-948-1148
Toll-Free: 877-250-7154

TTY: 800-465-7735
info@infc.gc.ca
www.infrastructure.gc.ca
Other Communication: Media Relations, Phone: 613-960-9251, E-mail: mediarelations.relationsmedias@infc.gc.ca
Infrastructure Canada is engaged in the following tasks to ensure modern public infrastructure for the benefit of Canadians: developing policies; establishing partnerships; fostering knowledge; making investments; & delivering programs.
To address local, regional, & national priorities, Infrastructure Canada works with municipalities, provinces & territories, other federal departments & agencies, as well as private companies & the non-profit sector to build & revitalize the infrastructure required by Canadians.

Minister, Transport, Infrastructure & Communities; Minister, Intergovernmental Affairs, Minister, Economic Development Agency of Canada for the Regions of Québec; President, Queen's Privy Council for Canada, Hon. Denis Lebel, P.C.
Tel: 61- 99- 070
Fax: 613-995-0327
mintc@tc.gc.ca
Minister's Office, Tower C
330 Sparks St.
Ottawa, ON K1A 0N5

Deputy Minister, Louis Lévesque
Tel: 613-990-4507
Fax: 613-991-0851
louis.levesque@tc.gc.ca

Associate Deputy Minister, Infrastructure, Marie Lemay
Tel: 613-948-8157
Fax: 613-948-2963
marie.lemay@infc.gc.ca

Parliamentary Secretary to the Minister, Transport, Infrastructure & Communities, & for the Federal Economic Development Agency for Southern Ontario, Pierre Poilievre
Tel: 513-992-2772
Fax: 613-992-1209
www.resultsforyou.ca
Social Media: www.facebook.com/pierre.poilievre
#680, La Promenade Buidling
111 Wellington St.
Ottawa, ON K1A 0A6

Senior Counsel, Legal Services, Richard Ouellet
Tel: 613-990-5783
Fax: 613-990-5777
ouellet.richard@tc.gc.ca

Audit & Evaluation Branch

#1100, 180 Kent St., Ottawa, ON K1P 0B6
Independent audits are conducted to ensure proper processes of Infrastructure Canada. Evaluation programs are also carried out to assess the value of the department's programs & initiatives. The work of the Audit & Evaluation Branch supports decision making within Infrastructure Canada.
Chief Audit & Evaluation Executive, Raymond Kunze
Tel: 613-954-4879
Fax: 613-941-5050
raymond.kunze@infc.gc.ca
Director, Evaluation, Alison Taylor
Tel: 613-954-7750
Fax: 613-941-5050
alison.taylor@infc.gc.ca
Director, Audit, Inanc Yazar
Tel: 613-946-8751
Fax: 613-941-5050
inanc.yazar@infc.gc.ca
Manager, Professional Practices, Vilma Youmaran
Tel: 613-960-9665
Fax: 613-960-8902
vilma.youmaran@infc.gc.ca

Corporate Services Branch

#1100, 180 Kent St., Ottawa, ON K1P 0B6
The Corporate Services Branch supports corporate functions & provides information management & technology services. Specific duties include administration, human resources services, procurement, financial services, & maintenance of the Shared Information Management System for Infrastructure.
Assistant Deputy Minister; Chief Financial Officer, David Miller
Tel: 613-948-9161
Fax: 613-960-6348
david.miller@infc.gc.ca
Director General, Human Resources, Security, & Administration, Nancy Martel
Tel: 613-948-3773
Fax: 613-948-3772
nancy.martel@infc.gc.ca
Director, Operational Support & Web Services, IM / IT Directorate, Patrick Boulé
Tel: 613-960-5661
Fax: 613-960-9648
pat.boule@infc.gc.ca
Director, Application Services, IM / IT Directorate, André Bourdon
Tel: 613-948-9719
Fax: 613-960-9423
andre.bourdon@infc.gc.ca
Director, Finance & Administration, Cynthia Cantlie
Tel: 613-948-4424
Fax: 613-960-6348
cynthia.cantlie@infc.gc.ca
Director, Planning, Standards, & Project Delivery, IM / IT Directorate, Mohamad Hamzeh
Tel: 613-960-6396
Chief Risk Officer, Denis Bouvier
Tel: 613-946-7874
Fax: 613-960-6348
denis.bouvier@infc.gc.ca
Chief, Financial Planning & Analysis, Danielle Byrne
Tel: 613-941-7955
Fax: 613-960-6348
danielle.byrne@infc.gc.ca
Chief Information Officer, Jennifer Dawson
Tel: 613-946-0509
Fax: 613-960-9649
jennifer.dawson@infc.gc.ca
Chief, Corporate Resourcing, Julie Parker
Tel: 613-948-7239
Fax: 613-960-6348
julie.parker@infc.gc.ca

Policy & Communications Branch

#1100, 180 Kent St., Ottawa, ON K1P 0B6
The following responsibilities are handled by the Policy & Communications Branch: identifying infrastructure priorities; conducting research that contributes to policy development; assessing investments; providing correspondence services; & coordinating communications on infrastructure & sharing knowledge.
Assistant Deputy Minister, Policy & Communications, Taki Sarantakis
Tel: 613-946-5188
Fax: 613-960-9648
taki.sarantakis@infc.gc.ca
Director General, Policy & Planning, Samantha Tattersall
Tel: 613-948-7237
Fax: 613-948-9393
samantha.tattersall@infc.gc.ca
Director General, Communications, Peter Wallace
Tel: 613-948-2940
Fax: 613-948-2963
peter.wallace@info.gc.ca
Director, Policy, Francis Bilodeau
Tel: 613-948-9160
Fax: 613-960-9648
francis.bilodeau@infc.gc.ca
Director, Special Projects, Louise Payette
Tel: 613-960-6807
Fax: 613-960-9289
louise.payette@infc.gc.ca
Director, Environmental Initiatives, Sonya Read
Tel: 613-960-9507
Fax: 613-960-9648
sonya.read@infc.gc.ca
Director, Reporting & Coordination, Tom Roberts
Tel: 613-946-9922
Fax: 613-960-9648
tom.roberts@infc.gc.ca
Director, Economic & Community Initiatives, Michael Rutherford
Tel: 613-952-3366
Fax: 613-960-6949
michael.rutherford@infc.gc.ca
Coordinator, Access to Information & Privacy, Veronique Vieira
Tel: 613-960-9622
Fax: 613-948-9393
veronique.vieira@infc.gc.ca

Program Operations Branch

#1100, 180 Kent St., Ottawa, ON K1P 0B6
The Program Operations Branch is responsible for the following activities: implementing programs; administering funding agreements; managing the federal Gas Tax transfer to Canadian municipalities to support environmentally sustainable infrastructure; & conducting environment assessments & program evaluations.
Assistant Deputy Minister, Program Operations, Natasha Rascanin
Tel: 613-948-8003
Fax: 613-960-9423
natasha.rascanin@infc.gc.ca
Director General, Program Integration, Claude Blanchette
Tel: 613-948-9392
Fax: 613-948-9394
claude.blanchette@infc.gc.ca
Director General, North, Atlantic, Ontario Program Operations, Deryck Trehearne
Tel: 613-960-6774
Fax: 613-960-9423
deryck.trehearne@infc.gc.ca
Director, West Region, Marie-Josée Lafleur
Tel: 613-948-1905
Fax: 613-948-2965
marie-josee.lafleur@infc.gc.ca
Director, Program Integration, Bogdan Makuc
Tel: 613-960-9247
Fax: 613-941-5050
bogdan.makuc@infc.gc.ca
Director, Québec Region, Isabel Romero
Tel: 613-960-6140
Fax: 613-960-9428
isabel.romero@infc.gc.ca
Director, North Program Operations, Paul Truant
Tel: 613-960-6802
Fax: 613-938-2965
paul.truant@infc.gc.ca
Deputy Director, Ontario Program Operations, Robert McCallum
Tel: 613-960-6790
Fax: 613-960-9423
robert.mccallum@infc.gc.ca
Manager, Atlantic Programs, Lucie Bergeron
Tel: 613-948-9465
Fax: 613-948-2965
lucie.bergeron@infc.gc.ca

International Development Research Centre (IDRC) / Centre de recherches pour le développement international (CRDI)

150 Kent St., PO Box 8500Ottawa, ON K1G 3H9
Tel: 613-236-6163
Fax: 613-238-7230
info@idrc.ca
www.idrc.ca
Helps scientists in developing countries identify long-term, practical solutions to pressing development problems. Support is given directly to scientists working in universities, private enterprise, government & non-profit-making organizations. Priority is given to research aimed at achieving equitable & sustainable development. One of the three program areas of focus is Environmental & Natural Resource Management. Initiatives in this area include a rural poverty & environment program initiative, an urban poverty & environment program, ecosystem approaches to human health, an international model forest network, biodiversity & regional water demand initiative.

Chair, Barbara McDougall
Tel: 613-236-6163 ext: 238
Fax: 613-565-8212
bmcdougall@idrc.ca

President, David M. Malone
Tel: 613-236-6163 ext: 259
Fax: 613-235-6391
dmalone@idrc.ca

Vice-President, Resources & Chief Financial Officer, Sylvain Dufour
Tel: 613-236-6163 ext: 218
Fax: 613-236-7293
sdufour@idrc.ca

Vice-President, Programs & Partnership Branch, Rohinton Medhora
Tel: 613-236-6163 ext: 231

Fax: 613-567-7748
rmedhora@idrc.ca

Director, Communications Division, Angela Prokopiak
Tel: 613-236-6163 ext: 259
Fax: 613-563-2476
aprokopiak@idrc.ca

Director, Environmental & Natural Resource Management, Jean Lebel
Tel: 613-236-6163 ext: 253
Fax: 613-567-7748
jlebel@idrc.ca

International Joint Commission (IJC) / Commission mixte internationale (CMI)

234 Laurier Ave. West, 22nd Fl., Ottawa, ON K1P 6K6
Tel: 613-947-1420
Fax: 613-993-5583
beckhoffb@ottawa.ijc.org
www.ijc.org
Other Communication: Great Lakes Water Quality Information: 519-257-6700
Established by the Boundary Waters Treaty of 1909 & is responsible for approving (by Order of Approval) certain works in boundary waters which affect levels & flows on both sides of the Canada-US border. The commission provides recommendations on matters along the common boundary which have been referred to the Commission by the governments. Also monitors & assesses the Great Lakes Water Quality Agreement (GLWQA) & is responsible for reviewing & commenting on Remedial Action Plans (RAPs) in coordination with eight US states & the province of Ontario.

Chair, Joseph Comuzzi

Commissioner, Lyall D. Knott

Commissioner, Pierre Trépanier

Great Lakes Regional Office
100 Ouellette Ave., 8th fl., Windsor, ON N9A 6T3
Tel: 519-257-6733
Fax: 519-257-6740
nevinj@windsor.ijc.org
Other Communication: Information: 519-257-6700
Director, Great Lakes Regional Office, Dr. Saad Y. Jasim
Tel: 519-257-6715
jasims@windsor.ijc.org

United States Section / Section des États-Unis
#615, 2000 L St., NW, Washington, DC 20440 USA
Tel: 202-736-9024
Fax: 202-643-2007
bevacquaf@washington.ijc.org

Marine Atlantic Inc. / Marine Atlantique

Corporate Office, Baine Johnston Centre, #302, 10 Fort William Pl., St. John's, NL A1C 1K4
Toll-Free: 800-897-2797
customer_relations@marine-atlantic.ca; marketing@marine-atlantic.ca
www.marine-atlantic.ca
Marine Atlantic is a Crown corporation that strives to provide safe & environmentally responsible ferry service between the island of Newfoundland & the province of Nova Scotia.
Two routes are available. A year round service is provided between Port aux Basques, Newfoundland & Labrador & North Sydney, Nova Scotia. The second route is available between mid-June & late September between Argentia, Newfoundland & Labrador & North Sydney, Nova Scotia.

Chair, Robert Crosbie

President & Chief Executive Officer, Paul John Griffin

Chief Information Officer, Colin Tibbo

Vice-President, Customer Experience, Donald Barnes

Vice-President, Human Resources, Rhona Green

Vice-President, Finance, Shawn Leamon

Director, Passenger Services, Neil Paterson

Manager, Marketing, Vicki Rose

National Battlefields Commission (NBC) / Commission des champs de bataille nationaux

390, av de Bernières, Québec, QC G1R 2L7
Tel: 418-648-3506
Fax: 418-648-3638
information@ccbn-nbc.gc.ca
www.ccbn-nbc.gc.ca
Other Communication: Communications, Phone: 418-649-6251; Customer Service: 418-649-6159; Archives: 418-648-2589; Finances: 418-648-4666; Activities: 418-648-4071
www.facebook.com/plainsofabraham
In 1908, an Act was passed to create the National Battlefields Commission. The purpose of the Commission is to acquire & preserve historical battlefields & to create national parks from these battlefields for the benefit of the public. The federal government agency, with its nine-member board of directors, operates under the portfolio of the Minister of Canadian Heritage. The Commission has a sustainable development policy for the conservation of the Plains of Abraham park.

Secretary - Director General, André Beaudet
Tel: 418-648-3553
Fax: 418-648-3638

Director, Administration; Financial Services Agent, Paule Veilleux
Tel: 418-648-4666
Fax: 418-649-6345

Chief, Security Service, Jean St-Pierre
Tel: 418-648-4655
Fax: 418-649-6152

Officer, Customer Service, Marie Cantin
Tel: 418-649-6159
Fax: 418-648-3809

Officer, Cultural & Technical Services, Martin Duchesneau
Tel: 418-648-4687
Fax: 418-648-2263

Officer, Development & Marketing, Benoit Gilbert
Tel: 418-648-4796
Fax: 418-648-3809

Officer, Material Management, Philippe Lafrenière
Tel: 418-648-4599
Fax: 418-649-6345

Officer, Communications, Joanne Laurin
Tel: 418-649-6251
Fax: 418-648-3809

Historian; Archivist, Hélène Quimper
Tel: 418-648-2589
Fax: 418-648-3638

Forest Engineer; Supervisor, Major Events, Marc Pelletier
Tel: 418-648-7052
Fax: 418-649-6576

Superintendent, Horticultural Services, Geneviève Thiboutot
Tel: 418-648-4664
Fax: 418-649-6576

Consultant, Landscape & Envrionment, Marc Boilard
Tel: 418-648-4795
Fax: 418-648-3809

National Capital Commission (NCC) / Commission de la capitale nationale (CCN)

#202, 40 Elgin St., Ottawa, ON K1P 1C7
Tel: 613-239-5000
Fax: 613-239-5063
Toll-Free: 800-465-1867
TTY: 866-661-3530
info@ncc-ccn.ca; contracts-contrats@ncc-ccn.ca (Contracting)
www.canadascapital.gc.ca
Other Communication: Emergency Service, Phone: 613-239-5353; Gatineau Park Visitor Centre: 819-827-2020; Volunteer Centre: 613-239-5373; Skateway: 613-239-5234; Sponsorship: 613-239-5625
www.youtube.com/user/nccvidccn
The National Capital Commission is a Crown corporation. It was established by Parliament in 1959 to act as a steward for federal buildings & lands in Canada's National Capital Region.
The Commission works to ensure that the region is a place of national significance & pride. It consists of the following corporate, advisory, & special committees: Executive; Audit; Governance; Advisory Committee on Planning, Design, & Realty; Advisory Committee on Communications, Marketing, & Programming; Advisory Committee on the Official Residences of Canada; & Canadiana Fund.
In accordance with the *National Capital Act*the Commission's board of directors is appointed by the Minister of Foreign Affairs, with the approval of the Governor-in-Council. The National Capital Commission is accountable to Parliament & reports through the Minister of Foreign Affairs.

Chair, Russell Andrew Mills

Chief Executive Officer, Jean-François Trépanier

Senior Vice-President, Public & Corporate Affairs Management, Diane Dupuis
Tel: 613-239-5363
Fax: 613-239-5007

Vice-President, Environment, Capital Lands, & Parks, Michelle Comeau
Tel: 613-239-5209
Fax: 613-239-5337

Vice-President, Finance & Procurement; Chief Financial Officer, Pierre Désautels
Tel: 613-239-5086
Fax: 613-239-5007

Vice-President, Capital Planning, François Lapointe
Tel: 613-239-5579
Fax: 613-239-5302

Vice-President, Real Estate Managemtn, Design, & Construction, Roland Morin
Tel: 613-239-5589
Fax: 613-239-5302

Vice-President, Human Resources, Manon Rochon
Tel: 613-239-5576
Fax: 613-239-5552

Director, Information Technologies & Geomatics Services, Martin Bernier
Tel: 613-239-5650
Fax: 613-239-5507

Director, Environmental Management & Protection, Steve Blight
Tel: 613-239-5583
Fax: 613-239-5336

Director, Digitial Communications Outreach & Youth Programs, Daniel Feeny
Tel: 613-239-5766
Fax: 613-239-5300

Director, Audit & Corporate Ethics; Chief Audit Executive, Jayne Hinchliff-Milne
Tel: 613-239-5629
Fax: 613-239-5695

Director, Marketing, Susan Kay
Tel: 613-239-5056
Fax: 613-239-5300

Director, Strategic Communications, Kathryn Keyes
Tel: 613-239-5636
Fax: 613-239-5758
kathryn.keyes@ncc-ccn.ca

Director, Official Residences, Art Marcotte
Tel: 613-993-2613
Fax: 613-993-8244

Director, Corporate Planning, Louise Mignault

Tel: 613-239-5734
Fax: 613-239-5039

Director, Public Affairs & Information Management, Sandra Pecek
Tel: 613-239-5155
Fax: 613-239-5274

Director, Design & Construction, Claude Robert
Tel: 613-239-5651
Fax: 613-239-5694

Director, Capital Celebrations & Program Operations, Guy Tanguay
Tel: 613-239-5245
Fax: 613-239-5013

Director, Capital Interpretation & Commemorations, Sylvie Tilden
Tel: 613-239-5242
Fax: 613-239-5333

General Counsel; Commission Secretary, Mark Dehler
Tel: 613-239-5102
Fax: 613-239-5404

Environmental Officer, Allison Myatt
Tel: 613-239-5019
Fax: 613-239-5336

Coordinator, Social Media, Judith Gadbois St-Cyr
Tel: 613-239-5708
judith.gadbois.st-cyr@ncc-ccn.ca

Department of National Defence & the Canadian Forces / Le Ministère de la Défense nationale et les Forces canadiennes

National Defence HQ, Major-General George R. Pearkes Bldg., 101 Colonel By Dr., Ottawa, ON K1A 0K2
Tel: 613-995-2534
Fax: 613-992-4739
TTY: 800-467-9877
DNDRecruitment-RecrutementMDN@forces.gc.ca (Civilian Careers)
www.forces.gc.ca
Other Communication: CF Recruiting, Phone: 1-800-856-8488; Access to Information, Phone: 613-992-0996; Media Inquiries, Phone: 613-996-2353 or 1-866-377-0811, Fax: 613-996-8330
twitter.com/CanadianForces
The Department of National Defence, the Canadian Forces, & related organizations provide services to defend Canada & Canadian interests.
The Defence Portfolio comprises the following organizations, which are the responsibility of the Minister of National Defence: The Office of the Legal Advisor to the Department of National Defence & the Canadian Forces; National Search & Rescue Secretariat; Defence Research & Development Canada; Communications Security Establishment; Cadets & Junior Canadian Rangers; Canadian Forces Housing Agency; Judge Advocate General; Military Police Complaints Commission; Canadian Forces Grievance Board; Office of the Chief Miltary Judge; The Office of the National Defence & Canadian Forces Ombudsman; & the Canadian Forces Personnel Support Agency.
Some of the Canadian Forces' current operations include Operation Attention in Afghanistan, Operation Artemis at sea, Operation Calumet in the Sinai Peninsula; Operation Proteus in Jerusalem, Operation Soprano in the Republic of South Sudan, Operation Sculpture in Sierra Leone, & Operation Crocodile in the Democratic Republic of the Congo.

Governor General; Commander-in-Chief of Canada, Right Hon. David Johnston, C.C., C.M.M., C.O.M., C.D.
Tel: 613-993-8200
Fax: 613-998-8760
TTY: 800-465-6890
Social Media: twitter.com/GGDavidJohnston, www.facebook.com/GGDavidJohnston
Rideau Hall
1 Sussex Dr.
Ottawa, ON K1A 0A1

Minister, National Defence, Hon. Peter Gordon MacKay, P.C., Q.C., B.A., LL.B.
Tel: 613-996-3100
Fax: 613-995-8189
dnd_mdn@forces.gc.ca
www.forces.gc.ca/site/minister-ministre/index-eng.asp
TTY: 800-467-9877

Associate Minister, National Defence, Hon. Kerry-Lynne D. Findlay, Q.C., B.A., LL.B.
Tel: 613-992-2957
Fax: 613-992-3589
kerry-lynne.findlay@parl.gc.ca
TTY: 800-467-9877
Social Media: twitter.com/KLDF2011, www.facebook.com/102431099842674
Note: Web Site: www.forces.gc.ca/site/minister-ministre/am-ma/index-eng.asp

Parliamentary Secretary to the Minister, National Defence, Chris Alexander
Tel: 613-995-8042
Fax: 613-996-1289
Chris.Alexander@parl.gc.ca
www.chrisalexander.ca
Social Media: twitter.com/calxandr

Chief of Defence Staff for the Canadian Forces, General Thomas Lawson
Tel: 613-992-7301
Fax: 613-992-3945
Note: On October 29, 2012, General Thomas Lawson was officially appointed as Canada's new Chief of the Defence Staff during a Change of Command ceremony held at the Canadian War Museum.

Vice-Chief of Defence Staff, V.-Adm. Bruce Donaldson
Tel: 613-992-6052
Fax: 613-992-3945
Other Communications: Secure Telephone: 613-995-0016

Chair, Defence Science Advisory Board, Wayne Williams
Tel: 613-992-4070
Fax: 613-996-9168

Ombudsman, Pierre Daigle
Tel: 613-996-2089
Fax: 613-996-3280
Other Communications: Secure Fax: 613-996-9562

Chief of Staff to the Minister, John MacDonell
Tel: 613-996-3100
Fax: 613-995-8189

Director, Access to Information & Privacy, Julie Jansen
Tel: 613-944-7225
Fax: 613-995-5777

Director, Strategic Corporate Services, Jane Lang
Tel: 613-996-3452
Fax: 613-947-3145

Director, Communications, Jay Paxton
Tel: 613-996-3100
Fax: 613-995-8189

Director, Communications to the Associate Minister, Pamela Stephens
Tel: 613-996-3100

Corporate Secretary, Larry Surtees
Tel: 613-996-6402
Fax: 613-992-0313

Associated Agencies, Boards & Commissions:
• Communications Security Establishment / Centre de la sécurité des telecommunications
1500 Bronson Ave.
PO Box 9703 Terminal
Ottawa, ON K1A OK2
Tel: 613-991-7600
Fax: 613-991-8514
www.cse-cst.gc.ca
The Communications Security Establishment is Canada's national cryptologic agency, providing the Government of Canada with two key services: foreign signals intelligence in support of defence & foreign policy, & the protection of electronic information & communication.
• Office of the Communications Security Establishment Commissioner / Bureau du Commissaire du Centre de la sécurité des télécommunications
PO Box 1984 B
Ottawa, ON K1P 5R5
Tel: 613-992-3044
www.ocsec-bccst.gc.ca
The Commissioner reviews the activities of the Communications Security Establishment for compliance with the law; advises the Minister of National Defence & the Attorney General of Canada of any CSE activity not in compliance with the law; receives complaints about CSE activities; carries out specific duties under the public interest provisions of the Security of Information Act.
• Military Police Complaints Commission / Commission d'examen des plaintes concernant la police militaire
270 Albert St., 10th Fl.
Ottawa, ON K1P 5G8
Tel: 613-947-5625
Fax: 613-947-5713
Toll-free: 800-632-0566
commission@mpcc-cppm.gc.ca
www.mpcc-cppm.gc.ca
Other Communication: Toll Free Fax: 1-877-947-5713
Quasi-judicial, independent civilian agency examines complaints arising from either the conduct of military police members in the exercise of policing duties or functions or from interference in or obstruction of their police investigations.

Infrastructure & Environment / Infrastructure et environnement
Assistant Deputy Minister, Scott Stevenson
Tel: 613-945-7545
Fax: 613-995-6653
Chief of Staff, M.Gen. Daniel Benjamin
Tel: 613-995-7243
Fax: 613-996-9527
Chief Executive Officer, Canadian Forces Housing Agency, Dominique Francoeur
Tel: 613-998-5904
Fax: 613-991-1988
Director General, Real Property, Susan Chambers
Tel: 613-995-0923
Fax: 613-995-1031
Acting Director General, Nuclear Safety, Sandy Dewar
Tel: 613-992-8546
Fax: 613-992-5537
Director General, Environment, Rose Kattackal
Tel: 613-995-5586
Fax: 613-995-1031
Director General & Chief, Military Engineering, Col. Sylvain Sirois
Tel: 613-995-2415
Fax: 613-995-8261

Judge Advocate General's Office / Juge-avocat général
Tel: 613-992-5678
Fax: 613-992-1211
Judge Advocate General, B.Gen. Ken Watkin
Tel: 613-992-3019
Fax: 613-992-5678

Science & Technology / Science et technologie
Assistant Deputy Minister, Dr. Robert Walker
Tel: 613-996-2020
Fax: 613-995-3402
Chief of Staff, René Larose
Tel: 613-996-7215
Fax: 613-995-3402
Director General, Defence Research & Development Canada - Centre for Security Science, Dr. Anthony Ashley
Tel: 613-944-8195
Fax: 613-995-0002
Director General, Research & Development Corporate Services, Colin McEwan
Tel: 613-992-6105
Fax: 613-996-0038
Director General, Defence Research & Development Canada - Centre for Operational Research & Analysis, Maria Rey
Tel: 613-992-5025
Fax: 613-992-3342
Director General, Science & Technology Operations, Rick Williams
Tel: 613-992-5776
Fax: 613-995-3402

Director, Science & Technology (Maritime), Keith Hendy
Tel: 613-992-7695
Fax: 613-996-7063
Director, Science & Technology (Human Performance), Kurtis Simpson
Tel: 613-947-7810
Fax: 613-990-1205
Director, Science & Technology (Land), Michel Szymaczak
Tel: 613-992-2608
Fax: 613-996-5177
Director, Science & Technology (Air), Joseph Templin
Tel: 613-992-4338
Fax: 613-996-5177
Director, Military Personnel Research & Analysis, Susan Truscott
Tel: 613-992-6162
Fax: 613-995-5785

National Energy Board (NEB) / Office national de l'énergie (ONE)

444 - 7 Ave. SW, Calgary, AB T2P 0X8
Tel: 403-292-4800
Fax: 403-292-5503
Toll-Free: 800-899-1265
TTY: 800-632-1663
info@neb-one.gc.ca
www.neb-one.gc.ca
Other Communication: Toll-free fax: 877-288-8803
Federal regulatory tribunal whose powers include: authorizing oil, natural gas & electricity exploration; certifying interprovincial & international pipelines & designated power lines; & setting tolls & tariffs for oil & gas pipelines under federal jurisdiction. The NEB reviews Canadian supply of all major commodities, with emphasis on electricity, oil, natural gas, & oil & natural gas by-products. It also reviews the demand for Canadian energy in Canada & in export markets. In addition to its regulatory role, the NEB is responsible for advising the government on the development & use of energy resources. Its responsibilities include regulating exploration, development & production of oil & gas on frontier lands in a manner that promotes worker safety, environmental protection & resource conservation. The NEB is responsible for environmental matters relating to the construction & operation of facilities & programs within its jurisdiction. Its environmental activities are carried out in three phases: The first phase involves evaluating the potential environmental effects of proposed projects. In the second phase, the environment is protected through monitoring & enforcement of terms & conditions attached to project approval. The third phase include s ongoing monitoring of operations to ensure that cleanup, restoration & maintenance of sites & rights of way are conducted to acceptable standards. The Board also verifies that emergency response plans are in place & that it or the operator can respond immediately to any incidents

Chair & Chief Executive Officer, Gaétan Caron
Tel: 403-299-2724
Fax: 403-299-5503
gaetan.caron@neb-one.gc.ca

Vice-Chair, Sheila Leggett
Tel: 403-221-3009
sheila.leggett@neb-one.gc.ca

Board Member, Kenneth Bateman
Tel: 403-229-3565
kenneth.bateman@neb-one.gc.ca

Board Member, Roland George
Tel: 403-299-3163
roland.goerge@neb-one.gc.ca

Board Member, Georgette Habib
Tel: 403-221-3004
georgette.habib@neb-one.gc.ca

Board Member, Rowland Harrison
Tel: 403-229-2736
rowland.harrison@neb-one.gc.ca

Board Member, Lyne Mercier
Tel: 403-229-3734
lyne.mercier@neb-one.gc.ca

Chief Operating Officer, Pradeep Kharé
Tel: 403-299-2700
pradeep.khare@neb-one.gc.ca

General Counsel, Legal Services, Rob Cohen
Tel: 403-292-6497
rob.cohen@neb-one.gc.ca

Professional Leader, Environment, Robert Steedman
Tel: 403-299-3178
rsteedman@neb-one.gc.ca

Strategic Leader, Regulatory Group, Sandy Lapointe
Tel: 403-299-3673
sandy.lapointe@neb-one.gc.ca

Strategic Leader, Business Integration Group, John McCarthy
Tel: 403-299-3646
john.mccarthy@neb-one.gc.ca

Team Leader, Planning, Coordination & Reporting, Lori-Ann Sharp
Tel: 403-299-1994
lori-ann.sharp@neb-one.gc.ca

National Research Council Canada (NRC) / Conseil national de recherches Canada (CNRC)

Building M-58, 1200 Montreal Rd., Ottawa, ON K1A 0R6
Tel: 613-993-9101
Fax: 613-952-9907
Toll-Free: 877-672-2672
TTY: 613-949-3042
info@nrc-cnrc.ca; media@nrc-cnrc.gc.ca
www.nrc-cnrc.gc.ca
Other Communication: Media Relations, Toll-free Phone: 1-855-282-1637; Human Resources, Phone: 613-993-9391; Recruitmenet Inquiries, E-mail: recruitment@nrc-cnrc.gc.ca
twitter.com/nrc_cnrc
www.youtube.com/researchcouncilcan
The National Research Council is the Government of Canada's agency for research & development. Reporting to Parliament is through the Minister of Industry. The Council works with partners & clients to meet industrial & societal needs, in accordance with the *National Research Council Act.*
Technical & advisory services are available to assist enterprises solve technical problems. The following are some examples of the specialized services available: analytical chemistry services, calibration services, cold regions techologies & services, molecular biology services, environmental hydraulics services, marine performance & evaluation services, flight test & evaluation services, surface transportation services, medical diagnostics, nuclear magnetic resonance services, & protein purification services.
The National Research Council encourages & engages in research & business partnerships. Licensing opportunities are available for research & development solutions.

President, John R. McDougall
Tel: 613-993-2024

Executive Vice-President; Secretary General, Patricia Mortimer
Tel: 613-998-3664
Fax: 613-998-3839

Vice-President, Human Resources, Isabelle Gingras
Tel: 613-993-9136
Fax: 613-952-6078

Vice-President, Corporate Management; Chief Financial Officer, Michel A. Piché
Tel: 613-991-5457
Fax: 613-952-1628

Vice-President, Engineering, Ian Potter
Tel: 613-949-5955
Fax: 613-949-5987

Vice-President, Life Sciences, Roman Szumski
Tel: 613-993-9244
Fax: 613-954-2066

Vice-President, Emerging Technologies, Danial D. Wayner
Tel: 613-998-5404
Fax: 613-949-1314

Executive Director, Program & Project Services, Gary J. Fudge
Tel: 613-949-0542

Executive Director, Strategic & Operational Planning, Judith C. Young
Tel: 613-993-4758
Fax: 613-941-0986

Director General, Knowledge Management, Pam Bjornson
Tel: 613-993-2341
Fax: 613-952-9112

Director General, Communications, Katharine Trim
Tel: 613-993-1357
Fax: 613-952-9907

Director, Audit & Evaluation, Alexandra Dagger
Tel: 613-993-9962
Fax: 613-941-0986

Director, Shared Services Canada Infrastructure Services, Ross Ogilvie
Tel: 613-990-0430
Fax: 613-954-2561

Senior Counsel, Legal Services, Michèle Hurteau
Tel: 613-998-8984
Fax: 613-952-2058

National Research Council Canada - Canada Institute for Scientific & Technical Information (NRC-CISTI) / l'Institut canadien de l'information scientifique et technique (ICIST)
Building M-55, 1200 Montreal Rd., Ottawa, ON K1A 0R6
Tel: 613-998-8544
Fax: 613-993-7619
Toll-Free: 800-668-1222
www.cisti-icist.nrc-cnrc.gc.ca
twitter.com/cisti_icist
www.facebook.com/cisti.icist
Also known as the National Research Council Canada National Science Library (Bibliothèque scientifique nationale), the Canada Institute for Scientific & Technical Information was founded in 1924. Under the *National Research Council Act*the Canada Institute for Scientific & Technical Information is mandated to operate & maintain a national library. The Institute supports Canada's research, innovation, & health communities by supplying resources & services to aid in discoveries & commercialization.
The main library, located in Ottawa, is open to the public. Library users have online access to the NRC-CISTI Public Catalogue in order to search for & order print & electronic holdings in the areas of science, technology, engineering, & medicine. The Institute also features "Discover", which is a web interface to search a database of more than twenty million peer reviewed scientific, technical, & medical journal articles. The National Research Council Archives offers information about the development of scientific research at the Council & the history of science in Canada.
The National Science Library is governed by a Director General & an Advisory Board that comprises national & international stakeholders from the library, publishing, academi c, & business sectors. Board members are appointed by the Council of the National Research Council Canada.
Chair, Advisory Board, Katherine Schultz
Director General, Pam Bjornson
Tel: 613-993-2341
Fax: 613-952-9112
Secretary, Christine A. Mattson
Tel: 613-993-1195
Fax: 613-941-1569

National Research Council Canada - Canada Institute for Scientific & Technical Information - Library Locations
Charlottetown
550 University Ave., Charlottetown, PE C1A 4P3
Tel: 902-566-7639
Chicoutimi
501, boul Université est, Chicoutimi, QC G7H 8C3
Service is by appointment only.
Fredericton
46 Dineen Dr., Fredericton, NB E3B 9W4
Tel: 506-444-0542
Halifax
1411 Oxford St., Halifax, NS B3H 3Z1

Tel: 902-426-8250
Montréal
6100, av Royalmount, Montréal, QC H4P 2R2
Tél: 514-496-6117
Penticton
Observatory, Herzberg Institute of Astrophysics, 717 White Lake Rd., PO Box 248Kaleden, BC VOH 1K0
Tel: 250-497-2311
Fax: 250-497-2355
St. John's
1 Kerwin Pl., St. John's, NL A1B 3T5
Tel: 709-772-2468
Vancouver
4250 Westbrook Mall, Vancouver, BC V6T 1W5
Tel: 604-221-3035
Victoria
Herzberg Institute of Astrophysics, 5071 West Saanich Rd., Victoria, BC V9E 2E7
Tel: 250-363-0020
Fax: 250-363-0045
Winnipeg
435 Ellice Ave., Winnipeg, MB R3B 1Y6
Tel: 204-984-2642

National Research Council Canada - Industrial Research Assistance Program (NRC-IRAP)
1200 Montreal Rd., Ottawa, ON K1A 0R6
Fax: 613-952-1086
Toll-Free: 877-994-4727
publicinquiries.irap-pari@nrc-cnrc.gc.ca
The Industrial Research Assistance Program offers advisory & funding services to help businesses with their research & development projects. Firms are assisted in both the development & commercialization of technologies.
For information about the Industrial Research Assistance Program or to consult an Industrial Technology Advisor, contact one of the regional offices located across Canada. Industrial Technology Advisors are available to support clients through each stage of their projects, by connecting firms with national & international industry experts & possible business partners.
Director General, Industrial Research Assistance Program, Bogdan Ciobanu
Tel: 613-993-0695
Fax: 613-954-0501
Executive Director, Industrial Research Assistance Program, Jason Charron
Tel: 613-998-2626
Fax: 613-952-1086
Director, Industrial Research Assistance Program Finance, Amina Bisbis
Tel: 613-949-0859
Fax: 613-952-1079
Director, Strategic & Operations Alignment, Byron D. De Kergommeaux
Tel: 613-993-0653
Fax: 613-952-1079
Manager, National Training, Cindy L. Almond
Tel: 613-990-7317
Fax: 613-952-1079
Manager, Portfolio Management, Kathleen Brière
Tel: 613-998-3744
Fax: 613-991-5758
Manager, Operational Policies, Alain Brizard
Tel: 613-990-9475
Fax: 613-952-1079
Manager, Strategic Planning & Performance Management, Margaret McKay
Tel: 613-991-6853
Fax: 613-952-1079
Co-Manager, Project Management, Marie-Claudy Nelson
Tel: 613-991-5505
Fax: 613-991-2594
Co-Manager, Project Management, Mamadou Samaké
Tel: 613-990-8951
Fax: 613-952-1086
Manager, Information Management & Information Technology, Brian C. Wilson
Tel: 613-993-4089
Fax: 613-952-1086
Executive Officer, Strategic Project Unit, Johanne H. Lavoie
Tel: 613-991-4699
Fax: 613-954-0501
Senior Officer, Communications & Marketing, Lesley L. Cushing
Tel: 613-990-1679
Fax: 613-952-1079

National Research Council Canada - Industrial Research Assistance Program - Regional Offices
Boucherville - Québec Region
#111P, 75, boul de Mortagne, Boucherville, QC J4B 6Y4
Tel: 450-641-5300
Fax: 450-641-5301
In Québec, Industrial Technology Advisors have expertise in important industrial sectors located in the province, such as manufacturing, communications, & the environment.
Executive Director, Claude Attendu
Tel: 450-641-5307
Fax: 450-641-5301
Director, Québec Periphery, Yves Lamarche
Tel: 450-641-5804
Fax: 450-641-5301
Director, Québec Montréal, Richard O'Shaughnessey
Tel: 514-496-1217
Manager, Québec Operations & Finances, Olga Bosak
Tel: 450-641-5395
Fax: 450-641-5301
Innovation & Network Advisor, Julie Guay
Tel: 450-641-5311
Fax: 450-641-5301
Calgary - West Region
3608 - 33rd St. NW, Calgary, AB T2L 2A6
Director, Robert Faulder
Tel: 403-292-6466
Fax: 403-292-6452
Charlottetown - Atlantic & Nunavut Region
550 University Ave., Charlottetown, PE C1A 4P3
Toll-Free: 877-994-4727
Edmonton - West Region
#208, 9650 - 20 Ave,, Edmonton, AB T6N 1G1
Tel: 780-495-6509
Fax: 780-495-6510
The Edmonton office serves Alberta & the Northwest Territories. Specialists are available for the following key industrial sectors in the western region: energy, environmental technologies, agricultural & food sciences, construction, transportation, telecommunications, advanced chemisty & manufacturing, & health care & pharmaceuticals.
Executive Director, West Region, Joan Barichello
Tel: 403-292-6460
Fax: 403-292-6452
Director, West Edmonton, Kashmir Gill
Tel: 780-495-2136
Fax: 780-495-6510
Manager, West Operations & Finance, Robin M. Tuson
Tel: 403-292-6446
Halifax - Atlantic & Nunavut Region
1411 Oxford St., Halifax, NS B3H 3Z1
Tel: 902-426-3138
Fax: 902-426-1624
Other Communication: New Brunswick, Phone: 1-877-994-4727
The expertise of Industrial Technology Advisors in the Atlantic & Nunavut area covers both established & developing industrial sectors. Examples of areas where assistance is available include aquaculture, agriculture, wood products, manufacturing, telecommunications, & biotechnology.
Executive Director, Bradley C. Goodyear
Tel: 902-426-1055
Fax: 902-426-1624
Manager, Atlantic Operations & Finance, Susan Simpson
Tel: 902-426-1939
Fax: 902-426-1624
Innovation & Network Advisor, Maritimes, Johannes Larsen
Tel: 506-778-2832
Fax: 506-778-2840
Markham - Ontario Region
Seneca College, #907, 10 Allstate Pkwy., Markham, ON L3R 5Y1
Tel: 905-479-9034
Fax: 416-973-4303
Director, Ontario Markham, Angelo Del Duca
Tel: 905-479-9034
Fax: 416-973-4303
Oakville - Ontario Region
#302, 690 Dorval Dr., Oakville, ON L6K 3W7
Regional Contribution Agreement Officer, Barbara Stevens
Tel: 905-849-9772
Fax: 905-849-3567
Ottawa - Ontario Region
3701 Carling Ave., Ottawa, ON K2H 8S2
Tel: 416-954-8331
Fax: 613-998-6947
Director, Ontario Ottawa, L.M. Plante
Tel: 613-998-6947
Fax: 613-949-0071
St. John's - Atlantic & Nunavut Region
Memorial University Campus, Arctic Ave., PO Box 12093St. John's, NL A1B 3T5
Tel: 709-772-5228
Fax: 709-772-5067
The St. John's office serves Newfoundland & Labrador & Nunavut.
Director, Kristi McBride
Tel: 709-772-6811
Fax: 709-772-5067
Toronto - Ontario Region
#903, 55 St. Clair Ave. East, Toronto, ON M4T 1M2
Tel: 416-973-4484
Fax: 416-973-4303
Industrial Technology Advisors are located at offices throughout Ontario. They offer a full range of expertise in areas such as manufacturing, construction, software, electronics, manufacturing, medical devices, life sciences, & aerospace.
Executive Director, Manfred Hubert
Tel: 416-952-4459
Fax: 416-973-4303
Director, Ontario St. Clair, Wiliam J. Dobson
Tel: 416-954-8330
Fax: 416-954-8331
Winnipeg - West Region
435 Ellice Ave., Winnipeg, MB R3B 1Y6
Tel: 204-983-0092
Fax: 204-983-8835
Other Communication: Saskatchewan, Toll-Free Phone: 1-877-994-4727
Director, Vivian Sullivan
Tel: 204-984-6477
Fax: 204-983-8835
Vancouver - Pacific Region
#650, 1185 West Georgia St., Vancouver, BC V6E 4E6
Tel: 604-666-6062
Fax: 604-666-7204
Toll-Free: 877-994-4727
British Columbia & the Yukon are served by Pacific region personnel. Expertise reflects the industrial activity in the area, such as mining, forestry, construction, industrial engineering, electronics, & information technologies.
Executive Director, Pacific Region, Christopher Ryan
Tel: 604-221-3163
Fax: 604-221-3101
Director, Pacific Kelowna, Olga Kargina
Tel: 604-666-6476
Fax: 604-666-7204
Director, Pacific Vancouver, James Wilkin
Tel: 604-666-6646
Fax: 604-666-7204
Innovation & Network Advisor, Diana Nacer-Cherif
Tel: 604-221-3109
Fax: 604-221-3101
International Science & Technology Advisor, Wei Ning
Tel: 604-294-9059
Fax: 604-291-6015
Waterloo - Ontario Region
Waterloo Research & Technology Park, 29 Hagey Blvd., Waterloo, ON N2L 6R5
Director, Ontario Waterloo, Tomas Matulis
Tel: 519-763-8046
Fax: 519-763-7217
Regional Contribution Agreement Officer, Michael Hibbert
Tel: 519-747-3513
Fax: 519-880-1360

National Research Council Canada - Research Facilities
The National Research Council provides Canadian businesses access to research facilities & research experts. The research infrastructure enables businesses to pursue research & development opportunities & to accelerate product development.

National Research Council Aerospace Manufacturing Technologies Centre (AMTC)
Campus Université de Montréal, 5145, av Decelles, Montréal, QC H3T 2B2
Industries are assisted in the implementation of advanced manufacturing methods for aerospace. Examples of technologies in-

vestigated include automation & robotics, metal forming & joining, fabrication of composite structures, & material removal.
Senior Communications Officer, Katia Jollez
Tel: 613-990-7480
Fax: 613-952-1628
Katia.Jollez@nrc-cnrc.gc.ca
Building M-3
#127, 1200 Montreal Rd.
Ottawa, ON K1A 0R6

National Research Council Anaerobic Bioprocessing Pilot Plant
c/o Montréal (av Royalmount) Research Facilities, 6100, av Royalmount, Montréal, QC H4P 2R2
The pilot plant works with engineering firms & their industrial & municipal clients. Equipment at the pilot plant is able to test methods to bioconvert organic feedstock to chemical or energy carriers. Other services include technology optimization, technology evaluation, kinetics assessment for model calibration, on-line control implementation, plus microbiological, chemical, & biochemical monitoring of processes.
Communications Advisor, Jacqueline Malboeuf
Tel: 613-993-3692
Fax: 613-991-2384
Jacqueline.Malboeuf@nrc-cnrc.gc.ca
Building M-12
#131, 1200 Montreal Rd.
Ottawa, ON K1A 0R6

National Research Council Animal Cell Pilot Plant
c/o Montréal (av Royalmount) Research Facilities, 6100, av Royalmount, Montréal, QC H4P 2R2
The pilot plant offers expertise in viral infection processes, virus recovery & purification, cell culture in bioreactors, & HPLC assays.
Strategic Communications Advisor, Anne-Marie Brugger
Tel: 613-990-2499
Fax: 613-952-1628
Anne-Marie.Brugger@nrc-cnrc.gc.ca
Communication Officer, Lise Lafontaine, BA, MLIS
Tel: 902-566-7403
Fax: 902-569-4289
Lise.Lafontaine@nrc-cnrc.gc.ca
#232, 550 University Ave.
Charlottetown, PE C1A 4P3

Canadian Centre for Housing Technology (CCHT) / Centre canadien des technologies résidentielles
c/o National Research Council Canada, Building M-20, 1200 Montreal Rd., Ottawa, ON K1A 0R6
construction@nrc-cnrc.gc.ca
www.ccht-cctr.gc.ca
Operated jointly by the National Research Council, Natural Resources Canada, & the Canada Mortgage & Housing Corporation, the Canadian Centre for Housing Technology offers research & demonstrations related to innovative technology in housing. The present focus is upon energy efficiency & energy conversion systems.
Facilities on the six acre site include two research houses, the InfoCentre, & four serviced lots to develop & build new concepts. The testing facilities are available to the construction industry on a fee-for-service basis.
Senior Advisor, Sylvie Dostaler
Tel: 613-998-9204
Fax: 613-941-0822
Sylvie.Dostaler@nrc-cnrc.gc.ca
Note: Contact Marianne Armstrong for general & project inquiries.
Research Council Officer, Marianne Armstrong, BSc, MSc
Tel: 613-991-0967
Fax: 613-991-0976
Note: Contact Marianne Armstrong for general & project inquiries.
Research Officer, Michael Swinton, BSc, MEng
Tel: 613-993-9708
Fax: 613-998-6802
Michael.Swinton@nrc-cnrc.gc.ca
Note: Contact Michael Swinton for information about research project initiation.
Communication Officer, Tracie Taylor-Labonté
Tel: 613-993-6755
Fax: 613-952-9907
Tracie.Taylor-Labonte@nrc-cnrc.gc.ca
Note: Media inquiries should be directed to Tracie Taylor-Labonté.

National Research Council Canadian Photonics Fabrication Centre (CPFC)
c/o National Research Council Canada, Building M-50, 1200 Montreal Rd., Ottawa, ON K1A 0R6
The Canadian Photonics Fabrication Centre has test & measurement capabilities for experts to assist companies in the diagnosis of material & fabrication related problems.
NRC-SIMS Business Development Officer, Orson L. Bourne
Tel: 613-990-0978
Orson.Bourne@nrc-cnrc.gc.ca
Senior Communication Advisor, Taylor Bildstein
Tel: 613-949-8680
Fax: 613-952-1628
Taylor.Bildstein@nrc-cnrc.gc.ca
Communication Officer, Cindy Goldberg
Tel: 902-426-6095
Fax: 902-426-9413
Cindy.Goldberg@nrc-cnrc.gc.ca
Acting Director, Research Programs, NCR, Charles-Antoine Gauthier
Tel: 613-993-8551
Fax: 613-952-7998
Charles-Antoine.Gauthier@nrc-cnrc.gc.ca

National Research Council Fire Resistance & Performance of Structures Testing Facilities
c/o National Research Council, 1200 Montreal Rd., Ottawa, ON K1A 0R6
construction@nrc-cnrc.gc.ca
Fire resistance testing facilities of the National Research Council serve the following purposes: to improve fire detection & suppression systems; to enhance the fire safety of structures & transportation systems; & to reduce the risk & cost of fire throughout Canada. Facilities include a Burn Hall / Smoke Tower Complex.
Senior Advisor, Sylvie Dostaler
Tel: 613-998-9204
Fax: 613-941-0822
Sylvie.Dostaler@nrc-cnrc.gc.ca
Senior Communication Officer, Katia Jollez
Tel: 613-990-7480
Fax: 613-952-1628
Katia.Jollez@nrc-cnrc.gc.ca

National Research Council Hydraulics Laboratories
c/o National Research Council, 1200 Montreal Rd., Ottawa, ON K1A 0R6
Toll-Free: 877-672-2672
www.climatechange.gc.ca
The National Research Council operates hydraulics laboratories for applied research & commercial studies. Studies focus upon civil engineering hydraulics, port & harbour developments, coastal science & engineering, & offshore energy projects.
Business Development Officer, Francois Moreau
Tel: 613-991-2206
Fax: 613-952-7679
Francois.Moreau@nrc-cnrc.gc.ca
Senior Advisor, Sylvie Dostaler
Tel: 613-998-9204
Fax: 613-941-0822
Sylvie.Dostaler@nrc-cnrc.gc.ca

National Research Council Indoor Environment Testing Facilities
c/o National Research Council, 1200 Montreal Rd., Ottawa, ON K1A 0R6
construction@nrc-cnrc.gc.ca
The National Research Council's indoor envrionment testing facilities include an indoor air testing facility, an indoor environment facility, a floor sound transmission testing facility, & a wall sound transmission testing facility. Through testing, industries can develop technologies for the design & operation of energy-efficient, cost-effective, & healthy indoor environments.
Sylvie Dostaler
Tel: 613-998-9204
Fax: 613-941-0822
Sylvie.Dostaler@nrc-cnrc.gc.ca

National Research Council Industrial Partnership Facility (IPF)
c/o Montréal (av Royalmount) Research Facilities, 6100, av Royalmount, Montréal, QC H4P 2R2
Tel: 514-496-6100
The scientific complex offers services to companies engaged in biotechnology research & development. Both large & small businesses have access to these advanced facilities & experts to create & test new technologies.
Liaison Officer, Louise Demers-Thorne
Tel: 514-496-1733
Fax: 514-496-5007
Louise.Demers-Thorne@cnrc-nrc.gc.ca

National Research Council Marine Performance Evaluation & Testing Facilities
c/o National Research Council, 1200 Montreal Rd., Ottawa, ON K1A 0R6
St. John's Research FacilitiesPO Box 12093 Sta.
St. John's, NL A1B 3T5
Marine performance evaluation & testing facilities in Ottawa, Ontario include the following: an ice tank, a large scale wave flume, a large area basin, a coastal wave basin, & a multidirectional wave basin.
The following facilities are located in St. John's Newfoundland & Labrador: cold room laboratories, a towing tank, an ice tank, & an offshore energy basin.
Research is conducted into problems involving marine environments, vessels, & structures.
Senior Advisor, Sylvie Dostaler
Tel: 613-998-9204
Fax: 613-941-0822
Sylvie.Dostaler@nrc-cnrc.gc.ca
Director, Business Development & External Relations, Richard Brommeland
Tel: 780-641-1620
Richard.Brommeland@nrc-cnrc.gc.ca
Director, Research Programs, Dr. Christopher J. Haugen
Tel: 780-641-1615
Chris.Haugen@nrc-cnrc.gc.ca
Research Officer, Nano Ethical, Environmental, Economic, Legal & Societal Issues (NEEELS), Michael D. Lounsbury
Tel: 780-492-1684
Fax: 780-492-3325
ml37@ualberta.ca

National Research Council Medical Device Facilities
Boucherville Research Facilities, 75, boul de Mortagne, Boucherville, QC J4B 6Y4
Tel: 450-641-5100
Secondary Address: 435 Ellice Ave.
Winnipeg Research Facilities
Winnipeg, MB R3B 1Y6
The National Research Council's medical device facilities offer assistance to healthcare organizations with research & development needs. Facilities are located in Boucherville Québec, Winnipeg Manitoba, & Halifax Nova Scotia.
The Boucherville site provides expertise in functional nanomaterials & virtual reality surgical planning for surgical oncology.
The Winnipeg facility's areas of interest include early stage disease diagnoses that are minially invasive & techology that reduces or eliminates hospital stays.
The Halifax locations focus upon translational neuroscience. Halifax's Neuroimaging Research Laboratory is situated at the QEII's Health Sciences Centre's Halifax Infirmary (#3900, 1796 Summer St, Halifax, NS B3H 3A7). The city's Clinicial Laboratory for Magnetoencephalography / Biomedical MRI Research is located at the IWK Health Centre (Goldbloom Pavillion, 5850 University Ave, Halifax, NS B3K 6R8).
Communication Officer, Valerie McPherson
Tel: 204-984-4890
Fax: 204-983-3154
Valerie.McPherson@nrc-cnrc.gc.ca
Winnipeg Research Facilities
#115, 435 Ellice Ave.
Winnipeg, MB R3B 1Y6
Director, Business & Corporate Services, Jeffrey P. Parker
Tel: 306-975-5568
Fax: 306-975-4839
Jeff.Parker@nrc-cnrc.gc.ca
Director, Research, Suzanne R. Abrams
Tel: 306-975-5569
Fax: 306-975-4191
Sue.Abrams@nrc-cnrc.gc.ca
Advisor, Strategic Communications, Anne-Marie Brugger
Tel: 613-990-2499
Fax: 613-952-1628
Anne-Marie.Brugger@nrc-cnrc.gc.ca

National Research Council Ocean Technology Enterprise Centre (OTEC)

PO Box 12093St. John's, NL A1B 3T5
Tel: 709-772-2469
Toll-Free: 877-672-2672
Opened in 2003, the Ocean Technology Enterprise Centre conducts ocean engineering research to benefit the Canadian marine industry. The Centre, which is housed within the National Research Council's Industry Partnership Facility on the campus of Memorial University, provides facilities & expertise to assist ocean technology companies in the development of technologies.
Communication Officer, Helene Letourneau
Tel: 613-949-0777
Fax: 613-952-9907
Helene.Letourneau@nrc-cnrc.gc.ca

National Research Council Performance Assessment of Civil Infrastructure & Related Structures Research Facilities
Water Quality Testing Facility, Research Innovation Centre, #508, 3737 Wascana Pkwy., Regina, SK S4S 0A2
Tel: 306-780-3208
construction@nrc-cnrc.gc.ca
Testing facilities are available to evaluate the design, performance, rehabilitation, & management of concrete structures & buried utilities.
The Water Quality Testing Facility in Regina, Saskatchewan has the capabilities to study water quality in distribution systems in order to develop improved infrastructure materials, treatment processes, & monitoring techniques.
Senior Advisor, Sylvie Dostaler
Tel: 613-998-9204
Fax: 613-941-0822
Sylvie.Dostaler@nrc-cnrc.gc.ca

National Research Council Single Domain Antibody Facility
c/o National Research Council, 1200 Montreal Rd., Ottawa, ON K1A 0R6
Established in 2008, the facility isolates single-domain antibodies. Access to the facility can be arranged for academic or industrial parners through collaborative research or service agreements.
Strategic Communications Advisor, Anne-Marie Brugger
Tel: 613-990-2499
Fax: 613-952-1628
Anne-Marie.Brugger@nrc-cnrc.gc.ca

National Research Council Surface Transportation Research Facilities
Ottawa Uplands Research Facilities, 2320 Lester Rd., Ottawa, ON K1V 1S2
Tel: 613-998-9639
Fax: 613-957-0831
inquiries.ST@nrc-cnrc.gc.ca
The Ottawa location of the National Research Council's Surface Transportation research facilities feature areas to test road, military, & rail vehicles & components. Examples of facilities include environmental chambers, the compression & tension facility, the heavy vehicle tilt facility, the rail vehicle impact facility, vibration testing facilities, as well as the railway, wheel, bearing, & brake facility.
Business Development Manager, Rail Program, Craig A. Ceppetelli, BSc., MBA
Tel: 613-998-9388
Fax: 613-957-0831
Craig.Ceppetelli@nrc-cnrc.gc.ca
Key Accounts Manager, Military, Kevin Hayes
Tel: 613-991-5024
Fax: 613-957-0831
Kevin.Hayes@nrc-cnrc.gc.ca
Key Accounts Manager, Commercial, Tony Jenkins
Tel: 613-990-8084
Fax: 613-957-0831
Tony.Jenkins@nrc-cnrc.gc.ca
Manager, Climatic Engineering, Donald J. LeBlanc, B.Sc., B.A.Sc.
Tel: 613-998-3979
Fax: 613-957-4159
Don.Leblanc@nrc.gc.ca
Key Accounts Manager, Rail Program, Jason Pierosara
Tel: 613-998-9378
Fax: 613-957-0831
Jason.Pierosara@nrc-cnrc.gc.ca
Manager, Vibration Testing Facilities, Bruce A. Playfair
Tel: 613-954-7968
Fax: 613-957-0831
Bruce.Playfair@nrc-cnrc.gc.ca
Manager, Business Development & Key Accounts Management, Rick Zaporzan, IMBA
Tel: 613-990-7249
Fax: 613-957-0831
Rick.Zaporzan@nrc-cnrc.gc.ca
Portfolio Communications Advisor, Sarah Mangione
Tel: 613-949-9660
Sarah.Mangione@nrc-cnrc.gc.ca

National Research Council SWCNT (Single-Wall Carbon Nanotubes) Technology Accelerator Centre
Montreal Road Campus, National Research Council, 1200 Montreal Rd., Ottawa, ON K1A 0R6
Tel: 613-993-9101
The SWCNT (Single-Wall Carbon Nanotubes) Technology Accelerator Centre works to fully understand the mechanical & physical properies of SWCNT modified polymers & fibrous composites, before application in components & structures. Some of the applications under investigation include protective sporting gear, light weight armour materials to protect soldiers & security personnel, nano-modified adhesives for bonding structures in the automotive & aerospace industries, & highly conductive SWCNT for energy efficient applications.

National Research Council Waste Biotreatability Facility
c/o National Research Council, 1200 Montreal Rd., Ottawa, ON K1A 0R6
The Waste Biotreatability Facility is engaged in the evaluation of organic waste for its biotreatability & its potential to produce energy such as hydrogen & methane. The facility is part of the National Research Council's Environmental Bioengineering Group, which specializes in bioenery production from organic matter.
Portfolio Communications Advisor, Jacqueline Malboeuf
Tel: 613-993-3692
Fax: 613-991-2384
Jacqueline.Malboeuf@nrc-cnrc.gc.ca

National Research Council Wind Tunnel Testing Facilities
c/o National Research Council, 1200 Montreal Rd., Ottawa, ON K1A 0R6
To support the research of government, industries, & universities, the National Research Council provides six wind tunnels, plus experties in aerodynamic noise measurement, pressure sensitive paint technology, & flow mapping.
Senior Communication Officer, Katia Jollez
Tel: 613-990-7480
Fax: 613-952-1628
Katia.Jollez@nrc-cnrc.gc.ca

National Research Council Zebrafish Screening Facility
c/o National Research Council, 1200 Montreal Rd., Ottawa, ON K1A 0R6
Testing services are available for pharmacological & toxicology activity. The National Research Council's Zebrafish Screening Facility can be accessed by companies & research organizations by entering into a technical service agreement or research collaboration.
Communication Officer, Lise Lafontaine, BA, MLIS
Tel: 902-566-7403
Fax: 902-569-4289
Lise.Lafontaine@nrc-cnrc.gc.ca
#232, 550 University Ave.
Charlottetown, PE C1A 4P3

National Round Table on the Environment & Economy (NRTEE) / Table ronde nationale sur l'environnement et l'économie (TRNEE)

#200, 344 Slater St., Ottawa, ON K1R 7Y3
Tel: 613-992-7189
Fax: 613-992-7385
info@nrtee-trnee.ca
www.nrtee-trnee.ca
The National Round Table on the Environment & the Economy is an independent agency of the federal government committed to providing decision makers & opinion leaders with reliable information & objective views on the current state of the debate on the environment & the economy. Working with stakeholders across Canada, the NRTEE carries out its mandate by identifying key issues with both environmental & economic implications, fully exploring these implications, & suggesting action designed to balance economic prosperity with environmental preservation. A multistakeholder approach, combined with impartiality & neutrality, are the hallmarks of the NRTEE's activities. By creating an atmosphere in which all points of view can be expressed freely & debated openly, the NRTEE has established a process whereby stakeholders themselves define the environment/economy interface within issues, determine areas of consensus & identify the reasons for disagreement in other areas. The NRTEE's programs focus on the following areas: energy & climate change; capital markets & sustainability; climate change adaptation

Acting President & Chief Executive Officer, Jim McLaughlin
Tel: 613-947-4507
jim.mclachlan@nrtee-trnee.gc.ca

Director, Policy & Research, René Drolet
Tel: 613-996-4501
rene.drolet@nrtee-trnee.gc.ca

Director, Communications & Public Affairs, Marie-Josée Lapointe
Tel: 613-943-2054
mariejosee.lapointe@nrtee-trnee.gc.ca

Manager, Human Resources & Administrative Services, Hélène Sutton
Tel: 613-992-7181

Manager, Finance & Contracts, Duane Wilson
Tel: 613-947-4421
duane.wilson@nrtee-trnee.gc.ca

Office & Facility Coordinator, Corporate Services, Kim Laforge
Tel: 613-947-4419
kim.laforge@nrtee-trnee.gc.ca

National Search & Rescue Secretariat / Secrétariat national de recherches et sauvetage

#400, 275 Slater St., Ottawa, ON K1A 0K2
Tel: 613-992-0054
Fax: 613-996-3746
Toll-Free: 800-727-9414
inquiry@nss.gc.ca
www.nss.gc.ca
Provides a central managerial role in the overall coordination of search & rescue. It addresses program & policy issues related to the National Search & Rescue Program, & advises the Lead Minister for search & rescue.

Executive Director, Géraldine Underdown
Tel: 613-992-0054
Fax: 613-996-3746

Communications Officer, Kim Fauteux
Tel: 613-992-3472
Fax: 613-996-3746

Natural Resources Canada (NRCan) / Ressources naturelles Canada (RNCan)

580 Booth St., Ottawa, ON K1A 0E4
Tel: 613-995-0947
Fax: 613-992-7211
TTY: 613-996-4397
www.nrcan-rncan.gc.ca/com/
Other Communication: Emergency Operations Centre: 613-995-5555, 613-943-0000
Advances development of Canada's economy by contributing to the development & use of Canada's mineral & energy resources in a manner consistent with federal environmental & social objectives; advances knowledge of the Canadian landmass through scientific & science-related activities.
Acts Administered:
Acts Administered in Part by Natural Resources Canada
Administration of Acts with respect to Changes in Provincial Boundaries
Alberta Act
Alberta/BC Boundary Act, 1974
Alberta/NWT Boundary Act, 1958
Arctic Shipping Pollution Prevention Regulations
Arctic Waters Experimental Pollution Regulations
Arctic Waters Pollution Prevention Act
Arctic Waters Pollution Prevention Act (Transport Canada/Indian & Northern Affairs)
Arctic Waters Pollution Prevention Regulations
BC-Yukon-NWT Boundary Act, 1967
British Columbia 1857, 1866
Canada Foundation for Sustainable Development Technology Act

Canada Lands Survey Act (Indian & Northern Affairs)
Canada Lands Surveys Examination Regulation
Canada Oil & Gas Certificate of Fitness Regulations
Canada Oil & Gas Diving Regulations
Canada Oil & Gas Drilling Regulations
Canada Oil & Gas Geophysical Operations Regulations
Canada Oil & Gas Installations Regulations
Canada Oil & Gas Operations Act (Indian Affairs & Northern Development)
Canada Oil & Gas Operations Regulations
Canada Oil & Gas Production & Conservation Regulations
Canada Petroleum Resources Act
Canada Petroleum Resources Act (Indian & Northern Affairs)
Canada-Newfoundland Atlantic Accord Implementation Act
Canada-Newfoundland Oil & Gas Spills & Debris Liability Regulations
Canada-Newfoundland Oil & Gas Spills & Debris Liability Regulations
Canada-Nova Scotia Offshore Petroleum Resources Accord Implementation Act
Canada-Nova Scotia Oil & Gas Spills & Debris Liability Regulations
Canadian Nuclear Safety Commission Rules of Procedure
Canadian Ownership & Control Determination Act
Cape Breton Development Corporation Act
Class I Nuclear Facilities Regulations
Class II Nuclear Facilities & Prescribed Equipment Regulations
Co-operative Energy Act
Department of Natural Resources Act
Energy Administration Act
Energy Efficiency Act
Energy Monitoring Act
Energy Supplies Emergency Act
Environmental Studies Research Fund Regions Regulations
Explosives Act
Forestry Act
Frontier Lands Petroleum Royalty Regulations
Frontier Lands Registration Regulations
General Nuclear Safety & Control Regulations
Gros Morne Forestry Timber Regulations
Hibernia Development Project Act
International Boundary Commission Act
Keewatin Act
Lancaster Sound Designated Area Regulations
Land Survey Tariff Regulations
Manitoba Boundaries Extension Act, 1912
Manitoba/Saskatchewan Boundary Act, 1966
Manitoba-NWT Boundary Act, 1966
Motor Vehicle Fuel Consumption Standards Act
National Energy Board Act
National Energy Board Act (Transport Canada)
National Energy Board Coast Recovery Regulations
National Energy Board Electricity Regulations
National Energy Board Export & Import Reporting Regulations
National Energy Board Pipeline Crossing Regulations, I & II
National Energy Board Processing Plant Regulations
National Energy Board Rules of Practice & Procedure
National Energy Board Substituted Service Regulations
New Brunswick, 1851
Newfoundland & Labrador Offshore Area Line Regulations
Newfoundland Offshore Area Oil & Gas Operations Regulations
Newfoundland Offshore Area Petroleum Diving Regulations
Newfoundland Offshore Area Petroleum Geophysical Operations Regulations
Newfoundland Offshore Area Petroleum Production & Conservation Regulations
Newfoundland Offshore Area Registration Regulations
Newfoundland Offshore Area Oil & Gas Operations Regulations
Newfoundland Offshore Area Petroleum Diving Regulations
Newfoundland Offshore Area Petroleum Geophysical Operations Regulations
Newfoundland Offshore Area Petroleum Production & Conservation Regulations
Newfoundland Offshore Area Registration Regulations
Newfoundland Offshore Certificate of Fitness Regulations
Newfoundland Offshore Petroleum Drilling Regulations
Newfoundland Offshore Petroleum Installations Regulations
Newfoundland Offshore Petroleum Drilling Regulations
Newfoundland Offshore Petroleum Installations Regulations
Newfoundland Offshore Petroleum Resource Revenue Fund Regulations
Newfoundland, 1949
Northern Pipeline Act
Northwest Territories, 1905
Nova Scotia Offshore Area Certificate of Fitness Regulations
Nova Scotia Offshore Area Petroleum Diving Regulations
Nova Scotia Offshore Area Petroleum Drilling Regulations
Nova Scotia Offshore Area Petroleum Geophysical Operations Regulations
Nova Scotia Offshore Area Petroleum Installations Regulations
Nova Scotia Offshore Area Petroleum Production & Conservation Regulations
Nova Scotia Offshore Area Production & Conservation Regulations
Nova Scotia Resources (Ventures) Ltd. Drilling Assistance Regulations
Nova Scotia Resources (Ventures) Limited Drilling Assistance Regulations
Nova Scotia, 1851
Nuclear Energy Control Act
Nuclear Fuel Waste Act, 2002
Nuclear Liability Act
Nuclear Non-Proliferation Import & Export Control Regulations
Nuclear Safety & Control Act
Nuclear Security Regulations
Nuclear Substances & Radiation Devices Regulations
Nunavut, 1993
Oil & Gas Spills & Debris Liability Regulations
Oil Substitution & Conservation Act
Onshore Pipeline Regulations
Ontario Boundaries Extension Act, 1912
Ontario, 1889
Ontario-Manitoba Boundary Act
Order Exempting the United States Coast Guard Icebreaker \Healy\" from the Application of the Arctic Shipping Pollution Prevention Regulations"
Orders Prohibiting the Issuance of Interests at Lapierre House Historic Site (Yukon) & Rampart House (Yukon)
Packaging & Transport of Nuclear Substances Regulations
Pipeline Arbitration Committee Procedure Rules
Power Line Crossing Regulations
Prince Edward Island, 1873
Québec Boundaries Extension Act, 1912
Radiation Protection Regulations
Report on the State of Canada's Forests Regulations
Resources & Technical Surveys Act (Fisheries & Oceans/Environment)
Saskatchewan, 1905
Saskatchewan/NWT Boundary Act, 1966
Shipping Safety Control Zones Order
Timber Regulations
Uranium Mines & Mills Regulations
Uranium Mines (Ontario) Occupational Health & Safety Regulations
Uranium Mines (Ontario) Occupational Health & Safety Regulations
Yukon, 1898

Minister, Natural Resources, Hon. Joe Oliver
Tel: 613-996-2007
Fax: 613-996-4516
Minister.Ministre@NRCan-RNCan.gc.ca

Deputy Minister, Serge Dupont
Tel: 613-992-3280
Fax: 613-992-3828
Serge.Dupont@NRCan-RNCan.gc.ca

Associate Deputy Minister, Karen Ellis
Tel: 613-996-9753
Fax: 613-992-3828
Karen.Ellis@NRCan-RNCan.gc.ca

Assistant Deputy Minister, Johanne Mongeon
Tel: 613-992-3457
Fax: 613-992-3828
Johanne.Mongeon@NRCan-RNCan.gc.ca

Chief Scientist, Geoff Munro
Tel: 613-947-1435
Fax: 613-944-4747
geoff.Munro@NRCan-RNCan.gc.ca

Chief Audit Executive, Joe Freamo
Tel: 613-996-4940
Fax: 613-992-8799
Joe.Freamo@NRCan-RNCan.gc.ca

Director General, Corporate Renewal Office, Sylvie Letellier
Tel: 613-947-7403
Fax: 613-992-8922
Sylvie.Letellier@NRCan-RNCan.gc.ca

Director General, External Relations, Mark Pearson
Tel: 613-996-6055
Fax: 613-996-0478
Mark.Pearson@NRCan-RNCan.gc.ca

Director, Communications, Chris McCluskey
Tel: 613-996-2007
Fax: 613-943-0662
Christopher.McCluskey@NRCan-RNCan.gc.ca

Associated Agencies, Boards & Commissions:
• National Energy Board
See Entry Name Index for detailed listing.

Canadian Forest Service (CFS) / Service canadien des forêts
Tél: 613-995-0947
Téléc: 613-947-1208
TTY: 613-996-4397
CFS-SCF@NRCan-RNCan.gc.ca
cfs.nrcan.gc.ca
Promotes the sustainable development of Canada's forests & competitiveness of the Canadian forest sector for the well-being of present & future generations of Canadians. It focuses on forest science & technology, & related national policy coordination. The CFS maintains five research centres across the country that share responsibility for research in the areas of biodiversity; biotechnology; climate change; ecology & ecosytems; entomology; forest conditions, monitoring & reporting; forest fires; forest & landscape management; pathology; silviculture & regeneration; & socioeconomics.
Assistant Deputy Minister, Tom Rosser
Tel: 613-947-7400
Fax: 613-947-7395
Tom.Rosser@NRCan-RNCan.gc.ca

Planning, Operations & Information Branch / Direction de la planification, des opérations et de l'information
Acting Director General, Terry Hatton
Tel: 613-947-7573
Fax: 613-947-9100
Director, Forest Knowledge & Information Management Division, Joanne Frappier
Tel: 613-947-9101
Fax: 613-947-0912
Acting Director, National & Departmental Relations Division, Benjamin Whelan
Tel: 613-947-9087
Fax: 613-947-9100
Benjamin.Whelan@NRCan-RNCan.gc.ca
Senior Policy Advisor, Planning & Renewal Division, Sylvia T. Boucher
Tel: 613-947-7371
Fax: 613-947-0912
SylviaT.Boucher@NRCan-RNCan.gc.ca

Policy, Economics & Industry Branch / Direction de la politique, de l'économie et de l'industrie
Director General, Glenn Mason
Tel: 613-947-7382
Fax: 613-947-7399
Glenn.Mason@NRCan-RNCan.gc.ca
Head, Finance & Administration, Janet Fahey
Tel: 613-947-9059
Fax: 613-947-7399
Janet.Fahey@NRCan-RNCan.gc.ca
Director, International Affairs, Peter Besseau
Tel: 613-947-7358
Fax: 613-947-9035
Peter.Besseau@NRCan-RNCan.gc.ca
Director, Economic Analysis Division, Darcie Booth
Tel: 613-947-9051
Fax: 613-947-9020
Darcie.Booth@NRCan-RNCan.gc.ca
Director, Strategic Analysis & Policy Development Division; Pulp & Paper Green Transformation Program, Glenn Hargrove
Tel: 613-947-9073
Fax: 613-947-9035
Glenn.Hargrove@NRCan-RNCan.gc.ca
Director, Industry & Trade Division, Robert Jones
Tel: 613-947-9041
Fax: 613-947-9035
Robert.Jones@NRCan-RNCan.gc.ca

Science & Programs Branch / Direction des sciences et des programmes
Director General, Mary Mes-Hartree
Tel: 613-947-8984
Fax: 613-947-9090
Director, Ecosystems Health Science Program, Maria Teresa Fernandez de Castro
Tel: 613-943-4215
Fax: 613-947-9090
MariaTeresa.FernandezdeCastro@NRCan-RNCan.gc.ca
Director, Forest Science Division, Mike Fullerton
Tel: 613-995-2332
Fax: 613-947-9035
Mike.Fullerton@NRCan-RNCan.gc.ca
Director, Science Policy Division, Jacques Gagnon
Tel: 613-947-9043
Fax: 613-947-9033
Jacques.Gagnon@NRCan-RNCan.gc.ca
Director, S&T Governance Division, Beth MacNeil
Tel: 613-943-1668
Fax: 613-992-5390
Beth.MacNeil@NRCan-RNCan.gc.ca
Acting Director, Programs Division, Trudy Samuel
Tel: 613-947-9053
Fax: 613-992-5390
Trudy.Samuel@nrcan-rncan.gc.ca
Atlantic Forestry Centre / Centre de foresterie de l'Atlantique
1350 Regent St. South, PO Box 4000Fredericton, NB E3B 5P7
Tel: 506-452-3500
Fax: 506-452-3525
cfs.nrcan.gc.ca/regions/afc
Responsible for the overall Canadian Forest Service operations & programs in the Atlantic region. Liaises & negotiates with provincial government, industry officials, & other sector-related senior management on behalf of the CFS in the region.
Acting Regional Director General, Derek MacFarlane
Tel: 506-452-3508
Derek.MacFarlane@NRCan-RNCan.gc.ca
Director, Forest Production & Protection, Derek MacFarlane
Tel: 506-452-3680
Derek.MacFarlane@NRCan-RNCan.gc.ca
Director, Science, Bruce Pendrel
Tel: 506-452-3505
Bruce.Pendrel@NRCan-RNCan.gc.ca
Canadian Wood Fibre Centre (CWFC) / Centre canadien sur la fibre de bois (CCFB)
580 Booth St., 8th Floor, Ottawa, ON K1A 0E4
Tel: 613-947-9001
Fax: 613-947-8863
cfs.nrcan.gc.ca/subsite/cwfc
The Canadian Wood Fibre Centre (CWFC) brings together forest sector researchers to develop solutions for the Canadian forest sector's wood fibre related industries in an environmentally responsible manner. Its mission is to create innovative knowledge to expand the economic opportunities for the forest sector to benefit from Canadian wood fibre.
Executive Director, George Alexande Bruemmer
Tel: 613-947-7331
Fax: 613-947-8863
GeorgeAlexande.Bruemmer@NRCan-RNCan.gc.ca
Great Lakes Forestry Centre / Centre de foresterie des Grands Lacs
1219 Queen St. East, PO Box 490Sault Ste Marie, ON P6A 2E5
Tel: 705-949-9461
Fax: 705-541-5700
cfs.nrcan.gc.ca/regions/glfc
Responsibilities include: forest research & regional forestry activities in Ontario; provides the primary federal focus for forestry in Ontario; emphasis on boreal mixed wood forest management & environmental impacts of pollutants & forestry practices; efforts also directed at the reduction of losses from insects, disease & fire; ecosystem dynamics & classification; nutrient problems & impacts from forestry practices; acid rain impacts (carbon dioxide/nitrogen oxide interactions).
Director General, Theodore Van Lunen
Tel: 705-541-5555
Theodore.VanLunen@NRCan-RNCan.gc.ca
Director, Forest Ecology & Productivity, David Nanang
Tel: 705-541-5558
David.Nanang@NRCan-RNCan.gc.ca
Director, Integrated Pest Management, Anthony Hopkin
Tel: 705-541-5568
Anthony.Hopkin@NRCan-RNCan.gc.ca
Director, Policy, Planning & Liaison, Rod Smith
Tel: 705-541-5561
Rod.CFS.Smith@NRCan-RNCan.gc.ca
Laurentian Forestry Centre / Centre de foresterie des Laurentides
1055, rue du PEPS, CP 10380 Succ Sainte-Foy, Québec, QC G1V 4C7
Tél: 418-648-3335
Téléc: 418-648-5849
lucie.labrecque@RNCan-NRCan-gc.ca
scf.rncan.gc.ca/regions/cfl
Responsibilities include: increasing scientific & technical knowledge in the area of forest biology which includes biodiversity, tree biotechnology & advanced genetics, pest management methods, & in the area of forest ecosystem which cover forest ecosystem processes, effects of forestry practices, landscape management & climate change.
Director General, Jacinthe Leclerc
Tel: 418-648-3957
Jacinthe.Leclerc@RNCan-NRCan.gc.ca
Director, Forest Biology Program, Lise Caron
Tel: 418-648-7616
Fax: 418-649-6956
Lise.Caron@NRCan-RNCan.gc.ca
Research Director, Forest Ecosystems, Vincent Roy
Tel: 418-648-3770
Fax: 418-649-6956
Vincent.Roy@NRCan-RNCan.gc.ca
Director, Planning & Development, Normand Laflamme
Tel: 418-648-2528
Fax: 418-648-2529
Normand.Laflamme@RNCan-NRCan.gc.ca
Northern Forestry Centre / Centre de foresterie du Nord
5320 - 122 St., Edmonton, AB T6H 3S5
Tel: 780-435-7210
Fax: 780-435-7359
cfs.nrcan.gc.ca/regions/nofc
Responsibilities include: socio-economics & forest sociology; fire ecology, environment, & advanced fire management & prediction systems; climate change & forest interactions; carbon budget modeling; forest health, insect, & disease monitoring & management systems; remote sensing applications & landscape level classification systems; ecosystems productivity; biodiversity. Regional coordination of national programs relating to Model Forests & First Nation Forestry. Responsible for the direction of forestry programs in the provinces of Alberta, Saskatchewan, Manitoba & the NWT, including R&D, & four federal-provincial partnership agreements in forestry.
Director General, Timothy Sheldan
Tel: 780-435-7202
Fax: 780-435-7396
Timothy.Sheldan@NRCan-RNCan.gc.ca
Director, Climate Change & Forests Research Program, Kelvin Hirsch
Tel: 780-435-7319
Kelvin.Hirsch@NRCan-RNCan.gc.ca
Director, Ecosystems Health Science Program, Maria Teresa Fernandez de Castro
Tel: 780-430-3848
MariaTeresa.FernandezdeCastro@NRCan-RNCan.gc.ca
Director, Strategic Policy & Planning Branch, Ken Mallett
Tel: 780-435-7201
Ken.Mallett@NRCan-RNCan.gc.ca
Pacific Forestry Centre / Centre de foresterie du Pacifique
506 West Burnside Rd., Victoria, BC V8Z 1M5
Tel: 250-363-0600
Fax: 250-363-0775
cfs.nrcan.gc.ca/regions/pfc
Responsibilities include: forest management of federal lands; first nations programs; first nations land claims resource analysis; economic analysis of the regional forest sector (value-added, labour costs, & industrial sustainability); national strategic planning for the forestry practices & landscape management networks; science & technology programs in both forest biology (ecosystems processes, climate change, pest management, & tree biotechnology). Advises the CFS ADM on all forestry matters relating to the Pacific & Yukon region. The Mountain Pine Beetle Action Plan 2005-2010 set out strategies for confronting the infestation.
Director General, Kami Ramcharan
Tel: 250-363-0608
Fax: 250-363-6088
Kami.Ramcharan@NRCan-RNCan.gc.ca
Director, Forest Information, Jeff Dechka
Tel: 250-363-0627
Jeff.Dechka@NRCan-RNCan.gc.ca
Director, Forest Resources Division, Jim Wood
Tel: 250-363-6008
Fax: 250-363-6004
Jim.Wood@NRCan-RNCan.gc.ca
Director, Forest Science, Judi Beck
Tel: 250-363-0705
Judi.BECK@NRCan-RNCan.gc.ca
Director, MPB Policy & Research, Bill Wilson
Tel: 250-363-0721
Fax: 250-363-6004
Bill.Wilson@NRCan-RNCan.gc.ca

Earth Sciences Sector / Secteur des sciences de la Terre
ess.nrcan.gc.ca/index_e.php
Provides Canadians with timely & reliable geomatics & geoscience knowledge, products & services of the highest standards & in the most cost-effective manner possible. The Earth Sciences Sector is a predominantly science- & technology-based sector & includes the Geological Survey of Canada, Geomatics Canada, & the Polar Continental Shelf Project. These groups are major contributors to the comprehensive geoscience knowledge base of Canada & provide surveying, mapping, remote sensing, & digital information services describing the Canadian landmass.
Assistant Deputy Minister, Brian Gray
Tel: 613-992-9983
Fax: 613-995-1509
brian.gray@NRCan-RNCan.gc.ca

Canada Centre for Remote Sensing - Geomatics Canada / Centre canadien de télédétection - Géomatique Canada
Director General, Douglas Bancroft
Tel: 613-947-1358
Fax: 613-947-1382
Douglas.Bancroft@NRCan-RNCan.gc.ca
Director, Data Acquisition Division, Caroline Cloutier
Tel: 613-995-0802
Fax: 613-947-1408
Caroline.Cloutier@NRCan-RNCan.gc.ca
Director, Earth Observation & GeoSolutions Divison, E. Paola de Rose
Tel: 613-947-1350
Fax: 613-947-1385
E.Paola.deRose@NRCan-RNCan.gc.ca
Director, Geodetic Survey Division, Denis Hains
Tel: 613-995-4282
Fax: 613-995-3215
Denis.Hains@NRCan-RNCan.gc.ca
Science Advisor, Terry Pultz
Tel: 613-947-1316
Fax: 613-947-1385
Terry.Pultz@NRCan-RNCan.gc.ca

Coordination & Strategic Issues Branch / Direction de la coordination et des enjeux stratégiques
Director General, Marian Campbell Jarvis
Tel: 613-992-5032
Marian.CampbellJarvis@NRCan-RNCan.gc.ca
Director, Strategic Issues Division, Alrick Huebener
Tel: 613-943-0997
Fax: 613-996-9670
Alrick.Huebener@NRCan-RNCan.gc.ca
Acting Director, Polar Continental Shelf Program, Michael Jordan
Tel: 613-947-1601
Fax: 613-947-1611
Michael.Jordan@NRCan-RNCan.gc.ca
Director, International Division, Kenneth Ko
Tel: 613-996-0441
Fax: 613-995-8737
Kenneth.Ko@NRCan-RNCan.gc.ca

Geological Survey of Canada (GSC) / Commission géologique du Canada
601 Booth St., Ottawa, ON K1A 0E8
Tel: 613-996-3919
Fax: 613-943-8742
esic@nrcan.gc.ca
gsc.nrcan.gc.ca
Other Communication: Bookstore: 613-995-4342
Geoscientific information & research, geoscience surveys, sustainable development of Canada's resources, environmental protection, technology innovation.

Director General, Central & Northern Canada Branch, Daniel Lebel
Tel: 613-992-1400
Fax: 613-996-6575
Daniel.Lebel@NRCan-RNCan.gc.ca
Chief Geologist, Canada Nunavut Geoscience Office, David Mate
Tel: 867-975-4412
Fax: 867-979-0708
David.Mate@NRCan-RNCan.gc.ca
Director, GSC Atlantic, Dr. Jacob Verhoef
Tel: 902-426-3448
Fax: 902-426-1466
Jacob.Verhoef@NRCan-RNCan.gc.ca
Challenger Drive
PO Box 1006
Dartmouth, NS B2Y 4A2 Canada
Acting Director, GSC Calgary, Godfrey Nowlan
Tel: 403-292-7079
Fax: 403-292-4691
Godfrey.Nowlan@NRCan-RNCan.gc.ca
#3303 - 33 St. NW
Calgary, AB T2L 2A7 Canada
Director, GSC Central Canada, Dr. Geneviève Béchard
Tel: 613-943-4119
Fax: 613-992-5694
Genevieve.Bechard@NRCan-RNCan.gc.ca
Director, GSC Northern Canada, Dr. David J. Scott
Tél: 613-992-3218
DavidJ.Scott@NRCan-RNCan.gc.ca
Director, GSC Pacific, Dr. Carmel Lowe
Tel: 250-363-6763
Fax: 250-363-6739
Carmel.Lowe@NRCan-RNCan.gc.ca
Director, GSC Québec, Donna Kirkwood
Tel: 418-654-2675
Fax: 418-654-2615
Donna.Kirkwood@RNCan-NRCan.gc.ca
490, rue de la Couronne
Québec, QC G1K 9A9 Canada
Program Officer, Atlantic & Western Branch, Dan Richardson
Tel: 613-996-9151
Fax: 613-996-6575
dan.richardson@NRCan-RNCan.gc.ca

Mapping Information Branch / Direction de l'information cartographique
Director General, Prashant Shukle
Tel: 613-947-0467
Fax: 613-994-6749
Prashant.Shukle@NRCan-RNCan.gc.ca
Director, Data Management Division, Michael Greskow
Tel: 613-943-3452
Fax: 613-947-2410
Michael.Greskow@NRCan-RNCan.gc.ca
Director, GeoConnections Division, David Harper
Tel: 613-943-5867
Fax: 613-947-2410
David.Harper@NRCan-RNCan.gc.ca
Director, Centre for Topographic Information - Sherbrooke, Eric Loubier
Tel: 819-564-5600 ext: 319
Fax: 819-564-5698
Eric.Loubier@RNCan-NRCan.gc.ca
Director, Data Dissemination Division, Ann Martin
Tel: 613-947-5849
Fax: 613-944-6749
Ann.Martin@NRCan-RNCan.gc.ca
Director, Centre for Topographic Information - Ottawa, Douglas O'Brien
Tel: 613-947-1287
Fax: 613-947-7948
Douglas.O'Brien@NRCan-RNCan.gc.ca
Technologist, Geo-Spatial/Data Services, Centre for Topographic Information - Ottawa, Alison Galloway
Tel: 613-992-4111
Alison.Galloway@NRCan-RNCan.gc.ca

Energy Sector / Secteur de la politique énergétique
Tel: 613-996-7432
Fax: 613-992-1405
www.nrcan-rncan.gc.ca/eneene/polpol/index-eng.php
Develops & promotes economic, regulatory & voluntary approaches to encourage sustainable development of energy resources to meet domestic needs & export markets. Advises the government on federal energy policies, strategies, emergency plans & activities; promotes efficient energy use.
Assistant Deputy Minister, Mark Corey
Tel: 613-947-2751
Mark.Corey@NRCan-RNCan.gc.ca

Innovation & Energy Technology Sector / Secteur de l'innovation et de la technologie énergétique
Assistant Deputy Minister & Chief Scientist, Geoff Munro
Tel: 613-947-1435
Fax: 613-944-4747
Geoff.Munro@NRCan-RNCan.gc.ca

CANMET Energy Technology Centre-Devon
1 Oil Patch Dr., #A202, PO Box 1280Devon, AB T9G 1A8
Tel: 780-987-8614
Fax: 780-987-8690
hamza@nrcan.gc.ca
canmetenergie.rncan.gc.ca
The federal government's primary research group for the development of hydrocarbon supply technologies & related environmental technologies, with an emphasis on oil sands & heavy oil. CWRC comprises of two S&T groups: Advanced Separation Technologies (AST) & the National Centre for Upgrading Technology (NCUT). CWRC conducts fee-for-service, cost-shared & task-shared S&T activities, & performs exploratory, public-good research in strategic areas such as environmental technologies. By developing hydrocarbon technologies that use less energy & have fewer environmental impacts, CWRC is helping to ensure that the oil industry is a sustainable, environmentally responsible contributor to Canada's energy supply.
Acting Director General, Dr. Hassan Hamza
Tel: 780-987-8614
Hassan.Hamza@nrcan-rncan.gc.ca

CANMET Energy Technology Centre-Ottawa (CETC)
1 Haanel Dr., Nepean, ON K1A 1M1
Tel: 613-996-8201
Fax: 613-995-9584
www.nrcan.gc.ca/es/etb/cetc/cetchome.htm
One of Canada's premier organizations in the field of energy science & technology. Fosters the research, development & deployment of innovative, environmentally responsible solutions for conventional, alternative & renewable energy technologies. Research carried out in renewable energy, energy-efficient technologies for industry, communities & buildings, alternative transportation fuels, district heating & cooling & integrated energy systems, advanced low-emission combustion technologies, processing & environmental catalysis for fuels production & hydrocarbon conversion, & energy-efficient metallurgical fuel products & technologies. Offers an Interlaboratory Sample Exchange Program (CANSPECS) for the characterization of standards, R&D testing services, technology & market assessments, & energy-related workshops.

CANMET Energy Technology Centre-Varennes (CEDRL)
1615, boul Lionel-Boulet, CP 4800Varennes, QC J3X 1S6
Tél: 450-652-4621
Téléc: 450-652-0999
Ligne sans frais: 800-322-8122
TTY: 613-996-4397
canmetenergy.nrcan.gc.ca
R&D & related technology transfer in efficiency technologies in the industrial & buildings sector; vehicle & engine efficiencies; alternative transportation fuels; renewable energy technology.
Director General, Gilles Jean
Tel: 450-652-6639
Fax: 450-652-5177

Minerals & Metals Sector (MMS) / Secteur des minéraux et des métaux
Tel: 613-947-6580
TTY: 613-996-4397
info-mms@nrcan-rncan.gc.ca
www.nrcan-rncan.gc.ca/mms-smm
MMS is the federal government's primary source of scientific & technological knowledge, & policy advice, on Canada's mineral & metal resources & on explosives regulation & technology. In addition to housing three scientific research institutions, MMS has the government lead in promoting sustainable development & responsible use of Canada's mineral & metal resources. The Sector is a leader in the generation & dissemination of knowledge on the Canadian minerals & metals industry, & collaborates with & provides research services to governmental, institutional & industrial clients for the development of new technology with economic, environmental & social benefits to Canadians.
Assistant Deputy Minister, Anil Arora
Tel: 613-992-2490
Fax: 613-996-7425
Anil.Arora@NRCan-RNCan.gc.ca
Director General, Minerals, Metals & Materials Policy Branch, Ginny Flood
Tel: 613-996-5309
Fax: 613-952-7501
Ginny.Flood@NRCan-RNCan.gc.ca
Director General, CANMET Materials Technology Laboratory, Dr. Jennifer Jackman
Tel: 613-995-8248
Fax: 613-992-8735
Jennifer.Jackman@NRCan-RNCan.gc.ca
Director General, Explosives Safety & Security Branch, Patrick O'Neill
Tel: 613-948-5181
Fax: 613-948-5195
Director General, Minerals, Metals & Materials Knowledge Branch, Christiane Villemure
Tel: 613-996-5525
Fax: 613-943-8453
Christiane.Villemure@NRCan-RNCan.gc.ca
Director & Chief Inspector, Explosives Regulatory Division, Christopher Watson
Tel: 613-948-5170
Fax: 613-948-5195
Christopher.Watson@NRCan-RNCan.gc.ca

Climate Change Impacts & Adaptation Division / Division sur les impacts et l'adaptation liés aux changements climatiques
601, rue Booth, Ottawa, ON K1A 0E8
Tel: 613-992-8302
Fax: 613-947-0126
adaptation@nrcan.gc.ca
adaptation.nrcan.gc.ca
Provides funding for research & activities to improve knowledge of Canada's vulnerability to climate change. Acts as facilitator between stakeholders & researchers through support of C-CIARN (Canadian Climate Impacts & Adaptation Research Network).
Executive Director, Niall O'Dea
Tel: 613-947-5723
Fax: 613-947-0126
Niall.O'Dea@NRCan-RNCan.gc.ca

Canada Centre for Remote Sensing - Geomatics Canada (CCRSO) / Centre canadien de télédétection (CCT)
588 Booth St., Ottawa, ON K1A 0Y7
Tel: 613-995-0947
Fax: 613-947-1382
TTY: 613-996-4397
ccrs.nrcan.gc.ca
Remote sensing data for Canada; development of remote sensing technology & applications in conjunction with the private sector, & in support of environmental monitoring; development of the Canadian geospatial data infrastructure for distribution of remote sensing & other geographical databases, in partnership with other departments; development of GIS applications.
Director General, Douglas Bancroft
Tel: 613-947-1358
Fax: 613-947-1382
Douglas.Bancroft@NRCan-RNCan.gc.ca
Director, Business, Policy & Planning, Gordon Deecker
Tel: 613-947-1280
Fax: 613-947-1408
Gordon.Deecker@NRCan-RNCan.gc.ca
Director, Data Acquisition Division, Caroline Cloutier
Tel: 613-995-0802
Fax: 613-947-1408
Caroline.Cloutier@NRCan-RNCan.gc.ca
Director, Earth Observation & GeoSolutions Divison, E. Paola de Rose
Tel: 613-947-1350
Fax: 613-947-1385
E.Paola.deRose@NRCan-RNCan.gc.ca
Director, Geodetic Survey Division, Denis Hains
Tel: 613-995-4282
Fax: 613-995-3215
Denis.Hains@NRCan-RNCan.gc.ca

Mapping Services Branch - Geomatics Canada
615 Booth St., Ottawa, ON K1A 0E9
Tel: 613-995-4945
Fax: 613-995-8737

Surveys Canadian lands & waters; prepares & distributes topographic, geographic, electoral & aeronautical maps & digital products, surveys federal-provincial boundaries; manages a national program for acquiring & using remote sensing data. Mapping Branch is responsible for the Canada Map Office, Geogrpahical Names Board of Canada & National Air Photo Library.
Director General, Jean Cooper
Tel: 613-947-0793

Mapping Information Branch / Direction de l'information cartographique
615 Booth St., Ottawa, ON K1A 0E9
Tel: 613-995-4945
Fax: 613-995-8737
Other Communication: Canada Map Office: 1-800-465-6277 or 613-952-7009; Help Desk: 613-996-5916
Director General, Prashant Shukle
Tel: 613-947-0467
Fax: 613-994-6749
Prashant.Shukle@NRCan-RNCan.gc.ca
Senior Policy Advisor, Wendy Ripmeester
Tel: 613-947-3736
Fax: 613-947-5977
wendy.ripmeester@nrcan-rncan.gc.ca
Director, Centre for Topographic Information - Ottawa, Douglas O'Brien
Tel: 613-947-1287
Fax: 613-947-7948
Douglas.O'Brien@NRCan-RNCan.gc.ca
Project Manager, Centre for Topographic Information - Ottawa, Sylvain Lemay
Tel: 613-992-3743
Fax: 613-995-4438
sylvain.lemay@nrcan-rncan.gc.ca
Director, Centre for Topographic Information - Sherbrooke, Eric Loubier
Tel: 819-564-5600 ext: 319
Fax: 819-564-5698
Eric.Loubier@RNCan-NRCan.gc.ca
Project Manager, Centre for Topographic Information - Sherbrooke, Denis Genest
Tel: 819-564-5600 ext: 230
Fax: 819-564-5698
denis.genest@nrcan-rncan.gc.ca
Director, Data Dissemination Division, Ann Martin
Tel: 613-947-5849
Fax: 613-944-6749
Ann.Martin@NRCan-RNCan.gc.ca
Director, GeoConnections Division, Yvan Désy
Tel: 613-947-0112
Fax: 613-947-2410
Yvan.Desy@NRCan-RNCan.gc.ca
Chair, Geographical Names Board of Canada, Bruce Amos
Fax: 613-943-8282
geonames@nrcan.gc.ca
Other Communications: URL: geonames.nrcan.gc.ca

Polar Continental Shelf Program (PCSP) / Étude du plateau continental polaire (EPCP)
#487, 615 Booth St., Ottawa, ON K1A 0E4
Tel: 613-947-1650
Fax: 613-947-1611
TTY: 613-996-4397
pcsp@nrcan-rncan.gc.ca
polar.nrcan.gc.ca
Other Communication: Resolute NWT Base: 867-252-3872; Fax: 867-252-3605
A logistics network that allows scientists to conduct research in the Arctic each year by providing ground & air transportation support, accommodations & communications. Maintains a comprehensive field logistical network, & promotes & coordinates scientific activities in the Canadian Arctic, including protecting the environment.
Acting Director, Michael Jordan
Tel: 613-947-1601
Fax: 613-947-1611
Michael.Jordan@NRCan-RNCan.gc.ca

Electricity Resources Branch / Direction des ressources en électricité
Legislative, policy & regulatory responsibilities for renewable energies, electricity, oil & gas, frontier lands activities. Provides leadership on policy on nuclear energy, uranium, radioactive waste & related environmental issues.
Director General, Jonathan Will
Tel: 613-947-8236
Fax: 613-947-4205
Jonathan.Will@NRCan-RNCan.gc.ca
Director, Nuclear Energy, Sylvana Guindon
Tel: 613-995-2870
Fax: 613-995-0087
Sylvana.Guindon@NRCan-RNCan.gc.ca
Director, Renewable & Electrical Energy Division, Anoop Kapoor
Tel: 613-996-5762
Fax: 613-947-4205
Anoop.Kapoor@NRCan-RNCan.gc.ca
Director, Uranium & Radioactive Waste, Dave McCauley
Tel: 613-996-4697
Fax: 613-947-4205
Dave.McCauley@NRCan-RNCan.gc.ca

Office of Energy Research & Development (OERD) / Bureau de recherche et développement énergétique (BRDE)
580 Booth St., 14th Fl., Ottawa, ON K1A 0E4
Tel: 613-947-1421
Fax: 613-995-6146
Coordinates the federal indepartmental program of Energy Research & Development (PERD) for research & development in energy efficiency & climate change, transportation, renewable energy, & coordinates & represents Canada in international collaboration energy R&D through international mechanisms such as the International Energy Agency & the MOU with US DOE International Energy Agency.
Director General, Dr. Marc D'Iorio
Tel: 613-947-1222
Fax: 613-995-6146
Marc.D'Iorio@NRCan-RNCan.gc.ca
Director, Energy S&T Programs, Milena Sejnoha
Tel: 613-947-1021
Milena.Sejnoha@NRCan-RNCan.gc.ca
Director, Energy Technolgy Policy, Claude Gauvin
Tel: 613-996-8635
Fax: 613-943-9215
Claude.Gauvin@NRCan-RNCan.gc.ca

Petroleum Resources Branch / Direction des ressources pétrolières
Legislative, policy & regulatory responsibilities for all sources of energy supplies, such as renewable energies, electricity, oil & gas, frontier lands activities.
Director General, Jeff Labonté
Tel: 613-992-8609
Fax: 613-992-8738
Jeff.Labonte@NRCan-RNCan.gc.ca
Director, Energy Infrastructure Protection Division, Dr. Felix Kwamena
Tel: 613-995-3190
Fax: 613-995-8463
Felix.Kwamena@NRCan-RNCan.gc.ca
Director, Frontier Lands Management Division, Drew Leyburne
Tel: 613-992-3794
Fax: 613-943-2274
Drew.Leyburne@NRCan-RNCan.gc.ca
Director, Oil Sands & Energy Security Division, Douglas Heath
Tel: 613-995-1525
Fax: 613-992-0614
Douglas.Heath@NRCan-RNCan.gc.ca
Director, Oil and Gas Policy & Regulatory Division, John Foran
Tel: 613-992-0287
Fax: 613-992-0614
John.Foran@NRCan-RNCan.gc.ca

Energy Policy Branch / Direction de la politique énergétique
Developing, planning and coordinating policy matters relating to the energy sector, including management of petroleum exploration and development, electricity markets and alternative energy, and the design or delivery of specific energy efficiency programs and services.

Office of Energy Efficiency / Office de l'éfficacité énergétique
Policy & programs in support of efficient use of energy, use of alternative energy & transportation fuels.
Director General, Carol Buckley
Tel: 613-944-7501
Fax: 613-996-6698
Carol.Buckley@NRCan-RNCan.gc.ca
Acting Director, Demand Policy & Analysis, Bob Blain
Tel: 613-943-1785
Fax: 613-947-4120
Bob.Blain@NRCan-RNCan.gc.ca
Director, Demand Policy & Analysis, Laura Oleson
Tel: 613-943-1785
Fax: 613-947-4120
Laura.Oleson@NRCan-RNCan.gc.ca
Director, Buildings Division, Philip Jago
Tel: 613-996-4079
Fax: 613-992-3161
Philip.Jago@NRCan-RNCan.gc.ca
Director, Housing Division, Kevin Lee
Tel: 613-947-2858
Fax: 613-943-1590
Kevin.Lee@NRCan-RNCan.gc.ca
Director, Fuels Policy & Programs, Paula Vieira
Tel: 613-996-1032
Paula.Vieira@NRCan-RNCan.gc.ca
Director, Equipment Division, John Cockburn
Tel: 613-996-4359
Fax: 613-947-5286
John.Cockburn@NRCan-RNCan.gc.ca
Director, Industrial Programs, Michael Burke
Tel: 613-996-6872
Fax: 613-992-3161
Michael.Burke@NRCan-RNCan.gc.ca
Director, Transportation Energy Use Division, Daniela DiBartolo
Tel: 613-960-7337
Daniela.DiBartolo@NRCan-RNCan.gc.ca

CANMET Mineral Technology Branch (MTB) / Direction de la technologie minérale
555 Booth St., Ottawa, ON K1A 0G1
Includes the Mining & Mineral Sciences Laboratories, the Materials Technology Laboratory & the Canadian Explosives Research Laboratory. R&D, technological solutions to reduce environmental liabilities.
Director General, Denis Lagacé
Tel: 613-995-7029
Denis.Lagace@nrcan-rncan.gc.ca
Director, CANMET Materials Technology Laboratory, Dr. Jennifer Jackman
Tel: 905-645-0698
Jennifer.Jackman@NRCan-RNCan.gc.ca

Natural Sciences & Engineering Research Council of Canada (NSERC) / Conseil des recherches en sciences naturelles et en génie du Canada (CRSNG)

Constitution Square, Tower II, 350 Albert St., Ottawa, ON K1A 1H5
Tel: 613-995-4273
Fax: 613-943-1624
marie-josee.duval@nserc-crsng.gc.ca
www.nserc.gc.ca
Science & Engineering Research Canada (NSERC) is a federal agency whose role is to make investments in people, discovery & innovation for the benefit of all Canadians. With an annual budget of more than $860 million, it supports more than 20,000 university students & postdoctoral fellows in their advanced studies. NSERC promotes discovery by funding more than 10,000 university professors every year & helps make innovation happen by encouraging more than 500 Canadian companies to participate & invest in university research projects.

President, Dr. Suzanne Fortier
Tel: 613-995-5840
suzanne.fortier@nserc-crsng.gc.ca

Vice-President, Research Grants & Scholarships Directorate, Isabelle Blain
Tel: 613-995-5833
isabelle.blain@nserc-crsng.gc.ca

Vice-President, Research Partnerships Programs Directorate, Janet Walden
Tel: 616-139-9215
Fax: 613-947-6371
janet.walden@nserc-crsng.gc.ca

Director, Communications Division, Jacqueline Couture
Tel: 613-995-5993
Jacqueline.Couture@nserc-crsng.gc.ca

Vice-President, Common Administrative Services Directorate, Jaime Pitfield
Tel: 613-995-3914

Fax: 613-991-0969
Jaime.Pitfield@nserc-crsng.gc.ca

Vice-President, Common Administrative Services, Michel Cavallin

Director, Finance & Awards Administration Division, Dominique Osterrath
Tel: 613-996-8269
dominique.osterrath@nserc-crsng.gc.ca

Commissioner, Serge Dupont
Tel: 613-992-3280
Fax: 613-992-3828

Assistant Commissioner & Comptroller, Christopher Cuddy
Tel: 613-995-4297
Fax: 613-996-5354

Parks Canada / Parcs Canada

25 Eddy St., Gatineau, QC K1A 0M5
Tel: 613-860-1251
Toll-Free: 888-773-8888
TTY: 866-787-6221
information@pc.gc.ca
www.pc.gc.ca
Responsible for the protection, management, operation & maintenance of national parks, historic sites, canals & other significant examples of Canada's natural & cultural heritage, for the benefit, understanding & enjoyment of Canadians. Administers one of the largest park systems in the world. Working towards establishing parks in each of 39 distinct natural regions. In addition to the national parks, national historic sites & national marine conservation areas, Parks Canada coordinates other heritage programs, including federal heritage buildings, heritage railway stations, grave sites of Canadian Prime Ministers, heritage rivers, archaeology programs, international programs.

Minister of Environment; Minister Responsible, Hon. Peter Kent
Tel: 613-992-0253
Fax: 613-992-0887
kentp@parl.gc.ca

Chief Executive Officer, Alan Latourelle
Tel: 819-997-9525
Fax: 819-953-9745

Chief Audit & Evaluation Executive, Office of Internal Audit & Evaluation, Brian Evans
Tel: 819-997-9928
Fax: 819-997-5285
Other Communications: Alt. Phone: 613-889-1675

Ombudsman, Luc Martin
Tel: 819-934-7000
Fax: 819-210-3645

Director General, National Parks, Ron Hallman
Tel: 819-994-2657
Fax: 819-994-5140

Director General, National Historic Sites, Larry S. Ostola
Tel: 819-994-1808
Fax: 819-934-1526

Communications Advisor, Joanne Huppé
Tel: 819-953-8699
Fax: 819-953-5523
Other Communications: Alt. Phone: 613-799-6269

Associated Agencies, Boards & Commissions:
• Historic Sites & Monuments Board of Canada / Commission des lieux et monuments historiques du Canada
Terrasses de la Chaudière
25 Eddy St.
Gatineau, QC K1A 0M5
Fax: 819-934-1115
Toll-free: 855-283-8730
hsmbc-clmhc@pc.gc.ca
www.pc.gc.ca/clmhc-hsmbc/
A seventeen-member advisory board which reports to the Minister of Environment & recommends whether persons, places or events are of national historic &/or architectural significance, & therefore warrant commemoration. The board also makes recommendations concerning the designation of heritage railway stations.

National Parks Directorate / Direction générale des parcs nationaux
Executive Director, Ecological Integrity, Mike P. Wong
Tel: 819-994-2639
Fax: 819-997-3380
Director, Parks Establishment, Kevin McNamee
Tel: 819-997-4908
Carillon
230, rue du Barrage, Saint-André-d'Argenteuil, QC J0V 1X0
Tel: 450-537-3534
Fax: 450-658-2428
parkscanada-que@pc.gc.ca
www.pc.gc.ca/canalcarillon
Chambly
1899, boul Périgny, Chambly, QC J3L 4C3
Tel: 450-658-6525
Fax: 450-658-2428
parkscanada-que@pc.gc.ca
www.pc.gc.ca/canalchambly
Other Communication: Lock #9 (Saint-Jean), Phone: 450-348-3392
Lachine
200, boul René-Lévesque ouest, tour Ouest, 6e étage, Montréal, QC H2Z 1X4
Tel: 514-283-6054
Fax: 514-496-1263
parcscanada-que@pc.gc.ca
www.pc.gc.ca/canallachine
Rideau
34 Beckwith St. South, Smiths Falls, ON K7A 2A8
Tel: 613-283-5170
Fax: 613-283-0677
RideauCanal-info@pc.gc.ca
www.pc.gc.ca/eng/lhn-nhs/on/rideau/index.aspx
Sainte-Anne-de-Bellevue
170, rue Sainte-Anne, Sainte-Anne, QC H9X 1N1
Tel: 514-457-5546
Fax: 450-658-2428
parkscanada-que@pc.gc.ca
www.pc.gc.ca/canalsteanne
Saint-Ours
2930, ch des Patriotes, Saint-Ours, QC J0G 1P0
Tél: 450-785-2212
Téléc: 450-658-2428
www.pc.gc.ca/canalstours
St. Peters
PO Box 8St Peters, NS B0E 3B0
Tel: 902-733-2280
Fax: 902-733-2362
information@pc.gc.ca
www.pc.gc.ca/stpeterscanal
Sault Ste Marie
1 Canal Dr., Sault Ste Marie, ON P6A 6W4
Tel: 705-941-6262
Fax: 705-941-6206
info-saultcanal@pc.gc.ca
www.pc.gc.ca/eng/lhn-nhs/on/ssmarie/index.aspx
Trent-Severn Waterway
PO Box 567Peterborough, ON K9J 6Z6
Tel: 705-750-4900
Fax: 705-742-9644
Toll-Free: 888-773-7777
TTY: 705-750-4949
Ont.Trentsevern@pc.gc.ca
www.pc.gc.ca/trentsevern

Alexander Graham Bell Historic Site of Canada
PO Box 159Baddeck, NS B0E 1B0
Tel: 902-295-2069
Fax: 902-295-3496
information@pc.gc.ca
www.pc.gc.ca/eng/lhn-nhs/ns/grahambell/index.aspx

Ardgowan National Historic Site of Canada
2 Palmer's Lane, Charlottetown, PE C1A 5V8
Tel: 902-566-7050
Fax: 902-566-7226
www.pc.gc.ca/eng/lhn-nhs/pe/ardgowan/index.aspx

Bank Fishery National Heritage Exhibit
PO Box 9080 Stn. A, Halifax, NS B3K 5M7
Tel: 902-426-5080
Fax: 902-426-4228
information@pc.gc.ca
www.pc.gc.ca/lhn-nhs/ns/bank/index.aspx

Boishébert & Beaubears Shipbuilding National Historic Sites of Canada
186, route 117, Kouchibouguac National Park, NB E4X 2P1
Tel: 506-876-2443
Fax: 506-876-4802
TTY: 506-876-4205
kouch.info@pc.gc.ca
www.pc.gc.ca/lhn-nhs/nb/boishebert/index.aspx

Canso Islands National Historic Site of Canada
PO Box 159Baddeck, NS B0E 1B0
Tel: 902-295-2069
Fax: 902-295-3496
information@pc.gc.ca
www.pc.gc.ca/lhn-nhs/ns/canso/index.aspx

Cape Breton Highlands National Park of Canada
Ingonish Beach, NS B0C 1L0
Tel: 902-224-2306
Fax: 902-285-2866
information@pc.gc.ca
www.pc.gc.ca/pn-np/ns/cbreton/index.aspx

Cape Spear National Historic Site of Canada
PO Box 1268St. John's, NL A1C 5M9
Tel: 709-772-5367
Fax: 709-772-6302
cape.spear@pc.gc.ca
www.pc.gc.ca/lhn-nhs/nl/spear/index.aspx

Carleton Martello Tower National Historic Site of Canada
454 Whipple St., Saint John, NB E2M 2R3
Tel: 506-636-4011
Fax: 506-636-4574
TTY: 506-887-6015
info.martello@pc.gc.ca
www.pc.gc.ca/lhn-nhs/nb/carleton/index.aspx

Castle Hill National Historic Site of Canada
PO Box 10, Jerseyside, Placentia Bay, NL A0B 2G0
Tel: 709-227-2401
Fax: 709-227-2452
castle.hill@pc.gc.ca
www.pc.gc.ca/lhn-nhs/nl/castlehill/index.aspx
Other Communication: Off-season: 709-772-5367, Fax: 709-772-6302

Fort Amherst/Port-La-Joye National Historic Site of Canada
2 Palmers Lane, Charlottetown, PE C1A 5V8
Tel: 902-566-7626
Fax: 902-566-8295
www.pc.gc.ca/lhn-nhs/pe/amherst/index.aspx
Other Communication: July 1-August 31 Phone: 902-675-2220

Fort Anne National Historic Site of Canada
PO Box 9Annapolis Royal, NS B0S 1A0
Tel: 902-532-2397
Fax: 902-532-2232
information@pc.gc.ca
www.pc.gc.ca/lhn-nhs/ns/fortanne/index.aspx
Other Communication: Off-season: 902-532-2321

Fort Beauséjour National Historic Site of Canada
111 Fort Beauséjour Rd., Aulac, NB E4L 2W5
Tel: 506-364-5080
Fax: 506-536-4399
fort.beausejour@pc.gc.ca
www.pc.gc.ca/lhn-nhs/nb/beausejour/index.aspx

Fort Edward National Historic Site of Canada
PO Box 9Annapolis Royal, NS B0S 1A0
Tel: 902-532-2321
Fax: 902-532-2232
www.pc.gc.ca/lhn-nhs/ns/edward/index.aspx
Other Communication: July & August: 902-798-4706

Fort McNab National Historic Site of Canada
PO Box 9080 Stn. A, Halifax, NS B3K 5M7
Tel: 902-426-5080
Fax: 902-426-4228

halifax.citadel@pc.gc.ca
www.pc.gc.ca/lhn-nhs/ns/mcnab/index.aspx

Fortress of Louisbourg National Historic Site
259 Park Service Rd., Louisbourg, NS B1C 2L2
Tel: 902-733-2280
Fax: 902-733-2362
TTY: 902-733-3607
information@pc.gc.ca
www.pc.gc.ca/lhn-nhs/ns/louisbourg/index.aspx

Fundy National Park of Canada
PO Box 1001Alma, NB E4H 1B4
Tel: 506-887-6000
Fax: 506-887-6008
TTY: 506-887-6015
fundy.info@pc.gc.ca
www.pc.gc.ca/pn-np/nb/fundy/index.aspx

Grand Pré National Historic Site of Canada
PO Box 150Grand Pré, NS B0P 1M0
Tel: 902-542-3631
Fax: 902-542-1691
Toll-Free: 866-542-3631
TTY: 902-532-7472
grandpre.info@pc.gc.ca; contact@grand-pre.com
www.pc.gc.ca/lhn-nhs/ns/grandpre/index.aspx;
www.grand-pre.com

Georges Island National Historic Site of Canada
PO Box 9080 Stn. A, Halifax, NS B3K 5M7
Tel: 902-426-5080
Fax: 902-426-4228
georges.island@pc.gc.ca
www.pc.gc.ca/lhn-nhs/ns/georges/index.aspx

Green Gables Heritage Place
2 Palmer's Lane, Charlottetown, PE C1A 5V6
Tel: 902-963-7874
greengables.info@pc.gc.ca
www.pc.gc.ca/lhn-nhs/pe/greengables/index.aspx

Gros Morne National Park of Canada
PO Box 130Rocky Harbour, NL A0K 4N0
Tel: 709-458-2417
Fax: 709-458-2059
TTY: 709-772-4564
grosmorne.info@pc.gc.ca
www.pc.gc.ca/pn-np/nl/grosmorne/index.aspx

Halifax Citadel National Historic Site of Canada
PO Box 9080 Stn. A, Halifax, NS B3K 5M7
Tel: 902-426-5080
Fax: 902-426-4228
halifax.citadel@pc.gc.ca
www.pc.gc.ca/lhn-nhs/ns/halifax/index.aspx

Hawthorne Cottage National Historic Site of Canada
PO Box 5542St. John's, NL A1C 5W4
Tel: 709-753-9262
Fax: 709-753-0879
info@historicsites.ca
www.pc.gc.ca/lhn-nhs/nl/hawthorne/index.aspx
Other Communication: Off-season: 709-528-4004

Kejimkujik National Park of Canada
PO Box 236Maitland Bridge, NS B0T 1B0
Tel: 902-682-2772
Fax: 902-682-3367
kejimkujik.info@pc.gc.ca
www.pc.gc.ca/pn-np/ns/kejimkujik/index_e.asp

Kouchibouguac National Park of Canada
186, Route 117, Kouchibouguac National Park, NB E4X 2P1
Tel: 506-876-2443
Fax: 506-876-4802
TTY: 506-876-4205
kouch.info@pc.gc.ca
www.pc.gc.ca/pn-np/nb/kouchibouguac/index.aspx

L'Anse aux Meadows National Historic Site of Canada
PO Box 70St-Lunaire-Griquet, NL A0K 2X0
Tel: 709-458-2417
Fax: 709-623-2028
viking.lam@pc.gc.ca
www.pc.gc.ca/lhn-nhs/nl/meadows/index.aspx

Marconi National Historic Site of Canada
PO Box 159Baddeck, NS B0E 1B0
Tel: 902-295-2069
Fax: 902-295-3496
information@pc.gc.ca
www.pc.gc.ca/lhn-nhs/ns/marconi/index.aspx

Monument Lefebvre National Historic Site of Canada
480 rue Centrale, Memramcook, NB E4K 3S6
Tel: 506-758-9808
Fax: 506-758-9813
monument@nbnet.nb.ca
www.pc.gc.ca/lhn-nhs/nb/lefebvre/index.aspx

Port-au-Choix National Historic Site of Canada
PO Box 140Port au Choix, NL A0K 4C0
Tel: 709-458-2417
Fax: 709-861-3827
pac-historic-site@pc.gc.ca
www.pc.gc.ca/lhn-nhs/nl/portauchoix/index.aspx
Other Communication: Seasonal: 709-861-3522

Port Royal National Historic Site of Canada
PO Box 9Annapolis Royal, NS B0S 1A0
Tel: 902-532-2898
Fax: 902-532-2232
information@pc.gc.ca
www.pc.gc.ca/lhn-nhs/ns/portroyal/index.aspx
Other Communication: Off-season: 902-532-2232

Prince Edward Island National Park of Canada
2 Palmers Lane, Charlottetown, PE C1A 5V8
Tel: 902-672-6350
Fax: 902-672-6370
TTY: 902-566-7061
pnipe.peinp@pc.gc.ca
www.pc.gc.ca/pn-np/pe/pei-ipe/index.aspx

Prince of Wales Tower National Historic Site
PO Box 9080 Stn. A, Halifax, NS B3K 5M7
Tel: 902-426-5080
Fax: 902-426-4228
halifax.citadel@pc.gc.ca
www.pc.gc.ca/lhn-nhs/ns/prince/index.aspx

Province House National Historic Site of Canada
2 Palmer's Lane, Charlottetown, PE C1A 5V8
Tel: 902-566-7626
Fax: 902-566-8295
information@pc.gc.ca
www.pc.gc.ca/lhn-nhs/pe/provincehouse/index.aspx

Red Bay National Historic Site of Canada
PO Box 103Red Bay, NL A0K 4K0
Tel: 709-920-2142
Fax: 709-458-2144
redbay.info@pc.gc.ca
www.pc.gc.ca/lhn-nhs/nl/redbay/index.aspx
Other Communication: Summer: 709-920-2051; Alt. Phone: 709-458-2417

Ryan Premises National Historic Site
PO Box 1451Bonavista, NL A0C 1B0
Tel: 709-468-1600
Fax: 709-468-1604
ryan.premises@pc.gc.ca
www.pc.gc.ca/lhn-nhs/nl/ryan/index.aspx

St. Andrews Blockhouse National Historic Site of Canada
454 Whipple St., Saint John, NB E2M 2R3
Tel: 506-636-4011
Fax: 506-636-4574
TTY: 506-887-6015
fundy.info@pc.gc.ca
www.pc.gc.ca/lhn-nhs/nb/standrews/index.aspx
Other Communication: Summer: 506-529-4270

St. Peters Canada National Historic Site of Canada
PO Box 8St Peters, NS B0E 3B0
Tel: 902-733-2280
Fax: 902-733-2362
information@pc.gc.ca
www.pc.gc.ca/lhn-nhs/ns/stpeters/index.aspx

Signal Hill National Historic Site of Canada
PO Box 1268St. John's, NL A1C 5M9
Tel: 709-772-5367
Fax: 709-772-6302
signal.hill@pc.gc.ca
www.pc.gc.ca/lhn-nhs/nl/signalhill/index.aspx

Terra Nova National Park of Canada
General Delivery, Glovertown, NL A0G 2L0
Tel: 709-533-2801
Fax: 709-533-2706
info.tnnp@pc.gc.ca
www.pc.gc.ca/pn-np/nl/terranova/index.aspx

York Redoubt National Historic Site of Canada
PO Box 9080 Stn. A, Halifax, NS B3K 5M7
Tel: 902-426-5080
Fax: 902-426-4228
halifax.citadel@pc.gc.ca
www.pc.gc.ca/lhn-nhs/ns/york/index.aspx

Battle of the Windmill National Historic Site of Canada
370 Vankoughnet St., PO Box 479Prescott, ON K0E 1T0
Tel: 613-925-2896
Fax: 613-925-1536
ont.wellington@pc.gc.ca
www.pc.gc.ca/lhn-nhs/on/windmill/index.aspx

Bellevue House National Historic Site of Canada
35 Centre St., Kingston, ON K7L 4E5
Tel: 613-545-8666
Fax: 613-545-8721
TTY: 613-545-8668
bellevue.house@pc.gc.ca
www.pc.gc.ca/lhn-nhs/on/bellevue/index.aspx

Bethune Memorial House National Historic Site of Canada
235 John St. North, Gravenhurst, ON P1P 1G4
Tel: 705-687-4261
Fax: 705-687-4935
ont-bethune@pc.gc.ca
www.pc.gc.ca/lhn-nhs/on/bethune/index.aspx

Bois Blanc Island Lighthouse National Historic Site of Canada
c/o Fort Malden N.H.S., 100 Laird Ave., PO Box 38Amherstburg, ON N9V 2Z2
Tel: 519-736-5416
Fax: 519-736-6603
ont.fort-malden@pc.gc.ca
www.pc.gc.ca/lhn-nhs/on/boisblanc/index.aspx

Bruce Peninsula National Park
PO Box 189Tobermory, ON N0H 2R0
Tel: 519-596-2233
Fax: 519-596-2298
bruce-fathomfive@pc.gc.ca
www.pc.gc.ca/pn-np/on/bruce/index.aspx

Butler's Barracks c/o Fort George National Historic Site
25 Eddy St., Gatineau, QB K1A 0M5
Tel: 905-468-6614
Fax: 905-468-4638
ont-niagara@pc.gc.ca
www.pc.gc.ca/lhn-nhs/on/fortgeorge/index.aspx

Fort George National Historic Site of Canada
25 Eddy St., Gatineau, QB K1A 0M5
Tel: 905-468-6614
Fax: 905-468-4638
ont-niagara@pc.gc.ca
www.pc.gc.ca/lhn-nhs/on/fortgeorge/index.aspx

Fathom Five National Marine Park of Canada
PO Box 189Tobermory, ON N0H 2R0
Tel: 519-596-2233
Fax: 519-596-2298
bruce-fathomfive@pc.gc.ca
www.pc.gc.ca/eng/amnc-nmca/on/fathomfive/index.aspx

Fort Malden National Historic Site
100 Laird Ave., PO Box 38Amherstburg, ON N9V 2Z2
Tel: 519-736-5416
Fax: 519-736-6603
ont.fort-malden@pc.gc.ca
www.pc.gc.ca/eng/lhn-nhs/on/malden/index.aspx

Fort Mississauga National Historic Site of Canada

26 Queen St., PO Box 787Niagara on the Lake, ON L0S 1J0
Tel: 905-468-6614
Fax: 905-468-4638
www.friendsoffortgeorge.ca

Fort St. Joseph National Historic Site of Canada
PO Box 220Richards Landing, ON P0R 1J0
Tel: 705-246-2664
Fax: 705-246-1796
fortstjoseph-info@pc.gc.ca
www.pc.gc.ca/lhn-nhs/on/stjoseph.aspx

Fort Wellington National Historic Site of Canada
PO Box 479Prescott, ON K0E 1T0
Tel: 613-925-2896
Fax: 613-925-1536
TTY: 613-925-2896
ont-wellington@pc.gc.ca
www.pc.gc.ca/lhn-nhs/on/wellington.aspx

Georgian Bay Islands National Park of Canada
901 Wye Valley Rd., PO Box 9Midland, ON L4R 4K6
Tel: 705-526-9804
Fax: 705-526-5939
info.gbi@pc.gc.ca
www.pc.gc.ca/eng/pn-np/on/georg/index.aspx

Inverarden House National Historic Site of Canada
370 Vankoughnet St., PO Box 479Prescott, ON K0E 1T0
Tel: 613-925-2896
Fax: 613-925-1536
ont-wellington@pc.gc.ca
www.pc.gc.ca/lhn-nhs/on/inverarden/index.aspx

Kingston Martello Towers
35 Centre St., Kingston, ON K7L 4E5
Tel: 613-545-8666
Fax: 613-545-8721
TTY: 613-545-8668
www.pc.gc.ca/lhn-nhs/on/bellevue/index.aspx

Laurier House National Historic Site of Canada
335 Laurier Ave. East, Ottawa, ON K1A 6R4
Tel: 613-992-8142
Fax: 613-947-4851
laurier-house@pc.gc.ca
www.pc.gc.ca/lhn-nhs/on/laurier.aspx

Point Clark Lighthouse National Historic Site of Canada
c/o Woodside National Historic Site, 528 Wellington St. North, Kitchener, ON N2H 5L5
Tel: 519-571-5684
Fax: 519-571-5286
ont-woodside@pc.gc.ca
www.pc.gc.ca/lhn-nhs/on/clark.aspx

Point Pelee National Park of Canada
407 Monarch Lane, RR#1, Leamington, ON N8H 3V4
Tel: 519-322-2365
Fax: 519-322-1277
pelee.info@pc.gc.ca
www.pc.gc.ca/fra/pn-np/on/pelee.aspx

Pukaskwa National Park of Canada
PO Box 212Heron Bay, ON P0T 1R0
Tel: 807-229-0801
Fax: 807-229-2097
ont-pukaskwa@pc.gc.ca
www.pc.gc.ca/pn-np/on/pukaskwa.aspx

Queenston Heights & Brock's Monument
26 Queen St., PO Box 787Niagara on the Lake, ON L0S 1J0
Tel: 905-468-4257
Fax: 905-468-4638
ont-niagara@pc.gc.ca
www.pc.gc.ca/lhn-nhs/on/queenston/index.aspx

St. Lawrence Islands National Park of Canada
2 County Rd. 5, RR#3, Mallorytown Landing, ON K0E 1R0
Tel: 613-923-5261
Fax: 613-923-1021
ont-sli@pc.gc.ca
www.pc.gc.ca/pn-np/on/lawren/index.aspx

Sir John Johnson National Historic Site of Canada
c/o Fort Wellington National Historic Site, 370 Vanhoughnet St., PO Box 479Prescott, ON K0E 1T0
Tel: 613-925-2896
Fax: 613-925-1536
ont.wellington@pc.gc.ca; sirjohnjohnson@sympatico.ca
www.pc.gc.ca/lhn-nhs/on/johnjohnson/index.aspx

Woodside National Historic Site of Canada
528 Wellington St. North, Kitchener, ON N2H 5L5
Tel: 519-571-5684
Fax: 519-571-5686
ont-woodside@pc.gc.ca
www.pc.gc.ca/lhn-nhs/on/woodside/index.aspx
Rob Watt

Artillery Park National Historic Site of Canada
2, rue d'Auteuil, CP 10 Succ B, Québec, QC G1K 7A1
Tél: 418-648-7016
Téléc: 418-648-2506
parkscanada-que@pc.gc.ca
www.pc.gc.ca/lhn-nhs/qc/artiller.aspx

Battle of the Châteauguay National Historic Site of Canada
2371, ch de la Rivière Châteauguay nord, CP 250Howick, QC J0S 1G0
Tél: 450-829-2003
Téléc: 450-829-3325
parkscanada-que@pc.gc.ca
www.pc.gc.ca/lhn-nhs/qc/chateauguay/index.aspx

Battle of the Restigouche National Historic Site of Canada
Route 132, CP 359Pointe-à-la-Croix, QC G0C 1L0
Tél: 418-788-5676
Téléc: 418-788-5895
parkscanada-que@pc.gc.ca
www.pc.gc.ca/lhn-nhs/qc/ristigouche.aspx

Carillon Barracks National Historic Site of Canada
1899, boul. Périgny, Chambly, QC J3L 4C3
Tel: 450-658-0681
Fax: 450-658-2428
parkscanada-que@pc.gc.ca
www.pc.gc.ca/lhn-nhs/qc/carillon/index.aspx

Cartier-Brébeuf National Historic Site of Canada
175, rue de l'Espinay, CP 10 Succ B, Québec, QC G1K 7A1
Tél: 418-648-4038
Téléc: 418-948-9181
parkscanada-que@pc.gc.ca
www.pc.gc.ca/lhn-nhs/qc/cartierbrebeuf.aspx

Coteau-du-Lac National Historic Site of Canada
308 A, ch du Fleuve, Coteau-du-Lac, QC J0P 1B0
Tél: 450-763-5631
Téléc: 450-763-1654
parkscanada-que@pc.gc.ca
www.pc.gc.ca/lhn-nhs/qc/coteaudulac.aspx

Forges du Saint-Maurice National Historic Site of Canada
10000, boul des Forges, Trois-Rivières, QC G9C 1B1
Tel: 819-378-5116
Fax: 819-378-0887
parkscanada-que@pc.gc.ca
www.pc.gc.ca/lhn-nhs/qc/saintmaurice.aspx

Forillon National Park of Canada
122, boul Gaspé, Gaspé, QC G4X 1A9
Tél: 418-368-5505
Téléc: 418-368-6837
parkscanada-que@pc.gc.ca
www.pc.gc.ca/pn-np/qc/forillon.aspx

Fort Chambly National Historic Site of Canada
2, rue de Richelieu, Chambly, QC J3L 2B9
Tel: 450-658-1585
Fax: 450-658-7216
parkscanada-que@pc.gc.ca
www.pc.gc.ca/lhn-nhs/qc/fortchambly/index.aspx

Fort Lennox National Historic Site of Canada
1 - 61e av, St-Paul-de-l'Ile-aux-Noix, QC J0J 1G0
Tél: 450-291-5700
Téléc: 450-291-4389
parkscanada-que@pc.gc.ca
www.pc.gc.ca/lhn-nhs/qc/lennox.aspx

Fort Témiscamingue National Historic Site of Canada
830, ch du Vieux-Fort, Duhamel ouest, QC J9V 1N7
Tél: 819-629-3222
Téléc: 819-629-2977
fort.temiscaminque@pc.gc.ca
www.pc.gc.ca/fra/lhn-nhs/qc/temiscamingue.aspx

Fortifications of Québec National Historic Site of Canada
2, rue d'Auteuil, PO Box 10 Stn. B, Québec, QC G1K 7A1
Tel: 418-648-7016
Fax: 418-648-2506
www.pc.gc.ca/lhn-nhs/qc/fortifications/index.aspx

Grosse Ile & the Irish Memorial National Historic Site of Canada
2 rue D'Auteuil, CP 10 Succ B, Québec, QC G1K 7A1
Tél: 418-234-8841
Téléc: 866-790-8991
parkscanada-que@pc.gc.ca
www.pc.gc.ca/lhn-nhs/qc/grosseile/index.aspx

La Mauricie National Park of Canada
702, 5e rue, CP 160 Succ Bureau-Chef, Shawinigan, QC G9N 6T9
Tél: 819-538-3232
Téléc: 819-536-3661
parkscanada-que@pc.gc.ca
www.pc.gc.ca/fra/pn-np/qc/mauricie.aspx

Lévis Forts National Historic Site of Canada
41, ch du Gouvernement, CP 10 Succ B, Québec, QC G1K 7A1
Tél: 418-835-5182
Téléc: 418-948-9119
parkscanada-que@pc.gc.ca
www.pc.gc.ca/lhn-nhs/qc/levis/index.aspx

Louis S. St-Laurent National Historic Site of Canada
6790, rte Louis-St-Laurent, Compton, QC J0B 1L0
Tel: 819-835-5448
Fax: 819-835-9101
parkscanada-que@pc.gc.ca
www.pc.gc.ca/fra/lhn-nhs/qc/stlaurent.aspx

Manoir Papineau National Historic Site of Canada
500, rue Notre-Dame, Montebello, QC J0V 1L0
Tél: 819-423-6965
Téléc: 819-423-6455
parkscanada-que@pc.gc.ca
www.pc.gc.ca/fra/lhn-nhs/qc/manoirpapineau/index.aspx

Mingan Archipelago National Park Reserve of Canada
1340, rue de la Digue, CP 1180Havre-Saint-Pierre, QC G0G 1P0
Tél: 418-538-3331
Téléc: 418-538-3595
parkscanada-que@pc.gc.ca
www.pc.gc.ca/pn-np/qc/mingan.aspx
Autres nombres: Information and/or Reservation: 418-538-3285; 418-949-2126

Pointe-au-Père Lighthouse National Historic Site of Canada
1034, rue du Phare, Pointe-au-Père, QC G5M 1L8
Tel: 418-724-6214
Fax: 418-721-0815
parkscanada-que@pc.gc.ca
www.pc.gc.ca/lhn-nhs/qc/pointaupere/index.aspx

Saguenay St. Lawrence Marine Park of Canada
182, rte de l'Église, CP 220Tadoussac, QC G0T 2A0
Tél: 418-235-4703
Téléc: 418-235-4686
parkscanada-que@pc.gc.ca
www.pc.gc.ca/amnc-nmca/qc/saguenay/default.aspx

Sir George-Étienne Cartier National Historic Site of Canada
458, rue Notre-Dame est, Montréal, QC H2Y 1C8
Tel: 514-283-2282
Fax: 514-283-5560
cartier.maison@pc.gc.ca
www.pc.gc.ca/lhn-nhs/qc/etiennecartier.aspx

Sir Wilfrid Laurier National Historic Site of Canada
#945, 12e av, St-Lin-Laurentides, QC J5M 2W4
Tél: 450-439-3702
Téléc: 450-439-5721
parkscanada-que@pc.gc.ca
www.pc.gc.ca/fra/lhn-nhs/qc/wilfridlaurier.aspx

The Fur Trade at Lachine National Historic Site of Canada
1255, boul Saint-Joseph, Lachine, QC H8S 2M2
Tel: 514-637-7433
Fax: 514-637-5325
parkscanada-que@pc.gc.ca
www.pc.gc.ca/lhn-nhs/qc/lachine/index.aspx
Other Communication: Winter, Phone: 514-283-6054; Fax: 514-496-1263

Aulavik National Park of Canada
PO Box 29Sachs Harbour, NT X0E 0Z0
Tel: 867-690-3904
Fax: 867-690-4808
inuvik.info@pc.gc.ca
pc.gc.ca/pn-np/nt/aulavik/index_e.asp

Auyuittuq National Park of Canada
PO Box 353Pangnirtung, NU X0A 0R0
Tel: 867-473-2500
Fax: 867-473-8612
nunavut.info@pc.gc.ca
www.pc.gc.ca/pn-np/nu/auyuittuq/index_e.asp

Banff National Park of Canada
PO Box 900Banff, AB T1L 1K2
Tel: 403-762-1550
Fax: 403-762-1551
banff.vrc@pc.gc.ca
www.pc.gc.ca/pn-np/ab/banff/index_e.asp

Banff Park Museum National Historic Site of Canada
PO Box 900Banff, AB T1L 1K2
Tel: 403-762-1558
Fax: 403-762-1565
banff.vrc@pch.gc.ca
www.pc.gc.ca/lhn-nhs/ab/banff/index_E.asp

Bar U Ranch National Historic Site of Canada
PO Box 168Longview, AB T0L 1H0
Tel: 403-395-2212
Fax: 403-395-2331
BarU.Info@pc.gc.ca
www.pc.gc.ca/lhn-nhs/ab/baru/index_e.asp
Ian Church

Batoche National Historic Site of Canada
RR#1 Box 1040, Wakaw, SK S0K 4P0
Tel: 306-423-6227
Fax: 306-423-5400
TTY: 306-423-5540
batoche@pc.gc.ca
www.pc.gc.ca/eng/lhn-nhs/sk/batoche/index.aspx

Cave & Basin National Historic Site of Canada
PO Box 900Banff, AB T1L 1K2
Tel: 403-762-1566
Fax: 403-762-1565
banff.vrc@pc.gc.ca
www.pc.gc.ca/lhn-nhs/ab/caveandbasin/index_e.asp

Chilkoot Trail National Historic Site of Canada
#205, 300 Main St., Whitehorse, YT Y1A 2B5
Tel: 867-667-3910
Fax: 867-393-6701
Toll-Free: 800-661-0486
whitehorse.info@pc.gc.ca
www.pc.gc.ca/lhn-nhs/yt/chilkoot/index_e.asp

Dawson Historical Complex National Historic Site of Canada
PO Box 390Dawson City, YT Y0B 1G0
Tel: 867-993-7200
Fax: 867-993-7203
dawson.info@pc.gc.ca
www.pc.gc.ca/lhn-nhs/yt/dawson/index_E.asp

Dredge No. 4 National Historic Site of Canada
PO Box 390Dawson City, YT Y0B 1G0
Tel: 867-993-7200
Fax: 867-993-7203
dawson.info@pc.gc.ca
www.pc.gc.ca/lhn-nhs/yt/klondike.aspx

Elk Island National Park of Canada
RR#1, Site 4, Fort Saskatchewan, AB T8L 2N7
Tel: 780-992-5790
Fax: 780-992-2951
elk.island@pc.gc.ca
www.pc.gc.ca/pn-np/ab/elkisland/index_e.asp
Other Communication: Administration: 780-992-2950

Fisgard Lighthouse National Historic Site of Canada
603 Fort Rodd Hill Rd., Victoria, BC V9C 2W8
Tel: 250-478-5849
Fax: 250-478-2816
fort.rodd@pc.gc.ca
www.pc.gc.ca/lhn-nhs/bc/fisgard/index_e.asp

Fort Battleford National Historic Site of Canada
PO Box 70Battleford, SK S0M 0E0
Tel: 306-937-2621
Fax: 306-937-3370
TTY: 306-937-3199
battleford-info@pc.gc.ca
www.pc.gc.ca/lhn-nhs/sk/battleford/index_e.asp

Fort Langley National Historic Site of Canada
23433 Mavis Ave., PO Box 129Fort Langley, BC V1M 2R5
Tel: 604-513-4777
Fax: 604-513-4798
fort.langley@pc.gc.ca
www.pc.gc.ca/lhn-nhs/bc/langley/index_e.asp

Fort Rodd Hill National Historic Site of Canada
603 Fort Rodd Hill Rd., Victoria, BC V9C 2W8
Tel: 250-478-5849
Fax: 250-478-2816
fort.rodd@pc.gc.ca
www.pc.gc.ca/lhn-nhs/bc/fortroddhill/index_e.asp

Fort St. James National Historic Site of Canada
PO Box 1148Fort St James, BC V0J 1P0
Tel: 250-996-7191
Fax: 250-996-8566
stjames@pc.gc.ca
www.pc.gc.ca/lhn-nhs/bc/stjames/index_e.asp

Fort Walsh National Historic Site of Canada
PO Box 278Maple Creek, SK S0N 1N0
Tel: 306-662-3590
Fax: 306-662-2711
TTY: 306-662-3124
fort.walsh@pc.gc.ca
www.pc.gc.ca/lhn-nhs/sk/walsh/index_e.asp
Other Communication: Administration: 306-662-2645

Gitwangak Battle Hill National Historic Site of Canada
PO Box 37Queen Charlotte, BC V0T 1S0
Tel: 250-559-8818
Fax: 250-559-8366
TTY: 250-559-8139
gwaii.haanas@pc.gc.ca
www.pc.gc.ca/lhn-nhs/bc/kitwanga/index_E.asp

Glacier National Park of Canada
PO Box 350Revelstoke, BC V0E 2S0
Tel: 250-837-7500
Fax: 250-837-7536
revglacier.reception@pc.gc.ca
www.pc.gc.ca/pn-np/bc/glacier/index_e.asp

Grasslands National Park of Canada
PO Box 150Val Marie, SK S0N 2T0
Fax: 306-298-2042
Toll-Free: 877-345-2257
grasslands.info@pc.gc.ca
www.pc.gc.ca/pn-np/sk/grasslands/index_e.asp

Gulf Islands National Park Reserve of Canada
2220 Harbour Rd., Sidney, BC V8L 2P6
Tel: 250-654-4000
Fax: 250-654-4014
Toll-Free: 866-944-1744
gulf.islands@pc.gc.ca
www.pc.gc.ca/pn-np/bc/gulf/index_E.asp

Gulf of Georgia Cannery National Historic Site of Canada
12138 Fourth Ave., Richmond, BC V7E 3J1
Tel: 604-664-9009
Fax: 604-664-9008
gog.info@pc.gc.ca
www.pc.gc.ca/lhn-nhs/bc/georgia/index_e.asp

Gwaii Haanas National Park Reserve & Haida Heritage Site of Canada
60 Second Beach Rd., PO Box 37Queen Charlotte, BC V0T 1S0
Tel: 250-559-8818
Fax: 250-559-8366
Toll-Free: 877-559-8818
gwaii.haanas@pc.gc.ca
www.pc.gc.ca/pn-np/bc/gwaiihaanas/index_e.asp

Ivvavik National Park of Canada
PO Box 1840Inuvik, NT X0E 0T0
Tel: 867-777-8800
Fax: 867-777-8820
inuvik.info@pc.gc.ca
www.pc.gc.ca/pn-np/yt/ivvavik/index_e.asp

Jasper National Park of Canada
PO Box 10Jasper, AB T0E 1E0
Tel: 780-852-6176
Fax: 780-852-6152
pnj.jnp@pc.gc.ca
www.pc.gc.ca/pn-np/ab/jasper/index_e.asp

Kluane National Park & Reserve of Canada
PO Box 5495Haines Junction, YT Y0B 1L0
Tel: 867-634-7250
Fax: 867-634-7208
kluane.info@pc.gc.ca
www.pc.gc.ca/pn-np/yt/kluane/index_e.asp

Kootenay National Park of Canada
PO Box 220Radium Hot Springs, BC V0A 1M0
Tel: 250-347-9505
Fax: 250-347-9980
kootenay.info@pc.gc.ca
www.pc.gc.ca/pn-np/bc/kootenay/index_e.asp

Lower Fort Garry National Historic Site of Canada
5925 Highway 9, St. Andrews, MB R1A 4A8
Tel: 204-785-6050
Fax: 204-482-5887
lfg.info@pc.gc.ca
www.pc.gc.ca/lhn-nhs/mb/fortgarry/index_e.asp

Motherwell Homestead National Historic Site of Canada
PO Box 70Abernethy, SK S0A 0A0
Tel: 306-333-2116
Fax: 306-333-2210
Motherwell.Homestead@pc.gc.ca
www.pc.gc.ca/lhn-nhs/sk/motherwell/index_e.asp

Mount Revelstoke National Park of Canada
PO Box 350Revelstoke, BC V0E 2S0
Tel: 250-837-7500
Fax: 250-837-7536
TTY: 866-787-6221
revglacier.reception@pc.gc.ca
www.pc.gc.ca/pn-np/bc/revelstoke/index_e.asp

Nahanni National Park Reserve of Canada
10002 - 100 St., PO Box 348Fort Simpson, NT X0E 0N0
Tel: 867-695-7750
Fax: 867-695-2446
nahanni.info@pc.gc.ca
www.pc.gc.ca/pn-np/nt/nahanni/index_e.asp

Pacific Rim National Park Reserve of Canada
2185 Ocean Terrace Rd., PO Box 280Ucluelet, BC V0R 3A0
Tel: 250-726-3500
Fax: 250-726-3520
pacrim.info@pc.gc.ca
www.pc.gc.ca/pn-np/bc/pacificrim/index_e.asp

Prince Albert National Park of Canada
PO Box 100Waskesiu Lake, SK S0J 2Y0
Tel: 306-663-4522
panp.info@pc.gc.ca
www.pc.gc.ca/pn-np/sk/princealbert/index_e.asp

Prince of Wales Fort National Historic Site of Canada
PO Box 127Churchill, MB R0B 0E0
Tel: 204-675-8863
Fax: 204-675-2026
mannorth.nhs@pc.gc.ca
www.pc.gc.ca/lhn-nhs/mb/prince/index_e.asp

Quttinirpaaq National Park of Canada
PO Box 278Iqaluit, NU X0A 0H0
Tel: 867-975-4673
Fax: 867-975-4674
nunavut.info@pc.gc.ca
www.pc.gc.ca/pn-np/nu/quttinirpaaq/index_e.asp

Riding Mountain National Park of Canada
Wasagaming, MB R0J 2H0
Tel: 204-848-7275
Fax: 204-848-2596
rmnp.info@pc.gc.ca
www.pc.gc.ca/pn-np/mb/riding/index_e.asp

Riel House National Historic Site of Canada
330 River Rd. (St. Vidal), PO Box 73Winnipeg, MB R2N 3X9
Tel: 204-257-1783
Fax: 204-983-2221
TTY: 866-787-6221
riel.info@pc.gc.ca
www.pc.gc.ca/lhn-nhs/mb/riel/index_E.asp
Other Communication: Winter: 204-983-6757

Rocky Mountain House National Historic Site of Canada
Site 127, Comp 6, RR#4, Rocky Mountain House, AB T4T 2A4
Tel: 403-845-2412
Fax: 403-845-5320
rocky.info@pc.gc.ca
www.pc.gc.ca/lhn-nhs/ab/rockymountain/index_E.asp

Sirmilik National Park of Canada
PO Box 300Pond Inlet, NU X0A 0S0
Tel: 867-899-8092
Fax: 867-899-8104
sirmilik.info@pc.gc.ca
www.pc.gc.ca/pn-np/nu/sirmilik/index_E.asp

SS Keno National Historic Site of Canada
PO Box 390Dawson City, YT Y0B 1G0
Tel: 867-993-7200
Fax: 867-993-7203
dawson.info@pc.gc.ca
www.pc.gc.ca/lhn-nhs/yt/sskeno/index_e.asp

SS Klondike National Historic Site of Canada
#205, 300 Main St., Whitehorse, YT Y1A 2B5
Fax: 867-393-6701
Toll-Free: 800-661-0486
whitehorse.info@pc.gc.ca
www.pc.gc.ca/lhn-nhs/yt/ssklondike/index_E.asp
Other Communication: Summer: 867-667-4511

St. Andrews Rectory National Historic Site of Canada
374, chemin River, St. Andrews, MB R1A 2Y1
Tel: 204-785-6050
Fax: 204-482-5887
lfg.info@pc.gc.ca
www.pc.gc.ca/lhn-nhs/mb/standrews/contact_e.asp

The Forks National Historic Site of Canada
401-25 Forks Market Rd., Winnipeg, MB R3C 4S8
Tel: 204-983-6757
Fax: 204-983-2221
forks.fourche@pc.gc.ca
www.pc.gc.ca/lhn-nhs/mb/forks/index_e.asp

Tuktut Nogait National Park of Canada
PO Box 91Paulatuk, NT X0E 1N0
Tel: 867-580-3233
Fax: 867-580-3234
inuvik.info@pc.gc.ca
www.pc.gc.ca/pn-np/nt/tuktutnogait/index_e.asp

Ukkusiksalik National Park of Canada
PO Box 220Repulse Bay, NU X0C 0H0
Tel: 867-462-4500
Fax: 867-462-4095
ukkusiksalik.info@pc.gc.ca
www.pc.gc.ca/pn-np/nu/ukkusiksalik/index_E.asp

Vuntut National Park of Canada
PO Box 19Old Crow, YT Y0B 1N0
Tel: 867-667-3910
Fax: 867-393-6701
vuntut.info@pc.gc.ca
www.pc.gc.ca/pn-np/yt/vuntut/index_E.asp

Wapusk National Park of Canada
Churchill Office, PO Box 127Churchill, MB R0B 0E0
Tel: 204-675-8863
Fax: 204-675-2026
wapusk.np@pc.gc.ca
www.pc.gc.ca/pn-np/mb/wapusk/index_e.asp

Waterton Lakes National Park of Canada
PO Box 200Waterton Park, AB T0K 2M0
Tel: 403-859-5133
Fax: 403-859-5152
waterton.info@pc.gc.ca
www.pc.gc.ca/pn-np/ab/waterton/index_E.asp

Wood Buffalo National Park of Canada
PO Box 750Fort Smith, NT X0E 0P0
Tel: 867-872-7900
Fax: 867-872-3910
TTY: 867-872-7961
wbnp.info@pc.gc.ca
www.pc.gc.ca/pn-np/nt/woodbuffalo/index_e.asp
Other Communication: 24 Hour Hotline: 867-872-7962

Yoho National Park of Canada
PO Box 99Field, BC V0A 1G0
Tel: 250-343-6783
Fax: 250-343-6012
yoho.info@pc.gc.ca
www.pc.gc.ca/pn-np/bc/yoho/index_E.asp

York Factory National Historic Site of Canada
PO Box 127Churchill, MB R0B 0E0
Tel: 204-675-8863
Fax: 204-675-2026
Toll-Free: 888-773-8888
TTY: 866-787-6221
mannorth.nhs@pc.gc.ca
www.pc.gc.ca/lhn-nhs/mb/yorkfactory/index_E.asp

Minister, Public Safety, Hon. Vic Toews
Tel: 613-992-3128
Fax: 613-995-1049
Toews.V@parl.gc.ca
Other Communications: Public Safety & Emergency Preparedness: 613-991-2924

Deputy Minister, François Guimont
Tel: 613-991-2895
Fax: 613-990-8312

Parliamentary Secretary to the Minister of Public Safety, Dave MacKenzie
Tel: 613-991-2924

Chief of Staff, Minister's Office, Andrew House
Tel: 613-991-2924

Assistant Inspector General, Canadian Security Intelligence Service (CSIS), Ian Blackie
Tel: 613-993-7431

Deputy Executive Director & Senior Counsel, Legal Services, Caroline Fobes
Tel: 613-949-9724

Senior Counsel & Strategic Policy Advisor, Mary-Anne Kirvan
Tel: 613-954-1067

Director, Internal Audit Directorate, Yolande Andrews
Tel: 613-990-3529

Director, Regional Affairs, Minister's Regional Office, Olivia Baldwin-Valainis
Tel: 204-983-7096

Director, Policy, Minister's Office, Jessica Oliver
Tel: 613-949-6473

Director, Communications, Minister's Office, Julie Carmichael
Tel: 613-991-2924

Director, Parliamentary Affairs, Minister's Office, Christena Stewart
Tel: 613-991-2863

Emergency Management & National Security Branch / Secteur de la gestion des urgences et de la sécurité nationale
340 Laurier Ave. West, Ottawa, ON K1A 0P8
The Emergency Management & National Security Branch consists of the following directorates & secretariat: Coordination Directorate; Emergency Management Policy Directorate; National Security Policy Directorate; Operations Directorate; Preparedness & Recovery Directorate; & the Cyber Security Strategy Secretariat.
Assistant Deputy Minister, Lynda Clairmont
Tel: 613-990-4976
Assistant Deputy Minister, Gina Wilson
Tel: 613-990-2743
Associate Assistant Deputy Minister, Daniel Lavoie
Tel: 613-990-2743
Director General, Science & Technology Policy, Ashley Anthony
Tel: 613-991-3376
Director General, Emergency Management Policy, Serge C. Beaudoin
Tel: 613-991-2944
Director General, National Security Policy, John Davies
Tel: 613-991-1970
Director General, Regional Operations Directorate, Jamie Deacon
Tel: 613-991-1699
Director General, National Cyber Security, Robert Dick
Tel: 613-990-2661
Director General, Preparedness & Recovery, Robert Lesser
Tel: 613-944-4853
Director General, National Security Operations, Michael MacDonald
Tel: 613-993-4595
Director General, Operations, Continuity of Government, Preparedness & Recovery, Richard Moreau
Tel: 613-990-7016
Director General, Critical Infrastructure & Strategic Coordination, Suki Wong
Tel: 613-991-3583
Associate Director General, Operations, Craig Oldham
Tel: 613-991-7728
Senior Director, Public Service Renewal, Kevin Phillips
Tel: 613-947-6492
Executive Director, Canadian Emergency Management College, Gary Donovan
Tel: 613-949-5000
Senior Analyst, National Cyber Security, Tom Campbell
Tel: 613-990-3577

Office of the Public Sector Integrity Commissioner of Canada (PSIC) / Commissariat à l'intégrité du secteur public du Canada (ISPC)

60 Queen St., 7th Fl., Ottawa, ON K1P 5Y7
Tel: 613-941-6400
Fax: 613-941-6535
TTY: 866-941-6400
www.psic-ispc.gc.ca
Other Communication: Secure Fax: 613-946-2151
A independent Agency of Parliament, established in 2007 under the Public Servants Disclosure Protection Act, that provides a means for public servants or members of the public to disclose possible wrongdoing in the federal public sector. The Commissioner reports directly to parliament.

Public Sector Integrity Commissioner of Canada, Mario Dion
Tel: 613-948-9178
Fax: 613-941-6535

Senior Investigator, Investigator, Investigations & Inquiries, Gail Gauvreau
Tel: 613-941-6764
Fax: 613-941-6535

Public Servants Disclosure Protection Tribunal (PSDPT) / Tribunal de la protection des fonctionnaires divulgateurs (TPFD)

#512, 90 Sparks St., Ottawa, ON K1P 5B4
Tel: 613-943-8310
Fax: 613-943-8325
tribunal@psdpt-tpfd.gc.ca
www.psdpt-tpfd.gc.ca

The Tribunal exists to hear reprisal complaints referred by the Public Sector Integrity Commissioner, & has the power to discipline persons who take reprisals while granting remedies to complainants.

Chair, Hon. Luc Marineau

Member, Hon. Marie-Josée Bédard

Member, Hon. Sean Harrington

Registrar & Deputy Head, Stuart Campbell
Tel: 613-943-8313
Fax: 613-943-8325

Public Works & Government Services Canada (PWGSC) / Travaux publics et services gouvernementaux

Place du Portage, Phase III, 11, rue Laurier, Ottawa, ON K1A 0S5
TTY: 800-926-9105
questions@tpsgc-pwgsc.gc.ca
www.tpsgc-pwgsc.gc.ca
twitter.com/PWGSC_TPSGC
Primary department responsible for purchasing goods & services for the Government of Canada. Purchases a variety of goods & services, construction, architectural, engineering & maintenance services & provides leasing services related to federal government works & facilities. Also maintains source lists of potential suppliers for some products. Ensures that the government's operational requirements are met in a cost-effective & timely manner, while taking into account the government's objectives including environmental considerations. As builders & caretakers of buildings, the department protects the environment by reducing solid waste, greening the construction & operation of buildings, conserving energy & water, improving fleet management, minimizing the effects of operations on climate change, & increasing environmental protection & conservation.

Acts Administered:
Anti-Personnel Mines Convention Implementation Act
Bridges Act
Expropriation Act
Federal District Commission to have acquired certain lands, An Act to Confirm the Authority of
Government Property Traffic Act
Ottawa River, Act Respecting Certain Works
Public Works & Government Services Act

Minister, Public Works & Government Services; Minister for Status of Women, Receiver General for Canada, Hon. Rona Ambrose
Tel: 819-997-5421
Fax: 819-956-8382
Rona.Ambrose@tpsgc-pwgsc.gc.ca

Parliamentary Secretary, Jacques Gourde
Tel: 613-992-2639
Fax: 613-992-1018
Gourdj@parl.gc.ca

Deputy Minister & Deputy Receiver General for Canada, Michelle d'Auray
Tel: 819-956-1706
Fax: 819-956-8280

Associate Deputy Minister, Renée Jolicoeur
Tel: 819-956-4472
Fax: 819-956-8280
renee.jolicoeur@tpsgc-pwgsc.gc.ca

Senior General Counsel & Executive Director, Legal Services Branch, Alain Vauclair
Tel: 819-956-0993
Fax: 819-953-3974
alain.vauclair@tpsgc-pwgsc.gc.ca

Director, Communications, Michelle Bakos
Tel: 819-997-5421
Fax: 819-956-8920
michelle.bakos@tpsgc-pwgsc.gc.ca

Press Secretary, Office of the Minister, Michael Bolkenius
Tel: 819-997-5421
Fax: 819-956-8920
michael.bolkenius@tpsgc-pwgsc.gc.ca

Associated Agencies, Boards & Commissions:
• **Canadian Wheat Board / Commission canadienne du blé**
See Entry Name Index for detailed listing.
• **Defence Construction Canada / Construction de Défense Canada**
See Entry Name Index for detailed listing.

Acquisitions Branch / Direction générale des approvisionnements

Provides departments & agencies with expert assistance at each stage of the supply cycle & offers tools that simplify & accelerate the acquisition of goods & services. It ensures that the government exercises due diligence & maintains the integrity of the procurement process. It is a primary service provider offering client departments a broad base of procurement solutions aimed at securing best value for their procurement dollar.
Assistant Deputy Minister, Tom Ring
Tel: 819-956-1711
Fax: 819-953-1058
tom.ring@tpsgc-pwgsc.gc.ca
Associate Assistant Deputy Minister, Pablo Sobrino
Tel: 819-953-6322
Fax: 819-953-1058
pablo.sobrino@tpsgc-pwgsc.gc.ca
Director General, Marine Sector, Scott Leslie
Tel: 613-943-3338
Fax: 613-944-7870
scott.leslie@tpsgc-pwgsc.gc.ca
Director General, Defence & Major Projects Sector, Cathy A. Sabiston
Tel: 819-956-0010
Fax: 819-956-9110
cathy.sabiston@tpsgc-pwgsc.gc.ca
Senior Director, Major Projects Services, Rami Acouri
Tel: 819-934-0960
Fax: 819-956-4944
rami.acouri@tpsgc-pwgsc.gc.ca
Senior Director, Major Projects Directorate - Sea, Christopher Boyle
Tel: 819-997-7607
Fax: 819-997-7607
Christopher.Boyle@tpsgc-pwgsc.gc.ca
Senior Director, Major Projects Directorate - Land, Sylvie Lalonde
Tel: 819-997-5368
Fax: 819-997-0786
sylvie.lalonde@tpsgc-pwgsc.gc.ca
Senior Director, Major Projects Directorate - Air, Lyne Lévesque-Schou
Tel: 819-997-6812
Fax: 819-997-1111
slyne.levesque-schou@tpsgc-pwgsc.gc.ca
Senior Director, Science Procurement Directorate, Suzanne Lorrain
Tel: 819-956-1788
Fax: 819-997-2229
suzanne.lorrain@tpsgc-pwgsc.gc.ca
Senior Director, Aerospace Equipment Program Directorate, Scott MacLure
Tel: 819-956-0236
Fax: 819-956-6897
scott.maclure@tpsgc-pwgsc.gc.ca
Senior Director, Logistics, Electrical, Fuel & Transportation Directorate, Lyne Rouillard
Tel: 819-956-3997
Fax: 819-953-2953
lyne.rouillard@tpsgc-pwgsc.gc.ca
Senior Director, Marine Systems Directorate, Mark Seely
Tel: 819-956-0684
Fax: 819-956-0040
mark.seely@tpsgc-pwgsc.gc.ca
Acting Senior Director, Operations Eastern Canada Division, Michel Violette
Tel: 819-956-8531
Fax: 819-956-8532
michel.violette@tpsgc-pwgsc.gc.ca

Corporate Services & Strategic Policy Branch / Direction générale des services ministériels et des politiques stratégiques

Assistant Deputy Minister, Caroline Weber
Tel: 819-956-4056
Fax: 819-956-5145
caroline.weber@tpsgc-pwgsc.gc.ca
Director General, Ministerial Services & Emergency Preparedness, Rupa Bhawal-Montmorency
Tel: 819-956-5132
Fax: 819-956-9538
Rupa.Bhawal-Montmorency@tpsgc-pwgsc.gc.ca
Director General, Office of Greening Government Operations, Robert Laframboise
Tel: 613-948-2422
Fax: 613-948-2393
Robert.Laframboise@tpsgc-pwgsc.gc.ca
Director, Corporate Emergency Preparedness Directorate, Bernadette Rudisuela
Tel: 819-956-4555
Fax: 819-956-4589
bernadette.rudisuela@tpsgc-pwgsc.gc.ca

Government Purchasing Information

Most federal government purchasing is centralized in the department of Public Works & Government Services Canada (PWGSC), which purchases all goods, certain services, & most construction. Individual departments work through PWGSC to obtain the supplies & some of the services they need. Contracting for the majority of services is done by individual departments. Federal departments & agencies are establishing purchasing practices to make government procurement more environmentally responsible, using online resources to identify products, services & companies that supply them: Agreements & Opportunities: Agreement on Internal Trade (AIT), which came into effect July 1, 1995, is designed to reduce barriers to trade within Canada. This agreement, between the federal government, the provinces & territories, opens up public procurement to all Canadian companies. Procurement for goods for $25,000, or more or service & construction contracts for $100,000 or more are covered by the AIT. These opportunities are advertised on MERX. World Trade Organization Agreement on Government Procurement (referred to as WTO-AGP) that expands on the General Agreement on Tariffs & Trade (GATT), also covers services. Service contracts of federal departments worth $245,000 or more & construction contracts worth $9.4 million or more are covered by WTO-AGP. These opportunities are also publicized through MERX. The North American Free Trade Agreement was the first international trade agreement signed by Canada to cover services, including construction-related services. In opening up the Mexican, U.S. & Canadian government service markets to each other's suppliers, NAFTA ensures equal treatment to all North American businesses. Service contracts worth $84,000 or more & construction contracts estimated at $10.9 million or more are covered by NAFTA when the purchases are made for government departments. For Crown corporations, NAFTA kicks in when service contracts are worth $420,000 or more & the estimated value of construction contracts is $13.4 million, or greater. Canadian opportunities affected by NAFTA are publicized through MERX. Mexican opportunities are advertised in that country's major daily newspapers & in the Diario Oficial de la Federaci¢n, as well as on MERX. U.S. purchases are published in the Commerce Business Daily (CBD). Extracts of the CBD appear on MERX

MERX

PO Box 11684 Stn. Centre-ville, Montreal, QC H3C 6H4
Tel: 613-727-4900
Fax: 888-235-5800
Toll-Free: 800-964-6379
merx@merx.com
www.merx.com
Other Communication: Agencies, Crown & Private Corporations, E-mail: priv@merx.com
The federal government's Government Electronic Tendering Service (GETS) contracts MERX to advertise government procurement opportunities online. Architectural & engineering consulting services, or services related to real property above $84,000 are advertised on MERX; below $84,000, they are handled through SELECT. Construction opportunities above $100,000 are advertised through MERX; below are handled through SELECT. MERX is used for printing services valued at $10,000 or above, & most goods & services valued at $25,000 or above. Below this level PWGSC uses a variety of bid solicitation methods: T-buys (purchasing by telephone when the product or service is required quickly & can easily be identified over the phone); RFQ (Request for Quotation); an Invitation to Tender (ITT) is used for straightforward requirements above $25,000 & where the lowest price will determine the awarding of the contract; RFP (Request for Proposal) for more complex requirements above $25,000; RFSO (Request for Standing Offer); RFSA (Request for Supply Arrangement); Sole-sourcing, subject to trade agreements & gov-

ernment contracting regulations. For products, individual departments have authority to buy up to $5,000 directly from suppliers; above $5,000, the department must go to PWGSC. Departments have authority to purchase nearly all their services; for program delivery services, departments may buy directly from suppliers up to $400,000 competitively or up to $100,000 without competition; they may also buy competitively up to $2 million when they advertise their requirements through MERX. Subscribers to MERX have access to an opportunity matching service, may view historical opportunities, review contract awards & international opportunities

Office of the Procurement Ombudsman / Bureau de l'ombudsman de l'approvisionnement
Constitution Square Bldg., #1150, 340 Albert St., 11th Fl., PO Box 151Ottawa, ON K1R 7Y6
Fax: 613-947-9800
Toll-Free: 866-734-5169
TTY: 800-926-9105
boa-opo@boa-opo.gc.ca
opo-boa.gc.ca
twitter.com/OPO_Canada
The Procurement Ombudsman reviews complaints with respect to awarded contracts for the acquisition of goods below $25,000 & services below $100,000; reviews complaints with respect to the administration of contracts, no matter the value; reviews departmental practices for acquiring goods & services; & helps provide an alternative dispute resolution process if agreeable to both parties.
Procurement Ombudsman, Frank Brunetta
Deputy Procurement Ombudsman, Lorenzo Ieraci

Real Property Branch / Biens immobiliers
Fax: 613-736-2789
Manages office space & other general-purpose property; acts as custodian for $7.6 billion of real property holdings; administers 2,000 lease contracts; provides working space for 241,000 public servants in 1,810 locations across Canada; provides professional & technical services to government departments & agencies. Government buildings are 34 per cent more energy efficient & 24 per cent more greenhouse gas efficient than in 1990. Green Leases address key environmental standards such as proper management of wastewater, indoor air quality, recycling, energy efficient lighting fixtures, greenhouse gas reduction. Works with other departments on the remediation of contaminated sites & is the federal lead in the cleanup of the Sydney Tar Ponds in Nova Scotia.
Assistant Deputy Minister, Pierre-Marc Mongeau
Tel: 819-956-3189
Fax: 819-956-7130
pierre-marc.mongeau@tpsgc-pwgsc.gc.ca
Director General, National Capital Area Operations Sector, Rick DeBenetti
Tel: 819-956-2469
Fax: 819-956-2720
rick.debenetti@tpsgc-pwgsc.gc.ca
Director General, Engineering Assets Strategy, Marilea Pirie
Tel: 604-666-5191
Fax: 604-775-6806
marilea.pirie@pwgsc-tpsgc.gc.ca
Director General, Major Crown Projects, Jean Vézina
Tel: 819-956-4935
Fax: 819-956-7384
jean.vezina@tpsgc-pwgsc.gc.ca
Senior Director, Energy Services Acquisition Program, Tomasz Smetny-Sowa
Tel: 613-947-9333
tomasz.smetny-sowa@tpsgc-pwgsc.gc.ca
Acting Director, Engineering Assets Portfolio, Rod Friesen
Tel: 604-666-8690
Fax: 604-775-6806
rod.friesen@pwgsc-tpsgc.gc.ca
Director, Esquimalt Graving Dock, Jim Milne
Tel: 250-363-3256
Fax: 250-363-8059
jim.milne@pwgsc-tpsgc.gc.ca
Director, Environmental Services Directorate, Jean-Rock Tourigny
Tel: 819-956-3875
jean-rock.tourigny@tpsgc-pwgsc.gc.ca
Director, Heritage Conservation Directorate, Jack Vandenberg
Tel: 819-997-6792
Fax: 819-953-7482
jack.vandenberg@tpsgc-pwgsc.gc.ca
Director, Alaska Highway Program Management - Fort Nelson, Paddy Whidden
Tel: 250-774-6956
Fax: 250-744-6365
paddy.whidden@pwgsc-tpsgc.gc.ca

Regional Offices
Atlantic
Dominion Public Bldg., 1713 Bedford Row, 7th Fl., Halifax, NS B3J 3C9
Fax: 902-496-5041
Regional Director General, Robert A. Wright
Tel: 902-496-5425
Fax: 902-496-5041
robert.a.wright@tpsgc-pwgsc.gc.ca
Ontario
Joseph Shepard Bldg., 4900 Yonge St., Toronto, ON M2N 6A6
Tel: 416-512-5500
Fax: 416-512-5615
Regional Director General, Pierre Vaillancourt
Tel: 416-512-5610
Fax: 416-512-5615
pierre.vaillancourt@pwgsc-tpsgc.gc.ca
Pacific
#641, 800 Burrard St., Vancouver, BC V6Z 2V8
Tel: 604-666-3995
Fax: 604-666-0398
Regional Director General, Alain G. Trépanier
Tel: 604-666-6983
Fax: 604-666-0398
alain.trepanier@pwgsc-tpsgc.gc.ca
Quebec
Place Bonaventure, #7300, 800 rue de la Gauchetière Ouest, Montréal, QC H5A 1L6
Fax: 514-496-3744
Acting Regional Director General, Richard Meroni
Tel: 514-496-3739
Fax: 514-496-3744
richard.meroni@tpsgc-pwgsc.gc.ca
Western
Telus Plaza North, 10025 Jasper Ave., 5th Fl., Edmonton, AB T5J 1S6
Tel: 780-497-3500
Fax: 780-497-3562
Regional Director General, Randal Cripps
Tel: 780-497-3556
randal.cripps@pwgsc-tpsgc.gc.ca

Procurement Allocation Directory (PAD) / Répertoire des attributions des approvisionnements (RAA)
pad.contractscanada.gc.ca
List of key purchasing contacts in PWGSC offices, & what products & services they buy.

Supplier Registration Information (SRI) / Données d'inscription des fournisseurs
Other Communication: URL: logiciels-software.tpsgc-pwgsc.gc.ca/secteur-prive-industry/dif-sri-eng.cfm
Companies register as potential suppliers to the government; used by federal government buyers to identify potential suppliers for purchases not subject to any trade agreements. Procurement Business Number (PBN) identifies a branch, division or office of a company & is used by PWGSC as a supplier identification code. Architectural & engineering consulting services, including environmental services, valued between $25,000 & $84,000 (construction up to $100,000) are handled through the online SELECT system, which contains a list of pre-qualified real property firms (architects, engineers, construction contractors) identified by their expertise or the service they provide. To get on the list, companies need to register in the SRI service. Supplier Registration Officers are located in regional offices across Canada.

Standards Council of Canada (SCC) / Conseil canadien des normes (CCN)

#200, 270 Albert St., Ottawa, ON K1P 6N7
Tel: 613-238-3222
Fax: 613-569-7808
info@scc.ca
www.scc.ca
Federal Crown corporation with the mandate to promote efficient & effective standardization. The organization reports to Parliament through the Minister of Industry & oversees Canada's National Standards System. The National Standards System comprises organizations & individuals involved in voluntary standards development, promotion & implementation. In addition, more than 400 organizations have been accredited by the Standards Council, including environmental management systems (EMS) registration organizations that perform registrations to ISO 14000 series standards. The Council offers accreditation to registration bodies for specialized environmental management systems in industry-specific areas, including sustainable forestry management (CAN/CSZ809-02). Manages the Program for the Accreditation of Laboratories - Canada (PALCAN) which seeks to identify & accredit competent testing laboratories. Initial assessment is made & regular follow-up audits are performed; accredited organizations are included in the Standards Council directory of accredited testing organizations. Users of testing services can eliminate or reduce their need to establish the competence of a prospective lab. In cooperation with the Canadian Association of Environmental Analy tical Laboratories (CAEAL), SCC operates an accreditation program for environmental analytical laboratories. SCC's website provides free access to a wide variety of standards information, including searchable databases containing information on Canadian, foreign & international standards, regulations & SCC-accredited organizations. More speacialized information is available through SCC's information & Research Service. Other accreditation programs include ones for registrars of ISO 14000 environmental management systems; environmental auditor certifiers & auditor training course providers.

Chair, Hugh Krentz
Tel: 613-238-3222
Fax: 613-569-7808

Executive Director, John Walter
Tel: 613-238-3222 ext: 400
Fax: 613-569-7808
jwalter@scc.ca

Manager, Communications, Pilar Castro
Tel: 613-238-3222 ext: 405
Fax: 613-569-7808
pcastro@scc.ca

Statistics Canada / Statistique Canada

R.H. Coats Bldg., Tunney's Pasture, 150 Tunney's Pasture Driveway, Ottawa, ON K1A 0T6
Tel: 613-951-8116
Fax: 877-287-4369
Toll-Free: 800-263-1136
TTY: 800-363-7629
infostats@statcan.ca
www.statcan.ca
Agency of the federal government, headed by the Chief Statistician of Canada which reports to Parliament through the Minister of Industry. As Canada's central statistical agency, it has a mandate to collect, compile, analyse, abstract & publish statistical information relating to the commercial, industrial, financial, social, economic & general activities & condition of the people of Canada; coordinates activities with its federal & provincial partners in the national statistical system to avoid duplication of effort & to ensure the consistency & usefulness of statistics. The agency profiles & measures both social & economic changes in Canada. It presents a comprehensive picture of the national economy through statistics on manufacturing, agriculture, retail sales, services, prices, productivity changes, trade, transportation, employment & unemployment, & aggregate measures such as gross domestic product. It also presents a comprehensive picture of social conditions through statistics on demography, health, areas.

Chief Statistician of Canada, Wayne Smith
Tel: 613-951-9757
Fax: 613-951-3880
Wayne.Smith@statcan.gc.ca

Environment Accounts & Statistics Division / Division des comptes et de la statistique de l'environnement
Fax: 613-951-0634
Statistical information on forests, air, water, animal & plant life, environment industry, environmental practices & pollution control. Learning resources for students. Publishes Human Activity & the Environment (annual overview of data on population, economic activities & the environment).
Acting Director, Rowena Orok
Tel: 613-951-4341
Fax: 613-951-0634
Acting Chief, Joan Forbes
Tel: 613-951-1801

Chief/Advisor, John Marshall
Tel: 613-951-0347
John.Marshall@statcan.gc.ca
Section Chief, Bruce Mitchell
Tel: 613-951-5347
Bruce.Mitchell@statcan.gc.ca
Section Chief, François Soulard
Tel: 613-951-1777
Francois.Soulard@statcan.gc.ca
Section Chief, Joe St Lawrence
Tel: 613-951-7709
Joe.St.Lawrence@statcan.gc.ca
Section Chief, Doug Trant
Tel: 613-951-3829
Doug.Trant@statcan.gc.ca

Minister, Public Works & Government Services; Minister for Status of Women, Hon. Rona Ambrose
Tel: 613-956-4000
Fax: 613-995-1761
minister-ministre@swc-cfc.gc.ca

Parliamentary Secretary for Status of Women, Susan Truppe
Tel: 613-992-0805
Fax: 613-992-9613

Transport Canada (TC) / Transports Canada

Place de Ville, 330 Sparks St., Tower C, Ottawa, ON K1A 0N5
Tel: 613-990-2309
Fax: 613-954-4731
Toll-Free: 866-995-9737
TTY: 888-675-6863
www.tc.gc.ca
Using EMS 14000 standards, Transport Canada incorporates environmental considerations in all decision-making to fulfill the department's sustainable development strategy. Working with airports & airlines to minimize environmental effects of de-icing fluids; working with Environment Canada & industry to more effectively manage road salt; participating with ICAO's Committee on Aviation Environmental Protection (CAEP) concerning aircraft emissions, noise & land use planning. Ongoing contaminated sites management program. The Moving on Sustainable Transportation (MOST) Program supports projects that educate, raise awareness & provide tools to understand, promote & encourage sustainable transportation, such as neighbourhood transit passes, idle-free workplaces, school walking routes. Development of strategies to reduce greenhouse gas emissions from freight transportation; information on fuel consumption. Urban Transportation Showcase Program aims to reduce greenhouse gas emissions through showcasing demonstrations in communities across Canada
(www.tc.gc.ca/eng/programs/environment-utsp-menu-964.htm)
Acts Administered:
Aeronautics Act
Arctic Waters Pollution Prevention Act (Indian & Northern Affairs)
Canada Marine Act
Canada Shipping Act, 2001 (Fisheries & Oceans)
Canada Transportation Act
Canadian Air Transport Security Authority Act
Department of Transport Act
Marine Transportation Security Act
Motor Vehicle Safety Act
Motor Vehicle Transport Act
Navigable Waters Projection Act
Pilotage Act
Railway Safety Act
Safe Containers Convention Act
Transportation Appeal Tribunal of Canada Act
Transportation of Dangerous Goods Act, 1992

Minister, Transport, Infrastructure, & Communities; Minister, Intergovernmental Affairs, Minister, Economic Development Agency of Canada for the Regions of Québec; President, Queen's Privy Council for Canada, Hon. Denis Lebel
Tel: 61- 99- 070
Fax: 613-995-0327
mintc@tc.gc.ca

Minister of State (Transport), Steven Fletcher
Tel: 613-991-0700

Deputy Minister, Yaprak Baltacioglu
Tel: 613-990-4507
Fax: 613-991-0851
yaprak.baltacioglu@tc.gc.ca

Associate Deputy Minister, Anita Biguzs
Tel: 613-949-2960
Fax: 613-991-0851
anita.biguzs@tc.gc.ca

Chief, Audit & Evaluation Executive, Laura Ruzzier
Tel: 613-990-5462
Fax: 613-990-6455
laura.ruzzier@tc.gc.ca

Integrity Officer, Transport Canada Office of Integrity, Ted Cherrett
Tel: 613-998-9654
ted.cherrett@tc.gc.ca

Director General, Corporate Secretariat, Natalie Bossé
Tel: 613-998-8058
Fax: 613-993-5146
natalie.bosse@tc.gc.ca

Director General, Communications & Marketing, Dan Dugas
Tel: 613-990-6138
Fax: 613-991-6719
dan.dugas@tc.gc.ca

Acting Executive Director to the Deputy Minister, Doreen Gagnon
Tel: 613-990-9002
Fax: 613-990-1878
doreen.gagnon@tc.gc.ca

Executive Director, Legal Services, Henry K. Schultz
Tel: 613-990-5768
Fax: 613-990-5777
henry.schultz@tc.gc.ca

Director, Communications, Michael Winterburn
Tel: 613-991-0700
Fax: 613-995-0327
mike.winterburn@tc.gc.ca

Associated Agencies, Boards & Commissions:
• **Atlantic Pilotage Authority Canada / Administration de pilotage de l'Atlantique Canada**
See Entry Name Index for detailed listing.
• **Canada Lands Company / Société Immobilière du Canada**
See Entry Name Index for detailed listing.
• **Canada Mortgage & Housing Corporation / Société canadienne d'hypothèques et de logement**
See Entry Name Index for detailed listing.
• **Canada Post Corporation / Société canadienne des postes**
See Entry Name Index for detailed listing.
• **Canadian Air Transport Security Authority (CATSA) / Administration canadienne de la sûreté du transport aérien (ACSTA)**
99 Bank St., 13th Fl.
Ottawa, ON K1P 6B9
Fax: 613-990-1295
Toll-free: 888-294-2202
TTY: 613-949-5534
www.catsa-acsta.gc.ca
CATSA secures critical elements of the air transportation system - from passenger screening to baggage screening - & encourages Canadians to Pack Smart for the benefit of all air travellers.
• **Canadian Transportation Agency / Office des transports du Canada**
See Entry Name Index for detailed listing.
• **Federal Bridge Corporation Limited (FBCL) / Société des ponts fédéraux Limitée**
#1210, 55 Metcalfe St.
Ottawa, ON K1P 6L5
Tel: 613-993-6880
Fax: 613-993-6945
info@federalbridge.ca
www.federalbridge.ca
The FBCL was incorporated in 1998 to assume the non-navigational management responsibilities of the St. Lawrence Seaway Authority, including the Jacques Cartier & Champlain Bridges Incorporated, & in a joint venture with its U.S. partner, the Seaway International Bridge Corporation, Ltd. At the same time, the FBCL assumed responsibility for the management of the Canadian portion of the Thousand Islands International Bridge. In 2000, the FBCL acquired the Canadian half of the Sault Ste. Marie International Bridge.
President & Chief Executive Officer, Micheline Dubé
Senior Vice-President, Engineering & Construction, Glenn W. Hewus
Director, Engineering & Construction, Thye Lee
• **Great Lakes Pilotage Authority / Administration de pilotage des Grands Lacs**
See Entry Name Index for detailed listing.
• **Laurentian Pilotage Authority / Administration de pilotage des Laurentides Canada**
See Entry Name Index for detailed listing.
• **Marine Atlantic Inc. / Marine Atlantique**
See Entry Name Index for detailed listing.
• **Pacific Pilotage Authority / Administration de Pilotage du Pacifique Canada**
See Entry Name Index for detailed listing.
• **Royal Canadian Mint / Monnaie royale canadienne**
See Entry Name Index for detailed listing.
• **Transportation Appeal Tribunal of Canada / Anciennement le Tribunal de l'aviation civile**
#1201, 333 Laurier Ave. West, 12th Fl.
Ottawa, ON K1A 0N5
Tel: 613-990-6906
Fax: 613-990-9153
info@tatc.gc.ca
www.tatc.gc.ca
The Tribunal provides an independent review process for anyone who has been given notice of an administrative or enforcement action taken by the Minister of Transport, railway safety inspectors or the Canadian Transportation Agency under various federal transportation Acts.
• **Transportation Safety Board of Canada / Bureau de la sécurité des transports du Canada**
See Entry Name Index for detailed listing.
• **VIA Rail Canada Inc.**
See Entry Name Index for detailed listing.
Director General, Linda Brouillette
Tel: 613-991-6317
linda.brouillette@tc.gc.ca
Chief, Diversity & Official Languages, Corporate HR Policy & Programs, Francine Charbonneau
Tel: 613-990-5690
Fax: 613-998-4614
francine.charbonneau@tc.gc.ca
Chief, Resources, Projects & Issues Management Branch, Patrice Faria
Tel: 613-993-7900
Fax: 613-998-4614
patrice.faria@tc.gc.ca
Chief, Values, Ethics & Wellness, Eric Saint-Onge
Tel: 613-949-1976
Fax: 613-998-1345
eric.saint-onge@tc.gc.ca
Senior Director, Human Resources Client Services, George Thwaites
Tel: 613-993-8976
Fax: 613-990-1880
george.thwaites@tc.gc.ca
Senior Director, Corporate, HR Policy, Programs, Planning & Systems, Robert Sincennes
Tel: 613-991-6485
Fax: 613-990-1880
robert.sincennes@tc.gc.ca
Director, Labour Relations, Compensation & Occupational Health & Safety, Richard Begin
Tel: 613-949-1453
Fax: 613-991-1850
richard.begin@tc.gc.ca
Director, Executive Ressourcing & Classification, Michèle Ouellette
Tel: 613-991-5913
Fax: 613-949-4202
michele.ouellette@tc.gc.ca
Acting Manager, HR Information Management Systems, HR Planning, Performance Measurement & Information Management, Suzanne Nichol
Tel: 613-991-6537
Fax: 613-993-1990
suzanne.nichol@tc.gc.ca
Exclusion & Designations Officer, Labour Relations, Compensation & Occupational Health & Safety, Bernise Lamoureux
Tel: 613-991-2995

Fax: 613-998-4065
bernise.lamoureux@tc.gc.ca
Director General, Chris Molinski
Tel: 613-998-6465
chris.molinski@tc.gc.ca
Director, Application Services, Tracey Boicey
Tel: 613-998-0739
Fax: 613-954-4493
tracey.boicey@tc.gc.ca
Director, IM/IT Architecture & Planning, Joël Comeau
Tel: 613-993-8040
Fax: 613-954-5858
joel.comeau@tc.gc.ca
Director, Computer Operations & Network Services, Rick Huard
Tel: 613-990-5380
rick.huard@tc.gc.ca
Director, Information Management, Diane Lavigne
Tel: 613-991-2867
Fax: 613-990-2469
diane.lavigne@tc.gc.ca
Director, IT/IM Security & Infrastructure Planning, Richard Ruta
Tel: 613-993-7066
Fax: 613-954-5858
richard.ruta@tc.gc.ca

Transportation Development Centre (TDC) / Centre de développement des transports
Tour Ouest, Complexe Guy-Favreau, 800, boul René-Lévesque ouest, 6e étage, Montréal, QC H3B 1X9
Tel: 514-283-0000
Fax: 514-283-7158
tdccdt@tc.gc.ca
www.tc.gc.ca/eng/innovation/tdc-menu.htm
Conducts research & development on new technologies in transportation to support Transport Canada's objectives of safety, security & economic competitiveness, as well as broader national concerns, such as accessibility, energy efficiency & the environment.
Director, Marc Prévost
Tel: 613-990-5437
Fax: 613-998-3987
marc.prevost@tc.gc.ca
Chief, Advanced Technology, Howard Posluns
Tel: 613-993-6254
Fax: 613-991-5928
howard.posluns@tc.gc.ca
Acting Chief, Technology Application, Deborah deGrasse
Tel: 613-998-1975
Fax: 613-991-5928
deborah.degrasse@tc.gc.ca
Director General, Transportation Technology & Innovation, Marc Fortin
Tel: 613-998-8242
Fax: 613-998-3987
marc.fortin@tc.gc.ca
Assistant Deputy Minister, Kristine Burr
Tel: 613-998-1880
Fax: 613-991-1440
kristine.burr@tc.gc.ca
Executive Director, Policy Initiatives, Marc Rioux
Tel: 613-993-1718
Fax: 613-991-6445
marc.rioux@tc.gc.ca
Director, Business Planning & Group Services, Malick Sidibé
Tel: 613-949-0245
Fax: 613-998-3987
malick.sidibe@tc.gc.ca
Human Resources Special Project Officer, Bruce Vo
Tel: 613-949-7272
Fax: 613-949-9415
bruce.vo@tc.gc.ca
Senior Policy Advisor, Félix Meunier
Tel: 613-998-1877
Fax: 613-991-6445

Air Policy / Politique du transport aérien
Fax: 613-991-6445
Director General, Brigita Gravitis-Beck
Tel: 613-993-0054
brigita.gravitis-beck@tc.gc.ca
Chief, Policy Analysis, Donald Park
Tel: 613-991-9082
donald.park@tc.gc.ca
Director, Airports & Air Navigation Services Policy, Dave Dawson
Tel: 613-991-2989
dave.dawson@tc.gc.ca
Director, National Air Services Policy, Colin Stacey
Tel: 613-993-4361
Fax: 613-991-6445
colin.stacey@tc.gc.ca
Canada's Permanent Representative to the International Civil Aviation Organization, Mark Allen
Tel: 613-991-6405
mark.allen@tc.gc.ca

Economic Analysis / Analyse économiques
Fax: 613-957-3280
Director General, Richard Thivierge
Tel: 613-998-1881
Fax: 613-957-3280
richard.thivierge@tc.gc.ca
Director, Forecasting & Modelling, Alexandre Gracovetsky
Tel: 613-949-0252
Fax: 613-957-3280
alexandre.gracovetsky@tc.gc.ca
Director, Economic & Environmental Analysis & Research, Bruno Jacques
Tel: 613-990-5340
Fax: 613-957-3280
bruno.jacques@tc.gc.ca
Director, Economic Analysis & Research, Louis-Paul Tardif
Tel: 613-991-6982
Fax: 613-957-3280
louis-paul.tardif@tc.gc.ca
Director, Transportation Statistics, Michel Villeneuve
Tel: 613-990-3825
michel.villeneuve@tc.gc.ca

Environmental Policy / Politiques environnementales
Director General, Pierre Marin
Tel: 613-949-2677
Fax: 613-949-9415
pierre.marin@tc.gc.ca
Director, Environmental Policy Analysis & Evaluation, Leigh Mazany
Tel: 613-949-6641
Fax: 613-949-9415
leigh.mazany@tc.gc.ca
Manager & Senior Policy Advisor, Environmental Policy & Climate Change, Christine Dufour
Tel: 613-993-6268
christine.dufour@tc.gc.ca
Manager, Climate Change, Environmental Policy Framework & Integration, Jeffrey Johnson
Tel: 613-998-6474
Fax: 613-949-9415
jeffrey.johnson@tc.gc.ca
Acting Manager & Senior Policy Advisor, International, Federal-Provincial & Sustainable Development, Elizabeth Smalley
Tel: 613-990-0364
Fax: 613-949-9415
elizabeth.smalley@tc.gc.ca

International & Intergovernmental Relations / Relations internationales et intergouvernementales
Director General, Arlene Turner
Tel: 613-991-6500
arlene.turner@tc.gc.ca
Chief, International & Intergovernmental Policy Coordination & Special Projects, Jennifer Little
Tel: 613-991-6505
jennifer.little@tc.gc.ca
Chief, Accessible Transportation, Intergovernmental Affairs & Accessibility, Barbara Nelson
Tel: 613-990-2269
Fax: 613-990-1719
barbara.nelson@tc.gc.ca
Director, Trade Policy, Les Ward
Tel: 613-998-0694
les.ward@tc.gc.ca
Manager & Senior Policy Advisor, International Relations, Paul Arvanitidis
Tel: 613-949-9597
Fax: 613-991-6422
paul.arvanitidis@tc.gc.ca
Manager & Senior Policy Advisor, Intergovernmental Affairs & Accessibility, Kimberly Ellard
Tel: 613-949-0615
Fax: 613-990-1719
kimberly.ellard@tc.gc.ca

Marine Policy / Politique maritime
Fax: 613-998-1845
Director General, Tim Meisner
Tel: 613-991-3536
Fax: 613-998-1845
tim.meisner@tc.gc.ca
Chief, International Marine Policy, Doug O'Keefe
Tel: 613-991-6526
doug.okeefe@tc.gc.ca
Executive Director, International Marine Policy & Liability, Jerry Rysanek
Tel: 613-998-0708
Fax: 613-998-1845
jerry.rysanek@tc.gc.ca
Director, Seaway & Domestic Ship Policy, Frank Cosentino
Tel: 613-991-6244
Fax: 613-998-1845
frank.cosentino@tc.gc.ca
Director, Seaway & Domestic Ship Policy, Valerie Devlin
Tel: 613-998-1843
Fax: 613-998-1845
valerie.devlin@tc.gc.ca
Director, Ferry Policy & Programs, Daniel Haché
Tel: 613-991-9509
Fax: 613-998-1845
daniel.hache@tc.gc.ca
Director, Ports Policy, Janet Kavanagh
Tel: 613-991-6428
janet.kavanagh@tc.gc.ca

Strategic Policy / Politiques stratégiques
Tel: 613-949-9596
Fax: 613-990-1719
Director General, Sandra LaFortune
Tel: 613-998-0402
Fax: 613-990-1719
sandra.lafortune@tc.gc.ca
Executive Director, Continental Gateway & System Analysis, Jacques Rochon
Tel: 613-991-2967
jacques.rochon@tc.gc.ca
Director, Policy Integration & Research, Craig Hutton
Tel: 613-949-7277
Fax: 613-990-1719
craig.hutton@tc.gc.ca
Director, Intergovernmental Affairs & Accessibility, Virgina Leung
Tel: 613-998-1930
Fax: 613-990-1719
virginia.leung@tc.gc.ca
Director, Atlantic Gateway, Calie McPhee
Tel: 613-949-2753
Fax: 613-990-1719
calie.mcphee@tc.gc.ca
Director, Policy Planning & Cabinet Affairs, Dawn L. Miller
Tel: 613-998-6475
Fax: 613-993-8674
dawn.miller@tc.gc.ca
Director, Pacific Gateway Coordination, Paul Sandhar-Cruz
Tel: 613-949-0654
Fax: 613-991-6422
paul.sandhar-cruz@tc.gc.ca

Surface Transportation Policy / Politiques de transport terrestre
Fax: 613-998-2686
Director General, Annette Gibbons
Tel: 613-998-2689
Fax: 613-998-2686
annette.gibbons@tc.gc.ca
Executive Director, Windsor Gateway Project Team, Sean O'Dell
Tel: 613-991-4702
Fax: 613-998-2686
sean.odell@tc.gc.ca
Director, Rail Policy, Carolyn Crook
Tel: 613-998-1918
Fax: 613-998-2686
carolyn.crook@tc.gc.ca
Director, Multimodal Investment Strategies, Eric H. Leroux
Tel: 613-990-9141
eric.leroux@tc.gc.ca
Director, Highway & Border Policy, Ted Mackay
Tel: 613-991-5981
ted.mackay@tc.gc.ca

Director, Urban Transportation & Motor Carrier Policy, Tom Oommen
Tel: 613-998-0674
Fax: 613-998-2686
tom.oommen@tc.gc.ca
Manager & Senior Policy Advisor, Freight Integration & Motor Carrier Policy, Monica Blaney
Tel: 613-949-4156
Fax: 613-998-2686
monica.blaney@tc.gc.ca

Transportation Technology & Innovation / Technologie des transports ed de l'innovation
Director General, Marc Fortin
Tel: 613-998-8242
Fax: 613-998-3987
marc.fortin@tc.gc.ca
Chief, Advanced Technology, Transportation Development Centre, Howard Posluns
Tel: 613-993-6254
Fax: 613-991-5928
howard.posluns@tc.gc.ca
Director, Innovation Policy, Jutta Paczulla
Tel: 613-998-2690
jutta.paczulla@tc.gc.ca
Director, Transportation Development Centre, Marc Prévost
Tel: 613-990-5437
Fax: 613-998-3987
marc.prevost@tc.gc.ca
Director, Intelligent Transportation System, Susan D. Spencer
Tel: 613-990-9681
susan.spencer@tc.gc.ca
Senior Policy Advisor, Intelligent Transportation Systems, Lorcan Scanlon
Tel: 613-990-6141
lorcan.scanlon@tc.gc.ca

Programs Group / Groupe des programmes
www.tc.gc.ca/eng/programs-menu.htm
Responsible for the transfer of ports, harbours & airports to communities & other interests; the oversight & lease management of divested facilities; the operation of facilities not yet divested; & real property management. Responsible for environmental programs & policies, including environmental management system, sustainable development strategies, environmental assessment & national environmental issues in transportation, such as climate change.

Airport & Port Programs / Programmes aeroportuaires et portuaires
Tel: 613-993-4466
Fax: 613-990-8889
Acting Director General, Marc Brazeau
Tel: 613-990-1340
Fax: 613-990-8889
marc.brazeau@tc.gc.ca
Senior Director, Authorities Management & Real Property, Richard Barbeau
Tel: 613-949-5721
Fax: 613-990-8889
richard.barbeau@tc.gc.ca
Director, Program Management, Michéle Bergevin
Tel: 613-991-3025
Fax: 613-990-8889
michele.bergevin@tc.gc.ca
Director, Bridge Policy & Programs, Brian E. Hicks
Tel: 613-998-1900
Fax: 613-990-8889
brian.hicks@tc.gc.ca
Acting Director, Operations & Special Projects, Jason Tom
Tel: 613-990-0505
jason.tom@tc.gc.ca

Environmental Affairs / Affaires environnementales
Fax: 613-957-4260
Director General, Catherine Higgens
Tel: 613-991-5995
Fax: 613-993-8674
catherine.higgens@tc.gc.ca
Chief, Energy & Advanced Vehicle Program, Nicole Galvin
Tel: 613-990-4321
nicole.galvin@tc.gc.ca
Senior Director, Environmental Management, Alec Simpson
Tel: 613-990-0512
alec.simpson@tc.gc.ca
Director, Aboriginal Consultation Unit, Nancy Harris
Tel: 613-990-0318
Fax: 613-993-8674
nancy.harris@tc.gc.ca
Manager, Administrative Services Directorate, Solange Azzi
Tel: 613-998-1933
solange.azzi@tc.gc.ca
Manager, Urban Transportation Programs, Environmental Initiatives, Eric Sévigny
Tel: 613-998-5693
Fax: 613-949-3874
eric.sevigny@tc.gc.ca

Surface Infrasturcture Programs / Programmes des infrastructures
Fax: 613-990-9639
Director General, Jane Weldon
Tel: 613-998-8137
Fax: 613-990-9639
jane.weldon@tc.gc.ca
Senior Director, Highways & Borders, Jim Lothrop
Tel: 613-998-1902
jim.lothrop@tc.gc.ca
Director, Transit Projects, John Hnatyshyn
Tel: 613-998-5162
Fax: 613-990-9639
john.hnatyshyn@tc.gc.ca
Director, Autoroute 30 & Quebec Projects, Marie-Hélène Lévesque
Tel: 613-998-2691
Fax: 613-990-9639
marie-helene.levesque@tc.gc.ca

Safety & Security Group / Groupe de sécurité et sûreté
The ADM, Safety & Security, directs the development of transportation safety & security legislation, regulations & national standards; is responsible for the uniform implementation of monitoring, testing, inspection, research & development, & subsidy programs in the aviation, marine, rail & road modes of transport; oversees the delivery of aircraft services to government & other transportation bodies; & is responsible for development & enforcement of regulations & standards under federal jurisdiction, to protect public safety in the transportation of dangerous goods, & to prevent unlawful interference in the aviation, marine & railways modes of transport, as well as ensuring that the department is prepared to respond to transportation & transportation-related emergencies.
Assistant Deputy Minister, Gerard A. McDonald
Tel: 613-990-3838
Fax: 613-990-2947
gerard.mcdonald@tc.gc.ca
Associate Assistant Deputy Minister, Laureen E. Kinney
Tel: 613-949-2394
Fax: 613-990-2947
laureen.kinney@tc.gc.ca
Chief, Ministerial Liaison & Strategic Issues Management, Christine Martel
Tel: 613-993-8803
Fax: 613-990-3994
christine.martel@tc.gc.ca
Chief, Corporate Services, Joseé L. Sabourin
Tel: 613-990-5492
Fax: 613-990-3894
josee.sabourin@tc.gc.ca

Aircraft Services / Services des aéronefs
Tel: 613-998-7991
Fax: 613-991-0365
Director General, Michel Gaudreau
Tel: 613-998-3316
Fax: 613-991-0365
michel.gaudreau@tc.gc.ca
Chief, Strategic Planning, Financial & Administrative Services, Lorraine Stairs
Tel: 613-998-8655
lorraine.stairs@tc.gc.ca
Chief, Flight Operations Training, Turbo-jet, Simon Pinsonneault
Tel: 613-949-5841
simon.pinsonneault@tc.gc.ca
Chief, Facilities Environmental & Site Safety, Sandra L. Phillips-McRae
Tel: 613-949-0559
Fax: 613-998-8235
sandra.phillips-mcrae@tc.gc.ca
Director, Flight Operations, Steve Buckles
Tel: 613-998-3419
Fax: 613-991-0365
steve.buckles@tc.gc.ca
Director, Engineering, Bohdan Goyaniuk
Tel: 613-998-4363
bohdan.goyaniuk@tc.gc.ca
Director, Technical Services, Gérald Toupin
Tel: 613-998-3403
Fax: 613-991-0365
gerald.toupin@tc.gc.ca

Aviation Security Directorate / Direction générale de la sûreté aérienne
Director General, Erin O'Gorman
Tel: 613-990-3651
Fax: 613-990-5046
erin.ogorman@tc.gc.ca
Director, Aviation Security Operations, Michel Béland
Tel: 613-990-1076
Fax: 613-996-6381
michel.beland@tc.gc.ca
Director, Operational Performance Framework, Nick Cartwright
Tel: 613-990-0239
Fax: 613-998-8238
nick.cartwright@tc.gc.ca
Director, Air Cargo Security, Shari Currie
Tel: 613-949-2385
Fax: 613-949-8502
shari.currie@tc.gc.ca
Director, Aviation Security Policy, Isabelle Desmartis
Tel: 613-998-6440
isabelle.desmartis@tc.gc.ca
Director, Aviation Security Regulatory Review, Jim Marriott
Tel: 613-990-5520
jim.marriott@tc.gc.ca
Director, Aviation Security Regulatory Review, Aaron McCrorie
Tel: 613-991-6477
aaron.mccrorie@tc.gc.ca
Director, Aviation Security Regulatory Affairs, James Pope
Tel: 613-990-8857
Fax: 613-990-5046
james.pope@tc.gc.ca
Acting Director, Strategic Planning & Business Direction, Madona Radi
Tel: 613-990-6621
madona.radi@tc.gc.ca
Director, Aviation Security Technology, Mario Saucier
Tel: 613-993-5539
Fax: 613-998-9010
mario.saucier@tc.gc.ca

Civil Aviation / Aviation civile
Tel: 613-990-1322
Fax: 613-957-4208
Director General, Martin J. Eley
Tel: 613-990-1322
martin.eley@tc.gc.ca
Acting Chief, Program Management, Standards, Brigitte Ouellet
Tel: 613-990-3716
Fax: 613-998-7416
brigitte.ouellet@tc.gc.ca
Director, International Operations, Shelley Chambers
Tel: 613-990-8177
Fax: 613-998-4860
shelley.chambers@tc.gc.ca
Director, Policy & Regulatory Services, Nicole Girard
Tel: 613-990-1224
nicole.girard@tc.gc.ca
Director, Civil Aviation Secretariat, Lucille Kamal
Tel: 613-991-9964
lucille.kamal@tc.gc.ca
Director, Management Services, Judy Rutherford
Tel: 613-990-1280
Fax: 613-993-7038
judy.rutherford@tc.gc.ca
Director, Medicine, David A. Salisbury
Tel: 613-990-1311
Fax: 613-990-6623
david.salisbury@tc.gc.ca
Director, National Operations, Jennifer Taylor
Tel: 613-991-9982
jennifer.taylor@tc.gc.ca
Director, National Aircraft Certification, David Turnbull
Tel: 613-952-4338
david.turnbull@tc.gc.ca
Manager, Technical & Administrative Services, Learning Services, Michelle Clark

Tel: 613-949-9593
Fax: 613-949-4219
michelle.clark@tc.gc.ca
Manager, Safety Promotion & Education, System Safety, Bryce Fisher
Tel: 613-998-4627
bryce.fisher@tc.gc.ca
Contact, International Operations, Douglas A. Tompkins
Tel: 613-991-5651
Fax: 613-991-5188
douglas.tompkins@tc.gc.ca
Administrative Assistant, General Aviation, Marie-Helene Boutin
Tel: 613-990-3054
Fax: 613-990-8889
marie-helene.boutin@tc.gc.ca
General Aviation Policy Advisor to the Director General, Manzur Huq
Tel: 613-990-1085
manzur.huq@tc.gc.ca

Marine Safety / Sécurité maritime
www.tc.gc.ca/marine/menu.htm
Responsible for the administration of national & international laws designed to ensure the safe operation, navigation, design & maintenance of ships, protection of life & property, & prevention of ship-source pollution. Transport Canada has assumed responsibility for environmental response from Fisheries & Oceans Canada. Strictly enforces pollution prevention regulations through the inspection of ships for compliance with pollution prevention regulations & through investigation of pollution incidents.
Director General, Donald Roussel
Tel: 613-998-0610
Fax: 613-954-1032
donald.roussel@tc.gc.ca
Chief, Marine Safety Application Management, Program & Technical Training Services, Lousie D. Gagné
Tel: 613-998-8310
louise.gagne@tc.gc.ca
Executive Director, Regulatory Services & Quality Assurance, Sylvian Lachance
Tel: 613-998-0600
Fax: 613-954-1032
sylvain.lachance@tc.gc.ca
Director, Operations & Environmental Programs, Richard Day
Tel: 613-991-3131
richard.day@tc.gc.ca
Director, Strategic Planning & Technical Training Services, David Delcorde
Tel: 613-991-3122
david.delcorde@tc.gc.ca
Director, Domestic Vessel Regulatory Oversight, Julie Gascon
Tel: 613-949-3819
julie.gascon@tc.gc.ca
Director, Operations & Environmental Programs, Yvette Myers
Tel: 613-991-3131
Fax: 613-998-0637
yvette.myers@tc.gc.ca
Director, Marine Personnel Standards & Pilotage, Naim Nazha
Tel: 613-990-4350
Fax: 613-990-1538
naim.nazha@tc.gc.ca
Manager, Marine Safety Executive Secretariat, Julia Cropley
Tel: 613-990-5915
Fax: 613-991-6719
julia.cropley@tc.gc.ca
Manager, Technical Review, Operations & Environmental Programs, Thomas Morris
Tel: 613-991-3170
Fax: 613-993-8196
thomas.morris@tc.gc.ca
Senior Marine Safety Inspector, Quality Assurance, Gerard G.M.K. Kruithof
Tel: 613-990-5941
Fax: 613-991-4818
gerard.kruithof@tc.gc.ca
Senior Marine Inspector - Small Vessel, Design, Equipment & Boating Safety, David Wallace
Tel: 613-998-0599
Fax: 613-993-8196
david.wallace@tc.gc.ca

Marine Security / Sûreté maritime
Director General, Fulvio Fracassi
Tel: 613-991-4173
Fax: 613-993-1714
fulvio.fracassi@tc.gc.ca
Director, Marine Security Regulatory Affairs, Susan Archer
Tel: 613-949-0655
susan.archer@tc.gc.ca
Director, Marine Security Policy, Allan R. Bartley
Tel: 613-949-1442
allan.bartley@tc.gc.ca
Director, Marine Security Operations, Dean Fuller
Tel: 613-990-1450
Fax: 613-949-3906
dean.fuller@tc.gc.ca
Acting Director, Marine Security Strategic & Business Direction, Shannon Lenahan
Tel: 613-949-0600
Fax: 613-949-3906
shannon.lenahan@tc.gc.ca
Director, Marine Security Contributions & Special Programs, Wendy Nixon
Tel: 613-990-1282
wendy.nixon@tc.gc.ca

Rail Safety / Sécurité ferroviaire
www.tc.gc.ca/rail/menu.htm
Administers the Railway Safety Act & associated regulations; provides funding for improvements to railway grade crossings; administers Part II of the Canada Labour Code, relating to the safety & health of employees; & ensures, for specific railway works, that environmental impacts are assessed in compliance with the Canadian Environmental Assessment Act.
Director General, Luc Bourdon
Tel: 613-998-2984
Fax: 613-990-2924
Chief Engineer, Rail Safety Operations, Engineering, Daniel Lafonatine
Tel: 613-990-4515
daniel.lafontaine@tc.gc.ca
Environmental Engineer, Ryan Rickard
Tel: 613-990-4517
Director, Equipment & Operations, Walter Carolson
Tel: 613-990-7745
walter.carlson@tc.gc.ca
Director, Audit & Quality Assurance, David Iezzi
Tel: 613-991-6777
david.iezzi@tc.gc.ca
Director, Regulatory Affairs, Don D. Pulciani
Tel: 613-990-8690
don.pulciani@tc.gc.ca
Director, Program Management, Karen Swol
Tel: 613-990-5631
karen.swol@tc.gc.ca
Director, Rail Safety Secretariat, Carla White-Taylor
Tel: 613-998-3434
carla.white-taylor@tc.gc.ca
Head, Resource Management, Program Analysis & Performance, Mary Callahan Bishop
Tel: 613-990-0198
Fax: 613-990-7767
mary.callahanbishop@tc.gc.ca
Manager, HR Planning & Training, Audit & Quality Assurance - Rail Safety, Francine Charron
Tel: 613-993-7030
Fax: 613-990-7767
francine.charron@tc.gc.ca
Senior Advisor, Public Education & Awareness, Funded & Partnership Programs, Jennifer Attack
Tel: 613-949-9194
jennifer.attack@tc.gc.ca

Road Safety & Motor Vehicle Registration / Direction de la sécurité routière et de la réglementation automobile
Tel: 613-998-8616
Toll-Free: 800-333-0371
www.tc.gc.ca/road/menu.htm
Administers the Motor Vehicle Safety Act by developing vehicle & motor vehicle equipment safety standards, emission standards & testing procedures; responds to public enquiries & complaints of alleged vehicle safety defects, emission defects & fuel consumption deficiencies; &, in conjunction with Natural Resources Canada, provides fuel consumption information through vehicle labels & the Fuel Consumption Guide. Also administers the Motor Vehicle Transport Act, which governs the safety fitness of extra-provincial trucks & buses. The enforcement of this act is largely delegated to the provinces.
Director General, Kash Ram
Tel: 613-993-6735
Acting Chief, Resources & Strategic Planning, Nicole MacIsaac
Tel: 613-991-3109
Fax: 613-998-4831
nicole.macisaac@tc.gc.ca
Director, Road Safety Programs, Kim Benjamin
Tel: 613-998-7851
kim.benjamin@tc.gc.ca
Director, Motor Vehicle Standards, Research & Development, Christian Lavoie
Tel: 613-998-2268
Fax: 613-990-2913
christian.lavoie@tc.gc.ca
Director, Motor Vehicle Regulation Enforcement, Stephanie Lines
Tel: 613-998-2157
Fax: 613-990-2915
stephanie.lines@tc.gc.ca
Director, Motor Vehicle Standards, Research & Development, Merz Rustom
Tel: 613-998-2268
Fax: 613-990-2913
merz.rustom@tc.gc.ca
Senior Financial Officer, Motor Vehicle - Test Centre, Quoc-Nam Tran
Tel: 450-430-7270
quoc-nam.tran@tc.gc.ca

Security Program Support / Soutien au programme de sûreté
Responsible for the development & enforcement of regulations & standards to prevent unlawful interference with air, rail & marine transportation; management of departmental security.
Director General, Emilia Warriner
Tel: 613-990-2208
Fax: 613-949-6637
emilia.warriner@tc.gc.ca
Chief, Security Education & Training Programs, Security Expertise Programs, Ginette Charlebois
Tel: 613-991-3095
Fax: 613-998-8238
ginette.charlebois@tc.gc.ca
Chief, Intelligence Security Screening Programs, Lise Ranger
Tel: 613-998-9773
Fax: 613-991-3205
lise.ranger@tc.gc.ca
Director, Security Expertise Programs, Angelo Boccanfuso
Tel: 613-990-1787
Fax: 613-998-9238
angelo.boccanfuso@tc.gc.ca
Director, Emergency Preparedness, Luc Brisebois
Tel: 613-947-5076
Fax: 613-957-6414
luc.brisebois@tc.gc.ca
Director, Security Intelligence & Assessments, Nicole Legault
Tel: 613-990-1812
Fax: 613-998-7906
nicole.legault@tc.gc.ca

Strategies & Integration / Strategies et intégration
Director General, Melanie Tod
Tel: 613-949-0864
Fax: 613-990-5058
melanie.tod@tc.gc.ca
Acting Chief, Administrative Services, Program Support, Nadine Vincent
Tel: 613-991-3022
Fax: 613-990-5058
nadine.vincent@tc.gc.ca
Director, Strategic Planning & Policy Coordination, France Bergeron
Tel: 613-990-3885
Fax: 613-990-5058
france.bergeron@tc.gc.ca
Director, Regulatory Affairs Coordination, Strategies & Integration, Michel Leclerc
Tel: 613-993-2721
michel.leclerc@tc.gc.ca

Surface & Inter-modal Security Directorate / Direction générale de la sûreté de transport terrestre et intermodal
Director General, Dominique Blanchard
Tel: 613-949-7778
Fax: 613-990-2015
dominique.blanchard@tc.gc.ca
Director, Program Operations, Peter Lavallee
Tel: 613-949-7792
Fax: 613-990-2015
peter.lavallee@tc.gc.ca

Director, Surface & Inter-modal Security Policy, Allan Van Dyk
Tel: 613-949-8192
Fax: 613-990-2015
allan.vandyk@tc.gc.ca

Transportation of Dangerous Goods / Transport des marchandises dangereuses

Regulatory development, information & guidance on dangerous goods transport for the public, industry & government. Represents Canada on international organizations responsible for establishing uniform international requirements, such as the United Nations Committee of Experts on the Transport of Dangerous Goods, Association of American Railroads (AAR) Tankcar Committee & International Civil Aviation Organization (ICAO) Dangerous Goods Panel. Branches are responsible for regulatory affairs, research, evaluation, compliance & response, review of remedial measures, development of training programs.

Director General, Marie-France Dagenais
Tel: 613-990-1147
Fax: 613-990-2917
marie-france.dagenais@tc.gc.ca
Director, Transportation of Dangerous Goods Secretariat, Nathalie Belliveau
Tel: 613-998-6546
nathalie.belliveau@tc.gc.ca
Director, Canada Transport Emergency Centre (CANUTEC), Michel Cloutier
Tel: 613-947-5052
michel.cloutier@tc.gc.ca
Director, Compliance & Response, Clive Law
Tel: 613-998-6540
Fax: 613-990-2917
clive.law@tc.gc.ca
Director, Research, Risk Evaluation & Systems, Geoffrey Oliver
Tel: 613-990-1139
Fax: 613-990-2917
geoffrey.oliver@tc.gc.ca
Director, Special Projects, Jacques Savard
Tel: 613-990-1154
Fax: 613-993-5925
jacques.savard@tc.gc.ca
Director, Regulatory Affairs, Joanne St-Onge
Tel: 613-990-1159
Fax: 613-990-2917
joanne.st-onge@tc.gc.ca
Manager, Resource Planning & Special Projects, Christiane Lamoureux
Tel: 613-990-1149
Fax: 613-993-5925
christiane.lamoureux@tc.gc.ca

Canada Transport Emergency Centre (CANUTEC) / Centre canadien d'urgence du Ministère des transports

Tel: 613-992-4624
Fax: 613-954-5101
canutec@tc.gc.ca
www.tc.gc.ca/canutec/

Assists emergency response personnel in handling dangerous goods emergencies; established a scientific data bank on chemicals manufactured, stored & transported in Canada; staffed by professional chemists specialized in emergency response & experienced in interpreting technical information; provides advice & serves as a communication link during emergencies; primary contact point for the Transport of Dangerous Goods Directorate; & provides assistance with regulations administration. Developed an Emergency Response Guide with the US Dept. of Transportation & the secretariat of Communications & Transportation of Mexico. The Guide is a reference source on chemical hazards and recommended responses to accidents involving dangerous goods.

Director, Michel Cloutier
Atlantic
Heritage Court, 95 Foundry St., 6th Fl., Moncton, NB E1C 5H7
Tel: 506-851-7131
Fax: 506-851-2563
Regional Director, Civil Aviation, Arthur W. Allan
Tel: 506-851-7220
arthur.allan@tc.gc.ca
Acting Regional Director, Coordination & Policy, Marthe Boissonnault
Tel: 506-851-7562
Fax: 506-851-7327
marthe.boissonnault@tc.gc.ca
Regional Director, Surface, Peter Fullarton
Tel: 506-851-7564
Fax: 506-851-7042
peter.fullarton@tc.gc.ca
Acting Regional Director, Communications & Marketing, Céline Gaudet
Tel: 506-851-2341
Fax: 506-851-7327
celine.gaudet@tc.gc.ca
Regional Director, Finance & Administration, Dianne Goguen
Tel: 506-851-7297
Fax: 506-851-3018
dianne.goguen@tc.gc.ca
Regional Director, Corporate Services, Richard Graves
Tel: 506-851-2857
Fax: 506-851-2568
richard.graves@tc.gc.ca
Regional Director, Marine, Scott E. Kennedy
Tel: 902-426-2060
Fax: 902-426-9049
scott.kennedy@tc.gc.ca
Regional Director, Programs, Maurice Landry
Tel: 506-851-3621
maurice.landry@tc.gc.ca
Regional Director, Transportation Security, Ross R. Munn
Tel: 902-431-8563
Fax: 902-407-7662
ross.munn@tc.gc.ca
Regional Director, Human Resources, Ginette Roy
Tel: 506-851-4614
ginette.roy@tc.gc.ca
Ontario
#300, 4900 Yonge St., Toronto, ON M2N 6A5
Tel: 416-952-0215
Fax: 416-952-0196
Regional Director General, Debra D. Taylor
Tel: 416-952-2170
Fax: 416-952-2174
debra.taylor@tc.gc.ca
Regional Director, Aviation Security, David Bayliss
Tel: 416-952-0519
Fax: 416-952-0189
david.bayliss@tc.gc.ca
Acting Regional Director, Pickering Lands, Rob Bergevin
Tel: 416-952-0489
Fax: 416-952-0516
rob.bergevin@tc.gc.ca
Acting Regional Director, Communications, Natacha A. Brun
Tel: 416-952-0156
Fax: 416-952-2174
natacha.brun@tc.gc.ca
Regional Director, Marine, Michael J. Dwyer
Tel: 519-383-1825
Fax: 519-464-5119
michaelj.dwyer@tc.gc.ca
Regional Director, Finance & Administration, Jason Gaetner
Tel: 416-952-0389
jason.gaertner@tc.gc.ca
Regional Director, Marine, Surface & Intermodal Security, Jack C. Goodman
Tel: 416-952-0184
jack.goodman@tc.gc.ca
Regional Director, Coordination & Policy, John G. Higham
Tel: 416-952-0168
john.higham@tc.gc.ca
Regional Director, Surface, Andre R. Lalonde
Tel: 416-954-9951
andre.lalonde@tc.gc.ca
Regional Director, Corporate Services, Shaun P. O'Reilly
Tel: 416-952-0460
Fax: 416-952-0370
shaun.oreilly@tc.gc.ca
Regional Director, Civil Aviation, Michael R. Stephenson
Tel: 416-952-2170
michael.stephenson@tc.gc.ca
Acting Regional Director, Civil Aviation, Joseph Szwalek
Tel: 416-952-0167
joseph.szwalek@tc.gc.ca
Pacific
#620, 800 Burrard St., Vancouver, BC V6Z 2J8
Tel: 604-666-5575
Fax: 604-666-4839
Regional Director General, Michael A. Henderson
Tel: 604-666-5849
michael.henderson@tc.gc.ca
Regional Director, Human Resources, Jasmir Basi
Tel: 604-666-4985
Fax: 604-666-5168
jasmir.basi@tc.gc.ca
Regional Director, Transportation Security, Brian Bramah
Tel: 604-666-4733
brian.bramah@tc.gc.ca
Regional Director, Finance & Administration, Marisol Grossling
Tel: 604-666-5350
Fax: 604-666-0725
marisol.grossling@tc.gc.ca
Regional Director, Corporate Services, Greg Gustavson
Tel: 604-666-5853
Fax: 604-666-0725
greg.gustavson@tc.gc.ca
Regional Director, Surface, Trevor Heryet
Tel: 604-666-0012
trevor.heryet@tc.gc.ca
Regional Director, Marine, James V.B. Lawson
Tel: 604-666-5470
james.lawson@tc.gc.ca
Regional Director, Communications, Rod Nelson
Tel: 604-666-1675
rod.nelson@tc.gc.ca
Regional Director, Civil Aviation, David J. Nowzek
Tel: 604-666-8317
Fax: 604-666-1175
david.nowzek@tc.gc.ca
Regional Director, Coordination & Policy, Mimi Sukhdeo
Tel: 604-666-5858
Fax: 604-666-7255
mimi.sukhdeo@tc.gc.ca
Acting Regional Director, Marine, To For Yeung
Tel: 604-666-9179
tofor.yeung@tc.gc.ca
Regional Director, Programs, Lori Young
Tel: 604-666-2387
lori.young@tc.gc.ca
Prairie & Northern
344 Edmonton St., 1st Fl., Winnipeg, MB R3C 0P6
Tel: 204-983-4341
Fax: 204-984-2069
Regional Director General, Michele Taylor
Tel: 204-984-8105
Fax: 204-984-8119
michele.taylor@tc.gc.ca
Regional Director, Finance & Administration, Sharon A. Bain
Tel: 204-983-4358
Fax: 204-983-0769
sharon.bain@tc.gc.ca
Acting Regional Director, Transportation Security, Steven P. Barker
Tel: 204-983-8330
steven.barker@tc.gc.ca
Regional Director, Human Resources, Claire Carriere
Tel: 204-983-3386
claire.carriere@tc.gc.ca
Regional Director, Surface, Mark Condrad
Tel: 204-983-2991
mark.conrad@tc.gc.ca
Regional Director, Civil Aviation, Kate M. Fletcher
Tel: 204-983-4373
kate.fletcher@tc.gc.ca
Regional Director, Coordination & Policy, Todd Frederickson
Tel: 204-984-6887
todd.frederickson@tc.gc.ca
Regional Director, Communications & Marketing, Susan A. McLennan
Tel: 204-983-6315
susan.mclennan@tc.gc.ca
Regional Director, Corporate Services, Scott Nichols
Tel: 204-984-3454
scott.nichols@tc.gc.ca
Regional Director, Programs, Harvey Nikkel
Tel: 204-983-4376
Fax: 204-983-5048
harvey.nikkel@tc.gc.ca
Regional Director, Marine, Desmond Raymond
Tel: 204-984-1624
Fax: 204-984-8417
desmond.raymond@tc.gc.ca
Regional Director, Marine, Peter Timonin
Tel: 613-998-0600
Fax: 613-991-5670
peter.timonin@tc.gc.ca
Québec
700, Leigh Capréol, 2e étage, Dorval, QC H4Y 1G7

Tel: 514-633-3580
Fax: 514-633-3585
Regional Director General, André Lapointe
Tel: 514-633-2717
Fax: 514-633-2720
andre.lapointe@tc.gc.ca
Regional Director, Marine, Michel Boulianne
Tel: 418-648-4618
Fax: 418-648-3790
michel.boulianne@tc.gc.ca
Regional Director, Finance & Administration, Susie Couto
Tel: 514-633-3032
Fax: 514-633-3705
susie.couto@tc.gc.ca
Regional Director, Surface Transportation, Hélène Gagnon
Tel: 514-633-2747
helene.gagnon@tc.gc.ca
Acting Director, Port & Airport, Ginette Gallant
Tel: 418-986-3785
Fax: 418-986-4751
ginette.gallant@tc.gc.ca
Regional Director, Coordination & Policy, Daniel Grochowalski
Tel: 514-633-2747
daniel.grochowalski@tc.gc.ca
Regional Director, Communications, Kim Hogan
Tel: 514-633-2741
kim.hogan@tc.gc.ca
Acting Regional Director, Programs, Vincent Jarry
Tel: 514-633-3254
Fax: 514-633-3250
vincent.jarry@tc.gc.ca
Regional Director, Transportation Security, Joanna Manger
Tel: 514-633-3557
joanna.manger@tc.gc.ca
Regional Director, Surface Transportation, Luciano Martin
Tel: 514-283-1774
Fax: 514-283-8234
luciano.martin@tc.gc.ca
Regional Director, Corporate Services, Adriana Mastrostefano
Tel: 514-633-3418
adriana.mastrostefano@tc.gc.ca
Regional Director, Human Resources, Mélanie Morier
Tel: 514-633-3500
melanie.morier@tc.gc.ca
Director, Sept-Îles Airport, Karen Young
Tel: 418-962-8212
Fax: 418-962-8262
karen.young@tc.gc.ca

Transportation Safety Board of Canada / Bureau de la sécurité des transports du Canada

200 Promenade du Portage, 4th Fl., Ottawa, ON K1A 1K8
Tel: 819-994-3741
Fax: 819-997-2239
Toll-Free: 800-387-3557
TTY: 819-953-7287
www.tsb.gc.ca
The Board is an independent agency reporting to Parliament through the President of the Queen's Privy Council. The formal name for the Board is the Canadian Transportation Accident Investigation & Safety Board. Its sole aim is the advancement of transportation safety in the marine, rail, pipeline & air modes of transport. The TSB conducts independent investigations into selected transportation occurences in order to make findings as to their causes & contributing factors; identifies safety deficiences, & makes recommendations designed to prevent further occurences. Because the Board is independent, its transportation accident investigations are completely separate from the regulatory agencies responsible for transportation. In making findings & recommendations it is not the function of the Board to assign fault or determine civil liability.

Chair, Wendy A. Tadros
Tel: 819-994-8000
Fax: 819-994-9759
Wendy.Tadros@tsb.gc.ca
Other Communications: Executive Assistant, Phone: 819-994-8002

Chief Operating Officer, Jean L. Laporte
Tel: 819-994-8004
Fax: 819-994-9759
Jean.Laporte@bst-tsb.gc.ca

Director, Investigations, Air, Mark Clitsome
Tel: 819-994-3813
Fax: 819-953-9586

Director, Investigations, Rail/Pipeline, Kirby Jang
Tel: 819-953-6470
Fax: 819-953-7876
Kirby.jang@bst-tsb.gc.ca
Other Communications: Administrative Assistant, Phone: 819-953-1646

Director, Investigations, Marine, Marc-André Poisson
Tel: 819-953-1398
Marc-Andre.Poisson@bst-tsb.gc.ca

Manager, Communications Products & Services, Publishing & Linquistic Services, Jacynthe Dubé
Tel: 819-934-1762
Fax: 819-953-1733
Jacynthe.Dube@bst-tsb.gc.ca

Acting Manager, Publishing & Linguistic Services, Chantal Laflamme
Tel: 819-994-8032
Fax: 819-953-1733
chantal.laflamme@bst-tsb.gc.ca

Corporate Services Directorate / Direction générale des services intégrés
Director General, Chantal Lemyre
Tel: 819-994-8003
Fax: 819-953-9648
chantal.lemyre@bst-tsb.gc.ca
Manager, Informatics, Peter Kusovac
Tel: 819-953-2636
Fax: 819-934-7479
peter.kusovac@bst-tsb.gc.ca
Manager, Finance & Administration, Brenda O'Reilly
Tel: 819-994-8001
Fax: 819-953-9648
brenda.oreilly@bst-tsb.gc.ca
Manager, Information Management, Jean-Louis Parent
Tel: 819-994-0385
Fax: 819-953-9648
Jean-Louis.Parent@bst-tsb.gc.ca
Manager, Human Resources, Lise Seguin
Tel: 819-994-8010
Fax: 819-994-8012
lise.seguin@bst-tsb.gc.ca

Operations Services Branch / Services à l'appui des opérations
Manager, Material Analysis & Structures, Dr. Sylvie Dionne
Tel: 613-949-3949
Fax: 613-998-5572
sylvie.dionne@bst-tsb.gc.ca
Manager, Human Factors & Macro Analysis, Leo Donati
Tel: 819-994-4420
Fax: 819-953-2160
Leo.Donati@bst-tsb.gc.ca
Manager, Systems & Engineering Services, Jim Foot
Tel: 613-990-0913
Fax: 613-998-5572
Jim.Foot@bst-tsb.gc.ca
Manager, Recorder & Vehicle Performance, Ted Givins
Tel: 613-998-3848
Fax: 613-998-5572
ted.givins@bst-tsb.gc.ca
Manager, Multi-Modal Training & Standards, Susan Greene
Tel: 819-934-5467
Fax: 819-934-7479
susan.greene@bst-tsb.gc.ca

Treasury Board of Canada / Conseil du Trésor du Canada

140 O'Connor St., Ottawa, ON K1A 0R5
Tel: 613-957-2400
Fax: 613-941-4000
Toll-Free: 877-636-0656
TTY: 613-957-9090
www.tbs-sct.gc.ca
The Treasury Board is a Cabinet Committee of government headed by the President of the Treasury Board. The committee constituting the Treasury Board includes, in addition to the President, the Minister of Finance & four other ministers appointed by the Governor-in-Council. The main role of the Treasury Board is the management of the government's financial, personnel & administrative responsibilities. The Treasury Board derives its authority primarily from the Financial Administration Act & is supported by the Treasury Board Secretariat.
Acts Administered:
Alternative Fuels Act
Federal Real Property & Federal Immovables Act

Minister, FedNor; President, Treasury Board, Hon. Tony Clement
Tel: 613-944-7740
Fax: 613-992-5092

Associated Agencies, Boards & Commissions:
• **Public Sector Pension Investment Board / Office d'investissement des régimes de pensions du secteur public**
#200, 440 Laurier Ave. West
Ottawa, ON K1R 7X6
Tel: 613-782-3095
Fax: 613-782-6864
info@investpsp.ca
www.investpsp.ca
Crown corporation established by Parliament by the Public Sector Pension Investment Board Act (September 1999). The mandate of PSP Investments is to manage employer & employee contributions made after April 1, 2000 to the federal Public Service, the Canadian Forces & the Royal Canadian Mounted Police pension funds.
• **Canada Public Service Agency (CPSA) / Agence de la fonction publique du Canada (AFPC)**
122 Bank St.
Ottawa, ON K1A 0R5
Created in 2003 to put in place a new human resources management regime in the public service of Canada. Formerly the Public Service Human Resources Management Agency of Canada (PSHRMAC).
• **Public Service Labour Relations Board / Commission des relations de travail dans la fonction publique**
CD Howe Building
240 Sparks St., 6th Fl.
PO Box 1525 B
Ottawa, ON K1P 5V2
Tel: 613-990-1800
Fax: 613-990-1849
Toll-free: 866-931-3454
mail.courrier@pslrb-crtfp.gc.ca
www.pslrb-crtfp.gc.ca
Independent, quasi-judicial statutory tribunal responsible for administering the collective bargaining & grievance adjudication systems in the federal Public & Parliamentary Service. Also provides mediation & conflict resolution services, compensation analysis & research services.

Office of the Commissioner of Lobbying
255 Albert St., 10th Fl., Ottawa, ON K1A 0R5
Tel: 613-957-2760
Fax: 613-957-3078
questionslobbying@ocl-cal.gc.ca
www.ocl-cal.gc.ca/eic/site/lobbyist-lobbyiste1.nsf/eng/Home
Includes all known federal contaminated sites for which federal departments & agencies (excluding Crown corporations) are accountable. Also includes some non-federal sites for which the government has accepted some or all responsibility. Sites are classified at the time of assessment for contaminants, in a system developed by the Canadian Council of Ministers of Environment.
Commissioner of Lobbying, Karen E. Shepherd
Tel: 613-941-9873
Fax: 613-957-3078
Other Communications: Executive Assistant, Phone: 613-941-3782
Deputy Commissioner, René Leblanc
Tel: 613-952-4250
Fax: 613-957-3078
Other Communications: Administrative Assistant, Phone: 613-941-7848
Chief Financial Officer, Johanne Blais
Tel: 613-952-4298
Fax: 613-957-3078
Chief Information Officer, Darquise Beauvais
Tel: 613-941-7883
Fax: 613-957-3078

Director, Registrations & Client Services, Gillian Cantello
Tel: 613-941-3394
Fax: 613-957-3078
Director, Investigations, Phil K. McIntosh
Tel: 613-948-1788
Fax: 613-957-3078

Minister, Veterans Affairs, Hon. Steven Blaney
Tel: 613-992-7434
Fax: 613-995-6856
steven.blaney@parl.gc.ca

VIA Rail Canada Inc.

#500, 3, Place Ville-Marie, Montréal, QC H3B 2C9
Tél: 514-871-6000
Téléc: 514-871-6104
Ligne sans frais: 888-842-7245
TTY: 800-268-9503
www.viarail.ca
twitter.com/VIA_Rail
www.facebook.com/viarailcanada
Established in 1977, VIA Rail Canada is a Crown corporation that manages the national passenger rail network. The corporation serves 450 communities throughout Canada. VIA works to offer safe, efficient, & environmentally responsible public transportation.
Environmental intiatives include a reduction in emissions & a reduce, re-use & recycle program. Under the capital investment plan, older locomotives & passenger cars are being rebuilt. The corporation also offers a Green Procurement Guide to promote the use of environmentally responsible products in all its activities.

Chair, Paul G. Smith

President & Chief Executive Officer, Marc Laliberté

Chief Information Officer, Yves Bourbonnais

Chief Human Resources Officer, Laurent F. Caron

Chief Marketing & Sales Officer, Steve Del Bosco

Chief Legal & Corporate Affairs Officer; Corporate Secretary, Yves Desjardins-Siciliano

Chief Customer Experience & Operating Officer, Denis Pinsonneault

Chief Financial & Administrative Officer, Robert St-Jean

Senior Director, Safety, Security, & Risk Management, Jean Tierney

Western Economic Diversification Canada (WD) / Diversification de l'économie de l'Ouest Canada (DEO)

Canada Place, #1500, 9700 Jasper Ave. NW, Edmonton, AB T5J 4H7
Tel: 780-495-4164
Fax: 780-495-4557
Toll-Free: 888-338-9378
TTY: 877-303-3388
www.wd-deo.gc.ca
Responsible for promoting economic growth & diversification in the West. By investing in innovation, fostering entrepreneurship & using partnerships to enhance community sustainability, WD is helping to create a more prosperous future for western Canadians.Invests in R&D & commercialization in environmental technologies as a focus area for innovation strategies.

Minister of State (Western Economic Diversification), Hon. Lynne Yelich
Tel: 613-952-2768
Fax: 613-952-1155
lynne.yelich@parl.gc.ca

Deputy Minister, Daphne Meredith
Tel: 780-495-5772
Fax: 780-495-6222
Other Communications: Ottawa: 613-952-9382

Chief of Staff, Office of the Minister, Stacey Gairdner
Tel: 613-952-2768
Fax: 613-957-1155

Director General, Planning & Programs, Nadean Langlois
Tel: 780-495-4973
Fax: 780-495-6876

Director General, Audit, Evaluation & Disclosure, Donald MacDonald
Tel: 780-495-8437
Fax: 780-495-6223

Director General, Finance & Management Accountability, Cathy Matthews
Tel: 780-495-6336
Fax: 780-495-4434

Executive Director, Alberta Federal Council, Marcel Préville
Tel: 780-495-5413

Executive Director, Finance & Corporate Management, Jim Saunderson
Tel: 780-495-4301
Fax: 780-495-7618
Other Communications: Administrative Assistant, Phone: 780-495-5791

Headquarters / Administration centrale
Tel: 780-495-4164
Fax: 780-495-5808
Director General, Planning & Programs, Nadean Langlois
Tel: 780-495-4873
Fax: 780-495-6876
Director General, Audit, Evaluation & Disclosure, Donald MacDonald
Tel: 780-495-8437
Fax: 780-495-6223
Director General, Finance & Management Accountability, Cathy Matthews
Tel: 780-495-6336
Fax: 780-495-4434
Executive Director, Policy Planning & Performance Measurement, Brant Popp
Tel: 780-495-6549
Fax: 780-495-6876
Executive Director, Finance & Corporate Management, Jim Saunderson
Tel: 780-495-4301
Fax: 780-495-7618
Alberta (Edmonton)
Canada Place, #1500, 9700 Jasper Ave. Northwest, Edmonton, AB T5J 4H7
Tel: 780-495-4164
Fax: 780-495-4557
Toll-Free: 888-338-9378
TTY: 877-303-3388
Assistant Deputy Minister, Doug Maley
Tel: 780-495-4168
Fax: 780-495-6222
Other Communications: Executive Assistant, Phone: 780-495-4960
Director General, Operations, David Woynorowski
Tel: 780-495-4970
Fax: 780-495-4557
Director, Policy, Planning & External Relations, Neil Kirkpatrick
Tel: 780-495-6796
Fax: 780-495-4557
British Columbia (Vancouver)
Price Waterhouse Bldg., #700, 333 Seymour St., Vancouver, BC V6B 5G9
Tel: 604-666-6256
Fax: 604-666-2353
Toll-Free: 888-338-9378
TTY: 877-303-3388
Assistant Deputy Minister, Gerry Salembier
Tel: 604-666-6366
Fax: 604-666-1510
Director General, Naina Sloan
Tel: 604-666-7011
Fax: 604-666-2353
Director, Innovation & Competitiveness, Tammy Schulz
Tel: 604-666-1889
Fax: 604-666-2353
Director, Policy, Planning & Performance Integration, Martin Sutherland
Tel: 604-666-4766
Fax: 604-666-2353
Calgary
#300, 639 - 5 Ave. SW, Calgary, AB T2P 0M9
Tel: 403-292-5458
Fax: 403-292-5487
Toll-Free: 888-338-9378
TTY: 877-303-3388
Acting Director, Neil Kirkpatrick
Tel: 403-292-4426
Fax: 403-292-5487
Manitoba (Winnipeg)
The Cargill Bldg., #620, 240 Graham Ave., Winnipeg, MB R3C 0J7
Tel: 204-983-4472
Fax: 204-983-3852
Toll-Free: 888-338-9378
TTY: 877-303-3388
Assistant Deputy Minister, Marilyn Kapitany
Tel: 204-983-5715
Fax: 204-983-0966
Other Communications: Executive Assistant, Phone: 204-983-4467
Executive Director, Manitoba Federal Council Secretariat, Cynthia Foreman
Tel: 204-984-6815
Fax: 204-984-0105
Director General, Operations, Derryl Millar
Tel: 204-983-4531
Fax: 204-983-1280
Director, Economic Recovery Branch, France Guimond
Tel: 204-984-2438
Fax: 204-983-1280
Director, Policy, Planning & External Relations, Tim Hibbard
Tel: 204-983-0689
Fax: 204-984-0360
Associate Director, Infrastructure Secretariat, Ivan Didiuk
Tel: 204-945-5557
Fax: 204-948-2035
Ottawa Liaison Office
#500, 141 Laurier Ave. West, Ottawa, ON K1P 5J3
Tel: 613-952-2768
Fax: 613-952-9384
TTY: 877-303-3388
Assistant Deputy Minister, James Meddings
Tel: 613-952-7096
Fax: 613-954-1044
Director, Strategic Policy & Advocacy, Francesco Del Bianco
Tel: 613-954-9640
Fax: 613-952-3434
Director, Consultation, Marketing & Communications, Peter G. Wallace
Tel: 613-952-7101
Fax: 613-952-6775
Saskatchewan (Saskatoon)
S.J. Cohen Bldg., #601, 119 - 4 Ave. South, PO Box 2025Saskatoon, SK S7K 3S7
Tel: 306-975-4373
Fax: 306-975-5484
Toll-Free: 888-338-9378
TTY: 877-303-3388
Assistant Deputy Minister, Sharon Lee Smith
Tel: 306-975-5858
Fax: 306-975-5484
Executive Director, Saskatchewan Federal Council, Rhonda Laing
Tel: 306-975-5944
Fax: 306-975-5484
Director General, Operations, Doug Zolinsky
Tel: 306-975-6988
Fax: 306-975-5484

Government of Alberta

Seat of Government: PO Box 1333Edmonton, AB T5J 2N2
Tel: 780-427-2711
Fax: 780-422-2852
Toll-Free: -310-0000
TTY: 800-232-7215
www.alberta.ca
Other Communication: TTY: 427-9999 (in Edmonton)
Alberta was proclaimed as a province on September 1, 1905. The province has an elected Legislative Assembly, consisting of 83 members. The Premier & the Cabinet exercise executive power. The representative of the Crown is the Lieutenant Governor, who is appointed by the Governor General. The population as of the census of 2011 was 3,645,257.

Federal/Provincial Government

Office of the Child & Youth Advocate
Peace Hills Trust Tower, #805, 10011 - 109 St., Edmonton, AB T5J 3S8
Tel: 780-422-6056
Fax: 780-644-8833
Toll-Free: 800-661-3446
www.alberta.ca/advocate
Other Communication: Southern Alberta Advocacy Services, Phone: 403-297-8435, Fax: 403-297-4456
Secondary Address: 301 - 14 St. NW
Southern Alberta Advocacy Services, Professional Bldg.
Calgary, AB T2N 2A1
As of April 1, 2012, the Child & Youth Advocate is an independent officer reporting to the Legislature under the newly created Child & Youth Advocate Act.
Acts Administered:
Child & Youth Advocate Act
Child, Youth & Family Enhancement Act
Protection of Sexually Exploited Children Act

Alberta Aboriginal Relations

Commerce Place, 10155 - 102 St., 20th Fl., Edmonton, AB T5J 4G8
Aboriginal Relations works with Aboriginal communities & other partners to enhance social & economic opportunities for Alberta's Aboriginal people.

Minister, Aboriginal Relations, Robin Campbell
Tel: 780-422-4144
Fax: 780-644-8389
Social Media: www.facebook.com/robin.campbell.3990
Legislature Building
#323, 10800 - 97 Ave.
Edmonton, AB T5K 2B6

Deputy Minister, Bill Werry
Tel: 780-643-9081
Fax: 780-422-2745
bill.werry@gov.ab.ca

Director, Communications, David Dear
Tel: 780-427-4210
Fax: 780-415-9548
david.dear@gov.ab.ca

Director, Business Integration & Strategy, Dale Unrau
Tel: 780-638-4331
Fax: 780-422-2745
dale.unrau@gov.ab.ca

Writer/Editor, Ministerial Correspondence Unit, Joanna Verhelst
Tel: 780-427-4627
Fax: 780-422-2745
joanna.verhelst@gov.ab.ca

Associated Agencies, Boards & Commissions:
• **Métis Settlements Appeal Tribunal (MSAT)**
14605 - 134 Ave. NW
Edmonton, AB T5L 4S9
Tel: 780-422-1541
Fax: 780-422-0019
Toll-free: 800-661-8864
Chair, Métis Settlements Appeal Tribunal, Don Cunningham
Tel: 780-422-4978
Fax: 780-422-0019
don.cunningham@gov.ab.ca
Director & Tribunal Secretary, Harold Robinson
Tel: 780-422-5152
Fax: 780-422-0019
harold.robinson@gov.ab.ca
Officer, Dispute Resolution, Harry Cunningham
Tel: 780-422-4362
Fax: 780-422-0019
harry.cunningham@gov.ab.ca
Officer, Dispute Resolution, Michael Gubbels
Tel: 780-422-5891
Fax: 780-422-0019
michael.gubbels@gov.ab.ca
Officer, Oil & Gas, Karen Mustus
Tel: 780-422-1739
Fax: 780-422-0019
karen.mustus@gov.ab.ca
Officer, Systems & Research, BJ Simpson
Tel: 780-422-5893
Fax: 780-422-0091
bj.simpson@gov.ab.ca
• **Métis Settlements Ombudsman Office**
#203, 10525 - 170 St.
Edmonton, AB T5P 4W2
Tel: 780-427-9828
Fax: 780-427-9962
Toll-free: 866-427-6813
Ombudsman, Harley Johnson
Tel: 780-427-9463
Fax: 780-427-9962
harley.johnson@gov.ab.ca
Team Lead / Senior Investigator, Joe Pendleton
Tel: 780-422-3054
Fax: 780-427-9962
joe.pendleton@gov.ab.ca
Investigator & Advisor, Keith Pink
Tel: 780-427-6835
Fax: 780-427-9962
keith.pink@gov.ab.ca

Consultation & Land Claims
Commerce Place, 10155 - 102 St., 20th Fl., Edmonton, AB T5J 4G8
Tel: 780-427-0417
Fax: 780-427-0401
Assistant Deputy Minister, Stan Rutwind, Q.C.
Tel: 780-643-1731
Fax: 780-427-0401
stan.rutwind@gov.ab.ca
Executive Director, Aboriginal Consultation, Cole Pederson
Tel: 780-427-8441
Fax: 780-427-0401
cole.pederson@gov.ab.ca
Director, Land Claims, Steven Andres
Tel: 780-427-6084
Fax: 780-427-0401
steven.andres@gov.ab.ca
Director, Aboriginal Consultation, Cory Enns
Tel: 780-644-1055
Fax: 780-427-0401
cory.enns@gov.ab.ca
Senior Manager, Consultation Policy & Regional Land Issues, Ashley Bodnar
Tel: 780-644-1036
Fax: 780-427-0401
ashley.bodnar@gov.ab.ca
Manager, Negotiation Support, Land Claims, Kathryn Coxson
Tel: 780-644-1003
Fax: 780-427-0401
kathryn.coxson@gov.ab.ca

First Nations & Metis Relations
Commerce Place, 10155 - 102 St., 19th Fl., Edmonton, AB T5J 4G8
Acting Assistant Deputy Minister, Cameron Henry
Tel: 780-427-2008
Fax: 780-427-4019
cameron.henry@gov.ab.ca
Executive Director, Policy & Planning, Vacant
Tel: 780-427-2008
Fax: 780-427-0401
Executive Director, Métis Relations, Thomas Droege
Tel: 780-427-9431
Fax: 780-427-4019
thomas.droege@gov.ab.ca
Executive Director, First Nations Relations, Cynthia Dunnigan
Tel: 780-415-6141
Fax: 780-427-1760
cynthia.dunnigan@gov.ab.ca
Director, First Nations Development Fund, Peter Croseen
Tel: 780-415-6142
Fax: 780-427-0401
peter.crossen@gov.ab.ca
Director, Aboriginal Economic Partnerships, Lanny Der
Tel: 780-644-1057
Fax: 780-427-1760
lanny.der@gov.ab.ca
Director, Métis Relations, Linda Lewis
Tel: 780-644-1004
Fax: 780-427-4019
linda.lewis@gov.ab.ca
Director, First Nations & Urban Initiatives, Kristina Midbo
Tel: 780-427-9394
Fax: 780-427-1760
kristina.midbo@gov.ab.ca
Director, Aboriginal Community Initiatives, Bronwyn Shoush
Tel: 780-427-3060
Fax: 780-427-4019
bronwyn.shoush@gov.ab.ca
Director, Planning & Research, Ellen Tian
Tel: 780-422-4061
Fax: 780-427-1760
ellen.tian@gov.ab.ca
Registrar, Métis Settlements Land Registry, Lisa Chartrand
Tel: 780-415-0168
Fax: 780-427-3656
lisa.chartrand@gov.ab.ca

Alberta Agriculture & Rural Development

JG O'Donoghue Bldg., #100A, 7000 - 113th St., Edmonton, AB T6H 5T6
Tel: 780-427-2727
Toll-Free: -310-3276
duke@gov.ab.ca
www.agric.gov.ab.ca
Alberta's Agriculture & Rural Development is engaged in the following key activities: facilitating sustainable industry growth, enhancing rural sustainability, & strengthening business risk management.
Acts Administered:
Agricultural Operations Practices Act
Agricultural Pests Act
Agricultural Service Board Act
Agricultural Societies Act
Agriculture Financial Services Act
Agriculture Satutes Repeal Act, 2008
Alberta Wheat & Barley Test Market Act
Animal Health Act
Animal Keepers Act
Animal Protection Act
Bee Act
Crop Liens Priorities Act
Crop Payments Act
Dairy Industry Act
Farm Implement Act
Farm Implement Dealerships Act
Feeder Associations Guarantee Act
Fuel Tax Act
Fur Farms Act
Gas Distribution Act
Government Accountability Act
Government Organization Act
Heating Oil & Propane Rebate Act
Horned Cattle Purchases Repeal Act
Irrigation Districts Act
Line Fence Act
Livestock & Livestock Products Act
Livestock Identification & Commerce Act
Livestock Industry Diversification Act
Marketing of Agricultural Products Act
Meat Inspection Act
Rural Electrification Loan Act
Rural Electrification Long-term Financing Act
Rural Utilities Act
Soil Conservation Act
Stray Animals Act
Vegetable Sales (Alberta) Repeal Act
Weed Control Act
Wheat Board Money Trust Act
Women's Institute Act

Minister, Agriculture & Rural Development, Hon. Verlyn Olson, QC
Constituency: Wetaskiwin-Camrose
Tel: 780-427-2137
Fax: 780-422-6035
olson.votepc.ca
Social Media: www.facebook.com/verlynolsonmla
Legislature Building
#228, 10800 - 97 Ave.
Edmonton, AB T5K 2B6

Deputy Minister, John Knapp
Tel: 780-427-2145
Fax: 780-415-6002
john.knapp@gov.ab.ca
JG O'Donoghue Building

7000 - 113 St., 3rd Fl.
Edmonton, AB T6H 5T6

Executive Director, Human Resource Services & Facilities Management Services, Heather K.M. Behman
Tel: 780-427-2430
Fax: 780-427-3398
heather.behman@gov.ab.ca
JG O'Donoghue Building
7000 - 113 St., 3rd Fl.
Edmonton, AB T6H 5T6

Acting Director, Communications Branch, David Hennig
Tel: 780-422-1177
Fax: 780-638-4477
david.hennig@gov.ab.ca

Executive Director/Senior Financial Officer, Financial & Business Planning Services Division, Anne Halldorson
Tel: 780-427-3216
Fax: 780-422-6529
anne.halldorson@gov.ab.ca

Associated Agencies, Boards & Commissions:
• Agricultural Products Marketing Council
JG O'Donoghue Bldg.
7000 - 113 St., 3rd Fl.
Edmonton, AB T6H 5T6
Tel: 780-427-2164
Fax: 780-422-9690
The Alberta Agricultural Products Marketing Council supports legislation & regulations & offers policy advice to the Minister of Agriculture & Rural Development & industry organizations.
General Manager, David Burdek
Tel: 780-427-4516
Fax: 780-422-9690
dave.burdek@gov.ab.ca
President & Managing Director, Brad Klak
Tel: 403-782-8225
Fax: 403-782-4226
brad.klak@afsc.ca
Other Communications: tammy.andruski@afsc.ca
• Alberta Grains Council (AGC)
JG O'Donoghue Bldg.
7000 - 113 St., 3rd Fl.
Edmonton, AB T6H 5T6
Tel: 780-427-7329
Fax: 780-422-9690
www1.agric.gov.ab.ca/$department/deptdocs.nsf/all/agc2620
The Alberta Grains Council makes recommendations to the Minister of Agriculture & Rural Affairs about issues in the grain industry.
Associate General Manager, Julie Toma
Tel: 780-427-3080
Fax: 780-422-9690
julie.toma@gov.ab.ca
General Manager, John Brown
Tel: 403-782-8033
Fax: 403-782-5514
john.brown@gov.ab.ca
Associate General Manager, Julie Toma
Tel: 780-427-3080
Fax: 780-422-9690
julie.toma@gov.ab.ca
• Alberta Livestock & Meat Agency (ALMA)
Ellwood Office Park South
#101, 1003 Ellwood Rd. SW
Edmonton, AB T6X 0B3
Tel: 780-638-1699
Fax: 780-638-6495
info@almaltd.ca
www.alma.alberta.ca
The provincial government agency was established to advance the Alberta Livestock & Meat Strategy. The goal of the Alberta Livestock & Meat Agency is to develop a profitable & competitive Alberta livestock & meat industry, by offering information & investment opportunities to the industry & the Government of Alberta.
Board Chair, Dr. David A. Chalack, DVM
President & Chief Executive Officer, Gordon Cove
Tel: 780-638-6489
Gordon.Cove@almaltd.ca
• Irrigation Council
Provincial Bldg.
200 - 5 Ave. South, 3rd Fl.
Lethbridge, AB T1J 4L1
Tel: 403-381-5176
Fax: 403-382-4406
www1.agric.gov.ab.ca/$department/deptdocs.nsf/all/irc9432
The Irrigation Council was established under Section 50 of the Irrigation Districts Act. The provincial agency reports to the Minister of Agriculture & Rural Development.
Chair, Peter Schuld
Vice-Chair, Richard Stamp
Council Member, David Ardell
Council Member, Casey Gouw, Jr.
Council Member, Brent Paterson
Council Member, Pat Shimbashi
• Office of the Farmers' Advocate
JG O'Donoghue Bldg.
7000 - 113 St.
Edmonton, AB T6H 5T6
Tel: 780-644-5365
Toll-free: -310-3276
www1.agric.gov.ab.ca/$department/deptdocs.nsf/all/ofa2621
The Farmers' Advocate Office offers rural consumer protection, rural opportunities, & fair process for rural Albertans. The Office supports programs to settle disputes or offer appeals privately.
Assistant Farmers' Advocate, Rural Affairs, Graham Gilchrist
Tel: 780-427-7956
graham.gilchrist@gov.ab.ca
Assistant Farmers' Advocate, Land & Energy, Carol Goodfellow
Tel: 780-427-2350
carol.goodfellow@gov.ab.ca
Assistant Farmers' Advocate, Communications & Programs, Janet Patriquin
Tel: 780-427-7950
janet.patriquin@gov.ab.ca
Assistant Farmers' Advocate & Farm Implement Inspector, Robert I. Martin
Tel: 780-415-1670
robert.i.martin@gov.ab.ca
Coordinator, Administration, Roseline Soparlo
Tel: 780-427-2389
roseline.soparlo@gov.ab.ca

Food Safety & Technology Sector
3rd fl. JG O'Donoghue Bldg., 7000 - 113 St., Edmonton, AB T6H 5T6
Tel: 780-427-6159

Food Safety & Animal Health Division
Agriculture & Rural Development, OS Longman Bldg., 6909 - 116 St., Edmonton, AB T6H 4P2
Tel: 780-427-6159
Executive Director, Food Safety & Animal Health Division, Greg Orriss
Tel: 780-427-6159
Fax: 780-427-1437
greg.orriss@gov.ab.ca

Office of the Chief Provincial Veterinarian
OS Longman Bldg., 6909 - 116 St., Edmonton, T6H 4P2
Tel: 780-427-3448
Fax: 780-415-0810
Chief Provincial Veterinarian, Dr. Gerald Hauer
Tel: 780-415-9503
Fax: 780-415-0810
gerald.hauer@gov.ab.ca
Program Veterinarian, Dr. Hernan Ortegon
Tel: 780-644-2148
Fax: 780-427-1437
hernan.ortegon@gov.ab.ca
Branch Head & Deputy Chief, Animal Health Branch, Dr. Chris Morley
Tel: 780-427-6406
Fax: 780-427-1437
chris.morley@gov.ab.ca
Unit Leader, Livestock Welfare, Michelle Follensbee
Tel: 780-644-3072
Fax: 780-415-0810
michelle.follensbee@gov.ab.ca

Information Management Division
JG O'Donoghue Bldg, 7000 - 113 St., 1st Fl., Edmonton, AB T6H 5T6
Tel: 780-427-2727
Fax: 780-427-2861
Director, Information Management, Gerard Vaillancourt
Tel: 780-422-6796
Fax: 780-427-2861
gerard.vaillancourt@gov.ab.ca
Division Administrator, Information Management, Rita Splawinski
Tel: 780-422-3375
Fax: 780-427-2861
rita.splawinski@gov.ab.ca

Information Technology Division
JG O'Donoghue Bldg., 7000 - 113 St., 2nd Fl., Edmonton, AB T6H 5T6
Executive Director, Information Technology, Rob Pungor
Tel: 780-422-6660
Fax: 780-422-4004
rob.pungor@gov.ab.ca
Manager, Business Services, Dean Pratt
Tel: 780-422-2142
Fax: 780-422-4004
dean.pratt@gov.ab.ca
Manager, Infrastructure, Chris Wright
Tel: 780-415-2361
Fax: 780-422-4004
chris.wright@gov.ab.ca

Regulatory Services Division
JG O'Donoghue Bldg., 7000 - 113 St., 3rd Fl., Edmonton, AB T6H 5T6
Tel: 780-422-7197
Fax: 780-422-4513
Executive Director, Regulatory Services Division, Cliff Munroe
Tel: 780-422-7249
Fax: 780-422-4513
cliff.munroe@gov.ab.ca
Branch Head, Meat Inspection Branch, Jake Kotowich
Tel: 780-644-2371
Fax: 780-422-4513
jake.kotowich@gov.ab.ca
Branch Head, Inspection & Investigation Branch, Lyle Marianchuk
Tel: 403-340-5320
Fax: 403-340-5870
yle.marianchuk@gov.ab.ca

Rural Utilities Division
JG O'Donoghue Bldg., 7000 - 113 St., 2nd Fl., Edmonton, AB T6H 5T6
Tel: 780-427-0125
Fax: 780-422-1613
Executive Director, Rural Utilities, Terry Holmes
Tel: 780-427-0134
Fax: 780-422-1613
terry.holmes@gov.ab.ca
Branch Head, Rural Electric & Information Systems Branch, Tom Kee
Tel: 780-427-0944
Fax: 780-422-1613
tom.kee@gov.ab.ca
Branch Head, Safety & Technical Services Branch, Bruce Partington
Tel: 780-427-0111
Fax: 780-422-1613
bruce.partington@gov.ab.ca

Industry & Market Development Sector
JG O'Donoghue Bldg., 7000 - 113 St., Edmonton, AB T6H 5T6
Assistant Deputy Minister, Jo-Ann Hall
Tel: 780-427-2439
Fax: 780-422-6317
jo-ann.hall@gov.ab.ca

Research & Innovation Division
JG O'Donoghue Bldg., 7000 - 113 St., 3rd Fl., Edmonton, AB T6H 5T6
Tel: 780-679-5172
Fax: 780-679-5175
Director, Research & Innovation, Connie Phillips
Tel: 780-644-8124
Fax: 780-427-1057
connie.phillips@gov.ab.ca
Branch Head, Livestock Research Branch, Wesley Johnson
Tel: 780-415-0828
Fax: 780-427-1057
wesley.johnson@gov.ab.ca
Branch Head, Bio-Industrial Opportunities Branch, Hong Qi
Tel: 780-644-8128

Fax: 780-638-3586
hong.qi@gov.ab.ca
Senior Manager, Pest Surveillance Branch, Paul Laflamme
Tel: 780-422-4911
Fax: 780-427-1057
paul.laflamme@gov.ab.ca
Branch Head, Food & Bio-Industrial Crops Branch, James Jones
Tel: 780-422-5028
Fax: 780-422-5028
james.jones@gov.ab.ca
Branch Head, Feed Crops Branch, Mark MacNaughton
Tel: 780-782-8033
Fax: 780-782-5514
mark.macnaughton@gov.ab.ca

Food Processing Division
Development Centre, 6309 - 45 St., Leduc, AB T9E 7C5
Tel: 780-986-4793
Fax: 780-986-5138
Executive Director, Food Processing Division, Ken Gossen
Tel: 780-980-4860
Fax: 780-986-5138
ken.gossen@gov.ab.ca
Senior Programs Manager, Programs Branch, Karen Erin
Tel: 780-980-4864
Fax: 780-986-5138
karen.erin@gov.ab.ca
Senior Operations Manager, Operations Branch, Robert Gibson
Tel: 780-980-4866
Fax: 780-980-4250
robert.gibson@gov.ab.ca

Rural Extension & Industry Development Division
Provincial Building, 4709 - 44 Ave., Stony Plain, AB T7Z 1N4
Tel: 780-968-3557
Fax: 780-963-4709
Executive Director, Rural Extension & Industry Development Division, Vacant
Tel: 780-968-3512
Fax: 780-963-4709
Branch Head, Crop Business Development Branch, James Calpas
Tel: 403-340-5329
Fax: 403-340-4896
james.calpas@gov.ab.ca
Branch Head, Agriculture Grant Programs Branch, Murray Greer
Tel: 780-980-4722
Fax: 780-980-4237
murray.greer@gov.ab.ca
Branch Head, Alberta Ag-Info Centre, Ross Hutchison
Tel: 403-742-7542
Fax: 403-742-7527
ross.hutchison@gov.ab.ca
Branch Head, Local / Domestic Market Expansion Branch, Shauna Johnston
Tel: 780-968-3553
Fax: 780-968-3554
shauna.johnston@gov.ab.ca
Branch Head, Livestock & Farm Business Branch, Carlyon Rod
Tel: 780-349-4466
Fax: 780-349-5240
rod.carlyon@gov.ab.ca
Branch Head, Ag-Industry Extension Branch, Barb Shackel-Hardman
Tel: 780-968-3550
Fax: 780-968-3554
barb.shackel.hardman@gov.ab.ca
Branch Head, 4-H Branch, Marguerite Stark
Tel: 403-948-8510
Fax: 780-948-2069
marguerite.stark@gov.ab.ca
Branch Head, Processing Industry Business Development Branch, Lynn Stegman
Tel: 403-340-7010
Fax: 403-340-4896
lynn.stegman@gov.ab.ca

Traceability Division
JG O'Donoghue Bldg., 7000 - 113 St., 3rd Fl., Edmonton, T6H 5T6
Tel: 780-643-1572
Fax: 780-422-3655
Executive Director, Traceability Division, John Brown
Tel: 780-427-2799
Fax: 780-422-3655
john.brown@gov.ab.ca
Coordinator, Traceability Education, Kelly Gordon
Tel: 780-638-3148
Fax: 780-422-3655
kelly.gordon@gov.ab.ca

Policy & Environment Sector
JG O'Donoghue Bldg., 7000 - 113 St., 3rd Fl., Edmonton, AB T6H 5T6
Assistant Deputy Minister, Colin Jeffares
Tel: 780-427-1957
Fax: 780-422-6317
colin.jeffares@gov.ab.ca

Economics & Competitiveness Division
JG O'Donoghue Bldg., 7000 - 113 St., 3rd Fl., Edmonton, AB T6H 5T6
Tel: 780-422-3771
Fax: 780-427-5220
Acting Executive Director, Economics & Competitiveness Division, Don Brown
Tel: 780-644-5634
Fax: 780-427-5220
don.brown@gov.ab.ca

Environmental Stewardship Division
JG O'Donoghue Bldg., 7000 - 113 St., 3rd Fl., Edmonton, AB T6H 5T6
Executive Director, Environmental Stewardship Division, Brenda Brindle
Tel: 780-427-0674
Fax: 780-422-9745
brenda.brindle@gov.ab.ca

Irrigation & Farm Water Division
Agriculture Centre, #100, 5401 - 1 Ave. South, Lethbridge, AB T1J 4V6
Executive Director, Irrigation & Farm Water Division, Brent Paterson
Tel: 403-381-5143
Fax: 403-381-5903
brent.paterson@gov.ab.ca
Branch Head, Basin Water Management Branch, Roger Hohm
Tel: 403-381-5152
Fax: 403-382-4406
roger.hohm@gov.ab.ca
Branch Head, Rural Water Program, Marshall Eliason
Tel: 780-427-4615
Fax: 780-422-9745
marshall.eliason@gov.ab.ca
Branch Head, Water Quality Branch, Andrea Kalischuk
Tel: 403-381-5883
Fax: 403-381-5765
andrea.kalischuk@gov.ab.ca

Policy, Strategy, & Intergovernmental Affairs Division
JG O'Donoghue Bldg., 7000 - 113 St., 2nd Fl., Edmonton, AB T6H 5T6
Tel: 780-422-9167
Fax: 780-427-5921
Executive Director, Dave Burdek
Tel: 780-427-3338
Fax: 780-427-5921
dave.burdek@gov.ab.ca
Branch Head, Policy Coordination & Research Branch, Dr. Shiferaw Adilu
Tel: 780-422-7196
Fax: 780-427-5921
shiferaw.adilu@gov.ab.ca
Branch Head, Strategy & Program Delivery Branch, Linda Hawk
Tel: 780-427-4463
Fax: 780-427-5921
linda.hawk@gov.ab.ca
Branch Head, Domestic & International Trade Policy Branch, Peter Kuperis
Tel: 780-415-8608
Fax: 780-427-5921
peter.kuperis@gov.ab.ca
Branch Head, Growing Forward Coordination & Program Policy Branch, Wendy McCormick
Tel: 403-340-5306
Fax: 403-340-4896
wendy.mccormick@gov.ab.ca

Rural Development Division
JG O'Donoghue Bldg., 7000 - 113 St., Edmonton, AB T6H 5T6
Tel: 780-427-2409
Fax: 780-427-4227
Executive Director, Rural Development Division, Ron Popek
Tel: 780-427-2409
Fax: 780-427-4227
ron.popek@gov.ab.ca
Senior Manager, Rural Initiatives & Research Unit, Robert Hornbrook
Tel: 780-427-4218
Fax: 780-427-4227
robert.hornbrook@gov.ab.ca

Human Resource Services & Facilities Management Services
JG O'Donoghue Bldg., 7000 -113 St., Edmonton, AB T6H 5T6
Tel: 780-427-2111
Fax: 780-427-3398
resumes@agric.gov.ab.ca
Executive Director, Human Resources Services and Facilities Management Services, Heather K.M. Behman
Tel: 780-427-2430
Fax: 780-427-3398
heather.behman@gov.ab.ca
Director, Human Resource Consulting Services, Helene Vegh
Tel: 780-427-2967
Fax: 780-427-3398
helene.vegh@gov.ab.ca
Coordinator, Facilities Management Unit, Rose Alwood
Tel: 780-422-4915
Fax: 780-427-4227
rose.alwood@gov.ab.ca
Manager, Workplace Health & Safety, Sandra Coventry
Tel: 780-422-5217
Fax: 780-427-3398
sandra.coventry@gov.ab.ca

Alberta Culture

Communications Branch, Standard Life Centre, 10405 Jasper Ave., 7th Fl., Edmonton, AB T5J 4R7
Tel: 780-427-6530
Toll-Free: 800-232-7215
TTY: 780-427-9999
ccs.communications@gov.ab.ca
www.culture.alberta.ca
Formerly known as Culture & Community Services, & before that Culture & Community Spirit, until name changes in 2011 & 2012 under Premier Redford, Alberta's Culture continues to support arts & cultural industries throughout Alberta. Financial assistance is provided to the non-profit sector, film, the arts, & heritage.
The following agencies, boards, & commissions report directly to the Minister: Alberta Foundation for the Arts, Alberta Historical Resources Foundation, Government House Foundation, & the Historic Resources Fund.

Minister, Culture, Hon. Heather Klimchuk
Tel: 780-422-3559
Fax: 780-427-7729
Social Media: twitter.com/heatherklimchuk, www.facebook.com/Heather.Klimchuk
Legislature Bldg.
#107, 10800 - 97 Ave.
Edmonton, AB T5K 2B6

Deputy Minister, Culture, Barry Day
Tel: 780-427-2921
Fax: 780-427-5362
barry.day@gov.ab.ca

Chief Information Officer, Culture & Community Services, Lorie Baddock
Tel: 780-427-7828
Fax: 780-427-0255
lorie.baddock@gov.ab.ca

Executive Director/Senior Financial Officer, Financial Services, Pam Arnston
Tel: 780-427-0120
Fax: 780-427-0255
pam.arnston@gov.ab.ca

Executive Director, Policy, Planning, & Legislative Services, Susan Cribbs
Tel: 780-422-1290
Fax: 780-427-0255
susan.cribbs@gov.ab.ca

Executive Director, Human Resources, Diane Dunn
Tel: 780-422-5779
Fax: 780-422-3142
diane.dunn@gov.ab.ca

Executive Director, Francophone Secretariat, Denis Tardif
Tel: 780-415-3232
Fax: 780-422-7533
denis.tardif@gov.ab.ca
Other Communications: Main Secretariat Number: 780-415-3348

Director, Legal & Legislative Services, Barbara Adamson
Tel: 780-644-7741
Fax: 780-427-0255
barbara.adamson@gov.ab.ca

Director, Planning & Performance Measurement, Brad Babiak
Tel: 780-644-3272
Fax: 780-427-0255
brad.babiak@gov.ab.ca

Director, Communications, John Tuckwell
Tel: 780-427-2395
Fax: 780-427-1496
john.tuckwell@gov.ab.ca

Director, Policy Coordination & Program Evaluation, David Middagh
Tel: 780-427-0617
Fax: 780-427-0255
david.middagh@gov.ab.ca

Acting Director, Financial Planning, Jeanette Stead
Tel: 780-644-8101
Fax: 780-427-0255
jeanette.stead@gov.ab.ca

Acting Director, Financial Reporting & Operations, Carmen Vidaurri
Tel: 780-644-5511
Fax: 780-427-0255
carmen.vidaurri@gov.ab.ca

Associated Agencies, Boards & Commissions:
• **Alberta Foundation for the Arts (AFA)**
10708 - 105 Ave.
Edmonton, AB T5H 0A1
Tel: 780-427-9968
Toll-free: -310-0000
www.affta.ab.ca
The Foundation supports the development of arts throughout Alberta. It works to maintain & expand the AFA art collection for Albertans.
• **Alberta Historical Resources Foundation (AHRF)**
Old St. Stephen's College
8820 - 112 St.
Edmonton, AB T6G 2P8
Tel: 780-431-2300
Fax: 780-427-5598
www.culture.alberta.ca/ahrf
Established through the Historical Resources Act, The Alberta Historical Resource Foundation raises awareness of Alberta's heritage.
• **Government House Foundation**
12845 - 102 Ave. NW
Edmonton, AB T5N 0M6
Tel: 780-427-2281
Fax: 780-422-6508
governmenthouseinfo@gov.ab.ca
Established in 1976, the Government House Foundation consist of a board of up to 12 directors. The Lieutenant Governor appoints the directors who are responsible to the Minister of Culture & Community Spirit.
The board of directors is engaged in the following activities: advising the Minister of Culture & Community Services about the preservation of Government House, raising public awareness of the architectural development of Government House, & soliciting property for display in Government House.
• **Historic Resources Fund**
c/o Culture & Community Spirit, Old St. Stephen's College
8820 - 112 St.
Edmonton, AB T6G 2P8
Tel: 780-431-2300
Fax: 780-427-5598
Under the authority of the Historical Resources Act, the Historic Resource Fund carries out its purpose to protect, enhance, display, & promote the historic resources of Alberta. It funds programs that are designated by the Lieutenant Governor.

Minister, Education, Hon. Thomas Lukaszuk
Tel: 780-427-5010
Fax: 780-427-5018
Social Media: twitter.com/lukaszukml, www.facebook.com/Thomas-A-Lukaszuk/662272836

Deputy Minister, Keray Henke
Tel: 780-427-3659
Fax: 780-427-7733
keray.henke@gov.ab.ca

Director, Communications, Kathy Telfer
Tel: 780-427-5423
Fax: 780-427-0591
kathy.telfer@gov.ab.ca

Parliamentary Assistant, Janice Sarich
Tel: 780-415-9462
Fax: 780-415-0951
keray.henke@gov.ab.ca

Alberta Energy

North Petroleum Plaza, 9945 - 108 St., Edmonton, AB T5K 2G6
Tel: 780-427-8050
Fax: 780-422-0698
Toll-Free: -310-0000
TTY: 780-427-9999
Library.Energy@gov.ab.ca
www.energy.gov.ab.ca
Other Communication: Calgary, Phone: 403-297-8955; TTY Toll-Free: 1-800-232-7215; Library Services, Phone: 780-415-0351
Alberta Energy is responsible for the development of Alberta's non-renewable resources & renewable energy. Non-renewable resources include natural gas, conventional oil & oil sands, coal, & minerals. Renewable resources include wind, solar, geothermal, & hydro.
Other responsbilities of Alberta Energy are as follows: establishing & administering fiscal & royalty systems; granting the right to explore & develop resources; promoting energy conservation; & encouraging investment to create economic prosperity.
Acts Administered:
Alberta Corporate Tax Act
Alberta Utilities Commission Act
Ammonite Shell Regulations
CO2 Projects Royalty Credit Regulation
Coal Conservation Act
Coal Sales Act
Electric Utilities Act
Electric Utilities Amendment Act, 2012
Energy Resources Conservation Act
Exploration Regulation
Flare Gas Generation Regulation
Freehold Mineral Rights Tax Act
Gas Processing Efficiency Assistance Regulation
Gas Resources Preservation Act
Gas Utilities Act
Hydro & Electric Energy Act
Independent Power & Small Power Regulation
Innovative Energy Technologies Regulation
Metallic & Industrial Minerals Exploration Regulation
Metallic & Industrial Minerals Regulation
Mineral Rights Compensation Regulation
Mines & Minerals Act
Natural Gas Marketing Act
Natural Gas Price Protection Act
Oil & Gas Conservation Act
Oil Sands Conservation Act
Oil Sands Tenure Regulation
Petroleum Marketing Act
Pipeline Act
Responsible Energy Development Act
Security Management Regulation
Small Power Research & Development Act
Turner Valley Unit Operations Act
Water, Gas & Electric Companies Act

Minister, Energy, Hon. Ken Hughes
Tel: 780-427-3740
Fax: 780-422-0195
minister.energy@gov.ab.ca
Legislature Building
10800 - 97th Ave.
Edmonton, AB T5K 2B6

Deputy Minister, Energy, Jim Ellis
Tel: 780-415-8434
Fax: 780-427-7737
jim.ellis@gov.ab.ca
Petroleum Plaza NT
9945 - 108 St.
Edmonton, AB T5K 2G5

Executive Director, Human Resources, Dave Prince
Tel: 780-427-6294
Fax: 780-422-4299
dave.prince@gov.ab.ca
Petroleum Plaza NT
9945 - 108 St.
Edmonton, AB T5K 2G5

Director, Communications, Janice Schroeder
Tel: 780-422-3667
Fax: 780-422-0698
janice.schroeder@gov.ab.ca
Petroleum Plaza NT
9945 - 108 St.
Edmonton, AB T5K 2G5

Manager, Planning & Communications, Matthew Good
Tel: 780-638-3812
Fax: 780-427-7737
matthew.good@gov.ab.ca

Associated Agencies, Boards & Commissions:
• **Alberta Utilities Commission (AUC)**
Fifth Avenue Place
425 - 1st St. SW, 4th Fl.
Calgary, AB T2P 3L8
Tel: 403-592-8845
Fax: 403-592-4406
Toll-free: -310-0000
info@auc.ab.ca; utilitiesconcerns@auc.ab.ca
www.auc.ab.ca
Other Communication: Edmonton Office, Phone: 780-427-4901; Edmonton Office, Fax: 780-427-6970
The Alberta Utilities Commission was established by the Government of Alberta as a quasi-judicial independent agency. It is responsible for regulating the utilities sector & the electricity & natural gas markets in Alberta to ensure that the delivery of utility service is responsible, fair, & in the public interest.
Chair, Willie Grieve
Vice-Chair, Carolyn Dahl Rees
Chief Executive, Bob Heggie
General Counsel & Executive Director, Law, Doug Larder, QC
Executive Director, Rates, Mike Hagan
Executive Director, Regulatory Policy, Fino Tiberi
Executive Director, Corporate Services, Jim Van Horne
Executive Director, Facilities, Wade Vienneau
• **Energy Resources Conservation Board (ERCB)**
#1000, 250 - 5 Ave. SW
Calgary, AB T2P 0R4
Tel: 403-297-8311
Fax: 403-297-7336
Toll-free: 855-297-8311
inquiries@ercb.ca; infoservices@ercb.ca; ADR@ercb.ca
www.ercb.ca
Other Communication: Appropriate Dispute Resolution Program, Phone: 403-297-6252; ERCB Applications Help Line, Phone: 403-297-4369; E-mail: Directive56.Help@ercb.ca
As an independent, quasi-judicial agency of the Government of Alberta, the Energy Resources Conservation Board is responsible for regulating the safe & responsible development of energy resources in Alberta. The province's energy resources include coal, natural gas, oil, & oil sands.
Chair, Dan McFadyen
Tel: 403-297-2215
Dan.McFadyen@ercb.ca
Chief Operating Officer, Trevor Dark
Tel: 403-297-6868
trevor.dark@ercb.ca

Chief Financial Officer, Tom Heywood
Tel: 403-297-2133
tom.heywood@ercb.ca
General Counsel, Patricia Johnston
Tel: 403-297-4439
patricia.johnston@ercb.ca
Board Secretariat, Paul Ferensowicz
Tel: 403-297-6895
paul.ferensowica@ercb.ca
Public Safety Officer, Marilyn Craig
Tel: 403-297-3194
marilyn.craig@ercb.ca

Clean Energy Division
Centre West Building, 10035 - 108 St., Edmonton, AB T5J 3E1
Assistant Deputy Minister, Clean Energy Division, John Donner
Tel: 780-638-4141
Fax: 780-638-4134
john.donner@gov.ab.ca
Director, Business Planning & Performance, Sandra Stemmer
Tel: 780-643-1438
Fax: 780-422-0800
sandra.stemmer@gov.ab.ca

Electricity, Alternative Energy, & Carbon Capture & Storage Division
Petroleum Plaza NT, 9945 - 108 St., 6th Fl., Edmonton, AB T5K 2G6
Assistant Deputy Minister, Sandra Locke
Tel: 780-644-7126
Fax: 780-427-7737
sandra.locke@gov.ab.ca
Executive Director, Carbon Capture & Storage Development / Energy Efficiency & Conservation Branch, Mikera Fernandez
Tel: 780-415-6414
Fax: 780-422-0229
mike.fernandez@gov.ab.ca
Executive Director, Infrastructure & Alternative Energy Branch, Ian McKay
Tel: 780-422-8726
Fax: 780-427-8065
ian.mckay@gov.ab.ca
Executive Director, Electricity Markets Branch, Kathryn Wood
Tel: 780-644-1232
Fax: 780-427-8065
kathryn.wood@gov.ab.ca

Oil Sands Strategy & Operations
Petroleum Plaza NT, 9945 - 108 St., 6th Fl., Edmonton, AB T5K 2G6
Chief Assistant Deputy Minister of Oil Sands Division, Jennifer Steber
Tel: 780-427-6370
Fax: 780-427-7737
jennifer.steber@gov.ab.ca
Executive Director, Oil Sands Strategy, Anne Denman
Tel: 780-422-9212
Fax: 780-427-8065
anne.denman@gov.ab.ca
Branch Head, External Relations & Advocacy, Lyn Bilida
Tel: 780-415-6187
Fax: 780-644-3234
lyn.bilida@gov.ab.ca
Branch Head, Operations, Steve Tkalcic
Tel: 780-422-9121
Fax: 780-422-0692
steve.tkalcic@gov.ab.ca
Branch Head, Business Design & Evaluation, Larry Ziegenhagel
Tel: 780-427-6384
Fax: 780-422-0692
larry.ziegenhagel@gov.ab.ca

Regulatory Enhancement Project Implementation
Petroleum Plaza NT, 9945 - 108 St., 10th Fl., Edmonton, AB T5K 2G6
Assistant Deputy Minister, John Buie
Tel: 780-427-2159
Fax: 780-644-1784
john.buie@gov.ab.ca
Executive Advisor, Robert Burwood
Tel: 780-427-4300
Fax: 780-644-1784
robert.burwood@gov.ab.ca
Executive Advisor, Charleen Schmidt
Tel: 780-427-2368
Fax: 780-644-1784
charleen.schmidt@gov.ab.ca

Resource Development Policy Division
Petroleum Plaza NT, 9945 - 108 St., Edmonton, AB T5K 2G6
Assistant Deputy Minister, Resource Development Policy Division, Martin Chamberlain
Tel: 780-422-1045
Fax: 780-427-7737
martin.chamberlain@gov.ab.ca
Executive Director, Resource Development, Sharla Rauschning
Tel: 780-427-6230
Fax: 780-644-3604
sharla.rauschning@gov.ab.ca

Revenue & Operations Division
Petroleum Plaza NT, 9945 - 108 St., 10th Fl., Edmonton, AB T5K 2G6
Assistant Deputy Minister, Revenue & Operations Division, Rhonda Wehrhahn
Tel: 780-422-9430
Fax: 780-422-1123
rhonda.wehrhahn@gov.ab.ca
Branch Head, Tenure, Brenda Allbright
Tel: 780-422-9393
Fax: 780-422-1123
brenda.allbright@gov.ab.ca
Branch Head, Petroleum Registry of Alberta (Edmonton / Calgary), Wally Goeres
Tel: 780-415-2079
Fax: 780-422-0229
wally.goeres@gov.ab.ca
Branch Head, Compliance & Assurance, Larry McGuinness
Tel: 403-297-6742
Fax: 403-297-5199
larry.mcguinness@gov.ab.ca
Branch Head, Royalty Operations, Salim Merali
Tel: 780-422-9124
Fax: 780-427-0865
salim.merali@gov.ab.ca
Branch Head, Petroleum Marketing & Valuation, & Site Services, Gale Robins
Tel: 403-297-5460
gale.robins@gov.ab.ca
Branch Head, Coal & Mineral Development, Gary V. White
Tel: 780-415-0349
Fax: 780-422-5447
gary.v.white@gov.ab.ca

Strategic Initiatives Division
Petroleum Plaza NT, 9945 - 108 St., 10th Fl., Edmonton, AB T5K 2G6
Assistant Deputy Minister, Mike Ekelund
Tel: 780-422-0813
Fax: 780-427-7737
mike.ekelund@gov.ab.ca
Director, Strategic Initiatives, Menzie McEachern
Tel: 780-638-4045
Fax: 780-427-7737
menzie.mceachern@gov.ab.ca

Strategic Services Division
Petroleum Plaza NT, 9945 - 108 St., 10th Fl., Edmonton, AB T5K 2G6
Director, Business Planning & Reporting, Sandra Stemmer
Tel: 780-643-1438
Fax: 780-422-0800
sandra.stemmer@gov.ab.ca
Branch Head, Finance & Business Services, Douglas Borland
Tel: 780-427-6223
Fax: 780-422-4281
douglas.borland@gov.ab.ca
Branch Head, FOIP & Records Management Branch, Marlene Bruyere
Tel: 780-644-3778
Fax: 780-644-3786
marlene.bruyere@gov.ab.ca
Branch Head, Information Management & Technology Services, Carol Anne Pasutto
Tel: 780-415-2083
Fax: 780-427-5696
carolanne.pasutto@gov.ab.ca

Alberta Enterprise & Advanced Education

Legislature Bldg., #324, 10800 - 97 Ave., Edmonton, AB T5K 2B6
Tel: 780-422-5400
Toll-Free: -310-0000
eae.alberta.ca
The key responsibilities of Enterprise & Advanced Education include post-secondary matters, apprenticeship & industry training, adult learning, research & innovation, economic development, immigration & labour attraction, & labour force development.
The following are some specific activities: funding public post-secondary institutions in Alberta; developing program standards with industry; counselling apprentices & employers; certifying apprentices & occupational trainees; providing student financial assistance; funding education providers; funding apprentices; working with various industry sectors, government councils, businesses, communities, & alliances to grow Alberta's economy; funding the Alberta Innovates programs; Facilitating technology commercialization & development; providing assistance to new immigrants; addressing & providing solutions for labour force issues

Associated Agencies, Boards & Commissions:
• **Access Advisory Council**
Sterling Place
9940 - 106 St., 4th Fl.
Edmonton, AB
Tel: 780-644-3183
The council is appointed by the Minister of Advanced Education & Technology. The role of the council is to offer advice regarding the Access to the Future Fund.
• **Alberta Apprenticeship & Industry Training Board**
Commerce Place
10155 - 102nd St., 10th Fl.
Edmonton, AB T5J 4L5
Tel: 780-427-8765
Fax: 780-422-7376
Toll-free: -310-0000
TTY: 780-427-9999
www.tradesecrets.gov.ab.ca
Other Communication: TTY Toll-Free: 1-800-232-7215
Board members are appointed by the Lieutenant Governor in Council, upon recommendation of the Minister of Advanced Education & Technology. The mission of the board is to maintain high quality training & certification standards in the apprenticeship & industry training system. The board offers recommendations to the Minister about the needs of the labour market in Alberta & the training & certification of persons in designated trades & occupations.
• **Alberta Council on Admissions & Transfer (ACAT)**
Commerce Place
10155 - 102 St., 11th Fl.
Edmonton, AB T5J 4L5
Tel: 780-422-9021
Fax: 780-422-3688
Toll-free: -310-0000
TTY: 780-427-9999
acat@gov.ab.ca
www.acat.gov.ab.ca
Other Communication: TTY Toll-Free: 1-800-232-7215
The independent body advocates for learners by working to ensure transferability of educational courses & programs to benefit students. The role of the council is to develop policies & procedures to facilitate transfer agreements among post-secondary institutions.
• **Alberta Economic Development Authority (AEDA)**
McDougall Centre
455 - 6th St. SW
Calgary, AB T2P 4E8
Tel: 403-297-3022
Fax: 403-297-6435
Toll-free: -310-0000
www.aeda.alberta.ca
Working in partnership with the provincial government, the Alberta Economic Development Authority offers recommendations on key economic issues. The Alberta Economic Development Authority consists of business, municipal, & academic leader from throughout Alberta.
• **Alberta Enterprise Corporation Board**
Alberta Enterprise Corporation
#1100, 10830 Jasper Ave.
Edmonton, AB T5J 2B3
Tel: 780-392-3901

The Alberta Enterprise Corporation Board was established in 2008 through the Alberta Enterprise Corporation Act. The Alberta Enterprise Fund is the corporation's fund that targets technology venture capital funds.

• Alberta Innovates - Bio Solutions (AI Bio)
Phipps McKinnon Bldg.
10020 - 101A Ave.
Edmonton, AB T5J 3G2
Tel: 780-427-1956
Fax: 780-427-3252
Toll-free: 877-828-0444
bio@albertainnovates.ca
www.albertainnovates.ca/bio
Other Communication: General inquiries related to research & innovation organizations throughout Alberta, Phone: 877-828-0444
Alberta Innovates Bio Solutions was established in 2010 under the Alberta Research & Innovation Act. It is part of the Alberta Innovates system, which reports to the Minister of Alberta Advanced Education & Technology. Investments are made in research & innovation to benefit Alberta's forestry, agriculture, & food sectors.
Chair, Art Froehlich
Chief Executive Officer, Stan Blade
Tel: 780-427-0367
stan.blade@albertainnovates.ca
Executive Director, Industry Challenges & Emerging Opportunities, Carol Bettac
Tel: 780-638-3721
carol.bettac@albertainnovates.ca
Executive Director, Value Chain Sustainability & Quality Food for Health, Cornelia Kreplin
Tel: 780-638-3678
cornelia.kreplin@albertainnovates.ca
Executive Director, Advancing the Bioeconomy, Cornelia Kreplin
Tel: 780-427-2567
steve.price@albertainnovates.ca
Director, Communications, Marie Cusack
Tel: 780-638-4060
marie.cusack@albertainnovates.ca
Director, Operations, Joan Unger
Tel: 780-422-5737
joan.unger@albertainnovates.ca

• Alberta Innovates - Energy & Environmental Solutions
AMEC Place
#2540, 801 - 6th Ave. SW
Calgary, AB T2P 3W2
Tel: 403-297-7089
ees@albertainnovates.ca
www.albertainnovates.ca/energy/introduction
The Alberta energy & environmental research organization works to develop innovative methods for the conversion of natural resources into environmentally responsible, market-ready energy.
Chair, Eric Newell
Vice-Chair, Kathy Sendall

• Alberta Innovates - Health Solutions (AIHS)
#1500, 10104 - 103 Ave.
Edmonton, AB T5J 4A7
Tel: 780-423-5727
Fax: 780-429-3509
Toll-free: 877-423-5727
health@albertainnovates.ca
www.ahfmr.ab.ca
Alberta Innovates - Health Solutions supports research & innovation for the improvement of Albertans' health & well-being. The organization also works to create health related social & economic benefits.

• Alberta Innovates - Technology Futures
250 Karl Clark Rd.
Edmonton, AB T6N 1E4
Tel: 780-450-5111
Fax: 780-450-5333
referral@albertainnovates.ca
www.albertatechfutures.ca
As part of the research & innovation system in Alberta, the organization works to build healthy, sustainable businesses. Technology Futures offers technical services, program funding, as well as regionally accessible commercialization support.

• Alberta Research & Innvoation Authority (ARIA)
Phipps-McKinnon Bldg.
#500, 101A Ave.
Edmonton, AB T5J 3G2
Tel: 780-427-1488
Fax: 780-427-0979
aria@albertainnovates.ca
www.albertainnovates.ca/research/introduction
The advisory body offers recommendations to the Government of Alberta about research, emerging technologies, & policy direction.
Executive Director, Lee Kruszewski
Tel: 780-638-3795
lee.kruszewski@gov.ab.ca
ARIA Secretariat, Chris Dambrowitz
Tel: 780-427-7461
chris.dambrowitz@gov.ab.ca

• Campus Alberta Quality Council (CAQC)
Commerce Place
10155 - 102 St., 11th Fl.
Edmonton, AB T5J 4L5
Tel: 780-427-8921
Fax: 780-427-4185
caqc@gov.ab.ca
www.caqc.gov.ab.ca
The arms-length quality assurance agency makes recommendations to the Minister of Advanced Education & Technology on applications from post-secondary institutions that want to offer new degree programs. All degree programs, except for degrees in divinity, offered by resident institutions & non-resident institutions in Alberta must be approved by the Minister.

• Northern Alberta Development Council (NADC)
Peace River Office, Provincial Building
#206, 9621 - 96 Ave.
PO Box 900-14
Peace River, AB T8S 1T4
Tel: 780-624-6274
Fax: 780-624-6184
Toll-free: -310-0000
nadc.council@gov.ab.ca
www.nadc.ca
Other Communication: Bursary Information, E-mail: nadc.bursary@gov.ab.ca
The Northern Alberta Development Council focuses on the advancement of the northern economy. The Council is engaged in projects involving tourism, transportation, educational initiatives, value-added agriculture, & inter-jurisdictional projects.

• Student Financial Assistance Appeal Committee
Students Finance
PO Box 28000 Main
Edmonton, AB T5J 4R4
Tel: 780-427-3722
Toll-free: 800-222-6485
The committees in Edmonton & Calgary hear appeals from students who were not provided the entire amount of financial assistance requested, or who had their application for assistance refused. The committees make a recommendation to the Minister, who make a decision on the appeal.

• Students Finance Board

Established in 1953, the Students Finance Board advises the Minister of Advanced Education & Technology about student financial assistance, including scholarships.

Advanced Technology Industries Division
Phipps-McKinnon Bldg., 10020 - 101A Ave., 5th Fl., Edmonton, AB T5J 3G2
Branches & sections in this division include the following: Emerging Technology Industries; Information & Technology Management; Innovation Client Services; & Technology Industry Development.
Assistant Deputy Minister, Mel Wong
Tel: 780-427-2084
Fax: 780-427-5924
mel.wong@gov.ab.ca
Executive Director & Chief Information Officer, Information & Technology Management Section, Leslie Sim-Kaiser
Tel: 780-415-0813
Fax: 780-422-0880
leslie.sim-kaiser@gov.ab.ca
Commerce Place
10155 - 102 St., 9th Fl.
Edmonton, AB T5J 4L5
Executive Director, Technology Industry Development Section, Robert Lai
Tel: 780-427-7722
Fax: 780-427-5924
robert.lai@gov.ab.ca
Director, Emerging Technology Industries Branch, Mathew Anil
Tel: 780-415-8751
Fax: 780-427-5924
mathew.anil@gov.ab.ca
Branch Head, Emerging Technology Industries Branch, Ryan Leskiw
Tel: 780-644-2587
Fax: 780-427-5924
ryan.leskiw@gov.ab.ca
Branch Head, Innovation Client Services Branch, Alex Umnikov
Tel: 780-427-6620
Fax: 780-427-5924
alex.umnikov@gov.ab.ca

Community, Learner & Industry Connections Division
Phipps-McKinnon Bldg., 10020 - 101A Ave., 5th Fl., Edmonton, AB T5J 3G2
Units of the Community Learner & Industry Connections Division include Apprenticeship & Industry Training & Learner Assistance.
Assistant Deputy Minister, Darlene Bouwsema
Tel: 780-422-1185
Fax: 780-422-2420
darlene.bouwsema@gov.ab.ca
Executive Director, Policy & Standards, Mark Douglas
Tel: 780-643-1466
Fax: 780-422-7376
mark.douglas@gov.ab.ca
Other Communications: General Apprentice Inquiries, Phone: 780-427-8517
Executive Director, Learner Assistance, Schubert Kwan
Tel: 780-422-4498
Fax: 780-422-4517
schubert.kwan@gov.ab.ca
Other Communications: Learner Assistance, Main Phone: 780-422-0555
Sterling Place
9940 - 106 St., 9th Fl.
Edmonton, AB T5K 2V1
Director, Program, Policy & Systens Support, Trudy Dupre
Tel: 780-422-1208
Fax: 780-422-4517
trudy.dupre@gov.ab.ca
Sterling Place
9940 - 106 St., 9th Fl.
Edmonton, AB T5K 2V1
Director, Financial Operations & Control Services, John Koehn
Tel: 780-422-5109
Fax: 780-422-4517
john.koehn@gov.ab.ca
Sterling Place
9940 - 106 St., 9th Fl.
Edmonton, AB T5K 1V1
Director, Learner Funding, Launa Lebeau
Tel: 780-427-9820
Fax: 780-422-4516
launa.lebeau@gov.ab.ca
Sterling Place
9940 - 106 St., 7th Fl.
Edmonton, AB T5K 1V1

Enterprise Division
Phipps-McKinnon Bldg., 10020 - 101A Ave., 6th Fl., Edmonton, AB T5J 3G2
Units of the Enterprise Division include Regional Development, the Alberta Economic Development Authority, Industry Development, Economic Development Policy & Analysis, & the Northern Alberta Development Council.
Assistant Deputy Minister, Justin Riemer
Tel: 780-427-6302
Fax: 780-422-0626
justin.riemer@gov.ab.ca
Executive Director, Industry Development, Kirsty Piquette
Tel: 780-427-6987
Fax: 780-422-2091
kirsty.piquette@gov.ab.ca
Executive Director, Economic Development Policy & Analysis, Duane Pyear
Tel: 780-427-0850
Fax: 780-422-0061
duane.pyear@gov.ab.ca
Executive Director, Regional Development, Diane Simsovic
Tel: 780-427-6656
Fax: 780-422-5804
diane.simsovic@gov.ab.ca
Senior Director, North Region & Regional Development Best Practices, George Brosseau

Tel: 780-427-0802
Fax: 780-422-5804
george.brosseau@gov.ab.ca
Senior Director, Productivity Alberta, Lori Schmidt
Tel: 780-422-0545
Fax: 780-422-2091
lori.schmidt@gov.ab.ca
Senior Director, South Region, Elvira Smid
Tel: 403-529-3733
Fax: 403-529-3140
elvira.smid@gov.ab.ca
Director, Metro Regions & Small Business Support, Karen Wronko
Tel: 780-422-8420
Fax: 780-422-5804
karen.wronko@gov.ab.ca
Team Lead, Energy & Value Added Development (EVAD), Jerry MacPherson
Tel: 780-427-6591
Fax: 780-422-2091
jerry.macpherson@gov.ab.ca

Immigration Division
Labour Building, 10808 - 99 Ave., 9th Fl., Edmonton, AB T5K 0G5
The main units of the Immigration Division are: Immigration Policy & Programs, Labour Force Development, & Strategic Marketing & Labour Attraction.

Post Secondary & Community Education Division
Commerce Place, 10155 - 102 St., 7th Fl., Edmonton, AB T5J 4L5
Campus Alberta Partnerships, Post-secondary Investments & Outcomes, & Strategic Directions make up the Post-secondary & Community Education Division.

Research & Innovation Division
Phipps-McKinnon Bldg., 10020 - 101A Ave., 5th Fl., Edmonton, AB T5J 3G2
The Research & Innovation Division consists of Cross Ministry Initiatives, Innovation Planning & Accountability, Alberta Research & Innovation Authority, Innovation Policy, & Alberta Innovates.
Executive Director, Innovation Planning & Accountability, Lisa Bowes
Tel: 780-422-3117
Fax: 780-427-1430
lisa.bowes@gov.ab.ca
Executive Director, Cross Ministry Initiatives, Daphne Cheel
Tel: 780-422-0054
Fax: 780-427-3252
daphne.cheel@gov.ab.ca
Director, Innovation Policy, Sandra Duxbury
Tel: 780-427-4498
Fax: 780-427-5924
sandra.duxbury@gov.ab.ca

Alberta Environment & Sustainable Resource Development

Oxbridge Place, 9820 - 106 St., Main Fl., Edmonton, AB T5K 2J6
Tel: 780-427-2700
Fax: 780-422-4086
Toll-Free: -310-0000
TTY: 780-427-9999
env.infocent@gov.ab.ca; srd.infocent@gov.ab.ca
environment.alberta.ca
Other Communication: 24-hour Environment Hotline (to report an environmental emergency or file a complaint): 1-800-222-6514; Media Enquiries, Phone: 780-427-6267; TTY: 1-800-232-7215
Alberta Environment & Sustainable Resource Development, created in 2012 by Premier Redford, works as a partner to protect & enhance the natural environment of Alberta.
The Minister of Environment & Sustainable Resource Development is repsonsible for the Environmental Appeals Board, & oversees the following agencies & boards: Alberta Recycling Management Authority, Alberta Used Oil Management Association, & the Beverage Container Management Board.
Acts Administered:
Boundary Surveys Act
Climate Change & Emissions Management Act
Environmental Protection & Enhancement Act
Expropriation Act (sections 25 to 28 & 72)
Fisheries (Alberta) Act
Forest & Prairie Protection Act
Forest Reserves Act
Forests Act
Government Organization Act (sections 4(2)(f) & (g) of Schedule 5, in common with the Minister of Environment & the Minister of Infrastructure)
Mines & Minerals Act (aections 108(g), (h), & (j), in common with the Minister of Energy)
Natural Resources Conservation Board Act (in common with the Minister of Environment)
Public Lands Act
Surface Rights Act
Surveys Act
Water Act
Wildlife Act

Minister, Environment & Sustainable Resource Development, Hon. Diana McQueen
Tel: 780-427-2391
Fax: 780-422-6259
Social Media: twitter.com/ministermcqueen, www.facebook.com/dianamcqueenmla, ca.linkedin.com/pub/diana-mcqueen/17/24/b62
Legislature Building
#204, 10800 - 97 Ave.
Edmonton, AB T5K 2B6

Deputy Minister, Environment & Sustainable Resource Development, Dana Woodworth
Tel: 780-427-1799
Fax: 780-415-9669
dana.woodworth@gov.ab.ca
Petroleum Plaza ST
9915 - 108 St., 10th Fl.
Edmonton, AB T5K 2G8

Director, Communications, Andy Weiler
Tel: 780-427-8122
Fax: 780-427-1874
andy.weiler@gov.ab.ca

Associated Agencies, Boards & Commissions:
• Alberta Environmental Appeals Board
Peace Hills Trust Tower
#306, 10011 - 109 St.
Edmonton, AB T5J 3S8
Tel: 780-427-6207
Fax: 780-427-4693
www.eab.gov.ab.ca
The Environmental Appeals Board strives to offer fair, impartial, & efficient resolutions to matters in order to advance the protection & enhancement of the environment in Alberta.
Chair, Justice Delmar Perras
General Counsel & Settlement Officer, Gilbert Van Nes
Registrar of Appeals, Valerie Myrmo
Board Secretary, Denise Black
• Alberta Recycling Management Authority (ARMA)
Scotia Tower 1
#1310, 10060 Jasper Ave.
PO Box 189
Edmonton, AB T5J 2J1
Tel: 780-990-1111
Fax: 780-990-1122
Toll-free: 888-999-8762
info@albertarecycling.ca
www.albertarecycling.ca
Other Communication: Toll-Free Fax: 1-866-990-1122; Electronics Recycling: electronics@albertarecycling.ca; Tire Recycling: tires@albertarecycling.ca; Paint: paint@albertarecycling.ca
Reporting to the Minister of Environment, the not-for-profit association manages tire, paint, & electronics recycling programs throughout Alberta.
Chair, Sid Hinton
• Alberta Used Oil Management Association (AUOMA)
Empire Building
#1008, 10080 Jasper Ave.
Edmonton, AB T5J 1V9
Tel: 780-414-1510
Fax: 780-414-1519
Toll-free: 866-414-1510
reception@usedoilrecycling.ca
www.usedoilrecycling.com/en/ab
Other Communication: Info Line (for information about the nearest Alberta Eco Centre / Collection Facility): 1-888-922-2298
The not-for-profit association encourages Albertans to return used oil, filters, & containers to collection facilities so they can be disposed of properly. The program is funded by an Environmental Handling Charge, & a Return Incentive is paid to private sector collectors.
Executive Director, Roger Jackson
rjackson@usedoilrecycling.ca
• Beverage Container Management Board (BCMB)
#750, 10707 - 100 Ave.
Edmonton, AB T5J 3M1
Tel: 780-424-3193
Fax: 780-428-4620
Toll-free: 888-424-7671
www.bcmb.ab.ca
The Beverage Container Management Board is an alliance of the Alberta Government, municipalities, beverage manufacturers, environmental organizations, & the public. It was established in 1997 as a management board, under the Beverage Container Recycling Regulation pursuant to Section 175 of the Environmental Protection & Enhancement Act.
The Beverage Container Management Board oversees the collection & recycling of beverage containers throughout Alberta. Its policy parameters are established by the Minister of Environment. Funding is through a levy based on the returns of beverage containers.
Compliance Manager, Jason London
jlondon@bcmb.ab.ca
• Disabled Hunter Review Committee
c/o Fish & Wildlife Div,, Sustainable Resource Development
9915 - 108 St., 11th Fl.
Edmonton, AB T5K 2G8
Toll-free: -310-0000
The Disabled Hunter Review Committee is engaged in hearing appeals & reviewing applications by persons who received a negative decision when attempting to obtain a licences or permit for hunting. Depending upon the number of applications, the Committee holds hearings annually.
• Environmental Response Centre
Twin Atria Bldg.
4999 - 98 Ave., 1st Fl.
Edmonton, AB T6B 2X3
Tel: 780-427-2700
Other Communication: Environment Hotline (for reporting an environmental emergency or filing a complaint): 1-800-222-6514
Complaints about contraventions of the Environmental Protection & Enhancement Act are investigated.
• Land Compensation Board (LCB)
1229 - 91 St. SW
Edmonton, AB T6X 1E9
srb.lcb@gov.ab.ca
www.landcompensation.gov.ab.ca
The Land Compensation Board listens to disputes & delivers a decision, within it legislated mandate, about the compensation for landowners or tenants when land is taken by an authority for public works projects. Applications to the Board can be made through forms found in the Expropriation Act Rules of Procedure & Practice.
Chair & Chief Executive Officer, Vern Hartwell
• Natural Resources Conservation Board (NRCB)
Sterling Place
9940 - 106 St.
Edmonton, AB T5K 2N2
Tel: 780-422-1977
Fax: 780-427-0607
Toll-free: 866-383-6722
info@nrcb.gov.ab.ca
www.nrcb.gov.ab.ca
Established in 1991 by the Government of Alberta, the Natural Resources Conservation Board carries out its responsibilities under the Natural Resources Conservation Board Act. The quasi-judicial agency, which is accountable to the Minister of Sustainable Resource Development, reviews non-energy natural resource projects. The Board considers environmental, economic, & social effects in deciding if a project is in the public interest.
In accordance with the Agricultural Operation Practices Act, the Natural Resources Conservation Board also has regulatory authority for confined feeding operations in Alberta. Its work in this area includes administering policies, fulfilling applications, & conducting board reviews.
Chair, Vern Hartwell
General Counsel, Bill Kennedy
Manager, Board Reviews, Susan Schlemko

• Surface Rights Board (SRB)
1229 - 91 St. SW
Edmonton, AB T6X 1E9
Tel: 780-427-2444
Fax: 780-427-5798
Toll-free: -310-0000
srb.lcb@gov.ab.ca
www.surfacerights.gov.ab.ca
The Surface Rights Board holds hearings on disputes related to energt activities & land access. The hearing usually involves a panel of three members of the Surface Rights Board. Members of the Board are appointed by an Order in Counsel, according to the Surface Rights Act. Affected parties may also participate in the hearings, which are open to the public.
The Board delivers decisions, within its legislated mandate, about compensation to landowners, surrounding issues such as oil & gas & power line activity. In determining compensation, the Board considers factors such as the value of the land, loss of use, inconvenience, nuisance, & noise, & adverse effects on remaining land.
Director, Surface Rights Board, Jill Mason
Tel: 780-427-9388
Fax: 780-427-5798
jill.mason@gov.ab.ca
Administrator, Debbie Thompson
Tel: 780-427-2444
Fax: 780-427-5798
debbie.thompson@gov.ab.ca
Team Lead, Decisions, Orders, & Legal Support, Anneliese Coutu
Tel: 780-427-7498
Fax: 780-427-5798
anneliese.coutu@gov.ab.ca

• Wildfire Costs Assessment Committee
c/o Office of the Farmer's Advocate, JG O'Donoghue Building
7000 - 113 St., 3rd Fl.
Edmonton, AB T6H 5T6
The Wildfire Costs Assessment Committee is administered by the Farmers' Advocate Office. When a party is deemed responsible for starting a wildfire, the Committee evaluates that party's ability to pay the cost of fighting the fire.

• Wildlife Predator & Shot Livestock Compensation Committee
c/o Fish & Wildlife Div., Sustainable Resource Development
9920 - 108 St., 3rd Fl.
Edmonton, AB T5K 2M4
The reimbursement paid to a livestock producer, when an animal has been injured by a wildlife predator, or shot, is determined by the Predator & Shot Livestock Compensation Committee of Alberta. Compensation provided to the livestock owner is based upon a schedule for losses or injury to specified livestock.

Clean Energy Division
Centre West Building, 10035 - 108 St., 8th Fl., Edmonton, AB T5J 3E1
Assistant Deputy Minister, John Donner
Tel: 780-638-4141
Fax: 780-638-4134
john.donner@gov.ab.ca
Acting Executive Director, Policy Management Office, Heather von Hauff
Tel: 780-638-4139
Fax: 780-638-4134
heather.vonhauff@gov.ab.ca
Senior Operations Manager, Chris Hunt
Tel: 780-644-1259
Fax: 780-638-4134
chris.hunt@gov.ab.ca

Corporate Services Division
Petroleum Plaza ST, 9915 - 108 St., 10th Fl, Edmonton, AB T5K 2G8
Tel: 780-643-0890
Fax: 780-644-8469
Assistant Deputy Minister, Tom Davis
Tel: 780-644-3205
Fax: 780-427-0923
tom.davis@gov.ab.ca
Chief Information Officer, Office of the CIO & Information Management & Technology Branch, Roger Burns
Tel: 780-644-5065
roger.burns@gov.ab.ca
Oxbridge Place
9820 - 106 St.
Edmonton, AB T5K 2J6
Chief Information Officer, Resource Information Management Branch, Sustainable Resource Development, James Greengrass
Tel: 780-422-5719
Fax: 780-422-0712
james.greengrass@gov.ab.ca
Oxbridge Place
9820 - 106 St.
Edmonton, AB T5K 2J6
Executive Director & Senior Financial Officer, Finance & Administration Branch, Mike Dalrymple
Tel: 780-427-9148
Fax: 780-427-0923
mike.dalrymple@gov.ab.ca
Executive Director & Senior Financial Officer, Finance & Administration Branch, Greg Kliparchuk
Tel: 780-638-3199
Fax: 780-427-2512
greg.kliparchuk@gov.ab.ca
Executive Director, Corporate Busines Support Branch, Scott Milligan
Tel: 780-422-0672
Fax: 780-644-4682
scott.milligan@gov.ab.ca
Director, Planning & Policy Coordination, Fiona Salkie
Tel: 780-422-0561
Fax: 780-644-4682
fiona.salkie@gov.ab.ca
Director, Information Communication Technology, Joe Vance
Tel: 780-644-8619
Fax: 780-427-7434
joe.vance@gov.ab.ca

Fish & Wildlife Division
Petroleum Plaza ST, 9915 - 108 St., 11th Fl., Edmonton, AB T5K 2G8
Assistant Deputy Minister, Rick Blackwood
Tel: 780-427-1139
Fax: 780-427-8884
rick.blackwood@gov.ab.ca
Executive Director, Wildlife Management, Ron Bjorge
Tel: 780-427-9503
Fax: 780-422-9557
ron.bjorge@gov.ab.ca
Director, Fisheries Management Branch, Travis Ripley
Tel: 780-427-7763
Fax: 780-422-9559
travis.ripley@gov.ab.ca

Forestry Division
Petroleum Plaza ST, 9915 - 108 St. 11th Fl., Edmonton, AB T5K 2G8
Assistant Deputy Minister, Bruce Mayer
Tel: 780-427-3542
Fax: 780-422-6068
bruce.mayer@gov.ab.ca
Executive Director, Wildfire Management Branch, Hugh Boyd
Tel: 780-442-7781
Fax: 780-415-1509
hugh.boyd@gov.ab.ca
Executive Director, Forest Management Branch, Darren Tapp
Tel: 780-427-5324
Fax: 780-427-0085
darren.tapp@gov.ab.ca
Executive Director, Forest Industry Development Branch, Dan Wilkinson
Tel: 780-427-6372
Fax: 780-644-5728
dan.wilkinson@gov.ab.ca
Director, Wildfire Operations Section, John Brewer
Tel: 780-427-7925
Fax: 780-422-7230
john.brewer@gov.ab.ca
Director, Wildfire Prevention Section, Herman Stegehuis
Tel: 780-415-9969
Fax: 780-427-0292

Land Use Secretariat
Centre West Building, 10035 - 108 St., Edmonton, AB T5J 3E1
Tel: 780-644-7972
Fax: 780-644-1034
luf@gov.ab.ca
www.landuse.alberta.ca
The Land Use Secretariat is a leader in the implementation of Alberta's Land-use Framework. The Secretariat assists regional advisory councils in offering advice to government about developing regional plans.
Executive Director, Regional Planning, Crystal Damer
Tel: 780-644-5014
Fax: 780-644-1034
crystal.damer@gov.ab.ca
Commissioner, Stewardship, Morris Seiferling
Tel: 780-644-7978
Fax: 780-644-1034
morris.seiferling@gov.ab.ca
Coordinator, Budget & Projects, Ursula Hung
Tel: 780-427-9195
Fax: 780-644-1034
ursula.hung@gov.ab.ca
Manager, Communications & Web, Tim Kulak
Tel: 780-415-9547
Fax: 780-644-1034
tim.kulak@gov.ab.ca

Lands Division
Petroleum Plaza ST, 9915 - 108 St., 11th Fl., Edmonton, AB T5K 2G8
Tel: 780-415-1396
Fax: 780-422-6068
Assistant Deputy Minister, Glenn Selland
Tel: 780-427-7061
Fax: 780-422-6068
glenn.selland@gov.ab.ca
Executive Director, Land Management Branch, Jeff Reynolds
Tel: 780-644-1752
Fax: 780-427-1185
jeff.reynolds@gov.ab.ca
Acting Executive Director, Rangeland Management Branch, Dan Smith
Tel: 780-427-3595
Fax: 780-422-0454
dan.smith@gov.ab.ca
Director, Land Dispositions Branch, Val Hoover
Tel: 780-427-3464
Fax: 780-422-2545
val.hoover@gov.ab.ca
Director, Project Management Branch, Todd Letwin
Tel: 780-427-4768
Fax: 780-644-1142
todd.letwin@gov.ab.ca

Monitoring & Science Division
Petroleum Plaza ST, 9915 - 108 St., 10th Fl., Edmonton, AB T5K 2G8
Assistant Deputy Minister, Bob Barraclough
Tel: 780-427-0029
Fax: 780-422-4192
bob.barraclough@gov.ab.ca
Acting Director, Data Monitoring & Validation Branch, Tom Dickson
Tel: 780-415-9367
Fax: 780-422-8606
tom.dickson@gov.ab.ca
Administrative Coordinator, Jannette Wombold
Tel: 780-427-8315
Fax: 780-427-6334
jannette.wombold@gov.ab.ca

Operations Division
Petroleum Plaza ST, 9915 - 108 St., Edmonton, AB T5K 2G8
Tel: 780-427-1335
Fax: 780-427-1335
Assistant Deputy Minister, Rick Brown
Tel: 780-427-1335
Fax: 780-422-5141
rick.brown@gov.ab.ca
Director, Water Management Operations, David Ardell
Tel: 780-297-5892
Fax: 780-297-6389
dave.ardell@gov.ab.ca
Director, Regional Integration Branch, Colin Blair
Tel: 780-427-8536
Fax: 780-422-4086
colin.blair@gov.ab.ca
Director, Environmental Support & Emergency Response Team, Greg Carter
Tel: 780-415-0989
Fax: 780-427-2278
greg.carter@gov.ab.ca

Acting Team Leader, Environmental Assessment, Environmental Impact Assessmnet Group, Corinne Kristensen
Tel: 780-427-9116
Fax: 780-427-9102
corinne.kristensen@gov.ab.ca

Policy Division
Petroleum Plaza ST, 9915 - 108 St., Edmonton, AB T5K 2G8
Tel: 780-415-8183
Fax: 780-415-6492
Assistant Deputy Minister, Shannon Flint
Tel: 780-422-8463
Fax: 780-427-0923
shannon.flint@gov.ab.ca
Acting Director, Policy & Legislation Innovation Branch, Janet McLean
Tel: 780-427-9888
Fax: 780-422-4192
janet.mclean@gov.ab.ca
Director, Clean Energy Policy Branch, Roger Ramcharita
Tel: 780-644-5290
Fax: 780-415-1718
roger.ramcharita@gov.ab.ca
Director, Water Policy Branch, Andy Ridge
Tel: 780-638-4198
Fax: 780-442-4192
andy.ridge@gov.ab.ca
Acting Director, Climate Change Secretariat, Bob Savage
Tel: 780-644-4918
Fax: 780-415-1718
robert.savage@gov.ab.ca
Office Coordinator, Air, Land, & Waste Policy Branch, Lynn Lockhart
Tel: 780-427-8249
Fax: 780-422-4192
lynn.lockhart@gov.ab.ca

Strategy Division
Petroleum Plaza ST, 9915 - 108 St., 10th Fl., Edmonton, AB T5K 2G8
Assistant Deputy Minister, Bev Yee
Tel: 780-427-6247
Fax: 780-427-1014
bev.yee@gov.ab.ca
Executive Director, SREM Aboriginal Affairs Branch (SAAB), Norman Calliou
Tel: 780-422-7898
Fax: 780-421-0028
norman.calliou@gov.ab.ca
Director, Strategy Development & Foresight, Stephanie Clarke
Tel: 780-422-1874
Fax: 780-644-7571
stephanie.clarke@gov.ab.ca
Director, Transboundary Secretariat, Robert Harrison
Tel: 780-427-9288
Fax: 780-638-3187
robert.harrison@gov.ab.ca
Acting Director, Systems Management, Christine Lazaruk
Tel: 780-422-9100
Fax: 780-422-5120
christine.lazaruk@gov.ab.ca

Alberta Health

PO Box 1360 Stn. Main, Edmonton, AB T5J 2N3
Tel: 780-427-7164
Fax: 780-427-1171
Toll-Free: -310-0000
TTY: 800-232-7215
www.health.alberta.ca; www.seniors.gov.ab.ca
Other Communication: Seniors Phone: 780-644-9992; Fax: 780-422-5954; Toll-Free: 1-877-644-9992
Formerly Alberta Health & Wellness, Alberta Health is involved in the following activities: establishing legislation, policy, & standards; supporting the health system; allocating resources; & administering provincial programs. As of 2012, Alberta Health also incorporates elements of the former Alberta Seniors.

Minister, Health, Hon. Fred Horne
Tel: 780-427-3665
Fax: 780-415-0961
health.minister@gov.ab.ca
Social Media: twitter.com/fredhornemla, www.facebook.com/FredHorne
Legislature Building
#208, 10800 - 97 Ave.
Edmonton, AB T5K 2B6

Associate Minister, Wellness, Hon. Dave Rodney
Tel: 780-415-0482
Fax: 780-415-2255
Legislature Building
#418, 10800 - 97 Ave.
Edmonton, AB T5K 2B6

Associate Minister, Seniors, Hon. George VanderBurg
Tel: 780-415-9550
Fax: 780-415-9411
Legislature Building
#227, 10800 - 97 Ave.
Edmonton, AB T5K 2B6

Deputy Minister, Health, Marcia Nelson
Tel: 780-422-0747
Fax: 780-427-1016
marcia.nelson@gov.ab.ca
Telus Plaza NT
10025 Jasper Ave., 22nd Fl.
Edmonton, AB T5J 1S6

Mental Health Patient Advocate, Fay Orr
Tel: 780-422-1812
Fax: 780-422-0695
fay.orr@gov.ab.ca
Centre West Building
10025 - 108 St., 12th Fl.
Edmonton, AB T5J 3E1

Associated Agencies, Boards & Commissions:
• Alberta Health Services (AHS)
Corporate Office, North Tower, Seventh Street Plaza
10030 - 107th St. NW, 14th Fl.
Edmonton, AB T5J 3E4
Tel: 780-342-2000
Fax: 780-342-2060
Toll-free: 888-342-2471
ahsb.admin@albertahealthservices.ca
www.albertahealthservices.ca
Other Communication: Board Office, Phone: 866-943-1120; Fax: 403-943-1124
Alberta Health Services was established in 2008, and became operational in 2009. The provincial health authority plans & delivers health services throughout Alberta.
• Health Quality Council of Alberta (HQCA)
#210, 811 - 14 St. NW
Calgary, AB T2N 2A4
Tel: 403-297-8162
Fax: 403-297-8258
info@hqca.ca
www.hqca.ca
Other Communication: Edmonton Office, Phone: 780-429-3008, Fax: 780-429-0985
The Health Quality Council of Alberta is legislated under the Regional Health Authorities Act. The Council's responsibilities are set forth in the Health Quality Council of Alberta Regulation. The independent organization strives to improve the health service quality, patient safety, & performance of the health system in Alberta.
• Office of the Chief Medical Officer of Health (OCMOH)
Telus Plaza NT
10025 Jasper Ave., 24th Fl.
Edmonton, AB T5J 1S6
Tel: 780-427-5263
The Office of the Chief Medical Officer of Health offers guidelines to Alberta Health Services about public health policy. The Office also provides information to the public about communicable diseases & public health programs.
The Chief Medical Officer of Health works under the authority of the Public Health Act to promote & protect the health of the people of Alberta.
• Seniors Advisory Council for Alberta
Standard Life Centre
#600, 10405 Jasper Ave., 6th Fl.
Edmonton, AB T5J 4R7
Tel: 780-422-2321
Fax: 780-422-8762
Toll-free: -310-0000
saca@gov.ab.ca
www.seniors.alberta.ca/services_resources/advisory_council
The Seniors Advisory Council for Alberta consults with senior citizens & seniors' organizations in communities throughout Alberta. The Council then informs the Government of Alberta, through the Minister of Seniors & Community Supports, about the issues that affect Alberta's seniors.
The Seniors Advisory Council for Alberta is also engaged in planning the Seniors' Week celebration each years, supporting workshops for frontline workers & seniors, & participating in research projects.

Alberta Aids to Daily Living (AADL)
Milner Building, 10040 - 104 St., 10th Fl., Edmonton, AB T5J 0Z2
Tel: 780-427-0731
Fax: 780-422-0968
www.seniors.gov.ab.ca/aadl
The AADL provides financial assistance to Albertans with long-term disabilities, chronic or terminal illnesses, who live at home, in lodges, or in group homes.
Acting Director, Barb Martini
Tel: 780-422-6985
Fax: 780-422-0968
barb.martini@gov.ab.ca
Manager, Medical & Surgical Benefits, Lauran Chittim
Tel: 780-422-4846
Fax: 780-422-0968
lauran.chittim@gov.ab.ca
Manager, Prosthetics & Orthotics, Seating & Footwear Benefits, Cathy Johnson
Tel: 780-422-6319
Fax: 780-422-0968
cathy.johnson@gov.ab.ca
Program Manager, Mobility & Large Equipment Benefits, Sheron Parmar
Tel: 780-422-8025
Fax: 780-422-0968
sheron.parmar@gov.ab.ca
Manager, AADL Business Unit, Erin Stevens
Tel: 780-422-7684
Fax: 780-422-0968
erin.stevens@gov.ab.ca
Manager, Hearing & Communication Benefits, Patti-Jo Sullivan
Tel: 780-422-6567
Fax: 780-422-0968
patti-jo.sullivan@gov.ab.ca
Respiratory Therapy Consultant, Respiratory Benefits, Mariana Chan
Tel: 780-422-4864
Fax: 780-422-0968
mariana.chan@gov.ab.ca

Family & Population Health Division
Telus Plaza NT, 10025 Jasper Ave., 24th Fl., Edmonton, AB T5J 1S6
Assistant Deputy Minister, Margaret King
Tel: 780-415-2783
Fax: 780-422-3671
margaret.king@gov.ab.ca
Executive Director, Health Protection, Dawn Friesen
Tel: 780-415-2818
Fax: 780-427-1470
dawn.friesen@gov.ab.ca
Executive Director, Wellness Branch, Neil MacDonald
Tel: 780-415-2759
Fax: 780-422-5474
neil.macdonald@gov.ab.ca
Executive Director, Surveillance & Assessment, Kathy Ness
Tel: 780-422-2561
Fax: 780-427-1470
kathy.ness@gov.ab.ca

Financial & Corporate Services Division
Telus Plaza NT, 10025 Jasper Ave., 19th Fl., Edmonton, AB T5J 1S6

Health Benefits & Compliance Division
Telus Plaza NT, 10025 Jasper Ave., 18th Fl., Edmonton, AB T5J 1S6

Health Information Technology & Systems Division
Telus Plaza NT, 10025 Jasper Ave., 21st Fl., Edmonton, AB T5J 1S6
Assistant Deputy Minister & Chief Information Officer, Health Information Technology & Systems Division, Mark Brisson
Tel: 780-427-1572

Fax: 780-422-5176
mark.brisson@gov.ab.ca
Executive Director, EHR Delivery Services, Susan Anderson
Tel: 780-415-2492
Fax: 780-415-2289
susan.anderson@gov.ab.ca
Executive Director, Information Systems Delivery Branch, Chris Kearney
Tel: 780-415-2704
Fax: 780-415-2289
chris.kearney@gov.ab.ca
Executive Director, Information Management Branch, Sue Kessler
Tel: 780-415-2788
Fax: 780-422-6663
sue.kessler@gov.ab.ca
Executive Director, Information Technology & Operations, Blaine Steward
Tel: 780-415-1562
Fax: 780-644-3091
blaine.steward@gov.ab.ca

Health Workforce Division
Telus Plaza NT, 10025 Jasper Ave., 10th Fl., Edmonton, AB T5J 1S6
Assistant Deputy Minister, Glenn Monteith
Tel: 780-415-2745
Fax: 780-415-8455
glenn.monteith@gov.ab.ca
Acting Executive Director, Innovative Compensation & Director, Academic Medicine, Sharon McCaughan
Tel: 780-427-8067
Fax: 780-422-5208
sharon.mccaughan@gov.ab.ca

Primary Health Care Division
Telus Plaza NT, 10025 Jasper Ave., 18th Fl., Edmonton, AB T5J 1S6
Assistant Deputy Minister, Susan A. Williams
Tel: 780-644-3086
Fax: 780-415-0570
susan.williams@gov.ab.ca
Executive Director, Acute/EMS Services Branch, Line Porfon
Tel: 780-415-2762
Fax: 780-422-1515
line.porfon@gov.ab.ca
Executive Director, Addictions & Mental Health, Silvia Vajushi
Tel: 780-422-1344
Fax: 780-422-6663
silvia.vajushi@gov.ab.ca
Executive Director, Clinical Advisory & Research Branch, & Acting Senior Provincial Clinical Advisor, Joan Berezanski
Tel: 780-422-9325
Fax: 780-422-4482
joan.berezanski@gov.ab.ca

Seniors Services & Continuing Care Division
Standard Life Centre, 10405 Jasper Ave., 6th Fl., Edmonton, AB T5J 4R7
Assistant Deputy Minister, Chi Loo
Tel: 780-422-3179
Fax: 780-422-5954
chi.loo@gov.ab.ca
Executive Director, Continuing Care Branch, Tyler James
Tel: 780-422-9678
Fax: 780-422-1515
tyler.james@gov.ab.ca
Executive Director, Seniors Financial Assistance Branch, John Cabral
Tel: 780-422-7270
Fax: 780-422-5954
john.cabral@gov.ab.ca
Director, Seniors Supplementary Supports Branch, Kindy Joseph
Tel: 780-644-8613
Fax: 780-422-5954
kindy.joseph@gov.ab.ca
Director, Seniors Policy & Community Partner Branch, Sarah Carr
Tel: 780-644-2975
Fax: 780-422-5954
sarah.carr@gov.ab.ca

Strategic Services Division
Telus Plaza NT, 10025 Jasper Ave., 22nd Fl., Edmonton, AB T5J 1S6
Assistant Deputy Minister, Linda Mattern
Tel: 780-422-2720
Fax: 780-643-9421
linda.mattern@gov.ab.ca
Executive Director, Deputy Minister Supports Branch, Shannon Haggarty
Tel: 780-415-0953
Fax: 780-643-9421
shannon.haggarty@gov.ab.ca
Executive Director, Information & Analysis, Dee-Jay King
Tel: 780-427-8596
Fax: 780-427-1577
dee-jay.king@gov.ab.ca
Acting Executive Director, Planning, Measuring & Reporting Branch, John Quince
Tel: 780-415-1505
Fax: 780-422-2880
john.quince@gov.ab.ca
Director, Strategic Policy Branch, Hilary Lynas
Tel: 780-643-0978
Fax: 780-422-1515
hilary.lynas@gov.ab.ca

Alberta Human Services

Office of the Minister, Legislature Building, #224, 10800 - 97 Ave., Edmonton, AB T5K 2B6
Tel: 780-644-5135
Toll-Free: 866-644-5135
www.humanservices.alberta.ca
Other Communication: Alberta Supports Contact Centre, Toll-Free Phone: 1-877-644-9992; Family Violence Info Line: 310-1818; Bullying Help Line: 1-888-456-2323
The Ministry of Human Services was created in 2011, under Premier Redford. The ministry is responsible for programs & services in the following areas: children & youth; employment & immigration; homelessness support; & Alberta Supports.
Children & youth services include the following: adoption, child care & early childhood development, child intervention, family support for children with disabilities, & the prevention of family violence & bullying.
Employment & immigration services oversee Alberta Works, employment standards, labour market information, labour relations, occupational health & safety, & immigration.
Homelessness support is involved in the administration of Alberta's Plan to End Homelessness, the Alberta Secretariat for Action on Homelessness, the Gunn Centre, & emergency shelters.
Alberta Supports includes the Alberta Supports Contact Centre.
As of 2012, Human Services is also responsible for programs relating to seniors & persons with disabilities.

Minister, Human Services; Government House Leader, Hon. David Hancock, QC
Tel: 780-643-6210
Fax: 780-643-6214
Social Media: twitter.com/davehancockmla, www.facebook.com/dave.hancock.376, www.linkedin.com/pub/dave-hancock/16/207/959
Legislature Building
#224, 10800 - 97 Ave.
Edmonton, AB T5K 2B6

Associate Minister, Services for Persons with Disabilities, Hon. Frank Oberle
Tel: 780-415-8700
Fax: 780-415-8738

Deputy Minister, Human Services, Steve MacDonald
Tel: 780-427-6448
Fax: 780-422-9044
steve.macdonald@gov.ab.ca

Executive Director, Alberta's Promise Secretariat, Ruth Copot
Tel: 780-403-2599
Fax: 780-297-6664
ruth.copot@gov.ab.ca

Executive Director, Human Resources, Rick Nisbet
Tel: 780-427-7274
Fax: 780-427-3937
rick.nisbet@gov.ab.ca

Executive Director, Organizational Renewal, Dawn White
Tel: 780-415-8964
Fax: 780-415-2003
dawn.white@gov.ab.ca

Director, Communications, Kathy Telfer
Tel: 780-415-6490
Fax: 780-422-3071
kathy.telfer@gov.ab.ca

Associated Agencies, Boards & Commissions:

- **Appeals Commission for Alberta Workers' Compensation**
Energy Square Building
#901, 10109 - 106th St.
Edmonton, AB T5J 3L7
Tel: 780-412-8700
Fax: 780-412-8701
webmaster1@appealscommission.ab.ca
www.appealscommission.ab.ca
Other Communication: Phone, Calgary: 403-508-8800
The Appeals Commission for Alberta Workers' Compensation strives to offer an independent, fair, & timely appeals process. The Commission works to operate consistently with legislation & policy.
Chief Appeals Commissioner, George Pheasey
Tel: 780-412-8735
Fax: 780-412-8701
george.pheasey@gov.ab.ca
Vice-Chair, Appeal Preparation, Rifath Mohanmmed
Tel: 780-412-8729
Fax: 780-412-8701
rifath.mohammed@gov.ab.ca
Vice-Chair, Hearings, Douglass Tadman
Tel: 780-412-8777
Fax: 780-412-8701
douglass.tadman@gov.ab.ca
General Counsel, Sandy Hermiston
Tel: 780-412-8709
Fax: 780-412-8701
sandy.hermiston@gov.ab.ca
Manager, Administrative Services, Sharon Moffat
Tel: 780-412-8740
Fax: 780-412-8701
sharon.moffat@gov.ab.ca
- **Calgary Citizens Appeal Panel**
Human Services, AMEC Pl.
801 - 6 Ave. SW
Calgary, AB T2P 3W2
Tel: 403-297-5636
- **Edmonton Citizens Appeal Panel**
Centre West Building
100335 - 108th St.
Edmonton, AB T5J 3E1
Tel: 780-427-2709
Fax: 780-422-1088
- **Labour Relations Board (ALRB)**
Labour Building
10808 - 99 Ave., 5th Fl.
Edmonton, AB T5K 0G5
Tel: 780-422-5926
Fax: 780-422-0970
Toll-free: 800-463-2572
alrbinfo@lab.gov.ab.ca
www.alrb.gov.ab.ca
The independent & impartial tribunal is involved in the application & interpretation of labour lawa in Alberta. The Alberta Labour Relations Board administers the Labour Relations Code to handle disputes between trade unions & employers.
Chair, Mark Asbell
Tel: 780-422-6707
Fax: 780-422-0970
mark.asbell@gov.ab.ca
Vice-Chair, Lyle Kanee
Tel: 780-422-6963
Fax: 780-422-0970
lyle.kanee@gov.ab.ca
Vice-Chair, Gerry Lucas
Tel: 780-644-5174
Fax: 780-422-0970
gerry.lucas@gov.ab.ca
Vice-Chair, Nancy Schlesinger
Tel: 780-422-6978
Fax: 780-422-0970
nancy.schlesinger@gov.ab.ca

Executive Director, Tannis Brown
Tel: 780-422-3657
Fax: 780-422-0970
tannis.brown@gov.ab.ca
Manager, Settlement, Labour Relations Board - South, Nancy McDermid
Tel: 403-297-4332
Fax: 403-297-5884
nancy.mcdermid@gov.ab.ca
Other Communications: Main Number: 403-297-4334
Tower 3, Deerfoot Junction
1212 - 31 Ave., 3rd Fl.
Calgary, AB T2E 7S8

• Lethbridge Citizens Appeal Panel
Human Services, Administration Building
#408, 909 - 3 Ave. North
Lethbridge, AB T1H 0H5

• Occupational Health & Safety Council (OHSC)
Labour Building
10808 - 99 Ave., 9th Fl.
Edmonton, AB T5K 0G5
Tel: 780-415-8690
Toll-free: 866-415-8690
Under the Occupational Health & Safety Act, the Occupational Health & Safety Council advises the Minister about matters related to the health & safety of Alberta's workers. Nine members serve on the Council, including the chair & representatives from employers, employees, & the public.
Chair, Tim Bennett
Tel: 780-415-0599
Fax: 780-422-8944

• Persons with Developmental Disabilities Community Boards
c/o PDD Program Branch, Peace Hills Trust Tower
10011 - 109 St., 4th Fl.
Edmonton, AB T5J 3S8
Tel: 780-427-1177
Fax: 780-427-1220
Toll-free: 800-310-0000
PDDinfo@gov.ab.ca
www.seniors.alberta.ca/pdd
Six Persons with Developmental Disabilities Community Boards were established by the Persons with Developmental Disabilities Community Governance Act. The boards deliver supports to adults with developmental disabilities. The following services are funded by the program: community living supports for persons in their home environment; employment supports to educate & train individuals; community access supports; & specialized community supports.

• Premier's Council on the Status of Persons with Disabilities
HSBC Building
10055 - 106 St., 11th Fl.
Edmonton, AB T5J 1G3
Tel: 780-422-1095
Toll-free: 800-272-8841
pcspd@gov.ab.ca
www.seniors.alberta.ca/PremiersCouncil
Established in 1988, the mandate for the Premier's Council on the Status of Persons with Disabilities is outlined in the Premier's Council on the Status of Persons with Disabilities Act. The Premier's Council consists of up to fifteen volunteer members who communicate the concerns of Alberta's disability community to the provincial government.

• Red Deer Citizens Appeal Panel
Human Services, Provincial Building
4920 - 51 St.
Red Deer, AB T4N 6K8

• Social Care Facilities Review Committee
Sterling Place
9940 - 106 St., 3rd Fl.
Edmonton, AB T5K 2N2
Other Communication: Complaint Line: 780-427-3010
Senior Manager, Social Care Facilities Review Committee, Beverly Sawicki
Tel: 780-644-2509
Fax: 780-644-6880
beverly.sawicki@gov.ab.ca
Manager, Misty Tryon
Tel: 780-422-1219
Fax: 780-644-6880
misty.tryon@gov.ab.ca

• Workers' Compensation Board (WCB)
9912 - 107 St.
Edmonton, AB T5J 2S5
Tel: 780-498-3999
Fax: 780-427-5863
Toll-free: 866-922-9221
TTY: 780-498-7895
www.wcb.ab.ca
Other Communication: Calgary, Phone: 403-517-6000; Toll-Free Phone, outside Alberta: 1-800-661-9608; Claims, Toll-Free Fax: 1-800-661-1993
The independent organization manages workers' compensation insurance, based on legislation. The Alberta Workers' Compensation Board compensates injured workers for costs such as lost income & health care.
President & Chief Executive Officer, Guy R. Kerr
Chief Financial Officer, R. Helmhold
Chief Audit Executive, A. Muchortow
Vice-President, Customer Service & Risk Management, D. Brunsch
Vice-President, Disability & Information Management, W. King
Vice-President, Employee & Corporate Services, R. Shulha-McKay
General Counsel & Secretary, D. Mah

Aboriginal Policy & Community Engagement Division
Sterling Place, 9940 - 106 St., 10th Fl., Edmonton, AB T5K 2N2

Child & Family Services Delivery Division
Sterling Place, 9940 - 106 St., 12th Fl., Edmonton, AB T5K 2N2
Services for Alberta's families & children are delivered from ten Child & Family Services Authorities located in regions throughout the province.

Child Intervention Program Quality & Supports Division
Sterling Pl., 9940 - 106 St., 10th Fl., Edmonton, AB T5K 2N2
Tel: 780-422-0305
Fax: 780-422-5415

Community Disability Services Division
Standard Life Centre, 10405 Jasper Ave., 3rd Fl., Edmonton, AB T5J 4R7
Assistant Deputy Minister, Brenda Lee Doyle
Tel: 780-427-2593
Fax: 780-427-1689
brendalee.doyle@gov.ab.ca
Acting Executive Director, Persons with Developmental Disabilities Program, Jim Menzies
Tel: 780-427-1216
Fax: 780-427-1220
jim.menzies@gov.ab.ca
Director, Family Support for Children with Disabilities (FSCD) Branch, Laura Alcock
Tel: 780-427-5869
Fax: 780-415-0651
laura.alcock@gov.ab.ca
Acting Director, Office of the Public Guardian, Shirley Peleshytyk
Tel: 780-422-2029
Fax: 780-422-6051
shirley.peleshytyk@gov.ab.ca
Other Communications: Main Number: 780-422-1868
Director, Program Development & Innovation, Tim Weinkauf
Tel: 780-427-1206
Fax: 780-427-1220
tim.weinkauf@gov.ab.ca
Public Trustee, Cindy Bentz
Tel: 780-422-3141
Fax: 780-422-9136
cindy.bentz@gov.ab.ca
Public Guardian - Calgary, Mohinder Bajwa
Tel: 403-297-3393
Fax: 403-297-3427
mohinder.bajwa@gov.ab.ca
Public Guardian - Central Region, Betty Lou Bowles
Tel: 403-340-5502
Fax: 403-340-7131
bettylou.bowles@gov.ab.ca
Public Guardian - South, Connie MacDonald
Tel: 403-381-5653
Fax: 403-381-5774
connie.macdonald@gov.ab.ca
Acting Public Guardian - North, Teresa Overgaard
Tel: 780-645-6296
Fax: 780-645-6260
teresa.overgaard@gov.ab.ca
Assistant Public Guardian - Edmonton, Debbie Urquhart
Tel: 780-422-7824
Fax: 780-422-9138
debbie.urquhart@gov.ab.ca

Community Strategies & Workforce Supports Division
Sterling Place, 9940 - 106 St., 10th Fl., Edmonton, AB T5K 2N2
Tel: 780-427-6428
Fax: 780-422-9045

Corporate Services Division
Standard Life Centre, 10405 Jasper Ave., 2nd Fl., Edmonton, AB T5J 4R7
Tel: 780-638-3560
Assistant Deputy Minister & Senior Financial Officer, Carol Ann Kushlyk
Tel: 780-422-8550
Fax: 780-644-2524
carolann.kushlyk@gov.ab.ca
Chief Information Officer, Vicki Ozaruk
Tel: 780-427-8398
Fax: 780-427-4310
vicki.ozaruk@gov.ab.ca
Executive Director & Senior Financial Officer, Shelley Engstrom
Tel: 780-427-0034
Fax: 780-422-2861
shelley.engstrom@gov.ab.ca
Executive Director & Chief Information Officer, Kevin Molcak
Tel: 780-644-1125
Fax: 780-427-9376
kevin.molcak@gov.ab.ca
Director, Appeals Secretariat, Kevin Young
Tel: 780-422-9079
Fax: 780-422-1088
kevin.young@gov.ab.ca

Disability Policy & Supports Division
Milner Building, 10040 - 104 St., 12th Fl., Edmonton, AB T5J 0Z2
Tel: 780-427-1245
Fax: 780-427-5148
Other Communication: Assured Income for the Severely Handicapped (AISH) Info Line: 1-866-477-8589
Assistant Deputy Minister, Donna Ludvigsen
Tel: 780-644-4555
Fax: 780-427-5148
donna.ludvigsen@gov.ab.ca
Executive Director, Assured Income for the Severely Handicapped (AISH) Delivery Services, Dale Beesley
Tel: 780-644-4731
Fax: 780-644-3299
dale.beesley@gov.ab.ca
Executive Director, Policy, Innovation & Partnerships, Sherri Wilson
Tel: 780-644-9910
Fax: 780-644-2315
sherri.wilson@gov.ab.ca
Director, Assured Income for the Severely Handicapped (AISH) Program & Disability Policy, Gisela Kwok
Tel: 780-422-0714
Fax: 780-644-2315
gisela.kwok@gov.ab.ca
Senior Manager, Finance & Contracting Services, Jackie Lee
Tel: 780-644-5179
Fax: 780-427-9145
jackie.lee@gov.ab.ca
Senior Manager, Fetal Alcohol Spectrum Disorder Initiatives/Children's Mental Health, Denise Milne
Tel: 780-415-0523
Fax: 780-415-0651
denise.milne@gov.ab.ca
Manager, Issues Management & Corporate Support, Susan West
Tel: 780-427-2065
Fax: 780-427-5148
susan.west@gov.ab.ca

Employment Services Delivery Division
Labour Building, 10808 - 99 Ave., 10th Fl., Edmonton, AB T5K 0G5
Tel: 780-415-2946
Fax: 780-427-7548

Family Violence Prevention & Homeless Supports Division
Capital Boulevard, #44, 10044 - 108 St., 3rd Fl., Edmonton, AB T5J 5E6

Tel: 780-643-6648
Fax: 780-644-5796

Service Delivery Transformation Initiative
Standard Life Centre, 10405 Jasper Ave., 4th Fl., Edmonton, AB T5J 4R7
Assistant Deputy Minister, Michele Kirchner
Tel: 780-427-5634
Fax: 780-638-2821
michele.kirchner@gov.ab.ca
Executive Director, Service Delivery Transformation Division, Carolann Regular
Tel: 780-643-1308
Fax: 780-638-2821
carolann.regular@gov.ab.ca
Director, Strategic Integration, Sherry Huston
Tel: 780-644-2230
Fax: 780-638-2381
sherry.huston@gov.ab.ca
Project Director, Business & Technical Integration, Felix Fridman
Tel: 780-427-2684
Fax: 780-638-2821
felix.fridman@gov.ab.ca
Project Director, Service Delivery Redesign, Linda Yargeau
Tel: 780-638-3527
Fax: 780-638-2821
linda.yargeau@gov.ab.ca

Strategic Services Division
Labour Building, 10808 - 99 Ave., 10th Fl., Edmonton, AB T5K 0G5
Tel: 780-427-4093
Fax: 780-422-8462

Workplace Standards Division
Labour Building, 10808 - 99 Ave., 9th Fl., Edmonton, AB T5K 0G5
Tel: 780-644-1500
Fax: 780-422-0014
Other Communication: Employment Standards Inquiries, Toll-Free Phone: 1-877-427-3731
The Division includes occupational health & saftety & employment standards program delivery.
Assistant Deputy Minister, Andrew Sharman
Tel: 780-643-1391
Fax: 780-422-0014
andrew.sharman@gov.ab.ca
Executive Director, Occupational Health & Safety Delivery, Brent McEwan
Tel: 780-415-0603
Fax: 780-644-1508
brent.mcewan@gov.ab.ca
Executive Director, Occupational Health & Safety Policy & Program Development, Ross Nairne
Tel: 780-644-8672
Fax: 780-422-0014
ross.nairne@gov.ab.ca
Executive Director, Employment Standards Program Delivery, Eric Reitsma
Tel: 780-422-5932
Fax: 780-644-5424
eric.reitsma@gov.ab.ca
Executive Director, Workplace Policy, Legislation & Program Development, Tim Thompson
Tel: 780-415-0527
Fax: 780-422-0014
tim.thompson@gov.ab.ca
Director, Parnerships in Injury Reduction, Rob Feagan
Tel: 780-415-0608
Fax: 780-427-5698
rob.feagan@gov.ab.ca
Director, Mediation Services (Labour Mediation), Bertha Greenstein
Tel: 780-415-0530
Fax: 780-427-6327
bertha.greenstein@gov.ab.ca
Manager/Registrar of Appeals & Employment Standards, Verna Carlson
Tel: 780-644-4517
Fax: 780-644-7173
verna.carlson@gov.ab.ca

Alberta Infrastructure

Infrastructure Building, 6950 - 113 St., Edmonton, AB T6H 5V7
Tel: 780-415-0507
Fax: 780-427-2187
Toll-Free: -310-0000
Infra.Contact.Us.m@gov.ab.ca
www.infrastructure.alberta.ca
The Ministry supports the provision of well designed, high quality public infrastructure for the people of Alberta.
Acts Administered:
Builders' Lien Act
Government Organization Act (section 3 of schedule 1; section 4(2) (f) & (g) & 9 of schedule 5; sections 4 to 8 of schedule 5; sections 1, 4, 5, 6-10, & 11-13 of schedule 11)
Hospitals Act (sections 28(1)(a), 42, & 43(h) to (j))
Land Assembly Project Area Act
Mental Health Act (section 53(1)(c))
Nursing Homes Act (sections 6, 11, 23(g) & (j), & 24(l))
Post-secondary Learning Act (sections 66(2) & (3), 67, 72(3) & (4), 73, 80, 99(1)(a) & (2) to (6))
Public Works Act
School Act (part 7, sections 195-206 & section 274)
Water, Gas & Electric Companies Act (section 4)

Minister, Infrastructure, Hon. Wayne Drysdale
Tel: 780-427-5041
Fax: 780-422-2002
Social Media: twitter.com/mla_w_drysdale, www.facebook.com/waynedrysdalemla, www.linkedin.com/pub/wayne-drysdale/1a/159/473
Legislature Building
#324, 10800 - 97 Ave.
Edmonton, AB T5K 2B6

Deputy Minister, Ray Gilmour
Tel: 780-427-3835
Fax: 780-422-6565
ray.gilmour@gov.ab.ca

Executive Director, Human Resources Branch, Dana Thompson
Tel: 780-422-4623
Fax: 780-422-5138
dana.thompson@gov.ab.ca

Director, Human Resources Consulting Services, Linda Flynn
Tel: 780-427-7371
Fax: 780-422-5138
linda.flynn@gov.ab.ca

Director, Communications, Sharon Lopatka
Tel: 780-644-8596
Fax: 780-427-2187
sharon.lopatka@gov.ab.ca

Capital Projects Division
Infrastructure Building, 6950 - 113 St., 2nd Fl., Edmonton, AB T6H 5V7
Tel: 780-427-3700
Assistant Deputy Minister, Diane Dagleish
Tel: 780-422-7436
Fax: 780-422-7599
diane.dalgleish@gov.ab.ca
Executive Director, Health Facilities Branch, Brian Fedor
Tel: 780-422-0616
Fax: 780-638-4158
brian.fedor@gov.ab.ca
Executive Director, Technical Services Branch, Tom O'Neill
Tel: 780-422-7447
Fax: 780-422-7479
Executive Director, Project Delivery Branch, Kent Phillips
Tel: 780-422-0770
Fax: 780-422-9749
kent.phillips@gov.ab.ca
Executive Director, Learning Facilities & Alternative Procurement Branch, Guy A. Smith
Tel: 780-422-7459
Fax: 780-427-5816
guy.smith@gov.ab.ca
Executive Director, Project Services Branch, Brian Soutar
Tel: 780-422-7461
Fax: 780-422-9594
brian.soutar@gov.ab.ca
Director, Divisional Coordination Branch, Lara McClelland
Tel: 780-638-4365
Fax: 780-422-7599
lara.mcclelland@gov.ab.ca

Properties Division
Infrastructure Building, 6950 - 113 St., 3rd Fl., Edmonton, AB T6H 5V7
Tel: 780-427-3881
Fax: 780-422-1389
Assistant Deputy Minister, John Enns
Tel: 780-427-3875
Fax: 780-422-1389
john.enns@gov.ab.ca
Executive Director, Reality Services Branch, Dave Bentley
Tel: 780-422-7489
Fax: 780-415-1641
dave.bentley@gov.ab.ca
Executive Director, Property Development Branch, Rod Dushnicky
Tel: 780-422-3597
Fax: 780-422-5832
rod.dushnicky@gov.ab.ca
Executive Director, Property Management Branch - North Region, Ken Grey
Tel: 780-427-9225
Fax: 780-422-0284
ken.grey@gov.ab.ca
Executive Director, Property Management Branch - South Region, George Tribe
Tel: 780-427-2710
Fax: 780-422-0284
george.tribe@gov.ab.ca
Director, Divisional Coordination Branch, Scott Beeby
Tel: 780-422-9591
Fax: 780-427-6905
scott.beeby@gov.ab.ca

Alberta International & Intergovernmental Relations

Commerce Place, 10155 - 102 St., 12th Fl., Edmonton, AB T5J 4G8
Tel: 780-422-1510
Toll-Free: -310-0000
www.international.alberta.ca
In 2012, under Premier Alison Redford, the new Ministry of International & Intergovernmental Relations was created.
International & Intergovernmental Relations coordinates Alberta's regional, national, & global relationships. The ministry also strives to facilitate trade & to attract investment.
Another responsibility of the ministry is the management of Alberta's international offices. The following international offices work to promote trade & to attract investment & other interests such as culture & education: Alberta China Office; Alberta Germany Office; Alberta Hong Kong Office; Alberta Japan Office; Alberta Korea Office; Alberta Mexico Office; Alberta Shanghai Office; Alberta Taiwan Office; Alberta United Kingdom Office; & Alberta Washington, D.C. Office.

Minister, International & Intergovernmental Relations, Hon. Cal Dallas
Tel: 780-643-6225
Fax: 780-643-6228
Social Media: twitter.com/CalDallas, www.facebook.com/caldallasmla, ca.linkedin.com/pub/cal-dallas/39/557/281
Legislature Building
#320, 10800 - 97 Ave.
Edmonton, AB T5K 2B6

Associate Minister, International & Intergovernmental Affairs, Hon. Teresa Woo-Paw
Tel: 780-415-2363
Fax: 780-422-0471
calgary.northernhills@assembly.ab.ca
Legislature Building
#130, 10800 - 97 Ave.
Edmonton, AB T5K 2B6

Deputy Minister, Roxanna Benoit
Tel: 780-415-0900
Fax: 780-415-6144
roxanna.benoit@gov.ab.ca

Director, Communications, David Sands
Tel: 780-422-2524
Fax: 780-422-2635
david.sands@gov.ab.ca

Senior Manager, Ministerial Issues & Correspondence, Allison Murphy
Tel: 780-422-7296
Fax: 780-422-2635
allison.murphy@gov.ab.ca

Alberta's Representative to Asia, Gary Mar
Tel: 780-427-6079
Fax: 780-427-0699
gary.mar@gov.ab.ca

Associated Agencies, Boards & Commissions:
• Asia Advisory Council (AAC)
www.international.alberta.ca/aac.cfm
Chair, Teresa Woo-Paw
Tel: 780-415-2363
Fax: 780-422-0871
Vice-Chair, Thomas Walter

Corporate Services
Commerce Place, 10155 - 102 St., 12th Fl., Edmonton, AB T5J 4G8
Tel: 780-427-6543
Fax: 780-427-0939
Assistant Deputy Minister, Lorne Harvey
Tel: 780-422-2429
Fax: 780-427-0939
lorne.harvey@gov.ab.ca
Executive Director, Human Resource Services, Pat Connolly
Tel: 780-422-1341
Fax: 780-427-1272
pat.connolly@gov.ab.ca
Executive Director, Finance & Administration, Howard Wong
Tel: 780-427-0793
Fax: 780-427-0939
howard.wong@gov.ab.ca
Director, FOIP, Gerry Kushlyk
Tel: 780-427-9658
Fax: 780-644-4939
gerry.kushlyk@gov.ab.ca
Director, IMIT, Carol Lawrence
Tel: 780-427-0269
Fax: 780-427-4625
carol.lawrence@gov.ab.ca
Director, Corporate Planning, Carol Mayers
Tel: 780-644-1160
Fax: 780-644-4939
carol.mayers@gov.ab.ca
Director, Financial Planning & Administration, Sharon Miskiw
Tel: 780-415-1941
Fax: 780-427-0939
sharon.miskiw@gov.ab.ca
Manager, Corporate Administration, Helen Stiles
Tel: 780-422-0980
Fax: 427-093-9625
helen.stiles@gov.ab.ca

Intergovernmental Relations
Commerce Place, 10155 - 102 St., 12th Fl., Edmonton, AB T5J 4G8
Tel: 780-427-6543
Fax: 780-427-0939
Assistant Deputy Minister, Garry Pocock
Tel: 780-422-0453
Fax: 780-427-0939
garry.pocock@gov.ab.ca
Executive Director, Trade Policy - International, Daryl Hanak
Tel: 780-422-1339
Fax: 780-427-0699
daryl.hanak@gov.ab.ca
Acting Executive Director, Immigration Policy, Don Kwas
Tel: 780-422-0487
Fax: 780-427-0939
don.kwas@gov.ab.ca
Executive Director, Trade Policy - Domestic, Shawn Robbins
Tel: 780-422-1129
Fax: 780-427-0699
shawn.robbins@gov.ab.ca
Executive Director, Federal / Provincial Relations, Bruce Tait
Tel: 780-422-1127
Fax: 780-427-0939
bruce.tait@gov.ab.ca
Executive Director, Social & Economic Policy, Gordon Vincent
Tel: 780-415-6548
Fax: 780-427-0939
gordon.vincent@gov.ab.ca
Director, Federalism, Constitutional Federal / Provincial Relations, Heather Edwards
Tel: 780-644-1223
Fax: 780-427-0939
heather.edwards@gov.ab.ca
Director, Economics & Resources, Randy Fischer
Tel: 780-422-0959
Fax: 780-427-0939
randy.fischer@gov.ab.ca
Director, Canadian Intergovernmental Policy, Clean Energy & Natural Resources / Social Policy, Carla White
Tel: 780-422-0937
Fax: 780-427-0939
carla.white@gov.ab.ca
Assistant Deputy Minister, Jason Krips
Tel: 780-422-5276
Fax: 780-427-0392
jason.krips@gov.ab.ca
Executive Director, Europe, US & International Offices, Chris Heseltine
Tel: 403-297-6377
Fax: 403-297-6168
chris.heseltine@gov.ab.ca
Standard Life Building
639 - 5 Ave. SW, 3rd Fl.
Calgary, AB T2P 0M9
Executive Director, Southern Hemisphere, Greg Jardine
Tel: 780-427-6368
Fax: 780-422-9127
greg.jardine@gov.ab.ca
Executive Director, North Asia & Business Planning, Yvette Ng
Tel: 780-422-2305
Fax: 780-427-0699
yvette.ng@gov.ab.ca
Executive Director, Advocacy, US Relations, & Mission Planning, Marvin Schneider
Tel: 780-422-2332
Fax: 780-422-5486
marvin.schneider@gov.ab.ca
Senior Director, Trade Investment, Middle East / North Africa, Norm Morrison
Tel: 780-427-6421
Fax: 780-422-9127
norm.morrison@gov.ab.ca
Senior Director, Southeast Asia & Oceania, Rahul Sharma
Tel: 780-427-6354
Fax: 780-422-9127
rahul.sharma@gov.ab.ca

International Relations - Alberta International Offices

Alberta has ten international offices. The manadate for each office is to meet the province's priorities in the region.
Alberta China Office Managing Director, Josephine Choi
josephine.choi@international.gc.ca
Other Communications: Phone: 011-86-10-5139-4272; Fax: 011-86-10-5139-4465
c/o Canadian Embassy
19 Dongzhimenwai Dajie, Chaoyang District
Beijing, 100600 China
Alberta Germany Office Commercial & Administrative Assistant, Ilka Jung
ilka.jung@international.gc.ca
Other Communications: Phone: 011-49-89-2199-5741; Fax: 011-49-89-2199-5745
Alberta Germany Office, Canadian Consulate
Tal 29
Munich, 80331 Germany
Alberta Hong Kong Office Trade Director, Christopher Liu
chris.liu@alberta.org.hk
Other Communications: Phone: 011-852-2528-4729; Fax: 011-852-2529-8115
Tower Two, Admiralty Centre
#1004, 18 Harcourt Rd.
Hong Kong, China
Alberta Japan Office Manager (Acting), Norihiro Saito
norihiro.saito@altanet.or.jp
Other Communications: Phone: 011-81-3-3475-1174; Fax: 011-81-3-3470-3939
Place Canada, 3rd Fl.
3-37 Akasaka 7 - chome Minato-ku
Tokyo, 107-0052 Japan
Alberta Korea Office Commercial Director, Won-il Chung
wonil.chung@international.gc.ca
Other Communications: Phone: 011-82-2-3783-6142; Fax: 011-82-2-3783-6147
c/o Embassy of Canada
21 Jeongdong-gil (Jeong-dong), Jung-gu
Seoul, 110-1202 South Korea
Alberta Mexico Office Managing Director, Tim Hazlett
Tel: 780-427-6679
Fax: 780-422-2091
tim.hazlett@gov.ab.ca
Alberta Taiwan Office Representative, Li-an Chen
lian.chen@international.gc.ca
Other Communications: Phone: 011-886-2-8789-2006; Fax: 011-886-2-8789-1878
Canadian Trade Office
6F, No. 1, Song Zhi Rd., ZinYi District
Taipei City, 11047 Taiwan
Alberta United Kingdom Office Managing Director, Jeffrey Sundquist
jeffrey.sundquist@international.gc.ca
Other Communications: Phone: 011-44-20-7258-6472; Fax: 011-44-20-7258-6309
Canadian High Commission, MacDonald House
1 Grosvenor Sq.
London, W1K 4AB UK
Alberta Washington DC Office Director, Alberta - USA Relations, Tristan Sanregret
Tel: 202-448-6474
Fax: 202-448-6477
tristan.sanregret@gov.ab.ca
Canadian Embassy
501 Pennsylvania Ave. NW
Washington, DC 20001 USA

Minister, Justice; Solicitor General, Hon. Jonathan Denis
Tel: 780-427-2339
Fax: 780-422-6621
calgary.acadia@assembly.ab.ca
Legislature Building
#403, 10800 - 97 Ave.
Edmonton, AB T5K 2B6

Deputy Minister, Justice; Deputy Attorney General, Ray Bodnarek, QC
Tel: 780-427-5032
Fax: 780-422-9639
ray.bodnarek@gov.ab.ca

Deputy Minister, Public Security; Deputy Solicitor General, Jay Ramotar
Tel: 780-427-3814
Fax: 780-427-0727
jay.ramotar@gov.ab.ca
John E. Brownlee Building
10365 - 97 St., 9th Fl
Edmonton, AB T5J 3W7
Assistant Deputy Minister, Denise Perret
Tel: 780-427-0912
Fax: 780-422-9639
denise.perret@gov.ab.ca

Alberta Municipal Affairs

Communications Branch, Commerce Place, 10155 - 102 St., 18th Fl., Edmonton, AB T5J 4L4
Tel: 780-427-2732
Fax: 780-422-1419
comments@gov.ab.ca
www.municipalaffairs.alberta.ca
In 2011, under Premier Redford, the Ministry of Municipal Affairs took on the responsibilities of the former Ministry of Housing & Urban Affairs.
Alberta's Ministry of Municipal Affairs is engaged in the following activities: assisting Alberta's municipalities in the provision of well-managed, accountable local government; managing municipal & library system boards; administering a safety system for the construction & maintenance of equipment & buildings; ensuring safe, affordable, & sustainable housing for Albertans; & assisting urban communities.
Acts Administered:
Alberta Housing Act
City of Lloydminster Act
Emergency Management Act
Government Organization Act
Libraries Act

Local Authorities Election Act
Municipal Government Act
New Home Buyer Protection Act
Parks Towns Act
Public Highways Development Act
Safety Codes Act
Social Care Facilities Licensing Act
Special Areas Act

Minister, Municipal Affairs, Hon. Doug Griffiths
Tel: 780-427-3744
Fax: 780-422-9550
Social Media: twitter.com/griffmla, www.facebook.com/Griffs4ABsFuture?sk=app_53267368995
Legislature Building
#104, 10800 - 97 Ave.
Edmonton, AB T5K 2B6

Associate Minister, Hon. Greg Weadick
Tel: 780-422-5627
Fax: 780-422-8983

Deputy Minister, Paul Whittaker
Tel: 780-427-4826
Fax: 780-422-9561
paul.whittaker@gov.ab.ca

Chief of Staff, Tim Morrison
Tel: 780-427-3744
Fax: 780-422-9550
tim.morrison@gov.ab.ca

Coordinator, Scheduling, Camille Hauck
Tel: 780-427-3744
Fax: 780-422-9550
camille.hauck@gov.ab.ca

Executive Director, Human Resource Services, Sandra Kraatz
Tel: 780-422-8681
Fax: 780-422-0214
sandra.kraatz@gov.ab.ca
HSBC Building
10055 - 106 St., 5th Fl.
Edmonton, AB T5J 1G3

Director, Communications, Cameron Traynor
Tel: 780-415-4758
Fax: 780-422-1419
cameron.traynor@gov.ab.ca

Director & Solicitor, Legal Services, Bill Nugent, Q.C.
Tel: 780-422-8795
Fax: 780-427-0996
bill.nugent@gov.ab.ca
Commerce Place
10155 - 102 St., 18th Fl.
Edmonton, AB T5J 4L4

Manager, Executive Correspondence, Chuck Costello
Tel: 780-422-9338
Fax: 780-422-1419
chuck.costello@gov.ab.ca

Associated Agencies, Boards & Commissions:
• Alberta Emergency Management Agency (AEMA)
c/o Alberta Municipal Affairs, Communications Branch
10155 - 102 St., 18th Fl.
Edmonton, AB T5J 4L4
Tel: 780-422-9000
Fax: 780-644-1044
Toll-free: -310-0000
aema@gov.ab.ca
www.aema.alberta.ca
Other Communication: Alberta Emergency Management Agency Response Readiness Centre, Phone: 1-866-618-2362
The Alberta Emergency Management Agency coordinates organizations, such as government, municipalities, & first responders, which are involved in the prevention, preparedness, & response to emergencies.
Managing Director, Colin Lloyd
Tel: 780-422-6591
Fax: 780-644-1044
colin.lloyd@gov.ab.ca
Executive Director, Provincial Operations, John Conrad
Tel: 780-422-6592
Fax: 780-422-1549
john.conrad@gov.ab.ca
Acting Director, Central Operations, Stephen Carr
Tel: 780-644-4407
Fax: 780-422-1549
stephen.carr@gov.ab.ca
Manager, Recovery Programs, Brad Ison
Tel: 780-415-9483
Fax: 780-422-1549
brad.ison@gov.ab.ca
Director, Public Safety Initiatives, Training & Policy Development, Len Hancock
Tel: 780-422-8682
Fax: 780-644-1044
len.hancock@gov.ab.ca
Executive Director, Public Safety Initiatives, Dave Galea
Tel: 780-415-0914
Fax: 780-644-1044
dave.galea@gov.ab.ca
• Capital Region Board
Bell Tower
#1405, 10104 - 103 Ave.
Edmonton, AB T5J 0H8
Tel: 780-638-6000
Fax: 780-638-6009
www.capitalregionboard.ab.ca
The Government of Alberta established the Capital Region Board in 2008. The Board consists of members from twenty-four participating municipalities. They serve on the following committees: land use; transit; Geographic Information Services; housing; & governance.
The following are the municipalities of the Capital Region Board: Town of Beaumont; Town of Bon Accord; Town of Bruderheim; Town of Calmar; Town of Devon; City of Edmonton; City of Fort Saskatchewan; Town of Gibbons; Lamont County; Town of Lamont; City of Leduc; Leduc County; Town of Legal; Town of Morinville; Parkland County; Town of Redwater; City of St. Albert; City of Spruce Grove; Town of Stony Plain; Strathcona County; Sturgeon County; Village of Thorsby; Village of Wabamun; & the Village of Warburg.
Chief Officer, Kathleen LeClair
Tel: 780-638-6002
kleclair@capitalregionboard.ab.ca
Manager, Regional Projects, Neal Sarnecki
Tel: 780-638-6003
nsarnecki@capitalregionboard.ab.ca
Manager, Regional Projects, Sharon Shuya
Tel: 780-638-6004
sshuya@capitalregionboard.ab.ca
• Gunn Centre
PO Box 130
Gunn, AB T0E 1A0
Tel: 780-967-2221
Fax: 780-967-3494
Since 1941, the Gunn Centre has offered services to disadvantaged men. The Centre provides temporary accommodation & support services to help men reestablish their lives.
Director, Homeless Support, Lynn Bell
Tel: 780-967-2221
Fax: 780-967-3494
lynn.bell@gov.ab.ca
Team Lead, Resident Incentive Program, David Daniel
Tel: 780-967-2221
Fax: 780-967-3494
david.daniel@gov.ab.ca
Team Lead, Administration, Susan Huberdeau
Tel: 780-967-2221
Fax: 780-967-3494
susan.huberdeau@gov.ab.ca
Team Lead, Resident Services, Peggy Massey
Tel: 780-967-2221
Fax: 780-967-3494
peggy.massey@gov.ab.ca
Team Lead, Medical Services, Genevieve Simmons
Tel: 780-967-2221
Fax: 780-967-3494
genevieve.simmons@gov.ab.ca
• Municipal Government Board (MGB)
Commerce Place
10155 - 102 St., 15th Fl.
Edmonton, AB T5J 4L4
Tel: 780-427-4864
Fax: 780-427-0986
Toll-free: -310-0000
mgbmail@gov.ab.ca
www.municipalaffairs.alberta.ca
Operating as an independent & impartial body, the Municipal Government Board decides upon certain appeals & disputes from the Municipal Government Act. Examples of issues dealt with by the Municipal Government Board are as follows: disputes between municipalities; annexation matters; linear property assessment complaints; & appeals about equalized assessment & subdivisions.
Chair, Ken Lesniak
Tel: 780-422-8655
Fax: 780-427-0986
ken.lesniak@gov.ab.ca
Director, Dennis Woolsey
Tel: 780-422-8080
Fax: 780-427-0986
dennis.woolsey@gov.ab.ca
• Safety Codes Council (SCC)
#1000, 10665 Jasper Ave. NW
Edmonton, AB T5J 3S9
Tel: 780-413-0099
Fax: 780-424-5134
Toll-free: 888-413-0099
sccinfo@safetycodes.ab.ca
www.safetycodes.ab.ca
Other Communication: Toll-Free Fax: 1-888-424-5134
The Safety Codes Council is a corporation that supports the Ministry of Municipal Affairs' administration of the Safety Codes Act. The Council has the following business units: Accreditation & Appeals; Administration; Certification & Policy; Electronic Business Solutions; & Training.
President & Chief Executive Officer, Brian Alford
Tel: 780-413-6054
Administrator, Accreditation, & Coordinator, Appeals, Gerald Baron
Tel: 780-413-6043
Administrator, Certification, Mike MacPherson
Tel: 780-413-6081
Coordinator, Research, Policy, & Investigations, Doug Clough
Tel: 780-969-1005
Manager, Electronic Business Solutions, Bruce Eckel
Tel: 780-413-6052
Manager, Training, Celia McDonagh
Tel: 780-413-6056
Controller, Louise Lalor
Tel: 780-969-1001
Officer, Communications, Christy McPhillamey
Tel: 780-424-7377
• Special Areas Board
Special Areas Board Administration
212 - 2nd Ave. West
PO Box 820
Hanna, AB T0J 1P0
Tel: 403-854-5600
Fax: 403-854-5527
specarea@telus.net
www.specialareas.ab.ca
Other Communication: Hanna, Phone: 403-854-5625; Oyen, Phone: 403-664-3618, Fax: 403-664-3320; Consort, Phone: 403-577-3523, Fax: 403-577-2446; Youngstown, Phone: 403-779-3733
The Special Areas Board is responsible for the management of public land in Alberta's three Special Areas. The Board also provides municipal services to eastern Alberta's dryland region.
The following are examples of programs & services offered by the Special Areas Board: protective & emergency services; construction & maintenance of local roads; provision of water services; management of public land; operation & maintenance of Special Areas recreational parks & community pastures; conservation programming; agricultural development; & economic development programs.
Chair, Jay J. Slemp

Corporate Strategic Services Division
Commerce Place, 10155 - 102 St., 18th Fl., Edmonton, AB T5J 4L4
Assistant Deputy Minister, Anthony Lemphers
Tel: 780-415-9099
Fax: 780-422-4923
anthony.lemphers@gov.ab.ca
Executive Director & Senior Financial Officer, Financial Services, Dan Balderston
Tel: 780-644-8098

Fax: 780-422-5840
dan.balderston@gov.ab.ca
Executive Director, Corporate Planning & Policy, Indira Breitkreuz
Tel: 780-422-7317
Fax: 780-422-4923
indira.breitkreuz@gov.ab.ca
Director, Information Technology, Heather Cox
Tel: 780-427-6097
Fax: 780-422-0776
heather.cox@gov.ab.ca
Director, Public Library Services, Diana Davidson
Tel: 780-415-0284
Fax: 780-415-8594
diana.davidson@gov.ab.ca
Director, Information Management, Legislative & Administrative Services, Wilma Sisk
Tel: 780-422-8834
Fax: 780-643-1090
wilma.sisk@gov.ab.ca

Housing & Urban Affairs
44 Capital Boulevard, 10044 - 108 St. 3rd Fl., Edmonton, AB T5J 5E6
Tel: 780-422-0122
Coordinator, Correspondence Management Unit, Dianne Singh
Tel: 780-422-8422
Fax: 780-644-5796
dianne.singh@gov.ab.ca
Program Advisor, Kelly Santarossa
Tel: 780-422-8240
Fax: 780-644-5796
kelly.santarossa@gov.ab.ca
#301, 7015 Macleod Trail South
Calgary, AB T2H 2K6
ARTS Administrator, Sherry Wynnyk
Tel: 780-644-5284
Fax: 780-644-5796
sherry.wynnyk@gov.ab.ca
Assistant Deputy Minister, Mike Leathwood
Tel: 780-638-3383
Fax: 780-422-8462
mike.leathwood@gov.ab.ca
Executive Director, Housing Development, Don Squire
Tel: 780-427-5786
Fax: 780-422-5124
don.squire@gov.ab.ca
Manager, Program Delivery, Walter Tauber
Tel: 780-427-8137
Fax: 780-422-5124
walter.tauber@gov.ab.ca
Director, Financial Monitoring & Contract Administration, Philip Henke
Tel: 780-422-8157
Fax: 780-422-5124
philip.henke@gov.ab.ca
Director, Financial Support, Peggy Kornega
Tel: 780-422-8255
Fax: 780-427-0418
peggy.kornega@gov.ab.ca
Administrator, Rent Supplement Program, Karen Butkowski
Tel: 780-422-8202
Fax: 780-422-8551
karen.butkowski@gov.ab.ca
Manager, North Operations, Bill Draper
Tel: 780-427-5785
Fax: 780-422-8551
bill.draper@gov.ab.ca
Manager, South Operations, David Staines
Tel: 780-297-5773
Fax: 780-297-6138
david.staines@gov.ab.ca
Manager, Special Operations, Lana Braidot
Tel: 780-415-1237
Fax: 780-415-9345
lana.braidot@gov.ab.ca

Local Government Services Division
Commerce Place, 10155 - 102 St., 17th Fl., Edmonton, AB T5J 4L4
Assistant Deputy Minister, Michael Merritt
Tel: 780-427-9660
Fax: 780-427-0453
michael.merritt@gov.ab.ca
Executive Director, Municipal Services Branch, Gary Sandberg
Tel: 780-422-8034
Fax: 780-420-1016
gary.sandberg@gov.ab.ca
Executive Director, Assessment Services Branch, Steve White
Tel: 780-422-1377
Fax: 780-422-3110
steve.white@gov.ab.ca
Director, Strategic Planning & Program Integration, James Acheson
Tel: 780-422-8908
Fax: 780-427-0453
james.acheson@gov.ab.ca
Director, Education Tax & Assessment Advisory, Lynda Downey
Tel: 780-422-8313
Fax: 780-422-3110
lynda.downey@gov.ab.ca
Director, Legislative Projects, Erin Foster-O'Riordan
Tel: 780-644-5684
Fax: 780-644-4941
safety.services@gov.ab.ca
Director, Assessment Audit, Brian Ferguson
Tel: 780-422-8396
Fax: 780-422-3110
brian.ferguson@gov.ab.ca
Director, Capacity Building, Colin Doupe
Tel: 780-427-9290
Fax: 780-420-1016
colin.doupe@gov.ab.ca
Director, Municipal Collaboration, Theresa Ostrum
Tel: 780-422-8053
Fax: 780-420-1016
theresa.ostrum@gov.ab.ca
Director, Linear Property Assessment, Chris Risling
Tel: 780-422-8414
Fax: 780-422-3110
chris.risling@gov.ab.ca
Executive Director, Grants & Education Property Tax Branch, Janice Romanyshyn
Tel: 780-415-0833
Fax: 780-422-9133
janice.romanyshyn@gov.ab.ca
Director, Planning & Policy Advisory, Bill Symonds
Tel: 780-422-8355
Fax: 780-422-8624
bill.symonds@gov.ab.ca
Director, Regulated Assessment Policy, Sheila Young
Tel: 780-422-8078
Fax: 780-644-4941
sheila.young@gov.ab.ca
Executive Director, Major Legislative Projects & Strategic Planning, Brandy Cox
Tel: 780-415-9786
Fax: 780-644-6941
brandy.cox@gov.ab.ca

Public Safety Division
Commerce Place, 10155 - 102 St., 16th Fl., Edmonton, AB T5J 4L4
Assistant Deputy Minister, Ivan Moore
Tel: 780-638-3245
Fax: 780-427-2538
ivan.moore@gov.ab.ca
Executive Director, Safety Services Branch, Chris Tye
Tel: 780-644-5691
Fax: 780-427-8686
safety.services@gov.ab.ca
Director, Legislation & Strategic Projects, Joan Armstrong
Tel: 780-427-2279
Fax: 780-427-2538
joan.armstrong@gov.ab.ca
Director, Risk Management & Finance, Diane McLean
Tel: 780-427-6133
Fax: 780-427-2538
diane.mclean@gov.ab.ca
Director, Safety Assurance Services, Alex Morrison
Tel: 780-644-1010
Fax: 403-297-4174
safety.services@gov.ab.ca
Director, Codes & Standards, James Orr
Tel: 780-644-1010
Fax: 780-427-8686
safety.services@gov.ab.ca
Director, Field Technical Services, Randy Paulson
Tel: 780-644-1010
Fax: 780-427-8686
safety.services@gov.ab.ca
Manager, Operational Support Services, Don Rebus
Tel: 780-644-1010
Fax: 780-427-8686
safety.services@gov.ab.ca
Project Coordinator, Tank Site Remediation Program, Stephen Hoare
Tel: 780-415-8665
Fax: 780-415-8664
stephen.hoare@gov.ab.ca
Assistant Deputy Minister, Bruce McDonald
Tel: 780-422-3188
Fax: 780-422-5124
bruce.mcdonald@gov.ab.ca
Chief Information Officer & Executive Director, Information Management & Technology, Dean Lussier
Tel: 780-427-1751
Fax: 780-427-0418
dean.lussier@gov.ab.ca
Executive Director & Senior Financial Officer, Finance & Administrative Services, Robert Lee
Tel: 780-643-1324
Fax: 780-427-0418
robert.lee@gov.ab.ca
Director, Strategic Planning & Legislative Program Services, Cynthia Evans
Tel: 780-422-8306
Fax: 780-422-5124
cynthia.evans@gov.ab.ca
Director, Strategic Policy & Urban Affairs, Patti Giberson
Tel: 780-644-2609
Fax: 780-422-5124
patti.giberson@gov.ab.ca
Director, Financial Services, Trevor Mireau
Tel: 780-643-1655
Fax: 780-427-0418
trevor.mireau@gov.ab.ca
Director, Financial Planning, Christine Oness
Tel: 780-427-2925
Fax: 780-427-0418
christine.oness@gov.ab.ca
Senior Manager, Federal - Provincial Relations, Kildy Yuen
Tel: 780-422-8133
Fax: 780-422-5124
kildy.yuen@gov.ab.ca
Advisor, Privacy & Information, Holly Simpson
Tel: 780-638-2979
Fax: 780-427-0418
holly.simpson@gov.ab.ca

Alberta Public Affairs Bureau (PAB)

Park Plaza, 10611 - 98 Ave., 6th Fl., Edmonton, AB T5K 2P7
Tel: 780-427-2754
Fax: 780-422-4168
Toll-Free: -310-0000
www.publicaffairs.alberta.ca
Communications are provided by the Public Affairs Bureau to support Alberta's government ministries. The Public Affairs Bureau provides information about government policies & programs to Albertans. The Bureau is also responsible for coordinating communications during public emergencies.

Managing Director, Lee Funke
Tel: 780-644-5655
Fax: 780-427-1010
lee.funke@gov.ab.ca

Service Alberta

Government of Alberta, PO Box 1333Edmonton, AB T5J 2N2
Tel: 780-427-4088
Toll-Free: -310-0000
service.alberta@gov.ab.ca
www.servicealberta.ca
Other Communication: Consumer Information, E-mail: cs@gov.ab.ca; Corporate Registry, E-mail: cr@gov.ab.ca; Land Titles, E-mail: lto@gov.ab.ca; Landlords & Tenants, E-mail: rta@gov.ab.ca
The Ministry of Service Alberta offers information, services, & products to Albertans. The following are examples of the ministry's services: delivery of shared services to ministries, such as printing documents & technical support; management of the government's vehicle fleet; administration of the Freedom of Information & Protection of Privacy legislation; provision of licensing

& registry services; & enforcement of high standards of consumer protection.

Minister, Service Alberta, Hon. Manmeet S. Bhullar
Tel: 780-422-6880
Fax: 780-422-2496
Social Media: twitter.com/manmeetsbhullar, www.facebook.com/manmeetbhullarmla
Legislature Building
#103, 10800 - 97 Ave.
Edmonton, AB T5K 2B6

Associate Minister of Accountability, Transparency & Transformation, Hon. Don Scott
Tel: 780-415-1356
Fax: 780-415-1711

Deputy Minister, Doug Lynkowski
Tel: 780-427-1990
Fax: 780-427-4999
doug.lynkowski@gov.ab.ca
Telus Plaza South
10020 - 100 St., 29th Fl.
Edmonton, AB T5J 0N3

Chief of Staff, Emir Mehinagic
Tel: 780-422-6880
Fax: 780-422-2496
emir.mehinagic@gov.ab.ca

Executive Director, Human Resource Services, Gerry Jacubo
Tel: 780-427-8352
Fax: 780-427-4999
gerry.jacubo@gov.ab.ca

Director, Communications, Gerald Kastendieck
Tel: 780-427-6699
Fax: 780-415-9816
gerald.kastendieck@gov.ab.ca

Manager, Ministry Advisory Services, Diane Carter
Tel: 780-644-4524
Fax: 780-422-0956
diane.carter@gov.ab.ca

Associated Agencies, Boards & Commissions:
• Alberta Funeral Services Regulatory Board (AFSRB)
11810 Kingsway Ave.
Edmonton, AB T5G 0X5
Tel: 780-452-6130
Fax: 780-452-6085
Toll-free: 800-563-4652
office@afsrb.ab.ca; complaints@afsrb.ab.ca; education@afsrb.ab.ca
www.afsrb.ab.ca
In 1992, the Alberta Funeral Services Regulatory Board was established under the Licensing of Trades & Businesses Act & the Funeral Services Business Licensing Regulation.
The Board provides the following services: establishing educational standards; licensing pre-need salespeople, funeral directors, embalmers, funeral businesses, & crematories; monitoring performance standards; & investigating consumer complaints.
Chair, Marlon Wombold
Vice-Chair & Member, Eucation Committee, Peter Portock
Administrator, Marilyn McPherson
administrator@afsrb.ab.ca
Inspector & Investigator, Wayne Konner
inspector@afsrb.ab.ca
Treasurer & Member, Complaints Committee, Ian Meikle
treasurer@afsrb.ab.ca
• Alberta Motor Vehicle Industry Council (AMVIC)
#303, 9945 - 50 St.
Edmonton, AB T6A 0L4
Tel: 780-466-1140
Fax: 780-462-0633
www.amvic.org
Other Communication: Investigations, Toll-Free Phone: 1-877-279-8200; Licensing, Toll-Free Phone: 1-877-979-8100
The Alberta Motor Vehicle Industry Council is responsible for the administration & enforcement of automotive industry regulations, under Alberta's Fair Trading Act.
Chair, Brian Heninger
Executive Director, Bob Hamilton
Director, Investigations, Bob Knight
Director, Licensing & Finance, Shannon DeLorey
• Money Mentors
Quikcard Centre
#175, 17010 - 102rd Ave.
Edmonton, AB T5S 1K7
Fax: 780-423-2791
Toll-free: 888-294-0076
info@moneymentors.ca
www.moneymentors.ca
Formerly known as Credit Counselling Services of Alberta, Money Mentors is a not-for-profit credit counselling & money coaching organization. It serves Albertans by educating them about personal money management & offering alternatives for those who encounter financial difficulties.
Chair, Gary Howitt
Executive Director, Jim Thorne
Legal Counsel, Monica Sharma
Coordinator, Community Relations, Wayne Coristine
Tel: 403-234-6198
wcoristine@moneymentors.ca
Secretary, Lynn Sande
• Real Estate Council of Alberta (RECA)
#350, 4954 Richard Rd. SW
Calgary, AB T3E 6L1
Tel: 403-228-2954
Fax: 403-228-3065
Toll-free: 888-425-2754
info@reca.ca
www.reca.ca
Operating under the Real Estate Act of Alberta, the Real Estate Council of Alberta is responsible for the regulation of professionals in the real estate, real estate appraisal, & mortgage broker industries. The Council is made up of the following committees: Audit, Finance, Governance, Hearings, & the Education Ad Hoc Committee.
Chair, Robert Telford

Strategic Planning & Financial Services
Commerce Place, 10155 - 102 St., 13th Fl., Edmonton, AB T5J 4G8
Tel: 780-422-8545
Executive Director & Senior Financial Officer, Strategic Planning & Financial Services, Althea Hutchinson
Tel: 780-415-8975
Fax: 780-427-0307
althea.hutchinson@gov.ab.ca
Director, Planning & Performance Measurement, Chrenan Borradaile
Tel: 780-427-0282
Fax: 780-427-0307
chrenan.borradaile@gov.ab.ca
Director, Financial Reporting & Policy, Rene Mella
Tel: 780-427-1882
Fax: 780-427-0307
rene.mella@gov.ab.ca
Manager, Shared Services Administration & Special Projects, Gerry Boily
Tel: 780-427-6622
Fax: 780-427-0307
gerry.boily@gov.ab.ca
Manager, Financial Planning & Analysis, Jennifer Gleave
Tel: 780-422-8167
Fax: 780-427-0307
jennifer.gleave@gov.ab.ca

Alberta Tourism, Parks, & Recreation

Communications Branch, Commerce Place, 10155 - 102 St., 6th Fl., Edmonton, AB T5J 4L6
Tel: 780-644-5589
TTY: 780-427-9999
TPR.Communications@gov.ab.ca
www.tpr.alberta.ca
Other Communication: TTY Toll-Free: 1-800-232-7215
Alberta's Ministry of Tourism, Parks, & Recreation was established in 2008.
The Ministry works to develop the tourism industry in Alberta by facilitating the profitability & sustainability of both existing & new tourism operations, positioning land for tourism, creating a positive policy environment, assisting with regulatory processes, & promoting tourism investment.
The Ministry of Tourism, Parks, & Recreation is also responsible for Alberta's network of parks & protected areas. These areas offer Albertans & tourists opportunities to appreciate the province's natural heritage & to participate in educational & recreational activities.
Promoting recreation & sports for healthy living & athletic excellence is another goal of the Ministry of Tourism, Parks, & Recreation. The government ministry works with recreation & sport associations & provides funding for recreation facilities across the province to achieve this goal.

Minister, Tourism, Parks, & Recreation, Hon. Christine Cusanelli
Tel: 780-427-4928
Fax: 780-427-0188
Legislature Building
#229, 10800 - 97 Ave.
Edmonton, AB T5K 2B6

Deputy Minister, Brad Pickering
Tel: 780-644-5139
Fax: 780-644-5145
brad.pickering@gov.ab.ca

Acting Director, Communications, Katrina Bluetchen
Tel: 780-427-8761
Fax: 780-644-5586
katrina.bluetchen@gov.ab.ca

Director, Issues Management, Paul Leeder
Tel: 780-415-1098
Fax: 780-644-5145
paul.leeder@gov.ab.ca

Coordinator, Correspondence, Rubena Hassan
Tel: 780-644-5139
Fax: 780-644-5145
rubena.hassan@gov.ab.ca

Associated Agencies, Boards & Commissions:
• Alberta Sport, Recreation, Parks, & Wildlife Foundation (ASRPWF)
Standard Life Centre
#903, 10405 Jasper Ave., 9th Fl.
Edmonton, AB T5J 4R7
Tel: 780-415-1167
Fax: 780-415-0308
Toll-free: -310-0000
www.cd.gov.ab.ca/asrpwf
Supported by the Alberta Lottery Fund, the Alberta Sport, Recreation, Parks, & Wildlife Foundation reports to the Minister of Alberta Tourism, Parks, & Recreation. The Foundation's objectives are provided in the Alberta, Sport, Recreation, Parks, & Wildlife Foundation Act.
The Alberta Sport, Recreation, Parks, & Wildlife Foundation develops partnerships with sport, recreation, active living, & parks & wildlife programs, in order to encourage & enhance athletic excellence, active lifestyles, & the conservation of natural areas.
The Foundation funds a variety of organizations throughout Alberta, such as Alberta Active Living agencies, the Percy Page Centre, sport & recreation associations, & sport development centres.
Chair, Kay Kenny
Vice-Chair, John Short
Contact, Sponsorship or Partner Programs, Dennis Allen
Tel: 403-297-2729
Fax: 403-297-6669
Dennis.Allen@gov.ab.ca
Contact, Arctic Winter Games, Cam Berwald
Tel: 780-422-7109
Fax: 780-427-5140
Cam.Berwald@gov.ab.ca
Contact, Development Initiatives Program, Marvin Dobish
Tel: 780-644-3616
Fax: 780-427-5140
Marvin.Dobish@gov.ab.ca
Contact, Alberta's Future Leaders, Scott Grevlund
Tel: 780-422-7110
Fax: 780-427-5140
Scott.Grevlund@gov.ab.ca
Contact, Event Support Program & Alberta Games & Marketing Branch, Jan Karakochuk
Tel: 403-297-2909
Fax: 403-297-6669
jan.karakochuk@gov.ab.ca
Contact, Park & Wildlife Ventures, Bernie MacDonald
Tel: 780-415-0266
Fax: 780-427-5140
Bernie.MacDonald@gov.ab.ca
Contact, Active Living, Chris Szabo
Tel: 780-415-0270

Fax: 780-427-5140
Chris.Szabo@gov.ab.ca
• Travel Alberta
2500
Edmonton, AB T5J 2Z4
Tel: 780-427-4321
Toll-free: 800-252-3782
travelinfo@TravelAlberta.com
www.travelalberta.com
Travel Alberta is a marketing organization that is engaged in the following activities: promotion of Alberta as a tourist destination; administration of the Tourism Information System; management of the Travel Alberta Contact / Distribution Centre; & the operation of a network of Visitor Information Centres.

Parks Division
Oxbridge Place, 9820 - 106 St., 2nd Fl., Edmonton, AB T5K 2J6
Tel: 780-427-3582
Fax: 780-427-5980
Toll-Free: 866-427-3582
Assistant Deputy Minister, Graham Statt
Tel: 780-644-4948
Fax: 780-427-5980
graham.statt@gov.ab.ca
Executive Director, Program Coordination, Parks & Protected Areas Program, Steve Donelon
Tel: 403-678-5500
Fax: 403-678-5505
steve.donelon@gov.ab.ca
Director, Policy & Strategic Support, Brian Kelly
Tel: 780-427-9382
Fax: 780-427-5980
brian.kelly@gov.ab.ca
Director, Land Management, Archie Landals
Tel: 780-427-9470
Fax: 780-427-5980
archie.landals@gov.ab.ca
Director, Parks Finance Section, Dale Schinkel
Tel: 780-427-8224
Fax: 780-427-5980
dale.schinkel@gov.ab.ca
Director, Operations, Learning, & Stewardship, Mark Storie
Tel: 780-427-9383
Fax: 780-427-5980
mark.storie@gov.ab.ca

Recreation & Sport Development Division
Standard Life Centre, 10405 Jasper Ave., 9th Fl., Edmonton, AB T5J 4R7
Assistant Deputy Minister, Tim Moorhouse
Tel: 780-422-3305
Fax: 780-415-0308
tim.moorhouse@gov.ab.ca
Executive Director, Sport Excellence Branch, Lloyd Bentz
Tel: 780-415-0263
Fax: 780-415-0308
lloyd.bentz@gov.ab.ca
Director, Marketing & Provincial Sport Branch, Dennis Allen
Tel: 403-297-2729
Fax: 403-297-6669
dennis.allen@gov.ab.ca
Director, Physical Activity Branch, Roger Kramers
Tel: 780-415-0272
Fax: 780-427-5140
roger.kramers@gov.ab.ca
Director, Outdoor Development Branch, Bernie MacDonald
Tel: 780-415-0268
Fax: 780-427-5140
bernie.macdonald@gov.ab.ca
Director, High Performance Sport Branch, Scott Fraser
Tel: 780-422-8310
Fax: 780-427-5140
scott.c.fraser@gov.ab.ca

Special Projects Division
Commerce Place, 10155 - 102 St., 6th Fl., Edmonton, AB T5J 4L6
Assistant Deputy Minister, Bob Scott
Tel: 780-415-0892
Fax: 780-427-0778
bob.scott@gov.ab.ca

Strategic Corporate Services Division
Commerce Place, 10155 - 102 St., Edmonton, AB T5J 4L6
Tel: 780-415-0257
Chief Information Officer & Executive Director, Information Management & Technology Services, Mark Diner
Tel: 780-427-1075
Fax: 780-644-1286
mark.diner@gov.ab.ca
Executive Director & Senior Financial Officer, Financial Services Branch, Cameron Steenveld
Tel: 780-644-2714
Fax: 780-644-5586
cameron.steenveld@gov.ab.ca

Alberta Transportation

Twin Atria Building, 4999 - 98 Jasper Ave., 2nd Fl., Edmonton, AB T6B 2X3
Tel: 780-427-2731
Toll-Free: -310-0000
Trans.Contact.Us.m@gov.ab.ca
www.transportation.alberta.ca
Alberta's Ministry of Transportation consists of the Department of Transportation & the Transportation Safety Board. The Ministry strives to provide a safe & sustainable transportation system & water management infrastructure throughout the province.
Key activities of the Department are as follows: leading the planning, construction & preservation of highways across Alberta; offering information & education about transportation safety services & enforcement programs; designing, building, & maintaining the water management infrastructure in the province; managing grant programs to assist municipalities; & representing Alberta at all levels of government to ensure regulatory harmonization.
Acts Administered:
Dangerous Goods Transportation & Handling Act
Government Organization Act (jointly with other ministries)
Highways Development & Protection Act
Provincial Parks Act (jointly with other ministries)
Railway (Alberta) Act
Regional Airports Authorities Act
Traffic Safety Act
Water Act (jointly with other ministries)
Water, Gas, & Electric Companies Act (jointly with other ministries)

Minister, Transportation, Hon. Ric McIver
Tel: 780-427-2080
Fax: 780-422-2722
Legislature Building
#204, 10800 - 97 Ave.
Edmonton, AB T5K 2B6

Deputy Minister, Tim Grant
Tel: 780-427-6912
Fax: 780-422-6515
tim.grant@gov.ab.ca

Director, Communications, Donna Babchishin
Tel: 780-415-1841
Fax: 780-466-3166
donna.babchishin@gov.ab.ca

Special Advisor on Highway 63, Mike Allen
Tel: 780-415-0361
Fax: 780-415-0951

Associated Agencies, Boards & Commissions:
• Transportation Safety Board
North Office, Twin Atria Building
4999 - 98 Ave., Main Fl.
Edmonton, AB T6B 2X3
Tel: 780-427-7178
Fax: 780-422-9739
Toll-free: -310-0000
www.atsb.alberta.ca
The Alberta Transportation Safety Board reports to the Minister of Transportation, through the Chair. The Board's members are chosen through a public recruitment process.
The Board hears appeals about licence suspensions & vehicle seizures. Its decisions are made in accordance with the Traffic Safety Act & the Railway (Alberta) Act.
Chair, Ron Smitten
Tel: 780-427-7178
Fax: 780-422-9739
ron.smitten@gov.ab.ca
Administrative Coordinator, Tammy Merenick
Tel: 780-427-7178
Fax: 780-422-9739
tammy.merenick@gov.ab.ca
Office Administrator, Calgary Office, Judith Esmail
Tel: 403-297-3466
Fax: 403-297-4139
judith.esmail@gov.ab.ca

Transportation & Civil Engineering Division
Twin Atria Building, 4999 - 98 Ave., 2nd Fl., Edmonton, AB T6B 2X3
Tel: 780-422-2184
Fax: 780-415-1268
The Transportation & Civil Engineering Division carries out the following functions: planning & delivering highway construction & rehabilitation projects & special projects throughout the province; managing highway maintenance activities; constructing & upgrading management facilities; & managing grant programs, such as the Canada-Alberta Municipal Rural Infrastructure Fund.
Assistant Deputy Minister, Bruno Zutautas
Tel: 780-422-2184
Fax: 780-415-1268
bruno.zutautas@gov.ab.ca

Transportation Safety Services Division
Twin Atria Building, 4999 - 98 Ave., Main Fl., Edmonton, AB T6B 2X3
Tel: 780-427-8901
Fax: 780-415-0782
Toll-Free: 800-666-5036
The Transportation Safety Services Division is responsible for the following services: monitoring the motor carrier industry & provincial railways; driver licensing & driver's licence enforcement; driver, vehicle, & road safety programs; impaired driving intervention programs; & dangerous goods control.
Assistant Deputy Minister, Shaun Hammond
Tel: 780-415-1146
Fax: 780-415-0782
shaun.hammond@gov.ab.ca
Chief Transport Officer, Commercial Vehicle Enforcement Branch, Steve Callahan
Tel: 403-340-5225
Fax: 403-340-5074
steve.callahan@gov.ab.ca
Executive Director, Office of Traffic Safety, Jeanette Espie
Tel: 780-427-6588
Fax: 780-422-3682
jeanette.espie@gov.ab.ca
Executive Director, Driver Programs, Mitch Fuhr
Tel: 780-644-4576
Fax: 780-427-0833
mitch.fuhr@gov.ab.ca
Director, Transport Engineering, Kim Durdle
Tel: 403-340-5189
Fax: 403-340-5092
kim.durdle@gov.ab.ca
Director, Dangerous Goods, Vehicle, & Rail Safety Branch, Terry Wallace
Tel: 780-427-7508
Fax: 780-422-9193
terry.wallace@gov.ab.ca

Government of British Columbia

Seat of Government: Parliament Bldgs., Victoria, BC V8V 1X4
Tel: 250-387-6121
Toll-Free: 800-663-7867
TTY: 800-661-8773
www.gov.bc.ca
Other Communication: Vancouver, Phone: 604-660-2421; Vancouver, TDD: 604-775-0303; Outside BC, Phone: 604-660-2421
The Province of British Columbia entered Confederation on July 20, 1871. According to the 2011 Census, the population of the province is 4,400,057. British Columbia's land area is 922,509.29 square kilometres.

Director, Operations & Management Services, Jerymy Brownridge
Tel: 250-387-2087

Premier, Hon. Christy Clark
Tel: 250-387-1715
Note: Although she lost her seat in Vancouver-Point Grey during the 2013 General Election, Christy Clark remains Premier & will likely run in a by-election to acquire a new riding.

Chief of Staff, Dan Doyle
Tel: 250-387-1715

Cabinet Ministers
Premier; President, Executive Council, Hon. Christy Clark
Tel: 250-387-1715
Fax: 250-387-0087
premier@gov.bc.ca
www.christyclark.ca
Note: Although she lost her seat in Vancouver-Point Grey during the 2013 General Election, Christy Clark remains Premier & will likely run in a by-election to acquire a new riding.
PO Box 9041 Prov Govt Sta.
Victoria, BC V8W 9E1
Deputy Premier; Minister, Energy, Mines, & Natural Gas; Minister Responsible, Housing, Hon. Rich Coleman
Tel: 250-387-5896
Fax: 250-356-2965
EMH.Minister@gov.bc.ca
www.gov.bc.ca/ener
Social Media: twitter.com/colemancountry
PO Box 9060 Prov Govt Sta.
Victoria, BC V8W 9E2
Minister, Finance; Government House Leader, Hon. Michael de Jong, Q.C.
Tel: 250-953-3547
Fax: 250-356-9587
FIN.Minister@gov.bc.ca
www.gov.bc.ca/fin
Social Media: twitter.com/mike_de_jong, www.facebook.com/michaeldejongbc
PO Box 9048 Prov Govt Sta.
Victoria, BC V8W 9E2
Minister, Agriculture, Hon. Norm Letnick
Tel: 250-387-1023
Fax: 250-387-1522
AGR.Minister@gov.bc.ca
www.gov.bc.ca/agri
Social Media: twitter.com/normletnick, www.facebook.com/normletnickmla, www.linkedin.com/pub/norm-letnick/15/8a0/589
PO Box 9043 Prov Govt Sta.
Victoria, BC V8W 9E2
Minister, Children & Family Development, Hon. Stephanie Cadieux
Tel: 250-387-9699
Fax: 250-387-9722
MCF.Minister@gov.bc.ca
www.gov.bc.ca/mcf
Social Media: twitter.com/mlacadieux, www.facebook.com/stephaniecadieuxsurrey
PO Box 9057 Prov Govt Sta.
Victoria, BC V8W 9E2
Minister, Citizens' Services & Open Government, Hon. Ben Stewart
Tel: 250-952-7623
Fax: 250-952-7628
CITZ.Minister@gov.bc.ca
www.gov.bc.ca/citz
Social Media: twitter.com/benstewart2013, www.facebook.com/benstewartBC
PO Box 9056 Prov Govt Sta.
Victoria, BC V8W 9E2
Minister, Community, Sport, & Cultural Development, Hon. Bill Bennett
Tel: 250-387-2283
Fax: 250-387-4312
CSCD.minister@gov.bc.ca
www.gov.bc.ca/cscd
Social Media: twitter.com/KootenayBill, www.facebook.com/kootenay.bill
PO Box 9056 Prov Govt Sta.
Victoria, BC V8W 9E2
Minister, Education, Hon. Don McRae
Tel: 250-387-1977
Fax: 250-387-3200
Minister.Educ@gov.bc.ca
www.gov.bc.ca/bced
Social Media: twitter.com/DonMcRaeMLA, www.facebook.com/donmcrae
PO Box 9045 Prov Govt Sta.
Victoria, BC V8W 9E2
Minister, Environment; Deputy House Leader, Hon. Terry Lake
Tel: 250-387-1187
Fax: 250-387-1356
ENV.Minister@gov.bc.ca
www.gov.bc.ca/env
Social Media: twitter.com/terrylake2013, www.facebook.com/teamterrylake
#247, Parliament Buildings
PO Box 9047 Prov Govt Sta.
Victoria, BC V8W 9E2
Minister, Forests, Lands, & Natural Resource Operations, Hon. Steve Thomson
Tel: 250-356-6211
Fax: 250-387-1040
FLNR.Minister@gov.bc.ca
www.gov.bc.ca/for
PO Box 9049 Prov Govt Sta.
Victoria, BC V8W 9E2
Minister, Justice; Attorney General, Hon. Shirley Bond
Tel: 250-387-1866
Fax: 250-387-6411
JAG.Minister@gov.bc.ca
www.gov.bc.ca/justice
Social Media: twitter.com/shirleybond, www.facebook.com/shirley.bond
PO Box 9044 Prov Govt Sta.
Victoria, BC V8W 9E2
Minister, Social Development, Hon. Dr. Moira Stilwell
Tel: 250-356-7750
Fax: 250-356-7292
SD.Minister@gov.bc.ca
www.gov.bc.ca/hsd
Social Media: twitter.com/DrMoiraStilwell
PO Box 9058 Prov Govt Sta.
Victoria, BC V8W 9E1
Minister, Transportation & Infrastructure, Hon. Mary Polak
Tel: 250-387-1978
Fax: 250-356-2290
Minister.Transportation@gov.bc.ca
www.gov.bc.ca/tran
Social Media: twitter.com/MaryPolakMLA, www.facebook.com/MLAPolak
PO Box 9055 Prov Govt Sta.
Victoria, BC V8W 9E2
Minister, Advanced Education, Innovation & Technology; Minister of State for Multiculturalism & Seniors, Hon. Ralph Sultan
Tel: 250-356-0179
Fax: 250-952-0260
AEIT.Minister@gov.bc.ca
Social Media: www.facebook.com/sultanralph
Minister of State for Small Business, Hon. Naomi Yamamoto
Tel: 250-356-0179
Fax: 250-952-0260
naomi.yamamoto.mla@leg.bc.ca
Social Media: twitter.com/naomiyamamoto, www.facebook.com/vote.yamamoto
Minister, Aboriginal Relations & Reconciliation, Vacant
www.gov.bc.ca/arr
Note: Former Minister Ida Chong was defeated in the May 13, 2013 General Election, & Premier Clark has yet to choose her new cabinet.
Minister, Health, Vacant
www.gov.bc.ca/health
Note: Former Minister Margaret MacDiarmid was defeated in the May 13, 2013 General Election, & Premier Clark has yet to choose her new cabinet.
Minister, Jobs, Tourism, & Skills Training; Minister Responsible, Labour, Vacant
www.gov.bc.ca/jti
Note: Former Minister Patrick Bell did not run in the May 13, 2013 General Election, & Premier Clark has yet to choose her new cabinet.

British Columbia Ministry of Agriculture

PO Box 9120 Stn. Prov Govt, Victoria, BC V8W 9E2
Tel: 250-387-5121
www.gov.bc.ca/agri
Other Communication: Agriculture Communications Office, Phone: 250-387-1693
The mission of the Ministry of Agriculture to stabilize & expand agrifoods production & incomes, to safeguard animal, plant, & human health, & to encourage environmental stewardship. Responsibilities include agriculture, acquacultures & food industry development, fish processing, meat processing policy, food safety & quality, & crop insurance.
Acts Administered:
Agricultural Land Commission Act
Agricultural Produce Grading Act
Agri-Food Choice & Quality Act
Agrologists Act
Animal Disease Control Act
Bee Act
Farm Income Insurance Act
Farm Practices Protection (Right to Farm) Act
Farmers & Womens Institutes Act
Farming & Fishing Industries Development Act
Fish Inspection Act
Fisheries Act (except Part 3 as it relates to the licensing of aquaculture)
Food Products Standards Act
Fur Farm Act
Game Farm Act
Insurance for Crops Act
Livestock Act
Livestock Identification Act
Livestock Lien Act
Local Government Act (ss. 916-919)
Milk Industry Act (s. 12 as it relates to tank milk receiver licences, & the remainder of the Act)
Ministry of Agriculture & Food Act
Ministry of Forestry & Range Act (s. 4 (d) (ii) & (e) as that provision relates to the portfolio of the Minister of Agriculture)
Natural Products Marketing (BC) Act
Plant Protection Act
Prevention of Cruelty to Animals Act
Range Act (ss. 39-41, 42 & 43; ss. 1 (2) & (3), 44, 45, 76, 79 & 80 as those provisions relate to the portfolio of the Minister of Agriculture)
Seed Potato Act
Special Accounts Appropriation & Control Act (s. 9.2)
Veterinarians Act
Veterinary Drugs Act

Minister, Agriculture, Hon. Norm Letnick
Tel: 250-387-1023
Fax: 250-387-1522
AGR.Minister@gov.bc.ca
Social Media: twitter.com/normletnick
PO Box 9043 Prov Govt Sta.
Victoria, BC V8W 9E2

Deputy Minister, Agriculture, Derek Sturko
Tel: 250-356-1800
Fax: 250-356-8392
PO Box 9120 Prov Govt Sta.
Victoria, BC V8W 9B4

Manager, Executive Operations, Sandra Roe
Tel: 250-356-5126
Fax: 250-356-8392
Sandra.Roe@gov.bc.ca

Operations, Project, & Administrative Coordinator, Correspondence Unit, Vacant
Tel: 250-356-1804
Fax: 250-356-8392

Associated Agencies, Boards & Commissions:
• **Agricultural Land Commission (ALC)**
#133, 4940 Canada Way
Burnaby, BC V5G 4K6
Tel: 604-660-7000
Fax: 604-660-7033
ALCBurnaby@Victoria1.gov.bc.ca
www.alc.gov.bc.ca
The independent Crown agency strives to preserve agricultural land in British Columbia. The Provincial Agricultural Land Commission also works to encourage & enable farm businesses throughout the province. The Commission's chief responsibility is the administration of the Agricultural Land Commission Act.
Executive Director, Strategic Planning & Corporate Policy, Brian Underhill
Brian.Underhill@gov.bc.ca
Executive Director, Regional Operations, Colin Fry
Colin.Fry@gov.bc.ca
• **British Columbia Broiler Hatching Egg Commission (BCBHEC)**
#180, 32160 South Fraser Way
Abbotsford, BC V2T 1W5
Tel: 604-850-1854
Fax: 604-850-1683
info@bcbhec.com
www.bcbhec.com
The British Columbia Broiler Hatching Egg Commission was formed in 1988 under the British Columbia Natural Products

Marketing Act, & seeks to promote a better understanding of the broiler hatching egg industry.
Chair, Peter Whitlock
whitlock@one-name.org
Vice-Chair, Chris den Hertog
chris@trine-enterprises.com
General Manager, Dave Cherniwchan
Tel: 604-854-4488
dave@bcbhec.com

• British Columbia Chicken Marketing Board (BCCMB)
#101, 32450 Simon Ave.
Abbotsford, BC V2T 4J2
Tel: 604-859-2868
Fax: 604-859-2811
info@bcchicken.ca
www.bcchicken.ca
The purpose of the BC Chicken Marketing Board is to monitor & regulate the production of chicken in British Columbia. The Board works closely with hatcheries, growers, truckers & processors, & carries out field inspections, to accomplish this.
Chair, Daphene Stancil
Vice-Chair, Greg Gauthier
General Manager, Bill Vanderspek
billvanderspek@bcchicken.ca

• British Columbia Cranberry Marketing Commission (BCCMC)
c/o #71, 4001 Old Clayburn Rd.
Abbotsford, BC V3S 1C5
Tel: 604-302-1046
cranberries@telus.net
www.bccranberries.com
Since 1968 the BCCMC has administered the British Columbia Cranberry Marketing Scheme, established under the Natural Products Marketing (BC) Act. The Commission reports to the British Columbia Farm Industry Review Board.

• British Columbia Egg Marketing Board (BCEMB)
#250, 32160 South Fraser Way
Abbotsford, BC V2T 1W5
Tel: 604-556-3348
Fax: 604-556-3410
bcemb@bcegg.com
www.bcegg.com
The BCEMB was established in 1967 in order to better regulate the price of eggs.
Chair, Richard King
Vice-Chair, Fred Krahn
Director, Amyn Alibhai

• British Columbia Farm Industry Review Board (BCFIRB)
780 Blanshard St.
PO Box 9129 Prov Govt
Victoria, BC V8W 9B5
Tel: 250-356-8945
Fax: 250-356-5131
firb@gov.bc.ca
www.firb.gov.bc.ca
The British Columbia Farm Industry Review Board is a statutory appeal body. It is engaged in the general supervision of marketing boards & commodity boards which operate in the agricultural & aquaculture sectors.
Chair, Ron Kilmury
Executive Director, Jim Collins

• British Columbia Hog Marketing Commission (BCHMC)
PO Box 8000-280
Abbotsford, BC V2S 6H1
Tel: 604-897-9252
Fax: 604-677-6058
dianned@bcpork.ca
www.bcpork.ca
The Commission seeks to promote BC-grown pork through the use of its logo on all BC pork products.
Chair, George Leroux

• British Columbia Milk Marketing Board (BCMMB)
#200, 32160 South Fraser Way
Abbotsford, BC V2T 1W5
Tel: 604-556-3444
Fax: 604-556-7717
info@milk-bc.com
bcmilkmarketing.worldsecuresystems.com/
The Board is reponsible for promoting, controlling & regulating the production, transportation, packing, storing & marketing of all BC milk products.
Chair, Jim Byrne
jbyrne@milk-bc.com
Vice-Chair, Ben Cuthbert
Tel: 250-245-3299
bcuthbert@milk-bc.com
Secretary-Treasurer, Ben Janzen
Tel: 604-855-8096
bjanzen@milk-bc.com
Acting General Manager/Controller, Robert Delange
Tel: 604-854-4475
rdelage@milk-bc.com

• British Columbia Turkey Marketing Board (BCTMB)
#106, 19329 Enterprise Way
Surrey, BC V3S 6J8
Tel: 604-534-5644
Fax: 604-534-3651
info@bcturkey.com
www.bcturkey.com
Established in 1966, the Board oversees the licensing of turkey farmers and processors; prices for live turkeys; maintaining of a quota system; & promoting turkey products, under the authority of the Natural Products Marketing (BC) Act.
General Manager/Marketing, Michel Benoit
mbenoit@bcturkey.com
Auditor/Grower Liaison, Susan Mallory
smallory@bcturkey.com

• British Columbia Vegetable Marketing Commission (BCVMC)
#207, 15252 32nd Ave.
Surrey, BC V3S 0R7
Tel: 604-542-9734
Fax: 603-542-9753
info@bcveg.com
The Commission is responsible for promoting controlled marketing for BC vegetable producers, under the authority of the Natural Products Marketing (BC) Act.
Chair, David Taylor
Vice-Chair, Peter Guichon
Secretary, Hugh Reynolds
General Manager, Tom Demma
Tel: 604-542-9734 ext: 25
tom@bcveg.com

Agriculture Science & Policy
PO Box 9120 Stn. Prov Govt, Victoria, BC V8W 9B4
Tel: 250-356-1816
Fax: 250-356-7279
Assistant Deputy Minister, Melanie Stewart
Tel: 250-356-1821
Melanie.J.Stewart@gov.bc.ca
Director, Innovation & Industry Development Branch, Alana Rosseker
Tel: 250-356-7057
Fax: 250-356-0358
Alana.Rosseker@gov.bc.ca
Director/Chief Veterinary Officer, Plant & Animal Health Branch, Abbotsford, Paul Kitching
Tel: 604-556-3038
Fax: 604-556-3010
Paul.Kitching@gov.bc.ca
Director, Agrifoods Policy & Legislative Branch, Grant Thompson
Tel: 250-356-8299
Fax: 250-387-0357
Grant.Thompson@gov.bc.ca
Assistant Director, Agrifoods Policy & Legislation Branch, Gavin Last
Tel: 250-356-7640
Fax: 250-387-0357
Gavin.Last@gov.bc.ca

Animal Health Center
Tel: 604-556-3003
Fax: 604-556-3010
Avian Pathologist, Dr. Victoria Bowes
Tel: 604-556-3041
Victoria.Bowes@gov.bc.ca
Veterinary Pathologist, Dr. Tara Arndt
Tel: 604-556-3037
Tara.Arndt@gov.bc.ca
Fish Pathologist, Dr. Gary Marty
Tel: 604-556-3123
Gary.Marty@gov.bc.ca
Veterinary Pathologist, Dr. Ann Britton
Tel: 604-556-3039
Ann.P.Britton@gov.bc.ca
Veterinary Virologist, Dr. John Robinson
Tel: 604-556-3036
John.H.Robinson@gov.bc.ca
Microbiologist, Supervisor, Dr. Sean Byrne
Tel: 604-556-3025
Sean.Byrne@gov.bc.ca
Poultry Health Veterinarian, Dr. William Cox
Tel: 604-556-3150
William.Cox@gov.bc.ca

Strategic Industry Partnerships Division
PO Box 9120 Stn. Prov Govt, Victoria, BC V8W 9B4
Tel: 250-356-1122
Fax: 250-356-7279
Assistant Deputy Minister, Grant Parnell
Tel: 250-356-1802
Grant.Parnell@gov.bc.ca
Director, Business Risk Management Branch, Gary Falk
Tel: 250-861-7206
Fax: 250-861-7490
Gary.Falk@gov.bc.ca
Director, Sustainable Agriculture Management, Ken Nickel
Tel: 604-556-3103
Fax: 604-556-3030
Ken.Nickel@gov.bc.ca
780 Blanshard St.
PO Box 9308 Prov Govt Sta.
Victoria, BC V8W 9N1
Director, Food Protection Branch, Jim Russell
Tel: 250-897-7561
Fax: 250-334-1410
Jim.Russell@gov.bc.ca
Assistant Director, Sustainable Agriculture Management, Leslie S. MacDonald
Tel: 604-556-3074
Fax: 604-556-3030
Leslie.MacDonald@gov.bc.ca
Agrologist, Business Risk Management Branch, Phil Croteau
Tel: 250-861-7419
Fax: 250-861-7490
Phil.Croteau@gov.bc.ca

British Columbia Centre for Disease Control (BCCDC)

655 West 12th Ave., Vancouver, BC V5Z 4R4
Tel: 604-707-2400
Fax: 604-707-2401
admininfo@bccdc.ca
www.bccdc.ca
www.twitter.com/cdcofbc
The BCCDC is both a provincial & national leader in public health as it detects, treats, & prevents diseases in its patients. Not only does it offer direct services for people with diseases & health concerns, but it also provides analytical & policy support to health authorities at all levels of government.

Provincial Executive Director & Scientific Director, Dr. Robert C. Brunham, MD, FRCP, OBC

Medical Director, Communicable Disease Prevention & Control Service, Dr. Bonnie Henry

Executive Assistant, Aja Dykes
aja.dykes@bccdc.ca

British Columbia Ministry of Citizens' Services

PO Box 9594 Stn. Prov Govt, Victoria, BC V8W 9E2
Tel: 250-952-7623
Fax: 250-952-7628
Toll-Free: 800-663-7867
EnquiryBC@gov.bc.ca
www.gov.bc.ca/citz
Other Communication: Victoria, Phone: 250-387-6121; Vancouver, Phone: 604-660-2421
The Ministry of Citizens' Services & Open Government oversees the following: Board Resourcing & Development Office; BC OnLine; BC Stats; Enquiry BC; government communications & public engagement; business & personal property registries; information & privacy policy; Queen's Printer; corporate accounting services; procurement & supply services; & telecommuciations infrastructure.
Acts Administered:
Legislative Assembly Privilege Act

Minister, Citizens' Services & Open Government, Hon. Ben Stewart
Tel: 250-952-7623
Fax: 250-952-7628

PO Box 9056 Prov Govt Sta.
Victoria, BC V8W 9E2

Deputy Minister, Citizens' Services & Open Government, Kim Henderson
Tel: 250-387-8852
Fax: 250-387-8561
PO Box 9440 Prov Govt Sta.
Victoria, BC V8W 9V3

Deputy Minister, Government Communications & Public Engagement, Athana Mentzelopoulos
Tel: 250-356-7398
Fax: 250-356-2872
Athana.Mentzelopoulos@gov.bc.ca
PO Box 9409 Prov Govt Sta.
Victoria, BC V8W 9V1

Manager, Communications, David Haslam
Tel: 250-387-0172
David.Haslam@gov.bc.ca

Coordinator, Administration, Yvette Marquis
Tel: 250-952-7623
Fax: 250-952-7628

Associated Agencies, Boards & Commissions:
• **Knowledge Network Corporation**
4355 Mathissi Pl.
Burnaby, BC V5G 4S8
Tel: 604-431-3222
Fax: 604-431-3387
Toll-free: 877-456-6988
info@knowledge.ca; hr@knowledge.ca (employment information)
www.knowledge.ca
Other Communication: Press, E-mail: press@knowledge.ca
The Knowledge Network Corporation is a provincial Crown agency, operating under British Columbia's Ministry of Citizens' Services & Open Government. The corporation is British Columbia's public broadcaster, which is licensed by the Canadian Radio-television & Telecommunications Commission.
Arts & culture & children's programs are featured through television & the Internet.
The network is commercial-free. Funds for the provision of educational broadcasting services are received the British Columbia provincial government, public supporters, & Knowledge Partners.

BC OnLine
Operations Centre, #400A, 4000 Seymour Pl., Victoria, BC V8X 5J8
Tel: 250-953-8250
Fax: 250-953-8222
Toll-Free: 800-663-6102
bconline@apicanada.com; bcolhelp@apicanada.com (support issues)
www.bconline.gov.bc.ca
Other Communication: Help Desk, Phone: 250-953-8200
BC OnLine serves government, legal, & business professionals by providing access to provincial government computer systems through the Internet. Examples of e-government services include Court Services Online, Land Title & Survey Authority Electronic Services, Personal Property Registry, Corporate Registry, Gas & Electrical Permits, & the Wills Registry.
Director, Operations, Allan Crawshaw
Tel: 250-953-8277
Fax: 250-953-8222
Allan.Crawshaw@apicanada.com
Chief Financial Officer, Harvey Coomber
Tel: 250-953-8276
Fax: 250-953-8222
Manager, Contract Administration, Bob Dearborn
Tel: 250-953-8266
Fax: 250-953-8222
Bob.Dearborn@apicanada.com
Coordinator, Client Support Services, Valeska Campbell
Tel: 250-953-8200
Fax: 250-953-8222
Valeska.Campbell@apicanada.com

BC Registry Services
PO Box 9431 Stn. Prov Govt, Victoria, BC V8W 9V3
Tel: 250-356-8661
Fax: 250-356-9422
www.bcregistryservices.gov.bc.ca
Other Communication: Corporations Unit, Phone: 250-356-8626; Societies & Cooperatives: 250-356-8609; OneStop Business Registry: 250-356-8689; Personal Property Registry: 250-952-7976
BC Registry Services support commerce by overseeing the Corporate Registry, the Personal Property Registry, the Manufactured Home Registry, & the OneStop Business Registry.
Manager, Registries Programs (Trade Agreements), Janice Gignac
Tel: 250-952-6025
Fax: 250-356-8923
Janice.Gignac@gov.bc.ca
Financial Analyst, Cassey Zhou
Tel: 250-356-8665
Fax: 250-356-9422
Cassey.Zhou@gov.bc.ca

BC Stats
553 Superior St., PO Box 9410 Stn. Prov Govt, Victoria, BC V8W 9V1
Tel: 250-387-0327
Fax: 250-387-0380
BC.Stats@gov.bc.ca
www.bcstats.gov.bc.ca
Operating under the direction of the Britisih Columbia Statistics Act, R.S.B.C. 1996, C. 439, BC Stats is the central statistical agency of the Province of British Columbia. The organization serves government & voluntary clients through the dissemination of general statistical information.
BC Stats carries out its activities through the following sections: Data Services; Business Statistics; Economic Statistics; Labour & Social Statistics; Demographic Analysis, & Public Sector Research & Evaluation.

Board Resourcing & Development Office

Tel: 604-660-1170
Fax: 604-775-0158
abc@gov.bc.ca
www.gov.bc.ca/brdo
The Board Resourcing & Development Office has the following responsibilities: forming guidelines for appointments to agencies; ensuring an open & consistent appointment process; & confirming that appointees to agencies receive orientation & continuing professional development.

Office of the Chief Information Officer (OCIO)
PO Box 9412 Stn. Prov Govt, Victoria, BC V8W 9V1
Tel: 250-387-0401
Fax: 250-387-5693
Toll-Free: 800-663-7867
ciowebcommunications@gov.bc.ca; CPIAadmin@gov.bc.ca (privacy help)
www.cio.gov.bc.ca
Other Communication: To report an information incident, such as a privacy breach, phone: 1-866-660-0811, option 3; BC Privacy Helpline, Phone: 250-356-1851, Fax: 250-953-0455
The Office of the Chief Information Officer guides & promotes the management of government information as an asset to business.
Examples of responsibilities include records management, legislation that governs the protection of privacy & personal information, freedom of information requests, & governance for corporate IM/IT policy, such as technology architecture & standards, data access, & information security.
Branches of the Office of the Chief Information Officer are as follows: Architecture & Standards; Community & External Initiatives; Corporate Operations & Finance; Knowledge & Information Services; Information Security; & Strategic Initiatives.

Communications & Media Relations Division
PO Box 9409 Stn. Prov Govt, Victoria, BC V8W 9V1
Tel: 250-387-3534
Assistant Deputy Minister, Communications & Media Relations, Kelly Gleeson
Tel: 250-356-8608
Fax: 250-356-2872
Kelly.Gleeson@gov.bc.ca
Director, Communications, Matt Gordon
Tel: 250-356-6482
Fax: 250-356-2872
Matt.Gordon@gov.bc.ca
Manager, Multicultural Communications, Pavan Bajwa
Tel: 250-387-5033
Fax: 250-387-6070
Pavan.Bajwa@gov.bc.ca
Manager, Media Relations, Karen Murry
Tel: 250-387-0779
Fax: 250-387-6070
Karen.Murry@gov.bc.ca
Manager, Media Monitoring Services, Scott Ryckman
Tel: 250-356-5735
Fax: 250-356-5901
Scott.Ryckman@gov.bc.ca

Corporate Services Division
PO Box 9409 Stn. Prov Govt, Victoria, BC V8W 9V1
Tel: 250-387-1449
Fax: 250-387-6687
The Corporate Services Division oversees facilities & administration, financial services, human resources, records management, & systems architecture.
Executive Director, Operations & Human Resources, Denise Champion
Tel: 250-953-4685
Fax: 250-387-3534
Denise.Champion@gov.bc.ca
Director, Systems Solutions & Architecture, Stephen Bamford
Tel: 250-217-6137
Fax: 250-387-6687
Stephen.Bamford@gov.bc.ca
Manager, Human Resources, Michelle Rowsell
Tel: 250-387-8067
Fax: 250-387-3534
Michelle.Rowsell@gov.bc.ca
Officer, Records Services, Bruce Foster
Tel: 250-812-2122
Fax: 250-387-6687
Bruce.Foster@gov.bc.ca
Officer, Administrative Services, Susan Smith
Tel: 250-387-1449
Fax: 250-387-6687
Susan.Smith@gov.bc.ca
Officer, Financial Services, Dawn Stewart
Tel: 250-356-8595
Fax: 250-387-6687
Dawn.Stewart@gov.bc.ca

Enquiry BC
PO Box 9594 Stn. Prov Govt, Victoria, BC V8W 9K4
Tel: 250-387-6121
Toll-Free: 800-663-7867
TTY: 800-661-8773
EnquiryBC@gov.bc.ca
Other Communication: Vancouver, Phone: 604-660-2421
Inquiries are handled about services provided by provincial governmen ministries, Crown corporations, & public agencies.
Program Manager, Catherine Wollner
Tel: 250-387-4845
Fax: 250-387-5633
Program Analyst, Craig Smith
Tel: 250-356-1487
Fax: 250-387-5633
Craig.Smith@gov.bc.ca

Queen's Printer
PO Box 9452 Stn. Prov Govt, Victoria, BC V8W 9V7
Tel: 250-387-3309
Fax: 250-356-6036
Toll-Free: 800-663-6105
QPGazette@gov.bc.ca (BC Gazette); QPLegalEze@gov.bc,ca
www.qp.gov.bc.ca
British Columbia's Queen's Printer provides printing & specialized scanning services, plus multimedia duplication to the province's government ministries & the public sector.
Senior Director, Queen's Printer / BC Mail Plus, Don Swagar
Tel: 250-387-6691
Fax: 250-356-7380
Don.Swagar@gov.bc.ca
Director, Queen's Printer, Sherry Brown
Tel: 250-356-6876
Fax: 250-387-0388
Sherry.Brown@gov.bc.ca
Manager, Crown Publications, Wendy Pope
Tel: 250-356-5392
Fax: 250-387-1120
Wendy.Pope@gov.bc.ca

Service BC

PO Box 9804 Stn. Prov Govt, Victoria, BC V8W 9W1
Tel: 250-387-6121
Fax: 250-387-5633
Toll-Free: 800-663-7867
TTY: 800-661-8773
www.servicebc.gov.bc.ca
Other Communication: Vancouver & outside B.C., Phone: 604-660-2421; Southeast Service BC Centre, Phone: 250-354-6109; Vancouver Island / South Coast Service BC Centre: 250-356-7302
Service BC provides frontline government services & information to businesses, residents, & visitors in British Columbia. Areas of service include education, training, employment & labour standards, doing business in the province, licensing & registration, taxation, health services, legal services, family support services, property, transportation, tourism, recreation, & publications. Service is available by phone, online, or in person at Service BC Centres throughout the province.
Assistant Deputy Minister, Service BC, Bette-Jo Hughes
Tel: 250-387-9170
Fax: 250-387-5633
Executive Director, Regional Operations, Ron Hinshaw
Tel: 250-356-2031
Fax: 250-387-5633
Ron.Hinshaw@gov.bc.ca
Director, Financial Operations, Tavish Annis
Tel: 250-387-0390
Fax: 250-387-5633
Tavish.Annis@gov.bc.ca
Director, Operations & Client Services, Brad Boquist
Tel: 250-356-2039
Fax: 250-387-5633
Brad.Boquist@gov.bc.ca
Project Director, John Hammond
Tel: 250-356-1356
Fax: 250-387-5633
John.Hammond@gov.bc.ca
Regional Director, Interior Northeast Service BC Centre, Deborah Lipscombe
Tel: 250-828-4545
Fax: 250-828-4542
Deborah.Lipscombe@gov.bc.ca
Regional Director, Northwest Service BC Centre, Perry Slump
Tel: 250-565-4488
Fax: 250-565-6638
Perry.Slump@gov.bc.ca
Manager, Clients & Special Projects, Kathy Ham-Rowbottom
Tel: 250-356-1444
Fax: 250-387-5633
Kathleen.HamRowbottom@gov.bc.ca
Executive Coordinator, Keri Merrick
Tel: 250-387-9170
Fax: 250-387-5633
Keri.Merrick@gov.bc.ca

Strategic Planning & Public Engagement Division
PO Box 9409 Stn. Prov Govt, Victoria, BC V8W 9V1
Tel: 250-356-2872
Assistant Deputy Minister, Strategic Planning & Public Engagement, John Paul Fraser
Tel: 250-356-8527
Fax: 250-356-2872
JohnPaul.Fraser@gov.bc.ca
Executive Director, Marketing & Communications Support Service, Mary Dila
Tel: 250-356-7823
Fax: 250-387-6070
Mary.Dila@gov.bc.ca
Executive Director, Citizen Engagement, Tanya Twynstra
Tel: 250-507-2163
Fax: 250-387-0718
Tanya.Twynstra@gov.bc.ca
Corporate Director, Public Engagement, Susan Ibbott
Tel: 250-356-7363
Fax: 250-387-6070
Susan.Ibbott@gov.bc.ca
Manager, Writing & Editorial Services, Jon Chant
Tel: 250-387-7194
Fax: 250-387-6687
Jon.Chant@gov.bc.ca
Manager, Engagement Programming, Jamieson Dunlop
Tel: 250-307-0291
Fax: 250-387-0718
Jamieson.Dunlop@gov.bc.ca
Manager, Social Media & Digital Services, Brooke Finnigan
Tel: 250-387-6693
Fax: 250-387-6070
Brooke.Finnigan@gov.bc.ca
Manager, Graphic Design Services, Andrew Pratt
Tel: 250-356-8120
Fax: 250-387-6070
Andrew.Pratt@gov.bc.ca
Manager, Advertising & Marketing Services, Adrienne Watt
Tel: 250-387-1374
Fax: 250-387-1435
Adrienne.Watt@gov.bc.ca

Columbia Power Corporation (CPC)

#200, 445 - 13th Ave., Castlegar, BC V1N 1G1
Tel: 250-304-6060
Fax: 250-304-6083
cpc.info@columbiapower.org
www.columbiapower.org
Columbia Power Corporation was established under the Company Act in 1994. A Crown corporation, it is wholly owned & controlled by the Province of British Columbia. On a joint venture basis with the Columbia Basin Trust, Columbia Power Corporation undertakes power project investments as the agent of the Province of British Columbia. Some power projects include the following: Arrow Lakes Generating Station, Brilliant Expansion Project, & Waneta Expansion Project.

Chair, Lee Doney

Vice-Chair, Tim Stanley

President/Chief Executive Officer, Jane Bird
Tel: 250-304-6040

Chief Technical Officer, Victor Jmaeff
Tel: 250-304-6023
Victor.Jmaeff@columbiapower.org

Vice-President, Human Resources & Corporate Services, Debbie Martin
Tel: 250-304-6055
debbie.martin@columbiapower.org

Vice-President, Project Development, Karim Hirji
Tel: 250-304-6070
cpc.info@columbiapower.org

Vice-President, Capital Projects, Giulio Ambrosone
Tel: 250-304-6065
giulio.ambrosone@columbiapower.org

Corporate Secretary, Don Rose
Tel: 604-640-4247
don.rose@columbiapower.org

British Columbia Ministry of Community, Sport, & Cultural Development

PO Box 9490 Stn. Prov Govt, Victoria, BC V8W 9N7
www.gov.bc.ca/cscd
Other Communication: Media Inquiries, Phone: 250-953-3677, Fax: 250-356-1070
Enabling local governments & citizens of British Columbia to build well-governed communities with opportunities to participate in the arts & sports is the goal of the Ministry of Community, Sport, & Cultural Development.
The following are examples of the ministry's responsibilities: providing policies & programs so that local governments can govern effectively; offering advice & funding for community economic growth; ensuring a fair & flexible property assessment system; & supporting the provincial sport system, cultural organizations, & artists.

Minister, Community, Sport, & Cultural Development, Hon. Bill Bennett
Tel: 250-387-2283
Fax: 250-387-4312
CSCD.minister@gov.bc.ca
Social Media: twitter.com/KootenayBill
PO Box 9056 Prov Govt Sta.
Victoria, BC V8W 9E2

Deputy Minister, Community, Sport, & Cultural Development, Don Fast
Tel: 250-387-4104
Fax: 250-387-7973
Don.Fast@gov.bc.ca

Administrative Coordinator, Connie Roberts
Tel: 250-387-2283
Fax: 250-387-4312

Executive Coordinator, Lee Valentine
Tel: 250-387-4104
Fax: 250-387-7973
Lee.Valentine@gov.bc.ca

Parliamentary Secretary for Rural Communities to the Minister, Community, Sport, & Cultural Development, Donna Barnett
Tel: 250-387-3820
Fax: 250-387-9066

Associated Agencies, Boards & Commissions:
• **British Columbia Assessment Authority (BCAA)**
#400, 3450 Uptown Blvd.
Victoria, BC V8Z 0B9
Tel: 250-595-6211
Fax: 250-595-6222
info@bcassessment.ca
www.bcassessment.bc.ca
The British Columbia Assessment Authority is an independent, provincial Crown corporation. Governed by a Board of Directors, the role of BC Assessment is the production of annual property assessments for each property owner in British Columbia. Area offices are located across the province.
Vice-President/Executive Financial Officer, Financial & Management Services, Andy Hoggarth
• **British Columbia Games Society**
#200, 990 Fort St.
Victoria, BC V8V 3K2
Tel: 250-387-1375
Fax: 250-387-4489
info@bcgames.org
www.bcgames.org
The BC Games Society is incorporated under the Societies Act. With responsibility to British Columbia's Minister of Healthy Living & Sport, the Crown Agency works with its partners to provide event management leadership. The Society strives to create development opportunities for athletes, coaches, & officials, sport organizations, & host communities.
Co-Chair (Vancouver), Cathy Priestner Allinger
Co-Chair (Fernie), Frank Lento
President & Chief Executive Officer, Kelly Mann
kellym@bcgames.org
• **Board of Examiners**
Tel: 250-387-4085
Fax: 250-387-7972
www.cscd.gov.bc.ca/lgd/gov_structure/board_examiners/index.htm
Office Manager, Deanna Battle
Tel: 250-356-0954
Fax: 250-387-6212
Deanna.Battle@gov.bc.ca
Administrator, Leta Hodge
• **Islands Trust**
#200, 1627 Fort St.
Victoria, BC V8R 1H8
Tel: 250-405-5151
Fax: 250-405-5155
information@islandstrust.bc.ca
www.islandstrust.bc.ca
Other Communication: Northern Office: 250-247-2063; Salt Spring Office: 250-537-9144
The Islands Trust area covers the following islands & waters between the British Columbia mainland & southern Vancouver Island: Bowen, Denman, Gabriola, Galiano, Gambier, Hornby, Lasqueti, Mayne, North Pender, Salt Spring, Saturna, South Pender, & Thetis. The Trust is a federation of independent local governments. The federation plans land use & regulates development to preserve & protect the area and its environment.
Chair, Kim Benson
smalcolmson@islandstrust.bc.ca
Chief Administrative Officer, Linda Adams
Tel: 250-405-5160
ladams@islandstrust.bc.ca
Director, Local Planning Services, David Marlor
Tel: 250-405-5169

Director, Trust Area Services, Lisa Gordon
Tel: 250-405-5174
lgordon@islandstrust.bc.ca
Director, Administrative Services, Craig Elder
Tel: 250-405-5150
celder@islandstrust.bc.ca

• Property Assessment Appeal Board (PAAB)
#10, 10551 Shellbridge Way
Richmond, BC V6X 2W9
Tel: 604-775-1740
Fax: 604-775-1742
Toll-free: 888-775-1740
office@paab.bc.ca
www.assessmentappeal.bc.ca
Other Communication: Toll-Free Fax: 1-888-775-1742
The Board assists with assessment appeals for all types of properties, dealing with issues such as market value, classification, and qualification for tax exemption.
Chair/Chief Executive Officer, Cheryl Vickers
Tel: 604-775-3117
Fax: 604-775-1742
Cheryl.Vickers@paab.bc.ca
Vice-Chair, Robert Fraser
Tel: 250-387-9195
Fax: 604-775-1742
Rob.Fraser@paab.bc.ca
Vice-Chair, Simmi Sandhu
Tel: 604-775-2001
Fax: 604-775-1742
Simmi.Sandhu@paab.bc.ca
Registrar/Administrator, Steve Guthrie
Tel: 604-775-3122
Fax: 604-775-1742
Steve.Guthrie@paab.bc.ca

• Provincial Capital Commission (PCC)
613 Pandora Ave.
Victoria, BC V8W 1N8
Tel: 250-953-8800
Fax: 250-386-1303
info.pcc@bcpcc.com
www.bcpcc.com
A Crown agency, the Provincial Capital Commission works to raise awareness of the Capital's history & character. The Commission's operations are funded through commercial revenues from provincially-owned properties & heritage buildings in the Capital region.
Manager, Outreach & Engagement, Kristine Anderson
Tel: 250-953-8826
Kris.Andersen@bcpcc.com

• British Columbia Film Commission
#201, 865 Hornby St.
Vancouver, BC V6Z 2G3
Tel: 604-660-2732
Fax: 604-660-4790
info@bcfilmcommission.com
www.bcfilmcommission.com
The British Columbia Film Commission's mission is to ensure that film & television production thrives for Canadian & international clients. As one of the largest production centres in North America, the province offers film producers & production companies a great range of services.

• Royal BC Museum Corporation
675 Belleville St.
Victoria, BC V8W 9W2
Tel: 250-356-7226
Fax: 250-387-5674
Toll-free: 888-447-7977
reception@royalbcmuseum.bc.ca
www.royalbcmuseum.bc.ca
The Royal BC Museum Corporation was created through the proclamation of the Museum Act. It is British Columbia's provincial museum & archives.

• Tourism British Columbia
1803 Douglas St., 3rd Fl.
Victoria, BC V8W 9W5
Tel: 250-356-6363
research@tourismbc.com; superhost@tourismbc.com
www.hellobc.com
Other Communication: Vancouver Phone: 604-660-2861; Research & Planning Phone: 250-387-1567; SuperHost Programs Phone: 250-387-1711
Tourism British Columbia is a Crown corporation which provides information for industry & the media. Its goals are increases in revenue, economic benefits, & employment in British Columbia, through the promotion of development & growth in the tourism industry. The organization is accountable to the Minister of Tourism, Culture & The Arts.

Arts, Culture, Gaming Grants & Sport
PO Box 9490 Stn. Prov Govt, Victoria, BC V8W 9N7
Tel: 250-356-6914
Fax: 250-387-7973
Assistant Deputy Minister, Arts, Culture & Sport, David Galbraith
Tel: 250-356-7139
Fax: 250-387-7973
David.Galbraith@gov.bc.ca
Executive Director, Arts & Culture Branch, Andrea Henning
Tel: 250-356-6614
Fax: 250-387-4099
Andrea.Henning@gov.bc.ca
Executive Director, Sport Branch, Margo Ross
Tel: 250-356-7168
Fax: 250-356-2842
Margo.Ross@gov.bc.ca
Executive Director, BC Arts Council, Gillian Wood
Tel: 250-356-1725
Fax: 250-387-4099
Gillian.Wood@gov.bc.ca
Commissioner, BC Film Commission, Susan Croome
Tel: 604-660-3235
Fax: 604-660-4790
susanc@bcfilmcommission.com
Policy Analyst/Sport Consultant, Sport Branch, Sharon White
Tel: 250-387-5651
Fax: 250-356-2842
Sharon.D.White@gov.bc.ca
Director, Sport Branch, Doug Wrean
Tel: 250-356-0364
Fax: 250-356-2842
Doug.Wrean@gov.bc.ca
Director, Arts, Culture, Gaming Grants & Sport Division, Robert Easton
Tel: 250-356-9416
Fax: 250-387-7973
Robert.Easton@gov.bc.ca

Integrated Policy, Legislation & Operations
PO Box 9847 Stn. Prov Govt, Victoria, BC V8W 9T2
Fax: 250-387-7973

Local Government
PO Box 9490 Stn. Prov Govt, Victoria, BC V8W 9N7
Tel: 250-356-6575
Fax: 250-387-7973
www.cd.gov.bc.ca/lgd
Working with a great range of partners, the Local Government Department develops communities that can manage change & offer affordable services to residents of British Columbia. The Department's programs include the following: developing local government legislation; facilitating partnerships with local governments & First Nations; fostering positive inter-governmental relations to facilitate community & regional planning; offering financial support; & providing information & advice.
Assistant Deputy Minister / Inspector of Municipalities, Julian C. Paine
Tel: 250-387-5312
Fax: 250-387-7973
Julian.Paine@gov.bc.ca
Executive Director, Local Government Division, Mark Tatchell
Tel: 250-217-8816
Fax: 250-387-7973
Mark.Tatchell@gov.bc.ca
Executive Director, Local Government Infrastructure & Finance, Glen Brown
Tel: 250-387-4067
Fax: 250-356-1873
Glen.T.Brown@gov.bc.ca
800 Johnson St., 4th Fl.
PO Box 9838 Prov Govt Sta.
Victoria, BC V8W 9T1
Executive Director, Intergovernmental Relations & Planning, Lois-Leah Goodwin
Tel: 250-356-1128
Fax: 250-387-6212
LoisLeah.Goodwin@gov.bc.ca
800 Johnson St., 6th Fl.
PO Box 9841 Prov Govt Sta.
Victoria, BC V8W 9T2

Minister, Education, Hon. Don McRae
Tel: 250-387-1977
Fax: 250-387-3200
Minister.Educ@gov.bc.ca
Social Media: twitter.com/DonMcRaeMLA, www.facebook.com/donmcrae
PO Box 9045 Prov Govt Sta.
Victoria, BC V8W 9E2

Deputy Minister, Education, James Gorman
Tel: 250-356-1234
Fax: 250-356-6007
dm.education@gov.bc.ca
PO Box 9179 Prov Govt Sta.
Victoria, BC V8W 9H8

Parliamentary Secretary for Independent School to the Minister of Education, Marc Dalton
Tel: 250-953-4769
Fax: 250-387-9100

Parliamentary Secretary for Student Support & Parent Engagement to the Minister of Education, Jane Thornthwaite
Tel: 250-387-2796
Fax: 250-387-9100

Executive Administrative Coordinator, Heather Langton
Tel: 250-387-2026
Fax: 250-356-6007
Heather.Langton@gov.bc.ca
PO Box 9179 Prov Govt Sta.
Victoria, BC V8W 9H8

Resource Management Division
PO Box 9151 Stn. Prov Govt, Victoria, BC V8W 9H1
Tel: 250-356-2588
Fax: 250-356-8332
www.bced.gov.bc.ca/departments/resource_man/

British Columbia Ministry of Energy, Mines, & Natural Gas (& Responsible for Housing)

PO Box 9053 Stn. Prov Govt, Victoria, BC V8W 9E2
www.gov.bc.ca/ener
In September 2012, changes were made to the Ministry of Energy & Mines to reinforce natural gas, which is an economic development priority of the provincial government.
The development of sustainable & competitive energy & mineral resource sectors in British Columbia is the focus of the Ministry of Energy, Mines, & Natural Gas. To develop legislation & guidelines, the ministry consults with other ministries & levels of government, as well as communities, First Nations, the public, energy & mining companies, & environmental organizations.
Acts Administered:
Assistance to Shelter Act
BC Hydro Public Power Legacy & Heritage Contract Act
Building Officials' Association Act
Clean Energy Act (except Part 6 & s. 38; s. 36 (2))
Coal Act
Coalbed Gas Act
Commercial Tenancy Act
Energy Efficiency Act
Gaming Control Act
Gas Utility Act
Geothermal Resources Act
Greenhouse Gas Reduction (Renewable & Low Carbon Fuel Requirements) Act
Homeowner Protection Act (except ss. 2 (2) & 10.1 & Part 9; (b) ss. 10, 32 & 36)
Hydro & Power Authority Act
Hydro Power Measures Act
Liquor Control & Licencing Act
Liquor Distribution Act
Local Government Act (ss. 692 & 693)
Manufactured Home Park Tenancy Act
Mineral Land Tax Act (except as it relates to (a) the collection of public money, as defined in section 1 of the Financial Administration Act, other than a fine, or (b) the administration of deposits & securities payable)
Mineral Tax Act (except as it relates to (a) the collection of public money, as defined in section 1 of the Financial Administration Act, other than a fine, or (b) the administration of deposits and securities payable)
Mineral Tenure Act
Mines Act
Mining Right of Way Act
Ministry of Energy & Mines Act

Ministry of Lands, Parks, & Housing Act (ss. 5 (c), 8.1 & 10)
Natural Gas Price Act
Oil & Gas Activities Act (except Division 2 of Part 2)
Petroleum & Natural Gas (Vancouver Island Railway Lands) Act
Petroleum & Natural Gas Act (except (a) ss 74-77; (b) except as it relates to (i) the collection of public money, as defined in section 1 of the Financial Administration Act, other than a fine, or (ii) the administration of deposits & securities payable)
Power for Jobs Development Act
Rent Distress Act
Residential Tenancy Act
Safety Authority Act
Safety Standards Act
Shelter Aid for Elderly Renters Act
Special Accounts Appropriation & Control Act (s. 9.3, s. 9.5)
Strata Property Act
Vancouver Island Natural Gas Pipeline Act

Minister; Energy, Mines, & Natural Gas; Minister Responsible for Housing; Deputy Premier, Hon. Rich Coleman
Tel: 250-387-5896
Fax: 250-356-2965
EMH.Minister@gov.bc.ca
Social Media: twitter.com/colemancountry
PO Box 9060 Prov Govt Sta.
Victoria, BC V8W 9E2

Deputy Minister, Energy, Mines, & Natural Gas, Steve Carr
Tel: 250-952-0504
Fax: 250-952-0269
Steve.Carr@gov.bc.ca
PO Box 9319 Prov Govt Sta.
Victoria, BC V8W 9N3

Director, Cabinet & Legislative Initiatives & Executive Operations, Rhonda De Champlain
Tel: 250-952-0253
Fax: 250-952-0269
Rhonda.DeChamplain@gov.bc.ca
PO Box 9319 Prov Govt Sta.
Victoria, BC V8W 9N3

Parliamentary Secretary for the Northeast to the Minister of Energy, Mines, & Natural Gas, Pat Pimm
Tel: 250-952-6784
Fax: 250-387-9100

Officer, Public Affairs, Jake Jacobs
Tel: 250-952-0628
Fax: 250-952-0627
Jake.Jacobs@gov.bc.ca

Associated Agencies, Boards & Commissions:

• British Columbia Lottery Corporation
74 West Seymour St.
Kamloops, BC V2C 1E2
Tel: 250-828-5500
Fax: 250-828-5631
Toll-free: 866-815-0222
www.bclc.com
Other Communication: Vancouver Phone: 604-215-0649

• British Columbia Pavilion Corporation (PavCo)
#850, 999 West Hastings St.
PO Box 16
Vancouver, BC V6C 2W2
Tel: 604-482-2200
Fax: 604-681-9017
info@bcpavco.com
www.bcpavco.com
A Provincial Crown Corporation of the Ministry of Tourism, Culture & The Arts, the BC Pavilion Corporation provides leadership in the meetings & events industry. It operates BC Place & The Vancouver Convention & Exhibition Centre.

• Building Code Appeal Board (BCAB)
c/o Building & Safety Standards Branch
PO Box 9844 Prov Govt
Victoria, BC V8W 1A4
Tel: 250-387-3133
Fax: 250-387-8164
Building.Safety@gov.bc.ca
www.housing.gov.bc.ca/bcab
Chair, George Humphrey

• Homeowner Protection Office (HPO)
c/o BC Housing
#650, 4789 Kingway
Burnaby, BC V5H 0A3
Tel: 604-646-7050
Fax: 604-646-7051
Toll-free: 800-407-7757
hpo@hpo.bc.ca
www.hpo.bc.ca
The Homeowner Protection Office seeks to protect buyers of new homes, to regulate the quality of residential construction, and to support residential construction research and education in British Columbia.

• Oil & Gas Commission (OGC)
#100, 10003 - 110 Ave.
Fort St John, BC V1J 6M7
Tel: 250-794-5200
Fax: 250-794-5375
www.bcogc.ca
Other Communication: Incident Reporting: 1-800-663-3456; Victoria: 250-419-4400; Dawson Creek: 250-795-2140
The Oil & Gas Commission was enacted under the Oil & Gas Commission Act, The Commission regulates British Columbia's oil & gas activities & pipelines.
Commissioner & Chief Executive Officer, Alex Ferguson
Tel: 250-419-4401
Alex.Ferguson@bcogc.ca
Deputy Commissioner, Regulatory Affairs & Stewardship, Paul Jeakins
Tel: 250-419-4411
Paul.Jeakins@bcogc.ca
Deputy Commissioner, Project Assessment & Compliance Assurance, James O'Hanley
Tel: 250-794-5226
James.OHanley@bcogc.ca
Deputy Commissioner, Operations Engineering Division, Lance Ollenberger
Tel: 250-794-5237
Lance.Ollenberger@bcogc.ca
Deputy Commissioner & Chief Engineer, Ken Paulson
Tel: 250-419-4404
Ken.Paulson@bcogc.ca

Electricity & Alternative Energy
PO Box 9314 Stn. Prov Govt, Victoria, BC V8W 9N1
Tel: 250-387-2814
Fax: 250-952-0258
Assistant Deputy Minister, Les MacLaren
Tel: 250-952-0204
Fax: 250-952-0926
Les.MacLaren@gov.bc.ca
Executive Director, Innovative Clean Energy (ICE) Fund, Dan Green
Tel: 250-952-0279
Fax: 250-952-0351
Dan.Green@gov.bc.ca
Executive Director, Electricity Transmission & Inter-Jurisdictional Branch; Electricity Generation & Regulation Branch, Derek Griffin
Tel: 250-952-0265
Fax: 250-952-0258
Derek.Griffin@gov.bc.ca
Executive Director, Columbia River Treaty (CRT) Review Team, Kathy Eichenberger
Tel: 250-952-3368
Fax: 250-952-0258
Kathy.Eichenberger@gov.bc.ca
Executive Director, Alternative Energy; Renewable Energy Development Branch, Paul Wieringa
Tel: 250-952-0651
Fax: 250-952-0657
Director, Electricity Transmission & Inter-Jurisdictional Branch, Scott Barillaro
Tel: 250-952-0267
Fax: 250-952-0258
Scott.Barillaro@gov.bc.ca
Director, Electricity Generation & Regulation Branch, Sue Bonnyman
Tel: 250-953-3365
Fax: 250-952-0258
Sue.Bonnyman@gov.bc.ca
Manager, Renewable Fuels, Michael Rensing
Tel: 250-952-0265
Fax: 250-952-0258
Michael.Rensing@gov.bc.ca
Director, Energy Efficiency Branch, Andrew Pape-Salmon
Tel: 250-952-0819
Fax: 250-952-0258
Andrew.PapeSalmon@gov.bc.ca
Director, ICE Fund, Liz Wouters
Tel: 250-387-2883
Fax: 250-952-0351
Liz.Wouters@gov.bc.ca

LNG Initiatives
PO Box 9319 Stn. Prov Govt, Victoria, BC V8W 9N3
Fax: 250-952-0269
Assistant Deputy Minister/Lead Negotiator, Brian Hansen
Tel: 250-952-0124
Brian.Hansen@gov.bc.ca
Executive Director, Regulatory & FN Engagement, LNG Initiative, Suzanne Manahan
Tel: 250-952-0729
Suzanne.Manahan@gov.bc.ca

Mines & Mineral Resources
PO Box 9319 Stn. Prov Govt, Victoria, BC V8W 9N3
Assistant Deputy Minister, David Morel
Tel: 250-952-0473
Fax: 250-952-0491
David.Morel@gov.bc.ca
Chief Inspector/Executive Director, Health & Safety, Health & Safety & Permitting Branch, Al Hoffman
Tel: 250-952-0494
Fax: 250-952-0491
Al.Hoffman@gov.bc.ca
Chief Geologist & Executive Director, British Columbia Geological Survey, Stephen Rowins
Tel: 250-952-0454
Fax: 250-952-0381
Stephen.Rowins@gov.bc.ca
Executive Director/Chief Gold Commissioner, Mineral Titles, May Mah-Paulson
Tel: 250-952-0335
May.Mah-Paulson@gov.bc.ca
Director, Mineral Development Office, Bruce Madu
Tel: 604-660-2094
Fax: 604-775-0313
Bruce.Madu@gov.bc.ca
Director, Resource Information Section, Larry Jones
Tel: 250-952-0386
Fax: 250-952-0381
Larry.Jones@gov.bc.ca
Director, Cordilleran Geoscience, Adrian Hickin
Tel: 250-953-3801
Fax: 250-952-0381
Adrian.Hickin@gov.bc.ca
Director, Mining Operations (Kamloops), Joe Seguin
Tel: 250-828-4448
Fax: 250-828-4154
Joe.Seguin@gov.bc.ca
Regional Director, Mining Operations (Victoria), Ed Taje
Tel: 250-952-0732
Fax: 250-952-0491
Eddy.Taje@gov.bc.ca
Executive Director, Policy, Stewart Guy
Tel: 250-952-0868
Fax: 250-952-0271
Stewart.Guy@gov.bc.ca

Office of Housing & Construction Standards
PO Box 9319 Stn. Prov Govt, Victoria, BC V8W 9N3
Fax: 250-952-0269
Assistant Deputy Minister, Jeff Vasey
Tel: 250-387-2001
Fax: 250-387-8164
Jeff.Vasey@gov.bc.ca
Executive Director, Building & Safety Standards Branch, Trudy Rotgans
Tel: 250-387-3754
Fax: 250-387-8164
Trudy.Rotgans@gov.bc.ca
Executive Director, Housing Policy Branch, Gregory Steves
Tel: 250-387-3087
Fax: 250-356-8182
Gregory.Steves@gov.bc.ca
Director, Crown Agency Liaison, Simon Clews
Tel: 250-387-1018
Fax: 250-356-8182
Simon.Clews@gov.bc.ca

Oil & Gas
PO Box 9323 Stn. Prov Govt, Victoria, BC V8W 9N3
Fax: 250-952-0926
Executive Director, GeoScience & Strategic Initiatives Branch, Linda Beltrano
Tel: 250-356-1183
Fax: 250-952-0255
Linda.Beltrano@gov.bc.ca
Executive Director, Petroleum & Natural Gas Titles Branch, Garth Thoroughgood
Tel: 250-952-6382
Fax: 250-952-0333
Garth.Thoroughgood@gov.bc.ca
Director, Policy & Planning, Geoff Turner
Tel: 250-952-0709
Fax: 250-952-0331
Geoff.Turner@gov.bc.ca
Acting Director, Resource Development, Sara Dickinson
Tel: 250-787-3426
Fax: 250-952-0331
Sara.Dickinson@gov.bc.ca
Director, Royalty & Policy, Aaron Nelson
Tel: 250-953-3740
Fax: 250-953-3770
Aaron.Nelson@gov.bc.ca
Acting Executive Director, Infrastructure & Development Section, Stephen Pal
Tel: 250-953-3738
Fax: 250-953-3770
Stephen.Pal@gov.bc.ca
Director, Tenure & Revenue Management, Debbie Fischer
Tel: 250-952-0336
Fax: 250-952-0331
Debbie.Fischer@gov.bc.ca
Director, GeoScience & Natural Gas Development Branch, Adrian Hickin
Tel: 250-953-3801
Fax: 250-953-3770
Adrian.Hickin@gov.bc.ca
Director, Best Practices & Strategic Planning, Olga Klimko
Tel: 250-953-3766
Fax: 250-952-0255
Olga.Klimko@gov.bc.ca
Director, Regulatory Policy Development, Michelle Schwabe
Tel: 250-387-1585
Fax: 250-952-0255
Michelle.Schwabe@gov.bc.ca
Acting Director, Infrastructure Development, Jennifer Purcell
Tel: 250-387-1584
Fax: 250-952-0255
Jennifer.Purcell@gov.bc.ca

British Columbia Ministry of Environment

PO Box 9339 Stn. Prov Govt, Victoria, BC V8W 9M1
Tel: 250-387-1161
Fax: 250-387-5669
envmail@gov.bc.ca
www.gov.bc.ca/env
Other Communication: Environmental Emergencies: 1-800-663-3456; Report All Poachers & Polluters (RAPP): 1-877-952-7277; Media Enquiries, Phone: 250-387-9973
The following responsibilities are handled by the Ministry of the Environment: establishment of standards; administration of legislation; promotion of stewardship & sustainability, through environmental protection; development of partnerships, by engaging stakeholders, First Nations, & citizens in policy & program development; & conservation, maintenance, & enhancement of ecosystems & native species.
Acts Administered:
College of Applied Biology Act
Ecological Reserve Act
Environmental Assessment Act
Environmental Management Act (except (a) s. 5 (f), as that provision relates to the portfolio of the Minister of Forests, Lands, & Natural Resource Operations; (b) Divisions 1 & 3 of Part 8)
Greenhouse Gas Reduction (Cap & Trade) Act
Greenhouse Gas Reduction (Vehicle Emissions Standards) Act
Greenhouse Gas Reduction Targets Act
Integrated Pest Management Act
Land Title Act (s. 219 (1), (2), (3) (a) & (b), (4)-(9.2), (10), (11) (a), (12) & (14), as that provision relates to the portfolio of the Minister of Environment)
Ministry of Environment Act (except s. 4 (2) (d); ss. 4 (2) (b), (e), (f) & (g) & 6.1 as those provisions relate to the portfolio of the Minister of Forests, Lands, & Natural Resource Operations)
Ministry of Lands, Parks, & Housing Act (ss. 5 (b), 6 & 9, as those provisions relate to the portfolio of the Minister of Environment)
Park Act
Protected Areas of British Columbia Act
Special Accounts Appropriation & Control (s. 9.6)
Sustainable Environment Fund Act
Wildlife Act (s. 3 (b), as that provision relates to the portfolio of the Minister of Environment; ss. 6 & 108 (2) (a))

Minister, Environment; Deputy House Leader, Hon. Terry Lake
Tel: 250-387-1187
Fax: 250-387-1356
ENV.minister@gov.bc.ca
Social Media: twitter.com/terrylakeMLA
PO Box 9047 Prov Govt Sta.
Victoria, BC V8W 9E2

Deputy Minister, Environment, Wes Shoemaker
Tel: 250-387-5429

Associated Agencies, Boards & Commissions:
- **British Columbia Environmental Assessment Office**

See Entry Name Index for detailed listing.

BC Parks & Conservation Officer Service
PO Box 9376 Stn. Prov Govt, Victoria, BC V8W 9M1
Tel: 250-356-9234
Fax: 250-356-9197
conservation.officer.service@gov.bc.ca
www.env.gov.bc.ca/cos/
Other Communication: Wildlife conflict: 1-877-952-7277
Chief Superintendent, Program Governance, Lance Sundquist
Tel: 250-751-3119
Fax: 250-751-7383
Lance.Sundquist@gov.bc.ca
Other Communications: Alternate Phone: 250-356-9121
Chief Superintendent, Provincial Operations, Barry Farynuk
Tel: 250-354-6336
Fax: 250-354-6277
Barry.Farynuk@gov.bc.ca

Climate Action Secretariat
PO Box 9486 Stn. Prov Govt, Victoria, BC V8W 9W6
Fax: 250-356-7286
climateactionsecretariat@gov.bc.ca
www.env.gov.bc.ca/cas//index.html
Head, James Mack
Tel: 250-387-9456
Fax: 250-356-7286
Chief Negotiator/Executive Director, Business Development, Tim Lesiuk
Tel: 250-387-9216
Fax: 250-356-7286
Other Communications: Cell Phone: 250-216-5893
Executive Director, Climate Policy, Liz Lilly
Tel: 250-356-7917
Fax: 250-356-7286
Liz.Lilly@gov.bc.ca
Executive Director, Carbon Neutral Government & Climate Action Outreach, Rob Abbott
Tel: 250-356-5826
Fax: 250-356-7286
Director, Business Development/Lead Negotiator, Jessica Verhagen
Tel: 604-836-1942
Fax: 250-356-7286
Jessica.Verhagen@gov.bc.ca
Manager, Business Partnerships, Diane Beattie
Tel: 250-953-4884
Fax: 250-356-7286
Diane.Beattie@gov.bc.ca

Environmental Assessment Office
PO Box 9426 Stn. Prov Govt, Victoria, BC V8W 9V1
Fax: 250-356-6448
eaoinfo@gov.bc.ca
Assistant Deputy Minister, Dave Nikolejsin
Tel: 250-356-7475
Fax: 250-356-6448
eaoinfo@gov.bc.ca
Executive Lead, Environmental Assessments, John Mazure
Tel: 250-387-2307
John_Mazure@gov.bc.ca
Executive Project Director, David "Archie" Riddell
Tel: 250-952-6507
David_Riddell@gov.bc.ca
Executive Director, Strategy and Quality Assurance, Michelle Carr
Tel: 250-387-6748
Michelle_Carr@gov.bc.ca
Director, Business Operations, Terri Starkes
Tel: 250-356-5770
Terri_Starkes@gov.bc.ca
Manager, Policy and Project Assessment, Tim Hicks
Tel: 250-387-6758
Tim_Hicks@gov.bc.ca
Director, Lands Policy, Dawna Harden
Tel: 250-356-7727
Dawna.Harden@gov.bc.ca

Environmental Protection Division
PO Box 9339Victoria, BC V8W 9M1
Tel: 250-387-1288
Fax: 250-387-5669
www.env.gov.bc.ca/epd/
Assistant Deputy Minister, Jim Standen
Tel: 250-387-1288
Fax: 250-387-5669
Jim.Standen@gov.bc.ca
Executive Director, Environmental Management, Jim Hofweber
Tel: 250-387-9971
Fax: 250-387-8897
Jim.Hofweber@gov.bc.ca
Executive Director, Environmental Standards Branch, David Ranson
Tel: 250-387-9933
Fax: 250-356-7197
David.Ranson@gov.bc.ca
Director, Regional Operations, Jennifer McGuire
Tel: 250-356-6027
Fax: 250-356-5496
Assistant Director, Regional Operations, Christa Zacharias-Homer
Tel: 250-490-8227
Fax: 250-356-5496
Christa.ZachariasHomer@gov.bc.ca
Regional Manager, Thompson Regional Office, Cassandra Caunce
Tel: 250-371-6225
Fax: 250-828-4000
Cassandra.Caunce@gov.bc.ca
1259 Dalhousie Dr.
Kamloops, BC V2C 5Z5
Director, Environmental Protection Division, West Coast Region, Randy Alexander
Tel: 250-751-3176
Fax: 250-751-3103
Randy.Alexander@gov.bc.ca
2080A Labieux Rd.
Nanaimo, BC V9T 6J9
Regional Manager, Environmental Protection, Lower Mainland Regional Office, Jonn Braman
Tel: 604-582-5284
Fax: 604-584-9751
Jonn.Braman@gov.bc.ca
10470 - 152nd St., 2nd Fl.
Surrey, BC V3R 0Y3
Regional Director, Omineca Regional Office, Edward Hoffman
Tel: 250-565-6443
Fax: 250-565-6629
Edward.Hoffman@gov.bc.ca
1011 - 4th Ave., 3rd Fl.
Prince George, BC V2L 3H9
Regional Director, Kootenay & Okanagan Regional Office, Robyn Roome
Tel: 250-354-6362
Fax: 250-354-6332
Robyn.Roome@gov.bc.ca
#401, 333 Victoria St.
Nelson, BC V1L 4K3
Regional Manager, Environmental Protection, Skeena Regional Office, Ian Sharpe
Tel: 250-847-7251
Fax: 250-847-7591
Ian.Sharpe@gov.bc.ca

3726 Alfred Ave.
PO Box 5000
Smithers, BC V0J 2N0
Section Head, Cariboo Regional Office, Douglas Hill
Tel: 250-398-4542
Fax: 250-398-4214
Doug.Hill@gov.bc.ca
#400, 640 Borland St.
Williams Lake, BC V2G 4T1
Director, Land Remediation, Mike Macfarlane
Tel: 250-356-0557
Mike.Macfarlane@gov.bc.ca
#400, 640 Borland St.
Williams Lake, BC V2G 4T1

Environmental Stewardship Division
PO Box 9339 Stn. Prov Govt, Victoria, BC V8W 9M1
Tel: 250-356-0121
Fax: 250-387-5669
Director, Regional Operations, Brian J. Clark
Tel: 250-356-0874
Fax: 250-356-9299
Brian.J.Clark@gov.bc.ca
Manager, First Nations Relations, Bryan Williams
Tel: 250-751-3155
Fax: 250-751-3208
Manager, Strategic Initiatives, Chris Tunnoch
Tel: 604-942-2224
Fax: 604-924-2244
Chris.Tunnoch@gov.bc.ca
Project Coordinator, BC Conservation Corps; Deputy Director, Wildlife, Mitch C. Kendall
Tel: 250-371-6251
Fax: 250-356-5104
Mitch.Kendall@gov.bc.ca
Regional Director, BC Parks & Conservation Officer Service Division, West Coast, Don Cadden
Tel: 250-751-3211
Fax: 250-751-3208
Don.Cadden@gov.bc.ca
Regional Director, Parks & Protected Areas, Thompson Regional Office, Jeff Leahy
Tel: 250-371-6304
Fax: 250-828-4000
Jeff.Leahy@gov.bc.ca
Section Head, Protected Areas, Peace Regional Office, Lisa Hardy
Tel: 250-787-3562
Fax: 250-787-3490
Lisa.Hardy@gov.bc.ca
Acting Regional Manager, Omineca Regional Office, Ted Zimmerman
Tel: 250-614-9904
Fax: 250-565-6940
Ted.Zimmerman@gov.bc.ca
Section Head, Ecosystems, Skeena Regional Office, Karen Diemert
Tel: 250-847-7300
Fax: 250-847-7728
Karen.Diemert@gov.bc.ca
Section Head, Recreation, Kootenay Regional Office, Glenn Campbell
Tel: 250-489-8595
Fax: 250-489-8506
Glenn.Campbell@gov.bc.ca
Section Head, Recreation, Cariboo Regional Office, Murray Carruthers
Tel: 250-398-4924
Fax: 250-398-4214
Murray.Carruthers@gov.bc.ca
Section Head, Planning - Squamish, Lower Mainland Regional Office, Vicki Haberl
Tel: 604-898-3678
Fax: 604-898-4171
Vicki.Haberl@gov.bc.ca
Section Head, Recreation, Okanagan Regional Office, Dave Richmond
Tel: 250-490-8259
Fax: 250-490-2231
Dave.Richmond@gov.bc.ca

Environmental Sustainability & Strategic Policy Division
PO Box 9335 Stn. Prov Govt, Victoria, BC V8W 9M1
Tel: 250-387-9666
Fax: 250-387-8894
Assistant Deputy Minister, Mark Zacharias
Tel: 250-356-0121
Fax: 250-387-5669
Executive Director, Strategic Policy Branch, Anthony J. Danks
Tel: 250-387-8483
Fax: 250-387-8894
Anthony.Danks@gov.bc.ca
Acting Director, Ecosystems Branch, Alec Dale
Tel: 250-387-9731
Fax: 250-356-5104
Alec.Dale@gov.bc.ca
Director, Knowledge Management Branch, Fern Schultz
Tel: 250-387-6722
Fax: 250-356-1202
Fern.Schultz@gov.bc.ca
Director, Water Protection & Sustainability Branch, Lynn Kriwoken
Tel: 250-387-9446
Fax: 250-356-1202
Lynn.Kriwoken@gov.bc.ca

Water Stewardship Division
PO Box 9339 Stn. Prov Govt, Victoria, BC V8W 9M1
Fax: 250-387-6003
Manager, Water Stewardship, Norm Bilodeau
Tel: 250-565-4457
Fax: 250-565-6629
Normand.Bilodeau@gov.bc.ca
Section Head, Nothern Region, Robert Piccini
Tel: 250-565-6441
Fax: 250-565-6629
Robert.Piccini@gov.bc.ca
Senior Flood Hazard Officer, Lyle Larsen
Tel: 250-565-6437
Fax: 250-565-6629
Lyle.Larsen@gov.bc.ca
Acts Administered:
Coastal Ferry Act

Minister, Finance; Government House Leader, Hon. Michael de Jong, Q.C.
Tel: 250-387-3751
Fax: 250-387-5594
FIN.Minister@gov.bc.ca; Michael.DeJong@gov.bc.ca
Social Media: twitter.com/mike_de_jong
PO Box 9048 Prov Govt Sta.
Victoria, BC V8W 9E2

Deputy Minister, Finance, Peter Milburn
Tel: 250-387-3184
Fax: 250-387-1655

Assistant Deputy Minister, Strategic Initiatives, Doug Foster
Tel: 250-387-9022
Fax: 250-387-1655
Doug.Foster@gov.bc.ca

Associate Deputy Minister, Sheila Taylor
Tel: 250-387-8499
Fax: 250-387-1655

Assistant Deputy Minister, Internal Audit & Advisory Services, Chris Brown
Tel: 250-387-8198
Fax: 250-356-2001
Chris.Brown@gov.bc.ca

Manager, Executive Operations, Shelley MacLean
Tel: 250-356-6696
Fax: 250-387-1655

British Columbia Ministry of Forests, Lands & Natural Resource Operations

PO Box 9352 Stn. Prov Govt, Victoria, BC V8W 9M1
Tel: 250-387-4809
Toll-Free: 877-855-3222
TTY: 800-661-8773
FLNRO.MediaRequests@gov.bc.ca
www.gov.bc.ca/for
Other Communication: Media Phone: 250-356-5261
The Ministry of Forests, Lands & Natural Resource Operations establishes policies for access to & use of British Columbia's forests, land, & natural resources. Services provided enable stewardship & sustainable management of the province's resources. Responsibilities of the ministry include Aboriginal consultation; Crown land administration policy; resource roads & bridges policy; forest, range, & grazing stewardship policy; pest & disease management policy; water use planning; timber supply & sales; fish, wildlife, & habitat management; licensing for hunting, trapping, & angling; recreation sites & trails; & wildfire management.
Acts Administered:
Boundary Act
Creston Valley Wildlife Act
Dike Maintenance Act
Drainage, Ditch & Dike Act
Environment & Land Use Act
Environmental Management Act (s. 5 (f), as that section relates to the portfolio of the Minister of Forests, Lands, & Natural Resource Operations)
Fish Protection Act
Fisheries Act (Part 3, as it relates to the licensing of aquaculture)
Flathead Watershed Area Conservation Act
Forest & Range Practices Act (except the collection of public money, as defined in the Financial Administration Act, other than a fine, or the administration of deposits & securities payable; & s. 166, as that relates to the Justice portfolio)
Forest Act (except the collection of public money, as defined in section 1 of the Financial Administration Act, other than a fine, or the administration of deposits & securities payable)
Forest Practices Code of British Columbia Act (except the collection of public money, as defined in section 1 of the Financial Administration Act, other than a fine, or the administration of deposits & securities payable; & Part 9)
Forest Stand Management Fund Act (except the collection of public money, as defined in section 1 of the Financial Administration Act, other than a fine, or the administration of deposits & securities payable)
Foresters Act
Forestry Revitalization Act
Forestry Service Providers Protection Act
Greenbelt Act
Heritage Conservation Act
Hunting & Fishing Heritage Act
Industrial Operation Compensation Act
Land (Spouse Protection) Act
Land Act
Land Survey Act
Land Surveyors Act
Land Title & Survey Authority Act
Land Title Act (except s. 77.2; s. 219 (1), (2), (3) (a) & (b), (4) - (9.2), (10), (11) (a), (12) & (14) as that provision relates to the portfolio of the Minister of Community, Sport, & Cultural Dev. or to the portfolio of the Minister of Environment)
Land Title Inquiry Act
Land Transfer Form Act
Libby Dam Reservoir Act
Ministry of Environment Act (s. 4 (2) (d); ss. 4 (2) (b), (e), (f) & (g) & 6.1 as those provisions relate to the portfolio of the Minister of Forests, Lands & Natural Resource Operations)
Ministry of Forests & Range Act (except the collection of public money, as defined in the Financial Administration Act, other than a fine, or the administration of deposits & securities payable; & s. 4 (d) (ii) & (e) as that relates to Agriculture)
Motor Vehicle (All Terrain) Act
Muskwa-Kechika Management Area Act
Natural Resource Compliance Act
Private Managed Forest Land Act
Protected Areas Forests Compensation Act
Railway Act (s. 33)
Range Act (except collection of public money, defined in the Financial Administration Act, other than a fine or the administration of deposits & securities payable; ss. 39, 41, 42 (1) & 43; (c) ss. 1 (2) & (3), 44, 45, 76, 79 & 80 related to Agriculture)
Resort Timber Administration Act
Skagit Environmental Enhancement Act
Special Accounts Appropriation & Control (s. 5)
Tugboat Worker Lien Act
University Endowment Land Act (ss. 2 (1) (a) & (d) & 3 (b))
Water Act
Water Protection Act
Water Utility Act
Weed Control Act
Wildfire Act (except as it relates to the collection of public money, as defined in section 1 of the Financial Administration Act, other than a fine, or the administration of deposits & securities payable)
Wildlife Act (except s. 3 (b) as that provision relates to the portfolio of the Minister of Environment; & ss. 6 & 108 (2) (a))

Woodworker Lien Act
Zero Net Deforestation Act

Minister, Forests, Lands, & Natural Resource Operations, Hon. Steve Thomson
Tel: 250-356-6211
Fax: 250-387-1040
FLNR.Minister@gov.bc.ca
PO Box 9049 Prov Govt Sta.
Victoria, BC V8W 9E2

Deputy Minister, Doug Konkin
Tel: 250-952-6500
Fax: 250-387-3291
1520 Blanshard St., 3rd Fl.
PO Box 9525 Prov Govt Sta.
Victoria, BC V8W 9C3

Parliamentary Secretary for Forestry to the Minister of Forests, Lands, & Natural Resource Operations, John Rustad
Tel: 250-953-4892
Fax: 250-387-9066

Associated Agencies, Boards & Commissions:
• Assayers Certification Board of Examiners (ACBE)
PO Box 9333 Prov Govt
Victoria, BC V8W 9N3
Tel: 250-952-0396
commons.bcit.ca/assayerscert/exam.html
The Board of Examiners administers the Assayers Certification Program, invigilate the examinations, grade papers, and recommend candidates for qualification to the Responsible Minister. The Board operates under the Ministry of Energy & Mines Act.
Chair, Manzur A. Chaudhry
Tel: 250-477-0979
manzur.chaudhry@bcassayer.com
• Forest Practices Board (FPB)
1675 Douglas St., 3rd Fl.
PO Box 9905 Prov Govt
Victoria, BC V8W 9R1
Tel: 250-213-4700
Fax: 250-213-4725
Toll-free: 800-994-5899
fpboard@gov.bc.ca
www.fpb.gov.bc.ca
Other Communication: Toll-Free Fax: 1-877-708-4607
British Columbia's Forest Practices Board is responsible for reporting to the government & public about compliance with the Forest & Range Practices Act. The Board engages in the following activities: Investigation of public complaints; Undertaking special investigations; Auditing forest practices of government, government enforcement of the Forest & Range Practices Act, & licence holders on public lands; Participation in appeals; & Provision of reports & recommendations.
Chair, Al Gorley
Tel: 250-213-4710
General Counsel, John Pennington
Tel: 250-213-4706
Executive Director, Fred Parker
Tel: 250-213-4702
Director, Audits, Chris Mosher
Tel: 250-213-4703
Director, Corporate Services, Peter Nagati
Tel: 250-213-4704
Director, Special Projects, Darlene Oman
Tel: 250-213-4705
Manager, Special Investigations, Marvin Eng
Tel: 250-213-4710
• Muskwa-Kechika Advisory Board (M-KAB)
coordinator@muskwa-kechika.com
www.muskwa-kechika.com
The Board oversees the preservation of the Muskwa-Kechika Management Area, & ensures that activities carried out within the area meet the standards set by the Muskwa-Kechika Management Plan.
Chair, Tom Briggs
Co-Vice-Chair, Bill Lux
Co-Vice-Chair, Jason Lee
• Timber Export Advisory Committee
PO Box 9514 Prov Govt
Victoria, BC V8W 9C2
Tel: 250-387-8916
Fax: 250-387-5050
Secretary, John R. Cook

Corporate Initiatives
PO Box 9352 Stn. Prov Govt, Victoria, BC V8W 9M1
Acting Executive Director, Ines Piccinino
Tel: 250-387-8885
Ines.Piccinino@gov.bc.ca
Acting Director, Strategic Initiatives, Gail Brewer
Tel: 250-356-5299
Fax: 250-953-3481
Director, Legislation, Richard Grieve
Tel: 250-387-8606
Fax: 250-356-7903
Richard.Grieve@gov.bc.ca
Acting Director, Major Projects, Brenda Hartley
Tel: 250-828-4443
Fax: 250-387-2335
Brenda.Hartley@gov.bc.ca
Director, Integrated Initiatives, Andrew Morgan
Tel: 250-953-4205
Andrew.Morgan@gov.bc.ca

Executive Operations
PO Box 9352 Stn. Prov Govt, Victoria, BC V8W 9M1
Fax: 250-387-3291
Acting Director, Jennifer Good
Tel: 250-356-2700
Jennifer.Goad@gov.bc.ca
Manager, Executive Services, Trevor Morrison
Tel: 250-356-5091
Trevor.Morrison@gov.bc.ca
Manager, Correspondence Services, Sonia Donison
Tel: 250-356-9638
Sonia.Donison@gov.bc.ca

Integrated Resource Operations Division
PO Box 9352 Stn. Prov Govt, Victoria, BC V8W 9M1
Tel: 250-356-1874
Fax: 250-387-2335
Assistant Deputy Minister, Gary Townsend
Tel: 250-356-1874
Fax: 250-387-2335
Executive Director, Field Operations, Jim Maxwell
Tel: 250-387-1236
Fax: 250-953-3687
Jim.Maxwell@gov.bc.ca
Executive Director, GeoBC; Integrated Resource Operations, Francesca Wheler
Tel: 250-387-3745
Francesca.Wheler@gov.bc.ca
Executive Director, Resort Development, Norman Lee
Tel: 250-952-0478
Norman.K.Lee@gov.bc.ca
Director, Compliance & Enforcement, Kevin Edquist
Tel: 250-387-8372
Fax: 250-387-2569
Kevin.Edquist@gov.bc.ca
Director, Recreation Sites & Trails BC, Bill Marshall
Tel: 250-953-3678
Bill.Marshall@gov.bc.ca
Director, Wildfire Management Headquarters, Brian Simpson
Tel: 250-387-6368
Fax: 250-387-5685
Brian.Simpson@gov.bc.ca
Director, Archaeology Branch, Justine Batten
Tel: 250-953-3355
Fax: 250-953-3340
Justine.Batten@gov.bc.ca
Director, Heritage Branch, Jennifer Iredale
Tel: 250-356-1431
Fax: 250-356-2842
Jennifer.Iredale@gov.bc.ca
Manager, Regional Service Delivery, GeoBC, Janet Adams
Tel: 250-952-5309
Fax: 250-356-5797
Janet.Adams@gov.bc.ca
Coast
2100 Labieux Rd., Nanaimo, BC V9T 6E9
Tel: 250-751-7001
Fax: 250-751-7190
Forests.CoastRegionOffice@gov.bc.ca
www.for.gov.bc.ca/rco
Assistant Deputy Minister, Craig Sutherland
Tel: 250-387-9773
Fax: 250-356-2150
Regional Executive Director, West Coast, Sharon Hadway
Tel: 250-751-7161
Fax: 250-751-7196
Sharon.Hadway@gov.bc.ca
Regional Executive Director, South Coast, Heather MacKnight
Tel: 604-586-2892
Fax: 604-586-4434
Heather.MacKnight@gov.bc.ca
Director, Resource Management (West Coast), Larry Barr
Tel: 250-751-7105
Fax: 250-741-5686
Larry.Barr@gov.bc.ca
Director, Pricing/Tenures/Mines (West Coast), Denis Collins
Tel: 250-751-7121
Fax: 250-751-7196
Denis.Collins@gov.bc.ca
Director, Authorizations (West Coast), Myles Mana
Tel: 250-751-7308
Fax: 250-751-7081
Myles.Mana@gov.bc.ca
Director, Resource Management (South Coast), Julia Berardinucci
Tel: 604-586-4433
Fax: 604-586-4434
Julia.Berardinucci@gov.bc.ca
Director, Resource Authorization (South Coast), Alec Drysdale
Tel: 604-586-4420
Fax: 604-586-4419
Alec.Drysdale@gov.bc.ca
Director, Resource Initiatives Office (South Coast), Kevin Haberl
Tel: 604-898-2145
Fax: 604-586-4434
Kevin Haberl@gov.bc.ca
Manager, Strategic Initiatives, Chris Tunnoch
Tel: 604-924-2224
Fax: 250-356-9299
Chris.Tunnoch@gov.bc.ca
Manager, Permit & Authorization Service Bureau, Yvonne Foxall
Tel: 250-387-3787
Fax: 250-387-1814
Yvonne.Foxall@gov.bc.ca
North Area
1011 - 4 Ave., 5th Fl., Prince George, BC V2L 3H9
Tel: 250-565-6100
www.for.gov.bc.ca/rni
Assistant Deputy Minister, Kevin Kriese
Tel: 250-952-0596
Executive Director, Butch Morningstar
Tel: 250-387-0844
Butch.Morningstar@gov.bc.ca
Executive Director, Strategic Projects, Gary Reay
Tel: 250-751-7007
Executive Coordinator, Leona Frenette
Tel: 250-356-5304
Regional Executive Director, Northeast, Dale Morgan
Tel: 250-784-1200
Dale.Morgan@gov.bc.ca
Regional Executive Director, Skeena, Eamon O'Donoghue
Tel: 250-847-7495
Fax: 250-847-7347
Eamon.ODonoghue@gov.bc.ca
Regional Executive Director, Omineca, Bill Warner
Tel: 250-565-6102
Fax: 250-565-6671
Bill.Warner@gov.bc.ca
Director, Authorizations (Prince George), Greg Rawling
Tel: 250-565-6234
Fax: 250-565-6671
Greg.Rawling@gov.bc.ca
Director, Resource Management (Omenica), Normand Bilodeau
Tel: 250-565-4457
Director, Major Projects (Northeast), Todd Bondaroff
Tel: 250-784-1245
Fax: 250-787-3219
Todd.Bondaroff@gov.bc.ca
Regional Director, Pricing & Tenures (Omineca), Heather Cullen
Tel: 250-565-6102
Fax: 250-565-6671
Heather.Cullen@gov.bc.ca
Director, Resource Management (Skeena), Jane Lloyd-Smith
Tel: 250-847-7340
Fax: 250-847-7728
Jane.LloydSmith@gov.bc.ca
Acting Director, Authorizations (Skeena), Nick Thomas
Tel: 250-847-7517
Fax: 250-847-7347
Nicholas.Thomas@gov.bc.ca

Director, Resource Authorizations (Northeast), Karrilyn Vince
Tel: 250-787-3534
Fax: 250-787-3219
Karrilyn.Vince@gov.bc.ca
District Manager, Resource Operations (Vanderhoof/Fort St. James), Lynda Currie
Tel: 250-996-5241
Fax: 250-996-5290
Lynda.Currie@gov.bc.ca
District Manager, Resource Operations (Mackenzie), Dave Francis
Tel: 250-997-2203
Fax: 250-997-2203
Dave.Francis@gov.bc.ca
District Manager, Resource Operations (Dawson Creek), Robert Kopecky
Tel: 250-784-1205
Fax: 250-784-1203
District Manager, Resource Operations (Fort Nelson), Steve Lindsey
Tel: 250-774-5520
Fax: 250-774-3704
Steve.Lindsey@gov.bc.ca
District Manager, Coast Mountains Resource District, Barry Dobbin
Tel: 250-638-5100
Fax: 250-638-5176
Barry.Dobbin@gov.bc.ca
District Manager, Nadina, Josh Pressey
Tel: 250-692-2224
Fax: 250-692-7461
Josh.Pressey@gov.bc.ca
South
441 Columbia St., Kamloops, BC V2C 2T3
Tel: 250-828-4131
Fax: 250-828-4154
www.for.gov.bc.ca/rsi
Assistant Deputy Minister, Richard Manwaring
Tel: 250-828-4449
Acting Executive Director, Madeline Maley
Tel: 250-828-4114
Other Communications: Alternate Phone: 250-371-3747
Regional Executive Director, Southern Interior Region, Kevin Dickenson
Tel: 250-828-4445
Fax: 250-828-4442
Kevin.Dickenson@gov.bc.ca
Regional Executive Director, Cariboo, Gerry MacDougall
Gerry.MacDougall@gov.bc.ca
Regional Executive Director, Kootenay Boundary, Tony Wideski
Tel: 250-426-1741
Fax: 250-426-1767
Tony.Wideski@gov.bc.ca
Director, Resource Management (Kootenay), Paul Rasmussen
Tel: 250-354-6947
Paul.Rasmussen@gov.bc.ca
Director, Resource Authorizations (Kamloops), Peter Lishman
Tel: 250-828-4239
Fax: 250-828-4442
Peter.Lishman@gov.bc.ca
Director, Resource Management (Kamloops), Dan Peterson
Tel: 250-828-4124
Fax: 250-828-4154
Dan.Peterson@gov.bc.ca
Director, Pricing & Tenures (Kamloops), Jim Schafthuizen
Tel: 250-828-4625
Fax: 250-828-4154
Jim.Schafthuizen@gov.bc.ca
Director, Resource Management (Cariboo), Rodger Stewart
Tel: 250-398-4549
Fax: 250-398-4214
Rodger.Stewart@gov.bc.ca
Other Communications: Cell Phone: 250-305-8536
Director, Resource Authorizations (Cariboo), Ken Vanderburgh
Tel: 250-398-4225
Fax: 250-398-4836
Ken.Vanderburgh@gov.bc.ca
District Manager, Natural Resource Operations (100 Mile House), Patrick Byrne
Tel: 250-395-7804
Fax: 250-395-7810
Pat.Byrne@gov.bc.ca
District Manager, Natural Resource Operations (Quensel), Steve Dodge
Tel: 250-992-4465
Fax: 250-992-4403
Steve.Dodge@gov.bc.ca
District Manager, Natural Resource Operations (Kamloops), Rick Sommer
Tel: 250-371-6501
Rick.B.Sommer@gov.bc.ca
District Manager, Natural Resource Operations (Okanagan Shuswap), Dave Hails
Tel: 250-558-1729
Fax: 250-549-5485
Dave.Hails@gov.bc.ca
District Manager, Natural Resource Operations (Cascades), Charles van Hemmen
Tel: 250-378-8402
Fax: 250-378-8481
Charles.vanHemmen@gov.bc.ca
Other Communications: Cell Phone: 250-315-3773
District Manager, Resource Operations (Central Cariboo/Chilcotin), Mike Pedersen
Tel: 250-398-4355
Fax: 250-398-4790
Mike.Pedersen@gov.bc.ca
Other Communications: Alternate Phone: 250-398-4345

Resource Stewardship Division
PO Box 9525 Stn. Prov Govt, Victoria, BC V8W 9C3
Tel: 250-387-1296
Fax: 250-953-3687
Assistant Deputy Minister, Tom Ethier
Tel: 250-356-0972
Fax: 250-356-2150
Chief Financial Officer, Water Allocation & Safety, Ron Simmons
Tel: 250-387-6308
Fax: 250-953-5124
Ron.Simmons@gov.bc.ca
Director, Tree Improvement Branch, Brian Barber
Tel: 250-356-0888
Fax: 250-356-8124
Brian.Barber@gov.bc.ca
Other Communications: URL: www.for.gov.bc.ca/hti/
Director & Comptroller, Water Rights, Water Management, Glen Davidson, P.Eng
Tel: 250-387-6949
Fax: 250-356-0605
Glen.Davidson@gov.bc.ca
Director, Resource Management Objectives, Allan Lidstone
Tel: 250-356-6255
Fax: 250-387-2410
Allan.Lidstone@gov.bc.ca
Director, Forest Analysis & Inventory Branch, Albert Nussbaum
Tel: 250-356-5958
Fax: 250-953-3838
Forests.ForestAnalysisBranchOffice@gov.bc.ca
Director, Resource Practices Branch, Jim D. Sutherland
Tel: 250-398-4527
Fax: 250-387-2136
Jim.D.Sutherland@gov.bc.ca
Other Communications: Alternate Phone: 250-387-0088
Director, Regional Operations, Water Stewardship, Brian Symonds
Tel: 250-490-8255
Fax: 250-490-2231
Brian.Symonds@gov.bc.ca
Director, Operations, Keith Thomas
Tel: 250-387-1742
Fax: 250-953-3687
Keith.Thomas@gov.bc.ca
Director, Fish, Wildlife & Habitat Management, Andrew Wilson
Tel: 250-387-5657
Fax: 250-387-9568
Andrew.Wilson@gov.bc.ca
Acting Deputy Director, Fish, Wildlife & Habitat Management, Yvonne Foxall
Tel: 250-356-0874
Fax: 250-387-9568
Yvonne.Foxall@gov.bc.ca
Director & Deputy Director's Assistant, Fish, Wildlife & Habitat Management, Diana McNeil
Tel: 250-387-3637
Fax: 250-387-9568
Diana.McNeill@gov.bc.ca

Tenures, Competitiveness & Innovation Division
PO Box 9352 Stn. Prov Govt, Victoria, BC V8W 9M1
Tel: 250-387-1057
Fax: 250-953-3603
Ensures that forestry laws are being followed in BC's public forests, & takes action where there is non-compliance. C&E staff enforce forest management laws & combat forest crimes such as theft, arson & mischief. Officials conduct more than 16,000 inspections a year to assess compliance with forest laws. Where there is evidence of a contravention, an investigation is conducted, which may lead to the issuance of a violation ticket, penalty or other enforcement action. The most serious forest crimes are prosecuted through the court system.
Chief Forester & Assistant Deputy Minister, Dave Peterson
Tel: 250-387-1057
Fax: 250-356-6791
Executive Lead, Forest Sector Initiatives, Susanna Laaksonen-Craig
Tel: 250-387-3162
Fax: 250-953-3603
Susanna.LaaksonenCraig@gov.bc.ca
Executive Director, Duncan Williams
Tel: 250-387-1810
Fax: 250-356-2150
Duncan.Williams@gov.bc.ca
Director, Compensation & Business Analysis Branch, Peter Jacobsen
Tel: 250-387-8643
Fax: 250-356-7903
Peter.Jacobsen@gov.bc.ca
Other Communications: Cell Phone: 250-415-6638
Director, Forest Tenures Branch, Doug Stewart
Tel: 250-387-8729
Fax: 250-387-6445
Doug.B.Stewart@gov.bc.ca
Director, Land Tenures Branch, Acting Director, Crown Land Opportunities & Restoration, Ward Trotter
Tel: 250-356-2166
Fax: 250-356-6791
Ward.Trotter@gov.bc.ca
Director, Competitiveness & Innovation Branch, Paul S. Knowles
Tel: 250-953-3988
Fax: 250-356-7903
Paul.S.Knowles@gov.bc.ca
Director, Compensation & Business Analysis Branch, Peter Jacobsen
Tel: 250-387-8643
Fax: 250-356-7903
Peter.Jacobsen@gov.bc.ca

Timber Operations & Pricing Division
PO Box 9525 Stn. Prov Govt, Victoria, BC V8W 9C3
Fax: 250-953-3687
Assistant Deputy Minister, Tom Jensen
Tel: 250-387-0902
Fax: 250-953-3687
Tom.Jensen@gov.bc.ca
Chief Engineer, Brian Chow
Tel: 250-953-4370
Fax: 250-953-3687
Brian.Chow@gov.bc.ca
Executive Director, Field Operations, Mike Falkiner
Tel: 250-387-8309
Fax: 250-953-3687
Mike.Falkiner@gov.bc.ca
Executive Director, Timber Operations & Pricing, Diane Nicholls
Tel: 250-356-9287
Fax: 250-953-3687
Diane.Nicholls@gov.bc.ca
Other Communications: Alternate Phone: 250-751-7196
Director, Resource Worker Safety, Tom Jackson
Tel: 250-956-5105
Fax: 250-956-5045
Tom.Jackson@gov.bc.ca
Director, First Nation Relations Branch, Darrell A. Robb
Tel: 250-387-6719
Fax: 250-356-6076
Darrell.Robb@gov.bc.ca
Director, Timber Pricing Branch, Murray Stech
Tel: 250-356-9807
Fax: 250-387-5670
Murray.Stech@gov.bc.ca
Director, Engineering Branch, Peter Wyatt
Tel: 250-387-1295
Fax: 250-953-3687
Peter.Wyatt@gov.bc.ca

Director, Business Management, BC Timber Sales Branch, Graham Archdekin
Tel: 250-387-2811
Fax: 250-356-6209
Graham.Archdekin@gov.bc.ca
Associate Director, Business Management, BC Timber Sales, Rob Bigalke
Tel: 250-953-3108
Fax: 250-387-5670
Rob.Bigalke@gov.bc.ca
Manager, Seedling Services Interior, Stephen Joyce
Tel: 250-260-4617
Fax: 250-260-4619
Stephen.Joyce@gov.bc.ca
Other Communications: Cell Phone: 250-503-8430
Manager, Timber Pricing Section, Grant Loeb
Tel: 250-387-8378
Fax: 250-387-8393
Grant.Loeb@gov.bc.ca
Manager, Seedling Services, Coast, Bob Merrell
Tel: 604-586-4347
Fax: 604-586-4353
Bob.Merrell@gov.bc.ca
Manager, Billing Operations & Support Section, Anne Preece
Tel: 250-387-8375
Fax: 250-387-9738
Anne.Preece@gov.bc.ca
Manager, Forecasting, Reporting & Planning, Glenn Rolph
Tel: 250-387-3904
Fax: 250-387-5670
Glenn.Rolph@gov.bc.ca
Acting Engineering Group Leader, Southern Engineering Group, Barry Trenholm
Tel: 250-398-4794
Fax: 250-828-4442
Barry.Trenholm@gov.bc.ca
Engineering Group Leader, Coastal Engineering Group, Gino Fournier
Tel: 250-716-5240
Fax: 250-751-7101
Gino.Fournier@gov.bc.ca
Acting Engineering Group Leader, Northern Engineering Group, Joseph Kenny
Tel: 250-565-4317
Fax: 250-565-6671
Joseph.Kenny@gov.bc.ca
Manager, Timber Measurements, Keith Tudor
Tel: 250-387-8357
Fax: 250-387-5670
Keith.Tudor@gov.bc.ca
Manager, First Nations Consultation, Stefan Tack
Tel: 250-387-0738
Fax: 250-356-6076
Forests.AboriginalAffairsBranchOffice@gov.bc.ca

Corporate Services for the Natural Resouces Sector
Director, Finance, Sandra Winter
Tel: 250-356-9227
Sandra.Winter@gov.bc.ca

Client Services Branch
PO Box 9352 Stn. Prov Govt, Victoria, BC V8W 9M1
Tel: 250-953-4745
Fax: 250-356-5797
Assistant Deputy Minister/Executive Financial Officer, Denise Bragg
Tel: 250-953-4745
Fax: 250-356-5797
Denise.Bragg@gov.bc.ca
Executive Director, Client Services Branch, Trish Dohan
Tel: 250-356-9221
Fax: 250-356-9239
Trish.Dohan@gov.bc.ca
Deputy Director, Client Services Branch, Wendy Byrnes
Tel: 250-371-6232
Wendy.Byrnes@gov.bc.ca
Director, Fleet, Facilities & Asset Management, Diane St. Hilair
Tel: 250-952-4944
Diane.StHilair@gov.bc.ca
Manager, Fleet & Assets, Kevin Doran
Tel: 250-952-4930
Fax: 250-952-4925
Kevin.Doran@gov.bc.ca
Manager, Warehousing & Fleet, Kim Pilotte
Tel: 250-952-4428
Fax: 250-952-4925
Kim.Pilotte@gov.bc.ca
Manager, Provincial Facilities & Operations, Rod Bergen
Tel: 250-952-4512
Rod.Bergen@gov.bc.ca

Financial Services Branch
PO Box 9339 Stn. Prov Govt, Victoria, BC V8W 9M1
Tel: 250-387-9878
Fax: 250-953-3414
Assistant Deputy Minister/Executive Financial Officer (Agriculture & Environment), Shauna Brouwer
Tel: 250-387-9878
Fax: 250-953-3414
Executive Director/Chief Financial Officer (Aboriginal Relations & Reconcilliation; Energy, Mines & Natural Gas), Ranbir Parmar
Tel: 250-953-3384
Ranbir.Parmar@gov.bc.ca
Acting Executive Director/Chief Financial Officer (Agriculture; Environment), Michael Lord
Tel: 250-356-9220
Michael.Lord@gov.bc.ca
Executive Director/Chief Financial Officer (Forests, Lands & Natural Resource Operations), Terry Gelinas
Tel: 250-387-4702
Terry.Gelinas@gov.bc.ca
Director, Financial Policy, Compliance, & Procurement, Diane Ross
Tel: 250-952-0560
Diane.Ross@gov.bc.ca
Director, Financial Planning & Reporting, Barb Searle
Tel: 250-387-4703
Director, Financial Planning, Systems & Reporting, Mary Myers
Tel: 250-952-0229
Fax: 250-387-5397
Mary.Myers@gov.bc.ca
Acting Director, Revenue, Cathy Gauthier
Tel: 250-387-5347
Fax: 250-356-9239

Information Management/Information Technology & Workplace Strategies
PO Box 9339 Stn. Prov Govt, Victoria, BC V8W 9M1
Tel: 250-356-8794
Fax: 250-953-3414
Assistant Deputy Minister/Executive Financial Officer (Aboriginal Relations & Reconciliation; Energy, Mines & Natural Gas), Neilane Mayhew
Tel: 250-356-8794
Fax: 250-953-3414
Chief Information Officer/Executive Director, Information Management Branch, Doug Say
Tel: 250-356-5216
Fax: 250-356-9836
Doug.Say@gov.bc.ca
Executive Director, People & Workplace Strategies, Mike R. Hykaway
Tel: 250-387-5953
Mike.Hykaway@gov.bc.ca
Executive Director, People & Workplace Strategies, Sonja Martins
Tel: 250-387-9299
Sonja.Martins@gov.bc.ca
Director, NRS Business Service Desk, Mike Kelley
Tel: 250-208-8944
Fax: 250-953-3752
Mike.Kelley@gov.bc.ca
Director, Projects, Tina St. Hilaire
Tel: 250-387-8809
Director, Client Business Solutions, Denise Rossander
Tel: 250-387-9648
Denise.Rossander@gov.bc.ca
Other Communications: Cell Phone: 250-213-5206
Director, Architecture, Fary Eriksson
Tel: 250-387-5277
Fary.Eriksson@gov.bc.ca
Director, Infrastructure Management, Terry Gunning
Tel: 250-387-9975
Fax: 250-356-9836
Terry.Gunning@gov.bc.ca
Director, Middle Tier & Database Administration, Colleen Coccola
Tel: 250-356-7743
Colleen.Coccola@gov.bc.ca
Director, Technology & Communication Services, Dave Rejminiak
Tel: 250-387-6358
Fax: 250-387-5132
Dave.Rejminiak@gov.bc.ca
Director, PMO, Strategic Planning & Info Security, Louise Anstey
Tel: 250-952-0944
Louise.Anstey@gov.bc.ca
Director, Communication Services, Keith Finnie
Tel: 250-217-4033
Keith.Finnie@gov.bc.ca

British Columbia Ministry of Health

1515 Blanshard St., Victoria, BC V8W 3C8
Toll-Free: 800-663-7100
hlth.health@gov.bc.ca
www.gov.bc.ca/health
Other Communication: Senior Health Care Support Line: 1-877-952-3181; Media Inquiries, Phone: 250-952-1887, Fax: 250-952-1883
The Ministry of Health is responsible for ensuring quality, timely, & cost effective health services for all citizens of British Columbia. To guide & enhance British Columbia's health services, the ministry works with health authorities, agencies, care providers, & other groups.
Acts Administered:
Access to Abortion Services Act
Anatomy Act
Community Care & Assisted Living Act (except ss. 8 & 34 (2) (h) & (h.1) & (6))
Continuing Care Act
Drinking Water Protection Act
E-Health Act (Personal Health Information Access & Protection of Privacy)
Emergency & Health Services Act
Food Safety Act
Forensic Psychiatry Act
Health & Social Services Delivery Improvement Act (except Part 3)
Health Act
Health Authorities Act
Health Care (Consent) & Care Facility (Admission) Act
Health Care Costs Recovery Act
Health Professions Act
Health Sector Partnerships Agreement Act
Health Special Account Act
Hospital Act
Hospital District Act
Hospital Insurance Act
Human Resource Facility Act (s. 1.1(d))
Human Tissue Gift Act
Marriage Act
Medicare Protection Act (except ss. 5 (1) (b), 7 (5), 8 (4), 8.1, 8.2 & 32)
Mental Health Act
Milk Industry Act (s. 12, except as that provision relates to tank milk receiver licences)
Ministry of Health Act
Name Act
Patient Care Quality Review Board Act
Pharmaceutical Services Act
Pharmacy Operations & Drug Scheduling Act
Public Health Act
Tobacco Control Act
Tobacco Damages & Health Care Costs Recovery Act
Wills Act (Part 2)

Minister, Health, Vacant
PO Box 9050 Prov Govt Sta.
Victoria, BC V8W 9E2

Deputy Minister, Health, Graham Whitmarsh
Tel: 250-952-1590
Fax: 250-952-1909
hlth.dmoffice@gov.bc.ca

Director, Executive Operations, Grace Foran
Tel: 250-952-1410
Fax: 250-952-1909
hlth.dmoffice@gov.bc.ca

Associated Agencies, Boards & Commissions:
• **British Columbia Ambulance Service (BCAS)**
PO Box 9600 Prov Govt
Victoria, BC V8W 9P1
Tel: 250-953-3298
Fax: 250-953-3119
www.bcas.ca

The BCAS operates under the Emergency Health Services Commission, legislated by the Emergency & Health Services Act.

• **Hospital Appeal Board (HAB)**
747 Fort St., 4th Fl.
PO Box 9425 Prov Govt
Victoria, BC V8W 9V1
Tel: 250-387-3464
Fax: 250-356-9923
Toll-free: 800-663-7867
hab@gov.bc.ca
www.hab.gov.bc.ca
The Hospital Appeal Board of British Columbia is an independent, quasi-judicial administrative appeal tribunal, which was created by the Hospital Act. The Board provides an appeal process for medical practitioners. The role of the Board is to review hospital board of management decisions concerning hospital privileges. Board members are appointed by British Columbia's Minister of Health.
Chair, Derek A. Brindle

• **Medical Services Commission (MSC)**
1515 Blanshard St., 3rd Fl.
Victoria, BC V8W 3C8
Tel: 250-952-3073
Fax: 250-952-3131
www.health.gov.bc.ca/msp/legislation/msc.html
The Medical Services Commission is a statutory body made up of nine members. In accordance with the Medicare Protection Act & Regulations, the Commission acts on behalf of the Government of British Columbia to manage the Medical Services Plan. The Commission works to ensure British Columbia residents have access to medical care, & to manage the provision & payment of medical services.

• **Mental Health Review Board (MHRB)**
Dogwood Building
2601 Lougheed Hwy.
Coquitlam, BC V3C 4J2
Tel: 604-524-7220
Fax: 604-524-7216

Emergency & Health Services Commission
PO Box 9600 Stn. Prov Govt, Victoria, BC V8W 9P1
Tel: 250-953-3298
Fax: 250-953-3119
President, Michael MacDougall
Tel: 250-953-3313
Executive Coordinator, Maureen Adams
Tel: 250-953-3313
CEO, BC Ambulance Service, Les Fisher
Tel: 250-953-3209

Organizational Development & Engagement
Fax: 250-952-2125
Assistant Deputy Minister, Barbara Walman
Tel: 250-952-1705
Fax: 250-952-1584
Executive Director, Business Management & Supplier Relations, Kelly Uyeno
Tel: 604-660-1303
Fax: 604-660-5405
Executive Director, Drug Intelligence, Eric Lun
Tel: 250-952-2272
Fax: 250-952-2790
Executive Director, Drug Use Optimization, Suzanne Taylor
Tel: 604-660-1217
Fax: 604-660-2108
Suzanne.Taylor@gov.bc.ca
Acting Executive Director, Policy, Outcomes Evaluation & Research, Mitch Moneo
Tel: 250-952-1187
Fax: 250-952-2790
Director, Business Management, Sophia Shin
Tel: 604-660-5420
Fax: 604-660-5405
Director, PharmaCare Operations & PharmaNet, Sorin Pop
Tel: 250-952-2288
Fax: 604-660-5405
Sorin.Pop@gov.bc.ca
Director, Clinical Decision Support, Elaine Chong
Tel: 604-657-5680
Fax: 250-952-2790
Director, Special Authority, Susan Galbraith
Tel: 250-952-1850
Fax: 250-952-2790
Director, Formulary Management, Tijiana Fazlagic
Tel: 250-952-1475
Fax: 250-952-2216
Director, Information, Walton Pang
Tel: 604-660-1245
Fax: 604-660-2108
Director, Evaluation & Coordinator, BC PAD Service, Terryn Naumann
Tel: 604-417-6473
Fax: 604-660-2108
Co-Director, Evaluation, Anne Nguyen
Tel: 604-660-1589
Fax: 604-660-2108
Director, Utilization, Barbara Gobis Ogle
Tel: 604-660-2292
Fax: 604-660-2108
Director, Economic Analysis, Christian Voggenreiter
Tel: 250-952-1450
Fax: 250-952-2790
Acting Director, Policy & Communications, John Capelli
Tel: 250-952-2642
Fax: 250-952-2790

British Columbia Hydro

6911 Southpoint Dr., Burnaby, BC V3N 4X8
Tel: 604-224-9376
Toll-Free: 800-224-9376
www.bchydro.com
Secondary Address: 333 Dunsmuir St.
Corporate Address
Vancouver, BC V6B 5R3
The Clean Energy Act consolidated BC Hydro & the BC Transmission Corporation in 2010. BC Hydro is a crown corporation that reports to the British Columbia Ministry of Energy, Mines, & Natural Gas. The mission of the corporation is the delivery of energy, in an envrionmentally & socially responsible manner, to meet the province's demand for electricity. Thirty-one hydroelectric facilities & three thermal generating plants are operated by BC Hydro.

President & Chief Executive Officer, Charles Reid

Chief Human Resources Officer & Senior Vice-President, Debbie Nagle

Chief Financial Officer & Executive Vice-President, Cheryl Yaremko

Executive Vice-President, Generation, Chris O'Riley

Executive Vice-President, Transmission & Distribution, Greg Reimer

Executive Vice-President, Site C Clean Energy Project, Susan Yurkovich

Senior Vice-President, Corporate Services & General Counsel, Ray Aldeguer

Associated Agencies, Boards & Commissions:

• **Powerex Corp.**
#1400, 666 Burrard St.
Vancouver, BC V6C 2X8
Tel: 604-891-5000
Fax: 604-891-6060
Toll-free: 800-220-4907
Brian.Moghadam@powerex.com
www.powerex.com
A wholly-owned subsidiary of BC Hydro, Powerex Corp. markets wholesale energy products & services to utilities, power pools, industrials, & power marketers in North America, particularly western Canada, the western United States.
Chair, Larry Blain
President/Chief Executive Officer, Teresa Conway
Chief Legal Officer, John Irving
Director, Risk Management, Amit Budhwar
Director, Finance, Janette Lyons
Director, Trade Policy, Mike MacDougall
Director, Human Resources, Julie Mantle

• **Powertech Labs Inc.**
12388 - 88 Ave.
Surrey, BC V8W 7R7
Tel: 604-590-7500
Fax: 604-590-6611
www.powertechlabs.com
A wholly owned subsidiary of BC Hydro, Powertech Labs offers environmental, mechanical, electrical, metallurgical, civil, chemical, gas technologies, & structural engineering to deal with technical problems with power equipment & systems.
Executive Chair, Bob Elton
President/Chief Executive Officer, Kathy Nguyen
kathy.nguyen@powertechlabs.com
Business Unit Director, Clean Transportation, Craig Webster
Tel: 604-590-7413
craig.webster@powertechlabs.com
Business Unit Director, Power Labs, Jan Zawadzki
Tel: 604-590-7487
Fax: 604-597-6656
jan.zawadzki@powertechlabs.com
Senior Advisor, Strategic Planning, Mari Nurminen
mari.nurminen@powertechlabs.com

British Columbia Ministry of Jobs, Tourism, & Skills Training (& Responsible for Labour)

PO Box 9071 Stn. Prov Govt, Victoria, BC V8W 9E2
EnquiryBC@gov.bc.ca; GCPE.JTI.Media.Requests@gov.bc.ca
www.gov.bc.ca/jti
Other Communication: Media Relations, Phone: 250-356-8177
In September 2012, the Ministry of Jobs, Tourism, & Innovation was reorganized to become the Ministry of Jobs, Tourism, & Skills Training. The minister of the ministry is also responsible for labour. The change was made to ensure citizens of British Columbia are equipped with useful skills to preserve a strong economy.
General responsibilities of the ministry are as follows: WorkBC; export market development; trade initiatives; the Canada-BC Business Service Centre; the Community Business Loans Program; labour relations; employment standards; regional economic & rural development; Rural BC Secretariat; tourism strategies; Aboriginal tourism; industry training; & occupational health & safety.

Acts Administered:
BC-Alcan Northern Development Fund Act
British Columbia Enterprise Corporation Act (as it relates to the B.C. Pavilion Corporation)
British Columbia Innovation Council Act
Columbia Basin Trust Act
Employee Investment Act
Hotel Guest Registration Act
Hotel Keepers Act
Industrial Development Act
Industry Training Authority Act
Labour Mobility Act
Ministry of International Business & Immigration Act
Miscellaneous Statutes Amendment Act (No. 3), 2010 (s. 40)
Multiculturalism Act
New West Partnership Trade Agreement Implementation Act
North Island-Coast Development Initiative Trust
Northern Development Initiative Trust Act
Small Business Venture Capital Act
Southern Interior Development Initiative Trust Act
Tourism Act
Trade, Investment, & Labour Mobility Agreement Implementation Act
Vancouver Tourism Levy Enabling Act
Wood First Act

Minister, Jobs, Tourism, & Skills Training; Minister Responsible, Labour, Vacant
PO Box 9067 Prov Govt Sta.
Victoria, BC V8W 9E9

Deputy Minister, Jobs, Tourism, & Skills Training, Dave Byng
Tel: 250-952-0103
Fax: 250-356-1195
Dave.Byng@gov.bc.ca
PO Box 9846 Prov Govt Sta.
Victoria, BC V8W 9T2

Manager, Correspondence, Darla Cooper
Tel: 250-387-4648
Darla.Cooper@gov.bc.ca

Manager, Small Business Roundtable Secretariat, Sean Murry
Tel: 250-387-9083
Fax: 250-952-0113

Parliamentary Secretary for Asia Pacific to the Minister of

Jobs, Tourism, & Skills Training, Richard T. Lee
Tel: 250-356-3052
Fax: 250-387-9100
Richard.Lee.MLA@leg.bc.ca

Director, Executive Operations, Maureen Yelovatz
Tel: 250-952-0104
Fax: 250-356-1195

Associated Agencies, Boards & Commissions:
• **British Columbia Labour Relations Board**
Oceanic Plaza
#600, 1066 West Hastings St.
Vancouver, BC V6E 3X1
Tel: 604-660-1300
Fax: 604-660-1892
information@lrb.bc.ca
www.lrb.bc.ca
The British Columbia Labour Relations Board is an independent, administrative tribunal. The Board is responsible for mediating & adjudicating employment & labour relations matters related to unionized workplaces.
Chair, Brent Mullin
Fax: 604-660-7321
BC.LRB@gov.bc.ca
Associate Chair, Adjudication, Mike Fleming
Registrar, Allison Matacheskie
• **Employment Standards Tribunal**
Oceanic Plaza
#650, 1066 West Hastings St.
Vancouver, BC V6E 3X1
Tel: 604-775-3512
Fax: 604-775-3372
registrar@bcest.bc.ca
www.bcest.bc.ca
Established under the Employment Standards Act, the Employment Standards Tribunal operates as an administrative tribunal. The responsibility of the Tribunal is to provide an independent appeal of Determinations made by the Director of Employment Standards.
Chair, Brent Mullin
Registry Administrator, Stephany Herzog
• **Forestry Innovation Investment Ltd. (FII)**
#1200, 1130 West Pender St.
Vancouver, BC V6E 4A4
Tel: 604-685-7507
Fax: 604-685-5373
info@bcfii.ca
www.bcfii.ca
British Columbia's Forestry Innovation Investment strives to support a prosperous & environmentally sustainable forest economy in the province. The role of the organization includes the following activities: Promotion of British Columbia's forest practices & wood products to international markets; Working in partnership with the forestry sector, the Government of British Columbia, & the Government of Canada; & Assisting the forestry sector with issues such as Mountain Pine Beetle outbreak.
Chair, Dana Hayden
Chief Executive Officer, Ken Baker
Tel: 604-685-7507
ken.baker@bcfii.ca
Vice-President, Operations, Michael Loseth
Tel: 604-685-7507
loseth@bcfii.ca
Vice-President, Finance & Administration, Doug Greig
Tel: 604-601-5301
doug.greig@bcfii.ca
Vice-President, China Operations, Mike Hogan
mike.hogan@bcfii.cn
• **Industry Training Authority (ITA)**
#1223, 13351 Commerce Pkwy.
Richmond, BC V6V 2X7
Tel: 604-214-8700
Fax: 604-214-8701
Toll-free: 866-660-6011
info@itabc.ca; customerservice@itabc.ca
www.itabc.ca
Other Communication: Customer Service: 778-328-8700
British Columbia's Industry Training Authority is a provincial government agency which oversees the province's training & apprenticeship system. The ITA works with industry, employers, training providers, trainees, & apprentices.
• **Leading Edge Endowment Fund Board (LEEF)**
1188 West Georgia St., 9th Fl.
Vancouver, BC V6E 4A2
Tel: 604-438-3220
contact@leefbc.ca
www.leefbc.ca
To encourage social & economic development in British Columbia, the provincial government established the Leading Edge Endowment Fund in 2002. The Fund establishes Leadership Research Chairs at the province's public, post-secondary institutions, & Regional Innovation Chairs through colleges, university-colleges, & institutes.
• **Northern Development Initiative Trust**
#301, 1268 Fifth Ave.
Prince George, BC V2L 3L2
Tel: 250-561-2525
Fax: 250-561-2563
info@northerndevelopment.bc.ca
northerndevelopment.bc.ca
The Northern Trust consists of a Board of Directors which makes funding decisions for programs of the Trust. According to provincial legislation, investments can be made in the following areas: agriculture, economic development, energy, forestry, mining, Olympic opportunities; pine beetle recovery, small business, tourism, & transportation.
Chair, Evan Saugstad
Chief Executive Officer, Janine North
Chief Financial Officer, Dennis Callaghan
dennis@northerndevelopment.bc.ca
Chief Financial Officer, Dennis Callaghan
dennis@northerndevelopment.bc.ca
Regional Director, Business Development, Renata King
renata@northerndevelopment.bc.ca
Regional Manager, Economic Development, Brodie Guy
brodie@northerndevelopment.bc.ca
Regional Manager, Economic Development, Dean McKinley
dean@northerndevelopment.bc.ca
• **Southern Interior Development Initiative Trust**
#204, 3131 29th St.
Vernon, BC V1T 5A8
Tel: 250-545-6829
Fax: 250-545-6896
admin@sidit-bc.ca
www.sidit-bc.ca
The government of British Columbia enacted legislation in 2006 to establish the Southern Interior Development Initiative Trust. The mission of the Trust is to grow & diversify the economy of the Southern Interior of British Columbia through investments in economic development projects that will benefit the area.
Chief Executive Officer, Luby Pow
ceo@sidit-bc.ca
• **Workers' Compensation Appeal Tribunal (WCAT)**
#150, 4600 Jacombs Rd.
Richmond, BC V6V 3B1
Tel: 604-664-7800
Fax: 604-664-7898
Toll-free: 800-663-2782
www.wcat.bc.ca
The Workers' Compensation Appeal Tribunal of British Columbia is an independent appeal tribunal, which was established by the Workers Compensation Amendment Act (No. 2), 2002. The Tribunal decides appeals from workers & employers from decisions of the Workers' Compensation Board (WorkSafeBC).
Chair, Jill Callan
Tel: 604-713-0424
Fax: 604-664-7899
Senior Vice-Chair & Registrar, Jane MacFadgen
Tel: 604-664-7922
Fax: 604-664-4898
Senior Vice-Chair & Tribunal Counsel, Teresa White

Competitiveness & Innovation
PO Box 9327 Stn. Prov Govt, Victoria, BC V8W 9N3
Fax: 250-952-0137

Investment Capital Branch
PO Box 9800 Stn. Prov Govt, Victoria, BC V8W 9V1
Fax: 250-952-0371
Senior Portfolio Manager, Venture Capital Programs, Ian Wong
Tel: 604-660-6396
Fax: 604-660-6812
Ian.Wong@gov.bc.ca
Senior Portfolio Manager, Venture Capital Programs, Matthew Brown
Tel: 250-952-0631
Fax: 250-952-0371
Matthew.J.Brown@gov.bc.ca

Economic Development Division
Assistant Deputy Minister, Shanna Mason
Tel: 250-952-6079
Shanna.Mason@gov.bc.ca
Executive Director, Economic Development, Trish Sterloff
Tel: 250-952-6268
Trish.Sterloff@gov.bc.ca
Executive Director, Economic Development, Chris Gilmore
Tel: 250-952-0139
Christopher.Gilmore@gov.bc.ca
Executive Director, Pine Beetle Epidemic Response Branch, Gord Borgstrom
Tel: 250-371-3741
Fax: 250-371-3735
Gordon.Borgstrom@gov.bc.ca
Executive Director, Regional Economic Policy & Projects, Greg Goodwin
Tel: 250-356-0778
Fax: 250-952-0351
Greg.Goodwin@gov.bc.ca
Executive Director, Economic Initiatives & Analysis, Dean Sekyer
Tel: 250-952-0409
Fax: 250-952-0646
Dean.Sekyer@gov.bc.ca
Acting Director, Community Economic Development (Williams Lake), Lisa Young
Tel: 250-819-2147
Fax: 250-371-3942
Lisa.Young@gov.bc.ca
Director, Pine Beetle Epidemic Response Branch (Fort St. James), Jim Burck
Tel: 250-996-5200
Fax: 250-387-1590
Jim.Burck@gov.bc.ca
Director, Pine Beetle Epidemic Response Branch (Williams Lake), Hugh Flinton
Tel: 250-398-4224
Fax: 250-371-3735
Hugh.Flinton@gov.bc.ca
Director, Pine Beetle Epidemic Response Branch (Kamloops), Marc Imus
Tel: 250-371-3937
Fax: 250-371-3942
Marc.Imus@gov.bc.ca
Senior Director, Economic Initiatives, Rob Pysden
Tel: 250-953-3790
Fax: 250-952-0646
Rob.Pysden@gov.bc.ca
Acting Director, Regional Economic Policy & Projects, Debra Larusson
Tel: 250-952-0643
Fax: 250-952-0351
Debra.Larusson@gov.bc.ca
Director, Land Use Initiatives & Analysis, Alison Coyne
Tel: 250-356-0807
Fax: 250-952-0137
Alison.Coyne@gov.bc.ca
Director, Business Analysis, Sylvia Selig
Tel: 250-387-7555
Fax: 250-952-0351
Sylvia.Selig@gov.bc.ca

Regional Economic Operations
PO Box 9837 Stn. Prov Govt, Victoria, BC V8W 9T1
Tel: 250-387-0220
Fax: 250-387-1407
Executive Director, Victoria, Sarah Fraser
Tel: 250-952-0644
Fax: 250-952-0351
Sarah.Fraser@gov.bc.ca
Director, Regional Economic Operations, Dale Richardson
Tel: 250-631-2959
Fax: 250-952-0351
Dale.Richardson@gov.bc.ca
Fort St. John
Fax: 250-787-3210
Regional Manager, Northeast, Tamara Danshin
Tel: 250-787-3351
Fax: 250-787-3210
Tamara.Danshin@gov.bc.ca
Kamloops
Fax: 250-828-4542
Regional Manager, Thompson/Okanagan, Myles Bruns
Tel: 250-371-3931

Fax: 250-828-4542
Myles.Bruns@gov.bc.ca
Other Communications: Cell Phone: 250-318-5150
Kootenay Boundary
Fax: 250-426-1253
Regional Manager, Kootenay, Diana Brooks
Tel: 250-426-1301
Fax: 250-426-1253
Diana.Brooks@gov.bc.ca
Nanaimo
Tel: 250-751-3227
Fax: 250-751-3245
Smithers
Tel: 250-847-7797
Fax: 250-847-7556
Regional Manager (on leave), Rick Braam
Tel: 250-847-7797
Fax: 250-847-7556
Rick.Braam@gov.bc.ca

Minister, Justice; Attorney General, Hon. Shirley Bond
Tel: 250-387-1866
Fax: 250-387-6411
JAG.Minister@gov.bc.ca
Social Media: twitter.com/shirleybond, www.facebook.com/shirley.bond

Deputy Minister, Justice, Richard Fyfe, QC
Tel: 250-356-0149
Fax: 250-387-6224
PO Box 9290 Prov Govt Sta.
Victoria, BC V8W 9J7

Deputy Minister, Justice, Lori Wanamaker
Tel: 250-356-0149
Fax: 250-387-6224
PO Box 9290 Prov Govt Sta.
Victoria, BC V8W 9J7

Assistant Deputy Minister, Management Services, Tara Faganello
Tel: 250-387-5258
Tara.Faganello@gov.bc.ca
Victoria, BC V8W 9J7

Executive Director, Business Intelligence & Performance Management, Allan Castle
Tel: 250-356-0111
Fax: 250-387-6224

Executive Advisor, Corporate Communications & Change Management, Barbara Greeniaus
Tel: 250-356-0169
Fax: 250-387-6224
Barbara.Greeniaus@gov.bc.ca

Executive Director, Organizational Development Team Office, Julie Spiteri
Tel: 250-387-6917
Fax: 250-356-6323
Julie.Spiteri@gov.bc.ca

Director, Investigation & Standards, Sydney Swift
Tel: 250-387-5948
Fax: 250-356-9875

Director, Security & Corporate Risk, Security & BCP, Betty-Ann Atherton
Tel: 250-356-5060
Fax: 250-356-8739
BettyAnn.Atherton@gov.bc.ca

Manager, Strategic Coordination, Darrion Campbell
Tel: 250-356-5203
Fax: 250-953-4072
Darrion.Campbell@gov.bc.ca

Executive Director, Facilities Services Division, Betty Chen-Mack
Tel: 250-356-7159
Fax: 250-356-9528
Betty.ChenMack@gov.bc.ca

Emergency Management BC
PO Box 9223 Stn. Prov Govt, Victoria, BC V8W 9J1
Tel: 250-953-4002
Fax: 250-953-4081
BC.CorSer@gov.bc.ca (Coroner); OFC@gov.bc.ca (Fire Commissioner)
www.pssg.gov.bc.ca/coroners; www.pssg.gov.bc.ca/firecom
Other Communication: Office of the Chief Coroner: 604-660-7745; Office of the Fire Commissioner Phone: 250-356-9000, Toll Free: 1-888-988-9488; Provincial Emergency Program: 250-952-4913
Emergency Management BC oversees the Coroners Service of British Columbia, the Office of the Fire Commissioner, & the Provincial Emergency Program (www.pep.bc.ca).
B.C. Coroners Service investigates all unexpected, unnatural, unexplained, & unattended deaths in the province. Improvements to public safety & recommendations to prevent similar deaths are made by the Coroners Service.
The Office of the Fire Commissioner administers & enforces fire safety legislation, trains local assistants to the fire commissioner, certifies fire fighters, provides public fire safety education, advises local governments, responds to major fires, & investigates fires.
The Provincial Emergency Program provides training & support to local governments.
Fire & Emergency Management Commissioner, Becky Denlinger
Tel: 250-953-4083
Fax: 250-387-4872
Becky.Denlinger@gov.bc.ca
Executive Officer, Cameron Lewis
Tel: 250-953-4036
Fax: 250-953-4081
Cameron.Lewis@gov.bc.ca
Executive Director, Corporate Services, David Curtis
Tel: 250-953-4034
Fax: 250-953-4081
David.Curtis@gov.bc.ca
Director, Flood Protection Program, Carol Loski
Tel: 250-953-4003
Fax: 250-953-4081

BC Coroners Service
Metrotower II, #800, 4720 Kingsway, Burnaby, BC V5H 4N2
Tel: 604-660-7745
Fax: 604-660-7766
BC.CorSer@gov.bc.ca
www.pssg.gov.bc.ca/coroners/
Chief Coroner, Lisa Lapointe
Tel: 604-660-7745
Fax: 604-660-7766
Deputy Chief Coroner, Norm Leibel
Tel: 604-660-7745
Fax: 604-660-7766
Norm.Leibel@gov.bc.ca
Executive Director, Public Accountability, Kellie Kilpatrick
Tel: 604-586-5695
Fax: 604-660-7766
Kellie.Kilpatrick@gov.bc.ca
Executive Coordinator to the Chief Civilian Director, Claire Leek
Tel: 604-586-5655
Fax: 604-660-7766
Claire.Leek@gov.bc.ca
Director, Legal Services & Inquests, Rodrick MacKenzie
Tel: 604-660-7745
Fax: 604-660-7766
Rodrick.MacKenzie@gov.bc.ca
Regional Coroner, Island, Matthew Brown
Tel: 250-952-4150
Fax: 250-951-4059
Matthew.G.Brown@gov.bc.ca
Regional Investigator, Interior, Mark D. Coleman
Tel: 604-586-2713
Fax: 250-861-7515
Mark.D.Coleman@gov.bc.ca
Senior Manager, Strategic Projects & Public Engagement, Vancouver Metro, Owen Court
Tel: 604-660-7708
Fax: 604-660-5290
Owen.Court@gov.bc.ca
Regional Coroner, Northern, Donita Kuzma
Tel: 250-565-6040
Fax: 250-565-6606
Regional Coroner, Fraser, Vincent Stancato
Tel: 604-775-1051
Fax: 604-930-7135
Vincent.Stancato@gov.bc.ca

Provincial Emergency Program
PO Box 9201 Stn. Prov Govt, Victoria, BC V8W 9J1
Tel: 250-952-4913
Fax: 250-952-4888
Toll-Free: 800-663-3456
www.pep.bc.ca
Executive Director, Emergency Coordination, Chris Duffy
Tel: 250-952-4544
Fax: 250-952-4888
Chris.Duffy@gov.bc.ca
Acting Executive Director, Mitigation Program, Carol McClintock
Tel: 250-952-4811
Fax: 250-952-4888
Carol.McClintock@gov.bc.ca
Executive Director, Strategic Planning, Policy & Legislation, Cam Filmer
Tel: 250-952-4881
Fax: 250-952-4888
Cam.Filmer@gov.bc.ca
Director, Integrated Public Safety Unit, Heather Lyle
Tel: 604-586-4358
Fax: 604-586-4334
Heather.Lyle@gov.bc.ca
Director, Integrated Planning, Aja Norgaard
Tel: 250-952-4854
Fax: 250-952-4888
Aja.Norgaard@gov.bc.ca
Senior Regional Manager/Assistant Director, Emergency Coordination, Northwest & Vancouver Island Regions, Ralph Mohrmann
Tel: 250-952-4895
Fax: 250-952-4888
Ralph.Mohrmann@gov.bc.ca
Other Communications: Vancouver Fax: 250-952-4304
Senior Regional Manager, Southwest Region, John Oakley
Tel: 604-586-4341
Fax: 604-586-4334
John.Oakley@gov.bc.ca
Senior Regional Manager, Central, Northeast & Southeast Regions, Peter Prendergast
Tel: 250-371-5240
Fax: 250-371-5246
Peter.Prendergast@gov.bc.ca
Other Communications: Northeast: 250-612-4172; Southeast: 250-371-5241

Office of the Fire Commissioner
PO Box 9201 Stn. Prov Govt, Victoria, BC V8W 9J1
Tel: 250-952-4913
Fax: 250-952-4888
Toll-Free: 888-988-9488
OFC@gov.bc.ca
www.pssg.gov.bc.ca/firecom/index.htm
Executive Director/Deputy Fire Commissioner, Mitigation, Kelly Gilday
Tel: 250-952-4919
Fax: 250-952-4888
Kelly.Gilday@gov.bc.ca
Deputy Fire Commissioner, Investigations, Rob Owens
Tel: 250-952-4913
Fax: 250-952-4888
Rob.Owens@gov.bc.ca
Fire Service Advisor, Lower Mainland Region, Tara Fraser
Tel: 604-250-6680
Fax: 250-952-4888
Tara.Fraser@gov.bc.ca
Fire Service Advisor, South East (Nelson) Region, Darrell Green
Tel: 250-354-5941
Fax: 250-354-6561
Darrell.Green@gov.bc.ca
Fire Service Advisor, Thompson Okanagan (Kamloops) Region, Rick Owens
Tel: 250-371-5253
Fax: 250-371-5246
Rick.Owens@gov.bc.ca
Fire Service Advisor, Vancouver Island Region, Gary McCall
Tel: 250-952-4307
Fax: 250-952-4888
OFC@gov.bc.ca
Fire Service Advisor, Northern Region, Terrance Ree
Tel: 250-612-4148
Fax: 250-612-4171
Terrance.Ree@gov.bc.ca

British Columbia Pavilion Corporation (PavCo)

#850, 999 West Hastings St., PO Box 16Vancouver, BC V6C 2W2
Tel: 604-482-2200
Fax: 604-681-9017
info@bcpavco.com
www.bcpavco.com
The BC Pavilion Corporation is a provincial crown corporation of British Columbia's Ministry of Energy, Mines, & Natural Gas. The corporation's divisions include Corporate Services, BC Place, & the Vancouver Convention Centre.

British Columbia Ministry of Transportation & Infrastructure

PO Box 9850 Stn. Prov Govt, Victoria, BC V8W 9T5
Tel: 250-387-3198
Fax: 250-356-7706
www.gov.bc.ca/tran
Other Communication: Media Enquiries, Phone: 250-387-7787, Fax: 250-356-2950
The mission of the Ministry of Transportation & Infrastructure is to plan tranportation networks, to establish policies, to provide transportation services & infrastructure, & to administer acts & regulations related to transportation & infrastructure.
Specific responsibilities include the following: working with partners to fund cost-effective public transit, ferry services, & cycling networks; managing funding for public infrastructure; maintaining highways; setting commercial vehicle operating standards & overseeing vehicle safety inspections; & licensing commercial passenger transporation.

Acts Administered:
British Columbia Rail Benefits (First Nations) Trust Act
British Columbia Railway Act
British Columbia Transit Act
Coastal Ferry Act (except Part 4 & ss. 70, 72 & 73)
Commercial Transport Act (s. 3; ss. 1, 4, 5, 8, 9, 11, & 12, as those provisions relate to highway infrastructure & weigh scales; & ss. 1, 4, 5, 8, 9, 11, 12, & 14, as those provisions relate to Commercial Vehicle Safety & Enforcement)
Industrial Roads Act
Land Title Act (s. 77.2)
Motor Vehicle Act (ss. 116.1, 118.94-118.992, 119-125.1, 126-135.1, 136-148.1, 149-169.1, 170-182, 185-209, 212-212.2, 213, 214, 216-218, 219, 223, 237, 239-240; ss. 1, 75-76, 78, 83, 83.1, 183 & 210; ss. 1, 66, 73, 75-76, 78, 82-83, 210, 211, 220, 238)
Passenger Transportation Act
Public Works Agreement Act
Railway Act (except s. 33)
Railway Safety Act
Significant Projects Streamlining Act
South Coast British Columbia Transportation Authority Act (except Part 7.1)
Transport of Dangerous Goods Act
Transportation Act
Transportation Investment Act

Minister, Transportation & Infrastructure, Hon. Mary Polak
Tel: 250-387-1978
Fax: 250-356-2290
Minister.Transportation@gov.bc.ca
Social Media: twitter.com/MaryPolakMLA, www.facebook.com/MLAPolak
PO Box 9055 Prov Govt Sta.
Victoria, BC V8W 9E2

Deputy Minister, Grant Main
Tel: 250-387-3280
Fax: 250-387-6431
Grant.Main@gov.bc.ca
PO Box 9850 Prov Govt Sta.
Victoria, BC V8W 9T5

Manager, Executive Operations, Vanessa Ginger
Tel: 250-387-3077
Fax: 250-387-6431
Vanessa.Ginger@gov.bc.ca

Information Officer, Katerina Anastasiadis
Tel: 250-660-5887
Fax: 250-660-6833

Coordinator, Documents, Elizabeth Nicholls
Tel: 250-356-1937
Fax: 250-387-6431
Elizabeth.Nicholls@gov.bc.ca

Associated Agencies, Boards & Commissions:
• British Columbia Ferry Services Inc.
See Entry Name Index for detailed listing.
• British Columbia Railway Company
#600, 221 West Esplanade
North Vancouver, BC V7M 3J3
Tel: 604-678-4735
Fax: 604-678-4736
westerhouts@bcrco.com
www.bcrco.com
President/Chief Executive Officer, Dave Byng
Tel: 250-387-7671
Chief Financial Officer/Vice-President, Finance, Kevin Steinberg
Tel: 604-678-4747
Vice-President, Operations & Corporate Affairs, Gordon Westlake
Tel: 604-678-4742
Corporate Secretary/Adminsitration Manager, Shelley Westerhout Hardman
Tel: 604-678-4737
• British Columbia Transit
520 Gorge Rd. East
Victoria, BC V8W 2P3
Tel: 250-385-2551
Fax: 250-995-5639
www.bctransit.com
Other Communication: Community transit information: transitinfo@bctransit.com; Media: pr@bctransit.com
A provincial crown agency, BC Transit coordinates the delivery of public transportation in British Columbia, outside the Greater Vancouver Regional District. The corporation's specific role, in accordance with the BC Transit Act, is the planning, acquisition, construction, operation, & maintenance of public passenger transportation systems & rail systems.
Chair, Kevin D. Mahoney
President/Chief Executive Officer, Manuel Achadinha
Tel: 250-385-2551
Fax: 250-995-5643
Chief Operating Officer, Mike Davis
Tel: 250-995-5617
Fax: 250-995-5689
Chief Financial Officer & Vice-President, Finance, Tony Sharp
Tel: 250-995-5602
Fax: 250-995-5643
Chief Information Officer & Vice-President, Business Development, Brian Anderson
Tel: 250-995-5614
Fax: 250-995-5639
Vice-President, Corporate & Human Resources, Debbie Nussbaum
Tel: 250-995-5730
Fax: 250-995-5664
Executive Director, Finance, Michael Kohl
Tel: 250-385-2551
Fax: 250-995-5639
Executive Director, Asset Management, Aaron Lamb
Tel: 250-995-5710
Fax: 250-995-5639
Director, Corporate & Strategic Planning, Erinn Pinkerton
Tel: 250-995-5663
Fax: 250-995-5643
Director, Regional Transit Systems, Peter Rantucci
Tel: 250-995-5732
Fax: 250-995-5689
Director, Business Services, Maureen Sheehan
Tel: 250-995-5605
Fax: 250-995-5641
• Passenger Transportation Board
#202, 940 Blanshard St.
PO Box 9850 Prov Govt
Victoria, BC V8W 9T5
Tel: 250-953-3777
Fax: 250-953-3788
ptboard@gov.bc.ca
www.ptboard.bc.ca
The Passenger Transportation Board carries out its responsibilities in accordance with the Passenger Transportation Act. The independent tribunal makes decisions regarding the operation of passenger directed vehicles and inter-city buses in British Columbia.
Director, Jan Broocke
Coordinator, Appeals & Operations, David Watling
Coordinator, Administration & Reseach, Kathleen Mitten
Manager, Policy & Communication, Michael McGee

Finance & Management Services Department
PO Box 9850Victoria, BC V8W 9T5
Tel: 250-387-3100
Fax: 250-387-6431
Assistant Deputy Minister, Finance & Management Services, Nancy Bain
Tel: 250-387-3100
Fax: 250-387-6431
Nancy.Bain@gov.bc.ca
Chief Financial Officer, Financial Management, Dave Stewart
Tel: 250-387-7897
Fax: 250-387-7645
Dave.Stewart@gov.bc.ca
Other Communications: Cell Phone: 250-818-5806
Executive Director, Crown Agencies, Carol Bishop
Tel: 250-387-1936
Fax: 250-356-7706
Carol.Bishop@gov.bc.ca
Other Communications: Cell Phone: 250-888-1251
Executive Director/Chief Information Officer, Information Management Branch, Debbie Fritz
Tel: 250-387-3580
Fax: 250-356-7184
Debbie.Fritz@gov.bc.ca
Director, Reporting & Analysis, Gail Silvestrini
Tel: 250-387-3104
Fax: 250-387-7645
Gail.Silvestrini@gov.bc.ca
Director, Finance (British Columbia Transportation Finance Authority), Gary So
Tel: 250-387-7873
Fax: 250-387-7645
Gary.So@gov.bc.ca
Manager, Finance & Administrative Services, Sharon Cowden
Tel: 250-387-5770
Fax: 250-387-5012
Sharon.Cowden@gov.bc.ca
Manager, Corporate Writing Services, Sara Haskett
Tel: 250-387-5705
Fax: 250-356-7706
Sara.Haskett@gov.bc.ca

Highways Department
PO Box 9850Victoria, BC V8W 9T5
Tel: 250-387-3260
Fax: 250-387-6431
Assistant Deputy Minister, Dave Duncan
Tel: 250-387-3260
Fax: 250-387-6431
Dave.Duncan@gov.bc.ca
Chief Bridge Engineer, Kevin Baskin
Tel: 250-387-7737
Fax: 250-387-7735
Kevin.Baskin@gov.bc.ca
Chief Traffic, Electricial, Highway Safety & Geometric Standards Engineer, Ed Miska
Tel: 250-387-7676
Fax: 250-387-7735
Ed.Miska@gov.bc.ca
Other Communications: Cell Phone: 250-213-8375
Chief Engineer, Dirk Nyland
Tel: 250-356-0723
Fax: 250-387-7735
Dirk.Nyland@gov.bc.ca
Other Communications: Cell Phone: 250-812-6645
Chief Environmental Officer, Greg Czernick
Tel: 250-387-7557
Fax: 250-356-8767
Greg.Czernick@gov.bc.ca
Other Communications: Cell Phone: 604-788-0741
Director, Provincial Field Services, Keith Callander
Tel: 250-828-4151
Fax: 250-828-4277
Keith.Callander@gov.bc.ca
Other Communications: Cell Phone: 604-880-2336
Director, Construction & Maintenance, Rodney Chapman
Tel: 250-387-7626
Fax: 250-356-8143
Rodney.Chapman@gov.bc.ca
Other Communications: Cell Phone: 250-213-7499
Director, Rehabilitation & Maintenance, Ian Pilkington
Tel: 250-387-7627

Fax: 250-356-7276
Ian.Pilkington@gov.bc.ca
Director, Social Media Branch, Russel Lolacher
Tel: 250-356-9682
Fax: 250-356-8767
Russel.Lolacher@gov.bc.ca
Other Communications: Cell Phone: 778-679-2482
Director, Commercial Vehicle Safety & Enforcement Branch, Brian Murray
Tel: 250-953-4024
Fax: 250-952-0578
Brian.Murray@gov.bc.ca
Other Communications: Cell Phone: 778-888-8436
Director, Business Management Services, Sandra Toth Nacey
Tel: 250-356-9768
Fax: 250-256-8767
Sandra.TothNacey@gov.bc.ca
Other Communications: Cell Phone: 778-679-2483
Director, Engineering Systems, Al Szczawinski
Tel: 250-387-7777
Fax: 250-387-8081
Al.Szczawinski@gov.bc.ca
Regional Director, South Coast Region, Patrick Livolsi
Tel: 604-660-8205
Fax: 604-660-0350
Patrick.Livolsi@gov.bc.ca
Regional Director, Northern Region, Kirsten Pedersen
Tel: 250-565-6479
Fax: 250-565-6065
Regional Director, Southern Interior Region, Mike Lorimer
Tel: 250-828-4220
Fax: 250-828-4204
Mike.Lorimer@gov.bc.ca

Partnerships Department
PO Box 9850 Stn. Prov Govt, Victoria, BC V8W 9T5
Tel: 250-356-1403
Fax: 250-387-6431
Assistant Deputy Minister, Doug Caul
Tel: 250-356-6225
Fax: 250-387-6431
Doug.Caul@gov.bc.ca
Director, Properties & Land Management Branch, Svein Haugen
Tel: 250-356-7904
Fax: 250-356-6970
Svein.Haugen@gov.bc.ca
Director, Transit Branch, Jim Hester
Tel: 250-387-6024
Fax: 250-387-5012
Jim.Hester@gov.bc.ca
Director, Real Esate, Richard Myhill Jones
Tel: 604-678-4703
Fax: 604-678-4702
Richard.MyhillJones@gov.bc.ca
Director, Procurement & Operations, Bruce McAllister
Tel: 250-356-7108
Fax: 250-356-6970
Bruce.McAllister@gov.bc.ca
Senior Manager, Project Governance & Corporate Initiative, Paul Squires
Tel: 250-356-9719
Fax: 250-387-6431
Paul.Squires@gov.bc.ca
Senior Manager, Transit Projects, Kevin Volk
Tel: 250-387-4851
Fax: 250-387-5012
Kevin.Volk@gov.bc.ca

Transportation Policy & Programs Department
PO Box 9850 Stn. Prov Govt, Victoria, BC V8W 9T5
Tel: 250-387-5062
Fax: 250-387-6431
Assistant Deputy Minister, Jacquie Dawes
Tel: 250-387-5062
Fax: 250-387-6431
Jacquie.Dawes@gov.bc.ca
Registrar/Director, Passenger Transportation Branch, Dawn Major
Tel: 604-453-4278
Dawn.Major@gov.bc.ca
Other Communications: Cell Phone: 604-992-9140
Executive Director, Pacific Gateway Branch, Lisa Gow
Tel: 250-387-2672
Fax: 250-387-5812
Lisa.Gow@gov.bc.ca
Executive Director, Transportation Policy Branch, Greg Gilks
Tel: 250-387-0882
Fax: 250-356-0897
Greg.Gilks@gov.bc.ca
Acting Director, Business Development, Fiona MacRaild
Tel: 250-387-2175
Fax: 250-387-5812
Fiona.MacRaild@gov.bc.ca
Project Director, Transportation Programs, Tom Greene
Tel: 250-356-0528
Fax: 250-387-6431
Tom.Greene@gov.bc.ca
Director, Strategic Outreach & Business Engagement, Linda Harmon
Tel: 250-356-0745
Fax: 250-387-5812
Linda.Harmon@gov.bc.ca
Director, Infrastructure Development, Southern Corridor, Helen Berthin
Tel: 250-356-9723
Fax: 250-387-5812
Helen.Berthin@gov.bc.ca
Director, Infrastructure Development, Northern Corridor, Brad Glazer
Tel: 250-356-9736
Fax: 250-387-5812
Brad.Glazer@gov.bc.ca
Director, Partnership & Project Development, Bob Steele
Tel: 250-356-2051
Fax: 250-356-2112
Bob.Steele@gov.bc.ca
Manager, Financial Services, Tammy Donison-McKay
Tel: 250-953-4961
Fax: 250-356-0897
Tammy.DonisonMcKay@gov.bc.ca

Infrastructure Department
PO Box 9850 Stn. Prov Govt, Victoria, BC V8W 9T5
Tel: 250-387-6742
Fax: 250-387-6431
Assistant Deputy Minister, Kevin Richter
Tel: 250-387-6742
Fax: 250-387-6431
Kevin.Richter@gov.bc.ca
Executive Director, Planning & Programming Branch, David Marr
Tel: 250-356-2100
Fax: 250-356-0897
David.Marr@gov.bc.ca
Acting Executive Project Director, Evergreen Line Project, Jon Buckle
Tel: 604-927-4452
Fax: 604-927-4453
Jon.Buckle@gov.bc.ca
Director, Marine Branch, Krik Handrahan
Tel: 250-952-0678
Fax: 250-356-0897
Kirk.Handrahan@gov.bc.ca
District Manager, Transportation, Renee Mounteney
Tel: 250-751-3282
Fax: 250-356-0897
Renee.Mounteney@gov.bc.ca
Other Communications: Cell Phone: 250-208-8876

British Columbia Utilities Commission

900 Howe St., 6th Fl., PO Box 250Vancouver, BC V6Z 2N3
Tel: 604-660-4700
Fax: 604-660-1102
Toll-Free: 800-663-1385
commission.secretary@bcuc.com
www.bcuc.com
The British Columbia Utilities Commission is an independent regulatory agency of the Provincial Government of British Columbia. The Commission's regulates the province's natural gas & electricity utilities. Other activities of the Utilities Commission include the regulation of universal compulsory automobile insurance & intra-provincial pipelines.
Acts Administered:
Utilities Commission Act

Chair/Chief Executive Officer, Len Kelsey
Tel: 604-660-4714
len.kelsey@bcuc.com

Commission Secretary, Erica Hamilton
Tel: 604-660-4727
Erica.Hamilton@bcuc.com

Director, Policy, Planning & Customer Relations, Alison Thorson
Tel: 604-660-4185
Fax: 604-660-1102
alison.thorson@bcuc.com

Director, Energy, Doug Chong
Tel: 604-660-4737
doug.chong@bcuc.com

Director, Rates, Philip W. Nakoneshny
Tel: 604-660-4736
philip.nakoneshny@bcuc.com

Director, Infrastructure, Mark Thomas
Tel: 604-660-4726
mark.thomas@bcuc.com

British Columbia Vital Statistics Agency

PO Box 9657 Stn. Prov Govt, Victoria, BC V8W 9P3
Tel: 250-952-2681
Fax: 250-952-9097
VSOFFCEO@gov.bc.ca
www.vs.gov.bc.ca
The Vital Statistics Agency operates under the Ministry of Health, and offers the following services: Birth registration; marriage certificates; death certificates; wills; name changes; and geneaology.

Chief Executive Officer, Jack Shewchuk
Tel: 250-952-9039
Fax: 250-952-9097
Jack.Shewchuk@gov.bc.ca

Manager, Business Operations, Support Services, Brenda Craven
Tel: 250-952-9035
Fax: 250-952-9045
Brenda.Craven@gov.bc.ca

Manager, Business Operations, Health Registries, Anita Malovec
Tel: 250-952-9129
Fax: 250-952-9038
anita.malovec@gov.bc.ca

Team Lead, Confidential Services, Renae Kinnee
Tel: 250-952-9057
Fax: 250-952-9044
VSCS@gov.bc.ca

Regional Manager, Greater Vancouver & Sunshine Coast, Mark Spearman
Tel: 250-952-9131
Fax: 604-660-2645
Mark.Spearman@gov.bc.ca

Regional Manager, Vancouver Island & Coast, Wanda Vincent
Tel: 250-952-9092
Fax: 250-952-9074
Wanda.Vincent@gov.bc.ca

Regional Manager, Kelowna, Ingrid Bloomfield
Tel: 250-712-3260
Fax: 250-712-7598
Ingrid.Bloomfield@gov.bc.ca

Workers' Compensation Board of British Columbia

PO Box 5350 Stn. Terminal, Vancouver, BC V6B 5L5
Tel: 604-276-3100
Fax: 604-276-3247
Toll-Free: 888-621-7233
www.worksafebc.com
Other Communication: Head Office Physical Address: 6951 Westminster Hwy., Richmond, BC; Claims: 604-231-8888, Fax: 604-233-9777; Employer services/Assessments: 604-244-6181
The Workers' Compensation Board of British Columbia, or WorkSafeBC, assists workers & employers in British Columbia by promoting health & safety in workplaces. WorkSafeBC's key responsiblities are as follows: consultation with & education of employers & workers; monitoring compliance with the Occupa-

tional Health & Safety Regulation; & provision of return-to-work compensation, rehabilitation, health care benefits, & other services for parties affected by work-related injuries or diseases.

Chair, George Morfitt

President/Chief Executive Officer, David Anderson

Chief Financial Officer/Senior Vice-President, Finance Division, Brian Erickson

Senior Vice-President, Human Resources & Corporate Affairs, Roberta Ellis

Senior Vice-President, Operations, Worker & Employer Services Division, Diana Miles

Chief Review Officer, Review Division, Pamela Cohen

Vice-President, Claims Services, Ian Munroe

Vice-President, Prevention Services, Betty Pirs

Vice-President, Industry Services & Sustainability, Donna Wilson

Vice-President, Marketing, Kevin LaFreniere

General Counsel & Secretary, Ed Bates

Government of Manitoba

Seat of Government: Legislative Building, Rm. 237, Winnipeg, MB R3C 0V8
Tel: 204-945-3636
Fax: 204-948-2507
clerkla@leg.gov.mb.ca
www.gov.mb.ca
The Province of Manitoba entered Confederation July 15, 1870. It has an area of 647,797 km2, & the StatsCan census population in 2011 was 1,208,268.

Manitoba Aboriginal & Northern Affairs

Legislative Bldg, 344-450 Broadway, Winnipeg, MB R3C OV8
Tel: 204-945-3719
Fax: 204-945-8374
anaweb@gov.mb.ca
www.gov.mb.ca/ana/
The goals of Manitoba's Aboriginal & Northern Affairs are as follows: to improve the quality of life & opportunities for Aboriginal & Northern people; to facilitate better services, opportunities & results for Manitoba's Aboriginal & northern people; to support the mental, emotional, physical & spiritual health of northern communities & Aboriginal people; to resolve outstanding provincial obligations to Aboriginal/northern communities; to foster self-determination, accountability & sustainable growth; & to strengthen the participation of Aboriginal & northern people in Manitoba's economy.
Acts Administered:
Manitoba Floodway and East Side Road Authority Act
Northern Affairs Act
Planning Act

Minister, Hon. Eric Robinson
Tel: 204-945-3719
Fax: 204-954-8374
minna@leg.gov.mb.ca

Deputy Minister, Harvey Bostrom
Tel: 204-945-0565
Fax: 204-945-1256
dmna@leg.gov.mb.ca

Executive Director, Aboriginal Affairs Secretariat, Joe Morrisseau
Tel: 204-945-8265

Associated Agencies, Boards & Commissions:
• Northern Affairs Capital Approval Board
PO Box 2532
The Pas, MB R9A 1M3
• Communities Economic Development Fund
15 Moak CRes.
Thompson, MB R8N 2B8
Tel: 204-778-4138
Fax: 204-778-4313
Toll-free: 800-561-4315
www.cedf.mb.ca
• MB Combative Sports Commission (MCSC)
#420, 213 Notre Dame Ave.
Winnipeg, MB R3B 1N3
Tel: 204-945-1788
Fax: 204-948-3649
www.manitobaboxingcommission.com
The Manitoba Combative Sports Commission regulates all professional contests or exhibitions of boxing, kick boxing and mixed martial arts, including the licensing and supervision of officials, athletes and promoters.
• Sport Manitoba
145 Pacific Ave.
Winnipeg, MB R3B 2Z6
Tel: 204-925-5600
Fax: 204-925-5916
info@sportmanitoba.ca
www.sportmanitoba.ca
Chair, Paul Robson

Local Government Development Division
59 Elizabeth Dr., PO Box 33Thompson, MB R8N 1X4
Tel: 204-677-6794
Fax: 204-677-6525
The Local Government Development Division provides support to 50 northern & remote communities, including public works, environmental services, & infrastructure development. It promotes cooperative, community-driven sustainable development.
Executive Director, Freda Albert
Tel: 204-677-6795
falbert@gov.mb.ca
Director, Program Planning & Development, Jeff Gordon
Tel: 204-945-1713
jgordon@gov.mb.ca

Manitoba Agriculture, Food & Rural Initiatives

Legislative Bldg., 165-450 Broadway, Winnipeg, MB R3C 0V8
Tel: 204-945-3722
Fax: 204-945-3470
minagr@leg.gov.mb.ca
www.gov.mb.ca/agriculture/
Acts Administered:
Animal Diseases Act
Animal Liability Act
Cattle Producers Association Act
Coarse Grain Marketing Control Act
Community development Bonds Act
Crown Lands Act, (in part) Sections 6, 7, 10, 12(1), 14, 16, 17, 18, 21, 23, 24 to 28 both inclusive
Farm Lands Ownership Act
Farm Practices Protection Act
Food Safety Act
Land Rehabilitation Act
Livestock & Livestock Products Act
Livestock Industry Diversification Act
Natural Products Marketing Act
Noxious Weeds Act
Organic Agricultural Products Act
Pesticides & Fertilizers Control Act
Plant Pests and Diseases Act
Property Tax and Insulation Assistance Act
Wildlife Act, (in part) Section 89(e)

Minister, Hon. Ron Kostyshyn
Tel: 204-945-3722
Fax: 204-945-3470

Deputy Minister, Barry Todd
Tel: 204-945-3734
Fax: 204-948-2095

Executive Director, Strategic Planning, Maurice Bouvier
Tel: 204-792-5406

Chief Veterinary Officer, Food Safety Knowledge Centre, Wayne Lees
Tel: 204-945-7685

Director, Crops Knowledge Centre, Mike Kagan
Tel: 204-745-5653

Director, Land Use Planning Knowledge Centre, Robert Fleming
Tel: 204-867-6551

Associated Agencies, Boards & Commissions:
• Agricultural Crown Lands Appeal Board
36 Armitage Ave.
PO Box 1286
Minnedosa, MB R0J 1E0
Tel: 204-867-6550
Fax: 204-867-6578
• Agricultural Producers' Organization Certification Agency
#812, 401 York Ave.
Winnipeg, MB R3C 0P8
Tel: 204-945-3854
Fax: 204-945-1489
• Agricultural Societies
1129 Queens Ave.
Brandon, MB R7A 1L9
Tel: 204-726-6195
Fax: 204-726-6260
Promotes improvement in agriculture & development of Manitoba agricultural products. Provide organizational assistance to rural & urban people.
Superintendent, Liz Roberts
liz.roberts@gov.mb.ca
• Agri-Food Research & Development Initiative Program Council (ARDI)
38 Birch Cres.
PO Box 72
Morris, MB R0G 1K0
• Animal Care Appeal Board
• Farm Machinery & Equipment Board
Norquay Bldg.
#812, 401 York Ave.
Winnipeg, MB R3C 0P8
Tel: 204-945-3856
Fax: 204-948-2844
Program Specialist, Randy Ozunko
Chair, Chuck Balmer
• Farm Practices Protection Board
c/o Boards, Commissions & Legislation
#812, 401 York Ave.
Winnipeg, MB R3C 0P8
Tel: 204-945-3854
Fax: 204-945-1489
• Manitoba Farm Mediation Board
c/o Boards, Commissions & Legislation Branch
#812, 401 York Ave.
Winnipeg, MB R3C 0P8
Tel: 204-945-0359
Fax: 204-945-1489
Toll-free: 800-282-8069
Mediates options to legal action by creditors when farmers cannot meet their obligations.
• Food Development Centre
810 Phillips St.
PO Box 1240
Portage la Prairie, MB R1N 3J9
Tel: 204-239-3150
Fax: 204-239-3180
Toll-free: 800-870-1044
www.gov.mb.ca/agriculture/fdc
The Food Development Centre (FDC) is a Special Operating Agency of Manitoba Agriculture, Food and Rural Initiatives (MAFRI). Its mandate is to assist the agri-food industry in the development and commercialization of conventional and functional foods and natural health products.
General Manager/COO, Lynda Lowry
Tel: 204-239-3624
Manager of Support Services, Mike Lalla
Tel: 204-871-5152
• Manitoba Agricultural Services Corporation (MASC)
#100, 1525 First St. South
Brandon, MB R7A 7A1
Tel: 204-726-6850
Fax: 204-726-6849
mailbox@masc.mb.ca
www.masc.mb.ca
Formerly the Manitoba Agricultural Credit Corporation & the Manitoba Crop Insurance Corporation. Manitoba Agricultural Services Corporation (MASC) fully supports the province's producers and rural communities, through innovative and targeted risk management and financial programs. MASC is represented across Manitoba by 19 insurance offices and 16 lending offices, with corporate offices located in Portage la Prairie and Brandon.
President/CEO, Neil Hamilton

• **Farm Lands Ownership Board**
#812, Norquay Bldg.
401 York Ave.
Winnipeg, MB R3C 0P8
Tel: 204-945-3149
Fax: 204-945-1489
Toll-free: 800-282-8069
Chair, Ken Caldwell
• **Farm Products Marketing Council**
c/o Boards, Commissions & Legislation Branch
#812, 401 York Ave.
Winnipeg, MB R3C 0P8
Tel: 204-945-4495
Fax: 204-948-2844
• **Manitoba Horse Racing Commission**
c/o Boards, Commissions & Legislation Branch
#812, 401 York Ave.
Winnipeg, MB R3C 0P8
Tel: 204-945-4495
Fax: 204-948-2844
Governs, directs, controls, & regulates horse racing & the operation of all race tracks in Manitoba.
• **Manitoba Milk Prices Review Commission**
c/o Boards, Commissions & Legislation Branch
#812, 401 York Ave.
Winnipeg, MB R3C 0P8
Tel: 204-945-3854
Fax: 204-948-2844
• **Veterinary Services Commission**
c/o Livestock Knowledge Centre
#204, 545 University Cres.
Winnipeg, MB R3T 5S6
Tel: 204-945-6311
Fax: 204-945-4327
Asst. Deputy Minister, Leloni Scott
Tel: 204-945-3735
Central Plains
Morris Ave., PO Box 532Gladstone, MB R0J 0T0
Tel: 204-871-4219
GO Team Leader, Dennis Beernaert
Eastman
20 First St. South, PO Box 50Beausejour, MB R0E 0C0
Tel: 204-268-6099
Fax: 204-268-6060
GO Team Manager, Shaunda Rossington
Tel: 204-268-6099
North Interlake
317 River Rd., PO Box 2000Arborg, MB R0C 0A0
Fax: 204-376-3311
GO Team Manager, Bob Penner
Tel: 204-641-4910
North Parkland
27 Second Ave. SW, Dauphin, MB R7N 3E5
Fax: 204-734-5271
GO Team Manager, Jana Schott
Tel: 204-648-3925
Pembina
279 Carlton St., PO Box 189Somerset, MB R0G 2L0
GO Team Leader, Shane Dobson
Red River
67 - 2 St. NE, PO Box 969Altona, MB R0G 0B0
Fax: 204-324-2803
GO Team Manager, Curtis Weeks
Tel: 204-304-0239
South Interlake
77 Main St., PO Box 70Teulon, MB R0C 3B0
Fax: 204-886-3657
GO Team Manager, Wray Whitmore
South Parkland
221 Elm St., Hwy 21 N, PO Box 50Hamiota, MB R0M 0T0
Southwest
247 Wellington St., PO Box 850Virden, MB R0M 2C0
Fax: 204-748-4775
GO Team Manager, John Corbey
Tel: 204-851-2442
Valleys North
120 - 6th Ave. North, PO Box 370Swan River, MB R0L 1Z0
Fax: 204-734-5271
GO Team Manager, Allen Muggaberg

Agri-Industry Development & Innovation Division
Acting Asst. Deputy Minister, Tracy Gilson
Tel: 204-945-3736
Chief Veterinary Officer, Wayne Lees
Tel: 204-945-7685

Manitoba Conservation & Water Stewardship

200 Saulteaux Cres., Winnipeg, MB R3J 3W3
Toll-Free: 800-214-6497
mws@gov.mb.ca
www.gov.mb.ca/conservation; www.gov.mb.ca/waterstewardship
Manitoba Conservation protects, conserves, manages & sustains development of forest, fisheries, wildlife, water, energy & Crown & Park land resources. It also protects environmental integrity, & ensures a high level of environmental quality.
The department is the lead agency for providing outdoor recreational opportunities for Manitobans & visitors.
It is a contributor to the economic development & well-being of the province, through resource-based harvesting operations, & in cooperation with other departments responsible for agriculture & tourism. Protecting people & property from floods, wildfires, & adverse effects of other natural occurrences, are also major roles.
The department administers legislation & regulations protecting the environment & public health, participates in approval, licensing & appeals for industrial development activities, administers waste reduction & pollution prevention activities, & monitors environmental quality.
Acts Administered:
Burning of Crop Residue & Non-Crop Herbage Regulation
Campgrounds Regulation
Classes of Development Regulation
Climate Change and Emissions Reductions Act
Conservation Agreement Forms Regulation
Conservation Agreements Act
Conservation Districts Act
Contaminated Sites Remediation Act
Crown Lands Act
Dangerous Goods Handling & Transportation Act
Dangerous Goods Handling & Transportation Fees Regulation
Dangerous Goods Handling & Transportation Regulation
Designation of Wild Animals Regulation
Designation of Wildlife Lands Regulation
Disposal of Whey Regulation
Drinking Water Safety Act, 2004
Dyking Authority Act
East Side Traditional Lands Planning and Special Protected Areas Act
Ecological Reserves Act
Ecological Reserves Designation Regulation
Eligible Conservation Agencies Regulation
Endangered Species Act
Environment Act
Environment Act Fees Regulation
Environmental Accident Reporting Regulation
Environmental Assessment Hearing Costs Recovery Regulation
Fisheries Act
Fishermen's Assistance & Polluter's Liability Act
Floodway Authority Act
Forest Act
Generator Registration & Carrier Licensing Regulation
Ground Water & Water Well Act
Ground Water & Water Well Act
High Level Radioactive Waste Act
Incinerators Regulation
Inco Ltd. & Hudson Bay Mining & Smelting Co., Ltd. Smelting Complex Regulation
International Peace Garden Act
Joint Environmental Assessment Regulation
Lake of the Woods Control Board Act
Litter Regulation
Livestock Manure & Mortalities Management Regulation
Manifest Regulation
Manitoba Hazardous Waste Management Corporation Act
Manitoba Natural Resources Transfer Act
Manitoba Natural Resources Transfer Act, Amendment Act
Manitoba Natural Resources Transfer Act, Amendment Act, 1963
Manitoba Natural Resources Transfer Act
Multi-Material Stewardship (Interim Measures) Regulation
Natural Resources Agreement Act
Onsite Wastewater Management Systems Regulation
Ozone Depleting Substances Act
Participant Assistance Regulation
PCB Storage Site Regulation
Peat Smoke Control Regulation
Pesticides Regulation
Plant Pests & Diseases Act
Polar Bear Protection Act, 2003
Protection of Water Resources Regulation
Provincial Parks Act
Public Health Act
Resource Tourism Operators Act
Rockwood Sensitive Area Regulation
Sanitary Areas Regulation
Special Waste (Shredder Residue) Regulation
Storage & Handling of Petroleum Products & Allied Products Regulation
Surveys Act (Part II)
Sustainable Development Act
Threatened, Endangered & Extirpated Species Regulation
Tire Stewardship Regulation
Used Oil, Oil Filters & Containers Stewardship Regulation
Waste Disposal Grounds Regulation
Waste Reduction & Prevention Act
Wastewater Management Systems Regulations
Water & Wastewater Facility Operators Regulation
Water Commission Act
Water Power Act
Water Resources Administration Act
Water Resources Conservation & Protection Act
Water Resources Conservation Act
Water Rights Act
Water Rights Act
Water Supplies Regulation
Water Supply Commissions Act
Water Works, Sewage & Sewage Disposal Regulations
Well Drilling Regulation
Wild Rice Act
Wildlife Act

Minister, Hon. Gord Mackintosh
Tel: 204-945-3730
Fax: 204-945-3586
minconws@leg.gov.mb.ca

Deputy Minister, Fred Meier
Tel: 204-945-3785
Fax: 204-948-2403
dmcon@leg.gov.mb.ca

Executive Director, Corporate Crown Lands Policy, Marlene Zyluk
Tel: 204-945-7370

Associated Agencies, Boards & Commissions:
• **Clean Environment Commission**
#305, 155 Carlton St.
Winnipeg, MB R3C 3H8
Tel: 204-945-0594
Fax: 204-945-0090
www.cecmanitoba.ca/
Arm's-length provincial agency that holds public hearings on the subject of the regulation of a broad range of private industry, municipal or provincial government operations. Investigates environmental matters or considers proposed abatement projects with public hearings. Reports to the Minister with advice & recommendations & acts as a mediator between two or more parties to an environmental dispute.
Chair, Terry Sargeant
• **Conservation Agreements Board**
c/o Manitoba Habitat Heritage Corporation
#200, 1555 St James St.
Winnipeg, MB R3H 1B5
Tel: 204-784-4350
• **Ecological Reserves Advisory Committee**
c/o Manitoba Conservation, Parks & Natural Areas Branch
200 Saulteaux Cres.
Winnipeg, MB R3J 3W3
Tel: 204-945-4148
Fax: 204-945-0012
Chair, David R. M. Hatch
• **Endangered Species Advisory Committee**
200 Saulteaux Cres.
PO Box 24
Winnipeg, MB R3J 3W3
Tel: 204-945-7465
Fax: 204-945-3077
Chair, James Duncan
• **Lake Winnipeg Stewardship Board**
PO Box 305
Gimli, MB R0C 1B0
Tel: 204-642-4899
www.lakewinnipeg.org
Established in 2003 to assist the government of Manitoba to achieve the main commitments in the Lake Winnipeg Action

Plan of reducing phosphorus & nitrogen in the lake to pre-1970 levels. The Lake Winnipeg Stewardship Board's Interim Report (Jan. 2005), contained 32 sets of recommendations & was followed by public discussions.
Chair, William Barlow
• **Lake of the Woods Control Board**
c/o Executive Engineer
Ottawa, ON K1A 0H3
Fax: 819-953-4666
Toll-free: 800-661-5922
secretariat@lwcb.ca
www.lwcb.ca
Chair, Gail Faven
• **Manitoba Conservation Districts Commission**
Secretariat c/o Planning & Coordination Branch
123 Main St.
PO Box 20000
Neepawa, MB R0J 1H0
Tel: 204-476-7033
Fax: 204-476-7539
The Conservation Districts Program has been delivering a comprehensive, sustainable approach to water & soil management for over 25 years. Conservation Districts are established under the authority of The Conservation District Act. There are 16 Conservation Districts covering approximately 60% of Agro-Manitoba. Individual district boundaries may vary depending on the needs of the people. Districts are usually based on the drainage basin or watershed of the major river in the area.
• **Manitoba Habitat Heritage Corporation**
#200, 1555 St. James St.
Winnipeg, MB R3H 1B5
Tel: 204-784-4350
Fax: 204-784-7359
mhhc@mhhc.mb.ca
www.mhhc.mb.ca
Chair, John Whitaker
• **Manitoba Hazardous Waste Management Corporation Board**
1803 Hekla Ave.
Winnipeg, MB R2R 0K3
• **Manitoba Round Table for Sustainable Development (MRT)**
#160, 123 Main St.
Winnipeg, MB R3C 1A5
Tel: 204-945-1869
Fax: 204-948-2357
mrtsd@gov.mb.ca
www.gov.mb.ca/conservation/susresmb/mrtsd
• **Manitoba Water Council**
200 Saulteaux Cres.
PO Box 27
Winnipeg, MB R3J 3W3
water.council@gov.mb.ca
www.manitobawatercouncil.ca
Assists rural residents outside Winnipeg in developing safe & sustainable water &/or sewerage facilities.
Chair, Jean Frieson

Administration & Finance Division

Climate Change & Environmental Protection
Assistant Deputy Minister, Dan McInnis
Tel: 204-296-4199
Director, Environmental Assessment & Licensing, Tracey Braun
Tel: 204-945-7071
Director, Climate Change, Neil Cunningham
Tel: 204-945-8793
Director, Environmental Programs & Strategies, Mike Gilbertson
Tel: 204-471-9338

Conservation Programs Division
Manages Manitoba's natural resources, parks, lands, forests, fish, wildlife, & the environment. Implements the principles of sustainable development.
Assistant Deputy Minister, Serge Scrafield
Tel: 204-945-7008
Chief Operating Officer, Green Manitoba, Christina McDonald
Tel: 204-945-1819
123 Main St. West
PO Box 20000
Neepawa, MB R0J 1H0
Director, Forestry, John Dojack
Tel: 204-945-7998
Director, GeoManitoba, Greg Carlson
Tel: 204-945-7952
123 Main St. West
PO Box 20000
Neepawa, MB R0J 1H0
Director, Wildlife & Ecosystem Protection, James Duncan
Tel: 204-945-7465

Corporate Policy Division
Executive Director, Jocelyn Baker
Tel: 204-945-6658
Director, Aboriginal Relations, Ron Missyabit
Tel: 204-945-7088
Director, Sustainable Resource & Policy Management, Charlotte Price
Tel: 204-945-6944

Ecological Services Division
Assistant Deputy Minister, Dwight Williamson
Tel: 204-945-7030
Director, Water Science & Management Branch, Nicole Armstrong
Tel: 204-945-3991
Director, Planning & Coordination, Rhonda McDougal
Tel: 204-945-8271
Director/Manager, Office of Drinking Water, Kim Philip
Tel: 204-945-7010
Senior Information Management Specialist, Fisheries Branch, Robert Moszynski
Tel: 204-945-2916

Manitoba Round Table for Sustainable Development (MRTSD)
#160, 123 Main St., Winnipeg, MB R3C 1A5
Tel: 204-945-1869
Fax: 204-948-2357
mrtsd@gov.mb.ca
www.gov.mb.ca/conservation/susresmb/mrtsd
The Manitoba Round Table for Sustainable Development is an advisory body to the provincial government. It provides advice & support to decision makers toward making responsible resource, land use, environment, social, & economic development decisions for the province.
Chair, Hon. Stan Struthers

Regional Services & Parks
Operates six regional offices in rural Manitoba & co-ordinated from Headquarters operations in Winnipeg. The Division co-ordinates the delivery of programs & services at the community level
Asst. Deputy Minister, Bruce Bremner
Tel: 204-945-4842
Director, Parks & Natural Areas, Barry J. Bentham
Tel: 204-945-4413
Director, Regional Support Services, Blair McTavish
Tel: 204-945-6647
Central (Gimli)
75 - 7th Ave., PO Box 6000Gimli, MB R0C 1B0
Tel: 204-642-6070
Fax: 204-642-6108
Regional Director, Rob Nedotiafko
Tel: 204-642-6096
Central (Winnipeg)
#160, 123 Main St., Winnipeg, MB R3C 1A5
Tel: 204-945-7100
Fax: 204-948-2338
Eastern
Provincial Hwy. #502, CP 4000Lac du Bonnet, MB R0E 1A0
Tél: 204-345-1431
Téléc: 204-345-1440
Chief of Park Operations, Don Hallett
Tel: 204-345-1480
Northeastern
59 Elizabeth Dr., PO Box 28Thompson, MB R8N 1X4
Tel: 204-677-6648
Fax: 204-677-6359
Regional Director, Pierce Roberts
Tel: 204-677-6893
Northwestern
3rd St. & Ross Ave., PO Box 2550The Pas, MB R9A 1M4
Tel: 204-627-8215
Fax: 204-623-5733
Regional Director, Wayde Roberts
Tel: 204-627-8399
Western
1129 Queens Ave., PO Box 13Brandon, MB R7A 1L9
Tel: 204-726-6441
Fax: 204-726-6301
Regional Director, Luke Peloquin
Tel: 204-726-6299

Manitoba Culture, Heritage & Tourism

Legislative Building, #118, 450 Broadway Ave., Winnipeg, MB R3C 0V8
Tel: 204-945-3729
Fax: 204-945-5223
mincht@leg.gov.mb.ca
www.gov.mb.ca/chc
Committed to the development & implementation of programs & services which promote & enhance the well-being, identity & creativity of Manitobans & which contribute to Manitoba's continued economic growth & steadily rising quality of life. Working with its partners in the community & with government, the Department raises the national & international profile of the talents & abilities of our people, encourages healthy active living, promotes pride of place, creates jobs & attracts & maintains investment in our province
Acts Administered:
Heritage Manitoba Act
Heritage Resources Act
Income Tax Act
Travel Manitoba Act

Minister, Hon. Florfina Marcelino
Tel: 204-945-3729
Fax: 204-945-5223
mincht@leg.gov.mb.ca

Deputy Minister, Cindy Stevens
Tel: 204-945-4136
Fax: 204-948-3102

Associated Agencies, Boards & Commissions:
• **Le Centre Culturel franco-manitobain/Franco-Manitoban Cultural Centre**
340, boul Provencher
St Boniface, MB R2H 0G7
Tel: 204-233-8972
Fax: 204-233-3324
ccfm@ccfm.mb.ca
www.ccfm.mb.ca
• **Heritage Grants Advisory Council**
213 Notre Dame Ave., 3rd Fl.
Winnipeg, MB R3B 1N3
Tel: 204-945-2213
Fax: 204-948-2086
• **Manitoba Arts Council**
#525, 93 Lombard Ave.
Winnipeg, MB R3B 3B1
Tel: 204-945-2237
Fax: 204-945-5925
Toll-free: 866-994-2787
info@artscouncil.mb.ca
www.artscouncil.mb.ca
An arms-length agency of the provincial government dedicated to artistic excellence. It offers a broad-based granting program for professional artists & arts organizations. It promotes, preserves, supports & advocates for the arts as essential to the quality of life of all the people of Manitoba.
• **Manitoba Centennial Centre Corporation**
555 Main St.
Winnipeg, MB R3B 1C3
Tel: 204-956-1360
Fax: 204-944-1390
inquiries@mbccc.ca
www.mbccc.ca
• **Manitoba Film Classification Board**
#216, 301 Weston St.
Winnipeg, MB R3E 3H4
Tel: 204-945-8962
Fax: 204-945-0890
Toll-free: 866-612-2399
MFCB@gov.mb.ca
www.gov.mb.ca/chc/mfcb/
• **Manitoba Heritage Council**
213 Notre Dame Ave., Main Fl.
Winnipeg, MB R3B 1N3
Tel: 204-945-2118
Fax: 204-948-2384
hrb@gov.mb.ca
www.gov.mb.ca/chc/hrb
Protects, interprets & promotes the heritage resources of the province; offers advice & recommendations on places & events

which should be protected by the department; protection of significant buildings & sites.
Chair, Sharon Reilly
• **Manitoba Museum / Musée du Manitoba**
190 Rupert Ave.
Winnipeg, MB R3B 0N2
Tel: 204-956-2830
Fax: 204-942-3679
info@manitobamuseum.mb.ca
www.manitobamuseum.mb.ca
Other Communication: Info Line:|204/943-3139
• **Manitoba Film & Music**
#410, 93 Lombard Ave.
Winnipeg, MB R3B 3B1
Tel: 204-947-2040
Fax: 204-956-5261
info@mbfilmmusic.ca
mbfilmmusic.ca
Pomotes the province's film & sound recording artists & industries.
• **Public Library Advisory Board**
#300, 1011 Rosser Ave.
Brandon, MB R7A 0L5
Tel: 204-726-6590
Fax: 204-726-6868
Toll-free: 800-252-9998
pls@gov.mb.ca
• **Venture Manitoba Tours Ltd.**
PO Box 1000
Riverton, MB R0C 2R0
Tel: 204-378-2769
Fax: 204-378-2734
vmt@mts.net

Communications Services Manitoba
155 Carlton St., 10th Fl., Winnipeg, MB R3C 3H8
Tel: 204-945-3765
Fax: 204-948-2147
Acting Assistant Deputy Minister, Debbie MacKenzie
Tel: 204-945-4271
Fax: 204-948-2219
Acting Director, Public Affairs, Angela Jamieson
Tel: 204-945-4971
Fax: 204-948-2147
Supervisor, Statutory Publications, Keith Holness
Tel: 204-945-3101
Fax: 204-945-7172
statpub@gov.mb.ca
200 Vaughan St.
Winnipeg, MB R3C 1T5

Culture & Heritage Programs Division
Assistant Deputy Minister, Veronica Dyck
Tel: 204-945-4078
Fax: 204-948-2739
Director, Historic Resources, Donna Dul
Tel: 204-945-4389
Fax: 204-948-2384

Tourism Secretariat
155 Carlton St., 7th Fl., Winnipeg, MB R3C 3H8
Toll-Free: 800-665-0040
www.travelmanitoba.com
Executive Director, Tourism Manitoba, Terry Welsh
Tel: 204-945-2449

Minister, Hon. Nancy Allan
Tel: 204-945-3720
Fax: 204-945-1291
minedu@leg.gov.mb.ca

Manitoba Entrepreneurship, Training & Trade

#1000, 259 Portage Ave, Winnipeg, MB R3B 3P4
Tel: 204-945-2475
Fax: 204-945-3977
minctt@leg.gov.mb.ca
www.gov.mb.ca/ctt
The mission of Manitoba's Entrepreneurship, Training & Trade is to support the growth of business in the province, to meet provincial labour demands, to increase training opportunities, & to expand global trade relations.
Acts Administered:
Biofuels Act
Drilling & Production Regulation
Economic Innovation & Technology Council Act
Energy Act
Gas Allocation Act
Gas Pipe Line Act
Greater Winnipeg Gas Distribution Act (S.M. 1988-89, C.40)
Mines & Minerals Act
Mining & Metallurgy Compensation Act
Oil & Gas Act
Oil & Gas Production Tax Act
Sustainable Development Act

Minister, Hon. Peter Bjornson
Tel: 204-945-0067
Fax: 204-945-4882
minett@leg.gov.mb.ca

Deputy Minister, Hugh Eliasson
Tel: 204-945-4076
Fax: 204-945-1561
dmett@leg.gov.mb.ca

Associated Agencies, Boards & Commissions:
• **Apprenticeship & Certification Board**
#1010, 401 York Ave.
Winnipeg, MB R3C 0P8
Tel: 204-945-3337
Fax: 204-948-2346
Toll-free: 877-978-7233
The Board is an advisory body which makes recommendations regarding the designation and regulation of trades and which approves apprenticeship training standards.
Chair, Leonard Harapiak
• **Convention Centre Corporation Board of Directors**
375 York Ave.
Winnipeg, MB R3C 3J3
Tel: 204-956-1720
Fax: 204-943-0310
Toll-free: 800-565-7776
audra@wcc.mb.ca
The Board manages and administers the affairs of the corporation.
Chair, Rennie Zegalski
• **Manitoba Development Corporation (MDC)**
#1040, 259 Portage Ave.
Winnipeg, MB R3B 3P4
Tel: 204-945-0141
Fax: 204-945-1193
The Board provides financial services and manages financial instruments on behalf of the Province of Manitoba to assist with economic development initiatives.
• **Manitoba Opportunity Fund (MOF)**
#600, 259 Portage Ave.
Winnipeg, MB R3B 2A9
Tel: 204-945-1872
MOF holds and invests the Provincial allocation of immigrants investments made through the Federal Department of Citizenship and Immigration Canada's Immigrant Investor Program.
• **Manitoba Trade & Investment Corporation (MTIC)**
#1100, 259 Portage Ave.
Winnipeg, MB R3B 3P4
Tel: 204-945-2466
Fax: 204-957-1793
MTIC is an administrative mechanism that supports the economic priorities of Building the Manitoba economy through increased exports and industry investments.
Chair, Hugh Eliasson
Director, Craig Halwachs
• **Manitoba Taking Charge! Inc**
276 Colony St.
Winnipeg, MB R3C 1W3
Tel: 204-945-1100
Taking Charge! Inc. is a non-profit organization under the leadership & direction of a Board of Directors that also oversees the employment programming & Taking Care, the licensed day care.
Co-chair, Susan Swan
Co-chair, Gail E. Watson
Executive Director, Jackie Lavallee

Manitoba Gaming Control Commission

#800, 215 Garry St., Winnipeg, MB R3C 3P3
Tel: 204-945-9400
Fax: 204-945-9450
Toll-Free: 800-782-0363
information@mgcc.mb.ca
www.mgcc.mb.ca
Established in 1969 under authority of the Financial Administration Act. Responsible for central accounting, payroll & financial reporting services for the government, consumer & corporate affairs & central financial control of cost-shared agreements. The ministry manages government borrowing programs & is responsible for federal-provincial relations.

Minister, Hon. David Chomiak
Tel: 204-945-9400

Chairperson, Darlene Dziewit

Vice-Chairperson, Lucille Cenerini

Commissioner, Barbara Bruce

Commissioner, Brenda Johnston

Commissioner, Dennis Meeches

Commissioner, Joe Stadnyk

Manitoba Health

#100, 300 Carlton St., Winnipeg, MB R3B 3M9
Tel: 204-786-7191
minhlt@leg.gov.mb.ca
www.gov.mb.ca/health/index.html
Responsible for the overall quality of the health system in the province, for maintaining the health system, & for ensuring that the health needs of Manitobans are met. Services are provided through regional delivery systems, hospitals & other health care facilities. The Department also makes insured benefits claims payments for residents of Manitoba related to the cost of medical, hospital, personal care, pharmacare & other health services. To lead the way to quality health care, built with creativity, compassion, confidence, trust & respect; empower Manitobans through knowledge, choices & access to the best possible health resources; & build partnerships & alliances for healthy & supportive communities. To foster innovation in the health care system. This is accomplished through: developing mechanisms to assess & monitor quality of care, utilization & cost effectiveness; fostering behaviours & environments which promote health; & promoting responsiveness & flexibility of delivery systems, & alternative & less expensive services.
Acts Administered:
Atmospheric Pollution Regulation
Collection & Disposal of Wastes Regulation
Fumigation & Pest Control Regulation
Protection of Water Sources Regulation
Public Health Act
Sanitation Regulation
Water Supplies Regulation
Water Works, Sewerage & Sewage Disposal Regulation
X-Ray Safety Regulation

Minister, Hon. Theresa Oswald
Tel: 204-945-3731
Fax: 204-945-0441
minhlt@leg.gov.mb.ca

Deputy Minister, Milton Sussman
Tel: 204-945-3771
Fax: 204-945-4564
dmhlt@leg.gov.mb.ca

Medical Officer of Health, STBBI, Dr. Jocelyn Reimer
Tel: 204-788-6614

Associated Agencies, Boards & Commissions:
• **Addictions Foundation of Manitoba (AFM) / Fondation manitobaine de lutte contre les dépendances**
1031 Portage Ave.
Winnipeg, MB R3G 0R8
Tel: 204-944-6200
Fax: 204-786-7768
library@afm.mb.ca
www.afm.mb.ca
• **Appeal Panel for Home Care**
#4012, 300 Carlton St.
Winnipeg, MB R3B 3M9
Tel: 204-788-6788
Fax: 204-948-2024
Toll-free: 800-491-4993
appeals@gov.mb.ca
www.gov.mb.ca/health/appealboard/appeals.html

• **CancerCare Manitoba**
Tel: 204-787-2197
Toll-free: 866-561-1026
www.cancercare.mb.ca
• **Health Information Privacy Committee**
#4043, 300 Carlton St.
Winnipeg, MB R3B 3M9
www.gov.mb.ca/health/hipc/index.html
• **Hearing Aid Board**
• **Manitoba Drug Standards & Therapeutics Committee (MDSTC)**
#1014, 300 Carlton St.
Winnipeg, MB R3B 3M9
Tel: 204-786-7317
Fax: 204-942-2030
www.gov.mb.ca/health/mdbif/review.html
• **Manitoba Health Appeal Board**
#4011, 300 Carlton St.
Winnipeg, MB R3B 3M9
Tel: 204-788-6704
Fax: 204-948-2024
Toll-free: 866-744-3257
Quasi-judicial body responsible for making decisions on appeals under The Health Services Insurance Act, The Ambulance Services Act & The Mental Health Act.
• **Medical Review Committee**
#200, 301 Weston St.
Winnipeg, MB R3E 3H4
Tel: 204-945-7350
Fax: 204-948-2682
www.gov.mb.ca/mit/boards/medical.html

Public Health & Primary Health Care
300 Carlton St., 2nd Floor, Winnipeg, MB R3B 3M9
Mission is to encourage the prevention of illness & injury, coordinate access to health care, & strengthen existing primary health care services with new initiatives
Executive Director, Public Health Programs & Strategies, Anita Moore
Tel: 204-788-6781

Regional Policy & Programs

Associated Agencies, Boards & Commissions:
• **Assiniboine Regional Health Authority**
192 - 1st Ave.
PO Box 579
Souris, MB R0K 2C0
Tel: 204-483-5000
Fax: 204-483-5005
Toll-free: 888-682-2253
assineboinerha@arha.ca
www.assiniboine-rha.ca
• **Brendon Regional Health Authority**
150 - 7th St.
Brandon, MB R7A 7M2
Tel: 204-578-2300
Fax: 204-578-2820
www.brandonrha.mb.ca
Chief Evecutive Officer, Brian Scoonbaert
• **Burntwood Regional Health Authority**
867 Thompson Dr. South
Thompson, MB R8N 1Z4
Tel: 204-677-5353
Fax: 204-677-5366
www.brha.mb.ca
Chief Executive Officer, Gloria King
• **Central Regional Health Authority**
180 Centennaire Dr.
Southport, MB R0H 1N0
Tel: 204-428-2720
Fax: 204-428-2779
Toll-free: 800-742-6509
www.rha-central.mb.ca
Chief Executive Officer, Kathy McPhail
• **Churchill Regional Health Authority**
Churchill Health Centre
Churchill, MB R0H 0E0
Tel: 204-675-8318
Fax: 204-675-2243
www.churchillrha.com
Chief Executive Officer, Derry Martens
• **Interlake Regional Health Authority**
589 - 3rd Ave. South
Stonewall, MB R0C 2Z0
Tel: 204-467-4742
Fax: 204-467-4750
Toll-free: 888-488-2299
www.irha.mb.ca
Chief Executive Officer, Randy Locke
• **Nor-Man Regional Health Authority**
84 Church St.
PO Box 130
Flin Flon, MB R8A 1M7
Tel: 204-687-1300
Fax: 204-687-6405
www.norman-rha.mb.ca
Chief Executive Officer, Drew Lockhart
• **North Eastman Regional Health Authority**
24 Aberdeen Ave.
PO Box 339
Pinawa, MB R0E 1L0
Tel: 204-753-3101
Fax: 204-753-2015
Toll-free: 800-753-2012
www.neha.mb.ca
Chief Executive Officer, Ron Van Denakker
• **Parkland Regional Health Authority**
625 Third St. SW
Dauphin, MB R7N 1R7
Tel: 204-638-2118
Fax: 204-622-6232
Toll-free: 800-259-7541
www.prha.mb.ca
Chief Executive Officer, Kevin McKnight
• **South Eastman Regional Health Authority**
PO Box 470
La Broquerie, MB R0A 0W0
Tel: 204-424-5880
Fax: 204-424-5888
Toll-free: 866-716-5633
www.sehealth.mb.ca
Chief Executive Officer, Monique Vielfaure Mackenzie
• **Winnipeg Regional Health Authority**
650 Main St.
Winnipeg, MB R3B 1E2
Tel: 204-926-7000
Fax: 204-926-7007
www.wrha.mb.ca
Chief Executive Officer, Arlene Wilgosh

Manitoba Healthy Child Office

332 Bannatyne Ave., 3rd Fl., Winnipeg, MB R3A 0E2
Tel: 204-945-2266
Toll-Free: 888-848-0140
healthychild@gov.mb.ca
www.gov.mb.ca/healthychild
Office provides leadership & encourages actions that address health concerns & reduces the need for medical care for children

Minister, Hon. Kevin Chief
Tel: 204-945-1373
Fax: 204-948-2703

Director, Programs, Susan Tessler
Tel: 204-945-1275

Manitoba Hydro

360 Portage Ave., PO Box 815 Stn. Main, Winnipeg, MB R3C 2P4
Tel: 204-474-3311
publicaffairs@hydro.mb.ca
www.hydro.mb.ca
Manitoba Hydro (MH) is a major energy utility. One of the largest electricity & natural gas utilities in Canada, it serves 521,600 electric customers throughout Manitoba & 261,150 gas customers in various communities throughout southern Manitoba. Virtually all electricity generated by the provincial Crown Corporation is from self-renewing water power. MH is the major distributor of natural gas in the province. Developing & implementing an environmental management system consistent with ISO standards. Actively pursuing a vairety or projects & programs aimed at reducing GHG & vehicle emissions, recycling, conserving energy, digging out contaminated soils, partnering with NGOs

Minister responsible, Hon. Dave Chomiak
Tel: 204-945-5356
Fax: 204-948-2692
miniem@leg.gov.mb.ca

President/CEO, Scott Thomson
Tel: 204-474-3600

Senior Vice-President, Finance & Administration & CFO, Vince Warden

Vice-President, Transmission, Ed Tymofichuk

Manitoba Immigration & Multiculturalism

Legislative Building, 317, 450 Broadway Ave., Winnipeg, MB R3C 0V8
Tel: 204-945-4079
Fax: 204-945-8312
minlab@leg.gov.mb.ca
www.gov.mb.ca/labour
Acts Administered:
Construction Industry Safety Regulation
Employment Standards Code
Fibrosis & Silicosis Regulation
Fires Prevention & Emergency Response Act
Forestry, Logging & Log Hauling Regulation
Gas & Oil Burner Act
Hearing Conservation & Noise Control Regulation
Minimum Wage & Working Conditions Regulation
Operation of Mines Regulation
Sanitary & Hygienic Welfare Regulation
Steam & Pressure Plants Act
Worker Recruitment and Protection Act
Workplace Hazardous Materials Information System Regulation
Workplace Health Hazard Regulation
Workplace Safety & Health Act
Workplace Safety & Health Committee Regulation
Workplace Safety Regulation

Minister, Christine Melnick
Tel: 204-945-4079
Fax: 204-945-8312
minimm@leg.gov.mb.ca

Deputy Minister, Hugh Eliasson
Tel: 204-945-4076

Director, Multiculturalism Secretariat, Tehani Jainarine
Tel: 204-945-2361

Associated Agencies, Boards & Commissions:
• **Advisory Council on Workplace Safety & Health (SAFE Work)**
#200, 401 York Ave.
Winnipeg, MB R3C 0P8
Tel: 204-945-3446
Fax: 204-945-4556
safemanitoba.com
The Advisory Council on Workplace Safety & Health was established in 1977 under the authority of the Workplace Safety & Health Act. The council reports directly to the Minister of Labour & Immigration. The council advises & makes recommendations to the Minister of Labour & Immigration concerning general workplace safety & health issues, protection of workers in specific situations & appointment of consultants & advisors.
Chair, Dennis Nikkel
• **Board of Electrical Examiners**
#500, 401 York Ave
Winnipeg, MB R3C 0P8
Tel: 204-945-3507
terry.rieger@gov.mb.ca
• **Gas Advisory Board**

Chair, Terry Reiger
terry.reiger@gov.mb.ca
• **Manitoba Ethnocultural Advisory & Advocacy Council (MEAAC)**
215 Notre Dame Ave. 4th Fl.
Winnipeg, MB R3B 1N3
Tel: 204-945-2339
Fax: 204-948-2323
Toll-free: 800-665-8332
meaac@gov.mb.ca
www.gov.mb.ca/immigration/multiculturalism/meaac.html
• **Multiculturalism Secretariat**
213 Notre Dame Ave., 9th Fl.
Winnipeg, MB R3B 1N3
Tel: 204-945-5632
multisec@gov.mb.ca
www.gov.mb.ca/immigration/multiculturalism

Manitoba Infrastructure & Transportation

Legislative Building, #203, 450 Broadway Ave., Winnipeg, MB R3C 0V8
Tel: 204-945-3723
Fax: 204-945-7610
www.gov.mb.ca/mit/
Acts Administered:
CentrePort Canada Act
Crown Lands Act
Drivers & Vehicles Act
Highway Traffic Act
Highways & Transportation Act
Highways Protection Act
Land Acquisition Act
Manitoba Floodway Authority Act
Manitoba Water Services Board Act
Off-Road Vehicles Act
Provincial Parks Act
Provincial Railways Act
Trans-Canada Highway Act
Water Resources Administration Act
Wild Rice Act

Minister, Hon. Steve Ashton
Tel: 204-945-3723
Fax: 204-945-7610
mininfratran@leg.gov.mb.ca

Deputy Minister, Doug McNeil
Tel: 204-945-4145

Associated Agencies, Boards & Commissions:
• Disaster Assistance Appeal Board
• Highway Traffic Board/Motor Transport Board
#200, 301 Weston St.
Winnipeg, MB R3E 3H4
Tel: 204-945-8912
Fax: 204-783-6529
www.gov.mb.ca/mit/boards/traffic.html
Chair, Alfred Rivers
• Manitoba Floodway Authority (MFA)
#200, 155 Carlton St.
Winnipeg, MB R3C 3H8
Tel: 204-945-4900
Fax: 204-948-2462
Toll-free: 866-356-6355
floodway@gov.mb.ca
www.floodwayauthority.mb.ca
Separate, independent, publicly accountable provincial agency that will manage the expansion & maintenance of the Red River Floodway on behalf of Manitobans.
CEO, Ernie Gilroy
• License Suspension Appeal Board/Medical Review Committee
#200, 301 Weston St.
Winnipeg, MB R3E 3H4
Tel: 204-945-7350
Fax: 204-948-2682
• Manitoba Land Value Appraisal Commission
#1144, 363 Broadway
Winnipeg, MB R3C 3N9
Tel: 204-945-5455
Fax: 204-948-2235
www.gov.mb.ca/mit/boards/land.html

Accommodation Services Division

1700 Portage Ave., Winnipeg, MB R3J 0E1
Asst. Deputy Minister, Chris Hauch
Tel: 204-945-7535
Fax: 204-945-2546
Acting Director, Corporate Services, Accommodation Policy & Planning, Don Armstrong
Tel: 204-945-2009

Emergency Measures Organization (EMO)

405 Broadway Ave., 15th Floor, Winnipeg, MB R3C 3L6
Tel: 204-945-4772
Fax: 204-945-4929
Toll-Free: 888-267-8298
emo@gov.mb.ca
www.manitobaemo.ca
Coordinates emergency response, municipal emergency planning & training, & disaster recovery programs
Executive Director, Chuck Sanderson
Tel: 204-945-4772
Fax: 204-945-4929

Supply & Services Division

270 Osborne St. North, Winnipeg, MB R3C 1V7
Asst. Deputy Minister, Tracey Danowski
Tel: 204-945-6340
Fax: 204-948-2509
Chief Operating Officer, Materials Distribution Agency, David Bishop
Tel: 204-945-6043
Fax: 204-948-3273
#7, 1715 St. James St.
Winnipeg, MB R3H 1H3

Transportation Policy Division

Legislative Bldg., #209, 450 Broadway, Winnipeg, MB R3C 0V8
Asst. Deputy Minister, John Spacek
Tel: 204-945-1025

Water Management & Structures Division

Assistant Deputy Minister, Doug McMahon
Tel: 204-945-3113
Director, Ron Richardson
Tel: 204-945-6494

Manitoba Floodway & East Side Road Authority

Manitoba Innovation, Energy & Mines

Tel: 204-945-3744
Toll-Free: 866-626-4862
mgi@gov.mb.ca
Acts Administered:
Gaming Control Act
Manitoba Hydro Act

Minister, Dave Chomiak
Tel: 204-945-5356

Deputy Minister, Grant Doak
Tel: 204-945-2771

Special Advisor to the Minister, Manitoba Hydro, Carolina Stecher
Tel: 204-945-3365

Associated Agencies, Boards & Commissions:
• Industrial Technology Centre
#200, 78 Innovation Dr.
Winnipeg, MB R3T 6C2
Tel: 204-480-3333
Fax: 204-480-0345
tech@itc.mb.ca
www.itc.mb.ca
Chair, John Clarkson
• Mining Board
#360, 1395 Ellice Ave.
Winnipeg, MB R3G 3P2
Tel: 204-489-0018
Arbitration of disputes between surface rights holders & mineral rights holders with respect to accessing of minerals other than oil & gas.
Presiding Member, Harvey J. Slobodzian
• Surface Rights Board
#360, 1395 Ellice Ave.
Winnipeg, MB R3G 3P2
Tel: 204-945-0731
Fax: 204-948-2578
Toll-free: 800-282-8069
Arbitrates disputes relating to right of entry or compensation for surface rights used by holders of oil & gas rights.
Presiding Member, Thomas Arthur Cowan
• Manitoba Education, Research & Learning Information Networks (MERLIN)
#100 - 135 Innovation Dr., University of Manitoba
Winnipeg, MB R3T 6A8
Tel: 204-474-7800
Fax: 204-474-7830
Toll-free: 800-430-6404
www.merlin.mb.ca
• Manitoba Health Research Council
#P216, 770 Bannatyne Ave.
Winnipeg, MB R3E 0W3
Tel: 204-775-1096
Fax: 204-786-5401
info@mhrc.mb.ca
mhrc.mb.ca
• Manitoba Gaming Control Commission
#800, 215 Garry St.
Winnipeg, MB R3C 3P3
Tel: 204-954-9400
Fax: 204-954-9450
Toll-free: 800-782-0363
information@mgcc.mb.ca
www.mgcc.mb.ca
Other Communication: Toll Free Fax: 1-866-999-6688
To regulate and control gaming activity in Manitoba by protecting the public interest, being proactive and responsive to Manitoba's evolving gaming environment and working in consultation with our clients, stakeholders and partners to establish fair, balanced and responsible gaming practices.

Administration & Finance

Executive Director, Financial & Administrative Services (Shared), Craig Halwachs
Tel: 905-945-3675
Director, Finance & Accountability, Peter Moreira
Tel: 204-945-7281
Supervisor of Accounting Services, Shirley Dimaala-Martin
Tel: 204-945-2176

Business Transformation & Technology

Asst. Deputy Minister, Gisela Rempel
Tel: 204-945-2692
Executive Director, ICT Management Services, Marion Guinn
Tel: 204-945-7629
Executive Director, ICT Strategic Services & Innovation, Ken K. Lamoureux
Tel: 204-945-7385

Legislative Building Information Systems

Acting Office Manager, Legislative Building Information Systems, Corazon Magnayon
Tel: 204-945-6219
Manager, Application Development, Bryan Lam
Tel: 204-945-0121
Manager, LBIS, Technical Services, Robert Bazzocchi
Tel: 204-945-0544
Senior Technical Specialist, Technical Services, Harry Van Ry
Tel: 204-945-0766

Mineral Resources Division

343 Legislative Bldg., 450 Broadway, Winnipeg, MB R3C 0V8
Fax: 204-948-2692
Assistant Deputy Minister, John Fox
Tel: 204-945-4317
Director, Manitoba Geological Survey, Ric Syme
Tel: 204-945-6556
Coordinator, Aboriginal Consultation, Minerals Policy & Business Development, Garry Courchene
Tel: 204-945-6563
Coordinator, Minerals Convention, Minerals Policy & Business Developments, Shirley Holgate
Tel: 204-945-2691
Director, Mines Branch, Ernie Armitt
Tel: 204-945-6505
Director, Petroleum Branch, Keith Lowdon
Tel: 204-945-6574

Science, Innovation & Business Development

343 Legislative Bldg., 450 Broadway, Winnipeg, MB R3C 0V8
Fax: 204-948-2692
Business Development Associate, Tim McIsaac
Tel: 204-945-0287
Director, Broadband Initiatives, Maurice Montreuil
Tel: 204-474-7098
Acting Director, Business Development, Knowledge Enterprises, Cindy Hodges
Tel: 204-945-6657
Senior Executive Director, Life Sciences, Douglas McCartney
Tel: 204-945-6298
Acts Administered:
Expropriation Act
Transboundary Pollution Reciprocal Access Act

Executive Director, Administration & Finance, Patrick J Sinnott
Tel: 204-945-2880

•
Chief Medical Examiner, Dr. Thambirajah Balachandra
•
Tel: 204-945-2703
Public Trustee, Joanna K. Knowlton
Tel: 204-945-2703

Manitoba Local Government

#301, 450 Broadway Ave., Winnipeg, MB R3C 0V8
Fax: 204-945-1383
mnia@leg.gov.mb.ca
www.gov.mb.ca/ia/
The mission is to improve the economic, social & environmental wellbeing of Manitoba communities & citizens. The Department serves individuals, local governments, community organizations & businesses; & establishes a legislative, financial, planning & policy framework that supports democratic, accountable, effective & financially efficient local government, & the sustainable development of our communities. Programs are aimed at meeting particular needs for training, on-going advice, technical analysis & funding related to community revitalization & development, infrastructure development, land management, business support & local governance. The Department functions as an advocate of community needs, a catalyst & co-ordinator of action, promotes & participates in partnerships with private sector & non-government organizations & intergovernmental alliances.
Acts Administered:
Emergency 911 Public Safety Answering Point Act
Emergency Measures Act
Municipal Act
Municipal Assessment Act
Planning Act (in part)
Prearranged Funeral Services Act
Regional Waste Management Authorities Act

Minister, Hon. Ron Lemieux
Tel: 204-945-3788
Fax: 204-945-1383
minlg@leg.gov.mb.ca

Deputy Minister, Intergovernmental Affairs, Linda McFadyen
Tel: 204-945-4309
Fax: 204-945-5255
dmlg@leg.gov.mb.ca

Associated Agencies, Boards & Commissions:
• **Manitoba Municipal Board**
#1144, 363 Broadway
Winnipeg, MB R3C 3N9
Tel: 204-945-2941
Fax: 204-948-2235
www.gov.mb.ca/municipalboard/index.html
Chair, Peter Diamant
Vice-Chair, Tanis Bjornson
• **Taxicab Board**
#200, 301 Weston St.
Winnipeg, MB R3E 3H4
Tel: 204-945-8919
Fax: 204-948-2315
Joan.Wilson@gov.mb.ca
www.gov.mb.ca/ia/taxicab/taxicab.html

Canada-Manitoba Infrastructure Secretariat
Tel: 204-945-4074
Fax: 204-945-2035
Toll-Free: 800-268-4883
infra@gov.mb.ca

Community Planning & Development
Assistant Deputy Minister, Ramona Mattix
Tel: 204-945-6117
Director, Community & Regional Planning, David Neufeld
Tel: 204-945-2192
Fax: 204-945-5059
Director, Planning Policy & Programs, Jon Gunn
Tel: 204-945-3864

Provincial-Municipal Support Services
#508, 800 Portage Ave., Winnipeg, MB R3G 0N4
Provincial Municipal Assessor, Assessment Branch, Mark Boreskie
Tel: 204-945-2604
Fax: 204-945-1994
assessment@gov.mb.ca
Other Communications: Web Site: www.gov.mb.ca/assessment

Manitoba Liquor Control Commission

1555 Buffalo Place, PO Box 1023Winnipeg, MB R3C 2X1
Tel: 204-284-2501
contact@mlcc.mb.ca
www.mlcc.mb.ca

Minister, Hon. Greg Selinger
Tel: 204-284-2501

Chair, Carmen Neufeld

Vice-Chair, Fran Frederickson

President & CEO, Ken Hildahl

Commissioner, Ed Azure

Commissioner, Janine Ballingall Scotten

Commissioner, Les Crisostomo

Commissioner, Garry Hammerback

Commissioner, Eugene Kostyra

Commissioner, Maria Moore

Commissioner, Aidan O'Brien

Commissioner, Myrna A. Phillips

Minister responsible, Steve Ashton

President/CEO, Winston Hodgins

Manitoba Workers' Compensation Board

333 Broadway Ave., Winnipeg, MB R3C 4W3
Tel: 204-954-4321
Fax: 204-954-4999
Toll-Free: 800-362-3340
wcb@wcb.mb.ca
www.wcb.mb.ca

President/CEO, Winston Maharaj

Vice President, Prevention, Assessments & Customer Service, Alice Sayant

Vice President, Rehabilitation & Compensation Services, Dave Scott

Director, Communications/SAFE Work, Warren Preece

Government of New Brunswick

Seat of Government: PO Box 6000Fredericton, NB E3B 5H1
www.gnb.ca
The Province of New Brunswick entered Confederation July 1, 1867. It has an area of 71,355.12 km2. The Statistics Canada census population in 2011 was 751,171.

New Brunswick Department of Agriculture, Aquaculture & Fisheries / Agriculture, Aquaculture et Pêches

Agricultural Research Station (Experimental Farm), PO Box 6000Fredericton, NB E3B 5H1
Tel: 506-453-2666
Fax: 506-453-7170
DAAF-MAAP@gnb.ca
www.gnb.ca/aquaculture
Acts Administered:
Agricultural Land Protection & Development Act
Agricultural Operation Practices Act
Agricultural Producers Registration and Farm Organizations Funding
Aquaculture Act
Farm Credit Corporation Assistance Act
Farm Improvement Assistance Loans Act
Farm Machinery Loans Act
Fish & Wildlife Act (in part)
Fisheries and Aquaculture Development Act
Inshore Fisheries Representation Act
Livestock Incentives Act
Livestock Operations Act
Marshland Reclamation Act
Mining Act
Natural Products Act
Plant Health Act
Potato Disease Eradication Act

Minister, Agriculture, Aquaculture, & Fisheries, Hon. Michael Olscamp
Tel: 506-453-2662
Fax: 506-453-3402
Mike.Olscamp@gnb.ca

Deputy Minister, Robert Rioux
Tel: 506-453-2450
Robert.Rioux@gnb.ca

Director, Communications, Gisèle Regimbal
Tel: 506-444-4218
Fax: 506-444-5022
Gisele.Regimbal@gnb.ca

Director, Policy & Planning, Shirley Stuible
Tel: 506-453-3451
Fax: 506-453-5210
shirley.stuible@gnb.ca

Associated Agencies, Boards & Commissions:
• **New Brunswick Agricultural Insurance Commission / Commission de L'assurance Agricole du Nouveau-Brunswick**
c/o Department of Agriculture, Aquaculture & Fisheries
PO Box 6000
Fredericton, NB E3B 5H1
Tel: 506-453-2185
Fax: 506-453-7406
daa-maa@gnb.ca
Agricultural Insurance Commission is responsible for administering the delivery to producers of an agricultural insurance plan to provide insurance protection against losses of production. This plan is funded through producer premiums and through contributions from the Province of New Brunswick and the Government of Canada.
• **New Brunswick Farm Products Commission / Commission des produits de ferme du Nouveau-Brunswick**
c/o Department of Agriculture, Aquaculture & Fisheries
PO Box 6000
Fredericton, NB E3B 5H1
Tel: 506-453-3647
Fax: 506-444-5969
Products Act. ment/administrative support to the Commission in the monitoring of commodity boards under the provisions of the Natural Products Act.
Chair, Bob Shannon
Tel: 506-453-3647
Bob.Shannon@gnb.ca
General Manager, Robert Goggin
Tel: 506-453-3647
robert.goggin@gnb.ca
Specialist, Dan Draper
Tel: 506-453-5920
Dan.Draper@gnb.ca
Analyst, Laura Poffenroth
Tel: 506-453-5918
Laura.Poffenroth@gnb.ca

Agriculture & Bio-Economy Division / Agriculture et Bioéconomie
DAAF-MAAP@gnb.ca
www.gnb.ca/agriculture
To encourage the development of a prosperous, globally competitive & sustainable agriculture & agri-food business using the latest technologies to produce & market innovative & safe food as well as other bio-products.
Asst. Deputy Minister, Kevin McKendy
Tel: 506-453-2366
Fax: 506-444-5022
kevin.mckendy@gnb.ca
Executive Director, Livestock Development, Michael Maloney
Tel: 506-453-2457
michael.maloney@gnb.ca
Director, Crop Development, Kevin McCully
Tel: 506-453-3481
kevin.mccully@gnb.ca
Director, Agricultural Financial Programs, Cathy Larochelle
Tel: 506-444-2728
cathy.larochelle@gnb.ca

Director, Land & Environment, Sandi McGeachy
Tel: 506-453-2109
sandi.mcgeachy@gnb.ca
Director, Regional Agri-Business Development, Gerry Chevrier
Tel: 506-453-2172
gerald.chevrier@gnb.ca
Manager, Veterinary Laboratory & Pathology Services, James Goltz
Tel: 506-453-5488
jim.goltz@gnb.ca
Manager, Food Safety & Quality, Clinton McLean
Tel: 506-453-6735
clint.mclean@gnb.ca

Fisheries Division / Pêches
DAAF-MAAP@gnb.ca
www.gnb.ca/agriculture
Asst. Deputy Minister, Perron Sadie
Tel: 506-457-6964
Fax: 506-444-5022
sadie.perron@gnb.ca
Executive Director, Fisheries Management & Operations, Yvon Chiasson
Tel: 506-453-8432
Fax: 506-462-5929
yvon.chiasson@gnb.ca
Director, Business Development, Louis Arsenault
Tel: 506-743-7222
louis.arsenault@gnb.ca
Director, Licensing & Technical Services, Ghislain Chiasson
Tel: 506-453-2252
ghislain.chiasson@gnb.ca
Bouctouche
26 Acadie St., Bouctouche, NB E4S 2T2
Tel: 506-743-7222
Fax: 506-743-7229
DAAF-MAAP@gnb.ca
Regional Director, Louis Arsenault
Caraquet
22 St-Pierre Blvd. East, Caraquet, NB E1W 1B6
Tel: 506-726-2400
Fax: 506-726-2419
MDP-DOF@gnb.ca
Regional Director, Mario Gaudet
Shippagan
104 Aquarium St., Shippagan, NB E8S 1H9
Tel: 506-336-3751
Fax: 506-336-3057
DAA-MAA@gnb.ca
Regional Director, Christian Noris

Minister, Economic Development; Minster Responsible for la Francophonie, Regional Development Corporation, Invest NB, the Northern New Brunswick Initiative & Rural Affairs; Deputy Premier; Government House Leader, Hon. Paul Robichaud
Tel: 506-453-5898
Fax: 506-453-6389
paul.robichaud@gnb.ca
Centennial Bldg.
670 King St.
PO Box 6000
Fredericton, NB E3B 5H1

Deputy Minister, Bill Levesque
Tel: 506-453-5897
bill.levesque@gnb.ca
•
Chair, Judy Head
Assistant Deputy Minister, Eric Beaulieu
Tel: 506-453-3412
eric.beaulieu@gnb.ca
Executive Director, Export Development, Joel Richardson
Tel: 506-453-3412
joel.richardson@gnb.ca
Director, Export Development, Michel Albert
Tel: 506-444-5053
michel.albert@gnb.ca
Manager, Knowledge Industries & Innovation, Jonathan Downey
Tel: 506-444-6758
Jon.downey@gnb.ca
Project Executive, Industry Services, Gilles Johnson
Tel: 506-444-2025
gilles.johnson@gnb.ca

Director, Information Technology, Doug Waugh
Tel: 506-457-7324
doug.waugh@gnb.ca
Manager, Financial Administration, Jean-Bernard Guignard
Tel: 506-453-3707
jean-bernard.guignard@gnb.ca
Supervisor, Records Management, Daphne MacKay
Tel: 506-453-8162
daphne.mackay2@gnb.ca

Northern Development Division
Harbourview Place, #400, 275 Main St., Bathurst, NB E2A 1A9
Tel: 506-547-2227
Fax: 506-547-2269
www.newbrunswick.ca
The Northern Development Division is engaged in the administration of financial programs.
Assistant Deputy Minister, Northern Development, Roger Robichaud
Tel: 506-547-2227
roger.robichaud@gnb.ca
Director, Northern Development, Rick Lloyd
Tel: 506-547-2227
rick.lloyd@gnb.ca
Director, Northern Development, Denis Roy
Tel: 506-547-2227
denis.roy2@gnb.ca
Financial Officer, Financial Programs, Sylvain Savoie
Tel: 506-547-2227
sylvain.savoie@gnb.ca

New Brunswick Department of Energy & Mines

Brunswick Square, #100M, 1 Germain St., Saint John, NB E2L 4V1
Tel: 506-658-3180
Fax: 506-643-2919
DOEweb@gnb.ca
www.gnb.ca/energy
The New Brunswick Department of Energy & Mines is responsible for the following: ensuring a reliable, secure, & cost effective energy supply; promoting economic efficiency in energy systems; encouraging economic development opportunities; protecting & improving the environment; & ensuring an effective regulatory regime.
Acts Administered:
Bituminous Shale
Electricity
Energy & Utilities Board
Energy Efficiency
Gas Distribution, 1999
Mining
Oil & Natural Gas
Ownership of Minerals
Petroleum Products Pricing
Pipeline
Underground Storage

Minister, Energy & Mines, Hon. Craig Leonard
Tel: 506-453-2240
Fax: 506-453-5329
Craig.Leonard@gnb.ca

Deputy Minster, Jean Finn
Tel: 506-658-3179
jean.finn@gnb.ca

Assistant Deputy Minster, Neil Jacobsen
Tel: 506-658-3132
neil.jacobsen@gnb.ca

Director, Communications, Tyler Campbell
Tel: 506-453-8420
tyler.campbell@gnb.ca

Alternative Energy & Energy Efficiency Division
Brunswick Square, #M100, 1 Germain St., Saint John, NB E2L 4V1
Tel: 506-658-3180
Fax: 506-658-3191
DOEweb@gnb.ca
www.gnb.ca/energy
The division focuses upon energy management initiatives to improve the use & diversity of energy resources. The work of the Alternative Energy & Energy Efficiency Division benefits the environment & the economy.
Director, Alternative Energy & Energy Efficiency Division, Bill Breckenridge
Tel: 506-658-3180
bill.breckenridge@gnb.ca
Policy Advisor, David Duplisea
Tel: 506-658-3180
David.Duplisea@gnb.ca
Policy Advisor, Keith Melvin
Tel: 506-658-3180
Keith.melvin@gnb.ca
Director, Electricity & Nuclear Energy, Stephen Waycott
Tel: 506-658-3126
stephen.waycott@gnb.ca
Policy Advisor, Heather Quinn
Tel: 506-658-3180
Heather.Quinn@gnb.ca
Policy Advisor, David Sollows
Tel: 506-658-3180
david.sollows@gnb.ca

Hydrocarbon Energy Legislative & Regulatory Affairs Division
Brunswick Square, #100M, 1 Germain St., Saint John, NB E2L 4V1
Tel: 506-658-3180
Fax: 506-658-3191
Doeweb@gnb.ca
Through ongoing infrastructure growth & regulatory reform, the Department of Energy works to develop & improve energy sources.
Director, Hydrocarbon Energy Legislative & Regulatory Affairs Division, Patrick Ervin
Tel: 506-658-3180
patrick.ervin@gnb.ca
Policy Advisor, Mary Ann Mann
Tel: 506-658-3180
maryann.mann@gnb.ca
Policy Advisor, Sacha Patino
Tel: 506-658-3180
sacha.patino@gnb.ca

New Brunswick Department of Environment & Local Government

Marysville Place, PO Box 6000Fredericton, NB E3B 5H1
Tel: 506-453-2690
Fax: 506-457-4994
elg/egl-info@gnb.ca
www2.gnb.ca/content/gnb/en/departments/elg.html
Other Communication: Toll-free phone to report pesicide, oil, chemical spills, & other environmental emergencies: 1-800-565-1633
The Departmemt of Environment & Local Government is responsible for environmental stewardship, Efficiency NB, & consultation with municipal governments & Local Service Districts concerning governance issues.
Acts Administered:
Agricultural Land Protection & Development (subsection 10(2) & section 11)
Assessment & Planning Appeal Board
Beverage Containers
Business Improvement Areas
Cemetery Companies (paragraph 5(1)(c))
Clean Air
Clean Environment
Clean Water
Community Planning
Control of Municipalities
Days of Rest
Edmundston Act, 1998
Environmental Trust Fund (except administration of fund)
Evidence (sections 88, 89 & 90)
Gas Distribution Act, 1999 (subsection 18(2), paragraph 32(1)(a), & subsection 39(1))
Highway (sections 58 to 62.1)
Metric Conversion
Mining (subsection 68(2))
Municipal Assistance
Municipal Capital Borrowing
Municipal Debentures
Municipal Thoroughfare Easements
Municipalities (other than subsection 19(8), 125(1), & 188(3))
New Brunswick Municipal Finance Corporation (section 14 & subsection 16(4))
Pesticides Control

Police (paragraph 17.05(2)(b), subsections 17.06(3), & (4), paragraph 17.2(3)(b), & subsections 17.4(3), & (4))
Real Property Tax (section 4 & subsection 5(10))
Service New Brunswick (paragraph 15.1(3)(b))
Society for the Prevention of Cruelty to Animals
Taxation of the LNG Terminal, An Act to Comply with the Request of The City of Saint John
Topsoil Preservation
Unsightly Premises

Minister, Environment & Local Government; Minister Responsible for the Energy Efficiency & Conservation Agency of NB, Hon. Bruce Fitch
Tel: 506-453-2807
Bruce.Fitch@gnb.ca

Deputy Minister, Environment & Local Government; President, Efficiency NB, Denis Caron
Tel: 506-453-3256
denis.caron@gnb.ca

Contact, Public Affairs, Marie-Claude Wedge
Tel: 506-453-3700
Fax: 506-453-3843
Marie-Claude.Wedge@gnb.ca

Associated Agencies, Boards & Commissions:
• Assessment & Plannning Appeal Board
City Centre
PO Box 6000
Fredericton, NB E3B 5H1
Tel: 506-453-2126
Fax: 506-444-4881
lg/gl-info@gnb.ca
The Assessment & Planning Appeal Board hears property assessment appeals, appeals of land use & planning decisions, & appeals of local heritage review board decisions. The board consists of eleven regional panels from across New Brunswick.
Chair, Scott MacGregor
Tel: 506-453-2126
scott.macgregor@gnb.ca
Administrative Assistant, Kathy Malcolm
Tel: 506-453-2126
kathy.malcolm@gnb.ca
• Efficiency NB
#101, 35 Charlotte St.
Saint John, NB E2L 2H3
Tel: 506-643-7826
Fax: 506-643-7835
Toll-free: 866-643-8833
www.efficiencynb.ca
Efficiency NB is a Crown Corporation established in 2005, mandated to promote energy efficiency for the residential, community & business sectors in the province of New Brunswick.
Minister Responsible, Hon. Bruce Fitch
bruce.fitch@gnb.ca
President & CEO, Margaret-Ann Blaney
margaret-ann.blaney@gnb.ca
Director, Residential Sector, Kate Butler
kate.butler@gnb.ca
Director, Commercial & Industrial Sectors, Beth Pollock
beth.pollock@gnb.ca
Director, Finance, Planning & Evaluation, Stephanie Wheaton
stephanie.wheaton@gnb.ca
• Royal District Planning Commission (RDPC)
#1, 49 Winter St.
Sussex, NB E4E 2W8
Tel: 506-432-7530
Fax: 506-432-7539
Toll-free: 888-245-9155
info@royaldpc.com
www.royaldpc.com
Established by a Ministerial Order under the Community Planning Act of the Province of New Brunswick, the Royal District Planning Commission is composed of board members who are appointed by the Minister of Environment & Local Government & municipal partners. It provides land use planning services to the municipalities & unincorporated areas.
The Commission oversees a staff that manages the daily work of the Commission, such as approving subdivision plans & developments; issuing building permits; inspecting new developments & buildings; administering & enforcing subdivision, building, & zoning by-laws; & providing planning advice to the Minister of Environment & Local Government, municipalities, & rural community committees.

Director, Patricia Munkittrick
Officer, Administration, Beverley Wilcox
Geomatic Analyst, Gerald Legacy

Community Planning & Environmental Protection Division
Marysville Place, PO Box 6000Fredericton, NB E3B 5H1
Tel: 506-444-5119
Fax: 506-457-7333
elg/egl-info@gnb.ca
The division is concerned with the state of the environment, sustainable development, impact evaluation & management, standard setting, & enforcement.
Executive Director, State of the Environment, David Schellenberg
Tel: 506-457-4844
dave.schellenberg@gnb.ca
Director, Standards Setting, Program Operations, & Enforcement, Mike Cormier
Tel: 506-444-3635
Mike.Cormier@gnb.ca
Director, Analytical Services, Peter McLaughlin
Tel: 506-453-2477
Peter.McLaughlin@gnb.ca
Director, Performance Excellence Process & Continuous Improvement, Colleen Mullin
Tel: 506-444-5119
Colleen.Mullin@gnb.ca
Director, Environmental Evaluation & Reporting, Darryl Pupek
Tel: 506-457-4844
Darryl.Pupek@gnb.ca
Director, Sustainable Development, Planning, & Impact Evaluation, Paul Vanderlaan
Tel: 506-444-4599
paul.vanderlaan@gnb.ca
Bathurst Regional Office
PO Box 5001Bathurst, NB E2A 3Z9
Tel: 506-547-2092
Fax: 506-547-7655
elg/egl-info@gnb.ca
Regional Director, Paul Fournier
Tel: 506-547-2092
Paul.Fournier@gnb.ca
Engineer, Gaétan Landry
Tel: 506-547-2092
Gaetan.Landry@gnb.ca
Fredericton Regional Office
Priestman Centre, PO Box 6000Fredericton, NB E3B 5H1
Tel: 506-444-5149
Fax: 506-453-2893
elg/egl-info@gnb.ca
Director, Serge Gagnon
Tel: 506-444-5149
Serge.Gagnon@gnb.ca
Engineer, Jennifer Bishop
Tel: 506-444-5149
jennifer.bishop@gnb.ca
Grand Falls Regional Office
PO Box 5001Grand Falls, NB E3Z 1G1
Tel: 506-473-7744
Fax: 506-475-2510
elg/egl-info@gnb.ca
Regional Director, Richard Keeley
Tel: 506-473-7744
Richard.Keeley@gnb.ca
Engineer, Roger Bélanger
Tel: 506-473-7744
Roger.Belanger@gnb.ca
Miramichi Regional Office
Industrial Park, 316 Dalton Ave., Miramichi, NB E1V 3N9
Tel: 506-778-6032
Fax: 506-778-6796
elg/egl-info@gnb.ca
Regional Director, Denis Daigle
Tel: 506-778-6032
Denis.Daigle@gnb.ca
Moncton Regional Office
PO Box 5001Moncton, NB E1C 8R3
Tel: 506-856-2374
Fax: 506-856-2370
elg/egl-info@gnb.ca
Regional Director, Laurie Collette
Tel: 506-856-2374
Laurie.Collette@gnb.ca
Saint John Regional Office
PO Box 5001Saint John, NB E2L 4Y9
Tel: 506-658-2558
Fax: 506-658-3046
elg/egl-info@gnb.ca
Director, Patrick Stull
Tel: 506-658-2558
patrick.stull@gnb.ca
Engineer, Barry Leger
Tel: 506-658-2558
Barry.Leger@gnb.ca
Biologist, Aaron Bennett
Tel: 506-658-2558
Aaron.Bennett@gnb.ca

Corporate Services, Community Funding & Technical Services Division
Marysville Place, PO Box 6000Fredericton, NB E3B 5H1
Tel: 506-453-2020
Fax: 506-457-7800
lg/gl-info@gnb.ca
The division oversees human resources & administrative services, information & technology management, corporate finance, & community funding.
Assistant Deputy Minister, Corporate Services, Community Funding, & Technical Services Division, Alan Roy
Tel: 506-453-6285
alan.roy@gnb.ca
Director, Community Funding & Technical Services, André Chenard
Tel: 506-457-4947
Andre.Chenard@gnb.ca
Director, Information & Technology Management, Laurie Robichaud
Tel: 506-453-2020
Laurie.Robichaud@gnb.ca
Director, Corporate Finance, Yvonne Samson
Tel: 506-453-2020
Yvonne.Samson@gnb.ca
Director, Human Resources & Administration, Mary Ellen Somerville
Tel: 506-453-2020
MaryEllen.Somerville@gnb.ca

Local Government Division
Marysville Place, PO Box 6000Fredericton, NB E3B 5H1
Tel: 506-453-2690
Fax: 506-457-4994
lg/gl-info@gnb.ca
The Local Government Division provides liaison services, financial support, & assistance with municipal functions. Examples of activities include overseeing the restructuring of municipalities & rural communities, & assisting Business Improvement Areas to improve downtown cores.
Assistant Deputy Minister, Local Government, Stephen Battah
Tel: 506-444-4423
stephen.battah@gnb.ca
Executive Director, Local & Regional Governance, Rob Kelly
Tel: 506-453-2154
Rob.Kelly@gnb.ca
Director, Local & Regional Governance, Susan Atkinson
Tel: 506-453-2154
susan.atkinson@gnb.ca
Director, Public Affairs, Ryan Donaghy
Tel: 506-444-4693
Ryan.Donaghy@gnb.ca
Director, Community Finances, Alexandra Ferris
Tel: 506-453-2154
Ali.Ferris@gnb.ca
Director, Special Projects, Sandra Jessop-Roach
Tel: 506-453-2154
Sandra.Roach@gnb.ca
Director, Capacity Building & Local Services, Peter Kavanagh
Tel: 506-444-4423
peter.kavanagh@gnb.ca
Director, Local Governance Policy, Christy Shaw
Tel: 506-453-3700
Christy.Shaw@gnb.ca

Partnerships & Innovation Division
Marysville Place, PO Box 6000Fredericton, NB E3B 5H1
Tel: 506-453-2862
Fax: 506-453-2265
elg/egl-info@gnb.ca
The Partnerships & Innovation Division manages the Climate Change Secretariat & the Green Economy Project.
The Climate Change Secretariat is concerned with greenhouse

gas emission reductions & adaptations. The secretariat also manages engagement with federal, provincial, territorial, & international jurisdictions on climate change issues. Public awareness & education programs are also produced.
The Green Economy Project focuses upon sustainable development & achieving a green economy.
Executive Director, Climate Change Secretariat & Green Economy Project, Darwin Curtis
Tel: 506-457-4844
Darwin.Curtis@gnb.ca
Coordinator, Adaptation, Robert Hughes
Tel: 506-457-4844
Robert.Hughes@gnb.ca
Community Planner, Paul Jordan
Tel: 506-457-4844
paul.jordan@gnb.ca

Policy & Strategic Initiatives Division
Marysville Place, PO Box 6000Fredericton, NB E3B 5H1
Tel: 506-453-3700
Fax: 506-453-7128
elg/egl-info@gnb.ca
The division is responsible for ensuring that policies & strategic planning intitiatives are developed & implemented to support the Department of Environment & Local Government.
Executive Director, Policy & Strategic Initiatives Division, Elizabeth Hayward
Tel: 506-453-8788
bebo.hayward@gnb.ca
Director, Stakeholder Education & Engagement, Michelle Daigle
Tel: 506-453-3700
Michelle.Daigle@gnb.ca
Director, Strategic Planning & Policy Development, Kim Hughes
Tel: 506-453-3700
kim.hughes@gnb.ca
Director, Environmental Policy, Katherine Lefeuvre
Tel: 506-453-3700
katherine.lefeuvre@gnb.ca
Director, Legislative Renewal & Legal Affairs, Denyse Smart
Tel: 506-453-3700
Denyse.Smart@gnb.ca
Director, Inter-governmental Affairs, Stephanie Whalen
Tel: 506-453-3700
Stephanie.Whalen@gnb.ca
Acts Administered:
Environmental Trust Fund (administration of fund)
Fishermen's Disaster Fund Act (functions vested in Provincial Secretary-Treasurer)
Gasoline & Motive Fuel Tax Act

Director, Communications, Brent Staeben
Tel: 506-453-6100
brent.staeben2@gnb.ca

Officer, Communications, Donna Leggatt
Tel: 506-453-3742
Donna.Leggatt@gnb.ca

New Brunswick Department of Health / Santé

PO Box 5100Fredericton, NB E3B 5G8
Tel: 506-457-4800
Fax: 506-453-5243
dh-ms@dh-ms.ca
www.gnb.ca/0051/index-e.asp
The mission of New Brunswick's Department of Health is to work with New Brunswickers in achieving well-being, by promoting self-sufficiency & personal responsibility, & providing approved services as required.
The development & delivery of health programs & services to New Brunswick residents is supported by a range of internal department functions, such as administration, planning & evaluation, & program support. The department provides the continuum of services to prevent illness & disability. Education & awareness raising initiatives promote the health & well-being of New Brunswickers of all ages, so that they can achieve their best potential, while enjoying an independent & healthy lifestyle for as long as possible.
Acts Administered:
Clean Air (Paragraph 8(2a) & Subsection 4)
Clean Water Act (in part)
Health Services Act
Motor Vehicle Act (in part)
Pesticides Control Act (in part)
Public Health
Smoke-Free Places Act, 2004
Tobacco Damages and Health Care Costs Recovery

Minister, Health, Hon. Hugh (Ted) Flemming
Tel: 506-848-5440
Fax: 506-453-5442
Hugh.Flemming@gnb.ca

Deputy Minister, Marc Léger
Tel: 506-475-4800
Marc.Leger@gnb.ca

Administrative Support, Kathy Densmore
Tel: 506-453-2536
Fax: 506-444-4697
kathy.densmore@gnb.ca

Associated Agencies, Boards & Commissions:
• **Psychiatric Patient Advocate Services Review Board**
c/o Dept. of Health, Psychiatric Patient Advocate Services
#505, 860 Main St.
Moncton, NB E1C 1G2
Tel: 506-869-6818
Fax: 506-869-6101
Toll-free: 888-350-4133
A senior lawyer, a psychiatrist (or a physician, if a psychiatrist is unavailable), & a lay person serve on the Psychiatric Patient Advocate Services Review Board, as required under section 30(2) of the Mental Health Act.
The Review Board is engaged in the following activities: granting certificates of detention; delivering an order to administer a treatment; reviewing a treatment; reviewing the status of an involuntary patient; reviewing a patient's competence to give consent; reviewing the patient's access to information regarding his treatment; reviewing a transfer to another jurisdiction; & reviewing the ability of an involuntary patient to manage his estate
• **Psychiatric Patient Advocate Services Tribunal**
c/o Dept. of Health, Psychiatric Patient Advocate Services
#505, 860 Main St.
Moncton, NB E1C 1G2
Tel: 506-869-6818
Fax: 506-869-6101
Toll-free: 888-350-4133
The Psychiatric Patient Advocate Services Tribunal is made up of a lawyer & two members of the public. The tribunal authorizes involuntary admission according to the Mental Health Act. It also authorize the treatment of involuntary patients.

Addiction, Mental Health, Primary Health Care & Extra Mural Services Division / Services de traitement des dépendances, de santé mentale, de soins de santé primaires et extra-muraux
HSBC Place, 520 King St., 5th Fl., PO Box 5100Fredericton, NB E3B 5G8
Tel: 506-457-4800
Fax: 506-453-5243
Health.Sante@gnb.ca
www.gnb.ca/0051/index-e.asp

Communications Branch / Communications
HSBC Place, 520 King St., 5th Fl., PO Box 5100Fredericton, NB E3B 6G3
Tel: 506-457-2356
Fax: 506-444-4697
Health.Sante@gnb.ca
www.gnb.ca/0051/index-e.asp
Public Health services are delivered through the province's seven health regions, under the management of Regional Directors. A Chief Medical Officer of Health & a Deputy Chief Medical Officer of Health oversee the development of policy & regulations, & provide medical operational support to the regional Medical Officers of Health. Public Health Services support healthy growth & development, foster healthy lifestyles, control communicable diseases, & protect the public from adverse health consequences of exposure to chemical, physical & biological agents.
Director, Tracy Burkhardt
Tel: 506-453-2536
tracy.burkhardt@gnb.ca
Media Relations Coordinator, Danielle Phillips
Tel: 506-453-2536
danielle.phillips@gnb.ca

Corporate Services / Services ministériels
HSBC Place, 520 King St., 5th Fl., PO Box 5100Fredericton, NB E3B 6G3
Tel: 506-457-2775
Fax: 506-453-5243
Health.Sante@gnb.ca
www.gnb.ca/0051/index-e.asp
Public Health services are delivered through the province's seven health regions, under the management of Regional Directors. A Chief Medical Officer of Health & a Deputy Chief Medical Officer of Health oversee the development of policy & regulations, & provide medical operational support to the regional Medical Officers of Health. Public Health Services support healthy growth & development, foster healthy lifestyles, control communicable diseases, & protect the public from adverse health consequences of exposure to chemical, physical & biological agents.

Human Resources Branch / Ressources humaines
HSBC Place, 520 King St., 4th Fl., PO Box 5100Fredericton, NB E3B 6G3
Tel: 506-453-2843
Fax: 506-453-2843
Health.Sante@gnb.ca
www.gnb.ca/0051/index-e.asp
Public Health services are delivered through the province's seven health regions, under the management of Regional Directors. A Chief Medical Officer of Health & a Deputy Chief Medical Officer of Health oversee the development of policy & regulations, & provide medical operational support to the regional Medical Officers of Health. Public Health Services support healthy growth & development, foster healthy lifestyles, control communicable diseases, & protect the public from adverse health consequences of exposure to chemical, physical & biological agents.

Institutional Services Division / Services en établissements
HSBC Place, 520 King St., 5th Fl., PO Box 5100Fredericton, NB E3B 6G3
Tel: 506-457-4800
Fax: 506-453-5243
Health.Sante@gnb.ca
www.gnb.ca/0051/index-e.asp
Public Health services are delivered through the province's seven health regions, under the management of Regional Directors. A Chief Medical Officer of Health & a Deputy Chief Medical Officer of Health oversee the development of policy & regulations, & provide medical operational support to the regional Medical Officers of Health. Public Health Services support healthy growth & development, foster healthy lifestyles, control communicable diseases, & protect the public from adverse health consequences of exposure to chemical, physical & biological agents.

New Brunswick Cancer Network / Réseau - Cancer Nouveau-Brunswick
HSBC Place, 520 King St., 2nd Fl., PO Box 5100Fredericton, NB E3B 6G3
Tel: 506-457-5521
Fax: 506-453-5522
Health.Sante@gnb.ca
www.gnb.ca/0051/index-e.asp
Public Health services are delivered through the province's seven health regions, under the management of Regional Directors. A Chief Medical Officer of Health & a Deputy Chief Medical Officer of Health oversee the development of policy & regulations, & provide medical operational support to the regional Medical Officers of Health. Public Health Services support healthy growth & development, foster healthy lifestyles, control communicable diseases, & protect the public from adverse health consequences of exposure to chemical, physical & biological agents.

Office of the Associate Deputy Minister of Health - Francophone Services Division / Bureau de la sous-ministre déléguée du ministère de la santé - Services aux francophones
HSBC Place, 520 King St., 5th Fl., PO Box 5100Fredericton, NB E3B 6G3
Tel: 506-453-2582
Fax: 506-453-5523
Health.Sante@gnb.ca
www.gnb.ca/0051/index-e.asp
Public Health services are delivered through the province's seven health regions, under the management of Regional Directors. A Chief Medical Officer of Health & a Deputy Chief Medical Officer of Health oversee the development of policy & regulations, & provide medical operational support to the regional Med-

ical Officers of Health. Public Health Services support healthy growth & development, foster healthy lifestyles, control communicable diseases, & protect the public from adverse health consequences of exposure to chemical, physical & biological agents.

Office of the Chief Medical Officer of Health Division / Bureau du Médecin-hygiéniste en chef du ministère de la santé - Services aux francophones
HSBC Place, 520 King St., 5th Fl., PO Box 5100Fredericton, NB E3B 6G3
Tel: 506-444-2112
Fax: 506-453-5243
Health.Sante@gnb.ca
www.gnb.ca/0051/index-e.asp
Public Health services are delivered through the province's seven health regions, under the management of Regional Directors. A Chief Medical Officer of Health & a Deputy Chief Medical Officer of Health oversee the development of policy & regulations, & provide medical operational support to the regional Medical Officers of Health. Public Health Services support healthy growth & development, foster healthy lifestyles, control communicable diseases, & protect the public from adverse health consequences of exposure to chemical, physical & biological agents.

Planning, Pharmaceutical Services & Privacy Division / Planification, services pharmaceutiques et protection de la vie privée
HSBC Place, 520 King St., 5th Fl., PO Box 5100Fredericton, NB E3B 6G3
Tel: 506-457-4800
Fax: 506-453-5523
Health.Sante@gnb.ca
www.gnb.ca/0051/index-e.asp
Public Health services are delivered through the province's seven health regions, under the management of Regional Directors. A Chief Medical Officer of Health & a Deputy Chief Medical Officer of Health oversee the development of policy & regulations, & provide medical operational support to the regional Medical Officers of Health. Public Health Services support healthy growth & development, foster healthy lifestyles, control communicable diseases, & protect the public from adverse health consequences of exposure to chemical, physical & biological agents.

New Brunswick Department of Natural Resources / Ressources naturelles

Hugh John Flemming Forestry Centre, PO Box 6000Fredericton, NB E3B 5H1
Tel: 506-453-3826
Fax: 506-444-4367
dnrweb@gnb.ca
www.gnb.ca/naturalresources
The Department of Natural Resources manages all natural resources within the province including fish & wildlife, timber, minerals, Crown lands, & water resources. It is also responsible for the development, protection, allocation, & utilization of resources in a way that is considered economically, environmentally, & socially acceptable.
Acts Administered:
Acts administered by an Associated Agency, Board, Commission or Corporation
Bituminous Shale Act
Conservation Easements Act
Crown Grant Restrictions Act
Crown Lands & Forests Act
Endangered Species Act
Fish & Wildlife Act
Forest Fires Act
Forest Products Act
Leasing Regulation
Maritime Forestry Complex Coporation Act
Mining Act (in part)
National Parks Act
Natural Products Act (in part)
Off-Road Vehicle Act
Oil & Natural Gas Act
Ownership of Minerals Act
Parks Act
Petroleum Act (except most of Part 13)
Protected Natural Areas Act, 2003
Quarriable Substances Act
Scalers Act
Territorial Divisions Act
Transportation of Primary Forest Products Act
Underground Storage Act

Minister, Natural Resources, Hon. Bruce Northrup
Tel: 506-453-2510
Fax: 506-444-5839
bruce.nortrup@gnb.ca

Deputy Minister, Phil LePage
Tel: 506-453-2501
Fax: 506-453-2930
Phil.Lepage@gnb.ca

Director, Communications, Steven Benteau
Tel: 506-453-2614
Fax: 506-457-4881
Steve.Benteau@gnb.ca

Executive Secretary, Ginette Delfrate
Tel: 506-453-2501
Fax: 506-457-4881
Ginette.Delfrate@gnb.ca

Associated Agencies, Boards & Commissions:
• New Brunswick Wildlife Council
c/o New Brunswick Wildlife Trust Fund
PO Box 30030
Fredericton, NB E3B 0H8
Tel: 506-453-6655
Fax: 506-462-5054
wildcoun@nbnet.nb.ca
www.nbwtf.ca/council-membership.asp
The New Brunswick Wildlife Council manages the New Brunswick Wildlife Trust Fund. The Fund was created by the Department of Natural Resources Minister in 1997. Under the Fish & Wildlife Act (O.C. 2002-49), the New Brunswick Wildlife Trust Fund evaluates project applications & advises the Department of Natural Resources Minister. The New Brunswick Wildlife Council is composed of seventeen members who represent environmental, naturalist, Aboriginal, hunting, angling, & trapping groups.
Chair, Robert Chiasson

Corporate Services Division / Services Généraux Division
Hugh John Flemming Forestry Centre, 3rd Fl, PO Box 6000Fredericton, NB E3B 5H1
Tel: 506-453-2178
Fax: 506-453-2930
Assistant Deputy Minister, Corporate Services, Janet Higgins
Tel: 506-453-2501
Fax: 506-453-2930
Janet.Higgins@gnb.ca
Director, Policy and Strategic Initiatives, Lesley Chenier-Aussant
Tel: 506-444-4688
lesley.chenier-aussant@gnb.ca
Director, Human Resource Services, Kathleen Good Waite
Tel: 506-453-2197
Kathleen.GoodWaite@gnb.ca
Director, Financial Services, Jean-Guy Leblanc
Tel: 506-453-3826
JeanGuy.LeBlanc@gnb.ca
Assistant Director, Employee Relations, Barb Macintosh
Tel: 506-453-3863
Barb.Macintosh@gnb.ca
Director, Information Services and Systems, Doris Wu
Tel: 506-457-4922
Doris.Wu@gnb.ca

Lands, Minerals & Petroleum Division / Terres, Minéraux et Pétrole Division
Hugh John Flemming Forestry Centre, PO Box 6000Fredericton, NB E3B 5H1
Tel: 506-453-2684
Fax: 506-453-2930
dnrweb@gnb.ca
www.gnb.ca/0078/minerals/index-e.asp
Asst. Deputy Minister, Samuel McEwan
Tel: 506-453-2684
Sam.McEwan@gnb.ca
Director, Crown Lands, Peter Macnutt
Tel: 506-453-6656
Peter.MacNutt@gnb.ca
Director, Geological Surveys Branch, Leslie Fyffe
Tel: 506-444-5005
Les.Fyffe@gnb.ca
Acting Director, Minerals & Petroleum Development, Endresen Keith
Tel: 506-444-2683
keith.endresen@gnb.ca

Renewable Resources / Ressources renouvelables
Hugh John Flemming Forestry Centre, Suite 310, Fl 3rd, PO Box 6000Fredericton, NB E3B 5H1
Tel: 506-453-2684
Fax: 506-453-2684
dnrweb@gnb.ca
www.gnb.ca/naturalresources
Asst. Deputy Minister, Paul Orser
Tel: 506-453-2684
Paul.Orser@gnb.ca
Executive Director, Regional Operations & Support Services, Julius Tarjan
Tel: 506-453-2684
Julius.Tarjan@gnb.ca

Fish & Wildlife Branch
Manages the province's fisheries & wildlife. By managing fish populations & habitats the Branch develops sport fisheries. Over 160 species of birds, mammals, reptiles & amphibians live in New Brunswick's forests. A Branch goal is to conserve the habitat to support these species. The staff develops environmental protection plans to ensure these resources are protected & maintained.
Director, Mike Sullivan
Tel: 506-453-2440
Fax: 506-453-6699
Manager, Big Game/Furbearer, Kevin Craig
Tel: 506-453-2440
Manager, Fisheries, Peter Cronin
Manager, Species at Risk, Pascal Giasson

Forest Management Branch
Tel: 506-453-2516
Fax: 506-453-6689
To manage Crown timber resource in accordance with Government Policy.
Director, Daniel Murphy
Tel: 506-453-2432
Fax: 506-453-6689
Manager, Robert Dick
Tel: 506-453-2516
Fax: 506-453-6689
robert.dick@gnb.ca
Manager, Forest Pest Management, Nelson Carter
Tel: 506-453-2516
Fax: 506-453-6689
nelson.carter@gnb.ca

New Brunswick Department of Post-Secondary Education, Training & Labour

Chestnut Complex, PO Box 6000Fredericton, NB E3B 5H1
Tel: 506-453-2597
Fax: 506-453-3618
dpetlinfo@gnb.ca
www.gnb.ca/post-secondary
New Brunswick's Department of Post-Secondary Education, Training, & Labour consists of the following divisions: Adult Learning & Employment; Communications; Corporate Services; Labour & Planning; Population Growth; & Post-Secondary Education.

Minister, Post-Secondary Education, Training & Labour, Hon. Danny Soucy
Tel: 506-453-2342
Danny.Soucy@gnb.ca

Deputy Minister, Tom Mann
Tel: 506-453-2343
Tom.Mann@gnb.ca

Adult Learning & Employment Division
Chestnut Complex, PO Box 6000Fredericton, NB E3B 5H1
Tel: 506-453-8202
Fax: 506-453-3038
dpetlinfo@gnb.ca
Adult Learning & Employment Division is composed of the following branches: Aprenticeship & Occupational Certification; Community Adult Learning Services; Employment Development; & the New Brunswick Library Service.
Assistant Deputy Minister, Adult Learning & Employment, Lily Fraser
Tel: 506-444-3479
lily.fraser@gnb.ca

Executive Director, New Brunswick Public Library Service, Sylvie Nadeau
Tel: 506-453-7141
sylvie.nadeau@gnb.ca
Director, Employment Programs & Services, Hélène Bouchard
Tel: 506-453-2814
helene.bouchard@gnb.ca
Director, Employment Development, Diane Hawkins
Tel: 506-453-8707
diane.hawkins@gnb.ca
Director, Community Adult Learning Services, Guy Lamarche
Tel: 506-444-4331
guy.lamarche@gnb.ca
Director, Employment Development Program Design & Support, Cindy Lanteigne
Tel: 506-444-5867
cindy.lanteigne@gnb.ca
Director, Apprenticeship & Occupational Certification, Daniel Mills
Tel: 506-444-3657
daniel.Mills@gnb.ca
Public Services Development Librarian, New Brunswick Public Library Service, Leah Brisco
Tel: 506-457-6713
leah.brisco@gnb.ca
Research & Planning Librarian, New Brunswick Public Library Service, Teresa Johnson
Tel: 506-453-3429
Teresa.Johnson@gnb.ca

Communications Division
Chestnut Complex, PO Box 6000Fredericton, NB E3B 5H1
Tel: 506-444-3465
Fax: 506-444-4314
dpetlinfo@gnb.ca
The Communications Division offers services to every branch & group within the Department of Post-Secondary Education, Training, & Labour. Employees in the division follow the directives of the Cabinet Policy on Communications.
Director, Communications, Marie-Josee Groulx
Tel: 506-444-3465
marie-josee.groulx@gnb.ca

Corporate Services Division
Chestnut Complex, PO Box 6000Fredericton, NB E3B 5H1
Tel: 506-453-3038
dpetlinfo@gnb.ca
Branches within the Corporate Services Division include the following: Corporate Information Management & Administrative Services; Financial Services: Information Technology Services; Facilities Management; Human Resource Services; Departmental Coordination; & Internal Audit & Portfolio Debt Management.
Executive Director, Corporate Services, Lyne Paquet
Tel: 506-453-2587
lyne.paquet@gnb.ca
Director, Information Technology Services, Suzanne Bourgeois
Tel: 506-453-2588
suzanne.bourgeois@gnb.ca
Director, Financial Services, Georges Breau
Tel: 506-444-5225
george.breau@gnb.ca
Director, Departmental Coordination, Linda Clayton
Tel: 506-453-8132
linda.clayton@gnb.ca
Director, Human Resource Services, Michael Murray
Tel: 506-453-8209
michael.murray@gnb.ca
Manager, Facilities Management, Michel Cormier
Tel: 506-453-8244
Michel.Cormier@gnb.ca
Supervisor, Administrative Services, Mavis Banks-Carr
Tel: 506-444-6750
mavis.banks-carr@gnb.ca
Librarian, Corporate Information Management, Mary Comeau
Tel: 506-453-8247
mary.comeau@gnb.ca
Auditor & Consultant, Internal Audit & Portfolio Debt Management, Erica Brown
Tel: 506-444-2157
Erica.Brown@gnb.ca

Labour & Planning Division
Chestnut Complex, PO Box 6000Fredericton, NB E3B 5H1
Tel: 506-453-8202
Fax: 506-453-3038
dpetlinfo@gnb.ca
The Labour & Planning Division consists of the following branches: Employers' Advocate; Employment Standards; Industrial Relations; Labour Market Analysis; Policy & Planning; & Workers' Advocate.
Assistant Deputy Minister, Gérin Girouard
Tel: 506-453-8202
gerin.girouard@gnb.ca
Director, Policy & Planning, Dianne Nason
Tel: 506-444-2071
dianne.nason@gnb.ca
Director, Industrial Relations & Employment Standards, Paula Ultican
Tel: 506-453-2261
paula.ultican@gnb.ca
Manager, Labour Market Analysis, Hope Brewer
Tel: 506-457-7891
Hope.Brewer@gnb.ca
Manager, Workers' Advocate, Guy Dagenais
Tel: 506-453-2149
guy.dagenais@gnb.ca
Manager, Employers' Advocate, Richard Fitzgerald
Tel: 506-457-3510
richard.fitzgerald@gnb.ca

Population Growth Division
Kings Place, PO Box 6000Fredericton, E3B 5H1
Tel: 506-457-7640
Fax: 506-453-3899
pgs-scd@gnb.ca
Issues such as immigration, attraction & repatriation, settlement & multiculturalism, & retention are handled by the Population Growth Division.
Assistant Deputy Minister, Charles Ayles
Tel: 506-444-5663
charles.ayles@gnb.ca
Director, Settlement & Multiculturalism, Ashraf Ghanem
Tel: 506-457-7644
ashraf.ghanem@gnb.ca
Director, Repatriation & Attraction, Ryan Jacobson
Tel: 506-457-7646
ryan.jacobson@gnb.ca
Manager, Immigration, Tammy Caseley
Tel: 506-444-5072
tammy.caseley@gnb.ca
Manager, Immigration, George Itoafa
Tel: 506-444-5055
george.itoafa@gnb.ca
Manager, Federal / Provincial / Territorial Relations & Research, Stephanie Eardley
Tel: 506-457-7642
Stephanie.Eardley@gnb.ca

Post-Secondary Education Division
Beaverbrook Building, PO Box 6000Fredericton, NB E3B 5H1
The Post-Secondary Division is made up of the College Support Service Branch, the University Relations Branch, the Private Occupational Training Branch, & Student Financial Services. The division also oversees the New Brunswick College of Craft & Design.
Director, College Admissions Service, Doris Adams
Tel: 506-789-2016
doris.adams@gnb.ca
Director, Student Financial Services, Michael Barnett
Tel: 506-453-3790
michael.barnett@gnb.ca
Director, New Brunswick College of Craft & Design, Donna Boudreau
Tel: 506-444-2435
donna.boudreau@gnb.ca
Director, University Relations, René Beaulieu
Tel: 506-462-5135
rene.boudreau@gnb.ca
Dean, New Brunswick College of Craft & Design, Keith McAlpine
Tel: 506-444-4056
keith.mcalpine@gnb.ca
Registrar, New Brunswick College of Craft & Design, Nancy Beaulieu
Tel: 506-453-6491
nancy.beaulieu@gnb.ca
Manager, Post-Secondary Education, Margie Layden-Oreto
Tel: 506-462-5127
margie.layden-oreto@gnb.ca

Manager, Financial Assistance Delivery, Gisèle Parkinson
Tel: 506-453-2025
gisele.parkinson@gnb.ca

New Brunswick Department of Public Safety / Sécurité publique

364 Argyle St., PO Box 6000Fredericton, NB E3B 5H1
Tel: 506-453-3992
Fax: 506-453-3870
DPS-MSP.Information@gnb.ca
www.gnb.ca/0276/index-e.asp
The Department of Public Safety provides leadership in the areas of public order & community safety.
It provides fair, accessible, community-focused, & coordinated public safety programs & services. The department also ensures effective inspection & enforcement of designated public safety programs & services. Acting in partnership with communities, the department works to prevent crime, assist victims, & create opportunities for offenders to change.
The Public Safety Department coordinates & cooperates with the federal government in the administration of correctional services & law enforcement in New Brunswick.
Acts Administered:
Boiler & Pressure Vessel Act
Elevators & Lifts Act
Emergency 911 Act
Emergency Measures Act
Fire Prevention Act
Gaming Control (except Part 2)
Industrial Relations (subsection 1(8.11))
Motor Vehicle Act
New Brunswick Building Code Act
Salvage Dealers Licensing Act
Transportation of Dangerous Goods Act

Minister, Public Safety; Solicitor General, Hon. Robert B. Trevors
Tel: 506-453-7414
Fax: 506-453-3870
robert.trevors@gnb.ca; robert.trevors.mla@bellaliant.com

Deputy Minister, Dale Wilson
Tel: 506-453-7412
Dale.Wilson@gnb.ca

Director, Communications & Public Awareness, Deborah Nobes
Tel: 506-444-3323
Deborah.Nobes@gnb.ca

Director, Financial Services, Deborah Carpenter
Tel: 506-453-5446
Fax: 506-444-4743
Deborah.Carpenter@gnb.ca

Director, Human Resources, Andrew Currie
Tel: 506-453-3903
Fax: 506-453-7481
andrew.currie@gnb.ca

Director, Information Technology, Virender Ambwani
Tel: 506-444-4433
Fax: 506-453-3321
vic.ambwani@gnb.ca

Executive Director, Jerome Connors
Tel: 506-453-5975
Jerome.Connors@gnb.ca

Safety Services / Direction des services de sécurité
Provides leadership in the areas of law enforcement & community safety in order to preserve & enhance the quality of life in New Brunswick.
Asst. Deputy Minister, Michael Cameau
Tel: 506-453-7142
Fax: 506-453-3870
michael.cameau@gnb.ca
Executive Director, Michael Johnston
Tel: 506-453-7472
Mike.Johnston@gnb.ca

Regional Development Corporation (RDC) / Société d'aménagement régional (SAR)

RDC Bldg., 836 Churchill Row, PO Box 428Fredericton, NB E3B 5R4

Tel: 506-453-2277
Fax: 506-453-7988
www2.gnb.ca/content/gnb/en/departments/regional_development.html
The Regional Development Corporation is a Crown corporation which carries out its mandate in accordance with the Regional Development Corporation Act. The following are responsibilities of the Corporation: administration & management of development agreements between the Province of New Brunswick & the federal government; assistance in the establishment & development of enterprises & institutions; assistance to municipalities in the planning & development of projects to benefit the public; assistance in the development of tourism & recreational facilities; planning, coordinating, & guiding regional development; & performing duties assigned by the Lieutenant-Governor-in-Council.

Minister Responsible, Hon. Paul Robichaud
Tel: 506-453-5898
Fax: 506-453-6389
paul.robichaud@gnb.ca

President, Denis Caron
Tel: 506-453-8542
denis.caron@gnb.ca

Corporate Secretary, Bruce Macfarlane
Tel: 506-444-4606
bruce.macfarlane@gnb.ca

New Brunswick Research & Productivity Council (RPC) / Conseil de la recherche et de la productivité du Nouveau-Brunswick (RPC)

921 College Hill Rd., Fredericton, NB E3B 6Z9
Tel: 506-452-1212
Fax: 506-452-1395
info@rpc.ca
www.rpc.ca
The New Brunswick Research & Productivity Council's vision is to excel in technological innovation, enabling its partners in business & industry to create wealth & high quality employment opportunities in New Brunswick.
The council works to steadily improve its capacity to develop & apply new technology, in partnership with firms in the private sector. It provides an expanding range of high quality technical services to clients in the global marketplace.
The Research & Productivity Council is registered to the ISO 9001:2000 International Standard.

Executive Director, Eric Cook, P.Eng.
Tel: 506-452-0585
eric.cook@rpc.ca

Chief Financial Officer, Stephen A. Fox
Tel: 506-452-1380
stephen.fox@rpc.ca

Head, Physical Metallurgy, John Aikens
Tel: 506-460-5766
john.aikens@rpc.ca

Head, Food, Fisheries & Aquaculture, Dr. Rachael Ritchie
Tel: 506-452-1365
rachael.ritchie@rpc.ca

Head, Inorganic Analytical Services, Ross Kean
Tel: 506-452-1399
ross.kean@rpc.ca

Head, Mechanical Systems & Diagnostics, John Aikens
Tel: 506-460-5766
john.aikens@rpc.ca

Manager, Organic Analytical Services, Bruce Phillips
Tel: 506-452-1369
bruce.phillips@rpc.ca

Manager, High Res Section, Dr. John Macaulay
Tel: 506-452-1369
john.macaulay@rpc.ca

Manager, Process Technology, Ross Gilders
Tel: 506-460-5672
ross.gilders@rpc.ca

Manager, Air Quality Services, Thelma Green
Tel: 506-452-0586
thelma.green@rpc.ca

Coordinator, Susi Chamberlain
Tel: 506-452-1244
susi.chamberlain@rpc.ca

Executive Assistant, Linda Horsman
Tel: 506-452-1363
Fax: 506-452-1386
linda.horsman@rpc.ca

Senior & Healthy Aging Secretariat

Sartain MacDonald Bldg., 4th Fl., PO Box 6000Fredericton, NB E3B 5H1
Tel: 506-453-2001
Fax: 506-453-2164
seniors@gnb.ca
www.gnb.ca/seniors
The Senior & Healthy Aging Secretariat has the following responsibilities: promoting the healthy aging & wellness of seniors; supporting the Minister Responsible for Seniors; overseeing initiatives under the Renewed Long Term Care Strategy; coordinating strategies that increase support for informal caregivers; producing & disseminating information for seniors; coordinating the Senior Goodwill Ambassador Program; & working with organizations related to seniors.

Minister, Social Development; Minister Responsible for Seniors, Housing, & Community Non-Profit Organizations, Hon. Sue Stultz
Tel: 506-453-2001
Fax: 506-453-2164
sue.stultz@gnb.ca

Deputy Minister, Edith Doucet
Tel: 506-453-2590
Fax: 506-453-2164
Edith.Doucet@gnb.ca

Director, Senior & Healthy Aging Secretariat, André Lepine
Tel: 506-457-6856
Fax: 506-453-2869
Andre.Lepine@gnb.ca

Manager, Communications, Judy Cole
Tel: 506-444-3522
Fax: 506-453-2164
judy.cole@gnb.ca

Advisor, Janice Clarke
Tel: 506-444-4076
Fax: 506-453-2869
janice.clarke@gnb.ca

New Brunswick Department of Tourism, Heritage & Culture

Centennial Building, PO Box 6000Fredericton, NB E3B 5H1
Tel: 506-444-5205
Fax: 506-457-4984
taponlinedirectory@gnb.ca
www2.gnb.ca/content/gnb/en/departments/cthl.html
The Department of Tourism, Heritage & Culture is engaged in facilitating community cultural development throughout New Brunswick and maximizing the profile of the province's tourism industry.

Minister, Tourism, Heritage & Culture, Hon. Trevor Holder
Tel: 506-453-3009
Fax: 506-457-4984
trevor.holder@gnb.ca

Deputy Minister, Kelly Cain
Tel: 506-453-3261
kelly.cain@gnb.ca

Director, Strategic Planning & Policy, Shannon Ferris
Tel: 506-462-5053
shannon.ferris@gnb.ca

Director, Communications, Jane Matthews-Clark
Tel: 506-444-4454
jane.matthews-clark@gnb.ca

Associated Agencies, Boards & Commissions:
• New Brunswick Arts Board / Conseil des arts Nouveau-Brunswick
61 Carleton St.
Fredericton, NB E3B 3T2
Tel: 506-444-4444
Fax: 506-444-5543
Toll-free: 866-460-2787
www.artsnb.ca
The New Brunswick Arts Board promotes the creation of art. The arts funding agency also administers funding programs for professional artists throughout New Brunswick.

Corporate Services
Centennial Building, 6th Fl., PO Box 6000Fredericton, NB E3B 5H1
Tel: 506-453-3115
Fax: 506-444-5760
taponlinedirectory@gnb.ca
Corporate services includes financial planning, monitoring, & consulting, plus human resource services to enhance individual & organizational effectiveness, & information technology services.
Director, Financial Services, Jo-Anne Lang
Tel: 506-444-5813
jo-anne.lang@gnb.ca
Director, Human Resource Services, Barbara Lapointe
Tel: 506-453-2198
barbara.legacy@gnb.ca
Director, Information Technology Services, Doug Waugh
Tel: 506-457-7324
doug.waugh@gnb.ca

Culture & Healthy Living
Place 2000, PO Box 6000Fredericton, NB E3B 5H1
Tel: 506-453-2909
Fax: 506-453-6668
WCScommunication@gnb.ca
Cultural responsiblities include development of the arts, heritage, cultural industries, & the New Brunswick Museum.
The province of New Brunswick also invests in improving health & wellness in homes, schools, workplaces, & communities.
Assistant Deputy Minister, Culture & Healthy Living, Ronald Durelle
Tel: 506-453-3989
Ron.durelle@gnb.ca
Chief Executive Officer, New Brunswick Museum, Jane Fullerton
Tel: 506-643-2346
jane.fullerton@nbm-mnb.ca
Director, Wellness, Michelle Bourgoin
Tel: 506-453-5526
michelle.bourgoin@gnb.ca
Director, Arts Devlopment, Nathalie Dubois
Tel: 506-453-2729
nathalie.dubois@gnb.ca
Director, Sport & Recreation, Roger Duval
Tel: 506-457-4950
roger.duval@gnb.ca
Director, Heritage, William Hicks
Tel: 506-444-5320
bill.hicks@gnb.ca

Marketing, Development & Operations
Centennial Building, 670 King St., 6th Fl., Fredericton, NB E3B 1G1
Tel: 506-444-6752
Fax: 506-453-2854
taponlinedirectory@gnb.ca
Activities include industry & media relations, as well as visit engagement through tourism communication & visitor information centres.
Assistant Deputy Minister, Kelly Cain
Tel: 506-444-4118
kelly.cain@gnb.ca
Director, Sales, Partnerships, & Business Development, Cindy Creamer Rouse
Tel: 506-444-4097
cindy.creamer-rouse@gnb.ca
Director, Product Development, Bruno Laplante
Tel: 506-444-3788
bruno.laplante@gnb.ca
Director, Marketing, Kim Matthews
Tel: 506-453-4284
kim.matthews@gnb.ca

Director, Content Development, Susan Morell
Tel: 506-453-5896
susan.morell@gnb.ca

Tourism Operations
Centennial Building, 6th Fl., PO Box 6000Fredericton, NB E3B 5H1
Tel: 506-444-6752
Fax: 506-453-2854
taponlinedirectory@gnb.ca
Tourism Operations oversees the following provincial parks & historical sites: De la République, Sugarloaf, Mactaquac, New River Beach, Herring Cove, Parlee Beach, Murray Beach, The Ancorage, Mount Carleton, Hopewell Rocks, Village Historique Acadien, Kings Landing, & Miscou.
Director, Tourism Operations, Alain Basque
Tel: 506-453-2170
alain.basque@gnb.ca
Assistant Director, Tourism Operations, Martin MacMullin
Tel: 506-444-5339
martin.macmullin@gnb.ca
Executive Director, Kings Landing Historical Site, Kevin Cormier
Tel: 506-363-4957
kevin.cormier@gnb.ca
Director, Village Historique Acadien, Gabriel Lebreton
Tel: 506-726-2600
gabriel.lebreton@gnb.ca
Director, Mactaquac Provincial Park, Neill Sandwith
Tel: 506-363-4905
neill.sandwith@gnb.ca
Manager, Herring Cove Provincial Park, Dorinda Anthony
Tel: 506-752-7010
Dorinda.Anthony@gnb.ca
Manager, Mount Carleton Provincial Park, Louis Comeau
Tel: 506-235-0793
Louis.Comeau@gnb.ca
Manager, Hopewell Rocks, Guy Daigle
Tel: 506-734-3538
guy.daigle2@gnb.ca
Manager, Sugarloaf Provincial Park, Greg Dion
Tel: 506-789-2366
greg.dion@gnb.ca
Manager, New River Beach Provincial Park & The Anchorage Provincial Park, Lenora Lomax
Tel: 506-755-4042
lenora.lomax@gnb.ca
Manager, New River Beach Provincial Park, Lenora Lomax
Tel: 506-755-4042
lenora.lomax@gnb.ca
Manager, Parlee Beach Provincial Park, Marcel Richard
Tel: 506-533-3363
marcel.richard2@gnb.ca
Manager, De la République Provincial Park, Jocelyne St. Onge
Tel: 506-735-2702
jocelyne.st-onge@gnb.ca
Supervisor, Murray Beach Provincial Park, M. Banks
Tel: 506-538-2628
murraybeach@gnb.ca

New Brunswick Department of Transportation & Infrastructure

Kings Place, PO Box 6000Fredericton, NB E3B 5H1
Tel: 506-453-3939
Fax: 506-453-2900
Transportation.Web@gnb.ca
www.gnb.ca/0113/index-e.asp
The mission of the Department of Transportation & Infrastructure is the maintenance of a safe transportation system & infrastructure within the province of New Brunswick's jurisdiction. The department also monitors & advises on transportation & infrastructure issues of federal jurisdiction.
Acts Administered:
Gas Distribution, 1999 (subsections 18(2) & 39(1))
Highway (except sections 58 to 62.1)
Motor Carrier Act (except licensing of motor carriers)
Public Landings
Public Works
Shortline Railways
Telephone Companies (Chief Highway Engineer under subsection 5(3))

Minister, Transportation & Infrastructure, Hon. Claude Williams
Tel: 506-457-7345
Fax: 506-453-7987
claude.williams@gnb.ca

Deputy Minister, Jean-Marc Dupuis
Tel: 506-453-2549
jean-marc.dupuis@gnb.ca

Director, Communications, Judy Cole
Tel: 506-453-5634
judy.cole@gnb.ca

Associated Agencies, Boards & Commissions:
• Vehicle Management Agency
Vehicle Management Center
PO Box 6000
Fredericton, NB E3B 5H1
Tel: 506-453-3939
Fax: 506-453-3628
Transportation.Web@gnb.ca
The Vehicle Management Agency provides vehicle maintenance & fleet management services to the Government of New Brunswick.
Director, Vehicle Management Agency, Kevin Richard
Tel: 506-453-2601
kevin.richard@gnb.ca
Superintendent, Vehicle Management Agency, Raymond Cashol
Tel: 506-453-2601
Raymond.Cashol@gnb.ca
Manager, Financial Services, Neil Haynes-MacDonald
Tel: 506-453-2601
neil.haynes-macdonald@gnb.ca
Engineer, Vehicle Management Agency, Gilles Beaulieu
Tel: 506-453-2601
gilles.beaulieu@gnb.ca

Buildings Division
Marysville Place, PO Box 6000Fredericton, NB E3B 5H1
Tel: 506-453-3742
Fax: 506-444-4400
Reception.Marysville@gnb.ca
The Building Division oversees the construction & maintenance of New Brunswick's provincial government buildings & leased premises. The division is also responsible for the acquisition & sale of government property.
Assistant Deputy Minister, Buildings Division, Robert Martin
Tel: 506-453-2228
bob.martin@gnb.ca
Executive Director, Design & Construction, Bob Daigle
Tel: 506-453-6118
Bob.Daigle@gnb.ca
Executive Director, Special Projects Development, Scott Gibson
Tel: 506-325-4520
Scott.Gibson@gnb.ca
Director, Planning & Project Development, Pam Barteaux
Tel: 506-453-2362
Pam.Barteaux@gnb.ca
Director, Design Services, Joel Bragdon
Tel: 506-444-5519
Joel.Bragdon@gnb.ca
Director, Property Management, Leah Essensa
Tel: 506-453-2221
Leah.Essensa@gnb.ca

Corporate Services & Fleet Management Division
Kings Place, PO Box 6000Fredericton, NB E3B 5H1
Tel: 506-453-3939
Fax: 506-453-7987
Transportation.Web@gnb.ca
The following services are provided by the Corporate Services & Fleet Management Division: administration; financial services; human resources; information technology services; & fleet management for the Government of New Brunswick.
Assistant Deputy Minister, Corporate Services & Fleet Management, Kim Daley
Tel: 506-453-3939
kim.daley@gnb.ca
Director, Human Resources, Myrna Belyea-Tracy
Tel: 506-444-5531
Myrna.Belyea-Taccy@gnb.ca
Director, Information Management & Technology, Colleen Boldon
Tel: 506-453-4498
colleen.boldon@gnb.ca
Director, Financial & Administrative Services, Charlotte Valley
Tel: 506-453-3389
Charlotte.Valley@gnb.ca

Engineering Services Division
Kings Place, PO Box 6000Fredericton, NB E3B 5H1
Tel: 506-453-3939
Fax: 506-453-7987
Transportation.Web@gnb.ca
Responsibilities of the Engineering Services Division are as follows: offering technical expertise; supporting the design of highway & bridge projects; & coordinating technical transportation research.
Assistant Deputy Minister, Dale Forster
Tel: 506-453-3939
dale.forster@gnb.ca
Executive Director, Operations, David Cogswell
Tel: 506-453-3939
david.cogswell@gnb.ca
Executive Director, Engineering Services, Carol MacQuarrie
Tel: 506-453-3939
carol.macquarrie@gnb.ca
Director, Planning & Land Management, Nancy Lynch
Tel: 506-453-5649
Nancy.Lynch@gnb.ca
Director, Maintenance & Traffic, Kevin Maclean
Tel: 506-444-2134
kevin.maclean@gnb.ca

Facilities Management Division
Marysville Place, PO Box 6000Fredericton, NB E3B 5H1
Tel: 506-453-3742
Fax: 506-444-4400
Reception.Marysville@gnb.ca
Responsibilities of the Facilities Management Division include the following: negotiating & administering leases; operating provincially-owned buildings; inspecting buildings; & offering technical support services to government departments, hospitals, & schools.
Executive Director, Facilities Management, Gary Lynch
Tel: 506-444-4527
gary.lynch@gnb.ca
Manager, Facilities Management Technical Services, Peter Davis
Tel: 506-444-4541
peter.davis@gnb.ca
Manager, Financial Administration & Space Management, Kimberly Lebritton
Tel: 506-444-4538
Kim.Lebritton@gnb.ca

Policy, Strategic Development, & Intergovernmental Relations Division
Kings Place, PO Box 6000Fredericton, NB E3B 5H1
Tel: 506-453-3939
Fax: 506-453-5859
Transportation.Web@gnb.ca
Transportation plans & policies are developed in consultation with provincial & federal governments, the transporation industry, & stakeholders.
Assistant Deputy Minister, Policy, Strategic Development, & Intergovernmental Relations Division, Margaret Grant-McGivney
Tel: 506-453-3939
margaret.grant-mcgivney@gnb.ca
Senior Policy Advisor, Strategic Development, John Weatherhead
Tel: 506-444-3185
john.weatherhead@gnb.ca

Workplace Health, Safety & Compensation Commission of New Brunswick (WHSCC) / La commission de la santé, de la sécurité et de l'indemnisation des accidents au travail du Nouveau-Brunswick

1 Portland St., PO Box 160Saint John, NB E2L 3X9
Tel: 506-632-2200
Toll-Free: 800-222-9775
communications@ws-ts.nb.ca
www.whscc.nb.ca
The Workplace Health, Safety & Compensation Commission (WHSCC) of New Brunswick is a crown corporation charged with overseeing the implementation & application of the New Brunswick Occupational Health & Safety Act, the Workers' Compensation Act of New Brunswick, & the Workplace Health, Safety & Compensation Commission Act of New Brunswick on behalf of the workers & employers of this province. The Commission administers no-fault workplace accident & disability insurance & comprehensive accident prevention health & safety initiatives for

employers & their workers, funded solely through premiums paid by employers.

Chair, Sharon Tucker

President/CEO, Peter Murphy

Chair, Appeals Tribunal, Ronald Gaffney

Member Representing Workers, Danny King

Member Representing Workers, Maureen Wallace

Member Representing Workers, Michéle Caron

Member Representing Employers, David Ellis

Member Representing Employers, Marty Martell

Government of Newfoundland & Labrador

Seat of Government: Confederation Bldg., St. John's, NL A1B 4J6
info@gov.nl.ca
www.gov.nl.ca
The Province of Newfoundland & Labrador entered Confederation March 31, 1949. It has an area of 370,494.89 km2, & the StatsCan census population in 2011 was 514,536.
Minister Responsible, Hon. Tom Hedderson
Tel: 709-729-2577
Fax: 709-729-0112
Director, Research & Evidence, Gerald Crane
Tel: 709-729-0379
Fax: 709-729-1119
geraldcrane@gov.nl.ca
Director, Government Relations, Alicia Sutton
Tel: 709-729-7955
aliciasutton@gov.nl.ca
Senior Engineer, Christopher House
Tel: 709-729-1394
christopherhouse@gov.nl.ca
Senior Policy Advisor, Climate Change, Jackie Janes
Tel: 709-729-7971
Fax: 709-729-1119
jackiejanes@gov.nl.ca
Senior Statistician, Patricia King
Tel: 709-729-0975
Fax: 709-729-1119
patriciaking@gov.nl.ca
Senior Policy Officer, Andrea McKenna
Tel: 709-729-3215
Fax: 709-729-1119
andreamckenna@gov.nl.ca

Minister, Hon. Joan Shea
Tel: 709-729-3580
Toll-free: 866-838-5620
Fax: 709-729-6996
joanshea@gov.nl.ca

Minister, Hon. Clyde Jackman
Tel: 709-729-5040
Toll-free: 866-838-5620
Fax: 709-729-0414
clydejackman@gov.nl.ca

Acting Deputy Minister, Janet Vivian-Walsh
Tel: 709-729-5086
janetvivianwalsh@gov.nl.ca

Newfoundland & Labrador Department of Environment & Conservation

Confederation Bldg., West Block, 4th Fl., PO Box 8700St. John's, NL A1B 4J6
Tel: 709-729-2664
Fax: 709-729-6639
Toll-Free: 800-563-6181
envcinquires@gov.nl.ca
www.env.gov.nl.ca
To protect, conserve & enhance the Province's environment through the management of water resources, the environmental assessment of undertakings & the control & management of substances & activities that may pollute the environment. The Department is actively working towards reducing the number of landfill sites & implementing the Provincial Waste Management Strategy.

Acts Administered:
Air Pollution Control Regulations, 2004
Dangerous Goods Transportation Act
Endangered Species Act
Environmental Assesment Act, 2000
Environmental Assessment Regulations, 2003
Environmental Control Water & Sewage Regulations
Environmental Protection Act
Gasoline Volatility Control Regulations, 2003
Geographical Names Board Act
Halocarbon Regulations
Heating Oil Storage Tank System Regulations
Land Surveyors Act
Lands Act
National Park Lands Act
Notices of Protected Water Supplies, Watershed Areas, Wellhead Protected Water Supplies
Ozone Depleting Substances Regulations, 2003
Pesticides Control Regulations, 2003
Provincial Parks Act
Species Status Advisory Committee Regulations
Storage & Handling of Gasoline & Associated Products Regulations, 2003
Storage of PCB Waste Regulations, 2003
Used Oil Control Regulations
Waste Management Regulations, 2003
Waste Material Disposal Areas Regulations
Water Power Rental Regulations, 2003
Water Resources Act
Well Drilling Regulations, 2003
Wild Life Act
Wild Life Park Order
Wild Life Park Regulations
Wild Life Regulations
Wild Life Reserve Regulations
Wilderness & Ecological Reserves Act

Minister, Hon. Thomas J. Hedderson
Tel: 709-729-2577
Fax: 709-729-0112
thedderson@gov.nl.ca

Deputy Minister, Bill Parrott
Tel: 709-729-2572
Fax: 709-729-0112
wparrott@gov.nl.ca

Assistant Deputy Minister, Natural Heritage (Corner Brook), Ross Firth
Tel: 709-637-2135
Fax: 709-637-2180
rossfirth@gov.nl.ca

Assistant Deputy Minister, Environment, Martin Goebel
Tel: 709-729-2559
Fax: 709-729-7413
mgoebel@gov.nl.ca

Assistant Deputy Minister, Lands, Peter Howe
Tel: 709-729-3236
Fax: 709-729-1930
phowe@gov.nl.ca

Environmental Engineer, Policy & Planning Division, Michael Carroll
Tel: 709-729-5550
Fax: 709-729-5818
michaelcarroll@gov.nl.ca

Associated Agencies, Boards & Commissions:
• C.A. Pippy Park Commission
Mount Scio House
15 Mount Scio Rd.
St. John's, NL A1B 3T2
Tel: 709-737-3655
Fax: 709-737-3303
info@pippypark.com
www.pippypark.com
C.A. Pippy Park was established by an Act of the Newfoundland Legislature in 1968. The Act created the C.A. Pippy Park Commission, a semi-autonomous Crown Corporation under the laws of the Province of Newfoundland & Labrador. The Commission currently reports to the Minister of Environment & Conservation.
Chair, Bernie Halloran

• Multi-Materials Stewardship Board (MMSB)
PO Box 8131 A
St. John's, NL A1B 3M9
Tel: 709-753-0948
Fax: 709-753-0974
Toll-free: 800-901-6672
inquiries@mmsb.nl.ca
www.mmsb.nf.ca
The Multi-Materials Stewardship Board is jointly run with the Department of Municipal Affairs.
Minister Responsible, Hon. Tom Hedderson
Tel: 709-729-2577
Fax: 709-729-0112
thedderson@gov.nl.ca
Chair & Chief Executive Officer, Leigh Puddester

Environment Branch
Other Communication: Spill Reporting (24 hours): 709-772-2083; Environmental Assessment: 1-800-563-6181
Assistant Deputy Minister, Martin Goebel
Tel: 709-729-2559
Fax: 709-729-7413
mgoebel@gov.nl.ca
Director, Environmental Assessment Division, Bas Cleary
Tel: 709-729-0673
Fax: 709-729-5518
clearyb@gov.nl.ca
Director, Water Resources, Hassen Khan
Tel: 709-729-2535
Fax: 709-729-0320
hkhan@gov.nl.ca
Director, Pollution Prevention, Derrick Maddocks
Tel: 709-729-5782
Fax: 709-729-6969
dmaddocks@gov.nl.ca
Manager, Waste Management, Craig Bugden
Tel: 709-729-0483
Fax: 709-729-6969
cbugden@gov.nl.ca
Manager, Petroleum Storage & Management, John Dutton
Tel: 709-729-2561
Fax: 709-729-6969
jdutton@gov.nl.ca
Manager, Groundwater, Dorothea Hanchar
Tel: 709-729-2539
Fax: 709-729-0320
dorotheahanchar@gov.nl.ca
Manager, Environmental Science & Monitoring, Peter Haring
Tel: 709-729-4147
Fax: 709-729-6969
pharing@gov.nl.ca
Manager, Pesticide Control Section, Karen Linfield
Tel: 709-729-3395
Fax: 709-729-6969
karenlinfield@gov.nl.ca
Manager, Investigations, Clyde McLean
Tel: 709-729-5713
Fax: 709-729-0320
clydemclean@gov.nl.ca
Manager, Industrial Projects, Dan Michielsen
Tel: 709-729-6697
Fax: 709-729-6969
michielsend@gov.nl.ca
Manager, Surfacewater Section, Robert Picco
Tel: 709-729-4290
Fax: 709-729-0320
rpicco@gov.nl.ca
Acting Manager, Industrial Compliance, Dexter Pittman
Tel: 709-729-6771
Fax: 709-729-6969
dpittman@gov.nl.ca

Lands Branch
Assistant Deputy Minister, Peter Howe
Tel: 709-729-3236
Fax: 709-729-1093
phowe@gov.nl.ca
Director, Surveys & Mapping Division, Allan Chafe
Tel: 709-729-0602
Fax: 709-729-0690
achafe@gov.nl.ca
Director, Crown Lands Administration Division, Robert Dicks
Tel: 709-729-3174
Fax: 709-729-4361
rdicks@gov.nl.ca

Director, Lands Management Division, Reginald Garland
Tel: 709-729-3844
Fax: 709-729-3923
rgarland@gov.nl.ca
Manager, Planning & Allocation, John Howley
Tel: 709-729-0501
Fax: 709-729-3923
jhowley@gov.nl.ca
Acting Manager, Crown Lands Administration, Andrew D. Pike
Tel: 709-729-3174
Fax: 709-729-4361
apike@gov.nl.ca
Senior Engineer, Surveys & Mapping Division, Bob Budgell
Tel: 709-729-3253
Fax: 709-729-0690
bbudgell@gov.nl.ca

Natural Heritage
Assistant Deputy Minister, Ross Firth
Tel: 709-637-2135
Fax: 709-637-2180
rossfirth@gov.nl.ca
Director, Wildlife Division, John Blake
Tel: 709-637-2008
Fax: 709-637-2180
johnblake@gov.nl.ca
Director, Parks & Natural Areas, Sian French
Tel: 709-637-4520
Fax: 709-635-4541
sianfrench@gov.nl.ca
Senior Manager, Game & Fur Management, Katherine Mehl
Tel: 709-637-2383
Fax: 709-637-2004
katherinemehl@gov.nl.ca
Senior Manager, Stewardship & Education, Vacant
Manager, Environmental Education & Promotion, Geoff Bailey
Tel: 709-637-4531
Fax: 709-635-4541
geoffbailey@gov.nl.ca
Manager, Conservation Services, Chris Baldwin
Tel: 709-637-2020
Fax: 709-637-2032
chrisbaldwin@gov.nl.ca
Manager, Licensing & Operations, Grant Dicks
Tel: 709-637-2045
Fax: 709-637-2099
gdicks@gov.nl.ca
Manager, Natural Areas, Jeri Graham
Tel: 709-635-4529
Fax: 709-635-4541
jerigraham@gov.nl.ca
Manager, Mistaken Point Ecological Reserve, Valerie Sullivan
Tel: 709-438-1012
valeriesullivan@gov.nl.ca

Sustainable Development & Strategic Science Branch
Executive Director, Policy & Legislation, Shane P. Mahoney
Tel: 709-729-2542
Fax: 709-729-7677
shanemahoney@gov.nl.ca
Director, Science, Monitoring & Data Synthesis, Rob Otto
Tel: 709-637-6200 ext: 639
Fax: 709-639-7591
rotto@gov.nl.ca
Research Manager, Corner Brook, Sabrina Ellsworth
Tel: 709-637-6200 ext: 700
Fax: 709-639-7591
sellsworth@swgc.mun.ca
Manager, Outreach & Education, Sharon Porter
Tel: 709-729-7417
Fax: 709-729-1747
sporter@gov.nl.ca
Research Manager, St. John's, Jackie Weir
Tel: 709-729-6648
Fax: 709-729-1747
jackieweir@gov.nl.ca
Senior Research Scientist, Keith Lewis
Tel: 709-729-2114
Fax: 709-729-1747
keith.lewis@gov.nl.ca
Senior Wildlife Biologist, Mariana Trindale
Tel: 709-729-1361
Fax: 709-729-1747
trindademariana@gov.nl.ca

Minister; President, Treasury Board, Hon. Jerome Kennedy, Q.C.
Tel: 709-729-3775
Fax: 709-729-2232
financeminister@gov.nl.ca

Taxation & Fiscal Policy Branch
Assistant Deputy Minister, Peter Au
Tel: 709-729-2944
Fax: 709-729-2070
peterau@gov.nl.ca
Director, Fiscal Policy, Chris Butt
Tel: 709-729-6714
cbutt@gov.nl.ca
Director, Tax Policy, Jay Griffin
Tel: 709-729-6847
jgriffin@gov.nl.ca
Director, Project Analysis, Brian Hurley
Tel: 709-729-3664
bhurley@gov.nl.ca
Director, Debt Management, Paul Myrden
Tel: 709-729-6848
Director, Tax Administration, Cathy M. Whalen
Tel: 709-729-6307
Fax: 709-729-2277
cathywhalen@gov.nl.ca

Newfoundland & Labrador Department of Fisheries & Aquaculture

Petten Bldg., 30 Strawberry Marsh Rd., PO Box 8700St. John's, NL A1B 4J6
Tel: 709-729-3723
Fax: 709-729-6082
fisheries@gov.nl.ca
www.fishaq.gov.nl.ca
Other Communication: Aquaculture Phone: 709-292-4100; Fax: 709-292-4113; Email: aquaculture@gov.nl.ca
twitter.com/FA_GovNL
Contributes to economic & community growth in the province by encouraging sustainable growth & development of the harvesting, processing, & distribution sectors; includes providing support for the marketing of fish & aquaculture products produced in Newfoundland & Labrador for domestic & export markets. Responsible for: setting & enforcing standards for the processing & sale of fish products in the province; licensing fish processing establishments; undertaking developmental initiatives in the harvesting, processing, & marketing sectors of the fishing industry; developing, promoting & licensing of aquaculture facilities; developing & maintaining strategic fisheries infrastructure; articulating policies & providing advice for the management & development of fisheries & aquaculture; providing statistical information.
Acts Administered:
Aquaculture Act
Fish Inspection Act
Fish Processing Licensing Board Act
Fisheries Act
Fishing Industry Collective Bargaining Act
Professional Fish Harvesters Act

Minister, Hon. Derrick Dalley
Tel: 709-729-3705
Fax: 709-729-0360
derrickdalley@gov.nl.ca

Deputy Minister, Alastair O'Rielly
Tel: 709-729-3707
Fax: 790-729-4219
aorielly@gov.nl.ca

Director, Compliance & Enforcement, Ron Brown
Tel: 709-729-1143
RonBrown@gov.nl.ca

Associated Agencies, Boards & Commissions:
• Fish Processing Licensing Board (FPLB)
c/o Fish Processing Licensing Board Secretariat
30 Strawberry Marsh Rd.
St. John's, NL A1B 4J6
fplbsecretariat@gov.nl.ca
Chair, Ted Lewis
Vice-Chair, David Woodman

• Professional Fish Harvesters Certification Board (PFHCB)
368 Hamilton Ave.
PO Box 8541
St. John's, NL A1B 3P2
Tel: 709-722-8170
Fax: 709-722-8201
pfh@pfhcb.com
www.pfhcb.com

Aquaculture Branch
58 Hardy Ave., PO Box 679Grand Falls-Windsor, NL A2A 2K2
Tel: 709-292-4100
Fax: 709-292-4113
aquaculture@gov.nl.ca
The Branch is responsible for licensing & aquaculture development.
Assistant Deputy Minister, Brian Meaney
Tel: 709-729-3710
Fax: 709-729-1882
bmeaney@gov.nl.ca
Director & Provincial Aquaculture Veterinarian, Dr. Daryl Whelan
Tel: 709-729-6872
Fax: 709-729-1882
darylswhelan@gov.nl.ca
Manager, Aquaculture Licencing & Inspections, Todd Budgell
Tel: 709-292-4106
Fax: 709-292-4113
tbudgell@gov.nl.ca

Fisheries Branch
Fax: 709-729-0360
fisheries@gov.nl.ca
This branch is responsible for fish processing operations, inspections, compliance & regulatory programs.
Assistant Deputy Minister, Shawn Robinson
Tel: 709-729-3723
Fax: 709-729-6082
Director, Licensing & Quality Assurance, Ian Burford
Tel: 709-729-3736
Fax: 709-729-5995
iburford@gov.nl.ca
Director, Innovation & Development, Mark Rumboldt
Tel: 709-729-3714
Fax: 709-729-1884
mrumboldt@gov.nl.ca

Marketing & Development Branch
Fax: 709-729-1884
fisheries@gov.nl.ca
This branch is responsible for promoting & supporting the diversification & development of the harvesting, processing, & marketing sectors of the seafood industry through public & private sector partnerships.
Assistant Deputy Minister, Marketing & Development, Gerry Donovan
Tel: 709-729-3718
Fax: 709-729-1884
gerrydonovan@gov.nl.ca
Director, Seafood Marketing & Support Services, Sean Barry
Tel: 709-729-3390
Fax: 709-729-1884
seanbarry@gov.nl.ca

Policy Development & Planning Branch
Fax: 709-729-0360
fisheries@gov.nl.ca
Provides policy & program planning services to the Department. Through the Sustainable Fisheries & Oceans Policy Division participates in oceans policy & governance issues, in addition to the resource assessment & management process of the federal Department of Fisheries & Oceans, including local, national, & international bodies responsible for fisheries conservation & management.
Assistant Deputy Minister, Mike Warren
Tel: 709-729-3708
Fax: 709-729-6082
mikewarren@gov.nl.ca
Director, Sustainable Fisheries & Oceans Policy, Tom Dooley
Tel: 709-729-0335
Fax: 709-729-6082
Acting Director, Fishing Industry Renewal & Adjustment, Paul Martin
Tel: 709-729-1073
Fax: 709-729-6082
pdmartin@gov.nl.ca

Director, Planning Services, Wandalee Wiseman
Tel: 709-729-3765
Fax: 709-729-6082
wandaleewiseman@gov.nl.ca
Eastern
PO Box 880Grand Bank, NL A0E 1W0
Tel: 709-832-2860
Fax: 709-832-1669
Supervisor, Fisheries, Brian Sullivan
Tel: 709-729-3784
briansullivan@gov.nl.ca
Northern
PO Box 3014 Stn. B, Happy Valley-Goose Bay, NL A0P 1E0
Tel: 709-896-3412
Fax: 709-896-3483
Regional Director, Craig Taylor
Tel: 709-896-3412
Fax: 709-896-3483
craigtaylor@gov.nl.ca
Western
PO Box 2006Corner Brook, NL A2H 6J8
Tel: 709-637-2955
Fax: 709-637-2908
Regional Director, Wilson Goosney
Tel: 709-637-2565
Fax: 709-637-2908

GSC Area Offices
Clarenville
#201, 8 Myers Ave., Clarenville, NL A5A 1T5
Tel: 709-466-4060
Fax: 709-466-4070
Director, Guy Perry
gperry@gov.nl.ca
Corner Brook
Sir Richard Squires Bldg., Mount Bernard Ave., PO Box 2006Corner Brook, NL A2H 6J8
Tel: 709-637-2204
Fax: 709-637-2681
Gander
Fraser Mall, 230 Airport Blvd., PO Box 2222Gander, NL A1V 2N9
Tel: 709-256-1420
Fax: 709-256-1438
Grand Bank
Buffett Buldg., Church St., PO Box 479Grand Bank, NL A0E 1W0
Tel: 709-632-2326
Fax: 709-632-1792
Grand Bank - Windsor
Provincial Bldg., 3 Cromer Ave., Grand Bank, NL A2A 1W9
Tel: 709-292-4206
Fax: 709-292-4149
Harbour Grace
7-9 Roddick Cres., PO Box 512Harbour Grace, NL A0A 2M0
Tel: 709-945-3107
Fax: 709-945-3114
Happy Valley-Goose Bay
2 Tenth St., PO Box 3014 Stn. B, Happy Valley-Goose Bay, NL A0P 1E0
Tel: 709-896-5428
Fax: 709-896-4340
Labrador City
118 Humphrey Rd., PO Box 1079Labrador City, NL A2V 2J8
Tel: 709-944-5282
Fax: 709-944-5630
Lewisporte
Porte Bldg., 224 Main St., PO Box 1136Lewisporte, NL A0G 3A0
Tel: 709-535-0262
Fax: 709-535-0284
Marystown
Industrial Park, 1 Harris Dr., PO Box 698Marytown, NL A0E 2M0
Tel: 709-279-0837
Port aux Basques
Provincial Bldg., Main St., PO Box 478Port Aux Basques, NL A0M 1C0
Tel: 709-695-2835
Fax: 709-695-2393
St Anthony
6-8 North St., PO Box 28St Anthony, NL A0K 4S0
Tel: 709-454-8833
Fax: 709-454-3206
St. John's
5 Mews Pl., PO Box 8700St. John's, NL A1B 4J5
Tel: 709-729-3699
Fax: 709-729-2071
Stephenville
35 Alabama Dr., Stephenville, NL A2N 3K9
Tel: 709-643-8650
Fax: 709-673-4232
Springdale
200 Main St., Springdale, NL A0J 1T0
Tel: 709-673-4218
Fax: 709-673-4232
Director, Jennifer Hooper
Tel: 416-314-8562

Newfoundland & Labrador Department of Health & Community Services (HCS)

West Block, Confederation Bldg., PO Box 8700St. John's, NL A1B 4J6
Tel: 709-729-4984
healthinfo@gov.nl.ca
www.health.gov.nl.ca
Other Communication: Senior Citizens Drug Program, Phone: 709-729-4984; Immunization Records, Phone: 709-729-0724; Medical Care Plan, Toll-Free: 1-800-563-1557; Avalon: 1-866-449-4459
Provides a leadership role in health & community service programs & policy development for the Province. This involves working in partnership with a number of key stakeholders including regional boards, community organizations, professional associations, post-secondary educational institutions, unions, consumer & other government departments.
Acts Administered:
Communicable Diseases Act
Food & Drug Act
Health & Community Services Act
Smoke-free Environment Act

Minister, Hon. Susan Sullivan
Tel: 709-729-3124
Toll-free: 800-514-9073
Fax: 709-729-0121
susansullivan@gov.nl.ca

Deputy Minister, Bruce Cooper
Tel: 709-729-3125
Fax: 709-729-0121

Associate Deputy Minister, Medical Services, Dr. Cathi Bradboury
Tel: 709-729-1574
Fax: 709-729-0121
cathibradbury@gov.nl.ca

Acting Assistant Deputy Minister, Beverly Griffiths
Tel: 709-729-3127
Fax: 709-729-4009
bgriffiths@gov.nl.ca

Assistant Deputy Minister, Michelle Jewer
Tel: 709-729-0620
Fax: 709-729-0640
michellejewer@gov.nl.ca

Assistant Deputy Minister, Pharmaceutical Services, Colleen Stockley
Tel: 709-729-1716
Fax: 709-729-0121
cstockley@gov.nl.ca

Assistant Deputy Minister, Denise Tubrett
Tel: 709-729-0580
Fax: 709-729-0640
dtubrett@gov.nl.ca

Director, Communications, Scott Barfoot
Tel: 709-729-1377
scottbarfoot@gov.nl.ca

Associated Agencies, Boards & Commissions:
• **Central Regional Health Authority**
21 Carmelite Rd.
Grand Falls-Windsor, NL A2A 1Y4
Toll-free: 888-799-2272
client.relations@centralhealth.nl.ca
www.centralhealth.nl.ca
Chief Operating Officer, Gander, Sherry Freake
Tel: 709-256-5531
sherry.freake@centralhealth.nl.ca
Chief Operating Officer, Grand Falls-Windsor, Sean Tulk
Tel: 709-292-2454
sean.tulk@centralhealth.nl.ca
Vice President, Professional Standards & Chief Nursing Officer, Trudy Stuckless
Tel: 709-292-2151
trudy.stuckless@centralhealth.nl.ca
• **Eastern Regional Health Authority**
Health Sciences Centre
#1345, Prince Philip Dr., Level 1
St. John's, NL A1B 3V6
Tel: 709-777-6500
Fax: 709-364-6460
Toll-free: 877-444-1399
client.relations@easternhealth.ca
www.easternhealth.ca
Other Communication: Toll-Free Healthline: 1-888-709-2929
Chair, Michael J. O'Keefe
President & CEO, Vickie Kaminski
Vice President, Cancer Care & Chief Nursing Officer, Katherine Chubbs
• **Health Research Ethics Authority (HREA)**
#200, 95 Bonaventure Ave., 2nd Fl.
St. John's, NL A1B 2X5
Tel: 709-777-6974
Fax: 709-777-8776
info@hrea.ca
www.lghealth.ca
The HREA is responsible for supervising all health research involving human subjects conducted in Newfoundland & Labrador.
Chair, Dr. Larry Felt
• **Labrador-Grenfell Regional Health Authority**
Administration Bldg.
Happy Valley-Goose Bay, NL A0P 1C0
Tel: 709-897-2267
Fax: 709-896-4032
www.lghealth.ca
Chair, Ray Norman
Chief Executive Officer, Tony Wakeham
• **Newfoundland & Labrador Centre for Health Information (NLCHI)**
70 O'Leary Ave.
St. John's, NL A1B 2C7
Tel: 709-752-6000
Fax: 709-752-6011
contact@nlchi.nl.ca
www.nlchi.nl.ca
• **Newfoundland & Labrador Health Boards Association (NLHBA)**
Beothuck Bldg.
20 Crosbie Pl., 2nd Fl.
St. John's, NL A1B 3Y8
Tel: 709-364-7701
Fax: 709-364-6460
www.nlhba.nl.ca
• **Western Regional Health Authority**
20 Farm Rd.
Deer Lake, NL A8A 1V2
Tel: 709-635-3541
westernhealth.nl.ca
Chair, Anthony Genge
Vice-Chair, Tom O'Brien
President & CEO, Dr. Susan Gillam
Vice President, Professional Practice, Chief Nursing Officer & Health Protection (Acting), Catherine McDonald

Corporate Services Branch
Regional Director, Audit & Claims Integrity, Glenn Budgell
Tel: 709-292-4009
Fax: 709-292-4052
gbudgell@gov.nl.ca
Director, Corporate Initiatives, Harry Hutchings
Tel: 709-729-0444
hhutchings@gov.nl.ca
Financial Manager, Financial Services, Pam Barnes
Tel: 709-729-5323
pbarnes@gov.nl.ca
Budgeting Manager, Financial Services, Linda Boland
Tel: 709-729-7956
Fax: 709-729-3151
lindaboland@gov.nl.ca

Manager, e-Health Transformation, Kevin Durdle
Tel: 709-729-1596
KevinDurdle@gov.nl.ca

Policy & Planning Branch
Acting Director, Chronic Disease Control, Linda Carter
Tel: 709-729-3117
Fax: 709-729-5824
lindacarter@gov.nl.ca
Director, Government Relations, Rosemary Boyd
Tel: 709-729-1775
rosemaryboyd@gov.nl.ca
Director, Policy Development, Wanda Legge
Tel: 709-729-5249
wlegge@gov.nl.ca
Secretary, Planning & Evaluation, Cindy Tucker
Tel: 709-729-3940
cmtucker@gov.nl.ca

Population Health Branch
Chief Medical Officer of Health, Public Health Division, Dr. Faith Stratton
Tel: 709-729-3430
fstratton@gov.nl.ca
Director, Environmental Public Health, Darryl Johnson
Tel: 709-729-3422
Fax: 709-729-0730
djohnson@gov.nl.ca
Director, Disease Control, Cathy O'Keefe
Tel: 709-729-5019
Fax: 709-729-5824
cokeefe@gov.nl.ca
Director, Health Promotion & Wellness, Eleanor Swanson
Tel: 709-729-5023

Professional Services
Assistant Deputy Minister, Colleen Janes
Tel: 709-729-1716
Fax: 709-729-5218
cjanes@gov.nl.ca
Chief Nurse & Director, Anita Ludlow
Tel: 709-729-2039
anitaludlow@gov.nl.ca
Provincial Director, Physician Services, Dr. Larry Alteen
Tel: 709-729-3531
LarryAlteen@gov.nl.ca
Provincial Director, Pathology & Laboratory Medicine, Beverly Carter
Tel: 709-729-7652
beverlycarter@gov.nl.ca
Director, Dental Services, Dr. Ed Williams
Tel: 709-758-1503
edwilliams@gov.nl.ca
Manager, Health Workforce Planning, Suellen Sheppard
Tel: 709-729-0117
Fax: 709-729-3416
suellensheppard@gov.nl.ca
Program & Policy Development Specialist, Darlene Ricketts
Tel: 709-729-0719
Fax: 709-729-7778
darlenericketts@gov.nl.ca

Newfoundland & Labrador Housing Corporation (NLHC)

Sir Brian Dunfield Bldg., 2 Canada Dr., PO Box 220St. John's, NL A1C 5J2
Tel: 709-724-3000
Fax: 709-724-3250
www.nlhc.nl.ca
twitter.com/nlhousing
www.facebook.com/NewfoundlandLabradorHousing
www.linkedin.com/company/newfoundland-&-labrador-housing

Minister Responsible, Hon. Paul Davis
Tel: 709-729-3679
Fax: 709-729-4285
pdavis@gov.nl.ca

Chair & Chief Executive Officer, Len Simms
Tel: 709-724-3054
lensimms@nlhc.nl.ca

Chief Financial Officer, Finance & Quality Assurance & Evaluation, Tom Lawrence

Executive Director, Human Resources & Engineering, Glenn Goss

Environmental Officer, Janet Rideout
Tel: 709-724-3101
Fax: 709-724-3250
jlrideout@nlhc.nl.ca

Newfoundland & Labrador Hydro

Hydro Place, 500 Columbus Dr., PO Box 12400St. John's, NL A1B 4K7
Tel: 709-737-1400
Fax: 709-737-1800
Toll-Free: 888-737-1296
hydro@nlh.nl.ca
www.nlh.nl.ca
Other Communication: Vendor Information, Phone: 709-737-1335; Fax: 709-737-1795; E-Mail: tenders@nlh.nl.ca; Customer Service, E-Mail: customerservices@nlh.nl.ca
Crown corporation, owned by the Province of Newfoundland & Labrador, & a subsidiary of Nalcor Energy. Hydro generates, transmits & distributes electrical power & energy to utility, residential & industrial customers throughout the province. Hydro is the parent company of the Hydro Group of Companies (Hydro Group), comprising Newfoundland & Labrador Hydro, Churchill Falls (Labrador) Corporation Limited (CF(L)Co), Lower Churchill Development Corporation Limited (LCDC), Gull Island Power Company Limited (GIPCo), & Twin Falls Power Corporation Limited (TwinCo). The Hydro Group's installed generating capacity is the fourth largest of all utility companies in Canada, consisting of ten hydroelectric plants, including the Churchill Falls hydraulic plant, which is the largest underground powerhouse in the world with a rated capacity of 5,428 megawatts (MW) of power, one oil-fired plant, four gas turbines & 26 diesel plants.

President & Chief Executive Officer, Ed Martin

Chief Financial Officer & Vice-President, Finance, Derrick Sturge

Vice-President, Regulated Operations, Jim Haynes

Vice-President, Human Resources & Organzational Effectiveness, Gerard McDonald

Churchill Falls (Labrador) Corporation Limited (CF(L)Co)
Hydro Place, 500 Columbus Dr., PO Box 12500St. John's, NL A1B 4K7
Tel: 709-737-1859
Fax: 709-737-1816
Churchill Falls (Labrador) Corporation operates a hydroelectric generating plant & transmission facilities.

Gull Island Power Co. Ltd. (GIPCo)

Lower Churchill Development Corporation Ltd. (LCDC)
PO Box 12700St. John's, NL A1B 3T5
Tel: 709-737-1400
Fax: 709-737-1400
The corporation seeks to develop the hydroelectric potential of the Lower Churchill basin. It is 49 per cent owned by the federal government.

Twin Falls Power Corporation (TwinCo)
PO Box 12500St. John's, NL A1B 3T5
Twin Falls Power Corporation has developed a hydroelectric generating plant on the Unknown River in Labrador. The plant has been inoperative since 1974.

Innovation
Assistant Deputy Minister, Mark Ploughman
Tel: 709-729-7101
Fax: 709-729-5124
markploughman@gov.nl.ca
Director, Information Management, Ruth Parsons
Tel: 709-729-1940
Fax: 709-729-5124
ruthparsons@gov.nl.ca
Director, Innovation & Advanced Technology, Sharon Tiller
Tel: 709-729-7068
stiller@gov.nl.ca

Ocean Technology Branch
Assistant Deputy Minister, Barry Dawe
Tel: 709-729-2820
barrydawe@gov.nl.ca
Director, Diane Taylor
Tel: 709-729-1684
dianetaylor@gov.nl.ca
Ocean Technology Advisor, Neil Gall
Tel: 709-729-4682
ngall@gov.nl.ca
Senior Technical Advisor, Darrell O'Neill
Tel: 709-729-0680
doneill@gov.nl.ca

Regional Development
Assistant Deputy Minister, Rita Malone
Tel: 709-637-2977
Fax: 709-639-7713
rmalone@gov.nl.ca
Acting Director, Regional Development, Gillian Skinner
Tel: 709-729-7451
Fax: 709-729-5124
gskinner@gov.nl.ca
Director, Fisheries Adjustment & Economic Diversification, Larry Weatherbie
Tel: 709-729-7125
Fax: 709-729-5124
lweather@gov.nl.ca

Strategic Industries & Business Development Branch
Acting Assistant Deputy Minister, Rita Malone
Tel: 709-637-2977
Fax: 709-729-4858
rmalone@gov.nl.ca
Director, Portfolio Management Division, Guy Edwards
Tel: 709-279-0213
Fax: 709-279-0218
gedwards@gov.nl.ca
Director, Business Analysis, Sharlene Jones
Tel: 709-729-7108
Fax: 709-729-4858
sharlenejones@gov.nl.va

Trade & Export Development Branch
Specializes in assisting provincial businesses develop an export plan to enter new markets, find export business partners & research national & international market opportunities.
Assistant Deputy Minister, Daryl Genge
Tel: 709-729-0882
Fax: 709-729-3484
darylgenge@gov.nl.ca
Director, Air Access, Fraser Howell
Tel: 709-729-6183
Fax: 709-729-5124
fraserhowell@gov.nl.ca
Director, Policy & Strategic Planning, Terry Johnstone
Tel: 709-729-4771
Fax: 709-729-5124
tjohnsto@gov.nl.ca
Director, European Union Trade Policy, Jacqueline Power
Tel: 709-729-5839
Fax: 709-729-5124
jpower@gov.nl.ca
Director, Marketing, Linda Spurrell
Tel: 709-729-7483
Fax: 709-729-5124
lspurrel@gov.nl.ca
Director, Business Investment, Darin Steeves
Tel: 709-729-3206
Fax: 709-729-5124
darinsteeves@gov.nl.ca
Manager, Ambassador Program, Sheila Fudge
Tel: 709-729-7019
Fax: 709-729-6627
sfudge@gov.nl.ca
Acts Administered:
Public Utilities Acquisition of Lands Act
Public Utilities Act

Minister, Hon. Darin T. King, Ph.D.
Tel: 709-729-2869
Fax: 709-729-0469
darinking@gov.nl.ca

Acting Deputy Minister; Deputy Attorney General, Paul Noble, Q.C.

Tel: 709-729-2872
Fax: 709-729-0469
pauln@gov.nl.ca

Director, Communications, Luke Joyce
Tel: 709-729-6985
Fax: 709-729-0469
lukejoyce@gov.nl.ca

Newfoundland & Labrador Department of Municipal Affairs

West Block, Main Fl., Confederation Bldg., PO Box 8700St. John's, NL A1B 4J6
Tel: 709-729-3046
Fax: 709-729-0943
mainfo@gov.nl.ca
www.ma.gov.nl.ca
Works with municipalities to ensure communities are properly managed & planned to ensure residents have a high standard of living in a clean, healthy & safe environment. The department is responsible for community-related activities such as the Office of the Fire Commissioner, the Emergency Measures Organization, Engineering & Land Use Planning.
Acts Administered:
Assessment Act, 2006
Building Standards Act
Emergency Services Act
Evacuated Communities Act
Fire Prevention Act, 1991
Municipalities Act, 1999
St. John's Municipal Council Parks Act
Urban & Rural Planning Act, 2000

Minister, Hon. Kevin O'Brien
Tel: 709-729-3046
Fax: 709-729-0943
kevinobrien@gov.nl.ca

Deputy Minister, Julia Mullaley
Tel: 709-729-2844
Fax: 709-729-0943
jmullaley@gov.nl.ca

Director, Communications, Hugh Donnan
Tel: 709-729-1983
Fax: 709-729-0943
hughdonnan@gov.nl.ca

Associated Agencies, Boards & Commissions:
• **Burin Peninsula Waste Management Corporation**
PO Box 510
Burin Bay Arm, NL A0E 1G0
Tel: 709-891-1717
Fax: 709-891-1727
info@burinpenwaste.com
burinpenwaste.com
Chair, Harold Murphy
Vice-Chair, Keith Keating
Secretary-Treasurer, Elaine Strowbridge
• **Central Newfoundland Waste Management Authority (CNMW)**
#3, 255 Majors Path
St. John's, NL A1A 0L5
Tel: 709-653-2900
Fax: 709-653-2920
info@cnwmc.com
www.cnwmc.com
Chair, Allan Scott
Tel: 709-651-5920
allanscott@nf.sympatico.ca
Manager, Edward Evans
ed@cnwmc.com
• **Eastern Waste Management Commission**
#3, 255 Majors Path
St. John's, NL A1A 0L5
Tel: 709-579-7960
Fax: 709-579-5392
info@easternwaste.ca
easternwaste.ca
Chair, Ed Grant
Vice-Chair, Harold Mullowney
• **Fire & Emergency Services**
25 Hallett Cres.
PO Box 8700
St. John's, NL A1B 4J6
Tel: 709-729-1608
Fax: 709-729-2524
www.gov.nl.ca/fes
Other Communication: Emergency Management: 709-729-3703 (Tel.), 709-729-3757 (Fax)
Minister Reponsible, Hon. Kevin O'Brien
Tel: 709-729-3048
Fax: 709-729-0943
kevinobrien@gov.nl.ca
Assistant Deputy Minister, Marilyn McCormack
Tel: 709-729-6794
Fax: 709-729-5609
marilynmccormack@gov.nl.ca
Fire Commissioner & Director, Fire Services, Derek Simmons
Tel: 709-635-4153
Fax: 709-635-4163
dsimmons@gov.nl.ca
Director, Emergency Services, David McCormack
Tel: 709-729-3830
davidmccormack@psnl.ca
Director, Emergency Services, Pamela Rodgers
Tel: 709-729-6794
Fax: 709-729-5609
prodgers@gov.nl.ca
• **Green Bay Waste Authority Inc.**
PO Box 116
South Brook, NL A0J 1S0
Tel: 709-657-2233
Fax: 709-657-2133
Toll-free: 877-657-2233
info@greenbaywaste.com
greenbaywaste.com
Coordinator, Waste Management, Glenda Fowlow
Supervisor, Site Operations, Glenn Rowsell
• **Northern Peninsula Regional Service Board**
PO Box 130
St. Anthony, NL A0K 4S0
Tel: 709-454-3110
Fax: 709-454-3818
nprsb@nf.aibn.com
norpenwaste.com
Chair, Doug Mills

Municipal Engineering & Planning
Assistant Deputy Minister, Cluney Mercer
Tel: 709-729-5326
Fax: 709-729-0477
mercerc@gov.nl.ca
Director, Engineering & Land Use Planning, Randy Dillon
Tel: 709-729-5334
Fax: 709-729-7491
rdillon@gov.nl.ca
Acting Director, Waste Management, Frank Huxter
Tel: 709-729-7482
fhuxter@gov.nl.ca
Manager, Land Use Planning, Corrie Davis
Tel: 709-729-5409
Fax: 709-729-7491
corriedavis@gov.nl.ca
Architect, Municipal Planning & Design Engineering, Dave Dewling
Tel: 709-729-1189
Fax: 709-729-7491
dewlingd@gov.nl.ca

Municipal Assessment Agency Inc.

75 O'Leary Ave., St. John's, NL A1B 2C9
Tel: 709-724-1532
Toll-Free: 877-777-2807
info@maa.ca
www.maa.ca
The agency provides property assessment & valuation services.

Chair, Fred Best

Vice-Chair, Dean Bell
Corner Brook - Western
PO Box 20051Corner Brook, NL A2H 7J5
Tel: 709-637-7150
Gander - Central
165 Roe Ave., PO Box 570Gander, NL A1V 2E1
Tel: 709-651-4460
Happy Valley-Goose Bay - Labrador
Elizabeth Goudie Bldg., PO Box 30141 Stn. B, Happy Valley-Goose Bay, NL A0P 1E0
Tel: 709-896-5393

Nalcor Energy

500 Columbus Dr., St. John's, NL A1E 2B2
Tel: 709-737-1400
Fax: 709-737-1800
www.nalcorenergy.com
twitter.com/NalcorEnergy
www.facebook.com/NalcorEnergy
www.youtube.com/user/NalcorEnergy
Crown corporation, founded in 2008 & owned by the Province of Newfoundland & Labrador. Nalcor is the parent company of Newfoundland & Labrador Hydro, which in turn is the parent of the Hydro Group of Companies. Nalcor's subsidiaries include: Newfoundland & Labrador Hydro, The Churchill Falls Generating Station, Lower Churchill Project, Oil & Gas & Bull Arm Fabrication.

President & Chief Executive Officer, Ed Martin

Chief Financial Officer & Vice-President, Finance, Derrick Sturge

Vice-President, Lower Churchill, Gilbert Bennett

Vice-President, Regulated Operations, Hydro, Jim Haynes

Vice-President, Regulated Operations, Hydro, Jim Hayes

Vice-President, Oil & Gas, Jim Keating

Vice-President, Strategic Planning & Business Development, Chris Kieley

Vice-President, Asset Management, Project Execution & Engineering Services, John MacIsaac

Vice-President, Churchill Falls, Andy MacNeill

Vice-President, Human Resources & Organizational Effectiveness, Gerard McDonald

Newfoundland & Labrador Department of Natural Resources

Natural Resources Bldg., 50 Elizabeth Ave., 7th Fl., PO Box 8700St. John's, NL A1B 4J6
Tel: 709-729-2920
Fax: 709-729-0059
www.nr.gov.nl.ca
Responsible for the management of the province's mineral, energy, land, forest & wildlife resources in a manner that will ensure optimum benefits for the people of the province.
Acts Administered:
Abitibi-Consolidated Inc. & Abitibi Partner Exemption Order, 2002
Abitibi-Consolidated Rights & Assets Act
Agricultural Products Marketing Board Appeal Regulations
Agricultural Products Marketing Board Order
Agrologists Act
Animal Health & Protection Act
Animal Protection Act
Assessment of Over-Marketing Regulations, 2009
Berry Regulations
Canada-Newfoundland & Labrador Atlantic Accord Implementation Newfoundland & Labrador Act
Canada-Newfoundland & Labrador Oil & Gas Spills & Debris Liability Newfoundland & Labrador Regulations
Chicken Farmers of Newfoundland & Labrador Licensing Regulations
Chicken Farmers of Newfoundland & Labrador Quota Regulations
Chicken Farmers of Newfoundland & Labrador Marketing Board Regulations
Churchill Falls (Labrador) Corporation Limited (Lease) Act, 1961
Consolidated Chicken Farmers of Newfoundland & Labrador Order
Control of Nurseries & Dealers in Nursery Stock Regulations
Copper-in-Concentrate Exemption Order, 2009
Corner Brook Pulp & Paper Limited Exemption Order
Crop Insurance Act
Cutting of Timber Regulations
Description of Lands Open for Staking in respect of which the Mineral Claims Recorder shall Issue only Map Staked Licenses Order
Designation of Inspectors Order

Directed Sale of Timber Regulations
Egg Regulations
Egg Scheme, 2000
Electrical Power Control Act, 1994
Endangered Species Act (jointly with Department of Environment and Conservation)
Energy Corporation Act
Energy Corporation of Newfoundland & Labrador Water Rights Act
Farm Practices Protection Act
Farm Products Corporation Act
Forest Fire Offence & Penalty Regulation
Forest Fire Regulations
Forest Fires Liability & Compensation Regulations
Forest Land Management & Taxation Regulations
Forest Management Districts Proclamation
Forest Protection Act
Forestry Act
Granite Canal Hydroelectric Project Exemption Order
Health & Community Services Act (jointly with Department of Health & Community Services)
Heritage Animals Act
Hydro Corporation Act, 2007
Labrador Hydro Project Exemption Order
Labrador Inuit Land Claims Agreement Act
Livestock Act
Livestock Health Act
Livestock Health Regulations
Livestock Regulations
Lower Churchill Development Act
Milk Regulations, 1998
Milk Scheme, 1998
Mill Regulations
Mineral Act
Mineral Act Baie Verte Area Exemption Regulations
Mineral Holdings Impost Act
Mineral Holdings Impost Regulations
Mineral Regulations
Mining Act
Mining Regulations
Miscellaneous Financial Provisions Act, 1975
Motorized Snow Vehicles & All-Terrain Vehicles Act (jointly with Government Services)
Motorized Snow Vehicles & All-Terrain Vehicles Regulations
Natural Products Marketing Act
Newfoundland & Labrador Chicken Marketing Scheme
Newfoundland & Labrador Hydro-Abitibi Consolidated Inc. Exemption Order
Newfoundland & Labrador Hydro-Abitibi Consolidated Inc. Stephensville Operations Exemption Order
Newfoundland & Labrador Hydro-Corner Brook Pulp & Paper Limited Exemption Order
Newfoundland & Labrador Power Commission (Water Power) Act
Newfoundland Pony Designation Order
Nickel-in-Concentrate Exemption Order, 2009
Offshore Area Oil & Gas Operations Regulations
Offshore Area Petroleum Diving Newfoundland & Labrador Regulations
Oil Royalty Regulations
Petroleum & Natural Gas Act
Petroleum Drilling Regulations
Petroleum Regulations
Plant Protection Act
Plant Quarantine Regulations
Plebiscite Regulations
Port au Port Peninsula Petroleum & Natural Gas Development Area Order
Quarry Leases Rental Order
Quarry Materials Regulations
Royalty Regulations, 2003
Seed Potato Regulations
Small Scale Operations Regulations
Timber Royalty Regulations
Timber Scaling Regulations
Undeveloped Minerals Areas Act
Undeveloped Minerals Areas Order
Voisey's Bay Nickel Company Limited Primary Production Order
Voisey's Bay Nickel Company Limited Matte Plant Exemption Order
Water Management Regulations

Minister & Minister Responsible for the Forestry & Agrifoods Agency, Hon. Thomas W. Marshall, Q.C.
Tel: 709-729-2920
Fax: 709-729-0059
tommarshall@gov.nl.ca

Deputy Minister, Charles Bown
Tel: 709-729-2766
Fax: 709-729-0059
cbown@gov.nl.ca

Assistant Deputy Minister, Keith Deering
Tel: 709-729-2488
Fax: 709-637-2461
keithdeering@gov.nl.ca

Chief Executive Officer, Forestry & Agrifoods Agency, James Evans
Tel: 709-637-2339
jevans@gov.nl.ca

Executive Director, Iron Ore Industry, Paul Carter
Tel: 709-944-7940
Fax: 709-944-7961
paulcarter@gov.nl.ca

Director, Communications, Diana Quinton
Tel: 709-729-5282
dianaquinton@gov.nl.ca

Associated Agencies, Boards & Commissions:
• Agricultural Land Consolidation Review Committee
The Committee administers the Agricultural Land Consolidation Program, which allows retiring farmers & non-farmer landowners to sell their granted land to the provincial government.
Chair, Robert Walsh
• Canada-Newfoundland & Labrador Offshore Petroleum Board (C-NLOPB)
TD Place
140 Water St., 5th Fl.
St. John's, NL A1C 6H6
Tel: 709-778-1400
Fax: 709-778-1473
information@cnlopb.nl.ca
www.cnlopb.nl.ca
Other Communication: Core Storage & Research Centre, Phone: 709-778-1500, E-mail: csrc@cnlopb.nl.na
Established in 1985, the Canada - Newfoundland & Labrador Offshore Petroleum Board applies the provisions of the *Atlantic Accord* & the *Atlantic Accord Implementation Acts.*
The Board regulates the oil & gas industrr for the Newfoundland & Labrador Offshore Area. Operator activity is overseen for legislative & regulatory compliance in the areas of environmental protection, resource management, offshore safety, & industrial benefits.
The role of the Canada - Newfoundland & Labrador Offshore Petroleum Board facilitates the exploration for & development of hydrocarbon resources.
Chair & CEO, Scott Tessier
Tel: 709-778-1455
Vice-Chair, Edward Williams
Tel: 709-778-1455
Manager, Legal & Land, John P. Andrews
Tel: 709-778-1458
Manager, Support Services, Mike Baker
Tel: 709-778-1464
Manager, Industrial Benefits, Jeffrey M. Bugden, P.Eng.
Tel: 709-778-1448
Manager, Environmental Affairs, Dave Burley
Tel: 709-778-1403
Manager, Exploration, Nicholle Carter, P.Geo.
Tel: 709-778-1428
Manager, Safety, Daniel B. Chicoyne, MSS
Tel: 709-778-4262
Manager, Public Relations, Sean Kelly
Tel: 709-778-1418
Fax: 709-689-0713
skelly@cnlopb.nl.ca
Manager, Resource Management, Jeff O'Keefe
Tel: 709-778-1406
Manager, Operations, Howard L. Pike, P.Eng.
Tel: 709-778-1412
• Chicken Farmers of Newfoundland & Labrador
Agriculture Canada Bldg. 6
308 Brookfield Rd.
PO Box 8098
St. John's, NL A1B 3M9
Tel: 709-747-1493
Fax: 709-747-0544
www.nlchicken.com
Chair, Ruth Noseworthy
Vice-Chair, Ed O'Reilly
Manager, Ron Walsh
• Farm Industry Review Board (FIRB)
Provincial Agriculture Bldg.
308 Brookfield Rd.
PO Box 8700
St. John's, NL A1B 4J6
Tel: 709-729-3799
Fax: 709-729-6568
www.nr.gov.nl.ca/NR/agrifoods/ic/firb
FIRB is responsible for controlling & directing the operations of the province's commodity boards, as well as providing farmers with protection against nuisance suits (as long as the farm in question is operating according to acceptable farm practices).
Manager, Roger Churchill
rogerchurchill@gov.nl.ca
• Forest Land Tax Appeal Board

The Forest Land Tax Appeal Board carried out its responsibilities under Part III of the Forestry Act as of March 31, 2008.
Chair, Sheri Wicks
• Mineral Rights Adjudication Board
PO Box 5955
St. John's, NL A1C 5X4
Tel: 709-726-3524
Fax: 709-726-9600
The Board is responsible for hearing & determining the outcome of questions, disputes & matters arising out of the application of the Minieral Act & the Mining Act & associated regulations.
Chair, Gregory F. Kirby
• Nalcor Energy
See Entry Name Index for detailed listing.
• Newfoundland & Labrador Crop Insurance Agency
Corner Brook, NL
Chair, Cynthia MacDonald, P.Ag.
• Newfoundland & Labrador Farm Products Corporation

The Farm Products Corporation was mandated to establish buildings & establishments necessary for the handling, preparation, processing & storage of farm products, both animal & vegetable. It is currently inactive, but can be reactivated in order to assist the Minister of Natural Resources with provincial sustainable development initiatives.
• Newfoundland & Labrador Livestock Owners Compensation Board

• St. John's Land Development Advisory Authority

Chair, Hazen Scarth
• St. John's Urban Region Agricultural Appeal Board

Chair, Peter Morris
• Timber Scalers Board

The Timber Scalers Board is currently inactive, with its mandate being fulfilled internally within the Department of Natural Resources. Its members remain on standby in the event the Minister required the board re-activated.
• Wooddale Land Development Advisory Authority

The Authority considers applications for development in the Wooddale Agriculture Development Area.
Chair, Cynthia MacDonald, P.Ag.

Energy Branch
Associate Deputy Minister, Energy Resources, Tracy English
Tel: 709-729-2349
Fax: 709-729-2871
tenglish@gov.nl.ca
Assistant Deputy Minister, Petroleum Development, Wes Foote
Tel: 709-729-2206
Fax: 709-729-2508
wesfoote@gov.nl.ca
Assistant Deputy Minister, Royalties & Benefits, Paul Carter
Tel: 709-729-1644
Fax: 709-729-2871
pcarter@gov.nl.ca
Director, Regulatory Affairs, Fred Allen
Tel: 709-729-2778
fredallen@gov.nl.ca

Director, Energy Economics, Wayne Andrews
Tel: 709-729-5899
wayneandrews@gov.nl.ca
Acting Director, Electricity & Alternative Energy, Paul Parsons
Tel: 709-729-5728
paulparsons@gov.nl.ca
Director, Petroleum Engineering, Keith Hynes
Tel: 709-729-7188
Fax: 709-729-2508
keithhynes@gov.nl.ca
Director, Royalties Administration & Monitoring, Craig Martin
Tel: 709-729-0463
Fax: 709-729-2508
cmartin@gov.nl.ca
Acting Director, Energy Policy, Planning & Coordination, Rob McGrath
Tel: 709-729-1421
robmcgrath@gov.nl.ca
Director, Petroleum Geoscience, David Middleton
Tel: 709-729-1821
davidmiddleton@gov.nl.ca
Director, Petroleum Marketing & Promotion, Darrell Spurrell
Tel: 709-729-0579
Fax: 709-729-4011
darrellspurrell@gov.nl.ca
Director, Industrial Benefits, Bryon Sparkes
Tel: 709-729-3906
Fax: 709-729-4011
bsparkes@gov.nl.ca

Forestry & Agrifoods Agency
Assistant Deputy Minister, Agrifoods, Keith Deering
Chief Executive Officer, James Evans
Tel: 709-637-2339
Fax: 709-637-2461
Chief, Special Investigations, Legislation & Compliance, Angus Head
Tel: 709-637-2037
Fax: 709-637-2083
angushead@gov.nl.ca
Executive Director, Policy & Planning, Tanya Noseworthy
Tel: 709-729-1466
Fax: 709-729-2871
tanyanoseworthy@gov.nl.ca
Director, Policy & Planning, Dena Parsons
Tel: 709-729-5029
Fax: 709-729-0973
denaparsons@gov.nl.ca
Manager, Center for Forest Science & Innovation, Barry Linehan
Tel: 709-489-3012
barrylinehan@gov.nl.ca

Agrifoods Development Branch
Provincial Agriculture Bldg., Brookfield Rd., PO Box 8700St. John's, NL A1B 4J6
Tel: 709-729-6588
Fax: 709-729-2674
To contribute to economic & rural development throughout the province by promoting the continued development, expansion & diversification of competitive & sustainable primary & value-added agrifood businesses.
Assistant Deputy Minister, Agrifoods, Keith Deering
Tel: 709-729-3787
Fax: 709-729-0973
keithdeering@gov.nl.ca
Director, Land Resource Stewardship, Carey Richard
Tel: 709-637-2081
Fax: 709-637-2586
rcarey@gov.nl.ca
Director, Animal Health Division & Chief Veterinary Officer, Dr. Hugh Whitney
Tel: 709-729-6879
Fax: 709-729-0055
hughwhitney@gov.nl.ca

Forestry Services Branch
Fortis Bldg., PO Box 2006Corner Brook, NL A2H 6J8
Tel: 709-637-2349
Fax: 709-637-2403
The Forestry Services Branch is responsible for managing and regulating the forest resources of the Province.
Assistant Deputy Minister, James Evans
Tel: 709-637-2339
Fax: 709-637-2461
Director, Legislation & Compliance, Stephen Balsom
Tel: 709-637-2041
stephenbalsom@gov.nl.ca
Director, Forest Ecosystem Management, Ivan Downton
Tel: 709-634-2284
idownton@gov.nl.ca

Soil, Plant & Feed Laboratory
308 Brookfield Rd., PO Box 8700St. John's, NL A1B 4J6
Tel: 709-729-6738
Fax: 709-729-6734
Research is focused on animal waste & soil conservation, environmental sustainability issues (ESI) & soil, plant & feed testing.
Chemist, Tom Fagner
tomfagner@gov.nl.ca
Chemist, Dr. Mridul Misra

Mines Branch
Promotes & facilitates the sustainable development of the province's mineral & energy resources through its resource assessment, management & development activities for the overall benefit of the citizens of Newfoundland & Labrador.
Assistant Deputy Minister, David Liverman
Tel: 709-729-2768
Fax: 709-729-2871
dliverman@gov.nl.ca
Director, Geological Survey Division, Lawrence Dickson
Tel: 709-729-2453
Fax: 709-729-4270
wldickson@gov.nl.ca
Director, Geochemical Laboratory, Chris Finch
Tel: 709-729-3312
chrisfinch@gov.nl.ca
Director, Mineral Lands Division, Jim Hinchey
Tel: 709-729-6425
Fax: 709-729-6782
jimhinchey@gov.nl.ca
Director, Mineral Development Division, Alex Smith
Tel: 709-729-6379
Fax: 709-729-3493
asmith@gov.nl.ca
Senior Geologist & Section Manager, Geochemistry/Geophysics & Terrain Sciences, Martin Batterson
Tel: 709-729-3419
martinbatterson@gov.nl.ca
Senior Geologist & Section Manager, Regional Geology, Alana Hinchey
Tel: 709-729-7725
alanahinchey@gov.nl.ca
Senior Geologist & Section Manager, Mineral Deposits, Andrew Kerr
Tel: 709-729-2164
andykerr@gov.nl.ca
Senior Geologist & Section Manager, Geoscience Data Management, Larry Nolan
Tel: 709-729-2168
larrynolan@gov.nl.ca
Senior Geologist & Section Manager, Geoscience Publications & Information, Sean O'Brien
Tel: 709-729-2775
seanobrien@gov.nl.ca
Manager, Mining Industry Analysis, Tony Burgess
Tel: 709-729-6445
tonyburgess@gov.nl.ca
Manager, Mineral Incentive Program, John Clarke
Tel: 709-729-5851
jclarke@gov.nl.ca
Manager, Quarry Material, Fred Kirby
Tel: 709-729-6447
fredkirby@gov.nl.ca
Manager, Mineral Rights, Justin Lake
Tel: 709-729-6437
justinwlake@gov.nl.ca
Manager, Engineering Analysis, Len Mandville
Tel: 709-729-6439
lenmandville@gov.nl.ca
Eastern
PO Box 2222Gander, NL A1V 5T4
Tel: 709-256-1450
Fax: 709-256-1459
Director, Special Projects, David Cheeks
Tel: 709-256-1462
Fax: 709-256-1459
Labrador
Elizabeth Goudie Bldg., PO Box 3014 Stn. B, Happy Valley-Goose Bay, NL A0P 1E0
Tel: 709-896-3405
Fax: 709-896-3747
Other Communication: Wildlife, Phone: 709-896-5107; Fax: 709-896-0188
Regional Compliance Manager, Derek J. LeBoubon
Tel: 709-896-3405 ext: 228
Fax: 709-896-3747
derekleboubon@gov.nl.ca
Western
Massey Drive Bldg., PO Box 2006Corner Brook, NL A2H 6J8
Tel: 709-637-2409
Fax: 709-639-1377
Special Projects Officer, Gord Fifield
Tel: 709-637-2298
gfifield@gov.nl.ca
Ecosystem Planner, Perry Benoit
Tel: 709-637-2692
Fax: 709-639-1377
pbenoit@gov.nl.ca
Bay D'Espoir
PO Box 179Milltown, NL A0H 1W0
Tel: 709-882-2200
Bishop Falls
PO Box 640Bishop Falls, NL A0H 1C0
Tel: 709-258-5334
Cartwright
PO Box 159Cartwright, NL A0K 1V0
Tel: 709-938-7362
Fax: 709-938-7399
Clarenville
#206, 97 Manitoba Dr., Clarenville, NL A5A 1K3
Tel: 709-466-7439
Fax: 709-466-3802
District Manager, Ed Stewart
Gambo
PO Box 25Gambo, NL A0G 2E0
Tel: 709-674-4625
Gander
PO Box 2222Gander, NL A1V 2N9
Tel: 709-256-1450
Lewisporte
PO Box 217Lewisporte, NL A0G 1A0
Tel: 709-535-2706
Massey Drive
PO Box 2006Corner Brook, NL A2H 6J8
Tel: 709-637-2370
Northwest River
PO Box 1200Northwest River, NL A0P 1B0
Tel: 709-497-8479
Fax: 709-497-8482
Paddy's Pond
PO Box 13036St. John's, NL A1B 3V8
Tel: 709-729-4180
District Manager, William Clarke
Pasadena
PO Box 340Pasadena, NL A0L 1K0
Tel: 709-686-2071
Port Saunders
PO Box 69Port Saunders, NL A0K 4H0
Tel: 709-861-3502
Roddickton
PO Box 250Roddickton, NL A0K 4P0
Tel: 709-457-2300
District Manager, George Gibbons
St. George's
PO Box 279St Georges, NL A0N 1Z0
Tel: 709-646-3720
Fax: 709-646-3729
District Manager, Hubert Smith
Springdale
PO Box 220Springdale, NL A0J 1T0
Tel: 709-673-3821
Fax: 709-673-4525
Wabush
PO Box 419Wabush, NL A0R 1D0
Tel: 709-282-6881

Newfoundland & Labrador Board of Commissioners of Public Utilities

Prince Charles Bldg., #E-210, 120 Torbay Rd., PO Box 21040St. John's, NL A1A 5B2

Tel: 709-726-8600
Fax: 709-726-9604
Toll-Free: 866-782-0006
ito@pub.nf.ca
www.pub.nf.ca
Regulates electrical utilities in Newfoundland & Labrador.

Chair & CEO, Andy Wells
Tel: 709-726-1133
awells@pub.nl.ca

Vice-Chair, Darlene Whalen
Tel: 709-726-0955
dwhalen@pub.nl.ca

Newfoundland & Labrador Research & Development Corporation (RDC)

68 Portugal Cove Rd., St. John's, NL A1B 2L9
Tel: 709-758-0913
Fax: 709-758-0927
info@rdc.org
www.rdc.org
Other Communication: Alternate E-mails: programs@rdc.org; application@rdc.org; careers@rdc.org
The RDC is a provincial Crown corporation established in 2009 to improve Newfoundland & Labrador's research & development capabilities.

Minister Responsible, Hon. Keith Hutchings
Tel: 709-729-4728
Fax: 709-729-0654
keithhutchings@gov.nl.ca

Chair, Jacqueline (Jackie) Sheppard, Q.C., M.A., L.L.B., B.A.

Chief Executive Officer, Glenn Janes
glennjanes@rdc.org

Director, Information Management, Debra Downing
debraldowning@rdc.org

Director, Business Development, Steve Mercer
Tel: 709-758-0984
stevemercer@researchnl.com

Director, Human Resources, Kimberly Spencer
kimberlyspencer@rdc.org

Director, Financial Operations, Joanne Whelan
joannewhelan@rdc.org

Director, Marketing & Communications, Vacant

Newfoundland & Labrador Department of Service NL

PO Box 8700St. John's, NL A1B 4J6
Tel: 709-729-4834
servicenlinfo@gov.nl.ca
www.servicenl.gov.nl.ca
Service NL provides a great range of services to the people of Newfoundland & Labrador. Areas of attention include public health, public safety, environmental protection, vital statistics, motor vehicles, printing services, provincially regulated financial institutions, the operation of Government Service Centres, consumer & commercial affairs, & occupational health & safety. The department works in accordance with more than 150 pieces of legislation, regulations, standards, & codes of practice.
Service NL operates as a single access point for the public to common government services, such as licencing, permitting, & inspecting. The department handles the following responsibilities: issuing birth, marriage, & death certificates; testing & issuing driver licenses; issuing vehicle registrations; mediating landlord & tenant issues; registering companies, deeds, & lobbyists; investigating workplace incidents; issuing charitable gaming licences; & protecting the interests of consumers.
Service NL strives to provide services with a staff of more than 500 people at over 30 locations throughout Newfoundland & Labrador.

Minister, Hon. Nick McGrath
Tel: 709-709-7294
Fax: 709-729-4754
nickmcgrath@gov.nl.ca

Deputy Minister, David Norman
Tel: 709-729-4752
Fax: 709-729-4754
davidnorman@gov.nl.ca

Director, Strategic Human Resource Management, Barbara Brenton
Tel: 709-729-5102
Fax: 709-729-6661
BarbaraBrenton@gov.nl.ca

Director, Policy & Strategic Planning, Megan Collins
Tel: 709-729-6470
Fax: 709-729-4754
megancollins@gov.nl.ca

Director, Communications, Vanessa Colman-Sadd
Tel: 709-729-4860
Fax: 709-729-4754
vanessacolmansadd@gov.nl.ca

Director, Information Management, Susanna Duke
Tel: 709-729-2544
Fax: 709-729-4754
susannaduke@gov.nl.ca

Associated Agencies, Boards & Commissions:
• Credit Union Deposit Guarantee Corporation
PO Box 340
Marystown, NL A0E 2M0
Tel: 709-279-0170
Fax: 709-279-0177
Toll-free: 877-279-0170
www.cudgcnl.com
The Credit Union Deposit Guarantee Corporation is a provincial Crown corporation. The corporation administers the Credit Union Act & Regulations. The Credit Union Deposit Guarantee Corporation is responsible for ensuring compliance with the Credit Union Act & Regulations by credit unions, & insuring deposits of credit union members & associate members in Newfoundland & Labrador.
Chief Executive Officer & Superintendent of Credit Unions, William Langthorne
Tel: 709-364-4791
billangthorne@gov.nl.ca
Manager, Operations & Deputy Superintendent of Credit Unions, Bob Piercey
Tel: 709-279-0175
robertpiercey@gov.nl.ca
Supervisor, Examinations, Penny Nolan
Tel: 709-279-0176
pennynolan@gov.nl.ca
Supervisor, Stabilization, Al Spencer
Tel: 709-279-0171
alspencer@gov.nl.ca
• Government Purchasing Agency
30 Strawberry Marsh Rd.
St. John's, NL A1B 4R4
Tel: 709-729-3348
Fax: 709-729-5817
tenders@gov.nl.ca
The Government Purchasing Agency is the Government of Newfoundland & Labrador's central procurement unit. The agency manages the procurement process for goods & services for all government departments. It administers the the Agreement on Internal Trade & the Atlantic Procurement Agreement.
Minister Responsible, Hon. Nick McGrath
Tel: 709-729-4712
Fax: 709-729-4754
nickmcgrath@gov.nl.ca
Chief Operating Officer, Larry Cahill
Tel: 709-729-3343
Fax: 709-729-5817
cahilll@gov.nl.ca
Director, Audit, Information, & Training, Joseph Day
Tel: 709-729-5429
dayj@gov.nl.ca
Director, Procurement & Development, Patricia Hearn
Tel: 709-729-3344
hearnp@gov.nl.ca
Director, Government Purchasing, Policy, & Administration, Wayne Hendry
Tel: 709-729-3347
Fax: 709-729-5817
hendryw@gov.nl.ca
Director, Planning & Administration, Sonya Payne
Tel: 709-729-3346
Fax: 709-729-5824
sonyapayne@gov.nl.ca

Government Services Branch

PO Box 8700St. John's, NL A1B 4J6
Other Communication: Engineering & Inspection Services, Phone: 709-729-2747
The Government Services Branch oversees the following: Government Service Centres; motor vehicle registration; the Office of the Queen's Printer; vital statistics; engineering & inspections; & program & support services. Government services staff handle matters related to vital statistics, public health & safety, environmental issues, accessibility, highway safety, as well as the processing of permits, licences, approvals, & inspections.
Government Service Centres are located in the following places, presented in alphabetical order:
Clarenville (709-466-4060);
Corner Brook (709-637-2204);
Gander (709-256-1420);
Grand Bank (709-832-2326);
Grand Falls-Windsor (709-292-4206);
Harbour Grace (709-945-3107);
Happy Valley-Goose Bay (709-896-5428);
Labrador City (709-944-5282);
Lewisporte (709-535-0262);
Marystown (709-279-0837);
Port aux Basques (709-695-2835);
St. Anthony (709-454-8833);
St. John's (709-729-3699);
Stephenville (709-643-8650);
Springdale (709-673-4218).
Newfoundland & Labrador's motor vehicle registration services are available in the following places:
Clarenville (1-877-636-6867);
Corner Brook (1-877-636-6867);
Gander (1-877-636-6867);
Grand Falls-Windsor (1-877-636-686);
Happy Valley-Goose Ba y (1-877-636-6867);
Harbour Grace (1-877-636-6867);
Labrador City (1-877-636-6867);
Mount Pearl (1-877-636-6867).

Occupational Health & Safety Branch

PO Box 8700St. John's, NL A1B 4J6
Other Communication: Safety Bulletins & Recalls, Toll-Free: 1-563-5471
The Occupational Health & Safety Branch of Service NL works to ensure the health & safety of employees in the workplace in Newfoundland & Labrador.
The branch oversees administration of the Occupational Health & Safety Act, the Radiation Health & Safety Act, & the Workplace Health, Safety, & Compensation Act. Related regulations include the following: Asebestos Abatement Regulations; the Asbestos Exposure Code Regulations; the Occupational Health & Safety Regulations; the Occupational Health & Safety First Aid Regulations; the Radiation Health & Safety Regulations; the Workplace Hazardous Materials Information System (WHMIS) Regulations; & the Workplace Health, Safety, & Compensation Regulations.
Responsibilities of the Occupational Health & Safety Branch are as follows: development of health & safety legislation; compliance inspections of provincially regulated workplaces; hygiene assessments in workplaces; inspection of radiation control measures in workplaces; investigation of workplace incidents; & enforcement of health & safety legislation.
Assistant Deputy Minister, Kim Dunphy
Tel: 709-729-5548
Fax: 709-729-4151
kdunphy@gov.nl.ca
Manager, Standards & Regulatory Review, Heather Clarke
Tel: 709-729-4196
Fax: 709-729-3445
heatherclarke@gov.nl.ca
Acts Administered:
Colonial Buildings Act
Historic Resources Act
Inkeepers Act
Tourist Establishments Act

Minister, Hon. Terry French
Tel: 709-729-0659
Toll-free: 877-787-0707
Fax: 709-729-0662
terryfrench@gov.nl.ca

Deputy Minister, Judith A. Hearn
Tel: 709-729-3555
Fax: 709-729-0662
judithhearn@gov.nl.ca

Culture & Recreation
The department administers archeology permits, the Art Procurement Program, the Heritage Foundation of Newfoundland & Labrador, provides grants to artists, arts organizations, museums & archives through the Newfoundland & Labrador Arts Council, provides grants to assists the Newfoundland & Labrador Film Development Corporation & administers provincial historic sites.
Assistant Deputy Minister, Mark Jones
Tel: 709-729-3609
Fax: 709-729-0870
markjones@gov.nl.ca
Acting Director, Heritage, Jerry Dick
Tel: 709-729-7393
Fax: 709-729-0870
jerrydick@gov.nl.ca

Tourism
Director, Tourism Product Development, Juanita Keel-Ryan
Tel: 709-729-1708
Fax: 709-729-0474
jkeelryan@gov.nl.ca
Director, Tourism Marketing Division, Carmela Murphy
Tel: 709-729-2831
Fax: 709-729-0057
carmelamurphy@gov.nl.ca
Director, Tourism Research Division, Michaela Roebothan
Tel: 709-729-6024
Fax: 709-729-0870
michaelaroebothan@gov.nl.ca

Newfoundland & Labrador Department of Transportation & Works

Confederation Bldg., West Block, 6th Fl., PO Box 8700St. John's, NL A1B 4J6
Tel: 709-729-3679
Fax: 709-729-4285
twminister@gov.nl.ca
www.tw.gov.nl.ca
To provide a safe, efficient & sustainable transportation system & to provide landlord services & support services such as leasing & mail services for all government departments. The department liaises with other agencies & the federal government to ensure the overall public works & transportation needs & interest of the province are fully provided & protected.
Acts Administered:
Expropriation Act
Highway Traffic Act
Local Road Boards Act
Motor Carrier Act
Rail Service Act
Transportation & Works Act

Minister, Hon. Paul Davis
Tel: 709-729-3679
Toll-free: 866-996-5670
Fax: 709-729-4285
pdavis@gov.nl.ca

Deputy Minister, Jamie Chippett
Tel: 709-729-3676
Fax: 709-729-4285
jamiechippett@gov.nl.ca

Director, Communications, Ed Moriarity
Tel: 709-729-3015
Fax: 709-729-4285
edmoriarity@gov.nl.ca

Marine Transportation Services
440 Main St., PO Box 97Lewisporte, NL A0G 3A0
Tel: 709-535-6202
Fax: 709-535-6245
Toll-Free: 888-638-5454
Assistant Deputy Minister, Max Harvey
Tel: 709-729-2767
maxharvey@gov.nl.ca
Director, Maintenance & Engineering, Greg Cuff
Tel: 709-535-6210
Fax: 709-535-6245
gregcuff@gov.nl.ca
Director, Ferry Operations, Walter Pumphrey
Tel: 705-535-6220
Fax: 709-535-6245
pumphrey@gov.nl.ca
Director, Vessel Replacement & Chief Operating Officer, Marine Services, Vacant
Tel: 709-729-3278
Fax: 709-729-3440

Road Transportation
Assistant Deputy Minister, Gary Gosse
Tel: 709-729-3796
Fax: 709-729-0283
gosseg@gov.nl.ca
Chief Bridge Engineer, Highway Design & Construction, Doug Power
Tel: 709-729-6508
Fax: 709-729-0283
Manager, Equipment Support, Murray Adams
Tel: 709-729-5308
Fax: 709-729-6934
adamsm@gov.nl.ca
Manager, Highway Design & Traffic Engineering, John Morrissey
Tel: 709-729-5493
Fax: 709-729-0283
Senior Bridge & Marine Design Engineer, Garfield Au
Tel: 709-729-6880
Fax: 709-729-0283
Senior Engineer, Highway Design, Bill Skanes
Tel: 709-729-5962
Fax: 709-729-0283
Senior Environmental Planner, Highway Design & Construction, Roger Pottle
Tel: 709-729-5379
Fax: 709-729-0646
Supervisor, Maintenance & Engineering Projects, Chris Parsons
Tel: 709-584-3974
Fax: 709-584-3895

Strategic & Corporate Services
Tel: 709-729-3019
Fax: 709-729-4658
Assistant Deputy Minister, Vacant
Tel: 709-729-3676
Fax: 709-729-3418
Director, Financial Operations, Kevin Antle
Tel: 709-729-5356
Fax: 709-729-0703
kantle@gov.nl.ca
Director, Policy, Planning & Evaluation, Lynn Bryant
Tel: 709-729-5344
Fax: 709-729-3418
lbryant@gov.nl.ca
Director, Human Resources, Cindy Hussey
Tel: 709-729-3292
cindyhussey@gov.nl.ca
Manager, Air Services, Glen Cooper
Tel: 709-257-1037
glencooper@gov.nl.ca

Works Branch
Tel: 709-729-3019
Fax: 709-729-4658
Assistant Deputy Minister, Cory Grandy
Tel: 709-729-5672
Fax: 709-729-5934
corygrandy@gov.nl.ca
Acting Director, Planning & Accommodations, Mariette Byrne
Tel: 709-729-4422
Fax: 709-729-4658
Director, Building Design & Construction, Paul Lahey
Tel: 709-729-3342
Fax: 709-729-0646
laheyp@gov.nl.ca
Deer Lake - Western
74 Old Bonne Bay Rd., Deer Lake, NL A8H 3H4
Tel: 709-635-4127
Fax: 709-635-2549
Gander - Central
Fraser Mall, PO Box 2222Gander, NL A1V 2N9
Tel: 709-256-1000
Fax: 709-256-1013
Happy Valley-Goose Bay - Labrador
PO Box 3014 Stn. B, Happy Valley-Goose Bay, NL A0P 1E0
Tel: 709-896-7840
Fax: 709-896-7840
St. John's - Avalon
West Block, Confederation Complex, PO Box 8700St. John's, NL A1B 4J6
Tel: 709-729-3362
Fax: 709-729-0036

Newfoundland & Labrador Workplace Health, Safety & Compensation Commission

146 - 148 Forest Rd., PO Box 9000St. John's, NL A1A 3B8
Tel: 709-778-1000
Fax: 709-738-1714
Toll-Free: 800-563-9000
general.inquiries@whscc.nl.ca
www.whscc.nf.ca
Other Communication: Grand Falls toll-free: 800-563-3448; Corner Brook toll-free: 800-563-2772
www.facebook.com/127058107367289
www.youtube.com/user/safeworknl
Utilizing skilled, professional employees, in partnership with workplace parties, the commission facilitates safe & healthy workplaces by assisting employers & workers to prevent accidents, & manage workplace injuries/illnesses & return-to-work processes. Operating as the administrator of the workers' compensation insurance program, the commission provides a reasonable level of benefits to injured workers & their dependents based on reasonable assessment rates for employers, while maintaining or exceeding service level performance when compared to other jurisdictions in Canada.

Minister Responsible, Hon. Nick McGrath
Tel: 709-729-4712
Fax: 709-729-4754
nickmcgrath@gov.nl.ca

Chair, Ralph Tucker

CEO, Leslie Galway

Chief Financial & Information Officer, Paul Kavanagh

Executive Director, Employer Services, Brenda Greenslade

Executive Director, Workers Services, Tom Mahoney
Corner Brook
Millbrook Mall, #201B, 2 Herald Ave., Corner Brook, NL A2H 6E6
Tel: 709-637-2700
Fax: 709-639-1018
Toll-Free: 800-563-2772
Grand Falls-Windsor
26 High St., Grand Falls-Windsor, NL A2A 2P7
Tel: 709-489-1600
Fax: 709-489-1616
Toll-Free: 800-563-3448

Government of the Northwest Territories

Seat of Government: PO Box 1320Yellowknife, NT X1A 2L9
www.gov.nt.ca
The Northwest Territories was reconstituted September 1, 1905. It has an area of 1,140,834.90 km2, & the StatsCan census in 2011 showed the population was 41,462. On April 1, 1999, the Northwest Territories was divided into two new territories: Nunavut Territories and the as yet unnamed territory (known as the Northwest Territories). The Northwest Territories is governed by a fully elected Legislative Assembly of 19 members elected for a four-year term. Government is by consensus rather than party politics. The Legislature elects the Premier & a seven-member Executive Council, which is charged with the operation of government & the establishment of program & spending priorities. The Commissioner of the Northwest Territories is appointed by the Federal Government, & serves a role similar to that of a Lieutenant Governor in provincial jurisdictions.

Northwest Territories Department of Aboriginal Affairs & Intergovernmental Relations

4910 - 52nd St., PO Box 1320Yellowknife, NT X1A 2L9
Tel: 867-873-7143
Fax: 867-873-0233
Toll-Free: 877-838-8194
nancy_gardiner@gov.nt.ca
www.daair.gov.nt.ca

The Department of Aboriginal Affairs & Intergovernmental Relations is charged with the following responsibilities: to negotiate, implement, & monitor land, resource & self-government agreements; to manage governmental relationships with Aboriginal, federal, provincial, & territorial governments, & with circumpolar countries; to provide advice on federal-provincial-territorial-Aboriginal relations; & to contribute to the political & constitutional development of the Northwest Territories.

Minister, Hon. Bob McLeod
Tel: 867-669-2311
Fax: 867-873-0385
bob_mcleod@gov.nt.ca

Acting Deputy Minister, Andy Bevan
Tel: 867-873-7143
Fax: 867-873-0233
andy_bevan@gov.nt.ca

Director, Implementation, Scott B. Alexander
Tel: 867-873-7149
Fax: 867-873-0540
scott_alexander@gov.nt.ca

Acting Director, Intergovernmental Relations, Jennifer Dallman-Sanders
Tel: 867-873-7112
Fax: 867-873-0233
jennifer_dallman-sanders@gov.nt.ca

Director, Negotiations, Fred Talen
Tel: 867-873-7388
Fax: 867-873-0593
fred_talen@gov.nt.ca

Aurora Research Institute (ARI)

191 MacKenzie Rd., PO Box 1450Inuvik, NT X0E 0T0
Tel: 867-777-3298
Fax: 867-777-4264
webmaster@nwtresearch.com
www.nwtresearch.com
Other Communication: Twitter: twitter.com/nwtresearch
A division of Aurora College that is dedicated to excellence, leadership & innovations in Northern education & research. Administers the research licencing provisions of the Northwest Territories Scientists Act & provides year round logistical assistance for researchers.

Director, Pippa Seccombe
Tel: 867-777-3298 ext: 235
pseccombe-hett@auroracollege.nt.ca

Manager, South Slave Research Centre, Sarah Rosolen
Tel: 867-872-4909
Fax: 867-872-5024
srosolen@auroracollege.nt.ca

Manager, Inuvik Research Centre, Jolie Gareis
Tel: 867-777-3298 ext: 232
jolie.gareis@auroracollege.nt.ca
50 Conibear Cr.
PO Box 45
Fort Smith, NT X0E 0P0 Canada

Manager, North Slave Research Centre, Dr. Pertice Moffitt
Tel: 867-920-3062
pmoffitt@auroracollege.nt.ca

Northwest Territories Business Development & Investment Corporation (BDIC)

#701, 5201 - 50th Ave., Yellowknife, NT X1A 3S9
Tel: 867-920-6455
Fax: 867-765-0652
www.bdic.ca
The BDIC provides access to business financing, support, & development assistance to communities throughout the Northwest Territories. Their focus is the small and mid-sized business sector.

Chair, Darrell Beaulieu

Chief Executive Officer, Pawan Chugh
Tel: 867-920-3348

Director, Policy, Planning & Operations, Ron Chiasson
Tel: 867-920-3355

Director, Finance & Subsidiaries, Leonard Kwong
Tel: 867-920-3339

Northwest Territories Department of Education, Culture & Employment (ECE)

PO Box 1320Yellowknife, NT X1A 2L9
Tel: 867-669-2399
Fax: 867-873-0431
Toll-Free: 866-606-5627
www.ece.gov.nt.ca
Other Communication: Jobs North Phone: 867-873-7690; Fax: 867-873-0636; Email: jobsnorth@gov.nt.ca
The Ministry's responsibilities cover the following areas: Early Childhood; Kindergarten to Grade 12; Adult & Post-Secondary Education; Career Development & Employment; Apprenticeship & Occupational Certification; Culture, Heritage & Languages; Income Security; & Labour Services.

Minister, Hon. Jackson Lafferty
Tel: 867-669-2399
Fax: 867-873-0274
jackson_lafferty@gov.nt.ca

Deputy Minister, Gabriela Eggenhofer
Tel: 867-920-6240
Fax: 867-873-0338
gabriela_eggenhofer@gov.nt.ca

Associate Deputy Minister, Gloria Iatridis
Tel: 867-920-6240
Fax: 867-873-0338
gloria_iatridis@gov.nt.ca

Associated Agencies, Boards & Commissions:
• Northwest Territories Apprenticeship, Trade & Occupations Certification Board (ATOCB)
PO Box 1320
Yellowknife, NT X1A 2L9
Tel: 867-873-7357
Fax: 867-873-0200
• NWT Arts Council
PO Box 1320 Main
Yellowknife, NT X1A 2L9
Tel: 867-920-6370
Fax: 867-873-0205
boris_atamanenko@gov.nt.ca
www.nwtartscouncil.ca

Northwest Territories Department of Environment & Natural Resources (ENR)

PO Box 1320Yellowknife, NT X1A 2L9
www.enr.gov.nt.ca
Operations cover a broad spectrum of activities directed at promoting a healthy environment that supports traditional lifestyles within a modern economy. The wise use & protection of natural resources are encouraged. The Department's activities are carried out through the following divisions: Environmental Protection, Forest Management, Policy, Legislation & Communications, Protected Areas Strategy, Informatics, & Wildlife.
Acts Administered:
Asphalt Paving Industry Emission Regulations
Beverage Container Regulations
Certification & Disposal of Wildlife Regulations
Critical Wildlife Areas Regulations
Environmental Protection Act
Environmental Rights Act
Forest Management Act
Forest Protection Act
Natural Resources Conservation Trust Act
Pesticide Act
Sale of Wildlife Regulations
Species At Risk NWT Act (Not in force)
Spill Contingency Planning & Reporting Regulations
Trapping Regulations
Used Oil & Waste Fuel Management Regulations
Waste Reduction & Recovery Act
Water Resources Agreement Act
Wildlife Act
Wildlife Export Regulations
Wildlife General Regulations
Wildlife Management Areas & Zones Regulations
Wildlife Preserves Regulations
Wildlife Sanctuaries Regulations

Minister, Hon. Michael Miltenberger
Tel: 867-669-2355
Fax: 867-873-0596
Michael_Miltenberger@gov.nt.ca

Deputy Minister, Ernie Campbell
Tel: 867-873-7401
ernie_campbell@gov.nt.ca

Assistant Deputy Minister, Operations, Jack Bird
Tel: 867-920-6389
jack_bird@gov.nt.ca

Assistant Deputy Minister, Corporate & Strategic Planning, Ray Case
Tel: 867-920-6389
ray_case@gov.nt.ca

Director, Environment, Lisa Dyer
Tel: 867-873-7654
Fax: 867-873-0221
lisa_dyer@gov.nt.ca

Director, Land & Water, Mary Tapsell
Tel: 867-920-8069
Fax: 867-873-4229
mary_tapsell@gov.nt.ca

Director, Policy & Strategic Planning, Field Support Unit, Evan Walz
Tel: 867-920-8046
evan_walz@gov.nt.ca
Deh Cho
Milton Bldg., 2nd Fl., PO Box 240Fort Simpson, NT X0E 0N0
Tel: 867-695-7450
Fax: 867-695-2381
Regional Superintendent, Carl Lafferty
Tel: 867-695-7451
carl_lafferty@gov.nt.ca
Inuvik
Semmler Bldg., 2nd Fl., Bag Service #1, Inuvik, NT X0E 0T0
Fax: 867-678-6699
Regional Superintendent, Stephen Charlie
Tel: 867-678-6690
stephen_charlie@gov.nt.ca
North Slave
PO Box 2668Yellowknife, NT X1A 2P9
Tel: 867-873-7184
Fax: 867-873-6230
Regional Superintendent, Fred Mandeville
Tel: 867-920-6114
fred_mandeville@gov.nt.ca
Sahtu
PO Box 130Norman Wells, NT X0E 0V0
Tel: 867-587-3500
Fax: 867-587-3516
Acting Regional Superintendent, Jeff Walker
Tel: 867-587-3532
jeff_walker@gov.nt.ca
Fort Smith (South Slave)
Sweetgrass Bldg., PO Box 390Fort Smith, NT X0E 0P0
Tel: 867-872-6400
Fax: 867-872-4250
Acting Regional Superintendent, Troy Vermillion
Tel: 867-872-6404
troy_vermillion@gov.nt.ca

Environment

Tel: 867-873-7654
Fax: 867-873-0221
To protect & enhance the environmental quality in the North. Departmental programs are designed to control the discharge of contaminants & reduce their impacts on the natural environment. This is a shared responsibility with federal, territorial, Aboriginal & municipal agencies, as well as every resident of the Northwest Territories. To promote energy conservation & the use of energy efficient technology in the Northwest Territories, identify & facilitate the development of alternative, local energy sources which strengthen community economies, & promote & facilitate energy planning.

Director, Lisa Dyer
Tel: 867-873-7654
lisa_dyer@gov.nt.ca
Manager, Environmental Protection, Harvey Gaukel
Tel: 867-873-7645
harvey_gaukel@gov.nt.ca
Manager, Climate Change Programs, Jim Sparling
Tel: 867-920-6396
jim_sparling@gov.nt.ca
Specialist, Hazardous Substances, Jamie Chambers
Tel: 867-873-7562
Specialist, Hazardous Waste, Gerald Enns
Tel: 867-920-8044
Specialist, Industrial Oil & Gas, Todd Paget
Tel: 867-873-7178
Specialist, Industrial Mining, Erika Nyyssonen
Tel: 867-920-3118
Specialist, Solid Waste, Diep Duong
Tel: 867-873-7178
Specialist, Alternative Energy, Bryan Pelley
Tel: 867-873-7123
Specialist, Adaptation Planning, Brian Sieben
Tel: 867-920-6592

Forest Management Division
PO Box 7Fort Smith, NT X0E 0P0
Fax: 867-874-2077
forestmanagement.enr.gov.nt/
Provides the policy, planning & regulatory framework for the stewardship, protection & sustainable management of forest resources on 33 million hectares of land in the Northwest Territories, eight per cent of Canada's entire forested area. Working with First Nations governments, communities, other governments & non-governmental agencies on such a vast land mass presents unique & complex challenges for forest managers. The FMD coordinates & facilitates the implementation of forest management programs & services among the five administrative regions of ENR. The regional offices have the primary responsibility for delivery of programs. Regional staff implement forest resource & fire management programs for the Department. Regional personnel receive applications for approval to harvest, supervise harvesting activities, ensure compliance with standards, support community protection planning efforts & carry out fire management activities under the direction of the Forest Management Division. The Forest Management
Director, William Mawdsley
Tel: 867-872-7725
Fax: 867-872-2148
william_mawdsley@gov.nt.ca
Officer, Material Management, Raymond Menard
Tel: 867-872-7732
Manager, Fire Operations, Frank Lepine
Tel: 867-872-7713
Manager, Aviation Services, Duane Sinclair
Tel: 867-872-7719
Manager, Forest Science, Kris Johnson
Tel: 867-872-7706
Forester, Forest and Fire Management, David Purchase
Tel: 867-870-7743
Forest Ecologist, Bob Decker
Tel: 867-874-2009
Manager, Forest Resources, Tom Lakusta
Tel: 867-874-2009
Acting Manager, Program Support Services, Jennifer Wilkinson
Tel: 867-872-7702

Policy & Strategic Planning
Fax: 867-873-0114
Provides services in the area of policy, legislation, environmental assessment, land claims & self-government, resource management & public affairs & communications.
Director, Policy & Strategic Planning, Evan Walz
Tel: 867-920-8046
Policy Analyst, Claire Singer
Tel: 867-873-7980
Policy Analyst, Aboriginal Relations, Jason McNeil
Tel: 867-920-3298
Manager, Public Affairs & Communication, Judy Mclinton
Tel: 867-873-7379

Wildlife
Fax: 867-874-2347
www.nwtwildlife.com/
Activities are directed towards maintaining productive populations of all native wildlife in their natural habitats, encouraging the wise use of wildlife populations within the limits of sustainable yield & encouraging the active participation of northern residents in the management of wildlife resources. In addition to assistance programs that are designed to support the hunting & trapping economy, the division provides support to organizations of resource users to allow them to become more involved in wildlife management.
Director, Lynda Yonge
Tel: 867-920-8043
Manager, Technical Support, Ray Case
Tel: 867-920-8067
ray_case@gov.nt.ca
Manager, Wildlife & Environment, Inuvik Region & Environmental Assessment Specialist, Marsha Branigan
Tel: 867-920-6315
Manager, Wildlife & Environment, South Slave Region, Tony Vermillion
Tel: 867-872-6404
Supervisor, Wildlife, Sahtu Region, Richard Popko
Tel: 867-587-3517
Manager, Biodiversity Conservation, Rob Gau
Tel: 867-920-6488
Manager, Wildlife Research & Management, Nicole McCutchen
Tel: 867-920-8067

Comptroller General, Warren St Germaine
Tel: 867-920-6196
Fax: 867-873-0296
warren_stgermaine@gov.nt.ca
Deh Cho
PO Box 246Fort Simpson, NT X0E 0N0
Tel: 867-695-3815
Fax: 867-695-2920
Tlicho
Bag #5, Behchoko, NT X0E 0Y0
Tel: 867-392-3000
Fax: 867-392-3001
Fort Smith
PO Box 1080Fort Smith, NT X0E 0P0
Tel: 867-872-6200
Fax: 867-872-6275
Hay River
3 Gaetz Dr., Hay River, NT X0E 0R8
Tel: 867-874-7100
Fax: 867-874-7118
Beaufort-Delta
Bag #2, 285 Mackenzie Rd., Inuvik, NT X0E 0T0
Tel: 867-777-8000
Fax: 867-777-8062
Sahtu
PO Box 340Norman Wells, NT X0E 0V0
Tel: 867-587-3650
Fax: 867-587-3436
Stanton
PO Box 10Yellowknife, NT X1A 2N1
Tel: 867-669-4224
Fax: 867-669-4128
www.srhb.org
Yellowknife
Jan Stirling Bldg., 4702 Franklin Ave., PO Box 608Yellowknife, NT X1A 2N5
Tel: 867-873-7276
Fax: 867-920-7025
yhssa@gov.nt.ca
www.yhssa.org

Northwest Territories Department of Health & Social Services

Centre Square Tower, PO Box 1320Yellowknife, NT X1A 2L9
Fax: 867-873-0266
www.hlthss.gov.nt.ca
The Department of Health & Social Services is mandated to provide a broad range of health & social programs & services to the residents of the NWT. Seven regional Health & Social Services Authorities plan, manage & deliver a full spectrum of community & facility-based services for health care & social services. Community health programs include daily sick clinics, public health clinics, home care, school health programs & educational programs. Visiting physicians & specialists routinely visit the communities.
Acts Administered:
Communicable Diseases Regulation
General Sanitation Regulations
Meat Inspection Regulations
Public Health Act
Public Sewerage Systems Regulation
Public Water Supply Regulations

Minister, Hon. Tom Beaulieu
Tel: 867-669-2315
Tom_Beaulieu@gov.nt.ca

Deputy Minister, Debbie DeLancey
Tel: 867-920-6173
Fax: 867-873-0266
debbie_delancey@gov.nt.ca

Community Wellness & Social Services
Fax: 867-873-7706
Director, Community Wellness & Social Services, Andy Langford
Tel: 867-920-7054
andy_langford@gov.nt.ca
Manager, Health Choices, Vacant
Tel: 867-920-6300
Public Guardian, Office of the Public Guardian, Beatrice Raddi
Tel: 867-920-8029
Manager, Prevention Services, Bethan Williams-Simpson
Tel: 867-920-6940
Territorial Nutritionist, Prevention Services, Elsie De Roose
Tel: 867-873-7925

Finance
Fax: 867-920-4969
Director, Jeannie Mathison
Tel: 867-873-7367
jeannie_mathison@gov.nt.ca
Assistant Director, Financial Planning & Analysis, Jeffrey Dalley
Tel: 867-873-7962
jeffrey_dalley@gov.nt.ca
Manager, Contracts/Purchasing, Joe Tkachuk
Tel: 867-873-7058
joe_tkachuk@gov.nt.ca
Comptroller, Finance, Kim Weir
Tel: 867-920-3003
kim_weir@gov.nt.ca

Information Services
Chief Information Officer, Michele Herriot
Tel: 867-920-8907
Manager, Application Systems, Jason Doiron
Tel: 867-920-3029
jason_doiron@gov.nt.ca
Acting Manager, Information Maangement, Val Ross
Tel: 867-920-6365
val_ross@gov.nt.ca

Policy, Legislation & Communications
Fax: 867-873-0484
Director, Denise Canuel
Tel: 867-920-3283
denise_canuel@gov.nt.ca
Manager, Policy & Legislation, Natasha Brotherton
Tel: 867-920-3334
Fax: 867-873-0204
natasha_brotherston@gov.nt.ca
Manager, Official Languages, Lisa Berthier
Tel: 867-920-3367
lisa_berthier@gov.nt.ca
Manager, Communications, Damien Healy
Tel: 867-920-8927
damien_healy@gov.nt.ca

Population Health
Fax: 867-873-0442
Director, Laura Seddon
Tel: 867-920-3231
laura_seddon@gov.nt.ca
Chief Environmental Health Officer, Duane Fleming
Tel: 867-873-2183
duane_fleming@gov.nt.ca
Manager, Health Protection, Wanda White
Tel: 867-920-3293
Fax: 867-873-0442
wanda_white@gov.nt.ca
Manager, Disease Registries/Territorial Epidemiologist, Marla Santos
Tel: 867-920-3241
marla_santos@gov.nt.ca

Territorial Health Services

Director, Donna Allen
Tel: 867-873-7403
donna_allen@gov.nt.ca
Manager, Primary Community Services, Scott Robertson
Tel: 867-920-6250
scott_robertson@gov.nt.ca
Manager, Health Systems Planning, Vicki Lafferty
Tel: 867-873-7060
vicki_lafferty@gov.nt.ca
Chief Public Health Officer, Office of the Chief Public Health Officer, Andre Corriveau
Tel: 867-920-5204
andre_corriveau@gov.nt.ca

Northwest Territories Department of Industry, Tourism & Investment (ITI)

PO Box 1320Yellowknife, NT X1A 2L9
Fax: 867-873-0306
info@iti.ca
www.iti.gov.nt.ca
The Department of Industry, Tourism & Investment promotes & supports economic prosperity & community self-reliance in the Northwest Territories by providing programs & services. Programs & services are available through the following departmental divisions: Diamonds; Energy Planning; Industrial Initiatives; Informatics; Investment & Economic Analysis; Mackenzie Valley Pipeline Office; Minerals, Oil & Gas; Policy, Legislation & Communications; & Tourism & Parks.
Acts Administered:
Herd & Fencing Act
Territorial Parks Act

Minister, Hon. David Ramsey
Tel: 867-669-2377
Fax: 867-873-0306
David_Ramsay@gov.nt.ca

Deputy Minister, Peter Vician
Tel: 867-920-8048
Fax: 867-873-0563
peter_vician@gov.nt.ca

Assistant Deputy Minister, Kelly Kaylo
Tel: 867-873-7115
kelly_kaylo@gov.nt.ca

Director, Energy Planning, Dave Nightingale
Tel: 867-920-3274
dave_nightingale@gov.nt.ca

Director, Policy, Legislation & Communications, Sonya Saunders
Tel: 867-873-7005
Fax: 867-873-0645
sonya_saunders@gov.nt.ca

Senior Contract Reporting Officer, The BIP Monitoring Office, Lori Gaukel
Tel: 867-873-7235
lori_gaukel@gov.nt.ca

Northwest Territories Geoscience Office

4601 B - 52 Ave., PO Box 1500Yellowknife, NT X1A 2R3
Tel: 867-669-2636
Fax: 867-669-2725
ntgo@gov.nt.ca
www.nwtgeoscience.ca
The Northwest Territories Geoscience Office (NTGO) advances the geoscience knowledge of the Northwest Territories for the benefit of northerners through: delivery of geoscience research; analysis of mineral & petroleum resources; excellence in data management. In collaboration with its partners, NTGO provides analysis, information & advice to individuals, communities, governments, & the mining & petroleum industry
Chief Geologist, AANDC Manager, Scott Cairns
Tel: 867-669-2479
scott_cairns@gov.nt.ca
Manager, Petroleum Geosciences, Kathryn Fiess
Tel: 867-669-2488
kathryn_fiess@gov.nt.ca
Manager, Geomatics & IT, Doug Irwin
Tel: 867-669-2482
doug_irwin@gov.nt.ca
Senior Geologist, GNWT Manager, John Ketchum
Tel: 867-669-2498
john_ketchum@gov.nt.ca
Geomatics Specialist, Kelly Pierce
Tel: 867-669-2484
kelly_pierce@gov.nt.ca

Mackenzie Valley Petroleum Planning Office

Coordinates the territorial government's planning & response related to the Mackenzie Gas Project, including the regulatory review & environmental assessment processes. Also handles the territorial government's communications with respect to the Mackenzie Gas Project, & will manage selective funding programs to help Aboriginal groups & communities to prepare for the project.
Director, Planning Coordination, Tim Coleman
Tel: 867-874-5405
Special Advisor, Ian Butters
Tel: 867-874-5404

Investment & Economic Analysis

Fax: 867-873-0101
With general responsibilities for strategies, plans & programs to develop the NWT business community, the division provides expert advice & support in the production & marketing of arts & crafts, & acts as a link to national & international businesses & organizations.
Director, John Colford
Tel: 867-873-7361
john_colford@gov.nt.ca
Trade Officer, Alexandrea Knight
Tel: 867-873-7003
alexandrea_knight@gov.nt.ca
Manager, Arts & Fine Crafts, Carla Wallis
Tel: 867-920-6130
carla_wallis@gov.nt.ca
Manager, Economic Planning & Analysis, Dan Westman
Tel: 867-873-7394
dan_westman@gov.nt.ca

Minerals, Oil & Gas Division

Fax: 867-873-0254
The Minerals, Oil & Gas Division develops & implements strategies to encourage & attract non-renewable resource investment in the Northwest Territories. It also provides advice on the geological potential, industrial activity & potential opportunities associated with mineral, oil & gas exploration in the Territory.
Director, Deb Archibald
Tel: 867-920-3222
Assistant Director, Pietro Debastiani
Tel: 867-920-3001

Tourism & Parks

Fax: 867-873-0163
Develops, operates & maintains facilities that include parks, visitor centres & interpretive displays. The division is also responsible for implementing the Protected Areas Strategy for the Northwest Territories, in conjunction with Canada's Federal Government & other stakeholders. The division also provides support for tourism marketing, research & product development.
Director, Richard Zieba
Tel: 867-873-7903
Manager, Research & Planning, Sarah Marsh
Tel: 867-920-3245
sarah_marsh@gov.nt.ca
Manager, Parks Operations, Benji Straker
Tel: 867-920-6206
benji_straker@gov.nt.ca
Acting Manager, Tourism Operations, Karen Taggart
Tel: 867-920-8848
karen_taggart@gov.nt.ca

Minister, Hon. Glen Abernethy
Tel: 867-669-2388
Glen_Abernethy@gov.nt.ca

Deputy Minister, Sylvia Haener
Tel: 867-920-6197
Fax: 867-873-0307
sylvia_haener@gov.nt.ca

Assistant Deputy Minister & Attorney General, Mark Aitken
Tel: 867-920-6197
mark_aitken@gov.nt.ca

Assistant Deputy Minister & Solicitor General, Shirley Kemeys-Jones
shirley_kemeysjones@gov.nt.ca

Chief Coroner, Coroner's Office, Cathy Menard
Tel: 867-973-7448
Fax: 867-873-0426
cathy_menard@gov.nt.ca

Chief Information Officer, Norm Embleton
Tel: 867-920-6100
Fax: 867-873-0197
norm_embleton@gov.nt.ca

Public Trustee, Public Trustee's Office, Brian Asmundson
Tel: 867-873-7464
Toll-free: 866-535-0423
Fax: 867-873-0184
larry_pontus@gov.nt.ca

Executive Director, Legal Services Board, Charlene Doolittle
Tel: 867-873-7450
Fax: 867-873-5320
charlene_doolittle@gov.nt.ca

Acting Director, Legislation Division, Kelly McLaughlin
Tel: 867-920-8778
Fax: 867-873-0234
kelly_mclaughlin@gov.nt.ca

Director, Corrections Services, Greg Debogorski
Tel: 867-920-8922
Fax: 867-873-0299
greg_debogorski@gov.nt.ca

Director, Court Services, Anne Mould
Tel: 867-920-8852
Fax: 867-873-0307
anne_mould@gov.nt.ca

Director, Community Justice & Community Policing, Parker Kennedy
Tel: 867-873-7002
Fax: 867-873-0199
parker_kennedy@gov.nt.ca

Director, Legal Registries, Gary MacDougall
Tel: 867-873-7490
Fax: 867-873-0243
gary.macdougall@gov.nt.ca

Director, Finance, Kim Schofield
Tel: 867-873-7641
Fax: 867-873-0173
kim_schofield@gov.nt.ca

Director, Policy & Planning, Glen Rutland
Tel: 867-920-3225
Fax: 867-873-0659
glen_rutland@gov.nt.ca

Director, Legal Division, Brad Patzer
Tel: 867-920-3248
Fax: 867-873-0234
brad_patzer@gov.nt.ca

Registrar, Land Titles, Tom Hall
Tel: 867-920-8986
Fax: 867-873-0243
tom_hall@gov.nt.ca

Registrar, Corporate Registries, Donald MacDougall
Tel: 867-920-8984
Fax: 867-873-0243
donald_macdougall@gov.nt.ca

Administrator, Commissioner for Oaths / Notary Public, Cindy Pettes
Tel: 867-920-8985
Fax: 867-873-0243
cindy_pettes@gov.nt.ca

Northwest Territories Department of Municipal & Community Affairs

PO Box 1320Yellowknife, NT X1A 2L9

Tel: 867-873-7118
Fax: 867-873-0309
www.maca.gov.nt.ca
Supports capable, accountable & self-directed community governments providing a safe, sustainable & healthy environment for community residents. Works with community governments & other partners in supporting community residents as they organize & manage democratic, responsible & accountable community governments. The Department assists municipalities with administrative services & infrastructure project management, provides expertise in engineering to communities & arranges for debentures on behalf of communities which are undertaking public works programs. Advisory services are supplied to community councils for the planning, development & administration of public lands within municipal boundaries. Technical expertise is provided for mapping, surveying & air photography & zoning by-law administration.
Acts Administered:
Area Development Act
Civil Emergency Measures Act
Commissioner's Land Act
Fire Prevention Act
Hamlets Act
Planning Act
Property Assessment & Taxation Act (jointly with Department of Finance)
Settlements Act

Minister, Hon. Robert C. McLeod
Tel: 867-669-2366
Robert_C_McLeod@gov.nt.ca

Deputy Minister, Tom R. Williams
Tel: 867-873-7118
Fax: 867-873-0309
tom_williams@gov.nt.ca

Assistant Deputy Minister, Regional Operations, Eleanor Young
Tel: 867-873-7118
Fax: 867-873-0309
eleanor_young@gov.nt.ca

Associated Agencies, Boards & Commissions:
• **Assessment Appeal Tribunal of the Northwest Territories**
#400, 5201 - 50th Ave.
PO Box 1320
Yellowknife, NT X1A 2L9
Tel: 867-873-7125
Fax: 867-873-0609
• **Territorial Board of Revision**
#400, 5201 - 50th Ave.
PO Box 1320
Yellowknife, NT X1A 2L9
Tel: 867-873-7125
Fax: 867-873-0609

Lands Administration
Tel: 867-873-7569
Fax: 867-920-6156
Responsible for the administration of Commissioner's lands in & around the communities of the Northwest Territories. Commissioner's lands make up about 2 percent of all land in the North. The Federal Government administers about 97 percent & municipal corporations administer the remaining 1 percent. Under the Lands Program, MACA is in the process of transferring certain lands from the Commissioner to municipalities. Land administration is being decentralized from MACA headquarters to regional offices or to the communities. As authority for land devolves, MACA will take on a training & advisory role, teaching & advising communities how to look after their own lands. The division supplies information & advice regarding land leases, surrenders, transfers, & mortgage registration for Commissioner's land & notifications.
Director, Emerald Murphy
Tel: 867-920-6284
emerald_murphy@gov.nt.ca
Manager, Lands Policy/Program Development, Michelle Chappell
Tel: 867-920-6318
michelle_chappell@gov.nt.ca

Northwest Territories Power Corporation

4 Capital Dr., Hay River, NT X0E 1G2
Tel: 867-874-5200
Fax: 867-874-5251
info@ntpc.com
www.ntpc.com
Other Communication: Fort Simpson: 800-288-4784; Fort Smith: 800-661-0855; Inuvik: 800-661-0856; Yellowknife: 800-661-0854
Made up of 28 separate power systems, the NWT Power Corporation serves approximately 42,000 people in communities across the Northwest Territories. Facilities include hydro-electric, diesel & natural gas generation plants, transmission systems, & several isolated electrical distribution systems. The Corporation works to provide environmentally sound, safe, reliable, cost-effective energy & related services in the territories.

Minister Responsible, Hon. Floyd K. Roland
Tel: 867-669-2311
Fax: 867-873-0169
Floyd_K_Roland@gov.nt.ca

Chief Financial Officer, Judith Goucher

Manager, Human Resources, Cheryle Donahue

Director, Thermal Region, Mike Ocko

Director, Transmission & Distribution, David Duncan

Director, Assets Management & Engineering, Dan Roberts

Director, Hydro Region, Robert Schmidt

Manager, Information Technology, Glenn Smith

Public Utilities Board of the Northwest Territories (PUB)

#203, 62 Woodland Dr., PO Box 4211Hay River, NT X0E 1G1
Tel: 867-874-3944
Fax: 867-874-3639
www.nwtpublicutilitiesboard.ca
The independent, quasi-judicial agency of the Government of the Northwest Territories is responsible for the regulation of public utilities in the territory. Its authority is from the Public Utilities Act. Issues are handled by an application & decision process.

Minister Responsible, Hon. Bob McLeod
Tel: 867-669-2388
Fax: 867-873-0431
Bob_McLeod@gov.nt.ca

Chair, Joe Acorn

Northwest Territories Department of Public Works & Services

PO Box 1320Yellowknife, NT X1A 2L9
www.pws.gov.nt.ca
Designs, constructs, maintains & operates territorial buildings; implements energy efficiency projects; provides essential petroleum products to the public where they are not available from the private sector; provides data systems & communication services to government departments.
Acts Administered:
Boilers & Pressure Vessels Act
Electrical Protection Act
Gas Protection Act
Purchasing Management Association Act

Minister, Hon. Glen Abernethy
Tel: 867-669-2388
glen_abernethy@gov.nt.ca

Deputy Minister, Paul Guy
Tel: 867-873-7114
Fax: 867-873-0226
paul_guy@gov.nt.ca

Asset Management Division
Stuart M. Hodgson Bldg., 5009 - 49th St., 3rd Fl., Yellowknife, NT X1A 2L9
Estimates the cost of building construction & renovation; consults in the plan of buildings so they meet program needs; reviews consultant designs of buildings & works; implements the Safe Drinking Water Initiatives.
Acting Assistant Deputy Minister, Mike Burns
Tel: 867-920-6142
Fax: 867-873-0226
mike_burns@gov.nt.ca
Director, Facility Management Section, Brian Nagel
Tel: 867-920-6465
Fax: 867-873-0226
brian_nagel@gov.nt.ca
Manager, Gas/Boilers & Electrical, Ron McRae
Tel: 867-920-8801
ron_mcrae@gov.nt.ca

Petroleum Products Division
Stuart M. Hodgson, 5009 - 49th St., 1st Fl., Yellowknife, NT X1A 2L9
Tel: 867-920-3447
Fax: 867-873-0100
Provides essential petroleum products to the public where they are not available from the private sector.
Director, John Vandenburg
Tel: 867-920-3447
Fax: 867-873-0100
john_vandenberg@gov.nt.ca
Senior Operations Officer, Mike Squirrel
Tel: 867-695-7257
Fax: 867-695-3034
mike_squirrel@gov.nt.ca
Coordinator, Fuel Operations, Susan Eveleigh
Tel: 867-873-7796
Fax: 867-920-6297
susan_eveleigh@gov.nt.ca

Northwest Territories Department of Transportation

Lahm Ridge Bldg., 4501 50 Ave., PO Box 1320Yellowknife, NT X1A 2L9
Tel: 867-920-3460
Fax: 867-873-0363
www.dot.gov.nt.ca
Acts Administered:
All-Terrain Vehicles Act
Deh Cho Bridge Act
Motor Vehicles Act
Public Airports Act
Public Highways Act
Transportation of Dangerous Goods Act, 1990
Transportation of Dangerous Goods Regulations

Minister, Hon. David Ramsay
Tel: 867-669-2377
Fax: 867-873-0388
David_Ramsay@gov.nt.ca

Deputy Minister, Russell Neudorf
Tel: 867-920-3460
Fax: 867-873-0363
russell_neudorf@gov.nt.ca

Assistant Deputy Minister, Daniel Auger
Tel: 867-920-3461
Fax: 867-873-0363
daniel_auger@gov.nt.ca

Highways & Marine
4510 - 50 Ave., 2nd fl., PO Box 1320Yellowknife, NT X1A 2L9
Tel: 867-920-8771
Fax: 867-873-0288
Director, Kevin McLeod
Tel: 867-873-7800
Fax: 867-873-0288
kevin_mcleod@gov.nt.ca
Head, Structures, Ann Kulmatycki
Tel: 867-920-8010
ann_lanteigne@gov.nt.ca

Northwest Territories Water Board

125 Mackenzie Rd., PO Box 2531Yellowknife, NT X0E 0T0
Tel: 867-678-2942
Fax: 867-678-2943
info@nwtwb.com
www.nwtwb.com
Responsible for the development, maintenance & conservation of water resources; administers licences for utilizing water or disposing of wastes into water under the Northwest Territories Waters Act; has federal/territorial jurisdiction.

Chair, Eddie T. Dillon

Executive Director, Mike Harlow

Tel: 867-678-8609
harlowm@nwtwb.com

Office & Finance Administrator, Freda Wilson
Tel: 867-678-2942
wilsonf@nwtwb.com

Vice-Chair, Rudy Cockney

Board Member, Mark Cleveland

Board Member, Peter Bannon

Northwest Territories & Nunavut Workers' Safety & Compensation Commission (WCB)

Centre Square Tower, 5022 - 49th St., 5th Fl., PO Box 8888Yellowknife, NT X1A 2R3
Tel: 867-920-3888
Fax: 867-873-4596
Toll-Free: 800-661-0792
www.wscc.nt.ca
Other Communication: Toll Free Fax: 1-866-277-3677; Incident/Accident Line: 1-800-661-0792
The Workers' Safety & Compensation Commission is engaged in the following activities: ensuring compensation & pensions are awarded to injured workers or their dependents; assessing sufficiently & fairly to meet obligations; maintaining balance in providing benefits to injured workers, while keeping costs to employers as low as possible; & promoting safe workplaces through education & enforcement.
Acts Administered:
Asbestos Safety Regulations
Environmental Tobacco Smoke Worksite Regulations
Explosives Use Act
Mine Health & Safety Act
Mine Health & Safety Regulations
Safety Act
Summary Convictions Procedures Act
Work Site Hazardous Materials Information System Regulations
Workers' Compensation Act

Minister Responsible, Hon. Robert C. McLeod
Tel: 867-669-2366
Robert_C_McLeod@gov.nt.ca

Vice-President, Prevention Services, Cara Benoit
Tel: 867-669-4407

Government of Nova Scotia

Seat of Government: Province House, 1726 Hollis St., Halifax, NS B3J 2T3
www.gov.ns.ca
The Province of Nova Scotia entered Confederation July 1, 1867. It has an area of 52,917,46 km2, & the StatsCan census population in 2011 was 921,727.

Nova Scotia Department of Agriculture

1741 Brunswick St., 3rd Fl., PO Box 2223Halifax, NS B3J 3C4
Tel: 902-424-4560
Fax: 902-424-4671
www.gov.ns.ca/nsafPO Box 550 Sta.
Truro, NS B2N 5E3 Canada
The Department of Agriculture has a legislated mandate to support & develop the agriculture & food industries, recognizing that these sectors are economic engines of Nova Scotia's rural communities. Fosters prosperous & sustainable agriculture & food industries through the delivery of quality public services for the betterment of rural communities in Nova Scotia.
Acts Administered:
Agriculture & Marketing Act
Agriculture Marshland Conservation Act
Animal Health & Protection Act
Animal Health & Protection Regulations
Animal Protection Act
Cattle Pest Control Act
Farm Practices Act
Health Protection Act (Food Regulations & Milk Production, Transportation & Pasteurization Regulations only)
Livestock Health Services Act
Livestock Health Services Regulations
Marsh Land Use Regulations: Bishop-Beckwith, Dentiballis, Dugau/Ryerson, Grand Pré, Lower Truro, Masstown, Victoria Diamond Jubilee, Wellington
Meat Inspection Act
Natural Products Act
Non-Agricultural Use Land Exemption Regulations
Potato Industry Act
Weed Control Act
Wildlife Act

Minister, Hon. John MacDonnell
Tel: 902-424-4388
Fax: 902-424-0699
min_dag@gov.ns.ca

Deputy Minister, Rosalind Penfound
Tel: 902-424-0301
Fax: 902-424-0698
rcpenfou@gov.ns.ca

Executive Director, Agriculture & Food Operations, Alan Grant
Tel: 902-893-6591

Executive Director, Legislation & Compliance, Leo Muise
Tel: 902-424-3664

Director, Policy & Planning, Scott Hosking
Tel: 902-424-8868
hoskinsp@gov.ns.ca

Director, Communications, Brett Loney
Tel: 902-424-0192
loneybm@gov.ns.ca

Executive Secretary, Yvelle Poirier
Tel: 902-424-4388
ypoirier@gov.ns.ca

Associated Agencies, Boards & Commissions:
• **Nova Scotia Crop & Livestock Insurance Commission**
MacRae Library Building
137 College Rd.
PO Box 1092
Truro, NS B2N 5G9
Tel: 902-424-4560
Fax: 902-895-4622
nsclic@gov.ns.ca
www.gov.ns.ca/agri/ci
Under the Crop & Livestock Insurance Act, the Commission is responsible for administering the program under the direction, supervision, & control of the Minister of Agriculture.
Chair, Avard Bentley
Chief Executive Officer, Bill MacLeod
Tel: 902-893-7755
macleojb@gov.ns.ca
• **Nova Scotia Farm Loan Board**
PO Box 550
Truro, NS B2N 5E3
Tel: 902-893-6506
Fax: 902-895-7693
flb@gov.ns.ca
www.gov.ns.ca/agri/farmlb/
Other Communication: Kentville location: Phone: 902-679-6009, Fax: 902-679-4997
The Nova Scotia Farm Loan Board operates as a Corporation of the Crown & supports the development of sustainable agriculture & agri-rural business in Nova Scotia through responsible lending.
Chief Executive Officer, Cheryl Burgess
Tel: 902-893-6500
burgescm@gov.ns.ca
Director, Jim MacAfee
Director, Lee Thompson
• **Nova Scotia Farm Practices Board**
PO Box 550
Truro, NS B2N 5E3
Tel: 902-893-7314
www.gov.ns.ca/agri/legislaton/fpb.shtml
The Farm Practices Board provides a structure to hear complaints & decide on normal farm practices. The Board provides a mechanism for resolving issues between farmers & their neighbours regarding odour, noise, dust, vibration, light, smoke or other disturbance resulting from a farming activity.
• **Nova Scotia Natural Products Marketing Council**
179 College Rd.
PO Box 550
Truro, NS B2N 5E3
Tel: 902-893-6306
Fax: 902-893-7579
www.gov.ns.ca/agri/npmc/
The Council, an agency of the NS Government, is responsible for the administration of the Natural Products Act & the Dairy Industry Act. Ten marketing boards are established under the Natural Products Act & the Dairy Farmers of Nova Scotia is established under the Dairy Industry Act. These boards are producer elected & the Council delegates or regulates authority to them specific to their farm product. The Council is a regulatory & supervisory body, a major role of which is to balance industry interests with teh broader public interest.
Chair, Dave Davies
General Manager, Elizabeth A. Crouse
Tel: 902-893-6511
crouseea@gov.ns.ca
• **Agricultural Marshland Conservation Commission**

www.gov.ns.ca/agri/legislation/amcc.shtml
The Commission advises the Minister of Agriculture on the conservation & protection of marshland, its development & use in agriculture.

Resource Stewardship Division
PO Box 550Truro, NS B2N 5E3
Encourages the best available management of agricultural resources to ensure sustainable & sound environmental farm practices. Environmental Management conducts research & technology adaptation initiatives that support a sustainable economic atmosphere for rural people. It also has a close working relationship with the Nova Scotia Federation of Agriculture & provides resources in support of the Environmental Farm Plan Program. Pest Management, Regulation & Environmental Coordination adapts & develops regulatory programs & related methods to prevent or minimize introduction & spread of designated diseases & pests of concern to agriculture; delivers enforcement of related regulations; conducts regular assessments to determine risk invasion of agricultural pests. Land Protection has the responsibilities to carry out maintenance work on system of tidal dykes in Nova Scotia. Staff of the Resource Stewardship Division also chair & provide administrative services to the Nova Scotia Soils Institute
Manager, Environmental Services, Marion MacAulay
Tel: 902-893-6518
macaulmt@gov.ns.ca
Manager, Regional Services, Arthur Pick
Tel: 902-893-6587
pickaa@gov.ns.ca
Engineer, Land Protection Services, Dave Browning
Tel: 902-893-6569
brownida@gov.ns.ca
Chief Inspector (Weed Control Act), Pest Management Regulation & Environmental Coordination, Joe Calder
Tel: 902-893-6549
calderjr@gov.ns.ca
Resource Management Specialist, Environmental Management, Lorne Crozier
Tel: 902-893-6548
crozielm@gov.ns.ca

Legislation & Compliance Services
www.gov.ns.ca/agri/department/divisions/legcom.shtml
Licenses meat processing, retail food outlets & restaurants, fur & game farms, oversees activities related to food & consumer safety, as well as on-farm quality evaluation. Responsible for monitoring & enforcing compliance with departmental regulations.
Executive Director, Leo Muise
Tel: 902-424-0337
muiselj@gov.ns.ca

Nova Scotia Agricultural College (NSAC)
PO Box 550Truro, NS B2N 5E3
Tel: 902-893-6600
Toll-Free: 888-700-6722
webmaster@snac.ca
www.nsac.ca
Co-President, Bernie MacDonald
Tel: 902-893-6034
Fax: 902-893-4601
bmacdonald@nsac.ca
Co-President, Leslie MacLaren
Tel: 902-893-6030
Acts Administered:
Heritage Property Act
Order of Nova Scotia Act
Peggy's Cove Commission Act
Schooner Bluenose Foundation Act

Special Places Protection Act (Ecological Site Designations: Abraham Lake, Bornish Hill, Duncans Cove, Great Barren & Quinan Lakes, Indian Man Lake, MacFarlane Woods, Panuke Lake, Ponhook Lake, Quinns Meadow, River Inhabitants, Roman Valley)

Minister, Hon. Leonard Preyra
Tel: 902-424-4889
Fax: 902-424-4872
min_cch@gov.ns.ca

Deputy Minister, Laura Lee Langley
Tel: 902-424-4938
Fax: 902-424-4872
langley@gov.ns.ca

Director, Communities, Natasha Jackson

Director, Programs, Craig Beaton

Director, Strategic Planning & Intergovernmental Relations, Peggy Tibbo-Cameron

Culture Division
#601, 1800 Argyle St., PO Box 456Halifax, NS B3J 2R5
Tel: 902-424-4510
Fax: 902-424-0710
culture@gov.ns.ca
www.gov.ns.ca/tch/culture_mandate.asp
Responsible for Nova Scotia museums which administer the Special Places Protection Act; preserves ecological sites in the province.
Interim Executive Director, Culture Division, Marcel Philip McKenough
Tel: 902-424-6393

Heritage Division
1747 Summer St., Halifax, NS B3H 3A6
Tel: 902-424-7344
Fax: 902-424-0560
Toll-Free: 800-632-1114
heritage@gov.ns.ca
www.gov.ns.ca/tch/heritage_mandate.asp
The mission of Heritage Division is to protect, enhance, & celebrate heritage for all Nova Scotians & for future generations.
Executive Director, Heritage Division, Bill Greenlaw
Tel: 902-424-4986
greenlbe@gov.ns.ca
Director & Chief Executive Officer, Art Gallery of Nova Scotia, Ray Cronin
Tel: 902-424-8458
croninr@gov.ns.ca
Director, Museum Operations, Calum Ewing
Tel: 902-424-7715
Director, Stewardship, Programs & Promotion, Jessica Kerrin
Tel: 902-424-2315
Director, Museum of Industry, Debra McNabb
Tel: 902-755-5425
Fax: 902-755-7045
Social Media: www.linkedin.com/pub/debra-mcnabb/34/7ba/57a

Secretary to Council, Don Osmond
Tel: 902-424-7600
•
Chair, Frank Balcom
Director, Racing, Paul Hogan
phogan@mphrc.ca

Minister, Hon. Percy Paris
Tel: 902-424-5790
Fax: 902-424-0514
econmin@gov.ns.ca

Associate Deputy Minister, Simon d'Entremont
Tel: 902-424-2901
Fax: 902-424-0619
dentrsp@gov.ns.ca

Executive Director, Tourism Division, John Somers
Tel: 902-424-4554
somersjh@gov.ns.ca

Director, Program Managment, Elizabeth D. Beck
Tel: 902-424-4641

Director, Robert Edwin Book
Tel: 902-424-7577

Director, Procurement, Rick Draper
Tel: 902-424-4557

Director, Communications, Jennifer Gavin
Tel: 902-424-4998
Fax: 902-424-7008
gavinjm@gov.ns.ca

Director, Decision Support, Liliani Kumaranayake
Tel: 902-424-4641

Director, Development Initiatives, Marvyn C. Robar
Tel: 902-424-3973

Nova Scotia Emergency Management Office (EMO)

PO Box 2581Halifax, NS B3J 3N5
Tel: 902-424-5620
Fax: 902-424-5376
Toll-Free: 866-424-5620
emo@gov.ns.ca
emo.gov.ns.ca
Coordinating agency of the Nova Scotia Government with the responsibility of assisting municipalities to plan & prepare for emergencies; responsible for the implementation of the province-wide 911 service. Coordinates emergency efforts of provincial & federal departments & agencies, as well as private health & social services, to provide assistance to disaster areas; sponsors the Ground Search & Rescue Program; maintains a professional planner at all offices. Coordinates all emergency preparedness training for municipal staff at the Emergency Preparedness College (Arnprior, ON) & through the Joint Emergency Preparedness Program (JEPP), which provides a federal government cost-sharing formula for emergency equipment for first-response agencies.
Acts Administered:
Emergency 911 Act
Emergency Management Act

Minister Responsible, Hon. Ross Landry
Tel: 902-424-4044
Fax: 902-424-0510
justmin@gov.ns.ca

Chief Executive Officer & Deputy Head, Marian Tyson
tysonmf@gov.ns.ca

Director, Emergency Services, Michael Myette
Tel: 902-424-6206

Advisor, Communications, Nicole Watkins-Campbell
Tel: 902-424-1906
watkinni@gov.ns.ca

Nova Scotia Department of Energy

Bank of Montreal Bldg., #400, 5151 George St., PO Box 2664Halifax, NS B3J 3P7
Tel: 902-424-4575
Fax: 902-424-0528
energyinfo@gov.ns.ca
www.gov.ns.ca/energy
To serve as the government's focal point in the development of the province's energy resources, as outlined in the Energy Strategy. Responsible for a wide range of initiatives in the following areas: energy transportation & utilization policy & analysis; resource assessment & royalties; climate change; business & technology; communications & public education.
Acts Administered:
Canada-Newfoundland Labrador Offshore Area Regulations
Canada-Nova Scotia Offshore Petroleum Resources Accord Implementation (Nova Scotia) Act
Electricity Act
Energy Resources Conservation Act
Energy-Efficient Appliances Act
Gas Distribution Act
Gas Plant Facility Regulations
Land Acquisition Regulations
Natural Gas Transmission Pipeline Assessment Regulations
Nova Scotia Offshore Area Certificate of Fitness Regulations
Nova Scotia Offshore Area Oil & Gas Spills & Debris Liability Regulations
Nova Scotia Offshore Area Petroleum Diving Regulations
Nova Scotia Offshore Area Petroleum Drilling Regulations
Nova Scotia Offshore Area Petroleum Geophysical Operations Regulations
Nova Scotia Offshore Area Petroleum Installations Regulations
Nova Scotia Offshore Petroleum Production & Conservation Regulations
Onshore Petroleum Drilling Regulations
Onshore Petroleum Geophysical Exploration Regulations
Onshore Petroleum Geophysical Exploration Regulations
Petroleum Resources Act
Petroleum Resources Removal Permit Act
Pipeline Act
Pipeline Benefits Plan Regulations
Pipeline Regulations
Sable Offshore Energy Project Regulations
Underground Hydrocarbons Storage Act

Minister, Hon. Charlie Parker
Tel: 902-424-7793
Fax: 902-424-3265
energyminister@gov.ns.ca

Deputy Minister, Murray Coolican
Tel: 902-424-4450
Fax: 902-424-3265
coolicm@gov.ns.ca

Executive Secretary to the Minister, Diane Bernard
Tel: 902-424-7793
Fax: 902-424-3265
bernardm@gov.ns.ca

Associated Agencies, Boards & Commissions:
• Utility & Review Board (UARB)
Summit Place
1601 Lower Water St., 3rd Fl.
PO Box 1692 M
Halifax, NS B3J 3S3
Tel: 902-424-4448
Fax: 902-424-3919
uarb.board@gov.ns.ca
www.nsuarb.ca
The Nova Scotia Utility & Review Board is an independent quasi-judicial body which has both regulatory adjudicative jurisdiction flowing from the Utility and Review Board Act.
Chair, Peter W. Gurnham, Q.C.
gurnhapw@gov.ns.ca

Business & Technology
www.gov.ns.ca/energy/what-we-do.asp#business-technology
Director, Charles Bernard MacDonald
Tel: 902-424-2704

Communications & Public Education
www.gov.ns.ca/energy/what-we-do.asp#communications
Director, Communications, Nancy Watson
Tel: 902-424-1195
watsonnm@gov.ns.ca

Energy Fiscal Affairs
Tel: 902-424-6673
www.gov.ns.ca/energy/what-we-do.asp#energy-fiscal
Director, Energy Markets, Reginald Scott McCoombs
Tel: 902-424-7305
Director, Chris Spencer

Energy Markets
www.gov.ns.ca/energy/what-we-do.asp#energy-markets

Petroleum Resources

Resource Assessment
www.gov.ns.ca/energy/what-we-do.asp#resource-assessment

Strategic Policy, Planning & Services
www.gov.ns.ca/energy/what-we-do.asp#spps

Nova Scotia Department of Environment

Terminal Bldg., 5151 Terminal Rd., 5th Fl., PO Box 697Halifax, NS B3J 2T8
Tel: 902-424-3600
Fax: 902-424-0503
Toll-Free: 877-936-8476
www.gov.ns.ca/nse
Major program responsibilities for Nova Scotia Environment are environmental & natural areas management, environmental

monitoring & compliance, & climate change. Pollution prevention, the NS Youth Conservation Corps., solid waste reduction & recycling, & environmental trade & innovation are all part of the new Nova Scotia Environment.
Acts Administered:
Court & Administrative Reform Act (Department of Justice)
Environment Act
Environmental Goals & Sustainable Prosperity Act
Health Protection Act
Non-essential Pesticides Control Act
Off-highway Vehicles Act
Special Places Protection Act
Wilderness Areas Protection Act

Minister, Hon. Sterling Belliveau
Tel: 902-424-3736
Fax: 902-424-1599
min_env@gov.ns.ca

Deputy Minister, Sara Jane Snook
Tel: 902-424-8150
Fax: 902-424-1599
snooksj@gov.ns.ca

Executive Secretary, Virginia Messervey
Tel: 902-424-3736
messerv@gov.ns.ca

Acting Director, Jason Hollett
Tel: 902-424-0784
holletjn@gov.ns.ca

Communications
www.gov.ns.ca/nse/dept/division.communications.asp
The Communications Division provides strategic communications planning & advice for the department. It is responsible for all external communications functions carried out for the department, including issues management, advertising, & media relations, & shares responsibility within the department for internal communications.
Director, Karen White
whitekl@gov.ns.ca

Environmental Monitoring & Compliance
Tel: 902-424-2547
Fax: 902-424-0569
Toll-Free: 877-936-8476
emc@gov.ns.ca
www.gov.ns.ca/nse/dept/division.emc.asp
The Environmental Monitoring Compliance Division is responsible for the majority of field operations relating to environmental protection.
Acting Executive Director, Regional & District Offices, Roger Munroe
Tel: 902-424-2547
Toll-free: 877-936-8476
Fax: 902-424-0569

Regional Offices

Central - HRM, East Hants, West Hants
Bedford Commons, #115, 30 Damascus Rd., Bedford, NS B4A 0C1
Tel: 902-424-7773
Fax: 902-424-0597
Eastern - Port Hawkesbury, Sydney
295 Charlotte St., Sydney, NS B1P 6H7
Tel: 902-563-2100
Fax: 902-563-2387
Regional Director, Roger Munroe
Tel: 902-563-2100
Fax: 902-563-2387
Eastern - Richmond Co., Southern Inverness, Mulgrave, Auld's Cove
#12, 218 MacSween St., Port Hawkesbury, NS B9A 2J9
Tel: 902-625-0791
Fax: 902-625-3722
District Manager, Terry MacPherson
Northern - Amherst, Antigosh, Truro, Pictou
#3, 36 Inglis Place, 2nd Fl., PO Box 824Truro, NS B2N 5G6
Tel: 902-667-6205
Fax: 902-667-6214
Northern - Antigosh, Guysborough Counties
#205, 155 Main St., Antigosh, NS B2N 2B6
Tel: 902-667-6205
Fax: 902-667-6214
District Manager, Paul Keats
Northern - Colchester County
Tel: 902-667-6205
Fax: 902-667-6214
District Manager, Wayne Faulkner
Northern - Cumberland County
71 East Victoria St., Amherst, NS B4H 1X7
Tel: 902-667-6205
Fax: 902-667-6214
District Manager, Brad Skinner
Northern - Colchester County
20 Pumphouse Rd., RR3, New Glasgow, NS B2H 5C6
Tel: 902-396-4194
Fax: 902-396-4765
District Manager, Penny McLeod
Western - Bridgewater, Kentville, Yarmouth
136 Exhibition St., Kentville, NS B4N 4E5
Tel: 902-679-6088
Fax: 902-679-6186
Regional Director, Adrian Fuller
District Manager, Jennifer Lonergan
Western - Digby, Yarmouth & Shelburne Counties
13 First St., Yarmouth, NS B5A 1S9
Tel: 902-742-8985
Fax: 902-742-7796
Western - Lunenberg & Queens Counties
60 Logan Rd., Bridgewater, NS B4V 3J8
Tel: 902-543-4685
Fax: 902-527-5480
District Manager, Kristen Martell

Environment & Sustainable Prosperity Partnerships
www.gov.ns.ca/nse/dept/division.espp.asp
The Division aims to provide leadership & coordination of community engagement activities in Environment (and more broadly) is responsible for delivery of major environmental service contracts with the private sector.

Environmental Science & Program Management
www.gov.ns.ca/nse/dept/division.espm.asp
The Environmental Science & Program Management Division promotes sustainable management & protection of the environment through both regulatory & non-regulatory means, including developing & implementing plans, standards, guidelines, & policies for the management & protection of Nova Scotia's air, water & terrestrial resources including protected areas, & by providing regionally-based regulatory approval, inspection, monitoring & enforcement.
Director, Kimberly MacNeil
Tel: 902-424-2386
Director, Water & Wastewater Branch, David Briggins
Tel: 902-424-2571
Director, Air Quality & Resource Management Branch, Andrew Murphy
Tel: 902-424-2177
Environmental Analyst, Helen MacPhail
Tel: 902-424-0126
Director, Vicki Dimick
Director, Michelle Lucas
Tel: 902-424-3731
Director, Steve Feindel
Tel: 902-424-2939
feindesj@gov.ns.ca
Director, Joyce McDonald
Tel: 902-424-7395
mcdonajm@gov.ns.ca
Director, Financial Accounting, Suzanne Wile
Tel: 902-424-7021
wilesm@gov.ns.ca

Nova Scotia Department of Fisheries & Aquaculture

1741 Brunswick St., 3rd Fl., PO Box 2223Halifax, NS B3J 3C4
Tel: 902-424-4560
Fax: 902-424-4671
www.gov.ns.ca/fish
The Department of Fisheries & Aquaculture's mission is to foster prosperous and sustainable fisheries, aquaculture and food industries through the delivery of quality public services for the betterment of coastal communities and of all Nova Scotians.
Acts Administered:
Fisheries & Coastal Resources Act
Fisheries Organizations Support Act
Wildlife Act (Fishing Regulations only)

Minister, Hon. Sterling Belliveau
Tel: 902-637-3200
Fax: 902-637-3530
min_dfa@gov.ns.ca
Other Communications: 902-875-9090 (Shelburne office)

Deputy Minister & Chief Executive Officer, Rosalind Penfound
Tel: 902-424-0300

Associate Deputy Minister, Gregory Roach
Tel: 902-424-0348
Fax: 902-424-1766
roachg@gov.ns.ca

Director, Communications, Celeste Sulliman
Tel: 902-424-0192
sullimcc@gov.ns.ca

Associated Agencies, Boards & Commissions:
• Fisheries & Aquaculture Loan Board
1741 Brunswick St., 3rd Fl.
PO Box 2223
Halifax, NS B3J 3C4
Tel: 902-424-0318
Fax: 902-424-3502
www.gov.ns.ca/nsaf/loanboards/fishlb/
Director, Bruce Cox
Tel: 902-424-0313
coxb@gov.ns.ca

Marine Division
Manager, Innovations & Field Services, Bruce Osborne
Tel: 902-424-0352
osbornbd@gov.ns.ca

Aquaculture Division
Director, Marshall Giles
Tel: 902-424-3664
gilesm@gov.ns.ca

Inland Fisheries Division
Director, Donald MacLean
Tel: 902-485-7021
macleand@gov.ns.ca

Minister, Hon. Dave Wilson
Tel: 902-424-3377
Fax: 902-424-0559
health.minister@gov.ns.ca

Deputy Minister, Kevin McNamara
Tel: 902-424-5818
Fax: 902-424-4570
mcnamakd@gov.ns.ca, Deputy.HealthandWellness@gov.ns.ca

Associate Deputy Minister, Frances Martin
Tel: 902-424-5818
Frances.Martin@gov.ns.ca

Executive Director, Strategic Financial Operations, Abram James Almeda
Tel: 902-424-4476

Executive Director, Health System Workforce, Carmelle d'Entremont
Tel: 902-424-8686

Executive Director, Policy & Planning, Tracey Williams
Tel: 902-424-7931

Senior Director, Labour Relations, Richard Anderson
Tel: 902-424-7730

Senior Director, Janet Braunstein
Tel: 902-424-5187

Senior Director, Sport & Research, Farida Gabbani
Tel: 902-424-7554

Chief Medical Director, Carman Giacomantonio
Tel: 902-473-6177

Senior Director, Physical Activity, Sport & Recreation, Farida Gabbani
Tel: 902-424-7554
gabbanfg@gov.ns.ca

Senior Director, Legislative Policy, Dennis Holland
Tel: 902-424-3351

Director, Communications, Sherri Aikenhead
Tel: 902-424-5579
sherri.aikenhead@gov.ns.ca

Director, Policy & Planning, Tracey Barbrick
Tel: 902-424-7337

Director, Acute & Tertiary Care, Lynn Edwards

Director, Health Intergovernmental Affairs, Vijay Bhashyakarla
Tel: 902-424-2842

Director, Heather Jane Christian
Tel: 902-424-5869

Director, Carolyn Davison
Tel: 902-424-7218
davisocj@gov.ns.ca

Director, Technical Operations, Anthony Eden
Tel: 902-424-4429

Director, Health Services, Kevin Elliott
Tel: 902-424-6869

Director, Acute Care, Katherine Fraser
Tel: 902-424-4878

Director, Active & Healthy Living, Rick Gilbert
Tel: 902-424-2772
Fax: 902-424-0520
gilberrf@gov.ns.ca

Director, Fin. & Admin. Internal Support, Gary Glessing
Tel: 902-424-6138

Director, Primary Health Care, Lisa Ruth Grandy
Tel: 902-424-4617

Director, Long Term Care, Dean Hirtle
Tel: 902-424-1797

Director, Chronic Disease & Injury Prevention, Nancy Hoddinott
Tel: 902-424-5840

Director, Lindsay Marja Hugenholtz
Tel: 902-490-3200

Director, Health Economics, Michael Joyce
Tel: 902-427-6879

Director, Health Privacy Office, Maria Lasheras
Tel: 902-424-8214

Director, Insured Services, Harold McCarthy
Tel: 902-424-7538

Director, Karen McDuff
Tel: 902-424-2635

Director, Environmental Health, Gary O'Toole
Tel: 902-424-1262

Director, AIDS Commission, Michelle Proctor-Simms
Tel: 902-424-4741

Director, Standards & Policy, Susan Stevens
Tel: 902-424-6857

Director, Emergency Managment Centre, Russell Stuart
Tel: 902-424-0000

Office of the Chief Public Health Officer
PO Box 488Halifax, NS B3J 2R8
The Office of the Chief Public Health Officer is responsible for the Department of Health's legislated responsibility to protect & promote the public's health in the following areas: communicable disease control, environmental health, emergency preparedness & response. In addition, staff in the Office of the Chief Public Health Officer, in collaboration with academic expertise at Dalhousie University, function as an expert resource in community health science & an epidemiological resource for the department, the health districts, & other relevant government & community groups.
Chief Public Health Officer/Chief Medical Officer of Health, Dr. Robert Strang
Tel: 902-424-2358
Fax: 902-424-4716
Deputy Chief Medical Officer of Health, Dr. Frank Atherton
Tel: 902-424-2358
Fax: 902-424-4716

Nova Scotia Department of Intergovernmental Affairs

Duke Tower, 5251 Duke St., 5th Fl., PO Box 1617Halifax, NS B3J 2Y3
Fax: 902-424-0728
iga@gov.ns.ca
www.gov.ns.ca/iga
Provides leadership in the development of corporate strategies for Nova Scotia's relations with governments & organizations.

Minister, Hon. Darrell Dexter
Tel: 902-424-6600
Toll-free: 800-267-1993
Fax: 902-424-7648
premier@gov.ns.ca

Deputy Minister/CEO, Catherine Blewett

Associate Deputy Minister, Scott Logan
Tel: 902-424-2094
logansm@gov.ns.ca

Director, Regional Relations, Darryl C. Eisan
Tel: 902-424-4535
dceisan@gov.ns.ca

Director, Strategic Policy, Norma MacIsaac
Tel: 902-424-7662
macisanj@gov.ns.ca

Director, Economic Policy & Analysis, André Moore
Tel: 902-424-7728
mooreac@gov.ns.ca

Director, Environmental & Social Affairs, Albert Walzak
Tel: 902-424-7748
walzakag@gov.ns.ca

General Counsel, Shanti Dogra

Minister & Attorney General, Hon. Ross Landry
Tel: 902-424-4044
Fax: 902-424-0510
justmin@gov.ns.ca

Deputy Minister, Judith Ferguson

Director, Regional & Canada US Relations, Daryl Eisan

Director, Contracts, Edward Kirby
Tel: 902-424-3178

Director, Emergency Programs, Andrew Lathem
Tel: 000-424-5620

Director, Economic Policy & Analysis, Andre Moore

Director, Emergency Services, Michael Myette
Tel: 902-424-6206

Director, Information Technology, Charles Purcell
Tel: 902-424-6349

Director, Social & Environmental Affairs, Albert Walzak
Tel: 902-563-5648

Minister, Hon. Marilyn More
Tel: 902-424-6647
Fax: 902-424-0575
min_lae@gov.ns.ca

Deputy Minister, Sandra McKenzie

Associate Deputy Minister, Jeff Conrad
Tel: 902-424-6270
conradja@gov.ns.ca

Director, Communications, Karen Stone
Tel: 902-424-2107
Fax: 902-424-0644
stonekk@gov.ns.ca

Nova Scotia Department of Natural Resources

Founder's Square, 1701 Hollis St., 3rd Fl., PO Box 698Halifax, NS B3J 2T9
Tel: 902-424-5935
Fax: 902-424-0594
Toll-Free: 800-565-2224
www.gov.ns.ca/natr
Responsible for the administration & management of provincial Crown lands, development of mineral & energy resources, protection & sustainable development of forest resources & operation & maintenance of parks system, & promoting the conservation & sustainable use of wildlife populations, habitat & ecosystems.Initiatives include: a State of the Forest report; working with other departments on State of the Environment report; leading the development of a provincial climate change strategy; implementing recovery plans for endangered & threatened wildlife species; & developing strategic land use plans for Crown lands using an integrated resource management planning process.
Acts Administered:
Act to Confer Certain Powers Upon the Lieutenant Governor in Council & to amend the Mines Act
Angling Act
Beaches Act
Blueberry Association Act
Bowater Mersey Agreement Act
Christmas Tree Grading Regulations
Christmas Tree Levy Regulations
Conservation Easements Act
Dutch Elm Disease Regulations
Endangered Species Act
Expropriation Act
Forest Fire Protection Regulations
Forest Sustainability Regulations
Forests Act
General Wildlife Regulations
Gypsum Mining Income Tax Act
Halifax Power & Pulp Company Limited Agreement Act, 1962
Indian Lands Act
Land Holdings Disclosure Act
Land Surveyors Act
Mineral Resources Act
Mines Act
Nova Scotia Federation of Anglers & Hunters Act
Off Highway Vehicles Act
Primary Forest Products Marketing Act
Private Ways Act
Provincial Parks Act
Registration & Statistical Returns Regulations
Scalers Act
Scott Maritimes Limited Agreement (1965) Act
Special Places Protection Act (jointly with Tourism, Culture & Heritage)
Stora Forest Industries Agreement Act
Timber Loan Board Regulations
Trails Act
Treasure Trove Act
Wildlife Act
Wildlife Habitat & Watercourses Protection Regulations

Minister, Hon. Charlie Parker
Tel: 902-424-4037
Fax: 902-424-0594
min_dnr@gov.ns.ca

Deputy Minister, Duff Montgomerie
Tel: 902-424-4121
Fax: 902-428-0594
montgodm@gov.ns.ca

Director, Communications, Dan Davis
Tel: 902-424-2354
Fax: 902-424-7735
davisds@gov.ns.ca

Associated Agencies, Boards & Commissions:

• Crown Land Information Management Centre
Founders Square
#501, 1701 Hollis St.
PO Box 698
Halifax, NS B3J 2T9
Tel: 902-424-3171
Registrar, Crown Lands & Land Holdings, Dean Benedict
Tel: 902-424-8681
bendida@gov.ns.ca
• NS Primary Forest Products Marketing Board
#804, 45 Alderney Dr.
Dartmouth, NS B2Y 2N6
Tel: 902-424-7598
Fax: 902-424-6965
www.gov.ns.ca/pfpmb/
Chair, Walter MacAlpine
Tel: 902-424-7598
Executive Assistant, Helen Benjamin
Tel: 902-424-7598
Fax: 902-424-6965

Land Services Branch
www.gov.ns.ca/natr/thedepartment/landservices.asp
The Land Services Branch management oversees, coordinates & approves all activities within the Branch relating to the administration of Crown land. The Branch provides advice on legislative revisions & advises & drafts policies relating to the administration of Crown land.
Executive Director, Gretchen Pohlkamp
Tel: 902-424-4267
pohlkagg@gov.ns.ca

Mineral Resources Branch
Fax: 902-424-7735
www.gov.ns.ca/natr/meb/
Implements policies & programs dealing with the exploration, development, management & efficient use of energy & mineral resources, promotes scientific studies of the geology of the province for use by government, industry & the public, provides a mineral rights tenure system to establish legal rights to minerals for exploration & development. Promotes concepts of environmental responsibility & sustainability.
Executive Director, Don James
Tel: 902-424-2523
Director, Mineral Management, Alan Davidson
Tel: 902-424-5618
Director, Geological Services, Rob Naylor
Tel: 902-424-8119

Policy, Planning & Support Services
Provides planning & policy coordination support to the Department, ensures that policies & plans developed in the Department are coordinated, supports the integrated management of natural resources. Also provides a range of administrative, planning, research, information management, information distribution, graphics, cartographic, communication, & occupational health & safety-related services.
Executive Director, Patricia Bernadette MacNeil
Tel: 902-424-4988
macneipb@gov.ns.ca

Regional Services Branch
Delivers departmental programs & services through a field office network, responsible for forest protection & planning, forest nurseries, research & development, enforcement, coordination of the hunter safety program, regional geological services, Crown land surveys, operation & maintenance of provincial parks, resource conservation, forest fire prevention & monitoring of forest insects & diseases.
Executive Director, Brian Stanley Gilbert
Tel: 902-424-3949
Director, Resource Management, Dan Eidt
Tel: 902-424-7594
Director, Enforcement Division, John Mombourquette
Tel: 902-424-5254
jamombou@gov.ns.ca
Director, Operations, William Smith
Tel: 902-424-4445
Director, Fleet Management, Ross Wickwire
Tel: 902-758-3438
Central
PO Box 68Truro, NS B2N 5B8
Tel: 902-893-6350
Fax: 902-893-5613
Secondary Address: 664 Prince St.
Arlington Place
Truro, NS B2N 1G6
Regional Director, J. Allan Eddy
Tel: 902-893-5627
Eastern
300 Mountain Rd., Sydney, NS B1L 1A9
Tel: 902-563-3370
Fax: 902-567-2535
Other Communication: Alternate Phone: 902-563-3372
Regional Director, Donald Feldman
Tel: 902-533-3370
Western
PO Box 6000Lunenberg, NS B0J 2C0
Tel: 902-634-7555
Fax: 902-634-7577
Secondary Address: 312 Green St.
Lunenburg, NS B0J 2C0
Regional Director, Gerald Joudrey
Tel: 902-543-0622
gtjoudre@gov.ns.ca

Renewable Resources
Executive Director, Julie Towers
Tel: 902-679-6139
Director, Forest Protection, Walter Fanning
Tel: 902-758-7236
Director, Forestry, Jonathan Kierstead
Tel: 902-893-5673
Director, Program Development, Peter MacQuarrie
Tel: 902-424-7708
gpmacqua@gov.ns.ca
Director, Wildlife, Robert Petrie
Tel: 902-679-4366

Nova Scotia Department of Service Nova Scotia & Municipal Relations

1505 Barrington St., PO Box 216Halifax, NS B3J 3K5
Tel: 902-424-5200
Fax: 902-424-0581
Toll-Free: 800-670-4357
TTY: 877-404-0720
askus@gov.ns.ca
www.gov.ns.ca/snsmr
Other Communication: Nova Scotia Business Registry: 1-800-670-4357
Provides leadership in the achievement of effective local government, assessment services, business licensing & registration, vehicle registration & driver licensing, taxation & revenue collection, vital statistics & an integrated land information management system to meet the needs of local & provincial agencies & residents of Nova Scotia.
Acts Administered:
Assessment Act
Land Registration Act
Motor Vehicle Act
Municipal Government Act
Municipal Government Act Resource Binder
Off-Highway Vehicles Act
Oil Refineries & L.N.G. Plants Municipal Taxation Act

Minister, Hon. John MacDonnell
Tel: 902-424-5550
Fax: 902-424-0581
snsmrmin@gov.ns.ca

Deputy Minister, Kevin Malloy
Tel: 902-424-4100
Fax: 902-424-0581
kdmalloy@gov.ns.ca

Executive Director, Strategic & Transition Planning, Cheryl Burgess
Tel: 902-424-5604
Fax: 902-424-0581

Executive Director, Human Resources Services & Client Support, Sharalyn Young
Tel: 902-424-0944
Fax: 902-424-0581

Director, Human Resources, Kimberley Aselstine
Tel: 902-424-3930
Fax: 902-424-0581

Director, Compensation & Benefits, John Campbell
Tel: 902-424-2824
Fax: 902-424-0581

Director, Audit & Evaluation, Katharine Cox-Brown
Tel: 902-424-8383
Fax: 902-424-0581

Director, Human Resources, Isabel Hache
Tel: 902-424-7840
Fax: 902-424-0581

Director, Human Resources, Catherine Francis Martin
Tel: 902-424-2751
Fax: 902-424-0581

Director, Communications, Penny McCormick
Tel: 902-424-6336
Fax: 902-424-0581

Director, Recruitment Services, Jocelyn Pletz
Tel: 902-722-1327
Fax: 902-424-0581

Director, Human Resources, Dale Rushton
Tel: 902-424-6498
Fax: 902-424-0581

Director, Human Resources, Leslie Shanahan
Tel: 902-424-8861
Fax: 902-424-0581

Director, Human Resources, Marica Mary Smythe
Tel: 902-424-3443
Fax: 902-424-0581

Director, Staff Relations, Cynthia Yazbek
Tel: 902-424-4588
Fax: 902-424-0581

Associated Agencies, Boards & Commissions:
• Nova Scotia Municipal Finance Corporation
Maritime Centre
1505 Barrington St., 10th Fl. South
PO Box 850 M
Halifax, NS B3J 2V2
Tel: 902-424-4590
Fax: 902-424-0525
www.gov.ns.ca/nsmfc
NSMFC issues pooled debentures that provide low-cost, long-term capital financing for municipal capital projects. The NSMFC issues in capital markets twice a year, generally in the spring & fall. On occasion the NSMFC will do a single issue, provided the size is large enough.
Chair, Kevin Malloy
Tel: 902-424-4100
kdmalloy@gov.ns.ca
Chief Executive Officer, Bob Houlihan, CGA
Tel: 902-424-4590
houlihra@gov.ns.ca

Land Programs
PO Box 1523Halifax, NS B3J 2Y3
Fax: 902-424-0639
Toll-Free: 866-518-4640
propertyonline@gov.ns.ca
Other Communication: www.gov.ns.ca/snsmr/access/land/land-services-information/land-registry.asp

Geomatics Centre
160 Willow St., Amherst, NS B4H 3W5
Tel: 902-667-7231
Fax: 902-667-6008
Toll-Free: 800-798-0706
geoinfo@gov.ns.ca
www.gov.ns.ca/snsmr/land/
Manager, Robert Neil Caldwell
Tel: 902-667-6287

Nova Scotia Department of Transportation & Infrastructure Renewal

Johnston Bldg., 1672 Granville St., 2nd Fl., PO Box 186Halifax, NS B3J 2N2
Tel: 902-424-2297
Fax: 902-424-0532
TTY: 888-432-3233

tpwpaff@gov.ns.ca
www.gov.ns.ca/tran
Provides a transportation network for the safe & efficient movement of people & goods; serves the building, property & accommodation needs of government departments & agencies; employs professional, dedicated people & offers a high level of customer service.
Acts Administered:
Dangerous Goods Transportation Act
Dangerous Goods Transportation Regulations
Ferries Act
Motor Carrier Act
Motor Vehicle Act
Off-Highway Vehicles Act
Public Highways Act
Railways Act
Surplus Crown Property Disposal Act

Minister, Hon. Maurice Smith
Tel: 902-424-5875
Fax: 902-424-0171
tirmin@gov.ns.ca

Deputy Minister, Paul Lafleche
Tel: 902-424-4036
Fax: 902-424-2014
plafleche@gov.ns.ca

Executive Director, John Bernard O'Connor
Tel: 902-424-2756

Executive Director, Human Resources & Client Support, Sharalyn Young
Tel: 902-424-0944
Social Media: www.linkedin.com/pub/sharalyn-young/39/794/112

Director, Information Technology, George Cooper
Social Media: www.linkedin.com/pub/george-cooper/21/864/338

Director, Policy & Planning, Brian Michael Gallivan
Tel: 902-424-2907

Director, Engineering, Design & Construction, Tom Gouthro
Tel: 902-860-2999
Fax: 902-861-4828
gouthrto@gov.ns.ca

Director, Central district, Peter Hackett
Tel: 902-860-5600
Social Media: www.linkedin.com/pub/peter-hackett/29/71a/820

Director, Eastern district, Gerard Jessome
Tel: 902-563-2250
Social Media: www.linkedin.com/pub/gerard-jessome/17/438/542

Director, Public Affairs & Communications, Cathy MacIsaac
Tel: 902-424-8978
Fax: 902-424-0532
macisacl@gov.ns.ca

Director, Western district, Stephen MacIsaac
Tel: 902-543-4121
Social Media: www.linkedin.com/pub/steve-macisaac/32/456/416

Director, Northern district, Peter Emile Merritt
Tel: 902-424-5328

Associated Agencies, Boards & Commissions:
• **Sydney Tar Ponds Agency**
1 Inglis St.
PO Box 1028 A
Sydney, NS B1P 6J7
Tel: 902-567-1035
Fax: 902-567-1032
www.tarpondscleanup.ca
Acting CEO, Kevin MacDonald, P.Eng.
Tel: 902-567-1037
kevin@tarpondscleanup.ca
Manager, Communications, Tanya Collier MacDonald
Tel: 902-567-2344
Fax: 902-567-1037
tanya@tarpondscleanup.ca
Director, Corporate Services, Corrie Stewart
Tel: 902-567-2734
Director, Engineering Services, Barbara Baillie, P.Eng.
Tel: 902-567-1035
Fax: 902-567-1037
Acting Director, Environmental Services, Wilfred Kaiser, P.Eng.
Tel: 902-567-3403
Fax: 902-567-2382

Highway Operations
www.gov.ns.ca/tran/highways
This division provides for provincial highway & bridge maintenance, as well as the operation of the Department's fleet management & a strategic planning section. District Services provides general services on primary & secondary roads & works with private sector contractors to provide the public with enhanced road systems.
Executive Director, Highway Engineering & Construction, Kevin Caines
Tel: 902-424-5687
Executive Director, Highway Maintenance & Operations, Charles Joseph MacDonald
Tel: 902-295-2700
Director, Highway / Engineering Services, Bernard Clancey
Tel: 902-424-4268

Public Works
www.gov.ns.ca/tran/works/
This division provides technical expertise & services required by the Department's highway, building & property divisions. The Highway Engineering Services section provides delivery of highway planning, geometric & structural design, traffic engineering, capital program maintenance & asset management business functions. The Engineering & Design section provides engineering, architectural, environmental & technical services & project management services for projects that are related to maintaining & constructing highway & building infrastructure. The Building Services & Operations section oversees the management, operation, maintenance & renovation of government buildings, infrastructure & properties, as well as the provision of trade & contract services in both leased & owned premises.
Executive Director, Strategiec Capital & Infrastructure Planning, Jane Fraser-Coutts
Tel: 902-424-8600
Director, Don Sutherland
Tel: 902-424-6038
Social Media: www.linkedin.com/pub/don-sutherland/21/610/696
Director, Building Services, Neil Whyte
Tel: 902-424-2883
Manager, Environmental Services, Chris Moir
Tel: 902-424-4725

Nova Scotia Utility & Review Board
Summit Place, 1601 Lower Water St., 3rd Fl., PO Box 1692 Stn. M, Halifax, NS B3J 3S3
Tel: 902-424-4448
Fax: 902-424-3919
uarb.board@gov.ns.ca
www.nsuarb.ca
The Board has a very broad mandate encompassing a number of Acts. Operations fall into two categories, regulatory & adjudicative. The regulatory category includes the regulation of public utilities, licensing of public passenger carriers, monitoring of automobile insurance rates, the approval of Halifax-Dartmouth bridge fares, & the regulation of natural gas distribution & pipelines. The Board conducts hearings relating to gaming control, liquor control & film classification. The adjudicative category includes appeals or applications relating to property assessments, expropriation compensation claims, planning & subdivisions, heritage properties, criminal injury compensation claims, municipal boundaries, municipal & school board electoral boundaries, as well as gasoline, diesel oil & tobacco taxes. The Board receives its authority from the Public Inquiries Act & the Utility & Review Board Act.
Acts Administered:
Fire Safety Act
Gas Distribution Act
Halifax-Dartmouth Bridge Commission Act
Motor Carrier Act (public passenger only)
Motor Vehicle Transport Act of Canada, 1987 (Federal)
Petroleum Products Pricing Act
Petroleum Resources Removal Permit Act
Pipeline Act
Public Utilities Act
Railways Act
Underground Hydrocarbons Storage Act
Utility & Review Board Act

Chair, Peter W. Gurnham, Q.C.
uarb.board@gov.ns.ca

Workers' Compensation Board of Nova Scotia
5668 South St., PO Box 1150Halifax, NS B3J 2Y2
Tel: 902-491-8999
Fax: 902-491-8002
Toll-Free: 800-870-3331
info@wcb.gov.ns.ca
www.wcb.ns.ca
Coordinates the workers' compensation system to assist injured workers & their employers by providing timely medical & rehabilitative support to help injured workers return to work. Also, to provide appropriate compensation for work-related injuries & illnesses.

Chair, Elaine Sibson

CEO, Nancy MacCready-Williams
Tel: 902-491-8300

Deputy Chair, Chris Power

Government of Nunavut
Seat of Government: PO Box 1200Iqaluit, NU X0A 0H0
Tel: 867-975-6000
Toll-Free: 877-212-6438
info@gov.nu.ca
www.gov.nu.ca
On April 1, 1999, Nunavut Territory was created as part of the Nunavut Land Claims Agreement signed in 1993. It has area of 1,877,787.62 km2, & the StatsCan census in 2011 showed the population was 31,906. Nunavut Territory is governed by a fully elected Legislative Assembly of 19 members elected for a five-year term. Government is by consensus rather than party politics. The Legislature elects the Premier & a seven-member Executive Council, which is charged with the operation of government & the establishment of program & spending priorities. Nunavut Territory acts under the same conditions as other territories in Canada. For an explanation of the difference between provinces & territories please see the Yukon Territory listing. The Commissioner of Nunavut Territory is appointed by the Federal Government, & serves a role similar to that of the Lieutenant Governor in provincial jurisdictions.

Director, Research, Policy & Library Services, Alex Baldwin
Tel: 867-975-5130
abaldwin@assembly.nu.ca

Director, Corporate Services, Michael Rafter
Tel: 867-975-5104
mrafter@assembly.nu.ca

Legislative Librarian, Yvonne Earle
Tel: 867-975-5134
yearle@assembly.nu.ca
PO Box 1200
Iqaluit, NU X0A 0H0 Canada

Nunavut Territory Department of Community & Government Services
W.G. Brown Bldg., 4th Fl., PO Box 1000 Stn. 700, Iqaluit, NU X0A 0H0
Tel: 867-975-5400
Fax: 867-975-5305
cgs.gov.nu.ca
Other Communication: 867-975-5306
To support the development, provision & maintenance of programs & services which affect the communities in all areas of municipal responsibility & transportation.
Acts Administered:
Area Development Act
Cities, Towns & Villages Act
Commissioner's Airport Lands Regulations
Commissioner's Land Act
Commissioner's Land Regulations
Consumer Protection Act
Dog Act
Emergency Measures Act
Fire Prevention Act
Fire Prevention Regulations
Fireworks Regulations
Gas Protection Act
Hamlets Act

Federal/Provincial Government

Iqaluit By-Law Exemption Order
Planning Act
Propane Cylinder Storage
Resolute Bay Development Area Regulations
Settlements Act
Strathcona Sound Development Area Regulations
Technical Standards & Safety Act
Town of Iqaluit Continuation Order

Minister, Hon. Lorne Kusuqak
Tel: 867-975-5003
Fax: 867-975-5095

Acting Deputy Minister, Roy Green
Tel: 867-975-5301
Fax: 867-975-5305

Assistant Deputy Minister, Darren Flynn
Tel: 867-645-8106
Fax: 867-645-8141

Corporate Chief Information Officer, Dean Wells
Tel: 867-975-6439
dwells@gov.nu.ca

Executive Director, Municipal Training Organization (MTO), Matthew Ayres
Tel: 867-975-5346
mayres@gov.nu.ca

Executive Director, NCIAC, Catherine Foo
Tel: 867-975-5336
cfoo@gov.nu.ca

Director, Community Infrastructure, Bu Lam
Tel: 867-975-5462
blam@gov.nu.ca

Director, Corporate Affairs & Support Services, Carmen Levi
Tel: 867-975-5332
clevi@gov.nu.ca

Director, Policy & Procedures, Lucy Magee
Tel: 867-975-5309
Fax: 867-975-5351
lmagee@gov.nu.ca

Director, Protection Services, Ed Zebedee
Tel: 867-975-5319
Fax: 867-975-5453
ezebedee@gov.nu.ca

Senior Manager, Operations & Networks, Jeff Bisson
Tel: 867-975-6474
jbisson@gov.nu.ca

Senior Manager, Procurement, Logistics & Contract Support Service, Mark McCulloch
Tel: 867-975-5427
Fax: 867-975-5450
mmcculloch@gov.nu.ca

Nunavut Territory Department of Culture, Language, Elders & Youth (CLEY)

PO Box 1000 Stn. 800, Iqaluit, NU X0A 0H0
Tel: 867-975-5500
Fax: 867-975-5504
Toll-Free: 866-934-2035
www.cley.gov.nu.ca
Responsible for the protection, preservation & promotion of Inuit languages. Cultural initiatives & departmental goals are reached in coordination with & in support of elder & youth groups. Acts in respect to issues concerning women & people with disabilities. The government is dedicated to preserving & promoting elements that make up the Inuit identity.

Minister, Hon. James Arreak
Tel: 867-975-5500
Fax: 867-975-5504
jarreak@assembly.nu.ca

Deputy Minister, Simon Awa
Tel: 867-975-5501
simon.awa@gov.nu.ca

Assistant Deputy Minister, Naullaq Arnaquq
Tel: 867-975-5532
Fax: 867-975-5504
narnaquq@gov.nu.ca

Nunavut Territory Department of Economic Development & Transportation

Bldg. 1104 A, Inuksugait Plaza, PO Box 1000 Stn. 1500, Iqaluit, NU X0A 0H0
Tel: 867-975-7800
Fax: 867-975-7870
Toll-Free: 888-975-5999
edt@gov.nu.ca
www.edt.gov.nu.ca
Acts Administered:
All-Terrain Vehicles Act
All-Terrain Vehicles Regulations
Carrier Fitness Regulations
Economic Development Agreements Act
Exemption of Motor Vehicles Act Regulations
Guide Exemption Regulations
Highway Designation & Classification Regulations
Highway Signs Regulations
Hours of Service Regulations
Large Vehicle Control Regulations
Motor Vehicle Equipment Regulations
Motor Vehicles Act
Nunavut Development Corporation
Outfitter Regulations
Public Highways Act
School Bus Regulations
Seasonal Highway Regulations
Special All-Terrain Vehicles Fees Regulations
Special All-Terrain Vehicles Helmet Regulations
Tourist Establishment Regulations
Transportation of Dangerous Goods Act
Transportation of Dangerous Goods Regulations
Travel & Tourism Act
Travel Development Area Regulations

Minister, Hon. Peter Taptuna
Tel: 867-975-5076
Fax: 867-975-5016

Deputy Minister, Robert Long
Tel: 867-975-7829
rlong@gov.nu.ca

Associated Agencies, Boards & Commissions:
• **Nunavut Business Credit Corporation**
Parnaivak Bldg.
#100
PO Box 2548
Iqaluit, NU X0A 0H0
Tel: 867-975-7891
Fax: 867-975-7897
Toll-free: 800-758-0038
credit@nbcc.nu.ca
www.nbcc.nu.ca

Economic Development
Assistant Deputy Minister, Gordon MacKay
Tel: 867-975-7822
gmackay@gov.nu.ca
Director, Community Operations, Kitikmeot, Dustin Fredlund
Director, Tourism & Cultural Industries, Karen Kabloona
Tel: 867-975-7856
kkabloona@gov.nu.ca
Director, Community Operations, Qikiqtaaluk, Rhoda Katsak
Tel: 867-899-7339
rkatsak@gov.nu.ca
Director, Community Operations, Kivalliq, Laura MacKenzie
Tel: 867-645-8458
lmackenzie@gov.nu.ca
Director, Minerals & Petroleum Resources, Eric Prosh
Tel: 867-975-7827
eprosh@gov.nu.ca

Transportation
Assistant Deputy Minister, Methusalah Kunuk
Tel: 867-975-7832
Fax: 867-975-7880
mkunuk@gov.nu.ca
Director, Motor Vehicles, Lorna Gee
Tel: 867-360-4614
lgee@gov.nu.ca
Director, Iqaluit International Airport, John Graham
Tel: 867-979-5224
jgraham@gov.nu.ca
Director, Nunavut Airports, Shawn Maley
Tel: 867-645-8203
smaley@gov.nu.ca
Interim Director, Transportation Policy & Planning, Art Stewart
Tel: 867-975-7826

Minister, Hon. Eva Aariak
Tel: 867-975-5050
Fax: 867-975-5051
Premier.Aariak@gov.nu.ca

Nunavut Emergency Management

PO Box 1000 Stn. 700, Iqaluit, NU X0A 0H0
Tel: 867-975-5403
Fax: 867-979-4221
Toll-Free: 800-693-1666
cgs.gov.nu.ca/en/commemergency.aspx
Other Communication: Headquarters Phone: 867-979-6262; Kitikmeot: 867-983-2542; Kivalliq: 867-645-3625; Qikiqtaaluk: 1-888-624-4043

Fire Marshall, Robert Prima
Tel: 867-975-5310
rprima@gov.nu.ca

Manager, Emergency Preparedness, Glen Higgins
Tel: 867-975-5403
Fax: 867-979-4221
ghiggins@gov.nu.ca

Officer, Emergency Preparedness Program, Jerry Anilniliak
Tel: 867-975-5319
janilniliak1@gov.nu.ca

Officer, Training & Logistics, Brenda Panipakoocho
Tel: 867-975-5353
bpanipakoocho@gov.nu.ca

Nunavut Territory Department of Environment

PO Box 1000 Stn. 1300, Iqaluit, NU X0A 0H0
Tel: 867-975-7700
Fax: 867-975-7742
environment@gov.nu.ca
env.gov.nu.ca
Acts Administered:
Asphalt Paving Industry Emission Regulations
Big Game Hunting Regulations
Birds of Prey Regulations
Certification & Disposal of Wildlife Regulations
Community Parks Order
Critical Wildlife Areas Regulations
Dempster Highway Special Management Area Regulations
Environmental Protection Act
Environmental Rights Act
Establishing Freshwater Fish Marketing Corporation Regulations
Flood Damage Reduction Agreements Act
Forest Management Act
Forest Management Regulations
Forest Protection Act
Freshwater Fish Marketing Act
Herd & Fencing Act
Heritage Parks, Natural Environment Parks & Recreation Parks Regulations
Historic Parks Order
Natural Environment Recreation Park Order
Nuisance Bison Control Regulations
Outdoor Recreation Parks Order
Outfitter Regulations
Pesticides Act
Polar Bear Defence Kill Regulations
Sale of Wildlife Regulations
Small Game Hunting Regulations
Spill Contingency Planning & Reporting
Territorial Parks Act
Territorial Parks Regulations
Tourist Establishment Regulations
Trapping Regulations
Travel & Tourism Act
Travel Development Area Regulation

Used Oil & Waste Fuel Management
Waste Reduction & Recovery Act
Water Resources Agreements Act
Wayside Parks Order
Wildlife Act
Wildlife Business Regulations
Wildlife Export Regulations
Wildlife General Regulations
Wildlife Licenses & Permits Regulations
Wildlife Management Barren Ground Caribou Area Regulation
Wildlife Management Grizzly Bear Area Regulations
Wildlife Management Muskox Areas Regulations
Wildlife Management Outfitter Area Regulations
Wildlife Management Polar Bear Areas Regulations
Wildlife Management Units Regulations
Wildlife Management Wood Bison Area Regulations
Wildlife Management Zones Regulations
Wildlife Preserves Regulations
Wildlife Regions Regulations
Wildlife Sanctuaries Regulations

Minister, Hon. James Arreak
Tel: 867-924-6423
Fax: 867-924-6429

Deputy Minister, David Akeeagok
Tel: 867-975-7705
dakeeagok@gov.nu.ca

Assistant Deputy Minister, Earle Baddaloo
Tel: 867-975-7704
ebaddaloo@gov.nu.ca

Director, Policy, Planning & Legislation, Steve Pinksen
Tel: 867-975-7718
Fax: 867-975-7740
spinksen@gov.nu.ca

Director, Fisheries & Sealing, Wayne Lynch
Tel: 867-975-7750
Fax: 867-975-7742
cegeni@gov.nu.ca

Environmental Protection
Tel: 867-975-5907
The government is working towards the development & implementation of a strategy to address climate change. Environmental protection ensures that all spills of hazardous substances are cleaned up properly by the party responsible. Major areas of the environment, such as persistent organic pollutants & other contaminants that threaten the traditional food chain will be monitored.
Director, Robert Eno
Tel: 867-975-7729
Fax: 867-975-7739
reno@gov.nu.ca
Manager, Land Use & Environmental Assessment, Michael Mifflin
Tel: 867-975-7732
mmifflin@gov.nu.ca

Parks & Conservation Areas
www.nunavutparks.com
Responsible for the planning, establishment, operations & the promotion of a system of territorial parks & conservation areas throughout Nunavut. In cooperation with Nunavummiut, Parks & Conservation Areas showcases Nunavut's protected areas locally, regionally, nationally, & internationally to ensure protected areas continue to reflect the Nunavut Territory's unique heritage & the spirit, principles & special relationships established through the Nunavut Land Claims Agreement & the Inuit Impact Benefit Agreements (IIBAs) for Territorial Parks.
Director, David Monteith
Tel: 867-975-5934
dmonteith@gov.nu.ca
Manager, Facility Planning & Operations, Cameron DeLong
Tel: 867-975-7725
cdelong@gov.nu.ca

Wildlife Management
Responsible for the management of terrestrial wildlife species in Nunavut. In addition to the Nunavut Wildlife Act, Wildlife Management is responsible for fulfilling responsibilities under a wide range of federal legislation & both national & international agreements & conventions.
Director, Drikus Gissing
Tel: 867-975-7734
dgissing@gov.nu.ca
Manager, South Baffin, Jason Aliqatuqtuq
Tel: 867-975-7900
jaliqatuqtuq@gov.nu.ca
Manager, Wildlife Reseach, Peter Hale
Tel: 867-934-2183
phale@gov.nu.ca

Regional Offices
Regional Offices

Baffin
PO Box 569Pond Inlet, NU X0A 0S0
Kitikmeot
PO Box 377Kugluktuk, NU X0B 0E0
Regional Wildlife Manager, Mathieu Dumond
Tel: 867-982-7441
mdumond@gov.nu.ca
Kivalliq
PO Box 120Arviat, NU X0C 0E0
Regional Wildlife Manager, David Vetra
Tel: 867-857-2828
Fax: 867-857-2986

Nunavut Territory Department of Executive & Intergovernmental Affairs

1084 Aeroplex bldg., PO Box 1000 Stn. 200, Iqaluit, NU X0A 0H0
Tel: 867-975-6000
Fax: 867-975-6099
www.eia.gov.nu.ca
The department provides advice & administrative support to Cabinet & the government, works to ensure that the Nunavut Land Claims Agreement & Nunavut's relationships with other governments in Canada & the circumpolar world are used to support common goals. The department compiles & communicates information & evaluates government programs & data.The Intergovernmental Affairs Division is responsible for the management & development of government strategies, policies & initiatives relating to federal, provincial, territorial, circumpolar & aboriginal affairs. This office participates in preparations for Intergovernmental activities such as the Western & Annual Premiers Conferences, First Ministers meetings & the Social Union Framework Agreement, the Arctic Council, the Nunavut Implementation Panel & the Clyde River Protocol.
Acts Administered:
Nunavut Power Corporation Assets Transfer Confirmation Act
Public Utilities Act
Public Utilities Regulations

Minister, Hon. Eva Aariak
Tel: 867-975-5050
Fax: 867-975-5051

Assistant Deputy Minister, Policy, Planning & Evaluation, Pauloosie Suvega
Tel: 867-975-6009
Fax: 867-975-6089

Commissioner, Commissioner's Office, Edna Elias
Tel: 867-975-5120
elias@gov.nu.ca

Deputy Commissioner, Commissioner's Office, Nellie Kusugak
Tel: 867-975-5122
nkusugakCOM@gov.nu.ca

Director, Communications, Pam Coulter
Tel: 867-975-6049
pcoulter2@gov.nu.ca

Director, Government Liaison Office, Hugh Lloyd
Tel: 867-975-6050

Director, Policy, Planning & Evaluation, Rachel Mark
Tel: 867-975-6029
Fax: 867-975-6029
rmark@gov.nu.ca

Director, Aboriginal & Circumpolar Affairs, Letia Obed
Tel: 867-975-6036
Fax: 867-975-6091
lobed@gov.nu.ca

Director, Devolution Division, Mark Thompson
Tel: 867-975-6070
mthompson1@gov.nu.ca

Manager, Access Information, Jessica Bell
Tel: 867-975-6044
jessica.bell@gov.nu.ca

Manager, Women's Secretariat, Tanya Campbell
Tel: 867-975-6018
tcampbell@gov.nu.ca

Manager, Administrative Services, Johnny Issaluk
Tel: 867-975-6051
jissaluk@gov.nu.ca

Manager, Finance, Angela Kabvitok
Tel: 867-975-6002
akabvitok@gov.nu.ca
Acts Administered:
Environmental Tobacco Smoke Work Site Reguations
Explosives Use Act
Mine Health & Safety Act
Safety Act
Technical Standards & Safety Act
Worker's Compensation Act

Nunavut Territory Department of Health & Social Services

PO Box 1000 Stn. 1000, Iqaluit, NU X0A 0H0
Tel: 867-975-5766
Fax: 867-975-5705
Toll-Free: 800-661-0833
www.hss.gov.nu.ca
The Environmental Health Specialist provides recommendations & direction, consultation, development of standards, monitoring, maintenance & evaluation of all environmental health programs within Nunavut. Reviews the Public Health Act & Regulations & environmental health standards & policies & makes recommendations for revisions. Guides the regional environmental health officers in development & implementation of programs & policies in prevention of diseases caused by environmental factors, including food, water, waste disposal, housing & the sanitation of public places, including schools, day cares & other institutional facilities. Guides the Regional Environmental Health Officers in water & food-borne related illness investigations & food recalls. Guides the regions in the monitoring of drinking water supplies. Assists with development of health education & promotional materials & activities related to environmental health.
Acts Administered:
Boards of Management Dissolution Act
Camp Sanitation Regulations
Communicable Diseases Regulations
Disease Registries Act
General Sanitation Exemption Regulations
General Sanitation Regulations
Meat Inspection Regulations
Public Health Act
Public Sewerage Systems Regulations
Public Water Supply Regulations
Reportable Diseases Order
Tobacco Control Act
Tourist Accomodation Health Regulations

Minister, Hon. Keith Peterson
Tel: 867-975-5005

Deputy Minister, Peter Ma
pma@gov.nu.ca

Acting Chief Medical Officer of Health, Dr. Maureen Baikie
Tel: 867-975-5743
mbaikie@gov.nu.ca

Executive Director, Population Health, Gogi Greeley
Tel: 867-975-5709
ggreeley@gov.nu.ca

Executive Director, Social Services, Lynn Ryan MacKenzie
Tel: 867-975-5947
lmackenzie@gov.nu.ca

Manager, Research & Special Projects, Janet Brewster

Tel: 867-975-5703
jbrewster@gov.nu.ca

Manager, Human Resources, Shawn Burke
Tel: 867-975-5749
sburke@gov.nu.ca

Manager, Public Health Strategy, Isabelle Dingemans
Tel: 867-975-5767
idingemans@gov.nu.ca

Environmental Health Consultant, Peter Workman
Tel: 867-975-5764
Fax: 867-975-5755
pworkman@gov.nu.ca

Regional Offices
Regional Offices
Tel: 867-983-4043
Fax: 867-983-4041
Baffin
Regional Director, Roy Inglangas
ringlangas@gov.nu.ca
Kitikmeot
Regional Director, Clara Evalik
cevalik@gov.nu.ca
Kivalliq
Regional Director, Debora Voth
dvoth@gov.nu.ca

Deputy Minister, Joe Adla Kunuk
Tel: 867-975-6213
Fax: 867-975-6216
jkunuk@gov.nu.ca
Acts Administered:
Engineers, Geologists & Geophysicists Act
Expropriation Act
Land Titles Act

Minister, Hon. Daniel Shewchuk
Tel: 867-975-5001
Fax: 867-975-5044

Deputy Minister, Norman Tarnow
Tel: 867-975-6332
ntarnow@gov.nu.ca

Northwest Territories & Nunavut Workers' Safety & Compensation Commission (WCB)

For a detailed listing please see Northwest Territories.

Government of Ontario

Seat of Government: Queen's Park, Toronto, ON M7A 1A2
Tel: 416-326-1234
Toll-Free: 800-267-8097
TTY: 800-268-7095
www.gov.on.ca
The Province of Ontario entered Confederation July 1, 1867. It has an area of 908,607.67 km2, & the StatsCan census population in 2011 was 12,851,821.

Secretary of the Cabinet & Head of the Ontario Public Service; Interim Chair, Ontario Lottery & Gaming Corporation, Peter Wallace
Tel: 416-325-7641
Fax: 416-314-8980
peter.wallace@ontario.ca

Deputy Minister, Policy & Delivery, Scott Thompson
Tel: 416-325-3759
Fax: 416-325-7631
scott.thompson@ontario.ca

Assistant Deputy Minister, Corporate Planning & Services, Linda Jackson
Tel: 416-314-0817
Fax: 416-325-2388
linda.jackson@ontario.ca

Minister, Hon. David Zimmer
Tel: 416-325-5110
Fax: 416-314-2701
dzimmer.mpp@liberal.ola.org

Ontario Ministry of Agriculture, Food & Rural Affairs (OMAFRA)

Ontario Government Bldg., 1 Stone Rd. West, Guelph, ON N1G 4Y2
Tel: 519-826-3100
Toll-Free: 888-466-2372
www.omafra.gov.on.ca
Secondary Address: 77 Grenville St., 11th Fl.
Toronto, ON M5S 1B3 Canada
twitter.com/atomafra
www.youtube.com/user/atomafra
The ministry works in partnership with an industry that employs over 640,000 people & contributes over $25 billion annually to the provincial economy. The ministry plays a key role in bringing a strong agricultural & rural perspective to provincial policies. The ministry works with other ministries to resolve local economic issues & assists rural communities in retaining & attracting business. Staff at the ministry's Guelph headquarters & across the province provide a wide range of agri-food & rural economic development programs & services to clients.
Acts Administered:
AgriCorp Act
Agricultural & Horticultural Organizations Act
Agricultural Employees Protection Act 2002
Agricultural Lands Regulations
Agricultural Research Institute of Ontario Act
Agricultural Tile Drainage Installation Act
Animals for Research Act
Drainage Act
Farm Products Container Act
Farm Products Marketing Act
Farming & Food Production Protection Act
Food Safety & Quality Act, 2001
Livestock & Livestock Products Act
Ministry of Agriculture, Food & Rural Affairs Act
Nutrient Management Act, 2002
Plant Diseases Act
Tile Drainage Act
Weed Control Act

Minister, Hon. Kathleen O. Wynne
Tel: 416-325-1941
Fax: 416-325-9895
minister.omaf@ontario.ca

Deputy Minister, Deb Stark
Tel: 416-326-3101
deb.stark@ontario.ca

Associated Agencies, Boards & Commissions:
• **Agricorp**
1 Stone Rd. West, 3rd Fl.
PO Box 3660 Central
Guelph, ON N1H 8M4
Fax: 519-826-4118
Toll-free: 888-247-4999
TTY: 877-275-1380
contact@agricorp.com
www.agricorp.com
Other Communication: AgriStability Fax: 519-826-4334
Responsible for delivering government & non-government priority products & services that assist Ontario's agri-food industry in managing risks.
Chair, Larry Skinner
Tel: 519-826-3280
Chief Executive Officer, Randy Jackiw
Tel: 519-826-4548
randy.jackiw@agricorp.com
• **Agricultural Research Institute of Ontario (ARIO)**
1 Stone Rd. West, 2nd Fl.
Guelph, ON N1G 4Y2
Tel: 519-826-4554
Toll-free: 888-466-2372
research.omafra@ontario.ca
www.omafra.gov.on.ca/english/research/ario/institute.htm
The role of ARIO is to enquire into programs of research with respect to agriculture, veterinary medicine & consumer studies, select & recommend areas of research for the betterment of agriculture, veterinary medicine & consumer studies, & stimulate interest in research as a means of developing a high degree of efficiency in the production & marketing of agricultural products in Ontario.
Chair, Stewart Cressman
Contact, Wilma Macfarlane
Tel: 519-826-4198
wilma.macfarlane@ontario.ca
• **Agriculture, Food & Rural Affairs Tribunal & Board of Negotiation**
1 Stone Rd. West, 2nd Fl.
Guelph, ON N1G 4Y2
Tel: 519-826-3433
Fax: 519-826-4232
Toll-free: 888-466-2372
appeals.tribunal@omafra.gov.on.ca
www.omafra.gov.on.ca/english/tribunal/index.html
Chair, Kirk Walstedt
Tel: 519-826-3433
• **College of Veterinarians of Ontario**
2106 Gordon St.
Guelph, ON N1L 1G6
Tel: 519-824-5600
Fax: 519-824-6497
Toll-free: 800-424-2856
inquiries@cvo.org
www.cvo.org
Other Communication: Toll-Free Fax: 1-888-662-9479
• **Grain Financial Protection Board**
1 Stone Rd. West, 1st Fl. Northeast
PO Box 3660 Central
Guelph, ON N1H 8M4
Tel: 519-826-3949
Fax: 519-826-3367
• **Livestock Financial Protection Board**
1 Stone Rd. West, 5th Fl. Northwest
Guelph, ON N1G 4Y2
Tel: 519-826-3886
Fax: 519-826-4375
Toll-free: 888-466-2372
Chair, Robert Brander
Contact, Jim Wideman
jim.wideman@ontario.ca
• **Livestock Medicines Advisory Committee**
1 Stone Rd. West, 3rd Fl. Northeast
Guelph, ON N1G 4Y2
Tel: 519-826-4110
Fax: 519-826-3254
ag.info.omafra@ontario.ca
Chair, Ian K. Russell
• **Normal Farm Practices Protection Board**
1 Stone Rd. West, 3rd Fl.
Guelph, ON N1G 4Y2
Tel: 519-826-4047
Fax: 519-826-3259
Toll-free: 877-424-1300
ag.info.omafra@ontario.ca
Chair, Glenn Walker
Tel: 519-826-3549
glenn.walker@ontario.ca
• **Ontario Farm Products Marketing Commission**
1 Stone Rd. West, 5th Fl. Southwest
Guelph, ON N1G 4Y2
Tel: 519-826-4220
Fax: 519-826-3400
www.omafra.gov.on.ca/english/farmproducts
Chair, Geri Kamenz
Tel: 519-826-3406
geri.kamenz@ontario.ca
• **Ontario Food Terminal Board**
165 The Queensway
Toronto, ON M8Y 1H8
Tel: 416-259-5479
Fax: 416-259-4303
oftboard@interlog.com
www.oftb.com
• **Rural Economic Development (RED) Panel**
1 Stone Rd. West, 4th Fl.
Guelph, ON N1G 4Y2
Fax: 519-826-4336
Toll-free: 888-588-4111
red.omafra@ontario.ca
www.ontario.ca/rural

Economic Development Division
Fax: 519-826-7819
Toll-Free: 877-424-1300
Other Communication: Northern Ontario, Toll-Free Phone: 1-800-461-6132

Assistant Deputy Minister, Bonnie Winchester
Tel: 519-826-3528
bonnie.winchester@ontario.ca

Food Safety & Environment Division
Tel: 519-826-4304
Fax: 519-826-4416
Assistant Deputy Minister, Dr. Dave Hope
Tel: 519-826-4301
Fax: 519-826-4416
dave.hope@ontario.ca

Office of the Chief Information Officer, Land & Resources I & IT Cluster
Fax: 416-314-6091
Chief Information Officer, James G. Hamilton
Tel: 416-314-1528
jim.hamilton@ontario.ca
Acting Director, Organizational Performance, Judy Tomarin
Tel: 416-212-7560
judy.tomarin@ontario.ca

Policy Division
Tel: 519-826-4020
Fax: 519-826-3492
Responsible for the ministry's policy processes, the administration & delivery of several farm business risk management programs & the management of the ministry's strategic partnership with AGRICORP.
Assistant Deputy Minister, Dave Antle
Tel: 519-826-4151
Fax: 519-826-3492
dave.antle@ontario.ca
Director, Strategic Policy, George McCaw
Tel: 519-826-4002
Fax: 519-826-3614
george.mccaw@ontario.ca

Research & Corporate Services Division
Tel: 519-826-4152
Fax: 519-826-3390
Acting Assistant Deputy Minister, Shelley Gibson
Tel: 519-826-4698
Fax: 519-826-3390
shelley.gibson@ontario.ca
Director, Strategic Solutions, Alan Hogan
Tel: 519-826-3739
alan.hogan@ontario.ca
Acts Administered:
Assessment Review Board Act
Expropriations Act
Transboundary Pollution Reciprocal Access Act
Acts Administered:
Fair Access to Regulated Professions Act
Holocaust Memorial Day Act
Holodomor Memorial Day Act
Ministry of Citizenship & Culture Act (in part)
Remembrance Day Observance Act
Vimy Ridge Day Act

Deputy Minister, Chisanga Puta-Chekwe
Tel: 416-325-6220
chisanga.puta-chekwe@ontario.ca

Parliamentary Assistant, Vacant

Director, Communications, Deborah Swain
Tel: 416-314-7606
Fax: 416-314-1061
deborah.swain@ontario.ca

Assistant Director & Manager, Program Communications Unit, Mary Dowding-Paré
Tel: 416-314-7230
mary.dowding-pare@ontario.ca

Ontario Ministry of Community Safety & Correctional Services (MCSCS)

George Drew Bldg., 25 Grosvenor St., 18th Fl., Toronto, ON M7A 1Y6
Tel: 416-326-5000
Fax: 416-326-0498
Toll-Free: 866-517-0571
TTY: 416-326-5511
mcscs.feedback@ontario.ca
www.mcscs.jus.gov.on.ca
Other Communication: Toll-Free TTY: 1-866-517-0572
The Ministry ensures that communities across the province are protected by safe, effective & accountable law enforcement & public safety systems. General responsibilities of the ministry are as follows: correctional services; public safety & security; & policing services.
Acts Administered:
Emergency Management & Civil Protection Act
Fire Protection & Prevention Act, 1997

Minister, Hon. Madeleine Meilleur
Tel: 416-326-5000
Toll-free: 866-517-0571
Fax: 416-325-6067
mmeilleur.mpp@liberal.ola.org

Deputy Minister, Community Safety, Ian Davidson
Tel: 416-326-5060
Fax: 416-327-0469
ian.davidson@ontario.ca

Associated Agencies, Boards & Commissions:
• Animal Care Review Board (ACRB)
77 Grenville St., 8th Fl.
Toronto, ON M5S 1B3
Tel: 416-314-5336
Fax: 416-314-5559
acrb.info@ontario.ca; acrb.registrar@ontario.ca
• Death Investigation Oversight Council (DIOC)
George Drew Bldg.
25 Grosvenor St., 1st Fl.
Toronto, ON M7A 1Y6
Tel: 416-212-4041
dioc@ontario.ca
www.sse.gov.on.ca/mcscs/dioc
• Fire Marshal's Public Fire Safety Council
Place Nouveau Bldg.
5775 Yonge St., 7th Fl.
Toronto, ON M2M 4J1
Tel: 416-325-3152
Fax: 416-325-3162
info@firesafetycouncil.com; orders@firesafetycouncil.com
www.firesafetycouncil.com
Chair, Patrick R. Burke
• Fire Safety Commission
Place Nouveau Bldg.
5775 Yonge St., 7th Fl.
Toronto, ON M2M 4J1
Tel: 416-325-3100
Fax: 416-314-1217
Chair, Richard D. Judge
• Ontario Civilian Police Commission (OCPC)
#605, 250 Dundas St. West
Toronto, ON M7A 2T3
Tel: 416-314-3004
Fax: 416-314-0198
Toll-free: 888-515-5005
www.ocpc.ca
Other Communication: Complaints (GTA): 416-326-1189; Toll-Free Fax: 1-888-311-7555
• Ontario Parole Board (OPB)
#1803, 415 Yonge St.
Toronto, ON M5B 2E7
Tel: 416-325-4480
Fax: 416-325-4485
Toll-free: 888-579-2888
www.operb.gov.on.ca
• Ontario Police Arbitration Commission (OPAC)
George Drew Bldg.
25 Grosvenor St., 1st Fl.
Toronto, ON M7A 1Y6
Tel: 416-314-3520
Fax: 416-314-3522
www.policearbitration.on.ca

Emergency Management Ontario
77 Wellesley St. West, PO Box 222Toronto, ON M7A 1N3
Tel: 416-314-3723
Fax: 416-314-3758
Toll-Free: 877-314-3723
Assistant Deputy Minister & Chief, Allison J. Stuart
Tel: 416-314-6186
allison.j.stuart2@ontario.ca

Ontario Ministry of Consumer Services (MCS)

Mowat Block, 900 Bay St., 6th Fl., Toronto, ON M7A 1L2
Tel: 416-327-8300
Fax: 416-326-1947
Toll-Free: 866-665-0662
TTY: 877-666-6545
infomcs@ontario.ca; consumer@ontario.ca
www.sse.gov.on.ca/mcs
Other Communication: Consumer Protection Branch Phone: 416-326-8800; Fax: 416-326-8665; TTY: 416-229-6086
twitter.com/ontarioconsumer
www.facebook.com/ontarioconsumer
The Ministry seeks to educate, protect & serve consumers in Ontario by maintaining a fair, safe & informed marketplace; providing modern information services; & regulating practices that serve the interests of Ontarians.

Minister, Hon. Tracy MacCharles
Tel: 416-327-8300
Fax: 416-326-1947
tmaccharles.mpp.co@liberal.ola.org

Deputy Minister, Giles Gherson
Tel: 416-314-1957
giles.gherson@ontario.ca

Director, Communications, Cindy Greeniaus
Tel: 416-326-7208
Fax: 416-326-7445
cindy.greeniaus@ontario.ca

Associated Agencies, Boards & Commissions:
• Ontario Film Review Board (OFRB)
#101B, 4950 Yonge St.
Toronto, ON M1N 6K1
Tel: 416-314-3626
Fax: 416-314-3632
www.ofrb.gov.on.ca

Ontario Ministry of Economic Development, Trade & Employment

Hearst Block, 900 Bay St., 8th Fl., Toronto, ON M7A 2E1
Tel: 416-325-6666
Fax: 416-325-6688
Toll-Free: 866-668-4249
TTY: 416-325-4402
info@edt.gov.on.ca
www.ontariocanada.com/ontcan/1medt/en/home_en.jsp
Other Communication: Toll-Free TTY: 1-877-408-3414
twitter.com/Onteconomy
www.facebook.com/ontarioinnovation
www.youtube.com/user/OntarioEconomy
Promotes economic development & job creation in Ontario by creating a climate for business to prosper & eliminate red tape as well as stimulating trade. This Ministry markets the province as a desirable place to live, work, invest & raise a family. It works with its private sector partners to ensure that its core responsibilities of employment & business development, investment & trade continue to help Ontario businesses compete globally; contribute to a highly-skilled, well-educated workforce; & generate prosperity for all Ontarians. In Northern Ontario, the Ministry is represented by the Northern Development Division of the Ministry of Northern Development & Mines.
Acts Administered:
Ministry of Industry, Trade & Technology Act
Research Foundation Act

Minister, Hon. Eric Hoskins
Tel: 416-656-0943
ehoskins.mpp.co@liberal.ola.org

Investment & Industry Division
Hearst Block, 900 Bay St., 5th fl., Toronto, ON M7A 2E1
Fax: 416-212-3658
Assistant Deputy Minister, Tony LaMantia
Tel: 416-325-6623
tony.lamantia@ontario.ca
Acting Manager, Manufacturing Investment Unit, John Millen
Tel: 416-325-6824
john.millen@ontario.ca
Manager, Aerospace & Materials Unit, Joseph Veloce
Tel: 416-325-6767
joe.veloce@ontario.ca

Acting Manager, Automotive Unit, Julie Washburn
Tel: 416-326-4908
julie.washburn@ontario.ca

Open for Business
#700, 375 University Ave., Toronto, ON M5G 2J5
Tel: 416-314-5072
Fax: 416-212-3288
Assistant Deputy Minister, Katherine Hewson
Tel: 416-212-3283
katherine.hewson@ontario.ca
Acting Director, Anne Bermonte
Tel: 416-212-3284
anne.bermonte@ontario.ca
Acting Director, Social Enterprise, Ryan Lock
Tel: 416-314-5525
ryan.lock@ontario.ca
Acting Manager, Andrea Bruce
Tel: 416-212-3284
andrea.bruce@ontario.ca

Policy & Strategy Division
Hearst Block, 900 Bay St., 3rd Fl., Toronto, ON M7A 2E7
Tel: 416-212-6653
Fax: 416-326-6393
Assistant Deputy Minister, John Whitehead
Tel: 416-325-4655
john.whitehead@ontario.ca

Research, Commercialization & Entrepreneurship Division
56 Wellesley St. West, 11th Fl., Toronto, ON M7A 2E7
Tel: 416-314-8474
Fax: 416-327-9573
Acting Assistant Deputy Minister, Bill Mantel
Tel: 416-327-2889
bill.mantel@ontario.ca
Director, Entrepreneurship Branch, Sam Boonstra
Tel: 416-314-3809
sam.boonstra@ontario.ca
Director, Commercialization Branch, George Cadete
Tel: 416-314-0670
Fax: 416-314-0680
george.cadete@ontario.ca

Ontario Capital Growth Corporation
#1701, 393 University Ave., Toronto, ON M5G 1E6
Tel: 416-314-8474
Fax: 416-212-0794
Toll-Free: 877-422-5818
www.ocgc.gov.on.ca
The OCGC was established by the Ontario Capital Growth Corporation Act, 2008. The Corporation's main focus is the management of the Government of Ontario's interests in the Ontario Venture Capital Fund LP and the Ontario Emerging Technologies Fund.
Acting President & Chief Executive Officer, John W. Marshall
Tel: 416-325-6644
john.w.marshall@ontario.ca
Acting Chief Financial Officer & Portfolio Manager, George Loo
Tel: 416-326-9623
george.loo@ontario.ca

Trade & Marketing Division
Hearst Block, 900 Bay St., 5th fl., Toronto, ON M7A 2E1
Tel: 416-325-9802
Fax: 416-325-5617
Toll-Free: 877-468-7233
Other Communication: North America Toll-Free: 1-800-819-8701
Assistant Deputy Minister, Cameron Sinclair
Tel: 416-325-9801
cameron.sinclair@ontario.ca

Ontario Ministry of Energy

Hearst Block, 900 Bay St., 4th Fl., Toronto, ON M7A 2E1
Tel: 416-327-6758
Fax: 416-325-8440
Toll-Free: 888-668-4636
TTY: 800-239-4224
write2us@ontario.ca
www.energy.gov.on.ca
twitter.com/OntMinEnergy
The Ministry of Energy's responsibility is to ensure that Ontario's electricity system functions at the highest level of reliability & productivity. The electricity system lies at the heart of the economy & way of life & by ensuring the system remains reliable, efficient & secure, the ministry is making sure Ontario remains one of the best places in the world in which to live, work, invest & raise a family. The Ministry of Energy is also focused on promoting ingenuity & innovation in the energy sector. By encouraging the development of new ideas & technologies it is helping to make Ontario a world leader in the global energy market. Protecting the environment is also a top priority for the Ministry. Developing renewable sources of energy, cleaner forms of fuel, as well as fostering a conservation culture, are all cornerstones of the Ministry's vision for Ontario's electricity future.
Acts Administered:
Hydro One Inc. Directors & Officers Act, 2002
Ministry of Energy Act, 2011
Ontario Energy Board Act
Power Corporation Act
Toronto District Heating Corporation Act

Minister, Hon. Bob Chiarelli
Tel: 416-327-6758
Fax: 416-327-6754
bchiarelli.mpp.co@liberal.ola.org

Deputy Minister, Serge Imbrogno
Tel: 416-327-6734
Fax: 416-327-6755
serge.imbrogno@ontario.ca

Parliamentary Assistant, Bob Delaney
Tel: 416-325-4140
Fax: 416-325-0818
bdelaney.mpp.co@liberal.ola.org

Associated Agencies, Boards & Commissions:
• **Hydro One Inc.**
See Entry Name Index for detailed listing.
• **Independent Electricity System Operator**
See Entry Name Index for detailed listing.
• **Ontario Energy Board (OEB)**
#2700, 2300 Yonge St.
Toronto, ON M4P 1E4
Tel: 416-481-1967
Fax: 416-440-7656
Toll-free: 888-632-6273
www.ontarioenergyboard.ca
Chair, Rosemarie T. Leclair
Tel: 416-440-7601
rosemarie.leclair@ontarioenergyboard.ca
Chief Operating Officer, Aleck Dadson
Tel: 416-440-8146
aleck.dadson@ontarioenergyboard.ca
• **Ontario Power Authority**
#1600, 120 Adelaide St. West
Toronto, ON M5H 1T1
Tel: 416-967-7474
Fax: 416-967-1947
Toll-free: 800-797-9604
info@powerauthority.on.ca
www.powerauthority.on.ca
Chair, James D. Hinds
Chief Executive Officer, Colin Anderson
• **Ontario Power Generation**
See Entry Name Index for detailed listing.

Corporate Development Division
880 Bay St., 5th Fl., Toronto, ON M7A 2C1
Tel: 416-327-7106
Fax: 416-314-3354
Provides a structure to identify strategic issues, to coordinate policy & program development; & to coordinate & integrate action by the Ministry & other governments.
Assistant Deputy Minister & Chief Administrative Officer, Vacant

Energy Supply, Transmission & Distribution Policy
880 Bay St., 3rd Fl., Toronto, ON M7A 2C1
Tel: 416-327-7353
Fax: 416-314-6224
Assistant Deputy Minister, Rick Jennings
Tel: 416-314-6190
rick.jennings@ontario.ca
Director, Energy Supply - Nuclear Branch, Cedric Jobe
Tel: 416-325-6545
Fax: 416-314-6224
cedric.jobe@ontario.ca
Director, Energy Supply & Competition, Garry McKeever
Tel: 416-325-8627
Fax: 416-314-6224
garry.mckeever@ontario.ca
Director, Transmission & Distribution Policy, Jonathan Norman
Tel: 416-326-1759
Fax: 416-314-6224
jonathan.norman@ontario.ca

Regulatory Affairs & Strategic Policy
Mowat Block, 900 Bay St., 5th Fl., Toronto, ON M7A 2E3
Tel: 416-325-6559
Fax: 416-325-7041
Provides strategic policy coordination & development for the ministry as well as policy analysis & advice related to energy conservation & efficiency, demand management, & conservation.
Acting Assistant Deputy Minister, Michael Reid
Tel: 416-325-6544
michael.reid@ontario.ca

Renewables & Energy Efficiency
880 Bay St., 6th Fl., Toronto, ON M7A 2C1
Tel: 416-314-6216
Fax: 416-325-3438
The branch provides analysis, advice & policy development on issues relating to energy efficiency, demand management & conservation as well as administering the Energy Efficiency Act.
Assistant Deputy Minister, Sue Lo
Tel: 416-327-8552
sue.lo@ontario.ca
Director, Energy Efficiency & Innovative Technology, Barry Beale
Tel: 416-326-4551
barry.beale@ontario.ca
Director, Renewables & Energy Facilitation, Pearl Ing
Tel: 416-327-3868
pearl.ing@ontario.ca
Acting Director, Project Management Office, Jennifer Block
Tel: 416-212-9267
jennifer.block@ontario.ca

Ontario Ministry of Environment (MOE)

135 St. Clair Ave. West, Toronto, ON M4V 1P5
Tel: 416-325-4000
Fax: 416-325-3159
Toll-Free: 800-565-4923
TTY: 800-515-2759
picemail.moe@ontario.ca
www.ene.gov.on.ca
Other Communication: Pollution Hotline: 1-866-MOE-TIPS (1-866-663-8477); Spills or Emergencies: 1-800-268-6060; Public Information: 1-800-565-4923
twitter.com/EnvironmentONT
www.facebook.com/OntarioEnvironment
The ministry is responsible for protecting clean & safe air, land & water to ensure healthy communities, ecological protection & sustainable development for present & future generations of Ontarians. Using stringent regulations, targeted enforcement & a variety of innovative programs & initiatives, the ministry continues to address environmental issues that have local, regional &/or global effects. The ministry has built a strong foundation of clear laws, stringent regulations, tough standards & rigorous permits & approvals. The ministry monitors pollution & restoration trends in an effort to determine the effectiveness of its activities & to assess risks to human health & the environment. This information is used to develop & implement environmental legislation, regulations, standards, policies, guidelines & programs to enhance environmental protection.
Acts Administered:
Adams Mine Lake Act, 2004
Additional Charges Regulation
Air Contaminants from Ferrous Foundries Regulation
Air Pollution - Local Quality Regulations
Airborne Contaminant Discharge Monitoring & Reporting Regulations
Ambient Air Quality Criteria Regulations
Blue Box Waste Regulations, 2002
Boilers Regulation
Capital Investment Plan Act
Certificates of Approval Exemptions Air Regulation
Certification of Drinking-Water System Operators & Water Quality Analysts
Classes of Contaminants Exemption Regulations
Classification & Exemption of Spills Regulations
Clean Water Act
Compliance & Enforcement
Containers Regulation
Deep Well Disposal Regulation

Definitions of "Deficiency" & "Municipal Drinking-Water System" Regulations
Definitions of Words & Expressions Used in the Act Regulations, 2003
Designation of Waste Regulation
Designations & Exemptions
Discharge of Sewage from Pleasure Boats Regulation
Disposable Containers for Milk Regulations
Disposable Paper Containers for Milk Regulations
Drinking-Water Systems Regulations, 2003
Drinking-Water Testing Services Regulations, 2003
Dry Cleaners Regulations
Effluent Monitoring & Effluent Limits Regulations
Electricity Projects Regulation
Emissions Trading Regulation
Environmental Assessment Act
Environmental Assessment General Regulations
Environmental Bill of Rights Act
Environmental Protection Act
Environmental Review Tribunal Act, 2000
Ethanol in Gasoline
Exemption Regulations
Gasoline Volatility Regulation
General Waste Management Regulation
Ground Source Heat Pumps Regulation
Halon Fire Extinguishing Equipment Regulation
Hot Mix Asphalt Facilities Regulation
Industrial, Commercial & Institutional Source Separation Programs Regulation
Industry Emissions - Nitrogen Oxides & Sulphur Dioxide
Lake Simcoe Protection Act
Lakeview Generating Station Regulations
Lambton Industry Meteorology Alert Regulation
Land Disposal Restrictions
Landfilling Sites Regulation
Licensing of Sewage Works Operators Regulations
Marinas Regulation
Ministry of the Environment Act
Mobil PCB Destruction Facilities Regulation
Motor Vehicles Regulation
Municipal Sewage & Water & Roads Class Environmental Assessment Project Regulation
Municipal Water & Sewage Transfer Act
Municipalities, Secured Creditors, Receivers, Trustees in Bankruptcy & Fiduciaries, Pt.XV.2 of the Act Regulations, 2002
Non-Residential & Non-Municipal Seasonal Residential Systems that do not Service Designated Facilities
Nutrient Management Act
Ontario Drinking-Water Quality Standards Regulations, 2003
Ontario Power Generation Regulations
Ontario Water Resources Act
Ozone Depleting Substances Regulation
Packaging Audits & Packaging Reduction Work Plans Regulation
Pesticides Act
Records of Site Condition, Pt.XV.1 of the Act Regulations, 2004
Recovery of Gasoline Vapour in Bulk Transfers Regulation
Recycling & Composting of Municipal Waste Regulation
Refillable Containers for Carbonated Soft Drink Regulation
Refrigerants Regulation
Reporting Requirements, Sulphur Levels in Gasoline Regulations
Safe Drinking Water Act, 2002
Schools, Private Schools & Day Nurseries Regulations, 2003
Secured Creditors, Receivers, Trustees in Bankruptcy Regulations, 2002
Sewage System Regulations & Exemptions
Sewage Works Subject to Approval under the Environmental Assessment Act Regulations
Solvents Regulation
Spills Regulation
Sterilants Regulation
Sulphur Content of Fuels Regulation
Sustainable Water & Sewage Systems Act, 2002
Toxins Reduction Act
Transitional Provisions Relating to the Repeal of Pt.VIII of the Environmental Protection Act Regulations
Used Oil Material Regulations, 2003
Used Tires Regulations, 2003
Waste Audits & Waste Reduction Workplans Regulation
Waste Disposal Sites & Waste Management Systems Subject to Approval under the Environmental Assessment Act Regulations
Waste Diversion Act, 2002
Waste Electrical & Electronic Equipment
Waste Management (PCBs) Regulation
Water Opportunities Act
Water Taking & Transfer Regulation
Wells Regulation

Minister, Hon. James J. Bradley
Tel: 416-314-6790
Fax: 416-314-6748
minister.moe@ontario.ca

Deputy Minister, Gail Beggs
Tel: 416-314-6753
Fax: 416-314-6791

Parliamentary Assistant, Phil McNeely
Tel: 416-325-0737
Fax: 416-314-6748
hjaczek.mpp.co@liberal.ola.org

Acting Director, Communications Branch, Michael Maddock
Tel: 416-325-9361
Fax: 416-314-6711
michael.maddock@ontario.ca

Director, Ontario Internal Audit, Resources & Labour Audit Team, Ray Masse
Tel: 416-314-9208
Fax: 416-314-3467
ray.masse@ontario.ca

Director, Legal Services Branch, Rand Roszell
Tel: 416-212-0853
Fax: 416-212-0863
rand.roszell@ontario.ca
Other Communications: Southwest Region Counsel Fax: 519-682-9539

Associated Agencies, Boards & Commissions:
• Advisory Council on Drinking Water Quality & Testing Standards (ODWAC)
40 St. Clair Ave. West, 3rd Fl.
Toronto, ON M4V 1M2
Tel: 416-212-7779
Fax: 416-212-7595
www.odwac.gov.on.ca
Chair, Jim Merritt
Tel: 416-414-3606
jim.merritt@ontario.ca
• Ontario Clean Water Agency (OCWA)
1 Yonge St., 17th Fl.
Toronto, ON M5E 1E5
Tel: 416-314-5600
Fax: 416-314-8300
Toll-free: 800-667-6292
www.ocwa.com
The Ontario Clean Water Agency (OCWA) was established as a Provincial Crown Agency in November 1993 & is committed to providing safe & reliable clean water services. The Agency is an established leader in the operation, maintenance & management of water & wastewater treatment facilities & their associated distribution & collection systems. OCWA operates hundreds of water & wastewater facilities, ranging in size from small wells & pumping stations to large-scale urban water & wastewater systems.
Chair, Michael R. Garrett
President & Chief Executive Officer, Jane Pagel
Tel: 416-314-0757
jpagel@ocwa.ca
• Pesticides Advisory Committee
135 St. Clair Ave. West, 15th Fl.
Toronto, ON M4V 1P5
Tel: 416-314-9230
Fax: 416-314-9237
www.opac.gov.on.ca
This committee advises the Minister of the Environment on matters pertaining to pesticides. It annually reviews the Pesticides Act & regulations, & government publications respecting pesticides & control of pests. The committee also recommends classifications for all new pesticide products prior to their marketing & use in Ontario, & publishes an annual report, which is available upon request. For other ministry publications on pests & pest control & information on pesticide licensing, contact the Standards Development Branch, Pesticides Section.
Chair, Dr. Frank Ingratta
Tel: 416-314-9233
• Walkerton Clean Water Centre
20 Ontario Rd.
PO Box 160
Walkerton, ON N0G 2V0
Tel: 519-881-2003
Fax: 519-881-4947
Toll-free: 866-515-0550
inquiry@wcwc.ca
www.wcwc.ca
Other Communication: Bell Relay Service: 1-800-267-6511
The vision of the Walkerton Clean Water Centre is to create a world-class intitute dedicated to safe & secure drinking water for the people of Ontario. Established by Ontario Regulation 304/04 as a crown agency of the Ministry of the Environment in October 2004, & governed by a 12-member board of directors, the Centre's work will complement & support that of the Ministry with a focus on ensuring that training, education & information is available & accessible to owners, operators & operating authorities of Ontario's drinking water systems, particularly in rural & remote communities.
Chief Executive Officer, Dr. Larry Moore
Tel: 519-881-2003 ext: 306
lmoore@wcwc.ca
Manager, WCWC Training Institute, Brian Jobb
Tel: 519-881-2003 ext: 399
brian.jobb@wcwc.ca
Manager, WCWC Research & Technology Institute, Dr. Souleymane Ndiongue
Tel: 519-881-2003 ext: 308
sndiongue@wcwc.ca

Corporate Management Division
135 St. Clair Ave. West, 14th Fl., Toronto, ON M4V 1P5
Tel: 416-314-6426
Fax: 416-314-6425
Assistant Deputy Minister & Chief Administrative Officer, Debra Sikora
Tel: 416-314-6424
debra.sikora@ontario.ca
Director, Business & Fiscal Planning, Rob W. Campbell
Tel: 416-314-7370
Fax: 416-314-7858
rob.w.campbell@ontario.ca
Director, Strategic Human Resources, Jacques LeGris
Tel: 416-314-9305
Fax: 416-314-9313
jacques.legris@ontario.ca
Director, Information Management & Access Branch, Jim Lewis
Tel: 416-314-3856
Fax: 416-314-6872
jim.d.lewis@ontario.ca
Director, Transition Office, Becky Taylor
Tel: 416-314-5606
Fax: 416-325-7962
becky.taylor@ontario.ca
Manager, Environmental Bill of Rights Office, Jacqueline Gallacher
Tel: 416-314-9615
Fax: 416-314-6872
jacqueline.gallacher@ontario.ca

Drinking Water Management Division
135 St. Clair Ave. West, 14th Fl., Toronto, ON M4V 1P5
Tel: 416-314-4475
Fax: 416-314-6935
The Drinking Water Management Division, led by the Chief Drinking Water Inspector, has lead responsibility for program & operational activities related to the protection & provision of safe drinking water in Ontario.
Assistant Deputy Minister & Chief Drinking Water Inspector, Paul Nieweglowski
Tel: 416-314-4463
paul.nieweglowski@ontario.ca
Director, Source Protection Programs, Ling Mark
Tel: 416-212-6459
Fax: 416-212-2757
ling.mark@ontario.ca
Director, Safe Drinking Water, Indra Prashad
Tel: 416-314-6437
Fax: 416-212-7576
indra.prashad@ontario.ca
Director, Drinking Water Programs, Orna Salamon
Tel: 416-212-2355

Fax: 416-314-9477
orna.salamon@ontario.ca
Manager, Certification, Training & Client Services, Brian Gildner
Tel: 416-212-7457
Fax: 416-314-9477
brian.gildner@ontario.ca
Acting Manager, Assessment, Evaluation & Best Practices, Eli Kane
Tel: 416-212-7317
Fax: 416-212-0607
eli.kane@ontario.ca
Supervisor, Approvals, Aziz Ahmed
Tel: 416-314-4625
Fax: 416-314-1037
aziz.ahmed@ontario.ca

Environmental Programs Division
135 St. Clair Ave. West, 14th Fl., Toronto, ON M4V 1P5
Tel: 416-326-7203
Fax: 416-327-8777
Assistant Deputy Minister, Jim Whitestone
Tel: 416-314-9530
jim.whitestone@ontario.ca
Director, Aboriginal Affairs, Mary Hennessy
Tel: 416-327-6953
Fax: 416-326-8114
mary.hennessy@ontario.ca
Director, Program Planning & Implementation, & Environmental Innovations, Kevin Perry
Tel: 416-327-9730
Fax: 416-325-8475
kevin.perry@ontario.ca
Director, Modernization of Approvals Project, Marcia Wallace
Tel: 416-327-9466
Fax: 416-325-7962
marcia.wallace@ontario.ca

Environmental Sciences & Standards Division
135 St. Clair Ave. West, 14th Fl., Toronto, ON M4V 1P5
Fax: 416-314-6358
The Environmental Sciences & Standards Division (ESSD) provides the best available science & technology to support decisions about the natural environment, & implements those decisions by developing & managing programs & partnerships, setting scientifically credible standards, monitoring the environment & providing valuable analytical & scientific expertise. Programs such as Drive Clean, that improve the environment & increase public awareness, are central to the ministry's efforts to strengthen environmental protection.
Assistant Deputy Minister, Anne Neary
Tel: 416-314-6310
anne.neary@ontario.ca
Director, Standards Development, Steve Klose
Tel: 416-314-1501
Fax: 416-327-2936
steve.klose@ontario.ca

Drive Clean Office
40 St. Clair Ave. West, 4th Fl., Toronto, ON M4V 1M2
Tel: 416-314-5856
Fax: 416-314-4160
www.driveclean.com
Director & Assistant Director/Manager, Program Design & Evaluation Section, Garth Napier
Tel: 416-314-3920
garth.napier@ontario.ca
Acting Manager, Drive Clean Contracts Section, Ron Seca
Tel: 416-314-3913
ron.seca@ontario.ca
Manager, Customer Service & Program Support Section, Mary-Ann Wong
Tel: 416-314-5936
mary-ann.wong@ontario.ca
Senior Technical Specialist, Drive Clean Facility Operations Section, Kirsten Lindgreen
Tel: 416-314-5929
kirsten.lindgreen@ontario.ca

Environmental Monitoring & Reporting Branch
West Wing, 125 Resources Rd., Toronto, ON M9P 3V6
Tel: 416-235-6300
Fax: 416-235-6235
Director, Ian Smith
Tel: 416-235-6160
ian.r.smith@ontario.ca
Manager, Air Quality Monitoring & Transboundary Air Sciences Section, Gary DeBrou
Tel: 416-235-6157
gary.debrou@ontario.ca
Manager, Regulatory & Environmental Data Management Section, Cynthia Carr
Tel: 416-235-6262
cynthia.carr@ontario.ca
Manager, Biomonitoring Section, Dr. Rachael Fletcher
Tel: 416-327-2935
rachael.fletcher@ontario.ca
Manager, Regulatory Program Reporting Section, Brian Whitehead
Tel: 416-235-6256
brian.whitehead@ontario.ca
Team Leader, Drinking Water Monitoring Unit, Patrick Cheung
Tel: 416-235-6236
patrick.cheung@ontario.ca
Supervisor, Great Lakes Monitoring Unit, Duncan Boyd
Tel: 416-235-6221
duncan.boyd@ontario.ca
Supervisor, Groundwater & Well Water Management Unit, Deborah Conrod
Tel: 416-235-6187
deborah.conrod@ontario.ca

Laboratory Services Branch
125 Resources Rd., Toronto, ON M9P 3V6
Tel: 416-235-5743
Fax: 416-235-5744
Director, Joseph Odumeru
Tel: 416-235-5747
joseph.odumeru@ontario.ca
Assistant Director, Dan Toner
Tel: 416-235-6310
dan.toner@ontario.ca
Manager, Toxic Organics, Dr. George Kanert
Tel: 416-235-5848
george.kanert@ontario.ca
Acting Manager, Organic Contaminants, David Morse
Tel: 416-235-5989
david.morse@ontario.ca
Manager, Spectroscopy & Physical Chemistry, Rusty Moody
Tel: 416-235-5863
rusty.moody@ontario.ca
Manager, Biological Analysis, Frank Tomassini
Tel: 416-235-5869
frank.tomassini@ontario.ca
Manager, Inorganic Chemical Analysis, Robert Tooley
Tel: 416-235-6094
robert.tooley@ontario.ca

Standards Development Branch
40 St. Clair Ave. West, 7th Fl., Toronto, ON M4V 1M2
Tel: 416-327-5519
Fax: 416-327-2936
Director, Steve Klose
Tel: 416-327-5543
steve.klose@ontario.ca
Manager, Water Standards, Minnie deJong
Tel: 416-314-3748
Fax: 416-327-6421
minnie.dejong@ontario.ca
Manager, Ecological Standards, Craig Kinch
Tel: 416-327-4460
Fax: 416-327-2936
craig.kinch@ontario.ca
Co-Manager, Pesticides Management Section, Wanda Michalowicz
Tel: 416-327-5934
Fax: 416-327-2936
wanda.michalowicz@ontario.ca
Co-Manager, Pesticides Management Section, Lorna Poff
Tel: 416-327-4138
Fax: 416-327-2936
lorna.poff@ontario.ca
Acting Manager, Technology Standards Section, Steven Radcliffe
Tel: 416-327-9064
Fax: 416-327-9187
steven.radcliffe@ontario.ca
Manager, Human Toxicology & Air Standards Section, Julie Schroeder
Tel: 416-325-3475
Fax: 416-327-2936
julie.schroeder@ontario.ca
Manager, Business Services, Una Wilton
Tel: 416-314-1988
Fax: 416-327-2936
una.wilton@ontario.ca
Coordinator, Issues Management Unit, Olga Lyssiakova
Tel: 416-327-4638
Fax: 416-327-2936
olga.lyssiakova2@ontario.ca

Integrated Environmental Policy Division
77 Wellesley St. West, 11th Fl., Toronto, ON M7A 2T5
Tel: 416-314-6338
Fax: 416-314-6346
Integrated Environmental Planning Division is responsible for integrating the overall policy development & planning functions of the Ministry. This involves integrating & synthesizing all information, data & perspectives on the many aspects of the Ministry's mandate. The division consults extensively on developing policies, strategies & programs that support the Ministry's core business of conservation & environmental protection.
Assistant Deputy Minister, Paul Evans
Tel: 416-314-6352
Fax: 416-314-6346
paul.evans@ontario.ca
Director, Land & Water Policy, Sharon Bailey
Tel: 416-314-7020
Fax: 416-314-7200
sharon.bailey@ontario.ca
Director, Environmental Intergovernmental Affairs, Brian Nixon
Tel: 416-212-1340
Fax: 416-212-3296
brian.nixon2@ontario.ca
Acting Director, Air Policy Instruments & Programs Design, Heather E. Pearson
Tel: 416-314-6419
heather.e.pearson@ontario.ca
Manager, Regional Air Issues, Karen Clark
Tel: 416-212-2747
Fax: 416-314-4128
karen.clark2@ontario.ca
Manager, Great Lakes, Carolyn O'Neill
Tel: 416-314-7833
Fax: 416-314-3918
carolyn.oneill@ontario.ca
Manager, Global Air Issues, Sarah Paul
Tel: 416-326-7999
Fax: 416-314-4128
sarah.paul@ontario.ca
Manager, Policy & Special Projects Section, Eileen Smith
Tel: 416-314-5135
Fax: 416-325-4233
eileen.smith@ontario.ca

Operations Division
135 St. Clair Ave. West, 8th Fl., Toronto, ON M4V 1P5
Tel: 416-314-6378
Fax: 416-314-6396
The Operations Division is the operations & program delivery arm of the ministry. It is responsible for delivering programs to protect air quality, to protect surface & ground water quality & quantity, to ensure appropriate management of wastes, to ensure an adequate quality of drinking water & to control the use of pesticides. In addition, the division is responsible for administering the ministry's approvals & licensing programs as well as an investigative & enforcement program to ensure compliance with environmental laws. The division has a province-wide network of regional, district & area offices.
Assistant Deputy Minister, Kevin French
Tel: 416-314-6366
Fax: 416-314-6396
kevin.french@ontario.ca
Assistant Director, Investigations & Enforcement, Don Earl
Tel: 416-326-4676
don.earl@ontario.ca
Assistant Director/Program Services Manager, Sector Compliance, Neera Shukla
Tel: 416-314-0782
Fax: 416-314-4464
neera.shukla@ontario.ca
Manager, Registrations & Application Evaluation, Millicent Dixon
Tel: 416-314-7135
millicent.dixon@ontario.ca
Acting Manager, Strategic Enforcement & Intelligence Unit, Jim Fry

Tel: 807-475-1714
jim.fry@ontario.ca
Acting Manager, Environmental Assessment Services, Ross Lashbrook
Tel: 416-314-7967
ross.lashbrook@ontario.ca
Manager, Spills Action Centre, Janet L. Woelfle
Tel: 416-314-6370
Toll-free: 866-663-8477
Fax: 416-325-3011
jan.woelfle@ontario.ca
Manager, Emergency Management Program Office, Gary Zikovitz
Tel: 416-325-1995
gary.zikovitz@ontario.ca
Barrie
#1201, 54 Cedar Pointe Dr., Barrie, ON L4N 5R7
Tel: 705-739-6441
Fax: 705-739-6440
Toll-Free: 800-890-8511
District Manager, Cindy Hood
Tel: 705-739-6436
cindy.hood@ontario.ca
Halton-Peel
#300, 4145 North Service Rd., Burlington, ON L7L 6A3
Tel: 905-319-3847
Fax: 905-319-9902
Toll-Free: 800-335-5906
District Manager, Tina Dufresne
Tel: 905-319-1870
tina.dufresne@ontario.ca
Toronto
Place Nouveau, 5775 Yonge St., 9th Fl., Toronto, ON M2M 4J1
Tel: 416-326-6700
Fax: 416-325-6345
Director, Regional Office, Dolly Goyette
Tel: 416-326-1825
dolly.goyette@ontario.ca
District Manager, Rod Adams
Tel: 416-326-5536
rod.adams@ontario.ca
York-Durham
230 Westney Rd. South, 5th Fl., Ajax, ON L1S 7J5
Tel: 905-427-5600
Fax: 905-427-5602
Toll-Free: 800-376-4547
District Manager, Dave Fumerton
Tel: 905-427-5626
dave.fumerton@ontario.ca
Belleville
345 College St. East, Belleville, ON K8N 5S7
Tel: 613-962-9208
Fax: 613-962-6809
Toll-Free: 800-860-2763
Area Supervisor, Christine E. Brown
Tel: 613-962-9459
christine.e.brown@ontario.ca
Cornwall
113 Amelia St., 1st Fl., Cornwall, ON K6H 3P1
Tel: 613-933-7402
Fax: 613-933-6402
Toll-Free: 800-860-2760
District Administrative Assistant, Suzanne Payette
Tel: 613-933-7611
suzanne.payette@ontario.ca
Kingston
#3, 1259 Gardiners Rd., PO Box 22032Kingston, ON K7M 8S5
Tel: 613-549-4000
Fax: 613-548-6908
Toll-Free: 800-267-0974
Director, Regional Office, Hollee Kew
Tel: 613-548-6901
Fax: 613-548-6911
hollee.kew@ontario.ca
District Manager, Trevor Dagilis
Tel: 613-548-6906
trevor.dagilis@ontario.ca
Ottawa
2430 Don Reid Dr., Ottawa, ON K1H 1E1
Tel: 613-521-3450
Fax: 613-521-5437
Toll-Free: 800-860-2195
District Manager, Steve Burns
Tel: 613-521-3450 ext: 224
steve.burns@ontario.ca
Peterborough
Robinson Place, South Tower, 300 Water St., 2nd Fl., Peterborough, ON K9J 8M5
Tel: 705-755-4300
Fax: 705-755-4321
Toll-Free: 800-558-0595
District Manager, Hope Boehm
Tel: 705-755-4315
hope.boehm@ontario.ca
North Bay
#16 & 17, 191 Booth Rd., North Bay, ON P1A 4K3
Tel: 705-497-6865
Fax: 705-497-6866
Toll-Free: 800-609-5553
Acting Supervisor, Liza Vandermeer
Tel: 705-497-6931
liza.vandermeer@ontario.ca
Kenora
808 Robertson St., PO Box 5150Kenora, ON P9N 3X9
Tel: 807-468-2718
Fax: 807-468-2735
Toll-Free: 888-367-7622
Acting Area Supervisor, Drew Stajkowski
Tel: 807-468-2730
drew.stajkowski@ontario.ca
Sault Ste Marie
289 Bay St., 3rd Fl., Sault Ste Marie, ON P6A 1W7
Tel: 705-942-6354
Fax: 705-942-6327
Toll-Free: 800-965-9990
Acting Area Supervisor, Trisha Westman
Tel: 705-942-6393
trisha.westman@ontario.ca
Sudbury
#1201, 199 Larch St., Sudbury, ON P3E 5P9
Tel: 705-564-3237
Fax: 705-564-4180
Toll-Free: 800-890-8516
District Manager, Brian Cameron
Tel: 705-564-3214
brian.cameron@ontario.ca
Thunder Bay
#331B, 435 James St. South, Thunder Bay, ON P7E 6S7
Tel: 807-475-1205
Fax: 807-475-1754
Toll-Free: 800-875-7772
Other Communication: District Office Phone: 807-475-1315; Alternate Fax: 807-473-3160
Director, Regional Office, John P. Taylor
Tel: 807-475-1690
john.p.taylor@ontario.ca
District Supervisor, Scott Sheriff
Tel: 807-475-1686
scott.sheriff@ontario.ca
Timmins
Government Complex, Hwy. 101 East, PO Bag 3080, South Porcupine, ON P0N 1H0
Tel: 705-235-1500
Fax: 705-235-1520
Toll-Free: 800-380-6615
District Manager, Dennis Durocher
Tel: 705-235-1506
denis.durocher@ontario.ca
London
733 Exeter Rd., London, ON N6E 1L3
Tel: 519-873-5000
Fax: 519-873-5020
Toll-Free: 800-265-7672
Director, Regional Office, Kanina Blanchard
Tel: 519-873-5001
kanina.blanchard@ontario.ca
District Manager, Mark Dunn
Tel: 519-873-5031
mark.dunn@ontario.ca
Owen Sound
101 - 17th St. East, 3rd Fl., Owen Sound, ON N4K 0A5
Tel: 519-371-2901
Fax: 519-371-2905
Toll-Free: 800-265-3783
District Manager, Rick Chappell
Tel: 519-371-6022
rick.chappell@ontario.ca
Sarnia
1094 London Rd., Sarnia, ON N7S 1P1
Tel: 519-336-4030
Fax: 519-336-4280
Toll-Free: 800-387-7784
District Manager, Mike Moroney
Tel: 519-383-3780
michael.moroney@ontario.ca
Windsor
#620, 4510 Rhodes Dr., Windsor, ON N8W 5K5
Tel: 519-948-1464
Fax: 519-948-2396
Toll-Free: 800-387-8826
Area Supervisor, Doug McDougall
Tel: 519-948-6024
doug.mcdougall@ontario.ca
Guelph
1 Stone Rd. West, 4th Fl., Guelph, ON N1G 4Y2
Tel: 519-826-4255
Fax: 519-826-4286
Toll-Free: 800-265-8658
District Manager, Jane Glassco
Tel: 519-826-4258
jane.glassco@ontario.ca
Hamilton
Ellen Fairclough Bldg., 119 King St. West, 9th Fl., Hamilton, ON L8P 4Y7
Tel: 905-521-7650
Fax: 905-521-7820
Toll-Free: 800-668-4557
Other Communication: Regional Office Phone: 905-521-7640
Director, Bill Bardswick
Tel: 905-521-7652
bill.bardswick@ontario.ca
District Manager, Geoffrey Knapper
Tel: 905-521-7642
geoffrey.knapper@ontario.ca
Niagara
#15, 301 St. Paul St., 9th Fl., St Catharines, ON L2R 7R4
Tel: 905-704-3900
Fax: 905-704-4015
Toll-Free: 800-263-1035
District Manager, Rich Vickers
Tel: 905-704-3904
richard.vickers@ontario.ca

Environmental Commissioner of Ontario (ECO)

#605, 1075 Bay St., Toronto, ON M5S 2B1
Tel: 416-325-3377
Fax: 416-325-3370
Toll-Free: 800-701-6454
commissioner@eco.on.ca
www.eco.on.ca
twitter.com/Ont_ECO
www.facebook.com/OntarioEnvironmentalCommissioner
www.youtube.com/user/EcoComms
An independent officer of the Legislative Assembly of Ontario, the Environmental Commissioner of Ontario promotes the values, goals & purposes of the Environmental Bill of Rights (EBR) to improve the quality of Ontario's natural environment. The ECO monitors & reports on the application of the EBR, provides public education to facilitate Ontario residents' participation in the EBR & reviews government accountability for environmental decision-making.

Commissioner, Gord Miller

Director, Operations, Peter Lapp
Tel: 416-325-3369
peter.lapp@eco.on.ca

Senior Manager, Climate Change, Chris Gates
Tel: 416-325-3373
chris.gates@eco.on.ca

Senior Manager, Policy Analysis, Ellen Schwartzel
Tel: 416-325-0559
ellen.schwartzel@eco.on.ca

Ontario Ministry of Government Services (MGS)

Ferguson Block, 77 Wellesley St. West, 8th Fl., Toronto, ON M7A 1N3
Tel: 416-326-8555
Toll-Free: 800-268-1142
TTY: 416-326-8566
www.mgs.gov.on.ca

Other Communication: Consumer Protection, Phone: 416-326-8800; Toll Free: 1-800-889-9768
MGS is responsible for the delivery of government services, the government workforce, procurement & technology resources. The ministry is engaged in the following main activities: providing government information to individuals & businesses, including distribution through Publications Ontario; protecting consumers through information about frauds & scams & mediating complaints about businesses; & issuing birth, death & marriage certificates, & managing Land Registry Offices throughout the province.
Acts Administered:
Boundaries Act

Minister, Hon. John Milloy
Tel: 416-325-7754
Fax: 416-325-7755
jmilloy.mpp@liberal.ola.org

Associated Agencies, Boards & Commissions:
• **Advertising Review Board**
Macdonald Block
#M2-56, 900 Bay St., 2nd Fl.
Toronto, ON M7A 1N3
Tel: 416-327-2183
Fax: 416-327-2179
• **Conflict of Interest Commissioner**
#1802, 2 Bloor St. East
Toronto, ON M4W 3J6
Tel: 416-325-1571
Fax: 416-325-4330
Commissioner, Sidney Linden
Tel: 416-212-1853
sidney.linden@ontario.ca
• **Licence Appeal Tribunal (LAT)**
#530, 20 Dundas St. West
Toronto, ON M5G 2C2
Tel: 416-314-4260
Fax: 416-314-4270
Toll-free: 800-255-2214
www.lat.gov.on.ca
Other Communication: Toll Free Fax: 1-800-720-5292
The LAT hears appeals when a decision or order to suspend or a proposal is made to cancel or to refuse to grant or renew a registration, certificate or a licence, or when a claim for compensation has been denied.
• **Ontario Pension Board (OPB)**
Sun Life Bldg.
#2200, 200 King St. West
Toronto, ON M5H 3X6
Tel: 416-364-8558
Fax: 416-364-7578
Toll-free: 800-668-6203
clientservice@opb.ca
www.opb.on.ca
• **Ontario Racing Commission (ORC)**
#400, 10 Carlson Crt.
Toronto, ON M9W 6L2
Tel: 416-213-0520
Fax: 416-213-7827
inquiry@ontarioracingcommission.ca
www.ontarioracingcommission.ca
• **OPSEU Pension Trust**
#1200, 1 Adelaide St. East
Toronto, ON M5C 3A7
Tel: 416-681-6161
Fax: 416-681-6175
Toll-free: 800-637-0024
www.optrust.com
Other Communication: Member & Pensioner Services: 416-681-6100
• **Provincial Judges Pension Board**
c/o Ontario Pension Board
#1100, 1 Adelaide St. East
Toronto, ON M5C 2X6
Tel: 416-327-8395
Fax: 416-366-0199
• **Public Service Commission**
Whitney Block
99 Wellesley St. West, 5th Fl.
Toronto, ON M7A 1W4
Tel: 416-325-1750
Chair, Kevin Costante
Tel: 416-327-2101
Secretariat Support, Janet Hannah
Tel: 416-325-8816
Secretariat Support, Kerry Pond
Tel: 416-325-1777
kerry.pond@ontario.ca

Ontario Shared Services
700 University Ave., 6th Fl., Toronto, ON M7A 2S4
Tel: 416-326-9300
Toll-Free: 866-979-9300
Associate Deputy Minister, Angela Coke
Tel: 416-325-5065
angela.coke@ontario.ca

Supply Chain Management
Tel: 413-212-0967
Fax: 416-327-3573
www.ontario.ca/supplychain
Develops & implements an integrated corporate procurement strategy to: leverage & optimize government procurement of goods & services; identify and implement procurement process improvements; enhance procurement controllership; provide strategic advice on large scale procurements; develop innovative policy frameworks to support service delivery through third party service providers.
Assistant Deputy Minister, Marian Macdonald
Tel: 416-327-7508
Fax: 416-327-3573
marian.macdonald@ontario.ca

Ontario Public Service Green Office
College Park, #16900, 777 Bay St., 16th Fl., Toronto, ON M7A 2J3
Tel: 416-325-4082
Assistant Deputy Minister, Neil Sentance
Tel: 416-327-3536
neil.sentance@ontario.ca
Manager, OPS Green Office Projects, Janice Fummerton
Tel: 416-325-4096
janice.fummerton@ontario.ca

Ontario Ministry of Health & Long-Term Care

Hepburn Block, 80 Grosvenor St., 10th Fl, Toronto, ON M7A 2C4
Tel: 416-327-4327
Toll-Free: 800-268-1153
TTY: 800-387-5559
www.health.gov.on.ca
twitter.com/ONThealth
www.facebook.com/217753654940869
www.youtube.com/user/ontariomohltc
The ministry is responsible for administering the health care system & providing services to the Ontario public through such programs as health insurance, drug benefits, assistive devices, care for the mentally ill, long-term care, home care, community & public health, & health promotion & disease prevention. It also regulates hospitals & nursing homes, operates psychiatric hospitals & medical laboratories, & co-ordinates emergency health services.
Acts Administered:
Brain Tumour Awareness Month Act, 2001
Chase McEachern Act (Heart Defibrillator Civil Liability), 2007
Commitment to the Future of Medicare Act, 2004
Excellent Care for All Act, 2010
Fluoridation Act
Healing Arts Radiation Protection Act
Health Protection & Promotion Act
Home Care & Community Services Act, 1994
Homeopathy Act, 2007
Katelyn Bedard Bone Marrow Awareness Month Act, 2010
Kinesiology Act
Local Health System Integration Act, 2006
Long-Term Care Homes Act, 2007
Medical Laboratory Technology Act
Medical Radiation Technology Act
Medicine Act
Ministry of Health & Long-Term Care Act
Ministry of Health & Long-Term Care Appeal & Review Boards Act
Narcotics Safety & Awareness Act
Natruopathy Act
Ontario Agency for Health Protection & Promotion Act, 2007
Patient Restraints Minimization Act
Personal Health Information Protection Act
Psychotherapy Act
Quality of Care Information Protection Act
Traditional Chinese Medicine Act
University Health Network Act
University of Ottawa Heart Institute Act

Minister, Hon. Deborah Matthews
Tel: 416-327-4300
Fax: 416-327-2679
dmatthews.mpp@liberal.ola.org

Deputy Minister, Saäd Rafi
Tel: 416-327-4496
Fax: 416-326-1570
saad.rafi@ontario.ca

Parliamentary Assistant, Helena Jaczek
Tel: 416-325-0710
Fax: 416-325-3862
hjaczek.mpp@liberal.ola.org

Parliamentary Assistant, Liz Sandals
Tel: 519-836-4190
lsandals.mpp.co@liberal.ola.org

Associated Agencies, Boards & Commissions:
• **Cancer Care Ontario (CCO)**
620 University Ave., 15th Fl.
Toronto, ON M5G 2L7
Tel: 416-971-9800
Fax: 416-971-6888
www.cancercare.on.ca
• **Chiropody Review Committee**
#2102, 180 Dundas St. West
Toronto, ON M5G 1Z8
Tel: 416-542-1333
Fax: 416-542-1666
Toll-free: 877-232-7653
A committee of the College of Chiropodists of Ontario that reviews accounts of podiatrists referred to it by the General Manager of the Ontario Health Insurance Plan.
• **Consent & Capacity Board**
151 Bloor St. West, 10th Fl.
Toronto, ON M5S 2T5
Tel: 416-327-4142
Fax: 416-924-8873
Toll-free: 866-777-7391
TTY: 877-301-0889
www.ccboard.on.ca
Other Communication: Toll-Free Fax: 1-866-777-7273
Hears appeals relating to involuntary placement in a psychiatric facility, capacity to make personal care & financial decisions & access to personal records from a psychiatric facility.
• **Dentistry Review Committee**
350 Rumsey Rd.
Toronto, ON M4G 1R8
Tel: 416-961-6555
A committee of the Royal College of Dental Surgeons that reviews accounts of dentists referred to it by the General Manager of the Ontario Health Insurance Plan.
• **Optometry Review Committee**
6 Crescent Rd, 3rd Fl.
Toronto, ON M4W 1T1
Tel: 416-962-4071
A committee of the College of Optometrists of Ontario that reviews accounts of optometrists referred to it by the General Manager of the Ontario Health Insurance Plan.
• **eHealth Ontario**
College Park
#701, 777 Bay St.
PO Box 148
Toronto, ON M5G 2C8
Tel: 416-586-6500
Fax: 416-586-4363
Toll-free: 888-411-7742
TTY: 855-645-3390
info@ehealthontario.on.ca; privacy@ehealthontario.on.ca
www.ehealthontario.on.ca
Other Communication: Privacy Office: 416-946-4767
• **Health Boards Secretariat**
151 Bloor St. West, 9th Fl.
Toronto, ON M5S 2T5
Tel: 416-327-8512
Fax: 416-327-8524
Toll-free: 866-282-2179
• **HealthForceOntario**
163 Queen St. East
Toronto, ON M5A 1S1

Tel: 416-862-2200
Toll-free: 800-596-4046
info@healthforceontario.ca;
accesscentre@healthforceontario.ca
www.healthforceontario.ca
Other Communication: International Toll-Free: 1-800-596-4046, ext. 4
HealthForceOntario seeks to identify & address the province's health human resource needs on behalf of the Ministry of Health & Long-Term Care, & the Ministry of Training, Colleges & Universities.
• Health Quality Ontario
#702, 130 Bloor St. West
Toronto, ON M5S 1N5
Tel: 416-323-6868
www.ohqc.ca
• Medical Eligibility Committee
370 Select Dr.
PO Box 168
Kingston, ON K7M 8T4
Tel: 613-536-3058
Deals with the eligibility of insured services as well as other matters assigned to it by the act or the regulation or by the minister; makes recommendations to the general manager with respect to these decisions.
• Ontario Mental Health Foundation (OMHF)
441 Jarvis St., 2nd Fl.
Toronto, ON M4Y 2G8
Tel: 416-920-7721
Fax: 416-920-0026
grants@omhf.on.ca
www.omhf.on.ca
• Ontario Review Board (ORB)
151 Bloor St. West, 10th Fl.
Toronto, ON M5S 2T5
Tel: 416-327-8866
Fax: 416-327-8867
TTY: 877-301-0889
orb@ontario.ca
www.orb.on.ca
• Public Health Ontario (PHO)
#300, 480 University Ave.
Toronto, ON M5G 1V2
Tel: 647-260-7100
Fax: 647-260-7600
Toll-free: 877-543-8931
info@oahpp.ca
www.oahpp.ca
• Trillium Gift of Life Network
#900, 522 University Ave.
Toronto, ON M5G 1W7
Tel: 416-363-4001
Fax: 416-363-4002
Toll-free: 800-263-2833
www.giftoflife.on.ca
Other Communication: Healthcare Professionals Organ & Tissue Referral: 416-363-4438; Toll-Free: 1-877-363-8456

Chief Medical Officer of Health
Hepburn Block, 80 Grosvenor St., 11th Fl., Toronto, ON M7A 1R3
Tel: 416-212-3831
Fax: 416-325-8412
Chief Medical Officer of Health, Dr. Arlene King
arlene.king@ontario.ca
Associate Chief Medical Officer of Health, Infrastructure & Systems (Transition), Dr. Robin Williams
Tel: 416-325-7672
dr.robin.williams@ontario.ca
Associate Chief Medical Officer of Health, Environmental Health, Vacant
Associate Chief Medical Officer of Health, Health Promotion, Chronic Diseases & Injury Prevention, Vacant
Associate Chief Medical Officer of Health, Health Protection & Prevention, Vacant
Executive Director, Public Health Division, Roselle Martino
Tel: 416-327-9555
Fax: 416-325-8412
roselle.martino@ontario.ca
Director, Public Health Policy & Programs, Nina Arron
Tel: 416-212-4873
nina.arron@ontario.ca
Director, Emergency Management, Gerilynne Carroll
Tel: 416-212-5229
gerilynne.carroll@ontario.ca
Director, Public Health Standards, Practice & Accountability, Sylvia Shedden
Tel: 416-327-7423
sylvia.shedden@ontario.ca
Director, Public Health Planning & Liaison, Elizabeth S. Walker
Tel: 416-212-6359
elizabeth.walker@ontario.ca
Assistant Deputy Minister, Patricia Li
Tel: 416-327-4845
Fax: 416-314-5915
patricia.li@ontario.ca
Director, Emergency Health Services (Land & Air), Malcolm Bates
Tel: 416-327-7909
Fax: 416-327-7879
malcolm.bates@ontario.ca
Director, Air Ambulance Program Oversight, Richard Jackson
Tel: 416-327-1535
richard.jackson@ontario.ca
Director, Assistive Devices Program, Susan Picarello
Tel: 416-212-5906
Toll-free: 800-268-6021
Fax: 416-327-8192
susan.picarello@ontario.ca
Other Communications: URL: www.health.gov.on.ca/adp
TTY: 800-387-5559
Acting Director, Psychiatric Patient Advocate Office, Susan Picarello
Tel: 416-212-5906
Fax: 416-327-7008
susan.picarello@ontario.ca
Other Communications: URL: www.ppao.gov.on.ca
Director, Claims Services, Dianne Wylie
Tel: 613-548-6454
Fax: 416-548-6320
dianne.wylie@ontario.ca

Hydro One Inc.

North Tower, 483 Bay St., 15th Fl., Toronto, ON M5G 2P5
Tel: 416-345-5000
Fax: 905-944-3251
Toll-Free: 877-955-1155
customercommunications@hydroone.com
www.hydroone.comPO Box 5700 Sta.
Markham, ON L3R 1C8

Chair, James Arnett

President & Chief Executive Officer, Laura Formusa

President & Chief Executive Officer, Hydro One Remotes Inc., Myles D'Arcey

President & Chief Executive Officer, Hydro One Telecom Inc., Paul Marchant

President & Chief Executive Officer, Hydro One Brampton Inc., Remy Fernandes

Senior Vice-President, Engineering & Project Delivery, Nairn McQueen

Vice-President, Health, Safety & Environment, John Macnamara

Independent Electricity System Operator (IESO)

PO Box 4474 Stn. A, Toronto, ON M5W 4E5
Tel: 905-403-6900
Fax: 905-403-6921
Toll-Free: 888-448-7777
customer.relations@ieso.ca
www.ieso.ca
Other Communication: Reception: 905-855-6100
twitter.com/ieso_tweets
www.facebook.com/OntarioIESO

Chair, Tim O'Neill

President & Chief Executive Officer, Paul Murphy
paul.murphy@ieso.ca

Vice-President, Resource Integration, Bruce Campbell
Tel: 416-506-2829
bruce.campbell@ieso.ca

Vice-President, Merger Integration, Ted Leonard
ted.leonard@ieso.ca

Vice-President, Organizational Development, Bill Limbrick
bill.limbrick@ieso.ca

Vice-President, Finance, Doug Thomas
doug.thomas@ieso.ca

Vice-President, Operations, Kim Warren
kim.warren@ieso.ca

Vice-President, Corporate Relations, Terry Young
terry.young@ieso.ca

General Counsel & Corporate Secretary, Human Resources, Roy Stewart
roy.stewart@ieso.ca

Ontario Ministry of Infrastructure (MOI)

Ferguson Block, 77 Wellesley St. West, Toronto, ON M7A 1Z8
Tel: 416-327-9200
Toll-Free: 888-668-4636
TTY: 800-239-4224
www.moi.gov.on.ca
twitter.com/ONinfra

Minister, Hon. Glen R. Murray
Tel: 416-327-9200
Fax: 416-327-9188
gmurray.mpp@liberal.ola.org

Deputy Minister, Drew Fagan
Tel: 416-212-0646
Fax: 416-212-0641

Parliamentary Assistant, Kevin Daniel Flynn
Tel: 416-327-0806
Fax: 416-327-9188
kflynn.mpp.co@liberal.ola.org

Associated Agencies, Boards & Commissions:
• Infrastructure Ontario
College Park
777 Bay St., 6th Fl.
Toronto, ON M5G 2C8
Tel: 416-327-6008
Fax: 416-326-9291
info@infrastructureontario.ca
www.infrastructureontario.ca
Management of complex infrastructure projects identified in the government's mulit-year capital plan as alternative financing & procurement projects.
Chair, Tony Ross
Tel: 416-325-1497
tony.ross@infrastructureontario.ca
President & Chief Executive Officer, Bert Clark
Tel: 416-325-4851
bert.clark@infrastructureontario.ca
Chief Administrative Officer, Dale Lawr
Tel: 416-212-6439
dale.lawr@infrastructureontario.ca
• Waterfront Toronto
#1310, 20 Bay St.
Toronto, ON M5J 2N8
Tel: 416-241-1344
Fax: 416-214-4591
info@waterfrontoronto.ca
www.waterfrontoronto.ca
Chair, Mark Wilson
President & Chief Executive Officer, John W. Campbell
jcampbell@waterfrontoronto.ca
Chief Operating Officer, David Kusturin
dkusturin@waterfrontoronto.ca
Chief Financial Officer, Chad McCleave
cmccleave@waterfrontoronto.ca
Chief Administrative Officer, Marisa Piattelli
mpiattelli@waterfrontoronto.ca
Vice-President, West Don Lands, Meg Davis
mdavis@waterfrontoronto.ca
Vice-President, Planning & Design, Christopher Glaisek
cglaisek@waterfrontoronto.ca

Corporate Development Division
880 Bay St, 5th Flr, Toronto, ON M7A 2C1

Tel: 416-327-7106
Fax: 416-314-3354
Assistant Deputy Minister, Vacant
Acting Director, Business & Resource Planning, Lourdes Valenton
Tel: 416-327-7227
lourdes.valenton@ontario.ca
Director, Service Management, Betty Morgan
Tel: 416-314-3309
Fax: 416-314-6654
betty.morgan@ontario.ca

Infrastructure Policy & Planning Division
Frost Bldg. South, 7 Queen's Park Cres., 6th Fl., Toronto, ON M7A 1Y7
Tel: 416-325-9411
Fax: 416-325-8851
Assistant Deputy Minister, Chris Giannekos
Tel: 416-325-5621
chris.giannekos@ontario.ca
Director, Capital Planning, Trevor Dauphinee
Tel: 416-325-8640
Fax: 416-326-9845
trevor.dauphinee@ontario.ca
Director, Economic Infrastructure, Joe Iannace
Tel: 416-325-3359
Fax: 416-326-9845
joe.iannace@ontario.ca
Acting Director, Finance Policy & Intergovernmental Relationships, & Social Infrastructure, Gladys Miu
Tel: 416-325-5311
Fax: 416-325-8851
gladys.miu@ontario.ca

Office of the Provincial Development Facilitator
College Park, 777 Bay St. 27th Flr Suite 2704, Toronto, ON M7A 2J8
Tel: 416-325-0835
Fax: 416-325-0209
www.moi.gov.on.ca
Provincial Development Facilitator, Paula Dill
Tel: 416-325-9764
paula.dill@ontario.ca
Project Manager, Linda Tam
Tel: 416-325-0255
linda.tam@ontario.ca
Acting Assistant to the Provincial Development Facilitator, Yasmin Nowsherwanji
Tel: 416-325-0835
yasmin.nowsherwanji@ontario.ca

Ontario Growth Secretariat
College Park, #425, 777 Bay St., Toronto, ON M5G 2E5
Tel: 416-325-1210
Fax: 416-325-7405
Toll-Free: 866-479-9781
Assistant Deputy Minister, Victor Severino
Tel: 416-325-5803
victor.severino@ontario.ca
Director, Growth Policy, Planning & Analysis, Tija Dirks
Tel: 416-325-1546
Fax: 416-325-7403
tija.dirks@ontario.ca
Director, Partnerships & Consultation, Hannah Evans
Tel: 416-325-5799
Fax: 416-325-7403
hannah.evans@ontario.ca

Regulatory Affairs & Strategic Policy
Mowat Block, 900 Bay St. 5th Flr, Toronto, ON M7A 2E3
Tel: 416-325-6559
Fax: 416-325-7041
Acting Assistant Deputy Minister, Michael Reid
Tel: 416-325-6544
michael.reid@ontario.ca
Acting Director, Planning & Agency Relations, Joanne Anderson
Tel: 416-326-5752
joanne.anderson2@ontario.ca
Director, Strategic Policy & Research, Kaili Sermat-Harding
Tel: 416-327-5555
kaili.sermat-harding@ontario.ca
Manager, First Nations & Metis Policy & Partnerships Office, Amy Gibson
Tel: 416-327-2116
amy.gibson@ontario.ca

Strategic Real Estate Asset Management
College Park, 777 Bay St., 4th Fl., Toronto, ON M5G 2E5
Tel: 416-327-5596
Fax: 416-325-4920
Assistant Deputy Minister, Bruce Singbush
Tel: 416-326-1766
bruce.singbush2@ontario.ca
Acting Director, Accommodation & Property Management, Maggie Allan
Tel: 416-212-1167
Fax: 416-212-4941
maggie.allan@ontario.ca
Director, Real Estate Policy, & Policy & Improvements, Mary Bartolomucci
Tel: 416-327-2900
Fax: 416-212-4941
mary.bartolomucci@ontario.ca
Director, Policy & Planning Branch, Barbara Ko
Tel: 416-327-2840
Fax: 416-212-4941
barbara.ko@ontario.ca

Ontario Ministry of Labour

400 University Ave., 14th Fl., Toronto, ON M7A 1T7
Tel: 416-326-7160
Toll-Free: 800-531-5551
TTY: 866-567-8893
www.labour.gov.on.ca
Other Communication: Health & Safety Contact Centre: 1-877-202-0008
twitter.com/OntMinLabour
www.facebook.com/OntarioMinistryofLabour
www.youtube.com/user/OntMinLabour
Advances safe, fair & harmonious workplace practices that are essential to the social & economic well-being of the people of Ontario. Through the ministry's key areas of occupational health & safety, employment rights & responsibilities, labour relations & internal administration, the ministry's mandate is to set, communicate & enforce workplace standards while encouraging greater workplace self-reliance. A range of specialized agencies, boards & commissions assist the ministry in its work.
Acts Administered:
Control of Exposure to Biological or Chemical Agents Regulations
Designated Substance Regulations (Various)
Occupational Health & Safety Act
Rights of Labour Act
Workplace Hazardous Materials Information System (WHMIS) Regulations
Workplace Safety & Insurance Act

Minister, Hon. Yasir Naqvi
Tel: 416-326-7600
Fax: 416-326-1449
ynaqvi.mpp.co@liberal.ola.org

Deputy Minister, Cynthia Morton
Tel: 416-326-7576
Fax: 416-326-0507

Parliamentary Assistant, Vic Dhillon
Tel: 416-325-5326
Fax: 416-325-5326
vdhillon.mpp.co@liberal.ola.org

Associated Agencies, Boards & Commissions:
• Grievance Settlement Board (GSB)
Dundas/Edward Ctr.
#600, 180 Dundas St. West
Toronto, ON M5G 1Z8
Tel: 416-326-1388
Fax: 416-326-1396
gsb.gsb@ontario.ca
www.psab.gov.on.ca/english/gsb
• Office of the Employer Advisor (OEA)
#704, 151 Bloor St. West.
Toronto, ON M5S 1S4
Tel: 416-327-0020
Fax: 416-327-0726
Toll-free: 800-387-0774
www.employeradviser.ca
Advise & represent employers with fewer than 100 employees in relation to worker's compensation issues at no cost to the employer.
• Office of the Worker Advisor (OWA)
#1300, 123 Edward St.
Toronto, ON M5G 1E2
Tel: 416-325-8570
Fax: 416-325-4830
Toll-free: 800-435-8980
TTY: 866-455-3092
www.owa.gov.on.ca
Other Communication: Toll-Free French: 1-800-661-6365
• Ontario Labour Relations Board (OLRB)
505 University Ave., 2nd Fl.
Toronto, ON M5G 2P1
Tel: 416-326-7500
Fax: 416-326-7531
Toll-free: 877-339-3335
TTY: 416-212-7036
www.olrb.gov.on.ca
• Pay Equity Commission
#300, 180 Dundas St. West
Toronto, ON M7A 2S6
Tel: 416-314-1896
Fax: 416-314-8741
Toll-free: 800-387-8813
www.payequity.gov.on.ca
• Public Service Grievance Board (PSGB)
Dundas/Edward Ctr.
#600, 180 Dundas St. West
Toronto, ON M5G 1Z8
Tel: 416-326-1388
Fax: 416-326-1396
Toll-free: 888-618-8846
TTY: 416-314-1787
psgb.psgb@ontario.ca
www.psab.gov.on.ca/english/psgb
• Workplace Safety & Insurance Appeals Tribunal (WSIAT)
505 University Ave., 7th Fl.
Toronto, ON M5G 2P2
Tel: 416-314-8800
Fax: 416-326-5164
Toll-free: 888-618-8846
TTY: 416-314-1787
www.wsiat.on.ca
• Workplace Safety & Insurance Board
See Entry Name Index for detailed listing.

Operations Division
400 University Ave., 14th Fl., Toronto, ON M7A 1T7
Tel: 416-326-7606
Fax: 416-212-4455
Assistant Deputy Minister, Sophie Dennis
Tel: 416-326-7665
sophie.dennis@ontario.ca
Acting Director, Occupational Health & Safety, Wayne De L'Orme
Tel: 416-326-7866
Fax: 416-326-7242
wayne.del'orme@ontario.ca
Associate Director, Information Management & Analysis, Carol Sackville-Duyvelshoff
Tel: 416-326-9615
Fax: 416-326-7242
carol.sackville-duyvelshoff@ontario.ca
Manager, Radiation Protection Service, Lothar Doehler
Tel: 416-235-5765
Fax: 416-235-5926
lothar.doehler@ontario.ca
Provincial Coordinator, Specialized Professional Services, Gabriel Mansour
Tel: 416-326-1404
Fax: 416-326-7761
gabriel.mansour@ontario.ca

Policy & Dispute Resolution Services Division
400 University Ave., 14th Fl., Toronto, ON M7A 1T7
Tel: 416-326-7558
Fax: 416-326-7599
Acting Assistant Deputy Minister, Reg J. Pearson
Tel: 416-326-7555
reg.pearson@ontario.ca
Acting Director, Employment, Labour & Corporate Policy, David Beaulieu
Tel: 416-326-7641
Fax: 416-326-7650
david.beaulieu@ontario.ca

Acting Director, Jobs Protection Office, Bob Onyschuk
Tel: 613-260-8363
Fax: 613-260-8369
bob.onyschuk@ontario.ca
Director, Health & Safety Policy, Maria Papoutsis
Tel: 416-326-7628
Fax: 416-326-7650
maria.papoutsis@ontario.ca
Acting Director, Dispute Resolution Services, Kirsten Watson
Tel: 416-326-7322
Fax: 416-314-8755
kirsten.watson@ontario.ca
Manager, Employment Rights & Responsibilities, Joel Gorlick
Tel: 416-326-7932
Fax: 416-326-7650
joel.gorlick@ontario.ca
Manager, Labour Relations, Careen Jones
Tel: 416-326-0809
Fax: 416-326-7650
careen.jones@ontario.ca

Prevention Office
400 University Ave., 14th Fl., Toronto, ON M7A 1T7
Chief Prevention Officer, George Gritziotis
Tel: 416-314-6342
george.gritziotis@ontario.ca
Director, Training & Safety Programs, Cordelia Clarke-Julien
Tel: 416-212-5301
cordelia.clarkejulien@ontario.ca
Director, Strategy & Integration, Brian Lewis
Tel: 416-327-6427
brian.lewis@ontario.ca
Director, Stakeholder & Partner Relations, David Zurawel
Tel: 416-212-5321
david.zurawel@ontario.ca
Senior Coordinator, Project Management, Frances Hobbs
Tel: 416-212-8996
frances.hobbs@ontario.ca

Ontario Ministry of Municipal Affairs & Housing (MAH)

College Park, 777 Bay St., 17th Fl., Toronto, ON M5G 2E5
Tel: 416-585-7041
Fax: 416-585-6470
Toll-Free: 866-220-2290
TTY: 866-220-2290
mininfo.mah@ontario.ca
www.mah.gov.on.ca
Other Communication: TTY: 416-585-6991
twitter.com/OntMMAH
www.youtube.com/user/ontariommah
Responsible for providing provincial leadership in defining the framework for governance, finances & management for the local government systems; as well as leadership in the development & administration of the legislative & policy framework for land use planning. It is also responsible for providing the operational, policy & accountability framework for local government to fund & administer social housing; policy & program instruments to create a competitive marketplace for rental housing; & the regulatory framework for buildings.
Acts Administered:
Designation of the Oak Ridges Moraine Area
Greenbelt Act
Housing Development Act
Ministry of Municipal Affairs & Housing Act
Municipal Act
Municipalities that are Required to Prepare & Adopt Official Plan Amendments
Oak Ridges Moraine Conservation Act
Oak Ridges Moraine Conservation Plan
Oak Ridges Moraine Protection Act, 2001
Planning Act
Public Utilities Act
Road Access Act
Shoreline Property Assistance Act
Toronto Islands Residential Community Stewardship Act

Minister, Hon. Linda Jeffrey
Tel: 416-585-7000
Fax: 419-585-6470
ljeffrey.mpp@liberal.ola.org

Deputy Minister, William Forward
Tel: 416-585-7100
william.forward@ontario.ca

Parliamentary Assistant, Bill Mauro
Tel: 416-585-6763
Fax: 416-585-4035
bmauro.mpp.co@liberal.ola.org

Parliamentary Assistant, Municipal Affairs, David Zimmer
Tel: 416-585-6768
Fax: 416-585-6777
dzimmer.mpp.co@liberal.ola.org

Associated Agencies, Boards & Commissions:
• **Building Code Commission (BCC)**
777 Bay St., 2nd Fl.
Toronto, ON M5G 2E5
Tel: 416-585-6666
Fax: 416-585-7531
codeinfo@ontario.ca
www.mah.gov.on.ca/Page7394.aspx
Works with the municipal & building sectors & consumer groups to improve & streamline the building regulatory system. This leads to efficient development & more construction jobs, while protecting public safety. The Branch administers the Building Code Act (BCA) & the Ontario Building Code (OBC), which govern the construction of new buildings & the renovation & maintenance of existing buildings. It provides enforcement officials & other building code users with advice & information so that they can apply building code requirements more consistently.
Manager, Code Development Unit, Alek Antoniuk
Tel: 416-585-6456
alek.antoniuk@ontario.ca
• **Building Materials Evaluation Commission (BMEC)**
777 Bay St., 2nd Fl.
Toronto, ON M5G 2E5
Tel: 416-585-4234
Fax: 416-585-7531
www.mah.gov.on.ca/Page8295.aspx

Local Government & Planning Policy Division
College Park, 777 Bay St., 13th Fl., Toronto, ON M5G 2E5
Tel: 416-585-6320
Fax: 416-585-6463
Assistant Deputy Minister, Janet Mason
Tel: 416-585-6320
janet.mason@ontario.ca

Ontario Ministry of Natural Resources (MNR)

300 Water St., PO Box 7000Peterborough, ON K9J 8M5
Tel: 705-755-2000
Fax: 705-755-1677
Toll-Free: 800-667-1940
TTY: 866-686-6072
mnr.nric.mnr@ontario.ca
www.mnr.gov.on.ca
Other Communication: www.flickr.com/photos/mnrcentral
twitter.com/mnrcentral
www.youtube.com/user/MNRcentralVideos
The MNR manages & protects natural resources in the province for wise use. Working with environmental organizations, private industries, fish & game associations, researchers, & other government agencies, the MNR is responsible for the following areas: science & information resources; forest management; fish & wildlife management; land & waters management; Ontario Parks; aviation & forest fire management; & geographic information.
Acts Administered:
Aggregate Resources Act
Algonquin Forestry Authority Act
Beds of Navigable Waters Act
Conservation Authorities Act
Conservation Bodies Land Regulation
Conservation Land Act
Crown Forest Sustainability Act
Designation of Parks
Endangered Species Act, 2007
Endangered Species Regulation
Fish & Wildlife Conservation Act
Forest Fires Prevention Act
Forestry Act
Gas & Oil Leases Act
Guides in Quetico Provincial Park
Heritage Hunting & Fishing Act, 2002
Indian Lands Act
Industrial & Mining Lands Compensation Act
Kawartha Highlands Signature Site Park Act
Lake of the Woods Control Board Act
Lakes & Rivers Improvement Act
Mining Act
Mining in Provincial Parks
Ministry of Natural Resources Act
Niagara Escarpment Planning & Development Act
North Georgian Bay Recreational Reserve Act
Oil, Gas & Salt Resources Act
Ontario Geographic Names Board Act
Ottawa River Water Powers Act
Possession, Buying & Selling of Wildlife
Public Lands Act
Surveys Act
Wild Rice Harvesting Act
Wilderness Areas Act
Wildlife in Captivity
Wildlife Management Units
Wildlife Schedules

Minister, Hon. David Orazietti
Tel: 416-314-2301
Fax: 416-325-5316
dorazietti.mpp@liberal.ola.org

Deputy Minister, David O'Toole
Tel: 416-314-2150
Fax: 416-314-2159
david.o'toole@ontario.ca

Parliamentary Assistant, Joe Dickson
jdickson.mpp@liberal.ola.org

Commissioner, Mining & Lands, Linda Kamerman
Tel: 416-314-2322
Fax: 416-314-2327
linda.kamerman@ontario.ca

Assistant Deputy Minister, Transformation Secretariat, Bill Thornton
Tel: 416-212-9593
bill.thornton@ontario.ca

Director, Communications, David Ayotte
Tel: 416-314-2119
Fax: 416-314-2102
david.ayotte@ontario.ca

Director, Legal Services, Anne Marie Gutierrez
Tel: 416-314-2025
Fax: 416-314-2030
annemarie.gutierrez@ontario.ca

Director, Ontario Internal Audit, Resources & Labour Audit Service Team, Ray Masse
Tel: 416-314-9208
Fax: 416-314-9220
ray.masse@ontario.ca

Director, Transformation, Rebecca Ramsarran
Tel: 416-212-9592
rebecca.ramsarran@ontario.ca

Associated Agencies, Boards & Commissions:
• **Academic & Experience Requirements Committee of the Association of Ontario Land Surveyors (AERC)**
1043 McNicoll Ave.
Toronto, ON M1W 3W6
Tel: 416-491-9020
Fax: 416-491-2576
• **Algonquin Forestry Authority - Huntsville**
222 Main St. West
Huntsville, ON P1H 1Y1
Tel: 705-789-9647
Fax: 705-789-3353
info@algonquinforestry.on.ca
www.algonquinforestry.on.ca
Ensures the viability of the local forest industry while preserving the soil & water resources, fish & wildlife habitat & recreational areas in the park.
General Manager, Danny Janke
Danny.Janke@algonquinforestry.on.ca
• **Algonquin Forestry Authority - Pembroke**
Victoria Centre
84 Isabella St., 2nd Fl.
Pembroke, ON K8A 5S5

Tel: 613-735-0173
Fax: 613-735-4192
info@algonquinforestry.on.ca
www.algonquinforestry.on.ca
Manager, Operations, Jeff Leavey
jeff.leavey@algonquinforestry.on.ca

• Association of Ontario Land Surveyors
1043 McNicoll Ave.
Toronto, ON M1W 3W6
Tel: 416-491-9020
Fax: 416-491-2576
Toll-free: 800-268-0718
www.aols.org

• Ontario Fish & Wildlife Heritage Commission
Robinson Pl.
300 Water St.
PO Box 7000
Peterborough, ON K9J 8M5
Tel: 705-755-1905
Fax: 705-755-1900
Chair, Thomas Brooke
Executive Director, Patrick Kennedy
Tel: 705-755-5088
patrick.kennedy@ontario.ca

• Ontario Geographic Names Board
Robinson Place
300 Water St., 2nd Fl.
PO Box 7000
Peterborough, ON K9J 8M5
Tel: 705-755-2132
The Board investigates the background of geographic names & recommends names to be used on maps.

• Ontario Moose & Bear Allocation Advisory Committee
PO Box 964
Sioux Lookout, ON P8T 1B3
Tel: 807-737-2615
Fax: 807-737-4173
An independent advisory committee to allocate moose & bear hunting opportunities provided by the Ministry of Natural Resources within the tourism industry in a manner which is ecologically sustainable & supports the economic viability of the industry in general & specific tourist establishments.

• Ottawa River Regulation Planning Board / Commission de planification de la régularisation de la rivière des Outaouais
351, boul St Joseph
Gatineau, QC J8Y 3Z5
Tel: 613-994-7079
Toll-free: 800-778-1246
secretariat@ottawariver.ca
www.ottawariver.ca
Established under the terms of a Canada-Ontario-Québec Agreement, it is responsible for the preparation & continuing review of policies, guidelines & criteria for the integrated management of the principal reservoirs of the Ottawa River Basin in order to reduce flood damages along the river, its tributaries & in the Montréal area; it is also responsible for the operation & coordination of inflow forecasting, flow routing & optimization models that will reduce flood damages while having the least possible impact on users of the basin.
Co-Chair, Patricia Clavet
Co-Chair, Rick Watchorn

• Rabies Advisory Committee
DNA Bldg, Trent University
2140 East Bank Dr.
Peterborough, ON K9J 7B8
Tel: 705-755-2273
Other Communication: Alternate Phone: 705-755-2272
Established in 1979 it advises the Minister on the development of suitable vaccines against rabies & an effective system for vaccinating wild animals.

• Shibogama Interim Planning Board
PO Box 105
Wunnumin, ON P0V 2Z0
Tel: 807-442-2559
Fax: 807-442-2627
Advises the province on land use & resource development in an 11,131-square-kilometre area south of Big Trout Lake in northwestern Ontario.

• Windigo Interim Planning Board
PO Box 299
Sioux Lookout, ON P8T 1A3
Tel: 807-737-1585
Fax: 807-737-3133
Advises the province on land use & resource development in two areas totalling 15,959 square kilometres south of Big Trout Lake.

Niagara Escarpment Commission (NEC)
232 Guelph St., Georgetown, ON L7G 4B1
Tel: 905-877-5191
Fax: 905-873-7452
www.escarpment.org
twitter.com/Escarpment_NEC
Responsible for implementing the Niagara Escarpment Planning & Development Act, which is designed to maintain the escarpment & surrounding area as a continuous natural environment & to ensure that all new development in the escarpment area is compatible with provincial goals of environmental protection & conservation. The commission is also the main source of information on the Niagara Escarpment & the Niagara Escarpment Plan.
Chair, Don Scott
Tel: 905-877-5594
Fax: 905-873-7452
don.scott@ontario.ca
Assistant Deputy Minister, Dana Richardson
Tel: 905-877-4810
Fax: 905-873-7452
dana.richardson@ontario.ca
Assistant Deputy Minister, David Lynch
Tel: 416-314-1939
Fax: 416-314-1994
david.lynch@ontario.ca
Other Communications: Alternate Phone: 705-755-2700
Director, Services & Infrastructure Management, Phil Cooke
Tel: 705-755-2532
Fax: 705-755-2508
phil.cooke@ontario.ca
300 Water St., 3rd Fl.
PO Box 7000
Peterborough, ON K9J 8M5 Canada

Forestry Division
Roberta Bondar Pl., #400, 70 Foster Dr., Sault Ste. Marie, ON P6A 6V5
Fax: 705-945-5977
Toll-Free: 800-667-1940
Acting Assistant Deputy Minister, Kathleen McFadden
Tel: 705-945-6660
bill.thornton@ontario.ca
Director, Forest Tenure & Economics, Mark Speers
Tel: 705-945-6636
mark.speers@ontario.ca
Acting Manager, Industry Development Section, Tom Hernden
Tel: 705-945-6769
Fax: 705-945-6796
tom.hernden@ontario.ca
Manager, Forestry Innovation & Market Development Section, Jason Koivisto
Tel: 705-945-6785
Fax: 705-945-6796
jason.koivisto@ontario.ca
Manager, Timber Allocation & Licensing Section, Sean Maguire
Tel: 705-945-6639
sean.maguire@ontario.ca
Manager, Wood Measurement Section, Walter Zagrobelny
Tel: 705-945-6643
Fax: 705-541-5111
walter.zagrobelny@ontario.ca

Policy Division
#6540, 99 Wellesley St. West, Toronto, ON M7A 1W3
Fax: 416-314-1994
Toll-Free: 800-667-1940
Provides assistance, advice & direction to ministry staff at all levels, on a variety of compliance & law enforcement matters. The branch is responsible for the development, coordination & delivery of an Integrated Provincial Compliance Program which focuses on the promotion, monitoring & enforcement aspects of compliance.
Assistant Deputy Minister, Rosalyn Lawrence
Tel: 416-314-6131
rosalyn.lawrence@ontario.ca
Director, Aboriginal, Karan Aquino
Tel: 705-755-1996
Fax: 705-755-1372
karan.aquino@ontario.ca
Director, Biodiversity Branch & Renewable Energy Program, Eric Boysen
Tel: 705-755-5999
Fax: 705-755-2901
eric.boysen@ontario.ca
Director, Strategic Policy & Economics, Craig Brown
Tel: 416-314-1923
Fax: 416-314-1948
craig.brown@ontario.ca
Director, Natural Heritage, Lands & Protected Spaces, Ray Pichette
Tel: 705-755-1241
Fax: 705-755-1971
ray.pichette@ontario.ca
Director, Species at Risk, Marc Rondeau
Tel: 416-314-1819
Fax: 705-755-5483
marc.rondeau@ontario.ca
Director, Forests, Chris M. Walsh
Tel: 705-945-6653
Fax: 705-945-6667
chris.m.walsh@ontario.ca
Manager, Lands & Non-Renewable Resources Section, Pauline Desrochers
Tel: 705-755-2140
Fax: 705-755-1267
pauline.desroches@ontario.ca
Manager, Forest Policy Section, Brian Hillier
Tel: 705-945-6601
Fax: 705-945-6667
brian.hillier@ontario.ca
Manager, Claims Negotiations Support Unit, David MacDonald
Tel: 705-755-1923
david.macdonald@ontario.ca
Manager, Wildlife Policy Section, Deb Stetson
Tel: 705-755-1925
Fax: 705-755-1957
deb.stetson@ontario.ca
Manager, Protection Section, Jason Travers
Tel: 705-755-1754
jason.travers@ontario.ca

Provincial Services Division
#6540, 99 Wellesley St. West, Toronto, ON M7A 1W3
Tel: 416-326-9504
The ministry's local presence in communities across the province, delivering integrated programs on resource management through 3 regions & 25 districts. The division delivers programs on provincial enforcement, native affairs, fisheries, forests & provincial lands, in addition to resources such as finance, facilities & engineering infrastructure, equipment & vehicles.
Assistant Deputy Minister, Tracey Mill
Tel: 416-326-9502
tracey.mill@ontario.ca
Director, Enforcement, Lois Deacon
Tel: 705-755-1750
Fax: 705-755-1757
lois.deacon@ontario.ca
Managing Director, Ontario Parks, Bradley Fauteux
Tel: 705-755-1702
Fax: 705-755-1701
bradley.fauteux@ontario.ca
Other Communications: URL: www.ontarioparks.com
Director, Fish & Wildlife Services, Mike Morencie
Tel: 519-873-4609
Fax: 705-755-1901
mike.morencie@ontario.ca
Director, Aviation, Forest Fire & Emergency Services, Al Tithecott
Tel: 705-945-5937
Fax: 705-945-5785
al.tithecott@ontario.ca
Manager, Marketing & Client Services Section, Jayne Best
Tel: 705-755-1803
Fax: 705-755-1900
jayne.best@ontario.ca
Manager, Response & Operations Section, Rob McAlpine
Tel: 705-945-5978
Fax: 705-945-5785
rob.mcalpine@ontario.ca
Manager, Intelligence & Investigations Section, Tim Moody
Tel: 705-755-1758
Fax: 705-755-3290
tim.moody@ontario.ca
Manager, Park Operations & Development Section, Bruce van Staalduinen
Tel: 705-755-1712
Fax: 705-755-1735
bruce.van staalduinen@ontario.ca

Regional Operations Division
#6610, 99 Wellesley St. West, Toronto, ON M7A 1W3
Fax: 416-314-2629
Toll-Free: 800-667-1940
Other Communication: Peterborough Fax: 705-755-5073
Acting Assistant Deputy Minister, Carrie Hayward
Tel: 416-314-2621
carrie.hayward@ontario.ca
Director, Far North Branch (South Porcupine), Dianne Corbett
Tel: 705-235-1284
Fax: 705-235-1106
dianne.corbett@ontario.ca
Director, Integration Branch, Dan Marinigh
Tel: 705-755-1620
Fax: 705-755-1201
dan.marinigh@ontario.ca
Manager, Strategic Divisional & Programs Services, Daryle Compardo
Tel: 705-755-5080
daryle.compardo@ontario.ca
Manager, Stewardship & Conservation Incentives Section, Neil Hayward
Tel: 705-755-1251
neil.hayward@ontario.ca
Manager, Land & Water Services Section, Peter Hulsman
Tel: 705-755-1278
Fax: 705-755-1267
peter.hulsman@ontario.ca
Acting Manager, Program Coordination, Monique Rolf von den Baumen-Clark
Tel: 705-755-1216
Fax: 705-755-1419
monique.rolfvondenbaumen@ontario.ca
Manager, Petroleum Operations Section, Joe Van Overberghe
Tel: 519-873-4635
Fax: 519-873-4645
joe.vanoverberghe@ontario.ca

Regional Offices
Northeast Region
Ontario Government Complex, 5520 Hwy. 101 East, PO Box 3020South Porcupine, ON P0N 1H0
Tel: 705-235-1157
Fax: 705-235-1246
Regional Director, Ginette Brindle
Tel: 705-235-1153
Fax: 705-235-1226
ginette.brindle@ontario.ca
Chapleau (Fire Management & Area Office)
190 Cherry St., Chapleau, ON P0M 1K0
Tel: 705-864-1710
Fax: 705-864-0681
District Manager, Paul Bernier
Tel: 705-864-3122
paul.bernier@ontario.ca
Fire Management Supervisor, Wes Woods
Tel: 705-864-3126
wesley.woods@ontario.ca
Cochrane (Fire Management Office)
#2, 4 Hwy. 11 South, PO Box 730Cochrane, ON P0L 1C0
Tel: 705-272-4365
Fax: 705-272-7183
District Manager, Martha P. Heidenheim
Tel: 705-372-2204
martha.heidenheim@ontario.ca
Hearst
Government Complex, 613 Front St., PO Box 670Hearst, ON P0L 1N0
Tel: 705-362-4346
Fax: 705-372-2245
District Manager, Martha Heidenheim
Tel: 705-273-2204
martha.heidenheim@ontario.ca
Kirkland Lake
10 Government Rd. East, PO Box 910Kirkland Lake, ON P2N 3K4
Tel: 705-568-3222
Fax: 705-568-3200
District Manager, Corrinne Nelson
Tel: 705-568-3201
corrinne.nelson@ontario.ca
North Bay
3301 Trout Lake Rd., North Bay, ON P1A 4L7
Tel: 705-475-5550
Fax: 705-475-5500
Acting District Manager, Corrinne Nelson
Tel: 705-457-5599
corrinne.nelson@ontario.ca
Sault Ste. Marie
64 Church St., Sault Ste Marie, ON P6A 3H3
Tel: 705-949-1231
Fax: 705-949-6450
District Manager, Marty Blake
Tel: 705-941-5120
marty.blake@ontario.ca
Fire Management Supervisor, Daryl Curran
Tel: 705-946-7855
daryl.curran@ontario.ca
Sudbury
#5, 3767 Hwy. 69 South, Sudbury, ON P3G 1E7
Tel: 705-564-7823
Fax: 705-564-7879
District Manager, Trevor Griffin
Tel: 705-564-7872
trevor.griffin@ontario.ca
Fire Management Supervisor, Ted Shannon
Tel: 705-564-6003
ted.shannon@ontario.ca
Timmins
Ontario Government Complex, 5520 Hwy. 101 East, PO Box 3090South Porcupine, ON P0N 1H0
Tel: 705-235-1490
Fax: 705-235-1377
Other Communication: Fire Fax: 705-755-1373; Warehouse Fax: 705-235-1331; Enforcement Fax: 705-235-1376
District Manager, Randy Pickering
Tel: 705-235-1325
randy.pickering@ontario.ca
Fire Management Supervisor, Anne-Marie Larivee
Tel: 705-235-1362
marie.larivee@ontario.ca
Wawa
48 Mission Rd. Hwy 101, PO Box 1160Wawa, ON P0S 1K0
Tel: 705-856-2396
Fax: 705-856-7511
Other Communication: Hornepayne Fax: 807-868-2842
District Manager, Paul Bernier
Tel: 705-856-4703
paul.bernier@ontario.ca
Forest Management Supervisor, CLUAH District Lead, Wendy LeClair
Tel: 705-856-4722
wendy.leclair@ontario.ca
Northwest Region
Ontario Government Bldg., #221A, 435 James St. South, Thunder Bay, ON P7E 6S8
Tel: 807-475-1261
Fax: 807-473-3023
Regional Director, Allan Willcocks
Tel: 807-475-1264
allan.willcocks@ontario.ca
Dryden
479 Government Rd., PO Box 730Dryden, ON P8N 2Z4
Tel: 807-223-3341
Fax: 807-223-2824
District Manager, Bert Hennessey
Tel: 807-223-7515
bert.hennessey@ontario.ca
Fire Management Supervisor, Rod Kellar
Tel: 807-937-7321
rod.kellar@ontario.ca
Fort Frances
922 Scott St., Fort Frances, ON P9A 1J4
Tel: 807-274-5337
Fax: 807-274-5553
Other Communication: Alternate Fax: 807-274-4438
District Manager, Greg Chapman
Tel: 807-274-8633
greg.chapman@ontario.ca
Acting Fire Management Supervisor, Harrold Boven
Tel: 807-274-8647
harrold.boven@ontario.ca
Kenora
808 Robertson St., PO Box 5080Kenora, ON P9N 3X9
Tel: 807-468-2501
Fax: 807-468-2736
District Manager, Deb Weedon
Tel: 807-468-2528
deb.weedon@ontario.ca
Fire Management Supervisor, Walt Lesenke
Tel: 807-548-8416
Nipigon
5 Wadsworth Dr., PO Box 970Nipigon, ON P0T 2J0
Tel: 807-887-5000
Fax: 807-887-2993
District Manager, Kim Groenendyk
Tel: 807-887-5013
kim.groenendyk@ontario.ca
Red Lake
227 Howey St., PO Box 5003Red Lake, ON P0V 2M0
Tel: 807-727-2253
Fax: 807-727-2861
Other Communication: Fire Headquarters Fax: 807-727-3182
District Manager, Graeme Swanwick
Tel: 807-727-1333
graeme.swanwick@ontario.ca
Acting Fire Management Supervisor, Randy Crampton
Tel: 807-727-2041
Sioux Lookout
49 Prince St., PO Box 309Sioux Lookout, ON P8T 1A6
Tel: 807-737-1140
Fax: 807-737-1813
District Manager, Bob David
Tel: 807-737-5026
Fax: 807-737-3581
bob.david@ontario.ca
Fire Management Supervisor, Darren McLarty
Tel: 807-737-5005
darren.mclarty@ontario.ca
Thunder Bay
Ontario Government Bldg., #B001, 435 James St. South, Thunder Bay, ON P7E 6S8
Tel: 807-475-1471
Fax: 807-475-1527
District Manager, Frank Miklas
Tel: 807-475-1174
frank.miklas@ontario.ca
Fire Management Supervisor, Dave Manol
Tel: 807-476-2230
Dave.Manol@ontario.vc
Southern Region
Robinson Place, South Tower, 300 Water St., 4th Fl. South, PO Box 7000Peterborough, ON K9J 8M5
Tel: 705-755-2000
Fax: 705-755-3233
Acting Regional Director, Jane Ireland
Tel: 705-755-3235
jane.ireland@ontario.ca
Aurora
50 Bloomington Rd. West, RR#2, Aurora, ON L4G 3G8
Tel: 905-713-7400
Fax: 905-713-7415
Other Communication: Enforcement Fax: 905-713-7429
District Manager, Debbie Pella Keen
Tel: 905-713-7372
debbie.pellakeen@ontario.ca
Aylmer
615 John St., Aylmer, ON N5H 2S8
Tel: 519-773-9241
Fax: 519-773-9014
District Manager, Mitch Wilson
Tel: 519-773-4710
mitch.wilson@ontario.ca
Bancroft
106 Monck St., PO Box 500Bancroft, ON K0L 1C0
Tel: 613-332-3940
Fax: 613-332-0608
District Manager, Vince Ewing
Tel: 613-332-3940 ext: 201
Fax: 613-332-3672
vince.ewing@ontario.ca
Guelph
1 Stone Rd. West, Guelph, ON N1G 4Y2
Tel: 519-826-4955
Fax: 519-826-4929
Other Communication: St. George Fax: 519-448-3105
District Manager, Ian Hagman
Tel: 519-826-4931
ian.hagman@ontario.ca

Kemptville
Provincial Government Bldg., 10 Campus Dr., PO Box 2002Kemptville, ON K0G 1J0
Tel: 613-258-8204
Fax: 613-258-3920
Other Communication: Brockville Fax: 613-342-7544; Cornwall Fax: 613-932-8969; Perth Fax: 613-267-7954
District Manager, Kenneth Durst
Tel: 613-258-8201
ken.durst@ontario.ca
Midhurst
2284 Nursery Rd., Midhurst, ON L0L 1X0
Tel: 705-725-7500
Fax: 705-725-7584
Other Communication: Bass Lake Fax: 705-329-6028
District Manager, Mark Shoreman
Tel: 705-725-7504
mark.shoreman@ontario.ca
Parry Sound
7 Bay St., Parry Sound, ON P2A 1S4
Tel: 705-746-4201
Fax: 705-746-8828
District Manager, Vacant
Tel: 705-773-4236
Pembroke
31 Riverside Dr., Pembroke, ON K8A 8R6
Tel: 613-732-3661
Fax: 613-732-2972
Other Communication: Secure Fax: 613-732-5539
District Manager, Rick Watchorn
Tel: 613-732-5520
rick.watchorn@ontario.ca
Peterborough
South Tower, 300 Water St., 1st Fl., PO Box 7000Peterborough, ON K9J 8M5
Tel: 705-755-2001
Fax: 705-755-3125
Other Communication: Enforcement Secure Fax: 705-755-1138
District Manager, Karen Bellamy
Tel: 705-755-3363
Fax: 705-755-3151
karen.bellamy@ontario.ca

Science & Information Resources Division
Roberta Bondar Pl., #400, 70 Foster Dr., Sault Ste Marie, ON P6A 6V5
Tel: 705-755-2000
Fax: 705-755-2802
Toll-Free: 800-667-1940
The division leads the development & application of scientific knowledge, information management systems & information technologies in support of the Ministry mandate. The division is responsible for ensuring operational decision-making requirements of the Ministry are supported by sound science & reliable data, by providing accurate, relevant & timely information to manage resources in an ecologically sustainable manner.
Assistant Deputy Minister, Frank Kennedy
Tel: 705-945-6703
Fax: 705-755-2802
frank.kennedy@ontario.ca
Acting Director, Science & Information, Cameron Mack
Tel: 705-755-1909
Fax: 705-945-6527
cameron.mack@ontario.ca
Director, Geographic Information, Brian J. Maloney
Tel: 705-755-2204
Fax: 705-755-2149
brian.j.maloney@ontario.ca
Director, Applied Research & Development, Vacant
Manager, Inventory Monitoring & Assessment Section, Joe Kapron
Tel: 705-755-1616
joe.kapron@ontario.ca
Manager, Office of the Surveyor General, Susan MacGregor
Tel: 705-755-2128
susan.macgregor@ontario.ca
Manager, Mapping & Geomatic Services, Tom Malone
Tel: 705-755-2130
tom.malone@ontario.ca
Manager, Land Information Ontario, Raphael Sussman
Tel: 705-755-2321
Fax: 705-755-2149
raphael.sussman@ontario.ca
Coordinator, Natural Heritage Information Centre, Jim S. Mackenzie
Tel: 705-755-1912
Fax: 705-755-2168
jim.s.mackenzie@ontario.ca

Ontario Ministry of Northern Development & Mines (MNDM)

159 Cedar St., Sudbury, ON P3E 6A5
Tel: 705-670-5755
Fax: 705-670-5818
Toll-Free: 888-415-9845
TTY: 866-349-1388
www.mndm.gov.on.ca
Secondary Address: #5630, 99 Wellesley St. West, 5th Fl. Whitney Block
Toronto, ON M7A 1W3
Fax: 416-327-0665
twitter.com/OntarioMNDM
www.facebook.com/OntarioMNDM
www.youtube.com/user/OntarioMNDM
The Ministry of Northern Development & Mines is the only regional ministry within the government & plays a central role in northern affairs. MNDM supports the mineral industry by providing it with valuable information about the province's geology. It also delivers & administers Ontario's Mining Act to improve the investment climate for mineral development. The ministry has a two-fold mandate, to promote northern economic development & support mineral sector competitiveness. The ministry is developing an initiative to help Ontario's Far North communities attract environmentally sound development, work with First Nation communities, partner ministries, the federal government, the mineral sector & private sector stakeholders to create opportunities for residents to help First Nation communities become more self-reliant. The ministry works with the Northern Ontario Heritage Fund Corporation & with the Ontario Northland Transportation Commission to bring much-needed service improvements to the northeast.
Acts Administered:
Mining Act
Ministry of Northern Development, Mines & Forestry Act
Ontario Northland Transportation Commission Act

Minister, Hon. Michael Gravelle
Tel: 416-327-0633
Fax: 416-327-0665
mgravelle.mpp@liberal.ola.org

Deputy Minister, George Ross
Tel: 416-212-2701
Fax: 416-327-0651
george.ross@ontario.ca

Parliamentary Assistant, Mike Colle
Tel: 416-327-0616
Fax: 416-327-0617
mcolle.mpp@liberal.ola.org

Associated Agencies, Boards & Commissions:
• **Ontario Northland**
555 Oak St. East
North Bay, ON P1B 8L3
Tel: 705-472-4500
Fax: 705-476-5598
Toll-free: 800-363-7512
info@ontarionorthland.ca; pr@ontarionorthland.ca
www.ontarionorthland.ca
• **Owen Sound Transportation Company Ltd. (OSTC)**
717875, Hwy. 6
Owen Sound, ON N4K 5N7
Tel: 519-376-8740
Toll-free: 800-265-3163
www.ontarioferries.com

Mines & Minerals Division
Willet Green Miller Centre, 933 Ramsey Lake Rd., Sudbury, ON P3E 6B5
Tel: 705-670-5755
Fax: 705-670-5818
Toll-Free: 888-415-9845
The Mines & Minerals Division works to generate new wealth & benefits for the residents of Ontario by providing basic geological information gathering & interpretation in support of Ontario's exploration, mine development & mining sectors & the administration of Ontario's Mining Act in a fair & consistent fashion. Collects, analyzes & publishes valuable information about the state of the mining & mineral industries, as well as specific information about the location & quality of mineral deposits. The field staff throughout the province provide consultative services to the industry through all phases of the mining sequence, & include resident geologists, mining recorders & mineral development officers.
Acting Assistant Deputy Minister, Cindy Blancher-Smith
Tel: 705-670-5820
Fax: 705-670-5818
cindy.blancher-smith@ontario.ca
Director, Aboriginal Relations, Bernie Hughes
Tel: 705-670-5743
Fax: 705-670-5818
bernie.hughes@ontario.ca
Acting Director, Diamond Sector Unit, Marc Leroux
Tel: 705-670-5609
Fax: 705-670-5818
marc.leroux@ontario.ca
Director, Mining Act Modernization, Robert Merwin
Tel: 705-670-5627
Fax: 416-327-0634
robert.merwin@ontario.ca

Mineral Development & Lands Branch
Willet Green Miller Centre, 933 Ramsey Lake Rd., Level B4, Sudbury, ON P3E 6B5
Tel: 705-670-5787
Fax: 705-670-5803
Toll-Free: 888-415-9845
Acting Director, Rob Ferguson
Tel: 705-670-5784
rob.ferguson@ontario.ca
Manager, Mineral Exploration & Development Section, Stephen DeVos
Tel: 705-670-5795
stephen.devos@ontario.ca
Manager, Mine Rehabilitation, Inspection & Compliance, Leslie Cooper
Tel: 705-670-5790
leslie.cooper@ontario.ca
Manager, Strategic Support Unit, Bruce Pollard
Tel: 705-670-3003
bruce.pollard@ontario.ca

Ontario Geological Survey
Willet Green Miller Centre, 933 Ramsey Lake Rd., Level B6, Sudbury, ON P3E 6B5
Tel: 705-670-5758
Fax: 705-670-5818
Toll-Free: 888-415-9845
Director, Dr. J. Andy Fyon
Tel: 705-670-5924
andy.fyon@ontario.ca
Senior Manager, Geoscience Laboratories, Ed Debicki
Tel: 705-670-5643
Fax: 705-670-3047
ed.debicki@ontario.ca
Senior Manager, Precambrian Geoscience, Jack Parker
Tel: 705-670-5976
Fax: 705-670-5905
jack.parker@ontario.ca
Acting Senior Manager, Resident Geologist Program, Tom Brown
Tel: 705-670-5955
Fax: 705-670-5905
tom.brown@ontario.ca
Acting Manager, Sedimentary Geoscience, Richard Dyer
Tel: 705-670-5916
Fax: 705-670-5905
richard.dyer@ontario.ca

Northern Development Division
Roberta Bondar Place, #200, 70 Foster Dr., Sault Ste Marie, ON P6A 6V8
Tel: 705-945-5900
Fax: 705-945-5931
Toll-Free: 800-461-2287
Other Communication: Delivery of Government Services: 705-945-5904
Responsible for promoting business, industrial, community & regional economic development & diversification; improving access to social & health services for northerners; planning & coordinating an integrated transportation system to meet private & commercial transportation needs at local, regional & provincial levels; coordinating the policies & programs of other ministries to ensure the special needs of northerners are addressed by government.

Assistant Deputy Minister, Cal McDonald
Tel: 705-564-7569
Fax: 705-945-5932
cal.mcdonald@ontario.ca
Executive Director, Northern Ontario Heritage Fund Corporation, Bruce Strapp
Tel: 705-945-6734
Fax: 705-564-7447
bruce.strapp@ontario.ca
Director, Transportation, Trade & Investment, Faye Johnson
Tel: 705-945-5903
Fax: 705-564-7597
faye.johnson@ontario.ca
Director, Regional Economic Development, Helen Mulc
Tel: 705-564-7134
Fax: 705-564-7582
helen.mulc@ontario.ca
Director, Strategic Coordination & Planning, Lisa Zanetti
Tel: 705-564-7016
lisa.zanetti@ontario.ca
Manager, Trade, Investment & Strategic Sectors Unit, Harold Dremin
Tel: 416-325-3379
harold.dremin@ontario.ca
Manager, Transportation & Infrastructure Unit, Tom Marcolini
Tel: 705-945-5836
Fax: 705-541-2140
tom.marcolini@ontario.ca
Senior Advisor, Northern Ontario Growth Plan Unit, Martin Broks
Tel: 705-564-7568
Fax: 705-564-7597
martin.broks@ontario.ca
Kenora
#104, 810 Robertson St., Kenora, ON P9N 4J2
Tel: 807-468-2937
Fax: 807-468-2930
Manager, Christine Hansen
Tel: 807-468-2938
christine.hansen@ontario.ca
North Bay
#203, 447 McKeown Ave., North Bay, ON P1B 9S9
Tel: 705-494-4045
Fax: 705-494-4069
Manager, Moe Dorie
Tel: 705-494-4176
moe.dorie@ontario.ca
Sault Ste. Marie
Roberta Bondar Place, #200, 70 Foster Dr., Sault Ste Marie, ON P6A 6V8
Tel: 705-945-5914
Fax: 705-945-5931
Acting Manager, Marl Melisek
Tel: 705-945-5839
mark.melisek@ontario.ca
Sudbury
#601, 159 Cedar St., Sudbury, ON P3E 6A5
Tel: 705-564-7517
Fax: 705-564-7583
Manager, Murray Morello
Tel: 705-564-7519
murray.morello@ontario.ca
Thunder Bay
Ontario Government Bldg., #332, 435 James St. South, Thunder Bay, ON P7E 6L3
Tel: 807-475-1648
Fax: 807-475-1589
Manager, John Guerard
Tel: 807-475-1573
john.guerard@ontario.ca
Timmins
Ontario Government Complex, E Wing, 5520 Hwy. 101 East, PO Box 3060South Porcupine, ON P0N 1H0
Tel: 705-235-1664
Fax: 705-235-1660
Manager, Brian Pountney
Tel: 705-235-1654
brian.pountney@ontario.ca

Office of the Chief Information Officer, Land & Resources I & IT Cluster
Whitney Block, #6601, 99 Wellesley St. West, 6th Fl., Toronto, ON M7A 1W3
Chief Information Officer, James G. Hamilton
Tel: 416-314-1528
jim.hamilton@ontario.ca
Acting Director, Organizational Performance, Judy Tomarin
Tel: 416-212-7560
judy.tomarin@ontario.ca

Ring of Fire Secretariat
Willet Green Miller Centre, 933 Ramsey Lake Rd., Level B2, Sudbury, ON P3E 6B5
Tel: 705-670-5755
Fax: 705-670-5818
Toll-Free: 888-415-9845
Assistant Deputy Minister, Christine Kaszycki
Tel: 705-670-5877
christine.kaszycki@ontario.ca
Director, Aboriginal Community & Stakeholder Relations, Harvey Yesno
Tel: 807-475-1587
Fax: 807-475-1120
harvey.yesno@ontario.ca
Senior Policy Advisor, Community Capacity & Economic Development, Lori Churchill
Tel: 705-670-5767
lori.churchill@ontario.ca
Senior Policy Advisor, Enviromental Assessment & Land Use Planning, Ariane Heisey
Tel: 416-327-0110
ariane.heisey@ontario.ca

Ontario Power Generation

700 University Ave., Toronto, ON M5G 1X6
Tel: 416-592-2555
Toll-Free: 877-592-2555
webmaster@opg.com
www.opg.com
Other Communication: Media Relations Email: media@opg.com; Investor Relations Email: investor.relations@opg.com
twitter.com/OntarioPowerGen
www.youtube.com/opgvideos
Mandate is to meet Ontario's requirements for electricity so as to result in the greatest overall benefit to the community & the lowest cost to the consumer, while operating in a safe & environmentally responsible manner. Assets include 3 nuclear generating stations, 5 fossil generating stations, 64 hydroelectric stations, 3 wind generating stations.

Chair, Hon. Jake Epp

President & Chief Executive Officer, Tom Mitchell

Chief Financial Officer, Donn W.J. Hanbridge, C.A.

Chief Nuclear Officer, Wayne Robbins

Senior Vice-President, Commercial Operations & Environment, Bruce Boland, MBA, CMA, ICD.D

Senior Vice-President, Hydro-Thermal Operations, Frank Chiarotto, BASc., P.Eng

Senior Vice-President, Law & General Counsel, Christopher F. Ginther

Executive Vice-President, Nuclear Projects, Albert Sweetnam

Ontario Ministry of Research & Innovation

Hearst Block, 900 Bay St., 8th Fl., Toronto, ON M7A 2E1
Tel: 416-325-6666
Fax: 416-325-6688
Toll-Free: 866-668-4249
TTY: 416-325-4402
info@edt.gov.on.ca
www.mri.gov.on.ca
Other Communication: Toll-Free TTY: 1-877-408-3414
twitter.com/OntInnovation
www.facebook.com/ontarioinnovation
www.youtube.com/OntarioInnovation
The Ministry supports research, commercialization & innovation in Ontario through programs & services such as the Ontario Research Fund, Innovation Demonstration Fund & Ontario Venture Capital Fund. The Ministry partners with universities, colleges, hospitals, entrepreneurs & business leaders in order to foster new scientific & technological discoveries that can be marketed to the world.

Minister, Reza Moridi
Tel: 416-326-9500
Fax: 416-326-2497
rmoridi.mpp@liberal.ola.org

Deputy Minister, Wendy Tilford
Tel: 416-325-6927
wendy.tilford@ontario.ca

Ontario Ministry of Rural Affairs

c/o Ministry of Agriculture & Food, 1 Stone Rd. West, Guelph, ON N1G 4Y2
Tel: 519-826-3100
Fax: 519-826-4335
Toll-Free: 888-466-2372
TTY: 519-826-7402
about.omafra@ontario.ca
www.omafra.gov.on.ca/english/rural
Other Communication: Media Hotline: 519-826-3145
twitter.com/atomafra
www.youtube.com/user/atomafra
The Ministry, which is attached to the Ministry of Agriculture & Food, seeks to strengthen Ontario's rural communities through funding programs, economic development programs, infrastructure & broadband internet access.

Minister, Hon. Jeff Leal
Tel: 416-326-3074
Fax: 416-326-3083
minister.mra@ontario.ca
Other Communications: Parliamentary E-mail: jleal.mpp.co@liberal.ola.org

Deputy Minister, Deb Stark
Tel: 416-326-3101
deb.stark@ontario.ca

Parliamentary Assistant, Grant Crack
Tel: 613-446-4010
gcrack.mpp.co@liberal.ola.org

Ontario Ministry of Tourism, Culture & Sport

Hearst Block, 900 Bay St., 9th Fl., Toronto, ON M7A 2E1
Tel: 416-326-9326
Fax: 416-314-7854
Toll-Free: 888-997-9015
TTY: 416-325-5807
www.mtc.gov.on.ca
Other Communication: Ontario Travel Information: 1-800-668-2746; Toll-Free TTY: 1-866-700-0040
twitter.com/ExploreON
Acts Administered:
AGO Act
Arts Council Act
Asian Heritage Act
Celebration of Portuguese Heritage Act
Centennial Centre of Science & Technology Act
Dutch Heritage Month Act
Emancipation Day Act
Foreign Cultural Objects Immunity from Seizure Act
George R. Gardiner Museum of Ceramic Art Act
German Pioneers Day Act
Historical Parks Act
Hotel Registration of Guests Act
Hummingbird Performing Arts Centre Corporation Act
Innkeepers Act
Irish Heritage Day Act
Italian Heritage Month Act
McMichael Canadian Art Collection Act
Metropolitan Toronto Convention Centre Act
Ministry of Citizenship & Culture Act
Ministry of Tourism & Recreation Act
Niagara Parks Act
Ontario Heritage Act
Ontario Place Corporation Act
Ontario Wine Week Act
Ottawa Convention Centre Corporation Act
Public Libraries Act
Royal Ontario Museum Act
Science North Act
South Asian Heritage Act
St. Lawrence Parks Commission Act
Status of Ontario Artists Act
Tartan Act
Ukrainian Heritage Day Act
United Empire Loyalists' Day Act

Minister, Hon. Michael Chan
Tel: 416-326-9326
Fax: 416-326-9338
mchan.mpp@liberal.ola.org

Associated Agencies, Boards & Commissions:
• Art Gallery of Ontario (AGO)
317 Dundas St. West
Toronto, ON M5T 1G4
Tel: 416-977-0414
Fax: 416-979-6669
Toll-free: 877-225-4246
www.ago.net
Other Communication: Art Rental & Sales: 416-977-4654; Donations: 416-979-6619; membership Information: 416-979-6620: Resource Centres: 416-979-6642; Image Resources: 416-979-6674
Honorary Chair, Charles Baillie
Tel: 416-979-6613
President, Tony Gagliano
Tel: 416-979-6613
Executive Director, Curatorial Affairs, Elizabeth Smith
• Conservation Review Board (CRB)
#1500, 655 Bay St.
Toronto, ON M5G 1E5
Tel: 416-212-6349
Fax: 416-326-6209
conservation.review.board@ontario.ca
www.crb.gov.on.ca
Executive Chair, Lynda Tanaka
Associate Chair, Peter Zakarow
• McMichael Canadian Art Collection
10365 Islington Ave.
Kelinburg, ON L0J 1C0
Tel: 905-893-1121
Fax: 905-893-0692
Toll-free: 888-213-1121
info@mcmichael.com
www.mcmichael.com
Chair, Board of Trustees, Upkar Arora
Chair, McMichael Canadian Art Foundation Board, Christopher Henley
Executive Director & CEO, Victoria Dickenson, FCMA, Ph.D.
• Metro Toronto Convention Centre Corporation (MTCC)
255 Front St. West
Toronto, ON M5V 2W6
Tel: 416-585-8120
Fax: 416-585-8198
info@mtccc.com; sales@mtccc.com
www.mtccc.com
• Minister's Advisory Council for Arts & Culture
400 University Ave., 5th Fl.
Toronto, ON M7A 2R9
Tel: 416-314-7621
Fax: 416-314-7635
Toll-free: 866-888-5829
macac@ontario.ca
Chair, Dr. James Fleck
• Niagara Parks Commission
Oak Hall Administration Bldg.
7400 Portage Rd. South
PO Box 150
Niagara Falls, ON L2E 6T2
Tel: 905-356-2241
Fax: 905-354-6041
Toll-free: 877-642-7275
corporateinfo@niagaraparks.com
www.niagaraparks.com
Chair, Janice Thomson
Tel: 905-356-2241 ext: 223
jthomson@niagaraparks.com
General Manager, John Lohuis
Tel: 905-356-2241 ext: 225
jlohuis@niagaraparks.com
Senior Director, Engineering & Planning, Marcelo Gruosso
Tel: 905-356-2241 ext: 240
mgruosso@niagaraparks.com
Senior Director, Parks, Deborah L. Whitehouse
Tel: 905-353-5410
dwhitehouse@niagaraparks.com
• Ontario Arts Council
151 Bloor St. West, 5th Fl.
Toronto, ON M5S 1T6
Tel: 416-961-1660
Fax: 416-961-7796
Toll-free: 800-387-0058
info@arts.on.ca
www.arts.on.ca
Chair, Martha Durdin
Tel: 416-969-7444
Director & CEO, Peter Caldwell
Tel: 416-969-7457
pcaldwell@arts.on.ca
Director, Granting Programs, Billyann Balay
Tel: 416-969-7458
bbalay@arts.on.ca
Coordinator, Information Services, Janice Lambrakos
Tel: 416-969-7429
jlambrakos@arts.on.ca
• Ontario Heritage Trust (OHT)
10 Adelaide St. East
Toronto, ON M5C 1J3
Tel: 416-325-5000
Fax: 416-325-5071
www.heritagetrust.on.ca
Other Communication: TTY: 711-416-325-5000
For more than three decades, the Ontario Heritage Trust has preserved, protected & promoted Ontario's rich & varied heritage. The Trust celebrates the people, places & events that have influenced & continue to shape our culture. As Ontario's lead heritage agency, the Trust's work extends to every corner of the province.
Chair, Dr. Thomas H.B. Symons
Tel: 416-314-4903
thomas.symons@heritagetrust.on.ca
Executive Director, Beth Hanna
Tel: 416-314-4901
beth.hanna@heritagetrust.on.ca
Acting Director, Heritage Programs & Operations, Wayne Kelly
Tel: 416-314-4913
programs@heritagetrust.on.ca
• Ontario Library Service - North (OLSN) / Service des bibliothèques de l'Ontario - Nord
334 Regent St.
Sudbury, ON P3C 4E2
Tel: 705-675-6467
Fax: 705-675-2285
Toll-free: 800-461-6348
www.olsn.ca
Other Communication: Toll-Free Fax: 1-800-461-6348
• Ontario Media Development Corporation (OMDC)
South Tower
#501, 175 Bloor St. East
Toronto, ON M4W 3R8
Tel: 416-314-6858
Fax: 416-314-6876
reception@omdc.on.ca
www.omdc.on.ca
Formerly the Ontario Film Development Corporation (OFDC).
• Ontario Place Corporation
955 Lake Shore Blvd. West
Toronto, ON M6K 3B9
Tel: 416-314-9900
Fax: 416-314-9989
Toll-free: 866-663-4386
www.ontarioplace.com
• Ontario Science Centre
770 Don Mills Rd.
Toronto, ON M3C 1T3
Tel: 416-696-1000
Fax: 416-696-3166
Toll-free: 888-696-1110
TTY: 416-696-3202
www.ontariosciencecentre.ca
• Ontario Tourism Marketing Partnership Corporation
#900, 10 Dundas St. East
Toronto, ON M7A 2A1
Tel: 416-212-0757
Fax: 416-325-6004
Toll-free: 800-668-2746
www.ontariotravel.net
• Ontario Trillium Foundation (OTF)
800 Bay St., 5th Fl.
Toronto, ON M5S 3A9
Tel: 416-963-4927
Fax: 416-963-8781
Toll-free: 800-263-2887
TTY: 416-963-7905
otf@otf.ca
www.otf.ca
The Ontario Trillium Foundation is an agency of the Ministry of Culture. Grants are provided to eligible not-for-profit & charitable organizations in the areas of arts & culture, sports and recreation, human & social services, & the environment.
Chief Executive Officer, Andrea Cohen
Tel: 416-963-4927
corpoffice@otf.ca
Vice-President, Finance & Administration, Anne Pashley
Tel: 416-963-7910
apashley@otf.ca
• Ottawa Convention Centre (OCC)
55 Colonel By Dr.
Ottawa, ON K1N 9J2
Tel: 613-563-1984
Fax: 613-563-7646
Toll-free: 800-450-0077
info@ottawaconventioncentre.com
www.ottawaconventioncentre.com
• Royal Botanical Gardens (RBG)
680 Plains Rd. West
Burlington, ON L7T 4H4
Tel: 905-527-1158
Fax: 905-577-0375
Toll-free: 800-694-4769
info@rbg.ca; auxiliary@rbg.ca
www.rbg.ca
Other Communication: GTA Toll-Free: 905-825-5040; RBG Auxiliary: 905-577-7771
Chair, Ian Brisbin
Tel: 905-527-1158 ext: 515
Chief Executive Officer & Director, Capital Projects, Mark C. Runciman
Tel: 905-527-1158 ext: 221
mrunciman@rbg.ca
Head, Science, Dr. David Galbraith
Tel: 905-527-1158 ext: 309
Head, Science, Dr. David Galbraith
Tel: 905-527-1158 ext: 309
dgalbraith@rbg.ca
Head, Conservation, Tys Theysmeyer
Tel: 905-527-1158 ext: 251
ttheysmeyer@rbg.ca
• Royal Ontario Museum (ROM)
100 Queen's Park Cres.
Toronto, ON M5S 2C6
Tel: 416-586-5549
Fax: 416-586-5685
info@rom.on.ca
www.rom.on.ca
• Science North
100 Ramsey Lake Rd.
Sudbury, ON P3E 5S9
Tel: 705-522-3701
Fax: 705-522-4954
Toll-free: 800-461-4898
contactus@sciencenorth.ca
www.sciencenorth.ca
Other Communication: Exhibit Fax: 705-522-1283
• Southern Ontario Library Service (SOLS)
#902, 111 Peter St.
Toronto, ON M5V 2H1
Tel: 416-961-1669
Fax: 416-961-5122
Toll-free: 800-387-5765
www.sols.org
• St. Lawrence Parks Commission
13740 County Rd. 2
Morrisburg, ON K0C 1X0
Tel: 613-543-3704
Fax: 613-543-2847
Toll-free: 800-437-2233
TTY: 613-543-4181
getaway@parks.on.ca
www.parks.on.ca
The St. Lawrence Parks Commission is an Ontario provincial agency established in 1955 to provide recreation, tourism, cultural & educational opportunities for residents of Ontario & visitors to the province through the presentation & interpretation of historical attractions & the development & operation of parks, campgrounds, scenic parkways & recreational areas.
Chair, Ian Wilson

Culture Division

#1800, 401 Bay St., Toronto, ON M7A 0A7
Tel: 416-314-7265
Fax: 416-314-7461
Assistant Deputy Minister, Kevin Finnerty
Tel: 416-314-7262
kevin.finnerty@ontario.ca
Director, Programs & Services, Peter Armstrong
Tel: 416-314-7342
Fax: 416-212-1802
peter.armstrong@ontario.ca
Acting Director, Culture & Strategic Policy, Dawn Landry
Tel: 416-212-7646
Fax: 416-314-7635
dawn.landry@ontario.ca
Acting Director, Culture Agencies, Suzanne Rowe Knight
Tel: 416-327-4305
suzanne.roweknight@ontario.ca

Office of the Chief Information Officer, Community Services I & IT Cluster
Mowat Block, 900 Bay St., 3rd Fl., Toronto, ON M7A 1L2
Assistant Deputy Minister & Chief Information Officer, Soussan Tabari
Tel: 416-326-8216
soussan.tabari@ontario.ca
Director, Case & Grants Management Solutions, Sanaul Haque
Tel: 416-585-6746
Fax: 416-585-7394
sanaul.haque@ontario.ca
Director, IAccess Solutions, Sanjay Madan
Tel: 416-325-2264
sanjay.madan@ontario.ca
Director, Strategic Planning & Business Relationship Management, Lolita Singh
Tel: 416-326-7942
Fax: 416-314-2561
lolita.singh@ontario.ca
Head, Data Collection & Decision Support Solutions, Michael Villani
Tel: 416-212-9709
Fax: 416-325-2262
michael.villani@ontario.ca

Ontario Internal Audit, Culture & Innovation Audit Service Team
College Park, 777 Bay St., 25th Fl., Toronto, ON M5G 2E5
Tel: 416-326-0800
Fax: 416-326-1712

Ontario Seniors' Secretariat
#601C, 777 Bay St., 6th Fl., Toronto, ON M7A 2J4
Fax: 416-326-7078
Toll-Free: 888-910-1999
TTY: 800-387-5559
infoseniors@ontario.ca
www.seniors.gov.on.ca
Minister Responsible, Hon. Mario Sergio
Tel: 416-314-9710
Fax: 416-325-4787
msergio.mpp@liberal.ola.org
Parliamentary Assistant, Vacant
Assistant Deputy Minister, Juanita Dobson
Tel: 416-326-7069
Fax: 416-326-7079
juanita.dobson@ontario.ca
Director, Retirement Homes Project, Abby Katz Starr
Tel: 416-325-2649
abby.katzstarr@ontario.ca

Regional & Corporate Services Division
400 University Ave., 2nd Fl., Toronto, ON M7A 2R9
Tel: 416-314-7311
Fax: 416-314-7313
Assistant Deputy Minister & Chief Administrative Officer, Robert M. Montgomery
robert.m.montgomery@ontario.ca
Central Region
400 University Ave., 4th Fl., Toronto, ON M7A 2R9
Tel: 416-314-6044
Fax: 416-314-2024
Toll-Free: 877-395-4105
Acting Manager, Mary Olijnyk
Tel: 416-314-6682
mary.olijnyk@ontario.ca
East Region
347 Preston St., 4th Fl., Ottawa, ON K1S 3J4
Tel: 613-742-3360
Fax: 613-742-5300
Toll-Free: 800-267-9340
Manager, Valerie Andrews
Tel: 613-742-3366
valerie.andrews@ontario.ca
North Region
#334, 435 James St. South, Thunder Bay, ON P7E 6S7
Tel: 807-475-1683
Fax: 807-475-1297
Toll-Free: 800-465-6861
Manager, Elaine Lynch
Tel: 807-475-1635
elaine.lynch@ontario.ca
West Region
2575 King St., 2nd Fl., Kitchener, ON N2P 2E9
Fax: 519-650-3425
Toll-Free: 800-265-2189
Manager, Chris Stack
Tel: 519-650-3421
chris.stack@ontario.ca

Sport, Recreation & Community Programs
College Park, 777 Bay St., 23rd Fl., Toronto, ON M7A 1S5
Tel: 416-326-4371
Fax: 416-314-7458
Assistant Deputy Minister, Phil Malcolmson
Tel: 416-212-8995
phil.malcolmson@ontario.ca
Director, Sport, Recreation & Community Programs, Rick Beaver
Tel: 416-314-7696
Fax: 416-314-7458
rick.beaver@ontario.ca
Manager, Community Programs, Pamela Bullard
Tel: 416-314-7684
pam.bullard@ontario.ca
Manager, Sport & Recreation Unit, Peter Evans
Tel: 416-314-7791
peter.evans@ontario.ca
Manager, Strategic Development, Gillian Steeve
Tel: 416-326-4370
gillian.steeve@ontario.ca

Tourism Planning & Operations Division
Hearst Block, 900 Bay St., 10th Fl., Toronto, ON M7A 2E2
Acting Assistant Deputy Minister, Morah Fenning
Tel: 416-325-2861
morah.fenning@ontario.ca
Director, Tourism Agencies, Dean Hustwick
Tel: 416-326-9579
Fax: 416-314-7003
dean.hustwick@ontario.ca
Director, Ontario Place Revitalization, Sevaun Palvetzian
Tel: 416-212-4861
Fax: 416-314-5060
sevaun.palvetzian@ontario.ca

Fort William Historical Park
1350 King Rd., Thunder Bay, ON P7K 1L7
Tel: 807-577-8461
Fax: 807-473-2327
info@fwhp.ca
www.fwhp.ca
Other Communication: Admissions: 807-473-2347; Admissions Fax: 807-473-2312; Reservations: 807-473-2344; Event Hotline: 807-473-2333; Emergency After Hours: 807-473-9750
twitter.com/FWHPtweets
www.facebook.com/fortwilliamhistoricalpark
General Manager, Sergio Buonocore
Tel: 807-473-2341
Fax: 807-473-2336
sergio.buonocore@ontario.ca
Manager, Maintenance & Facility Services, Joe Hagdu
Tel: 807-473-2329
joe.hagdu@ontario.ca

Huronia Historical Parks
16164 Hwy. 12, PO Box 160Midland, ON L4R 4K8
Tel: 705-526-7838
Fax: 705-526-9193
TTY: 705-528-7697
www.hhp.on.ca
General Manager, Jan Gray
Tel: 705-528-7690
jan.gray@ontario.ca

Tourism Policy & Development Division
Hearst Block, 900 Bay St., 10th Fl., Toronto, ON M7A 2E1
Tel: 416-326-9326
Fax: 416-325-6985
Assistant Deputy Minister, Richard McKinnell
Tel: 416-325-6961
richard.mckinnell@ontario.ca
Director, Investment & Development Office, Michael Langford
Tel: 416-314-7105
Fax: 416-327-2506
michael.langford@ontario.ca
Acting Director, Tourism Policy & Research, Diane Wise
Tel: 416-325-6055
Fax: 416-314-7341
diane.wise@ontario.ca
Manager, Regional Tourism Unit, Neil Coburn
Tel: 416-327-8824
Fax: 416-327-7947
neil.coburn@ontario.ca
Manager, Capital Grants Unit, Karen L. Drake
Tel: 416-314-1685
Fax: 416-314-1382
karen.l.drake@ontario.ca
Acting Grants Administration Officer, Product Development & Investment Services, Joan Marquis
Tel: 416-326-6894
Fax: 416-327-2506
joan.marquis@ontario.ca

Ontario Ministry of Transportation (MTO)

Ferguson Block, 77 Wellesley St. West, 3rd Fl., Toronto, ON M7A 1Z8
Tel: 416-235-4686
Fax: 905-704-2001
Toll-Free: 800-268-4686
TTY: 905-704-2426
www.mto.gov.on.ca
Other Communication: TTY Toll-Free: 1-866-471-8929; Driver & Vehicle Licensing: 1-800-387-3445; Road Test Booking: 1-888-570-6110
The Ministry performs the following functions: planning, designing & building highways; performing environmental assessments; rehabilitating existing highways to increase their efficiency & safety; performing ongoing highway maintenance; developing standards, operational guidelines & policies relating to highways; & researching & introducing new technologies for more effective highway management. MTO commits to providing & promoting transportation services in a way that sustains a healthful environment through the Ministry's Statement of Environmental Values. The Ministry applies & integrates environmental concerns, along with prevailing social, economic, scientific & other considerations when conducting its business activities.
Acts Administered:
Airports Act
Dangerous Goods Transportation Act
Highway Traffic Act
Improving Customer Service for Road Users Act
Ministry of Transportation Act
Motor Vehicle Transportation Act
Motorized Snow Vehicles Act
Northern Transportation Commission Act
Off-Road Vehicles Act
Ontario Highway Transport Board Act
Ontario Transportation Development Corporation Act
Photo Card Act
Public Service Works on Highways Act
Public Transportation & Highway Improvement Act
Public Vehicles Act
Railways Act

Minister, Hon. Glen R. Murray
Tel: 416-327-9200
Fax: 416-327-9188
gmurray.mpp@liberal.ola.org

Deputy Minister, Carol Layton
Tel: 416-327-9162
Fax: 416-327-9185
carol.layton@ontario.ca

Parliamentary Assistant, Kevin Daniel Flynn

Tel: 416-327-0806
Fax: 416-327-9188
kflynn.mpp.co@liberal.ola.org

Associated Agencies, Boards & Commissions:
• **Metrolinx**
#600, 20 Bay St.
Toronto, ON M5J 2W3
Tel: 416-874-5900
Fax: 416-869-1755
www.metrolinx.com
Metrolinx serves the Greater Toronto Area & Hamilton, & operates the following companies & programs: GO Transit; Air Rail Link; PRESTO; Smart Commute; & the Transit Procurement Initiative (TPI).
Chair, J. Robert S. Pritchard
President & CEO, Bruce McCuaig
Tel: 416-874-5903
ceo@metrolinx.com
President, Air Rail Link, Kathy M. Haley
President, GO Transit, Gary McNeil
Tel: 416-869-3600 ext: 550
Fax: 416-869-1755
gary.mcneil@gotransit.com
Other Communications: URL: www.gotransit.com
Chief Information Officer, Executive Vice-President & Managing Director, PRESTO, Robert Hollis
Tel: 647-789-0320
robert.hollis@prestocard.ca
Other Communications: URL: www.prestocard.ca
• **Ontario Highway Transport Board (OHTB)**
151 Bloor St. West, 10th Fl.
Toronto, ON M5S 2T5
Tel: 416-326-6732
Fax: 416-326-6738
ohtb@mto.gov.on.ca
www.ohtb.gov.on.ca
Chair, Gary R. Stanley
Tel: 416-326-5634
gary.stanley@ontario.ca
Board Secretary & Manager, Felix D'Mello
Tel: 416-326-5640
Assistant Deputy Minister, John Lieou
Tel: 416-327-8521
john.lieou@ontario.ca
Director, Transportation Planning, Patricia Boeckner
Tel: 905-585-7238
Fax: 416-585-7324
patricia.boeckner@ontario.ca
Director, Aboriginal Relations, Bob Goulais
Tel: 416-585-7329
Fax: 416-585-6876
bob.goulais@ontario.ca
Acting Director, Transportation Policy, Elizabeth Kay-zorowski
Tel: 416-585-7177
Fax: 416-585-7204
elizabeth.kay-zorowski@ontario.ca
Director, Transit Policy, Andrew Posluns
Tel: 416-585-7347
Fax: 905-704-2445
andrew.posluns@ontario.ca
Director, Strategic Policy & Transportation, Economics, David Ward
Tel: 416-212-1893
Fax: 416-212-2351
david.ward@ontario.ca
Assistant Deputy Minister, Gerry Chaput
Tel: 416-327-9044
Fax: 416-327-9226
gerry.chaput@ontario.ca
Manager, Bridge Office, Dino Bagnariol
Tel: 905-704-2341
Fax: 905-704-2060
dino.bagnariol@ontario.ca
Manager, Traffic Office, Roger Degannes
Tel: 905-704-2940
Fax: 905-704-2888
roger.degannes@ontario.ca
Manager, Geomatics Office, Russ Hogan
Tel: 905-704-2328
Fax: 905-704-2051
russ.hogan@ontario.ca
Manager, Materials Engineering & Research Office, Tom Kazmierowski
Tel: 416-235-3512
Fax: 416-235-3487
tom.kazmierowski@ontario.ca
Acting Manager, Design & Contract Standards Office, Heather McClintock
Tel: 905-704-2199
Fax: 905-704-2051
heather.mcclintock@ontario.ca

Road User Safety Division
Bldg A, #191, 1201 Wilson Ave., Downsview, ON M3M 1J8
Tel: 416-235-2999
Fax: 416-235-4153
The division sets safety standards, develops policies, legislation & regulation, & educates road users about road user safety. Responsibilities include evaluating the effectiveness of safety measures, inspecting, monitoring & enforcing compliance with standards, testing, licenses & drivers, & registering vehicles. Through public education, legislation & enforcement, the government strives to ensure all motorists take responsibility for their driving behaviour. The Assistant Deputy Minister, Road User Safety, is responsible for the co-ordination of all Road User Safety activities for the province & acts as the Registrar of Motor Vehicles for Ontario.
Assistant Deputy Minister, Rob Fleming
Tel: 416-235-4453
Fax: 416-235-4153
rob.fleming@ontario.ca
Director, Licencing Services, Paul Brown
Tel: 416-235-4392
Fax: 416-235-4378
paul.h.brown@ontario.ca
Director, RUS Modernization Project, Linda Dunstall
Tel: 416-235-4628
linda.dunstall@ontario.ca
Director, Regional Operations, Tony Foster
Tel: 416-235-3526
Fax: 416-235-4670
tony.foster@ontario.ca
Director, Safety Policy & Education, Heidi Francis
Tel: 416-235-4050
Fax: 416-235-5139
heidi.francis@ontario.ca
Director, Program Development & Evaluation, Paul Harbottle
Tel: 416-235-4199
Fax: 416-235-4111
paul.harbottle@ontario.ca
Director, Carrier Safety & Enforcement, Peter Hurst
Tel: 416-235-2501
Fax: 905-704-2530
paul.harbottle@ontario.ca
Director, Service Delivery Partnerships, Kim Lambert
Tel: 416-235-5312
Fax: 416-235-4433
kim.lambert@ontario.ca
Director, Oranizational Development, Barbara Maher
Tel: 416-235-4864
Fax: 416-235-3939
barbara.maher@ontario.ca

Workplace Safety & Insurance Board (WSIB)

200 Front St. West, Ground Fl., Toronto, ON M5V 3J1
Tel: 416-344-1000
Fax: 416-344-4684
Toll-Free: 800-387-0750
TTY: 800-387-0050
wsibcomm@wsib.on.ca; prevention@wsib.on.ca (training programs)
www.wsib.on.ca
Other Communication: eServices Inquiries, Phone: 1-888-243-1569; Forms Order Line: 416-344-3862; Collections, Phone: 1-800-268-0929
www.facebook.com/youngworkersafety
www.youtube.com/ontariowsib
The Workplace Safety & Insurance Board is involved in Ontario's occupational health & safety system. The Board's responsibilities are as follows: administering no-fault workplace insurance in Ontario for employers & workers; providing disability benefits; monitoring the quality of healthcare; & assisting workers who have been injured on the job or persons who have contracted an occupational disease in an early & safe return to work.

Chair, Elizabeth Witmer

President & Chief Executive Officer, David Marshall
Tel: 416-344-4009

Chief Prevention & Corporate Strategy Officer, Tom Beegan
Tel: 416-344-4446
tom_beegan@wsib.on.ca

Acting Chief Financial Officer, Dan Hogg
Tel: 416-344-6147
dan_hogg@wsib.on.ca

Chief Operating Officer, John Slinger
Tel: 416-344-4450
john_slinger@wsib.on.ca

Chief Corporate Services Officer, Tom Teahen
Tel: 416-344-6129
tom_teahen@wsib.on.ca

Chief Strategy Officer, Susanna Zagar
Tel: 416-344-6188
susanna_zagar@wsib.on.ca

Contact, Media Relations, Christine Arnott
Tel: 416-344-4202
Fax: 416-344-4800
christine_arnott@wsib.on.ca

Government of Prince Edward Island

Seat of Government: Island Information Service, PO Box 2000Charlottetown, PE C1A 7N8
Tel: 902-368-4000
island@gov.pe.ca
www.gov.pe.ca
Other Communication: Tourism Information, Toll-Free Phone: 1-800-463-4734
twitter.com/infopei
www.facebook.com/govpe
youtube.com/user/govpeca; flickr.com/photos/peigov
The Province of Prince Edward Island entered Confederation on July 1, 1873. It has an area of 5,685.73 km2, with a population of 140,204, according to the 2011 national census.

Minister, Agriculture & Forestry; Deputy Premier, Hon. George T. Webster
Tel: 902-368-4820
Fax: 902-368-4846
gtwebster@gov.pe.ca
Other Communications: Department Phone: 902-368-4880; Fax: 902-368-4857
Note: Web Site: www.gov.pe.ca/agriculture (Department of Agriculture)
Department of Agriculture, Jones Bldg.
11 Kent St., 5th Fl.
PO Box 2000
Charlottetown, PE C1A 7N8

Minister, Fisheries, Aquaculture, & Rural Development, Hon. Ron W. MacKinley
Tel: 902-368-5120
Toll-free: 877-407-0187
Fax: 902-368-5385
rwmackinley@gov.pe.ca
Other Communications: Department Phone: 902-838-0910; Fax: 902-838-0975
Note: Web Site: www.gov.pe.ca/fard (Department of Fisheries, Aquaculture, & Rural Development)
Department of Fisheries, Aquaculture, & Rural Development
548 Main St.
PO Box 1180
Montague, PE C0A 1R0

Minister, Health & Wellness, Hon. Doug W. Currie
Tel: 902-368-5152
Fax: 902-368-4910
dwcurrie@gov.pe.ca
Other Communications: Department Phone: 902-368-6414; Fax: 902-368-4121
Social Media: twitter.com/DougCurrie, www.facebook.com/doug.w.currie
Note: Web Sites: www.gov.pe.ca/health (Department of Health & Wellness); www.dougcurrie.ca (Personal Website)
Department of Health & Wellness
105 Rochford St., North, 4th Fl.
PO Box 2000
Charlottetown, PE C1A 7N8

Minister, Finance, Energy & Municipal Affairs, Hon. Wesley J. Sheridan
Tel: 902-368-4050
Fax: 902-368-6575
wjsheridan@gov.pe.ca
Other Communications: Department Phone: 902-368-4000; Fax: 902-368-5544
Social Media: www.facebook.com/wes.sheridan.9
Note: Web Site: www.gov.pe.ca/finance (Department of Finance & Municipal Affairs)
Department of Finance & Municipal Affairs, Shaw Bldg.
95 Rochford St. South, 2nd Fl.
PO Box 2000
Charlottetown, PE C1A 7N8

Minister, Community Services, Seniors & Labour; Minister Responsible, Status of Women, Hon. Valerie E. Docherty
Tel: 902-368-4330
Toll-free: 86- 59- 377
Fax: 902-368-4348
vedocherty@assembly.pe.ca
Other Communications: Department Phone: 902-620-3777; Fax: 902-368-4740
Social Media: www.facebook.com/valerie.docherty.5
Note: Web Site: www.gov.pe.ca/sss (Department of Community Services, Seniors, & Labour)
Department of Community Services, Seniors, & Labour, Jones Bldg.
11 Kent St., 2nd Fl.
PO Box 2000
Charlottetown, PE C1A 7N8

Minister, Environment, Labour & Justice; Attorney General, Hon. Janice A. Sherry
Tel: 902-368-4930
Fax: 902-368-4974
jasherry@gov.pe.ca
Other Communications: Department Phone: 902-368-5000; Fax: 902-368-5830
Social Media: www.facebook.com/janice.sherry.16
Note: Web Site: www.gov.pe.ca/eef (Department of Environment, Energy, & Forestry)
Department of Environment, Energy, & Forestry, Jones Bldg.
11 Kent St., 4th Fl.
PO Box 2000
Charlottetown, PE C1A 7N8

Minister, Transportation & Infrastructure Renewal, Hon. Robert S. Vessey
Tel: 902-368-4801
Fax: 902-368-5277
rsvessey@gov.pe.ca
Other Communications: Department Phone: 902-368-5100; Fax: 902-368-5395
Note: Web Site: www.gov.pe.ca/tir (Department of Transportation & Infrastructure Renewal)
Department of Transportation & Infrastructure Renewal, Jones Bldg.
11 Kent St., 3rd Fl.
PO Box 2000
Charlottetown, PE C1A 7N8

Prince Edward Island Department of Agriculture & Forestry

Jones Bldg., 11 Kent St., PO Box 2000Charlottetown, PE C1A 7N8
Tel: 902-368-4880
Fax: 902-368-4857
www.gov.pe.ca/af
Prince Edward Island's Department of Agriculture provides programs & services to farmers. Programs are developed within the context of the Sustainable Resource Policy, which protects the province's land, water, & air.
The following are some examples of program categories: AgriFlexibility; Buy PEI;, Crop Production; Food Safety, Biosecurity, & Traceability; Forestry; Innovation & Applied Research; Laboratory Services; Livestock; Organic; & Training.
Acts Administered:
Agricultural Crop Rotation Act
Agricultural Insurance Act
Agricultural Products Standards Act
Agrologists Act
Animal Health & Protection Act
Artificial Insemination Act
Companion Animal Protection Act
Dairy Industry Act
Dairy Producers Act
Dog Act
Environmental Protection Act
Farm Machinery Dealers & Vendors Act
Farm Practices Act
Farm Registration & Farm Organization Funding Act
Fire Prevention Act
Forest Management Act
Gasoline Tax Act
Grain Elevators Corporation Act
Lands Protection Act, P.E.I.
Livestock Community Auction Sales Act
Natural Areas Protection Act
Natural Products Marketing Act
Occupational Health & Safety Act
PEI Farm Safety Code of Practice
Pesticides Control Act
Planning Act
Plant Health Act
Public Forest Council Act
Real Property Assessment Act
Real Property Tax Act
Revenue Tax Axt
Smoke Free Places Act
Stray Livestock Act
Veterinary Profession Act
Weed Control Act
Women's Institute Act

Minister; Deputy Premier, Hon. George T. Webster
Tel: 902-368-4820
Fax: 902-368-4846
gtwebster@gov.pe.ca
Other Communications: Department Phone: 902-368-4880; Fax: 902-368-4857

Deputy Minister, John MacQuarrie
Tel: 902-368-4830
Fax: 902-368-4846
jamacquarrie@gov.pe.ca

Associated Agencies, Boards & Commissions:
• **Agricultural Insurance Corporation**
29 Indigo Cres.
PO Box 1600
Charlottetown, PE C1A 7N3
Tel: 902-368-4842
Fax: 902-368-6677
www.gov.pe.ca/growingforward
Production insurance is administered by the Prince Edward Island Agricultural Insurance Corporation. It provides production risk protection to producers who may sustain crop losses due to natural hazards.
Programs administered by the Corporation are as follows: AgriStability, AgriInvest, AgriInsurance, & AgriRecovery.
Manager, David Aiton
Tel: 902-368-4843
Fax: 902-368-6677
draiton@gov.pe.ca
Supervisor, AgriStability Program, Michael Gill
Tel: 902-620-3172
Fax: 902-368-6677
mggill@gov.pe.ca
Supervisor, Production Insurance, Melis Visser
Tel: 902-368-4853
Fax: 902-569-7745
mvisser@gov.pe.ca
Area Supervisor, East Position, Bev Francis
Tel: 902-315-0230
Fax: 902-569-7745
bmfrancis@gov.pe.ca
Area Supervisor, West Position, Ken Malone
Tel: 902-315-0226
Fax: 902-836-8921
kdmalone@gov.pe.ca
• **Agricultural Insurance Corporation Appeal Board**
Chair, James Toombs
• **Animal Health Advisory Committee**
• **Farm Practices Review Board**
The Farm Practices Review Board is responsible for reviewing concerns from the public about farm practices.
Chair, Alvin Keenan
• **Grain Elevators Corporation**
7 Gerald McCarville Dr.
PO Box 250
Kensington, PE C0B 1M0
Tel: 902-836-8935
Fax: 902-836-8926
www.peigec.com
The Prince Edward Island Grain Elevators Corporation is a leader in the province's cereal & protein sector.
For growers who want the pooled return, the Corporation operates grain marketing pools. Producers may also sell part of their crop to the Corporation at daily market prices.
Grain & products marketed throughout Prince Edward Island & Atlantic Canada.
President, Dave Thompson
Tel: 902-628-7200
Vice-President, Gary Robinson
Tel: 902-672-2649
Secretary-Treasurer, Tracey MacEwen
Tel: 902-836-2432
• **Marketing Council**

Chair, Gordon MacBeath
Officer, Marketing Council, Murray Myles
Tel: 902-569-7575
Fax: 902-569-7745
mamyles@gov.pe.ca
29 Indigo Cres.
PO Box 1600
Charlottetown, PE C1A 7N3
• **Natural Areas Advisory Committee**

• **Natural Products Appeals Tribunal**

• **Pesticides Advisory Committee**

• **Public Forest Council (PFC)**
c/o PEI Department of Agriculture & Forestry
Forests, Fish & Wildlife Division
PO Box 2000
Charlottetown, PE C1A 7N8
Fax: 902-368-4713
publicforest@gov.pe.ca
www.gov.pe.ca/forestry/PFC
The Public Forest Council is made up of six private sector members & three public sector members, who are appointed by the Lieutenant Governor in Council. Council members foster discussion about the potential for provincial woodlands. The council is especially interested in non-traditional, non-consumptive uses of public forests.
Chair, John Rowe
Manager, Public Lands, Vacant
Manager, Fish & Wildlife, Gerald MacDougall
Tel: 902-368-5111
Fax: 902-368-4713
dgmacdougall@gov.pe.ca
• **Species at Risk Advisory Committee**
The Species at Risk Advisory Committee performs the following tasks: assessing the province's wildlife resources; advising the Minister of Environment, Energy, & Forestry about the species that should be listed at risk; analyzing the effects of land use on wildlife & their habitat; & making recommendations about the conservation of wildlife & its habitat.
Chair; Natural Areas Biologist, Rosemary Curley
Tel: 902-368-4807
Fax: 902-368-5830
frcurley@gov.pe.ca
J. Frank Gaudet Tree Nursery
Upton Rd.
PO Box 2000
Charlottetown, PE C1A 7N8
• **Veterinary College Advisory Council**
• **Veterinary Medical Association Licensing Board**
• **Wildlife Conservation Fund Advisory Committee**

Agriculture Policy & Regulatory Division

Jones Bldg., 11 Kent St., 5th Fl., Charlottetown, PE C1A 7N8
The Agriculture Policy & Regulatory Division oversees areas such as the following: research; administration of industry development programs; community pastures; on-farm food safety; food quality; marketing legislation; domestic & foreign trade; traceability; foreign animal disease; & emergency preparedness.
Director, Shane Murphy
Tel: 902-620-3084
srmurphy@gov.pe.ca

Executive Director, Women's Institute, Ellen D. MacPhail
Tel: 902-368-4860
Fax: 902-368-4439
edmacphail@gov.pe.ca
Other Communications: URL: www.peiwi.ca
Administrative Director, 4-H, Emily Brown
Tel: 902-368-4836
Fax: 902-368-6289
eabrown@gov.pe.ca
Manager, Agriculture Regulatory Programs, Brian Matheson
Tel: 902-368-5087
Fax: 902-368-4857
bgmatheson@gov.pe.ca
Acting Officer, Marketing Council, Murray Myles
Tel: 902-569-7575
Fax: 902-569-7745
mamyles@gov.pe.ca

Agriculture Resource Division
Research Station, University Ave., PO Box 1600Charlottetown, PE C1A 7N3
Tel: 902-368-4145
Fax: 902-368-5661
The Agriculture Resource Division delivers sustainable resource & farm extension programs & services.
Acting Director, Tracy Wood
Tel: 902-368-5645
Fax: 902-368-5661
tmwood@gov.pe.ca
Manager, Agriculture Information, Sandra MacKinnon
Tel: 902-368-5647
Fax: 902-368-5729
sjmackinnon@gov.pe.ca
Manager, Agriculture Innovation, Lynda MacSwain
Tel: 902-368-4815
Fax: 902-368-5729
lemacswain@gov.pe.ca
Manager, Sustainable Agriculture Resources, Barry Thompson
Tel: 902-368-6366
Fax: 902-368-5661
blthompson@gov.pe.ca

Corporate & Financial Services Division
Jones Bldg., 11 Kent St., 5th Fl., PO Box 2000Charlottetown, PE C1A 7N8
Tel: 902-368-4880
Fax: 902-368-4857
Financial, administrative, & human resources services are provided by the Corporate & Financial Services Division.
Director, Jerry Gavin
Tel: 902-368-5741
Fax: 902-368-4857
jpgavin@gov.pe.ca
Manager, Human Resources, Tory Kennedy
Tel: 902-368-6694
Fax: 902-368-4857
tkkennedy@gov.pe.ca
Financial Services Officer, Janet Doyle
Tel: 902-368-4837
Fax: 902-368-4857
jedoyle@gov.pe.ca

Forests, Fish, & Wildlife Division
J. Frank Gaudet Tree Nursery, 183 Upton Rd., PO Box 2000Charlottetown, PE C1A 7N8
Tel: 902-368-4700
Fax: 902-368-4713
The Forests, Fish, & Wildlife Division oversees the following programs & services: the provincial forests; the private forest program; production development; resource inventory & modelling; & wildlife & fish.
Director, Kate E. MacQuarrie
Tel: 902-368-4705
Fax: 902-368-4713
kemacquarrie@gov.pe.ca
Senior Manager, Dan McAskill
Tel: 902-368-6730
Fax: 902-368-4713
jdmcaskill@gov.pe.ca
Manager, Private Forests, Brian Brown
Tel: 902-368-6431
Fax: 902-368-4713
bmbrown@gov.pe.ca
Manager, Fish & Wildlife, Gerald MacDougall
Tel: 902-368-5111
Fax: 902-368-4713
dgmacdougall@gov.pe.ca
Manager, Production Development, Vacant
Manager, Public Lands, Vacant
Provincial Forest Supervisor, Eastern District, Reg Conohan
Tel: 902-961-7296
Fax: 902-961-7298
rwconohan@gov.pe.ca
Provincial Forest Supervisor, Central District, Vacant
Provincial Forest Supervisor, Western District, Vacant
Information Officer, Ken Mayhew
Tel: 902-368-6450
Fax: 902-368-4713
khmayhew@gov.pe.ca
Inventory Forester, Resource Inventory & Modelling, Mike Montigny
Tel: 902-368-4709
mmontigny@gov.pe.ca

Prince Edward Island Analytical Laboratories
23 Innovation Way, Charlottetown, PE C1E 0B7
Tel: 902-368-4190
Prince Edward Island Analytical Laboratories include the Dairy Laboratory, the Soil, Feed, & Water Chemistry Testing Laboratory, & the Water Microbiology Laboratory.
The Dairy Laboratory works in support of the Prince Edward Island Dairy Industry Act & Regulations. It also provides services to VALACTA in Prince Edward Island, Nova Scotia, & New Brunswick.
The Soil, Feed, & Water Chemistry Testing Laboratory provides analytical information for farmers & the public.
Acting Laboratory Manager, Anna Marie MacFarlane
Tel: 902-368-4190
Fax: 902-368-4486
ammacfarlane@gov.pe.ca
Supervisor, Soil, Feed, & Water Chemistry Testing Laboratory, Lori C. Connolly-Brine
Tel: 902-368-5671
Fax: 902-368-6299
lcconnolly@gov.pe.ca
Acting Supervisor, Dairy Lab & Water Microbiology Laboratory; Mass Spectrometry Technologist, April M. Driscoll
Tel: 902-314-2811
amdriscoll@gov.pe.ca
Quality Assurance Officer, Marlene MacNeill
Tel: 902-368-5622
Fax: 902-569-7778
mcmacneill@gov.pe.ca
Diagnostician (Part Time), Plant Disease, Marleen Clark
Tel: 902-836-8922
Fax: 902-836-8921
mmclark@gov.pe.ca

Prince Edward Island Department of Community Services & Seniors

Jones Bldg., 11 Kent St., 2nd Fl., PO Box 2000Charlottetown, PE C1A 7N8
Tel: 902-620-3777
Fax: 902-894-0242
Toll-Free: 866-594-3777
www.gov.pe.ca/sss
The Department of Community Services & Seniors strives to develop healthy & self-reliant individuals & to support vulnerable members of the province. Programs & services are offered to promote social & economic prosperity & the creation of work environments that contribute to a safe, healthy, & engaged workforce.
Acts Administered:
Labour Act
North American Labour Cooperation Agreement Implementation Act
Occupational Health & Safety Act
Pay Equity Act
Rehabilitation of Disabled Persons Act
Social Assistance Act
Social Work Act
Youth Employment Act

Minister; Minister Responsible, Status of Women, Hon. Valerie E. Docherty
Tel: 902-368-4330
Toll-free: 866-594-3777
Fax: 902-368-4348
vedocherty@assembly.pe.ca
Social Media: www.facebook.com/valerie.docherty.5

Deputy Minister, Carol Ann Duffy
Tel: 902-368-6520
Fax: 902-368-4740
caduffy@gov.pe.ca

Communications Officer, Beth P. Johnston
Tel: 902-620-3409
Fax: 902-894-0242
bpjohnston@gov.pe.ca

Associated Agencies, Boards & Commissions:
• Advisory Council on the Status of Women
Sherwood Business Centre
161 St. Peter's Rd., Main Level
PO Box 2000
Charlottetown, PE C1A 7N8
Tel: 902-368-4510
Fax: 902-368-3269
peistatusofwomen@eastlink.ca; info@peistatusofwomen.ca
www.gov.pe.ca/acsw; eiacsw.wordpress.com
The Prince Edward Island Advisory Council on the Status of Women consists of nine members. Members are appointed by government to serve on the government advisory agency. The Council advises the Minister Responsible for the Status of Women & works to support equality & the participation of women in economic, political, legal, & cultural activities.
Minister Responsible, Status of Women; Minister, Community Services & Seniors, Hon. Valerie E. Docherty
Tel: 902-368-4330
Fax: 902-368-4348
vedocherty@assembly.pe.ca; valerie.docherty@liberal.pe.ca
Social Media: www.facebook.com/valerie.docherty.5
Executive Director, Michelle Jay
Researcher & Policy Analyst, Jane Ledwell
• Alberton Housing Authority
Chair, Michael King
• Charlottetown Area Housing Authority
Chair, Don MacRae
• Disability Action Council
The 19 member Council is responsible for consulting with & advising the provincial government on legislation, policies, programs & services that affect people with disabilities.
• Georgetown Housing Authority
Chair, Gerry MacKenzie
• Montague Housing Authority
Chair, Flora Martin
• Mount Stewart Housing Authority
Chair, Colleen Mullen-Doyle
• O'Leary Housing Authority
Chair, Robert Luxton
• PEI Social Work Registration Board (PEISWRB)
81 Prince St.
Charlottetown, PE C1A 4R3
Tel: 902-368-7337
Fax: 902-368-7180
registrar@socialworkpei.ca
socialworkpei.ca
Regulatory body for the social work profession on Prince Edward Island, seeking to protect the public from preventable harm.
• Premier's Action Committee on Family Violence Prevention
c/o Child and Family Services Division
161 St. Peters Rd.
PO Box 2000
Charlottetown, PE C1A 7N8
Tel: 902-368-5984
Fax: 902-368-6186
mrgill@ihis.org
www.stopfamilyviolence.pe.ca
Chair, Dr. Philip Smith
Resource Person, Dr. Wendy Verhoek-Oftedahl
• Seniors' Secretariat
c/o Office of Seniors
11 Kent St.
Charlottetown, PE C1A 7N8
Chair, Mary Hughes
• Social Assistance Appeals Panel
• Souris Housing Authority
Chair, Mary Lang
• Summerside Housing Authority
Chair, Brian Wedge
• Tignish Housing Authority
Chair, June Watterson

Child & Family Services
Jones Bldg., 11 Kent St., 2nd Fl., PO Box 2000Charlottetown, PE C1A 7N8
Tel: 902-368-5294
The Child & Family Services Division offers a wide range of programs & services to care for Prince Edward Island's children & families. Examples of programs include child protection, foster care, & adoption services.
Director, Child & Family Services, Rona Smith
Tel: 902-368-5396
Fax: 902-368-4258
ronasmith@gov.pe.ca
Director, Child Protection, Wendy L. McCourt
Tel: 902-368-6515
Fax: 902-620-3776
wlmccourt@gov.pe.ca
Provincial Coordinator, Residential Services, Barry L. Chandler
Tel: 902-368-6180
Fax: 902-620-3362
blchandler@gov.pe.ca
Provincial Coordinator, Child Protection, Maureen G. MacEwen
Tel: 902-368-6161
Fax: 902-620-3362
mgmacewen@gov.pe.ca
Coordinator, Family Violence Prevention & Community Development, Premier's Action Committee on Family Violence Prevention, Dr. Wendy Verhoek-Oftedahl
Tel: 902-368-6712
Fax: 902-368-6169
wverhoekoftedahl@gov.pe.ca

Housing, Seniors & Corporate Support
Jones Bldg., 11 Kent St., 2nd Fl., PO Box 2000Charlottetown, PE C1A 7N8
Fax: 902-894-0242
The Corporate & Financial Services Division is responsible for the following areas: finance, administration, human resources, communications, French language services, intergovernmental & external relations, records information management, & emergency social services.
Director, Housing, Seniors & Corporate Support, W. Lorne Clow
Tel: 902-368-6109
Fax: 902-894-0242
wlclow@gov.pe.ca
Manager, Financial Services & Audit, Sonya L. Cobb
Tel: 902-620-3408
Fax: 902-894-0242
slcobb@gov.pe.ca
Coordinator, Corporate Support, Jennifer Burgess
Tel: 902-368-5199
Fax: 902-894-0242
jmburgess@gov.pe.ca
Coordinator, Provincial Housing, Bill Fleming
Tel: 905-368-5779
Fax: 902-894-5471
bhfleming@gov.pe.ca

Interministerial Women's Secretariat
Jones Bldg., 11 Kent St., 2nd Fl., PO Box 2000Charlottetown, PE C1A 7N8
Tel: 902-368-6494
Fax: 902-892-0242
The role of the Interministerial Women's Secretariat is to assist the Minister Responsible for the Status of Women to protect & promote gender equality.
Director, Michelle Harris-Genge
Tel: 902-368-5557
Fax: 902-892-0242
mdharris-genge@gov.pe.ca

Social Programs
Jones Bldg., 11 Kent St., 2nd Fl., PO Box 2000Charlottetown, PE C1A 7N8
The Social Programs & Housing Division provides services related to social assistance, disability support, & housing.
Director, Social Programs, Bob D. Creed
Tel: 902-368-6446
Fax: 902-620-3553
bdcreed@gov.pe.ca
Coordinator, Social Assistance & Disability Support Programs (East), Rhea M. Jenkins
Tel: 902-368-5904
Fax: 902-368-6443
rmjenkins@ihis.org
Coordinator, Social Assistance & Disability Support Programs (West), Pat W. MacDonald
Tel: 902-888-8149
Fax: 902-888-8398
pwmacdonald@ihis.org
Supervisor, Social Assistance & Disability Support Programs (Central), Ann L. Drake
Tel: 902-368-4039
Fax: 902-368-6443
aldrake@ihis.org
Supervisor, Social Assistance & Disability Support Programs (West), Karen H. Murray
Tel: 902-888-8128
Fax: 902-888-8398
khmurray@ihis.org
Temporary Supervisor, Social Assistance & Disability Support Programs (Montague/Souris), Adam J. Peters
Tel: 902-838-0710
Fax: 902-838-0727
ajpeters@ihis.org
Administrative Officer, Social Assistance & Disability Support Programs (Summerside), Rosemary C. Jenkins
Tel: 902-888-8121
Fax: 902-888-8398
rcjenkins@gov.pe.ca

Minister, Hon. J. Alan McIsaac
Tel: 902-368-4330
Fax: 902-368-4348
jamcisaac@assembly.pe.ca
Social Media: www.facebook.com/alan.mcisaac.3

Deputy Minister, Dr. Alex (Sandy) MacDonald
Tel: 902-438-4876
Fax: 902-438-4150
agmacdonald@edupe.ca

Communications Officer, Laura Steeves
Tel: 902-368-6449
lcsteeves@gov.pe.ca

Communications Officer, Major Stewart
Tel: 902-438-4873
Fax: 902-438-4150
mbstewart@gov.pe.ca

Prince Edward Island Department of Environment, Labour & Justice

Shaw Bldg. South, 95 Rochford St., 4th Fl., PO Box 2000Charlottetown, PE C1A 7N8
Tel: 902-368-6410
Fax: 902-368-6488
www.gov.pe.ca/jps
Other Communication: Corporations: 902-368-4550

Minister, Hon. Janice A. Sherry
Tel: 902-368-6410
Fax: 902-368-6488
jasherry@gov.pe.ca
Social Media: www.facebook.com/janice.sherry.16

Deputy Minister & Deputy Attorney General, Shauna Sullivan Curley, Q.C.
Tel: 902-368-5152
Fax: 902-368-4910
sscurley@gov.pe.ca

Senior Communications Officer, Ron Ryder
Tel: 902-620-3774
Fax: 902-368-4242
rrryder@gov.pe.ca

Associated Agencies, Boards & Commissions:
• Boilers & Pressure Vessels Advisory Board
Chair, Lloyd Cudmore
• Court Transcribers Examining Board
• Credit Union Deposit Insurance Corporation (CUDIC)
#209, 281 University Ave.
Charlottetown, PE C1A 4M3
Tel: 902-628-6280
Fax: 902-628-8147
info@peicudic.com
www.peicudic.com
Chair, James Blanchard
Registrar of Credit Unions, Katharine Tummon
CEO, Richard Kenny
Tel: 902-628-8194
rkenny@peicudic.com
• Electrical Contractors Examining Board
• Employment Standards Board
Sherwood Business Centre
161 St. Peters Rd., 2nd Fl.
Charlottetown, PE C1A 7N8
Tel: 902-368-5550
Fax: 902-368-5476
Toll-free: 800-333-4362
The Employment Standards Board listens to appeals from employers regarding alleged violations of the Employment Standards Act. The Employment Standards Board is also responsible for presenting recommendations about the Minimum Wage Order to the Lieutenant Governor in Council.
Chair, Donald F. MacCormac
Vice-Chair, Brian L.A. Watts
Secretary, Hazel Walsh
• Environmental Advisory Council
11 Kent St., 4th Fl.
PO Box 2000
Charlottetown, PE C1A 7N8
www.gov.pe.ca/environment/eac
The Environmental Advisory Council advises the Minister responsible for the environment about environmental concerns. Members of the council are appointed by the Lieutenant Governor in Council.
Chair, Richard Davies
Vice-Chair, Dean Stewart
• Judicial Remuneration Review Commission
• Labour Relations Board
Sherwood Business Centre
161 St. Peters Rd., 2nd Fl.
PO Box 2000
Charlottetown, PE C1A 7N8
Tel: 902-368-5550
Fax: 902-368-5476
Toll-free: 800-333-4362
www.gov.pe.ca/sss
The Labour Relations Board works to resolve applications received from labour or management, in accordance with Prince Edward Island's Labour Act.
Chair, Nancy Birt
Vice-Chair, Patrick Alyward
Vice-Chair, Matthew MacFarlane
Vice-Chair, Karen MacLeod
Chief Executive Officer, Shawn Shea
Tel: 902-368-5565
Toll-free: 800-333-4362
Fax: 902-368-5476
smshea@gov.pe.ca
• Law Society of Prince Edward Island Council (LSPEI)
49 Water St.
PO Box 128
Charlottetown, PE C1A 7K2
Tel: 902-566-1666
Fax: 902-368-7557
lawsociety@lspei.pe.ca
www.lspei.pe.ca/council.php
• Prince Edward Island Criminal Code Review Board
Chair, Elizabeth Reagh
• Prince Edward Island Human Rights Commission
See Entry Name Index for detailed listing.
• Prince Edward Island Workers Compensation Board
See Entry Name Index for detailed listing.
• Office of the Police Commissioner
114 Kent St.
PO Box 427
Charlottetown, PE C1A 7K7
Tel: 902-368-7200
Fax: 902-368-1123
Toll-free: 877-541-7204
www.policecommissioner.pe.ca
The Office of the Police Commissioner investigates & resolves complaints about the unprofessional conduct of police, other than the RCMP. Under the Police Act, a person who is 18 years of age & over, who has been directly affected by the conduct of municipal police officer, may make a complaint. The Office of the Police Commissioner also handles complaints about a chief of a municipal police service, a director or instructing officer at the Atlantic Police Academy, or a security police officer at the University of Prince Edward Island. The independent statutory office works to carry out its mission in a timely & impartial manner.

Persons must call the Office of the Police Commissioner to book an appointment.
• **Power Engineers Board of Examiners**
• **Public Trustee Advisory Committee**
• **Sewage Disposal Regulations Board of Examiners**
• **Supreme Court Finance Committee**
• **Victim Services Advisory Committee**
Chair, Donna Langille
• **Workers Compensation Appeal Tribunal (WCAT)**
161 St. Peters Rd., 1st Fl.
PO Box 2000
Charlottetown, PE C1A 7N8
Established under Prince Edward Island's Worker's Compensation Act, the Workers Compensation Appeal Tribunal operates as an independent quasi-judicial administrative tribunal. Workers or employers who are dissatisfied with a decision made by the Internal Reconsideration Officer can appeal it through the Workers Compensation Appeal Tribunal. The appeal body is the last level of appeal for workers' compensation matters.
The Office of the Workers Compensation Appeal Tribunal Coordinator is responsible for administrative duties related to the tribunal. The coordinator attends all hearings, but is not part of the decision making process.
Chair, Wendy E. Reid, Q.C.
Vice-Chair, Jordan K.M. Brown, Q.C.
Vice-Chair, John L. Ramsay, Q.C.
Tribunal Coordinator, Judy Burke
Tel: 902-894-0278
Fax: 902-620-3477
jaburke@gov.pe.ca

Community Safety & Justice Policy
Shaw Bldg., 105 Rochford St., 4th Fl., Charlottetown, PE C1A 7N8
Tel: 902-368-6620
Fax: 902-368-5283
The Policy, Policing, & Crime Prevention Division is comprised of the following sections: Justice Resource Service; Policing Services; & Access & Privacy Services.
The Justice Resource Service supports government & community organizations in justice issues, with a focus on community & social development.
The Police Act is administerd by the Policing Services Section.
The Access & Privacy Services Section offers advice regarding the operation of the Freedom of Information & Protection of Privacy (FOIPP) Act & its regulations.

Office of Public Safety
National Bank Tower, #600, 134 Kent St., 6th Fl., PO Box 2000Charlottetown, PE C1A 7N8
Tel: 902-894-0385
Fax: 902-368-6362
www.gov.pe.ca/jps/index.php3?number=1004340&
twitter.com/PEIPublicSafety
www.facebook.com/PEIPublicSafety
The Office of Public Safety includes the following sections: 911 Administration Office; Emergency Measures Organization; Fire Marshal's Office; & the Office for Business Continuity Management Planning.
Director, Aaron Campbell
Tel: 902-894-0385
Fax: 902-368-6362
acampbell@gov.pe.ca
Fire Marshal, Fire Marshal's Office, David Rossiter
Tel: 902-368-4869
Fax: 902-368-5526
derossiter@gov.pe.ca
Deputy Fire Marshal, Fire Marshal's Office, Robert Arsenault
Tel: 902-368-4893
Fax: 902-368-5526
robarsenault@gov.pe.ca
Provincial Coordinator, 911 Call Answer & Transfer Service, Pat J. Kelly
Tel: 902-894-0299
Fax: 902-368-6362
pjkelly@gov.pe.ca
Provincial Emergency Management Coordinator, Emergency Measures Organization, Tanya Mullally
Tel: 902-368-5980
Fax: 902-368-6362
tlmullally@gov.pe.ca
Coordinator, Civic Addressing, 911 Call Answer & Transfer Service, D. Steven Dickie
Tel: 902-368-6361
Fax: 902-368-6362
dsdickie@gov.pe.ca
Project Manager, Public Safety Radio, Larry Avery
Tel: 902-368-4073
Fax: 902-368-6362
jlavery@gov.pe.ca
Senior Business Continuity Planner, Office for Business Continuity Management Planning, Brian McFeely
Tel: 902-438-4174
Fax: 902-432-2659
bcmcfeely@gov.pe.ca

Environment
Jones Bldg., 11 Kent St., 4th Fl., PO Box 2000Charlottetown, PE C1A 7N8
Tel: 902-368-5044
Fax: 902-368-5830
Toll-Free: 866-368-5028
The Environment Division oversees programs that protect the province's environement, including the following elements: groundwater; inland surface water & coastal estuaries; drinking water; the ozone layer; & air quality.
The division is also involved in waste management activities, such as the handling of litter, beverage containers, hazardous wastes, used oil, petroleum storage tanks, lead-acid batteries, tires, & derelict vehicles.
Director, Environment, Jim Young, P.Eng
Tel: 902-368-5034
Fax: 902-368-5830
jjyoung@gov.pe.ca
Manager, Climate Change & Air Management, Erin Taylor
Tel: 902-368-6111
Fax: 902-368-5830
eotaylor@gov.pe.ca
Acting Manager, Administrative & Customer Services, Roxanne Larter
Tel: 902-368-5561
Fax: 902-368-5526
rmlarter@gov.pe.ca
Manager, Inspection Services, Glenda MacKinnon-Peters, P.Eng.
Tel: 902-368-4874
Fax: 902-368-5526
gcmackinnon-peters@gov.pe.ca
Manager, Watershed & Subdivision Planning, Bruce Raymond
Tel: 902-368-5054
Fax: 902-368-5830
bgraymond@gov.pe.ca
Manager, Drinking Water & Wastewater Management, George Somers
Tel: 902-368-5046
Fax: 902-368-5830
ghsomers@gov.pe.ca
Manager, Environmental Land Management, Greg Wilson
Tel: 902-368-5274
Fax: 902-368-5830
gbwilson@gov.pe.ca
Chief Inspector, Elevator, Lifts & Amusement Devices, Eric MacArthur
Tel: 902-368-6561
Fax: 902-368-5526
ermacarthur@gov.pe.ca
Chief, Safety Standards, Alan Robison
Tel: 902-368-4892
Fax: 902-368-5526
amrobison@gov.pe.ca
Chief Engineer, Building Standards, Garth Simmons
Tel: 902-569-7746
Fax: 902-368-5830
gssimmons@gov.pe.ca
Chief Officer, Boiler, Pressure Vessel, LP Gas, Plumbing & Home Heat Tank, Steve Townsend
Tel: 902-368-5567
Fax: 902-368-5526
srtownsend@gov.pe.ca
Coordinator, Pesticide Monitoring & Control, Thane Clarke
Tel: 902-368-5599
Fax: 902-368-5830
ktclarke@gov.pe.ca
Coordinator, Alternative Land Use Services (ALUS) Program, Shawn Hill
Tel: 902-620-3725
Fax: 902-368-5830
sjhill@gov.pe.ca
Environmental & Regulatory Coordinator, Barrie Jackson
Tel: 902-368-5173
Fax: 902-368-5830
bajackson@gov.pe.ca
Director, Mary Kinsman
Tel: 902-368-5032
Fax: 902-368-5830
makinsman@gov.pe.ca
Manager, Human Resources, Charlotte A. Murray
Tel: 902-368-4629
Fax: 902-368-5830
camurray@gov.pe.ca
Manager, Finance, Michele Koughan
Tel: 902-368-6688
Fax: 902-368-5830
makoughan@gov.pe.ca
Clerk, Records Management, Anne Proud
Tel: 902-368-5305
Fax: 902-368-5830
paproud@gov.pe.ca

Policy & Administration Division
Shaw Bldg., 105 Rochford St., 4th Fl., PO Box 2000Charlottetown, PE C1A 7N8
Tel: 902-368-4865
Fax: 902-368-5335
The Policy & Administration Division provides financial administration & human resource management services for the Department of Justice & Public Safety.
Director, Kevin Barnes, CA
Tel: 902-368-4865
Fax: 902-368-4224
kcbarnes@gov.pe.ca

Prince Edward Island Department of Finance, Energy & Municipal Affairs

Shaw Bldg., 95 Rochford St. South, 2nd Fl., PO Box 2000Charlottetown, PE C1A 7N8
Tel: 902-368-4000
Fax: 902-368-5544
www.gov.pe.ca/finance
The Department of Finance & Municipal Affairs facilitates the management of the Government of Prince Edward Island's human & financial resources.

Minister, Hon. Wesley J. Sheridan
Tel: 902-368-4050
Fax: 902-368-6575
wjsheridan@gov.pe.ca
Social Media: www.facebook.com/wes.sheridan.9

Deputy Minister, David Arsenault
Tel: 902-368-4053
Fax: 902-368-6575
davidarsenault@gov.pe.ca

Associated Agencies, Boards & Commissions:
• **Child & Youth Services Commissioner**
Homan Bldg.
#101, 250 Water St.
Summerside, PE C1N 1B6
Tel: 902-438-4872
Fax: 902-438-4874
www.gov.pe.ca/childandyouth
The Child & Youth Services Commissioner deals with issues that affect children & youth in Prince Edward Island. The following legislation in Prince Edward Island affects children & youth: Child Protection Act; Mental Health Act; School Act; & Youth Justice Act.
Commissioner, Child & Youth Services, Jeff Clow
jaclow@gov.pe.ca
• **Classification Appeal Committee**
• **Commission on the Land & Local Governance**
Aubin Arsenault Bldg.
3 Brighton Rd.
Charlottetown, PE C1A 8T6
Tel: 902-620-3558
Fax: 902-569-7545
www.gov.pe.ca/landandlocalgovernance
Commissioner, Ralph Thompson
Director, Implementation, Christine MacKinnon
Tel: 902-368-5282
Fax: 902-569-7545
cgmackinnon@gov.pe.ca

• **Lotteries Commission**
• **Maritime Geomatics Committee**
• **Maritime Provinces Harness Racing Commission**
Member, Fred Paynter
Member, Lowell Stead
• **Northumberland Strait Crossing Advisory Group**
• **Prince Edward Island Energy Corporation**
Jones Bldg.
11 Kent St., 4th Fl.
PO Box 2000
Charlottetown, PE C1A 7N8
The Prince Edward Island Energy Corporation promotes the development, generation, transmission, & distribution of energy in an economic & efficient manner.
Chief Executive Officer, Wayne MacQuarrie
Tel: 902-894-0289
Fax: 902-894-0290
dwmacquarrie@gov.pe.ca
Coordinator, Special Projects, Mark Victor
Tel: 902-368-6098
Fax: 902-894-0290
mevictor@gov.pe.ca
• **Prince Edward Island Master Trust Investment Advisory Committee**
• **Public Service Commission (PSC)**
Shaw Bldg. North
105 Rochford St., 1st Fl.
PO Box 2000
Charlottetown, PE C1A 7N8
Tel: 902-368-4080
Fax: 902-368-4383
www.gov.pe.ca/psc
The independent & impartial agency coordinates human resources in the public sector of Prince Edward Island. All government departments & agencies, health authorities, & other public sector employers are served by Prince Edward Island's Public Service Commission. Examples of services include recruitment, selection, occupational health & safety, payroll & benefits administration, & the employee assistant program.
Chief Executive Officer, Aidan Sheridan
Tel: 902-368-4207
Fax: 902-368-4383
ajsheridan@gov.pe.ca
Director, Classification & Employee Relations, Allan O'Keefe
Tel: 902-368-4188
Fax: 902-368-4383
awokeefe@gov.pe.ca
Director, Staffing & Human Resource Planning, Andrew M. Thompson
Tel: 902-368-4204
Fax: 902-368-4383
amthompson@gov.pe.ca
• **Self-Insurance & Risk Management Fund Advisory Committee**

Wind Energy Institute of Canada (WEICan)
21741 Rte. 12, North Cape, PE C0B 2B0
Tel: 902-882-2746
Fax: 902-882-3823
info@weican.org
www.weican.ca
The Wind Energy Institute of Canada (WEICan) has evolved from the Atlantic Wind Test Site (AWTS), which had been a cornerstone of Canada's wind energy R&D program for the last 25 years. Located at North Cape, the northernmost tip of Prince Edward Island, the site offers one of the harshest environments in the world for the testing of wind technology. Its mission is to support the development of safe, reliable, efficient, sustainable & affordable wind power generation in Canada & the development of wind energy-related products & services for Canadian & export markets. Major funders of WEICan include Natural Resources Canada, the Atlantic Canada Opportunities Agency, & the PEI Energy Corporation.
Chair, Richard Hassard
CEO, Scott Harper
Tel: 902-882-4125
scott.harper@weican.ca
Director, Technology, Ken Montgomery
Tel: 902-882-4127
ken.montgomery@weican.ca

Energy & Minerals Division
Jones Bldg., 4th Fl., PO Box 2000Charlottetown, PE C1A 7N8
Tel: 902-894-0288
Fax: 902-894-0290
The Energy & Minerals Division is engaged in the following activities: developing & managing energy policies & programs; overseeing the development of mineral resources; & supporting gas exploration.
Director, Wayne MacQuarrie
Tel: 902-894-0289
Fax: 902-894-0290
dwmacquarrie@gov.pe.ca
Manager, Office of Energy Efficiency, Mike Proud
Tel: 902-620-3792
Fax: 902-620-3796
mpproud@gov.pe.ca
Other Communications: URL: www.gov.pe.ca/oee
Officer, Energy Programs, Andy Collier
Tel: 902-620-3794
Fax: 902-620-3796
ajcollier@gov.pe.ca
Officer, Sustainable Operations Program, George Meggison
Tel: 902-620-3793
Fax: 902-620-3796
gemeggison@gov.pe.ca
Energy Advisor, Ronald Estabrooks
Tel: 902-368-5011
Fax: 902-894-0290
rgestabr@gov.pe.ca

Information Technology Shared Services Division
Sullivan Bldg., 5th Fl., PO Box 2000Charlottetown, PE C1A 7N8
Tel: 902-620-3470
Information Technology Shared Services consists of the following sections: Client Services; Information Technology Infrastructure Support; Corporate, Operations, Finance & Policy Planning; Business Systems; & Enterprise Architecture Services.
Chief Operating Officer, Norman MacDonald
ncmacdonald@gov.pe.ca

Municipal Affairs & Provincial Planning Division
3 Brighton Rd., PO Box 2000Charlottetown, PE C1A 7N8
Tel: 902-620-3558
Fax: 902-569-7545
Municipal Affairs acts as the liaison with municipalities & municipal interest groups on municipal matters. Consulting services are available regarding governance, administration, operations, & municipal land use planning.
Provincial Planning works in accordance with Prince Edward Island's Planning Act & Lands Protection Act related to land use & development in the province. Efforts are made to achieve sustainable development in the province.
Director, Municipal Affairs & Provincial Planning, Albert MacDonald
Tel: 902-368-5582
Fax: 902-569-7545
Manager, Implementation, Land Use & Local Governance, Christine MacKinnon
Tel: 902-368-5282
Fax: 902-569-7545
cgmackinnon@gov.pe.ca
Manager, Municipal Affairs, Samantha J. Murphy
Tel: 902-368-5892
Fax: 902-569-7545
sjmurphy@gov.pe.ca
Director, Provincial Planning, Vacant
Acting Manager, Provincial Planning, Dale McKeigan
Tel: 902-620-3634
Fax: 902-569-7545
dfmckeigan@gov.pe.ca
Acting Senior Provincial Planner, Patrick J. Carroll
Tel: 902-620-3459
Fax: 902-569-7545
pjcarroll@gov.pe.ca

Office of the Comptroller
Shaw Bldg., 95 Rochford St., 2nd Fl., PO Box 2000Charlottetown, PE C1A 7N8
Tel: 902-368-4201
Fax: 902-368-6661
The Office of the Comptroller carries out the following responsibilities: operating the government's corporate accounting system; providing advice related to financial management; administering the corporate procurement service for departments & agencies; managing a corporate fleet information system; & producing the province's public accounts.
Comptroller, Doug Clow, CA
Tel: 902-368-4201
Fax: 902-368-6661
dmclow@gov.pe.ca
Manager, Administration Services, Lane Pineau
Tel: 902-569-7559
Fax: 902-368-6661
lepineau@gov.pe.ca

Taxation & Property Records Division
Shaw Bldg., 95 Rochford St., 1st Fl., PO Box 2000Charlottetown, PE C1A 7N8
Tel: 902-368-4070
Fax: 902-368-6164
The role of the Taxation & Property Records Division is to ensure equity in the collection of provincial tax revenues & in the production of both provincial & municipal real property assessment rolls. Services are coordinated with federal, provincial, & municipal governments.
Provincial Tax Commissioner, Elizabeth (Beth) Gaudet
Tel: 902-368-5686
Fax: 902-368-6584
eagaudet@gov.pe.ca
Manager, Tax Compliance Services, Mary Hennessey, CA
Tel: 902-368-4174
Fax: 902-368-6584
mihennessey@gov.pe.ca

Prince Edward Island Department of Fisheries, Aquaculture & Rural Development

548 Main St., PO Box 1180Montague, PE C0A 1R0
Tel: 902-838-0910
Fax: 902-838-0975
Toll-Free: 877-407-0187
www.gov.pe.ca/fard
The Department of Fisheries, Aquaculture, & Rural Development is guided by the following federal legislation: Aboriginal Communal Fishing Licences Regulations; Atlantic Fishery Regulations, 1985; Canada's Species at Risk Act; Federal Fisheries Act; Fishery Health Protection Regulations; Fishery (General) Regulations; Management of Contaminated Fisheries Regulations; Maritime Provinces Fishery Regulations; & the Navigable Waters Protection Act. The department carries out its mission through its divisions.
The Marine Fisheries & Seafood Services Division provides information to clients & advocates on behalf of the marine fisheries industry.
The Aquaculture Division offers assistance to the aquaculture & estuarial shellfish fisheries.
The Rural Development Division serves rural clients through community development & the delivery of employment programs.
Access PEI offers provincial government programs, services, & information to residents of Prince Edward Island. Examples of Access PEI's services include purchasing a fishing license or obtaining a drivers license.

Minister, Hon. Ron W. MacKinley
Tel: 902-838-0976
Toll-free: 877-407-0187
Fax: 902-838-0972
rwmackinley@gov.pe.ca

Deputy Minister, Richard Gallant
Tel: 902-838-0983
Fax: 902-838-0972
rkgallant@gov.pe.ca

Officer, Communications, Kim Devine
Tel: 902-368-5286
Fax: 902-368-5830
kmdevine@gov.pe.ca

Associated Agencies, Boards & Commissions:
• **Employment Development Agency**
548 Main St.
PO Box 1180
Montague, PE C0A 1R0
Tel: 902-838-0910
Fax: 902-838-0975
Toll-free: 877-407-0187
Director, Brian Schmeisser
Tel: 902-838-0662
beschmeisser@gov.pe.ca
Coordinator, Prince County, Elliot Deighan
Tel: 902-888-8032

Fax: 902-432-2634
eldeighan@gov.pe.ca
Coordinator, Queens & King Counties, Daryl Macdonald
Tel: 902-838-0652
Fax: 902-838-0975
dgmacdonald@gov.pe.ca
Clerk/Receptionist, Montague, Michelle Johnston
mejohnston@gov.pe.ca

Aquaculture Division
548 Main St., PO Box 1180Montague, PE C0A 1R0
Tel: 902-838-0828
Fax: 902-838-0975
Toll-Free: 877-407-0187
The Aquaculture Division delivers the following services: advice & information to the provinces's aquaculture industry; financial programs to assist in aquaculture development; & biological & technical services to the shellfish & finfish sectors on the Island.
Director, Aquaculture Division, Neil MacNair
Tel: 902-838-0685
Toll-free: 877-407-0187
Fax: 902-838-0975
ngmacnair@gov.pe.ca
Aquaculture Biologist, Kim Gill
Tel: 902-838-0859
Fax: 902-838-0975
klgill@gov.pe.ca
Aquaculture Biologist, Aaron Ramsay
Tel: 902-838-0827
Fax: 902-838-0975
apramsay@gov.pe.ca
Mussel Technician, Brian Gillis
Tel: 902-838-0895
Fax: 902-838-0975
blgillis@gov.pe.ca
Shellfish Technician, Mark MacLeod
Tel: 902-368-5268
mtmacleod@gov.pe.ca
Shellfish Technician, Gary Smith
Tel: 902-838-5287
Fax: 902-838-0975
gbsmith@gov.pe.ca
Contact, Warehouse, Jeff MacEwen
Tel: 902-368-5268

Marine Fisheries & Seafood Services Division
548 Main St., PO Box 1180Montague, PE C0A 1R0
Tel: 902-838-0910
Fax: 902-838-0975
Toll-Free: 877-407-0187
The Marine Fisheries & Seafood Services Division is engaged in the following activities: advocating for Prince Edward Island's fishing industry; offering programs to support new technology & value-added processing of seafood; supporting development of emerging species; undertaking biological research in support of major fish species; issuing licences for fish buying, fish peddling, & fish processing; managing & maintaining shellfish launching sites around the province; enforcing regulations under Prince Edward Island's Fish Inspection Act & Fisheries Act; overseeing the dead mammal removal program from the province's shore line; & compiling statistics about the fishing industry.
Director, Barry MacPhee
Tel: 902-838-0625
Toll-free: 877-407-0187
Fax: 902-838-0975
jbmacphee@gov.pe.ca
Manager, Marine Fisheries, David MacEwen
Tel: 902-838-0635
Fax: 902-838-0975
dgmacewen@gov.pe.ca
Manager, Seafood Services, David McGuire
Tel: 902-838-0691
Fax: 902-838-0975
dpmcguire@gov.pe.ca
Lobster Biologist, Robert MacMillan
Tel: 902-838-0699
Fax: 902-838-0975
rjmacmillan@gov.pe.ca
Fisheries Technician, Michelle Dixon
Tel: 902-838-0819
Fax: 902-838-0975
madixon@gov.pe.ca
Officer, Program Statistics, Cheryl Campbell
Tel: 902-838-0826
Fax: 902-838-0975
cherylcampbell@gov.pe.ca
Officer, Seafood Marketing, Kaley E. MacDonald
Tel: 902-838-0627
Fax: 902-838-0975
kemacdonald@gov.pe.ca

Rural Development Division
548 Main St., PO Box 1180Montague, PE C0A 1R0
Tel: 902-838-0910
Fax: 902-838-0975
Toll-Free: 877-407-0187
The responsibilities of the Rural Development Division are as follows: implementing action items in the Rural Action Plan; overseeing the delivery of the Island Community Fund; & ensuring the effectiveness of the Seasonal Hiring Centre & the Employment Development Agency.
Director, Brian Schmeisser
Tel: 902-838-0662
Fax: 902-838-0975
beschmeisser@gov.pe.ca
Community Development Officer, Giselle Bernard
Tel: 902-854-3680
Fax: 902-854-3099
gbbernard@gov.pe.ca
Community Development Officer, Eastern Kings, Chris Blaisdell
Tel: 902-687-7083
Fax: 902-687-7091
cwblaisdell@gov.pe.ca
Community Development Officer, Southern Kings, Stephen Lewis
Tel: 902-838-0618
Fax: 902-838-0975
sjlewis@gov.pe.ca
Community Development Officer, East Prince, Kellie Mulligan
Tel: 902-887-3975
Fax: 902-887-2400
kamulligan@gov.pe.ca
Community Development Officer, Rural Queens, Nancy Murphy
Tel: 902-894-0347
Fax: 902-368-5542
nkmurphy@gov.pe.ca
Community Development Officer, West Prince, Brenda Profit
Tel: 902-853-0104
Fax: 902-853-3839
bfprofit@gov.pe.ca
Rural Plan Officer, Kim Klein
Tel: 902-838-0670
Fax: 902-838-0975
keklein@gov.pe.ca

Single Window Service / Access PEI
548 Main St., PO Box 1180Montague, PE C0A 1R0
Tel: 902-838-0910
Fax: 902-838-0975
TTY: 877-407-0187
www.gov.pe.ca/accesspei
Prince Edward Island Provincial Government services are available at government service centres, known as Access PEI locations. At the eight Access PEI centres across Prince Edward Island, citizens obtain information about the Provincial Government & its programs.
The Access PEI Centres are situated in the following places:
Alberton (902-853-8622);
Charlottetown (902-368-5200);
Montague (902-838-0600);
O'Leary (902-859-8800);
Souris' Johnny Ross Young Service Centre (902-687-7000);
Summerside (902-888-8000;
Tignish (902-882-7351); &
Wellington (902-854-7250).
Director, Tim G. Garrity
Tel: 902-838-0651
Fax: 902-838-0975
tggarrity@gov.pe.ca
Manager, Access PEI Summerside & PEI Wellington, Cindy Lou Andrews
Tel: 902-888-8001
Fax: 902-888-8306
clandrews@gov.pe.ca
Other Communications: Access PEI Wellington: accesspeiwellington@gov.pe.ca
Access PEI Summerside
120 Harbour Dr.
Summerside, PE C1N 5L2
Manager, Access PEI Montague & Access PEI Souris, Eleanor Avery
Tel: 902-687-7050
Fax: 902-687-7091
emavery@gov.pe.ca
Other Communications: Access PEI Souris, E-mail: accesspeisouris@gov.pe.ca
Access PEI Souris, Johnny Ross Young Services Centre
15 Green St.
PO Box 550
Souris, PE C0A 2B0
Manager, Access PEI Alberton, Access PEI O'Leary, & Access PEI Tignish, Martha Dawson
Tel: 902-859-8801
Fax: 902-859-8709
accesspeialberton@gov.pe.ca
Other Communications: Access PEI Tignish E-mail: accesspeitignish@gov.pe.ca
Access PEI O'Leary
45 East Dr.
PO Box 8
O'Leary, PE C0B 1V0
Manager, Access PEI Charlottetown, Paulette Gallant
Tel: 902-368-6847
Fax: 902-569-7560
plgallant@gov.pe.ca
Other Communications: Access PEI Charlottetown, Fax: 902-569-7560
Access PEI Charlottetown, Highway Safety Bldg.
33 Riverside Dr.
PO Box 2000
Charlottetown, PE C1A 7N8

Prince Edward Island Department of Health & Wellness

105 Rochford St. North, 4th Fl., PO Box 2000Charlottetown, PE C1A 7N8
Tel: 902-368-6414
Fax: 902-368-4121
www.gov.pe.ca/health
The Department of Health & Wellness carries out the following responsibilities: ensuring quality health care to the citizens of Prince Edward Island; providing leadership in policy, programs, & operations; maintaining & improving the health of citizens; playing a leadership role in innovation; coordinating the implementation of the Healthy Living Strategy; providing regulatory services to the health system; acting as a central contact for Aboriginal organizations; & promoting cooperation on governmental matters related to Aboriginal affairs.

Minister; Minister Responsible, Aboriginal Affairs, Hon. Doug W. Currie
Tel: 902-368-5152
Fax: 902-368-4910
dwcurrie@gov.pe.ca
www.dougcurrie.ca
Social Media: twitter.com/DougCurrie, www.facebook.com/doug.w.currie

Deputy Minister, Dr. Michael Mayne
Tel: 902-368-5290
Fax: 902-368-4121
mbmayne@gov.pe.ca

Communications Officer, Autumn Tremere
Tel: 902-368-5610
Fax: 902-368-4224
agtremere@gov.pe.ca

Communications Officer, April Winchester
Tel: 902-368-5512
Fax: 902-368-4224
awinchester@gov.pe.ca

Associated Agencies, Boards & Commissions:
• **Community Care Facilities & Nursing Homes Board**
16 Garfield St.
Charlottetown, PE C1A 7N8
Tel: 902-368-4953
Fax: 902-368-6136
The Board issues licenses to community care facilities & nursing homes.

• Council of the Association of Registered Nurses of PEI (ARNPEI)
53 Grafton St.
Charlottetown, PE C1A 1K8
Tel: 902-368-3764
Fax: 902-368-1430
www.arnpei.ca
President, Vacant
• Council of the College of Physicians & Surgeons of PEI (CPSPEI)
14 Paramount Dr.
Charlottetown, PE C1E 0C7
Tel: 902-566-3861
Fax: 902-566-3986
cpspei.ca
President, Dr. McLean
Registrar, Dr. C. Moyse
cmoyse@cpspei.ca
Deputy Registrar, Dr. G. Johnston
gjohnston@cpspei.ca
• Council of the Denturist Society of PEI
• Council of the PEI Chiropractic Association
Member, Dr. Darren MacLean
Member, Dr. Murray Rusk
Member, Dr. Michael Sider
• Council of the PEI College of Physiotherapists (PEICPT)
PO Box 20078
Charlottetown, PE C1A 9E3
Tel: 902-894-2490
www.peicpt.com
• Dietitians Registration Board (PEIDRB)
153 Spring St.
Summerside, PE C1N 3G2
Tel: 902-436-2438
peidrb@pei.sympatico.ca
Contact, Katherine Schaefer
• Dispensing Opticians Board
PO Box 20140 Sherwood
Charlottetown, PE C1A 9E3
• Emergency Medical Services Board
• Financial Assistance Appeal Panel
Member, Marie MacAulay
Member, Phil Matusiewicz
Member, Doris White
• Health PEI
See Entry Name Index for detailed listing.
• Licensed Practical Nurses Registration Board (LPNA)
PO Box 20058
Charlottetown, PE C1E 1E9
Tel: 902-566-1512
Fax: 902-892-6315
info@lpna.ca
www.lpna.ca
Executive Director & Registrar, Alana Essery
Tel: 902-566-1512 ext: 1
aessery@lpna.ca
• Medical Advisory Committee
• Mental Health Review Board
Chair, Michael Drake
• Nurse Practitioner Diagnostic & Therapeutics Committee
• Prince Edward Island College of Optometrists
• Prince Edward Island Occupational Therapists Registration Board
PO Box 2248 Central
Charlottetown, PE C1A 8B9
Tel: 902-892-1266
rbregistrar@peiot.org
www.peiot.org
Chair, Colleen MacPherson
Registrar, Manon Gallant
• Prince Edward Island Pharmacy Board (PEIPB)
20454 Trans Canada Hwy.
PO Box 89
Crapaud, PE C0A 1J0
Tel: 902-658-2780
Fax: 902-658-2198
info@pepharmacists.ca
www.pepharmacists.ca
The Prince Edward Island Pharmacy Board regulates the practice of pharmacy in Prince Edward Island. Its goal is to promote high standards of pharmaceutical service for the welfare of the public.
Registrar, Neila Auld
nauld@pepharmacists.ca
Assistant Registrar, Michelle Wyand
mwyand@eastlink.ca
Administrative Assistant, Rachel Lowther-Doiron
r.lowtherdoiron@pei.aibn.com
• Prince Edward Island Psychologists Registration Board (PEIPRB)
c/o Dept. of Psychology, UPEI
550 University Ave.
Charlottetown, PE C1A 4P3
Tel: 902-566-0549
smithp@upei.ca
www.peipsychology.org/peiprb
Chair, Jason Doiron, Ph.D., C.Psych.
Registrar, Philip Smith, Ph.D., C.Psych.
• Pharmaceutical Information Program Advisory Committee
• Physician Resource Planning Committee
President, Dr. George Carruthers
• Provincial Canada Games Committee

Chief Public Health Office
PO Box 2000Charlottetown, PE C1A 7N8
Tel: 902-368-4996
Fax: 902-620-3354
The Chief Health Office administers & enforces the Public Health Act. The office also delivers services in the following areas: environmental health, epidemiology, reproductive care, & vital statistics.
Chief Public Health Officer, Dr. Heather G. Morrison
Tel: 902-368-4996
Fax: 902-620-3354
hgmorrison@gov.pe.ca
Deputy Chief Public Health Officer, Dr. Lamont Sweet
Tel: 902-368-4996
Fax: 902-620-3354
lesweet@ihis.org
Manager, Environmental Health, Joe Bradley
Tel: 902-368-4792
Fax: 902-368-6468
joebradley@ihis.org
Acting Manager, Vital Statistics, Jo-Anne H. Larsen
Tel: 902-838-0884
Fax: 902-838-0883
jhlarsen@ihis.org
Provincial Epidemiologist, Dr. Carolyn J. Sanford
Tel: 902-368-4964
Fax: 902-620-3354
cjsanford@gov.pe.ca
Coordinator, Provincial Infection Control Program, Stacey L. Burns
Tel: 902-368-4934
Fax: 902-620-3354
slburns@ihis.org
Coordinator, Communicable Disease & Immunization, Anne M. Neatby
Tel: 902-368-6114
Fax: 902-620-3354
amneatbty@ihis.org
Coordinator, Infection Control Services, Corrine A. Rowswell
Tel: 902-368-6190
Fax: 902-620-3354
carowswell@ihis.org

Finance & Corporate Management Division
Shaw Bldg., 105 Rochford St. North, 4th Fl., PO Box 2000Charlottetown, PE C1A 7N8
The Finance & Corporate Management Division supports the Department of Health & Wellness in the areas of finances, human resources, communications, & the administration of the Freedom of Information & Protection of Privacy Act.
Director, Kevin Barnes, CA
Tel: 902-368-4865
Fax: 902-368-4224
kcbarnes@gov.pe.ca
Manager, Finance & Administration, Kelli Spence
Tel: 902-368-4897
Fax: 902-368-4224
kcspence@gov.pe.ca
Manager, Human Resources, Michael Ready
Tel: 902-569-0549
Fax: 902-368-4224
mcready@gov.pe.ca

Health System Planning & Development Division
Sullivan Bldg., 16 Fitzroy St., 3rd Fl., PO Box 2000Charlottetown, PE C1A 7N8
The Health System Planning & Development Division supports the Department of Health & Wellness. It includes the Health Recruitment & Retention section.
Acting Director, Kevin Barnes, CA
Tel: 902-368-4865
Fax: 902-368-4224
kcbarnes@gov.pe.ca
Manager, Health Recruitment & Retention, Marney MacRae
Tel: 902-620-3874
Fax: 902-620-3875
mjmacrae@gov.pe.ca
Manager, Policy & Planning, FPT Relations & FOIPP Coordinator, Shaun MacNeill
Tel: 902-368-6117
Fax: 902-368-4224
smacneill@gov.pe.ca
Coordinator, Physician Recruitment, Sheila MacLean
Tel: 902-368-6302
Fax: 902-620-3875
smmaclean@gov.pe.ca
Consultant, Pharmacy, Roy Cairns
Tel: 902-368-4907
Fax: 902-368-4905
brcairns@gov.pe.ca
Consultant, Dietetic Services, Diane M. Clow
Tel: 902-368-6262
Fax: 902-569-7656
mdclow@ihis.org
Consultant, Community Care Facilities & Nursing Homes, Mary P. MacSwain
Tel: 902-368-4953
Fax: 902-569-7656
mpmacswain@ihis.org
Legislative Specialist, Nichola M. Hewitt
Tel: 902-368-6681
Fax: 902-620-3081
nmhewitt@gov.pe.ca

Sport, Recreation, & Healthy Living Division
Shaw Bldg., 105 Rochford St. North, 4th Fl., PO Box 2000Charlottetown, PE
www.teampei.ca
The main role of the Sport, Recreation & Healthy Living Division is to encourage citizens of Prince Edward Island to be active. Sport, recreation, & other physical activities are promoted. Consultation services & grants are available for community, regional, & provincial groups.
Director, John Morrison
Tel: 902-894-0283
Fax: 902-368-4224
jwmorris@gov.pe.ca
Officer, Health Promotion & Chronic Disease Prevention, Laraine Poole
Tel: 902-368-4926
Fax: 902-620-3081
lfpoole@gov.pe.ca
Coordinator, Healthy Living, Mary Acorn
Tel: 902-368-6523
Fax: 902-620-3081
mracorn@gov.pe.ca
Coordinator, Central Region, Francois R. Caron
Tel: 902-432-2706
Fax: 902-888-8023
frcaron@gov.pe.ca
Coordinator, Eastern Region, Neil A. Kinsman
Tel: 902-687-7041
Fax: 902-368-4224
nakinsman@gov.pe.ca
Coordinator, Healthy Living, Nancy Malcolm-Sharratt
Tel: 902-368-4955
Fax: 902-368-6136
nmsharratt@gov.pe.ca
Coordinator, Amateur Sport, Lewis R. Page
Tel: 902-368-4783
Fax: 902-368-4224
lrpage@gov.pe.ca
Coordinator, Western Region, Joanne P. Wallace
Tel: 902-859-8861
Fax: 902-859-8709
jpwallace@gov.pe.ca

Health PEI

PO Box 2000Charlottetown, PE C1A 7N8
Tel: 902-368-6130
Fax: 902-368-6136

healthinput@gov.pe.ca
www.healthpei.ca
twitter.com/Health_PEI
When the Health Services Act was proclaimed in 2010, Health PEI took on responsibility for the operation & delivery of health services in the province.
The main goals of Health PEI are to improve access to quality health care across Prince Edward Island & to develop more consistent standards & practices for health services

Chair, Leo Steven
Tel: 902-368-5810
Fax: 902-368-5835
lsteven@gov.pe.ca

Interim Chief Executive Officer, Dr. Richard Wedge
Tel: 902-368-4935
Fax: 902-368-4974
rhwedge@gov.pe.ca

Vice-Chair, Gordon MacKay

Administrative Assistant, Barb Buell
Tel: 902-368-4637
Fax: 902-368-4974
healthpeiboard@gov.pe.ca

Community Hospitals & Primary Health Care Division
16 Garfield St., 1st Fl., PO Box 2000Charlottetown, PE C1A 6A5
Tel: 902-368-6157
Fax: 902-569-0579
Executive Director, Community Hospitals & Primary Health Care, Deborah Bradley
Tel: 902-368-6157
Fax: 902-569-0579
mdbradley@gov.pe.ca
Director, Primary Care Networks & Chronic Desease Prevention & Management, Marilyn A. Barrett
Tel: 902-569-7640
Fax: 902-569-0579
mabarrett@gov.pe.ca
Director, Public Health Programs, Kathy Jones
Tel: 902-894-0247
Fax: 902-569-0579
kljones@gov.pe.ca
Director, Mental Health & Addictions, Margaret Kennedy
Tel: 902-368-6197
Fax: 902-569-0579
mmkennedy@gov.pe.ca
Administrator, Community Hospitals East, Terry S. Campbell
Tel: 902-687-7150
Fax: 902-687-7175
tscampbell@gov.pe.ca
Administrator, Community Hospitals West, Cathy D. DesRoches
Tel: 902-853-8660
cddesroches@gov.pe.ca
Manager, Chronic Disease Prevention & Management, Pat Charlton
Tel: 902-368-6721
Fax: 902-368-6936
pccharlton@gov.pe.ca
Senior Dental Consultant, Dental Health Program, Dr. Albert O. Adegbembo
Tel: 902-368-4915
Fax: 902-368-4922
aoadegbembo@gov.pe.ca

Corporate Development & Innovation Division
16 Garfield St., 2nd Fl., PO Box 2000Charlottetown, PE C1A 6A5
Tel: 902-368-4927
Fax: 902-368-4969
Executive Director, Pamela Trainor
Tel: 902-368-5804
Fax: 902-368-4969
pjtrainor@gov.pe.ca
Director, Quality & Access Management, Joanne Donahoe
Tel: 902-368-5815
Fax: 902-368-4969
jmdonahoe@gov.pe.ca
Director, Human Resources, Karen MacDonald
Tel: 902-368-6257
Fax: 902-368-4969
karenmacdonald@gov.pe.ca
Director, Strategy & Performance; Manager, Planning & Evaluation, Una Hassenstein
Tel: 902-368-4932
Fax: 902-368-4969
uehassenstein@gov.pe.ca
Manager, Communications, Brad Chatfield
Tel: 902-368-6135
Fax: 902-368-4969
bpchatfield@gov.pe.ca
Lead, Organizational Development, Garth Waite
Tel: 902-368-5806
Fax: 902-368-4969
glwaite@gov.pe.ca

Financial Services Division
16 Garfield St., 1st Fl., PO Box 2000Charlottetown, PE C1A 6A5
Tel: 902-368-6196
Fax: 902-368-6136
Executive Director, Denise Lewis Fleming
Tel: 902-368-6125
Fax: 902-368-6136
dmlewis@gov.pe.ca
Director, Fiscal Planning, Analysis, & Audit, Kellie C. Hawes
Tel: 902-569-0506
Fax: 902-368-6136
kchawes@ihis.org
Director, Materials Management, Todd Gillis
Tel: 902-894-2097
Fax: 902-894-2384
gtgillis@ihis.org
Comptroller, Business Office, Pat G. Ryan
Tel: 902-368-4921
Fax: 902-368-6136
pgryan@gov.pe.ca
Manager, Medicare Services, Charles Allan
Tel: 902-838-0931
Fax: 902-838-0940
cballen@ihis.org

Health Information Management Division
16 Garfield St., 1st Fl., PO Box 2000Charlottetown, PE C1A 6A5
Tel: 902-368-4637
Fax: 902-368-6136
The Health Information Management Division oversees the following areas: eHealth implementation; eHealth operations; eHealth strategy; health information; IM & IT planning; & privacy & information access.
Executive Director, Liam Whitty
Tel: 902-620-3165
Fax: 902-368-6136
lwhitty@gov.pe.ca
Project Manager, iEHR & eHealth Project Implementation, Brenda Campbell
Tel: 902-368-6517
Fax: 902-620-3061
bccampbell@gov.pe.ca
Manager, Health Information, Vacant
Coordinator, Privacy & Information Access, Marina Fay
Tel: 902-368-4942
Fax: 902-368-4969
mafay@ihis.org
Information Technology Architect, Jackie Irwin
Tel: 902-620-3229
Fax: 902-368-6136
jirwin@gov.pe.ca
Information Technology Architect, Trevor Waugh
Tel: 902-894-2463
Fax: 902-894-2279
tawaugh@gov.pe.ca

Home-Based & Long-Term Care Division
16 Garfield St., 1st Fl., PO Box 2000Charlottetown, PE C1A 6A5
Tel: 902-894-0337
Fax: 902-368-6136
Executive Director, Cecil Villard
Tel: 902-894-0337
Fax: 902-368-6136
cfvillard@gov.pe.ca
Director, Home Care, Mary Sullivan
Tel: 902-888-8005
Fax: 902-432-2610
mksullivan@gov.pe.ca
Administrator, Long Term Care, East, Jean Fallis
Tel: 902-838-0643
Fax: 902-838-5294
njfallis@gov.pe.ca
Administrator, Long Term Care, East Prince, Gayle Lamont
Tel: 902-888-8350
Fax: 902-888-8369
gdlamont@gov.pe.ca
Administrator, Long Term Care, Queens, Andrew MacDougall
Tel: 902-368-5773
Fax: 902-368-6764
asmacdougall@gov.pe.ca
Administrator, Long Term Care, West Prince, John Martin
Tel: 902-859-8734
Fax: 902-859-8774
jmartin@gov.pe.ca
Coordinator, Provincial Geriatric Services, Elaine Campbell
Tel: 902-432-2861
Fax: 902-432-2859
eecampbell@ihis.org
Coordinator, Renal Program, Lanea Harris
Consultant, Seniors' Mental Health Services, Debye Macdonald Connolly
Tel: 902-368-4602
Fax: 902-368-6136
damacdonald-connolly@ihis.org

Medical Affairs Division
16 Garfield St., 2nd Fl., PO Box 2000Charlottetown, PE C1A 6A5
Tel: 902-368-6261
Fax: 902-620-3072
Executive Director, Medical Affairs, Dr. Richard Wedge
Tel: 902-368-6261
Fax: 902-620-3072
rhwedge@gov.pe.ca
PHC Medical Director, Summerside, Dr. Andre Celliers
acelliers@ihis.org
PHC Medical Director, Kings, Dr. David Hambly
jdhambly@ihis.org
PHC Medical Director, Queens (East & West), Dr. Alf Morais
Tel: 902-569-7625
Fax: 902-620-3072
jamorais@ihis.org
Manager, Physician Services, Johanne Irwin
Tel: 902-368-6736
Fax: 902-620-3072
jcirwin@gov.pe.ca

Prince County Hospital (PCH)
65 Boates Ave., PO Box 3000Summerside, PE C1N 2A9
Tel: 902-438-4510
Fax: 902-438-4381
www.healthpei.ca/pch
Executive Director, Prince County Hospital, Arlene Gallant-Bernard
Tel: 902-438-4514
Fax: 902-438-4381
algallant-bernard@gov.pe.ca
Director, Hospital Services, Cynthia Bryanton
Tel: 902-438-4519
Fax: 902-438-4381
clbryanton@gov.pe.ca
Director, Administration & Support Services, Margie Kays
Tel: 902-438-4530
Fax: 902-438-4381
mrkays@gov.pe.ca
Director, Medical Services, Dr. Wassim Salamoun
Tel: 902-438-4518
Fax: 902-438-4381
wsalamoun@ihis.org
Director, Nursing Services, Brenda Worth
Tel: 902-438-4516
Fax: 902-438-4381
baworth@gov.pe.ca
Coordinator, Physician Services, Kelly Waite
Tel: 902-438-4518
Fax: 902-438-4381
kdwaite@ihis.org

Provincial Clinical Services Division
16 Garfield St., 3rd Fl., PO Box 2000Charlottetown, PE C1A 6A5
Tel: 902-569-7768
Fax: 902-368-5444
Executive Director, Jamie MacDonald
Tel: 902-894-2277

Fax: 902-894-2276
jamiemacdonald@ihis.org
Director, Provincial Laboratory Services, Bill Bylhouwer
Tel: 902-894-2064
Fax: 902-894-2385
bjbylhouwer@ihis.org
Director, Provincial Diagnostic Imaging Services, Theresa Callaghan
Tel: 902-894-2979
Fax: 902-894-2416
tkcallaghan@gov.pe.ca
Director, Provincial Pharmacy Services, Iain Smith
Tel: 902-894-2024
idsmith@gov.pe.ca
Manager, Provincial Pharmacare Program, Faye E. Campbell
Tel: 902-368-6338
Fax: 902-368-4905
fecampbell@ihis.org
Manager, Emergency Health Services, Alan Toombs
Tel: 902-368-6719
Fax: 902-368-6136
altoombs@gov.pe.ca
Coordinator, Pharmaceutical Information Program, Vacant

Queen Elizabeth Hospital
60 Riverside Dr., PO Box 6600Charlottetown, PE C1A 8T5
Tel: 902-894-2351
Fax: 902-894-2416
TTY: 902-894-2204
www.healthpei.ca/qeh
Executive Director, Rick Adams
Tel: 902-894-2351
Fax: 902-894-2416
radams@gov.pe.ca
Director, Nursing Services, Marion H. Dowling
Tel: 902-894-2356
Fax: 902-894-2926
mhdowling@gov.pe.ca
Director, Medical Services, Dr. Rosemary Henderson
Tel: 902-894-2411
Fax: 902-894-2416
rfhenderson@gov.pe.ca
Director, Hospital Services, Kelley Rayner
Tel: 902-894-2364
Fax: 902-894-0138
kjrayner@gov.pe.ca
Director, Support Services, David J. White
Tel: 902-894-2353
Fax: 902-894-2416
jdwhite@gov.pe.ca

Prince Edward Island Department of Innovation & Advanced Learning (IAL)

Shaw Bldg., 105 Rochford St., 5th Fl., PO Box 2000Charlottetown, PE C1A 7N8
Tel: 902-368-4240
Fax: 902-368-4242
www.gov.pe.ca/ial
The role of Prince Edward Island's Department of Innovation & Advanced Learning is to manage the implementation of The Island Prosperity Strategy, A Focus for Change. This is the provincial government's economic strategy. It is the goal of the government to improve post-secondary opportunities for Islanders to ensure a strong workforce prepared for the present economy.

Minister, Hon. Allen F. Roach
allen.roach@liberal.pe.ca
Social Media: www.facebook.com/allen.roach.127

Deputy Minister, Melissa MacEachern
Tel: 902-368-4250
Fax: 902-368-5277
mamaceachern@gov.pe.ca

Communications Officer, Amber Caseley
Tel: 902-620-3774
Fax: 902-368-4242
amcaseley@gov.pe.ca

Associated Agencies, Boards & Commissions:

• **Anne of Green Gables Licensing Authority Inc.**
94 Euston St.
PO Box 910
Charlottetown, PE C1A 7L9
Tel: 902-569-7787
Fax: 902-368-6301
kobaker@gov.pe.ca; aggla@bellnet.ca
Other Communication: Toronto Office, Phone: 416-971-7473
The Anne of Green Gables Licensing Authority Inc. controls the use of Anne of Green Gables & related trademarks, protects the integrity of Anne images, & preserves the legacy of L.M. Montgomery & her works. The authority is jointly owned by the Province of Prince Edward Island, Ruth Macdonald, & David Macdonald.

• **BIO|FOOD|TECH**
101 Belvedere Ave.
PO Box 2000
Charlottetown, PE C1A 7N8
Tel: 902-368-5548
Fax: 902-368-5549
Toll-free: 877-368-5548
biofoodtech@biofoodtech.ca
www.biofoodtech.ca
Formerly known as the PEI Food Technology Centre, BIO|FOOD|TECH operates as a contract research & analytical services company. It serves companies & entrepreneurs in the food & bioprocessing sectors.
Executive Director, James (Jim) Smith, PhD, MBA, FIFST
Tel: 902-368-5548
Fax: 902-368-5549
jsmith@gov.pe.ca
Manager, Laboratory; Senior Microbiologist, Ebo Budu-Amoako, PhD
Tel: 902-368-5769
Fax: 902-368-5549
ebamoako@gov.pe.ca
Manager, Food & Bioscience Technology, Edward A. Charter, Ph.D.
Tel: 902-368-5912
Fax: 902-368-5549
eacharter@gov.pe.ca
Project Secretary, Administration & Building Services, Karen Devine
Tel: 902-368-5146
Fax: 902-368-5549
kadevine@gov.pe.ca

• **Charlottetown Area Development Corporation (CADC)**
4 Pownal St.
PO Box 786
Charlottetown, PE C1A 7L9
Tel: 902-892-5341
Fax: 902-368-1935
www.cadcpei.com
The Charlottetown Area Development Corporation operates as a self-financed entity that aims to attract private sector development to the Greater Charlottetown area. To carry out its work, the Charlottetown Area Development Corporation partners with the Province of Prince Edward Island, the City of Charlottetown, & the Town of Stratford.
General Manager, Ron Waite
rwaite@cadcpei.com
Manager, Properties, Wade Arsenault
warsenault@cadcpei.com
Manager, Parking, Susan Connell
sconnell@cadcpei.com
Comptroller, George Brammer
gbrammer@cadcpei.com
Landscape Architect, Ernie Morello
emorello@cadcpei.com

• **Charlottetown Civic Centre Management Inc.**
46 Kensington Rd.
Charlottetown, PE C1A 5H7
Tel: 902-629-6600
Fax: 902-629-6650
www.civiccentre.pe.ca
The Charlottetown Civic Centre is a multi-purpose facility.
General Manager, Dave McGrath
Tel: 902-629-6618
gm@civiccentre.pe.ca
Manager, Operations, Stu Dunn
Tel: 902-629-6621
sdunn@civiccentre.pe.ca

• **Innovation PEI**
94 Euston St.
PO Box 910
Charlottetown, PE C1A 7L9
Tel: 902-368-6300
Fax: 902-368-6301
Toll-free: 800-563-3734
innovation@gov.pe.ca
www.innovationpei.com
Innovation PEI strives to advance economic development in Prince Edward Island. It promotes small business development, business improvement, employment creation, research, innovation, market access, & trade. Through the Island Prosperity Strategy, Innovation PEI focuses upon the following sectors: renewable energy, aerospace, information technology, & bioscience.

• **Island Investment Development Inc. (IIDI)**
94 Euston St., 2nd Fl.
Charlottetown, PE C1A 7M8
Tel: 902-620-3628
Fax: 902-368-5886
peinominee@gov.pe.ca
www.gov.pe.ca/immigration; www.opportunitiespei.ca
The Island Investment Development Inc. is a crown corporation. Its business name is Immigration Services. The organization oversees the Prince Edward Island Provincial Nominee Program.

• **Prince Edward Island Lending Agency**
Homburg Financial Tower
98 Fitzroy St., 2nd Fl.
Charlottetown, PE C1A 1R7
Tel: 902-368-6200
Fax: 902-368-6201
Assistance is provided by the Lending Agency to new & growing businesses. Loans are available for organizations with export potential in the following industries: agriculture, fisheries & aquaculture, tourism, manufacturing & processing, information technology, & small business.
Chief Executive Officer, Peter Wilson
Tel: 902-368-6211
Fax: 902-620-3011
pawilson@gov.pe.ca
Account Manager, Fisheries & Aquaculture, Don Aitken
Tel: 902-368-6207
Fax: 902-368-6201
dcaitken@gov.pe.ca
Account Manager, Agriculture, Kelly R. MacDonald
Tel: 902-368-6240
Fax: 902-368-6201
krmacdonald@gov.pe.ca
Account Manager, Small Business & Tourism, Information Technology, Manufacturing, & Processing, Peter Whitlock
Tel: 902-368-6223
Fax: 902-368-6201
pgwhitlock@gov.pe.ca
Officer, Finance, Melissa Rennie
Tel: 902-569-7677
Fax: 902-368-6201
mrennie@gov.pe.ca

• **Summerside Regional Development Corporation Ltd. (SRDC)**
268 Water St.
Summerside, PE C1N 1B6
Tel: 902-436-2246
Fax: 902-436-9269
www.summersidewaterfront.com
Formerly known as the Summerside Waterfront Development Corporation, the Summerside Regional Development Corporation works to facilitate economic development in Summerside & the surrounding region. Shareholders of the corporation include the Province of Prince Edward Island, the City of Summerside, & the Greater Summerside Development Inc.

Economic, Trade, Policy & Strategy
Shaw Bldg., 105 Rochford St., 5th Fl., PO Box 2000Charlottetown, PE C1A 7N8
Secretary, Sandy Stewart
Tel: 902-368-4505
Fax: 902-368-4242
swstewart@gov.pe.ca
Director, Strategic Initiatives, Dan Campbell
Tel: 902-620-3357
Fax: 902-368-6118
dmcampbell@gov.pe.ca
Director, Policy & Strategy, Jane Mallard
Tel: 902-569-7556
Fax: 902-368-4252
jmallard@gov.pe.ca
Director, Trade & Economic Policy, Kal Whitnell
Tel: 902-368-4228
Fax: 902-368-4242
kbwhitnell@gov.pe.ca

Officer, Policy & Strategy, Erin Docherty
Tel: 902-368-5127
Fax: 902-368-4242
ecdocherty@gov.pe.ca

Finance & Administration Division
105 Rochford St., PO Box 2000Charlottetown, PE C1A 7N8
Tel: 902-368-5878
Fax: 902-368-7087
Responsibilities include financial management, administration, the Prince Edward Island Business Development Inc., & human resource management.

Post-Secondary & Continuing Education
Atlantic Technology Centre, #212, 90 University Ave., 2nd Fl., Charlottetown, PE C1A 4K9
Director, Susan A. MacKenzie
Tel: 902-368-4615
Fax: 902-368-6144
samackenzie@gov.pe.ca
Manager, Student Financial Services, Vacant
Manager, Apprenticeship Training, Susan LeFort
Tel: 902-368-4625
Fax: 902-368-6144
sflefort@gov.pe.ca
Manager, Literacy Secretariat, Barbara Macnutt
Tel: 902-368-6286
Fax: 902-368-6144
bemacnutt@edu.pe.ca
Senior Officer, Financial Services, Barry Gosby, CMA
Tel: 902-368-4897
Fax: 902-368-6144
bbgosby@gov.pe.ca
Apprenticeship Officer, Roger MacInnis
Tel: 902-368-4461
Fax: 902-368-6144
rjmacinnis@edu.pe.ca
Coordinator, Youth Apprenticeship, Paula MacKay
Tel: 902-368-4463
Fax: 902-368-4463
pamackay@gov.pe.ca

SkillsPEI
Atlantic Technology Centre, #212, 90 University Ave., Charlottetown, PE C1A 4K9
Tel: 902-368-6290
Fax: 902-368-6340
Toll-Free: 877-491-4766
www.skillspei.com
Skills PEI manages the delivery of training & skills development programs. The programming is funded by the Labour Market Agreement & the Canada-Prince Edward Island Labour Market Development Agreement. Examples of programs include Training PEI, Employ PEI, Self Employ PEI, Community Internship, Immigrant Work Experience, & Labour Market Partnerships. SkillsPEI offices are located across Prince Edward Island.
Director, Birt MacKinnon
Tel: 902-368-4244
Fax: 902-368-6580
bwmackinnon@gov.pe.ca
Director, Labour Market Unit, Scot MacDonald
Tel: 902-368-6521
Fax: 902-368-6340
dsmacdonald@gov.pe.ca
Manager, Service Delivery, Kings & Queens County, Blair Aitken
Tel: 902-368-4178
Fax: 902-368-6580
abaitken@gov.pe.ca
Manager, Service Delivery, Prince County, Mary Hunter
Tel: 902-438-4110
Fax: 902-438-4096
mehunter@gov.pe.ca
Manager, Labour Mobility, Jeannie Pitts
Tel: 902-368-5825
Fax: 902-368-6340
jpitts@gov.pe.ca
Coordinator, Provincial Employment, Heather Berrigan
Tel: 902-368-5908
Fax: 902-368-5909
heberrigan@gov.pe.ca
Coordinator, Marketing, Passport to Employment Program, Yvonne Doyle
Tel: 902-620-3857
Fax: 902-368-5909
ymdoule@gov.pe.ca
Coordinator, Passport to Employment Program, Maitland MacIsaac
Tel: 902-368-4466
Fax: 902-368-5909
mamacisaac@gov.pe.ca
Coordinator, Foreign Qualifications Recognition Project, Rebecca Murphy
Tel: 902-620-3082
Fax: 902-368-6340
romurphy@gov.pe.ca

Prince Edward Island Regulatory & Appeals Commission (IRAC) / Commission de réglementation et d'appels

National Bank Tower, #501, 134 Kent St., PO Box 577Charlottetown, PE C1A 7L1
Tel: 902-892-3501
Fax: 902-566-4076
Toll-Free: 800-501-6268
info@irac.pe.ca
www.irac.pe.ca
Prince Edward Island's Regulatory & Appeals Commission was established in 1991, with the amalgamation of the Office of the Director of Residential Property, the Public Utilities Commission, & the Land Use Commission.
Operating under the authority of the Island Regulatory & Appeals Commission Act, the Regulatory & Appeals Commission works at arms-length from the provincial government to administer statutes dealing with economic regulation. The quasi-judicial tribunal also listens to appeals dealing with property & revenue sales tax, land use, & unsightly premises.
The Regulatory & Appeals Commission reports to the Legislative Assembly of Prince Edward Island through the Minister of Education & Early Childhood Development.

Chair & Chief Executive Officer, F. Maurice (Moe) Rodgerson

Vice-Chair, Allan Rankin

Full-time Commissioner, John Broderick

Director, Land, Corporate & Appellate Services Division, Eileen Callaghan
mecallaghan@irac.pe.ca

Director, Residential Rental Property, Cathy Flanagan
cflanagan@irac.pe.ca

Director, Technical & Regulatory Services Division, Allison MacEwen
amacewen@irac.pe.ca

Prince Edward Island Department of Transportation & Infrastructure Renewal (TIR)

Jones Bldg., 11 Kent St., 3rd Fl., PO Box 2000Charlottetown, PE C1A 7N8
Tel: 902-368-5100
Fax: 902-368-5395
www.gov.pe.ca/tir
Prince Edward Island's Department of Transportation & Infrastructure Renewal maintains & enhances transportation systems & services throughout the province to ensure the safe & efficient movement of people, goods, & services.
The department also works to provide necessary infrastructure for the efficient operation of government. The department is therefore involved in crown land management & building construction & maintenance.
Acts Administered:
Closing of Roads Regulations
Highway Access Regulations
Public Utility Easement (Fees) Regulation
Vehicle Weights & Dimensions Regulations

Minister, Hon. Robert S. Vessey
Tel: 902-368-4801
Fax: 902-368-5277
rsvessey@gov.pe.ca

Deputy Minister, Brian Douglas
Tel: 902-368-5130
Fax: 902-368-5385
bwdouglas@gov.pe.ca

Communications Officer, Mary Moszynski
Tel: 902-368-5112
Fax: 902-368-5385
mamoszynski@gov.pe.ca

Associated Agencies, Boards & Commissions:
- **100099 P.E.I. Inc.**
- **C.V.C. Management Inc.**
- **Crown Building Corporation**
- **Island Waste Management Corporation (IWMC)**
110 Watts Ave.
Charlottetown, PE C1E 2C1
Tel: 902-894-0330
Fax: 902-894-0331
Toll-free: 888-280-8111
info@iwmc.pe.ca
www.iwmc.pe.ca
Other Communication: Customer Service Fax: 902-882-0520
The Island Waste Management Corporation is a provincial Crown Corporation that was formed in 1999, according to the Environmental Act R.S.P.E.I. 1988, Cap. E-9. Conducting business throughout Prince Edward Island, the corporation administers & provides solid waste management services to both commercial & residential sectors.
One of the Island Waste Management Corporation's successful environmental programs is Waste Watch. Everyone in Prince Edward Island must separate waste into one of three categories: compost, marketable recyclable material, & waste. Waste Watch Drop-Off Centres also accept household hazardous waste free of charge.
In addition to operating the Waste Watch Drop-Off Centres, the Island Waste Management Corporation also operates or oversees the following facilities: Central Compost Facility, East Prince Waste Management Facility, & the Energy from Waste Facility.
Chair, Mark McLane
Chief Executive Officer, Gerry Moore
Tel: 902-894-0333
Fax: 902-894-0331
gmoore@iwmc.pe.ca
- **Land Surveyors Board of Examiners**

Capital Projects Division
Jones Bldg., 11 Kent St., 3rd Fl., Charlottetown, PE C1A 7N8
Tel: 902-368-5180
Fax: 902-368-5425
The following sections make up the Capital Projects Division: Engineering Services; Highway Construction; Materials Lab; & Planning & Design. Staff take care of the design & construction of highways & building infrastructure.
Director & Chief Engineer, Stephen J. Yeo, P.Eng.
Tel: 902-368-5105
Fax: 902-368-5425
sjyeo@gov.pe.ca
Senior Manager, Materials Lab, Terry Kelly, P.Eng.
Tel: 902-676-7979
Fax: 902-676-7994
jtkelly@gov.pe.ca
Manager, Design & Bridge Maintenance, Darrell Evans, P.Eng.
Tel: 902-569-0578
Fax: 902-368-5395
djevans@gov.pe.ca
Manager, Engineering Services, Dan MacDonald
Tel: 902-368-5158
Fax: 902-368-5425
wdmacdonald@gov.pe.ca
Manager, Traffic Data Collection & Analysis, Orooba H. Mohammed
Tel: 902-368-5107
Fax: 902-368-5425
ohmohammed@gov.pe.ca
Engineer, Traffic Operations, Alan Aitken, P.Eng.
Tel: 902-368-5006
Fax: 902-368-5425
aaaitken@gov.pe.ca
Regional Engineer, Eastern Highway Construction, Matt Collins, P.Eng.
Tel: 902-652-8998
Fax: 902-652-8981
mscollins@gov.pe.ca
Regional Engineer, Western Highway Construction, Mark Sherren, P.Eng.
Tel: 902-368-6195
Fax: 902-368-5425
mesherren@gov.pe.ca

Finance & Human Resources Division
Jones Bldg., 11 Kent St., 2nd Fl., Charlottetown, PE C1A 7N8

Tel: 902-368-5100
Fax: 902-368-5395
The fiscal matters & human resources issues of the Department of Transportation & Infrastructure Renewal are handled by the Finance & Human Resources Division.
Director, Finance & Human Resource Division, Wendy L. MacDonald, CA
Tel: 902-368-5126
Fax: 902-368-5395
wlmacdonald@gov.pe.ca
Manager, Human Resources, Anne MacAulay
Tel: 902-620-3356
Fax: 902-894-0368
ammacaulay@gov.pe.ca
Manager, Finance, Vacant

Highway Maintenance Division
Park St. & Riverside Dr. Provincial Headquarters, PO Box 2000Charlottetown, PE C1A 7N8
Tel: 902-368-5090
Fax: 902-368-6244
The Highway Maintenance Division is responsible for the upkeep of the total provincial highway system.
Director, Darren Chaisson, P.Eng
Tel: 902-368-5103
Fax: 902-368-6244
ddchaisson@gov.pe.ca
Manager, Light Fleet, Mechanical Branch, Tina L. Lowther
Tel: 902-368-4758
Fax: 902-368-5994
tllowther@gov.pe.ca
Manager, Fleet, Mechanical Branch, Wilfred J. MacDonald
Tel: 902-368-5222
Fax: 902-368-5994
wjmacdonald@gov.pe.ca
Manager, Inventory Control, Provincial Headquarters, Robert A. MacKinnon
Tel: 902-368-4746
Fax: 902-368-6244
ramackinnon@gov.pe.ca
Superintendent, Western Highway Maintenance, Mike Berrigan
Tel: 902-888-8282
Fax: 902-888-8291
mjberrigan@gov.pe.ca
Superintendent, Central Highway Maintenance, Gordie Lund
Tel: 902-368-5172
Fax: 902-368-6244
gllund@gov.pe.ca
Superintendent, Eastern Highway Maintenance, Gerard F. Morrison
Tel: 902-652-8971
Fax: 902-652-8978
gfmorrison@gov.pe.ca

Highway Safety Division
33 Riverside Dr., Charlottetown, PE C1A 9R9
Tel: 902-368-5228
Fax: 902-368-5236
Safety issues from the province's highways are handled by the Highway Safety Division.
Director, John B. MacDonald
Tel: 902-368-5225
Fax: 902-368-5236
jbmacdonald@gov.pe.ca
Registrar, Highway Safety Operations, Graham L. Miner
Tel: 902-368-5223
Fax: 902-368-5236
glminer@gov.pe.ca
Coordinator, Safety, Doug J. MacEwen
Tel: 902-368-5219
Fax: 902-368-5236
djmacewen@gov.pe.ca

Infrastructure Division
#303, 75 Fitzroy St., PO Box 2000Charlottetown, PE C1A 7N8
Fax: 902-620-3383
Toll-Free: 888-240-4411
cpei-infrastructure@gov.pe.ca
Infrastructure is a joint initiative between the Government of Prince Edward Island & the Government of Canada.
Provincial Manager, Darlene Rhodenizer
Tel: 902-368-6213
Fax: 902-620-3383
dlrhodenizer@gov.pe.ca
Federal Manager, Pat MacAulay
Tel: 902-368-0987
Fax: 902-620-3383
pat.macaulay@acoa-apeca.gc.ca
Provincial Project Officer, John Arsenault
Tel: 902-368-4882
Fax: 902-620-3383
jearsenault@gov.pe.ca
Federal Project Officer, Stacey Ward
Tel: 902-620-3380
Fax: 902-620-3383
stacey.ward@acoa-apeca.gc.ca
Director, Kim D. Horrelt
Tel: 902-620-3799
Fax: 902-368-5385
kdhorrelt@gov.pe.ca

Land & Environment Division
Jones Bldg., 11 Kent St., 3rd Fl., PO Box 2000Charlottetown, PE C1A 7N8
Tel: 902-368-5221
Fax: 902-368-5395
The Land & Environment Division is responsible for provincial lands. Environmental services are also provided by the Land & Environment Division for projects related to transportation & public works. Staff members ensure compliance with provincial & federal environmental legislation & regulations during highway construction & maintenance projects.
Director, Brian F. Thompson, P.Eng.
Tel: 902-368-5185
Fax: 902-368-5395
bfthompson@gov.pe.ca
Chief Surveyor, David R.J. Morris, P.Eng, PEILS, CLS
Tel: 902-368-5143
Fax: 902-620-3033
drjmorris@gov.pe.ca
Manager, Properties, Leo J. Creamer
Tel: 902-368-5134
Fax: 902-368-5395
jlcreamer@gov.pe.ca
Supervisor, Land Administration, Carol Craswell, BBA
Tel: 902-368-6119
Fax: 902-368-5395
cmcraswell@gov.pe.ca
Supervisor, Provincial Roads, Sharon N. Slauenwhite, BA
Tel: 902-368-6387
Fax: 902-368-5395
snslauenwhite@gov.pe.ca
Acting Environmental Coordinator, Shelley Cole-Arbing
Tel: 902-368-5095
Fax: 902-368-5395
slcole@gov.pe.ca

Public Works & Planning Division
Jones Bldg., 11 Kent St., 3rd Fl., Charlottetown, PE C1A 7N8
Tel: 902-368-5100
Fax: 902-368-5395
The Public Works & Planning Division is engaged in the following activities: analyzing long term transportation requirements; planning & designing construction projects; implementing major projects; & maintaining buildings.
Director, Alan Maynard, P.Eng.
Tel: 902-368-5147
Fax: 902-569-0590
aemaynard@gov.pe.ca
Provincial Manager, Infrastructure Secretariat, Darlene Rhodenizer
Tel: 902-368-6213
Fax: 902-620-3383
dlrhodenizer@gov.pe.ca
Manager, Policy & Planning, Paul Godfrey, P.Eng.
Tel: 902-368-4849
Fax: 902-569-0590
jpgodfrey@gov.pe.ca
Manager, General Services, Shawn Heron
Tel: 902-368-5116
Fax: 902-368-5395
sjheron@gov.pe.ca
Manager, Building Maintenance & Accommodation, Holly Hinds
Tel: 902-368-4854
Fax: 902-368-5395
hahinds@gov.pe.ca
Manager, Building Construction Contract Administration, Kevin Kennedy
Tel: 902-368-5148
Fax: 902-368-5395
kjkennedy@gov.pe.ca
Manager, Building Design & Construction, Tyler Richardson, P.Eng.
Tel: 902-368-4249
Fax: 902-569-0590
ttrichardson@gov.pe.ca
Assistant Manager, Building Maintenance, Central Region, Keith Peters
Tel: 902-368-5128
Fax: 902-368-5395
kjpeters@gov.pe.ca

Prince Edward Island Workers Compensation Board (WCB)

14 Weymouth St., PO Box 757Charlottetown, PE C1A 7L7
Tel: 902-368-5680
Fax: 902-368-5696
Toll-Free: 800-237-5049
www.wcb.pe.ca
Other Communication: Customer Liaison Service, Toll-Free Phone: 1-866-460-3074; Employer Services, Fax: 902-368-5705
The Workers Compensation Board of Prince Edward Island operates as an independent, non-profit organization. Prince Edward Island employers provide funding for the board. Both workers & employers are served by the Workers Compensation Board through the promotion of workplace health & safety & the provision of workplace injury & illness insurance.
Acts Administered:
Occupational Health & Safety Act
Workers Compensation Act

Chief Executive Officer, Sharon Cameron
Tel: 902-368-5688
secameron@wcb.pe.ca

Director, Corporate Development, Bonnie Blakney
Tel: 902-620-3478
blblakney@wcb.pe.ca

Director, Client Services, Wendy McIsaac
Tel: 902-368-5687
wlmcisaac@wcb.pe.ca

Director, Occupational Health & Safety, Bill Reid
Tel: 902-368-5562
bkreid@wcb.pe.ca

Director, Corporate Services, Tammy Turner
Tel: 902-368-4102
teturner@wcb.pe.ca

Manager, Case Management, Dawn Bradley
Tel: 902-368-6044
dbradley@wcb.pe.ca

Manager, Employer Services, Greg MacCallum
Tel: 902-368-5679
ggmaccallum@wcb.pe.ca

Manager, Information Technology Services, Darren MacDonald
Tel: 902-368-5669
dpmacdonald@wcb.pe.ca

Manager, Intake & Entitlement, Kate Marshall
Tel: 902-368-6358
kmarshall@wcb.pe.ca

Manager, Human Resources, Luanne Gallant
Tel: 902-894-0315
lmgallant@wcb.pe.ca

Manager, Facilities & Procurement, Larry Phelan
Tel: 902-368-4091
ljphelan@wcb.pe.ca

Manager, OHS, Ian Rodd
Tel: 902-368-5575
ihrodd@wcb.pe.ca

Gouvernement du Québec / Government of Québec

Siege du gouvernement: Hôtel du Parlement, 1045, rue des Parlementaires, Québec, QC G1A 1A3

Tél: 418-643-7239
Téléc: 418-646-4271
Ligne sans frais: 866-337-8837
www.gouv.qc.ca; www.assnat.qc.ca
La Province de Québec est entrée dans la Confédération le 1ère juillet, 1867. Terre: 1,356,366.78 km2. Population: 7,903,001 (2011)
•
Président, Denis Marsolais

Ministère des Affaires municipales, des Régions et de l'Occupation du territoire / Municipal Affairs, Regions & Land Occupancy

Aile Chaveau, 10, rue Pierre-Olivier-Chauveau, 3e étage, Québec, QC G1R 4J3
Tél: 418-691-2019
Téléc: 418-643-7385
communications@mamrot.gouv.qc.ca
www.mamrot.gouv.qc.ca
A la charge de conseiller le gouvernement & d'assurer la coordination interministérielle dans ces domaines; a pour mission de favoriser la mise en place & le maintien d'un cadre de vie & de services municipaux de qualité pour des citoyens/citoyennes; le développement des régions & des milieux ruraux; & le progrès & le rayonnement de la métropole; intervient auprès des municipalités locales, régionales de comté, des communautés métropolitaines de Montréal & de Québec, & de l'administration régionale Kativik
Lois administrèes:
Code municipal du Québec
Loi concernant la réglementation municipale des édifices publics
Loi sur l'aménagement et l'urbanisme
Loi sur la Régie du logement
Loi sur la Société québécoise d'assainissement des eaux
Loi sur les abus préjudiciables à l'agriculture
Loi sur les cités et villes
Loi sur les conseils intermunicipaux de transport dans la région de Montréal
Loi sur les immeubles industriels municipaux
Loi sur les travaux municipaux

Ministre, L'hon. Sylvain Gaudreault
Tél: 418-691-2030
Téléc: 418-643-1795
ministre@mamrot.gouv.qc.ca

Sous-ministre, Sylvain Boucher
Tél: 418-691-2040
Téléc: 418-643-7708

Sous-ministre adjoint, Métropole, Claire Deronzier
Tél: 514-873-8395

Sous-ministre adjoint, Infrastructures & finances municipales, Frédéric Guay
Tél: 418-691-2040

Sous-ministre adjointe, Territoires, Linda Morin
Tél: 418-691-2040

Sous-ministre adjoint, Politiques, Jérôme Unterberg
Tél: 418-691-2040

Secrétariat général, Stéphanie Jourdain
Tél: 418-691-2040

Directeur, Affaires juridiques, Nicolas Paradis
Tél: 418-691-2022

Infrastructures et finances municipales / Infrastructures & Municipal Financing
Sous-ministre adjoint, Frédéric Guay
Tél: 418-691-2040
Directeur général, Infrastructures, Pierre Aubé
Tél: 418-691-2005
Directeur général, Finances municipales, Jean Monfet
Tél: 418-691-2007

Métropole / Metropolitan Regions
800, rue du Square-Victoria, bureau 2.17, CP 83Montréal, QC H4Z 1B7
Tél: 514-873-8246
Téléc: 514-864-7082
Sous-ministre adjoint, Claire Deronzier
Tél: 514-873-8395
Directeur, Développement régional & métropolitain, Hubert De Nicolini
Tél: 514-873-6992
Directrice métropolitaine, Aménagement et des affaires municipales, Lucie Tremblay
Tél: 514-873-8246

Politiques / Policy
Sous-ministre adjoint, Jérôme Unterberg
Tél: 418-691-2040
Directrice générale, Urbanisme/Aménagement du territoire, Marie-Lise Côté
Tél: 418-691-2015
Directrice générale, Politiques, Jocelyn Savoie
Tél: 418-691-2015 ext: 352

Services à la gestion / Administrative Services
Directeur général, Raymond Sarrazin
Tél: 418-691-2015
Directrice (par intérim), Ressources humaines/Performance organisationnelle, Kathleen Dumont
Tél: 418-691-2025
Directrice, Ressources financières et matérielles, Sylvie Plante
Tél: 418-691-2001

Territoires / Regions
Sous-ministre adjointe, Linda Morin
Tél: 418-691-2040
Directeur général, Information territoriale, Dominique Jodoin
Tél: 418-691-2088
Directrice générale, Affaires territoriales, Marie-Claude Samuel
Directeur, Géomatique, et de la statistique, Sylvain Goulet
Directeur, Économie numérique, Daniel Roberge
Directeur (par intérim), Régional, rural, et de l'économie sociale, Yannick Routhier
Tél: 418-691-2078
Abitibi-Témiscamingue
#105, 170, av Principale, 1er étage, Rouyn-Noranda, QC J9X 4P7
Tél: 819-763-3582
Téléc: 819-763-3803
dr.abitibi-temis@mamrot.gouv.qc.ca
Directeur, Denis Moffet
Tél: 519-763-3582
Bas-Saint-Laurent
337, rue Moreault, 2e étage, Rimouski, QC G5L 1P4
Tél: 418-727-3629
Téléc: 418-727-3537
dr.bas-st-laur@mamrot.gouv.qc.ca
Directeur, Gilles Julien
Tél: 418-727-3629
Capitale-Nationale
Aile Chauveau, 10, rue Pierre-Olivier-Chauveau, 3e étage, Québec, QC G1R 4J3
Tél: 418-691-2016
Téléc: 418-643-2206
dr.capnat@mamrot.gouv.qc.a
Directeur, Jean Dionne
Tél: 418-691-2060
Centre-du-Québec
le Chauveau, 62, rue Saint-Jean-Baptiste, #S-05, Québec, QC G6P 4E3
Tél: 819-752-2453
Téléc: 819-795-3673
dr.centre-quebec@mamrot.gouv.qc.a
Directeur, Gaétan Désilets
Tél: 819-752-2453
Chaudière-Appalaches
#102, 1100, boul Frontenac est, Thetford Mines, QC G6G 6H1
Tél: 418-338-4624
Téléc: 418-338-1908
dr.chaud-app@mamrot.gouv.qc.ca
Directrice, Danie Croteau
Tél: 418-338-4624
Côte-Nord
625, boul Laflèche, #RC-708, Baie-Comeau, QC G5C 1C5
Tél: 418-295-4241
Téléc: 418-295-4955
dr.cotenord@mamrot.gouv.qc.ca
Directeur, Jacques Tremblay
Tél: 418-295-4241
Estrie
#4.04, 200, rue Belvédère nord, Sherbrooke, QC J1H 4A9
Tél: 819-820-3244
Téléc: 819-820-3979
dr.estrie@mamrot.gouv.qc.ca
Directeur, Pierre Poulin
Tél: 819-820-3244
Gaspésie—Iles-de-la-Madeleine
#10B, 500, av Daigneault, Chandler, QC G0C 1K0
Tél: 418-689-5024
Téléc: 418-689-4823
dr.gaspe-ilesmad@mamrot.gouv.qc.ca
Directeur, Michel Gionest
Tél: 418-689-5024
Lanaudière
#3200, 40, rue Gauthier sud, Joliette, QC J6E 4J4
Tél: 450-752-8080
Téléc: 450-752-8087
dr.lanaudiere@mamrot.gouv.qc.ca
Directeur, Jean Ouellet
Tél: 450-752-8060
Laurentides
#210, 161, rue de la Gare, Saint-Jérôme, QC J7Z 2B9
Tél: 450-569-7646
Téléc: 450-569-3131
dr.laurentides@mamrot.gouv.qc.ca
Directeur, Jean Ouellet
Tél: 450-569-7646
Mauricie
#321, 100, rue Laviolette, 3e étage, Trois-Rivières, QC G9A 5S9
Tél: 819-371-6653
Téléc: 819-371-6953
dr.mauricie@mamrot.gouv.qc.ca
Directeur, Pierre Robert
Tél: 819-371-6653
Montérégie
#403, 201, place Charles-Le Moyne, Longueuil, QC J4K 2T5
Tél: 450-928-5670
Téléc: 450-928-5673
dr.monteregie@mamrot.gouv.qc.ca
Directeur, Robert Sabourin
Tél: 450-926-5670
Nord-du-Québec
#1, 215, 3e Rue, Chibougamau, QC G8P 1N3
Tél: 418-748-7737
Téléc: 418-748-7841
nord-du-quebec@mamrot.gouv.qc.ca
Directeur, Richard Leclerc
Tél: 418-748-7738
Outaouais
#9.300, 170, rue de l'Hôtel-de-Ville, Gatineau, QC J8X 4C2
Tél: 819-772-3006
Téléc: 819-772-3989
dr.outaouais@mamrot.gouv.qc.ca
Directeur (par intérim), Yannick Gignac
Tél: 819-772-3006
Saguenay—Lac-Saint-Jean
227, rue Racine est, #RC.03, Chicoutimi, QC G7H 7B4
Tél: 418-698-3523
Téléc: 418-698-3526
dr.sag-lac@mamrot.gouv.qc.ca
Directeur, Jean Dionne
Tél: 418-698-3523

Ministère de l'Agriculture, des Pêcheries et de l'Alimentation (MAPAQ) / Agriculture, Fisheries & Food

200, ch Sainte-Foy, Québec, QC G1R 4X6
Tél: 418-380-2110
Ligne sans frais: 888-222-6272
www.mapaq.gouv.qc.ca
www.youtube.com/user/mapaquebec
Le Ministère influence et appuie l'essor de l'industrie bioalimentaire québécoise dans une perspective de développement durable; réalise des interventions en production, transformation, commercialisation & consommation des produits agricoles, marins & alimentaires; & joue un rôle important en matière de recherche & de développement, d'enseignement & de formation
Lois administrèes:
Loi sur l'acquisition de terres agricoles par des non-résidants/An Act governing the acquisition of farm land by non-residents
Loi sur l'aquaculture commerciale/ An Act respecting commercial aquaculture
Loi sur l'assurance-récolte/Crop Insurance Act
Loi sur la commercialisation des produits marins/An Act respecting the marketing of marine products

Loi sur la conservation et la mise en valeur de la faune/An Act respecting the conservation & development of wildlife
Loi sur la protection des plantes/Plant Protection Act
Loi sur la protection sanitaire des animaux/Animal Health Protection Act
Loi sur le ministère de l'Agriculture, des Pêcheries et de l'Alimentation/An Act respecting the Ministère de l'Agriculture, des Pêcheries et de l'Alimentation
Loi sur les abus préjudiciables à l'agriculture/Agricultural Abuses Act
Loi sur les cités et villes/Cities & Towns Act (certain sections)
Loi sur les terres agricoles du domaine de l'État/An Act respecting agricultural lands in the domain of the state

Ministre, L'hon François Gendron
Tél: 418-380-2525
Téléc: 418-380-2184
ministre@mapaq.gouv.qc.ca

Sous-ministre, Norman Johnston

Agences, Conseils et Commissions Associés/ Associated Agencies, Boards & Commissions:

• Commission de protection du territoire agricole du Québec (CPTAQ) / Agricultural Land Preservation Commission
200, ch Ste-Foy, 2e étage
Québec, QC G1R 4X6
Tél: 418-643-3314
Téléc: 418-643-2261
Ligne sans frais: 800-667-5294
info@cptaq.gouv.qc.ca
www.cptaq.gouv.qc.ca
Présidente, Marie-Josée Gouin
• La financière agricole de Québec (FADQ) / Farm Financial Québec
1400, boul de la Rive-Sud
Saint-Romuald, QC G6W 8K7
Tél: 418-838-5602
Téléc: 418-833-3871
Ligne sans frais: 800-749-3646
financiereagricole@fadq.qc.ca
www.fadq.qc.ca
• Régie des marchés agricoles et alimentaires du Québec (RMAAQ) / Québec Agriculture & Food Marketing Board
201, boul Crémazie est, 5e étage
Montréal, QC H2M 1L3
Tél: 514-873-4024
Téléc: 514-873-3984
www.rmaaq.gouv.qc.ca
Présidente, Françoise Gauthier
Directeur générale, Yves Lapierre

Développement régional et développement durable / Regional Development/Sustainable Development
Sous-ministre adjoint, Michel Bonneau

Directions régionales/Regional Offices
Abitibi-Témiscamingue - Nord-du-Québec
#2.01, 180, boul Rideau, Rouyn-Noranda, QC J9X 1N9
Tél: 819-763-3287
Téléc: 819-763-3359
Directrice régionale, Line Charland
Bas-Saint-Laurent
335, rue Moreault, Rimouski, QC G5L 9C8
Tél: 418-727-3615
Téléc: 418-727-3967
Capitale Nationale
#RC.22, 1685, boul Wilfrid-Hamel ouest, Québec, QC G1N 3Y7
Tél: 418-643-0033
Téléc: 418-644-8263
Directrice régionale, Suzanne Pilote
Centre-du-Québec
460, boul Louis-Fréchette, 2e étage, Québec, QC J3T 1Y2
Tél: 819-293-8501
Téléc: 819-293-8446
Directeur régional, Luc Couture
Chaudière-Appalaches
#100, 675, route Cameron, Sainte-Marie, QC G6E 3V7
Tél: 418-386-8116
Téléc: 418-386-8345
castemarie@mapaq.gouv.qc.ca
Directrice régionale, Renée Caron
Estrie
Directeur régional, Alain Roy
Gaspésie—îles-de-la-Madeleine
34, boul Perron ouest, CP 524Caplan, QC G0C 1H0
Tél: 418-388-2282
Téléc: 418-388-2834
Ligne sans frais: 877-221-7038
dr11@mapaq.gouv.qc.ca
Directeur régional, Louis Bigaouette
Laurentides
#100, 617, boul Labelle, Blainville, QC J7C 2J1
Tél: 450-971-5110
Téléc: 450-971-5069
blainville@mapaq.gouv.qc.ca
Directeur régional (par intérim), Michel Boisclair
Mauricie
#102, 5195, boul des Forges, Trois-Rivières, QC G8Y 4Z3
Tél: 819-371-6761
Téléc: 819-371-6976
Ligne sans frais: 866-943-3012
dr04m@mapaq.gouv.qc.ca
Directeur régional, Norman Houle
Montérégie Est
#3300, 1355, rue Johnson ouest, Saint-Hyacinthe, QC J2S 8W7
Tél: 450-778-6530
Téléc: 450-778-6540
Directeur régional, Jean-Pierre Lessard
Montérégie Ouest
#201, 177, rue Saint-Joseph, Sainte-Martine, QC J0S 1V0
Tél: 450-427-2000
Téléc: 450-427-0407
Directeur régional, Robert Beaulieu
Montréal-Laval-Lanaudière
#1.01, 867, boul de l'Ange-Gardien, L'Assomption, QC J5W 1T3
Tél: 450-589-5781
Téléc: 450-589-7812
bureau.assomption@mapaq.gouv.qc.ca
Directeur régional, François Perron
Outaouais
Galeries de Buckingham, 999, rue Dollard, Local 01, Gatineau, QC J8L 3E6
Tél: 819-986-8544
Téléc: 819-986-9299
Directeur régional, Yves Lévesque
Saguenay—Lac-Saint-Jean
801, ch du Pont-Taché nord, Alma, QC G8B 5W2
Tél: 418-662-6457
Téléc: 418-668-8694
Ligne sans frais: 866-727-6584
Directeur régional, Sylvie Denis

Pêches et aquaculture commerciales / Commercial Fishing & Aquaculture
Sous-ministre adjointe, Michel Gagnon
Directeur, Analyses et politiques, Abdoul Aziz Niang
Directeur, Aquaculture et développement durable, Paul Morin

Directions régionales/Regional Offices
Côte-Nord
466, av Arnaud, Sept-îles, QC G4R 3B1
Tél: 418-964-8521
Téléc: 418-964-8744
drcn@mapag.gouv.qc.ca
Directeur régional, Alain Côté
Gaspésie
#205, 96, montée de Sandy Beach, Gaspé, QC G4X 2V6
Tél: 418-368-7630
Téléc: 418-360-8851
drg@mapaq.gouv.qc.ca
Directeur régional, Marcel Roussy
îles-de-la-Madeleine
Édifice Réjean-Richard, 101-125, ch du Parc, Cap-aux-Meules, QC G4T 1B3
Tél: 418-986-2098
Téléc: 418-986-4421
drim@mapaq.gouv.qc.ca
Directeur régional, Donald Arseneau

Institut de technologie agroalimentaire / Institute of Food Technology
Directrice général, Rosaire Ouellet
Directeur, Direction campus de Saint-Hyacinthe, Alain Couture
Directeur, Services administratifs, Joseé Garant
Directeur, Direction des études, Sylvain Gingras
Directeur, Direction campus de la Pocatière, Jean-Marc Tardiff

Politiques agroalimentaires / Food Policy
Sous-ministre adjoint, Bernard Verret
Directeur, Appui à la reschercge et à l'innovation, Claude Bernard
Directrice, Études et perspectives économiques, Hélène Boivin
Directeur, Planification et priorités stratégiques, Daniel Bouchard
Directrice, Politiques et analyses sectorielles, Hélène Brassard
Directeur (par intérim), Développement et initiatives économiques, Yvon Forest
Directeur, Politiques commerciales et intergouvernementales, Laval Poulin

Santé animale & inspection des aliments / Animal Health & Food Inspection
dgsaia@mapaq.gouv.qc.ca
Sous-ministre adjointe, Madeleine Fortin
Directeur, Inspection des aliments - Secteur Est et Ouest, Guy Caron
Directeur, Soutien à l'inspection, Michel Houle
Directrice, Coordination administrative et Services à la clientèle, Michèle Lavoie
Directrice, Laboratoire d'expertises, Ginette Levesque
#C 2.105, 2700, rue Einstein
Sainte-Foy, QC G1P 3W8 Canada

Transformation Alimentaire et des Marchés / Food Processing Québec
Sous-ministre associé, Dominique Fortin

Ministère de la Culture et Communications / Culture & Communications

225, Grande Allée est, Québec, QC G1R 5G5
Ligne sans frais: 888-380-8882
www.mcc.gouv.qc.ca
Lois administrèes:
Loi sur les musées nationaux

Ministre, L'hon. Maka Kotto
Tél: 418-380-2310
Téléc: 418-380-2311
ministre@mcc.gouv.qc.ca

Sous-ministre, Rachel Laperriere
Tél: 418-380-2330
Téléc: 418-380-2391

Sous-ministre adjointe, Politiques, patrimoine, muséologie et communications, France Dionne
Tél: 418-380-2330
Téléc: 418-380-2331
france.dionne@mcccf.gouv.qc.ca

Directrice, Ressources humaines, gestion immobilière et communication interne, Marc Tremblay
Tél: 418-380-2358
Téléc: 418-380-2364

Directeur, Financement des sociétés d'État, Patrick Tessier

Commission des biens culturels du Québec (CBCQ) / Québec Cultural Property Commission
Bloc A-RC, 225, Grande Allée est, Québec, QC G1R 5G5
Tél: 418-643-8378
Téléc: 418-643-8591
info@cbcq.gouv.qc.ca
www.cbcq.gouv.qc.ca
Président, Yves Lefebvre
Vice-présidente, Ann Mundy

Ministère du Développement durable, de l'Environnement, de la Faune, et des Parcs / Sustainable Development, Environment, Wildlife & Parks

Édifice Marie-Guyart, 675, boul René-Lévesque est, 29e étage, Québec, QC G1R 5V7
Tél: 418-521-3911
Téléc: 418-643-4143
Ligne sans frais: 800-561-1616
info@mddep.gouv.qc.ca
www.mddep.gouv.qc.ca
www.facebook.com/MDDEFP
www.youtube.com/user/MDDEPQuebec
A pour mission d'assurer la protection de l'environnement & des écosystèmes naturels; de promouvoir le développement durable & d'assurer à la population un environnement sain en harmonie

avec le développement économique & le progrès social du Québec

Lois administrées:

Agricultural Operations Regulation, 2002
Groundwater Catchment Regulation, 2002
Land Protection & Rehabilitation Regulation, 2003
Loi portant restrictions à l'élevage de porcs/Act to Impose Restrictions on Pig Farming, 2002
Loi portant sur la délimitation de la ligne des hautes eaux du Fleuve Saint-Laurent sur le territoire de la municipalité régionale de comté de la Côte-de-Beaupré/An Act to delimit the high water mark of the St. Lawrence River in the territory of Municipa
Loi sur la conservation du patrimoine naturel/Natural Heritage Conservation Act
Loi sur la conservation et la mise en valeur de la faune/Act respecting the Conservation & Development of Wildlife (in part)
Loi sur la protection des arbres/Tree Protection Act
Loi sur la provocation artificielle de la pluie/Act respecting the artificial inducement of rain
Loi sur la qualité de l'environnement/Environment Quality Act
Loi sur la sécurité des barrages/Dam Safety Act
Loi sur la Société des établissements de plein air du Québec
Loi sur la Société québécoise de récupération et de recyclage
Loi sur la vente et la distribution de bière et de boissons gazeuses dans des contenants à remplissage unique/Act respecting the Sale & Distribution of Beer & Soft Drinks in Non-returnable Containers
Loi sur le développement durable
Loi sur le ministère du Développement durable, de l'Environnement et des Parcs
Loi sur le parc de la Mauricie et ses environs
Loi sur le Parc Forillon et des environs
Loi sur le parc marin du Saguenay—Saint-Laurent
Loi sur le régime des eaux/Watercourses Act
Loi sur les espèces menacées ou vulnérables/Act respecting Threatened or Vulnerable Species
Loi sur les parcs
Loi sur les pesticides/Pesticides Act
Loi visant la préservation des ressources en eau/Water Resources Preservation Act
Pesticides Management Code, 2003
Regulation respecting certain bodies for the protection of the environment and social milieu of the territory of James Bay and Northern Québec
Regulation respecting Compensation for Municipal Services Provided to Recover & Reclaim Residual Materials
Regulation respecting Environmental Impact Assessments & review applicable to part of Northeastern Québec
Regulation respecting Halocarbons
Regulation respecting Hazardous Materials
Regulation respecting Hot Mix Asphalt Plants
Regulation respecting Industrial Depollution Attestations
Regulation respecting Motor Vehicle Traffic in Certain Fragile Environments
Regulation respecting Permits & Certificates for the Sale & Use of Pesticides
Regulation respecting Pits & Quarries
Regulation respecting Prevention of Water Pollution in Livestock Operations
Regulation respecting Public Swimming & Wading Pools
Regulation respecting Pulp & Paper Mills
Regulation respecting Sanitary Conditions in Industrial or other Camps
Regulation respecting Snow Elimination Sites
Regulation respecting Solid Waste
Regulation respecting the Application of the Environment Quality Act
Regulation respecting the Artificial Inducement of Rain
Regulation respecting the Burial of Contaminated Soils
Regulation respecting the environmental and social impact assessment and review procedure applicable to the territory of James Bay and Northern Québec
Regulation respecting the environmental impact assessment and review applicable to a part of the northeastern Québec region
Regulation respecting the Liquid Effluents of Petroleum Refineries
Regulation respecting the Quality of Drinking Water
Regulation respecting the Quality of the Atmosphere
Regulation respecting the Recovery & Reclamation of Discarded Paint Containers & Paints
Regulation respecting the Recovery & Reclamation of Used Oils, Oil or Fluid Containers & Used Filters
Regulation respecting the Water Property in the Domain of the State, 2003
Regulation respecting threatened or vulnerable plant species and their habitats
Regulation respecting Used Tire Storage
Regulation Respecting Waste Water Disposal Systems for Isolated Dwellings
Regulation respecting Waterworks & Sewer Services
Rules of internal management of the James Bay Advisory Committee on the Environment
Rules of internal management of the Kativik Environmental Advisory Committee

Ministre, L'hon. Yves-François Blanchet
Tél: 418-521-3911
Téléc: 418-643-4143
ministre.mddefp@gouv.qc.ca

Sous-ministre, Clément D'Astous

Directeur du Cabinet, François Émond
Tél: 418-521-3911

Sous-ministre adjointe, Services à la gestion & au milieu terrestre, Brigitte Portelance

Sous-ministre adjoint, Changements climatiques, à l'air & à l'eau, Charles Larochelle

Sous-ministre adjoint, Développement durable, Léopold Gaudreau

Sous-ministre adjoint, Expertise hydrique, analyse et évaluations environnementales, Jacques Dupoint

Sous-ministre adjoint, Analyse & expertise régionales/Centre de contrôle environnemental du Québec, Michel Rousseau

Secrétaire générale et Directrice, Vérification interne, Caroline Drouin
Tél: 418-521-3810
Téléc: 418-646-4762

Directeur, Bureau des renseignements, de l'accès à l'information et des plaintes sur la qualité des services, Lise Rodrigues

Directrice, Affaires juridiques, Monique Rousseau
Tél: 418-521-3816 ext: 454
Téléc: 418-646-0908

Directeur, Communications, Jérôme Thibaudeau

Agences, Conseils et Commissions Associés/ Associated Agencies, Boards & Commissions:

• Bureau d'audiences publiques sur l'environnement (BAPE) / Environmental Public Hearing Board
Édifice Lomer-Gouin
#2.10, 575, rue Saint-Amable
Québec, QC G1R 6A6
Tél: 418-643-7447
Téléc: 418-643-9474
Ligne sans frais: 800-463-4732
communication@bape.gouv.qc.ca
www.bape.gouv.qc.ca
Président, Pierre Renaud
Vice-président, Pierre Fortin

• Comité consultatif de l'environnement Kativik (CCEK) / Kativik Environmental Advisory Committee (KEAC)
CP 930
Kuujjuaq, QC J0M 1C0
Tél: 819-964-2961
Téléc: 819-964-0694
keac-ccek@krg.ca
www.keac-ccek.ca
Présidente, Sylvie Létourneau
Secrétaire éxecutive, Stéphanie Benoit

• Société des établissements en plein air du Québec (SÉPAQ)
Place de la Cité, Tour Cominar
#250, 2640, boul Laurier, 2e étage
Québec, QC G1V 5C2
Tel: 418-890-6527
Fax: 418-528-6025
Toll-free: 800-665-6527
inforeservation@sepaq.com
www.sepaq.com
Président, Conseil d'administration, Daniel Deslauriers
Président-directeur général, Raymond Desjardins
Secrétaire générale et directrice, Services juridiques, Nelly Rodrigue
Vice-président, Ressources humaines, Pierre Bélanger
Vice-présidente, Administration et finances, Guylaine Berthiaume
Vice-président, Marketing, Alain Brochu
Vice-président, Exploitation, Secteurs faunique et touristique, Jean-Charles Morin
Vice-président, Exploitation, Parcs Québec, Martin Soucy

• Société québécoise de récupération et de recyclage (RECYC-QUÉBEC)
#200, 420, boul Charest est
Québec, QC G1K 8M4
Tél: 418-643-0394
Téléc: 418-643-6507
Ligne sans frais: 866-523-8290
info@recyc-quebec.gouv.qc.ca
www.recyc-quebec.gouv.qc.ca
Autres numéros: Infoline: 1-800-807-0678; Montréal: 514-351-7835
Présidente-directrice générale, Ginette Bureau
Other Communications: poste 2249
Vice-présidente, Communications, Marie Cloutier
Other Communications: poste 2288

Analyses environnementales et aux technologies de l'information / Environmental Analysis & Information Technology
Sous-ministre adjoint, Michel Gagnon
Directeur général, Technologies de l'information, Yvan Déry
Directeur général, Centre d'expertise en analyse environnementale du Québec, Guy Chouinard
Directeur, Solutions d'affaires, Yvan Béliveau
Directeur, Laboratoire des pollutions industrielles; Analyse et de l'étude de la qualité du milieu, Claude Laliberté
Directeur, Accréditation etdes relations externes, Louis Martel
Directeur, Technologies et de l'exploitation, Patrice Tremblay
Directrice, Pilotage des systèmes et de l'assistance aux utilisateurs, Céline Villeneuve

Analyse et expertise régionales / Regional Analysis & Expertise
Édifice Marie-Guyart, 675, boul René-Lévesque est, 30e étage, Québec, QC G1R 5V7
Tél: 418-521-3861
Téléc: 418-646-1800
La mission est d'assurer l'analyse & la délivrance d'autorisations environnementales & d'offrir une expertise professionnelle en matière d'environnement
Sous-ministre adjoint, Michel Rousseau
Tél: 418-521-3861
Téléc: 418-646-1800
Baie-Comeau
20, boul Comeau, Baie-Comeau, QC G4Z 3A8
Tél: 418-294-8888
Téléc: 418-294-8018
cote-nord@mddep.gouv.qc.ca
Directeur, Alain Gaudreault
Gatineau
#7.340, 170, rue de l'Hôtel-de-Ville, Gatineau, QC J8X 4C2
Tél: 819-772-3434
Téléc: 819-772-3952
outaouais@mddep.gouv.qc.ca
Directeur, Marc Dubreuil
Laval
850, boul Vanier, Laval, QC H7C 2M7
Tél: 450-661-2008
Téléc: 450-661-2217
laval@mddep.gouv.qc.ca
Directeur, Pierre Robert
Longueuil
201, Place Charles-Le Moyne, 2e étage, Longueuil, QC J4K 2T5
Tél: 450-928-7607
Téléc: 450-928-7625
monteregie@mddep.gouv.qc.ca
Directeur adjoint, Pierre Paquin
Montréal
#3860, 5199, rue Sherbrooke est, Montréal, QC H1T 3X9

Tél: 514-873-3636
Téléc: 514-873-5662
montreal@mddep.gouv.qc.ca
Directeur, Pierre Robert
Nicolet
1579, boul Louis-Fréchette, Nicolet, QC J3T 2A5
Tél: 819-293-4122
Téléc: 819-293-8322
centre-du-quebec@mddep.gouv.qc.ca
Directeur, Luc St-Martin
Québec
#100, 1175, boul Lebourgneuf, Québec, QC G2K 0B7
Tél: 418-644-8844
Téléc: 418-646-1214
capitale-nationale@mddep.gouv.qc.ca
Directrice, Isabelle Olivier
Repentigny
100, boul Industriel, Repentigny, QC J6A 4X6
Tél: 450-654-4355
Téléc: 450-654-6131
lanaudiere@mddep.gouv.qc.ca
Directeur, Pierre Robert
Rimouski
212, av Belzile, Rimouski, QC G5L 3C3
Tél: 418-727-3511
Téléc: 418-727-3849
bas-saint-laurent@mddep.gouv.qc.ca
Directeur, Jean-Marie Dionne
Rouyn-Noranda
180, boul Rideau, 1er étage, Rouyn-Noranda, QC J9X 1N9
Tél: 819-763-3333
Téléc: 819-763-3202
abitibi-temiscamingue@mddep.gouv.qc.ca
Directrice, Édith van de Walle
Saguenay
3950, boul Harvey, 4e étage, Saguenay, QC G7X 8L6
Tél: 418-695-7883
Téléc: 418-695-7897
saguenay-lac-saint-jean@mddep.gouv.qc.ca
Directrice, Édith Tremblay
Sainte-Anne-des-Monts
124, 1re av ouest, Sainte-Anne-des-Monts, QC G4V 1C5
Tél: 418-763-3301
Téléc: 418-763-7810
gaspesie-iles-de-la-madeleine@mddep.gouv.qc.ca
Directeur, Jean-Marie Dionne
Sainte-Marie
#200, 675, rte Cameron, Sainte-Marie, QC G6E 3V7
Tél: 418-386-8000
Téléc: 418-386-8080
chaudiere-appalaches@mddep.gouv.qc.ca
Directrice, Isabelle Olivier
Sainte-Thérèse
#80, 300, rue Sicard, Sainte-Thérèse, QC J7E 3X5
Tél: 450-433-2220
Téléc: 450-433-1315
laurentides@mddep.gouv.qc.ca
Directeur, Pierre Robert
Sept-îles
818, boul Laure, Sept-îles, QC G4R 1Y8
Tél: 418-964-8888
Téléc: 418-964-8023
cote-nord@mddep.gouv.qc.ca
Directeur, Alain Gaudreault
Sherbrooke
770, rue Goretti, Sherbrooke, QC J1E 3H4
Tél: 819-820-3882
Téléc: 819-820-3958
estrie@mddep.gouv.qc.ca
Directeur, Pierre Paquin
Trois-Rivières
#102, 100, rue Laviolette, Trois-Rivières, QC G9A 5S9
Tél: 819-371-6581
Téléc: 819-371-6987
mauricie@mddep.gouv.qc.ca
Directeur, Luc St-Martin

Changements climatiques, de l'air et de l'eau / Climate Change
675, boul René-Lévesque est, 30e étage, Québec, QC G1R 5V7
Tél: 418-521-3861
Téléc: 418-643-9990
Sous-ministre adjoint, Charles Larochelle
Tél: 418-521-3868
Téléc: 418-646-4920
Directeur, Politiques de l'eau, Marcel Gaucher
Directeur, Politiques de la qualité de l'atmosphère, Michel Goulet
Directrice, Bureau des changements climatiques, Geneviève Moisan
Directrice, Relations intergouvernementales, Danielle Pronovost

Centre de contrôle environnemental du Québec
Édifice Marie-Guyart, 675, boul René-Lévesque est, 30e étage, Québec, QC G1R 5V7
Tél: 418-521-3861
Téléc: 418-646-1800
Sous-ministre adjoint, Michel Rousseau
Baie-Comeau
20, boulevard Comeau, Baie-Comeau, QC G4Z 3A8
Tél: 418-294-8888
Téléc: 418-294-8018
cote-nord@mddep.gouv.qc.ca
Directrice, Nathalie Chouinard
Gatineau
7.340, 170, rue de l'Hôtel-de-Ville, Gatineau, QC J8X 4C2
Tél: 819-772-3434
Téléc: 819-772-3952
outaouais@mddep.gouv.qc.ca
Directeur, Alexandre Iracà
Nicolet
1579, boul Louis-Fréchette, Nicolet, QC J3T 2A5
Tél: 819-293-4122
Téléc: 819-293-8322
centre-du-quebec@mddep.gouv.qc.ca
Directeur, Pierre Boucher
Rimouski
212, av Belzile, Rimouski, QC G5L 3C3
Tél: 418-727-3511
Téléc: 418-727-3849
bas-saint-laurent@mddep.gouv.qc.ca
Directeur, Jules Boulanger
Rouyn-Noranda
180, boul Rideau, 1er étage, Rouyn-Noranda, QC J9X 1N9
Tél: 819-763-3333
Téléc: 819-763-3202
abitibi-temiscamingue@mddep.gouv.qc.ca
Directrice (par intérim), Hélène Iracà
Saguenay
3950, boul Harvey, 4e étage, Saguenay, QC G7X 8L6
Tél: 418-695-7883
Téléc: 418-695-7897
saguenay-lac-saint-jean@mddep.gouv.qc.ca
Directeur, Daniel Labrecque
Sainte-Marie
#200, 675, rte Cameron, Sainte-Marie, QC G6E 3V7
Tél: 418-386-8000
Téléc: 418-386-8080
chaudiere-appalaches@mddep.gouv.qc.ca
Directeur, Jean-Marc Lachance
Sherbrooke
770, rue Goretti, Sherbrooke, QC J1E 3H4
Tél: 819-820-3882
Téléc: 819-820-3958
estrie@mddep.gouv.qc.ca
Directeur, Émile Grieco
Montréal
#3860, 5199, rue Sherbrooke est, Montréal, QC H1T 3X9
Tél: 514-873-3636
Téléc: 514-873-5662
montreal@mddep.gouv.qc.ca
Directrice (par intérim), Hélène Proteau

Développement durable / Sustainable Development
Tél: 418-521-3861
Téléc: 418-646-5883
Sous-ministre adjoint, Léopold Gaudreau
Tél: 418-521-3861
Téléc: 418-646-5883
Directeur, Patrimoine écologique et des parcs, Patrick Beauchesne
Tél: 418-521-3907
Téléc: 418-646-6169
Directrice, Suivi de l'état de l'environnement, Linda Tapin
Tél: 418-521-3820
Téléc: 418-643-9591
Directeur, Bureau de Coordination du développement durable, Luc Vézina
Tél: 418-521-3848
Téléc: 418-646-6169

Expertise hydrique et aux évaluations environnementales / Water & Environmental Assessments
Sous-ministre adjoint, Jacques Dupont
Tél: 418-521-3861
Téléc: 418-643-7812
Directeur général, Centre d'expertise hydrique du Québec, Yvon Gosselin
Directrice, Expertise hydriques, Paula Bergeron
Directeur, Sécurité des barrages, Michel Dolbec
Directrice, Évaluations environnementales, Marie-Josée Lizotte
Directrice, Bureau de coordination sur les évaluations stratégiques, Yvon Maranda
Directrice, Domaine hydrique de l'État, Peter Stevenson

Services à la gestion & au milieu terrestre / Administrative Services & Earth Environment
Tél: 418-521-3861
Téléc: 418-643-9990
Sous-ministre adjoint et directrice générale (par intérim), Brigitte Portelance
Tél: 418-521-3861
Téléc: 418-643-9990
Directrice, Ressources humaines, Sylvie Beaulieu
Tél: 418-521-3811
Téléc: 418-646-6498
Directeur, Analyse et des instruments économiques, André G. Bernier
Directeur, Matières résiduelles & lieux contaminés, Mario Bérubé
Tél: 418-521-3950
Téléc: 418-644-3386
Directeur, Secteur agricole & pesticides, Didier Bicchi
Tél: 418-521-3950
Téléc: 418-644-8562
Directeur, Ressources financières et matérielles, Sophie Boisvert

Centre d'expertise en analyse environnementale du Québec (CEAEQ)
#E-2-220, 2700, rue Einstein, Sainte-Foy, QC G1P 3W8
Tél: 418-643-1301
Téléc: 418-528-1091
ceaeq@mddep.gouv.qc.ca
www.ceaeq.gouv.qc.ca
La mission: garantir la disponibilité, la qualité & la continuité de l'expertise & de l'information analytique pour les besoins de protection de l'environnement, & de conservation des ressources
Directeur général, Guy Chouinard

Centre d'expertise hydrique du Québec
Tél: 418-521-3866
Téléc: 418-643-6900
cehq@mddep.gouv.qc.ca
www.cehq.gouv.qc.ca
A pour mission de gérer le régime hydrique de Québec avec une préoccupation de sécurité, d'équité & de développement durable, & d'assurer la régularisation du régime des eaux
Directeur général, Yvon Gosselin
Directrice, Expertise hydrique, Paula Bergeron
Directeur, Barrages publics, VACANT
Directeur, Sécurité des barrages, Michel Dolbec
Directeur, Gestion du domaine hydrique de l'État, Peter Stevenson

Ministère du Développement économique, de l'Innovation et de l'Exportation / Economic Development, Innovation & Export Trade

710, place D'Youville, 3e étage, Québec, QC G1R 4Y4
Tél: 418-691-5950
Téléc: 418-644-0118
Ligne sans frais: 866-680-1884
www.mdeie.gouv.qc.ca
twitter.com/MFE_Economie
A pour mission de soutenir le développement économique, l'innovation & l'exportation; d'offrir des services-conseils; de promouvoir l'image du Québec à l'étranger auprès des investisseurs

Ministre, L'hon. Sam Hamad

Sous-ministre, Christyne Tremblay

Directeur, Accords internationaux et mandit spécial, Patrick Muzzi

Directeur, Politique commerciale, Jean-François Raymond

Directrice, Communications, Johanne Pelletier

Secrétaire générale, Geneviève Masse

Agences, Conseils et Commissions Associés/ Associated Agencies, Boards & Commissions:

• Centre de recherche industrielle du Québec (CRIQ) / Industrial Research Centre of Québec
333, rue Franquet
Québec, QC G1P 4C7
Tél: 418-659-1550
Ligne sans frais: 800-667-2386
infocriq@criq.qc.ca
www.criq.qc.ca
Recherche industrielle appliquée; services de RD pour des entreprises
Président-directeur général, Georges Archambault, ing., M.Sc.A., MBA

• Fonds québécois de la recherche sur la nature et les technologies (FQRNT) / Québec Fund for Research on Nature and Technologies
#450, 140, Grande Allée est
Québec, QC G1R 5M8
Tél: 418-643-8560
Téléc: 418-643-1451
info.nt@frq.gouv.qc.ca
www.fqrnt.gouv.qc.ca
Président du conseil d'administration et Scientifique en chef du Québec, Fonds de recherche du Québec, Rémi Quirion, Ph.D., CQ, OC, MSRC
remi.quirion@frq.gouv.qc.ca
Directrice scientifique, Maryse Lassonde

• Fonds québécois de la recherche sur la société et la culture (FQRSC) / Québec Fund for Research on Society and Culture
#470, 140, Grande Allée est
Québec, QC G1R 5M8
Tél: 418-643-7582
Téléc: 418-644-5248
frq.sc@frq.gouv.qc.ca
www.fqrsc.gouv.qc.ca

• Fonds de la recherche en santé du Québec / Québec Health Research Fund
#800, 500, rue Sherbrooke ouest
Montréal, QC H3A 3C6
Tél: 514-873-2114
Téléc: 514-873-8768
www.frsq.gouv.qc.ca

• Investissement Québec / Investment Québec
#500, 1200, rte de l'Église
Québec, QC G1V 5A3
Tél: 418-643-5172
Ligne sans frais: 866-870-0437
www.investquebec.com

• Innovatech Québec
#410, 888, rue St-Jean
Québec, QC G1R 5H6
Tél: 418-528-9770
Téléc: 418-528-9783
Ligne sans frais: 866-605-1676
www.innovatechquebec.com
Présidente-directrice générale (par intérim), Chantal Brunet, Ph.D., MBA, ASC
Tel: 418-528-9774
cbrunet@innovatechquebec.com

Affaires économiques internationales (AEI) / International Economic Affairs
Sous-ministre adjoint, Jean Séguin
Directeur général, Export Québec, Alain Proulx
Directeur, Occasions d'affaires mondiales, Chantal Castonguay
Directrice, Asie-Pacifique et Océanie, Marie-ève Jean
Directeur, Amérique du Nord et Europe, Yves Lafortune
Directrice, Information, promotion, et investissements internationaux, Isabelle Phaneuf
Directeur, Amérique latine, Afrique et Moyen-Orient, Rafaël Sanchez

Bureau de la Capitale-Nationale / National Capital Office

Industries stratégiques (IS) / Strategic Industries
Sous-ministre adjointe, Suzanne Lévesque
Directrice, Technologies de l'information et des communications, Diane Hastie
Directrice, Santé et biotechnologies, Michèle Houpert
Directeur, Technologies vertes et entreprises de service, Gaétan Poiré

Politiques économiques (PE) / Economic Policies
Sous-ministre adjoint et directeur (par intérim), Politiques économiques, Alain Veilleux
Directrice, Développement de l'entrepreneuriat, Lyne Fournier
Directeur, Développement des coopératives, Michel Jean
Directrice, Analyse économique, Denise Lacroix
Directeur, Évaluation de programmes et planification stratégique, François Maxime Langlois

Projets économiques majeurs et sociétés d'État (PEMSE) / Major Economic Projects & Crown Corporations
Sous-ministre adjoint, Mario Bouchard
Directeur général, Interventions stratégiques, Pierre Dupont
Directeur, Produits industriels, Clément Drolet
Directrice, FDE et programmes, Lise Mathieu
Directrice, Interventions financières, Michèle Robert
Directrice, Coordination, analyse et sociétés d'État, Lisette Seyer
Directeur, Projets économiques, Frédéric Simard

Recherche, innovation et science citoyenne (RISC) / Research, Innovation, & Social Science
Sous-ministre adjoint et directeur général (par intérim), Reserche Québec, Jean Belzile
Directeur, Financement des infrastructures de recherche, Gaston Beaudoin
Directrice, Collaborations internationales, Marie-Josée Blais
Directeur, Recherche industrielle, Marco Blouin
Directeur (par intérim), Recherche universitaire & collégiale, Martin Doyon
Directrice, Promotion de la science citoyenne, Christian Desbiens
Directrice, Coordination & concertation, Marie-Odile Koch
Directrice, Soutien à l'innovation technologique et sociale, Monique La Rue

Services à la gestion / Administrative Services
Directrice générale, Carole Lafond
Directrice, Ressources humaines et matérielles, Nicole Lévesque
Directeur, Ressources informationnelles, Guy Leclerc
Directeur, Ressources financières, Francis Mathieu

Services aux entreprises et affaires territoriales (SEAT) / Business Services & Territorial Affairs
Sous-ministre adjoint, Jean-Marc Sauvé
Directeur général, Affaires économiques métropolitaines, Mario Limoges
Directeur, Pôles et créneaux d'excellence, Xavier Fonteneau
Directrice (par intérim), Coordination régionale, Michèle Robert
Directeur, Développement des entreprises, Bertrand Verbruggen
Directeur, Jean-François Talbot
Directeur, Roch Delagrave

Ministre, L'hon. Marie Malavoy
Tél: 418-644-0664
Téléc: 418-646-7551
ministre@mels.gouv.qc.ca

Hydro-Québec

75, boul René-Lévesque ouest, Montréal, QC H2Z 1A4
Tél: 514-289-2211
www.hydroquebec.com

Président, Conseil d'administration, Michael Louis Turcotte

Président-directeur général, Thierry Vandal

Président, Hydro-Québec TransÉnergie, André Boulanger

Président, Hydro-Québec Production, Richard Cacchione

Présidente, Hydro-Québec Distribution, Isabelle Courville

Protectrice de la personne, Joëlle Thibault

Développement durable / Sustainable Development
www.hydroquebec.com/developpementdurable/
Président-directeur général, Thierry Vandal

Subsidiaries/Filiales
Subsidiaries/Filiales

Société d'énergie de la Baie-James (SEBJ) / James Bay Energy
888, de Maisonneuve est, 6e étage, Montréal, QC H2L 5B2
Tél: 514-286-2020
www.hydroquebec.com/sebj
Directeur, Projets de l'Eastmain, Yvan David
Chef, Transport, services généraux et gestion des actifs, Denis Lalonde
Chef, Projet Northern Pass Transmission, Ghislain Lévesque
Chef de service, Réclamations et fermeture de contrats, Victor Gauvin
Chef de service, Construction et contrôle de projet, Jean-Pierre Motard
Chef de chantier, Centrale la Sarcelle, Laurent Busque
Chef de chantier, Centrale EM-1-A, Denis Groleau

Innovation technologique / Technological Innovation
www.hydroquebec.com/technologie/index.html

Ministère des Ressources naturelles / Natural Resources

880, ch Sainte-Foy, Québec, QC G1S 4X4
Tél: 418-627-8600
Téléc: 418-644-6513
Ligne sans frais: 866-248-6936
services.clientele@mrnf.gouv.qc.ca
www.mrn.gouv.qc.ca
twitter.com/mrn_Quebec
www.facebook.com/fetedelapeche;
www.facebook.com/QuebecMines
youtube.com/mrnfquebec; flickr.com/photos/mrnfquebec

Lois administrées:
Lands in the Domain of the State Designated for Development of Wildlife Resources Regulation
Loi approuvant la convention de la Baie-James et du nord québécois/An Act approving the Agreement concerning James Bay and Northern Québec
Loi approuvant la convention du nord-est québécois/An Act approving the Northeastern Québec Agreement
Loi assurant la mise en oeuvre de l'entente concernant une nouvelle relation entre le gouvernement du Québec et les Cris du Québec/An Act to ensure the implementation of the Agreement Concerning a New Relationship Between the Government of Québec and the
Loi concernant les droits sur les mines/Mining Duties Act
Loi de 1994 sur la convention concernant les oiseaux migrateurs
Loi favorisant la réforme du cadastre québécois/An Act to promote the reform of the cadastre in Québec
Loi sur Hydro-Québec/Hydro-Québec Act
Loi sur l'exportation de l'électricité/An Act respecting the exportation of electric power
Loi sur la conservation et la mise en valeur de la faune/Act respecting the conservation and development of wildlife
Loi sur la division territoriale/Territorial Division Act
Loi sur la Régie de l'énergie/An Act respecting the Régie de l'énergie
Loi sur la société de développement autochtone de la Baie James/An Act respecting the James Bay Native Development Corporation
Loi sur la société Eeyou de la Baie-James/An Act respecting the James Bay Eeyou Corporation
Loi sur la société nationale de l'amiante/An Act respecting the Société nationale de l'amiante
Loi sur le cadastre/Cadastre Act
Loi sur le développement et l'organisation municipale de la région de la Baie-James/James Bay Region Development and Municipal Organization Act
Loi sur le ministère des ressources naturelles et de la faune/An Act respecting the Ministère des Ressources naturelles et de la Faune
Loi sur le programme d'aide aux Inuits bénéficiaires de la convention de la Baie-James et du nord québécois pour leurs activités de chasse, de pêche et de piégeage/An Act respecting the support program for Inuit beneficiaries of the James Bay and Norther
Loi sur le régime des eaux/Watercourses Act
Loi sur le régime des terres dans les territoires de la Baie-James et du Nouveau-Québec/An Act respecting the land regime in the James Bay and New Québec territories
Loi sur les arpentages/An Act respecting land survey
Loi sur les bureaux de la publicité des droits/An Act respecting registry offices
Loi sur les clubs de chasse et de pêche/Fish and Game Clubs Act

Loi sur les compagnies de flottage/Timber-Driving Companies Act
Loi sur les droits de chasse et de pêche dans les territoires de la Baie James et du Nouveau-Québec/An Act respecting hunting and fishing rights in the James Bay and New Québec territories
Loi sur les espèces menacées ou vulnérables/An Act respecting threatened or vulnerable species
Loi sur les forêts/Forest Act
Loi sur les mesurers de bois/Cullers Act
Loi sur les mines/Mining Act
Loi sur les Pêches
Loi sur les systèmes municipaux et les systèmes privés d'électricité/An Act respecting municipal and private electric power systems
Loi sur les terres du domaine de l'état/An Act respecting the lands in the domain of the State
Loi sur les titres de propriété dans certains districts électoraux/An Act respecting land titles in certain electoral districts
Règlement sur l'application de dispositions législatives par les agents de protection de la faune/Regulation respecting enforcement of certain legislative & regulatory provisions respecting protection of environment by wildlife protection officers
Règlement sur le domaine hydrique de l'État/Regulation respecting the water property in the domain of the State
Règlement sur les produits pétroliers/Petroleum Products Regulation
Règlement sur les zones d'exploitation contrôlée de chasse et de pêche/Regulation respecting hunting & fishing controlled zones
Regulation respecting aquaculture and the sale of fish
Regulation respecting wildlife habitats
Regulation respecting wildlife sanctuaries

Ministre, L'hon. Martine Ouellet
Tél: 418-643-7295
Téléc: 418-643-4318
ministre@mrnf.gouv.qc.ca

Ministre délégué, L'hon. Patrick Déry

Sous-ministre, Patrick Déry
Tél: 418-627-6370
Téléc: 418-643-1443

Directeur général, Administration/Connaissance géographique, Ubald Gagné
Tél: 418-627-6260
Téléc: 418-646-2614

Agences, Conseils et Commissions Associés/ Associated Agencies, Boards & Commissions:

• Agence de l'efficacité énergétique / Energy Efficiencies Agency
#B406, 5700, 4e av ouest
Québec, QC G1H 6R1
Tél: 418-627-6379
Téléc: 418-643-5828
Ligne sans frais: 877-727-6655
efficaciteenergetique@mrn.gouv.qc.ca
www.efficaciteenergetique.mrn.gouv.qc.ca
Promotes the efficient use of all forms of energy, in all sectors of activity, for the benefit of the people of Québec. The Agency achieves this through demonstration projects, which highlight new technologies, new approaches or new applications that save energy; design, management & evaluation of energy efficient programs; information, training & educational materials; technical & organizational support for export of products & services; review, commentary on proposed amendments to applicable laws & regulations.

• Comité conjoint de chasse, de pêche et de piégeage / Hunting, Fishing & Trapping Joint Committee
#C220, 383 rue Saint-Jacques
Montréal, QC H2Y 1N9
Tél: 514-284-2151
Téléc: 514-284-0039
infohftcc@cccpp-hftcc.com
www.cccpp-hftcc.com
Président, Denis Vandal

• Fondation de la faune du Québec / Québec Wildlife Foundation
Place Iberville II
#420, 1175, av Lavigerie
Québec, QC G1V 4P1
Tél: 418-644-7926
Téléc: 418-643-7655
Ligne sans frais: 877-639-0742
ffq@fondationdelafaune.qc.ca
www.fondationdelafaune.qc.ca
Non-profit organization whose mission is to enhance the value & promote the conservation of wildlife & its habitats.
Président-directeur général, André Martin
Tél: 418-644-7926 ext: 138
direction@fondationdelafaune.qc.ca

• Hydro Québec
See Entry Name Index for detailed listing.

• Régie de l'énergie / Energy Regulation Board
Tour de la Bourse
#2.55, 800, Place Victoria
Montréal, QC H4Z 1A2
Tél: 514-873-2452
Téléc: 514-873-2070
Ligne sans frais: 888-873-2452
secretariat@regie-energie.qc.ca; greffe@regie-energie.qc.ca
www.regie-energie.qc.ca
An economic regulation agency, its mission is to reconcile the public interest, consumer protection, & fair treatment of the electricity carrier & distributors.
Président, Jean-Paul Théorêt

• Société de développement de la Baie James (SDBJ) / James Bay Development Society
110, boul Matagami
CP 970
Matagami, QC J0Y 2A0
Tél: 819-739-4717
Téléc: 819-739-4329
mat@sdbj.gouv.qc.ca
www.sdbj.gouv.qc.ca
Developed in 1971, this organization uses its resources & vast knowledge of the territory, contributors, & development projects to promote & maintain activities in the James Bay area, with a perspective of integrated economic development & harmonious cohabitation with territorial residents.
Président-directeur général et administrateur, Raymond Thibault

Énergie / Energy
#B401, 5700, 4e av ouest, Québec, QC G1H 6R1
Tél: 418-627-6377
Téléc: 418-643-0701
Le gouvernement québécois prévoit le lancement des projets hydoélectriques représentant 4,500 MW, qui susciteront des investissements de l'ordre de 25m de dollars, et la création d'environ 70,000 emplois sur six ans. Il mise sur le développement du potential existant d'énergie éolienne, avec l'objectif de 4,000 MW d'ici 2015, et prend plusieurs moyens afin de renforcer la sécurité des approvisionnements en pétrole et gaz naturel
Sous-ministre associé, Mario Gosselin
Directrice générale, Électricité, Julie Grignon
Tél: 418-627-6386 ext: 819
Directeur général, Hydrocarbures et Bioarburants, Alain Lefebvre
Tél: 418-627-6385 ext: 825
Directeur général (par intérim), Efficacité et innovation énergétiques, J. E. Alain Daneau
Directeur, Grands projets et réglementation, Philippe-Pierre Nazon

Faune Québec / Wildlife Québec
RC-120, 880, ch Sainte-Foy, Québec, QC G1S 4X4
Tél: 418-627-8652
Sous-ministre associée, Nathalie Camden
Tél: 418-627-8652 ext: 400
Directeur général, Protection de la faune, Guy Nadeau
Tél: 418-627-8688 ext: 751
Directeur, Expertise sur la faune et ses habitats, Pierre Bérubé
Tél: 418-627-8694 ext: 741
Directeur, Développement socio-économique, partenariats et éducation, Jacob Martin-Malus
Tél: 418-627-8691 ext: 736
Chef, Réglementation, tarification et permis, Lucie Aubin
Chef (par intérim), Biodiversité et maladies de la faune, Francis Bouchard
Chef, Faune aquatique, Jessy Dynes
Chef, Mise en valeur de la ressource et des territories fauniques, Serge Goulet
Chef, Faune terrestre et avifaune, Danielle St-Pierre

Foncier Québec / Québec Lands
5700, 4e av ouest, Québec, QC G1H 6R1
Tél: 418-643-3582
Téléc: 418-528-8721
Ligne sans frais: 866-226-0977
assistance.clientele@mrnf.registrefoncier.gouv.qc.ca
Sous-ministre associée, Louise Ouellet
Tél: 418-627-6252 ext: 308
Téléc: 418-643-3954
Directeur général, Arpentage et cadastre, Julien Arsenault
Tél: 418-627-6267
Téléc: 418-646-7405
Directeur général, Clientèle et technologies d'affaires, Marc Lainé
Directrice générale, Registre Foncier, Line Drouin
Tél: 418-627-6264 ext: 380
Directeur, Évolution du registre foncier et centre d'opérations de Québec, Guy Cantin
Directeur, Service a la clientèle, Marc Desgagné
Directrice, Intégration et innovation, Isabelle Godbout
Directeur, Enregistrement Cadastral, Marc Lasnier
Directeur, Technologies, Josée Morency
Directrice, Systèmes, Lucie Quintal
Directeur (par intérim), Gestion du fonds d'information foncière, Isabelle Godbout
Directeur (par intérim), Bureau de l'appenteur général du Québec, Julien Arsenault
Directeur, Projet de service en ligne de réquisitions d'inscription, Alain Simard
Directeur, Renovation cadastrale, Jean Thibault

Forestier en chef / Chief Forester
845, boul Saint-Joseph, Roberval, QC G8H 2L4
Tél: 418-275-7770
Téléc: 418-275-8884
bureau@forestierenchef.gouv.qc.ca
www.forestierenchef.gouv.qc.ca
Forestier en chef, Gérard Szaraz
Sous-ministre associé (par intérim), Directeur, Dévelopment stratégique, Marc Plante
Directeur, Calcul des possibilités forestiéres, Jean Girard

Forêt Québec / Québec Forests
880, ch Ste-Foy, #RC 120, Québec, QC G1S 4X4
Tél: 418-627-8652
Téléc: 418-528-1278
foretquebec@mrnf.gouv.qc.ca
Sous-ministre associé, Richard Savard
Directrice, Orientations stratégiques et administration, Francis Forcier
Directeur, Bureau de la coordination du régime forestier, Alain Sénéchal
Directrice générale, Connaissance et gestion de l'information forestière, Elisabeth Bossert
Directeur, Recherche forestière, Robert Jobidon
Directeur, Gestion de l'information forestière, Denis Robitaille
Directeur, Inventaires forestiers, Luc Tellier
Directeur général, Attribution des bois et développement industriel, Réal Paris
Directeur, Développement de l'industrie et des produits forestiers, André Denis
Directeur, Gestion des stocks ligneux, Réal Paris
Directeur général, Aménagement durable des forêts/Bureau de mise en marché des bois, Mario Gibeault
Directeur, Évaluations économiques et opérations financières, Jean-Pierre Adam
Directeur, Aménagement et environnement forestiers, Ronald Brizard
Directeur, Protection des forêts, Paul Lamirande
Directeur, Opérations territoriales de mise en marché, François Trottier

Mines
Centre de service des Mines, 1685, boul Wilfrid Hamel ouest, 1er étage, Québec, QC G1N 3Y7
Tél: 418-627-6278
Téléc: 418-644-8960
Ligne sans frais: 800-363-7233
service.mines@mrnf.gouv.qc.ca
Sous-ministre associé, Mines, Robert Marquis
Tél: 418-627-8652

Directeur général (par intérim), Géologie Québec, Robert Giguère
Tél: 819-354-4514 ext: 232
Directrice générale, Gestion du milieu minier, Lucie Ste-Croix
Tél: 418-627-6292 ext: 538
Directeur général, Développement de l'industrie minérale, Renée Garon
Tél: 418-627-6292 ext: 505
Directeur (par intérim), Information géologique de Québec, Luc Charbonneau
Directrice, Restauration des sites miniers, Johanne Cyr
Directeur, Titres miniers et systémes, Roch Gaudreau
Directeur, Politiques, coordination et affaires intergouvernementales, Robert Giguère
Directeur (par intérim), Bureau de l'exploration géologique du Québec, Patrice Roy
Directrice, Imposition minière, Jocelyne Lamothe
Abitibi-Témiscamingue
70, av Québec, Rouyn-Noranda, QC J9X 6R1
Tél: 819-763-3388
Téléc: 819-763-3186
Directeur (par intérim), Jean-Pierre Lessard
Bas-Saint-Laurent
#207, 92, 2e rue ouest, Rimouski, QC G5L 8B3
Tél: 418-727-3710
Téléc: 418-727-3735
Directeur, Dominic Gagnon
Capitale-Nationale—Chaudière-Appalaches
8400, av Sous-le-Vent, Charny, QC G6X 3S9
Tél: 418-832-7222
Téléc: 418-832-1827
Directeur, André Jutras
Mauricie—Centre-du-Québec
#207, 100 rue Laviolette, Trois-Rivières, QC G9A 5S9
Tél: 819-371-6151
Téléc: 819-371-6978
Ligne sans frais: 866-821-4625
Directeur, Réjean Rioux
Côte-Nord
456, av Arnaud, 1er étage, Sept-îles, QC G4R 3B1
Tél: 418-964-8300
Téléc: 418-964-8506
cote-nord@mrnf.gouv.qc.ca
Directeur, David Erdely
Estrie—Montréal—Montérégie
770, rue Goretti, Sherbrooke, QC J1E 3H4
Tél: 819-820-3883
Téléc: 819-820-3747
Directeur, Claude Beauchemin
Gaspésie—Iles-de-la-Madeleine
124, 1re Avenue ouest, Sainte-Anne-des-Monts, QC G4V 1C5
Tél: 418-763-3302
Téléc: 418-764-2378
Directeur (par intérim), Dominic Gagnon
Laval—Lanaudière—Laurentides
#1.50B, 999, rue Nobel, Saint-Jérôme, QC J7Z 7A3
Tél: 450-569-3113
Téléc: 450-469-7568
Directeur (par intérim), Benoît Levert
Nord-du-Québec
1121, boul Industriel, CP 159Lebel-sur-Quévillon, QC J0Y 1X0
Tél: 819-755-4838
Téléc: 819-755-3541
nord-du-quebec@mrnf.gouv.qc.ca
Directeur, Michel Bergeron
Outaouais
#RC 100, 16, impasse de la Gare-Talon, Gatineau, QC J8T 0B1
Tél: 819-246-4827
Téléc: 819-246-5049
outaouais@mrnf.gouv.qc.ca
Directeur, Benoît Levert
Saguenay—Lac-Saint-Jean
3950, boul Harvey, 4e étage, Jonquière, QC G7X 8L6
Tél: 418-695-8125
Téléc: 418-695-8436
saguenay-lac-saint-jean@mrnf.gouv.qc.ca
Directrice (par intérim), Jasmin Larouche
Abitibi-Témiscamingue
70, av Québec, Rouyn-Noranda, QC J9X 6R1
Tél: 819-763-3388
Téléc: 819-763-3216
abitibi-temiscamingue@mrnf.gouv.qc.ca
Directeur général, Martin Gingras
Bas-Saint-Laurent
#207, 92, 2e Rue ouest, Rimouski, QC G5L 8B3
Tél: 418-727-3710
Téléc: 418-727-3735
bas-saint-laurent@mrnf.gouv.qc.ca
Directeur général, Paul St-Laurent
Capitale-Nationale—Chaudières-Appalaches
#1.14, 1685, boul Wilfrid Hamel ouest, Québec, QC G1N 3Y7
Tél: 418-643-4680
Téléc: 418-644-8960
capitale-nationale@mrnf.gouv.qc.ca
Autres nombres: chaudiere-appalaches@mrnf.gouv.qc.ca
Côte-Nord
#RC 702, 625, boul Laflèche, Baie-Comeau, QC G5C 1C5
Tél: 418-295-4676
Téléc: 418-295-4682
cote-nord.@mrnf.gouv.qc.ca
Directeur général (par intérim), Linda Tremblay
Gaspésie—Iles-de-la-Madeleine
195, boul Perron est, Caplan, QC G0C 1H0
Tél: 418-388-2125
Téléc: 418-388-2444
gaspesie-iles-de-la-madeleine@mrnf.gouv.qc.ca
Directeur général, Bernard Landry
Mauricie—Centre-du-Québec
#207, 100, rue Laviolette, Trois-Rivières, QC G9A 5S9
Tél: 418-371-6151
Téléc: 418-371-6978
Ligne sans frais: 866-821-4625
mauricie@mrnf.gouv.qc.ca
Autres nombres: centreduquebec@mrnf.gouv.qc.ca
Directeur général, Alain Simard
Estrie—Montréal—Montérégie et Laval—Lanaudière—Laurentides
545, boul Crémazie est, 8e étage, Montréal, QC H2M 2V1
Tél: 514-873-2140
Téléc: 514-873-8983
estrie@mrnf.gouv.qc.ca
Autres nombres: montreal@mrnf.gouv.qc.ca; monteregie@mrnf.gouv.qc.ca; laval@mrnf.gouv.qc.ca; lanaudiere@mrnf.gouv.qc.ca; laurentides@mrnf.gouv.qc.ca
Directeur général, André B. Lemay
Nord-du-Québec
1121, boul Industriel, CP 159Lebel-sur-Quévillon, QC J0Y 1X0
Tél: 819-755-4838
Téléc: 819-755-3541
nord-du-quebec@mrnf.gouv.qc.ca
Directeur général, Guy Hétu
Outaouais
#RC 100, 16, impasse de la Gare-Talon, Gatineau, QC J8T 0B1
Tél: 819-246-4827
Téléc: 819-246-5049
outaouais@mrnf.gouv.qc.ca
Directeur général, Pierre Ménard
Saguenay—Lac-Saint-Jean
3950, boul Harvey, 3e étage, Jonquière, QC G7X 8L6
Tél: 418-695-8125
Téléc: 418-695-8133
saguenay-lac-saint-jean@mrnf.gouv.qc.ca
Directeur général, Alain Thibeault

Territoire
#A313, 5700, 4e av ouest, Québec, QC G1H 6R1
Tél: 418-627-6256
Téléc: 418-528-2075
Le Ministère favorise une utilisation du territoire qui rejoint les préoccupations économiques, sociales & environnementales des Québécois
Sous-ministre associé (par intérim), Plan Nord et Territoire, Patrick Déry
Tél: 418-627-6370 ext: 357
Directeur général, Affaires stratégiques et territoire, André Auclair
Tél: 418-627-6256 ext: 312
Directrice, Coordination du Plan Nord, Andrée Bélanger
Tél: 418-627-6368 ext: 295
Directeur, Environnement et Coordination, Marcel Grenier
Tél: 418-627-6256 ext: 312
Directeur, Affaires autochtones, François Dupuis
Tél: 418-627-6254 ext: 309
Directeur (par intérim), Politiques et Intégité du territoire, Benoit Trudel
Tél: 418-627-6362 ext: 260

Ministère de la Santé et des Services sociaux / Health & Social Services

Direction des communications, 1075, ch Sainte-Foy, 16e étage, Québec, QC G1S 2M1
Tél: 418-643-9395
Téléc: 418-643-4768
regisseur.web@msss.gouv.qc.ca
www.msss.gouv.qc.ca
Lois administrées:
Loi sur la protection de la santé publique/Public Health Protection Act
Loi sur la santé publique/Public Health Act
Loi sur le tabac/Tobacco Act

Ministre, Santé et des services sociaux et Ministre responsable des aînés, L'hon. Réjean Hébert
Tél: 418-266-7171
Téléc: 418-266-7197
ministre@msss.gouv.qc.ca

Ministre déléguée, Santé publique et à la Protection de la jeunesse, L'hon. Véronique Hivon
Tél: 418-266-7181
Téléc: 418-266-7199
Ministre.deleguee@msss.gouv.qc.ca

Sous-ministre, Jacques Cotton
Tél: 418-266-8989
Téléc: 418-266-8990

Agences, Conseils et Commissions Associés/ Associated Agencies, Boards & Commissions:

• **Commissaire à la santé et du bien-être (CSBE) / Health & Welfare Commission**
#700, 1020, rte de l'Église
Québec, QC G1V 3V9
Tél: 418-643-3040
Téléc: 418-644-0654
csbe@csbe.gouv.qc.ca
www.csbe.gouv.qc.ca
• **Corporation d'hébergement du Québec (CHQ) / Long Term Care Facilities Corporation of Québec**
2535, boul Laurier, 5e étage
Québec, QC G1V 4M3
Tél: 418-644-3600
Téléc: 418-644-3609
Ligne sans frais: 877-747-9911
clientele.sante@siq.gouv.qc.ca
www.chq.gouv.qc.ca
• **Institut national d'excellence en santé et en services sociaux (INESSS) / National Institute for Excellence in Health & Social Services**
#10.083, 2021, av Union
Montréal, QC H3A 2S9
Tél: 514-873-2563
Téléc: 514-873-1369
inesss@inesss.qc.ca
www.inesss.qc.ca
• **Institut national de santé publique du Québec / National Public Health Institute of Québec**
945, av Wolfe
Québec, QC G1V 5B3
Tél: 418-650-5115
Téléc: 418-646-9328
info@inspq.qc.ca
www.inspq.qc.ca
Autres numéros: Poste: 5336
Président-directeur général, Luc Boileau
• **Modernisation des centres hospitaliers universitaires de Montréal, CHUM, CUSM, CHU Sainte-Justine / Modernization of Montréal's University Health Centres CHUM, MUHC and Sainte-Justine UHC**
#10.049, 2021, rue Union
Montréal, QC H3A 2S9
Tél: 514-864-9883
Téléc: 514-873-7362
info.construction3chu@msss.gouv.qc.ca
construction3chu.msss.gouv.qc.ca
• **Office des personnes handicapées du Québec / Office for Handicapped Persons**
309, rue Brock
Drummondville, QC J2B 1C5
Téléc: 819-475-8753
Ligne sans frais: 800-567-1465

TTY: 800-567-1477
aide@ophq.gouv.qc.ca
www.ophq.gouv.qc.ca
• **Régie de l'assurance maladie du Québec (RAMQ) / Québec Health Insurance Board**
1125, Grande Allée ouest
Québec, QC G1S 1E7
Tél: 418-646-4636
Ligne sans frais: 800-561-9749
www.ramq.gouv.qc.ca
• **Secrétariat à l'accès aux services en langue anglaise et aux communautés ethnoculturelles / English Language & Ethnocultural Communities Services Secretariat**
#840, 2021, av Union
Montréal, QC H3A 2S9
Tél: 514-873-5163
Téléc: 514-873-9876
www.msss.gouv.qc.ca/ministere/saslacc
• **Urgences-santé Québec / Emergency Health Services Québec**
3232, rue Bélanger
Montréal, QC H1Y 3H5
Tél: 514-723-5600
info@urgences-sante.qc.ca
www.urgences-sante.qc.ca

Cabinet du Sous-ministre / Office of the Deputy Minister

Coordination, financement, immobilisations et budget / Coordination, funding & capital budget
Sous-ministre associé, Michel Fontaine
Tél: 418-266-8850
Directeur général adjointe, Budget et des politiques des financement, François Dion
Tél: 418-266-5965
Directeur général adjointe, Coordination et aux ententes de gestion, Pierre Laflamme
Tél: 418-266-5812
Directeur général adjointe, Investissements, Sylvain Périgny
Tél: 418-266-5830
Directeur, Gestion budgétaire et comptable ministérielle, André Bolduc
Tél: 418-266-5986
Directeur, Gestion financière - réseau, Guylaine Lajoie
Tél: 418-266-5920
Directeur, Ressources matérielles, François Lamarre
Tél: 418-266-8760
Directeur, Allocation des ressources, Vacant
Tél: 418-266-7111
Directeur, Ententes de gestion, Vacant
Tél: 418-266-5980
Directeur, Secrétariat à l'accès aux services en langue anglaise et aux communautés culturelles, Ronald McNeil
Tél: 514-873-2292
Directeur (par intérim), Affaires autochtones, ethnoculturelles et régions nordiques, Louise Rondeau
Tél: 418-266-7128
Directeur, Relations institutionnelles, Martin Simard
Tél: 418-266-5800
Directeur, Inspection, Jean-François Therrien
Tél: 418-643-6084
Directrice, Investissements du financement, Marlène Sinclair
Tél: 418-266-5850
Directeur, Gestion intégrée de l'information, Alain Saucier
Tél: 418-266-8399
Directrice, Logistique sociosanitaire, Caroline Imbeau
Tél: 418-266-5835
Directeur, Expertise et de la normalisation, Pierre Gauthier
Tél: 418-266-5956

Planification, performance et qualité / Planning, Performance and Quality
Sous-ministre adjoint, Luc Castonguay
Tél: 418-266-5990
Directeur général adjointe, Performance, Éric Fournier
Tél: 418-266-7025
Directrice, Qualité, Sylvie Bernier
Tél: 418-266-7505
Directeur, Évaluation, Vacant
Tél: 418-266-7030
Directeur, Études et des analyses, Harold Côté
Tél: 418-266-7025
Directrice, Planification et orientations stratégiques, Andrée Quenneville, 2010-09-13
Tél: 418-266-7088
Directrice, Recherche, innovation et transfert des connaissances, Manon St-Pierre
Tél: 418-266-7056
Directrice, Affaires pharmaceutiques et du médicament, Hélène Beaulieu
Tél: 418-266-8810
Directrice, Affaires intergouvernementales et de la coopération internationale, Anne Marcoux
Tél: 418-266-8740

Santé publique / Public Health
Sous-ministre adjoint, Horacio Arruda
Tél: 514-873-1587
Directrice, Planification, évaluation et développement en santé publique, Lyne Jobin
Tél: 418-266-6780
Directeur, Développement des individus et de l'environnement social, André Dontigny
Tél: 418-266-6714
Directrice, Prévention des maladies chroniques et des traumatismes, Marie Rochette
Tél: 418-266-6750
Directrice, Protection de la santé publique, Danielle Auger
Tél: 514-864-2755
Directrice (par intérim), Surveillance de l'état de santé, Lyne Jobin
Tél: 418-266-6780

Services de santé et médecine universitaire / Health Services & Academic Medicine
Sous-ministre adjoint, Services de santé et médecine universitaire, Jean Rodrigue
Tél: 418-266-6930
Directrice, Main d'oeuvre médicale, Isabelle Savard
Tél: 418-266-6975
Directeur (par intérim), Organisation des services médicaux et technologiques, Yves Jalbert
Tél: 418-266-6946
Directrice, Services médicaux généraux, Jeannine Auger
Tél: 418-266-5827
Directeur, Affaires universitaires, Louis R. Dufresne
Tél: 418-266-7500
Directrice, Organisation des services de première ligne intégrés, Yolaine Galarneau
Tél: 418-266-6976
Directeur, Santé mentale, André Delorme
Tél: 418-266-6835
Directeur nationale, Urgences, services de traumatologie & services préhospitaliers d'urgence, Daniel Lefrançois
Tél: 418-266-5811
Directeur, Biovigilance, Yves Jalbert
Tél: 418-266-6946
Directeur, Soins infirmiers, Danielle Fleury
Tél: 418-266-8485

Services sociaux / Social Services
Sous-ministre adjoint, Sylvain Gagnon
Tél: 418-266-6800
Directeur général adjointe, Personnes ayant une déficience, des dépendances et de la coordination du soutien à domicile, Vacant
Tél: 418-266-6818
Directrice générale, Personnes âgées, Chantal Maltais
Tél: 418-266-6818
Directrice, Secrétariat à l'adoption internationale, Luce de Bellefeuille
Tél: 514-873-4747
Directeur (par intérim), Services sociaux généraux/Activités communautaires, Mario Frechette
Tél: 418-266-6936
Directrice (par intérim), Jeunes et des familles, Natalie Rosebush
Tél: 418-226-6840
Directrice, Dépendances et de l''itinérance, Lynne Duguay
Tél: 418-266-6830
Directrice, Presonnes ayant une déficience, Josette Chouinard
Tél: 418-266-6874

Technologies de l'information / Information Technology
Sous-ministre associée, Technologies de l'information, Lise Verrault
Tél: 418-266-8770
Directeur général adjoint, Projets, Vacant
Tél: 418-266-8770
Directeur, Relations d'affaires avec les clientèles, Clermont Saucier
Tél: 418-266-6935
Directeur (par intérim), Relations avec les partenaires et les mandataires, Clermont Saucier
Tél: 418-266-6935
Directrice, Sécurité des technologies de l'information, Sonia Roy
Tél: 418-266-6935
Directeur, Service financiers & administratif, Philippe Moss
Tél: 418-266-7118
Directeur, Soutien ministériel & infrastructures communes, Michel Rochette
Tél: 418-266-2287

Secrétariat aux aînés / Seniors

Commission de la santé et de la sécurité du travail du Québec (CSST) / Québec Occupational Health & Safety Commission

425, rue du Pont, CP 4900 Succ Terminus, Québec, QC G1K 7S6
Téléc: 418-266-4015
Ligne sans frais: 866-302-2778
www.csst.qc.ca
twitter.com/laCSST
www.facebook.com/laCSST
www.youtube.com/user/LaCSST
A pour mission de soutenir aux travailleurs & aux employeurs dans leurs démarches pour éliminer les dangers présents dans leur milieu de travail, inspecter des lieux de travail, & promouvoir la santé & sécurité du travail

Président & Chef de la direction, Michel Després

Vice-président, Opérations, Gaétan Thériault

Ministère de la Sécurité publique / Ministry of Public Security

Tour des Laurentides, 2525, boul Laurier, 5e étage, Québec, QC G1V 2L2
Tél: 418-643-2112
Téléc: 418-646-6168
Ligne sans frais: 866-644-6826
www.securitepublique.gouv.qc.ca
Secondary Address: #11.39, 10, rue Saint-Antoine est
Bureau de Montréal
Montréal, QC H2Y 1A2
Téléc: 514-873-6597
A pour mission d'assurer la sécurité publique au Québec
Lois administrées:
Loi sur la sécurité civile/Civil Protection Act
Loi sur la sécurité incendie/Fire Safety Act
Loi sur le ministère de la Sécurité publique/An Act respecting the Ministère de la Sécurité publique
Loi sur les bombes lacrymogènes/Act respecting tear bombs
Loi sur les explosifs/An Act respecting explosives

Ministre, L'hon. Stéphane Bergeron
Tél: 418-643-2112
Téléc: 418-646-6168
ministre@msp.gouv.qc.ca
Note: www.securitepublique.gouv.qc.ca

Sous-ministre, Martin Prud'homme

Agences, Conseils et Commissions Associés/ Associated Agencies, Boards & Commissions:

• **Bureau du coroner / Office of the Coroner**
Édifice le Delta 2
#390, 2875, boul Laurier
Québec, QC G1V 5B1
Tél: 418-643-1845
Téléc: 418-643-6174
Ligne sans frais: 866-312-7051
clientele.coroner@msp.gouv.qc.ca
www.coroner.gouv.qc.ca
• **Comité de déontologie policière / Police Ethics Committee**
Tour du Saint-Laurent
#A-200, 2525, boul Laurier, 2e étage
Québec, QC G1V 4Z6
Tél: 418-646-1936
Téléc: 418-528-0987
comite.deontologie@msp.gouv.qc.ca
www.deontologie-policiere.gouv.qc.ca

• Commissaire à la déontologie policière / Police Ethics Commissioner
#1-40, 1200, rte de l'Église
Québec, QC G1V 4Y9
Tél: 418-643-7897
Téléc: 418-528-9473
Ligne sans frais: 877-237-7897
deontologie-policiere.quebec@msp.gouv.qc.ca
www.deontologie-policiere.gouv.qc.ca

• Commissaire à la lutte contre la corruption (Unité permanente anticorruption) (UPAC) / Commissioner in the Fight Against Corruption
#UA8010, 600, rue Fullum
Montréal, QC H2K 3L6
Tél: 514-228-3098
Téléc: 514-873-0177
Ligne sans frais: 855-567-8722
upac@upac.gouv.qc.ca
www.upac.gouv.qc.ca

• Commissariat des incendies / Fire Commissioner
455, rue Dupont
Québec, QC G1K 6N2
Tél: 418-529-5706
Téléc: 418-529-9922
www.securitepublique.gouv.qc.ca/securite-incendie.html
Commissaire-enquêteur, Cyrille Delâge
cdelage@notarius.net

• Commission québecoise des libérations conditionnelles (CQLC) / Parole Board
#1.32A, 300, boul Jean-Lesage
Québec, QC G1K 8K6
Tél: 418-646-8300
Téléc: 418-643-7217
cqlc@msp.gouv.qc.ca
www.cqlc.gouv.qc.ca

• Direction générale de la Sûreté du Québec / Provincial Police
1701, rue Parthenais
Montréal, QC H2K 3S7
Tél: 514-598-4141
Téléc: 514-598-4242
www.sq.gouv.qc.ca

• École nationale de police du Québec (ENPQ) / National Police School of Québec
350, rue Marguerite-d'Youville
Nicolet, QC J3T 1X4
Tél: 819-293-8631
Téléc: 819-293-8630
courriel@enpq.qc.ca
www.enpq.qc.ca

• École nationale des pompiers du Québec (ENPQ) / Québec National Fire Fighters School
#3.08, 2800, boul Saint-Martin ouest
Laval, QC H7T 2S9
Tél: 450-680-6800
Téléc: 450-680-6818
Ligne sans frais: 866-680-3677
www.enpq.gouv.qc.ca
Directeur général, Michel Richer

• Régie des alcools, des courses et des jeux (RACJ) / Liquor, Gaming & Racing Board
560, boul Charest est
Québec, QC G1K 3J3
Tél: 418-643-7667
Téléc: 418-643-5971
Ligne sans frais: 800-363-0320
www.racj.gouv.qc.ca

Sécurité civile et Sécurité incendie / Public Safety & Fire Services
Sous-ministre associé & directeur général, Guy Laroche
Tél: 418-643-3500
Téléc: 418-643-0275
Directeur, Opérations, Éric Houde
Tél: 418-646-6777 ext: 400
Téléc: 418-646-5426
Directeur (par intérim), Prévention et de la planification, Raynald Chassé
Directeur (par intérim), Service de l'analyse et des politiques, Marc Morin
2525, boul Laurier, 6e étage
Sainte-Foy, QC G1V 2L2 Canada
Directeur, Rétablissement, Denis Landry
Tél: 418-646-6638
Téléc: 418-646-6628
Bas-Saint-Laurent, Gaspésie et Iles-de-la-Madeleine
#60, 70, rue Saint-Germain est, Rimouski, QC G5L 7J9
Tel: 418-727-3589
Fax: 418-727-3643
securite.civile01@msp.gouv.qc.ca
Directeur, Jacques Bélanger
Capitale-Nationale, Chaudière Appalaches et Nunavik
#200, 1122, Grande-Allée ouest, Québec, QC G1S 1E5
Tél: 418-643-3244
Téléc: 418-644-2080
securite.civile03@msp.gouv.qc.ca
Directrice, France-Sylvie Loisel
Estrie et Montérégie
165, rue Jacques-Cartier nord, Saint-Jean-sur-Richelieu, QC J3B 6S9
Tél: 450-346-3200
Téléc: 450-346-5856
securite.civile16@msp.gouv.qc.ca
Directrice, Christine Savard
Mauricie et Centre-du-Québec
4000, rue Louis-Pinard, Trois-Rivières, QC G8Y 4L9
Tel: 819-371-6703
Fax: 819-371-6983
securite.civile04@msp.gouv.qc.ca
Directeur, Sébastien Doire
Montréal, Laval, Lanaudière et Laurentides
RC #23, 5100, rue Sherbrooke est, Montréal, QC H1V 3R9
Tél: 514-873-1300
Téléc: 514-864-8654
securite.civile06@msp.gouv.qc.ca
Autres nombres: securite.civile13@msp.gouv.qc.ca; securite.civile14@msp.gouv.qc.ca; securite.civile15@msp.gouv.qc.ca
Directeur, Louis Métivier
Outaouais, Abitibi-Témiscamingue et Nord-du-Québec
817, boul St-René ouest, Gatineau, QC J8T 8M3
Tel: 819-772-3737
Fax: 819-772-3954
securite.civile07@msp.gouv.qc.ca
Directeur, Jacques Viger
Saguenay-Lac-Saint-Jean et Côte-Nord
RC #01, 3950, boul Harvey, Saguenay, QC G7X 8L6
Tel: 418-695-7872
Fax: 418-695-7875
securite.civile02@msp.gouv.qc.ca
Directeur, Pierre Dassylva

Services Québec

Bureau de la qualité, 800, place D'Youville, 20e étage, Québec, QC G1R 3P4
Tél: 418-644-4545
Ligne sans frais: 877-644-4545
TTY: 800-361-9596
www.gouv.qc.ca/portail/quebec/servicesquebec
Autres nombres: Montréal: 514-644-4545

Présidente, Monique L. Bégin

Président-directeur général (par intérim) et vice-président, Développement des services et au partenariat, Pierre E. Rodrigue

Vice-présidente, Relations avec les citoyens et les entreprises, Jean Audet

Directrice générale, Secrétariat, de l'administration et des communications, Réjeanne Lachance

Ministère du Tourisme / Tourism Québec

#400, 900, boul René-Lévesque est, Québec, QC G1R 2B5
Tél: 418-643-5959
Téléc: 418-646-8723
Ligne sans frais: 800-482-2433
www.tourisme.gouv.qc.ca

Ministre, L'hon. Pascal Bérubé
Tél: 418-528-8063
Téléc: 418-528-8066
ministre@tourisme.gouv.qc.ca

Sous-ministre, Suzanne Giguère
Tél: 418-643-5959 ext: 503

Secrétariat, David Belgue
Tél: 418-643-5959 ext: 349

Agences, Conseils et Commissions Associés/ Associated Agencies, Boards & Commissions:

• Régie des installations olympiques/Parc olympique Québec / Québec Olympic Park
4141, av Pierre-De Coubertin
Montréal, QC H1V 3N7
Tél: 514-252-4141
Téléc: 514-252-0372
Ligne sans frais: 877-997-0919
rio@rio.gouv.qc.ca
www.parcolympique.qc.ca

• Société du Centre des congrès de Québec / Québec City Convention Centre
1000, boul René-Lévesque est
Québec, QC G1R 5T8
Tél: 418-644-4000
Téléc: 418-644-6455
Ligne sans frais: 888-679-4000
www.convention.qc.ca

• Société du Palais des congrès de Montréal / Montréal City Convention Centre
159, rue Saint-Antoine ouest, 9é étage
Montréal, QC H2Z 1H2
Tél: 514-871-8122
Téléc: 514-871-9389
Ligne sans frais: 800-268-8122
info@congresmtl.com
congresmtl.com
Sous-ministre adjoint, Georges Vacher
Tél: 514-873-7977 ext: 560
Directeur général, Services à la clientèle touristique, Sylvain Lacombe
Directrice générale, Marketing, Sylvie Quenneville
Directeur, Stratégie et de la mise en marché, Alain Dupont
Directeur, Opérations, Julien Cormier
Directrice, Renseignements par téléphone et Internet, Brigitte Hernando
Directrice, Centre d'affaires électroniques, Michèle Morel

Ministère des Transports (MTQ) / Transportation

700, boul René-Lévesque est, 28e étage, Québec, QC G1R 5H1
Tél: 418-643-6980
Téléc: 418-643-2033
Ligne sans frais: 888-355-0511
communications@mtq.gouv.qc.ca
www.mtq.gouv.qc.ca
Autres nombres: Au Québec: 5-1-1
Secondary Address: 500, boul René-Lévesque ouest, 16e étage
Montréal, QC H4Z 1W7
Téléc: 514-864-2836

Lois administrées:
Code de la sécurité routière/Highway Safety Code
Loi concernant les partenariats en matière d'infrastructures de transport/Act respecting transport infrastructure partnerships
Loi concernant les propriétaires et exploitants de véhicules lourds/Act respecting owners and operators of heavy vehicles
Loi sur l'expropriation/Expropriation Act
Loi sur la sécurité du transport terrestre guidé/Act to ensure safety in guided land transportation
Loi sur la voirie/Act respecting roads
Loi sur les chemins de fer/Railway Act
Loi sur les sociétés de transport en commun/Act respecting public transit authorities
Loi sur les véhicules hors route/Act respecting off-highway vehicles

Ministre, L'hon. Sylvain Gaudreault
Tél: 418-643-6980
Téléc: 418-643-2033
ministre@mtq.gouv.qc.ca

Directeur, Cabinet du ministre, Thierry St-Cyr
Tél: 418-643-6980

Agences, Conseils et Commissions Associés/ Associated Agencies, Boards & Commissions:

• Agence métropolitaine de transport
700, rue De La Gauchetière Ouest, 26e étage
Montréal, QC H3B 5M2
Tél: 514-287-2464
www.amt.qc.ca

• **Commission de la capitale nationale du Québec**
Edifice Hector-Fabre
525 boul René-Lévesque Est, RC
Québec, QC G1R 5S9
Tél: 418-528-0773
Téléc: 418-528-0833
Ligne sans frais: 800-442-0773
commission@capitale.gouv.qc.ca
www.capitale.gouv.qc.ca
• **Commission des transports du Québec / Québec Transport Commission**
200, ch Sainte-Foy, 7e étage
Québec, QC G1R 5V5
Téléc: 418-644-8034
Ligne sans frais: 888-461-2433
www.ctq.gouv.qc.ca
Président, Daniel Bureau
Tel: 418-266-0350
• **Société de l'assurance automobile du Québec (SAAQ)**
333, boul Jean-Lesage
CP 19600 Terminus
Québec, QC G1K 8J6
Tél: 418-643-7620
Téléc: 418-644-0339
Ligne sans frais: 800-361-7620
TTY: 800-565-7763
courrier@saaq.gouv.qc.ca
www.saaq.gouv.qc.ca
• **Société des traversiers du Québec / Ferries Québec**
250, rue Saint-Paul
Québec, QC G1K 9K9
Tél: 418-643-2019
Téléc: 418-643-7308
stq@traversiers.gouv.qc.ca
www.traversiers.gouv.qc.ca
Président et directeur général, Georges Farrah
• **Société du port ferroviaire Baie-Comeau-Hauterive / Baie-Comeau-Hauterive Railway Station**
18, rte Maritime
Baie-Comeau, QC G4Z 2L6
Tél: 418-296-6785
Téléc: 418-296-2377
societeduport@globetrotter.net
www.sopor.ca

Bureau de la sous-ministre / Office of the Deputy Minister
Sous-ministre, Dominique Savoie
Tél: 418-643-6740

Infrastructures et technologies / Infrastructure & Technologies
Directrice générale et sous-ministre adjointe, Anne-Marie Leclerc
Tél: 418-528-0808
Directeur, Structures, Daniel Bouchard
Tél: 418-643-6906
Directeur, Soutien aux opérations, Éric Breton
Tél: 418-643-9298
Directeur, Parcs routiers, Claude Marquis
Tél: 418-646-8301
Directeur, Environnement et recherche, Christian Therrien
Tél: 418-643-8326
Directeur, Laboratoire des chaussées, Guy Tremblay
Tél: 418-643-6618

Politiques et sécurité en transport / Transportation Policy & Security
Directeur général et sous-ministre adjoint, André Meloche
Tél: 418-528-0808
Directeur, Transport routier des marchandises, Benoît Cayouette
Tél: 418-528-0631
Directrice, Transport terrestre des personnes, France Dompierre
Tél: 418-644-0324
Directrice, Transport maritime, aérien et ferroviaire, Josée Hallé
Tél: 418-643-1864
Directeur, Sécurité en transport, Claude Morin
Tél: 418-643-1564

Services à la gestion et de la surveillance des marchés / Administrative Services & Market Oversight
Directrice générale et directrice (par intérim), Contrats et ressources matérielles, Josée Dupont
Tél: 418-528-0808
Directrice générale adjointe, Ressources humaines financières et informationnelles, Danièle Cantin
Tél: 418-646-9934
Directrice, Enquêtes et analyse de marché, Chantale Brouillet
Tél: 418-643-6840
Directeur, Planification budgétaire et expertise immobilière, Raymond Cloutier
Tél: 418-644-2182
Directrice, Gestion financière et information, Brigitte Duchesne
Tél: 418-646-9932
Directrice, Ressources humaines, Mireille Parent
Tél: 418-646-4157
Directeur, Technologies de l'information, Louis Potvin
Tél: 418-643-4431

Territoires / Territories
Directeur général et sous-ministre adoint, André Caron
Tél: 418-528-0808
Directrice générale adjointe, Planification et de la coordination territoriale, Chantal Gingras
Tél: 514-864-1850
Directrice générale adjointe, Projets stratégiques, Ginette Sylvain
Tél: 514-864-1850
Directeur, Programmation, ressources, et opérations, Mario Bergeron
Tél: 418-643-7726
Directeur, Projet Turcot, Alain Marc Dubé
Tél: 514-873-3838
Directeur, Planification et suivi des projets, Fadi Moubayed
Tél: 514-864-1730
Directeur, Projets routiers et de transport collectif, Maroun Shaneen
Tél: 514-873-7781
Directrice, Gouvernance des projets stratégiques et des partenariats public-privé, Sandra Sultana
Tél: 514-873-4377
Abitibi-Témiscamingue
80, av Québec, Rouyn-Noranda, QC J9X 6R1
Tél: 819-763-3271
Téléc: 819-763-3493
dat@mtq.gouv.qc.ca
Bas-Saint-Laurent—Gaspésie—Îles-de-la-Madeleine
#101, 92, 2e rue ouest, Rimouski, QC G5L 8E6
Tél: 418-727-3674
Téléc: 418-727-3673
dtbgi@mtq.gouv.qc.ca
Capitale-Nationale
475, boul de l'Atrium, 2e étage, Québec, QC G1H 7H9
Tél: 418-643-1911
Téléc: 418-646-0003
dcnat@mtq.gouv.qc.ca
Chaudière-Appalaches
1156, boul de la Rive-Sud, Saint-Romuald, QC G6W 5M6
Tél: 418-839-5581
Téléc: 418-834-7338
dtca@mtq.gouv.qc.ca
Côte-Nord
#110, 625, boul Laflèche, Baie-Comeau, QC G5C 1C5
Tél: 418-295-4765
Téléc: 418-295-4766
cotenord@mtq.gouv.qc.ca
Est-de-la-Montérégie
201, place Charles-Lemoyne, 5e étage, Longueuil, QC J4K 2T5
Tél: 450-677-3413
Téléc: 450-442-1317
dtem@mtq.gouv.qc.ca
Estrie
#2.02, 200, rue Belvédère nord, Sherbrooke, QC J1H 4A9
Tél: 819-820-3280
Téléc: 819-820-3118
dte@mtq.gouv.qc.ca
Île-de-Montréal
500, boul René-Lévesque ouest, 12e étage, CP 5Montréal, QC H2Z 1W7
Tél: 514-873-7781
Téléc: 514-864-3867
dtim@mtq.gouv.qc.ca
Laurentides-Lanaudière
222, rue Saint-Georges, 2e étage, Saint-Jérôme, QC J7Z 4Z9
Tél: 450-569-3057
Téléc: 450-569-3072
dll@mtq.gouv.qc.ca
Laval-Mille-Îles
1725, boul Le Corbusier, Laval, QC H7S 2K7
Tél: 450-680-6330
Téléc: 450-973-4959
dtlmi@mtq.gouv.qc.ca
Mauricie—Centre-du-Québec
100, rue Laviolette, 4e étage, Trois-Rivières, QC G9A 5S9
Tél: 819-371-6896
Téléc: 819-371-6136
dmcq@mtq.gouv.qc.ca
Ouest-de-la-Montérégie
#200, 180, boul d'Anjou, Châteauguay, QC J6K 1C4
Tél: 450-698-3400
Téléc: 450-698-3452
dtom@mtq.gouv.qc.ca
Outaouais
#5.110, 170, rue de l'Hôtel-de-Ville, Gatineau, QC J8X 4C2
Tél: 819-772-3849
Téléc: 819-772-3338
dto@mtq.gouv.qc.ca
Saguenay—Lac-Saint-Jean—Chibougamau
3950, boul Harvey, Jonquière, QC G7X 8L6
Tél: 418-695-7916
Téléc: 418-695-7926
dt.slsjc@mtq.gouv.qc.ca

Ministère du Travail / Labour

200, ch Sainte-Foy, 5e étage, Québec, QC G1R 5S1
Tél: 418-644-4545
Téléc: 418-528-0559
Ligne sans frais: 800-643-4817
www.travail.gouv.qc.ca
Lois administrées:
Loi sur la santé et la sécurité du travail/Occupational Health & Safety Act
Loi sur les accidents du travail et les maladies professionnelles/Act respecting accidents at work & professional illness or sickness

Ministre, L'hon. Agnès Maltais
Tél: 418-643-5297
Téléc: 418-644-0003
ministre@mess.gouv.qc.ca

Sous-ministre, Brigitte Pelletier
Tél: 418-643-2902
Téléc: 418-643-0735

Directeur, Communications, Gervais Fortier
Tél: 418-646-2642

Agences, Conseils et Commissions Associés/ Associated Agencies, Boards & Commissions:

• **Commission de la construction du Québec (CCQ) / Québec Construction Commission**
8485, av Christophe-Colomb
Montréal, QC H2M 0A7
Ligne sans frais: 888-842-8282
www.ccq.org
• **Commission de l'équité salariale (CES) / Pay Equity Commission**
200, ch Ste-Foy, 4e étage
Québec, QC G1R 6A1
Tél: 418-528-8765
Téléc: 418-528-6999
Ligne sans frais: 888-528-8765
equite.salariale@ces.gouv.qc.ca
www.ces.gouv.qc.ca
• **Commission des lésions professionnelles (CLP) / Work-Related Injuries Commission**
#700, 900, Place d'Youville
Québec, QC G1R 3P7
Tél: 418-644-7777
Téléc: 418-644-6443
Ligne sans frais: 800-463-1591
www.clp.gouv.qc.ca
Administrative tribunal that is the last recourse for employers or workers who contest a decision made by the Commission de la santé et de la sécurité du travail.
Présidente et juge administratif en chef, Marie Lamarre
Tél: 418-643-5643
Téléc: 418-528-9042
Vice-président, Opérations, Bernard Lemay
Vice-présidente, Qualité et de la cohérence, Lucie Nadeau
• **Commission des normes du travail (CNT) / Labour Standards Commission**
Hall Est
400, boul Jean-Lesage, 7e étage
Québec, QC G1K 8W1

Tél: 514-873-7061
Ligne sans frais: 800-265-1414
www.cnt.gouv.qc.ca
Présidente-directrice générale (par intérim), Marie-Claude Champoux

• **Commission des relations du travail (CRT) / Labour Relations Commission**
900, boul René-Lévesque est, 5e étage
Québec, QC G1R 6C9
Tél: 418-643-3208
Téléc: 418-643-8946
Ligne sans frais: 866-864-3646
crtm@crt.gouv.qc.ca
www.crt.gouv.qc.ca
Président, Robert Côté
Tél: 514-864-1890

• **Commission de la santé et de la sécurité du travail (CSST) / Occupational Health & Safety Commission**
See Entry Name Index for detailed listing.

• **Conseil consultatif du travail et de la main d'oeuvre (CCTM) / Advisory Council on Labour & Manpower**
#17.100, 500, boul René-Lévesque ouest
Montréal, QC H2Z 1W7
Tél: 514-873-2880
Téléc: 514-873-1129
cctm@cctm.gouv.qc.ca
www.cctm.gouv.qc.ca

• **Régie du bâtiment du Québec (RBQ) / Québec Construction Companies Board**
545, boul Crémazie est, 4e étage
Montréal, QC H2M 2V2
Tél: 514-873-0976
Téléc: 514-864-2903
Ligne sans frais: 800-361-0761
crc@rbq.gouv.qc.ca
www.rbq.gouv.qc.ca

Politiques et recherche / Policy & Research
Sous-ministre adjoint, Normand Pelletier
Directeur, Politiques du travail, Steeve Audet
Directeur, Information sur le travail, Charles Bélanger
Directeur (par intérim), Recherche et innovation en milieu de travail, Martine Poulin

Relations du travail / Labour Relations
Sous-ministre adjointe, Suzanne Thérien
Directeur générale, Daniel Cholette
Directeur (par intérim), Médiation-conciliation & prévention (Montréal), Robert Dupuis
Directeur, Médiation-conciliation, prévention & arbitrage (Québec), Jean Poirier
Directeur, Bureau d'évaluation médicale, Dr André Perron

Ministre responsable de l'Administration gouvernementale & Présidente du Conseil du trésor, et ministre responsable de la région du Saguenay-Lac-Saint-Jean, L'hon. Stéphane Bédard
Tél: 418-643-5926
Téléc: 418-643-7824
cabinet@sct.gouv.qc.ca
Secrétaire associé, Julie Blackburn
Tél: 418-643-0875 ext: 490

Government of Saskatchewan

Seat of Government: Regina, SK S4S 0B3
www.gov.sk.ca
The Province of Saskatchewan entered Confederation on September 1, 1905. It has an area of 588,276.09 km2, & the StatsCan census population in 2011 was 1,033,381.

Assistant Deputy Minister, Employment, Immigration and Training, Rupen Pandya
Tel: 306-787-6846
Fax: 306-798-0975
Rupen.Pandya@gov.sk.ca

Saskatchewan Agriculture (AG)

Walter Scott Bldg., 3085 Albert St., Regina, SK S4S 0B1
Toll-Free: 866-457-2377
aginfo@gov.sk.ca
www.agriculture.gov.sk.ca
The Ministry's mandate is to foster, in partnership with individuals, communities, industry, & government, a commercially viable, self-sufficient, & sustainable agricultural sector in Saskatchewan. The Ministry addresses needs of individual farmers & ranchers, encourages & develops higher value production & processing, & promotes sustainable economic development in rural areas of the province. Some responsibilities are as follows: agri-business development through provision of agriculture-based business experts & technical support; agricultural research to promote development & diversification; corporate services to support the Information Technology Office & the Rural Economic Co-operative Development; crop development; financial programs; inspection & administration of regulations for food & crop protection, animal disease surveillance, environmental reviews, licenses, registrations, & complaint resolution; irrigation development; promotion of sustainable use of Crown land; livestock development; provision of food safety, quality, policy, regulatory, market & business development programs; policy analysis, strategies, & agricultural information services; & delivery of Saskatchewan Crop Insurance Corporation programs & services.

Acts Administered:
Agri-Food Act, 2004
Agri-Food Innovation Act
Animal Products Act
Bacterial Ring Rot Control Regulations
Department of Agriculture, Food & Rural Revitilization Act
Disease of Animals Act
Dutch Elm Disease Control Regulations
Expropriation (Rehabilitation Projects) Act
Farming Communities Land Act
Irrigation Act
Line Fence Act
Pastures Act
Pest Control Act
Pest Control Products (Saskatchewan) Act
Provincial Lands Act
Sale or Lease of Certain Lands Act
Saskatchewan Wetland Conservation Corporation Land Regulation
Soil Drifting Control Act
Weed Control Act

Minister, Agriculture; Minister Responsible, Saskatchewan Crop Insurance Corporation, Hon. Lyle Stewart
Tel: 306-787-0338
Fax: 306-787-0630
minister.ag@gov.sk.ca
Social Media:
www.facebook.com/group.php?gid=182442928469194
Office of the Minister of Agriculture, Legislative Bldg.
#334, 2405 Legislative Dr.
Regina, SK S4S 0B3

Deputy Minister, Agriculture, Alanna Koch
Tel: 306-787-5170
Fax: 306-787-2393
alanna.koch@gov.sk.ca

Assistant Deputy Minister, Rick Burton
Tel: 306-787-8077
Fax: 306-787-2393
rick.burton@gov.sk.ca

Executive Director, Corporate Services, Raymond Arscott
Tel: 306-787-5211
Fax: 306-787-0600
raymond.arscott@gov.sk.ca

Executive Director, Policy, Scott Brown
Tel: 306-787-5961
Fax: 306-787-5134
Scott.Brown@gov.sk.ca

Executive Director, Saskatchewan 4-H Council, Valerie Pearson
Tel: 306-933-7729
Fax: 306-933-7730
valerie.pearson@gov.sk.ca

Director, Regional Services, Lee Auten
Tel: 306-787-5018
Fax: 306-787-9623
lee.auten@gov.sk.ca

Director, Crops, Doug Billett
Tel: 306-787-8061
Fax: 306-787-0428
doug.billett@gov.sk.ca

Director, Lands, Wally Hoehn
Tel: 306-787-1045
Fax: 306-787-5180
Wally.Hoehn@gov.sk.ca

Director, Agriculture Research, Abdul Jalil
Tel: 306-787-5960
Fax: 306-787-2654
abdul.jalil@gov.sk.ca

Director, Livestock, Paul Johnson
Tel: 306-787-6423
Fax: 306-787-1315
paul.johnson@gov.sk.ca

Associated Agencies, Boards & Commissions:

• **Agri-Food Council**
#302, 3085 Albert St.
Regina, SK S4S 0B1
Tel: 306-787-5978
Fax: 306-787-5134
corey.ruud@gov.sk.ca
www.agriculture.gov.sk.ca/Agri-Food-Council
The Agri-Food Council is an independent board appointed by the provincial government. The Council is accountable to the Minister of Agriculture for the supervision of all agencies established under The Agri-Food Act, 2004.
Chair, Robert Tyler

• **Agricultural Implements Board**
#202, 3085 Albert St.
Regina, SK S4S 0B1
Tel: 306-787-4693
Fax: 306-787-1315
Chair, Jeffrey Wheaton
Secretary, Don Brooks

• **Farm Stress Unit**
#125, 3085 Albert St.
Regina, SK S4S 0B1
Tel: 306-787-5196
Fax: 306-798-3042
Toll-free: 800-667-4442

• **Farmland Security Board**
#207, 3988 Albert St.
Regina, SK S4S 3R1
Tel: 306-787-5047
Fax: 306-787-8599
General Manager, Mark Folk
Tel: 306-787-5153
Fax: 306-787-8599
mfolk@farmland.gov.sk.ca
Manager, Farm Foreclosure/Home Quarter Protection, Dick Wellman
Tel: 306-787-5181
Fax: 306-787-8599
dwellman@farmland.gov.sk.ca

• **Prairie Agricultural Machinery Institute (PAMI)**
Hwy 5 West
PO Box 1150
Humboldt, SK S0K 2A0
Tel: 306-682-2555
Fax: 306-682-5080
Toll-free: 800-567-7264
humboldt@pami.ca
www.pami.ca
PAMI works for the advancement of technology in agriculture through research and development.

• **Saskatchewan Crop Insurance Corporation**
484 Prince William Dr.
PO Box 3000
Melville, SK S0A 2P0
Tel: 306-728-7200
Fax: 306-728-7202
Toll-free: 888-935-0000
customer.service@scic.gov.sk.ca
www.saskcropinsurance.com
The provincial Crown Corporation provides responsive & flexible risk management tools. Crop insurance programs are as follows: Multi-Peril Insurance; Organic Insurance; Forage Insurance; & Weather Based Insurance.
Minister Responsible, Hon. Bob Bjornerud
minister.ag@gov.sk.ca
Chair, Alanna Koch

• **Saskatchewan Egg Producers (SEP)**
496 Hoffer Dr.
PO Box 1263
Regina, SK S4P 3B8
Tel: 306-924-1505
Fax: 306-924-1515
sep@saskegg.ca
www.saskegg.ca
• **Saskatchewan Lands Appeal Board (SLAB)**
#202, 3085 Albert St.
Regina, SK S4S 0B1
Tel: 306-787-4693
Fax: 306-787-1315
Donald.Brooks@gov.sk.ca
Secretary, Donald Brooks
Tel: 306-787-4693
Fax: 306-787-8599
• **Saskatchewan Milk Marketing Board (SMMB)**
444 McLeod St.
Regina, SK S4N 4Z3
Tel: 306-949-6999
Fax: 306-949-2605
www.saskmilk.ca
• **Saskatchewan Sheep Development Board**
2213C Hanselman Crt.
Saskatoon, SK S7L 6A8
Tel: 306-933-5200
Fax: 306-933-7182
sheepdb@sasktel.net; gordsheepdb@sasktel.net
www.sksheep.com
Executive Director, Gord Schroeder
Tel: 306-933-5582
• **Saskatchewan Turkey Producers Marketing Board**
502 - 45th St. West, 2nd Fl.
Saskatoon, SK S7L 6H2
Tel: 306-931-1050
Fax: 306-931-2825
saskaturkey@sasktel.net
The STP manages the supply management system in Saskatchewan & raises levies in order to submit their own levy to the Canadian Turkey Marketing Agency (CTMA). The STP negotiates the province's quota levels with the CTMA, negotiates price levels with local processors, & develops a long-term strategy for the turkey industry in Saskatchewan.
Chair, Kevin Pulvermacher
Tel: 306-369-2952
Director, Jelmer Wiersma
Tel: 306-256-3494

Saskatchewan Assessment Management Agency (SAMA)

#200, 2201 - 11th Ave., Regina, SK S4P 0J8
Tel: 306-924-8000
Fax: 306-924-8070
Toll-Free: 800-667-7262
info.request@sama.sk.ca
www.sama.sk.ca
SAMA is an independent agency with responsibility to develop & maintain the province's assessment policies, standards & procedures, audit assessments, & review & confirm municipal assessment rolls & provide property valuation services to local governments (municipalities & school boards).

Chair, Neal Hardy

Chief Executive Officer, Irwin Blank
Tel: 306-924-8046
Fax: 306-924-8060

Managing Director, Finance, George Dobni
Tel: 306-924-8025
Fax: 306-924-8060

Managing Director, Assessment Services, Brad Korbo
Tel: 306-924-8017
Fax: 306-924-8070

Managing Director, Administration, Betty Rogers
Tel: 306-924-8032
Fax: 306-924-8060

Managing Director, Quality Assurance, Gordon Senz
Tel: 306-924-8008
Fax: 306-924-8067

Managing Director, Technical Standards & Policy, Steve Suchan
Tel: 306-924-8024
Fax: 306-924-8060

Director, Technical Standards, Shaun Cooney
Tel: 306-924-8030
Fax: 306-924-8070

Director, Information Services, Mike Kraus
Tel: 306-540-9681
Fax: 306-924-8070

Director, Liaison & Policy, Gord Larson
Tel: 306-924-8049
Fax: 306-924-8070

Accommodation Services Division

The Municipal Relations Division strengthens Saskatchewan communities by providing the legal framework, organizational support, financial assistance & other services for the operation of municipalities. Working in partnership with municipal organizations & other communities, the Division encourages cooperation, understanding & self-reliance.
Assistant Deputy Minister, Asset Management, Allen Mullen
Tel: 306-787-8018
Fax: 306-798-0370
allen.mullen@gov.sk.cas
Assistant Deputy Minister, Facility Management, Richard Murray
Tel: 306-787-9586
Fax: 306-798-0371
richard.murray@gov.sk.ca
Director, Sustainability & Energy Management, Howard Arndt
Tel: 306-787-2033
Fax: 306-787-1980
Howard.Arndt@gov.sk.ca
Director, Real Estate Services, Alf Bernstein
Tel: 306-787-6959
Fax: 306-787-1980
alf.bernstein@gov.sk.ca
Director, Project Delivery North, Ivan Francis
Tel: 306-933-5676
Fax: 306-933-6999
ivan.francis@gov.sk.ca
Director, Capital & Infrastructure Management, Todd Godfrey
Tel: 306-787-2253
Fax: 306-787-1980
todd.godfrey@gov.sk.ca
Director, Project Delivery South, Paul Nepper
Tel: 306-787-0990
Fax: 306-798-0370
paul.nepper@gov.sk.ca
Acts Administered:
Architects Act, 1996
Interior Designers Act
Public Works & Services Act
Purchasing Act, 2004
Assistant Deputy Minister, Project Management & Delivery, Allen Mullen
Tel: 306-787-8018
Fax: 306-798-0370
allen.mullen@gov.sk.ca
#1420, 1855 Victoria Ave.
Regina, SK S4P 3T2 Canada
Assistant Deputy Minister, Property Management, Richard Murray
Tel: 306-787-9586
Fax: 306-798-0371
richard.murray@gov.sk.ca
#1420, 1855 Victoria Ave.
Regina, SK S4P 3T2 Canada
Executive Director, Commercial Services, Greg Lusk
Tel: 306-787-7842
Fax: 306-787-1061
Greg.Lusk@gov.sk.ca
#1420, 1855 Victoria Ave.
Regina, SK S4P 3T2 Canada
Director, Pricing & Data Management Services, Garth Belanger
Tel: 306-787-9680
Fax: 306-787-1980
garth.belanger@gov.sk.ca
#1420, 1855 Victoria Ave.
Regina, SK S4P 3T2 Canada
Director, Realty, Alf Bernstein
Tel: 306-787-6959
Fax: 306-787-1980
alf.bernstein@gov.sk.ca
#1420, 1855 Victoria Ave.
Regina, SK S4P 3T2 Canada
Director, Infrastructure Support, Dave Bryanton
Tel: 306-787-0959
Fax: 306-787-2019
Dave.Bryanton@gov.sk.ca
#1420, 1855 Victoria Ave.
Regina, SK S4P 3T2 Canada
Director, Sustainability, Rob Clarke
Tel: 306-787-6332
Fax: 306-787-1980
Rob.Clarke@gov.sk.ca
#1420, 1855 Victoria Ave.
Regina, SK S4P 3T2 Canada
Director, Mail Services, Carol Halvorson
Tel: 306-787-6866
Fax: 306-787-1873
carol.halvorson@gov.sk.ca
#1420, 1855 Victoria Ave.
Regina, SK S4P 3T2 Canada
Director, Protective Services, Glynn Mitchell
Tel: 306-787-9280
Fax: 306-787-9495
glynn.mitchell@gov.sk.ca
#1420, 1855 Victoria Ave.
Regina, SK S4P 3T2 Canada
Director, Executive Air Services, Chris Oleson
Tel: 306-787-7717
Fax: 306-787-1424
chris.oleson@gov.sk.ca
#1420, 1855 Victoria Ave.
Regina, SK S4P 3T2 Canada
Director, Strategic Portfolio Management, Loreen Porter
Tel: 306-787-4241
Fax: 306-787-1980
loreen.porter@gov.sk.ca
#1420, 1855 Victoria Ave.
Regina, SK S4P 3T2 Canada
Director, Central Vehicle Agency Business Process & Systems Implementation, Paul Radigan
Tel: 306-787-9046
Fax: 306-787-1061
paul.radigan@gov.sk.ca
#1420, 1855 Victoria Ave.
Regina, SK S4P 3T2 Canada
Director, Air Ambulance Services, Lee Smith
Tel: 306-933-6501
Fax: 306-933-5480
Lee.Smith@gov.sk.ca
#1420, 1855 Victoria Ave.
Regina, SK S4P 3T2 Canada

Saskatchewan Corrections & Policing (CPSP)

1874 Scarth St., Regina, SK S4P 4B3
Tel: 306-787-7872
communicationsCPSP@gov.sk.ca
www.cpsp.gov.sk.ca
The Ministry of Corrections, Public Safety & Policing promotes safe communities in Saskatchewan. Adult correction & young offender programs & services are delivered that serve individuals in conflict with the law. Public safety is also addressed through the following programs & services: protection & emergency planning & communication; monitoring of building standards; fire prevention & disaster assistance programs; & licensing & inspections services.

Minister Responsible, Corrections & Policing, Hon. Christine Tell
Tel: 306-787-4377
Fax: 306-787-5331
minister.cp@gov.sk.ca
Social Media: www.facebook.com/christinetellsp
Office of the Minister Responsible, Corrections & Policing, Legislative Building
#345, 2045 Legislative Dr.
Regina, SK S4S 0B3

Deputy Minister, Corrections & Policing, Dale McFee
Tel: 306-787-8065
Fax: 306-798-0270
dale.mcfee@gov.sk.ca

Executive Director, Strategic Systems & Innovation, Ron Anderson
Tel: 306-787-8062
Fax: 306-798-0270
ron.anderson@gov.sk.ca

Executive Director, Research & Evidence-based Excellence, Brian Rector
Tel: 306-787-3892
Fax: 306-798-0270
brian.rector@gov.sk.ca

Chief Information Officer, Darrel Treppel
Tel: 306-787-5651
Fax: 306-787-6979
darrel.treppel@gov.sk.ca

Director, Information Management, Cathy Drader
Tel: 306-787-9512
Fax: 306-787-6979
cathy.drader@gov.sk.ca

Chief Privacy & Access Officer, Freedom of Information & Privacy, Tom Young
Tel: 306-787-3316
Fax: 306-798-9007
tom.young@gov.sk.ca

Acting Director, Privacy, Access & Risk Management, Dawn Campbell
Tel: 306-798-0334
Fax: 306-798-9007
dawn.campbell@gov.sk.ca

Director, Clinical Services (Saskatoon), Delphine Gossner
Tel: 306-933-7383
Fax: 306-798-0270
delphine.gossner@gov.sk.ca

Director, Clinical Services (Regina CC), Terri Simon
Tel: 306-924-9973
Fax: 306-798-0270
terri.simonr@gov.sk.ca

Associated Agencies, Boards & Commissions:
• **Saskatchewan Police College (SkPC)**
217 College West Bldg., University of Regina
3737 Wascana Pkwy.
Regina, SK S4S 0A2
Tel: 306-787-8870
Fax: 306-787-8876
www.uregina.ca/police
• **Saskatchewan Police Commission**
1850 - 1881 Scarth St.
Regina, SK S4P 4K9
Tel: 306-787-6518
Fax: 306-787-0136
www.cpsp.gov.sk.ca/Saskatchewan-Police-Commission
The Commission promotes crime prevention, improved police relationships with communities, & effective policing throughout Saskatchewan by working closely with police services & Boards of Police Commissioners.

Energy & Resources (ER)

#300, 2103 - 11th Ave., Regina, SK S4P 3Z8
Tel: 306-787-2528
www.er.gov.sk.ca
To build an innovative, diversified, & sustainable economy for Saskatchewan, the Energy & Resources unit develops, implements, & promotes policies & programs related to the province's energy, mineral, & forestry sectors.
The following mineral resource databases are available: Saskatchewan Mineral Assessment Database; Saskatchewan Mineral Deposit Index; & Saskatchewan Kimberlite Indicator Minerals.
Minister Responsible, Energy & Resources; Minister Responsible, Tourism Saskatchewan; Minister Responsible, Trade; Minister Responsible, SaskEnergy Incorporated, Hon. Tim McMillan
Tel: 306-787-9124
Fax: 306-787-0395
minister.er@gov.sk.ca
Social Media: www.facebook.com/timmcmillanmla
Office of the Minister Responsible, Energy & Resources / Tourism Saskatchewan, Legislative Building
#346, 2405 Legislative Dr.
Regina, SK S4S 0B3
Assistant Deputy Minister, Petroleum & Natural Gas, Ed Dancsok
Tel: 306-787-2591
Fax: 306-787-2478
Ed.Dancsok@gov.sk.ca
Assistant Deputy Minister, Minerals, Lands, & Resource Policy, Hal Sanders
Tel: 306-787-3524
Fax: 306-787-2198
Hal.Sanders@gov.sk.ca

Minerals, Lands & Resource Policy

Tel: 306-787-8178
Fax: 306-787-2198
Assistant Deputy Minister, Hal Sanders
Tel: 306-787-3524
Fax: 306-787-2198
Hal.Sanders@gov.sk.ca
Chief Geologist, Gary Delaney
Tel: 306-787-1160
Fax: 306-787-1284
gary.delaney@gov.sk.ca
Executive Director, Lands & Mineral Tenure, Doug MacKnight
Tel: 306-787-2082
Fax: 306-787-7338
Doug.Macknight@gov.sk.ca
Executive Director, Energy Policy, Floyd Wist
Tel: 306-787-2477
Fax: 306-787-2198
Floyd.Wist@gov.sk.ca
Executive Director, Forestry Development - Prince Albert, Shane Vermette
Tel: 306-953-3797
Fax: 306-953-3733
shane.vermette@gov.sk.ca
Director, Energy Economics, Mike Balfour
Tel: 306-787-2479
Fax: 306-787-2198
Mike.Balfour@gov.sk.ca
Director, Mineral Tenure, Mike Detharet
Tel: 306-787-2139
Fax: 306-798-0047
Mike.Detharet@gov.sk.ca
Director, Mineral Policy, Cory Hughes
Tel: 306-787-3628
Fax: 306-787-2198
Cory.Hughes@gov.sk.ca
Director, Energy Development & Climate Change, Howard Loseth
Tel: 306-787-3379
Fax: 306-787-2198
Howard.Loseth@gov.sk.ca
Assistant Chief Geologist, Petroleum Geology, Melinda Yurkowski
Tel: 306-787-0650
Fax: 306-787-4608
melinda.yurkowski@gov.sk.ca

Petroleum & Natural Gas Division

Tel: 306-787-2592
Fax: 306-787-2478
Assistant Deputy Minister, Ed Dancsok
Tel: 306-787-2591
Fax: 306-787-2478
Ed.Dancsok@gov.sk.ca
Director, Petroleum Development, Todd Han
Tel: 306-787-2221
Fax: 306-787-2478
todd.han@gov.sk.ca
Director, Petroleum Royalties, Mike Ferguson
Tel: 306-787-2605
Fax: 306-787-2478
mike.ferguson@gov.sk.ca
Director, Petroleum Tenure Branch, Paul Mahnic
Tel: 306-787-5385
Fax: 306-787-0620
Paul.Mahnic@gov.sk.ca
Director, Petroleum Data Management & Compliance, Bruce Lerner
Tel: 306-798-9507
Fax: 306-787-8236
bruce.lerner@gov.sk.ca
Director, Engineering Services Branch, Bert West
Tel: 306-787-2318
Fax: 306-787-2478
bert.west@gov.sk.ca
Geodata Supervisor, Sedimentary Geodata Branch, Catherine Syrota
Tel: 306-787-2550
Fax: 306-787-2488
catherine.syrota@gov.sk.ca

Enterprise Saskatchewan

#200, 3085 Albert St., Regina, SK S4S 0B1
Tel: 306-787-4484
Fax: 306-798-0629
invest@gov.sk.ca
www.enterprisesaskatchewan.ca
Enterprise Saskatchewan promotes investment in the province. The following are some of the programs & services offered: Invest in Saskatchewan Program; Small Business Loans Association Program; Ethanol Fuel Grant Program; Business Infosource; Inventory of Major Projects in Saskatchewan; Saskatchewan Manufacturers Guide; Saskbiz.ca; & the Aborignal Business Directory.

Minister, Economy; Minister Responsible, Global Transporation Hub; Minister Responsible, SK Power Corporation, Enterprise SK, Innovation SK, Uranium Development Partnership, & SK Research Council, Hon. Bill Boyd
Tel: 306-787-0804
Fax: 306-798-2009
Bill.Boyd@gov.sk.ca
Office of the Minister of Economy, Legislative Building
#340, 2405 Legislative Dr.
Regina, SK S4S 0B3

Chief Financial Officer, Investment & Corporate Services, Denise Haas
Tel: 306-787-2756
Fax: 306-798-0629
denise.haas@enterprisesask.ca

Vice-President, Sector Development, Tony Baumgartner
Tel: 306-787-3435
Fax: 306-787-3989
Tony.Baumgartner@enterprisesask.ca

Vice-President, Entrepreneurial Development Services, Ernest Heapy
Tel: 306-787-2561
Fax: 306-787-7559
Ernest.Heapy@enterprisesask.ca

Vice-President, Competitiveness & Strategy, Angela Schmidt
Tel: 306-933-8223
Fax: 306-933-8244
Angela.Schmidt@enterprisesask.ca

Director, Business Services Improvement, Joseph Carson
Tel: 306-787-8865
Fax: 306-787-3989
Joe.Carson@enterprisesask.ca

Director, Economic Analysis & Strategy, Bryan Dilling
Tel: 306-933-7599
Fax: 306-933-8244
Bryan.Dilling@enterprisesask.ca

Director, Investment Attraction, Alex Fallon
Tel: 306-933-7210
Fax: 306-933-8244
Alex.Fallon@enterprisesask.ca

Director, Resources, Kim Lonsdale
Tel: 306-933-7164
Fax: 306-933-8244
Kim.Lonsdale@enterprisesask.ca

Director, Sector & Regional Policy, Michael Mitchell
Tel: 306-787-0572
Fax: 306-787-3989
Michael.Mitchell@enterprisesask.ca

Director, Corporate Services & Financial Programs, Andrea Terry Munro

Tel: 306-787-8024
Fax: 306-798-0796
andrea.terrymunro@enterprisesask.ca

Director, Advanced Technology & Services, Bill Spring
Tel: 306-787-2225
Fax: 306-787-3989
Bill.Spring@enterprisesask.ca

Saskatchewan Environment (ENV)

3211 Albert St., 2nd Fl., Regina, SK S4S 5W6
Tel: 306-787-2584
Fax: 306-787-9544
Toll-Free: 800-567-4224
Centre.Inquiry@gov.sk.ca
www.environment.gov.sk.ca
Other Communication: Parkwatch Line: 1-800-667-1788; Firewatch Line: 1-800-667-9660; Spill Control Centre: 1-800-667-7525; TIP (Turn in Poachers: 1-800-667-7561
Saskatchewan Environment protects & mananges the province's environmental & natural resources by offering the following programs & services: compliance & enforcement to protect the public's interests in the management of air, land, water & natural resources; protection & management of forest ecosystems; wildfire management; Green Strategy; environmental assessment; legislation, & policies to ensure that Crown land is used in ways that respect environmental, economic & social values; fishing & fisheries management; hunting management; licensing & guiding the trapping industry; protection of wildlife; recycling; waste management; & water resource & treatment plant operations management.
Acts Administered:
Assiniboine Slopes Provincial Ecological Reserves Regulations
Buffalograss Ecological Reserve Regulations
Captive Wildlife Regulations
Clean Air Act
Clean Air Regulation
Commercial Activities Regulations
Commercial Fishing Production Incentive Regulations
Conservation Easements Act
Crown Resource Lands Regulations, 1989
Dog Training Regulations
Drainage Control Regulations
Dutch Elm Disease Regulations
Ecological Reserves Act
Environmental Assessment Act
Environmental Management & Protection Act, 2002
Environmental Spill Control Regulations
Fisheries Act
Fisheries Regulations
Forest Resources Management Act
Forest Resources Management Regulations
Forestry Professions Act
Government Land Reserves Regulation
Grasslands National Park Act
Groundwater Regulations
Halocarbon Control Regulations
Hazardous Substances & Dangerous Goods Regulations
Historic Sites Regulations
Indian Treaty Obligations Regulations
Litter Control Act
Mineral Industry Environmental Protection Regulations
Municipal Refuse Management Regulations
Natural Resources Act
Open Seasons Game Regulations
Outfitter & Guide Regulations, 1996
Ozone-Depleting Substances Control Regulations
Park Land Reserve Regulations
Park Land Reserves Regulations
Parks Act
Parks Regulations
PCB Waste Storage Regulations
Potash Refining Air Emissions Regulations
Prairie & Forest Fires Act, 1982
Provincial Ecological Reserves Regulation
Provincial Lands Act
Provincial Lands Regulations
Qu'Appelle Coulee Provincial Ecological Reserves Regulations
Recreation Site Regulations, 1991
Representative Area Ecological Reserve Regulations
Reservoir Development Area Regulations
Reservoir Development Area Regulations
Resource Protection & Development Services Regulations
Sale or Lease of Certain Lands Act
Saskatchewan Watershed Authority Act 2005
Scrap Tire Management Regulations
State of the Environment Report Act
Surface Lease Agreement Regulations: Beaverlodge, Cigar Lake, Cluff Lake, Jolu Project, Key Lake, Konuto Project, McArthur River Operation, McClean Lake, Midwest Joint, Rabbit Lake
Surface Rights Regulations (Grasslands Park, Komis Project, Parks Lake Uranium Mining, Seabee)
Treaty Land Entitlement Withdrawal Regulations
Used Oil Collection Regulations
Waste Electronic Equipment Regulations
Waste Paint Management Regulations
Water Appeal Board Act
Water Regulations
Wild Rice Regulations
Wild Species at Risk Regulations
Wildlife Act, 1998
Wildlife Habitat Lands Designation Regulations
Wildlife Habitat Lands Disposition & Alteration Regulations
Wildlife Habitat Protection Act
Wildlife Landowner Assistance Regulations, 1991
Wildlife Management Zones & Special Areas Boundaries Regulations, 1990
Wildlife Regulations, 1981
Withdrawal of Land from Forests; Historical Interest Regulations

Minister, Environment; Minister Responsible, Saskatchewan Watershed Authority; Minister Responsible, Hon. Ken Cheveldayoff
Tel: 306-787-0393
Fax: 306-787-1669
minister.env@gov.sk.ca
Social Media:
www.facebook.com/pages/Ken-Cheveldayoff/52760912740
Office of the Minister of the Environment, Legislative Building #315, 2405 Legislative Dr.
Regina, SK S4S 0B3

Deputy Minister, Environment, Liz Quarshie
Tel: 306-787-2930
Fax: 306-787-2947
liz.quarshie@gov.sk.ca

Executive Director, Strategic Planning & Performance Improvement, Greg Leake
Tel: 306-787-5511
Fax: 306-787-2947

Director, Communications Services, Dorma Everett
Tel: 306-787-2770
Fax: 306-787-3941
Everett.Dorma@gov.sk.ca

Manager, Correspondence, Krista Campbell
Tel: 306-787-5796
Fax: 306-787-3941
krista.campbell@gov.sk.ca

Associated Agencies, Boards & Commissions:
• Saskatchewan Conservation Data Centre
3211 Albert St.
Regina, SK S4S 5W6
Tel: 306-787-9038
Fax: 306-787-9544
www.biodiversity.sk.ca
The SKCDC was formed as a co-operative venture between the province, The Nature Conservancy USA & The Nature Conservancy of Canada. The SKCDC gathers, interprets & distributes scientific information on the ecological status of provincial wild species & communities. The SKCDC is committed to conserving biological diversity; producing scientific reports & being the provincial clearinghouse for threatened & endangered species information.
Data Manager, Ben Sawa
ben.sawa@gov.sk.ca
Aquatics Biodiversity Specialist, Jeff Keith
jeff.keith@gov.sk.ca
• Water Appeal Board
#217, 3085 Albert St.
Regina, SK S4S 0B1
Tel: 306-798-7462
Fax: 306-787-8558
www.gov.sk.ca/wb
Secretary, Maggie Linton

Environmental Protection & Audit Division
3211 Albert St., 5th Fl., Regina, SK S4S 5W6
Tel: 306-787-2947
Protects human health & ecosystem integrity.
Assistant Deputy Minister, Environmental Protection & Audit, Mark Wittrup
Tel: 306-787-5419
Fax: 306-787-2947
mark.wittrup@gov.sk.ca
Chief Engineer, Technical Resources Branch, Kevin McCullum
Tel: 306-787-2739
Fax: 306-787-2947
Kevin.McCullum@gov.sk.ca
Executive Director, Municipal Branch, Sam Ferris
Tel: 306-787-6193
Fax: 306-787-0197
sam.ferris@gov.sk.ca
Executive Director, Industrial Branch, Wes Kotyk
Tel: 306-933-6542
Fax: 306-933-8442
Wes.Kotyk@gov.sk.ca
Director, Environmental Protection Services Section, Thon Phommavong
Tel: 306-787-9986
Fax: 306-787-0197
Thon.Phommavong@gov.sk.ca
Senior Geo Scientist, Science Support Unit, Lynn Kelley
Tel: 306-787-7147
Fax: 306-787-0024
lynn.kelley@gov.sk.ca

Wildfire Management Branch
Hwy. #2 North, PO Box 3003Prince Albert, SK S6V 6G1
Tel: 306-953-3473
Fax: 306-953-3575
Executive Director, Steve Roberts
Tel: 306-953-2206
Steve.Roberts@gov.sk.ca

Environmental Support Division
3211 Albert St., 5th Fl., Regina, SK S4S 5W6
Fax: 306-787-2947
Assistant Deputy Minister, Environmental Support, Lori Uhersky
Tel: 306-787-5737
Fax: 306-787-2947
lori.uhersky@gov.sk.ca
Acting Director, Information Management & Geomatics Services, Ginny Nisbet
Tel: 306-787-2913
Fax: 306-787-3913
ginny.nisbet@gov.sk.ca
Executive Director, Finance & Administration, Laurel Welsh
Tel: 306-787-2484
Fax: 306-787-8441
Laurel.Welsh@gov.sk.ca
Director, Financial Management, Susan Loewen
Tel: 306-787-7609
Fax: 306-787-8441
Susan.Loewen@gov.sk.ca
Director, Aboriginal Affairs, Jennifer McKillop
Tel: 306-787-9643
Fax: 306-787-0197
Jennifer.Mckillop@gov.sk.ca
Director, Financial & Property Management, Zachery Solomon
Tel: 306-798-3904
Fax: 306-787-8441
zachery.solomon@gov.sk.ca
Acting Director, Budget & Fiscal Planning Section, Lynette Halvorsen
Tel: 306-787-8922
Fax: 306-787-8441

Resource Management & Compliance Division
3211 Albert St., 5th fl., Regina, SK S4S 5W6
Fax: 306-787-2947
Assistant Deputy Minister, Resource Management & Compliance, Kevin Murphy
Tel: 306-787-8567
Fax: 306-787-2947
Kevin.Murphy@gov.sk.ca
Executive Director, Fish & Wildlife, Lyle Saigeon
Tel: 306-787-2309
Fax: 306-787-9544
Lyle.Saigeon@gov.sk.ca

Acting Director, Lands, Todd Olexson
Tel: 306-953-2586
Fax: 306-953-2684
Todd.Olexson@gov.sk.ca
Director, Field Services, Brent Webster
Tel: 306-446-7424
Fax: 306-446-7464
Brent.Webster@gov.sk.ca
Director, Compliance & Enforcement Section, Ken Aube
Tel: 306-953-2993
Fax: 306-953-2999
ken.aube@gov.sk.ca
Director, Client Service, Kim Clark
Tel: 306-953-2786
Fax: 306-953-2684
kim.clark@gov.sk.ca

Regional Operations
Compliance Manager, Dennis Daigneault
Tel: 306-288-4713
Fax: 306-288-4717
Dennis.Daigneault@gov.sk.ca
Compliance Manager, Bill Zimmer
Tel: 306-953-2945
Fax: 306-953-2999
Bill.Zimmer@gov.sk.ca

SaskEnergy Incorporated

1777 Victoria Ave., Regina, SK S4P 4K5
Tel: 306-777-9225
Toll-Free: 800-567-8899
www.saskenergy.com
Other Communication: Emergency & safety Line: 1-888-700-0427; Line Locates: 1-866-828-4888
The provincial Crown corporation provides natural gas to residential, farm, commercial, & industrial customers in 92% of Saskatchewan's communities.
Acts Administered:
SaskEnergy Act

Minister Responsible, Energy & Resources; Minister Responsible, Tourism Saskatchewan; Minister Responsible, Trade; Minister Responsible, SaskEnergy Incorporated, Hon. Tim McMillan
Tel: 306-787-9124
Fax: 306-787-0395
minister.er@gov.sk.ca
Social Media: www.facebook.com/timmcmillanmla
Office of the Minister Responsible Energy & Resources / SaskEnergy Incorporated
#346, 2405 Legislative Dr.
Regina, SK S4S 0B3

Chair, Rob Pletch
Tel: 306-777-9901

President & CEO, Doug Kelin
Tel: 306-777-9901
Fax: 306-522-2217

Distribution Utility
Tel: 306-777-9994
Fax: 306-522-2217
Executive Director, Distribution Customer Service, Randy Greggains
Tel: 306-777-9233
Fax: 306-522-2217
rgreggains@saskenergy.com
Director, Distribution Engineering, Perry Blazic
Tel: 306-975-8567
Fax: 306-975-8698
pblazic@saskenergy.com
Director, Customer Solutions, Jacquie Kerr
Tel: 306-777-9049
Fax: 306-522-2217
jkerr@saskenergy.com
Director, Construction Services, Derwin Zelinski
Tel: 306-975-8665
Fax: 306-543-9808
dzelinski@saskenergy.com

Gas Supply & Business Development
Tel: 306-777-9354
Fax: 306-569-3522
Executive Vice-President, Dean Reeve
Tel: 306-777-9354
Fax: 306-525-3488
Executive Director, Gas Supply, Marketing & Rates, Lori Christie
Tel: 306-777-9361
Fax: 306-569-3522
lchristie@saskenergy.com
Director, Gas Supply & Marketing, Dan Parent
Tel: 306-777-9374
Fax: 306-525-3488
dparent@saskenergy.com
Director, Business Development, Deidre Donaldson Meyer
Tel: 306-777-9032
Fax: 306-777-9877

Minister, Finance; Deputy Premier, Hon. Ken Krawetz
Tel: 306-787-6060
Fax: 306-787-6055
minister.fin@gov.sk.ca
Legislative Building
#312, 2405 Legislative Dr.
Regina, SK S4S 0B3

Saskatchewan Government Relations (GR)

1855 Victoria Ave., Regina, SK S4P 3T2
Tel: 306-787-8885
www.gr.gov.sk.ca
Municipal relations, public safety, & First Nations, Métis, & northern affairs are the main responsibilities of the Ministry of Government Relations. The Ministry aims to ensure effective governance, to provide emergency management programs, & to fulfill obligations under Treaty Land Entitlement.

Minister, Government Relations; Minister Responsible, First Nations, Métis, & Northern Affairs, Hon. Jim Reiter
Tel: 306-787-6100
Fax: 306-787-0399
minister.gr@gov.sk.ca
Social Media: twitter.com/jim_reiter, www.facebook.com/pages/Jim-Reiter/207539405959289
Office of the Minister of Government Relations, Legislative Building
#348, 2405 Legislative Dr.
Regina, SK S4S 0B3

Deputy Minister, Government Relations, Alan Hilton
Tel: 306-787-1925
Fax: 306-787-1987
Alan.Hilton@gov.sk.ca

Assistant Deputy Minister, Keith Comstock
Tel: 306-787-5765
Fax: 306-787-1987
Keith.Comstock@gov.sk.ca

Associated Agencies, Boards & Commissions:
• **Saskatchewan Municipal Board (SMB)**
#480, 2151 Scarth St.
Regina, SK S4P 2H8
Tel: 306-787-6221
Fax: 306-787-1610
info@smb.gov.sk.ca
www.smb.gov.sk.ca

Central Management Services
#1410, 1855 Victoria Ave., Regina, SK S4P 3T2
Tel: 306-787-0325
Fax: 306-787-4161
Executive Director, Central Management Services, Wanda Lamberti
Tel: 306-787-1640
Fax: 306-787-4161
Wanda.Lamberti@gov.sk.ca
Director, Financial Planning, Marj Abel
Tel: 306-787-4172
Fax: 306-787-4161
Marj.Abel@gov.sk.ca
Director, Financial Services, Janie Markewich
Tel: 306-787-6408
Fax: 306-787-4161
janie.markewich@gov.sk.ca
Manager, Corporate Planning, Garett Murray
Tel: 306-798-6093
Fax: 306-787-4161
Garett.Murray@gov.sk.ca

Communications
#1530, 1855 Victoria Ave., Regina, SK S4P 3T2
Tel: 306-787-4181
Executive Director, Communications, Jeff Welke
Tel: 306-787-6156
Fax: 306-787-4181
jeff.welke@gov.sk.ca
Co-Director, Communications, Bob Ellis
Tel: 306-787-2709
Fax: 306-787-4181
robert.ellis@gov.sk.ca
Co-Director, Communications, Nicole Fellinger
Tel: 306-787-2687
Fax: 306-787-4181
Nicole.Fellinger@gov.sk.ca
Manager, Content & Internet Coordinator, Lorrie Guillaume
Tel: 306-787-4340
Fax: 306-787-4181
Lorrie.Guillaume@gov.sk.ca

Community Planning
#420, 1855 Victoria Ave., Regina, SK S4P 3T2
Tel: 306-787-9411
Fax: 306-798-0194
Executive Director, Community Planning, Ralph Leibel
Tel: 306-787-7672
Fax: 306-798-0194
Ralph.Leibel@gov.sk.ca
Director, Community Planning (Regina), Barry Braitman
Tel: 306-787-2893
Fax: 306-798-0194
Barry.Braitman@gov.sk.ca
Director, Community Planning (Saskatoon), Len Kowalko
Tel: 306-933-6118
Fax: 306-933-7720
Len.Kowalko@gov.sk.ca
#978, 122 - 3rd Ave. North, 9th Fl.
Saskatoon, SK S7K 2H6

First Nations, Métis, & Northern Affairs (FNMR)
#1020, 1855 Victoria Ave., Regina, SK S4P 3T2
Tel: 306-787-6680
Fax: 306-798-0083
The organization strives to improve the economic & social circumstances for First Nations & Métis people & northerners. The following are programs & services offered: First Nations & Métis Community Initiative; First Nations & Métis Women's Initiative; Treaty Land Entitlement; Northern Development Fund; Northern Saskatchewan Environmental Quality; & Mineral Surface Lease Agreements.
Minister, Government Relations; Minister Responsible, First Nations, Métis, & Northern Affairs, Hon. Jim Reiter
Tel: 306-787-6100
Fax: 306-787-0399
minister.gr@gov.sk.ca
Social Media: twitter.com/jim_reiter, www.facebook.com/pages/Jim-Reiter/207539405959289
Office of the Minister Responsible, First Nations, Métis, & Northern Affairs, Legislative Building
#348, 2405 Legislative Dr.
Regina, SK S4S 0B3
Assistant Deputy Minister, First Nations, Métis, & Northern Affairs, Hon. James Froh
Tel: 306-787-7405
Fax: 306-798-0083
James.Froh@gov.sk.ca
Assistant Deputy Minister, Northern Affairs, Giselle Marcotte
Tel: 306-425-4204
Fax: 306-425-4349
Giselle.Marcotte@gov.sk.ca
Executive Director, Lands & Consultation, Trisha Delormier-Hill
Tel: 306-787-6681
Fax: 306-798-0004
Trisha.Delormier-Hill@gov.sk.ca
Executive Director, Relationship & Policy, Alethea Foster
Tel: 306-787-5176
Fax: 306-787-5832
Alethea.Foster@gov.sk.ca
Executive Director, Northern Regional Economic Development, Doug Howorko
Tel: 306-798-5167
Fax: 306-787-6014
Doug.Howorko2@gov.sk.ca
Executive Director, Northern Social Development, Mark LaRocque

Tel: 306-787-6400
Fax: 306-787-6014
Mark.LaRocque@gov.sk.ca
Executive Director, Strategic Initiatives, Seonaid MacPherson
Tel: 306-787-8142
Fax: 306-798-0083
Seonaid.MacPherson@gov.sk.ca
Executive Director, Northern Industry & Resource Development, Richard Turkheim
Tel: 306-787-2143
Fax: 306-787-6014
Richard.Turkheim@gov.sk.ca
Director, Finance, Accountability & Corporate Services, Kerry Gray
Tel: 306-787-2123
Fax: 306-798-0004
Kerry.Gray@gov.sk.ca
Director, Communications, Cathe Offet
Tel: 306-787-5701
Fax: 306-798-0083
Cathe.Offet@gov.sk.ca
Director, Gaming Trust & Grants, Sam Swan
Tel: 306-787-1695
Fax: 306-798-0004
Sam.Swan@gov.sk.ca

Grant Administration & Financial Management
#410, 1855 Victoria Ave., Regina, SK S4P 3T2
Tel: 306-787-8808
Fax: 306-787-3641
Executive Director, Grant Administration & Financial Management, Kathy Rintoul
Tel: 306-787-8887
Fax: 306-787-3641
Kathy.Rintoul@gov.sk.ca
Director, New Deal Secretariat, Teri Kitney
Tel: 306-787-9699
Fax: 306-787-3641
teri.kitney@gov.sk.ca
Director, Grant Administration, Kyle Toffan
Tel: 306-787-7994
Fax: 306-787-3641
kyle.toffan@gov.sk.ca

Northern Municipal Services
Mistasinihk Pl., #2700, 1328 La Ronge Ave., PO Box 5000La Ronge, SK S0J 1L0
Tel: 306-425-4320
Fax: 306-425-2401
Toll-Free: 800-663-1555
Northern Municipal Services administers the Northern Municipal Account. Administrative support & operational assistance are given to Saskatchewan's northern municipalities through municipal management functions, training, & advisory services.
Executive Director, Northern Municipal Services, Brad Henry
Tel: 306-425-4322
Fax: 306-425-2401
brad.henry@gov.sk.ca
Manager, Northern Municipal Administration, Colleen Digness
Tel: 306-425-4325
Fax: 306-425-2401
Colleen.Digness@gov.sk.ca
PO Box 69
Buffalo Narrows, SK S0M 0J0
Manager, Financial Services, Ken Kowalczyk
Tel: 306-425-4328
Fax: 306-425-2401
ken.kowalczyk@gov.sk.ca
PO Box 69
Buffalo Narrows, SK S0M 0J0
Northern District Planner, Dee Johns
Tel: 306-425-6642
Fax: 306-425-2401
Dee.Johns@gov.sk.ca
PO Box 69
Buffalo Narrows, SK S0M 0J0

Policy Development
#1540, 1855 Victoria Ave., Regina, SK S4P 3T2
Tel: 306-787-2653
Fax: 306-787-5822
Executive Director, Policy Development, John Edwards
Tel: 306-787-2665
Fax: 306-787-5822
john.edwards2@gov.sk.ca
Director, Property Assessment & Taxation, Norm Magnin
Tel: 306-787-2895
Fax: 306-787-5822
Norm.Magnin@gov.sk.ca
Director, Legislation & Regulations, Rod Nasewich
Tel: 306-798-7048
Fax: 306-787-5822
Rod.Nasewich@gov.sk.ca
Manager, Policy Analysis, Ryan Cossitt
Tel: 306-787-2780
Fax: 306-787-5822
Ryan.Cossitt@gov.sk.ca

Provincial Disaster Assistance Program (PDAP)
PO Box 227Regina, SK S4P 2Z6
Tel: 306-787-7800
Fax: 306-798-2318
Toll-Free: 866-632-4033
Assistance is provided to recover from natural disasters such as tornadoes, plow winds, flooding, & other severe weather. The Provincial Disaster Assistance Program serves the following people & organizations of Saskatchewan: residents, communal organizations, agricultural operations, nonprofit organizations, small businesses, parks, & communities.
Executive Director, Provincial Disaster Assistance Program, Margaret Anderson
Tel: 306-798-8470
Fax: 306-798-6356
Margaret.Anderson@gov.sk.ca
Director, Policy, Kevin Roche
Tel: 306-798-8020
Fax: 306-798-2318
Kevin.Roche@gov.sk.ca
Manager, Program, Tamie Folwark
Tel: 306-798-0590
Fax: 306-798-2318
Tamie.Folwark@gov.sk.ca
Manager, Finances, Noel McAvena
Tel: 306-798-0583
Fax: 306-798-2318
noel.mcavena@gov.sk.ca
Manager, Contracts, Lee Moyse
Tel: 306-787-9532
Fax: 306-798-2318
lee.moyse@gov.sk.ca

Strategy & Sector Relations
#1010, 1855 Victoria Ave., Regina, SK S4P 3T2
Tel: 306-798-2568
Executive Director, Strategy & Sector Relations, Sheldon Green
Tel: 306-787-7883
Fax: 306-798-2568
Sheldon.Green@gov.sk.ca
Director, Strategy & Sector Relations, Randy McAfee
Tel: 306-787-9641
Fax: 306-798-2568
randy.mcafee@gov.sk.ca
Manager, Sector Relations, Dustin Austman
Tel: 306-787-2740
Fax: 306-798-2568
Dustin.Austman@gov.sk.ca
Manager, Strategic Initiatives, Chris Gunningham
Tel: 306-787-4984
Fax: 306-798-2568
Chris.Gunningham@gov.sk.ca

Saskatchewan Health (HE)

T.C. Douglas Bldg., 3475 Albert St., Regina, SK S4S 6X6
Tel: 306-787-0146
Toll-Free: 800-667-7766
info@health.gov.sk.ca
www.health.gov.sk.ca
Other Communication: Family Health Benefits: 1-800-266-0695; HealthLine: 1-877-800-0002; Health Registration / Health Card: 1-800-667-7551; Prescription Drug Plan: 1-800-667-7581
Saskatchewan Health offers the following programs & services: continuing care to help people live independently; e-health & information systems for access to medical information; emergency services; health benefits; recruitment & retention of healthcare providers; promotion of mental health & treatment for mental illness & addictions; personal health services; prescription drug coverage; public health programs; privacy of health information; services for people with long term disabilities or illnesses; surgery & diagnostics initiatives; & vital statistics.
Acts Administered:
Department of Health Act
Public Health Act
Tobacco Control Act

Minister, Health, Hon. Dustin Duncan
Tel: 306-787-7345
Fax: 306-787-0237
minister.he@gov.sk.ca
Social Media: twitter.com/dustin_duncan
Office of the Minister of Health, Legislative Building
#204, 2405 Legislative Dr.
Regina, SK S4S 0B3

Minister Responsible, Rural & Remote Health, Hon. Randy Weekes
Tel: 306-798-9014
Fax: 306-798-9013
minister.rrhe@gov.sk.ca
Social Media: www.facebook.com/pages/Randy-Weekes-MLA/356610274367735?sk=info
Office of the Minister Responsible for Rural & Remote Health, Legislative Building
#208, 2405 Legislative Dr.
Regina, SK S4S 0B3

Deputy Minister, Dan Florizone
Tel: 306-787-3041
Fax: 306-787-4533
dan.florizone@health.gov.sk.ca

Associate Deputy Minister, Max Hendricks
Tel: 306-787-4695
Fax: 306-787-4533
max.hendricks@health.gov.sk.ca

Associated Agencies, Boards & Commissions:
• **Health Quality Council**
241, 111 Research Dr.
Saskatoon, SK S7N 3R2
Tel: 306-668-8810
Fax: 306-668-8820
info@hqc.sk.ca
www.hqc.sk.ca
• **Saskatchewan Health Research Foundation**
#253, 111 Research Dr.
Saskatoon, SK S7N 3R2
Tel: 306-975-1680
Fax: 306-975-1688
Toll-free: 800-975-1699
www.shrf.ca
Chair, Terry Baker
Chief Executive Officer, June Bold
Director, Finance & Operations, Deborah Fortosky
Chief Medical Health Officer, Dr. Saqib Shahab
Tel: 306-787-4722
Fax: 306-787-3237
Chief Population Health Epidemiologist, Dr. Valerie Mann
Tel: 306-787-4086
Fax: 306-787-3823
vmann@health.gov.sk.ca
Executive Director, Rick Trimp
Tel: 306-787-8847
Fax: 306-787-3237
rtrimp@health.gov.sk.ca
Executive Director, Health Promotion, Ron Knaus
Tel: 306-787-3329
Fax: 306-787-3823
ron.knaus@health.gov.sk.ca
Director, Health Promotion, Tami Denomie
Tel: 306-787-7110
Fax: 306-787-3823
tami.denomie@health.gov.sk.ca
Director, Epidemiology & Research, Winanne Downey
Tel: 306-787-7625
Fax: 306-787-3237
Director, Corporate Services, Paul Leech
Tel: 306-787-6544
Fax: 306-787-3237
pleech@health.gov.sk.ca
Director, Environmental Health, Tim Macaulay
Tel: 306-787-7128
Fax: 306-787-3237
tmacaulay@health.gov.sk.ca

Director, Disease Prevention, Jim Myres
Tel: 306-787-1580
Fax: 306-787-3823
jim.myres@health.gov.sk.ca
Executive Director, Rick Trimp
Tel: 306-787-3129
Fax: 306-787-1525
rtrimp@health.gov.sk.ca
Associate Executive Director, Niki Coffin
Tel: 306-787-1522
Fax: 306-787-1525
ncoffin@health.gov.sk.ca
Medical Director, Dr. Greg Horsman
Tel: 306-787-8316
Fax: 306-787-1525
ghorsman@health.gov.sk.ca
Director, Environmental Services, Dr. Phillip Bailey
Tel: 306-787-3140
Fax: 306-787-1525
pbailey@health.gov.sk.ca
Director, Screening & Reference Testing, Jeff Eichhorst
Tel: 306-787-3284
Fax: 306-798-0955
jeichhorst@health.gov.sk.ca
Director, Operations, Joyce Kirsch
Tel: 306-787-9404
Fax: 306-787-1525
joyce.kirsch@health.gov.sk.ca
Acting Director, Bacteriology, Dr. David Alexander
Tel: 306-798-4154
Fax: 306-787-1525
dalexander@health.gov.sk.ca
Director, Administration, Debra Ulrich
Tel: 306-787-3033
Fax: 306-787-1525
dulrich@health.gov.sk.ca
Section Manager, Molecular Diagnostics (DNA), Dr. Nick Antonishyn
Tel: 306-787-7744
Fax: 306-787-9122
nantonishyn@health.gov.sk.ca
Section Manager, Materials Management, Cary Legien
Tel: 306-787-3383
Fax: 306-798-0071
clegien@health.gov.sk.ca
Section Manager, Specimen Management Centre, Darlene Miller
Tel: 306-787-3238
Fax: 306-787-9122
dmiller@health.gov.sk.ca
Section Manager, Biomedical Equipment Services, Ken Sperlie
Tel: 306-787-7179
Fax: 306-787-9122
ksperlie@health.gov.sk.ca
Section Manager, Bacteriology, Mycology, Parasitology, Rosanne Kitzul
Tel: 306-787-8634
Fax: 306-787-9122
Section Manager, Immunoserology, Jim Putz
Tel: 306-787-4948
Fax: 306-787-9122
Section Manager, Virology, Ken Brandt
Tel: 306-798-3102
Fax: 306-787-9122

Saskatchewan Highways & Infrastructure (HI)

Victoria Tower, 1855 Victoria Ave., Regina, SK S4P 3T2
Tel: 306-787-4800
communications@highways.gov.sk.ca
www.highways.gov.sk.ca
Other Communication: Road Information Hotline: 306-933-8333
twitter.com/skgovhwyhotline
www.facebook.com/SaskatchewanHighwayHotline
The Ministry of Highways & Infrastructure is concerned with transportation in Saskatchewan as it relates to the social & economic development of the province. Business areas include ministry services & standards information, plning & policy development, & regional services.
The following are some programs & services offered through the Ministry: Urban Highway Connector Program; Adopt a Highway; Assistance to Motorists; Preservation Program; & Community Airport Partnership Program. In May 2012, Don McMorris became the new Minister of Highways & Infrastructure. He is also the Minister Responsible for SaskBuilds. SaskBuilds is a new government agency that plans, designs, funds, & implements infrastructure projects for the government as well as third-party projects that are government funded, such as hospitals & schools.
Acts Administered:
Dangerous Goods Transportation Act
Highway Traffic Act
Highways & Transportation Act, 1997
Railway Act

Minister, Highways & Infrastructure; Minister Responsible, Saskatchewan Telecommunications; Minister Responsible, Saskatchewan Transportation Company; Minister Responsible, Information Services Corporation; Minister Responsible, Saskatchewan Gaming Corp., Hon. Don McMorris
Tel: 306-787-6447
Fax: 306-787-1736
minister.hi@gov.sk.ca
Social Media: twitter.com/dmcmorrissp, www.facebook.com/DonMcMorrisSP
Minister's Office, Legislative Building
#302, 2405 Legislative Dr.
Regina, SK S4S 0B3

Deputy Minister, Highways & Infrastructure, Rob Penny
Tel: 306-787-4949
Fax: 306-787-9777
Rob.Penny@gov.sk.ca

Associated Agencies, Boards & Commissions:
• Global Transportation Hub Authority
#350, 1777 Victoria Ave.
Regina, SK S4P 4K5
Tel: 306-787-4842
Fax: 306-798-4600
www.gtha.ca
The Hub Authority was created in June 2009, & is the primary agency in charge of planning, developing, constructing & promoting the Global Transportation Hub - a transportation & logistics centre encompassing 2,000 acres of serviced land.
• Saskatchewan Grain Car Corporation
#1210, 1855 Victoria Ave.
Regina, SK S4P 3T2
Tel: 306-787-1137
Fax: 306-798-0931
www.sgcc.gov.sk.ca
The SGCC works with farmers, community groups, shippers, & railroads to maximize the efficiency and effectiveness of transporting grain across the province.
President, Bob Mason
Tel: 306-787-1848
Fax: 306-798-0931
bmason@sgcc.gov.sk.ca
Vice-President, Operations, Kelly Moskowy
Tel: 306-787-0551
Fax: 306-798-0931
kmoskowy@sgcc.gov.sk.ca
Manager, Finance & Administration, Shannon Lindholm
Tel: 306-787-1137
Fax: 306-798-0931
slindholm@sgcc.gov.sk.ca
• Saskatchewan Highway Traffic Board
1550 Saskatchewan Dr.
Regina, SK S4P 0E4
Tel: 306-775-6674
contactus@highwaytrafficboard.sk.ca
www.highwaytrafficboard.sk.ca
The Highway Traffic Board's mandate is to establish & to administer legislation relating to the safe & legal operations of private vehicles, the bus-truck industry & the short line rail industry in Saskatchewan, where specifically legislated to do so.
Chair, David Wilton
Tel: 306-775-6665
Fax: 306-775-6618
htbchairperson@highwaytrafficboard.sk.ca
Manager, Traffic Board Secretariat, Jason Nystrom
Tel: 306-775-6661
Assistant Deputy Minister, Ministry Services & Standards, Jennifer Ehrmantraut
Tel: 306-787-4859
Fax: 306-787-9777
Jennifer.Ehrmantraut@gov.sk.ca
Executive Director, Technical Standards, Dave Stearns
Tel: 306-787-2295
Fax: 306-787-4836
Director, Earth Sciences & Research, Magdy Beshara
Tel: 306-787-4922
Fax: 306-787-4582
Magdy.Beshara@gov.sk.ca
Director, Financial Services, Gary Diebel
Tel: 306-787-4794
Fax: 306-787-8700
Gary.Diebel@gov.sk.ca
Director, Corporate Support, Wayne Gienow
Tel: 306-787-1355
Fax: 306-787-8700
wayne.gienow@gov.sk.ca
Director, Design & Traffic Engineering, Sukhy Kent
Tel: 306-787-4945
Fax: 306-787-4836
Sukhy.Kent@gov.sk.ca
Director, Preservation & Operations Standards, Frass Len
Tel: 306-933-5226
Fax: 306-933-7090
Director, Construction Standards, Bill Pacholka
Tel: 306-787-4917
Fax: 306-787-4836
Bill.Pacholka@gov.sk.ca
Director, Bridge Standards, Howard Yea
Tel: 306-787-4830
Fax: 306-787-4836
Howard.Yea@gov.sk.ca
Manager, Forecasting, Judy A. Adams
Tel: 306-787-4796
Fax: 306-787-8700
Judy.Adams@gov.sk.ca
Manager, Property Rights & Registration, Neil Daku
Tel: 306-787-4884
Fax: 306-787-4100
Neil.Daku@gov.sk.ca
Manager, IT Systems, Robert Gee
Tel: 306-787-4824
Fax: 306-787-8700
Robert.Gee@gov.sk.ca
Manager, TLE & Property Preservation, Peter Gennutt
Tel: 306-787-4045
Fax: 306-787-4100
Peter.Gennutt@gov.sk.ca

Planning & Policy Division

Tel: 306-787-4904
Assistant Deputy Minister, George Stamatinos
Tel: 306-787-5028
Fax: 306-787-9777
george.stamatinos@gov.sk.ca
Executive Director, Systems Planning & Management, Miranda Carlberg
Tel: 306-787-0825
Fax: 306-787-3963
Miranda.Carlberg@gov.sk.ca
Executive Director, Strategic Planning & Policy, Harold Hugg
Tel: 306-787-5311
Fax: 306-787-3963
Harold.Hugg@gov.sk.ca
Director, Legislation & Administration, Reg Cox
Tel: 306-964-9241
Fax: 306-787-3963
Director, Trucking Policy & Regulation, Andrew Cipywnyk
Tel: 306-787-6998
Fax: 306-787-3963
Director, Transportation Infrastructure, Andrew Liu
Tel: 306-787-4784
Fax: 306-787-3963
Andrew.Liu@gov.sk.ca
Director, Strategic Business Planning, Cathy Lynn Borbely
Tel: 306-787-4787
Fax: 306-787-3963
CathyLynn.Borbely@gov.sk.ca
Director, Multimodal, Trade & Logistics, Michael Makowsky
Tel: 306-787-7664
Fax: 306-787-3963
Michael.Makowsky@gov.sk.ca
Director, Rail Services, Ed Zsombor
Tel: 306-787-5847
Fax: 306-787-3963
Ed.Zsombor@gov.sk.ca
Director, Systems Management, Ben Liu
Tel: 306-787-4121
Fax: 306-787-3963

Director, Transportation Planning, Harold Retzlaff
Tel: 306-787-4758
Fax: 306-787-3963

Regional Services Division
Assistant Deputy Minister, Ted Stobbs
Tel: 306-787-9287
Ted.Stobbs@gov.sk.ca
Executive Director, Major Projects Unit, Zvjezdan Lazic
Tel: 306-933-6203
Fax: 306-933-5188
Zvjezdan.Lazic@gov.sk.ca

Northern Region
L.F. McIntosh Bldg., 800 Central Ave., PO Box 3003Prince Albert, SK S6V 6G1
Tel: 306-953-3500
Fax: 306-953-3533
Executive Director, Doug Hansen
Tel: 306-953-3503
Fax: 306-953-3533
Doug.Hansen@gov.sk.ca
Director, Operations, Northern Region, Larry Young
Tel: 306-953-3518
Fax: 306-953-3533
larry.young@gov.sk.ca
Director, Regional Design & Construction, Ray Connoly
Tel: 306-933-6117
Fax: 306-933-6161
ray.connoly@gov.sk.ca
Director, Operations, Regional Logistics, Barry Gallivan
Tel: 306-953-3564
Fax: 306-953-3533
barry.gallivan@gov.sk.ca
Director, Regional Asset Management, Doug Neis
Tel: 306-953-3516
Fax: 306-953-3533
doug.neis@gov.sk.ca
Bridge Crew Manager, Bridges, Bert Campbell
Tel: 306-953-3524
Fax: 306-953-3533
Bert.Campbell@gov.sk.ca

Central Region
#18, 3603 Millar Ave., Saskatoon, SK S7P 0B2
Tel: 306-933-5186
Fax: 306-933-5188
Regional Executive Director, Allan Churko
Tel: 306-933-6225
Fax: 306-933-5188
Allan.Churko@gov.sk.ca
Director, Regional Logistics, Mike Burnett
Tel: 306-933-8058
Fax: 306-933-5188
mike.burnett@gov.sk.ca
Director, Regional Design & Construction, Tracy Danielson
Tel: 306-933-6211
Fax: 306-933-5188
Tracy.Danielson@gov.sk.ca
Director, Fleet Services, Rock Gorlick
Tel: 306-933-5225
Fax: 306-933-5188
Rock.Gorlick@gov.sk.ca
Director, Regional Asset Management, Brandon Harris
Tel: 306-933-5197
Fax: 306-933-5188
Brandon.Harris@gov.sk.ca
Director, Operations, Central Region, Goran Saric
Tel: 306-933-6217
Fax: 306-933-5188
Goran.Saric@gov.sk.ca

Southern Region
1630 Park St., Regina, SK S4N 2G1
Tel: 306-787-4969
Fax: 306-787-4910
Executive Director, Ron Gerbrandt
Tel: 306-787-4973
Fax: 306-787-4910
Ron.Gerbrandt@gov.sk.ca
Director, Regional Logistics, Tom Davies
Tel: 306-787-4751
Fax: 306-787-4910
Tom.Davies@gov.sk.ca
Director, Regional Operations, Dave Smith
Tel: 306-787-0109
Fax: 306-787-4910
dave.smith@gov.sk.ca
Director, Regional Asset Management, Brent Miller
Tel: 306-787-2735
Fax: 306-787-1007
Brent.Miller@gov.sk.ca
Director, Regional Design & Construction, Doug Kelly
Tel: 306-787-1700
Fax: 306-787-4910
Doug.Kelly@gov.sk.ca
Acts Administered:
Alberta-Saskatchewan Boundary Act, 1939
Expropriation Act
Land Surveys Act, 2000
Land Titles Act, 2000

Minister, Justice & Attorney General; Deputy Government House Leader, Hon. Gordon Wyant, Q.C.
Tel: 306-787-5353
Fax: 306-787-1232
minister.ju@gov.sk.ca
Social Media: twitter.com/GordWyant
Office of the Minister of Justice & Attorney General, Legislative Buiding
#355, 2405 Legislative Dr.
Regina, SK S4S 0B3

Deputy Minister, Justice; Deputy Attorney General, Gerald Tegart
Tel: 306-787-5352
Fax: 306-787-3874
gerald.tegart@gov.sk.ca

Executive Director, Civil Law Division, Rick Hischebett
Tel: 306-787-6642
Fax: 306-787-0581
Rick.Hischebett@gov.sk.ca
Other Communications: URL: www.justice.gov.sk.ca/civillaw

Executive Director, Policy, Planning & Evaluation, Betty Ann Pottruff, Q.C.
Tel: 306-787-8954
Fax: 306-787-9008
bettyann.pottruff@gov.sk.ca

Executive Director, Corporate Services, Dave Tulloch
Tel: 306-787-5472
Fax: 306-787-5830
dave.tulloch@gov.sk.ca

Director, Financial & Resource Planning, Mindy Gudmundson
Tel: 306-787-5580
Fax: 306-787-5830
mindy.gudmundson@gov.sk.ca

Director, Assurance & Financial Reporting, Brad Gurash
Tel: 306-798-5112
Fax: 306-787-5830
brad.gurash2@gov.sk.ca

Director, Communications, Linsay Rabyj
Tel: 306-787-0775
Fax: 306-787-3874
Linsay.Rabyj@gov.sk.ca
Executive Director, Susan Amrud, Q.C.
Tel: 306-787-8990
susan.amrud@gov.sk.ca

Saskatchewan Labour Relations & Workplace Safety (LRWS)

#300, 1870 Albert St., Regina, SK S4P 4W1
Tel: 306-787-7404
webmaster@lab.gov.sk.ca
www.lrws.gov.sk.ca
The Ministry is responsible for labour standards, labour support services, labour relations, mediation, occupational health & safety, & workers' advocacy.
Acts Administered:
Mines Regulation
Occupational Health & Safety Act, 1993
Occupational Health & Safety Regulations, 1996
Radiation Health & Safety Act, 1985
Radiation Health & Safety Regulations
Worker's Compensation Act
Worker's Compensation Act Exclusion Regulations
Worker's Compensation General Regulations, 1985

Minister, Advanced Education; Minister, Labour Relations & Workplace Safety; Minister Responsible, Saskatchewan Workers' Compensation Board, Hon. Don Morgan, Q.C.
Tel: 306-787-0613
Fax: 306-787-6946
minister.ae@gov.sk.ca
Social Media:
www.facebook.com/pages/Don-Morgan/48835718931?sk=info
Office of the Minister of Advanced Education / Labour Relation & Wokoplace Safety, Legislative Bldg.
#361, 2405 Legislative Dr.
Regina, SK S4S 0B3

Deputy Minister, Labour Relations & Workplace Safety, Mike Carr
Tel: 306-787-7424
Fax: 306-798-5190
Mike.Carr@gov.sk.ca

Executive Director, Corporate Services (Shared Services), Karen Allen
Tel: 306-787-5654
Fax: 306-787-7392
karen.allen@gov.sk.ca

Executive Director, Central Services, Laurier Donais
Tel: 306-787-8078
Fax: 306-798-5190
laurier.donais@gov.sk.ca

Executive Director, Labour Relations & Mediation, Doug Forseth
Tel: 306-787-9106
Fax: 306-787-1064
doug.forseth@gov.sk.ca

Acting Executive Director, Marketing & Communications (Shared Services), Rikki Bote
Tel: 306-787-4156
Fax: 306-798-5021
rikki.bote@gov.sk.ca

Director, Policy & Central Services, Pat Parenteau
Tel: 306-787-8409
Fax: 306-798-5190

Associated Agencies, Boards & Commissions:
• **Labour Relations Board**
#1600, 1920 Broad St.
Regina, SK S4P 3V2
Tel: 306-787-2406
Fax: 306-787-2664
www.sasklabourrelationsboard.com
An independent, quasi-judicial tribunal charged with the responsibility of adjudicating disputes that arise under The Trade Union Act, The Construction Industry Labour Relations Act, 1992 & The Health Labour Relations Reorganization Act
• **Minimum Wage Board**
#400, 1870 Albert St.
Regina, SK S4P 4W1
www.aeei.gov.sk.ca/minimum-wage-board-review-reporting
Makes recommendations respecting minimum employment standards including: the minimum wage, minimum age, maximum work periods, maximum rates for room & board & minimum rest periods.
• **Office of the Worker's Advocate**
#300, 1870 Albert St.
Regina, SK S4P 4W1
Tel: 306-787-2456
Fax: 306-787-0249
Toll-free: 877-787-2456
www.lrws.gov.sk.ca/wao
The Office of the Worker's Advocate provides free assistance to workers who are experiencing difficulties with workers' compensation claims. The Office offers information about the following programs & services: wage loss, benefits, survivor's benefits, medical aid, rehabilitation, & retraining. Working with advocacy groups & unions, The Office of the Worker's Advocate strives to improve service to injured workers. Workers' Compensation Board (WCB) decisions about claims can be reviewed & appealed.
Director, Denise Klotz
Tel: 306-787-2459

Fax: 306-787-0249
denise.klotz@gov.sk.ca
Early Resolution Officer, Luke McWilliams
Tel: 306-787-2455
Fax: 306-787-0249
luke.mcwilliams@gov.sk.ca
• **Saskatchewan Workers' Compensation Board**
See Entry Name Index for detailed listing.

Labour Standards
Tel: 306-787-2438
Fax: 306-787-4780
Toll-Free: 800-667-1783
www.lrws.gov.sk.ca/ls
Executive Director, Greg Tuer
Tel: 306-787-2432
Fax: 306-787-4780
greg.tuer@gov.sk.ca
Director, Compliance & Investigations (Saskatoon), Glen McRorie
Tel: 306-933-5087
Fax: 306-787-4780
glen.mcrorie@gov.sk.ca
Director, Legal & Education Services, Daniel Parrott
Tel: 306-787-9454
Fax: 306-787-4780
daniel.parrott@gov.sk.ca

Occupational Health & Safety Division
Tel: 306-787-4496
Fax: 306-787-2208
Toll-Free: 800-567-7233
www.lrws.gov.sk.ca/ohs
Executive Director, Glennis Bihun
Tel: 306-787-4481
Fax: 306-787-2208
glennis.bihun@gov.sk.ca
Chief Mines Inspector, Mines Safety, Neil Crocker
Tel: 306-933-5106
Fax: 306-933-7339
neil.crocker@gov.sk.ca
Director, Health Services, Rita Coshan
Tel: 306-787-4539
Fax: 306-787-2208
rita.coshan@gov.sk.ca
Director, Safety Services, Ray Anthony
Tel: 306-787-4502
Fax: 306-787-2208
ray.anthony@gov.sk.ca

Saskatchewan Parks, Culture, & Sport (PCS)

1919 Saskatchewan Dr., 4th Fl., Regina, SK S4P 4H2
Tel: 306-787-5729
Fax: 306-798-0033
Toll-Free: 800-205-7070
info@tpcs.gov.sk.ca
www.pcs.gov.sk.ca
Other Communication: Park Watch (Emergency & Security Issues), Toll-Free Phone: 1-800-667-1788
The Ministry is concerned with Saskatchewan's quality of life, tourism, & economic growth.
The following are some of the goals of the Ministry of Parks, Culture, & Sport: to enhance the province's parks by offering recreational activities & focussing upon natural resources that appeal to residents & visitors; to conserve heritage resources & ecosystems; to protect the province's history & culture; to promote Saskatchewan's cultural & artistic communities; & to encourage residents to be healthy & active through participation in sports & recreational events.
Some of the programs & services available through the Ministry include the Developers' Online Screening Tool, the provision of Archaeological/Palaeontological Permits, the maintenance of the Saskatchewan Register of Heritage Property, the operation of the Royal Saskatchewan Museum, competitive games information, the operation of the Canadian Sport Centre Saskatchewan, & the Active Families Benefit.
Ministry publications available through the provincial government's publication centre include the annual *Parks GuideA Physically Active Saskatchewan: A Strategy to get Saskatchewan People in Motion*& *Conserving Your Historic Places.*

Minister, Parks, Culture, & Sport; Minister Responsible, Provincial Capital Commission, Hon. Kevin Doherty
Tel: 306-787-0354
Fax: 306-798-0264
minister.pcs@gov.sk.ca
Social Media:
www.facebook.com/KevinDohertyforReginaNorthEast, ca.linkedin.com/pub/kevin-doherty/21/125/6b1
Office of the Minister, Parks, Culture, & Sport, Legislative Building
#38, 2405 Legislative Dr.
Regina, SK S4S 0B3

Deputy Minister, Parks, Culture, & Sport, Wynne Young
Tel: 306-787-5050
Fax: 306-798-0033
Wynne.Young@gov.sk.ca

Associate Deputy Minister, Parks, Culture, & Sport; Chief Executive Officer, Provincial Capital Commission, Lin Gallagher
Tel: 306-798-3905
Fax: 306-798-0033
Lin.Gallagher@gov.sk.ca

Manager, Executive Services, Wendy Searcy
Tel: 306-787-1062
Fax: 306-798-0033
Wendy.Searcy@gov.sk.ca

Associated Agencies, Boards & Commissions:
• **Conexus Arts Centre**
200A Lakeshore Dr.
Regina, SK S4S 7L3
Tel: 306-565-4500
Toll-free: 800-667-8497
cac.admin@conexusartscentre.ca
www.conexusartscentre.ca
Other Communication: Box Office, Phone: 306-525-9999
Formerly known as the Saskatchewan Centre of the Arts, the Conexus Arts Centrs is a performing arts & theatre complex. The Centre's mandate is to provide facilities, services, & programs to educate & entertain the people of Saskatchewan.
• **Provincial Capital Commission (PCC)**
4607 Dewdney Ave.
Regina, SK S4T 1B7
Tel: 306-787-9261
www.opcc.gov.sk.ca
The Provincial Capital Commission aims to provide education about the history of Saskatchewan. The Commission creates tourism & economic development opportunities, through the preservation & promotion of the province's heritage & culture.
The following Acts & Regulations guide the work of the Provincial Capital Commission:
Air, Army, Sea, & Navy League Cadets Recognition Day Act;
Archives Act, 2004;
Culture & Recreation Act, 1993;
Government House Foundation Regulations;
Heritage Property Act;
Historic Properties Foundations Act;
Provincial Capital Commission Regulations;
National Peacekeepers Recognition Day Act;
Recognition of John George Diefenbaker Day Act;
Recognition of Telemiracle Week Act;
Saskatchewan Centre of the Arts Act, 2000;
Saskatchewan Heritage Foundation Act;
Tartan Day Act;
Tommy Douglas Day Act;
Wascana Centre Act.
Minister, Parks, Culture, & Sport; Minister Responsible, Provincial Capital Commission, Hon. Kevin Doherty
Tel: 306-787-0354
Fax: 306-798-0264
minister.pcs@gov.sk.ca
Social Media:
www.facebook.com/KevinDohertyforReginaNorthEast, ca.linkedin.com/pub/kevin-doherty/21/125/6b1
Office of the Minister Responsible, Provincial Capital Commission
#38, 2405 Legislative Dr.
Regina, SK S4S 0B3
Associate Deputy Minister, Parks, Culture, & Sport; Chief Executive Officer, Provincial Capital Commission, Lin Gallagher
Tel: 306-798-3905
Fax: 306-798-0033
Lin.Gallagher@gov.sk.ca
Executive Director, Government House, Carrie Ross
Tel: 306-787-5720
Fax: 306-787-5714
carrie.ross2@gov.sk.ca
Director, Operations, Gwen Jacobson
Tel: 306-787-6863
Fax: 306-787-5714
Gwen.Jacobson@gov.sk.ca
Manager, Visitor Experience, Government House, Amanda Girardin
Tel: 306-787-5773
Fax: 306-787-5714
amanda.girardin@gov.sk.ca
• **Wascana Centre Authority**
2900 Wascana Dr.
PO Box 7111
Regina, SK S4P 3S7
Tel: 306-522-3661
Fax: 306-565-2742
wca@wascana.ca
www.wascana.ca
The Wascana Centre is committed to the conservation of the environment, the enhancement of educational & research opportunities, the improvement of recreational facilities, & the advancement of cultural arts. The Centre's vision, mission, & mandate are guided by The Wascana Centre Act.
Chief Executive Officer, Bernadette McIntyre
Tel: 306-347-1846
Fax: 306-347-1875
bernadette.mcintyre@wascana.ca
Chief Financial Officer, Rachel Ratch
Tel: 306-347-1829
Fax: 306-565-2742
rachel.ratch@wascana.ca
Director, Operations, Ken Dockham
Tel: 306-347-1812
Fax: 306-565-2742
ken.dockham@wascana.sk.ca
Manager, Infrastructure, Patrick Coulthard
Tel: 306-347-1814
Fax: 306-565-2742
patrick.coulthard@wascana.ca
Manager, Human Resources, Ranae McKenzie
Tel: 306-347-1828
Fax: 306-565-2742
ranae.mckenzie@wascana.ca
Manager, Safety, Jim Morgan
Tel: 306-347-1839
Fax: 306-565-2742
jim.morgan@wascana.ca
Manager, Maintenance, Nelson Quevillon
Tel: 306-347-1834
Fax: 306-565-2742
nelson.quevillon@wascana.ca
Manager, Community Relations, Carissa Robb
Tel: 306-347-1870
Fax: 306-565-2742
carissa.robb@wascana.ca
Manager, Horticulture & Forestry, D'Arcy Schenk
Tel: 306-347-1838
Fax: 306-565-2742
darcy.schenk@wascana.ca
Naturalist, Jared Clarke
Tel: 306-347-1811
Fax: 306-565-2742
jared.clarke@wascana.ca
• **Western Development Museum (WDM)**
Curatorial Centre
2935 Melville St,
Saskatoon, SK S7J 5A6
Tel: 306-934-1400
Fax: 306-934-4467
Toll-free: 800-363-6345
info@wdm.ca; curatorial@wdm.ca
www.wdm.ca
Other Communication: Moose Jaw WDM, Phone: 306-693-5989; North Battleford WDM, Phone: 306-445-8033; Saskatoon WDM, Phone: 306-931-1910; Yorkton WDM, Phone: 306-783-8361
There are locations in Moose Jaw (50 Diefenbaker Dr., Moose Jaw, SK S6J 1L9), North Battleford (PO Box 183, Hwy. 16 & 40, North Battleford SK S9A 2Y1), Saskatoon (2610 Lorne Ave. South, Saskatoon, SK S7J 0S6), & Yorkton (PO Box 98, Hwy. 16 West, Yorkton, SK S3N 2V6).
Executive Director, Curatorial Centre WDM, Joan Champ
jchamp@wdm.ca
Social Media: twitter.com/SaskWDM, www.facebook.com/skwdm?ref=ts

Director, Administration, Cal Glasman
cglasman@wdm.ca
Director, Marketing, Jan Olsen
jolsen@wdm.ca
Manager, Conservation, Thom Cholowski
tcholowski@wdm.ca
Manager, Moose Jaw WDM, Katherine Fitton
Tel: 306-693-5989
Fax: 306-691-0511
kfitton@wdm.ca; moosejaw@wdm.ca
Manager, Corporate Development, Josh Hourie
jhourie@wdm.ca
Manager, Yorkton WDM, Susan Mandziuk
Tel: 306-783-8361
Fax: 306-782-1027
smandziuk@wdm.ca; yorkton@wdm.ca
Manager, North Battleford WDM, Joyce Smith
Tel: 306-445-8033
Fax: 306-445-7211
jsmith@wdm.ca; nbattleford@wdm.ca
Manager, Facilities, Terry Thompson
tthompson@wdm.ca
Manager, Saskatoon WDM, Jason Wall
Tel: 306-931-1910
Fax: 306-934-0525
jwall@wdm.ca; saskatoon@wdm.ca
Curator, Collections, Ruth Bitner
rbitner@wdm.ca
Curator, Exhibits, Warren Clubb
wclubb@wdm.ca

Communications
1919 Saskatchewan Dr., 4th Fl., Regina, SK S4P 4H2
Tel: 306-787-0346
Fax: 306-798-0033
Other Communication: Inquiry Line: 306-787-5729; Marketing, Phone: 306-787-7828, Fax: 306-798-0033
Director, Communications, Jennifer Johnson
Tel: 306-787-0619
Fax: 306-798-0033
jennifer.johnson@gov.sk.ca
Manager, Communications, Linda Smith
Tel: 306-787-3506
Fax: 306-798-0033
Linda.Smith@gov.sk.ca
Executive Coordinator, Helen Petrovitch
Tel: 306-787-0346
Fax: 306-798-0033
Helen.Petrovitch@gov.sk.ca
Coordinator, Website, Steve Tompkins
Tel: 306-787-5164
Fax: 306-798-0033
steve.tompkins@gov.sk.ca

Cultural Planning & Development
1919 Saskatchewan Dr., 2nd Fl., Regina, SK S4P 4H2
Tel: 306-787-5877
Fax: 306-798-3177
Other Communication: Policy Analysis, Phone: 306-787-6880, Fax: 306-798-3177
It is the goal of the Ministry to increase the social & economic benefits of culture. The Ministry is guided by the following plan in its decision-making related to cultural policy: *Pride of Saskatchewan: A Policy Where Culture, Community & Commerce Meet.* The following programs & events are supported by the Ministry: artsVest Saskatchewan; Creative Industry Growth & Sustainability; Culture on the Go; Culture Days; & Prairie Scene.
Executive Director, Cultural Planning & Development, Gerald Folk
Tel: 306-787-8527
Fax: 306-798-3177
gerry.folk@gov.sk.ca
Analyst, Culture & Heritage, Shannon Chernick
Tel: 306-787-1360
Fax: 306-798-3177
shannon.chernick@gov.sk.ca
Analyst, Policy, Grace Hrycyshen
Tel: 306-787-8580
Fax: 306-798-3177
grace.hrycyshen@gov.sk.ca

Operations
1919 Saskatchewan Dr., 4th Fl., Regina, SK S4P 4H2
Tel: 306-798-0697
Fax: 306-798-0033
Other Communication: Heritage Conservation, Phone: 306-787-2817, Fax: 306-787-0069
Responsibilities of the Operations division include corporate services, heritage conservation, oversight of the Saskatchewan Heritage Foundation & the Royal Saskatchewan Museum, & park services.
Heritage conservation involves the protection of the province's heritage legacy, through inventories, research, & consultative services. Resources are available to help municipalities manage their historic places. One program is known as Main Street Saskatchewan, which works to revitalize historic downtown commercial districts.
The Saskatchewan Heritage Foundation was established by provincial legislation as an agent of the Crown. Its mission is to conserve heritage resources for the benefit of present & future generations.
The Royal Saskatchewan Museum in Regina presents Saskatchewan's geological & natural history, as well as a look at First Nations' cultures of the past & present.
Saskatchewan has a provincial parks & protected areas network. The Ministry provides programs & services to conserve, protect, & enhance the province's natural & cultural resources in its parks & protected areas.
Executive Director, Park Services, Cindy MacDonald
Tel: 306-787-0731
Toll-free: 800-205-7070
Fax: 306-787-7000
Cindy.MacDonald@gov.sk.ca
www.saskparks.net
Other Communications: Parks Service, Phone: 306-787-8676, Fax: 306-787-7000
Social Media: www.facebook.com/saskparks
Park Services Operations
3211 Albert St., 2nd Fl.
Regina, SK S4S 5W6
Director, Royal Saskatchewan Museum, Harold Bryant
Tel: 306-787-2813
Fax: 306-787-2820
Harold.Bryant@gov.sk.ca
www.royalsaskmuseum.ca
Other Communications: Royal Saskatchewan Museum, Phone: 306-787-2815
Social Media: twitter.com/royalsaskmuseum, www.facebook.com/Royal.Saskatchewan.Museum
Royal Saskatchewan Museum
2445 Albert St.
Regina, SK S4P 4W7
Director, Heritage Conservation, Carolos Germann
Tel: 306-787-5772
Fax: 306-787-0069
Carlos.Germann@gov.sk.ca
Heritage Conservation
1919 Saskatchewan Dr., 9th Fl.
Regina, SK S4P 4H2
Director, Southern Park Operations & Planning, Marty Halpape
Tel: 306-787-7621
Fax: 306-787-7000
Marty.Halpape@gov.sk.ca
Southern Park Operations & Planning
3211 Albert St., 2nd Fl.
Regina, SK S4S 5W6
Director, Facilities, Park Services, Bob Lalonde
Tel: 306-787-2783
Fax: 306-787-4218
Bob.Lalonde@gov.sk.ca
Facilities, Park Services
3211 Albert St., 2nd Fl.
Regina, SK S4S 5W6
Director, Corporate Services, Melinda Leibel
Tel: 306-787-5896
Fax: 306-798-0033
Melinda.Leibel@gov.sk.ca
Corporate Services
1919 Saskatchewan Dr., 4th Fl.
Regina, SK S4P 4H2
Director, Park Management Services, Bob McEachern
Tel: 306-787-2948
Fax: 306-787-7000
Bob.McEachern@gov.sk.ca
Park Management Services
3211 Albert St., 2nd Fl.
Regina, SK S4S 5W6
Director, Northern Park Operations & Planning, Randy Zielke
Tel: 306-953-2884
Fax: 306-953-2502
Randy.Zielke@gov.sk.ca
Northern Park Operations & Planning, L.F. McIntosh Building
800 Central Ave., 6th Fl.
PO Box 3003
Prince Albert, SK S6V 6G1
Senior Project Manager, Facilities, Park Services, Byron Davis
Tel: 306-787-3035
Fax: 306-787-4218
Byron.Davis@gov.sk.ca
Facilities, Park Services
3211 Albert St., 2nd Fl.
Regina, SK S4S 5W6
Manager, Business Development & Leasing, Park Management Services, Kevin Engel
Tel: 306-787-1285
Fax: 306-787-7000
Kevin.Engel@gov.sk.ca
Park Management Services
3211 Albert St., 2nd Fl.
Regina, SK S4S 5W6
Manager, Research & Collections, Royal Saskatchewan Museum, Ray Poulin
Tel: 306-787-2801
Fax: 306-787-2645
ray.poulin@gov.sk.ca
Royal Saskatchewan Museum
2340 Albert St.
Regina, SK S4P 2V7
Manager, Saskatchewan Heritage Foundation, Garth Pugh
Tel: 306-787-4188
Fax: 306-787-0069
Garth.Pugh@gov.sk.ca
Saskatchewan Heritage Foundation
1919 Saskatchewan Dr., 9th Fl.
Regina, SK S4P 4H2
Manager, Exhibits & Public Programs, Royal Saskatchewan Museum, John Snell
Tel: 306-787-2811
Fax: 306-787-2645
john.snell@gov.sk.ca
Other Communications: Public Programs, Phone: 306-787-9054
Royal Saskatchewan Museum
2445 Albert St.
Regina, SK S4P 4W7
Manager, Visitor Experiences, Park Services, Mary-Anne Wihak
Tel: 306-787-7826
Fax: 306-787-7000
Mary-Anne.Wihak@gov.sk.ca
Visitor Experiences, Park Services
3211 Albert St., 2nd Fl.
Regina, SK S4S 5W6
Curator of Palaeontology, Royal Saskatchewan Museum Fossil Research Station, Tim Tokaryk
Tel: 306-295-4701
Fax: 306-295-4702
Tim.Tokaryk@gov.sk.ca
Royal Saskatchewan Museum Fossil Research Station
1 T-Rex Dr.
PO Box 460
Eastend, SK S0N 0T0
Senior Archaeologist, Nathan Friesen
Tel: 306-787-5774
Fax: 306-787-0069
Nathan.Friesen@gov.sk.ca
Heritage Conservation
1919 Saskatchewan Dr., 9th Fl.
Regina, SK S4P 4H2
Heritage Architect, Patricia Glanville
Tel: 306-787-1588
Fax: 306-787-0069
Heritage Conservation
1919 Saskatchewan Dr., 9th Fl.
Regina, SK S4P 4H2

Policy, Planning, & Evaluation
1919 Saskatchewan Dr., 4th Fl., Regina, SK S4P 4H2
Tel: 306-787-0346
Fax: 306-798-0033
The Policy, Planning, & Evaluation unit carries out the following functions: provision of professional development activities to assist in the policy & program decision-making process; performance of primary research & evaluation studies; provision of technical assistance to external consultants; & analysis of secondary data to support policy & program development.

Executive Director, Policy, Planning, & Evaluation, Leanne Thera
Tel: 306-798-8762
Fax: 306-798-0033
Leanne.Thera@gov.sk.ca
Director, Strategic Alignment, Nancy Martin
Tel: 306-787-2834
Fax: 306-798-0033
nancy.martin@gov.sk.ca
Project Manager, Colin McAllister
Tel: 306-787-8448
Fax: 306-798-3177
Manager, Legislative Services, Janet Peters
Tel: 306-787-4967
Fax: 306-798-0033
Janet.Peters@gov.sk.ca
Senior Policy Analyst, Denise Hildebrand
Tel: 306-787-8170
Fax: 306-798-0033
denise.hildebrand@gov.sk.ca

Sport, Recreation, & Stewardship
1919 Saskatchewan Dr., 9th Fl., Regina, SK S4P 4H2
Tel: 306-787-7451
Fax: 306-787-0069
Ministry staff work with a variety of organizations to ensure that Saskatchewan's citizens have access to sports & recreational programs & services.
Consultative & technical services are also available through the Ministry for the staging of multi-sport competitive games in the province, such as the Saskatchewan Summer & Winter Games, the Saskatchewan Indian Summer & Winter Games, the Northern Games & Cultural Festival, & the 55+ Senior Games.
Executive Director, Sport, Recreation, & Stewardship, Darin Banadyga
Tel: 306-787-0685
Fax: 306-787-0069
Darin.Banadyga@gov.sk.ca
Senior Policy Analyst, Nancy Porter
Tel: 306-787-3828
Fax: 306-787-0069
Nancy.Porter@gov.sk.ca
Senior Policy Analyst, Elizabeth Verrall
Tel: 306-787-5734
Fax: 306-787-0069
Elizabeth.Verrall@gov.sk.ca

Tourism Initiatives
1919 Saskatchewan Dr., 2nd Fl., Regina, SK S4P 4H2
Tel: 306-787-8985
Fax: 306-798-3177
Executive Director, Ken Dueck
Tel: 306-787-7871
Fax: 306-798-3177
Ken.Dueck@gov.sk.ca
Executive Coordinator, Mag Massier
Tel: 306-787-8985
Fax: 306-798-3177
Mag.Massier@gov.sk.ca
Senior Policy Analyst, Tyler Lloyd
Tel: 306-787-5728
Fax: 306-798-3177
Tyler.Lloyd@gov.sk.ca
Tourism Analyst, Travis McLellan
Tel: 306-787-5946
Fax: 306-798-3177
Travis.McLellan@gov.sk.ca
Tourism Analyst, Spencer Roberton
Tel: 306-787-7741
Fax: 306-798-0033
Spencer.Roberton@gov.sk.ca

Saskatchewan Power Corporation (SaskPower)

2025 Victoria Ave., Regina, SK S4P 0S1
Tel: 306-566-3306
Fax: 800-757-6937
Toll-Free: 888-757-6937
www.saskpower.com
Other Communication: Media phone: 306-536-2886
A Crown Corporation which provides services to over 439,000 customers over 652,000 square kilometres of diverse terrain in Saskatchewan; operates 15 generating facilities including, four base-load thermal stations, seven hydroelectric stations, three gas-fired peaking stations, & the Cypress Wind Power facility; capacity of 3,655 megawatts. The SaskPower Environmental policy maintains a commitment to environmental responsibility. The policy includes compliance with relevant environmental legislation, regulations & corporate environmental committees; continual improvement of environmental management systems & prevention of pollution. SaskPower's management system is ISO 14001 registered.

Minister Responsible, Hon. Bill Boyd
Tel: 306-787-0341
Fax: 306-787-6946
minister.aeei@gov.sk.ca

President/Chief Executive Officer, NorthPoint Energy Solutions, Grant Ring
Tel: 306-566-3577

Vice-President, Power Production, John Lebersback
Tel: 306-566-3228
jlebersback@saskpower.com

Vice-President, Transmission & Distribution, Mike Marsh
Tel: 306-566-3271
mmarsh@saskpower.com

Vice-President, Customer Services, Judy May
Tel: 306-566-2161

Vice-President, Clean Coal Technology, Michael Monea
Tel: 306-566-3132
mmonea@saskpower.com

Vice-President, Law, Land & Regulatory Affairs, Rachelle Verret Morphy
Tel: 306-566-3139
rverretmor@saskpower.com

General Manager, Corporate Relations, Keith Moon
Tel: 306-566-3421

SaskPower Shand GreenHouse
PO Box 280Estevan, SK S4A 2A3
Tel: 306-634-9771
Fax: 306-634-6682
greenhouse@saskpower.com
www.saskpower.com/shandgreenhouse/index.shtml
Environmentally advanced power station, completed in July of 1992; burns high-quality lignite coal; flyash is removed by an electrostatic precipitator; a calcium-bearing sorbent injection system removes sulphur dioxide; burner temperature & air quality controls nitrogen oxide formations; Rafferty reservoir & Estevan sewage are the primary water sources for cooling. The Shand Power Station is a Zero discharge plant. Fully operational in 1996.

Saskatchewan Research Council (SRC)

#125, 15 Innovation Blvd., Saskatoon, SK S7N 2X8
Tel: 306-933-5400
Fax: 306-933-7446
info@src.sk.ca
www.src.sk.ca
Research activities include: gas emissions testing; indoor environment testing; groundwater pesticides testing; indoor air quality & source testing for rayon & asbestos; spray drift research; vegetation studies for range, forestry, conservation; aquatic monitoring & assessment methods; climate impact assessment for environmental economic & urban stormwater management; development of plant bioassays for assessing the effects of hazardous materials in aquatic ecosystems; radiochemistry, chromatographic analysis, water analysis; parenting verification centre for the Canadian livestock industry; develops the optimum engine & fuel system for natural gas operation; bioprocessing technology; emulsions research; studies to support mineral exploration; analyses various sample material used in mineral exploration; geoenvironmental research. SRC's Biofuels Test Centre opened in September, 2006.

President/Chief Executive Officer, Dr. Laurier Schramm
Tel: 306-933-5402
schramm@src.sk.ca

Vice-President, Environment, Joe Muldoon
Tel: 306-933-5439
Fax: 306-933-7299
muldoon@src.sk.ca

Vice-President, Mining & Minerals, Craig Murray
Tel: 306-933-5482
Fax: 306-933-7446
murray@src.sk.ca

Vice-President, Energy, Ernie S. Pappas
Tel: 306-787-9351
Fax: 306-787-8811
pappas@src.sk.ca

Vice-President, Agriculture & Biotechnology, Phillip Stephan
Tel: 306-933-8199
Fax: 306-933-7662
stephan@src.sk.ca

Saskatchewan Water Corporation (SaskWater)

#200, 111 Fairford St. East, Moose Jaw, SK S6H 1C8
Fax: 306-694-3207
Toll-Free: 888-230-1111
comm@saskwater.com; customerservice@saskwater.com
www.saskwater.com
Other Communication: SaskWater Customer Emergencies: 1-800-667-5799
SaskWater, a provincial Crown corporation, is Saskatchewan's water utility service provider. Lines of business are as follows: supply of potable & non-potable water; treatment & management of wastewater; & certified operations & maintenance. SaskWater is responsible for designing, building, & operating transmission, regional, & stand-alone water supply & wastewater systems. All systems must meet regulatory requirements.
Acts Administered:
Saskatchewan Water Corporation Act, 2002

Minister Responsible, Hon. Ken Cheveldayoff
Tel: 306-787-0393
Fax: 306-787-1669
minister.env@gov.sk.ca
Social Media:
www.facebook.com/pages/Ken-Cheveldayoff/52760912740
Office of the Minister, Legislative Building
#315, 2405 Legislative Dr.
Regina, SK S4S 0B3

President, Doug Matthies
Tel: 306-694-3903
Fax: 306-694-3207
doug.matthies@saskwater.com

Vice-President, Operations & Engineering, Jeff Mander
Tel: 306-694-3880
Fax: 306-694-3207
jeff.mander@saskwater.com

Vice President, Business Development & Corporate Services, Marie Alexander
Tel: 306-694-3916
Fax: 306-694-3207
marie.alexander@saskwater.com

Director, Engineering, Eric Light
Tel: 306-694-3920
Fax: 306-694-3207
eric.light@saskwater.com

Director, District Operations, Jeff Mander
Tel: 306-694-3880
Fax: 306-694-3207
jeff.mander@saskwater.com

Saskatchewan Watershed Authority (SWA)

111 Fairford St. East, Moose Jaw, SK S6H 7X9
Tel: 306-694-3900
Fax: 306-694-3944
comm@swa.ca
www.swa.ca
Other Communication: Provincial Water Inquiry Line: 866-727-5420
Saskatchewan Watershed Authority is a Crown corporation that is responsible for managing water resources in Saskatchewan. The Authority works to ensure reliable water supplies & safe drinking water sources.
The following regulations are administered by the Saskatchewan Watershed Authority: Conservation & Development; Drainage Control; Ground Water; & Reservoir Development Area.

Acts Administered:
Conservation & Development Act
Saskatchewan Watershed Authority Act, 2005
The Water Power Act
Watershed Associations Act

Minister, Environment; Minister Responsible, Saskatchewan Watershed Authority; Minister Responsible, Saskatchewan Water Corporation, Hon. Ken Cheveldayoff
Tel: 306-787-0393
Fax: 306-787-1669
minister.env@gov.sk.ca
Social Media:
www.facebook.com/pages/Ken-Cheveldayoff/52760912740
Office of the Minister, Legislative Building
#315, 2405 Legislative Dr.
Regina, SK S4S 0B3

President, Wayne Dybvig
Tel: 306-694-7739
Fax: 306-694-3991
wayne.dybvig@swa.ca

Vice-President, Corporate Services, Bob Carles
Tel: 306-694-7737
Fax: 306-694-3465
bob.carles@swa.ca

Executive Director, Dam Safety & Major Structures, Bill Duncan
Tel: 306-694-3990
Fax: 306-694-3944
bill.duncan@swa.ca

Executive Director, Integrated Water Services, Jim Gerhart
Tel: 306-694-3952
Fax: 306-694-3944
jim.gerhart@swa.ca

Executive Director, Policy & Communications, Dale Hjertaas
Tel: 306-787-0726
Fax: 306-787-0780
dale.hjertaas@swa.ca

Director, Hydrology & Groundwater Services, John Fahlman
Tel: 306-694-3954
Fax: 306-694-3944
john.fahlman@swa.ca

Director, Business Information & Technology Systems, Jan Franken
Tel: 306-694-3961
Fax: 306-694-3465
jan.franken@swa.ca

Director, Policy & Risk Management, Terry Hanley
Tel: 306-787-9982
Fax: 306-787-0780
terry.hanley@swa.ca

Director, Parnerships & Plan Implementation, Tom Harrison
Tel: 306-694-3973
Fax: 306-694-3616
tom.harrison@swa.ca

Director, Financial Services, Irene Hrynkiw
Tel: 306-694-3960
Fax: 306-694-3465
irene.hrynkiw@swa.ca

Director, Human Resources & Workplace Services, Joe Maciag
Tel: 306-694-3878
Fax: 306-694-3465
joe.maciag@swa.ca

Director, Licensing & Water Use, Jim Waggoner
Tel: 306-694-3966
Fax: 306-694-3944
jim.waggoner@swa.ca

Saskatchewan Workers' Compensation Board

#200, 1881 Scarth St., Regina, SK S4P 4L1
Tel: 306-787-4370
Fax: 306-787-4311
Toll-Free: 800-667-7590
internet_clientsvc@wcbsask.com
www.wcbsask.com
Other Communication: Injury Reports: 1-800-787-9288; Employer Inquiries: reainquiry@wcbsask.com; Health Care Provider Inquiries: internet_healthcare@wcbsask.com; Appeal Fax: 306-787-1116
Secondary Address: 129 Third Ave. North
Saskatoon, SK S7K 2H6
Fax: 306-787-4311
The Saskatchewan's Workers' Compensation Board was created by the following provincial legislation in Saskatchewan: the Workers' Compensation Act 1979, General Regulations, & Exclusion Regulations. The Board is an independent body that administers a no-fault compensation system to protect employers and workers against the result of work injuries. The WCB provides financial protection, medical benefits. & rehabilitation services to injured workers & their dependents in cases of injury or death arising from, & in the course of, employment.

Minister, Advanced Education; Minister, Labour Relations & Workplace Safety; Minister Responsible, Saskatchewan Workers' Compensation Board, Hon. Don Morgan, Q.C.
Tel: 306-787-0613
Fax: 306-787-6946
minister.ae@gov.sk.ca
Social Media:
www.facebook.com/pages/Don-Morgan/488357189317sk=info
Office of the Minister of Advanced Education / Labour Relation & Workplace Safety, Legislative Bldg.
#361, 2405 Legislative Dr.
Regina, SK S4S 0B3

Chairman, David Eberle
Tel: 306-787-4379
Fax: 306-787-0213

Chief Executive Officer, Peter Federko
Tel: 306-787-7398
Fax: 306-787-0213
pfederko@wcbsask.com

Vice-President, Human Resources & Team Support, Donna Kane
Tel: 306-787-4440
Fax: 306-787-0213
dkane@wcbsask.com

Vice-President, Prevention, Finance & Information Technology, Gail Kruger
Tel: 306-787-2475
Fax: 306-787-0213
gkruger@wcbsask.com

Vice-President, Operations, Graham Topp
Tel: 306-787-4371
Fax: 306-787-7582
gtopp@wcbsask.com

Director, Planning & Communications, Janice Siekawitch
Tel: 306-787-4386
Fax: 306-787-3915
jsiekawitch@wcbsask.com

Government of the Yukon Territory

Seat of Government: PO Box 2703Whitehorse, YT Y1A 2C6
Tel: 867-667-5811
Toll-Free: 800-661-0408
TTY: 867-393-7460
www.gov.yk.ca
The Yukon was created as a separate territory June 13, 1898. It has an area of 474,711.02 km2, & StatsCan's census in 2011 showed the population was 32,897. A federally appointed commissioner (similar to a provincial lieutenant-governor) oversees federal interests in the territory, but the day-to-day operation of the government rests with the wholly elected executive council (cabinet). The territorial legislature has power to make acts on generally all matters of a local nature in the territory, including the imposition of local taxes, property & civil rights & the administration of justice, education & health & social services. Legislative powers vested in the provinces but not available to the territory include control of unoccupied Crown land, renewable & non-renewable resources (except wildlife & sport fisheries) & the power to amend the Yukon Act, a federal statute.
Acts Administered:
Raven Act
Waters Act (jointly with Environment & Energy, Mines & Resources)
Yukon Environmental & Socio-Economic Assessment Act
Yukon Land Claim Final Agreements Act

Yukon Community Services

PO Box 2703Whitehorse, YT Y1A 2C6
Tel: 867-667-5811
Fax: 867-393-6295
Toll-Free: 800-661-0408
TTY: 867-393-7460
inquiry@gov.yk.ca
www.community.gov.yk.ca
The main purpose of the department is to serve Yukoners & their communities by providing access to services to strengthen communities. The department focuses on community affairs & municipal relations within government on behalf of Yukon communities & acts as a liaison between community groups & government departments.
Acts Administered:
Animal Protection Act (jointly with Energy, Mines & Resources)
Area Development Act
Assessment & Taxation Act
Building Standards Act
Civil Emergency Measures Act
Fire Prevention Act
Forest Protection Act (jointly with Department of Energy, Mines & Resources)
Gasoline Handling Act
Miner's Lien Act
Motor Vehicles Act (jointly with Highways & Public Works)
Municipal Act
Recreation Act

Minister, Elaine Taylor, Hon.
Tel: 867-667-8641
Fax: 867-393-6252
elaine.taylor@gov.yk.ca

Deputy Minister, Harvey Brooks
Tel: 867-456-6512
Fax: 867-633-7957
harvey.brooks@gov.yk.ca

Director, Communications, Matt King
Tel: 867-456-6580
Fax: 867-393-6404
matt.king@gov.yk.ca

Director, Corporate Policy, Caitlin Kerwin
Tel: 867-456-5524
Fax: 867-393-6404
caitlin.kerwin@gov.yk.ca

Director, Finance, Systems & Administration, Christine Mahar
Tel: 867-667-5311
Fax: 867-393-6264
christine.mahar@gov.yk.ca

Manager, Information Management, Craig Brooks
Tel: 867-667-3451
Fax: 867-393-6264
craig.brooks@gov.yk.ca

Manager, Finance, Beth Fricke
Tel: 867-667-5921
Fax: 867-393-6264
beth.fricke@gov.yk.ca

Director, Human Resources, Les Hudson
Tel: 867-667-5667
Fax: 867-393-6933
Les.Hudson@gov.yk.ca

Associated Agencies, Boards & Commissions:
• **Assessment Appeal Board**
Tel: 867-668-6598
Fax: 867-633-2640
• **Driver Control Board**
2130 Second Ave., 3rd Fl.
PO Box 2703
Whitehorse, YT Y1A 2C6
Tel: 867-667-5111
Fax: 867-667-3609

dcb@gov.yk.ca
www.community.gov.yk.ca/dcb
Other Communication: 800-661-0408 (ext. 5111)
• Yukon Lottery Commission
312 Wood St.
Whitehorse, YT Y1A 2E6
Tel: 867-633-7890
Fax: 867-668-7561
lotteriesyukon@gov.yk.ca
www.lotteriesyukon.com

Safety Resources
91790 Alaska Hwy., Whitehorse, YT Y1A 5X7
Fax: 867-456-6567

Community Development
The branch assists, advises & organizes municipal & unincorporated communities, provides funding by administering the comprehensive municipal grants & grants in lieu of taxes, assesses properties, collects property taxes & administers the Rural Electrification & Telecommunication program & the Home Owner Grant program. The branch collaborates with communities for the planning, design, & construction of land development projects & includes residential, rural residential, commercial, industrial, & cottage lots. The branch is responsible for regulatory approvals & design, managing construction capital works projects, such as upgrading roads, water & sewage treatment facilities & solid waste disposal sites & assists communities in developing land use plans, working closely with the Yukon Municipal Board & the Association of Yukon Communities. The branch is responsible for the operation of Yukon Government owned facilities for water supply & distribution, sewage treatment & solid waste disposal.
Assistant Deputy Minister, Paul Moore
Tel: 867-667-3534
Fax: 867-393-6216
paul.moore@gov.yk.ca

Emergency Measures Organization (EMO)
Combined Services Bldg., 2nd Fl., 60 Norseman Rd, Airport, Whitehorse, YT Y1A 2C6
Tel: 867-667-5220
Fax: 867-393-6266
Toll-Free: 800-661-0408
emo.yukon@gov.yk.ca
www.community.gov.yk.ca/emo
Responsible for coordinating the Territory's preparedness for, response to, & recovery from, major emergencies & disasters. EMO provides authority to ensure that contingency plans are in place to deal with foreseeable risks & hazards. The Yukon EMO is divided into 13 geographical preparedness areas, mirroring the RCMP detachment boundaries. Eight of these areas have incorporated Municipalities that have appointed a Municipal EMO Coordinator to chair the local Emergency Planning Committee. In the remaining areas, the Emergency Measures Branch appoints a co-ordinator.
Manager, Michael Templeton
Tel: 867-667-5220
Fax: 867-393-6266
michael.templeton@gov.yk.ca

Consumer Services & Information Development
Berska Bldg., 2nd Fl., 307 Black St., Whitehorse, YT
Fax: 867-393-6943
Assistant Deputy Minister, Dan Boyd
Tel: 867-667-5486
Fax: 867-393-6251
dan.boyd@gov.yk.ca

Protective Services
91790 Alaska Hwy., Whitehorse, YT Y1A 5X7
Fax: 867-456-6567

Emergency Medical Services
Yukon Electrical Bldg., #200, 1100 First Ave., Whitehorse, YT
www.community.gov.yk.ca/ems

Fire Marshal's Office
91790 Alaska Hwy., Whitehorse, YT Y1A 5X7
Tel: 867-667-5811
Fax: 867-667-3165
inquiry@gov.yk.ca
www.community.gov.yk.ca/fireprotection/contact.html
The Fire Marshal's Office works to reduce the loss of life & property due to fire & is responsible for public education & fire fighter training, as well as for funding & administering volunteer fire departments in Yukon unincorporated communities. Staff carry out fire & life safety inspections on hotels, motels, public assembly buildings, schools, day care centers, homes for special care, restaurants, etc. throughout Yukon. The Office inspects & permits underground fuel storage tank installations.

Wildlife Fire Management
91790 Alaska Hwy., Whitehorse, YT Y1A 5X7
Tel: 867-456-3845
Fax: 867-667-3191
www.community.gov.yk.ca/firemanagement

Yukon Development Corporation (YDC)

#2 Miles Canyon Rd., PO Box 5920Whitehorse, YT Y1A 6S7
Tel: 867-393-5337
Fax: 867-393-5401
www.ydc.yk.ca
The Yukon Development Corporation (YDC) assists with implementation of energy policies from the Department of Energy, Mines & Resources, by designing & delivering related energy programs. YDC facilitates the generation, production, transmission & distribution of energy in a manner consistent with sustainable development. YDC has investments in electricity & related energy infrastructure & acts as the primary vehicle for delivery of territorial energy programs & services. YDC owns two subsidiary corporations, Yukon Energy Corporation, YEC, & the Energy Solutions Centre Inc., ESC. YEC is the primary producer & transmitter of electrical energy in the territory & operates under the Yukon Utilities Board & the Public Utilities Act. ESC provides technical services, promotes efficiency & renewable energy technologies, co-ordinates & delivers federal & territorial energy programs to households, businesses, institutions, First Nation & public governments.

Minister responsible, Brad Cathers
Tel: 867-667-8625
Fax: 867-456-6741
brad.cathers@gov.yk.ca

Chief Executive Officer, David Morrison
Tel: 867-393-5400
Fax: 867-393-5401
david.morrison@gov.yk.ca

Yukon Energy Corporation
2 Miles Canyon Rd., PO Box 5920Whitehorse, YT Y1A 6S7
Tel: 867-393-5300
Toll-Free: 866-926-3749
communications@yukonenergy.ca
www.yukonenergy.ca
The YEC distributes electricity to wholesale & industrial customers. YEC acts in an environmentally responsible manner while developing & maintaining energy infrastructure & services consistent with the principles of sustainable development. Sources of energy include solar power, wind power, geo-thermal power, hydro power & diesel power. YEC is also involved in fish ladder & hatchery.
Minister responsible, Brad Cathers
Tel: 867-667-8625
Fax: 867-456-6741
brad.cathers@gov.yk.ca
President/CEO, David Morrison
Vice-President, Operations & Engineering, David MacDonald

Yukon Economic Development

PO Box 2703Whitehorse, YT Y1A 2C6
Tel: 867-393-7191
Fax: 867-393-6412
Toll-Free: 800-661-0408
ecdev@gov.yk.ca
www.economicdevelopment.gov.yk.ca
The Department works with the Yukon business community & with other governments to support business development, trade & investment opportunities, & partnerships for the development of the Yukon economy. It co-ordinates & facilitates the Yukon Government's economic development agenda. The Department is focused on creating a positive business climate in Yukon & is committed to First Nation business development in the territory. Economic Development markets Yukon as a great place to do business.

Minister, Currie Dixon, Hon.
Tel: 867-667-5800
Fax: 867-393-6252
currie.dixon@gov.yk.ca

Deputy Minister, Harvey Brooks
Tel: 867-393-7191
Fax: 867-667-3159
harvey.brooks@gov.yk.ca

Assistant Deputy Minister, Operations, Terry Hayden
Tel: 867-456-3912
Fax: 867-667-3159
terry.hayden@gov.yk.ca

Director, Finance & Information Services, Karen Mason
Tel: 867-667-5933
Fax: 867-393-7199
karen.mason@gov.yk.ca

Director, Policy, Planning & Research, Stephen Rose
Tel: 867-667-8416
Fax: 867-393-6412
stephen.rose@gov.yk.ca

Executive Assistant to the Minister, Valerie Boxall
Tel: 867-667-8628
Fax: 867-393-7400
valerie.boxall@gov.yk.ca

Executive Assistant to the Deputy Minister, Judith Voswinkel
Tel: 867-393-7191
Fax: 867-667-3159
judith.voswinkel@gov.yk.ca

Yukon Energy, Mines & Resources

PO Box 2703Whitehorse, YT Y1A 2C6
Tel: 867-667-3130
Fax: 867-456-3965
Toll-Free: 800-661-0408
TTY: 867-393-7460
emr@gov.yk.ca
www.emr.gov.yk.ca
The territory has extensive mineral deposits, oil & gas potential, with two producing gas wells, which rank among the top producing wells in Canada, forest reserves & local manufacturing of wood products, such as furniture, wood laminate stock & lumber. The territory has abundant & diverse energy resources due to the presence of fossil fuel reserves, numerous lakes & rivers, windy & mountainous terrain, broad forest cover & sunny conditions. The Yukon is one of the few places left in Canada where Crown land can be obtained for agricultural purposes.
Acts Administered:
Agriculture Development Act
Animal Health Act (jointly with Environment)
Forest Protection Act (jointly with Community Services)
Lands Act
Oil & Gas Act
Oil & Gas Disposition Regulations
Oil & Gas Drilling & Production Regulations
Oil & Gas Geoscience & Exploration Regulations
Oil & Gas Licence Administration Regulations
Placer Mining Act
Quartz Mining Act
Subdivision Act
Territorial Lands (Yukon) Act
Waters Act (jointly with Environment & the Executive Council Office)

Minister, Brad Cathers, Hon.
Tel: 867-667-8625
Fax: 867-456-6741
brad.cathers@gov.yk.ca

Deputy Minister, Angus Robertson
Tel: 867-667-5417
Fax: 867-393-7167
angus.robertson@gov.yk.ca

Assistant Deputy Minister, Energy, Corporate Policy & Communications, Shirley Abercrombie
Tel: 867-667-3187
Fax: 867-393-7421
shirley.abercrombie@gov.yk.ca

Executive Director, Yukon Placer Secretariat, Robert Thomson
Tel: 867-667-3136

Fax: 867-667-3632
robert.thomson@gov.yk.ca

Director, Corporate Services, Ross McLachlan
Tel: 867-456-3960
Fax: 867-456-3965
ross.mclachlan@gov.yk.ca

Director, Communications, Mark Roberts
Tel: 867-667-5307
Fax: 867-393-7421
mark.roberts@gov.yk.ca

Agriculture
Tel: 867-667-5838
Fax: 867-393-6222
agriculture@gov.yk.ca
www.emr.gov.yk.ca/agriculture/index.html
Other Communication: 800-661-0408, ext. 5838 (toll-free)
Director, Tony Hill
tony.hill@gov.yk.ca

Assessment & Abandoned Mines
Assessment Centre, #2C, 4114 4th Ave., Whitehorse, YT Y1A 2C6
Tel: 867-393-7098
Fax: 867-456-6780
yukonabandonedmines@gov.yk.ca
www.emr.gov.yk.ca
Other Communication: 800-661-0408, ext. 7098 (toll-free)
Director, Stephen Mead
Tel: 867-393-6904
stephen.mead@gov.yk.ca

Client Services & Inspections
www.emr.gov.yk.ca/csi/index.html
Director, Robert Thomson
Tel: 867-667-3136
Fax: 867-667-3199
robert.thomson@gov.yk.ca

Energy Solutions Centre
206A Lowe St., 1st Fl., Whitehorse, YT Y1A 1W6
Tel: 867-393-7063
Fax: 867-393-7061
esc@gov.yk.ca
www.energy.gov.yk.ca
The ESC is a non-profit organization that works in partnership with Natural Resources Canada (NRCan) to promote renewable energy programs & assist Yukon businesses, institutions, & municipal governments implement renewable energy solutions.
Director, Shane Andre
Tel: 867-393-7070
sharon.andre@gov.yk.ca

Forestry
Mile 918 Alaska Hwy., PO Box 2703Whitehorse, YT Y1A 2C6
Tel: 867-456-3999
Fax: 867-667-3138
forestry@gov.yk.ca
www.emr.gov.yk.ca/forestry
Acting Director, Pat MacDonell
Tel: 867-633-7917
patrick.macdonnell@gov.yk.ca

Human Resources
230-300 Main St., PO Box 2703Whitehorse, YT Y1A 2C6
Tel: 867-667-3007
Fax: 867-393-7422
www.emr.gov.yk.ca/hr
Other Communication: 800-661-0408, ext. 3007 (toll-free)
Director, Ingrid Fawcus
Tel: 867-667-3549
ingrid.fawcus@gov.yk.ca

Land Services
#320, 300 Main St., Whitehorse, YT Y1A 2C6
Tel: 867-667-5215
www.emr.gov.yk.ca/lands
Director, Land Planning, George Stetkiewicz
Tel: 867-667-3530
Fax: 867-393-6340
george.stetkiewicz@gov.yk.ca
Manager, Programs & Policy Support, Mike Draper
Tel: 867-667-3185
Fax: 867-393-6340
mike.draper@gov.yk.ca
Manager, Land Use, Marg White
Tel: 867-667-3173
Fax: 867-667-3214
marg.white@gov.yk.ca
Manager, Land Client Services, John Cole
Tel: 867-667-5882
Fax: 867-667-3214
john.cole@gov.yk.ca

Library
Elijah Smith Building, #335, 300 Main St., Whitehorse, YT Y1A 2B5
Tel: 867-667-3111
Fax: 867-456-3888
emrlibrary@gov.yk.ca
www.emr.gov.yk.ca/library
Manager, Aimee Ellis
Tel: 867-667-3108
aimee.ellis@gov.yk.ca

Mining
#400, 211 Main St., Whitehorse, YT Y1A 2B2
Tel: 867-633-7952
Fax: 867-456-3899
mining@gov.yk.ca
www.emr.gov.yk.ca/mining
Other Communication: 800-661-0408, ext. 7952 (toll-free)
Director, Mineral Resources, Bob Holmes
Tel: 867-667-3126
robert.holmes@gov.yk.ca

Oil & Gas Mineral Resources
#300, 211 Main St., Whitehorse, YT Y1A 2B2
Tel: 867-667-5087
Fax: 867-393-6262
oilandgas@gov.yk.ca
www.emr.gov.yk.ca/oilandgas
Other Communication: 800-661-0408, ext. 5087 (toll-free)

Yukon Geological Survey
Elijah Smith Building, #102-300 Main St., Whitehorse, YT
Tel: 867-667-5097
Fax: 867-393-6262
oilandgas@gov.yk.ca
www.emr.gov.yk.ca/oilandgas
Other Communication: 800-661-0408, ext. 5087 (toll-free)
Also located at the Professional Building at 2099-2nd Ave.
Director, Carolyn Relf
Tel: 867-667-8892
carolyn.relf@gov.yk.ca

Yukon Geological Survey
Tel: 867-667-8508
Fax: 867-393-6232
geosales@gov.yk.ca
www.geology.gov.yk.ca
Director, Carolyn Relf
Tel: 867-667-8892
carolyn.relf@gov.yk.ca
Environmental Geologist, Karen Pelletier
Tel: 867-456-3808
karen.pelletier@gov.yk.ca

Forest Management Branch
Mile 918 Alaska Highway, PO Box 2703Whitehorse, YT Y1A 2C6
Tel: 867-456-3999
Fax: 867-667-3138
Toll-Free: 800-661-0408
forestry@gov.yk.ca
Oversees the development & management of Yukon's forest resources. The services & responsibilities include: taking inventory of & managing Yukon forests, conduct environmental assessments of proposed timber harvesting projects, forest renewal, forest management planning, identifying & allocating timber harvesting areas, issuing permits to harvest timber, conducting environmental assessments of proposed forest activities, collecting stumpage revenues; auditing activities, consultation, forestry legislations, forest practices planning & liaison, & maintaining & improving forestry GIS & mapping capabilities.
Director, Diane Reed
Tel: 867-456-3838

Yukon Environment

PO Box 2703Whitehorse, YT Y1A 2C6
Tel: 867-667-5652
Fax: 867-393-7197
environment.yukon@gov.yk.ca
www.env.gov.yk.ca
Other Communication: 800-661-0408, ext. 5652 (toll-free)
The department is responsible for legislation, regulations licensing, management, policies, programs, services, education & information regarding the natural environment in three program areas: fish & wildlife, environmental protection & assessment & parks & protection areas. The department's branches educate resource users & the general public, develop & enforce policies, regulations, & legislation & assist other departments in the sustainable use & management of the territory's natural resources. The department supports land claims negotiations & assists in implementing land claims agreements. The department represents the Yukon government at national & global environmental forums on issues such as climate change & biodiversity conservation.Through the Environmental Awareness Fund the government provides funding to assist registered non-government organizations to promote environmental education or awareness, resource planning & sustainable development in the Yukon.
Acts Administered:
Activities Requiring Environmental Assessment (Inclusion List) Regulations
Administrative Regulation
Air Emissions Regulations
Animal Health Act (jointly with Energy, Mines & Resources)
Beverage Container Regulation
Campground Regulations
Coal River Springs Ecological Reserve
Comprehensive Study List Regulation
Concession & Compensation Review Board Regulations
Conservation Fund Regulations
Contaminated Sites Regulations
Coordination of Environmental Assessment Procedures & Requirement Regulations
Designated Materials
Environment Act
Establish Ni'iinlii Njik (Fishing Branch) Ecological Reserve
Establish Ni'iinlii Njik (Fishing Branch) Wilderness Preserve
Exclusion List Regulation
Game Farm Regulations
Game Management Sub-zone Regulations
Herschel Island Nature Preserve
Herschel Island Park Regulations
Law List Regulation
Mackenzie River Basin Agreement Act
Outfitting Concession Area Boundary Regulations
Ozone Depleting Substances & Other Halocarbons Regulation
Parks & Land Certainty Act
Pesticides Regulations
Recycling Fund Regulation
Solid Waste Regulations
Special Waste Regulations
Spills Regulations
Storage Tank Regulations
Tombstone Territorial Park Regulations
Trapping Concession Area Boundary Regulations
Trapping Regulations
Waters Act (jointly with Energy, Mines & Resources & the Executive Council Office)
Waters Regulation
Wilderness Tourism Licensing Act
Wildlife Act
Wildlife Sanctuary Regulation
Yukon Council on the Economy & the Environment Regulation
Yukon River Basin & Alsek River Basin Agreements Act

Minister, Currie Dixon, Hon.
Tel: 867-667-5800
Fax: 867-393-6252
currie.dixon@gov.yk.ca

Deputy Minister, Kelvin Leary
Tel: 867-667-5460
Fax: 867-393-6213
kelvin.leary@gov.yk.ca

Associated Agencies, Boards & Commissions:
• Alsek Renewable Resource Council (ARRC)
PO Box 2077
Haines Junction, YT Y0B 1L0
Tel: 867-634-2524
Fax: 867-634-2527
www.alsekrrc.ca/www.alsekrrc.ca

A voice for local community members in managing renewable resources, such as fish, wildlife and forests, ARRC was formed in 1995 with the signing of the Champagne & Aishihik First Nations (CAFN) Final Agreement.

• Carcross/ Tagish Renewable Resource Council
PO Box 70
Tagish, YT Y0B 1T0
Tel: 867-399-4923
Fax: 867-399-4978
carcrosstagishrrc@gmail.com
Co-Chair, Albert James
Co-Chair, Ken Reeder
Secretariat, Wendy Huffman

• Carmacks Renewable Resource Council
PO Box 122
Carmacks, YT Y0B 1C0
Tel: 867-863-6838
Fax: 867-863-6429
carmacksrrc@northwestel.net
Other Communication: www.yfwmb.ca/rrc/carmacks

• Dan Keyi Renewable Resource Council
PO Box 50
Burwash Landing, YT Y0B 1V0
Tel: 867-841-5820
Fax: 867-841-5821
dankeyirrc@northwestel.net
Co-Chair, Louise Bouvier
Co-Chair, Peter Upton
Secretariat, Wendy Lastiwka

• Dawson District Renewable Resource Council
PO Box 1380
Dawson City, YT Y0B 1G0
Tel: 867-993-6976
Fax: 867-993-6093
dawsonrrc@northwestel.net
www.yfwmb.ca/rrc/dawson

• Laberge Renewable Resource Council
#202, 102 Copper Rd.
Whitehorse, YT Y1A 2Z6
labergerrc@northwestel.net
Co-Chair, Dorothy Bradley
Co-Chair, Frances Woolsey
Secretariat, Charlotte O'Donnell

• Mayo District Renewable Resources Council
PO Box 249
Mayo, YT Y0B 1M0
Tel: 867-996-2942
Fax: 867-996-2948
mayorrc@yknet.yk.ca

• North Yukon Renewable Resources Council
PO Box 80
Old Crow, YT Y0B 1N0
Tel: 867-966-3034
Fax: 867-966-3036
vgrrc@yknet.yk.ca
www.yfwmb.ca/rrc/northyukon

• Selkirk Renewable Resources Council
PO Box 32
Pelly Crossing, YT Y0B 1P0
Tel: 867-537-3937
Fax: 867-537-3939
selkirkrrc@yknet.yk.ca
www.yfwmb.ca/rrc/selkirk

• Teslin Renewable Resource Council
PO Box 186
Teslin, YT Y0A 1B0
Tel: 867-390-2323
Fax: 867-390-2919
teslinrrc@northwestel.net
www.yfwmb.ca/rrc/teslin

• Yukon Fish & Wildlife Management Board
106 Main St., 2nd Fl.
Whitehorse, YT Y1A 5P7
Tel: 867-667-3754
Fax: 867-393-6947
officemanager@yfwmb.ca
www.yfwmb.ca
The Board focuses its efforts on territorial policies, legislation & other measures to help guide management of fish & wildlife, conserve habitat & enhance the renewable resources economy. The Board influences management decisions through public education & by making recommendations to Yukon, Federal and First Nations governments. Recommendations & positions are based on the best technical, traditional & local information available.
Chair, Richard Sidney
Vice Chair, Shirley Ford

• Yukon Land Use Planning Council
#201, 307 Jarvis St.
Whitehorse, YT Y1A 2H3
Tel: 867-667-7397
Fax: 867-667-4624
ylupc@planyukon.ca
www.planyukon.ca/
The Yukon Land Use Planning Council assists government & Yukon First Nationsto co-ordinate efforts to conduct community based regional land use planning. This planning is necessary to resolve land use & resource conflicts. The plans ensure that use of lands & resources is consistent with social, cultural, economic & environmental values. These plans build upon traditional knowledge & experience of the residents of each region.
Director, Ron Cruikshank
ron@planyukon.ca
Acting Chairperson, Ian Robertson
ian@planyukon.ca
First Nation Policy & Planning Advisor, Gerald Isaac
gerald@planyukon.ca
Land & Resource Planner, Shawn Francis
shawn@planyukon.ca
Planning & GIS Advisor, Jeff Hamm
jeff@planyukon.ca

Climate Change Secretariat
Tel: 867-456-5544
Fax: 867-456-5543
Toll-Free: 800-661-0408
ClimateChange@gov.yk.ca
Other Communication:
www.env.gov.yk.ca/monitoringenvironment/climate_change_secretariat.php
The Secretariat has the lead role in ensuring Yukon government actions support a healthy & resilient Yukon in a changing climate. It strives to identify needs, opportunities & priorities; promote & support action; & monitor & report on progress.
Director, Eric Schroff
Tel: 867-633-7971
eric.schroff@gov.yk.ca

Conservation Officer Services
Tel: 867-667-8005
Fax: 867-393-6206
Toll-Free: 800-661-0408
coservicesgov.yk.ca
www.env.gov.yk.ca/branches/conservation_officer_services.php
Other Communication: T.I.P. line: 800-661-0525
The Branch provides environmental education, environmental youth camps & projects, provides hunting, fishing & trapping licences, provides hunter & trapper education, resource management support, wildlife safety for the public & provides enforcement & compliance.
Director, John Russell
Tel: 867-667-5786
Fax: 867-393-6206
john.russell@gov.yk.ca
Manager, Enforcement & Compliance, Kris Gustafson
Tel: 867-667-5115
Fax: 867-393-6206
kris.gustafson@gov.yk.ca
Manager, Field Operations, Torrie Hunter
Tel: 867-993-5492
torrie.hunter@gov.yk.ca

Corporate Services
Tel: 867-667-5652
Fax: 867-393-7197
Toll-Free: 800-661-0408
environmentyukon@gov.yk.ca
www.env.gov.yk.ca/branches/corporate_services.php
Provides support services to the Department of Environment.
Director, Mindy Crayford
Tel: 867-667-8486
Fax: 867-393-7012
mindy.crayford@gov.yk.ca
Manager, Client Services, Dee Balsam
Tel: 867-667-5797
Fax: 867-393-7197
dee.balsam@gov.yk.ca
Manager, Information Management & Technology, Beth Hawkings
Tel: 867-667-8137
Fax: 867-393-7003
beth.hawkings@gov.yk.ca
Manager, Financial Services Branch, Darrell Branch
Tel: 867-667-5160
Fax: 867-393-6219
darrell.branch@gov.yk.ca
Manager, Communications, Dennis Senger
Tel: 867-667-5237
Fax: 867-393-6213
dennis.senger@gov.yk.ca

Environmental Programs
Tel: 867-667-5683
Fax: 867-393-6213
Toll-Free: 800-661-0408
envprot@gov.yk.ca
www.env.gov.yk.ca/branches/environmental_programs.php
Formed in 1994, the Branch is responsible for development of regulations & standards under the Environment Act & programs associated with everyday waste management, contaminated sites, air quality & pesticides. The Branch is also responsible for monitoring & inspection of permits, spill cleanup & environmental assessments of development projects, recycling education & promotion, public education & awareness.
Director, Jon Bowen
Tel: 867-667-8177
Fax: 867-393-6213
jon.bowen@gov.yk.ca
Manager, Site Assessment & Remediation Unit, Ruth Hall
Tel: 867-667-5851
Fax: 867-456-6124
ruth.hall@gov.yk.ca
Manager, Hydrology, Richard Janowicz
Tel: 867-667-3223
richard.janowicz@gov.yk.ca
Manager, Standards & Approvals, Shannon Jensen
Tel: 867-667-8787
Fax: 867-393-6205
shannon.jensen@gov.yk.ca
Manager, Environmental Affairs, Randy Lamb
Tel: 867-667-5409
Fax: 867-667-3641
randy.lamb@gov.yk.ca
Manager, Monitoring & Inspections, Bryan Levia
Tel: 867-667-3436
Fax: 867-393-6205
bryan.levia@gov.yk.ca

Fish & Wildlife
Tel: 867-667-5715
Fax: 867-393-6405
Toll-Free: 800-661-0408
fish.wildlife@gov.yk.ca
www.env.gov.yk.ca/branches/fish_wildlife.php
The Branch maintains the ecosystem based on sound management of fish, wildlife & their habitats, preserves the sustainability of fish & wildlife populations, works with First Nations & community relations to preserve & enhance the ecosystem, develops management plans, provides policy & planning, collects, assesses & disseminates natural resource data & provides public education for resource users.
Director, Dan Lindsey
Tel: 867-667-5715
Fax: 867-393-6405
dan.lindsey@gov.yk.ca
Biologist, Fisheries Management, Nathan Millar
Tel: 867-667-5117
nathan.millar@gov.yk.ca
Acting Manager, Habitat Programs, Karen Clyde
Tel: 867-667-5464
Fax: 867-393-6405
karen.clyde@gov.yk.ca
Manager, Species Programs, Rob Florkiewicz
Tel: 867-667-5177
Fax: 867-393-6263
rob.florkiewicz@gov.yk.ca
Manager, Biodiversity Programs, Todd Powell
Tel: 867-456-6572
Fax: 867-393-6263
todd.powell@gov.yk.ca

Human Resources
10 Burns Rd., Whitehorse, YT
Fax: 867-393-7012

Parks
PO Box 2703 V-4Whitehorse, YT Y1A 2C6
Tel: 867-667-5648
Fax: 867-393-6223
Toll-Free: 800-661-0408
yukon.parks@gov.yk.ca
www.environmentyukon.gov.yk.ca/parks/parks.html
Director, Erik Val
Tel: 867-667-5639
Fax: 867-393-6223
erik.val@gov.yk.ca
Regional Superintendent, Klondike Region, Gordon MacRae
Tel: 867-993-6850
Fax: 867-993-6548
gordon.macrae@gov.yk.ca
Regional Superintendent, Kluane Region, George Nassiopoulos
Tel: 867-634-2026
Fax: 867-634-2435
george.nassiopoulos@gov.yk.ca
Regional Superintendent, Liard Region, Gary Vantell
Tel: 867-667-5282
Fax: 867-393-6223
gary.vantell@gov.yk.ca

Policy & Planning
10 Burns Rd., Whitehorse, YT
Fax: 867-393-6213

Water Resources
Tel: 867-667-3171
Fax: 867-667-3195
Toll-Free: 800-661-0408
water.resources@gov.yk.ca
www.env.gov.yk.ca/monitoringenvironment/aboutwaterresources.php
Director, Kevin McDonnell
Tel: 867-667-3145
Fax: 867-667-3195
kevin.mcdonnell@gov.yk.ca
Manager, Richard Janowicz
Tel: 867-667-3223
richard.janowicz@gov.yk.ca

Yukon Finance

PO Box 2703Whitehorse, YT Y1A 2C6
Tel: 867-667-5343
Fax: 867-393-6217
fininfo@gov.yk.ca
www.finance.gov.yk.ca

Minister, Darrell Pasloski
Tel: 867-667-8660
Fax: 867-393-6252
premier@gov.yk.ca

Deputy Minister, David Hrycan
Tel: 867-667-3571
Fax: 867-393-6217
david.hrycan@gov.yk.ca

Director, Finance & Administration, Bill Curtis
Tel: 867-667-5276
Fax: 867-393-6217
bill.curtis@gov.yk.ca

Yukon Health & Social Services

PO Box 2703Whitehorse, YT Y1A 2C6
Tel: 867-667-3673
Fax: 867-667-3096
hss@gov.yk.ca
www.hss.gov.yk.ca
Committed to quality health & social services for Yukoners by helping individuals acquire the skills to live responsible, healthy & independent lives; & providing a range of accessible, affordable services that assist individuals, families & communities to reach their full potential.
Acts Administered:
Public Health & Safety Act
Regulations to Establish Butylnitrite as Regulated Matter
Rubbish Disposal
Sewage Disposal Systems Regulations

Minister, Doug Graham, Hon.
Tel: 867-667-5800
Fax: 867-393-6252
doug.graham@gov.yk.ca

Deputy Minister, Stuart Whitley
Tel: 867-667-5770
Fax: 867-667-3096
stuart.whitley@gov.yk.ca

Executive Director, Strategic Social Initiatives, Michael McCann
Tel: 867-667-5700
Fax: 867-667-3096
michael.mccann@gov.yk.ca

Executive Director, Social Strategic Initiatives, Christine Paradis
Tel: 867-667-8087

Executive Director, Wellness Strategy Initiatives, Dr. Paula Pasquali
Tel: 867-393-6305

Director, Communications & Social Marketing, Pat Living
Tel: 867-667-3673
Fax: 867-667-3096
patricia.living@gov.yk.ca

Director, Human Resources, John Periera
Tel: 867-667-3031
john.periera@gov.yk.ca

Associated Agencies, Boards & Commissions:
• Health & Social Service Council
This advisory body makes recommendations to the government relating to issues of health, social services, education & justice.
• Yukon Child Care Board
This advisory body makes recommendations to the Minister of Health & Social Services, on any issues that pertain to child care.
Chair, June Cable
june.cable@gov.yk.ca

Continuing Care
307 Black St., Whitehorse, YT Y1A 2N1
Tel: 867-667-5945
www.hss.gov.yk.ca/continuing.php
Other Communication: 800-661-0408, ext. 5945 (toll-free)
Provides residential, home care & regional therapy services for the citizens of the Yukon Territory.
Assistant Deputy Minister, Cathy Morton-Bielz
Tel: 867-667-8922
Fax: 867-456-6545
cathy.morton-bielz@gov.yk.ca
Director, Safety & Clinical Excellence, Nancy Kidd
Tel: 867-667-8750
Fax: 867-456-6545
nancy.kidd@gov.yk.ca
Director, Extended Care, Willy Shippey
willy.shippey@gov.yk.ca
Director, Care & Community, Liris Smith
Tel: 867-456-6839
liris.smith@gov.yk.ca

Coporate Services
www.hss.gov.yk.ca/corporate.php
Plays a key role in ensuring that Yukon residents have accurate, up-to-date information about the territory's health & social programs, services & systems.
Assistant Deputy Minister, Birgitte Hunter
Tel: 867-667-8309
Fax: 867-393-6457
birgitte.hunter@gov.yk.ca
Director, Finance, Systems & Administration, Warren Holland
warren.holland@wgh.yk.ca
Director, Policy & Program Development, Brian Kitchen
Tel: 867-667-5688
Fax: 867-667-3096
brian.kitchen@gov.yk.ca
Director, Corporate Strategic Initiatives & Priorities, Cynthia Lyslo
Tel: 867-667-5673
cynthia.lyslo@gov.yk.ca
Director, Quality & Risk Management, Karen Archbell
Tel: 867-667-5943
karen.archbell@gov.yk.ca

Health Services
Financial Plaza, 204 Lambert St., 4th Fl., Whitehorse, YT Y1A 3T2
Fax: 867-393-6486
www.hss.gov.yk.ca/healthservices.php
Responsible for a variety of health care, disease prevention & treatment services which assist eligible Yukon residents in attaining maximum individual independence within their community.
Assistant Deputy Minister, Health Services, Sherri Wright
Tel: 867-667-5689
Fax: 867-667-3096
Director, Insured Health & Hearing Services, Paul Gudatis
Tel: 867-667-5209
Fax: 867-393-6486
Director, Community Nursing, Joy Kajiwara
Tel: 867-667-8324
Fax: 867-667-8338
Director, Community Health Programs, Cathy Stannard
Tel: 867-667-8340
Fax: 867-456-6502
cathy.stannard@gov.yk.ca

Social Services
www.hss.gov.yk.ca/socialservices.php
Consists of Adult Community Services, Alcohol & Drug Services, Family & Children's Services, Regional Services, Senior Services, Seniors & Elder Abuse, Services for People With Disabilities, & Social Assistance.
Assistant Deputy Minister, Dorothea Warren
dorothea.warren@gov.yk.ca
Acting Director, Michele McDonnell
Tel: 867-667-3705
Fax: 867-393-6926
michele.mcdonnell@gov.yk.ca
Supervisor, Dale Gordon
Tel: 867-393-6913
Fax: 867-667-8471
dale.gordon@gov.yk.ca
Supervisor, Marg Render
Tel: 867-667-5819
Fax: 867-667-5669
marg.render@gov.yk.ca
Manager, Community Audit Services Unit, Tim Brady
Tel: 867-667-5691
Fax: 867-393-6278
Manager, Seniors' Services/ Adult Protection, Kelly Cooper
Tel: 867-456-3948
Fax: 867-393-6926
Acting Manager, Program Management, Sandy Schmidt
Tel: 867-667-5056
Fax: 867-667-8471

Yukon Highways & Public Works

PO Box 2703Whitehorse, YT Y1A 2C6
Tel: 867-393-7193
Fax: 867-393-6218
Toll-Free: 800-661-0408
TTY: 867-393-7460
hpw-info@gov.yk.ca
www.hpw.gov.yk.ca
The Department of Highways & Public Works is responsible for ensuring safe & efficient public highways, airstrips, buildings & information systems.
Acts Administered:
Dangerous Goods Transportation Act
Highways Act
Motor Vehicles Act (jointly with Community Services)

Minister, Wade Istchenko, Hon.
Tel: 867-667-5800
Fax: 867-393-6252
wade.istchenko@gov.yk.ca

Deputy Minister, Mike Johnson
Tel: 867-667-3732
Fax: 867-393-6218
mike.johnson@gov.yk.ca

Aviation
Tel: 867-634-2450
Fax: 867-634-2131
aviation@gov.yk.ca
Other Communication: 800-661-0408, ext. 2450 (toll-free)

Corporate Services
Tel: 867-667-5128
Other Communication: 800-661-0408, ext. 5128 (toll-free)

Information & Communications Technology
Tel: 867-667-5397
Fax: 867-667-5304
Other Communication: 800-661-0408, ext. 5397 (toll-free)

Property Management Agency
Tel: 867-667-5879
Fax: 867-667-5349
Other Communication: 800-661-0408, ext. 5879 (toll-free)

Supply Services
Tel: 867-667-5432
Fax: 867-667-2958
hpw-info@gov.yk.ca
Other Communication: 800-661-0408, ext. 5432 (toll-free)
Director, Carl Rumscheidt
Tel: 867-667-5289
Fax: 867-667-2958
carl.rumscheidt@gov.yk.ca
Manager, Procurement Services, David Knight
Tel: 867-393-6387
Fax: 867-667-2958
david.knight@gov.yk.ca

Transportation
Other Communication: 800-661-0408, ext. 7193 (toll-free)
Assistant Deputy Minister, Allan Nixon
Tel: 867-667-5196
Fax: 867-393-6218
allan.nixon@gov.yk.ca
Director, Transportation Maintenance, Don Hobbis
Tel: 867-667-5761
Director, Transportation Engineering, Robin Walsh
Tel: 867-633-7928
Fax: 867-393-6447
Director, Transport Services Branch, Vern Janz
Tel: 867-667-5833
Fax: 867-667-5799

Driver Control Board
307 Black St., Whitehorse, YT Y1A 2C6
Tel: 867-667-5111
Fax: 867-667-3609
dcb@gov.yk.ca
www.community.gov.yk.ca/dcb

Minister responsible, Scott Kent, Hon.
Tel: 867-667-5800
Fax: 867-393-6252
scott.kent@gov.yk.ca

President, Ron Macmillan
Tel: 867-667-5155
Fax: 867-393-6274
ron.macmillan@gov.yk.ca

Director, Systems & Administration, Mark Davey
Tel: 867-667-8773
Fax: 867-393-6399
mark.davey@gov.yk.ca

Director, Capital Development, Mike Fraser
Tel: 867-456-6190
Fax: 867-393-6441
mike.fraser@gov.yk.ca

Director, Policy & Communications, JoAnne Harach
Tel: 867-456-6802
Fax: 867-393-6274
joanne.harach@gov.yk.ca

Director, Community & Industry Partnering, Allyn Lyon
Tel: 867-667-3773
Fax: 867-393-6441
allyn.lyon@gov.yk.ca

Director, Program Delivery, Marc Perreault
Tel: 867-393-7154
marc.perreault@gov.yk.ca

Director, Human Resources, Sue Richards
Tel: 867-667-8272
Fax: 867-393-6933
sue.richards@gov.yk.ca
Acts Administered:
Expropriation Act
Land Titles Act
Public Guardian & Trustee Act
Public Utilities Act

Minister, Mike Nixon
Tel: 867-667-5800
Fax: 867-393-6252
mike.nixon@gov.yk.ca

Deputy Minister, Dennis Cooley
Tel: 867-667-5959
Fax: 867-393-5790
jus.dm@gov.yk.ca

Director, Finance, Systems & Administration, Luda Ayzenberg
Tel: 867-667-5615
Fax: 867-667-5790
luda.ayzenberg@gov.yk.ca

Director, Policy & Communications, Dan Cable
Tel: 867-667-3508
Fax: 867-677-5790
dan.cable@gov.yk.ca

Director, Human Resources, Brian Farrell
Tel: 867-667-5105

Executive Assistant to the Deputy Minister, Charmaine Hall
Tel: 867-667-5959
Fax: 867-667-5790
charmaine.hall@gov.yk.ca

Executive Assistant to the Minister, Christopher Young
Tel: 867-633-7973
Fax: 867-393-7400
christopher.young@gov.yk.ca

Yukon Tourism & Culture

100 Hanson St., Whitehorse, YT Y1A 2C6
Tel: 867-667-5036
Fax: 867-667-3546
www.tc.gov.yk.ca/
The department focuses on business, tourism, cultural industries & technology/telecommunications to develop & promote economic capacity & entrepreneurial skills to stimulate economy. The department works with the Yukon's diverse arts communities to foster creativity & quality of life & with heritage interests to preserve & interpret heritage resources.
Acts Administered:
Archives Act
Arts Act
Historical Resources Act
Scientists & Explorers Act

Minister, Mike Nixon, Hon.
Tel: 867-667-5800
Fax: 867-393-6252
mike.nixon@gov.yk.ca

Deputy Minister, Joy Waters
Tel: 867-667-5430
Fax: 867-667-8844

Corporate Services
Provides a range of central support services within the Department of Tourism & Culture. These include human resources, information technology, administration, information management, & finance.

Cultural Services
Tel: 867-667-8589
Toll-Free: 800-661-0408
TTY: 867-393-6456
Dedicated to the preservation, development, interpretation of Yukon's heritage resources & to fostering the growth & mpact of the territory's visual, literary, & performing arts.

Policy & Communications
Tel: 867-667-8304
Fax: 867-393-8844
Toll-Free: 800-661-0408
Provides legislative & policy support for Tourism & Culture & coordinates the communications efforts of the department.

Tourism Branch
Tel: 867-667-3053
Fax: 867-667-3546
The Tourism Branch directs the development, implementation, & evaluation of the Yukon's tourism marketing programs to promote the Yukon as a travel destination.
Director, Pierre Germain
Tel: 867-667-3087

Tourism & Culture
Tel: 867-667-3053
Toll-Free: 800-661-0408
Engages in tourism marketing, product development, & research in order to bring the scenic natural beauty and rich & diverse cultural heritage of Yukon to the attention of potential visitors.

Yukon Workers' Compensation Health & Safety Board (YWCHSB)

401 Strickland St., Whitehorse, YT Y1A 5N8
Tel: 867-667-5645
Fax: 867-393-6279
Toll-Free: 800-661-0443
worksafe@gov.yk.ca
wcb.yk.ca/
The Yukon Workers' Compensation Health & Safety Board (YWCHSB) administers workers' compensation & occupational health & safety in the Yukon.
Acts Administered:
Occupational Health & Safety Act
Workplace Hazardous Materials Information System (WHMIS) Regulations

Minister responsible, Doug Graham
Tel: 867-667-5800
Fax: 867-393-6252
doug.graham@gov.yk.ca

President & Chief Executive Officer, Valerie Royle
Tel: 867-667-8983
Fax: 867-393-6419
valerie.royle@gov.yk.ca

Municipal Governments

Alberta

Alberta Environment carries out its work under the authority of the Environmental Protection & Enhancement Act (EPEA), the Climate Change & Emissions Management Act & the Water Act. The EPEA mandate is to maintain air, land & water quality so that ecosystems & public health are protected. The Climate Change & Emissions Management Act provides the legislative backing for Alberta's Climate Change Program. The Water Act supports the conservation & management of water in the province.

Alberta Environment is organized into four main business divisions: Environmental Stewardship, Environmental Assurance, Environmental Management and Oil Sands Environmental Management. Each division is supported by People Services, Communications, Legal Services, Finance and Administration and the Strategic Planning Secretariat.

Alberta's air quality is maintained through a management system comprising protection, enforcement, monitoring & modelling.

Municipal waterworks, wastewater, storm drainage & solid waste disposal facilities may be municipally or privately owned. Alberta Municipal Management Facility guidelines require most facilities to demonstrate the financial capability to reclaim the site after its closure. Waste collection is the responsibility of the municipality. Those who operate or propose developments are subject to requirements that detail their environmental responsibilities. Alberta's Municipal Waste Action Plan calls for the Waste Management Stakeholder Group, comprising non-profit waste management associations in the province, to communicate waste management initiatives to interested parties, and to prepare recommendations.

"Water for Life: Alberta's Strategy for Sustainability" is mandated to establish a water management policy to ensure safe drinking water, healthy aquatic ecosystems & a reliable water supply-municipalities are active partners in this initiative. The Alberta Water Council was formed in April, 2004, to guide the implementation of the Strategy. The Strategy was renewed in 2008 & continues to be implemented in 2013.

EPEA establishes a legislated process for environmental assessments. This process will ensure that potential environmental impacts are identified early during planning. A company will submit one comprehensive application to Alberta Environment. A designated director coordinates the preparation of a single, integrated approval for the project.

The EPEA regulates the beverage container collection program, which diverts containers from landfill to recycling. Containers are collected through over 200 privately owned beverage container depots. There is an 80-85% recovery rate from regulated containers. An electronics recycling program is dedicated to recovering televisions, computers & other electronics with fees ranging from $5 to $15 per item-this is being managed by the Alberta Recycling Management Authority (which also operates Tire Recycling, Paint Recycling & Household Hazardous Waste disposal).

The municipal energy efficiency program (ME! First) provides interest-free loans to municipalities to achieve energy savings. More than $15.9 million out of the $100-million program has been made available for 34 projects that will reduce greenhouse gas emissions by more than 27,000 tonnes. The Municipal Sponsorship Program provides municipalities with populations of 20,000 or under with grants. The program provided funding for projects such as the provision of solar energy sources for existing municipal buildings and the construction of new facilities. The Alberta Municipal Infrastructure Program provides financial assistance for core capital municipal infrastructure projects through Alberta Infrastructure & Transportation. Under the federal government's New Deal for Cities, Alberta received $477 million in federal gas tax funding from 2005 to 2010 for municipal infrastructure projects. In addition, the Alberta Infrastructure Program provided $600 million annually for the same period.

Counties & Municipal Districts in Alberta

Clearwater County

P.O. Box 550
4340 - 47th Ave.
Rocky Mountain House, AB T4T 1A4
403-845-4444
Fax: 403-845-7330
admin@county.clearwater.ab.ca
www.county.clearwater.ab.ca
Population: 12,278 *Census Year:* 2011
Number of Households: 4,649
Joe Baker, Manager, Planning / West Country, email: jbaker@county.clearwater.ab.ca
Kim Nielsen, Manager, Agricultural Services, email: knielsen@county.clearwater.ab.ca
Marshall Morton, Manager, Public Works, email: mmorton@county.clearwater.ab.ca
Water & Wastewater Treatment:
Nordegg water treatment plant plus sewer systems in Nordegg, Leslieville & Condor maintained by county public works department
Other Initiatives:
Green zone development

Foothills No. 31

P.O. Box 5605
309 Macleod Trail
High River, AB T1V 1M7
403-652-2341
Fax: 403-652-7880
Emergencies: 1-888-808-3722
mdfthlls@mdfoothills.com
www.mdfoothills.com
Population: 21,258 *Census Year:* 2011
Number of Households: 6,159
Graham Clark, Fire Chief, Protective Services, email: graham.clark@mdfoothills.com
Tom Gillis, Director, Public Works & Engineering, email: tom.gillis@mdfoothills.com
Nasir Sheikh, Municipal Engineer, email: nasir.sheikh@mdfoothills.com
Judy Gordon, Coordinator, Planning & Development, email: judy.gordon@mdfoothills.com
Marilyn Gordon-Cooper, Contact, Property Tax & Utilities Department, email: marilyn.gordon-cooper@mdfoothills.com
Heather Hemingway, Contact, Environment Committee, email: heather.hemingway@mdfoothills.com
Ken McKay, Contact, Building Safety Codes & Bylaw Enforcement, email: ken.mckay@mdfoothills.com
Waste Management:
Number of landfill sites: 1
Solid Waste Disposal Fees: $39/tonne (over 200 kg); $58/tonne (hard to handle garbage)
Transfer Station(s): Priddis - 264 St. West & 178 Ave.; Black Diamond/Turner Valley - 168 St. West & 402 Ave.
Recycling: Depot; Foothills Regional Waste Management Facility, Secondary Hwy. 783, south of Okotoks
Hazardous Waste Depot or Facility: Foothills Regional Waste Management Facility, 403/938-5224
Composters subsidized: Yes
Water & Wastewater Treatment:
Aldersyde, Blackie & Cayley Waterworks Systems
Other Initiatives:
Salvage Centre for reusable items at Regional Waste Management Facility, solidwaste@platinum.ca

Grande Prairie No. 1

10001 - 84 Ave.
Clairmont, AB TOH OWO
780-532-9722
Fax: 780-539-9880
info@countygp.ab.ca
www.countygp.ab.ca
Population: 20,347 *Census Year:* 2011
Number of Households: 5,597
John Simpson, Director, Planning, 780-513-3950, email: plan@countygp.ab.ca
Everett Cooke, Fire Chief, 780-567-5590, email: fire@countygp.ab.ca
Steve Madden, Manager, Environment, 780-532-7393
Herb Pfau, Superintendent, Public Works, 780-532-7393, email: pubwks@countygp.ab.ca
Waste Management:
Waste collection contracted to Prairie Disposal, 780/539-5950
Number of landfill sites: 4
Solid Waste Disposal Fees: $52/tonne (county commercial & non-county)
Recycling: Depot; 6 recycle bin locations at LaGlace, Teepee Creek, Bezanson, Clairmont, Elmworth & Valhalla
Other Initiatives:
Electronics recycling program at regional landfill

Lacombe County

RR#3
Lacombe, AB T4L 2N3
403-782-6601
Fax: 403-782-3820
info@lacombecounty.com
www.lacombecounty.com
Population: 10,312 *Census Year:* 2011
Number of Households: 3,790
Terry Hager, County Commissioner, email: thager@lacombecounty.com
Keith Boras, Manager, Agriculture Services, email: kboras@lacombecounty.com
Dale Freitag, Manager, Planning Services, email: dfreitag@lacombecounty.com
Julian Veuger, County Constable, Disaster Services, email: jveuger@lacombecounty.com
Dale Freitaq, Planner & Development Officer, email: dfreitaq@lacombecounty.com
Dale Kary, Project Coordinator, Public Works, email: dkary@lacombecounty.com
Phil Lodermeier, Supervisor, Public Works, email: plodermeier@lacombecounty.com
Waste Management:
Waste management responsibility of Lacombe Regional Solid Waste Authority, 403/782-6601; Daily operations of Authority responsibility of county public works department
Number of landfill sites: 1
Solid Waste Disposal Fees: $20/tonne (dry rubble)
Transfer Station(s): Bentley, Spruceville, Prentice, Eckville, Blackfalds & Alix/Mirror transfer stations
Other Initiatives:
Environmental program to assist agricultural producers; Household hazardous waste roundup; Electronics recycling accepted at Prentiss transfer station

Leduc County

#101, 1101 - 5 St.
Nisku, AB T9E 2X3
780-955-3555
Fax: 780-955-3444
Toll free: 1-800-379-9052
shaunaf@leduc-county.com
www.leduc-county.com
Population: 13,541 *Census Year:* 2011
Number of Households: 4,758
Michael MacLean, Director, Public Works & Engineering, 780-955-6416, email: michael@leduc-county.com
Phil Newman, Director, Planning & Development, 780-955-6413, email: phil@leduc-county.com
Dean Ohnysty, Director, Parks & Recreation, 780-955-4535, email: dean@leduc-county.com
Garett Broadbent, Director, Agricultural Services, 780-955-6404, email: garett@leduc-county.com
Bob Galloway, Chief, Fire, 780-955-7099, email: bobg@leduc-county.com
Deryld Dublanko, Manager, Maintenance & Materials Supply, 780-955-2469, email: deryld@leduc-county.com
Janis Fong, Manager, Public Works & Infrastructure
Des Mryglod, Manager, Engineering
Dave McPhee, Officer, Utilities, 780-955-4541, email: dave@leduc-county.com
Waste Management:
Number of landfill sites: 1*Landfill Capacity:* 14+ years
Solid Waste Disposal Fees: $27/tonne (regular residential waste)

Clean Fill Fee: No
Transfer Station(s): New Sarepta; Rollyview; Looma; Thorsby; Mission Beach; Sunnybrook; Warburg; St. Francis
Recycling: Depot; Materials Recovery Facility at Leduc & District Regional Landfill
Hazardous Waste Depot or Facility: Materials Recovery Facility at Leduc & District Regional Landfill
Water & Wastewater Treatment:
Capital Region Southwest Water Services Commission provides water service to the county
Other Initiatives:
Agricultural Services Dept. provides the following services: weed control, pest control, water management, sustainable agriculture & soil conservation information

Mountain View County

P.O. Box 100
1408 Twp Rd. 320
Didsbury, AB T0M 0W0
403-335-3311
Fax: 403-335-9207
Toll Free Phone: 1-877-264-9754
info@mountainviewcounty.com
www.mountainviewcounty.com
Population: 12,359 *Census Year:* 2011
Number of Households: 4,851
Doug Plamping, CAO, email: doug.plamping@mountainviewcounty.com
Steve McInnis, Director, Operational Services, email: steve.mcinnis@mountainviewcounty.com
Tony Martens, Director, Legislative & Community Services, email: tony.martens@mountainviewcounty.com
Jeff Holmes, Manager, Agriculture & Parks Services, email: jeff.holmes@mountainviewcounty.com
Waste Management:
Waste management responsibility of Mountain View Regional Waste Management Commission, Email: wastemgmt@mountainview-ab.com
Solid Waste Disposal Fees: $100/tonne
Transfer Station(s): Olds, Sundre, Water Valley, Reed Ranch & Carstairs
Recycling: Depot; Recycle Centres located at Village of Cremona, Town of Carstairs, Town of Didsbury, Town of Olds (2), Town of Sundre & Eagle Hill
Hazardous Waste Depot or Facility: Eco Site Centres located at Olds, Sundre, Water Valley & Didsbury MVRWMC Landfill
Water & Wastewater Treatment:
Water services responsibility of Mountain View Regional Water Services Commission
Other Initiatives:
Environmental farm plan workshops

Parkland County

53109A Sec Hwy. 779
Parkland County, AB T7Z 1R1
780-968-8888
Fax: 780-968-8413
Toll Free: 1-888-880-0858
inquiries@parklandcounty.com
www.parklandcounty.com
Population: 30,568 *Census Year:* 2011
Number of Households: 10,444
Mark Cardinal, Manager, Agricultural Services, email: mcardinal@parklandcounty.com
Andy Haden, Manager, Planning & Development Services, email: ahaden@parklandcounty.com
Rob McGowan, Manager, Engineering Services, email: rmcgowan@parklandcounty.com
Daryl Phillips, Manager, Public Works, email: dphillips@parklandcounty.com
Ken Saulit, Manager, Protective Services, email: ksaulit@parklandcounty.com
Ken Van Buul, Manager, Recreation & Parks Services, email: kvanbuul@parklandcounty.com
Janette Szucs, Coordinator, Purchasing, email: jszucs@parklandcounty.com
Trent Tompkins, Coordinator, Solid Waste, email: ttompkins@parklandcounty.com
Kevin Bryant, Supervisor, Utilities & Waste Services, email: kbryant@parklandcounty.com
Brian Rimmer, Supervisor, Environmental Services, email: brimmer@parklandcounty.com
Grace Horsfield, Officer, Development, email: ghorsfield@parklandcounty.com
Waste Management:
Number of landfill sites: 3
Clean Fill Fee: No
Transfer Station(s): 3
Hazardous Waste Depot or Facility: Yes
Water & Wastewater Treatment:
Water systems: Acheson Industrial Area Water Distribution System, Big Lake Water Distribution System, Entwistle Water Treatment & Distribution System. Wastewater systems: Acheson Industrial Area Sanitary Sewer System, Big Lake Water Sanitary Sewer System, Tomahawk Sanitary Sewer System, Duffield Sanitary Sewage System, Regional Sewage Transfer Stations, Entwistle Sewage Collection System & Lagoon.
Other Initiatives:
Development of a municipal based conservation plan.

Red Deer County

Red Deer County Centre
38106 Range Rd. 275
Red Deer County, AB T4S 2L9
403-350-2150
Fax: 403-346-9840
info@rdcounty.ca
http://rdcounty.ca
Population: 18,351 *Census Year:* 2011
Number of Households: 7,302
Curtis Herzberg, County Manager, email: cherzberg@reddeercounty.ab.ca
Harry Harker, Director, Planning & Development, email: hharker@reddeercounty.ab.ca
Ric Henderson, Director, Community & Protective Services, email: rhenderson@reddeercounty.ab.ca
Frank Peck, Director, Operations Services, email: fpeck@reddeercounty.ab.ca
Cliff Fuller, Fire Chief, email: cfuller@reddeercounty.ab.ca
Don Bardonnex, Manager, Fire Services, email: dbardonnex@reddeercounty.ab.ca
Joe D'Onofrio, Manager, Land, email: jd'onofrio@reddeercounty.ab.ca
Linda Henrickson, Manager, Rural Planning, email: lhenrickson@reddeercounty.ab.ca
Johan van der Bank, Manager, Urban Planning, email: jvanderbank@reddeercounty.ab.ca
Marty Campbell, Coordinator, Engineering, email: mcampbell@reddeercounty.ab.ca
Jo-Ann Symington, Coordinator, Community Services, email: jsymington@reddeercounty.ab.ca
Andrew Treu, Coordinator, Environmental Services, email: atreu@reddeercounty.ab.ca
Donna Trottier, Coordinator, Conservation
Dawna Barnes, Specialist, Community Development, email: dbarnes@reddeercounty.ab.ca
Art Preachuk, Fieldman, Agricultural Services, email: apreachuk@reddeercounty.ab.ca
Waste Management:
Waste management responsibility of Central Alberta Regional Waste Commission
Transfer Station(s): Horne Hill, Kevisville, Lousana & Innisfail Solid Waste Transfer Stations
Recycling: Depot; Burnt Lake Business Park, Spruce View, Bowden, Delburne & Innisfail Recycling Depots
Special Bans/by-laws: Land Use Bylaw
Water & Wastewater Treatment:
County has a utility management agreement with EPCOR to operate water & wastewater systems in the following 5 communities: Springbrook, Spruce View, Benalto, South Hills & Lousana
Other Initiatives:
Reeve's Task Force on Land Use Planning & Sustainable Agriculture; County partnered with Alberta Environmentally Sustainable Agriculture to provide farmers & ranchers with a conservation program; Household hazardous waste roundup

Rocky View County

911 - 32 Ave. NE
Calgary, AB T2E 6X6
403-230-1401
Fax: 403-277-5977
comments@rockyview.ca
www.rockyview.ca
Population: 36,461 *Census Year:* 2011
Number of Households: 10,350
Brian Jobson, Director, Transportation Services, email: bjobson@gov.mdrockyview.ab.ca
Frank Misura, Manager, Development/Utility Services
Linda Ratzlaff, Coordinator, Policy Planning, 403-520-8166
Tim Dietzler, Fieldman, Agriculture, 403-520-1271
Waste Management:
Municipality operates 4 transfer sites. There are no landfill sites in the municipality. Residents may use City of Calgary landfill sites. Hazardous waste is not accepted at transfer stations.
Solid Waste Disposal Fees: No
Recycling: Facility locations: Wintergreen Road NE., Bragg Creek, AB, Railway Ave., Langdon AB, Range Rd. 33, Springbank, AB
Water & Wastewater Treatment:
Wastewater collection & treatment utility, Hamlet of Langdon, administered by Municipality; Domestic water co-ops & private water distribution companies own & operate distribution systems.
Other Initiatives:
62 Environmental reserve parcels protected under municipal government act.

Strathcona County

2001 Sherwood Dr.
Sherwood Park, AB T8A 3W7
780-464-8111
Fax: 780-464-8050
info@strathcona.ab.ca
www.strathcona.ab.ca
Population: 92,490 *Census Year:* 2011
Number of Households: 24,528
Robyn W. Singleton, Q.C., Chief Commissioner, 780-464-8100, email: singleton@strathcona.ab.ca
Peter Vana, Associate Commissioner, Infrastructure & Planning Services, 780-464-8188, email: vana@strathcona.ab.ca
Denise Exton, Associate Commissioner, Community Services, 780-464-8291, email: exton@strathcona.ab.ca
Waste Management:
Waste disposal handled by City of Edmonton Waste Management Centre's Clover Bar Landfill; Waste transfer handled by City of Fort Saskatchewan's Transfer Station & Beaver Regional Waste Commission's Lindbrook Transfer Station
Recycling: Both Curbside & Depot; Streambank Avenue Recycling Centre, 420 Streambank Ave., Sherwood Park; Baseline Rd. Recycling Station, 624 Bethel Dr., Sherwood Park; Josephburg Recycling Station, Moyer Recreation Centre; Ardrossan Recycling Station, Ardrossan Recreation Complex; South Cooking Lake Recycling Station, Fire Hall
Compost Sites: Yes *Composters subsidized:* Yes
Water & Wastewater Treatment:
Water treatment handled by EPCOR Water which operates 2 water treatment plants in Edmonton; Wastewater treatment handled by Alberta Capital Region Wastewater Commission
Other Initiatives:
Freecycle program in Sherwood Park

Sturgeon County

9613 - 100 St.
Morinville, AB T8R 1L9
780-939-4321
Fax: 780-939-3003
Toll free: 1-866-939-9303
sturgeonmail@sturgeoncounty.ab.ca
www.sturgeoncounty.ab.ca
Population: 19,578 *Census Year:* 2011
Number of Households: 5,821
Ian McKay, General Manager, Infrastructure Services, 780-939-8337, email: imckay@sturgeoncounty.ab.ca
Peter Tarnawsky, General Manager, Public Services, 780-939-8344, email: ptarnawsky@sturgeoncounty.ab.ca
Bart Clark, Manager, Protective Services, 780-939-0600, email: bclark@sturgeoncounty.ab.ca
Collin Steffes, Manager, Planning & Development, 780-939-8275, email: csteffes@sturgeoncounty.ab.ca
Roy Lidgren, Manager, Transportation Services, 780-939-8250, email: rlidgern@sturgeoncounty.ab.ca
Quentin Bochar, Manager, Agriculture Services, 780-939-8325, email: qbochar@sturgeoncounty.ab.ca
Mike Hittinger, Coordinator, Municipal Conservation, 780-939-8339, email: nwaci@sturgeoncounty.ab.ca
Waste Management:
Landfill site is the Roseridge Landfill, Roseridge Waste Management Services Commission; Free permits are issued to county residents to use the landfill
Number of landfill sites: 1*Landfill Capacity:* 100 years
Solid Waste Disposal Fees: $58.50/tonne
Recycling: Depot; Landfill site

Special Bans/by-laws: Each household is permitted 8,000 kg of garbage per year; If limit is exceeded, fee is $30/tonne
Water & Wastewater Treatment:
Water supply attained via City of Edmonton or municipal treated water; Capital Region Wastewater Sewer Commission
Other Initiatives:
Agricultural services include conservation programs, pest & weed control & water management.

Wetaskiwin County No. 10
P.O. Box 6960
Wetaskiwin, AB T9A 2G5
780-352-3321
Fax: 780-352-3486
Toll Free: 1-800-661-4125
fcoutney@county.wetaskiwin.ab.ca
www.county.wetaskiwin.ab.ca
Population: 10,866 *Census Year:* 2011
Number of Households: 4,670
Ken Carlson, Director, Disaster Services, 780-361-6340, email: kcarlson@county.wetaskiwin.ab.ca
Dave Dextraze, Director, Public Works, 780-361-6230, email: ddextraze@county.wetaskiwin.ab.ca
Steve Majek, Director, Agricultural Services, 780-361-6226, email: smajek@county.wetaskiwin.ab.ca
Waste Management:
Landfill is serviced by the West Dried Meat Lake Regional Landfill, located within the County of Camrose
Landfill Capacity: 100 years
Water & Wastewater Treatment:
2 independent water systems serving the Hamlet of Winfield & Mulhurst Bay's Lakeview subdivision are serviced by the county; Wastewater systems are Gwynne, Falun, Mulhurst Bay, Winfield & Alder Flats Wastewater System

Wood Buffalo
9909 Franklin Ave.
Fort McMurray, AB T9H 2K4
780-743-7000
Fax: 780-743-7028
Toll Free: 1-800-973-9663
communications@woodbuffalo.ab.ca
www.woodbuffalo.ab.ca
Population: 65,565 *Census Year:* 2011
Number of Households: 16,151
Wes Holodniuk, Manager, Operations & Maintenance, 780-743-7931, Fax: 780-799-5909, email: wes.holodniuk@woodbuffalo.ab.ca
Salem Abushawashi, Superintendent, Fort Chipewyan, 780-697-3600, email: salem.abushawashi@woodbuffalo.ab.ca
Guy Jette, Acting Superintendent, Operations & Facilities Maintenance, 780-799-7486, email: guy.jette@woodbuffalo.ab.ca
Darcy Elder, Superintendent, Infrastructure, 780-799-7475, email: darcy.elder@woodbuffalo.ab.ca
Michel Savard, Superintendent, Environment, 780-799-7490, email: michel.savard@woodbuffalo.ab.ca
Dwayne Harvie, Project Engineer, 780-743-7855, email: dwayne.harvie@woodbuffalo.ab.ca
Waste Management:
Landfill & composting is at the Fort McMurray Regional Landfill site; Regional landfill design for 6-8 communities; Contracted to Fort McMurray, Conklin & Janvier; Contract for hamlet waste collection; First Nations & industry responsible for their waste management & sewage treatment facilities
Number of landfill sites: 7*Landfill Capacity:* 4-10 years
Solid Waste Disposal Fees: $21.21 - 64/tonne (household refuse & commercial waste); $50/tonne (waste requiring special handling)
Transfer Station(s): Shift to transfer stations for hamlets
Recycling: Depot; Depots located at Timberlea, Thickwood, Downtown: Planning 6 more in 2008
Special Bans/by-laws: Animal waste in residential collection; Natural oil in Oilsands; Hydro-carbon contaminations
Hazardous Waste Depot or Facility: Fort McMurray Landfill
Compost Sites: Yes *Composters subsidized:* Yes
Water & Wastewater Treatment:
Water treatment plants located at Conklin, Chard, Anzac, Fort McMurray, Fort McKay, Fort Chipewyan
Other Initiatives:
Fort McMurray water treatment plant optimization; Trunkline water supply designed for Anzac; Membrane treatment for Fort MacKay; BNR sewage treatment designed for Fort McMurray; New truck fill at McMurray, phase II Fort McMurray Intake; Fort McKay LIFTS station; Conklin water treatment expansion

Major Municipalities in Alberta

City of Airdrie
400 Main St. SE
Airdrie, AB T4B 3C3
403-948-8800
Fax: 403-948-6567
information.systems@airdrie.ca
www.airdrie.ca
Population: 42,564 *Census Year:* 2011
Number of Households: 6,897
George Keene, City Manager, email: george.keen@airdrie.ca
Mark Locking, Director, Engineering & Public Works
Jeff Greene, City Planner & Team Leader, 403-948-8848, email: planning.development@airdrie.ca
Dave Rimes, Leader, Parks, 403-948-8402, email: parks@airdrie.ca
Mary Grace Curtis, Coordinator, Recycling & Composting, 780-948-0246, email: environmental.services@airdrie.ca
Darryl Wolski, Coordinator, Solid Waste, 403-948-0246, email: pubwrks@airdrie.ca

Emergency Services
Airdrie, AB T4B 3G1
403-948-8880
emergency.services@airdrie.ca
Waste Management:
Hauled by contractor & disposed of at Calgary landfills.
Solid Waste Disposal Fees: Transfer site fee $20/ truckload (3/4 tonne)
Clean Fill Fee: No
Transfer Station(s): Yes
Recycling: Located at 15 East Lake Hill. Compost, grass & plant clippings accepted in the spring
Hazardous Waste Depot or Facility: Toxic Roundup May 1 to Sept 30
Composters subsidized: Yes
Other Initiatives:
Use-pay garbage collection system; Airdrie Environmental Education Centre.

City of Brooks
P.O. Box 880
201 - 1 Ave. West
Brooks, AB T1R 0Z6
403-362-3333
Fax: 403-362-4787
admin@brooks.ca
www.brooks.ca
Population: 13,676 *Census Year:* 2011
Number of Households: 4,379
Kevin Stephenson, City Manager, email: kstephenson@brooks.ca
Neil Hollands, Director, Engineering & Property Services, email: nhollands@brooks.ca
Kevin Swanson, Director, Protective Services, 403-362-2331
Terry Walsh, Director, Parks & Recreation, email: twalsh@brooks.ca
Maurice Landry, Manager, Development Services, email: mlandry@brooks.ca
Bill Prentice, Manager, Public Works, 403-362-3146, email: bprentice@brooks.ca
Gord Shaw, Manager, Planning Services, email: gshaw@brooks.ca
Water & Wastewater Treatment:
Town of Brooks Water Treatment System
Other Initiatives:
Surface irrigation system supplies untreated water, pumped through a piped network to homes & parks to reduce consumption of treated water for irrigation; WTP treated storage & high-lift design & construction.

City of Calgary
P.O. Box 2100 M
800 Macleod Trail SE
Calgary, AB T2P 2M5
403-268-2489
Fax: 403-538-6111
TTY: 403-268-4889
www.calgary.ca
Population: 1,096,833 *Census Year:* 2011
Number of Households: 481,900
J. Bernie Trahan, Director, Fleet Services, 403-268-1122, Fax: 403-266-2496, email: btrahan@calgary.ca
Anne Charlton, Director, Parks, 403-268-3888
Mac Logan, General Manager, Transportation
Mary Axworthy, Director, Land Use Planning & Policy
David L. Day, Director, Environmental & Safety Management, 403-268-3668
Dave Griffiths, Director, Waste & Recycling Services
Allyn Humber, Director, Water Services, 403-268-2702, email: waterworks@calgary.ca
Ian Norris, Director, Transportation Infrastructure, 403-974-4876
Wolf Keller, Director, Water Resources, 403-268-6752
W. Bruce Burrell, Fire Chief, 403-287-4255, Fax: 403-243-1490
Tom Sampson, Deputy Chief, Calgary Emergency Management Agency, email: tom.sampson@calgary.ca
Rolin Stanley, General Manager, Planning Development & Assessment, 403-268-2601
Rob Pritchard, General Manager, Utilities & Environmental Protection, 403-268-2042, Fax: 403-537-3023
Sharon E. Young, Manager, Environmental & Safety Management, 403-268-4699
Bruce Cullen, Manager, Infrastructure & Information Services
Waste Management:
Number of landfill sites: 3*Landfill Capacity:* 45 years
Solid Waste Disposal Fees: $64.00/tonne
Recycling: 52 residential depot locations
Special Bans/by-laws: Sewer service by-law; waste by-law; unsightly premises by-law
Hazardous Waste Depot or Facility: 3 landfill sites; 38 fire stations; 2 HazMat response vehicles
Compost Sites: Yes *Composters subsidized:* Yes
Water & Wastewater Treatment:
Bonnybrook Water Treatment Plant; Fish Creek Water Treatment Plant
Other Initiatives:
Calgary Waste & Recycling Services was the first public waste management system to achieve ISO 14001 certification; Fleet & Supply Management Services, golf courses & the Calgary Fire Dept. achieved ISO 14001 certification in 2001. City of Calgary Climate Change Action Plan includes emission reduction initiatives, such as streetlight & traffic signal head retrofitting. Mayor's Environmental Expo, an environmental forum & community outreach opportunity, is hosted annually by the city. Calgro Program is the biosolids-to-land initiative established in 1983.

City of Camrose
City Hall
5204 - 50 Ave.
Camrose, AB T4V 0S8
780-672-4426
Fax: 780-672-2469
admin@camrose.ca
www.camrose.ca
Population: 17,286 *Census Year:* 2011
Number of Households: 6,340
Brian Hamblin, P.Eng., City Manager, email: bhamblin@camrose.ca
Jeremy Enarson, Acting City Engineer, Engineering Services
Chris Clarkson, Director, Parks, 780-672-9195
Jim Kupka, Director, Public Works, 780-672-5513
Darrell Kambeitz, Police Chief
Peter Krich, Fire Chief/Deputy Director, Emergency Management
Brenda Hisey, Director, Planning & Development, 780-672-4428
Doug Delmage, Chief Building Inspector, 780-672-4428
Waste Management:
Camrose Regional Sanitary Landfill; Waste collection contracted to Waste Services Inc., 780/679-0409
Number of landfill sites: 1
Solid Waste Disposal Fees: $24.00/tonne
Clean Fill Fee:
Recycling: Depot; Centra Cam Recycling Depot, 4402 - 51 Ave., for regular paper, plastics & glass recyclable, as well as paint, batteries, computers & televisions, fluorescent tubes; Universal Bottle Depot& ECO-Centre, 5501 - 52 Ave.; Public Works Yard, 4202 - 51 Ave.; for other reusable goods, Restore at 5007 - 46 St.
Hazardous Waste Depot or Facility: Camrose Regional Sanitary Landfill, south of Camrose on 50 St., for hazardous waste & scrap metals, used appliances, tires
Compost Sites: Yes *Composters subsidized:* Yes
Water & Wastewater Treatment:
Camrose Water Treatment Plant; Camrose Wastewater Treatment Plant
Other Initiatives:
Composting workshop each spring; Emergency Clothing &

Furniture Depot, 780/672-9282; Tire Recycling Management Association, 1-880-999-8767; Hazardous Waste Round-Up & Paint Exchange twice each year

City of Canmore

902 - 7 Ave.
Canmore, AB T1W 3K1
403-678-1500
Fax: 403-678-1524
info@canmore.ca
www.canmore.ca
Population: 12,288 *Census Year:* 2011
Number of Households: 5,043
Don Kochan, Director, Environmental Services, email: donkochan@canmore.ca
Doug Townsend, Manager, Facilities, 403-678-1586
Kevin Van Vliet, Manager, Engineering, 403-678-1545, Fax: 403-678-1534

Waste Management:
Number of landfill sites: 1
Solid Waste Disposal Fees: Varies
Clean Fill Fee: Yes; Varies
Recycling: Depot; 2 depots located at 115 Boulder Cres. & Sobeys; Canmore Bottle Depot located at 103 Boulder Cres.
Special Bans/by-laws: Waste Control Bylaw

Water & Wastewater Treatment:
Managed by EPCOR Water Services, Phone 403/609-6400.

Other Initiatives:
Francis Cooke Regional Class III Landfill Site, operated by Bow Valley Waste Management Commission; Animal Proof Waste Handling System (no curbside waste collection); Residential toxic round-up & paint exchange events; Community Clean Up; eWaste Recycling Program at Boulder Recycling Depot; Leaf & Grass Collection Program

City of Cochrane

P.O. Box 10
101 Ranche House Rd.
Cochrane, AB T4C 2K8
403-851-2505
Fax: 403-851-2581
cochrane@cochrane.ca
www.cochrane.ca
Population: 17,580 *Census Year:* 2011
Number of Households: 4,067
Jim Anderson, Director, Operational Services, 403-851-2560, email: jim.anderson@cochrane.ca
Lori Leipnitz, Director, Corporate Services, 403-851-2510, email: lori.leipnitz@cochrane.ca
Ian Smith, Director, Community & Protective Services, 403-851-2530, email: ian.smith@cochrane.ca
Frank Wesseling, Director, Planning & Engineering, 403-851-2570, email: frank.wesseling@cochrane.ca
Elise Harnick, Engineer, Subdivision & Development, 403-851-2575, email: elise.harnick@cochrane.ca

Waste Management:
Waste collection is contracted out & transported to a landfill site in Calgary.
Recycling: Town of Cochrane Recycling Plant. 413/932-2742

Water & Wastewater Treatment:
Town of Cochrane Water Treatment Plant. Six sewage lift stations in operation in town, with a pipeline to the Bonnybrook Wastewater Treatment plant in Calgary.

Other Initiatives:
Residents are restricted to 3 bags of garbage per week; Toxic-Round-Up

City of Cold Lake

5513 - 48 Ave.
Cold Lake, AB T9M 1A1
780-594-4494
Fax: 780-594-3480
city@coldlake.com
www.coldlake.com
Population: 13,839 *Census Year:* 2011
Number of Households: 4,709
Gordon Frank, CAO, email: gfrank@coldlake.com
Allan Weiss, Chief, Fire, 780-594-4494
Carry Grant, Manager, Operations, 780-594-3776, email: cgrant@coldlake.com
George McIntosh, Foreman, Utilities, 780-639-3604, email: wtp@coldlake.com
John McLean, Foreman, Parks & Facilities, 780-594-3776, email: parks@coldlake.com

RCMP Inquiries
780-594-3302

Public Works Shop
780-639-3776
knagoya@coldlake.com

Waste Management:
Waste Management of Canada Corp., 1-800-648-3433
Number of landfill sites: 1*Landfill Capacity:* 2.5 years
Solid Waste Disposal Fees: $40/tonne
Recycling: Depot; North: 8th Ave./13th St.; South: west of curling rink; 4 Wing: MFRC building
Compost Sites: Yes *Composters subsidized:* No

Water & Wastewater Treatment:
Regional water plant, 780/639-3604; Water treatment, 102 - 10th St. NW; Cold Lake Regional Utilities Services Commission

Other Initiatives:
Toxic Round-Up; Undertaking a water treatment plant improvement, expansion & lagoon upgrade to conform to Alberta legislation; Toxic waste roundup June; Beginning transition to regional waste management model by 2007.

City of Edmonton

City Hall
1 Sir Winston Churchill Sq., 3rd Fl.
Edmonton, AB T5J 2R7
Fax: 780-496-8210
Telephone: 311 in Edmonton; or 780-442-5311
311@edmonton.ca
www.edmonton.ca
Population: 812,201 *Census Year:* 2011
Number of Households: 324,386
Dave Galea, Director, Office of Emergency Preparedness, 780-944-6420, Fax: 780-496-3062, email: david.galea@edmonton.ca
Doug Costigan, Director, Asset Management & Public Works, Parks Branch, 780-496-4956, Fax: 780-496-4978, email: doug.costigan@edmonton.ca
John Hodgson, Manager, Drainage Services, 780-496-5658, Fax: 780-496-3629
Gerald W. Goodall, Consultant, Corporate Services, Materials Management Branch, 780-496-3729, Fax: 780-496-5015, email: gerry.goodall@edmonton.ca
Audra Jones, Director, Transportation Planning, 780-496-1790, Fax: 780-496-4287
Gary Klassen, General Manager, Planning & Development, 780-496-6050, Fax: 780-496-6916, email: gary.klassen@edmonton.ca
Bob Boutilier, General Manager, Transportation, 780-496-2808, Fax: 780-496-2803, email: transportation@edmonton.ca
Peter Muller, EMT-P, ABCP, Emergency Management Officer (Planning), Office of Emergency Preparedness, 780-496-1530, Fax: 780-496-3062, email: peter.muller@edmonton.ca
Grant Pearsell, Director, Asset Management & Public Works, Parks Branch, 780-496-6080, Fax: 780-496-5636, email: grant.pearsell@edmonton.ca
Garth Clyburn, Planner II, Planning & Development, Planning & Policy Branch, 780-496-6209, Fax: 780-496-6299, email: garth.clyburn@edmonton.ca
Roy Neehall, Manager, Waste Management, 780-496-5405, Fax: 780-496-5657

Waste Management:
Half of waste collection contracted to Waste Services Inc., 780/464-9400 & other half to City crews, 780/496-5678. Automated collection BFI, FM & WSI. Weekly (special winter collection schedule) pickup of waste & recyclables.
Number of landfill sites: 2*Landfill Capacity:* 5 years ea.; Cloverbar Landfill (city), now at capacity; Integrat
Solid Waste Disposal Fees: $58/tonne for householder refuse; $65/tonne for commercially hauled refuse
Clean Fill Fee: Yes; $5/tonne, city owned landfill
Transfer Station(s): Yes
Recycling: Both Curbside & Depot; 23 depot locations throughout the city
Hazardous Waste Depot or Facility: Year-round Eco stations accept household hazardous wastes & other recyclables, 3 depot locations
Compost Sites: Yes *Composters subsidized:* Yes

Water & Wastewater Treatment:
Rossdale Water Treatment Plant in city centre; E.L. Smith Water Treatment Plant on western outskirts, with a 3-year upgrade completed in 2008; Gold Bar Waste Water Treatment Plant in east

Other Initiatives:
Brownfield redevelopment grant pilot project, $500,000 to be used for development of 5 sites to encourage redevelopment & cleanup of contaminated sites in Edmonton. Blue Bag program serves 156,904 single family residents (84% participation rate). 20 community recycling depots for multi-dwelling residents. A new direct recycling collection for the multi-family sector (approx. 126,087 households) began March, 2002. Master Composter/Recycler Program trains 30 community volunteers per year. Approximately 20-30,000 Christmas trees collected annually, chipped & used for park trails. Multi-purpose Eco Stations which accept HHW & a wide variety of recyclables & waste, attracting 89,531 visitors in 2003—the first of its kind in Canada. Edmonton Composting Facility opened in March 2000 & has a capacity of accepting 22,500 dewatered tonnes of bio-solids & 200,000 tonnes of municipal solid waste. Materials Recovery Facility opened in April, 1999 & has processing capabilities of 40,000 tonnes per year. Various public education programs & events, garbage fairs. Energy Management Program in place for over 10 years with a $5 million revolving fund in place to finance energy retrofit projects. Energy & water use tracked & reported for all city-owned facilities. Administration working closely with the Alberta Clean Air Strategic Alliance (CASA) process in developing air quality management initiatives for the Edmonton area. Water treatment pilot plant used to test innovative treatment processes. North Saskatchewan River Valley lands protected by by-law. An environmental impact assessment is required prior to development. Policy developed for protection of other environmentally sensitive & natural areas. Environmental Strategic Plan developed & approved by City Council in July, 1999. eEdmonton's first Report on Environmental Performance was published in May, 2001. Second report was published in October 2002. The third published in March 2004. The reports provide an accounting of the implementation of the City's Environmental Strateigc Plan, summarizing the City's environmental mission & vision. Greenhouse Gas Emissions Reduction Plan for City Operations developed & approved by Council in October, 1999. Community-wide Greenhouse Gas Reducation & Energy Strategy was developed with many external stake-holders. The strategy was approved by City Council in December, 2001. A 10-year strategy to develop a 62-kilometre network of multi-use trail corridors was approved by City Council in March, 2002. The trail corridor network will be a comprehensive system for self-propelled transportation through the City that links residential districts with the downtown, University & the river valley.

City of Fort Saskatchewan

10005 - 102 St.
Fort Saskatchewan, AB T8L 2C5
780-992-6200
Fax: 780-998-4774
lrosen@fortsask.ca
www.fortsask.ca
Population: 19,051 *Census Year:* 2011
Number of Households: 4,806
Scott Mack, Director, Planning, 780-992-6573, email: smack@fortsask.ca
Todd Burge, Manager, Corporate Services, 780-992-6255, email: tburge@fortsask.ca
Richard Hobson, Manager, Community & Protective Services, 780-992-6205, Fax: 780-992-0192, email: rhobson@fortsask.ca
Dave Worman, Manager, Planning & Public Works, 780-992-6207, email: dworman@fortsask.ca
Ken Lura, Superintendent, Public Works, 780-992-6247, email: klura@fortsask.ca
Gale Katchur, Contact, Environmental Awareness Committee, email: gkatchur@fortsask.ca

Waste Management:
Garbage disposal, 780/992-6248; Recycling/Waste Transfer station, 780/992-6152; There is a regional landfill centre; Waste collection contracted to Waste Services Inc., 780/464-9401
Recycling: Depot; Recycling/Waste Transfer Station, 8609 - 111 St.
Compost Sites: Yes *Composters subsidized:* Yes

Water & Wastewater Treatment:
Water is purified at the Capital Region Northeast Water Services Commission, 780/992-6229; Wastewater is processed at the Alberta Capital Regional Wastewater Commission, 780/467-8655

Other Initiatives:
Diversion of grass clippings & yard waste from landfill to produce compost, which is marketed to the general public; Annual Toxic Round-Up

City of Grande Prairie
P.O. Box 4000
10205 - 98 St.
Grande Prairie, AB T8V 6V3
780-538-0300
Fax: 780-538-0746
www.cityofgp.com
Population: 55,032 *Census Year:* 2011
Number of Households: 13,997
Greg Scerbak, City Manager, 780-538-0312, Fax: 780-814-7560, email: gscerbak@cityofgp.com
Frank Daskewech, Director, Public Works, 780-538-0350, Fax: 780-538-4667, email: fdaskewech@cityofgp.com
Josy Burrough, Manager, Parks, 780-538-0476, Fax: 780-532-7588, email: jburrough@cityofgp.com
Michael MacIntyre, Planning Manager, Development Services, 780-538-0440, Fax: 780-538-0746, email: mmacintyre@cityofgp.com
Valerie Norris-Kirk, Development Coordinator, Development Services, 780-513-5236, Fax: 780-538-0746, email: vnorrisk@cityofgp.com
Uli Wolf, Solid Waste Services Supervisor, Aquatera Utilities Inc., 780-538-0360, Fax: 780-830-7060, email: uwolf@aquatera.ca
Amy Horne, Recycling Coordinator, Aquatera Utilities Inc., 780-538-0452, Fax: 780-830-7060, email: ahorne@aquatera.ca
Mark Simpson, Operations Coordinator, Aquatera Utilities Inc., 780-538-0442, Fax: 780-830-7430, email: msimpson@aquatera.ca
Dan Lemieux, Sr. Deputy Fire Chief, 780-538-0398, Fax: 780-538-0395, email: dlemieux@cityofgp.com
Waste Management:
Waste management responsibility of Aquatera Utilites Inc., a regional utility corporation, 780/538-0452; Waste collection contracted by Aquatera to Waste Management, waste@aquatera.ca
Recycling: Recycling services provided by Aquatera Utilities Inc.; the Eco Centre accepts recyclables from commercial and residential customers.
Hazardous Waste Depot or Facility: Household hazardous waste may be taken to the Eco Centre, 10431 96 Ave.
Water & Wastewater Treatment:
Water & wastewater treatment responsibility of Aquatera Utilities Inc., 780/538-0348
Other Initiatives:
Aboriginal Workforce Participation Initiative

City of Leduc
1 Alexandra Park
Leduc, AB T9E 4C4
780-980-7177
Fax: 780-980-7127
info@leduc.ca
www.leduc.ca
Population: 24,279 *Census Year:* 2011
Number of Households: 5,480
Paul Benedetto, City Manager, email: pbenedetto@leduc.ca
Kevin Cole, Director, Public Services
Doug Parrish, Director, Planning & Development, 780-980-7124, email: dparrish@leduc.ca
Rick Sereda, Fire Chief & Director, Protective Services
Allan Yamashita, City Engineer & General Manager, Operations
Waste Management:
Waste collection contracted to Canadian Waste; Leduc & District Regional Landfill, 780/986-4202
Number of landfill sites: 1
Recycling: Both Curbside & Depot; Recycling depot located at 61 Ave. & 46 St., Leduc, 780/986-9494
Hazardous Waste Depot or Facility: Materials Recovery Facility, Leduc & District Regional Landfill Site
Composters subsidized: Yes
Water & Wastewater Treatment:
Capital Region Southwest Water Services Commission provides water service to city
Other Initiatives:
Limit of 4 bags/cans of garbage each pickup; Large item collection each spring; Yard waste pickup each spring & fall; Christmas tree collection program; Annual residential toxic waste round-up held in Sept.; Composting sites at the recycling depot & Lede Park

City of Lethbridge
City Hall
910 - 4 Ave. South
Lethbridge, AB T1J 0P6
403-329-7355
Fax: 403-320-7575
info@lethbridge.ca
www.lethbridge.ca
Population: 83,417 *Census Year:* 2011
Number of Households: 24,756
Brian Cornforth, Fire Chief, 403-320-3800, Fax: 403-327-3503, email: astrandlund@lethbridge.ca
Byron Buzunis, M.Eng., PMP, P.Eng., Urban Construction Manager, 403-320-3975
Warren Andrews, Manager, Public Operations, email: wandrews@lethbridge.ca
Kevin Viergutz, Manager, Transportation Operations, email: kviergutz@lethbridge.ab.ca
Bary Beck, Director, Corporate Initiatives
John King, Manager, Transit, 403-320-3884, Fax: 403-380-3876, email: jking@lethbridge.ca
Craig Milley, Manager, Purchasing, 403-320-3961, email: cmilley@lethbridge.ca
Kevin Theodore, Manager, Waste & Recycling, 403-320-3088, email: ktheodore@lethbridge.ab.ca
Don Bulpitt, Manager, Water & Wastewater Operations, email: dbulpitt@lethbridge.ca
Kevin Jensen, Coordinator, Parks, 403-330-5108, email: kjensen@lethbridge.ab.ca
George Kuhl, Senior Planner, Development Services, 403-327-3926, Fax: 403-327-6571, email: gkuhl@lethbridge.ca
Waste Management:
City responsible for waste collection, 403/320-3850; For landfill fees, recycling depot locations, hazardous waste disposal locations & composting, contact 403/329-7367
Number of landfill sites: 1 *Landfill Capacity:* 23 years
Solid Waste Disposal Fees: $37-52/tonne
Clean Fill Fee: Yes; $0-27/load
Recycling: Depot; 7 depot locations
Hazardous Waste Depot or Facility: 1430 - 33 St. North
Compost Sites: Yes
Water & Wastewater Treatment:
For information about water & wastewater treatment, contact 403/320-3850
Other Initiatives:
Sponsors Environment Week; Cleanup projects; Christmas tree recycling; Electronics recycling program

City of Lloydminster
City Hall
4420 - 50 Ave.
Lloydminster, AB T9V 0W2
780-875-6184
Fax: 780-871-8345
jkeeley@lloydminster.ca
www.lloydminster.ca
Population: 18,032 *Census Year:* 2011
Number of Households: 5,160
Adam Homes, Deputy CAO, Infrastructure Services, 780-875-8332, email: ahomes@lloydminster.ca
Ken Coleman, Deputy CAO, Community Services, 780-875-4529, email: kcoleman@lloydminster.ca
Don Newlin, Deputy CAO, Finance, 780-871-8330, email: dnewlin@lloydminster.ca
Brent Stasiuk, Deputy CAO, Protective Services, 780-874-9054, email: bstasiuk@lloydminster.ca
Waste Management:
Waste collection contracted to Quik Pick Waste Disposal, 780/875-4100; Blue box recycling contracted to Bea Fisher Enterprises, 306/825-9777
Number of landfill sites: 1
Solid Waste Disposal Fees: $10/tonne
Recycling: Both Curbside & Depot; Depot located at 1215 - 50 Ave.
Special Bans/by-laws: Boulevard tree planting (Bylaw 21-2002); Cardboard ban at landfill (Bylaw 24-2001); Higher tire disposal fees at landfill (Bylaw 09-2002)
Composters subsidized: Yes
Water & Wastewater Treatment:
Lloydminster Water Treatment Plant, 4701 - 67 St., 306/625-2437
Other Initiatives:
Hazardous household waste roundup; Computer recycling program; Pitch-in week

City of Medicine Hat
City Hall
580 - 1 St. SE
Medicine Hat, AB T1A 8E6
403-529-8115
Fax: 403-529-8182
clerk@medicinehat.ca
www.medicinehat.ca
Population: 60,005 *Census Year:* 2011
Number of Households: 21,504
Gerry Labas, COO, 403-529-8222, email: gerlab@medicinehat.ca
Ron Robinson, Fire Chief, 403-502-8006, Fax: 403-526-1352
John Komanchuk, Commissioner, Development & Infrastructure, 403-529-8354, email: johjo@medicinehat.ca
Dwight Brown, General Manager, Planning, Building & Development Services
John Fedoruk, General Manager, Environmental Utilities, 403-529-8176, Fax: 403-528-4955, email: eu@medicinehat.ca
Tony Klauwers, General Manager, Municipal Works
Dave Panabaker, General Manager, Gas Utility, 403-529-8288, email: davepan@medicinehat.ca
Kendall Woodacre, General Manager, Electric Utility, 403-502-8081, email: kenwoo@medicinehat.ca
R. Vizbar, General Manager, Parks & Outdoor Recreation, 403-529-8312, Fax: 403-527-4798, email: parks@medicinehat.ca
Russ Smith, Manager, Environment Management, 403-529-8188, email: russmi@medicinhat.ca
Frank Wetsch, Manager, Water & WasteWater Treatment, 403-529-8227
S. Schentag, Coordinator, Recycling Development, 403-502-8593
Ron Davis, Officer, Health & Safety, 403-529-8359, email: rondav@medicine-hat.ca
Waste Management:
Recycling program operated in partnership with REDI Recycle, 403/504-1322; Residential yard waste in biodegradable paper bags or marked containers is picked up with regular garbage from April to October; Composting facility is operated at City landfill site, 403/527-1718
Number of landfill sites: 1 *Landfill Capacity:* 15-30 years
Solid Waste Disposal Fees: $15/tonne
Recycling: Depot; 4 depots
Hazardous Waste Depot or Facility: City Landfill site
Composters subsidized: Yes
Water & Wastewater Treatment:
City operated

City of Okotoks
P.O. Box 20 Main
5 Elizabeth St.
Okotoks, AB T1S 1K1
403-938-4404
Fax: 403-938-7387
info@okotoks.ca
www.okotoks.ca
Population: 24,511 *Census Year:* 2011
Number of Households: 3,804
Rick Quail, Municipal Manager, 403-938-8900, email: municipalmanager@okotoks.ca
Ken Thevenot, Fire Chief, 403-938-4066, email: fire@okotoks.ca
Marley Oness, Municipal Engineer, 403-938-8930, email: municipalengineer@okotoks.ca
Dave Robertson, Manager, Operations, 403-938-8952, email: operations@okotoks.ca
Waste Management:
Okotoks Operations Dept. responsible for waste collection, composting & recycling; Waste disposal at Municipality of Foothills Landfill; Email: solidwaste@okotoks.ca; Phone: 403/938-8054
Recycling: Both Curbside & Depot; Recycling Depot 3730 - 32 St., Okotoks, 403/938-2652
Water & Wastewater Treatment:
Okotoks Wastewater Treatment Plant; Water services handled by EPCOR Water Services, Inc.
Other Initiatives:
Town operates a drop off center for composting of grass & leaves; Toxic round-up drop-off locations are Okotoks Fire Station or the regional landfill

City of Red Deer
City Hall
P.O. Box 5008
4914 - 48th Ave.
Red Deer, AB T4N 3T4
403-342-8111
Fax: 403-346-6195

feedback@reddeer.ca
www.reddeer.ca
Population: 90,564 *Census Year:* 2011
Number of Households: 27,136
Frank Colosimo, Manager, Public Works, 403-342-8238, Fax: 403-343-7074, email: publicworks@reddeer.ca
Kevin Joll, Manager, Transit, 403-342-8225, Fax: 403-342-8116, email: transit@reddeer.ca
Paul Meyette, Director, Planning Division
Greg Scott, Manager, Recreation, Parks & Culture, 403-342-8159, Fax: 403-342-8222
Dave Matthews, Supervisor, Planning & Technical Services
Tom Marstaller, Superintendent, Environmental Services, 403-342-8238, Fax: 403-343-7074, email: publicworks@reddeer.ca
Waste Management:
Yard waste collection from April to October
Number of landfill sites: 1
Recycling: Curbside; Blue Box program in effect; unlimited amount of recyclables permitted, to be collected weekly
Special Bans/by-laws: 5-unit limit on residential garbage collection
Hazardous Waste Depot or Facility: Waste Management Facility, 1709 - 40 Ave., Red Deer, 403/340-2583
Compost Sites: No *Composters subsidized:* Yes
Water & Wastewater Treatment:
Water & wastewater treatment plants operated by city
Other Initiatives:
Parks Department administers biological pest control; Habitat conservation; Backyard composting; Naturalization of park trees; Tree planting; Office paper recycling depot located at 5420 - 47 St., Red Deer, 403/340-2583; Yard waste collection program in effect; Electronics recycling

City of St. Albert

5 St. Anne St.
St. Albert, AB T8N 3Z9
780-459-1500
Fax: 780-460-2394
stalbert@st-albert.net
www.stalbert.ca
Population: 61,466 *Census Year:* 2011
Number of Households: 18,638
Gail Barrington-Moss, General Manager, Community & Protective Services
N. Jamieson, General Manager, Planning & Engineering Services
C. Cundy, Director, Planning & Development
D. Irving, Manager, Planning
Tracy Young, Administrative Resources Coordinator, Fire & Emergency Medical Services, 780-458-2020, Fax: 780-459-7636
Waste Management:
Waste collection contracted to Canadian Waste Management, 780/440-1700; St. Albert residents may use Northwest ECOstation in Edmonton
Recycling: Depot; St. Albert Recycling depot located at 7 Chevigny St. Campbell Industrial Park, 780/459-1557
Special Bans/by-laws: No open air burning of waste
Hazardous Waste Depot or Facility: Eco Station, 40 Bellrose Dr., St. Albert
Composters subsidized: Yes
Other Initiatives:
Establishment of Environment Advisory Committee; Pay-as-you-throw waste management system subscription; Annual Take It or Leave It event in June to dispose of unwanted usable items; Residents may pick up free compost material in spring & fall; Christmas tree collection in January; 2 bottle depots; Green cart pick up in summer months; St. Albert Compost Depot located on Veness Rd.; St. Albert residents may also use Eco Stations in Edmonton for household hazardous waste; Expansion of the Lacombe Park Water Reservoir

City of Spruce Grove

315 Jespersen Ave.
Spruce Grove, AB T7X 3E8
780-962-2611
Fax: 780-962-2526
info@sprucegrove.org
www.sprucegrove.org
Population: 26,171 *Census Year:* 2011
Number of Households: 5,632
Ken Luck, Director, FCSS & Recreation
Jackie Araujo, General Manager, Community Services, 780-962-7617
David Hales, General Manager, Planning & Infrastructure, 780-962-7622
Robert Kosterman, Chief, Fire, 780-962-4496
Jeff Mustard, Superintendent, Engineering, 780-962-7624
Paul Hanlan, Supervisor, Planning & Development
Jane Holmes, Coordinator, Sustainable Development
Waste Management:
Waste collection contracted to Waste Management of Canada Corporation, 780-440-1700
Transfer Station(s): 10 Alberta Ave., Spruce Grove, 780/962-9383
Recycling: Depot; Recycling Centre located at 10 Alberta Ave., Spruce Grove, 780/962-9383, operated by KC Environmental Group Ltd.
Water & Wastewater Treatment:
Water services handled by Capital Region Parkland Water Services Commission; Town Public Works department responsible for system maintenance
Other Initiatives:
Organic collection program; Spring toxic roundup; Electronic (e-waste) recycling program; Rechargeable Battery Recycling program; Annual fall home & yard clean up pickup; Business BEST (Building an Environmental & Social Trust), a program where businesses commit to environmental & community considerations in their operations; Partners for Climate Protection program; Urban forest management; Sale of compost from Spruce Grove Recycling Centre

City of Wetaskiwin

P.O. Box 6210
4705 - 50th Ave.
Wetaskiwin, AB T9A 2E9
780-361-4400
Fax: 780-352-0930
Toll Free Phone: 1-800-989-6899
reception@wetaskiwin.ca
www.wetaskiwin.ca
Population: 12,525 *Census Year:* 2011
Number of Households: 4,707
Ted Gillespie, City Manager
Merlin Klassen, Fire Chief, 780-361-4429, Fax: 780-352-6261, email: fireservices@wetaskiwin.ca
Waste Management:
Waste management handled by Wetaskiwin Operational Services dept.; Landfill site is Wetaskiwin Regional Sanitary Landfill.
Number of landfill sites: 1
Solid Waste Disposal Fees: $53/tonne for residents, $95/tonne for non-residents.
Clean Fill Fee: No
Recycling: Depot; Recycling depot located at 5707-51st St., Wetaskiwin, 780/361-4431
Composters subsidized: Yes
Water & Wastewater Treatment:
Water Treatment Plant located in Coal Lake, AB, 780/361-4415; Sewage treatment provided by a series of lagoons
Other Initiatives:
User pay approach to waste handling; Spring & fall clean-up; Annual household toxic round-up; E-waste drop-off at recycling depot

Other Municipalities in Alberta

Alberta Capital Region Wastewater Commission

23262 Township Rd. 540
Fort Saskatchewan, AB T8L 4A2
780-467-8655
Fax: 780-467-5398
Gordon Thompson, General Manager
Water & Wastewater Treatment:
Responsible only for wastewater transmission & treatment for cities of St. Albert, Leduc, Spruce Grove & Fort Saskatchewan, towns of Morinville, Stony Plain, Beaumont, Bon Accord & Gibbons, counties of Strathcona, Leduc & Parkland, & Sturgeon.

Athabasca Regional Waste Management Services Commission

P.O. Box 90
Athabasca, AB T9S 2A2
780-675-1117
Fax: 780-675-8881
arwmsc@telusplanet.net
Robert Smith, Manager

Beaver Regional Waste Management Services Commission

P.O. Box 322
Ryley, AB T0B 4A0
780-663-2038
Fax: 780-663-2006
brwmsccc@telusplanet.net
www.brwmsc.com
Forrest Wright, CAO

Beaver River Regional Waste Management Commission

Bag 1010
Bonnyville, AB T9N 2J7
780-826-3951
Fax: 780-826-5064
Marco Schroeninger, Manager

Big Country Waste Management Commission

P.O. Box 1906
Hanna, AB T0J 1P0
403-854-5600
Fax: 403-854-5527
Greg R. Sheppard, Operations Manager
Waste Management:
Members include Special Areas 2, 3, & 4, Towns of Hanna & Oyen, Villages of Cereal, Consort, Empress, Veteran & Youngstown; Youngstown regional landfill, 403/779-3890
Composters subsidized: No

Bow Valley Waste Management Commission

Wild Earth Associates Inc.
185 Carey
Canmore, AB T1W 2R7
403-609-7229
Fax: 403-609-0320
bvwmc@wildearth.ab.ca
John Stutz, Chair

Capital Region Northeast Water Services Commission

10005 - 102 St.
Fort Saskatchewan, AB T8L 2C5
780-992-6207
Fax: 780-992-1375
Dave Worman, Manager
Water & Wastewater Treatment:
Member areas: County of Strathcona #20, Municipal District of Sturgeon #90, Towns of Redwater, Gibbons, Fort Saskatchewan & Bon Accord

Capital Region Parkland Water Services

c/o 315 Jesperson Ave.
Spruce Grove, AB T7X 3E8
780-962-2611
Water & Wastewater Treatment:
Capital Region Parkland Water Services serves the following municipalities: County of Parkland No. 31, Town of Spruce Grove & Town of Stony Plain; Water supplied from Epcor Water Services Inc.

Capital Region Southwest Water Services Commission

#101, 1101 - 5 St.
Nisku, AB T9E 2X3
780-955-3555
Fax: 780-955-3444
Darryl Rubis, Manager

Capital Region Vegreville Corridor Water Services Commission

P.O. Box 176
Chipman, AB T0B 0W0
780-363-3982
Fax: 780-363-2386
chipmanab@primus.ca
Pat Tomkow, Manager
Water & Wastewater Treatment:
Water is purchased & transported via pipeline from Edmonton to the counties of Lamont & Strathcona, towns of Bruderheim, Lamont, Mundare & Vegreville, & the village of Chipman.

Central Peace Regional Waste Management Commission
c/o Saddle Hills County
P.O. Box 69
Spirit River, AB T0H 3G0
780-864-3760
Fax: 780-864-3904
Cliff Travis, Chair

Cold Lake Regional Utility
5513 - 48 Ave.
Cold Lake, AB T9M 1A1
780-594-4494
Fax: 780-594-3480
Water & Wastewater Treatment:
Member areas: City of Cold Lake, Cold Lake Indian Reserve #149, Cold Lake Armed Forces Base, Municipal District of Bonnyville #87

Evergreen Regional Waste Management Services Commission
5015 - 49 Ave.
St Paul, AB T0A 3A4
780-645-3301
Fax: 780-645-3104
Dennis Bergheim, Manager

Foothills Regional Services
P.O. Box 5605
High River, AB T1V 1M7
403-652-2341
Fax: 403-652-7880
Bill Robinson, Sec.-Treas.
Waste Management:
Number of landfill sites: 1*Landfill Capacity:* 80 years
Solid Waste Disposal Fees: $33/tonne
Clean Fill Fee: No
Recycling: Depot; Depots located in area's towns
Hazardous Waste Depot or Facility: Depots in each town
Composters subsidized: Yes
Water & Wastewater Treatment:
Responsible for municipal district of Foothills & towns & hamlets of Blackie, Cayley & Aldersyde.

Greenview Regional Waste Management Commission
P.O. Box 115
Valleyview, AB T0H 3N0
780-524-7601
Fax: 780-524-4432
Gordon Frank, Acting Administrator

Henry Kroeger Regional Water Services Commission
P.O. Box 25
Youngstown, AB T0J 3P0
403-779-3904
Fax: 403-779-2279
Evelyn Manion, Manager
Water & Wastewater Treatment:
Members include towns of Hanna & Oyen, villages of Youngstown, Cereal & Delia, Starland County & Special Areas 2, 3, & 4.

Highway 14 Regional Water Services
P.O. Box 322
Ryley, AB T0B 4A0
780-663-2039
Fax: 780-663-2006
brwmsccc@telusplanet.net
Forrest Wright, CAO

Highway 43 East Waste Commission Services
P.O. Box 219
Sangudo, AB T0E 2A0
780-785-3411
Fax: 780-785-2359
bweldon@vennercs.com
Ron Kidd, Chair
Waste Management:
Members include Lac Ste. Anne County, Villages of Alberta Beach, Onoway & Sangudo, Town of Mayerthorpe, Summer Villages of Birch Cove, Castle Island, Nakamun Park, Ross Haven, Sandy Beach, Silver Sands, South View, Sunrise Beach, Sunset Point, Val Quentin, West Cove & Yellowstone.

Kneehill Regional Water Services Commission
P.O. Box 592
Acme, AB T0M 2A0
403-546-3783
Fax: 403-546-3014
vacme@telus.net
John Van Doesburg, Manager

Lakeland Regional Waste Management Services Commission
P.O. Box 387
Lac La Biche, AB T0A 2C0
780-623-4323
Fax: 780-623-3510
townlib@telusplanet.net
Gordon Elliott, Chair

Lamont County Regional Solid Waste Commission
General Delivery
Lamont, AB T0B 2R0
780-895-2233
Fax: 780-895-7404
John Stribling, Chair

Lesser Slave Lake Regional Waste Management Services Commission
P.O. Box 722
Slave Lake, AB T0G 2A0
780-369-2590
Fax: 780-369-2599
md124@md124.ca
www.md124.ca
George Snider, Interim Manager

Lethbridge Regional Waste Management Services
P.O. Box 1594
Lethbridge, AB T1J 4K3
403-732-4722
Fax: 403-732-4328
rsnowdon@county.lethbridge.ab.ca
Eugene Wauters, Chair
Waste Management:
Commission serves the following municipalities: County of Lethbridge, Town of Picture Butte & Village of Nobleford; City of Lethbridge Regional Landfill is used
Transfer Station(s): Picture Butte; Nobleford; Coaldale; Iron Springs

Lethbridge Regional Water Services Commission
c/o County of Lethbridge
#100, 905 - 4 Ave. South
Lethbridge, AB T1J 4E4
403-328-5525
Fax: 403-328-5602
rrobinson@county.lethbridge.ab.ca
Rick Robinson, Commission Manager

Long Lake Regional Waste Management Commission
P.O. Box 178
Grimshaw, AB T0H 1W0
780-971-2200
Fax: 780-971-2200
llrwmsc@telusplanet.net
Elzina Vance, Acting Manager

Mackenzie Regional Waste Management Commission
9813 - 102 St.
High Level, AB T0H 1Z0
780-926-2201
Fax: 780-926-2899
landfill@highlevel.ca
Ron Pelensky, Manager

Mountain View Regional Waste Management Commission
1230
Didsbury, AB T0M 0W0
403-335-2005
Fax: 403-335-8132
nrkivell@telusplanet.net
Dave Derksen, Chair

Mountain View Regional Water Services
Site 22, Box 1, RR#1
Innisfail, AB T4G 1T6
403-227-5828
Fax: 403-227-5831
mtnwater@telusplanet.net
John Van Doesburg, Administrator

North 43 Lagoon Commission
14403 - 110 Ave.
Edmonton, AB T5N 1J7
780-454-9414
Fax: 780-452-2322
Mark Anker, Manager

North Forty Mile Regional Waste Management Services Commission
P.O. Box 276
Bow Island, AB T0K 0G0
403-833-3805
Population:
Number of Households: 1,400
Bill Ressler, Chair
Waste Management:
Commission serves the following municipalities: Town of Bow Island & County of Forty Mile
Number of landfill sites: 1

North Peace Regional Landfill Commission
P.O. Box 2654
Fairview, AB T0H 1L0
780-835-2576
Fax: 780-835-2579
info@nprlandfill.com
www.nprlandfill.com
Darren Lubeck, Manager

North Red Deer River Water Services Commission
5432 - 56 Ave.
Lacombe, AB T4L 1E9
403-391-0270
Judy Gordon, Chair

Northeast Pigeon Lake Regional Services Commission
P.O. Box 6960
Wetaskiwin, AB T9A 2G5
780-352-3321
Fax: 780-352-3486
fcoutney@telusplanet.net
Frank Coutney, Manager

Roseridge Waste Management Services Commission
P.O. Box 19
Site 1, RR#1
Morinville, AB T8R 1P4
780-939-8369
Fax: 780-939-4788
sbberry@sturgeoncounty.ab.ca
Randy Boyd, Chairperson
Waste Management:
Number of landfill sites: 1
Solid Waste Disposal Fees: $38.50/tonne
Recycling: Depot; at landfill site

Smoky River Regional Waste Management Commission
P.O. Box 155
Falher, AB T0H 1M0
780-837-2257
Fax: 780-837-2647
admin@town.falher.ab.ca
Donna Buchinski, Chairperson

Smoky River Regional Water Management Commission
P.O. Box 155
Falher, AB T0H 1M0
780-837-2257
Fax: 780-837-2647
srwater@telus.net
Donna Buchinski, Chairperson

South Forty Waste Services Commission
P.O. Box 307
Foremost, AB T0K 0X0
403-647-7572
Fax: 403-867-2663
Bryne Lengyel, Chairperson

Thorhild Regional Waste Management Services Commission
P.O. Box 10
Thorhild, AB T0A 3J0
780-398-3741
Fax: 780-398-3748
Debbie Hamilton, Acting Commission Manager

Thorhild Regional Water Services Commission
P.O. Box 310
Thorhild, AB T0A 3J0
780-398-3688
Fax: 780-398-2100
dhamilton@telusplanet.net
Debbie Hamilton, Manager

Tri Village Regional Sewage Services
Box 16, Site 1, RR#2
Carvel, AB T0E 0H0
780-963-4211
Fax: 780-963-4260
Don Boudreaux, Chair

Two Hills Regional Waste Management Commission
P.O. Box 8
Two Hills, AB T0B 4K0
780-567-2016
Darren Banack, Operations Manager

Vulcan District Waste Commission
P.O. Box 180
Vulcan, AB T0L 2B0
403-485-2241
Fax: 403-482-2920
countyadmin@vulcancounty.ab.ca
www.vulcancounty.ab.ca
Merle Wyatt, Chair

Westend Regional Sewage Services
P.O. Box 330
Turner Valley, AB T0L 2A0
403-933-4744
Fax: 403-933-5377
Sharlene Brown, Chair

Westlock Regional Waste Management Commission
10336 - 106 St.
Westlock, AB T7P 2G1
780-349-3346
Fax: 780-349-2012
Vacant, Manager

Willow Creek Regional Waste Management Services Commission
P.O. Box 2820
Claresholm, AB T0L 0T0
403-687-2603
Fax: 403-287-2602
wcrwmsc@telusplanet.net
Gerry McGueire, Chair

British Columbia

Sewage & wastewater is provincially regulated. This is split between the Ministry of Environment for regional districts & the Ministry of Health for individual septic tank systems. Under the Municipal Sewage Regulations, municipalities, commercial entities & industries are responsible for treating sewage, generating & using reclaimed water & disposing of wastewater. British Columbia enacted the Municipal Sewage Regulation that replaces a permit system & provides rules for treating sewage, generating & using reclaimed water, & disposing of effluent that cannot be re-used. Grants of up to $10,000 are available to local governments through the Water & Sewer Infrastructure Planning Grant Program to study proposed sewer, water, groundwater or stormwater drainage facilities.

The Drinking Water Protection Act is administered by the Ministry of Health, as is the Sewerage System Regulation, dealing with on-site wastewater management in rural and regional municipalities. Community Water Improvement Program has been allocated $80 million to improve drinking water & wastewater management, with local governments responsible for an additional $40 million.

Regional districts were set up to initiate programs & develop regulations to reduce the amount of solid waste being sent to the 125 landfills in the province. The province has reduced the amount of solid waste being sent to landfills by 36%. The Environmental Management Act (July, 2004) accelerates & simplifies the process of rehabilitating low-risk contaminated sites. The Liquid Waste Management Plan provides guidance to local government seeking an approved liquid waste plant. The Organic Matter Recycling Regulation governs the production, quality and application of certain types of organic matter.

Product stewardship programs exist for beverage containers, based on deposit refunds; lead acid batteries, funded from a $5 levy on the sale of all new vehicle type lead acid batteries weighing more than 2 kg; medications; paints; scrap tires, funded through a $3 levy on new tires; solvents, flammable liquids or gases, pesticides; used lubricating oil; household hazardous waste.

The Greenhouse Gas Action Guide assists local governments carry out initiatives to decrease greenhouse gases. Vancouver has implemented the Greenest City 2020 Action Plan in order to improve carbon output, waste systems & the ecosystem, & become the greenest city in the world.

Counties & Municipal Districts in British Columbia

Alberni-Clayoquot
3008 - 5 Ave.
Port Alberni, BC V9Y 2E3
250-720-2700
Fax: 250-723-1327
mailbox@acrd.bc.ca
www.acrd.bc.ca
Population: 31,061 *Census Year:* 2011
Number of Households: 13,603
Vacant, Manager, Environmental Services
Mike Irg, Manager, Planning & Development, 250-720-2710, email: mirg@acrd.bc.ca
Waste Management:
Number of landfill sites: 2
Solid Waste Disposal Fees: $65/tonne (residential); $82.50/tonne (land clearing debris)
Composters subsidized: Yes

Bulkley-Nechako
P.O. Box 820
37, 3rd Ave.
Burns Lake, BC V0J 1E0
250-692-3195
Fax: 250-692-3305
Toll Free Phone: 1-800-320-3339
inquiries@rdbn.bc.ca
www.rdbn.bc.ca
Population: 39,208 *Census Year:* 2011
Number of Households: 16,896
Jason Llewellyn, Director, Planning, email: jason.llewellyn@rdbn.bc.ca
Janine Dougall, Director, Environmental Services, 250-692-3195, email: janine.dougall@rdbn.bc.ca
Richard Wainwright, C.A., Chief Building Inspector, email: richard.wainwright@rdbn.bc.ca
Rory McKenzie, Supervisor, Field Operations, Environmental Services, email: rory.mckenzie@rdbn.bc.ca
Waste Management:
Operates landfill sites & transfer stations for the Regional District.
Number of landfill sites: 7
Recycling: Depot locations: Smithers/Telkwa Transfer Station, Landfills: Knockholt, Granisle, Burns Lake, Fraser Lake, Fort Fraser, Fort St. James, Vanderhoof, Southside Transfer Station
Special Bans/by-laws: Ban on tires in landfill
Hazardous Waste Depot or Facility: Smithers/Telkiva Transfer Station.
Composters subsidized: Yes
Other Initiatives:
Implementation of noxious weed control program; Re-use sheds for public use.

Capital Regional District
625 Fisgard St.
Victoria, BC V8W 1R7
250-360-3000
Mailing address: PO Box 1000, Victoria, BC V8W 2S6
www.crd.bc.ca
Population: 359,991 *Census Year:* 2011
Number of Households: 151,461
Larissa Hutcheson, General Manager, Environmental Sustainability, 250-360-3085
Jack Hull, General Manager, Integrated Water Services, 250-474-9604
Robert Lapham, General Manager, Planning & Protective Services, 250-360-3285
Dan Telford, Senior Manager, Environmental Engineering, 250-360-3064
Glenn Harris, Senior Manager, Environmental Protection, 250-360-3090
Russ Smith, Senior Manager, Environmental Resource Management, 250-360-3083
Tim Tanton, Senior Manager, Infrasturcture Engineering, 250-474-9611
Maurice Rachwalski, Senior Manager, Health & Capital Planning Strategies, 250-360-3114
Ian Hennigar, Senior Manager, Peninsula Recreation Commission/Panorama Recreation, 250-655-2170
Margaret Misek-Evans, Senior Manager, Regional Planning, 250-360-3244
Ted Robbins, Senior Manager, Water Management, 250-360-3061
Stewart Irwin, Senior Manager, Water Quality, 250-474-9603
Gordon Joyce, Senior Manager, Watershep Protection, 250-474-9621
Waste Management:
Collection of recyclables contracted to International Paper Industries Ltd. For more information contact CRD Recycling hotline 250/360-3030, or Email: hotline@crd.bc.ca
Number of landfill sites: 1
Solid Waste Disposal Fees: $90/tonne (general refuse)
Recycling: Both Curbside & Depot; Hartland Landfill & Recyling Area, northwest of Victoria; a multi-purpose facility for residential & commercial customers, to handle recycling, yard & garden waste, household hazardous waste, and salvageable items. Depots under contract to the CRD, Southern Gulf Islands & Salt Spring Island
Special Bans/by-laws: Landfill restricted wastes: aggregate, asphalt, biomedical waste, clean soil, concrete, corrugated cardboard, directories, lead acid batteries, PCBs, drywall, hazardous wastes, liquids, radioactive & reactive waste, ignitable wastes, motor vehicle bodies & farm implements, scrap metal, tires, white goods
Hazardous Waste Depot or Facility: Hartland Landfill & Recyling Area
Composters subsidized: Yes
Water & Wastewater Treatment:
Water treatment plants: Japan Gulch Treatment Plant; Charters Creek Treatment Plant. Wastewater treatment plants: Saanich Peninsula Treatment Plant; Port Renfrew Treatment Plant, Vancouver Island; Ganges Harbour Treatment Plant, Salt Spring Island; Maliview Treatment Plant, Salt Spring Island; Schooner Way Treatment Plant, Pender Island; Cannon Crescent Treatment Plant, Pender Island. For more information contact water@crd.bc.ca
Other Initiatives:
Environmental education & awareness through publications & promotional campaigns; Composting initiatives; Liquid waste management plan; Stewardship intiatives; Air quality working group; Stormwater, harbours & watersheds program; Sooke reservoir expansion

Cariboo
180 North 3rd Ave., #D
Williams Lake, BC V2G 2A4
250-392-3351
Fax: 250-392-2812
Toll Free Phone: 1-800-665-1636
mailbox@cariboord.bc.ca
www.cariboord.bc.ca
Population: 62,392 *Census Year:* 2011
Number of Households: 30,048
Mitch Minchau, Manager, Utilities/Solid Waste Management, email: mminchau@cariboord.bc.ca
Rick Brundrige, Manager, Planning Services, email: rbrundrige@cariboord.bc.ca

Darron Campbell, Manager, Community Services/Recreation/Airports, email: dcampbell@cariboord.bc.ca
Rowena Bastien, Manager, Protective Services, email: rbastien@cariboord.bc.ca
Waste Management:
Cities of Quesnel & Williams Lake operate their landfills
Number of landfill sites: 14
Transfer Station(s): 15 transfer stations
Recycling: Curbside; Depot locations: 100 Mile House, Williams Lake, Quesnel
Water & Wastewater Treatment:
Cities within the region are responsible for their own water & wastewater treatment; regional district is responsible for the following water systems: Alexis Creek, Lac La Hache, Forest Grove & 108 Mile
Other Initiatives:
Institutional, commercial & industrial waste exchange program; landfill & transfer station upgrading program; wood waste management program

Central Kootenay
P.O. Box 590
202 Lakeside Dr.
Nelson, BC V1L 5R4
250-352-6665
Fax: 250-352-9300
Toll Free Phone: 1-800-268-7325
info@rdck.bc.ca
www.rdck.bc.ca
Population: 58,441 *Census Year:* 2011
Number of Households: 27,089
Jim Gustafson, Chief Administrative Officer, 250-352-8152, email: jgustafson@rdck.bc.ca
Uli Wolf, General Manager, Environmental Services, 250-352-8163, email: uwolf@rdck.bc.ca
Waste Management:
Waste collection responsibility of member areas
Number of landfill sites: 4
Solid Waste Disposal Fees: Yes
Transfer Station(s): 9 transfer stations in the region
Recycling: Depot; 28 recycling depots in the region
Water & Wastewater Treatment:
8 water systems in the region

Central Okanagan
1450 KLO Rd.
Kelowna, BC V1W 3Z4
250-763-4918
Fax: 250-763-0606
info@cord.bc.ca
www.cord.bc.ca
Population: 179,839 *Census Year:* 2011
Number of Households: 62,675
Dan Plamondon, Director, Development Services, 250-868-5227, email: planning@cord.bc.ca
Murray Kopp, Director, Parks Services
Peter Rotheisler, Manager, Regional Waste Reduction Office, 250-469-6250, Fax: 250-762-7011, email: recycle@cord.bc.ca
Waste Management:
Waste collection contracted to OK Environmental Waste Systems, 250/868-3211 & Waste Management, 250/861-8788; Recycling collection contracted to Canadian Waste Services
Number of landfill sites: 2
Solid Waste Disposal Fees: $50/tonne
Transfer Station(s): Westside Rd.; Whiteman Creek Forest Service Rd.
Recycling: Both Curbside & Depot; Depots: Kirschner Rd. Recycling, 1988 Kirschner Rd.; Metro Materials Recovery Recycling Depot, 144 Cambro Rd.; Glenmore Landfill, Glenmore Dr.; Westside Landfill, Asquith Rd.
Special Bans/by-laws: Bylaw to reduce emissions from open burning, camp fires, & wood burning appliances to ensure good air quality
Composters subsidized: Yes
Water & Wastewater Treatment:
Westside Regional Waste Water Treatment Plant, south end of Gellatly Rd.; Regional district administers 8 water distribution systems
Other Initiatives:
Residential grasscycling promotion; Composting workshops & education garden; Technical assistance in starting up recycling & waste reduction programs at home & work; Recycling directories for residential, commercial & construction, demolition & renovation; Spring & fall yard waste pick-up; Annual household hazardous waste round-up; Private depots collect pesticides, oil, flammable liquids, batteries, paint & computers; Recycling at work program, 250/846-6250, recycle@cord.bc.ca; Joe Rich Creek Watershed Restoration; Protection of environmentally sensitive areas, watercourses, water quality & endangered species

Columbia-Shuswap
P.O. Box 978
781 Marine Park Dr. NE
Salmon Arm, BC V1E 4P1
250-832-8194
Fax: 250-832-3375
Toll Free Phone: 1-888-248-2773
enquiries@csrd.bc.ca
www.csrd.bc.ca
Population: 50,512 *Census Year:* 2011
Number of Households: 24,726
Gerald Christie, Manager, Development Services, 250-833-5919, email: gchristie@csrd.bc.ca
Gary Holte, Manager, Environment & Engineering Services, 250-833-5935, email: gholte@csrd.bc.ca
Jack Blair, Co-ordinator, Fire Services, 250-833-5945, email: jblair@csrd.bc.ca
Hamish Kassa, Co-ordinator, Environment Services, 250-833-5942, email: hkassa@csrd.bc.ca
Terry Langois, Co-ordinator, Water Systems, 250-833-5941, email: tlanglois@csrd.bc.ca
Ben Van Nostrand, Co-ordinator, Waste Management, 250-833-5940, email: bvannostrand@csrd.bc.ca
Waste Management:
Regional landfills located in the following areas: Golden, Revelstoke, Salmon Arm, Sicamous & Skimikin
Number of landfill sites: 5
Solid Waste Disposal Fees: $60/tonne
Transfer Station(s): Falkland; Glenemma; Scotch Creek; Seymour Arm; Malakwa; Trout Lake; Parson
Recycling: Depot; 17 depots located throughout region
Special Bans/by-laws: Land Use
Water & Wastewater Treatment:
Community waterworks at Cedar Heights, Eagle Bay Estates & Falkland
Other Initiatives:
Elimination of small disposal sites in rural areas; Implementation of refuse disposal fees

Comox Valley
600 Comox Rd.
Courtenay, BC V9N 3P6
250-334-6000
Fax: 250-334-4358
Toll Free Phone: 1-800-331-6007
administration@comoxvalleyrd.ca
www.comoxvalleyrd.ca
Population: 63,538 *Census Year:* 2011
Number of Households: 44,153
Ian Smith, General Manager, Community Services
Kevin Lorette, General Manager, Property Service Branch
Waste Management:
Number of landfill sites: 4
Solid Waste Disposal Fees: $65/tonne
Transfer Station(s): Cortes Island, Gold River, Hornby Island
Recycling: Depot; 16 depots throughout the region
Special Bans/by-laws: Water Conservation Bylaw, Noise Control Bylaw, Noxious Weed Bylaw, Fire Control Bylaws, Floodplain Management Bylaw
Compost Sites: Yes *Composters subsidized:* Yes
Water & Wastewater Treatment:
Comox Valley Water Pollution Control Centre
Other Initiatives:
Compost education centres in Comox Valley & Campbell River; E-waste drop-off events; School & youth recycling education programs; Liquid waste management planning; Pesticide awareness & pesticide disposal at Campbell River Refund Centre; Promotion & education about household hazardous waste provincial programs

Cowichan Valley
175 Ingram St.
Duncan, BC V9L 1N8
250-746-2500
Toll Free Phone: 1-800-665-3955
cvrd@cvrd.bc.ca
www.cvrd.bc.ca
Population: 80,332 *Census Year:* 2011
Number of Households: 31,149
Brian Dennison, General Manager, Engineering & Environment, 250-746-2532, email: bdennison@cvrd.bc.ca
Ron Austen, General Manager, Parks, Recreation & Culture, 250-746-2635, email: rausten@cvrd.bc.ca
Tom R. Anderson, General Manager, Planning & Development, 250-746-2601, email: tanderson@cvrd.bc.ca
Waste Management:
Waste transported from transfer station to Cache Creek Landfill, near Kamloops
Solid Waste Disposal Fees: $110/tonne
Transfer Station(s): Bings Creek Waste Transfer Station
Recycling: Both Curbside & Depot; Depot locations: Peerless Road Recycling Drop-off Depot, Ladysmith; Meade Creek Recycling Drop-off Depot, Lake Cowichan; Bings Creek Solid Waste Management Complex, North Cowichan; 9 CVRD multi-product neighbourhood bin locations; For more information contact CVRD Recycling Hotline, 1-800-665-3955
Special Bans/by-laws: Waste stream management licensing bylaw
Water & Wastewater Treatment:
Region responsible for collection & disposal of sewage for the following sewer systems: Shawnigan Beach Estates, Maple Hills, Cowichan Bay, Eagle Heights, Mesachie Lake, Kerry Village & Creekside Resort; Engineering department maintains operations of the following water systems: Shawnigan Lake North, Cherry Point Estates, Honeymoon Bay, Mesachie Lake, Saltair Water System, Lakeside Estates, Kerry Village & Youbou Water System

East Kootenay
19 - 24 Ave. South
Cranbrook, BC V1C 3H8
250-489-2791
Fax: 250-489-3498
Toll Free Phone: 1-888-478-7335
info@rdek.bc.ca
www.rdek.bc.ca
Population: 56,685 *Census Year:* 2011
Number of Households: 28,649
Dan McNeill, Manager, Building & Protective Services, email: dmcneill@rdek.bc.ca
Loree Duczek, Manager, Communications, email: lduczek@rdek.bc.ca
Shannon Moskal, Manager, Community Services, email: smoskal@rdek.bc.ca
Brian Funke, Manager, Engineering Services, email: bfunke@rdek.bc.ca
Kevin Paterson, Manager, Environmental Services, email: kpaterson@rdek.bc.ca
Lori Engler, Manager, Human Resources, email: lengler@rdek.bc.ca
Andrew McLeod, Manager, Planning & Development Services, email: amcleod@rdek.bc.ca
Waste Management:
Number of landfill sites: 2
Solid Waste Disposal Fees: No charge for household refuse; User fees apply at staffed facilities on most other loads
Transfer Station(s): 4 covered transfer stations, Cranbrook, Kimberley, Sparwood & Elkford; 15 rural transfer stations, across the region
Recycling: Depot; Yellow bin program for mixed recyclables; Glass recycling program; Blue bin program for household plastics; Elkford, Sparwood & Fernie have their own programs
Hazardous Waste Depot or Facility: Consumer Stewardship Program depot: Purcell Recycling, 125 Slater Rd., Cranbrook
Water & Wastewater Treatment:
Region manages sewage collection & disposal systems at Holland Creek (Kinbasket Sewage Treatment Plant), Edgewater; Region operates water systems in Elko, Moyie, Windermere, Timber Ridge, Holland Creek & Edgewater
Other Initiatives:
Paint & used oil depots across the region

Fraser Valley
#1, 45950 Cheam Ave.
Chilliwack, BC V2P 1N6
604-702-5000
Fax: 604-792-9684
Toll Free Phone: 1-800-528-0061
info@fvrd.bc.ca
www.fvrd.com
Population: 277,593 *Census Year:* 2011
Number of Households: 90,799
Tareq Islam, P.Eng., Director, Engineering, 604-702-5026, email: tislam@fvrd.bc.ca

Lance Lilley, Planner, Watershed, email: llilley@fvrd.bc.ca
Waste Management:
Waste collection & recycling services in electoral areas A, B, C, F & G & several First Nations Reserves responsibility of region; Collection of recyclables in certain areas contracted to R&R Recycling, 604/869-3328
Number of landfill sites: 1
Solid Waste Disposal Fees: $163.50/tonne (residents outside Electoral Area A)
Transfer Station(s): Sunshine Valley Station; Harrison Mills Station, 14050 Chehalis Forest Service Rd.; Hemlock Valley Station, Laurel Rd.; Sylve
Recycling: Both Curbside & Depot; Depots: Chaumox Landfill, North Bend, Electoral Area A; Sunshine Valley Transfer Station, Electoral Area B; Harrison Mills Transfer Station, 14050 Chehalis Forest Service Rd., Electoral Area C; Sylvester Rd. Transfer Station, Electoral Area F
Composters subsidized: Yes
Water & Wastewater Treatment:
Operatation of 10 water systems & 3 sewer systems responsibility of region's engineering services department
Other Initiatives:
Free stores at 3 transfer stations for exchange of used items; Air quality monitoring

Fraser-Fort George

155 George St.
Prince George, BC V2L 1P8
250-960-4400
Toll Free Phone: 1-800-667-1959
district@rdffg.bc.ca
www.rdffg.bc.ca
Population: 91,879 *Census Year:* 2011
Number of Households: 38,897
Waste Management:
Responsibility of the regional district; municipalities (Prince George, MacKenzie, McBride & Valemount) carry out the waste collection.
Number of landfill sites: 6
Solid Waste Disposal Fees: $42/tonne
Recycling: Depot locations: Prince George, MacKenzie, McBride, Dunster & Valemount
Hazardous Waste Depot or Facility: Household depot location Product Care Assn. Depot, 1922 First Ave., Prince George.
Composters subsidized: Yes
Other Initiatives:
Upgrading or closing of landfill sites. \Swap Shed\"" waste exchange areas. Industrial, commercial & institutional recycling processing plant, 1015 Great St., Prince George is operated by Metro Materials. Developed \""Prince George Air Quality Management Plan\"".""

Kitimat-Stikine

#300, 4545 Lazelle Ave.
Terrace, BC V8G 4E1
250-615-6100
Fax: 250-635-9222
Toll Free Phone: 1-800-663-3208
info@rdks.bc.ca
www.rdks.bc.ca
Population: 37,361 *Census Year:* 2011
Number of Households: 16,340
Andrew Webber, Manager, Planning & Economic Development, email: awebber@rdks.bc.ca
Roger Tooms, Manager, Works & Services, email: rtooms@rdks.bc.ca
Waste Management:
Number of landfill sites: 6*Landfill Capacity:* 5-30 years
Solid Waste Disposal Fees: $12.50 - $50.00 (truck volume)
Special Bans/by-laws: Special wastes, waste oil, ozone-depleting substances & tires banned from landfill
Hazardous Waste Depot or Facility: Terrace Bottle Depot, Terrace BC
Composters subsidized: Yes
Water & Wastewater Treatment:
Thornhill Water System; Queensway Sewage System
Other Initiatives:
Re-use area at landfill where items such as lawnmowers, bicycles, small engines etc. are available for others to salvage; Help Minimize Waste; Making Compost brochures on www.rdks.bc.ca; Kelse Lake/Jackpine Flats liquid waste management plan

Kootenay Boundary

#202, 843 Rossland Ave.
Trail, BC V1R 4S8
250-368-9148
Fax: 250-368-3990
Toll Free Phone: 1-800-355-7352 (BC only)
Population: 31,138 *Census Year:* 2011
Number of Households: 15,733
Alan Stanley, Director, Environmental Services, email: astanley@rdkb.com
Gerry Gardner, Director, Finance, email: ggardner@rdkb.com
Mark Andison, Director, Planning & Development, email: mandison@rdkb.com
Dale Green, Manager, Information Services, email: dgreen@rdkb.com
Waste Management:
Collection responsibility of the member municipalities; regional district responsible for recycling & disposal
Number of landfill sites: 5
Solid Waste Disposal Fees: $60/tonne or $9/cubic metre; fees in effect at all sites
Recycling: Both Curbside & Depot; 16 depots across the district
Special Bans/by-laws: Ban on cardboard, paper fibre, beverage containers, all recyclable glass, metal, plastics, compostable yard & garden waste in effect
Hazardous Waste Depot or Facility: Trail, Grand Forks, Greenwood, Beaverdell
Composters subsidized: Yes
Water & Wastewater Treatment:
Water & wastewater treatment contracted to City of Trail's Columbia Pollution Control Centre, 250/368-3822
Other Initiatives:
Increase in tipping fees in 2006

Metro Vancouver

4330 Kingsway
Burnaby, BC V5H 4G8
604-432-6200
Fax: 604-436-6901
icentre@metrovancouver.org
www.metrovancouver.org
Population: 2,313,328 *Census Year:* 2011
Number of Households: 786,277
Johnny Carline, Chief Administrative Officer/Commissioner
Jim Rusnak, Chief Financial Officer
Tim Jervis, P.Eng., Manager, Engineering & Construction
Doug Humphris, P.Eng., Manager, Operations & Maintenance
Mitch Sokalski, Acting Manager, Regional Parks
Waste Management:
One mass burn MSW incinerator with energy recovery
Number of landfill sites: 2*Landfill Capacity:* 5-10 & 30+ years
Solid Waste Disposal Fees: $65/tonne
Transfer Station(s): Six waste transfer facilities
Special Bans/by-laws: Disposal bans on gypsum, used oil filters, corrugated cardboard; voluntary Code of Practice for source separation of designated recyclable materials, waste audits & waste reduction plans for all businesses
Hazardous Waste Depot or Facility: No
Water & Wastewater Treatment:
District operates 5 wastewater treatment plants

Mount Waddington

P.O. Box 729
2044 McNeill Rd.
Port McNeill, BC V0N 2R0
250-956-3301
Fax: 250-956-3232
Alternate Phone: 250-956-3161
info@rdmw.bc.ca
www.rdmw.bc.ca
Population: 11,506 *Census Year:* 2011
Number of Households: 6,012
Joe MacKenzie, Treasurer
Neil Smith, Manager, Economic Development/Parks
Patrick Donaghy, Manager, Operations
Jeff Long, Manager, Planning
Bonnie Danyk, Financial Clerk
Paddy Hinton, Supervisor, Parks
Waste Management:
Contracted to 4B Enterprises
Number of landfill sites: 1*Landfill Capacity:* 20 years
Solid Waste Disposal Fees: $2/can or bag (residential), $80/tonne (construction, demolition, woodwaste)
Clean Fill Fee: Yes; $5/tonne
Recycling: Depot; Depot 7-Mile Landfill & Recycling Facility
Hazardous Waste Depot or Facility: Household waste 7-Mile Landfill & Recycling; BC Paint Care Drop-Off & Exchange.
Water & Wastewater Treatment:
Region administers sewer & water services in rural communities. Sewage collection & treatment are provided in: Coal Harbour, Quatsino First Nation, Sointula, Woss, Quatse Lake. Contracted to PG Enterprises 250/949-7075.
Other Initiatives:
Biosolids composted & reused. Sale of reusable items & construction materials at 7-Mile site.

Nanaimo

6300 Hammond Bay Rd.
Nanaimo, BC V9T 6N2
250-390-4111
Fax: 250-390-4163
Toll Free Phone: 1-877-607-4111
corpsrv@rdn.bc.ca
www.rdn.bc.ca
Population: 146,574 *Census Year:* 2011
Number of Households: 58,238
Neil Connelly, General Manager, Community Services, 250-390-6510
John Finnie, General Manager, Regional & Community Utilities, 250-390-6560
Wendy Idema, Acting General Manager, Finance & Information Services, 250-390-4111, email: widema@rdn.bc.ca
Tom Osborne, General Manager, Recreation & Parks Services, email: recparks@rdn.bc.ca
Paul Thorkelsson, General Manager, Development Services, 250-390-6530
Dennis Trudeau, General Manager, Transportation & Solid Waste, 250-390-6565
Waste Management:
Number of landfill sites: 1
Solid Waste Disposal Fees: $95/tonne (solid waste); $190/tonne (controlled waste)
Transfer Station(s): Church Road Transfer Station, 860 Church Rd., Parksville
Recycling: Both Curbside & Depot
Composters subsidized: Yes
Water & Wastewater Treatment:
Region operates the following Water Local Service Areas: Nanoose, Fairwinds, Arbutus Park, West Bay, Driftwood, Madrona, Wall Beach, San Pareil, Decourcey, Englishman River, Melrose Terrace, Surfside & French Creek; Wastewater treatment plants in the region: Greater Nanaimo Water Pollution Control Centre, French Creek Water Pollution Control Centre, Nanoose Water Pollution Control Centre, Duke Point Water Pollution Control Centre
Other Initiatives:
Garbage limitations; Landfill project to reduce greenhouse gases; Food waste diversion program; Organics diversion strategy; Directory available of recycling depots throughout region

North Okanagan

9848 Aberdeen Rd.
Coldstream, BC V1B 2K9
250-550-3700
Fax: 250-550-3701
info@nord.ca
www.nord.ca
Population: 81,237 *Census Year:* 2011
Number of Households: 31,977
Leah Mellott, Acting General Manager, Corporate & Electoral Area Services, 250-550-3722, email: leah.mellott@rdno.ca
Al McNiven, General Manager, Greater Vernon Parks, Recreation & Culture, 250-550-3664
Ron Baker, Manager, Comunity Protective Services, email: doug.buchholz@rdno.ca
Nicole Kohnert, Regional Manager, Engineering Services, 250-550-3674, email: nicole.kohnert@rdno.ca
Dale Danallanko, Manager, Recycling & Disposal Facilities Operations, 250-550-3744, email: dale.danallanko@rdno.ca
Al Cotsworth, Manager, Utilities, 250-550-3674, email: al.cotsworth@rdno.ca
Renee Clark, Manager, Water Quality, 250-550-3747, email: renee.clark@rdno.ca
Greg Routley, Planner, Development Services, 250-550-3734, email: greg.routley@rdno.ca
Marnie Skobalski, Planner, Development Services, 250-550-3737, email: marnie.skobalski@rdno.ca
Waste Management:
Number of landfill sites: 4

Solid Waste Disposal Fees: $57/tonne; $22.25/cubic metre compacted; $7.40/cubic metre loose
Transfer Station(s): King Fisher at Mabel Lake & Silver Star Mountain
Recycling: Both Curbside & Depot; Recycling & Disposal Facilities in Greater Vernon, Armstrong/Spallumcheen, Lumby & Cherryville
Special Bans/by-laws: Recyclable Materials Separation Bylaw; Open Burning/Fire Regulation Bylaw
Hazardous Waste Depot or Facility: Chasers Bottle Depot, 4612 - 27 St., Vernon
Composters subsidized: Yes
Water & Wastewater Treatment:
Silver Star Water Utility; Whitevale Water Utility; Grinwold Water Utility
Other Initiatives:
Recyclable glass program; Bagged organics programs; Annual household hazardous waste round-up

Okanagan-Similkameen
101 Martin St.
Penticton, BC V2A 5J9
250-492-0237
Toll Free Phone: 1-877-610-3737
info@rdos.bc.ca
www.rdos.bc.ca
Population: 80,742 *Census Year:* 2011
Number of Households: 36,824
Mark Woods, Manager, Community Services, 250-490-4132, email: mwoods@rdos.bc.ca
Donna Butler, Manager, Development Services, 250-490-4109, email: dbutler@rdos.bc.ca
Warren Everton, BA, CMA, Manager, Finance, 250-490-4105
Patty Tracy, Manager, Human Resources, 250-490-4138, email: pderkach@rdos.bc.ca
Tim Bouwmeester, Manager, Information Services
Doug French, P.Eng., Manager, Public Works, 250-490-4103
Waste Management:
Collection of recyclables contracted to OK Environmental, 250/492-4707; Waste collection contracted to Canadian Waste, 250/492-0089
Number of landfill sites: 4
Solid Waste Disposal Fees: $43/tonne
Recycling: Both Curbside & Depot; Main recycling depots at the following landfill sites: Campbell Mountain, Okanagan Falls, Keremeos, Oliver
Water & Wastewater Treatment:
Region responsible for the following water systems: Apex; Faulder; Naramato
Other Initiatives:
User pay principle for garbage collection services; Environmental education programs; Okanagan Falls landfill in process of becoming a Regional Service Area Centre for demolition, land clearing & construction waste

Peace River
P.O. Box 810
1981 Alaska Ave.
Dawson Creek, BC V1G 4H8
250-784-3200
Fax: 250-784-3201
Toll-Free Phone: 1-800-670-7773
prrd.dc@prrd.bc.ca
prrd.bc.ca
Population: 60,082 *Census Year:* 2011
Number of Households: 22,755
Bruce Simard, General Manager, Development Services, 250-784-3204
Shannon Anderson, General Manager, Environmental Services, 250-784-3203
Trish Morgan, Manager, Community Services, 250-784-3218
Jeff Rahn, Manager, Solid Waste Services, 250-784-3226
Waste Management:
Contracted to Canadian Waste, 250/262-7183 & DC Waste Disposal, 250/784-3333
Number of landfill sites: 4*Landfill Capacity:* 8 years
Solid Waste Disposal Fees: $30/tonne or $2/cubic metre
Clean Fill Fee: No
Recycling: Depot; Depots at Dawson Creek, Fort St. John, Chetwynd, Tumbler Ridge
Hazardous Waste Depot or Facility: No
Water & Wastewater Treatment:
Wastewater treatment plants: Kelly Lake, Rolla, Fort St. John Airport Water & Sewer Utility, Charlie Lake Sewer Utility, Chilton Subdivision Sewer Utility

Other Initiatives:
Solid waste management plan; implementation of a regional disposal & reduction system

Powell River
5776 Marine Ave.
Powell River, BC V8A 2M4
604-483-3231
Fax: 604-483-2229
administration@powellriverrd.bc.ca
www.powellriverrd.bc.ca
Population: 19,906 *Census Year:* 2011
Number of Households: 10,286
Malcolm Fraser, Chief Administrative Officer
Sean McGinn, Manager, Community Services
Linda Greenan, Manager, Financial Services
Shawn Gullette, Foreman, Parks & Properties
Don Turner, Senior Planner
Other Initiatives:
Myrtle Pond Water Study; Texada Island Shoreline Hazards Study; Savary Island Dune & Shoreline Study

Skeena-Queen Charlotte
100 - 1st Ave. East
Prince Rupert, BC V8J 1A6
250-624-2002
Fax: 250-627-8493
Toll Free Phone: 1-888-301-2002
musgrave@sqcrd.bc.ca
www.sqcrd.bc.ca
Population: 18,784 *Census Year:* 2011
Number of Households: 9,500
Waste Management:
All aspects of waste management on the Queen Charlotte Islands & recycling in all areas responsibility of the regional district
Number of landfill sites: 1
Transfer Station(s): 3 island transfer stations
Recycling: Depot; Depot locations: Prince Rupert Envirocenter, Port Edward Drop-Off station, 2 mainland urban drop-off stations, 3 island drop-off locations with limited recycling
Other Initiatives:
Waste management user fees policies; Waste collection limit for each island household; Agricultural Land Reserve, Queen Charlotte Islands; Recycling education & training

Squamish-Lillooet
P.O. Box 219
1350 Aster St.
Pemberton, BC V0N 2L0
604-894-6371
Fax: 604-894-6526
Toll Free Phone: 1-800-298-7753
info@slrd.bc.ca
www.slrd.bc.ca
Population: 38,171 *Census Year:* 2011
Number of Households: 18,649
Steven Olmstead, Manager, Planning & Development, 604-894-6371
Janis Netzel, Director, Utilities & Environmental Services, 604-894-6371, email: rdsouza@slrd.bc.ca
Waste Management:
Number of landfill sites: 3
Solid Waste Disposal Fees: $65-80/tonne & $10/cubic metre
Clean Fill Fee: Yes
Transfer Station(s): 3 sites
Water & Wastewater Treatment:
Devine Water System, D'Arcy; Pemberton North Water System, Pemberton; Bralorne Water System, Bralorne Sewage System, Bralorne; Furry Creek Water & Sewage System, Furry Creek.
Other Initiatives:
Squamish Coast demonstration garden; Subsidized vermibins, with training session; 3Rs educator community workshops, plus composting & household hazardous waste community outreach programs; Composting facility feasibility study for southern region; Study to reduce construction & demolition waste; Application to construct new transfer station & recycling centre, south of Pemberton

Strathcona
#301, 990 Cedar St.
Campbell River, BC V9W 7Z8
250-830-6700
Fax: 250-830-6710
Toll Free Phone: 1-877-830-2990
administration@strathconard.ca
www.strathconard.ca
Population: 43,252 *Census Year:* 2011

Sunshine Coast
1975 Field Rd.
Sechelt, BC V0N 3A1
604-885-6800
Fax: 604-885-7909
Toll Free Phone: 1-800-687-5753
info@scrd.ca
www.scrd.ca
Population: 28,619 *Census Year:* 2011
Number of Households: 14,444
John France, Chief Administrative Officer
Randy Brown, Manager, Human Resources, email: randy.brown@scrd.ca
Angie Legault, Manager, Legislative Services
David Rafael, Senior Planner, 604-885-6804, email: david.rafael@scrd.ca
Waste Management:
SCRD contracts for residential garbage collection
Number of landfill sites: 2
Solid Waste Disposal Fees: $60/tonne
Recycling: Depot; Sechelt & Pender Harbour Landfills offer recycling programs
Water & Wastewater Treatment:
Region operates & maintains sewage treatment facilities in West Howe Sound, Elphinstone, Halfmoon Bay & Pender Harbour; Water purification & treatment facilities are at Chapman Creek & Gray Creek
Other Initiatives:
1 garbage can/household/week; Fee for extra garbage; After July 2002 all toilets installed in SCRD water service area meet low-flow requirements; Water Efficiency Award Program for non-residential buildings; Free mulch available from yard waste drop off at landfills; Paint Care Depot & Product Care Depot at Sechelt Landfill site; Sharesheds at Sechelt & Pender Harbour Landfills; Annual Spring Cleanup program

Thompson-Nicola
#300, 465 Victoria St.
Kamloops, BC V2C 2A9
250-377-8673
Fax: 250-372-5048
Toll Free Phone: 1-877-377-8673
admin@tnrd.bc.ca
www.tnrd.bc.ca
Population: 128,473 *Census Year:* 2011
Number of Households: 52,190
Greg Toma, Chief Administrative Officer, 250-377-8673, email: gtoma@tnrd.bc.ca
Vicci Weller, Executive Director, Film Commission, 250-377-7058, email: vweller@tnrd.bc.ca
Lyle Huntley, Clerk/Director, Corporate & Community Services, 250-377-7052, email: lhuntley@tnrd.bc.ca
Regina Sadilkova, Director, Development Services, 250-377-7060, email: rsadilkova@tnrd.bc.ca
Peter Hughes, Director, Environmental Services, email: phughes@tnrd.bc.ca
Sukh Gill, Director/Deputy Administrator, Finance & Information Technology, 250-377-8673, email: sgill@tnrd.bc.ca
Kevin Kierans, Director, Libraries, 250-374-8866, email: kevink@tnrdlib.bc.ca
Ron Popoff, Manager, Building Inspection Services, 250-377-7062, email: rpopoff@tnrd.bc.ca
Don May, Manager, Environmental Health Services, 250-377-7057, email: dmay@tnrd.bc.ca
Bob Finley, Manager, Planning Services, 250-377-7062, email: bfinley@tnrd.bc.ca
Arden Bolton, Manager, Utility Services, 250-377-7056, email: abolton@tnrd.bc.ca
Waste Management:
Responsible for waste management in the regional district, except for the City of Kamloops. Region has 32 container sites. Five of the landfill sites & twelve of the container sites are controlled access.
Number of landfill sites: 5
Solid Waste Disposal Fees: $31-$103/load, depending on size of load (demolition & land clearing debris only)
Special Bans/by-laws: Landfills not authorized to accept special wastes, biomedical wastes, waste oil or raw sewage

Major Municipalities in British Columbia

City of Abbotsford
32315 South Fraser Way
Abbotsford, BC V2T 1W7
604-853-2281
Fax: 604-853-1934
Toll Free Phone: 1-866-853-2281
www.abbotsford.ca; twitter.com/City_Abbotsford
Population: 133,497 *Census Year:* 2011
Number of Households: 41,352
Frank Pizzuto, City Manager, 604-864-5501, email: fpizzuto@abbotsford.ca
Jim Gordon, P.Eng., General Manager, Engineering & Regional Utilities, 604-864-5514, email: eng-info@abbotsford.ca
Mark Taylor, General Manager, Parks, Recreation & Culture, 604-859-3134, email: prcoffice@abbotsford.ca
Jay Teichroeb, General Manager, Economic Development/Development Services, 604-864-5586, email: econdev@abbotsford.ca
Karen Sinclair, Director, Strategic Planning & Business Improvement, 604-865-5640, email: ksinclair@abbotsford.ca
Don Beer, Fire Chief, 604-853-3566, email: fire-info@abbotsford.ca
Waste Management:
Waste hauled to Cache Creek landfill
Transfer Station(s): Matsqui Transfer Station, 33621 Valley Rd., operated under contract with the Greater Vancouver Regional District.
Recycling: Both Curbside & Depot; Abbotsford Mission Recycling Depot, 33670 Valley Rd.; curbside collection, with no limit on number of Blue Bags, & no sorting of recyclables required; yard waste is collected on a biweekly basis (to be contained in kraft paper yard waste bags only)
Hazardous Waste Depot or Facility: Household hazardous waste can be handled at Abbotsford Mission Recycling Depot, & other locations in Abbotsford which are designated as Product Care Paint Plus Facilities
Compost Sites: No *Composters subsidized:* Yes
Water & Wastewater Treatment:
Wastewater treatment is the responsibility of Fraser Valley Regional District; Small urban area serviced by Clearbrook Waterworks, a private utility
Other Initiatives:
Food waste collection pilot program launched in Dec., 2009

City of Burnaby
4949 Canada Way
Burnaby, BC V5G 1M2
604-294-7944
postmaster@burnaby.ca
www.city.burnaby.bc.ca
Population: 223,218 *Census Year:* 2011
Number of Households: 80,130
Robert H. Moncur, City Manager, 604-294-7101
Chad Turpin, Deputy City Manager
Lambert Chu, Director, Engineering, 604-294-7460
D. Ellenwood, Director, Parks, Recreation & Cultural Services, 604-294-7450, email: parks@burnaby.ca
Basil Luksun, Director, Planning & Building, 604-294-7400, Fax: 604-294-7220
Patrick Shek, P.Eng, Chief Building Inspector
Bob Cook, Fire Chief, 604-294-7195
Waste Management:
Waste collection responsibility of city; Disposal responsibility of Greater Vancouver Regional District
Transfer Station(s): Still Creek, Burnaby
Recycling: Both Curbside & Depot; Depot located at Still Creek
Special Bans/by-laws: Watercourse bylaw prohibits fouling, destructing or impeding watercourses in Burnaby; Pesticide notification bylaw
Hazardous Waste Depot or Facility: Still Creek Depot, Burnaby
Compost Sites: Yes *Composters subsidized:* Yes
Water & Wastewater Treatment:
Water provided by Greater Vancouver Regional District & distributed by the City; Wastewater collection by the city, treatment by Greater Vancouver Regional District
Other Initiatives:
Alternative stormwater management approaches; watershed-based planning initiatives/stormwater management plans (Brunette Basin, Byrne Creek, Stoney Creek); management/area plans & OPCs with comprehensive environmental sections; \streamkeepers\"" projects; urban noise remediation; State of the Environment Report; integrated pest management; Environment & Waste Management Committee""

City of Campbell River
301 St. Ann's Rd.
Campbell River, BC V9W 4C7
250-286-5700
info@campbellriver.ca
www.campbellriver.ca
Population: 31,186 *Census Year:* 2011
Number of Households: 12,128
Laura Ciarniello, General Manager, Corporate Services, 250-286-5759, email: laura.ciarniello@campbellriver.ca
Ross Milnthorp, General Manager, Parks, Recreation & Culture, 250-286-5797, email: ross.milnthorp@campbellriver.ca
Dave Morris, General Manager, Facilities & Supply Management, 250-286-5739, email: dave.morris@campbellriver.ca
Ron Neufeld, General Manager, Operations Services, 250-286-5765, email: ron.neufeld@campbellriver.ca
Andrew Bailey, Manager, Facilities - Property, 250-286-5709, email: andrew.bailey@campbellriver.ca
Jason Hartley, Manager, Capital Works, 250-286-5790, email: jason.hartley@campbellriver.ca
Dean Spry, Fire Chief, 250-286-6266, email: dean.spry@campbellriver.ca
Waste Management:
Waste collection contracted to International Paper Industries (250/286-0211); Recycling & landfill responsibility of Comox Strathcona Regional District
Number of landfill sites: 1
Solid Waste Disposal Fees: Schedule depending on type of waste (from no fee to $350/tonne)
Clean Fill Fee: No
Recycling: Depot; Private & regional district depots
Special Bans/by-laws: Restrictions on burning; sanitary sewer source control by-law; cardboard disposal surcharge
Hazardous Waste Depot or Facility: Privately run depot
Composters subsidized: Yes
Water & Wastewater Treatment:
One re-chlorination station; Two wastewater treatment plants: Industrial Park Treatment Plant (lagoon); Norm Wood Environmental Centre (two secondary oxidation ditches with secondary clarifiers)
Other Initiatives:
Biosolids reuse project; Hybrid poplar plantation on land at Norm Wood Environmental Centre; 2005 plan changes to water bylaw to place more emphasis on water conservation

City of Chilliwack
8550 Young Rd
Chilliwack, BC V2P 8A4
604-792-9311
Fax: 604-795-8443
www.chilliwack.com
Population: 77,936 *Census Year:* 2011
Number of Households: 25,119
Janet Demarcke, Manager, Environmental Services, 604-792-2907, Fax: 604-795-8443
Erik Leidekker, Manager, Information Technology, 604-793-2912, Fax: 604-793-1812
Rod Sanderson, Manager, Transportation & Drainage, 604-793-2907
Karen Stanton, Manager, Long Range Planning, 604-793-2906
Paul Whitehouse, Manager, Purchasing, 604-793-2809, Fax: 604-795-2963
David Blain, Director, Engineering, 604-793-2907, Fax: 604-793-2285
Kurt Houlden, Director, Planning & Strategic Initiatives, 604-793-2906
Glen MacPherson, Director, Public Works, 604-792-2810, Fax: 604-793-2997
Gordon Pederson, Director, Parks, Recreation & Culture, 604-793-2996, Fax: 604-793-8443
Rick Ryall, Fire Chief, 604-792-8713, Fax: 604-702-5087
Waste Management:
Municipality responsible for waste management. Waste collection contracted to Waste Management of Canada Corp. Household hazardous waste handled by BC Product Care Association at Chilliwack Bottle Depot.
Number of landfill sites: 1
Solid Waste Disposal Fees: $73/tonne; $115/tonne (for gypsum)
Recycling: Depot; Municipal Recycling Depot; Green Bin Recycling Depots
Hazardous Waste Depot or Facility: Annual household hazardous waste day
Compost Sites: Yes *Composters subsidized:* Yes
Water & Wastewater Treatment:
Water Pollution Control Plant, 44280 Wolfe Rd.
Other Initiatives:
Adopt a River & Adopt a Road programs; Christmas Tree Disposal & Spring Pitch-In campaigns

City of Colwood
3300 Wishart Rd.
Victoria, BC V9C 1R1
250-478-5541
Fax: 250-478-7516
generalinquiry@colwood.ca
colwood.ca
Population: 16,093 *Census Year:* 2011
Number of Households: 4,966
Dan Brazier, Manager, Public Works, 250-474-4133, Fax: 250-474-6977, email: dbrazier@colwood.ca
Alan Haldenby, Director, Planning, email: ahaldenby@colwood.ca
Flo Pikula, Chief Building Inspector, email: fpikula@colwood.ca
Russ Cameron, Fire Chief, 250-478-8321, Fax: 250-478-8032, email: rcameron@colwood.bc.ca
Waste Management:
Responsibility of Capital Regional District
Recycling: Curbside
Water & Wastewater Treatment:
Responsibility of Capital Regional District

City of Comox
Town Hall
1809 Beaufort Ave.
Comox, BC V9M 1R9
250-339-2202
Fax: 250-339-7110
town@comox.ca
www.comox.ca
Population: 13,627 *Census Year:* 2011
Number of Households: 4,873
Richard Kanigan, Chief Administrative Officer
Donald Jacquest, Director, Finance
Jim Stevenson, Director, Recreation, 250-339-2255
Allan Fraser, Superintendent, Parks, 250-339-2421
Glenn Westendorp, Superintendent, Public Works, 250-339-5410, Fax: 250-890-0698
Marvin Kamenz, Municipal Planner, 250-339-1118
Gord Schreiner, Fire Chief, 250-339-2432, Fax: 250-339-1988
Waste Management:
Waste collection & collection of recyclables responsibility of town; Compost site located at town's Public Works Yard; Waste disposal responsibility of Comox-Strathcona Regional District; Pidgeon Lake Regional Landfill is used
Recycling: Curbside
Composters subsidized: Yes
Water & Wastewater Treatment:
Responsibility of Comox-Strathcona Regional District
Other Initiatives:
Comox Return Centre for beverage containers & paint & paint products

City of Coquitlam
3000 Guildford Way
Coquitlam, BC V3B 7N2
604-927-3000
feedback@coquitlam.ca
www.coquitlam.ca
Population: 126,456 *Census Year:* 2011
Number of Households: 41,481
Peter Steblin, City Manager, 604-927-2006, email: managersoffice@coquitlam.ca
Lori MacKay, General Manager, Parks, Recreation & Culture Services, 604-927-3538, email: prcs@coquitlam.ca
Jim McIntyre, General Manager, Planning & Development, 604-927-3400, Fax: 604-927-3405, email: planninganddevelopment@coquitlam.ca
Bill Susak, General Manager, Engineering & Public Works, 604-927-2504, Fax: 604-927-3505, email: engineeringandpublicworks@coquitlam.ca
Karen Basi, Manager, Emergency Programs, 604-927-3481
Michelle Hunt, Manager, Corporate Planning, 604-927-3531, Fax: 604-927-3015
Waste Management:
Responsibility of Greater Vancouver Regional District; Collection contracted to International Paper Industries (IPI)

Solid Waste Disposal Fees: $65/tonne
Compost Sites: Yes
Water & Wastewater Treatment:
Responsibility of Greater Vancouver Regional District

City of Courtenay
830 Cliffe Ave.
Courtenay, BC V9N 2J7
250-334-4441
Fax: 250-334-4241
info@courtenay.ca
www.courtenay.ca
Population: 24,099 *Census Year:* 2011
Number of Households: 8,549
Peter Crawford, Director, Planning Services, email: planning@courtenay.ca
Kevin Lagan, Director, Operational Services
Tillie Manthey, Director, Financial Services, email: finance@courtenay.ca
Lis Pedersen, Director, Human Resources
John Ward, Director, Corporate Services
Randy Wiwchar, Director, Community Services
Waste Management:
Responsibility of the Regional District of Comox Strathcona; Collection contracted to West Coast Waste, 250/336-2172
Recycling: Curbside
Water & Wastewater Treatment:
Responsibility of the Regional District of Comox Strathcona
Other Initiatives:
Tree management & protection; Weekly garbage limit is a 121 litre can

City of Cranbrook
40 - 10th Ave. South
Cranbrook, BC V1C 2M8
250-426-4211
Fax: 250-426-4026
Toll Free Phone: 1-800-728-2726
info@cranbrook.ca
www.cranbrook.ca
Population: 19,319 *Census Year:* 2011
Number of Households: 7,872
Roy Hales, Director, Corporate Services, email: hales@cranbrook.ca
Joe McGowan, Director, Public Works, email: mcgowan@cranbrook.ca
Chris Zettel, Corporate Communications Officer, email: zettel@cranbrook.ca
Jamie Hodge, City Engineer, email: hodge@cranbrook.ca
Wayne Price, Coordinator, Emergency Program, email: price@cranbrook.ca
Waste Management:
Responsibility of the Regional District of East Kootenay
Water & Wastewater Treatment:
Cranbrook Water Treatment Plant

City of Dawson Creek
P.O. Box 150
10105 - 12A St.
Dawson Creek, BC V1G 4G4
250-784-3600
Fax: 250-782-3203
General Fax: 250-782-3352
admin@dawsoncreek.ca
www.dawsoncreek.ca
Population: 11,583 *Census Year:* 2011
Number of Households: 4,690
Greg Dobrowolski, Manager, Special Projects, 250-784-3619, email: gdobrowolski@dawsoncreek.ca
Chante Patterson Elden, Manager, recreation Facilities, 250-782-2229, email: celden@dawsoncreek.ca
Darcy Perrin, Manager, Parks Facilities, 250-784-3632, email: rharmon@dawsoncreek.ca
Gordon (Shorty) Smith, Fire Chief, 250-784-3635, email: shorty@dawsoncreek.ca
Waste Management:
Waste collection contracted to Canadian Waste, 250/782-6488; Landfill the responsibility of the Peace River Regional District; Recycling handled by Recycle Plus
Water & Wastewater Treatment:
City of Dawson Creek Water Treatment Plant; Wastewater treatment plant

City of Fort St. John
10631 - 100 St.
Fort St John, BC V1J 3Z5
250-787-8150
Fax: 250-787-8181
info@fortstjohn.ca
www.fortstjohn.ca
Population: 18,609 *Census Year:* 2011
Number of Households: 6,385
Sarah Cockerill, Director, Community Services, email: scockerill@fortstjohn.ca
Don Demers, Director, Public Works & Utilities, email: ddemers@fortstjohn.ca
Grace Fika, Director, Corporate Affairs & Human Resources, email: gfika@fortstjohn.ca
Horacio Galanti, Director, Planning & Engineering, email: hgalanti@fortstjohn.ca
Jim Rogers, Director, Facilities & Protective Services, email: jrogers@forststjohn.ca
Laura Sanders, Director, Finance, email: lsanders@forststjohn.ca
Victor Shopland, Director, Infrastructure & Capital Works, email: vshopland@forststjohn.ca
Fred Burrows, Fire Chief, 250-785-4333, Fax: 250-785-0080, email: fburrows@fortstjohn.ca
Waste Management:
Waste management responsibility of Peace River Regional District; Waste collection responsibility of City
Water & Wastewater Treatment:
South Sewage Treatment Lagoons; North Sewage Treatment Lagoons; Fort St. John Water Treatment Plant & Bulk Water Station, West Bypass Rd.
Other Initiatives:
Creation of Liquid Waste Management Plan

City of Kamloops
City Hall
7 Victoria St. West
Kamloops, BC V2C 1A2
250-828-3311
info@kamloops.ca
www.kamloops.ca
Population: 85,678 *Census Year:* 2011
Number of Households: 32,076
Randy H. Diehl, Chief Administrative Officer, 250-828-3498, email: rdiehl@kamloops.ca
David Duckworth, Director, Public Works & Sustainability, 250-828-3348, email: publicworks@kamloops.ca
Byron McCorkell, Director, Parks, Recreation & Culture Services, 250-828-3400, email: parks@kamloops.ca
David A. Trawin, Director, Development & Engineering Services, 250-828-2561, email: devadmin@kamloops.ca
Neill Moroz, Fire Chief, Fire & Rescue Services, 250-372-5131, Fax: 250-372-1447, email: fireinfo@kamloops.ca
Waste Management:
Number of landfill sites: 3
Solid Waste Disposal Fees: $25/tonne (loads greater than 250 kgs)
Clean Fill Fee: No
Recycling: Depot; Mission Flats Recycling Service; Recycling bins located throughout city
Special Bans/by-laws: Backyard burning ban
Hazardous Waste Depot or Facility: Mission Flats landfill site, Consumer Product Stewardship Program
Composters subsidized: Yes
Water & Wastewater Treatment:
Kamloops Centre for Water Quality water treatment plant; Kamloops Wastewater Treatment Centre
Other Initiatives:
Partners for Climate Protection Program; TravelSmart Plan; WaterSmart Program

City of Kelowna
City Hall
1435 Water St.
Kelowna, BC V1Y 1J4
250-469-8500
Fax: 250-862-3399
ask@kelowna.ca
www.kelowna.ca
Population: 117,312 *Census Year:* 2011
Number of Households: 41,604
Ronald Mattiussi, City Manager
Jim Paterson, General Manager, Community Sustainability
Signe Bagh, Director, Policy & Planning
Mo Bayat, Director, Development Services
William J. Berry, Director, Design & Construction Services
Randy Cleveland, Director, Infrastructure Planning
Charlene Covington, Director, Human Resources
Joe Creron, Director, Civic Operations
Jim Gabriel, Director, Recreation & Cultural Services
Shelley Gambacort, Director, Land Use Management
Doug Gilchrist, Director, Real Estate & Building Services
Rob Mayne, Director, Corporate Services
Ron W. Westlake, Director, Regional Services
Steve Kinsey, Fire Chief
Waste Management:
Glenmore Landfill accepts recyclables, organic waste, household and commercial waste, yard waste, tires, metals, wood, concrete and asphalt. The facility uses a state-of-the-art microturbine, the first of its kind in British Columbia, to convert gas into electricity for use at the landfill
Number of landfill sites: 2
Solid Waste Disposal Fees: $55/tonne
Recycling: Depot; Recycling bin system, with no sorting of recyclables required; automated curbside collection. The Regional Waste Reduction Office oversees recycling, yard waste, and garbage collection, in cooperation with the Regional Districts of Kelowna, Peachland, Lake Country and Westide. Depots located at Kirschner Road Depot, 1988 Kirchner Rd.; Glenmore Landfill, 2105 Glenmore Rd.
Water & Wastewater Treatment:
Kelowna Joint Water Committee includes city's 5 major water suppliers, 250/861-4200; Kelowna Wastewater Treatment Facility, Raymer Ave., 250/469-8502; Bardenpho Wastewater Treatment Facility
Other Initiatives:
Ogogrow composting program; Christmas tree drop-off; Water smart program: watersmart@look.ca; Wetland protection; Environmental education & events

City of Langford
877 Goldstream Ave., 2nd Fl.
Victoria, BC V9B 2X8
250-478-7882
www.cityoflangford.ca
Population: 29,228 *Census Year:* 2011
Number of Households: 7,215
John Manson, City Engineer
Matthew Baldwin, City Planner
Waste Management:
Waste collectors hired by property owners; Waste management responsibility of Capital Regional District
Water & Wastewater Treatment:
Sewer construction & maintenance responsibility of City Engineering Department; Water & wastewater treatment responsibility of Capital Regional District

City of Langley
20399 Douglas Cres.
Langley, BC V3A 4B3
604-514-2800
Fax: 604-530-4371
www.city.langley.bc.ca
Population: 25,081 *Census Year:* 2011
Number of Households: 10,343
Carolyn Bonnick, Manager/Corporate Officer, Legislative Services
Judy Hale, Manager, Human Resources
Gerald Minchuk, Director, Development Services & Economic Development
Gary Vlieg, Director, Engineering, Parks & Environment
Rory Thompson, Fire Chief
Waste Management:
Responsibility of the Greater Vancouver Regional District; waste collection contracted to Canadian Waste Services, 604/520-7800.
Transfer Station(s): Langley Transfer Station, 1070 - 272 St., Aldergrove
Recycling: Curbside; Depots at City of Langley Works Yard, 5713 - 198 St.; Langley Transfer Station; Willowbrook Recycling, 6001 - 196A St.; Masonville Plastics, 19402 - 56 Ave.; Aldergrove Landfill, 1070 - 272 St.; Enviro Wood Waste, 2460 - 192 St.
Hazardous Waste Depot or Facility: JR Bottle Depot, #224, 9640 - 201 St.; Langley Bottle Depot, 20137 Industrial Ave.
Water & Wastewater Treatment:
Responsibility of the Greater Vancouver Regional District.

City of Nanaimo
455 Wallace St.
Nanaimo, BC V9R 5J6

250-754-4251
legislativeservices.office@nanaimo.ca
www.nanaimo.ca
Population: 83,810 *Census Year:* 2011
Number of Households: 32,422
Alastair (Al) Kenning, City Manager, 250-755-4401, email: alastair.kenning@nanaimo.ca
Tom Hickey, General Manager, Community Services, 250-756-5301, email: tom.hickey@nanaimo.ca
Ted Swabey, General Manager, Development Services, 250-755-4451, email: ted.swabey@nanaimo.ca
Jeff Ritchie, Senior Manager, Parks, 250-755-7503, email: jeff.ritchie@nanaimo.ca
Brian Denbigh, Manager, Roads & Traffic Services, 250-756-5303
John Elliot, Manager, Utilities, 250-756-5305, email: john.elliot@nanaimo.ca
Kurtis Felker, Manager, Purchasing & Stores, 250-756-5317, email: kurtis.felker@nanaimo.ca
Gary Franssen, Manager, Sanitation, Recycling & Cemeteries, 250-756-5307, email: gary.franssen@nanaimo.ca
Rick Kroeker, Manager, Occupational Health & Rehabilitation, 250-755-4508, email: rick.kroeker@nanaimo.ca
Bob Prokopenko, Manager, Engineering Services, 250-755-4495, email: bob.prokopenko@nanaimo.ca
Richard Harding, Director, Parks, Recreation & Culture, 250-755-7516, email: richard.harding@nanaimo.ca
Andrew Tucker, Director, Planning, 250-755-4450, email: andrew.tucker@nanaimo.ca
Ron Lambert, Fire Chief, 250-755-4555, email: ron.lambert@nanaimo.ca
Waste Management:
Operation of regional landfill responsibility of Regional District of Nanaimo; Waste collection responsibility of City of Nanaimo
Recycling: Both Curbside & Depot; Collection contracted to Waste Services Inc., 250/758-5360; Depot located at centralized recycling facility, operated by Nanaimo Recycling Exchange, 2477 Kenworth Rd.
Special Bans/by-laws: Tree Protection By-law
Water & Wastewater Treatment:
Water treatment responsibility of city; Chlorine & treatment plants, located in the Village of South West Extension & the City of Nanaimo
Other Initiatives:
Water quality protection program; Watershed management; Wise use of water program; Reuse rendezvous

City of New Westminster

511 Royal Ave.
New Westminster, BC V3L 1H9
604-521-3711
Fax: 604-521-3895
postmaster@newwestcity.ca
www.city.new-westminster.bc.ca
Population: 65,976 *Census Year:* 2011
Number of Households: 26,624
Paul Daminato, City Administrator, email: pdaminato@newwestcity.ca
Rod Carle, General Manager, Electric Utility, email: rcarle@newwestcity.ca
Dean Gibson, Director, Parks, Culture & Recreation, email: dgibson@newwestcity.ca
Jim Lowrie, Director, Engineering Services, email: jlowrie@newwestcity.ca
Lisa Spitale, Director, Development Services, email: lspitale@newwestcity.ca
Dave Jones, Police Chief, Police Services, email: djones@nwpolice.org
Tim Armstrong, Fire Chief, Fire & Rescue Services, email: tarmstrong@newwestcity.ca
Waste Management:
Responsibility of Greater Vancouver Regional District.
Recycling: Both Curbside & Depot; New Westminster Recycling Depot at 6th Ave. & McBride Blvd.
Water & Wastewater Treatment:
Responsibility of Greater Vancouver Regional District.
Other Initiatives:
Development of greenways.

City of North Vancouver

141 - 14 St. West
North Vancouver, BC V7M 1H9
604-985-7761
Fax: 604-985-9417
info@cnv.org
www.cnv.org
Population: 48,196 *Census Year:* 2011
Number of Households: 21,217
Francis Caouette, Director, Corporate Services, 604-990-4221, Fax: 604-985-7492, email: fcaouette@cnv.org
Richard White, Director, Community Development, 604-990-4215, Fax: 604-985-0576, email: rwhite@cnv.org
Wolfgang Beier, Manager, Purchasing, 604-983-7392, Fax: 604-985-1573, email: wbeier@cnv.org
Navin Chad, Manager, Financial Planning, 604-983-7320, Fax: 604-985-1573, email: nchand@cnv.org
Janice Irwin, Manager, Financial Services, 604-983-7300, Fax: 604-985-1573, email: jirwin@cnv.org
Nikii Hoglund, Manager, Operations, 604-983-7388, Fax: 604-987-5379, email: nhoglund@cnv.org
Mike Hunter, Manager, Environment & Parks, 604-983-7335, Fax: 604-985-8439, email: mhunter@cnv.org
Percy Melville, Manager, Inspections, 604-983-7375, Fax: 604-985-0576, email: pmelville@cnv.org
David Nelson, Manager, Information Technology, 604-983-7318, Fax: 604-985-7492, email: dnelson@cnv.org
Connie Rabold, Manager, Communications, 604-983-7383, Fax: 604-985-5971, email: crabold@cnv.org
Glenn Stainton, Manager, City Facilities, 604-983-7305, Fax: 604-985-1573, email: gstainton@cnv.org
Steven Ono, City Engineer, 604-983-7336, Fax: 604-985-8439, email: sono@cnv.org
Emilie K. Adin, City Planner, 604-982-3922, Fax: 604-985-0576
Barrie Penman, Fire Chief, 604-904-5201, Fax: 604-980-8544, email: bpenman@cnv.org
Waste Management:
Waste collection responsibility of city; Waste disposal responsibility of Greater Vancouver Regional District
Transfer Station(s): North Shore Transfer Station, 30 Riverside Dr., North Vancouver
Recycling: Both Curbside & Depot; Collection contracted to Waste Management of Canada, 604/929-3416; North Shore Recycling Drop-off Depot, 29 Riverside Dr., North Vancouver
Hazardous Waste Depot or Facility: North Shore Transfer Station Hazardous Household Waste Collection Depot
Compost Sites: Yes *Composters subsidized:* Yes
Water & Wastewater Treatment:
Responsibility of Greater Vancouver Regional District
Other Initiatives:
Environmental Protection Program; Curbside yard trimmings collection; Pesticide Management Plan; Parks & Greenways Strategic Plan

City of Parksville

P.O. Box 1390
100 Jensen Ave. East
Parksville, BC V9P 2H3
250-248-6144
Fax: 250-248-6650
www.parksville.ca
Population: 11,977 *Census Year:* 2011
Number of Households: 5,030
Fred Manson, Chief Administrative Officer, 250-954-4666, email: fmanson@city.parksville.bc.ca
Lucy Butterworth, Director, Finance, 250-954-3063, email: lbutterworth@parksville.ca
Robert Harary, Director, Engineering & Operations, 250-951-2477, email: rharary@parksville.ca
Gayle Jackson, Director, Community Planning, 250-954-4656, email: gjackson@city.parksville.bc.ca
Doug Banks, Fire Chief, 250-954-4671, email: dbanks@parksville.ca
Waste Management:
Responsibility of Nanaimo Regional District
Water & Wastewater Treatment:
Responsibility of Nanaimo Regional District
Other Initiatives:
Wood chipping program

City of Penticton

171 Main St.
Penticton, BC V2A 5A9
250-490-2400
Fax: 250-490-2402
www.penticton.ca
Population: 32,877 *Census Year:* 2011
Number of Households: 14,745
Chuck Loewen, General Manager, Recreation, 250-490-2445
Cathy Ingram, Manager, Purchasing, 250-490-2555
Gillian Kenny, Manager, Human Resources, 250-490-2470
Ken Kunka, Manager, Building & Permitting, 250-490-2505
Dave Lieskovsky, Manager, Facilities, 250-490-2433
Eric Livolsi, Manager, Electric Utility, 250-490-2537
Peter Ord, Manager, Museum, 250-490-2452
Len Robson, Manager, Public Works, 250-490-2500
Kristin Wilkes, Manager, Information Technology, 250-490-2499
Mitch Moroziuk, Director, Operations, 250-490-2515
Brent Edge, Supervisor, Water, email: brent.edge@penticton.ca
Berne Udala, Supervisor, Water Quality, 250-490-2564
Carolyn Stewart, Environmental Coordinator, Water Treatment Plant, 250-490-2562
Wayne Williams, Fire Chief, 250-490-2309
Waste Management:
Waste management responsibility of Regional District of Okanagan-Similkameen; Waste collection responsibility of city; Waste collection contracted to Waste Services Inc., 250/490-3888
Water & Wastewater Treatment:
City of Penticton Water Treatment Plant, 1900 Penticton Ave., 250/490-2560, Email: wtp@city.penticton.bc.ca; Advanced Wastewater Treatment Plant, 459 Waterloo Ave., 250/490-2550, Email:wwtp@city.penticton.bc.ca
Other Initiatives:
Upgrades to Advanced Wastewater Treatment Plant; Updates to Liquid Waste Management Plan; Yard waste pickup, 4 times/yr.

City of Pitt Meadows

Municipal Hall
12007 Harris Rd.
Pitt Meadows, BC V3Y 2B5
604-465-5454
Fax: 604-465-2404
info@pittmeadows.bc.ca
www.pittmeadows.bc.ca
Population: 17,736 *Census Year:* 2011
Number of Households: 5,397
Kelly Swift, General Manager, Community Development, Parks & Recreation, 604-467-7337
Kim Grout, Director, Operations & Development Services, 604-465-2428
Don Jolley, Fire Chief, Protective Services, 604-465-2401
Dave Walsh, Superintendent, RCMP, 604-463-6251
Waste Management:
Waste collection contracted to Canadian Waste Services, 604/520-7806
Recycling: Curbside
Composters subsidized: Yes
Water & Wastewater Treatment:
Maintenance of water supply system & wastewater system responsibility of District Municipality's Operations Centre; Water & wastewater treatment responsibility of Greater Vancouver Regional District
Other Initiatives:
Agricultural Land Reserve; Watercourse & tree preservation; Ongoing education to reduce, reuse & recycle; Compost site located at 18020 Kennedy Rd., 604/465-1311; Hazardous waste handled by BC Recycling

City of Port Alberni

4850 Argyle St.
Port Alberni, BC V9Y 1V8
250-723-2146
Fax: 250-723-1003
citypa@portalberni.ca
www.portalberni.ca
Population: 17,743 *Census Year:* 2011
Number of Households: 7,985
Ken Watson, City Manager, 250-720-2824, email: ken_watson@portalberni.ca
Scott Kenny, Director, Parks & Recreation, 250-720-2507, email: scott_kenny@portalberni.ca
Jean McIntosh, Director, 250-720-2501, email: jean_mcintosh@portalberni.ca
Randy Fraser, Superintendent, Streets, 250-720-2845, email: randy_fraser@portalberni.ca
Brian Mousley, Superintendent, Utilities, 250-720-2849, email: brian_mousley@portalberni.ca
Guy Cicon, City Engineer, 250-720-2838, email: guy_cicon@port-alberni.ca
Scott Smith, City Planner, 250-720-2808, email: scott_smith@port-alberni.ca
Tim Pley, Fire Chief, 250-720-2540, email: tim_pley@portalberni.ca

Waste Management:
Alberni-Clayoquot Regional district responsible for waste disposal; municipality responsible for collection
Water & Wastewater Treatment:
Chlorination stations: Bainbridge Pumpstation, Johnston Pumpstation & Somass Pump/Intake; Sewage Treatment Facility: aeration Lagoon, south side of Somass River
Other Initiatives:
Developing a liquid waste management plan with Associated Engineering & the Ministry of the Environment

City of Port Coquitlam
2580 Shaughnessy St.
Port Coquitlam, BC V3C 2A8
604-927-5411
Fax: 604-927-5360
info@portcoquitlam.ca
www.portcoquitlam.ca
Population: 56,342 *Census Year:* 2011
Number of Households: 18,248
Susan Rauh, CMC, Corporate Officer/City Clerk, 604-927-5421, Fax: 604-927-5402, email: corporateoffice@portcoquitlam.ca
Tony Chong, P. Eng., Chief Administrative Officer, 604-927-5410, Fax: 604-927-5331, email: chongt@portcoquitlam.ca
Kathleen Vincent, Director, Legislative & Administrative Services, 604-927-5335, email: vincentk@portcoquitlam.ca
Igor Zahynacz, P. Eng., Director, Engineering & Operations, 604-927-5453, email: zahynaczi@portcoquitlam.ca
Karen Laustrup, Manager, Purchasing, 604-927-5430, Fax: 604-927-5408, email: laustrupk@portcoquitlam.ca
Brian North, Manager, Revenues & Collections, 604-927-5426, Fax: 604-927-5401, email: northb@portcoquitlam.ca
Pardeep Purewal, Manager, Communications & Administrative Services, 604-927-5335, Fax: 604-927-5331, email: purewalp@portcoquitlam.ca
Terry Hochstetter, Acting Fire Chief, 604-927-5494, email: hochstettert@portcoquitlam.ca
Waste Management:
Waste management responsibility of Greater Vancouver Regional District.; Waste collection responsibility of city
Recycling: Curbside
Hazardous Waste Depot or Facility: Biggar Bottle Depot, 2577 Kingsway Ave.
Water & Wastewater Treatment:
Water treatment responsibility of Greater Vancouver Regional District; Maintenance of watermain & sewer system responsibility of city
Other Initiatives:
Tree bylaw; Waterways protection; Reduction of road salt; Anti-idling program; Watershed management plan; Water conservation; Pitch in for PoCo pride; Seasonal green waste collection

City of Port Moody
P.O. Box 36
100 Newport Dr.
Port Moody, BC V3H 3E1
604-469-4500
Fax: 604-469-4550
info@cityofportmoody.com
www.cityofportmoody.com
Population: 32,975 *Census Year:* 2011
Number of Households: 8,767
Ron Higo, Director, Community Services
Lynne Russell, Director, Library Services
Jim Weber, Acting Director, Development Services
Mary De Paoli, Manager, Planning, 604-469-4540, email: planning@portmoody.ca
Devin Jain, Manager, Cultural Services
D. Kidd, Manager, Operations
J. LaCroix, Manager, Recreation
Angie Parnell, Manager, Human Resources
Julie Pavey, Manager, Parks & Environmental Services
Cory Day, City Engineer
Brad Parker, Chief Constable, Police Services
Remo Faedo, Fire Chief, email: pmfd.info@portmoody.ca
Waste Management:
Waste disposal responsibility of Greater Vancouver Regional District; Collection contracted by the City to International Paper industries, 604/520-3157
Recycling: Curbside
Compost Sites: Yes
Water & Wastewater Treatment:
Responsibility of Greater Vancouver Regional District

Other Initiatives:
Environmentally Sensitive Areas Management Strategy; Creeks & streams stewardship; Composting & Rain Collection Program

City of Powell River
6910 Duncan St.
Powell River, BC V8A 1V4
604-485-6291
Fax: 604-485-2913
info@cdpr.bc.ca
www.powellriver.ca
Population: 13,165 *Census Year:* 2011
Number of Households: 5,854
Marie Claxton, City Clerk, 604-485-8601, Fax: 604-485-8628
Stan Westby, Chief Administrative Officer, 604-485-8601, Fax: 604-485-8628
Tor Birtig, Manager, Operational Division, 604-485-6291, Fax: 604-485-2913, email: tbirtig@cdpr.bc.ca
Mike Elvy, Manager, Arena & Sport, 604-485-2891, Fax: 604-485-2162, email: parksrec@cdpr.bc.ca
Barb Mohan, Manager, Human Resources, 604-485-8638, Fax: 604-485-2913
Regina Sadilkova, Manager, Development Services, 604-485-8612, Fax: 604-485-2913
Vacant, City Engineer
Charlie Kregel, Chief Librarian, Fire & Emergency Services, 604-485-8661, Fax: 604-485-5320, email: ckregel@powellriverlibrary.ca
Dan Ouellette, Fire Chief/Director, Fire & Emergency Services, 604-485-4431
Waste Management:
Recycling: Both Curbside & Depot; Augusta Recyclers Depot, 7346 Hwy. 101, Powell River
Water & Wastewater Treatment:
Westview Sewage Treatment Plant; Wildwood Sewage Lagoon Plant; Halsam Lake System (chlorinating, screening); Powell Lake System (chlorinating), townsite sewage treatment
Other Initiatives:
Bag & tag system in place for all curbside collection

City of Prince George
City Hall
1100 Patricia Blvd.
Prince George, BC V2L 3V9
250-561-7600
cityclerk@city.pg.bc.ca
princegeorge.ca
Population: 71,974 *Census Year:* 2011
Number of Households: 29,345
Derek Bates, City Manager, 250-561-7607, Fax: 250-561-0183
Dan Milburn, Acting Director, Planning & Development Contracts, 250-561-7614, Fax: 250-561-7721
Colleen Van Mook, Director, Community Services, 250-561-7675, Fax: 250-561-7718
Rob Whitwham, Director, Public Safety & Civic Facilities, 250-561-7608, Fax: 250-561-0183
Dan Adamson, Manager, Environment, 250-561-7698, Fax: 250-561-7721
Frank Blues, Asset Manager, Downtown Projects, 250-561-7503, Fax: 250-561-7721
Scott Bone, Manager, Supply & Fleet Services, 250-561-7511, Fax: 250-612-5603
Marco Fornari, Manager, Utilities, 250-561-7573, Fax: 250-561-7519
Flavio Viola, Manager, Parks & Solid Waste Services, 250-561-7575, Fax: 250-612-5612
Dave Dyer, Chief Engineer, 250-561-7663, Fax: 250-561-7721
Glenn Stanker, Engineer, Transportation, 250-561-7757
John Lane, Fire Chief, 250-561-7667, Fax: 250-561-7703
Waste Management:
Waste management, including operation of the Foothills Blvd. Regional Landfill, drop-depot recycling system & composting, responsibility of Regional District of Fraser Fort George; Waste collection responsibility of city
Transfer Station(s): 18th & Quinn Streets; Vanway Firehall
Special Bans/by-laws: Clean Air Bylaw
Water & Wastewater Treatment:
Waste Water Treatment Centre, 250/562-4578
Other Initiatives:
Air Quality Management Plan prepared by the Prince George Airshed Technical Management Committee; Stream stewardship; Spring clean up; Urban forest management & stewardship plan; Water conservation plan

City of Prince Rupert
424 - 3rd Ave. West
Prince Rupert, BC V8J 1L7
250-627-0934
Fax: 250-627-0999
cityhall@princerupert.ca
www.princerupert.ca
Population: 12,508 *Census Year:* 2011
Number of Households: 6,149
Gord Howie, City Manager
Z. Krekic, City Planner
Dave Mckenzie, Fire Chief, 250-624-5115, email: dave.mckenzie@princerupert.ca
Waste Management:
Waste collection responsibility of City; Recycling & waste management responsibility of Skeena-Queen Charlotte Regional District
Number of landfill sites: 1
Solid Waste Disposal Fees: $85/tonne
Other Initiatives:
Adopt a Green Space & Adopt a Trail programs

City of Richmond
6911 No. 3 Rd.
Richmond, BC V6Y 2C1
604-276-4000
TTY: 604-276-4311
www.richmond.ca
Population: 190,473 *Census Year:* 2011
Number of Households: 58,272
Mike Kirk, Deputy Chief Administrative Officer, Corporate Services, 604-276-4147, email: corporateservices@richmond.ca
Cathryn Carlile, General Manager, Community Services, 604-276-4068, email: cathryn.carlile@richmond.ca
Jeff Day, P.Eng., General Manager, Project Development & Facility Management, 604-276-4019, email: jeff.day@richmond.ca
Joe Erceg, General Manager, Planning & Development, 604-276-4214, email: planningdevelopment@richmond.ca
Robert Gonzalez, P. Eng., General Manager, Engineering & Public Works, 604-276-4150, email: robert.gonzalez@richmond.ca
Andrew Nazareth, General Manager, Business & Finance Services, 604-276-4095, email: finance@richmond.ca
Jane Fernyhough, Director, Arts, Culture & Heritage Services, 604-276-4288, email: jane.fernyhough@richmond.ca
Dave Semple, Director, Operations, 604-244-1206, email: dave.semple@richmond.ca
Greg Buss, Chief Librarian, 604-231-6418, email: greg.buss@rpl.richmond.bc.ca
William (John) McGowan, Fire Chief, 604-303-2719, email: fire@richmond.ca
Waste Management:
Disposal responsibility of Greater Vancouver Regional District; Waste collection contracted to International Paper Industries, 604/599-8151
Number of landfill sites: 1*Landfill Capacity:* 25 years; private site, owned by Ecowaste Industries
Solid Waste Disposal Fees: $65/tonne
Transfer Station(s): Yes
Recycling: Both Curbside & Depot; Depot at 5555 Lynas Lane
Special Bans/by-laws: Solid waste & recycling regulation bylaw; ESA bylaw; storm sewer bylaw; pollution prevention
Hazardous Waste Depot or Facility: paint, pesticides & solvents only to depot at 5555 Lynas Lane.
Compost Sites: Yes *Composters subsidized:* Yes
Water & Wastewater Treatment:
Responsibility of Greater Vancouver Regional District
Other Initiatives:
Programs include: Advisory Committee on Environment; Environmental Purchasing Policy & Guideline; Partners for Beautification; State of Environment Report; Environmental Project Handbook; Partners for Climate Protection

City of Salmon Arm
P.O. Box 40
500 - 2nd Ave. NE
Salmon Arm, BC V1E 4N2
250-803-4000
Fax: 250-803-4041
cityhall@salmonarm.ca
www.salmonarm.ca
Population: 17,464 *Census Year:* 2011
Number of Households: 6,503

Carl Bannister, Chief Administrative Officer, email: cbannistser@salmonarm.ca
Dale McTaggart, Director, Engineering & Public Works, email: dmctaggart@salmonarm.ca
Corey Paiement, Director, Development Services, email: cpaiement@salmonarm.ca
Betty Hiebert, Manager, Financial Services, email: bhiebert@salmonarm.ca
Maurice Roy, Manager, Permits/Licensing, email: mroy@salmonarm.ca
John Rosenberg, Manager, Public Works, email: jrosenberg@salmonarm.ca
Donna Shultz, Manager, Human Resources, email: dshultz@salmonarm.ca
Brad Shirley, Fire Chief, 250-803-4060, email: bshirley@salmonarm.ca
Waste Management:
Responsibility of the Columbia Shuswap Regional District
Water & Wastewater Treatment:
Water sources are East Canoe Creek & Shuswap Lake; Storage & distribution form pump stations & 11 reservoirs; Sewage treatment at Waste Water Treatment Plant, 250/832-3500
Other Initiatives:
SCADA computer program to monitor water & sewer systems

City of Sidney
Municipal Hall
2440 Sidney Ave.
Sidney, BC V8L 1Y7
250-656-1184
Fax: 250-655-4508
www.sidney.ca
Population: 11,178 *Census Year:* 2011
Number of Households: 5,278
Rob Hall, P.Eng., Director, Engineering & Works, 250-656-4502
Wendy Taylor, Manager, 250-656-1139
Mike van der Linden, Manager, Engineering, 250-655-5416
Shari Holmes-Saltzman, Municipal Planner, 250-655-5419
Jim Marshall, Senior Building Official, 250-655-5412
Dan Holder, Fire Chief, 250-655-5421
Waste Management:
Waste collection & composting pickup contracted to Evergreen Industries (Alpine Disposal), 250/474-5145; Waste management & recycling responsibility of Capital Regional District
Special Bans/by-laws: Tree Preservation Bylaw; Backyard burning ban
Water & Wastewater Treatment:
Responsibility of the Capital Regional District

City of Surrey
14245 - 56th Ave.
Surrey, BC V3X 3A2
604-591-4011
Fax: 604-591-8731
www.surrey.ca
Population: 468,251 *Census Year:* 2011
Number of Households: 118,529
Laurie Cavan, General Manager, Parks, Recreation & Culture, 604-598-5760, Fax: 604-598-5781
Vincent Lalonde, P.Eng., General Manager, Engineering, 604-591-4314, Fax: 604-591-8693
Jean Lamontagne, General Manager, Planning & Development, 604-591-4441, Fax: 604-591-2507
Jeff Arason, P. Eng., Manager, Utilities, 604-591-4367
Jamie Boan, P. Eng., Manager, Transportation, 604-591-4514
Sam Chauhan, Manager, Operational Health & Safety, 604-591-4658
Sam Lau, P. Eng., Acting Manager, Land Development, 604-591-4276
Violet McGregor, CMA, C.P.P., Manager, Purchasing & Payments, 604-591-4011
Gerry McKinnon, Manager, Operations, 604-590-7211
Sheila McKinnon, Manager, Arts, 604-591-5127
Mary Ann Smith, Senior Economic Development Officer, 604-591-4333, email: masmith@surrey.ca
Beth Barlow, Chief Librarian, 604-598-7304, email: babarlow@surrey.ca
Len Garis, Fire Chief, 604-541-4011
W. Fraser MacRae, Assistant Commissioner/Officer in Charge, RCMP Surrey Detachment, 604-599-0502, Fax: 604-599-8894
Waste Management:
Waste management responsibility of Greater Vancouver Regional District; Collection of garbage, recyclables & yard waste responsibility of city; Waste collection contracted to Waste Management Inc., 604/520-7800
Solid Waste Disposal Fees: $65/tonne
Transfer Station(s): Surrey Transfer Station, 9770 - 192 St., Surrey; Coquitlam Transfer Station, 1200 United Blvd., Coquitlam; Waste trucked to C
Recycling: Both Curbside & Depot
Hazardous Waste Depot or Facility: Metro Material Recovery; International Paper Industries; Willowbrook Recycling Depot
Water & Wastewater Treatment:
Water treatment responsibility of Greater Vancouver Regional District; Maintenance & operation of sanitary sewer system responsibility of city
Other Initiatives:
Environmental education programs; Large item collections; Water conservation; Protection of environmentally sensitive areas; Adopt a street neighbourhood litter stewardship program; Partners in Parks programs; Releaf program tree planting initiative; Stream restoration projects; Reduction in use of chemical fertilizers, pesticides & herbicides

City of Terrace
3215 Eby St.
Terrace, BC V8G 2X8
250-635-6311
Fax: 250-638-4777
cityhall@terrace.ca
www.terrace.ca
Population: 11,486 *Census Year:* 2011
Number of Households: 4,611
Herb Dusdal, Director, Public Works, 250-615-4030, email: hdusdal@terrace.ca
Marvin Kwiatkowski, Director, Development Services, 250-615-4041, email: mkwiatkowski@terrace.ca
Brad Hansen, Manager, Information Systems Manager, 250-638-4701, email: bhansen@terrace.ca
David Block, City Planner, 250-615-4028, email: dblock@terrace.ca
John Klie, Fire Chief, 250-638-4742, email: jklie@terrace.ca
Dana Hart, Officer in Charge, RCMP Terrace Detachment, 250-638-7400
Lyle Marleau, Foreman, Environmental Health, 250-635-6871, email: lmarleau@terrace.ca
Waste Management:
Disposal responsibility of the regional district. Waste collection contracted to Residential City Collection, 250/635-6311.
Number of landfill sites: 1
Recycling: Depot; Terrace Bottle Depot, 3098 Kofoed Dr
Hazardous Waste Depot or Facility: Paint & Consumer Product Stewardship Program; Terrace Bottle Depot, 250/635-6909
Composters subsidized: Yes
Water & Wastewater Treatment:
Sewage treatment plant, 5123 Graham Ave.; fluoridation & chlorination water treatment facilities.
Other Initiatives:
Curbside collection of compost; free spring & fall cleanup collection; re-use area at Terrace Landfill, Kalum Lake Dr.; water conservation program, including publication of household guide to water efficiency.

City of Vancouver
453 West 12th Ave.
Vancouver, BC V5Y 1V4
604-873-7000
Telephone locally: 311; TTY: 711
info@vancouver.ca
www.vancouver.ca
Population: 603,502 *Census Year:* 2011
Number of Households: 253,210
Penny Ballem, City Manager
Patrice Impey, General Manager & Chief Financial Officer, Financial Services Group
Peter Judd, General Manager, Engineering Services
John McKearney, General Manager & Fire Chief, Fire & Rescue Services, 604-873-7000, email: vfrscommunications@vancouver.ca
Annette Klein, Director, Operational Information & Planning
Kevin Wallinger, Director
Waste Management:
Number of landfill sites: 1*Landfill Capacity:* 40 years
Solid Waste Disposal Fees: $82/tonne
Transfer Station(s): Vancouver South Transfer Station, 377 West Kent Ave. North, Vancouver
Recycling: Both Curbside & Depot; Depots located at Vancouver South Transfer Station; Recycling Depot & Yard Trimmings Drop Off, 377 West Kent Ave. North
Special Bans/by-laws: Gypsum ban; paper products; garbage collection fees are based on the size of container, ranging from $89/yr for 75 litre containers to $194 for 360 litre container; city stickers available for purchase for extra garbage; all residential properties are billed annually for recycling, ranging from $29 for single unit house to $3174 for building complexes with 150 units.
Hazardous Waste Depot or Facility: A list of companies accepting various hazardous & other types of refuse & recyclable material is accessible on the City's website. See "Alternative Disposal & Recycling Locations".
Compost Sites: Yes *Composters subsidized:* Yes
Water & Wastewater Treatment:
Iona Island Sewage Treatment Plant, owned & operated by Greater Vancouver Sewage & Drainage District
Other Initiatives:
Keep Vancouver Spectacular annual cleanup campaign; annual leaf removal program; apartment recycling service; sale of compost from Yard & Garden Trimmings Composting Facility at Vancouver landfill; rain barrel program; demonstration gardens to promote water conservation, backyard composting, worm bins; industrial water conservation programs; landfill gas cogeneration system 5.5 megawatts, heats tomato green house; automated garbage & yard trimmings collection, fee based on container size, since Fall 2005.

City of Vernon
3400 - 30th St.
Vernon, BC V1T 5E6
250-545-1361
Fax: 250-545-7876
admin@vernon.ca
www.vernon.ca
Population: 38,150 *Census Year:* 2011
Number of Households: 15,288
Patti Bridal, City Clerk & Manager, Corporate Services
Leon Gous, Chief Administrative Officer, 250-550-3515, email: lgous@vernon.ca
Rob Dickinson, Manager, Engineering
Kim Flick, Manager, Planning, Development & Engineering Services
Shirley Koenig, Manager, Operations
Tony Kopp, Manager, Utilities, 250-549-6757
James Rice, Manager, Public Works, email: jrice@vernon.ca
Ed Stranks, Manager, Engineering Development
Keith Green, Fire Chief, 250-550-3561, email: fire@vernon.ca
Waste Management:
Disposal responsibility of North Okanagan Regional District; Waste collection contracted to O.K. Environmental Waste System Ltd., 250/549-3234
Recycling: Collection contracted to Alson Waste Systems, 1-888-547-6961
Water & Wastewater Treatment:
City of Vernon Water Reclamation Plant, 2400 - 43 St., Vernon, 250/542-9825; Greater Vernon Water Utility oversees supply & distribution, 250/542-8410; City's utilities division is responsible for wastewater treatment
Other Initiatives:
Two-bag non-recyclable garbage limit per week; Spring chipping program; Spring & fall collection of leaves & garden refuse; Christmas Tree Disposal

City of Victoria
1 Centennial Sq.
Victoria, BC V8W 1P6
250-385-5711
Fax: 250-361-0214
publicsrv@victoria.ca
www.victoria.ca
Population: 80,017 *Census Year:* 2011
Number of Households: 42,359
Gail Stephens, City Manager, 250-361-0202
Kevin Greig, General Manager, Corporate Services, 250-361-0247
Peter Sparanese, General Manager, Operations, 250-361-0292
Deborah Day, Director, Planning & Development, 250-361-0511
Kate Friars, Director, Parks, Recreation & Community Development, 250-361-0355
Pete Sparanese, Acting Director, Sustainability, 250-361-0292
Glen Oberg, Manager, Supply Management Services, 250-361-0271
John Basey, City Solicitor, 250-361-0588, Fax: 250-361-0348
Doug Angrove, Fire Chief, 250-920-3353
Waste Management:
Residential collecion by the City of Victoria; Commercial waste collection contracted out by owners of property
Number of landfill sites: 1*Landfill Capacity:* 44 years, Hartland

Landfill
Solid Waste Disposal Fees: $128/tonne
Recycling: Both Curbside & Depot; Pickup by Ellice Recycle; Depots at Hartland Landfill & Ellise Recycle
Special Bans/by-laws: Stormwater quality
Hazardous Waste Depot or Facility: Hartland Landfill & Ellice Recycle
Composters subsidized: Yes
Water & Wastewater Treatment:
Responsibility of Capital Regional District
Other Initiatives:
Victoria Harbour Environmental Protection Plan; Pilot program in conjunction with Capital Regional District to enhance composting by removing kitchen waste

City of White Rock
15322 Buena Vista Ave.
White Rock, BC V4B 1Y6
604-541-2100
Fax: 604-541-2118
whiterockcouncil@city.whiterock.bc.ca
www.city.whiterock.bc.ca
Population: 19,339 *Census Year:* 2011
Number of Households: 9,397
Rob Thompson, Director, Municipal Operations, 604-541-2181, email: rthompson@city.whiterock.bc.ca
Paul Stanton, Director, Development Services, 604-541-2142, email: pstanton@city.whiterock.bc.ca
Sylvia Yee, Acting Director, Development Services, 604-541-2173, email: syee@city.whiterock.bc.ca
Jacquie Johnstone, Director, Human Resources, 604-541-2157, email: jjohnstone@city.whiterock.bc.ca
Chris Zota, Manager, Information Technology, 604-541-2113, email: czota@city.whiterock.bc.ca
Phil Lemire, Fire Chief, 604-541-2122, email: plemire@city.whiterock.bc.ca
Lesli Roseberry, White Rock RCMP Detachment Commander, 604-541-5101, email: lesli.roseberry@rcmp-grc.gc.ca
Waste Management:
Waste collection responsibility of city operations department; Collection of recyclables for multi-family & commercial properties contracted to Encorp Pacific (Canada), 604/473-2400
Recycling: Both Curbside & Depot; Four cardboard recycling depots
Water & Wastewater Treatment:
Responsibility of Epcor White Rock Water Inc., 604/536-7556
Other Initiatives:
Branch chipping, rubbish removal & collection of green waste for fee; Tree management

City of Williams Lake
450 Mart St.
Williams Lake, BC V2G 1N3
250-392-2311
Fax: 250-392-4408
corporateservices@williamslake.ca
www.williamslake.ca
Population: 10,832 *Census Year:* 2011
Number of Households: 4,629
Kevin Goldfuss, Director, Municipal Services, 250-392-1783, email: kgoldfuss@williamslake.ca
Geoff Goodall, Director, Development Services, 250-392-1766, email: ggoodall@williamslake.ca
Patricia Higgins, Director, Financial Services, 250-392-1762, email: phiggins@williamslake.ca
Randy Isfeld, Director/Fire Chief, Protective Services, 250-392-1779, email: risfeld@williamslake.ca
Geoff Paynton, Director, Community Services, 250-392-1786, email: gpaynton@williamslake.ca
Cindy Bouchard, Manager, Legislative Services, email: cbouchard@williamslake.ca
Joe Engelberts, Manager, Water/Sewer Division, email: jengelberts@williamslake.ca
Waste Management:
Waste management responsibility of Cariboo Regional District
Transfer Station(s): Central Cariboo Transfer Station, 5025 Frizzi Rd., 250/392-6379
Recycling: Curbside
Special Bans/by-laws: Water Management Bylaw
Water & Wastewater Treatment:
Water management responsibility of City Municipal Services Dept., Water & Sewer Division
Other Initiatives:
Share Shed

Other Municipalities in British Columbia

Central Saanich
1903 Mt. Newton Cross Rd.
Saanichton, BC V8M 2A9
250-652-4444
Fax: 250-652-0135
www.centralsaanich.ca
Population: 15,936 *Census Year:* 2011
Number of Households: 6,047
Waste Management:
Responsibility of Capital Regional District.
Water & Wastewater Treatment:
Responsibility of Capital Regional District.

Delta
4500 Clarence Taylor Cres.
Delta, BC V4K 3E2
604-946-4141
www.corp.delta.bc.ca
Population: 99,863 *Census Year:* 2011
Number of Households: 33,366
Waste Management:
Waste collection contracted to Remple Disposal, 604/580-3379
Recycling: Curbside
Special Bans/by-laws: Two-can limit on curbside garbage collection
Water & Wastewater Treatment:
Responsibility of Greater Vancouver Regional District
Other Initiatives:
Annual Spring Clean-up; Christmas tree chipping; Various drop off locations throughout area for household hazardous waste & recyclables; Streamside & tree protection; Watershed creek restoration; Agricultural land stewardship

Esquimalt
1229 Esquimalt Rd.
Victoria, BC V9A 3P1
250-414-7100
Fax: 250-414-7111
www.esquimalt.ca
Population: 16,209 *Census Year:* 2011
Number of Households: 7,847
Waste Management:
Waste collection responsibility of Township; Collection of recyclables responsibility of Capital Regional District; CRD Recycling Hotline: 250/360-3030; Waste management responsibility of Capital Regional District; Hartland Landfill is used
Composters subsidized: Yes
Water & Wastewater Treatment:
Design, inspection & technical supervision of water distribution systems responsibility of City of Victoria; Maintenance & upgrading of sewer system & sewage pump stations responsibility of Township; Sewage treatment responsibility of Capital Regional District
Other Initiatives:
Canteen Composting located at 605 Canteen Rd.; Phone: 250/386-3343

Kitimat
270 City Centre
Kitimat, BC V8C 2H7
250-632-8900
Fax: 250-632-4995
feedback@kitimat.ca
www.kitimat.ca
Population: 8,335 *Census Year:* 2011
Number of Households: 4,230
Waste Management:
Number of landfill sites: 1
Recycling: Depot; 316 Railway Ave.; Depot operated by Kitimat Understanding the Environment (KUTE), 250/632-6633
Water & Wastewater Treatment:
Kitimat Pollution Control Centre

Langley
20338 - 65 Ave.
Langley, BC V2Y 3J1
604-534-3211
info@tol.ca
www.tol.ca
Population: 104,177 *Census Year:* 2011
Number of Households: 30,269
Waste Management:
Responsibility of Greater Vancouver Regional District, contracted to International Paper Industries, 604/530-3939
Solid Waste Disposal Fees: $65/tonne
Recycling: Curbside
Hazardous Waste Depot or Facility: Depot locations in Langley, through the Paint & Consumer Product Stewardship Program
Compost Sites: Yes
Water & Wastewater Treatment:
Water treatment is the responsiblity of the Greater Vancouver Regional District, Aldergrove Water Treatment Plant, 27540 - 28 Ave.; Wastewater treatment is the responsibility of the Greater Vancouver Regional District & the Fraser Valley Regional District

Maple Ridge
11995 Haney Pl.
Maple Ridge, BC V2X 6A9
604-463-5221
Fax: 604-467-7329
enquiries@mapleridge.ca
www.mapleridge.ca
Population: 76,052 *Census Year:* 2011
Number of Households: 23,788
Waste Management:
Responsibility of the Greater Vancouver Regional District
Transfer Station(s): Maple Ridge Transfer Station, 236th & River Rd.
Recycling: Both Curbside & Depot; Maple Ridge
Special Bans/by-laws: Bylaws on soil deposit, tree preservation, water preservation, watercourse protection
Composters subsidized: Yes
Water & Wastewater Treatment:
2 reservoirs on the Greater Vancouver Regional District system
Other Initiatives:
Green waste drop-off program; Community compost demonstration garden; Collection of flammable liquids, pesticides & gasoline at recycling depot

Mission
P.O. Box 20
8645 Stave Lake St.
Mission, BC V2V 4L9
604-820-3700
Fax: 604-820-3715
info@mission.ca
www.mission.ca
Population: 36,426 *Census Year:* 2011
Number of Households: 10,993
Waste Management:
Waste collection contracted to Smithrite Disposal Ltd., 604/299-4030.
Number of landfill sites: 1
Solid Waste Disposal Fees: $60/tonne
Recycling: Both Curbside & Depot; No collection for rural residents; 6 depots
Water & Wastewater Treatment:
Responsibility of the Central Fraser Valley Water Commission.

North Cowichan
P.O. Box 278
7030 Trans Canada Hwy.
Duncan, BC V9L 3X4
250-746-3100
Fax: 250-746-3133
info@northcowichan.bc.ca
www.northcowichan.bc.ca
Population: 28,807 *Census Year:* 2011
Number of Households: 10,929
Waste Management:
Responsibility of Cowichan Valley Regional District; collection & recycling programs responsibility of the municipality.
Recycling: Both Curbside & Depot; Collection is contracted to Active Disposal & Recycling; Depot located at Bing's Creek Depot, Drinkwater Rd., 250/701-0092; Multi-product bins provided by regional district
Water & Wastewater Treatment:
Chemainus Waste Treatment Treatment Plant, 9575 Bare Point Rd., Chemainus; Crofton Wastewater Treatment Plant, 1575 Chaplin St., Crofton; North Cowichan-Duncan Joint Utilities Sewage Lagoons Wastewater Treatment Plant.

North Saanich
1620 Mills Rd.
North Saanich, BC V8L 5S9
250-656-0781
Fax: 250-656-3155

admin@northsaanich.ca
www.northsaanich.ca
Population: 11,089 *Census Year:* 2011
Number of Households: 4,279

North Vancouver
355 West Queens Rd.
North Vancouver, BC V7N 4N5
604-990-2311
infoweb@dnv.org
www.dnv.org
Population: 84,412 *Census Year:* 2011
Number of Households: 29,528

Health Department
North Vancouver, BC V7M 1A2
604-983-6701
Fax: 604-983-6839
Waste Management:
Waste management responsibility of Greater Vancouver Regional District; Waste collection responsibility of District's Solid Waste Dept.
Transfer Station(s): 30 Riverside Dr., North Vancouver
Recycling: Both Curbside & Depot; North Shore Recycling Program, 604/984-9730; North Shore Recycling Drop-off Depot, 75 Riverside Dr., North Vancouver
Special Bans/by-laws: Environmental Protection & Preservation By-law; Regulations regarding water courses, trees, soils, sloping land
Hazardous Waste Depot or Facility: Drop off at transfer station
Compost Sites: Yes *Composters subsidized:* Yes
Water & Wastewater Treatment:
Responsibility of Greater Vancouver Regional District
Other Initiatives:
Sediment & erosion control; Stream & waterfront setbacks

Oak Bay
2167 Oak Bay Ave.
Victoria, BC V8R 1G2
250-598-3311
Fax: 250-598-9108
obcouncil@oakbay.ca
www.oakbaybc.org
Population: 18,015 *Census Year:* 2011
Number of Households: 7,745
Waste Management:
Waste management responsibility of the Capital Regional District; Waste collection responsibility of the municipality
Recycling: Curbside
Special Bans/by-laws: Land development & tree protection
Water & Wastewater Treatment:
Responsibility of Capital Regional District
Other Initiatives:
Regulation totes & blue boxes; Annual garden refuse pickup; Sale of compost

Quesnel
410 Kinchant St.
Quesnel, BC V2J 7J5
250-992-2111
Fax: 250-992-2206
cityhall@quesnel.ca
www.quesnel.ca
Population: 10,007 *Census Year:* 2011
Number of Households: 4,408
Waste Management:
Residential, commercial & industrial waste collection responsibility of city
Number of landfill sites: 1
Solid Waste Disposal Fees: $15/1 ton truck
Transfer Station(s): Carson Pitt Rd., 250/992-3817
Recycling: Depot; City of Quesnel Landfill Site & Recycling Depot, Carson Pitt Rd., 250/992-2426
Other Initiatives:
Quesnel Air Quality Roundtable; Community Action on Energy Efficiency

Saanich
770 Vernon Ave.
Victoria, BC V8X 2W7
250-475-1775
www.saanich.ca
Population: 109,752 *Census Year:* 2011
Number of Households: 42,905
Waste Management:
Capital Regional District responsible for waste disposal & recycling; Saanich responsible for collection
Special Bans/by-laws: Watercourse; tree preservation; deposit of fill; floodplane development permit area; streamside development permit area; urban outdoor burning ban
Water & Wastewater Treatment:
Responsibility of Capital Regional District
Other Initiatives:
Production of an environmentally significant areas atlas; Saanich Native Plant Salvage Program; Curbside Pickup program; Paint can & garden waste drop off; Transportation demand management; Environmental management plan; Garry Oak Restoration Program; LEED Gold or Silver rating for new municipal buildings; Pesticide Reduction Initiative

Squamish
P.O. Box 310
37955 Second Ave.
Squamish, BC V0N 3G0
604-892-5217
Fax: 604-892-1083
www.squamish.ca
Population: 17,158 *Census Year:* 2011
Number of Households: 5,411
Waste Management:
Waste collection contracted to Carney's Waste Systems, 604/892-5604
Number of landfill sites: 1
Solid Waste Disposal Fees: $80/tonne
Recycling: Both Curbside & Depot
Water & Wastewater Treatment:
Water source is Powerhouse Springs; Mashiter Creek & Stawamus River are emergency water sources; Water treatment includes chlorination; Wastewater treatment at Mamquam & Central plants, operated & maintained by municipal crews
Other Initiatives:
Water conservation strategy; Expansion of Mamquam (wastewater) plant; Squamish estuary management plan

Summerland
P.O. Box 159
11321 Henry Ave.
Summerland, BC V0H 1Z0
250-494-6451
Fax: 250-494-1415
info@summerland.ca
www.summerland.ca
Population: 11,280 *Census Year:* 2011
Number of Households: 4,669
Waste Management:
Number of landfill sites: 1
Solid Waste Disposal Fees: $55/tonne
Recycling: Depot; Depot at 9119 Peach Orchard Rd.
Composters subsidized: Yes
Water & Wastewater Treatment:
Trout Creek Chlorinator; Garnett Valley Chlorinator; Wastewater Treatment Plant, Trout Creek
Other Initiatives:
Establishment of Agricultural Advisory Committee, committee@summerland.ca

West Kelowna
2760 Cameron Rd.
West Kelowna, BC V1Z 2T6
778-797-1000
Fax: 778-797-1001
info@districtofwestkelowna.ca
www.districtofwestkelowna.ca
Population: 30,892 *Census Year:* 2011

West Vancouver
750 - 17 St.
West Vancouver, BC V7V 3T3
604-925-7000
Fax: 604-925-5999
info@westvancouver.ca
www.westvancouver.ca
Population: 42,694 *Census Year:* 2011
Number of Households: 17,299
Waste Management:
Collection & disposal responsibility of municipality's Engineering & Transportation Division
Solid Waste Disposal Fees: Yes
Recycling: Both Curbside & Depot; North Shore Recyling Drop-off Depot
Composters subsidized: Yes
Water & Wastewater Treatment:
Responsibility of Greater Vancouver Regional District
Other Initiatives:
Opening of Citrus Wynd Wastewater Treatment Plant; Product Care organization responsible for collection of hazardous waste; East Lake Micro-generation Project

Manitoba

The Manitoba Conservation & Water Stewardship office administers the Environment Act for the province. Each municipality in the province is individually licensed & responsible for sewage & wastewater management under the guidelines of the Act.

There are approximately 270 landfill sites in the province. Some transfer stations burn brush & plain wood. There are no incinerators or open pit burning.

Under the Waste Reduction & Prevention Act, the Manitoba Product Stewardship Corporation was created & mandated to establish & administer a waste reduction & prevention program for designated materials for Manitoba. As of 2010, that mandate has shifted to the newly created Multi-Material Stewardship Manitoba (MMSM), which in its first year of operation saw a 2 percent increase in material recovery over the previous year. Recycling is supported by the province, with the municipalities paying 20% of the cost. MMSM's Municipal Services Program, introduced in 2010, allows participating communities (including First Nations) to create recycling programs to suit their needs. All municipalities are responsible for establishing & maintaining their own recycling programs. There are over 200 community recycling programs in Manitoba. In 2012, MMSM provided $9,453,943 in funding to municipalities. Ninety-two percent of the population of Manitoba recycles; glass, bottles, cans & paper are recycled at transfer stations. Beverage container recycling is encouraged with consumers paying an extra 2 cents per bottle as part of a non-refundable recycling fee.

Manitoba Water Stewardship manages the province's water resources. The Drinking Water Safety Act created the Office of Drinking Water, established to provide a regulatory & advisory function. The Act also provides regulations regarding livestock, waste systems, and other measures to ensure the drinking water supply. The Water Protection Act (2005) was designed to protect water at its source & includes standards regarding treatment of municipal waste, watershed management plans, water management zones, & the establishment of the Manitoba Water Council. The first standard to be introduced related to municipal waste. Municipal water conservation is promoted through the Water Efficiency Program, which created the Manitoba Water Protection Handbook.

Municipalities are eligible for the Sustainable Development Innovations Fund, which supports the development, implementation & promotion of environmental innovation & sustainable development projects. In 2011/2012, approximately $900,000 was expended under this fund. Current programs under the Fund are the Waste Production & Pollution Prevention Fund, the Manitoba Climate Change Action Fund & the Water Stewardship Fund.

Major Municipalities in Manitoba

City of Brandon
410 - 9th St.
Brandon, MB R7A 6A2
204-729-2186
Fax: 204-729-8244
cityclerk@brandon.ca
www.brandon.ca
Population: 46,061 *Census Year:* 2011
Number of Households: 17,509
Brent Dane, Fire Chief, 204-729-2404, Fax: 204-729-2153, email: b.dane@brandon.ca
Rick Bailey, Director, Public Works, email: r.bailey@brandon.ca
Brian Kayes, Director, Emergency Coordination, email: best@brandon.ca
Jeff Roziere, Director, Sanitation, 204-573-6480, email: j.roziere@brandon.ca
Cathy Snelgrove, General Manager, Operations, 204-729-2145, Fax: 204-729-2191, email: c.snelgrove@brandon.ca
Ted Snure, General Manager & City Engineer, Development Services, 204-729-2214, Fax: 204-725-3235, email: t.snure@brandon.ca
Ian Christiansen, Manager, Engineering Services & Water Resources, email: i.christiansen@brandon.ca

Sandy Trudel, Officer, Economic Development, email: s.trudel@brandon.ca
Vivianne Lockerby, CPP, Supervisor, Purchasing, email: v.lockerby@brandon.ca
Waste Management:
Household waste in black-lid cart for curbside collection
Number of landfill sites: 1*Landfill Capacity:* 50 years
Solid Waste Disposal Fees: $34/tonne
Clean Fill Fee: Yes; $1.30/tonne
Recycling: Both Curbside & Depot; Household recyclables in blue-lid cart; household/yard waste depot locations: 1st St. & Richmond Ave.; Rideau Park, 400 Block Franklin; Kirkcaldy Boat Launch; 34th St. & Victoria Ave.; Westridge Community Centre; Landmark Capitol Theatre; Eastview Landfill Site, 3000 Victoria Ave. E.
Special Bans/by-laws: Pesticide Use Bylaw
Hazardous Waste Depot or Facility: Household hazardous waste on 2 days/year, in Spring & Fall; depot located behind the Civic Services Complex, 900 Richmond Ave. East
Compost Sites: No *Composters subsidized:* Yes
Water & Wastewater Treatment:
City of Brandon Water Treatment Plant, 108 - 26th St. North, 204/729-2190,; Municipal Wastewater Treatment Facility, 4040 Victoria Ave. East; Industrial Wastewater Treatment Facility, Richmond Ave. E.; email: wwtp@brandon.ca
Other Initiatives:
Implementation of City's Green Space Master Plan; Two hazardous waste days/year in May & Oct. at Civic Works Complex; Spring & Fall Clean Up; Community Clean-up events; Methane gas recovery; Bio-Diesel program; Vegetable (Grocer) Composting

City of Portage La Prairie
97 Saskatchewan Ave. East
Portage la Prairie, MB R1N 0L8
204-239-8337
Fax: 204-239-1532
swilliams@city-plap.com
www.city-plap.com
Population: 12,996 *Census Year:* 2011
Number of Households: 5,386
Kelly Braden, Director, Operations, 204-239-8350, Fax: 204-857-7275, email: kbraden@city-plap.com
Kathy McGregor, Administrative Assistant, Economic & Community Development, email: kmcgregor@city-plap.com
Phil Carpenter, Chief, Fire & Emergency, 204-239-8340, Fax: 204-239-5154, email: sharont@city-plap.com
Doug Campbell, Manager, Water Treatment, 204-239-8373, email: dcampbell@city-plap.com
Dave Green, Manager, Parks, 204-239-8325, email: dgreen@city-plap.com
Ian Milne, Manager, Engineering, 204-239-8349, email: imilne@city-plap.com
Brian Taylor, Manager, Public Works, 204-239-8352, email: btaylor@city-plap.com
Wayne Wall, Manager, Water Pollution Control Facility, 204-239-8359, email: wwall@city-plap.com
Waste Management:
Waste collection contracted to International Paper Industries.
Number of landfill sites: 1*Landfill Capacity:* 40 years
Solid Waste Disposal Fees: $25/tonne
Recycling: Both Curbside & Depot; Depot located at 700 Phillips St., 204/239-8346. Operation of recycling depot contracted to Portage & District Recycling Inc.
Special Bans/by-laws: User pay waste collection; two-bag limit per five-day cycle, extra bags must have a $1.00 waste collection tag
Hazardous Waste Depot or Facility: Yes
Compost Sites: Yes *Composters subsidized:* Yes
Water & Wastewater Treatment:
Responsibility of the city; Water pollution control facility at 400 River Rd.; Water treatment plant at 120 - 130 Yellowquill Trail; Water Pollution Control, 204/239-8360, Fax: 204/239-8364; Water Treatment Plant, 204/239-8374, Fax: 204/239-8371
Other Initiatives:
Tree disposal site; Christmas Tree collection program; Annual household hazardous waste day; Annual spring & fall curbside yard waste pickup

City of Thompson
226 Mystery Lake Rd.
Thompson, MB R8N 1S6
204-677-7910
Fax: 204-677-7981
rpatrick@city.thompson.mb.ca
www.thompson.ca
Population: 12,829 *Census Year:* 2011
Number of Households: 5,208
Ian Thompson, Fire Chief, 204-677-7915, email: fchief@city.thompson.mb.ca
Gary Ceppetelli, Director, Planning & Community Development, email: gceppetelli@city.thompson.mb.ca
Wayne Koversky, Director, Public Works, email: koversky@city.thompson.mb.ca
Mike Webb, Technician, Water & Sewer, email: mwebb@city.thompson.mb.ca
Ken Ament, Technician, Buildings & Roads, email: kament@city.thompson.mb.ca
Joyce Kopp, Agent, Purchasing, email: jkopp@city.thompson.mb.ca
Waste Management:
Waste disposal site is owned & operated by the local government district of Mystery Lake; Waste collection responsibility of city
Recycling: Both Curbside & Depot; Thompson Recycling Centre, 204/677-7991, Fax: 204/778-7844; Several depots throughout the city
Water & Wastewater Treatment:
Water treatment plant is owned & operated by Inco Ltd.; Water distribution responsibility of city; City of Thompson Sewage Treatment Plant, Nelson Rd.
Other Initiatives:
Spring Cleanup Program

City of Winnipeg
City Hall
510 Main St.
Winnipeg, MB R3B 1B9
204-986-6432
Fax: 204-947-3452
Phone or Fax: 311 for information on city services
www.winnipeg.ca
Population: 633,617 *Census Year:* 2011
Number of Households: 264,224
Jim Brennan, Chief, Winnipeg Fire Paramedic Service
Bill Larkin, Director, Public Works
Barry MacBride, Director, Water & Waste
Deepak Joshi, Director, Planning, Property & Development
Dave Wardrop, Director, Winnipeg Transit
Brad Sacher, Manager, Transportation
Waste Management:
Brady Road Landfill for household & commercial waste
Number of landfill sites: 1
Solid Waste Disposal Fees: $22.50/tonne
Recycling: Both Curbside & Depot; 7 depot locations; Recycling & Garbage Info Line: call 311, or 204/986-8888, Code 9819
Hazardous Waste Depot or Facility: Collection depot: Miller Environmental Corporation, 1803 Hekla Ave., Winnipeg; 204/925-9615
Composters subsidized: Yes
Water & Wastewater Treatment:
Wastewater treatment plant located at Deacon Reservoir is a state-of-the-art facility that began operations on late 2009; treatment capacity of 400m litres of water per day; anticipated active service life of approx. 75 years
Other Initiatives:
Septic waste hauler licensing & monitoring; Abandoned landfill monitoring; Bio-solid application service offered to agricultural land holders; Ozone-depleting substance appliance collection & disposal; Christmas tree, bulk metal & used tire recycling programs; Flood control education; Land drainage collection; Dead animal collection & disposal

Rural Municipality

Hanover
P.O. Box 1720
28 Westland Dr.
Steinbach, MB R5G 1N4
204-326-4488
Fax: 204-326-4830
www.hanovermb.ca
Population: 14,026 *Census Year:* 2011
Number of Households: 3,199
Waste Management:
Number of landfill sites: 1
Recycling: Both Curbside & Depot
Composters subsidized: No
Water & Wastewater Treatment:
Region owns & operates water systems in Grunthal & Kleefeld Co-Op

St. Andrews
P.O. Box 130
500 Railway Ave.
Clandeboye, MB R0C 0P0
204-738-2264
Fax: 204-738-2500
info@rmofstandrews.com
www.rmofstandrews.com
Population: 11,875 *Census Year:* 2011
Number of Households: 4,055
Waste Management:
Number of landfill sites: 2
Recycling: Depot locations: Earl Grey Road Landfill, Clandeboye (Bell Road) Landfill, Harry's Foods, Hwy 9 & St. Andrews Rd.)

Springfield
P.O. Box 219
628 Main St.
Oakbank, MB R0E 1J0
204-444-3321
Fax: 204-444-2137
ltetrault@rmofspringfield.ca
www.rmofspringfield.ca
Population: 14,069 *Census Year:* 2011
Number of Households: 4,335
Waste Management:
Contracted to BI (204/633-9730), Canadian Waste (204/956-6360) & G.H. Sanitation (204/866-3200)
Solid Waste Disposal Fees: $22.50/tonne
Recycling: Both Curbside & Depot; Hillside & Oakwood transfer stations
Water & Wastewater Treatment:
Oakbank & Dugald water treatment stations

New Brunswick

The goal of New Brunswick's Department of Environment & Local Government is to protect, maintain or improve the water quality of its lakes & rivers, the quality of the air breathed & to provide appropriate reduction & disposal of waste. The Department relies on the Clean Air Act, the Clean Environment Act and the Clean Water Act to achieve these goals. All three stipulate that anyone discharging a contaminant needs approval from the Minister.

Municipalities oversee solid waste collection for their municipality & its surrounding area. The Province contracts with local haulers for waste collection in rural areas. There are six sanitary landfill sites, with five transfer stations that complete the province-wide waste management network. The Provincial government provides legislation, regulations & guidelines to manage the environment appropriately. Solid waste commissions, their establishment & operation, & the conditions under which they may accept solid waste, are outlined in the Clean Environment Act and the Regional Solid Waste Commissions Regulation. New Brunswick's rate of diversion of materials from landfills between 2004 and 2008 was 36%, up 12% from the 2004 rate.

Water & wastewater systems are owned & operated by municipalities, the province & private companies. Under the Municipal Drinking Water Program established in 2003, certificates of approval for municipal water treatment & water distribution facilities are required to safeguard drinking water systems. The certificates cover training, certification, monitoring and reporting requirements. The Wellfield Protection Program & the Watershed Protection Programs are designed to ensure safe drinking water for municipalities that rely on groundwater for drinking water by designating the area that needs to be protected from industries or activities operating in the area of a wellfield or watershed. The Canada/New Brunswick Infrastructure Framework Agreement provides New Brunswick with $61.490 million through the Building Canada Fund between 2007-08 and 2013-14 and $225.276 million through the Gas Tax Fund between 2014-15 and 2018-19. These funds will contribute to long-term plans to address infrastructure needs in the areas of water, wastewater, public transit & green energy.

The Beverage Containers Program was devised to reduce the amount of waste going into landfills, or littered along roadsides & waterways. Each beverage distributor is responsible for their containers by refilling or recycling them. Scrap tires & used oil programs exist as well.

Major Municipalities in New Brunswick

City of Bathurst
150 St. George St.
Bathurst, NB E2A 1B5
506-548-0400
Fax: 506-548-0581
city@bathurst.ca
www.bathurst.ca
Population: 12,275 *Census Year:* 2011
Number of Households: 6,017
Paul Godin, Manager, Operational Planning (acting), Operational Services, 506-548-0444, Fax: 506-548-0581
Vincent Wood, General Foreman, Utilities, 506-548-0444, email: Vincent.Wood@bathurst.ca
Paul Godin, General Foreman Engineer
Barry Veniot, Supervisor, Purchasing, 506-548-0700, email: Barry.Veniot@bathurst.ca
Lucien Cormier, Building Inspector, email: Lucien.Cormier@bathurst.ca
Donald McLaughlin, Technician, Planning
Dave Moran, General Foreman, Above Ground Operational Services
Waste Management:
Waste collection responsibility of city above ground operational services department; Waste management responsibility of the Commission des déchets solides de Nepisiguit-Chaleur
Water & Wastewater Treatment:
Water treatment plant & waste water treatment plant operations responsibility of city utilities department

City of Dieppe
333, av Acadie
Dieppe, NB E1A 1G9
506-877-7900
Fax: 506-877-7910
info@dieppe.ca, communications@dieppe.ca
www.dieppe.ca
Population: 23,310 *Census Year:* 2011
Number of Households: 5,771
Jacques LeBlanc, Director, Public Works
Isabelle LeBlanc, Director, Communications, email: communications@dieppe.ca
Luc St-Jules, Director, Municipal Buildings and Environment, email: luc.stjules@dieppe.ca
Charles LeBlanc, Fire Chief, Fire Department, 506-877-7970, email: charles.leblanc@dieppe.ca
Nicole Melanson, Coordinator, Planning and Development, 506-877-7855
Waste Management:
Waste management responsibility of Westmorland-Albert Solid Waste Corporation; Waste collection responsibility of city
Special Bans/by-laws: Water conservation bylaw; Backwater valver bylaw
Water & Wastewater Treatment:
Management, operation & maintenance of water distribution responsibility of city public works department; Maintenance of sanitary & storm sewer components responsibility of city
Other Initiatives:
Three special waste collections & two hazardous waste collections each year; Construction of second water reservoir; Increased pump capacity & pumping station improvements in 2005

City of Edmundston
7 Canada Rd.
Edmundston, NB E3V 1T7
506-739-4636
Fax: 506-737-6902
communication@edmundston.ca
www.ville.edmundston.nb.ca
Population: 16,032 *Census Year:* 2011
Number of Households: 7,725
Paul Dionne, Director, Public Works and Environment, 506-739-2103
Waste Management:
Waste collection contracted to Gallant Entreprises Ltée, 506/739-9390.
Hazardous Waste Depot or Facility: Fire & Rescue Dept., 7 Canada Rd.
Water & Wastewater Treatment:
Wastewater treatment lagoon
Other Initiatives:
Special collections each month

City of Fredericton
City Hall
P.O. Box 130
397 Queen St.
Fredericton, NB E3B 4Y7
506-460-2020
Fax: 506-460-2042
www.fredericton.ca
Population: 56,224 *Census Year:* 2011
Number of Households: 21,987
Paul R. Stapleton, City Administrator, email: cityadmin@fredericton.ca
Philip E. Toole, Fire Chief & Deputy Director, Emergency Measures Organization, 506-460-2500, email: fire@fredericton.ca
W. Frank Flanagan, Director, Development Services, email: planning@fredericton.ca
Murray Jamer, P.Eng., Director, Engineering & Public Works, email: publicworks@fredericton.ca
Wayne Tallon, Director, Community Services, email: wayne.tallon@fredericton.ca
Ken Forrest, Manager, Policy & Planning, 506-460-2110, Fax: 506-460-2894
Sandy MacNeill, Manager, Transit, 506-460-2200, email: transit@fredericton.ca
Andy Holyoke, Superintendent, Water & Sewer, email: publicworks@fredericton.ca
Brian Cochrane, Superintendent, Parks & Trees Division, 506-460-2230, email: recreation@fredericton.ca
Waste Management:
Responsibility of Fredericton Region Solid Waste Commission; Fall leaf pickup; Christmas tree pickup; Spring cleanup
Number of landfill sites: 1
Solid Waste Disposal Fees: $61/tonne (household, ICI); $30.50/tonne (segregated construction & demolition waste)
Recycling: Both Curbside & Depot; Blue Box program for metal food cans, plastics; Grey Box program for newsprint, cardboard/boxboard, & paper; Beverage container redemption centres at 213 Macfarlane St., 70 Timothy Ave. South, & at SWC Recycling on Wilsey Rd.; Recycling Hotline: 506/453-9938
Hazardous Waste Depot or Facility: Depot at Fredericton Landfill, Alison Blvd.; HHW Info: 506/453-9938
Water & Wastewater Treatment:
Water Treatment Plant, off Woodstock Rd., operated by the city's water & sewer division; Barker St. Treatment Plant is operated by Fredericton Area Pollution Control Commission; City's water & sewer division also operates 2 sewage treatment facilities
Other Initiatives:
Backyard Composting Display Site at Fredericton Region Sanitary Landfill, 1775 Alison Blvd., Fredericton

City of Miramichi
141 Henry St.
Miramichi, NB E1V 2N5
506-623-2200
Fax: 506-623-2201
jim.lamkey@miramichi.org
www.miramichi.org
Population: 17,811 *Census Year:* 2011
Number of Households: 7,911
Darlene O'shea, City Treasurer, Finance, 506-623-2200, Fax: 506-623-2434
Ian Gavet, Fire Chief, 506-623-2225, Fax: 506-623-2226
Csaba Kazamer, Clerk, Engineering, 506-623-2021, Fax: 506-623-2201
Suzanne Watters, Clerk, Community Wellness and Recreation, 506-623-2300, Fax: 506-623-2306
Waste Management:
Responsibility of the Northumberland Waste Commission; waste collection responsibility of the city; waste is transported to the Red Pine Solid Waste Disposal Site in Allardville
Water & Wastewater Treatment:
Water & Wastewater treatment plants
Other Initiatives:
Consulting Engineers of Canada Award of Merit for the Paul J. Hayes Wastewater Treatment Plant project

City of Moncton / Ville de Moncton
655 Main St.
Moncton, NB E1C 1E8
506-853-3333
Fax: 506-389-5904
info@moncton.ca
www.moncton.ca
Population: 69,074 *Census Year:* 2011
Number of Households: 27,126
Eric Arsenault, Fire Chief, 506-857-8800, Fax: 506-856-4353, email: info.fire@moncton.ca
Bill Budd, Director, District Planning
D. Morehouse, Director, Engineering Operations, email: info.engineering@moncton.ca
A. Richard, Director, Design & Construction
S. Sparks, Director, Building Inspection, email: info.inspection@moncton.ca
Kevin Silliker, Director, Economic Development, 506-853-3516
Tanya Carter, Manager, Purchasing, 506-853-3535, email: info.purchasing@moncton.ca
Waste Management:
Responsibility of the Westmorland Albert Solid Waste Corporation.
Number of landfill sites: 1 *Landfill Capacity:* 100 years
Solid Waste Disposal Fees: $53.60/tonne
Recycling: Wet/Dry waste separation program: blue or green transparent bags are mandatory for all Moncton residents; over half of all Moncton residential waste is recycled or composted.
Special Bans/by-laws: Waste Collection By-Law P-406
Hazardous Waste Depot or Facility: Westmorland Albert Solid Waste Corporation sponsors collection events twice per year.
Composters subsidized: Yes
Water & Wastewater Treatment:
Wastewater management is the responsibility of the Greater Moncton Sewage Commission, Riverview NB; Water treatment facility is located at Turtle Creek, NB.
Other Initiatives:
Annual spring clean-up week; Christmas tree mulching program.

City of Quispamsis
P.O. Box 21085
12 Landing Ct.
Quispamsis, NB E2E 4Z4
506-849-5778
Fax: 506-849-5799
quispamsis@quispamsis.ca
www.quispamsis.ca
Population: 17,886 *Census Year:* 2011
Number of Households: 4,596
Chris Vriezen, Superintendent, Utility, 506-849-5734, email: cvriezen@quispamsis.ca
Phil Shedd, Superintendent, Works, 506-849-5742, email: pshedd@quispamsis.ca
Margie McGrath, Secretary, Planning Advisory Committee, 506-849-5745, email: mmcgrath@quispamsis.ca
Paul Kirkpatrick, Fleet Foreman, Kennebecasis Valley Fire Dept., 506-849-5726
Gary Losier, Director, Engineering & Works, 506-849-5749, email: glosier@quispamsis.ca
Waste Management:
Town issues licenses to private collectors for waste collection. Town supports recycling & composting programs of the Fundy Region Solid Waste Commission. Fundy Region Solid Waste Commission serves town through operation of the Crane Mountain Landfill, 506/738-1200, Fax: 506/738-1207.
Water & Wastewater Treatment:
Responsibility of the municipality; 13 wastewater pumping stations; 1 expanded & enlarged wastewater treatment plant

City of Riverview
30 Honour House Ct.
Riverview, NB E1C3Y9
506-387-2020
Fax: 506-387-2033
www.townofriverview.ca
Population: 19,128 *Census Year:* 2011
Number of Households: 6,456
Tina Smith, Director, Human Resources, 506-387-2163
Cole Gerry, Director, Parks, Recreation & Community Relations, 506-387-2031
Denis Pleau, Chief, Fire & Rescue, 506-387-2201, email: rivefire@nbnet.nb.ca
Michel Ouellet, Director, Works & Engineering, 506-387-2220
Waste Management:
Serviced by Westmoreland-Albert Solid Waste Corporation
Other Initiatives:
Spring & Fall Clean Ups; Christmas Tree Pick Up

City of Rothesay
70 Hampton Rd.
Rothesay, NB E2E 5L5

506-848-6600
Fax: 506-848-6677
info@rothesay.ca
www.rothesay.ca
Population: 11,947 *Census Year:* 2011
Number of Households: 4,333
Charles Jensen, Director, Recreation, email: charlesjensen@rothesay.ca
Gay Drescher, Director, Development Services, email: gaydrescher@rothesay.ca
Corinne Bexson, Senior GIS Technician, Engineering, email: corrinebexson@rothesay.ca
Waste Management:
Waste collection contracted to Dominion Refuse, 506/633-8986; Waste management responsibility of Fundy Region Solid Waste Commission, which manages Crane Mountain Landfill, 506/738-1212, Fax: 506/738-1207
Water & Wastewater Treatment:
Water Treatment Plant; Two wastewater treatment lagoons & 11 wastewater pumping stations; Water operations monitoring is contracted to Rutter Engineering & Automation Inc. & Zenon Environmental Inc.
Other Initiatives:
Curbside collection of compost

City of Saint John
City Hall
P.O. Box 1971
15 Market Sq.
Saint John, NB E2L 4L1
506-649-6000
inquiries@saintjohn.ca
www.saintjohn.ca
Population: 70,063 *Census Year:* 2011
Number of Households: 31,684
Vacant, Commissioner, Urban Environment Services, 506-658-2835, Fax: 506-658-2837
Vacant, Commissioner, Water, 506-658-4455, Fax: 506-658-4740
Jacqueline Hamilton, Commissioner, Strategic Services, email: strategicservices@saintjohn.ca
Rob Simonds, Fire Chief, 506-658-2910, Fax: 506-658-2916, email: fire@saintjohn.ca
Shayne Galbraith, Director, Works, 506-658-2852, email: works@saintjohn.ca
Peter J. Hanlon, P.Eng., Manager, Water & Sewerage Services, 506-658-2811, Fax: 506-658-4740, email: waterandsewerage@cityofsaintjohn.com
David Logan, Purchasing Agent, Material & Fleet Management, 506-658-2930, Fax: 506-658-4742, email: mat-man@saintjohn.ca
Waste Management:
City issues licenses to waste collectors; Fundy Region Solid Waste Commission serves the city through the operation of the Crane Mountain landfill, a recycling depot program & a community composting program (506/738-1200; Fax: 506/738-1207)
Recycling: Recycling & compostable waste are handled by the Fundy Region Solid Waste Commission (www.fundyrecycles.com); for household appliances, the White Goods Drop Off Program is free & is offered 4x/yr, call 506-658-4455

Other Municipalities in New Brunswick

Commission de gestion des déchets solides de la péninsule Acadienne (COGEDES)
#4, 149, boul St-Pierre ouest
Caraquet, NB E1W 1B6
506-726-2911
Fax: 506-726-2912
cogedes@nbnet.nb.ca
www.cogedes.com
Jean-Marie Gionet, Président
Waste Management:
Responsible for the municipalities of Caraquet, Tracadie-Sheila, St-Isidore, Shippagan, Lamèque, Maisonnette, Grande-Anse, Bas-Caraquet, Paquetville, Saint-Léolin & Bertrand; Waste is transported to Red Pine landfill in Allardville, in Nepisiguit-Chaleur Solid Waste Commission region
Transfer Station(s): Station operated by MDI
Other Initiatives:
Special household hazardous waste collection days

Commission de gestion enviro ressources du Nord-Ouest (COGERNO)
248, ch Clément Roy
Rivière-Verte, NB E7C 2W7
506-263-3470
Fax: 506-263-3476
jean@cogerno.com
www.cogerno.com
Gildard Lavoie, Président
Waste Management:
Number of landfill sites: 1
Solid Waste Disposal Fees: Yes
Recycling: Depot; 30 recycling depots throughout the region
Other Initiatives:
Annual household hazardous waste day

Fredericton Region Solid Waste Commission
P.O. Box 21 A
Fredericton, NB E3B 4Y2
506-453-9930
Fax: 506-453-9933
gordon@frswc.ca
www.frswc.ca
Waste Management:
Serves the following areas: Fredericton Junction, Nackawic, Millville, Keswick, Dumfries, New Maryland, Chipman, Estey Bridge, Stanley, Cambridge Narrows, Lincoln, Oromocto, Tracy, Gagetown, Fredericton, Minto.
Number of landfill sites: 1
Solid Waste Disposal Fees: $59/tonne (residential/ICI); $29.50/tonne (construction/demolition material)
Recycling: Both Curbside & Depot; 5 depots in Oromocto, Minto, Stanley, Cambridge-Narrows, Fredericton
Hazardous Waste Depot or Facility: Depot at Fredericton landfill, 790 Wilsey Rd. South
Other Initiatives:
Recycling at Work program in the Fredericton & Oromocto areas.

Fundy Region Solid Waste Commission
P.O. Box 3032
Grand-Bay Westfield, NB E5K 4V3
506-738-1212
Fax: 506-738-1207
hotline@fundyrecycles.com
www.fundyrecycles.com
Pat Gallagher Jette, Chair
Waste Management:
Commission serves the following municipalities: Saint John, Grand Bay-Westfield, Hampton, Quispamsis, Rothesay, St. Martins, plus 10 parishes
Number of landfill sites: 1
Solid Waste Disposal Fees: $108/tonne (municipal & commerical waste); $28/tonne (construction & demolition waste); $45/tonne (compostable material)
Recycling: Depot; 23 recycling depots located throughout the region
Hazardous Waste Depot or Facility: Crane Mountain Landfill, 10 Crane Mountain Rd., Saint John
Composters subsidized: Yes
Other Initiatives:
Sale of compost

Kent County Solid Waste Commission
#210,211 boul Irving
Bouctouche, NB E4S 2B9
506-743-1818
Fax: 506-743-8640
kentsolidwaste@yahoo.ca
Neil Leblanc, Chair
Waste Management:
Waste is transported to the Westmorland-Albert Regional Wet/Dry Processing Facility & Sanitary Landfill, Berry Mills.
Transfer Station(s): Located at Bouctouche, operated by Tiru NB, Inc.
Recycling: Westmorland-Albert Solid Waste Corporation Dry plant
Hazardous Waste Depot or Facility: WASWC Household Hazardous Waste Depot
Composters subsidized: Yes
Other Initiatives:
Compost (wet waste) is sent to the WASWC Wet plant; Recycling wet/dry program; WASWC Mobile Household Hazardous Waste Unit

Kings County Region Solid Waste Commission
P.O. Box 4861
Sussex, NB E4E 5L9
506-433-6502
Fax: 506-432-1122
kingssolidwaste@nb.aibn.com
Marc Thorne, Chair
Waste Management:
Waste from transfer station is transported to the Westmorland-Albert Solid Waste Corporation's sanitary landfill site
Transfer Station(s): Yes

Nepisiguit-Chaleur Solid Waste Commission
1300, rte 360
Allardville, NB E8L 1H5
506-725-2402
Fax: 506-725-2410
redpine@nb.sympatico.ca
Waste Management:
NCSWC operates the Red Pine landfill at Red Pine Station which accepts waste from the following commissions: Nepisiguit-Chaleur Solid Waste Commission, Northumberland Solid Waste Commission, COGEDES Transfer Station, Restigouche Solid Waste Corporation
Number of landfill sites: 1

Northumberland Solid Waste Commission
505 Old King George Hwy.
Miramichi, NB E1V 1J8
506-778-6646
Fax: 506-778-6642
nswc@nb.aibn.com
www.nswc-cdsn.ca
Waste Management:
Waste is transported to the Red Pine Sanitary Landfill in the Nepisiguit-Chaleur Solid Waste Commission region
Recycling: Depot
Other Initiatives:
Paper, cardboard, plastic & metal can recyclying program, with depots located in the city of Miramichi & throughout Northumberland County

Restigouche Solid Waste Corporation
P.O. Box 93
162B Water St.
Campbellton, NB E3N 3G1
506-789-2111
Fax: 506-789-2111
Waste Management:
Waste from the Restigouche Transfer Station is transported to the Red Pine landfill site in Allard
Transfer Station(s): Transfer station operated by MDI
Recycling: Depot; 9 recycling depots throughout region for cardboard & paper

South West Solid Waste Commission
P.O. Box 70
St Stephen, NB E3L 2W9
506-466-7830
Fax: 506-466-7833
crww@nbnet.nb.ca
www.swswc.com
Waste Management:
Commission serves the following: Blacks Harbour, St. Andrews, St. George, St. Stephen, Grand Manan, Canterbury, Harvey, McAdam, Meductic, Charlotte County, York County, Carleton County. Waste collection contracted to private companies. Contracting is the responsibility of the municipality or local municipal services representative.
Number of landfill sites: 1
Solid Waste Disposal Fees: $68.50/tonne (household waste); $20/tonne (construction/demolition material)
Recycling: Depot; 12 locations
Hazardous Waste Depot or Facility: Hemlock Knoll Landfill Site Lawrence Station
Composters subsidized: Yes
Other Initiatives:
Compost demonstration site, at Hemlock Knoll landfill site. Construction of new recycling plant.

Valley Solid Waste Commission
#102, 633 rue Main
Woodstock, NB E7M 2C6

506-325-4388
Fax: 506-325-4389
Toll Free Phone: 1-866-312-8800
vswc@nb.sympatico.ca
www.valleysolidwaste.com
James Kennedy, Président
Waste Management:
Waste disposal with two NB landfills & 1 transfer station contracted to commission
Recycling: Depot; Several community recycling depots
Other Initiatives:
Household hazardous waste round-up events

Westmorland-Albert Solid Waste Corporation

P.O. Box 1397
Moncton, NB E1C 8T6
506-877-1050
Fax: 506-877-1060
bslater@nbnet.nb.ca
www.westmorlandalbert.com
Bill Slater, General Manager
Waste Management:
Serves the following areas: Alma, Cap-Péle, Dieppe, Dorchester, Hillsborough, Moncton, Memramcook, Petitcodiac, Port Elgin, Riverside-Albert, Riverview, Sackville, Salisbury, Shediac; Waste collection is the responsibility of municipalities
Number of landfill sites: 1
Solid Waste Disposal Fees: $53.58/tonne (mixed waste); $20/tonne (construction & demolition waste)
Transfer Station(s): Yes
Hazardous Waste Depot or Facility: Mobile HHW recovery unit operates in the spring & fall
Other Initiatives:
Christmas tree mulching; Wet/dry source separation program includes curbside collection & transportation to WASWC Waste Management Facility; Electronic recycling program; Rechargeable battery recycling program

Newfoundland & Labrador

The Environmental Protection Act prohibits the pollution of air, water & soil. There are provisions in the act for the management of sewage, wastewater, landfills, solid waste, recycling & water quality.

The Water Resources Management department is in charge of the protection, enhancement & utilization of all water resources in the province. This division monitors drinking water & groundwater resources, conducts studies & regulates water systems.

The Environment Branch is also responsible for several waste management programs within the province. The Waste Management Section takes care of the management, collection and disposal of solid waste, hazardous & special waste. Its duties include developing environmental standards that comply with the Waste Management Strategy, managing waste, disposing harmful waste and regulating environmental standards. They have implemented a program that works to safely dispose of asbestos, which is a health hazard and a danger to the environment.

The Climate Change Action Plan 2011 outlined two initiatives relevant to municipalities specifically-assessing vulnerabilities of local communities to climate change & educating municipalities on the impacts of climate change & the development of adaptation strategies.

Major Municipalities in Newfoundland & Labrador

City of Conception Bay South

106 Conception Bay Hwy.
Conception Bay South, NL A1W 3A5
709-834-6500
Fax: 709-834-8337
jmiller@conceptionbaysouth.ca
www.conceptionbaysouth.ca
Population: 24,848 *Census Year:* 2011
Number of Households: 7,142
Elaine Mitchell, Director, Planning, 709-834-6553
Ron Franey, Director, Public Works, 709-834-6523
Dave Tibbo, Director, Recreation & Leisure Services, 709-834-6534
Todd Brophy, Fire Chief, Fire Department, 709-834-6543
Waste Management:
Waste collection contracted to Bishop's Service Ltd.
Water & Wastewater Treatment:
Topsail sewage treatment plant, Goodland Rd.
Other Initiatives:
Bulk garbage bins at Topsail Treatment Plant

City of Corner Brook

City Hall
P.O. Box 1080
Corner Brook, NL A2H 6E1
709-637-1500
Fax: 709-637-1625
cityhall@cornerbrook.com
www.cornerbrook.com
Population: 19,886 *Census Year:* 2011
Number of Households: 8,296
Neville Wheaton, Fire Chief, 709-637-1615, email: nmwheaton@cornerbrook.com
Gerry Cole, Supervisor, Recreational Services, 709-637-1232, email: gcole@cornerbrook.com
Steve May, Director, Operational Services, 709-637-1541, Fax: 709-637-1502, email: smay@cornerbrook.com
Todd Pickett, Land Management Officer, 709-637-1544, email: tpickett@cornerbrook.com
Colleen Humphries, Supervisor, Planning, 709-637-1553, email: chumphries@cornerbrook.com
James Warford, P.Eng., Coordinator, Engineering Services, 709-637-1626, email: jwarford@cornerbrook.com
Keith Costello, Superintendent, Water & Sewer, 709-637-1595, email: kcostello@cornerbrook.com
Barry Ellsworth, Manager, Public Works, 709-637-1509, email: bellsworth@cornerbrook.com
Percy Joyce, Officer, Land Management, 709-637-1544, email: pjoyce@cornerbrook.com
Deon Rumbolt, Supervisor, Development & Inspection, 709-637-1552, email: drumbolt@cornerbrook.com
Rhea Hutchings, Sustainable Development Officer, Operational Services, 709-637-1574, email: rhutchings@cornerbrook.com
Craig Kennedy, Superintendent, Public Works, 709-637-1607, email: ckennedy@cornerbrook.com
Waste Management:
Wild Cove Landfill; Waste collection is contracted to Murphy Bros. Ltd., 709/634-3345
Number of landfill sites: 1*Landfill Capacity:* 11 years
Solid Waste Disposal Fees: Schedule as per type of vehicle & cubic meters
Recycling: Both Curbside & Depot; Curbside recycling collection/blue bag program: info 709-637-1630; Green Depot operating by Scotia Recycling Ltd. located at 55 Maple Valley Rd., call 709-634-2025; household yard waste/leaves & Christmas tree recycling program in Fall/Winter.
Special Bans/by-laws: Voluntary pesticide ban
Hazardous Waste Depot or Facility: Household hazardous waste collection in Spring and Fall; household metals recycling can be dropped off free of charge at the Wild Cove Landfill; disposal of used tires can be arranged through Multi Materials Stewardship Board, call 709-753-0948
Water & Wastewater Treatment:
Treatment contracted to City of Cornerbrook, 709/637-1595; Chlorine treatment plants located in Trout Pond, Second Pond, Burnt Pond
Other Initiatives:
Spring Cleanup in May.

City of Grand Falls-Windsor

P.O. Box 439
Grand Falls-Windsor, NL A2A 2J8
709-489-0412
Fax: 709-489-0465
jrowsell@grandfallswindsor.com
www.grandfallswindsor.com
Population: 13,725 *Census Year:* 2011
Number of Households: 5,253
Michael Pinsent, Town Manager, 709-487-0407, Fax: 709-292-0018, email: mpinsent@grandfallswindsor.com
Jeff Saunders, Director, Engineering Works, 709-489-0427, Fax: 709-489-0465, email: jsaunders@grandfallswindsor.com
Vince J. McKenzie, Fire Chief, 709-489-0431, Fax: 709-489-0885, email: firechief@grandfallswindsor.com
Dave Nichols, Director, Parks & Recreation, 709-489-0450, Fax: 709-489-0454, email: dnichols@grandfallswindsor.com
Robert Thompson, Supervisor, Engineering & Works, 709-489-0421, Fax: 709-489-0467, email: rthompson@grandfallswindsor.com
Mark Kelly, Clerk, Purchasing, 709-489-0422, Fax: 709-489-0465, email: purchasing@grandfallswindsor.com
Waste Management:
Trans Canada Hwy. Landfill closed; New Bay Rd. Regional Landfill site, managed by Exploits Regional Services Board, now serves the town
Recycling: Curbside
Other Initiatives:
Spring Clean-up; Household Hazardous Waste Collection program handled by the Multi-Materials Stewardship Board

City of Mount Pearl

3 Centennial St.
Mount Pearl, NL A1N 1G4
709-748-1006
Fax: 709-748-1150
info@mtpearl.nf.ca
www.mountpearl.ca
Population: 24,284 *Census Year:* 2011
Number of Households: 9,131
Stephen Jewczyk, Director, Planning & Development, 709-748-1029, email: sjewczyk@mountpearl.ca
Scott Lush, Director, Infrastructure & Public Works, 709-748-1028, email: slush@mountpearl.ca
Brian Chmarney, Director, Community Services, 709-748-1027, email: bchmarney@mountpearl.ca
Bronda Aylward, Director, Economic Development, 709-748-1096, email: baylward@mountpearl.ca
Jason Silver, Director, Corporate Services, 709-748-1026, email: jsilver@mountpearl.ca
Norm Snelgrove, Manager, Finance, 709-748-1159, email: nsnelgrove@mountpearl.ca
Colleen Butler, Manager, Human Resources, 709-748-1095, email: cbutler@mountpearl.ca
Blair Tilley, Superintendent, Municipal Enforcement, 709-748-1068, email: btilley@mountpearl.ca
Waste Management:
Recycling: Curbside
Hazardous Waste Depot or Facility: 59 Clyde Ave.
Water & Wastewater Treatment:
Mt. Pearl's water supplied by Bay Bulls Big Pond Water Treatment Plant; Regional water system administered by Regional Water Authority
Other Initiatives:
Water conservation program; Energy management control system for major city facilities; Household hazardous waste collection twice a year; Adopt-a-Park; Slam Dunk your Junk; Community clean-ups; Bulk garbage collection; Construction of sewage treatment plant for Mount Pearl, St. John's & Paradise

City of St. John's

City Hall
P.O. Box 908
10 New Gower St.
St. John's, NL A1C 5M2
709-754-2489
Fax: 709-576-7688
311 for city services
council@stjohns.ca
www.stjohns.ca
Population: 106,172 *Census Year:* 2011
Number of Households: 42,443
Ronald Penney, City Solicitor & City Manager, 709-576-8557, Fax: 709-576-8561, email: legal@stjohns.ca
Walt Mills, Director, Engineering, 709-576-8658, Fax: 709-576-8625
David Blackmore, Director, Building & Property Management, 709-576-8701, Fax: 709-576-8160
Cliff Johnston, Director, Planning, 709-576-8383, Fax: 709-576-8625
Elizabeth Lawrence, Director, Economic Development, Tourism & Culture, 709-576-8203, Fax: 709-576-8246
Paul Mackey, Director, Public Works & Parks, 709-576-8303, Fax: 709-576-8026
Jim Clarke, Manager, Streets & Parks, 709-576-8541, Fax: 709-576-8026
P.J. (Jim) Ford, Manager, Regulatory Services, 709-576-8294, Fax: 709-576-8160
Geraldine King, Manager, Environmental Initiatives, 709-576-8613, Fax: 709-576-8625
Joe Sampson, Manager, Development
Bob Wilson, Manager, Energy Efficiency, 709-576-8238, Fax: 709-576-8160
Robin King, Transportation Engineer, 709-576-8232, Fax: 709-576-8625
Waste Management:
Number of landfill sites: 1*Landfill Capacity:* 30+ years

Solid Waste Disposal Fees: $23/tonne
Clean Fill Fee: No
Recycling: Robin Hood Bay Integrated Waste Management Facility, 340 East White Hills Rd.; the site handles regular commercial & residential recycling & compostables, solid waste, & household hazardous waste; Christmas tree mulching; leaf disposal
Hazardous Waste Depot or Facility: Robin Hood Bay Integrated Waste Management Facility handles household hazardous waste, & collects & processes leachate & methane gas
Composters subsidized: No
Water & Wastewater Treatment:
Bay Bulls Big Pond Regional Water Facility, 709/745-1870; Windsor Lake Water Treatment Facility, 709/576-8391; Ruby Line, & Kenmount Pumping Stations; Mount Pearl, & Mundy Pond Reservoirs
Other Initiatives:
St. John's Harbour Clean-up; Waste Diversion Pilot Project; Well Aware Program; Idle Free St. John's (climate change initiative); pesticide reduction initiative; St. John's Clean & Beautiful litter clean-up program

Other Municipalities in Newfoundland & Labrador

Gander
100 Elizabeth Dr.
Gander, NL A1V 1G7
709-651-2930
Fax: 709-256-5809
info@gandercanada.com
www.gandercanada.com
Population: 11,054 *Census Year:* 2011
Number of Households: 3,689
Waste Management:
Number of landfill sites: 1
Solid Waste Disposal Fees: No
Clean Fill Fee: No
Recycling: Depot
Special Bans/by-laws: Municipal wildlife stewardship agreement
Compost Sites: Yes
Water & Wastewater Treatment:
Beaverwood Sewage Treatment Plant, Navy Rd.; Gander Bay Road Wastewater Treatment Plant, Gander Bay Rd.
Other Initiatives:
Household hazardous waste day; Cleanup Week

Northwest Territories

The Government of the Northwest Territories funds & manages the water & wastewater, & waste management programs for small non-tax based communities. Major tax-based municipalities are fully responsible for the management & partially responsible for the funding for their municipal programs. The Environmental Protection Division of the Dept. of Environment & Natural Resources is responsible for programs that cover hazardous substances, waste management, air quality & environmental impact assessment. The Water Resources Agreement provides for the conservation and use of water; research, collection and publication of data pertaining to water resources; regulating quality and quantity control of water; and establishing an intergovernmental committee for further action.

Major Municipalities in Northwest Territories

City of Yellowknife
P.O. Box 580
4807 - 52 St.
Yellowknife, NT X1A 2N4
867-920-5600
Fax: 867-920-5649
Alt. E-mail: council@yellowknife.ca
cityclerk@yellowknife.ca
www.yellowknife.ca
Population: 19,234 *Census Year:* 2011
Number of Households: 6,514
Dennis Kefalas, Senior Administrative Officer, 867-920-5685, email: dkefalas@yellowknife.ca
Darcy Hernblad, Fire Chief, 867-766-5501, email: dhernblad@yellowknife.ca
Chris Greenhorn, Director, Public Works, 867-920-5637, email: cgreencorn@yellowknife.ca
Jeffrey Humble, Director, Planning & Development, 867-920-5624, email: jhumble@yellowknife.ca
Dennis Marchiori, Director, Public Safety, 867-920-5685, email: dmarchiori@yellowknife.ca
Nalini Naidoo, Director, Communications & Economic Development, 867-920-5660, email: nnaidoo@yellowknife.ca
Grant White, Director, Community Services, 867-920-5624, email: gwhite@yellowknife.ca
Devin Lake, Acting Manager, Planning & Lands, 867-920-5674, email: dlake@yellowknife.ca
Waste Management:
User fees for waste collection for commercial & multi-family residences; 3 bag limit for residential pickup, with additional bags requiring a $1 tag; waste collection contracted to Kavanaugh Bros Ltd. Waste Removal Services, 403-873-2811.
Number of landfill sites: 1
Solid Waste Disposal Fees: $75/tonne (commercial waste); $45/tonne (construction & demolition waste); $5/load for mixed residential waste
Clean Fill Fee: No
Recycling: Depot; Recyclables must be sorted, and taken to depot locations: Yellowknife Landfill, Co-op parking lot; Pool/Arena parking lot; Schooldraw Ave. & Franklin Ave., 52nd Ave., & Extra Foods on Old Airport Rd. For fee-based curbside pickup, call Yellowknife Recycling Services.
Water & Wastewater Treatment:
Department of Public Works & Engineering is responsible for water treatment & sewage disposal facilities.
Other Initiatives:
Used motor oil collected at baling facility at the Solid Waste Management Facility; Annual Spring & Fall clean up; Adopt-A-Street; Environmental Spill Line, 867-820-8130; Community energy plan

Nova Scotia

Municipalities are responsible for waste management, water treatment & supply, & wastewater treatment.

The province is divided into seven solid waste management regions. The provincial Department of Environment's Solid Waste Resource Management Branch is responsible for a number of initiatives, including recycling, composting, disposal bans & the province's Solid Waste Strategy. The private, not-for-profit Resource Recovery Fund Board funds municipal & regional waste diversion programs. Fifty-three of 55 municipalities have centralized composting facilities for the business sector. Ninety-nine percent of residents have access to curbside recycling programs. Draft regulations have been drawn up to ban electronics from landfills. All landfills are required to have containment landfill systems (liners). The current number of landfills has been reduced to nine.

Under the Drinking Water Strategy (2002), the province is auditing all municipal water systems to assess that all comply with provincial standards. Clarification & simplification of regulations regarding operation of water & wastewater facilities are under review. Standards regarding the treatment & application of sewage sludge on lands were established in 2004. A further commitment was made in 2010 under the Environmental Goals and Sustainable Prosperity Act to ensure an integrated approach to managing water resources.

Through the federal government's Gas Tax Fund, outlined in Economic Action Plan 2013, Nova Scotia will be allocated $276,776,000 between 2014 and 2019 for municipal infrastructure projects that focus on clean air, water and reducing greenhouse gas emissions.

Counties & Municipal Districts in Nova Scotia

Cape Breton
Civic Centre
320 Esplanade
Sydney, NS B1P 7B9
902-563-5005
Fax: 902-564-0481
cbrm@cbrm.ns.ca
www.cbrm.ns.ca
Population: 97,398 *Census Year:* 2011
Number of Households: 45,491
Marie Walsh, Chief Administrative Officer, 902-563-5005, Fax: 902-564-0481
Malcolm Gillis, Director, Planning, 902-563-5027, Fax: 902-564-0481, email: mggillis@cbrm.ns.ca
Bernie MacKinnon, Director, Fire Services, 902-563-5132
Francis Campbell, Manager, Solid Waste, 902-563-5182, email: solidwaste@cbrm.ns.ca
Waste Management:
Incinerator, off Sydney Port Access Rd., 902/563-5592
Recycling: Both Curbside & Depot; Green Island Recycling Facility, Sydport Industrial Park
Compost Sites: Yes
Water & Wastewater Treatment:
The municipality manages 10 water treatment & pumping facilities at the following locations: Sydney, Glace Bay, New Waterford, North Sydney, Louisbourg, Birch Grove, Port Morien, Donkin, Former Radar Base & Coxheath; Water Treatment: 902/562-5509
Other Initiatives:
Water conservation program; Mandatory blue bag recycling program; 5 garbage bag limit per household

Halifax Regional Municipality
P.O. Box 1749
1841 Argyle St.
Halifax, NS B3J 3A5
902-490-4000
Fax: 902-490-4208
Toll Free Phone: 1-800-835-6428
www.halifax.ca
Population: 390,096 *Census Year:* 2011
Number of Households: 153,328
Larry Munroe, Municipal Auditor General, Business Systems & Control
Richard Butts, Chief Administrative Officer, 902-490-6430
Bill Mosher, Chief Director, Fire & Emergency Services
Ken Reashor, Director, Transportation & Public Works
Phillip Townsend, Director, Infrastructure & Asset Management
Vacant, Director, Community Development
Alan Brady, Manager, Wastewater Treatment, 302-835-9566
Gord Helm, Manager, Solid Waste Resources, 902-490-6606
John P. Sheppard, P.Eng., Manager, Environmental Engineering Services, 902-490-6958, Fax: 902-490-4858, email: sheppaj@halifax.ca
John Sibbald, Coordinator, Pollution Prevention, 902-490-5527, email: sibbalj@halifax.ca
Carl Yates, Manager, Halifax Water, 902-490-4827, Fax: 902-490-4808, email: general.manager@hrwc.ca
Waste Management:
Household hazardous waste depot located behind Material Recycling Facility, Bayers Lake Industrial Park; No curbside pickup
Number of landfill sites: 1*Landfill Capacity:* 22 years
Solid Waste Disposal Fees: $125/tonne; Otter Lake Processing & Disposal Facility; composting facilities located at Gloria McCluskey Ave., Burnside & Evergreen Pl., & Ragged Lake
Recycling: Both Curbside & Depot; 22 Enviro-Depots in municipality. Material Recycling Facility, Bayer's Lake Industrial Park, 20 Horseshoe Dr., Halifax, 902/490-6640
Special Bans/by-laws: Pesticides, solid waste, construction & demolition materials recycling & disposal.
Hazardous Waste Depot or Facility: The Household Hazardous Waste (HHW) Depot is located at the Bayer's Lake Industrial Park, 20 Horseshoe Lake Dr., Halifax
Compost Sites: Yes *Composters subsidized:* Yes
Water & Wastewater Treatment:
Wastewater Treatment Division of Environmental Management Services operates & maintains the following municipal facilities: Water Pollution Control Plants at Eastern Passage, Mill Cove, Lakeside/Timberlea, Lockview-MacPherson, Springfield Lake, Middle Musquodoboit, North Preston, Uplands Park & Aerotech; Sewage treatment plants at Steeves Subdivision, Frame Subdivision, Lively Subdivision, Leachate Treatment Facility, Aerotech Water Treatment Plant & Aerotech Biosolids Lagoon; 2004 contract sign
Other Initiatives:
The Sustainable Environment Management Office has initiatives in the areas of Clean Land, Clean Air, Clean Water, & Clean Energy: long term policy & planning for water quality, open space, affordable housing, transit, waste management, pesticide use reduction, climate change adaptation strategy, corporate & community greenhouse gas emission reduction, use of bio-fuels, Corporate Smart Car Program, the Harbour Solutions Project, road salt management, wastewater/stormwater management strategies, Wind Energy Master Plan & other initiatives for geothermal energy, solar energy, LED street & traffic lights, heat recovery, & methane gas recovery. In addition, the HRM participates in Earth Day & other community projects to promote sustainable use of energy & the safeguarding of the environment; Bennery Lake Watershed protection project;

ClimAdapt: private & public sector agencies coming together to develop strategies to adapt to the effects of climate change; & the Compost Research Trial

Major Municipalities in Nova Scotia

City of Truro
P.O. Box 427
695 Prince St.
Truro, NS B2N 5C5
902-895-4484
Fax: 902-893-0501
town@truro.ca
www.truro.ca
Population: 12,059 *Census Year:* 2011
Number of Households: 5,583
Chuck Roberts, Senior Engineer
Doug MacKenzie, Director, Parks & Recreation Committee, 902-893-6078, Fax: 902-893-6099, email: dmackenzie@truro.ca
Tom Bremner, Chief, Fire, 902-895-8645, Fax: 902-895-8063
Juanita Bigelow, Administrator, Planning, 902-895-1148, Fax: 902-893-6091
Waste Management:
Responsibility shared by Truro & Colchester County
Number of landfill sites: 1*Landfill Capacity:* 35 years
Water & Wastewater Treatment:
Victoria Park Water Treatment Plant; Central Colchester Wastewater Treatment Plant
Other Initiatives:
Spring Clean-up

Other Municipalities in Nova Scotia

Kings County
P.O. Box 100
87 Cornwallis St.
Kentville, NS B4N 3W3
902-678-6141
Fax: 902-678-9279
1-888-337-2999
inquiry@county.kings.ns.ca
www.county.kings.ns.ca
Population: 60,589 *Census Year:* 2011
Number of Households: 22,197
Waste Management:
Waste management handled by Valley Waste Resource Management, 902/679-1325, Toll free 1-877/927-8300
Water & Wastewater Treatment:
Public Works operates & maintains the Greenwood Water Utility (supplier to village of Greenwood & an area of Aylesford); Wastewater treatment plants: Hants Border, Avonport, Canning, Aldershot, New Minas, Waterville, Aylesford, Greenwood

Rural Municipality

Annapolis County
P.O. Box 100
752 George St.
Annapolis Royal, NS B0S 1A0
902-532-2331
Fax: 902-532-2096
Alt. Phone: 902-825-2005
info@annapoliscounty.ns.ca
www.annapoliscounty.ca
Population: 20,756 *Census Year:* 2011
Number of Households: 8,801
Waste Management:
Waste collection & disposal responsibility of Valley Waste Resource Management Authority
Water & Wastewater Treatment:
Water supply & sewer systems responsibility of municipality's engineering services

Antigonish County
285 Beech Hill Rd.
Antigonish, NS B2G 0B4
902-863-1117
Fax: 902-863-5751
clerk@antigonishcounty.ns.ca
www.antigonishcounty.ns.ca
Population: 19,589 *Census Year:* 2011
Number of Households: 6,631
Waste Management:
Number of landfill sites: 1
Solid Waste Disposal Fees: $45/tonne
Clean Fill Fee: No
Recycling: Curbside

Chester District
P.O. Box 369
151 King St.
Chester, NS B0J 1J0
902-275-3554
Fax: 902-275-4771
administration@district.chester.ns.ca
www.chester.ca
Population: 10,599 *Census Year:* 2011
Number of Households: 5,848
Waste Management:
For information about waste collection contact G.E.'s All Trucking, 1-866-303-1103
Number of landfill sites: 1
Recycling: Curbside
Hazardous Waste Depot or Facility: Kaizer Meadow Landfill, 450 Kaizer Meadow Rd.
Other Initiatives:
Adopt-a-Highway; Environment Week; Green Cart program for organics; Composting/Recycling Workshops; Plant-a-Row; Grow & Row; Derelict Vehicle Removal

Colchester County
P.O. Box 697
1 Church St.
Truro, NS B2N 5E7
902-897-3160
Fax: 902-843-4066
866-728-5144 (toll-free)
www.colchester.ca
Population: 50,968 *Census Year:* 2011
Number of Households: 18,943
Waste Management:
Number of landfill sites: 1*Landfill Capacity:* 70 years (Regional Balefill & Composting Facility, Kemptown)
Solid Waste Disposal Fees: $60/tonne (mixed garbage)
Recycling: Both Curbside & Depot; Enviro-Depot locations: John Ross & Sons, Truro; Subway Bottle Exchange, Bible Hill; TNT Recycling, Stewiacke; Tatamagouche Recycling, Tatamagouche; Colchester Materials Recovery Facility, Kemptown
Hazardous Waste Depot or Facility: Clean Harbours, 640 McElmon Rd., Debert
Compost Sites: Yes *Composters subsidized:* Yes
Water & Wastewater Treatment:
Wastewater treatment facility handles wastewater from central region areas of Truro, Valley, Salmon River, Bible Hill, Hilden, Lower Truro, Truro Heights & part of Onslow; County also maintains wastewater treatment plants in Tatamagouche, Great Village & Brookfield; Wastewater treatment information, 902/897-3175; Municipality manages only the Tatamagouche Water Utility
Other Initiatives:
Free compost for residents; Spring & Fall clean ups; Christmas tree collection; Free annual removal of derelict vehicles for recycling; Residents are supplied with green carts & small mini-bins for composting; Backyard earth machines are also for sale; In vessel composting program at Waste Management Park in Kemptown; Educational programs

Cumberland County
E.D. Fullerton Municipal Bldg.
1395 Blair Lake Rd., RR#6
Amherst, NS B4H 3Y4
902-667-2313
Fax: 902-667-1352
Toll Free Phone: 1-888-756-6262
info@cumberlandcounty.ns.ca
www.cumberlandcounty.ns.ca
Population: 31,353 *Census Year:* 2011
Number of Households: 13,346
Waste Management:
Cumberland Central Landfill operated by Cumberland Joint Services Management Authority, 902/667-5141
Number of landfill sites: 1
Transfer Station(s): Yes
Recycling: Depot; Cumberland Central Recycling Facility, 2052 Littleforks Rd., Littleforks, NS
Special Bans/by-laws: Open Burning Bylaw
Compost Sites: Yes *Composters subsidized:* Yes
Water & Wastewater Treatment:
Amherst Marsh Ultra Violet Treatment Building; Pugwash Sewage Treatment Plant
Other Initiatives:
Enviro-Depots for beverage container refunds, unused paint & automotive batteries; Scheduled collections for household hazardous waste

Hants East District
P.O. Box 190
230 - 15 Commerce Ct.
Elmsdale, NS B2S 3K5
902-883-2299
Fax: 888-684-5912
1-866-758-2299
info@easthants.ca
www.easthants.ca
Population: 22,111 *Census Year:* 2011
Number of Households: 8,176
Waste Management:
Solid waste collection & transportation contracted to Miller Waste Systems, 902/883-4561
Number of landfill sites: 1
Solid Waste Disposal Fees: Yes
Water & Wastewater Treatment:
2 water utilities & 3 sewage collection & treatment systems are operated by the municipality's public works department for the following communities: Enfield, Elmsdale, Lantz, Milford & Shubenacadie
Other Initiatives:
Water conservation program; Household hazardous waste & paint events; Christmas tree collection; Derelict vehicle removal program; Compost give-away events; Community clean-ups

Inverness County
Municipal Bldg.
P.O. Box 179
375 Main St.
Port Hood, NS B0E 2W0
902-787-2274
Fax: 902-787-3110
www.invernesscounty.ca
Population: 17,947 *Census Year:* 2011
Number of Households: 7,416
Waste Management:
Contracted to Leo S. Bourgeois Inc., c/o Terry Bennett, 902/224-1600
Solid Waste Disposal Fees: $75/tonne
Clean Fill Fee: Yes; $30/tonne
Recycling: Curbside
Compost Sites: Yes *Composters subsidized:* Yes
Water & Wastewater Treatment:
Inverness, Judique, Mabour, Port Hood, Whycocomagh
Other Initiatives:
New regional sewage treatment plant & wastewater collection system, replacing two sewage treatment plants in Port Hawkesbury & Port Hastings

Lunenburg District
P.O. Box 200
210 Aberdeen Rd.
Bridgewater, NS B4V 2W8
902-543-8181
Fax: 902-543-7123
info@modl.ca
www.modl.ca
Population: 25,118 *Census Year:* 2011
Number of Households: 12,906
Waste Management:
Number of landfill sites: 1
Solid Waste Disposal Fees: $110/tonne
Recycling: Both Curbside & Depot; Lunenburg Regional Recycling & Composting Facility, 908 Mullock Rd., Whynott's Settlement, 902/543-2991, Email: recycle@lunrecycle.ns.ca
Hazardous Waste Depot or Facility: Lunenberg Regional Recycling & Composting Facility
Composters subsidized: Yes
Water & Wastewater Treatment:
Municipality collected septage & treatment system, located at Lunenburg Regional Recycling & Composting Facility; Sewage treatment plants, located at New Germany & Conquerall Bank; Public community sewer system at Hebbville is connected to Town of Bridgewater sewage treatment plant
Other Initiatives:
Closure of landfill at Lunenburg Regional Recycling &

Composting Facility; New landfill to be located in Chester; Transfer station at Recycling & Composting Facility to operate in 2006

Pictou County

P.O. Box 910
46 Municipal Dr.
Pictou, NS B0K 1H0
902-485-4311
Fax: 902-485-6475
902-752-1530
cmacintosh@county.pictou.ns.ca
www.county.pictou.ns.ca
Population: 45,643 *Census Year:* 2011
Waste Management:
Number of landfill sites: 1
Solid Waste Disposal Fees: $75/metric tonne; $55/tonne organics
Recycling: Both Curbside & Depot; Enviro-Depot locations: Johns Bottle & Recycling Depot, Pictou; Bill Stewart Metal & Bottle, New Glasgow; Golden Penney, New Glasgow
Hazardous Waste Depot or Facility: Mount William Landfill Site, Mount William, NS
Composters subsidized: Yes
Water & Wastewater Treatment:
Central Sewage Treatment Plant (part of East River Pollution Abatement System)

Richmond County

P.O. Box 120
2357 Hwy. 206
Arichat, NS B0E 1A0
902-226-2400
Fax: 902-226-1510
www.richmondcounty.ca
Population: 9,293 *Census Year:* 2011
Number of Households: 3,994
Waste Management:
Sorting of recyclables responsibility of Green Island Recycling Ltd.
Number of landfill sites: 1
Solid Waste Disposal Fees: $35/tonne (sorted material); $70/tonne (unsorted material)
Recycling: Curbside
Water & Wastewater Treatment:
Arichat/Petit de Grat Water Treatment Plant; Evanston Sewage Treatment Plant; Petit de Grat Sewage Treatment Plant; Operation & maintenance of the municipality's water & sewer services responsibility of county public works department
Other Initiatives:
Free curbside collection of \heavy collection\"" in May & Sept.""

West Hants

P.O. Box 3000
76 Morrison Dr.
Windsor, NS B0N 2T0
902-798-8391
Fax: 902-798-8553
west.hants@westhants.ca
www.westhants.ca
Population: 14,165 *Census Year:* 2011
Number of Households: 5,858
Waste Management:
Waste collection contracted to Waste Management of Canada Corp., 902/798-0910
Number of landfill sites: 1*Landfill Capacity:* .5 year
Solid Waste Disposal Fees: $40/tonne
Clean Fill Fee: No
Recycling: Curbside
Hazardous Waste Depot or Facility: Cogmagun Landfill, 1379 Walton Woods Rd.
Compost Sites: Yes
Water & Wastewater Treatment:
Wastewater treatment plant, Falmouth Water Treatment Plant, 242 Eldridge Rd., Falmouth, NS
Other Initiatives:
Public/private partnership for solid waste disposal

Yarmouth District

P.O. Box 21
932, Hwy 1
Hebron, NS B0W 1X0
902-742-7159
Fax: 902-742-3164
admin@district.yarmouth.ns.ca
www.district.yarmouth.ns.ca
Population: 10,105 *Census Year:* 2011
Number of Households: 5,112
Waste Management:
Landfill sites have been closed & municipal waste is now deposited at the transfer station, to be shipped to Queens Co., located in the Municipality of the District of Yarmouth; Waste collection is contracted to Wasteco Ltd., 902/742-7707
Solid Waste Disposal Fees: $100/tonne; $79/tonne for compost; $9,118/month for handling recyclables
Water & Wastewater Treatment:
Water & wastewater treatment plant in Port Maitland, Yarmouth County

Nunavut

One of Nunavut's challenges is the lack of well-developed infrastructure. There are very few roads in Nunavut, which makes up one-fifth of Canada's land mass, none of which connect the territory to the rest of Canada. The only paved road is in Iqaluit, but it does not have any traffic lights. As the population grows there will be an increasing need to further develop infrastructure, particularly in such environmental areas as water quality & waste management.

There are 26 active landfill sites for solid waste, one for each community in Nunavut. Each landfill site allows open pit burning. In municipalities, there is residential diversion of plastics & metals from the landfill sites.

The territory is in the process of devising a recycling & diversion program for all municipalities. The Department of Environment launched three pilot recycling projects in Iqaluit, Kugluktuk and Rankin Inlet from 2007-2010, which resulted in beverage containers diverting 2-3 percent of the waste from the landfill, and establishing a recycling plan in Nunavut would cost $18.2 million to start, with an additional cost for operating and maintenance costs.

Drinking water, collection, treatment & distribution is a territorial function. Regulated by the territory through the Public Health Water Supply Regulations for public drinking water, this dictates distribution & quality.

Nunavut is reviewing the regulations to bring them up to standard & to align them with the requirements of the territory.

Each municipality disposes of its own sewage & wastewater by deep ocean discharge, or primary treatment in a sewage lagoon followed by deep ocean discharge where the municipality can do so. Sewage & wastewater discharge requires a license supplied by the Nunavut Water Board. The department of Community and Government Services as well as the Department of Environment will develop a solid waste management system that will develop a way to dispose of solid waste. Issues such as land, fencing, environmental concerns, sequestration, composting and back-hauling will be focused on in order to develop the best possible system.

Major Municipalities in Nunavut

City of Iqaluit

P.O. Box 460
Iqaluit, NU X0A 0H0
867-979-5600
Fax: 867-979-5922
Hotline: 867-979-5677
info@city.iqaluit.nu.ca
www.city.iqaluit.nu.ca
Population: 6,699 *Census Year:* 2011
Number of Households: 2,105
Waste Management:
City's Public Works Dept. responsible for waste collection & management of the municipal landfill in the West 40, as well as for the delivery of trucked water & sewer services to clients not serviced by the Utilidor facility
Number of landfill sites: 1
Solid Waste Disposal Fees: $5/half ton pick-up truck
Recycling: Both Curbside & Depot; Blue bin recycling was launched in 2001, however by 2004 the program's future was uncertain. The City received a federal grant to promote recycling in 2003, however currently the City does not indicate if curbside recycling collection is provided. An alternative is the Inuit-owned Northern Collectables company, located at Bldg. 1324, which will accept beverage cans & bottles, as well as car batteries - www.facebook.com/pages/Recycling-In-Iqaluit/113492523009.
Special Bans/by-laws: Noise by-law; All-terrain vehicle by-law
Water & Wastewater Treatment:
Utilidor responsible for maintenance of Water Treatment Plant & Sewage Treatment Facility, Phone: 867/979-5648, Fax: 867/979-4166

Ontario

Ontario's Environmental Protection Act (EPA) is the Act that governs water & waste management for the province.

Bill 90 Waste Diversion Act was passed June, 2002. The Act promotes reduction, reuse & recycling of waste by creating Waste Diversion Ontario (WDO), a permanent non-crown, multi-stakeholder corporation with industry, municipal, non-government & Ministry of the Environment representatives on its board of directors. WDO develops, implements & funds waste diversion programs in the province. The legislation seeks to increase diversion of waste materials, such as organics, scrap tires, used oil, household special wastes, electronics, pharmaceutical products, fluorescent lighting tubes & batteries. The first phase of the Waste Electrical & Electronic Equipment Program was approved by the Minister on July 10, 2008, and commenced on April 1, 2009. Since then, over 170,000 tonnes of electronic & electrical waste has been processed, according to the WDO. The Used Tires Program Plan was approved on April 9, 2009, & commenced on September 1, 2009. In its first year the program recycled 95% of all the used tires generated. However, the newly proposed Bill 91 Waste Reduction Act, 2013, seeks to combat low diversion rates in the industrial, commercial & institutional sectors by repealing the Waste Diversion act & creating a revamped Waste Reduction Authority.

Sewage & wastewater management has been transferred to municipalities by the province. Most municipal governments own & operate their own sewage & wastewater systems. Certificates of approval under the Ontario Water Resources Act (OWRA) are issued by the Ministry for the treatment & disposal of sewage by municipal & private systems. Certificates of approval are required for facilities that discharge contaminants to groundwater & surface water.

Municipal residential drinking water systems are required to be tested regularly and meet stringent provincial standards. More than 99.83 percent of over 700,000 recent tests conducted on these systems met the standards set out in the Safe Drinking Water Act, 2002. In 2010-11, 99.87 percent of municipal residential drinking water systems met the provincial standards. In the same year, there were 14 convictions for cases of drinking water violations, resulting in total fines of $199,300. To date, the Ontario Drinking Water Stewardship Program has funded over 2,000 local initiatives to protect community drinking water.

The Greenbelt Act, 2005 protects about 1.8 million acres of environmentally sensitive land & agricultural land in the Golden Horseshoe from urban development & sprawl.

Under the federal government's New Deal for Cities, Ontario was allocated $1.865 billion in federal gas tax funding between 2005 & 2010 for municipal infrastructure projects.

Counties & Municipal Districts in Ontario

Brant

P.O. Box 160
26 Park Ave.
Burford, ON N0E 1A0
519-449-2451
Fax: 519-449-2454
Toll Free Phone: 1-888-250-2297
brant@county.brant.on.ca
www.brant.ca
Population: 35,638 *Census Year:* 2011
Number of Households: 11,203
Cynthia Compeau, Director, Public Works
David Johnston, Director, Development Services
Paul Boissonneault, Fire Chief
Kathy Ballantyne, Manager, Parks & Facilities
Alex Davidson, Manager, Water Division
Lee Robinson, Manager, Infrastructure Services
Ed Sharp, Manager, Environmental Services
Mike Tout, Manager, Roads Operations
Waste Management:
5 bag limit for curbside garbage collection; Biggars Lane Landfill
Number of landfill sites: 1
Solid Waste Disposal Fees: $71.50/tonne
Recycling: Both Curbside & Depot; Single stream recycling:

residents may put all of their recyclables into one box. Recycling services provided by Emterra Environmental.
Hazardous Waste Depot or Facility: No
Water & Wastewater Treatment:
St. George Water Supply System, 60 Church St.; Cainsville Distribution System (Brantford WTP); Brant County Airport Water Works, 9 Airport Rd.; Mt. Pleasant Water Supply System, 320 Maple Ave.; Paris Water Supply System, 319 Grand River St. North, 166 West River Rd. & 57 Schuyler St.

Bruce

P.O. Box 70
30 Park St.
Walkerton, ON N0G 2V0
519-881-1291
Fax: 519-881-1619
www.brucecounty.on.ca
Population: 66,102 *Census Year:* 2011
Number of Households: 35,043
Doug Harris, Director, Human Resources
Chris LaForest, Director, Planning
Doug Smith, Director, Emergency Services
Brian Knox, County Engineer
Waste Management:
County responsible for waste management planning; Member municipalities responsible for waste diversion & disposal
Water & Wastewater Treatment:
Responsibility of member municipalities

Dufferin

51 Zina St.
Orangeville, ON L9W 1E5
519-941-2816
Fax: 519-941-4565
Toll-Free Phone: 1-877-941-6991
info@dufferincounty.on.ca; treasury@dufferincounty.on.ca
www.dufferincounty.on.ca
Population: 56,881 *Census Year:* 2011
Number of Households: 16,790
Trevor Lewis, Director, Public Works, email: directorofpublicworks@dufferincounty.on.ca
Michael A. Giles, Chief Building Official, email: cbo@dufferincounty.on.ca
Mark Bialkowski, Manager, Human Resources, email: hr@dufferincounty.on.ca
Melissa Kovacs-Reid, Coordinator, Waste Management, email: wastemgmt@dufferincounty.on.ca
Shara Bagnell, Officer, Health & Safety, email: health&safety@dufferincounty.on.ca
Waste Management:
Member municipalities responsible for waste management
Other Initiatives:
Organization of household hazardous waste days in partnership with local municipalities; Annual Dufferin Environment Day features litter clean-up of roads & community areas; County awarded consulting contract, in 2002, for the Dufferin County Alternative Waste Diversion & Disposal Plan; Waste Management Forum & Roundtable discussions organized; Pilot project in process - Dufferin Composts; Weigh our Waste program initiated

Durham

P.O. Box 623
605 Rossland Rd. East
Whitby, ON L1N 6A3
905-668-7711
Fax: 905-668-9963
Toll-Free Phone: 1-800-372-1102
info@durham.ca; cishelp@durham.ca (Corporate Information)
www.durham.ca
Population: 608,124 *Census Year:* 2011
Number of Households: 175,738
Cliff Curtis, Commissioner, Works Department, Fax: 905-668-2051, email: works@durham.ca
Alex L. Georgieff, Commissioner, Planning Department, Fax: 905-666-6208, email: planning@durham.ca
Garth S. Johns, Commissioner, Human Resources, Fax: 905-666-3327
Robert J. Kyle, Commissioner, Health Department & Medical Officer of Health, Fax: 905-666-3327, email: health@durham.ca
Ivan Ciuciura, Director, Durham Emergency Management Office, 905-430-2792, Fax: 905-430-8635, email: demo@durham.ca
Ted Galinis, General Manager, Durham Region Transit, Fax: 905-666-6193, email: transit@durham.ca
Waste Management:
Region responsible for disposal of residential solid waste, waste reduction programs, operation of five waste management facilities including a recycling processing centre, as well as blue box collection & marketing of recyclables; Area municipalities responsible for garbage & yard waste collection
Number of landfill sites: 1 *Landfill Capacity:* 25 years
Solid Waste Disposal Fees: $90/tonne for garbage & mixed loads; No charge for source-separated blue box materials & HHW
Recycling: Both Curbside & Depot; 4 depots
Special Bans/by-laws: Regional sewer use
Hazardous Waste Depot or Facility: Oshawa, Port Perry & Brock; Hazardous waste/paint exchange site at Oshawa waste management
Compost Sites: Yes
Water & Wastewater Treatment:
Water supply plants: Ajax, Bowmanville, Newcastle, Oshawa & Whitby; Water pollution control plants: Corbett Creek, Duffin Creek, Newcastle, Harmony Creek, Pringle Creek, Port Darlington & Lake Simcoe
Other Initiatives:
Region operates a 34,000 tonne/year recycling centre; Spring & Fall Newsletter "Durham Works"; Daily radio messages on local stations to promote 3Rs; Mall displays & tours of recycling centres; Electronics recycling; Blue box sales events; Compost giveaways; Wellhead protection program for groundwater supply systems

Elgin

450 Sunset Dr.
St Thomas, ON N5R 5V1
519-631-1460
Fax: 519-633-7661
www.elgin-county.on.ca
Population: 87,461 *Census Year:* 2011
Number of Households: 30,970
Rob Bryce, Director, Human Resources
Clayton Watters, Director, Engineering Services
Waste Management:
Responsibility of member municipalities
Water & Wastewater Treatment:
Responsibility of member municipalities

Essex

360 Fairview Ave. West
Essex, ON N8M 1Y6
519-776-6441
Fax: 519-776-4455
Planning Department, Fax: 519-776-1253
www.countyofessex.on.ca
Population: 388,782 *Census Year:* 2011
Number of Households: 149,744
Greg Schlosser, Director, Human Resources
Bill King, Manager, Planning Services
Tom Bateman, County Engineer
Phillip Berthiaume, Planner, Emergency Measures
Waste Management:
Waste management responsibility of Essex-Windsor Solid Waste Authority, Fax: 519/776-6370, Email: info@ewswa.org; Waste collection responsibility of member municipalities
Number of landfill sites: 1
Solid Waste Disposal Fees: $48.50-$54.50/tonne (industrial, commercial & institutional); $7.80/100 kg (residential)
Transfer Station(s): 3460 North Service Rd. East, Windsor; 2021 County Rd. 31, Municipality of Kingsville
Recycling: Both Curbside & Depot; Recycling Centre, 3560 North Service Rd. East, Windsor
Special Bans/by-laws: Pallets, radioactive, biomedical & chemical waste, yard waste, white goods (metal items), tires
Hazardous Waste Depot or Facility: 3450 North Service Rd. East, Windsor; County Rd. 31, Municipality of Kingsville
Composters subsidized: Yes
Water & Wastewater Treatment:
Responsibility of member municipalities
Other Initiatives:
Public education programs; Waste reduction programs; White goods collection & recycling; Reuse Centre, 3450 North Service Rd. East, Windsor; Compost sales; Christmas tree recycling

Frontenac

2069 Battersea Rd., RR#1
Glenburnie, ON K0H 1S0
613-548-9400
Fax: 613-546-8460
info@frontenaccounty.ca
www.frontenaccounty.ca
Population: 149,738 *Census Year:* 2011
Number of Households: 61,801
Paul Charbonneau, Director, Emergency & Transportation Services & Chief, Paramedics
Waste Management:
Responsibility of member municipalities
Water & Wastewater Treatment:
Responsibility of member municipalities

Grey

County Administration Bldg.
595 Ninth Ave. East
Owen Sound, ON N4K 3E3
519-376-2205
Toll-Free Phone: 1-800-567-4739
www.greycounty.ca
Population: 92,568 *Census Year:* 2011
Number of Households: 42,527
Randy Scherzer, BES, MCIP, RPP, Director, Planning & Development, email: randy.scherzer@grey.ca
Grant McLevy, Director, Human Resources, email: grant.mclevy@grey.ca; employment@grey.ca
Waste Management:
Waste long-term management strategy responsibility of county
Other Initiatives:
Grey-Owen Sound Waste Management Plan Study carried out by county & city of Owen Sound; Grey County Forest Stewardship Network, established to encourage wise use of forests & natural resources

Haldimand

Cayuga Administration Bldg.
45 Munsee St. North
Cayuga, ON N0A 1E0
905-318-5932
Fax: 905-772-3542
www.haldimandcounty.on.ca
Population: 44,876 *Census Year:* 2011
Number of Households: 15,565
Craig Manley, General Manager, Planning & Economic Development, email: cmanley@haldimandcounty.on.ca
Paul Mungar, Director, Environemtnal Services & Fleet & Facility Asset Management, email: pmungar@haldimandcounty.on.ca
Waste Management:
Waste collection contracted to HGC Management
Number of landfill sites: 1
Solid Waste Disposal Fees: $55/1-100 tonnes/month
Transfer Station(s): Canborough Transfer Station
Recycling: Curbside
Water & Wastewater Treatment:
County's Environmental Services Division administers contracts for water & wastewater; Water treatment plants are the responsibility of Ontario Clean Water Agency; Nanticoke Water Treatment Plant; Dunnville Water Treatment Plant; City of Hamilton supplies Caledonia & Cayuga with treated water; Wastewater treatment responsibility of Veolia Water Canada
Other Initiatives:
Household hazardous waste days; Electronic equipment recycling at Tom Howe Landfill

Haliburton

P.O. Box 399
11 Newcastle St.
Minden, ON K0M 2K0
705-286-1333
Fax: 705-286-4829
Toll-Free: 1-866-886-8815
aballe@county.haliburton.on.ca
www.haliburtoncounty.ca
Population: 17,026 *Census Year:* 2011
Number of Households: 20,700
Pat Kennedy, Director, Emergency Services, email: pkennedy@county.haliburton.on.ca
Doug Ray, Director, Public Works, email: dray@county.haliburton.on.ca
Jane Tousaw, Director, Planning, email: jtousaw@county.haliburton.on.ca
Roy Haig, Manager, Engineering & 911 Services, email: rhaig@county.haliburton.on.ca
Jim Young, Manager, Operations, email: jyoung@county.haliburton.on.ca
Waste Management:
Special Bans/by-laws: Tree Cutting By-Law enforces

sustainable, low impact harvesting operations
Other Initiatives:
Adopt-a-Road; Wetland assessment project; Groundwater/source protection project

Halton
1151 Bronte Rd.
Oakville, ON L6M 3L1
905-825-6000
Fax: 905-825-9010
Toll-Free Phone: 1-866-442-5866; TTY: 905-827-9833
accesshalton@halton.ca
www.halton.ca
Population: 501,669 *Census Year:* 2011
Number of Households: 136,668
Mark Meneray, Commissioner, Legislative & Planning Services & Corporate Counsel
Robert Nosal, Commissioner & Medical Officer of Health
M. Zamojc, Commissioner, Public Works
Waste Management:
Waste collection responsibility of region; Waste & recyclables collection contracted to Halton Recycling Limited, 1-888-403-3333
Number of landfill sites: 1*Landfill Capacity:* 38 years
Solid Waste Disposal Fees: $98/tonne
Clean Fill Fee: Yes; $98/tonne
Special Bans/by-laws: Landfill ban on all blue box materials as well as drywall, tires, scrap metal & hazardous waste
Hazardous Waste Depot or Facility: Halton Waste Management Site
Composters subsidized: Yes
Water & Wastewater Treatment:
Water purification plants: Burlington (3249 Lakeshore Rd.), Georgetown (241 Maple Ave.), Oakville (21 Kerr St.), Kelso (Tremaine Rd./3rd Side Rd.); Wastewater treatment plants: Burlington (1125 Lakeshore Rd.), Acton (202 Churchill Rd. S.), Georgetown (275 Mountainview Rd. S.), Oakville (2195 North Service Rd., 2497 Lakeshore Rd. E., 1385 Lakeshore Rd. W.), Milton (161 Fulton St.)
Other Initiatives:
Construction of new Burloak Water Purification Plant; Development of a blueprint for the Halton Durable Plan: Building our Future; Implementation of the initiatives identified in the new 2006-2010 Halton Waste Management Strategy; Water conservation

Hastings
County Administration Bldg.
P.O. Box 4400
235 Pinnacle St.
Belleville, ON K8N 3A9
613-966-1319
Fax: 613-966-2574
Toll-Free Phone: 1-800-510-3306
www.hastingscounty.com
Population: 134,934 *Census Year:* 2011
Number of Households: 58,257
Shaune Lightfoot, Director, Human Resources
Brian McComb, Director, Planning
Waste Management:
Responsibility of member municipalities
Water & Wastewater Treatment:
Responsibility of member municipalities

Huron
1 Court House Sq.
Goderich, ON N7A 1M2
519-524-8394
Fax: 519-524-2044
Toll-Free Phone: 1-888-524-8394 (in 519 area)
huronadmin@huroncounty.ca
www.huroncounty.ca
Population: 59,100 *Census Year:* 2011
Number of Households: 26,612
Dave Laurie, Director, Public Works
Scott Tousaw, Director, Planning & Development
Nancy Cameron, Medical Officer of Health
Waste Management:
County responsible for waste management planning
Special Bans/by-laws: Forestry Conservation By-law
Water & Wastewater Treatment:
Responsibility of member municipalities
Other Initiatives:
Household hazardous waste disposal program; Water Protection Steering Committe; Huron Clean Water Project; Aggregates Strategy

Lambton
P.O. Box 3000
789 Broadway St.
Wyoming, ON N0N 1T0
519-845-0801
Fax: 519-845-3160
Toll-Free Phone: 1-866-324-6912
www.lambtononline.com
Population: 126,199 *Census Year:* 2011
Number of Households: 53,281
Jim Kutyba, P.Eng., General Manager, Infrastructure & Development Services, email: jim.kutyba@county-lambton.on.ca
Jason Cole, P.Eng., Manager, Public Works, email: jason.cole@county-lambton.on.ca
Waste Management:
County responsible for waste disposal; Member municipalities responsible for composting, recycling & collection; Waste disposal contracted to Canadian Waste Services Inc.
Number of landfill sites: 6*Landfill Capacity:* County contracts with 2 active private landfills
Solid Waste Disposal Fees: $35/tonne
Clean Fill Fee: No
Hazardous Waste Depot or Facility: Clean Harbours Facility
Water & Wastewater Treatment:
Responsibility of member municipalities
Other Initiatives:
6 household Hazardous Waste collection events; Adopt-a-County Road program

Lanark
County Administration Bldg.
P.O. Box 37
99 Christie Lake Rd.
Perth, ON K7H 3E2
613-267-4200
Fax: 613-267-2964
Toll-Free Phone: 1-888-952-6275
info@county.lanark.on.ca
www.county.lanark.on.ca
Population: 65,667 *Census Year:* 2011
Number of Households: 27,667
Lisa Crosbie-Larmon, Director, Human Resources
Waste Management:
Local municipalities responsible for their own waste & recycling
Water & Wastewater Treatment:
Responsibility of local municipalities

Lennox & Addington
P.O. Box 1000
97 Thomas St. East
Napanee, ON K7R 3S9
613-354-4883
Fax: 613-354-3112
www.lennox-addington.on.ca
Population: 41,824 *Census Year:* 2011
Number of Households: 17,205
Mark Schjerning, Chief, Emergency Services
Bill Bishop, Director, Human Resources, email: bbishop@lennox-addington.on.ca
Brian Elo-Shepherd, Director, Social Services
Stephen Paul, Manager, Economic Development
Waste Management:
Responsibility of area municipalities

Middlesex
399 Ridout St. North
London, ON N6A 2P1
519-434-7321
Fax: 519-434-0638
www.middlesex.ca
Population: 439,151 *Census Year:* 2011
Number of Households: 170,915
Steve Evans, Director, Planning & Economic Development
Neal Roberts, Director, Emergency Services
Chris Traini, County Engineer
Doug Spettigue, Human Resource Officer
John Trott, Woodlands Conservation Officer & Weed Inspector
Waste Management:
Responsibility of area municipalities
Special Bans/by-laws: Woodlands Conservation By-law; Liquid Manure Transfer
Other Initiatives:
Clean Water Program, a rural water quality initiative; County residents use City of London Household Hazardous Waste Drop-off Depot

Muskoka
70 Pine St.
Bracebridge, ON P1L 1N3
705-645-2231
Fax: 705-645-5319
Toll-Free Phone: 1-800-461-4210 (In 705 area code)
info@muskoka.on.ca
www.muskoka.on.ca
Population: 57,047 *Census Year:* 2011
Number of Households: 42,843
Tony White, Commissioner, Engineering & Public Works, 705-645-6764
Geoff Bache, Director, Environmental Services
Terri Burton, Director, Emergency Services
Herman Clemens, Director, Water & Sewer Operations
Anna Landry, Director, Human Resources, email: alandry@muskoka.on.ca
Waste Management:
Waste management responsibility of the district municipality
Number of landfill sites: 3
Solid Waste Disposal Fees: $95/tonne
Transfer Station(s): Lake of Bays Township: Baysville, Dorset, Sinclair, Dwight; Muskoka Lakes Township: Eveleigh Road; Georgian Bay Township: Tow
Recycling: Curbside
Hazardous Waste Depot or Facility: Hazardous waste day services provided by Brendar Environmental Inc.
Water & Wastewater Treatment:
District municipality's water & sewer operations division is responsible for operation & maintenance of water & sewage treatment plants; Kirby's Beach Water Treatment Plant, Bracebridge Water Works; Gravenhurst Water Treatment Plant, Gravenhurst Water Works; Highway 60 Water Treatment Plant, Huntsville Water Works; Clarke Crescent Well Water System, Port Sydney Water Works; Ferndale Water Treatment Plant, Port Carling Water Works; Beech Avenue Water Treatment Plant, MacTier Water Works; Bala Wat
Other Initiatives:
Household hazardous waste depots: Town of Bracebridge Landfill, Town of Huntsville Madill Church Works Yard, Township of Lake of Bays Dwight Transfer Site, Town of Gravenhurst Landfill, Township of Muskoka Lakes Eveleigh Road Transfer Site, Township of Georgian Bay Baxter Transfer Site; Reuse buildings at most landfills & transfer stations

Niagara
P.O. Box 1042
2201 St. David's Rd.
Thorold, ON L2V 4T7
905-685-1571
Fax: 905-687-4977
Toll-Free Phone: 1-800-263-7215; TTY: 905-984-3613
www.niagararegion.ca
Population: 431,346 *Census Year:* 2011
Number of Households: 170,876
Patrick Robson, Commissioner, Integrated Community Planning
Valerie Jaeger, Commissioner, Public Health & Medical Officer of Health
Ken Bothers, Commissioner, Public Works
Andrew Pollock, Director, Waste Management Services
Waste Management:
Waste collection contracted to Canada Waste Services, 905/687-6687; Modern Corporation, 905/262-6000; Household hazardous waste permanent location: Niagara Road 12 Landfill Site, West Lincoln; 7 temporary household hazardous waste locations: Niagara Falls, St. Catharines, Port Colborne, Welland, Fort Erie, Wainfleet & Niagara-on-the-Lake
Number of landfill sites: 5*Landfill Capacity:* 6-25 years, various sites
Solid Waste Disposal Fees: $60/tonne
Clean Fill Fee:
Recycling: Both Curbside & Depot; Depot locations: Bridge Street Landfill, Fort Erie; Elm Street, Port Colborne; Niagara Road 12, West Lincoln; Humberstone Landfill, Welland; Residential Waste Drop-Off Depot, Walker Industries, Thorold; Niagara Recycling, Niagara Falls
Hazardous Waste Depot or Facility: Niagara Road 12; temporary depots
Compost Sites: Yes *Composters subsidized:* Yes
Water & Wastewater Treatment:
Water & Wastewater Division operates the following water treatment plants: Niagara Falls Water Treatment Plant, 3599

Macklem St., Niagara Falls; Port Colborne Water Treatment Plant, 323 King St., Port Colborne; Grimsby Water Treatment Plant, 300 N. Service Rd., Grimsby; Wastewater treatment plants: Niagara Falls Water Pollution Control Plant (WPCP), 3450 Stanley Ave., Niagara Falls; Port Dalhousie WPCP, 40 Lighthouse Rd., St. Catharines; Port Weller WPCP, 27 Lombardy St., St. Catharines; Welland
Other Initiatives:
Organics curbside residential collection

Norfolk

50 Colborne St. South
Simcoe, ON N3Y 4N5
519-426-5870
Fax: 519-426-8573
Delhi Customer Service Ctr., Phone: 519-582-2100
www.norfolkcounty.on.ca
Population: 62,175 *Census Year:* 2011
Number of Households: 25,359
Christopher D. Baird, CET, CMMIII, Ec.D., General Manager, Planning & Economic Development, email: chris.baird@norfolkcounty.ca
Eric R. D'Hondt, P.Eng., General Manager, Public Works & Environmental Services, Fax: 519-582-4571, email: eric.dhondt@norfolkcounty.ca
Patti Moore, General Manager, Health & Social Services, email: patti.moore@haldimand-norfolk.org
Bob Fields, Manager, Environmental Services, email: bob.fields@norfolkcounty.ca
John Hamilton, Manager, Engineering, email: john.hamilton@norfolkcounty.ca
Marlene L. Ireland, Manager, Fleets & Facilities, email: marlene.ireland@norfolkcounty.ca
Terry Dicks, Fire Chief, 519-426-4115, Fax: 519-426-4140, email: terry.dicks@norfolkcounty.ca
Waste Management:
100% of waste collection is contracted to Norfolk Disposal, 519/443-8022
Number of landfill sites: 2*Landfill Capacity:* 12 years
Solid Waste Disposal Fees: $55/tonne
Transfer Station(s): 2 sites
Recycling: Both Curbside & Depot; Material Recovery Facility, 28 Grigg Dr., Simcoe
Special Bans/by-laws: Leaves & Christmas trees banned from landfill
Hazardous Waste Depot or Facility: yearly from 4 depots
Compost Sites: Yes *Composters subsidized:* Yes
Water & Wastewater Treatment:
Water & wastewater facilities in Simcoe, Waterford, Port Dover, Delhi, Port Rowan & Courtland; Contracted to Veolia, 519/583-0612
Other Initiatives:
Curbside bulky pickup tri-annually

Northumberland

555 Courthouse Rd.
Cobourg, ON K9A 5J6
905-372-3329
Fax: 905-372-1746
Toll-Free Phone: 1-800-354-7050
www.northumberlandcounty.ca
Population: 82,126 *Census Year:* 2011
Number of Households: 32,395
Bill Pyatt, Chief Administrative Officer, email: pyattb@northumberlandcounty.ca
James Rogers, By-Law Officer, Forest Conservation, 705-799-2470
Ken Stubbings, Coordinator, Emergency Management, email: stubbingsk@northumberlandcounty.ca
Waste Management:
Responsibility of county; Collection of waste & recyclables contracted to National Waste Services; Waste & Recycling Hot Line: 1-866-293-8379
Number of landfill sites: 2
Solid Waste Disposal Fees: $85/tonne
Transfer Station(s): Bewdley Transfer Station; Hope Transfer Station
Recycling: Both Curbside & Depot; Depot is the County of Northumberland Material Recovery Facility, Edwardson Rd., Grafton
Special Bans/by-laws: Tree Conservation By-law
Hazardous Waste Depot or Facility: Cobourg HHW Depot; Bewdley HHW Depot; Seymour HHW Depot; Brighton HHW Depot
Compost Sites: Yes *Composters subsidized:* Yes
Water & Wastewater Treatment:
Responsibility of the area municipalities
Other Initiatives:
Maintenance of 6 closed landfills; Electronics waste disposal; Large item disposal program; Sale of compost; Northumberland Forest Users Committee; Weed control; Salt management

Peel

70 Peel Centre Dr.
Brampton, ON L6T 4B9
905-791-7800
Fax: 905-791-7871
Toll-Free Phone: 1-888-919-7800
info@peelregion.ca
www.peelregion.ca
Population: 1,296,814 *Census Year:* 2011
Number of Households: 313,650
Kent Gillespie, Commissioner, Employee & Business Services
Dan Labrecque, Commissioner, Public Works
Janette Smith, Commissioner, Health Services
Janet Menard, Commissioner, Human Services
David Mowat, Medical Officer of Health
Arvin Prasad, Director, Planning Policy & Research
Norman Lee, Director, Waste Management
Waste Management:
Collection contracted to Sandhill Waste Collection & Recycling (rural collection); Waste haulage & disposal contracted to Wilson Logistic Inc.; Republic Service Inc. contracted to haul waste to Michigan for disposal; Information about waste management Wasteline, 905/791-9499
Number of landfill sites: 1
Recycling: Both Curbside & Depot; Depot locations: Bolton Community Recycling Centre, Caledon Public Waste & Recycling Depot, Brampton Community Recycling Centre, Britannnia Public Waste & Recycling Depot, Mississauga
Hazardous Waste Depot or Facility: Brampton CRC, 395 Chrysler Dr.; Caledon Public Waste & Recycling Depot, 1795 Quarry Dr.
Compost Sites: Yes *Composters subsidized:* Yes
Water & Wastewater Treatment:
Public Works Dept. operates & maintains 2 water treatment plants, 2 wastewater treatment plants & 80 pumping stations
Other Initiatives:
Three Bag Standard for garbage collection; Environment Days for drop off of unwanted materials; Outdoor water efficiency kits & rain barrels available from the Region; Organics demonstration project; Reuse stores at Bolton CRC; Electronics recycling program; Peel Odour Management Strategy; Water Smart Peel conservation program; Algonquin Power Energy from waste facility; Expansion of Lakeview Wastewater Treatment Facility, Clarkson Wastewater Treatment Facility & Lakeview Water Treatment Facility by 2006; 2005 completion of community recycling centres: Clarkson, 2307 Lakeshore Rd.West, Heart Lake, Railside Dr.; 2007 completion of Lakeview Community Recycling Centre, 1300 Lakes

Perth

Courthouse
1 Huron St.
Stratford, ON N5A 5S4
519-271-0531
Fax: 519-271-6265
www.perthcounty.ca
Population: 75,112 *Census Year:* 2011
Number of Households: 27,777
Matt Ash, Director, Public Works, email: mash@perthcounty.ca
Dave Hanly, Director, Planning & Development, email: dhanly@perthcounty.ca
Linda Rockwood, Director, Emergency Medical Services, email: lrockwood@perthcounty.ca
Cliff Eggleton, Manager, EMS Operations, email: ceggleton@perthcounty.ca
Ann McKnight Duralia, Manager, Human Resources, email: amcknight@perthcounty.ca
Waste Management:
Responsibility of area municipalities
Special Bans/by-laws: Bylaw to regulate nutrient management for certain livestock operations; Bylaw to restrict & regulate destruction of trees
Water & Wastewater Treatment:
Responsibility of area municipalities
Other Initiatives:
Perth County groundwater study

Peterborough

County Court House
470 Water St.
Peterborough, ON K9H 3M3
705-743-0380
Fax: 705-876-1730
Toll-Free Phone: 1-800-710-9586
www.county.peterborough.on.ca
Population: 134,933 *Census Year:* 2011
Number of Households: 61,355
Chris Bradley, Director, Public Works, email: cbradley@county.peterborough.on.ca
Patti Kraft, Director, Human Resources, email: pkraft@county.peterborough.on.ca
Bryan Weir, Director, Planning, email: bweir@county.peterborough.on.ca
Laurie Westaway, Manager, Environmental Services, email: lwestaway@county.peterborough.on.ca
Bill Linnen, Manager, Operations, email: blinnen@county.peterborough.on.ca
Bob English, Chief, Emergency Medical Services (EMS), email: benglish@county.peterborough.on.ca
Mark Cross, Specialist, Waste Diversion Operations, email: mcross@county.peterborough.on.ca
Waste Management:
Recycling: Both Curbside & Depot; County provides recycling depots at all waste depots & transfer stations; Recycling information 705/743-0380, ext.777, Email: rrr@county.peterborough.on.ca
Hazardous Waste Depot or Facility: Belmont Transfer Stn, Anstruther Lake, City/Cty HHW facility, Buckhorn Landfill, Bobcaygeo
Compost Sites: No
Water & Wastewater Treatment:
Responsibility of individual member municipalities
Other Initiatives:
Adopt-A-Road program; Free reuse area at household waste depots for paints & stains; Annual White Goods Days, when unwanted appliances & scrap metal are accepted for re-use or recycling; Drop-off locations for Christmas trees

Prince Edward

332 Main St.
Picton, ON K0K 2T0
613-476-2148
Fax: 613-476-8356
council@pecounty.on.ca
www.pecounty.on.ca
Population: 25,258 *Census Year:* 2011
Number of Households: 11,712
Barry Braun, Commissioner, Recreation, Parks, & Culture Department, email: bbraun@pecounty.on.ca
Robert McAuley, Commissioner, Public Works Department, email: rmcauley@pecounty.on.ca
Kimberly Pierce, Manager, Human Resources, Corporate Services & Finance, email: kpierce@pecounty.on.ca
Scott Manlow, Fire Chief, email: smanlow@pecounty.on.ca

Renfrew

9 International Dr.
Pembroke, ON K8A 6W5
613-735-7288
Fax: 613-735-2081
Toll-Free Phone: 1-800-273-0183
info@countyofrenfrew.on.ca
www.countyofrenfrew.on.ca
Population: 101,326 *Census Year:* 2011
Number of Households: 43,487
Bruce Beakley, Director, Human Resources
Dave Darch, Director, Public Works & Engineering
Michael Nolan, Director, Emergency Services
Jeff Muzzi, Manager, Forestry Services, 613-735-3204, email: jmuzzi@countyofrenfrew.on.ca
Water & Wastewater Treatment:
Responsibility of area municipalities
Other Initiatives:
Adopt-a-road program; Forest operating plan; Regional groundwater & aquifer study

Simcoe

County of Simcoe Administration Centre
1110 Hwy. 26
Midhurst, ON L0L 1X0
705-735-6901
Fax: 705-719-4626

Toll-Free Phone: 1-800-263-3199
info@simcoe.ca
www.simcoe.ca
Population: 446,063 *Census Year:* 2011
Number of Households: 142,868
Jane Sinclair, General Manager, Health & Emergency Services, email: jane.sinclair@simcoe.ca
Dawn Hipwell, Director, Procurement, Fleet & Property, email: dawn.hipwell@simcoe.ca
Jim Hunter, Director, Transportation Construction, email: jim.hunter@simcoe.ca
Bryan MacKell, Director, Planning, Development & Tourism, email: bryan.macKell@simcoe.ca
Michael Moffatt, Director, Human Resources, email: michael.moffatt@simcoe.ca
Waste Management:
Waste collection, recycling & operation of several waste disposal facilities responsibility of county
Number of landfill sites: 8
Transfer Station(s): North Simcoe Transfer Station, 1700 Golflink Rd., Tiny Twp.; New Tecumseth Transfer Station, 5917 - 7th Line, New Tecumseth
Recycling: Curbside
Hazardous Waste Depot or Facility: Nottawasaga Landfill Site, 5715 - 30/31 Sideroad; North Simcoe & New Tecumseth Transfer St
Water & Wastewater Treatment:
Water & wastewater treatment responsibility of member municipalities
Other Initiatives:
Household hazardous waste days; Curbside organics collection pilot program; Leaf, yard waste & metal item special collections; Management of closed landfill sites; Forest management, including tree cutting bylaw

Waterloo
Regional Administration Bldg.
P.O. Box 9051 C
150 Frederick St.
Kitchener, ON N2G 4J3
519-575-4400
Fax: 519-575-4481
Phone, Regional Councillors: 519-575-4581
regionalinquiries@region.waterloo.on.ca
www.region.waterloo.on.ca
Population: 507,096 *Census Year:* 2011
Number of Households: 166,813
Rob Horne, Commissioner, Planning, Housing & Community Services
Thomas Schmidt, Commissioner, Transportation & Environmental Services
Penny Smiley, Commissioner, Human Resources
Jon Arsenault, Director, Waste Management
Amanda Kutler, Director, Community Planning
Eric Gillespie, Director, Transit Services
Nancy Kodousek, Director, Water Services
Ellen McGaghey, Director, Facilities Management & Fleet Services
Graham Vincent, Director, Transportation Planning
Liana Nolan, Medical Officer of Health
Waste Management:
Waste disposal & recycling responsibility of regional municipality
Number of landfill sites: 2*Landfill Capacity:* 30 years (Waterloo), 8 years (Cambridge Waste Management Centre)
Solid Waste Disposal Fees: Commercial $50/tonne; Residential $65/tonne
Clean Fill Fee: Yes; first 50 kg free & $3/100 kg therea
Transfer Station(s): Elmira, Ayr, Wilmot, Wellesley
Hazardous Waste Depot or Facility: Waterloo & Cambridge landfill sites
Compost Sites: Yes *Composters subsidized:* Yes
Water & Wastewater Treatment:
Water treatment responsibility of the Region; Water & wastewater treatment contracted to Ontario Clean Water Agency, 1-800-667-OCWA; Mannheim Water Treatment Plant, 2069 Ottawa St. South, Kitchener
Other Initiatives:
Currently undertaking a comprehensive ground & surface water protection strategy; Evaluating long-term water supply; Water conservation devices easily available region-wide (ie., toilet replacement program, using six-litre ultra-low flush unit); Area municipalities required to enact by-laws for lawn watering regulation; Environmental sampling/testing

Wellington
74 Woolwich St.
Guelph, ON N1H 3T9
519-837-2600
Fax: 519-837-1909
Toll-Free Phone: 1-800-663-0750
finance@county.wellington.on.ca (Treasury)
www.wellington.ca
Population: 208,360 *Census Year:* 2011
Number of Households: 72,055
Andrea Lawson, Administrator, Human Resources, Fax: 519-837-8882, email: andreal@county.wellington.on.ca
Gary Cousins, Director, Planning, Fax: 519-823-1694, email: garyc@wellington.ca
Linda Dickson, Coordinator, Community Emergency Management, 519-846-8058, Fax: 519-846-8482, email: lindad@wellington.ca
Rob Johnson, Coordinator, Forestry
Waste Management:
The City of Guelph operates its own recycling, disposal & transfer facilities
Number of landfill sites: 3
Solid Waste Disposal Fees: $60/tonne
Transfer Station(s): 3 transfer stations
Recycling: Both Curbside & Depot; Drop off locations Aberfoyle, Riverstown, Harriston, Rothsay, Belwood, Elora, Hillsburgh
Special Bans/by-laws: Tree cutting by-law
Hazardous Waste Depot or Facility: Guelph Household Hazardous Waste Depot, 110 Dunlop Dr., Guelph.
Other Initiatives:
Curbside user pay garbage program; Household hazardous waste event days; Curbside Christmas tree collection; Adopt-A-Road program; Tire recycling; Appliance collection areas at landfill sites & transfer stations; Wood & brush diversion programs; Pilot Reuse Center at Aberfoyle Landfill site

York
17250 Yonge St.
Newmarket, ON L3Y 6Z1
905-895-1231
Fax: 905-895-1238
Toll-Free Phone: 1-877-464-9675
info@york.ca; twgeneral@york.ca (Transportation & Works)
www.york.ca
Population: 1,032,524 *Census Year:* 2011
Number of Households: 229,239
Kathleen Llewellyn-Thomas, Commissioner, Transportation Services
Erin Mahoney, Commissioner, Environmental Services
Adelina Urbanski, Commissioner, Community & Health Services
John Walker, Acting Commissioner, Planning & Development Services
Karen Close, Director, Human Resources
Karim Kurji, Medical Officer of Health & Director, Public Health Programs
Waste Management:
Waste from transfer stations is transported to the Green Lane Landfill in southwestern Ontario & the Onyx Arbor Hills Landfill & Carleton Farms Landfill in Michigan; Contact: garbage@region.york.on.ca
Solid Waste Disposal Fees: $70/tonne (residential); $86/tonne (industrial, commercial & institutional)
Clean Fill Fee: Yes; $7/load (up to 500 kg)
Transfer Station(s): Georgina Waste Transfer Station (Household Hazardous Waste & Recycling Depot), 23068 Warden Ave., Town of Georgina
Recycling: Both Curbside & Depot; York Region Waste Management Centre (Household Hazardous Waste & Recycling Depot), 100 Garfield Wright Blvd., East Gwillimbury; York Region Waste Transfer Station (Household Hazardous Waste & Recycling Depot), 23068 Warden Ave., Georgina; Contact: recycling@region.york.on.ca
Hazardous Waste Depot or Facility: Georgina (Warden); Markham (Rodick Rd); East Gwillimbury (Garfield Wright); Vaughan (Ruthe
Composters subsidized: Yes
Water & Wastewater Treatment:
City of Toronto supplies water from its water treatment plants to urban areas of Markham, Richmond Hill & Vaughan; Water treatment plants owned & operated by the region: Georgina, Keswick; Wastewater treatment plants owned & operated by region: Stouffville, Mount Albert, Holland Landing, Schomberg, Kleinburg, Keswick, Sutton; York Durham Sewage System: Duffin Creek Water Pollution Control Plant in Pickering serves Newmarket, Aurora, Richmond Hill, Vaughan & Markham; Contact: waterwastewater@regi
Other Initiatives:
In addition to the region's Georgina Waste Transfer Station, waste is accepted at City of Toronto transfer stations & Miller Waste Systems' Transfer Station (a private facility); In addition to the region's 2 recycling locations, Markham, Aurora & Whitchurch-Stouffville operate their own recycling depots

Major Municipalities in Ontario

City of Barrie
P.O. Box 400
70 Collier St.
Barrie, ON L4M 4T5
705-726-4242
Fax: 705-739-4243
TTY: 705-792-7910; Council Info: 705-739-4204
cityinfo@barrie.ca
www.barrie.ca; www.facebook.com/cityofbarrie
Population: 135,711 *Census Year:* 2011
Number of Households: 38,191
Richard Forward, M.Sc., P.Eng., General Manager, Infrastructure, Development & Culture Division
J.W. (Jim) Sales, General Manager, Community Operations
G. Allison, Director, Building Services & Chief Building Official
Sandy Coulter, B.Sc., Acting Director, Operations - Water, Wastewater & Environmental
Dave Friary, Acting Director, Operations - Roads, Parks & Fleet Operations
Wendell McArthur, Director, Engineering
Barbara Roth, Director, Leisure, Transit & Facilities
J. Taylor, Director, Planning Services Department
John Lynn, Fire Chief
Bruce L. Griffin, Community Emergency Planner
Waste Management:
Garbage, recyclable & yard waste collection contracted to Frith Regional Waste, 705-733-1200; 1 garbage bag per dwelling per week, with additional bags to be tagged
Number of landfill sites: 1*Landfill Capacity:* 10 years
Solid Waste Disposal Fees: $118.45/tonne; $55.70/tonne (leaf & yard waste)
Recycling: Curbside; Blue & Grey Box programs for recyclables; household & commercial curbside collection; leaf & yard waste collection every other week, weekly for the months of Sept., Oct., & Nov.; leaf & yard waste may be taken to the city's landfill site as well; organics collection program (green bin) requires compostable bin liners, with city approved labels; bulky items such as household appliances are accepted at the Habitat for Humanity Huronia ReStore at $25 per item
Hazardous Waste Depot or Facility: HHW Depot at Barrie's Environmental Centre, 272 Ferndale Dr. North; Saturdays from 9:00 a.m. to 4:00 p.m.
Compost Sites: No *Composters subsidized:* Yes
Water & Wastewater Treatment:
13 wells; 3 reservoirs, 3 water towers & 5 booster stations in 5 pressure zones; Water Pollution Control Centre, 249 Bradford St. Barrie
Other Initiatives:
Low flow toilet rebate program; 1 garbage container limit, cost for additional containers; Organics collection to all single family residences

City of Belleville
City Hall
169 Front St.
Belleville, ON K8N 2Y8
613-968-6481
Fax: 613-967-3206
TTY: 613-967-3768
www.city.belleville.on.ca
Population: 49,454 *Census Year:* 2011
Number of Households: 20,031
Mark Fluhrer, Director, Recreation Culture & Community Services, email: mfluhrer@city.belleville.on.ca
Rod Bovay, Acting Director, Engineering & Development Services, email: rbovay@city.belleville.on.ca
John Martin, Director, Human Resources, email: jmartin@city.belleville.on.ca
Brad Wilson, Director, Environmental & Operational Services, email: bwilson@city.belleville.on.ca
Ted Marecak, Chief Building Official, email: tmarecak@city.belleville.on.ca
Rhéaume Chaput, Fire Chief, email: rchaput@city.belleville.on.ca

Peter Hodgson, Manager, Transit Operations, email: phodgson@city.belleville.on.ca
Art MacKay, Manager, Policy Planning, email: amackay@city.belleville.on.ca
Pat McNulty, Manager, Transportation, email: pmcnulty@city.belleville.on.ca
Richard Reinert, Manager, Environmental Services (Water Operations), email: rreinert@city.belleville.on.ca
Waste Management:
Household hazardous waste disposal responsibility of Quinte Waste Solutions, 613/394-6266
Number of landfill sites: 2
Solid Waste Disposal Fees: $99/tonne
Recycling: Curbside; Recyclable collection contracted to Quinte Waste Solutions
Hazardous Waste Depot or Facility: 75 Wallbridge Cres.
Water & Wastewater Treatment:
Belleville Water Distribution & Services, 195 College St. West, PO Box 939, Belleville, 613/966-3651, Fax: 613/969-1944; Belleville Water Treatment, 2 Sidney St., Belleville
Other Initiatives:
Special collections for leaf & yard waste; User-pay garbage system

City of Brampton
2 Wellington St. West
Brampton, ON L6Y 4R2
905-874-2000
Fax: 905-874-2119
E-mail, Economic Development: edo@brampton.ca
cityhall@brampton.ca; tourism@brampton.ca (Tourism)
www.brampton.ca
Population: 523,911 *Census Year:* 2011
Number of Households: 98,753
John Corbett, Commissioner, Planning, Design & Development
Jamie Lowery, Commissioner, Community Services
Tom Mulligan, Commissioner, Works & Transportation
Julian Patteson, Commissioner, Buildings & Property Management
Waste Management:
Responsibility of the Regional Municipality of Peel
Water & Wastewater Treatment:
Responsibility of the Regional Municipality of Peel
Other Initiatives:
"Harvest Cleanup" in Oct.; "Spring Cleanup" in April

City of Brantford
City Hall
P.O. Box 818
100 Wellington Sq.
Brantford, ON N3T 2M3
519-759-4150
webmaster@brantford.ca
www.brantford.ca
Population: 93,650 *Census Year:* 2011
Number of Households: 34,881
Greg Dworak, Acting General Manager, Engineering & Operational Services
Dan Temprile, General Manager, Public Health, Safety, & Social Services
Waste Management:
Waste collection contracted to Capital Environmental, 519/756-4444; Recycling processing & WSI
Number of landfill sites: 1 *Landfill Capacity:* 60 years
Solid Waste Disposal Fees: $60/tonne; $140/tonne for mixed loads of wood, metal, cardboard, house
Recycling: Both Curbside & Depot
Special Bans/by-laws: Recently enacted bylaw to allow for maximum of $1,000 financial assistance to rectify private drain cross connections where current home owner not responsible & original builder/developer not available to correct
Hazardous Waste Depot or Facility: Landfill site
Compost Sites: Yes *Composters subsidized:* Yes
Water & Wastewater Treatment:
Water treatment plant operated by city staff after PUC amalgamation; New pre-treatment system for raw water in 1998; New residual management facility added in 2003; Brantford Water Pollution Control Plant owned by city & operated by Ontario Clean Water Agency; 2006 Water rate is 68 cents/cubic metre; 2006 Sewage rate is 65 cents/cubic metre with residential bill capped at 30 cubic metres/month

City of Brockville
Victoria Bldg.
P.O. Box 5000
1 King St. West
Brockville, ON K6V 7A5
613-342-8772
Fax: 613-342-8780
info@brockville.com; tourism@brockvillechamber.com
www.brockville.com
Population: 21,870 *Census Year:* 2011
Number of Households: 10,154
Jim Baker, Director, Human Resources, email: jbaker@brockville.com
Maureen Pascoe Merkley, Director, Planning, email: mpmerkley@brockville.com
Peter Raabe, Director, Environmental Services, email: praabe@brockville.com
Harry Jones, Fire Chief, email: hjones@brockville.com
Waste Management:
Waste collection contracted to Waste Services Inc., 613/345-2442
Transfer Station(s): Refuse Transfer Station, 4800 Development Dr., Brockville, 613/345-2442
Recycling: Both Curbside & Depot
Compost Sites: Yes *Composters subsidized:* Yes
Water & Wastewater Treatment:
City of Brockville Water Treatment Plant, 20 Rivers Ave., Brockville; City of Brockville Water Pollution Control Centre, 1807 Hwy. 2 East, Brockville
Other Initiatives:
Annual household hazardous waste collection days; 1 container/week refuse limit

City of Burlington
City Hall
P.O. Box 5013
426 Brant St.
Burlington, ON L7R 3Z6
905-335-7600
Fax: 905-335-7881
Toll-Free Phone: 1-877-213-3609
cob@burlington.ca
www.burlington.ca
Population: 175,779 *Census Year:* 2011
Number of Households: 59,020
Waste Management:
Responsibility of Regional Municipality of Halton
Water & Wastewater Treatment:
Responsibility of Regional Municipality of Halton
Other Initiatives:
Preparation of environmental management plan for the city; Adoption of Halton Public Sector Smog Response Plan; Development of a healthy green spaces strategy for public land; Maintenance of tree protection standards; Reduction of road salt & pesticide usage; Use of natural creek channel design; EnerGuide for houses program; Partners for climate protection; Idling awareness campaign

City of Cambridge
P.O. Box 669
50 Dickson St.
Cambridge, ON N1R 5W8
519-623-1340
Fax: 519-740-3011
E-mail, Corporate Services: corpserv@cambridge.ca
questions@cambridge.ca; csd@cambridge.ca (Community Svs.)
www.cambridge.ca
Population: 126,748 *Census Year:* 2011
Number of Households: 40,061
Janet Babcock, Commisssioner, Planning Services
George Elliott, Commisssioner, Transportation & Public Works
Kent McVittie, Commisssioner, Community Services
Bill Chesney, Fire Chief
Waste Management:
Responsibility of Regional Municipality of Waterloo
Water & Wastewater Treatment:
Responsibility of Regional Municipality of Waterloo
Other Initiatives:
City Green Strategy is a community action plan for environmental initiatives; Establishment of Cambridge Trails Advisory Committee, which reviews riverbank & greenbelt development; Groundwater Guardian is a volunteer-led groundwater education initiative; Cambridge Environmental Advisory Committee established to advise council

City of Clarence-Rockland
1560 Laurier St.
Rockland, ON K4K 1P7
613-446-6022
Fax: 613-446-1497
www.clarence-rockland.com
Population: 23,185 *Census Year:* 2011
Number of Households: 6,793
Thérèse Lefaivre, Director, Community Services, email: tlefaivre@clarence-rockland.com
Michael Michaud, Director, Planning, email: mmichaud@clarence-rockland.com
Yves Rivard, Director, By-law Enforcement, email: yrivard@clarence-rockland.com
Yves Rousselle, Director, Physical Services, email: yrousselle@clarence-rockland.com
Pierre Sabourin, Fire Chief, email: psabourin@clarence-rockland.com
Denis Longpré, Manager, Environment, email: dlongpre@clarence-rockland.com
Waste Management:
Number of landfill sites: 1
Solid Waste Disposal Fees: $70/1-7 ton truck
Transfer Station(s): Industrielle St., Rockland
Recycling: Curbside
Special Bans/by-laws: Watering By-law
Hazardous Waste Depot or Facility: Landfill site, 2335 Lalonde Rd., Bourget
Composters subsidized: Yes
Water & Wastewater Treatment:
Rockland Water Treatment Plant, Edwards St., Rockland; Sewage treatment facility, Industrielle St., Rockland.; Sewage treatment facility operated by Ontario Clean Water Agency
Other Initiatives:
Tags for additional refuse over 3 containers; Spring & fall clean-ups

City of Cornwall
P.O. Box 877
360 Pitt St.
Cornwall, ON K6H 5T9
613-932-6252
Fax: 613-932-8145
www.cornwall.ca
Population: 46,340 *Census Year:* 2011
Number of Households: 20,450
Stephen Alexander, General Manager, Planning, Parks & Recreation Services
Norm Levac, General Manager, Infrastructure & Municipal Works
Jean Cousineau, Division Manager, Municipal Works
Morris McCormick, Division Manager, Environment
Len Tapp, Division Manager, Transit
Myles Cassidy, Fire Chief & Manager, Emergency Services
Patrick Carrière, Supervisor, Waste Water Treatment Facility
Owen O'Keefe, Supervisor, Water Purification Plant
Waste Management:
Curbside solid waste & recycling contracted to HGC Management Inc., 613/936-6072
Number of landfill sites: 1 *Landfill Capacity:* 35 years
Solid Waste Disposal Fees: $50/tonne (regular waste, scrap metal & white goods)
Recycling: Both Curbside & Depot; Recycling Plant, located at City of Cornwall Landfill site, 613/933-6953
Hazardous Waste Depot or Facility: City of Cornwall Landfill & Household Special Waste Facility, 2590 Cornwall Centre Rd. W.,
Composters subsidized: Yes
Water & Wastewater Treatment:
Cornwall Water Purification Plant, 861 Second St. West; Cornwall Wastewater Treatment Plant, 2800 Montreal Rd. East
Other Initiatives:
Autumn collection of leaf & yard waste; Hazardous waste days; Christmas tree collection; White goods collection for fee; Free compost

City of Elliot Lake
45 Hillside Dr. North
Elliot Lake, ON P5A 1X5
705-848-2287
www.cityofelliotlake.com
Population: 11,348 *Census Year:* 2011
Number of Households: 6,202
Paul Officer, Fire Chief
Waste Management:
Number of landfill sites: 1
Water & Wastewater Treatment:
Water treatment plant on Spine Rd., Elliot Lake; Wastewater treatment plant on Scott Rd., Elliot Lake

City of Greater Napanee
P.O. Box 97
124 John St.
Napanee, ON K7R 3L4
613-354-3351
Fax: 613-354-6545
E-mail, Programs: recreation@greaternapanee.com
info@greaternapanee.com; roads@greaternapanee.com
www.greaternapanee.com
Population: 15,511 *Census Year:* 2011
Number of Households: 6,574
Vern Amey, Director, Public Works, email: vamey@greaternapanee.com
Kevin Hill, Director, Parks, Recreation & Culture, email: khill@greaternapanee.com
Charles McDonald, Director, Development Services, email: cmcdonald@greaternapanee.com
Terry Gervais, Fire Chief, email: tgervais@greaternapanee.com
Ron Vankoughnet, Supervisor, Roads & Landfill
Waste Management:
Garbage & recycling collection contracted to Waste Management, Canadian Waste, 613/549-7100
Number of landfill sites: 3
Solid Waste Disposal Fees: $10/utility trailers, cars, 1/2 & 3/4 ton trucks
Recycling: Curbside
Other Initiatives:
Waste Reduction Week

City of Greater Sudbury / Grand Sudbury
Tom Davies Square
P.O. Box 5000 A
200 Brady St.
Sudbury, ON P3A 5P3
705-671-2489
Fax: 705-671-8118
Phone, Local Calls: 3-1-1
www.greatersudbury.ca
Population: 160,274 *Census Year:* 2011
Number of Households: 68,690
Greg Clausen, P. Eng, General Manager, Infrastructure Services, email: greg.clausen@greatersudbury.ca
Bill Lautenbach, General Manager, Growth & Development, email: bill.lautenbach@greatersudbury.ca
Catherine Matheson, General Manager, Community Development, email: catherine.matheson@greatersudbury.ca
Tim P. Beadman, Chief, Emergency Services, email: tim.beadman@greatersudbury.ca
Marc Leduc, Fire Chief, email: marc.leduc@greatersudbury.ca
Nick Benkovich, Director, Water & Wastewater, email: nick.benkovich@greatersudbury.ca
Robert Falcioni, Director, Roads & Transportation, email: robert.falcioni@greatersudbury.ca
Guido Mazza, Director, Building Services, email: guido.mazza@greatersudbury.caa
Roger Sauvé, Director, Greater Sudbury Transit, email: roger.sauve@greatersudbury.ca
Kevin Shaw, Director, Engineering Services, email: kevin.shaw@greatersudbury.ca
Waste Management:
Number of landfill sites: 4
Solid Waste Disposal Fees: $63/tonne
Recycling: Both Curbside & Depot; Blue Box for recyclables; Green Cart program for organics; leaf & yard waste; Recycling Centre, 1825 Frobisher St.
Hazardous Waste Depot or Facility: Household hazardous waste can be disposed of at no charge; depot located at 1853 Frobisher St., or call Toxic Taxi for free home collection service; see city website for schedule of dates
Composters subsidized: Yes
Water & Wastewater Treatment:
10 wastewater treatment plants; 4 sewage treatment lagoons; David Street Water Treatment Plant; Wanapitei Water Treatment Plant; For more information, 705/560-2022
Other Initiatives:
Adopt-a-road; Derelict motor vehicle removal & recycling program; Annual clean-up blitz; Waste optimization study; Leaf & yard trimmings collection; Garbage bag limit; Landfill diversion areas for items such as scrap metal & white goods, reusable cloth items & electronic waste; Land reclamation program

City of Guelph
City Hall
1 Carden St.
Guelph, ON N1H 3A1
519-822-1260
Fax: 519-763-1269
TTY: 519-826-9771
info@guelph.ca; communications@guelph.ca
www.guelph.ca
Population: 121,688 *Census Year:* 2011
Number of Households: 42,479
Mark Amorosi, Executive Director, Human Resources & Legal Services, email: mark.amorosi@guelph.ca
Janet Laird, Executive Director, Environmental Services, email: janet.laird@guelph.ca
Derek McCaughan, Executive Director, Operations, email: operations@guelph.ca
Shawn Armstrong, General Manager, Emergency Services
Waste Management:
Number of landfill sites: 1
Solid Waste Disposal Fees: $70/tonne
Recycling: Both Curbside & Depot; Waste Resource Innovation Centre, 110 Dunlop Dr.
Hazardous Waste Depot or Facility: Waste Resource Innovation Centre, 110 Dunlop Dr.
Composters subsidized: Yes
Water & Wastewater Treatment:
F.M. Woods Pumping Station, 29 Waterworks Place, waterworks@guelph.ca; Wastewater Treatment Plant, 530 Wellington St., wastewater@guelph.ca
Other Initiatives:
User-pay bulky item collection program; Formation of an environmental advisory committee & pesticide review committee; Outside water use program; City of Guelph Green Plan; Waste Reduction Week; Formation of anti-litter team; Paint plus reuse program; Recycling programs for industries & apartments; Air quality monitoring station; Natural heritage strategy

City of Hamilton
Hamilton City Centre
P.O. Box 2040 LCD1
#220, 77 James St. North
Hamilton, ON L8R 2K3
905-546-2489
Fax: 905-546-2095
E-mail, Dev.: economicdevelopment@hamilton.ca
askCITY@hamilton.ca; communications@hamilton.ca
www.hamilton.ca
Population: 519,949 *Census Year:* 2011
Number of Households: 194,154
Jim Kay, General Manager, Hamilton Emergency Services
Tim McCabe, General Manager, Planning & Economic Development
Scott Stewart, C.E.T., General Manager, Public Works
Waste Management:
Contractors include AIM Environmental Group, & Maple Reinders (composting); Canada Fibres Ltd. (recycling); Community Living Hamilton (Mountain Community Recycling Centre's Re-use Store); Hotz Environmental Services Inc.; National Waste Services Inc. (green cart, garbage, blue box, multi-residential pick-up); BFI (recycling); Waste Management of Canada Corp. (Glanbrook Landfill Site); & Waste Services Inc. (paper bin from multi-residential sites). Email: wastemanagement@city.hamilton.on.ca
Number of landfill sites: 1
Recycling: Both Curbside & Depot; Three Community Recycling Centres handle household recycling, leafe & yard waste, scrap metal, & household hazardous waste; Depots located at Dundas CRC, Kenora CRC, & Mountain CRC
Hazardous Waste Depot or Facility: Contract with Hotz Environmental Services Inc., 239 Lottridge St. North; depots located at the Community Recycling Centres
Composters subsidized: Yes
Water & Wastewater Treatment:
The following are owned by the city: Woodward Ave. Water Treatment Facility, 700 Woodward Ave.; Wastewater Treatment Facility, King St.; Wastewater Treatment Facility, Dundas; Main St. Wastewater Treatment Facility, Waterdown. For more information, email water-quality@hamilton.ca. The City also maintains an environmental laboratory for water, wastewater & landfill leachate testing
Other Initiatives:
Lead Pipe Service Replacement Program; Wise Water Use Public Education & Outreach Program; Water & Wastewater Master Plan; Biosolid Master Plan; Children's Water Festival; Spring clean-up week; Earth Week; City greening iniatives & tree planting program; Hamilton Renewable Power Incorporated Cogeneration Facility will promote sustainable green energy

City of Huntsville
37 Main St. East
Huntsville, ON P1H 1A1
705-789-1751
Fax: 705-789-6689
TTY: 705-789-1768
administration@huntsville.ca
www.huntsville.ca
Population: 19,056 *Census Year:* 2011
Number of Households: 9,089
Mike Gooch, Director, Building & Chief Building Official
Steve Hernen, Director, Protective Services & Fire Chief
Steve Keeley, Director, Public Works
Colleen MacDonald, Manager, Parks & Cemeteries
Lisa Smith, Manager, Human Resources
Waste Management:
Responsibility of District Municipality of Muskoka, 905/645-6764
Water & Wastewater Treatment:
Water & wastewater treatment responsibility of District Municipality of Muskoka

City of Kawartha Lakes
P.O. Box 9000
26 Francis St.
Lindsay, ON K9V 5R8
705-324-9411
Fax: 705-324-8110
Toll-Free Phone: 1-888-822-2225
info@city.kawarthalakes.on.ca
www.city.kawarthalakes.on.ca
Population: 73,214 *Census Year:* 2011
Number of Households: 34,637
Michelle Hendry, Director, Public Works, email: mhendry@city.kawarthalakes.on.ca
Ron Taylor, Director, Development Services, email: rtaylor@city.kawarthalakes.on.ca
Bob Knight, Director, Health & Social Services, email: bknight@city.kawarthalakes.on.ca
Mark Pankhurst, Fire Chief, email: mpankhurst@city.kawarthalakes.on.ca
Waste Management:
Waste collection contracted to National Waste Services, 1-866-344-1544
Number of landfill sites: 5*Landfill Capacity:* 25 years
Solid Waste Disposal Fees: $85/tonne
Recycling: Curbside
Hazardous Waste Depot or Facility: Household Hazardous Waste Depot, Fenelon Waste Facility, 341 Mark Rd.
Compost Sites: Yes *Composters subsidized:* Yes
Water & Wastewater Treatment:
The city operates water treatment facilities in Birch Point, Highview Acres, Kinmount, Lindsay, Norland, Palmina, Sonya, Southview Estates, Springdale Gardens, Sturgeon Park & Western Trent; Ontario Clean Water Agency (OCWA) operates water treatment facilities in Bobcaygeon, Canadiana Shores, Fenelon Falls, Janetville, King's Bay, Manorview/Bethany, Mariposa Estates, Oakwood Estates, Omemee, Pinewood/Pontypool, Pleasant Point, Sandwood, Sunny Acres, Victoria Place, Woodfield, Woods of Manilla &
Other Initiatives:
Reuse Centre plus Electronics Recycling Depot, located at Fenelon Waste Facility

City of Kingston
City Hall
216 Ontario St.
Kingston, ON K7L 2Z3
613-546-0000
Fax: 613-546-5232
TTY: 613-546-4889
www.cityofkingston.ca
Population: 123,363 *Census Year:* 2011
Number of Households: 50,755
Cynthia Beach, Commissioner, Sustainability & Growth
Paul MacLatchy, Director, Strategy, Environment, & Communications
Mark Van Buren, Director, Engineering
Damon Wells, Director, Public Works
Terry Willing, Director, Building & Licensing
Harold Tulk, Fire Chief
John Cross, Manager, Emergency Planning
John Giles, Manager, Solid Waste
George Wallace, Project Manager, Sustainability & Growth
Waste Management:
Number of landfill sites: 1*Landfill Capacity:* 2 years

Solid Waste Disposal Fees: $110/tonne
Transfer Station(s): Yes
Recycling: Both Curbside & Depot; Kingston Area Recycling Centre, 196 Lappan's Lane
Hazardous Waste Depot or Facility: 196 Lappan's Lane
Compost Sites: Yes *Composters subsidized:* Yes
Water & Wastewater Treatment:
Kingston Central Water Treatment Plant, 302 King St. West; Kingston West Water Treatment Plant, 80 Sunny Acres Rd.; Ravensview Water Pollution Control Plant, Hwy. #2; Kingston West Water Pollution Control Plant, Days Rd.

City of Kingsville

2021 Division Rd. North
Kingsville, ON N9Y 2Y9
519-733-2305
Fax: 519-733-8108
www.kingsville.ca
Population: 21,362 *Census Year:* 2011
Number of Households: 7,246
Andrew Plancke, C.E.T., Director, Municipal Services, email: aplancke@kingsville.ca
Michael Arthur, Chief Building Official, email: marthur@kingsville.ca
Bob Kissner, Fire Chief, email: bkissner@kingsville.ca
Andy Coghill, Manager, Public Works, email: acoghill@kingsville.ca
Dan Wood, Manager, Parks & Recreation, email: dwood@kingsville.ca
Waste Management:
Waste management responsibility of Essex County; Public Works Dept. is responsible for waste collection
Water & Wastewater Treatment:
Ontario Clean Water Agency operates the Lakeshore West Wastewater Treatment Plant & the Waste Treatment Lagoon
Other Initiatives:
Special collections for grass clippings, brush, leaves & Christmas trees

City of Kitchener

City Hall
P.O. Box 1118
200 King St. West
Kitchener, ON N2G 4G7
519-741-2345
TTY: 1-866-969-9994
www.kitchener.ca
Population: 219,153 *Census Year:* 2011
Number of Households: 74,127
Jeff Willmer, General Manager, Development & Technical Services
Grant Murphy, Director, Engineering Services
Alain Pinard, Director, Planning
Mike Seiling, Director, Building
Tim Beckett, Fire Chief, 519-741-2495
Waste Management:
Responsibility of the Regional Municipality of Waterloo
Other Initiatives:
Environmental Strategic Plan: identifying a number of issues & initiatives in the areas of water resources, waste management, growth management, energy systems, resource consumption, natural areas, education & public awareness

City of London

City Hall
P.O. Box 5035
300 Dufferin Ave.
London, ON N6A 4L9
519-661-4500
Fax: 519-661-4892
webmaster@london.ca
www.london.ca
Population: 366,151 *Census Year:* 2011
Number of Households: 146,976
Veronica McAlea Major, Chief Human Resources Officer, email: vmcaleamajor@london.ca
Ross Fair, Executive Director, Community Services, email: rfair@london.ca
Patrick McNally, P.Eng., Executive Director, Planning, Environmental & Engineering Services
William Coxhead, Director, Parks & Recreation, email: bcoxhead@london.ca
Ronald Standish, Director, Wastewater & Treatment, email: rstandis@london.ca
Jay Stanford, Director, Environmental Programs & Solid Waste, email: jstanfor@london.ca
Waste Management:
W12A Landfill, located at 3502 Manning Dr. for household waste; 4-container limit for curbside collection
Recycling: Blue Box recyclables and yard waste may be taken to the Oxford St. Community or Clarke Rd. Community EnviroDepots; these locations also accept tires, batteries, propane tanks, & empty oil containers, as well as used electronics (except for televisions & monitors), & scrap metal
Hazardous Waste Depot or Facility: Household hazardous waste may be taken to the depot at the W12A Landfill, located at 3502 Manning Dr.
Water & Wastewater Treatment:
The city operates the following Water Pollution Control Plants: Greenway, Pottersburg, Vauxhall, Adelaide, Oxford, Westminster & Lambeth (Southland Park)

City of Markham

Markham Civic Centre
101 Town Centre Blvd.
Markham, ON L3R 9W3
905-477-7000
Fax: 905-479-7771
Customer Service: 905-477-5530
customerservice@markham.ca; webmaster@markham.ca
www.markham.ca
Population: 301,709 *Census Year:* 2011
Number of Households: 61,618
Jim Baird, Commissioner, Development Services, 905-475-4875, email: jbaird@markham.ca
Brenda Librecz, Commissioner, Community & Fire Services, 905-479-7761, email: blibrecz@markham.ca
Bill Snowball, Fire Chief, Fire & Emergency Services, 905-305-5982, email: bsnowball@markham.ca
Alan Brown, Director, Engineering, 905-415-7507, email: abrown@markham.ca
Sharon Laing, Director, Human Resources, 905-475-4725, email: slaing@markham.ca
Peter Loukes, Director, Operations, 905-475-4894, email: ploukes@markham.ca
Tim Moore, Director, Building Standards, 905-475-4712, email: tmoore@markham.ca
Claudia Marsales, Senior Manager, Waste Management & Environment, email: cmarsales@markham.ca
Waste Management:
Waste collection responsibility of city waste management division; Waste management responsibility of the Region of York
Recycling: Both Curbside & Depot; Depot locations: Unionville Recycling Depot, Thornhill Recycling Depot, Markham Recycling Depot & Milliken Mills Drop-Off Centre
Water & Wastewater Treatment:
City receives treated water from 4 plants owned & operated by the City of Toronto

City of Mississauga

Civic Centre
300 City Centre Dr.
Mississauga, ON L5B 3C1
905-615-4311
Fax: 905-615-4081
TTY: 905-896-5151
public.info@mississauga.ca
www.mississauga.ca
Population: 713,443 *Census Year:* 2011
Number of Households: 198,235
Paul Mitcham, Commissioner, Community Services
Martin Powell, Commissioner, Transportation & Works
Ed Sajecki, Commissioner, Planning & Building
John McDougall, Fire Chief
Waste Management:
Responsibility of Regional Municipality of Peel
Special Bans/by-laws: Erosion & sediment control bylaw; Storm sewer use bylaw; Noise bylaw; Debris bylaw; Tree permit bylaw
Water & Wastewater Treatment:
Responsibility of Regional Municipality of Peel
Other Initiatives:
Tree preservation; Leaf collection service; Street tree planting & management of woodlands; Ecological restoration; Parkland naturalization of parks & open spaces; Natural areas survey; Integrated turf management/pesticide reduction program; Bicycle pathways program; City plan environmental policies; Energy management plan; Stormwater channel stabilization & erosion control monitoring; Subwatershed plans; Earth Days & Litter Not campaign; Displays of city & community environmental programs; Street lighting program (high-efficiency streetlights); Creek restoration projects; Water conservation; Anti-idling campaign; Mayor's Megawatt Challenge; Smart Commute; Environmental awards

City of Newmarket

P.O. Box 328
395 Mulock Dr.
Newmarket, ON L3Y 4X7
905-895-5193
Fax: 905-953-5100
info@newmarket.ca
www.newmarket.ca
Population: 79,978 *Census Year:* 2011
Number of Households: 21,589
Lynn Georgeff, Director, Human Resources
Brian Jones, Director, Public Works Services
Jim Koutroubis, Director, Engineering Services, email: engineering@newmarket.ca
Rick Nethery, BES, MCIP, RPP, Director, Planning, 905-953-5321, Fax: 905-953-5140, email: planning@newmarket.ca
David Potter, Chief Building Official, email: buildings@newmarket.ca
Waste Management:
Waste management responsibility of the Regional Municipality of York; Waste collection responsibility of Town
Recycling: Curbside
Water & Wastewater Treatment:
Responsibility of the Regional Municipality of York
Other Initiatives:
Yard waste collection; Ccurbside give-away days; Eestablishment of Environmental Advisory Committee with the following subcommittees: education, outreach & stewardship, terrestrial planning & policy, & atmospheric; Green series seminars; Reduction in road salting; Identification of green space areas; Appliance collection

City of Niagara Falls

City Hall
P.O. Box 1023
4310 Queen St.
Niagara Falls, ON L2E 6X5
905-356-7521
Fax: 905-356-9083
www.niagarafalls.ca
Population: 82,997 *Census Year:* 2011
Number of Households: 32,447
Alex Herlovitch, Director, Planning & Development, email: planning@niagarafalls.ca
Geoffrey Holman, Director, Municipal Works
Lee Smith, Fire Chief
Waste Management:
Responsibility of Regional Municipality of Niagara
Water & Wastewater Treatment:
Responsibility of Regional Municipality of Niagara
Other Initiatives:
Woodlot study to promote stewardship

City of North Bay

City Hall
P.O. Box 360
200 McIntyre St. East
North Bay, ON P1B 8H8
705-474-0400
Fax: 705-495-4353
Toll-Free Phone: 1-800-465-1882
info@cityofnorthbay.ca
www.city.north-bay.on.ca
Population: 53,651 *Census Year:* 2011
Number of Households: 22,973
Alan Korell, Managing Director, Engineering, Environmental & Works, email: alan.korell@cityofnorthbay.ca
David Euler, Director, Sewer & Water, email: david.euler@cityofnorthbay.ca
Jamie Houston, Director, Parks, Recreation, & Leisure Services, email: jamie.houston@cityofnorthbay.ca
Lea Janisse, Director, Human Resources, email: lea.janisse@cityofnorthbay.ca
John Severino, Manager, Environmental Services, email: john.severino@cityofnorthbay.ca
Dorothea Carvell, Manager, Transit, email: dorothea.carvell@cityofnorthbay.ca
Joe Germano, Manager, Road & Traffic, email: joe.germano@cityofnorthbay.ca

Ian Kilgour, Manager, Planning Services, email: ian.kilgour@cityofnorthbay.ca
Shawn Killins, Chief Building Official, email: shawn.killins@cityofnorthbay.ca
Peter Leckie, City Solicitor, email: peter.leckie@cityofnorthbay.ca
Grant Love, Fire Chief, email: grant.love@cityofnorthbay.ca
Waste Management:
Waste collection contracted to Miller Waste Systems
Number of landfill sites: 1
Solid Waste Disposal Fees: $20/minimum load; $45/tonne (ICI)
Clean Fill Fee: No
Recycling: Both Curbside & Depot; Recycling Centre, 112 Patton St.; Organic drop-off area
Special Bans/by-laws: Household hazardous waste, corrugated cardboard, tires, liquid waste, pathological waste banned from Merrick landfill; ban on grass collection
Hazardous Waste Depot or Facility: Facility at 112 Patton St.
Water & Wastewater Treatment:
North Bay WPCP, 650 Memorial Dr.; Water treatment plant, 248 Lakeside Dr.; Both facilities are operated by the Ontario Clean Water Agency

City of Oakville

1225 Trafalgar Rd.
Oakville, ON L6J 5A6
905-845-6601
Fax: 905-815-2025
TTY: 905-338-4200
publicinquiry@oakville.ca; communications@oakville.ca
www.oakville.ca
Population: 182,520 *Census Year:* 2011
David Bloomer, Commissioner, Infrastructure & Transportation Services, email: dbloomer@oakville.ca
Jane Clohecy, Commissioner, Planning & Development Services, email: jclohecy@oakville.ca; planning@oakville.ca
Elizabeth Bourns, Director, Human Resources, email: ebourns@oakville.ca; humanresources@oakville.ca
Barry Cole, Director, Transit Services, email: bcole@oakville.ca; transit@oakville.ca
Daniel Cozzi, P.Eng., Director, Roads & Works Operations, email: dcozzi@oakville.ca
Darnell Lambert, C.E.T., Director, Engineering & Construction, email: dlambert@oakville.ca
Chris Mark, Director, Parks & Open Space, email: cmark@oakville.ca; parks@oakville.ca
Cindy Toth, Director, Environmental Policy, email: ctoth@oakville.ca; environment@oakville.ca
Sheldon Switzer, Director, Building Services & Chief Building Official, email: sswitzer@oakville.ca; building@oakville.ca
John McNeil, Manager, Forestry & Cemetery Services, email: jmcneil@oakville.ca; forestry@oakville.ca
Richard Boyes, Fire Chief, email: rboyes@oakville.ca; fire@oakville.ca
Waste Management:
Responsibility of Regional Municipality of Halton; Halton Waste Management Services
Recycling: Halton Waste Management Site is a multi-purpose facility for recyclables, yard waste, household hazardous waste, & garbage; located at 5400 Regional Rd. 25, Milton
Water & Wastewater Treatment:
Responsibility of Regional Municipality of Halton
Other Initiatives:
Blueprint Oakville included the Environmental Strategic Plan (at the implementation stage); Development Charges By-law Study; Subwatershed Studies; Transportation Master Plan; anti-litter programs; pesticide awareness; anti-idling; air quality; Oakville Conserves awareness program; past programs have included: Doors Closed Campaign, 20/20 The Way to Clean Air, Rain Water Barrels, Purchase Hybrid Vehicles & LED Traffic Signal Replacement; Earth Hour; Energy Conservation Week; Watt Not Waste Not

City of Orillia

Administration Office
#300, 50 Andrew St. South
Orillia, ON L3V 7T5
705-325-1311
Fax: 705-325-5178
corporate@city.orillia.on.ca
www.orillia.ca
Population: 30,586 *Census Year:* 2011
Number of Households: 12,152
Lori Bolton, Director, Human Resources, email: lbolton@orillia.ca
Peter Dance, Director, Public Works, email: publicworks@orillia.ca; pdance@orillia.ca
Ray Merkley, Director, Parks & Recreation, email: parks@orillia.ca; rmerkley@orillia.ca
Craig Metcalf, Director, Culture & Heritage, email: cmetcalf@orillia.ca
Ian Sugden, Director, Planning & Development, email: planning@orillia.ca; isugden@orillia.ca
Ralph Dominell, Fire Chief, email: ofd@orillia.ca; rdominelli@orillia.ca
Kelly Smith, Chief Building Official, email: ksmith@orillia.ca
Jack Green, Manager, Transportation, email: jgreen@orillia.ca
Andrew Schell, Manager, Environmental Services, email: aschell@orillia.ca
Percival Thomas, Manager, Water & Wastewater Systems, email: pthomas@orillia.ca
Waste Management:
Number of landfill sites: 1
Recycling: Both Curbside & Depot; Depot located at Recycling Depot, Waste Diversion Site, 100 Kitchener St., Orillia
Hazardous Waste Depot or Facility: Depot at 100 Kitchener St., Orillia
Composters subsidized: Yes
Water & Wastewater Treatment:
Water Filtration Plant at 200 Bay St., Orillia; Wastewater Treatment Centre at 40 Kitchener St., Orillia
Other Initiatives:
Garbage tag program; Compostable waste collected year-round; Paint reuse depot; Tree planting rebate; Water efficiency rebate program; Upgrades to Water Filtration Plant

City of Oshawa

City Hall
50 Centre St. South
Oshawa, ON L1H 3Z7
905-436-3311
Fax: 905-436-5642
Toll-Free Phone: 1-800-667-4292; TTY: 905-436-5627
service@oshawa.ca
www.oshawa.ca
Population: 149,607 *Census Year:* 2011
Number of Households: 53,298
Tom Hodgins, Commissioner, Development Services Department
Jacqueline Long, Director, Human Resource Services, email: humanresources@oshawa.ca
Gary Carroll, Director, Engineering Services
Craig Kelly, Director, Works & Transportation Services
Paul Ralph, Director, Planning Services
Mike Leonard, Chief Building Official, email: buildings@oshawa.ca
Steve Meringer, Fire Chief
Waste Management:
Waste diversion & management responsiblity of Durham Region; Waste collection responsibility of city's public works services
Water & Wastewater Treatment:
Responsibility of Durham Region
Other Initiatives:
Christmas tree, yard waste & green bin collection programs; Forestry & environmental stewardship programs

City of Ottawa

City Hall
110 Laurier Ave. West
Ottawa, ON K1P 1J1
613-580-2400
Fax: 613-560-1380
Toll Free Phone: 1-866-261-9799; or 311
info@ottawa.ca
www.ottawa.ca
Population: 883,391 *Census Year:* 2011
Number of Households: 144,451
Catherine Frederick, Director, Human Resources
Donna L. Gray, Director, Organizational Development & Performance
Johanne Levesque, Director, Community Sustainability
Wayne Newell, Director, Infrastructure Services
Dan Chenier, General Manager, Parks, Recreation & Cultural Service
Susan Jones, General Manager, Emergency & Protective Services
John Manconi, General Manager, Public Works
Alain Mercier, General Manager, Transit Services
John Moser, General Manager, Planning & Growth Management
Dixon A. Weir, General Manager, Environmental Services
Isra Levy, Medical Officer of Health
Michel Chevalier, Manager, Wastewater & Drainage Operations
Felice Petti, Manager, Strategic & Environmental Services
Tammy Rose, Manager, Drinking Water Services
Waste Management:
Waste collection responsibility of city & private contractors
Number of landfill sites: 2*Landfill Capacity:* 30 years
Solid Waste Disposal Fees: $89.46/tonne
Clean Fill Fee: Yes; $20/tonne
Recycling: Green Bin program for residential organic waste (greenbinottawa.ca); residential scrap steel & tire drop off: Waste Management Residential Recycling Centre, 2301 Carp Rd.
Hazardous Waste Depot or Facility: Household hazardous waste only, with commercial depots across the city accepting waste on scheduled dates; check city website for details
Composters subsidized: Yes
Water & Wastewater Treatment:
Lemieux Island Water Purification Plant; Britannia Water Purification Plant; Robert O. Pickard Environmental Centre, a wastewater treatment facility
Other Initiatives:
Plasma gasification pilot project (75 tonnes of MSW converted to electrical energy), start-up at end 2006; Travelwise, a program to promote healthier alternatives to driving; Take it Back, a program to return hazardous waste products to participating retailers; Reduction of pesticide/herbicide use; Sewer Use Program, in conjunction with the sewer use by-law, to protect water through pollution prevention; Air Quality & Climate Change Management Plan; One day household hazardous waste depots; Natural areas protection; Sub-watershed planning; Sustainable indicators program; Adopt-a-park/Adopt-a roadway program; Tree protection; Greenspace Master Plan; Rural clean water program; Zerofootprint Ottawa interactive website encourages residents & organizations to reduce their carbon footprint & greenhouse gas emissions to fight global warming; WaterWise: Ottawa's Water Efficiency Strategy; TREE Program, 2007-2010, tree planting throughout the city; Community Environmental Projects Grants Program; National Capital Air Quality Mapping Pilot Project, 2007-2009; anti-idling initiative

City of Owen Sound

City Hall
808 - 2nd Ave. East
Owen Sound, ON N4K 2H4
519-376-1440
Fax: 519-371-0511
cityadmin@e-owensound.com; communityservices@e-owensound.com
www.owensound.ca
Population: 21,688 *Census Year:* 2011
Number of Households: 9,532
John D. Johnston, C.E.T., Director, Operations, email: jdjohnson@e-owensound.com
Chris Webb, P.Eng., Manager, Engineering Services
Ed Nowak, Fire Chief, email: enowak@e-owensound.com
Waste Management:
Garbage collection every other week, to coincide with Blue Box recycling collection; 4 bag limit every two weeks, garbage bags must be labeled with purchased $2.00 bag tags. Household and commercial leaf and yard waste may be taken to the compost site located at the corner of 28th Ave. East and 26th St. East, northeast of the Heritage Place Mall.
Number of landfill sites: 1
Solid Waste Disposal Fees: $47.50/tonne, domestic waste; $70/tonne, commercial or industrial general waste
Clean Fill Fee:
Transfer Station(s):
Recycling: Both Curbside & Depot; Recycling Drop-of Depot: Miller Waste Transfer Station, 2085 - 20th St. East; call 519-372-1855. For electronics disposal/recycling, the Habitat for Humanity ReStore, located on Grey Rd. 11, just off Hwy. 26, accepts your used electronics
Hazardous Waste Depot or Facility: Household hazardous waste only; fryer oil now accepted; Owen Sound Public Works Building, HHW Depot, 1900 20th St. East; hours from 9 a.m. to 3 p.m. on designated days only, from April through October
Compost Sites: Yes
Water & Wastewater Treatment:
Richard H. Neath Water Treatment Plant, 2600 - 3rd Ave. East, Owen Sound

City of Pembroke

1 Pembroke St. East
Pembroke, ON K8A 3J5

613-735-6821
Fax: 613-735-3660
pembroke@pembroke.ca
www.pembroke.ca
Population: 14,360 *Census Year:* 2011
Number of Households: 6,298
Susan Ellis, Manager, Economic Development, Recreation, & Tourism, email: sellis@pembroke.ca
Colleen Sauriol, Coordinator, Emergency Management, email: csauriol@pembroke.ca
Douglas Sitland, Manager, Operations, email: dsitland@pembroke.ca
Daniel Herback, Fire Chief, email: dherback@pembroke.ca
Robert Hughes, Chief Building Official, email: rhughes@pembroke.ca
Ron Conroy, Supervisor, Parks & Facilities, email: rconroy@pembroke.ca
Chris Mantha, Supervisor, Roads & Fleet, email: cmantha@pembroke.ca
Curtis Mick, Supervisor, Water & Sewer, email: cmick@pembroke.ca
Waste Management:
Responsibility of City of Pembroke, in partnership with the Township of Laurentian Valley, the Town of Petawawa, the Township of North Algoma-Wilberforce & the Township of Bonnechere Valley; Landfill site located on Woito Station Rd., Pembroke
Number of landfill sites: 1
Solid Waste Disposal Fees: $65.87/tonne
Recycling: Both Curbside & Depot; Material Recovery Facility at Ottawa Valley Waste Recovery Centre, 900 Woito Station Rd., Pembroke
Hazardous Waste Depot or Facility: Ottawa Valley Waste Recovery Centre, 900 Woito Station Rd., Pembroke
Composters subsidized: Yes
Water & Wastewater Treatment:
Water Purification Plant, 1 Riverside Dr., Pembroke, 613/735-0309; Pollution Control Plant, 98 Rankin St. Pembroke, 613/735-0409
Other Initiatives:
Upgrades to Water Purification Plant & Pollution Control Plant; Spring & fall special garbage collection

City of Peterborough

500 George St. North
Peterborough, ON K9H 3R9
705-742-7777
Fax: 705-742-4138
E-mail, Human Resources: hr@peterborough.ca
cityptbo@peterborough.ca; clerk@peterborough.ca
www.peterborough.ca
Population: 78,698 *Census Year:* 2011
Number of Households: 30,804
Ken Doherty, Director, Community Services, email: kdoherty@peterborough.ca
Malcolm Hunt, Director, Planning & Development Services, email: mhunt@peterborough.ca
Wayne Jackson, Director, Utility Services & Deputy CAO, email: wjackson@peterborough.ca
Trent Gervais, Fire Chief
Waste Management:
Handled by the city
Number of landfill sites: 1*Landfill Capacity:* 25 years
Solid Waste Disposal Fees: $70/tonne
Recycling: Both Curbside & Depot; Depots: Materials Recycling Facility, Peterborough; Peterborough County/City Landfill site; Electronics Drop-Off Depot, Peterborough
Special Bans/by-laws: Garbage limit 2/household/week, 4/business/week; Following items banned from Peterborough County/City landfill site: blue box recyclables, tires, green wastes, hazardous materials, biomedical wastes, radioactive wastes, liquid wastes, materials from outside County of Peterborough
Hazardous Waste Depot or Facility: 400 Pido Rd., Peterborough
Composters subsidized: Yes
Water & Wastewater Treatment:
City of Peterborough Wastewater Treatment Plant, 425 Kennedy Rd., Peterborough; City of Peterborough Water Treatment Plant, 1230 Water St. North, Peterborough
Other Initiatives:
Clean Stream Waste Management Program; Curbside collection of household food wastes; Hope to expand the organics collection to all households

City of Pickering

1 The Esplanade
Pickering, ON L1V 6K7
905-420-2222
Toll-Free Phone: 1-866-683-2760; TTY: 905-420-1739
info@cityofpickering.com; customercare@cityofpickering.com
www.cityofpickering.com
Population: 88,721 *Census Year:* 2011
Number of Households: 27,924
Everett Buntsma, Director, Community Services, 905-420-4624, email: ebuntsma@cityofpickering.com
Neil Carroll, Director, Planning & Development, 905-420-4617, email: ncarroll@cityofpickering.com
Thomas E. Melymuk, Director, Office of Sustainability, 905-420-4636, email: tmelymuk@cityofpickering.com
Richard W. Holborn, Division Head, Engineering Services Division, 90-542-2049, email: rholborn@cityofpickering.com
Jennifer Parent, Division Head, Human Resources, 905-420-2160
William T. Douglas, Fire Chief, 905-839-9968, Fax: 905-839-6327, email: fire@cityofpickering.com
Kyle Bentley, Chief Building Official, 905-420-2070, email: kbentley@cityofpickering.com
Waste Management:
Responsibility of Regional Municipality of Durham, waste@region.durham.on.ca
Special Bans/by-laws: Waste management by-law; Anti-idling by-law
Water & Wastewater Treatment:
Responsibility of Regional Municipality of Durham

City of Port Colborne

66 Charlotte St.
Port Colborne, ON L3K 3C8
905-835-2900
Fax: 905-834-5746
www.portcolborne.ca
Population: 18,424 *Census Year:* 2011
Number of Households: 8,411
Dan Aquilina, Director, Planning & Development, email: danaquilina@portcolborne.ca
Ron Hanson, Director, Engineering & Operations, email: hanson@portcolborne.cane.ca
Peter Senese, Director, Community & Corporate Services, email: petersenese@portcolborne.ca
Thomas Cartwright, Fire Chief, email: firechief@portcolborne.ca
Ernie Cronier, Chief Building Official, email: erniecronier@portcolborne.ca
Randy Chamberlain, Coordinator, Health & Safety, email: randychamberlain@portcolborne.ca
Rick Marshall, Coordinator, Human Resources, email: rickmarshall@portcolborne.ca
Darlene Suddard, Coordinator, Water & Waste Water Compliance, email: darlenesuddard@portcolborne.ca
Waste Management:
Responsibility of the Regional Municipality of Niagara
Water & Wastewater Treatment:
Responsibility of the Regional Municipality of Niagara

City of Quinte West

P.O. Box 490
7 Creswell Dr.
Trenton, ON K8V 5R6
613-392-2841
Fax: 613-392-5608
Toll-Free Phone: 1-866-485-2841
www.city.quintewest.on.ca
Population: 43,086 *Census Year:* 2011
Number of Households: 16,212
Chris Angelo, Director, Public Works & Environmental Services
Charlie Murphy, Director, Planning & Development Services
Tim Colasante, Manager, Engineering Services
Matt Tracey, Manager, Water & Wastewater
Tim Osborne, Manager, Human Resources
Phillip Lappan, Chief Building Official
John Whelan, Fire Chief
Waste Management:
Waste management in the Frankford ward responsibility of city's public works department; Waste management contracts in the Murray, Sidney & Trenton wards overseen by city's public works department
Number of landfill sites: 1
Recycling: Curbside; Administered by Centre & South Hastings Waste Services Board
Water & Wastewater Treatment:
Water treatment & distribution plus sewage collection & treatment responsibility of city's public works department; Treatment plants include: Trenton Water Treatment Plant, 20 Chester Rd.; Trenton Ward Wastewater Treatment Plant, Bay St.; Bayside Water Treatment Plant, Aikins Rd.; Frankford Water & Sewage Treatment Plant, North Trent St.; Batawa Water & Sewage Treatments Plants, Batawa
Other Initiatives:
Bag tag garbage program; Information about recycling, household hazardous waste disposal & composting, contact Quinte Waste Solutions, 613/394-6266; Yard waste site, Frankford Landfill; Designated depots for disposal of large & bulky items

City of Richmond Hill

225 East Beaver Creek Rd.
Richmond Hill, ON L4B 3P4
905-771-8800
Fax: 905-771-2500
www.richmondhill.ca
Population: 185,541 *Census Year:* 2011
Number of Households: 41,966
A. Bassios, Commissioner, Planning, email: planning@richmondhill.ca
Italo Brutto, Commissioner, Environment & Infrastructure Services, 905-771-8830, email: eis@richmondhill.ca
J. DeVries, Director, Building Services, & Chief Building Official
P. Lee, Director, Planning Policy
Waste Management:
Town is responsible for collection of garbage & recyclables; Regional Municipality of York is responsible for household hazardous waste depot & compost facility; Waste disposal handled by Region of York & City of Toronto transfer stations
Recycling: Curbside
Compost Sites: Yes
Water & Wastewater Treatment:
Water supply from Lake Ontario is treated by City of Toronto Metro Works; Regional Municipality of York accepts the water from the City of Toronto; Town is responsible for maintenance of the water distribution system; Town is responsible for maintenance & operation of sewage collection system; Durham & York Region sewage systems treat sewage
Other Initiatives:
Clean air initiatives include the following programs: walk to school day, clean air local business award, telework, & development of sustainable transportation policies; Lake Wilcox remediation strategy; Planting of native trees & plants; Natural heritage strategy; Yard waste & Christmas tree collection; No clear plastic bags accepted for yard waste; Introduction of green bins for organic waste; Spring clean-up program; Salt management plan; Water conservation practices

City of St. Catharines

City Hall
P.O. Box 3012
50 Church St.
St Catharines, ON L2R 7C2
905-688-5600
Fax: 905-682-3631
TTY: 905-688-4889
info@stcatharines.ca
www.stcatharines.ca
Population: 131,400 *Census Year:* 2011
Number of Households: 55,815
Paul Chapman, Director, Planning Services
Mark Mehlenbacher, Director, Fire & Emergency Management Services, email: fs@stcatharines.ca
Paul Mustard, Director, Transportation & Environmental Services, email: tes@stcatharines.ca
David Oakes, Director, Economic Development & Tourism Services, email: edt@stcatharines.ca
Waste Management:
Responsibility of Regional Municipality of Niagara, 905/356-4141
Water & Wastewater Treatment:
Responsibility of Regional Municipality of Niagara
Other Initiatives:
Flood alleviation program; Green Ribbon Trail Eco-Tour

City of St. Thomas

City Hall
P.O. Box 520
545 Talbot St.
St Thomas, ON N5P 3V7
519-631-1680
www.city.st-thomas.on.ca

Population: 37,905 *Census Year:* 2011
Number of Households: 13,842
Graham Dart, Director, Human Resources, email: gdart@city.st-thomas.on.ca
John Dewancker, Director, Environmental Services, & City Engineer, email: jdewancker@city.st-thomas.on.ca
Patrick Keenan, Director, Planning, email: pkeenan@city.st-thomas.on.ca
Brian Clement, Manager, Engineering, email: bclement@city.st-thomas.on.ca
Edward Soldo, Manager, Operations & Compliance, email: esoldo@city.st-thomas.on.ca
Ross Tucker, Director, Parks & Recreation, email: rtucker@city.st-thomas.on.ca
Rob Broadbent, Fire Chief, email: rbroadbent@city.st-thomas.on.ca
Leon Bach, Chief Building Official, email: lbach@city.st-thomas.on.ca
Cyril McCready, Supervisor, Water & Wastewater, email: cmccready@city.st-thomas.on.ca
Dave White, Supervisor, Roads & Transportation, email: dwhite@city.st-thomas.on.ca
Waste Management:
Waste collection contracted to Green Lane Environmental Group Ltd., 519/631-7970
Recycling: Curbside
Water & Wastewater Treatment:
St. Thomas Secondary Water System is operated by American Water Services Canada Corp., under contract to St. Thomas Secondary Water Board; Elgin-Middlesex Pumping Station treatment facility, Lot 9, Concession 9, Former township of Yarmouth
Other Initiatives:
Curbside composting

City of Sarnia

City Hall
P.O. Box 3018
255 North Christina St.
Sarnia, ON N7T 7N2
519-332-0330
TTY: 519-332-2664
clerks@sarnia.ca; bylaws@sarnia.ca; legal@sarnia.ca
www.sarnia.ca
Population: 72,366 *Census Year:* 2011
Number of Households: 30,859
Kim Bresee, Director, Planning & Building, email: planning@sarnia.ca; kim.bresee@sarnia.ca
Ian Smith, Director, Community Services, email: comserv@sarnia.ca; ian.smith@sarnia.ca
Jim Stevens, Director, Transit, email: transit@sarnia.ca; jim.stevens@sarnia.ca
Chris Armstrong, Manager, Human Resources, email: hr@sarnia.ca; chris.armstrong@sarnia.ca
Andre Morin, City Engineer, email: engineer@sarnia.ca; andre.morin@sarnia.ca
Doug Robertson, Superintendent, Public Works Department, email: doug.robertson@sarnia.ca
Pat Cayen, Fire Chief, Fire Rescue Services, email: firerescue@sarnia.ca; pat.cayen@sarnia.ca
Waste Management:
Waste collection contracted to Marcotte Disposal, 519/339-9988; Recycling services contracted to Halton Recycling, 1-866-628-0735
Recycling: Curbside
Composters subsidized: Yes
Water & Wastewater Treatment:
Water supplied to the city by the Lambton Area Water Supply System, operated by the Ontario Clean Water Agency; Water distribution system is maintained by the City of Sarnia Engineering & Public Works Dept.
Other Initiatives:
Household Hazardous Waste Days provided by the County of Lambton

City of Sault Ste. Marie

Civic Centre
P.O. Box 580
99 Foster Dr.
Sault Ste Marie, ON P6A 5N1
705-759-2500
Fax: 705-759-2310
webmaster@cityssm.on.
www.cityssm.on.ca
Population: 75,141 *Census Year:* 2011
Number of Households: 32,822
Nicholas J. Apostle, Commissioner, Community Services, email: n.apostle@cityssm.on.ca
Jerry Dolcetti, Commissioner, Engineering & Planning, email: j.dolcetti@cityssm.on.ca
John R. Luszka, Commissioner, Human Resources, email: j.luszka@cityssm.on.ca
Larry Girardi, Commissioner, Public Works & Transportation, email: l.girardi@cityssm.on.ca
Marcel Provenzano, Fire Chief, email: m.provenzano@cityssm.on.ca
Waste Management:
Industrial, commercial & institutional waste collection & disposal provided by Sault Ste. Marie Disposals, 705/945-7554 & Canadian Waste Services, 705/254-5050
Number of landfill sites: 1
Solid Waste Disposal Fees: $27.50/tonne; $55/tonne
Recycling: Curbside; Depot located at Sault Ste. Marie Recycling Depot, McNabb St. Operated by Canadian Waste Services, 705/254-5050
Hazardous Waste Depot or Facility: Household Special Waste Depot, 115 Industrial Pk., Cres.

City of Stratford

City Hall
P.O. Box 818
1 Wellington St.
Stratford, ON N5A 6W1
519-271-0250
Fax: 519-273-5041
TTY: 519-271-5241
general@city.stratford.on.ca
www.city.stratford.on.ca
Population: 30,886 *Census Year:* 2011
Number of Households: 12,662
George Bowa, Director, Engineering & Public Works
Barbara Dembek, Director, Building & Planning
David St. Louis, Director, Community Services
Rick Young, Fire Chief
Jeff Bannon, City Planner
Waste Management:
Waste collection contracted to BFI, 519/681-4040
Number of landfill sites: 1
Solid Waste Disposal Fees: $58/tonne
Recycling: Both Curbside & Depot; Recycling Depot at Stratford Landfill, 777 Romeo St. South
Hazardous Waste Depot or Facility: Household Hazardous Waste Depot at Stratford Landfill, 777 Romeo St. South
Composters subsidized: Yes
Water & Wastewater Treatment:
Water Pollution Control Plant, West Gore St., owned by the city & operated by Ontario Clean Water Agency
Other Initiatives:
Pay as You Waste garbage system

City of Thorold

Thorold City Hall
P.O. Box 1044
3540 Schmon Pkwy.
Thorold, ON L2V 4A7
905-227-6613
Fax: 905-227-5590
E-mail, Deputy City Clerk: depclerk@thorold.com
secr@thorold.com (Administrative Assistant)
www.thorold.com
Population: 17,931 *Census Year:* 2011
Number of Households: 7,273
Adele Arbour, Director, Planning & Building Services, email: aarbour@thorold.com
Mike Sauchuk, Director, Operations, 905-227-3535, email: theoreng@thorold.com
Jeff Menard, A.Sc.T., B.Tech, Chief Building Official, email: jmenard@thorold.com
Dave Akrigg, Manager, Parks, Cemetary & Arena Operations, 905-227-1911, email: dave@thorold.com
Waste Management:
Responsibility of the Regional Municipality of Niagara, 905/356-4141
Water & Wastewater Treatment:
Responsibility of the Regional Municipality of Niagara, www.regional.niagara.on.ca

City of Thunder Bay

City Hall
P.O. Box 800
500 Donald St. East
Thunder Bay, ON P7C 5K4
807-625-2230
Fax: 807-623-5468
TTY: 807-625-2230
cityinfo@thunderbay.ca
www.thunderbay.ca
Population: 108,359 *Census Year:* 2011
Number of Households: 47,889
Alan Fydirchuk, General Manager, Facililties & Fleet, 807-684-2774, Fax: 807-345-1909, email: afydirchuk@thunderbay.ca
Darrell Matson, General Manager, Transportation & Works, email: dmatson@thunderbay.ca
Mark Smith, General Manager, Development Services, 807-625-2544, Fax: 807-625-2206, email: msmith@thunderbay.ca
Norm Gale, Chief, Emergency Medical Services, 807-625-3259, Fax: 807-625-2698, email: ngale@thunderbay.ca
John Hay, Fire Chief, email: jhay@thunderbay.ca
Brad Loroff, Manager, Transit, 807-684-2187, email: bloroff@thunderbay.ca
Alan Hjorth, Manager, Human Resources, 807-625-2585, Fax: 807-625-3585, email: ahjorth@thunderbay.ca
Kerri Marshall, Manager, Environment, 807-625-2836, Fax: 807-625-3588, email: kmarshall@thunderbay.ca
Pat Mauro, Manager, Engineering, 807-625-3022, Fax: 807-625-3588, email: pmauro@thunderbay.ca
Waste Management:
Weekly garbage collection is the responsibility of the Roads Division.
Number of landfill sites: 1
Solid Waste Disposal Fees: $34.65/tonne
Recycling: Both Curbside & Depot; Collection provided by Recool Canada Inc., 807/577-0411; Depots: Mountdale Ave., Front St., John St. Landfill site
Special Bans/by-laws: Refrigeration units containing CFCs not accepted at depots
Hazardous Waste Depot or Facility: John St. Landfill site, open Saturdays only between May & October.
Composters subsidized: Yes
Water & Wastewater Treatment:
Water treatment plants: RR#13 Bare Point Rd., 807/683-8141 & Loch Lomond Rd.; Water Pollution Control plant at 901 Atlantic Ave., 807/625-3370
Other Initiatives:
Spring & fall leaf & yard collection; St. John Landfill site composting facility

City of Timmins

220 Algonquin Blvd. East
Timmins, ON P4N 1B3
705-264-1331
Fax: 705-360-2674
www.timmins.ca
Population: 43,165 *Census Year:* 2011
Number of Households: 19,284
Luc Duval, Director, Public Works & Engineering
Mike Pintar, Fire Chief
Waste Management:
Recycling: Both Curbside & Depot; Depot locations: Deloro Landfill Site; Tisdale Landfill Site; German Township Disposal Site
Water & Wastewater Treatment:
City of Timmins Water Filtration Plant, 15 Feldman Rd.; Whitney & Tisdale Waste Water Treatment Plant, 6th Ave., Porcupine, serves South Porcupine & Porcupine; Mattagami River Waste Water Treatment Plant, 837 Airport Rd., serves Timmins, Mountjoy & Schumacher
Other Initiatives:
Upgrades to operational & maintenance systems at Water Filtration Plant; Waste container limit

City of Toronto

City Hall
100 Queen St. West
Toronto, ON M5H 2N2
416-392-2489
Fax: 416-338-0685
In Toronto: 311; TTY: 416-338-0889
311@toronto.ca
www.toronto.ca

Population: 2,615,060 *Census Year:* 2011
Number of Households: 965,554
Bruce L. Anderson, Executive Director, Human Resources, 416-397-4112, Fax: 416-392-1524
Ann Borooah, Executive Director, Toronto Building, & Chief Building Official, 416-397-4446, Fax: 416-397-4383
Tracey Cook, Executive Director, Municipal Licensing & Standards, 416-392-8445, Fax: 416-397-5463
Jennifer Keesmaat, Executive Director, City Planning, & Chief Planner, 416-392-8772, Fax: 416-392-8115
Elaine Baxter-Trahair, General Manager, Children's Services, 416-392-8134, Fax: 416-392-4576
Stephen Buckley, General Manager, Transportation Services, 416-392-8431, Fax: 416-392-4455
Lou Di Gironimo, General Manager, Toronto Water, 416-392-8200, Fax: 416-302-4540
Jim Harnum, General Manager, Solid Waste Management Services, 416-392-4715, Fax: 416-392-4754
Jim Hart, General Manager, Parks, Forestry, & Recreation, 416-392-8182, Fax: 416-392-8565, email: parks@toronto.ca
J.W. (Jim) Sales, General Manager, Fire Services & Fire Chief, 416-338-9051, Fax: 416-338-9060
Michael H. Williams, General Manager, Economic Development & Culture, 416-397-1970, Fax: 416-397-5314
David McKeown, Medical Officer of Health, 416-338-7820, Fax: 416-392-0713, email: publichealth@toronto.ca
Paul Raftis, Chief, Emergency Medical Services, 416-397-9240, Fax: 416-392-2115
Waste Management:
Waste from transfer stations transported to Carlton Farms Landfill in Michigan
Solid Waste Disposal Fees: Yes
Transfer Station(s): Bermondsey; Commissioners; Disco; Ingram, Scarborough; Victoria Park
Recycling: Both Curbside & Depot; The City of Toronto maintains blue bin & green bin recycling programs; Solid Waste Drop-off Depots: Bermondsey, 188 Bermondsey Rd., 416/392-3133; Commissioners, 400 Commissioners St., call 311; Disco, 120 Disco Rd.; Dufferin, 35 Vanley Cres., 416/392-3161 (tires only); Ingram, 50 Ingram Dr., 416/392-5592; Scarborough, 1 Transfer Pl., 416/392-3019; Victoria Park, 3350 Victoria Park Ave., 416/392-3025
Special Bans/by-laws: The City of Toronto has a number of solid waste collection by-laws pertaining to residential & commercial collection; packaging by-law; Transfer Station By-law - Muncipal Code Ch. 846 re prohibited wastes
Hazardous Waste Depot or Facility: Bermondsey; Commissioners; Disco; Ingram; Scarborough; Victoria Park
Compost Sites: Yes *Composters subsidized:* Yes
Water & Wastewater Treatment:
Wastewater treatment plants: Highland Creek, Ashbridges Bay, North Toronto, Humber Bay; Water filtration plants: R.C. Harris, R.L. Clark, Frank J. Horgan, Island
Other Initiatives:
Composting demonstration sites; Green bin program for organics collection, greenbin@toronto.ca; Yellow bag program, a waste management program for commercial customers, yellowbag@toronto.ca; Establishment of the Energy Efficient Office, 416/392-1110; Toxics Taxi will pick up more than 10 litres of hazardous waste from a residence, 416/392-4330; HHW Reuse Centres at Bermondsey, Disco, Ingram & Scarborough Depots; Computer drop-off at Commissioners, Disco, Ingram, Scarborough & Victoria Park depots; Adopt-a-bin program; Leaf & yard waste collection; Environment Days events, 416/392-9585; Water pollution control projects; ReUseIt program, reuseit@toronto.ca; Construction of a residue managementfacility

City of Vaughan
2141 Major Mackenzie Dr.
Vaughan, ON L6A 1T1
905-832-2281
Fax: 905-832-8535
Phone (Automated): 905-832-8585
clerks@vaughan.ca; humanresources@vaughan.ca
www.vaughan.ca
Population: 288,201 *Census Year:* 2011
Number of Households: 54,359
Paul Jankowski, Commissioner, Engineering & Public Works
John Zipay, Commissioner, Planning, email: john.mackenzie@vaughan.ca
Marjie Fraser, Director, Parks & Forestry Operations, email: parks@vaughan.ca
Jack Graziosi, Director, Engineering Services, email: jack.graziosi@vaughan.ca
Leo Grellette, Director, Building Standards, email: leo.grellette@vaughan.ca
Andrew D. Pearce, Director, Development & Transportation Engineering, email: andrew.pearce@vaughan.ca
Gregory R. Senay, Fire Chief, email: firerescue@vaughan.ca
Waste Management:
Responsibility of the Regional Municipality of York
Water & Wastewater Treatment:
Majority of water supply & treatment by City of Toronto; Well water supply & treatment in Kleinberg area responsibility of Regional Municipality of York; Sewage treatment responsibility of Dufferin Creek Treatment Plant
Other Initiatives:
Adopt-a-park program; Free mulch day; Greening Vaughan programs, including organics (green bin) collection, greeningvaughan@vaughan.ca; Anti-idling program; Vaughan manufacturers' sustainability program

City of Waterloo
City Hall
100 Regina St. South
Waterloo, ON N2J 4A8
519-886-1550
Fax: 519-747-8500
TTY Toll Free: 1-866-786-3941
www.city.waterloo.on.ca
Population: 98,780 *Census Year:* 2011
Number of Households: 35,437
Cameron Rapp, General Manager, Development Services
Mark Dykstra, Director, Environment & Parks Services
Bill Garibaldi, Director, Water Services
Phil Hewitson, Director, Transportation
Murray Kieswetter, Manager, Parks Operations, 519-747-8607, Fax: 519-886-5788
Mary Thorpe, Manager, Human Resources
John DeHooge, Fire Chief
Waste Management:
Responsibility of the Regional Municipality of Waterloo
Water & Wastewater Treatment:
Responsibility of the Regional Municipality of Waterloo; Waterloo Utilities is responsible for operation of the water distribution & wastewater collection systems
Other Initiatives:
Partners in Parks program; Environmental Lands Acquisition & Maintenance Policy; Protective measures for trees; Green space naturalization & rehabilitation; Watershed monitoring program; Adopt-a-Road program; Storm water management; Waste reduction with all city facilities; Energy & water conservation; Reduction of road salt use; Pesticide reduction campaign; Green roof project

City of Welland
60 East Main St.
Welland, ON L3B 3X4
905-735-1700
Fax: 905-732-1919
www.welland.ca
Population: 50,631 *Census Year:* 2011
Number of Households: 20,577
Bill Fenwick, General Manager, Parks, Facilities & Leisure Services, email: bill.fenwick@welland.ca
Sal Iannello, General Manager, Engineering, Public Works, & Transportation Svs., email: sal.iannello@welland.ca
Rosanne Mantesso, General Manager, Human Resources, email: rosanne.mantesso@welland.ca
Donald Thorpe, General Manager, Planning & Development Services, email: don.thorpe@welland.ca
Mike Mantesso, Chief Building Official, email: mike.mantesso@welland.ca
Denys Prevost, Fire Chief, email: denys.prevost@welland.ca
Waste Management:
Waste management responsibility of Region of Niagara
Water & Wastewater Treatment:
Responsibility of Region of Niagara; City's Public Works Division maintains sewers & waterworks

City of Windsor
City Hall
P.O. Box 1607
350 City Hall Sq. West
Windsor, ON N9A 6S1
Fax: 519-255-6868
Phone: 311; Toll Free Phone: 1-877-746-4311
311@city.windsor.on.ca; hrdiv@city.windsor.on.ca (HR Dept.)
www.citywindsor.ca
Population: 210,891 *Census Year:* 2011
Number of Households: 88,533
Michael Duben, General Manager, Community & Protective Services
Dev Tyagi, General Manager, Public Works, email: pubwork@city.windsor.on.ca
Ronna Warsh, General Manager, Social & Health Services, email: socserv@city.windsor.on.ca
Thom Hunt, MCIP, RPP, City Planner, email: thunt@city.windsor.on.ca
Mario Sonego, P. Eng., City Engineer, email: engineeringdept@city.windsor.on.ca
David T. Fields, Fire Chief, Windsor Fire & Rescue Service, 519-253-6573, Fax: 519-255-6832
Josette Eugeni, Manager, Transportation Planning
Bill Lacasse, Manager, Lou Romano Water Reclamation Plant, 519-253-7217
Jack MacRae, Manager, Little River Pollution Control Plant, 519-948-1751
Jim Yanchula, MCIP, RPP, Manager, Urban Design & Community Development, email: jyanchula@city.windsor.on.ca
Waste Management:
Yard waste collected on scheduled garbage collection days
Number of landfill sites: 1
Solid Waste Disposal Fees: $60/tonne (garbage & household waste); $42/tonne (yard waste)
Recycling: Both Curbside & Depot; The city maintains a Blue Box (materials such as food cans & cartons, aluminum foil, plastics, glass bottles & jars) & a Red Box (newspapers, cardboard, mixed paper, cardboard) recycling program; residential applicance & metal collection service is free to Windsor residents: call 311 to arrange pickup; Public Drop Off Depot, E.C. Row & Central Ave., 519/974-1010
Special Bans/by-laws: Various sewer usage by-laws
Hazardous Waste Depot or Facility: Household Chemical Waste Depot & Reuse Centre, E.C. Row & Central Ave.
Water & Wastewater Treatment:
Lou Romano Water Reclamation Plant, 519/253-7217; Little River Pollution Control Plant, 519/948-1751; City's Environmental Services also maintains 32 pumping stations
Other Initiatives:
City of Windsor Apartment Recycling Initiative

City of Woodstock
City Hall
P.O. Box 1539
500 Dundas St.
Woodstock, ON N4S 7W5
519-539-1291
aash@city.woodstock.on.ca (Assistant to Mayor & CAO)
www.city.woodstock.on.ca
Population: 37,754 *Census Year:* 2011
Number of Households: 13,733
Len Magyar, Commissioner, Development, email: lmagyar@city.woodstock.on.ca
Harold deHaan, City Engineer, email: hdehaan@city.woodstock.on.ca
Filippo D'Emilio, Engineer, Development, email: fdemilio@city.woodstock.on.ca
Scott Tegler, Fire Chief, email: stegler@city.woodstock.on.ca
Laird Crooks, Manager, Human Resources, email: lcrooks@city.woodstock.on.ca
Alex Piggott, Superintendent, Works, email: apiggott@city.woodstock.on.ca
Terry Harrington, Supervisor, Water Distribution, email: tharrington@city.woodstock.on.ca
Dan Major, Supervisor, Parks, email: dmajor@city.woodstock.on.ca
Waste Management:
Waste & recycling collection responsibility of city
Special Bans/by-laws: By-law #7138-94 makes recycling mandatory for certain items; Waste limit 3 bags/week/residence; Extra bags will not be collected
Composters subsidized: Yes
Water & Wastewater Treatment:
Water Pollution Control Plant, 519/537-8531
Other Initiatives:
Paint Swap; Appliance Drop-Off Day; Household Hazardous Waste days

Other Municipalities in Ontario

Adjala-Tosorontio
7855 Sideroad 30, RR#1
Alliston, ON L9R 1V1
705-434-5055
Fax: 705-434-5051
www.townshipadjtos.on.ca
Population: 10,603 *Census Year:* 2011
Number of Households: 3,281
Waste Management:
Waste collection, management & recycling responsibility of County of Simcoe
Water & Wastewater Treatment:
Water & wastewater treatment responsibility of township public works department, water sector; Township's water systems include Colgan, Everett, Hockley, Lisle, Loretto Heights, Rosemont & Weca

Ajax
65 Harwood Ave. South
Ajax, ON L1S 2H9
905-683-4550
Fax: 905-683-1061
Corporate Communications: 905-619-2529, ext. 3362
contactus@townofajax.com; info@townofajax.com
www.townofajax.com
Population: 109,600 *Census Year:* 2011
Number of Households: 23,642
Waste Management:
Responsibility of Regional Municipality of Durham, 905/579-5264, 1-800-667-5671
Recycling: Both Curbside & Depot
Hazardous Waste Depot or Facility: Yes
Water & Wastewater Treatment:
Responsibility of Region of Durham
Other Initiatives:
Anti-Idling policy applies to all town staff when using town equipment/vehicles (2 min. idle time), Scott Glew, Fleet Manager, 905/683-3949; Plant health care program, minimize/eliminate use of selective herbicides through aggressive aeration, over seeding/top dragging program, Jeff Stewart, Parks, 905/683-2957

Alnwick-Haldimand
P.O. Box 70
10836 County Rd. No. 2
Grafton, ON K0K 2G0
905-349-2822
Fax: 905-349-3259
Phone, Roseneath Satellite Office: 905-352-3949
alnhald@alnwickhaldimand.ca
www.alnwickhaldimand.ca
Population: 6,617 *Census Year:* 2011

Amherstburg
271 Sandwich St. South
Amherstburg, ON N9V 2A5
519-736-0012
Fax: 519-736-5403
TTY: 519-736-9860
www.amherstburg.ca
Population: 21,556 *Census Year:* 2011
Number of Households: 7,603
Waste Management:
Contracted to D.W. Crowder Trucking
Water & Wastewater Treatment:
Amherstburg Water Treatment Plant; Boblo Island Water Treatment Plant
Other Initiatives:
Yard Waste Depot, 512 Sandwich St. South

Aurora
P.O. Box 1000
100 John Way West
Aurora, ON L4G 6J1
905-727-1375
Fax: 905-726-4738
Alternative Phone: 905-727-3123; TTY: 905-726-4766
info@aurora.ca
www.aurora.ca
Population: 53,203 *Census Year:* 2011
Number of Households: 13,247
Waste Management:
Waste collection contracted to Miller Waste Systems, 1-800-465-5914; Waste management responsibility of York Region
Recycling: Curbside
Water & Wastewater Treatment:
Water & wastewater treatment responsibility of York Region

Bracebridge
1000 Taylor Ct.
Bracebridge, ON P1L 1R6
705-645-5264
Fax: 705-645-1262
Fax, Public Works: 705-645-7525
www.bracebridge.ca
Population: 15,409 *Census Year:* 2011
Number of Households: 7,392
Waste Management:
Operation of domestic waste collection & landfill site responsibility of District of Muskoka
Water & Wastewater Treatment:
Water & sewer operations responsibility of the District of Muskoka

Bradford West Gwillimbury
Administration Centre
P.O. Box 100
100 Dissette St.
Bradford, ON L3Z 2A7
905-775-5366
Fax: 905-775-0153
www.town.bradfordwestgwillimbury.on.ca
Population: 28,077 *Census Year:* 2011
Number of Households: 7,522
Waste Management:
Waste management is the responsibility of the County of Simcoe
Water & Wastewater Treatment:
7 municipal wells plus pump house treatment facilities; Waste water treatment, 225 Dissette St., Bradford
Other Initiatives:
Leaf & yard waste collection; Fall brush collection

Brock
P.O. Box 10
1 Cameron St. East
Cannington, ON L0E 1E0
705-432-2355
Fax: 705-432-3487
Toll-Free Phone: 1-866-223-7668
brock@townshipofbrock.ca
www.townshipofbrock.ca
Population: 11,341 *Census Year:* 2011
Number of Households: 4,858
Waste Management:
Responsibility of Regional Municipality of Durham
Water & Wastewater Treatment:
Responsibility of Regional Municipality of Durham

Caledon
Town Hall
6311 Old Church Rd.
Caledon, ON L7C 1J6
905-584-2272
Fax: 905-584-4325
Toll-Free Phone: 1-888-225-3366
www.caledon.ca
Population: 59,460 *Census Year:* 2011
Number of Households: 16,662
Waste Management:
Responsibility of Regional Municipality of Peel
Special Bans/by-laws: Healthy Horticultural Landscapes By-Law
Water & Wastewater Treatment:
Responsibility of Regional Municipality of Peel
Other Initiatives:
Environmental Progress Office to develop & promote environmental initiatives; Membership in Partners for Climate Protection Program; Smog Response Strategy; Wind Solutions Business Case Committee; Salt & chloride management

Central Elgin
450 Sunset Dr.
St Thomas, ON N5R 5V1
519-631-4860
Fax: 519-631-4036
www.centralelgin.org
Population: 12,743 *Census Year:* 2011
Number of Households: 4,797
Waste Management:
Waste & recyclable collection contracted to Green Lane Environmental Group Ltd.
Recycling: Curbside
Water & Wastewater Treatment:
Belmont Water System; Water treatment lagoons, Belmont

Centre Wellington
P.O. Box 10
1 MacDonald Sq.
Elora, ON N0B 1S0
519-846-9691
Fax: 519-846-2190
www.centrewellington.ca
Population: 26,693 *Census Year:* 2011
Number of Households: 8,728
Waste Management:
Responsibility of Wellington County
Water & Wastewater Treatment:
Enviro-Test Laboratories Ltd. performs & analyzes samples collected by the township from Elora & Fergus water supply systems
Other Initiatives:
Leaf collection & Christmas tree pick-up by township's Public Works Department

Chatham-Kent
Civic Centre
P.O. Box 640
315 King St. West
Chatham, ON N7M 5K8
519-360-1998
Fax: 519-436-3237
Toll-Free Phone: 1-800-714-7497
ckinfo@chatham-kent.ca
www.chatham-kent.ca
Population: 103,671 *Census Year:* 2011
Number of Households: 45,241
Waste Management:
Collection of recyclables by contractor
Solid Waste Disposal Fees: $60/tonne (Ridge Landfill); $55/tonne (Blenheim Landfill)
Transfer Station(s): Yes
Recycling: Both Curbside & Depot
Composters subsidized: Yes
Water & Wastewater Treatment:
The following Sewage Treatment Plants are located in Chatham-Kent: Chatham, Dresden, Ridgetown, Thamesville, Wallaceburg & Wheatley; For further information, contact Chatham-Kent Public Utilities Commission, 325 Grand Ave., East, Chatham, Phone: 519/436-0119, Email: CKpuc@chatham-kent.ca
Other Initiatives:
Annual household hazardous waste days; Leaf & yard waste collection plus 7 depots

Clarington
40 Temperance St.
Bowmanville, ON L1C 3A6
905-623-3379
Fax: 905-623-6506
Toll-Free Phone: 1-800-563-1195
info@clarington.net; communications@clarington.net
www.clarington.net
Population: 84,548 *Census Year:* 2011
Number of Households: 23,619
Waste Management:
Operations Dept. administers waste disposal & recycling contracts
Water & Wastewater Treatment:
Responsibility of Regional Municipality of Durham

Clearview
P.O. Box 200
217 Gideon St.
Stayner, ON L0M 1S0
705-428-6230
Fax: 705-428-0288
www.clearview.ca
Population: 13,734 *Census Year:* 2011
Number of Households: 5,388
Waste Management:
Responsibility of the County of Simcoe
Water & Wastewater Treatment:

Township owns & manages 6 water systems & 6 community center water systems; Water systems with well supplies include Stayner, Creemore, New Lowell, Buckingham Woods, Colling-Woodlands & McKean

Cobourg
55 King St. West
Cobourg, ON K9A 2M2
905-372-4301
Fax: 905-372-7421
Toll-Free Phone: 1-888-262-6874
webmaster@cobourg.ca
www.cobourg.ca
Population: 18,519 *Census Year:* 2011
Number of Households: 7,171
Waste Management:
Responsibility of the County of Northumberland
Water & Wastewater Treatment:
Operation of the water system contracted by the town to Lakefront Utility Services Inc., 207 Division St., Cobourg; Town of Cobourg Water Treatment Plant; Town responsible for wastewater treatment; Water Pollution Control Plant #1, end of University Ave., west shore of Cobourg Creek; Water Pollution Control Plant #2 - Lucas Point, west side of Normar Rd., on shore of Lake Ontario

Cochrane
Cochrane, ON
www.cdssab.on.ca
Population: 81,122 *Census Year:* 2011
Number of Households: 37,733

Collingwood
P.O. Box 157
97 Hurontario St.
Collingwood, ON L9Y 3Z5
705-445-1030
Fax: 705-445-2448
www.collingwood.ca
Population: 19,241 *Census Year:* 2011
Number of Households: 8,331
Waste Management:
Waste management responsibility of Simcoe County
Water & Wastewater Treatment:
Raymond A. Barker Ultra-Filtration Water Treatment Plant, 2 Raglan St.; Ted Carmichael Reservoir; Water facilities operated by Collingwood Public Utilities

East Gwillimbury
19000 Leslie St.
Sharon, ON L0G 1V0
905-478-4282
Fax: 905-478-2808
Alternate Fax: 905-478-8545
town@eastgwillimbury.ca; engineering@eastgwillimbury.ca
www.eastgwillimbury.ca
Population: 22,473 *Census Year:* 2011
Number of Households: 6,601
Waste Management:
Waste management is the responsibility of the Regional Municipality of York; Waste collection contracted to LaRue's, 905/478-1940
Compost Sites: Yes
Water & Wastewater Treatment:
Responsibility of the Regional Municipality of York
Other Initiatives:
Garbage bag/can limit; Annual clean-up green-up day

Elizabethtown-Kitley
6544 New Dublin Rd., RR#2
Addison, ON K0E 1A0
613-345-7480
Fax: 613-345-7235
Toll-Free Phone: 1-800-492-3175
mail@elizabethtown-kitley.on.ca
www.elizabethtown-kitley.on.ca
Population: 9,724 *Census Year:* 2011
Number of Households: 3,779
Waste Management:
Number of landfill sites: 1
Solid Waste Disposal Fees: $22.50/quarter to half ton truck or 8 foot trailer
Recycling: Depot; Located at waste disposal site, 8468 County Rd. 7
Water & Wastewater Treatment:
Township of Elizabethtown-Kitley Water Distribution System; City of Brockville Water Treatment Plant, 20 Rivers Ave., Brockville, serves a portion of Elizabethtown-Kitley
Other Initiatives:
User-pay waste collection & disposal services; Upgrades to water treatment plant; Pitch-In Elizabeth-Kitley Program to clean up roadside garbage

Erin
5684 Wellington Rd., RR#2
Hillsburgh, ON N0B 1Z0
519-855-4407
Fax: 519-855-4821
Toll-Free Phone: 1-877-818-2888
council@erin.ca; cao@erin.ca (Town Manager)
www.erin.ca
Population: 10,770 *Census Year:* 2011
Number of Households: 3,890
Waste Management:
Responsibility of the County of Wellington
Special Bans/by-laws: Nutrient Management for Certain Livestock Operations

Essa
5786 County Rd. 21
Utopia, ON L0M 1T0
705-424-9770
Fax: 705-424-2367
TTY: 705-424-5302
info@essatownship.on.ca
www.essatownship.on.ca
Population: 18,505 *Census Year:* 2011
Number of Households: 4,726
Waste Management:
Responsibility of County of Simcoe, 705/735-6901
Water & Wastewater Treatment:
Water treatment contracted to Ontario Clean Water Agency, 1-866-775-7712

Essex
33 Talbot St. South
Essex, ON N8M 1A8
519-776-7336
Fax: 519-776-8811
www.essex.ca
Population: 19,600 *Census Year:* 2011
Number of Households: 8,103
Waste Management:
Responsibility of the Essex-Windsor Solid Waste Authority (519/776-6441), an agency created by the County of Essex & the City of Windsor
Water & Wastewater Treatment:
Operation of the Union Water Treatment Plant & the Harrow/Colchester South Water Treatment Plant contracted to Ontario Clean Water Agency

Fort Erie
1 Municipal Centre Dr.
Fort Erie, ON L2A 2S6
905-871-1600
Fax: 905-871-4022
Fax, Corporate Services: 905-871-9984
www.forterie.on.ca
Population: 29,960 *Census Year:* 2011
Number of Households: 13,581
Waste Management:
Responsibility of the Region of Niagara
Water & Wastewater Treatment:
Responsibility of the Region of Niagara
Other Initiatives:
Transportation environmental study report

Georgian Bluffs
177964 Grey Rd. 18, RR#3
Owen Sound, ON N4K 5N5
519-376-2729
Fax: 519-372-1620
office@georgianbluffs.on.ca
www.georgianbluffs.on.ca
Population: 10,404 *Census Year:* 2011
Number of Households: 4,499
Waste Management:
Waste collection contracted to Bruce Service Sales & Rentals, 519/363-3811; Recycling collection contracted to Miller Waste Services, 519/373-1855
Number of landfill sites: 1
Solid Waste Disposal Fees: $70/tonne (sorted domestic, commercial & industrial materials); $95/tonne (unsorted)
Recycling: Curbside
Water & Wastewater Treatment:
Responsibility of Veolia Water Canada, 519/376-4640
Other Initiatives:
2005 Environmental Study Report for provision of expanded municipal water supply system; Residential energy efficiency program; 2 bag garbage limit; Bale wrap recycling program for farmers

Georgina
Georgina Civic Centre
26557 Civic Centre Rd., RR#2
Keswick, ON L4P 3G1
905-476-4301
Fax: 905-476-8100
Alternative Phones: 905-722-6516; 705-437-2210
info@georgina.ca; events@georgina.ca
www.georgina.ca
Population: 43,517 *Census Year:* 2011
Number of Households: 15,328
Waste Management:
Waste management responsibility of the Regional Municipality of York; Waste & blue box collection contracted to Miller Waste Limited, 1-800-465-5914
Water & Wastewater Treatment:
Responsibility of the Regional Municipality of York

Gravenhurst
3 - 5 Pineridge Gate
Gravenhurst, ON P1P 1Z3
705-687-3412
Fax: 705-687-7016
reception@gravenhurst.ca
www.gravenhurst.ca
Population: 11,640 *Census Year:* 2011
Number of Households: 7,598
Waste Management:
Responsibility of District of Muskoka
Water & Wastewater Treatment:
Responsibility of District of Muskoka

Grimsby
160 Livingston Ave.
Grimsby, ON L3M 4G3
905-945-9634
Fax: 905-945-5010
www.town.grimsby.on.ca
Population: 25,325 *Census Year:* 2011
Number of Households: 7,792
Waste Management:
Responsibility of Region of Niagara, 1-800-594-5542 or 905/687-9595
Water & Wastewater Treatment:
Grimsby Water Treatment Plant, 905/945-2840; Maintenance & operation of drinking water distribution system & wastewater collection system responsibility of town environmental services department

Guelph / Eramosa
P.O. Box 700
8348 Wellington Rd. 124
Rockwood, ON N0B 2K0
519-856-9951
Fax: 519-856-2240
Toll-Free Phone: 1-800-267-1465
general@get.on.ca
www.get.on.ca
Population: 12,380 *Census Year:* 2011
Number of Households: 3,652
Waste Management:
Responsibility of County of Wellington, wasteinfo@county.wellington.on.ca
Special Bans/by-laws: Water Use Bylaw; Nutrient Management Bylaw
Water & Wastewater Treatment:
Operation of Rockwood water system (2 wells, a pumping station & standpipe) & Hamilton hamlet water system (3 wells, 3 pumping stations & standpipe) responsibility of township; Wastewater system, with a pre-treatment plant, operated in Rockwood, with further treatment at City of Guelph treatment plant

Halton Hills
1 Halton Hills Dr.
Georgetown, ON L7G 5G2

905-873-2600
Fax: 905-873-2347
TTY: 905-873-0644
www.haltonhills.ca
Population: 59,008 *Census Year:* 2011
Number of Households: 17,000
Waste Management:
Responsibility of the Regional Municipality of Halton
Special Bans/by-laws: Smoking Bylaw
Water & Wastewater Treatment:
Responsibility of the Regional Municipality of Halton
Other Initiatives:
Adopt A Road program; Community Clean Up Days; Water resource management

Hamilton
P.O. Box 1060
8285 Majestic Hills Dr.
Cobourg, ON K9A 4W5
905-342-2810
Fax: 905-342-2818
info@hamiltontownship.ca
www.hamiltontownship.ca
Population: 10,702 *Census Year:* 2011
Number of Households: 4,483
Waste Management:
Responsibility of Northumberland County, 905/372-3329
Special Bans/by-laws: Outside water use restrictions
Water & Wastewater Treatment:
Town of Cobourg Water Treatment Plant; Camborne Water Treatment Plant; Creighton Heights Water Treatment Plant

Hawkesbury
600 Higginson St.
Hawkesbury, ON K6A 1H1
613-632-0106
www.hawkesbury.ca
Population: 10,551 *Census Year:* 2011
Number of Households: 4,644
Water & Wastewater Treatment:
Water pollution control plant, located on Main St. East, is operated by the Ontario Clean Water Agency; Town manages water filtration plant, located at 670 Main St. West
Other Initiatives:
Major upgrade to water pollution control plant

Ingersoll
130 Oxford St., 2nd Fl.
Ingersoll, ON N5C 2V5
519-485-0120
Fax: 519-485-3543
www.ingersoll.ca
Population: 12,146 *Census Year:* 2011
Number of Households: 4,337
Waste Management:
Waste management responsibility of the County of Oxford
Recycling: Curbside
Water & Wastewater Treatment:
Responsibility of Oxford County, Public Works Department
Other Initiatives:
Annual Special Waste Day for household hazardous waste; Collections for spring rubbish, leaves & Christmas trees

Innisfil
2101 Innisfil Beach Rd.
Innisfil, ON L9S 1A1
705-436-3710
Fax: 705-436-7120
www.innisfil.ca
Population: 33,079 *Census Year:* 2011
Number of Households: 11,707
Waste Management:
All aspects of waste management responsibility of Simcoe County
Recycling: Curbside
Water & Wastewater Treatment:
Water treatment facilities owned & operated by town: Lakeshore Water Filtration Plant, 2155 - 25th Sideroad, Innisfil ON L9S 4V3; Wastewater treatment plant, 1578 St. John's Rd., Innisfil ON L9S 4T9
Other Initiatives:
Two-bag garbage limit, extra bags require $1.25 tags; Special collection for yard waste, brush, large items & Christmas trees

Kenora
Kenora District Services Board Admin Office
#1, 211 Princess St.
Dryden, ON P8N 3L5
807-223-2100
Fax: 807-223-6500
kdsb@kdsb.on.ca
www.kdsb.on.ca
Population: 64,419 *Census Year:* 2011
Number of Households: 30,797

Kincardine
1475 Conc. 5, RR#5
Kincardine, ON N2Z 2X6
519-396-3468
Fax: 519-396-8288
ssmith@kincardine.net
www.kincardine.net
Population: 11,174 *Census Year:* 2011
Number of Households: 5,329
Waste Management:
Waste collection is contracted to Bruce Area Solid Waste Recycling, 1-800-794-9770
Number of landfill sites: 3
Recycling: Curbside
Water & Wastewater Treatment:
Municipality of Kincardine & Ontario Clean Water Agency responsible for Kincardine Water Treatment Plant & sewage treatment plants
Other Initiatives:
Upgrades to 8 municipal water systems

King
2075 King Rd.
King City, ON L7B 1A1
905-833-5321
Fax: 905-833-2300
online@king.ca
www.king.ca
Population: 19,899 *Census Year:* 2011
Number of Households: 6,330
Waste Management:
Waste collection handled by Sandhill Disposal & Recycling Services, 905/505-5252; Region of York provides waste management services for township
Number of landfill sites: 1
Solid Waste Disposal Fees: $5/vehicle
Water & Wastewater Treatment:
Responsibility of Region of York

Lakeshore
419 Notre Dame Rd.
Belle River, ON N0R 1A0
519-728-2700
Fax: 519-728-9530
webmaster@lakeshore.ca
www.lakeshore.ca
Population: 34,546 *Census Year:* 2011
Number of Households: 10,418
Waste Management:
Waste management responsibility of Essex-Windsor Solid Waste Authority, 1-800-563-3377
Recycling: Curbside
Water & Wastewater Treatment:
Belle River Water Treatment Plant, 493 Lakeview Dr.; Stoney Point Water Treatment Plant, 6011 St. Clair Rd.; Wheatley Water Treatment Plant (supplier to the Lighthouse Cove Water Distribution system, through an agreement with the Municipality of Chatham-Kent for water supply); Tecumseh Water Treatment Plant, 9725 Riverside Dr. Windsor (supplier to the Tecumseh Water Service Area, through an agreement with the Town of Tecumseh for water supply); Union Water Treatment Plant, Kingsville; Belle Rive
Other Initiatives:
Monthly collection of white goods; Organic waste collection

Lambton Shores
P.O. Box 610
7883 Amtelecom Pkwy.
Forest, ON N0N 1J0
519-786-2335
Fax: 519-786-2135
Toll-Free Phone: 1-877-786-2335
administration@lambtonshores.ca
www.lambtonshores.ca
Population: 10,656 *Census Year:* 2011
Number of Households: 6,705
Waste Management:
Waste management responsibility of Lambton County; Waste collection responsibility of City's Community Services Dept.; Recycling handled by Bluewater Recycling Association, 519/228-6678
Composters subsidized: Yes
Water & Wastewater Treatment:
Water & wastewater services managed, operated & maintained by Operations Management International Canada Inc.

LaSalle
5950 Malden Rd.
Lasalle, ON N9H 1S4
519-969-7770
Fax: 519-969-4469
webmaster@town.lasalle.on.ca
www.town.lasalle.on.ca
Population: 28,643 *Census Year:* 2011
Number of Households: 8,504
Waste Management:
Waste management responsibility of Essex-Windsor Solid Waste Authority, 519/776-6441; Waste collection provided by Windsor Disposal, 519/944-8009
Water & Wastewater Treatment:
Water received from ENWIN Utilities Ltd., 519/255-2727

Leamington
111 Erie St. North
Leamington, ON N8H 2Z3
519-326-5761
Fax: 519-326-2481
E-mail, Public Works: publicworks@leamington.ca
info@leamington.ca
www.leamington.ca
Population: 28,403 *Census Year:* 2011
Number of Households: 9,845
Waste Management:
Waste management responsibility of Essex-Windsor Solid Waste Authority, 1-800-563-3377; Waste collection responsibility of Operations Deptartment
Clean Fill Fee:

Water & Wastewater Treatment:
Leamington is a member municipality of the Union Water Treatment Plant, 1615 Union Ave., Ruthven, operated by the Ontario Clean Water Agency; Leamington Pollution Control Centre

Leeds & Grenville
#100, 25 Central Ave. West
Brockville, ON K6V 4N6
613-342-3840
Fax: 613-342-2101
Toll-Free Phone: 1-800-770-2170
www.uclg.ca
Population: 99,306 *Census Year:* 2011
Number of Households: 44,618
Waste Management:
Member municipalities without active landfills have private waste disposal agreements
Water & Wastewater Treatment:
Responsibility of area municipalities
Other Initiatives:
County-wide groundwater management study

Lincoln
4800 South Service Rd.
Beamsville, ON L0R 1B1
905-563-8205
Fax: 905-563-6566
info@lincoln.ca
www.lincoln.ca
Population: 22,487 *Census Year:* 2011
Number of Households: 7,275
Waste Management:
Responsibility of Region of Niagara
Water & Wastewater Treatment:
Responsibility of Region of Niagara

Loyalist
P.O. Box 70
263 Main St.
Odessa, ON K0H 2H0

613-386-7351
Fax: 613-386-3833
www.loyalisttownship.ca
Population: 16,221 *Census Year:* 2011
Number of Households: 5,394
Waste Management:
Waste collection contracted to Canadian Waste Services, 613/549-7100; Recycling services contracted to Kingston Area Recycling Centre, operated by the City of Kingston
Number of landfill sites: 2
Solid Waste Disposal Fees: $105/tonne
Recycling: Both Curbside & Depot
Special Bans/by-laws: Open air burning restrictions; Lawn watering restrictions
Hazardous Waste Depot or Facility: 70 Lappan's Lane, Kingston
Composters subsidized: Yes
Water & Wastewater Treatment:
Fairfeld Water Treatment Plant, servicing Amhertsview, Odessa, Harewood & Brooklands; Bath Water Treatment Plant; Bath Water Pollution Control Plant; Amherstview Water Pollution Control Plant; Odessa Waste Water Treatment Plant, owned & operated by the township
Other Initiatives:
Pay-as-you-throw bag tag program; Large item & free drop-off days at Violet Landfill & Amherst Island Landfill sites; Spring & fall yard waste collections; Disposal of CFC units, subsidized composters; Transit Services (Amherstview to City of Kingston)

Manitoulin
Gore Bay, ON

Population: 13,048 *Census Year:* 2011
Number of Households: 9,213

Meaford
21 Trowbridge St. West
Meaford, ON N4L 1A1
519-538-1060
Fax: 519-538-5240
Alternate Fax: 519-538-1556
www.meaford.ca
Population: 11,100 *Census Year:* 2011
Number of Households: 5,100
Waste Management:
Waste collection contracted to North Grey Sanitation Services, 519/376-0440
Number of landfill sites: 1*Landfill Capacity:* 9 years
Solid Waste Disposal Fees: $48-78/tonne
Clean Fill Fee: Yes; $48-48/tonne
Recycling: Both Curbside & Depot; Miller St. depot
Hazardous Waste Depot or Facility: 20th St. East, Owen Sound
Compost Sites: Yes *Composters subsidized:* Yes
Water & Wastewater Treatment:
Meaford Water Treatment Plant, 574 Grandview Dr.; Leith Water Treatment Plant, 359466 Bayshore Rd.; Meaford Wastewater Treatment Plant, 35 Grant Ave., Meaford; Wastewater contracted to OCWA, 519/538-3311

Middlesex Centre
10227 Ilderton Rd., RR#2
Ilderton, ON N0M 2A0
519-666-0190
Fax: 519-666-0271
Toll-Free Phone: 1-800-220-8968
cormans@middlesexcentre.on.ca
www.middlesexcentre.on.ca
Population: 16,487 *Census Year:* 2011
Number of Households: 5,299
Waste Management:
Township public works & engineering department responsible for recycling, waste collection & waste disposal; Waste collection contracted to Bluewater Recycling Association, 1-800-265-9799
Recycling: Curbside
Composters subsidized: Yes
Water & Wastewater Treatment:
Operation of all township water & sewer systems responsibility of Ontario Clean Water Agency, 519/641-2116
Other Initiatives:
Hazardous waste & clean-up days

Midland
575 Dominion Ave.
Midland, ON L4R 1R2
705-526-4275
Fax: 705-526-9971
TTY: 705-526-4276, ext. 2824
clerks@midland.ca
www.midland.ca
Population: 16,572 *Census Year:* 2011
Number of Households: 6,847
Waste Management:
Responsibility of County of Simcoe
Water & Wastewater Treatment:
Water distribution system, including wells, booster pumping stations, storage reservoir sites & a lift station operated & maintained by town; Sewage treatment facility operated by town

Milton
150 Mary St.
Milton, ON L9T 6Z5
905-878-7252
Fax: 905-878-6995
info@milton.ca
www.milton.ca
Population: 84,362 *Census Year:* 2011
Number of Households: 13,933
Waste Management:
Responsibility of Regional Municipality of Halton

Mississippi Mills
P.O. Box 400
3131 Old Perth Rd., RR#2
Almonte, ON K0A 1A0
613-256-2064
Fax: 613-256-4887
Toll-Free Phone: 1-888-779-8666
town@mississippimills.ca
www.mississippimills.ca
Population: 12,385 *Census Year:* 2011
Number of Households: 4,481
Waste Management:
Waste collection contracted to Topps Waste Management, Carleton Place, 613/257-2955 or 1-800-387-5710
Number of landfill sites: 1
Solid Waste Disposal Fees: $80/tonne
Recycling: Both Curbside & Depot; Recycling Transfer Station, Pakenham Landfill Site
Hazardous Waste Depot or Facility: Carleton Place depot
Compost Sites: Yes
Water & Wastewater Treatment:
Ontario Clean Water Agency operates the sewage lagoon & 5 wells

New Tecumseth
Town Administration Centre
P.O. Box 910
10 Wellington St. East
Alliston, ON L9R 1A1
705-435-6219
Fax: 705-435-2873
Alternative Phone: 905-729-0057
www.town.newtecumseth.on.ca
Population: 30,234 *Census Year:* 2011
Number of Households: 9,244
Waste Management:
Responsibility of County of Simcoe
Water & Wastewater Treatment:
Town provides water & sewer services for the Alliston Water System & the Hillcrest Water System; Wastewater treatment facilities: Sir Frederick Banting WPCP, Regional WPCP, Tottenham WPCP; Contracted to Town of New Tecumseh 705/435-3900

Niagara-on-the-Lake
P.O. Box 100
1593 Four Mile Creek Rd.
Virgil, ON L0S 1T0
905-468-3266
Fax: 905-468-2959
webinquiry@notl.org
www.notl.org
Population: 15,400 *Census Year:* 2011
Number of Households: 5,642
Waste Management:
Waste management responsibility of Regional Municipality of Niagara, 1-800-594-5542
Water & Wastewater Treatment:
Responsibility of the Regional Municipality of Niagara
Other Initiatives:
Reduction in salt use in winter control operations

Nipissing
District Social Services Administration Bd.
P.O. Box 750
200 McIntyre St. East
North Bay, ON P1B 8J8

Population: 84,736 *Census Year:* 2011
Number of Households: 38,145

North Dundas
P.O. Box 489
636 St. Lawrence St.
Winchester, ON K0C 2K0
613-774-2105
Fax: 613-774-5699
Toll-Free Phone: 1-800-795-0437
info@northdundas.com
www.northdundas.com
Population: 11,225 *Census Year:* 2011
Number of Households: 4,174
Waste Management:
Number of landfill sites: 2
Solid Waste Disposal Fees: $10/cubic yard
Recycling: Curbside
Water & Wastewater Treatment:
Chesterville Water System; Winchester Water System; Ontario Clean Water Agency, 613-448-3098, inspects new service
Other Initiatives:
Hazardous Household Waste Days

North Glengarry
P.O. Box 700
90 Main St. South
Alexandria, ON K0C 1A0
613-525-1110
Fax: 613-525-1649
www.northglengarry.ca
Population: 10,251 *Census Year:* 2011
Number of Households: 4,575
Waste Management:
Number of landfill sites: 2
Solid Waste Disposal Fees: $50/ton, commercial & industrial waste
Recycling: Depot; Alexandria Recycling (R.A.R.E. Plant), 265 Industrial Blvd., Alexandria
Special Bans/by-laws: Bonfire By-law

North Grenville
P.O. Box 130
285 County Rd. 44
Kemptville, ON K0G 1J0
613-258-9569
Fax: 613-258-9620
www.northgrenville.ca
Population: 15,085 *Census Year:* 2011
Number of Households: 5,375
Waste Management:
Number of landfill sites: 1
Recycling: Curbside; Depot at Kemptville Landfill Site, 190 County Rd. 44
Water & Wastewater Treatment:
Municipality of North Grenville Wastewater Treatment Plant, Hwy. 43, 613/258-7400
Other Initiatives:
Oxford Mills Brush Depot, 699 Crozier Rd.; Leaf & yard waste depot, Ferguson Forest Centre County Rd. 43

North Perth
330 Wallace Ave. North
Listowel, ON N4W 1L3
519-291-2950
Toll-Free Phone: 1-888-714-1993
town@northperth.ca
www.northperth.ca
Population: 12,631 *Census Year:* 2011
Number of Households: 4,529
Waste Management:
Recycling handled by Bluewater Recycling Association, 1-800-265-9799
Number of landfill sites: 3
Solid Waste Disposal Fees: $50/1 ton truck, household waste
Recycling: Both Curbside & Depot; Listowel Landfill, 905 Louise Ave. North, accepts some recyclables
Water & Wastewater Treatment:
Bowman, Gowanstown, Listowel & Smith drinking water systems

owned by town
Other Initiatives:
User pay system for waste

Norwich
P.O. Box 100
210 Main St. East
Otterville, ON N0J 1R0
519-863-2709
Fax: 519-879-6385
Alternative Phone: 519-879-6568
www.twp.norwich.on.ca
Population: 10,721 *Census Year:* 2011
Number of Households: 3,536
Waste Management:
Responsibility of County of Oxford
Water & Wastewater Treatment:
Responsiblity of County of Oxford
Other Initiatives:
Household hazardous waste day; White goods & scrap metal collection depots; Large article collection

Orangeville
87 Broadway St.
Orangeville, ON L9W 1K1
519-941-0440
Fax: 519-941-9033
Toll-Free Phone: 1-866-941-0440; TTY: 519-943-0782
info@orangeville.ca
www.orangeville.ca
Population: 27,975 *Census Year:* 2011
Number of Households: 8,877
Waste Management:
Solid Waste Disposal Fees: $85/tonne
Recycling: Curbside; Depot at Dufferin Transfer & Recycling Facility, County Rd. 11
Special Bans/by-laws: Residents may have up to 3 bags per week for curbside collection, additional waste is charged $1 per bag
Hazardous Waste Depot or Facility: Yes
Compost Sites: Yes
Water & Wastewater Treatment:
Water Pollution Control Plant operated by Ontario Clean Water Agency

Oro-Medonte
148 Line 7 South
Oro, ON L0L 2X0
705-487-2171
Fax: 705-487-0133
www.oro-medonte.ca
Population: 20,078 *Census Year:* 2011
Number of Households: 7,634
Waste Management:
Responsibility of Simcoe County
Water & Wastewater Treatment:
Water systems in 11 locations are owned & operated by the municipality

Oxford
P.O. Box 1614
21 Reeve St.
Woodstock, ON N4S 7Y3
519-539-9800
www.oxfordcounty.ca
Population: 105,719 *Census Year:* 2011
Number of Households: 35,735
Waste Management:
County responsible for all waste management (waste collection & recycling); Area municipalities look after some customer service associated with waste management
Number of landfill sites: 1*Landfill Capacity:* 18 years
Solid Waste Disposal Fees: $45/tonne
Recycling: Curbside
Special Bans/by-laws: Water Use; Sewer Use; Water Rate
Hazardous Waste Depot or Facility: Special hazardous waste days; Woodstock-WPCP; Ingersoll - Cami Auto; Tillsonburg - Public
Compost Sites: Yes *Composters subsidized:* Yes
Water & Wastewater Treatment:
County responsible for all water systems & wastewater treatment facilities, including planning, design & construction, maintenance, monitoring & operations; Wastewater systems in Drumbo, Ingersoll, Norwich, Plattsville, Tavistock, Thamesford, Tillsonburg & Woodstock; Water treatment plants in Beachville-Loweville, Bright, Brownsville, Dereham Centre, Drumbo, Embro, Hickson-King, Ingersoll, Innerkip, Lakeside, Mount Elgin, Norwich, Otterville, Plattsville, Princeton, Springford, Sweaburg-Oxford
Other Initiatives:
Thornton/Tabor Well Field Study; Groundwater Pilot Project.

Parry Sound
District Social Services Administration Bd.
1 Beechwood Dr., 2nd Fl.
Parry Sound, ON P2A 1J2
705-746-7777
Fax: 705-746-7783
Population: 42,162 *Census Year:* 2011
Number of Households: 34,931

Pelham
P.O. Box 400
20 Pelham Town Sq.
Fonthill, ON L0S 1E0
905-892-2607
www.pelham.ca
Population: 16,598 *Census Year:* 2011
Number of Households: 5,793
Waste Management:
Responsibility of the Regional Municipality of Niagara
Water & Wastewater Treatment:
Responsibility of the Regional Municipality of Niagara

Perth East
P.O. Box 455
25 Mill St. East
Milverton, ON N0K 1M0
519-595-2800
Fax: 519-595-2801
township@pertheast.on.ca
www.pertheast.on.ca
Population: 12,028 *Census Year:* 2011
Number of Households: 4,006
Waste Management:
Number of landfill sites: 2
Water & Wastewater Treatment:
Township's public works dept. operates 2 water supply systems in Milverton & Shakespeare, plus 1 wastewater treatment system in Milverton

Petawawa
1111 Victoria St.
Petawawa, ON K8H 2E6
613-687-5536
Fax: 613-687-5973
www.petawawa.ca
Population: 15,988 *Census Year:* 2011
Number of Households: 4,000
Waste Management:
Responsibility of the Town of Petawawa, in partnership with the Township of Laurentian Valley, the City of Pembroke, the Township of North Algona-Wilberforce & the Township of Bonnechere Valley; Landfill site located at 1076 Woito Station Rd., in the township of Laurentian Valley
Number of landfill sites: 1
Hazardous Waste Depot or Facility: Ottawa Valley Waste Recovery Centre, 900 Woito Station Rd, Twp of Laurentian Valley, 613/7
Water & Wastewater Treatment:
Town of Petawawa Water Pollution Control Plant & water treatment plant, operated by Ontario Clean Water Agency, 613/687-7512

Port Hope
Town Hall
56 Queen St.
Port Hope, ON L1A 3Z9
905-885-4544
Fax: 905-885-7698
admin@porthope.ca
www.porthope.ca
Population: 16,214 *Census Year:* 2011
Number of Households: 6,138
Waste Management:
Responsibility of Northumberland County
Water & Wastewater Treatment:
Water purification plant, Marsh St. Port Hope; Sewage treatment plant, 100 Lake St., Port Hope
Other Initiatives:
Construction of new water treatment plant, www.porthopewatertreatment.ca

Prescott & Russell
P.O. Box 304
59 Court St.
L'Orignal, ON K0B 1K0
613-675-4661
Fax: 613-675-2519
Toll-Free Phone: 1-800-667-6307
support@prescott-russell.on.ca
www.prescott-russell.on.ca
Population: 85,381 *Census Year:* 2011
Number of Households: 28,039
Waste Management:
Responsibility of area municipalities
Water & Wastewater Treatment:
Responsibility of area municipalities

Rainy River
District Social Services Administration Bd.
450 Scott St.
Fort Frances, ON P9A 1H2
807-274-5349
Fax: 807-274-0678
Toll-Free Phone: 1-800-265-5349
Population: 20,370 *Census Year:* 2011
Number of Households: 11,212

Russell
717 Notre Dame St.
Embrun, ON K0A 1W1
613-443-3066
Fax: 613-443-1042
Bylaws, E-mail: bylaws.reglements@russell.ca
info@russell.ca; publicworks.voirie@russell.ca
www.russell.ca
Population: 15,247 *Census Year:* 2011
Number of Households: 4,110
Waste Management:
Contracted to Malex Waste Systems, 819/778-5237
Number of landfill sites: 1*Landfill Capacity:* 20 years
Solid Waste Disposal Fees: $12.50/cu metre
Clean Fill Fee: Yes; $12.50/cu metre
Recycling: Curbside
Hazardous Waste Depot or Facility: Depot at the landfill site
Composters subsidized: Yes
Water & Wastewater Treatment:
Township of Russell, Utilities Services, 851 Rte. 400, Embrun, ON, K0A 1W1

St. Clair
Civic Centre
1155 Emily St.
Mooretown, ON N0N 1M0
519-867-2021
Fax: 519-867-5509
Toll-Free Phone: 1-800-809-0301 (Sombra & Lambton)
webmaster@twp.stclair.on.ca; publicworks@twp.stclair.on.ca
www.twp.stclair.on.ca
Population: 14,515 *Census Year:* 2011
Number of Households: 5,877
Waste Management:
Waste collection responsibility of township public works & operations department; Collection of yard waste in urbanized areas; Collection of recyclables contracted to Halton Recycling; Waste management responsibility of County of Lambton
Recycling: Curbside
Special Bans/by-laws: Water restrictions
Compost Sites: Yes
Water & Wastewater Treatment:
St. Clair Distribution System operated by township; Majority of water supply from Lambton Area Water Supply System

Saugeen Shores
P.O. Box 820
600 Tomlinson Dr.
Port Elgin, ON N0H 2C0
519-832-2008
Fax: 519-832-2140
www.saugeenshores.ca
Population: 12,661 *Census Year:* 2011
Number of Households: 6,268
Waste Management:
Bruce Solid Waste Recycling Association responsible for recycling pickup
Number of landfill sites: 2
Recycling: Depot; Services provided by Bruce Area Solid Waste

Recycling, 519/797-5557.
Water & Wastewater Treatment:
Sewage treatment plant, Lehnen St.; Southhampton Water Treatment Plant
Other Initiatives:
Goods Exchange Days; Hazardous Waste Disposal Day; Leaf Collection

Scugog
P.O. Box 780
181 Perry St.
Port Perry, ON L9L 1A7
905-985-7346
Fax: 905-985-9914
www.scugog.ca
Population: 21,569 *Census Year:* 2011
Number of Households: 7,616
Waste Management:
Responsibility of Regional Municipality of Durham
Water & Wastewater Treatment:
Responsibility of Regional Municipality of Durham

Severn
P.O. Box 159
1024 Hurlwood Lane
Orillia, ON L3V 6J3
705-325-2315
Fax: 705-327-5818
severn@encode.com
www.townshipofsevern.com
Population: 12,377 *Census Year:* 2011
Number of Households: 5,937
Waste Management:
Responsibility of County of Simcoe
Special Bans/by-laws: Littering By-law; Clean & Clear Yards By-law
Water & Wastewater Treatment:
The following municipal drinking water systems & water treatment plants are owned and operated by the township: Bass Lake Woodlands Well Supply & Distribution; Coldwater Well Supply & Distribution; Sandcastle Estates Water Treatment Plant; Severn Estates Well Supply & Distribution; Washago Water Treatment Plant; Westshore Water Treatment Plant
Other Initiatives:
Westshore Water & Sewer Project completed in 2006

Smith-Ennismore-Lakefield
P.O. Box 270
1310 Centre Line, RR#4
Bridgenorth, ON K0L 1H0
705-292-9507
Fax: 705-292-8964
Toll-Free Phone: 1-877-213-7419 (in 705 area code)
www.smithennismorelakefield.on.ca
Population: 16,846 *Census Year:* 2011
Number of Households: 7,722
Waste Management:
Waste collection is contracted to Capital Environmental, 705/742-4268; County of Peterborough is responsible for recycling & disposal of hazardous waste
Number of landfill sites: 2
Solid Waste Disposal Fees: Yes
Composters subsidized: Yes
Water & Wastewater Treatment:
Township has agreement with Peterborough Utilities Services Inc. to maintain operations of Lakefield Water Works & Woodland Acres Water Works; Private wells & septic systems serve other areas
Other Initiatives:
Major appliances & large household furniture day at Smith Landfill Site

South Dundas
P.O. Box 160
4296 County Rd. 31
Williamsburg, ON K0C 2H0
613-535-2673
Fax: 613-535-2099
Toll-Free Phone: 1-800-265-0619
mail@southdundas.com
www.southdundas.com
Population: 10,794 *Census Year:* 2011
Number of Households: 4,412
Waste Management:
Collection of waste & recyclables plus waste disposal responsibility of township public works department
Number of landfill sites: 2
Solid Waste Disposal Fees: $10/ 1/2 or 3/4 ton pick-up; $50/construction material
Recycling: Curbside
Composters subsidized: Yes
Water & Wastewater Treatment:
St. Lawrence River is township water source; Regional water treatment facility; Sewage treatment facilities
Other Initiatives:
Limit of 2 bags of garbage/week; Stickers for additional bags of garbage cost $1.25 each; Participation with township of North Dundas in its household hazardous waste program; Landfill sites are located in Williamsburg & Matilda wards; Upgrades to water distribution system

South Frontenac
P.O. Box 100
4432 George St.
Sydenham, ON K0H 2T0
613-376-3027
Fax: 613-376-6657
Toll-Free Phone: 1-800-559-5862
admin@township.southfrontenac.on.ca
www.township.southfrontenac.on.ca
Population: 18,113 *Census Year:* 2011
Number of Households: 8,748
Waste Management:
Landfills/waste disposal sites located in Bedford, Loughborough, Portland & Storrington
Solid Waste Disposal Fees: Yes
Recycling: Both Curbside & Depot; Depots at the following waste disposal sites: Bradshaw, Green Bay, Salem & Massassauga
Other Initiatives:
Hazardous waste disposal tickets may be purchased & turned into the City of Kingston Hazardous Waste Disposal Site; Garbage bag limits

South Glengarry
6 Oak St.
Lancaster, ON K0C 1N0
613-347-1166
info@southglengarry.com
www.southglengarry.com
Population: 13,162 *Census Year:* 2011
Number of Households: 5,329
Waste Management:
Recycling handled by R.A.R.E. Recycling
Number of landfill sites: 2
Solid Waste Disposal Fees: $10/van, pickup truck, private car, utility trailer; $50/1 ton vehicle
Water & Wastewater Treatment:
Glen Walter Water Treatment Plant, 18352 County Rd.2, in Glen Walter
Other Initiatives:
Adopt-a-Road program; Household hazardous waste day

South Huron
P.O. Box 759
322 Main St. South
Exeter, ON N0M 1S6
519-235-0310
Fax: 519-235-3304
Toll-Free: 1-877-204-0747
info@southhuron.ca
www.southhuron.ca
Population: 9,945 *Census Year:* 2011
Number of Households: 4,372
Waste Management:
Blue Water Recycling, 519/228-6678
Number of landfill sites: 1*Landfill Capacity:* 100 years
Solid Waste Disposal Fees: $75.00/tonne
Recycling: Curbside; Recycling handled by Bluewater Recycling Assoc.
Hazardous Waste Depot or Facility: 82 Nelson St., Exeter
Water & Wastewater Treatment:
Lake Huron Water Plant, Hwy. 21, 683 South Huron
Other Initiatives:
Special pick-up for brush, furniture, fixtures, appliances & compostable garden waste; User pay system for garbage; Special depots, at certain times for household hazardous waste

South Stormont
P.O. Box 84
2 Mille Roches Rd.
Long Sault, ON K0C 1P0
613-534-8889
Fax: 613-534-2280
Toll-Free Phone: 1-800-265-3915
info@southstormont.ca
www.southstormont.ca
Population: 12,617 *Census Year:* 2011
Number of Households: 4,569
Waste Management:
Number of landfill sites: 1
Solid Waste Disposal Fees: $5/car; $15/pick up truck; $20/1 ton truck; $30/white goods containing freon; $22/tractor & loader tires; $15/large truck tire; $5/car & light truck t
Recycling: Curbside
Water & Wastewater Treatment:
Township's Public Works Dept. responsible for waterworks at Ingleside & Long Sault (South Stormont Regional Water Treatment Plant), Rosedale/St. Andrews, Newington & Osnabruck Centre; Wastewater handled at Ingleside & Long Sault
Other Initiatives:
Household garbage limit; Household hazardous waste accepted at City of Cornwall Landfill Site on specific dates; Water system upgrades

Springwater
Township of Springwater Administrative Ctr.
2231 Nursery Rd.
Minesing, ON L0L 1Y2
705-728-4784
Fax: 705-728-6957
info@springwater.ca; council@springwater.ca
www.springwater.ca
Population: 18,223 *Census Year:* 2011
Number of Households: 5,599
Waste Management:
Responsibility of the County of Simcoe
Water & Wastewater Treatment:
Township's Public Works Dept. is responsible for the operation of water systems in the following areas: Anten Mills, Elmvale, Hillsdale, Midhurst, Midhurst - Carson Rd., Minesing, Snow Valley, Vespra Downs & Sunnidale Rd.; Systems include the following: wells, pumping stations, towers, reservoirs, booster stations, generator sets, watermain & metered units; Operation of the Elmvale Sewage Treatment Plant & 2 pumping stations is contracted to the Ontario Clean Water Agency
Other Initiatives:
Environmental assessment regarding a municipal water system to serve Phelpston

Stormont, Dundas & Glengarry
26 Pitt St.
Cornwall, ON K6J 3P2
613-932-1515
Fax: 613-936-2913
Toll-Free Phone: 1-800-267-7158
info@sdgcounties.ca
www.sdgcounties.ca
Population: 111,164 *Census Year:* 2011
Number of Households: 45,478
Waste Management:
Responsibility of area municipalities; County involved in waste management planning only
Water & Wastewater Treatment:
Responsibility of area municipalities
Other Initiatives:
Designation of open spaces in urban settlement areas; Adopt-a-road program; Designation of agricultural resource lands for protection; Policies to control operational impacts of extractive resouce lands; Designation of provincially significant wetlands

Strathroy-Caradoc
52 Frank St.
Strathroy, ON N7G 2R4
519-245-1070
Fax: 519-245-6353
general@strathroy-caradoc.ca
www.strathroy-caradoc.ca
Population: 20,978 *Census Year:* 2011
Number of Households: 7,237
Waste Management:
Garbage collection contracted to Bluewater Recycling Association, 1-800-265-9799
Recycling: Curbside
Water & Wastewater Treatment:

Strathroy-Caradoc Wastewater Treatment Plant, Pike Rd., Strathroy

Sudbury District
c/o Manitoulin-Sudbury District Services Bd
210 Mead Blvd.
Espanola, ON P5E 1R9
www.msdsb.net
Population: 21,196 *Census Year:* 2011
Number of Households: 13,322

Tay
P.O. Box 100
450 Park St.
Victoria Harbour, ON L0K 2A0
705-534-7248
Fax: 705-534-4493
taytownship@tay.ca
www.tay.ca
Population: 9,736 *Census Year:* 2011

Tecumseh
917 Lesperance Rd.
Tecumseh, ON N8N 1W9
519-735-2184
Fax: 519-735-6712
info@tecumseh.ca
www.tecumseh.ca
Population: 23,610 *Census Year:* 2011
Number of Households: 8,544

Thames Centre
4305 Hamilton Rd.
Dorchester, ON N0L 1G3
519-268-7334
Fax: 519-268-3928
Toll-Free Phone: 1-866-425-7306
inquiries@thamescentre.on.ca
www.thamescentre.on.ca
Population: 13,000 *Census Year:* 2011
Number of Households: 4,347
Waste Management:
Waste collection & collection of recyclables contracted to Halton Recycling, 519/690-2796
Number of landfill sites: 1
Solid Waste Disposal Fees: $100/tonne, oversized non-recyclable waste; $20/recyclable waste
Clean Fill Fee: No
Recycling: Both Curbside & Depot; Landfill Site, 2015 Crampton Dr.
Special Bans/by-laws: Water use restictions
Composters subsidized: Yes
Water & Wastewater Treatment:
Dorechester Water Treatment Facility; Thorndale Well Supply System
Other Initiatives:
Garbage bag tag system; Township residents can use the City of London Household Special Waste Drop-Off Depot; Open air burning regulated

The Nation
958 Rte. 500 West
Casselman, ON K0A 1M0
613-764-5444
Fax: 613-764-3310
Toll-Free Phone: 1-800-475-2855
mmccuaig@nationmun.ca
www.nationmun.ca
Population: 11,668 *Census Year:* 2011
Number of Households: 3,797
Waste Management:
Waste removal contracted to Mike's Waste Disposal; Household waste is hauled to the Lafleche Environmental Site in the Township of North Stormont
Number of landfill sites: 3*Landfill Capacity:* 50 years
Recycling: Curbside
Water & Wastewater Treatment:
Limoges Water Treatment Plant; St.Isidore Water Treatment Plant; Ontario Clean Water Agency, 613/443-2195

Thunder Bay
District Social Services Administration Bd.
34 North Cumberland St., 4th Fl.
Thunder Bay, ON P7A 8B9
Population: 146,057 *Census Year:* 2011
Number of Households: 69,857

Tillsonburg
200 Broadway St., 2nd Fl.
Tillsonburg, ON N4G 5A7
519-842-9200
Fax: 519-688-0759
www.tillsonburg.ca
Population: 15,301 *Census Year:* 2011
Number of Households: 6,138
Waste Management:
Responsibility of County of Oxford
Water & Wastewater Treatment:
Responsibility of County of Oxford
Other Initiatives:
Town's public works department is responsible for leaf collection; Leaf, grass, concrete & asphalt recycling; Transfer station operation

Timiskaming
District Social Services Administrative Bd.
P.O. Box 310
29 Duncan Ave. North
Kirkland Lake, ON P2N 3H7
705-567-9366
Toll-Free Phone: 1-888-544-5555
Population: 32,634 *Census Year:* 2011
Number of Households: 16,852

Trent Hills
P.O. Box 1030
66 Front St. South
Campbellford, ON K0L 1L0
705-653-1900
Fax: 705-653-5203
Public Works Emergency, Phone: 705-653-2610
info@trenthills.ca
www.trenthills.ca
Population: 12,604 *Census Year:* 2011
Number of Households: 6,434
Waste Management:
Waste & recycling collection & management responsibility of County of Northumberland, Department of Transportation & Waste Office, 905/372-3329
Water & Wastewater Treatment:
Water treatment responsibility of town; Campbellford Water Treatment Plant; Hastings Water Treatment Plant; Warkworth Water Treatment Plant; Trentview Estates Water Distribution System; Wastewater treatment contracted to Ontario Clean Water Agency; Campbellford Wastewater Treatment Plant; Hastings Wastewater Treatment Plant

Uxbridge
P.O. Box 190
51 Toronto St. South
Uxbridge, ON L9P 1T1
905-852-9181
Fax: 905-852-9674
info@town.uxbridge.on.ca
www.town.uxbridge.on.ca
Population: 20,623 *Census Year:* 2011
Number of Households: 6,116
Waste Management:
Responsibility of Region of Durham
Water & Wastewater Treatment:
Responsibility of Region of Durham
Other Initiatives:
Established Uxbridge Brook Watershed Committee to enhance & protect water resources

Wasaga Beach
30 Lewis St.
Wasaga Beach, ON L9Z 1A1
705-429-3844
Fax: 705-429-7603
www.wasagabeach.com
Population: 17,537 *Census Year:* 2011
Number of Households: 8,068
Waste Management:
Responsibility of Simcoe County
Water & Wastewater Treatment:
Powerline Road Water Plant/Water Pollution Control Plant & Janetta Well Site, operated by Ontario Clean Water Agency

Wellington North
P.O. Box 125
7490 Sideroad 7 West
Kenilworth, ON N0G 2E0
519-848-3620
Toll-Free Phone: 1-866-848-3620
township@wellington-north.com
www.wellington-north.com
Population: 11,477 *Census Year:* 2011
Number of Households: 4,358
Waste Management:
Responsibility of County of Wellington
Special Bans/by-laws: Nutrient Management By-Law
Water & Wastewater Treatment:
Kenilworth Well Water Supply System; Damascus Hall Well Water Supply System; Operation of Arthur Wastewater Treatment Plant & Mount Forest Wastewater Treatment Plant contracted to Ontario Clean Water Agency
Other Initiatives:
Annual tree planting; Brush collection; Salt management plan

West Grey
402813 Grey Rd., RR#2
Durham, ON N0G 1R0
519-369-2200
Fax: 519-369-5962
Toll-Free Phone: 1-800-538-9647
info@westgrey.com
www.westgrey.com
Population: 12,286 *Census Year:* 2011
Number of Households: 5,096
Waste Management:
Number of landfill sites: 3
Recycling: Curbside
Other Initiatives:
Waste bag tag system; Goods exchange day; Household hazardous waste program through Owen Sound Public Works Depot

West Lincoln
P.O. Box 400
318 Canborough St.
Smithville, ON L0R 2A0
905-957-3346
Fax: 905-957-3219
Toll-Free Phone: 1-800-350-3876; TTY: 905-957-0680
reception@westlincoln.ca
www.westlincoln.ca
Population: 13,837 *Census Year:* 2011
Number of Households: 3,940
Waste Management:
Waste management responsibility of the Regional Municipality of Niagara
Water & Wastewater Treatment:
Water & wastewater treatment responsibility of the Regional Municipality of Niagara

West Nipissing
Municipal Office
#101, 225 Holditch St.
Sturgeon Falls, ON P2B 1T1
705-753-2250
Fax: 705-753-3950
www.westnipissingouest.ca
Population: 14,149 *Census Year:* 2011
Number of Households: 6,943
Waste Management:
Municipality administers landfill sites owned by Field, Caldwell, Sturgeon Falls & the Ministry of Natural Resources
Number of landfill sites: 7
Water & Wastewater Treatment:
Sturgeon Falls & Cache Bay Water Treatment Facility, 705/753-5287; Verner Water Treatment Facility, 705/594-2763; Sturgeon Falls, Cache Bay & Field Sewage Treatment Facility/Pumping Station, 705/753-3210; Verner Sewage Treatment Facility/Pumping Station, 705/753-2763

Whitby
575 Rossland Rd. East
Whitby, ON L1N 2M8
905-668-5803
Fax: 905-686-7005
TTY: 905-430-1942
www.whitby.ca
Population: 122,022 *Census Year:* 2011
Number of Households: 29,530
Waste Management:
Waste disposal responsibility of Durham Region; Whitby's Public Works Dept. responsible for waste, compost & special collections; Recyclables collected by Miller Waste Systems

Water & Wastewater Treatment:
Responsibility of Durham Region
Other Initiatives:
Garbage Bag Tag program, 4 item (bag/can) limit; Use of kraft bags for leaf & yard waste collection; Fee for special collection for items containing CFCs

Whitchurch-Stouffville

111 Sandiford Dr.
Stouffville, ON L4A 0Z8
905-640-1900
Fax: 905-640-7957
Toll-Free Phone: 1-855-642-8696
www.townofws.com
Population: 37,628 *Census Year:* 2011
Number of Households: 7,984
Waste Management:
Waste collection contracted to Miller Waste Systems, 905/475-6356; Composting facilities responsibility of York Region Waste Management Division, 1-877-464-4675, ext.5717
Recycling: Both Curbside & Depot; Whitchurch-Stouffville Recycling Depot, off Burkholder St.
Special Bans/by-laws: Waste collection limit of 3 containers; Waste stickers available at $2.00 for each bag above three & up to a maximum of six
Water & Wastewater Treatment:
Treatment responsibility of the Region of York; Operation & maintenance of water distribution & sewer collection systems responsibility of town
Other Initiatives:
Large article, yard waste & Christmas tree collection

Wilmot

60 Snyder's Rd. West
Baden, ON N3A 1A1
519-634-8444
Fax: 519-634-5522
Toll-Free Phone: 1-800-469-5576
info@wilmot.ca
www.wilmot.ca
Population: 19,223 *Census Year:* 2011
Number of Households: 5,208
Waste Management:
Responsibility of Regional Municipality of Waterloo
Water & Wastewater Treatment:
Responsibility of Regional Municipality of Waterloo

Woolwich

P.O. Box 158
24 Church St. West
Elmira, ON N3B 2Z6
519-669-1647
Fax: 519-669-1820
Phone from 648 exchange: 519-664-2613
woolwich.mail@woolwich.ca
www.woolwich.ca
Population: 23,145 *Census Year:* 2011
Number of Households: 6,300
Waste Management:
Responsibility of the Regional Municipality of Waterloo
Water & Wastewater Treatment:
Regional Municipality of Waterloo responsible for water & wastewater treatment; Township responsible for collection & local distribution

Prince Edward Island

The Prince Edward Island Department of Environment, Labour & Justice is responsible for The Prince Edward Island Department of Environmental Protection Act.

The entire municipal population of 29 island communities is served by central wastewater treatment plants. Municipal wastewater includes household wastewater, waste from shopping malls, office buildings, hospitals, schools & some manufacturing plants. The central wastewater treatment system cleans the water until it is safe to return to the environment via rivers & harbours.

The Waste Resource Management Regulations are for the construction & operation of all facilities that handle solid waste in the province. This includes landfill sites & recycling facilities. Materials diverted from landfill sites are compost, paper, plastic, glass, cans & dry cell batteries. The entire province, including rural areas, has curbside recycling pickup. Solid waste that is not compostable or recyclable is sent to one of three landfill sites in the province. There is one incinerator in Charlottetown, which powers a hospital.

The Drinking Water Strategy is an updated action plan with new & tighter regulations, implemented summer of 2002. This provincial action plan ensures that PEI drinking water stays clear from the ground to the glass. In PEI, 57% of the population depends on private wells for drinking water & approximately 40% has onsite sewage disposal systems for wastewater treatment.

Under the Renewable Energy Act, given Royal Assent in December 2004, the province established a guaranteed selling price for electricity supplied to the provincial utility from a community or cooperative wind system, & gave residents the opportunity to invest in local wind energy projects.

Under the federal government's New Deal for Cities, Prince Edward Island was allocated $37.5 million in federal gas tax funding between 2005 and 2010 for municipal infrastructure projects.

Major Municipalities in Prince Edward Island

City of Charlottetown

P.O. Box 98
199 Queen St.
Charlottetown, PE C1A 4B7
902-566-5548
Fax: 902-566-4701
city@city.charlottetown.pe.ca
www.city.charlottetown.pe.ca
Population: 34,562 *Census Year:* 2011
Number of Households: 14,175
Joseph Coady, Director, Public Services, email: jcoady@city.charlottetown.pe.ca
Phil Handrahan, Director, Fiscal & Development Services, email: phandrahan@city.charlottetown.pe.ca
Craig Walker, Manager, Water & Sewer Utility, 902-629-4014, email: cwalker@city.charlottetown.pe.ca
Bill Clair, Works Superintendent, Water & Sewer Utility, 902-629-4015, email: bclair@city.charlottetown.pe.ca
Herman Van Omme, Superintendent, Waste Water Treatment Plant, 902-628-6647, Fax: 902-628-6684, email: hvanomme@city.charlottetown.pe.ca
Ron Atkinson, Economic Development Officer, Economic Development, Tourism & Events, email: ratkinson@city.charlottetown.pe.ca
Don Poole, Manager of Planning, Planning & Development, email: dpoole@city.charlottetown.pe.ca
Vada Fernandez, Purchasing Officer, Finance, email: vfernandez@city.charlottetown.pe.ca
Mel Cheverie, Chief Building Inspector, Planning & Development, email: mcheverie@city.charlottetown.pe.ca
Jim Molyneux, Field Works Coordinator, Public Works, email: jmolyneux@city.charlottetown.pe.ca
Blair Kinch, Sr. Superintendent, Public Works, email: bkinch@city.charlottetown.pe.ca
Lance Jones, Streets Maintenance Supervisor, Public Works, email: ljones@city.charlottetown.pe.ca
Nancy McMinn, Parks Superintendent, Parks & Recreation, email: nmcminn@city.charlottetown.pe.ca
Randy MacDonald, Fire Chief, Fire Services, email: rmacdonald@city.charlottetown.pe.ca
Paul Johnston, Manager, Public Works, 902-894-5208, email: pjohnston@city.charlottetown.pe.ca
Sue Hendricken, Manager, Parks & Recreation, 902-368-1025, email: shendricken@city.charlottetown.pe.ca
Waste Management:
Waste collection services provided by Island Waste Management Corporation, 902/894-0330, URL: www.iwmc.pe.ca, Email: info@iwmc.pe.ca
Recycling: Residential & commercial waste, compostables, & recyclables collection managed by Island Waste Management Corporation; recyclables collected once a month; drop-off centre located at 7 Superior Cres.,
Special Bans/by-laws: Tree Maintenance Bylaw; Water and Sewer Utility Bylaw; Dangerous, Hazardous and Unsightly Premises Bylaw
Hazardous Waste Depot or Facility: Household hazardous waste, tires, & other special items handled by Island Waste Management Corporation
Water & Wastewater Treatment:
Water sources include the Brackley, Suffolk & Union main wellfields & the smaller Brookdale & Hunter Green systems; Malpeque pumping station is a water supply used as required; Sewage treatment facilities include the Riverside Drive Treatment Plant, East Royalty Lagoon & sewer pumping stations at Dorchester Street, Navy Quay, West Royalty & West Royalty Industrial Park
Other Initiatives:
Establishment of Department of Urban Beautification & Forestry

City of Summerside

275 Fitzroy St.
Summerside, PE C1N 1H9
902-432-1230
Fax: 902-436-9296
cityhall@city.summerside.pe.ca
www.city.summerside.pe.ca
Population: 14,751 *Census Year:* 2011
Number of Households: 5,981
Terry Murphy, Chief Administrative Officer, email: tmurphy@city.summerside.pe.ca
Paul Gallant, Program & Scheduling Coordinator, Community Services, Recreation, 902-432-1294, email: pgallant@city.summerside.pe.ca
James Peters, Director, Fire Services, 902-432-1224, email: jpeters@city.summerside.pe.ca
Michael Thususka, Director, Economic Development, 902-432-1255, email: miket@city.summerside.pe.ca
Aaron MacDonald, Director, Technical Services, 902-432-1258, email: aaronmac@city.summerside.pe.ca
Waste Management:
Waste collection responsibility of Waste Management Commission

Québec

Garbage collection is conducted by municipalities; recycling & waste management is carried out by municipalities & upper tier level governments. Water & wastewater treatment is similarly the responsibility of municipalities & upper tier level governments. Municipalities may enter into agreements with one another in the management & delivery of these services. With the exception of garbage collection, all the above services are subsidized in part by the provincial government.

Funding was made available to communities under the Strategy & Action Plan on Biological Diversity 2004-2007. Rural municipal infrastructure funding ($390 million) is a federal-provincial initiative.

Through the federal government's Gas Tax Fund, outlined in Economic Action Plan 2013, Québec will be allocated $2,382,738,000 between 2014 and 2019 for municipal infrastructure projects that focus on clean air, water and reducing greenhouse gas emissions.

Major Municipalities in Québec

City of Alma

140, rue St-Joseph
Alma, QC G8B 3R1
418-669-5000
Fax: 418-669-5019
info@ville.alma.qc.ca
www.ville.alma.qc.ca
Population: 30,904 *Census Year:* 2011
Number of Households: 10,774
Jocelyn Fradette, Conseillère, 418-450-1359, email: jocelyn.fradette@ville.alma.qc.ca, Wards: 2
Jean-Yves Lessard, Directeur, 418-669-5001, Fax: 418-669-5180, email: jeanyves.lessard@ville.alma.qc.ca
Waste Management:
Recycling: Both Curbside & Depot

City of Amos

182, 1re Rue est
Amos, QC J9T 2G1
819-732-3254
Fax: 819-727-9792
master@ville.amos.qc.ca
www.ville.amos.qc.ca
Population: 12,671 *Census Year:* 2011
Number of Households: 5,536
Sébastien D'Astous, Conseiller, Infrastructures & services aux citoyens, Wards: 1
Amélie Mercier, Conseillère, Environnement, culture & services à la population, Wards: 2

Régis Fortin, Directeur, Service de l'environnement, 819-732-3254, Fax: 819-732-9675
Waste Management:
Contracted to Sanimos Inc., 819/732-8833
Solid Waste Disposal Fees: $60.00
Recycling: Both Curbside & Depot; Depot centre is for three regions
Special Bans/by-laws: Institutions, businesses & plants are required to recycle materials using blue & grey boxes
Hazardous Waste Depot or Facility: Sorting area with the materials forwarded to specialized centres
Water & Wastewater Treatment:
Drinking water from well #1 & #2 purified through a filter system

City of Baie-Comeau
19, av Marquette
Baie-Comeau, QC G4Z 1K5
418-296-4931
Fax: 418-296-3759
vbc@ville.baie-comeau.qc.ca
www.ville.baie-comeau.qc.ca
Population: 22,113 *Census Year:* 2011
Number of Households: 10,254
Ghislain Gauthier, Directeur, Service des travaux publics, 418-296-8180, Fax: 418-296-3095, email: ggauthier@ville.baie-comeau.qc.ca
Waste Management:
Recycling: Curbside

City of Beaconsfield
303, boul Beaconsfield
Beaconsfield, QC H9W 4A7
514-428-4400
Fax: 514-428-4424
info@beaconsfield.ca
www.beaconsfield.ca
Population: 19,505 *Census Year:* 2011

City of Beauharnois
#100, 660, rue Ellice
Beauharnois, QC J6N 1Y1
450-429-3546
Fax: 450-429-2478
direction.generale@ville.beauharnois.qc.ca
www.ville.beauharnois.qc.ca
Population: 12,011 *Census Year:* 2011
Number of Households: 2,770
Yves Magnan, Directeur, Travaux publics, 450-225-0650, email: yves.magnan@ville.beauharnois.qc.ca
Daniel Leblanc, Directeur, Environnement, 450-429-3959, email: daniel.leblanc@ville.beauharnois.qc.ca
Waste Management:
Recycling: Both Curbside & Depot

City of Bécancour
1295, av Nicolas-Perrot
Bécancour, QC G9H 1A1
819-294-6500
Fax: 819-294-6535
becancour@ville.becancour.qc.ca
www.becancour.net
Population: 12,438 *Census Year:* 2011
Number of Households: 4,690
Water & Wastewater Treatment:
Centrale de traitement d'eau, (155, av. Godefroy), 819/233-2147

City of Beloeil
777, rue Laurier
Beloeil, QC J3G 4S9
450-467-2835
Fax: 450-464-5445
info@ville.beloeil.qc.ca
www.ville.beloeil.qc.ca
Population: 20,783 *Census Year:* 2011
Number of Households: 7,254
Waste Management:
Recycling: Both Curbside & Depot

City of Blainville
1000, ch du Plan-Bouchard
Blainville, QC J7C 3S9
450-434-5200
Fax: 450-434-8295
accueil@ville.blainville.qc.ca
www.ville.blainville.qc.ca
Population: 53,510 *Census Year:* 2011
Number of Households: 12,783
Waste Management:
Waste collection contracted to Entreprise Sanitaire F.A. Ltée, 514/661-5080; Recyclables collection contracted to La Régie Intermunicipale d'Argenteuil Deux-Montagnes, 450/562-0778; Dry material depot: 60, boul de la Seigneurie Est, Blainville, 450/434-5348
Transfer Station(s): Corporation régionale de Centre de Tri-CFER, 450/562-4488
Hazardous Waste Depot or Facility: 60, boul de la Seigneurie
Water & Wastewater Treatment:
Responsibility of the city of Ste-Thérèse

City of Boisbriand
940, boul de la Grande-Allée
Boisbriand, QC J7G 2J7
450-435-1954
Fax: 450-435-6398
www.ville.boisbriand.qc.ca
Population: 26,816 *Census Year:* 2011
Number of Households: 9,495
Waste Management:
Waste collection responsibility of Régie intermunicipale Argenteuil Deux Montagnes; Treatment under CFER Lachute
Water & Wastewater Treatment:
Responsiblility of town of Ste-Thérèse

City of Candiac
100, boul Montcalm nord
Candiac, QC J5R 3L8
450-444-6000
Fax: 450-444-6009
info@ville.candiac.qc.ca
www.ville.candiac.qc.ca
Population: 19,876 *Census Year:* 2011
Number of Households: 5,100
Waste Management:
Responsibility of the MRC (Roussillon)
Recycling: Both Curbside & Depot
Water & Wastewater Treatment:
Water treatment plant located at 62, Marie-Victorin, operated by Ville de Candiac, 450/444-6000

City of Chambly
56, rue Martel
Chambly, QC J3L 1V3
450-658-8788
Fax: 450-447-4525
information@ville.chambly.qc.ca
www.ville.chambly.qc.ca
Population: 25,571 *Census Year:* 2011
Number of Households: 7,567
Waste Management:
Waste collection contracted to Intersan; Chambly residents can drop off construction debris at a dry materials site located at 2400, boul Industriel
Number of landfill sites: 1
Hazardous Waste Depot or Facility: Yes
Water & Wastewater Treatment:
Water treatment contracted to SECTEAU, 514/658-1112
Other Initiatives:
Collection of leaves & yard waste for composting

City of Châteauguay
5, boul d'Youville
Châteauguay, QC J6J 2P8
450-698-3000
Fax: 450-698-3019
info@ville.chateauguay.qc.ca
www.ville.chateauguay.qc.ca
Population: 45,904 *Census Year:* 2011
Number of Households: 15,682
Waste Management:
Recycling: Curbside
Water & Wastewater Treatment:
Wastewater Treatment Plant located in Saint-Bernard; Pumping stations: Jean-Louis Chèvrefils, Joseph-Chèvrefils, Marchard & Alonzo-Béliveau
Other Initiatives:
Household hazardous waste collected annually

City of Cowansville
220, place Municipale
Cowansville, QC J2K 1T4
450-263-0141
Fax: 450-263-9357
hoteldeville@ville.cowansville.qc.ca
www.ville.cowansville.qc.ca
Population: 12,489 *Census Year:* 2011
Number of Households: 5,164
Waste Management:
Responsible for waste collection; Collection of toxic materials
Hazardous Waste Depot or Facility: Landfill stie, 2500, rang St-Joseph, Cowansville, 450/263-2351
Other Initiatives:
Pick-up of composting materials

City of Deux-Montagnes
803, ch d'Oka
Deux-Montagnes, QC J7R 1L8
450-473-2796
Fax: 450-473-2417
info@ville.deux-montagnes.qc.ca
www.ville.deux-montagnes.qc.ca
Population: 17,552 *Census Year:* 2011
Number of Households: 6,522
Waste Management:
Recycling: Curbside

City of Dolbeau-Mistassini
1100, boul Wallberg
Dolbeau-Mistassini, QC G8L 1G7
418-276-0160
Fax: 418-276-8312
hotelville@ville.dolbeau-mistassini.qc.ca
www.ville.dolbeau-mistassini.qc.ca
Population: 14,384 *Census Year:* 2011
Number of Households: 6,045

City of Drummondville
CP 398
415, rue Lindsay
Drummondville, QC J2B 6W3
819-478-6550
communications@ville.drummondville.qc.ca
www.ville.drummondville.qc.ca
Population: 71,852 *Census Year:* 2011
Number of Households: 21,783
Waste Management:
Recycling: Both Curbside & Depot
Water & Wastewater Treatment:
Water treatment plant at 60, rue Poirier, 819/478-6576, Fax: 819/474-8824, Email: ute@cgocable.ca
Other Initiatives:
Pick-up of composting materials

City of Gaspé
25, rue de l'Hôtel-de-Ville
Gaspé, QC G4X 2A5
418-368-2104
Fax: 418-368-8532
direction.generale@ville.gaspe.qc.ca
www.ville.gaspe.qc.ca
Population: 15,163 *Census Year:* 2011
Number of Households: 5,801
Charles Aspirault, Conseiller, Wards: 2
Waste Management:
Waste collection & management responsibility of the city; Some contracts are undertaken by private companies under the supervision of the public works superintendent

City of Gatineau
CP 1970 Hull
25, rue Laurier
Gatineau, QC J8X 3Y9
819-595-2002
info@gatineau.ca
www.ville.gatineau.qc.ca
Population: 265,349 *Census Year:* 2011
Number of Households: 40,259
Stefan Psenak, Conseiller, email: psenak.stefan@gatineau.ca, Wards: 1. Aylmer
Patrice Martin, Conseiller, email: martin.patrice@gatineau.ca, Wards: 5. Wright—Parc-de-la-Montagne
Mireille Apollon, Conseillère, email: apollon.mireille@gatineau.ca, Wards: 6. Orée-du-Parc
Suzanne Ouellet, Greffière, 819-595-7180, Fax: 819-595-7192, email: ouellet.suzanne@ville.gatineau.qc.ca
Marco Lalonde, Directeur, Service des travaux publics
Louise Lavoie, Directrice, Service de l'environnement

Municipal Governments

Marie-Claude Martel, Directrice, Service de l'urbanisme et du développement durable
Mario Harel, Directeur, Service de police
Waste Management:
Waste collection responsibility of the city
Recycling: Both Curbside & Depot
Hazardous Waste Depot or Facility: 860, boulevard de la CarriSre
Other Initiatives:
Composting materials pick-up in Aylmer & Hull region in 2007 & other regions in 2008

City of Granby
87, rue Principale
Granby, QC J2G 2T8
450-776-8282
Fax: 450-776-8231
communication@ville.granby.qc.ca
www.ville.granby.qc.ca
Population: 63,433 *Census Year:* 2011
Number of Households: 20,379
André Jean, Directeur, Travaux publics, 450-776-8366, Fax: 450-776-8370, email: travaux.publics@ville.granby.qc.ca
Pierre Lacombe, Directeur, Incendies, 450-776-8344, Fax: 450-839-0370, email: incendie@ville.granby.qc.ca
Claude Ouimette, Coordonnateur, Station d'épuration des eaux usées, 450-776-8371, Fax: 450-776-8373, email: epuration@ville.granby.qc.ca
Waste Management:
Recycling: Curbside
Water & Wastewater Treatment:
Station d'épuration des eaux usées, 1250, boul Industriel; Centrale de traitement d'eau potable, 91, rue Robitaille

City of Joliette
614, boul Manseau
Joliette, QC J6E 3E4
450-753-8000
Fax: 450-753-8199
www.ville.joliette.qc.ca
Population: 19,621 *Census Year:* 2011
Number of Households: 8,444
François Pépin, Directeur, Travaux publics et services techniques, 450-753-8080, email: francois.pepin@ville.joliette.qc.ca
Terry Rousseau, Directeur, Incendies, 450-753-8154, email: service.incendies@ville.joliette.qc.ca

City of L'Assomption
399, rue Dorval
L'Assomption, QC J5W 1A1
450-589-5671
Fax: 450-589-4512
information@ville.lassomption.qc.ca
www.ville.lassomption.qc.ca
Population: 20,065 *Census Year:* 2011
Number of Households: 5,796
Waste Management:
Construction materials collected through Groupe EBI, 450/836-2546
Recycling: Curbside
Hazardous Waste Depot or Facility: 134, ch des Commissaires
Water & Wastewater Treatment:
Jean Perreault Water Treatment Plant, 450, boul l'Ange-Gardien; Wastewater pumping stations at Thouin & St-Ours; 8 pumping stations; Directeur: Christian Sauvageau

City of La Prairie
#400, 170, boul Taschereau
La Prairie, QC J5R 5H6
450-444-6600
Fax: 450-444-6636
info@ville.laprairie.qc.ca
www.ville.laprairie.qc.ca
Population: 23,357 *Census Year:* 2011
Number of Households: 7,486
Guy Trahan, Directeur, Travaux publics, 450-444-6684, Fax: 450-444-6692, email: tp@ville.laprairie.qc.ca
Waste Management:
Recycling: Both Curbside & Depot
Water & Wastewater Treatment:
Filtration plant, 310, rue Ignace, La Prairie J5R 1E5, 450/444-6694

City of La Tuque
375, rue St-Joseph
La Tuque, QC G9X 1L5
819-523-8200
Fax: 819-523-5419
dg@ville.latuque.qc.ca
www.ville.latuque.qc.ca
Population: 11,227 *Census Year:* 2011
Number of Households: 5,319

City of Lachute
380, rue Principale
Lachute, QC J8H 1Y2
450-562-3781
Fax: 450-562-1431
lachute@ville.lachute.qc.ca
www.ville.lachute.qc.ca
Population: 12,551 *Census Year:* 2011
Number of Households: 5,245
Waste Management:
Wastewater plant, 550, boul de l'Aéroparc
Water & Wastewater Treatment:
Water filtration plant, 1950, ch Thomas-Gore, 450-562-9302

City of Laval
Hôtel de Ville
CP 422 St-Martin
1, Place du Souvenir
Laval, QC H7V 3Z4
450-978-8000
Fax: 450-978-5943
info@ville.laval.qc.ca
www.ville.laval.qc.ca
Population: 401,553 *Census Year:* 2011
Number of Households: 135,661
Gaétan Turbide, Directeur général, 450-978-3676
Gilles Benoit, Directeur, Environnement, 450-978-8000
Gérard Poirier, Directeur, Ingénierie, 450-680-2999
Lise Poirier, Directrice, Systèmes & technologies, 450-662-4040
Michel Toutant, Directeur, Travaux publics, 450-978-8000
Sylvain Dubois, Directeur, Urbanisme, 450-680-5500
Waste Management:
Waste collection contracted to Intersan, Clément Riberdy, 450/438-5604; Recyclables collection contracted to Rebuts Solides Canadiens, Michel Leboeuf, 514/593-8555
Solid Waste Disposal Fees: $33.72/tonne
Clean Fill Fee: No
Transfer Station(s): Yes
Recycling: Curbside
Hazardous Waste Depot or Facility: Collection days
Compost Sites: No *Composters subsidized:* Yes
Water & Wastewater Treatment:
Water treatment plants: Usine Chomedey, 3810, boul Lévesque; Usine Pont-Viau, 45, rue St-Hubert; Usine Ste-Rose, 4, rue Hotte; Wastewater treatment plants: Station d'épuration Fabreville, 3985, rue Séguin; Station d'épuration Auteuil, 8985, boul des Laurentides; Station d'épuration Lapinière, 1133, Montée Masson
Other Initiatives:
First 3 streams collection system in Québec, carts & composting; Distribution of 9,000 subsidized household composters; Household composting demonstration site; Christmas tree collection; Waste education programs; Water-use education program; Lawn watering control; Wastewater sludge agricultural utilization after drying & granulation; Leaf collection & composting pilot program; Collects 3 streams from 6,000 households - garbage, recyclables & compostables; Herbicylage program; Ecological landscaping demonstration area; Environmental law management guide; Ecological lawn maintenance workshop

City of Lavaltrie
1370, rue Notre-Dame
Lavaltrie, QC J0K 1H0
450-586-2921
Fax: 450-586-3939
mairie@ville.lavaltrie.qc.ca
www.ville.lavaltrie.qc.ca
Population: 13,267 *Census Year:* 2011
Number of Households: 2,070
Yvon Mousseau, Directeur général, 450-586-2921, Fax: 450-586-3939, email: ymousseau@ville.lavaltrie.qc.ca
André Houle, Directeur, Travaux publics, 450-586-2921, Fax: 450-586-3540, email: travauxpublics@ville.lavaltrie.qc.ca

City of Lévis
2175, ch du Fleuve
Lévis, QC G6W 7W9
418-839-2002
Fax: 418-839-5548
levis@ville.levis.qc.ca
www.ville.levis.qc.ca
Population: 138,769 *Census Year:* 2011
Number of Households: 18,610
Jean Dubé, Directeur général, 418-839-2002, email: jdube@ville.levis.qc.ca
Marcel Rodrigue, Trésorier, 418-839-2002, Fax: 418-835-8522
René Tremblay, Directeur, Culture et des loisirs
Alain Francoeur, Directeur, Travaux publics
Pierre Boulay, Directeur, Environnement
André Matte, Vérificateur général
Robert Cooke, Directeur, Urbanisme
Philippe Meurant, Directrice, Planification et du développement
Yves Després, Directeur, Sécurité incendie
Waste Management:
Incinérateur municipal: 259, ch des Iles; Déchetterie de St-Lambert: 517, rue St-Aimé, St-Lambert-de-Lauzon
Recycling: Both Curbside & Depot
Water & Wastewater Treatment:
Four filtration plants (Charny, Lévis, Lauzon, St-Romuald)

City of Longueuil
4250, ch de la Savane
Longueuil, QC J3Y 9G4
450-463-7000
Fax: 450-463-7403
www.longueuil.ca
Population: 231,409 *Census Year:* 2011
Number of Households: 59,445
Guy Benedetti, Directeur général
Alain Cyr, Directeur, Travaux publics
Francine Brunette, Vérificatrice générale
Waste Management:
Recycling: Curbside
Hazardous Waste Depot or Facility: Yes
Water & Wastewater Treatment:
Filtration plant Le Royer (Brossard, Greenfield Park, St-Lambert-Le Moyne); Water/wastewater treatment plant Rive-Sud (Saint-Hubert); 3 plants in Longueuil
Other Initiatives:
Leaf drop-off bins

City of Magog
7, rue Principale est
Magog, QC J1X 1Y4
819-843-6501
Fax: 819-843-1091
info@ville.magog.qc.ca
www.ville.magog.qc.ca
Population: 25,358 *Census Year:* 2011
Number of Households: 6,655
Armand Comeau, Directeur général, 819-843-2880, email: dg@ville.magog.qc.ca
Waste Management:
Recycling: Both Curbside & Depot
Hazardous Waste Depot or Facility: 520, rue St-Luc
Water & Wastewater Treatment:
Wastewater treatment plant, 819/843-0215, Fax: 819/843-9036

City of Mascouche
3034, ch Ste-Marie
Mascouche, QC J7K 1P1
450-474-4133
Fax: 450-474-6401
www.ville.mascouche.qc.ca
Population: 42,491 *Census Year:* 2011
Number of Households: 10,102
Luc Tremblay, Directeur général, 450-474-4133
Michel Gobeil, Trésorier, Finances, 450-474-4133
Waste Management:
Recycling: Both Curbside & Depot

City of Matane
230, av St-Jérôme
Matane, QC G4W 3A2
418-562-2333
Fax: 418-562-4869
mairie@ville.matane.qc.ca
www.ville.matane.qc.ca

Population: 14,462 *Census Year:* 2011
Number of Households: 5,573
Michel Barriault, Directeur général, 418-562-2333, email: m.barriault@ville.matane.qc.ca
Waste Management:
Landfill at 330, rue des Goélands, 418-562-5023
Number of landfill sites: 1
Recycling: Both Curbside & Depot

City of Mirabel
14111, rue Saint-Jean
Mirabel, QC J7J 1Y3
450-475-8653
Fax: 450-475-7195
communications@ville.mirabel.qc.ca
ville.mirabel.qc.ca
Population: 41,957 *Census Year:* 2011
Number of Households: 10,067
Louis Prud'homme, Directeur général, 450-475-2000, Fax: 450-475-2013, email: l.prud'homme@ville.mirabel.qc.ca
Denis Maurice, Directeur adjoint, Sécurité incendie, 450-475-2010, email: d.maurice@ville.mirabel.qc.ca
Waste Management:
4 Écocentres: St-Justin, St-Canut, St-Janvier, Ste-Scholastique
Recycling: Both Curbside & Depot

City of Mont-Laurier
485, rue Mercier
Mont-Laurier, QC J9L 3N8
819-623-1221
Fax: 819-623-4840
info@villemontlaurier.qc.ca
www.villemontlaurier.qc.ca
Population: 13,779 *Census Year:* 2011
Number of Households: 3,260

City of Mont-St-Hilaire
100, rue du Centre-Civique
Mont-Saint-Hilaire, QC J3H 3M8
450-467-2854
Fax: 450-467-6460
information@villemsh.ca
www.ville.mont-saint-hilaire.qc.ca
Population: 18,200 *Census Year:* 2011
Number of Households: 5,514
Waste Management:
Recycling: Both Curbside & Depot
Other Initiatives:
Collection & composting of leaves; Annual collection of household hazardous waste

City of Montmagny
143, rue St-Jean-Baptiste est
Montmagny, QC G5V 1K4
418-248-3361
Fax: 418-248-4870
info@ville.montmagny.qc.ca
www.ville.montmagny.qc.ca
Population: 11,491 *Census Year:* 2011
Number of Households: 5,094
Félix Michaud, Greffier, 418-248-3362, email: felix.michaud@ville.montmagny.qc.ca
Bernard Létourneau, Directeur général, 418-248-3362, email: bernard.letourneau@ville.montmagny.qc.ca
Yves Chayer, Directeur, Protection contre les incendies, 418-248-5813, Fax: 418-248-2266, email: yves.chayer@ville.montmagny.qc.ca

City of Montréal
Hôtel de Ville
275, rue Notre-Dame est
Montréal, QC H2Y 1C6
514-872-3142
Fax: 514-872-5655
www.ville.montreal.qc.ca
Population: 1,649,519 *Census Year:* 2011
Number of Households: 805,820
Louis Roquet, Directeur général
Jean Yves Hinse, Directeur, Service du capital humain

Bureau du vérificateur général
#1201, 1550, rue Metcalfe
Montréal, QC H3A 3P1
514-872-2209
Fax: 514-872-6950
verificateurgeneral@ville.montreal.qc.ca
www.ville.montreal.qc.ca

Service de sécurité incendie de Montréal
Montréal, QC H2W 1S8
514-872-4684
sim@ville.montreal.qc.ca
www.ville.montreal.qc.ca

Service du capital humain
Montréal, QC H2X 1R9
514-872-5809
Fax: 514-872-9619
preid@ville.montreal.qc.ca

Direction générale
Hôtel de ville
275, rue Notre-Dame est
Montréal, QC H2Y 1C6

Service de police de la Ville de Montréal
1441, rue Saint-Urbain
Montréal, QC H2X 2M6
514-280-2000
Fax: 514-280-2008
www.spvm.qc.ca; www.ville.montreal.qc.ca
Waste Management:
Complexe environnemental Saint-Michel (CESM) 2235, rue Michel-Jurdant; 514-872-1226
Water & Wastewater Treatment:
Station d'épuration 12001, Maurice Duplessis; 514/280-4400; Fax: 514/280-4387
Other Initiatives:
Guide du réemploi de Montréal: guide pratique permet de trouver des moyens pour contribuer à la protection de l'environnement en diminuant la quantité des matières acheminées vers les sites d'enfouissement.

City of Pincourt
919, ch Duhamel
Pincourt, QC J7V 4G8
514-453-8981
Fax: 514-453-8401
pincourtinfo@videotron.ca
www.villepincourt.qc.ca
Population: 14,305 *Census Year:* 2011
Number of Households: 3,608
Michel Perrier, Directeur général, 514-453-8981, Fax: 514-453-0934
Nathalie Boisvert, Trésorière, 514-453-8981
Waste Management:
Responsibility of the MRC (Vaudreil-Soulanges), 450/455-5753
Recycling: Curbside
Special Bans/by-laws: Pesticide ban in effect for the months of July & August; Water restrictions
Water & Wastewater Treatment:
Usine de Pincourt, 707, Cardinal-Léger, Pincourt QC J7V 6W9, 514/425-2622
Other Initiatives:
Household hazardous waste collection every 2 years

City of Québec
Hôtel de Ville
CP 700 Haute-Ville
2, rue des Jardins
Québec, QC G1R 4S9
418-641-6000
Fax: 418-641-6463
renseignements@ville.quebec.qc.ca
www.ville.quebec.qc.ca
Population: 516,622 *Census Year:* 2011
Number of Households: 90,799
Alain Marcoux, Directeur général, 418-641-6373, email: directiongenerale@ville.quebec.qc.ca
Jacques Grantham, Directeur, Environnement, 418-641-6189, email: environnement@ville.quebec.qc.ca
Fernand Martin, Directeur, Aménagement du territoire, 418-641-6160, email: amenageterrit@ville.quebec.qc.ca
Marcel Roy, Directeur, Travaux publics, 418-641-6240, email: travauxpublics@ville.quebec.qc.ca
Daniel Lessard, Directeur, Ingénierie, 418-641-6217, email: ingenierie@ville.quebec.qc.ca
Richard Poitras, Directeur, Protection contre l'incendie, 418-641-6231, email: protectionincendie@ville.quebec.qc.ca
Daniel Maranda, Directeur, Service des approvisionnements, 418-641-6164, email: approvisionnements@ville.quebec.qc.ca

Service de la planification stratégique & du développement organisationnel
2, rue des Jardins
Québec, QC G1R 4S9
418-641-6373
directiongenerale@ville.quebec.qc
Waste Management:
Dry waste drop-off site: 336, rue Charles-Marchand; Paint: Centre de rénovation Prud'homme, 444, rue Notre-Dame
Recycling: Both Curbside & Depot
Hazardous Waste Depot or Facility: No
Water & Wastewater Treatment:
Water treatment: 535, rue La Traverse, 450-470-3870; Wastewater plant: 45, rue Lebel, 450-470-3880

City of Repentigny
435, boul Iberville
Repentigny, QC J6A 2B6
450-470-3000
Fax: 450-470-3082
communication@ville.repentigny.qc.ca
www.ville.repentigny.qc.ca
Population: 82,000 *Census Year:* 2011
Number of Households: 20,499
Daniel L'Écuyer, Directeur général, 450-470-3110, email: direction-generale@ville.repentigny.qc.ca
David Legault, Directeur, Permis, inspections et urbanisme, 450-470-3840, email: permis@ville.repentigny.qc.ca
Denis Larose, Directeur, Incendie, 450-470-3620, email: incendie@ville.repentigny.qc.ca
Sylvie Bouchard, Directrice, Travaux publics, 450-470-3800, email: travaux-publics@ville.repentigny.qc.ca
Sylviane DiFolco, Directrice, Loisirs, culture et vie communautaire, 450-470-3400, email: loisirs@ville.repentigny.qc.ca
Ghislain Bélanger, Directeur, Développement économique et services techniques, 450-470-3150, email: belangerg@ville.repentigny.qc.ca
Waste Management:
Transfer Station(s): 139, de la rue Louvain
Hazardous Waste Depot or Facility: 134, ch des Commissaires, L'Assomption
Composters subsidized: Yes
Water & Wastewater Treatment:
Water treatment at 535, rue de la Traverse, 450/654-2369; Wastewater treatment at 428, rue Notre-Dame, 450/654-2468
Other Initiatives:
Dye or paint products can be dropped off at Centre de rénovation Prud-homme, 444, rue Notre-Dame

City of Rimouski
CP 710
205, av de la Cathédrale
Rimouski, QC G5L 7C7
418-724-3126
Fax: 418-724-3183
communications@ville.rimouski.qc.ca
www.ville.rimouski.qc.ca
Population: 46,860 *Census Year:* 2011
Number of Households: 15,159
Waste Management:
Contracted to Sanibelle Inc., 418/724-6447
Number of landfill sites: 2*Landfill Capacity:* 50 years
Solid Waste Disposal Fees: $38.30/capita
Recycling: Both Curbside & Depot; Colisee depot
Special Bans/by-laws: Pesticide ban, water restrictions
Hazardous Waste Depot or Facility: Annual collection
Water & Wastewater Treatment:
Household water is treated
Other Initiatives:
New Eco-centre; New landfill

City of Rivière-du-Loup
CP 37
65, rue de l'Hôtel-de-Ville
Rivière-du-Loup, QC G5R 3Y7
418-867-6700
Fax: 418-862-2817
www.ville.riviere-du-loup.qc.ca
Population: 19,447 *Census Year:* 2011
Number of Households: 8,254
Gérald Tremblay, Directeur, Travaux publics, 418-862-2121, Fax: 418-867-6096, email: gerald.tremblay@ville.riviere-du-loup.qc.ca

Municipal Governments

Éric Côté, Directeur, Environnement et développement durable, 418-867-6663, email: eric.cote@ville-riviere-du-loup.qc.ca
Waste Management:
Sanibele, 418/862-9017
Number of landfill sites: 1 *Landfill Capacity:* 50 years
Solid Waste Disposal Fees: $43.50/tonne
Hazardous Waste Depot or Facility: No
Compost Sites: Yes *Composters subsidized:* No
Water & Wastewater Treatment:
Usine de filtration, eau potable, 100, rue Delage; E'tangs aérés, 300, Bellevue

City of Roberval
851, boul St-Joseph
Roberval, QC G8H 2L6
418-275-0202
Fax: 418-275-5031
vroberval@ville.roberval.qc.ca
www.ville.roberval.qc.ca
Population: 10,227 *Census Year:* 2011
Number of Households: 4,386
Water & Wastewater Treatment:
Water treatment: Usine d'eau potable, 770, boul de la Traversée, Roberval; Wastewater: Usine de prétraitement, 201, rue Côté, Roberval

City of Rosemère
100, rue Charbonneau
Rosemère, QC J7A 3W1
450-621-3500
Fax: 450-621-7601
info@ville.rosemere.qc.ca
ville.rosemere.qc.ca
Population: 14,294 *Census Year:* 2011
Number of Households: 4,839
Michel Gagné, Directeur général, 450-621-3500, email: mgagne@ville.rosemere.qc.ca
Luce Jacques, Trésorière, 450-621-3500, email: ljacques@ville.rosemere.qc.ca
Waste Management:
Waste collection contracted to Entr. Sanitaire F.A. Ltée., 514/661-5080
Solid Waste Disposal Fees: $23/tonne
Special Bans/by-laws: Regulations on pesticide use; drinking water, runoff.
Hazardous Waste Depot or Facility: 190, rue Charbonneau
Water & Wastewater Treatment:
Water treatment plant, 450-621-6630; Wastewater treatment plant, Rosemère-Lorraine, 450-621-6630

City of Rouyn-Noranda
CP 220
100, rue Taschereau est
Rouyn-Noranda, QC J9X 5C3
819-797-7110
Fax: 819-797-7108
www.ville.rouyn-noranda.qc.ca
Population: 41,012 *Census Year:* 2011
Number of Households: 13,967
Denis Charron, Directeur général, 819-797-7110, Fax: 819-797-7108
Noël Lanouette, Directeur, Travaux publics et services techniques, 819-797-7110, Fax: 819-797-7153
Waste Management:
Large items accepted at Éco-centre; Motor oil accepted at Canadian Tire; Fluorescents accepted at Norama Industries; Batteries accepted at La Sources; Expired drugs accepted at pharmacies
Recycling: Both Curbside & Depot
Hazardous Waste Depot or Facility: Éco-centre Arthur Gagnon, 210, av Marcel Baril
Water & Wastewater Treatment:
Water filtration plant located at 2, 9e rue
Other Initiatives:
Opération grand nettoyage in the fall

City of Saguenay
CP 129
201, rue Racine est
Chicoutimi, QC G7H 5B8
418-698-3000
Fax: 418-541-4524
info@ville.saguenay.qc.ca
www.ville.saguenay.qc.ca
Population: 144,746 *Census Year:* 2011
Jean-François Boivin, Directeur général, 418-698-3320, Fax: 418-541-4524
Sylvie Jean, Directrice, Approvisionnements, 418-698-3055, Fax: 418-546-2114
Denis Coulombe, Directeur, Aménagement du territoire et urbanisme, 418-698-3130, Fax: 418-698-1158
Claude Bouchard, Directeur, Hydro-Jonquière, 418-698-3370, Fax: 418-546-2068
Jean Morneau, Directeur, Immeubles et équipements motorisés, 418-698-3060, Fax: 418-698-3069
Pierre Racine, Directeur, Sports et du plein air, 418-698-3000, Fax: 418-699-6095
Carol Girard, Directeur, Sécurité incendie, 418-698-3380, Fax: 418-698-3389
Denis Simard, Directeur, Travaux publics, 418-698-3180, Fax: 418-698-3189
Waste Management:
Waste collection contracted to Matrec, 418/549-8074 & Service Sanitaire R. Bonneau, 1-800-590-2615
Solid Waste Disposal Fees: $66/tonne
Recycling: 5 depots
Hazardous Waste Depot or Facility: No
Compost Sites: Yes *Composters subsidized:* Yes
Water & Wastewater Treatment:
Water filtration plants at Chicoutimi, Arvida & Jonquière; Wastewater plants at Chicoutimi, Jonquière & La Baie
Other Initiatives:
Plan de gestion des matieres residuelles sera mis á jour dans les proclaires mors

City of Saint-Basile-le-Grand
204, rue Principale
Saint-Basile-le-Grand, QC J3N 1M1
450-461-8000
Fax: 450-461-8029
communciations@ville.saint-basile-le-grand.qc.ca
www.ville.saint-basile-le-grand.qc.ca
Population: 16,736 *Census Year:* 2011
Number of Households: 4,392
Jean-Marie Beaupré, Directeur général, 450-461-8000, Fax: 450-461-8039, email: direction.generale@ville.saint-basile-le-grand.qc.
Marc-André Lehoux, Directeur, Loisirs, culture et vie communautaire
Waste Management:
Recycling: Both Curbside & Depot
Hazardous Waste Depot or Facility: Édifice Léon-Taillon, yearly drop-off, 450-461-8046

City of Saint-Constant
147, rue St-Pierre
Saint-Constant, QC J5A 2G2
450-638-2010
Fax: 450-638-5919
communications@ville.saint-constant.qc.ca
www.ville.saint-constant.qc.ca
Population: 24,980 *Census Year:* 2011
Number of Households: 7,720
Vacant, Responsable, Travaux publics, 450-638-2010, Fax: 450-632-0072, email: travaux_publics@ville.saint-constant.qc.ca
Jean Gariépy, Directeur et chef, Brigade des pompiers
Sylvain Boulianne, Coordonnateur, Mesures d'urgence
Waste Management:
Éco-centre: 25, montée Lasaline
Recycling: Depot
Other Initiatives:
Bac roulant de 360 litres

City of Saint-Eustache
145, rue St-Louis
Saint-Eustache, QC J7R 1X9
450-974-5000
Fax: 450-974-5229
communications@ville.saint-eustache.qc.ca
www.ville.saint-eustache.qc.ca
Population: 44,154 *Census Year:* 2011
Number of Households: 15,821
Ginette Lacoix, Trésorière, 450-974-5070, Fax: 450-974-5077
Stéphanie Bouchard, Directrice, Communications, 450-974-5220, Fax: 450-974-5223, email: communications@ville.saint-eustache.qc.ca
Waste Management:
Waste collection cntracted to Rebus Canada, 514/648-8815
Solid Waste Disposal Fees: $23/tonne
Clean Fill Fee: Yes; $5/cubic metre
Hazardous Waste Depot or Facility: Garage municipal
Compost Sites: Yes
Water & Wastewater Treatment:
Wastewater treatment plant at 50, 25e av; Filtration plant at 45, rue Chénier; Water treatment contracted to Simo Management Inc., 514/384-5660

City of Saint-Félicien
CP 7000
1209, boul Sacré-Coeur
Saint-Félicien, QC G8K 2R5
418-679-0251
Fax: 418-679-1449
dir.general@ville.stfelicien.qc.ca
www.ville.stfelicien.qc.ca
Population: 10,278 *Census Year:* 2011
Number of Households: 4,251
Olivier de Launière, Directeur, Protection contre les incendies, 418-679-0313, Fax: 418-679-8217, email: sincendie@ville.st-felicien.qc.ca
Jacynthe Duplain, Secrétaire administrative, Aménagement et entretien du territoire, 418-679-2100, Fax: 418-679-4083, email: urbanisme@ville.stfelicien.qc.ca

City of Saint-Georges
11700, boul Lacroix
Saint-Georges, QC G5Y 1L3
418-228-5555
Fax: 418-228-3855
www.ville.saint-georges.qc.ca
Population: 31,173 *Census Year:* 2011
Number of Households: 9,149
Marcel Grondin, Directeur général, email: marcel.grondin@ville.saint-georges.qc.ca
Waste Management:
Responsibility of the Régie intermunicipale du comté de Beauce-Sud; Collection contracted to GS Gestion des déchets
Recycling: Curbside
Hazardous Waste Depot or Facility: No
Water & Wastewater Treatment:
Water treatment contracted to Aquatech, 418/228-6640; Water treatment plant, 14800, 1ère av, St-Georges, 418/228-6640; Wastewater treatment plant, 400, av Chaudière, St-Georges, 418/228-4841

City of Saint-Hyacinthe
CP 10
700, av de l'Hôtel-de-Ville
Saint-Hyacinthe, QC J2S 5B2
450-778-8300
Fax: 450-778-8628
communications@ville.st-hyacinthe.qc.ca
www.ville.st-hyacinthe.qc.ca
Population: 53,236 *Census Year:* 2011
Number of Households: 18,279
Hélène Beauchesne, Greffière, 450-778-8317, Fax: 450-778-2514
Louis Bilodeau, Directeur général, email: louis.bilodeau@ville.st-hyacinthe.qc.ca
Chantal Frigon, Directrice générale adjointe, 450-778-8304, email: chantal.frigon@ville.st-hyacinthe.qc.ca
Yvan Gatien, Directeur, Urbanisme, 450-778-8321, Fax: 450-778-5820, email: urbanisme@ville.st-hyacinthe.qc.ca
Daniel Dubois, Directeur, Sécurité incendie, 450-778-8550, Fax: 450-778-5853, email: daniel.dubois@ville.st.hyacinthe.qc.ca
Waste Management:
Recycling: Both Curbside & Depot
Hazardous Waste Depot or Facility: No
Water & Wastewater Treatment:
Sewage & wastewater treatment plant, Email: usine-epuration@ville.st.-hyacinthe.qc.ca; Water filtration plant, 450/778-8373, Email: usine-filtration@ville.st.-hyacinthe.qc.ca

City of Saint-Jean-sur-Richelieu
CP 1025
188, rue Jacques-Cartier nord
Saint-Jean-sur-Richelieu, QC J3B 7B2
450-357-2100
Fax: 450-357-2362
info@ville.saint-jean-sur-richelieu.qc.ca
www.ville.saint-jean-sur-richelieu.qc.ca
Population: 92,394 *Census Year:* 2011
Number of Households: 33,897
Roch Arbour, Directeur, Travaux publics, 450-357-2238, Fax: 450-357-2290

Luc Castonguay, Directeur, Urbanisme, email: urbanisme@ville.saint-jean-sur-richelieu.qc.ca

City of Saint-Jérôme
#301, 10, rue St-Joseph
Saint-Jérôme, QC J7Z 7G7
450-436-1511
Fax: 450-436-6626
info@vsj.ca
www.ville.saint-jerome.qc.ca
Population: 68,456 *Census Year:* 2011
Number of Households: 12,141
Éric Lachapelle, Directeur général
Fernand Boudreault, Directeur, Travaux publics
Richard St-Jean, Directeur, Urbanisme
Waste Management:
Écocentre, rue Lajeunesse & de l'Industrie; Tricentris, 601, ch Félix-Touchette, Lachute J8H 2C5, 450-562-4488
Recycling: Both Curbside & Depot
Hazardous Waste Depot or Facility: No
Other Initiatives:
Cèdres Recyclés (cedar trees pick up); Composting program

City of Saint-Lazare
1960, ch Ste-Angélique
Saint-Lazare, QC J7T 3A3
450-424-8000
Fax: 450-455-4712
info@ville.saint-lazare.qc.ca
www.ville.saint-lazare.qc.ca
Population: 19,295 *Census Year:* 2011
Number of Households: 4,361
Nathaly Rayneault, Greffière
Claude La Rue, Directeur, Travaux publics
Waste Management:
Recycling: Both Curbside & Depot
Hazardous Waste Depot or Facility: No
Other Initiatives:
Since Nov. 2000, the Town of St. Lazare prohibits the use of pesticides for cosmetic purposes. Since that time, residents dealing with major infestation problems must apply for a temporary spraying permit with the town's Urban Planning & Zoning departments.

City of Saint-Lin-Laurentides
900, 12e av
Saint-Lin-Laurentides, QC J5M 2W2
450-439-3130
Fax: 450-439-1525
saint-lin-laurentides.com
Population: 17,463 *Census Year:* 2011
Number of Households: 4,864
André Héroux, Directeur, Travaux publics
Jean-Pierre Desjardins, Directeur, Incendies
Waste Management:
Construction material drop-off, Ste-Sophie (1-800-267-1251), Service fee
Recycling: Both Curbside & Depot
Hazardous Waste Depot or Facility: No

City of Sainte-Anne-des-Plaines
139, boul Ste-Anne
Sainte-Anne-des-Plaines, QC J0N 1H0
450-478-0211
Fax: 450-478-5660
info@ville.ste-anne-des-plaines.qc.ca
www.ville.ste-anne-des-plaines.qc.ca
Population: 14,535 *Census Year:* 2011
Number of Households: 4,282
Paul Fournier, Directeur, Travaux publics
Water & Wastewater Treatment:
Water treatment at 3, boul Ste-Anne, 450/478-5373; Municipal aqueduct at 146, rue Chaumont, 450/478-0414

City of Sainte-Catherine
5465, boul Marie-Victorin
Sainte-Catherine, QC J5C 1M1
450-632-0590
Fax: 450-632-3298
information@ville.sainte-catherine.qc.ca
www.ville.sainte-catherine.qc.ca
Population: 16,762 *Census Year:* 2011
Number of Households: 5,891

City of Sainte-Julie
1580, ch du Fer-à-Cheval
Sainte-Julie, QC J3E 2M1
450-922-7111
Fax: 450-922-7108
communications@ville.sainte-julie.qc.ca
www.ville.sainte-julie.qc.ca
Population: 30,104 *Census Year:* 2011
Number of Households: 9,455
Pierre Bernardin, Directeur général, 450-922-7102, email: dirgen@ville.sainte-julie.qc.ca
Denyse Journault, Directrice, Communications, 450-922-7092, email: communications@ville.sainte-julie.qc.ca
Pierre-Luc Blanchard, Directeur, Urbanisme, 450-922-7142, email: urbanisme@ville.sainte-julie.qc.ca
Waste Management:
Contact: 100, rue de Murano
Hazardous Waste Depot or Facility: No
Other Initiatives:
Computer information, c/o Club informatique, 450-653-4871

City of Sainte-Marie
270, av Marguerite-Bourgeoys
Sainte-Marie, QC G6E 3Z3
418-387-2301
Fax: 418-387-2454
info@sainte-marie.ca
www.ville.sainte-marie.qc.ca
Population: 12,889 *Census Year:* 2011
Number of Households: 4,442
Louis Normand, Directeur général, 418-387-2301
Maurice Mercier, Directeur, Travaux publics, 418-387-6111

City of Sainte-Thérèse
CP 100
6, rue de l'Église
Sainte-Thérèse, QC J7E 4H7
450-434-1440
Fax: 450-434-1499
info@sainte-therese.ca
www.ville.sainte-therese.qc.ca
Population: 26,025 *Census Year:* 2011
Number of Households: 10,879
Waste Management:
Recycling: Curbside
Compost Sites: Yes
Water & Wastewater Treatment:
111, boul Curé-Labelle, Rosemère J7A 4C1
Other Initiatives:
No pesticides/herbicides allowed - free consulting service

City of Salaberry-de-Valleyfield
61, rue Ste-Cécile
Salaberry-de-Valleyfield, QC J6T 1L8
450-370-4300
communications@ville.valleyfield.qc.ca
www.ville.valleyfield.qc.ca
Population: 40,077 *Census Year:* 2011
Number of Households: 12,350
Pierre Chevrier, Directeur général, 450-370-4800, Fax: 450-370-4343, email: pierre.chevrier@ville.valleyfield.qc.ca
Michel Ménard, Directeur, Sécurité incendie, 450-370-4750, Fax: 450-370-4755, email: securiteincendie@ville.valleyfield.qc.ca
Denis Larochelle, Directeur, Eau et environnement/Travaux publics, 450-370-4820, Fax: 450-370-4370, email: gestionduterritoire@ville.valleyfield.qc.ca
Danielle Prieur, Coordonnatrice, 450-370-4875, Fax: 450-370-4343, email: communications@ville.valleyfield.qc.ca
Waste Management:
Contact: 978 & 1000 boul Cadieux, 450-370-4230
Recycling: Both Curbside & Depot
Water & Wastewater Treatment:
Water treatment plant: 64, av du Centenaire

City of Sept-îles
546, av De Quen
Sept-îles, QC G4R 2R4
418-962-2525
Fax: 418-964-3213
info@ville.sept-iles.qc.ca
www.ville.sept-iles.qc.ca
Population: 25,686 *Census Year:* 2011
Number of Households: 10,738

City of La Corporation de protection de l'environnement de Sept-Iles (CPESI)
498, av Brochu
Sept-Iles, QC G4R 2W8
418-962-1316
Fax: 418-968-4176
cpesi@cgocable.ca
www.ville.sept-iles.qc.ca
Waste Management:
Recycling: Both Curbside & Depot

City of Shawinigan
CP 400
550, av de l'Hôtel-de-Ville
Shawinigan, QC G9N 6V3
819-536-7200
Fax: 819-536-7255
information@shawinigan.ca
www.shawinigan.ca
Population: 50,060 *Census Year:* 2011
Number of Households: 9,373
Gaétan Béchard, Directeur général, 819-536-7211, email: directiongenerale@shawinigan.ca
Réal Beauchamp, Directeur général adjoint, 819-536-7211, email: directiongenerale@shawinigan.ca
Vacant, Directeur, Aménagement et de l'environnement, 819-536-7211, email: urbanisme@shawinigan.ca
François St-Onge, Directeur, Communications, 819-536-7211, email: fstonge@shawinigan.ca
Pierre Godin, Directeur, Travaux publics, 819-536-7211, email: travauxpublics@shawinigan.ca
Claude Larocque, Directeur, Techniques, 819-536-7211, email: servicestechniques@shawinigan.ca
François Lelièvre, Directeur, Sécurité incendie, 819-538-2248, email: incendie@shawinigan.ca
Waste Management:
La Ressourcerie, 2132, av de la Transmission, 819-537-8737; Éco-centre
Recycling: Both Curbside & Depot

City of Sherbrooke
CP 610
191, rue du Palais
Sherbrooke, QC J1H 5H9
819-821-5500
Fax: 819-822-6064
www.ville.sherbrooke.qc.ca
Population: 154,601 *Census Year:* 2011
Number of Households: 40,473
Gaétan Labbé, Directeur, Protection des incendies, 819-821-5514, Fax: 819-821-5516, email: protection.incendies@ville.sherbrooke.qc.ca

Arrondissement de Jacques-Cartier
Water & Wastewater Treatment:
Water & wastewater treatment plant operated by Régie intermunicipale des eaux usées, 2275, Claude Giffard, Sherbrooke, 819/823-5562, Email: info@raers.qc.ca

City of Sorel-Tracy
CP 368
71, rue Charlotte
Sorel-Tracy, QC J3P 7K1
450-780-5600
Fax: 450-780-5625
info@ville.sorel-tracy.qc.ca
www.ville.sorel.qc.ca
Population: 34,600 *Census Year:* 2011
Number of Households: 15,676
Mario Lazure, Directeur général, 450-780-5600
Alain Rouleau, Directeur, Sécurité incendie, 450-780-5600
Waste Management:
Construction materials: c/o Conporec, 746-9996, service fee
Other Initiatives:
Implementation of wheeled containers for garbage

City of Terrebonne
775, rue St-Jean-Baptiste
Terrebonne, QC J6W 1B5
450-961-2001
Fax: 450-471-4482
information@ville.terrebonne.qc.ca
www.ville.terrebonne.qc.ca
Population: 106,322 *Census Year:* 2011
Number of Households: 16,301
Denis Lévesque, Directeur général
Jacques Bérubé, Directeur, Incendie
Michel Sarrazin, Directeur, Travaux publics

Other Initiatives:
Environmental policy: Plan vert

City of Thetford Mines
CP 489
144, rue Notre-Dame sud
Thetford Mines, QC G6G 5T3
418-335-2981
Fax: 418-335-7089
infos@ville.thetfordmines.qc.ca
www.ville.thetfordmines.qc.ca
Population: 25,709 *Census Year:* 2011
Number of Households: 7,864
René Soucy, Directeur général, email: dirgen@ville.thetfordmines.qc.ca
Waste Management:
Transport ordurier de la région de L'Amiante; 2951 2076 Québec inc.; Services Sanitaires Denis Fortier
Recycling: Curbside
Other Initiatives:
Centre de tri: Récupération Frontenac inc., 418/338-8551

City of Trois-Rivières
CP 368
1325, place de l'Hôtel-de-Ville
Trois-Rivières, QC G9A 5H3
819-374-2002
Fax: 819-372-4631
info@v3r.net
www.v3r.net
Population: 131,338 *Census Year:* 2011
Number of Households: 25,400
Michel Byette, Directeur général, 819-372-4608, Fax: 819-372-4631, email: directiongenerale@v3r.net
Pierre Desjardins, Directeur, Aménagement, gestion et développement durable du territoire, 819-372-4626, Fax: 819-375-5865, email: urbanisme@v3r.net
Vincent Fortier, Directeur, Techniques, 819-372-4627, Fax: 819-374-6646
Ghislain Lachance, Directeur, Travaux publics, 819-379-3733

City of Val-d'Or
CP 400
855, 2e av
Val-d'Or, QC J9P 4P4
819-824-9613
Fax: 819-825-6650
info@ville.valdor.qc.ca
www.ville.valdor.qc.ca
Population: 31,862 *Census Year:* 2011
Number of Households: 10,580
Guy Faucher, Directeur général, 819-824-9613
Waste Management:
Recycling: Both Curbside & Depot
Hazardous Waste Depot or Facility: No
Water & Wastewater Treatment:
Usine d'épuration, 1500, chemin des Eaux-Nettes, Val-d'Or, QC, J9P 4N7, phone & fax: 819/874-8722
Other Initiatives:
Info-Récup, 819/874-8378

City of Varennes
CP 5000
175, rue Ste-Anne
Varennes, QC J3X 1T5
450-652-9888
Fax: 450-652-2655
general@ville.varennes.qc.ca
ville.varennes.qc.ca
Population: 20,994 *Census Year:* 2011
Number of Households: 7,019
Denis Guay, Directeur, Travaux publics
Denis Marchand, Directeur, Urbanisme
Waste Management:
Waste collection responsibility of the MRC de Lajemmerais; Waste collection contracted to Services Matrec Inc.
Hazardous Waste Depot or Facility: 1850 Marie-Victorin (once a year)
Water & Wastewater Treatment:
Water treatment responsibility of the Régie intermunicipale de l'eau potable Varennes - Sainte-Julie - Saint-Amable, 514/652-2052; Usine de filtration, 1870 boul Marie-Victorin, Varennes; Wastewater treatment responsibility of the city

City of Vaudreuil-Dorion
#200, 2555, rue Dutrisac
Vaudreuil-Dorion, QC J7V 7E6
450-455-3371
Fax: 450-424-8540
courriel@ville.vaudreuil-dorion.qc.ca
www.ville.vaudreuil-dorion.qc.ca
Population: 33,305 *Census Year:* 2011
Number of Households: 8,078
Luc Duval, Directeur, Travaux publics
Waste Management:
Contact: 325, rue Marie-Curie
Hazardous Waste Depot or Facility: No
Water & Wastewater Treatment:
Contact: 2530, ch Paul-Gérin-Lajoie, 450-424-7802

City of Victoriaville
CP 370
1, rue Notre-Dame ouest
Victoriaville, QC G6P 6T2
819-758-1571
Fax: 819-758-9292
info@ville.victoriaville.qc.ca
www.ville.victoriaville.qc.ca
Population: 43,462 *Census Year:* 2011
Number of Households: 16,764
Martin Lessard, Directeur général, email: martin.lessard@ville.victoriaville.qc.ca
André Charest, Directeur, Travaux publics, 819-758-0651, email: andre.charest@ville.victoriaville.qc.ca
Jean Demers, Directeur, Gestion du territoire, 819-758-1571, email: jean.demers@ville.victoriaville.qc.ca
Waste Management:
Contact: 350, rue de la Bulstrode, 819-357-8666
Recycling: Both Curbside & Depot
Hazardous Waste Depot or Facility: No
Water & Wastewater Treatment:
Usine d'épuration des eaux Achille-Gagnon, 555, boul Jutras ouest
Other Initiatives:
3 containers: green (recyclable materials), brown (organic matters), grey (solid waste)

Other Municipalities in Québec

Abitibi
CP 214
571, 1re Rue est
Amos, QC J9T 2H3
819-732-5356
Fax: 819-732-9607
mrc@mrcabitibi.qc.ca
www.mrcabitibi.qc.ca
Population: 24,354 *Census Year:* 2011
Number of Households: 9,998
Waste Management:
Many contractors
Number of landfill sites: 12
Recycling: Curbside; 80% of households have collection
Hazardous Waste Depot or Facility: 50% of households have collection

Abitibi-Ouest
#105, 6, 8e Av est
La Sarre, QC J9Z 1N6
819-339-5671
Fax: 819-339-5400
mrcao@mrcao.qc.ca
www.mrc.ao.ca
Population: 21,003 *Census Year:* 2011
Number of Households: 9,916
Other Initiatives:
Plan de gestion des matières résiduelles; service de collecte et traitement des boues des fosses septiques

Acton
CP 99
1037, rue Beaugrand
Acton Vale, QC J0H 1A0
450-546-3256
Fax: 450-546-0525
mrc@mrcacton.qc.ca
www.mrcacton.qc.ca
Population: 15,381 *Census Year:* 2011
Number of Households: 6,443
Huguette St-Pierre-Beaulac, Préfète
Waste Management:
Several centers & organizations accept recyclable materials, composting materials & hazardous waste
Recycling: Both Curbside & Depot
Water & Wastewater Treatment:
7 centres to treat sludge
Other Initiatives:
3 collections: regular household waste, recyclable waste, organic materials

Antoine-Labelle
425, rue du Pont
Mont-Laurier, QC J9L 2R6
819-623-3485
Fax: 819-623-5052
administration@mrc-antoine-labelle.qc.ca
www.mrc-antoine-labelle.qc.ca
Population: 35,159 *Census Year:* 2011
Number of Households: 20,803

Argenteuil
430, rue Grace
Lachute, QC J8H 1M6
450-562-2474
Fax: 450-562-1911
mrc@argenteuil.qc.ca
www.argenteuil.qc.ca
Population: 32,117 *Census Year:* 2011
Number of Households: 16,069
Water & Wastewater Treatment:
Responsibility of MRC
Other Initiatives:
Implementation of Plan de gestion des matières résiduelles

Arthabaska
40, rte de la Grande-Ligne
Victoriaville, QC G6T 0E6
819-752-2444
Fax: 819-752-3623
info@mrc-arthabaska.qc.ca
www.mrc-arthabaska.qc.ca
Population: 69,237 *Census Year:* 2011
Number of Households: 27,471

Avignon
CP 128
470, rue Francoeur
Nouvelle, QC G0C 2E0
418-794-2221
Fax: 418-794-2076
info@mrcavignon.com
www.mrcavignon.com
Population: 15,246 *Census Year:* 2011
Number of Households: 7,093

Batiscan
395, rue Principale
Batiscan, QC G0X 1A0
418-362-2421
Fax: 418-362-3174
municipalite@batiscan.ca
www.batiscan.ca
Population: 940 *Census Year:* 2011

Beauce-Sartigan
2727, 6e Av
Saint-Georges, QC G5Y 3Y1
418-228-8418
Fax: 418-228-3709
mrcbsart@globetrotter.net
Population: 50,962 *Census Year:* 2011
Number of Households: 19,293

Beauharnois-Salaberry
#200, 660, rue Ellice
Beauharnois, QC J6N 1Y1
450-225-0870
Fax: 450-225-0872
info@mrc-beauharnois-salaberry.com
www.mrc-beauharnois-salaberry.com
Population: 61,950 *Census Year:* 2011
Number of Households: 25,986
Yves Daoust, Préfet

Waste Management:
Number of landfill sites: 1
Hazardous Waste Depot or Facility: No
Composters subsidized: Yes
Water & Wastewater Treatment:
Responsibility of MRC
Other Initiatives:
Implementation of Plan de gestion des matières résiduelles; Automated collection of recyclable materials; Promotion of composting; New garbage containers for household waste

Bécancour
#1, 3689, boul Bécancour
Bécancour, QC G9H 3W7
819-298-2070
Fax: 819-298-2041
info@mrcbecancour.qc.ca
Population: 20,081 *Census Year:* 2011
Number of Households: 8,500

Bellechasse
100, rue Monseigneur-Bilodeau
Saint-Lazare-de-Bellechasse, QC G0R 3J0
418-883-3347
Fax: 418-883-2555
clement@mrcbellechasse.qc.ca
www.mrcbellechasse.qc.ca
Population: 35,318 *Census Year:* 2011
Number of Households: 13,109
Waste Management:
Waste management responsibiltiy of MRC de Bellechasse; Garbage trucks belong to the MRC; Collection handled by Campor inc. for MRC de Bellechasse, Montmagny & Les Etchemins; Landfill site in Armagh

Bonaventure
CP 310
51, rue Notre-Dame
New Carlisle, QC G0C 1Z0
418-752-6601
Fax: 418-752-6657
mrcbonav@globetrotter.net
www.mrcbonaventure.com
Population: 18,000 *Census Year:* 2011
Number of Households: 7,808
Water & Wastewater Treatment:
All municipal water responsibility of MRC

Brome-Missisquoi
749, rue Principale
Cowansville, QC J2K 1J8
450-266-4900
Fax: 450-266-6141
administration@mrcbm.qc.ca
www.brome-missisquoi.ca
Population: 55,621 *Census Year:* 2011
Number of Households: 22,500
Arthur Fauteux, Préfet
Waste Management:
Landfill operated by Régie Intermunicipale d'Élimination de Déchets Solides de Brome-Missisquoi
Other Initiatives:
Implementation of Plan de gestion des matières résiduelles; Publications: Guide pratique de la récupération, Prendre en main nos déchets, Dépliant sur l'herbicyclage

Charlevoix
#201, 4, place de l'Église
Baie-Saint-Paul, QC G3Z 1T2
418-435-2639
Fax: 418-435-2666
mrc@charlevoix.net
www.mrc-charlevoix.com
Population: 13,338 *Census Year:* 2011
Number of Households: 5,924
Dominic Tremblay, Préfet
Waste Management:
Waste management responsibility of the MRC; Landfill operated by the MRC

Charlevoix-Est
172, boul Notre-Dame
Clermont, QC G4A 1G1
418-439-3947
Fax: 418-439-2502
direction@mrccharlevoixest.ca
www.mrccharlevoixest.ca
Population: 16,240 *Census Year:* 2011
Number of Households: 6,893

Coaticook
294, rue St-Jacques nord
Coaticook, QC J1A 2R3
819-849-9166
Fax: 819-849-4320
secretariat@mrcdecoaticook.qc.ca
www.mrcdecoaticook.qc.ca
Population: 18,847 *Census Year:* 2011
Number of Households: 7,764
Waste Management:
Number of landfill sites: 1*Landfill Capacity:* 30 years
Recycling: Curbside
Other Initiatives:
Implementation of an Eco-centre; Septic tank policy for municipalities; Implementation of Plan de gestion des matières résiduelles; Environmental brochures; Metal containers for paint cans

D'Autray
CP 1500
550, rue De Montcalm
Berthierville, QC J0K 1A0
450-836-7007
Fax: 450-836-1576
mrcautray@mrcautray.com
www.mrcautray.com
Population: 41,650 *Census Year:* 2011
Number of Households: 17,733
Gaétan Gravel, Préfet
Waste Management:
Landfill owned by Groupe EBI
Hazardous Waste Depot or Facility: No
Other Initiatives:
Implementation of Plan de gestion des matières résiduelles; Septic tank policy; Collection of composting materials

Deux-Montagnes
1, place de la Gare
Saint-Eustache, QC J7R 0B4
450-491-1818
Fax: 450-491-3040
info@mrc2m.qc.ca
Population: 95,670 *Census Year:* 2011
Number of Households: 31,295

Drummond
436, rue Lindsay
Drummondville, QC J2B 1G6
819-477-2230
Fax: 819-477-8442
courriel@mrcdrummond.qc.ca
www.mrcdrummond.qc.ca
Population: 98,681 *Census Year:* 2011
Number of Households: 38,271
Francine Ruest Jutras, Préfète
Other Initiatives:
Implementation of Plan de gestion des matières résiduelles: En vert et avec tous; No new landfill will be authorized; Reuse & recycle 65% of solid waste

Joliette
632, rue De Lanaudière
Joliette, QC J6E 3M7
450-759-2237
Fax: 450-759-2597
info@mrcjoliette.qc.ca
www.mrcjoliette.qc.ca
Population: 63,551 *Census Year:* 2011
Number of Households: 23,191

Kamouraska
CP 1120
425, av Patry
Saint-Pascal, QC G0L 3Y0
418-492-1660
Fax: 418-492-2220
info@mrckamouraska.com
www.kamouraska.com
Population: 21,492 *Census Year:* 2011
Number of Households: 10,074

L'Assomption
300A, rue Dorval
L'Assomption, QC J5W 3A1
450-589-2288
Fax: 450-589-9430
mrcinfo@mrclassomption.qc.ca
www.mrclassomption.qc.ca
Population: 119,840 *Census Year:* 2011
Number of Households: 38,815
Waste Management:
Hazardous Waste Depot or Facility: No
Other Initiatives:
Implementation of Plan de gestion des matières résiduelles; High waste recovery objectives; Promotion of recycling & composting

L'Érable
#300, 1783, av St-Édouard
Plessisville, QC G6L 3S7
819-362-2333
Fax: 819-362-9150
info@mrc-erable.qc.ca
www.mrc-erable.qc.ca
Population: 23,366 *Census Year:* 2011
Number of Households: 10,294
Other Initiatives:
Implementation of Plan de gestion des matières résiduelles; Reclaim 65% of recoverable residual material; Promote recycling, reusing, reducing & composting; Establish a waste sorting & recovery centre

L'Islet
34-A, rue Fortin
Saint-Jean-Port-Joli, QC G0R 3G0
418-598-3076
Fax: 418-598-6880
administration@mrclislet.com
www.mrclislet.com
Population: 18,517 *Census Year:* 2011
Number of Households: 8,944

La Côte-de-Beaupré
3, rue de la Seigneurie
Château-Richer, QC G0A 1N0
418-824-3444
Fax: 418-824-3917
info@mrccotedebeaupre.qc.ca
Population: 26,172 *Census Year:* 2011
Number of Households: 10,969

La Côte-de-Gaspé
#208, 19, rue Adams
Gaspé, QC G4X 1E5
418-368-7000
Fax: 418-368-8181
mrc@cotedegaspe.ca
mrc.cotedegaspe.ca
Population: 17,985 *Census Year:* 2011
Number of Households: 7,910

La Haute-Côte-Nord
#101, 26, rue de la Rivière
Les Escoumins, QC G0T 1K0
418-233-2102
Fax: 418-233-3010
info@mrchcn.qc.ca
www.mrchcn.qc.ca
Population: 11,546 *Census Year:* 2011
Number of Households: 5,449

La Haute-Gaspésie
464, boul Ste-Anne ouest
Sainte-Anne-des-Monts, QC G4V 1T5
418-763-7791
Fax: 418-763-7737
mrchg.rdeschenes@globetrotter.net
www.hautegaspesie.com
Population: 12,088 *Census Year:* 2011
Number of Households: 5,999

La Haute-Yamaska
#100, 142, rue Dufferin
Granby, QC J2G 4X1
450-378-9975
Fax: 450-378-2465

mrc@mrchauteyamaska.qc.ca
www.haute-yamaska.ca
Population: 85,042 *Census Year:* 2011
Number of Households: 34,103
Water & Wastewater Treatment:
Water management responsibility of MRC
Other Initiatives:
Implementaion of Plan de gestion des matières rèsiduelles; Reduce the use of landfills by 60% through reuse, recycling & composting

La Jacques-Cartier
60, rue St-Patrick
Shannon, QC G0A 4N0
418-844-2160
Fax: 418-844-2664
mrcjc@mrc.lajacquescartier.qc.ca
www.mrc.lajacquescartier.qc.ca
Population: 36,883 *Census Year:* 2011
Number of Households: 12,302
Jacques Marcotte, Préfet

La Matapédia
#501, 123, rue Desbiens
Amqui, QC G5J 3P9
418-629-2053
Fax: 418-629-3195
administration@mrcmatapedia.qc.ca
www.lamatapedia.com/mrc
Population: 18,573 *Census Year:* 2011
Number of Households: 8,575

La Mitis
300, av du Sanatorium
Mont-Joli, QC G5H 1V7
418-775-8445
Fax: 418-775-9303
mrc.mitis@cgocable.ca
www.lamitis.ca
Population: 18,942 *Census Year:* 2011
Number of Households: 9,437
Waste Management:
MRC responsible for landfill used by 11 municipalities
Other Initiatives:
Centre de formation en entreprise et récupération (CFER) managed by MRC

La Nouvelle-Beauce
#B, 700, rue Notre-Dame nord
Sainte-Marie, QC G6E 2K9
418-387-3444
Fax: 418-387-7060
mrc.lanouvellebeauce@nouvellebeauce.com
www.nouvellebeauce.com
Population: 35,107 *Census Year:* 2011
Number of Households: 9,761
Waste Management:
CRGD (Centre de récupération et de gestion des déchets), 418/397-5402; Info-environnement: 418/387-3441

La Rivière-du-Nord
#200, 161, rue de la Gare
Saint-Jérôme, QC J7Z 2B9
450-436-9321
Fax: 450-436-1977
info@mrcrivieredunord.qc.ca
www.mrcrivieredunord.qc.ca
Population: 115,165 *Census Year:* 2011
Number of Households: 40,308

La Vallée-de-l'Or
42, place Hammond
Val-d'Or, QC J9P 3A9
819-825-7733
Fax: 819-825-4137
info@mrcvo.qc.ca
www.mrcvo.qc.ca
Population: 42,896 *Census Year:* 2011
Number of Households: 18,445
Fernand Trahan, Préfet
Other Initiatives:
Implementation of Plan de gestion des matières résiduelles, Vert un mode de vie; Reduce waste by 65%, through waste reduction, recycling, reuse, composting & special collections; Septic tanks policies

La Vallée-de-la-Gatineau
7, rue de la Polyvalente
Gracefield, QC J0X 1W0
819-463-3241
Fax: 819-463-3632
info@mrcvg.qc.ca
www.mrcvg.qc.ca
Population: 20,530 *Census Year:* 2011
Number of Households: 12,828
Water & Wastewater Treatment:
Sludge from septic tanks is treated at Kazabazua purification plant, responsibility of MRC
Other Initiatives:
Implementation of Plan de gestion des matières résiduelles; Reduce use of landfills by 60% through recycling, reducing & composting

La Vallée-du-Richelieu
#100, 255, boul Laurier
McMasterville, QC J3G 0B7
450-464-0339
Fax: 450-464-3827
info@mrcvr.ca
www.vallee-du-richelieu.ca
Population: 116,773 *Census Year:* 2011
Number of Households: 45,096
Water & Wastewater Treatment:
All waters on territory managed by the MRC

Lac-Saint-Jean-Est
625, rue Bergeron ouest
Alma, QC G8B 1V3
418-668-3023
Fax: 418-668-5112
sabin.larouche@mrclac.qc.ca
www.mrclacsaintjeanest.qc.ca
Population: 52,520 *Census Year:* 2011
Number of Households: 20,367

Le Domaine-du-Roy
901, boul St-Joseph
Roberval, QC G8H 2L8
418-275-5044
Fax: 418-275-4049
administration@mrcdomaineduroy.ca
www.domaineduroy.ca
Population: 31,870 *Census Year:* 2011
Number of Households: 13,126

Le Fjord-du-Saguenay
3110, boul Martel
Saint-Honoré, QC G0V 1L0
418-673-1705
Fax: 418-673-7205
mrcdufjord@mrc-fjord.qc.ca
www.mrc-fjord.qc.ca
Population: 20,465 *Census Year:* 2011
Number of Households: 71,728

Le Granit
5090, rue Frontenac
Lac-Mégantic, QC G6B 1H3
819-583-0181
Fax: 819-583-5327
administration@mrcgranit.qc.ca
www.mrcgranit.qc.ca
Population: 22,259 *Census Year:* 2011
Number of Households: 10,237

Le Haut-Richelieu
380, 4e av
Saint-Jean-sur-Richelieu, QC J2X 1W9
450-346-3636
Fax: 450-346-8464
info@mrchr.qc.ca
mrchr.qc.ca
Population: 114,344 *Census Year:* 2011
Number of Households: 43,617
Other Initiatives:
Partnership with Comp-Haut-Richelieu; Recycling information: www.compo-haut-richelieu.qc.ca/cgi-bin/index.cgi

Le Haut-St-François
85, rue du Parc
Cookshire, QC J0B 1M0
819-875-5451
Fax: 819-875-3135
dominic.provost@hsfqc.ca
www.mrchsf.com
Population: 22,065 *Census Year:* 2011
Number of Households: 9,217
Other Initiatives:
Establish a waste sorting and recovery centre; Collection of hazardous waste; Promote composting; Public awareness program

Le Haut-St-Laurent
#400, 10, rue King
Huntingdon, QC J0S 1H0
450-264-5411
Fax: 450-264-6885
mrchsl@mrchsl.com
www.mrchsl.com
Population: 21,197 *Census Year:* 2011
Number of Households: 10,805

Le Rocher-Percé
CP 128
129, boul René-Lévesque ouest
Chandler, QC G0C 1K0
418-689-4313
Fax: 418-689-5807
mrc@rocherperce.qc.ca
www.mrcrocherperce.qc.ca
Population: 17,979 *Census Year:* 2011
Number of Households: 8,630

Le Val-St-François
CP 3160
810, montée du Parc
Richmond, QC J0B 2H0
819-826-6505
Fax: 819-826-3484
mrc@val-saint-francois.qc.ca
www.val-saint-francois.qc.ca
Population: 29,654 *Census Year:* 2011
Number of Households: 12,398
Waste Management:
All waste management, including landfill management, by the Société de gestion, d'élimination et de mise en valeur des matières résiduelles du Val-Saint-François

Les Appalaches
3830, boul Frontenac ouest
Thetford Mines, QC G6H 2L8
418-423-2757
Fax: 418-423-5122
info@mrcdesappalaches.ca
www.mrcdesappalaches.ca
Population: 43,120 *Census Year:* 2011
Number of Households: 20,795
Other Initiatives:
Implementation of Plan de gestion des matières résiduelles; Reduce waste by 65% through waste reduction, recycling, composting, increased collections, waste sorting & recovery centres

Les Basques
#400, 2, rue Jean-Rioux
Trois-Pistoles, QC G0L 4K0
418-851-3206
Fax: 418-851-3171
mrc@mrcdesbasques.com
www.mrcdesbasques.com
Population: 9,142 *Census Year:* 2011

Les Chenaux
630, rue Principale
Saint-Luc-de-Vincennes, QC G0X 3K0
819-840-0704
Fax: 819-295-5117
info@mrcdeschenaux.ca
www.mrcdeschenaux.ca
Population: 17,865 *Census Year:* 2011
Waste Management:
Régie de gestion des matières résiduelles de la Mauricie
Water & Wastewater Treatment:
All waters on the territory responsibility of the MRC
Other Initiatives:
Implementation of Plan de gestion des matières résiduelles

managed by Régie de gestion des matières résiduelles de la Mauricie

Les Collines-de-l'Outaouais
216, ch Old Chelsea
Chelsea, QC J9B 1J4
819-827-0516
Fax: 819-827-4669
gpoulin@mrcdescollines.com
www.mrcdescollines.com
Population: 46,393 *Census Year:* 2011
Number of Households: 17,364
Robert Bussière, Préfet
Water & Wastewater Treatment:
Septic tank program in collaboration with municipalities
Other Initiatives:
Implementation of Plan de gestion des matières résiduelles; Waste sorting & recovery centre managed by Cascades Récupération; Reclaim 65% of recoverable residual material; Initiate composting program

Les Etchemins
1137, rte 277
Lac-Etchemin, QC G0R 1S0
418-625-9000
Fax: 418-625-9005
mrcetchemins@sogetel.net
www.mrcetchemins.qc.ca
Population: 17,254 *Census Year:* 2011
Number of Households: 7,477

Les Jardins-de-Napierville
1767, rue Principale
Saint-Michel, QC J0L 2J0
450-454-0559
Fax: 450-454-0560
info@mrcjardinsdenapierville.ca
mrcjardinsdenapierville.ca
Population: 26,234 *Census Year:* 2011
Number of Households: 9,046

Les Laurentides
1255, ch des Lacs
Saint-Faustin-Lac-Carré, QC J0T 1J2
819-425-5555
Fax: 819-688-6590
adm@mrclaurentides.qc.ca
www.mrclaurentides.qc.ca
Population: 45,157 *Census Year:* 2011
Number of Households: 29,523
Waste Management:
Managed by Régie intermunicipale de Récupération des Hautes-Laurentides & Régie intermunicipale des déchets de la Rouge for 13 municipalities
Other Initiatives:
Implementation of Plan de gestion des matières résiduelles; Reclaim 65% of recoverable residual material; Establish a Complexe interrégional de traitement & an éco-centre; Composting program; Special attention given to tourist areas

Les Maskoutains
805, av du Palais
Saint-Hyacinthe, QC J2S 5C6
450-774-3141
Fax: 450-774-7161
admin@mrcmaskoutains.qc.ca
www.mrcmaskoutains.qc.ca
Population: 84,248 *Census Year:* 2011
Number of Households: 33,761
Waste Management:
Managed by the Régie intermunicipale de gestion des déchets de la région maskoutaine
Hazardous Waste Depot or Facility: No
Other Initiatives:
Implementation of Plan de gestion des matières résiduelles in collaboration with MRC d'Acton; Use of 3 containers: green (recyclable materials); grey (household refuse); brown (organic matter)

Les Moulins
148, rue St-André
Terrebonne, QC J6W 3C3
450-471-9576
Fax: 450-471-8193
info@mrclesmoulins.ca
www.mrclesmoulins.ca
Population: 148,813 *Census Year:* 2011
Number of Households: 39,107

Les Pays-d'en-Haut
1014, rue Valiquette
Sainte-Adèle, QC J8B 2M3
450-229-6637
Fax: 450-229-5203
info@mrcpdh.org
www.mrcpdh.com
Population: 40,331 *Census Year:* 2011
Number of Households: 23,268
Water & Wastewater Treatment:
MRC responsible for all waters on its territory
Other Initiatives:
Implementation of Plan de gestion des matières résiduelles; Recover 65% of residual materials that can be recuperated; Promotion of reduce, reuse, recycle & compost; Increase efficiency of green waste collection

Les Sources
309, rue Chassé
Asbestos, QC J1T 2B4
819-879-6643
Fax: 819-879-5188
mrcdessources@mrcdessources.com
www.mrcdessources.com
Population: 14,756 *Census Year:* 2011
Number of Households: 6,915
Jacques Hémond, Préfet
Other Initiatives:
Implementation of La Brigade verte: mrcasbestos.com/brigadeverte/index.htm

Lotbinière
6375, rue Garneau
Sainte-Croix, QC G0S 2H0
418-926-3407
Fax: 418-926-3409
info@mrclotbiniere.org
www.mrclotbiniere.org
Population: 29,617 *Census Year:* 2011
Number of Households: 11,332
Water & Wastewater Treatment:
Site d'enfouissement, 1450, rang Pointe-du-Jour, 418/728-5554, Fax: 418/728-5554

Manicouagan
768, rue Bossé
Baie-Comeau, QC G5C 1L6
418-589-9594
Fax: 418-589-6383
info@mrcmanicouagan.qc.ca
www.mrcmanicouagan.qc.ca
Population: 32,012 *Census Year:* 2011
Number of Households: 14,898

Marguerite-D'Youville
609, rte Marie-Victorin
Verchères, QC J0L 2R0
450-583-3301
Fax: 450-583-3592
info@margueritedyouville.ca
www.margueritedyouville.ca
Population: 74,416 *Census Year:* 2011
Number of Households: 37,274
Waste Management:
Garage municipal de Contrecoeur, 4884, rang du Ruisseau
Hazardous Waste Depot or Facility: No
Water & Wastewater Treatment:
Plant: 533, rue de l'Aqueduc; All waters under the jurisdiction of the MRC
Other Initiatives:
Collection of recyclable & green materials; Promotion of composting; Publications: Guide pratique de la récupération domestique; Water conservation; Pesticides policies

Maria-Chapdelaine
173, boul St-Michel
Dolbeau-Mistassini, QC G8L 4N9
418-276-2131
Fax: 418-276-7043
portail@mrcmaria.qc.ca
www.mrcdemaria-chapdelaine.ca
Population: 25,279 *Census Year:* 2011
Number of Households: 10,513

Maskinongé
651, boul St-Laurent est
Louiseville, QC J5V 1J1
819-228-9461
Fax: 819-228-2193
mrcinfo@mrc-maskinonge.qc.ca
www.mrc-maskinonge.qc.ca
Population: 36,286 *Census Year:* 2011
Number of Households: 11,261

Matane
145, rue Soucy
Matane, QC G4W 2E1
418-562-6734
Fax: 418-562-7265
mrcmatane@mrcdematane.qc.ca
Population: 21,786 *Census Year:* 2011
Number of Households: 11,025

Matawinie
3184, 1re Av
Rawdon, QC J0K 1S0
450-834-5441
Fax: 450-834-6560
administration@matawinie.org
www.matawinie.org
Population: 49,516 *Census Year:* 2011
Number of Households: 31,868
Waste Management:
Responsibility of the municipalities

Mékinac
560, rue Notre-Dame
Saint-Tite, QC G0X 3H0
418-365-5151
Fax: 418-365-7377
mrcmekinac@mrcmekinac.com
www.regionmekinac.com
Population: 12,924 *Census Year:* 2011
Number of Households: 6,026

Memphrémagog
#200, 455, rue MacDonald
Magog, QC J1X 1M2
819-843-9292
Fax: 819-843-7295
info@mrcmemphremagog.com
www.mrcmemphremagog.com
Population: 48,551 *Census Year:* 2011
Number of Households: 24,173
Other Initiatives:
Septic tank policies; Regulations for protection of lake waters from pleasure boat waste & sewage discharges; Implementation of Plan de gestion des matières résiduelles; Recovery of residual material; Promote reduce, reuse & recycle; Composting program; Public awareness campaigns; Promote composting; Regulations for pesticide use; Forestry preservation plan

Montcalm
1540, rue Albert
Sainte-Julienne, QC J0K 2T0
450-831-2182
Fax: 450-831-2647
info@mrcmontcalm.com
www.mrcmontcalm.com
Population: 48,378 *Census Year:* 2011
Number of Households: 17,528
Waste Management:
Contracted to EBI in St-Thomas-de-Joliette
Recycling: Curbside; Contracted to EBI
Hazardous Waste Depot or Facility: Sainte-Julienne
Water & Wastewater Treatment:
Not the responsibility of the MRC

Montmagny
159, rue Saint-Louis
Montmagny, QC G5V 1N5
418-248-5985
Fax: 418-248-4624
mrc@montmagny.com
www.montmagny.com
Population: 22,877 *Census Year:* 2011
Number of Households: 10,617
Other Initiatives:
Implementation of Plan de gestion des matières résiduelles; Reclaim 65% of recoverable residual material

Nicolet-Yamaska
#257, 1, rue de Mgr-Courchesne
Nicolet, QC J3T 2C1
819-293-2997
Fax: 819-293-5367
mrcny@mrcnicolet-yamaska.qc.ca
www.mrcnicolet-yamaska.qc.ca
Population: 22,798 *Census Year:* 2011
Number of Households: 10,228
Waste Management:
Waste collection outsourced to several organizations, but managed by Régie intermunicipale de gestion intégrée des déchets Bécancour Nicolet-Yamaska & Bas-St-François
Other Initiatives:
Implementation of Plan de gestion des matières résiduelles; Increase services offered; Public awareness campaigns

Papineau
266, rue Viger
Papineauville, QC J0V 1R0
819-427-6243
Fax: 819-427-8318
info@mrcpapineau.com
www.mrcpapineau.com
Population: 22,541 *Census Year:* 2011
Number of Households: 14,174
Other Initiatives:
Implementation of Plan de gestion des matières résiduelles; Recycling residual materials from forestry industry

Pierre-De Saurel
50, rue du Fort
Sorel-Tracy, QC J3P 7X7
450-743-2703
Fax: 450-743-7313
mrc@pierredesaurel.com
www.soreltracyregion.net
Population: 50,900 *Census Year:* 2011
Number of Households: 23,120
Waste Management:
Waste collection contracted to Conporec Inc., 514/746-9996
Hazardous Waste Depot or Facility: No
Other Initiatives:
Implementation of Plan de gestion des matières résiduelles; Reclaim 65% of recoverable residual material; Provide a waste sorting & recovery centre; Promote recycling, reusing & composting; Increase collections & number of containers per household

Pontiac
602, rte 301
Campbell's Bay, QC J0X 1K0
819-648-5689
Fax: 819-648-5810
mrc@mrcpontiac.qc.ca
www.mrcpontiac.qc.ca
Population: 14,358 *Census Year:* 2011
Number of Households: 8,845

Portneuf
185, rte 138
Cap-Santé, QC G0A 1L0
418-285-3744
Fax: 418-285-1703
portneuf@mrc-portneuf.qc.ca
www.portneuf.com
Population: 49,370 *Census Year:* 2011
Number of Households: 22,597
Waste Management:
Waste collections done by Service sanitaire Donat Pagé, Services sanitaires NGCDA & Services Matrec; Landfill managed by Régie intermunicipale de l'Est de Portneuf
Other Initiatives:
Septic tank policies; Implementation of Plan de gestion des matières résiduelles; Increase recycling initiatives & green waste collections; Inform & educate citizens on source reduction & reuse of residual materials; Establish a waste sorting & recovery centre; Increase household containers capacity

Régie d'aqueduc de Grand Pré
3000, Rang des chutes
Saint-Édouard-de-Maskinongé, QC J0K 2H0
819-228-0181
Fax: 819-228-0807
Population:
Number of Households: 2,000
Eve Masson, Sec.-Trés.

Régie d'aqueduc intermunicipale des Moulins
775, rue St-Jean-Baptiste
Terrebonne, QC J6W 1B5
450-471-4192
Fax: 450-471-2594
Claude Therrien, Operator

Régie d'aqueduc intermunicipale paroisse St-Pie et Notre-Dame-de-St-Hyacinthe
4740, rue Gouyn
Saint-Hyacinthe, QC J2S 1E1
450-773-3720
Fax: 450-773-5611
Jean-Luc Giard, Sec.-Trés.

Régie d'aqueduc Richelieu-Centre
765A, rue St-Joseph
Saint-Louis, QC J0G 1K0
450-788-2544
Fax: 450-788-4003
rarc@mtic.qc.ca
Ronald Jacques, Coordonateur

Régie d'assainissement des Coteaux
65, rte 338
Les Côteaux, QC J7X 1A2
450-763-0980
Fax: 450-763-1410
filt.coteau@qc.aira.com
Jacques Legault, Agent de liaison

Régie d'assainissement des eaux de Chandler, Pabos et Pabos Mills
CP 459
35, rue Commerciale ouest
Chandler, QC G0C 1K0
418-689-2221
Fax: 418-689-4963
Léandre Savoie, Sec.-Trés.

Régie d'assainissement des eaux de la région sherbrookoise
CP 610
555, rue des Grandes-Fourches sud, bloc
Sherbrooke, QC J1H 5H9
819-823-5562
Fax: 819-823-8207
info@raers.qc.ca
Population:
Number of Households: 50,000
André-P. Robert, Ing., dsa., Directeur-général, Assainissement des eaux usées
Water & Wastewater Treatment:
Responsible for the treatment of wastewater only; Wastewater treatment is contracted to Jean-Francois Audet, Aquatech, 819/566-1150, poste 202

Régie d'assainissement des eaux de la Vallée du Richelieu
300, ch Brunet
Mont-Saint-Hilaire, QC J3G 4S6
450-464-0041
Jean Tremblay, Sec.-Trés.

Régie d'assainissement des eaux du bassin de la Prairie
5000, boul Marie-Victorin
Sainte-Catherine, QC J5C 1L9
450-638-2163
Fax: 450-638-6567
Gilbert Samson, Sec.-Trés.

Régie d'assainissement des eaux du Haut-Richelieu
CP 1025
188, rue Jacques-Cartier nord
Saint-Jean-sur-Richelieu, QC J3B 7B2
450-348-2667
Fax: 450-357-2285
Jacques Jutras, Secrétaire

Régie d'assainissement des eaux Richelieu/Saint-Laurent
390, boul Poliquin
Sorel, QC J3P 5N3
Fax: 450-743-4132
Louis Cardin, Sec.-Trés.

Régie d'assainissement des eaux usées de Boischatel, L'Ange-Gardien, Château-Richer
9, côte de l'Eglise
Boischatel, QC G0A 1H0
418-822-4500
Fax: 418-822-4512
Jacques Villeneuve, Sec.-Trés.
Waste Management:
Waste collection contracted to C.S. Matrec, 418/628-8666
Composters subsidized: Yes
Water & Wastewater Treatment:
Water treatment at Regie d'assainissement des eaux usees, 66010, boul Ste-Anne, L'Ange-Guardien, G0A 2K0

Régie d'assainissement des eaux usées de la Basse-Lièvre
CP 670
57, ch de Montréal est
Masson-Angers, QC J8M 1K7
Fax: 819-986-9539
Pierre Hayes, Sec.-Trés.

Régie d'assainissement des eaux usées de Piedmont, St-Sauveur et St-Sauveur-des-Monts
2125, ch Jean Adam
Saint-Sauveur, QC J0R 1R2
450-227-2668
Fax: 450-227-8564
Patrice Normand, Sec.-Trés.

Régie d'assainissement des eaux usées Rougemont/St-Césaire
#4, 1111, av St-Paul
Saint-Césaire, QC J0L 1T0
450-469-0651
Fax: 450-469-5275
regie1996@bellnet.ca
Susie Dubois, Sec.-Trés.
Water & Wastewater Treatment:
Water management contracted to Aquatech Inc., 450/646-5270; Station d'épuration inter-municipale, 1372, rte 112, Rougemont, QC

Régie d'assainissement des eaux usées Terrebonne/Mascouche
199, ch de la Cabane Ronde
Mascouche, QC J7K 1P1
450-474-4133
Population:
Number of Households: 10,000
Luc Tremblay, Sec.-Trés.

Régie de l'eau de l'Ile Perrot
1244, boul Perrot
Notre-Dame-de-l'Ile-Perrot, QC J7V 7P2
514-425-2244
Fax: 514-425-2252
Jacob Céline, Sec.-Trés.

Régie Intermunicipale Argenteuil-Deux-Montagnes
Complex Environnemental
651, ch Félix-Touchette
Lachute, QC J8H 2C5
450-562-0778
Fax: 450-562-8482
info@riadm.ca
Daniel Mayer, Président

Régie intermunicipale d'alimentation en eau potable du Bas-St-François
CP 429
39, rue Aly
Pierreville, QC J0G 1M0
450-568-7160
Fax: 450-568-7160
Diane Précourt, Sec.-Trés.

Régie intermunicipale d'approvisionnement en eau potable de l'île centrale
CP 1170
1589, ch L'Étand-du-Nord
L'Étand-du-Nord, QC G0B 1E0

Elphège LeBlanc, Sec.-Trés., Responsable de l'alimentation en eau potable

Régie intermunicipale d'approvisionnement en eau potable Henryville/Venise
559, rue Dussault
Saint-Sébastien, QC J0J 2C0
450-244-5813
Fax: 450-244-5813
Suzanne Ouellet, Sec.-Trés.

Régie intermunicipale d'aqueduc de la vallée de Châteauguay
527, rang St-Joseph
Saint-Paul-de-Chateauguay, QC J0S 1V0
450-427-3703
Fax: 450-427-2548
Léopold Vanier, Secrétaire

Régie intermunicipale d'aqueduc du Bas-Richelieu
737, ch des Patriotes
Saint-Denis-sur-Richelieu, QC J0H 1K0
450-787-2101
Fax: 450-787-3857
Pierre Bélanger, Directeur-général

Régie intermunicipale d'aqueduc et d'égout de Lotbinière-Centre
121, rue St-André
Laurier-Station, QC G0S 1N0
418-728-3852
Fax: 418-728-4801
Jean-Paul Lemay, Usine d'épuration des eaux, 418-728-3976

Régie intermunicipale d'aqueduc Richelieu-Yamaska
517, ch Ste-Victoire
Sainte-Victoire-de-Sorel, QC J0G 1T0
450-782-3111
Fax: 450-782-2687
Michel St-Martin, Sec.-Trés.

Régie intermunicipale d'assainissement de Daveluyville
CP 187
337, rue Principale
Daveluyville, QC G0Z 1C0
819-367-3395
Fax: 819-367-3395
Gaston Bélanger, Sec.-Trés.

Régie intermunicipale d'assainissement de la Haute-Bécancour
144, rue Notre-Dame sud
Thetford Mines, QC G6G 5T3
418-423-2773
Fax: 418-335-7089
Denise Veilleux, Secrétaire

Régie intermunicipale d'assainissement des eaux usées des Desjardins
225, côte du Passage
Lévis, QC G6V 5T4
418-838-4000
Denis Fradette, Sec.-Trés.

Régie intermunicipale d'assainissement des eaux de Sainte-Thérèse et Blainville
500, rue Omer-deSerres
Blainville, QC J7C 5N6
450-435-9090
Fax: 450-435-8839
assainissement.stb@videotron.net
Diane Dubé, Sec.-Trés.
Water & Wastewater Treatment:
Régie intermunicipale d'assainissement des eaux usées de Sainte-Thérese et Blainville; Contracted to Simo Management, 514/281-1010

Régie intermunicipale d'assainissement des eaux du Trois-Rivières Métropolitain
CP 368
1325, place de l'Hôtel-de-Ville
Trois-Rivières, QC G9A 5H3
819-374-3521
Fax: 819-372-4631
Claude Doucet, Sec.-Trés.

Régie intermunicipale d'assainissement des eaux de Rosemère et de Lorraine
100, rue Charbonneau
Rosemère, QC J7A 3W1
450-621-3500
Fax: 450-621-7601
Chantal Gauvreau, Sec.-Trés.
Water & Wastewater Treatment:
Centrale de traitement de l'eau de Rosemère; Usine d'épuration de Rosemère et de Lorraine

Régie intermunicipale d'assainissement du canton de Metgermette
CP 249
735, 15e rue
Saint-Zacharie, QC G0M 2C0
418-593-3185
Fax: 418-593-3085
Sophie Fortin, Sec.-Trés.

Régie intermunicipale d'élimination de déchets solides de Brome-Missisquoi
2500 Rang St-Joseph
Cowansville, QC J2K 3G6
450-263-2351
Fax: 450-263-4977
info@riedsbm.ca
www.riedsbm.ca
Gaetan Martel, Directeur operations

Régie intermunicipale d'enfouissement sanitaire de Manicouagan
768, rue Bossé
Baie-Comeau, QC G5C 1L6
418-589-0762
Fax: 418-589-6450

Régie intermunicipale d'enfouissement sanitaire de Charlevoix-Est
119, ch Snigoll
Clermont, QC G4A 1B1
418-439-3051
Fax: 418-439-3051

Régie intermunicipale de gestion des déchets solides de Saint-Vianney et Saint-Tharcisius
CP 39
170, av Centrale
Saint-Vianney, QC G0J 3J0
418-629-4082
Fax: 418-629-4821
Adrien Beaupré, Sec.-Trés.

Régie intermunicipale de gestion des déchets solides des Etchemins
CP 10
167, route 204
Sainte-Justine, QC G0R 1Y0
418-383-5397
Fax: 418-383-5398
sjustine@sogetel.net
www.stejustine.net/
Marcel Morissette, Maire
Waste Management:
Responsibility of the Régie des déchets de CJLLR, 418/383-5397
Water & Wastewater Treatment:
Not the responsibility of the Régie

Régie intermunicipale de gestion des déchets solides de la région de Coaticook
98, rue Norton
Coaticook, QC J1A 2S8
819-849-6668
Fax: 819-849-6668
Yves Morissette, Sec.-Trés.

Régie intermunicipale de gestion des déchets de la région Maskoutaine
#201, 2200, av Pratte
Saint-Hyacinthe, QC J2S 4B6
450-774-2350
Fax: 450-774-9737
rigdrm@ntic.qc.ca
www.regiedesdechets.qc.ca
Lynda Charest, Directrice générale

Régie intermunicipale de gestion des déchets de la Mauricie
1, boul de la Gabelle
Saint-Étienne-des-Grès, QC G0X 2P0
819-373-3130
Fax: 819-694-1004

Régie intermunicipale de gestion des déchets des Chutes-de-la-Chaudière
114, rue du Pont
Saint-Lambert-de-Lauzon, QC G0S 2W0
418-889-8662
Fax: 418-889-5157
rigdcc@chutes.chaudiere.com
www.chaudiere.com/regie-dechets
Lois Fleury, Sec.-Treas.

Régie intermunicipale de gestion des déchets de la Rive-Sud de Québec
259, ch des Iles
Saint-David, QC G6V 7M5
418-837-3361
Fax: 418-837-1103
Alexandre Faber, Sec.-Trés.

Régie intermunicipale de gestion des déchets de l'Islet-Sud
366, rue Principale
Sainte-Perpétue-de-l'Islet, QC G0R 3Z0
418-359-2966
Fax: 418-359-2707
Marie-Claude Chouinard, Sec.-Trés.

Régie intermunicipale de gestion des déchets solides de l'Anse-à-Gilles
284, boul Nilus-Leclerc, Local 2
L'Islet, QC G0R 2C0
418-247-3884
Fax: 418-247-3885
Martine Fortin, Secrétaire

Régie intermunicipale de gestion des déchets solides de New Richmond, Caplan et Maria
CP 338
99, place Suzanne-Guité
New Richmond, QC G0C 2B0
418-392-5602
Fax: 418-392-5331
Benoît Roussy, Sec.-Trés.

Régie intermunicipale de gestion des déchets solides des Anses
CP 939
108, rue de l'Hôtel-de-Ville
Grande-Rivière, QC G0C 1V0
418-385-2282
Fax: 418-385-2290
Denis Beaudin, Sec.-Trés.

Régie intermunicipale de gestion des déchets du Bas St-François
38, rue Notre-Dame
Saint-François-du-Lac, QC J0G 1M0
450-568-7013
Fax: 450-568-7015

Régie intermunicipale de gestion intégrée des déchets Bécancour-Nicolet-Yamaska
8405, rue Desormeaux
Bécancour, QC G9H 2X3
819-294-2999
Fax: 819-294-2966
Manon Poliquin, Sec.-Trés.

Régie intermunicipale de l'aqueduc de Saint-Antoine
105, av Saint-Laurent
Louiseville, QC J5V 2L6

Régie intermunicipale de l'eau de Deux-Montagnes
101, 26e av
Deux-Montagnes, QC J7R 5T3
450-473-4502
Denis Berthellette, Directeur d'Exploitation
Water & Wastewater Treatment:
Responsible for water treatment for the municipalities of Deux-Montagnes, St-Marthe-sur-le-Lac, St-Joseph-du-Lac, & Pointe-Calumet since the formation of the Régie in 1987

Régie intermunicipale de l'eau de la Vallée du Richelieu
1348, ch des Patriotes
Otterburn Park, QC J3H 2B3
450-464-0348
Fax: 450-464-3827
Claude Giroux, Sec.-Trés.

Régie intermunicipale de l'eau potable Varennes, Ste-Julie, St-Amable
1870, boul Marie-Victorin
Varennes, QC J3X 1R3
450-652-2052
Fax: 450-652-3808
Normand Massicotte, Sec.-Trés.
Water & Wastewater Treatment:
Responsible for water treatment for Varennes, Sainte-Julie & Saint-Amable; Usine de filtration, 1870 Marie-Victorin, Varennes; usine d'épuration, 2630 Ste-Anne, Varennes

Régie intermunicipale de l'Est de Portneuf
212, rue Dupont est
Pont-Rouge, QC G3H 1A1
418-873-4481
Fax: 418-873-3494
Paul-Eugène Parent, Président

Régie intermunicipale de récuperation des Hautes-Laurentides
402, route 117 sud
Marchand, QC J0T 1T0
819-275-3516
Fax: 819-275-3925

Régie intermunicipale de traitement de l'eau potable Saint-Romuald/Saint-Jean
CP 43100
2175, ch du Fleuve
Saint-Romuald, QC G6W 7W9
418-839-4141
Fax: 418-839-5548
Marcel Deslandes, Directeur

Régie intermunicipale de traitement des déchets de Matawinie
3184, 1e av
Rawdon, QC J0K 1S0
450-834-5441
Fax: 450-834-6560

Régie intermunicipale des déchets de CJLLR
CP 10
Sainte-Justine, QC G0R 1Y0
418-383-5397
Fax: 418-383-5398
Gilles Vézina, Sec.-Trés.

Régie intermunicipale des déchets de la Rouge
400 Route 117 Sud
Marchand, QC J0T 1T0
819-275-3205
Fax: 819-275-2139
ridrouge@lannon.qc.ca
Johanne Bock, Directrice-générale
Waste Management:
Waste collection contracted to Intersan & Service environnementaux Lachute
Number of landfill sites: 1*Landfill Capacity:* 5 years
Solid Waste Disposal Fees: $35/tonne
Hazardous Waste Depot or Facility: Landfill site

Régie intermunicipale des déchets solides de la Lièvre
CP 160
1064, boul Industriel
Mont-Laurier, QC J9L 3G9
819-623-7382
Jimmy Brisebois, Directeur-général
Waste Management:
Waste collection contracted to Laidlaw & Service environnement taux Lachute

Régie intermunicipale du comté de Beauce-Sud
695 rang St-Joseph
Saint-Côme Linière, QC G0M 1J0
418-685-2230
Fax: 418-685-3952
Roger Turcotte, Sec.-Trés.
Waste Management:
Contracted to SSDF Inc., 418/228-7877
Number of landfill sites: 1
Solid Waste Disposal Fees: $100/tonne
Clean Fill Fee: Yes; $100/tonne
Hazardous Waste Depot or Facility: Let St. Couric Liniec
Water & Wastewater Treatment:
Regie intermunicipale du comite du Beauce Sud

Rimouski-Neigette
#220, 23, rue de l'Évêché ouest
Rimouski, QC G5L 4H4
418-724-5154
Fax: 418-725-4567
administration@mrcrimouskineigette.qc.ca
Population: 55,095 *Census Year:* 2011
Number of Households: 24,991

Rivière-du-Loup
310, rue St-Pierre
Rivière-du-Loup, QC G5R 3V3
418-867-2485
Fax: 418-867-3100
administration@mrc-riviere-du-loup.qc.ca
www.mrc-rdl.qc.ca
Population: 34,375 *Census Year:* 2011
Number of Households: 14,723

Robert-Cliche
111A, 107e Rue
Beauceville, QC G5X 2P9
418-774-9828
Fax: 418-774-4057
mrc.robert.cliche@beaucerc.com
www.beaucerc.com
Population: 19,288 *Census Year:* 2011
Number of Households: 7,598
Jean-Rock Veilleux, Préfet
Other Initiatives:
Implementation of Plan de gestion des matières résiduelles; Increase services throughout the region; Update infrastructure; Increase capacity of household containers; Promote composting; Establish a waste sorting and recovery centre; Educate citizens

Roussillon
#200, 260, rue Saint-Pierre
Saint-Constant, QC J5A 2A5
450-638-1221
Fax: 450-638-4499
admin@mrcroussillon.qc.ca
www.mrcroussillon.qc.ca
Population: 162,187 *Census Year:* 2011
Number of Households: 51,425
Waste Management:
Services Matrec, Boucherville
Other Initiatives:
Publication: Journal La Vie d'ange; 16 schools participate in composting program

Rouville
#100, 500 rue Desjardins
Marieville, QC J3M 1E1
450-460-2127
Fax: 450-460-7169
mrcrouville@on.aira.com
www.mrcrouville.qc.ca
Population: 35,690 *Census Year:* 2011
Number of Households: 11,760
Michel Picotte, Préfet
Waste Management:
Waste management responsibility of MRC; Waste management contracted to Matrec/Transvick Inc., 514/641-3070
Hazardous Waste Depot or Facility: No
Composters subsidized: Yes
Water & Wastewater Treatment:
Wastewater treatment plant located in Ange-Gardien
Other Initiatives:
Implementation of Plan de gestion des matières résiduelles; Green waste collections; Paint disposal program in collaboration with local businesses; Used oil program in collaboration with Canadian Tire

Saint-Charles-Borromée
370, rue de la Visitation
Saint-Charles-Borromée, QC J6E 4P3
450-759-4415
Fax: 450-759-3393
info@st-charles-borromee.org
www.st-charles-borromee.org
Population: 13,321 *Census Year:* 2011
Number of Households: 4,245
Water & Wastewater Treatment:
Water treatment at 1020, rue de la Visitation

Sept-Rivières
#400, 106, rue Napoléon
Sept-×les, QC G4R 3L7
418-962-1900
Fax: 418-962-3365
dg.mrc7riv@globetrotter.net
Population: 39,500 *Census Year:* 2011
Number of Households: 17,510
Waste Management:
Responsibility of the Ville de Sept-Iles & Ville de Port-Cortice

Témiscamingue
#209, 21, rue Notre-Dame-de-Lourdes
Ville-Marie, QC J9V 1X8
819-629-2829
Fax: 819-629-3472
mrc@mrctemiscamingue.qc.ca
www.temiscamingue.net
Population: 16,425 *Census Year:* 2011
Number of Households: 7,791
Waste Management:
Waste collection contracted to Transport Larouche et Beauregard
Number of landfill sites: 19
Recycling: Depot; 21 dépôts in Ville-Marie
Water & Wastewater Treatment:
Wastewater treatment plant at Ville-Marie

Témiscouata
5, rue de l'Hôtel de Ville, 2e étage
Notre-Dame-du-Lac, QC G0L 1X0
418-899-6725
Fax: 418-899-2000
admin@mrctemis.ca
www.mrctemiscouata.qc.ca
Population: 20,572 *Census Year:* 2011
Number of Households: 10,638

Thérèse-de-Blainville
479, boul Adolphe-Chapleau
Bois-des-Filion, QC J6Z 1J9
450-621-5546
Fax: 450-621-2628
reception@mrc-tdb.org
www.mrctheresedeblainville.qc.ca
Population: 154,144 *Census Year:* 2011
Number of Households: 48,045

Vaudreuil-Soulanges
420, av Saint-Charles
Vaudreuil-Dorion, QC J7V 2N1
450-455-5753
Fax: 450-455-0145
info@mrcvs.ca
www.mrcvs.ca
Population: 139,353 *Census Year:* 2011
Number of Households: 39,977
Guy-Lin Beaudoin, Directeur général
Waste Management:
Waste collection done by Rebuts Solides Canadiens & Robert Daoust; Waste processing outside the MRC

Other Initiatives:
Implementation of Plan de gestion des matières résiduelles; Improve existing collection services; Increase reduce, reuse & recycle practices; Establish a composting site

Saskatchewan

Saskatchewan Environment's mandate is to manage, enhance & protect Saskatchewan's natural & environmental resources for conservation, recreation, social, & economic purposes & to ensure they are sustained for future generations.

The department regulates municipal or communal drinking water systems. Communities own & operate their own water treatment facilities. SaskWater is working with 63 communities & 7 rural municipalities to provide a sustainable, reliable, safe & clean supply of drinking water. The Safe Drinking Water Strategy focuses on waterworks operator certification; assisting northern municipalities through the Northern Water & Sewer Program, & the Northern Emergency Water & Sewer Program. Municipal waterworks rate & capital investment bylaws were put in place July 1, 2006 to ensure that waterworks revenue covers expenses & capital debt payments. The Planning & Development Act (2007) required municipalities to have land use bylaws to protect watersheds.

There are over 600 waste disposal sites in Saskatchewan. Eight regional waste authorities have been created to consolidate & streamline waste management. Eighty percent of $20 million in infrastructure funding from the federal & provincial governments went for green municipal projects in the province. In the department's Performance Plan for 2004-05, key actions were outlined in the areas of developing a provincial strategy for municipal solid waste, developing & implementing recycling programs for electronics & new paint. In 2011-12, the province provided approximately $13 million in funding to environmental projects through the Go Green Fund.

Sewage lagoons are designed & operated to treat sewage to a quality acceptable for release into the environment. Treated effluent from domestic sewage holding tanks or septic tanks is becoming a resource (fertilizer, a source of moisture) rather than a pollutant. Where access to sewage systems or lagoons is unavailable, disposal of liquid sewage by haulers is an option.

In terms of recycling, the consumer pays a deposit for containers & an Environmental Handling Charge (EHC) on refillable & non-refillable containers. When the refillable container is returned, the consumer receives a refund. EHCs are not refundable & help to fund the province-wide transportation, processing & marketing system. There are 71 SARCAN recycling centres in 63 communities across the province. %). A Multi-Material Recycling Program was introduced in 2010 through Multi-Material Stewardship Western (MMSW) Inc. The corporation will submit a Program Management Plan to the Minister of Environment in August 2013. Once the plan is approved, the new recycling program can proceed, with an implementation date of 2014.

Under the federal government's New Deal for Cities, Saskatchewan received $147 million in federal gas tax funding from 2005 to 2010 for municipal infrastructure projects.

In the department's Annual Report for 2010-11, strategies for meeting the demands of economic & population growth were outlined, including the implementation of the following new environmental acts: The Environmental Assessment Act; The Forest Resources Management Act; The Environmental Management & Protection Act; & The Management & Reduction of Greenhouse Gases Act.

Major Municipalities in Saskatchewan

City of Estevan
1102 - 4 St.
Estevan, SK S4A 0W7
306-634-1800
Fax: 306-634-9790
citymanager@estevan.ca
www.estevan.ca
Population: 11,054 *Census Year:* 2011
Number of Households: 4,355
James Puffalt, City Manager, 306-634-1803
Tim Leson, Treasurer
Trina Sieben, Assessor
Waste Management:
City's Engineering Services Division manages third party contracts for residential waste collection
Number of landfill sites: 1
Water & Wastewater Treatment:
City of Estevan Water Treatment Plant, River Rd., 306/634-1822; City of Estevan Wastewater Treatment Plant, southern city limits
Other Initiatives:
Paint recycle program

City of Lloydminster
City Hall
4420 - 50 Ave.
Lloydminster, SK T9V 0W2
306-875-6184
Fax: 306-871-8346
info@lloydminster.ca
www.lloydminster.ca
Population: 27,804 *Census Year:* 2011
Number of Households: 8,106

City of Moose Jaw
228 Main St. North
Moose Jaw, SK S6H 3J8
306-694-4400
Fax: 306-694-4480
www.moosejaw.ca
Population: 33,274 *Census Year:* 2011
Number of Households: 14,403
Waste Management:
Number of landfill sites: 1
Recycling: Depot; EcoCentre Recycling, sanitary landfill site, northeastern city limits
Hazardous Waste Depot or Facility: Hazardous Waste Collection Site, sanitary landfill site, northeastern city limits
Water & Wastewater Treatment:
Advanced Waste Water Treatment & Disposal Project, Baildon Irrigation Area; Buffalo Pound Water Treatment Plant
Other Initiatives:
Community Clean Up Week; Annual household hazardous waste collection day; Paint exchange day; Municipal Advisory Committee on the Environment; Parks & Recreation Dept. green space & urban forest area maintenance

City of North Battleford
P.O. Box 460
1291 - 101st St.
North Battleford, SK S9A 2Y6
306-445-1700
Fax: 306-445-0411
www.cityofnb.ca
Population: 13,888 *Census Year:* 2011
Number of Households: 5,976
Tim LaFreniere, City Planner, email: tlafreniere@citynb.ca
Stewart Schafer, Director, Public Works
Keith Anderson, Director, Parks & Recreation, email: kanderson@cityofnb.ca
Pat MacIsaac, Fire Chief, email: pmacisaac@cityofnb.ca
Waste Management:
Waste collection contracted to K&B Construction, 306/445-3900.
Number of landfill sites: 1*Landfill Capacity:* 50 years
Solid Waste Disposal Fees: $40/tonne
Recycling: Depot; 2 main & 35 paper only depots
Hazardous Waste Depot or Facility: Various depots
Composters subsidized: Yes
Water & Wastewater Treatment:
City owns: #1 Water Treatment Plant, FE Holliday Water Treatment Plant & a Wastewater Treatment Plant, 306/445-1766
Other Initiatives:
Newly renovated water treatment plants with UV; New wastewater plant with UV; Impressed current trial for well maintenance; Recycling & water conservation education programs

City of Prince Albert
City Hall
1084 Central Ave.
Prince Albert, SK S6V 7P3
306-953-4884
www.citypa.ca
Population: 35,129 *Census Year:* 2011
Number of Households: 13,763
Les Karpluk, Fire Chief, 306-953-4200, email: lkarpluk@citypa.com
Dale McFee, Police Chief, 306-953-4222
Waste Management:
Number of landfill sites: 1*Landfill Capacity:* 100 years
Solid Waste Disposal Fees: $30/tonne
Recycling: Both Curbside & Depot; Depots throughout the city
Composters subsidized: Yes
Water & Wastewater Treatment:
Water treatment plant, 655 River St. West, Prince Albert; Wastewater treatment plant, J.W. Oliver Pollution Control Centre, 2100 1st St., Prince Albert
Other Initiatives:
Composting facility in operation at landfill; Annual Paint Recycling Day; Hazardous Waste Collection Day

City of Regina
City Hall
P.O. Box 1790
2476 Victoria Ave.
Regina, SK S4P 3C8
306-777-7000
www.regina.ca
Population: 193,100 *Census Year:* 2011
Number of Households: 74,814
Jason Carlston, B.A., M.A., General Manager, Planning & Development
Dorian Wandzura, P.Eng., General Manager, Public Works Division
Waste Management:
Number of landfill sites: 1
Recycling: Programs include Big Blue Bin, Tinsel Mulch, White Metal Goods Recycling Program, Xeriscaping, Composting, paint donation program, & glass recycling at the Fleet St. landfill; refundable glass bottles may be recycled at SARCAN
Water & Wastewater Treatment:
Buffalo Pound Water Treatment Plant, northeast of Moose Jaw, co-owned & operated by cities of Regina & Moose Jaw; City of Regina sewage treatment plant, Engineer, 306/777-7440; Supervisor, 306/777-7692
Other Initiatives:
Big Blue Bin program features big blue recycling bins in 13 city neighbourhoods; Waste paper from bins is transported to city's Paper Recycling Depot, operated by an NPO under contract with the city; Cool Down the City program, encourages reduction of greenhouse gas emissions, Program Coordinator, 306/777-7639; Paint it Recycled program collects & recycles paint & paint cans; Tinsel Mulch Christmas Tree Recycling & Tinsel Mulch Give-Away programs; Water Conservation Program includes a Xeriscape Demonstration Site & free xeriscape landscaping classes; White Metal Goods Recycling program at landfill site; Developed a Solid Waste Management Plan; Commuter Challenge for workers to use green modes of transportation

City of Saskatoon
City Hall
222 - 3rd Ave. North
Saskatoon, SK S7K 0J5
306-975-3200
www.saskatoon.ca
Population: 222,189 *Census Year:* 2011
Number of Households: 84,281
Brian Bentley, General Manager, Fire & Protective Services, 306-975-2575, Fax: 306-975-2689, email: fire.protective.services@city.saskatoon.sk.ca
Paul Gauthier, General Manager, Community Services
Mike Gutek, General Manager, Infrastructure Services
Brenda Wallace, General Manager, Utility Services
Brian Bentley, Fire Chief
Waste Management:
Number of landfill sites: 1
Solid Waste Disposal Fees: $55/tonne, & per schedule; Solid Waste Hotline: 306-975-2486; Landfill located on Dundonald Ave.
Clean Fill Fee: No
Recycling: The Saskatoon Waste & Recycling Plan (2007) established guidelines for recycling initiatives; ongoing public consultation & re-evaluation of options going forward; 6 recycling depots accept newsprint, mixed papers, cardboard, bottles & cans
Hazardous Waste Depot or Facility: Household hazardous waste only may be taken to Envirotec, 100 Cory Rd., Saskatoon; consult the city website for collection dates
Water & Wastewater Treatment:
Water treatment plant at 1030 Ave. H South; Wastewater treatment plant, 470 Whiteswan Dr.
Other Initiatives:
Paint exchange program; Cosmo Bins for newspaper & magazine recycling & Can-Man bins for tin can recycling, located throughout city; Eco Centre, located at Saskatoon landfill, offers

recycling opportunities; Christmas tree drop-off locations open each January; Rideshare Week in October encourages carpooling; Waste Reduction Week, also in October; Commuter Week, & National Environment Week in June

City of Swift Current

P.O. Box 340
Swift Current, SK S9H 3W1
306-778-2777
admin@swiftcurrent.ca
www.swiftcurrent.ca
Population: 15,503 *Census Year:* 2011
Number of Households: 6,891
Mac Forster, Director, Engineering, 306-778-2740, email: eng@swiftcurrent.ca
Dean Robson, Director, Recreation & Parks, 306-778-2787
Trevor Feicht, Manager, Engineering Services, 306-778-2740
Andy Toth, Manager, Parks, 306-778-2787
Denis Pilon, Fire Chief, 306-778-2760
Waste Management:
Waste collection contracted to Waste Management
Number of landfill sites: 1
Solid Waste Disposal Fees: $20/tonne
Recycling: Depot; Green Stop recycling depots locations: Wheatland Mall, Swift Current Mall, Fairview Arena, Civic Centre, 10th St. NW & Chaplin St., & North Railway St. East
Composters subsidized: Yes
Water & Wastewater Treatment:
Water source is Duncairn Dam; Swift Current Water Treatment Plant; Swift Current Wastewater Treatment Plant
Other Initiatives:
Community composting program, including compost collection; Household hazardous waste day; Christmas tree pickup program; 2006 litter campaign; Water conservation program, including sale of water saving devices; Renovations & upgrades to water treatment plant

City of Yorkton

37 - 3rd Ave. North
Yorkton, SK S3N 2W3
306-786-1700
Fax: 306-786-6880
www.yorkton.ca
Population: 15,669 *Census Year:* 2011
Number of Households: 6,773
David Putz, City Manager, 306-786-1703, email: dputz@yorkton.ca
Michael Buchholzer, Director, Water Works, 306-828-2470, email: mbuchholzer@yorkton.ca
Lonnie Kaal, Director, Finance, 306-786-1721, email: lkaal@yorkton.ca
Trent Mandzuk, Director, Public Works, 306-786-1762, email: tmanzuk@yorkton.ca
Gord Shaw, Director, Planning & Engineering, 306-786-1730, email: gshaw@yorkton.ca
Brant Hryhorczuk, Manager, Building Services, 306-786-1710, email: bhryhorczuk@yorkton.ca
Faisal Anwar, Officer, Economic Development, 306-786-1747, email: fanwar@yorkton.ca
Dean Clark, Fire Chief, Fire Protective Services, 306-786-1795, email: dclark@yorkton.ca
Waste Management:
Waste collection contracted to Ottenbriet Waste Systems Ltd., 306/783-3867
Number of landfill sites: 1
Solid Waste Disposal Fees: Yes
Clean Fill Fee:
Recycling: Depot; Sask. Abilities Council, 162 Ball Rd., 306/782-7844
Special Bans/by-laws: Smoking in public & work places within the city of Yorkton
Water & Wastewater Treatment:
City owns & operates the H.M. Bailey Water Pollution Control Plant, secondary wastewater treatment facility, located east of Hwy. 9, 1 km north of the city, 306/786-1774; City owns & operates 3 water treatment plants, which are being upgraded; Contact Michael Buchholzer, 306/786-1771

Yukon Territory

The Yukon Environmental Protection & Assessment Branch is responsible for environment impact analysis, contaminated sites monitoring, permits for regulated activities/substances, recycling education & promotion, public education & awareness.

Municipalities are responsible for their own water quality, clean drinking water, waste management, water & wastewater treatment. There is a Yukon Water Board which consists of four to nine people who have been appointed by the Commissioner in Executive Council. The Board provides conservation, development and utilization of water that will be beneficial for all residences.

The Government of Yukon developed an environmentally safe waste management system, which has shut down all 20 open waste burning facilities. New facilities are full service sites that have bins to separate domestic waste, recyclable, refundable and hazardous materials. This is part of the Solid Waste Action Plan, which has plans for installing compaction systems, as well as an educational campaign for more information about recycling and composting. The Solid Waste Action Plan is developing a 10 year waste management plan for solid waste facilities. They will also install garbage compaction systems at Marsh Lake, Mount Lorne, Carcross and Tagish in hopes of tripling the volume of waste that can be transferred at once. The Plan is also going to improve hazardous waste areas and install groundwater monitoring wells at remaining sites.

Yukon's Waste Reduction and Recycling Initiative funds small projects that aim to provide positive and lasting benefits to the environment by reducing waste generation, recycling materials without collecting a surcharge and/or increasing diversion of compostable materials from landfills. Projects can earn a grant up to $10,000 for funding.

Major Municipalities in Yukon Territory

City of Whitehorse

2121 Second Ave.
Whitehorse, YT Y1A 1C2
867-667-6401
mayorandcouncil@whitehorse.ca
www.city.whitehorse.yk.ca
Population: 23,276 *Census Year:* 2011
Number of Households: 7,831
Mike Gau, Director, Development Services, 867-335-4455, email: mike.gau@whitehorse.ca
Linda Rapp, Director, Community & Recreation Services, 867-668-8329, email: linda.rapp@whitehorse.ca
Cheri Malo, Manager, Transit, 867-668-8391, email: cheri.malo@whitehorse.ca
Dave Muir, Manager, Operations, 867-668-8302, email: dave.muir@whitehorse.ca
Dave Pruden, Manager, Bylaw Services, 867-334-1082, email: dave.pruden@whitehorse.ca
Wayne Tuck, Manager, Engineering Services, 867-668-8306, email: wayne.tuck@whitehorse.ca
Clive Sparks, Fire Chief, 867-668-8383, email: clive.sparks@whitehorse.ca
Waste Management:
Waste collection is the responsibility of the Whitehorse Public Works department
Number of landfill sites: 1
Solid Waste Disposal Fees: $5.50/pick-up truck load for residential solid waste; see city website fee schedule for other categories
Recycling: Both Curbside & Depot; Whitehorse does not have a blue box program, however recyclables may be taken to 2 commercial depots in the city; Whitehorse Landfill, Alaska Hwy.; 3 privately operated depots
Special Bans/by-laws: All-terrain vehicle bylaw; Snowmobile bylaw; Dangerous Goods bylaw; Green Space bylaw; Protected Area bylaw; Solid Waste bylaw; Zoning bylaw; Limit of 1 garbage cart per household per curbside garbage collection; no limit on properly sorted compostables
Hazardous Waste Depot or Facility: No
Water & Wastewater Treatment:
Water & sewer systems are the responsibility of the city's Public Works department; One main lagoon system, plus one minor lagoon system to serve Crestview
Other Initiatives:
Habitat conservation & stewardship program; Compostables may be dropped off at Whitehorse Landfill, Alaska Hwy., 867/668-1621; Waste Watch initiative ensures city operations are conducted in an environmentally sound manner; Local Action Plan for Climate Change

Intergovernmental Offices & Councils

Arctic Council

Foreign Affairs & International Trade Canada, 125 Sussex Dr., Ottawa ON K1A 0G2
Tel: 613-995-1874; *Fax:* 613-644-1852
e-mail: media@international.gc.ca
URL: www.arctic-council.org
Chief Officer(s):
Magnus Johannesson, Director of the Secretariat
magnus@arctic-council.org
Description: Intergovernmental forum for addressing common concerns & challenges by the member states of Canada, Denmark (including Greenland & the Faroe Islands), Finland, Iceland, Norway, the Russian Federation, Sweden & the U.S. Its objective is to be a regional forum for sustainable development mandated to address environmental, social & economic issues. The scientific work of the Council is carried out in six expert working groups focusing on such issues as monitoring, assessing & preventing pollution in the Arctic, climate change, biodiversity conservation & sustainable use, emergency preparedness & prevention. The six working groups are: Sustainable Development Working Group; Arctic Monitoring & Assessment Programme; Protection of the Marine Environment; Conservation of Arctic Flora & Fauna; Emergency, Prevention, Preparedness & Response; Arctic Contaminants Action Program. The Council meets every two years; the secretariat rotates among the member states.

Canada-Newfoundland Offshore Petroleum Board

TD Place, 140 Water St., 5th Fl., St. John's NL A1C 6H6
Tel: 709-778-1400; *Fax:* 709-778-1473
e-mail: information@cnlopb.nl.ca
URL: www.cnlopb.nl.ca
Chief Officer(s):
Max Ruelokke, P.Eng, Chair & Chief Conservation Officer
David Wells, Deputy Chief Executive Officer
John P. Andrew, Manager, Legal & Land
709-776-1458
Description: The Canada-Newfoundland Offshore Petroleum Board manages the petroleum resources in the Nlfd. offshore area on behalf of the Government of Canada & the Government of N.L. The Board's authority is derived from the legislation implementing the 1985 Atlantic Accord between the two governments. The Environmental Affairs department ensures that offshore oil & gas industrial activities proceed in an environmentally acceptable manner & evaluates the effect of the offshore environment upon the safety of offshore activities & by ensuring protection of the environment during the conduct of these activities. Working in close consultation with the Operations & Safety department, Environmental Affairs assesses the effects of environmental conditions, such as winds, waves & ice conditions, in the Nfld. offshore area upon the safety of operations. Environmental Affairs reviews operators' plans for collecting the weather, oceanographic & ice data that they are required to measure at offshore drilling & production sites. The Board reviews proposals for all physical activities offshore to identify their potential effects upon the natural environment or upon other users of that environment, such as the fishery. It evaluates measures that are proposed to prevent or mitigate these effects. This activity includes reviewing operators' contingency plans for environmental emergencies, especially oil spills, to ensure there are adequate response measures.

Canada-Nova Scotia Offshore Petroleum Board

TD Centre, 1791 Barrington St., 18th Fl., Halifax NS B3J 3K9
Tel: 902-422-5588; *Fax:* 902-422-1799
e-mail: postmaster@cnsopb.ns.ca
URL: www.cnsopb.ns.ca
Social media: twitter.com/CNSOPB
Chief Officer(s):
Stuart Pinks, CEO
spinks@cnsopb.ns.ca
Steve Bigelow, Chief Conservation Officer
sbigelow@cnsopb.ns.ca
Keith Landra, Director, Operations
klandra@cnsopb.ns.ca
Description: CNSOPB is responsible for protection of the environment during all phases of offshore petroleum activities, from initial exploration to abandonment. The Board is a Federal Authority under the Canadian Environmental Assessment Act. The environmental assessment process starts at the Call for Bids stage. At this stage, a strategic or broad environmental assessment is conducted which identifies environmental concerns or issues. All subsequent projects, including seismic programs & exploratory wells, must undergo an environmental assessment prior to approval by the CNSOPB. The Board also uses class screenings or generic assessments to streamline the regulatory process. These more in-depth environmental assessments, usually jointly funded by a number of petroleum companies, provide more detailed overviews of potential environmental effects, research priorities & mitigation measure than can be accomplished in a single project-specific environmental assessment. Applications from the petroleum industry for work authorizations must include an environmental assessment, environmental contingency plan & spill contingency plan. The Board consults with FEAC on environmental & fisheries-related matters. The Board is also involved in initiatives led by the Department of Fisheries & Oceans (DFO) related to marine protected areas & integrated management planning under the Oceans Act. The Board has signed memorandums of understanding with both the DFO & Environment Canada.

Canadian Council of Forest Ministers (CCFM) / Conseil canadien des ministres des forêts

c/o Policy, Economics & Industry Branch, Natural Resources Canada, 580 Booth St., 11th Fl, Ottawa ON K1A 0E4
Tel: 613-947-9099; *Fax:* 613-947-9033
URL: www.ccfm.org
Chief Officer(s):
Martine Ouellet, Ministre, Natural Resources & Wildlife
ministre@mrnf.gouv.gc.ca
Mario Gibeault, Sous-ministre
mario.gibeault@bmmb.gouv.qc.ca
Description: The Canadian Council of Ministers (CCFM) was established in 1985 to give sufficient attention to forest issues. CCFM stimulates the development of policies & initiatives for strengthening the forest sector, including the forest resource & its use. It provides leadership, addresses national & international issues & sets the direction for stewardship & sustainable management of Canada's forests. The CCFM is composed of the fourteen federal, provincial & territorial ministers responsible for forests. The CCFM undertakes activities primarily through ad hoc fora, committees & working groups. At present there are 9 committees. CCFM initiatives include: International Forest Issues Working Group; International Forestry Partnerships Program; Sustainable Forest Management Working Group; Canadian Wildland Fire Strategy; National Forest Information System; National Forestry Database Program; Science & Technology Working Group; Forest Communities Working Group. The Council also cooperates with the Canadian Wildland Fire Strategy Declaration, a federal-provincial-territorial initiative to address the management of wildland fires. National Forestry Database Program: nfdp.ccfm.org/; National Forest Information System: nfis.org

Canadian Council of Ministers of the Environment (CCME) / Conseil canadien des ministres de l'environnement

#360, 123 Main St., Winnipeg MB R3C 1A3
Tel: 204-948-2090; *Fax:* 204-948-2125
Toll-Free: 800-805-3025
e-mail: info@ccme.ca
URL: www.ccme.ca
Chief Officer(s):
James Arreak, President
Michael Goeres, Executive Director
mgoeres@ccme.ca
David Akeeagok, Chair, Mgmt & Deputy Ministers Committees
Finances: *Annual Operating Budget:* $1.5 Million-$3 Million; *Funding Sources:* Federal, provincial & territorial governments
Staff: 8 staff member(s)
Membership: 1-99; *Committees:* Environmental Planning & Protection
Description: CCME is comprised of the environment ministers from the federal, provincial and territorial governments. These 14 ministers normally meet at least once a year to discuss national environmental priorities and determine work to be carried out under the auspices of CCME. The Council seeks to achieve positive environmental results, focusing on issues that are national in scope and that require collective attention by a number of governments. CCME aims to assist its members to meet their mandate of protecting Canada's environment. As with any association, each member can accomplish more by working together than by working alone. CCME serves as a principal forum for members to develop national strategies, norms, and guidelines that each environment ministry across the country can use. Since environment is constitutionally speaking an area of shared jurisdiction, it makes sense to work together to promote effective results. CCME is not another level of government regulator, but a council of government ministers holding similar responsibilities.

Canadian Intergovernmental Conference Secretariat (CICS) / Secrétariat des conférences intergouvernementales canadiennes

PO Box 488, Stn. A, Ottawa ON K1N 8V5
Location/Deliveries: 222 Queen St. 10th Fl., Ottawa ON K1P 5V9
Tel: 613-995-2341; *Fax:* 613-996-6091
e-mail: info@scics.gc.ca
URL: www.scics.gc.ca
Chief Officer(s):
André McArdle, Secretary, 613-995-2344
Louise Seaward-Gagnon, Director
louise.seaward-gagnon@scics.gc.ca
Description: CICS was established in 1973 by the First Ministers as an agency of the federal & provincial governments. Governments recognized a need for a mechanism to serve on a continuing basis, conferences of First Ministers & a growing number of intergovernmental meetings. CICS serves federal-provincial First Ministers' meetings, the Annual Premiers' Conference, the Eastern Canadian Premiers' & New England Governors' Conference & the Western Premiers' Conference. The core of the Secretariat's work is providing services to multilateral meetings of Ministers & Deputy Ministers in virtually every sector of government activity. The Secretariat's services are available to federal, provincial & territorial departments that are called upon to organize & chair such meetings. The agency's mandate & sole program are designed to relieve its clients of the numerous & various technical & administrative tasks associated with the planning & conduct of senior level intergovernmental conferences. The CICS maintains through its Information Services section, a document archives for the use of governments & the general public. Containing over 25,000 conference-related documents spanning every sector of conference activity, this collection is unique. The information contained in the archives is made available, as appropriate, to government institutions at the federal, provincial & territorial levels while unclassified material is also available to the public on request.

Commission for Environmental Cooperation (CEC) / Commission Coopération Environnementale

Secretariat, #200, 393 rue St-Jacques ouest, Montréal QC H2Y 1N9
Tel: 514-350-4300; *Fax:* 514-350-4314
e-mail: info@cec.org
URL: www.cec.org
Chief Officer(s):
Irasema Coronado, Executive Director
Orlando Cabrera-Rivera, Program Manager, Air Quality & PRTR, 514-350-4323
ocabrera@cec.org
Marco Antonio Heredia Fragoso, Program Manager, Environmental Law, 514-350-4302
maheredia@cec.org
Description: The Commission for Environmental Cooperation (CEC) is an international organization created by Canada, Mexico & the United States under the North American Agreement on Environmental Cooperation (NAAEC). The CEC was established to address regional environmental concerns, help prevent potential trade & environmental conflicts & to promote the effective enforcement of environmental law. The Agreement complements the environmental provisions of the North American Free Trade Agreement (NAFTA).

Commission on Sustainable Development

#405, 42nd St. East, New York NY 10017 USA
Tel: 212-963-8102; *Fax:* 212-963-4260
e-mail: dsd@un.org
URL: sustainabledevelopment.un.org
Chief Officer(s):

Seth Nikhil, Director
Member Profile: Permanent Mission of Canada to the UN: 1 Dag Hammarskjold Plaza, New York NY 10017 212/848-1100; Fax: 212/848-1195; Email: canada@un.it
Description: Functional commission of the UN Economic & Social Council, composed of members elected for terms of office for three years. An intergovernmental body, members are elected by the Economic & Social Council from member states of the United Nations & its specialized agencies. The Commission meets annually; a multi-year (2004-2017) program of work outlines seven two-year cycles, with each two-year cyle focused on themes. For 2010-2011, the themes centre on poverty eradication, changing unsustainable patterns of consumption and production, protecting and managing the natural resource base of economic and social development, sustainable development in a globalizing world, health and sustainable development, sustainable development of SIDS, sustainable development for Africa, other regional initiatives, means of implementation, institutional framework for sustainable development, gender equality, and education. The role of the Commission as a high level forum on sustainable development, includes reviewing progress at the international, regional & national levels in the implementation of recommendations & commitments contained in Agenda 21 & the Rio Declaration on Environment & Development; elaborates policy & options for future activities to follow up the Johannesburg Plan of Implementation & achieve sustainable development; promotes dialogue & builds partnerships for sustainable development with governments, the international community & the major groups who have a role to play in the transition towards sustainable development, including women, youth, indigenous peoples, non-governmental organizations, local authorities, workers & trade unions, business & industry, the scientific community & farmers.

Conference of New England Governors & Eastern Canadian Premiers

Council Secretariat, PO Box 2044, #1006, 5161Halifax NS B3J 2Z1
Tel: 902-424-7590; *Fax:* 902-424-8976
e-mail: info@cap-cpma.ca
URL: www.cap-cpma.ca
Description: Established in 1973, & is composed of the premiers of the Atlantic provinces, Québec & governors of six New England States. Initiatives include the expansion of economic ties among the states & provinces; the fostering of energy exchanges; the forceful advocacy of environmental issues & sustainable development; & the coordination of numerous policies & programs in such areas as transportation, forest management, tourism, small-scale agriculture & fisheries. At annual conferences the Governors & Premiers discuss issues of common interest & concern, & enact policy resolutions that call on actions by the state & provincial governments, as well as by the two national governments. During the year, the Conference convenes meetings of state & provincial officials, organizes roundtables & workshops, & prepares reports & studies of issues of regional import. The Committee on the Environment adopted an acid rain action plan & a mercury action plan. The Northeast International Committee on Energy monitors & acts on common issues in the northeast region, such as electric restructuring; natural gas developments; resource & infrastructure development;collaboration with environmental departments & agencies; new technologies. At its most recent meeting, Aug. 2006, the conference resolved to create an Oceans Working Committee for ocean management, to develop a long term strategy to explore regional governance issues, to mitigate future growth in energy, increase amount of new renewable energy.

Council of Atlantic Premiers (CAP)

Council Secretariat, PO Box 2044, #1006, 5161 George St., Halifax NS B3J 2Z1
Tel: 902-424-7590; *Fax:* 902-424-8976
e-mail: info@cap-cpma.ca
URL: www.cap-cpma.ca
Chief Officer(s):
Tim Porter, Secretary to Council, 902-424-7600
tporter@cap-cpma.ca
Description: The mandate of the Council is also to promote Atlantic Canadian interests on national issues. To accomplish this, the Council seeks to establish common views & positions to ensure that Atlantic Canadians & their interests are well represented in national debates. The work of the Council of Atlantic Premiers builds on the ongoing work of the Council of Maritime Premiers & the Conference of Atlantic Premiers. The premiers are committed to work together on behalf of Atlantic Canadians to strengthen the economic competitiveness of the region, improve the quality of public services to Atlantic Canadians and/or improve the cost-effectiveness of delivering public services to Atlantic Canadians. In June 2005, CAP released their Atlantic Action Plan 2005-2008. Environmental priorities include establishing a Council of Atlantic Ministers of the Environment to better communicate & collaborate on issues, collaborate on pest management education initiatives through the Atlantic Working Group in Pest Management Education & Training Standards, explore extended producer responsibility programs to address common solid waste resource management issues. The Atlantic Energy Ministers Forum commits to developing an energy efficiency awareness campaign & a regional electricity sector approach which takes into account energy efficiency & renewable energy technologies. The Forum will also examine developing regional air emissions reduction models applicable to sulphur dioxides & nitrous oxides.

Great Lakes Commission / Commission des Grands Lacs

Eisenhower Corporate Park, #100, 2805 S. Industrial Way, Ann Arbor MI 48104-6791 USA
Tel: 734-971-9135; *Fax:* 734-971-9150
URL: www.glc.org
Chief Officer(s):
Tim Eder, Executive Director
teder@glc.org
Description: The Great Lakes Commission is a binational public agency dedicated to the use, management & protection of water, land & other natural resources of the Great Lakes-St. Lawrence system. In partnership with 8 Great Lakes states & provinces of Ontario & Québec, the Commission applies sustainable development principles addressing issues of resource management, environmental protection, transportation & sustainable development. The Commission provides accurate & objective information on public policy issues; an effective forum for developing & coordinating public policy; & a unified, system wide voice to advocate member interests.

Office of Greening Government Operations

Tel: 416-241-4000, ext. 221
URL: www.greeninggovernment.ca
Chief Officer(s):
Nigel Marsh, President
nigel.marsh@govpages.ca
Description: GreeningGovernment is an electronic information system developed by the Government of Canada for the internet. It is designed to provide a one-window access to sustainable development in government operations knowledge in the Government of Canada. This web site was developed to support the Sustainable Development in Government Operations (SDGO) initiative, whose purpose is to coordinate the federal effort to green government operations & encourage the report of concrete results among the departments & agencies that prepare Sustainable Development Strategies (SDSs). There are seven priority areas of operations: Energy Efficiency/Buildings, Human Resources Management, Land Use Management, Procurement, Vehicle Fleet Management, Waste Management & Water Conservation & Wastewater Management.

Gulf of Maine Council on the Marine Environment

c/o New Brunswick Dept. of Environment & Local Government, PO Box 6000, 850 Lincoln Rd., Fredericton NB E3B 5H1
Tel: 506-457-8946; *Fax:* 506-457-7823
URL: www.gulfofmaine.org
Chief Officer(s):
Robert Capozi, New Brunswick Contact
robert.capozi@gnb.ca
Sophia Foley, Nova Scotia Contact
foleys@gov.ns.ca
Description: A U.S.-Canadian partnership of government & non-government organizations working to maintain & enhance environmental quality in the Gulf of Maine to allow for sustainable resource use. The Council organizes conferences & workshops; offers grants & recognition awards; conducts environmental monitoring; provides science translation to management; raises public awareness about the Gulf. The secretariat rotates annually among the member jurisdictions. Initiatives include Gulf of Maine Mapping Initiative (GOMMI), comprehensive seafloor imaging, mapping & biological & geological surveys; habitat restoration grants program (U.S. only); Action Plan grants program; annual recognition awards; Gulf of Maine Times, a quarterly newspaper; Gulfwatch Monitoring Program, which helps to assess the fate & impacts of toxic contaminants in the Gulf of Maine.

North American Bird Conservation Initiative Canada (NABCI)

c/o Canadian Wildlife Service, Environment Canada, 3rd floor, 351 St. Joseph Boulevard, Gatineau, Quebec, Canada, K1A 0H3.
Tel: 819-994-0512; *Fax:* 819-994-4445
e-mail: nabci@ec.gc.ca
URL: www.nabci.net
Description: The NABCI is a coordinated effort among Canada, the United States & Mexico to maintain the diversity & abundance of all North American birds. National coordination of this effort in Canada occurs through the NABCI Canada Council, chaired by the Asst. Deputy Minister of Environment Canada's Environmental Conservation Service. Council members include representatives from provincial governments, non-government organizations, four bird plans (waterfowl, landbirds, shorebirds, waterbirds), & habitat joint ventures. In Canada, the joint venture conservation projects has three habitat joint ventures (Pacific Coast, Prairie Habitat, Eastern Habitat) & three species (Arctic Goose, Black Duck, Sea Duck).

North American Waterfowl Management Plan (NAWMP) / Le plan nord-américain de gestion de la sauvagine

c/o Canadian Wildlife Service, Place Vincent Massey, 7th fl., 351, boul St. Joseph, Hull QC K1A 0H3
Tel: 819-934-6036; *Fax:* 819-934-6017
e-mail: nawmp@ec.gc.ca
URL: www.nawmp.ca
Chief Officer(s):
Tasha Sargent, Coordinator
tasha_sargent@pcjv.org
Description: The North American Waterfowl Management Plan is an international action plan to conserve migratory birds throughout the continent. The Plan's goal is toreturn waterfowl populations to their 1970's levels by conserving wetland and upland habitat. Canada & the United States signed the Plan in 1986 in reaction to critically low numbers of waterfowl. Mexico joined in 1994 making it a truly continental effort. The Plan is a partnership of federal, provincial/state & municipal governments, non-governmental organizations, private companies & many individuals, all working towards achieving better wetland habitat for the benefit of migratory birds, other wetland-associated species & people. The Plan's unique combination of biology, landscape conservation & partnerships comprise its exemplary conservation legacy. Plan projects are international in scope, but implemented at regional levels. These projects contribute to the protection of habitat & wildlife species across the North American landscape. In fact, the North American Waterfowl Management Plan is considered one of the most successful conservation initiatives in the world.

Arctic Goose Joint Venture

e-mail: agjv@ec.gc.ca
URL: www.agjv.ca

Black Duck Joint Venture

URL: www.blackduckjv.org
Contact:
Brigitte Collins
Coordinator, BDJV
Environment Canada
Canadian Wildlife Service
335 River Road
Ottawa, Ontario K1A0H3
613-949-8254
brigitte.collins@ec.gc.ca
Patrick Devers
Science Coordinator, BDJV
U.S. Fish and Wildlife Service
11410 American Holly Drive
Laurel, MD 20708
301-497-5549
patrick_devers@fws.gov

Eastern Habitat Joint Venture

URL: www.ehjv.ca
Contact:
Patricia Edwards, Coordinator
patricia.edwards@ec.gc.ca

Prairie Habitat

URL: www.pcjv.org
Contact:
Tasha Sargent, Coordinator
tasha_sargent@pcjv.org

Pacific States/British Columbia Oil Spill Task Force
Environmental Emergencies Branch, BC Ministry of Environment
P. O. Box 9377 Stn. Prov. Govt, Victoria, BC, Canada V8W 9M6
Tel: 250-356-8383; *Fax:* 250-387-9935
URL: www.oilspilltaskforce.org
Chief Officer(s):
Sarah Brace, Executive Coordinator
sarah@vedaenv.com
Description: The Pacific States/British Columbia Oil Spill Task Force was authorized by a Memorandum of Cooperation signed in 1989 by the Governors of Alaska, Washington, Oregon, and California and the Premier of British Columbia following the Nestucca and Exxon Valdez oil spills. These events highlighted their common concerns regarding oil spill risks and the need for cooperation across shared borders. In June 2001 a revised Memorandum of Cooperation was adopted to include the State of Hawaii and expand our focus to spill preparedness and prevention needs of the 21st century. Now in our second decade, we provide a forum where Task Force Members can work with stakeholders from the Western US and Canada to implement regional initiatives that protect 56,660 miles of coastline from Alaska to California and the Hawaiian archipelago. The Task Force Members are senior executives from the environmental agencies with oil spill regulatory authority in the states of Alaska, Washington, Oregon, California and Hawaii and the Province of British Columbia. Oil spill program managers from each member agency comprise the Task Force's Coordinating Committee, which oversees activities and projects as authorized by the Members when they adopt a Five Year Strategic Plan and Annual Work Plans. The Coordinating Committee convenes four times a year. The Task Force Members hold their Annual Meetings each summer, rotating locations among member jurisdictions.

Environmental Trade Representatives Abroad

People's Democratic Republic of Algeria
Canadian Embassy, PO Box 48, Alger-Gare, 16035 Algeria
011-213-7008-3000, Fax: 011-213-7008-3070,
alger-td@international.gc.ca
www.international.gc.ca/world/embassies/algeria/
Amel Ait Mahiout Benrejdal, Trade Commissioner, Environmental Industries

Argentine Republic
Canadian Embassy, Casilla de Correo 1598, Correa Central, Buenos Aires, C1000WAP Argentine
011-54-11-4808-1000, Fax: 011-54-11-4808-111,
bairs-commerce@international.gc.ca
www.buenosaires.gc.ca
Ana Garasino, Trade Commissioner, Environmental Industries

Commonwealth of Australia
Canadian High Commission, Commonwealth Ave., Canberra, ACT 2600 Australia
61-2-6270-4000, Fax: 61-2-6270-3585,
sydny-td@international.gc.ca
www.canada.org.au
Angela Dark, Trade Commissioner, Environmental Industries

Republic of Austria
Canadian Embassy, Laurenzerberg 2, Vienna, A-1010 Austria
43-1-531-38-3321, Fax: 43-1-531-38-3910,
vienn-td@international.gc.ca
www.dfait-maeci.gc.ca/canadaeurope/austria
Roland Rossi, Trade Commissioner, Environmental Industries, roland.rossi@international.gc.ca

People's Republic of Bangladesh
Canadian High Commission, GPO Box 569, Dhaka, 1212 Bangladesh
88-2-988-7091, Fax: 88-2-882-3043,
dhaka-td@international.gc.ca
www.bangladesh.gc.ca
Mortoza Tarafder, Sr. Trade Commissioner, Environmental Industries, mortoza.tarafder@international.gc.ca

Barbados
Canadian High Commission, PO Box 404, Bridgetown, Barbados
246-429-3550, Fax: 246-429-3780,
bdgtn-td@international.gc.ca
Tammy Griffith, Trade Commissioner, Environmental Industries

Kingdom of Belgium
Canadian Embassy, 2, av de Tervuren, Brussels, 1040 Belgium
32-2-741-0611, Fax: 32-2-741-0643,
bru.td-infocentre@international.gc.ca
www.ambassade-canada.be
Fabienne De Kimpe, Trade Commissioner, Environmental Industries, fabienne.de-kimpe@international.gc.ca

Brazil
Canadian Trade Commissioner Service
Avenida das Nações Unidas, 12901 CENU Torre Norte, 16th floor, São Paulo, SP, 04578-000
55-11-5509-4321, Fax: 55-11-5509-4317
commerce.br@international.gc.ca
www.tradecommissioner.gc.ca/br
Mariangela Lima, Trade Commissioner, Environmental Industries

Brunei Darussalam
Canadian High Commission, PO Box 2808, Bandar Seri Begawan, BS8675 Brunei Darussalam
673-2-220-043, Fax: 673-2-220-040,
bsbgn-td@international.gc.ca
www.dfait-maeci.gc.ca/brunei
Eva Eng Chin Ng, Trade Commissioner, Environmental Industries

Burkina Faso
Canadian Embassy, 316, Ave. Prof. Joseph Ki-Zerbo, Ouagadougou, Burkina Faso
011-226-50 31 18 94, Fax: 011-226-50 31 19 00,
ouaga@international.gc.ca
www.tradecommissioner.gc.ca/bf
Adama Soro, Trade Commissioner

Republic of Cameroon
Canadian High Commission, Immeuble SCI-TOM (formerly Stamatiades), PO Box 572, Yaoundé, Cameroon
011-237-2223-2311, Fax: 011-237-2222-1090,
yunde-td@international.gc.ca
Jude Bijingsi, Trade Commissioner, Environmental Industries, jude.bijingsi@international.gc.ca

Republic of Chile
Canadian Embassy, Cassilla 139, Correo 10, Santiago, Chile
56-2-652-3800, Fax: 56-2-652-3912,
santiago.commerce@international.gc.ca
www.chile.gc.ca
Margot Edwards, Trade Commissioner, Environmental Industries

People's Republic of China
Canadian Embassy, 19 Dong Zhi Men Wai St., Chao Yang Dist., Beijing, 100600 China
011-86-10-5139-4000, Fax: 011-86-10-5139-4454,
infocentrechina@international.gc.ca
www.beijing.gc.ca
Josiane Simon, Trade Commissioner, Environmental Industries

Republic of Colombia
Canadian Embassy, Apartado Aereo 110067, Bogota, Colombia
57-1-657-9800, Fax: 57-1-657-9912,
bgota-td@international.gc.ca
www.bogota.gc.ca
Edmund Lee, Senior Trade Commissioner

Republic of Costa Rica
Canadian Embassy, Apartado Postal 351-1007 Centro Colon, San José, Costa Rica
506-2242-4400, Fax: 506-2242-4410,
sjcra-td@international.gc.ca
www.costarica.gc.ca
Adolfo Quesada, Trade Commissioner, Environmental Industries, adolfo.quesada@international.gc.ca

Republic of Croatia
Canadian Trade Commissioner Service
Prilaz Gjure Dezelica #4, Zagreb, 10 000 Croatia
385-1-488-1200, Fax: 385-1-488-1230,
Synthia Dodig, Trade Commissioner, Environmental Industries, synthia.dodig@international.gc.ca

Republic of Cuba
Canadian Embassy, Calle 30, No. 518, Esquina 7a, Miramar, Havana, Cuba
53-7-204-2516, Fax: 53-7-204-9772,
havan-td@international.gc.ca
www.dfait-maeci.gc.ca/cuba
Francisco Rodriguez, Trade Commissioner, Environmental Industries

Republic of Cyprus
15, Themistokles Dervis St.
Canadian Trade Commissioner Service
Nicosia, 1066 Cyprus
357-22- 775508 Fax: 357-22- 779 905
athns-td@international.gc.ca
www.tradecommissioner.gc.ca/cy
Rhea Pelides, Trade Commissioner, Environmental Industries

Czech Republic
Canadian Embassy, Muchova 6, 160 00, Prague, 6 Czech Republic
420 272 101 800, Fax: 420 272 101 898,
prgue-td@dfait-maeci.gc.ca
www.canada.cz
Martina Taxova, Trade Commissioner, Environmental Industries

Kingdom of Denmark
Canadian Embassy, Kr. Bernikows Gade 1, Copenhagen, DK-1105 Denmark
45-33-48-32-00, Fax: 45-33-48-32-20,
copen-td@international.gc.ca
www.denmark.gc.ca
David Horup, Trade Commissioner, Environmental Industries

Dominican Republic
Canadian Embassy, PO Box 2054, Santo Domingo, Dominican Republic
809-685-1136, Fax: 809-682-2691,
sdmgo-td@international.gc.ca
www.santodomingo.gc.ca
Regis Batista-Lemaire, Trade Commissioner, Environmental Industries, regis.barista@international.gc.ca

Republic of Ecuador
Canadian Embassy, PO Box 17-11-6512, Quito, Ecuador
593-2-2455-499, Fax: 593-2-2277-672,
quito-td@international.gc.ca
www.ecuador.gc.ca
Patricia Bustamante, Trade Commissioner, Environmental Industries

Egypt
Canadian Embassy, Cairo, Egypt
26 Kamel El Shenawy St., Garden City, Cairo
011-20-2-2791-8700, Fax: 011- 20- 2-2791-8865
cairo-td@international.gc.ca
www.tradecommissioner.gc.ca/eg
Joseph Tadros, Trade Commissioner, Environmental Industries

Republic of El Salvador
Canadian Embassy, Edificio Centro Financiero Gigante, Alameda Roosevelt y 63 Avenida Sur, Nivel Lobby 2, Loca, San Salvador, El Salvador
503-2279-4655, Fax: 503-2279-0765
www.sansalvador.gc.ca
Romeo Calderon, Trade Commissioner, Environmental Industries, romeo.calderon@international.gc.ca

Federal Democratic Republic of Ethiopia
Canadian Embassy, PO Box 1130, Addis Ababa, Ethiopia
251-1-71-30-22, Fax: 251-1-71-30-33,
addis@international.gc.ca
Baharnesh Mesfin Teshome, Trade Commissioner, Environmental Industries,
baharneshmesfin.teshome@international.gc.ca

Republic of Finland
Canadian Embassy, PO Box 779, Helsinki, FIN-00101 Finland
358-9-228-530, Fax: 358-9-601-060,
hsnki-td@international.gc.ca
www.canada.fi
Seppo Vihersaari, Trade Commissioner, Environmental Industries, seppo.vihersaari@international.gc.ca

French Republic
Canadian Embassy, 35 - 37, av Montaigne, Paris, 75008 France
33-1-44-43-29-00, Fax: 33-1-44-43-29-99,
france-td@international.gc.ca
www.international.gc.ca/canada-europa/france
Yannick Dheilly, Trade Commissioner, Environmental Industries

Federal Republic of Germany
Canadian Embassy, Leipziger Platz 17, Berlin, 10117 Germany
41-30-20-312-0, Fax: 49-30-20-312-590,
deutschland.commerce@international.gc.ca
www.dfait-maeci.gc.ca/canada-europa/germany
Arndt Ulland, Trade Commissioner, Environmental Industries

Republic of Guatemala
Canadian Embassy, PO Box 400, Guatemala City, 1001 Guatemala
502-2363-4348, Fax: 502-2365-1210,
gtmla-td@international.gc.ca
www.guatemala.gc.ca
Christine Luttmann, Trade Commissioner, Environmental Industries

Republic of Guyana
Canadian Trade Commissioner Service
High and Young Streets, Georgetown
011-592-227-2081/2085, Fax: 011-592-225-8380
grgtn-td@international.gc.ca
www.tradecommissioner.gc.ca/gy
Nicole Johnson, Trade Commissioner, Environmental Industries, nicole.johnson@international.gc.ca

Hong Kong
The Canadian Consulate General, Special Administrative Region, PRC

11th-14th Floors, Tower One, Exchange Square, 8 Connaught Place, Central
Hong Kong, Hong Kong
011-852-2847-7414, Fax: 011-852-2847-7441
infocentrechina@international.gc.ca
www.tradecommissioner.gc.ca/hk
Fatima Lai, Trade Commissioner, Environmental Industries

Haiti
Canadian Trade Commissioner Service
Delmas Road, between Delmas 71 and 75
Port-au-Prince
011-509-2812-9000, Fax: 011-509-2812-9922
www.tradecommissioner.gc.ca/ht
Emmanuel Choute, Trade Commissioner, Environmental Industries, emmanuel.choute@international.gc.ca

Republic of Hungary
Canadian Embassy, Ganz U. 12-14, Budapest, 10 1027 Hungary
36-1-392-3360, Fax: 36-1-392-3390,
bpest-td@international.gc.ca
www.canadaeuropa.gc.ca/hungary
Zsuzsanna Matyus, Trade Commissioner, Environmental Industries, zsuzsanna.matyus@international.gc.ca

Republic of Iceland
Canadian Embassy, PO Box 1510, Reykjavik, 121 Iceland
354-575-6500, Fax: 354-575-6501,
kristbjorg.agustsdottir@international.gc.ca
www.canada.is
Olof Sigridur Bjornsdottir, Trade Commissioner, Environmental Industries

Republic of India
Canadian Embassy, Indiabulls Finance Centre, Tower 2, 21st Floor, Senapati Bapat Marg, Elphinstone Road (West), Mumbai, Maharashtra
400 013 India
91-22-6749-4444 , Fax: 91-22-6749-4454 ,
india.commerce@international.gc.ca
www.india.gc.ca
Yasmine Dubash, Trade Commissioner, Environmental Industries

Republic of Indonesia
Canadian Embassy, PO Box 8324/JKS.MP, Jakarta, 12083 Indonesia
62-21-2550-7800, Fax: 62-21-2550-7811,
jkrta-td@international.gc.ca
www.jakarta.gc.ca
Dian Martosoebroto, Trade Commissioner, Environmental Industries

Republic of Ireland
Canadian Embassy, 7-8 Wilton Terrace, Dublin 2, Ireland
353-1-234-4000, Fax: 353-1-234-4101,
dubln-td@international.gc.ca
www.canada.ie
Gerry Mongey, Trade Commissioner, Environmental Industries, gerry.mongey@international.gc.ca

State of Israel
Canadian Embassy, PO Box 9442, 3 Nirim St., 4th Fl., Tel Aviv, 67060 Israel
011-972-3-636-3300, Fax: 011-972-3-636-3380,
taviv-td@international.gc.ca
Israel.gc.ca
Mona Ashkar, Trade Commissioner, Environmental Industries

Italian Republic
Canadian Embassy, Villa Grazioli, Via Salaria 243, Rome, 00199 Italy
39-06-85444-1, Fax: 39-06-85444-3947,
ital-td@international.gc.ca
www.canada.it
Patrizia Giuliotti, Trade Commissioner, Environmental Industries

Republic of Ivory Coast
Canadian Embassy, Immeuble Trade Centre, 23, av Nogues, 6th & 7th Fls., Le Plateau, Abidjan, 01 Ivory Coast
225-20 30 07 00, Fax: 225-20 30 07 20,
abdjn-td@international.gc.ca
www.canadainternational.gc.ca/cotedivoire
Laetitia Gadegbeku, Trade Commissioner, Environmental Services, jean-claude.diplo@international.gc.ca

Jamaica
Canadian High Commission, PO Box 1500, Kingston, 10 Jamaica
876/926-1500-7, Fax: 876/511-3494,
kngtn-td@international.gc.ca
www.kingston.gc.ca
Yasmin Chong, Trade Commissioner, Environmental Industries, yasmin.chong@international.gc.ca

Japan
Canadian Embassy, 7-3-38 Akasaka, Minato-ku
Tokyo, 107-8503
011-81-3-5412-6200, Fax: 011-81-3-5412-6254
jpn.commerce@international.gc.ca
www.tradecommissioner.gc.ca/jp
Stéphane Beaulieu, Sr. Trade Commissioner, Environmental Industries

Hashemite Kingdom of Jordan
Canadian Embassy, PO Box 815403, Amman, 11180 Jordan
962-6-520-3300, Fax: 962-6-520-3390,
amman-td@international.gc.ca
www.amman.gc.ca
Wafa Herzallah, Trade Commissioner, Environmental Industries, wafa.herzallah@international.gc.ca

Republic of Kazakhstan
Canadian Embassy, 34 Karasai Batir St., Almaty, 050010 Kazakhstan
73-27-250-11-51, Fax: 73-27-258-24-93,
astna-td@international.tc.ca
www.infoexport.gc.ca/kz
Steven Basadur, Sr. Trade Commissioner

Kenya
The Canadian High Commission
Limuru Road, Gigiri
Nairobi
011-254 20-366-3000, Fax: 011-254 20-366-3900
nrobi-td@international.gc.ca
www.tradecommissioner.gc.ca/ke
Benjamin Wamahiu, Trade Commissioner, Environmental Industries, benjamin.wamahiu@international.gc.ca

Republic of Korea
Canadian Embassy, 16-1 Jeong-dong, Jung-gu, Seoul, Korea
82-2-3783-6000, Fax: 82-2-3783-6239,
seoul-td@international.gc.ca
www.korea.gc.ca
Hyun Ju Lim, Trade Commissioner, Environmental Industries, hyun-ju.lim@international.gc.ca

State of Kuwait
Canadian Embassy, PO Box 25281, Safat, Kuwait City, 13113 Kuwait
965-2256-3025, Fax: 965-2256-0173,
kwait-td@international.gc.ca
www.infoexport.gc.ca/kw
Yolande Lansing, Trade Commissioner, Environmental Industries

Republic of Latvia
Canadian Embassy, 20/22 Baznicas St., 6th Fl., Riga, LV-1010 Latvia
371-6781-3945, Fax: 371-6781-3960
www.balticstates.gc.ca
Irena Cirule, Trade Commissioner, Environmental Industries, irena.cirule@international.gc.ca

Lebanese Republic
Canadian Embassy, 43 Autostrade Jal El Dib, Beirut, Lebanon
961-4-713-900, Fax: 961-4-710-595,
berut-td@international.gc.ca
www.dfait-maeci.gc.ca/beirut/
Grace Dib, Trade Commissioner, Environmental Industries, grace.dib@international.gc.ca

Socialist People's Libyan Arab Jamahiriya
Canadian Embassy, PO Box 93392, Al-Fateh Tower, 7th Fl., Tripoli, Libya
218-21-335-1633, Fax: 218-21-335-1630,
trpli-td@international.gc.ca
Libya.gc.ca
Hesham Ganem, Trade Commissioner, Environmental Industries, hesham.ganem@international.gc.ca

Lithuania
Canadian Trade Commissioner Service
Business centre 2000 Jogailos g. 4
Vilnius, LT - 01116
370-5249-0950, Fax: 370-5249-7865
vilnius@canada.lt
www.tradecommissioner.gc.ca/lt
Egle Jurkeviciene, Trade Commissioner, Environmental Industries

Federation of Malaysia
Canadian High Commission, PO Box 10990, Kuala Lumpur, Malaysia
60-3-2718-3333, Fax: 60-3-2718-3399,
klmpr-td@international.gc.ca
www.international.gc.ca/missions/malaysia-mala isie/
Sharon Fam, Trade Commissioner, Environmental Industries, sharon.fam@international.gc.ca

Republic of Mali
Canadian Embassy, PO Box 198, Route de Koulikoro, Immeuble séméga, Bamako, Mali
223-2021-2236, Fax: 223-2021-4362,
www.bamako.gc.ca
Ernest Akpoue, Trade Commissioner, Environmental Industries, ernest.akpoue@international.gc.ca

United States of Mexico
Canadian Embassy, Apartado Postal 105-05, Mexico City, 11580 Mexico
52-57-24-7900, Fax: 52-57-24-7980,
mexico.commerce@international.gc.ca
www.mexico.gc.ca
Other information: Emergency: 1-800-703-2900
Paula Caldwell, Senior Trade Commissioner, mexico.commerce@international.gc.ca
Rosalba Cruz, Trade Commissioner, Environmental Industries

Kingdom of Morocco
Canadian Embassy, PO Box 709, Rabat-Agdal, Morocco
212-37-68-74-00, Fax: 212-37-68-74-30,
rabat-td@international.gc.ca
www.rabat.gc.ca
Asmae Amrouche, Trade Commissioner, Environmental Industries

Republic of Mozambique
Canadian High Commission, PO Box 1578, 1138, Kenneth Kaunda Ave., Maputo, Mozambique
258-21-492-623, Fax: 258-21-492-667,
mputo@international.gc.ca
Lurdes Magneli, Trade Commissioner, Environmental Industries lurdes.magneli@international.gc.ca

Kingdom of the Netherlands
Canadian Embassy, Sophialaan 7, The Hague, 2514 JP The Netherlands
31-70-311-1600, Fax: 31-70-311-1620,
hague-td@international.gc.ca
www.canada.nl
Judith Baguley, Trade Commissioner, Environmental Industries

New Zealand
Level 9, 48 Emily Place, Auckland, 1010
011-64-9-309-3690, Fax: 011-64-9-307-3111
aklnd@international.gc.ca
www.tradecommissioner.gc.ca/nz
Pierre Delorme, Sr. Trade Commissioner, Environmental Industries

Nigeria
4 Anifowoshe Street
Victoria Island, Lagos, Nigeria
011-234-1-271-5650/62, Fax: 011-234-1-271-5651/3
lagos-td@international.gc.ca
www.tradecommissioner.gc.ca/ng
Sylvia Koleva, Trade Commissioner, Environmental Industries, sylvia.koleva@international.gc.ca

Kingdom of Norway
Canadian Embassy, Wergelandsveien 7, Oslo, 0244 Norway
47-2299-5300, Fax: 47-2299-5301,
oslo-td@international.gc.ca
www.canada.no
John Winterbourne, Trade Commissioner, Environmental Industries, john.winterbourne@international.gc.ca

Pakistan
Canadian Trade Commissioner Service
336, Beach Luxury Hotel M.T. Khan Road
Karachi, Sindh, 74000
011-92-21-3564-0560, Fax: 011-92-21-3564-0561
isbad-td@international.gc.ca
www.tradecommissioner.gc.ca/pk

Athar Moeen Khan, Trade Commissioner, Environmental Industries, athar.khan@international.gc.ca

Republic of Panama
Canadian Embassy, Apartado Postal 0832-2446, Estafata World Trade Centre, Panama City, Panama
011-507-264-9731, Fax: 011-507-263-8083, panam.commerce@international.gc.ca
www.panama.gc.ca
Luis Cedeno, Trade Commissioner, Environmental Industries, luis.cedeno@international.gc.ca

Republic of Peru
Canadian Embassy, Calle Bolognesi 228, Miraflores, Lima, Peru
511-319-3200, Fax: 511-446-4912, lima.commerce@international.gc.ca
Sandra Shaddick, Sr. Trade Commissioner

Republic of the Philippines
Canadian Embassy, PO Box 2098, Makati Central Post Office, Makati City, 1200 Philippines
63-2-857-9000, Fax: 63-2-843-1082, infocentre-manila@international.gc.ca
Philippines.gc.ca
Dodjie Fabian, Trade Commissioner, Environmental Industries, ramon.yazon@international.gc.ca

Republic of Poland
Canadian Embassy, ul. Jana Matejiki 1/5, Warsaw, 00-481 Poland
48-22-584-3100, Fax: 48-22-584-3192, wsaw-td@international.gc.ca
www.canada.pl
Rouslan Kats, Trade Commissioner, Environmental Industries

Portuguese Republic
Canadian Embassy, Avenida da Liberdade, 196-200, 3rd Fl., Lisbon, 1269-121 Portugal
351-21-316-4600, Fax: 351-21-316-4691, lsbon-td@international.gc.ca
www.portugal.gc.ca
Eurico Nobre, Trade Commissioner, Environmental Industries

Republic of Romania
Canadian Embassy, 1-3 Tuberozelor Str., Bucharest, 011411 Romania
40-21-307-5000, Fax: 40-21-307-5010, bucst-td@international.gc.ca
www.dfait-maeci.gc.ca/bucharest
Octavian Bonea, Trade Commissioner, Environmental Industries

Russian Federation
Canadian Embassy, 23 Starokonyushenny Pereulok, Moscow, 119002 Russian Federation
7-495-925-6000, Fax: 7-495-925-6025, rus.commerce@international.gc.ca
Laura Lumsden, Trade Commissioner, Environmental Industries

Kingdom of Saudi Arabia
Canadian Embassy, PO Box 94321, Riyadh, 11693 Saudi Arabia
966-1-488-2288, Fax: 966-1-488-1997, ryadh-td@international.gc.ca
Richard Dubuc, Sr. Trade Commissioner

Republic of Senegal
Canadian Embassy, PO Box 3373, Dakar, Senegal
221-33-889-4700, Fax: 221-33-889-4720, dakar-td@international.gc.ca
www.dakar.gc.ca
Aminata Ly Faye, Trade Commissioner, Environmental Industries, aminata.ly@international.gc.ca

Serbia
Canadian Trade Commissioner Service
Kneza Milosa 75, Belgrade, 11000
011-381-11-306-3070, Fax: 011-381-11-306-3035
bgrad-td@international.gc.ca
www.tradecommissioner.gc.ca/rs
Djurdjevka Ceramilac, Trade Commissioner, Environmental Industries, djurdjevka.ceramilac@international.gc.ca

Republic of Singapore
Canadian High Commission, PO Box 845, Singapore, 901645 Singapore
65 68545900, Fax: 65 68545930, spore-td@international.gc.ca
www.dfait-maeci.gc.ca/singapore/
Paula Murphy-Ives, Trade Commissioner

Slovak Republic
Canadian Embassy, Mostova 2, Bratislava, 811 02 Slovak Republic
421-259-204-031, Fax: 421-254-434-227
www.ocanada.sk
Milan Harustiak, Trade Commissioner, Environmental Industries milan.harustiak@international.gc.ca

South Africa
Canadian Trade Commissioner Service
Cradock Place, 1st Floor, 10 Arnold Road, Rosebank
Johannesburg, 2196
011-27-11-442-3130, Fax: 011-27-11-442-3325
jobrg@international.gc.ca
www.tradecommissioner.gc.ca/za
Trindard Makunike, Trade Commissioner, Environmental Industries

Kingdom of Spain
Canadian Embassy, Apartado 587, Madrid, 28080 Spain
34-9-423-3250, Fax: 34-9-423-3251, espana@international.gc.ca
www.spain.gc.ca
Amaya Jauregui, Trade Commissioner, Environmental Industries

Democratic Socialist Republic of Sri Lanka
Canadian High Commission, PO Box 1006, Colombo, 7 Sri Lanka
94-11-522-6232, Fax: 94-11-522-6299, clmbo-td@international.gc.ca
Megan Foster, Sr. Trade Commissioner

Kingdom of Sweden
Canadian Embassy, PO Box 16129, Stockholm, 103 23 Sweden
46-8-453-3000, Fax: 46-8-453-3016, stkhm-commerce@international.gc.ca
www.canadaeuropa.gc.ca/sweden
Inga-Lill Olsson, Trade Commissioner, Environmental Industries

Swiss Confederation
Canadian Embassy, Kirchenfeldstrasse 88, Bern, CH-3005 Switzerland
41-31-357-3200, Fax: 41-31-357-3210, bern-td@international.gc.ca
www.switzerland.gc.ca
Annie Dube, Sr. Trade Commissioner

Syrian Arab Republic
Canadian Embassy, PO Box 3394, Damascus, Syria
963-11-611-6692, Fax: 963-11-611-4000, dmcus@international.gc.ca
www.international.gc.ca/syria
Stéphane Beaulieu, Counsellor (Commercial) & Sr. Trade Commissioner, stephane.beaulieu@international.gc.ca
*This office has suspended business temporarily due to the poor security situation. Trade inquiries should be directed to the Canadian Embassy in Amman.

Taiwan
Canadian Trade Commissioner Service
6F, No. 1, Song Zhi Rd., Xinyi District
Taipei, 11047
011-886-2-8723-3000, Fax: 011-886-2-8723-3595
tapei-td@international.gc.ca
www.tradecommissioner.gc.ca/tw
Brendan Murphy, Trade Commissioner, Environmental Industries, Brendan.Murphy@international.gc.ca

United Republic of Tanzania
Canadian High Commission, PO Box 1022, Dar-es-Salaam, Tanzania
255-22-216-3300, Fax: 255-22-211-6897, dslam-td@international.gc.ca
www.dfait-maeci.gc.ca/tanzania
Specioza Lugazia, Trade Commissioner, specioza.lugazia@international.gc.ca

Kingdom of Thailand
Canadian Embassy, PO Box 2090, Bangkok, 10501 Thailand
66-2-636-0540, Fax: 66-2-636-0566, bngkk-td@international.gc.ca
www.thailand.gc.ca
Ekasit Chunlakittiphan, Trade Commissioner, Environmental Industries, ekasit.chunlakittiphan@international.gc.ca

Republic of Trinidad & Tobago
Canadian High Commission, PO Box 1246, Port of Spain, Trinidad
868-622-6232, Fax: 868-628-2581, pspan-commerce@international.gc.ca
www.trinidadandtobago.gc.ca
Michaeline Narcisse, Trade Commissioner, Environmental Industries, michaeline.narcisse@international.gc.ca

Republic of Tunisia
Canadian Embassy, PO Box 31, Tunis, 1002 Tunisia
216-71-104-000, Fax: 216-71-104-191, tunis-td@international.gc.ca
www.dfait-maeci.gc.ca/tunisia
Lassaad Bourguiba, Trade Commissioner, Environmental Industries, lassaad.bourguiba@international.gc.ca

Republic of Turkey
Canadian Embassy, Cinnah Caddesi 58, Cankaya, Ankara, 06690 Turkey
90-312-409-2700, Fax: 90-312-312-409-2810, ankra-td@international.gc.ca
www.dfait-maeci.gc.ca/canadaeuropa/turkey/menu -en.asp
Loc Pham, Second Secretary (Commercial) & Trade Commissioner

Ukraine
Canadian Embassy, 31 Yaroslaviv Val, Kyiv, 1901 Ukraine
380-44-590-3100, Fax: 380-44-590-3109, kyiv-td@international.gc.ca
www.kyiv.gc.ca
Yury Mardak, Trade Commissioner, Environmental Industries, yury.mardak@international.gc.ca

United Arab Emirates
Canadian Embassy, PO Box 6970, Abu Dhabi, United Arab Emirates
971-2-694-0300, Fax: 971-2-694-0399, uae-eau.infocentre@international.gc.ca
www.uae.gc.ca
Imad Arafat, Trade Commissioner, Environmental Industries

United Kingdom of Great Britain & Northern Ireland
Canadian High Commission, MacDonald House, One Grosvenor Sq., London, W1K 4AB United Kingdom
44-20-7258-6600, Fax: 44-20-7258-6384, ldn-td@international.gc.ca
www.london.gc.ca
Daniel Tibbetts, Trade Commissioner, Environmental Industries

United States of America
Consulate General of Canada
1251 Avenue of the Americas
New York, New York
10020-1175
212-596-1650, Fax: 212-596-1793
cngny-td@international.gc.ca
www.tradecommissioner.gc.ca/us
Regine Clement, Trade Commissioner, Environmental Industries

Eastern Republic of Uruguay
Canadian Embassy, #102, Plaza Independencia 749, C.P. 11100, Montevideo, Uruguay
598-2-902-2030, Fax: 598-2-902-2029, mvdeo-td@international.gc.ca
www.montevideo.gc.ca
Patricia Wilson, Trade Commissioner, Environmental Industries

Republic of Venezuela
Canadian Embassy, Apartado Postal 62302, Caracas, 1060A Venezuela
58-212-600-3000, Fax: 58-212-263-8326, crcas-td@international.gc.ca
www.caracas.gc.ca
Daniela Oyague, Trade Commissioner, Environmental Industries

Socialist Republic of Vietnam
Canadian Embassy, 31 Huong Vuong St., Hanoi, Vietnam
84-4-3734-5000, Fax: 84-4-3734-5049, vietnam-infocentre@international.gc.ca
www.vietnam.gc.ca
Dang-Anh Thu, Trade Commissioner, Environmental Industries

Republic of Zambia
Canadian High Commission, PO Box 31313, Lusaka, 10101 Zambia
260-1-25-08-33, Fax: 260-1-25-41-76, lsaka@international.gc.ca
www.international.gc.ca/world/embassies/zambia /
Solomon Milimbo, Trade Commissioner, Environmental Industries, solomon.milimbo@international.gc.ca

Zimbabwe
Canadian Trade Commissioner Service
45 Baines Avenue
Harare
011-263-4-252-181/5, Fax: 011-263-4-252-186
hrare-td@international.gc.ca
www.tradecommissioner.gc.ca/zw
C.J. Scott, Sr. Trade Commissioner

Associations Subject Index

Associations Acronym Index

A

B

C

D

DUC - Ducks Unlimited Canada, 741

E

EAC - Ecology Action Centre, 744
EACO - Environmental Abatement Council of Ontario, 747
EAGE - European Association of Geoscientists & Engineers, 750
EAP - Ecological Agriculture Projects, 743
EAWLS - East African Wild Life Society, 743
EBA - Environmental Bankers Association, 747
ECO-PEI - Environmental Coalition of Prince Edward Island, 747
ECOS - Eastern Canada Orchid Society, 743
EDA - Electricity Distributors Association, 745
EDC - Earth Day Canada, 742
EEAY - Environmental Education Association of the Yukon, 748
EECOM - Canadian Network for Environmental Education & Communication, 711
EEON - Environmental Education Ontario, 748
EEPSA - Environmental Educators' Provincial Specialist Association, 748
EEQ - Éco Entreprises Québec, 743
EESC - Earth Energy Society of Canada, 742
EFC - Egg Farmers of Canada, 744
EFC - Electro-Federation Canada Inc., 745
EFO - Ecological Farmers of Ontario, 743
EFWC - Eskasoni Fish & Wildlife Commission, 750
EGS - European Geosciences Union, 750
EHA Ontario - Environmental Health Association of Ontario, 748
EHABC - Environmental Health Association of British Columbia, 748
EHANS - Environmental Health Association of Nova Scotia, 748
EHFC - Environmental Health Foundation of Canada, 748
EIA - Environmental Industry Associations, 748
EIC - The Engineering Institute of Canada, 746
EII - Earth Island Institute, 742
EIS - Ecoforestry Institute Society, 743
ELC - The Environmental Law Centre (Alberta) Society, 748
EMABC - Environmental Managers Association of British Columbia, 749
EMC - Electric Mobility Canada, 744
EnerACT - Energy Action Council of Toronto, 745
EPRF - Energy Probe Research Foundation, 745
ESA - Ecological Society of America, 743
ESA - Entomological Society of Alberta, 746
ESAA - Environmental Services Association of Alberta, 749
ESAC - Environmental Studies Association of Canada, 749
ESANS - Environmental Services Association of Nova Scotia, 749
ESBC - Entomological Society of British Columbia, 746
ESC - Earthsave Canada, 742
ESM - Entomological Society of Manitoba Inc., 747
ESO - Entomological Society of Ontario, 747
ESS - Entomological Society of Saskatchewan, 747
ESSF - Edmonton Space & Science Foundation, 744
EVCO - Electric Vehicle Council of Ottawa, 744
EVS - Electric Vehicle Society of Canada, 745
EWB - Engineers Without Borders, 746
EWC - EcoWatch Canada, 744
EYA - Environmental Youth Alliance, 749

F

FABQ - Fédération d'agriculture biologique du Québec, 751
FAN - Federation of Alberta Naturalists, 752
FAN - Forest Action Network, 755
FAQ - Fédération des agricultrices du Québec, 751
FARMS - Foreign Agricultural Resource Management Services, 755
FBC - Fraser Basin Council, 757
FBCN - British Columbia Nature (Federation of British Columbia Naturalists), 676
FBD - Fur-Bearer Defenders, 760
FBO - Field Botanists of Ontario, 753
FC - Flowers Canada, 754
FCA - Freight Carriers Association of Canada, 757
FCC - Federation of Calgary Communities, 752
FCC - Fisheries Council of Canada, 754
FCC - The Fur Council of Canada, 760
FCM - Federation of Canadian Municipalities, 752
FCPC - Food & Consumer Products of Canada, 755
FEC - Foundation for Environmental Conservation, 756
FER - Friends of Ecological Reserves, 758
FFFH - Friends of the Forestry Farm House Inc., 759
FFGA - Foothills Forage & Grazing Association, 755
FFGA - Fredericton Fish & Game Association, 757
FFQ - Fondation de la faune du Québec, 754
FFSBC - Freshwater Fisheries Society of British Columbia, 757
FIC - Fur Institute of Canada, 760
FIELD - Foundation for International Environmental Law & Development, 756
FMRG - Friends of Mount Revelstoke & Glacier National Parks, 758
FNA - Farmers of North America, 751
FNA-SAG - Farmers of North America Strategic Agriculture Institute, 751
FoA - Friends of Animals, 757
FOCA - Federation of Ontario Cottagers' Associations, 752
FOCS - Friends of Clayoquot Sound, 758
FoE - Friends of the Earth Canada, 759
FoEI - Friends of the Earth International, 759
FOF - Fresh Outlook Foundation, 757
FONOM - Federation of Northern Ontario Municipalities, 752
FOR - Friends of the Oldman River, 759
FOS - Friends of the Stikine Society, 759
FOTCSI - Friends of the Coves Subwatershed Inc., 759
FPAC - Forest Products Association of Canada, 755
FPANS - Forest Products Association of Nova Scotia, 756
FPBQ - La Fédération des producteurs de bois du Québec, 751
FPC - Fire Prevention Canada, 753
FPC - Food Processors of Canada, 755
FPCCQ - Fédération des producteurs de cultures commerciales du Québec, 751
FPEIM - Federation of Prince Edward Island Municipalities Inc., 752
FPEP - Fédération du personnel de l'enseignement privé, 751
FPI - Foodservice & Packaging Institute, 755
FQCC - Fédération québécoise de camping et de caravaning inc., 753
FQCF - Fédération québécoise des coopératives forestières, 753
FQCK - Fédération québécoise du canot et du kayak, 753
FQM - Fédération Québécoise des Municipalités, 753
FQME - Fédération québécoise de la montagne et de l'escalade, 753
FQSA - Fédération québécoise pour le saumon atlantique, 753
FRC - Fish Harvesters Resource Centres, 754
FSHÉQ - Fédération des sociétés d'horticulture et d'écologie du Québec, 751
FSRS - Fishermen and Scientists Research Society, 754
FSSRA - Federation of Saskatchewan Surface Rights Association, 752
FTSW - Friends of the Trent-Severn Waterway, 759
FWKP - The Friends of West Kootenay Parks Society, 759

G

GAC - Geological Association of Canada, 761
GBR - The Green Brick Road, 763
GCC - Green Communities Canada, 763
GCO - The Garden Clubs of Ontario, 760
GEAPS - Grain Elevator & Processing Society, 762
GEOEC - Global, Environmental & Outdoor Education Council, 762
GHTA - Ganaraska Hiking Trail Association, 760
GIAC - Geomatics Industry Association of Canada, 761
GLIER - Great Lakes Institute for Environmental Research, 763
GLRC - The Great Lakes Research Consortium, 763
GLU - Great Lakes United, 763
GMCS - Gem & Mineral Club of Scarborough, 760
GMWSRS - Grand Manan Whale & Seabird Research Station, 762
GN - Grasslands Naturalists, 762
GPAC - Gas Processing Association Canada, 760
GPBC - Green Party Political Association of British Columbia, 764
GPC - Green Party of Canada, 763
GPI - Glass Packaging Institute, 761
GPO - The Green Party of Ontario, 764
GRCF - Grand River Conservation Foundation, 762
GRESOC - Groupe de recherche en écologie sociale, 765
GRHC - Green Roofs for Healthy Cities, 764
GRO - Gateway Research Organization, 760
GSE - Geotechnical Society of Edmonton, 761
GTWGHS - Greater Toronto Water Garden & Horticultural Society, 763
GWFA - Grey Wooded Forage Association, 765

H

HAC - Helicopter Association of Canada, 767
HAT - Habitat Acquisition Trust, 765
HCF - Heritage Canada Foundation, 767
HCQ - L'Héritage canadien du Québec, 768
HFN - Halifax Field Naturalists, 765
HFNL - Heritage Foundation of Newfoundland & Labrador, 768
HFP - Council of the Haida Nation - Haida Fisheries Program, 739
HIEA - Hamilton Industrial Environmental Association, 765
HIP - Healthy Indoors Partnership, 766
HIT - Hamilton Technology Centre, 765
HM - Héritage Montréal, 768
HMANA - Hawk Migration Association of North America, 766
HNC - Hamilton Naturalists' Club, 765
HORT NS - Horticulture Nova Scotia, 769
HRAI - Heating, Refrigeration & Air Conditioning Institute of Canada, 766
HRMSC - H.R. MacMillan Space Centre Society, 769
HSAA - Health Sciences Association of Alberta, 766
HSAS - Health Sciences Association of Saskatchewan, 766
HSCSA - Health & Safety Conference Society of Alberta, 766
HTNS - Heritage Trust of Nova Scotia, 768
HW - Heritage Winnipeg Corp., 768

I

IAAE - International Association of Agricultural Economists, 775
IAEA - International Atomic Energy Agency, 776
IAEAC - International Association of Environmental Analytical Chemistry, 775
IAEE - International Association for Earthquake Engineering, 774
IAEH - International Association for Environmental Hydrology, 774
IAEWP Canada - International Association of Educators for World Peace, 775
IAF - British Columbia Investment Agriculture Foundation, 676
IAFF - International Association of Fire Fighters (AFL-CIO/CLC), 775
IAGLR - International Association for Great Lakes Research, 774
IAH - International Association of Hydrogeologists, 775
IAH-CNC - International Association of Hydrogeologists - Canadian National Chapter, 775
IAHE - International Association for Hydrogen Energy, 774
IAIA - International Association for Impact Assessment, 774
IAP2 - International Association for Public Participation, 775
IAPO - Indian Agricultural Program of Ontario, 769
IAS - International Association of Sedimentologists, 776
IASC - International Arctic Science Committee, 774
IASTED - International Association of Science & Technology for Development, 775
IATA - International Air Transport Association, 773
IATAL - International Society of Limnology, 784
IAVGO - Industrial Accident Victims Group of Ontario, 769
IBA - International Association for Bear Research & Management, 774
IBWA - International Bottled Water Association, 776
ICA - International Cooperative Alliance, 777
ICAM - International Council for Applied Mineralogy, 777
ICASE - International Council of Associations for Science Education, 777
ICAZ - International Council for Archaeozoology, 777
ICCE - International Centre for Conservation Education, 776
ICEL - International Council of Environmental Law, 777
ICFA - International Coalition of Fisheries Associations, 776
ICID - International Commission on Irrigation & Drainage, 776
ICLAS - International Council for Laboratory Animal Science, 777
ICLEI - International Council for Local Environmental Initiatives, 777
ICOH - International Commission on Occupational Health, 777
ICOMOS - International Council on Monuments & Sites, 778
ICRP - International Commission on Radiological Protection, 777
ICSC - International Centre for Sustainable Cities, 776
ICTAC - International Confederation for Thermal Analysis & Calorimetry, 777
ICURR - Intergovernmental Committee on Urban & Regional Research, 773
IDRC - International Development Research Centre, 778
IECA - International Erosion Control Association, 778
IEEE - Institute of Electrical & Electronics Engineers Inc., 771
IEF - International Energy Foundation, 778

IEPF - Institut de l'énergie et de l'environnement de la Francophonie, 770
IFAW - International Fund for Animal Welfare Canada, 779
IFCB - International Federation for Cell Biology, 778
IFF - International Flying Farmers, 779
IFHP - International Federation for Housing & Planning, 778
IFLA - International Federation of Landscape Architects, 779
IFMBE - International Federation for Medical & Biological Engineering, 778
IFOAM - International Federation of Organic Agriculture Movements, 779
IFS - International Federation of Surveyors, 779
IFT - Institute of Food Technologists, 772
IGF - International Genetics Federation, 779
IGS - International Geosynthetics Society, 779
IGU - International Geographic Union, 779
IGUA - Industrial Gas Users Association Inc., 769
IHHA - International Heavy Haul Association, 780
IHSA - Infrastructure Health & Safety Association, 770
IIASA - International Institute for Applied Systems Analysis, 780
IIC - International Institute for Conservation of Historic & Artistic Works, 780
IICPH - International Institute of Concern for Public Health, 780
IIE - Institute of Industrial Engineers, 772
IIEC - International Institute for Energy Conservation, 780
IIFET - International Institute of Fisheries Economics & Trade, 780
IISD - International Institute for Sustainable Development, 780
ILDC - Independent Lumber Dealers Co-operative, 769
ILSR - Institute for Local Self-Reliance, 771
IMAC - Innovation Management Association of Canada, 770
IMechE - Institution of Mechanical Engineers, 773
IMO - International Maritime Organization, 780
INEM - International Network for Environmental Management, 781
INLA - International Nuclear Law Association, 781
INT - Island Nature Trust, 787
INTECOL - International Association for Ecology, 774
IOI - International Ocean Institute, 781
IOIC - International Oceans Institute of Canada, 781
IOPA - Islands Organic Producers Association, 787
IoPP - Institute of Packaging Professionals, 772
IPA - International Permafrost Association, 781
IPE - Institute of Power Engineers, 772
IPNI - International Plant Nutrition Institute, 782
IPPL - International Primate Protection League, 782
IPPS - International Plant Propagators Society, Inc., 782
IPPSA - Independent Power Producers Society of Alberta, 769
IPS - International Peat Society, 781
IRBV - Institut de recherche en biologie végétale, 770
IRDA - Research & Development Institute for the Agri-Environment, 841
IRG - International Research Group on Wood Protection, 782
IRR - Institute for Risk Research, 771,
IRSST - Institut de recherche Robert-Sauvé en santé et en sécurité du travail, 771
ISAS - Institute of Space & Atmospheric Studies, 772
ISB - International Society of Biometeorology, 783
ISC - International Society of Citriculture, 783
ISEB - International Society for Environmental Biotechnology, 782
ISEE - International Society for Ecological Economics, 782
ISEE - International Society for Environmental Epidemiology, 782
ISEE - International Society for Environmental Ethics, 783
ISEEESA - Institute for Sustainable Energy, Economy & Environment Student's Association, 771
ISEM - International Society for Ecological Modelling, 782
ISEP - International Society for Evolutionary Protistology, 783
ISES - International Solar Energy Society, 784
ISIAQ - International Society of Indoor Air Quality & Climate, 784
ISO - International Organization for Standardization, 781
ISRI - Institute of Scrap Recycling Industries, Inc., 772
ISRIC - International Soil Reference & Information Centre, 784
ISRM - International Society for Rock Mechanics, 783
ISSA - International Sanitary Supply Association, Inc., 782
ISSMGE - International Society for Soil Mechanics & Geotechnical Engineering, 783
ISWA - International Solid Waste Association, 784
ITA - Industrial Truck Association, 769
ITA - International Titanium Association, 784
ITE - Institute of Transportation Engineers, 773
IUBS - International Union of Biological Sciences, 785
IUCN - International Union for Conservation of Nature, 785
IUFoST - International Union of Food Science & Technology, 785
IUFRO - International Union of Forest Research Organizations, 785
IUGG - International Union of Geodesy & Geophysics, 785
IUPAC - International Union of Pure & Applied Chemistry, 786
IUS - Institute of Urban Studies, 773
IUSBSE - International Union of Societies for Biomaterials Science & Engineering, 786
IUSS - International Union of Soil Sciences, 786
IVMA of BC - Integrated Vegetation Management Association of British Columbia, 773
IWA - International Water Association, 786
IWC - International Whaling Commission, 786
IWC - International Wildlife Coalition, 786
IWH - Institute for Work & Health, 771
IWRC - International Wildlife Rehabilitation Council, 786

J

JEA - Jasper Environmental Association, 787
JFAO - Junior Farmers' Association of Ontario, 787
JGI - The Jane Goodal Institute of Canada, 787
JZQ - Jardin zoologique du Québec, 787

K

KAP - Keystone Agricultural Producers, 788
KFN - Kingston Field Naturalists, 788
KNC - Kamloops Naturalist Club, 788
KWIC - Kawartha World Issues Centre, 788

L

LAEA - Lloydminster Agricultural Exhibition Association, 790
LANTA - Landscape Alberta Nursery Trades Association, 789
LARA - Lakeland Agricultural Research Association, 789
LBMAO - Lumber & Building Materials Association of Ontario, 791
LFN - Langley Field Naturalists Society, 789
LGMA - Local Government Management Association of British Columbia, 790
LNL - Landscape Newfoundland & Labrador, 789
LOHTA - Landscape Ontario Horticultural Trades Association, 789
LORDA - Lansdowne Outdoor Recreational Development Association, 789
LSF - Learning for a Sustainable Future, 789
LTA - Land Trust Alliance, 789
LWI - Lambton Wildlife Inc., 789

M

MABC - Mining Association of British Columbia, 797
MAC - Mineralogical Association of Canada, 796
MAC - Mining Association of Canada, 797
MALA - Manitoba Association of Landscape Architects, 791
MAMI - Mining Association of Manitoba Inc., 797
MARA - Mackenzie Applied Research Assciation, 791
MCA - Manitoba Camping Association, 791,
MCABC - Mechanical Contractors Association of British Columbia, 795
MCAC - Mechanical Contractors Association of Canada, 795
MCAM - Mechanical Contractors Association of Manitoba, 795
MCAO - Mechanical Contractors Association of Ontario, 795
MCAS - Mechanical Contractors Association of Saskatchewan Inc., 795
MCIC - Manitoba Council for International Cooperation, 792
MCPA - Manitoba Cattle Producers Association, 791
MCTGA - Manitoba Christmas Tree Growers Association, 792
MEA - Municipal Engineers Association, 798
MEIA - Manitoba Environmental Industries Association Inc., 792
MEN - Manitoba Eco-Network Inc., 792
MEOA - Manitoba Environment Officers Association Inc., 792
MetSoc - Metallurgy & Materials Society of the Canadian Institute of Mining, Metallurgy & Petroleum, 796
MFA - Middlesex Federation of Agriculture, 796
MFNL - Model Forest of Newfoundland & Labrador, 797
MGMC - Montréal Gem & Mineral Club, 797
MHBA - Manitoba Home Builders' Association, 793
MHCA - Manitoba Heavy Construction Association, 792
MIA - Manitoba Institute of Agrologists, 793
MIHR - Mining Industry Human Resources Council, 797
MNS - Nature Manitoba, 803
MOPIA - Manitoba Ozone Protection Industry Association, 793
MPHA - Manitoba Public Health Association, 793
MPPI - Manitoba Professional Planners Institute, 793
MRA - Muskoka Ratepayers' Association, 798
MRAS - Millarville Racing & Agricultural Society, 796
MSCCA - Mining Suppliers, Contractors & Consultants Association of BC, 797
MSM - Mineral Society of Manitoba, 796
MSPEI - Medical Society of Prince Edward Island, 796
MTA - Manitoba Trucking Association, 794
MUC - Manitoba Underwater Council, 794
MVA - Meewasin Valley Authority, 796
MWA - Municipal Waste Association, 798
MWF - Manitoba Wildlife Federation, 794
MWWA - Manitoba Water & Wastewater Association, 794
MWWA - Manitoba Water Well Association, 794

N

NAAEE - North American Association for Environmental Education, 808
NABCI - North American Bird Conservation Initiative Canada, 808
NACE - NACE International, 798
NAEE - National Association for Environmental Education (UK), 799
NAEM - National Association for Environmental Management, 799
NAEP - National Association of Environmental Professionals, 799
NAFA - National Aboriginal Forestry Association, 799
NAIA - Newfoundland Aquaculture Industry Association, 807
NAID - National Association for Information Destruction, 799
NANPS - North American Native Plant Society, 808
NAPCOR - National Association for PET Container Resources, 799
NAPEG - Northwest Territories & Nunavut Association of Professional Engineers & Geoscientists, 810
NARRA - North American Recycled Rubber Association, 809
NAS - National Audubon Society, Inc., 800
NASOH - North American Society for Oceanic History, 809
NATaT - National Association of Towns & Townships, 800
NAWMP - North American Waterfowl Management Plan, 809
NBEC - National Building Envelope Council, 800
NBEIA - New Brunswick Environment Industry Association, 804
NBEN - New Brunswick Environmental Network, 804
NBFPA - New Brunswick Forest Products Association Inc., 804
NBIA - New Brunswick Institute of Agrologists, 804
NBMS - New Brunswick Medical Society, 805
NBSC - New Brunswick Salmon Council, 805
NBSCETT - New Brunswick Society of Certified Engineering Technicians & Technologists, 805
NBSCIA - New Brunswick Soil & Crop Improvement Association, 805
NBWF - New Brunswick Wildlife Federation, 805
NCAMP - National Coalition Against the Misuse of Pesticides, 800
NCAP - Northwest Coalition for Alternatives to Pesticides, 810
NCC - The Nature Conservancy of Canada, 802
NCLGA - North Central Local Government Association, 809
NCSE - National Council for Science & the Environment, 800
NDG - The New Directions Group, 805
NECA - National Energy Conservation Association Inc., 800
NEHA - National Environmental Health Association, 800
NEIA - Newfoundland & Labrador Environmental Industry Association, 806
NER - National Electricity Roundtable, 800
NEW - Nipissing Environmental Watch, 808
NFA - Native Fishing Association, 801
NFN - Norfolk Field Naturalists, 808
NFNC - Niagara Falls Nature Club, 807
NFU - National Farmers Union, 800
NGWA - National Ground Water Association, 801
NHA - Nunavut Harvesters Association, 813
NHPCA - Natural Health Practitioners of Canada Association, 802
NIRS - Nuclear Information & Resource Service, 813
NIVMA - Northern Interior Vegetation Management Association, 810
NLALA - Newfoundland & Labrador Association of Landscape Architects, 805
NLATC - Newfoundland & Labrador Association of Technology Companies, 805
NLCA - Newfoundland & Labrador Construction Association, 806
NLEN - Newfoundland & Labrador Environment Network, 806

O

P

Q

R

RA - Rainforest Alliance, 839
RAC - The Rubber Association of Canada, 843
RACCA-BC - Refrigeration & Air Conditioning Contractors Association of British Columbia, 840
RAN - Rainforest Action Network, 839
RAWF - Royal Agricultural Winter Fair Association, 843
RBC - Rare Breeds Canada, 839
RBG - Royal Botanical Gardens, 843
RCA - Recycling Council of Alberta, 839
RCBC - Recycling Council of British Columbia, 839
RCC - Retail Council of Canada, 841
RCEN - Canadian Environmental Network, 696
RCGS - The Royal Canadian Geographical Society, 843
RCM - Green Action Centre, 763
RCO - Recycling Council of Ontario, 840
RDLC - Regina & District Labour Council, 840
RDRN - Red Deer River Naturalists, 840
REAL - Rideau Environmental Action League, 842
REAP Canada - Resource Efficient Agricultural Production, 841
REAPS - Prince George Recycling & Environmental Action Planning Society, 835
RGS - Resources for Global Sustainability, 841
RHAM - The Regional Health Authorities of Manitoba, 840
RHN - Richmond Hill Naturalists, 842
RISA - Resource Industry Suppliers Association, 841
RMA - Rubber Manufacturers Association, 843
RMAA - Rural Municipal Administrators' Association of Saskatchewan, 844
RMI - The Rocky Mountain Institute, 842
RNRF - Renewable Natural Resources Foundation, 841
RPFANS - Registered Professional Foresters Association of Nova Scotia, 840
RQGE - Réseau québécois des groupes écologistes, 841
RSC - Rhododendron Society of Canada, 842
RSC - The Royal Society of Canada, 843
RSES Canada - Refrigeration Service Engineers Society (Canada), 840
RTA - Rideau Trail Association, 842
RVCA - Rideau Valley Conservation Authority, 842
RVFN - Rideau Valley Field Naturalists, 842
RVLT - Ruiter Valley Land Trust, 844
RWF - Regina Wildlife Federation, 840

S

SAASE - Saskatchewan Association of Agricultural Societies & Exhibitions, 845
SABNES - Salmon Arm Bay Nature Enhancement Society, 845
SALA - Saskatchewan Association of Landscape Architects, 845
SARA - Farming Smarter, 751
SARDA - Smoky Applied Research & Demonstration Association, 852
SARM - Saskatchewan Association of Rural Municipalities, 845
SASTT - Saskatchewan Applied Science Technologists & Technicians, 845
SBC - Sustainable Buildings Canada, 858
SCA - Saskatchewan Camping Association, 846
SCB - Society for Conservation Biology, 854
SCC - Sierra Club of Canada, 851
SCCC - Soil Conservation Council of Canada, 856
SCCWS - Swift Current Creek Watershed Stewards, 859
SCI - Society of Chemical Industry - Canadian Section, 855
SCNHS - Sunshine Coast Natural History Society, 858
SCO - Society of Canadian Ornithologists, 855
SCSA - Saskatchewan Construction Safety Association Inc., 846
SCWIST - Society for Canadian Women in Science & Technology, 854
SDTC - Sustainable Development Technology Canada, 858
SEA - Southeast Environmental Association, 857
SEGD - Society for Environmental Graphic Design, 854
SEI - Stockholm Environment Institute, 858
SEIMA - Saskatchewan Environmental Industry & Managers' Association, 846
SEN - Saskatchewan Eco-Network, 846
SEPAQ - Société des établissements de plein air du Québec, 853
SEQ - Société d'entomologie du Québec, 852
SER - Society for Ecological Restoration International, 854
SES - Saskatchewan Environmental Society, 846
SESCI - Solar & Sustainable Energy Society of Canada Inc., 856
SETAC - Society of Environmental Toxicology & Chemistry, 855
SFA - Saskatchewan Forestry Association, 846
SFN - Sydenham Field Naturalists, 859,
SFNCC - Seniors for Nature Canoe Club, 850
SFPE - Society of Fire Protection Engineers, 855,
SFPIRG - Simon Fraser Public Interest Research Group, 851
SGWA - Saskatchewan Ground Water Association, 847
SHEP - Société d'Horticulture et d'Écologie de Prévost, 852
SILGA - Southern Interior Local Government Association, 857
SIO - Social Investment Organization, 852
SJCAB - St. John's Clean & Beautiful, 844
SKSA - Saskatchewan Katahdin Sheep Association Inc., 847
SLA - Saskatchewan Livestock Association, 847
SLEA - Sarnia-Lambton Environmental Association, 845
SLF - Strategic Leadership Forum, The Toronto Society for Strategic Management, 858
SLSA - Saskatchewan Land Surveyors' Association, 847
SMA - Saskatchewan Medical Association, 847
SMA - Saskatchewan Mining Association, 847
SMACNA - Sheet Metal & Air Conditioning Contractors' National Association, 850
SMCAA - Sheet Metal Contractors Association of Alberta, 851
SMRA - St Mary's River Association, 845
SNLA - Saskatchewan Nursery Landscape Association, 848
SOCODEVI - Société de coopération pour le développement international, 853
SoDC - Seeds of Diversity Canada, 850
SODES - Société de développement économique du Saint-Laurent, 853
SOEEA - Saskatchewan Outdoor & Environmental Education Association, 848
SOOPA - Similkameen Okanagan Organic Producers Association, 851
SOS - Save Ontario Shipwrecks, 849
SOSN - Southern Ontario Seismic Network, 857
SOT - Society of Toxicology, 856
SPAWN - Salmon Preservation Association for the Waters of Newfoundland, 845
SPE - Society of Petroleum Engineers, 855
SPEA - Society of Professional Engineers & Associates, 855
SPEC - Society Promoting Environmental Conservation, 856
SPES - Stanley Park Ecology Society, 858
SPHNC - Société Provancher d'histoire naturelle du Canada, 853
SPI - Society of the Plastics Industry, Inc., 856
SPMABC - Structural Pest Management Association of British Columbia, 858
SPMAO - Structural Pest Management Association of Ontario, 858
SPNC - South Peel Naturalists' Club, 857
SPRA - Saskatchewan Parks & Recreation Association, 848
SQDA - Société québécoise pour la défense des animaux, 854
SQHH - Société québécoise des hostas et des hémérocalles, 854
SQS - Société québécoise de spéléologie, 853
SRI - Steel Recycling Institute, 858
SRLS - Sudbury Rock & Lapidary Society, 858
SSCA - Saskatchewan Soil Conservation Association, 848
SSCS - Sea Shepherd Conservation Society, 849
SSCS - Sea Shepherd Conservation Society - USA, 850
SSEA - Severn Sound Environmental Association, 850
SSGA - Saskatchewan Stock Growers Association, 848
SSM - Safety Services Manitoba, 844
SSNB - Safety Services New Brunswick, 844
SSNS - Safety Services Nova Scotia, 844
SSS - Society for Socialist Studies, 854
STA - Saskatchewan Trucking Association, 848
STC - Society of Toxicology of Canada, 856
STEP - Saskatchewan Trade & Export Partnership Inc., 848
SUDA - Sustainable Urban Development Association, 859
SUMA - Saskatchewan Urban Municipalities Association, 849
SWANA - Solid Waste Association of North America, 857
SWCS - Soil & Water Conservation Society, 856
SWF - Saskatchewan Wildlife Federation, 849
SWRC - Saskatchewan Waste Reduction Council, 849
SYC - Sierra Youth Coalition, 851

T

TAC - Transportation Association of Canada, 861
TAC - Tunnelling Association of Canada, 862
TBFN - Thunder Bay Field Naturalists, 860
TBI - Toronto Biotechnology Initiative, 860
TCS - The Cousteau Society, 740
TCTF - Trans Canada Trail Foundation, 861
TCYHA - Trans Canada Yellowhead Highway Association, 861
TEA - Toronto Entomologists Association, 860
TEA - Toronto Environmental Alliance, 860
TEAC - Temiskaming Environmental Action Committee, 859
TECA - Thermal Environmental Comfort Association, 859
TFN - Toronto Field Naturalists, 860
TIANB - Tourism Industry Association of New Brunswick Inc., 861
TLA - Truck Loggers Association, 862
TOC - Toronto Ornithological Club, 860
TOGA - The Ontario Greenhouse Alliance, 818
TREA - Thames Region Ecological Association, 859
TREC - Toronto Renewable Energy Co-operative, 860
TSBC - Tire Stewardship BC Association, 860
TSMCA - Toronto Sheet Metal Contractors Association, 860
TTS - Toronto Transportation Society, 860
TUC - Trout Unlimited Canada, 862
TWS - Toxics Watch Society of Alberta, 861

U

UASBC - Underwater Archaeological Society of British Columbia, 862
UBCM - Union of British Columbia Municipalities, 862
UCA - Utility Contractors Association of Ontario, Inc., 865
UCA - Uxbridge Conservation Association, 865
UCFO - Union des cultivateurs franco-ontariens, 862
UDI - Urban Development Institute of Canada, 864
UIA - Union internationale des architectes, 862
UMAAS - Urban Municipal Administrators' Association of Saskatchewan, 864
UMQ - Union des municipalités du Québec, 862
UNAC - United Nations Association in Canada, 863
UNCTAD - United Nations Conference on Trade & Development, 863
UNDP - United Nations Development Programme, 863
UNEP - United Nations Environment Programme, 864
UNEP-WCMC - UNEP - World Conservation Monitoring Centre, 862
UNIDO - United Nations Industrial Development Organization, 864
UNSM - Union of Nova Scotia Municipalities, 863
UPA - Union des producteurs agricoles, 862
URISA - Urban & Regional Information Systems Association, 864

V

VBGA - VanDusen Botanical Garden Association, 865
VEVA - Vancouver Electric Vehicle Association, 865
VGAM - Vegetable Growers' Association of Manitoba, 865
VI - The Vinyl Institute, 866
VLMS - Victoria Lapidary & Mineral Society, 866
VRCA - Vancouver Regional Construction Association, 865
VTA - Voyageur Trail Association, 866
VWS - Valhalla Wilderness Society, 865

W

WAITRO - World Association of Industrial & Technological Research Organizations, 871
WAS - World Aquaculture Society, 871
WBCC - Wild Bird Care Centre, 869
WBCSD - World Business Council for Sustainable Development, 871
WBEA - Wood Buffalo Environmental Association, 870
WBFN - Willow Beach Field Naturalists, 870
WCA - Wilderness Canoe Association, 869
WCEL - West Coast Environmental Law, 867
WCF - World Citizen Foundation, 871
WCFA - West Central Forage Association, 867
WCI - World Coal Institute, 872
WCSC - Western Canadian Shippers' Coalition, 868
WCTD - Western Canada Tire Dealers Association, 868
WCWC - Western Canada Wilderness Committee, 868
WCWWA - Western Canada Water, 868
WEAO - Water Environment Association of Ontario, 866
WEC - World Energy Council, 872
WEDO - Women's Environment & Development Organization, 870
WEF - Water Environment Federation, 866
WESTAC - Western Transportation Advisory Council, 869
WETT - Wood Energy Technology Transfer Inc., 870
WFM - World Federalist Movement, 872
WFS - World Future Society, 872
WFUES - World Federation of Ukrainian Engineering Societies, 872
WHC - Wildlife Habitat Canada, 869
WHO - World Health Organization, 872

Y

Associations Publications Index

D

E

Q

R

S

T

U

V

W

Y

Educational Programs Index

Foundations & Grants Index

Law Firms Index

N

O

P

R

S

T

W

Y

Libraries & Resource Centres Index

D

E

F

G

H

I

J

K

L

M

N

O

P

Q

R

S

T

U

V

W

X

Y

Research Centres Index

I

J

K

L

M

N

O

P

Q

R

S

T

U

V

W

Y

Entry Name Index

For Federal Government Offices see Quick Reference Guide on page 1057

B

For Federal Government Offices see Quick Reference Guide on page 1057

For Federal Government Offices see Quick Reference Guide on page 1057

For Federal Government Offices see Quick Reference Guide on page 1057

D

For Federal Government Offices see Quick Reference Guide on page 1057

For Federal Government Offices see Quick Reference Guide on page 1057

F

For Federal Government Offices see Quick Reference Guide on page 1057

H

For Federal Government Offices see Quick Reference Guide on page 1057

J

K

L

M

For Federal Government Offices see Quick Reference Guide on page 1057

N

For Federal Government Offices see Quick Reference Guide on page 1057

O

For Federal Government Offices see Quick Reference Guide on page 1057

P

Q

R

For Federal Government Offices see Quick Reference Guide on page 1057

S

For Federal Government Offices see Quick Reference Guide on page 1057

T

For Federal Government Offices see Quick Reference Guide on page 1057

W

For Federal Government Offices see Quick Reference Guide on page 1057

Executive Name Index

A

A., Muchortow, Chief Audit Executive, 1190
Aaron, McCrorie, Director, Aviation Security Regulatory Review, 1175
Aaron, Nelson, Director, Royalty & Policy, 1203
Aaron, Lamb, Executive Director, Asset Management, 1211
Aaron, Bennett, Biologist, 1221
Aaron, Campbell, Director, 1268
Aaron, Ramsay, Aquaculture Biologist, 1270
Abbot, Sue, Vice-President, 803
Abbott, Amy, Associate, Ackroyd LLP Barristers & Solicitors, 906
Abby, Hoffman, Assistant Deputy Minister, 1146
Abby, Katz Starr, Director, Retirement Homes Project, 1263
Abdel-Aziz, Ahab, Partner, Heenan Blaikie LLP - Toronto, 931
Abdel-Barr, B.Comm., J.D., LL.B., Khaled S., Partner, Lawson Lundell LLP - Vancouver, 913
Abdoul Aziz, Niang, Directeur, Analyses et politiques, 1277
Abdul, Jalil, Director, Agriculture Research, 1286
Abdula, Amyn M., Stikeman Elliott LLP - Vancouver, 914
Abeytunga, Patabendi K., Vice-President, 691
Ableson, Serena, Assistant Law Librarian, Akitsiraq Law School, Diana M. Priestly Law Library, 968
Ablog-Morrant, Kelly, Director, 676
Abouchar, Juli, Partner, Willms & Shier Environmental Lawyers LLP, 937
Abraham, Brian E., Dentons Canada LLP - Vancouver, 912
Abram, Sean, Chair, 664
Abram James, Almeda, Executive Director, Strategic Financial Operations, 1242
Abrametz, Peter V., Abrametz & Eggum, 946
Abriel, Katie, Manager, 730
Abushawashi, Salem, Superintendent, Wood Buffalo, 1305
Abusow, Kathy, President & Chief Executive Officer, 699
Abusow, Kathy, President & CEO, 859
Accardi, P.Eng, Joe, Executive Director, 824
Accursi, Chad, Partner, Cassels Brock & Blackwell LLP, 928
Aceto, Silvana, Specialist, 689
Achim, Guy, Monty Coulombe s.e.n.c. - Sherbrooke, 946
Ackman, Elizabeth K., Partner, Miller Thomson LLP - Toronto, 934
Acres, Trace, Vice-President, 678
Acton, Gordon P., Senior Business Partner, Wishart Law Firm LLP, 927
Adam, Robert-André, Associé, Cain Lamarre Casgrain Wells - Val-d'Or, 946
Adam, Arlene, Executive Assistant, Saskatchewan Watershed Authority, 1031
Adam, Fancy, Contact, Intergovernmental Affairs, 1136
Adam, Taylor, Director, Communications & Forward Planning, 1143
Adam J., Peters, Temporary Supervisor, Social Assistance & Disability Support Programs (Montague/Souris), 1267
Adamik, David, Treasurer, 704
Adams, Richard H.G., Thompson Dorfman Sweatman LLP - Winnipeg, 916
Adams, Alison, Librarian, Cornwall Campus, 985
Adams, Karen, Director of Libraries, University of Manitoba Libraries, 972
Adams, Karen, Director, Library Services & Information Resources, University of Alberta, 956
Adams, Kelly, Chief Operating Officer, Central Newfoundland Regional Health Centre, 977
Adams, Patricia, President, Energy Probe Research Foundation, 1002
Adams, Virgina, Dept Head, Library Public Services, Vancouver Community College, 967
Adams, Patricia, Executive Director, 836
Adams, David C., President, 661
Adams, Patricia, President, 745
Adamson, Dan, General Manager, 795
Adamson, Lee, Manager, 780
Adamson, Dan, Manager, Prince George, 1317
Adams-Webber, Tamsin, Librarian, Hospital for Sick Children, 1003
Adant, Pierre, Responsable, Bibliothèque des sciences et de génie, 1029
Adant, Pierre, Responsable, Bibliothèque sciences et génie, Université de Sherbrooke, 1030
Addario, Martin J., Partner, Hicks Morley Hamilton Stewart Storie LLP - Toronto, 932
Addison, Emily, Membership Coordinator, 824
Adelberg, Ellen, Director, 713
Adele, Shaughnessy, Director, Financial Guarantee Programs Division, 1120
Adin, Emilie K., City Planner, North Vancouver, 1316
Adjibade, Aboudou Karim, Regional Director, 778
Adkin, Rob, Secretary-Treasurer, 757
Adkins, Robert J.M., Thompson Dorfman Sweatman LLP - Winnipeg, 916
Adkins, Sam, McCarthy Tétrault LLP - Vancouver, 913
Adler, Monica, Vice-President, 684
Adrian, Boyd, Director, Policy, 1118
Adrian, Hickin, Director, Cordilleran Geoscience, 1202
Adrian, Hickin, Director, GeoScience & Natural Gas Development Branch, 1203
Adrian, Fuller, Regional Director, 1242
Adriana, Mastrostefano, Regional Director, Corporate Services, 1178
Adrienne, Watt, Manager, Advertising & Marketing Services, 1200
Affonso, Amanda, Director, 696
L'Africain, Daniel, Joli-Coeur Lacasse Avocats - Montréal, 940
Agar, Glen W., Thompson Dorfman Sweatman LLP - Winnipeg, 916
Agathe, Jérôme, Chief, Management & Liaison Services, 1132
Aggas, Roger, Registrar, 840
Agioritis, John, MacPherson Leslie & Tyerman LLP - Saskatoon, 947
Agnès, Maltais, Ministre, 1285
Agnew, Jocelyne, Bibliotechnicienne, La Cité Collégiale, 994
Agnew, Wilma, Executive Director, 851
Ahearn, Margaret, Head Librarian, Natural Resources Canada Library, 996
Ahearn, Brian, Vice-President, 700
Ahmed, Fatimah, Librarian, The Scarborough Hospital - Grace Campus, 1007
Ahmed, Fatimah, Manager, Health Information Resource Centre, The Scarborough Hospital - General Campus, 1007
Ahmed, A. Karim, Sec.-Treas., 800
Ahuja, Kelley, CAO, 772
Aïda, Warah, Acting Director, Pollutant Inventories & Reporting, 1135
Aidan, O'Brien, Commissioner, 1219
Aidan, Sheridan, Chief Executive Officer, 1269
Aiken, Tim, Chairman, 808
Aime, Rachelle, Vice-President, 794
Aime, Dimatteo, Director General, 1154
Aimee, Ellis, Manager, 1299
Ainley, William M., Senior Partner, Davies Ward Phillips & Vineberg LLP, 929
Ainsworth, Jon, Senior Analyst/Programmer, 757
Aird, Judy, Volunteer Director, 865
Aitchison, Chrissy, Marketing Manager, 706
Aitken, Cindy, Manager, 651
Aja, Dykes, Executive Assistant, 1198
Aja, Norgaard, Director, Integrated Planning, 1210
Akeeagok, David, Chair, 694
Akermann, Markus, CEO, 871
Akrigg, Dave, Manager, Parks, Cemetary & Arena Operations, Thorold, 1337
Al, Hoffman, Chief Inspector/Executive Director, Health & Safet, Health & Safety & Permitting Branch, 1202
Al, Gorley, Chair, 1205
Al, Szczawinski, Director, Engineering Systems, 1212
Al, Spencer, Supervisor, Stabilization, 1234
Al, Tithecott, Director, Aviation, Forest Fire & Emergency Services, 1258
Alain, Jacques, Directeur Exécutif, 656
Alain, Marjorie, Responsable des relations publiques, 753
Alain, Giguère, Director, Operations, 1121
Alain, Houde, Director, Operations, 1122
Alain, Beaudet, President, 1130
Alain, Dufresne, Manager, Environmental Services - Québec, 1133
Alain, Vézina, Regional Director, Science, 1141
Alain, Brizard, Manager, Operational Policies, 1159
Alain, Vauclair, Senior General Counsel & Executive Director, Legal Services Branch, 1171
Alain, Basque, Director, Tourism Operations, 1226
Alain, Roy, Directeur régional, 1277
Alain, Côté, Directeur régional, 1277
Alain, Couture, Directeur, Direction campus de Saint-Hyacinthe, 1277
Alain, Brochu, Vice-président, Marketing, 1278
Alain, Gaudreault, Directeur, 1278
Alain, Gaudreault, Directeur, 1279
Alain, Proulx, Directeur général, Export Québec, 1280
Alain, Veilleux, Sous-ministre adjoint et directeur (par intérim), Politiques économiques, 1280
Alain, Lefebvre, Directeur général, Hydrocarbures et Bioarburants, 1281
Alain, Simard, Directeur, Projet de service en ligne de réquisitions d'inscription, 1281
Alain, Sénéchal, Directeur, Bureau de la coordination du régime forestier, 1281
Alain, Simard, Directeur général, 1282
Alain, Thibeault, Directeur général, 1282
Alain, Saucier, Directeur, Gestion intégrée de l'information, 1283
Alain, Dupont, Directeur, Stratégie et de la mise en marché, 1284
Alain G., Trépanier, Regional Director General, 1172
Alain Marc, Dubé, Directeur, Projet Turcot, 1285
Alaire, Dominique, Responsable, Collège Montmorency, 1014
Alan, Ehrlich, Acting Manager, Environmental Impact Assessment, 1117
Alan, Schlachter, Director, Market Access Secretariat-Asia & Oceania, 1120
Alan, Parkinson, Director General, Community Pastures Program, 1120
Alan, Wilde, Departmental Advisor, Americas, 1143
Alan, Minz, Regional Director & Senior Trade Commissioner, 1144
Alan, Johnston, President, 1154
Alan, Latourelle, Chief Executive Officer, 1166
Alan, Roy, Assistant Deputy Minister, Corporate Services, Com, 1221
Alan, Grant, Executive Director, Agriculture & Food Operations, 1240
Alan, Davidson, Director, Mineral Management, 1244
Alan, Hogan, Director, Strategic Solutions, 1249
Alan, Robison, Chief, Safety Standards, 1268
Alan, Toombs, Manager, Emergency Health Services, 1273
Alan, Aitken, Engineer, Traffic Operations, 1274
Alan, Maynard, Director, 1275
Alan, Hilton, Deputy Minister, Government Relations, 1290
Alan J., Stewart, Senior Soil Resource Specialist, Land & Soil Resources Unit, 1119
Alana, Rosseker, Director, Innovation & Industry Development Branch, 1198
Alana, Hinchey, Senior Geologist & Section Manager, Regional Geology, 1233
Alana, Essery, Executive Director & Registrar, 1271
Alanna, Koch, Deputy Minister, Agriculture, 1286
Alanna, Koch, Chair, 1286
Alastair, O'Rielly, Deputy Minister, 1228
Alati, John M., Davies Howe Partners LLP, 929
Alati-it, Julie, Information Specialist, Women's Health Knowledge Centre, 953
Alavy, Sam, President & Chief Executive Officer, 715
Albarella, Umberto, Secretary, 777
Albert, Johanne, Secrétaire, Campus d'Edmundston, 973
Albert, Thorassie, Chair, 1117
Albert, Asztalos, Supervisor, Farm Services, Delhi Research Farm, 1123
Albert, Nussbaum, Director, Forest Analysis & Inventory Branch, 1206
Albert, Walzak, Director, Environmental & Social Affairs, 1243
Albert, Walzak, Director, Social & Environmental Affairs, 1243
Albert, Sweetnam, Executive Vice-President, Nuclear Projects, 1261
Albert, MacDonald, Director, Municipal Affairs & Provincial Planning, 1269
Albert, James, Co-Chair, 1300

Albert J., Middleton, Manager, Stavely Research Substation Site, 1122
Albert O., Adegbembo, Senior Dental Consultant, Dental Health Program, 1272
Alder, Sheridan L., Head Librarian, Southern Crop Protection & Food Research Centre, 1010
Alec, Simpson, Senior Director, Environmental Management, 1175
Alec, Dale, Acting Director, Ecosystems Branch, 1204
Alec, Drysdale, Director, Resource Authorization (South Coast), 1205
Aleck, Dadson, Chief Operating Officer, 1250
Alek, Antoniuk, Manager, Code Development Unit, 1257
Alethea, Foster, Executive Director, Relationship & Policy, 1290
Alex, Li, Director, Maritime Safety Systems, 1140
Alex, Thompson, Deputy Director, Commercial Aerospace, 1154
Alex, Umnikov, Branch Head, Innovation Client Services Branch, 1185
Alex, Morrison, Director, Safety Assurance Services, 1194
Alex, Ferguson, Commissioner & Chief Executive Officer, 1202
Alex, Smith, Director, Mineral Development Division, 1233
Alex, Baldwin, Director, Research, Policy & Library Services, 1245
Alex, Fallon, Director, Investment Attraction, 1288
Alex (Sandy), MacDonald, Deputy Minister, 1267
Alexander, Lawrence, Heenan Blaikie LLP - Victoria, 915
Alexander, Megan, Associate, Cox & Palmer - St. John's, 918
Alexander, Timothy P., Blaney McMurtry LLP, 928
Alexander, Aruna, President, 863
Alexander, Sasha, Director, 854
Alexander, Steve, Executive Director, 663
Alexander, Denny, Officer, 699
Alexander, Stephen, General Manager, Planning, Parks & Recreation Serv, Cornwall, 1332
Alexander, Smith, Director, Communications, 1123
Alexander-Smith, Janet, Emery Jamieson LLP, 907
Alexanderson, Miguel Benedetto, President, 799
Alexandra, Sutton, Director General, Communications, 1138
Alexandra, Dagger, Director, Audit & Evaluation, 1158
Alexandra, Ferris, Director, Community Finances, 1221
Alexandre, Misty, Partner, Robertson Stromberg LLP, 947
Alexandre, Gracovetsky, Director, Forecasting & Modelling, 1174
Alexandre, Iracà, Directeur, 1279
Alexandrea, Knight, Trade Officer, 1238
Alexandrowicz, John-Paul, Partner, Hicks Morley Hamilton Stewart Storie LLP - Toronto, 932
Alexeev, Lev, Stikeman Elliott LLP - Montréal, 943
Aleyaseen, Val, Chair, 855
Alf, Morais, PHC Medical Director, Queens (East & West), 1272
Alf, Bernstein, Director, Real Estate Services, 1287
Alf, Bernstein, Director, Realty, 1287
Alford, Larry, Chief Librarian, University of Toronto Libraries, 1008
Alfred, Rivers, Chair, 1218
Ali Khan, Abbas, Partner, Dentons Canada LLP - Toronto, 930
Alice, Wong, Minister of State (Seniors), 1147
Alice, Sayant, Vice President, Prevention, Assessments & Customer Service, 1219
Alicia, Sutton, Director, Government Relations, 1227
Aline, Dimitri, Director, Executive Support & Coordination, 1129
Alison, McDermott, Acting Director General, Program Coordination Branch, 1154
Alison, Taylor, Director, Evaluation, 1155
Alison, Galloway, Technologist, Geo-Spatial/Data Services, Centre for Topographic Information - Ottawa, 1164
Alison, Coyne, Director, Land Use Initiatives & Analysis, 1209
Alison, Thorson, Director, Policy, Planning & Customer Relations, 1212
Allaire-Hébert, Marie-Eve, Coordonnatrice, 713
Allan, John, President & Chief Executive Officer, 739
Allan, Steve, Manager, 641
Allan, Pope, Chief Review Officer, 1138
Allan, Van Dyk, Director, Surface & Inter-modal Security Policy, 1177
Allan, Crawshaw, Director, Operations, 1199
Allan, Lidstone, Director, Resource Management Objectives, 1206
Allan, Castle, Executive Director, Business Intelligence & Perfor, 1210
Allan, Chafe, Director, Surveys & Mapping Division, 1227
Allan, Scott, Chair, 1231
Allan, Willcocks, Regional Director, 1259
Allan, O'Keefe, Director, Classification & Employee Relations, 1269
Allan, Rankin, Vice-Chair, 1274
Allan, Churko, Regional Executive Director, 1293
Allan, Nixon, Assistant Deputy Minister, 1302
Allan D., MacLean, Director General, Conservation & Protection, 1140
Allan R., Bartley, Director, Marine Security Policy, 1176
Allard, Jean R., Senior Partner, Norton Rose Fulbright Canada LLP - Montréal, 942
Allard, André, Responsable, Centre hospitalier de l'Université de Montréal Hôtel-Dieu, 1017
Allard, Louise, Chef, Division du Traitement des fonds documentair, Université Laval, 1025
Allard, Louis-Paul, Président, 755
Allard Strutt, Suzanne, Chief Executive Officer, 677
Allardyce, Laura, Officer, 711
Allen, Greg J., Alexander Holburn Beaudin & Lang, LLP, 910
Allen, Michael S., Partner, Stikeman Elliott LLP - Vancouver, 914
Allen, Clara, Petroleum Products & Records Administrator, Northwest Territories Public Works & Services, 979
Allen, Neil, Ciculation Supervisor, Engineering & Computer Science Library, 1002
Allen, Brian, President, 821
Allen, Mary, CEO, 644
Allen, Mary, Regional Coordinator, 644
Allen, Muggaberg, GO Team Manager, 1214
Allen, Mullen, Assistant Deputy Minister, Asset Management, 1287
Allen, Mullen, Assistant Deputy Minister, Project Management & De, 1287
Allen F., Roach, Minister, 1273
Allen, FEC, P.Eng., Kim, CEO, 746
Alleyne-Martin, Natasha, Manager, 859
Allford, R. Bruce, Partner, Burnet, Duckworth & Palmer LLP, 902
Allingham, Jana, Library Assistant, Campbell River Campus Library, 959
Allison, Andrea, Librarian, John B. Ridley Research Library, 983
Allison, G., Director, Building Services & Chief Building Offic, Barrie, 1331
Allison, Webb, Acting Director, US & Asia/Pacific Regional Affairs, 1141
Allison, Myatt, Environmental Officer, 1157
Allison, Murphy, Senior Manager, Ministerial Issues & Correspondenc, 1192
Allison, Matacheskie, Registrar, 1209
Allison, MacEwen, Director, Technical & Regulatory Services Division, 1274
Allison J., Stuart, Assistant Deputy Minister & Chief, 1249
Allyn, Lyon, Director, Community & Industry Partnering, 1302
Alrick, Huebener, Director, Strategic Issues Division, 1163
Alter, Lloyd, President, 652
Althea, Hutchinson, Executive Director & Senior Financial Officer, Str, 1195
Alton, Michelle A., Associate, Hicks Morley Hamilton Stewart Storie LLP - Toronto, 932
Alvarenga, Rosibel, Contact, 856
Alvarez, Héctor, Chef des services publics, Université de Moncton, 975
Alvarez, Pierre, Chair, 691
Alvarez, Isis, Office Coordinator, 759
Alvin, Keenan, Chair, 1265
Alyea, Alexis, Davis LLP - Toronto, 930
Am Rhyn, Jost, Executive Director, 723
Amanda, Murphy, Advisor, Parliamentary Affairs & Issues Management, 1143
Amanda, McNaughton, Senior Trade Commissioner, Bio-Industries, Health Industries & Investment Promotion, 1144
Amanda, Girardin, Manager, Visitor Experience, Government House, 1294
Amano, Yukiya, Director General, 776
Amantea, Joseph B., Partner, Warren Tettensor Amantea LLP, 906
Amar, Serge, Associé, Langlois Kronström Desjardins, 940
Amber, Caseley, Communications Officer, 1273
Ambrozy, Samantha, Heenan Blaikie LLP - Toronto, 931
Ament, Ken, Technician, Thompson, 1321
Ames, Doris, President, 802
Amey, Vern, Director, Public Works, Greater Napanee, 1333
Amina, Bisbis, Director, Industrial Research Assistance Program F, 1159
Amit, Budhwar, Director, Risk Management, 1208
Amm, David, Chair, 737
Amnotte, Céline, Directrice, Développement collections et acquisiti, Université de Montréal, 1021
Amonson, Carla, Manager, 867
Amorosi, Mark, Executive Director, Human Resources & Legal Servic, Guelph, 1333
Amsterdam, Cynthia, Partner, Heenan Blaikie LLP - Calgary, 904
Amsterdam, Cynthia, Partner, Heenan Blaikie LLP - Toronto, 931
Amy, Gibson, Manager, First Nations & Metis Policy & Partnerships Office, 1256
Amyn, Alibhai, Director, 1198
Anand, Gita, Partner, Miller Thomson LLP - Toronto, 934
Andersen, Harold K., Partner, Stikeman Elliott LLP - Calgary, 905
Andersen, Donna, Library Assistant, Brandon University, 969
Andersen, Erica, Director, 861
Anderson, Danny R., Partner, MacPherson Leslie & Tyerman LLP - Saskatoon, 947
Anderson, John F., Partner, Stikeman Elliott LLP - Vancouver, 914
Anderson, Robert S., Farris, Vaughan, Wills & Murphy LLP, 912
Anderson, Dean, General Manager & Chief Operating Officer, Farm Safety Association Inc., 985
Anderson, Karen H., Library Assistant, Brandon University, 969
Anderson, Megan, Librarian, Data, Access & Media, Fanshawe College, 989
Anderson, Shirley, Library Technician, Northern Lakes College, 957
Anderson, Stephen, Contact, Career Centre Reference Library, 1001
Anderson, Charles F., President, 650
Anderson, Mary, Manager, 696
Anderson, Kjelti, Coordinator, 713
Anderson, Scott, Contact, 761
Anderson, Brian, Manager, 818
Anderson, Dean, Chair, 683
Anderson, Patti, President, 807
Anderson, Ian, Chair, 771
Anderson, Bill, Treasurer & Vice-President, 804
Anderson, Bill, Président, 654
Anderson, Bruce L., Executive Director, Human Resources, Toronto, 1338
Anderson, Jim, Director, Cochrane, 1306
Anderson, Keith, Director, North Battleford, 1359
Anderson, Shannon, General Manager, Peace River, 1313
Anderson, Tom R., General Manager, Cowichan Valley, 1311
Andersson, Roland, Executive Director, 728
Andersson, Luke, Coordinator, 728
Andison, Mark, Director, Kootenay Boundary, 1312
Andrahennadi, Ruwandi, President, 747
Andre, Corriveau, Chief Public Health Officer, Office of the Chief Public Health Officer, 1238
Andre, Moore, Director, Economic Policy & Analysis, 1243
Andre, Celliers, PHC Medical Director, Summerside, 1272
André, Charron, Director, Business Programs, 1123
André, Régimbald, Director General, Nuclear Substance Regulation, 1131
André, Bernier, Senior Director, Aerospace, 1154
André, Bourdon, Director, Application Services, IM / IT Directorat, 1155
André, Beaudet, Secretary - Director General, 1156
André, Lapointe, Regional Director General, 1178
André, Chenard, Director, Community Funding & Technical Services, 1221
André, Lepine, Director, Senior & Healthy Aging Secretariat, 1225
André, Moore, Director, Economic Policy & Analysis, 1243
André, Boulanger, Président, Hydro-Québec TransÉnergie, 1280
André, Martin, Président-directeur général, 1281
André, Denis, Directeur, Développement de l'industrie et des produits forestiers, 1281
André, Jutras, Directeur, 1282
André, Auclair, Directeur général, Affaires stratégiques et territoire, 1282
André, Bolduc, Directeur, Gestion budgétaire et comptable ministérielle, 1283
André, Dontigny, Directeur, Développement des individus et de l'environnement social, 1283
André, Delorme, Directeur, Santé mentale, 1283

André, Meloche, Directeur général et sous-ministre adjoint, 1285
André, Caron, Directeur général et sous-ministre adoint, 1285
André, Perron, Directeur, Bureau d'évaluation médicale, 1286
André B., Lemay, Directeur général, 1282
André G., Bernier, Directeur, Analyse et des instruments économiques, 1279
Andre J., Talbot, Director, Aquatic Ecosystem Protection Research, 1135
Andre R., Lalonde, Regional Director, Surface, 1177
Andrea, Shelley, Director, 639
Andrea, Lyon, Associate Deputy Minister, 1134
Andrea, Raper, Director, Real Property, Long Term Capital Management, 1140
Andrea, Kalischuk, Branch Head, Water Quality Branch, 1182
Andrea, Henning, Executive Director, Arts & Culture Branch, 1201
Andrea, McKenna, Senior Policy Officer, 1227
Andrea, Bruce, Acting Manager, 1250
Andrea, Cohen, Chief Executive Officer, 1262
Andrea Terry, Munro, Director, Corporate Services & Financial Programs, 1288
Andrée, Chevrier, Director, Operational Support, 1128
Andrée, Bélanger, Directrice, Coordination du Plan Nord, 1282
Andrée, Quenneville, Directrice, Planification et orientations stratégiques, 1283
Andreeff, Monica, Executive Director, 658
Andres, Gerd, Manager, 640
Andrew, Hart, Contact, 680
Andrew, Gail, Treasurer, 866
Andrew, Murray, Executive Director, 847
Andrew, Ferguson, Principal, Sustainable Development Strategies, Aud, 1124
Andrew, House, Chief of Staff, Minister's Office, 1170
Andrew, Sharman, Assistant Deputy Minister, 1191
Andrew, Pratt, Manager, Graphic Design Services, 1200
Andrew, Pape-Salmon, Director, Energy Efficiency Branch, 1202
Andrew, Morgan, Director, Integrated Initiatives, 1205
Andrew, Wilson, Director, Fish, Wildlife & Habitat Management, 1206
Andrew, Currie, Director, Human Resources, 1224
Andrew, Kerr, Senior Geologist & Section Manager, Mineral Deposits, 1233
Andrew, Murphy, Director, Air Quality & Resource Management Branch, 1242
Andrew, Lathem, Director, Emergency Programs, 1243
Andrew, Posluns, Director, Transit Policy, 1264
Andrew, MacDougall, Administrator, Long Term Care, Queens, 1272
Andrew, Cipywnyk, Director, Trucking Policy & Regulation, 1292
Andrew, Liu, Director, Transportation Infrastructure, 1292
Andrew D., Pike, Acting Manager, Crown Lands Administration, 1228
Andrew M., Thompson, Director, Staffing & Human Resource Planning, 1269
Andrew P.W., Bennett, Ambassador of Religious Freedom, 1142
Andrews, Kurtis R., Donald R. Good & Associates, 925
Andrews, Mark R., Partner, Ottenheimer Baker, 919
Andrews, John P., Manager, 681
Andrews, Warren, Manager, Lethbridge, 1307
Andrews, Q.C., Robert B., Partner, Ottenheimer Baker, 919
Andrychuk, Q.C., Leonard D., Partner, MacPherson Leslie & Tyerman LLP - Regina, 946
Andy, Weiler, Director, Communications, 1186
Andy, Ridge, Director, Water Policy Branch, 1188
Andy, Hoggarth, Vice-President/Executive Financial Officer, Financial & Management Services, 1200
Andy, MacNeill, Vice-President, Churchill Falls, 1231
Andy, Wells, Chair & CEO, 1234
Andy, Bevan, Acting Deputy Minister, 1236
Andy, Langford, Director, Community Wellness & Social Services, 1237
Andy, Collier, Officer, Energy Programs, 1269
Angela, Bogdan, Chief of Protocol of Canada, Office of Protocol, 1143
Angela, Prokopiak, Director, Communications Division, 1156
Angela, Jamieson, Acting Director, Public Affairs, 1216
Angela, Kabvitok, Manager, Finance, 1247
Angela, Coke, Associate Deputy Minister, 1254
Angela, Schmidt, Vice-President, Competitiveness & Strategy, 1288
Angelo, Chris, Director, Public Works & Environmental Services, Quinte West, 1336
Angelo, Ottoni, Vice-President, Corporate Services & CFO, 1132
Angelo, Del Duca, Director, Ontario Markham, 1159
Angelo, Boccanfuso, Director, Security Expertise Programs, 1176
Angrove, Doug, Fire Chief, Victoria, 1318
Angus, Iain, Vice-President, 811
Angus, Head, Chief, Special Investigations, Legislation & Compliance, 1233
Angus, Robertson, Deputy Minister, 1298
Anil, Arora, Assistant Deputy Minister, 1164
Anita, Ploj, Director, Office of Intellectual Property & Commercialization, 1121
Anita, Biguzs, Associate Deputy Minister, 1173
Anita, Malovec, Manager, Business Operations, Health Registries, 1212
Anita, Moore, Executive Director, Public Health Programs & Strategies, 1217
Anita, Ludlow, Chief Nurse & Director, 1230
Anker, Mark, Manager, North 43 Lagoon Commission, 1309
Ann, Bonner, Executive Director, Strategic Services Directorate, 1147
Ann, Martin, Director, Data Dissemination Division, 1164
Ann, Martin, Director, Data Dissemination Division, 1165
Ann, Britton, Veterinary Pathologist, 1198
Ann, Kulmatycki, Head, Structures, 1239
Ann, Mundy, Vice-présidente, 1277
Ann L., Drake, Supervisor, Social Assistance & Disability Support Programs (Central), 1267
Anna, Romano, Acting Director General, Policy Development & Anal, 1123
Anna Marie, MacFarlane, Acting Laboratory Manager, 1266
Anne, Breau, Chief, 1131
Anne, Morin, Executive Assistant to the ADM, 1136
Anne, Gauthier, Manager, Coordination Office St Lawrence Plan, Strategic Integration & Partnerships, 1136
Anne, Lapierre, Director, Strategic Planning, Financial & Business Operations, 1146
Anne, Lamar, Assistant Deputy Minister, 1146
Anne, Halldorson, Executive Director/Senior Financial Officer, Financial & Business Planning Services Division, 1181
Anne, Denman, Executive Director, Oil Sands Strategy, 1184
Anne, Preece, Manager, Billing Operations & Support Section, 1207
Anne, Nguyen, Co-Director, Evaluation, 1208
Anne, Mould, Director, Court Services, 1238
Anne, Bermonte, Acting Director, 1250
Anne, Neary, Assistant Deputy Minister, 1252
Anne, Pashley, Vice-President, Finance & Administration, 1262
Anne, Proud, Clerk, Records Management, 1268
Anne, MacAulay, Manager, Human Resources, 1275
Anne, Marcoux, Directrice, Affaires intergouvernementales et de la coopération international, 1283
Anne M., Neatby, Coordinator, Communicable Disease & Immunization, 1271
Anne Marie, Gutierrez, Director, Legal Services, 1257
Anneliese, Coutu, Team Lead, Decisions, Orders, & Legal Support, 1187
Anne-Marie, Robinson, Associate Deputy Minister, Associate Deputy Minister's Office, 1145
Anne-Marie, Brugger, Strategic Communications Advisor, 1160
Anne-Marie, Brugger, Advisor, Strategic Communications, 1160
Anne-Marie, Brugger, Strategic Communications Advisor, 1161
Anne-Marie, Larivee, Fire Management Supervisor, 1259
Anne-Marie, Leclerc, Directrice générale et sous-ministre adjointe, 1285
Annesley, Janet, Vice-President, 687
Annette, Gibbons, Director General, 1174
Annibale, Quinto M., Loopstra Nixon LLP Barristers & Solicitors, 932
Annis, Eleanor, Catalogue Librarian, University of Northern British Columbia, 963
Anoma, Patirana, Senior Policy Advisor, Sustainability Division, 1136
Anoop, Kapoor, Director, Renewable & Electrical Energy Division, 1165
Ansell, Wendy, Administrator, 684
Anselmo, Hélène, Supervisor of Processing, Laurentian University, 1000
Anthony, Gregory M., Partner, Cox & Palmer - St. John's, 918
Anthony, McLevey, Senior Trade Commissioner, 1144
Anthony, Sangster, Director General, Emergency Preparedness & Occupational Health, 1146
Anthony, Ashley, Director General, Defence Research & Development Canada - Centre for Security Scien, 1157
Anthony, Hopkin, Director, Integrated Pest Management, 1163
Anthony, Lemphers, Assistant Deputy Minister, 1193
Anthony, Genge, Chair, 1229
Anthony, Eden, Director, Technical Operations, 1243
Anthony J., Danks, Executive Director, Strategic Policy Branch, 1204
Anthony-Malone, Kristin, Manager, 689
Antill, Sally, Administrator, 787
Antler, Denise, Ring Registrar, 671
Antler, Susan, Executive Director, 733
Antonet, Svircev, Research Scientist, Vineland Research Farm, 1122
Antoniw, Karna, Reference Librarian, King's University College, 955
Antony, Jen, Coordinator, 846
Anwar, Faisal, Officer, Yorkton, 1360
Apollon, Mireille, Conseillère, Gatineau, 1347
Apolphe, Dale, Executive Director, 717
Apostle, Nicholas J., Commissioner, Community Services, Sault Ste. Marie, 1337
Apostolatos, Gerry, Associé, Langlois Kronström Desjardins, 940
Appleby, Lianne, Manager, 815
Applejohn, Andrew, Institute Director, Aurora College. Aurora Research Institute, 979
Appleron, Rob, Executive Director, 769
Apps, Ellen, Library Assistant, St Joseph's Health Care, London, 990
Apps, Stephen, Contact, 706
April, Winchester, Communications Officer, 1270
April M., Driscoll, Acting Supervisor, Dairy Lab & Water Microbiology Laboratory; Mass Spectrometry Tech, 1266
Aquilina, Dan, Director, Planning & Development, Port Colborne, 1336
Aquin, CAE, Elizabeth, Senior Vice-President, 832
Araoz, Gustavo, President, 778
Arason, P. Eng., Jeff, Manager, Surrey, 1318
Araujo, Jackie, General Manager, Spruce Grove, 1308
Arbour, Judith, Executive Director, 700
Arbour, Adele, Director, Planning & Building Services, Thorold, 1337
Arbour, Roch, Directeur, Saint-Jean-sur-Richelieu, 1350
Arbuck, Jason, Partner, Cassels Brock & Blackwell LLP, 928
Arbuckle, Alan, Chair, 842
Arcand, MaryAnne, Executive Director, 727
Archambault, Julien, Davis LLP - Montréal, 939
Archambault, Peter, Weaver, Simmons LLP, 927
Archambault, Benoît, Directeur adjoint aux études, Collège Lionel-Groulx, 1028
Archambault, Marc, Chef entreposage et exploitation des fonds documen, Hydro-Québec, 1019
Archambault, Daniel, 841
Archer, Cynthia, University Librarian, York University Libraries, 1009
Archer-Cournoyer, Joan, Beaudry, Bertrand, s.e.n.c.r.l., 938
Archibald, Megan, Associate Director, 663
Archibald, Valerie, Associate Director, 699
Archibald, Dale, President, 845
Archibald, Helen, Secretary, 673
Archie, Landals, Director, Land Management, 1196
Argue, Andrea V., Kanuka Thuringer LLP, Barristers & Solicitors, 947
Argue, Bob, Executive Director, 744
Argue, Charlotte, Assistant Manager, 757
Arguin, Chantal, President, 761
Ariane, Plourde, Regional Director, Regional Science Branch, 1142
Ariane, Heisey, Senior Policy Advisor, Enviromental Assessment & Land Use Planning, 1261
Arisman, Audrey, Executive Director, 868
Ariss, Margaret, President, 687
Arkell, Tracy, HGR Graham Partners LLP - Barrie, 922
Arklie, Sandra, Library Supervisor, Stoney Creek Campus, 999
Arlene, Turner, Director General, 1174
Arlene, Wilgosh, Chief Executive Officer, 1217
Arlene, King, Chief Medical Officer of Health, 1255
Arlene, Gallant-Bernard, Executive Director, Prince County Hospital, 1272
Armbruster, Walter J., Sec.-Treas., 775
Armitage, Maureen, Executive Director, 702
Armstrong, Niall, Counsel, Fasken Martineau - Calgary, 903

B

Baltazar, Diana, Sylvestre & Associés Avocats S.E.N.C., 945
Baltgailis, Karen, Executive Director, 874
Bamber, Audrey, Agrologist, 728
Banach, Isaiah, Davies Howe Partners LLP, 929
Banack, Hart, President, 674
Banack, Darren, Operations Manager, Two Hills Regional Waste Management Commission, 1310
Banasch, Barb, Supervisor, Circulation & AV, Medicine Hat College, 957
Bancroft, Bob, President, 803
Bancroft, Q.C., James, Davis LLP - Calgary, 903
Bandow, James H., Executive Director, 684
Bandow, Donna, Coordinator, 684
Banfai, Geza R., Blaney McMurtry LLP, 928
Banfai, Geza, Partner, Heenan Blaikie LLP - Toronto, 931
Bangma, Janet, Head Librarian, Health Sciences Library, 1033
Banham, Fred, President, 790
Banks, Susannah, General Manager, 805
Banks, Doug, Fire Chief, Parksville, 1316
Banman, Janis, Coordinator, 791
Bannister, Carl, Chief Administrative Officer, Salmon Arm, 1318
Banno, Robert T., Partner, Davis LLP - Vancouver, 911
Bannon, David J., Partner, Norton Rose Fulbright Canada LLP - Toronto - Royal Bank Plaza, 934
Bannon, Keith A., Partner, Glaholt LLP, 931
Bannon, Jeff, City Planner, Stratford, 1337
Banting, Pamela, President, 658
Bapna, Manish, Exec. Vice-President & Managing Dir, 873
Baqi, Anowara, CFO, 851
Baratta, Lisa, Director, 869
Barb, Shackel-Hardman, Branch Head, Ag-Industry Extension Branch, 1182
Barb, Martini, Acting Director, 1188
Barb, Searle, Director, Financial Planning & Reporting, 1207
Barb, Macintosh, Assistant Director, Employee Relations, 1223
Barb, Buell, Administrative Assistant, 1272
Barbara, Kreider, Executive Assistant, Strategic Integration & Partnerships, 1136
Barbara, Richardson, Director General, Consular Operations Bureau, 1143
Barbara, McDougall, Chair, 1155
Barbara, Stevens, Regional Contribution Agreement Officer, 1159
Barbara, Nelson, Chief, Accessible Transportation, Intergovernmental Affairs & Accessibility, 1174
Barbara, Adamson, Director, Legal & Legislative Services, 1183
Barbara, Walman, Assistant Deputy Minister, 1208
Barbara, Gobis Ogle, Director, Utilization, 1208
Barbara, Greeniaus, Executive Advisor, Corporate Communications & Chan, 1210
Barbara, Bruce, Commissioner, 1216
Barbara, Lapointe, Director, Human Resource Services, 1225
Barbara, Brenton, Director, Strategic Human Resource Management, 1234
Barbara, Baillie, Director, Engineering Services, 1245
Barbara, Ko, Director, Policy & Planning Branch, 1256
Barbara, Maher, Director, Oranizational Development, 1264
Barbara, Macnutt, Manager, Literacy Secretariat, 1274
Barbeau, François, Joli-Coeur Lacasse Avocats - Québec, 944
Barbeau, Marc B., Associé, Stikeman Elliott LLP - Montréal, 943
Barber, Daniel, Singleton Urquhart LLP, 914
Barber, Wendy, Coordinator of Library Services, Conservation & Environment Library, 970
Barber, Q.C., Darryl J., Partner, Bennett Jones LLP - Calgary, 901
Barberini, Ivano, President, 777
Barbero, Kim, Executive Director, 676
Barbieri, Jamie, Secretary-Treasurer, 715
Barbosa-Canovas, Gustavo, Chair, 785
Barclay, William W., Partner, Reynolds Mirth Richards & Farmer LLP, 909
Barclay, Howden, Director General, Regulatory Improvement & Major Projects Management, 1131
Bardai, Naheed, Partner, MacPherson Leslie & Tyerman LLP - Saskatoon, 947
Barden, Nancy, Region Coordinator, 706
Bardonnex, Don, Manager, Red Deer County, 1304
Bareil, Sylvie, Responsable, Bibliothèque de musique, 1029
Barenie, Mark, CFO, 772
Baribeau, Pierre-L., Lavery, de Billy - Montréal, 941
Barich, Phyllis, Coordinator, Off Campus & Media Services, Red River College, 972
Baril, Cécile, Agente de bureau, Collège Laflêche, 1030
Barker, Susan, Digital Services & Reference Librarian, Bora Laskin Law Library, 1001
Barker, Steve, CFO & Vice-President, 873
Barkusky, Michaeln, Treasurer, 714
Barlee, Gwen, Director, 868
Barlow, W. Thomas, Partner, Fasken Martineau - Toronto, 930
Barlow, Beth, Chief Librarian, Surrey, 1318
Barnes, Brandon, Burnet, Duckworth & Palmer LLP, 902
Barnes, Jim, Executive Director, 651
Barnes, Ross D., General Manager, 736
Barnes, Steven, President, 714
Barnes, Jacqui, Director, 651
Barnes, Dawna, Specialist, Red Deer County, 1304
Barnett, Chris, Davis LLP - Toronto, 930
Barnett, Linda, Head of Public Services, Health Sciences Library, 978
Barnett, Ian, Director, 742
Barnett, Ian, Vice-President, 802
Barnett, Sheriden, Program Director, 836
Barnsley, Joseph D., Pitblado LLP, 916
Baron, Mireille, Secrétaire, CÉGEP de l'Outaouais, 1013
Barr, Bill, President, 792
Barr, Judy, Contact, 801
Barraclough, Joe, Director, 749
Barré, Louis, Vice-President, 703
Barrett, Ann, Administration, W.K. Kellogg Health Sciences Library, 982
Barrett, Hyacinth, Contact, Circulation Services, King's University College, 955
Barrett, Lynn, Access Services Generalist, Noranda Earth Sciences Library, 1005
Barrett, Wanda, Manager, 814
Barrett, Lynda, Director, 702
Barrett, Rob, Region President, 706
Barrett, Betty, Officer, 805
Barrette, Bruno, Associé, Stikeman Elliott LLP - Montréal, 943
Barrette, Katharine, Collections Librarian, Mount Royal University, 951
Barriault, Michel, Directeur général, Matane, 1349
Barrie, Jackson, Environmental & Regulatory Coordinator, 1268
Barrington-Moss, Gail, General Manager, St. Albert, 1308
Barry, Jennifer, Membership/Events Coordinator, 706
Barry, Robert, Secretary, 807
Barry, Day, Deputy Minister, Culture, 1182
Barry, Farynuk, Chief Superintendent, Provincial Operations, 1203
Barry, Dobbin, District Manager, Coast Mountains Resource District, 1206
Barry, Trenholm, Acting Engineering Group Leader, Southern Engineering Group, 1207
Barry, Todd, Deputy Minister, 1213
Barry, Leger, Engineer, 1221
Barry, Dawe, Assistant Deputy Minister, 1230
Barry, Linehan, Manager, Center for Forest Science & Innovation, 1233
Barry, Beale, Director, Energy Efficiency & Innovative Technology, 1250
Barry, Thompson, Manager, Sustainable Agriculture Resources, 1266
Barry, MacPhee, Director, 1270
Barry, Gosby, Senior Officer, Financial Services, 1274
Barry, Braitman, Director, Community Planning (Regina), 1290
Barry, Gallivan, Director, Operations, Regional Logistics, 1293
Barry J., Bentham, Director, Parks & Natural Areas, 1215
Barry L., Chandler, Provincial Coordinator, Residential Services, 1267
Barry W., Grace, Director, Research & Development, 1122
Barry, Q.C., T. Arthur, General Counsel, Stewart McKelvey - Halifax, 922
Barsalou, Michel, Executive Vice-President, 692
Barss, Bob, President, 638
Barsy, Paul W., Associate, D'Arcy & Deacon LLP - Winnipeg, 916
Bartel, Patricia, Library Staff, Ontario Ministry of Transportation, 999
Bartello, Peter, President, 710
Bartle, Bart, Chair, 824
Bartlett, Linda, Executive Director, 806
Bartman, Elizabeth, President, 652
Bartolcic, Allan, Executive Director, 841
Barton, Tony, Chair, 678
Bartoshewski, Pam, Controller, 848
Bartosiewicz, László, President, 777
Bas, Cleary, Director, Environmental Assessment Division, 1227
Basey, John, City Solicitor, Victoria, 1318
Basi, Karen, Manager, Coquitlam, 1314
Basile, van Havre, Director, Population Conservation & Management, 1135
Baskin, Mary, Manager, 760
Bassios, A., Commissioner, Planning, Richmond Hill, 1336
Bastien, Rowena, Manager, Cariboo, 1311
Baston, Rosie, Coorindator, 855
Bate, Lisa, Chair, 681
Bateman, Robert, Honorary Chair, 766
Bateman, Lisa, Coordinator, 730
Bateman, Tom, County Engineer, Essex, 1328
Bates, Jack, President, 678
Bates, Derek, City Manager, Prince George, 1317
Bath, Selina, Associate, Wickwire Holm, 922
Bathe, Ravi, President, 674
Battagliotti, A., General Manager, 769
Bauer, Jack, Contact, 796
Baumann, Roland, President, 674
Bausinger, Lynda, Acting General Manager, 745
Baxter, Leona V., Pushor Mitchell LLP, Lawyers & Trade-Mark Agents, 910
Baxter, Stephanie, Senior Director, 689
Baxter-Trahair, Elaine, General Manager, Children's Services, Toronto, 1338
Bayat, Mo, Director, Kelowna, 1315
Bayer, R. Martin, Weaver, Simmons LLP, 927
Bayley, Liz, Director, Health Sciences Library, 986
Bayne, Chad, Partner, Osler, Hoskin & Harcourt LLP - Toronto, 935
Baynes, Tina, Chapter Chair, 712
Bayo Aregbesola, Emmanuel, Manager, Canadian Forest Service, 973
Bazin, Q.C., Jean, Dentons Canada LLP - Montreal, 939
Beach, Cynthia, Commissioner, Sustainability & Growth, Kingston, 1333
Beadman, Tim P., Chief, Emergency Services, Greater Sudbury / Grand Sudbury, 1333
Beakley, Bruce, Director, Human Resources, Renfrew, 1330
Beaman, Roger T., Thomson, Rogers, 936
Beamish, Peter, Co-Director, 727
Beamish, Christine, Co-Director, 727
Bean, Stephen, Victoria Office Contact, Thurber Group, 969
Beard, Mark R., Pitblado LLP, 916
Beard, Colleen, Map Librarian, University Map Library, 999
Beardsley, Gisele, Bookkeeper & Translator, 834
Beasley, Gerald, University Librarian, Concordia University Libraries, 1018
Beatch, Rebecca, Alexander Holburn Beaudin & Lang, LLP, 910
Beate, Schiffer-Graham, Director, Incorporation & Information Products & Services Directorate, 1154
Beatrice, Raddi, Public Guardian, Office of the Public Guardian, 1237
Beattie, Leslie, Librarian, Red Deer College, 958
Beattie, Norman, Coordinator, Reference, Red River College, 972
Beattie, Al, Chief Executive Officer & President, 770
Beatty, Rob, Vice-President, 670
Beatty, Perrin, President & CEO, 692
Beaubier, Aidan, Head Librarian, Semi-Arid Prairie Agricultural Research Centre, 1034
Beauchamp, John, Norton Rose Fulbright Canada LLP - Toronto - Royal Bank Plaza, 934
Beauchamp, Luc, Secretary-Treasurer, 717
Beauchamp, Benoît, Executive Director, 652
Beauchamp, Denis, Directeur général et secrétaire, 827
Beauchamp, Réal, Directeur général adjoint, Shawinigan, 1351
Beauchemin, Patrick, Tremblay Bois Mignault Lemay S.E.N.C.R.L., 945
Beauchemin, Raymond, Region President, 706
Beauchesne, Éric, Joli-Coeur Lacasse Avocats - Trois-Rivières, 946
Beauchesne, Hélène, Greffière, Saint-Hyacinthe, 1350
Beaudet, Thérèse, Membership Secretary, 855
Beaudin, Geneviève, Heenan Blaikie LLP - Montréal, 939
Beaudin, Denis, Sec.-Trés., Régie intermunicipale de gestion des déchets solides des Anses, 1357
Beaudoin, Pierre, Partner, Lavery, de Billy - Québec, 944
Beaudoin, Guy-Lin, Directeur général, Vaudreuil-Soulanges, 1358
Beaudry, Marie-Andrée, Associée, Stikeman Elliott LLP - Montréal, 943
Beaudry, Guylaine, Director, R. Howard Webster Library, 1020

Beaudry, Marie-Claude, Technicienne en documentation, ILL, CÉGEP Limoilou, 1022
Beaudry, Rene, President, 865
Beaudry, Q.C., Harold P., Counsel, Weaver, Simmons LLP, 927
Beaulac, Claude, Directeur général, 827
Beaulieu, Hugo, Joli-Coeur Lacasse Avocats - Montréal, 940
Beaulieu, Pierre, Partner, Heenan Blaikie S.E.N.C.R.L./SRL - Québec, 944
Beaulieu, R. Luc, Senior Partner, Norton Rose Fulbright Canada LLP - Montréal, 942
Beaulieu, Daniel, Bibliothécaire de référence, Collège universitaire de St-Boniface, 970
Beaulieu, Maryna, Chef de bibliothèque, Bibliothèque de chimie, 1016
Beaulieu, Maryna, Chef de bibliothèque, Bibliothèque de physique, 1016
Beaulieu, Solange, Responsible, Prêt, CÉGEP de St-Jérôme, 1027
Beaumont, D. Robert, Partner, Osler, Hoskin & Harcourt LLP - Toronto, 935
Beaumont, Huguette, Technicienne en documentation, Centre de recherche industrielle du Québec, 1022
Beaupré, Denis, Bélanger, Sauvé, 938
Beaupré, Anne, University Librarian, Algoma University, 998
Beaupré, Jean-Marie, Directeur général, Saint-Basile-le-Grand, 1350
Beaupré, Adrien, Sec.-Trés., Régie intermunicipale de gestion des déchets solides de Saint-Via, 1357
Beauregard, Nathalie, Partner, Osler, Hoskin & Harcourt S.E.N.C.R.L./LLP, 943
Beauregard, Robert, Chair, 666
Beavers, Janet, Librarian, Northern Lights College, 960
Bechard, Mary Ellen, Coordinator, Library Services, Windsor Regional Hospital - Metropolitan Campus, 1011
Béchard, Anne-Marie, Cain Lamarre Casgrain Wells - Québec, 943
Béchard, Gaétan, Directeur général, Shawinigan, 1351
Beck, Joan, Partner, Cassels Brock & Blackwell LLP, 928
Beck, Marlene, Library Technician, Interlibrary Loans & Special N, Humber College Institute of Technology & Advanced Learning, 1003
Beck, Bary, Director, Lethbridge, 1307
Becker, Joanna, Head, Technical Services, AMEC Inc., 949
Becker Brookes, Kelsey L., Partner, Reynolds Mirth Richards & Farmer LLP, 909
Beckett, George, Associate University Librarian, Health Sciences, Health Sciences Library, 978
Beckett, Tim, Fire Chief, Kitchener, 1334
Beckman, Kimberly L., Davies Howe Partners LLP, 929
Beckwith, Gaye, President, 788
Becky, Denlinger, Fire & Emergency Management Commissioner, 1210
Becky, Taylor, Director, Transition Office, 1251
Bédard, Jean-Paul, Directeur, 787
Beddome, James, President, 764
Beddome, James R., Party Leader, 764
Bede, Gilbert, Librarian, Systems & Acquisitions, Okanagan College, 961
Bedford, Jill, Contact, Library Services, H. G. Thode Library of Science & Engineering, 986
Bedi, Shailoo, Head, Access Services, University of Victoria Libraries, 969
Bedritsky, Alexander I., President, 872
Beeman, Robb D., Partner, Heenan Blaikie LLP - Calgary, 904
Been, Jenny, Section Secretary/Treasurer, 798
Beer, Don, Fire Chief, Abbotsford, 1314
Beggs, Paul, President, 783
Behie, Q.C., Peter C.P, Partner, Ramsay Lampman Rhodes, 910
Behnam, Awni, President, 781
Behrens, Elizabeth, Associate University Librarian, Sir Wilfred Grenfell College, 976
Beier, Wolfgang, Manager, North Vancouver, 1316
Beke, Paul A., Burnet, Duckworth & Palmer LLP, 902
Bélair, Sylvain, Bélanger, Sauvé, 938
Bélair, Jo-Anne, Secteur du répertoire de vedettes-matière, Université Laval, 1025
Bélair, J., Office Manager, 651
Bélair, Marc, President, 864
Belanger, Linda, Library Secretary, Donald-Petzel Memorial Library, 1023
Bélanger, Anne, Lavery, de Billy - Montréal, 941
Bélanger, Guy, Beaudry, Bertrand, s.e.n.c.r.l., 938
Bélanger, Jacques, Robinson Sheppard Shapiro LLP, 943
Bélanger, Louis P., Associé, Stikeman Elliott LLP - Montréal, 943
Bélanger, Lyne, Chef de bibliothèque, Bibliothèque d'aménagement, 1015
Bélanger, Pierre, Technicien en documentation, CÉGEP de Marie-Victorin, 1017
Bélanger, Éric, Conseiller technique, 667
Bélanger, Étienne, Manager, 756
Bélanger, Ghislain, Directeur, Repentigny, 1349
Bélanger, Gaston, Sec.-Trés., Régie intermunicipale d'assainissement de Daveluyville, 1357
Bélanger, Pierre, Directeur-général, Régie intermunicipale d'aqueduc du Bas-Richelieu, 1357
Bélanger-Cadieux, Nicole, Responsable, acquisitions, CÉGEP de Marie-Victorin, 1017
Belcher, Pam, Resource Worker, Saskatchewan Environmental Society, 1033
Belich, Mel, Chairman, 865
Belinda, White, Chief of Staff, Office of the Deputy Minister, 1153
Belisle, André, Président, 668
Bélisle, Amélie, Heenan Blaikie LLP - Montréal, 940
Bell, Bruce C., Partner, Cassels Brock & Blackwell LLP, 928
Bell, Donald R.M., Davis LLP - Toronto, 930
Bell, Donald R.M., Partner, Davis LLP - Vancouver, 911
Bell, John, Shibley Righton LLP, 936
Bell, Allan, Associate University Librarian, Information Techno, University of Waterloo, 1010
Bell, Connie, Manager, Oil Museum of Canada, 992
Bell, Judith, Support Services, Woodstock Campus, 1011
Bell, Sarah Jane, Coordinator, 857
Bell, Patricia, Senior Community Energy Planner, 733
Bell, Jeff, President, 794
Bell, Janis, Vice-President, 790
Belland, Grégoire, Executive Director, 713
Bellavance, Pierre C., Partner, Heenan Blaikie S.E.N.C.R.L./SRL - Québec, 944
Belleau, Pascale, Coordinator, 695
Bellefleur, P.Eng., Mark, Vice-President, 664
Bellefontaine, Ronda, President, 835
Bellemare, Marie-Claude, Fasken Martineau - Montréal, 939
Bellemare, Marie-Claude, Partner, Heenan Blaikie LLP - Montréal, 939
Belley, Dominic C., Partner, Norton Rose Fulbright Canada LLP - Montréal, 942
Belley, Johanne, Directrice, Université du Québec à Chicoutimi, 1012
Belley Perron, Julie, McCarthy Tétrault LLP - Montréal, 941
Bellinger, Deborah A., Nelligan O'Brien Payne, 926
Bellissimo, Eva, Partner, Cassels Brock & Blackwell LLP, 928
Belliveau, Melanie, Information Services, Rockyview General Hospital Knowledge Centre, 952
Belliveau, Q.C., Robert G., McInnes Cooper - Halifax, 921
Belrose, Jim, Vice-President, 819
Belton, Tracey, Senior Records Analyst, Northwest Territories Public Works & Services, 979
Belton, Mark, Director, 693
Beltzner, Klaus, Treasurer, 861
Belzile, Sylvie, Directrice, Université de Sherbrooke, 1030
Ben, Berry, Deputy Director, Trade Show Strategy & Delivery, 1120
Ben, Stewart, Minister, Citizens' Services & Open Government, 1197
Ben, Cuthbert, Vice-Chair, 1198
Ben, Janzen, Secretary-Treasurer, 1198
Ben, Stewart, Minister, Citizens' Services & Open Government, 1198
Ben, Sawa, Data Manager, 1289
Ben, Liu, Director, Systems Management, 1292
Benaissa, Becky, Director, 723
Benedetti, Guy, Directeur général, Longueuil, 1348
Benedetto, Paul, City Manager, Leduc, 1307
Benham, Karie Ann, Lawrence, Lawrence, Stevenson LLP, 923
Benjamin, Whelan, Acting Director, National & Departmental Relations Division, 1162
Benjelloun, Rida, Secteur recherche et développements numériques, Université Laval, 1025
Benji, Straker, Manager, Parks Operations, 1238
Benkovich, Nick, Director, Water & Wastewater, Greater Sudbury / Grand Sudbury, 1333
Bennett, Chris, Partner, McMillan LLP - Toronto, 933
Bennett, Clarence L., Stewart McKelvey - Fredericton, 917
Bennett, Mark, Partner, Cassels Brock & Blackwell LLP, 928
Bennett, Peter, Chair, 651
Bennett, John, Executive Director, 851
Bennett, Ben, Manager, 798
Bennett, P.Eng, Tony, President, 746
Benoit, Manon, Agente de bureau, Comptoir de prêt, CÉGEP St-Jean-sur-Richelieu, 1027
Benoit, Gil, Treasurer, 858
Benoit, Denis, Deuxième Vice-Président, 752
Benoit, Gilles, Directeur, Laval, 1348
Benoit, Gilbert, Officer, Development & Marketing, 1156
Benoit, Trudel, Directeur (par intérim), Politiques et Intégité du territoire, 1282
Benoît, Marcotte, Director General, Corporate Services, 1132
Benoît, Levert, Directeur (par intérim), 1282
Benoît, Levert, Directeur, 1282
Benoît, Cayouette, Directeur, Transport routier des marchandises, 1285
Benson, Matthew, Heenan Blaikie LLP - Toronto, 931
Bentley, Lynne, Director, Humber College Institute of Technology & Advanced Learning, 1003
Bentley, Sam, President, 761
Bentley, Brian, Fire Chief, Saskatoon, 1359
Bentley, Brian, General Manager, Saskatoon, 1359
Bentley, Kyle, Chief Building Official, Pickering, 1336
Bentzen, Eric, Treasurer, 820
Bercier, Pierre, Président, 862
Bercov, Q.C., Sydney A., Emery Jamieson LLP, 907
Berdnikoff, Loïc, Lavery, de Billy - Montréal, 941
Berdowski, Ted, President, 858
Beresford, Q.C., Harvey A., Partner, Hicks Morley Hamilton Stewart Storie LLP - Toronto, 932
Bergen, Kristina, Executive Director, 717
Berger, Craig M., Director, 854
Bergeron, Jean-Sébastien, Cain Lamarre Casgrain Wells - Saguenay, 938
Bergeron, Martine, Langlois Kronström Desjardins, 940
Bergeron, Richard, Associé, Cain Lamarre Casgrain Wells - Saguenay, 938
Bergeron, Christine, Technicienne en documentation, CÉGEP St-Jean-sur-Richelieu, 1027
Bergeron, Marthe, Responsable, Référence et periodiques, CÉGEP de la Pocatière, 1014
Bergeron, André, Site Contact, 767
Bergeron, André, Directeur général, 738
Bergeson, Cara, Publisher & Conference Manager, 841
Bergheim, Dennis, Manager, Evergreen Regional Waste Management Services Commission, 1309
Bergin, Patrick J., CEO, 635
Bergkamp, Ger, Interim Executive Director, 786
Bergner, B.A., LL.B., Keith, Partner, Lawson Lundell LLP - Vancouver, 913
Beriau, Tania, Development Director, 851
Berkenbosch, Wendy-Anne, Davis LLP - Edmonton, 907
Berliner, QC, Lloyd I., Patterson Law, 921
Bernadette, Sereda, Manager, 832
Bernadette, Rudisuela, Director, Corporate Emergency Preparedness Directorate, 1171
Bernadette, McIntyre, Chief Executive Officer, 1294
Bernard, Max R., Partner, Heenan Blaikie LLP - Montréal, 940
Bernard, Yann, Associé, Langlois Kronström Desjardins, 940
Bernard, Magalie, Agente, 753
Bernard, Valcourt, Minister, Aboriginal Affairs & Northern Developmen, 1117
Bernard, Funston, Chair, 1132
Bernard, Madé, Director, Chemical Production, 1134
Bernard, Clancey, Director, Highway / Engineering Services, 1245
Bernard, Verret, Sous-ministre adjoint, 1277
Bernard, Landry, Directeur général, 1282
Bernard, Lemay, Vice-président, Opérations, 1285
Bernard (Butch), Postma, Senior Trade Commissioner, Aerospace & Defence, Ag, Environmental Industries, Health Industries, Service Industries &, 1144
Bernardin, Pierre, Directeur général, Sainte-Julie, 1351
Bernas, Luke R., Associate, D'Arcy & Deacon LLP - Winnipeg, 916
Bernatchez, Anik, Heenan Blaikie S.E.N.C.R.L./SRL - Québec, 944
Bernhardt-Lowdon, Margaret, Executive Director & Director, 793
Bernie, MacDonald, Contact, Park & Wildlife Ventures, 1195
Bernie, MacDonald, Director, Outdoor Development Branch, 1196
Bernie, Halloran, Chair, 1227
Bernie, MacDonald, Co-President, 1240
Bernie, Hughes, Director, Aboriginal Relations, 1260

Bernier, Diane, Technicienne, Référence, catalogage, et PEB, CÉGEP de Saint-Félicien, 1026
Bernier, Hélène, Bibliothécaire, Bibliothèque des sciences et de génie, 1029
Bernier, Jean-Luc, Officer, 653
Bernier, Monique, Chair, 716
Bernier, Janice, President, 840
Bernier, Danielle, Présidente, 853
Bernier, André, Chair, 837
Bernise, Lamoureux, Exclusion & Designations Officer, Labour Relations, Compensation & Occupational Health & Safety, 1173
Berns-McGown, Rima, President, 739
Bernstein, Roger D., Vice-President, 646
Berry, William J., Director, Kelowna, 1315
Bersabel, Ephrem, Director General, International Affairs, 1146
Bert, Clark, President & Chief Executive Officer, 1255
Bert, Hennessey, District Manager, 1259
Bert, West, Director, Engineering Services Branch, 1288
Bert, Campbell, Bridge Crew Manager, Bridges, 1293
Bertel-Rault, Bernadette, Secretary General, 778
Bertha, Greenstein, Director, Mediation Services (Labour Mediation), 1191
Berthellette, Denis, Directeur d'Exploitation, Régie intermunicipale de l'eau de Deux-Montagnes, 1358
Berthelot, Jean-Marie, Vice-President, 703
Berthiaume, Phillip, Planner, Emergency Measures, Essex, 1328
Bertossi, Henry, Partner, Heenan Blaikie LLP - Toronto, 931
Bertrand, Jean G., Managing Partner, Norton Rose Fulbright Canada LLP - Montréal, 942
Bertrand, Justin, Heenan Blaikie LLP - Ottawa, 925
Bertrand, Gordon, Coordinator, Library Technology, Grant MacEwan University, 954
Bertrand, Sylvie, Reader's Services Assistant, Canada Science & Technology Museum, 993
Bertrand, Michèle, Présidente, 863
Bertrand, Verbruggen, Directeur, Développement des entreprises, 1280
Bérubé, Andrée-Claude, McCarthy Tétrault LLP - Montréal, 942
Bérubé, François, Associé, Cain Lamarre Casgrain Wells - Amqui, 938
Bérubé, Marie-Eve, Secrétaire, 853
Bérubé, Jacques, Directeur, Terrebonne, 1351
Bérubé-Gagné, Joanne, President, 861
Bespalko, Jenny, Contact, 653
Best, Erin, Associate, Cox & Palmer - St. John's, 919
Beswick, Bette, Registrar, 642
Beth, Pieterson, Director General, Environmental & Radiation Health Sciences, 1145
Beth, MacNeil, Director, S&T Governance Division, 1163
Beth, Pollock, Director, Commercial & Industrial Sectors, 1221
Beth, Hanna, Executive Director, 1262
Beth, Fricke, Manager, Finance, 1297
Beth, Hawkings, Manager, Information Management & Technology, 1300
Beth P., Johnston, Communications Officer, 1266
Bethan, Williams-Simpson, Manager, Prevention Services, 1237
Betker, Terry, President, 693
Bette-Jo, Hughes, Assistant Deputy Minister, Service BC, 1200
Betti, Mirko, Secretary-Treasurer, 704
Betts, John, Executive Director, 869
Betty, Chen-Mack, Executive Director, Facilities Services Division, 1210
Betty, Pirs, Vice-President, Prevention Services, 1213
Betty, Morgan, Director, Service Management, 1256
Betty, Rogers, Managing Director, Administration, 1287
Betty Ann, Pottruff, Executive Director, Policy, Planning & Evaluation, 1293
Betty Lou, Bowles, Public Guardian - Central Region, 1190
Betty-Ann, Atherton, Director, Security & Corporate Risk, Security & BCP, 1210
Beutler, Joseph, Section Chair, 799
Bev, Yee, Assistant Deputy Minister, 1188
Bev, Francis, Area Supervisor, East Position, 1265
Bevan Baker, Peter, Party Leader, 764
Beveridge, Keith, President, 858
Beverley, Wilcox, Officer, Administration, 1221
Beverly, Sawicki, Senior Manager, Social Care Facilities Review Comm, 1190
Beverly, Griffiths, Acting Assistant Deputy Minister, 1229
Beverly, Carter, Provincial Director, Pathology & Laboratory Medicine, 1230
Bexson, Corinne, Senior GIS Technician, Rothesay, 1323
Bhagwant, Sandhu, Executive Director, Legislation & Regulatory Affairs, 1141
Bhat, Rama B., President, 719
Bhojani, Zeenat, Specialist, Informaton Technology, Farm Safety Association Inc., 985
Bialkowski, Mark, Manager, Human Resources, Dufferin, 1328
Bickell, Jana, Library Technician, Videos/DVD Booking, Orillia Campus, 992
Bickford, Frederick J.W., Partner, Weiler, Maloney, Nelson, 928
Biderman, Matthew A., Paterson, MacDougall LLP, Barristers, Solicitors, 936
Biderman, David, General Counsel & Director, 801
Bidyk, Brian, Partner, Heenan Blaikie LLP - Calgary, 904
Bieganek, Q.C., Darren R., Managing Partner, Duncan Craig LLP - Edmonton, 907
Biesenthal, Betty, Director of Publicity, 758
Bigelow, Juanita, Administrator, Truro, 1326
Bigelow, P.Eng., Steve, Chief Conservation Officer & Director, 681
Biggs Brock, Heidi, President, 644
Bigioni, Rob, HGR Graham Partners LLP - Barrie, 922
Bignell, Robert, Executive Director, 825
Bigué, Ann M., McCarthy Tétrault LLP - Montréal, 941
Bilek, Ian B., Partner, Cox & Palmer - Halifax, 921
Bill, Currie, Director, Strategic Project, 1117
Bill, Teeter, Vice-President, Business Transformation, 1129
Bill, Hawkins, Chief of Staff, 1143
Bill, James, Superintendent of Bankruptcy, 1154
Bill, Wilson, Director, MPB Policy & Research, 1163
Bill, Werry, Deputy Minister, 1180
Bill, Kennedy, General Counsel, 1186
Bill, Nugent, Director & Solicitor, Legal Services, 1193
Bill, Draper, Manager, North Operations, 1194
Bill, Symonds, Director, Planning & Policy Advisory, 1194
Bill, Bennett, Minister, Community, Sport, & Cultural Development, 1197
Bill, Vanderspek, General Manager, 1198
Bill, Bennett, Minister, Community, Sport, & Cultural Development, 1200
Bill, Lux, Co-Vice-Chair, 1205
Bill, Marshall, Director, Recreation Sites & Trails BC, 1205
Bill, Warner, Regional Executive Director, Omineca, 1205
Bill, Levesque, Deputy Minister, 1220
Bill, Breckenridge, Director, Alternative Energy & Energy Efficiency D, 1220
Bill, Parrott, Deputy Minister, 1227
Bill, Skanes, Senior Engineer, Highway Design, 1235
Bill, MacLeod, Chief Executive Officer, 1240
Bill, Greenlaw, Executive Director, Heritage Division, 1241
Bill, Mantel, Acting Assistant Deputy Minister, 1250
Bill, Bardswick, Director, 1253
Bill, Limbrick, Vice-President, Organizational Development, 1255
Bill, Mauro, Parliamentary Assistant, 1257
Bill, Thornton, Assistant Deputy Minister, Transformation Secretariat, 1257
Bill, Fleming, Coordinator, Provincial Housing, 1267
Bill, Bylhouwer, Director, Provincial Laboratory Services, 1273
Bill, Reid, Director, Occupational Health & Safety, 1275
Bill, Boyd, Minister, Economy; Minister Responsible, Global Tr, SK Power Corporation, Enterprise SK, Innovation SK, Uranium Devel, 1288
Bill, Spring, Director, Advanced Technology & Services, 1289
Bill, Zimmer, Compliance Manager, 1290
Bill, Pacholka, Director, Construction Standards, 1292
Bill, Boyd, Minister Responsible, 1296
Bill, Duncan, Executive Director, Dam Safety & Major Structures, 1297
Bill, Curtis, Director, Finance & Administration, 1301
Bill R., Schroeder, Research Manager, 1121
Billings, Laurie, Executive Director, 642
Billington, Charles, Executive Director, 842
Billyann, Balay, Director, Granting Programs, 1262
Bilodeau, Sandra, Morency Société d'Avocats - Québec, 944
Bilodeau, Yvan, Président-directeur général, 853
Bilodeau, Denis, Second Vice President General, 683
Bilodeau, Louis, Directeur général, Saint-Hyacinthe, 1350
Bilodeau, ing., Stéphane, Vice-président, 827
Bindraban, Ir P.S., Director, 784
Birch, Jennifer, Vice-President, 683
Birchall, Charles, Partner, Willms & Shier Environmental Lawyers LLP, 937
Bird, Alison J., Associate, Cox & Palmer - Halifax, 921
Bird, Kathryn J., Associate, Hicks Morley Hamilton Stewart Storie LLP - Toronto, 932
Bird, Jason, Director, Sault College, 999
Birgitte, Hunter, Assistant Deputy Minister, 1301
Birns, Larry, Director, 740
Biron, Yvan, Lavery, de Billy - Montréal, 941
Biron, Sylvain, Président, 657
Birrell, Sandy, Sec.-Treas., 665
Birt, MacKinnon, Director, 1274
Birthistle, Anne, Director, 651
Birtig, Tor, Manager, Powell River, 1317
Birtz, Frédéric, Directeur des opérations, 667
Bischoff, Ralph, Executive Director, 857
Bischoff, Angela, Director, 816
Bishop, Jeff, Coordinator, 756
Bishop, Gary, President/Treasurer, 806
Bishop, Gart, Chair, 788
Bishop, Bill, Director, Human Resources, Lennox & Addington, 1329
Bisset, Laura K., Davis LLP - Toronto, 930
Bisson, Robert, Treasurer, 679
Bisson, Barry, President, 850
Bittorf, Brad, Executive Vice-President, 780
Bizimana, Bernard, Directeur, Services techniques & informatisés, HEC Montréal, 1019
BJ, Simpson, Officer, Systems & Research, 1180
Bjeld, Lis, Executive Director, 720
Bjergso, Eric, General Manager, 693
Bjornson, Pam, Director, Business Affairs, Canadian Institute for Scientific & Technical Information (CISTI), 994
Black, Michael J., Heenan Blaikie LLP - Calgary, 904
Black, Michael, Partner, Fasken Martineau - Calgary, 903
Black, Robert N., Davis LLP - Toronto, 930
Black, Margaret, Librarian, Cataloguing & Interlibrary Loans, Dawson College, 1018
Black, Nancy E., Manager, Access & Information Services, University of Northern British Columbia, 963
Black, John, President & Director, 817
Black, Q.C., Douglas J., Dentons Canada LLP - Calgary, 903
Blackburn, John, Vice-President & Secretary, 662
Blackburn, Diane, Manager, 840
Blackburn, Ronald, Président, 656
Blackburn, Jacquie, Secretary, 742
Blackett, Glenn C., Partner, Carscallen LLP, 902
Blacklock, Don, President, 648
Blackmore, David, Director, St. John's, 1324
Blaikie, Peter M., Founding Partner, Heenan Blaikie LLP - Montréal, 940
Blain, David, Director, Chilliwack, 1314
Blaine, Steward, Executive Director, Information Technology & Opera, 1189
Blair, David F., Partner, Heenan Blaikie S.E.N.C.R.L./SRL - Québec, 944
Blair, K. Alan, Gowling Lafleur Henderson LLP - Vancouver, 912
Blair, Iain, Administrative Officer, Institute for the Study of International Development, 1019
Blair, Jack, Co-ordinator, Columbia-Shuswap, 1311
Blair, Hodgson, Chief of Staff to the Deputy Minister, 1139
Blair, McTavish, Director, Regional Support Services, 1215
Blair, Aitken, Manager, Service Delivery, Kings & Queens County, 1274
Blais, Carole, Reference & Collections Officer, Canadian Nuclear Safety Commission, 994
Blais, Renaud, Administrator, 650
Blakney, John F., Dentons Canada LLP - Ottawa, 925
Blanchard, Emma, Borden Ladner Gervais LLP - Ottawa, 925
Blanchard, Carmel, Technicienne en administration, Québec Ministère des ressources naturelles et de la faune, 1024
Blanchard, Laurie, Hospital Librarian, Misericordia Health Centre, 972
Blanchard, Pierre-Luc, Directeur, Sainte-Julie, 1351
Blanchet, Nicolas, CFES President, 698
Blanchette, Denis, Gowling Lafleur Henderson S.E.N.C.R.L./LLP, 939
Blanchette, Frédéric, Associé, Lapointe Rosenstein Marchand Melançon, 941
Blanchette, Shirley, Library Technician, Saskatoon City Hospital, 1034
Blaney, Paul, President, 788
Blazina, Sandy, Document Delivery Specialist, Gallagher Library of Geology & Geophysics, 951
Bleaney, Bob, Vice-President, 687
Bleskie, Jeanette, Manager, Records & Information Technology, Vale Inco, 1009

Boutin, Louise, Associée, Langlois Kronström Desjardins, 940
Boutin, Bernard, Trésorier du conseil, 657
Bouvier, Ellen, Office Coordinator, 803
Bouwmeester, Tim, Manager, Okanagan-Similkameen, 1313
Bovay, Rod, Acting Director, Engineering & Development Service, Belleville, 1331
Bowa, George, Director, Engineering & Public Works, Stratford, 1337
Bowdridge, Paula, Library Technician, Newfoundland & Labrador Department of Natural Resources, 978
Bower, Scott H.D., Partner, Bennett Jones LLP - Calgary, 901
Bower, Bill, President, 828
Bower, Tim, 799
Bowing, Scott, Section Chair, 798
Bowker, QC, George E., Counsel, Duncan Craig LLP - Edmonton, 907
Bowler, Aaron J., Aikins, MacAulay & Thorvaldson LLP, 915
Bowles, Brendan D., Managing Partner, Glaholt LLP, 931
Bowles, Nigel, Executive Director, 789
Bowles, Ron, Treasurer, 790
Bowlin, Michael E., Partner, Cox & Palmer - Fredericton, 917
Bowman, Corin, McMillan LLP - Vancouver, 913
Bowman, Michael H.D., Partner, Osler, Hoskin & Harcourt LLP - Toronto, 935
Bowman, Jerry, Vice-President, 772
Bowser, Dara, Secretary, 767
Boxall, James, Secretary-Treasurer, 686
Boyce, William C., Manager, 664
Boyce, Jane, Chair, 864
Boychuk, Nelson, Vice-President, 639
Boychuk, Q.C., Christopher C., McDougall Gauley - Saskatoon, 947
Boyd, William C., Managing Partner, Ottenheimer Baker, 919
Boyd, Alastair, Head, Cataloguing, University of Toronto Libraries, 1008
Boyd, Lynne, Head Librarian, Canadian Agriculture Library - Summerland, 964
Boyd, Roger, President, 871
Boyd, Ralph, President, 669
Boyd, Randy, Chairperson, Roseridge Waste Management Services Commission, 1309
Boyd, Q.C., Keith D., Kanuka Thuringer LLP, Barristers & Solicitors, 946
Boyer, Douglas J., Partner, McLennan Ross LLP - Edmonton, 908
Boyer, Daniel, Head Librarian, Nahum Gelber Law Library, 1020
Boyer, Greg, Executive Director, 763
Boyer, Jason, Executive Manager, 813
Boyes, Richard, Fire Chief, Oakville, 1335
Boykiw, Donald, Partner, Osler, Hoskin & Harcourt LLP - Calgary, 905
Boyle, Glenn J., Executive Director, 870
Brace, Sarah, Executive Coordinator, 829
Brad, Tinney, Director, Infrastructure/Operations (PC/RDI), 1140
Brad, Klak, President & Managing Director, 1181
Brad, Babiak, Director, Planning & Performance Measurement, 1183
Brad, Ison, Manager, Recovery Programs, 1193
Brad, Pickering, Deputy Minister, 1195
Brad, Boquist, Director, Operations & Client Services, 1200
Brad, Glazer, Director, Infrastructure Development, Northern Corridor, 1212
Brad, Patzer, Director, Legal Division, 1238
Brad, Skinner, District Manager, 1242
Brad, Chatfield, Manager, Communications, 1272
Brad, Korbo, Managing Director, Assessment Services, 1287
Brad, Henry, Executive Director, Northern Municipal Services, 1291
Brad, Gurash, Director, Assurance & Financial Reporting, 1293
Brad, Cathers, Minister responsible, 1298
Brad, Cathers, Minister responsible, 1298
Brad, Cathers, Minister, 1298
Braden, Kelly, Director, Portage La Prairie, 1321
Bradet, Denis, Grondin, Poudrier, Bernier, 944
Bradford, P. Ross, Executive Director, 642
Bradley, Gordon M., McCaffery Mudry Pritchard LLP, Barristers & Solicitors, 904
Bradley, Janet, Partner, Borden Ladner Gervais LLP - Ottawa, 925
Bradley, Monica, Treasurer, 637
Bradley, David H., President, 826
Bradley, Kevin, President, 808
Bradley, Rinnie, Executive Director, 834
Bradley, Francis, Vice-President, 695
Bradley, Chris, Director, Public Works, Peterborough, 1330
Bradley, Fauteux, Managing Director, Ontario Parks, 1258
Bradley C., Goodyear, Executive Director, 1159
Bradstreet, Michael, Vice-President, 802
Brady, David W., Partner, Hicks Morley Hamilton Stewart Storie LLP - Toronto, 932
Brady, Joan, Women's President, 800
Brady, Allyson, Executive Director, 846
Brady, Emily, President, 783
Brady, Alan, Manager, Halifax Regional Municipality, 1325
Braid, Ron, Head, Reference, Trinity Western University, 961
Braithwaite, Jack, Counsel, Weaver, Simmons LLP, 927
Braley, Damian, Secretary, 826
Brander, R. Bruce, Burnet, Duckworth & Palmer LLP, 902
Brandon, Harris, Director, Regional Asset Management, 1293
Brandy, Cox, Executive Director, Major Legislative Projects & S, 1194
Brant, Cherie, Partner, Willms & Shier Environmental Lawyers LLP, 937
Brant, William J., Chair, 769
Brant, Popp, Executive Director, Policy Planning & Performance Measurement, 1179
Brasier, CAE, Steven, Executive Director, 705
Brassard, Monique, Lavery, de Billy - Montréal, 941
Brassard, Raynald, Cain Lamarre Casgrain Wells - Saguenay, 938
Braton, Andrew, Secretary, 666
Brattinga, Denise, Manager, 640
Braul, Waldemar, Dentons Canada LLP - Vancouver, 912
Braun, John R., Aikins, MacAulay & Thorvaldson LLP, 915
Braun, Barry, Commissioner, Recreation, Parks, & Culture Departm, Prince Edward, 1330
Braun-Jackson, Jeff, Office Manager & Researcher, 822
Brayford, Susan, Manager, Library Operations, Southern Alberta Institute of Technology, 952
Brazeau, Luce, Bibliothécaire, Bibliothèque de physique, 1016
Brazeau, Marc, President & CEO, 670
Brazier, Warren G., Clark Wilson LLP, 911
Brazier, Dan, Manager, Colwood, 1314
Brearley, Scott, Singleton Urquhart LLP, 914
Breault, Alain, McMillan LLP - Calgary, 905
Brebeau, Martine, Head, Information Resources, FPInnovations, 1022
Breier, Liz, Library Technician, Sir Mortimer B. Davis Jewish General Hospital, 1021
Brekke, Kris, Executive Director, 714
Bremner, Janet, President, 789
Bremner, Tom, Chief, Truro, 1326
Brenda, Cherniawsky, Director, Planning & Corporate Services, 1117
Brenda, Morehouse, Director, Office of Environmental Coordination, 1140
Brenda, Côté, Director General, Africa Bureau, 1143
Brenda, O'Reilly, Manager, Finance & Administration, 1178
Brenda, Brindle, Executive Director, Environmental Stewardship Divi, 1182
Brenda, Allbright, Branch Head, Tenure, 1184
Brenda, Hartley, Acting Director, Major Projects, 1205
Brenda, Craven, Manager, Business Operations, Support Services, 1212
Brenda, Johnston, Commissioner, 1216
Brenda, Greenslade, Executive Director, Employer Services, 1235
Brenda, Panipakoocho, Officer, Training & Logistics, 1246
Brenda, Profit, Community Development Officer, West Prince, 1270
Brenda, Campbell, Project Manager, iEHR & eHealth Project Implementa, 1272
Brenda, Worth, Director, Nursing Services, 1272
Brenda Lee, Doyle, Assistant Deputy Minister, 1190
Brennan, Nola, Librarian, Institute of Technology Campus, 981
Brennan, Mary Ellen, Director, 646
Brennan, Shirley, Executive Director, 729
Brennan, Elizabeth, Coordinator, 790
Brennan, Krystal, Coordinator, 870
Brennan, Joe, Chair, 834
Brennan, Jim, Chief, Winnipeg, 1321
Brenner, Pamela, Chair, 674
Brennick, John, President, 680
Brent, Montgomery, Vice-Chair, 1119
Brent, Wilson, Acting Director, Technical Trade Policy Division, 1120
Brent, Montgomery, Vice-Chair, 1138
Brent, Paterson, Council Member, 1181
Brent, Paterson, Executive Director, Irrigation & Farm Water Divisi, 1182
Brent, McEwan, Executive Director, Occupational Health & Safety D, 1191
Brent, Mullin, Chair, 1209
Brent, Mullin, Chair, 1209
Brent, Staeben, Director, Communications, 1222
Brent, Webster, Director, Field Services, 1290
Brent, Miller, Director, Regional Asset Management, 1293
Brenton, Janelle, Cataloguer, Nova Scotia Agricultural College, 983
Brenton, Janelle, Library Staff, Nova Scotia Dept. of Natural Resources, 981
Bresee, Kim, Director, Planning & Building, Sarnia, 1337
Breton, Patrice, Director, 858
Brett, Jerry, President, 639
Brett, Matthew, Secretary & Moderator, 855
Brett, Loney, Director, Communications, 1240
Breu, Michael, President, 748
Brewer, Andrea, Norton Rose Fulbright Canada LLP - Toronto - Royal Bank Plaza, 934
Breyfogle, Donna, Associate Director, Collections, University of Manitoba Libraries, 972
Brian, Aglukark, Director, Regional Planning, 1118
Brian, Baron, Site Supervisor, Canada-Manitoba Crop Diversification Centre, 1119
Brian, Freeze, Director, Operations, 1122
Brian, Smithon, Executive Director, Audit, Evaluation & Risk Oversight, 1129
Brian, Spurling, Director General, 1153
Brian, Gear, Assistant Deputy Minister & Director General, 1154
Brian, Gray, Assistant Deputy Minister, 1163
Brian, Evans, Chief Audit & Evaluation Executive, Office of Internal Audit & Evaluation, 1166
Brian, Bramah, Regional Director, Transportation Security, 1177
Brian, Fedor, Executive Director, Health Facilities Branch, 1191
Brian, Soutar, Executive Director, Project Services Branch, 1191
Brian, Alford, President & Chief Executive Officer, 1193
Brian, Ferguson, Director, Assessment Audit, 1194
Brian, Heninger, Chair, 1195
Brian, Kelly, Director, Policy & Strategic Support, 1196
Brian, Underhill, Executive Director, Strategic Planning & Corporate Policy, 1197
Brian, Hansen, Assistant Deputy Minister/Lead Negotiator, 1202
Brian, Simpson, Director, Wildfire Management Headquarters, 1205
Brian, Barber, Director, Tree Improvement Branch, 1206
Brian, Symonds, Director, Regional Operations, Water Stewardship, 1206
Brian, Chow, Chief Engineer, 1206
Brian, Anderson, Chief Information Officer & Vice-President, Business Development, 1211
Brian, Murray, Director, Commercial Vehicle Safety & Enforcement Branch, 1212
Brian, Erickson, Chief Financial Officer/Senior Vice-President, Finance Division, 1213
Brian, Scoonbaert, Chief Evecutive Officer, 1217
Brian, Hurley, Director, Project Analysis, 1228
Brian, Meaney, Assistant Deputy Minister, 1228
Brian, Sullivan, Supervisor, Fisheries, 1229
Brian, Sieben, Specialist, Adaptation Planning, 1237
Brian, Asmundson, Public Trustee, Public Trustee's Office, 1238
Brian, Nagel, Director, Facility Management Section, 1239
Brian, Jobb, Manager, WCWC Training Institute, 1251
Brian, Gildner, Manager, Certification, Training & Client Services, 1252
Brian, Whitehead, Manager, Regulatory Program Reporting Section, 1252
Brian, Nixon, Director, Environmental Intergovernmental Affairs, 1252
Brian, Cameron, District Manager, 1253
Brian, Lewis, Director, Strategy & Integration, 1257
Brian, Hillier, Manager, Forest Policy Section, 1258
Brian, Pountney, Manager, 1261
Brian, Matheson, Manager, Agriculture Regulatory Programs, 1266
Brian, Brown, Manager, Private Forests, 1266
Brian, Wedge, Chair, 1266
Brian, McFeely, Senior Business Continuity Planner, Office for Bus, 1268
Brian, Schmeisser, Director, 1269

Buchinski, Donna, Chairperson, Smoky River Regional Water Management Commission, 1309
Buck, Gordon A., Alexander Holburn Beaudin & Lang, LLP, 910
Buck, William D., Registrar, 663
Buckingham, Janice, Partner, Osler, Hoskin & Harcourt LLP - Calgary, 905
Buckingham, Laura, Associate, Field LLP - Calgary, 903
Buckley, Valdene, President, 793
Buckley, Stephen, General Manager, Transportation Services, Toronto, 1338
Bucknell, Ruth, Treasurer, 770
Budd, David, Partner, Cassels Brock & Blackwell LLP, 928
Budd, Bill, Director, Moncton / Ville de Moncton, 1322
Budney, Heather, President, 761
Bueti, Vincent J., Pullan Kammerloch Frohlinger, 916
Buettner, Adele, Executive Director, 693
Bugden, Lydia S., Partner, Stewart McKelvey - Halifax, 922
Bugden, P.Eng., Jeffrey M., Manager, 681
Bugg, Angie, Coordinator, 846
Buhlman, J.M., WeirFoulds LLP, 936
Buholzer, Bill, Young, Anderson, 914
Buijs, Adriaan, President, 711
Bujold, John, Gorman Nason Lawyers, 918
Bujold, Yvan, Associé, Cain Lamarre Casgrain Wells - Rimouski, 945
Bujold, Lise, Director, 705
Bujold, Monette, Secrétaire adjointe-administrative, 735
Buker, Mike, Chair, 685
Bulat, Drazen F., Partner, Miller Thomson LLP - Toronto, 934
Bull, Natalie, Executive Director, 767
Bullen, Jason K.S., Partner, Cassels Brock & Blackwell LLP, 928
Bullock, Timothy, Managing Partner, SimpsonWigle LAW LLP, 923
Bullock, Paul, Treasurer, 721
Bullock, Greg, President, 819
Bullough, Vaughn, President, 792
Bulpitt, Don, Manager, Lethbridge, 1307
Bumbaru, Dinu, President, 769
Buntsma, Damien M.E., Lawrence, Lawrence, Stevenson LLP, 923
Buntsma, Everett, Director, Community Services, Pickering, 1336
Bur, Justin, VP East, 861
Burak, Monika, Coordinator, 642
Burak, Rob, President, 715
Burden, Bill, Librarian, Prince Edward Island Dept. of Provincial Treasury, 1011
Bureau, Paul, Delorme, LeBel, Bureau, Savoie, 945
Bureau, Suzanne, Director, Collection & Metadata Services, Canadian Institute for Scientific & Technical Information (CISTI), 994
Bureau, Ginette, Président-directeur général, 853
Burge, Todd, Manager, Fort Saskatchewan, 1306
Burgess, John, Director, Library, Keyano College, 956
Burgoyne, Ryan P., Associate, Cox & Palmer - Fredericton, 917
Burhenne, Wolfgang E., Executive Governor, 778
Burke, D. Kevin, Partner, Cox & Palmer - Halifax, 921
Burke, Joseph F., Partner, Cox & Palmer - Halifax, 921
Burke, Kelly, Librarian, Borrower Services, SIAST Kelsey Campus, 1034
Burke, Sabrina, Library Technician, Champlain College Saint-Lambert, 1028
Burke, John, President, 755
Burkett, Brian W., Senior Partner, Heenan Blaikie LLP - Toronto, 931
Burkholder, Forrest, Chair, 686
Burley, Dave, Manager, 681
Burnell, John, Chair, 685
Burnett, Marian, Librarian, Corner Brook Campus, 976
Burnett, Q.C., William J., Thompson Dorfman Sweatman LLP - Winnipeg, 916
Burns, Michael, Partner, McMillan LLP - Toronto, 933
Burns, Angela, Librarian, Energy Resources Conservation Board (ERCB), 950
Burns, Chris, Research Support & Data Librarian, Kwantlen Polytechnic University, 964
Burns, Dave, President, 665
Burns, Jeremy, President, 642
Burns, Tim, Press Secretary, 775
Burns, Maggy, Internal Director, 744
Burns, Sandra, Manager, 696
Burone, Federico, Regional Director, 778
Burpee, Terry, Sec.-Treas., 804
Burpee, Jim, President & CEO, 695
Burrell, Carol Ann, Executive Director, 704
Burrell, W. Bruce, Fire Chief, Calgary, 1305
Burrough, Josy, Manager, Grande Prairie, 1307
Burrows, Will, Executive Director, 731
Burrows, Holly-Ann, Manager, 677
Burrows, Fred, Fire Chief, Fort St. John, 1315
Burston, Merle, Chair, 824
Burt, Patricia, Library Director, Red River College, 972
Burtnick, Diane, Treasurer, 639
Burton, Alstair H. A., Thomson, Rogers, 936
Burton, Andrew J.G., Davis LLP - Toronto, 930
Burton, Andrew J.G., Partner, Davis LLP - Vancouver, 911
Burton, Melody, Deputy University Librarian, University of British Columbia, 967
Burton, Terri, Director, Emergency Services, Muskoka, 1329
Busby, Lorraine, Associate University Librarian, Information Resour, Western University Libraries, 990
Bushman, Jonathan, President, 648
Bushway, Christine, Executive Director, 828
Buss, Greg, Chief Librarian, Richmond, 1317
Bussière, Hélène, Bibliothécaire, Bibliothèque centrale, 1015
Bussière, Jean, Research Editor, 684
Bussière, Robert, Préfet, Les Collines-de-l'Outaouais, 1355
Butch, Morningstar, Executive Director, 1205
Butkus, Mavis, McKenzie Lake Lawyers, 924
Butler, Jenelle R., Associate, Brownlee LLP - Edmonton, 906
Butler, Scott, Manager, 818
Butler, Al, President, 864
Butler, Kim, Supervisor, 658
Butler, Colleen, Manager, Mount Pearl, 1324
Butler, Donna, Manager, Okanagan-Similkameen, 1313
Buttenham, D.O., CEO, 814
Butters, David, President, 663
Butterworth, Lucy, Director, Parksville, 1316
Buttigieg, Bryan J., Partner, Miller Thomson LLP - Toronto, 934
Butts, Richard, Chief Administrative Officer, Halifax Regional Municipality, 1325
Buwalda, Sandie, Coordinator, 639
Buzunis, M.Eng., PMP, P.Eng., Byron, Urban Construction Manager, Lethbridge, 1307
Bych, Casper, McMillan LLP - Vancouver, 913
Byers, Barbara, Executive Vice-President, 707
Byette, Michel, Directeur général, Trois-Rivières, 1352
Bynum, Laura, Contact, 716
Byres, Nicole M., Clark Wilson LLP, 911
Byrne, Mary-Louise, Secretary-Treasurer, 686
Byrne, Melissa, Coordinator, 807
Byron, Irvine, Director, Operations, 1121
Byron, Davis, Senior Project Manager, Facilities, Park Services, 1295
Byron D., De Kergommeaux, Director, Strategic & Operations Alignment, 1159
Byrtus, Lilly, Regional Coordinator, 644

C

C., Moyse, Registrar, 1271
Cabrera-Rivera, Orlando, Program Manager, 732
Cacciani, Antonietta, Manager, 775
Cade, James R., Senior Partner, Norton Rose Fulbright Canada LLP - Toronto - Royal Bank Plaza, 934
Cade-Menun, Barbara, Secretary, 721
Cadieux, Michel, Directeur général, 853
Cadigan, Robert, President & CEO, 808
Cadman, David, President, 777
Caetano, Lucy, Commis, Bibliothèque de géographie, 1016
Caetano, Vincent, Documentation Technician, Royal Victoria Hospital, 1020
Cafaro, Philip J., Vice-President, 783
Cahill, William T., Associate, Cox & Palmer - St. John's, 919
Cahill, Robert B., Executive Director, 760
Caines, Jennifer, Treasurer, 807
Cairns, Peter, President, 851
Cairns, Malcolm, Executive Vice-President, 722
Caitlin, Workman, Spokesperson, Media Relations, Outreach & E-Communications Division, 1144
Caitlin, Kerwin, Director, Corporate Policy, 1297
Cajic, Natalie, Specialist, 701
Cal, Dallas, Minister, International & Intergovernmental Relati, 1191
Cal, McDonald, Assistant Deputy Minister, 1261
Cal, Glasman, Director, Administration, 1295
Caldwell, Fran, President, 673
Caldwell, Paul, President, 726
Calich, Michael J., Loopstra Nixon LLP Barristers & Solicitors, 932
Calie, McPhee, Director, Atlantic Gateway, 1174
Calla, Andrea, President, 662
Callaghan, Cathy, Information Services Librarian, University of Prince Edward Island, 1011
Callbreath, Deborah, Chair, 701
Callen, Cammie, Specialist, 856
Callihoo, Cheryl, Secretary, 639
Caloren, Noëlle, Borden Ladner Gervais LLP - Ottawa, 925
Calum, Ewing, Director, Museum Operations, 1241
Calvert, Mitch, Coordinator, 736
Cam, Berwald, Contact, Arctic Winter Games, 1195
Cam, Filmer, Executive Director, Strategic Planning, Policy & Legislation, 1210
Camago, Javier, Chair, 864
Came, Frank, President, 675
Cameron, David A., Burchells LLP, 920
Cameron, George, HGR Graham Partners LLP - Barrie, 922
Cameron, Glenn, Partner, Stikeman Elliott LLP - Calgary, 905
Cameron, Hugh J., Partner, Stewart McKelvey - Fredericton, 917
Cameron, Claudia, Contact, Buffalo Lake Naturalists Club, 958
Cameron, Susan, Special Collections Librarian, St Francis-Xavier University, 980
Cameron, Grantland M., Executive Director, 641
Cameron, Patricia, Executive Director, 763
Cameron, Nancy, Medical Officer of Health, Huron, 1329
Cameron, Russ, Fire Chief, Colwood, 1314
Cameron, Prince, Vice-President, Inspection Modernization, 1129
Cameron, Henry, Acting Assistant Deputy Minister, 1180
Cameron, Traynor, Director, Communications, 1193
Cameron, Steenveld, Executive Director & Senior Financial Officer, Fin, 1196
Cameron, Lewis, Executive Officer, 1210
Cameron, DeLong, Manager, Facility Planning & Operations, 1247
Cameron, Sinclair, Assistant Deputy Minister, 1250
Cameron, Mack, Acting Director, Science & Information, 1260
Camille, Mageau, Director, Oceans Policy & Planning, 1141
Camille, Hauck, Coordinator, Scheduling, 1193
Campbell, A.Neil, Partner, McMillan LLP - Toronto, 933
Campbell, Allen A., Boyne Clarke LLP, 920
Campbell, J. Andrew D., Partner, Cox & Palmer - Summerside, 938
Campbell, Jennifer, Partner, Cassels Brock & Blackwell LLP, 928
Campbell, Margaret, Librarian, Chatham-Kent Health Alliance, 985
Campbell, Neil A., Law Librarian & Associate Professor, Diana M. Priestly Law Library, 968
Campbell, Neil, Associate University Librarian, Law, University of Victoria Libraries, 969
Campbell, Rita, Special Projects Librarian, St Francis-Xavier University, 980
Campbell, Robert, Director, Library Services, Cape Breton University, 982
Campbell, Sandy, Collection Coordinator, Cameron Science & Technology Library, 954
Campbell, Suzzette, Library Assistant, DeVry Institute of Technology, 950
Campbell, Chris, Exective Director, 794
Campbell, Bruce, Executive Director, 691
Campbell, David W., President, 791
Campbell, Noel, Manager, 723
Campbell, Anne, Officer, 728
Campbell, Cathy, President, 685
Campbell, Carolyn, Executive Director, 677
Campbell, Darron, Manager, Cariboo, 1311
Campbell, Doug, Manager, Portage La Prairie, 1321
Campbell, Francis, Manager, Cape Breton, 1325
Campbell, Marty, Coordinator, Red Deer County, 1304
Campbell, QC, Daniel M., Partner, Cox & Palmer - Halifax, 921
Campbell, QC, Jocelyn M., Partner, Cox & Palmer - Halifax, 921
Campbell, QC, Karen A., Cox & Palmer - Charlottetown, 937
Campeau, Stephanie, Director, 670
Campion, John A., Senior Partner, Fasken Martineau - Toronto, 930
Campos, Anna, Officer, 693
Campsall, Mitch, President, 809
Canfield, Brian R., Farris, Vaughan, Wills & Murphy LLP, 912

Canham, Robin, Librarian, Services Assessment, Saskatchewan Institute of Applied Science & Technology, 1032
Cannan, Kevin, Treasurer, 748
Cannon, Charles A., President/CEO, 843
Cantello, Geoffrey, Nelligan O'Brien Payne, 926
Cantin, Jacques, Joli-Coeur Lacasse Avocats - Québec, 944
Cantin, Marie-Claude, Partner, Lavery, de Billy - Montréal, 941
Cantin, Michel, Bélanger, Sauvé, 938
Cantrell, Rick, Vice-President & COO, 859
Cao, Siv Kham, Bibliothécaire, Bibliothèque paramédicale, 1017
Caouette, Pierre, Cain Lamarre Casgrain Wells - Québec, 943
Caouette, Francis, Director, North Vancouver, 1316
Cape, Geoff, Executive Director, 750
Caplan, Tyana R., Stewart McKelvey - Halifax, 922
Capobianco, John, President, 837
Capozi, Robert, New Brunswick Contact, 765
Capuano, Mike, Chair, 709
Cara, Benoit, Vice-President, Prevention Services, 1240
Carbert, Blair R., Founding Partner, Stones Carbert Waite Wells LLP, 906
Carbonaro, David, Senior Partner, Heenan Blaikie LLP - Toronto, 931
Carbone, Cecilia, Secretary General, 777
Carbonneau, Lise, Region Coordinator, 706
Cardin, Louis, Sec.-Trés., Régie d'assainissement des eaux Richelieu/Saint-Laurent, 1356
Cardinal, Julie, Directrice, Traitement et accès aux documents, Université de Montréal, 1021
Cardinal, Mark, Manager, Parkland County, 1304
Cardozo, Paula, Librarian, Nippissing University & Canadore College of Applie Arts & Technol, 992
Cardwell, Linda, Contact, Library Services, H. G. Thode Library of Science & Engineering, 986
Cardy, Eileen, Library Technician, Alberta Hospital Edmonton, 953
Careen, Jones, Manager, Labour Relations, 1257
Carey, Richard, Director, Land Resource Stewardship, 1233
Caricofe, Erin, Program Assistant, 767
Carissa, Robb, Manager, Community Relations, 1294
Carl, Girard, Acting Director General, Infrastructure Operations Directorate, 1134
Carl, Lafferty, Regional Superintendent, 1236
Carl, Rumscheidt, Director, 1302
Carla, White-Taylor, Director, Rail Safety Secretariat, 1176
Carla, White, Director, Canadian Intergovernmental Policy, Clean Energy & Natural Resources / Social Policy, 1192
Carla, Wallis, Manager, Arts & Fine Crafts, 1238
Carle, Michel G., Senior Partner, Norton Rose Fulbright Canada LLP - Montréal, 942
Carle, Rod, General Manager, New Westminster, 1316
Carlile, Cathryn, General Manager, Richmond, 1317
Carline, Johnny, Chief Administrative Officer/Commissioner, Metro Vancouver, 1312
Carlson, Darren W., McDougall Gauley - Regina, 946
Carlson, Harold, Chairperson, 637
Carlson, Christine, Administrator, 673
Carlson, Matthew, Officer, 806
Carlson, Ken, Director, Wetaskiwin County No. 10, 1305
Carlston, B.A., M.A., Jason, General Manager, Regina, 1359
Carlyon, Rod, Branch Head, Livestock & Farm Business Branch, 1182
Carman, Giacomantonio, Chief Medical Director, 1242
Carmel, Lowe, Director, GSC Pacific, 1164
Carmela, Murphy, Director, Tourism Marketing Division, 1235
Carmelle, d'Entremont, Executive Director, Health System Workforce, 1242
Carmen, Vidaurri, Acting Director, Financial Reporting & Operations, 1183
Carmen, Neufeld, Chair, 1219
Carmen, Levi, Director, Corporate Affairs & Support Services, 1246
Carol, Najm, Acting Assistant Deputy Minister, 1135
Carol, Buckley, Director General, 1165
Carol, Goodfellow, Assistant Farmers' Advocate, Land & Energy, 1181
Carol, Bettac, Executive Director, Industry Challenges & Emerging, 1185
Carol, Lawrence, Director, IMIT, 1192
Carol, Mayers, Director, Corporate Planning, 1192
Carol, Loski, Director, Flood Protection Program, 1210
Carol, McClintock, Acting Executive Director, Mitigation Program, 1210
Carol, Bishop, Executive Director, Crown Agencies, 1211
Carol, MacQuarrie, Executive Director, Engineering Services, 1226
Carol, Sackville-Duyvelshoff, Associate Director, Information Management & Analysis, 1256
Carol, Layton, Deputy Minister, 1263
Carol, Craswell, Supervisor, Land Administration, 1275
Carol, Halvorson, Director, Mail Services, 1287
Carol Ann, Kushlyk, Assistant Deputy Minister & Senior Financial Offic, 1190
Carol Ann, Duffy, Deputy Minister, 1266
Carol Anne, Pasutto, Branch Head, Information Management & Technology S, 1184
Carolann, Regular, Executive Director, Service Delivery Transformatio, 1191
Carole, Girard, Senior Director, Regulatory Approvals & Compliance Directorate, 1132
Carole, Lemay, Director, Executive Group Services & Management Development, 1135
Carole, Lafond, Directrice générale, 1280
Carolina, Stecher, Special Advisor to the Minister, Manitoba Hydro, 1218
Caroline, Ladanowski, Director, Wildlife Program Support Division, 1135
Caroline, Ladanowski, Director, Water Quality Monitoring & Surveillance, 1135
Caroline, Blais, Director, Electricity & Combustion, 1136
Caroline, Cloutier, Director, Data Acquisition Division, 1163
Caroline, Cloutier, Director, Data Acquisition Division, 1164
Caroline, Fobes, Deputy Executive Director & Senior Counsel, Legal Services, 1170
Caroline, Weber, Assistant Deputy Minister, 1171
Caroline, Drouin, Secrétaire générale et Directrice, Vérification interne, 1278
Caroline, Imbeau, Directrice, Logistique sociosanitaire, 1283
Carolos, Germann, Director, Heritage Conservation, 1295
Carolyn, Babcock, Manager, Canadian Collection of Fungal Cultures, Biodiversity & Collections, 1121
Carolyn, Crook, Director, Rail Policy, 1174
Carolyn, Dahl Rees, Vice-Chair, 1183
Carolyn, Davison, Director, 1243
Carolyn, O'Neill, Manager, Great Lakes, 1252
Carolyn, Relf, Director, 1299
Carolyn, Relf, Director, 1299
Carolyn J., Sanford, Provincial Epidemiologist, 1271
Caron, Monique, Hutchins Caron & Associés, 940
Carothers, Leslie, President, 749
Carpenter, A.W. (Sandy), Partner, Fasken Martineau - Calgary, 903
Carpenter, Phil, Chief, Portage La Prairie, 1321
Carr, Alison, Loopstra Nixon LLP Barristers & Solicitors, 932
Carr, Hilary, Assistant Director, Knowledge & Research Program, Halifax Office, 981
Carr, Jonathan, Director, 670
Carr, John, Board Member, 744
Carr, Susan, General Manager, 834
Carrasco, Erika, Associate, Field LLP - Calgary, 903
Carrie, Hayward, Acting Assistant Deputy Minister, 1259
Carrie, Ross, Executive Director, Government House, 1294
Carrier, Geneviève, Cain Lamarre Casgrain Wells - Québec, 943
Carrier, Hélène, Cain Lamarre Casgrain Wells - Québec, 943
Carrier, Jean, Associé, Stikeman Elliott LLP - Montréal, 943
Carrier, Pierre, Secteur de la consultation, Bibliothèque des sciences humaines et sociales, 1022
Carrier, Gilles, President, 855
Carrière, Louis, Partner, Heenan Blaikie S.E.N.C.R.L./SRL - Québec, 944
Carrière, Mathilde, Dentons Canada LLP - Montreal, 939
Carrière, Jean-Marc, Vice-President, 660
Carrière, Ghislaine, Manager, 769
Carrière, Patrick, Supervisor, Waste Water Treatment Facility, Cornwall, 1332
Carringon, Heather, Coordinator, 763
Carroll, Daniel P., Managing Partner, Field LLP - Edmonton, 908
Carroll, Joanna, Blaney McMurtry LLP, 928
Carroll, Gary, Vice-President, 798
Carroll, Gary, Director, Engineering Services, Oshawa, 1335
Carroll, Neil, Director, Planning & Development, Pickering, 1336
Carruthers, Amy J., Partner, Lawson Lundell LLP - Vancouver, 913
Carscallen, Q.C., Stanley, Partner, Carscallen LLP, 902
Carson, Lorne, Partner, Osler, Hoskin & Harcourt LLP - Calgary, 905
Carson, Tim, Chief Executive Officer, 637
Carsten, Tudor, Davis LLP - Toronto, 930
Carteaux, William R., President & CEO, 856
Carter, Mae, Reference Resource Specialist, Great Lakes Regional Office, 1010
Carter, Josh, President, 760
Carter, David C., Executive Director & Registrar, 665
Carter, Fran, President, 675
Carter, Simon, Regional Director, 778
Carter, Tanya, Manager, Moncton / Ville de Moncton, 1322
Carter, FEC, P.Eng., Marie, COO, 746
Carter, P.Geo., Nicholle, Manager, 681
Cartwright, Barbara, CEO, 698
Cartwright, Thomas, Fire Chief, Port Colborne, 1336
Caruk, Kelly, MacPherson Leslie & Tyerman LLP - Saskatoon, 947
Caruso, Colette, Coordinator, 818
Carvalho, Hernandez F., Secretary General, 778
Carvell, Dorothea, Manager, Transit, North Bay, 1334
Cary, Legien, Section Manager, Materials Management, 1292
Casabon, François, Directeur du service, Campus Notre-Dame-de-Foy, 1026
Casaubon, Marie-Josée, Présidente, 655
Casavant, Ginette, Technicienne, Université du Québec Institut national de la recherche scientifiq, 1025
Casey, Brian P., Associate, Boyne Clarke LLP, 920
Casey, Andrew, Vice-President, 755
Casey, Susan, Coordinator, 806
Casey, Andrew, President & CEO, 672
Casey, Gouw, Council Member, 1181
Casey, QC, Michael, Counsel, Field LLP - Calgary, 903
Cash, Colleen, Co-Chair, 718
Cashman, Danette, Loopstra Nixon LLP Barristers & Solicitors, 932
Cass, Fred D., Aird & Berlis LLP, 928
Cassandra, Caunce, Regional Manager, Thompson Regional Office, 1203
Cassell, Chris, Secretary-Treasurer, 688
Casselman, Daniel, Coordinator, 696
Casselman, Alice, President, 658
Cassey, Zhou, Financial Analyst, 1199
Cassidy, Myles, Fire Chief & Manager, Emergency Services, Cornwall, 1332
Castell, Barb, Staff, 796
Castellan, Dan, Contact, 648
Castonguay, Luc, Directeur, Saint-Jean-sur-Richelieu, 1351
Catana, Ruth, Chief Operating Officer, 802
Catania, Peter J., Chair, 778
Catelin, Milton, Chief Executive, 872
Catellier, Maryse, Vice-président exécutif, 681
Cathe, Offet, Director, Communications, 1291
Catherine, MacInnis, Executive Director, Prince Edward Island Federal C, 1123
Catherine, Higgens, Director General, 1175
Catherine, Wollner, Program Manager, 1199
Catherine, McDonald, Vice President, Professional Practice, Chief Nursi, 1229
Catherine, Blewett, Deputy Minister/CEO, 1243
Catherine, Foo, Executive Director, NCIAC, 1246
Catherine, Syrota, Geodata Supervisor, Sedimentary Geodata Branch, 1288
Catherine Francis, Martin, Director, Human Resources, 1244
Cathi, Bradboury, Associate Deputy Minister, Medical Services, 1229
Cathro, Mike, President, 788
Cathryn, Taubman, Director, Human Resources Operations - National Capital Region, 1140
Cathy, Banic, Acting Manager, Experimental Studies Section, 1135
Cathy, Matthews, Director General, Finance & Management Accountability, 1179
Cathy, Matthews, Director General, Finance & Management Accountability, 1179
Cathy, Johnson, Manager, Prosthetics & Orthotics, Seating & Footwe, 1188
Cathy, Gauthier, Acting Director, Revenue, 1207
Cathy, Larochelle, Director, Agricultural Financial Programs, 1219
Cathy, O'Keefe, Director, Disease Control, 1230
Cathy, Menard, Chief Coroner, Coroner's Office, 1238
Cathy, MacIsaac, Director, Public Affairs & Communications, 1245
Cathy, Flanagan, Director, Residential Rental Property, 1274
Cathy, Drader, Director, Information Management, 1288
Cathy, Lynn Borbely, Director, Strategic Business Planning, 1292

Cathy, Morton-Bielz, Assistant Deputy Minister, 1301
Cathy, Stannard, Director, Community Health Programs, 1301
Cathy A., Sabiston, Director General, Controlled Substances & Tobacco, 1145
Cathy A., Sabiston, Director General, Defence & Major Projects Sector, 1171
Cathy D., DesRoches, Administrator, Community Hospitals West, 1272
Cathy M., Whalen, Director, Tax Administration, 1228
Cathy Priestner, Allinger, Co-Chair (Vancouver), 1200
Cattaneo, Joseph J., President, 762
Cauz, Carrie, Resource Centre Coordinator, Environmental Commissioner of Ontario, 1003
Cavan, Scott, Program Director, 836
Cavan, Laurie, General Manager, Surrey, 1318
Cavanaugh, Darlene, Director, 639
Cavanaugh, Barry, CEO & General Counsel, 666
Cave, Christine, Administrative Officer, 798
Cayen, Pat, Fire Chief, Fire Rescue Services, Sarnia, 1337
Cayouette, Heather, Program Manager, 660
Ceccolini, Bruna, Assistant to the Trenholme Dean of Libraries, McGill University, 1020
Cecil, Villard, Executive Director, 1272
Cedric, Jobe, Director, Energy Supply - Nuclear Branch, 1250
Celeste, Sulliman, Director, Communications, 1242
Celia, McDonagh, Manager, Training, 1193
Céline, Jacob, Sec.-Trés., Régie de l'eau de l'Ile Perrot, 1356
Céline, Gaudet, Acting Regional Director, Communications & Marketing, 1177
Céline, Villeneuve, Directrice, Pilotage des systèmes et de l'assistance aux utilisateurs, 1278
Centa, Andrea L., Partner, Fasken Martineau - Toronto, 930
Ceppetelli, Gary, Director, Thompson, 1321
Cerit, Errol, Senior Director, 755
Cernile, Carol, Research Library Technician, U.S. Steel Canada, 987
Chabot, Josiane, Présidente, 657
Chabot, Annie, Directrice générale, 657
Chad, Navin, Manager, North Vancouver, 1316
Chad, McCleave, Chief Financial Officer, 1255
Chafe, David, President, 840
Chaillez, Lise, Bibliothécaire, École nationale d'aérotechnique, 1027
Chaîné, Yves, Bélanger, Sauvé, 938
Chaisson, J. Robert, Vice-President, 804
Chalker, Bob, Executive Director, 798
Chalker, George, Executive Director, 768
Chalmers, Ben, Vice-President, 797
Chamaschuk, Shelly K., Reynolds Mirth Richards & Farmer LLP, 909
Chamberlain, Marijoel, Coordinator, Member Services, & Manager, 679
Chamberlain, Randy, Coordinator, Health & Safety, Port Colborne, 1336
Chamberland, Geneviève, Heenan Blaikie S.E.N.C.R.L/SRL - Sherbrooke, 945
Chamberland, Patricia, Bibliotechnicienne, CHUQ-CHUL, 1023
Chambers, Stuart W., Partner, McLennan Ross LLP - Edmonton, 908
Chambers, B.Comm., LL.B., Gordon R., Partner, Lawson Lundell LLP - Vancouver, 913
Champagne, Pierre, Partner, Heenan Blaikie LLP - Ottawa, 925
Champagne, Sylvain, Directeur, Services à la clientèle, HEC Montréal, 1019
Champion, Q.C., Jeffrey B., Bishop & McKenzie LLP, 906
Champoux, Hugo, Delorme, LeBel, Bureau, Savoie, 945
Chan, J. Christopher, Burns Fitzpatrick Rogers & Schwartz LLP, Barristers & Solicitors, 911
Chan, Margaret, Director General, 872
Chandel, Vikram Singh, Contact, Midland Campus, 990
Chang, Phillis, Director, 819
Channan, Omkar Nath, Founding President & Governor, 873
Chantal, Claude, Président, 656
Chantal, Lafontaine, Officer, Communications, 1138
Chantal, Laflamme, Acting Manager, Publishing & Linguistic Services, 1178
Chantal, Lemyre, Director General, 1178
Chantal, Brunet, Présidente-directrice générale (par intérim), 1280
Chantal, Castonguay, Directeur, Occasions d'affaires mondiales, 1280
Chantal, Maltais, Directrice générale, Personnes âgées, 1283
Chantal, Gingras, Directrice générale adjointe, Planification et de la coordination territoriale, 1285
Chantal D., Dallaire, Executive Assistant, Program Development & Engagement, 1135
Chantale, Brouillet, Directrice, Enquêtes et analyse de marché, 1285
Chapman, Shad A., Partner, Brownlee LLP - Edmonton, 906
Chapman, Bruce, Executive Director, 765
Chapman, G.A., Treasurer, 690
Chapman, Paul, Director, Planning Services, St. Catharines, 1336
Chapman, QC, Anthony L., Partner, Cox & Palmer - Halifax, 921
Chappell, Charles L., Aikins, MacAulay & Thorvaldson LLP, 915
Chaput, Marie, Présidente, 727
Chaput, Rhéaume, Fire Chief, Belleville, 1331
Charanduk, Brian, Treasurer, 637
Charbonneau, George, President, 688
Charbonneau, Mathieu, Directeur général adjoint, 668
Charbonneau, Paul, Director, Emergency & Transportation Services & Ch, Frontenac, 1328
Charest Knoetze, Claire, Technicienne en documentation, Campus d'Edmundston, 973
Charest, André, Directeur, Victoriaville, 1352
Charest, Lynda, Directrice générale, Régie intermunicipale de gestion des déchets de la région Maskout, 1357
Charette, Jules, Senior Partner, Norton Rose Fulbright Canada LLP - Montréal, 942
Charette, Louis, Partner, Lavery, de Billy - Montréal, 941
Charland, Roger, Bibliothécaire, CÉGEP de Trois-Rivières, 1030
Charland-Lallier, Maryève, Présidente, 735
Charleen, Schmidt, Executive Advisor, 1184
Charlene, Gaudet, Director, Communications, 1128
Charlene, Doolittle, Executive Director, Legal Services Board, 1238
Charles, Lambert, Regional Director, 1127
Charles, Ouellette, Chief Information Officer, 1132
Charles, Larabie, Director, Cleantech, Infrastructure & Life Sciences Practices Division, 1143
Charles, Tremblay, Deputy Director, Investment Cooperation Program Division, 1143
Charles, Mojsej, Director General, Strategic Communications, 1146
Charles, Vincent, Senior Director, Planning & Programming Directorate, 1154
Charles, van Hemmen, District Manager, Natural Resource Operations (Cascades), 1206
Charles, Reid, President & Chief Executive Officer, 1208
Charles, Ayles, Assistant Deputy Minister, 1224
Charles, Bown, Deputy Minister, 1232
Charles, Purcell, Director, Information Technology, 1243
Charles, Baillie, Honorary Chair, 1262
Charles, Allan, Manager, Medicare Services, 1272
Charles, Larochelle, Sous-ministre adjoint, Changements climatiques, à l'air & à l'eau, 1278
Charles, Larochelle, Sous-ministre adjoint, 1279
Charles, Bélanger, Directeur, Information sur le travail, 1286
Charles A., Lin, Director General, Atmospheric Science & Technology, 1135
Charles Bernard, MacDonald, Director, 1241
Charles Joseph, MacDonald, Executive Director, Highway Maintenance & Operations, 1245
Charles-Antoine, Gauthier, Acting Director, Research Programs, NCR, 1160
Charlie, Parker, Minister, 1241
Charlie, Parker, Minister, 1243
Charlotte, Price, Director, Sustainable Resource & Policy Management, 1215
Charlotte, Valley, Director, Financial & Administrative Services, 1226
Charlotte, O'Donnell, Secretariat, 1300
Charlotte A., Murray, Manager, Human Resources, 1268
Charlton, Anne, Director, Calgary, 1305
Charmaine, Hall, Executive Assistant to the Deputy Minister, 1302
Charney, Richard J., Senior Partner, Norton Rose Fulbright Canada LLP - Toronto - Royal Bank Plaza, 934
Charron, Lyne, Responsable, PEB, La Cité Collégiale, 994
Charron, Noëlline, Technicienne en documentation, Collège Jean-de-Brébeuf, 1018
Charron, Danielle, Executive Director, 662
Charron, Denis, Directeur général, Rouyn-Noranda, 1350
Chartier, Michelle, Responsable, services techniques, Collège Édouard-Montpetit, 1015
Chartrand, Melanie, Lavery, de Billy - Montréal, 941
Chase, Lindsay, President, 833
Chassé, Gabriel, Tremblay Bois Mignault Lemay S.E.N.C.R.L., 945
Chatwin, Randall C., Lawson Lundell LLP - Vancouver, 913
Chauhan, Sam, Manager, Surrey, 1318
Chauvin, James, Director, 716
Chayer, Yves, Directeur, Montmagny, 1349
Chayra, Melanie, Secretariat, 709
Chaytor, QC, Sandra R., Partner, Cox & Palmer - St. John's, 919
Cheal, Lauren, Contractor, 763
Cheatle, Andrew, Vice-President, 665
Cheesman, Norman, Chief Executive Officer, 823
Cheng, Siu Mee, Exeuctive Director, 822
Chenier, Dan, General Manager, Parks, Recreation & Cultural Serv, Ottawa, 1335
Chénier, Marc, Sec.-Treas., 692
Chenoweth, Brian, Manager, Novelis Inc., 988
Cheodore, Bill, National Coordinator, 703
Chernis, Terry, Manager, Sir F.G. Banting Research Centre, 997
Chernos, David P., Torys LLP - Toronto, 936
Cheryl, Bertrand, Acting Director General, Integrated Enterprise Services, 1135
Cheryl, Ringor, Director, Compliance & Policy Branch, 1154
Cheryl, Vickers, Chair/Chief Executive Officer, 1201
Cheryl, Yaremko, Chief Financial Officer & Executive Vice-President, 1208
Cheryl, Burgess, Chief Executive Officer, 1240
Cheryl, Burgess, Executive Director, Strategic & Transition Planning, 1244
Cheryl, Campbell, Officer, Program Statistics, 1270
Cheryl A., Devine, Executive Assistant, Science & Technology Integration Division, 1135
Cheryl L., Meek, Director, Strategic Communications & Employee Enga, 1148
Cheryle, Donahue, Manager, Human Resources, 1239
Cheskey, Ted, Manager, 802
Chesney, Bill, Fire Chief, Cambridge, 1332
Chester, Simon, Partner, Heenan Blaikie LLP - Toronto, 931
Cheung, Rich, President, 855
Chevalier, Michel, Manager, Wastewater & Drainage Operations, Ottawa, 1335
Chevarie, Veronique, Agente de bureau, Campus des Iles-de-la-Madeleine, 1014
Cheverie, Mel, Chief Building Inspector, Charlottetown, 1346
Chevrier, Pierre, Directeur général, Salaberry-de-Valleyfield, 1351
Chi, Loo, Assistant Deputy Minister, 1189
Chiarello, Gene P., Associate, Cohen Highley LLP - London, 924
Chiasson, Derek G., Partner, Norton Rose Fulbright Canada LLP - Montréal, 942
Chiasson, Christine, Digital Services Technican, Brantford Campus, 984
Chiasson, Claude, Associate Director, Bathurst Campus, 973
Chiasson, John, President, 741
Chiasson, Cindy, Executive Director, 749
Chick, Diane, McKenzie Lake Lawyers, 924
Chick, Timothy P., Davis LLP - Calgary, 903
Chicoyne, MSS, Daniel B., Manager, 681
Childress, Amy, President, 660
Chilton, John, Executive Manager, 775
Chin, Ron A., Farris, Vaughan, Wills & Murphy LLP, 912
Chipeur, Q.C., Gerald D., Partner, Miller Thomson LLP - Calgary, 905
Chisanga, Puta-Chekwe, Deputy Minister, 1249
Chisholm, Damon, McMillan LLP - Vancouver, 913
Chisholm, Cathy, Information Services Librarian, Cape Breton University, 982
Chislett, Michelle, Chair, 721
Chisman, Dennis, Treasurer, 777
Chiu, Jung-Kay, Partner, Norton Rose Fulbright Canada LLP - Toronto - Royal Bank Plaza, 935
Chiu, P.Eng, Stella, Chair, 664
Chivers, George (Joe) F., Partner, Brownlee LLP - Edmonton, 906
Chmarney, Brian, Director, Mount Pearl, 1324
Cho, Raymond, Chair, 861
Cho, CGA, Jennifer, Director, 663
Chochinov, CET, Robert B., Registrar, 727
Chomlak, Kerra, Executive Director, 729
Chong, P. Eng., Tony, Chief Administrative Officer, Port Coquitlam, 1317

Cooke, Jason, Burchells LLP, 920
Cooke, Carol, Acting Hospital Librarian, St Boniface General Hospital, 972
Cooke, Murray, Vice-President, 855
Cooke, Everett, Fire Chief, Grande Prairie No. 1, 1303
Cooke, Robert, Directeur, Lévis, 1348
Cooley, Ken, Associate University Librarian, IT & Technical Ser, University of Victoria Libraries, 969
Coombs, Michael T., Associate, Brownlee LLP - Edmonton, 906
Coombs, Shannon, Executive Director, 693
Coon, David, Party Leader, 764
Cooney, Adam, President, 749
Cooper, George L., Managing Partner, Cox & Palmer - Moncton, 917
Cooper, Rosalind H., Partner, Fasken Martineau - Toronto, 930
Cooper, Beverley, Secretary, 777
Cooper, Graham, Executive Director, 651
Cooper, Kathleen, Senior Researcher, 696
Cooper, Mark, Director, 849
Cooper, Wendy, Executive Director, 737
Copestake, Peter, President, 672
Copley, Darren, President, 866
Copley, Christine, Senior Manager, 872
Corazon, Magnayon, Acting Office Manager, Legislative Building Information Systems, 1218
Corbett, Leland P., Partner, Stikeman Elliott LLP - Calgary, 905
Corbett, John, Commissioner, Planning, Design & Development, Brampton, 1332
Cordeau, Q.C., John F., Partner, Bennett Jones LLP - Calgary, 901
Cordeiro, Sonia, Eccleston LLP, 930
Cordelia, Clarke-Julien, Director, Training & Safety Programs, 1257
Corenblum, Bruce, Associate, D'Arcy & Deacon LLP - Calgary, 903
Corinne, Guénette, Director, Advisory Services Group, 1153
Corinne, Kristensen, Acting Team Leader, Environmental Assessment, Envi, 1188
Corless, Pat, Waterous, Holden, Amey, Hitchon LLP, 923
Cormack, Alison, Information Services Officer, British Columbia Utilities Commission, 965
Cormack, Mike, Treasurer, 743
Cormier, Elizabeth K., Patton Cormier & Associates, 924
Cormier, Mathieu, Adjoint au directeur des études, CÉGEP de Saint-Laurent, 1028
Cormier, Chantal, Vice-President, 685
Cormier, Lucien, Building Inspector, Bathurst, 1322
Cornelia, Kreplin, Executive Director, Value Chain Sustainability & Q, 1185
Cornelia, Kreplin, Executive Director, Advancing the Bioeconomy, 1185
Cornelius, Jim, Chair, 693
Cornett, BSc, OLS, Sarah, Executive Director, 836
Cornforth, Brian, Fire Chief, Lethbridge, 1307
Cornish, Barbara, Partner, Singleton Urquhart LLP, 914
Coronado, Irasema, Executive Director, 732
Corr, Tom, President & CEO, 815
Corrie, Davis, Manager, Land Use Planning, 1231
Corrie, Stewart, Director, Corporate Services, 1245
Corrine A., Rowswell, Coordinator, Infection Control Services, 1271
Corrinne, Nelson, District Manager, 1259
Corrinne, Nelson, Acting District Manager, 1259
Corriveau, Marie-Josée, Joli-Coeur Lacasse Avocats - Montréal, 940
Corriveau, Josée, Conseillère pédagogique, Collège de Rosemont, 1017
Corriveau, Robert, President, 704
Corriveau, Robert, Director, 834
Corry, Julie, Hutchins Caron & Associés, 940
Corso, Nathalie, Coordonnatrice, 827
Cortis, William, Partner, Miller Thomson LLP - Toronto, 934
Cory, Enns, Director, Aboriginal Consultation, 1180
Cory, Grandy, Assistant Deputy Minister, 1235
Cory, Hughes, Director, Mineral Policy, 1288
Cosgrove, Julie, Coordinator, Kawartha World Issues Centre, 997
Cosgrove, Julie, Coordinator, 788
Cosman, Robert W., Partner, Fasken Martineau - Toronto, 930
Cossarini, Danielle, Librarian, Selkirk College, 960
Costa, Glenda, Vice-President, 755
Costachescu, Irina, Tradeshow Operations Manager, 698
Costello, Eileen, Treasurer & Secretary, 687
Costello, Cecily, Treasurer, 774
Costello, Keith, Superintendent, Corner Brook, 1324
Costelo, Debbie, Public Services Librarian, Nova Scotia Community College, 981
Costigan, Doug, Director, Edmonton, 1306
Costin, Abraham, Partner, McCarthy Tétrault LLP - Toronto, 933
Cote, Larry, President, Chief Executive Officer, & Journal Cont, Canadian Institute for NDE, 986
Cote, Larry, President & CEO, 704
Côté, Lise, Joli-Coeur Lacasse Avocats - Québec, 944
Côté, Louis-Antoine, Heenan Blaikie S.E.N.C.R.L./SRL - Québec, 944
Côté, Marie-José, Grondin, Poudrier, Bernier, 944
Côté, MArie-José, Joli-Coeur Lacasse Avocats - Québec, 944
Côté, Andrée, Librarian, Faculty of Social Sciences, 995
Côté, Frédéric, directeur général, 859
Côté, Connie, Senior Director, 707
Côté, Marc-André, Directeur, 751
Côté, Éric, Directeur, Rivière-du-Loup, 1350
Cotsworth, Al, Manager, North Okanagan, 1312
Cott, Shaun, Manager, 671
Cotter, Catherine, Reference & Instruction Librarian, Gerard V. La Forest Law Library, 974
Cotter, Thomas, Secretary, 691
Cotton, Helen, Vice-Chair, 847
Cottrell, Cathy, Sr. Energy Efficiency Advisor, Yukon Energy Solutions Centre, 1035
Cottrell, Lois, Library Technician, St Joseph's Hospital (Hamilton), 987
Cottrell, Tom, IWMP Coordinator, 809
Coughlan-Lambly, Judith, Technical Services Librarian, W.K. Kellogg Health Sciences Library, 982
Coulombe, Louis, Associé, Cain Lamarre Casgrain Wells - Saguenay, 938
Coulombe, Solange, Technicienne en documentation, CÉGEP de Trois-Rivières, 1030
Coulombe, Robert, Président, 862
Coulombe, Denis, Directeur, Saguenay, 1350
Coulter, Laverne, Chapter President, 767
Coulter, B.Sc., Sandy, Acting Director, Operations - Water, Wastewater &, Barrie, 1331
Coumans, Catherine, Research Coordinator, 797
Coupland, Steve, Director, 711
Courcelles, Michel, Bibliothécaire, INRS - Institut Armand-Frappier, 1015
Cournoyer-Proulx, Magali, Partner, Heenan Blaikie LLP - Montréal, 940
Courtemanch, Edgar, Vice-Chairman, 728
Courtemanche, Guy, Bibliothécaire, Bibliothèque centrale, 1015
Cousineau, Marie, Heenan Blaikie LLP - Montréal, 940
Cousineau, Kenneth S., Executive Director, 701
Cousineau, Jean, Division Manager, Municipal Works, Cornwall, 1332
Cousins, Gary, Director, Planning, Wellington, 1331
Cousteau, Francine, President, 740
Coutney, Frank, Manager, Northeast Pigeon Lake Regional Services Commission, 1309
Couto, Sandra, Manager, 677
Couture, Karine, Responsable, Bibliothèque droit et publications go, Université de Sherbrooke, 1030
Couture, Yves, Directeur, 727
Couture, Céline, Secrétaire-Réceptionniste, 651
Covey, John, Vice-President, 687
Covich, Alan P., President, 774
Covington, Charlene, Director, Kelowna, 1315
Cowan, David J., McMillan LLP - Vancouver, 913
Cowan, J.G., WeirFoulds LLP, 936
Cowan, Dale, Treasurer, 814
Cowan, John, Vice-President, 762
Coward, Deryk W., Partner, D'Arcy & Deacon LLP - Winnipeg, 916
Cowles, Roger, President, 666
Cox, Louise, Présidente, 862
Cox, William, Chair, 811
Cox, Bryan, Executive Director, 874
Cox, Bruce, Executive Director, 764
Coxhead, William, Director, Parks & Recreation, London, 1334
Coxworthy, Paul L., Partner, Stewart McKelvey - St. John's, 919
Coylits, Ed, Executive Director, 728
Coysh, Sarah, Head Librarian, York University Glendon College Campus, 1009
Cozzi, P.Eng., Daniel, Director, Roads & Works Operations, Oakville, 1335
Crabbe, Darrell, Executive Director, 849
Cracknell, Linda, Head, Acquisitions & Serials, Wilfrid Laurier University, 1010
Craib, Linda, Admin Coordinator & Sr. Researcher, 735
Craig, John H., Partner, Cassels Brock & Blackwell LLP, 929
Craig, John N., Partner, Bennett Jones LLP - Calgary, 901
Craig, Gordon, President, 671
Craig, Levangie, Vice-President & Area Manager, 1125
Craig, Morris, Deputy Director, F-35 Industrial Participation, 1154
Craig, Oldham, Associate Director General, Operations, 1170
Craig, Hutton, Director, Policy Integration & Research, 1174
Craig, Smith, Program Analyst, 1199
Craig, Elder, Director, Administrative Services, 1201
Craig, Sutherland, Assistant Deputy Minister, 1205
Craig, Webster, Business Unit Director, Clean Transportation, 1208
Craig, Halwachs, Director, 1216
Craig, Halwachs, Executive Director, Financial & Administrative Services (Shared), 1218
Craig, Leonard, Minister, Energy & Mines, 1220
Craig, Bugden, Manager, Waste Management, 1227
Craig, Taylor, Regional Director, 1229
Craig, Martin, Director, Royalties Administration & Monitoring, 1233
Craig, Beaton, Director, Programs, 1241
Craig, Kinch, Manager, Ecological Standards, 1252
Craig, Brown, Director, Strategic Policy & Economics, 1258
Craig, Murray, Vice-President, Mining & Minerals, 1296
Craig, Brooks, Manager, Information Management, 1297
Craig A., Ceppetelli, Business Development Manager, Rail Program, 1161
Craig, B.A., LL.B., Gordon M., Partner, Lawson Lundell LLP - Vancouver, 913
Craik, Bill, Executive Director, 766
Crain, Kirsten, Partner, Borden Ladner Gervais LLP - Ottawa, 925
Cramer, Albert, Vice-President, 640
Cran, Bruce, President, 738
Crane, Rebecca, Norton Rose Fulbright Canada LLP - Toronto - Royal Bank Plaza, 935
Crane, Ron, HGR Graham Partners LLP - Midland, 924
Crang, Catherine A., Partner, Carscallen LLP, 902
Cranna, Derek A., Field LLP - Edmonton, 908
Craven, Jim, Treasurer, 700
Crawford, Dean, Partner, Heenan Blaikie LLP - Vancouver, 912
Crawford, Kara L., Thompson Dorfman Sweatman LLP - Winnipeg, 916
Crawford, Elizabeth, Librarian, New Brunswick Community College, 975
Crawford, Linda, Supervisor, CRL Library, Atomic Energy of Canada Ltd., 985
Crawford, Patricia, Head of Library, British Columbia Hydro, 959
Crawford, Donna, Administrative Coordinator, 769
Crawford, Alayne, Manager, 689
Crawford, Marie, Associate Executive Director, 863
Crawford, Marie, Director, 651
Crawford, Peter, Director, Courtenay, 1315
Creber, Ross, President & Secretary, 741
Cree, Lysane, Hutchins Caron & Associés, 940
Creech, Lori, Manager, 638
Cregan, Q.C., James E., Partner, Ackroyd LLP Barristers & Solicitors, 906
Creighton, QC, J. Ronald, Patterson Law, 921
Crenna, David, Director, 702
Crépault, Hubert, Cain Lamarre Casgrain Wells - Québec, 943
Creron, Joe, Director, Kelowna, 1315
Cressman, Doug, CEO, 862
Crewe, Heather, Manager, 818
Crichton, Chad, Coordinator, Reference, Research & Instruction, University of Toronto, Scarborough, 1009
Crim, Liz, Library Clerk, Circulation & Student Assistants, Lakeshore Campus, 1004
Criscenti, Louise, Treasurer, 761
Crocker, David I., Davis LLP - Toronto, 930
Crocker, Stephanie, Associate Director, 744
Crockett, Maureen, Treasurer, 767
Croft, Rosie, University Librarian, Royal Roads University, 968
Croitoru, Nancy, President & Chief Executive Officer, 755
Cron, Charles, President, 813
Cronier, Ernie, Chief Building Official, Port Colborne, 1336
Crook, Alice, President & Chair, 651
Crooks, Brent, Vice-President, 811
Crooks, Terry, CFO & Treasurer, 642

D

Daniel, McNaughton, Director, 1129
Daniel, Jean, Deputy Minister, 1129
Daniel, Bezalel Richardsen, Press Secretary, 1130
Daniel, Boulet, Director General, Enterprise Solution Branch, 1153
Daniel, Feeny, Director, Digitial Communications Outreach & Youth, 1156
Daniel, Benjamin, Chief of Staff, 1157
Daniel, Lebel, Director General, Central & Northern Canada Branch, 1164
Daniel, Lavoie, Associate Assistant Deputy Minister, 1170
Daniel, Haché, Director, Ferry Policy & Programs, 1174
Daniel, Lafonatine, Chief Engineer, Rail Safety Operations, Engineering, 1176
Daniel, Grochowalski, Regional Director, Coordination & Policy, 1178
Daniel, Murphy, Director, 1223
Daniel, Mills, Director, Apprenticeship & Occupational Certificat, 1224
Daniel, Auger, Assistant Deputy Minister, 1239
Daniel, Shewchuk, Minister, 1248
Daniel, Roberge, Directeur, Économie numérique, 1276
Daniel, Bouchard, Directeur, Planification et priorités stratégiques, 1277
Daniel, Deslauriers, Président, Conseil d'administration, 1278
Daniel, Labrecque, Directeur, 1279
Daniel, Lefrançois, Directeur nationale, Urgences, services de traumatologie & services préhospitaliers d', 1283
Daniel, Bureau, Président, 1285
Daniel, Bouchard, Directeur, Structures, 1285
Daniel, Cholette, Directeur générale, 1286
Daniel, Parrott, Director, Legal & Education Services, 1294
Daniel B., Chicoyne, Manager, Safety, 1232
Daniela, DiBartolo, Director, Transportation Energy Use Division, 1165
Daniele, Dionne, Vice-President, Corporate Services & Adjudication Branch, 1145
Danièle, Cantin, Directrice générale adjointe, Ressources humaines financières et informationnelles, 1285
Danielle, Lacasse, Director General, Business Policy, 1135
Danielle, Dubois, Director, Operations, 1145
Danielle, Byrne, Chief, Financial Planning & Analysis, 1155
Danielle, Phillips, Media Relations Coordinator, 1222
Danielle, Pronovost, Directrice, Relations intergouvernementales, 1279
Danielle, St-Pierre, Chef, Faune terrestre et avifaune, 1281
Danielle, Auger, Directrice, Protection de la santé publique, 1283
Danielle, Fleury, Directeur, Soins infirmiers, 1283
Daniels, Caroline, Systems, Web & ILL Librarian, Kwantlen Polytechnic University, 964
Daniels, Terry, Managing Director, 727
Dankowich, Stephen, Executive Director, 813
Danni, Bonnie, Director, 763
Danny, Soucy, Minister, Post-Secondary Education, Training & Lab, 1223
Danny, King, Member Representing Workers, 1227
Danny, Janke, General Manager, 1257
Danyk, Bonnie, Financial Clerk, Mount Waddington, 1312
Danyliw, Jason, President, 648
Daoud, Alexandra, Partner, Norton Rose Fulbright Canada LLP - Montréal, 942
Daoust, Nathalie, Secretary, 732
Daoust, Yves, Préfet, Beauharnois-Salaberry, 1352
Daphene, Stancil, Chair, 1198
Daphne, Meredith, Deputy Minister, 1179
Daphne, Cheel, Executive Director, Cross Ministry Initiatives, 1186
Daphne, MacKay, Supervisor, Records Management, 1220
Darby, Gail, Librarian, New Brunswick Dept. of Environment, 974
Darch, Dave, Director, Public Works & Engineering, Renfrew, 1330
Darcie, Booth, Director, Economic Analysis Division, 1162
Darin, Steeves, Director, Business Investment, 1230
Darin, Banadyga, Executive Director, Sport, Recreation, & Stewardsh, 1296
Darin T., King, Minister, 1230
Darla, Cooper, Manager, Correspondence, 1208
Darlene, Bouwsema, Assistant Deputy Minister, 1185
Darlene, Oman, Director, Special Projects, 1205
Darlene, Dziewit, Chairperson, 1216
Darlene, Ricketts, Program & Policy Development Specialist, 1230
Darlene, Whalen, Vice-Chair, 1234
Darlene, Rhodenizer, Provincial Manager, 1275
Darlene, Rhodenizer, Provincial Manager, Infrastructure Secretariat, 1275
Darlene, Miller, Section Manager, Specimen Management Centre, 1292
Darquise, Beauvais, Chief Information Officer, 1178
Darrel, Treppel, Chief Information Officer, 1288
Darrell, Green, Fire Service Advisor, South East (Nelson) Region, 1210
Darrell, O'Neill, Senior Technical Advisor, 1230
Darrell, Spurrell, Director, Petroleum Marketing & Promotion, 1233
Darrell, Beaulieu, Chair, 1236
Darrell, Dexter, Minister, 1243
Darrell, Evans, Manager, Design & Bridge Maintenance, 1274
Darrell, Branch, Manager, Financial Services Branch, 1300
Darrell, Pasloski, Minister, 1301
Darrell A., Robb, Director, First Nation Relations Branch, 1206
Darren, Ramlal, Director, Risk Management Office, 1121
Darren, Pollock, Supervisor, Indian Head Research Farm, 1122
Darren, Schemmer, Vice-President, 1130
Darren, Goetze, Director, Partnerships Division, 1135
Darren, Williams, Acting Director, Oceans & Species at Risk, Policies & Strategies, 1141
Darren, Tapp, Executive Director, Forest Management Branch, 1187
Darren, Flynn, Assistant Deputy Minister, 1246
Darren, McLarty, Fire Management Supervisor, 1259
Darren, MacLean, Member, 1271
Darren, Chaisson, Director, 1275
Darren, MacDonald, Manager, Information Technology Services, 1275
Darrion, Campbell, Manager, Strategic Coordination, 1210
Darryl, Pupek, Director, Environmental Evaluation & Reporting, 1221
Darryl, Johnson, Director, Environmental Public Health, 1230
Darryl C., Eisan, Director, Regional Relations, 1243
Dart, Graham, Director, Human Resources, St. Thomas, 1337
Darwin, Curtis, Executive Director, Climate Change Secretariat & G, 1222
Daryell, Nowlan, Senior Vice-President, 1123
Daryl, Hanak, Executive Director, Trade Policy - International, 1192
Daryl, Whelan, Director & Provincial Aquaculture Veterinarian, 1228
Daryl, Genge, Assistant Deputy Minister, 1230
Daryl, Eisan, Director, Regional & Canada US Relations, 1243
Daryl, Curran, Fire Management Supervisor, 1259
Daryl, Macdonald, Coordinator, Queens & King Counties, 1270
Daryle, Compardo, Manager, Strategic Divisional & Programs Services, 1259
Daryll, Hedman, Vice-Chair, Operations, 1117
Dash, Cheryl, Secretary, 834
Dashney, Brenda, Chief Financial Officer, 684
Daskewech, Frank, Director, Grande Prairie, 1307
Daunais, Pierre-Paul, Stikeman Elliott LLP - Montréal, 943
Dauncey, Guy, President, 677
Dave, Smith, Treasurer, 743
Dave, Burrows, Vice-President, Client Relations & Communications, 1119
Dave, Dancoisne, Manager, Feed Mill, 1122
Dave, McCauley, Director, Uranium & Radioactive Waste, 1165
Dave, MacKenzie, Parliamentary Secretary to the Minister of Public, 1170
Dave, Dawson, Director, Airports & Air Navigation Services Policy, 1174
Dave, Burdek, Executive Director, 1182
Dave, Prince, Executive Director, Human Resources, 1183
Dave, Rodney, Associate Minister, Wellness, 1188
Dave, Bentley, Executive Director, Reality Services Branch, 1191
Dave, Galea, Executive Director, Public Safety Initiatives, 1193
Dave, Cherniwchan, General Manager, 1198
Dave, Nikolejsin, Assistant Deputy Minister, 1203
Dave, Richmond, Section Head, Recreation, Okanagan Regional Office, 1204
Dave, Francis, District Manager, Resource Operations (Mackenzie), 1206
Dave, Hails, District Manager, Natural Resource Operations (Okanagan Shuswap), 1206
Dave, Peterson, Chief Forester & Assistant Deputy Minister, 1206
Dave, Rejminiak, Director, Technology & Communication Services, 1207
Dave, Byng, Deputy Minister, Jobs, Tourism, & Skills Training, 1208
Dave, Byng, President/Chief Executive Officer, 1211
Dave, Stewart, Chief Financial Officer, Financial Management, 1211
Dave, Duncan, Assistant Deputy Minister, 1211
Dave, Chomiak, Minister responsible, 1217
Dave, Chomiak, Minister, 1218
Dave, Scott, Vice President, Rehabilitation & Compensation Services, 1219
Dave, Dewling, Architect, Municipal Planning & Design Engineering, 1231
Dave, Burley, Manager, Environmental Affairs, 1232
Dave, Nightingale, Director, Energy Planning, 1238
Dave, Davies, Chair, 1240
Dave, Browning, Engineer, Land Protection Services, 1240
Dave, Wilson, Minister, 1242
Dave, Hope, Assistant Deputy Minister, 1249
Dave, Antle, Assistant Deputy Minister, 1249
Dave, Fumerton, District Manager, 1253
Dave, Manol, Fire Management Supervisor, 1259
Dave, Thompson, President, 1265
Dave, McGrath, General Manager, 1273
Dave, Bryanton, Director, Infrastructure Support, 1287
Dave, Stearns, Executive Director, Technical Standards, 1292
Dave, Smith, Director, Regional Operations, 1293
Dave, Tulloch, Executive Director, Corporate Services, 1293
Dave A., Kiely, Manager, Irrigation & Drainage Engineering, Development, 1121
Davey, David, President, 670
David, Marie-Claude, Stikeman Elliott LLP - Montréal, 943
David, Camil, Technicien en documentation, Bibliothèque des sciences, 1016
David, Geneviève, Chargée de projet en communication, 657
David, Wall, Director, Operations, 1121
David, Hubbard, Director, Financial Management Services, 1123
David, Brophy, Manager, Computer Systems & Services, 1128
David, Morrison, Senior Vice-President, 1130
David, Stevenson, Director General, Global Initiatives Directorate, 1130
David, Kendall, Director General, Space Science, 1132
David, Grimes, Assistant Deputy Minister, 1135
David, Morin, Acting Director General, 1135
David, Balfour, Senior Assistant Deputy Minister, 1140
David, Millette, Director General, Aboriginal Programs & Governance, 1140
David, Gillis, Director General, Ecosystem Science, 1140
David, Burden, Acting Regional Director General, 1141
David, Butler-Jones, Chief Public Health Officer, 1145
David, Mowat, Deputy Chief Public Health Officer, Public Health Practice & Regional Operations, 1145
David, Dunbar, Senior General Counsel & Executive Director, Legal Services, 1153
David, Campbell, Chief, Patent Branch - General Chemistry & Organic Division, 1153
David, Miller, Assistant Deputy Minister; Chief Financial Officer, 1155
David, Johnston, Governor General; Commander-in-Chief of Canada, 1157
David, Nanang, Director, Forest Ecology & Productivity, 1163
David, Mate, Chief Geologist, Canada Nunavut Geoscience Office, 1164
David, Harper, Director, GeoConnections Division, 1164
David, Turnbull, Director, National Aircraft Certification, 1175
David, Delcorde, Director, Strategic Planning & Technical Training Services, 1176
David, Wallace, Senior Marine Inspector - Small Vessel, Design, Equipment & Boating Safety, 1176
David, Iezzi, Director, Audit & Quality Assurance, 1176
David, Bayliss, Regional Director, Aviation Security, 1177
David, Woynorowski, Director General, Operations, 1179
David, Dear, Director, Communications, 1180
David, Hennig, Acting Director, Communications Branch, 1181
David, Burdek, General Manager, 1181
David, Ardell, Council Member, 1181
David, Middagh, Director, Policy Coordination & Program Evaluation, 1183
David, Ardell, Director, Water Management Operations, 1187
David, Hancock, Minister, Human Services; Government House Leader, 1189
David, Sands, Director, Communications, 1191
David, Daniel, Team Lead, Resident Incentive Program, 1193
David, Staines, Manager, South Operations, 1194
David, Taylor, Chair, 1198

David, Haslam, Manager, Communications, 1199
David, Marlor, Director, Local Planning Services, 1200
David, Galbraith, Assistant Deputy Minister, Arts, Culture & Sport, 1201
David, Morel, Assistant Deputy Minister, 1202
David, Ranson, Executive Director, Environmental Standards Branch, 1203
David, Curtis, Executive Director, Corporate Services, 1210
David, Watling, Coordinator, Appeals & Operations, 1211
David, Marr, Executive Director, Planning & Programming Branch, 1212
David, Anderson, President/Chief Executive Officer, 1213
David, Chomiak, Minister, 1216
David, Bishop, Chief Operating Officer, Materials Distribution Agency, 1218
David, Neufeld, Director, Community & Regional Planning, 1219
David, Duplisea, Policy Advisor, 1220
David, Sollows, Policy Advisor, 1220
David, Schellenberg, Executive Director, State of the Environment, 1221
David, Cogswell, Executive Director, Operations, 1226
David, Ellis, Member Representing Employers, 1227
David, Woodman, Vice-Chair, 1228
David, McCormack, Director, Emergency Services, 1231
David, Middleton, Director, Petroleum Geoscience, 1233
David, Liverman, Assistant Deputy Minister, 1233
David, Cheeks, Director, Special Projects, 1233
David, Norman, Deputy Minister, 1234
David, Purchase, Forester, Forest and Fire Management, 1237
David, Ramsey, Minister, 1238
David, Duncan, Director, Transmission & Distribution, 1239
David, Ramsay, Minister, 1239
David, Briggins, Director, Water & Wastewater Branch, 1242
David, Akeeagok, Deputy Minister, 1247
David, Monteith, Director, 1247
David, Vetra, Regional Wildlife Manager, 1247
David, Zimmer, Minister, 1248
David, Morse, Acting Manager, Organic Contaminants, 1252
David, Kusturin, Chief Operating Officer, 1255
David, Beaulieu, Acting Director, Employment, Labour & Corporate Policy, 1256
David, Zurawel, Director, Stakeholder & Partner Relations, 1257
David, Zimmer, Parliamentary Assistant, Municipal Affairs, 1257
David, Orazietti, Minister, 1257
David, O'Toole, Deputy Minister, 1257
David, Ayotte, Director, Communications, 1257
David, Lynch, Assistant Deputy Minister, 1258
David, MacDonald, Manager, Claims Negotiations Support Unit, 1258
David, Galbraith, Head, Science, 1262
David, Galbraith, Head, Science, 1262
David, Ward, Director, Strategic Policy & Transportation, Economics, 1264
David, Marshall, President & Chief Executive Officer, 1264
David, Aiton, Manager, 1265
David, Rossiter, Fire Marshal, Fire Marshal's Office, 1268
David, Arsenault, Deputy Minister, 1268
David, MacEwen, Manager, Marine Fisheries, 1270
David, McGuire, Manager, Seafood Services, 1270
David, Hambly, PHC Medical Director, Kings, 1272
David, Erdely, Directeur, 1282
David, Belgue, Secrétariat, 1284
David, Alexander, Acting Director, Bacteriology, 1292
David, Wilton, Chair, 1292
David, Eberle, Chairman, 1297
David, Morrison, Chief Executive Officer, 1298
David, Morrison, President/CEO, 1298
David, MacDonald, Vice-President, Operations & Engineering, 1298
David, Hrycan, Deputy Minister, 1301
David, Knight, Manager, Procurement Services, 1302
David "Archie", Riddell, Executive Project Director, 1203
David A., Salisbury, Director, Medicine, 1175
David A., Chalack, Board Chair, 1181
David G., Faulkner, Special Advisor to the Commissioner, 1140
David J., Scott, Director, GSC Northern Canada, 1164
David J., Nowzek, Regional Director, Civil Aviation, 1177
David J., White, Director, Support Services, 1273
David L., Bowlby, Manager, Farm, Innovation & Renewal, 1121
David M., Kelly, Manager, Strategic Analysis & Policy, 1136
David M., Malone, President, 1155
David R. M., Hatch, Chair, 1214
David R.J., Morris, Chief Surveyor, 1275
Davidson, Catherine, Associate University Librarian, Collections, York University Libraries, 1009
Davidson, Maureen, Library Technician (Cataloguing & Acquisitions), College of the Rockies, 960
Davidson, Ian, Executive Director, 802
Davidson, Valerie, Chair, NSERC/HP CWSE, 813
Davidson, Sarah, Administrator, 674
Davidson, Susan, President, 674
Davidson, Alex, Manager, Water Division, Brant, 1327
Davidson-Fisher, Irene, CEO, 861
Davie, James, President, 719
Davies, Don, McCarthy Tétrault LLP - Calgary, 904
Davies, Jeffrey L., Davies Howe Partners LLP, 929
Davies, Marianne (Chuck), Bennett Jones LLP - Calgary, 901
Davies, Michael, Partner, Heenan Blaikie LLP - Toronto, 931
Davies, Todd R., Alexander Holburn Beaudin & Lang, LLP, 910
Davies, Paul, Treasurer, 819
Davies, Peter, Director General, 873
Davies, Terrence, Acting Director, 700
Davis, Carl, Conway Davis Gryski, 929
Davis, Roxanne M., Stones Carbert Waite Wells LLP, 906
Davis, Terry R., Partner, Parlee McLaws LLP, 905
Davis, Thomas R.M., Partner, Norton Rose Fulbright Canada LLP - Montréal, 942
Davis, Alexandra, Librarian, Civic Campus, 995
Davis, Susan, Coordinator, 875
Davis, Seth, Manager, 761
Davis, Bill, President, 648
Davis, Robin, President, 662
Davis, Marie-danielle, Corporate Secretary/Director, 711
Davis, Lisa, Project Coordinator, 833
Davis, Swep, Chair, 647
Davis, Martha, President, 742
Davis, Troy, President, 871
Davis, Ron, Officer, Medicine Hat, 1307
Davison, Betty, Office Manager, 676
Davreux, Cam, Vice-President, 740
Dawe, Karen, Director, 761
Dawe, David, Executive Director, 795
Dawe, PAg, Corrina, President, 636
Dawes, Wendy, Secretary, 788
Dawn, Pearcey, Acting Director, Resource Management - National, 1140
Dawn, Friesen, Executive Director, Health Protection, 1188
Dawn, White, Executive Director, Organizational Renewal, 1189
Dawn, Stewart, Officer, Financial Services, 1199
Dawn, Major, Registrar/Director, Passenger Transportation Branch, 1212
Dawn, Landry, Acting Director, Culture & Strategic Policy, 1263
Dawn, Bradley, Manager, Case Management, 1275
Dawn, Campbell, Acting Director, Privacy, Access & Risk Management, 1288
Dawn L., Miller, Director, Policy Planning & Cabinet Affairs, 1174
Dawna, Harden, Director, Lands Policy, 1203
Dawson, John A.R., Partner, McCarthy Tétrault LLP - Toronto, 933
Dawson, Scott A., Farris, Vaughan, Wills & Murphy LLP, 912
Dawson, Kelly, Library Assistant, Canadian Agriculture Library - Saskatoon, 1033
Day, Jill, Manager, Cataloguing and Acquisitions, Grant MacEwan University, 954
Day, Gordon W., President & CEO, 771
Day, Brian A., Executive Director, 808
Day, Robert D., Executive Director, 841
Day, Cory, City Engineer, Port Moody, 1317
Day, David L., Director, Calgary, 1305
Day, Deborah, Director, Victoria, 1318
Day, P.Eng., Jeff, General Manager, Richmond, 1317
Day-Boutilier, Nadine, Circulation/Document Delivery/Reference Librarian, W.K. Kellogg Health Sciences Library, 982
Daynard, Kelly, Program Manager, 636
Daysh, Zena, Executive Vice-Chair, 733
De Andrade, Annemarie, Program Manager, 680
De Batist, Marc, Treasurer, 776
de Beaupré, Beryl, Treasurer, 712
de Boer, Dirk, President, 686
de Boer, Poppe, President, 776
De Caria, Joseph, Executive Secretary, 635
De Champlain, Karine, Associate, Ackroyd LLP Barristers & Solicitors, 906
De Giovanni, Vivian, Executive Director, 798
de Henry, Patrick, Treasurer, 785
De Koster, Christophe, Partner, Heenan Blaikie LLP - Montréal, 940
de la Chevrotière, François, Directeur, CÉGEP de l'Abitibi-Témiscamingue, 1026
de Launière, Olivier, Directeur, Saint-Félicien, 1350
de Marsh, Peter, President, 698
De Paoli, Mary, Manager, Port Moody, 1317
de Repentigny, France, Secrétaire, 668
De Vita, Bruno, Alexander Holburn Beaudin & Lang, LLP, 910
de Vries, Joanne, CEO, 757
de Waal, L., Chairman, 787
Deacon, QC, John E., Associate, D'Arcy & Deacon LLP - Winnipeg, 916
Dean, Ed, Treasurer, 724
Dean, Knudson, Director General, Americas, 1135
Dean, Fuller, Director, Marine Security Operations, 1176
Dean, Pratt, Manager, Business Services, 1181
Dean, Lussier, Chief Information Officer & Executive Director, In, 1194
Dean, McKinley, Regional Manager, Economic Development, 1209
Dean, Sekyer, Executive Director, Economic Initiatives & Analysis, 1209
Dean, Bell, Vice-Chair, 1231
Dean, Hirtle, Director, Long Term Care, 1243
Dean, Benedict, Registrar, Crown Lands & Land Holdings, 1244
Dean, Wells, Corporate Chief Information Officer, 1246
Dean, Hustwick, Director, Tourism Agencies, 1263
Dean, Stewart, Vice-Chair, 1267
Dean, Reeve, Executive Vice-President, 1290
Dean L., Vey, Regional Director, 1120
Deana, Lemke, Secretariat, 1118
Deanna, Dixon, Coordinator, 1137
Deanna, Dixon, Coordinator, 1138
Deanna, Battle, Office Manager, 1200
Deans, Rosemary, Coordinator, 792
Dearborn, Diane, Librarian, A.D. Allen Chemistry Library, 1001
Dearborn, Dylanne, Physics Librarian, Physics Library, 1006
Dearth, Betty, Librarian, Industrial Technology Centre, 971
Deb, Archibald, Director, 1238
Deb, Stark, Deputy Minister, 1248
Deb, Stetson, Manager, Wildlife Policy Section, 1258
Deb, Weedon, District Manager, 1259
Deb, Stark, Deputy Minister, 1261
DeBaker, April, Director, 650
Debbah, Karim, Bibliothécaire, Bibliothèque des sciences, 1016
Debbie, Palecek, Technical Assistant, 659
Debbie, Audet, Regional Coordinator, 1137
Debbie, Beresford-Green, Acting Senior Director General, Programs, 1146
Debbie, Thompson, Administrator, 1187
Debbie, Urquhart, Assistant Public Guardian - Edmonton, 1190
Debbie, Martin, Vice-President, Human Resources & Corporate Services, 1200
Debbie, Fischer, Director, Tenure & Revenue Management, 1203
Debbie, Nagle, Chief Human Resources Officer & Senior Vice-Presid, 1208
Debbie, Nussbaum, Vice-President, Corporate & Human Resources, 1211
Debbie, Fritz, Executive Director/Chief Information Officer, Information Management Branch, 1211
Debbie, MacKenzie, Acting Assistant Deputy Minister, 1216
Debbie, DeLancey, Deputy Minister, 1237
Debbie, Pella Keen, District Manager, 1259
Debbie L., Reid, Senior Director General, 1145
Debenham, David, McMillan LLP - Ottawa, 926
Debicki, Ed, Secretary, Sudbury Rock & Lapidary Society, 1009
Debicki, Ruth, Vice-President & Librarian, Sudbury Rock & Lapidary Society, 1009
Debicki, Ed, Secretary, 858
Debnath, Samir C., President, 718
Debnath, Samir, Registrar, 806
Debora, Voth, Regional Director, 1248
Deborah, Price, Director, Strategic Aboriginal Policy, 1141
Deborah, deGrasse, Acting Chief, Technology Application, 1174
Deborah, Lipscombe, Regional Director, Interior Northeast Service BC C, 1200
Deborah, Nobes, Director, Communications & Public Awareness, 1224
Deborah, Carpenter, Director, Financial Services, 1224
Deborah, Swain, Director, Communications, 1249
Deborah, Conrod, Supervisor, Groundwater & Well Water Management Unit, 1252

Desjardins, Pierre-Marcel, Directeur exécutif, 654
Desjardins, Jean-Pierre, Directeur, Saint-Lin-Laurentides, 1351
Desjardins, Pierre, Directeur, Trois-Rivières, 1352
Deslandes, Moira, Executive Director, 775
Deslandes, Marcel, Directeur, Régie intermunicipale de traitement de l'eau potable Saint-Romual, 1358
Desmeules, Nathalie, Secrétaire, CÉGEP de Saint-Félicien, 1026
Desmeules, Justine, 751
Desmond, Raymond, Regional Director, Marine, 1177
Després, Yves, Directeur, Lévis, 1348
Desrochers, Caroline, Analyst, Cartographic Metadata, Geographic, Statistical & Government Information Centre, 995
Desrochers, Johanne, Présidente-directrice générale, 657
Desrochers, Mélissa, Vice-présidente, 655
Deutsch, Thomas J., McMillan LLP - Vancouver, 913
Devereaux, Sarah, Treasurer, 857
Devereux, Jeremy J., Partner, Norton Rose Fulbright Canada LLP - Toronto - Royal Bank Plaza, 935
Deverman, Ron, President, 799
Devine, Patrick J., Partner, Dentons Canada LLP - Toronto, 930
Devion, Catherine, Coordinator, Circulation & Access, University of Toronto, Scarborough, 1009
Devitt, Crosby, Manager, 762
Devlin, Corbin D., Partner, McLennan Ross LLP - Edmonton, 908
Devlin, Lori, Director, 725
DeVries, Warren, Secretary-Treasurer, 648
DeVries, Andrew, Director, 756
DeVries, J., Director, Building Services, & Chief Building Offi, Richmond Hill, 1336
Dewancker, John, Director, Environmental Services, & City Engineer, St. Thomas, 1337
Dewar, Edgar, Chair, 857
Dewey, John, Executive Director, 752
DeWolfe, Michelle, Secretary, 796
Dex, Daniel D., McMillan LLP - Vancouver, 913
Dexter, Pittman, Acting Manager, Industrial Compliance, 1227
Dextraze, Dave, Director, Wetaskiwin County No. 10, 1305
Dey Nuttall, Anita, Associate Director, 692
DeYoung, Marie, University Librarian, Saint Mary's University, 982
Dhaliwal, Raj, Osler, Hoskin & Harcourt LLP - Toronto, 935
Di Campo, Pierre, Head Librarian, Centre de recherche et de développement sur les aliments, 1027
Di Gironimo, Lou, General Manager, Toronto Water, Toronto, 1338
Di Lallo, Robert, Daniel & Partners LLP, 927
Di Persio, Barb, Director HR, Northern Lights Regional Health Centre, 956
Di Ruggiero, Erica, Chair, 716
Dia Touré, Fatimata, Directrice, 770
Diamond, Denise, Chef de bibliothèque, Bibliothèque paramédicale, 1017
Diamond, Corey, Managing Director, 858
Diamond, Dorothy, Secretary, 804
Diana, Nacer-Cherif, Innovation & Network Advisor, 1159
Diana, McQueen, Minister, Environment & Sustainable Resource Devel, 1186
Diana, Davidson, Director, Public Library Services, 1194
Diana, McNeil, Director & Deputy Director's Assistant, Fish, Wildlife & Habitat Management, 1206
Diana, Brooks, Regional Manager, Kootenay, 1210
Diana, Miles, Senior Vice-President, Operations, Worker & Employer Services Division, 1213
Diana, Quinton, Director, Communications, 1232
Diane, Massicotte, Director, Human Resources, 1130
Diane, Jacovella, Vice-President, 1130
Diane, Orange, Assistant Deputy Minister, 1140
Diane, Séguin-Guérette, Director, Corporate Compensation Branch, 1140
Diane, Ablonczy, Minister of State, Foreign Affairs (Americas & Con, 1143
Diane, Finley, Minister, Human Resources & Skills Development, 1146
Diane, Finley, Minister, Human Resources & Skills Development, 1147
Diane, Dupuis, Senior Vice-President, Public & Corporate Affairs, 1156
Diane, Lavigne, Director, Information Management, 1174
Diane, Dunn, Executive Director, Human Resources, 1183
Diane, Simsovic, Executive Director, Regional Development, 1185
Diane, Dagleish, Assistant Deputy Minister, 1191
Diane, McLean, Director, Risk Management & Finance, 1194
Diane, Carter, Manager, Ministry Advisory Services, 1195
Diane, Beattie, Manager, Business Partnerships, 1203
Diane, Nicholls, Executive Director, Timber Operations & Pricing, 1206
Diane, St. Hilair, Director, Fleet, Facilities & Asset Management, 1207
Diane, Ross, Director, Financial Policy, Compliance, & Procurement, 1207
Diane, Hawkins, Director, Employment Development, 1224
Diane, Taylor, Director, 1230
Diane, Bernard, Executive Secretary to the Minister, 1241
Diane, Wise, Acting Director, Tourism Policy & Research, 1263
Diane, Hastie, Directrice, Technologies de l'information et des communications, 1280
Diane, Reed, Director, 1299
Diane E., Campbell, Director General, Weather & Environmental Prediction & Services, 1135
Diane M., Clow, Consultant, Dietetic Services, 1271
Dianne, Caldbick, Executive Director, Science, Technology & Innovation Council Secretariat, 1154
Dianne, Goguen, Regional Director, Finance & Administration, 1177
Dianne, Singh, Coordinator, Correspondence Management Unit, 1194
Dianne, Nason, Director, Policy & Planning, 1224
Dianne, Wylie, Director, Claims Services, 1255
Dianne, Corbett, Director, Far North Branch (South Porcupine), 1259
DiBarbora, Lisa, Virtual Services Librarian, Humber College Institute of Technology & Advanced Learning, 1003
Dick, Wellman, Manager, Farm Foreclosure/Home Quarter Protection, 1286
Dickhout, Roger, Chair, 873
Dickie, Christopher, President, 699
Dickie, Q.C., Gregory W., Partner, Ottenheimer Baker, 919
Dickinson, Evan, Stikeman Elliott LLP - Calgary, 905
Dickinson, Jan, Executive Director, 791
Dickinson, Rob, Manager, Vernon, 1318
Dicks, Terry, Fire Chief, Norfolk, 1330
Dickson, James M., Partner, Stewart McKelvey - Halifax, 922
Dickson, Louise, Library Technician, Nexen Inc., 952
Dickson, Linda, Coordinator, Community Emergency Management, Wellington, 1331
DiClemente, Warren, Chief Operating Officer & VP, 819
Didier, Bicchi, Directeur, Secteur agricole & pesticides, 1279
Diehl, Randy H., Chief Administrative Officer, Kamloops, 1315
Diemer, Ulli, Head, Connexions Information Sharing Services, 1002
Diemer, Ulli, Coordinator, 734
Diep, Duong, Specialist, Solid Waste, 1237
Dietrich, Mike, President, 638
Dietrich, Mark, CEO, 824
Dietrick, Linda, Acting University Librarian, University of Winnipeg, 973
Dietzler, Tim, Fieldman, Rocky View County, 1304
DiFolco, Sylviane, Directrice, Repentigny, 1349
Digby, Wayne, Executive Director, 699
Diges, Carmen, Partner, McMillan LLP - Toronto, 933
DiGiovanni, Tony, Executive Director, 789
Dignan, Annette, Librarian, Metro Vancouver (formerly Greater Vancouver Regional District), 959
Dilhari, Fernando, Director General, Strategic Policy & Priorities, 1141
Dillon, Patricia, Chair, 797
Dinel, Sean, Chapter Secretary, 767
Dingman, Wally, Chair, 671
Dino, Chiesa, Chair, 1127
Dino, Bagnariol, Manager, Bridge Office, 1264
DiNovo, Cheri, Contact, 844
Dinsdale, Henry Y., Partner, Heenan Blaikie LLP - Toronto, 931
DiNucci, Mary, Coordinator, 769
Dion, Chantale, Documentaliste, Gazoduc Trans Québec & Maritimes Inc., 1012
Dion, Sylvia, Contact, Library Services, Mills Memorial Library, 986
Dion, Martine, Première Vice-Présidente, 752
Dionne, Paul, Director, Edmundston, 1322
Dionne, Filiatrault, Executive Director, 1118
Diotte, Marie-Josée, Responsable, Service du prêt, Campus de Shippagan, 976
DiPietro, Barbara, CFO, 735
Dipple, John A., Partner, MacPherson Leslie & Tyerman LLP - Regina, 946
Dirk, Pat, President, 658
Dirk, Nyland, Chief Engineer, 1211
Dirom, Gavin C., President & CEO, 658
Dirszowsky, Randy, Secretary-Treasurer, 686
Dishan, Brad, Medical Librarian, St Joseph's Health Care, London, 990
Distasio, Jino, Director, 773
Dixon, Evan W., Associate, McLennan Ross LLP - Calgary, 905
Dixon, Peggy, Vice-President, 635
Dixon, Dwight, President, 869
Dixon, Bill, Executive Director, 795
Dixon, Deanna, Coordinator, 809
Dixon, Deanna, 809
Dixon, P.Eng., FEC, Denis, President, 836
Djoghlaf, Ahmed, Executive Secretary, 864
Doan-Crider, Diana, Secretary, 774
Dobbin, Bradley S., Stones Carbert Waite Wells LLP, 906
Dobell, Darcy, Vice-President, 873
Dobrowolski, Doug, President, 662
Dobrowolski, Greg, Manager, Dawson Creek, 1315
Dobson, Mary, Technical Services Librarian, Cape Breton University, 982
Dobson, Kelly, President, 801
Dodd, Doreen, Contact, 797
Dodge, Carman, President, 803
Doehler, Joachim G., President, 763
Doelle, Meinhard, Counsel, Stewart McKelvey - Halifax, 922
Doerksen, Darlene, Chief Executive Officer, 875
Doherty, Barbara R.C., Senior Partner, Miller Thomson LLP - Toronto, 934
Doherty, Bob, President, 811
Doherty, Mark, Contact, 759
Doherty, Ken, Director, Community Services, Peterborough, 1336
Doiron, Micheline, Associate, Stewart McKelvey - Moncton, 917
Dolbec, Jean-François, Partner, Heenan Blaikie S.E.N.C.R.L./SRL - Québec, 944
Dolcetti, Jerry, Commissioner, Engineering & Planning, Sault Ste. Marie, 1337
Dolezsar, Richard, Executive Director, 864
Dolly, Goyette, Director, Regional Office, 1253
Dolter, Sean, General Manager, 797
Dolyniuk, Bob, General Manager, 794
Dominell, Ralph, Fire Chief, Orillia, 1335
Dominic, Gagnon, Directeur, 1282
Dominic, Gagnon, Directeur (par intérim), 1282
Dominique, Brian P., Partner, Cassels Brock & Blackwell LLP, 929
Dominique, Francoeur, Chief Executive Officer, Canadian Forces Housing Agency, 1157
Dominique, Osterrath, Director, Finance & Awards Administration Division, 1166
Dominique, Blanchard, Director General, 1176
Dominique, Jodoin, Directeur général, Information territoriale, 1276
Dominique, Fortin, Sous-ministre associé, 1277
Dominique, Savoie, Sous-ministre, 1285
Don, Margaret, Membership Secretary, 829
Don, Cunningham, Chair, Métis Settlements Appeal Tribunal, 1180
Don, Brown, Acting Executive Director, Economics & Competitive, 1182
Don, Kwas, Acting Executive Director, Immigration Policy, 1192
Don, Squire, Executive Director, Housing Development, 1194
Don, Rebus, Manager, Operational Support Services, 1194
Don, Scott, Associate Minister of Accountability, Transparency, 1195
Don, McRae, Minister, Education, 1197
Don, Swagar, Senior Director, Queen's Printer / BC Mail Plus, 1199
Don, Rose, Corporate Secretary, 1200
Don, Fast, Deputy Minister, Community, Sport, & Cultural Deve, 1200
Don, McRae, Minister, Education, 1201
Don, Cadden, Regional Director, BC Parks & Conservation Officer Service Division, West Coast, 1204
Don, Hallett, Chief of Park Operations, 1215
Don, Armstrong, Acting Director, Corporate Services, Accommodation Policy & Planning, 1218
Don, Osmond, Secretary to Council, 1241
Don, James, Executive Director, 1244
Don, Sutherland, Director, 1245
Don, Earl, Assistant Director, Investigations & Enforcement, 1252

Dubé, Martin, Conseiller pédagogique en bibliothéconomie, CÉGEP de Drummondville, 1012
Dubé, Sylvie, Référence-PEB, CÉGEP de Lévis-Lauzon, 1015
Dubé, Normand, Président, 655
Dubé, Jean, Directeur général, Lévis, 1348
Dubé, Diane, Sec.-Trés., Régie intermunicipale d'assainissement des eaux de Sainte-Thérèse, 1357
Dubeau, Colin, Nelligan O'Brien Payne, 926
Duben, Michael, General Manager, Community & Protective Services, Windsor, 1338
Dublanko, Deryld, Manager, Leduc County, 1303
Dubois, Joël M., Partner, Perley-Robertson, Hill & McDougall LLP / s.r.l., 926
Dubois, Claire, Directrice, Bibliothèque de géographie, 1016
Dubois, Lyne, Merlicom, 841
Dubois, Daniel, Directeur, Saint-Hyacinthe, 1350
Dubois, Sylvain, Directeur, Laval, 1348
Dubois, Susie, Sec.-Trés., Régie d'assainissement des eaux usées Rougemont/St-Césaire, 1356
Dubuc, Marie-France, Directrice, Information stratégique, Investissement Québec, 1019
Ducas, Ada, Head Librarian, Neil John Maclean Health Sciences Library, 972
Duchesne, Benoit M., Partner, Heenan Blaikie LLP - Ottawa, 925
Duchesne, Caroline, Directrice, 735
Duchesneau, Pierre, Coordonnateur des ressources didactiques et docume, CÉGEP de Marie-Victorin, 1017
Duck, Glen, Executive Director, 845
Duckworth, Harry, President, 759
Duckworth, David, Director, Kamloops, 1315
Duclos, Claudette, Directrice générale, 658
Duczek, Loree, Manager, East Kootenay, 1311
Dudar, Michael P., Vice Président-CCE, 734
Dudas, Janice, Library Technician, Metro Vancouver (formerly Greater Vancouver Regional District), 959
Dudley, Michael, Research Associate, Institute of Urban Studies, 971
Dueck, Annette E.F., Stikeman Elliott LLP - Vancouver, 914
Duff, Sheila, Technical Files Clerk, Canada-Newfoundland Offshore Petroleum Board, 977
Duff, Montgomerie, Deputy Minister, 1243
Duffet, Charles, Senior Vice-Presient & CIO Advisor, 682
Duffy, Jane, Dean of Libraries, Grant MacEwan University, 954
Duffy, April, Coordinator, 682
Dufour, Marie-Christine, Grondin, Poudrier, Bernier, 944
Dufour, Marie-Hélène, Dentons Canada LLP - Montreal, 939
Dufour, Jules, Président, 863
Dufour, Denis, Coprésident, 653
Dufresne, Danielle, Agente de bureau, Matériauthèque, 1030
Dugas, Ginette, Librarian, Comité national de recherche sur le logement, 1018
Dugas, Marie-Eve, Bibliothécaire, Université du Québec Institut national de la recherche scientifiq, 1025
Dugas, Marjolaine, Director, 705
Dugas, Arnold, Directeur général, 668
Duguay, Pat, Library Administration/Admin. Assistant, University of Winnipeg, 973
Duguid, Owen, O'Connor MacLeod Hanna LLP, 925
Duimovich, George, Manager, Geomatics, Maps & Special Collections Library, 995
Duimovich, George, Manager, Minerals & Materials Sciences Information Centre, 996
Duimovich, George, Manager, Policy, Management & Economics Information Centre, 996
Duin, Margret, Administrator, 674
Dujardin, Michael, Controller, 702
Dujmovich, Christine-Louise, Librarian, Reference & Electronic Resources, Justice Institute of British Columbia, 962
Duke, Laura E., Lawson Lundell LLP - Vancouver, 913
Dukes, Nancy Jean, Manager, Great Lakes Forestry Centre, 999
Dulude, France, Associée, Robinson Sheppard Shapiro LLP, 943
Dumont, Marie-Claude, Technicienne en documentation, Bibliothèque de botanique - L'Institut de recherche en biologie v, 1015
Dumont, Richard, Directeur général, Université de Montréal, 1021
Dumouchel, Bernard, Director General, Canadian Institute for Scientific & Technical Information (CISTI), 994
Dunbar, Brian, President, 743
Dunberry, Éric, Partner, Norton Rose Fulbright Canada LLP - Montréal, 942
Duncan, Pierre, Professionnel, Institut de technologie agro-alimentaire de la Pocatière, 1014
Duncan, Williams, Executive Director, 1206
Duncan, Boyd, Supervisor, Great Lakes Monitoring Unit, 1252
Dunfield, Jessica, Vice-Chair, 704
Dungen, Ellen, Regional Manager, 859
Dunk, Carol, President, 819
Dunlop, David R., Partner, McMillan LLP - Toronto, 933
Dunlop, Paula, Director, 700
Dunn, Ashley P., Associate, Cox & Palmer - Halifax, 921
Dunn, Julia Marko, Newsletter Editor, 753
Dunn, Burgandy, Counsel, 696
Dunn, Barbara M., President, 719
Dunn, Tanya, Executive Assistant, 815
Dunn Lee, Janice, Deputy Director General, 776
Dunning, Marc, Associate, Wickwire Holm, 922
Dunphy, Gerard, Treasurer, 771
Dunphy, QC, Michael E., Partner, Cox & Palmer - Halifax, 921
Dunsky, Ilan, Partner, Heenan Blaikie LLP - Montréal, 940
Dupas, Lorraine, Coordinator, 664
Duplain, Jacynthe, Secrétaire administrative, Saint-Félicien, 1350
Dupont, Patrice, Information Specialist, NRC Information Centre, 1012
Dupont, Denise, Présidente, 656
Dupras, George, Director, 651
Dupuis, John, Acting Associate University Librarian, Informtion, York University Libraries, 1009
Dupuis, Marie-Hélène, Conseillère principale, développement des services, École polytechnique de Montréal, 1018
Dupuis, Norm, Director, 639
Dupuis, Todd, Executive Director, 670
Duquette, Lise, Chair, 681
Durand, Simon, Directeur général, 862
Durando, Paola, Librarian, Public Services, Bracken Health Sciences Library, 987
Durdle, Ron, Chair, 673
Durisin, Michael N., Bratty & Partners, LLP Barristers & Solicitors, 937
Durocher, André, Partner, Fasken Martineau - Montréal, 939
Durocher, Normand, Coprésident, 653
Duron, Bill, CEO, 843
Dusdal, Herb, Director, Terrace, 1318
Dussault, Chantal, Head, Archives, Records & Library, Canadian Museum of Nature, 985
Dussault, Louis-Marie, Directrice, Collège Édouard-Montpetit, 1015
Dustin, Fredlund, Director, Community Operations, Kitikmeot, 1246
Dustin, Austman, Manager, Sector Relations, 1291
Dustin, Duncan, Minister, Health, 1291
Dutchak, Kathleen, Services & Systems Librarian, British Columbia Institute of Technology, 959
Dutton, Craig, Library Technician, Halifax Office, 981
Duval, Marc, Bibliothécaire consultant, Rio Tinto Fer et Titane inc, 1030
Duval, Luc, Directeur, Vaudreuil-Dorion, 1352
Duval, Luc, Director, Public Works & Engineering, Timmins, 1337
Dwight, Williamson, Assistant Deputy Minister, 1215
Dworak, Greg, Acting General Manager, Engineering & Operational, Brantford, 1332
Dwyer, Denis, Treasurer, 732
Dwyer, PhD, Lianne, Vice-President, 636
Dye, Beth, Secretary, 843
Dyer, Fiona, Manager, Library Services, Lethbridge Community College, 957
Dyer, Lynn M., President, 756
Dyer, Dave, Chief Engineer, Prince George, 1317
Dykes, Barbara, Manager, 772
Dykstra, Mark, Director, Environment & Parks Services, Waterloo, 1338
Dysart, J.E. Britt, Partner, Stewart McKelvey - Fredericton, 917
Dysart, Robert, Partner, Stewart McKelvey - Moncton, 917

E

E. Paola, de Rose, Director, Earth Observation & GeoSolutions Divison, 1163
E. Paola, de Rose, Director, Earth Observation & GeoSolutions Divison, 1164
Eades, Kyle, Library Technician, Labrador West Campus, 977
Eagles, Michelle, Chair, 845
Eamon, O'Donoghue, Regional Executive Director, Skeena, 1205
Earl, Geddes, Chief Executive Officer, 1119
Earle, Baddaloo, Assistant Deputy Minister, 1247
Earthy, Daron L., Loopstra Nixon LLP Barristers & Solicitors, 932
East, Ron, Director, 793
Easthope, John, Treasurer, 779
Eastwell, Doug, Registrar, 665
Eaton, John, Head Librarian, E.K. Williams Law Library, 971
Eaton, Bob, Director, 673
Eaton, Q.C., J. David B., McInnes Cooper - St. John's, 919
Ebbett, Gwendolyn, University Librarian, University of Windsor, 1011
Eberts, Derrek, Secretary-Treasurer, 686
Ebo, Budu-Amoako, Manager, Laboratory; Senior Microbiologist, 1273
Eccleston, Marion, President, 829
Eckman, Chuck, Dean of Library Services, Simon Fraser University, 959
L'Écuyer, Isabelle, Heenan Blaikie S.E.N.C.R.L./SRL - Québec, 944
L'Écuyer, Daniel, Directeur général, Repentigny, 1349
Ed, Coulthard, Director, Research & Development, 1122
Ed, Taje, Regional Director, Mining Operations (Victoria), 1202
Ed, Miska, Chief Traffic, Electricial, Highway Safety & Geome, 1211
Ed, Bates, General Counsel & Secretary, 1213
Ed, Tymofichuk, Vice-President, Transmission, 1217
Ed, Azure, Commissioner, 1219
Ed, Williams, Director, Dental Services, 1230
Ed, Martin, President & Chief Executive Officer, 1230
Ed, Grant, Chair, 1231
Ed, Martin, President & Chief Executive Officer, 1231
Ed, O'Reilly, Vice-Chair, 1232
Ed, Stewart, District Manager, 1233
Ed, Moriarity, Director, Communications, 1235
Ed, Zebedee, Director, Protection Services, 1246
Ed, Debicki, Senior Manager, Geoscience Laboratories, 1260
Ed, Dancsok, Assistant Deputy Minister, Petroleum & Natural Gas, 1288
Ed, Dancsok, Assistant Deputy Minister, 1288
Ed, Zsombor, Director, Rail Services, 1292
Eddie, Jean-Marc, Partner, Perley-Robertson, Hill & McDougall LLP / s.r.l., 926
Eddie T., Dillon, Chair, 1239
Eddy, Jamie, Managing Partner, Cox & Palmer - Fredericton, 917
Eder, Tim A., Executive Director, 763
Edge, Brent, Supervisor, Penticton, 1316
Edgecombe, Don, Operations Manager, 832
Edie, Q.C., Donald C., Counsel, Carscallen LLP, 903
Edinger, H. David, Partner, Heenan Blaikie LLP - Vancouver, 912
Edith, Doucet, Deputy Minister, 1225
Édith, van de Walle, Directrice, 1279
Édith, Tremblay, Directrice, 1279
Edmée, Métivier, Executive Vice-President, Financing & Consulting, 1124
Edmond, James G., Thompson Dorfman Sweatman LLP - Winnipeg, 916
Edmonds, Ernie, President, 673
Edmondson, Debra E., Librarian, ADI Group, 973
Edmunds, Eileen, Liaison Librarian & Regional Campus Coordinator, Cowichan Campus, 960
Edmunds, Eileen, Liaison Librarian & Regional Campus Coordinator, Powell River Campus, 963
Edna, Elias, Commissioner, Commissioner's Office, 1247
Edward, Hurley, Director, Operations, 1122
Edward, Fast, Minister, International Trade; Minister, Asia-Paci, 1142
Edward, Fast, Minister, International Trade; Minister, Asia-Paci, 1143
Edward, Hoffman, Regional Director, Omineca Regional Office, 1203
Edward, Evans, Manager, 1231
Edward, Williams, Vice-Chair, 1232
Edward, Kirby, Director, Contracts, 1243
Edward A., Charter, Manager, Food & Bioscience Technology, 1273
Edwards, Cheryl A., Partner, Heenan Blaikie LLP - Toronto, 931
Edwards, Robert C., Erickson & Partners, Barristers, Solicitors, Notaries, 927
Edwards, Jean Marc, Associate University Librarian, Information System, Concordia University Libraries, 1018
Edwards, Gord, Executive Director, 643

F

Frank, Balcom, Chair, 1241
Frank, Atherton, Deputy Chief Medical Officer of Health, 1243
Frank, Ingratta, Chair, 1251
Frank, Tomassini, Manager, Biological Analysis, 1252
Frank, Miklas, District Manager, 1259
Frank, Kennedy, Assistant Deputy Minister, 1260
Frank, Chiarotto, Senior Vice-President, Hydro-Thermal Operations, 1261
Franklin, Sharon, Finance/Administrative Director, 726
Frankling, Freddie, Vice-President, 762
Franks, Maria, Executive Director, Legal Information Society of Nova Scotia, 981
Frankum, Ken, Chair, 745
Franssen, Gary, Manager, Nanaimo, 1316
Franz, Klingender, Curator, Agriculture, 1128
Franzin, Bill, President, 646
Fraser, Andrew, Partner, Stewart McKelvey - Halifax, 922
Fraser, Blair C., Partner, Cox & Palmer - Moncton, 917
Fraser, Janet, Bibliographic & Collection Services Librarian, Ward Chipman Library, 975
Fraser, Terri, Head, Regional Library & Records Services, Prairie & Northern Region - Edmonton, 955
Fraser, Duncan, Secretary, 804
Fraser, Robert, Manager, 822
Fraser, Margo, Executive Director, 659
Fraser, Allan, Superintendent, Comox, 1314
Fraser, Malcolm, Chief Administrative Officer, Powell River, 1313
Fraser, Marjie, Director, Parks & Forestry Operations, Vaughan, 1338
Fraser, Randy, Superintendent, Port Alberni, 1316
Fraser, Howell, Director, Air Access, 1230
Frass, Len, Director, Preservation & Operations Standards, 1292
Frawley, Nigel, Secretary General, 732
Frayne, Les, Project Manager, 850
Fred, Gorrell, Director General, Market Access Secretariat, 1119
Fred, Brandenburg, Deputy Director, 1120
Fred, Horne, Minister, Health, 1188
Fred, Krahn, Vice-Chair, 1198
Fred, Parker, Executive Director, 1205
Fred, Meier, Deputy Minister, 1214
Fred, Best, Chair, 1231
Fred, Allen, Director, Regulatory Affairs, 1232
Fred, Kirby, Manager, Quarry Material, 1233
Fred, Talen, Director, Negotiations, 1236
Fred, Mandeville, Regional Superintendent, 1236
Fred, Paynter, Member, 1269
Freda, Albert, Executive Director, 1213
Freda, Wilson, Office & Finance Administrator, 1240
Frede, Carla, Webmaster, 865
Frédéric, Seppey, Director General, Trade Agreements & Negotiations, 1119
Frédéric, Guay, Sous-ministre adjoint, Infrastructures & finances municipales, 1276
Frédéric, Guay, Sous-ministre adjoint, 1276
Frédéric, Simard, Directeur, Projets économiques, 1280
Frederick, G. Marcille, Director of Library Services, King's University College, 955
Frederick, Catherine, Director, Human Resources, Ottawa, 1335
Frederiksen, Penny, Partner, Ackroyd LLP Barristers & Solicitors, 906
Fredrickson, Bryan, Head, Acquisitions, Law Library, 1033
Freedman, Robert C., Cook Roberts LLP, 915
Freedman, Allan, Executive Director, 855
Freelan, Jeffery L., Blaney McMurtry LLP, 928
Freeman, Lynne, Secretary & Director, 817
Freitag, Dale, Manager, Lacombe County, 1303
Freitaq, Dale, Planner & Development Officer, Lacombe County, 1303
Frelick, Kathryn M., Partner, Miller Thomson LLP - Toronto, 934
French, Harry, Director, 825
French, David, Treasurer, 744
French, Lew, Treasurer, 814
French, Ruth, Development & Outreach Coordinator, 837
French, P.Eng., Doug, Manager, Okanagan-Similkameen, 1313
Frenette, Marie-Christine, Heenan Blaikie LLP - Montréal, 940
Frenette, Philippe M., Associate, Cox & Palmer - Fredericton, 917
Frenette, Guy, Bibliotechnicien, Jardin Botanique de Montréal, 1019
Frenette, Ed, Manager, 835
Frenkel, Brian, Second Vice-President, 809
Frère, Philippe, Partner, Lavery, de Billy - Montréal, 941
Freund, Cliff, President, 792
Freund, Dorothy, Treasurer, 792
Friars, Kate, Director, Victoria, 1318
Friary, Dave, Acting Director, Operations - Roads, Parks & Fleet, Barrie, 1331
Fricker, Marc, Vice-President, 722
Fridman, Richard, Partner, Davies Ward Phillips & Vineberg LLP, 929
Friedman, Kelly, Davis LLP - Toronto, 930
Friedman, Michael, Partner, McMillan LLP - Toronto, 933
Friend, Q.C., Anthony L., Partner, Bennett Jones LLP - Calgary, 901
Friesen, Debbie, Office Administrator, Nature Manitoba, 972
Friesen, Kyle, President, 794
Friesen, Bob, CEO, 751
Friesen, Wally, Secretary, 713
Friesen, Erin, Chair, 675
Frigon, Florence, Présidente, 852
Frigon, Chantal, Directrice générale adjointe, Saint-Hyacinthe, 1350
Frise, Peter, CEO & Scientific Director, 670
Fritz, Linda, Head, Research Services, University of Saskatchewan, 1034
Fritz, Richard (Rick) D., Executive Director, 645
Friz, Peter, Treasurer, 761
Froese, Andrea L., Partner, Bennett Jones LLP - Calgary, 901
Frohlinger, Thomas G., Pullan Kammerloch Frohlinger, 916
Fromme, Tom, Specialist, 809
Fruitman, Mel, Vice-President, 738
Fruitman, Mel, Vice-President, 755
Fry, Kathleen, Acting Manager, 678
Fry, Jean-Pierre, President, 670
Fryer, W. Mark, Loopstra Nixon LLP Barristers & Solicitors, 932
Fryer, Brian, Contact, 763
Fuchs, Dieter R., President, 871
Fudge, John, Executive Director, 660
Fulford, Allison, Assistant Design & Technology Librarian, Sexton Design & Technology Library, 982
Fuller, Ana, Coordinator, 790
Fuller, James, Chairman, 754
Fuller, Cliff, Fire Chief, Red Deer County, 1304
Fulton, Abigail, Vice-President, 674
Fulton, B.A., LL.B., Brian D., Partner, Lawson Lundell LLP - Vancouver, 913
Fultz, R. Christopher H., Associate, D'Arcy & Deacon LLP - Winnipeg, 916
Fulvio, Fracassi, Director General, 1176
Fumagalli, Laurie A., Associate, McLennan Ross LLP - Edmonton, 908
Fung, Aileen, Research Services Coordinator, EPCOR, 954
Funke, Brian, Manager, East Kootenay, 1311
Funt, Christopher R.C., Lawson Lundell LLP - Vancouver, 913
Furey, William, President, 806
Furgiuele-Percy, Karen, Director, 714
Furlan, Stephen, Partner, McCarthy Tétrault LLP - Toronto, 933
Fydirchuk, Alan, General Manager, Facililties & Fleet, Thunder Bay, 1337
Fyfe, Trina, Northern Health Sciences Librarian, University of Northern British Columbia, 963

G

G., Johnston, Deputy Registrar, 1271
Gaal, Mary-Lynn, Research Librarian, Merck Canada Inc., 1014
Gabel, Marianne, Chair, 833
Gabor, Q.C., Robert T., Aikins, MacAulay & Thorvaldson LLP, 915
Gaboury, Gilles, Président, 853
Gabriel, Jim, Director, Kelowna, 1315
Gabriel, Piette, Director, Research & Development, 1122
Gabriel, Lebreton, Director, Village Historique Acadien, 1226
Gabriel, Mansour, Provincial Coordinator, Specialized Professional Services, 1256
Gabriela, Eggenhofer, Deputy Minister, 1236
Gabrielle, Blais, Director General, Canadian Heritage Information Network (CHIN), 1130
Gadonneix, Pierre, Chair, 872
Gadoury, Lynda, Directrice des bibliothèques, Université du Québec à Montréal, 1021
Gadoury, Lynda, Directrice, Bibliothèque des arts et musique (par, Université du Québec à Montréal, 1021
Gaedecke, Gabrielle, Library Technician, Laboratories Library, 1004
Gaerdes, Fritz C., Alexander Holburn Beaudin & Lang, LLP, 910
Gaétan, Caron, Chair & Chief Executive Officer, 1158
Gaétan, Landry, Engineer, 1221
Gaétan, Désilets, Directeur, 1276
Gaétan, Poiré, Directeur, Technologies vertes et entreprises de service, 1280
Gaétan, Thériault, Vice-président, Opérations, 1283
Gage, Darren, Treasurer, 673
Gagné, Jean M., Fasken Martineau - Québec, 943
Gagné, Jocelyne, Partner, Lavery, de Billy - Montréal, 941
Gagné, Martin R., Fasken Martineau - Québec, 943
Gagné, Michel, McCarthy Tétrault LLP - Montréal, 942
Gagné, Simon, Partner, Heenan Blaikie LLP - Montréal, 940
Gagné, Pierre, Vice-président, 656
Gagné, Michel, Directeur général, Rosemère, 1350
Gagne-Lalonde, Lyne, Library Associate, Collège d'Alfred, 983
Gagnon, Julie, Partner, Reynolds Mirth Richards & Farmer LLP, 909
Gagnon, Marie-Andrée, Lavery, de Billy - Montréal, 941
Gagnon, Nicolas, Partner, Lavery, de Billy - Montréal, 941
Gagnon, Pierre, Joli-Coeur Lacasse Avocats - Québec, 944
Gagnon, Annie, Responsable, Périodiques, CÉGEP de Chicoutimi, 1012
Gagnon, Frederic, Bibliothécaire, Commission de toponymie du Québec, Bibliothèque (Library), 1023
Gagnon, Hélène, Specialist, Scientific Information, Boehringer Ingelheim (Canada) Ltd., 1012
Gagnon, Lucille, Technicienne en informatique, Atelier multimédia e, CÉGEP de Drummondville, 1012
Gagnon, Yolande, Senior Library Assistant, Circulation & Serials Ma, Gerard V. La Forest Law Library, 974
Gagnon, Cathy, Adjointe administrative, 753
Gagnon, Gilles R., Président, 672
Gagnon, Michel, Président, 667
Gagnon-Bourget, Marianne, Cain Lamarre Casgrain Wells - Amos, 938
Gagnon-Mountzouris, Vicky, Personne-ressource, endnote, formation, Université du Québec École de technologie supérieure, 1021
Gail, Shea, Minister for the Atlantic Canada Opportunities Age, 1123
Gail, Moser, Director, Policy, Advocacy, & Coordination, 1123
Gail, Shea, Minister, National Revenue; Minister for the Atlan, 1128
Gail, Faulkner, Director, Regional Oceans Operations, 1140
Gail, Gauvreau, Senior Investigator, Investigator, Investigations & Inquiries, 1170
Gail, Brewer, Acting Director, Strategic Initiatives, 1205
Gail, Silvestrini, Director, Reporting & Analysis, 1211
Gail, Faven, Chair, 1215
Gail, Beggs, Deputy Minister, 1251
Gail, Kruger, Vice-President, Prevention, Finance & Information Technology, 1297
Gail E., Watson, Co-chair, 1216
Gair, Janice, Director, Human Resources & Administration, International Institute for Sustainable Development, 971
Galal, Osman, Secretary General, 786
Galambos, Michael, Ganapathi & Company, 912
Galanti, Horacio, Director, Fort St. John, 1315
Galardo, Catherine, Langlois Kronström Desjardins, 941
Galardo, Pierre, Associé, Langlois Kronström Desjardins, 941
Galbraith, David, Head, Scientific Development, Royal Botanical Gardens, 984
Galbraith, Shayne, Director, Saint John, 1323
Gale, Francis, Contact, 807
Gale, Norm, Chief, Emergency Medical Services, Thunder Bay, 1337
Gale, Robins, Branch Head, Petroleum Marketing & Valuation, & Si, 1184
Galea, Dave, Director, Edmonton, 1306
Galinis, Ted, General Manager, Durham Region Transit, Durham, 1328
Gall, Q.C., Peter A., Partner, Heenan Blaikie LLP - Vancouver, 912
Gall, Q.C., Peter A., Partner, Heenan Blaikie LLP - Victoria, 915
Gallagher Jette, Pat, Chair, Fundy Region Solid Waste Commission, 1323
Gallagher, Q.C., Daniel T., Partner, Bennett Jones LLP - Calgary, 901
Gallant, Bryan L., Stones Carbert Waite Wells LLP, 906
Gallant, Heather, Associate, Duncan Craig LLP - Edmonton, 907
Gallant, Maryse, CÉGEP de Sept-Iles, 1028

Georgescu, Adina-Cristina, Miller Thomson LLP - Montréal, 942
Georgette, Habib, Board Member, 1158
Georgetti, Ken, President, 707
Georgieff, Alex L., Commissioner, Planning Department, Durham, 1328
Geraghty, Dennis, Lalonde Geraghty Riendeau Lapierre Avocats, 945
Gerald, Keddy, Parliamentary Secretary to the Minister, Internati, for the Atlantic Canada Opportunities Agency & for the Atlantic G, 1142
Gerald, Hauer, Chief Provincial Veterinarian, 1181
Gerald, Baron, Administrator, Accreditation, & Coordinator, Appea, 1193
Gerald, Kastendieck, Director, Communications, 1195
Gerald, Legacy, Geomatic Analyst, 1221
Gerald, Crane, Director, Research & Evidence, 1227
Gerald, Enns, Specialist, Hazardous Waste, 1237
Gerald, Joudrey, Regional Director, 1244
Gerald, MacDougall, Manager, Fish & Wildlife, 1265
Gerald, MacDougall, Manager, Fish & Wildlife, 1266
Gerald, Tegart, Deputy Minister, Justice; Deputy Attorney General, 1293
Gerald, Folk, Exeuctive Director, Cultural Planning & Developmen, 1295
Gerald, Isaac, First Nation Policy & Planning Advisor, 1300
Gérald, Toupin, Director, Technical Services, 1175
Géraldine, Underdown, Executive Director, 1161
Gerard, Vaillancourt, Director, Information Management, 1181
Gerard, McDonald, Vice-President, Human Resources & Organzational Effectiveness, 1230
Gerard, McDonald, Vice-President, Human Resources & Organizational Effectiveness, 1231
Gerard, Jessome, Director, Eastern district, 1245
Gérard, Étienne, Vice-President, Human Resources, 1129
Gérard, Szaraz, Forestier en chef, 1281
Gerard A., McDonald, Assistant Deputy Minister, 1175
Gerard F., Morrison, Superintendent, Eastern Highway Maintenance, 1275
Gerard G.M.K., Kruithof, Senior Marine Safety Inspector, Quality Assurance, 1176
Gerbig, Shelleen, Agrologist, 852
Gerhardt McLuckie, Cheryl, Beament Green, 925
Geri, Kamenz, Chair, 1248
Gerilynne, Carroll, Director, Emergency Management, 1255
Gérin, Girouard, Assistant Deputy Minister, 1224
Germain, Marc-André, Heenan Blaikie S.E.N.C.R.L/SRL - Trois-Rivières, 946
Germain, Lizette, Bibliothécaire, CHUQ-CHUL, 1023
Germanakos, Chris N., Partner, McMillan LLP - Toronto, 933
Germano, Joe, Manager, Road & Traffic, North Bay, 1334
Gerry, Cole, Director, Riverview, 1322
Gerry, Ritz, Minister, Agriculture & Agri-Food; Minister, Canad, 1118
Gerry, Frappier, Director General, Assessment & Analysis, 1131
Gerry, Salembier, Assistant Deputy Minister, 1179
Gerry, Lucas, Vice-Chair, 1189
Gerry, Kushlyk, Director, FOIP, 1192
Gerry, Jacubo, Executive Director, Human Resource Services, 1195
Gerry, Boily, Manager, Shared Services Administration & Special, 1195
Gerry, MacDougall, Regional Executive Director, Cariboo, 1206
Gerry, Chevrier, Director, Regional Agri-Business Development, 1220
Gerry, Donovan, Assistant Deputy Minister, Marketing & Development, 1228
Gerry, Chaput, Assistant Deputy Minister, 1264
Gerry, MacKenzie, Chair, 1266
Gerry, Moore, Chief Executive Officer, 1274
Gerspacher, Melvin, Managing Partner, Robertson Stromberg LLP, 947
Gervais, Melissa, President, 637
Gervais, Terry, Fire Chief, Greater Napanee, 1333
Gervais, Trent, Fire Chief, Peterborough, 1336
Gervais, Fortier, Directeur, Communications, 1285
Ghaouti, Loubna, Chef, Bibliothèque des sciences humaines et social, Bibliothèque des sciences humaines et sociales, 1022
Ghaouti, Loubna, Directrice, Université Laval, 1025
Gherbaz, Sabrina A., Torys LLP - Toronto, 936
Ghislain, Blanchard, Director General, Industry Regulation & Determinations Branch, 1132
Ghislain, Chiasson, Director, Licensing & Technical Services, 1220
Ghislain, Lévesque, Chef, Projet Northern Pass Transmission, 1280
Ghosh, Prabal, Secretary, 704
Giard, Jean-Luc, Sec.-Trés., Régie d'aqueduc intermunicipale paroisse St-Pie et Notre-Dame-de-, 1356
Giaschi, Christopher J., President, 708
Gibbon, Brian, Treasurer, 817
Gibbon, Brian, Contact, 673
Gibbons, Jack, Chair, 816
Gibbs, Lee-Ann, Davis LLP - Toronto, 930
Gibbs, Lois Marie, Executive Director/Founder, 726
Gibeau, Guy, Adjoint au directeur des études, CÉGEP de Saint-Laurent, 1028
Gibeault, Mario, Sous-ministre, 694
Gibney, Laura, Manager, 755
Gibson, Kevin D., McInnes Cooper - Halifax, 921
Gibson, Steve, McKenzie Lake Lawyers, 924
Gibson, Janine, Chapter Chair, 712
Gibson, Ken, Executive Director, 639
Gibson, Dean, President, 677
Gibson, Brent, Contact, 763
Gibson, Jean, Treasurer, 803
Gibson, Monika, Regional Coordinator, 644
Gibson, Dean, Director, New Westminster, 1316
Gichohi, Helen W., President, 635
Gick, Natialie, Acting Campus Librarian, Fraser Valley Real Estate Board Academic Library (Surrey), 964
Gierczak, P. Eng., Eugene J.A., Partner, Miller Thomson LLP - Toronto, 934
Giersch, Lynn, Business Manager, 794
Giffin, Todd, President, 866
Gifford, CAE, Terry, Executive Director, 727
Gigi, Mandy, Director, Canada Health Act Division, 1146
Gignac, Éric, Président du conseil, 657
Gignac, Andrée, Directrice, 730
Giguère, Robert, Monty Coulombe s.e.n.c. - Lac-Mégantic, 938
Giguère, Claude, President, 736
Gilbert, Annick, Fasken Martineau - Québec, 943
Gilbert, Cheryl, Heenan Blaikie S.E.N.C.R.L/SRL - Sherbrooke, 945
Gilbert, Eric, Chair, 825
Gilbert, Jane, Chief Communications Officer, 802
Gilbert, Brunet, Director, Meteorological Research, 1135
Gilbert, Van Nes, General Counsel & Settlement Officer, 1186
Gilbert, Bennett, Vice-President, Lower Churchill, 1231
Gilbert-Collet, Alice, Bibliotechnicienne, Acquisitions, Collège universitaire de St-Boniface, 970
Gilby, Stuart C.B., Burchells LLP, 920
Gilchrist, Peter G., Associate, Brownlee LLP - Edmonton, 906
Gilchrist, Doug, Director, Kelowna, 1315
Giles, Vicki L., Partner, McLennan Ross LLP - Edmonton, 908
Giles, Robert, Secretary, 860
Giles, John, Manager, Solid Waste, Kingston, 1333
Giles, Michael A., Chief Building Official, Dufferin, 1328
Giles, Gherson, Deputy Minister, 1249
Gill, Kabal, Coordinator, 852
Gill, Vijay, Vice-President Program/Publications, 722
Gill, Alison, 779
Gill, Harvinder, Manager, 839
Gill, Alex, Executive Director, 817
Gill, Bruce, President, 747
Gill, Sukh, Director/Deputy Administrator, Thompson-Nicola, 1313
Gilles, Saindon, Associate Assistant Deputy Minister, 1121
Gilles, Leclerc, Director General, Space Exploration, 1132
Gilles, Vinet, Vice-President, Program Development Directorate, 1154
Gilles, Jean, Director General, 1164
Gilles, Johnson, Project Executive, Industry Services, 1220
Gilles, Beaulieu, Engineer, Vehicle Management Agency, 1226
Gilles, Julien, Directeur, 1276
Gillespie, Michelle, Vice-President, 684
Gillespie, Robert, Secretary, 679
Gillespie, Eric, Director, Transit Services, Waterloo, 1331
Gillespie, Kent, Commissioner, Employee & Business Services, Peel, 1330
Gillespie, Ted, City Manager, Wetaskiwin, 1308
Gillian, Cantello, Director, Registrations & Client Services, 1179
Gillian, Wood, Executive Director, BC Arts Council, 1201
Gillian, Skinner, Acting Director, Regional Development, 1230
Gillian, Steeve, Manager, Strategic Development, 1263
Gilligan, Amy, Treasurer, 636
Gillihan, Scott, Executive Director, 647
Gilliland, William G., Dentons Canada LLP - Calgary, 903
Gillis, Mary, Circulation Clerk, Defence R & D Canada - Atlantic, 981
Gillis, Derek, Coordinator, 730
Gillis, Rayna, Manager, 818
Gillis, Malcolm, Director, Cape Breton, 1325
Gillis, Tom, Director, Foothills No. 31, 1303
Gillis, QC, Rodney J., Partner, Gilbert McGloan Gillis, 918
Gillis-Bowers, Rosemary, Sec.-Treas., 686
Gillott, Roger, Partner, Osler, Hoskin & Harcourt LLP - Toronto, 935
Gilmore, Carolyn, Coordinator, Dawson College, 1018
Gilmour, Brad, Partner, Bennett Jones LLP - Calgary, 901
Gilmour, Darren, Executive Director, 843
Gina, Sinclair, Director, Oceans & Species at Risk, Policies & Strategies, 1141
Gina, Wilson, Assistant Deputy Minister, 1170
Ginette, Trahan, Director General, Outreach Services, 1154
Ginette, Charlebois, Chief, Security Education & Training Programs, Security Expertise Programs, 1176
Ginette, Roy, Regional Director, Human Resources, 1177
Ginette, Gallant, Acting Director, Port & Airport, 1178
Ginette, Delfrate, Executive Secretary, 1223
Ginette, Brindle, Regional Director, 1259
Ginette, Levesque, Directrice, Laboratoire d'expertises, 1277
Ginette, Bureau, Présidente-directrice générale, 1278
Ginette, Sylvain, Directrice générale adjointe, Projets stratégiques, 1285
Gingras, Vincent, Joli-Coeur Lacasse Avocats - Québec, 944
Gingras, Serge, Technicien en audiovisuel, Campus Notre-Dame-de-Foy, 1026
Ginny, Flood, Director General, Minerals, Metals & Materials Policy Branch, 1164
Ginny, Nisbet, Acting Director, Information Management & Geomatics Services, 1289
Gino, Fournier, Engineering Group Leader, Coastal Engineering Group, 1207
Ginter, Marvyl, Library Technician, Conservation & Environment Library, 970
Gionet, André, Head Librarian, Potato Research Centre, 974
Gionet, Jean-Marie, Président, Commission de gestion des déchets solides de la péninsule Acadien, 1323
Giraldi, Julie, Chief Human Resources & Officer, 819
Girard, Jean-Claude, Morency Société d'Avocats - Québec, 945
Girard, Patrick, Associé, Stikeman Elliott LLP - Montréal, 943
Girard, Diane, Personne-ressource, génie de la production automat, Université du Québec École de technologie supérieure, 1021
Girard, Betty, Executive Director, 732
Girard, Brian, Treasurer, 855
Girard, Jean-François, Président, 727
Girard, Carol, Directeur, Saguenay, 1350
Girardi, Larry, Commissioner, Public Works & Transportation, Sault Ste. Marie, 1337
Giroday, Lesley A., Ratcliff & Company LLP, 910
Girouard, Sylvie, Bibliothécaire, Bibliothèque des sciences juridiques, 1016
Giroux, Pierre, Tremblay Bois Mignault Lemay S.E.N.C.R.L., 945
Giroux, Ghislaine, Web & Library Assistant, International Civil Aviation Organization, 1019
Giroux, Jeanette, Contact, Thames Campus, 985
Giroux, Michael, President, 725
Giroux, Eric, Président, 668
Giroux, Claude, Sec.-Trés., Régie intermunicipale de l'eau de la Vallée du Richelieu, 1358
Girvitz, Ronald S., Wilson Laycraft, 906
Gisela, Kwok, Director, Assured Income for the Severely Handicap, 1190
Gisela, Rempel, Asst. Deputy Minister, 1218
Gisèle, Regimbal, Director, Communications, 1219
Gisèle, Parkinson, Manager, Financial Assistance Delivery, 1224
Giselle, Bernard, Community Development Officer, 1270
Giselle, Marcotte, Assistant Deputy Minister, Northern Affairs, 1290
Gish, Ann, Access Services Librarian, Grande Prairie Regional College, 956
Gislason, Thora, Librarian, Metro Vancouver (formerly Greater Vancouver Regional District), 959
Giuffre, R. Michael, President, 640
Giulio, Ambrosone, Vice-President, Capital Projects, 1200
Giustini, Dean, Reference Librarian, Biomedical Branch Library, 965
Gladwin, Cathy, Contact, 641

Granger, Lucie, Directrice Générale, 667
Granosik, Lukasz, Partner, Norton Rose Fulbright Canada LLP - Montréal, 942
Grant, Bradley B., Partner, Stikeman Elliott LLP - Calgary, 905
Grant, Janet L., Stewart McKelvey - St. John's, 919
Grant, Anna, Archivist, Old Library, 1011
Grant, Laura, Contact, 763
Grant, Lee, Treasurer, 686
Grant, Carla, Executive Director, 818
Grant, Glenn, Operations Manager, 788
Grant, Carry, Manager, Cold Lake, 1306
Grant, Hogg, Director, Environmental Emergencies, 1134
Grant, Manuge, Associate Assistant Deputy Minister, 1143
Grant, Thompson, Director, Agrifoods Policy & Legislative Branch, 1198
Grant, Parnell, Assistant Deputy Minister, 1198
Grant, Loeb, Manager, Timber Pricing Section, 1207
Grant, Main, Deputy Minister, 1211
Grant, Doak, Deputy Minister, 1218
Grant, Dicks, Manager, Licensing & Operations, 1228
Grant, Crack, Parliamentary Assistant, 1261
Grant, Ring, President/Chief Executive Officer, NorthPoint Energy Solutions, 1296
Grant, Q.C., Bruce C., Partner, Stewart McKelvey - St. John's, 919
Grant, Q.C., Robert G., Partner, Stewart McKelvey - Halifax, 922
Grantham, Jacques, Directeur, Québec, 1349
Grapentine, Ray, Manager, 640
Gratton, Luc, Associé, Miller Thomson LLP - Montréal, 942
Gratton, Pierre, President & CEO, 797
Gratton, Pierre, President/CEO, 797
Grauer, Shanon O.N., Partner, McCarthy Tétrault LLP - Toronto, 933
Gravel, Michel, Executive Director, 861
Gravel, Ned, Manager, 684
Gravel, Gaétan, Préfet, D'Autray, 1353
Gravelle, Diane, Agente de bureau, Campus Félix-Leclerc, 1013
Gravenor, Gaël C., Fasken Martineau - Montréal, 939
Graves, Brian C., Partner, McCarthy Tétrault LLP - Toronto, 933
Graves, David A., McInnes Cooper - Halifax, 921
Graves, Charles, President, 844
Gray, Alison J., Bennett Jones LLP - Calgary, 901
Gray, Brian W., Senior Partner, Norton Rose Fulbright Canada LLP - Toronto - Royal Bank Plaza, 935
Gray, Brian, Osler, Hoskin & Harcourt LLP - Toronto, 935
Gray, Marge, Reference Library Technician, South Campus, 956
Gray, Vince, Data Librarian, Department of Geography, 989
Gray, Donna L., Director, Organizational Development & Performance, Ottawa, 1335
Graziosi, Jack, Director, Engineering Services, Vaughan, 1338
Greaves, Susan, GIS/Map Librarian, Maps, Data & Government Information Centre (MADGIC), 988
Grebmeier, Jackie, Vice-President, 774
Greco, Patrick, Partner, Miller Thomson LLP - Toronto, 934
Green, Bram J., Partner, McCarthy Tétrault LLP - Toronto, 933
Green, E. Marshall, HGR Graham Partners LLP - Barrie, 922
Green, Ilja, Technical Services Assistant, Canadian Urban Transit Association, 1001
Green, Clay, Secretary, 867
Green, Susan, Coordinator, 794
Green, Gus, President, 857
Green, Dale, Manager, Kootenay Boundary, 1312
Green, Dave, Manager, Portage La Prairie, 1321
Green, Jack, Manager, Transportation, Orillia, 1335
Green, Keith, Fire Chief, Vernon, 1318
Green, Q.C., John M., McInnes Cooper - St. John's, 919
Greenan, Linda, Manager, Powell River, 1313
Greenberg, Jonathan D., Counsel, Heenan Blaikie LLP - Vancouver, 912
Greenberg, Arlene, Chief Medical Librarian, Sir Mortimer B. Davis Jewish General Hospital, 1021
Greene, Don, Executive Director, 772
Greene, Dale, General Manager/Secretary, 842
Greene, Jeff, City Planner & Team Leader, Airdrie, 1305
Greenfield, Donald E., Partner, Bennett Jones LLP - Calgary, 901
Greenhorn, Chris, Director, Yellowknife, 1325
Greenwood, Kelly L., Burchells LLP, 920
Greenwood, Aletela, Acting Head, Woodward Library and Hospital Branch, Woodward Library, 967
Greer, John, Chair, 692
Greetham, Georgia, Office Coordinator, Yukon Conservation Society, 1035
Greetham, Georgia, Coordinator, 874
Greg, Meredith, Assistant Deputy Minister, 1123
Greg, Stain, Director General, Research & Analysis Directorate, 1123
Greg, Rzentkowski, Director General, Power Reactor Regulation, 1131
Greg, Stevens, Manager, Community Programs, 1136
Greg, Gustavson, Regional Director, Corporate Services, 1177
Greg, Orriss, Executive Director, Food Safety & Animal Health Di, 1181
Greg, Kliparchuk, Executive Director & Senior Financial Officer, Fin, 1187
Greg, Carter, Director, Environmental Support & Emergency Respon, 1187
Greg, Jardine, Executive Director, Southern Hemisphere, 1192
Greg, Weadick, Associate Minister, 1193
Greg, Gauthier, Vice-Chair, 1198
Greg, Rawling, Director, Authorizations (Prince George), 1205
Greg, Reimer, Executive Vice-President, Transmission & Distribut, 1208
Greg, Goodwin, Executive Director, Regional Economic Policy & Projects, 1209
Greg, Czernick, Chief Environmental Officer, 1211
Greg, Gilks, Executive Director, Transportation Policy Branch, 1212
Greg, Carlson, Director, GeoManitoba, 1215
Greg, Selinger, Minister, 1219
Greg, Dion, Manager, Sugarloaf Provincial Park, 1226
Greg, Cuff, Director, Maintenance & Engineering, 1235
Greg, Debogorski, Director, Corrections Services, 1238
Greg, Chapman, District Manager, 1259
Greg, Wilson, Manager, Environmental Land Management, 1268
Greg, MacCallum, Manager, Employer Services, 1275
Greg, Lusk, Executive Director, Commercial Services, 1287
Greg, Leake, Executive Director, Strategic Planning & Performan, 1289
Greg, Horsman, Medical Director, 1292
Greg, Tuer, Executive Director, 1294
Gregg, Mora, Head of Library, William R. Newman Library, 973
Gregoire, Louis-Pierre, Blaney McMurtry LLP, 928
Grégoire, Louis-Pierre, Heenan Blaikie LLP - Ottawa, 925
Gregoire, P.Eng., Michael, Officer, 664
Gregorchuk, John, Managing Secretary, 710
Gregorwich, Don, Secretary, 639
Gregorwich, Joan, Contact, 639
Gregory, Sara J., Lawson Lundell LLP - Vancouver, 913
Gregory, Gabe, Chair, 691
Gregory, Steves, Executive Director, Housing Policy Branch, 1202
Gregory, Roach, Associate Deputy Minister, 1242
Gregory F., Kirby, Chair, 1232
Greig, Kevin, General Manager, Victoria, 1318
Grellette, Leo, President, 699
Grellette, Leo, Director, Building Standards, Vaughan, 1338
Grenier, Glenn, Partner, McMillan LLP - Toronto, 933
Grenier, Richard-Alexandre, Joli-Coeur Lacasse Avocats - Trois-Rivières, 946
Grenier, Paul, Chair, 824
Grenier, Yan, Président, 650
Greta, Bossenmaier, Senior Executive Vice-President, 1131
Gretchen, Pohlkamp, Executive Director, 1244
Gretener, Nicholas M., Partner, Bennett Jones LLP - Calgary, 901
Gretton, Michael, President, 863
Greund Summerfield, Wendy, Manager, 792
Grey, Deb, Reference Librarian, John & Dotsa Bitove Family Law Library, 989
Grier, David, 1st Vice-President, 871
Griffin, Gilly, Director, 695
Griffin, Helen, Vice-President, 725
Griffin, Bruce L., Community Emergency Planner, Barrie, 1331
Griffith, Gillian, Librarian, Outreach Services, Bracken Health Sciences Library, 987
Griffith, FEC, P.Eng, ing, Gordon, Director, 746
Griffiths, Dave, Director, Calgary, 1305
Grills, Tracy, Treasurer, 702
Grimaud, Andrea, Officer, 718
Grimoldby-Campbell, Heather, Manager, 766
Grimsmo, Oivind, Deputy Secretary, 732
Gripp, Roger D., Partner, D'Arcy & Deacon LLP - Winnipeg, 916
Grisley, Kerry, Co-Manager, 639
Griss, Paul, Coordinator, 805
Griswold, Elizabeth, Executive Director, 690
Grivicic, Mike, Administrative Contact, 867
Groat, Lee A., Vice-President, 796
Grobe, Matt, Manager, 761
Groff, Libby, Chair, 823
Grof-Iannelli, Martie, Manager, Library & Media Services, Fanshawe College, 989
Groleau, Jean, Dentons Canada LLP - Montreal, 939
Groleau, Marcel, Président, 862
Groleau, Marcel, Présidente, 751
Grondin, François, McCarthy Tétrault LLP - Montréal, 942
Grondin, Julie, Lavery, de Billy - Montréal, 941
Grondin, Myrian, Bibliothécaire, Bibliothèque paramédicale, 1017
Grondin, Marcel, Directeur général, Saint-Georges, 1350
Grondines, Lousie, Spécialiste en moyens et techniques d'enseignement, CÉGEP de Victoriaville, 1031
Gross, Benjamin David, Partner, Lavery, de Billy - Montréal, 941
Gross, Margaret, Manager, MDA Space, 1028
Grosse, April D., Partner, Bennett Jones LLP - Calgary, 901
Grossklaus, Jennifer, Partner, Davies Ward Phillips & Vineberg LLP, 929
Grossman, Andrew, Partner, Norton Rose Fulbright Canada LLP - Toronto - Royal Bank Plaza, 935
Grosvold, Leann, Coordinator, 730
Ground, Colin, Partner, Cassels Brock & Blackwell LLP, 929
Grout, Kim, Director, Pitt Meadows, 1316
Grove, Margaret, University Librarian, Brock University, 999
Grove-McClement, Tammy W., Magwood, Van De Vyvere, Thompson, & Grove-McClement LLP, 937
Groves, Brett, President, 859
Gruber, Sandra, President-Elect, 709
Gruending, Dennis, Contact, 707
Grugeon, James, Chief Executive Officer, 749
Grundberg, Jeneane S., Partner, Brownlee LLP - Edmonton, 906
Grushcow, Jeremy, Partner, Norton Rose Fulbright Canada LLP - Toronto - Royal Bank Plaza, 935
Grynol, CAE, Susie, Vice-President, 660
Gryski, Chester, Conway Davis Gryski, 929
Guard, Lyle G., Bennett Jones LLP - Calgary, 901
Guay, Denis, Directeur, Varennes, 1352
Guderley, Helga, Secretary, 721
Guénette, Jean-Sébastien, Directeur général, 841
Guenther, Mary Ann, Coordinator, Library Services, North Island College Library, 960
Guenther, Mary Anne, Coordinator, Library Services, Port Alberni Regional Campus Library, 963
Guglielmo, Vincent, Vice-President, 671
Guilbaud-Cox, Elisabeth, Senior Programme Officer & Head, 864
Guild, Don, President, 727
Guillaume, Bernard, President, 871
Guillou, Christian, Electronic Resources Librarian, Douglas College, 962
Guimond, Lucie, Partner, Heenan Blaikie LLP - Montréal, 940
Gulamhusein, Alifeyah, Associate, Brownlee LLP - Edmonton, 906
Güldner, Ralf, Vice-Chairman, 873
Gulkan, Polat, President, 774
Gullberg, Edward W., Partner, McLennan Ross LLP - Yellowknife, 920
Gullette, Shawn, Foreman, Powell River, 1313
Gulliford, Jim, Executive Director, 856
Gullino, M. Lodovica, President, 783
Gunn, Brian, President, 869
Gurley, Angela, Secretary, 760
Gurnett, Amy, Secretary-Treasurer, 791
Gurnsey, D.L., President, 847
Gurria, Angel, Secretary General, 828
Gurses, Elif Aytek, Manager, Acquisitions & York University Libraries, York University Libraries, 1009
Gus, van Helvoort, Executive Director, Fisheries Modernization Initiative, 1140
Gustafson, Jim, Chief Administrative Officer, Central Kootenay, 1311
Gustafson, Q.C., Karl E., Managing Partner, McMillan LLP - Vancouver, 913
Gustavson, John, President & CEO, 708
Gutek, Mike, General Manager, Saskatoon, 1359
Guy, Rob, Senior Director, 721
Guy, Boulet, Manager, Greenhouse Crops, Experimental Farms & Greenhouses, 1121

Guy, Boulet, Manager, Greenhouse, 1122
Guy, Mc Kenzie, Deputy Minister & President, 1127
Guy, Beaupré, Director General, Aquaculture Management, 1141
Guy, Tanguay, Director, Capital Celebrations & Program Operation, 1157
Guy, Lamarche, Director, Community Adult Learning Services, 1224
Guy, Dagenais, Manager, Workers' Advocate, 1224
Guy, Daigle, Manager, Hopewell Rocks, 1226
Guy, Perry, Director, 1229
Guy, Edwards, Director, Portfolio Management Division, 1230
Guy, Caron, Directeur, Inspection des aliments - Secteur Est et Ouest, 1277
Guy, Chouinard, Directeur général, Centre d'expertise en analyse environnementale du Québec, 1278
Guy, Chouinard, Directeur général, 1279
Guy, Leclerc, Directeur, Ressources informationnelles, 1280
Guy, Nadeau, Directeur général, Protection de la faune, 1281
Guy, Cantin, Directeur, Évolution du registre foncier et centre d'opérations de Québec, 1281
Guy, Hétu, Directeur général, 1282
Guy, Laroche, Sous-ministre associé & directeur général, 1284
Guy, Tremblay, Directeur, Laboratoire des chaussées, 1285
Guy A., Smith, Executive Director, Learning Facilities & Alternat, 1191
Guy R., Kerr, President & Chief Executive Officer, 1190
Guylaine, Boisvert, Acting Chief, Translation Bureau, 1153
Guylaine, Berthiaume, Vice-présidente, Administration et finances, 1278
Guylaine, Lajoie, Directeur, Gestion financière - réseau, 1283
Gwen, Jacobson, Director, Operations, 1294
Gwen C.B., Goodier, Acting Director, Outreach, 1134
Gwyn, Graham, Manager, Water Management & Indicators, 1136
Gysbers, Jeannette, Chair, 713
Gysel, Lisa, Librarian, Interior Health Authority, 961

H

Haaf, Chad M., McDougall Gauley - Saskatoon, 947
Haaksma, Wynne, Contact, Library, Manitoba Eco-Network Inc., 971
Haas, Jennifer, Department Head, Information Services & Resources,, Davis Centre Library, 1010
Haase, Martin R., Executive Secretary, 759
Habenicht, Gerfried, Manager, 784
Habib, George, President & Chief Executive Officer, 820
Hacault, Antoine F., Thompson Dorfman Sweatman LLP - Winnipeg, 916
Hacault, Marcel L., Executive Director, 683
Haché, Nicole, Library Coordinator, Champlain College Saint-Lambert, 1028
Hackman, Arlin, Chief Conservation Officer & Vice-President, 873
Haddad, April, Institute Librarian, Justice Institute of British Columbia, 962
Haden, Andy, Manager, Parkland County, 1304
Hadjigeorgiou, John, Chair, 717
Haffner, Jan, Vice-President, 847
Haga, Rick, Executive Director, 725
Hagar, Idlout-Sudlovenick, Executive Director, Nunavut Federal Council, 1131
Hagen, Peter, Soloway, Wright LLP - Ottawa, 926
Hager, Terry, County Commissioner, Lacombe County, 1303
Hagerman, Steve, Records Manager, Northwest Territories Public Works & Services, 979
Haggarty, Penny, Collections Librarian, Thompson Rivers University, 961
Haggerty, John, Secretary-Treasurer, 640
Hahn, Niels Jorn, President, 784
Haig, Roy, Manager, Engineering & 911 Services, Haliburton, 1328
Haigh, Liz, Director, 650
Haigh, Q.C., David R., Partner, Burnet, Duckworth & Palmer LLP, 902
Hailes, Chellie, Secretary, 836
Haines, Margaret, University Librarian, Carleton University, 994
Haines, Keith, Vice-President, 826
Hainsworth, Lynn, Executive Director, 846
Hainsworth, Ray, Secretary, 726
Haire, David, Vice-President, 708
Hakier, Anne, Bibliothécaire, Bibliothèque de géographie, 1016
Hal, Sanders, Assistant Deputy Minister, Minerals, Lands, & Reso, 1288
Hal, Sanders, Assistant Deputy Minister, 1288
Hal M., Howie, Executive Director, Community Services - Western C, 1147
Haldenby, Alan, Director, Colwood, 1314
Hale, Alison, Librarian, Library Services, Canadian Transportation Agency, 1013
Hale, Ivan, Executive Director, 838
Hale, Robin, President, 688
Hale, Judy, Manager, Langley, 1315
Hales, David, General Manager, Spruce Grove, 1308
Hales, Roy, Director, Cranbrook, 1315
Halfyard, Laura, President, 813
Halfyard, Job, President, 807
Halkai, Errol, Executive Director, 697
Hall, Tracy L., Bennett Jones LLP - Calgary, 901
Hall, Karin, Collections Development Librarian, Capilano University, 962
Hall, Linda, Manager, Library Services, Explosives & Energy Technology Infomration Centre, 995
Hall, Nancy, Head, Monograph Acquisitions, York University Libraries, 1009
Hall, M. Barry, President, 754
Hall, Don, President, 849
Hall, Andrew, Director, 766
Hall, Randy, Secretary, 832
Hall, P.Eng., Rob, Director, Sidney, 1318
Hallett, Sandra, Librarian, Prince Philip Drive Campus Library, 978
Halliday, Karen, Health Sciences and Community Studies Librarian, Georgian College of Applied Arts & Technology, 984
Halliday, Sandra, Librarian, Public Services/Circulation Supervisor, Bracken Health Sciences Library, 987
Halliday, Jim, Director, 868
Hallsor, Bruce, Crease Harman & Company, 915
Halperin, Jesse, Lindsay Kenney LLP - Vancouver, 913
Hamann, Maria, Office Manager, 676
Hamblin, P.Eng., Brian, City Manager, Camrose, 1305
Hamel, Lucie, Directrice, CÉGEP de Trois-Rivières, 1030
Hamel, Gérard, Director, 705
Hamel, Denis, Director General, 729
Hamelin, Tara L., Partner, Bishop & McKenzie LLP, 906
Hamer, Howard, President, 813
Hamilton, Arthur, Partner, Cassels Brock & Blackwell LLP, 929
Hamilton, Douglas, Partner, McCarthy Tétrault LLP - Toronto, 933
Hamilton, Rachel J., Managing Partner, Davis LLP - Edmonton, 907
Hamilton, Scott E., Loopstra Nixon LLP Barristers & Solicitors, 932
Hamilton, Don, Information Technology Manager, Wilfrid Laurier University, 1010
Hamilton, Janice, Treasurer, 693
Hamilton, Gord, President, 665
Hamilton, Gary, Executive Director, 869
Hamilton, Peter, Founder, 790
Hamilton, Ron, President, 826
Hamilton, Janice, Executive Director, 792
Hamilton, Jacqueline, Commissioner, Saint John, 1323
Hamilton, John, Manager, Engineering, Norfolk, 1330
Hamilton, Debbie, Acting Commission Manager, Thorhild Regional Waste Management Services Commission, 1310
Hamilton, Debbie, Manager, Thorhild Regional Water Services Commission, 1310
Hamilton Upham, Jennifer J., Patterson Law, 921
Hamlyn, Angela, Director, 705
Hamm, Frank P., Gorman Nason Lawyers, 918
Hamm, Rita R., CEO, 774
Hamoodi, Mary, Director, 850
Hancock, Kimberly, Director, Library Services, Western Health Care Corporation, 976
Hancock, Bruce, Executive Director, 652
Hancock, Brent, President, 868
Hand, Jeffrey A., Partner, Singleton Urquhart LLP, 914
Handley, Gerald, President, 804
Handley, Philip, President, 778
Handlon, Richard J., Pitblado LLP, 916
Handrahan, Phil, Director, Charlottetown, 1346
Handzic, Kember, Emery Jamieson LLP, 907
Hanert, Caireen E., Partner, Heenan Blaikie LLP - Calgary, 904
Haney, Ted, President, 681
Hanick, David, Partner, Osler, Hoskin & Harcourt LLP - Toronto, 935
Hankey, Aleksandra, Librarian, POS Bio-sciences, 1033
Hanlan, Paul, Supervisor, Spruce Grove, 1308
Hanley, Jim, Manager, 669
Hanlon, Ward, Vice-President, 698
Hanlon, Mark, National Director, 851
Hanlon, P.Eng., Peter J., Manager, Saint John, 1323
Hanly, Dave, Director, Planning & Development, Perth, 1330
Hanmer, Gregory P., Miller Thomson LLP - Waterloo, 937
Hanna, W. Brad, Partner, McMillan LLP - Toronto, 933
Hanna, Suzanne, Secretary, Clean North, 998
Hannah, Evans, Director, Partnerships & Consultation, 1256
Hansen, Sarah D., Partner, Miller Thomson LLP - Vancouver, 914
Hansen, Linda, Electronic Services Librarian, Ward Chipman Library, 975
Hansen, Judy, Vice-President, 835
Hansen, Glen, Treasurer, 865
Hansen, Brad, Manager, Terrace, 1318
Hanson, David, Program Manager, 840
Hanson, Ron, Director, Engineering & Operations, Port Colborne, 1336
Harary, Robert, Director, Parksville, 1316
Harasen, Paul J., Kanuka Thuringer LLP, Barristers & Solicitors, 946
Harbottle, Cammie, Youth President, 800
Hardacre, Elizabeth, Librarian, Science Library, 959
Hardel, Frederic, Responsable, Services aux usagers, CÉGEP de Rimouski, 1025
Harder, Brian, President, 757
Hardie, Kristy, Administrative Assistant, 662
Hardie, Ken, Manager, 804
Harding, Gregory S., Partner, Stewart McKelvey - Saint John, 918
Harding, Reece, Young, Anderson, 914
Harding, John, Chair, 688
Harding, Bill, Vice-President, 821
Harding, Richard, Director, Nanaimo, 1316
Hardy, John L., Director, Educational Resources, George Brown College of Applied Arts & Technology, 1003
Hardy, Pamela, Library Technician II, Port aux Basques Campus Library, 977
Hardy, Paula, Library Technician, Interior Health Authority, 961
Hardy, Lisa, Executive Director, 637
Hare, Rob, President, 817
Harel, Mario, Directeur, Gatineau, 1348
Hargreaves, Tara, Scientist & Coordinator, 838
Hargrove, Lyle, President, 813
Harju, Mel, Director, 791
Harker, Harry, Director, Red Deer County, 1304
Harkness, Michelle, Coordinator, 643
Harley, Jayne, Library Assistant, Homewood Health Centre, 985
Harley, Johnson, Ombudsman, 1180
Harling, Ann, Secretary-Treasurer, 716
Harman, Donna A., President & Chief Executive Officer, 646
Harman, L., Vice President, 746
Harmsworth Dow, Joan, Library Technician, Regina Qu'Appelle Health Region - Wascana Rehabilitation Centre, 1032
Harney, Margo, Library Technician, Aurora College, 979
Harnick, Elise, Engineer, Cochrane, 1306
Harnum, Jim, General Manager, Solid Waste Management Services, Toronto, 1338
Harold, Robinson, Director & Tribunal Secretary, 1180
Harold, Murphy, Chair, 1231
Harold, Mullowney, Vice-Chair, 1231
Harold, McCarthy, Director, Insured Services, 1243
Harold, Dremin, Manager, Trade, Investment & Strategic Sectors Unit, 1261
Harold, Côté, Directeur, Études et des analyses, 1283
Harold, Hugg, Executive Director, Strategic Planning & Policy, 1292
Harold, Retzlaff, Director, Transportation Planning, 1293
Harold, Bryant, Director, Royal Saskatchewan Museum, 1295
Harop, Lori, Executive Director, 755
Harpley, Paul, President, 857
Harquail, J. Paul M., Partner, Stewart McKelvey - Saint John, 918
Harricks, Paul H., Lead, Energy, Infra. & Miningu, Gowling Lafleur Henderson LLP - Toronto, 931
Harrington, Terry, Supervisor, Water Distribution, Woodstock, 1338
Harris, Elizabeth A,, Partner, Morelli Chertkow LLP, Lawyers - Kamloops, 909
Harris, Judith E., Senior Partner, Osler, Hoskin & Harcourt LLP - Toronto, 935
Harris, Donna, Support Librarian, Acquisitions, Dawson College, 1018

Henwood, Nancy, Chair, Library Services & Media Librarian, Camosun College, 968
Henze, Harald, Treasurer, 745
Heppler, Em (Matthew), Coordinator, 823
Hepworth, Lorne, President, 740
Herback, Daniel, Fire Chief, Pembroke, 1336
Herbert, Jason K., Partner, Davis LLP - Vancouver, 911
Herchenson, Lorna, Int'l Corresponding Secretary, 675
Herd, Larry, Vice-President, 720
Herdrich, Peter, CEO, 652
Heredia Fragoso, Marco Antonio, Program Manager, 732
Herle, Neil, Osler, Hoskin & Harcourt LLP - Calgary, 905
Herlovitch, Alex, Director, Planning & Development, Niagara Falls, 1334
Herman, Alexander, Langlois Kronström Desjardins, 941
Herman, Lawrence L., Partner, Cassels Brock & Blackwell LLP, 929
Herman, Stegehuis, Director, Wildfire Prevention Section, 1187
Hermanutz, Roni, Manager, 766
Hermenegilde, Twagiramungu, Director, Sustainable Water Management, 1134
Hernan, Ortegon, Program Veterinarian, 1181
Hernblad, Darcy, Fire Chief, Yellowknife, 1325
Hernden, Ken, University Librarian, Algoma University, 998
Hernen, Steve, Director, Protective Services & Fire Chief, Huntsville, 1333
Herny, Meredith, Vice-President, 844
Herone, Marilee, Manager, 849
Héroux, André, Directeur, Saint-Lin-Laurentides, 1351
Herridge, Lesley, Contact, 863
Herron, Terese, National Secretary, 703
Herschorn, Joseph, Associate, Cox & Palmer - Halifax, 921
Herscovici, Alan, Executive Director, 760
Herscovitch, Pearl, Chairperson, Mount Royal University, 951
Hervieux, Margot, Contact, 831
Herzberg, Curtis, County Manager, Red Deer County, 1304
Herzig, Elise, President & Chief Executive Officer, 816
Hesler, Q.C., William, Senior Partner, Norton Rose Fulbright Canada LLP - Montréal, 942
Hétu, Marie-Josée, Partner, Heenan Blaikie S.E.N.C.R.L/SRL - Trois-Rivières, 946
L'Heureux, Karine, Monty Coulombe s.e.n.c. - Sherbrooke, 946
L'Heureux, Brigitte, Bibliotechnicienne, Référence et service du prêt, Collège universitaire de St-Boniface, 970
L'Heureux, Rob, Treasurer, 761
L'Heureux, Gervais, Directeur général, 668
Heuser, Ken, Vice-President, 866
Hewitson, Phil, Director, Transportation, Waterloo, 1338
Hewitt, Dianne, Web Development Librarian, Douglas College, 962
Hewitt, Khadijah, Coordinator, 684
Heyman, George, Executive Director, 851
Hibma, Dick, Chair, 735
Hicik, Andrew, Treasurer, 791
Hick, Cindy, Vice-President, 703
Hicken, Curt, Executive Director, 661
Hickerson, H. Thomas, University Librarian, University of Calgary, 952
Hickey, Tom, General Manager, Nanaimo, 1316
Hickman, Stephanie, Partner, Cox & Palmer - St. John's, 919
Hicks, Barb, President, 842
Hicks, Larry, Secretary-Treasurer, 761
Hiebert, Brian F., Managing Partner, Davis LLP - Vancouver, 911
Hiebert, Betty, Manager, Salmon Arm, 1318
Higdon, Terri C., Associate, Cox & Palmer - St. John's, 919
Higginbotham, Ken, Chair, 739
Higgins, Caroline J., Gorman Nason Lawyers, 918
Higgins, Charles L.K., Fasken Martineau - Toronto, 930
Higgins, Patricia, Director, Williams Lake, 1319
Highley, Frank, Counsel, Cohen Highley LLP - London, 924
Higo, Ron, Director, Port Moody, 1317
Hik, David, President, 774
Hilary, Geller, Assistant Deputy Minister, 1145
Hilary, Lynas, Director, Strategic Policy Branch, 1189
Hildebrandt, Karen, Access Services Coordinator, Concordia University College of Alberta, 954
Hildebrandt, Kalamity, Coordinator, 852
Hill, Krista F., Torys LLP - Toronto, 936
Hill, Terrence H., Daniel & Partners LLP, 927
Hill, Elizabeth, Data Librarian, Department of Geography, 989
Hill, Chris, President & CEO, 744
Hill, Jim, President, 639
Hill, Terry, President, 781
Hill, Bruce C., President, 672
Hill, Michael, Director, 715
Hill, Caitlin, Coordinator, 743
Hill, Michael, President, 849
Hill, Violet, Executive Director, 802
Hill, Claude, Directeur général, 755
Hill, Kevin, Director, Parks, Recreation & Culture, Greater Napanee, 1333
Hill, QC, David H., Partner, Perley-Robertson, Hill & McDougall LLP / s.r.l., 926
Hiller, Marc, Conseiller principal, développement des collection, École polytechnique de Montréal, 1019
Hillier, Jacob, Director of Membership, 686
Hilliker, Arthur, Vice President, 719
Himbeault, Donald, Executive Vice-President, 803
Hines, Michael A., Partner, Hicks Morley Hamilton Stewart Storie LLP - Toronto, 932
Hinse, Jean Yves, Directeur, Montréal, 1349
Hinton, Julie, Administrator, 851
Hinton, Paddy, Supervisor, Mount Waddington, 1312
Hipwell, Dawn, Director, Procurement, Fleet & Property, Simcoe, 1331
Hirning, Lorraine, Serials Technician, Athabasca University, 949
Hirst, Christopher E., Alexander Holburn Beaudin & Lang, LLP, 910
Hiscocks, Mandy, Coordinator, 823
Hisey, Brenda, Director, Camrose, 1305
Hitchins, Nancy, Director, 693
Hitchon, Jay, Waterous, Holden, Amey, Hitchon LLP, 923
Hittinger, Mike, Coordinator, Sturgeon County, 1304
Hivon, Marie-Christine, Partner, Norton Rose Fulbright Canada LLP - Montréal, 942
Hjertaas, Dale, President, 803
Hjorth, Alan, Manager, Human Resources, Thunder Bay, 1337
Hnatick, Lynn E., Partner, MacPherson Leslie & Tyerman LLP - Saskatoon, 947
Ho, Carrie G., Kanuka Thuringer LLP, Barristers & Solicitors, 946
Ho, Winnie, Library Assistant, The Michener Institute for Applied Health Sciences, 1005
Hobbs, Randy, Director, 714
Hobbs, Brian, Director, 735
Hobday, Tina, Associée, Langlois Kronström Desjardins, 941
Hobday, Ed, Administrative Director, 847
Hobin, Morgan, Acting Manager, 830
Hobin, Bruce, President, 819
Hobson, Richard, Manager, Fort Saskatchewan, 1306
Hocher, Josef, Partner, Osler, Hoskin & Harcourt LLP - Calgary, 905
Hochstein, Sandra, Information Literacy Librarian, Douglas College, 962
Hochstetter, Terry, Acting Fire Chief, Port Coquitlam, 1317
Hochu, Carol, President & CEO, 715
Hockin, Jeremy H.H., Partner, Parlee McLaws LLP, 908
Hodes, Jonathan L.S., Clark Wilson LLP, 911
Hodge, Jamie, City Engineer, Cranbrook, 1315
Hodgett, Simon, Partner, Osler, Hoskin & Harcourt LLP - Toronto, 935
Hodgins, Robert A., Partner, Singleton Urquhart LLP, 914
Hodgins, Margaret, Campus Librarian, Vernon Campus, 967
Hodgins, E. David, President, 753
Hodgins, Tom, Commissioner, Development Services Department, Oshawa, 1335
Hodgson, James A., Senior Partner, Norton Rose Fulbright Canada LLP - Toronto - Royal Bank Plaza, 935
Hodgson, Glen, Sr. VP & Chief Economist, 734
Hodgson, Chris, President, 820
Hodgson, John, Manager, Edmonton, 1306
Hodgson, Peter, Manager, Transit Operations, Belleville, 1332
Hoefer, Tom, Executive Director, 811
Hoekenga, Virginia, Deputy Director, 799
Hoeppner, Christine, Digital Resources & Aquisitions Coordinator, University of Winnipeg, 973
Hoffer, Joseph, Partner, Cohen Highley LLP - London, 924
Hoffman, Derek D., McDougall Gauley - Saskatoon, 947
Hoffman, Jay M., Partner, Miller Thomson LLP - Toronto, 934
Hofman, Wayne, Coordinator, LR Computer Services, Northern Alberta Institute of Technology, 955
Hogan, Gregory, Partner, Cassels Brock & Blackwell LLP, 929
Hogan, John J., Associate, Cox & Palmer - St. John's, 919
Hogan, Chris, Executive Director, 806
Hogarth, William, Chair, 786
Hogarth, Mary, Director, 661
Hogg, Linda J., McMillan LLP - Vancouver, 913
Hogg, QC, John M., Partner, Morelli Chertkow LLP, Lawyers - Kamloops, 909
Hoglund, Nikii, Manager, North Vancouver, 1316
Hogue, Marie-Josée, Partner, Heenan Blaikie LLP - Montréal, 940
Hogue, Edward E., Vice-President, 873
Holborn, Richard W., Division Head, Engineering Services Division, Pickering, 1336
Holden, Michelle, Agronomist, 760
Holder, William D., Clark Wilson LLP, 911
Holder, Barbara, Librarian, FP Innovations Forintek Division, 966
Holder, Dan, Fire Chief, Sidney, 1318
Holland, Roger E., Partner, Singleton Urquhart LLP, 914
Holland, Dan, President, 780
Holländer, Tibor, Partner, Heenan Blaikie LLP - Montréal, 940
Hollands, Neil, Director, Brooks, 1305
Hollebone, Jean, President, 829
Hollee, Kew, Director, Regional Office, 1253
Hollett, Karen, Co-Chair, 744
Hollinger, Martha, Contact, 849
Hollingsworth, Janet, Library Coordinator, Lakeshore Campus, 1004
Hollis, Robert, Chief Information Officer, Ontario Ministry of Environment, 1005
Holloway, R. Ivan, Partner, D'Arcy & Deacon LLP - Winnipeg, 916
Holloway, Kate, Director, 825
Holly, Simpson, Advisor, Privacy & Information, 1194
Holly, Hinds, Manager, Building Maintenance & Accommodation, 1275
Holman, Geoffrey, Director, Municipal Works, Niagara Falls, 1334
Holme, Allan L., Partner, Carscallen LLP, 903
Holmes, Marcia, Technical Services Technician, Portage College, 957
Holmes, Robert, Administrative Director, 682
Holmes, Mark, Manager, 818
Holmes, Jonathan, Executive Director, 825
Holmes, Elizabeth, General Manager, 743
Holmes, Jane, Coordinator, Spruce Grove, 1308
Holmes, Jeff, Manager, Mountain View County, 1304
Holmes-Saltzman, Shari, Municipal Planner, Sidney, 1318
Holodniuk, Wes, Manager, Wood Buffalo, 1305
Holt, Cynthia, Associate University Librarian, Collection Service, Concordia University Libraries, 1018
Holte, Gary, Manager, Columbia-Shuswap, 1311
Holyoke, Francesca, Head Librarian, Science & Forestry Library, 974
Holyoke, Andy, Superintendent, Fredericton, 1322
Holz, Christian, Executive Director, 730
Holzschuster, Alfred, Manager, 784
Homes, Adam, Deputy CAO, Lloydminster, 1307
Hong, Peter, Partner, Davies Ward Phillips & Vineberg LLP, 929
Hong, S. Len, President/CEO, 691
Hong, Qi, Branch Head, Bio-Industrial Opportunities Branch, 1181
Honsberger, Dave, Managing Director, 823
Honsinger, Sandra, Library Technician, Boehringer Ingelheim (Canada) Ltd., 1012
Hood, Gerry, Secretary, 781
Hood, David, Chair, 836
Hoogkamer, Dawne, Library Technician, Government Documents/Statistic, Humber College Institute of Technology & Advanced Learning, 1003
Hook, Alexandra, Librarian, Aurora College, 979
Hook, Sheril, Coordinator of Instructional Services, University of Toronto at Mississauga, 991
Hooles, Richard, Vice-President, 860
Hooley, QC, David W., Partner, Cox & Palmer - Charlottetown, 937
Hooper, Elizabeth, Executive Director, 719
Hooper, Ron, President, 803
Hooper, Jaye E., President, 725
Hooper, Q.C., John G.M., McMillan LLP - Ottawa, 926
Hoover, Barry, Vice-President, 744
Hope, Corinne, Access Services Coordinator, Keyano College, 956
Hope, David, President, 694
Hope, Brewer, Manager, Labour Market Analysis, 1224
Hope, Boehm, District Manager, 1253
Hopkins, Timothy M., Gorman Nason Lawyers, 918
Hopkins, Tony, President, 679
Hopkins, Susan, 733
Horacio, Arruda, Sous-ministre adjoint, 1283

Horgan, Pat, Chair, 692
Hornby, Kathryn, Head, Woodward Library, 967
Horne, Bonnie, Librarian, Resource Sharing & Access Services Unit, Gerstein Science Information Centre, 1003
Horne, Wraychel, Executive Director, 682
Horne, Amy, Recycling Coordinator, Grande Prairie, 1307
Horne, Rob, Commissioner, Planning, Housing & Community Servic, Waterloo, 1331
Horner, Kim, Library Technician, Prince Albert Campus Library, 1031
Hornung, Robert, President, 725
Horosko, Barry A., Bratty & Partners, LLP Barristers & Solicitors, 937
Horrocks, Maureen, Coordinator, 849
Horsfield, Grace, Officer, Parkland County, 1304
Horst, Roger, Blaney McMurtry LLP, 928
Horst, Scot, Senior Vice-President LEED, 865
Horswill, Jeffrey D., Davis LLP - Vancouver, 911
Hortie, R. Tyler, Partner, Cohen Highley LLP - Kitchener, 924
Hortie, Phyllis, Contact, 856
Hosack, R. Paul, Cline Backus Nightingale McArthur, 927
Hotchkiss, Tricia, Library Services Assistant, Fort St. John Campus, 960
Houde, France, Responsable, Comptoir du prêt, CÉGEP de Chicoutimi, 1012
Houde, Annie, Regional Office Manager, 827
Hough, Jeanna, Contact, Halton Healthcare Services Corporation, 992
Hough, Merlyn L., President, 636
Hough, Lucy, Director, 868
Houghton, Ed, President, 821
Houlden, Kurt, Director, Chilliwack, 1314
Houle, Louis, Associate Director, Client Services, Sciences, Hea, Schulich Library of Science & Engineering, 1020
Houle, Sylviane, Bibliothécaire, CÉGEP de Saint-Hyacinthe, 1027
Houle, André, Directeur, Lavaltrie, 1348
Hounsell, Terry, Director, Acquisitions/Accounts, College of New Caledonia, 963
Hourdequin, Marion, Treasurer, 783
House, Betty, Coordinator, 669
Houston, Mark T., Partner, Burnet, Duckworth & Palmer LLP, 902
Houston, Jamie, Director, Parks, Recreation, & Leisure Services, North Bay, 1334
Houyoux, Éve-Marie, Directrice adjointe - gestion du prêt et des colle, Université du Québec à Trois-Rivières, 1030
Hovdebo, Harold S., President, 724
Howard, Paul, Howard Ryan Kelford Knott & Dixon - Smiths Falls, 927
Howard, Jack, Librarian, H.H. Mu Far Eastern Library, 1003
Howard, Linda, Librarian, Surrey Memorial Hospital, 964
Howard, Peter, President & Chief Executive Officer, 696
Howard, Rick, President, 815
Howard, John, Chair, 688
Howard, Posluns, Chief, Advanced Technology, 1174
Howard, Posluns, Chief, Advanced Technology, Transportation Development Centre, 1175
Howard, Wong, Executive Director, Finance & Administration, 1192
Howard, Arndt, Director, Sustainability & Energy Management, 1287
Howard, Loseth, Director, Energy Development & Climate Change, 1288
Howard, Yea, Director, Bridge Standards, 1292
Howard L., Pike, Manager, Operations, 1232
Howarth, Janet, Reference Assistant, Map Library, 1004
Howatt, Wayne, Burchells LLP, 920
Howcroft, Ian, Vice-President, 708
Howes, Hilary, Executive Director, 736
Howie, Gord, City Manager, Prince Rupert, 1317
Howland, Sharon, Vice-President, 839
Howse, Mary Anne, Manager, Library Services, Women's College Hospital, 1009
Hoyles, John, Chief Executive Officer, 689
Hoyt, Kevin, Treasurer, 844
Hoyt, Q.C., Leonard T., McInnes Cooper - Fredericton, 917
Hryhorczuk, Brant, Manager, Yorkton, 1360
Hsu, Annie, Vice-President, 740
Huard, Marie-Douce, Cain Lamarre Casgrain Wells - Québec, 943
Huart, Michel, Langlois Kronström Desjardins, 941
Hubberten, Hans-W., President, 781
Hubert, Mark, Vice-President, 756
Hubert, Smith, District Manager, 1233
Hubert, De Nicolini, Directeur, Développement régional & métropolitain, 1276
Hubick, Lisa, Public Relations Librarian, Kwantlen Polytechnic University, 964
Hudon, Caroline, Library Assistant, Centre de recherche et de développement sur les sols et les grand, 1028
Hudson, Benjamin, Stikeman Elliott LLP - Calgary, 905
Hudson, Roy H., Davis LLP - Calgary, 903
Hudson, John A., President, 783
Hudson, Victoria, Treasurer, 704
Huebel, Norm, Regional Director, 692
Huebert, Ed, Executive Vice President, 797
Huff, Robert, Chief Information Officer, 650
Huff, Greg, Manager, 792
Hugh, Robertson, Director General, Information Management & Technology, 1131
Hugh, Krentz, Chair, 1172
Hugh, Boyd, Executive Director, Wildfire Management Branch, 1187
Hugh, Reynolds, Secretary, 1198
Hugh, Flinton, Director, Pine Beetle Epidemic Response Branch (Williams Lake), 1209
Hugh, Eliasson, Deputy Minister, 1216
Hugh, Eliasson, Chair, 1216
Hugh, Eliasson, Deputy Minister, 1217
Hugh, Donnan, Director, Communications, 1231
Hugh, Whitney, Director, Animal Health Division & Chief Veterinary Officer, 1233
Hugh, Lloyd, Director, Government Liaison Office, 1247
Hugh (Ted), Flemming, Minister, Health, 1222
Hughes, Nicholas R., McCarthy Tétrault LLP - Vancouver, 913
Hughes, Terrance M., McCarthy Tétrault LLP - Calgary, 904
Hughes, Lynn, Library Technician (Copyright), College of the Rockies, 960
Hughes, Philip, Instructor/Librarian, Maritime College of Forest Technology, 974
Hughes, Tom, President, 697
Hughes, Shawn, Vice-President, 814
Hughes, Peter, Director, Thompson-Nicola, 1313
Hughes, Robert, Chief Building Official, Pembroke, 1336
Hugonnier, Bernard, Directeur, 753
Hui, Katherina, Librarian, Edmonton Planning & Development Dept. Library, 954
Hull, Jack, General Manager, Capital Regional District, 1310
Humber, Allyn, Director, Calgary, 1305
Humble, Jeffrey, Director, Yellowknife, 1325
Humes, Paul, Vice President, 801
Hummel, Monte, President Emeritus, 873
Humphries, Colleen, Supervisor, Corner Brook, 1324
Humphris, P.Eng., Doug, Manager, Metro Vancouver, 1312
Hunston, Jeff, Secretary-Treasurer, 683
Hunt, Jeffrey R., Patterson Law, 921
Hunt, Raymond G., Walsh Wilkins Creighton LLP, 906
Hunt, Susan, Program Manager, 832
Hunt, Murray, Treasurer, 842
Hunt, Daryl, President, 842
Hunt, Malcolm, Director, Planning & Development Services, Peterborough, 1336
Hunt, Michelle, Manager, Coquitlam, 1314
Hunt, MCIP, RPP, Thom, City Planner, Windsor, 1338
Hunter, Amanda J., Partner, Hicks Morley Hamilton Stewart Storie LLP - Toronto, 932
Hunter, Brenden, Associate, Fasken Martineau - Calgary, 903
Hunter, Clay, Paterson, MacDougall LLP, Barristers, Solicitors, 936
Hunter, Jennifer, Library Assistant, Marine Campus, 963
Hunter, Kenneth W., Treasurer, 872
Hunter, Peg, Chair, 708
Hunter, Nigel Derek, Executive Director, 743
Hunter, Jim, Director, Transportation Construction, Simcoe, 1331
Hunter, Mike, Manager, North Vancouver, 1316
Huntley, Lyle, Clerk/Director, Thompson-Nicola, 1313
Hupfer, Raymond D., Partner, McLennan Ross LLP - Edmonton, 908
Hurd, Michael, Chair, 824
Hurlburt, Kate L., Emery Jamieson LLP, 907
Hurlburt, Kate, Vice-Chair, 637
Hurlburt, QC, William H., Counsel, Reynolds Mirth Richards & Farmer LLP, 909
Hurley, John, Gowling Lafleur Henderson S.E.N.C.R.L./LLP, 939
Hurrell, Christie, Libararian, Rockyview General Hospital Knowledge Centre, 952
Hurst, Michael A., Dentons Canada LLP - Calgary, 903
Hurst, Russel, Managing Director, 740
Hurtubise, Marc, Grondin, Poudrier, Bernier, 944
Hussain, Azim, Partner, Norton Rose Fulbright Canada LLP - Montréal, 942
Hustins, Donald, President, 670
Huston, Dale, Reference Librarian, Champlain College Saint-Lambert, 1028
Hutchens, Lisa A., Manager, 832
Hutcherson, Christine, Director, 801
Hutcheson, Larissa, General Manager, Capital Regional District, 1310
Hutchings, Deborah L.J., McInnes Cooper - St. John's, 919
Hutchings, Rhea, Sustainable Development Officer, Corner Brook, 1324
Hutchins, Peter W., Associé, Hutchins Caron & Associés, 940
Hutchinson, Fred, Executive Director, 662
Hutt, David, Burchells LLP, 920
Hutt, Howard W., President, 745
Hutton, Susan M., Partner, Stikeman Elliott LLP - Ottawa, 926
Hutton, Jon, Director, 862
Huxtable, David, Treasurer, 855
Hwang, Dianna S., Alexander Holburn Beaudin & Lang, LLP, 910
Hyder Ali, Amyn, Financial Officer, 867
Hyland, Maureen, Collections Development & Technical Services Libra, Humber College Institute of Technology & Advanced Learning, 1003
Hynes, Theresa, Library Technician, Martin Gallant Bldg., College of the North Atlantic, 979
Hynick, Derrill, Executive Director & Service Provider, 857
Hyvarinen, Joy, Director, 756
Hyvärinen, Anne, Secretary, 784

I

Iacovelli, Antonio, Miller Thomson LLP - Montréal, 942
Iain, Smith, Director, Provincial Pharmacy Services, 1273
Ian, Walker, Manager, Onefour Research Substation Site, 1122
Ian, Alexander, Chief Veterinary Officer, 1129
Ian, Graham, Vice-President, Knowledge Translation & Public Outreach, 1130
Ian, Macleod, Manager, Aboriginal Affairs, 1136
Ian, Burney, Assistant Deputy Minister, 1143
Ian, Shugart, Deputy Minister, Human Resources & Skills Developm, 1147
Ian, Potter, Vice-President, Engineering, 1158
Ian, Church, 1169
Ian, Blackie, Assistant Inspector General, Canadian Security Intelligence Service (CSIS), 1170
Ian, McKay, Executive Director, Infrastructure & Alternative E, 1184
Ian, Meikle, Treasurer & Member, Complaints Committee, 1195
Ian, Sharpe, Regional Manager, Environmental Protection, Skeena Regional Office, 1203
Ian, Wong, Senior Portfolio Manager, Venture Capital Programs, 1209
Ian, Pilkington, Director, Rehabilitation & Maintenance, 1211
Ian, Munroe, Vice-President, Claims Services, 1213
Ian, Burford, Director, Licensing & Quality Assurance, 1228
Ian, Butters, Special Advisor, 1238
Ian, Davidson, Deputy Minister, Community Safety, 1249
Ian, Smith, Director, 1252
Ian, Hagman, District Manager, 1259
Ian, Brisbin, Chair, 1262
Ian, Wilson, Chair, 1262
Ian, Rodd, Manager, OHS, 1275
Ian, Robertson, Acting Chairperson, 1300
Ian D., Campbell, Director, Science & Technology Quality Assurance & Programs, 1121
Ian D., Rutherford, Executive Director, Canada Meteorological & Oceanographic Society, 1140
Ian K., Russell, Chair, 1248
Iannello, Sal, General Manager, Engineering, Public Works, & Tran, Welland, 1338
Iatridis, Kristos J., Bennett Jones LLP - Calgary, 901
Iavicoli, Sergio, Secretary General, 777
Ibrahimi, Ali, Manager, 860
Icharia, David, Director, 678
Idee, Inyangudor, Director, Policy, 1130
Idema, Wendy, Acting General Manager, Nanaimo, 1312
Iezzoni, Véronique, Partner, Heenan Blaikie LLP - Montréal, 940
Ikert, Chad, Logistics Coordinator, 666
Ilka, Jung, Alberta Germany Office Commercial & Administrative, 1192

Illsey, Karen L., Partner, Bennett Jones LLP - Calgary, 901
Ilnyckyj, Oleh W., Partner, Miller Thomson LLP - Vancouver, 914
Ilona, Rehberg, Director General, 1154
Imata, Katsuji, Deputy Secretary General, 729
Imomoh, Egbert, President, 855
Impey, Patrice, General Manager & Chief Financial Officer, Vancouver, 1318
Inanc, Yazar, Director, Audit, 1155
Indira, Breitkreuz, Executive Director, Corporate Planning & Policy, 1194
Indra, Prashad, Director, Safe Drinking Water, 1251
Ines, Piccinino, Acting Executive Director, 1205
Ingelson, Allan, Executive Director, Canadian Institute of Resources Law, 950
Ingelson, Allan, Executive Director, 706
Ingersoll, QC, Daniel W., Partner, Cox & Palmer - Halifax, 921
Ingham, April, Executive Director, 829
Inglis, R.G., Saxe, Dianne, 936
Ingram, Sarah, Programs Manager, 865
Ingram, Cathy, Manager, Penticton, 1316
Ingrid, Bloomfield, Regional Manager, Kelowna, 1212
Ingrid, Fawcus, Director, 1299
Ings, Joanne, Executive Director, 835
Inkinen, Tomi, Library Technician, Library (Burnaby), 959
Innes, John, Regional Director, 732
Ip, Samantha, Clark Wilson LLP, 911
Iredale, Q.C., John N., Gowling Lafleur Henderson LLP - Calgary, 904
Ireland, Michael, Acting Director, Information Access & Delivery, Canadian Institute for Scientific & Technical Information (CISTI), 994
Ireland, Marlene L., Manager, Fleets & Facilities, Norfolk, 1330
Irene, Hrynkiw, Director, Financial Services, 1297
Irene V., Gendron, General Counsel & Executive Director, Legal Services, 1128
Irg, Mike, Manager, Alberni-Clayoquot, 1310
Irizawa, Naomi, Treasurer, 662
Irvin, William Robert (Bob), President, 647
Irvine, Seana, Chief Operating officer, 750
Irving, Catherine, Librarian, Coady International Institute, 980
Irving, D., Manager, St. Albert, 1308
Irving, QC, Harold K., Associate, D'Arcy & Deacon LLP - Winnipeg, 916
Irwin, Jason J., Miles, Davison LLP, 905
Irwin, Elizabeth, Library Assistant, Powertech Labs Inc., 964
Irwin, David, President, 823
Irwin, Sandy, Executive Director, 796
Irwin, Tracey, Manager, 847
Irwin, Janice, Manager, North Vancouver, 1316
Irwin, Stewart, Senior Manager, Capital Regional District, 1310
Irwin, Blank, Chief Executive Officer, 1287
Isaac, Thomas F., McCarthy Tétrault LLP - Calgary, 904
Isaac, Thomas F., McCarthy Tétrault LLP - Vancouver, 913
Isaac, Thomas, Partner, McCarthy Tétrault LLP - Toronto, 933
Isaac, Kim, University Librarian, University of the Fraser Valley, 958
Isaacson, P.Eng., PhD, Michael, President, 663
Isaak, Kim, Secretary, 790
Isabel, Romero, Director, Québec Region, 1155
Isabel, Hache, Director, Human Resources, 1244
Isabella, Louis, Treasurer, 644
Isabelle, Dupuis, Acting Director, First Nations Land Management Directorate, 1118
Isabelle, Bérard, Director General, Planning, Operations & Specialists Directorate, 1130
Isabelle, Gingras, Vice-President, Human Resources, 1158
Isabelle, Blain, Vice-President, Research Grants & Scholarships Directorate, 1165
Isabelle, Desmartis, Director, Aviation Security Policy, 1175
Isabelle, Dingemans, Manager, Public Health Strategy, 1248
Isabelle, Olivier, Directrice, 1279
Isabelle, Olivier, Directrice, 1279
Isabelle, Phaneuf, Directrice, Information, promotion, et investissements internationaux, 1280
Isabelle, Courville, Présidente, Hydro-Québec Distribution, 1280
Isabelle, Godbout, Directrice, Intégration et innovation, 1281
Isabelle, Godbout, Directeur (par intérim), Gestion du fonds d'information foncière, 1281
Isabelle, Savard, Directrice, Main d'oeuvre médicale, 1283
Isdell, Neville, Chair, 874
Isfeld, Randy, Director/Fire Chief, Williams Lake, 1319
Islam, P.Eng., Tareq, Director, Fraser Valley, 1311
Ismail-Zadeh, Alik, Secretary General, 785
Issa, Antonia, Communications Manager, 843
Ivan, Didiuk, Associate Director, Infrastructure Secretariat, 1179
Ivan, Moore, Assistant Deputy Minister, 1194
Ivan, Downton, Director, Forest Ecosystem Management, 1233
Ivan, Francis, Director, Project Delivery North, 1287
Ivanoff, Paul, Partner, Osler, Hoskin & Harcourt LLP - Toronto, 935
Ivey, Rosamond, Chair, 842
Ivey, Richard W., Secretary-Treasurer, 842
Ivy, Chan, Director, Environmental Public Health, Primary Health Care & Public Health, 1145
Iwaniw, Aubrey, Acting Manager, 852

J

J. Alan, McIsaac, Minister, 1267
J. Allan, Eddy, Regional Director, 1244
J. Andy, Fyon, Director, 1260
J. E. Alain, Daneau, Directeur général (par intérim), Efficacité et innovation énergétiques, 1281
J. Robert, Keeley, Senior Technical & Policy Advisor, 1142
J. Robert S., Pritchard, Chair, 1264
Jabbour, Raymond, Chief Financial Officer & Director, 838
Jacinta, Berthier, Director, Conservation & Protection, Enforcement Policies & Standards, 1140
Jacinthe, Leclerc, Director General, 1163
Jack, Don, Partner, Heenan Blaikie LLP - Toronto, 931
Jack, Ian, Managing Director, 689
Jack, Vandenberg, Director, Heritage Conservation Directorate, 1172
Jack, Shewchuk, Chief Executive Officer, 1212
Jack, Bird, Assistant Deputy Minister, Operations, 1236
Jack, Parker, Senior Manager, Precambrian Geoscience, 1260
Jack C., Goodman, Regional Director, Marine, Surface & Intermodal Security, 1177
Jackie, Olsen, Acting Regional Director General, 1136
Jackie, Lee, Senior Manager, Finance & Contracting Services, 1190
Jackie, Lavallee, Executive Director, 1216
Jackie, Janes, Senior Policy Advisor, Climate Change, 1227
Jackie, Weir, Research Manager, St. John's, 1228
Jackie, Irwin, Information Technology Architect, 1272
Jacklin, Marcie, Director, 817
Jackson, Patricia D. S. (Trisha), Torys LLP - Toronto, 936
Jackson, Kathryn, Manager, HECS Library, 996
Jackson, Susan, Head, Maps, Data & Government Information Centre (, Carleton University, 994
Jackson, John, Coordinator, 729
Jackson, Craig, Coordinator, 825
Jackson, Ian, Coordinator, 825
Jackson, Fawn, Manager, 691
Jackson, Scott, Manager, 818
Jackson, Andrew, Director, 707
Jackson, John, Executive Director & Director, 763
Jackson, Lois, Chairman of the Board, 869
Jackson, Tim, President, 652
Jackson, Viki, Executive Director, 795
Jackson, Gayle, Director, Parksville, 1316
Jackson, Wayne, Director, Utility Services & Deputy CAO, Peterborough, 1336
Jackson, Lafferty, Minister, 1236
Jacob, Gibby, Chair, 742
Jacob, Verhoef, Director, GSC Atlantic, 1164
Jacob, Martin-Malus, Directeur, Développement socio-économique, partenariats et éducation, 1281
Jacobs, Neil L., Partner, Stewart McKelvey - St. John's, 919
Jacobs, Paul, President, 875
Jacobsohn, Alice, Director, 801
Jacoby-Hawkins, Erich, Board Member, 747
Jacome, José, Directeur général, 708
Jacqueline, Bannister, Director, Communications Directorate, 1132
Jacqueline, Gonçalves, Director General, 1140
Jacqueline, Malboeuf, Communications Advisor, 1160
Jacqueline, Malboeuf, Portfolio Communications Advisor, 1161
Jacqueline, Couture, Director, Communications Division, 1165
Jacqueline, Power, Director, European Union Trade Policy, 1230
Jacqueline, Gallacher, Manager, Environmental Bill of Rights Office, 1251
Jacqueline (Jackie), Sheppard, Chair, 1234
Jacques, Mélanie, Dentons Canada LLP - Montreal, 939
Jacques, Luce, Trésorière, Rosemère, 1350
Jacques, Ronald, Coordonateur, Régie d'aqueduc Richelieu-Centre, 1356
Jacques, Surprenant, Director, Research & Development, 1121
Jacques, Suprenant, Director, Research & Development, 1122
Jacques, Greffe, Vice-President, Contract Management & Procurement, 1128
Jacques, Gagnon, Director, Science Policy Division, 1163
Jacques, Gourde, Parliamentary Secretary, 1171
Jacques, Rochon, Executive Director, Continental Gateway & System Analysis, 1174
Jacques, Savard, Director, Special Projects, 1177
Jacques, LeGris, Director, Strategic Human Resources, 1251
Jacques, Tremblay, Directeur, 1276
Jacques, Dupoint, Sous-ministre adjoint, Expertise hydrique, analyse et évaluations environnementales, 1278
Jacques, Dupont, Sous-ministre adjoint, 1279
Jacques, Cotton, Sous-ministre, 1282
Jacques, Bélanger, Directeur, 1284
Jacques, Viger, Directeur, 1284
Jacques J., Laprise, Executive Director, Strategic & Communications Ser, 1147
Jacquest, Donald, Director, Comox, 1314
Jacquie, Manchevsky, Director General, Call Centre Directorate, 1147
Jacquie, Dawes, Assistant Deputy Minister, 1212
Jacquie, Kerr, Director, Customer Solutions, 1290
Jacynthe, Dubé, Manager, Communications Products & Services, Publishing & Linquistic Services, 1178
Jaeger, Valerie, Commissioner, Public Health & Medical Officer of H, Niagara, 1329
Jail, Louis-Noël, Chef du service, Information et documentation, Institut de l'Énergie et de l'environnement de la francophonie, 1023
Jaime, Caceres, Acting Director General, Operations Integration, 1140
Jaime, Pitfield, Vice-President, Common Administrative Services Directorate, 1165
Jaimeson, John, Executive Director, 835
Jain, Devin, Manager, Port Moody, 1317
Jairam, Andy C., Loopstra Nixon LLP Barristers & Solicitors, 933
Jake, Kotowich, Branch Head, Meat Inspection Branch, 1181
Jake, Jacobs, Officer, Public Affairs, 1202
Jake, Epp, Chair, 1261
Jakola, Roy, Director, 687
Jamer, P.Eng., Murray, Director, Fredericton, 1322
James, Dennis J., Patterson Law, 921
James, Robert P., Partner, Parlee McLaws LLP, 908
James, Eric, Reference Specialist, Noranda Earth Sciences Library, 1005
James, Tina, Associate Director, Facilities & Administration, University of Alberta, 956
James, Victoria, Coordinator, 810
James, Gord, Chair, 713
James, McKenzie, Principal, Sustainable Development Strategies, Aud, 1124
James, Moore, Minister, Canadian Heritage & Official Languages, 1129
James, Greene, Chief, Resource & Environmental Taxation, 1139
James, Smith, Director, Certification & Sustainability Reporting, 1141
James, Wilkin, Director, Pacific Vancouver, 1159
James, Pope, Director, Aviation Security Regulatory Affairs, 1175
James, Meddings, Assistant Deputy Minister, 1179
James, Jones, Branch Head, Food & Bio-Industrial Crops Branch, 1182
James, Calpas, Branch Head, Crop Business Development Branch, 1182
James, Greengrass, Chief Information Officer, Resource Information Ma, Sustainable Resource Development, 1187
James, Acheson, Director, Strategic Planning & Program Integration, 1194
James, Orr, Director, Codes & Standards, 1194
James, Gorman, Deputy Minister, Education, 1201
James, O'Hanley, Deputy Commissioner, Project Assessment & Compliance Assurance, 1202
James, Mack, Head, 1203
James, Duncan, Chair, 1214
James, Duncan, Director, Wildlife & Ecosystem Protection, 1215
James, Goltz, Manager, Veterinary Laboratory & Pathology Services, 1220
James, Evans, Chief Executive Officer, Forestry & Agrifoods Agency, 1232
James, Evans, Chief Executive Officer, 1233

James, Evans, Assistant Deputy Minister, 1233
James, Arreak, Minister, 1246
James, Arreak, Minister, 1247
James, Arnett, Chair, 1255
James, Fleck, Chair, 1262
James, Toombs, Chair, 1265
James, Blanchard, Chair, 1267
James, Froh, Assistant Deputy Minister, First Nations, Métis, &, 1290
James (Jim), Smith, Executive Director, 1273
James D., Crawford, Executive Director, 1129
James D., Hinds, Chair, 1250
James G., Hamilton, Chief Information Officer, 1249
James G., Hamilton, Chief Information Officer, 1261
James J., Bradley, Minister, 1251
James Michael (Jim), Flaherty, Minister, Finance, 1139
James S., Paul, President & Chief Executive Officer, 1132
James V.B., Lawson, Regional Director, Marine, 1177
Jamie, Deacon, Director General, Regional Operations Directorate, 1170
Jamie, Chippett, Deputy Minister, 1235
Jamie, Chambers, Specialist, Hazardous Substances, 1237
Jamie, MacDonald, Executive Director, 1272
Jamieson, Elisha C., Associate, Hicks Morley Hamilton Stewart Storie LLP - Toronto, 932
Jamieson, JoAnn P., Partner, Lawson Lundell LLP - Calgary, 904
Jamieson, N., General Manager, St. Albert, 1308
Jamieson, Dunlop, Manager, Engagement Programming, 1200
Jamison, Kelly, Director, 720
Jan, Dyer, Director General, Sustainability Directorate, 1136
Jan, Karakochuk, Contact, Event Support Program & Alberta Games & M, 1195
Jan, Zawadzki, Business Unit Director, Power Labs, 1208
Jan, Broocke, Director, 1211
Jan, Gray, General Manager, 1263
Jan, Olsen, Director, Marketing, 1295
Jan, Franken, Director, Business Information & Technology System, 1297
Jana, Schott, GO Team Manager, 1214
Jancik, Milos, President/CEO, 745
Jane, Rooney, Trade Commissioner, 1144
Jane, Hazel, Director General, Marketing & Communications Services, 1146
Jane, Lang, Director, Strategic Corporate Services, 1157
Jane, Weldon, Director General, 1175
Jane, Bird, President/Chief Executive Officer, 1200
Jane, Thornthwaite, Parliamentary Secretary for Student Support & Pare, 1201
Jane, Lloyd-Smith, Director, Resource Management (Skeena), 1205
Jane, MacFadgen, Senior Vice-Chair & Registrar, 1209
Jane, Matthews-Clark, Director, Communications, 1225
Jane, Fullerton, Chief Executive Officer, New Brunswick Museum, 1225
Jane, Fraser-Coutts, Executive Director, Strategiec Capital & Infrastructure Planning, 1245
Jane, Pagel, President & Chief Executive Officer, 1251
Jane, Glassco, District Manager, 1253
Jane, Ireland, Acting Regional Director, 1259
Jane, Ledwell, Researcher & Policy Analyst, 1266
Jane, Mallard, Director, Policy & Strategy, 1273
Jane-Ann, Graham, Administrative Assistant, Science Policy Division, 1135
Janega, Ann, Vice President, 708
Janes, Robert J.M., Cook Roberts LLP, 915
Janes, Erica, Coordinator, 714
Janet, King, Assistant Deputy Minister, 1118
Janet, Dorey, Deputy Director, 1120
Janet, Steele, Regional Director, 1120
Janet, Gagnon, Vice-President, New Brunswick, 1123
Janet, Fahey, Head, Finance & Administration, 1162
Janet, Walden, Vice-President, Research Partnerships Programs Directorate, 1165
Janet, Kavanagh, Director, Ports Policy, 1174
Janet, Patriquin, Assistant Farmers' Advocate, Communications & Prog, 1181
Janet, McLean, Acting Director, Policy & Legislation Innovation B, 1188
Janet, Adams, Manager, Regional Service Delivery, GeoBC, 1205
Janet, Higgins, Assistant Deputy Minister, Corporate Services, 1223
Janet, Vivian-Walsh, Acting Deputy Minister, 1227
Janet, Rideout, Environmental Officer, 1230
Janet, Braunstein, Senior Director, 1242
Janet, Brewster, Manager, Research & Special Projects, 1247
Janet, Hannah, Secretariat Support, 1254
Janet, Mason, Assistant Deputy Minister, 1257
Janet, Doyle, Financial Services Officer, 1266
Janet, Peters, Manager, Legislative Services, 1296
Janet L., Woelfle, Manager, Spills Action Centre, 1253
Janette, Lyons, Director, Finance, 1208
Janice, Sarich, Parliamentary Assistant, 1183
Janice, Schroeder, Director, Communications, 1183
Janice, Romanyshyn, Executive Director, Grants & Education Property Ta, 1194
Janice, Gignac, Manager, Registries Programs (Trade Agreements), 1199
Janice, Clarke, Advisor, 1225
Janice, Fummerton, Manager, OPS Green Office Projects, 1254
Janice, Thomson, Chair, 1262
Janice, Lambrakos, Coordinator, Information Services, 1262
Janice, Siekawitch, Director, Planning & Communications, 1297
Janice A., Sherry, Minister, Environment, Labour & Justice; Attorney, 1265
Janice A., Sherry, Minister, 1267
Janie, Markewich, Director, Financial Services, 1290
Janine, North, Chief Executive Officer, 1209
Janine, Ballingall Scotten, Commissioner, 1219
Janisse, Lea, Director, Human Resources, North Bay, 1334
Jankowski, Paul, Commissioner, Engineering & Public Works, Vaughan, 1338
Jannette, Wombold, Administrative Coordinator, 1187
Janower, Lori, Library Services Coordinator, Manitoba Dept. of Science, Technology, Energy & Mines, 971
Janssens, John Paul, Partner, Reynolds Mirth Richards & Farmer LLP, 909
Jantzen, Andrew, Coordinator, 812
Jantzi, Leanna, Electronic Resources Librarian, Capilano University, 963
Jardine, Marjory, Librarian, Vancouver Coastal Health Authority, 967
Jardine, Marjory, Librarian, Reference & Instruction, Justice Institute of British Columbia, 962
Jared, Clarke, Naturalist, 1294
Jarnagin, Ronald, President, 647
Jarvis, Danielle R., Davis LLP - Vancouver, 911
Jarvis, Darrell, Partner, Fasken Martineau - Toronto, 930
Jarvis, Julie, Librarian, MacDonald Dettwiler & Associates Ltd., 963
Jasim, Saad, President, 826
Jasmin, Larouche, Directrice (par intérim), 1282
Jasmir, Basi, Regional Director, Human Resources, 1177
Jason, Kenney, Minister, Citizenship, Immigration, & Multicultura, 1132
Jason, Wood, Manager, Policy Development, 1145
Jason, Charron, Executive Director, Industrial Research Assistance, 1159
Jason, Pierosara, Key Accounts Manager, Rail Program, 1161
Jason, Tom, Acting Director, Operations & Special Projects, 1175
Jason, Gaetner, Regional Director, Finance & Administration, 1177
Jason, London, Compliance Manager, 1186
Jason, Krips, Assistant Deputy Minister, 1192
Jason, Lee, Co-Vice-Chair, 1205
Jason, McNeil, Policy Analyst, Aboriginal Relations, 1237
Jason, Doiron, Manager, Application Systems, 1237
Jason, Hollett, Acting Director, 1242
Jason, Aliqatuqtuq, Manager, South Baffin, 1247
Jason, Koivisto, Manager, Forestry Innovation & Market Development Section, 1258
Jason, Travers, Manager, Protection Section, 1258
Jason, Doiron, Chair, 1271
Jason, Nystrom, Manager, Traffic Board Secretariat, 1292
Jason, Wall, Manager, Saskatoon WDM, 1295
Jason A., Vanrobaeys, LUMDS Senior Land Resource Specialist, Landscape Integration Unit, 1119
Jason K., Cameron, Director General, Strategic Planning, 1131
Jasper, Marianna, Lawson Lundell LLP - Vancouver, 913
Javaid, Saqib, Director, 704
Javier A., Gracia-Garza, Director General, 1135
Jay, Parsons, Director, Aquaculture Science Branch, 1140
Jay, Paxton, Director, Communications, 1157
Jay, Ramotar, Deputy Minister, Public Security; Deputy Solicitor, 1192
Jay, Griffin, Director, Tax Policy, 1228
Jay J., Slemp, Chair, 1193
Jayne, Hinchliff-Milne, Director, Audit & Corporate Ethics; Chief Audit Ex, 1156
Jayne, Best, Manager, Marketing & Client Services Section, 1258
Jean, Claude, Tremblay Bois Mignault Lemay S.E.N.C.R.L., 945
Jean, Paré, Director, 723
Jean, Louis-Joseph, Directeur général, 750
Jean, Michel, Directeur général, 753
Jean, André, Directeur, Granby, 1348
Jean, Sylvie, Directrice, Saguenay, 1350
Jean, Goulet, Chief Audit Executive, 1130
Jean, Lauriault, Environmental Specialist, 1131
Jean, Langlais, Director, Biosphere, 1134
Jean, Picard, Manager, Aboriginal & Corporative Affairs, Strategic Integration & Partnerships, 1136
Jean, Landry, Director, Fish Population Science, 1140
Jean, Pruneau, Acting Executive Director, Office of Pharmaceuticals Management Strategies, 1146
Jean, Lafortune, Acting Vice-President, Engineering & Laboratory Services, 1154
Jean, Lebel, Director, Environmental & Natural Resource Management, 1156
Jean, St-Pierre, Chief, Security Service, 1156
Jean, Cooper, Director General, 1165
Jean, Vézina, Director General, Major Crown Projects, 1172
Jean, Tierney, Senior Director, Safety, Security, & Risk Manageme, 1179
Jean, Frieson, Chair, 1215
Jean, Finn, Deputy Minster, 1220
Jean, Fallis, Administrator, Long Term Care, East, 1272
Jean, Monfet, Directeur général, Finances municipales, 1276
Jean, Dionne, Directeur, 1276
Jean, Ouellet, Directeur, 1276
Jean, Ouellet, Directeur, 1276
Jean, Dionne, Directeur, 1276
Jean, Séguin, Sous-ministre adjoint, 1280
Jean, Belzile, Sous-ministre adjoint et directeur général (par in, Reserche Québec, 1280
Jean, Thibault, Directeur, Renovation cadastrale, 1281
Jean, Girard, Directeur, Calcul des possibilités forestiéres, 1281
Jean, Rodrigue, Sous-ministre adjoint, Services de santé et médecine universitaire, 1283
Jean, Audet, Vice-présidente, Relations avec les citoyens et les entreprises, 1284
Jean, Poirier, Directeur, Médiation-conciliation, prévention & arbitrage (Québec), 1286
Jean Guy, d'Entremont, Chair, 1140
Jean J., Gagnon, Chief, Data Management & Client Services Division, 1142
Jean L., Laporte, Chief Operating Officer, 1178
Jean-Bernard, Guignard, Manager, Financial Administration, 1220
Jean-Charles, Morin, Vice-président, Exploitation, Secteurs faunique et touristique, 1278
Jeanes, David, President, 861
Jeanette, Stead, Acting Director, Financial Planning, 1183
Jeanette, Espie, Executive Director, Office of Traffic Safety, 1196
Jean-François, Trépanier, Chief Executive Officer, 1156
Jean-François, Raymond, Directeur, Politique commerciale, 1279
Jean-François, Talbot, Directeur, 1280
Jean-François, Therrien, Directeur, Inspection, 1283
Jean-Guy, Leblanc, Director, Financial Services, 1223
Jean-Louis, Parent, Manager, Information Management, 1178
Jean-Marc, Lafrenière, Acting Director, Audit Operations Division, 1130
Jean-Marc, Comtois, Chief of the Astronauts, 1132
Jean-Marc, Dupuis, Deputy Minister, 1226
Jean-Marc, Tardiff, Directeur, Direction campus de la Pocatière, 1277
Jean-Marc, Lachance, Directeur, 1279
Jean-Marc, Sauvé, Sous-ministre adjoint, 1280
Jean-Marie, Beaulieu, Senior Science Advisor, 1132
Jean-Marie, Dionne, Directeur, 1279
Jean-Marie, Dionne, Directeur, 1279
Jeanne E., Inch, Director General, Canadian Conservation Institute & Chief Operating Officer, 1130
Jeannie, Smith, Chief of Staff, Office of the Minister of State (Science & Technology), 1153
Jeannie, Mathison, Director, 1237
Jeannie, Pitts, Manager, Labour Mobility, 1274
Jeannine, Auger, Directrice, Services médicaux généraux, 1283

Johnston, Anna, Acting Associate Dean: Libraries & Learning, Mohawk College of Applied Arts & Technology, 987
Johnston, Don, Senior Director, 702
Johnston, Karen, Manager, 761
Johnston, Heather, President, 726
Johnston, Lynne, Contact, 834
Johnston, Wesley, Director, 721
Johnston, Bill, President, 787
Johnston, Gord, President, 737
Johnston, John, Sec.-Treas., 789
Johnston, Lindsay, Circumpolar Librarian & Public Service Mgr, 692
Johnston, Cliff, Director, St. John's, 1324
Johnston, David, Director, Development Services, Brant, 1327
Johnston, Paul, Manager, Charlottetown, 1346
Johnston, C.E.T., John D., Director, Operations, Owen Sound, 1335
Johnstone, Betty A., Aikins, MacAulay & Thorvaldson LLP, 915
Johnstone, Heather, Chair, 751
Johnstone, Jacquie, Director, White Rock, 1319
Jolene, Head, Director, Lands & Environmental Operational Policy, 1118
Joli-Coeur, André, Joli-Coeur Lacasse Avocats - Québec, 944
Jolicoeur, Darquise, Partner, Beaudry, Bertrand, s.e.n.c.r.l., 938
Jolicoeur, Manon, Partner, Heenan Blaikie LLP - Montréal, 940
Jolicoeur, Marc, Regional Managing Partner, Borden Ladner Gervais LLP - Ottawa, 925
Jolicoeur, Catherine, Bibliothécaire responsable, CÉGEP du Vieux-Montréal, 1017
Jolicoeur, Pierre, Comptroller, 700
Jolicoeur, Elizabeth, General Manager, 680
Jolie, Gareis, Manager, Inuvik Research Centre, 1236
Joll, Kevin, Manager, Red Deer, 1308
Jolley, Don, Fire Chief, Pitt Meadows, 1316
Jollineau, Marilyn, President, 686
Joly, Linda, Commis bibliothèque, Université du Québec Institut national de la recherche scientifiq, 1025
Jon, Gee, Manager, Areas of Concern, Great Lakes Division, 1136
Jon, Gee, Manager, Environment Office, 1136
Jon, Chant, Manager, Writing & Editorial Services, 1200
Jon, Buckle, Acting Executive Project Director, Evergreen Line Project, 1212
Jon, Gunn, Director, Planning Policy & Programs, 1219
Jon, Bowen, Director, 1300
Jonathan, Will, Director General, 1165
Jonathan, Denis, Minister, Justice; Solicitor General, 1192
Jonathan, Downey, Manager, Knowledge Industries & Innovation, 1220
Jonathan, Kierstead, Director, Forestry, 1244
Jonathan, Norman, Director, Transmission & Distribution Policy, 1250
Jones, Ian C., Singleton Urquhart LLP, 914
Jones, Lindsay M., McDougall Gauley - Saskatoon, 947
Jones, Peter F.M., Paterson, MacDougall LLP, Barristers, Solicitors, 936
Jones, Charlene, Program & Service Manager, Red Deer College, 958
Jones, Wayne, Head, Technical Services, Queen's University, 988
Jones, Beth, Associate Director & Manager, 763
Jones, Twlya, Chair, 640
Jones, Wendy, Director, 838
Jones, Peter, Treasurer, 688
Jones, Dan, Region President, 706
Jones, Linda, Secretary-Treasurer, 707
Jones, Sarah, Vice-President, 791
Jones, Yolanda, Coordinator, 823
Jones, Lee Anne E., Vice-President, 826
Jones, Christopher, Vice-President, 739
Jones, Audra, Director, Edmonton, 1306
Jones, Brian, Director, Public Works Services, Newmarket, 1334
Jones, Dave, Police Chief, New Westminster, 1316
Jones, Harry, Fire Chief, Brockville, 1332
Jones, Lance, Streets Maintenance Supervisor, Charlottetown, 1346
Jones, Susan, General Manager, Emergency & Protective Services, Ottawa, 1335
Jones, BA LLB, Fred L., President & Chief Executive Officer, 767
Jongerden, Harry, Garden Director, 865
Jonn, Braman, Regional Manager, Environmental Protection, Lower Mainland Regional Office, 1203
Jonson, Derek, Partner, Ramsay Lampman Rhodes, 910
Jordan, Nicole, President, 780
Jordan K.M., Brown, Vice-Chair, 1268
Jorgensen, Sven E., President, 782
Jorgenson, Amanda, Executive Director, 854
Joseé, Garant, Directeur, Services administratifs, 1277
Josée, Lanctôt, Director, Forestry, Agriculture & Aquaculture, 1134
Josée, De Menezes, Acting Director, Sanitary & Phytosanitary Measures Division, 1143
Josée, Morency, Directeur, Technologies, 1281
Josée, Hallé, Directrice, Transport maritime, aérien et ferroviaire, 1285
Josée, Dupont, Directrice générale et directrice (par intérim), Contrats et ressources matérielles, 1285
Joseé L., Sabourin, Chief, Corporate Services, 1175
Joseph, Dion, Director, Rail, Air & Marine Disputes Directorate, 1132
Joseph, Lavoie, Director, Strategic Communications & New Media, 1143
Joseph, Comuzzi, Chair, 1156
Joseph, Templin, Director, Science & Technology (Air), 1158
Joseph, Szwalek, Acting Regional Director, Civil Aviation, 1177
Joseph, Kenny, Acting Engineering Group Leader, Northern Engineering Group, 1207
Joseph, Day, Director, Audit, Information, & Training, 1234
Joseph, Veloce, Manager, Aerospace & Materials Unit, 1249
Joseph, Odumeru, Director, 1252
Joseph, Carson, Director, Business Services Improvement, 1288
Josephine, Choi, Alberta China Office Managing Director, 1192
Josette, Chouinard, Directrice, Presonnes ayant une déficience, 1283
Josh, Pressey, District Manager, Nadina, 1206
Josh, Hourie, Manager, Corporate Development, 1295
Joshi, Sanjay, Partner, Norton Rose Fulbright Canada LLP - Toronto - Royal Bank Plaza, 935
Joshi, Deepak, Director, Winnipeg, 1321
Josy, Parrotta-Marck, Deputy Director, Regional Coordination & Correspon, 1120
Journault, Denyse, Directrice, Sainte-Julie, 1351
Jovanovic, D. Stephen, Bartlet & Richardes LLP, 937
Jowett, Ed, President, 707
Jowsey, Cathy, Regional Manager, 859
Joy, Jodi, Manager, 802
Joy, Kajiwara, Director, Community Nursing, 1301
Joy, Waters, Deputy Minister, 1302
Joyal, Gentiane, Dentons Canada LLP - Montreal, 939
Joyal, Colin, President, 857
Joyce, Erin, Contact, Library Services, Mills Memorial Library, 987
Joyce, Martha, Liasion and Instruction Librarian, Fanshawe College, 989
Joyce, Gordon, Senior Manager, Capital Regional District, 1310
Joyce, Percy, Officer, Corner Brook, 1324
Joyce, McDonald, Director, 1242
Joyce, Kirsch, Director, Operations, 1292
Joyce, Smith, Manager, North Battleford WDM, 1295
Juanita, Keel-Ryan, Director, Tourism Product Development, 1235
Juanita, Dobson, Assistant Deputy Minister, 1263
Juarez, Lorenzo, President, 871
Juárez, Manuel, Sec.-Treas., 709
Judd, Peter, General Manager, Vancouver, 1318
Judge, Ross, Counsel, Weiler, Maloney, Nelson, 928
Judi, Beck, Director, Forest Science, 1163
Judith, Hamel, Senior Economist, Economic Research & Liaison, 1136
Judith, St. George, Director General, Trade Commissioner Service Operations & Trade Strategy Bureau, 1143
Judith, Gadbois St-Cyr, Coordinator, Social Media, 1157
Judith, Esmail, Office Administrator, Calgary Office, 1196
Judith, Goucher, Chief Financial Officer, 1239
Judith, Ferguson, Deputy Minister, 1243
Judith, Voswinkel, Executive Assistant to the Deputy Minister, 1298
Judith A., Hearn, Deputy Minister, 1235
Judith C., Young, Executive Director, Strategic & Operational Planni, 1158
Judson, David, Partner, Miller Thomson LLP - Toronto, 934
Judy, Rutherford, Director, Management Services, 1175
Judy, Head, Chair, 1220
Judy, Cole, Manager, Communications, 1225
Judy, Cole, Director, Communications, 1226
Judy, Mclinton, Manager, Public Affairs & Communication, 1237
Judy, Tomarin, Acting Director, Organizational Performance, 1249
Judy, Tomarin, Acting Director, Organizational Performance, 1261
Judy, Burke, Tribunal Coordinator, 1268
Judy, May, Vice-President, Customer Services, 1296
Judy A., Adams, Manager, Forecasting, 1292
Juie, Philippe, Manager, ADM's Office, 1136
Jules, Boulanger, Directeur, 1279
Julia, Cropley, Manager, Marine Safety Executive Secretariat, 1176
Julia, Berardinucci, Director, Resource Management (South Coast), 1205
Julia, Mullaley, Deputy Minister, 1231
Julian, Fantino, Minister, International Cooperation, 1130
Julian C., Paine, Assistant Deputy Minister / Inspector of Municipal, 1201
Julie, Boyer, Executive Director, IPY 2012 Conference Secretariat, 1118
Julie, Leese, Executive Director, Grants & Contributions Delivery Project (GCDP), 1120
Julie, Grimard, Assistant Director, Industry Development Division, 1120
Julie, Carrière, Senior Advisor, Regulatory Innovation & Management Systems, 1134
Julie, Lalonde, Director, Conflict Management, 1135
Julie, Stewart, Director, Pacific Integrated Commercial Fisheries Initiative, 1140
Julie, Insley, Director & Senior Trade Commissioner, 1144
Julie, Vaillancourt, Sepcial Advisor to the Director General, 1154
Julie, Parker, Chief, Corporate Resourcing, 1155
Julie, Jansen, Director, Access to Information & Privacy, 1157
Julie, Guay, Innovation & Network Advisor, 1159
Julie, Carmichael, Director, Communications, Minister's Office, 1170
Julie, Gascon, Director, Domestic Vessel Regulatory Oversight, 1176
Julie, Toma, Associate General Manager, 1181
Julie, Toma, Associate General Manager, 1181
Julie, Mantle, Director, Human Resources, 1208
Julie, Spiteri, Executive Director, Organizational Development Team Office, 1210
Julie, Towers, Executive Director, 1244
Julie, Washburn, Acting Manager, Automotive Unit, 1250
Julie, Schroeder, Manager, Human Toxicology & Air Standards Section, 1252
Julie, Grignon, Directrice générale, Électricité, 1281
Julie, Blackburn, Secrétaire associé, 1286
Julien, Marc, Responsable, Campus de Charlesbourg, 1022
Julien, Arsenault, Directeur général, Arpentage et cadastre, 1281
Julien, Arsenault, Directeur (par intérim), Bureau de l'appenteur général du Québec, 1281
Julien, Cormier, Directeur, Opérations, 1284
Julius, Tarjan, Executive Director, Regional Operations & Support Services, 1223
June, Watterson, Chair, 1266
June, Bold, Chief Executive Officer, 1291
June, Cable, Chair, 1301
Jung, Jason, Manager, 651
Junkin, Belinda, President/CEO, 713
Justin, Riemer, Assistant Deputy Minister, 1185
Justin, Lake, Manager, Mineral Rights, 1233
Justine, Batten, Director, Archaeology Branch, 1205
Juteau, Nathalie, Présidente, 668
Jutras, Jacques, Secrétaire, Régie d'assainissement des eaux du Haut-Richelieu, 1356
Jutta, Paczulla, Director, Innovation Policy, 1175
Jóhannesson, Magnus, Director of the Secretariat, 652

K

Kaai, Wanjiku, Librarian, Public Services, Lakeland College, 958
Kaal, Lonnie, Director, Yorkton, 1360
Kaarsemaker, Neil, Director, 708
Kaemingh, Dale, Chair, 819
Kagan, Jamie A., Thompson Dorfman Sweatman LLP - Winnipeg, 917
Kagan, Rachel, Vice-President, 755
Kaili, Sermat-Harding, Director, Strategic Policy & Research, 1256

Kaiser, Miranda M., Chair, 646
Kakabadse, Yolanda, President, 874
Kakar, Shahaa, Coordinator, 852
Kal, Whitnell, Director, Trade & Economic Policy, 1273
Kaley E., MacDonald, Officer, Seafood Marketing, 1270
Kalmakoff, David, Hutchins Caron & Associés, 940
Kalvee, Debbie, Associate University Librarian, Services, Brock University, 999
Kambeitz, Darrell, Police Chief, Camrose, 1305
Kamelchuk, Dave, Treasurer, 638
Kamennof-Sine, Lana, Librarian, Kingstec Campus, 982
Kamenz, Kris, Director, 793
Kamenz, Marvin, Municipal Planner, Comox, 1314
Kami, Ramcharan, Director General, 1163
Kammerer, Joan, Resource Support Services, Allyn & Betty Taylor Library, 989
Kampitsch, Ronald E., Merchant Law Group LLP - Calgary, 905
Kampitsch, Ronald E., Merchant Law Group LLP - Edmonton, 908
Kanani, Karima, Partner, Miller Thomson LLP - Toronto, 934
Kanani, Zahida, Manager, 762
Kane, Mary Lynn, Managing Partner, Cox & Palmer - Summerside, 938
Kane, Tom, President, 816
Kane, Q.C., T. Gregory, Partner, Stikeman Elliott LLP - Ottawa, 926
Kane, QC, Mary Lynn, Managing Partner, Cox & Palmer - Alberton, 937
Kane, QC, Mary Lynn, Managing Partner, Cox & Palmer - Charlottetown, 938
Kane, QC, Mary Lynn, Managing Partner, Cox & Palmer - Montague, 938
Kane, QC, Mary Lynn, Managing Partner, Cox & Palmer - Morell, 938
Kaneshalingam, Mythili, Interim Librarian, Coordinator, Pembrook Campus, 997
Kanigan, Richard, President, 791
Kanigan, Richard, Chief Administrative Officer, Comox, 1314
Kanina, Blanchard, Director, Regional Office, 1253
Kantrowitz, Ted, Vice-President, 700
Kapa, Dubravka, Director, Georges P. Vanier Library, 1019
Kapac, Tom, Program Manager, 840
Kapesi-Miller, Kimberly M., Bennett Jones LLP - Calgary, 901
Kaplun, Rolf N., Partner, Davis LLP - Vancouver, 911
Kapsales, Tom, Partner, Cassels Brock & Blackwell LLP, 929
Kapur, Sandy, Vice-President, 719
Karami, Hisham, Director, 704
Karan, Aquino, Director, Aboriginal, 1258
Karayannides, George J., Partner, Heenan Blaikie LLP - Toronto, 931
Karch, Danny, Director, 859
Kardash, Adam, Partner, Heenan Blaikie LLP - Toronto, 931
Karen, Spierkel, Director, Communications & Marketing, 1130
Karen, Turcotte, Acting Director General, Corporate Management, 1135
Karen, Mailhiot, Director, Program Integration, 1135
Karen, Richardson, Program Manager, Environmental Information, 1138
Karen, Dodds, Executive Director, 1145
Karen, Lloyd, Director, Environmental Assessment Division, 1145
Karen, Lloyd, Director, Planning & Administrative Services, Safe Environments, 1145
Karen, Jackson, Senior Associate Deputy Minister, Human Resources, 1147
Karen, Corkery, Executive Director, Industrial Technologies Office, 1154
Karen, Corkery, Executive Director, Knowledge Infrastructure Progr, Science Partnerships Team, 1154
Karen, Ellis, Associate Deputy Minister, 1162
Karen, Swol, Director, Program Management, 1176
Karen, Young, Director, Sept-Îles Airport, 1178
Karen, Mustus, Officer, Oil & Gas, 1180
Karen, Erin, Senior Programs Manager, Programs Branch, 1182
Karen, Wronko, Director, Metro Regions & Small Business Support, 1186
Karen, Butkowski, Administrator, Rent Supplement Program, 1194
Karen, Murry, Manager, Media Relations, 1199
Karen, Diemert, Section Head, Ecosystems, Skeena Regional Office, 1204
Karen, Linfield, Manager, Pesticide Control Section, 1227
Karen, Taggart, Acting Manager, Tourism Operations, 1238
Karen, White, Director, 1242
Karen, McDuff, Director, 1243
Karen, Stone, Director, Communications, 1243
Karen, Kabloona, Director, Tourism & Cultural Industries, 1246
Karen, Clark, Manager, Regional Air Issues, 1252
Karen, Bellamy, District Manager, 1260
Karen, MacLeod, Vice-Chair, 1267
Karen, MacDonald, Director, Human Resources, 1272
Karen, Devine, Project Secretary, Administration & Building Servi, 1273
Karen, Allen, Executive Director, Corporate Services (Shared Services), 1293
Karen, Mason, Director, Finance & Information Services, 1298
Karen, Pelletier, Environmental Geologist, 1299
Karen, Clyde, Acting Manager, Habitat Programs, 1300
Karen, Archbell, Director, Quality & Risk Management, 1301
Karen E., Shepherd, Commissioner of Lobbying, 1178
Karen H., Murray, Supervisor, Social Assistance & Disability Support Programs (West), 1267
Karen L., Dodds, Assistant Deputy Minister, 1135
Karen L., Drake, Manager, Capital Grants Unit, 1263
Karg, Ludwig, Chair, 781
Kargut, Sigrid, AV Collection Librarian & Chair, Faculty Library, Kwantlen Polytechnic University, 964
Karie, Petz, Executive Assistant to the Director General, 1135
Kariel, Douglas, Head, Technical Services & Systems, Athabasca University, 949
Karim, Hirji, Vice-President, Project Development, 1200
Kariya, Paul, Executive Director, 730
Karkut, Neil N., McDougall Gauley - Regina, 947
Karl, Volkmar, Director, Operations, 1122
Karl K., Primmer, Director, Infrastructure Operations (Networks/Telephony), 1140
Karpluk, Les, Fire Chief, Prince Albert, 1359
Karrilyn, Vince, Director, Resource Authorizations (Northeast), 1206
Karst, Amanda, President, 714
Karsten, Tammie, Coordinator, Marketing, Farm Safety Association Inc., 985
Kary, Dale, Project Coordinator, Lacombe County, 1303
Kash, Ram, Director General, 1176
Kashmir, Gill, Director, West Edmonton, 1159
Kassa, Hamish, Co-ordinator, Columbia-Shuswap, 1311
Kassirer, Jay, President, 766
Katchur, Gale, Contact, Fort Saskatchewan, 1306
Kate, Butler, Director, Residential Sector, 1221
Kate, Marshall, Manager, Intake & Entitlement, 1275
Kate E., MacQuarrie, Director, 1266
Kate M., Fletcher, Regional Director, Civil Aviation, 1177
Katerina, Daniel, Director, Intergovernmental Affairs, 1141
Katerina, Daniel, Director, Atlantic & Americas Regional Affairs, 1141
Katerina, Anastasiadis, Information Officer, 1211
Kath, Shelley L., Fasken Martineau - Montréal, 939
Katharine, Trim, Director General, Communications, 1158
Katharine, Cox-Brown, Director, Audit & Evaluation, 1244
Katharine, Tummon, Registrar of Credit Unions, 1267
Katherine, Schultz, Chair, Advisory Board, 1158
Katherine, Lefeuvre, Director, Environmental Policy, 1222
Katherine, Mehl, Senior Manager, Game & Fur Management, 1228
Katherine, Chubbs, Vice President, Cancer Care & Chief Nursing Office, 1229
Katherine, Fraser, Director, Acute Care, 1243
Katherine, Hewson, Assistant Deputy Minister, 1250
Katherine, Schaefer, Contact, 1271
Katherine, Fitton, Manager, Moose Jaw WDM, 1295
Katherine E., Locke, Director, Parliamentary Affairs & Issues Managemen, 1143
Kathleen, Heppell-Masys, Director General, Safety Management, 1131
Kathleen, Roussel, Senior General Counsel & Executive Director, Legal Services, 1135
Kathleen, Fischer, Director General, Special Projects, 1140
Kathleen, Brière, Manager, Portfolio Management, 1159
Kathleen, LeClair, Chief Officer, 1193
Kathleen, Mitten, Coordinator, Administration & Reseach, 1211
Kathleen, Good Waite, Director, Human Resource Services, 1223
Kathleen, McFadden, Acting Assistant Deputy Minister, 1258
Kathleen, Dumont, Directrice (par intérim), Ressources humaines/Performance organisationnelle, 1276
Kathleen O., Wynne, Minister, 1248
Kathol, Neil, Partner, Field LLP - Calgary, 904
Kathol, Todd, Partner, Field LLP - Calgary, 904
Kathryn, Emmett, Executive Director, 1129
Kathryn, Keyes, Director, Strategic Communications, 1156
Kathryn, Coxson, Manager, Negotiation Support, Land Claims, 1180
Kathryn, Wood, Executive Director, Electricity Markets Branch, 1184
Kathryn, Fiess, Manager, Petroleum Geosciences, 1238
Kathy, Couturier, Deputy Director & Area Management Advisor, Area Management Office - Investment, Innovation & Sectors, 1143
Kathy, Telfer, Director, Communications, 1183
Kathy, Sendall, Vice-Chair, 1185
Kathy, Ness, Executive Director, Surveillance & Assessment, 1188
Kathy, Telfer, Director, Communications, 1189
Kathy, Ham-Rowbottom, Manager, Clients & Special Projects, 1200
Kathy, Eichenberger, Executive Director, Columbia River Treaty (CRT) Review Team, 1202
Kathy, Nguyen, President/Chief Executive Officer, 1208
Kathy, McPhail, Chief Executive Officer, 1217
Kathy, Malcolm, Administrative Assistant, 1221
Kathy, Densmore, Administrative Support, 1222
Kathy, Jones, Director, Public Health Programs, 1272
Kathy, Rintoul, Executive Director, Grant Administration & Financi, 1291
Kathy M., Haley, President, Air Rail Link, 1264
Katia, Jollez, Senior Communications Officer, 1160
Katia, Jollez, Senior Communication Officer, 1160
Katia, Jollez, Senior Communication Officer, 1161
Katie, Durling, Senior Policy Advisor, 1154
Katrina, Bluetchen, Acting Director, Communications, 1195
Katz, Perry, Partner, Miller Thomson LLP - Toronto, 934
Kaufman, Amy, Head, Law Library, William R. Lederman Law Library, 988
Kaufman, Rocky, President, 672
Kavanagh, Benjamin J., Benson Myles, 918
Kavanagh, Shawn M., Partner, Cox & Palmer - St. John's, 919
Kavanaugh, O.J., President, 832
Kay, Jim, General Manager, Hamilton Emergency Services, Hamilton, 1333
Kay, Kenny, Chair, 1195
Kay, Q.C., H. Martin, Counsel, Bennett Jones LLP - Calgary, 901
Kaye, Barbara, Manager, Canada Revenue Agency, 993
Kayes, Brian, Director, Brandon, 1320
Kayler, Grant, Librarian, John Alexander Weir Memorial Law Library, 954
Kazamer, Csaba, Clerk, Miramichi, 1322
Kazaz, Charles, Fasken Martineau - Montréal, 939
Kazaz, Charles, Partner, Fasken Martineau - Toronto, 930
Kean, Roni, Coordinator, 818
Keaney, P. Berk, Weaver, Simmons LLP, 927
Kearns, Stephanie A., Ratcliff & Company LLP, 910
Keeble, Ron, Registrar, 822
Keeley, Steve, Director, Public Works, Huntsville, 1333
Keen, Matthew, Osler, Hoskin & Harcourt LLP - Calgary, 905
Keenan, Patrick, Director, Planning, St. Thomas, 1337
Keene, George, City Manager, Airdrie, 1305
Keeping, Janet, Party Leader, 750
Keesing, Don, Administrative Coordinator, 813
Keesmaat, Jennifer, Executive Director, City Planning, & Chief Planner, Toronto, 1338
Kefalas, Dennis, Senior Administrative Officer, Yellowknife, 1325
Kehar, Raj, Davies Howe Partners LLP, 929
Kehler, Connie, Executive Director, 847
Keirstead, Robin, University Archivist, Western University Libraries, 990
Keith, John A., Partner, Cox & Palmer - Halifax, 921
Keith, Ward, President, 694
Keith, Paul, President, 719
Keith, Ross, Chair, 767
Keith, Ashfield, Minister, Fisheries & Oceans, 1139
Keith, Hendy, Director, Science & Technology (Maritime), 1158
Keith, Pink, Investigator & Advisor, 1180
Keith, Thomas, Director, Operations, 1206
Keith, Tudor, Manager, Timber Measurements, 1207
Keith, Finnie, Director, Communication Services, 1207
Keith, Callander, Director, Provincial Field Services, 1211
Keith, Holness, Supervisor, Statutory Publications, 1216
Keith, Lowdon, Director, Petroleum Branch, 1218
Keith, Melvin, Policy Advisor, 1220
Keith, McAlpine, Dean, New Brunswick College of Craft & Design, 1224

Khatter, Kapil, President, 688
Khaw, Michael, President, 648
Khayutin, Mila, Contact, Library Services, Mills Memorial Library, 987
Kheng-Lian, Koh, Director, 653
Khoraych, Mireille, Associate, Hicks Morley Hamilton Stewart Storie LLP - Toronto, 932
Kidd, Bob, President, 867
Kidd, May, World President, 654
Kidd, D., Manager, Port Moody, 1317
Kidd, Ron, Chair, Highway 43 East Waste Commission Services, 1309
Kiebuzinski, Ksenya, Head, PJRC & Slavic Resources Coordinator, Petro Jacyk Central & East European Resource Centre, 1006
Kiell, David, Executive Director, 789
Kielly, Carole, Manager, 663
Kieper, P.Ag., Richard, President, 793
Kierans, Kevin, Director, Thompson-Nicola, 1313
Kiernan, Thomas C., President, 801
Kieswetter, Murray, Manager, Parks Operations, Waterloo, 1338
Kilback, Keith D., Managing Partner, Kanuka Thuringer LLP, Barristers & Solicitors, 946
Kildy, Yuen, Senior Manager, Federal - Provincial Relations, 1194
Kilgour, Ian, Manager, Planning Services, North Bay, 1335
Killick-Dzenick, Cherisse N., Partner, Reynolds Mirth Richards & Farmer LLP, 909
Killins, Shawn, Chief Building Official, North Bay, 1335
Killoran, Maureen, Managing Partner, Osler, Hoskin & Harcourt LLP - Calgary, 905
Kilmury, Ron, Chair, 675
Kilty, Colleen, Manager, 707
Kim, Sooin, Faculty Services Librarian, Bora Laskin Law Library, 1001
Kim, Soohyun, Specialist, 864
Kim, Hibbeln, National Director, Enforcement Services, 1134
Kim, Colavecchia, Community Program Officer, Strategic Integration & Partnerships, 1136
Kim, Laforge, Office & Facility Coordinator, Corporate Services, 1161
Kim, Fauteux, Communications Officer, 1161
Kim, Benjamin, Director, Road Safety Programs, 1176
Kim, Hogan, Regional Director, Communications, 1178
Kim, Durdle, Director, Transport Engineering, 1196
Kim, Henderson, Deputy Minister, Citizens' Services & Open Governm, 1199
Kim, Benson, Chair, 1200
Kim, Pilotte, Manager, Warehousing & Fleet, 1207
Kim, Philip, Director/Manager, Office of Drinking Water, 1215
Kim, Hughes, Director, Strategic Planning & Policy Development, 1222
Kim, Matthews, Director, Marketing, 1225
Kim, Daley, Assistant Deputy Minister, Corporate Services & FI, 1226
Kim, Dunphy, Assistant Deputy Minister, 1234
Kim, Weir, Comptroller, Finance, 1237
Kim, Schofield, Director, Finance, 1238
Kim, Warren, Vice-President, Operations, 1255
Kim, Groenendyk, District Manager, 1259
Kim, Lambert, Director, Service Delivery Partnerships, 1264
Kim, Devine, Officer, Communications, 1269
Kim, Gill, Aquaculture Biologist, 1270
Kim, Klein, Rural Plan Officer, 1270
Kim, Lonsdale, Director, Resources, 1288
Kim, Clark, Director, Client Service, 1290
Kim D., Horrelt, Director, 1275
Kimber, Jeanne, Group Leader, Information Centre, EnCana Corporation, 950
Kimberley, Aselstine, Director, Human Resources, 1244
Kimberly, Leach, Principal, Sustainable Development Strategies, Aud, 1124
Kimberly, Empey, Vice-President, Operations Branch, 1145
Kimberly, Ellard, Manager & Senior Policy Advisor, Intergovernmental Affairs & Accessibility, 1174
Kimberly, Lebritton, Manager, Financial Administration & Space Manageme, 1226
Kimberly, Spencer, Director, Human Resources, 1234
Kimberly, MacNeil, Director, 1242
Kimmel, Terry, Vice-President, 702
Kimnach, Kim, Executive Director, 649
Kinar, Karen, Treasurer, 766
Kinch, Blair, Sr. Superintendent, Charlottetown, 1346
Kinchlea, Richard, Director, 691
Kindred, P.Eng., FEC, Patti, Director, 665
Kindy, Joseph, Director, Seniors Supplementary Supports Branch, 1189
King, Bruce H., Pitblado LLP, 916
King, Derek J., Partner, Brownlee LLP - Calgary, 902
King, Jay, Partner, Cassels Brock & Blackwell LLP, 929
King, Richard J., Partner, Norton Rose Fulbright Canada LLP - Toronto - Royal Bank Plaza, 935
King, Barbara, Library Technician, D.S.B. Fowlow Bldg., College of the North Atlantic, 979
King, Jean, Head, Acquisitions Unit, Health Canada, 995
King, Patricia, General Manager, 754
King, Carl, Councilor, 836
King, Catherine, Manager, 698
King, Peter, Executive Director, 716
King, Bruce, 1st National Vice President, 772
King, Peter, Executive Director, 647
King, Shelley, Secretary, 652
King, Bill, Manager, Planning Services, Essex, 1328
King, Geraldine, Manager, St. John's, 1324
King, John, Manager, Lethbridge, 1307
King, Robin, Transportation Engineer, St. John's, 1324
King, Q.C., Roger B., Campbell Marr, 916
Kinghan, Robert P., Partner, Perley-Robertson, Hill & McDougall LLP / s.r.l., 926
Kingsmill, Terry, Registrar, 819
Kingston, Brad, Chair, 791
Kingston, Joan, Director, 728
Kinnaird, Helga, Manager, Technology & Curriculum Innovation Operat, Northern Alberta Institute of Technology, 955
Kinsey, Steve, Fire Chief, Kelowna, 1315
Kirby, C.W. Daniel, Partner, Osler, Hoskin & Harcourt LLP - Toronto, 935
Kirby, Sarah M., McInnes Cooper - Halifax, 921
Kirby, Heather, Manager, 763
Kirby, Jang, Director, Investigations, Rail/Pipeline, 1178
Kirchner, Matthew F., Partner, Ratcliff & Company LLP, 910
Kirk, Mike, Deputy Chief Administrative Officer, Richmond, 1317
Kirk, Walstedt, Chair, 1248
Kirkpatrick, Paul, Fleet Foreman, Quispamsis, 1322
Kirkwood, Bonnie, Administrative Assistant, 867
Kirsh, Harvey, Counsel, Glaholt LLP, 931
Kirsh, Harvey, Senior Partner, Osler, Hoskin & Harcourt LLP - Toronto, 935
Kirsten, Pedersen, Regional Director, Northern Region, 1212
Kirsten, Lindgreen, Senior Technical Specialist, Drive Clean Facility Operations Section, 1252
Kirsten, Watson, Acting Director, Dispute Resolution Services, 1257
Kirsty, Piquette, Executive Director, Industry Development, 1185
Kiru, Tony, Partner, Heenan Blaikie LLP - Toronto, 931
Kirwin, Mark M., Kirwin LLP, 908
Kiselbach, Daniel L., Partner, Miller Thomson LLP - Vancouver, 914
Kissinger, S.A., 791
Kissner, Bob, Fire Chief, Kingsville, 1334
Kitamura, Yutaka, Secretary, 776
Kitchen, Hugh, Vice President, 874
Klassen, Krista, Associate, D'Arcy & Deacon LLP - Winnipeg, 916
Klassen, Peter W., Crease Harman & Company, 915
Klassen, Gary, General Manager, Edmonton, 1306
Klassen, Merlin, Fire Chief, Wetaskiwin, 1308
Klauwers, Tony, General Manager, Medicine Hat, 1307
Kleb, Heather, Acting President & Chief Executive Officer, 711
Klein, Annette, Director, Vancouver, 1318
Klie, John, Fire Chief, Terrace, 1318
Knight, Anthony H.S., McMillan LLP - Vancouver, 914
Knight, Mel, President, 800
Knight, Wade, Executive Director, 827
Knight, Bob, Director, Health & Social Services, Kawartha Lakes, 1333
Knoss, Calvin, President, 848
Knowler, Sandra M., McMillan LLP - Vancouver, 914
Knox, D. Anthony, McCarthy Tétrault LLP - Vancouver, 913
Knox, John, Vice-President, 708
Knox, John, Executive Director, 742
Knox, Brian, County Engineer, Bruce, 1328
Knox, Q.C., Andrew C., O'Connor MacLeod Hanna LLP, 925
Knutson, P.C., Gar, Borden Ladner Gervais LLP - Ottawa, 925
Ko, Patty P., Associate, Bishop & McKenzie LLP, 906
Kochan, Don, Director, Canmore, 1306
Kodousek, Nancy, Director, Water Services, Waterloo, 1331
Koe, Ed, President, 855
Koehler, Marlaine, Executive Director, Waterfront Regeneration Trust, 1009
Koenig, Shirley, Manager, Vernon, 1318
Koepke, Jocelyne, Manager, 693
Kogi, Kazutaka, President, 777
Kohnert, Nicole, Regional Manager, North Okanagan, 1312
Kokiw, Michael, Executive Director, Yukon Chamber of Mines, 1034
Kokoszka, Monika, Coordinator, 744
Kolaitis, Gerry, VP Finance/Treasurer, 722
Kolesniak, Greg, Director, 678
Koller, Hermann, Managing Director, 784
Kolstad, Randy, President, 706
Kolybabi, Deanie, Executive Director, 742
Komanchuk, John, Commissioner, Medicine Hat, 1307
Kompter, Gerhard, Interim President, 727
Kondro, J. Trina, Partner, Ackroyd LLP Barristers & Solicitors, 906
Konge, Niels, Vice-President, 811
Konkle, Wynnie, Contact, 839
Kooistra, Jennifer, Treasurer, 790
Koopmans, Sim, Treasurer, 832
Koostachin, Katherine, Associate, Willms & Shier Environmental Lawyers LLP, 937
Kopach, Chad, Blaney McMurtry LLP, 928
Kopan, Marsha, Secretariat, 782
Kopp, Joyce, Agent, Thompson, 1321
Kopp, Murray, Director, Central Okanagan, 1311
Kopp, Tony, Manager, Vernon, 1318
Koppe, Maxine, Executive Director, 809
Kopperson, Brent, Executive Director, 870
Korell, Alan, Managing Director, Engineering, Environmental & Wo, North Bay, 1334
Koropatnick, P.Eng., Grant, Executive Director & Registrar, 664
Korosis, Harry, Chown, Cairns LLP, 927
Korossy, Marika, Librarian, Surrey Place Centre, 1007
Kort, Kees, Partner, Hicks Morley Hamilton Stewart Storie LLP - Kingston, 923
Kortright, Bob, President, 860
Kosak, Alvin R., Partner, Brownlee LLP - Edmonton, 907
Koscak, Brian, Partner, Cassels Brock & Blackwell LLP, 929
Koslowsky, Ron, Vice-President, 708
Kosmidis, Elizabeth, Associate, Hicks Morley Hamilton Stewart Storie LLP - Toronto, 932
Kosolowski, John A., Partner, Duncan Craig LLP - Edmonton, 907
Kosten, April, Stikeman Elliott LLP - Calgary, 905
Kosterman, Robert, Chief, Spruce Grove, 1308
Kostic, Kosta, Partner, Heenan Blaikie LLP - Montréal, 940
Kotak, Brian, General Manager, 793
Kotkas, Alex, Partner, Fasken Martineau - Calgary, 903
Kott, Olivier F., Senior Partner, Norton Rose Fulbright Canada LLP - Montréal, 942
Koughan, William S., Partner, Russell, Christie LLP, 925
Koul, Krishna P., Bennett Jones LLP - Calgary, 901
Koutoulakis, Tom, Partner, Cassels Brock & Blackwell LLP, 929
Koutroubis, Jim, Director, Engineering Services, Newmarket, 1334
Kovach, M. Janine, Partner, Cassels Brock & Blackwell LLP, 929
Kovacs-Reid, Melissa, Coordinator, Waste Management, Dufferin, 1328
Kovats, Ava, Sr. Finance Officer, 756
Koversky, Wayne, Director, Thompson, 1321
Kovich, Tammy, Coordinator, 823
Kowal, Robert, Chair, 704
Kowbel, Christine J., Lawson Lundell LLP - Vancouver, 913
Kozak, QC, Fred, Partner, Reynolds Mirth Richards & Farmer LLP, 909
Kraag, Scott, Torys LLP - Toronto, 936
Kraenzle, Christina, Director, Canadian Centre for German & European Studies, 1001
Kraft, Kenneth David, Partner, Heenan Blaikie LLP - Toronto, 931
Kraft, Patti, Director, Human Resources, Peterborough, 1330
Kramar, Lev, Bennett Jones LLP - Calgary, 901
Kramer, Charlene, Librarian, SaskTel, 1032
Krannitz, Pam, Canadian Board Member, 854
Krause, Dietmar, Chairperson, 723
Krauss, Lindsay, Davis LLP - Toronto, 930
Krauss, Angela, Executive Director, 848
Kregel, Charlie, Chief Librarian, Powell River, 1317
Krejci, David, Executive Vice-President, 762

L

Landry, Isabelle, Heenan Blaikie S.E.N.C.R.L./SRL - Québec, 944
Landry, P. John, Partner, Davis LLP - Vancouver, 911
Landry, Cédric, Conseiller en documentation, Campus de Shippagan, 975
Landry, Nicole, Technicienne en documentation, Services techniques, CÉGEP de Drummondville, 1012
Landry, Paul, President/CEO, 723
Landry, Pierre, President, 804
Landry, Daniel, Secretary, 694
Landry, Alain, General Manager, 810
Landry, Anna, Director, Human Resources, Muskoka, 1329
Landry, Maurice, Manager, Brooks, 1305
Lane, Christopher J., Partner, McLennan Ross LLP - Edmonton, 908
Lane, Cynthia, Director, 650
Lane, Jill, Manager, 637
Lane, Neil G., Executive Director, 832
Lane, Tom, Director, 710
Lane, John, Fire Chief, Prince George, 1317
Lane, Pineau, Manager, Administration Services, 1269
Lanea, Harris, Coordinator, Renal Program, 1272
Lang, F. Stuart, Alexander Holburn Beaudin & Lang, LLP, 910
Lang, Peter, General Manager, 869
Langian, Mark, President, 670
Langille, Donna, Manager, 812
Langille, Robin, President, 811
Langlais, Michel, Tremblay Bois Mignault Lemay S.E.N.C.R.L., 945
Langlands, Sandra, Director, Gerstein Science Information Centre, 1003
Langley, Charles H., Secretary-General, 779
Langlois, Pierre, Partner, Heenan Blaikie LLP - Montréal, 940
Langlois, Bruno, Responsable, Analyste information, Université du Québec à Rimouski, 1026
Langlois, Alain, Directeur général, 666
Langois, Terry, Co-ordinator, Columbia-Shuswap, 1311
Languedoc, Geoff, Executive Director, 682
Lanigan, Carrie, Librarian, Brockville Campus, 984
Lanny, Der, Director, Aboriginal Economic Partnerships, 1180
Lanouette, Noël, Directeur, Rouyn-Noranda, 1350
Lansbergen, Paul, Director, 756
Lantagne, Réjean, Directeur général, 853
Lanthier, Clément, President & CEO, 680
Lantuit, Hugues, International Secretariat, 781
Lapham, Robert, General Manager, Capital Regional District, 1310
Lapierre, Denis, Lalonde Geraghty Riendeau Lapierre Avocats, 945
Lapierre, Mireille, Bibliothécaire, Bibliothèque des sciences de la santé, 1029
Lapierre, Rhona, Corporate Librarian, Manitoba Hydro, 971
Lapierrière, Marc, Bélanger, Sauvé, 939
Laplante, Maurice, Cain Lamarre Casgrain Wells - Drummondville, 938
Laplante, Michaël, Sylvain Parent Gobeil Simard S.E.N.C.R.L., 945
Laplante, Debbie, Head, Information Management, Canadian Heritage, 1013
Laplante, Élise, Technicienne en documentation, CÉGEP de Granby, 1013
Laplante, Mario, Directeur général adjointé, 841
Laplume, John A., CEO, 741
Lapointe, Julie, Cain Lamarre Casgrain Wells - Sept-Iles, 945
Lapointe, Manon, Service du prêt, Université du Québec en Abitibi-Témiscamingue, 1026
Lapointe, Pierre, Directeur général, 667
Lapointe, ing., Martin, Vice-président, 827
Laporte, Manon, Présidente-directrice générale, 747
Lappan, Phillip, Chief Building Official, Quinte West, 1336
Lappin, Barry, President, 702
Laprise, Lucie, Responsable, Acquisition et périodique, Université du Québec en Abitibi-Témiscamingue, 1026
Laprise, Lucie, Responsable, acquisitions/périodique, CÉGEP de l'Abitibi-Témiscamingue, 1026
Lara, McClelland, Director, Divisional Coordination Branch, 1191
Laraine, Poole, Officer, Health Promotion & Chronic Disease Preven, 1271
Lardjane, Mahmoud, Manager, 718
Larkin, Bill, Director, Winnipeg, 1321
Larmand, Andrew J., Martin Sheppard Fraser LLP - Niagara Falls, 924
Larner, Caren, Librarian, E.I. duPont Canada Company, 990
Laroche, Jacques, Président-directeur général, 655
Laroche, Ben, President, 739
Larochelle, Daniel, Responsable de la bibliothèque, École des pêches et de l'aquaculture du Québec, 1013
Larochelle, Denis, Directeur, Salaberry-de-Valleyfield, 1351
Larocque, Reno, Serials Assistant, Portage College, 957
Larocque, Dave, President, 810
Larocque, Nicole, Administrative Assistant, 683
Larocque, Claude, Directeur, Shawinigan, 1351
Laroque, Colin, President, 686
Larose, Diane, Bélanger, Sauvé, 939
Larose, Denis, Directeur, Repentigny, 1349
Larouche, Marguerite, Vice-président, 730
Larrivée, Nelson, Joli-Coeur Lacasse Avocats - Québec, 944
Larrivée, Pierre, Partner, Heenan Blaikie S.E.N.C.R.L./SRL - Québec, 944
Larry, Nentwig, Chief Financial Officer, 1119
Larry, Maio, Facility Manager, Kamloops Range Research Unit, 1122
Larry, McMillan, Manager, Farm, 1122
Larry, Surtees, Corporate Secretary, 1157
Larry, Ziegenhagel, Branch Head, Business Design & Evaluation, 1184
Larry, McGuinness, Branch Head, Compliance & Assurance, 1184
Larry, Jones, Director, Resource Information Section, 1202
Larry, Barr, Director, Resource Management (West Coast), 1205
Larry, Blain, Chair, 1208
Larry, Felt, Chair, 1229
Larry, Alteen, Provincial Director, Physician Services, 1230
Larry, Weatherbie, Director, Fisheries Adjustment & Economic Diversification, 1230
Larry, Nolan, Senior Geologist & Section Manager, Geoscience Data Management, 1233
Larry, Cahill, Chief Operating Officer, 1234
Larry, Skinner, Chair, 1248
Larry, Moore, Chief Executive Officer, 1251
Larry, Avery, Project Manager, Public Safety Radio, 1268
Larry, Phelan, Manager, Facilities & Procurement, 1275
Larry, Young, Director, Operations, Northern Region, 1293
Larry A., Braul, Manager, Water & Wastewater Technologies, Development, 1121
Larry P., Hildebrand, Manager, Sustainable Communities & Ecosystems, ATL Head - Integrated Ecosystem & Public Engagement Programs, 1136
Larry S., Ostola, Director General, National Historic Sites, 1166
Larson, Scott N., Associate, Gilbert McGloan Gillis, 918
Larson, Roger L., President, 698
Larue, Marie, Présidente/Directrice générale, 771
Lash, Jonathan, President, 873
Lashuk, PAg, Lynn, President, 636
Last, Iva, Executive Director, 794
Latchford, Shea-Lea, Administrative Assistant, 820
Latimer, QC, Kevin, Managing Partner, Cox & Palmer - Halifax, 921
Latko, Mary Ann, Director, 646
Latraverse, Pierre, Président, 753
Latta, Bud, Treasurer, 857
Latter, Rob, Chair, 693
Latyszewskyj, Maria, Head, Library Services, Environment Canada Library, Downsview, 1002
Lau, P. Eng., Sam, Acting Manager, Surrey, 1318
Launa, Lebeau, Director, Learner Funding, 1185
Laura, Collier, Senior Manager, Canada Business Network Operations, 1126
Laura, Richards, Regional Director, Science Branch, 1141
Laura, Richards, Regional Director, Science Branch, 1142
Laura, Oleson, Director, Demand Policy & Analysis, 1165
Laura, Ruzzier, Chief, Audit & Evaluation Executive, 1173
Laura, Alcock, Director, Family Support for Children with Disabil, 1190
Laura, Poffenroth, Analyst, 1219
Laura, Seddon, Director, 1237
Laura, MacKenzie, Director, Community Operations, Kivalliq, 1246
Laura, Formusa, President & Chief Executive Officer, 1255
Laura, Steeves, Communications Officer, 1267
Laura Lee, Langley, Deputy Minister, 1241
Lauran, Chittim, Manager, Medical & Surgical Benefits, 1188
Laureen E., Kinney, Associate Assistant Deputy Minister, 1175
Laurel, Herwig, Executive Director, Strategic Communication, 1129
Laurel, Welsh, Executive Director, Finance & Administration, 1289
Laurent, Pellerin, Chair, 1119
Laurent, Pellerin, Chair, 1138
Laurent, Busque, Chef de chantier, Centrale la Sarcelle, 1280
Laurent F., Caron, Chief Human Resources Officer, 1179
Laurie, Dave, Director, Public Works, Huron, 1329
Laurie, Buckland, Polar Research Analyst, 1132
Laurie, Collette, Regional Director, 1221
Laurie, Robichaud, Director, Information & Technology Management, 1221
Laurier, Donais, Executive Director, Central Services, 1293
Laurier, Schramm, President/Chief Executive Officer, 1296
Laurin, Pierre, Tremblay Bois Mignault Lemay S.E.N.C.R.L., 945
Laurin, Jean-Michel, Vice-President, 708
Laustrup, Karen, Manager, Port Coquitlam, 1317
Lautenbach, Bill, General Manager, Growth & Development, Greater Sudbury / Grand Sudbury, 1333
Lauzon, Johanne, Bibliothécaire & Chef d'équipe, Commission de la santé et de la securité du travail, 1018
Lauzon, Jules, Regional Director, 692
Lauzon, Hélène, Présidente, 735
Lauzone, Marie-Christine, Heenan Blaikie LLP - Montréal, 940
Laval, Poulin, Directeur, Politiques commerciales et intergouvernementales, 1277
LaVallee, Gene, Treasurer, 638
Lavallée, Chantal, Associée, Cain Lamarre Casgrain Wells - Saguenay, 938
Lavallée, Myriam, Heenan Blaikie S.E.N.C.R.L/SRL - Trois-Rivières, 946
Lavallée, Alexandra, Responsable, CÉGEP Limoilou, 1022
Lavallée, Lise, Adjointe, Bibliothèque, Centre de recherche et de développement en horticulture, 1027
Laverdière, Philippe, Sylvestre & Associés Avocats S.E.N.C., 945
Laverdure, Paul, Director, Library & Archives, University of Sudbury, 1000
Lavergne, F. Albert X., Partner, Reynolds Mirth Richards & Farmer LLP, 909
Laverick, Jennifer, Kay McVey Smith & Carlstrom LLP - Grande Prairie, 909
Lavers, John W., Partner, Ottenheimer Baker, 919
Laverty, Cory, Acting Head, Reference, Queen's University, 988
Lavictoire, Suzanne, Director, 723
Lavoie, Manon, Joli-Coeur Lacasse Avocats - Montréal, 940
Lavoie, Suzanne, Adjointe administrative, 655
Lavoie, Marc, President, 701
Lavoie, Louise, Directrice, Gatineau, 1347
Lavoie, Gildard, Président, Commission de gestion enviro ressources du Nord-Ouest (COGERNO), 1323
Law, Daniel R., Partner, Fasken Martineau - Toronto, 930
Law, Margaret, Associate Director Libraries, Cameron Science & Technology Library, 954
Law, John, President, 861
Lawless, Justin, Coordinator, 834
Lawrence, Elizabeth, Director, St. John's, 1324
Lawrence, Hanson, Director General, Strategic Policy Directorate, 1136
Lawrence, Dickson, Director, Geological Survey Division, 1233
Laws, James M., Executive Director, 709
Lawson, Tim, Partner, Heenan Blaikie LLP - Toronto, 931
Lawson, Steve, Coordinator, 754
Lawson, Jennifer, Executive Assistant, 805
Lawson, Carol, 635
Lawson, Andrea, Administrator, Human Resources, Wellington, 1331
Lawton, Catherine, Librarian, Fisheries & Marine Institute, 977
Lawton, Jane, CEO, 787
Lawton, Jane, Executive Director, 787
Laycock, Anthony, Executive Director, 871
Laycraft, Dennis, Executive Director, 691
Laycraft, Q.C., James B., Founding Partner, Wilson Laycraft, 906
Layzell, Rick, Chair, 801
Lazar, Avrim, President & Chief Executive Officer, 755
Lazarnko, David, President, 683
Lazea, Ioana, Manager, 725
Lazier, Kate, Partner, Miller Thomson LLP - Toronto, 934
Lazure, Mario, Directeur général, Sorel-Tracy, 1351
Leah, Canning, Director, Policy, 1144
Leah, Brisco, Public Services Development Librarian, New Brunswi, 1224
Leah, Essensa, Director, Property Management, 1226
Leamen, Paull N., Soloway, Wright LLP - Ottawa, 926
Lean, Q.C., Ralph E., Partner, Cassels Brock & Blackwell LLP, 929

Leanne, Thera, Executive Director, Policy, Planning, & Evaluation, 1296
Leape, James P., Director General, 874
Leard, Jeffrey H., Partner, Cox & Palmer - Summerside, 938
Leard, Neal L.D., Partner, Stewart McKelvey - Saint John, 918
Leary, Kelvin, Chair, 694
Leask, W.C., Executive Vice-President, 717
Leathers, Mike, Vice President, 816
Leavitt, Beverly J., President & CEO, 681
Lebeau, Marvin, Chair, 686
LeBel, Louis, President, 859
Lebel, Carol, Executive Director, 748
Lebel, PMP, Daniel, Président, 827
LeBlanc, George H., Partner, Cox & Palmer - Moncton, 917
LeBlanc, Karine, Associate, Stewart McKelvey - Moncton, 917
LeBlanc, Fred, President, 822
LeBlanc, Kim, Secretary, 673
LeBlanc, Charles, Fire Chief, Dieppe, 1322
LeBlanc, Isabelle, Director, Dieppe, 1322
LeBlanc, Jacques, Director, Dieppe, 1322
LeBlanc, Elphège, Sec.-Trés., Responsable de l'alimentation en eau p, Régie intermunicipale d'approvisionnement en eau potable de l'île, 1357
Leblanc, Carole, Agente de bureau, Comptoir de prêt, CÉGEP St-Jean-sur-Richelieu, 1027
Leblanc, Diane, Agente de bureau, Campus de Carleton-sur-mer, 1012
Leblanc, Nadine, Technicienne en documentation, Institut maritime du Québec, 1025
Leblanc, Pierre, Specialist, Cartographic & GIS Support, Geographic, Statistical & Government Information Centre, 995
Leblanc, Rachelle, Technicienne en documentation, Service des documen, CÉGEP de Drummondville, 1012
Leblanc, Daniel, Directeur, Beauharnois, 1347
Leblanc, Neil, Chair, Kent County Solid Waste Commission, 1323
LeBlanc-Comeau, Réjeanne, Acquisitions, Université Sainte-Anne, 980
LeBlond, Isidore J., CEO, 694
LeBlond, Q.C., Charles, Stewart McKelvey - Moncton, 917
Lebo, Q.C., James L., Partner, McLennan Ross LLP - Calgary, 905
Leboeuf, Marie-Josée, Chef de service, Prêt et traitement des collection, Bibliothèque des sciences de la santé, 1016
LeBourdais, Maureen, Regional Manager & Sr. Program Manager, 757
Lebrun, Gilles, Contact, 866
Lebrun, Mario, Directeur général, 672
Lebrun-Ginn, Lucie, Office Administrator, 705
LeCain, Peter, Associate, Cox & Palmer - Halifax, 921
Lechner, Bill, President, 710
Leckie, Peter, City Solicitor, North Bay, 1335
Leclair, Ginette, Directrice, Ressources matérielles, CÉGEP d'André-Laurendeau, 1014
Leclair-Ghosh, Amar, Partner, Norton Rose Fulbright Canada LLP - Montréal, 942
Leclerc, Liette, Responsable, Traitement documentaire, Université du Québec en Abitibi-Témiscamingue, 1026
Leclerc, Marc, Coordonnateur, CÉGEP de Saint-Hyacinthe, 1027
Leclerc, Patrick, Director, 723
Lecompte, Claire, Bibliothécaire responsable, Bibliothèque de droit et publications gouvernementales, 1029
Ledingham, G. Brett, McDougall Gauley - Regina, 947
Ledi-Thom, Arlene, Vice-President, 766
Leduc, Pierre-Yves, Associé, Stikeman Elliott LLP - Montréal, 943
Leduc, Marc, Fire Chief, Greater Sudbury / Grand Sudbury, 1333
Ledwon, P.Geo., Anatasia, Chair, 664
Lee, Andrea, Partner, Glaholt LLP, 931
Lee, Lora H., Associate, Bishop & McKenzie LLP, 906
Lee, Raelene L., Partner, Ottenheimer Baker, 919
Lee, Serena, SimpsonWigle LAW LLP, 923
Lee, Diana, Librarian, Harriet Tubman Resource Centre, 1003
Lee, Don K., President, 785
Lee, Jack, President, 737
Lee, Eric, Senior Director, 693
Lee, Stephen, Region President, 706
Lee, Norman, Director, Waste Management, Peel, 1330
Lee, P., Director, Planning Policy, Richmond Hill, 1336
Lee, Kruszewski, Executive Director, 1185
Lee, Funke, Managing Director, 1194
Lee, Doney, Chair, 1200
Lee, Valentine, Executive Coordinator, 1200
Lee, Thompson, Director, 1240
Lee, Auten, Director, Regional Services, 1286
Lee, Smith, Director, Air Ambulance Services, 1287
Lee, Moyse, Manager, Contracts, 1291
Lee, BSc.,B.A.,M.A.,LL.B., Michael L., Partner, Lawson Lundell LLP - Vancouver, 913
Leech, Robin, Executive Director, 642
Leech, AScT, CAE, John E., Executive Director, 651
Leeman, Ed, Secretary, 673
Leeney, Peter, President, 679
Leenhouts, Pieter, President, 827
Leese, Dave, Contact, 789
Leeson, Jon, Region President, 706
Lefaivre, Thérèse, Director, Community Services, Clarence-Rockland, 1332
Lefebre, Michelle, Secretary, 637
Lefebvre, Denis, Davis LLP - Edmonton, 907
Lefebvre, Madeleine, Chief Librarian, Ryerson University, 1007
Lefebvre, Kellie, Coordinator, 846
Lefebvre, François, Président, 854
Lefler, Leaf, Contact, 753
Lefrançois, Guy, Bibliothécaire/Directeur, Campus d'Edmundston, 973
Lefton, Jay A., Senior Partner, Norton Rose Fulbright Canada LLP - Toronto - Royal Bank Plaza, 935
Legault, Francine, Partner, Heenan Blaikie LLP - Montréal, 940
Legault, Pierre, Gowling Lafleur Henderson S.E.N.C.R.L./LLP, 939
Legault, Gilles, Chair, 728
Legault, Angie, Manager, Sunshine Coast, 1313
Legault, David, Directeur, Repentigny, 1349
Legault, Jacques, Agent de liaison, Régie d'assainissement des Coteaux, 1356
Legé, Christine, Stikeman Elliott LLP - Montréal, 943
Léger, M.Sc., MLIS, Lori W., Manager of Library Services, Horizon Health Network, 975
Leger, QC, Franklin O., Counsel, Cox & Palmer - Saint John, 918
Legge, John A., Partner, Heenan Blaikie LLP - Vancouver, 912
Leggieri, Dan, Manager, 698
Leggott, Mark, University Librarian, University of Prince Edward Island, 1011
Lehoux, Marc-André, Directeur, Saint-Basile-le-Grand, 1350
Leibel, Carmen, Regional Vice President, 803
Leidekker, Erik, Manager, Chilliwack, 1314
Leigh, Tamara, Vice-President, 697
Leigh, Mazany, Director, Environmental Policy Analysis & Evaluation, 1174
Leigh, Puddester, Chair & Chief Executive Officer, 1227
Leighton, Catherine, Coordinator, 840
Leipnitz, Lori, Director, Cochrane, 1306
Leising, Ken, Manager Rate Research/Development, 757
Leisk, Signe, Partner, Cassels Brock & Blackwell LLP, 929
Leiske, Ryan, President, 830
Leitch, Frederick E., Thoman Soule LLP, Lawyers, 923
Leitold, Daina, Tour Manager, 763
LeLievre, Conrad, President, 648
Lelievre, Steve, Head Librarian, Engineering Library, 974
Lelièvre, François, Directeur, Shawinigan, 1351
Leloni, Scott, Asst. Deputy Minister, 1214
Lemaire, Marc, Tremblay Bois Mignault Lemay S.E.N.C.R.L., 945
LeMay, William L., Partner, Hicks Morley Hamilton Stewart Storie LLP - Toronto, 932
Lemay, André, Tremblay Bois Mignault Lemay S.E.N.C.R.L., 945
Lemay, Margaret G., Partner, Bennett Jones LLP - Calgary, 901
Lemay, Mireille, Tremblay Bois Mignault Lemay S.E.N.C.R.L., 945
Lemay, Jean-Paul, Régie intermunicipale d'aqueduc et d'égout de Lotbinière-Centre, 1357
LeMesurier, James F., Partner, Stewart McKelvey - Saint John, 918
Lemieux, John F., Dentons Canada LLP - Montreal, 939
Lemieux, Lisa A., Donald R. Good & Associates, 925
Lemieux, Martine, Secteur du soutien informatique, Université Laval, 1025
Lemieux, Pierre, President, 841
Lemieux, Dan, Sr. Deputy Fire Chief, Grande Prairie, 1307
Lemire, Phil, Fire Chief, White Rock, 1319
LeMoine, Jeff, Consultant, 689
Len, Hancock, Director, Public Safety Initiatives, Training & Po, 1193
Len, Kelsey, Chair/Chief Executive Officer, 1212
Len, Simms, Chair & Chief Executive Officer, 1230
Len, Mandville, Manager, Engineering Analysis, 1233
Len, Kowalko, Director, Community Planning (Saskatoon), 1290
Lenders, Taryn, Manager, Health Information Network Calgary, 951
Lenfesty, Tracy, Head librarian, Nova Scotia Dept. of Natural Resources, 981
Lengyel, Bryne, Chairperson, South Forty Waste Services Commission, 1310
Lenhardt, Larry, 828
Lennox, David M., Partner, Bennett Jones LLP - Calgary, 901
Lenora, Lomax, Manager, New River Beach Provincial Park & The Anc, 1226
Lenora, Lomax, Manager, New River Beach Provincial Park, 1226
Lenz, Andrew J.F., Partner, Perley-Robertson, Hill & McDougall LLP / s.r.l., 926
Lenz, Kenneth T., Partner, Bennett Jones LLP - Calgary, 901
Leo, Donati, Manager, Human Factors & Macro Analysis, 1178
Leo, Muise, Executive Director, Legislation & Compliance, 1240
Leo, Muise, Executive Director, 1240
Leo, Steven, Chair, 1272
Leo J., Creamer, Manager, Properties, 1275
Leon, Barry, Head International Arbitration, Perley-Robertson, Hill & McDougall LLP / s.r.l., 926
Leona, Aglukkaq, Minister, Canadian Northern Economic Development A, 1131
Leona, Aglukkaq, Minister, Health, 1144
Leona, Frenette, Executive Coordinator, 1205
Leonard, Wish, Manager, Circulation Services, Resource Sharing, University of Waterloo, 1010
Leonard, Mike, Chief Building Official, Oshawa, 1335
Leonard, Harapiak, Chair, 1216
Leonard, Kwong, Director, Finance & Subsidiaries, 1236
Leonard, Preyra, Minister, 1241
Léopold, Gaudreau, Sous-ministre adjoint, Développement durable, 1278
Léopold, Gaudreau, Sous-ministre adjoint, 1279
LePage, Pierre, Bélanger, Sauvé, 939
Lepage, André, Partner, Heenan Blaikie S.E.N.C.R.L./SRL - Québec, 944
Lepage, Jean-François, Partner, Lavery, de Billy - Montréal, 941
Lepage, Michel, Secrétaire, 853
Leprette, Hannah, Library Assistant, Port Alberni Regional Campus Library, 963
Lerat, Phyllis G., Head Librarian, First Nations University of Canada, 1031
Leroux, Anny, Secrétaire, CÉGEP de Drummondville, 1012
Leroux, Michèle, Bibliothécaire, Bibliothèque de droit, 1016
Leroux, Gary, Executive Director, 659
Leroy, Denise, Manager, Library Services, Northern Forestry Centre, 955
Les, Ward, Director, Trade Policy, 1174
Les, MacLaren, Assistant Deputy Minister, 1202
Les, Fisher, CEO, BC Ambulance Service, 1208
Les, Crisostomo, Commissioner, 1219
Les, Hudson, Director, Human Resources, 1297
Leshner, Alan I., Chief Executive Officer, 645
Lesieur, Vicky, Coodonnatrice générale, 727
Lesiuk, Steven L., Singleton Urquhart LLP, 914
Lesley, Chenier-Aussant, Director, Policy and Strategic Initiatives, 1223
Lesley L., Cushing, Senior Officer, Communications & Marketing, 1159
Leslie, Edward F., Executive Director, 805
Leslie, Cass, Manager, Pesticide Risk Reduction, Risk Reduction, 1121
Leslie, Norton, Director General, International Humanitarian Assistance Directorate, 1130
Leslie, Sim-Kaiser, Executive Director & Chief Information Officer, In, 1185
Leslie, Fyffe, Director, Geological Surveys Branch, 1223
Leslie, Galway, CEO, 1235
Leslie, MacLaren, Co-President, 1240
Leslie, Shanahan, Director, Human Resources, 1244
Leslie, Cooper, Manager, Mine Rehabilitation, Inspection & Compliance, 1260
Leslie S., MacDonald, Assistant Director, Sustainable Agriculture Management, 1198
Leson, Tim, Treasurer, Estevan, 1359
Lessard, Jocelyn, Directeur général, 753
Lessard, Daniel, Directeur, Québec, 1349
Lessard, Jean-Yves, Directeur, Alma, 1346

Lin, Gallagher, Associate Deputy Minister, Parks, Culture, & Sport, 1294

Lochhead, Mary, Head Librarian, Architecture & Fine Arts Library, 970
Lochhead, Sara, University Librarian, Acadia University, 983
Locke, Michelle, Chair, Public Education Committee, Entomological Society of Ontario, 995
Lockerby, CPP, Vivianne, Supervisor, Brandon, 1321
Locking, Mark, Director, Airdrie, 1305
Lockwood, Bob, Chair, 791
Lodermeier, Phil, Supervisor, Lacombe County, 1303
Loewen, Chuck, General Manager, Penticton, 1316
Loewenberg, Madeleine L.S., Norton Rose Fulbright Canada LLP - Toronto - Royal Bank Plaza, 935
Logan, Penny, Manager, Library Services, Capital Health, 981
Logan, Tracy, Contact, 752
Logan, Kim, 638
Logan, David, Purchasing Agent, Saint John, 1323
Logan, Mac, General Manager, Calgary, 1305
Lohmann, Megan, Senior Energy Planner, 733
Lohuis, Jennifer, Associate, Weiler, Maloney, Nelson, 928
Lois, Brown, Parliamentary Secretary to the Minister of Interna, 1130
Lois, Brown, Parliamentary Secretary to the Minister, Internati, 1142
Lois, Deacon, Director, Enforcement, 1258
Loiselle, Rick, President, 818
Lois-Leah, Goodwin, Executive Director, Intergovernmental Relations & Planning, 1201
Lok, Jonathan, President, 738
Lolita, Singh, Director, Strategic Planning & Business Relationship Management, 1263
Lombardi, Paula, Siskind LLP - London, 924
Lommer, Josh, MacPherson Leslie & Tyerman LLP - Saskatoon, 947
London, Jason, President, 839
London, Q.C., Jack R., Counsel, Pitblado LLP, 916
Lonergan, Robert M., Fasken Martineau - Vancouver, 912
Long, Cindy, Assistant to the Exec. Director, 647
Long, Jacqueline, Director, Human Resource Services, Oshawa, 1335
Long, Jeff, Manager, Mount Waddington, 1312
Longard, Sharon, Reference, Dalhousie University Libraries, 981
Longo, Leo F., Senior Partner, Aird & Berlis LLP, 928
Longpré, Elise, Delorme, LeBel, Bureau, Savoie, 945
Longpré, Denis, Manager, Environment, Clarence-Rockland, 1332
Longstaff, Holly, Officer, 690
Loopstra, QC, Charles M.K. (Chuck), Loopstra Nixon LLP Barristers & Solicitors, 933
Lorcan, Scanlon, Senior Policy Advisor, Intelligent Transportation Systems, 1175
Lord, Andrew, Davis LLP - Toronto, 930
Lord, Guy, Partner, Osler, Hoskin & Harcourt S.E.N.C.R.L./LLP, 943
Loreen, Porter, Director, Strategic Portfolio Management, 1287
Lorenc, Christopher, President, 792
Lorenzo, Ieraci, Deputy Procurement Ombudsman, 1172
Lorette, Kevin, General Manager, Comox Valley, 1311
Lori, Dawe, Director, Parliamentary Affairs, 1134
Lori, Brooks, Acting Director, Policy & Operations, 1145
Lori, Young, Regional Director, Programs, 1177
Lori, Schmidt, Senior Director, Productivity Alberta, 1186
Lori, Wanamaker, Deputy Minister, Justice, 1210
Lori, Gaukel, Senior Contract Reporting Officer, The BIP Monitoring Office, 1238
Lori, Churchill, Senior Policy Advisor, Community Capacity & Economic Development, 1261
Lori, Uhersky, Assistant Deputy Minister, Environmental Support, 1289
Lori, Christie, Executive Director, Gas Supply, Marketing & Rates, 1290
Lori C., Connolly-Brine, Supervisor, Soil, Feed, & Water Chemistry Testing Laboratory, 1266
Lori-Ann, Sharp, Team Leader, Planning, Coordination & Reporting, 1158
Lorie, Baddock, Chief Information Officer, Culture & Community Ser, 1182
Lorincz, Tamara, Executive Director, 812
Lorion, Johanne, Technicienne en documentation, CÉGEP St-Jean-sur-Richelieu, 1027
Lorna, Gee, Director, Motor Vehicles, 1246
Lorna, Poff, Co-Manager, Pesticides Management Section, 1252
Lorne, Harvey, Assistant Deputy Minister, 1192
Lorne, Crozier, Resource Management Specialist, Environmental Management, 1240
Lorne, Kusuqak, Minister, 1246
Loroff, Brad, Manager, Transit, Thunder Bay, 1337
Lorraine, Davison, Manager, Chemical Services, 1128
Lorraine, Cameron, Manager, Intergovernmental & International Affairs, 1136
Lorraine, Stairs, Chief, Strategic Planning, Financial & Administrative Services, 1175
Lorri, Biesenthal, Director General, Strategic Services Directorate, 1147
Lorrie, Guillaume, Manager, Content & Internet Coordinator, 1290
Lorrie L., Marchand, Manager, Science Planning & Reporting, 1121
Losier, Gary, Director, Quispamsis, 1322
Lothar, Doehler, Manager, Radiation Protection Service, 1256
Loucks, John, Vice President, 745
Louer, Alain, Secretary, 803
Loughlin, Rita, Records/Information Manager, Sproule Associates Limited, 952
Loughlin, Thomas G., Executive Director, 648
Loughlin, Katherine, Manager, 640
Louis, Vallée, Director, Environmental & Engineering Services, 1119
Louis, LaPierre, Review Officer, 1138
Louis, Marcotte, Director General, Office of the Chief Trade Commissioner, 1143
Louis, Beauséjour, Assistant Deputy Minister, Integrity Services, 1147
Louis, Lévesque, Deputy Minister, 1155
Louis, Arsenault, Director, Business Development, 1220
Louis, Arsenault, Regional Director, 1220
Louis, Comeau, Manager, Mount Carleton Provincial Park, 1226
Louis, Bigaouette, Directeur régional, 1277
Louis, Martel, Directeur, Accréditation etdes relations externes, 1278
Louis, Métivier, Directeur, 1284
Louis, Potvin, Directeur, Technologies de l'information, 1285
Louis R., Dufresne, Directeur, Affaires universitaires, 1283
Louise, Boucher, Manager, Integrated Services, Senator Hervé J Mich, 1122
Louise, Henderson, Manager, Human Resources, 1128
Louise, Knox, Director, 1128
Louise, Métivier, Director General, Strategic Priorities, 1134
Louise, Power, Director, Compliance Promotion & Analysis, 1134
Louise, Lesage, Executive Assistant, 1135
Louise, Levonian, Associate Deputy Minister, 1139
Louise, Girouard, Director General, Communications, 1139
Louise, Baird, Senior Director, Public Affairs & Ministerial Services, 1153
Louise, Payette, Director, Special Projects, 1155
Louise, Mignault, Director, Corporate Planning, 1156
Louise, Demers-Thorne, Liaison Officer, 1160
Louise, Lalor, Controller, 1193
Louise, Anstey, Director, PMO, Strategic Planning & Info Security, 1207
Louise, Ouellet, Sous-ministre associée, 1281
Louise, Rondeau, Directeur (par intérim), Affaires autochtones, ethnoculturelles et régions nordiques, 1283
Louise, Bouvier, Co-Chair, 1300
Louis-Paul, Tardif, Director, Economic Analysis & Research, 1174
Loukes, Peter, Director, Operations, Markham, 1334
Lounds, John, President & Chief Executive Officer, 802
Lourdes, Valenton, Acting Director, Business & Resource Planning, 1256
Lourenço, Mary, Library Supervisor, Nahum Gelber Law Library, 1020
Lourie, Bruce, President, 842
Lousie D., Gagné, Chief, Marine Safety Application Management, Program & Technical Training Services, 1176
Lovatt, Carol J., Sec.-Treas., 783
Love, Geoff, President, 759
Love, David, Executive Director, 735
Love, Grant, Fire Chief, North Bay, 1335
Lovegrove, Wendy, Secretary, 673
Lovelace, W. Scott, CEO, 780
Loveless, Evan, Executive Director, 869
Lovelock, Marty, Chief Librarian, Health Canada, 995
Low, Sarah, McKenzie Lake Lawyers, 924
Lowden, Brenda, Senior Vice-President, 674
Lowe, John E., Partner, Burnet, Duckworth & Palmer LLP, 902
Lowell, Cathie, IEEE Canada Administrator, 771
Lowell, Stead, Member, 1269
Lowery, Jamie, Commissioner, Community Services, Brampton, 1332
Lowrie, Jim, Director, New Westminster, 1316
Lowry, Mark, President, 814
Luanne, Gallant, Manager, Human Resources, 1275
Lubeck, Darren, Manager, North Peace Regional Landfill Commission, 1309
Lubinski, Robert, Treasurer, 860
Luby, Pow, Chief Executive Officer, 1209
Luc, Portelance, President, 1126
Luc, Martin, Ombudsman, 1166
Luc, Marineau, Chair, 1171
Luc, Bourdon, Director General, 1176
Luc, Brisebois, Director, Emergency Preparedness, 1176
Luc, Couture, Directeur régional, 1277
Luc, St-Martin, Directeur, 1279
Luc, St-Martin, Directeur, 1279
Luc, Vézina, Directeur, Bureau de Coordination du développement durable, 1279
Luc, Tellier, Directeur, Inventaires forestiers, 1281
Luc, Charbonneau, Directeur (par intérim), Information géologique de Québec, 1282
Luc, Boileau, Président-directeur général, 1282
Luc, Castonguay, Sous-ministre adjoint, 1283
Luce, de Bellefeuille, Directrice, Secrétariat à l'adoption internationale, 1283
Luciano, Martin, Regional Director, Surface Transportation, 1178
Lucie, Bergeron, Manager, Atlantic Programs, 1155
Lucie, Tremblay, Directrice métropolitaine, Aménagement et des affaires municipales, 1276
Lucie, Aubin, Chef, Réglementation, tarification et permis, 1281
Lucie, Quintal, Directrice, Systèmes, 1281
Lucie, Ste-Croix, Directrice générale, Gestion du milieu minier, 1282
Lucie, Nadeau, Vice-présidente, Qualité et de la cohérence, 1285
Lucienne, Godbout, Director General, Enterprise Development, 1123
Lucille, Kamal, Director, Civil Aviation Secretariat, 1175
Lucille, Cenerini, Vice-Chairperson, 1216
Luck, Ken, Director, Spruce Grove, 1308
Lucky, Donald C.I., Partner, Reynolds Mirth Richards & Farmer LLP, 909
Lucy, Magee, Director, Policy & Procedures, 1246
Luda, Ayzenberg, Director, Finance, Systems & Administration, 1302
Ludwig, Paula, Library Technician, Vancouver Coastal Health Authority, 967
Luff, David, Treasurer, 691
Lui, Laurel, Bennett Jones LLP - Calgary, 901
Lui, Javis, Manager, 702
Luke, Peloquin, Regional Director, 1215
Luke, Joyce, Director, Communications, 1231
Luke, McWilliams, Early Resolution Officer, 1294
Lukian, Maegan, Secretary, 839
Luksun, Basil, Director, Burnaby, 1314
Lunau, Karey, Managing Partner, Conway Davis Gryski, 929
Lund, Galan T., Partner, Brownlee LLP - Edmonton, 907
Lunden, Susan, COO, 800
Lundrigan, Jennifer E., Stewart McKelvey - St. John's, 919
Luoto, Robert A. (Bob), Chair, 859
Lura, Ken, Superintendent, Fort Saskatchewan, 1306
Luscombe, Sandra, President, 807
Lush, Scott, Director, Mount Pearl, 1324
Lussier, Serge, Secretary-Treasurer, 688
Lussier, Richard, Controller, 695
Luszka, John R., Commissioner, Human Resources, Sault Ste. Marie, 1337
Lutes, Jon, Associate, Cox & Palmer - Moncton, 917
Luther, Ritu, Office Administrator, 855
Lutz, Douglas, McInnes Cooper - Halifax, 921
Luyben, Jean, Liaison Librarian, Trent University, 998
Luymes, Martin, Vice-President, 766
Luzak, Bruno, President, 654
Lyall D., Knott, Commissioner, 1156
Lyle, Marianchuk, Branch Head, Inspection & Investigation Branch, 1181
Lyle, Kanee, Vice-Chair, 1189
Lyle, Larsen, Senior Flood Hazard Officer, 1204
Lyle, Stewart, Minister, Agriculture; Minister Responsible, Saska, 1286
Lyle, Saigeon, Executive Director, Fish & Wildlife, 1289

Lyn, Bilida, Branch Head, External Relations & Advocacy, 1184
Lynda, Danquah, Acting Director, Trading Regimes, 1134
Lynda, Clairmont, Assistant Deputy Minister, 1170
Lynda, Downey, Director, Education Tax & Assessment Advisory, 1194
Lynda, Currie, District Manager, Resource Operations (Vanderhoof/Fort St. James), 1206
Lynda, Lowry, General Manager/COO, 1213
Lynda, Yonge, Director, 1237
Lynda, Tanaka, Executive Chair, 1262
Lynda, MacSwain, Manager, Agriculture Innovation, 1266
Lyne, Mercier, Board Member, 1158
Lyne, Lévesque-Schou, Senior Director, Major Projects Directorate - Air, 1171
Lyne, Rouillard, Senior Director, Logistics, Electrical, Fuel & Transportation Directorate, 1171
Lyne, Paquet, Executive Director, Corporate Services, 1224
Lyne, Fournier, Directrice, Développement de l'entrepreneuriat, 1280
Lyne, Jobin, Directrice, Planification, évaluation et développement en santé publique, 1283
Lyne, Jobin, Directrice (par intérim), Surveillance de l'état de santé, 1283
Lynette, Cox, Assistant Deputy Minister, 1135
Lynette, Halvorsen, Acting Director, Budget & Fiscal Planning Section, 1289
Lynkowski, Debra, Chief Executive Officer, 716
Lynn, John, Fire Chief, Barrie, 1331
Lynn, Stewart, Director, Food Regulatory Issues Division, 1120
Lynn, Renaud, Director, Industry Development Division, 1120
Lynn, Lovett, Executive Director & Senior General Counsel, Legal Services Unit, 1139
Lynn, Stegman, Branch Head, Processing Industry Business Developm, 1182
Lynn, Lockhart, Office Coordinator, Air, Land, & Waste Policy Bran, 1188
Lynn, Bell, Director, Homeless Support, 1193
Lynn, Sande, Secretary, 1195
Lynn, Kriwoken, Director, Water Protection & Sustainability Branch, 1204
Lynn, Bryant, Director, Policy, Planning & Evaluation, 1235
Lynn, Edwards, Director, Acute & Tertiary Care, 1243
Lynn, Kelley, Senior Geo Scientist, Science Support Unit, 1289
Lynn Ryan, MacKenzie, Executive Director, Social Services, 1247
Lynne, Guerrette, Director, AgriMarketing, 1120
Lynne, Beairsto, Director, Corporate Programs & Services, 1123
Lynne, Yelich, Minister of State (Western Economic Diversificatio, 1179
Lynne, Duguay, Directrice, Dépendances et de l''itinérance, 1283
Lyons, Audrey, Acquisitions/Cataloguing, Vegreville Knowledge Centre, 958

M

M., Banks, Supervisor, Murray Beach Provincial Park, 1226
Maaskant, John, Chairman, 817
Macaluso, Charlie, President & CEO, 745
MacArthur, Q.C., Colin R., Aikins, MacAulay & Thorvaldson LLP, 915
Macaulay, David J., Partner, Bennett Jones LLP - Calgary, 901
Macaulay, Elizabeth, Manager, 695
MacBride, Barry, Director, Winnipeg, 1321
Macchione, Luigi, Partner, McMillan LLP - Toronto, 933
MacCready-Williams, Nancy, CEO, 741
MacDonald, Gavin D.F., Partner, Cox & Palmer - Halifax, 921
MacDonald, Randy, Matheson & Murray, 938
MacDonald, Ross A., Managing Partner, Stikeman Elliott LLP - Vancouver, 914
MacDonald, Sophie, Matheson & Murray, 938
MacDonald, Carol, Associate University Librarian Systems and Informa, University of Regina, 1032
MacDonald, James, Digital Initiatives Librarian, University of Northern British Columbia, 963
MacDonald, Tim, College Librarian, Northwest Community College Library, 965
MacDonald, Nathan B., Director, 745
MacDonald, John P., Chair, 670
MacDonald, Tom, Registrar, 660
MacDonald, Shelagh, Program Director, 698
MacDonald, Monique, Manager, 698
MacDonald, Alex, Manager, 802
MacDonald, Watson, Contact, 835
MacDonald, Mary, Contact, 795
MacDonald, Tom, Executive Director, 790
MacDonald, Betty, Executive Director, 863
MacDonald, Troy, Director, 681
MacDonald, Ron, President, 718
MacDonald, Martin, President, 834
MacDonald, Aaron, Director, Summerside, 1346
MacDonald, Colleen, Manager, Parks & Cemeteries, Huntsville, 1333
MacDonald, Randy, Fire Chief, Charlottetown, 1346
Macdonald, Cameron, Director, Publishing (NRC Research Press), Canadian Institute for Scientific & Technical Information (CISTI), 994
Macdonald, Kerry, Hospital Librarian, Seven Oaks General Hospital, 972
Macdonald, Brock, Executive Director, 839
Macdonald, Ian, President, 665
MacDonald, Q.C., George W., McInnes Cooper - Halifax, 921
MacDonald, QC, Alexander (Sandy), Managing Partner, Cox & Palmer - St. John's, 919
MacDonald, QC, Ian, Partner, Field LLP - Calgary, 904
MacDonald-Pratt, Elizabeth, Co-ordinator, Circulation & Reserve, Bracken Health Sciences Library, 987
MacDougall, Cynthia, Partner, McCarthy Tétrault LLP - Toronto, 933
MacDougall, P.J., Librarian, University of Toronto, Massey College, 1008
MacDougall, Bruce, President, 752
MacDougall, Kim, Vice President, 718
MacDougall, Colleen, Executive Director & Registrar, 802
MacDougall, Peter, Treasurer, 836
MacEachern, Jane E., Associate, Cox & Palmer - Saint John, 918
MacEachern, Carna, Executive Director, 870
MacEwen, Kathy, Information & Promotion Assistant, Prince Edward Island Food Technology Centre, 1011
MacEwen, Philip, President, 719
MacEwen, P.Eng., Brian, Manager, 836
Macey, Anne, Secretary, 712
Macfarlane, Gary, President, 644
MacGillivray, John J., Gorman Nason Lawyers, 918
MacGillivray, Cameron, President & CEO, 746
Macgregor, Alex, Secretary General, 783
Machida, N.K., Machida Mack Shewchuk Meagher LLP, 904
Machum, D. Geoffrey, Partner, Stewart McKelvey - Halifax, 922
MacInnis, Debbie, Head of Circulation, Cape Breton University, 982
MacIntosh, Glenn, Section Chair, 799
Macintosh, Don, Partner, Dentons Canada LLP - Toronto, 930
MacIntyre, Scott, Area Membership Chairman, 798
MacIntyre, Michael, Planning Manager, Grande Prairie, 1307
MacIsaac, Gary, Executive Director, 863
MacIsaac, Pat, Fire Chief, North Battleford, 1359
MacIver, John A., Partner, Carscallen LLP, 903
Maciver, Robert, Vice-President & Director, 817
Mack, Timothy C., President, 872
Mack, Lis, Manager, 830
Mack, Andrew, Vice-President, 827
Mack, Scott, Director, Fort Saskatchewan, 1306
MacKay, Andrew S., Alexander Holburn Beaudin & Lang, LLP, 910
MacKay, Krista J., Partner, Cox & Palmer - Summerside, 938
MacKay, Barry Kent, Director, 651
MacKay, Art, Manager, Policy Planning, Belleville, 1332
MacKay, Lori, General Manager, Coquitlam, 1314
Mackay, Stuart, McKenzie Lake Lawyers, 924
Mackay, Tara A., Torys LLP - Toronto, 936
Mackay, Crystal, Executive Director, Farm & Food Care Ontario, 985
Mackay, Crystal, Executive Director, 817
MacKay, Q.C., R. Neil, Partner, MacPherson Leslie & Tyerman LLP - Saskatoon, 947
MacKay, Q.C., O.C., Harold H., Counsel, MacPherson Leslie & Tyerman LLP - Regina, 946
MacKell, Bryan, Director, Planning, Development & Tourism, Simcoe, 1331
MacKenzie, Douglas J., Campbell Marr, 916
MacKenzie, Cyndy, Health Sciences Librarian, Northern Ontario School of Medicine, 1000
MacKenzie, Doug, Director, Truro, 1326
MacKenzie, Joe, Treasurer, Mount Waddington, 1312
Mackenzie, Judy, Librarian, FPInnovations - Paprican Division, Vancouver, 966
Mackenzie, Kimberley, Executive Director, 789
Mackenzie, Ken, Vice-President, 638
Mackenzie, Ann, President, 828
Mackey, Paul, Director, St. John's, 1324
MacKinnon, Corey, Heenan Blaikie LLP - Toronto, 931
MacKinnon, Collin, Senior Vice-President & Chief Risk Officer, 674
MacKinnon, Barbara, President & Chief Executive Officer, 805
MacKinnon, Rob, Secretary-Treasurer, 819
MacKinnon, Bernie, Director, Cape Breton, 1325
MacLachlan, Thomas B., MacLachlan McNab Hembroff LLP, 909
MacLachlan, Ian, Editor, 686
MacLachlan, Ph.D., P.Geo., Kate, Director, 665
MacLaren, Keith A., Perley-Robertson, Hill & McDougall LLP / s.r.l., 926
MacLatchy, Paul, Director, Strategy, Environment, & Communications, Kingston, 1333
MacLean, Amy, Coordinator, Library Services, Marianopolis College, 1020
MacLean, Elaine, Collection Librarian, St Francis-Xavier University, 980
MacLean, Lana, Librarian, Strait Area Campus, 982
MacLean, Michael, Director, Leduc County, 1303
Maclean, James R., Heenan Blaikie LLP - Calgary, 904
MacLeod, Malcolm J., Loopstra Nixon LLP Barristers & Solicitors, 933
MacLeod, Beverly, Executive Director, 738
MacLeod, Linda, Registrar, 815
MacLeod, Peter, Vice-President, 740
MacLeod, Mark, President, 820
MacLeod, Florence, Coordinator, 837
MacLeod, Iain, Chair, 766
Macleod, April, 788
Macleod, Angela, Corporate Secretary, 695
MacMaster, Ken, Vice-President, 794
MacMillan, Sue, Program Manager, 706
Macnab, Kevin, Chair, 842
MacNeil, James D., Managing Partner, Boyne Clarke LLP, 920
MacNeill, Kevin D., Partner, Heenan Blaikie LLP - Ottawa, 925
MacNeill, Kevin D., Partner, Heenan Blaikie LLP - Toronto, 931
MacNeill, Sandy, Manager, Fredericton, 1322
MacPhail, Don, Treasurer, 844
MacPherson, Natalie, Information Resources Manager, Nova Scotia Environment & Labour, 981
MacPherson, Chad, General Manager, 848
MacPherson, Glen, Director, Chilliwack, 1314
MacPherson, AScT, Bill, President, 651
MacRae, Wayne C., Executive Director, 701
MacRae, Susan (Sue), President, 690
MacRae, Jack, Manager, Little River Pollution Control Plant, Windsor, 1338
MacRae, W. Fraser, Assistant Commissioner/Officer in Charge, Surrey, 1318
Mac-Seing, Valérie, Associée, Stikeman Elliott LLP - Montréal, 943
MacWilliam, Alexander G., Dentons Canada LLP - Calgary, 903
Madaire, Patricia, Head Librarian, Eastern Cereal & Oilseed Research Centre Library, 995
Maddalena, Michael A., Burchell MacDougall Lawyers - Truro, 922
Madden, Steve, Manager, Grande Prairie No. 1, 1303
Maddigan, Matilda, Manager, 832
Maddox, Sean, Director, 731
Maddox, Peter, Regional Manager, 716
Maddy, Jim, President & CEO, 650
Madeleine, Meilleur, Minister, 1249
Madeleine, Fortin, Sous-ministre adjointe, 1277
Madeline, Maley, Acting Executive Director, 1206
Madill, QC, Havelock B., Counsel, Brownlee LLP - Edmonton, 907
Madona, Radi, Acting Director, Strategic Planning & Business Direction, 1175
Madonna, Kent, Director General, Advocacy & Industrial Benefits, 1123
Madorin, Q.C., W.H.P., Managing Partner, Madorin, Snyder LLP, 924
Madryga, Jack, 1st Vice-President, 788
Madsen, Randy, Partner, Lawson Lundell LLP - Calgary, 904
Maekawan, Takaaki, Secretary General, 776
Mag, Massier, Executive Coordinator, 1296
Magdy, Beshara, Director, Earth Sciences & Research, 1292
Maggie, Allan, Acting Director, Accommodation & Property Management, 1256
Maggie, Linton, Secretary, 1289
Magjarevic, Ratko, Vice President, 779

Marg, White, Manager, Land Use, 1299
Marg, Render, Supervisor, 1301
Margaret, Buist, Director General, Lands & Environmental Management, 1118
Margaret, Fairbairn, Director, 1128
Margaret, Biggs, President, 1131
Margaret, Kenny, Director General, Chemicals Sector, 1134
Margaret, Meroni, Executive Director, Oil, Gas & Alternative Energy, 1136
Margaret, McKay, Manager, Strategic Planning & Performance Manageme, 1159
Margaret, King, Assistant Deputy Minister, 1188
Margaret, Grant-McGivney, Assistant Deputy Minister, Policy, Strategic Devel, 1226
Margaret, Kennedy, Director, Mental Health & Addictions, 1272
Margaret, Anderson, Executive Director, Provincial Disaster Assistance, 1291
Margaret-Ann, Blaney, President & CEO, 1221
Margherita, Conti, Director General, Re-evaluation Management, 1146
Margie, John, Partner, Glaholt LLP, 931
Margie, Layden-Oreto, Manager, Post-Secondary Education, 1224
Margie, Kays, Director, Administration & Support Services, 1272
Margo, Ross, Executive Director, Sport Branch, 1201
Marguerite, Stark, Branch Head, 4-H Branch, 1182
Mari, Nurminen, Senior Advisor, Strategic Planning, 1208
Maria, Rodriguez, Director, Operations, 1121
Maria, Rey, Director General, Defence Research & Development Canada - Centre for Operational Re, 1157
Maria, Moore, Commissioner, 1219
Maria, Lasheras, Director, Health Privacy Office, 1243
Maria, Papoutsis, Director, Health & Safety Policy, 1257
Maria Teresa, Fernandez de Castro, Director, Ecosystems Health Science Program, 1163
Maria Teresa, Fernandez de Castro, Director, Ecosystems Health Science Program, 1163
Mariage, Frank, Associé, Miller Thomson LLP - Montréal, 942
Marian, Campbell Jarvis, Director General, 1163
Marian, Tyson, Chief Executive Officer & Deputy Head, 1241
Marian, Macdonald, Assistant Deputy Minister, 1254
Mariana, Chan, Respiratory Therapy Consultant, Respiratory Benefi, 1188
Mariana, Trindale, Senior Wildlife Biologist, 1228
Marianne, Armstrong, Research Council Officer, 1160
Marica Mary, Smythe, Director, Human Resources, 1244
Marie, Wilson, Commissioner, 1118
Marie, Lemay, Associate Deputy Minister, Infrastructure, 1155
Marie, Cantin, Officer, Customer Service, 1156
Marie, Cusack, Director, Communications, 1185
Marie, MacAulay, Member, 1271
Marie, Cloutier, Vice-présidente, Communications, 1278
Marie, Malavoy, Ministre, 1280
Marie, Rochette, Directrice, Prévention des maladies chroniques et des traumatismes, 1283
Marie, Lamarre, Présidente et juge administratif en chef, 1285
Marie, Alexander, Vice President, Business Development & Corporate Services, 1296
Marie-Claude, Guerard, Chief Financial Officer, 1132
Marie-Claude, Wedge, Contact, Public Affairs, 1221
Marie-Claude, Samuel, Directrice générale, Affaires territoriales, 1276
Marie-Claude, Champoux, Présidente-directrice générale (par intérim), 1286
Marie-Claudy, Nelson, Co-Manager, Project Management, 1159
Marie-ève, Jean, Directrice, Asie-Pacifique et Océanie, 1280
Marie-France, Dagenais, Director General, 1177
Marie-Helene, Boutin, Administrative Assistant, General Aviation, 1176
Marie-Hélène, Légaré, Acting Senior Director, S&T Policy Advice Directorate, 1154
Marie-Hélène, Lévesque, Director, Autoroute 30 & Quebec Projects, 1175
Marie-Josee, Groulx, Director, Communications, 1224
Marie-Josée, Noël, Trésorerie, 752
Marie-Josée, Couture, Director, Strategic Integration & Partnerships, 1136
Marie-Josée, Thivierge, Assistant Deputy Minister, 1154
Marie-Josée, Lafleur, Director, West Region, 1155
Marie-Josée, Lapointe, Director, Communications & Public Affairs, 1161
Marie-Josée, Bédard, Member, 1171
Marie-Josée, Gouin, Présidente, 1277
Marie-Josée, Lizotte, Directrice, Évaluations environnementales, 1279
Marie-Josée, Blais, Directrice, Collaborations internationales, 1280
Marie-Lise, Côté, Directrice générale, Urbanisme/Aménagement du territoire, 1276
Marie-Odile, Koch, Directrice, Coordination & concertation, 1280
Mariette, Fyfe-Fortin, Vice-President, Strategy & Organizational Development, 1128
Mariette, Byrne, Acting Director, Planning & Accommodations, 1235
Marilea, Pirie, Director General, Engineering Assets Strategy, 1172
Marilyn, Denton, Trade Commissioner, Ocean Technologies, 1144
Marilyn, Kapitany, Assistant Deputy Minister, 1179
Marilyn, Craig, Public Safety Officer, 1184
Marilyn, McPherson, Administrator, 1195
Marilyn, McCormack, Assistant Deputy Minister, 1231
Marilyn, More, Minister, 1243
Marilyn A., Barrett, Director, Primary Care Networks & Chronic Desease, 1272
Marina, Fay, Coordinator, Privacy & Information Access, 1272
Mario, Pelletier, Assistant Commissioner, 1140
Mario, Dion, Public Sector Integrity Commissioner of Canada, 1170
Mario, Saucier, Director, Aviation Security Technology, 1175
Mario, Gaudet, Regional Director, 1220
Mario, Sergio, Minister Responsible, 1263
Mario, Bérubé, Directeur, Matières résiduelles & lieux contaminés, 1279
Mario, Bouchard, Sous-ministre adjoint, 1280
Mario, Limoges, Directeur général, Affaires économiques métropolitaines, 1280
Mario, Gosselin, Sous-ministre associé, 1281
Mario, Gibeault, Directeur général, Aménagement durable des forêts/Bureau de mise en marché des bois, 1281
Mario, Frechette, Directeur (par intérim), Services sociaux généraux/Activités communautaires, 1283
Mario, Bergeron, Directeur, Programmation, ressources, et opérations, 1285
Marion, Law, Chief Registrar, 1146
Marion, Guinn, Executive Director, ICT Management Services, 1218
Marion, MacAulay, Manager, Environmental Services, 1240
Marion H., Dowling, Director, Nursing Services, 1273
Mariotte, Michael, Executive Director, 813
Marisa, Piattelli, Chief Administrative Officer, 1255
Marisol, Grossling, Regional Director, Finance & Administration, 1177
Marit, David, President, 846
Marj, Abel, Director, Financial Planning, 1290
Mark, Alan, Senior Partner, Norton Rose Fulbright Canada LLP - Toronto - Royal Bank Plaza, 935
Mark, Chris, Director, Parks & Open Space, Oakville, 1335
Mark, Hodges, Director, Operations, 1121
Mark, Dallaire, Director General, Regulatory Policy, 1131
Mark, Cauchi, Director, Transportation, 1137
Mark, Lyng, Contact, 1141
Mark, Bailey, Director General, Middle East & Maghreb Bureau, 1143
Mark, Schaan, Director, Pharmaceutical Sector Directorate, 1154
Mark, Dehler, General Counsel; Commission Secretary, 1157
Mark, Pearson, Director General, External Relations, 1162
Mark, Corey, Assistant Deputy Minister, 1164
Mark, Seely, Senior Director, Marine Systems Directorate, 1171
Mark, Allen, Canada's Permanent Representative to the Internati, 1174
Mark, Condrad, Regional Director, Surface, 1177
Mark, Clitsome, Director, Investigations, Air, 1178
Mark, MacNaughton, Branch Head, Feed Crops Branch, 1182
Mark, Douglas, Executive Director, Policy & Standards, 1185
Mark, Brisson, Assistant Deputy Minister & Chief Information Offi, 1188
Mark, Asbell, Chair, 1189
Mark, Storie, Director, Operations, Learning, & Stewardship, 1196
Mark, Diner, Chief Information Officer & Executive Director, In, 1196
Mark, Tatchell, Executive Director, Local Government Division, 1201
Mark, Zacharias, Assistant Deputy Minister, 1204
Mark, Thomas, Director, Infrastructure, 1212
Mark, Spearman, Regional Manager, Greater Vancouver & Sunshine Coast, 1212
Mark, Boreskie, Provincial Municipal Assessor, Assessment Branch, 1219
Mark, Rumboldt, Director, Innovation & Development, 1228
Mark, Ploughman, Assistant Deputy Minister, 1230
Mark, Jones, Assistant Deputy Minister, 1235
Mark, Aitken, Assistant Deputy Minister & Attorney General, 1238
Mark, Cleveland, Board Member, 1240
Mark, McCulloch, Senior Manager, Procurement, Logistics & Contract Support Service, 1246
Mark, Thompson, Director, Devolution Division, 1247
Mark, Dunn, District Manager, 1253
Mark, Wilson, Chair, 1255
Mark, Speers, Director, Forest Tenure & Economics, 1258
Mark, Shoreman, District Manager, 1260
Mark, Victor, Coordinator, Special Projects, 1269
Mark, MacLeod, Shellfish Technician, 1270
Mark, McLane, Chair, 1274
Mark, Sherren, Regional Engineer, Western Highway Construction, 1274
Mark, Folk, General Manager, 1286
Mark, Wittrup, Assistant Deputy Minister, Environmental Protectio, 1289
Mark, LaRocque, Executive Director, Northern Social Development, 1290
Mark, Roberts, Director, Communications, 1299
Mark, Davey, Director, Systems & Administration, 1302
Mark A., Bonnell, Senior Science Advisor, Ecological Assessment, 1135
Mark C., Runciman, Chief Executive Officer & Director, Capital Projects, 1262
Mark D., Coleman, Regional Investigator, Interior, 1210
Marketa, Evans, Corporate Social Responsibiltiy Counsellor for the, 1142
Markou, Chris, Lawrence, Lawrence, Stevenson LLP, 923
Marks, Linda, Secretary, 813
Marks, Raissa, Coordinator, 804
Marks, Scott, Asst. to President, 775
Markwell, Jason C., Partner, Norton Rose Fulbright Canada LLP - Toronto - Royal Bank Plaza, 935
Marl, Melisek, Acting Manager, 1261
Marla, Santos, Manager, Disease Registries/Territorial Epidemiologist, 1237
Marleau, Lyle, Foreman, Terrace, 1318
Marleen, Clark, Diagnostician (Part Time), Plant Disease, 1266
Marlene, Elliot, Contact, Pacific Environment Centre Office, 1136
Marlene, Bruyere, Branch Head, FOIP & Records Management Branch, 1184
Marlene, Zyluk, Executive Director, Corporate Crown Lands Policy, 1214
Marlene, MacNeill, Quality Assurance Officer, 1266
Marlène, Sinclair, Directrice, Investissements du financement, 1283
Marlon, Wombold, Chair, 1195
Marney, MacRae, Manager, Health Recruitment & Retention, 1271
Marotz, Karen, Head Librarian, Samuel & Frances Belzberg Library, 966
Maroun, Shaneen, Directeur, Projets routiers et de transport collectif, 1285
Marquis, Daniel, Bibliothécaire professionnel, CÉGEP de Granby, 1013
Marquis, Dany, Technicienne en documentation, Campus d'Edmundston, 973
Marquis, Robert, Contact, 761
Marriott, Thomas D., Managing Partner, Brownlee LLP - Edmonton, 907
Marsales, Claudia, Senior Manager, Waste Management & Environment, Markham, 1334
Marsh, Nigel, President & Conference Director, 814
Marsha, Branigan, Manager, Wildlife & Environment, Inuvik Region & Environmental Assessment, 1237
Marshall, Andrew, Associate, D'Arcy & Deacon LLP - Winnipeg, 916
Marshall, Karen, Director, Library, Western University Libraries, 990
Marshall, Lisa, College Librarian, D.S.B. Fowlow Bldg., College of the North Atlantic, 979
Marshall, David, Executive Director, 757
Marshall, Jim, Senior Building Official, Sidney, 1318
Marshall, Kerri, Manager, Environment, Thunder Bay, 1337

Marshall, Rick, Coordinator, Human Resources, Port Colborne, 1336
Marshall, Eliason, Branch Head, Rural Water Program, 1182
Marshall, Giles, Director, 1242
Marstaller, Tom, Superintendent, Red Deer, 1308
Martel, Catherine, Partner, Norton Rose Fulbright Canada LLP - Montréal, 942
Martel, Line, Agente de bureau, Service de prêts, CÉGEP de Drummondville, 1012
Martel, Jean-Pierre, Sr. Vice-President, 755
Martel, Claude, Directeur, 851
Martel, Marie-Claude, Directrice, Gatineau, 1348
Martel, Gaetan, Directeur operations, Régie intermunicipale d'élimination de déchets solides de Brome-M, 1357
Martell, Art, Chair, 672
Martens, Christine, Specialist, Scientific Information, Boehringer Ingelheim (Canada) Ltd., 1012
Martens, Marilyn, Office Manager, 848
Martens, Tony, Director, Mountain View County, 1304
Martha, Heidenheim, District Manager, 1259
Martha, Durdin, Chair, 1262
Martha, Dawson, Manager, Access PEI Alberton, Access PEI O'Leary,, 1270
Martha P., Heidenheim, District Manager, 1259
Marthe, Boissonnault, Acting Regional Director, Coordination & Policy, 1177
Martial, Pagé, Director General, North America Policy Bureau, 1143
Martin, Christopher D., Lindsay Kenney LLP - Vancouver, 913
Martin, David H., Research Director, Nuclear Awareness Project, 1009
Martin, Joan, Chief, Information Services, Western Region, Canadian Agriculture Library - Saskatoon, 1033
Martin, Angela, President, 758
Martin, Derek, Secretary General, 778
Martin, Jean, Secretary-Treasurer, 782
Martin, Glenn, Executive Director, 737
Martin, Glen, Executive Director, 737
Martin, Blain W., Executive Director, 663
Martin, Ted, Treasurer, 823
Martin, Robert F., Principal Editor, 796
Martin, André, Président-directeur général, 754
Martin, Kathy, President, 743
Martin, Rhonda, Executive Assistant, 787
Martin, Dave, Contact, 865
Martin, Luciano, Executive Director, 635
Martin, Fernand, Directeur, Québec, 1349
Martin, John, Director, Human Resources, Belleville, 1331
Martin, Patrice, Conseiller, Gatineau, 1347
Martin, Bolduc, Associate Vice-President, 1126
Martin, Zablocki, Vice-President/Chief Financial Officer, Risk & Finance, 1128
Martin, Rubenstein, Director, Evaluations, Internal Audit & Risk Management, 1130
Martin, Damus, Canadian Coordinator, 1134
Martin, Damus, Contact, 1136
Martin, Loken, Chief Air Negotiator & Director General, IP & Serv, 1143
Martin, Jensen, Director, Investment Cooperation Program Division, 1143
Martin, Barratt, Deputy Director & Trade Commissioner, Building Products, Forest Industries, 1144
Martin, Tomkin, Director General, Compliance, Lab Services & Regional Operations, 1146
Martin, Duchesneau, Officer, Cultural & Technical Services, 1156
Martin, Bernier, Director, Information Technologies & Geomatics Ser, 1156
Martin, Sutherland, Director, Policy, Planning & Performance Integration, 1179
Martin, Chamberlain, Assistant Deputy Minister, Resource Development Po, 1184
Martin, MacMullin, Assistant Director, Tourism Operations, 1226
Martin, Goebel, Assistant Deputy Minister, Environment, 1227
Martin, Goebel, Assistant Deputy Minister, 1227
Martin, Batterson, Senior Geologist & Section Manager, Geochemistry/Geophysics & Terrain Sciences, 1233
Martin, Broks, Senior Advisor, Northern Ontario Growth Plan Unit, 1261
Martin, Soucy, Vice-président, Exploitation, Parcs Québec, 1278
Martin, Doyon, Directeur (par intérim), Recherche universitaire & collégiale, 1280
Martin, Gingras, Directeur général, 1282
Martin, Simard, Directeur, Relations institutionnelles, 1283
Martin, Prud'homme, Sous-ministre, 1283
Martin J., Eley, Director General, 1175
Martin, QC, Noella, Partner, Wickwire Holm, 922
Martine, Dubuc, Chief Food Safety Officer, 1129
Martine, Ouellet, Ministre, 1281
Martine, Poulin, Directeur (par intérim), Recherche et innovation en milieu de travail, 1286
Martineau, Yves, Associé, Stikeman Elliott LLP - Montréal, 943
Martinez, Karla, Manager, 663
Martinez, Ana Maria, Program Coordinator, 658
Martinez Uriarte, Desiree, President, 779
Martini-Wong, Saskia, Manager, Operations & Finance, 737
Marty, Martell, Member Representing Employers, 1227
Marty, Blake, District Manager, 1259
Marty, Halpape, Director, Southern Park Operations & Planning, 1295
Marty L., Leonard, Chair, 1134
Maruca, Rodolphe, Sylvestre & Associés Avocats S.E.N.C., 945
Marvin, Hare, Director, Lands & Environmental Operations Directorate, 1118
Marvin, Schneider, Executive Director, Advocacy, US Relations, & Miss, 1192
Marvin, Dobish, Contact, Development Initiatives Program, 1195
Marvin, Eng, Manager, Special Investigations, 1205
Marvyn C., Robar, Director, Development Initiatives, 1241
Mary, Karamanos, Senior Vice President, Human Resources, 1124
Mary, Komarynsky, Executive Vice-President, Office of the President, 1129
Mary, Taylor, Director, Conservation Service Delivery & Permitting, 1135
Mary, Pender, Manager, Community Programs, 1136
Mary, Mitchell, Director General, Environmental Assessment, 1146
Mary, Gregory, Executive Director, Industrial & Regional Benefit Directorate, 1154
Mary, Mes-Hartree, Director General, 1163
Mary, Callahan Bishop, Head, Resource Management, Program Analysis & Performance, 1176
Mary, Polak, Minister, Transportation & Infrastructure, 1197
Mary, Dila, Executive Director, Marketing & Communications Sup, 1200
Mary, Myers, Director, Financial Planning, Systems & Reporting, 1207
Mary, Polak, Minister, Transportation & Infrastructure, 1211
Mary, Comeau, Librarian, Corporate Information Management, 1224
Mary, Tapsell, Director, Land & Water, 1236
Mary, Dowding-Paré, Assistant Director & Manager, Program Communications Unit, 1249
Mary, Hennessy, Director, Aboriginal Affairs, 1252
Mary, Bartolomucci, Director, Real Estate Policy, & Policy & Improvements, 1256
Mary, Olijnyk, Acting Manager, 1263
Mary, Hughes, Chair, 1266
Mary, Lang, Chair, 1266
Mary, Kinsman, Director, 1268
Mary, Hennessey, Manager, Tax Compliance Services, 1269
Mary, Acorn, Coordinator, Healthy Living, 1271
Mary, Sullivan, Director, Home Care, 1272
Mary, Hunter, Manager, Service Delivery, Prince County, 1274
Mary, Moszynski, Communications Officer, 1274
Mary Ann, Mann, Policy Advisor, 1220
Mary Ellen, Somerville, Director, Human Resources & Administration, 1221
Mary Jean, Comfort, Director, Regional Oceans Operations, 1140
Mary P., MacSwain, Consultant, Community Care Facilities & Nursing Ho, 1271
Mary-Ann, Wong, Manager, Customer Service & Program Support Section, 1252
Mary-Anne, Kirvan, Senior Counsel & Strategic Policy Advisor, 1170
Mary-Anne, Wihak, Manager, Visitor Experiences, Park Services, 1295
Maryniuk, Jill, Manager, Marketing & Communications, 849
Maryse, Lassonde, Directrice scientifique, 1280
Masi, D. Tomas, Associate, D'Arcy & Deacon LLP - Winnipeg, 916
Masi, Joe, Executive Director, 662
Maskell, Cathy, Associate University Librarian, University of Windsor, 1011
Mason, Andrew M., Scott Phelps & Mason Barristers & Solicitors, 947
Mason, Mary, Associate Librarian, Queen's University, 988
Mason, Diane, Contact, 717
Masse, Martin G., McMillan LLP - Ottawa, 926
Massé, David, Stikeman Elliott LLP - Montréal, 943
Massicotte, Samuel, Heenan Blaikie S.E.N.C.R.L./SRL - Québec, 944
Massicotte, Hugues, President, 690
Massicotte, Normand, Sec.-Trés., Régie intermunicipale de l'eau potable Varennes, Ste-Julie, St-Am, 1358
Massie, Dominique, Executive Director, 838
Masson, Louis, Joli-Coeur Lacasse Avocats - Québec, 944
Masson, Marie-Geneviève, Associée, Langlois Kronström Desjardins, 941
Masson, Stéphane, Coordonateur scientifique, Parc Aquarium du Québec, 1023
Masson, Eve, Sec.-Trés., Régie d'aqueduc de Grand Pré, 1356
Masson, P.Eng, Brendon, Chair, 664
Masswohl, John, Director, 691
Masterson, Bob, Vice-President, 692
Mastragostino, Marelene, Administrator, McMaster University, 986
Mastropietro, Jean, Président, 668
Masztalar, Blaire, Chapter President, 766
Masztalar, Blaire, President, 840
Matesic, Gina, Guelph-Humber Librarian, Humber College Institute of Technology & Advanced Learning, 1003
Mather, Duane, Chair, 746
Matheson, Ginette, Head, Acquisitions, Royal Military College of Canada, 988
Matheson, Catherine, General Manager, Community Development, Greater Sudbury / Grand Sudbury, 1333
Mathew, Anil, Director, Emerging Technology Industries Branch, 1185
Mathie, Denise, Contact, 769
Mathieu, Dumond, Regional Wildlife Manager, 1247
Matichuk, Adam, Coordinator, 849
Matlock, Matt, Executive Director, 868
Matson, Darrell, General Manager, Transportation & Works, Thunder Bay, 1337
Matt, Jones, Director, Air Emissions Priorities, 1134
Matt, Gordon, Director, Communications, 1199
Matt, Collins, Regional Engineer, Eastern Highway Construction, 1274
Matt, King, Director, Communications, 1297
Matte, Simon, Président-directeur général, 657
Matte, André, Vérificateur général, Lévis, 1348
Mattheos, Sarantos, Thompson Dorfman Sweatman LLP - Winnipeg, 917
Matthew, Spence, Director General, 1131
Matthew, King, Deputy Minister, 1139
Matthew, Good, Manager, Planning & Communications, 1183
Matthew, Brown, Senior Portfolio Manager, Venture Capital Programs, 1209
Matthew, Brown, Regional Coroner, Island, 1210
Matthew, Ayres, Executive Director, Municipal Training Organization (MTO), 1246
Matthew, MacFarlane, Vice-Chair, 1267
Matthews, Mary, Reference Services Librarian, Douglas College, 962
Matthews, Fay, President, 807
Matthews, Karen, General Manager, 808
Matthews, Dave, Supervisor, Red Deer, 1308
Mattiussi, Ronald, City Manager, Kelowna, 1315
Matton, Dalie, Bibliothécaire, Référence, dévelopment des collect, Bibliothèque de didacthèque, 1016
Matwick, Stacy, Information Centre Assistant, International Institute for Sustainable Development, 971
Mauch, Anne, Director, 739
Maunaga, Suzana, Head, Cataloguing, Trinity Western University, 961
Mauraises, Joelle, Beaudry, Bertrand, s.e.n.c.r.l., 938
Maureen, Adams, Executive Coordinator, 1208
Maureen, Yelovatz, Director, Executive Operations, 1209
Maureen, Sheehan, Director, Business Services, 1211
Maureen, Wallace, Member Representing Workers, 1227
Maureen, Baikie, Acting Chief Medical Officer of Health, 1247
Maureen G., MacEwen, Provincial Coordinator, Child Protection, 1267
Maurer, Amy, Contact, 673
Maurice, Andréanne, Joli-Coeur Lacasse Avocats - Québec, 944
Maurice, Joe, Vice-President, 814
Maurice, Denis, Directeur adjoint, Mirabel, 1349

Maurice, Egan, Director, Food Industry Division, 1119
Maurice, Portelance, Head Herdsman, Kapuskasing Beef Research Farm, 1122
Maurice, Landry, Regional Director, Programs, 1177
Maurice, Bouvier, Executive Director, Strategic Planning, 1213
Maurice, Montreuil, Director, Broadband Initiatives, 1218
Maurice, Smith, Minister, 1245
Mauro, Pat, Manager, Engineering, Thunder Bay, 1337
Maves, Michael D., Exec. Vice President & CEO, 647
Maville, Tom, Treasurer, 728
Mavis, Banks-Carr, Supervisor, Administrative Services, 1224
Mavko, Tim, Partner, Reynolds Mirth Richards & Farmer LLP, 909
Mavrinac, Mary Ann, Chief Librarian, University of Toronto at Mississauga, 991
Mawhinney, Tara, Liaison Librarian, Atmospheric & Oceanic Science,, Schulich Library of Science & Engineering, 1020
Max, Harvey, Assistant Deputy Minister, 1235
Max, Hendricks, Associate Deputy Minister, 1291
Maxime, Bernier, Minister, State (Small Business & Tourism), 1152
Maxine S., Kingston, Director, Local Outreach Office - Ontario, 1121
May, Stephen J., Partner, Cox & Palmer - St. John's, 919
May, Francine, Coordinator, Technical Services, Mount Royal University, 951
May, Peter, President, 782
May, Shelley, Coordinator, 821
May, Elizabeth, Leader, 764
May, Chris, Sec.-Treas., 837
May, Ian, Chair, 868
May, Don, Manager, Thompson-Nicola, 1313
May, Steve, Director, Corner Brook, 1324
May, Mah-Paulson, Executive Director/Chief Gold Commissioner, Mineral Titles, 1202
Mayer, Elizabeth, Davis LLP - Vancouver, 911
Mayer, Peter, Executive Director, 785
Mayer, Daniel, Président, Régie Intermunicipale Argenteuil-Deux-Montagnes, 1356
Maynard, Elizabeth, Sec.-Treas., 835
Maynard, Hugh, Secretary-Treasurer, 697
Mayne, Rob, Director, Kelowna, 1315
Maynes, Clifford, Executive Director, 763
Mazur, Paulette, Cataloguing Technician, Manitoba Hydro, 971
Mazur, P.Eng, Piotr, Chair, 664
Mazza, Guido, Director, Building Services, Greater Sudbury / Grand Sudbury, 1333
McAlea Major, Veronica, Chief Human Resources Officer, London, 1334
McAllister, David, President, 660
McAnulty, David, Administrative Director, 859
McArdle, André, Secretary, 707
McArdle, Betty, President, 810
McAree, Marc, Partner, Willms & Shier Environmental Lawyers LLP, 937
McArthur, Peter J.G., Partner, Miller Thomson LLP - Vancouver, 914
McArthur, Melissa, Administrator, 704
McArthur, Ian, President, 680
McArthur, Wendell, Director, Engineering, Barrie, 1331
McAskill, James, O'Connor MacLeod Hanna LLP, 925
McAskill, Bill, Librarian, Casa Loma Campus, 1001
McAskill, Bill, Librarian, Casa Loma ESL Resource Centre, 1001
McAuley, Robert, Commissioner, Public Works Department, Prince Edward, 1330
McAusland, Linda, Vice-President Meetings, 722
McAvoy, Lynette, Director, 766
McBain, Ann, Director, 686
McBeath, Suzanne, Librarian, Teck Resources, 966
McBeath, James, Sec.-Treas., 811
McBride, Ian R., Partner, Davies Ward Phillips & Vineberg LLP, 929
McBride, Kathryn, Administrator, 707
McCabe, Don, President, 856
McCabe, Don, Vice-President, 817
McCabe, Larry, Administrative Member, 824
McCabe, Tim, General Manager, Planning & Economic Development, Hamilton, 1333
McCagg, Darrell, Chapter President, 767
McCaig, Kim, Vice-President & Chief Operating Officer, 696
McCall, Carol E., Paterson, MacDougall LLP, Barristers, Solicitors, 936
McCall, Jeremy, Executive Director, 814
McCallum, Larry, Web Services Librarian, Thompson Rivers University, 961
McCallum, Jan, Communications Director, 829
McCallum, Don, President, 844
McCance, John, Secretary:, 822
McCann-Hiltz, Diane, Secretary, 637
McCarney, Carolyn, O'Connor MacLeod Hanna LLP, 925
McCarrick, Toby, Executive Director, 739
McCarter, Katherine S., Executive Director, 744
McCarthy, Don, President, 669
McCarthy, Keith, Chair, 806
McCarthy, John, President, 845
McCaughan, Derek, Executive Director, Operations, Guelph, 1333
McCauley, Karen, Treasurer & Membership Secretary, 780
McClaymont, Terri, Executive Director, 835
McClenaghan, Theresa, Executive Director & Counsel, 696
McClure, Neville J., Partner, Stikeman Elliott LLP - Vancouver, 914
McClure, Marlene, Director, 704
McCollum, Vicki, Librarian, Yukon Department of Environment, 1035
McComb, Brian, Director, Planning, Hastings, 1329
McConnell, James R., Associate, Cox & Palmer - Saint John, 918
McConnell, Mary, Associate University Librarian, Planning & Adminis, University of Calgary, 953
McConnell, Merle, Chief, Health Canada, Health Products & Food Branch, 995
McCord, Katherine, Chapter Chair, 712
McCorkell, Byron, Director, Kamloops, 1315
McCormack, Stuart C., Managing Partner, Stikeman Elliott LLP - Ottawa, 926
McCormack, Karl, President, 835
McCormack, Neil, Business Manager, 821
McCormick, Gary, Reference Librarian, Bishop's University, 1029
McCormick, Bev, Treasurer, 835
McCormick, Morris, Division Manager, Environment, Cornwall, 1332
McCormick, Q.C., Carman G., Partner, Stewart McKelvey - Halifax, 922
McCotter, Damien, Associate, Glaholt LLP, 931
McCoy, Elaine, President, 791
McCracken, Lynn, Library Technician, Information/ILL, Loyalist College of Applied Arts & Technology, 984
McCray, Kevin, Executive Director, 801
McCrea, QC, J. Craig, Partner, Cox & Palmer - Halifax, 921
McCready, Cate, Vice-President, External Affairs, Canadian Institute of Biotechnology, 994
McCready, Jim, President, 743
McCready, Cyril, Supervisor, Water & Wastewater, St. Thomas, 1337
McCreary, Andrew J., Partner, Hicks Morley Hamilton Stewart Storie LLP - Ottawa, 925
McCrory, Russ, Librarian, 673
McCuaig, Cathie, Executive Director, 642
McCue, Robert D., McCarthy Tétrault LLP - Calgary, 904
McCue, Richard, Systems Administrator, Diana M. Priestly Law Library, 968
McCulloch, Sandra L., Patterson Law, 921
McCullogh, Elaine, Treasurer, 813
McCullogh, Q.C., Kenneth B., Partner, Stewart McKelvey - Saint John, 918
McCullough, William, Partner, McCarthy Tétrault LLP - Toronto, 933
McCullough, Elizabeth, General Manager, 706
McCurdy, Earle, President, 694
McCutcheon, David, Partner, Dentons Canada LLP - Toronto, 930
McCutcheon, Christine, Chief, Library Services, Environment Canada, 1013
McDade, Q.C., Greg J., Managing Partner, Ratcliff & Company LLP, 910
McDaniel, Lon S., CEO, 873
McDavid, Cara, Secretary, 766
McDermid, Erin, McKenzie Lake Lawyers, 924
McDermid, Meaghan, Davies Howe Partners LLP, 929
McDermid, Gary, Secretary, 767
McDermott, Robert K., Partner, McMillan LLP - Toronto, 933
McDermott, Dan, Director, 851
McDoland, Ed, President, 851
McDonald, Paul M., Partner, Cox & Palmer - St. John's, 919
McDonald, Barbara, Associate University Librarian, Collections & Liai, Brock University, 999
McDonald, Carol, Director of Admin. & Human Resources, Ecojustice Canada, 965
McDonald, Connie, Library Technician, Information, Loyalist College of Applied Arts & Technology, 984
McDonald, Linda, Executive Director, 658
McDonald, Cory, Vice-President, 814
McDonald, Scott, Executive Director, 676
McDonald, Peter, President, 679
McDonald, Jamie D., Manager, 796
McDonald, Lisa J., Chief Operations Officer, 836
McDonald, Kate, Energy Coordinator, 747
McDonald, Melanie, President, 752
McDonald, Charles, Director, Development Services, Greater Napanee, 1333
McDonald, P.Eng., FEC, LL, Bob, Director, 665
McDonald, Q.C., Daniel J., Partner, Burnet, Duckworth & Palmer LLP, 902
McDonell, Robert J., Farris, Vaughan, Wills & Murphy LLP, 912
McDonnell, John C., Partner, Brownlee LLP - Edmonton, 907
McDonnell, Paul A., Partner, Miller Thomson LLP - Vancouver, 914
McDonnell, John, Executive Director, 713
McDougall, Ian F., Associate, Ackroyd LLP Barristers & Solicitors, 906
McDougall, T. Micheal, Kanuka Thuringer LLP, Barristers & Solicitors, 946
McDougall, Mike, President, 788
McDougall, Terry, Executive Director, 807
McDougall, John, Fire Chief, Mississauga, 1334
McDougall, QC, Thomas A., Founding Partner, Perley-Robertson, Hill & McDougall LLP / s.r.l., 926
McDowell, Lisa A., Partner, Stikeman Elliott LLP - Calgary, 905
McDowell, Mary, Map Library Assistant, Map Library, 1004
McElhanney, William L., Partner, Ackroyd LLP Barristers & Solicitors, 906
McElman, Joshua J.B., Managing Partner, Cox & Palmer - Saint John, 918
McElman, Melody, President, 844
McEwan, Q.C., J. Kenneth, Farris, Vaughan, Wills & Murphy LLP, 912
McEwen, Blair, President, 725
McEwen, Veronica, Contact, 741
McEwen, Q.C., David F., Alexander Holburn Beaudin & Lang, LLP, 910
McFadden, Michael G., Partner, Norton Rose Fulbright Canada LLP - Toronto - Royal Bank Plaza, 935
McFadyen, Marissa, Coordinator, 676
McFarlane, Andrew J., Partner, Stewart McKelvey - Halifax, 922
McFarlane, George, National President, 703
McFarlane, Mary, Programs Officer, 769
McFarlane, Anne, Vice-President, 703
McFarlane, Q.C., John S., Partner, Stewart McKelvey - Halifax, 922
McFayden, Ross A., Thompson Dorfman Sweatman LLP - Winnipeg, 917
McFayden, Lee, Director, 851
McFee, Dale, Police Chief, Prince Albert, 1359
McGaghey, Ellen, Director, Facilities Management & Fleet Services, Waterloo, 1331
McGee, David, Manager, Canada Science & Technology Museum, 993
McGee, Jasmine, Contact, Okanagan College, 961
McGeoghegan, Michael, President, 835
McGill, James D., Executive Director, 684
McGillivray, Douglas A., Partner, Burnet, Duckworth & Palmer LLP, 902
McGinn, Sean, Manager, Powell River, 1313
McGinnis, Gregs T., Partner, Heenan Blaikie LLP - Toronto, 931
McGovern, Susan, Assistant Executive Director, 824
McGowan, John, CEO, 642
McGowan, Wade, Vice-Chair, 687
McGowan, Joe, Director, Cranbrook, 1315
McGowan, Rob, Manager, Parkland County, 1304
McGowan, William (John), Fire Chief, Richmond, 1317
McGrath, Beth M.W., Ottenheimer Baker, 919
McGrath, Rosalie E., Partner, Ottenheimer Baker, 919
McGrath, Karen, Manager, Library Services, Niagara College Libraries & Learning Commons, 1010
McGrath, Margie, Secretary, Quispamsis, 1322
McGreal, Shirley, Executive Director, 782
McGregor, Kathy, Administrative Assistant, Portage La Prairie, 1321
McGregor, CMA, C.P.P., Violet, Manager, Surrey, 1318

Mercier, Guy, Président, 667
Mercier, Alain, General Manager, Transit Services, Ottawa, 1335
Mercier, Amélie, Conseillère, Amos, 1346
Mercier, Maurice, Directeur, Sainte-Marie, 1351
Mercier-Filteau, Nathalie, Stikeman Elliott LLP - Montréal, 943
Mercury, Q.C., A.J. (Telly), Aikins, MacAulay & Thorvaldson LLP, 915
Meredith, Jane, Contact, 788
Meredith, Mimi, Manager, 855
Mereu, R.F., Administrator, 857
Meringer, Steve, Fire Chief, Oshawa, 1335
Merkley, Ray, Director, Parks & Recreation, Orillia, 1335
Meronek, QC, Brian J., D'Arcy & Deacon LLP - Winnipeg, 916
Merrick, Paul, Bratty & Partners, LLP Barristers & Solicitors, 937
Mersereau, Jennifer, Client Services Officer, NRC Information Centre - St John's, 978
Merz, Rustom, Director, Motor Vehicle Standards, Research & Development, 1176
Messely, Maryse, Responsable, Bibliothèque, Collège Mérici, 1023
Messely, Louis, Secrétaire, 730
Mestinsek, Michael, Partner, Stikeman Elliott LLP - Calgary, 906
Metallic, Naiomi W., Burchells LLP, 920
Metcalf, Craig, Director, Culture & Heritage, Orillia, 1335
Metcalfe, S.A., WeirFoulds LLP, 936
Metcalfe, Selina, President, 748
Méthé, Charles, Vice-président, 635
Méthot, Josée, Présidente-directrice générale, 658
Methusalah, Kunuk, Assistant Deputy Minister, 1246
Metzger, Thom, Director, 801
Metzler, Susan Adam, Partner, Miller Thomson LLP - Toronto, 934
Meulien, Pierre, President & CEO, 761
Meunier, Pierre B., Fasken Martineau - Montréal, 939
Meunier, Sylvain, Directeur, École polytechnique de Montréal, 1018
Meurant, Philippe, Directrice, Lévis, 1348
Meyer, Gail, Manager, 849
Meyers, Brad, Secretary Manager, 643
Meyette, Paul, Director, Red Deer, 1308
Mezzano, Lucas, Chair, 832
Micallef, Barry, Secretary, 721
Michael, Wernick, Deputy Minister, 1117
Michael, Metson, Deputy Director, 1120
Michael, Ferguson, Auditor General, 1124
Michael, Bloor, Regional Director, 1131
Michael, Binder, President, 1131
Michael, Keenan, Assistant Deputy Minister, 1136
Michael, Goffin, Acting Regional Director General, 1136
Michael, Olsen, Director General, Executive Secretariat, 1141
Michael, Pearson, Director General, International Affairs, 1141
Michael, Gillen, Chief, Patent Branch - Biotechnology Division, 1153
Michael, Rutherford, Director, Economic & Community Initiatives, 1155
Michael, Hibbert, Regional Contribution Agreement Officer, 1159
Michael, Swinton, Research Officer, 1160
Michael, Jordan, Acting Director, Polar Continental Shelf Program, 1163
Michael, Greskow, Director, Data Management Division, 1164
Michael, Jordan, Acting Director, 1165
Michael, Burke, Director, Industrial Programs, 1165
Michael, MacDonald, Director General, National Security Operations, 1170
Michael, Bolkenius, Press Secretary, Office of the Minister, 1171
Michael, Winterburn, Director, Communications, 1173
Michael, Gubbels, Officer, Dispute Resolution, 1180
Michael, Merritt, Assistant Deputy Minister, 1194
Michael, de Jong, Minister, Finance; Government House Leader, 1197
Michael, Rensing, Manager, Renewable Fuels, 1202
Michael, de Jong, Minister, Finance; Government House Leader, 1204
Michael, Lord, Acting Executive Director/Chief Financial Officer, 1207
Michael, MacDougall, President, 1208
Michael, Loseth, Vice-President, Operations, 1209
Michael, Kohl, Executive Director, Finance, 1211
Michael, McGee, Manager, Policy & Communication, 1211
Michael, Olscamp, Minister, Agriculture, Aquaculture, & Fisheries, 1219
Michael, Maloney, Executive Director, Livestock Development, 1219
Michael, Murray, Director, Human Resource Services, 1224
Michael, Barnett, Director, Student Financial Services, 1224
Michael, Cameau, Asst. Deputy Minister, 1224
Michael, Johnston, Executive Director, 1224
Michael, Carroll, Environmental Engineer, Policy & Planning Division, 1227
Michael, Miltenberger, Minister, 1236
Michael, Myette, Director, Emergency Services, 1241
Michael, Joyce, Director, Health Economics, 1243
Michael, Myette, Director, Emergency Services, 1243
Michael, Rafter, Director, Corporate Services, 1245
Michael, Mifflin, Manager, Land Use & Environmental Assessment, 1247
Michael, Reid, Acting Assistant Deputy Minister, 1250
Michael, Maddock, Acting Director, Communications Branch, 1251
Michael, Reid, Acting Assistant Deputy Minister, 1256
Michael, Gravelle, Minister, 1260
Michael, Chan, Minister, 1262
Michael, Villani, Head, Data Collection & Decision Support Solutions, 1263
Michael, Langford, Director, Investment & Development Office, 1263
Michael, Gill, Supervisor, AgriStability Program, 1265
Michael, King, Chair, 1266
Michael, Mayne, Deputy Minister, 1270
Michael, Sider, Member, 1271
Michael, Drake, Chair, 1271
Michael, Ready, Manager, Human Resources, 1271
Michael, Mitchell, Director, Sector & Regional Policy, 1288
Michael, Makowsky, Director, Multimodal, Trade & Logistics, 1292
Michael, Monea, Vice-President, Clean Coal Technology, 1296
Michael, Templeton, Manager, 1298
Michael, McCann, Executive Director, Strategic Social Initiatives, 1301
Michael A., Henderson, Regional Director General, 1177
Michael D., Lounsbury, Research Officer, Nano Ethical, Environmental, Economic, Legal & Societal Issues (N, 1160
Michael J., Horgan, Deputy Minister, 1139
Michael J., Alexander, Regional Director General, 1141
Michael J., Dwyer, Regional Director, Marine, 1177
Michael J., O'Keefe, Chair, 1229
Michael Louis, Turcotte, Président, Conseil d'administration, 1280
Michael M., Weis, Manager, Electron Microscopy & Imaging Labratory, Bioproducts & Bioprocesses, 1121
Michael R., Stephenson, Regional Director, Civil Aviation, 1177
Michael R., Garrett, Chair, 1251
Michael, Q.C., Paul D., Partner, Campbell Lea Barristers & Solicitors, 937
Michaela, Roebothan, Director, Tourism Research Division, 1235
Michal, Jacob-Fletcher, Manager, Aboriginal & Environmental Programming, 1120
Michalsky, Sue, Chair, 713
Michaud, Charles, Delorme, LeBel, Bureau, Savoie, 945
Michaud, Christian E., Partner, Cox & Palmer - Moncton, 917
Michaud, Denis, Lavery, de Billy - Québec, 944
Michaud, Jean-François, Partner, Norton Rose Fulbright Canada LLP - Montréal, 942
Michaud, Ginette, Responsable, Services techniques, CÉGEP de Rimouski, 1025
Michaud, Josée, Coordinator, 653
Michaud, Odette, Secrétaire de l'Ordre, 827
Michaud, Hélène, Chair, 820
Michaud, Roland, President, 805
Michaud, Steve, General Manager, 741
Michaud, Gerard, 852
Michaud, Félix, Greffier, Montmagny, 1349
Michaud, Michael, Director, Planning, Clarence-Rockland, 1332
Michaud-Oystryk, Nicole, Head, Elizabeth Dafoe Library, 971
Michel, Falardeau, Director, Real Property & Building Operations, 1119
Michel, Têtu, Director General, Trade & Investment, 1123
Michel, Cavallin, Vice-President/CSB & Chief Financial Officer, Corporate Services Branch, 1131
Michel, Jean, Director General, Weather & Environmental Monitoring, 1135
Michel, Mitchell, Manager, Ocean Sciences, 1142
Michel, Lamarre, Acting Deputy Director & Trade Commissioner (InfoC, 1144
Michel, Roy, Assistant Deputy Minister, 1145
Michel, Patenaude, Chief, International Affairs, Policy, International Affairs & Research Office, 1153
Michel, Galipeau, Acting Senior Director, Strategic Planning & Management Services, 1154
Michel, Szymaczak, Director, Science & Technology (Land), 1158
Michel, Cavallin, Vice-President, Common Administrative Services, 1166
Michel, Violette, Acting Senior Director, Operations Eastern Canada Division, 1171
Michel, Villeneuve, Director, Transportation Statistics, 1174
Michel, Gaudreau, Director General, 1175
Michel, Béland, Director, Aviation Security Operations, 1175
Michel, Leclerc, Director, Regulatory Affairs Coordination, Strategies & Integration, 1176
Michel, Cloutier, Director, Canada Transport Emergency Centre (CANUTEC), 1177
Michel, Cloutier, Director, 1177
Michel, Boulianne, Regional Director, Marine, 1178
Michel, Benoit, General Manager/Marketing, 1198
Michel, Albert, Director, Export Development, 1220
Michel, Cormier, Manager, Facilities Management, 1224
Michel, Gionest, Directeur, 1276
Michel, Bonneau, Sous-ministre adjoint, 1277
Michel, Boisclair, Directeur régional (par intérim), 1277
Michel, Gagnon, Sous-ministre adjointe, 1277
Michel, Houle, Directeur, Soutien à l'inspection, 1277
Michel, Rousseau, Sous-ministre adjoint, Analyse & expertise régionales/Centre de contrôle environnemental, 1278
Michel, Gagnon, Sous-ministre adjoint, 1278
Michel, Rousseau, Sous-ministre adjoint, 1278
Michel, Goulet, Directeur, Politiques de la qualité de l'atmosphère, 1279
Michel, Rousseau, Sous-ministre adjoint, 1279
Michel, Dolbec, Directeur, Sécurité des barrages, 1279
Michel, Dolbec, Directeur, Sécurité des barrages, 1279
Michel, Jean, Directeur, Développement des coopératives, 1280
Michel, Bergeron, Directeur, 1282
Michel, Fontaine, Sous-ministre associé, 1283
Michel, Rochette, Directeur, Soutien ministériel & infrastructures communes, 1283
Michel, Després, Président & Chef de la direction, 1283
Michel, Richer, Directeur général, 1284
Michel A., Piché, Vice-President, Corporate Management; Chief Financ, 1158
Michel C., Doré, Assistant Deputy Minister, 1146
Michel G., Vermette, Deputy Commissioner, Vessel Procurement, 1140
Michele, Taylor, Regional Director General, 1177
Michele, Kirchner, Assistant Deputy Minister, 1191
Michele, Herriot, Chief Information Officer, 1237
Michele, Koughan, Manager, Finance, 1268
Michele, McDonnell, Acting Director, 1301
Michéle, Bergevin, Director, Program Management, 1175
Michéle, Caron, Member Representing Workers, 1227
Michèle, Marcotte, Director, Research & Development, 1122
Michèle, Hurteau, Senior Counsel, Legal Services, 1158
Michèle, Ouellette, Director, Executive Ressourcing & Classification, 1173
Michèle, Lavoie, Directrice, Coordination administrative et Services à la clientèle, 1277
Michèle, Houpert, Directrice, Santé et biotechnologies, 1280
Michèle, Robert, Directrice, Interventions financières, 1280
Michèle, Robert, Directrice (par intérim), Coordination régionale, 1280
Michèle, Morel, Directrice, Centre d'affaires électroniques, 1284
Micheline, Leduc, Director General, Small Craft Harbours, 1140
Micheline, Dubé, President & Chief Executive Officer, 1173
Michelle, Soucie, Deputy Director, 1120
Michelle, Kaminski, Manager, Global Environment & Climate Finance Unit, 1130
Michelle, Kovacevic, Associate Assistant Deputy Minister, 1146
Michelle, Comeau, Vice-President, Environment, Capital Lands, & Park, 1156
Michelle, d'Auray, Deputy Minister & Deputy Receiver General for Cana, 1171
Michelle, Bakos, Director, Communications, 1171
Michelle, Clark, Manager, Technical & Administrative Services, Learning Services, 1175
Michelle, Follensbee, Unit Leader, Livestock Welfare, 1181
Michelle, Rowsell, Manager, Human Resources, 1199

Michelle, Schwabe, Director, Regulatory Policy Development, 1203
Michelle, Carr, Executive Director, Strategy and Quality Assurance, 1203
Michelle, Daigle, Director, Stakeholder Education & Engagement, 1222
Michelle, Bourgoin, Director, Wellness, 1225
Michelle, Jewer, Assistant Deputy Minister, 1229
Michelle, Chappell, Manager, Lands Policy/Program Development, 1239
Michelle, Lucas, Director, 1242
Michelle, Proctor-Simms, Director, AIDS Commission, 1243
Michelle, Jay, Executive Director, 1266
Michelle, Harris-Genge, Director, 1267
Michelle, Johnston, Clerk/Receptionist, Montague, 1270
Michelle, Dixon, Fisheries Technician, 1270
Michelle, Wyand, Assistant Registrar, 1271
Michelle A., Harland, Chief, Land & Soil Resources, 1119
Michelyne, Paulin, Director, Atlantic Region, Economic & Trade Policy, 1144
Michnik, Brad, Executive Director, 848
Michrowski, Andrew, President, 833
Mick, Curtis, Supervisor, Water & Sewer, Pembroke, 1336
Middlebrook, Ken, Manager, 684
Middler, Anne, Coordinator, 874
Middleton, Janice, Contact, 760
Miedema, Robert L., Partner, Boyne Clarke LLP, 920
Mielke, Brent W., Emery Jamieson LLP, 907
Mierau, Phyllis, Executive Director, 685
Mighetto, Lisa, Executive Director, 647
Migicovsky, David, Head, Litigation Group, Perley-Robertson, Hill & McDougall LLP / s.r.l., 926
Mihailidi, Helen A., Bratty & Partners, LLP Barristers & Solicitors, 937
Mike, Atkinson, Director, 1128
Mike, Minuk, Director General, Major Projects & Supercomputing Directorate, 1134
Mike, Beale, Associate Assistant Deputy Minister, 1134
Mike, Jamieson, Executive Assistant to the Director, Science & Technology Liaison, 1135
Mike, Norton, Acting Regional Director General, 1136
Mike, Renouf, Executive Director, Transboundary Waters Unit, 1136
Mike, Fullerton, Director, Forest Science Division, 1163
Mike, Hagan, Executive Director, Rates, 1183
Mike, Ekelund, Assistant Deputy Minister, 1184
Mike, Dalrymple, Executive Director & Senior Financial Officer, Fin, 1187
Mike, MacPherson, Administrator, Certification, 1193
Mike, Leathwood, Assistant Deputy Minister, 1194
Mike, Allen, Special Advisor on Highway 63, 1196
Mike, Macfarlane, Director, Land Remediation, 1204
Mike, Pedersen, District Manager, Resource Operations (Central Cariboo/Chilcotin), 1206
Mike, Falkiner, Executive Director, Field Operations, 1206
Mike, Kelley, Director, NRS Business Service Desk, 1207
Mike, MacDougall, Director, Trade Policy, 1208
Mike, Fleming, Associate Chair, Adjudication, 1209
Mike, Hogan, Vice-President, China Operations, 1209
Mike, Davis, Chief Operating Officer, 1211
Mike, Lorimer, Regional Director, Southern Interior Region, 1212
Mike, Kagan, Director, Crops Knowledge Centre, 1213
Mike, Lalla, Manager of Support Services, 1213
Mike, Gilbertson, Director, Environmental Programs & Strategies, 1215
Mike, Cormier, Director, Standards Setting, Program Operations, &, 1221
Mike, Sullivan, Director, 1223
Mike, Warren, Assistant Deputy Minister, 1228
Mike, Baker, Manager, Support Services, 1232
Mike, Ocko, Director, Thermal Region, 1239
Mike, Burns, Acting Assistant Deputy Minister, 1239
Mike, Squirrel, Senior Operations Officer, 1239
Mike, Harlow, Executive Director, 1239
Mike, Moroney, District Manager, 1253
Mike, Morencie, Director, Fish & Wildlife Services, 1258
Mike, Colle, Parliamentary Assistant, 1260
Mike, Montigny, Inventory Forester, Resource Inventory & Modelling, 1266
Mike, Proud, Manager, Office of Energy Efficiency, 1269
Mike, Berrigan, Superintendent, Western Highway Maintenance, 1275
Mike, Kraus, Director, Information Services, 1287
Mike, Balfour, Director, Energy Economics, 1288
Mike, Detharet, Director, Mineral Tenure, 1288
Mike, Ferguson, Director, Petroleum Royalties, 1288
Mike, Burnett, Director, Regional Logistics, 1293
Mike, Carr, Deputy Minister, Labour Relations & Workplace Safe, 1293
Mike, Marsh, Vice-President, Transmission & Distribution, 1296
Mike, Draper, Manager, Programs & Policy Support, 1299
Mike, Johnson, Deputy Minister, 1301
Mike, Fraser, Director, Capital Development, 1302
Mike, Nixon, Minister, 1302
Mike, Nixon, Minister, 1302
Mike P., Wong, Executive Director, Ecological Integrity, 1166
Mike R., Hykaway, Executive Director, People & Workplace Strategies, 1207
Mikera, Fernandez, Executive Director, Carbon Capture & Storage Devel, 1184
Miki, Raymond (Guy) G., Partner, Brownlee LLP - Edmonton, 907
Mikulasik, Mark, Associate, Weiler, Maloney, Nelson, 928
Milani, Q.C., Michael W., McDougall Gauley - Regina, 947
Milburn, Dan, Acting Director, Prince George, 1317
Milena, Sejnoha, Director, Energy S&T Programs, 1165
Mill, Carolyn, Office Manager, EarthSave Canada, 965
Mill, Carolyn, Office Manager, 742
Millan, Larry, Vice-President, 794
Millar, Cynthia A., Partner, Davis LLP - Vancouver, 911
Millar, Kristin J., Bennett Jones LLP - Calgary, 901
Millar, W.A.D., WeirFoulds LLP, 936
Millard, Michele, Coordinator, Centre for Refugee Studies, 1002
Millbank, Jennifer, Ramsay Lampman Rhodes, 910
Miller, Greg S., Partner, Lindsay Kenney LLP - Vancouver, 913
Miller, Keith F., Partner, Burnet, Duckworth & Palmer LLP, 902
Miller, Michael M., Partner, Russell, Christie LLP, 925
Miller, Robert J., McCarthy Tétrault LLP - Vancouver, 913
Miller, Todd A., Partner, McMillan LLP - Toronto, 933
Miller, Barb, Information Technician, EnCana Corporation, 950
Miller, Jim, Director, Canadian Outdoor Leadership Training, Strathcona Park Lodge & Outdoor Education Centre, 959
Miller, Sarah, Coordinator and Researcher, The Resource Library for the Environment and the Law, 1006
Miller, Sherree, Circulation Assistant, Nova Scotia Agricultural College, 983
Miller, Mark E., Executive Director, 793
Miller, Rock E., International President, 773
Miller, Moreen, CEO, 825
Miller, Christine, Manager, 792
Miller, Barb, Director, 665
Miller, Jennifer, Vice-President, 847
Miller, Chris, National Manager, 713
Miller, Chris, Biologist, 713
Miller, Doug, Chief Financial Officer, 819
Miller, George, 847
Miller, Chris, Vice-President, 680
Miller, Thomas H., General Secretary-Treasurer, 775
Miller, Ray, Secretary-Treasurer, 826
Miller, M.Eng., P.Eng., Nadine, President & Chair, 824
Miller, Q.C., David A., Partner, Stewart McKelvey - Halifax, 922
Miller-Sanford, Brenda, Manager, 762
Millette, Réjean, Président, 854
Milley, Gary, Executive Director, 839
Milley, Craig, Manager, Lethbridge, 1307
Millicent, Dixon, Manager, Registrations & Application Evaluation, 1252
Milligan, Louise, President, 721
Millington, Dinara, Director, 696
Mills, Douglas G., Partner, Burnet, Duckworth & Palmer LLP, 902
Mills, Elizabeth, CEO, 871
Mills, John, Vice-President, 701
Mills, Sarah, Manager, 840
Mills, Walt, Director, St. John's, 1324
Milman, Warren B., McCarthy Tétrault LLP - Vancouver, 913
Milne, Ian, Manager, Portage La Prairie, 1321
Milnthorp, Ross, General Manager, Campbell River, 1314
Milojevic, Alex, Secretary, 823
Milsom, David, Director, 818
Milton, David G., President & Secretary, 820
Milton, Sussman, Deputy Minister, 1216
Milton, Q.C., Claire E., Boyne Clarke LLP, 920
Mimi, Fortier, Director General, Northern Oil & Gas Branch, 1118
Mimi, Sukhdeo, Regional Director, Coordination & Policy, 1177
Minato, David, Coordinator, 677
Minchau, Mitch, Manager, Cariboo, 1310
Minchuk, Gerald, Director, Langley, 1315
Mindy, Gudmundson, Director, Financial & Resource Planning, 1293
Mindy, Crayford, Director, 1300
Miner, Richard, Partner, McCarthy Tétrault LLP - Toronto, 933
Miner, Kirk W., Executive Director, 787
Mingay, Cameron, Partner, Cassels Brock & Blackwell LLP, 929
Mingie, Christine, McMillan LLP - Vancouver, 914
Mingo, Verna, Head, Acquisitions/Serials, Nova Scotia Agricultural College, 983
Minicola, David, Manager, 858
Minion, Robin, Director, Library Services, Olds College, 958
Minnie, deJong, Manager, Water Standards, 1252
Minty, Eden, Director, 698
Min-yang Wang, Eric, Secretary General, 778
Miranda, Carlberg, Executive Director, Systems Planning & Management, 1292
Mirau, Dan, Library Director, Concordia University College of Alberta, 954
Mireille, Parent, Directrice, Ressources humaines, 1285
Mirth, QC, E. (Sonny), Partner, Reynolds Mirth Richards & Farmer LLP, 909
Mirynech, John E., Chown, Cairns LLP, 927
Misek-Evans, Margaret, Senior Manager, Capital Regional District, 1310
Misfeldt, Rian, Librarian, Marketing, Saskatchewan Institute of Applied Science & Technology, 1032
Mish, Janette, Vice-President, 847
Misra, Kara, Manager, 677
Mistry, Reena, Chair, 675
Misty, Tryon, Manager, 1190
Misura, Frank, Manager, Rocky View County, 1304
Mitch, Bloom, Vice-President, Policy, Planning, Communications & NPMO, 1131
Mitch, Davies, Associate Assistant Deputy Minister, 1154
Mitch, Fuhr, Executive Director, Driver Programs, 1196
Mitch, Moneo, Acting Executive Director, Policy, Outcomes Evaluation & Research, 1208
Mitch, Wilson, District Manager, 1259
Mitch C., Kendall, Project Coordinator, BC Conservation Corps; Deputy, Wildlife, 1204
Mitcham, Paul, Commissioner, Community Services, Mississauga, 1334
Mitchell, Angus B., Partner, Bennett Jones LLP - Calgary, 901
Mitchell, Brad S., McDougall Gauley - Saskatoon, 947
Mitchell, Don, Conway Davis Gryski, 929
Mitchell, Lynn, Partner, Heenan Blaikie LLP - Toronto, 931
Mitchell, Joan, Archives Librarian, Wilfrid Laurier University, 1010
Mitchell, Mark, Manager, 643
Mitchell, Parker, Co-CEO, 746
Mitchell, Stacy, Senior Researcher, 771
Mitchell, Elaine, Director, Conception Bay South, 1324
Mitchell, P.Eng., Peter, Director, 663
Mitchelmore, P.Eng., Perry, President, 746
Mittermeier, Russell A., President, 735
Mitton, Donald, Project Director, 684
Moar, Joe, Manager, 730
Moe, Matthew, Contact, 828
Moe, Dorie, Manager, 1261
Moen-Nijssen, Phyllis, Library Technician, Cameco Corporation, 1032
Moffatt, Michael, Director, Human Resources, Simcoe, 1331
Mohamad, Hamzeh, Director, Planning, Standards, & Project Delivery,, 1155
Mohamed, Munaf, Partner, Bennett Jones LLP - Calgary, 901
Mohan, Barb, Manager, Powell River, 1317
Mohinder, Bajwa, Public Guardian - Calgary, 1190
Mohr, Gary, Executive Vice-President, 691
Moira, Stilwell, Minister, Social Development, 1197
Moisan, Jérémie-Nicolas, McCarthy Tétrault LLP - Montréal, 942
Mokhtar, Suriati, Deputy Secretary-General, 871
Molgat, Lucie, Director, Csi Project Managment Office, Canadian Institute for Scientific & Technical Information (CISTI), 994
Molinari, Patrick A., Heenan Blaikie LLP - Montréal, 940
Moller, Dave, Vice-President, 665
Molnar, L. Frank, Partner, Field LLP - Calgary, 904
Moloci, Matthew G., Scarfone Hawkins LLP, 923
Molson, John, Président, 768
Molyneux, Jim, Field Works Coordinator, Charlottetown, 1346
Mona M., Taylor, Senior Trade Commissioner, 1144
Monaghan, William, Secretary-Treasurer, 700

Monasterios, Ingrit, Acting Director, Agriculture & Agri-Food Canada, 993
Monck, Grant, National Director, 741
Moncur, Robert H., City Manager, Burnaby, 1314
Money, J. Stuart, Burnet, Duckworth & Palmer LLP, 902
Monge, Todd, Manager, 868
Mongeau, Éric, Associé, Stikeman Elliott LLP - Montréal, 943
Mongeau, René, Président, 827
Monica, Blaney, Manager & Senior Policy Advisor, Freight Integration & Motor Carrier Policy, 1175
Monica, Sharma, Legal Counsel, 1195
Monière, Lynda, Coordinator, 838
Monique, Bourassa, Senior Administrative Officer, Directorate Operations Unit, 1135
Monique, Vielfaure Mackenzie, Chief Executive Officer, 1217
Monique, Rolf von den Baumen-Clark, Acting Manager, Program Coordination, 1259
Monique, Rousseau, Directrice, Affaires juridiques, 1278
Monique, La Rue, Directrice, Soutien à l'innovation technologique et sociale, 1280
Monique L., Bégin, Présidente, 1284
Monro, Joanne, Officer, 766
Monro, H. Alec B., President, 870
Monson, Cathie, Coordinator, 643
Monster, Tamara, Contact, Library Services, Mills Memorial Library, 987
Montague, Barrie, Senior Policy Advisor, 826
Montgomery, Janet, Manager, 789
Montpellier, Ryan, Executive Director, 797
Montpetit, Chantal, Director, 693
Montwieler, William, Executive Director, 770
Moody, Robert, Executive Director, 675
Moon, Joshua P., Partner, Perley-Robertson, Hill & McDougall LLP / s.r.l., 926
Moon, Jeffrey, Head, Maps, Data & Government Information Centre, Maps, Data & Government Information Centre (MADGIC), 988
Moons, John, Vice-President, 673
Moore, J. Alexander, Partner, Davies Ward Phillips & Vineberg LLP, 929
Moore, Deirdre, Manager, Laurentian Forestry Centre, 1023
Moore, Kathryn, Head Librarian, Lacombe Research Centre, 957
Moore, Pat, Associate University Librarian & Head, Systems, Carleton University, 994
Moore, Angela, Coordinator, 664
Moore, Mike, President, 793
Moore, Larry, Vice-President, 745
Moore, Monica, Founding Executive Director, 831
Moore, Walter, Vice-President, 646
Moore, Patti, General Manager, Health & Social Services, Norfolk, 1330
Moore, Tim, Director, Building Standards, Markham, 1334
Moores, Gregory A.C., Partner, Stewart McKelvey - St. John's, 919
Moores, Richard, Executive Director, 754
Moore-Stewart, Robert, Moore-Stewart, Robert, 915
Moorhouse, Richard, Executive Director, 819
Morah, Fenning, Acting Assistant Deputy Minister, 1263
Moran, M. Patrick, Partner, Hicks Morley Hamilton Stewart Storie LLP - Toronto, 932
Moran, Hugh, Executive Director, 821
Moran, Rod, President, 803
Moran, Dave, General Foreman, Bathurst, 1322
Morand, Pierre-Étienne, Heenan Blaikie S.E.N.C.R.L./SRL - Québec, 944
Morasiewicz, Ryan W., Miller Thomson LLP - Vancouver, 914
Morassutti, Paul J., Partner, Osler, Hoskin & Harcourt LLP - Toronto, 935
Morawski, Matthew M., Miller Thomson LLP - Vancouver, 914
Moreau, Gilles, Moreau Avocats inc., 945
Morehouse, D., Director, Moncton / Ville de Moncton, 1322
Moreira, William, Partner, Stewart McKelvey - Halifax, 922
Morgan, Trish, Library Systems Support, Bracken Health Sciences Library, 987
Morgan, Lloyd, President, 812
Morgan, Trish, Manager, Peace River, 1313
Morhart, EIT, Adel, Chair, 664
Moridi, R., Vice-President, 838
Morin, Jean, Grondin, Poudrier, Bernier, 944
Morin, Jean, Joli-Coeur Lacasse Avocats - Québec, 944
Morin, Véronique, Lavery, de Billy - Montréal, 941
Morin, Denise, Bibliotechnicienne, CHUQ-CHUL, 1023
Morin, Sue, Library Technician, Sault College, 999
Morin, Andrew, Director, 661
Morin, Dave, Président, 649
Morin, Andre, City Engineer, Sarnia, 1337
Morin-Corbeil, Johanne, Bibliothécaire responsable, Université de Hearst, 987
Morisset, Charles, Joli-Coeur Lacasse Avocats - Québec, 944
Morisset, Philippe, Joli-Coeur Lacasse Avocats - Québec, 944
Morisset, Sacha, Stewart McKelvey - Moncton, 917
Morissette, Benoit, Lalonde Geraghty Riendeau Lapierre Avocats, 945
Morissette, Miriam, Joli-Coeur Lacasse Avocats - Montréal, 940
Morissette, Brenda, Library Technician, Haileybury Campus, 986
Morissette, Marcel, Maire, Régie intermunicipale de gestion des déchets solides des Etchemin, 1357
Morissette, Yves, Sec.-Trés., Régie intermunicipale de gestion des déchets solides de la région, 1357
Morley B., Knight, Regional Director General, 1141
Morneau, Jean, Directeur, Saguenay, 1350
Moroskat, Sharon, Manager, 737
Moroz, Michele, President, 685
Moroz, Neill, Fire Chief, Kamloops, 1315
Moroziuk, Mitch, Director, Penticton, 1316
Morrell, Louis M., Chair, 645
Morris, Christopher P., Associate, Perley-Robertson, Hill & McDougall LLP / s.r.l., 926
Morris, Dan G., McDougall Gauley - Regina, 947
Morris, Bob, Second Vice-President, 724
Morris, Lawrence B., President, 838
Morris, Sara R., Secretary, 647
Morris, David, Vice-President, 771
Morris, Andrew, Manager, 684
Morris, Ross, Secretary-Treasurer, 829
Morris, Dave, General Manager, Campbell River, 1314
Morris, Seiferling, Commissioner, Stewardship, 1187
Morrison, Gary D.D., Partner, Heenan Blaikie LLP - Montréal, 940
Morrison, Harvey L., McInnes Cooper - Halifax, 921
Morrison, John D., McMillan LLP - Vancouver, 914
Morrison, Stephen, Partner, Cassels Brock & Blackwell LLP, 929
Morrison, Laurie, Head, Liaison Services, Brock University, 999
Morrison, Kelly, Vice-President, 832
Morrison, Jamie, Treasurer, 699
Morrison, Don, President, 857
Morrison, Brian, Secretary-Treasurer, 834
Morrison, Matt, Executive Director, 829
Morrissette, Mike, President, 741
Morrissey, Krista, Executive Director, Conservation Council of New Brunswick, 973
Morrissey, Renee, Reference Librarian, Alberta Innovates - Technology Futures, 953
Morrow, Stuart B., Senior Partner, Davis LLP - Vancouver, 911
Mortimer, Simon E., Partner, Hicks Morley Hamilton Stewart Storie LLP - Toronto, 932
Mortimer, Burke, Sr. Reference Librarian & Circulation Supervisor, Athabasca University, 949
Mortimer-Gibson, Shana, 635
Mortimore, Amy A., Clark Wilson LLP, 911
Morton, Cheryl, Director, 646
Morton, Marshall, Manager, Clearwater County, 1303
Moser, John, General Manager, Planning & Growth Management, Ottawa, 1335
Mosher, Scott, President, 789
Mosher, Bill, Chief Director, Halifax Regional Municipality, 1325
Moskal, Shannon, Manager, East Kootenay, 1311
Mosky, Nick, Secretary, 766
Moss, Janet, Head Law Librarian, Gerard V. La Forest Law Library, 974
Moss, Brian, President, 784
Moss, Eileen, Vice-President, 788
Mostowich, John, Boughton Law Corporation, 911
Mostyn, Matthew, Eccleston LLP, 930
Mostyn, Mitchell, Davis LLP - Toronto, 930
Motard, Pauline, McCarthy Tétrault LLP - Québec, 944
Mougeot, Laurent, CEO, 849
Mouland, Tracy, Library Technician, Bonavista Campus Learning Resource Centre, 976
Moulin, Elsa, Technicienne en documentation, CÉGEP de la Gaspésie et des Iles, 1012
Moulton, Alexis N., Partner, McLennan Ross LLP - Calgary, 905
Moulton, Angie, Coordinator, 728
Moulton Tennison, Melissa, Burnet, Duckworth & Palmer LLP, 902
Moura, Antonio Divino, 3rd Vice-President, 872
Mousley, Brian, Superintendent, Port Alberni, 1316
Mousseau, Yvon, Directeur général, Lavaltrie, 1348
Moutsatsos, Steve S., Weaver, Simmons LLP, 927
Moutsatsos, Tom, Partner, Hicks Morley Hamilton Stewart Storie LLP - Toronto, 932
Mowat, Sheila, General Manager, 791
Mowat, Farley, Honorary Chair, 850
Mowat, David, Medical Officer of Health, Peel, 1330
Mowers, Susan, Librarian, Data, Geographic, Statistical & Government Information Centre, 995
Moyaert, Leon, President, 835
Moyneur, Monique, Responsable, Acquisitions, CÉGEP de l'Outaouais, 1013
Moysa, Susan, Reference Coordinator, Cameron Science & Technology Library, 954
Mozayani, Natalia, Program Manager, 838
Mozes, Erika, Events Chair, 837
Mozur, Mike, Executive Director, 855
Mridul, Misra, Chemist, 1233
Mryglod, Des, Manager, Leduc County, 1303
Muchnik, Paul, Partner, Cassels Brock & Blackwell LLP, 929
Muchynski, Joe, Site Contact, 767
Mucklestone, Connie, Director, 836
Mudry, T. Thomas, Managing Partner, McCaffery Mudry Pritchard LLP, Barristers & Solicitors, 904
Muecke, Cristin, President, 716
Muir, J. Brent, Associé, Miller Thomson LLP - Montréal, 942
Muir, Robert, Blaney McMurtry LLP, 928
Muir, Dave, Manager, Whitehorse, 1360
Mukasa, Samuel, Vice-President, 761
Mulhern, Vanessa, Associate, D'Arcy & Deacon LLP - Winnipeg, 916
Mulholland, Lindsay M., Associate, D'Arcy & Deacon LLP - Winnipeg, 916
Mullan, Q.C., Derek J., Clark Wilson LLP, 911
Mullaney, Carol, Treasurer, 840
Muller, Robert D., Associate, McLennan Ross LLP - Edmonton, 908
Muller, Joy, Manager, Teaching, Learning & Copyright Services, Markham Campus, 990
Muller, Joy, Manager, Teaching, Learning & Copyright Services, Seneca@York Campus, 1007
Muller, EMT-P, ABCP, Peter, Emergency Management Officer (Planning), Edmonton, 1306
Mulligan, Brock, Director, 639
Mulligan, Terry B., Executive Director, 797
Mulligan, Tom, Commissioner, Works & Transportation, Brampton, 1332
Mullin, Pat, Chair, 740
Mullinder, John, President & CEO, 693
Mulroney, P.C., C.C., LL.D., Brian, Senior Partner, Norton Rose Fulbright Canada LLP - Montréal, 942
Multamaki, Hartley, Vice-Chair, 819
Munday, Brian, Executive Director, Alberta Land Surveyors' Association, 953
Munday, Brian, Executive Director, 640
Munden, L. Martina, Patterson Law, 921
Mundle, Todd, Associate University Librarian, Simon Fraser University, 959
Mundle, Todd, University Librarian, Kwantlen Polytechnic University, 964
Mungar, Paul, Director, Haldimand, 1328
Munn, D. Lawrence, Clark Wilson LLP, 911
Munn, Chris, President, 666
Munoz, Eeva, Assistant University Librarian, Allyn & Betty Tayl, Allyn & Betty Taylor Library, 989
Munoz, Alfredo, President, 648
Munro, James R., McMillan LLP - Vancouver, 914
Munro, Shawn M., Partner, Bennett Jones LLP - Calgary, 901
Munro, Marian, Vice-President, 690
Munro, Margaret, President, 835
Munro, John, Sec.-tres., 816
Munro, Zoë, Program Manager, 739
Munroe, Larry, Municipal Auditor General, Halifax Regional Municipality, 1325
Munton, Barb, Membership Sec.-Treas., 717
Murison, Laurie, Managing Director, 762
Murjani, Maria, Customer Service Representative, 706
Murkin, Henry, National Director, 741
Murphy, James D., Burnet, Duckworth & Palmer LLP, 902
Murphy, Kathleen C., Thompson Dorfman Sweatman LLP - Winnipeg, 917
Murphy, Robert S., Partner, Davies Ward Phillips & Vineberg LLP, 929

Murphy, Suzanne, McCarthy Tétrault LLP - Toronto, 933
Murphy, Timothy John, Partner, McMillan LLP - Toronto, 933
Murphy, Colleen, Associate University Librarian Academic Liaison an, University of Regina, 1032
Murphy, Lynne, University Librarian, St Francis-Xavier University, 980
Murphy, Martha, Librarian, Office of the Fire Marshal, 1005
Murphy, Paul, Director, Paul Martin Law Library, 1010
Murphy, Judy, President & CEO, 844
Murphy, James, Coordinator, 793
Murphy, Jill, Director, 730
Murphy, Maureen, Executive Director, 764
Murphy, Suzanne, Treasurer, 786
Murphy, Raymond, President, 797
Murphy, Charlie, Director, Planning & Development Services, Quinte West, 1336
Murphy, Grant, Director, Engineering Services, Kitchener, 1334
Murphy, Terry, Chief Administrative Officer, Summerside, 1346
Murphy, Q.C., George L., Partner, Poole Althouse, Barristers & Solicitors, 918
Murray, Jeffrey D.A., Partner, Stringer LLP, 936
Murray, Jeffrey, Osler, Hoskin & Harcourt LLP - Toronto, 935
Murray, Patty G., Partner, Hicks Morley Hamilton Stewart Storie LLP - Toronto, 932
Murray, Annie, Digital & Special Collections Librarian, Georges P. Vanier Library, 1019
Murray, Susan, Head, Life Sciences Library, Life Sciences Library, 1019
Murray, Keith, Director, 639
Murray, Mary Lou, Registrar, 699
Murray, Susan, Executive Director, 756
Murray, Linda, President, 679
Murray, Cassandra, Contact, 741
Murray, Pat, Treasurer, 807
Murray, Mike, Secretary-Treasurer, 835
Murray, Sinclair, Chair, 1118
Murray, Greer, Branch Head, Agriculture Grant Programs Branch, 1182
Murray, Carruthers, Section Head, Recreation, Cariboo Regional Office, 1204
Murray, Stech, Director, Timber Pricing Branch, 1206
Murray, Adams, Manager, Equipment Support, 1235
Murray, Coolican, Deputy Minister, 1241
Murray, Morello, Manager, 1261
Murray, Myles, Officer, Marketing Council, 1265
Murray, Myles, Acting Officer, Marketing Council, 1266
Murray, Rusk, Member, 1271
Murray, Q.C., M. Lynn, Matheson & Murray, 938
Murry, Sean, Treasurer, 710
Murtland, Dave, President, 767
Mustard, Cameron, President & Senior Scientist, 771
Mustard, Jeff, Superintendent, Spruce Grove, 1308
Mustard, Paul, Director, Transportation & Environmental Services, St. Catharines, 1336
Mutimer, David, Contact, Centre for International & Security Studies, 1002
Muys, Kenneth J., Associate, D'Arcy & Deacon LLP - Winnipeg, 916
Muzzi, Jeff, Manager, Forestry Services, Renfrew, 1330
Myers, Sidney, Technical Services Librarian, Capilano University, 962
Myers, Jayson, President & Chief Executive Officer, 708
Myles, Mana, Director, Authorizations (West Coast), 1205
Myles, Bruns, Regional Manager, Thompson/Okanagan, 1209
Myles, D'Arcey, President & Chief Executive Officer, Hydro One Remotes Inc., 1255
Myles, Q.C., R. Wayne, Benson Myles, 918
Myles, QC, Wayne, Counsel, Cox & Palmer - St. John's, 919
Myner, Louise, Sec.-trés., 656
Myre, Stéphanie, Présidente-directrice générale, 841
Myrna, Belyea-Tracy, Director, Human Resources, 1226
Myrna A., Phillips, Commissioner, 1219
Myrol, David G., Partner, McLennan Ross LLP - Edmonton, 908
Mysak, Michael D., Partner, Bennett Jones LLP - Calgary, 901

N

Nadalutti, Rob, Director, 760
Nadean, Langlois, Director General, Planning & Programs, 1179
Nadean, Langlois, Director General, Planning & Programs, 1179
Nadeau, Charles, Associé, Stikeman Elliott LLP - Montréal, 943
Nadeau, Nicole, Responsable, Québec Ministère du développement économique, de l'innovation et, 1024
Nadeau, Marie-José, Présidente, 754
Nadeau, Pierre, Directeur, 657
Nadeau, Patrick, Directeur général, 713
Nadeau, Steven, Administrator, 825
Nadel, Steven, Executive Director, 646
Nadia, Kostiuk, Acting Vice-President, Business Modernization Initiative, 1131
Nadia, Bouffard, Director General, Fisheries & Aboriginal Policy, 1141
Nadiger, Bill, Librarian, Transportation, British Columbia Institute of Technology, 959
Nadiger, Bill, Reference Librarian, Aerospace Technology Campus, 963
Nadiger, Bill, Reference Librarian, Marine Campus, 963
Nadine, Vincent, Acting Chief, Administrative Services, Program Support, 1176
Nadon, Jean-François, Joli-Coeur Lacasse Avocats - Montréal, 940
Naffin, Daron K., Partner, Bennett Jones LLP - Calgary, 901
Naftzger, David, Executive Director, 739
Nagelbach, Melissa, Singleton Urquhart LLP, 914
Nagus, Judy, Executive Director, 795
Naidoo, Kumi, Executive Director, 764
Naidoo, Kumi, International Executive Director, 765
Naidoo, Nalini, Director, Yellowknife, 1325
Naim, Nazha, Director, Marine Personnel Standards & Pilotage, 1176
Naina, Sloan, Director General, 1179
Nairn, McQueen, Senior Vice-President, Engineering & Project Delivery, 1255
Nalbone, Jennifer, Director, 763
Nancy, Ives, Director, Finance & Management Services, 1123
Nancy, Edwards, Scientific Director, 1130
Nancy, Roberts, Acting Director General, Intergovernmental & Stakeholder Relations Directorate, 1136
Nancy, Horsman, Assistant Deputy Minister, 1139
Nancy, Martel, Director General, Human Resources, Security, & Adm, 1155
Nancy, Harris, Director, Aboriginal Consultation Unit, 1175
Nancy, Schlesinger, Vice-Chair, 1189
Nancy, McDermid, Manager, Settlement, Labour Relations Board - South, 1190
Nancy, Bain, Assistant Deputy Minister, Finance & Management Services, 1211
Nancy, Allan, Minister, 1216
Nancy, Beaulieu, Registrar, New Brunswick College of Craft & Design, 1224
Nancy, Lynch, Director, Planning & Land Management, 1226
Nancy, Watson, Director, Communications, 1241
Nancy, Hoddinott, Director, Chronic Disease & Injury Prevention, 1243
Nancy, MacCready-Williams, CEO, 1245
Nancy, Birt, Chair, 1267
Nancy, Murphy, Community Development Officer, Rural Queens, 1270
Nancy, Malcolm-Sharratt, Coordinator, Healthy Living, 1271
Nancy, Martin, Director, Strategic Alignment, 1296
Nancy, Porter, Senior Policy Analyst, 1296
Nancy, Kidd, Director, Safety & Clinical Excellence, 1301
Nanubhai, Veena, Coordinator, 678
Naomi, Sterling, Acting Director, Operations & Corporate Communications, 1153
Naomi, Yamamoto, Minister of State for Small Business, 1197
Nash, David, McKenzie Lake Lawyers, 924
Natacha A., Brun, Acting Regional Director, Communications, 1177
Natalie, Deschamps, Senior Policy Analyst, Legislative & Regulatory Affairs, 1128
Natalie, Bossé, Director General, Corporate Secretariat, 1173
Natalie, Rosebush, Directrice (par intérim), Jeunes et des familles, 1283
Natasha, Mozes, Director, Resource Planning & Financial Services, 1118
Natasha, Rascanin, Assistant Deputy Minister, Program Operations, 1155
Natasha, Brotherton, Manager, Policy & Legislation, 1237
Natasha, Jackson, Director, Communities, 1241
Natasha Kay, Brenders, Director General, Infrastructure Operations, 1139
Nathalie, Durand, Director, Americas Division, 1119
Nathalie, Daoust, Council Secretary, 1138
Nathalie, Vanasse, Council Secretary; Registrar, 1138
Nathalie, Tremblay, Chief, Patent Branch - Electrical Division, 1153
Nathalie, Belliveau, Director, Transportation of Dangerous Goods Secretariat, 1177
Nathalie, Dubois, Director, Arts Devlopment, 1225
Nathalie, Chouinard, Directrice, 1279
Nathalie, Camden, Sous-ministre associée, 1281
Nathan, Friesen, Senior Archaeologist, 1295
Nathan, Millar, Biologist, Fisheries Management, 1300
Nathanael, Olson, Director, Centre of Program Excellence, 1120
Nathwani, Jay, Osler, Hoskin & Harcourt LLP - Toronto, 935
Nattrass, Bradley J., Associate, Brownlee LLP - Edmonton, 907
Naud, Dominique, Manager, 731
Naullaq, Arnaquq, Assistant Deputy Minister, 1246
Nauss, Kim, Director, 681
Navarro, Luis, President, 783
Nayler, Tanya, Davies Howe Partners LLP, 929
Nazareth, Andrew, General Manager, Richmond, 1317
Neal, Sarnecki, Manager, Regional Projects, 1193
Neal, Hardy, Chair, 1287
Neals-Bolinger, Sarah, Research Technician, Compliance Manager, & Archivi, Ecologistics Research Services, 1000
Neary, Ron, Region President, 706
Neary, Rhonda, President & Chief Operating Officer, 806
Neas, Gisèle, Responsable, Audiovidéothèque, Université du Québec en Abitibi-Témiscamingue, 1026
Neath, Greg, Chair, 741
Ned T., Brooks, Program Manager, Chemicals Management, 1138
Neeb, Gerald, President, 789
Neehall, Roy, Manager, Edmonton, 1306
Neeland, Donald K., Field LLP - Edmonton, 908
Neely, Colleen, Head, Technical Services, Carleton University, 994
Neera, Shukla, Assistant Director/Program Services Manager, Sector Compliance, 1252
Negenman, Paul, Partner, Lawson Lundell LLP - Calgary, 904
Neifer, Shane, Williams Lake Campus Library Contact, Williams Lake Campus Library, 969
Neighbor, Mark, McMillan LLP - Vancouver, 914
Neil, Joan, Contact, 868
Neil, Bouwer, Vice-President, Policy & Programs, 1129
Neil, Desai, Chief of Staff, 1130
Neil, O'Rourke, Director, Operational Restructuring, 1140
Neil, Reeder, Director General, Latin America & Caribbean Bureau, 1143
Neil, Paterson, Director, Passenger Services, 1156
Neil, Kirkpatrick, Director, Policy, Planning & External Relations, 1179
Neil, Kirkpatrick, Acting Director, 1179
Neil, MacDonald, Executive Director, Wellness Branch, 1188
Neil, Hamilton, President/CEO, 1213
Neil, Cunningham, Director, Climate Change, 1215
Neil, Jacobsen, Assistant Deputy Minster, 1220
Neil, Haynes-MacDonald, Manager, Financial Services, 1226
Neil, Gall, Ocean Technology Advisor, 1230
Neil, Whyte, Director, Building Services, 1245
Neil, Sentance, Assistant Deputy Minister, 1254
Neil, Hayward, Manager, Stewardship & Conservation Incentives Section, 1259
Neil, Coburn, Manager, Regional Tourism Unit, 1263
Neil, MacNair, Director, Aquaculture Division, 1270
Neil, Daku, Manager, Property Rights & Registration, 1292
Neil, Crocker, Chief Mines Inspector, Mines Safety, 1294
Neil A., Kinsman, Coordinator, Eastern Region, 1271
Neila, Auld, Registrar, 1271
Neilane, Mayhew, Assistant Deputy Minister/Executive Financial Offi, 1207
Neill, Sandwith, Director, Mactaquac Provincial Park, 1226
Nellie, Kusugak, Deputy Commissioner, Commissioner's Office, 1247
Nelligan, Q.C., LSM, D.U., John, Nelligan O'Brien Payne, 926
Nelly, Rodrigue, Secrétaire générale et directrice, Services juridiques, 1278
Nelson, Larry J., Fasken Martineau - Vancouver, 912
Nelson, Ronald R., Partner, Brownlee LLP - Edmonton, 907
Nelson, Judy, Librarian, South Campus, 956
Nelson, Gordon, Chair, 726
Nelson, Peter, Executive Director, 669
Nelson, Trenholm, President, 718
Nelson, David, Manager, North Vancouver, 1316
Nelson, Carter, Manager, Forest Pest Management, 1223
Nelson, Quevillon, Manager, Maintenance, 1294
Nemetz, Q.C., Bradley G., Partner, Bennett Jones LLP - Calgary, 901
Nerbas, Tim, President, 848

Nerman, Howard P., Pitblado LLP, 916
Néron, Bruno, Grondin, Poudrier, Bernier, 944
Néron, Marie-Claude, Cain Lamarre Casgrain Wells - Saguenay, 938
Néron, Véronique, Joli-Coeur Lacasse Avocats - Trois-Rivières, 946
Nethery, BES, MCIP, RPP, Rick, Director, Planning, Newmarket, 1334
Nettleton, Gordon, Partner, Osler, Hoskin & Harcourt LLP - Calgary, 905
Netzel, Janis, Director, Squamish-Lillooet, 1313
Neu, Joseph, Vice-President, 745
Neuburger, David, 1st Vice-President, 847
Neufeld, Richard A., Dentons Canada LLP - Calgary, 903
Neufeld, Stephanie, President, 640
Neufeld, Ron, General Manager, Campbell River, 1314
Neuheimer, Joel, Director, 756
Neuman, Teresa, Communications Specialist, 701
Neuman, Jamie, Secretary, 637
Neumann, Randy, Secretary, 749
Neumann, Linda, Treasurer, 866
Neveu, Marie-Josée, Manager, Energy Technology Library, 1030
Neville, Richard R., Davis LLP - Toronto, 930
Nevin, John, Public Information Officer, Great Lakes Regional Office, 1010
Newell, Peter S., Senior Partner, Norton Rose Fulbright Canada LLP - Toronto - Royal Bank Plaza, 935
Newell, Wayne, Director, Infrastructure Services, Ottawa, 1335
Newkirk, Ingrid E., President, 831
Newland, Helen, Partner, Dentons Canada LLP - Toronto, 930
Newlin, Don, Deputy CAO, Lloydminster, 1307
Newman, David G., Pitblado LLP, 916
Newman, Diane, Circulation Clerk, Commerce Court Educational Resources, 991
Newman, Paul J., Executive Director, 739
Newman, Angela, Treasurer, 666
Newman, Louise, Manager, 718
Newman, Phil, Director, Leduc County, 1303
Newton, Murray, President, 769
Newton, Paul, President, 868
Newyear-Ramirez, Jo Anne, Assist. University Librarian, Collections & Schola, University of British Columbia, 967
Ng, Judy, Library Technician, The Scarborough Hospital - General Campus, 1007
Ng, Carmen, Executive Director, 744
Niall, O'Dea, Executive Director, 1164
Nichiporik, Kellie, Coordinator, 789
Nichol, Kevin, President, 860
Nichola M., Hewitt, Legislative Specialist, 1271
Nicholas, Winfield, Director, Habitat Program Policy Branch, 1141
Nicholas, Trudel, Director General, Branch Management Services, 1146
Nicholle, Carter, Manager, Exploration, 1232
Nicholls, Pat, Head, Systems, University of Manitoba Libraries, 972
Nichols, Sarah, Information Specialist, Ontario Ministry of Municipal Affairs & Housing, 1005
Nichols, Dave, Director, Grand Falls-Windsor, 1324
Nicholson, Kelly, Partner, Field LLP - Calgary, 904
Nicholson, Peter D., Chown, Cairns LLP, 927
Nicholson, S., Contact, BMT Fleet Technology Limited, 987
Nicholson, Sindy, President, 846
Nicholson, Ensor, Chair, 669
Nick, Cartwright, Director, Operational Performance Framework, 1175
Nick, Thomas, Acting Director, Authorizations (Skeena), 1205
Nick, McGrath, Minister, 1234
Nick, McGrath, Minister Responsible, 1234
Nick, McGrath, Minister Responsible, 1235
Nick, Antonishyn, Section Manager, Molecular Diagnostics (DNA), 1292
Nickel, William A., McDougall Gauley - Saskatoon, 947
Nickerson, Susan L., Partner, Hicks Morley Hamilton Stewart Storie LLP - Toronto, 932
Nickles, Chelsea L., Bennett Jones LLP - Calgary, 901
Nicol, Lynda, Coordinator, 685
Nicol, Michele, Director Business Programs, 723
Nicol, Michele, Director, 678
Nicolas, Paradis, Directeur, Affaires juridiques, 1276
Nicole, Bouchard-Steeves, Executive Director, 1129
Nicole, Davidson, Director, Emerging Priorities, 1135
Nicole, Galvin, Chief, Energy & Advanced Vehicle Program, 1175
Nicole, Girard, Director, Policy & Regulatory Services, 1175
Nicole, MacIsaac, Acting Chief, Resources & Strategic Planning, 1176
Nicole, Legault, Director, Security Intelligence & Assessments, 1176
Nicole, Armstrong, Director, Water Science & Management Branch, 1215
Nicole, McCutchen, Manager, Wildlife Research & Management, 1237
Nicole, Watkins-Campbell, Advisor, Communications, 1241
Nicole, Lévesque, Directrice, Ressources humaines et matérielles, 1280
Nicole, Fellinger, Co-Director, Communications, 1290
Nielsen, Juliet, Librarian, Distance Education, Saskatchewan Institute of Applied Science & Technology, 1032
Nielsen, Fran, Vice-President, 698
Nielsen, Peter, Secretary, 829
Nielsen, Leah, Coordinator, 692
Nielsen, Kim, Manager, Clearwater County, 1303
Nielsen, Q.C., Rex M., Emery Jamieson LLP, 907
Nieuwenburg, Roy A., Clark Wilson LLP, 911
Nighbor, Derek, Senior Vice-President, 755
Nihei, Kathy, Founder, 869
Nijman, Gary M., Alexander Holburn Beaudin & Lang, LLP, 910
Niki, Coffin, Associate Executive Director, 1292
Nikiforov, Dmitry, Acting Manager, Systems & Media, Centennial College, 1002
Nikkel, Terry, Director, Information Services & Systems, Ward Chipman Library, 975
Nilsen, Christina, Borrower & Data Services Librarian, Thompson Rivers University, 961
Nilsson, Ulrika, Associate Public Information Officer, Biosafety, Secretariat of the Convention on Biological Diversity, 1021
Nina, Frid, Director General, Dispute Resolution Branch, 1132
Nina, Arron, Director, Public Health Policy & Programs, 1255
Nirenberg, Jami, Coordinator, 755
Nisbet, Ginny, Director, Information Management / Geomatics, Saskatchewan Environment, 1032
Nisbet, Charles, President, 645
Nishimura, Doug, Partner, Burnet, Duckworth & Palmer LLP, 902
Nissan, Sandra, Partner, Norton Rose Fulbright Canada LLP - Toronto - Royal Bank Plaza, 935
Niven, Q.C., Michael B., Partner, Carscallen LLP, 903
Njagi Runguma, Sebastian, Manager, 729
Nnadi, Emeka, President, 791
Noakes, Jamie, Contact, 680
Nobert, Conrad, President, 861
Noble, CJ, Executive Director, 713
Noble, Owen, President, 790
Nobrega, Michael J., Chair, 815
Nocera, Joe, Vice-President, 855
Noel, Glen L.C., Partner, Cox & Palmer - St. John's, 919
Noel, Greg, Acting Executive Director, 806
Noel, Kivimaki, Acting Director, Federal/Provincial Relations, 1146
Noel, McAvena, Manager, Finances, 1291
Noël, QC, Denis R., Counsel, Reynolds Mirth Richards & Farmer LLP, 909
Nol, Erica, President, 855
Nolan, Philip, Partner, Lavery, de Billy - Montréal, 941
Nolan, Stephen, Librarian, Carbonear Campus Library, 976
Nolan, Fergal, President & Chief Executive Officer, 838
Nolan, Mark, Registrar, 637
Nolan, Liana, Medical Officer of Health, Waterloo, 1331
Nolan, Michael, Director, Emergency Services, Renfrew, 1330
Nols, Jacques, Partner, Lavery, de Billy - Montréal, 941
Noonan, Lisa, Senior Manager, 798
Noone, Fran, Information Specialist, Teck Metals Ltd., 965
Noorian, Ali Mohammad, 1st Vice-President, 872
Nordheim, Alfred, President, 779
Nordin, Dave, Director, 720
Norihiro, Saito, Alberta Japan Office Manager (Acting), 1192
Norm, Morrison, Senior Director, Trade Investment, Middle East / N, 1192
Norm, Letnick, Minister, Agriculture, 1197
Norm, Letnick, Minister, Agriculture, 1197
Norm, Bilodeau, Manager, Water Stewardship, 1204
Norm, Leibel, Deputy Chief Coroner, 1210
Norm, Embleton, Chief Information Officer, 1238
Norm, Magnin, Director, Property Assessment & Taxation, 1291
Norma, Gibson-MacDonald, Manager, General Health & Safety Services, 1128
Norma, MacIsaac, Director, Strategic Policy, 1243
Norman, Richard W., Associate, Cox & Palmer - Halifax, 921
Norman, Jackie, Executive Director, 844
Norman, Calliou, Executive Director, SREM Aboriginal Affairs Branch, 1188
Norman, Lee, Executive Director, Resort Development, 1205
Norman, Tarnow, Deputy Minister, 1248
Norman, MacDonald, Chief Operating Officer, 1269
Norman, Johnston, Sous-ministre, 1277
Norman, Houle, Directeur régional, 1277
Normand, Jérôme, Directeur général, 750
Normand, Louis, Directeur général, Sainte-Marie, 1351
Normand, Patrice, Sec.-Trés., Régie d'assainissement des eaux usées de Piedmont, St-Sauveur et, 1356
Normand, Laflamme, Director, Planning & Development, 1163
Normand, Bilodeau, Director, Resource Management (Omenica), 1205
Normand, Pelletier, Sous-ministre adjoint, 1286
Norrie, Jenn, CAMA AB Treasurer, 683
Norris, Robin-Lee, Miller Thomson LLP - Waterloo, 937
Norris, Christopher, Manager of Technical Services, Canadian Urban Transit Association, 1001
Norris, Paul, President, 826
Norris, Ian, Director, Calgary, 1305
Norris-Kirk, Valerie, Development Coordinator, Grande Prairie, 1307
Nortcliff, Stephen, Secretary General, 786
North, Brian, Manager, Port Coquitlam, 1317
North Hryko, Leah, President, 674
Northcott, Teri, Chair, 767
Norton, Michele, Circulation Assistant, Portage College, 957
Norton, Debbie, President, 810
Nosal, Robert, Commissioner & Medical Officer of Health, Halton, 1329
Nosko, Mike, Executive Director, 717
Nott, Mel, Executive Director, 793
Nouvet, Dominique A., Cook Roberts LLP, 915
Novak, Patrick, President, 749
Novecosky, Joe, Contact, 769
Novinger Grant, Louise, Partner, Burnet, Duckworth & Palmer LLP, 902
Nowak, Ed, Fire Chief, Owen Sound, 1335
Nugent, Q.C., Ross A.L., Thompson Dorfman Sweatman LLP - Winnipeg, 917
Nunn, Cara, Administrator, 809
Nyland, Jennifer S., Lawson Lundell LLP - Vancouver, 913
Nyokong, Loraine, National Director, 741

O

O'Brien, Allan R., Nelligan O'Brien Payne, 926
O'Brien, Siobhan, Associate, Hicks Morley Hamilton Stewart Storie LLP - Ottawa, 925
O'Brien, Sean, Senior Geologist, Newfoundland & Labrador Department of Natural Resources, 978
O'Brien, Robert, Founder/Chair, 814
O'Bryan, Raymond J., Chief Financial Officer & CAO, 646
O'Byrne, Brian A., Partner, Fasken Martineau - Toronto, 930
O'Callaghan, Kevin, Fasken Martineau - Vancouver, 912
O'Connell, QC, James K., Partner, Cox & Palmer - Saint John, 918
O'Connor, Jo-ann, Library Technician, Owen Sound Campus, 997
O'Connor, Kirsi, Director, 693
O'Connor, John G., National Vice-President, 708
O'Connor, Glenn, President, 815
O'Dea, John V., McInnes Cooper - St. John's, 919
O'Dell, Irene, Office Coordinator, 685
O'Hara, Sean, Head Librarian, Canadian Agriculture Library - Winnipeg, 970
O'Hara, Sean, Librarian, Canadian Grain Commission, 970
O'Keefe, Darren D., Associate, Cox & Palmer - St. John's, 919
O'Keefe, Kristen, Executive Director, 837
O'Keefe, Jeff, Manager, 681
O'Keefe, Owen, Supervisor, Water Purification Plant, Cornwall, 1332
O'Leary, Dennis M., Aird & Berlis LLP, 928
O'Loughlin, Chloe, Executive Director, 714
O'Loughlin, Chloe, Executive Member, 677
O'Neil, Robert D., Coordinator, Library Services, SIAST Kelsey Campus, 1034
O'Neil, Peter J., Executive Director, 646
O'Neil, Maureen, President, 699
O'Neill, Garth, Partner, Weiler, Maloney, Nelson, 928
O'Neill, Sean, McMillan LLP - Vancouver, 914
O'Regan, Fred, President, 779
O'Reilly, Adrienne A., Heenan Blaikie LLP - Calgary, 904

O'Rourke, Kim, Administrative Assistant, 806
O'shea, Darlene, City Treasurer, Miramichi, 1322
O'Sullivan, Siobhan, McMillan LLP - Vancouver, 914
Oake, Audrey, Circulation Clerk, Keyano College, 956
Oakes, David, Director, Economic Development & Tourism Services, St. Catharines, 1336
Oates, Sara, CFO & Vice-President, 873
Obal, T., President, 666
Oberg, Glen, Manager, Victoria, 1318
Obermann, Elisa, Atlantic Director, 794
Oberth, Ron, President, 828
Oblin, Rhonda, General Manager, 866
Odell, Marion, Contact, 780
Odnokon, Quinten, President, 865
Oeyangen, Marina, Manager, 828
Officer, Paul, Fire Chief, Elliot Lake, 1332
Ogale, Aruna, Executive Director, 815
Ogilvie, R., Vice President, 746
Ogilvie, Louise, Vice-President, 703
Ogryzlo, Jon, Sec.-Treas., 747
Ogunmefun, Bola, HGR Graham Partners LLP - Barrie, 922
Ohnysty, Dean, Director, Leduc County, 1303
Okabe, CET, Robert, Chair, 694
Okita, Kerry Lynn, Associate, Bishop & McKenzie LLP, 902
Olafson, David, Contact, 835
Olasker, Patricia L., Partner, Davies Ward Phillips & Vineberg LLP, 929
Oleniuk, Terri-Lee V., Osler, Hoskin & Harcourt LLP - Calgary, 905
Olexiuk, Paula, Partner, Osler, Hoskin & Harcourt LLP - Calgary, 905
Olfert, Jon, President, 638
Olga, Bosak, Manager, Québec Operations & Finances, 1159
Olga, Kargina, Director, Pacific Kelowna, 1159
Olga, Klimko, Director, Best Practices & Strategic Planning, 1203
Olga, Lyssiakova, Coordinator, Issues Management Unit, 1252
Olguin, Eugenia, President, 782
Oliphant, Monica V., President, 784
Olivastri, Beatrice, CEO, 759
Oliver, Joan, Library Technician, St Clair College of Applied Arts & Technology - Main Campus, 1010
Oliver, John, Treasurer, 704
Oliver, Bob, CEO, 833
Olivia, Baldwin-Valainis, Director, Regional Affairs, Minister's Regional Office, 1170
Olley, Stuart M., Partner, Stikeman Elliott LLP - Calgary, 906
Olmstead, Steven, Manager, Squamish-Lillooet, 1313
Olsen, Clarinda, Head, Science/Engineering Library, ILL & Reference, Massey Library (Science & Engineering), 988
Olsiak, Catherine A., SimpsonWigle LAW LLP, 923
Olsmats, Carl, General Secretary, 873
Olson, Christyann, Director, Alberta Wilderness Resource Centre, 949
Olson, Kathryn H., Library Assistant, Semi-Arid Prairie Agricultural Research Centre, 1034
Olson, Stan, Head, Acquisitions & Systems, Trinity Western University, 961
Olson, Christyann, Executive Director, 643
Olson, Ph.D., P.Eng., James, Director & Professor, 837
Olson, Q.C., E. William, Thompson Dorfman Sweatman LLP - Winnipeg, 917
Olyan, Arnold, Burnet, Duckworth & Palmer LLP, 902
Olychick, Deesh, Associate Director, 663
Olynyk, John M., Partner, Lawson Lundell LLP - Calgary, 904
Olyslager, Patricia E., Burnet, Duckworth & Palmer LLP, 902
Omkar, Atul, Partner, Reynolds Mirth Richards & Farmer LLP, 909
Omokanye, Akim, Coordinator, 830
Oness, Marley, Municipal Engineer, Okotoks, 1307
Ono, Herbert I., McMillan LLP - Vancouver, 914
Ono, Steven, City Engineer, North Vancouver, 1316
Ontko, Ken, Senior Vice-President & CIO, 674
Opadeyi, Jacob, President, 732
Ord, Peter, Manager, Penticton, 1316
Ordyniec, Krystyn, Scarfone Hawkins LLP, 923
Oresnik, Ivan, President, 720
Orlandini, Rosa, Map Librarian, Map Library, 1004
Orlando, Cabrera-Rivera, Program Manager, Air Quality & PRTR, 1138
Orna, Salamon, Director, Drinking Water Programs, 1251
Ornyik, Roman, Registrar, 666
Orooba H., Mohammed, Manager, Traffic Data Collection & Analysis, 1274
Orson L., Bourne, NRC-SIMS Business Development Officer, 1160
Ortenburg, Nancy, Director, 723
Orzech, Jamie, Partner, McCarthy Tétrault LLP - Toronto, 933
Osborne, Zack, Head Librarian, Toronto Botanical Garden, 1008
Osborne, Tim, Manager, Human Resources, Quinte West, 1336
Osborne, Tom, General Manager, Nanaimo, 1312
Osepchook, Felicity, Head, New Brunswick Museum, 975
Osler, William S., Partner, Bennett Jones LLP - Calgary, 901
Osther, Jennifer, Librarian, IBI Group, 1004
Ostrander, Ingrid, President, 866
Ostrowski, Richard, Manager, Ontario Petroleum Institute Inc., 989
Oswald, Patricia, President, 725
Oswick-Kearney, Tammy, Provincial Coordinator, Quebec Young Farmers' 4H Association, 1031
Oswick-Kearney, Tammy, Provincial Coordinator, 838
Oswick-Kearney, Tammy, Officer, 682
Osyany, Andrew, Secretary, 824
Oszust, Steve, President, 845
Oud, Joanne, Collections & Acquistions Dept. Head, Wilfrid Laurier University, 1010
Ouellet, Pierre, Grondin, Poudrier, Bernier, 944
Ouellet, Diane, Technicienne à la référence, aux périodiques et au, CÉGEP de Rivière-du-Loup, 1026
Ouellet, Martine, Minister, 694
Ouellet, Alison, Director, 717
Ouellet, Michel, Director, Riverview, 1322
Ouellet, Suzanne, Greffière, Gatineau, 1347
Ouellet, Suzanne, Sec.-Trés., Régie intermunicipale d'approvisionnement en eau potable Henryvil, 1357
Ouellett, Iris, Library Manager, Defence R & D Canada - Atlantic, 981
Ouellette, Colin D., Emery Jamieson LLP, 907
Ouellette, Dana, Information Services Librarian, Concordia University College of Alberta, 954
Ouellette, Dan, Fire Chief/Director, Powell River, 1317
Ouimet, François H., Associé, Stikeman Elliott LLP - Montréal, 943
Ouimette, Claude, Coordonnateur, Granby, 1348
Oulton, Daniel L., Partner, Burchell MacDougall Lawyers - Wolfville, 922
Oulton, David, Chair, 811
Overbeek, Christian, Président, 751
Owen, Brian, Associate University Librarian, Simon Fraser University, 959
Owen, Victoria, Head Librarian, University of Toronto, Scarborough, 1009
Owen, John, President, 673
Owen, Olfert, Acting Director, Operations, 1122
Owen, Teo, Director, Office of the Deputy Director, Internati, 1143
Owen, Court, Senior Manager, Strategic Projects & Public Engage, Vancouver Metro, 1210
Owens, Geoff, Coordinator, Media, Mount Royal University, 951
Oxford, Susan, Assistant Director, Library Services, Slave Lake Campus Library, 958
Oyhenart, Greg, Sr. VP & Chief Member Experience Officer, 674
Ozao, Riko, Membership Secretary, 777
Ozaruk, Janet, President, 788
Ozolins, Dorothy, Librarian, KSH Solutions Inc. (KSH), 1019

P

Pablo, Sobrino, Associate Assistant Deputy Minister, 1171
Pace, Michael J., Partner, Miller Thomson LLP - Toronto, 934
Pace, William R., Executive Director, 872
Pach, Beata, Manager, Library Services, Public Health Ontario, 1006
Paddock, Gwen, President, 814
Paddock, P.Eng., FEC, Dennis, Executive Director & Registrar, 665
Paddy, Whidden, Director, Alaska Highway Program Management - Fort Nelson, 1172
Padwick, James, Norton Rose Fulbright Canada LLP - Toronto - Royal Bank Plaza, 935
Page, Devon, Executive Director, Ecojustice Canada, 965
Page, Victoria, Sec.-Treas., 637
Page, Devon, Executive Director, 743
Pagé, Frédéric, Lavery, de Billy - Montréal, 941
Pagé, Jean-François, Partner, Heenan Blaikie S.E.N.C.R.L/SRL - Sherbrooke, 945
Pagé, Karin, Associate, Perley-Robertson, Hill & McDougall LLP / s.r.l., 926
Paiement, Bertrand, Associé, Lapointe Rosenstein Marchand Melançon, 941
Paiement, Corey, Director, Salmon Arm, 1318
Paillard, Cedric, Vice-President, 637
Paine, Jeffrey D., Templeman Menninga LLP, 923
Pakenham, Dennis, Morency Société d'Avocats - Québec, 945
Pakenham, Robert E., Counsel, LLF Lawyers LLP, 927
Pakosh, Maureen, Library Contact, Lyndhurst Centre, 1004
Pakosh, Maureen, Library Contact, Rumsey Centre - Cardiac, 1006
Pakosh, Maureen, Library Contact, Rumsey Centre - Neurorehabilitation, 1006
Pakrul, Robert W., Alexander Holburn Beaudin & Lang, LLP, 910
Palayew, Dan, Partner, Heenan Blaikie LLP - Ottawa, 925
Paleczny, Kelly, Chair, 823
Palin, Marie-France, Secretary-Treasurer, 719
Palleson, Martin L., Gowling Lafleur Henderson LLP - Vancouver, 912
Palm, W. Ian, Partner, McCarthy Tétrault LLP - Toronto, 933
Palmay, Frank, Partner, McMillan LLP - Toronto, 934
Palmer, Barb, Manager, Library Services, Portage College, 957
Palov, Joey D., Partner, Cox & Palmer - Halifax, 921
Palozzi, BA, MBA, ICD.D, Dina, Chair, 689
Pam, Bjornson, Director General, Knowledge Management, 1158
Pam, Bjornson, Director General, 1158
Pam, Arnston, Executive Director/Senior Financial Officer, Finan, 1182
Pam, Barteaux, Director, Planning & Project Development, 1226
Pam, Barnes, Financial Manager, Financial Services, 1229
Pam, Coulter, Director, Communications, 1247
Pamela, Stephens, Director, Communications to the Associate Minister, 1157
Pamela, Cohen, Chief Review Officer, Review Division, 1213
Pamela, Rodgers, Director, Emergency Services, 1231
Pamela, Bullard, Manager, Community Programs, 1263
Pamela, Trainor, Executive Director, 1272
Pammett, Dianne, Information Specialist/Head, NRC Information Centre - Saskatoon, 1033
Panabaker, Dave, General Manager, Medicine Hat, 1307
Pandit, Ph.D., Nitin, President, 780
Panetta, Vince M., Partner, Hicks Morley Hamilton Stewart Storie LLP - Kingston, 923
Pangman, Jill, Chair, 714
Panitchpakdi, Supachai, Secretary General, 863
Pankhurst, Mark, Fire Chief, Kawartha Lakes, 1333
Pankratz, Darryl G., Alexander Holburn Beaudin & Lang, LLP, 910
Pankratz, H., President, 737
Panneton, Alexandre, Heenan Blaikie LLP - Montréal, 940
Pantazis, Sig, Beament Green, 925
Paolo, Solano, Legal Officer, Submission on Enforcement Matters Unit, 1138
Paon, Michelle, Vice-President, 813
Papadopoulos, John, Chief Librarian, Bora Laskin Law Library, 1001
Papavinasam, Sankara, Section Chair, 799
Pappas, Q.C., Chrys, Thompson Dorfman Sweatman LLP - Winnipeg, 917
Paquet, Claude, Partner, Heenan Blaikie LLP - Montréal, 940
Paquet, Caroline, Présidente, 648
Paquette, René, Associé, Langlois Kronström Desjardins, 941
Paquin, Pierre B., Bélanger, Sauvé, 939
Paquin, Chantal, Technician, INRS - Université du Québec, CGC - Québec, 1023
Paquin, Chantal, Technicienne, Université du Québec Institut national de la recherche scientifiq, 1025
Paradis, Michel, Joli-Coeur Lacasse Avocats - Québec, 944
Paradis, Paul D., Partner, Ross & McBride LLP, 923
Paradis, Brigitte, Client Services Officer, NRC Information Centre, 1012
Paradis, Louise, Bibliothécaire, Bibliothèque paramédicale, 1017
Paradise, Connie, Director, 646
Paraszczak, Jacek, Director, 791
Parent, Jean-Guy, Sylvain Parent Gobeil Simard S.E.N.C.R.L., 945
Parent, Ingrid, University Librarian, University of British Columbia, 967
Parent, Diane, Directrice générale, 666
Parent, Erick, Secrétaire général, 738

Parent, Jennifer, Division Head, Human Resources, Pickering, 1336
Parent, Paul-Eugène, Président, Régie intermunicipale de l'Est de Portneuf, 1358
Parets, Otto, Vice-President, 641
Park, Jason, Partner, Dentons Canada LLP - Toronto, 930
Park, Stephen, Directeur, Bibliothèque centrale, 1015
Park, Stephen, Directeur, Bibliothèque centrale, Université du Québec à Montréal, 1021
Park, Chad, Executive Director, 802
Parker, Glenn G., Chown, Cairns LLP, 927
Parker, Linda G., McCarthy Tétrault LLP - Vancouver, 913
Parker, Nick, Partner, Reynolds Mirth Richards & Farmer LLP, 909
Parker, Sean D., Associate, McLennan Ross LLP - Edmonton, 908
Parker, Martin, President, 831
Parker, Douglas, Executive Director, 821
Parker, Pamela, Executive Director, 669
Parker, Elaine M., Vice-President, 719
Parker, Bruce J., President & CEO, 748
Parker, Scott D., Executive Director, 808
Parker, Bruce J., President & Chief Executive Officer, 801
Parker, Brad, Chief Constable, Port Moody, 1317
Parker, Kennedy, Director, Community Justice & Community Policing, 1238
Parkes, Lisa, Vice-President, 790
Parks, Nick, President & CEO, 689
Parnell, Angie, Manager, Port Moody, 1317
Parra, Mariela, Corporate Librarian, Devon Energy Corporation (Canada), 950
Parrish, Doug, Director, Leduc, 1307
Parrott, Denise, Technical Services Librarian, Nova Scotia Community College, 981
Parsad, Asvin, Treasurer, 768
Parsons, Sue, Information Resources Officer, Canadian Institute of Resources Law, 950
Parsons, Carolyn, President, 635
Parsons, Katharine, Vice-President, 867
Parsons, Marlene, Director, 730
Partington, Lynne, Head, Bibliographic Control, University of Manitoba Libraries, 972
Pascal, Giasson, Manager, Species at Risk, 1223
Pascal, Bérubé, Ministre, 1284
Pascoe Merkley, Maureen, Director, Planning, Brockville, 1332
Pascolo, Rita, Library Technician, Engineering Branch, 985
Pascucci, Vincenzo, General Secretary, 776
Pasieka, James, Partner, Heenan Blaikie LLP - Calgary, 904
Pat, MacAulay, Director, Infrastructure Programs, 1123
Pat, Falletta, Manager, 1137
Pat, Shimbashi, Council Member, 1181
Pat, Connolly, Executive Director, Human Resource Services, 1192
Pat, Pimm, Parliamentary Secretary for the Northeast to the M, 1202
Pat, Charlton, Manager, Chronic Disease Prevention & Management, 1272
Pat, MacAulay, Federal Manager, 1275
Pat, Parenteau, Director, Policy & Central Services, 1293
Pat, MacDonell, Acting Director, 1299
Pat, Living, Director, Communications & Social Marketing, 1301
Pat G., Ryan, Comptroller, Business Office, 1272
Pat J., Kelly, Provincial Coordinator, 911 Call Answer & Transfer, 1268
Pat Roy, Mooney, Executive Director, 750
Pat W., MacDonald, Coordinator, Social Assistance & Disability Suppor, 1267
Patabendi K., Abeytunga, Vice-President, 1128
Patelos, Effie, Acting Librarian, John H. Daniels Faculty of Architecture, Landscape & Design, 1004
Paterson, Brent, President, 711
Paterson, Heather, Treasurer, 704
Paterson, Jim, General Manager, Kelowna, 1315
Paterson, Kevin, Manager, East Kootenay, 1311
Paton, Jason, Partner, Lawson Lundell LLP - Calgary, 904
Paton, Richard, President & CEO, 692
Patrice, Simon, Director, Environment & Biodiversity Science, 1140
Patrice, Faria, Chief, Resources, Projects & Issues Management Branch, 1173
Patrice, Tremblay, Directeur, Technologies et de l'exploitation, 1278
Patrice, Roy, Directeur (par intérim), Bureau de l'exploration géologique du Québec, 1282
Patricia, Field, Director, Communications, 1123
Patricia, Chambers, Acting Director, Aquatic Ecosystem Impacts Research, 1135
Patricia, Malikail, Director General, Africa Bureau, 1143
Patricia, Elliott, Director & Senior Trade Commissioner, 1144
Patricia, Alferez, Deputy Superintendent, 1154
Patricia, Mortimer, Executive Vice-President; Secretary General, 1158
Patricia, Johnston, General Counsel, 1184
Patricia, Munkittrick, Director, 1221
Patricia, King, Senior Statistician, 1227
Patricia, Hearn, Director, Procurement & Development, 1234
Patricia, Li, Assistant Deputy Minister, 1255
Patricia, Clavet, Co-Chair, 1258
Patricia, Boeckner, Director, Transportation Planning, 1264
Patricia, Glanville, Heritage Architect, 1295
Patricia Bernadette, MacNeil, Executive Director, 1244
Patrick, Susan, Head, Special Collections & Archives, Ryerson University, 1007
Patrick, Janna, Administrative Assistant, 823
Patrick, Dorsey, Vice-President, Prince Edward Island & Tourism, 1123
Patrick, Borbey, Deputy Minister & President, 1131
Patrick, Hum, Director, Resource Manufacturing Directorate, 1154
Patrick, Boulé, Director, Operational Support & Web Services, IM /, 1155
Patrick, O'Neill, Director General, Explosives Safety & Security Branch, 1164
Patrick, Byrne, District Manager, Natural Resource Operations (100 Mile House), 1206
Patrick, Livolsi, Regional Director, South Coast Region, 1212
Patrick, Ervin, Director, Hydrocarbon Energy Legislative & Regulat, 1220
Patrick, Stull, Director, 1221
Patrick, Cheung, Team Leader, Drinking Water Monitoring Unit, 1252
Patrick, Kennedy, Executive Director, 1258
Patrick, Alyward, Vice-Chair, 1267
Patrick, Tessier, Directeur, Financement des sociétés d'État, 1277
Patrick, Beauchesne, Directeur, Patrimoine écologique et des parcs, 1279
Patrick, Muzzi, Directeur, Accords internationaux et mandit spécial, 1279
Patrick, Déry, Ministre délégué, 1281
Patrick, Déry, Sous-ministre, 1281
Patrick, Déry, Sous-ministre associé (par intérim), Plan Nord et Territoire, 1282
Patrick, Coulthard, Manager, Infrastructure, 1294
Patrick J, Sinnott, Executive Director, Administration & Finance, 1218
Patrick J., Carroll, Acting Senior Provincial Planner, 1269
Patrick R., Burke, Chair, 1249
Patry, Catherine, Spécialiste, Moyen et techniques d'enseignement, Collège Shawinigan, 1028
Patsy, Thompson, Director General, Environmental & Radiation Protection & Assessment, 1131
Patterson, Janet M., Associate, McLennan Ross LLP - Edmonton, 908
Patterson, Robert L., Partner, Paterson Patterson Wyman & Abel, 915
Patterson, Brian J., President & General Manager, 824
Patterson, Tracy, Vice-President, 707
Patterson, Gina, Director, 730
Patterson, James, Coordinator, 635
Patterson Elden, Chante, Manager, Dawson Creek, 1315
Patteson, Julian, Commissioner, Buildings & Property Management, Brampton, 1332
Patti, Giberson, Director, Strategic Policy & Urban Affairs, 1194
Patti-Jo, Sullivan, Manager, Hearing & Communication Benefits, 1188
Pattimore, John, Executive Director, 666
Pattison, Scott, Officer, 766
Pattison, Eric, President, 768
Patton, Alan R., Patton Cormier & Associates, 924
Patton, Ed, Secretary, 791
Patton, John, President, 831
Pau, Tiffany, Library Coordinator, MFL Occupational Health Centre, 971
Pau Woo, Yuen, President & CEO, 653
Paul, Marlena (Marny), Brownlee LLP - Calgary, 902
Paul, Sacha R., Thompson Dorfman Sweatman LLP - Winnipeg, 917
Paul, France, Responsable, Services techniques, Université de Sherbrooke, 1030
Paul, Vera, President, 767
Paul, Stephen, Manager, Economic Development, Lennox & Addington, 1329
Paul, Rose, Senior Marketing & Trade Officer, Newfoundland & Labrador Operations, 1120
Paul, McCaughey, Director, Research & Development, 1122
Paul, Kelly, Director, 1124
Paul, Buron, Executive Vice-President & Chief Financial Officer, 1124
Paul, Samson, Director General, Multilateral Development Institutions Directorate, 1130
Paul, Kluckner, Regional Director General, 1136
Paul, Rochon, Associate Deputy Minister & G-7 Deputy for Canada, 1139
Paul, Steele, Director General, Conservation & Protection, 1140
Paul, Sprout, Regional Director General, 1141
Paul, McKinstry, Director, Strategic Relations, Strategic Policy, Planning & Analysis, 1145
Paul, Glover, Assistant Deputy Minister, 1145
Paul, Thompson, Assistant Deputy Minister, Processing & Payment Se, 1147
Paul, Truant, Director, North Program Operations, 1155
Paul, Arvanitidis, Manager & Senior Policy Advisor, International Relations, 1174
Paul, Sandhar-Cruz, Director, Pacific Gateway Coordination, 1174
Paul, Laflamme, Senior Manager, Pest Surveillance Branch, 1182
Paul, Ferensowicz, Board Secretariat, 1184
Paul, Whittaker, Deputy Minister, 1193
Paul, Leeder, Director, Issues Management, 1195
Paul, Kitching, Director/Chief Veterinary Officer, Plant & Animal Health Branch, Abbotsford, 1198
Paul, Jeakins, Deputy Commissioner, Regulatory Affairs & Stewardship, 1202
Paul, Wieringa, Executive Director, Alternative Energy; Renewable Energy Development Branch, 1202
Paul, Rasmussen, Director, Resource Management (Kootenay), 1206
Paul, Squires, Senior Manager, Project Governance & Corporate Initiative, 1212
Paul, Robson, Chair, 1213
Paul, Vanderlaan, Director, Sustainable Development, Planning, & Imp, 1221
Paul, Fournier, Regional Director, 1221
Paul, Jordan, Community Planner, 1222
Paul, Orser, Asst. Deputy Minister, 1223
Paul, Robichaud, Minister Responsible, 1225
Paul, Myrden, Director, Debt Management, 1228
Paul, Martin, Acting Director, Fishing Industry Renewal & Adjustment, 1228
Paul, Davis, Minister Responsible, 1230
Paul, Noble, Acting Deputy Minister; Deputy Attorney General, 1230
Paul, Carter, Executive Director, Iron Ore Industry, 1232
Paul, Carter, Assistant Deputy Minister, Royalties & Benefits, 1232
Paul, Parsons, Acting Director, Electricity & Alternative Energy, 1233
Paul, Davis, Minister, 1235
Paul, Lahey, Director, Building Design & Construction, 1235
Paul, Kavanagh, Chief Financial & Information Officer, 1235
Paul, Guy, Deputy Minister, 1239
Paul, Hogan, Director, Racing, 1241
Paul, Keats, District Manager, 1242
Paul, Lafleche, Deputy Minister, 1245
Paul, Nieweglowski, Assistant Deputy Minister & Chief Drinking Water I, 1251
Paul, Evans, Assistant Deputy Minister, 1252
Paul, Marchant, President & Chief Executive Officer, Hydro One Telecom Inc., 1255
Paul, Murphy, President & Chief Executive Officer, 1255
Paul, Bernier, District Manager, 1259
Paul, Bernier, District Manager, 1259
Paul, Brown, Director, Licencing Services, 1264
Paul, Harbottle, Director, Program Development & Evaluation, 1264
Paul, Godfrey, Manager, Policy & Planning, 1275
Paul, Morin, Directeur, Aquaculture et développement durable, 1277
Paul, Lamirande, Directeur, Protection des forêts, 1281
Paul, St-Laurent, Directeur général, 1282
Paul, Johnson, Director, Livestock, 1286
Paul, Nepper, Director, Project Delivery South, 1287

Paul, Radigan, Director, Central Vehicle Agency Business Process, 1287
Paul, Mahnic, Director, Petroleum Tenure Branch, 1288
Paul, Leech, Director, Corporate Services, 1291
Paul, Moore, Assistant Deputy Minister, 1298
Paul, Gudatis, Director, Insured Health & Hearing Services, 1301
Paul G., Smith, Chair, 1179
Paul J., LeBlanc, Deputy Minister & President, 1123
Paul J., LeBlanc, Chair, 1123
Paul John, Griffin, President & Chief Executive Officer, 1156
Paul R., Gully, Deputy Chief Public Health Officer, Infectious Disease & Emergency Preparedness, 1145
Paul S., Knowles, Director, Competitiveness & Innovation Branch, 1206
Paula, Isaak, Director General, Natural Resources & Environment Branch, 1118
Paula, Vieira, Director, Fuels Policy & Programs, 1165
Paula, Ultican, Director, Industrial Relations & Employment Standa, 1224
Paula, Dill, Provincial Development Facilitator, 1256
Paula, MacKay, Coordinator, Youth Apprenticeship, 1274
Paula, Bergeron, Directrice, Expertise hydriques, 1279
Paula, Bergeron, Directrice, Expertise hydrique, 1279
Paula, Pasquali, Executive Director, Wellness Strategy Initiatives, 1301
Paule, Veilleux, Director, Administration; Financial Services Agent, 1156
Paulette, Gallant, Manager, Access PEI Charlottetown, 1270
Pauline, Desrochers, Manager, Lands & Non-Renewable Resources Section, 1258
Pauloosie, Suvega, Assistant Deputy Minister, Policy, Planning & Evaluation, 1247
Paulovich, Nora, Manager & Coordinator, 809
Paulson, Dianne, Secretary, 766
Pauzé, Lee, General Manager, 757
Pavan, Bajwa, Manager, Multicultural Communications, 1199
Pavelich, Craig, Coordinator, 852
Pavey, Julie, Manager, Port Moody, 1317
Pawan, Chugh, Chief Executive Officer, 1236
Pawlyk, Jerritt R., Partner, Bishop & McKenzie LLP, 906
Pawsey, Deryk, Secretary, 677
Pawson, Owen D., Partner, Miller Thomson LLP - Vancouver, 914
Payne, Christopher J., Associate, Cox & Palmer - St. John's, 919
Payne, Peter, Director, 678
Payne, Keith, Executive Director, 807
Payne, Jr., Tom, 2nd Vice President, 794
Paynton, Geoff, Director, Williams Lake, 1319
Pazdzior, Josie, President, 829
Peach, Brenda, Library Technician, Carbonear Campus Library, 976
Peacock, Ken, Chief Economist & Vice-President, 680
Peana, Cornel, Singleton Urquhart LLP, 914
Pearce, Ann, Contact, Library Services, Innis Library, 986
Pearce, Tim, Director, Lambton College of Applied Arts & Technology, 998
Pearce, David, Treasurer & Financial Agent, 764
Pearce, Andrew D., Director, Development & Transportation Engineering, Vaughan, 1338
Pearl, Ing, Director, Renewables & Energy Facilitation, 1250
Pearsell, Grant, Director, Edmonton, 1306
Pearson, Anna, Research & Systems Librarian, Yukon Department of Energy, Mines & Resources, 1035
Pearson, Jean, Contact, Anadarko Canada Corp., 949
Pearson, Don, General Manager, 735
Pearson, Valerie, Executive Director, 682
Pearson, Cindy, Vice-President & Chief Operating Officer, 678
Pearson, Ronald H., Secretary, 743
Pearson, Keith, President, 873
Peat, John P., President, 702
Peck, Steven, President, 764
Peck, Frank, Director, Red Deer County, 1304
Peddigrew, Christopher J., Partner, Cox & Palmer - St. John's, 919
Pedersen, Leigh, Partner, Morelli Chertkow LLP, Lawyers - Kamloops, 909
Pedersen, Soren, President, 776
Pedersen, Lis, Director, Courtenay, 1315
Pederson, Lori, Library Assistant, Aerospace Technology Campus, 963
Pederson, Gordon, Director, Chilliwack, 1314
Peever, Jacynthe, Business Administrator, 788
Peever, Dick, President, 673
Peggy, Massey, Team Lead, Resident Services, 1193
Peggy, Kornega, Director, Financial Support, 1194
Peggy, Tibbo-Cameron, Director, Strategic Planning & Intergovernmental Relations, 1241
Pegoraro, Liz, Coordinator, Information Support, Northern Alberta Institute of Technology, 955
Pelchat, Caroline, Tremblay Bois Mignault Lemay S.E.N.C.R.L., 945
Pelchat, Carole, Archiviste, Gestionnaire de documents, Collège universitaire de St-Boniface, 970
Pelensky, Ron, Manager, Mackenzie Regional Waste Management Commission, 1309
Pelland, Philippe, Agent, 753
Pelletier, Mélanie, Monty Coulombe s.e.n.c. - Sherbrooke, 946
Pelletier, Francine, Bibliothécaire, CÉGEP de Sherbrooke, 1029
Pelletier, Joanne, Bibliotechnicienne, Service du prêt entre biblioth, Collège universitaire de St-Boniface, 970
Pelletier, Josée, Coordonnatrice, serv. d'accès information/document, Université du Québec à Rimouski, 1026
Pelletier, Louise, Pilote du système Unicorn, Université Laval, 1025
Pelletier, Noël, Président, 667
Pelletier, Claude A., Directeur général, 814
Pelletier-Giroux, Dominique, Cain Lamarre Casgrain Wells - Québec, 943
Pelletier-Giroux, Dominique, Monty Coulombe s.e.n.c. - Sherbrooke, 946
Pellicer, Fernando, President & Chair, 687
Pelzer, Paul, Birchall Northey, 928
Pelzowski, Mike, Secretary/Treasurer, 826
Peng, Christopher R., Partner, Heenan Blaikie LLP - Calgary, 904
Penhorwood, Jan, Public Services Librarian, Kwantlen Polytechnic University, 964
Penman, Barrie, Fire Chief, North Vancouver, 1316
Penna, Phillip, Coordinator, 817
Pennell, Tim, Second Vice-President, 857
Penner, Nancy M., Counsel, Parlee McLaws LLP, 905
Penney, Geoffrey K., Partner, Ottenheimer Baker, 919
Penney, Jacqueline A.M., McInnes Cooper - St. John's, 919
Penney, Stephen F., Partner, Stewart McKelvey - St. John's, 919
Penney, Greg, Director, 716
Penney, Ronald, City Solicitor & City Manager, St. John's, 1324
Penny, David J., Marketing Manager, 738
Penny, Joss, Executive Director, 676
Penny, Nolan, Supervisor, Examinations, 1234
Penny, McLeod, District Manager, 1242
Penny, McCormick, Director, Communications, 1244
Penrose, Robert, President, 714
Pépin, Hubert, Partner, Heenan Blaikie S.E.N.C.R.L/SRL - Sherbrooke, 945
Pépin, François, Directeur, Joliette, 1348
Pe-Piper, G., Contact, 669
Peppas, Nicholas A., President, 786
Pepper, David, Director, Library Services, British Columbia Institute of Technology, 959
Peraya, Michael, Singleton Urquhart LLP, 914
Percival, Michael J., Partner, Miller Thomson LLP - Vancouver, 914
Percival, Robert L., Partner, Norton Rose Fulbright Canada LLP - Toronto - Royal Bank Plaza, 935
Percy, John, Party Leader, 764
Percy, Paris, Minister, 1241
Perelman, Dell, Chief of Staff & General Counsel, 646
Perkins, Kevin, Executive Director, 751
Perkovic, Ines, Contact, Library Services, Innis Library, 986
Perks, Warren, Vice-President & Director, 674
Perl, Amanda, Vice-President, 772
Peros, Matthew, President, 687
Perreault, Rhéaume, Partner, Heenan Blaikie LLP - Montréal, 940
Perreault, Sophie, Partner, Norton Rose Fulbright Canada LLP - Montréal, 942
Perreault, Kimberly, Coordinator, 678
Perrier, Michel, Directeur général, Pincourt, 1349
Perrin, Robert, Davis LLP - Calgary, 903
Perrin, Janne, President, 728
Perrin, Darcy, Manager, Dawson Creek, 1315
Perron, Jacques, Partner, Lavery, de Billy - Montréal, 941
Perron, Nicolas, Président, 668
Perron, Sadie, Asst. Deputy Minister, 1220
Perry, David G., Partner, Singleton Urquhart LLP, 914
Perry, Jane, Librarian, Union Gas Ltd., a Spectra Energy Company, 985
Perry, Kevin, Chair, 799
Perry, Joan, Secretary, 675
Perry, Slump, Regional Director, Northwest Service BC Centre, 1200
Perry, Benoit, Ecosystem Planner, 1233
Perry, Blazic, Director, Distribution Engineering, 1290
Persad, Vashti, Administrative Coordinaor, Centre for Women & Trans People - Ontario Public Interest Researc, 1002
Pertice, Moffitt, Manager, North Slave Research Centre, 1236
Peskett, Daniel R., Partner, Brownlee LLP - Edmonton, 907
Pete, Diponio, Regional Director General, Windsor - St. Clair Reg, 1126
Petelle, Pierre, Contact, 865
Petelle, Pierre, Executive Director, 740
Peter, Gaudet, Director, Operations & Emergency Management Divisi, 1119
Peter, Hogan, Vice-President, Nova Scotia (acting), 1123
Peter, Hogan, Director General, Regional Operations, 1123
Peter, Everson, Vice-President, Corporate Management, 1129
Peter, Bruce, Acting Vice-President, Information Management & Information Technology, 1129
Peter, Rinaldi, Acting Director General, Operations, 1131
Peter, Kent, Minister, Environment, 1133
Peter, Beaman, General Counsel & Director, Environment Canada Regulations, 1135
Peter, McGovern, Assistant Deputy Minister & Chief Trade Commission, 1143
Peter, MacArthur, Director General, South, Southeast Asia & Oceania, 1143
Peter, Chan, Director General, Health Evaluation, 1146
Peter, Simeoni, Assistant Deputy Minister, Citizen Services, 1147
Peter, Wallace, Director General, Communications, 1155
Peter, Besseau, Director, International Affairs, 1162
Peter, Kent, Minister of Environment; Minister Responsible, 1166
Peter, Lavallee, Director, Program Operations, 1176
Peter, Fullarton, Regional Director, Surface, 1177
Peter, Timonin, Regional Director, Marine, 1177
Peter, Kusovac, Manager, Informatics, 1178
Peter, Croseen, Director, First Nations Development Fund, 1180
Peter, Schuld, Chair, 1181
Peter, Kuperis, Branch Head, Domestic & International Trade Policy, 1182
Peter, Portock, Vice-Chair & Member, Eucation Committee, 1195
Peter, Whitlock, Chair, 1198
Peter, Guichon, Vice-Chair, 1198
Peter, Milburn, Deputy Minister, Finance, 1204
Peter, Nagati, Director, Corporate Services, 1205
Peter, Lishman, Director, Resource Authorizations (Kamloops), 1206
Peter, Jacobsen, Director, Compensation & Business Analysis Branch, 1206
Peter, Jacobsen, Director, Compensation & Business Analysis Branch, 1206
Peter, Wyatt, Director, Engineering Branch, 1206
Peter, Prendergast, Senior Regional Manager, Central, Northeast & Southeast Regions, 1210
Peter, Rantucci, Director, Regional Transit Systems, 1211
Peter, Bjornson, Minister, 1216
Peter, Moreira, Director, Finance & Accountability, 1218
Peter, Diamant, Chair, 1219
Peter, McLaughlin, Director, Analytical Services, 1221
Peter, Kavanagh, Director, Capacity Building & Local Services, 1221
Peter, Macnutt, Director, Crown Lands, 1223
Peter, Cronin, Manager, Fisheries, 1223
Peter, Davis, Manager, Facilities Management Technical Services, 1226
Peter, Murphy, President/CEO, 1227
Peter, Howe, Assistant Deputy Minister, Lands, 1227
Peter, Haring, Manager, Environmental Science & Monitoring, 1227
Peter, Howe, Assistant Deputy Minister, 1227
Peter, Au, Assistant Deputy Minister, 1228
Peter, Morris, Chair, 1232
Peter, Vician, Deputy Minister, 1238
Peter, Bannon, Board Member, 1240
Peter, MacQuarrie, Director, Program Development, 1244
Peter, Hackett, Director, Central district, 1245
Peter, Taptuna, Minister, 1246

Pletch, Q.C., Robert B., Chairman, MacPherson Leslie & Tyerman LLP - Regina, 946
Plett, Kathy, Library Director, College of New Caledonia, 963
Pley, Tim, Fire Chief, Port Alberni, 1316
Plitt, Cameron N., Chief Financial Officer, 640
Plotkin, Ella, Partner, Fasken Martineau - Toronto, 930
Plourde, Marcel, Secteur du catalogage, Université Laval, 1025
Plourde, Alain, Directeur général, 653
Plumridge, Nancy, Director, 662
Pockey, Michelle, Fasken Martineau - Vancouver, 912
Podowski, Darrell W., Fasken Martineau - Vancouver, 912
Podowski, Darrell W., McMillan LLP - Vancouver, 914
Podruzny, David, Vice-President, 692
Poffenroth, Q.C., Robert W., Dentons Canada LLP - Calgary, 903
Pohorecky, Michael, Partner, Birchall Northey, 928
Pohrebnuk, Patricia, Executive Director, 792
Poirier, Michel, Partner, Heenan Blaikie LLP - Montréal, 940
Poirier, Sylvain, Partner, Heenan Blaikie LLP - Montréal, 940
Poirier, Gilberte, Responsable, Centre hospitalier universitaire de Sherbrooke Hôtel-Dieu, 1029
Poirier, Gilberte, Responsable, CHUS Hôtel-Dieu, 1030
Poirier, Marc, Director, 704
Poirier, Stephanie, CWPCP, 725
Poirier, Ghislain, Président, 655
Poirier, Gérard, Directeur, Laval, 1348
Poirier, Lise, Directrice, Laval, 1348
Poitras, Yvon, Treasurer, 677
Poitras, Richard, Directeur, Québec, 1349
Polard, Sharna, Manager, Learning Resources, Covenant Health, 954
Polard, Sharna, Manager, Library Services, Misericordia Community Hospital, 955
Poley, Ralph D., Gorman Nason Lawyers, 918
Poling, Jan, Vice-President, General Counsel & Secretary, 646
Poliquin, Manon, Sec.-Trés., Régie intermunicipale de gestion intégrée des déchets Bécancour-N, 1357
Polk, Josephine, 635
Pollett, Craig, Executive Director, 798
Pollock, Alana, Manager, Minerals & Metals Information Centre, 987
Pollock, Andrew, Director, Waste Management Services, Niagara, 1329
Polowin, Stephen R., Soloway, Wright LLP - Ottawa, 926
Polson, Rory G., Partner, Burnet, Duckworth & Palmer LLP, 902
Polster, David, President, 707
Polunin, Nicholas V.C., Editor, 756
Pon, Leola W., Associate, Hicks Morley Hamilton Stewart Storie LLP - Toronto, 932
Pontbriand, France, Bibliothécaire, Centre de santé et de services sociaux de Laval, 1014
Ponting, Arlene, CEO, 849
Poole, Jeremy M., Alexander Holburn Beaudin & Lang, LLP, 910
Poole, Grace, Treasurer, 829
Poole, Don, Manager of Planning, Charlottetown, 1346
Poon, Debra, Counsel, McCarthy Tétrault LLP - Calgary, 904
Poot, Peter, Secretary, 763
Pope Hutson, Mary, Exec. Vice President, 789
Popham, Heather, Program Manager, 759
Popoff, Ron, Manager, Thompson-Nicola, 1313
Poretti, Marco S., Partner, Reynolds Mirth Richards & Farmer LLP, 909
Porlier, Pascal, Cain Lamarre Casgrain Wells - Val-d'Or, 946
Portelli, Steven, Waterous, Holden, Amey, Hitchon LLP, 923
Porteous, Suzanne M., Counsel, Carscallen LLP, 903
Porteous, Murray, President, 702
Porter, Claire B.N., Associate, Gilbert McGloan Gillis, 918
Porter, Dean A., Partner, Poole Althouse, Barristers & Solicitors, 918
Porter, Linda, 682
Porter, Tim, Secretary to Council, 739
Porter, Karen, Treasurer, 757
Portner, Christopher, Partner, Osler, Hoskin & Harcourt LLP - Toronto, 935
Poruchny, Rita, President, 762
Poschmann, Finn, Vice-President, 726
Postl, Brian D., Chair, 699
Poston, Brian C., MacKenzie Fujisawa LLP, 913
Pothier, Marc, Associé, Miller Thomson LLP - Montréal, 942
Pothier-Comeau, Cécile, Bibliothécaire, Université Sainte-Anne, 980
Pott, Derek, Manager, Client Services, 736
Potter, John, President, 831
Potter, David, Chief Building Official, Newmarket, 1334
Pottier, Anne, Associate University Librarian, Library Services, McMaster University, 986
Pottinger, Fhara, Associate, Weiler, Maloney, Nelson, 928
Potts, Robert J., Blaney McMurtry LLP, 928
Potts, Michael, President & CEO, 842
Potvin, Jacinthe, Assistante, Institut de l'Énergie et de l'environnement de la francophonie, 1023
Potvin, ing., Éric, Vice-président, 827
Pouleur, Stéphan, Trésorier, 853
Poulin, Roger, Vice-President, 822
Poulin, Jacques, Président, 656
Poulin, Martin, Treasurer, 709
Poulin, Roger, President, 858
Pouliot, Renée, Technicienne en documentation, Collège Shawinigan, 1029
Pouyot, Frederic, President, 857
Pow, Virginia, Map Librarian, William C. Wonders Map Collection, 956
Powell, Charles, Associate, Glaholt LLP, 931
Powell, Mark S., Partner, Bennett Jones LLP - Calgary, 901
Powell, Sarah V., Partner, Davies Ward Phillips & Vineberg LLP, 929
Powell, Helen, Design & Technology Librarian, Sexton Design & Technology Library, 982
Powell, Jim, Executive Director/Secretary, 636
Powell, Charles, President, 704
Powell, Dave, President, 724
Powell, Debbie, Manager, 858
Powell, Glenn, Director, 826
Powell, Martin, Commissioner, Transportation & Works, Mississauga, 1334
Power, Gregory J., Associate, Hicks Morley Hamilton Stewart Storie LLP - Toronto, 932
Powers, Linda, Contact, Yukon Workers' Compensation Health & Safety Board, 1035
Powers, Vincent, Contact, 712
Powers, QC, R. Greg, Partner, Fasken Martineau - Calgary, 903
Prabhu, Mohan, Contact, 733
Pradeep, Kharé, Chief Operating Officer, 1158
Pranger, John, Director, 651
Prasad, Arvin, Director, Planning Policy & Research, Peel, 1330
Prashant, Shukle, Director General, 1164
Prashant, Shukle, Director General, 1165
Praski, Sheri, Executive Director, 857
Prather, Valerie R., Partner, Bennett Jones LLP - Calgary, 901
Pratt, Tracy A., Partner, Fasken Martineau - Toronto, 930
Pratt, Robert L., Chair, 780
Preachuk, Art, Fieldman, Red Deer County, 1304
Prebble, Peter, Director, 846
Précourt, Diane, Sec.-Trés., Régie intermunicipale d'alimentation en eau potable du Bas-St-Fra, 1356
Preda, Adina, Associate, Brownlee LLP - Edmonton, 907
Prefontaine, Gabrielle, University Archivist/FIPPA Coordinator, University of Winnipeg, 973
Préfontaine, André, Executive Director, 843
Prégent, Sophie, Lavery, de Billy - Montréal, 941
Prénoveau, Marie-Andrée, Directrice, 743
Prentice, Bill, Manager, Brooks, 1305
Pressman, Amy, Davis LLP - Toronto, 930
Presta, John, Treasurer, 866
Preston, Carolyn, CEO & Executive Director, 712
Preston, Q.C., Bill D., Robertson Stromberg LLP, 947
Pretty-Straathof, Debra, Vice-President, 817
Prevost, Denys, Fire Chief, Welland, 1338
Prévost, Marc, Associé, Robinson Sheppard Shapiro LLP, 943
Prévost, Simon, Président, 708
Prévost, Pierre, Directeur général par intérim, 862
Price, Cairns E., Bennett Jones LLP - Calgary, 901
Price, Maureen, Campus Librarian, Mohawk-McMaster Institute for Applied Health Sciences, 987
Price, Gordon, President, 721
Price, Audrey, Region Coordinator, 706
Price, Ray, First Vice President-Treasurer, 709
Price, Anita, Managing Director, 662
Price, Jill, Executive Director, 653
Price, Wayne, Coordinator, Cranbrook, 1315
Price, P.Eng., MBA, Michael, Acting CEO & Registrar, 836
Price, QC, Francis C.R., Partner, Reynolds Mirth Richards & Farmer LLP, 909
Priestley, Charles, Chair, 672
Priestley, Lisa Takats, Executive Director, 672
Prieur, Danielle, Coordonnatrice, Salaberry-de-Valleyfield, 1351
Prince, Matthew, Delorme, LeBel, Bureau, Savoie, 945
Prince, Metzi, Manager, 832
Princz, Marina, Librarian, VanDusen Gardens Library, 967
Pringle, Sherri, Library Technician, Owen Sound Campus, 997
Pritchard, J. Prescott, Managing Partner, McCaffery Mudry Pritchard LLP, Barristers & Solicitors, 904
Pritchard, Rob, General Manager, Calgary, 1305
Privett, Lisa, Coordinator, 730
Procyk, Christine, Secretary, 740
Profit, Talia C., Cox & Palmer - Moncton, 917
Prokop, Valerie, Manager, 700
Prokopchuk, Shauna, Coordinator, 642
Prokopenko, Bob, Manager, Nanaimo, 1316
Prokopiuk, Denise M., Partner, McLennan Ross LLP - Edmonton, 908
Pronovost, Janet, Office Manager, 799
Prosofsky, Patti, President, 766
Prosser, Christopher, Secretary, 791
Prosser, Q.C., Leslie W., Managing Partner, Robertson Stromberg LLP, 947
Prosterman, Paul S., Partner, Norton Rose Fulbright Canada LLP - Montréal, 942
Proudfoot, Jessica, Associate, McLennan Ross LLP - Edmonton, 908
Proudfoot, LL.B., LL.M., Clifford G., Partner, Lawson Lundell LLP - Vancouver, 913
Proudfoot, Q.C., Gordon F., Boyne Clarke LLP, 920
Proulx, Mario, Cain Lamarre Casgrain Wells - Montréal, 939
Prouse, Dennis, Vice-President, 740
Prout, Tom, General Manager/Sec.-Treas., 670
Provenzano, Marcel, Fire Chief, Sault Ste. Marie, 1337
Prud'homme, Louis, Directeur général, Mirabel, 1349
Pruden, Connie, Region Coordinator, 706
Pruden, Dave, Manager, Whitehorse, 1360
Pruski, Ph.D., Kris, Secretary-Treasurer, 718
Pryce, David, Vice-President, 688
Pryor, Miranda, Executive Director, 807
Prysliak, JeanAnne, Coordinator, 849
Psenak, Stefan, Conseiller, Gatineau, 1347
Psge, Steve, Chair, 758
Psomopoulos, Panayis, Secretary General/Treasurer, 873
Puchalski, Irene, Librarian (on leave 2012-2013), John H. Daniels Faculty of Architecture, Landscape & Design, 1004
Puetter, Juergen, Chair, 858
Puffalt, James, City Manager, Estevan, 1359
Puhvel, Kris, Executive Director, 758
Pulkkinen, Tuija, President, 750
Pullan, QC, Gordon Morris, Pullan Kammerloch Frohlinger, 916
Punia, Gulu, Partner, Fasken Martineau - Calgary, 903
Punidadas, Piyasena, Director, Operations, 1122
Purcell, Michelle, Librarian, Ottawa Hospital, 996
Purcell, Carl, President, 670
Purcell, Carl, President, 812
Purdy, Q.C., Tore M., Associate, Brownlee LLP - Edmonton, 907
Purdy, QC, Raymond C., Partner, Brownlee LLP - Edmonton, 907
Purdy, QC, Robert M., Patterson Law, 921
Purewal, Pardeep, Manager, Port Coquitlam, 1317
Purin, Sam, Director, 869
Purser, Don, National Secretary, 772
Purslow, Peter, President, 709
Putz, David, City Manager, Yorkton, 1360
Pyatt, Bill, Chief Administrative Officer, Northumberland, 1330
Pybus, Kathy L., Partner, Burnet, Duckworth & Palmer LLP, 902

Q

Quaiattini, Gordon, President, 717
Quail, Rick, Municipal Manager, Okotoks, 1307
Quattrocchi, Nancy, Vice-President, 699
Quenneville, Mathieu, Lavery, de Billy - Montréal, 941
Quenneville, Richard, Sec.-Treas., 813
Quesnel, Alicia K., Partner, Burnet, Duckworth & Palmer LLP, 902
Quesnel, Normand, Partner, Heenan Blaikie LLP - Montréal, 940
Quick, Jim, President & CEO, 635
Quigg, Janice L., Eccleston LLP, 930
Quinlan, Maureen, Partner, Heenan Blaikie LLP - Toronto, 931
Quinn, Bernard P., Partner, Norton Rose Fulbright Canada LLP - Montréal, 942
Quinn, Peter D., Partner, McCarthy Tétrault LLP - Toronto, 933

Quinn, Glenna, Reference & Research Services Librarian, St Francis-Xavier University, 980
Quinn, Barry, Secretary-Treasurer, 822
Quinn, Carolyn, Director, 767
Quintal, Michel, Trésorier, 753
Quinton-Campbell, Patricia, Partner, Burnet, Duckworth & Palmer LLP, 902
Quirie, Margaret, Director, Library Services, Ottawa Hospital, 996
Quirion, Diane, Responsable, Bibliothèque sciences humaines, Université de Sherbrooke, 1030
Quirion, France, Registrar/Director, Student Affairs, Cambrian College of Applied Arts & Technology, 999
Quoc-Nam, Tran, Senior Financial Officer, Motor Vehicle - Test Centre, 1176
Quoika-Stanka, Wanda, Acting Librarian, John Alexander Weir Memorial Law Library, 955

R

R., Helmhold, Chief Financial Officer, 1190
R., Shulha-McKay, Vice-President, Employee & Corporate Services, 1190
Raabe, Peter, Director, Environmental Services, Brockville, 1332
Rabinovitch, Paul, HGR Graham Partners LLP - Barrie, 922
Rabold, Connie, Manager, North Vancouver, 1316
Raccah, William, Administrator, 641
Racette, Jim, Managing Director, 720
Rachael, Ritchie, Head, Food, Fisheries & Aquaculture, 1225
Rachael, Fletcher, Manager, Biomonitoring Section, 1252
Rachel, Mark, Director, Policy, Planning & Evaluation, 1247
Rachel, Lowther-Doiron, Administrative Assistant, 1271
Rachel, Laperriere, Sous-ministre, 1277
Rachel, Ratch, Chief Financial Officer, 1294
Rachelle, Saumure, Executive Assistant to the ADM, 1154
Rachelle, Verret Morphy, Vice-President, Law, Land & Regulatory Affairs, 1296
Rachold, Volker, Executive Secretary, 774
Rachwalski, Maurice, Senior Manager, Capital Regional District, 1310
Racicot, Patrice, Partner, Lavery, de Billy - Montréal, 941
Racine, Lynda, Technicienne en documentation, Québec Ministère des ressources naturelles et de la faune, 1024
Racine, Pierre, Directeur, Saguenay, 1350
Radecki, Jack, Executive Director, 826
Radford, Phil, Executive Director, 765
Radman, Ljiljana, Library Technician, Hatch, 990
Rae, Robert, President, 805
Raeside, Rob, Chair, 849
Rafael, David, Senior Planner, Sunshine Coast, 1313
Rafaël, Sanchez, Directeur, Amérique latine, Afrique et Moyen-Orient, 1280
Raftis, Paul, Chief, Emergency Medical Services, Toronto, 1338
Rager, Dave E., Treasurer, 650
Raglon, Rebecca, Secretary, 685
Rahn, Emily S., Associate, Perley-Robertson, Hill & McDougall LLP / s.r.l., 926
Rahn, Jeff, Manager, Peace River, 1313
Rahul, Sharma, Senior Director, Southeast Asia & Oceania, 1192
Raikes, Russell M., McKenzie Lake Lawyers, 924
Railer, Carol E., Manager, Production & Advertising for Geomatica, Canadian Institute of Geomatics, 994
Rainville, Simon, Cain Lamarre Casgrain Wells - Québec, 943
Rainville, Guy, Chef, 830
Rajani, Kamal, Chief Financial Officer, 802
Rajaselvan, Lucinda, Librarian, Birchmount Campus, 1001
Rajotte, Laurence, Chef de bibliothèque, Bibliothèque de didacthèque, 1016
Ralph, Paul, Director, Planning Services, Oshawa, 1335
Ralph, Sultan, Minister, Advanced Education, Innovation & Technol, 1197
Ralph, Mohrmann, Senior Regional Manager/Assistant Director, Emerge, Northwest & Vancouver Island Regions, 1210
Ralph, Tucker, Chair, 1235
Ralph, Thompson, Commissioner, 1268
Ralph, Leibel, Executive Director, Community Planning, 1290
Ramakrishnan, MBA, P.Eng, Ravee, Chair, 664
Raman, Meena, Chair, 759
Ramarui, Jennifer, Executive Director, 814
Ramey, Bev, President, 676
Rami, Acouri, Senior Director, Major Projects Services, 1171
Ramirez, Rue, Associate University Librarian, Library Systems &, University of British Columbia, 967
Rammlmair, Dieter, Secretary General, 777
Ramona, Mattix, Assistant Deputy Minister, 1219
Ramos, Ben, Manager, 839
Ramotar, Karam, Co-Chair, 718
Ramsay, David B.N., Pitblado LLP, 916
Ramsay, Michael, Matheson & Murray, 938
Ramsey, Virginia, Executive Director, 770
Ramshaw, Spencer, Director, 687
Ramundo, Merika, Officer, Communications, McGill University, 1020
Ramzi, Jammal, Executive Vice-President/Chief Regulatory Operatio, 1131
Rana, Kulbir, Secretary-Treasurer, 674
Ranae, McKenzie, Manager, Human Resources, 1294
Ranalli, Melissa, Manager, 803
Ranbir, Parmar, Executive Director/Chief Financial Officer (Aborig, 1207
Rancourt, Gilles, Heenan Blaikie S.E.N.C.R.L./SRL - Québec, 944
Rand, Roszell, Director, Legal Services Branch, 1251
Randa, Lorne I., Associate, Brownlee LLP - Edmonton, 907
Randal, Cripps, Regional Director General, 1172
Randall, Meades, Director General, Public & Resources Sectors, 1134
Randell, Edward, President, 719
Randle, Larry, President, 791
Randy, McGee, Vice-President, Operations, 1132
Randy, Larkin, Acting Director General, Finance Directorate, 1135
Randy, Kamp, Parliamentary Secretary to the Minister of Fisheri, 1139
Randy, Kamp, Parliamentary Secretary to the Minister, Fisheries, 1142
Randy, Fischer, Director, Economics & Resources, 1192
Randy, Paulson, Director, Field Technical Services, 1194
Randy, Alexander, Director, Environmental Protection Division, West Coast Region, 1203
Randy, Ozunko, Program Specialist, 1213
Randy, Locke, Chief Executive Officer, 1217
Randy, Dillon, Director, Engineering & Land Use Planning, 1231
Randy, Jackiw, Chief Executive Officer, 1248
Randy, Pickering, District Manager, 1259
Randy, Crampton, Acting Fire Management Supervisor, 1259
Randy, Greggains, Executive Director, Distribution Customer Service, 1290
Randy, McAfee, Director, Strategy & Sector Relations, 1291
Randy, Weekes, Minister Responsible, Rural & Remote Health, 1291
Randy, Zielke, Director, Northern Park Operations & Planning, 1295
Randy, Lamb, Manager, Environmental Affairs, 1300
Rangam, Mary Ann, Executive Director, 822
Rangeley, Robert, Vice-President, 873
Rangi, Aneel, Director, 693
Ranjana, Sharma, Director, Operations, 1122
Ranjit, Kathryn, Librarian, Peter Lougheed Knowledge Centre, 952
Rankin, Jude, National President, 772
Rankin, Leo, Secretary, 747
Rankin Nash, Erin, McKenzie Lake Lawyers, 924
Rankin, Q.C., T. Murray, Partner, Heenan Blaikie LLP - Vancouver, 912
Rankin, Q.C., T. Murray, Partner, Heenan Blaikie LLP - Victoria, 915
Rao, Pingfan, President, 785
Raoul R., Awad, Director General, Security & Safeguards, 1131
Raphael, Sussman, Manager, Land Information Ontario, 1260
Raphaël, Dina, Partner, Lavery, de Billy - Montréal, 941
Rapp, Cameron, General Manager, Development Services, Waterloo, 1338
Rapp, Linda, Director, Whitehorse, 1360
Raschke, Vera, Legislative Librarian, Northwest Territories Legislative Assembly, 979
Rashid, Humayun, Reference Librarian & Cataloguer, Bora Laskin Law Library, 1001
Rashid, Shahida, Manager, College Library Services, College of the Rockies, 960
Raskin, Paul, President, 859
Rassam, Gus, Executive Director, 646
Ratté, Hélène, Bibliotechnicienne, La Cité Collégiale, 994
Ratté, Jasmine, Service aux membres, 864
Rattray, Rita, Office Administrator, 805
Ratzlaff, Linda, Coordinator, Rocky View County, 1304
Rauh, CMC, Susan, Corporate Officer/City Clerk, Port Coquitlam, 1317
Rauser, Erika, Coordinator, 760
Rautenkranz, Frank, Librarian, Canadian Nuclear Safety Commission, 994
Ravinsky, Carl M., Partner, Lavery, de Billy - Montréal, 941
Rawlings, Fran, Secretary, 768
Rawlusyk, Ross, President, 642
Rawson, Julie, Executive Director, 810
Ray, Geoff, Executive Director, 811
Ray, Doug, Director, Public Works, Haliburton, 1328
Ray, Edwards, Director General, Service & Program Excellence Directorate, 1120
Ray, Gilmour, Deputy Minister, 1191
Ray, Bodnarek, Deputy Minister, Justice; Deputy Attorney General, 1192
Ray, Aldeguer, Senior Vice-President, Corporate Services & Genera, 1208
Ray, Norman, Chair, 1229
Ray, Case, Assistant Deputy Minister, Corporate & Strategic Planning, 1236
Ray, Case, Manager, Technical Support, 1237
Ray, Cronin, Director & Chief Executive Officer, Art Gallery of Nova Scotia, 1241
Ray, Masse, Director, Ontario Internal Audit, Resources & Labour Audit Team, 1251
Ray, Masse, Director, Ontario Internal Audit, Resources & Labour Audit Service Team, 1257
Ray, Pichette, Director, Natural Heritage, Lands & Protected Spaces, 1258
Ray, Connoly, Director, Regional Design & Construction, 1293
Ray, Anthony, Director, Safety Services, 1294
Ray, Poulin, Manager, Research & Collections, Royal Saskatchewa, 1295
Ray T., Alisauskas, Research Scientist, Wildlife Research, 1136
Rayment, Jennifer, Library Technician, Periodicals, Humber College Institute of Technology & Advanced Learning, 1003
Raymond, Geneviève, Lalonde Geraghty Riendeau Lapierre Avocats, 945
Raymond, Kathryn A., Boyne Clarke LLP, 920
Raymond, Paul, Partner, Norton Rose Fulbright Canada LLP - Montréal, 942
Raymond, Gallant, Executive Director, New Brunswick Federal Council, 1123
Raymond, Kunze, Chief Audit & Evaluation Executive, 1155
Raymond, Cashol, Superintendent, Vehicle Management Agency, 1226
Raymond, Menard, Officer, Material Management, 1237
Raymond, Sarrazin, Directeur général, 1276
Raymond, Desjardins, Président-directeur général, 1278
Raymond, Thibault, Président-directeur général et administrateur, 1281
Raymond, Cloutier, Directeur, Planification budgétaire et expertise immobilière, 1285
Raymond, Arscott, Executive Director, Corporate Services, 1286
Raynald, Chassé, Directeur (par intérim), Prévention et de la planification, 1284
Raynard, Melissa, Hospital Librarian, Concordia Hospital, 970
Rayneault, Nathaly, Greffière, Saint-Lazare, 1351
Rayner, Wally, President, 822
Read, John, Beament Green, 925
Read, Gayle, Contact, 801
Read, Steve, Chair, 866
Reader, Mike, Executive Director, 817
Ready, Suzanne, Chargée de l'information, 668
Ready, Q.C., Kenneth A., McDougall Gauley - Regina, 947
Réal, Paris, Directeur général, Attribution des bois et développement industriel, 1281
Réal, Paris, Directeur, Gestion des stocks ligneux, 1281
Rea-Rosseker, Linda, Coordinator, 846
Reashor, Ken, Director, Halifax Regional Municipality, 1325
Reback, Andrew M., Partner, Cassels Brock & Blackwell LLP, 929
Rebbapragada, Aditya, Norton Rose Fulbright Canada LLP - Toronto - Royal Bank Plaza, 935
Rebecca, Rogers, Manager, Forward Planning & Events, 1143
Rebecca, Ramsarran, Director, Transformation, 1257
Rebecca, Murphy, Coordinator, Foreign Qualifications Recognition Pr, 1274
Rebelo, Lucie, Directeur, Bibliothèque sciences juridiques, Université du Québec à Montréal, 1021

Rebelo, Lucie, Directrice, Bibliothèque des sciences juridiques, 1016
Recalma, Mark, Co-Chair, 802
Reddekopp, Neil, Associate, Ackroyd LLP Barristers & Solicitors, 906
Reddigan, Linda, Librarian, Placentia Campus Learning Resource Centre, 977
Redekopp, Michelle R., Aikins, MacAulay & Thorvaldson LLP, 915
Reder, Eric, Campaign Director, 868
Redmond, David A., Partner, Cassels Brock & Blackwell LLP, 929
Redmond, Margaret, President & CEO, 653
Reece, Karen, Sr. Library Technician, Technical Services & Sched, Lakeshore Campus, 1004
Reed, Wendy S., Counsel, Heenan Blaikie LLP - Toronto, 931
Reed, Darryl, President, 684
Reedman, June, Technician in Charge, Acquisitions, University of the Fraser Valley, 958
Rees, Terry, Executive Director, 752
Reesor, Lauri A., Associate, Hicks Morley Hamilton Stewart Storie LLP - Toronto, 932
Reeves, Delbert, Treasurer, 660
Reeves, Andrew, Coordinator, 840
Reg, Conohan, Provincial Forest Supervisor, Eastern District, 1266
Reg, Cox, Director, Legislation & Administration, 1292
Reg J., Pearson, Acting Assistant Deputy Minister, 1256
Regan, Ron, Executive Director, 661
Regehr, Bradley D., Associate, D'Arcy & Deacon LLP - Winnipeg, 916
Reggi, Nick, Secretary, 840
Regi, Mathew, Director General, Legislative & Regulatory Policy, 1146
Reginald, Garland, Director, Lands Management Division, 1228
Reginald Scott, McCoombs, Director, Energy Markets, 1241
Regis, Romy, Coordonnatrice, 841
Reicher, Philippe, Vice-President, 696
Reichert, Patricia, Chapter Chair, 712
Reid, Brian P., Bennett Jones LLP - Calgary, 901
Reid, David R., Partner, Davis LLP - Vancouver, 911
Reid, James R., Partner, Davies Ward Phillips & Vineberg LLP, 930
Reid, Twila E., Partner, Stewart McKelvey - St. John's, 919
Reid, Brian, President, 863
Reid, John, President & CEO, 682
Reid, Jen, Coordinator, 674
Reid, David, Chair, 851
Reid, Anne, President, 709
Reid, Jeff, General Manager, 850
Reid, Kenneth D., Executive Vice President, 650
Reid, Sirrs, Director General, International Operations, 1131
Reid, QC, Wendy E., Cox & Palmer - Charlottetown, 938
Reilly, Terry, Director, Archives & Special Collections, University of Calgary, 952
Reilly-King, Fraser, Policy Analyst, 693
Reimer, Garth P., Campbell Marr, 916
Reimer, Eleanor, Supervisor, Architecture & Fine Arts Library, 970
Reimer, Michael, Acting Executive Director, 794
Reinert, Richard, Manager, Environmental Services (Water Operations), Belleville, 1332
Reinhart, Heidi, Norton Rose Fulbright Canada LLP - Toronto - Royal Bank Plaza, 935
Reinhart, Ellen, Contact, 870
Reiss, Warren, President, 809
Reithmayer, Sheila, Administrator, 857
Réjean, Rioux, Directeur, 1282
Réjean, Hébert, Ministre, Santé et des services sociaux et Ministre responsable des aînés, 1282
Réjeanne, Lachance, Directrice générale, Secrétariat, de l'administration et des communications, 1284
Rémi, Quirion, Président du conseil d'administration et Scientifi, Fonds de recherche du Québec, 1280
Rémillard, Gil, Counsel, Dentons Canada LLP - Montreal, 939
Rempel, Sharon, Founder & Project Manager, 760
Remtulla, Tariq, Bennett Jones LLP - Calgary, 901
Remy, Fernandes, President & Chief Executive Officer, Hydro One Brampton Inc., 1255
Renae, Kinnee, Team Lead, Confidential Services, 1212
Renata, King, Regional Director, Business Development, 1209
Renaud, Fernande, Responsable, Périodiques, La Cité Collégiale, 995
Renaud, Marie-Eve, Technicienne en documentation, Collège d'Alma, 1011
Renaud, Sophie, Responsable, Université du Québec Institut national de la recherche scientifiq, 1025
Renaud, QC, Philip J., Partner, Duncan Craig LLP - Edmonton, 907
Rene, Mella, Director, Financial Reporting & Policy, 1195
René, Jean-Charles, Partner, Norton Rose Fulbright Canada LLP - Montréal, 942
René, Béliveau, Principal, 1124
René, Larose, Chief of Staff, 1157
René, Drolet, Director, Policy & Research, 1161
René, Leblanc, Deputy Commissioner, 1178
René, Beaulieu, Director, University Relations, 1224
Renee, Mounteney, District Manager, Transportation, 1212
Renée, Sauvé, Director, Global Marine & Northern Affairs, 1141
Renée, Jolicoeur, Associate Deputy Minister, 1171
Renée, Caron, Directrice régionale, 1277
Renée, Garon, Directeur général, Développement de l'industrie minérale, 1282
Renick, J. James, Renick, Jim Law Office, 922
Renita, Jenkins, Head, Communications, 1117
Renkema, Karen, Director, 823
Rennehan, George, Vice-President, 813
Rennie, Elizabeth, Instruction & Outreach Librarian, Thompson Rivers University, 961
Rennie, Zegalski, Chair, 1216
Rentmeister, Trina, Secretary-Treasurer, 811
Reny, Gilles, Grondin, Poudrier, Bernier, 944
Renzo, Bertolini, Manager, Inquiries & Client Services, 1128
Repa, Ed, Director, 801
Resch, Peter, Associate University Librarian Planning and Assess, University of Regina, 1032
Ressler, Bill, Chair, North Forty Mile Regional Waste Management Services Commission, 1309
Reuse, Mary, Contact, 824
Rex, Doug, Executive Director, 806
Rex, Newkirk, Vice-President, Research & Innovation, 1119
Reyes, Katrina, Heenan Blaikie LLP - Toronto, 931
Reyners, Patrick, Secretary General, 781
Reynolds, Stéphane, Monty Coulombe s.e.n.c. - Sherbrooke, 946
Reynolds, Jennifer, President, 713
Reynolds, Lynne, Executive Director, 752
Reynolds, Harry, Vice-President, 774
Reza, Moridi, Minister, 1261
Rhainds, Marc, Vice-président, 657
Rhea M., Jenkins, Coordinator, Social Assistance & Disability Suppor, 1267
Rhoda, Katsak, Director, Community Operations, Qikiqtaaluk, 1246
Rhodes, Gerald, Executive Director, 638
Rhona, Green, Vice-President, Human Resources, 1156
Rhonda, Laing, Executive Director, Saskatchewan Federal Council, 1179
Rhonda, Wehrhahn, Assistant Deputy Minister, Revenue & Operations Di, 1184
Rhonda, De Champlain, Director, Cabinet & Legislative Initiatives & Exec, 1202
Rhonda, McDougal, Director, Planning & Coordination, 1215
Rhyno, Art, Head, Systems Department, University of Windsor, 1011
Ribière, Michelle, Bibliothécaire, CÉGEP de Sainte-Foy, 1022
Ric, McIver, Minister, Transportation, 1196
Ric, Syme, Director, Manitoba Geological Survey, 1218
Rice, David, Counsel, Miller Thomson LLP - Vancouver, 914
Rice, James, Manager, Vernon, 1318
Rich, John R., Partner, Ratcliff & Company LLP, 910
Rich, Coleman, Deputy Premier; Minister, Energy, Mines, & Natural, 1197
Rich, Coleman, Minister; Energy, Mines, & Natural Gas; Minister R, 1202
Rich, Vickers, District Manager, 1253
Richard, Joan, Vice President, 679
Richard, Monik, Executive Director, 729
Richard, A., Director, Moncton / Ville de Moncton, 1322
Richard, Edjericon, Chair, 1117
Richard, Séguin, Acting Regional Director, 1120
Richard, Butts, Director General, Cross-Sectoral Strategic Direction, 1121
Richard, Gagné, Director General, Corporate Services, 1128
Richard, Vermette, Director, Fisheries Protection Program, 1140
Richard, Nadeau, Regional Director General, 1141
Richard, Aucoin, Chief Registrar, 1145
Richard, Aucoin, Executive Director, 1146
Richard, Ouellet, Senior Counsel, Legal Services, 1155
Richard, O'Shaughnessey, Director, Québec Montréal, 1159
Richard, Brommeland, Director, Business Development & External Relations, 1160
Richard, Moreau, Director General, Operations, Continuity of Govern, Preparedness & Recovery, 1170
Richard, Meroni, Acting Regional Director General, 1172
Richard, Begin, Director, Labour Relations, Compensation & Occupational Health & Safety, 1173
Richard, Ruta, Director, IT/IM Security & Infrastructure Planning, 1174
Richard, Thivierge, Director General, 1174
Richard, Barbeau, Senior Director, Authorities Management & Real Property, 1175
Richard, Day, Director, Operations & Environmental Programs, 1176
Richard, Graves, Regional Director, Corporate Services, 1177
Richard, Stamp, Vice-Chair, 1181
Richard, King, Chair, 1198
Richard, Grieve, Director, Legislation, 1205
Richard, Manwaring, Assistant Deputy Minister, 1206
Richard, Fyfe, Deputy Minister, Justice, 1210
Richard, Keeley, Regional Director, 1221
Richard, Fitzgerald, Manager, Employers' Advocate, 1224
Richard, Popko, Supervisor, Wildlife, Sahtu Region, 1237
Richard, Zieba, Director, 1238
Richard, Anderson, Senior Director, Labour Relations, 1242
Richard, Jackson, Director, Air Ambulance Program Oversight, 1255
Richard, Dyer, Acting Manager, Sedimentary Geoscience, 1260
Richard, McKinnell, Assistant Deputy Minister, 1263
Richard, Kenny, CEO, 1267
Richard, Davies, Chair, 1267
Richard, Hassard, Chair, 1269
Richard, Gallant, Deputy Minister, 1269
Richard, Wedge, Interim Chief Executive Officer, 1272
Richard, Wedge, Executive Director, Medical Affairs, 1272
Richard, Leclerc, Directeur, 1276
Richard, Cacchione, Président, Hydro-Québec Production, 1280
Richard, Savard, Sous-ministre associé, 1281
Richard, Murray, Assistant Deputy Minister, Facility Management, 1287
Richard, Murray, Assistant Deputy Minister, Property Management, 1287
Richard, Turkheim, Executive Director, Northern Industry & Resource D, 1291
Richard, Sidney, Chair, 1300
Richard, Janowicz, Manager, Hydrology, 1300
Richard, Janowicz, Manager, 1301
Richard D., Judge, Chair, 1249
Richard Myhill, Jones, Director, Real Esate, 1212
Richard T., Lee, Parliamentary Secretary for Asia Pacific to the Mi, 1208
Richard, Q.C., André G., Stewart McKelvey - Moncton, 917
Richards, Lisa, Ritch Durnford, Lawyers, 921
Richards, Michael D., Partner, D'Arcy & Deacon LLP - Winnipeg, 916
Richards, Pat, Team Leader, St Michael's Hospital, 1007
Richards, Sarah, Manager, 702
Richards, Greg, President, 796
Richards, Bruce J., President, 835
Richardson, Douglas, Partner, Stikeman Elliott LLP - Calgary, 906
Richardson, Iris, Head, Circulation, John W. Scott Health Sciences Library, 955
Richardson, Glenn, President, 860
Richardson, Douglas, Executive Director, 659
Richardson, Hartley, Chair, 653
Richardson, Mark, Sec.-Manager, 695
Richelhoff, Jerald, Treasurer, 766
Richèr, Pierrette, Bibliothécaire, Bibliothèque centrale, 1015
Richer La Flèche, Erik, Associé, Stikeman Elliott LLP - Montréal, 943
Richmond, Mike, Partner, McMillan LLP - Toronto, 934
Rick, W. John, Managing Partner, Rick & Associates, 926
Rick, Ashton, Assistant Director, Community Pastures Program, 1120
Rick, Comerford, Regional Director General, Niagara Region, 1126
Rick, Roth, Press Secretary, 1143
Rick, Rinholm, Chief Informatics Officer, 1154
Rick, Williams, Director General, Science & Technology Operations, 1157
Rick, Zaporzan, Manager, Business Development & Key Accounts Manag, 1161

Roberts, Neal, Director, Emergency Services, Middlesex, 1329
Roberts Jones, Bonnie, Heenan Blaikie LLP - Toronto, 931
Roberts, Q.C., Darrell W., Counsel, Miller Thomson LLP - Vancouver, 914
Robertson, Tiffany, Burchells LLP, 920
Robertson, Helen Lee, Liaison/Document Delivery, Health Sciences Library, 951
Robertson, Marie, Directrice, La Cité Collégiale, 994
Robertson, Marlene, Librarian, Nexen Inc., 952
Robertson, Grant, Chair, 674
Robertson, Craig, President, 749
Robertson, D., 791
Robertson, Dave, Manager, Okotoks, 1307
Robertson, Doug, Superintendent, Public Works Department, Sarnia, 1337
Robertson, Q.C., Reynold A., Robertson Stromberg LLP, 947
Robichaud, Karine, Technicienne en documentation, Matériauthèque, 1030
Robichaud, Karen, Treasurer, 660
Robichaud, Réal, Executive Director, 861
Robichaud, Anne-Marie, Secrétaire, 727
Robin, Jackie, Director, Communications, Ag-West Bio Inc., 1032
Robin, Brown, Manager, Ocean Sciences Directorate, 1142
Robin, Dubeau, Director General, Emergency Management Bureau, 1143
Robin, McNabb, Trade Commissioner, 1144
Robin, Campbell, Minister, Aboriginal Relations, 1180
Robin, Williams, Associate Chief Medical Officer of Health, Infrastructure & Systems (Transition), 1255
Robin, Walsh, Director, Transportation Engineering, 1302
Robin M., Tuson, Manager, West Operations & Finance, 1159
Robins, David L., Sutts, Strosberg LLP, 937
Robins, Clayton, Executive Director, 682
Robins, Anne, Vice-President, 766
Robinson, Brent, MacPherson Leslie & Tyerman LLP - Saskatoon, 947
Robinson, Dusty L., McDougall Gauley - Saskatoon, 947
Robinson, Lawrence (Lanny) N., Alexander Holburn Beaudin & Lang, LLP, 910
Robinson, Marion, Regional Manager, 757
Robinson, Charla, Executive Director, 811
Robinson, Lucy, Manager, 840
Robinson, Joanna, President, 856
Robinson, John, President, 805
Robinson, Carla, Administrative Director, 850
Robinson, Peter, CEO, 741
Robinson, Lee, Manager, Infrastructure Services, Brant, 1327
Robinson, Ron, Fire Chief, Medicine Hat, 1307
Robinson, Bill, Sec.-Treas., Foothills Regional Services, 1309
Robinson, Rick, Commission Manager, Lethbridge Regional Water Services Commission, 1309
Robinson, Q.C., Christopher C., McInnes Cooper - Halifax, 921
Robison, Alan, Vice-President, 660
Robitaille, Charles-Antoine, Gowling Lafleur Henderson S.E.N.C.R.L./LLP, 939
Robitaille, Steeve, Associé, Stikeman Elliott LLP - Montréal, 943
Robitaille, Anne, Responsable des acquisitions, Université du Québec Institut national de la recherche scientifiq, 1025
Robitaille, Anne, Technician, INRS - Université du Québec, CGC - Québec, 1023
Robitaille, Claude, Region Coordinator, 706
Robson, William B.P., President & CEO, 726
Robson, Dean, Director, Swift Current, 1360
Robson, Len, Manager, Penticton, 1316
Robson, Patrick, Commissioner, Integrated Community Planning, Niagara, 1329
Robyn, Roome, Regional Director, Kootenay & Okanagan Regional Office, 1203
Rocca, Dino, Director, Communiations & Public Affairs, Ontario Ministry of Economic Development & Innovation, 1005
Roch, Delagrave, Directeur, 1280
Roch, Gaudreau, Directeur, Titres miniers et systémes, 1282
Roche, Michael V., Alexander Holburn Beaudin & Lang, LLP, 910
Rochefort, Terry, Executive Director, 681
Rochelle, Anna, Director, 839
Rochester, Lawlor, Counsel, Glaholt LLP, 931
Rochette, Louis, Partner, Lavery, de Billy - Québec, 944
Rock, Gorlick, Director, Fleet Services, 1293
Rockwell, Alan T., McInnes Cooper - Fredericton, 917
Rockwood, Linda, Director, Emergency Medical Services, Perth, 1330
Rod, Smith, Director, Policy, Planning & Liaison, 1163
Rod, Friesen, Acting Director, Engineering Assets Portfolio, 1172
Rod, Nelson, Regional Director, Communications, 1177
Rod, Dushnicky, Executive Director, Property Development Branch, 1191
Rod, Bergen, Manager, Provincial Facilities & Operations, 1207
Rod, Adams, District Manager, 1253
Rod, Kellar, Fire Management Supervisor, 1259
Rod, Nasewich, Director, Legislation & Regulations, 1291
Roddy C., Pratt, Manager, Research Operations, 1121
Rodenberg, Frances, Secretary, 651
Rodenburg, Frances, Manager, 636
Rodenburg, Frances, General Manager, 636
Rodger, Stewart, Director, Resource Management (Cariboo), 1206
Rodgers, Steve, President, 671
Rodier, Ryan, MacPherson Leslie & Tyerman LLP - Saskatoon, 947
Rodney, Dlugos, Regional Director, 1120
Rodney, Chapman, Director, Construction & Maintenance, 1211
Rodrick, MacKenzie, Director, Legal Services & Inquests, 1210
Rodrigue, Sylvie, Partner, Norton Rose Fulbright Canada LLP - Montréal, 942
Rodrigue, Nicole, Chair, 704
Rodrigue, Marcel, Trésorier, Lévis, 1348
Roe, Brock A.F., Davis LLP - Edmonton, 907
Roebuck, L. David, Partner, Heenan Blaikie LLP - Toronto, 931
Roger, Andrew, President, 783
Roger, Riverin, Acting Deputy Director, 1120
Roger, Chagnon, Director, Operations, 1122
Roger, Hohm, Branch Head, Basin Water Management Branch, 1182
Roger, Jackson, Executive Director, 1186
Roger, Burns, Chief Information Officer, Office of the CIO & Inf, 1187
Roger, Ramcharita, Director, Clean Energy Policy Branch, 1188
Roger, Kramers, Director, Physical Activity Branch, 1196
Roger, Robichaud, Assistant Deputy Minister, Northern Development, 1220
Roger, Bélanger, Engineer, 1221
Roger, Duval, Director, Sport & Recreation, 1225
Roger, Churchill, Manager, 1232
Roger, Pottle, Senior Environmental Planner, Highway Design & Construction, 1235
Roger, Munroe, Acting Executive Director, Regional & District Offices, 1242
Roger, Munroe, Regional Director, 1242
Roger, Degannes, Manager, Traffic Office, 1264
Roger, MacInnis, Apprenticeship Officer, 1274
Rogers, David N., Partner, Gilbert McGloan Gillis, 918
Rogers, John E., Burns Fitzpatrick Rogers & Schwartz LLP, Barristers & Solicitors, 911
Rogers, Karen M., Partner, Heenan Blaikie LLP - Montréal, 940
Rogers, Linda, Collection Development Librarian, Kwantlen Polytechnic University, 964
Rogers, James E., Chairman, President & CEO, 871
Rogers, Ben, President, 714
Rogers, Gary, President, 834
Rogers, James, By-Law Officer, Forest Conservation, Northumberland, 1330
Rogers, Jim, Director, Fort St. John, 1315
Rohinton, Medhora, Vice-President, Programs & Partnership Branch, 1155
Rokolj, Téa, Librarian, Government Information, Geographic, Statistical & Government Information Centre, 995
Roland, Morin, Vice-President, Real Estate Managemtn, Design, & C, 1156
Roland, George, Board Member, 1158
Rollins, Caron, Associate Law Librarian, Diana M. Priestly Law Library, 968
Rollo, Sean, Treasurer, 714
Roman, Andrew J., Partner, Miller Thomson LLP - Toronto, 934
Roman, Ann, Librarian, Akerley Campus, 980
Roman, Lori, President, 845
Roman, Szumski, Vice-President, Life Sciences, 1158
Romanick, Dana L., Alexander Holburn Beaudin & Lang, LLP, 910
Romaniuk, David C., Partner, Duncan Craig LLP - Edmonton, 907
Romanko, Patti, Instructional Services Librarian, Douglas College, 962
Ron, Roach, Chair, 1117
Ron, Wonneck, Acting Deputy Director, 1120
Ron, Wheeler, Manager, Research Support, 1122
Ron, de Vries, Senior Vice-President, Operations, 1132
Ron, Meighan, Director General, Benefits Processing, 1147
Ron, Hallman, Director General, National Parks, 1166
Ron, Popek, Executive Director, Rural Development Division, 1182
Ron, Bjorge, Executive Director, Wildlife Management, 1187
Ron, Smitten, Chair, 1196
Ron, Kilmury, Chair, 1198
Ron, Hinshaw, Executive Director, Regional Operations, 1200
Ron, Simmons, Chief Financial Officer, Water Allocation & Safety, 1206
Ron, Kostyshyn, Minister, 1213
Ron, Missyabit, Director, Aboriginal Relations, 1215
Ron, Van Denakker, Chief Executive Officer, 1217
Ron, Richardson, Director, 1218
Ron, Lemieux, Minister, 1219
Ron, Brown, Director, Compliance & Enforcement, 1228
Ron, Walsh, Manager, 1232
Ron, Chiasson, Director, Policy, Planning & Operations, 1236
Ron, McRae, Manager, Gas/Boilers & Electrical, 1239
Ron, Seca, Acting Manager, Drive Clean Contracts Section, 1252
Ron, Ryder, Senior Communications Officer, 1267
Ron, Waite, General Manager, 1273
Ron, Anderson, Executive Director, Strategic Systems & Innovation, 1288
Ron, Knaus, Executive Director, Health Promotion, 1291
Ron, Gerbrandt, Executive Director, 1293
Ron, Cruikshank, Director, 1300
Ron, Macmillan, President, 1302
Ron W., MacKinley, Minister, Fisheries, Aquaculture, & Rural Developm, 1264
Ron W., MacKinley, Minister, 1269
Rona, Ambrose, Minister of State (Status of Women), 1129
Rona, Ambrose, Minister, Public Works & Government Services; Mini, 1171
Rona, Ambrose, Minister, Public Works & Government Services; Mini, 1173
Rona, Smith, Director, Child & Family Services, 1267
Ronald, Durelle, Assistant Deputy Minister, Culture & Healthy Livin, 1225
Ronald, Gaffney, Chair, Appeals Tribunal, 1227
Ronald, Estabrooks, Energy Advisor, 1269
Ronald, Brizard, Directeur, Aménagement et environnement forestiers, 1281
Ronald, McNeil, Directeur, Secrétariat à l'accès aux services en langue anglaiuse et aux com, 1283
Ronalds, Jennifer, Associate, Stewart McKelvey - Moncton, 917
Ronan, Paul, Executive Director, 821
Roney, Michael, Chair, 780
Rooke, Greg, Coordinator, 846
Rooney, Kevin, Partner, Heenan Blaikie LLP - Toronto, 931
Rooney, Mike, Contact, 797
Roos, Hank, President, 727
Roquet, Louis, Directeur général, Montréal, 1349
Rosa, Orlando M., Managing Partner, Wishart Law Firm LLP, 927
Rosaire, Ouellet, Directrice général, 1277
Rosalind, Penfound, Deputy Minister, 1240
Rosalind, Penfound, Deputy Minister & Chief Executive Officer, 1242
Rosalyn, Lawrence, Assistant Deputy Minister, 1258
Rosanne, Kitzul, Section Manager, Bacteriology, Mycology, Parasitology, 1292
Rosato, Melissa, Associate Executive Director, 754
Roschlau, Michael W., President & Chief Executive Officer, 723
Rose, Mark, Information Services Manager, Intergovernmental Committee on Urban & Regional Research (ICURR), 1004
Rose, Ramona, Head, Archives/Special Collections, University of Northern British Columbia, 963
Rose, Frank, Treasurer, 807
Rose, Bonnie, President, 722
Rose, Tammy, Manager, Drinking Water Services, Ottawa, 1335
Rose, McParland, Deputy Director, Canada Brand Integration, 1120
Rose, Kattackal, Director General, Environment, 1157
Rose, Alwood, Coordinator, Facilities Management Unit, 1182
Rose, R.P.F., Craig D., Davis LLP - Edmonton, 907
Roseberry, Lesli, White Rock RCMP Detachment Commander, White Rock, 1319
Roseline, Soparlo, Coordinator, Administration, 1181

Roselle, Martino, Executive Director, Public Health Division, 1255
RoseMarie, Ramsingh, Executive Director, Office of Community Medicine, 1145
Rosemarie T., Leclair, Chair, 1250
Rosemary, Boyd, Director, Government Relations, 1230
Rosemary, Curley, Chair; Natural Areas Biologist, 1265
Rosemary, Henderson, Director, Medical Services, 1273
Rosemary C., Jenkins, Administrative Officer, Social Assistance & Disability Support Programs (Summerside), 1267
Rosen, Hartley, Managing Director, 749
Rosen, Michael, President, 861
Rosenberg, Paul S., Rosenberg & Rosenberg, 914
Rosenberg, Sheryl A., Thompson Dorfman Sweatman LLP - Winnipeg, 917
Rosenberg, John, Manager, Salmon Arm, 1318
Rosenberg, QC, David M., Rosenberg & Rosenberg, 914
Rosengarten, Joanna, Counsel, McCarthy Tétrault LLP - Toronto, 933
Rosenstein, Mark M., Associé, Lapointe Rosenstein Marchand Melançon, 941
Rosenthal, Susan, Davies Howe Partners LLP, 929
Rosin, Jason, Manager, 792
Roslyn, MacVicar, Regional Director General, Pacific Region, 1126
Ross, D. Alan, Bennett Jones LLP - Calgary, 901
Ross, David J., McMillan LLP - Vancouver, 914
Ross, M. David, Associate, Hicks Morley Hamilton Stewart Storie LLP - Toronto, 932
Ross, Stephen R., Partner, Miller Thomson LLP - Vancouver, 914
Ross, Alexandra, Liaison Librarian, Lakeshore Campus, 1004
Ross, Amanda, Librarian, Outreach Services, Bracken Health Sciences Library, 988
Ross, Cathy, Coordinator, Information Resources, Talisman Energy Inc., 952
Ross, Brian D., President, 640
Ross, Delaney, Manager, 685
Ross, F.A. (Rick), Executive Director & Editor, 724
Ross, William, President, 683
Ross, John, President, 840
Ross, Thompson, Secretary-Treasurer, 1117
Ross, Welsman, Director, Atlantic Region, Business Operations - Atlantic Region, 1132
Ross, Ogilvie, Director, Shared Services Canada Infrastructure Se, 1158
Ross, Hutchison, Branch Head, Alberta Ag-Info Centre, 1182
Ross, Nairne, Executive Director, Occupational Health & Safety P, 1191
Ross, Kean, Head, Inorganic Analytical Services, 1225
Ross, Gilders, Manager, Process Technology, 1225
Ross, Firth, Assistant Deputy Minister, Natural Heritage (Corner Brook), 1227
Ross, Firth, Assistant Deputy Minister, 1228
Ross, Landry, Minister Responsible, 1241
Ross, Landry, Minister & Attorney General, 1243
Ross, Wickwire, Director, Fleet Management, 1244
Ross, Lashbrook, Acting Manager, Environmental Assessment Services, 1253
Ross, McLachlan, Director, Corporate Services, 1299
Ross R., Munn, Regional Director, Transportation Security, 1177
Ross, QC, David J., Partner, McLennan Ross LLP - Edmonton, 908
Rossall, QC, Jonathan P., Partner, McLennan Ross LLP - Edmonton, 908
Rosseker, Al, Executive Director, 849
Rosser, William S., Partner, McLennan Ross LLP - Edmonton, 908
Rosser, Lloyd, Director General, Business Risk Management Programs Directorate, 1120
Rosseth, Lynn, Director, 755
Rossi, Kimberly, Director Marketing, 826
Ross-Smith, Denny, Executive Director, 852
Roter, George, Co-CEO, 746
Roth, Bernie J., Dentons Canada LLP - Calgary, 903
Roth, Dennis B., Partner, Ackroyd LLP Barristers & Solicitors, 906
Roth, Jason D., Partner, Bennett Jones LLP - Calgary, 901
Roth, Barbara, Director, Leisure, Transit & Facilities, Barrie, 1331
Rothberg, Daniel A., Partner, Miller Thomson LLP - Toronto, 934
Rotheisler, Peter, Manager, Central Okanagan, 1311
Rothschild, David W., Davis LLP - Montréal, 939
Rotterdam, Markus, Legal Researcher, Glaholt LLP, 931
Rouben, Denise, Office Manager, 711
Roudsari, Abdul, Director, University of Victoria School of Health Information Science, 969
Rougvie, Carol, Secretariat, 782
Rouillard, René, Secrétaire du conseil, 657
Rouleau, Alain, Directeur, Sorel-Tracy, 1351
Rouse, Anderson, Coordinator, 819
Rousseau, André, Associé, Lapointe Rosenstein Marchand Melançon, 941
Rousseau, Philippe C., Partner, Davies Ward Phillips & Vineberg LLP, 930
Rousseau, Yvonne, Regional Coordinator, 644
Rousseau, Terry, Directeur, Joliette, 1348
Roussel, Céline, Responsable, Catalogage et classification, CÉGEP de Chicoutimi, 1012
Rousselle, Yves, Director, Physical Services, Clarence-Rockland, 1332
Roussy, Benoît, Sec.-Trés., Régie intermunicipale de gestion des déchets solides de New Richm, 1357
Routhier, Paul, Joli-Coeur Lacasse Avocats - Québec, 944
Routledge, Doug, Vice-President, 739
Routley, Greg, Planner, North Okanagan, 1312
Roux-Guindon, Johanne, Library Technician, Ontario Ministry of Northern Development & Mines, 1000
Rouzier, Michael, Bibliothécaire, La Cité Collégiale, 994
Rowan, Ann, Chair, 764
Rowe, Karen, Librarian/Website Administrator, Gander Campus Library & Career Exploration Centre, 977
Rowe, Kevin, Librarian, Canadian Forces Northern Area Headquarters, 979
Rowe, Steven, President, 815
Rowena, Orok, Acting Director, 1172
Rowland, Betony, Burchells LLP, 920
Rowland, Harrison, Board Member, 1158
Rowlands, William A., Partner, McMillan LLP - Toronto, 934
Rowley, P.Eng, Lee, Chair, 664
Roxana, Orué, Executive Assistant, Science & Technology Priorities & Planning, 1135
Roxanna, Benoit, Deputy Minister, 1191
Roxanne, Dubé, Director General, North America Programs & Operati, 1143
Roxanne, Larter, Acting Manager, Administrative & Customer Services, 1268
Roxburgh, Bruce, Manager, 763
Roy, Jeffrey, Partner, Cassels Brock & Blackwell LLP, 929
Roy, Nicolas, Dentons Canada LLP - Montreal, 939
Roy, Stéphane, Associé, Lapointe Rosenstein Marchand Melançon, 941
Roy, Claude, Directeur, Études, Campus Notre-Dame-de-Foy, 1026
Roy, Diane, Coordinator, Documentation, Rheinmetall Canada Inc., 1027
Roy, Diane, Library Assistant, Canadian Agriculture Library - Sherbrooke, 1029
Roy, Marlene, Research and Learning Resources, International Institute for Sustainable Development, 971
Roy, Suzie, Bibliothécaire, CÉGEP de Sorel-Tracy, 1030
Roy, Lisa, Chair, 790
Roy, André, Dean, 749
Roy, Roger, President, 804
Roy, Marcel, Directeur, Québec, 1349
Roy, Maurice, Manager, Salmon Arm, 1318
Roy, Kwiatkowski, Director, Environmental Health Research, Primary Health Care & Public Health, 1145
Roy, Green, Acting Deputy Minister, 1246
Roy, Inglangas, Regional Director, 1248
Roy, Stewart, General Counsel & Corporate Secretary, Human Resources, 1255
Roy, Cairns, Consultant, Pharmacy, 1271
Royce, Diana, Chief Operating Officer & Managing Director, 643
Royer, Lucien, Director, 707
Roy-McDougall, Vanessa, Executive Director, 803
Rozhon, Jon, Senior Researcher, 696
Roziere, Jeff, Director, Brandon, 1320
Ruaro, Carol Ann, Document Control/Library, AMEC Inc., 949
Rubena, Hassan, Coordinator, Correspondence, 1195
Rubin, Nancy G., Partner, Stewart McKelvey - Halifax, 922
Rubin, Mark A., Executive Director, 855
Rubinoff, Fred, Partner, McCarthy Tétrault LLP - Toronto, 933
Rubis, Darryl, Manager, Capital Region Southwest Water Services Commission, 1308
Rudd, Diane, Membership Contact, 675
Rudi, Marilynn J., Archivist/Librarian, Bedford Institute of Oceanography, 980
Rudiak, Ron, Secretary, Red River Apiarists' Association, 969
Rudolph, Karlah, Coordinator, 831
Rudy, Harold, Executive Director, 825
Rudy, Husny, Press Secretary, 1143
Rudy, Cockney, Vice-Chair, 1240
Rudyk, Marta, Manager, Communications & Coordinator, 643
La Rue, Antoine, Joli-Coeur Lacasse Avocats - Québec, 944
La Rue, Claude, Directeur, Saint-Lazare, 1351
Ruel, Simon, Heenan Blaikie S.E.N.C.R.L./SRL - Québec, 944
Ruelokke, P.Emg, Max, Chair, CEO, & Chief Conservation Officer, 681
Ruest Jutras, Francine, Préfète, Drummond, 1353
Ruff, John, President, 772
Ruggero, Sue, Administrator, 824
Rumboldt, Bernie, Contact, 807
Rumbolt, Deon, Supervisor, Corner Brook, 1324
Rumscheidt, Peter C., Partner, Cox & Palmer - Halifax, 921
Runciman, Mark, CEO, Royal Botanical Gardens, 984
Runciman, Mark C., CEO, 843
Rung, Sandy, Chair, 867
Runighan, Dawn, Vice-President, 835
Rupa, Bhawal-Montmorency, Director General, Ministerial Services & Emergency Preparedness, 1171
Rupasinghe, H.P. Vasantha, Secretary-Treasurer, 704
Rupen, Pandya, Assistant Deputy Minister, Employment, Immigration and Training, 1286
Rushowick, Geoffrey, President, 804
Rusk, Richard J., Associé, Stikeman Elliott LLP - Montréal, 943
Rusnak, Jim, Chief Financial Officer, Metro Vancouver, 1312
Russ, Hogan, Manager, Geomatics Office, 1264
Russel, Lolacher, Director, Social Media Branch, 1212
Russell, Chris, Associate, LLF Lawyers LLP, 927
Russell, Janet E., Partner, Scott Venturo LLP, 905
Russell, Jeremy A.J., Bennett Jones LLP - Calgary, 901
Russell, Mark A., Associate, Cox & Palmer - St. John's, 919
Russell, W. Ben, Counsel, Bishop & McKenzie LLP, 906
Russell, Shari, Coordinator, 692
Russell, Steve, Vice-President, 646
Russell, Lynne, Director, Port Moody, 1317
Russell, Neudorf, Deputy Minister, 1239
Russell, Stuart, Director, Emergency Managment Centre, 1243
Russell Andrew, Mills, Chair, 1156
Russell, QC, W.D (Rusty), Counsel, Russell, Christie LLP, 925
Russon, Nicholas N., Stewart McKelvey - Fredericton, 917
Rusty, Moody, Manager, Spectroscopy & Physical Chemistry, 1252
Ruth, Copot, Executive Director, Alberta's Promise Secretariat, 1189
Ruth, Parsons, Director, Information Management, 1230
Ruth, Noseworthy, Chair, 1232
Ruth, Bitner, Curator, Collections, 1295
Ruth, Hall, Manager, Site Assessment & Remediation Unit, 1300
Rutherford, Ian D., Executive Director, 710
Rutherford, John, President, 813
Ruttan, Stephen, Vice-President, 758
Ruttman, Kelly, Manager, 748
Ryall, Rick, Fire Chief, Chilliwack, 1314
Ryan, Aisling, Associate, Reynolds Mirth Richards & Farmer LLP, 909
Ryan, Dennis J., Partner, Stewart McKelvey - St. John's, 919
Ryan, Dennis, Fasken Martineau - Vancouver, 912
Ryan, Kieran F., Bennett Jones LLP - Calgary, 901
Ryan, Maureen E., Partner, Stewart McKelvey - St. John's, 919
Ryan, Susan, Contact, Library Services, H. G. Thode Library of Science & Engineering, 986
Ryan, Elizabeth, Manager, 799
Ryan, Lacey, Agrologist, 728
Ryan, Loretta, Manager, 822
Ryan, Jim, President, 761
Ryan, Barry, Executive Director, 1117
Ryan, Rickard, Environmental Engineer, 1176
Ryan, Leskiw, Branch Head, Emerging Technology Industries Branch, 1185
Ryan, Donaghy, Director, Public Affairs, 1221
Ryan, Jacobson, Director, Repatriation & Attraction, 1224
Ryan, Lock, Acting Director, Social Enterprise, 1250
Ryan, Cossitt, Manager, Policy Analysis, 1291
Ryan, Q.C., William L. (Mick), Partner, Stewart McKelvey - Halifax, 922
Ryan, QC, Michael S., Counsel, Cox & Palmer - Halifax, 921
Rykse, Harriet, Research & Instructional Services, Allyn & Betty Taylor Library, 989

Savoie, Léandre, Sec.-Trés., Régie d'assainissement des eaux de Chandler, Pabos et Pabos Mills, 1356
Saw, Janine, Executive Director, 674
Sawatzky, Q.C., Murray R., McDougall Gauley - Regina, 947
Sawh, Dianne, Librarian, CH2M Hill Canada Limited, 1002
Saxberg, Kris M., Partner, D'Arcy & Deacon LLP - Winnipeg, 916
Sbert, Carla, Manager, 802
Scammell, Janice, Head, Reference Services, Carleton University, 994
Scapillati, Nicholas, Execxutive Director, 751
Scarcello, Shawn C., Associate, D'Arcy & Deacon LLP - Winnipeg, 916
Scarfo, Maria, Blaney McMurtry LLP, 928
Scarfone, James A., Scarfone Hawkins LLP, 923
Scarlett, James D., Torys LLP - Toronto, 936
Scarlett, Rod, Executive Director, 869
Scarth, Ian B., Associate, D'Arcy & Deacon LLP - Winnipeg, 916
Scerbak, Greg, City Manager, Grande Prairie, 1307
Schachter, Debbie, Director, Douglas College, 962
Schaer, Lilian, Executive Director, 636
Schafer, Steve, Director, Library Services, Athabasca University, 949
Schafer, Lore, President, 817
Schafer, Stewart, Director, North Battleford, 1359
Schafers, Val, Vice-President, 641
Schaffer, Thane, Section Chair, 798
Schafler, Michael, Partner, Dentons Canada LLP - Toronto, 930
Schaitberger, Harold A., General President, 775
Schanck, Daniel, Directeur général, 656
Schatz, Leah A., Partner, MacPherson Leslie & Tyerman LLP - Saskatoon, 947
Schedler, Mike, Technical Advisor, 799
Schell, Andrew, Manager, Environmental Services, Orillia, 1335
Schellenberg, David, Chair, 635
Schemenauer, Robert, Executive Director, 754
Schentag, S., Coordinator, Medicine Hat, 1307
Schepper, Josée, Manager, Merck Canada Inc., 1014
Scherman, Chris S., Stikeman Elliott LLP - Calgary, 906
Scherzer, BES, MCIP, RPP, Randy, Director, Planning & Development, Grey, 1328
Schindelka, Dana, Davis LLP - Calgary, 903
Schjerning, Mark, Chief, Emergency Services, Lennox & Addington, 1329
Schlegl, Heide, Director Engineering, 826
Schlosser, Greg, Director, Human Resources, Essex, 1328
Schmaltz, Valerie, Sec.-Treas., 642
Schmelzl, Eric, President, 685
Schmid, Taryn, Campus Librarian, Salmon Arm Campus, 964
Schmidt, Mark A., Managing Partner, Davis LLP - Vancouver, 911
Schmidt, Jane, Collections Team Manager, Ryerson University, 1007
Schmidt, Thomas, Commissioner, Transportation & Environmental Servi, Waterloo, 1331
Schmitt, Douglas G., Alexander Holburn Beaudin & Lang, LLP, 910
Schmuck, Derek A., Partner, SimpsonWigle LAW LLP, 923
Schneider, Linda, Director, Conestoga College Institute of Technology & Advanced Learning, 989
Schneider, Richard, Executive Director, 638
Schneider, Gary, Co-Chair, 748
Schneider, Marilyn, Secretary-Treasurer, 794
Schnurr, Amy, Executive Director, 680
Schoen, Carol, Secretary-Treasurer, 681
Schoenhoeffer, Frank, President, 679
Scholl-Buckwald, Steve, CFO & Managing Director, 831
Schoonover, Kristin, Librarian, Archives & Digitization, SIAST Kelsey Campus, 1034
Schoonover, Jason, Communications Director, 750
Schramm, Laurier L., President & CEO, Saskatchewan Research Council, 1034
Schramm, B.Comm., LL.B., Jerrold W., Partner, Lawson Lundell LLP - Vancouver, 913
Schreiber, Yvonne, President, 857
Schreiner, Mike, Leader, 764
Schreiner, Gord, Fire Chief, Comox, 1314
Schrenk, Manfred, Treasurer, 783
Schroeninger, Marco, Manager, Beaver River Regional Waste Management Commission, 1308
Schrum, Mike, Secretary, 748
Schryver, Donna, Secretary, 847
Schubert, John, Chair, 692
Schubert, Kwan, Executive Director, Learner Assistance, 1185
Schuck, Thomas A., Nimegeers Schuck Wormsbecker Bobbitt, 947
Schultz, Nick, Vice-President, 688
Schultz, Caroline, Executive Director, 821
Schultz, Robert, Treasurer, 864
Schultz, Tom, Treasurer, 831
Schulz, Al, Regional Director, 692
Schumilas, T., Contact, 712
Schwanky, T.J., Executive Director, 829
Schwann, Pamela, Executive Director, 847
Schwartz, Bryan P., Associate Counsel, Pitblado LLP, 916
Schwartz, Jeremy D., Partner, Stringer LLP, 936
Schwartz, Mark D., Secretary, 783
Schwartz, Sandra, Vice-President, 695
Schwartz, Q.C., Charles J., Partner, Miller Thomson LLP - Toronto, 934
Schwartzkopf-Genswein, Karen, President, 719
Schwass, Dave, President, 641
Schweiger, Larry J., President & CEO, 801
Schymon, Karen N., Associate, Morelli Chertkow LLP, Lawyers - Kamloops, 909
Scigliano, Marisa, Technical Services Librarian, Trent University, 998
Sclar, Casey, Interim Executive Director, 647
Scoler, Joel M., Partner, McCarthy Tétrault LLP - Toronto, 933
Scollan, Anna-Léa, Vice-présidente, 727
Scollie, Theodore L., Erickson & Partners, Barristers, Solicitors, Notaries, 927
Scot, MacDonald, Director, Labour Market Unit, 1274
Scott, Anne, Librarian, Cataloguing, Acquisitions & Library Sys, Dawson College, 1018
Scott, Dan, Systems Librarian, Laurentian University, 1000
Scott, Laurie, Acting Head, Engineering & Science Library, 988
Scott, Linda, Manager, Library Services, Alberta Government Library, 953
Scott, Wendy, Library & Resources Manager, H.H. Angus & Associates Limited Consulting Engineers, 1003
Scott, Michel, Board Chair, 652
Scott, Sue Ann, Vice-President, 670
Scott, Tony, President, 660
Scott, John F.T., President & Chief Executive Officer, 698
Scott, Frank, Chair, 847
Scott, Lorne, President, 803
Scott, Sean, Executive Director, 736
Scott, Dale, Chair, 794
Scott, Bill, President, 806
Scott, William, President, 799
Scott, Greg, Manager, Red Deer, 1308
Scott, Roy, Director, Water Infrastructure Divison, 1119
Scott, Patterson, Acting Regional Director, 1120
Scott, Vaughan, Commissioner, Environment & Sustainable Developmen, 1124
Scott, Vasudev, Chief, Patent Administrative Policy, Classification & International Affa, 1153
Scott, Stevenson, Assistant Deputy Minister, 1157
Scott, Leslie, Director General, Marine Sector, 1171
Scott, MacLure, Senior Director, Aerospace Equipment Program Directorate, 1171
Scott, Nichols, Regional Director, Corporate Services, 1177
Scott, Milligan, Executive Director, Corporate Busines Support Bran, 1187
Scott, Beeby, Director, Divisional Coordination Branch, 1191
Scott, Grevlund, Contact, Alberta's Future Leaders, 1195
Scott, Fraser, Director, High Performance Sport Branch, 1196
Scott, Ryckman, Manager, Media Monitoring Services, 1199
Scott, Barillaro, Director, Electricity Transmission & Inter-Jurisdictional Branch, 1202
Scott, Thomson, President/CEO, 1217
Scott, MacGregor, Chair, 1221
Scott, Gibson, Executive Director, Special Projects Development, 1226
Scott, Barfoot, Director, Communications, 1229
Scott, Tessier, Chair & CEO, 1232
Scott, Robertson, Manager, Primary Community Services, 1238
Scott, Cairns, Chief Geologist, AANDC Manager, 1238
Scott, Hosking, Director, Policy & Planning, 1240
Scott, Logan, Associate Deputy Minister, 1243
Scott, Thompson, Deputy Minister, Policy & Delivery, 1248
Scott, Sheriff, District Supervisor, 1253
Scott, Harper, CEO, 1269
Scott, Brown, Executive Director, Policy, 1286
Scott, Kent, Minister responsible, 1302
Scott B., Alexander, Director, Implementation, 1236
Scott E., Kennedy, Regional Director, Marine, 1177
Scott, Q.C., Graham W.S., Senior Partner, McMillan LLP - Toronto, 934
Scott, QC, Glen B., Partner, Brownlee LLP - Calgary, 902
Scrivener, Yvetter, Regional Manager, 859
Scruton, Steven A., Stewart McKelvey - St. John's, 919
Scull, John, Vice-President, 740
Seager, John, President & CEO, 833
Seale, Linda, Head, Information Services, John W. Scott Health Sciences Library, 955
Sealy, Jean, Librarian, Atlantic Region, 980
Sean, Malone, Acting Director General, Business Development & Competitiveness Directorate, 1120
Sean, Harrington, Member, 1171
Sean, O'Dell, Executive Director, Windsor Gateway Project Team, 1174
Sean, Byrne, Microbiologist, Supervisor, 1198
Sean, Murry, Manager, Small Business Roundtable Secretariat, 1208
Sean, Barry, Director, Seafood Marketing & Support Services, 1228
Sean, Tulk, Chief Operating Officer, Grand Falls-Windsor, 1229
Sean, Kelly, Manager, Public Relations, 1232
Sean, O'Brien, Senior Geologist & Section Manager, Geoscience Publications & Information, 1233
Sean, Maguire, Manager, Timber Allocation & Licensing Section, 1258
Searle, Yvonne, Contact, 796
Searles Jones, Janis, President & CEO, 813
Sears, Allison M., Bennett Jones LLP - Calgary, 902
Sears, EIT, Eric, Chair, 664
Seaward-Gagnon, Louise, Director, 707
Sebastiano, Rocco M., Partner, Osler, Hoskin & Harcourt LLP - Toronto, 935
Sébastien, Doire, Directeur, 1284
Secord, Richard C., Partner, Ackroyd LLP Barristers & Solicitors, 906
Secord, Richard, President, 643
See, Jonathan D., Partner, McCarthy Tétrault LLP - Toronto, 933
Seebruch, Carol A., Information Resources Coordinator, Jacobs Canada Inc., 951
Segal, Elizabeth (Betsy), Singleton Urquhart LLP, 914
Seguin, Sylvain, Vice-President & Director, 767
Séguin, Benoit, Directeur du Service de la bibliothèque, Université du Québec à Trois-Rivières, 1030
Séguin, Lise, Supervisor of Circulation, Laurentian University, 1000
Seib, Gary, General Manager, 803
Seidel, Q.C., Robert A., National Managing Partner, Davis LLP - Calgary, 903
Seidel, Q.C., Robert A., National Managing Partner, Davis LLP - Edmonton, 907
Seifert, Mike, Membership Chair, 724
Seifner, Gerhard J., Partner, McLennan Ross LLP - Edmonton, 908
Seiling, Mike, Director, Building, Kitchener, 1334
Sekimizu, Koji, Secretary General, 780
Selcho, Laura, Training Course Registrar, 643
Seldman, Neil, President, 771
Seligmann, Peter, Chairman/Chief Executive Officer, 735
Sell, Stephen, President, 816
Semenchuk, Lisa K., Associate, McLennan Ross LLP - Edmonton, 908
Semenchuk, Glen, Executive Director, 740
Semple, Dave, Director, Richmond, 1317
Senay, Gregory R., Fire Chief, Vaughan, 1338
Senécal-Tremblay, Marie, Directrice générale, 768
Senese, Peter, Director, Community & Corporate Services, Port Colborne, 1336
Senesi, Trudy, President, 679
Senft, Barry, Chief Executive Officer, 762
Senkovich, Vlado, President/Director General, 873
Senkow, Barb, Library Technician, Canadian Agriculture Library - Regina, 1031
Seonaid, MacPherson, Executive Director, Strategic Initiatives, 1291
Sereda, Rick, Fire Chief & Director, Leduc, 1307
Serge, Theriault, Regional Director General, 1141
Serge, Thériault, Regional Director General, 1141
Serge, Dupont, Deputy Minister, 1162
Serge, Dupont, Commissioner, 1166
Serge, Scrafield, Assistant Deputy Minister, 1215
Serge, Gagnon, Director, 1221
Serge, Imbrogno, Deputy Minister, 1250

Serge, Goulet, Chef, Mise en valeur de la ressource et des territories fauniques, 1281
Serge C., Beaudoin, Director General, Emergency Management Policy, 1170
Sergio, Buonocore, General Manager, 1263
Servant, Michel, Partner, Lavery, de Billy - Montréal, 941
Servos, Mark, Scientific Director, 724
Seth, Nikhil, Director, 732
Sevalrud, ICD.D., David L., Partner, Carscallen LLP, 903
Sevaun, Palvetzian, Director, Ontario Place Revitalization, 1263
Severino, John, Manager, Environmental Services, North Bay, 1334
Sévigny, Martin, Directeur, Bureau systèmes, Université de Montréal, 1021
Seviour, Colm St. Roch, Partner, Stewart McKelvey - St. John's, 920
Seward Carpenter, Kerri Lynn, Matheson & Murray, 938
Sewerin, Cristina, Instruction & Reference Librarian, Engineering & Computer Science Library, 1002
Seyed Mahmoud, Donna, Associate University Librarian, University of Lethbridge, 957
Sgrazzutti, William, University Librarian, University of Regina, 1032
Shaffina, Kassam, Acting Manager, Policy & Aboriginal Relations, 1136
Shahab, Saqib, President, 848
Shalini, Anand, Deputy Director, Office of the Deputy Minister, In, 1143
Shallow, Sandra, Library Technician, Burin Campus Library, 976
Shamie, Stephen J., Managing Partner, Hicks Morley Hamilton Stewart Storie LLP - Toronto, 932
Shan, Umesh (Mason), Heenan Blaikie LLP - Calgary, 904
Shane, Michael P., Partner, Richards Buell Sutton LLP, 914
Shane, Dobson, GO Team Leader, 1214
Shane, Murphy, Director, 1265
Shane, Vermette, Executive Director, Forestry Development - Prince Albert, 1288
Shane, Andre, Director, 1299
Shane P., Mahoney, Executive Director, Policy & Legislation, 1228
Shanna, Mason, Assistant Deputy Minister, 1209
Shannon, Glenn, Director General, Policy Branch, 1154
Shannon, Lenahan, Acting Director, Marine Security Strategic & Business Direction, 1176
Shannon, Flint, Assistant Deputy Minister, 1188
Shannon, Haggarty, Executive Director, Deputy Minister Supports Branc, 1189
Shannon, DeLorey, Director, Licensing & Finance, 1195
Shannon, Ferris, Director, Strategic Planning & Policy, 1225
Shannon, Lindholm, Manager, Finance & Administration, 1292
Shannon, Chernick, Analyst, Culture & Heritage, 1295
Shannon, Jensen, Manager, Standards & Approvals, 1300
Shanti, Dogra, General Counsel, 1243
Shantz, Paul D., Counsel, Dentons Canada LLP - Toronto, 930
Shantz, J. David, Executive Director, 798
Sharalyn, Young, Executive Director, Human Resources Services & Client Support, 1244
Sharalyn, Young, Executive Director, Human Resources & Client Support, 1245
Sharek, Q.C., W. Paul, Emery Jamieson LLP, 907
Shari, Currie, Director, Air Cargo Security, 1175
Shariff, Nashina, Chair, 639
Sharla, Rauschning, Executive Director, Resource Development, 1184
Sharlene, Jones, Director, Business Analysis, 1230
Sharma, Atul, Director, 715
Sharon, Ehaloak, Executive Director, 1118
Sharon, Reedyk, Manager, Water Quality Impacts, Development, 1121
Sharon, Babaian, Curator, Transportation, 1128
Sharon, Ashley, Director General, Ecosystem Management, 1140
Sharon, Ford, Director, Aquaculture Regulatory Policy, 1141
Sharon, McGladdery, Station Director & SABS Division Manager, 1142
Sharon, Watts, President & Chief Executive Officer, 1145
Sharon, Irwin, Acting Director, Defence & Marine, 1154
Sharon, Lee Smith, Assistant Deputy Minister, 1179
Sharon, McCaughan, Acting Executive Director, Innovative Compensation, 1189
Sharon, Moffat, Manager, Administrative Services, 1189
Sharon, Lopatka, Director, Communications, 1191
Sharon, Miskiw, Director, Financial Planning & Administration, 1192
Sharon, Shuya, Manager, Regional Projects, 1193
Sharon, White, Policy Analyst/Sport Consultant, Sport Branch, 1201
Sharon, Hadway, Regional Executive Director, West Coast, 1205
Sharon, Cowden, Manager, Finance & Administrative Services, 1211
Sharon, Reilly, Chair, 1216
Sharon, Tucker, Chair, 1227
Sharon, Porter, Manager, Outreach & Education, 1228
Sharon, Tiller, Director, Innovation & Advanced Technology, 1230
Sharon, Bailey, Director, Land & Water Policy, 1252
Sharon, Cameron, Chief Executive Officer, 1275
Sharon A., Bain, Regional Director, Finance & Administration, 1177
Sharon N., Slauenwhite, Supervisor, Provincial Roads, 1275
Sharp, Phillip A., President, 645
Sharp, Ed, Manager, Environmental Services, Brant, 1327
Sharp, BA, Anne, Manager, Marketing & Exec. Dir., 651
Sharpe, Gilbert, Partner, Fasken Martineau - Toronto, 931
Sharpe, Jeff, Partner, Burnet, Duckworth & Palmer LLP, 902
Sharpe, Doreen, President, 758
Sharpe, Elizabeth A., Executive Director, 720
Sharpe, Vicky J., President & Chief Executive Officer, 858
Sharren, Martin, Executive Vice-President, 639
Shaughnessy, Richard, President, 784
Shaun, Hammond, Assistant Deputy Minister, 1196
Shaun, MacNeill, Manager, Policy & Planning, FPT Relations & FOIPP, 1271
Shaun, Cooney, Director, Technical Standards, 1287
Shaun P., O'Reilly, Regional Director, Corporate Services, 1177
Shauna, Johnston, Branch Head, Local / Domestic Market Expansion Bra, 1182
Shauna, Brouwer, Assistant Deputy Minister/Executive Financial Offi, 1207
Shauna, Sullivan Curley, Deputy Minister & Deputy Attorney General, 1267
Shaunda, Rossington, GO Team Manager, 1214
Shaw, Blair M., Partner, Davis LLP - Vancouver, 911
Shaw, Karen, Osler, Hoskin & Harcourt S.E.N.C.R.L./LLP, 943
Shaw, William J., McDougall Gauley - Saskatoon, 947
Shaw, Glen, Executive Director, 856
Shaw, Len, Executive Director, 688
Shaw, Tracy, Manager, 688
Shaw, Mary-Pat, Acting President & Chief Executive Officer, 707
Shaw, David E., Treasurer, 645
Shaw, James F., President, 715
Shaw, Robert, Treasurer, 865
Shaw, Gord, Director, Yorkton, 1360
Shaw, Gord, Manager, Brooks, 1305
Shaw, Kevin, Director, Engineering Services, Greater Sudbury / Grand Sudbury, 1333
Shawn, Leamon, Vice-President, Finance, 1156
Shawn, Robbins, Executive Director, Trade Policy - Domestic, 1192
Shawn, Robinson, Assistant Deputy Minister, 1228
Shawn, Maley, Director, Nunavut Airports, 1246
Shawn, Burke, Manager, Human Resources, 1248
Shawn, Shea, Chief Executive Officer, 1267
Shawn, Hill, Coordinator, Alternative Land Use Services (ALUS), 1268
Shawn, Heron, Manager, General Services, 1275
Shawn, Francis, Land & Resource Planner, 1300
Shea, Frank, Conway Davis Gryski, 929
Shea, Peter D., Partner, Cox & Palmer - St. John's, 919
Shea, Shelley, President, 641
Sheahan, Ann-Marie, McCarthy Tétrault LLP - Montréal, 942
Sheahan, Cillian D., Partner, Poole Althouse, Barristers & Solicitors, 918
Sheahan, Grant, Vice-President, 823
Shearman, Tim, President, 689
Shearmur, Richard, Vice-président, 654
Sheaves, David, President, 805
Shedd, Regina, Reference Specialist, Gallagher Library of Geology & Geophysics, 951
Shedd, Phil, Superintendent, Quispamsis, 1322
Shedden, Callum, Daniel & Partners LLP, 927
Sheehan, Deirdre A., Partner, Bennett Jones LLP - Calgary, 902
Sheehy, Paul, Treasurer, 764
Sheikh, Nasir, Municipal Engineer, Foothills No. 31, 1303
Sheila, Bourque, Director, 710
Sheila, Jones, Director, Horticulture & Cross Sectoral Division, 1119
Sheila, Leggett, Vice-Chair, 1158
Sheila, Young, Director, Regulated Assessment Policy, 1194
Sheila, Taylor, Associate Deputy Minister, 1204
Sheila, Fudge, Manager, Ambassador Program, 1230
Sheila, MacLean, Coordinator, Physician Recruitment, 1271
Sheila M., Barth, Acting Director, Trade Commissioner & Market Devel, 1119
Shek, P.Eng, Patrick, Chief Building Inspector, Burnaby, 1314
Shelagh Jane, Woods, Director, Primary Health Care & Public Health, 1145
Sheldon, Lani, Team Leader, 870
Sheldon, Jordan, National Director, Wildlife Enforcement, 1134
Sheldon, Green, Executive Director, Strategy & Sector Relations, 1291
Shelford, Jeremy, McMillan LLP - Vancouver, 914
Shelley, Monlezun, Director, International Policy & Coordination Divi, 1119
Shelley, Manning, Deputy Director, Nova Scotia Operations, 1120
Shelley, Chambers, Director, International Operations, 1175
Shelley, Engstrom, Executive Director & Senior Financial Officer, 1190
Shelley, MacLean, Manager, Executive Operations, 1204
Shelley, Gibson, Acting Assistant Deputy Minister, 1249
Shelley, Cole-Arbing, Acting Environmental Coordinator, 1275
Shelley Westerhout, Hardman, Corporate Secretary/Adminsitration Manager, 1211
Shelly, David R., Nelligan O'Brien Payne, 926
Shelly, Neil, Executive Director, 639
Shepherd, Jennifer M., Associate, Fasken Martineau - Calgary, 903
Shepherd, Andrew, Director, 670
Sheppard, Marie Leigh, Library Technician, Northern College of Applied Arts & Technology, 1000
Sheppard, Maureen, Librarian, Coordinator Selection, Algonquin College of Applied Arts & Technology, 993
Sheppard, Steve, Executive Director, 719
Sheppard, Diane, Accountant, 757
Sheppard, Greg R., Operations Manager, Big Country Waste Management Commission, 1308
Sheppard, P.Eng., John P., Manager, Halifax Regional Municipality, 1325
Shepstone, Carol, Director of Library Services, Mount Royal University, 951
Shepstone, Carol, Head, Access Services, University of Saskatchewan, 1034
Sheri, Wicks, Chair, 1232
Sheridan, William J.V., Partner, McMillan LLP - Toronto, 934
Sherlock, Dave, Vice-Chair, 823
Sherman, Keith, Executive Director, 850
Sherman D., Nelson, Director, AgroClimate, Geomatics & Earth Observations Division, 1121
Sheron, Parmar, Program Manager, Mobility & Large Equipment Benefi, 1188
Sherri, Wilson, Executive Director, Policy, Innovation & Partnersh, 1190
Sherri, Aikenhead, Director, Communications, 1243
Sherri, Wright, Assistant Deputy Minister, Health Services, 1301
Sherrott, Geoffrey M., Partner, Edwards, Kenny & Bray LLP, 912
Sherry, Huston, Director, Strategic Integration, 1191
Sherry, Wynnyk, ARTS Administrator, 1194
Sherry, Brown, Director, Queen's Printer, 1199
Sherry, Freake, Chief Operating Officer, Gander, 1229
Sherven, Dan, Manager, 846
Sheward, Jill L.A., Associate, Brownlee LLP - Edmonton, 907
Shewchuk, B.Comm., Heather, Director, 666
Shields, Barbara M., Aikins, MacAulay & Thorvaldson LLP, 915
Shields, Douglas G., Partner, Davis LLP - Vancouver, 911
Shields, Deborah, Director, 707
Shields, Tiffany, Administrator, 721
Shiels, A. Carl, Executive Director & Registrar, 847
Shier, Donna, Partner, Willms & Shier Environmental Lawyers LLP, 937
Shier, E. Mitchell, Counsel, Heenan Blaikie LLP - Calgary, 904
Shier, Roger, Interim Chief Executive Officer, 682
Shier, Catherine, Executive Director, 713
Shiferaw, Adilu, Branch Head, Policy Coordination & Research Branch, 1182
Shiff, Arthur, Partner, Davies Ward Phillips & Vineberg LLP, 930

Stephany, Herzog, Registry Administrator, 1209
Stephen, Van Dine, Director General, Devolution & Territorial Relations, 1118
Stephen, Lavergne, Director, Grains & Oilseeds Division, 1119
Stephen, Baker, Vice-President, Operations, 1129
Stephen, Salewicz, Director, Humanitarian Assistance Division, 1130
Stephen, de Boer, Director General, Climate Change International, 1135
Stephen, Stephen, Director, Biotechnology & Aquatic Animal Health Sciences, 1140
Stephen, Locke, Director, Natural Resources Canada - Geological Survey of Canada (Atlantic), 1141
Stephen, Carr, Acting Director, Central Operations, 1193
Stephen, Hoare, Project Coordinator, Tank Site Remediation Program, 1194
Stephen, Bamford, Director, Systems Solutions & Architecture, 1199
Stephen, Rowins, Chief Geologist & Executive Director, British Columbia Geological Survey, 1202
Stephen, Pal, Acting Executive Director, Infrastructure & Development Section, 1203
Stephen, Joyce, Manager, Seedling Services Interior, 1207
Stephen, Waycott, Director, Electricity & Nuclear Energy, 1220
Stephen, Battah, Assistant Deputy Minister, Local Government, 1221
Stephen, Balsom, Director, Legislation & Compliance, 1233
Stephen, Charlie, Regional Superintendent, 1236
Stephen, MacIsaac, Director, Western district, 1245
Stephen, DeVos, Manager, Mineral Exploration & Development Section, 1260
Stephen, Lewis, Community Development Officer, Southern Kings, 1270
Stephen, Rose, Director, Policy, Planning & Research, 1298
Stephen, Mead, Director, 1299
Stephen A., Fox, Chief Financial Officer, 1225
Stephen B., Snell, Chief of Staff, 1143
Stephen D., Morgan Jones, Director General, Prairie/Boreal Plain Ecozone, 1121
Stephen G., Karpyshin, Director, Western Region, Environmental Services - Western Region, 1133
Stephen J., Yeo, Director & Chief Engineer, 1274
Stephens, Kristian, Senior Manager, 698
Stephens, Gail, City Manager, Victoria, 1318
Stephenson, Darrell J., Partner, Stewart McKelvey - Saint John, 918
Stephenson, Cheryl, Senior Information Specialist, 3M Canada Company, 990
Stephenson, Linda M., Regional Vice President, 802
Stephenson, Kevin, City Manager, Brooks, 1305
Stephenson, Q.C., Rod E., Aikins, MacAulay & Thorvaldson LLP, 915
Steranka, Marilyn, Executive Director, 663
Steringa, Erinn, Coordinator, 867
Sterk, Jane, Leader, 764
Sterling, Belliveau, Minister, 1242
Sterling, Belliveau, Minister, 1242
Steve, Suttie, Acting Executive Director, Canadian Pari-Mutuel Ag, 1119
Steve, Dunnigan, Director, Science Policy Integration, 1121
Steve, Burgess, Executive Director, Project Reviews, 1128
Steve, Irwin, Vice-President, Operations, 1132
Steve, McCauley, Director General, Energy & Transportation, 1134
Steve, McCauley, Director General, 1136
Steve, Burgess, Acting Director General, Ecosystem Programs Policy, 1141
Steve, Blight, Director, Environmental Management & Protection, 1156
Steve, Buckles, Director, Flight Operations, 1175
Steve, Del Bosco, Chief Marketing & Sales Officer, 1179
Steve, Tkalcic, Branch Head, Operations, 1184
Steve, MacDonald, Deputy Minister, Human Services, 1189
Steve, White, Executive Director, Assessment Services Branch, 1194
Steve, Donelon, Executive Director, Program Coordination, Parks &, 1196
Steve, Callahan, Chief Transport Officer, Commercial Vehicle Enforc, 1196
Steve, Thomson, Minister, Forests, Lands, & Natural Resource Opera, 1197
Steve, Guthrie, Registrar/Administrator, 1201
Steve, Carr, Deputy Minister, Energy, Mines, & Natural Gas, 1202
Steve, Thomson, Minister, Forests, Lands, & Natural Resource Opera, 1205
Steve, Lindsey, District Manager, Resource Operations (Fort Nelson), 1206
Steve, Dodge, District Manager, Natural Resource Operations (Quensel), 1206
Steve, Ashton, Minister, 1218
Steve, Ashton, Minister responsible, 1219
Steve, Mercer, Director, Business Development, 1234
Steve, Feindel, Director, 1242
Steve, Pinksen, Director, Policy, Planning & Legislation, 1247
Steve, Klose, Director, Standards Development, 1252
Steve, Klose, Director, 1252
Steve, Burns, District Manager, 1253
Steve, Townsend, Chief Officer, Boiler, Pressure Vessel, LP Gas, Pl, 1268
Steve, Suchan, Managing Director, Technical Standards & Policy, 1287
Steve, Roberts, Executive Director, 1289
Steve, Tompkins, Coordinator, Website, 1295
Steven, Bigras, Executive Director, 1132
Steven, MacLean, President & Chief Astronaut, 1132
Steven, Fletcher, Minister of State (Transport), 1173
Steven, Blaney, Minister, Veterans Affairs, 1179
Steven, Andres, Director, Land Claims, 1180
Steven, Benteau, Director, Communications, 1223
Steven, Radcliffe, Acting Manager, Technology Standards Section, 1252
Steven P., Barker, Acting Regional Director, Transportation Security, 1177
Stevens, Jacquelyn, Associate, Willms & Shier Environmental Lawyers LLP, 937
Stevens, Cindy, Tech Services Assistant, Nova Scotia Agricultural College, 983
Stevens, Spencer, Information Specialist, Alberta Children's Hospital Knowledge Centre, 949
Stevens, Kristopher, Executive Director, 825
Stevens, Nathan, Interim Manager & Director, 728
Stevens, Emile, Contact, 745
Stevens, Sharon, Info-activee Coordinator, 653
Stevens, Jim, Director, Transit, Sarnia, 1337
Stevenson, David, Vice-President, 666
Stevenson, Roberta, Executive Director, 677
Stevenson, Jim, Director, Comox, 1314
Stewart, Christopher, Partner, Stewart McKelvey - Moncton, 917
Stewart, Greg, Donnelly & Murphy Lawyers, 923
Stewart, John C., Partner, D'Arcy & Deacon LLP - Winnipeg, 916
Stewart, Robert C., Stewart & Turner, 920
Stewart, Robert M., Partner, Miller Thomson LLP - Toronto, 934
Stewart, Andrea, Director, Library Services, Nova Scotia Community College, 981
Stewart, Linda, Executive Director, 661
Stewart, John, Director, 711
Stewart, Basil L., President, 752
Stewart, Dave, Executive Director, 815
Stewart, Donna, Regional Vice President, 802
Stewart, Murray J., President, 745
Stewart, Janice, Secretary, 824
Stewart, Caylee, Coordinator, 678
Stewart, Kim, Chair, 822
Stewart, Fraser, Executive Director, 745
Stewart, Don, President, 796
Stewart, Carolyn, Environmental Coordinator, Penticton, 1316
Stewart, Guy, Executive Director, Policy, 1202
Stewart, Cressman, Chair, 1248
Stewart, C.E.T., Scott, General Manager, Public Works, Hamilton, 1333
Steynen, Marc, President, 835
St-Hilaire, André, Trésorier, 853
Stickney, Melinda, Vice-President, 791
Stikker, Szabi, Educational Technology, Douglas College, 962
Stiles, Paul, Assistant Manager, 815
Still, Rebecca, Museum Manager, 767
Stirling, Jim, Chair, 765
Stitt, AScT, Robert, Manager, 651
Stiver, Lisa J., Thompson Dorfman Sweatman LLP - Winnipeg, 917
St-Jacques, André, Directeur des opérations, 753
St-Jean, Monique, Directrice, Bibliothèque des sciences de la santé, 1016
St-Jean, Richard, Directeur, Saint-Jérôme, 1351
St-Jules, Luc, Director, Dieppe, 1322
St-Laurent, Jacques, Commis specialisé en approvisionnements, Université du Québec à Rimouski, 1026
St-Louis, Chantal, Chef, services-conseils en ressources documentaire, Bibliothèque des sciences humaines et sociales, 1022
St-Louis, Pierre, Vice-président, 668
St-Martin, Michel, Sec.-Trés., Régie intermunicipale d'aqueduc Richelieu-Yamaska, 1357
St-Maurice, J.-P., Chair, 772
Stobbe, Richard, Associate, Field LLP - Calgary, 904
Stobbs, Bob, Executive Director, 692
Stobo, Gerry, Borden Ladner Gervais LLP - Ottawa, 925
Stocco, Paul V., Partner, Brownlee LLP - Edmonton, 907
Stock, Emily A., Alexander Holburn Beaudin & Lang, LLP, 910
Stocker, Simon, Director, 750
Stokes, Alex, Contact, 639
Stoll, Scott, Aird & Berlis LLP, 928
Stoltz, Keith, 1st Vice-Chair, 681
Stolz, Angela, McDougall Gauley - Regina, 947
Stone, Aingeal, Information Coordinator, ENR-ITI Shared Services Departmental Library, 979
Stone, Lauren, Policy Analyst, 791
Stone, David, Executive Director, 862
Stone, Jeff, President, 788
Stoner, Ruth, Librarian, Niagara Parks Botanical Gardens School of Horticulture, 991
St-Onge, François, Directeur, Shawinigan, 1351
Stopforth, Sylvia, Head, Archives, Trinity Western University, 961
Stougiannos, Lampros, Heenan Blaikie LLP - Montréal, 940
Stout, Bruce, President, 865
Stovell, Alan, President, 676
Stovin, Elaine, Coordinator, 674
Stoyanova, Penka, Health Sciences Librarian, Credit Valley Hospital, 990
St-Pierre, Rébecca, Langlois Kronström Desjardins, 941
St-Pierre, Sylvie, Bibliothécaire, Bibliothèque centrale, 1015
St-Pierre-Beaulac, Huguette, Préfète, Acton, 1352
Stradiotti, Leo, President, 739
Strain, Kerry, Library Assistant, Campbell River Campus Library, 959
Strand, David H., Partner, Burnet, Duckworth & Palmer LLP, 902
Les Strange, Terrell, Corporate Records Manager, British Columbia Ferry Services Inc., 967
Strange, Rebecca, Librarian Specialist, Peel Public Health, 991
Stranks, Ed, Manager, Vernon, 1318
Strater, Crowfoot, Chief Executive Officer & Executive Director, 1117
Stratton, Susan, President, 750
Stratton, Q.C., David J., Davis LLP - Calgary, 903
Stratton, Q.C., David J., Davis LLP - Edmonton, 907
Strauss, Stephen, President, 717
Stribling, John, Chair, Lamont County Regional Solid Waste Commission, 1309
Strickland, Cecily Y., Partner, Stewart McKelvey - St. John's, 920
Stringer, Mike, President, 706
Stringham, Greg, Vice-President, 688
Strong, Ward, President, 747
Stroock, Lucy, 733
Stroock, Lucy, Sec.-Treas., 733
Strugnell, Jillian B., Associate, Cox & Palmer - Halifax, 921
Stu, Dunn, Manager, Operations, 1273
Stuart, Campbell, Registrar & Deputy Head, 1171
Stuart, Whitley, Deputy Minister, 1301
Stubbings, Ken, Coordinator, Emergency Management, Northumberland, 1330
Stuhldreier, Lucia M., Aikins, MacAulay & Thorvaldson LLP, 915
Stumph, David, Executive Director, 739
Sturchio, Neil, Secretary, 761
Sturm, Peter, President, 721
Stutz, John, Chair, Bow Valley Waste Management Commission, 1308
Suarez, Steve, Partner, Osler, Hoskin & Harcourt LLP - Toronto, 935
Subba, Bhim, Director, 763
Suddard, Darlene, Coordinator, Water & Waste Water Compliance, Port Colborne, 1336
Sue, Milburn-Hopwood, Director General, Environmental Protection Operations, 1134
Sue, Kessler, Executive Director, Information Management Branch, 1189

Sue, Bonnyman, Director, Electricity Generation & Regulation Branch, 1202
Sue, Stultz, Minister, Social Development; Minister Responsible, 1225
Sue, Lo, Assistant Deputy Minister, 1250
Sue, Richards, Director, Human Resources, 1302
Suellen, Sheppard, Manager, Health Workforce Planning, 1230
Sugden, Lori, Map Curator, Map Library, 968
Sugden, Ian, Director, Planning & Development, Orillia, 1335
Sukhy, Kent, Director, Design & Traffic Engineering, 1292
Suki, Wong, Director General, Critical Infrastructure & Strategic Coordination, 1170
Sullivan, Lori K., Partner, Davies Ward Phillips & Vineberg LLP, 930
Sullivan, Peter J., Partner, Lazier Hickey Langs O'Neal, 923
Sullivan, Gerry, President, 682
Sullivan, Leah, Vice-President, 847
Sullivan, Brian, General Manager, 722
Sullivan, Gerry, Coordinator, 806
Summer, Janet, Executive Director, 714
Summers, James, Editor, 704
Summers, P.Eng, Richard, Chair, 664
Sun, Wei Kiat, Singleton Urquhart LLP, 914
Sun, Karen, Secretary, 735
Sunderland, Laura, Vice-President, 707
Suppa, Ralph, President & General Manager, 706
Surette, Marc, Executive Director, 812
Surgeoner, Gord, President, 814
Surprenant, Richard, President & Chair, 642
Susak, Bill, General Manager, Coquitlam, 1314
Susan, Winkelaar, Associate Director, Global Analysis, 1120
Susan, Zimmerman, Executive Director, Secretariat on Research Ethics, 1130
Susan, Steffen, Acting Regional Director General, West & Central Africa, 1130
Susan, Wild, Director, MSC Regional Operations Renewal, 1134
Susan, Anzolin, Director General, Innovation & Economic Development, 1139
Susan, Mojgani, Director, Species at Risk Program Management, 1140
Susan, Waters, Director, Aboriginal Programs, 1140
Susan, Farlinger, Regional Director General, 1141
Susan, Hart, Director General, Audit & Evaluation, 1153
Susan, Kay, Director, Marketing, 1156
Susan, Chambers, Director General, Real Property, 1157
Susan, Truscott, Director, Military Personnel Research & Analysis, 1158
Susan, Simpson, Manager, Atlantic Operations & Finance, 1159
Susan, Truppe, Parliamentary Secretary for Status of Women, 1173
Susan, Archer, Director, Marine Security Regulatory Affairs, 1176
Susan, Greene, Manager, Multi-Modal Training & Standards, 1178
Susan, Cribbs, Executive Director, Policy, Planning, & Legislativ, 1182
Susan, Schlemko, Manager, Board Reviews, 1186
Susan, Anderson, Executive Director, EHR Delivery Services, 1189
Susan, West, Manager, Issues Management & Corporate Support, 1190
Susan, Huberdeau, Team Lead, Administration, 1193
Susan, Mallory, Auditor/Grower Liaison, 1198
Susan, Smith, Officer, Administrative Services, 1199
Susan, Ibbott, Corporate Director, Public Engagement, 1200
Susan, Croome, Commissioner, BC Film Commission, 1201
Susan, Galbraith, Director, Special Authority, 1208
Susan, Yurkovich, Executive Vice-President, Site C Clean Energy Proj, 1208
Susan, Swan, Co-chair, 1216
Susan, Tessler, Director, Programs, 1217
Susan, Atkinson, Director, Local & Regional Governance, 1221
Susan, Morell, Director, Content Development, 1226
Susan, Sullivan, Minister, 1229
Susan, Gillam, President & CEO, 1229
Susan, Eveleigh, Coordinator, Fuel Operations, 1239
Susan, Stevens, Director, Standards & Policy, 1243
Susan, Picarello, Director, Assistive Devices Program, 1255
Susan, Picarello, Acting Director, Psychiatric Patient Advocate Office, 1255
Susan, MacGregor, Manager, Office of the Surveyor General, 1260
Susan, Connell, Manager, Parking, 1273
Susan, LeFort, Manager, Apprenticeship Training, 1274
Susan, Loewen, Director, Financial Management, 1289
Susan, Amrud, Executive Director, 1293
Susan, Mandziuk, Manager, Yorkton WDM, 1295
Susan A., McLennan, Regional Director, Communications & Marketing, 1177
Susan A., Williams, Assistant Deputy Minister, 1189
Susan A., MacKenzie, Director, 1274
Susan D., Spencer, Director, Intelligent Transportation System, 1175
Susanna, Laaksonen-Craig, Executive Lead, Forest Sector Initiatives, 1206
Susanna, Duke, Director, Information Management, 1234
Susanna, Zagar, Chief Strategy Officer, 1264
Susi, Chamberlain, Coordinator, 1225
Susie, Miller, Director General, Sector Development & Analysis Di, 1119
Susie, Couto, Regional Director, Finance & Administration, 1178
Sutcliffe, John, Executive Director, 694
Sutherland, Robert, Manager, Library, Archives & Record Management, Yukon College, 1035
Sutherland, Bonnie, Executive Director, 812
Sutherland, Tyrone W., 2nd Vice-President, 872
Sutherland, Helen, Contact, 755
Sutherland, John, Region Coordinator, 706
Sutherland, Janet, Director, 708
Sutherland, John K., Executive Secretary, 669
Sutin, Richard S., Senior Partner, Norton Rose Fulbright Canada LLP - Toronto - Royal Bank Plaza, 935
Sutton, Roxanne, Librarian, Labrador West Campus, 977
Sutton, Chris, Director, 802
Sutton, Stephanie, Executive Assistant, 712
Sutts, Q.C., Clifford N., Sutts, Strosberg LLP, 937
Suzanne, Keating, Director, Commercialization & Environmental Programs Division, 1120
Suzanne, Chevalier, Branch Administration Officer, Management Services, 1134
Suzanne, Beaudoin, Correspondence Officer, 1136
Suzanne, Fortier, President, 1165
Suzanne, Lorrain, Senior Director, Science Procurement Directorate, 1171
Suzanne, Nichol, Acting Manager, HR Information Management Systems, HR Planning, Performance Measurement & Information Management, 1173
Suzanne, Manahan, Executive Director, Regulatory & FN Engagement, LNG Initiative, 1202
Suzanne, Taylor, Executive Director, Drug Use Optimization, 1208
Suzanne, Bourgeois, Director, Information Technology Services, 1224
Suzanne, Wile, Director, Financial Accounting, 1242
Suzanne, Payette, District Administrative Assistant, 1253
Suzanne, Rowe Knight, Acting Director, Culture Agencies, 1263
Suzanne, Pilote, Directrice régionale, 1277
Suzanne, Lévesque, Sous-ministre adjointe, 1280
Suzanne, Giguère, Sous-ministre, 1284
Suzanne, Thérien, Sous-ministre adjointe, 1286
Suzanne R., Abrams, Director, Research, 1160
Suzie, Da Costa, Senior Administrative Officer, Branch Planning & Coordination Team, 1121
Suzuki, David, Chair, 741
Svarich, Brigitte, Director, 745
Svein, Haugen, Director, Properties & Land Management Branch, 1212
Svend, Holm, Director, Area Management Office - Trade Policy & Negotiations Branch, 1143
Swabey, Ted, General Manager, Nanaimo, 1316
Swainson, Jillian, Associate, Brownlee LLP - Edmonton, 907
Swanepoel, Marinus, University Librarian, University of Lethbridge, 957
Swanson, Marnie, University Librarian, University of Victoria Libraries, 969
Swanson, Kevin, Director, Brooks, 1305
Swaren, Kristine, Librarian, Canadian Organic Growers Inc., 994
Swayzer, Natalie, Executive Director, 711
Sweeney, Tara M., Soloway, Wright LLP - Ottawa, 926
Sweeney Marsh, Joan, Manager, Library Services, Sheridan College Institute of Technology & Advanced Learning, 992
Sweetland, Mary Beth, Vice-President, 831
Sweetland, Barb, Manager, 638
Sweetlove, Jim A., Chair, 735
Swick, Brenda C., Partner, McCarthy Tétrault LLP - Toronto, 933
Swift, Leah, Researcher, R.V. Anderson Associates Limited, 1006
Swift, Roger, President, 786
Swift, Kelly, General Manager, Pitt Meadows, 1316
Swinimer, Hope, Founder & Director, 769
Switzer, Doug, Manager Government Relations, 826
Switzer, Sheldon, Director, Building Services & Chief Building Offic, Oakville, 1335
Sydenham, Gina, Chair, 867
Sydney, Swift, Director, Investigation & Standards, 1210
Syed, Farzana, Regional Manager, 859
Sykes, Stephanie J., Partner, Heenan Blaikie LLP - Toronto, 932
Sylvain, Paradis, Director General, Applied Research & Analysis, 1146
Sylvain, Laporte, Commissioner, Patents; Registrar, Trademarks; Chie, 1153
Sylvain, Dufour, Vice-President, Resources & Chief Financial Officer, 1155
Sylvain, Sirois, Director General & Chief, Military Engineering, 1157
Sylvain, Lemay, Project Manager, Centre for Topographic Information - Ottawa, 1165
Sylvain, Savoie, Financial Officer, Financial Programs, 1220
Sylvain, Gaudreault, Ministre, 1276
Sylvain, Boucher, Sous-ministre, 1276
Sylvain, Goulet, Directeur, Géomatique, et de la statistique, 1276
Sylvain, Gingras, Directeur, Direction des études, 1277
Sylvain, Périgny, Directeur général adjointe, Investissements, 1283
Sylvain, Gagnon, Sous-ministre adjoint, 1283
Sylvain, Lacombe, Directeur général, Services à la clientèle touristique, 1284
Sylvain, Gaudreault, Ministre, 1284
Sylvana, Guindon, Director, Nuclear Energy, 1165
Sylvester, Bruce, Vice-President, 838
Sylvestre, Chantal, Partner, Heenan Blaikie LLP - Montréal, 940
Sylvestre, Frédéric, Sylvestre & Associés Avocats S.E.N.C., 945
Sylvestre, Michel G., Senior Partner, Norton Rose Fulbright Canada LLP - Montréal, 942
Sylvia, Selig, Director, Business Analysis, 1209
Sylvia, Haener, Deputy Minister, 1238
Sylvia, Shedden, Director, Public Health Standards, Practice & Accountability, 1255
Sylvia T., Boucher, Senior Policy Advisor, Planning & Renewal Division, 1162
Sylvian, Lachance, Executive Director, Regulatory Services & Quality Assurance, 1176
Sylvie, Dubreuil, Acting Director, Operations, Canadian Pari-Mutuel Agency, 1119
Sylvie, Millette LeDuc, Director, Industry Engagement Division, 1119
Sylvie, Renaud, Regional Director, 1131
Sylvie, Lapointe, Associate Director General, International Affairs, 1141
Sylvie, Stachenko, Deputy Chief Public Health Officer, Health Promotion & Chronic Disease, 1145
Sylvie, Tilden, Director, Capital Interpretation & Commemorations, 1157
Sylvie, Dostaler, Senior Advisor, 1160
Sylvie, Dostaler, Senior Advisor, 1160
Sylvie, Dostaler, Senior Advisor, 1160
Sylvie, Dostaler, 1160
Sylvie, Dostaler, Senior Advisor, 1160
Sylvie, Dostaler, Senior Advisor, 1161
Sylvie, Letellier, Director General, Corporate Renewal Office, 1162
Sylvie, Lalonde, Senior Director, Major Projects Directorate - Land, 1171
Sylvie, Dionne, Manager, Material Analysis & Structures, 1178
Sylvie, Nadeau, Executive Director, New Brunswick Public Library S, 1224
Sylvie, Plante, Directrice, Ressources financières et matérielles, 1276
Sylvie, Denis, Directeur régional, 1277
Sylvie, Létourneau, Présidente, 1278
Sylvie, Beaulieu, Directrice, Ressources humaines, 1279
Sylvie, Bernier, Directrice, Qualité, 1283
Sylvie, Quenneville, Directrice générale, Marketing, 1284
Symington, Jo-Ann, Coordinator, Red Deer County, 1304

Symmonds, Philip D. A., Partner, Torys LLP - Toronto, 936
Symon, Forbes, Vice-President, 826
Symons, Elisabeth, Partner, Miller Thomson LLP - Toronto, 934
Syms, Laura, Business & Data Services Librarian, Cape Breton University, 983
Synnott, Matthew, Stikeman Elliott LLP - Calgary, 906
Szel, Marcella, Chairman (Executive Committee), 869
Szep, Jutta, Librarian, Walker, Nott, Dragicevic Associates Limited, 1009
Szkotnicki, Jean, President, 683
Szot-Sacawa, Anna, Circulation Coordinator, Bora Laskin Law Library, 1001
Szott, Tara, Associate, Duncan Craig LLP - Edmonton, 907
Szucs, Janette, Coordinator, Parkland County, 1304

T

Tachuk, Rick, Director, 694
Tagami, Reiko, Information & Resolutions Coordinator, Union of British Columbia Municipalities, 964
Tai, George, Partner, Carscallen LLP, 903
Tai, Sabrina, Contact, 648
Tait, B. Douglas, Thompson Dorfman Sweatman LLP - Winnipeg, 917
Tait, Glenn D., Partner, McLennan Ross LLP - Yellowknife, 920
Taitinger, Jeremy D., Partner, Reynolds Mirth Richards & Farmer LLP, 909
Tak, John W., President & Chief Executive Officer, 702
Tak, Devendra, Manager, 729
Takeda, Sadao, Vice-President, 781
Taki, Sarantakis, Assistant Deputy Minister, Policy & Communications, 1155
Takishita, Faith, Coordinator, Special Collections & Archives, Vancouver Island University, 962
Talbot, Richard, Tremblay Bois Mignault Lemay S.E.N.C.R.L., 945
Talbot, Steve, Executive Director, 756
Tallon, Gregory J., Thompson Dorfman Sweatman LLP - Winnipeg, 917
Tallon, Jan, Manager, Learning Centres & LRC Operations, Centennial College, 1002
Tallon, Wayne, Director, Fredericton, 1322
Tam, Bill, President & Chief Executive Officer, 678
Tamara, Parschin-Rybkin, Vice-President/Legal General Counsel & Corporate S, Legal Services, 1128
Tamara, Danshin, Regional Manager, Northeast, 1209
Tami, Denomie, Director, Health Promotion, 1291
Tamie, Folwark, Manager, Program, 1291
Tammy, Schulz, Director, Innovation & Competitiveness, 1179
Tammy, Merenick, Administrative Coordinator, 1196
Tammy, Donison-McKay, Manager, Financial Services, 1212
Tammy, Caseley, Manager, Immigration, 1224
Tammy, Turner, Director, Corporate Services, 1275
Tamura-O'Connor, Bernadita, Counsel, Lawson Lundell LLP - Calgary, 904
Tan, Darlene, Reference Librarian, Fisheries & Oceans Canada, 995
Tandon, Nidhi, President, 821
Tanguay, Denis, President & Chief Executive Officer, 700
Tanis, Bjornson, Vice-Chair, 1219
Tannen, Lesley, Executive Director, 676
Tanner, Richard C., Scott Venturo LLP, 905
Tanner, Annette, Contact, 868
Tannis, Brown, Executive Director, 1190
Tanton, Tim, Senior Manager, Capital Regional District, 1310
Tanya, Dagenais, Acting Executive Advisor to the Senior ADM, 1141
Tanya, Twynstra, Executive Director, Citizen Engagement, 1200
Tanya, Noseworthy, Executive Director, Policy & Planning, 1233
Tanya, Collier MacDonald, Manager, Communications, 1245
Tanya, Campbell, Manager, Women's Secretariat, 1247
Tanya, Mullally, Provincial Emergency Management Coordinator, Emerg, 1268
Tanzola, Christopher J., Partner, McCarthy Tétrault LLP - Toronto, 933
Tapp, Len, Division Manager, Transit, Cornwall, 1332
Tappenden, Kristen, President, 761
Tara, Arndt, Veterinary Pathologist, 1198
Tara, Faganello, Assistant Deputy Minister, Management Services, 1210
Tara, Fraser, Fire Service Advisor, Lower Mainland Region, 1210
Tardif, Hélène, Bibliothécaire, Bibliothèque de botanique - L'Institut de recherche en biologie v, 1015
Tardiff, Deb, Coordinator, 792
Tarini, Natalie, Manager, 725
Tarita, Teri, Librarian, Pacific Salmon Commission, 966
Tarnawsky, Peter, General Manager, Sturgeon County, 1304
Tarnowsky, Gordon L., Dentons Canada LLP - Calgary, 903
Tarry, Greg, Manager, 688
Taschuk, QC, Peter P., Partner, McLennan Ross LLP - Edmonton, 908
Tasha, Sargent, Coordinator, 1137
Tastad, Mary, Reference Librarian, Law Library, 1033
Tate, James P., Partner, Ratcliff & Company LLP, 910
Tatsumi, Kazuyuki, President, 786
Tattenbach, Franz, President/CEO, 780
Tavender, Q.C., E. David D., Dentons Canada LLP - Calgary, 903
Tavish, Annis, Director, Financial Operations, 1200
Tay, Derrick C., Senior Partner, Norton Rose Fulbright Canada LLP - Toronto - Royal Bank Plaza, 935
Taylor, Allison L., Counsel, Stringer LLP, 936
Taylor, Blair S., O'Connor MacLeod Hanna LLP, 925
Taylor, G. Bruce, Aikins, MacAulay & Thorvaldson LLP, 915
Taylor, John K., Partner, Burnet, Duckworth & Palmer LLP, 902
Taylor, Paul S., Associate, Brownlee LLP - Calgary, 902
Taylor, Robert C., Blaney McMurtry LLP, 928
Taylor, Leslie, Reference/Technical Services Librarian, William R. Lederman Law Library, 988
Taylor, Lorelle, Chief Information Officer, Ontario Ministry of Health & Long-Term Care, 1005
Taylor, R. N. (Neil), Secretary General, 783
Taylor, Crispin, Executive Director, 649
Taylor, Curtis, President, 661
Taylor, Nick, President, 774
Taylor, Bill, President & Chief Executive Officer, 670
Taylor, Rolster, Tradeshow Manager, 698
Taylor, Brian, Chair, 826
Taylor, Janice, Director, 725
Taylor, Dana, Executive Vice President, 795
Taylor, Donna, Vice President, 666
Taylor, Ron, Chief Executive Officer, 805
Taylor, Peter, Chair, 675
Taylor, Brian, Manager, Portage La Prairie, 1321
Taylor, J., Director, Planning Services Department, Barrie, 1331
Taylor, Mark, General Manager, Abbotsford, 1314
Taylor, Ron, Director, Development Services, Kawartha Lakes, 1333
Taylor, Wendy, Manager, Sidney, 1318
Taylor, Bildstein, Senior Communication Advisor, 1160
Taylor, DipBM, Karen, Manager, 651
Taylor-Snow, Dianne, Chair, 782
Tchegus, R.P., Cunningham, Swan, Carty, Little & Bonham LLP, 923
Teal, Jeffrey C., Scarfone Hawkins LLP, 923
Teasdale, Guy, Directeur, Bibliothèques numérique et technologies, Université Laval, 1025
Teatero, Barbara, Associate Librarian, Queen's University, 988
Ted, Jennex, Manager, Community Outreach, ATL Head - Integrated Ecosystem & Public Engagement Programs, 1136
Ted, Menzies, Minister of State (Finance), 1139
Ted, Cherrett, Integrity Officer, Transport Canada Office of Integrity, 1173
Ted, Mackay, Director, Highway & Border Policy, 1174
Ted, Givins, Manager, Recorder & Vehicle Performance, 1178
Ted, Zimmerman, Acting Regional Manager, Omineca Regional Office, 1204
Ted, Lewis, Chair, 1228
Ted, Leonard, Vice-President, Merger Integration, 1255
Ted, Shannon, Fire Management Supervisor, 1259
Ted, Stobbs, Assistant Deputy Minister, 1293
Teed, QC, William H., Partner, Cox & Palmer - Saint John, 918
Tegler, Scott, Fire Chief, Woodstock, 1338
Tehani, Jainarine, Director, Multiculturalism Secretariat, 1217
Teichman, Brad, Partner, McCarthy Tétrault LLP - Toronto, 933
Teichroeb, Jay, General Manager, Abbotsford, 1314
Teitelbaum, Michael S., Partner, Hughes, Amys LLP, 932
Telego, Tacy, Co-Executive Director, 747
Telego, D. Jeffrey, Co-Executive Director, 747
Telford, Laura, Executive Director, 712
Telford, Dan, Senior Manager, Capital Regional District, 1310
Temple, Laurie, Secretary, 840
Templeton, J. Alex, Associate, Cox & Palmer - St. John's, 919
Templeton, Jamie, Stikeman Elliott LLP - Vancouver, 914
Temprile, Dan, General Manager, Public Health, Safety, & Social S, Brantford, 1332
Tenaille, France M., Partner, Cassels Brock & Blackwell LLP, 929
Tenerife, Wilmer, Library Technician, Canadian University College, 957
Teo, CheeHai, President, 779
Teresa, Overgaard, Acting Public Guardian - North, 1190
Teresa, Woo-Paw, Associate Minister, International & Intergovernmen, 1191
Teresa, Woo-Paw, Chair, 1192
Teresa, Conway, President/Chief Executive Officer, 1208
Teresa, White, Senior Vice-Chair & Tribunal Counsel, 1209
Teresa, Johnson, Research & Planning Librarian, New Brunswick Publi, 1224
Teri, Kitney, Director, New Deal Secretariat, 1291
Terrance, Ree, Fire Service Advisor, Northern Region, 1210
Terri, Starkes, Director, Business Operations, 1203
Terri, Simon, Director, Clinical Services (Regina CC), 1288
Terry, Campbell, Director, PAN - Institute Affairs & Initiatives, 1130
Terry, Jamieson, Vice-President, Technical Support Branch, 1131
Terry, Hatton, Acting Director General, 1162
Terry, Pultz, Science Advisor, 1163
Terry, Holmes, Executive Director, Rural Utilities, 1181
Terry, Wallace, Director, Dangerous Goods, Vehicle, & Rail Safety, 1196
Terry, Lake, Minister, Environment; Deputy House Leader, 1197
Terry, Lake, Minister, Environment; Deputy House Leader, 1203
Terry, Gelinas, Executive Director/Chief Financial Officer (Forest, 1207
Terry, Gunning, Director, Infrastructure Management, 1207
Terry, Sargeant, Chair, 1214
Terry, Welsh, Executive Director, Tourism Manitoba, 1216
Terry, Reiger, Chair, 1217
Terry, Johnstone, Director, Policy & Strategic Planning, 1230
Terry, French, Minister, 1234
Terry, MacPherson, District Manager, 1242
Terry, Young, Vice-President, Corporate Relations, 1255
Terry, Kelly, Senior Manager, Materials Lab, 1274
Terry, Baker, Chair, 1291
Terry, Thompson, Manager, Facilities, 1295
Terry, Hanley, Director, Policy & Risk Management, 1297
Terry, Hayden, Assistant Deputy Minister, Operations, 1298
Terry S., Campbell, Administrator, Community Hospitals East, 1272
Terryn, Naumann, Director, Evaluation & Coordinator, BC PAD Service, 1208
Tersigni, John, Executive Director, 763
Teskey, John, Director of Libraries, University of New Brunswick, 974
Tessier, Céline, McMillan LLP - Calgary, 905
Tessier, Philippe-André, Associé, Robinson Sheppard Shapiro LLP, 943
Tétreault, Jean-Claude, Executive Director, 659
Tezcucano, Aline, Chair, 704
Thaker, Sailesh, Vice-President, 858
Tham, Carmen, Lindsay Kenney LLP - Vancouver, 913
Thambirajah, Balachandra, Chief Medical Examiner, 1219
Thane, Clarke, Coordinator, Pesticide Monitoring & Control, 1268
Thapa, Rekha, Secretary, 864
Thelma, Green, Manager, Air Quality Services, 1225
Theodorakis, Tom, McMillan LLP - Vancouver, 914
Theodore, Kevin, Manager, Lethbridge, 1307
Theodore, Van Lunen, Director General, 1163
Theresa, Ostrum, Director, Municipal Collaboration, 1194
Theresa, Oswald, Minister, 1216
Theresa, Callaghan, Director, Provincial Diagnostic Imaging Services, 1273
Theriault, Reg D., Loopstra Nixon LLP Barristers & Solicitors, 933
Thériault, Lyne, Joli-Coeur Lacasse Avocats - Québec, 944
Thériault, Martin, Partner, Norton Rose Fulbright Canada LLP - Montréal, 942
Theroux, Michael P., Partner, Bennett Jones LLP - Calgary, 902
Therriault, Dominique, Technicienne agricole, Institut de technologie agro-alimentaire de la Pocatière, 1014
Therrien, Carole, President, 789
Therrien, Claude, Operator, Régie d'aqueduc intermunicipale des Moulins, 1356
Thevenot, Ken, Fire Chief, Okotoks, 1307
Thibault, Charles Olivier, Heenan Blaikie LLP - Montréal, 940
Thibault, Josée, Delorme, LeBel, Bureau, Savoie, 945
Thibault, Julie, Heenan Blaikie LLP - Ottawa, 925

Tom, Beegan, Chief Prevention & Corporate Strategy Officer, 1264
Tom, Teahen, Chief Corporate Services Officer, 1264
Tom, Young, Chief Privacy & Access Officer, Freedom of Information & Privacy, 1288
Tom, Davies, Director, Regional Logistics, 1293
Tom, Harrison, Director, Parnerships & Plan Implementation, 1297
Tom R., Williams, Deputy Minister, 1239
Toma, Ward, General Manager, 638
Toma, Greg, Chief Administrative Officer, Thompson-Nicola, 1313
Tomandi, Stan, Co-Chair, 759
Tomas, Matulis, Director, Ontario Waterloo, 1159
Tomasini, Chris, Librarian, Orillia Campus, Orillia Library, 992
Tomasz, Smetny-Sowa, Senior Director, Energy Services Acquisition Program, 1172
Tomihiro, Ken, Contact, 706
Tomkow, Pat, Manager, Capital Region Vegreville Corridor Water Services Commission, 1308
Tomm, Ian, Executive Director, 689
Tompkins, Trent, Coordinator, Parkland County, 1304
Tomsons, Sandra, Vice-President, 719
Toncon, Dan, President, 864
Toner, Pat, President, 804
Toni, Ana, Chair, 764
Tony, Richard, Director General, Financial Management & Strategic Services, 1118
Tony, Young, Director General, Economic Analysis Directorate, 1136
Tony, Clement, Minister, FedNor; President, Treasury Board, 1154
Tony, Jenkins, Key Accounts Manager, Commercial, 1161
Tony, Clement, Minister, FedNor; President, Treasury Board, 1178
Tony, Wideski, Regional Executive Director, Kootenay Boundary, 1206
Tony, Sharp, Chief Financial Officer & Vice-President, Finance, 1211
Tony, Wakeham, Chief Executive Officer, 1229
Tony, Burgess, Manager, Mining Industry Analysis, 1233
Tony, Vermillion, Manager, Wildlife & Environment, South Slave Region, 1237
Tony, LaMantia, Assistant Deputy Minister, 1249
Tony, Ross, Chair, 1255
Tony, Gagliano, President, 1262
Tony, Foster, Director, Regional Operations, 1264
Tony, Baumgartner, Vice-President, Sector Development, 1288
Tony, Hill, Director, 1299
Toole, Philip E., Fire Chief & Deputy Director, Fredericton, 1322
Toomey, Sarah, Chief Librarian, Royal Military College of Canada, 988
Tooms, Roger, Manager, Kitimat-Stikine, 1312
Topp, Christina, Vice-President, 873
Topping Jr., John C., President/CEO, 730
Torfs, Marijke, International Coordinator, 759
Torn, Rebecka, Manager Communications, 826
Torrance, Michael, Norton Rose Fulbright Canada LLP - Toronto - Royal Bank Plaza, 935
Torrie, Hunter, Manager, Field Operations, 1300
Tory, Kennedy, Manager, Human Resources, 1266
Toth, Brenda, Secretary, 724
Toth, Andy, Manager, Swift Current, 1360
Toth, Cindy, Director, Environmental Policy, Oakville, 1335
Touchette, Gilles, Senior Partner, Norton Rose Fulbright Canada LLP - Montréal, 943
Touchette, Diane, Director, 691
Tougas, François E.J., McMillan LLP - Vancouver, 914
Toupin, Sylvain, Cain Lamarre Casgrain Wells - Montréal, 939
Toupin, Harley P., CEO, 848
Tourangeau, Michel, Associé, Lapointe Rosenstein Marchand Melançon, 941
Touré, Kathryn, Regional Director, 778
Tourigny, R. Michael, McMillan LLP - Vancouver, 914
Tourigny, Thérèse, Directrice générale, 751
Tourond-Townsend, Margaret, Chapter Chair, 712
Tousaw, Jane, Director, Planning, Haliburton, 1328
Tousaw, Scott, Director, Planning & Development, Huron, 1329
Tout, Mike, Manager, Roads Operations, Brant, 1327
Toutant, Michel, Directeur, Laval, 1348
Town, Marion, Senior Regional Manager, 757
Town, Marion, Senior Regional Manager, 757
Townsend, Jack K., Associate, Cox & Palmer - Halifax, 921
Townsend, James S., Secretary, 718
Townsend, Doug, Manager, Canmore, 1306
Townsend, Phillip, Director, Halifax Regional Municipality, 1325
Townsley, John, President, 720
Tracey, Karen, Executive Director, 810
Tracey, Matt, Manager, Water & Wastewater, Quinte West, 1336
Tracey, Boicey, Director, Application Services, 1174
Tracey, Braun, Director, Environmental Assessment & Licensing, 1215
Tracey, Danowski, Asst. Deputy Minister, 1218
Tracey, Williams, Executive Director, Policy & Planning, 1242
Tracey, Barbrick, Director, Policy & Planning, 1243
Tracey, Mill, Assistant Deputy Minister, 1258
Tracey, MacEwen, Secretary-Treasurer, 1265
Tracie, Taylor-Labonté, Communication Officer, 1160
Tracogna, John, Chief Executive Officer, 861
Tracy, Patty, Manager, Okanagan-Similkameen, 1313
Tracy, Gilson, Acting Asst. Deputy Minister, 1214
Tracy, Burkhardt, Director, 1222
Tracy, English, Associate Deputy Minister, Energy Resources, 1232
Tracy, MacCharles, Minister, 1249
Tracy, Wood, Acting Director, 1266
Tracy, Danielson, Director, Regional Design & Construction, 1293
Trafford, Richard J., Miller Thomson LLP - Waterloo, 937
Trafford, Joyce, General Manager, 726
Trafton, Jackie, Administrator, 679
Trahan, Guy, Directeur, La Prairie, 1348
Trahan, J. Bernie, Director, Calgary, 1305
Trahan, Fernand, Préfet, La Vallée-de-l'Or, 1354
Traini, Chris, County Engineer, Middlesex, 1329
Tranberg, Janice, Vice-President, 740
Trask, Ruth E., Stewart McKelvey - St. John's, 920
Trask, Robert, Coordinator, 832
Trasolini, Franco E., Davis LLP - Vancouver, 911
Trattner, Paula, Partner, Osler, Hoskin & Harcourt LLP - Toronto, 935
Traub, Jennifer, Partner, Cassels Brock & Blackwell LLP, 929
Travis, Cliff, Chair, Central Peace Regional Waste Management Commission, 1309
Travis, Ripley, Director, Fisheries Management Branch, 1187
Travis, McLellan, Tourism Analyst, 1296
Travors, Mark, Provincial President, 860
Trawin, David A., Director, Kamloops, 1315
Traynor, Marian, Manager, Library Service, Davis Campus, 984
Treacy, Heather L., Dentons Canada LLP - Calgary, 903
Trebych, Debbie, Contact, Library Services, Mills Memorial Library, 987
Treffry, Keith, Director, 742
Treichel, Audrey, Coordinator, 791
Tremblay, André, Cain Lamarre Casgrain Wells - Montréal, 939
Tremblay, Annie, Cain Lamarre Casgrain Wells - Saguenay, 938
Tremblay, Chantal C., McCarthy Tétrault LLP - Montréal, 942
Tremblay, Dominic, Cain Lamarre Casgrain Wells - Saguenay, 938
Tremblay, Jacques, Morency Société d'Avocats - Québec, 945
Tremblay, Louis-Michel, Associé, Miller Thomson LLP - Montréal, 942
Tremblay, Marc A., Partner, Norton Rose Fulbright Canada LLP - Montréal, 943
Tremblay, Marc, Partner, Norton Rose Fulbright Canada LLP - Montréal, 943
Tremblay, Martine, Cain Lamarre Casgrain Wells - Alma, 938
Tremblay, Philippe, Partner, Heenan Blaikie LLP - Montréal, 940
Tremblay, Jeannine, Agente de bureau, Institut maritime du Québec, 1025
Tremblay, Lino, Bibliothécaire des systèmes et des ressources élec, Université du Québec à Chicoutimi, 1012
Tremblay, Madeleine, Documentaliste, Campus de Carleton-sur-mer, 1012
Tremblay, Wayne, Sec.-Treas., 663
Tremblay, Pierrette, Managing Editor, 797
Tremblay, André, Président-CEO, 734
Tremblay, Dawn, Program Coordinator, 744
Tremblay, Donald, Responsable, 655
Tremblay, Gérald, Directeur, Rivière-du-Loup, 1349
Tremblay, Luc, Directeur général, Mascouche, 1348
Tremblay, René, Directeur, Lévis, 1348
Tremblay, Dominic, Préfet, Charlevoix, 1353
Tremblay, Jean, Sec.-Trés., Régie d'assainissement des eaux de la Vallée du Richelieu, 1356
Tremblay, Luc, Sec.-Trés., Régie d'assainissement des eaux usées Terrebonne/Mascouche, 1356
Tremblay, ing., Marc, Président du Conseil, 657
Trépanier, Nicole, Président, 853
Treu, Andrew, Coordinator, Red Deer County, 1304
Trevor, Thibault, Director, Strategic Management Directorate, 1118
Trevor, Sinclair, Executive Director, Northwest Territories Federal Council, 1131
Trevor, Swerdfager, Assistant Deputy Minister, 1141
Trevor, Heryet, Regional Director, Surface, 1177
Trevor, Dark, Chief Operating Officer, 1183
Trevor, Mireau, Director, Financial Services, 1194
Trevor, Morrison, Manager, Executive Services, 1205
Trevor, Holder, Minister, Tourism, Heritage & Culture, 1225
Trevor, Dagilis, District Manager, 1253
Trevor, Dauphinee, Director, Capital Planning, 1256
Trevor, Griffin, District Manager, 1259
Trevor, Waugh, Information Technology Architect, 1272
Trew, David, Executive Director, 809
Trider, Dillon, Associate, Wickwire Holm, 922
Trifon, Larry R., Bratty & Partners, LLP Barristers & Solicitors, 937
Trihey, Stephan H., Partner, Heenan Blaikie LLP - Montréal, 940
Trillo, Sandi, Secretary, 764
Trimble, Richard, Executive Director, 738
Trimble, Richard, Registrar, 665
Tripp, Douglas, President, 703
Trippler, Aaron, Director, 646
Trish, MacQuarrie, Director General, Policy, Communications & Regulatory Affairs, 1146
Trish, Dohan, Executive Director, Client Services Branch, 1207
Trish, Steroff, Executive Director, Economic Development, 1209
Trisha, Westman, Acting Area Supervisor, 1253
Trisha, Delormier-Hill, Executive Director, Lands & Consultation, 1290
Tristan, Sanregret, Alberta Washington DC Office Director, Alberta - U, 1192
Trogdon, Eric, Executive Director, 821
Trojan, Bogusia, Director, Library Services, University Health Network, 1008
Trott, Guy, Library Manager, Calgary Library & Information Centre, 950
Trott, John, Woodlands Conservation Officer & Weed Inspector, Middlesex, 1329
Trottier, Jean-Guy, Directeur général, 667
Trottier, Donna, Coordinator, Red Deer County, 1304
Troup, Lynda K., Thompson Dorfman Sweatman LLP - Winnipeg, 917
Trowsdale-Mutafov, Deanna, Manager, 803
Troy, Vermillion, Acting Regional Superintendent, 1236
Trudeau, Marie-Josée, Cain Lamarre Casgrain Wells - Montréal, 939
Trudeau, Mélanie, Cain Lamarre Casgrain Wells - Sept-Iles, 945
Trudeau, Dennis, General Manager, Nanaimo, 1312
Trudel, Raymonde, Bibliothécaire responsable, CÉGEP de St-Jérôme, 1027
Trudel, Colette, Directrice générale, 666
Trudel, Pierre, Directeur général, 753
Trudel, Sylvie, Director, 763
Trudel, Amélie, Vice-présidente, 668
Trudel, Sandy, Officer, Brandon, 1321
Trudy, Samuel, Acting Director, Programs Division, 1163
Trudy, Dupre, Director, Program, Policy & Systens Support, 1185
Trudy, Rotgans, Executive Director, Building & Safety Standards Branch, 1202
Trudy, Stuckless, Vice President, Professional Standards & Chief Nur, 1229
Truesdale, Margaret, Research Director, Perley-Robertson, Hill & McDougall LLP / s.r.l., 926
Trump, Grant S., President/CEO, 747
Truswell, Jon C., Partner, Bennett Jones LLP - Calgary, 902
Trzaska, Karen, O'Connor MacLeod Hanna LLP, 925
Trzyna, Thaddeus C., President, 680
Tsakopoulos, Tom C., HGR Graham Partners LLP - Barrie, 922
Tse, Mark, Chair, 832
Tuck, Wayne, Manager, Whitehorse, 1360
Tucker, Tracy, Manager, 696
Tucker, Andrew, Director, Nanaimo, 1316
Tucker, Ross, Director, Parks & Recreation, St. Thomas, 1337
Tufts, Gordon E., VP Organization/Development, 722
Tugwell, Cindy, Executive Director, 768

Tulk, Harold, Fire Chief, Kingston, 1333
Tumach, Trevor, President, 845
Tume, Vincent, Secretary, 855
Tunteng, Verki, Heenan Blaikie LLP - Toronto, 932
Turbide, Gaétan, Directeur général, Laval, 1348
Turcotte, Mathieu, Associé, Miller Thomson LLP - Montréal, 942
Turcotte, Dawna, Campus Librarian, Fort St. John Campus, 960
Turcotte, Roger, Sec.-Trés., Régie intermunicipale du comté de Beauce-Sud, 1358
Turenne, Roger, President, 803
Turgeon, Yves, Partner, Heenan Blaikie LLP - Montréal, 940
Turkstra, Herman, Partner, Turkstra Mazza Associates, 923
Turmel, André, Fasken Martineau - Montréal, 939
Turnbull, Alex, Treasurer, 861
Turnbull, Greg, Chair, 680
Turnbull, Wendy, Specialist, 678
Turner, Frank, Partner, Osler, Hoskin & Harcourt LLP - Calgary, 905
Turner, Greg J., Stewart & Turner, 920
Turner, John, Partner, Fasken Martineau - Toronto, 931
Turner, Thomas W., Pitblado LLP, 916
Turner, Wendy, Manager, Legal Information Services, Legal Information Society of Nova Scotia, 981
Turner, Monika, Director, 662
Turner, Donna, Association Manager, 688
Turner, Don, Senior Planner, Powell River, 1313
Turney, Lisa, Coordinator, 815
Turpin, Chad, Deputy City Manager, Burnaby, 1314
Turrittin, Tony, Secretary, 861
Tutty, Paddy, Administrator, 846
Tuytel, Neo J., Bernard & Partners, 911
Twa, Q.C., Allan R., Partner, Burnet, Duckworth & Palmer LLP, 902
Tweedie, Jim, Director, 700
Tweedie, James, Director, 726
Tyagi, Avinash C., Secretary General, 777
Tyagi, Dev, General Manager, Public Works, Windsor, 1338
Tyler, Robert L., Aikins, MacAulay & Thorvaldson LLP, 915
Tyler, Tony, Director General, 774
Tyler, Susan, Administrator, 827
Tyler, James, Executive Director, Continuing Care Branch, 1189
Tyler, Campbell, Director, Communications, 1220
Tyler, Richardson, Manager, Building Design & Construction, 1275
Tyler, Lloyd, Senior Policy Analyst, 1296
Tyner, Ross, Director, Library Services, Okanagan College, 961
Tys, Theysmeyer, Head, Conservation, 1262
T›th, Krisztián, Partner, Fasken Martineau - Toronto, 931

U

Uauy, Richard, President, 786
Ubald, Gagné, Directeur général, Administration/Connaissance géographique, 1281
Udala, Berne, Supervisor, Penticton, 1316
Ufholz, Lee-Anne, Director, Bibliothèque des sciences de la santé, 993
Ugarenko, Len, President, 870
Uleryk, Elizabeth, Director, Hospital for Sick Children, 1003
Ulmer, Sandra, Contact, 755
Umlah, James, Chair, 636
Una, Wilton, Manager, Business Services, 1252
Una, Hassenstein, Director, Strategy & Performance; Manager, Plannin, 1272
Unka, Magnolia, Associate, Field LLP - Yellowknife, 920
Unrau, Martin, President, 691
Unvoas, Arlene, Executive Director, 859
Upenieks, Edwin G., Lawrence, Lawrence, Stevenson LLP, 923
Upkar, Arora, Chair, Board of Trustees, 1262
Urbanoski, Larry, Director, 710
Urbanski, Adelina, Commissioner, Community & Health Services, York, 1331
Urquhart, Sharon M., Alexander Holburn Beaudin & Lang, LLP, 910
Urquhart, Brian, President, 762
Urquhart, Gail, Vice President, 861
Urquhart, Q.C., Glenn A., Counsel, Singleton Urquhart LLP, 914
Ursula, Hung, Coordinator, Budget & Projects, 1187
Ursulak, Nick, Acting Manager, Borrower Services, Grant MacEwan University, 954
Usher, Kathleen, Contact, 750

V

Vaadeland, Gord, Executive Director, 713
Vaccaro, Angie, Reference Librarian, Manitoba Hydro, 971
Vachon, Claire, Partner, Heenan Blaikie LLP - Toronto, 932
Vadeboncoeur, Mélanie, Lavery, de Billy - Ottawa, 926
Vaillancourt, Cindy, McCarthy Tétrault LLP - Montréal, 942
Vaillancourt, Lise, Respiratory Therapist & Coordinator, 838
Vaillancourt, Jean-Guy, Directeur, 765
Vaillant, Nathalie, Joli-Coeur Lacasse Avocats - Québec, 944
Vaisey, Douglas, Librarian, Reference & Research, Saint Mary's University, 982
Val, Hoover, Director, Land Dispositions Branch, 1187
Val, Ross, Acting Manager, Information Maangement, 1237
Valade, Gilles, Treasurer, 869
Valasek, Martin J., Partner, Norton Rose Fulbright Canada LLP - Montréal, 943
Valente, Michael J., Scarfone Hawkins LLP, 923
Valenti, Alysha, Partner, McCarthy Tétrault LLP - Toronto, 933
Valeri, Andrew J., Associate, Gilbert McGloan Gillis, 918
Valerie, Gideon, Director General, Strategic Policy, Planning & Analysis, 1145
Valerie, McPherson, Communication Officer, 1160
Valerie, Devlin, Director, Seaway & Domestic Ship Policy, 1174
Valerie, Myrmo, Registrar of Appeals, 1186
Valerie, Sullivan, Manager, Mistaken Point Ecological Reserve, 1228
Valerie, Andrews, Manager, 1263
Valerie, Pearson, Executive Director, Saskatchewan 4-H Council, 1286
Valerie, Mann, Chief Population Health Epidemiologist, 1291
Valerie, Boxall, Executive Assistant to the Minister, 1298
Valerie, Royle, President & Chief Executive Officer, 1302
Valerie E., Docherty, Minister, Community Services, Seniors & Labour; Mi, 1265
Valerie E., Docherty, Minister; Minister Responsible, Status of Women, 1266
Valerie E., Docherty, Minister Responsible, Status of Women; Minister, C, 1266
Valeska, Campbell, Coordinator, Client Support Services, 1199
Vallée, Kim, Senior Library Technician, Orillia Library, 992
Vallée, Michel, President, 705
Vallega, Adalberto, President, 779
Vallières, Dominique, Lavery, de Billy - Montréal, 941
Valmstead, Liv, Reference Librarian, Architecture & Fine Arts Library, 970
Valo, Michael, Associate, Glaholt LLP, 931
Valverde, Sharon, Vice-President, 747
Van Buren, Mark, Director, Engineering, Kingston, 1333
Van Buul, Ken, Manager, Parkland County, 1304
van Bylandt, Katrina, Manager, 676
Van Dam, Anne, Director, 708
Van de Voort, Colleen, Circulation/AV Librarian, Kwantlen Polytechnic University, 964
van der Bank, Johan, Manager, Red Deer County, 1304
van der Bliek, Rob, Music Librarian, Sound & Moving Image Library, 1007
van der Lee, Jean C., Partner, Field LLP - Calgary, 904
van der Leest, Michel, Office Coordinator, 787
van der Linden, Mike, Manager, Sidney, 1318
Van Doesburg, John, Administrator, Mountain View Regional Water Services, 1309
Van Doesburg, John, Manager, Kneehill Regional Water Services Commission, 1309
Van Dorpe, Bertrand, President, 688
Van Eerden, Evert, Chair, 757
Van Egdom, Susan, Accounting Coordinator, 723
van Gelder, Ezra B., Associate, Cox & Palmer - Halifax, 921
Van Gyzen, Sharon, Chair, 644
Van Heyningen, Anthony, Senior Director, 689
van Hierden, John, Vice-President, 701
Van Iterson, Andrew, Manager, 802
van Manen, Frank, President, 774
Van Mook, Colleen, Director, Prince George, 1317
Van Nostrand, Ben, Co-ordinator, Columbia-Shuswap, 1311
Van Omme, Herman, Superintendent, Charlottetown, 1346
Van Overberghe, Joe, Trustee, Ontario Petroleum Institute Inc., 989
Van Tongerloo, Robert, Treasurer, 766
van Veen, Misha, Program Manager, 833
van Veen, Misha, Program Manager, 833
van Veen, Allard W., Founder, 833
Van Vliet, Kevin, Manager, Canmore, 1306
Van Wachem, Yolanda S., Associate, McLennan Ross LLP - Edmonton, 908
van Walsum, Nell, Secretary, 775
Vana, Peter, Associate Commissioner, Strathcona County, 1304
VanBerkum, Melissa E., Conway Davis Gryski, 929
Vance, Bradley N., Counsel, MacPherson Leslie & Tyerman LLP - Regina, 946
Vance, Elzina, Acting Manager, Long Lake Regional Waste Management Commission, 1309
Vandeloo, Joe, Assistant University Librarian, Administrative Ser, Western University Libraries, 990
Vander Aa, Diana, Coordinator, 664
Vanderberghe, Jason, President, 648
Vanderburgh, Eileen E., Alexander Holburn Beaudin & Lang, LLP, 910
Vanderdrift, Ron, Vice-President, 677
VanDerMeulen, Jackie, Heenan Blaikie LLP - Toronto, 932
Vandervecht, Dylan, Osler, Hoskin & Harcourt LLP - Calgary, 905
VanderWielen, Henry, President, 671
VanderZwaag, Rolf, Manager Maintenance/Tech. Issues, 826
Van-Dyk, Dale, Contact, Customer Service, Owen Sound Campus, 997
Vanessa, Ginger, Manager, Executive Operations, 1211
Vanessa, Colman-Sadd, Director, Communications, 1234
VanGenderen, Albert, Secretary Treasurer, 701
Vanier, Léopold, Secrétaire, Régie intermunicipale d'aqueduc de la vallée de Châteauguay, 1357
Vanini, Pat, Executive Director, 662
VanKessel, Karla, Manager, London Health Sciences Centre, 989
Vankoughnet, Ron, Supervisor, Roads & Landfill, Greater Napanee, 1333
VanZant, Paul, Vice-President, 814
Vaska, Marcus, Librarian, Cancer Care Knowledge Centres, 950
Vasseur, Liette, Contact, 669
Vassileva, Julita, NSERC/Cameco CWSE, 813
Vaudry, Peter, Director, 641
Vaughan, Steve, Partner, Heenan Blaikie LLP - Toronto, 932
Vaughan, Sarah, Manager, 678
Vavrek, Jean, Executive Director, 705
Vecchiarelli, Cindy, Administrator, 671
Vehrs, Mary Anne, Sales/Marketing, 757
Veillard, Jeremy, Vice-President, 703
Veilleux, Charles A., Morency Société d'Avocats - Québec, 945
Veilleux, Marie-Claude, Monty Coulombe s.e.n.c. - Sherbrooke, 946
Veilleux, Roland, Monty Coulombe s.e.n.c. - Sherbrooke, 946
Veilleux, Ruth, Associée, Lapointe Rosenstein Marchand Melançon, 941
Veilleux, Denise, Secrétaire, Régie intermunicipale d'assainissement de la Haute-Bécancour, 1357
Veilleux, Jean-Rock, Préfet, Robert-Cliche, 1358
Vejvoda, Berenica, Data Librarian, Map & Data Library, 1004
Veldboom, Edward B., Partner, Russell, Christie LLP, 925
Venditto, Christine, Trésorière, 668
Veniot, Barry, Supervisor, Bathurst, 1322
Verbeek, Linda, President, 644
Verge, Robert, Managing Director, 691
Verhaeghe, Amanda, Pullan Kammerloch Frohlinger, 916
Verheul, Michiel, President, 640
Verkerk, Anne, Library & Bookshop Contact, Silver King Campus, 962
Verleun, Peter, Chair, 834
Verlinden, Emily, Coordinator, 695
Verlyn, Olson, Minister, Agriculture & Rural Development, 1180
Vermette, Maryse, Présidente-directrice générale, 743
Vern, Christensen, Executive Director, 1117
Vern, Hartwell, Chair & Chief Executive Officer, 1186
Vern, Hartwell, Chair, 1186
Vern, Janz, Director, Transport Services Branch, 1302
Verna, Carlson, Manager/Registrar of Appeals & Employment Standard, 1191
Vernon, David, Osler, Hoskin & Harcourt LLP - Toronto, 935
Veronica, McGuire, Executive Director, Corporate Secretariat, 1129
Veronica, Dyck, Assistant Deputy Minister, 1216
Veronique, Vieira, Coordinator, Access to Information & Privacy, 1155
Véronique, Bouchet, Acting Director, Air Quality Research Division, 1135
Véronique, Hivon, Ministre déléguée, Santé publique et à la Protection de la jeunesse, 1282
Verschueren, Christian, Director General, 740
Versteeg, Edward, Sec.-Treas., 669
Vervoort, Rudy, Contact, 810

Vetter, Mary A., Secretary-Treasurer, 687
Vettese, John, Partner, Cassels Brock & Blackwell LLP, 929
Veuger, Julian, County Constable, Lacombe County, 1303
Vezina, Guy, Secretary, 724
Vézina, Jean-François, Dentons Canada LLP - Montreal, 939
Vézina, Sébastien, Partner, Lavery, de Billy - Montréal, 941
Vézina, Chantal, Secteur des acquisitions, Université Laval, 1025
Vézina, Gilles, Sec.-Trés., Régie intermunicipale des déchets de CJLLR, 1358
Veziroglu, T. Nejat, President, 774
Veziroglu, Ayfer, Comptroller, 774
Vic, Toews, Minister, Public Safety, 1126
Vic, Toews, Minister, Public Safety, 1170
Vic, Dhillon, Parliamentary Assistant, 1256
Vice, John, Chair, 735
Vicki, Rose, Manager, Marketing, 1156
Vicki, Ozaruk, Chief Information Officer, 1190
Vicki, Haberl, Section Head, Planning - Squamish, Lower Mainland Regional Office, 1204
Vicki, Lafferty, Manager, Health Systems Planning, 1238
Vicki, Dimick, Director, 1242
Vickie, Kaminski, President & CEO, 1229
Victor, Mark E., President, 665
Victor, Jmaeff, Chief Technical Officer, 1200
Victor, Severino, Assistant Deputy Minister, 1256
Victor, Gauvin, Chef de service, Réclamations et fermeture de contrats, 1280
Victoria, Bowes, Avian Pathologist, 1198
Victoria, Dickenson, Executive Director & CEO, 1262
Vidershpan, Valery, Manager, 694
Vidrascu, Emil, Partner, Lavery, de Billy - Montréal, 941
Vidya, ShankarNarayan, Director General, Service Transformation, 1154
Viegas, CMA, CAE, Norman, Director, 666
Viergutz, Kevin, Manager, Lethbridge, 1307
Vietz, Gordana, Library Services/Systems Coordinator, Niagara College Libraries & Learning Commons, 1010
Vigeant, Virginie, Heenan Blaikie LLP - Montréal, 940
Viglas, Catherine, President, 706
Vigneau, Isabelle, Agente de bureau, Campus des Iles-de-la-Madeleine, 1014
Vigneault, Diane, Présidente, 853
Vigon, Carolyne, Administrator, 699
Vigon, Bruce, Manager, 855
Vija, Poruks, Assistant Commissioner, Canadian Coast Guard, 1140
Vijay, Bhashyakarla, Director, Health Intergovernmental Affairs, 1243
Villavicencio, George, Systems Librarian, Capilano University, 963
Villecourt, Guy, President, 851
Villeneuve, Claude, Partner, Heenan Blaikie S.E.N.C.R.L/SRL - Sherbrooke, 945
Villeneuve, Denis, Président, 827
Villeneuve, Jacques, Sec.-Trés., Régie d'assainissement des eaux usées de Boischatel, L'Ange-Gardi, 1356
Villiard, Luc, Partner, Lavery, de Billy - Montréal, 941
Vilma, Youmaran, Manager, Professional Practices, 1155
Vince, Joanna, Associate, Willms & Shier Environmental Lawyers LLP, 937
Vince, Warden, Senior Vice-President, Finance & Administration & CFO, 1217
Vince, Ewing, District Manager, 1259
Vincent, Julie A., Executive Administrator, 866
Vincent, Graham, Director, Transportation Planning, Waterloo, 1331
Vincent, Kathleen, Director, Port Coquitlam, 1317
Vincent, DaLuz, Chief Audit Executive, 1147
Vincent, Roy, Research Director, Forest Ecosystems, 1163
Vincent, Jarry, Acting Regional Director, Programs, 1178
Vincent, Stancato, Regional Coroner, Fraser, 1210
Vincent, Q.C., Robert G., Partner, Stewart McKelvey - Saint John, 918
Vincze, Georgette, Librarian, Abbott Laboratories Limited, 1028
Viola, Flavio, Manager, Prince George, 1317
Virender, Ambwani, Director, Information Technology, 1224
Virgina, Leung, Director, Intergovernmental Affairs & Accessibility, 1174
Virginia, Poter, Director General, 1134
Virginia, Messervey, Executive Secretary, 1242
Virtue, Steve, Director, 836
Vivian, Sullivan, Director, 1159
Vizbar, R., General Manager, Medicine Hat, 1307
Vlasak, Yanick, Partner, Heenan Blaikie S.E.N.C.R.L/SRL - Sherbrooke, 945
Vlavianos, George M., Partner, Bennett Jones LLP - Calgary, 902
Vlieg, Gary, Director, Langley, 1315
Voce, Graham, Executive Secretary, 780
Vodicka, Christy, President, 796
Vogel, Paul G., Partner, Cohen Highley LLP - London, 924
Vogel, Martin, Executive Director, 847
Vogler, Connie, Library Technician, Westmount Campus, 956
Vogt, Greg, Managing Director, 784
Voigt, Herbert F., President, 779
Voisine, Pierre, Secretary, 686
Volkanova, Victoria, Chef du service des systèmes informatisés, Université de Moncton, 975
Volpatti, Michael C., Bratty & Partners, LLP Barristers & Solicitors, 937
von Sass, Carola, Director, 640
von Winterfeldt, Detlof, Director, 780
Voordouw, Jan, Executive Director, 830
Voss, Brigitte, Présidente, 713
Voyer, John, Executive Director, 643
Vrbanovic, Berry, President, 752
Vriezen, Chris, Superintendent, Quispamsis, 1322
Vuicic, George G., Partner, Hicks Morley Hamilton Stewart Storie LLP - Ottawa, 925
Vukelic, Snezana, Manager, Information Services, Association of Municipalities of Ontario, 1001

W

W., King, Vice-President, Disability & Information Managemen, 1190
W. Lorne, Clow, Director, Housing, Seniors & Corporate Support, 1267
W.A. Sam, Shaw, Interim Chair, 1153
Waddell, Bonnie R., Chief Librarian, Nova Scotia Agricultural College, 983
Waddell, Linda, Vice President, 801
Waddy, Susan, Manager, 652
Wade, Catherine, Partner, Heenan Blaikie LLP - Vancouver, 912
Wade, David, Secretary, 747
Wade, Joy, Vice-President, 652
Wade, Aucoin, Acting Director General, Community Development, 1123
Wade, Spurrell, Director General, Operations, 1140
Wade, Vienneau, Executive Director, Facilities, 1183
Wade, Arsenault, Manager, Properties, 1273
Wade, Istchenko, Minister, 1301
Wade, QC, Deirdre L., Partner, Cox & Palmer - Saint John, 918
Waggott, George, Partner, McMillan LLP - Toronto, 934
Wagner, Sarah, Executive Director, 839
Wagner, Belinda, General Manager, 847
Wainwright, C.A., Richard, Chief Building Inspector, Bulkley-Nechako, 1310
Waite, Michael A., Partner, Stones Carbert Waite Wells LLP, 906
Waite, Les, Secretary-Treasurer, 638
Waito, Barry, Chair, 699
Wake, Tyler, MacPherson Leslie & Tyerman LLP - Saskatoon, 947
Wakulowsky, Lydia, Partner, McMillan LLP - Toronto, 934
Walbourne, Holly, Erickson & Partners, Barristers, Solicitors, Notaries, 927
Walden, Pam, Aerial Photograph & Serials Technician, Yukon Department of Energy, Mines & Resources, 1035
Walden, Thorn, Senior Economist, 696
Walden, Tracy, Director, 695
Waldie, Shelley, Assistant, Douglas College, 962
Waldy, Brian, Secretary General, 732
Wales, Mark, President, 817
Wales, Don, President, 840
Walker, Cheryl A., Thompson Dorfman Sweatman LLP - Winnipeg, 917
Walker, John, HGR Graham Partners LLP - Midland, 924
Walker, Keith, Director, Library Services, Brooks Campus, 949
Walker, Keith, Director, Library Services, Medicine Hat College, 957
Walker, Janet, President, 780
Walker, Jeff, Vice-President & Chief Strategy Officer, 689
Walker, Ryan, Treasurer, 663
Walker, Bill, President & CEO, 844
Walker, Craig, Manager, Charlottetown, 1346
Walker, John, Acting Commissioner, Planning & Development Servic, York, 1331
Walker, BAH, BEd, MLIS, Jennifer, Head Librarian, 725
Walker, Q.C., Philip H.G., Partner, McCarthy Tétrault LLP - Toronto, 933
Wall, John, Chair, 787
Wall, Wayne, Manager, Portage La Prairie, 1321
Wallace, Ian C., Partner, Stewart McKelvey - St. John's, 920
Wallace, Brenda, General Manager, Saskatoon, 1359
Wallace, George, Project Manager, Sustainability & Growth, Kingston, 1333
Walling, Mary Ellen, Executive Director, 677
Wallinger, Kevin, Director, Vancouver, 1318
Wallis, Katherine, Director, Learning Resource Centres, Georgian College of Applied Arts & Technology, 984
Wallis, Peter C., President & CEO, 865
Walls, Barbara, Director, 805
Walls, Michael P., Vice-President, 646
Wally, Goeres, Branch Head, Petroleum Registry of Alberta (Edmont, 1184
Wally, Hoehn, Director, Lands, 1286
Walpac, Elizabeth A., President, 813
Walsh, Kimberley A., Partner, Stewart McKelvey - St. John's, 920
Walsh, Susan, Executive Director, 865
Walsh, Rose, Program Coordinator, 754
Walsh, Robert, Executive Director, 693
Walsh, Dave, Superintendent, Pitt Meadows, 1316
Walsh, Marie, Chief Administrative Officer, Cape Breton, 1325
Walsh, Terry, Director, Brooks, 1305
Walsh Craig, Peggy, Managing Director, 712
Walt, Lesenke, Fire Management Supervisor, 1259
Walter, Scott, Executive Director, 731
Walter, Carolson, Director, Equipment & Operations, 1176
Walter, Tauber, Manager, Program Delivery, 1194
Walter, Pumphrey, Director, Ferry Operations, 1235
Walter, MacAlpine, Chair, 1244
Walter, Fanning, Director, Forest Protection, 1244
Walter, Zagrobelny, Manager, Wood Measurement Section, 1258
Walters, Wanda, Administrator, 725
Walthert, Henry, Executive Director, 871
Walthert, Henry, Executive Director, 725
Walton, Valerie, Library Technician, Reference, Periodicals, & Gove, Lakeshore Campus, 1004
Walton, Pang, Director, Information, 1208
Wamala, George, Manager, 756
Wanda, Vincent, Regional Manager, Vancouver Island & Coast, 1212
Wanda, Legge, Director, Policy Development, 1230
Wanda, White, Manager, Health Protection, 1237
Wanda, Michalowicz, Co-Manager, Pesticides Management Section, 1252
Wanda, Lamberti, Executive Director, Central Management Services, 1290
Wandalee, Wiseman, Director, Planning Services, 1229
Wandzura, P.Eng., Dorian, General Manager, Regina, 1359
Wang, Ningyan (Sandy), McMillan LLP - Vancouver, 914
Wang, Jiabin, Head of Library, Engineering & Computer Science Library, 1002
Wang, Kangmei, Library Technician, H.H. Mu Far Eastern Library, 1003
Wang, Ren, Director, 737
Waram, Cheryl, Associate, Hicks Morley Hamilton Stewart Storie LLP - Ottawa, 925
Ward, Aaron, Associate, Wickwire Holm, 922
Ward, Sean, Partner, Reynolds Mirth Richards & Farmer LLP, 909
Ward, John, Vice President, 769
Ward, John, Director, Courtenay, 1315
Ward, Trotter, Director, Land Tenures Branch, Acting Director, Crown Land Opportunities & Restoration, 1206
Wardle, Richard, Vice-President, 761
Wardrop, Dave, Director, Winnipeg, 1321
Wareham, Wendy, Manager, Health Resource Centre, Brandon Regional Health Centre, 969
Warford, P.Eng., James, Coordinator, Corner Brook, 1324
Warner, Patrick, Head, Lending Services Division, Memorial University of Newfoundland, 978
Warner, Ralph, Director, 843
Warner, Jim, President, 860
Warner, Donna, Program Coordinator, 711
Warner, William, Senior Editor, 864
Warner, Q.C., J. Philip, Senior Partner, Bishop & McKenzie LLP, 906

White, Andy, Chairman, 873
White, Gil, President, 840
White, Chris, Contact, 712
White, Adam, President, 661
White, Tanya T., Director, 681
White, Mildred, Director, 843
White, Peter, President, 855
White, Judy, Office Manager, 715
White, Kathryn, Executive Director, 863
White, Liz, Director, 651
White, Gord, CEO, 665
White, Dave, Supervisor, Roads & Transportation, St. Thomas, 1337
White, Grant, Director, Yellowknife, 1325
White, Richard, Director, North Vancouver, 1316
White, Tony, Commissioner, Engineering & Public Works, Muskoka, 1329
White, P. Eng., Leo, Director, 836
White, P.Eng., Len, Chief Executive Officer & Registrar, 746
White, Q.C., Robert B., Davis LLP - Edmonton, 907
White, QC, George L., Patterson Law, 921
Whiteford, Ken, Contact, 770
Whitehall, Q.C., Ivan G., Counsel, Heenan Blaikie LLP - Ottawa, 925
Whitehead, Martha, University Librarian, Queen's University, 988
Whitehead, Brian, Vice-President, 637
Whitehead, Lois, Executive Director, 849
Whitehead, Karen, Treasurer, 762
Whitehead, Bob, President, 661
Whitehouse, Caroline, Treasurer, 746
Whitehouse, Paul, Manager, Chilliwack, 1314
Whitelaw, Bill, Secretary, 702
Whitemarsh, M.J., CEO, 702
Whiteway, Kenneth, Law Librarian, Law Library, 1033
Whitfield, Paul H., Co-Editor, 724
Whiting, Michael J., Partner, Carscallen LLP, 903
Whitley, Moriah, Library Office Assistant, Technical Services, Royal Roads University, 968
Whitney, Greg, Chef, Services techniques et systèmes informatisés, École polytechnique de Montréal, 1019
Whittaker, Brady, President & Chief Executive Officer, 639
Whittaker, Sean, Vice-President, 725
Whittaker, Rick, Chief Technology Officer & Vice-President, 858
Whittingham, Ed, Executive Director, 831
Whitwham, Rob, Director, Prince George, 1317
Whyte, Ian, Deputy Chief Librarian, University of Toronto at Mississauga, 991
Whyte, Pat, Operations Manager, Georgian College of Applied Arts & Technology, 984
Wiazowski, Peter J., Partner, Norton Rose Fulbright Canada LLP - Montréal, 943
Wickett, Robert V., MacKenzie Fujisawa LLP, 913
Wickett, Sarah, Health Informatics Librarian, Bracken Health Sciences Library, 988
Wickham, Daniel A.J., Partner, Shook, Wickham, Bishop & Field, 909
Wickins, Hélène, Library Assistant, North Island College Library, 960
Wicks, Sheri H., Partner, Ottenheimer Baker, 919
Wickwire, Levi, Coordinator, 854
Wiebe, Victor G., Engineering Librarian, Engineering Library, 1033
Wiebe, Reg, Coordinator, 794
Wiebe, John D., President & Chief Executive Officer, 762
Wiener, Neil, Partner, Heenan Blaikie LLP - Montréal, 940
Wiener, Robin K., President, 772
Wiens, David, Chair, 741
Wiercinska, Grazyna, Library Technician, Women's College Hospital, 1009
Wiercinski, Henry, Partner, McCarthy Tétrault LLP - Toronto, 933
Wight, Wanda, President, 839
Wigle, Q.C., Wendell S., Senior Partner, Hughes, Amys LLP, 932
Wijesinghe, Anna-Maria, Manager, 863
Wijewickreme, Nilmini, Chair, 675
Wilbur, Stephen P., Wilbur & Wilbur, 918
Wilbur, Sara, Executive Director, 762
Wilcox, Ian, General Manager/Sec.-Treas., 864
Wild, Ray, President, 849
Wildfong, Bob, Executive Director, 850
Wiley, Sarah, Executive Director, 829
Wilfred, Kaiser, Acting Director, Environmental Services, 1245
Wilfred J., MacDonald, Manager, Fleet, Mechanical Branch, 1275
Wiliam J., Dobson, Director, Ontario St. Clair, 1159
Wilker, Jeffrey J., Thomson, Rogers, 936
Wilkes, David, Senior Vice-President, 842
Wilkes, Kristin, Manager, Penticton, 1316
Wilkin, T.J., Cunningham, Swan, Carty, Little & Bonham LLP, 923
Wilkins, Pamela G., Librarian, Institute of Ocean Sciences, 964
Wilkins, Robert C., Secretary-Treasurer, 708
Wilkinson, Andrew, Associate, Field LLP - Calgary, 904
Wilkinson, Anna, Norton Rose Fulbright Canada LLP - Toronto - Royal Bank Plaza, 935
Wilkinson, Geoff, Executive Director, 823
Wilkinson, Chris, Coordinator, 735
Wilkinson, Donna, Executive Director, 846
Wilkinson, Cathy, President & Chair, 743
Willcock, Michael, Partner, D'Arcy & Deacon LLP - Winnipeg, 916
Willcocks, Gordon, Partner, McCarthy Tétrault LLP - Toronto, 933
Willcox Whetung, Linda, Whetung Law Office, Barristers & Solicitors, Notarie Public, 927
Willey, John C., Chown, Cairns LLP, 927
William, Crosbie, Assistant Deputy Minister & Chief Security Officer, 1143
William, Cox, Poultry Health Veterinarian, 1198
William, Barlow, Chair, 1215
William, Hicks, Director, Heritage, 1225
William, Clarke, District Manager, 1233
William, Langthorne, Chief Executive Officer & Superintendent of Credit, 1234
William, Mawdsley, Director, 1237
William, Smith, Director, Operations, 1244
William, Forward, Deputy Minister, 1257
William J., Woods, Senior Executive Director, Citizen Services & Prog, 1147
Williams, Darren G., Merchant Law Group LLP - Victoria, 915
Williams, Jack, Partner, Field LLP - Yellowknife, 920
Williams, Matthew G., Ritch Durnford, Lawyers, 921
Williams, Nicholas C., Partner, Davies Ward Phillips & Vineberg LLP, 930
Williams, R. Blake, Bennett Jones LLP - Calgary, 902
Williams, Tammy, Partner, LLF Lawyers LLP, 927
Williams, Terry J., Dentons Canada LLP - Edmonton, 907
Williams, Gary, Chairman/President, 871
Williams, Sue, General Manager, 755
Williams, Rachael, Technical Manager, 784
Williams, Craig, Vice-President, 708
Williams, Lesley, Program Manager, 836
Williams, Kai, Executive Director, 786
Williams, Elaine, Executive Director, 870
Williams, Bruce, Chair, 760
Williams, Laura, General Manager, 726
Williams, Christine, Secretary, 727
Williams, Michael H., General Manager, Economic Development & Culture, Toronto, 1338
Williams, Wayne, Fire Chief, Penticton, 1316
Williams, QC, Pamela J., Cox & Palmer - Charlottetown, 938
Williamson, Barry, Young, Anderson, 914
Williamson, Vicki, Dean, University of Saskatchewan, 1034
Williamson, Randy, President, 864
Willie, Grieve, Chair, 1183
Willing, Terry, Director, Building & Licensing, Kingston, 1333
Willingshofer, Pamela, Secretary, 757
Willis, Hugh, Emery Jamieson LLP, 908
Willison, Martin, President & Chair, 713
Willmer, Jeff, General Manager, Development & Technical Services, Kitchener, 1334
Willms, John, Partner, Willms & Shier Environmental Lawyers LLP, 937
Willson, Julie, Contact, Library Services, H. G. Thode Library of Science & Engineering, 986
Willy, Shippey, Director, Extended Care, 1301
Wilm, Angela, Chair, Academic Services, Lakeland College, 958
Wilma, Sisk, Director, Information Management, Legislative & Ad, 1194
Wilma, Macfarlane, Contact, 1248
Wilson, David S., Blaney McMurtry LLP, 928
Wilson, Donald J., Davis LLP - Edmonton, 907
Wilson, Paul C., Fasken Martineau - Vancouver, 912
Wilson, June E., Information Broker, Ontario Ministry of Transportation, 999
Wilson, Liane, Content Administrator, R.V. Anderson Associates Limited, 1007
Wilson, Patti, Collections Librarian, University of the Fraser Valley, 958
Wilson, Linda, Directrice générale, 655
Wilson, Christopher, Director, 708
Wilson, Mathew, Vice-President, 708
Wilson, Bill, President, 768
Wilson, Todd, 2nd Vice-President, 819
Wilson, Rob, Secretary, 804
Wilson, Ed, President & CEO, 743
Wilson, Mark, Treasurer, 848
Wilson, Bill, Co-Chair, 802
Wilson, Geoff, President, 775
Wilson, Don, Executive Director, 641
Wilson, Barry, Vice-President, 858
Wilson, Bob, Manager, St. John's, 1324
Wilson, Brad, Director, Environmental & Operational Services, Belleville, 1331
Wilson, Goosney, Regional Director, 1229
Wilson, Q.C., Donald K., Managing Partner, MacPherson Leslie & Tyerman LLP - Regina, 946
Wilton, Littlechild, Commissioner, 1118
Wimmer, P.Eng., Chris, Director, 665
Winanne, Downey, Director, Epidemiology & Research, 1291
Winch, Jordan D., Partner, Norton Rose Fulbright Canada LLP - Toronto - Royal Bank Plaza, 935
Winnitoy, David M., Partner, Russell, Christie LLP, 925
Winser, Nigel, Executive Director, 743
Winsor, Roderick S.W., Blaney McMurtry LLP, 928
Winston, Fogarty, Executive Director & General Counsel, Legal Services Division, 1130
Winston, Hodgins, President/CEO, 1219
Winston, Maharaj, President/CEO, 1219
Winter, Jennifer S., Associate, D'Arcy & Deacon LLP - Winnipeg, 916
Winter, Chris, Executive Director, 735
Winterbottom, Marcia, Acting Manager, Toronto Rehabilitation Institute, 1008
Winters, W.H., Partner, Burnet, Duckworth & Palmer LLP, 902
Wipperman, Kristy, Office Manager, 727
Wise, Rick, Vice-President & Chair, 830
Wise, Mandi, Coordinator, 641
Wisebrod, QC, Herbert L., Bratty & Partners, LLP Barristers & Solicitors, 937
Wishart, Ian, President, 788
Wishart, Rick, Treasurer, 711
Wismer, Beth, General Manager, 769
Wisner, Robert, Partner, McMillan LLP - Toronto, 934
Wisniewski, Jeremy, Heenan Blaikie LLP - Montréal, 940
Withrow, Cory J., Burchells LLP, 920
Wivcharuk, Jody L., Partner, Burnet, Duckworth & Palmer LLP, 902
Wiwchar, Randy, Director, Courtenay, 1315
Wobschall, Pete, Chair, 736
Wolbaum, Dianne, Director, 848
Wolf, Uli, General Manager, Central Kootenay, 1311
Wolf, Uli, Solid Waste Services Supervisor, Grande Prairie, 1307
Wolff, Erin, MacPherson Leslie & Tyerman LLP - Regina, 946
Wolski, Darryl, Coordinator, Airdrie, 1305
Womack Kolton, Anne, Vice-President, 646
Wong, Andrew, Partner, Osler, Hoskin & Harcourt LLP - Toronto, 935
Wong, Richard, Partner, Osler, Hoskin & Harcourt LLP - Toronto, 936
Wong, Joyce, Department Chair, Langara College, 966
Wong, Kevin, Coordinator, 706
Wong, Debora, Manager, 676
Wong, Kevin, Executive Director, 724
Wong, Nancy, Director, 865
Wong-Chor, Trevor, Managing Partner, Davis LLP - Calgary, 903
Wong-Martinez, Carlos, Coordinator, Technical Services & Systems, Red River College, 972
Won-il, Chung, Alberta Korea Office Commercial Director, 1192
Wood, David M., Partner, Stikeman Elliott LLP - Calgary, 906
Wood, Alberta Auringer, Secretary, 690
Wood, James, Chapter President, 767
Wood, Julie, Vice-President, 802
Wood, Brian, President, 816
Wood, Dan, Manager, Parks & Recreation, Kingsville, 1334
Wood, Vincent, General Foreman, Bathurst, 1322
Wood Edwards, Linda, Region Coordinator, 706
Woodacre, Kendall, General Manager, Medicine Hat, 1307

Woodcock, Linda, Technical Services & Public Services Librarian, Kwantlen Polytechnic University, 964
Woodcock, Loretta, Executive Member, 677
Woodford, Bernadette, Library Clerk, Seal Cove Campus Library, 976
Woodin, Melanie, Secretary, 714
Woodland, Chris A., Partner, MacPherson Leslie & Tyerman LLP - Saskatoon, 947
Woodley, Matthew A., Reynolds Mirth Richards & Farmer LLP, 909
Woodley, Alison, National Director, 713
Woods, Cheryl, Data Librarian, Department of Geography, 989
Woods, Doug, Director, 818
Woods, Reid, President, 794
Woods, Mark, Secretary, 783
Woods, James, Director, 858
Woods, Mark, Manager, Okanagan-Similkameen, 1313
Woodward, Christina, Manager, Trillium Health Centre - Mississauga Site, 991
Woodward, Nina, Librarian, St Anthony Campus Library, 977
Woodward, Renata, Executive Director, 804
Woodworth, Scott, President, 723
Wookey, Russell G., Associate, D'Arcy & Deacon LLP - Winnipeg, 916
Wooldridge, Edward A., Partner, Heenan Blaikie LLP - Calgary, 904
Woolley, Jonathan M., Thompson Dorfman Sweatman LLP - Winnipeg, 917
Woolley, Linda A., Acting President & CEO, 741
Worden, Tom, President, 741
Worden, Sean, Treasurer, 803
Worman, Dave, Manager, Fort Saskatchewan, 1306
Worman, Dave, Manager, Capital Region Northeast Water Services Commission, 1308
Worrall, Edward, 1st Vice-President, 845
Worsley, Julian, Partner, Heenan Blaikie LLP - Toronto, 932
Worte, Charley, Manager, 735
Worth, Ann, Executive Director, 834
Worthington, Heidi, Sr. Vice-President & Chief Marketing Officer, 674
Wortley, Stephen D., McMillan LLP - Vancouver, 914
Woudsma, Carole Ann, Secretary, 722
Wrathall, Gary, President, 679
Wray, Shannon L., Partner, Burnet, Duckworth & Palmer LLP, 902
Wray, Whitmore, GO Team Manager, 1214
Wren, Michael J., Partner, Miller Thomson LLP - Toronto, 934
Wrezel, Mira, Librarian, Golder Associates Ltd., 990
Wright, Andrew, Siskind LLP - London, 924
Wright, Carolyn A., Burnet, Duckworth & Palmer LLP, 902
Wright, Douglas, Associate, Cox & Palmer - St. John's, 919
Wright, Michael J.G., Associate, Fasken Martineau - Calgary, 903
Wright, Nicola, Executive Director, 673
Wright, Elizabeth, Secretary, 807
Wright, John, President & Chief Executive Officer, 703
Wright, Nancy, Vice-President, 762
Wright, Christa, Coordinator, 806
Wright, Forrest, CAO, Beaver Regional Waste Management Services Commission, 1308
Wright, Forrest, CAO, Highway 14 Regional Water Services, 1309
Wright Eastley, Teresa, Librarian, SaskPower Corporation, 1032
Wu, PhD, Xiaohua, Treasurer, 746
Wulf, Warren, Librarian, Information Management, Environment Canada Library Saskatoon, 1033
Wunderlich, Richard, Chair, 800
Wurzer, Greg, Reference Librarian, Law Library, 1033
Wyatt, Merle, Chair, Vulcan District Waste Commission, 1310
Wynick, Robert H., MacKenzie Fujisawa LLP, 913
Wynne, Young, Deputy Minister, Parks, Culture, & Sport, 1294

X

Xavier, Fonteneau, Directeur, Pôles et créneaux d'excellence, 1280
Xénopoulos, Ianny, Fasken Martineau - Québec, 943
Xiaoyuan, Geng, Manager, Soil Landscape Analysis & Application, Environmental Health, 1121
Xinsheng, Zhang, President, 785
Xiwu, Zhang, Chair, 872

Y

Yada, Rickey, Scientific Director, 635
Yada, Rickey, President-Elect, 785
Yake, Marianne, President, 842
Yako, Louise, Director Policy/Communications, 723
Yako, Louise, President & Chief Executive Officer, 678
Yale, Darcie C., Partner, D'Arcy & Deacon LLP - Winnipeg, 916
Yamashita, Colleen, Scarfone Hawkins LLP, 923
Yamashita, Allan, City Engineer & General Manager, Leduc, 1307
Yanch, E. Helen, Operations Manager, 758
Yanchula, MCIP, RPP, Jim, Manager, Urban Design & Community Development, Windsor, 1338
Yannick, Routhier, Directeur (par intérim), Régional, rural, et de l'économie sociale, 1276
Yannick, Gignac, Directeur (par intérim), 1276
Yanofsky, Deena, Coordinator & Liaison Librarian, Maps & Geospatial, Walter Hitschfeld Geographic Information Centre, 1022
Yap, Derek, Cataloguing Librarian, Yukon College, 1035
Yap, George, Executive Director, 867
Yap, George, Program Director, 867
Yaprak, Baltacioglu, Deputy Minister, 1173
Yarnold, David, President & CEO, 800
Yasir, Naqvi, Minister, 1256
Yasmin, Nowsherwanji, Acting Assistant to the Provincial Development Fac, 1256
Yates, Carl, Manager, Halifax Regional Municipality, 1325
Yaworski, Q.C., Brian, Davis LLP - Calgary, 903
Yeager, Penny L., MacPherson Leslie & Tyerman LLP - Saskatoon, 947
Yee, Brenda, Technical Services Librarian, College of New Caledonia, 963
Yee, John, Chief Information Manager, International Joint Commission, 996
Yee, Sylvia, Acting Director, White Rock, 1319
Yefang, Jiang, Senior Hydrogeologist, Water Quality & Geoenvironment Unit, 1119
Yergeau, Michel, Partner, Lavery, de Billy - Montréal, 941
Yingling, Cathie, President, 866
Yobp, Vicky, Director, 646
Yolaine, Galarneau, Directrice, Organisation des services de première ligne intégrés, 1283
Yoland, Mallet, Chief, Creative Services, 1153
Yolande, Andrews, Director, Internal Audit Directorate, 1170
Yorke-Slader, Q.C., Blair C., Partner, Bennett Jones LLP - Calgary, 902
Yoshimura, Manabu, Secretary General, 774
Young, Christopher M., Associate, Brownlee LLP - Edmonton, 907
Young, Daina, Associate, Reynolds Mirth Richards & Farmer LLP, 909
Young, David Duncan, McInnes Cooper - Fredericton, 917
Young, David M.W., Partner, McMillan LLP - Toronto, 934
Young, Jessica A.N., Stringer LLP, 936
Young, Joan M., McMillan LLP - Vancouver, 914
Young, Landon P., Managing Partner, Stringer LLP, 936
Young, Mark I., Partner, Cassels Brock & Blackwell LLP, 929
Young, Raymond E., Young, Anderson, 914
Young, Belle, Library Technician, First Nations University of Canada, 1031
Young, Patricia, Librarian, Vancouver Coastal Health Authority, 967
Young, Wayne D., General Manager, 788
Young, Jane, Treasurer, 690
Young, Jim, Head, 831
Young, Don A., Executive Vice-President, 742
Young, Lorna, Regional Director, 692
Young, David, Chair, 869
Young, Ken, Treasurer, 828
Young, Jim, Manager, Operations, Haliburton, 1328
Young, Rick, Fire Chief, Stratford, 1337
Young, Sharon E., Manager, Calgary, 1305
Young, Tracy, Administrative Resources Coordinator, St. Albert, 1308
Young, Q.C., John A., Firm Chair, Boyne Clarke LLP, 920
Younge, Val, Librarian, Emergent Technologies, Saskatchewan Institute of Applied Science & Technology, 1032
Younger, Zoe, Vice-President, 797
Youngman, Colin J., Associate, Hicks Morley Hamilton Stewart Storie LLP - Kingston, 923
Younker, Jonathan, Head, Library Systems & Technologies, Brock University, 999
Yousuf Esha, Samina, President, 823
Yu, Veronica, President & CEO, 712
Yumkella, Kandeh K., Director General, 864
Yussuff, Hassan, Secretary-Treasurer, 707
Yvan, Désy, Director, GeoConnections Division, 1165
Yvan, Déry, Directeur général, Technologies de l'information, 1278
Yvan, Béliveau, Directeur, Solutions d'affaires, 1278
Yvan, David, Directeur, Projets de l'Eastmain, 1280
Yvan M., Déry, Director, Policy & Research, 1130
Yvelle, Poirier, Executive Secretary, 1240
Yves, Plante, Acting Director, Reserch & Development - South, 1122
Yves, Leboeuf, Vice-President, Operations, 1128
Yves, Robineau, Chief Financial Officer & Director, Corporate Services, 1131
Yves, Saulnier, Chief, Human Resources Officer, 1132
Yves, Gagnon, Senior Policy Advisor, 1143
Yves, Lamarche, Director, Québec Periphery, 1159
Yves, Bourbonnais, Chief Information Officer, 1179
Yves, Desjardins-Siciliano, Chief Legal & Corporate Affairs Officer; Corporate, 1179
Yves, Lapierre, Directeur générale, 1277
Yves, Lévesque, Directeur régional, 1277
Yves, Lefebvre, Président, 1277
Yves, Lafortune, Directeur, Amérique du Nord et Europe, 1280
Yves, Jalbert, Directeur (par intérim), Organisation des services médicaux et technologiques, 1283
Yves, Jalbert, Directeur, Biovigilance, 1283
Yves-François, Blanchet, Ministre, 1278
Yvette, Myers, Director, Operations & Environmental Programs, 1176
Yvette, Ng, Executive Director, North Asia & Business Planning, 1192
Yvette, Marquis, Coordinator, Administration, 1199
Yvon, Chiasson, Executive Director, Fisheries Management & Operations, 1220
Yvon, Forest, Directeur (par intérim), Développement et initiatives économiques, 1277
Yvon, Gosselin, Directeur général, Centre d'expertise hydrique du Québec, 1279
Yvon, Maranda, Directrice, Bureau de coordination sur les évaluations stratégiques, 1279
Yvon, Gosselin, Directeur général, 1279
Yvonne, Foxall, Manager, Permit & Authorization Service Bureau, 1205
Yvonne, Foxall, Acting Deputy Director, Fish, Wildlife & Habitat Management, 1206
Yvonne, Samson, Director, Corporate Finance, 1221
Yvonne, Earle, Legislative Librarian, 1245
Yvonne, Doyle, Coordinator, Marketing, Passport to Employment Pro, 1274

Z

Zabrovsky, Andrew N., Associate, Hicks Morley Hamilton Stewart Storie LLP - Toronto, 932
Zaccarelli, Wayne, Sec.-Treas., 645
Zachery, Solomon, Director, Financial & Property Management, 1289
Zacks, Nadine S., Associate, Hicks Morley Hamilton Stewart Storie LLP - Toronto, 932
Zahynacz, P. Eng., Igor, Director, Port Coquitlam, 1317
Zakutney, Tim J., Chair, 709
Zalmanowitz, Q.C., Barry, Dentons Canada LLP - Edmonton, 907
Zamojc, M., Commissioner, Public Works, Halton, 1329
Zamprogna Ballès, Julie, McKenzie Lake Lawyers, 924
Zaozirny, Q.C., John B., McCarthy Tétrault LLP - Calgary, 905
Zaugg, Ruth, Secretary, 808
Zawadski, Brian, Executive Director, 813
Zdebiak, Rodney J., Partner, Stewart McKelvey - St. John's, 920
Zealand, Gord, Executive Director, 875
Zed, Peter T., Associate, Cox & Palmer - Halifax, 921
Zella, Osberg, Manager, Clean Air Agenda, 1136
Zerr, Nadine, Library Officer, Technical Library, 1032
Zettel, Chris, Corporate Communications Officer, Cranbrook, 1315
Zhang, Judy, Manager, 678
Zhao, Jennifer, Liaison Librarian, Electrical & Computer Engineeri, Schulich Library of Science & Engineering, 1021
Zhu, Yun, Bennett Jones LLP - Calgary, 902
Ziegler, Kenneth K.E., Robertson Stromberg LLP, 947
Zikovsky, claire, Associée, Stikeman Elliott LLP - Montréal, 943

CANADA'S INFORMATION RESOURCE CENTRE (CIRC)

Access all these great resources Online, all the time, at Canada's Information Resource Centre (CIRC)
http://circ.greyhouse.ca

Canada's Information Resource Centre (CIRC) integrates all of Grey House Canada's award-winning reference content into one easy-to-use online resource. With over 100,000 Canadian organizations, contacts, facts and figures, it is the most comprehensive resource for specialized database content in Canada!

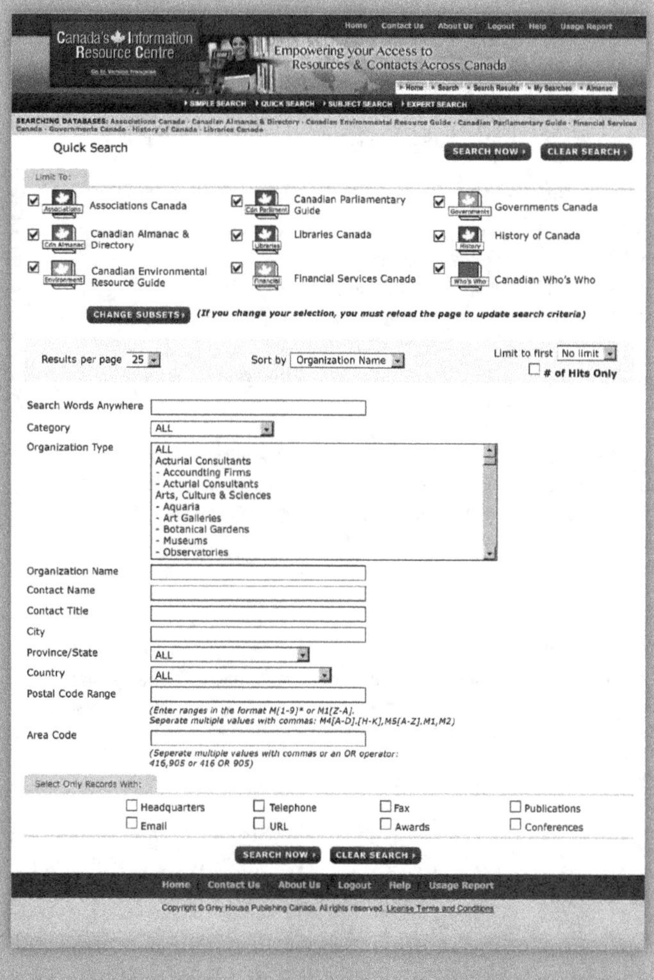

KEY ADVANTAGES OF CIRC:

- seamlessly cross-database search content from select databases
- save search results for future reference
- link directly to websites or email addresses
- clear display of your results make compiling and adding to your research easier than ever before

DESIGN YOUR OWN CUSTOM CONTACT LISTS!

CIRC gives you the option to define and extract your own lists in seconds. Whether you need contact, mail or e-mail lists, CIRC can pull together the information quickly and export it in a variety of formats.

CHOOSE BETWEEN QUICK AND EXPERT SEARCH!

With CIRC, you can choose between Expert and Quick search to pinpoint information. Designed for both novice and advanced researchers, you can conduct simple text searches as well as powerful Boolean searches.

SEARCH THE DATABASE USING COMMON OR UNIQUE FIELDS SUCH AS:

- organization type - area code - number of employees
- affiliations - founding year - language
- category - city - branch name
- contact name - contact title - postal code

ONLY GREY HOUSE DIRECTORIES PROVIDE SPECIAL CONTENT YOU WON'T FIND ANYWHERE ELSE!

- **Associations Canada:** finances/funding sources, activities, publications, conferences, membership, awards, member profile
- **Canadian Parliamentary Guide:** private and political careers of elected members, complete list of constituencies and representatives
- **Canadian Environmental Resouce Guide:** products/services/areas of expertise, working languages, domestic markets, type of ownership, revenue sources
- **Financial Services:** type of ownership, number of employees, year founded, assets, revenue, ticker symbol
- **Libraries Canada:** staffing, special collections, services, year founded, national library symbol, regional system
- **Governments Canada:** municipal population
- **Canadian Who's Who:** birth city, publications, education (degrees, alma mater), career/occupation and employer

CIRC provides easier searching and faster, more pinpointed results of all of our great resources in Canada, from Associations and Government to Major Companies to Zoos and everything in between. Whether you need fully detailed information on your contact or just an email address, you can customize your search query to meet your needs. Contact us now for a free trial subscription or visit **http://circ.greyhouse.ca**. You'll be amazed at how much data can be right at your fingertips 24/7!

GREY HOUSE PUBLISHING CANADA
For more information please contact Grey House Publishing Canada
Tel.: (866) 433-4739 or (416) 644-6479 Fax: (416) 644-1904 | info@greyhouse.ca | www.greyhouse.ca

CENTRE DE DOCUMENTATION DU CANADA (CDC)

Consultez en tout temps toutes ces excellentes ressources en ligne grâce au Centre de documentation du Canada (CDC) à http://circ.greyhouse.ca

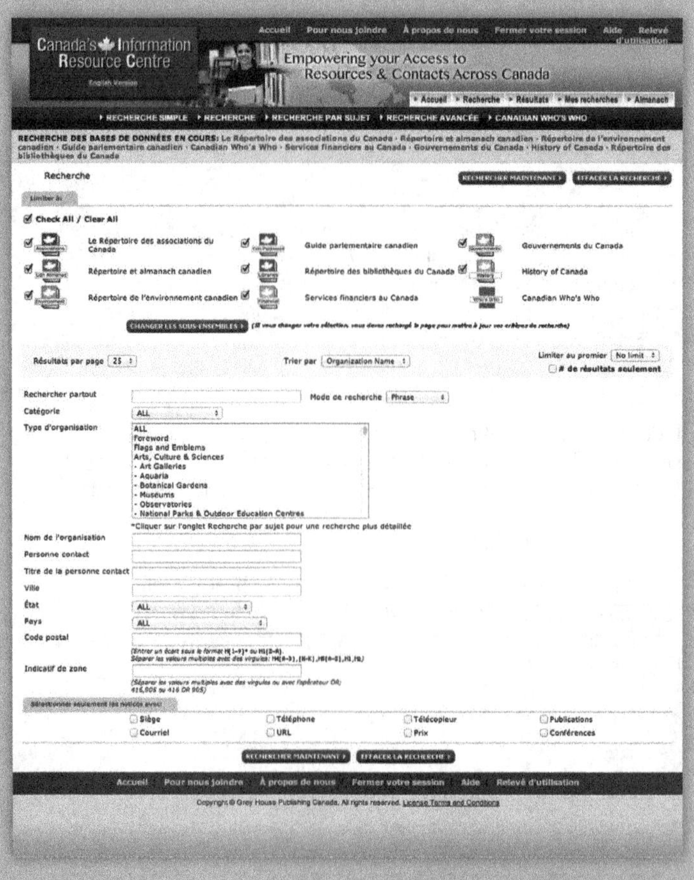

Le Centre de documentation du Canada (CDC) regroupe sous une seule ressource en ligne conviviale tout le contenu des ouvrages de référence primés de Grey House Canada. Répertoriant plus de 100 000 entreprises canadiennes, personnes-ressources, faits et chiffres, il s'agit de la ressource la plus complète en matière de bases de données spécialisées au Canada.

PRINCIPAUX AVANTAGES DU CDC

- Recherche transversale efficace dans le contenu des bases de données
- Sauvegarde des résultats de recherche pour consultation future
- Lien direct aux sites Web et aux adresses électroniques
- Grâce à l'affichage lisible de vos résultats, il est dorénavant plus facile de compiler les résultats ou d'ajouter des critères à vos recherches.

CONCEPTION PERSONNALISÉE DE VOS LISTES DE PERSONNES-RESSOURCES!

Le CDC vous permet de définir et d'extraire vos propres listes, et ce, en quelques secondes. Que vous ayez besoin d'une liste de coordonnées, de distribution ou de courriels, le CDC peut rassembler l'information rapidement et l'exporter en plusieurs formats.

CHOISISSEZ ENTRE LA RECHERCHE RAPIDE ET CELLE D'EXPERT!

Grâce au CDC, vous pouvez choisir entre une recherche d'expert ou rapide pour localiser l'information avec précision. Vous avez la possibilité d'effectuer des recherches en texte simple ou booléennes puissantes – les recherches sont conçues à l'intention des chercheurs débutants et avancés.

RECHERCHE DANS LA BASE DE DONNÉES À L'AIDE DE CHAMPS COMMUNS OU SPÉCIAUX

- Type d'organisation – indicatif régional – nombre d'employés
- Affiliations – année de la fondation – langue
- Catégorie – ville – nom de la succursale
- Nom de la personne-ressource – titre de la personne-ressource – code postal

SEULS LES RÉPERTOIRES DE GREY HOUSE VOUS OFFRENT UN CONTENU PARTICULIER QUE VOUS NE TROUVEREZ NULLE PART AILLEURS!

- **Le répertoire des associations du Canada** : sources de financement, activités, publications, congrès, membres, prix, profil de membre
- **Guide parlementaire canadien** : carrières privées et politiques des membres élus, liste complète des comtés et des représentants
- **Guide des ressources environnementales canadiennes** : produits/services/domaines d'expertise, langues de travail, marchés nationaux, type de propriétaire, sources de revenus
- **Services financiers** : type de propriétaire, nombre d'employés, année de la fondation, immobilisations, revenus, symbole au téléscripteur
- **Bibliothèques Canada** : personnel, collections particulières, services, année de la fondation, symbole de bibliothèque national, système régional
- **Gouvernements du Canada** : population municipale
- **Canadian Who's Who** : ville d'origine, publication, formation (diplômes et alma mater), carrière/emploi et employeur

Le nouveau CDC facilite la recherche au sein de toutes nos ressources au Canada et procure plus rapidement des résultats plus poussés – des associations au gouvernement en passant par les principales entreprises et les zoos, sans oublier tout un éventail d'organisations! Que vous ayez besoin d'information très détaillée au sujet de votre personne-ressource ou d'une simple adresse électronique, vous pouvez personnaliser votre requête afin qu'elle réponde à vos besoins. Communiquez avec nous pour obtenir une inscription d'essai GRATUITE ou visitez le http://circ.greyhouse.ca. Vous serez agréablement surpris de constater que les renseignements sont à portée de main, et ce, 24 heures sur 24, 7 jours sur 7!

GREY HOUSE PUBLISHING CANADA

Pour obtenir plus d'information, veuillez contacter Grey House Publishing Canada

par tél. : 1 866 433-4739 ou 416 644-6479 par téléc. : 416 644-1904 | info@greyhouse.ca | www.greyhouse.ca

Guide canadien de la santé

Un manuel informatif au sujet des services en santé au Canada

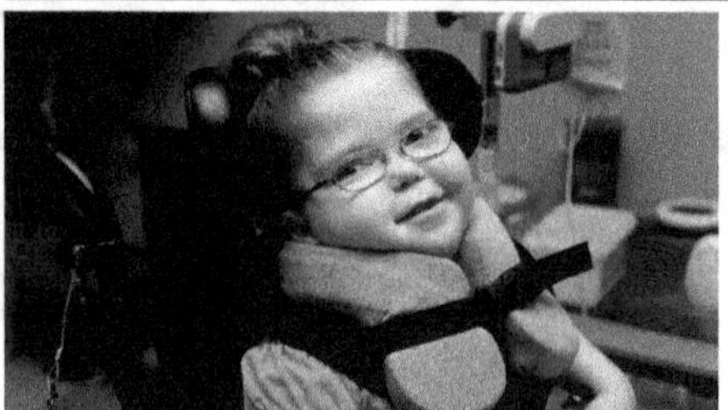

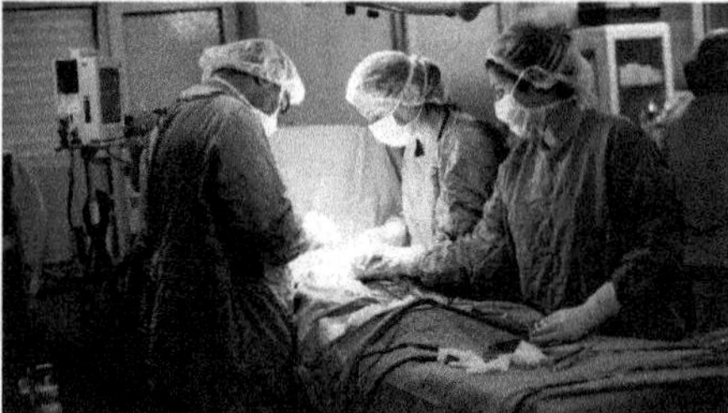

Le *Guide canadien de la santé : un manuel informatif au sujet des maladies chroniques et mentales de même que des services en santé au Canada* donne un aperçu exhaustif de 99 maladies chroniques et mentales, de la maladie d'Addison à celle de Wilson. Chaque chapitre comprend une description médicale facile à comprendre, une vaste gamme de services de soutien particuliers à l'état et des ressources documentaires qui portent sur diverses questions relatives aux personnes qui sont aux prises avec une maladie chronique ou mentale et à ceux qui soutiennent la communauté liée à cette maladie.

Le *Guide canadien de la santé* contient des milliers de moyens pour composer avec divers aspects d'une maladie chronique ou d'un problème de santé mentale. Il comprend des associations, des organismes gouvernementaux, des bibliothèques et des centres de documentation, des services d'éducation, des hôpitaux et des publications. En plus des chapitres qui portent sur des états chroniques ou mentaux, un chapitre traite de l'industrie de la santé en général; d'autres abordent les fondations qui réalisent des rêves, les groupes de soutien axés sur le décès et le deuil, la médecine homéopathique, les questions autochtones et les sports pour les personnes handicapées. Les sections incluent

- Matériel didactique
- Section I : Les maladies chroniques ou mentales
- Section II : Les ressources génériques
- Section III : Les annexes
- Section IV : Les statistiques

Chaque entrée comprend une description, une adresse (y compris le site Web, le courriel et les liens des médias sociaux, lorsque possible), les noms et titres des directeurs de même que plusieurs détails particuliers à ce type d'organisme.

Les membres du personnel des hôpitaux et des centres médicaux peuvent trouver, au même titre que parents et familles, le soutien dont ils ont besoin dans le cadre de leur travail ou de leurs études. Le *Guide canadien de la santé* est rempli de ressources capitales pour les personnes qui souffrent d'une maladie chronique alors qu'elles passent du diagnostic au retour à la maison, de la maison au travail et du travail à la vie au sein de la communauté.

OFFERT EN FORMAT PAPIER OU EN LIGNE—UN ACCÈS RAPIDE ET FACILE À TOUS LES RENSEIGNEMENTS DONT VOUS AVEZ BESOIN!

Offert sous couverture souple ou en format électronique grâce au web, le *Guide canadien de la santé* donne invariablement un accès instantané aux personnes et aux faits dont vous avez besoin. Si la version imprimée est vérifiée et mise à jour annuellement, des changements continus sont apportés mensuellement à la base de données en ligne. Servez-vous de la version en ligne afin de circonscrire vos recherches grâce à des champs spéciaux de l'index comme le nom de l'organisation ou son type, le sujet, l'emplacement, le nom de la personne-ressource ou son titre et le code postal.

LE GUIDE CANADIEN DE LA SANTÉ VOUS AIDERA À TROUVER CE DONT VOUS AVEZ BESOIN GRÂCE À CES OUTILS DE REPÉRAGE PRÉCIEUX!

Répertoire nominatif—une list alphabétique offrant un moyen rapide et facile d'accéder à toute liste de cette edition.

Onglets—les sections principals possèdent un onglet pour une consultation facile. Les notes en tête de chaque page vous aident à trouver les données voulues.

Créez vos propres listes! Les abonnés au service en ligne peuvent générer instantanément leurs propres listes de contacts et les exporter en format feuille de calcul pour une utilisation approfondie – une solution de rechange géniale aux services dispendieux d'un commissionnaire en publipostage.

Pour obtenir plus d'information, veuillez contacter Grey House Publishing Canada

par tél. : 1 866 433-4739 ou 416 644-6479 par téléc. : 416 644-1904 | info@greyhouse.ca | www.greyhouse.ca

Associations du Canada

La recherche d'organisations simplifiée

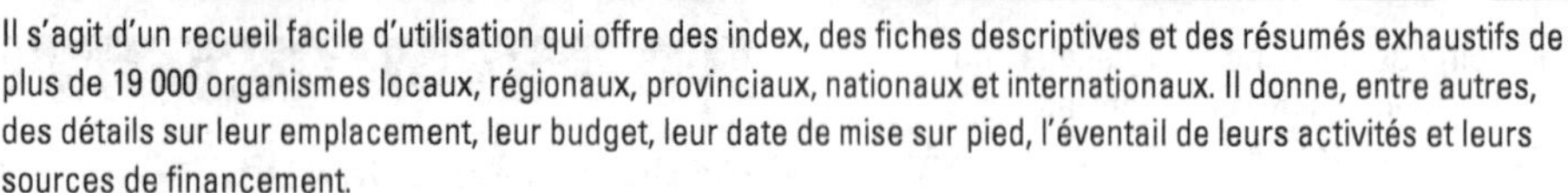

Il s'agit d'un recueil facile d'utilisation qui offre des index, des fiches descriptives et des résumés exhaustifs de plus de 19 000 organismes locaux, régionaux, provinciaux, nationaux et internationaux. Il donne, entre autres, des détails sur leur emplacement, leur budget, leur date de mise sur pied, l'éventail de leurs activités et leurs sources de financement.

En plus d'affecter plus d'un milliard de dollars annuellement aux frais de transport, à la participation à des congrès et à la mise en marché, *Associations du Canada* débourse des millions de dollars dans sa quête pour répondre aux intérêts de ses membres.

DES INDEX PUISSANTS QUI VOUS AIDENT À CIBLER LES ORGANISATIONS VOULUES

Vous pouvez vous servir de plusieurs critères pour cibler des organisations précises. C'est avec l'utilisateur en tête qu'*Associations du Canada* a été divisé en plusieurs index pour vous aider à trouver, rapidement et facilement, ce que vous cherchez.

- **Index des sujets**—liste des sièges sociaux d'associations canadiennes et étrangères; sujets classés en ordre alphabétique et mot-clé.
- **Index des acronymes**—liste alphabétique des acronymes et des associations canadiennes et étrangères équivalentes; présenté dans les deux langues officielles.
- **Index des budgets**—associations canadiennes classées en ordre alphabétique parmi huit catégories de budget.
- **Index des congrès**—rencontres commanditées par des associations canadiennes et étrangères; classées en ordre alphabétique selon le titre de l'événement.
- **Index des directeurs**—liste alphabétique des principales personnes-ressources des associations canadiennes, aux sièges sociaux et aux succursales.
- **Index géographique**—liste des sièges sociaux, des succursales, des sections régionales et des divisions des associations canadiennes; ordre alphabétique au sein des provinces et des villes.
- **Index des listes de distribution**—liste des associations qui offrent des listes de distribution; en ordre alphabétique selon le sujet.
- **Index des œuvres de bienfaisance enregistrées**—liste des associations enregistrées en tant qu'œuvres de bienfaisance; en ordre alphabétique selon le sujet.

OFFERT EN FORMAT PAPIER OU EN LIGNE—UN ACCÈS RAPIDE ET FACILE À TOUS LES RENSEIGNEMENTS DONT VOUS AVEZ BESOIN!

Offert sous couverture rigide ou en format électronique grâce au web, *Associations du Canada* donne invariablement un accès instantané aux personnes et aux faits dont vous avez besoin. Si la version imprimée est vérifiée et mise à jour annuellement, des changements continus sont apportés mensuellement à la base de données en ligne. Servez-vous de la version en ligne afin de circonscrire vos recherches grâce à des champs spéciaux de l'index comme le nom de l'organisation ou son type, le sujet, l'emplacement, le nom de la personne-ressource ou son titre et le code postal.

Créez vos propres listes! Les abonnés au service en ligne peuvent générer instantanément leurs propres listes de contacts et les exporter en format feuille de calcul pour une utilisation approfondie – une solution de rechange géniale aux services dispendieux d'un commissionnaire en publipostage.

ASSOCIATIONS DU CANADA OFFRE UN ACCÈS COMPLET À CES MARCHÉS HAUTEMENT LUCRATIFS

Voyage et tourisme

- Renseignez-vous sur les hôtes des événements... sur les dates et les endroits.
- Consultez les événements trois ans au préalable.

Journalisme et médias

- Recherche authentique—quel est leur centre d'activité? Qui est la personne responsable? Quel est leur budget?
- Vérifiez les faits et sources en une seule étape.

Bibliothèques

- Orientez les chercheurs vers la référence la plus complète en ce qui concerne les associations canadiennes.

Commerce

- Ciblez votre marché, faites une recherche selon vos sujets de prédilection, compilez des profils et recensez des listes des membres.
- Préparez votre sollicitation au hasard en obtenant les renseignements dont vous avez besoin pour offrir votre produit ou service.
- Obtenez un aperçu de vos clients potentiels selon les budgets, les intérêts au marché ou l'emplacement géographique.

Directeurs d'associations

- Recherchez des alliances stratégiques avec des associations partageant vos intérêts.
- Repérez des occasions ou des conflits dans le cadre de la planification des congrès.

Recherche et gouvernement

- Parcourez les groupes d'intérêts ou identifiez les organismes de bienfaisance de votre domaine d'intérêt.
- Consultez les sites Web, les publications et vérifiez la disponibilité des conférenciers.
- Évaluez les mandats, les affiliations et le champ d'application.

Pour obtenir plus d'information, veuillez contacter Grey House Publishing Canada

par tél. : 1 866 433-4739 ou 416 644-6479 par téléc. : 416 644-1904 | info@greyhouse.ca | www.greyhouse.ca

Guide parlementaire canadien

Votre principale source d'information en matière de résultats d'élections fédérales!

Publié annuellement depuis avant la Confédération, le *Guide parlementaire canadien* est une source fondamentale de notices biographiques des membres élus et nommés aux gouvernements fédéral et provinciaux. Il y est question, notamment, d'établissements gouvernementaux comme la résidence du gouverneur général, le Conseil privé et la législature canadienne. Ce recueil exhaustif présente les résultats historiques et actuels accompagnés de données statistiques, provinciales et politiques.

LE GUIDE PARLEMENTAIRE CANADIEN EST DIVISÉ EN CINQ CATÉGORIES EXHAUSTIVES:

La monarchie—des renseignements biographiques sur Sa Majesté la reine Elizabeth II, la famille royale et le gouverneur général.

Le gouvernement fédéral—un chapitre distinct pour chacun des sujets suivants: Conseil privé, sénat, Chambre des communes (y compris une brève description de l'institution, son historique sous forme de textes et de graphiques et une liste des membres actuels) suivi de notes biographiques sans pareil.*

Les élections fédérales

1867–2008

- Les renseignements sont présentés en ordre alphabétique par province puis par circonscription.
- Les notes de chaque circonscription comprennent : La date d'établissement, la date d'abolition, l'ancienne circonscription, les circonscriptions ultérieures, etc. puis l'année d'élection ainsi que le nom et le parti des candidats élus.
- Viennent ensuite des renseignements sur l'élection partielle.

2011

- Les renseignements de l'élection 2011 sont organisés de la même manière, mais comprennent également de l'information sur tous les candidats qui se sont présentés dans chaque circonscription, leur appartenance politique et le nombre de voix récoltées.

Gouvernements provinciaux et territoriaux—Chaque chapitre portant sur le gouvernement provincial comprend :

- des renseignements statistiques
- une description de l'Assemblée législative
- des notes biographiques sur le lieutenant-gouverneur ou le commissaire
- une liste des ministres actuels
- les dates de périodes législatives depuis la Confédération
- une liste des membres et des circonscriptions
- des notes biographiques*
- les résultats des élections générales et partielles

Cours : fédérale—chaque chapitre comprend : une description de la cour (suprême, fédérale, cour d'appel fédérale, cour d'appel de la cour martiale et cour de l'impôt), son histoire, une liste des juges qui y siègent ainsi que des notes biographiques.*

* Les notes biographiques respectent un format concis, bien qu'approfondi :

Renseignements personnels—lieu de naissance, formation, renseignements familiaux

Carrière politique—cheminement politique et service public

Carrière privée—antécédents professionnels, membre d'organisations, antécédents militaires

OFFERT EN FORMAT PAPIER ET DÉSORMAIS ÉLECTRONIQUE!

Offert sous couverture rigide ou en format électronique grâce au web, le *Guide parlementaire canadien* donne invariablement un accès instantané aux représentants du gouvernement et aux faits qui font l'objet de vos recherches. Si la version imprimée est vérifiée et mise à jour annuellement, des changements continus sont apportés mensuellement à la base de données en ligne. Servez-vous de la version en ligne afin de circonscrire vos recherches grâce aux champs spéciaux de l'index comme l'institution, la province et le nom.

Créez vos propres listes! Les abonnés au service en ligne peuvent générer instantanément leurs propres listes de contacts et les exporter en format feuille de calcul pour une utilisation approfondie – une solution de rechange géniale aux services dispendieux d'un commissionnaire en publipostage!

Pour obtenir plus d'information, veuillez contacter Grey House Publishing Canada

par tél. : 1 866 433-4739 ou 416 644-6479 par téléc. : 416 644-1904 | info@greyhouse.ca | www.greyhouse.ca

Répertoire et almanach canadien

La ressource de référence au sujet des données et des faits relatifs au Canada

Le *Répertoire et almanach canadien* constitue le guide canadien le plus rigoureux depuis 166 ans. Publié annuellement depuis 1847, il est toujours grandement utilisé dans le monde des affaires, les bureaux gouvernementaux, par les spécialistes de l'information, les chercheurs, les éditeurs ou quiconque est à la recherche d'information actuelle et accessible sur tous les sujets imaginables à propos des gens qui vivent et travaillent au Canada.

À la fois répertoire et guide, le *Répertoire et almanach canadien* dresse le tableau le plus complet du Canada, des caractéristiques physiques jusqu'aux revues économique et commerciale, en passant par les loisirs et les activités récréatives. Il combine des documents textuels, des représentations graphiques, des photographies en couleurs et des listes de répertoires accompagnées de profils détaillés. Autant d'information pointue et organisée de manière à ce qu'elle soit facile à obtenir. Le *Répertoire et almanach canadien* foisonne de renseignements généraux. Il présente des statistiques nationales sur la population, l'emploi, l'IPC, l'importation et l'exportation ainsi que des images des prix nationaux, des symboles canadiens, des drapeaux, des emblèmes et des leaders parlementaires canadiens.

Si vous cherchez des personnes-ressources essentielles un peu partout au Canada, peu importe qu'il s'agisse de projets d'affaires ou d'une question factuelle anecdotique, le Répertoire et almanach canadien vous fournira les pistes dont vous ignoriez l'existence – rapidement et facilement!

TOUTE L'INFORMATION DONT VOUS AUREZ BESOIN, ORGANISÉE EN 17 CATÉGORIES DISTINCTES POUR UNE CONSULTATION FACILE!

Almanach—un aperçu informatif du Canada, notamment l'histoire, la géographie, l'économie et les statistiques essentielles.

Arts et culture—comprends 9 sujets, des galeries aux zoos.

Associations—des milliers d'organisations classées selon 139 sujets différents, de l'actuariat au zoo.

Radiodiffusion—les principales sociétés de radiodiffusion au Canada, les stations radiophoniques et de télévision ainsi que les entreprises de câblodistribution et les diffuseurs thématiques.

Commerce et finance—comptabilité, services bancaires, assurances, principales entreprises et bourses canadiennes.

Éducation—organisé par province et comprend les arrondissements scolaires, les organismes gouvernementaux, les écoles spécialisées et indépendantes, les universités et les établissements techniques.

Gouvernement—s'étend sur trois sections et comprend un guide de référence, des listes fédérales et provinciales, les comtés et arrondissements municipaux ainsi que les cours canadiennes.

Santé—organismes gouvernementaux, hôpitaux, centres de santé communautaires, établissements de soins pour personnes retraitées et de soins de santé mentale.

Sociétés d'avocats—toutes les principales sociétés d'avocats, suivies des sociétés plus petites, classées par province et en ordre alphabétique.

Bibliothèques—la bibliothèque et les archives principales du Canada ainsi que les bibliothèques des ministères, suivis des listes provinciales et des systèmes régionaux.

Édition—livres, magazines et journaux classés par province, y compris leur fréquence et les données relatives à leur diffusion.

Religion—information générale au sujet des groupes religieux et des associations religieuses de 21 dénominations.

Sports—associations de 93 sports distincts; comprend des listes de ligues et d'équipes.

Transport—des listes complètes des principaux modes de transport.

Services publics—associations, organismes gouvernementaux et entreprises de services publics provinciales.

FORMAT PAPIER OU EN LIGNE— ACCÈS RAPIDE À TOUS LES RENSEIGNEMENTS DONT VOUS AVEZ BESOIN!

Offert sous couverture rigide ou en format électronique grâce au web, le *Répertoire et almanach canadien* offre invariablement un accès instantané aux représentants du gouvernement et aux faits qui font l'objet de vos recherches.

La version imprimée du Répertoire et almanach canadien est vérifiée et mise à jour annuellement. La version en ligne est mise à jour mensuellement. Cette version vous permet de circonscrire la recherche grâce aux champs de l'index comme le nom ou le type d'organisme, le sujet, l'emplacement, le nom ou le titre de la personne-ressource et le code postal.

Les abonnés au service en ligne peuvent générer instantanément leurs propres listes de contacts et les exporter en format feuille de calcul pour une utilisation approfondie – une solution de rechange géniale aux services dispendieux d'un commissionnaire en publipostage.

Pour obtenir plus d'information, veuillez contacter Grey House Publishing Canada

par tél. : 1 866 433-4739 ou 416 644-6479 par téléc. : 416 644-1904 | info@greyhouse.ca | www.greyhouse.ca

Gouvernements du Canada

Le guide le plus complet et exhaustif pour trouver des personnes et des programmes au Canada

Ce répertoire offre des fiches descriptives mises à jour régulièrement au sujet des ministères fédéraux, provinciaux et territoriaux, des bureaux et des agences du gouvernement de partout au pays. Les directions générales et les bureaux régionaux en font également partie, tout comme les organismes associés, les conseils, les commissions et les sociétés de la Couronne.

Les fiches descriptives comprennent les noms de personnes-ressources, l'adresse complète, les numéros de téléphone et de télécopieur de même que les courriels. Vous pouvez compter sur notre engagement envers la précision et l'indexation de qualité supérieure.

VOUS AVEZ AINSI ACCÈS AUX DÉCIDEURS CLÉS À TOUS LES PALIERS DE GOUVERNEMENT, NOTAMMENT :

- Conseils des ministres/conseils exécutifs
- Représentants élus
- Gouverneur général/lieutenants gouverneurs/ commissaires territoriaux
- Premiers ministres/premiers ministres provinciaux/ leaders du gouvernement
- Vérificateur général du Canada/vérificateurs provinciaux
- Fonctionnaires électoraux
- Ministères/organismes et administration publique

CES INDEX PUISSANTS ET FACILES D'UTILISATION SONT CONÇUS POUR VOUS AIDER À OBTENIR DES RÉSULTATS RAPIDES ET DIGNES DE FOI, PEU IMPORTE VOTRE RECHERCHE.

- **Table des matières de noms communs**—un seul index unifié pour toutes les juridictions.
- **Guide éclair des sujets**—une liste détaillée accompagnée de références sur plus de 170 sujets d'intérêt.
- **Faits saillants des changements importants**—une liste des principaux changements importants récemment apportés au sein du gouvernement.
- **Personnes-ressources**—un outil irremplaçable de réseautage et de ventes grâce à plus de 130 pages de coordonnées complètes.
- **Listes de sites Web et de courriels**—classées par gouvernement et ministère.
- **Acronymes**—une liste alphabétique des acronymes les plus utilisés.

GOUVERNEMENTS DU CANADA EST L'OUTIL ESSENTIEL DES PROFESSIONNELS POUR TROUVER:

Des groupes de revendication—trouvez les bonnes personnes pour avoir une conversation productive sur des questions-clés.

Des avocats, des comptables et des conseillers—obtenez les noms et les adresses les plus courants des personnes-ressources clés de chaque bureau gouvernemental.

Des bibliothécaires—épargnez du temps de recherche grâce à cet outil de référence complet.

Des ambassades et des consulats—trouvez la bonne personne-ressource ou le bon fonctionnaire en matière de présentation partout au Canada.

Des employés du gouvernement—consultez les faits et renseignements faciles à obtenir à tous les paliers gouvernementaux.

Des fournisseurs du gouvernement—trouvez les décideurs afin de cibler vos produits et services.

Pour obtenir plus d'information, veuillez contacter Grey House Publishing Canada

par tél. : 1 866 433-4739 ou 416 644-6479 par téléc. : 416 644-1904 | info@greyhouse.ca | www.greyhouse.ca

Services financiers au Canada

Une couverture sans pareille de l'industrie des services financiers canadiens

Grâce à plus de 17 000 organisations et renseignements commerciaux rares, *Services financiers du Canada* est la source la plus à jour de noms et de coordonnées de professionnels, de membres de la haute direction, de gestionnaires de portefeuille, de conseillers financiers, de fonctionnaires et de représentants élus de l'industrie.

Services financiers du Canada intègre les plus récentes modifications à l'industrie afin de vous offrir les détails les plus à jour au sujet de chaque entreprise, notamment le nom, le titre, l'organisation, les numéros de téléphone et de télécopieur, le courriel et l'adresse du site Web. Servez-vous de la base de données en ligne et raffinez votre recherche selon le symbole, le revenu, l'année de création, les immobilisations, le type de propriété ou le nombre d'employés.

DES INDEX PUISSANTS VOUS AIDENT À TROUVER LES RENSEIGNEMENTS FINANCIERS ESSENTIELS DONT VOUS AVEZ BESOIN.

C'est avec l'utilisateur en tête que Services financiers au Canada a été conçu; il contient des listes catégorisées et quatre index faciles d'utilisation :

Alphabétique—les organisations financières apparaissent en ordre alphabétique, selon le nom de l'entreprise.

Géographique—les institutions financières et leurs succursales sont détaillées par ville.

Nom de directeur—tous les agents, directeurs et cadres supérieurs sont classés en ordre alphabétique, selon leur nom de famille.

Classe d'assurance—toutes les entreprises selon leur type d'assurance.

Passez moins de temps à préparer des listes, à faire des recherches ou à chercher des contacts et des courriels. Que vous soyez intéressé à contacter un avocat en droit des affaires au sujet de projets conjoints internationaux et nationaux, que vous ayez besoin de générer une liste des banques étrangères au Canada ou que vous souhaitiez communiquer avec la Bourse de Toronto, *Services financiers au Canada* vous permet de trouver toutes les données dont vous avez besoin.

OFFERT EN FORMAT PAPIER OU EN LIGNE – UN ACCÈS RAPIDE ET FACILE À TOUS LES RENSEIGNEMENTS DONT VOUS AVEZ BESOIN!

Offert sous couverture rigide ou en format électronique grâce au Web, Services financiers du Canada donne invariablement un accès instantané aux personnes et aux faits dont vous avez besoin. Si la version imprimée est vérifiée et mise à jour annuellement, des changements continus sont apportés mensuellement à la base de données en ligne. Servez-vous de la version en ligne afin de circonscrire vos recherches grâce à des champs spéciaux de l'index comme le nom de l'organisation ou son type, le sujet, l'emplacement, le nom de la personne-ressource ou son titre et le code postal.

Créez vos propres listes! Les abonnés au service en ligne peuvent générer instantanément leurs propres listes de contacts et les exporter en format feuille de calcul pour une utilisation approfondie – une solution de rechange géniale aux services dispendieux d'un commissionnaire en publipostage.

ACCÉDEZ AUX LISTES ACTUELLES...

Banques et institutions de dépôt

- Banques nationales et d'épargne
- Banques étrangères et leurs succursales
- Bureaux des représentants de banques étrangères
- Sociétés de fiducie
- Coopératives d'épargne et de crédit

Établissements financiers

- Entreprises de notation des obligations
- Agences de placement
- Compagnies de carte de crédit
- Sociétés de financement et de prêt
- Syndics de faillite

Sociétés de gestion de placements, y compris les valeurs et marchandises

- Entreprises de planification financière et de gestion des investissements
- Maisons de courtage de valeurs
  Courtiers en épargne collective
- Entreprises de gestion de la pension/de trésorerie
- Bourses
- Sociétés de portefeuille

Compagnies d'assurance, fédérales et provinciales

- Compagnies de réassurance
- Sociétés fraternelles
- Sociétés de secours mutuel
- Échanges selon la formule de réciprocité — comptabilité et droit
- Comptables
- Cabinets d'actuaires-conseils
- Cabinets d'avocats (spécialisés en finance)
- Principales entreprises canadiennes
- Principaux contacts financiers pour les sociétés de capitaux publiques, privées et de la Couronne
- Gouvernement
- Personnes-ressources aux paliers fédéral, provinciaux et territoriaux

Annexe de publications

- Principales publications qui desservent l'industrie des services financiers

Pour obtenir plus d'information, veuillez contacter Grey House Publishing Canada

par tél. : 1 866 433-4739 ou 416 644-6479 par téléc. : 416 644-1904 | info@greyhouse.ca | www.greyhouse.ca

Mailing List Services

As a boutique provider of mailing lists, Grey House Publishing Canada specializes in the areas below to ensure a high level of accuracy. Our clients return to us time and time again because of the reliability of our information and great customer service. We'll work with you to develop a campaign that provides results. No other list services will work as closely as we do to meet your unique needs.

Associations—the most extensive list of Canadian associations available, featuring all professional, trade and business organizations together with not-for-profit groups.

Arts & Culture—the definitive source of key prospects in various Canadian arts and cultural outlets.

Education—the most comprehensive list of educational institutions and organizations in Canada.

Health Care / Hospitals—includes all major medical facilities with chief executives.

Lawyers—key prospects for a number of direct mail offers.

Media—the definitive source of key prospects in various Canadian media outlets, offering the top business managers and/or publishers.

Environmental—a complete profile of the Canadian Environmental scene, constantly revised for the annual Canadian Environmental Resource Guide.

Financial Services—a list of key contacts from the full range of Canada's financial services industry.

Government Key Contacts—a list of key Government contacts, maintained by the Canadian Almanac & Directory, Canada's standard institutional reference for 165 years.

Libraries—the most unique and complete list of government, special and public libraries available.

Major Canadian Companies—listings of Canada's largest private, public and Crown corporations with major key contacts of the top business decision-makers.

AVAILABILITY

Lists are available on CD, labels and via e-mail. They are provided on a one-time use basis or for a one-year lease. For a quotation on tailor-made lists to suit your needs, inquire using the contact information listed below.

GREY HOUSE PUBLISHING CANADA

For more information please contact Grey House Publishing Canada

Tel.: (866) 433-4739 or (416) 644-6479 Fax: (416) 644-1904 | info@greyhouse.ca | www.greyhouse.ca

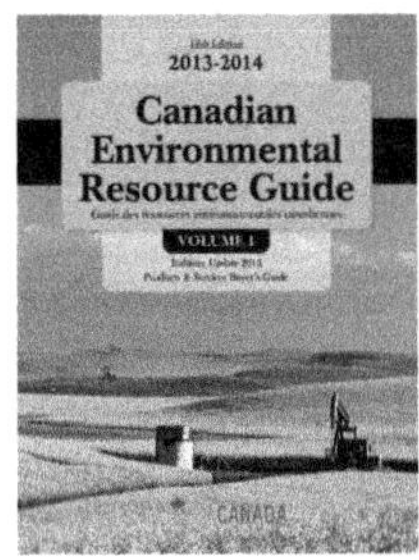

Canadian Environmental Resource Guide

Grey House Publishing Canada
555 Richmond Street West, Suite 301
Toronto, Ontario M5V 3B1

Fax completed forms to: (416) 644-1904

FREE LISTING & UPDATE
Be sure your organization appears in Canadian Environmental Resource Guide

Canadian Environmental Resource Guide is Canada's complete guide to environmental affairs and includes government agencies, associations, special libraries, law firms, companies providing environmental products and services, conferences and more.

This listing is **FREE**. To ensure a complete and accurate listing in the upcoming edition, simply fill in the questionnaire and return it by **fax or by mail**. Include any relevant information such as phone, fax or toll free numbers, website and email addresses, and official translations (if applicable).

If you have any questions, please call Tannys Williams at (416) 644-6476 or 1-866-433-4739. You can return this form either by **fax**: (416) 644-1904, by **mail** to the address above, or **email** info@greyhouse.ca

Is your organization already listed in this publication? Yes, we're updating existing information______ No, we're new_____

Completed by: ____________________ Phone: __________________ Email: ______________________________

ORGANIZATION

Name: ____

Street Address: ____

Phone: ____________________

Toll Free: ____________________

Fax: ____________________

Email: ________________________________

Website: ________________________________

Translated Name: ____

Also known as: ____

Acronym: ____________________

Founded: ____________________

CHIEF OFFICERS/STAFF

President - ____

Secretary - ____

Treasurer - ____

Vice-President - ____

Other Staff: please see following page

Number of staff: ______________; Volunteers: ______________

Contact: ____

FOUNDED:

Firm Type: ____

Products/ Services/ Areas of Expertise: ____

____

ISO: ____

Recently Completed/ Ongoing Projects: ____

____

Type of Ownership: ____

Revenue: ____

Revenue Resources: ____

ADDITIONAL INFORMATION

SUBJECT FOCUS:

i. ______________________ ii. ______________________

iii. ______________________ iv. ______________________

SCOPE OF ACTIVITY:

- ❑ International
- ❑ National
- ❑ Provincial/Territorial
- ❑ Local
- ❑ Regional

MARKETS SOUGHT: ______________________

MISSION STATEMENT/GOALS/MANDATE:

____

____

____

ANNUAL OPERATING BUDGET:

- ❑ Less than $50,000
- ❑ $50,000 - $99,999
- ❑ $100,000 - $249,999
- ❑ $250,000 - $499,999
- ❑ $500,000 - $1,499,999
- ❑ $1,500,000 - $2,999,999
- ❑ $3,000,000 - $4,999,999
- ❑ Over $5,000,000

DO YOU:			
	Rent your Mailing Lists?	❑ Yes	❑ No
	Have a Speakers Service?	❑ Yes	❑ No
	Have an Internship Program?	❑ Yes	❑ No

OTHER STAFF: (attach list if necessary)

Name: ______________________ Title: ______________________

Telephone: ______________________ Email: ______________________

Name: ______________________ Title: ______________________

Telephone: ______________________ Email: ______________________

Name: ______________________ Title: ______________________

Telephone: ______________________ Email: ______________________

CANADIAN BRANCHES:

Name: ______________________

Address: ______________________

Name: ______________________

Address: ______________________

Name: ______________________

Address: ______________________

Name: ______________________

Address: ______________________

INTERNATIONAL BRANCHES:

Name: ______________________

Address: ______________________

Name: ______________________

Address: ______________________

Name: ______________________

Address: ______________________

WE THANK YOU FOR TAKING THE TIME TO PROVIDE YOUR VALUABLE INFORMATION.